简明
英汉词典

A CONCISE
ENGLISH—CHINESE
DICTIONARY

《新英汉词典》编写组编
泛太平洋词典编委会改编

生活·讀書·新知三联书店香港分店
JOINT PUBLISHING COMPANY (Hong Kong Branch)

泛太平洋书业(星)私人有限公司
PAN PACIFIC BOOK DISTRIBUTORS (S) PTE LTD

┌─ 鸣 谢 ─────────────────────────

承蒙卢绍昌先生、黄守坚先生协助改编本词典，
谨此致谢。

We would like to express our sincere thanks to both
Mr. Loo Shaw Chang and Mr. Wong Chow Keng for their
help in bringing out this dictionary.

Acknowledgements ─┘

简 明 英 汉 词 典
A CONCISE ENGLISH – CHINESE DICTIONARY

Original edition under the title
A New English — Chinese Dictionary
first published 1975 by
© **Joint Publishing Company (Hong Kong Branch)**
10th floor 9 Queen Victoria Street Hong Kong

原版《 新英汉词典 》由
生活 • 读书 • 新知三联书店香港分店出版

This edition first published 1981
Reprinted 1982
© **Pan Pacific Book Distributors (S) Pte Ltd**
597 Havelock Road Singapore 0316

此改编本由
泛太平洋书业(星)私人有限公司改编出版

Printed by Koon Wah Printing Pte Ltd

ISBN 9971-63-187-3

前　言

　　《简明英汉词典》是根据1975年三联书店香港分店出版的《新英汉词典》改编的。该书由上海复旦大学外语系等单位的七十多名专家学者合力编成。

　　《新英汉词典》收词丰富，解释精当，举例繁多，是一部具有崭新内容而又切合实用的大型工具书。泛太平洋书业（星）私人有限公司决定和香港三联书店合作，将原来的大型词典改编成为一部中型词典，以适合新马一带广大读者的需求。

　　改编后的《简明英汉词典》仍然保留原有的特色和精华，只是删去原词典里比较罕用的、专门的或缩略的词目，以及一些内容不适宜的例句。不过，改编本增加了一百多张插图，使词典生色不少。

　　《简明英汉词典》收词约五万五千余条，包括基本词汇、派生词、复合词、一般词汇、科技术语、缩略语、外来语、地名等。此外，书末附有不规则动词表、常用符号、度量衡表等附录。

　　《简明英汉词典》不但是一部简明、好用的工具书，同时也容易携带，是老师、学生和各阶层读者可以信赖的参考书。

FOREWORD

A Concise English-Chinese Dictionary is adapted from the 1975 edition of *A New English-Chinese Dictionary* which was compiled by a team of more than seventy specialists and scholars from the Foreign Languages Department of Futan University, Shanghai, and published by Joint Publishing Co. (Hong Kong Branch).

A New English-Chinese Dictionary has collected a very wide range of English words, idioms and phrases and their Chinese equivalents. It contains many examples on their uses. In more respects than one, it is a very useful reference. However, it is a little bulky to carry about and is also not very suitable for the general reader. Hence, we have adapted it to the present volume in the hope that it will meet the requirements of the general reader in Singapore and Malaysia.

Although words not in frequent use and special terms not usually required have been omitted, many of the original, essential features have been retained in **A Concise English-Chinese Dictionary**. Other than that, examples unsuitable to our local context have also been deleted and some 100 illustrations added to help in the understanding of certain words or phrases. ·

Despite the fact that this volume is said to be "concise", there are altogether 55 000 entries including the basic vocabulary, their derivatives and compounds, general terms, scientific and technical terms, idiomatic expressions, abbreviations and contractions, foreign words, geographical names, etc. At the end there are some addenda which the reader may also find useful, like the lists on irregular verbs, on common marks and symbols; and the tables on measures and weights.

In short, this present volume of **A Concise English-Chinese Dictionary** is not only a handy reference book, but also one which teachers, students and the general reader may use confidently to their advantage.

目 录

CONTENTS

体 例 说 明

(一) 词　　条

一个词条的主要部分是**本词**和**释义**,有的词条还收有**习语**、**派生词**、**复合词**等。

(二) 本　　词

1. 本词用黑正体印刷, 有些习惯上斜写的外来词语用黑斜体印刷。 拼法相同、词源及词义不同的词, 分立词条, 在右上角标以 1、2 等数码。一个词有不同拼法时,若拼法接近,排在同一词条内,中间用逗号隔开;若拼法相差较大,分立词条,但释义只出现于一处,另一处注明等于某词。

2. 本词后用国际音标注明发音。词缀、构词成分及缩写词语等一般不注发音。

3. 音标后注明词性。 一个词若有几种不同词性,各词性前分别标以罗马数字 I、II 等(及物动词、不及物动词等加标 ❶、❷ 等)。词性用英语缩写形式注出,共分十类: 名词 (*n.*), 动词(包括及物动词 *vt.*、不及物动词 *vi.*、助动词 *v. aux.* 等),代词 (*pron.*), 数词 (*num.*),形容词 (*a.*),副词 (*ad.*),前置词 (*prep.*),连接词 (*conj.*),感叹词 (*int.*),冠词 (*art.*)。分写的复合词不注词性。

4. 不规则动词的变化形式、名词复数的不规则变化形式、形容词及副词各比较级的不规则变化形式,均加以注明。 规则变化中需重复词尾辅音字母或拼法、发音等有较大变动的,也加以注明。各变化形式一般注在词性前。 如:

> **go** [gou] **I** (went [went], gone [gɔn]) ❶ *vi.* . . .
> **bind** [baind] **I** (bound [baund]) ❶ *vt.* . . .
> 　　* 只注一个变化形式的,表示过去式和过去分词同形。
> **life** [laif] ([复] lives [laivz]) *n.* . . .
> **good** [gud] **I** (better ['betə], best [best]) *a.* . . .
> **shrug** [ʃrʌg] **I** (shrugged; shrugging) *vt. & vi.* . . .

5. 名词是复数形式或单复同形的,在词性前加以注明(放在方括号内)。如:

> **earnings** ['ə:niŋz] [复] *n.* . . .
> **species** ['spi:ʃi:z] [单复同] *n.* . . .

(三) 释　　义

1. 一个词(包括派生词、复合词)或一个习语有多条不同的释义时,各条释义分别列出,前面标以 ①、② 等数码。 大体相同的若干释义则列在同一条内,词义较近的用逗号分隔,稍远的用分号分隔。

2. 名词释义前所注的[复]、[常用复]、[只用单]等表示对该名词的数的要求；[用作复]、[用作单]等表示对后接谓语动词的数的要求。如：

feature ... *n.* ... ②[复]面貌,相貌…
　　* 表示该名词释作"面貌,相貌"时需用复数形式 features。
letter[2] ... *n.* ... ③信,函件;[常用复]证书,许可证…
　　* 表示该名词释作"证书,许可证"时常用复数形式 letters。
physics ... *n.* [用作单或复] ①物理学…
　　* 表示该名词作主语时,后面的谓语动词可用单数也可用复数形式。

3. 释义后根据需要收入词组或句子作为例证,例证后附汉语译文。作为例证的名词词组,按需要加注冠词,但科技术语一般不加冠词。

4. 例证分别放在有关释义后,但有时也将结构类似或难以归在某一释义后的若干例证集中排列在几条释义后作为"独立例证"。"独立例证"按首字母次序(冠词除外)排列,用白斜体印刷。

5. 例证中在使用或搭配等方面要求读者加以注意的词或词组,常用白斜体印刷。

6. 例证中用 one, one's 分别指本人(或自己),本人的(或自己的);用 sb., sb.'s 分别指某人(或别人),某人的(或别人的)。如：

redouble one's efforts加倍努力
　　* 例中的 one's 在人称上与动作主体一致, 如 *I* redoubled *my* efforts. 或 *He* redoubled *his* efforts.
make an apology to sb. for sth. 为某事向某人道歉
　　* 例中的 sb. 在人称上与动作主体不一致,如 *I* made an apology to *him* for sth.

（四）习　　语

1. 习语(其中包括谚语,下文中提到的习语也兼指谚语)用黑斜体印刷,按首字母次序(包括冠词、用代字号代表的词等)排列。

2. 习语的归属按下述原则处理：

(1) 动词与名词、前置词与名词、形容词与名词等组成的习语,一般收在名词词条内。如：

take place　　入 **place** 词条
look sb. in the face　　入 **face** 词条
by way of　　入 **way** 词条
a black sheep　　入 **sheep** 词条

(2) 动词与副词、动词与前置词、动词与代词等组成的习语,一般收在动词词条内。如:

go over　入 **go** 词条
look for　入 **look** 词条
make it　入 **make** 词条

(3) 动词与形容词组成的习语,一般收在形容词词条内。如:

come true　入 **true** 词条

(4) 前置词与代词组成的习语,一般收在代词词条内。如:

at that　入 **that** 词条

(5) 句子或从句形式的习语,一般收在主语的词条内;主语为代词时,收在其他起关键作用的词的词条内。如:

Practice makes perfect.　入 **practice** 词条
He laughs best who laughs last.　入 **laugh** 词条
as matters stand　入 **matter** 词条

(6) 不属于上述情况的,一般收在习语第一个词(冠词除外)的词条内或收在习语中起关键作用的词的词条内。如:

a man of letters　入 **man** 词条
day and night　入 **day** 词条
as soon as　入 **soon** 词条
ever since　入 **since** 词条

3. 有的习语除收入 2. 条规定的词条外,也同时收在其他别的有关词的词条内。释义一般只出现于一处,另一处注明见某词。

4. 习语中 one、one's、sb.、sb.'s 的用法,与例证中相同。

(五) 派生词及复合词

1. 派生词及复合词大部分列在词条内部,少数由于较常用或释义、用法较复杂等原因,单独列为词条。

2. 列在词条内部的派生词及复合词用黑正体印刷,按首字母次序排列,其本词部分用代字号代表。但有些派生词的本词部分的拼法起了变化,有些复合词的本词部分的重音不在第一音节上,其本词部分仍全部拼出。如:

bright 词条内的 brightness 印成 **~ness**
above 词条内的 above-mentioned 印成 **a'bove-'mentioned**

3．列在词条内部的派生词及复合词的注音问题，见《注音说明》。

4．列在词条内部的派生词均注明词性；复合词除分写的以外，也均注明词性。某些带后缀 -ly, -ness, -tion, -al, -y 等的派生词，若释义相当于词条本词的释义，不再注出释义。

（六）若干符号的用法

1．平行号(‖)用于表示词条内习语、派生词、复合词、"独立例证"等部分的开始。

2．斜线号(/)用于分隔例证与例证、习语与习语、派生词与派生词、复合词与复合词。

3．代字号(～)用于代表词条的本词。

4．双连字号(＝)用于复合词的移行，表示移行处原有连字号。如：

> all-powerful 在移行时印成 all-
> powerful

5．圆括号(‹ ›)用于：

(1) 注明词形变化。如：

> **cut** 词条内的 (cut; cutting)

(2) 加注内容或意义等方面的补充性说明。如：

> **毫米**(千分之一米，略作 mm.)
> (文章、讲话、乐曲等的)一段，一节
> (目光等)洞察的，锐利的
> 元素氧(oxygen)的符号
> (楼房的)底层 (＝[美] first floor)

(3) 括去可以省略的部分。如：

> **neighbo(u)r**
> People think him (to be) a good cadre.
> (*as*) *thick as hail*
> 渗(透)压(力)
> 电话(号码)簿

(4) 括出代换的部分。如：

> *shift gears* . . . ②改变方式(或办法、速度等)
> 　　* 表示"*shift gears*"可释作"改变方式"、"改变办法"、"改变速度"等。
> *off* (或 *away from*) *the point* 不切题，离题
> 　　* 表示"*off the point*"、"*away from the point*"都释作"不切题，离题"。

a new (an old, a green) hand 新(老,生)手

    * 表示可分为 "a new hand 新手"、"an old hand 老手"、"a green hand 生手" 三条。

in (*out of*) *position* 在(不在)适当的位置

    * 表示可分为 "*in position* 在适当的位置"、"*out of position* 不在适当的位置" 两条。

(5) 在某些及物动词或不及物动词的释义中注明宾语或主语。如：

set ... **❶** *vt.* ... ⑮定(日期、限度、价格等)；制定(规则等)…

lead[1] ... **❶** *vt.* ... ②带领，引导；走在(队伍等)的最前头…

fall ... **❶** *vi.* ... ②(温度、价格等)下降…

(6) 在某些动词、形容词、名词等的释义中注明常用的后接副词或前置词。如：

kick[1] ... *vt.* ... ④…驱逐(*out*) ...

dependent ... *a.* ①依靠的；依赖的(*on, upon*) ...

(7) 归并某些词的相近的释义。如：

rich ... *a.* ... ⑧(近乎)纯的…

    * 表示释义为"近乎纯的"和"纯的"。

6. 方括号([ ])用于：

(1) 注明音标。

(2) 注明词源或修辞色彩。如：

[法]；[主英]；[俚]；[贬]；[委婉语]

(3) 注明地名的有关说明。如：

坦桑尼亚[非洲]；巴黎[法国首都]；密西西比河[美国]

(4) 加注语法或使用等方面的补充性说明。如：

[总称]

[常用被动语态]

[P-]

    * 表示第一个字母 P 要大写。

[the ~]

    * 表示该词前要加定冠词。

[~ oneself]

    * 表示该词后接反身代词。

7. 鱼尾号(【 】)用于注明学科等。

注 音 说 明

(一) 注 音 方 式

本词典用国际音标注音,采用宽式注音法。音标注在本词后,放在方括号内。重音符号(')标在重读音节的左上方,如:teacher ['ti:tʃə];在多音节单词中如有两个或两个以上的重读音节,主重音符号 (') 标在左上方,次重音符号 (ˌ) 标在左下方,如:possibility [ˌpɔsə'biliti]。

(二) 同词异音的标注

1. 一个词一般只标注一种发音,有时也选收较常用的异读音,放在同一方括号内,用逗号隔开。如:

    direct [di'rekt, dai'rekt]

2. 斜体音标表示该音素可读可不读。如:

    presume [pri'zju:m]

       * 表示可读作 [pri'zju:m] 或 [pri'zu:m]。

3. 音标后面若有带括号的长音符号 (ː),表示该音素可读作长音或短音。如:

    museum [mju(ː)'ziəm]

       * 表示可读作 [mjuː'ziəm] 或 [mju'ziəm]。

4. 一个词的发音若有强式和弱式两种,在音标前分别加注强弱两字,中间用分号隔开。如:

    a [强 ei; 弱 ə], **an** [强 æn; 弱 ən, n]

    them [强 ðem; 弱 ðəm]

5. 一个词因词性或释义不同而发音不同时,注音方式有如下两种:

(1) 在发音有变化的有关词性或释义前另行注音。如:

    inland ['inlənd] **I** *a.* . . . **II** *n.* . . . **III** [in'lænd] *ad.* . . . ‖~**er** *n.* . . .

       * 表示 **inland** 作形容词和名词时读作 ['inlənd], 作副词时读作 [in'lænd]; 派生词 ~**er** 读作 ['inləndə]。

    second[1] ['sekənd] **I** *num.* . . . **V** *vt.* ①… ⑧[si'kɔnd][英]【军】调任,调派…

(2) 分别在各词性或释义前注音。如:

    implant **I** [im'plɑːnt] *vt.* . . . **II** ['im-plɑːnt] *n.* . . .

6．与英国发音有规律性对应变化的美国发音，一般不另行标注(可参见*14*页《英美发音差异例释》)。与英国发音差别较大的美国发音，在同一方括号内加注，用分号隔开。如：

schedule ['ʃedjuːl; 美 'skedʒul] ...
militarily ['militərili; 美 ,mili'terili] ...

7．外来词语如果标注的是未经英语化的发音，则在音标前注明原语种。如：

madame ['mædəm; 法 madam] ...
　　* 表示 ['mædəm] 是英语化的发音，[madam] 是法语的发音。

（三）派生词及复合词的注音

1．列在词条内部的派生词，凡按本词的注音加上后缀部分的注音(见 *13* 页《常见后缀发音表》)发音者，一般不注音。但重音或音素起变化者，则在该词后注出音标。如：

main [mein] ... ‖~**ly** ...
　　* ~**ly** 不注音，应读作 ['meinli]。
industrialize [in'dʌstriəlaiz] ... ‖**industrialization** [in,dʌstriəlai'zeiʃən] ...
　　* 因重音起变化，**industrialization** 的音标全部注出。

2．列在词条内部的复合词，一般只在该词的重读音节前标注重音符号(分写的不标)。但音素起变化者，则在该词后注出音标。如：

work [wəːk] ... ‖'~,**basket** ...
　　* 只标重音，发音参照 work 和 basket 两词条。
above [ə'bʌv] ... ‖a'bove'board ...
　　* 因本词部分的重音不在第一音节上，全词拼出后加标重音。
three [θriː] ... ‖~**penny** ['θrepəni] ...
　　* 因音素起变化，~**penny** 的音标全部注出。

（四）其　它

1．例证、习语、复合词等中若出现本词典未收作词条的词，在该词后直接注出音标。如：

coup [kuː] ... ‖~ *d'état* [dei'tɑː] ...

2．音标中有时使用隔音符号分隔两个音节，表示两侧邻接的音素要按音节构成位置分别读出。如：

outskirt ['aut-skəːt] ...
　　* 表示 [t] 和 [s] 都要分别读出，全词不能读作 ['auts-kəːt]。

略 语 表

（以下四类略语分别以笔划为序排列）

[日]日语　　　　　　　　　[阿拉伯]阿拉伯语　　　　　　[爱尔兰]爱尔兰语
[汉]汉语　　　　　　　　　[英]英国特有用语　　　　　　[斯瓦希里]斯瓦希里语
[印地]印地语　　　　　　　[拉]拉丁语　　　　　　　　　[意]意大利语
[西]西班牙语　　　　　　　[法]法语　　　　　　　　　　[德]德语
[苏格兰]苏格兰语　　　　　[俄]俄语　　　　　　　　　　[澳]澳大利亚特有用语
[希]希腊语　　　　　　　　[美]美国特有用语

[口]口语　　　　　　　　　[贬]贬义　　　　　　　　　　[谚]谚语
[方]方言　　　　　　　　　[诗]诗歌用语　　　　　　　　[喻]比喻
[古]古语　　　　　　　　　[俚]俚语　　　　　　　　　　[蔑]蔑称
[讽]讽刺语　　　　　　　　[俗]俗语
[罕]罕用　　　　　　　　　[谑]戏谑语

【心】心理学　　　　　　　【罗神】罗马神话　　　　　　【哲】哲学
【史】历史　　　　　　　　【宗】宗教　　　　　　　　　【逻】逻辑学
【军】军事　　　　　　　　【经】经济　　　　　　　　　【商】商业
【戏】戏剧　　　　　　　　【律】法律　　　　　　　　　【摄】摄影
【体】体育　　　　　　　　【音】音乐
【希神】希腊神话　　　　　【语】语言学

【工】工业　　　　　　　　【地】地质学；地理学　　　　【空】航空
【无】无线电　　　　　　　【机】机械工程　　　　　　　【建】建筑工程
【天】天文学　　　　　　　【自】自动控制　　　　　　　【药】药物；药物学
【化】化学　　　　　　　　【交】交通运输　　　　　　　【测】测量
【气】气象学　　　　　　　【宇】宇宙空间技术　　　　　【原】原子能
【水】水利　　　　　　　　【农】农业　　　　　　　　　【海】航海
【电】电工；电学　　　　　【医】医学　　　　　　　　　【船】造船
【印】印刷　　　　　　　　【冶】冶金　　　　　　　　　【植】植物；植物学
【生】生物学　　　　　　　【纺】纺织工业　　　　　　　【微】微生物学
【生化】生物化学　　　　　【矿】矿业；矿物学　　　　　【解】解剖学
【讯】电信　　　　　　　　【物】物理学　　　　　　　　【数】数学
【动】动物；动物学　　　　【油】石油工业；石油化学

说明：① 略语用于注明词源、修辞色彩、学科等。
　　　② 有些以本表略语为基础构成的略语，不再收入本表。如：[美俚]（指美国俚语）；[主方]（指
　　　　 主要用于方言）；【英史】（指英国历史）等。
　　　③ 未经缩略、意义自明的，也不收入本表。如：[委婉语]；【会计】；【基督教】等。

国际音标和韦氏音标①对照表

国际音标	韦氏音标	例 词	国际音标注音	韦氏音标注音	其 他 例 词
iː	'ē, ˌē	see	[siː]	['sē]	even, bleed, amoeba, people, machine, field, key, Caesar, quay, beat, receive
i	ē, i	easy	['iːzi]	['ēzē, -zi]	city, this, busy, build, English
e	e	bed	[bed]	['bed]	desk, bread, leopard
æ	a	map	[mæp]	['map]	add, plaid
ɑː	ä, ȧ	father	['fɑːðə(r)]	['fäthə(r), 'fȧthə(r)]	saga, cart, heart, sergeant, calm, aunt
ɔ	ä	hot	[hɔt]	['hät]	clock, waddle
ɔː	ȯ	all	[ɔːl]	['ȯl]	saw, shore, walk, author, fought, taught, board, door, pour, order
u	u̇	book	[buk]	['bu̇k]	good, put, wolf, should
uː	ü	rule	[ruːl]	['rül]	food, two, soup, blue, move, grew, manoeuvre
ʌ	'ə, ˌə	custom	['kʌstəm]	['kəstəm]	sun, son, couple, humdrum, abut, flood
əː	ər, ə̄	bird	[bəːd]	['bərd, 'bə̄d]	fur, work, term, learn, myrtle
ə	ə(r)	sister	['sistə]	['sistə(r)]	worker, actor
ə	ə	about	[ə'baut]	[ə'bau̇t]	China, possible, gallop, circus
ə	°	botany	['botəni]	['bät°nē]	
ei	ā	day	[dei]	['dā]	name, rain, veil, obey, eight, break
ai	ī	side	[said]	['sīd]	ice, fly, either, aisle, height
ou②, ou	ō	go	[gou]	['gō]	note, low, toe, sew, road, soul, beau, omit, November
au	au̇	now	[nau]	['nau̇]	out, how, bough
ɔi	ȯi	boy	[bɔi]	['bȯi]	coin, noisy, destroy, buoy
iə	i(ə)r, iə	here	[hiə]	['hi(ə)r, -iə]	ear, deer, weird
ɛə	e(ə)r, a(ə)r	care	[kɛə]	['ke(ə)r, 'ka(ə)r]	dare, their, pear, there, air
ɔə③	ō(ə)r, ȯ(ə)r	door	[dɔə]	['dō(ə)r, 'dȯ(ə)r]	pour, more

国际音标	韦氏音标	例 词	国际音标注音	韦氏音标注音	其 他 例 词
uə	u̇(ə)r	p**oor**	[puə]	['pu̇(ə)r]	**tour, moor**
ju:	yü	**you**th	[ju:θ]	['yüth]	**use, few, view, cue, feud, beauty, queue**
p	p	**p**en	[pen]	['pen]	**pepper, lip, speak**
b	b	**b**aby	['beibi]	['bābē]	**cab, hobby**
t	t	**t**ime	[taim]	['tīm]	**talked, bottom, thyme**
d	d	**d**esk	[desk]	['desk]	**did, ladder**
k	k	**c**ook	[kuk]	['ku̇k]	**kick, car, acquaint, character, account, picturesque, liquor**
g	g	**g**o	[gou]	['gō]	**big, egg, ghost, guard, vague**
m	m	**m**ap	[mæp]	['map]	**him, bomb, hymn, hammer**
n	n	**n**ine	[nain]	['nīn]	**own, knife, pneumonia, gnaw, runner**
ŋ	ŋ	si**ng**	[siŋ]	['siŋ]	**ink, English, tongue**
l	l	**l**ittle	['litl]	['litᵊl]	**lily, world, tall**
f	f	**f**ifty	['fifti]	['fiftē]	**five, cuff, photo, rough**
v	v	**v**ery	['veri]	['verē]	**vivid, of, Stephen,**
θ	th	**th**in	[θin]	['thin]	**three, bath**
ð	t͟h	**th**en	[ðen]	['t͟hen]	**this, with, bathe**
s	s	**s**ix	[siks]	['siks]	**source, city, scene, loss**
z	z	**z**ero	['ziərou]	['zērō, 'zi(ə)rō]	**zone, was, drizzle, scissors, xenophobe**
ʃ	sh	**sh**oe	[ʃu:]	['shü]	**ship, ocean, machine, sugar, social, portion, pension, conscience, mission**
ʒ	zh	plea**s**ure	['pleʒə]	['plezhər]	**vision, rouge, azure, measure**
r	r	**r**ight	[rait]	['rīt]	**radio, rhythm, parrot, wrong**
h	h	**h**at	[hæt]	['hat]	**ahead, who**
tʃ	ch	**ch**urch	[tʃə:tʃ]	['chərch]	**catch, future, question, righteous**
dʒ	j	**j**oin	[dʒɔin]	['jȯin]	**judge, gem, sandwich, soldier**
w	w	**w**e	[wi:]	['wē]	**well, quiet, choir**
ʍw	hw	**wh**eat	[ʍwi:t]	['hwēt]	**when**
j	y	**y**es	[jes]	['yes]	**yet, union, hallelujah**

注: ① 韦氏音标指 Merriam-Webster Pronunciation Symbols。
　　② 双元音 [ou] 的主要变读音为 [əu]、[o]、[ə] 等，[o] 和 [ə] 主要出现在非重读音节中。
　　③ 双元音 [ɔə] 是 [ɔ:] 的变读音。如 **door** 可读作 [dɔ:] 或 [dɔə]。

常见后缀发音表

-able [-əbl]

-age [-idʒ]

-al [-əl]

-ally [-əli]

-an [-ən]

-ance [-əns]

-ancy [-ənsi]

-ant [-ənt]

-ard [-əd]

-ary [-əri]

-ate 构成名词或形容词读作 [-it];
构成动词读作 [-eit]

-ation [-'eiʃən]

-crat [-kræt]

-cy [-si]

-dom [-dəm]

-ed 在除 [d] 外的浊辅音和元音后读作 [-d];
在除 [t] 外的清辅音后读作 [-t];
在 [t]、[d] 后读作 [-id]

-en [-ən]

-ence [-əns]

-ency [-ənsi]

-ent [-ənt]

-er [-ə]

-ery [-əri]

-es 在 [s]、[z]、[ʃ]、[tʃ] 等辅音后读作 [-iz];
在元音和辅音 [v] 后读作 [-z]

-ess [-is]

-fold [-fould]

-ful 构成形容词读作 [-ful];
构成名词读作 [-ful]

-fully [-fuli, -fəli]

-fy [-fai]

-gram [-græm]

-graph [-grɑːf]

-hood [-hud]

-ial [-iəl]

-ian [-jən, -iən]

-ible [-əbl, -ibl]

-ic [-ik]

-ical [-ikəl]

-ing [-iŋ]

-ise [-aiz]

-ish [-iʃ]

-ism [-izəm]

-ist [-ist]

-ite [-ait]

-ity [-iti]

-ive [-iv]

-ize [-aiz]

-kin [-kin]

-less [-lis]

-let [-lit]

-like [-laik]

-ling [-liŋ]

-ly [-li]

-ment [-mənt]

-ness [-nis]

-or [-ə]

-ous [-əs]

-ry [-ri]

-s 在 [s]、[z]、[ʃ]、[ʒ]、[tʃ]、[dʒ] 等辅音后读作 [-iz];在
除 [z]、[ʒ]、[dʒ] 外的浊辅音和元音后读作 [-z];
在除 [s]、[ʃ]、[tʃ] 外的清辅音后读作 [-s]

-ship [-ʃip]

-sion [-ʃən, -ʒən]

-some [-səm]

-tion [-ʃən]

-tious [-ʃəs]

-tress [-tris]

-trix [-triks]

-ure [-ə]

-ward(s) [-wəd(z)]

-ways [-weiz]

-wise [-waiz]

-y [-i]

英美发音差异例释

英	美	例　　词	注　　音 英	注　　音 美
a:—æ		glass	[glɑ:s]	[glæs]
		can't	[kɑ:nt]	[kænt]
iər—i(:)r		hero	['hiərou]	['hi:ro:]
		appearance	[ə'piərəns]	[ə'pirəns]
ɔ—a		shop	[ʃɔp]	[ʃap]
		dollar	['dɔlə]	['dalər]
ɔ—ɔ:		dog	[dɔg]	[dɔ:g]
		moth	[mɔθ]	[mɔ:θ]
ɔ:—o:		editorial	[ˌedi'tɔ:riəl]	[ˌedi'to:riəl]
		orient	['ɔ:riənt]	['o:riənt]
uər—ur		assurance	[ə'ʃuərəns]	[ə'ʃurəns]
		curious	['kjuəriəs]	['kjuriəs]
ʌr—ə:r		hurry	['hʌri]	['hə:ri]
		worry	['wʌri]	['wə:ri]
ju:—u:		duly	['dju:li]	['du:li]
		nuclear	['nju:kliə]	['nu:kliər]
ə—ə		ration	['ræʃən]	['ræʃən]
		medical	['medikəl]	['medikəl]
ai—i		agile	['ædʒail]	['ædʒil]
		fragile	['frædʒail]	['frædʒil]

说明: ① 在美国发音中,只要单词中有 **r** 字母,就需发相应的 [r] 音,如: **work** [wə:rk], **far** [fɑ:r]。而在英国发音中,[r] 音只出现在元音前。

② 以上例释只表示英美发音中某些对应性的差异。英美发音中一致或类似之处均不在本表内反映,如 **saga** 在英美发音中都读作 ['sɑ:gə], **all** 在英美发音中都读作 [ɔ:l]。

非英语语音例释

音　　　标	例　　　　　　　　　词	
a	*agrément*	[法 agremã]
y	*brut*	[法 bryt]
ø	*à deux*	[法 a dø]
œ	*jeune*	[法 ʒœn]
ɛ̃	*pince-nez*	['pɛ̃:nsnei]
ɐ̃	*são*	[葡 sɐ̃u]
ã	*en*	[法 ã]
ɔ̃	Gabon	[法 gabɔ̃]
ɯ	ugh	[ɯ:x]
ɲ	Gdańsk	[波 g'daɲsk]
ɸ	faugh	[pɸ:]
ç	*ewigkeit*	['eiviçkait]
x	loch	[lɔx]
ɥ	nuance	[法 nɥɑ̃:s]
ɱ	hem	[ɱm]

A

a [强 ei; 弱 ə], **an** [强 æn; 弱 ən, n] [a 用于以辅音音素开始的词前; an 用于以元音音素开始的词前] *art.* [不定冠词] ① (非特指的) 一 (个): *a high building* 一座高楼 / *an hour* 一个小时 / *a foreign guest* 一位外宾 ②(一类事物中的)任何一个: *A square has four sides.* 正方形有四条边。③每一(个): *sixty km an hour* 每小时六十公里 ④ 同一(个): *Things of a kind come together; people of a mind fall into the same group.* 物以类聚,人以群分。⑤[用于两件通常配在一起的东西前]: *a knife and fork* 一副刀叉 ⑥[用于某些复数名词前,表示一个单位]: *spend an additional two weeks* 再花两星期 ⑦[用于不可数的抽象名词前,表示一种、某种]: *a deep hatred for the enemies* 对敌人的深仇大恨 ⑧[用于某些物质名词前,表示一种、一客等]: *a green tea* 一种绿茶 / *an ice cream* 一客冰淇淋 ⑨[用于专有名词前,表示类似的一个或某一个]: *A Mr Lin is looking for you.* 一位姓林的在找你。⑩[用于专有名词前,表示某人的一部作品、一件艺术品,或某厂的一件产品]: *a complete Lu Hsun* 一套鲁迅全集 [注意下列句子和短语中 a 或 an 的位置: How profound *a* lesson (或 What *a* profound lesson) 多么深刻的一课! / on so grand *an* occasion (或 on such *a* grand occasion) 在这样隆重的场合 / It is too difficult *a* book for beginners. 对初学的人说来这本书太难了。]

aback [ə'bæk] *ad.* ①向后 ②[海]逆帆 ‖*be taken ~* 吃了一惊

abacus ['æbəkəs] ([复] abaci ['æbəsai] 或 abacuses) *n.* ①算盘: use (或 work) an ~ 打算盘 ②[建] (圆柱顶部的) 顶板

abacus

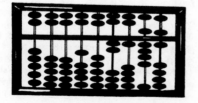

abandon [ə'bændən] **I** *vt.* ① 抛弃,放弃: ~ smoking 戒烟 / In his early days he ~*ed* medicine *for* literature. 他早年弃医学文。/ ~ an attempt 放弃尝试 / ~ sb. *to* the mercy of 听任某人由…摆布 ②离弃(家园、船只、飞机等) ③叛离,丢弃(信仰等) ④遗弃(妻、女等) **II** *n.* 放任,纵情; 无拘无束: with ~ 恣意地,放肆地 ‖~ *oneself to sth.* 沉湎于某事; ~ *oneself to despair* 陷入绝望 ‖~*ed* *a.* ①被抛弃的; 被遗弃的 ② 自我放任的; 极恶的 ③无约束的,无度的 / ~*ee* [ə,bændə'ni:] *n.* 【律】受领人(或主张有权受领)被遗弃财物者;(海运保险中)由保险人委以海损财物全部权利的承保人 / ~*ment* *n.* ①放弃,抛弃; 遗弃 ②放任,放纵

abase [ə'beis] *vt.* 使谦卑,使降低地位(或身分等) ‖~ *oneself* 谦卑 ‖~*ment* *n.*

abash [ə'bæ∫] *vt.* 使羞愧,使窘迫 ‖~*ment* *n.*

abate [ə'beit] ❶ *vt.* ①减少,减轻,减退;降(价) ②废除,撤销(法令等);除去(妨碍等) ❷ *vi.* ①(洪水、风暴、病痛等)减少,减轻,减退: His anger has ~*d*. 他的怒气消了。②(法令等)被废除,成为无效 ‖~*ment* *n.*

abattoir ['æbətwɑ:] *n.* [法]屠场

abbess ['æbis] *n.* 女修道院院长

abbey ['æbi] *n.* ① 修道院,大寺院,大教堂; 全院修道士(或修道女) ②[the A-] 威斯敏斯特教堂 (=Westminster Abbey)

abbot ['æbət] *n.* 男修道院院长;大寺院住持 ‖*the Abbot of Misrule* (英国) 主持圣诞节狂欢会的人(尤指十五、十六世纪时)

abbreviate [ə'bri:vieit] : *vt.* ① 缩写; 简略: "Monday" is ~*d* to "Mon." "Monday" 被缩写成 "Mon."。/ "AF" is ~*d from* "air force". "AF" 是 "air force" 的缩写。②缩短 (访问等);节略(读物等): The ceremony was ~*d* by rain. 因为下雨,仪式举行得很简短。‖**abbreviation** [ə,bri:vi'ei∫ən] *n.* ① 缩写;缩短;节略 ②缩写式;缩写词 / **abbreviator** *n.* 缩写者;节略者

abdicate ['æbdikeit] ❶ *vt.* 退(位),放弃(职位、权力等) ❷ *vi.* (国王)退位 ‖**abdication** [,æbdi'kei∫ən] *n.* / **abdicator** *n.* 退位者

abdomen ['æbdəmen, æb'doumen] *n.* 腹(部)

abduct [æb'dʌkt] *vt.* ① 诱拐,劫持 ②【生】外展 ‖~**ion** [æb'dʌk∫ən] *n.* / ~**or** *n.* ① 诱拐者,拐子 ②【解】外展肌 (= ~or muscle)

abet [ə'bet] (abetted; abetting) *vt.* ①教唆,唆使;煽动 ②帮助,支持 ‖~**ment** *n.* / **abettor, abetter** *n.* 唆使者;煽动者

abeyance [ə'beiəns] *n.* 中止，暂搁；(所有权等的) 未定: The matter is kept in ～. 这事暂被搁置起来。/ statutes fallen into ～ 已失效的法令

abhor [əb'hɔ:] (abhorred; abhorring [əb'hɔ:riŋ]) *vt.* 憎恶，厌恶 ‖**abhorrer** [əb'hɔ:rə] *n.* 憎恶者 厌恶者

abide [ə'baid] (abode [ə'boud] 或 abided) ❶ *vi.* ① 遵守(法律、诺言、决定等)；坚持(意见等) (by): ～ by the consequences 承担后果 ②持续 ③[古] 逗留，住 (at, in) ❷ *vt.* ①[常用于否定句和疑问句]忍受，容忍: I can't ～ such people. 对这种人我不能容忍。②顶住 ③等候 ‖**abidance** *n.* ①遵守 ②持续 ③居住 / **abiding** *a.* 持久的，永久的

ability [ə'biliti] *n.* ①能力: the ～ to speak a foreign language 说一种外语的能力 ②才能，才智；[复]技能: a man of ～ 有才能的人 / leadership ～ 领导才干 / manifold *abilities* 多方面的才能 / to the best of one's ～ 尽最大努力

abject ['æbdʒekt] *a.* ①(情况等)可怜的，凄惨的: ～ poverty 赤贫 ②(人或行为)卑下的；卑鄙的 ‖～**ion** [æb'dʒekʃən] *n.* / ～**ly** *ad.*

abjure [əb'dʒuə] *vt.* 发誓断绝；公开放弃(意见等) ‖**abjuration** [,æbdʒuə'reiʃən] *n.*

ablaze [ə'bleiz] *a.* [常作表语] & *ad.*①着火 ②闪耀: be ～ with lights 灯火辉煌 ③兴奋，激昂: His face was ～ with anger. 他满面怒容。

able ['eibl] *a.* ①有能力的；有才干的，能干的: an ～ leader 有才干的领导者 ②显示出才智的: an ～ portrait 笔法娴熟的肖像画 ③【律】有法定资格的 ‖*be ～ to* ... 能，会 (=can, 常用以表示 can 所不能表示的未来或完成的概念): We shall *be ～ to* finish the work tomorrow. 我们可以在明天完成这工作。/ He has not *been ～ to* come. 他没有能来。/ *spell* ～ [美俚] 有能力，干练 ‖'～-'**bodied** *a.* 体格健全的，强壮的 / '～-'**minded** *a.* 能干的 / ～ **seaman**【军】(英)二等水兵；[海]一等水手 (=～-bodied seaman)

ablution [ə'blu:ʃən] *n.* ①[常用复]沐浴；【宗】沐浴(仪式)，洗手(仪式) ②沐浴(或洗手)仪式用的水

abnormal [æb'nɔ:məl] *a.* 反常的，变态的，不规则的 ‖～**ity** [,æbnɔ:'mæliti] *n.* ① 反常，变态，不规则 ②反常的事物；畸形 / ～**ly** *ad.* ‖～ **psychology** (以精神病患者等为研究对象的)病态心理学

aboard [ə'bɔ:d] *I ad.* ①在船(或飞机、车)上；上船 (或飞机、车) ②沿船边 *II prep.* 在(船、飞机、车)上；上(船、飞机、车) ‖**All** ～! 请上船(或上飞机、上车)! 开船啦! (或: 开车啦! 飞机要起飞啦!) / **close** (或 **hard**) ～ 紧靠船边 / **fall** ～ 与(他船)碰撞 / **lay** ～ (为了进行海战等而)靠近(他船) / **Welcome** ～! 请上船(或上飞机、上车)!

abode[1] [ə'boud] *n.* 住所: make one's ～ 居住 / take up one's ～ with sb. 开始与某人一起居住

abode[2] [ə'boud] abide 的过去式和过去分词

abolish [ə'bɔliʃ] *vt.* 废除(法律、习惯等)；取消：

able. *a.* 可废除的 / ～**er** *n.* 废除者 / ～**ment** *n.*

abolition [,æbə'liʃən] *n.* (法律、习惯等的)废除；取消

abominable [ə'bɔminəbl] *a.* ① 可恶的，讨厌的 ② [口](天气、食物等)极坏的 ‖**abominably** *ad.* ‖**Abominable Snowman** 雪人 (传说生存在喜马拉雅山上的一种动物，据信是熊)

abominate [ə'bɔmineit] *vt.* 厌恶，憎恨；[口]不喜欢 ‖**abomination** [ə,bɔmi'neiʃən] *n.* ①厌恶，憎恨: hold sth. in *abomination* 厌恶某事物 ②令人讨厌的事物

aboriginal [,æbə'ridʒənl] *I a.* 土著的 *II n.* 土著居民；土生动植物 ‖～**ly** *ad.*

aborigines [,æbə'ridʒini:z] [复] *n.* 土著居民；土生动植物

abortion [ə'bɔ:ʃən] *n.* ①流产，小产，早产: induced ～ 人工流产 / threatened ～ 先兆流产 / habitual ～ 习惯性流产 ②(计划等的)失败，夭折: prove an ～ 终于失败 ③流产的胎儿(或胎)；畸形的人(或动物) ④【生】(动植物器官的)发育不全; 败育; 发育不全的动植物器官 ‖～**ist** *n.* 为人堕胎者

abortive [ə'bɔ:tiv] *a.* ①(药)有堕胎作用的; (药等)使病程中断的 ②流产的，早产的; (计划等)失败的，夭折的 ③【生】发育不全的 ‖～**ly** *ad.* / ～**ness** *n.*

abound [ə'baund] *vi.* ①(物产)丰富: Natural resources ～ in our country. 我国自然资源丰富。②盛产，富于; 多，充满 (with, in): That region ～*s with* rain all the year round. 那个地区终年多雨。

about [ə'baut] *I prep.* ① 在…周围，在…附近，在…身边: Have you a pen ～ you? 你带着笔吗? ② 在…各处，去…各处: take the foreign guests ～ the campus 带外宾参观校园 ③ 关于: What is all this ～? 这是怎么回事? ④(时刻、大小、数量等)近于: We left there ～ six o'clock. 我们大约六点钟离开那里的。/ That's ～ it. 差不多。⑤ 从事于: What are you ～? 你在干什么? *II ad.* ①周围，附近; 到处: ten miles ～ 周围十哩 / Don't drop cigarette ashes ～. 不要乱弹烟灰。②大约; 差不多: ～ two years ago 大约两年前 / The work is ～ finished. 工作快完了。③(转到)相反方向: *About* turn! (或 [美] *About* face!) 向后转! / go a long way ～ 兜了一个大圈 ④轮转: take turns ～ 轮流(做某事) ⑤(活动; 疾病)流行; 传开: The patient is up and ～ again. 病人已能起来走动了。/ The news is going ～. 消息正在传开。‖*be ～ to* ... 即将…: Autumn harvest *is ～ to* start. 快要秋收了。/ *How ～* ...? 见 how / *What* ～ ...? 见 what ‖～-**face** *n.* [ə'bautfeis] 向后转; (态度、意见等的)大改变: make a 180° ～-**face** 来一个一百八十度的大转弯 *vi.* [ə,baut'feis] 向后转; (在态度、意见等方面)作重大改变 / **a,bout-'ship** *vi.* [海]改变航向 / **a'bout-sledge** *n.* 大铁锤 / ～-**turn** [英] *n.* [ə'bauttə:n] =～-face (n.) *vi.*

[ə,baut'tə:n] =~-face (*vi.*)

above [ə'bʌv] **I** *prep.* ①[表示位置、职位等]在… 上面: 1,000 metres ~ sea level 海拔一千米 ② 在…的上游: The waterfall is ~ the bridge. 瀑 布在桥的上游一侧。③[表示数量、年龄等]在… 以上: It weighs ~ five tons. 这东西有五吨多 重。④[表示品质、行为、能力等]超出…之外: a man ~ vulgar interests 一个脱离了低级趣味 的人 / ~ all praise 赞扬不尽 / ~ reproach 无 可指责 / The problem is ~ me. 这个问题我不 懂(或不能解决)。/ We must not be ~ asking questions about things we do not understand. 不懂的事情,不要怕提出来问。**II** *ad.* ①在上面; 以上: His room is just ~. 他的房间就在上面。 ②在上游 ③上述: as (has been) indicated ~ 如 上面所指出 / the Powers ~ 【宗】天上 的众神 **III** *a.* 上面的;上述的: for the ~ reasons 根据上述的理由 **IV** *n.* ①上面; 上述 ② 上级: We should rely on our own efforts instead of asking help from ~. 我们应当自力更生,不要 向上级伸手。③【宗】上天, 天 ‖~ all 见 all / ~ oneself 自高自大;兴高采烈 ‖a'bove'board *a.* [常作表语] & *ad.* 公开(地),光明正大(地) / a'bove-'cited *a.* 上面所引的 / a'bove-ground *ad.* 在地上;还活着 / a'bove-'mentioned *a.* 上述的

abrasion [ə'breiʒən] *n.* ①擦掉;磨损 ②(皮肤等 的)擦伤处;磨损处 ③【地】磨蚀,浪蚀,海蚀

abrasive [ə'breisiv] **I** *a.* 有研磨(或磨蚀)作用的 **II** *n.* 研磨料(如金刚砂、砂纸等),磨蚀剂

abreast [ə'brest] *ad.* 相并,并肩: walk six ~ 六人 并肩而行 ‖*keep* (或 *be*) ~ *of* (或 *with*) 保持 与…并列: *keep* ~ *of* the times 与时代并进

abridge [ə'bridʒ] *vt.* ① 节略: an ~d edition 节 本 ②剥夺: ~ sb. *of* his rights 剥夺某人的权利 ‖**abridg(e)ment** *n.* ①节略 ②节本 ③(权利、 自由等)剥夺

abroad [ə'brɔ:d] *ad.* ①到国外;在国外: go ~ 出 国 / return from ~ 从国外回来 / at home and ~ 国内外 ②到处; 广泛: The happy tidings soon got (或 spread) ~. 喜讯不久就传开来。 ‖*be all* ~ ①感到莫明其妙 ②不中肯,离题

abrogate ['æbrougeit] *vt.* 取消,废除(法令、条约、 习惯等) ‖**abrogation** [,æbrou'geiʃən]

abrupt [ə'brʌpt] *a.* ① 突然的, 出其不意的: The road is full of ~ turns. 这条路有许多急转弯。 an ~ departure 突然离去 ②陡峭的,险峻的: an ~ slope 陡峭的斜坡 ③ 粗鲁的,无礼的: an ~ manner 无礼的态度 ④(讲话、文章等)不连 贯的,支离的 ‖~ion [ə'brʌpʃən] *n.* 突然分离,分 裂,断裂 / ~ly *ad.* / ~ness *n.*

abscond [əb'skɔnd] *vi.* (为躲避罪责、债务等)潜逃 ‖~ence *n.*

absence ['æbsəns] *n.* ①不在,缺席: ~ *from* classes 缺课 / an ~ rate 缺勤率 / leave of ~ 请假许 可;获准的假期 / during sb.'s ~ *in* Shanghai 在

某人暂去上海的期间 / during sb.'s ~ *from* Shanghai 在某人暂离上海的期间 ②缺乏: in the ~ of these conditions 在缺乏这些条件的情况下 ‖*of mind* 心不在焉

absent ['æbsənt] **I** *a.* ①不在,缺席: He is ~ *from* France. 他不在法国。/ He is ~ *in* France. 他 外出了,暂时在法国。/ go ~ without leave 擅离 职守(尤指军队中开小差);[美俚]越狱, 逃亡 ② 缺乏的 ③不在意的,漫不经心的: in an ~ sort of way 有些心不在焉地 **II** [æb'sent] *vt.* [~ oneself] 缺席: ~ onese'f *from* a meeting on some pretext 借故不去开会 / ~ly *ad.*

absentee [,æbsən'ti:] *n.* 不在者,缺席者; 外住者 ‖~ism *n.* 旷课; 旷工 ‖~ ballot 缺席选举人票 (指缺席者预先交给选举机构的票)

absent-minded ['æbsənt'maindid] *a.* 心不在焉的 ‖~ly *ad.* / ~ness *n.*

absolute ['æbsəlju:t] **I** *a.* ①绝对的: ~ equal- itarianism 绝对平均主义 / ~ ceiling 【空】绝对 升限 / ~ zero 【物】绝对零度 (约为摄氏零下 273.16度) ②专制的,独裁的: ~ monarchy 君 主专制政体; 专制君主国 ③纯粹的,完全的: ~ alcohol 无水酒精 ④【语】独立的: an ~ participle 独立分词 / an ~ construction 独立结构 ⑤确实 的,的确如此的: an ~ fact 确确实实的事实 **II** *n.* 绝 对 ‖*the Absolute* ①【哲】绝对 ②【宗】上帝,神 ‖~ly *ad.* / ~ness *n.* / **absolutism** *n.* ①专 制主义 ②绝对论 / **absolutist** *n.* ① 专制主义 者 ②绝对论者 *a.* ①专制主义的 ②绝对论的

absolution [,æbsə'lju:ʃən] *n.* ①(罪、惩罚、责任的) 免除;赦免 ②【宗】忏悔式;赦罪礼

absolve [əb'zɔlv] *vt.* ①解除;赦免,宽恕: ~ sb. *from* sin 【宗】赦免某人的罪 ②免除,开脱: ~ sb. *from* an obligation 免除某人的一项责任

absorb [əb'sɔ:b] *vt.* ①吸收(水、热、光等);(无反 冲地)承受(震动等)②吸引(注意);使专心,使精 神贯注: ~ed in thoughts 在沉思中 ③并入,同 化 ④承担(费用等) ‖~er *n.* 吸收器: a shock ~er 减震器 / ~ing *a.* 非常吸引人的,引人入 胜的

abstain [əb'stein] *vi.* ①戒,避免,避开 (*from*): ~ *from* wine (或 drinking) 戒酒,不喝酒 / ~ *from* speaking 默不作声 ②弃权 (*from*): ~ *from* voting 弃权,不投票 ‖~er *n.* 戒…的人 (尤指不喝酒的人)

abstention [æb'stenʃən] *n.* ①戒,避免,避开 (*from*) ②弃权: ~ *from* voting 投票时弃权 / six votes for, four against, and three ~s 六票 赞成,四票反对,三票弃权

abstract ['æbstrækt] **I** *a.* ①抽象的: an ~ noun 【语】抽象名词 / an ~ number 【数】不名数,抽象数 ②理论性的,无实际意义的 ③难解的,深奥的 ④(艺术上)抽象派的 **II** *n.* ①摘要,概括: make an ~ of 把…的要点摘录下来 ②抽象; 抽象物, 抽象观念 ③【化】提出物,萃取物 **III** [æb'strækt] *vt.* ① 提取,抽取: ~ metal from ore 从矿石提

取金属 ②[口]窃取 ③使抽象(化) ④摘录…的要点 ⑤ 转移 (注意等): Nothing can ~ his mind while he works. 他工作时，什么也不能分散他的心思。‖in the ~ 抽象地; 理论上 ‖**~ly** *ad.* / **~ness** *n.*

abstracted [æb'stræktid] *a.* 分心的, 心不在焉的; 抽出了的: with an ~ air 出神地, 心不在焉地 ‖**~ly** *ad.*

abstraction [æb'strækʃən] *n.* ①抽象(化); 抽象作用: scientific ~ 科学的抽象 ②抽象观念; 抽象词语 ③出神, 心不在焉: an air of ~ 心不在焉的神态 ④抽象派的艺术品 ⑤ 提取; 分离 ‖**~ism** *n.* 抽象派艺术 / **~ist** 抽象派艺术家, 抽象派艺术爱好者

abstruse [æb'struːs] *a.* 难解的, 深奥的 ‖**~ly** *ad.* / **~ness** *n.*

absurd [əb'səːd] *a.* 不合理的, 荒谬的, 可笑的, 愚蠢的 ‖**~ity** *n.* 荒谬; 谬论; 荒唐(或愚蠢)的行为: sink into ~ity 做荒唐(或愚蠢)的事; 陷入荒谬 / a glaring ~ity 荒谬绝伦的言论(或行动) / **~ly** *ad.* / **~ness** *n.*

abundance [ə'bʌndəns] *n.* 丰富, 充裕: a year of ~ 丰年 / grain in ~ 充足的粮食 / an ~ of sunshine 充足的阳光 / ~ of the heart 感情的丰富

abundant [ə'bʌndənt] *a.* ①丰富的, 充裕的: an ~ year 丰年 / an ~ harvest 丰收 / ~ in petroleum deposits 石油蕴藏量丰富的 ② 充分的: ~ proof 充分的证据 ‖**~ly** *ad.*

abuse I [ə'bjuːz] *vt.* ①滥用, 妄用: ~ one's authority (power) 滥用职权(权力) ②[古]虐待, 凌辱 ③辱骂 ④[古][常用被动语态]欺骗 II [ə'bjuːs] *n.* ①滥用, 妄用 ②[古]虐待, 凌辱 ③辱骂: personal ~ 人身攻击 / heap ~ on sb. 肆意漫骂某人 ④陋习, 弊病: remedy an ~ 纠正陋习

abusive [ə'bjuːsiv] *a.* ①辱骂性的; 骂人的 ②滥用的; 被滥用的 ③陋习性的 ‖**~ly** *ad.* / **~ness** *n.*

abysmal [ə'bizməl] *a.* 无底的, 深不可测的: ~ ignorance 完全无知

abyss [ə'bis] *n.* ① 深渊 ② 阴间, 地狱 ‖**~al** *a.* ①深渊的, 深不可测的: ~al rock 【地】深成岩 ②(深度超过 300 呎的) 深海的

academic [ˌækə'demik] I *a.* ①(高等)专科院校的; 研究院的; 学会的 ②学术的: an ~ degree 学位 / ~ discussion 学术讨论 ③学究的, 书生气的; 空谈的 II *n.* ①大学生; 大学教师; 学究式人物 ②[复]空论

academy [ə'kædəmi] *n.* ①(高等)专科院校; 中等学校: a military ~ 陆军军官学校; 军事学院 ②研究院; 学会 ③[A-]学园(柏拉图讲哲学的地方); 柏拉图哲学(或学派)

accede [æk'siːd] *vi.* ①答应, 同意 (to) ②就任 (to) ③加入 (to)

accelerate [æk'seləreit] ❶ *vt.* 加速, 加快; 促进 ❷ *vi.* 增加速度 ‖**~d** 【物】加速的: ~d

motion 加速运动 / **acceleration** [ækˌseləˈreiʃən] *n.* ①加速, 促进 ②[物]加速度; 加速(作用)

accelerative [æk'selərətiv] *a.* 加速的, 促进的

accelerator *n.* ①加速者 ②[物]加速器, 加速装置; 加速电极 ③[化]加速剂, 促进剂, 催速剂

accent I ['æksənt] *n.* ① 重音: a primary (secondary) ~ 主(次)重音 ②重音符号 ③音调; 腔调; 口音: without an ~ 不带任何特殊的口音(指发音正确地) / with a strong (或 marked) Shanghai ~ 带有很重的上海口音 ④特征, 特点 ⑤ 着重 (on) II [æk'sent] *vt.* ① 重读 ②在…上加重音符号 ③ 使特别显著 ‖**~ual** [æk'sentjuəl] *a.* (关于)重音的

accentuate [æk'sentjueit] *vt.* ①重读 ②在…上加重音符号 ③ 强调, 着重指出 ‖**accentuation** [ækˌsentjuˈeiʃən] *n.*

accept [ək'sept] ❶ *vt.* ①接受, 领受: ~ criticism with an open mind 虚心接受批评 ②承认, 认可: ~ the truth of a statement 认为某句话不错 ③【商】承兑(票据等) ❷ *vi.* 同意, 承认; 认付, 承兑 (of) ‖**~ed** *a.* 公认的 / **~er**, **~or** *n.* ①领受人, 受主 ②【商】(票据的)承兑人 ③【无】接受器; 受主 ④[化]接受体; 被诱物

acceptable [ək'septəbl] *a.* 可接受的, 合意的, 受到欢迎的 ‖**acceptability** [əkˌseptə'biliti] *n.* / **~ness** *n.* / **acceptably** *ad.*

acceptance [ək'septəns] *n.* ①接受, 领受; 接收; 验收: an ~ test 验收试验 ②承认, 认可 ③【商】(票据等的)承兑 ‖**~ speech** [美]总统候选人接受政党提名时所作的演讲

access ['ækses] *n.* ①接近; 进入; 通路: a place easy (difficult) of ~ 易于(难以)进入的地方 / the ~ to a building 到达(或进入)大楼的通路 ②接近(或进入)的方法(或权利、机会等): You can easily get ~ to him. 你很容易接近(或见到)他。/ He is easy of ~. 他是易于接近的。③发作: an ~ of fever (rage) 发热(怒) ④增加, 增长 ‖**~ time** 【自】存取时间

accessary [æk'sesəri] I *n.* ①同谋, 帮凶, 从犯(美国常用 accessory) ②附件, 附属品 II *a.* ①同谋的 ②附属的, 附加的

accessible [æk'sesəbl] *a.* ①易接近的, 能进去的 (to): a place ~ to the public 公众可以进入的地方 ②易受影响的 (to) ③可以理解的 (to): easily ~ to beginners 易于为初学者理解的 ‖**accessibility** [ækˌsesiˈbiliti] *n.* / **accessibly** *ad.*

accession [æk'seʃən] I *n.* ①到达 (to); 接近: ~ to manhood 成年 ② 就职, 就任 (to) ③增加; 增加物 (to); 【律】财产自然增益 ④同意 II *vt.* 把(新书等)登记入册 ‖**~al** *a.* 附加的

accessory [æk'sesəri] I *n.* ① 附件, 附属品: the accessories of a car 汽车附件 ②[美]同谋, 帮凶, 从犯: an ~ before (after) the fact 【律】事前(后)从犯 ③[复]妇女全套衣饰中的小配件(指提包、手套等) II *a.* ①附属的, 附加的: an ~ factory 附属工厂 / a set of ~ equipment 一套

附带设备 / ~ fruit【植】附果 ②同谋的 ‖**accessorial** [ˌæksə'sɔːriəl] *a.* 附属的

accident ['æksidənt] *n.* ①意外的事, 偶然的事: a mere ~ 纯粹是偶然的事 ②事故: a traffic ~ 交通事故 ③【地】褶皱; 地形不平 ‖*Accidents will happen in the best regulated families.* [谚] 家规再严, 丑事难免。/ **by** ~ 偶然 / *without* ~ 安全地 ‖~ **insurance** 事故保险 / '~-'**prone** *a.* (因粗枝大叶而)特别易出事故的 / '~-'**proneness** *n.* (因粗枝大叶而)特别易出事故

accidental [ˌæksi'dentl] I *a.* ①偶然的, 意外的 ②附属的 II *n.* ①非本质的属性 ②【音】(升、降、还原)临时符 ‖~**ly** *ad.* 偶然地

acclaim [ə'kleim] I *vt.* ①向…欢呼, 为…喝采: be widely ~ed 受到广泛的赞扬 ②以欢呼声拥戴(或推举、承认): He was ~ed (as) the winner. 在欢呼声中他被承认为得胜者。❷ *vi.* 欢呼, 喝采 II *n.* 欢呼, 喝采

acclamation [ˌæklə'meiʃən] *n.* ①欢呼, 喝采 ②鼓掌欢呼表示通过: carry a motion by ~ 以欢呼或鼓掌(指不用投票)通过一项动议

acclimatize [ə'klaimətaiz] ❶ *vt.* 使服水土, 使适应气候: You will soon get ~d (对新环境、气候等)你很快就会适应的。❷ *vi.* 服水土, 适应气候 ‖**acclimatization** [əˌklaimətai'zeiʃən] *n.*

accommodate [ə'kɔmədeit] ❶ *vt.* ①容纳, 接纳: This university auditorium can ~ over three thousand people. 这座大学礼堂能容纳三千余人。/ ~ sb. for the night 留某人过夜 ②供应, 供给; 提供: ~ sb. *with* lodging (a loan) 向某人提供住宿(贷款) / a well ~d hotel 设备良好的旅馆 ③使适应, 使迁就; 调节: ~ oneself *to* new conditions 适应新的情况 ④调停(争端等) ❷ *vi.* 适应 ‖**accommodating** *a.* 与人方便的; 随和的 / **accommodator** *n.* (帮佣的)替工

accommodation [əˌkɔmə'deiʃən] *n.* ①[美常用复] 招待设备, 膳宿供应; 居住舱室: This hospital has ~(s) for 300 patients. 这所医院有三百张病床。/ an ~ deck 舱室甲板 ②提供便利的设备(或用具): office ~s 办公用具 ③适应, 调节 (*to*) ④(争端等的)和解, 调停 ⑤贷款 ‖~ **bill** 通融汇票 / ~ **bridge** 专用桥梁; 特设桥梁 / ~ **ladder** 舷梯 / ~ **road** 专用道路 / ~ **train** [美]慢车

accompaniment [ə'kʌmpənimənt] *n.* ①伴随物; 附属物 ②伴奏; 伴唱; (声音)伴随: sing to the ~ of the accordion 由手风琴伴奏着歌唱

accompany [ə'kʌmpəni] ❶ *vt.* ①伴随, 陪同: ~ a foreign visitor to the airport (station) 送外宾去机场(车站) / one's speech with gestures 以手势帮助说话 ②为…伴奏: The singer was *accompanied* at the piano by Mr Wang. 王先生为歌唱家担任钢琴伴奏。❷ *vi.* 伴奏 ‖~**ing** *a.* 随同的, 附见的: an ~**ing** diagram 附图

accomplice [ə'kɔmplis] *n.* 同谋, 同犯, 帮凶

accomplish [ə'kɔmpliʃ] *vt.* 完成(任务等) ‖~**ed** *a.* ①完成了的, 竣工的 ②有才艺的, 有造诣的: ~ed *in* 擅长… / ~**ment** *n.* ①完成 ②成就 ③[复]才艺, 造诣, 技能

accord [ə'kɔːd] I ❶ *vt.* ①使一致 ②给予(欢迎、称颂等): ~ sb. a warm welcome 向某人表示热烈欢迎 ❷ *vi.* 符合, 调和, 一致 (*with*): ~ *with* the fundamental interests of the people 符合人民的基本利益 II *n.* ①一致, 调和, 符合 ②'(国家之间的)协议 ③【音】和弦 ‖*in* ~ *with* 同…一致 / *of one's own* ~ 自愿地, 主动地 / *out of* ~ *with* 同…不一致 / *with one* ~ 一致地

accordance [ə'kɔːdəns] *n.* ①一致 ②给予 ‖*in* ~ *with* 与……一致; 按照, 依据: *in* ~ *with* the principle of consultation on an equal footing 根据平等协商的原则

according [ə'kɔːdiŋ] *ad.* [只用于下列两个习语中] ‖~ *as* [后接从句]根据…而…, 按照…而…… / ~ *to* 按照; 根据…所说; 随着…的不同(而不同): ~ *to* today's papers 根据今天的报纸 / from each ~ *to* his ability 各尽所能

accordingly [ə'kɔːdiŋli] *ad.* ①照着(办、做等); 相应地: We must ascertain the actual conditions and arrange ~. 我们必须了解具体情况, 作出相应安排。②因此; 从而: The weather has changed suddenly, and we must alter our plans for rush-harvesting ~. 天气突然变了, 因而我们必须改变抢收计划。

accordion [ə'kɔːdjən] I *n.* 手风琴 II *a.* (象手风琴一样)可折迭的 ‖~**ist** *n.* 手风琴手

accordion

accost [ə'kɔst] *vt.* ① 走上前去跟(某人)讲话 ②(妓女等)勾引

account [ə'kaunt] I *n.* ①帐, 帐目; 帐户: keep (cast) ~s 记(算)帐 / charge (或 put) it to sb.'s ~ 把它记在某人帐上 ②算帐: be quick at ~s 算帐很快 ③(关于事件、人物等的)报道, 叙述, 描写: by sb.'s own ~ 根据某人自己所讲 ④原因, 理由: on this ~ 由于这个原因 / on (或 for) sb.'s ~ 因为某人的缘故 ⑤重要性; 价值; 考虑: a matter of great ~ 一件很重要的事 / hold … in no ~ 对…不重视 ⑥利润; 利益: find one's ~ in 在…中得到好处 ‖an ~ book 帐簿 / an

~ *payable* (*receivable*) 应付(收)帐 / *an ~ rendered* 结欠清单 / *an ~ sale* 代办交易细帐*; 赊销 / *an ~ stated* (债务人认为无误的) 确定清单 / *a current ~* (略作 a/c, A/C 或 C/A) 往来帐户; 活期存款帐户 / *an open ~* 未结算的帐目 **II ❶ vi.** [与 for 连用] ①说出(钱等的)用途: ~ *to sb. for the expenditure* 向某人汇报开支 ②说明(原因等): *That ~s for the delay of the train.* 那就是火车晚点的原因。/ *There is no ~ing for tastes.* 人各有所好。③[指数量等]占 ④捕捉; 杀死; 击落; 解决 **❷ vt.** 认为 ‖*a money of ~* 计算货币 / *balance ~s with* 与…结清帐目 / *be much* (*little*) *~ed of* 被重(轻)视 / *by* (或 *from*) *all ~s* 根据大家所说 / *call* (或 *bring*) *to ~* 责问 / *cast up ~s* [口] [谑] 呕吐 / *for ~ of* 为…代销 / *give a good ~ of oneself* ①付清帐 ②为自己辩护 ③[口] 干得好 / *go to one's ~* 死 / *hand in one's ~s* [美口]死 / *have an ~ to settle with sb.* 要跟某人算帐; 要责问某人 / *hold to ~* 使承担责任 / *in ~ with* 与…有帐务往来 / *lay one's ~ with* 把…计算在内; 期望 / *leave out of ~* 不考虑 / *make much* (*little*) *~ of* 重(轻)视 / *on ~ of* 因为/ *on all ~s* (或 *on every ~*) 无论如何 / *on no ~* (或 *not on any ~*)决不/*on one's own ~* ①为自己的利益 ②自行负责 ③依靠自己 / *pay on ~* 先付…(作为部分付款) / *render* (或 *yield*) *an ~* 报帐; 汇报 / *settle* (或 *square*) *an ~ with* 与…结清帐目/*take an ~ of* 把…列表; 把…登帐 / *take into ~* 考虑; 重视 / *take* (*no*) *~ of* (不)考虑; (不)重视 / *the great ~* 【宗】最后审判日 / *turn to* (*good*) *~* 利用

accountable [ə'kauntəbl] *a.* ①有说明义务的; 负有责任的: *He is ~ to us for this action.* 他对我们负有说明这一行动的责任。②可说明的 ‖**accountability** [ə,kauntə'biliti] *n.* / **accountably** *ad.*

accountant [ə'kauntənt] *n.* 会计: *a chartered ~* [英]会计师 / *a certified public ~* [美]会计师 ‖**accountancy** *n.* 会计工作 / **~ship** *n.* 会计职务 ‖*~-'general n.* 会计主任

accounting [ə'kauntiŋ] *n.* ①会计学 ②借贷对照表 ③清算帐目

accredit [ə'kredit] *vt.* ①相信; 认可 ②委任, 任命(大使等) ③把…归咎: ~ *a remark to sb.* 认为某句话是某人说的 / ~ *sb. with an action* 认为某个行动是某人做的 ④鉴定…为合格 ‖**~ation** [ə,kredi'teiʃən] *n.* ①大使等的任命 ②鉴定

accrue [ə'kru:] *vi.* (利息等) 自然增长

accumulate [ə'kju:mjuleit] **❶ vt.** 积累, 积聚: ~ *funds for* 为…积累资金 / ~ *a large amount of river mud for fertilizer* 积大量河泥作肥料 **❷ vi.** 积累; 堆积 ‖**accumulation** [ə,kju:mju'leiʃən] *n.* ①积累, 积聚 ②堆积物, 积聚物 / **accumulator** *n.* ①积聚者 【机】储蓄

器; [英]【电】蓄电池; [自]累加器, 存储器; [无]储能电路

accumulative [ə'kju:mjulətiv] *a.* ①积累的, 堆积的 ②喜欢积累的, 贪得的 ‖**~ly** *ad.*

accuracy ['ækjurəsi] *n.* 准确, 精确; 准确度; 【机】精(密)度

accurate ['ækjurit] *a.* 准确的; 精确的 ‖**~ly** *ad.*

accursed [ə'kə:sid], **accurst** [ə'kə:st] *a.* ①被诅咒的, 不幸的 ②可憎的, 可恶的

accusation [,ækju(:)'zeiʃən] *n.* ①责备, 谴责 ②控告, 起诉, 告发 ③(被告发的) 罪名 ‖*be under an ~* 被控告 / *bring an ~ against* 对…起诉, 谴责

accuse [ə'kju:z] *vt.* ①指责, 谴责: ~ *sb. of carelessness* 指责某人粗枝大叶 ②控诉, 控告: ~ *sb. of a crime* 控告某人犯罪 ‖*the ~d* 被告 ‖*~r n.* 谴责者, 起诉者

accustom [ə'kʌstəm] *vt.* 使习惯: ~ *oneself to* 使自己习惯于 / *be ~ed to work* (或 *to working*) *hard* 习惯于努力工作 / *be ~ed to hard work* 习惯于艰苦的工作 ‖**~ed** *a.* 惯常的

ace [eis] **I n.** ①(纸牌、骰子的)一点; 一点的纸牌, "A" 牌 ②(开赛车或飞机的)王牌驾驶员; (任何一行中的)能手, 专家 ③少许, 毫厘 ④(网球等运动中的) 发球得分; 得一分的发球 **II a.** 第一流的, 头等的 **III vt.** (在网球等运动中)以发球赢…一分 ‖*an ~ in the hole* ①正面朝下的 "A" 牌 ②秘藏的法宝, 备而未用的王牌 / *have an ~ up one's sleeve* 手中握有王牌; 有应急的妙计 / *trump sb.'s ~* 以王牌打某人的 "A" 牌; 向某人还击 / *within an ~ of* 离…只差一点儿 ‖*~-'high a.* 受崇敬的; 被喜爱的

acetic [ə'si:tik] *a.* 醋的; 醋酸的: ~ *acid* 醋酸(又称乙酸)

ache [eik] **I vi.** ①痛: *His head ~s.* 他头痛。/ *I am aching all over.* 我浑身疼痛。② [口]想念; 渴望: ~ *for sb.* 想念某人 **II n.** (连续固定的) 疼痛

achieve [ə'tʃi:v] *vt.* ①完成 ②达到(目的), 得到(胜利) ‖**achievable** *a.* 能作成的; 能达到的

achievement [ə'tʃi:vmənt] *n.* ①完成; 达到: *the ~ of one's object* 达到目的 ②成就, 成绩

acid ['æsid] **I a.** ①酸的, 酸味的 ②【化】酸的, 酸性的 ③[喻]尖刻的 **II n.** ①酸味物质 ②【化】酸 ③[美俚]麻醉药物(尤指麦角酸二乙基酰胺) ‖*'~proof a.* 耐酸的: *~proof stoneware* 耐酸缸器 / ~ *reaction* 酸性反应 / *'~-re'sistant a.* 耐酸的, 抗酸的 / *n.* 耐酸物, 抗酸物 / ~ *test* ①酸性试验 ②严峻的考验

acknowledge [ək'nɔlidʒ] *vt.* ①承认: *It is universally ~d that ....* …是大家所公认的。/ ~ *oneself beaten* 认输 ②告知收到(信件、礼物等): ~ (*receipt of* 或 *the receipt of*) *sb.'s letter* 向某人表示来信已收到 ③对(某人所做的事) 表示感谢 ④对(人)打招呼(表示认识)

acknowledg(e)ment [ək'nɔlidʒmənt] *n.* ①承认 ②收到的通知: *We have had no ~ of our letter.*

我们尚未接到对方的收函通知。③感谢: in ~ of sb.'s help 对某人的帮助表示感谢 / wave to the cheering crowd in ~ 向欢呼的群众招手致意

acme ['ækmi] *n.* 顶点,极度: the ~ of perfection 尽善尽美

acorn ['eikɔ:n] *n.* 【植】橡树子(果) ‖~ **cup** 橡果的壳斗 / ~ **shell** 【动】藤壶(属贝类) / ~ **tube** 橡实形(电子)管

acoustic(al) [ə'ku:stik(əl)] *a.* 听觉的; 传音的;声学的: ~ **engineering** 声工程学 / an ~ **magnetic mine** 【军】音响磁性水雷 / an ~ **torpedo** 【军】音响鱼雷 / an ~ **radiator** 【军】音响辐射器 / ~ **waves** 声波 / ~ **nerve** 【解】听神经 ‖**acoustically** *ad.*

acoustics [ə'ku:stiks] [复] *n.* ①[用作单] 声学 ② (礼堂、剧院等的)音响装置;音响效果: The ~ of the hall are excellent. 这座礼堂的音响效果极好。

acquaint [ə'kweint] *vt.* 使认识,使了解;通知 ‖~ **oneself with** (或 **of**) 开始知道 / ~ **sb. with** (或 **of, that**...) 把…通知某人 / **get ~ed with** 开始认识(某人);开始了解(某事) / **make sb. ~ed with** 把…告知某人;使某人认识…

acquaintance [ə'kweintəns] *n.* ①相识;了解: a steel worker of my ~ 我认识的一个钢铁工人 / He has some ~ with French but does not speak it fluently. 他懂得一点法语,但讲得不流利。② 相识的人,熟人: a mere ~, not a friend 只是相识,不是朋友 ‖a **nodding** ~ 点头之交 / a **speaking** ~ 见了面谈几句的朋友 / **drop an** ~ 断绝来往 / **have a nodding** ~ ①和…有点头之交 ②对…略知一二 / **make the ~ of sb.** (或 **make sb.'s** ~) 结识某人 / **scrape (up) an** ~ **with sb.** 硬要同某人交朋友 ‖~**ship** [ə'kweintənsʃip] *n.* 相识

acquiesce [,ækwi'es] *vi.* 默认,默许 (in): ~ **in** a suggestion (plan) 默然同意一项建议 (计划)

acquiescence [,ækwi'esns] *n.* 默认,默许

acquiescent [,ækwi'esnt] *a.* 默认的,默许的 ‖~**ly** *ad.*

acquire [ə'kwaiə] *vt.* ①取得,获得,得到: ~ a completely new mental outlook 思想面貌焕然一新 ② 学到(知识等)~ (a knowledge of) English 学到英语(知识) ‖~**d** *a.* 后天的,(通过学习、经历等)获得的;已成习惯的: ~**d immunity** 【医】后天免疫性 / ~**d character** 【生】获得性 / ~**ment** *n.* ①获得;学到 ②学到的东西: one's ~**ments** 某人的学识(或技能)等

acquisition [,ækwi'ziʃən] *n.* ①获得 ②(有价值的)获得物: He is a valuable ~ to the team. 他是该球队一个不可多得的新队员。③【无】探测

acquisitive [ə'kwizitiv] *a.* (对知识、财富等)渴望得到的;能够获得的: ~ **of** knowledge 渴望得到知识的 ‖~**ly** *ad.* / ~**ness** *n.*

acquit [ə'kwit] (acquitted; acquitting) *vt.* ①宣判…无罪: ~ **sb.** (**of** a crime) 宣判某人无罪 ②[~ **oneself**] 表现;履行,完成: ~ **oneself** well (ill)

表现好 (不好) / ~ **oneself of** a promise 履行诺言 / They have *acquitted themselves of* various duties splendidly. 他们出色地完成了各项任务。 ‖**acquittal** *n.* ①宣判无罪 ②(职责的)履行 ③ (债务的)清偿 / **acquittance** *n.* ①(债务的)清偿 ②清欠收据

acre ['eikə] *n.* ①英亩(等于 40.47 公亩或 6.07 亩) ②[复] 田地;地产: broad ~**s** 宽广的田地 ③ [复][口]大量 ‖**God's** ~ 墓地 / ~**age** ['eikəridʒ] *n.* ① 英亩数 ② 土地的面积: the ~**age** under cultivation 耕种面积

acrid ['ækrid] *a.* ① (气味等) 辛辣的; 腐蚀性的 ②(语言等)刻毒的 ‖~**ity** [ə'kriditi] *n.* / ~**ness** *n.*

acrimonious [,ækri'mounjəs] *a.* (语言、态度、脾气等)刻毒的,讥刺的,苛刻的 ‖~**ly** *ad.* / ~**ness** *n.*

acrobat ['ækrəbæt] *n.* ① 杂技演员(尤指走钢丝者) ②政治见解变化无常的人 ‖~**ic** [,ækrə'bætik] *a.* 杂技的: an ~**ic flight** 【军】特技飞行 / ~**ics** [,ækrə'bætiks] *n.* [用作单或复] ①杂技;[喻]技艺 ②【军】特技飞行 / ~**ism** *n.* 杂技

acrobat

across [ə'krɔs] **I** *prep.* ① 横过,穿过: Let's help push the cart ~ the bridge. 我们帮着把车子推过桥吧。② 在…的另一边: The post office is just ~ the street. 邮局就在马路对过。/ From the fields came cheers of the crowd. 从田野的那一边传来群众的欢呼声。③交叉: with a rifle ~ one's shoulder 肩上扛着枪 ④经过(一整段时期): ~ the century 历时整整一个世纪 **II** *ad.* ①横过,穿过; 从一边到另一边: Lay the two reinforcement bars ~ and tie them up. 把两根钢筋交叉扎起来。③横,阔: The river is 400 metres ~. 河宽四百米。 ‖~ **from** [美]在…对过: The co-op is ~ **from** the bookstore. 合作社在书店对面。/ **It is** ~ **to you.** [美口]这是你的事了。 ‖a'**cross-the-'board** *a.* ①全面的,包括一切的: an across-the-board **tax cut** 全面的减税 ②(电台或电视节目)在固定时间内播送的

act [ækt] **I** *n.* ①行为,动作: an ~ of justice 正义行动 ②法令;条例 ③【戏】幕;(马戏、杂耍中的)一段表演: a play in three ~**s** 三幕剧 / Act I, Scene ii 第一幕第二场 **II** ❶ *vi.* ①行动;做,做事: Think carefully before you ~. 你在行动前必须仔细想一想。②【戏】表演; (剧本等)适于

上演③[与 as 连用]担当: ~ *as* interpreter 当口译 ④起作用; 尽职责: The brakes refused to ~. 刹车不灵了。⑤假装: ~ tired 假装疲倦了 ❷ *vt.* ①扮演(角色); 演出(戏) ②表现出…的样子; 装作: Don't ~ the fool. 别傻气了。(或: 别装傻。) ‖~ *against* 违反 / ~ *and deed* 有约束力的契约 / ~ *for* 代理 / ~ *on* (或 *upon*) ①(药等)对…起作用 ②按照…行动: ~ *on* sb.'s advice 听从某人的劝告 / ~ *one's age* 举止与年龄相称(尤指有大人气) / ~ *up* [美口]调皮; 捣蛋 / ~ *up to* 遵照(原则等)办事; 做与(自己的声望等)相称的事 / *an ~ of God* 不可抗力(如风暴、地震等) / *an Act of Grace* (或 *Oblivion*) 大赦令 / *an ~ of grace* ①恩典 ②大赦令 / *get into the ~* (为了想得到好处)插手, 参加 / *in the* (*very*) ~ (*of*) 正在…时: He injured his foot *in the ~ of* saving the child. 他在救孩子时脚受了伤。/ *put on an ~* [口]装腔; 炫耀自己 / *read the Riot Act* (向骚动 的群众)宣读骚动取缔法令(以示警告) / *The Acts* (*of the Apostles*) (基督教《圣经·新约全书》中的)《使徒行传》‖**able** *a.* 能上演的

acting ['æktiŋ] I *a.* ①代理的: the *Acting* Minister of Foreign Affairs 代理外交部长 ②适于演出的; 演戏用的: an ~ copy (或 version)【戏】脚本 II *n.* ①演戏 ②表演; 演技 ③假装 ‖~ **sublieutenant** (英)海军少尉

action ['ækʃən] *n.* ①行动; 行为; 活动: a man of ~ 实行家, 活动家 / an ~ radius【军】(飞机的)活动半径 ②【军】战斗: a zone of ~ 战斗地带 ③作用: the ~ of an acid on metal 酸对金属所起的作用 ④(钢琴等的)机械装置 ⑤(小说等的)情节 ⑥(运动员、演员等的)姿势 ⑦诉讼: bring an ~ against sb. 对某人起诉 ⑧[美俚]刺激性的活动; 赌博 ‖~ *of the first impression*【律】新诉(无以前判例的诉讼) / *Actions speak louder than words.* [谚]行动比语言更响亮。(或: 百说不如一干。) / *amicable ~*【律】合意诉讼(两造同意静候法庭裁判) / *bring* (或 *call*) *into ~* 使行动起来, 使开始工作 / *go into ~* 投入战斗 / *in ~* ①在活动 ②在运转 ③在战斗中; be killed *in ~* 阵亡 / *put* (或 *set*) *in ~* 使行动起来, 使开始工作 / *put out of ~* 使失去效用; 使失去战斗力: *put* the enemy's machine guns *out of ~* 把敌人的机关枪打哑 / *see ~* 经历战斗 / *suit the ~ to the word* 怎么说就怎么做 (尤指威胁) / *take ~* ①采取行动: take concerted ~ 采取一致行动 ②提出诉讼 ‖~**able** *a.* 可控诉的 ‖~ **painting** 一种抽象派绘画(以乱洒颜料等为特征)

activate ['æktiveit] *vt.* ①使活动: ~ public opinion 使舆论活跃起来 ② 正式成立(部队等) ③【化】使活化, 使激活: ~*d* carbon 活性炭 ④【原】使产生放射性 ‖**activation** [,ækti'veiʃən] *n.* ①【化】激活; 活(性); 敏化; 活性化 ②军事单位的建成 / **activator** *n.*【化】活化剂

active ['æktiv] *a.* ①有活动力的, 灵敏的; 积极的, 能动的 / ~ in one's movements 动作灵敏的 ②在活动中的, 现行的; 现役的: an ~ volcano 活火山 / ~ capital 流动资本 / on ~ service【军】服现役的 ③主动的: the ~ voice【语】主动语态 / ~ radar homing【军】主动式雷达寻的 / ~ memory【无】主动式存储器; 快速存储器 ④【化】活性的; 【原】放射性的: ~ carbon 活性炭 (= activated carbon) ⑤【物】有功的; 【无】有源的: ~ component (交流电的)有功部分 / ~ element 有源元件 ⑥【医】速效的: ~ remedy 速效药物 ‖*an ~ aircraft inventory*【军】现役作战飞机总数 / ~ *defence*【军】积极防御 / *an ~ list*【军】现役名册 / *an ~ military unit* 实际军队 / *an ~ runway* 正在使用的跑道 / *an ~ weapon*【军】编制武器 ‖~**ly** *ad.* / ~**ness** *n.* ‖~ **duty**, ~ **service** 现役

activity [æk'tiviti] *n.* ①活动性; 能动性; 活跃, 敏捷; 【化】活度: be in ~ (火山等)在活动中 / subjective ~ 主观能动性 / an athlete's ~ 运动员的敏捷 ②[常用复]活动, 所做的事情: practical *activities* 实践活动 / political *activities* 政治活动 / extracurricular *activities* 课外活动 / social *activities* 社会活动; 文娱活动

actor ['æktə] *n.* ①男演员 ②行动者 ③【化】两级作用物, 原动质 ‖*a bad ~* [美]做坏事的人; 不择手段的危险人物

actress ['æktris] *n.* 女演员

actual ['æktjuəl, 'æktʃuəl] *a.* 实际的, 现实的, 事实上的: the ~ conditions 实际情况 / the ~ state 现状 / in ~ fact 事实上 / the ~ range【军】实际投弹距离(飞机投弹点与弹着点的水平距离); (火炮)实际射程 ‖~**ist** *n.* 实际家; 现实论者 / ~**ity** [,æktju'æliti, ,æktʃu'æliti] *n.* ①现实; 现实性 ②[复]现状 / ~**ly** *ad.* ①实际上 ②竟然: He ~*ly* said so. 他竟然这样说。③如今

actuate ['æktjueit] *vt.* ①开动(机器等): an ~*d* mine【军】待发地雷 ②激励, 驱使: What motives ~*d* him? 什么动机使他这样做的? ‖**actuation** [,æktju'eiʃən] *n.* / **actuator** *n.* ①【机】促动器; trigger **actuator** 枪机 ②【电】调节器, 传动装置; 传动机构 ③【电】(电磁铁)螺线管 ④【自】执行机构; 激励器

acute [ə'kju:t] *a.* ①尖锐的, 锐利的; 【植】急尖的: an ~ angle 锐角 ②敏锐的: an ~ observer 敏锐的观察家 / ~ eyesight 敏锐的目光 ③ 剧烈的, 严重的; 【医】急性的: ~ class struggle 激烈的阶级斗争 ④高音的, 刺耳的 ‖~**ly** *ad.* / ~**ness** *n.*

AD, A. D. [缩] ① active duty 现役 ② assembly district 选区 ③ [拉] *Anno Domini* 公元

adage ['ædidʒ] *n.* 谚语; 格言

adamant ['ædəmənt] I *n.* 坚硬的东西; 【地】硬石(指金刚石、刚玉等) II *a.* ①坚硬的 ②不动摇的, 坚强不屈的

adapt [ə'dæpt] ❶ *vt.* ①使适应, 使适合: ~ one's thinking *to* the new conditions 使自己的思想适

应新的情况 / ～ sth. *for* a particular use 使某物适合某一特殊用途 ②改编,改写: books ～*ed for* middle-school students 为中学生改写的书 / a play ～*ed from* a novel 由小说改编的剧本 *vi.* 适应 (to) ||～**er,** ～**or** *n.* ①改编者 ②【机】接合器,接头 ③【无】拾音器;附加器;接续器

adaptable [ə'dæptəbl] *a.* ①能适应的,适应性强的 ②可改编的 ||**adaptability** [ə,dæptə'biliti] *n.*

adaptation [,ædæp'teiʃən] *n.* ①适应,适合: ～ *to* the ground 【军】适应地形 ②改编本;改制物 ③【生】适应性的变化

add [æd] ❶ *vt.* ①加,增加,添加: Three ～*ed to* four makes seven. 三 加 四 等于 七。②进而讲(或写): Then he ～*ed* that .... 接着,他又说(或写)道… ❷ *vi.* 增添 (to); 做加法: Fireworks ～*ed to* the attraction of the festival night. 烟火使节日之夜更加生色。/ an ～*ing* machine 加法机 ||～ *sth. in* 把某物包括在内 / ～ *up* (或 *together*) 加算,合计 / ～ *up to* ①合计达 ②[口]总起来就意味着: All this ～*s up to* a new concept of the universe. 这一切意味着对宇宙的一种新看法。

addendum [ə'dendəm] ([复] addenda [ə'dendə]) *n.* ①补遗;附录 ②附加物 ③【机】(齿轮轮齿的)齿顶高

adder ['ædə] *n.* 【动】蝰蛇(一种小毒蛇) ||*the flying* ～ 蜻蜓 ||'～'**s-mouth** *n.* 【植】沼兰属植物 / '～'**s-tongue** *n.* 【植】①赤莲属植物 ②瓶尔小草属植物

addict I [ə'dikt] *vt.* 使沉溺,使醉心: ～ oneself *to* (或 be ～*ed to*) 沉溺于,醉心于 ②使吸毒成瘾 II ['ædikt] *n.* 有瘾的人: a drug ～ 吸毒上瘾的人 / a work ～ 对工作入迷的人 ||～**ion** [ə'dikʃən] *n.* ①沉溺 ②吸毒成瘾 / ～**ive** [ə'diktiv] *a.* ①使成瘾的 ②上瘾的.

addition [ə'diʃən] *n.* ①加;【数】加法 ②增加;增加物;(建筑物等的)增建部分: ～ compound 【化】加成化合物 / valuable ～*s to* the library 图书馆中新增的有价值的书刊 ③【律】(加在姓名后的)头衔,称号 ||*in* ～ 另外 / *in* ～ *to* 除…之外

additional [ə'diʃənl] *a.* 附加的,追加的;另外的: an ～ tax 附加税 / It will take an ～ two weeks to finish the work. 还得再花两星期才能完成这项工作。||～**ly** *ad.*

addle ['ædl] I *a.* ① 变质腐坏的: an ～ egg 臭蛋 ②(思想等)混乱的,糊涂的 II ❶ *vt.* ①使腐坏 ②使混乱,使糊涂: ～ one's head over figures 被数字搞昏了头 ❷ *vi.* ①(蛋等)腐坏 ②变混乱,变糊涂 ||'～**brained,** '～**pated** *a.* 思想糊涂的,昏头昏脑的, '～**head** *n.* 糊涂虫

address [ə'dres] I *vt.* ①向…讲话;写信给: ～ the rally 在群众大会上讲话 ②讲(话等),提出(抗议、请愿等) (to) ③在(信封、包裹等)上写姓名地址; 致(函等) ④称呼 ⑤向(女子)求爱 II *n.* ①演说,讲话: deliver an opening ～ 致开幕词 ②地址: a return ～ 回信地址 / a cable ～

电报挂号 ③谈吐,风度 ④灵巧,熟练 ⑤[复]求爱;殷勤: pay one's ～*es to* a lady 向女子献殷勤 ||～ *oneself to* ①[用于正式场合]向…讲话;与…通信 ②(在讲演中)论述,谈到 ③致力于;着手 / a form of ～ 称呼 / an inside ～ 在信纸左上角的收信人姓名、地址 / direct ～ 【语】呼语 ||～**ee** [,ædre'si:] *n.* 收信人,收件人 / ～**er,** ～**or** *n.* 发言人;发信人 / ～**ograph** [ə'dresəgrɑ:f] *n.* 姓名地址印写机

adduce [ə'dju:s] *vt.* 引证,提出(理由等): He ～*d* a lot of facts to support his argument. 他引用许多事实来证明自己的论点。

adept ['ædept, ə'dept] I *a.* 熟练的,内行的: be ～ *in* (或 *at*) figures 善于计算 II *n.* 内行,能手: an ～ in photography 照相能手 ||～**ly** *ad.* / ～**ness** *n.*

adequacy ['ædikwəsi] *n.* ①适合,恰当 ②充分,足够

adequate ['ædikwit] *a.* ① 适当的;充分的,足够的: take ～ measures 采取适当措施 / The supply is not ～ *to* the demand. 供不应求。 ② 可以胜任的 ||～**ly** *ad.* / ～**ness** *n.*

adhere [əd'hiə] *vi.* ①粘附,胶着 (to) ②追随,依附 (to) ③坚持 (to)

adherence [əd'hiərəns] *n.* ①信奉,依附 ②坚持,固执

adherent [əd'hiərənt] I *a.* 粘着的;附着的 II *n.* 信徒,追随者;拥护者

adhesion [əd'hi:ʒən] *n.* ①粘着;附着;【医】粘连 ②【物】粘着力,附着力 ③支持;信奉,追随: give one's ～ *to* a plan 支持一项计划 ④ 同意加入(条约等)

adhesive [əd'hi:siv] I *a.* ① 粘着的: an ～ stamp 背面有胶水的邮票(或印花) / ～ plaster 橡皮膏 / ～ disc 【动】吸盘;【植】粘着盘 ②带粘性的,有附着力的 II *n.* 胶粘剂

adieu [ə'dju:] I *int.* 再见 II ([复] adieus 或 adieux [ə'dju:z]) *n.* 告别 ||bid sb. ～ 向某人告别 / make (或 take) one's ～ 辞行

adjacent [ə'dʒeisənt] *a.* ① 邻近的;毗连的: ～ rooms 邻近的房间 / ～ angles 【数】邻角 ②紧接着的: a music programme ～ *to* the news 紧接在新闻广播前(或后)的音乐节目

adjectival [,ædʒek'taivəl] *a.* 形容词的 ||～**ly** *ad.*

adjective ['ædʒiktiv] I *n.* 【语】形容词;修饰语 II *a.* ① 形容词的;修饰性的: an ～ phrase 形容词短语 ②辅助的,从属的: ～ dyes 间接染料,需要媒染剂的染料 ③【律】有关程序的: ～ law 程序法 ||～**ly** *ad.*

adjoin [ə'dʒɔin] ❶ *vt.* 贴近;毗连: The cotton field ～*s* the paddy field. 棉田与稻田相接。 ❷ *vi.* 靠近;毗邻着 ||～**ing** *a.* 毗邻的: an ～*ing* room 邻室

adjourn [ə'dʒə:n] ❶ *vt.* 使中止;休(会): The meeting will be ～*ed to* (或 *till*) next Monday.

会议暂停，下星期一继续举行。/ The meeting was ~ed for a week. 休会一周。❷ vi. ①休会；闭会：~ without (a) day (或 ~ sine die) 无限期休会 / The meeting ~ed at 5 o'clock. 会议在五时休会。②[口] 移动；(与会者) 移动会场：Let's ~ to the campus. 我们到校园去吧。/ They ~ed to the classroom. 他们移到教室继续开会。‖~ment n. 休会；闭会

adjudicate [ə'dʒu:dikeit] ❶ vt. 【律】判决，宣判；裁定：~ a claim 裁决一起关于权利的要求 ❷ vi. 判决；审断 (upon) ‖**adjudication** [ə,dʒu:di-'keiʃən] n. 判决；审断；裁定；宣告 / **adjudicative** a. 判决的 / **adjudicator** n. 判决者；(音乐比赛等的) 评判员

adjunct ['ædʒʌŋkt] I n. ①附属品，附属物 (to) ②助手，副手 ③【语】附加语，修饰语 ④【逻】非本质属性 II a. 附属的 ‖~**ion** [æ'dʒʌŋkʃən] n. ①添加，附加 ②【数】附益，附加 ‖~ **professor** (美国某些高等学校的) 副教授

adjure [ə'dʒuə] vt. ①使…起誓 ②恳求 ‖**adjuration** [,ædʒuə'reiʃən] n. ①誓言 ②恳求，祈求 / **adjuratory** [ə'dʒuərətəri] a. ①誓言的 ②恳求的

adjust [ə'dʒʌst] ❶ vt. ①调整，调节；整顿：~ the pillows on the bed 把床上枕头弄松放好 ②校准；对准：~ the errors 校正误差 / ~ one's watch 把表拨准 ③【军】修正(炮火等)：~ a gun 修正枪炮的射角(或射向) ④(保险业中)评定(赔偿要求) ⑤【军】调整；校准：the ~ing point (炮兵的) 试射点 ⑥适应于 (to) ‖~ oneself to 使自己适应于 ‖~able a. 可调整的；可校准的 / ~er, ~or n. ①调整者；调停者 ②【机】调整器 / ~ment n. 调整，调节；校正：~ment curve【建】缓和曲线

adjutant ['ædʒutənt] I n. ①【军】副官，人事行政参谋 ②助手 II a. 辅助的 ‖**adjutancy** n. 副官职位 ‖~ **general** ①【军】副官长；人事行政参谋主任 ②[美] [the A- G-] 陆军副官长；副官署署长

administer [əd'ministə] ❶ vt. ①管理，支配 ②执行，施行，实施：~ justice 执法 / ~ relief 施舍 ③给与，用(药等)：~ medicine to a patient 给病人吃药 ④提出(誓言等)：~ an oath to sb. 使某人宣誓 ❷ vi. ①管理(upon) ②有助于(to)：Physical exercise ~s to the circulation of the blood. 体操有助于血液的流通。

administration [əd,minis'treiʃən] n. ①管理，经营；【律】遗产管理 ②行政；行政机关，局(或署、处等)；[A-] (总统制国家的) 政府：civil (military) ~ 民(军)政 ③(行政官员或机关的) 任职期 ④【军】后方勤务 ⑤执行；施行；(药的)服法，用法；给与

administrative [əd'ministrətiv] a. 行政的；管理的；后方勤务的：an ~ division 行政区域 / simplify the ~ structure 精简机构 / ~ services (英美军队中的) 非战斗性行政勤务；行政勤务部

队(指副官队、宪兵队、牧师队等) / an ~ organ (post) 行政机关(职务) ‖~ly ad.

administrator [əd'ministreitə] n. ①管理人；【律】遗产管理人 ②行政官员 ③给(药等)的人 ④代管教区的牧师

admirable ['ædmərəbl] a. ①令人钦佩的，令人赞美的 ②极妙的，极好的 ‖**admirably** ad.

admiral ['ædmərəl] n. ①海军将军；海军上将 ②舰队司令 ③[英] 渔船船长 ④商船队长 ⑤蛱蝶 ‖~ of the fleet (英国)海军元帅 / the ~'s bridge (军舰的)司令舰桥 / the ~'s superintendent (英国)海军总监 / a fleet ~ (美国)海军五星上将 / a full ~ (美国)海军上将 / a vice ~ 海军中将 / a rear ~ 海军少将

admiralty ['ædmərəlti] n. ①海军上将的职位 ②[A-] 英国海军部：the First Lord of the Admiralty 英国海军大臣 ③海事法，海事法庭 ‖an ~ chart 海图 / an ~ court 海事法庭

admiration [,ædmə'reiʃən] n. ①钦佩，赞美，羡慕：in ~ of 怀着对…的赞美 / express ~ for 对…表示钦佩 ②引人赞美的人(或物) ‖do sth. to ~ 把某事做得极好

admire [əd'maiə] vt. ①钦佩，羡慕 ②[美口]想要，喜欢：~ to do sth. 很想做某事 ‖~r [əd'maiərə] n. 赞赏者；爱慕某一女子的男人

admissible [əd'misəbl] a. ①可采纳的；【律】(证据)可接受的 ②有资格加入的 ‖**admissibility** [əd,misə'biliti] n.

admission [əd'miʃən] n. ①允许进入：an ~ ticket 入场券 / ~ to a school 准许入学 / Admission by ticket only. 凭票入场。/ Admission free. 免费入场。/ ~ valve【机】进入阀，进气阀 ②入场费 ③承认

admit [əd'mit] (admitted; admitting) ❶ vt. ①让…进入；让…享有 (to) ②接纳；招收 ③容纳：Our auditorium ~s 3,000 persons. 我们的礼堂可以容纳三千人。④承认(事实、错误等) ❷ vi. ①容许有 (of)：The matter ~s of no delay. 这件事不容拖延。②开向：This gate ~s to the yard. 这道门通向院子。③承认 (to)

admittance [əd'mitəns] n. ①进入；允许进入(尤指非公共场所)：gain (或 get) ~ to a place 准入某处；进入某处 / No ~ except on business. 非公莫入。②【建】通道 ③【物】导纳

admittedly [əd'mitidli] ad. 公认地

admonish [əd'məniʃ] vt. ①告诫：~ sb. of a danger 警告某人当心危险 ②劝告，忠告：~ sb. to do sth. 劝某人做某事 ‖~ment n.

admonition [,ædmə'niʃən] n. ①告诫；劝告 ②温和的责备

ado [ə'du:] n. 忙乱；费力，艰难 ‖make (或 have) much ~ 费尽力气：make much ~ about nothing 无事空忙 / with much ~ 费煞心血 / without more (或 further) ~ 不再嗦苏，立即，干脆

adolescence [,ædou'lesns], **adolescency** [,ædou-'lesnsi] n. 青春期；青春

adolescent [,ædou'lesnt] **I** *a.* 青春期的 **II** *n.* 青少年

adopt [ə'dɔpt] *vt.* ① 采用，采纳；采取(态度等)：~ed words 外来词 ②选定(道路、职业等) ③ 收养：an ~ed son 养子 ④ 正式通过：~ a resolution 通过一个决议 ‖~able *a.* 可采用的；可收养的 / ~ion [ə'dɔpʃən] *n.*

adorable [ə'dɔːrəbl] *a.* ①值得崇拜的；值得敬慕的 ②[口]极可爱的 ‖~ness *n.* / **adorably** *ad.*

adoration [,ædɔ'reiʃən] *n.* 崇拜；敬慕

adore [ə'dɔː] *vt.* ①崇拜(上帝)；敬慕 ②[口]很喜欢 ‖~r [ə'dɔːrə] *n.* 崇拜者；敬慕者

adorn [ə'dɔːn] *vt.* 装饰；使生色：~ a building *with* multi-coloured lamps and flags 用彩色电灯和旗帜把大楼装饰起来 / ~ oneself *with* 佩戴着…(装饰品) ‖~ment *n.* 装饰；装饰品

adrift [ə'drift] *a.* [常作表语] & *ad.* ① 漂浮；漂流 ②[喻]漂泊 ‖*be all* ~ 不知所措，茫然若失 / *get* (或 *go*) ~ (船等)随波逐流；[喻]脱节：*go* ~ from the subject 离题 / *set a boat* ~ 使船漂去 / *turn sb.* ~ 逐出某人；使某人漂泊流浪；辞退某人

adroit [ə'drɔit] *a.* 灵巧的；机敏的 (*in, at*) ‖~ly *ad.* / ~ness *n.*

adsorb [æd'sɔːb] *vt.* 【化】吸附 ‖~ate [æd'sɔːbit] *n.* 被吸附物 / ~ent *a.* 吸附的 *n.* 吸附剂

adult ['ædʌlt] **I** *a.* 已成人的，成年的；已成熟的 **II** *n.* ①成年人：~ education 成人教育 ②【生】成体；成虫 ‖~hood *n.* 成年 / ~ly *ad.* / ~ness *n.*

adulterate [ə'dʌltəreit] **I** *vt.* 掺杂，掺假：~ wine *with* water 酒中掺水 **II** *a.* ①掺假的 ②通奸的 ‖**adulteration** [ə,dʌltə'reiʃən] *n.* ①掺杂，掺假 ②劣等货，掺假货 / **adulterator** *n.* 掺假的人，造假货的人

advance [əd'vɑːns] **I** ❶ *vt.* ①推进；促进：~ the movement *to* a new stage 把运动推到一个新阶段 / ~ the growth of wheat 促进小麦生长 ②提出(建议、看法、理论等) ③提前：The date of the meeting has been ~d from Friday to Wednesday. 会议日期已从星期五提前到星期三。④ 提高(价格等)；提升(某人)④预付(货款)：~ money *to* sb. 预先付钱(或贷款)给某人 / ~ sb. some money 预付(或贷给)某人一些钱 ❷ *vi.* ①前进；进展：~ *against* the enemy 向敌人进击 / ~ *on* a place 向某地进击 ②(物价)上涨；(质量、地位等方面)提高，提升 **II** *n.* ①前进，进展：make a mighty ~ (或 mighty ~s) 取得很大进展 ②(价格、工资、年龄等的)增长，增高 ③预付；预付款；贷款：make an ~ to sb. 贷款给某人 ④[复]友好表示；求爱：make ~s to sb. (为交友或求爱而)接近某人 **III** *a.* [只作定语] ①前进的：an ~ base【军】前进基地 ②先头的：an ~ guard【军】前卫 / an ~ agent 先遣人员；打前站的 ③预先的：an ~ copy (发行前的)新书样本 / an ~ notice 预告 ‖*be on the* ~ (物价)在上涨

中 / *in* ~ ①在前面 ②预先：pay (receive) *in* ~ 预付(收) / *in* ~ *of* 在…的前面；超过 ‖~ment *n.*

advanced [əd'vɑːnst] *a.* ①在前面的：an ~ post 前哨 ②(年)老的；(夜)深的：He is ~ in years. 他年纪已经很大了。③高级的；先进的：~ algebra 高等代数 / ~ experience 先进经验 / the ~ 先进的人们

advantage [əd'vɑːntidʒ] **I** *n.* ①有利条件；优点：This school has many ~s. 这个学校具有很多优点。/ This hall combines the ~s of a dining room and of a meeting place. 这个大厅既可作食堂，又可作会场。②优势；好处，利益：At the end of an hour's play the ~ lay definitely with him. 经过一个小时的比赛，他已肯定取得优势。③(网球)打成平手后一方赢得的第一分 **II** *vt.* 使有利，有助于：In what way will it ~ them? 这在哪一方面将对他们有利？/ an ~d social position 有利的社会地位 ‖*gain* (或 *have, win*) *an* ~ *over* 胜过，优于 / *have the* ~ *of* 胜过，占优势：You *have the* ~ *of* me there. 你比我强。/ You *have the* ~ *of* me. (客套用语)你倒认识我，我还不认识你呢！/ *take* ~ *of sb.* 欺骗(或捉弄)某人 / *take* ~ *of sth.* 趁机利用某事(或某物) / *take sb. at* ~ 乘某人不备 / *to* ~ (用比较、衬托等)使优点突出：The painting is seen *to* better ~ from a distance. 这幅画从远处看格外好。/ *to sb.'s* ~ (或 *to the* ~ *of sb.*) 对某人有利 / *turn to* ~ 使转化为有利

advantageous [,ædvən'teidʒəs] *a.* 有利的，有助的 ‖~ly *ad.* / ~ness *n.*

advent ['ædvənt] *n.* ① (事件、时期等的)出现，到来：before the ~ of the coldest season 在最寒冷的季节到来之前 ② [A-]【宗】基督降临节：the Second *Advent* 基督再临

adventitious [,ædven'tiʃəs] *a.* ① 外来的；偶然的 ②【医】偶发的；异位的，不定的 ③【生】不定的；获得的(指非遗传的) ‖~ly *ad.*

adventure [əd'ventʃə] **I** *n.* ① 冒险，冒险活动：military ~s 军事冒险 ② (人性格上的)冒险性 ③ 惊险活动，奇遇 ④ 投机活动 **II** ❶ *vt.* ①拿…冒险 ② 大胆进行，大胆表示：~ an opinion 大胆提出一个意见 ❷ *vi.* 冒险 ‖~r [əd'ventʃərə] *n.* 冒险家，投机家 / ~some [əd'ventʃəsəm] *a.* 爱冒险的 / ~ss [əd'ventʃəris] *n.* 女冒险家；女骗子

adventurous [əd'ventʃərəs] *a.* ① 喜欢冒险的 ② 冒险的，有危险性的 ‖~ly *ad.* / ~ness *n.*

adverb ['ædvəːb] *n.*【语】副词：a relative ~ 关系副词 / an interrogative ~ 疑问副词

adverbial [əd'vəːbjəl] **I** *a.* 副词的；状语的：an ~ modifier 状语 / an ~ clause (phrase) 状语从句(短语) **II** *n.*【语】状语 ‖~ly *ad.* 作状语

adversary ['ædvəsəri] *n.* 对手；敌手

adverse ['ædvəːs] *a.* ①(在位置或方向上)逆的，相反的；敌对的：an ~ wind (current) 逆风(流) / ~ criticism 非难 / an opinion ~ *to* sb.'s 与

某人(意见)相反的意见 ② 不利的, 有害的: ~ circumstances 逆境 / an ~ balance of trade 入超 / an ~ balance of payments 支付逆差 ③【植】(叶子等) 朝着茎的; 对生的 ‖~ly ad. / ~ness n.

adversity [əd'və:siti] n. ①逆境, 不幸 ②苦难, 灾难

advertise, advertize ['ædvətaiz; 美 ,ædvə'taiz] ❶ vt. ①通知 ②为…做广告; 大肆宣扬: ~ the goods 为商品做广告 / extravagantly ~ sb. 大肆吹捧某人 ❷ vi. 登广告, 做广告: ~ for sth. 登广告征求(或寻找)某物 ‖~ment [əd'və:tismənt; 美 ,ædvə'taizmənt] n. 做广告, 登广告; 广告; 公告 / ~r n. 登广告的人

advice [əd'vais] n. ①劝告, 忠告; (医师、顾问等的)意见, 指点: a piece (或 word) of ~ (一个)劝告 / do sth. by (或 on) sb.'s ~ 按某人的劝告(或意见)做某事 / ask for sb.'s ~ (或 ask ~ of sb.) 向某人征求意见 / give (或 tender) ~ 提出劝告 / follow (或 take) sb.'s ~ 接受某人的意见 / seek medical ~ 请医生诊视, 向医生询问有关健康的问题 / I want your ~ on this work. 我希望你对这件工作提出意见。②通知; [常用复]报道, 消息: a letter of ~ 通知信, 报告信 / an ~ note 通知单

advisable [əd'vaizəbl] a. 可取的, 适当的; 贤明的: This course of action is ~. 这个办法是可取的。 / Do you think it ~ to try again? 再试一下你看好不好? ‖**advisability** [əd,vaizə'biliti] n. / ~ness n. / advisably ad.

advise [əd'vaiz] ❶ vt. ①劝告; 向…提意见: ~ sb. to do sth. 劝某人做某事 / ~ sb. against the danger 劝某人提防危险 / ~ sb. against doing sth. 劝某人不要做某事 / Be ~d! 接受意见吧! ②建议: We ~ that steps be taken at once. 我们建议立即采取措施。 / We ~ (an) immediate decision. 我们认为应立即作出决定。 / ~ going slower 建议进行得慢一些 ③通知, 告知: ~ sb. of sth. 把某事通知某人 / We are to ~ you that the matter is under consideration. 此事已在讨论中, 特此通知。 ❷ vi. ①提出意见; 作顾问: Will you ~ on these points? 关于这几点请你提提意见好吗? ②商量: ~ with sb. on (或 about) sth. 同某人商量某事 ‖~ment n. ①深思熟虑: take sth. under ~ment 对某事进行周密考虑 ②劝告; 意见; 提供劝告(或意见) / ~r, advisor n. 劝告者; 顾问: an ~r on legal affairs to the committee 委员会的法律顾问 / an ~r in agriculture 农业顾问

advisory [əd'vaizəri] I a. ①劝告的, 忠告的: words of an ~ nature 劝告性的意见 (指无约束力) ②顾问的, 谘询的: in an ~ capacity 以顾问资格(或身分) / an ~ body 顾问团 / an ~ committee 谘询委员会 II n. 报告(尤指气象方面的报告)

advocacy ['ædvəkəsi] n. 辩护; 拥护, 提倡

advocate I ['ædvəkit] n. ①辩护者; 律师 ②鼓吹者, 拥护者, 提倡者: a warm (lukewarm) ~ of a theory 一个理论的热烈的(不起劲的)鼓吹者 II ['ædvəkeit] vt. 拥护, 提倡 ‖ the devil's ~ ①(天主教中)负责指出申请加入圣列者缺点的教吏; [喻]吹毛求疵的人 ②明知不对而坚持错误观点争论不休的人 / the judge ~【军】军法官 ‖advocator ['ædvəkeitə] n. 提倡者, 拥护者

aerate ['eiəreit] vt. ①使暴露于空气中, 使通空气 充气于; 充注碳酸气于: ~d water(s) (各种) 汽水 ③通过呼吸供给氧气给(血液) ‖aeration [eiə'reiʃən] n. 通风, 通气;【化】充气; 吹风;【医】曝气: aeration cell 充气电池, 氧气电池 / aerator n. 充气器

aerial ['ɛəriəl] I a. ①空气的; 大气的 ②航空的 ③高耸空中的, 架空的 ④生存在空中的;【植】气生的 ⑤无形的, 空想中的 ‖ ~ acrobatics 特技飞行 / an ~ attack 空中攻击, 空袭 / an ~ barrage 空中气球阻塞网 / ~ blitz(krieg) 空中闪击战 / an ~ cable 架空电缆 / an ~ car 气球吊篮; 高架铁道车 / an ~ chart 航行图 / ~ defence 防空 / an ~ depth charge 空投深水炸弹 / an ~ flare 空中照明弹 / an ~ fleet 大机群 / an ~ gunnery range 空中射击靶场 / an ~ ladder (救火车上的) 架空消防梯 / an ~ line 航空线 / ~ liner 定期民航机 / an ~ man(o)euver 空中机动; 空中演习 / an ~ mosaic 航空照片镶嵌图 / an ~ observation 空中观察 / ~ photograph interpretation 航空照片判读 / ~ photo reconnaissance 空中照相侦察 / an ~ picket 空中巡逻飞机 / an ~ port 空运港, 空运场 / an ~ railway 高架铁道 / an ~ review 空中阅兵式 / an ~ ropeway 架空索道 / ~ spotting 弹着空中观察(修正) / an ~ survey 航空测量 / an ~ torpedo 空投鱼雷 / an ~ train 空中列车(指飞机牵引一架或数架滑翔机构成的队列) / ~ warfare 空战 II n. [英][无]天线 (=~ wire) ‖~ist n. 高空杂技演员 / ~ly ad.

aerodrome ['ɛərədroum] n. 飞机场

aeronaut ['ɛərənɔ:t] n. 飞艇(或气球)的驾驶员; 飞艇(或气球)的乘客

aeroplane ['ɛərəplein] n. [英]飞机: go by ~ 乘飞机去

aesthetic(al) [i:s'θetik(əl); 美 es'θetik(əl)] a. ①美学的 ②审美的 ③美的, 艺术的 ‖**aesthetically** ad.

aesthetics [i:s'θetiks; 美 es'θetiks] [复] n. [用单]美学

afar [ə'fɑ:] ad. 在远处; 从远处: 遥远地: ~ off 远远地 / come from ~ 从远处来

affable ['æfəbl] a. ①和蔼可亲的 ②(天气等)宜人的, 使人愉快的 ‖**affability** [,æfə'biliti] n. / **affably** ad.

affair [ə'fɛə] n. ①事, 事情, 事件: a public (private) ~ 公(私)事 / a got-up ~ 故意造成(或预谋)的事件, 圈套 ②[复]事务; 事态: the ~s of state 国

家大事 / current ~s 时事 / family ~s 家事 / the Ministry of Foreign *Affairs* 外交部 / a state of ~s 事态,形势 / How do ~s stand? 情况怎样? ③不正当的恋爱事件,私通事件 ④[口] 东西,物: This machine is a complicated ~. 这部机器很复杂。

affect[1] [ə'fekt] *vt.* ①影响: The climate ~ed the amount of the rainfall. 气候影响了雨量。②感动: The audience was deeply ~ed. 听众深受感动。③(疾病)侵袭: be ~ed by heat 中暑 / be ~ed with high fever 发高烧 / the ~ed part (人体的)患部 II ['æfekt] *n.* 【心】感情,情感;引起感情的因素

affect[2] [ə'fekt] *vt.* ①假装: ~ ignorance 假装不知道 / to be uninterested 装作漠然的样子 ②喜爱,老是爱用(或穿);老是往…去: He ~s an exaggerative way of speaking. 他说话老爱夸张。/ This is the table they ~ in the dining room. 在食堂里他们一般总在这张桌上吃饭。③倾向于

affectation [,æfek'teiʃən] *n.* 假装;做作,装模作样的言行): without ~ 直率地,不做作地

affected [ə'fektid] *a.* ①假装的;做作的,不自然的: ~ manners 矫揉造作的举止 ②倾向于…的 (to) ||~ly *ad.* / ~ness *n.*

affecting [ə'fektiŋ] *a.* 令人感动的,动人的 ||~ly *ad.*

affection [ə'fekʃən] *n.* ①慈爱,爱: have an ~ for (或 towards) sb. 喜欢某人 ②[常用复]爱慕,钟爱之情: set one's ~s on (或 upon) sb. 钟爱某人 / become the object of sb.'s ~s 成为某人钟爱的对象 ③【心】感情

affectionate [ə'fekʃnit] *a.* 充满深情的,出于柔情的 ||~ly *ad.* Yours ~ly (或 *Affectionately* yours) 你的亲爱的(英美人写家信时的结尾用语)

affective [ə'fektiv] *a.* ①感情方面的;由感情引起的 ②表达感情的

affidavit [,æfi'deivit] *n.*【律】宣誓书

affiliate I [ə'filieit] ❶ *vt.* ① 接纳…为会员(或分支机构): an ~d middle school 附属中学 / an ~d society (company) 分会(公司) ②[常接oneself 或用被动语态]使隶属(或附属): ~ oneself with (或 to) 加入…作为成员 / Lumbering and its ~d activities form the city's chief industry. 伐木业及与此有关的事业是该城市的主要工业。③追溯…的来源;【律】把(私生子等)的父亲确认出来: ~ Greek art upon Egypt 把希腊艺术溯源于埃及 ❷ *vi.* 交往;有关 (with) II [ə'filiit] *n.* [美]会员;分支机构 ||**affiliation** [ə,fili'eiʃən] *n.*

affinity [ə'finiti] *n.* ①姻亲关系;密切关系 ②共鸣;吸引;有吸引力的人: an ~ between A and B 甲与乙的共鸣(或相互吸引) / develop an ~ for sth. 逐渐被某事所吸引,逐渐爱好某事 ③(语言等的)类同,近似: English has a close ~ to French. 英语同法语很相近。④【化】亲合性,亲和力 ⑤【数】仿射性

affirm [ə'fə:m] ❶ *vt.* ① 断言,肯定地说 (that) ②证实;批准 ③【律】不经宣誓而证明 ❷ *vi.* ①断言 ②(上级法院)维持下级法院的判决 ③【律】不经宣誓而提供正式证词 ||~able *a.* 可断言的,可肯定的 / ~ance *n.*

affirmation [,æfə'meiʃən] *n.* ① 断言,肯定 ②证实;批准 ③【律】不经宣誓而作出的正式证词

affirmative [ə'fə:mətiv] I *a.* 肯定的 ~, not a negative, answer 一个肯定的而不是否定的回答 II *n.* ①肯定词(如英语中的"yes");肯定语(如英语中的"that's so"): answer in the ~ 作肯定的回答 / A: Are the strikes still going on? B: *Affirmative.* (无线电通话用语)甲: 罢工还在继续吗? 乙: 是的。② 赞成的方面: All the votes were in the ~. 全体投赞成票。||~ly *ad.*

affix I [ə'fiks] *vt.* ① 粘上,贴上: ~ a stamp to an envelope 把邮票贴在信封上 ② 签署;盖(印章): ~ one's signature to an agreement 在协议上签名 ③附添,加(附言) II ['æfiks] *n.* ①附加物,附件 ②【语】词缀 ||~ation [,æfik'seiʃən] *n.* ①附加 ②【语】词缀法,附加法 / ~ture [ə'fikstʃə] *n.* 粘上,贴上;附加

afflict [ə'flikt] *vt.* 使苦恼,折磨: be ~ed with a disease 害病 ||~ion [ə'flikʃən] *n.* ① 苦恼,折磨 ②苦事 / ~ive *a.* 使人苦恼的,折磨人的

affluence ['æfluəns] *n.* ① 流入,涌入 ② 丰富;富裕

affluent ['æfluənt] I *a.* 丰富的,丰饶的;富裕的: be ~ in minerals 矿产丰富 II *n.* 支流 ||~ly *ad.*

afford [ə'fɔːd] *vt.* ①[常接在 can, be able to 后]担负得起(…的费用、损失、后果等);抽得出(时间): ~ (to buy) sth. 买得起某物 / In accomplishing our task, we cannot ~ the waste of a single minute. 我们在完成任务的时候,一分钟也不能浪费。②提供,给予;出产 / History ~s us lessons that merit attention. 历史给我们提供了值得注意的经验教训。

afforest [æ'fɔrist] *vt.* 造林于: an ~ed area 造林区 ||~ation [æ,fɔris'teiʃən] *n.* 造林

affray [ə'frei] *n.* 吵架,打架,闹事(尤指在公共场所)

affright [ə'frait] [古] I *vt.* 恐吓,使害怕 II *n.* 恐怖,恐惧

affront [ə'frʌnt] I *vt.* ① 当众侮辱;有意冒犯 ②(挑战似地)面对 II *n.* 当众侮辱: put an ~ upon sb. (或 offer an ~ to sb.) 当众侮辱某人

afield [ə'fiːld] *ad.* ①在野外;在田里;下地 ②在战场上;上战场: letters from fighters ~ 战地来信 ③远离;远离家(乡): Your remarks are far ~. 你的话离题太远了。

afire [ə'faiə] *a.* [常作表语] & *ad.* 燃烧着: with heart ~ 热血沸腾地

aflame [ə'fleim] *a.* [常作表语] & *ad.* ① 燃烧着 ②发着火光;发亮;发红: ~ with blushes 涨红了脸

afloat [ə'flout] *a.* [常作表语] & *ad.* ① 浮着,漂浮不定 ②在水上;在船上: cargo ~ 在水运中的货物 / life ~ 船员生活 ③(甲板等)浸满水 ④

(经济上)应付自如;【商】(票据等)可流通 ⑤活动起来;在进行中: get a newspaper ～ 创办一种报纸 ⑥(消息、谣言等)在流传中

afoot [ə'fut] *a.* [常作表语] & *ad.* ①徒步 ②活动着;在进行中: set a project ～ 开始执行计划 / The work is well ～. 工作在顺利进行中。

afore [ə'fɔ:] *ad.* & *prep.* ①在(…)前 ②[古]以前,早先 ‖**a'fore'mentioned** *a.* 前面提到的 / **a'foresaid** *a.* 上述的 / **a'forethought** *a.* [常放在所修饰的名词之后]故意的;预谋的 / **a'fore-time** *ad.* 从前,早先

afraid [ə'freid] *a.* [常作表语] ①怕,害怕: He handled the test tube with care, because he was ～ of breaking it. 他小心地拿着试管,怕把它打碎。②[口]恐怕: I'm ～ I am late. 我恐怕迟到了吧! / I'm ～ (that) I'll be late. 我恐怕要迟到了! / I am ～ not. (或 Afraid not!) 恐怕不是这样吧!

afresh [ə'freʃ] *ad.* 重新: learn ～ 重新学习 / start ～ 重新开始;改弦更张

aft [ɑ:ft] *ad.* & *a.* 在船尾,近船尾,向船尾: fore and ～ 从船头到船尾;在(或向)船头与船尾

after ['ɑ:ftə] **I** *prep.* ①(时间)在…以后;(位置)…后面: (the) day ～ tomorrow 后天 / ～ school 放学后 / half ～ six [美]六点半(=half past six) / Shut the door ～ you. 随手关门。[注意: 表示位置时,用 behind 比用 ～ 更为普通] ②(顺序)跟在…后面,次于: After you! [口] (客套语)您先请! / After you with the paper, please. 您看完报纸给我看。③(一个)接着(一个): day ～ day 一天又一天 / time ～ time 再三,常常 / bus ～ bus 一辆公共汽车接着一辆公共汽车 ④由于,因为;尽管…(但): After what has happened, he won't go. 既然发生了这一切,他就不去了。/ After all our advice, he insists on going. 尽管我们劝阻他,他仍然坚持要去。⑤[与某些动词连用]追;探求: What are you ～? 你追求什么? (或:你在找什么?) / run ～ sb. 追踪某人 / ask (或 inquire) ～ sb. 询问某人的情况 / look ～ sb. 照料某人 ⑥仿照;依照: a play ～ Shakespeare 一个模仿莎士比亚的剧本 **II** *conj.* 在…以后: After the work was done, we sat down to sum up experience. 工作结束后,我们坐下来总结经验。**III** *ad.* ①(一段时间)以后;后来: He left on Monday and returned two days ～ (或 ～ two days). 他星期一走的,两天后回来了。[注意: two days ～ 等短语作用于将来时] ②后来;以后;后面: What comes ～? 后来怎样? (=What comes next?) ②后面: look before and ～ 向前看再向后看;瞻前顾后 **IV** *a.* ①以后的: in ～ years 在以后的岁月里 ②靠近后部的(尤指船的后部): an ～ cabin 后舱 ‖*a fashion* 见 **fashion** / *～ all* 见 **all** / *～ one's (own) heart* 见 **heart** / *one ～ another* 见 **one** / *one ～ the other* 见 **one** ‖*most* 最后面的;最靠近船尾的 / ‖*～birth* *n.* 胞衣,胎盘,胎膜 /

～,**body** *n.* 船体后部 / '*～*,**burner** *n.* 【空】(涡轮喷气发动机的)补燃器,加力燃烧室 / '*～*,**burning** *n.* (涡轮喷气发动机的)补燃,加力燃烧;脉动燃烧 / '*～***care** *n.* ①(病后或产后的)调养 ②(罪犯释放后的)安置 / '*～***clap** *n.* 节外生枝的事件 / '*～*,**cooler** *n.* 【机】后冷却机 / '*～***crop** *n.* 【农】第二次收割 / '*～***damp** *n.* 矿山火灾(或爆炸后)形成的毒气 / '*～***deck** *n.* 【船】后甲板 / '*～***ef,fect** *n.* 后效;后来的影响,副作用 / '*～***glow** *n.* 余辉,夕照 / '*～***grass** *n.* 再生草 / '*～*,**image** *n.* 【心】余象,余感 / '*～***life** *n.* ①(迷信者所说的)来世 ②下半生 / '*～***light** *n.* ①余辉,夕照 ②后面的领悟 / '*～***math** *n.* ①再生草 ②后果(尤指灾祸) / '*～***pains** [复] *n.* 【医】产后痛 / '*～***piece** *n.* 剧终余兴 / '*～*,**ripening** *n.* 【生】后熟作用 / '*～***shock** *n.* (地震的)余震,后震 / '*～***taste** *n.* 回味,余味 / '*～***thought** *n.* 事后的思考(或想法) / '*～***wit** *n.* 事后聪明 / '*～***word** *n.* 跋;编后记

afternoon ['ɑ:ftə'nu:n] *n.* ①下午,午后: Good ～! 你好! (午后见面时用;午后分别时也可用,表示"再见") / this (tomorrow, yesterday) ～ 今天(明天,昨天)下午 [作状语用] / in (或 during) the ～ 在下午 / on Monday ～ 在星期一下午 ②后半期: the ～ of life 后半生 ‖*of an* ～ 往往在下午(指动作的习惯性) ‖*～s* *ad.* [美]每天下午;在任何下午

afterward(s) ['ɑ:ftəwəd(z)] *ad.* 后来;以后

Ag 【化】元素银 (silver) 的符号,由拉丁名 argentum 而来

again [ə'gein] *ad.* ①又,再: Try ～. 再试一下。/ Say it ～, please. 请再说一遍。/ See you ～. 再见。/ be oneself ～ 病好了;恢复常态 ②倍: as much ～ as 比…多一倍 / half as long ～ as 比…长一半 ③[常接在 then 等后用]而且,其次,还有: Then ～, we must consider the other aspects of the problem. 另外,我们还得考虑问题的其他方面。④ 一方面: He might go and ～ he might not. 他可能去,也可能不去。‖*～ and ～* 再三地,反复地 / *ever and ～* 时时,不时地 / *now and ～* 常常,不时地 / *time and ～* 一次又一次地,反复地

against [ə'geinst] *prep.* ①逆;反对: advance ～ difficulties 迎着困难上 / No one is ～ this proposal. 没有人反对这个提议。/ The resolution was adopted by a vote of 92 in favour to 9 ～ (it). 决议案以九十二票对九票获得通过。②撞击,碰击: hit one's head ～ a brick wall 碰壁 ③倚在;紧靠: Place the ladder ～ the wall. 把梯子靠在墙上。④防备: be prepared ～ war and natural disasters 备战备荒 ⑤以…为背景;与…对比,与…对照: be tested ～ reality 受客观实际检验 ⑥用…交换,用…抵付: the rates ～ U.S. dollars 美元兑换率 ‖*a rainy day* 未雨绸缪地 / *over* ～ 见 **over**

agape [ə'geip] *a.* [常作表语] & *ad.* ①(惊奇、害怕得)张大着嘴,目瞪口呆 ②洞开着,张开着: A blast of wind blew the window ~. 一阵风吹开了窗子.

age [eidʒ] **I** n. ①年龄: at the ~ of 在…岁时 / a school-~ child 学龄儿童 / attain full ~ 到达成年 / They two are of an ~. 他们两人同年. / live to a great ~ 活到很大年纪 ② 寿命: mine~ 矿山寿命(指其可采期) ③成年: be under ~ 未成年 ④老年 ⑤时期,时代: the Stone *Age* 石器时代 ⑥[常用复][口]很长一段时间: I haven't seen you *for* ~s (或 *for* an ~). 好久没看到你了. **II** (ag(e)ing) vt. & vi. ①(使)变老 ②(使)变陈;(使)成熟:【化】(使)老化 ‖*act one's* ~ 举止与年龄相称(尤指有大人气) / *a dog's* ~ [口]好久 / *be of* ~ 成年 / *come of* ~ 到达法定年龄 / *over* ~ 超龄 ‖~**less** a. 不会老的; 永恒的 / ~**r** n. 蒸化机; 熟化器 ‖'~-ˌbracket n. ① 某一年龄范围 ② 某一年龄范围内的人们 / '~-grade n. 同一年龄的人们,年龄相仿的人们 / '~-group n. [英]=~-grade / '~-ˌhardening n. [冶]时效硬化 / '~-long a. 长久的,久远的 / '~-old a. 古老的;久远的

aged a. ① ['eidʒid] [作定语用] 年老的, 老的; 陈年的: ~ wine 陈酒 / the ~ 老年的人们 ② [eidʒd] [常作表语]…岁的: a boy ~ ten (years) 十岁的男孩 ‖~**ness** ['eidʒidnis] n.

agency ['eidʒənsi] n. ①功能(力)作用: *through* human ~ 由人力所致 ②媒介; 经办,代理;代理权: *by* (或 *through*) the ~ of 由于…的作用;由于…的帮助 / the sole ~ 独家经理(权) ③ 代理处 ④ 机构: News *Agency* 通讯社 ‖~ **shop** 工会代理制企业(指企业全体雇员,不管是否工会会员,均向工会缴纳经费并一律由工会出面代表)

agenda [ə'dʒendə] n. ①议事日程: Now let's come to the next item on the ~. 现在让我们讨论议事日程上的下一个项目. / place (或 put) sth. on the ~ 把某事提到日程上来 ②记事册

agent ['eidʒənt] n. ①(发生作用或影响的)动因,力量: a natural ~ 自然力(如风、水等) ② 代理商; 代理人: a shipping ~ 运货代理商 / an enemy ~ 敌特 ③【化】剂: drying ~ 干燥剂 ‖~**ial** [ei'dʒenʃəl] a.

aggravate ['ægrəveit] vt. ①加重(病情、负担、罪行等),使更恶化 ②[口]激怒,使恼火 ‖**aggravating** a. / **aggravation** [ˌægrə'veiʃən] n.

aggregate ['ægrigit] **I** a. 聚集的 **II** a. ①合计;聚集;聚集体;【地】集合体 ③【建】(混凝土等的)集料, 粒料; 骨料: ~ chips 石屑 **III** ['ægrigeit] vt. & vi. ① (使) 聚集 ② 总计 ‖**aggregation** [ˌægri'geiʃən] n. 聚集; 聚集物,聚集体 / **aggregative** ['ægrigeitiv] a. 聚集的,聚集而成的

aggression [ə'greʃən] n. ①侵略 ②侵略行为;侵犯行为: an ~ *upon* sb.'s rights 对某人权利的侵犯

aggressive [ə'gresiv] a.①侵略的②爱寻衅的;(行为等)过分的, 放肆的 ③ 敢作敢为的,不是缩手缩脚的;有进取心的 ‖~**ly** ad. / ~**ness** n.

aggressor [ə'gresə] n. 侵略者: ~ troops 侵略军

aggrieve [ə'gri:v] vt. [常用被动语态] ①使悲痛 ②使委屈;侵害: feel ~d at (by) sth. 对某事(因某事)愤愤不平

aghast [ə'gɑ:st] a. [常作表语]吓呆的, 惊呆的: stand ~ at sth. 被某事吓呆

agile ['ædʒail] a. 敏捷的, 灵活的 ‖~**ly** ad. / **agility** [ə'dʒiliti] n.

agitate ['ædʒiteit] ❶ vt. ① 鼓动; 煽动 ② 搅动, 摇动(液体等) ③使不安定,使焦虑: be ~d *about* sth. 对某事感到焦急 ④热烈讨论,激烈辩论(问题、计划等) ❷ vi. 进行鼓动: ~ *for* sth. 为某事进行鼓动

agitation [ˌædʒi'teiʃən] n. ①鼓动; 煽动 ②(液体等的)搅动, 摇动 ③激动不安,焦虑 ‖~**al** a. 鼓动性的

agitator ['ædʒiteitə] n. ① 鼓动者,鼓动家 ② 搅拌器

aglow [ə'glou] a. [常作表语] & ad. 发亮,发红,灼热: be ~ *with* health 容光焕发

agnostic [æg'nɔstik] 【哲】**I** n. 不可知论者 **II** a. 不可知论的 ‖~**ism** [æg'nɔstisizəm] n. 不可知论

ago [ə'gou] ad. [常和一般过去时的动词连用]以前: I met him a few minutes ~. 我在几分钟前碰到他. / six years ~ 六年以前 / long ~ 很久以前

agonize ['ægənaiz] ❶ vt. 使极度痛苦, 折磨 ❷ vi. ①感到极度痛苦 ②拚命挣扎 ‖~**d** a. 感到(或表示)极度痛苦的 / **agonizing** a. 使人极度痛苦的

agony ['ægəni] n. ① 极度痛苦 ②痛苦的挣扎 ③(感情上)突然、强烈的爆发: in an ~ of joy 高兴到极点 ‖*pile up* (或 *on*) the ~ 渲染悲痛的事情 ‖~ **column** (报刊上)登载寻人、离婚等通告的专栏 (也作 personal column)

agree [ə'gri:] ❶ vi. ①同意, 赞同: I quite ~ *with* you. 我很同意你. / I quite ~ *with* what you say. 我很同意你所说的. / Do you ~ *to* this arrangement? 你赞成这个安排吗? / We are all ~d *that* the proposal is a good one. 我们都认为这个建议很好. / *Agreed!* 同意! ②应允: He ~d *to* help us. 他答应帮助我们. ③确定, 约定: The two sides have ~d on the date of negotiations. 双方商定了谈判的日期. ④(性情等)投合; (意见等)一致;【语】(人称、数、性、动词时态等)呼应, 一致 ⑤(气候、食物等)适合(*with*) ❷ vt. 同意; 认为(帐目)正确无误: It is unanimously ~d *that* .... 一致同意… / I ~d *that* .... 我同意…

agreeable [ə'griəbl] a. ①惬意的,令人愉快的: ~ weather 舒适的天气 / an ~ voice 悦耳的声音 / ~ *to* sb.'s tastes 适合某人爱好的 ②(欣然)同意的: Are you ~? 你同意吗? / be ~ *to* a plan 欣然赞同一项计划 / I am ~ to do what you suggest. 我乐意照你的建议去做. ③一致的,符合的 (*to*) ‖~**ness** n. / **agreeably** ad.

agreement [ə'gri:mənt] *n.* ①同意，一致；【语】呼应，一致：be in ~ with what sb. says 同意某人所说的 / be in ~ on (或 about, upon) sth. 对某事意见一致 ②(口头或书面)协定，协议：come to (或 arrive at, make) an ~ with 与…达成协议 ‖*a gentleman's* (或 *gentlemen's*) ~ 君子协定

agricultural [ˌægri'kʌltʃərəl] *a.* 农业的；农艺的，农学的：~ economy 农业经济 / ~ machinery 农业机械 / ~ pharmacology 农药学 / ~ products 农产品 ‖**~ist** *n.* 农学家

agriculture ['ægrikʌltʃə] *n.* ①农业；农艺 ②农学 ‖**agriculturist** [ˌægri'kʌltʃərist] *n.* 农学家

aground [ə'graund] *a.* [常作表语] & *ad.* ①地面上 ②搁浅：be (或 go, run) ~ (船)搁浅；触礁

ah [ɑ:] *int.* 啊! [表示恳求、懊悔、藐视、威胁、欢乐等]

ahead [ə'hed] *a.* [常作表语] & *ad.* ①在前：There is an infinitely bright future ~ of us. 我们有无限光明的前途。/ tasks for the period ~ 今后的任务 ②向前：Full speed ~! 全速前进! / set the clock ~ 把时钟指针拨向前 / look ~ 向前看；展望未来 ③提前：fulfil the plan ~ of schedule (或 time) 提前完成计划 ‖*be* ~ [口] 赢钱，赚钱 / *get* ~ 见 get / *go* ~ 见 go

ahoy [ə'hɔi] *int.* 喂! 啊嗨! (海员招呼船只或人的喊声)

aid [eid] **I** *vt.* 援助，帮助 **II** *n.* ①援助，帮助；救护：come (或 go) to sb.'s ~ 帮助某人 / call in sb.'s ~ 请某人援助 / first ~ 急救 / an ~ post 救护所 ②助手；助力，辅助物：a hearing ~ (或 an ~ to hearing) 助听器 ‖*~ and abet* 【律】伙同作(案)，同谋 / *pray in* ~ of 见 pray / *What's (all) this in* ~ of? [口]你是什么意思? ‖'**~man** *n.* 战地医务急救员 / ~ **station** 前线救护站

aide-de-camp ['eiddə'kɑ:ŋ] ([复] aides-de-camp) *n.* [法]副官；随从参谋

ail [eil] **❶** *vt.* 使受病痛；使苦恼：What ~s the child? 这孩子哪里不舒服? **❷** *vi.* 有病痛，生病 ‖**~ment** *n.* 失调(指较轻微的病)；精神不适

aim [eim] **I ❶** *vi.* ①瞄准；针对 (at) ②目的在于：~ high 力争上游 / What are you ~ing at? 你的用意何在? **❷** *vt.* 把…瞄准；把…对准 **II** *n.* ①瞄准：take ~ 瞄准 ②目标；目的：achieve (或 attain) one's ~ 达到目的 / miss one's ~ 打不中目标；达不到目的

aimless ['eimlis] *a.* 无目标的，无目的的 ‖**~ly** *ad.* / **~ness** *n.*

ain't [eint] ①[口] =are not, am not, is not ②[俗] =has not, have not

air [ɛə] **I** *n.* ①空气；大气：fresh air 新鲜空气 / an ~ compressor 空气压缩机 ②空中，天空：mastery of the ~ 制空权 / the open ~ 露天，户外 ③微风 ④歌曲，曲调 ⑤外观，神态：an important ~ (或 an ~ of importance) 煞有介事

的神态 ⑥[常用复]做作的姿态，架子：do away with apathetic, arrogant, bureaucratic and finicky ~s 打掉暮气、骄气、官气、娇气 / sanctified ~s 装出的神圣不可侵犯的气派 **II** *vt.* ①晾(衣服、被褥等)；烘干 ②使(房间等)通气 ③发表(意见、理论等)；炫耀：~ one's views freely 大鸣大放 / ~ one's grievances against the old society 诉旧社会的苦 ④(用无线电、电视)播送 ⑤[后常接 oneself] 到户外呼吸新鲜空气 ‖*~s and graces* 做作的姿态，装腔作势 / *beat the* ~ 白费气力，徒劳 / *by* ~ 通过航空途径：go by ~ 坐飞机去 / send the mail by ~ 由航空寄发邮件 / *clear the* ~ ①使空气流通 ②澄清真相 ③消除误会(或紧张、猜疑气氛) / *fan the* ~ 打个空，扑个空 / *fish in the* ~ =plough the ~ / *get the* ~ [美俚]被解雇 / *give* ~ *to* 发表(意见等) / *give oneself* ~s =put on ~s / *give sb. the* ~ [美俚]解雇某人 / *go off the* ~ 停止广播 / *go on the* ~ 开始广播 / *go up in the* ~ [美俚]①发怒，突然发火 ②演员突然忘记台词 / *hang in the* ~ 未完成；未证实；未正式核准 / *hot* ~ [口]夸夸其谈，吹牛 / *in the* ~ ①在空中. castles *in the* ~ 空中楼阁 ②(问题、计划等)未定，悬而未决 ③(意见、谣言等)在流传中 ④【军】未设防的，没有掩护的 / *into thin* ~ 无影无踪 / *leave in the* ~ 使悬而不决 / *live on* ~ 不吃东西 / *make the* ~ *blue* 诅咒 / *on the* ~ (正在)广播 / *out of thin* ~ 无中生有地 / *plough the* ~ 白费气力 / *put on* ~s 摆架子 / *saw the* ~ 挥舞手臂 / *take* ~ (事等)传开 / *take the* ~ 到户外(呼吸新鲜空气) / *up in the* ~ (问题、计划等)未定，悬而未决 / *walk on* ~ (或 *tread on* ~) 洋洋得意 ‖'~ **action**, ~ battle 空战 / ~ **alarm** 空袭警报 / ~ **alert** ①空袭警报(期间) ②【军】空中待机 / '~-**atomic** ['ɛər-ə'tɔmik] *a.* 能通过空间发射核武器的：~-atomic power 空间核力量 / ~ **attack** 空中攻击，空袭 / ~ **base** 航空基地，空军基地 / ~ **bath** 空气浴；空气浴装置 / '~-**bed** *n.* 空气床垫 / ~ **bladder** 【生】鳔；气泡 / ~ **blast** ①空中爆炸 ②气喷净法 / '~,**blower** *n.* 【机】鼓风机 / '~**boat** *n.* 气艇 / '~**borne** *a.* ①空降的：an ~borne division 空降师 ②空运的，机载的 ③空中的，(飞机)在飞行中的：~borne fire-control equipment 飞机炮火控制设备 ④(飞机)离开了地面的：We were soon ~borne. 很快我们就起飞了。⑤通过无线电播送的，通过电视播送的 / ~ **brake** ①【空】空气制动器 ②【机】气闸，风闸 / ~ **brick** 空心砖(特通通风透气用的) / '~-**bridge** *n.* 空运线 / '~**brush** *n.* (喷漆等用的)喷枪 *vt.* 用喷枪喷 / '~**bus** *n.* [口]大型客机，"空中公共汽车" / ~ **cargo** 空运货物，空运邮件 / ~ **castle** 空中楼阁 / ~ **cell** 气胞 / ~ **chamber** 气室 / ~ **coach** 二等客机 / ~ **command** 空军司令部 / '~-**condition** *vt.* 在…上装空气调节器；调节…的空气 / ~ **conditioner** 空气调节器 / ~ **control-**

man 海军空中交通管理调配员 / '∼-cool vt. 用空气冷却 / '∼-,cooler n. 空气冷却器 / ∼ corridor 空中走廊 / ∼ cover = ∼ umbrella / '∼craft [单复同] n. 航空器；飞机，飞艇：an ∼craft carrier 航空母舰 / ∼craft(s)man ['ɛə-kra:ft(s)mən] n. 空军士兵：a senior (leading) ∼craft(s)man (英) 空军一等(二等)兵 / '∼crew n. 空勤人员 / ∼ cushion 气垫 / ∼ defence 防空 / '∼dent n. 气喷磨牙机 / ∼ division [美]空军师 / ∼ drill 风钻 / '∼drome n. [美]飞机场 / '∼-drop vt. & n. 空投 / '∼-dry vt. & a. 晾干(的) / ∼ express ①包裹空运 ②空运的包裹 / ∼field n. 飞机场 / ∼ flight 航空小队 / '∼flow n. 气流 / '∼-flue n. 气道，烟道，风道 / ∼foil【空】翼(剖)面；机翼,方向舵 / ∼ force 空军 / '∼freight n.①空中货运②空中货运费 vt. 由空中运输 / '∼,freighter n. 货运飞机 / ∼ ga(u)ge 气压计 / '∼glow n. [气]气辉 / '∼-ground n. 陆空的：an ∼-ground operation 陆空协同作战 / ∼ group 空军大队 / ∼ gun 气枪 / ∼ hammer 气锤 / ∼ harbo(u)r 航空港 / '∼head n. 空降场 / ∼ hole ①气孔②(结冰的河、池中的)不冰冻部分③【空】空中陷阱,气潭 / ∼ hostess 客机上的女服务员,空中小姐 / ∼ jacket ①空气救生衣②气套 / ∼ jet ①空气喷射②空气喷口 / '∼land vt.【军】机降 / ∼ lane 航空路线 / '∼-launch vt. 空中发射 / ∼ letter 航空信；航空邮笺 / '∼lift n. 空中补给线 vt. 空运 / '∼line n. ①航空系统②航空公司③航线④大圆航线 / '∼,liner n. 客机,班机 / ∼ lock 气塞 / '∼-lock vt. 用气塞堵住 / ∼ log ①航空日记②空哩计 / '∼mail n. ①航空邮件②航空邮政③航空邮票 vt. 航空邮寄 a. 航空邮件的；航空邮政的 / ∼ man n. ①航空兵：an ∼man apprentice 见习航空兵 / an Airman First (Second, Third) Class (美) 空军一(二, 三)等兵②飞行员 / '∼manship n. 飞行技术；导航技术 / ∼ map 由空中摄影制成的地图 / ,mapping aeroplane 测绘飞机 / '∼-minded a. 热心于航空的 / ∼ mobile ['ɛərəmɔbi:l] a. 空中机动的：∼mobile warfare 空中机动战 / '∼plane n. [美]飞机 / ∼ pocket【空】空中陷阱,气潭 / '∼port n. 机场,航空站 / '∼post n. = ∼mail (n.) / ∼ power 空中力量 / '∼proof a. 不漏气的,密封的. 使不漏气,使密封 / ∼ propeller 飞机螺旋桨 / ∼ pump 气泵 / ∼ raid 空袭：an ∼-raid warning 空袭警报 / an ∼-raid shelter 防空洞 / '∼-,raider n. 空袭飞机 / ∼ rifle 气枪 / ∼ sac (动植物的)气囊 / '∼scape n. 空中鸟瞰图 / ∼ scout ①对空监视哨②侦察机 / '∼screw n. [英]飞机螺旋桨 / '∼sea n. 海空的：an ∼-sea rescue 海空搜索救援 / ∼ shaft ①【矿】风井②【建】通风孔 / '∼ship n. 飞艇 / ∼ show 航空表演 / ∼ shower【物】空气簇射 (宇宙线穿过大气时形成的簇射) / '∼sick a. 晕

机的 / '∼,sickness n. 晕机 / '∼-slake vt. 风化 / ∼ sleeve, ∼ sock 风标 / '∼ space n. ①空域；领空：a restricted ∼space 空中禁区②广播时间 / '∼speed n. 空速：an ∼speed indicator (或 meter) 空速计 / '∼-spray a. 气喷的 / ∼ squadron 空军中队 / ∼ station 航空维修站 / '∼stop n. 直升飞机航空站 / '∼stream n. 气流 / ∼ strike 空袭 / '∼strip n. 简易机场 / '∼tight a. ①不漏气的,密封的②(防守等)严密的；(论点等)无懈可击的 / '∼,tightness n. 密封性 / ∼ time 广播时间 / '∼-to-' a. 空对空的 / '∼-to-'ground a. 空对地的 / '∼-to-'surface a. 空对面(地面或水面)的 / '∼-to-'underwater a. 空对水下的 / ∼ transport ①空运②运输机(尤指军用的) / ∼ umbrella 空中掩护(幕) / ∼ vehicle 空中运载工具(如飞机、导弹等) / ∼ warden 防空队长 / '∼wave n. ①电波②波长 / '∼way n. ①【矿】通风道,风巷②航路③[复]航空公司 / ∼ wave 波长 / ∼ well【建】通风井 / ∼ wing (美、英军)的空军联队 / '∼,worthiness n. 适航性；飞行性能 / ,worthy a. 适航的；飞行性能良好的 / ∼ zero 原子弹空中爆炸中心

airily ['ɛərili] ad. ①活泼地,轻盈地②快活地,逍遥自在地③轻率地

airy ['ɛəri] a. ①空气的②空中的③通风的；(织物)使人凉爽的④空想的,不实际的,虚无飘渺的⑤活泼的,轻盈的⑥快活的,逍遥自在的⑦轻率的⑧[口]做作的,摆架子的 ‖ ∼-'fairy a. ①象童话中仙子一般的②空想的,不实际的

aisle [ail] n. (教堂、戏院等的)侧廊, 通道, 走廊；楼间,耳堂 ‖ roll in the ∼s [美]捧腹大笑 ‖ ∼-'sitter n. 剧评家

ajar [ə'dʒɑ:] a. [常作表语] & ad. (门等) 微开着,半开着

akimbo [ə'kimbou] a. [常作表语] & ad. 叉着腰：stand (with arms) ∼ 双手叉腰立着

akin [ə'kin] a. [常作表语] ①同族的,有血族关系的②同类的,相近似的 (to)

alabaster ['æləbɑ:stə] I n. 雪花石膏 II a. 雪花石膏制的；雪花石膏似的

alacrity [ə'lækriti] n. ①乐意,欣然②轻捷

alarm [ə'lɑ:m] I n. ①警报：an air-raid ∼ 空袭警报 / sound the ∼ 发警报,敲警钟 / a false ∼ 假警报②报警器③惊恐：take (或 feel) ∼ at 因…而惊恐 II vt. ①向…报警,使警觉②使惊恐：There is nothing to get ∼ed about. 没什么可大惊小怪的。 ‖ ∼ bell 警铃, 警钟 / ∼ call【军】紧急号 / ∼ clock 闹钟：set the ∼ clock for 5 o'clock 把闹钟拨到五点钟 / ∼ post【军】紧急集合场所

alarming [ə'lɑ:miŋ] a. 使人惊恐的；用以引起惊恐的：an ∼ report 故意用来吓人的虚假 ‖ ∼ly ad.

albatross ['ælbətrɔs] ([复] albatross(es)) n.【动】信天翁

album ['ælbəm] n. ①粘贴簿：a photo (stamp,

autograph) ~ 照相(集邮,题词)簿 ②(照相簿式
的)唱片套,片套;唱片集 ③ 文选;歌曲选;画片
选;摄影选

albumen ['ælbjumin] *n.* ①蛋白 ②【生化】白朊,
白蛋白 ③【植】胚乳

alchemy ['ælkimi] *n.* 炼金术,炼丹术 ||**alchem-
ic(al)** [æl'kemik(ə)b] *a.* / **alchemist** *n.* 炼金术
士,炼丹术士

alcohol ['ælkəhol] *n.* ①【化】酒精,乙醇;醇: an ~
lamp 酒精灯 ② 含有酒精的饮料 ||**-ic** [ælkə-
'holik] *a.* ①酒精的;含酒精的 ②酒精中毒的 *n.*
饮酒过度的人: *Alcoholics* Anonymous 嗜酒者互
诫协会 / **~ism** *n.* 酒精中毒

alert [ə'lə:t] **I** *a.* ①警惕的,警觉的 ②活跃的,机
灵的 **II** *n.* ①警报 ②警戒状态;警戒期间 ③【军】
待命行动: No. one ~ 一级战备 / the ~ station
空中待机区 **III** *vt.* 使警觉;使…处于待命状态:
~ sb. *to* the fact that . . . 提醒某人注意…的事
实 ||**on the ~** 警惕着,警觉着 ||**~ly** *ad.* / **~-
ness** *n.*

algebra ['ældʒibrə] *n.* 代数学

alias ['eiliæs] **I** *n.* 别名; 化名 **II** *ad.* 别名叫; 化
名为

alibi ['ælibai] **I** *n.* ①【律】不在犯罪现场: establish
(或 prove) an ~ 提出不在犯罪现场的证据 ②
[口]借口,托辞 **II** ❶ *vi.* [口]辩解 ❷ *vt.* [口]
~ oneself 为…辩解

alien ['eiljən] **I** *a.* ①外国的;异己的: an ~ friend
友好国家侨民 / ~ property 外国人的财产 ②相
异的;不相容的: It is ~ *to* the principles of
economy. 这是违反节约原则的。 **II** *n.* ①外侨
②外人 **III** *vt.* 【律】转让,让渡(所有权)

alight[1] [ə'lait] (alighted 或 alit [ə'lit]) *vi.* ①(从
马车中,车、飞机等处)下来 (*from*) ②(鸟等)飞落;
(飞机等)降落 (*on*): A sparrow ~*ed on* the
branch. 一只麻雀飞落在树枝上。 / the ~*ing*
deck (航空母舰上的)降落甲板 ② 偶然发现,偶
然碰见 (*upon, on*)

alight[2] [ə'lait] *a.* [常作表语] ①点着的,烧着的
②照亮的: wear a face ~ *with* happiness 脸上
喜气洋洋

align [ə'lain] ❶ *vt.* ①使成一线,使成一行: ~ the
sights and bull's-eye 瞄准靶心 ② 使结盟;使密
切合作: a non-~*ed* country 不结盟国家 / ~
oneself with sb. 同某人结盟 ③【物】匹配;调准,
校直 ❷ *vi.* ① 成一线,排成一行;排队,列队 ②
结盟 (*with*)

alignment [ə'lainmənt] *n.* ①队列,一直线: in
(out of) ~ 成 (不成)一直线 ②结盟;联合,组
合 ③【测】定线;准线 ④【物】调准,校直

alike [ə'laik] **I** *a.* [常作表语]相同的,相象的: The
two brothers are very much ~. 这两兄弟非常
相象。 / All music is ~ to Tom. 各种音乐在汤
姆听来全是一样 (指没有鉴赏能力)。 **II** *ad.* 一
样地,相似地: treat ~ 同样对待 / think ~
同样想法

alive [ə'laiv] *a.* [常作表语] ①活着的,存在的,在
世的: the happiest children ~ 当代最幸福
的孩子们 ②有活力的,有生气的: ~ in every
fibre 浑身是劲 ③ 热闹的; 充满着…的 (*with*):
The whole square was ~ *with* singing and
rejoicing. 整个广场歌声嘹亮,喜气洋洋。 / The
lake is ~ *with* fish. 湖里鱼多得很。 ④敏感的,
感觉到的,注意到的 (*to*): be fully ~ *to* the
danger of 充分注意到…的危险 ⑤【电】通有电流
的,加有电压的 ||**~ and kicking** 活蹦活跳的 /
any man ~ 任何人 / *Man* (或 *Heart*) ~!
[口]哎呀! 我的天呀! / ~ *come* ① 活跃起
来; 觉悟起来 ②显得象真的似的 / *Look* ~! 快
些! / *skin* ~ ①活活地剥去(人或动物)的皮 ②
[口]严厉申斥,严厉责罚 ③[口]决定性地击败

alkali ['ælkəlai] ([复] alkali(e)s) *n.* 【化】碱;强碱
||**~fy** ['ælkəlifai] *vt.* & *vi.* (使)碱化;加碱(于) /
~ze *vt.* 使碱化

all [ɔ:l] **I** *a.* ①一切的,所有的;整个的,全部的:
do good ~ one's life 一辈子做好事 / ~ (the)
day 全天 / ~ the year (round) 全年 / *All* the
idioms are not (或 Not ~ the idioms are)
illustrated. 不是每一个习语都有例证。 / be ~
attention 聚精会神 / be ~ eyes 双目注视,全神
贯注 ② 极度的: with ~ speed 以最高的速度
③任何的: beyond ~ doubt 不容许任何怀疑 ④
[俚] 耗尽,用完: The tea was ~. 茶全喝光了。
II *ad.* ①[加强语气]完全地,十分: I am ~ for
adopting the new technique. 我十分赞成采用这
项新技术。 ②[接 the 和比较级]更加: Well I know that
there's danger ahead, but I am ~ *the more* set
on driving forward. 明知征途有艰险,越是艰险
越向前。 ③ (球赛等) 双方得分相等的,打平的:
The score was two ~. 比分是两平。 **III** *pron.* 一
切;全部;大家,全体: Say ~ you know and say
it without reserve. 知无不言, 言无不尽。 / *All*
are agreed. 一致同意。 / Are you ~ here? 你
们全来了吗? / *All* of us are of the opinion that
. . . . 我们大家都认为…[注意:代词 all 只用来指
三个或三个以上的人或物;指两个用 both] / It
was ~ I could do not to laugh. 我差点笑出来。
IV *n.* [与物主代词连用]所有的一切: give one's
~ *to* the nation 把自己的一切献给国家
||*above* ~ 首先,首要/ *after* ~ 毕竟;终究: Don't
get discouraged by setbacks, we are new to the
work *after* ~. 别因挫折而灰心,这工作对我们
说来毕竟还是新的。 / ~ *alone* ①独个儿 ②独
立地 / ~ *along* 始终,一直,一贯 / ~ *and
singular* 悉,皆,全体,一律 / ~ *and sundry* 全
部;所有的人 / ~ *around* (在…)周围;各处:
shake hands ~ *around* 和大家一一握手 / ~ *at
once* ①突然 ②同时 / ~ *but* 几乎,差一点: I
~ *but* stumbled. 我差一点摔跤。 / ~ *but
impossible* 几乎不可能 / ~ *clear* (空袭)解
除警报 / ~ *dressed up and nowhere to
go* 打扮得整整齐齐却无处可去炫耀 / ~ *for*

naught 徒然,无用 / **~ get-out** [美俚]非常: big as ~ *get-out* 极大 / work like ~ *get-out* 拼命干 / **~ in** [口]疲乏到极点 / **~ in ~** ①总的说来: *All in ~*, it was a success. 总的说来,这事是成功的。 / take it ~ *in ~* 总而言之 ②头等重要的(东西);最心爱的(东西),一切的一切: be ~ *in ~* to sb. 对某人说来,是一切的一切(或是无价之宝) / *All is not gold that glitters.* [谚]发亮的东西不一定都是金子。(或:好看的东西不一定都有用处。) / **~ of** 实足 / **~ of a . . .** 见 *of*[1] / **~ one knows** ①所能知道的一切 ②尽所能,尽全力 / **~ one to** 对…说来都一样: It is ~ *one to* me whether he comes or not. 他来不来,对我说来都一样。 / **~ out** 竭尽全力: go ~ *out* 鼓足干劲 / **~ over** ① 全部结束;完蛋: Glad (或 I'm glad) it's ~ *over*. 这事全部结束了,好得很。 / It's ~ *over* with him. 他完蛋了。②浑身;到处: I'm wet ~ *over*. 我浑身都湿了。 / I have looked ~ *over* for him. 我到处都找过他了。 / We have friends ~ *over* the world. 我们的朋友遍天下。③[口](行为)十足(是某人)的特点: That's Young Li ~ *over*. 小李就是这种脾气。 / **~ right** ①行,好;(健康状况)良好: It's (quite) ~ *right*. 没有关系! (或:很不错!) / Is it ~ *right* with you? 这对你方便吗? ②顺利,圆满;无误 ③[加强语气]确实: You have read the book ~ *right*, but the point is that you haven't studied it critically. 不错,这本书你是读过了,但问题是没有用批判的眼光去分析。 / *All's well that ends well.* [谚]结果好就一切都好。 / **~ the more** 更加,益发 / **~ there** ①[口][常用于否定句]头脑清醒的: He doesn't seem to be ~ *there*. 他看来是头脑不清的。②[俚]机警的,富于机智的 / **~ through** 一直,从来就 / **~ together** ①一道,同时 ②总共(= altogether) 总共,合计 / **~ told** 总共,合计 / **~ to nothing** 见 **nothing** / **~ up** 无望,彻底完蛋: It's ~ *up* with the enemy. 敌人彻底完蛋了。 / **and ~** 连同其他一切 / **at ~** [常用于否定句和条件从句以加强语气]根本: Do it well if you do it at ~. 要做就要做得好。 / **for ~** 尽管 / **for ~ I care** 与我无关: He may leave at once *for ~ I care*. 他尽可立刻离开,我才不管呢。 / **for ~ I know** 亦未可知: *For ~ I know*, the matter may have been settled. 这事也许早解决了,谁知道呢。 / **Grasp ~, lose ~.** 见 **grasp** / **in ~** 总共 / **not at ~** ①根本不;一点也不 ②(客套语)别客气: A: Thank you very much. B: *Not at ~*. 甲:谢谢你。乙:别客气。 / **of ~ . . .** 见 *of*[1] / **over ~** 遍;从一头到另一头 / **sweep before one** 见 **sweep** / **the ~ and the one** 全部,整体 / **when ~ comes to ~** 通盘考虑后 / **when ~ is said and done** 结果,毕竟 // **a'round** *a.* [美] = ~-round / **~-'rounder** *n.* [美] = ~-rounder / **'~-'conquering** *a.* 所向无敌的 / **'~-'day** *a.* 全天的 / **'~-em'bracing**

a. 包括一切的 / **'~-'fired** *a.* & *ad.* [俚]该死的,该死要命(表示诅咒): ~-*fired* hot 热得要命 / **'~-im'portant** *a.* 十分重要的 / **'~-'in** *a.* ①包括一切的: an ~-*in* 10-day tour 包括一切的十天游览旅行 ②(摔角)自由式的 / **'~-'in'clusive** *a.* 包括一切的 / **'~-'mains** *a.* [只作定语](收音机)适应各种电压的 / **'~-night** *a.* 通宵的: This shop gives ~-*night* service. 这家商店通宵服务。 / **'~-or-'none** *a.* 全或无的 / **'~-or-'nothing** *a.* 占有一切或一无所有的;孤注一掷的: an ~-*or-nothing* attitude 全归我或全不要的态度 / play an ~-*or-nothing* game 玩全败的赌局 / **'~-'out** *a.* 全力的;没有保留的: ~-*out* support 全力支持 / **'~-'overish** *a.* ①心中不安的 ②浑身不舒服的 / **'~-per'vasive** *a.* 无孔不入的 / **'~-pos'sessed** *a.* [美口]中了邪似的,入了迷的 / **'~-'powerful** *a.* 最强大的;无所不能的 / **'~-'purpose** *a.* 适于各种用途的: ~-*purpose* aircraft 通用飞机 / **'~-'red** *a.* (航线、海底电线等)全在英联邦范围内的 / **'~='round** *a.* ①(看法等)全面的 ②才能多方面的 ③(工具等)适于各种用途的;综合性的 / **'~='rounder** *n.* 多面手;全能运动员 / **'~-'seed** *a.* 多种子植物 / **'~-'sided** *a.* 全面的 / **'~-'sidedly** *ad.* 全面地 / **'~-'sidedness** *n.* 全面性 / **'~-spice** *n.* [植]多香果 / **'~-'time** *a.* ①空前的: hit (或 reach) an ~-*time* high in grain output 达到粮食产量的最高记录 ②全部时间的;专职的 / **'~-'up weight** (飞机包括机务员、乘客、货物等在内的)空中总重量 / **'~-'wave** *a.* (收音机)全波段的 / **'~-'way** *a.* 从所有方向和向所有方向运动的: an ~-*way* airfield 多跑道飞机场 / **'~-'weather** *a.* 适应各种气候的;【空】全天候的: an ~-*weather* interceptor 全天候截击机

allay [ə'lei] *vt.* 减轻(痛苦、疼痛、忧虑等)

allegation [æle'geiʃən] *n.* 断言,主张,辩解(尤指提不出证明的)

allege [ə'ledʒ] *vt.* ①断言,宣称(尤指在提不出证明的情况下): It is ~*d* that . . . . 据说… ②(作为事实、理由、借口、辩解)提出: ~ sth. as a reason 提出某事作为理由

alleged [ə'ledʒd] *a.* 被说成的,被指称的 ‖**-ly** [ə'ledʒidli] *ad.* This is ~*ly* the case. 据说情况是这样。

allegiance [ə'li:dʒəns] *n.* (对国家、政府、事业、个人等的)忠诚: give ~ *to* 忠诚于,效忠于

allegory ['æligəri] *n.* 讽喻,比方;寓言 ‖**allegorist** *n.* 寓言作家;讽喻家 / **allegorize** ['æligəraiz] *vt.* 用讽喻方式叙述 *vi.* 作寓言

alleluia [,æli'lu:jə] *n.* & *int.* 哈利路亚(犹太教和基督教的欢呼语,意为"赞美神"; =hallelujah)

allergy ['ælədʒi] *n.* ①[医]变(态反)应性,变态反应,过敏症 ②反感,憎恶: have an ~ *to* 讨厌…;对某事物感到说不出的厌恶 ‖**allergic** [ə'lə:dʒik] *a.* ①[医]变应性的,过敏性的 ②[口]过敏的;(对某事物)感到说不出的厌恶的 (to) / **allergist** *n.* 过敏症专家

alleviate [ə'li:vieit] **vt.** 减轻(痛苦等); 缓和: ~ the patient's suffering 减轻病人的痛苦 ‖**alleviation** [ə,li:vi'vieiʃən] **n.** / **alleviative** a. 减轻痛苦的; 起缓和作用的 **n.** 解痛药; 缓和物 / **alleviator** **n.** 解痛药; 缓和物 / **alleviatory** [ə'li:vietəri] a. 减轻痛苦的; 起缓和作用的

alley ['æli] **n.** 胡同, 小巷, 弄堂; 公园(或庭园)中的小径 ‖a blind ~ 死胡同 / up (或 down) sb.'s ~ [俚]合某人胃口(或才能)的‖'~way n. [美]小弄

alliance [ə'laiəns] **n.** ① 联盟, 同盟, 联合 ②联姻 ③【植】群落属 ‖enter into (an) ~ with 与…结成联盟, 与…联合

allied [ə'laid, 'ælaid] a. ① 联合的, 同盟的 ② [A-] (第一次世界大战中)协约国的; (第二次世界大战中)同盟国的 ③ 联姻的 ④ 同源的: The English language is ~ to the German language. 英语和德语同出一源。 ⑤ 性质上有密切联系的: the rapid development of electronics and ~ sciences in our country 电子学和有关各门科学在我国的迅速发展

alligator ['æligeitə] **n.** ①短吻鳄, 鼍; (泛指)一般鳄鱼 ②短吻鳄皮 ③水陆平底军用车 ④鳄式碎石机, 鳄式压轧机

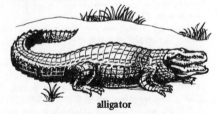

alligator

allocate ['æləkeit] **vt.** ①分配, 分派; 配给: ~ duties to certain persons 分配任务给某些人 ② 把(物资、资金等)划归: ~ materials and facilities for a new construction project 调拨材料和设备给新的建设项目 ‖**allocation** [,ælə'keiʃən] **n.** ①分配, 分派; 配给: allocation of materials 物资分配 ②配给物: an additional budget allocation for education 教育事业的追加预算

allot [ə'lɔt] (allotted; allotting) **vt.** ①(按股或按规定)分配, 配给 (to): A part of this urgent task was allotted to us. 这项紧急任务的一部分分配给了我们。②(为特定用途而)拨给 ③规定, 派定: We accomplished the work within the allotted time. 我们在规定时间内完成了工作。 ‖~ment **n.** / allot(t)ee [,ælə'ti:] **n.** 接受分配的人, 接受拨给物资的人员(或机构等)

allow [ə'lau] **❶ vt.** ①允许, 准许; 任, 由: No smoking (或 Smoking not) ~ed. 禁止吸烟。②允给, 让…得到: ~ an hour for lunch 规定一小时的午饭时间 / ~ sb. a monthly subsidy 按月发给某人津贴 ③[方]认为, 承认 ④酌加; 酌减: ~ one percent for leakage 少算百分之一作为漏损 ⑤

[方]打算, 计划: ~ to do sth. 打算做某事 **❷ vi.** ①考虑到, 估及; 体谅 (for): It takes about an hour to get there, ~ing for possible traffic delays. 把路上可能的耽搁算进去, 大约一个小时可到那里。/ We must ~ for his inexperience. 我们必须考虑到他的缺乏经验。②容许, 容得 (of): The overhauling of the lathe ~s of no delay. 这台车床非马上检修不可。

allowance [ə'lauəns] **I n.** ①允许, 准许 ②被允许的东西(如限额、限期等): What is the ~ of luggage? 行李的重量限额是多少? / ask for an ~ of three days 要求给三天时间 ③津贴, 补助费(或粮等): a separation ~ 政府发给出征军人妻子的津贴 / a traffic ~ 车贴, 交通费 ④(体育比赛中)按规则给对方的让步 ⑤【商】折扣: ~s and rebates 折让和回扣 ⑥【机】(配合)容差; (加工)留量 **II vt.** ①定量供应(物品) ②发津贴给 ③把物品定量发给 ‖make ~(s) 留出余地 / make ~(s) for ①扣除, 估及, 为…留出余地(或余量) ②考虑到…(而原谅)

alloy **I** ['ælɔi] **n.** ①合金, 齐: an ~ of copper and (或 with) zinc 铜和锌的合金, 铜锌齐 / ~ steel 合金钢 ②(金属的)成色, 纯度 ③与金、银熔合的其他金属; [喻]搀杂物 **II** [ə'lɔi] **❶ vt.** ①合铸(金属);用其他金属熔合(贵金属): ~ silver and copper 合铸银和铜 / ~ silver with copper 用铜熔合银 ②减低(金属)的成色; 减低(乐趣等) **❷ vi.** 合铸; (易于)熔合: Iron ~s well. 铁易于熔合。

allude [ə'lju:d] **vi.** 暗指; (间接)提到 (to)

allure [ə'ljuə] **I vt.** 诱惑, 引诱, 吸引: ~ sb. from 诱使某人离开… / ~ sb. into 诱使某人陷入… **II n.** 诱惑力, 魅力, 吸引力 ‖~ment **n.** 诱惑; 魅力; 诱惑物 / **alluring** [ə'ljuəriŋ] a. 诱惑的, 迷人的, 引人向往的

allusion [ə'lju:ʒən] **n.** ① 暗指, (间接)提到 (to): make (an) ~ to (不明言地)提及 / in ~ to 针对…而提的 ②引喻

alluvial [ə'lju:vjəl] **I** a. 冲积的, 淤积的: an ~ cone 冲积锥 / ~ soil 冲积土, 淤积土 **II** n. 冲积土, 淤积土; 冲积层, 冲积矿床

ally **I** ['ælai, ə'lai] **n.** ①同盟国, 同盟者: the Allies 第一次世界大战中的协约国; 第二次世界大战中的同盟国 ②伙伴; 助手 ③同源的动物(或植物) **II** [ə'lai, æ'lai] **❶ vt.** ①使结盟, 使联姻 ② 与…(在起源或性质上)关联: Diamond is chemically allied to coal. 金刚石与煤在化学上是同类的。 **❷ vi.** 结盟: ~ with another country 与另一国结盟

almanac ['ɔ:lmənæk] **n.** 历书, 历本; 年历, 年鉴: a nautical ~ 天文年鉴(航海、测量用)

almighty [ɔ:l'maiti] **I** a. ①全能的: the Almighty (=Almighty God) 【基督教】全能者, 上帝 ②[俚]槽糕透的: in an ~ fix 处境槽糕透了 **II** ad. [俚]极, 非常: ~ cold 极冷 ‖**almightiness** n. 全能 / **almightily** ad.

almond ['ɑ:mənd] **n.** 杏仁; 扁桃, 巴旦杏 ‖'~-eyed a. 杏眼的(指眼部呈椭圆形、眼梢细长) / ~ oil 杏仁油 / ~ paste 杏仁糊

almost ['ɔ:lmoust, 'ɔ:lməst] **I** *ad.* 几乎，差不多: It was ~ midnight when we heard the good news over the radio. 我们从收音机里听到这个好消息已是快半夜了。/ *Almost* no one took any rest. 几乎没有一个人歇过一下。**II** *a.* [罕] 几乎是…(的): be in a state of ~ collapse 处于接近垮台的状态

alms [ɑ:mz] [单复同] *n.* 施舍物，救济金 ‖~-**house** *n.* 贫民所，救济院 / ~**man** ['ɑ:mzmən] *n.* 领教济金者，受施舍者

aloft [ə'lɒft] *ad.* ①高高地；向上 ②【海】在桅杆(或帆索)高处

alone [ə'loun] **I** *ad.* ① 单独地；独自: I went ~. 我是一个人去的。/ He did it all ~. 这事是他一个人干的。②[用在名词或代词后面]只，只有: He ~ is not responsible for it. 这件事只有他一人毫无责任。**II** *a.* [用作表语] 单独，独一无二: I am not ~ in this opinion. 不只是我一个人有这想法。‖*leave* ~ 见 **leave**[1] / *let* ~ 见 **let**[1] / *let well* ~ 见 **well**[2] / *stand* ~ *in* 在…方面独一无二

along [ə'lɒŋ] **I** *prep.* 沿着: "Pass ~ the car, please!" said the conductor. 售票员说: "请往里走!" **II** *ad.* ①沿: trees ~ by the river 沿河的树 ②向前: Move ~, please! 请向前走!(不要阻塞交通) / pass the note ~ 把条子传过去 ③一道，一起: He took his sister ~ (*with* him). [美] 他带了妹妹一同去。/ Come ~! 跟我来! ④[美](时间)够: The morning was well ~. 近中午了。⑤在手边: He took his umbrella ~. 他带着伞。‖*all* ~ 始终，一直，一贯 / ~ *of* (或 *on*) [方]因为 / *be* ~ 来到: He will soon *be* ~. 他快要来了。/ *get* ~ 见 **get** / *go* ~ 见 **go** / *right* ~ 继续地，不断地 ‖**a'long'shore** *ad.* 沿岸: There are many trees ~*shore*. 沿岸有许多树。*a.* 沿岸的: ~*shore* currents 沿岸的水流

alongside [ə'lɒŋ'said] **I** *prep.* 在…旁边；横靠；与…并肩: ships anchored ~ a dock 停泊在码头边的船 **II** *ad.* 并排地；并肩地 ‖~ *of* 在…旁边；与…并肩

aloof [ə'lu:f] **I** *ad.* 离开，避开，远离: Never stand (或 hold, keep) ~ from the masses. 千万不可脱离群众。**II** *a.* [常作表语] ① 远离的，孤零的: an ~ building 一幢孤零零的房屋 ② 冷淡的: His manner was ~. 他的态度冷淡。‖~**ness** *n.*

aloud [ə'laud] *ad.* 出声地；大声地: read ~ 朗读

alpha ['ælfə] **I** *n.* ① 希腊语的第一个字母 (A, α) ②最初，开始 ③第一位的东西；【天】主星，α星 (星座中最亮的星) **II** *a.* 【化】(有机化合物分子中离特定基团或原子) 第一位的, α 位的 ‖*the* ~ *and omega* 始终，全部 ‖~ **iron** [冶] α-铁 / ~ **particle** [物] α 粒子 / ~ **ray** [物] ① α 粒子 ② α 射线

alphabet ['ælfəbit] *n.* ①字母表，字母系统: the Roman (或 Latin) ~ 拉丁字母表 ②初步，入门 ‖~**ize** ['ælfəbətaiz] *vt.* ① 用字母标示，拼音化 ②依字母顺序排列

alphabetic(al) [,ælfə'betik(əl)] *a.* 字母(表)的，依字母顺序的 ‖**alphabetically** *ad.* 依字母顺序地

alpine ['ælpain] **I** *a.* ① 高山的: an ~ belt 高山带 / ~ light 紫外线(或人工日光) / an ~ plant 高山植物 ② [A-] 阿尔卑斯山脉的；阿尔卑斯山区居民的 **II** *n.* ① 高山植物 ②登山软帽 ‖**alpinist** ['ælpinist] *n.* [常作 A-] 登山运动员，登山运动家

already [ɔ:l'redi] *ad.* 已经: They continued working, though it was ~ near midnight. 虽然时间已近半夜,他们还是继续工作下去。/ Are you back ~? 你怎么已经回来了? ‖~ *in* 早在…时候

also ['ɔ:lsou] **I** *ad.* ①也,同样: He ~ asked to go. 他也要求去。/ *Also* present (at the meeting) are ... 出席(会议)的还有… ②而且,(除此之外)还 **II** *conj.* [口]还: His style is terse, ~ vivacious. 他的文体既简明又活泼。‖*not only ... but* ~ 不但…而且… ‖~-**ran** *n.* (赛马中)落选的马; [喻]竞争失败的人(或东西)

altar ['ɔ:ltə] *n.* 祭坛, (基督教教堂内的)圣坛 ‖*lead sb. to the* ~ 娶某人为妻(指在教堂结婚)

alter ['ɔ:ltə] ❶ *vt.* ①改变,改动: The ship ~*ed* her course. 这艘船改变了航线。/ The design of this lathe must be ~*ed* to meet the new requirements. 这台车床的设计必须改动,以适应新的要求。②改做(衣服) ③[美方]阉割 ❷ *vi.* 变样,改变

alterable ['ɔ:ltərəbl] *a.* 可改变的, 可改动的 ‖**alterability** [,ɔ:ltərə'biliti] *n.* 可变性 / **alterably** *ad.*

alteration [,ɔ:ltə'reiʃən] *n.* ① 改变, 改动: make ~s for the better 作出改进 ②[美方]阉割

alternate [ɔ:l'tə:nit] **I** *a.* ①交替的,轮流的;交错的: He and I go to the spare-time school on ~ days. 他和我隔天轮流上业余学校(如: 他一、三、五去,我二、四、六去)。(此句也可译作: 他和我是隔一天上业余学校。)/ ~ angles【数】(一对)错角 ②预备的,候补的 **II** *n.* ①代理人,代表人 ②比较方案 **III** ['ɔ:ltə:neit] ❶ *vt.* 使交替,使轮流:On the school farm they ~ crops. 在校办农场里他们实行作物轮种。/ We ~ mechanical with chemical treatment. 我们交替地进行机械和化学处理。❷ *vi.* 交替,轮流: Mechanical treatment ~s with chemical. 机械处理和化学处理交替进行。/ The weather ~s between sunshine and rain. 时而天晴,时而下雨。‖~**ly** *ad.* / **alternation** [,ɔ:ltə'neiʃən] *n.* / **alternating** ['ɔ:ltə:neitiŋ] **current** 【电】交变电流, 交流电(略作 AC)

alternative [ɔ:l'tə:nətiv] **I** *a.* ① 两者(或两者以上)挑一的: ~ ways 可选择的两种(或两种以上)方法 ② 选择的: ~ conjunctions 【语】选择连词(如 either, or 等) **II** *n.* ①两者挑一,取舍,抉择: the ~ of going or staying 去留之间的抉择 / We have no ~ in the matter. 在这件事上,我们没有挑选的余地。②替换物;选择对象;

可供选择的办法（或方案）: You may say *lighted* or *lit* or *alight*; there is no other ~. 你可以说 lighted 或 lit 或 alight, 其他的说法没有了。/ That's the only ~. （除此之外）那是唯一一可供选择的。‖*have no ~ but . . .* 除…外别无选择 ‖~ly *ad.* 两者挑一地: go by ship or ~ly by rail 乘船去, 或者乘火车去

although [ɔːl'ðou] *conj.* 尽管, 虽然: *Although* (he was) seriously wounded, (yet) he flatly refused to quit the battle line. 他虽然身负重伤, 但坚决不下火线。[注意: 句中的 "yet" 不能改用 "but"]

altimeter ['æltimiːtə] *n.* 测高计, 高度表

altitude ['æltitjuːd] *n.* ① 高, 高度 (尤指海拔): an ~ of 20,000 metres above sea level 海拔二万米 / ~ flight 高空飞行 (=high-~ flight) / ~ sickness 【医】高空病 / grab for ~ (空战中) 抢占高度 ② [常用复] 高处, 高地: the mountain ~s 山的高处 ③ 高级 (指等级、地位等) ④【数】顶垂线, 高线

alto ['æltou] 【音】 **I** *n.* ① 女低音; 男声最高音; 中音部 ② 中提琴 (=viola) **II** *a.* 中音部的: an ~ horn 中音萨克号

altogether [,ɔːltə'geðə] **I** *ad.* ① 完全, 全然, 全部地: an ~ new aspect 崭新的面貌 / He felt not ~ satisfied. 他并不完全满意。② 总起来说, 总而言之: *Altogether*, our achievements are very great. 总的说来, 我们的成绩是很大的。③ 总共: There are ten people here ~. 这里总共有十个人。 **II** *n.* 总共, 全体 ‖*the* ~ [口] 裸体

altruism ['æltruizəm] *n.* 利他主义 ‖**altruist** *n.* 利他主义者

aluminium [,ælju'minjəm] *n.* 【化】铝

always ['ɔːlwəz, 'ɔːlweiz] *ad.* ① 永远, 始终 ② 一直, 总是, 老是: A: Do you stay at home in the evening? B: Not ~. 甲: 你晚上总在家吗? 乙: 不一定。/ The boy is ~ asking whys. 这男孩子老是问这问问那没个完。

am [强 æm; 弱 əm] 见 be

amalgam [ə'mælgəm] *n.* ①【冶】汞齐, 汞合金 ② 混合物

amalgamate [ə'mælgəmeit] ❶ *vt.* ①【冶】使 (金属) 汞齐化 ② 使混合, 使合并 ❷ *vi.* ① (金属) 汞齐化 ② 混合, 合并, 合成一体 ‖**amalgamation** [ə,mælgə'meiʃən] *n.* 汞齐化 (作用); 混合, 合并; 混合物 / **amalgamative** *a.* 有混合倾向的 / **amalgamator** *n.* 【化】(混汞) 提金器; 混汞者; 混合者

amass [ə'mæs] *vt.* 积累, 积聚 ‖~**er** *n.* 积聚者 / ~**ment** *n.*

amateur ['æmətə:, 'æmətjuə] **I** *n.* ① 业余活动者 (指对文娱、体育、艺术、科学 等有爱好者): a radio ~ 无线电业余爱好者 / an ~ in table tennis 乒乓球业余爱好者 / (泛指) 非专业性人员 **II** *a.* 业余的: an ~ storyteller 业余故事员 / an ~ troupe 业余文工团 ‖~**ism** ['æmətə:rizəm, 'æmətjuərizəm] *n.* 业余活动; 业余性质

amaze [ə'meiz] **I** *vt.* 使惊奇, 使惊愕: Visitors were ~d at the soaring drive of our shipbuilders. 参观者对我国造船工人的冲天干劲感到惊奇。/ I am ~d by what you have told me. 我听了你说的话, 感到惊愕。 发现 (看见, 听到) 某事物感到惊奇 **II** *n.* [诗] 惊奇, 惊愕 ‖~d to find (see, hear) sth. [诗] 惊奇, 惊愕 ‖~**dly** [ə'meizidli] *ad.* 惊奇地, 愕然

amazement [ə'meizmənt] *n.* 惊奇, 诧异: stand in ~ 愣住 / be filled with ~ 大为惊奇 / to sb.'s ~ 使某人感到诧异的 (是…)

ambassador [æm'bæsədə] *n.* 大使, 使节: an ~-at-large 巡回大使, 无任所大使 / an ~ extraordinary and plenipotentiary 特命全权大使 ‖~**ial** [æm,bæsə'dɔːriəl] *a.* 大使的; 大使一级的: ~ial talks 大使级会谈

amber ['æmbə] **I** *n.* ① 琥珀 ② 琥珀色 ③【军】线状无烟火药 (弹) **II** *a.* ① 琥珀做成的 ② 琥珀色的 **III** *vt.* 使成琥珀色

ambiguity [,æmbi'gju(ː)iti] *n.* ① 可作两种 (或多种) 解释; 意义不明确 ② 可作两种 (或多种) 解释的话, 模棱两可的话, 意义不明确的话

ambiguous [æm'bigjuəs] *a.* ① 可能有两种 (或多种) 解释的, 模棱两可的, 意义不明确的 ② 分歧的: ~ case 【数】分歧情况, 歧例 ‖~**ly** *ad.* / ~**ness** *n.*

ambition [æm'biʃən] **I** *n.* ① 志向, 志气, 抱负 ② 野心, 奢望: the ~ for fame and gain 名利野心 ③ (具体的) 抱负目标: achieve one's ~(s) 达到抱负 ④ 劲头 **II** *vt.* 妄想获得

ambitious [æm'biʃəs] *a.* ① 有雄心的; 野心勃勃的 ② 劲头十足的; 热望的: ~ to do sth. 热望做某事 / be ~ of (或 for) sth. 热望得到某物 ③ 炫耀的 ‖~**ly** *ad.*

amble ['æmbl] **I** *vi.* ① (马) 溜花蹄, 缓驰 ② 从容轻松地行走 ③ 骑马缓行 **II** *n.* ① 溜花蹄, 侧对步 ② 轻松的步伐

ambulance ['æmbjuləns] *n.* ① 救护车 ② 野战医院, 流动医院 ③ 救护船; 救护飞机 ‖~ **corps** 救护队

ambulant ['æmbjulənt] *a.* ① 走动的; 流动的: an ~ radio station 流动电台 / ~ blisters 移动性水疱 ②【医】非卧床的; 适宜于下床走动的

ambush ['æmbuʃ] **I** *n.* 伏击; 设伏地点; 伏兵: lay (或 make, set) an ~ (for) 埋伏下来 (等待…) / be (或 lie, hide) in ~ 埋伏着 / fall into an ~ 中 (埋) 伏 **II** ❶ *vt.* 埋伏下: He ~ed his platoon in the woods. 他把他的那一排人埋伏在树林里。② 伏击 ❷ *vi.* 埋伏下来 ‖~**ment** *n.*

ameliorate [ə'miːljəreit] ❶ *vt.* 改善, 改进, 改良 ❷ *vi.* 变好 ‖**ameliorator** *n.* 改良者; 改良物

amen ['ɑːmen, 'eimen] *int.* (基督教祈祷或圣歌的结束语) 阿们! (="So be it!" "诚心所愿!")

amenable [ə'miːnəbl] *a.* ① 有义务 (或责任) 的: be ~ to discipline 有遵守纪律的义务 ② 顺从的, 服理的: be ~ to reason 讲理, 服理 / be ~ to counsel 听从劝告 ③ 经得起检验 (或考查) 的: ~

data 经得起检验的数据 / be ～ to the laws of physics 经得起物理定律的检验 ‖**amenability** [ə,miːnə'biliti] *n.* / **amenably** *ad.*

amend [ə'mend] ❶ *vt.* ① 改正, 修正 (议案等): ～ a bill 修正议案 ②改好, 改进: ～ one's ways 改过自新 ❷ *vi.* 改过自新 ‖**～able** *a.* 可改正的, 可修正的

amendment [ə'mendmənt] *n.* ①改正, 修正; 改善 ②(议案等的)修正案 ③改良土壤的物质 (指不含氮、磷、钾的物质, 如石灰、石膏等)

amends [ə'mendz] [复] *n.* 赔偿; 赔罪: make ～ for one's crimes by good deeds 将功赎罪 / make ～ to sb. for sth. 为某事向某人赔偿(或赔罪)

amenity [ə'miːniti] *n.* ①(环境、气候的)舒服, (性情等的)愉快: the ～ of the climate 气候的温和宜人 ②[复]令人愉快的举动(或事情等); (社交)礼节: an exchange of *amenities* 相互的致意, 寒暄

amethyst ['æmiθist] *n.* 【矿】紫晶, 水碧, 紫水晶 ‖**～ine** [,æmi'θistain] *a.* 紫晶色的

amiable ['eimjəbl] *a.* 亲切的; 和蔼可亲的: Do you really want to go or are you merely being ～? 你是真想去呢还是仅仅为了表示友好? ‖**amiability** [,eimjə'biliti] *n.* / **～ness** *n.* / **amiably** *ad.*

amicable ['æmikəbl] *a.* ① 友好的, 和睦的: ～ relations 友谊关系 / ～ settlement 和解 / in an ～ way 用友好的方式 ② 温和的 ‖**amicability** [,æmikə'biliti] *n.* / **amicably** *ad.*

amid [ə'mid] *prep.* 在…中, 在…当中: *Amid* warm applause the honoured guests mounted the rostrum. 在热烈的掌声中贵宾们登上了主席台。

amidship(s) [ə'midʃip(s)] *ad.* 在(或朝着)船舰中部; [船]在纵中线上

amidst [ə'midst] *prep.* ＝amid

amiss [ə'mis] I *ad.* ①偏, 歪 ②错误地, 有缺陷地: You judge ～. 你判断错了。③不恰当地: speak ～ 说得不恰当, 说话唐突 II *a.* [常作表语]有差错的, 有缺陷的; 不恰当的: Is there anything ～ with the machine? 机器有什么毛病吗? / It is not ～ to do so. 这样做是可以的。‖**come ～** 不称心; 有妨碍 / **go ～** 出岔子; 不顺当 / **take sth. ～** 因某事见怪: Don't *take* my words ～. 我的话请别见怪。

ammunition [,æmju'niʃən] I *n.* ①弹药: an ～ bag (belt) 弹药袋(带) / an ～ clip 子弹夹 / an ～ depot 弹药库 / an ～ park 弹药场 ②进攻(或防御)手段 II *vt.* & *vi.* 供弹药(给); 装弹药(于)

amnesty ['æmnesti] I *n.* 大赦 II *vt.* 对…实行大赦; 赦免

amoeba [ə'miːbə] ([复] amoebae [ə'miːbiː] 或 amoebas) *n.* 变形虫, 阿米巴 ‖**amoebic** [ə'miːbik] *a.* 变形虫(性)的

amok [ə'mɔk] *ad.* & *a.* ＝amuck

among [ə'mʌŋ] *prep.* 在…中间, 在…之中[注意: between 一般指"在两者之中"; among 一般指"在三者(或三者以上)之中"]: a village ～ the

hills 群山中的村庄 / *Among* those present were …. 出席的人有… / They settled the dispute ～ themselves. 他们自己把这个争论解决了。‖**one ～ a thousand** 千中挑一的人, 罕见的人

amongst [ə'mʌŋst] *prep.* ＝among

amorous ['æmərəs] *a.* ①色情的 ②多情的 ③恋爱的; 有关爱情的 ‖**～ly** *ad.* / **～ness** *n.*

amorphous [ə'mɔːfəs] *a.* ①无定形的; 非结晶的 ② 难以名状的; 乱七八糟的: an ～ mass of fugitive soldiers 一群混乱的逃兵 ③ 无一定方向(或目的)的

amount [ə'maunt] I *vi.* ①合计, 总共达 (to): The annual output of the steel plant ～s to … tons. 这家钢铁厂的年产量达…吨。②相当于, 等于, 就是 (to): His answer ～s to a refusal. 他的回答等于拒绝。II *n.* ①总数; 【数】和 ②数量, 数额: accumulate a huge ～ of manure 大量积肥 / in large (small) ～s 大 (少)量地 / ～ of crown 【建】(路面)拱度 / a considerable ～ of prejudice 相当大的成见 / No ～ of lies can cover it up. 再多的谎言也掩盖不了这一点。/ pay the ～ in full 全部付清 ③总的意思; 重要性, 价值: The ～ of his remarks is that … 他的话总的意思是… / be of little ～ 不重要, 无价值 ‖**any ～ (of)** ① 任何数量(的…) ②大量(的…)

ampere ['æmpɛə] *n.* 【电】安培 ‖**～-hour** ['æmpɛər'auə] *n.* 安培小时, 安时 / '～,meter *n.* 电流计, 安培计 / '～-'turn *n.* 安匝(数)

amphibian [æm'fibiən] I *a.* 两栖的; 水陆(或水空)两用的: an ～ detachment 两栖分遣队 / an ～ personnel carrier 水陆两用人员输送车 II *n.* ① 两栖动物(或植物) ② 水陆飞机; 水陆两栖车 ③面目不清的人; 性质不明的东西

amphibious [æm'fibiəs] *a.* ①两栖的; 水陆(或水空)两用的: an ～ plant 两栖植物 / ～ operations (或 warfare) 两栖作战 / an ～ vessel 两栖作战舰艇, 登陆舰艇 ② 具有双重性的 ‖**～ly** *ad.* / **～ness** *n.*

amphitheatre, amphitheater ['æmfi,θiətə] *n.* ①圆形剧场(或竞技场); 比赛场; 大会堂 ②倾斜的看台; (现代戏院中)半圆形的梯形楼座 ③圆形凹地 ④(供观看外科手术等的)附有梯形座位的房间

ample ['æmpl] *a.* ①充分的, 足够的; 富裕的: ～ time 充裕的时间 / ～ evidence 充分证据 / an ～ basket of fruit 满满一篮水果 ② 宽敞的, 宽大的: ～ space 宽敞的空间 ‖**～ness** *n.* / **amply** *ad.*

amplification [,æmplifi'keiʃən] *n.* ①扩大, 放大; 加强 ②扩充; 详述

amplifier ['æmplifaiə] *n.* ① 放大器 ② 扩音机 ‖an audio-frequency ～ 音频放大器 / a power ～ 功率放大器 / a radio-frequency ～ 射频放大器 / a video ～ 视频放大器

amplify ['æmplifai] ❶ *vt.* ①放大, 增强: ～ a radio signal 增强无线电讯号 ②扩大; 详述: ～ one's statement 对自己的说法作进一步发挥 ❷ *vi.* 引伸, 作进一步阐述 (on, upon)

amputate ['æmpjuteit] *vt.* ①【医】切断，截（肢）② 砍掉；删除 ‖**amputation** [,æmpju'teiʃən] *n.* 截肢；砍除 / **amputator** *n.* 施行截肢手术者

amuck [ə'mʌk] I *ad.* 杀气腾腾地；疯狂地，狂暴地 II *a.* 有杀人狂的 ‖ *run* ～ 乱砍乱杀；胡作为非：The sea *ran* ～. 海上风暴大作。

amulet ['æmjulit] *n.* 护（身）符

amuse [ə'mju:z] *vt.* ①给…娱乐（或消遣）：～ oneself *by*（或 *with*）以…自娱 ② 逗…乐，逗…笑：You ～ me. 嘻，你这人真有趣。/ *feel* ～*d at*（或 *by, with*）对…感到有趣 / *be* ～*d to* learn (hear) 得知（听到）…觉得有趣 / *with an* ～*d look* 带着感到有趣的神情

amusement [ə'mju:zmənt] *n.* ①娱乐，消遣；乐趣 ②娱乐活动：an ～ park（或 ～ grounds）公共游乐场

an [强 æn；弱 ən, n] *art.* 见 **a**

anachronism [ə'nækrənizəm] *n.* ① 时代错误（指与时代不合而引起的错误）；弄错年代 ② 与时代不合的人（或事物）

anaemia [ə'ni:mjə] *n.* =anemia

anaesthesia [,ænis'θi:zjə] *n.*【医】①感觉缺失，麻木 ② 麻醉（法）：local ～ 局部麻醉 / acupuncture ～ 针刺麻醉

anaesthetic [,ænis'θetik] I *a.* 麻木的；麻醉的 II *n.* 麻醉剂

anagram ['ænəgræm] *n.* ① 变移单词（或短语）中字母位置而构成的另一单词（或短语）（例如将 now 的字母变移位置而构成的 won）② [复] 字（或词）谜游戏 ‖**anagrammatic(al)** [,ænəgrə'mætik(əl)] *a.* / **anagrammatize** [,ænə'græmətaiz] *vt.* 把…作成字（或词）谜

analogous [ə'næləgəs] *a.* 类似的，相似的 (to)；【自】模拟的：～ organs【生】同功器官 ‖～**ly** *ad.* / ～**ness** *n.*

analogy [ə'nælədʒi] *n.* ①类似，相似：bear (show) some ～ *to*（或 *with*）具有（显示出）与…的某种相似之处 / trace an ～ between the two 发现两者之间有相似之处 ②比拟；类推：a forced ～ 勉强的类推，牵强附会 ③【语】类推法 ‖*by* ～ 用类推的方法 / *on the* ～ *of* 根据…类推

analyse ['ænəlaiz] *vt.* ①分析；分解；解析：～ the causes of success and failure 分析成功和失败的原因 / ～ cast iron for phosphorus 分析铸铁是否含磷 / ～ a sentence 对句子作语法分析 ②[美] =psychoanalyse ‖**analysable** *a.* 可分析的；可分解的，可解析的 / ～**r** *n.* 分析者

analysis [ə'næləsis] ([复] analyses [ə'næləsi:z]) *n.* ①分析；分解；解析：class ～ 阶级分析 / qualitative (quantitative) ～【化】定性（定量）分析 ②[美] =psychoanalysis ‖*in the final*（或 *last*）～ 归根到底

analyst ['ænəlist] *n.* ①分析者；善于分析者；分解者；化验员：a news ～ 新闻分析员 ②[美] = psychoanalyst

anarchy ['ænəki] *n.* 无政府状态；混乱；无秩序 ‖**anarchic(al)** [æ'nɑ:kik(əl)] *a.* 无政府主义

的；不守法的 / **anarchism** *n.* 无政府主义 / **anarchist** *n.* 无政府主义者

anathema [ə'næθimə] *n.* ①【宗】诅咒；革出教门 ②诅咒，强烈的谴责；被诅咒的人（或物）③十分讨厌的人（或物）‖～**tize**, ～**tise** *vt. & vi.* 诅咒，强烈谴责

anatomy [ə'nætəmi] *n.* ① 解剖；分解；分析 ② 解剖学 ③解剖学论文（或书籍）④解剖体；解剖模型 ⑤人体，骨骼 ‖**anatomist** *n.* ① 解剖学者 ② 解剖者；剖析者 / **anatomize, anatomise** [ə'nætəmaiz] *vt. & vi.* ①解剖 ②剖析，分析

ancestry ['ænsistri] *n.* ① [总称]祖先，列祖 ②家世，世系 ③名门出身

anchor ['æŋkə] I *n.* ① 锚，锚状物：a kedge ～ 小锚 / a sheet ～ 备用大锚；[喻]危难时可依靠的人（或物）②【军】桩（如在陆地上用以固定铁丝网的装具）；支撑点（或物）；[喻]依靠 ③制动器（尤指车辆的紧急制动器）④ 团体比赛中位置（或顺序）排在最后的运动员 II ❶ *vt.* 抛锚泊（船）；把…固定住：～ papers on the desk with a paperweight 用镇纸压住桌上的文件 ❷ *vi.* 抛锚；固定 ‖*be*（或 *lie, ride*）*at* ～ 抛了锚，停泊着 / *cast*（或 *drop*）～ 抛锚；[喻]定居下来 / *come to (an)* ～ 抛锚 / *swallow the* ～ 脱离航海生活 / The ～ *has come home.* ①脱锚啦！②事情失败了。/ *weigh* ～ 起锚；[喻]起动，离去 ‖～ **gear**【海】（抛）起锚设备 / ～ **ground**【海】锚地 / ～ **ice** 底冰 / ～ **man** ①团体比赛中位置（或顺序）排在最后的运动员 ②负责安排广播的新闻广播员 / ～ **plate**【建】锚定板 / ～ **watch**【海】锚更

ancient ['einʃənt] I *a.* ①古代的；古老的；老式的：an ～ city 一座古城 / ～ history 古代史 ②年高德劭的；（因年事高而）足智多谋的 II *n.* ①古年的人 ②老年人 ‖*the* ～*s* ①古代民族，古人（尤指希腊、罗马时代的人）②古典作家，古典艺术家 ‖～**ly** *ad.* / ～**ness** *n.* / ～**ry** *n.* 古代；古老；古风

ancillary [æn'siləri] I *a.* 辅助的；附属的 (to) II *n.* [英]助手，随从

and [强 ænd；弱 ənd, ən] *conj.* ①[表示并列或对称的关系，用来连接词、短语或句子]和，与，及，同；又；并；兼 ②[强调连续、反复]接连，又：There are books ～ books. 有各种各样的书。(意指：书有好坏之分。) / many ～ many a time 多次 ③[用来连接数词]加：one hundred ～ twenty 一百二十 / Five ～ six is（或 are）eleven. 五加六等于十一。④那末：Come early ～ you will see him. 早些来，那末你就会见到他了。/ Knit your brows ～ you will hit upon a stratagem. 眉头一皱，计上心来。⑤[位于句首，用来承上启下打手；而且：*And* you may now say that things are all right. 因此你现在可以说一切都好。⑥ [口] [用来表示目的]：Go ～ tell him. 去告诉他。‖～ *all that* 诸如此类 / ～ *how* [美俚][加强语气]是了，难道还有问题! A: Were you on duty? B: *And how!* 甲：你那时在

值班吗? 乙: 可不是! / ~/or 与(或): That may be done by men ~/or women. 那事可由男子和(或)妇女来做。/ ~ others 以及其他等等 / ~ so on (或 ~ so forth, ~ so on ~ so forth, ~ the like) 等等 / ~ that 而且 / ~ then 于是, 然后 / ~ what not 诸如此类, 等等: paper clips, pins, ~ what not 回形针、大头针等等 / ~ yet 可是, 但

anecdote ['ænikdout] *n.* 轶事 ‖**anecdotist** *n.* 收集轶事者; 好谈轶事者

aneroid ['ænəroid] **I** *a.* 无液的, 不用液体的 **II** *n.* 【气】空盒气压表 (= ~ barometer)

anew [ə'nju:] *ad.* 再; 重新: repent and start ~ 悔过自新

angel ['eindʒəl] **I** *n.* ① 天使; 神差: ~(s') visits [喻] 难得碰上的事情 ②守护神 ③安琪儿, 可爱的人 ④[俚] 后台老板 **II** *vt.* ①[俚] 出钱资助(演出等) ‖*entertain* ~ *an unawares* 接待名人、要人而不知其身分; 无意中为名人、要人做了好事 / *Speak of* ~*s, and you will hear their wings.* [谚] 说到某人, 某人就到。‖ ~ **cake** *n.* [美] 蛋糕 / '~**fish** *n.* 【动】扁鲨

anger ['æŋgə] **I** *n.* 怒, 愤怒: speak in ~ 气冲冲地说话 / be filled with ~ 满腔怒火 / in a moment of ~ 在发怒的时候, 一时性起 **II** ❶ *vt.* 使发怒, 激怒: be ~ed by (或 at) 因…而发怒 / The little boy's mischief ~ed his parents. 这个小男孩的顽皮使他的父母生气。❷ *vi.* 发怒: a young man who ~s easily 一个容易发怒的年轻人 ‖*bluster oneself into* ~ 勃然大怒

angle[1] ['æŋgl] **I** *n.* ① 角, 角位, 角的度数: a dead ~ of fire 射击死角 ②[喻]角度, 方面: view sth. at a different ~ 从另一角度来观察某事 / discuss all ~s of a problem 讨论一个问题的各个方面 ③[美口] 诡计, 手段; 隐蔽的个人动机 ‖*an actual* ~ *of attack* 【军】实际冲角, 实际攻角 / *an acute* (或 *a sharp*) ~ 锐角 / *an alternate* ~ 错角 / *an* ~ *of incidence* 入射角 / *an* ~ *of reflection* 反射角 / *an* ~ *of refraction* 折射角 / *an* ~ *of site* 【军】炮目高低角 / *an auxiliary* ~ 补角 / *an external* (或 *exterior*) ~ 外角 / *an internal* (或 *interior*) ~ 内角 / *an obtuse* ~ 钝角 / *an opposite vertical* ~ 对顶角 / *a right* ~ 直角 / *a straight* ~ 平角 / *a subsidiary* (或 *supplementary*) ~ 补角 **II** ❶ *vt.* ① 使转一角度: ~ a camera (摄影时)对角度 ②从某一角度报道(新闻等), 使(报道等)带上色彩: ~ the news 带着偏见报道新闻 ❷ *vi.* 转变角度 ‖~ **iron** 角铁 / '~-,table *n.* 【建】托座; 角撑架

angle[2] ['æŋgl] *vi.* ① 钓鱼 ②(用不正当手段)攫取; 追逐 (*for*): ~ *for* compliments 博取夸奖 ‖~**r** *n.* ① 钓鱼者; 追逐…的人 (*for*) ②【动】鮟鱇 / **angling** *n.* 钓鱼(术)

Anglican ['æŋglikən] **I** *a.* ① 英国国教的, 英国圣公会的: the ~ Church 英国圣公会 ②[美]英国的 **II** *n.* 英国圣公会教徒 ‖**-ism** *n.* ① 英国圣公会教义 ②英国风度; 英国方式

Anglicize ['æŋglisaiz] *vt. & vi.* (在语言和风俗习惯方面)(使)英国化

angostura [,æŋgos'tjuərə] *n.* 产于南美北部的一种树皮 (= ~ bark, 可制滋补、退热药品)

angry ['æŋgri] *a.* ① 发怒的, 愤怒的: be ~ at (或 about) sth. 因某事而生气 / be ~ with (或 at) sb. 对某人发怒 ②(风雨等)狂暴的: ~ waves 怒涛 / ~ winds 狂风 ③(患处)肿痛发炎的 ‖*young men* 愤怒的年轻人 (指五十年代英国一部分对现实不满的青年作家) ‖**angrily** *ad.*

anguish ['æŋgwiʃ] **I** *n.* 极度的痛苦; 苦恼: be in ~ 感到极度痛苦 **II** *vt. & vi.* (使)感到极度痛苦; (使)苦恼 ‖**-ed** *a.*

angular ['æŋgjulə] *a.* ① 有角的; 角形的; 尖的 ② 用角量度的: ~ frequency (velocity) 【物】角频率(速度) / ~ distance 【数】角距离 ③骨瘦如柴的 ④不灵活的, 生硬的 ‖**-ity** [,æŋgju'læriti] *n.* ① 成角度; 棱角 ② (样子、衣着等的)难看; 生硬 ③【机】斜度 / **-ly** *ad.*

animal ['æniməl] **I** *n.* ①动物; 兽; 牲畜: a wild ~ 野兽 / a domestic ~ 家畜 / a draught ~ 耕畜, 驮畜 / ~ breeding 家畜饲养 / ~ husbandry 畜牧业; 畜牧学 / the ~ kingdom 动物界 ②畜牲般的人 **II** *a.* 动物的, 兽的; 肉体的: ~ food 肉食, 荤腥 / ~ charcoal 兽炭, 骨灰 / ~ spirits 生气, 活泼、轻快精神 ‖**-ly** *ad.* 肉体上

animate **I** ['ænimeit] *vt.* ① 使有生命 ②使活泼, 使生气勃勃 ③激励: The old worker's words ~d us *to* greater efforts. 这位老工人的话激励我们作出更大努力。**II** ['ænimit] *a.* ① 有生命的: ~ and inanimate objects 生物与非生物 ② 有生气的, 生气勃勃的

animated ['ænimeitid] *a.* ① 栩栩如生的: an ~ piece of sculpture 栩栩如生的雕塑品 ②生气勃勃的, 活跃的: an ~ discussion 一场热烈的讨论 ③受鼓舞的 ‖**-ly** *ad.* ‖~ **cartoon**, ~ **drawing** 动画片

animosity [,æni'mositi] *n.* 仇恨, 憎恶, 敌意

annals ['ænəlz] [复] *n.* ① 编年史 ② 历史记载 ③ 学会(或学科等)的年刊

anneal [ə'ni:l] *vt.* ①[冶] 退火, 焖火, 韧炼 ②[喻] 锻炼(意志等)

annex **I** [ə'neks] *vt.* ① 附加; 添加; 附带: ~ a condition *to* a contract 在合同中附加一项条件 ② 并吞, 兼并(领土等) **II** ['æneks] *n.* ① 附加物; 附件, 附录 ②【建】附属建筑物, 群房

annexment [ə'neksmənt] *n.* 附加物; 并吞物

annihilate [ə'naiəleit] *vt.* 歼灭, 消灭: ~ the enemy 歼灭敌人 ‖**annihilator** *n.* ①歼灭者 ②【数】零化子

anniversary [,æni'və:səri] **I** *n.* ①周年纪念日; 周年纪念 ②结婚周年 **II** *a.* 周年的; 周年纪念的

annotate ['ænouteit] *vt. & vi.* 注解, 注释 ‖**annotator** *n.* 注解者, 注释者

annotation [,ænou'teiʃən] *n.* 注解, 注释: an ~ *on* a word 关于一个词的注释 / ~*s on* the text 正文的注解 / The ~ of the book took him ten days. 这本书的注解工作花了他十天的时间。

announce [ə'nauns] ❶ *vt.* ①宣布，宣告，发表：It has been ~d that .... 已宣布… ②报告…的来到 ③预告 ④(不通过言语)使…被知道：Footsteps ~d his return. 听见脚步声，知道他回来了。⑤当(节目、比赛等)的报幕员(或播音员等) ❷ *vi.* ①当报幕员(或播音员) ②宣布参加竞选(*for*) (在竞选中)宣布支持某人(*for*) ‖~ment *n.* 宣布，宣告；通告，布告；预告：An ~ment will be made soon. 一项通告即将发表。/ a broadcast ~ment 广播通知 / ~ment of new books 新书预告 / ~r *n.* ①宣告者 ②(电台)播音员；(戏剧等的)报幕员；(比赛等的)讲解员

annoy [ə'nɔi] *vt.* 使烦恼；使生气；打搅：be ~ed (*with* sb.) *for* (或 *at*) (对某人)为…而生气 / He was ~ed to learn that he would not be able to catch the train. 他听到赶不上火车，心里感到烦恼。

annual ['ænjuəl] I *a.* ①每年的，年度的：the ~ output 年产量 / an ~ report 年度报告 / an ~ revenue (expenditure) 岁入(出) ②年生的；季生的 II *n.* ①年报，年刊，年鉴 ②年生(或季生)的植物(或其他生物) ‖~ly *ad.* ‖~ ring 【植】年轮

annuity [ə'nju(:)iti] *n.* ①年金；年金享受权：a life ~ 终身年金 ②年金保险 ③每年得到固定收入的一笔投资

annul [ə'nʌl] (annulled; annulling) *vt.* 废除，取消(法令、合同等)，宣告…无效 ‖~ment *n.*

anoint [ə'nɔint] *vt.* ①涂油于(尤指一种宗教仪式) ②用油擦，用油润 ‖the (Lord's) Anointed ①[宗]基督，救世主 ②神权帝王 ‖~ment *n.*

anomalous [ə'nɔmələs] *a.* 不规则的，异常的，破格的：an ~ verb 【语】不规则动词，变态动词(例如 be, have, do, shall, can 等) ‖~ly *ad.* ‖~ness *n.*

anomaly [ə'nɔməli] *n.* ①破格，不按常规；异常；反常：gravity ~ 重力异常 / thermal ~ 热的反常 ②畸形物 ③【天】近点角，近点距离

anonymous [ə'nɔniməs] *a.* ①匿名的，无名的，不知名的：an ~ author 无名氏作者 / an ~ letter 匿名信 ②无个性特征的 ‖~ly *ad.* ~ness *n.*

Anopheles [ə'nɔfili:z] *n.*【动】疟蚊属

anorak ['ɑ:nəræk] *n.* (北方严寒地带人穿的)带风帽的厚茄克，皮猴

another [ə'nʌðə] I *a.* ①再一，另一：Don't lose heart. Have a ~ try. 别灰心，再试一次。/ in ten days 再过十天 ②别的；不同的：That's quite ~ matter. 那完全是另外一回事。③类似的 II *pron.* 另一个；类似的一个：I don't like this one; please show me a ~. 我不喜欢这个，请另拿一个给我看看。/ risk one's life for ~ 舍己为人 / in one way or ~ 用这样或那样的方法 ‖one after ~ 见 one / one ~ 见 one / taken (或 taking) one with ~ 总的看来

answer ['ɑ:nsə] I *n.* ①回答，答复；应答：Have you had an ~ to your letter? 你接到复信了吗？②答案：The ~ to 3×4 is 12. 三乘以四等于十二。③答辩；抗辩 II ❶ *vt.* ①回答，答复；应答：

~ a question (letter) 答复一个问题(一封信) / Answer me. 回答我! / ~ the door 应声开门 / ~ the telephone 接电话 / ~ the helm (船)随着舵转动 ②以…作答：He ~ed nothing. 他没有回答。/ She ~ed that .... 她回答说… ③响应 ④适应，适合；与…相符，符合：~ sb.'s hopes 符合某人的愿望 / It is a project that ~s many purposes. 这项设计适用于多方面的需要。⑤答辩 ❷ *vi.* ①回答 ②负责，保证 ③成功，奏效：Our experiment has ~ed. 我们的实验成功了。④适应；符合：~ to a description 与描述相符 / ~ for sb.'s purpose 符合某人的需要 ‖~ (sb.) back (向某人)回嘴，(与某人)顶撞 / ~ to the name of 名叫，叫作 / ~ up 应对迅速 / in ~ to [作状语用]回答；应答；响应：The electrician went at once in ~ to the phone call. 电工师傅一接到电话马上就去了。/ *one who knows all the ~s* [美俚] ①自命万事通的人 ②(对一切缺乏热情的)老于世故的人 / *The ~'s a lemon.* [口](对无意义或不能回答问题的答复语) ①没有回答的必要。②这倒是个问题。

answerable ['ɑ:nsərəbl] *a.* ①可答复的；可驳斥的：questions ~ in one word 用一句话(或一个字)即可回答的问题 ②应负责任的：be ~ for sth. 应对某事负责 / an advisory body directly ~ to the head of the government 对政府首脑直接负责的顾问机构

ant [ænt] *n.* 蚁 ‖have ~s in one's pants (因焦急、气愤等而)坐立不安，急欲行动 ‖~ bear 大食蚁兽 / '~,eater *n.* 食蚁兽 / '~hill *n.* 蚁冢；人口稠密的地方

antagonize, antagonise [æn'tægənaiz] ❶ *vt.* ①对…起反作用，中和，抵销 ②(无意识地)引起…的对抗(或反感等)，招…的怨 ③[美]对抗，反抗 ❷ *vi.* 引起对抗(或反感等)，招怨

antecedent [,ænti'si:dənt] I *a.* ①先行的，先时的；先前的；[地]先成的 ②【逻】前提的，前件的 II *n.* ①前例，前事 ②【语】先行词；【数】前项；【逻】前提，前件 ③[复]经历，履历；学历；祖先 ‖~ly *ad.*

antedate ['ænti'deit] I *vt.* ①在(信、文件等)上写上比实际书写日期早的日期：~ a letter by three days 在信上写上比实际书写日期早三天的日期 ②把(事件)发生的日期说成比实际际早：~ a historical event by several years 把某历史事件的发生日期说早了几年 ③先于，前于：That event ~d World War II. 那事件发生在第二次世界大战以前。④使提前发生 II *n.* 比实际早的日期(或时期)

antelope ['æntiloup] ([复] antelope(s)) *n.* ①羚羊 ②羚羊皮

antenna [æn'tenə] ([复] antennae [æn'teni:] 或 antennas) *n.* ①【生】触角 ②【无】天线(英国一般用 aerial)：directional ~ 定向天线 ‖~l [æn'tenl], ~ry [æn'tenəri] *a.* ①触角的 ②天线的

anterior [æn'tiəriə] *a.* ①前面的 ②先前的，先于的 (*to*) ‖~ity [æn,tiəri'ɔriti] *n.* ①在前面 ②先前 / ~ly *ad.*

anthem ['ænθəm] *n.* ①【宗】赞美诗；圣歌 ②颂歌，赞歌 ③国歌：the national ~ 国歌 ④校歌

anther ['ænθə] *n.* 花药（花的带花粉部分）‖**~al** ['ænθərəl] *a.*

anthology [æn'θɔlədʒi] *n.* (诗、文、曲、画等的)选集 ‖**anthologist** *n.* 选集的编者

anthracene ['ænθrəsiːn] *n.*【化】蒽

anthracite ['ænθrəsait] *n.* 无烟煤，白煤，硬煤

anthropology [ˌænθrə'pɔlədʒi] *n.* 人类学 ‖**anthropologic(al)** [ˌænθrəpə'lɔdʒik(əl)] *a.* / **anthropologist** *n.* 人类学者

anthropotomy [ˌænθrə'pɔtəmi] *n.* 人体解剖(学)

antibiotic ['æntibai'ɔtik] I *n.*【微】抗菌素，抗生素 II *a.* 抗菌的，抗生的 ‖**~ally** *ad.*

antibody ['ænti,bɔdi] *n.*【生】抗体

antic ['æntik] I *n.* ①[常用复]滑稽动作（或姿态）；古怪行为 ②[古]丑角，小丑 II *a.* ①[古]古怪的 ②丑角般的 ③嬉戏的；狂欢的 III (anticked; anticking) *vi.* 做滑稽动作

anticipate [æn'tisipeit] *vt.* ①预期，期望：We ~ (the pleasure of) hearing from you again. (或 We ~ *that* we shall hear from you again.) 我们期待再接到你们的来信。②抢…之先；占…之先：~ the enemy 先发制敌 / ~ the crisis 预先采取措施来防止危机 ③行动在(请求、吩咐等)之前：~ the members' demands 因预见到成员们的要求而满足在前 ④提前使用：~ one's wages 提前使用工资，寅吃卯粮 ⑤ 使提前发生：~ payment 先期付款 ‖**anticipator** *n.* ①期望者 ②抢先者；占先者 ③[无]预器器，预测器

anticipation [æn,tisi'peiʃən] *n.* ①预期，期望，预料：in ~ of an early reply 期待早复 / Thanks in ~. 预致谢意。②预知，预觉

anticlimax ['ænti'klaimæks] *n.* ①(修辞学中的)突降法（指说话或写作中从有重大意义的内容突然转入平淡或荒谬的内容）②虎头蛇尾

anticyclone ['ænti'saikloun] *n.*【气】反气旋；高(气)压

antidote ['æntidout] *n.* ①解毒药 (*for, against, to*) ②矫正方法；除害物 ‖**antidotal** *a.* 解毒的，有解毒功效的

antimacassar ['æntimə'kæsə] *n.* 椅子(或沙发等)背(或扶手处)的套子

antinomy [æn'tinəmi] *n.* ①法律上的自相矛盾；两种法律间的矛盾 ②两种表面上"合理"的原则之间的矛盾 ③自相矛盾的话

antipathy [æn'tipəθi] *n.* ①不相容 ②反感，厌恶：have an ~ *to* 对…有反感，厌恶… ③被人厌恶的事物

antipersonnel ['ænti,pə:sə'nel] *a.* 杀伤性的：an ~ bomb 杀伤炸弹

antipodes [æn'tipədi:z] [复] *n.* ①对跖点，地球上相反的地区；[英][A-]新西兰和澳大利亚 ②[古]对跖人 ③[用作单或复]恰恰相反的事物 (*of, to*)

antiquary ['æntikwəri] *n.* ①文物工作者，古物收藏者 ②古董商

antique [æn'ti:k] I *a.* ①古时的；自古就有的 ②

古希腊的，古罗马的 ③古风的，古式的 II *n.* ①古物，古器，古玩 ②[the ~]古式(尤指古希腊、古罗马的雕刻、建筑等) ③【印】黑体字，粗体字；凹凸体 ‖**~ly** *ad.* / **~ness** *n.*

antiquity [æn'tikwiti] *n.* ①古代(尤指中世纪前)，古：a city of great ~ 一座很古的城 ②古人们 ③[常用复]古物，古物；古代的风俗习惯

antiseptic [ˌænti'septik] I *a.* ①防腐的：~ gauze 防腐纱布，消毒纱布 ②用防腐剂的 ③不受传染的 ④异常整洁的：an ~ room 异常整洁的房间 ⑤冷静的；客观的，不掺杂个人情感的 II *n.* 防腐剂，抗菌剂

antisocial [ˌænti'souʃəl] *a.* ①厌恶社交的，孤僻的 ②反对社会组织的，反社会的

antithesis [æn'tiθisis] ([复] antitheses [æn'tiθisi:z]) *n.* ①(修辞学中的)对语，对偶，对句(例如 You are going; I am staying.) ②(对语中的)后半部 ③对照，对立，对立面：*Smallness* is the ~ of *largeness*. 小是大的对立面。‖**antithetic(al)** [ˌænti'θetik(əl)] *a.*

antitoxin ['ænti'tɔksin] *n.*【生】抗毒素

antler ['æntlə] *n.* 鹿角

antonym ['æntənim] *n.* 反义词：*Far* is the ~ of *near*. "远"是"近"的反义词。

anvil ['ænvil] *n.* ①铁砧 ②【解】砧骨 ‖**on the ~** 在准备中；在讨论中

anxiety [æŋg'zaiəti] *n.* ①忧虑，担心 ②忧虑的事：be relieved of one's *anxieties* 消除忧虑 ③渴望，热望：~ *to* do sth. 急于想做某事的愿望 / ~ *for* sth. 对某事的渴望 / He expressed ~ *that* it should be done in no time. 他急切希望这事能立即做好。‖**an'xiety-'ridden** *a.* 忧心忡忡的

anxious ['æŋkʃəs] *a.* ①忧虑的，担心的，焦急的：We are ~ *about* (或 *for*) his safety. 我们为他的安全而忧虑。②令人忧虑的；在焦急中度过的：His ill health has been a very ~ business. 他身体不好使人十分担心。/ an ~ moment焦急不安的时刻 ③渴望的，急要的：He is ~ *to* go. 他急切想去。/ We are ~ *that* he (should) do his bit. 我们极力希望他能尽到自己的本分。‖**~ly** *ad.* / **~ness** *n.*‖**~ seat, ~ bench** ①教堂内离布道讲坛最近的座位（常由急于忏悔的教徒占坐）②焦急不安：be kept on the ~ *seat* 被弄得焦急不安

any ['eni] I *a.* ①[常用于疑问句、否定句、条件从句中，或与含有疑问、否定意义的词连用]什么；一些：*Any* suggestions? 有什么建议吗？/ There isn't ~ sign of immediate rain. 没有马上要下雨的迹象。/ There are scarcely ~ flies left around here. 这一带苍蝇已基本消灭。/ I wonder if this idea of mine is ~ good. 不知道我这个想法是否可行。②任何的；(三个或三个以上的人或物中)任一的：You may take ~ one of these. 这些当中你可以随便拿一个。[试比较：You may take *either* (one) of the two. 这两者之中你可以随便拿一个。] II *pron.* (无论)那一个，(无论)那些；一个，一些：Do(es) ~ of you know his address? 你们中间有谁知道他的地址吗？/ I can't find ~. 我一个也找不到。/ We need some tools. Have you got ~? 我们需要一些工具。你们有吗？**III** *ad.* [常与比较级连用]稍，丝毫: Is he ~ *better* today? 他(的健康状况)今天好些吗？/ I didn't hurt myself ~. [美]我一点也没受伤。‖ *at* ~ *rate* 见 rate[1] / *if* ~ 若有的话: Correct the errors in his composition, *if* ~. 如果他的作文里有错，请你改正。/ *in* ~ *case* 见 case[1] / (*not*) ~ *longer* (不)再 / (*not*) ~ *more* ①(不)再 ②(并不)较…多些 (*than*)

anybody ['eni,bodi] **I** *pron.* ①[用于疑问句、否定句、条件从句中]任何人: Did you see ~ there? 你在那儿看见任何人吗？[对应的肯定句中用 somebody: I saw *somebody* there. 我在那儿看见某人。]②无论什么人，任何人: As we are all comrades here, you may ask ~ for help when you meet with difficulties. 因为我们这里都是同志，你有困难时可以请求任何人帮助。**II** *n.* 重要人物: I ain't ~. 我不是什么重要人物。

anyhow ['enihau] *ad.* ①不管怎样，无论如何: *Anyhow* I must finish this work today. 无论如何，我今天必须完成这项工作。②不论用何种方法: It seemed as if I couldn't think of the right word ~. 我似乎怎么也想不出恰当的字眼来了。③随随便便，马马虎虎，杂乱无章: We ought to criticize him for doing his work ~. 他工作马马虎虎，我们就该批评他。

anymore ['eni'mɔ:] *ad.* [一般只用于否定句中，或与含有否定意义的词连用]现在: He rarely comes here ~. 现在他难得来这儿。

anyone ['eniwʌn] *pron.* =anybody (*pron.*)

anything ['eniθiŋ] *pron.* ①[常用于疑问句、否定句、条件从句中，或与含有疑问、否定意义的词连用]什么事(物)；任何事(物): Can I do ~ for you? 我能帮你点什么忙吗？/ *Anything* else? 还有什么要说(或做)的吗？/ He didn't say ~. 他啥也没说。/ If there is ~ *the matter with* the machine, please let us know. 机器如果发生什么毛病，请通知我们。/ There was scarcely ~ mentioned about that point. 关于那一点几乎没提到什么。②任何事(物)，一切 ‖ *but* 除…以外任何事(物)，根本不…: I will do ~ *but* that. 我决不干那件事。/ That's ~ *but* true. 那决不是真的。/ ~ *like* 象…那样的事(物)，全然(不)…: I cannot give ~ *like* a fair description of the exciting scene. 我真无法描绘那激动人心的场面。/ ~ *of* ①一点儿: I have not seen ~ *of* him just lately. 近来我连他的影子也没见到过。②一点…的味儿: Is he ~ *of* a sportsman? 他有些运动员风度吗？/ *as* ~ 象什么似地，非常猛地；拼命地 / *for* ~ 无论如何: I will not give up halfway *for* ~. 我决不半途而废。/ *for* ~ *I know* 据我所知 / *if* ~ 如果(稍)有区别的话 / *like* ~ 见 like[2]

anytime ['enitaim] *ad.* 在任何时候

anyway ['eniwei] *ad.* =anyhow

anywhere ['eniwsə] **I** *ad.* ①无论那里 ②在任何一点上: ~ from forty to fifty minutes 在四十与五十分钟之间 ③[口][用于否定句]根本: He never came ~ near to knowing what it was. 他根本不懂得这是什么。**II** *n.* 任何地方 ‖ *get* ~ [口][用于否定句](使)进展: It won't *get* you ~. (你)这样是行不通的。/ *not* (或 *never*) *go* ~ 过隐居生活

apace [ə'peis] *ad.* 飞快地，迅速地: The news of victory spread ~. 胜利的消息迅速传开。

apart [ə'pɑ:t] *ad.* ①相隔，相距: The two villages are five *li* ~. 两村相距五里。②离开，离去: The railway station stands ~ from the town. 火车站在镇外。③除去，撇开: *Apart from* this consideration (或 This consideration ~), there is no reason why we should not do so. 除非考虑这一点，否则我们就没有理由不这样做。④拆开: take a machine ~ 把机器拆开 ⑤区别，分别: I can't tell these two things ~. 我对这两件东西无从区分。‖ *fall* ~ 崩溃，土崩瓦解 / *joking* (或 *jesting*) ~ [口]言归正传，说正经话 / *set* (或 *put*) ~ 留开，拨出

apartheid [ə'pɑ:theit, ə'pɑ:thaid] *n.* 种族隔离，种族隔离法(尤指南非反动当局对有色人，特别是黑人，实行的一种种族歧视政策)

apartment [ə'pɑ:tmənt] *n.* ①房间 ②[英][复]一套房间(特指置有家具，供短期出租的) ③[美]一套公寓房间(英国称 flat): an ~ house (或 building) [美]公寓 (=[英] a block of flats) ‖ *have got* ~*s to let* [英俚]脑筋有点儿不清楚，有几分傻 ‖*-al* [ə,pɑ:t'mentl] *a.*

apathy ['æpəθi] *n.* 无感情，无感觉 ②冷淡，漠然

ape [eip] **I** *n.* ①无尾猿；类人猿 ②模仿者，学样的人 ③粗野的大汉 **II** *vt.* 模仿，学…的样 ‖*go* ~ [俚]发疯；变得狂热 / *play the* ~ 模仿，学样 ‖*~r* *n.* 模仿者，学样的人 ‖*'~-man* *n.* 猿人

ape

aperture ['æpətjuə] *n.* ①孔，隙缝，孔眼 ②口径，(照相透镜等的)孔径，孔径阑的直径

apex ['eipeks] ([复] apices ['eipisi:z] 或 apexes) *n.* ①顶，顶点: the ~ of a triangle 三角形的顶点 ②【天】奔赴点(=the ~ of the sun's motion) ③[无]反射点 ④[矿]脊，矿脉顶

aphorism ['æfərizəm] *n.* 格言，警句

apiece [ə'pi:s] *ad.* 每个,每人,各: be produced at the cost of five *fen* ~ 以每个五分钱的成本生产出来 / They took two hours ~ to do the experiment. 他们每人花了两小时进行这次实验。

apologetic [ə,pɔlə'dʒetik] **I** *a.* ①辩护的,辩解的 ②道歉的 **II** *n.* 正式的道歉;[常用复]辩护(尤指对基督教教义的辩护) ‖~**ally** *ad.*

apologize [ə'pɔlədʒaiz] *vi.* ①道歉,谢罪: ~ to sb. *for* sth. 为某事向某人道歉 / ~ *for* the delay in replying to a letter 因为没有及早复信而表示歉意 ②解释,辩护

apology [ə'pɔlədʒi] *n.* ①道歉,认错,谢罪: make (或 offer) an ~ *to* sb. *for* sth. 为某事向某人道歉 / accept an ~ 接受道歉 / I owe you an ~. 我该向你道歉。/ *Apologies!* (我向你)道歉! / I give you my *apologies*. 我向你道歉。②(为信仰等进行的)辩护,辩解 ③勉强代用的东西,聊以充数的东西: a mere ~ for ... 勉强充作…的东西

apostle [ə'pɔsl] *n.* ①[常用 A-]【基督教】使徒;传道者 ②热心的倡导者,鼓吹者,改革家 ‖**apostolic** [,æpəs'tɔlik] *a.* ①使徒的: *apostolic* succession 使徒传统(指主教等的权力是由使徒开始各代相传而来的) ②按使徒教义(或行为)的 ③关于罗马教皇的

apostrophe [ə'pɔstrəfi] *n.* [表示所有格和复数]撤号,省字号(即 ')[如 the people's 人民的 / don't (do not 的省略形式) / '72 (1972 的省略形式) / these five *a*'s 这五个 *a* 字 / the 1970's (读作 the nineteen seventies) 二十世纪七十年代] ‖**apostrophic** [,æpəs'trɔfik] *a.*

apparatus [,æpə'reitəs] ([复]apparatus(es)) *n.* ①器械,仪器;设备,装置: an ~ (或 a piece of ~) 一件器械 / cooling ~ 冷却器,冷却设备 / heating ~ 加热器;暖室装置 / medical ~ 医疗器械 / remote control ~ 遥控装置 ②器官: the digestive ~ 消化器官 ③机构,机关: the ~ of political power 政权机构 / the government ~ 政府机构 / the state ~ 国家机器 ④政党组织;地下活动组织 ⑤学术著作中的注解(或索引等) ‖~ **criticus** ['kritikəs] 书中所附供比较的材料

apparel [ə'pærəl] **I** *n.* ①衣服,衣着;服饰 ②装饰物;外表,外观: the white ~ of winter 冬天的一片白色的外景 ③船上的用具(如索具、锚等) **II** (apparel(l)ed; apparel(l)ing) *vt.* 给…穿衣;给…修饰

apparent [ə'pærənt] *a.* ①明显的,显而易见的: This is ~ to all. 这是大家都明了的。②表面上的,貌似的,外观上的 ③【物】表观,视,外显: expansion 表观膨胀,视膨胀 / ~ angle 【地】视角 / ~ dip 【地】视倾角 / ~ solar time 【天】视太阳时 ‖~**ly** *ad.*

apparition [,æpə'riʃən] *n.* ①幻象(或怪影、鬼怪等)的出现;神奇的现象 ②鬼怪,幽灵 ③(行星、彗星等隐没后的)初现

appeal [ə'pi:l] **I** ❶ *vi.* ① 呼吁; 要求: ~ to sb.

for sth. 为某事向某人呼吁 / ~ *to* sb. to do sth. 呼吁某人做某事 ② 诉(诸),求助(于): ~ *to* arms 诉诸武力 / ~ *to* reason 用理智,讲道理 ③【律】上诉: ~ *to* a higher court 向上级法院上诉 ④ (作品等) 有感染力,有吸引力; 投人所好 ❷ *vt.* 控诉; 把(案件)上诉 **II** *n.* ① 呼吁; 要求: make an ~ *to* sb. (*for* sth.) 向某人提出呼吁 ②【律】上诉: lodge an ~ 提出上诉 ③感染力; 号召力 ‖~ **to the country** (英)(解散国会后)诉诸舆论,诉诸国民的公断 ‖~**able** *a.* (案件)可上诉的

appealing [ə'pi:liŋ] *a.* ① 有感染力的,吸引人的 ② 哀诉的,恳求似的: an ~ tone 恳求的音调 ‖~**ly** *ad.* / ~**ness** *n.*

appear [ə'piə] *vi.* ①出现,显露: ②来到; 露面: He didn't ~ until six. 他六点钟才来。/ ~ in court 出庭,到案 / ~ on the stage 上台演出 ③出版,发表 ④看来 (好像): Everybody ~s (to be) well prepared. 看来大家都准备好了。/ It ~s to me that .... 据我看来,似乎… / It ~s not. 看来不象是这么一回事。

appearance [ə'piərəns] *n.* ①出现,显露;来到;露面: Poisonous weeds must be uprooted as soon as they *make their* ~. 毒草一出笼就必须铲除。②出版,发表 ③出庭,到案 ④外貌,外观;外表: There is every ~ of rain. 看来肯定要下雨了。/ Don't judge by ~s. 不要根据外表来判断。⑤出现物;[古]幽灵,幻象 ⑥【哲】现象 ‖*at first* ~ 初看起来 / *by all* ~s 显然 / *enter an* ~ 到场 / *for* ~' *sake* 为了装点门面 / *in* ~ 在外表上 / *keep up* ~s 装门面 / *put in an* ~ 露(一下)面;到场一会儿 / *put on the* ~ *of* 装出…的样子 / *save* ~s 保全面子 / *to all* ~(*s*) 显然

appease [ə'pi:z] *vt.* ①平息,抚慰,使息怒 ②绥靖;姑息,对…让步 ③充(饥);解(渴);满足(好奇心): Water ~s thirst. 水能解渴。‖**appeasable** *a.* 可平息的,可满足的 / ~**ment** *n.* an ~ment policy 绥靖政策

append [ə'pend] *vt.* ①附加: ~ notes *to* a drawing 在图样上附加注解 / ~ a seal (signature) *to* an agreement 在协定上盖印(签名) ②贴上;挂上

appendage [ə'pendidʒ] *n.* ① 附属物;附加物 ② 【生】附器;附肢

appendicitis [ə,pendi'saitis] *n.* 【医】阑尾炎

appendix [ə'pendiks] ([复]appendices [ə'pendisi:z] 或 appendixes) *n.* ①附录;附属物,附庸: two *appendices* to a book 一本书的两个附录 ②【医】阑尾,蚓突

appertain [,æpə(:)'tein] *vi.* ①属于;关于(*to*): the duties ~ing *to* one's post 应尽的职责 ②适合于(*to*)

appetite ['æpitait] *n.* ①食欲,胃口: have a poor (good) ~ 胃口不好(好) / lose one's ~ 食欲减退 ②欲望;爱好: have an ~ *for* 爱好… / to sb.'s ~ 投某人之好,合某人的口味 ‖**appetitive** [ə'petitiv] *a.* 关于食欲的

appetizing, appetising ['æpitaiziŋ] *a.* ①促进食欲的,开胃的,鲜美的: an ~ smell 开胃的香味 / ~ dishes 鲜美的菜肴 ②刺激欲望的,诱人的

applaud [ə'plɔːd] ❶ *vt.* 鼓掌欢迎;欢呼;向…喝采;称赞;赞成: I ~ your decision. 我赞成你的决定。❷ *vi.* 鼓掌欢迎;欢呼

applause [ə'plɔːz] *n.* 鼓掌欢迎;欢呼;喝采;称赞;赞成: win the ~ of the masses 得到群众的赞扬

apple ['æpl] *n.* ① 苹果;苹果树 ②形似苹果的果实: a custard ~ 番荔枝 / a love ~ (或 an ~ of love) 番茄 / an oak ~ 栎五倍子 / a Persian ~ 枸橼 / an ~ of Peru 假酸浆(大千生) / a cherry ~ 山荆子 / a mad ~ 茄子 ③【美俚】炸弹;手榴弹;(棒球的)球 ④【美俚】人,家伙: a smooth ~ 讨人喜欢的人 / a wise ~ 傲慢的年轻人 ‖ an ~ of discord 争端,祸根 (原意为希腊神话中各女神争夺的金苹果) / an ~ of Sodom ['sɔdəm] (或 a Dead Sea ~) ①(古代传说中) 一种外表美丽、摘下便成灰烬的果子 ②外表华丽而实无价值的东西; 外强中干的东西 / the ~ of one's (或 the) eye ①瞳孔 ②珍爱物;珍爱的人;宝贝 ‖~ butter ①苹果酱 ②[美方]闲谈, 聊天 / '~cart *n.* 苹果小贩手推车: upset sb.'s ~cart 破坏某人的计划 / ~ head [美俚]笨汉 / '~jack 苹果白兰地,苹果酒 / ~ knocker [美俚]①采水果的临时工 ②庄稼汉 ③生手 ④老实人 / '~-pie *n.* 苹果饼 *a.* ①苹果饼状的: an ~-pie bed 铺迭得使人不得伸直腿的床 ②完美无缺的: in ~-pie order 整整齐齐 / '~-,polish [美俚] 拍马屁 *vt.* 拍…的马屁 / ~sauce *n.* ①苹果酱 ②[美俚]假话,胡说 / '~wife *n.* 卖苹果的女人

appliance [ə'plaiəns] *n.* ①应用,适用 ②用具,器具;器械,装置: an office ~ 办公用具 / a medical ~ 医疗器械 / an ~ for opening cans 开罐头用的器具

applicable ['æplikəbl] *a.* ①能应用的,可适用的 (to): The rule is ~ to this case. 这条规则可适用于这种情况。②适当的,合适的 ‖**applicability** [,æplikə'biliti] *n.* (可)应用性,适用性 / ~ness *n.* / applicably *ad.*

applicant ['æplikənt] *n.* 申请人,请求者

application [,æpli'keiʃən] *n.* ①应用,适用;运用: the ~ of new technology to printing and dyeing 印染业中新工艺的应用 ②施用,敷用;搽剂: the ~ of fertilizer to the subsoil 施底肥 / for external ~ (药)供外用 ③请求,申请;申请表: an ~ form 申请书(或表格) / make an ~ to sb. for help 请求某人帮助 / Catalogues will be sent on ~. 目录函索即寄。④用功,专心: The work demands close ~. 这项工作要求思想高度集中。

applied [ə'plaid] *a.* 应用的,实用的: ~ chemistry 应用化学

apply [ə'plai] ❶ *vt.* ①应用,实施;运用,使用: ~

a theory to practice 把理论应用于实际 / ~ the brake(s) 使用刹车 ②把…应用于 (to): ~ fertilizer to the paddy fields 给稻田施肥 / a match to an alcohol lamp 用火柴点酒精灯 / ~ a plaster to a wound 给伤口涂上膏药 ❷ *vi.* ①适用: The principle of diligence and frugality applies to all undertakings. 勤俭节约的原则适用于一切事业。② 提出申请(或要求等): ~ for a visa 申请护照签证 / ~ to sb. for help 请求某人帮助 / For particulars, ~ to the information desk. 详情请向问讯台询问。‖~ oneself to 致力于 / ~ one's mind to 专心于…

appoint [ə'point] *vt.* ① 任命,委任: ~ sb. to a post 派某人任某职 ②约定,指定(时间、地点): The time ~ed for the mass meeting was 2 p.m. 群众大会定于下午二时召开。/ They ~ed a place to exchange experience. 他们约定一个地方交流经验。③命令: ~ that sth. (shall) be done 命令完成某事 ④【律】处置(财产) ⑤给…提供设备,装备 ‖~ee [əpoin'tiː] *n.* 被任命人;【律】被指定人 / ~ive *a.* 委任的(非选举的): an ~ive office 委任的职位 / ~or *n.* 【律】指定人

appointment [ə'pointmənt] *n.* ①任命,选派: the ~ of a proper person to an office 任命一个适当的人担任某个职务 ②职位: take up an ~ 就职 ③约会,约定,约: by ~ 按照约定的时间(和地点) / keep (break) one's ~ 守(违)约 / make (或 fix) an ~ with sb. 与某人约会 ④[复]家具;设备(尤指旅馆和船的) ⑤【律】指定(接受财产人) ‖~ call [讯] 定人定时呼叫

apportion [ə'pɔːʃən] *vt.* 分配;按比例(或计划)分配 ‖~ment *n.*

apposition [,æpə'ziʃən] *n.* ①并置,并列 ②【语】同位,同格 ‖~al *a.*

appreciable [ə'priːʃiəbl] *a.* 可估计的;(大得)可以看到(或感觉到)的: an ~ increase in current strength 电流强度的明显增加 ‖**appreciably** *ad.*

appreciate [ə'priːʃieit] ❶ *vt.* ①欣赏,鉴赏;赏识: ~ works of art 欣赏艺术作品 ②正确评价,鉴别 ③感谢,感激: We greatly ~ your timely help. 我们非常感谢你们的及时帮助。/ We shall ~ hearing from you again. 我们将乐于再收到你的信。④ 意识到,懂得: We ~ your difficulty. 我们意识到你们的困难。⑤ 抬高…的价格 ❷ *vi.* 涨价;增值;增多 ‖**appreciator** *n.* 欣赏者,鉴赏者

appreciation [ə,priːʃi'eiʃən] *n.* ①欣赏,鉴赏;赏识: *Appreciation* of works of art is bound to be dominated by a particular world outlook. 对于艺术作品的欣赏必然受到一定世界观的支配。②正确评价,鉴别 ③感谢,感激: We take this opportunity of expressing (或 to express) our sincere ~ of your help. 对于你们的帮助,我们趁这个机会向你们表示衷心的感谢。④涨价

appreciative [ə'priːʃjətiv] *a.* ① 有眼力的,有欣赏力的;欣赏的: an ~ audience 表示欣赏的听众(或观众) ②感激的 ‖~ly *ad.*

apprehend [,æpri'hend] ❶ *vt.* ① 理解, 领悟; 认识: At last, I ~ed his meaning. 最后, 我领会了他的意思。② 逮捕, 拘押 ③ 畏惧, 忧虑: ~ danger in every sound 风声鹤唳 / Do you ~ any difficulty? 你担心会有困难吗? ❷ *vi.* 理解, 了解: 认识

apprehension [,æpri'hen∫ən] *n.* ① 理解, 领悟: be quick (slow 或 dull) of ~ 理解敏捷 (迟钝) ② 逮捕, 拘押 ③ [常用复] 恐惧, 忧虑, 担心, 挂念: entertain (或 have) some ~ of 对…有点担心 / be filled with ~ 充满恐惧 / be under some ~s about sth. 对某事有所忧虑

apprehensive [,æpri'hensiv] *a.* ① 有理解力的, 善于领会的; 聪明的, 敏捷的 ② 担心的, 忧惧的/ be ~ for sb.'s safety 担心某人的安全 / be ~ that ... 担心将会发生… ‖~ly *ad.* / ~ness *n.*

apprentice [ə'prentis] I *n.* 艺徒, 学徒, 徒弟; 初学者, 生手: an ~ carpenter 学木工的艺徒 / be bound ~ to sb. 做某人的徒弟 II *vt.* 使当学徒: He was ~d to a blacksmith when he was only ten years old. 他在十岁时就去跟一个铁匠当学徒。‖~ship *n.* ① 学徒身分; 学徒年限: serve one's ~ship with sb. 跟某人当学徒 / be through one's ~ship 当学徒期满 ② 训练; 训练期 ‖~ seaman (美) 海军三等兵

approach [ə'prout∫] I ❶ *vt.* ① 向…靠近; 接近, 近似: ~ completion (perfection) 接近完成 (完美) ② 与…打交道: ~ sb. on (或 about) sth. 为某事同某人打交道 / ~ sb. with a proposal 向某人提出建议 / He is easy to ~. 他平易近人。③ 探讨; 看待; 处理 (问题等) ④ [美] 企图贿赂 ❷ *vi.* 靠近, 临近; 接近, 近似: National Day is ~ing. 国庆节即将来临。 II *n.* ① 靠近, 临近; 接近, 近似: be easy (difficult) of ~ (指地方) 容易 (难) 到达的; (指人) 易于 (难于) 接近的 ② 进路; 入门: the ~ to a bridge (或 the ~ span) 引桥 / This book provides a good ~ to electronics. 这是一本很好的电子学入门书。③ [常用复] 亲近的表示: make ~es to sb. 想亲近某人; 想与某人打交道 ④ 探讨; 处理; 态度; 方法: a correct ~ to the subject 研究这个问题的正确方法 ⑤ [军] 战斗前进 ⑥ [空] 进场 (指飞机进入机场时的飞行); 进入 (指轰炸机向投弹点接近的飞行)

approbation [,æprə'bei∫ən] *n.* ① 认可, 批准 ② 感觉满意 ‖on ~ [俚] (商品) 供试用的, 包退包换的

appropriate [ə'proupriit] I *a.* 适当的, 恰如其分的: at an ~ time 在适当的时间 / take ~ measures 采取适当的措施 / a remark ~ to (或 for) the occasion 适合时宜的话 / a style ~ to the subject matter 合乎题材的文体 II [ə'prouprieit] *vt.* ① 拨出 (款项等): a sum for capital construction 拨出一笔款子作基本建设用 ② 占用; 盗用, 挪用 ‖~ly *ad.* / ~ness *n.* / **appropriator** [ə'prouprieitə] *n.* 拨款者; 盗用者; 【宗】拥有转让圣俸的宗教团体

appropriation [ə,proupri'ei∫ən] *n.* ① 拨给; (一笔) 拨款: make an ~ for the building programme 拨出一笔款子供造屋计划用 ② 占用; 盗用, 挪用 ③ 【宗】圣俸的转让; 转让的圣俸

approval [ə'pru:vəl] *n.* ① 批准; 认可 ② 赞成, 同意: meet with general ~ 获得一致同意 ‖on ~ [俚] (商品) 供试用的, 包退包换的

approve [ə'pru:v] ❶ *vt.* ① 批准, 通过: The session ~d the report. 会议批准了这个报告。 / The resolution was ~d 68 to 10 with 28 abstentions. 决议以六十八票对十票通过, 二十八票弃权。② 赞成, 称许, 满意 ❷ *vi.* 赞成, 称许, 满意 (of): ~ of what sb. has done 赞成某人已做的事 ‖~r *n.* ① 批准者; 赞成者 ② [英] 告密者 / **approvingly** *ad.* 赞成地, 称许地 ‖~d school (英国的) 少年罪犯教养院

approximate [ə'prɔksimit] I *a.* 近似的, 大约的: an ~ reading 近似读数 / an ~ value 近似值 / an ~ estimate 约略的估计 / a value ~ to the standard 接近标准的数值 II [ə'prɔksimeit] ❶ *vt.* ① 近似, 接近: The design ~s perfection. 这个设计几乎是完美的。② 使接近 (to): ~ the operating temperature to the optimum value 使工作温度接近最佳值 ❷ *vi.* 近于 (to): The yearly output ~s to 500,000 tons. 年产量约计五十万吨。 ‖~ly *ad.*

approximation [ə,prɔksi'mei∫ən] *n.* ① 近似: That is a very close ~ to the truth. 那非常接近事实真相。② 近似值; 略计; 近似法

apricot ['eiprikɔt] *n.* ① [A-] 【植】李属 ② 杏; 杏树 ③ 杏黄色

April ['eiprəl] *n.* 四月 (略作 Apr.) ‖~ fool 愚人节中的受愚弄者 (或愚弄的行为) / ~ Fools' Day 愚人节 (每年四月一日) (=All Fools' Day)

apron ['eiprən] I *n.* ① 围裙, 工作裙 ② 【机】挡板; 机床 (刀座下的) 拖板箱 (或溜板箱); (输送机的) 平板; 唇 ~ 刀座 / ~ conveyer 裙式运输机 ③ 【空】停机坪 ④ 【地】冰川前的砂砾层: ~ plain 冰前平原, 冰川沉积平原 ⑤ (船) 船头的护船木, (木船) 副艏材 ⑥ 【军】(炮的) 口罩 ⑦ 【军】屋顶形铁丝网面; 伪装天幕 ⑧ 台口 (戏台的幕前部分) II *vt.* 用围裙围住 ‖~ful *n.* 满满一围裙 (的数量): an ~ful of pears 满满一围裙的梨子 ‖~ strings 围裙带: be tied to one's mother's (wife's) ~ strings 受母亲 (妻子) 的控制

apropos ['æprəpou] I *ad.* ① 恰当地, 中肯地; 及时地: Your letter comes ~ as usual. 你的信象往常一样来得正好。② 顺便说一说 (=by the way): *Apropos*, do you find the new radio set satisfactory? 顺便问一声, 你对那架新的收音机满意吗? II *a.* 恰当的, 中肯的: make ~ comments 作恰当的评语 III *prep.* [口] 关于: ~ what you were saying 关于你刚才所说的话 ‖~ of 关于, 至于, 就…说来 / ~ity [,æprou'pɔsiti] *n.* 恰当, 贴切

apt [æpt] *a.* ① 恰当的, 贴切的: an ~ example 适例 / an ~ remark 恰当的话 ② 聪明的, 灵巧的: This boy is ~ to learn. 这男孩善于学习。 / She is ~ at languages. 她善于学习语言。③ 易于…的, 有…倾向的: Food is ~ to deteriorate in summer. 食物在夏天容易变质。‖**~ly** *ad.* / **~ness** *n.*

aptitude ['æptitju:d] *n.* ①自然倾向 (*for*): Beavers have an ~ *for* building dams. 水獭有筑坝的习性。②能力,才能 (*for*) ③敏悟,颖悟

aqualung ['ækwəlʌŋ] *n.* 水中呼吸器(指潜水员背的氧气瓶连同戴的面罩)

aqueduct ['ækwidʌkt] *n.* ①沟渠;导水管;高架渠;水管桥 ②【解】导管

arable ['ærəbl] **I** *a.* 适于耕作的,可耕的 **II** *n.* 耕地;可耕地

arbitrary ['ɑ:bitrəri] *a.* 任意的;专断的,专横的: an ~ decision 任意的决定,武断 ‖**arbitrarily** ['ɑ:bitrərili; 美 ‚ɑ:bi'trərili] *ad.* / **arbitrariness** *n.*

arbitrate ['ɑ:bitreit] ❶ *vt.* ①仲裁,公断: ~ a dispute 对争端进行仲裁 ②把(争端等)交付仲裁,使听任公断 ❷ *vi.* 进行仲裁,进行公断: ~ between two parties 在两方间进行仲裁 ‖**arbitration** [‚ɑ:bi'treiʃən] *n.* 仲裁,公断 / **arbitrator** *n.*【律】仲裁人,公断人

arc [ɑ:k] *n.* ①弧;弓形(物);拱(洞) ②【电】弧光 ‖~ **furnace** 电弧炉 / ~ **lamp** 弧光灯 / ~ **light** 弧光;弧光灯 / '~-‚over *n.*【物】闪络,飞弧,电弧放电 / ~ **welding** (电)弧焊

arcade [ɑ:'keid] *n.* ①【建】连拱廊 ②有拱顶的走道(两旁常设商店) ‖~**d** *a.* 有拱顶的

arch[1] [ɑ:tʃ] **I** *n.* ①【建】拱;拱门;弓形结构: an ~ bridge 拱桥 / an ~ dam 拱坝 / an ~ roof 拱形屋顶 ②弓形;半圆形;弓形门;牌楼;弓状物: the ~ of the heavens 天穹 **II** ❶ *vt.* ①用拱连接,用拱覆盖: A bridge ~*es* the canal. 一座桥横跨在运河之上。②使成弓形 ❷ *vi.* 拱起;成为弓形 ‖~**ed** *a.* ①弓形的;弓形结构的 ②拱起的

arch[2] [ɑ:tʃ] *a.* 狡黠的,调皮的: an ~ look 一脸调皮相 ‖~**ly** *ad.*

archaeology [‚ɑ:ki'ɔlədʒi] *n.* 考古学 ‖**archaeological** [‚ɑ:kiə'lɔdʒikəl] *a.* 考古学的 / **archaeologist** *n.* 考古学家

archaic [ɑ:'keiik] *a.* ①古代的;古风的 ②(语言上)古体的,陈旧的 ‖~**ally** *ad.*

archer ['ɑ:tʃə] *n.* ①弓箭手;射箭运动员 ②[A-]【天】人马座;人马宫 ‖'~**fish** *n.* 射水鱼(一种产于东南亚的淡水鱼)

archery ['ɑ:tʃəri] *n.* ①射箭(术) ②[总称]射箭用器 ③[总称]弓箭手;射箭运动员

archipelago [‚ɑ:ki'peligou] ([复] archipelago(e)s) *n.* ①群岛 ②多岛屿的海

architect ['ɑ:kitekt] *n.* ①建筑师;设计师 ②[喻]缔造者 ‖~**ive** *a.* 关于建筑的;关于建设的

architectural [‚ɑ:ki'tektʃərəl] *a.* 关于建筑的,建筑上的,建筑学的: ~ engineering 建筑工程学 ‖~**ly** *ad.* 建筑(学)上;有一定结构地

architecture ['ɑ:kitektʃə] *n.* ①建筑学: civil ~ 民用建筑 / naval ~ 造船学 ②[总称]建筑物;建筑式样,建筑风格 ③结构,组织

archive ['ɑ:kaiv] *n.* [常用复] ①档案馆,档案室 ②档案,案卷: secret ~s 机密档案 ‖**archival** [ɑ:'kaivəl] *a.* 关于档案的;档案中的 / **archivist** ['ɑ:kivist] *n.* 档案保管员

arctic ['ɑ:ktik] **I** *a.* ①北极的; 北极区的: the Arctic Circle 北极圈 / the Arctic Ocean 北冰洋 / the Arctic Regions 北极地区 ②极冷的: ~ weather 极冷的气候 **II** *n.* ①北极; 北极圈; 北极区 ②[美][常用复](御寒防水的)橡胶套鞋 ‖~**ally** *ad.*

ardent ['ɑ:dənt] *a.* ①热情的,热烈的 ②炽热的 ③强烈的,烈性的: ~ spirits 烈性酒 ‖~**ly** *ad.*

ardo(u)r ['ɑ:də] *n.* ①热情,热心: ~ for study 对于学习的热情 ②炽热

arduous ['ɑ:djuəs] *a.* ①艰巨的,艰苦的: an ~ task 艰巨的任务 / be tempered under ~ conditions 在艰苦的条件下经受锻炼 ②努力的,勤奋的: make ~ efforts 努力奋斗 ③陡峭的,险峻的 ‖~**ly** *ad.* / **~ness** *n.*

are [强 ɑ:; 弱 ɑ, ə] 见 **be**

area ['eəriə] *n.* ①空地;地面 ②面积: the ~ of a triangle 三角形的面积 ③地区;区域 ④范围,领域: an ~ of fire 【军】射界 / the ~ of scientific investigation 科学研究的领域 ⑤[英]地下室前的空地 ‖~ **bombing**【军】面积轰炸 / ~ **code**(美、加等国)电话分区的三位数代号 / *a base* ~ 根据地 / *a loading* ~ (码头的)装卸区 / *a military* ~ 军区 / *a motor* ~ 【解】(大脑皮层的)运动区 / *a mountainous* ~ 山区 / *a pasturing* ~ 牧区 / *a rear* ~ 后方 / *a rural* ~ 农村地区 / *a special administrative* ~ 专区 ‖~**l** *a.* (关于)地区的 / '~**way** *n.* ①地下室前的空地 ②(建筑物之间的)通道

arena [ə'ri:nə] *n.* ①(古罗马圆形剧场中央的)竞技场地;(一般的)竞技场 ②活动场所;竞争场所: an ~ of warfare 战场 / a political ~ 政治舞台 ‖~ **theatre** 表演场设在观众座席中央的剧院

aren't [ɑ:nt] ①=are not ②[口]=am not (用于问句)

argue ['ɑ:gju:] ❶ *vi.* 争辩,争论,辩论: ~ *with* (或 *against*) sb. *about* (或 *on*) sth. 与某人辩论某事 / ~ *against* (*for*) 为反对(赞成)…而辩论 / ~ *to the contrary* 提出相反的意见 ❷ *vt.* ①辩论,争论: ~ one's case 为自己的意见作辩解 / ~ a matter *out* 把事情辩个水落石出 / ~ sth. *away* (或 *off*) 找理由把某事辩解过去 ②说服: ~ sb. *into* (*out of*) doing sth. 说服某人做(不做)某事 ③用辩论证明: He ~*d that* the experiment could be done in another way. 他论证说这项实验可以换一种方法进行。④表明,证明: His accent ~s him to be a southerner 或 ~s *that* he is a southerner. 他的口音表明他是个南方人。‖~**r** ['ɑ:gjuə] *n.* 争辩者,辩论者

argument ['ɑ:gjumənt] *n.* ①争论,辩论: It is beyond ~ that . . . . …是无可争辩的。/ be engaged in an ~ 参加一场辩论 / a principled ~ 原则上的争论 ②论据,论点;理由: What is his ~? 他的论据是什么? / put forward an

提出论点 / an ～ *against* (*for* 或 *in favour of*) 反对 (赞成)…的理由　③(文学作品等的)概要,梗概;主题　④【逻】(三段论中的)中项,中词　⑤【数】幅角;宗量,宗数,自变量 ‖***ram an ～ home*** 反复说明论点使对方接受

arid ['ærid] *a.* ①干旱的,(土地)贫瘠的: an ～ area 干旱地区　②枯燥无味的,无生气的 ‖**～ity** [æ'riditi] *n.* / **～ly** *ad.* / **～ness** *n.*

aright [ə'rait] *ad.* 正确地: put (或 set) sth. ～ 把某事搞正确 / If I hear (remember) ～, … . 假使我听得(记得)不错的话,…

arise [ə'raiz] (arose [ə'rouz], arisen [ə'rizn]) *vi.* ①起来;升起　②出现,呈现: A new problem has ～n. 出现了一个新的问题。　③由…而引起,由…而产生(*from*): Development ～*s from* the contradictions inside a thing. 事物的发展起因于它内部的矛盾。

aristocracy [,æris'tɔkrəsi] *n.* ①贵族统治;寡头政治　②贵族政府;贵族统治的国家　③[总称]贵族　④[总称](从封建贵族观点看来在智力等方面)最优等的人

aristocrat ['æristəkræt] *n.* ①贵族中的一员;有贵族派头的人　②贵族政治论者 ‖**～ism** [,æris'tɔkrətizəm] *n.* 贵族(政治)主义;贵族作风

aristocratic [,æristə'krætik] *a.* ①贵族的;(主张)贵族政治的　②贵族式的[注意: 此义可引伸作"高贵的"或"势利的"] ‖**～ally** *ad.*

arithmetic [ə'riθmətik] *n.* ①算术;计算: mental ～ 心算 / business ～ 商业算术　②算术教科书;算术论著

arithmetic(al) [,æriθ'metik(əl)] *a.* 算术的: an ～ average (或 mean) 算术平均数 / *arithmetic progression* 算术级数,等差级数 ‖**arithmetically** *ad.* 用算术方法

ark [ɑːk] *n.* ①(基督教《圣经》中的)方舟; [喻]避难所　②(基督教《圣经》中的)约柜　③[美](笨重的)大平底船 ‖**Noah's ～** ①挪亚方舟(基督教《圣经》中挪亚为避洪水而造的方形大船)　②装有各种动物的玩具船

arm¹ [ɑːm] *n.* ①臂; (动物的)前肢,肢: have a child *in* one's ～*s* 抱着一个孩子 / carry a parcel *under* one's ～ (腋下)挟着一只包裹　②臂状物(如树枝、机器的曲柄、海湾等): the ～ of a derrick 起重机的吊臂 / an ～ of the sea 海湾　③【机】(轮)辐; 【电】线担,支架,支路; 电唱头臂　④袖子　⑤(椅子的)扶手,靠肘　⑥[喻]权力: the ～ of the law 法律之权 ‖**～ *in* ～** 臂挽臂(地) / ***by the strong ～*** 强制地 / ***chance one's ～*** [英口]冒险一试 / ***in ～s*** (婴孩)怀抱着的(指向不会走路) / ***Justice has long ～.*** [谚]天网恢恢,疏而不漏。 / ***keep at ～'s length*** 避免同…亲近 / ***make a long ～*** 伸臂(攫取);奋力(抛掷) / ***put the ～ on sb.*** 向某人要钱;抢劫某人 / ***talk sb.'s ～ off*** [俚]对某人说个不停,对某人唠叨不休 / ***the ～ of flesh*** 人力,人的努力 / ***twist sb.'s ～*** 倒扭某人的手臂; [喻]向某人施加压力;强迫某人 / ***with folded ～s*** 两臂交叉于胸前:

look on with folded ～*s* 袖手旁观 / *with open* ～*s* 张着双臂(欢迎);热情地 ‖**～ful** *n.* 一抱: an ～*ful* of firewood 一抱柴火 ‖**'～band** *n.* 臂章 / **'～chair** *n.* 扶手椅 *a.* 坐在椅子里空想的: an ～*chair* strategist 空想的战略家 / **'～hole** *n.* 袖孔 / **'～pit** *n.* 腋窝 / **'～rest** *n.* 靠手

arm² [ɑːm] Ⅰ *n.* ①[常用复]武器(尤指枪支): small ～*s* 轻兵器(指手枪、步枪、机枪等) / ～*s* expansion and war preparations 扩军备战 / To ～*s*! 准备战斗! (指要求人员携带武装紧急集合的口令或号音) / Take ～*s*! 取枪! / Trail (或 Port) ～*s*! 持枪! / Shoulder (或 Left shoulder) ～*s*! 枪上肩! / Order ～*s*! 枪放下! / Secure ～*s*! 挟枪! / Stack ～*s*! 架枪! ②兵种: combined ～*s* 联合兵种 / all services and ～*s* 各军、兵种　③[复]纹章 Ⅱ ❶ *vt.* ①武装; 装备　②打开(雷等)的.保险: an ～*ed* fuze 打开了保险的引信 / an ～*ed* mine 待发雷 ❷ *vi.* 武装起来 ‖***a call to ～s*** 战斗的号令 / ***appeal to ～s*** 诉诸武力 / ***bear ～s*** 当兵 / ***be ～ed to the teeth*** 武装到牙齿 / ***fly to ～s*** 急切地拿起武器(或诉诸武力) / ***go to ～s*** 诉诸武力 / ***lay down ～s*** 放下武器(指投降或停止战斗): *Lay down your* ～*s, or we'll fire!* 缴枪不杀! / ***rest on one's ～s*** 暂事休息(指随时可以恢复作战或行动) / ***take up ～s*** 拿起武器 / ***under ～s*** ①在备战状态中②在服兵役期间 / ***up in ～s*** 起来进行武装斗争;竭力反对

armada [ɑː'mɑːdə] *n.* ①舰队: the Invincible (或 Spanish) *Armada* (十六世纪西班牙的)无敌舰队　②(飞机)机群: an air ～ 大机群

armament ['ɑːməmənt] *n.* ①军队　②[常用复](一国的) 武力量　③(一个作战单位中所有的)军械,武器　④武装,备战　⑤(动植物的)防护器官(如甲壳、皮刺等)　⑥【军】军舰(或要塞)的火炮　⑦战斗部(指导弹的弹头、引信和保险装置系统三者的组合件)

armed [ɑːmd] *a.* ①武装的: ～ struggle 武装斗争 / ～ forces 武力量,武装部队(指一国的全部军队) / ～ neutrality 武装中立　②(动植物)有防护器官(如甲壳、皮刺等)的

armistice ['ɑːmistis] *n.* 停战,休战: an ～ agreement 停战协定 / a military ～ commission 军事停战委员会 ‖**Armistice Day** 第一、二次世界大战的停战纪念日(十一月十一日)

armo(u)r ['ɑːmə] Ⅰ *n.* ①盔甲: a suit of ～ 一整套盔甲　②[总称](军舰、车辆等的) 装甲(钢)板

armo(u)r

③[总称] 装甲部队，装甲兵(种)　④(动植物的)防护器官；潜水人的防护服: flyer's ~ 防弹飞行服 / submarine ~ 潜水服 ⑤(覆盖在电线外的)铠装 II *vt.* 为…盔甲；为…装甲 ‖'~-'clad *a.* 穿戴盔甲的；装甲的 / '~-piercing *a.* 穿甲的: an ~-*piercing* bullet (或 shell) 穿甲弹 / '~-plate *n.* 装甲(钢)板 / '~-'plated *a.* 装甲的

armo(u)red ['ɑːməd] *a.* ①穿戴盔甲的 ②装甲的: ~ corps (或 forces, troops) 装甲部队 / an ~ car (或vehicle) 装甲车辆 ‖~ cable 铠装电缆 / ~ concrete 钢筋混凝土

army ['ɑːmi] *n.* ①军队；陆军: join (或 enter) the ~参军 / serve in the ~ 服兵役 ②军；野战军；集团军；兵团 ③大军: a labour ~ 一支劳动大军 ④大群: an ~ of bees 一大群蜜蜂 ‖*an Army and Navy Store* (英军)军人消费合作社 / *Army Aviation* (美军)陆军航空兵 / *the Army Council* (英军)陆军委员会 / *the Army Department* (美国)陆军部 / *an Army Serial Number* 军号,入伍编号(每一军事人员入伍时所勘定的号数) / *the Army Service Forces* 陆军后勤部队 / *the Blue Ribbon Army* (英国)禁酒团 / *a field* ~ 野战军 / *a group* ~ 集团军 / *a regular* ~ 正规军 / *the Salvation Army*【宗】救世军 / *Secretary of the Army* (美国)陆军部长 / *a standing* ~ 常备军 ‖'~-ci'vilian *a.* 军民(联合)的: ~-*civilian* defence 军民联防 / ~ corps 军 / group 集团军群 / '~-list *n.* [英]陆军军官名册 / '~-man *n.* 军人 / '~-worm *n.*【动】粘虫

aroma [ə'roumə] *n.* ①芳香,香味 ②(艺术品的)风味,韵味

aromatic [ˌærou'mætik] I *a.* ①芳香的,有香味的: an ~ plant 芳香植物 ②【化】芳香族的: ~ hydrocarbon 芳(族)烃 II *n.* ①芳香植物 ②[常用复]芳香族化合物；芳香剂

arose [ə'rouz] arise 的过去式

around [ə'raund] [around 和 round 作前置词和副词时的意义基本相同, around 多用于美国, round 多用于英国] I *prep.* ①在…周围；环绕着: The earth moves ~ the sun. 地球绕着太阳转。②绕过: steer a ship ~ reefs 使船绕过暗礁 ③在…各处；在…附近: ~ here 在这一带 ④大约: ~ two o'clock 两点钟左右 II *ad.* ①在周围,在附近；存在着,活着 ②各处: The good news soon got ~. 好消息很快就传开了。③整整一圈；回转；返回: The track is 400 metres ~. 跑道一圈有四百米长。/ pass the note ~ 传阅字条 ④到(彼此知道的)某一地点: Come ~ this evening if you have time. 今晚有空到我那儿去。‖all ~ 见 all / bring ~ 见 bring / get ~ 见 get / go ~ 见 go / have been ~ (a lot) [口]阅历(很)多；世故(很)深 / the other way ~ [美]从相反方向；用相反的方式 ‖a'round-the-'clock *a.* [美]连续二十四小时的；连续不停的

arouse [ə'rauz] ❶ *vt.* ①唤醒: ~ sb. *from* sleep

唤醒某人 ②唤起,激起,引起 ❷ *vi.* 睡醒

arraign [ə'rein] *vt.* ①传讯,提审 ②控告 ③指责,责难 ‖~ment *n.*

arrange [ə'reindʒ] ❶ *vt.* ①整理,分类,排列: ~ tools in order 把工具整理好 / ~ troops for battle 部署作战部队 ②筹备,安排: Everything has been ~d. 一切都准备好了。/ an X-ray examination for next week 在下周安排一次 X 光检查 ③调解,调停(纠纷、分歧等) ④改编(乐曲等) ❷ *vi.* ①安排,准备: ~ *with* sb. *for* (或 *about*) sth. 与某人商定某事

arrangement [ə'reindʒmənt] *n.* ①整理,排列；布置 ②[常用复]安排,准备: *Arrangements* have been made to give the foreign guests a warm welcome. 为热烈欢迎外宾作好了准备工作。/ proper ~ of work and rest 劳逸结合 ③商定；调解 ④(乐曲等的)改编；改编的乐曲

arrant ['ærənt] *a.* 彻头彻尾的；臭名昭著的: an ~ knave 大坏蛋 / ~ nonsense 彻头彻尾的谬论 ‖~ly *ad.*

array [ə'rei] I *vt.* ①使…排列成阵势: ~ troops for battle 使军队排列成战斗队形 ②装扮,打扮: ~ oneself in all one's finery 穿上盛装 ③排列(陪审员)的名单 II *n.* ①(军队等的)列阵: be ready in full battle ~ 严阵以待 ②衣服；盛装: The whole city is in holiday ~. 整个城市披上了节日盛装。③(排列整齐的)一批；大量: a whole ~ of tools (排列整齐的)一批工具 / an ~ of facts (proofs) 一系列的事实(证据) ④陪审员名单

arrear [ə'riə] *n.* ①[常用复](过期未付的)欠款(未付清款项的)尾数；剩留的部分: ~s of rent 欠租 / ~s of work (correspondence) 剩下未做完的工作(未复的信件) / work off ~s 扫尾 ②落后,拖延 ‖*in* ~(s) 拖欠；拖延: be *in* ~s with one's payment 拖欠款项 / I am two or three letters *in* ~s. 我还有两三封信搁着未复。

arrest [ə'rest] I *vt.* ①逮捕；拘留；扣留(船只、货物等) ②阻止,抑制 ③吸引: ~ sb.'s attention (或 eye) 引起某人注意 II *n.* ①逮捕；拘留: be put (或 placed, held) under ~ 被逮捕 / under house ~ 在软禁中 ②阻止；制动装置 ‖~ee [əres'tiː] *n.* 被逮捕者 / ~er, ~or *n.* ①逮捕者 ②制动装置 ③避雷器 / ~ing *a.* 引人注意的 / ~ment *n.* [罕]①逮捕 ②阻止

arrival [ə'raivəl] *n.* ①到来；到达: on sb.'s ~ 当某人到达时 / ~ at a conclusion 得出结论 ②到达者；到达物: a new ~ 新来的人(或新生小孩)；新到货物 / an ~ form 来客登记表

arrive [ə'raiv] *vi.* ①到,来到: ~ *at* a station (destination) 到达车站(目的地) / ~ *on* (或 *upon*) the scene 到场 ②(时间)到来: The time has ~d for departure. 出发的时间到了。③达到；得出 (*at*): ~ *at* a conclusion (decision) 作出结论(决定) / ~ *at* manhood 成年 ④成功,成名 ‖~r *n.* 到达者

arrogance ['ærəgəns] *n.* 骄傲自大,傲慢: Guard

against ~. 力戒骄傲。/ feed sb.'s ~ 助长某人的气焰

arrogant ['ærəgənt] *a.* 骄傲自大的,傲慢的 ‖~**ly** *ad.*

arrow ['ærou] *n.* ① 箭: shoot the ~ at the target 有的放矢 ② 箭状物; 箭号(即→): a traffic ~ 交通箭头标志 / a broad ~ [英]宽箭形戳记(用于标明英国政府财产的官印) ‖*have an ~ left in one's quiver* 还有本钱;还有办法 ‖~**root** ['ærəru:t] *n.* ①[植]竹芋; 葛 ②竹芋粉; 葛粉; 藕粉 / '~**wood** *n.* [植]荚蒾(产于北美,印第安人常用来制箭)

arsenic I ['ɑ:snik] *n.* [化] ① 砷 ② 三氧化二砷(俗称砒霜, =white ~) II [ɑ:'senik] *a.* 砷的; 含砷的; 五价砷的 ‖~**al** [ɑ:'senikəl] *a.* 砷的; 含砷的 *n.* 含砷制剂(用于杀虫等)

arson ['ɑ:sn] *n.* 放火, 纵火 ‖~**ist** *n.* 放火犯, 纵火犯

art[1] [ɑ:t] [古] be 的现在式单数第二人称, 与 thou 连用 (thou ~ =you are)

art[2] [ɑ:t] *n.* ①艺术;美术:a work of ~ 艺术品;美术品 ②技术, 技艺: the healing ~ 医术 / the military ~ 军事艺术 / the ~ of writing 写作技巧 ③[复](人文)学科: Bachelor of *Arts* 文学士 / Master of *Arts* 文学硕士 ④人工(指与自然相对而言) ⑤奸计,诡计 ‖*an ~ gallery* 美术馆 / ~ *paper* 铜版纸 / *an ~ school* 美术学校 / *the black* ~ 魔术,妖术 / *the fine ~s* 美术(指诗歌、音乐、绘画、雕塑、建筑等) / *the industrial ~s* 工艺美术 / *the liberal ~s* 人文学科 / *the useful ~s* 手艺,工艺 ‖'~ *and part* 策划并参与 / ~ *for ~'s sake* 为艺术而艺术, 艺术至上主义 ‖'~**ware** *n.* [总称]工艺品

arterial [ɑ:'tiəriəl] *a.* ① 动脉的;象动脉的: ~ blood 动脉血 ②干线的: an ~ railway (highway) 铁道(公路)干线

artery ['ɑ:təri] *n.* ①[解]动脉 ② 干线: economic *arteries* 经济命脉

artesian [ɑ:'ti:zjən] *a.* 自动流出的: an ~ spring 自流泉 / an ~ well 自流井, 深井

article ['ɑ:tikl] I *n.* ①文章, 论文: a leading (或 an editorial) ~ 社论 / a feature ~ 特写;重点文章 ②物品,物件;商品: And the next ~? (店员问顾客的用语)您还要买什么? / three ~s of luggage 三件行李 / a bamboo (straw) ~ 竹(草)器 ③项目,条款: ~s of an agreement 协定的条款 / *Article* 1 第一条(略作 Art. 1) / ~s of association 公司章程 / *Articles* of War 陆军法规 / the Thirty-nine *Articles* 英国国教的三十九条教规 ④[语]冠词: the definite ~ 定冠词(指 the) / the indefinite ~ 不定冠词 (指 a, an) ⑤ [俚] 人,家伙(尤指精明的、善于钻营的人): a smooth (或 slick) ~ 圆滑的人,八面玲珑的人 II *vt.* ①将…逐条罗列;列举(罪状) ②控告 ③用条款约束; 订约将…收为徒弟: be ~d to an attorney 订约给律师当徒弟 / an ~d pupil 订有

工读合同的学生, 工读生 ‖*in the ~ of death* 在临死时

articulate [ɑ:'tikjulit] I *a.* ①接合起来的;[生]有(关)节的 ②(讲话等)发音清晰的 ③(人)表达力强的; (论据等)表达得清楚有力的 ④能说话的: As a result of new acupuncture-therapy, the deaf-mutes are now ~. 由于进行了新针治疗, 聋哑人现在会讲话了。⑤ 可以发音的,有发言权的 II *n.* [动] 环节动物 III [ɑ:'tikjuleit] ❶ *vt.* ① (用关节)连接;使接合: an ~d trailer (用铰链连接的)拖车 ② 把(字句)清晰地发出音来; 明确表达 ③[语]把…发音 ❷ *vi.* ①连接起来,接合起来 ②清楚地讲话; 清晰地发音 ③[语]发音 ‖~**ly** *ad.* / ~**ness** *n.*

articulation [ɑ:,tikju'leiʃən] *n.* ① 连接,接合; 连接(或接合)方式 ② (清楚的)发音;[语]发音动作; 发出的音(尤指辅音) ③ (骨头等的)关节; [植]节 ④[无]清晰度,可懂度

artifice ['ɑ:tifis] *n.* ① 技巧,技能;机智 ② 巧计, 计谋, 诡计: acquire sth. by ~ 耍手段获得某物 ‖~**r** *n.* ①工匠;[军]工匠兵, 技工 ②发明家, 设计者

artificial [,ɑ:ti'fiʃəl] *a.* ① 人工的, 人造的; 假的: ~ brain [自]人工脑 / ~ rainfall (respiration) 人工降雨 (呼吸) / ~ insemination (selection) [生]人工受精(选择) / ~ fibre (silk) 人造纤维(丝) / ~ horizon [空]航空地平仪 / an ~ earth satellite 人造地球卫星 ② 矫揉造作的, 不自然的: an ~ smile 做作的微笑 ‖~**ly** *ad.* / ~**ness** *n.*

artillery [ɑ:'tiləri] *n.* ①[总称] 火炮, 大炮: a piece of ~ 一门大炮 / ~ salute 礼炮 ②[the ~] [总称]炮兵(部队) ③炮术 ④[总称][俚]防身武器(尤指小枪等) ⑤[美国](注射麻醉剂成瘾者用语)皮下注射针 ⑥[喻]辩才 ‖*antiaircraft* ~ 高射炮 / *field* ~ 野战炮 / *long-range* ~ 远程炮 / *mountain* ~ 山地炮 ‖**artillerist** *n.* 炮兵;炮手; 精通炮术的人 ‖**ar'tilleryman** *n.* ①炮兵 ②[俚]醉汉

artisan, artizan [,ɑ:ti'zæn] *n.* 手工业工人,手艺人, 工匠

artist ['ɑ:tist] *n.* ①艺术家; 美术家 (尤指画家): ~s' colours 画家用的颜料 ② (某方面的) 能手: an ~ in words 善于运用语言的人 / a hot-air ~ 惯于夸夸其谈的人 ③玩弄诈术的人 ‖~'**s proof** [印]雕版的初印稿

artiste [ɑ:'ti:st] *n.* ① 艺人 ②[谑](擅长某项手艺的)能手, 大师

artistry ['ɑ:tistri] *n.* ①艺术性; 艺术效果 ②艺术才能; 艺术技巧

as [强 æz; 弱 əz] I *ad.* [表示程度]同样地: ~ firm as a rock 坚如磐石[注意: 在 "as...as..." 结构中, 第一个 as 是副词, 第二个 as 是连接词或关系代词] / I guessed ~ much. 我料到是这么一回事。 II *conj.* ① [表示比较]象…一样: The work is *not so* easy ~ you imagine. 这

工作决不象你想象的那么简单。 / John is very healthy, ~ are his sisters.约翰的身体很健康,他的姊妹也一样。②[表示方式]按照;如同: state the facts ~ they are 如实地陈述事实／English ~ (it is) spoken in Australia 在澳大利亚所讲的英语 ③[表示时间]当…的时候④[表示原因]由于,鉴于: As he was not well, I decided to go without him. 因为他身体不好,我决定独自去了。⑤[表示结果或目的]以至于: Be so good ~ to come and join us. 务请来参加我们的活动。/ He raised his voice so ~ to be heard. 他提高了嗓门,好让别人听到。⑥[表示让步]虽然,尽管: Much ~ I like it, I will not buy it. 虽然我很喜欢这东西,但不想买它。**III pron.** ①[用在 "such as", "the same as", "as ... as ..." 等结构中]象…样的人(或物);凡是…的人(或物): There is no *such* thing ~ art for art's sake. 根本不存在什么为艺术的艺术。/ My home town is no longer *the same* ~ it was. 我的家乡同过去不一样了。/ as many people ~ are present 所有在场的人们 ②这一点: The statement reads in full ~ follows: .... 声明全文如下: … **IV prep.** 作为;如同 ‖**~far** ~ 见 **far** / **~ for** 至于,就…方面说 / **~ from** 从…时起 / **~ if** 好象,仿佛: He works with such enthusiasm ~ *if* he never knew fatigue. 他工作热情这么高,好象从不知道疲倦似的。/ *As if* he would ever go! 他才不会去呢! / **~ is** 照现在的样子(指不再作修理或改进) / **~ it is** (或 *was*) 见 **it** / **~ it were** 见 **it** / **~ long ~** 见 **long**[1] / **~ of** 在…时;到…时为止;从…时起: *As of* this writing, no reply has been received. 到写这封信时为止,还没有得到回音。/ The agreement takes effect ~ *of* June 5. 协定从六月五日起生效。/ **~ ... ~**, *so* ..., *so* ~ 象…那样,…也就…; 随着…,也就…: *As* you sow, *so* will you reap. 种瓜得瓜,种豆得豆。/ **~ though =** **~ if** / **~ to** ①至于 ②关于 / **~ well** (**~**) 见 **well**[2] / **~ yet** 至今,迄今[多用于否定句中] / *such* ~ 见 **such**

ascend [ə'send] ❶ **vi.** ①登高;上升,升高 ②追溯(到某个时间) (to): ~ to the prehistorical period 追溯到史前时期 ③【天】向天顶上升 ❷ **vt.** 攀登;登上: ~ a hill (ladder) 登山(梯) / ~ the throne 登上王位 ‖**~ing a.** 上升的;向上的;【解】上行的

ascendancy, ascendency [ə'sendənsi] **n.** 优势;支配地位: gain ~ over 对…占优势 / ensure the ~ of 保证…的支配地位

ascendant, ascendent [ə'sendənt] **I a.** ①上升的;向上的: an ~ stem 向上的枝干 ②占优势的;占支配地位的 ③【天】向天顶上升的 **II n.** ①优势 ②[罕]祖先 ③(占星术的)星位;(诞生时的)运星,命宫 ‖*be in the* ~ ①走运,吉星高照 ②占优势;蒸蒸日上

ascension [ə'senʃən] **n.** ①上升,升高 ② [the A-]

【基督教】耶稣升天 ‖**~al a.** 上升的 ‖**Ascension Day** 耶稣升天节(复活节后四十天以后的第一个星期四)

ascent [ə'sent] **n.** ① 上升,升高 ② 登高,爬坡: make an ~ of the mountain 登山 ③(声望或社会地位的)提高 ④斜坡,(一段)阶梯;坡度,斜度: a rapid (gentle) ~ 陡(缓)坡 / The road has an ~ of five degrees. 这条路的坡度是五度。⑤上溯,追溯

ascertain [ˌæsə'tein] **vt.** 查明,弄清,确定: ~ the true situation 查明真实情况 / ~ where the trouble lies 弄清毛病所在 ‖**~able a.** 可查明的,可弄清的 / **~ment n.**

ascetic [ə'setik] **I a.** 苦行的;禁欲(主义)的 **II n.** 苦行者;禁欲主义者 ‖**~ism** [ə'setisizəm] **n.** 苦行主义;禁欲主义

ascribe [əs'kraib] **vt.** 把…归于 (to): One should not ~ one's errors *to* objective conditions.一个人不应把自己的错误归咎于客观条件。‖**ascribable a.** 可归于…的;起因于…的 (to)

asdic ['æzdik] **n.** [英]潜艇探测器

ash[1] [æʃ] **n.** ①灰,灰末;[常用复]灰烬: ~ fertilizer 灰肥 / fly ~ 煤灰,飞灰 / ~ test 【化】灰分试验 ②[复]骨灰; 遗体 ③[复]废墟 ④[复]死灰色 ‖*in dust and* ~*es* (或 *in sackcloth and* ~*es*) 【宗】哀悔,悲切忏悔 / *lay in* ~*es* 使化为灰烬,使全部消灭 / *reduce* (*burn*) *to* ~*es* 把…化(烧)为灰烬 ‖**~less a.** 无灰的: ~*less* filter paper 【化】无灰滤纸 ‖**~ bin** ①[英]垃圾箱 ②[俚]深水炸弹 / '**~cake n.** 用灰火焙制的玉米饼 / '**~can a.** 如实地描绘城市生活的(尤指其中的阴暗面) / **~ can** ①[美]垃圾箱 ②[俚]深水炸弹 / **~ cart** 垃圾车 / '**~ fire** 灰火;余烬 / '**~man n.** 除灰工 / '**~pan n.** (火炉里的)炉灰盘 / '**~tray n.** 烟灰缸,烟灰盘 / **Ash Wednesday** 【基督教】圣灰星期三(四旬节的第一天)

ash[2] [æʃ] **n.** 【植】①梣,白蜡树;梣木,秦皮 ②桉树

ashamed [ə'ʃeimd] **a.** [常作表语]羞耻,惭愧,害臊: be (或 feel) ~ to do sth. 对做某事感到害臊 / be (或 feel) ~ of oneself 为自己感到害臊 / feel ~ for sb. 替某人感到羞愧

ashore [ə'ʃɔ:] **ad.** 在岸上,在陆上;上岸,上陆: go (或 come) ~ 上岸 / The ship ran (或 was driven) ~. 那条船在岸边搁浅了。

aside [ə'said] **I ad.** ①在旁边,在一边;到(或向)旁边,到(或向)一边: stand ~ 站开,靠边站,站在一边 / lay sth. ~ 把某物放在一边;把某物搁置起来 / put sth. ~ for sb. 把某物留起来给某人 / speak ~ 旁白 ②[常用于句首独立结构中](暂且)撇开不谈: Joking ~, ... 不开玩笑(正经地说),… / Small problems ~, the exhibition was a success. 除了一些小问题,那展览会是成功的。**II n.** ①(戏剧等中的)旁白 ②离题的话 ‖*from* [美]除…以外

ask [ɑ:sk] ❶ **vt.** ①问,询问: ~ the way 问路 / ~ (sb.) a question 问(某人)一个问题 ②要求,

请求: May I ~ a favour *of* you? 能 不能请你帮我一个忙? ③邀请,请: ~ sb. *to* a meeting 邀请某人到会 / *Ask* him in. 请他进来。④讨(价等) ⑤需要: The matter ~*s* immediate attention. 这件事需要立即予以注意。❷ *vi.* ①要求,请求 ②问: ~ *about* the efficiency of the new machine 询问新机器的效能 / If you don't know, just ~. 你要是不懂,就问好了。‖~ *after* 探问,询问: ~ *for* ①请求; 向…要: *Ask* the barren land *for* grain. 向荒地要粮。② 通过询问来寻找(人等): Did anyone ~ *for* me? 有人来找过我吗? / ~ *for it* [口]自找麻烦,自讨苦吃 / ~ *for trouble* 自找麻烦,自讨苦吃 ‖~*ing* n. ①询问 ②索取: You may have it *for* the ~*ing*. 只要你愿意要,就把它拿去好了。/ the ~*ing* price 卖主的开叫价

askance [əsˈkæns], **askant** [əsˈkænt] *ad.* 横眼(看),斜眼(看): look ~ at sb. 斜眼看某人(常表示蔑视、怀疑、厌恶等情绪)

askew [əsˈkjuː] *ad. & a.* [常作表语]斜(的),歪(的): look ~ at sb. 斜着看某人 / hang a picture ~ 把图画挂歪 / cut sth. ~ 斜切(或劈)某物 / have one's hat on ~ 歪戴着帽

aslant [əˈslɑːnt] **I** *ad. & a.* [常作表语]倾斜: with head ~ 歪着头 **II** *prep.* 倾斜地横过: lie ~ sth. 斜横在某物上 / run ~ sth. 与某事物相抵触

asleep [əˈsliːp] *a.* [常作表语]①睡着,睡熟: drop ~ 入睡 / lie ~ 躺着熟睡 / be fast ~ 熟睡 ②(四肢)发麻,麻木: My arm is ~. 我的手臂发麻。③静止(状态);发呆: The sea is ~. 海上风平浪静。④长眠,已死 ‖~ *at the switch* 玩忽职守;错过机会 / fall ~ ①入睡 ②长眠,死 ③懈怠,玩忽职守 ④静止不动;(指陀螺转动)稳得使人看不出转动

asparagus [əsˈpærəgəs] *n.* 【植】① [A-] 天门冬属 ②石刁柏,芦笋

aspect [ˈæspekt] *n.* ①样子,外表,面貌: take on (或 assume) an entirely new ~ 面貌一新 / general ~*s* 概况 ②(问题、事物等的)方面: We should consider a problem in all its ~*s*. 我们应该全面地考虑问题。③(建筑物等的)方向,方位: The house has a southern ~. 这所房子朝南。④【语】(动词的)体 ‖~ **ratio** 纵横比;(飞机的)展弦比

asperity [æsˈperiti] *n.* ①粗糙;(气候的)严酷;(声音的)刺耳 ②(性格、语言等的)粗暴,严厉: speak with ~ 严厉地说 ③[常用复]严酷的气候;艰苦的条件;粗暴的话语: the *asperities* of northern winter 北方冬季的严寒 / an exchange of *asperities* 对骂

asperse [əsˈpəːs] *vt.* ①洒水于;【宗】洒圣水于 ②诽谤,中伤,破坏(名誉等)

asphalt [ˈæsfælt], **asphaltum** [æsˈfæltəm] **I** *n.* (地)沥青;(铺路用)沥青混合料: ~ felt 油毛毡 / an ~ road 沥青路,柏油路 **II** *vt.* 铺沥青于 ‖**asphaltic** [æsˈfæltik] *a.* 沥青的,含沥青的 ‖~ **jungle** "柏油丛林"

asphyxiate [æsˈfiksieit] *vt. & vi.* (使)窒息 ‖**asphyxiation** [æsˌfiksiˈeiʃən] *n.* 窒息 / **asphyxiator** *n.* 窒息装置,动物窒息试验器 ‖**asphyxiating gas** 窒息性气体

aspiration [ˌæspəˈreiʃən] *n.* ① 志气,抱负; 渴望 (*after, for*): an ~ *to* do sth. 渴望做某事 ②发送气音;送气音 ③吸出

aspire [əsˈpaiə] *vi.* 渴望,追求(知识、名誉等)(*to, after, at*) ‖~**r** [əsˈpaiərə] *n.* 渴望者,追求者

aspirin [ˈæspərin] *n.* 阿司匹林(解热镇痛药);阿司匹林药片: take two ~(*s*) for a headache 服两片阿司匹林治头痛

ass [æs] *n.* ①驴 ②傻瓜,蠢人: make an ~ of sb. 愚弄某人 / make an ~ of oneself 干蠢事;使自己出洋相 ③[俗]屁股 ‖*an ~ in a lion's skin* 说大话的胆小鬼,色厉内荏的人 / *an ~ with two panniers* 两臂各挽一女人在街上行走的男人 / *on one's* ~ [美俚]处境困难;破产 / *The ~ waggeth his ears.* [谚]驴子摇耳朵,傻瓜装聪明。/ *till the ~ ascends the ladder* 决不能,永不能 ‖~**es' bridge** 笨人难过的桥(指欧几里得《几何学》第一卷第五命题;因初学者难懂,故有此谑称) / **'~-,kisser** *n.* [美俚]拍马屁的无耻之尤

assail [əˈseil] *vt.* ① 攻击,袭击: ~ sb. with blows (reproaches, questions) 殴打 (责备, 质问) 某人 ②毅然应付,着手解决(任务、难题等): ~ a task 毅然着手去完成任务 ‖~**able** *a.* 易受攻击的 / ~**ant** *n.* 攻击者

assassin [əˈsæsin] *n.* ①暗杀者,行刺者(常指政治性的) ② [A-] 【史】暗杀十字军中基督徒的穆斯林秘密团体成员 ‖~ **bug** 食虫椿象科昆虫(一种寄生于他虫并吸其血的益虫)

assassinate [əˈsæsineit] *vt.* ①暗杀,行刺 ②中伤,破坏(名誉等)

assassination [əˌsæsiˈneiʃən] *n.* 暗杀,行刺

assault [əˈsɔːlt] **I** *n.* ①(武力或口头上的)攻击,袭击: make a surprise ~ *on* 对…进行突然袭击 / take a town by ~ 强行攻占城镇 【军】冲击,突击,强击: a bayonet ~ 白刃战(肉搏) / a converging ~ 围攻 / an ~ boat (两栖作战用的)强击艇,突击舟 / an ~ force 突击队 / river crossing ~ 强渡 【律】殴打(尤指未遂的殴打),(用言语等的)威胁 ④[委婉语]强奸 **II** ❶ *vt.* ①突击,攻击,袭击 ②殴打 ③[委婉语]强奸 ❷ *vi.* 动武 ‖~ *and battery* 【律】殴打(已遂);人身攻击 ‖~**able** *a.* 可攻击的,可袭击的

assay [əˈsei] **I** *n.* ①试金(指分析矿石和合金的成分);化验,(药物等的)分析,检定: ~ balance 【化】试金天平 / ~ ton 【化】化验吨 (29.1667 克) ②被分析物,被化验物 ③化验报告 ④[古]企图,尝试 **II** ❶ *vt.* ①化验,分析,检定 ②企图,尝试: ~ to do sth. 试图做某事 ❷ *vi.* 被验明成分: The ore ~*s* high in gold. 这种矿石被验明含金量很高。‖~**er** *n.* 化验者,分析者;尝试者 / ~**ing** *n.* 试金;化验(法)

assemblage [əˈsemblidʒ] *n.* ①集合;【机】装配;装

配而成的大件 ②一群人，会众；集合物：I was one of the ~. 我是与会者中的一个。/ an ~ of colours 五彩缤纷

assemble [ə'sembl] ❶ vt. ①集合；调集：~ forces 调集兵力 ②装配：~ a machine 装配机器 / an assembling shop 装配车间 ❷ vi. 集合 ‖~r n. 装配工

assembly [ə'sembli] n. ①集合：an ~ point 集合地点 ②集会；[总称]与会者：freedom of speech and ~ 言论和集会的自由 / hold an ~ 举行集会 / an ~ hall 会议厅 / There was a large ~ yesterday. 昨天到会的人很多。③[A-] 议会；(美国某些州的)州议会众议院：the National Assembly【法史】国民议会 / General Assembly 联合国大会;(长老会等宗教团体的)最高司法(或管理)机构；[美]州议会 ④装配；装配车间；供装配的零件：an ~ shop 装配车间 / an ~ line (生产上一环接一环的)装配线 / an ~ line method (生产上的)流水作业法 ⑤【军】集合信号 ⑥(统计力学中的)系集 ‖**as'semblyman** n. ①议员;(美国某些州的)州议会众议员 ②装配工

assent [ə'sent] I n. 同意，赞成 (to)：give one's ~ to a proposal 对建议表示同意 / nod ~ 点头表示同意 / by common ~ 经一致同意 / with one ~ 一致同意地 II vi. 同意，赞成 (to) ‖~or n. 同意者，赞成者

assert [ə'sə:t] vt. ①宣称；断言：He ~ed that this could be done. 他宣称这是可行的。/ ~ sth. to be true 断言某事是真实的 ②维护，坚持(权利等)：~ national independence 维护民族独立 ‖~ oneself 坚持自己的权利；表明(或表现)自己 ‖~or, ~er n. 断言者；维护者

assertion [ə'sə:ʃən] n. ①主张，断言：stand to one's ~ 坚持自己的主张 ②维护，坚持

assertive [ə'sə:tiv] a. ①断言的，肯定的：speak in an ~ tone 以肯定的语气说话 / an ~ sentence 【语】陈述句 ②过分自信的，武断的 ‖~ly ad. / ~ness n.

assess [ə'ses] vt. ①对(财产等)进行估价(作为征税根据) ②确定(税款、罚款等)的金额：~ damages at 把赔偿金额定为… ③征收(税款、罚款等) (on, upon)；向…征税(或罚款)：~ a tax of 100 dollars upon sb. (sth.) 向某人(对某物)征收一百元的税款 / ~ sb. at ten pounds 向某人征收十镑 ④对(人物、工作等)进行评价 ‖~able a. 可估价的，可估计的；可征税的 / ~ment n. ①估价；评价：a correct ~ment of historical figures 对历史人物的正确评价 ②估价(或评价)法 ③估计数 / ~or n. ①估价财产的人；确定税款(或罚款)的人 ②(法官、官方委员会等的)技术顾问；助理，助理 ③陪审推事

asset ['æset] n. ①(单项)财产：enemy ~s 敌产 ②宝贵的人(或物) ③[复]资产，财产：a statement of ~s and liabilities 资产负债表

assiduity [,æsi'dju(:)iti] n. ①刻苦，勤奋：with ~ 兢兢业业地 ②[常用复]殷勤 (to)

assiduous [ə'sidjuəs] a. ①刻苦的，勤奋的 (in, at)；②殷勤的 (over) ‖~ly ad. / ~ness n.

assign [ə'sain] I ❶ vt. ①分配；把…分配给 (to)：~ homework 指定家庭作业 / ~ two rooms to sb. 把两间房屋分配给某人 / He was ~ed an important mission. 他分配到一个重要任务。②委派，指派：He has been ~ed to a new post. 他被派到新的工作岗位。/ ~ sb. to do a difficult task 派某人去完成一项艰巨的任务 ③指定(时间、地点)：Experts ~ the temple to 150 B. C. 专家们确定该庙宇是公元前一五〇年的建筑物。/ ~ a day for a meeting 确定开会日期 / an ~ed position 指定的地点 ④把…归因于 (to, for) ⑤【律】把…转让给 (to) ❷ vi.【律】转让财产 II n. [常用复]受让人，接受转让的人 ‖~able a. 可分配的；可指派的；可指定的；(原因等)可指出的；可转让的 / ~ee [,æsi'ni:] n.【律】①受让人 ②代理人，受托者 / ~er, ~or n. 分配者；委派者；【律】转让者

assignment [ə'sainmənt] n. ①分配；委派：the country of ~ (大使等)被派往的国家 ②(分派的)任务；指定的(课外)作业：What are today's ~? 今天的作业(或任务)是什么？③【律】(财产、权利的)转让；转让证书 ④(理由、动机等的)说明，陈述

assimilate [ə'simileit] ❶ vt. ①吸收(食物、思想、文化等) ②同化(民族、语言成分等) ③使相似，使相同(to, with) ④把…比作(to, with) ❷ vi. ①被吸收 ②被同化 ③成为相似(或相同) ‖**assimilator** n. 吸收者；同化者

assimilation [ə,simi'leiʃən] n. ①吸收(作用) ②同化(作用)

assist [ə'sist] I ❶ vt. ①援助，帮助：~ sb. with sth. 帮助某人做某事 ②搀扶：~ sb. from the saddle 搀某人下马 / ~ sb. to his feet 扶某人站起来 ❷ vi. ①援助，帮忙：~ in a department store 在百货店里帮忙 ②出席，参加：~ at a ceremony 出席仪式 II n. 援助，帮助 ‖~or n. 帮助者；加力器，助推器

assistance [ə'sistəns] n. 援助，帮助：give (或render, extend) ~ to sb. 给某人以帮助 / come to sb.'s ~ 帮助某人 / be of ~ to sb. 有助于某人

assistant [ə'sistənt] I a. 辅助的；助理的：an ~ engineer 助理工程师 / an ~ manager 副经理，协理，襄理 II n. ①助手，助理：a shop ~ 店员，营业员 ②助教：be appointed as ~ in English 被指派为英语助教 ③辅助物；(染色的)助剂

assize [ə'saiz] n. ①立法会议，行政会议；(立法、行政等会议制定的)法令，条令 ②[常用复](英国各郡的)巡回审判；大审 ③(对商品的规格、价格等制定的)法定标准

associate [ə'souʃieit] I ❶ vt. ①使发生联系，使联合 (with)：~ oneself (或 be ~d) with sb. in an enterprise 与某人联合从事一项事业 / ~ oneself with a proposal (an opinion) 赞成一项提议(一种

意见) / personnel ~d *with* the work of the exhibition 展览会工作的有关人员 ② 把…联想起来: ❷ *vi.* 交往, 结交(*with*) II [ə'souʃiit] *n.* ①合伙人;同事;朋友 ②(协会、社团等内只有部分权利的)非正式会员 ③相关物 III [ə'souʃiit] *a.* ①合伙的;有联系的,有关的 ②副的: an ~ editor (professor) [美]副主编(教授) ‖~d *a.* 联合的: the *Associated* Press (略作 AP 或 A.P.) 联合通讯社(简称美联社)(美国)

association [ə,sousi'eiʃən] *n.* ① 联合, 联系;联盟;合伙; 交际, 交往: a deed of ~ [英]有限公司的合伙契约 ②联想: an ~ of ideas 联想 ③协会, 社团 ④【化】缔合(作用) ⑤ 英式足球 (= ~ football) ‖~al *a.* ①协会的, 社团的 ②联想的 ‖~ **book** 因与名人有关(如由名人赠送等)而受珍视的书

assorted [ə'sɔːtid] *a.* ①各式各样的, 混杂的: ~ biscuits 什锦饼干 / ~ rubber goods 各式橡胶制品 ②相配的, 相称的: a well-~ couple 一对佳偶 ③分了类的;分类排列的

assortment [ə'sɔːtmənt] *n.* ①分类 ②花色品种, 各种各类的聚合: a rich (或 large) ~ of goods 一批花色齐全的货物

assuage [ə'sweidʒ] *vt.* ① 缓和, 减轻(病痛等): ~ pain 止痛 ② 使安静;平息(愤怒等) ③充(饥);解(渴) ‖~ment *n.*

assume [ə'sju:m] ❶ *vt.* ①假定, 设想: ~ a statement to be correct 假定一种说法是正确的 / *assuming* that ... 假定… ②担任;承担;接受: ~ office 就职 / ~ a leading position 担任领导职务 / ~ responsibility 承担责任 / ~ the reins of government 开始执政 ③采取;呈(某种形式、面貌): The motion of matter always ~s certain forms. 物质的运动总是表现为一定的形式。/ ~ a new aspect 呈现新的面貌 / ~ the offensive 采取攻势 ④装出: ~ the airs of 摆出…架子 ⑤侵占,僭取 ❷ *vi.* 专擅;僭越

assuming [ə'sju:miŋ] *a.* 僭越的;自负的, 傲慢的 ‖~ly *ad.*

assumption [ə'sʌmpʃən] *n.* ①假定, 设想: on the ~ that ... 以…的设想为根据 ②担任;承担;采取;假装 ③自负, 傲慢;僭越 ④[常作 A-] (基督教)圣母升天(节)

assurance [ə'ʃuərəns] *n.* ①把握, 信念: I have full ~ of the reliability of his words. 我充分相信他的话是可靠的。② 自信: speak with ~ 很自信地讲话 ③自大, 狂妄: He had the ~ to claim that ... 他竟狂妄地宣称… ④ 保证, 断言: give an ~ (或 the ~ 或 ~s) that ... 保证… ⑤[英]保险(主要用于 life ~ 人寿保险) ⑥【律】财产转让(书)

assure [ə'ʃuə] *vt.* ①使确信;使放心: Investigations ~d us of the soundness of the plan. 调查研究使我们确信这个计划是可行的。/ ~ oneself of sth. 弄清楚某事 / The news ~d me. 这消息使我放心了。②向…保证: I can ~ you *of* the

reliability of the information. 我可以向你保证这消息是可靠的。③保证获得;保障: ~ national security 保障国家安全 ④对…进行保险(主要用于人寿保险) ‖~r [ə'ʃuərə] *n.* 保证者;保险商

assured [ə'ʃuəd] I *a.* ①确定的;有保证的: an ~ income 有保证的收入 ②自信的;自大的, 自满的 ③感到有把握的,感到放心的: be ~ of the merits of the new method 确信新方法的优越性 / You may *rest* ~ that .... 对…你尽可放心。II *n.* [the ~(s)] 被保险人 ‖~ly [ə'ʃuəridli] *ad.* ①确定地, 无疑问地 ②自信地, 有把握地 / ~ness *n.*

asterisk ['æstərisk] I *n.* ① 星号(即*) ②星状物 II *vt.* 加星号于

astern [əs'tə:n] *ad.* ①在船(或飞机)的尾部;向船(或飞机)的尾部 ② 在后;向后: Full speed ~! 全速后退! ‖~ *of* 在…的后面 / *fall* (或 *drop*) ~ 落在(他船)后面

asthma ['æsmə] *n.* 气喘(病)

asthmatic [æs'mætik] I *a.* 气喘的, 患气喘病的 II *n.* 气喘病患者 ‖~ally *ad.*

astigmatism [æs'tigmətizəm] *n.* ① 散光, 乱视 ②【物】象散性, 象散现象

astir [ə'stə:] *ad. & a.* [常作表语] ① 动起来;轰动起来;骚动起来: The whole school was ~ when the good news came. 喜讯传来, 全校都轰动起来。②已起床: be ~ early 起得早

astonish [əs'təniʃ] *vt.* 使惊讶: His words ~ed all. 他的话使大家感到惊讶。/ be ~ed *to see* ... 见到…感觉惊讶 / be ~ed at sth. 对某事感到惊讶

astonishment [əs'təniʃmənt] *n.* ① 惊讶: watch with openmouthed ~ 目瞪口呆地看着 / say in ~ (因) 感到惊讶而说 / To my ~, he was so opinionated. 使我吃惊的是, 他竟如此固执己见。②使人惊讶的事物(或人)

astound [əs'taund] *vt.* 使震惊,使大吃一惊

astray [əs'trei] *ad.* 迷路;入歧途,离开正道;犯错误: go ~ 走入迷路;走上歧途 / lead sb. ~ 把某人引入歧途

astride [əs'traid] I *a.* [常作表语] & *ad.* 两脚分开着: sit ~ *of* a chair 两脚分开跨坐在椅上 / ride a horse ~ 跨马 II *prep.* 跨着: ~ a river (road) 横跨河流(道路)的两旁

astringent [əs'trindʒənt] I *a.* ①收缩的;收敛的;止血的 ②严厉的,严峻的 II *n.* 【药】收敛剂;止血药 ‖~ly *ad.*

astrology [əs'trɔlədʒi] *n.* 星占学,占星术

astronomy [əs'trɔnəmi] *n.* 天文学: radio ~ 射电天文学

astute [əs'tju:t; 美 əs'tju:t] *a.* ①敏锐的, 精明的, 聪明的 ②狡猾的, 诡计多端的 ‖~ly *ad.* / ~ness *n.*

asunder [ə'sʌndə] *a.* [常作表语] & *ad.* ①(向不同方向)分开: as wide ~ as the poles 象南北两极那样分隔得很远,南辕北辙 ②散;碎: tear (或 break) sth. ~ 把某物扯得粉碎 / fall ~ 崩溃

asylum [ə'sailəm] *n.* ①收容所, 救济院: a lunatic

~ 精神病院 / an orphan ~ 孤儿院 ②避难所, 庇护所 ③避难;政治避难权,庇护权: seek ~ in a neutral nation 要求在一中立国避难

at [强 æt; 弱 ət] *prep.* ①[表示空间]在…,在…上: ~ the station 在车站 / enter ~ the front door 从前门进入 ②[表示时间]在…时(刻);一经…: ~ five o'clock 在五点钟 / ~ the age of fifteen 在十五岁的时候 / ~ regular intervals 定期地 / ~ the mere mention (thought) of ... 一提(想)到… ③[表示状态]在…中: ~ war (peace) 在交战(和平)状态中 ④在…方面: good ~ learning 善于学习的 ⑤针对着,向: shoot the arrow ~ the target 有的放矢 / keep on ~ sb. 跟某人纠缠不休 ⑥[表示速度、价格等]以: The train runs ~ fifty kilometres an hour. 火车以每小时五十公里的速度行驶。/ ~ a trot 小跑着 / mass-produce sth. ~ a low cost 以低成本大规模生产某种产品 ⑦从事于: What is he ~? 他正在干什么? ⑧因为,由于: rejoice ~ others' achievements 为别人的成就感到高兴

ate [et; 美 eit] eat 的过去式

atheism ['eiθiizəm] *n.* 无神论 ‖**atheist** *n.* 无神论者

athlete ['æθli:t] *n.* ①运动员,体育家; [英]田径运动员 ②身强力壮的人 ‖~'s foot 脚癣,香港脚

athletic [æθ'letik] *a.* ①运动的,体育的; 运动员的,体育家的: an ~ meeting 运动会 / sports 体育运动,竞技 ②体格健壮的; 行动敏捷的; 活跃的 ‖~ally *ad.* ~ism [æθ'letisizəm] *n.* 运动练习

athletics [æθ'letiks] [复] *n.* ①[用作单或复]体育运动,竞技; [英]田径运动 ②[用作单]体育(课); 运动技巧

atlas ['ætləs] *n.* ①地图册; 图表集 ②大张绘图纸 ③【解】寰椎,第一颈椎 ④[A-]【希神】阿特拉斯(顶天的巨神) ⑤[喻]身负重担的人 ⑥[A-]阿特拉斯山脉 [非洲] (=the Atlas Mountains)

atmosphere ['ætməsfiə] *n.* ①大气; 大气层 ②空气: a moist ~ 潮湿的空气 ③【物】大气压力; 大气压(压力单位): absolute ~ 绝对气压 ④【化】雾(各种物体周围的介质): ion ~ 离子雾 / electron ~ 电子云 ⑤气氛,环境: a cordial and friendly ~ 亲切友好的气氛 / a new and dynamic ~ 生气勃勃的新气象 ⑥(艺术品的)基调 ‖clear the ~ 消除误会(或紧张、猜疑气氛)

atmospheric [,ætməs'ferik] *a.* ①大气的,空气的; 大气中的; 大气层的: an ~ test 大气层试验 ②大气所引起的: ~ pressure 大气压力 / ~ discharge 【电】大气放电 ③产生某种气氛的; 有美感(或感情气氛)的

atoll ['ætɔl] *n.* 【地】环礁,环状珊瑚岛: ~ lake 环礁湖

atom ['ætəm] *n.* ①原子: tagged (或 labelled) ~ 【原】示踪原子,显迹原子 ②微粒: smash (或 break) sth. to ~s 某物打得粉碎 ③微量: have not an ~ of 一点也没有… ‖the ~ 原子能

‖~less *a.* 无原子武器的 ‖~ bomb 原子弹 / '~-bomb *vt.* 用原子弹轰炸 / '~-,bomber *n.* 原子轰炸机 / '~-'free *a.* 无原子武器的: an ~-free zone 无原子武器区 / '~-'powered *a.* 原子动力的: an ~-powered plane (submarine) 原子动力飞机 (潜艇) / ~ smasher 【原】核粒子加速器 / '~-'stricken *a.* 受原子爆炸污染的 / '~-'tipped *a.* 装有原子弹头的: an ~-tipped missile 装有原子弹头的导弹

atomic [ə'tɔmik] *a.* ①原子的 ②原子能的 ③原子武器的 ④【化】以原子形式存在的,分裂为原子的 ⑤极微的 ⑥强大的: an ~ effort 巨大的努力 ‖the ~ age 原子时代 / an ~ aircraft carrier 原子动力航空母舰 / an ~ arms race 原子军备竞赛 / an ~ attack (或 strike) 原子袭击 / an ~ base 原子基地 / an ~ battery 原子能电池 / an ~ bomb 原子弹 / ~ capability 使用原子武器的能力 / an ~ clock 原子钟 / ~ cloud 原子云 / an ~ cocktail [俚] 含放射性物质的吞服剂(用于癌症等的诊断和治疗) / an ~ defence unit 原子防护部队 / ~ diplomacy 原子外交 / ~ energy 原子能 / ~ formation 原子条件下的战斗队形 / ~ fuel 原子燃料 / an ~ guided missile 原子导弹 / ~ hypothesis 【化】原子假说 / an ~ icebreaker 原子破冰船 / ~ monopoly 原子垄断 / ~ nucleus 【物】原子核 / ~ number 【化】原子序(数) / an ~ pile (或 reactor) 原子反应堆 / ~ power 原子动力 / an ~ power plant (或 station) 原子能发电站 / ~ protection 原子防护 / ~ stockpile 原子储备 / ~ structure 【物】原子结构 / ~ volume 【化】原子体积 / an ~ war 原子战争 / an ~ warhead 原子弹头 / ~ weight 【化】原子量 ‖a'tomic-,bearing *a.* 携带原子弹的: ~-bearing capacity 携带原子弹的能力 / a'tomic-,cosmic *a.* 掌握原子能和宇宙空间技术的 / a'tomic-proof *a.* 防原子的: an ~-proof hideout 防原子掩蔽部 / a'tomic-'tipped *a.* 装有原子弹头的: ~-tipped rockets 装有原子弹头的火箭

atone [ə'toun] *vi.* 赎回; 偿还(for): perform merits to ~ for one's misdeeds 立功赎罪 ‖~ment *n.*

atrocious [ə'trouʃəs] *a.* ①凶恶的,残暴的: ~ exploitation 残酷的剥削 ②[口] 糟透的,恶劣的: ~ weather 恶劣的天气 / ~ manners 粗暴的举止 ‖~ly *ad.* / ~ness *n.*

atrocity [ə'trɔsiti] *n.* ①凶恶,残暴; 暴行 ②[口] 庸俗不堪的东西; 令人不愉快的事物

atrophy ['ætrəfi] **I** *n.* ①萎缩,虚脱,衰退 ②【医】萎缩症; 【植】萎缩,减缩 **II** *vt.* & *vi.* (使)萎缩,(使)虚脱

attach [ə'tætʃ] ❶ *vt.* ①缚,系; 贴: ~ a cable 连接缆索 / ~ labels to the luggage 把标签系(或贴)在行李上 ②附加; 隶属: aid with no conditions ~ed 无附加条件的援助 / a bedroom with a bathroom ~ed 附有浴室的卧室 ③把(重点等)放在 (to) ④使喜爱,使依恋 (to) ⑤任命 ⑥逮

捕;扣押,查封 ⑦【军】配属 ❷ vi. 系,缚;附;归属 ‖~ *oneself to* 依附;参加(党派) / *be ~ed to* ①附属于 ②喜爱;爱慕,爱恋 ‖~able a. 可结上的;可附上的;可拘留的 / ~ment n. ① 连接物;附属品;附件;附加装置 ②依恋 ③逮捕;扣押财产

attack [ə'tæk] **I** ❶ vt. ① 攻击,进攻 ②非难,抨击 ③(干劲十足地)投入,着手: ~ a task 干劲十足地投入工作 ④ (疾病)侵袭: be ~ed with a disease 害病 ❷ vi. 攻击 **II** n. ① 攻击,进攻: launch (或 make) an ~ on (或 upon) 对…发动进攻 / an ~ order【军】攻击令/ an ~ plane 攻击机 / a converging ~ 【军】分进合击 / a feint ~ 佯攻 / a hit-and-run ~ 即打即离(或打了就跑)的进攻 / a nibbling ~ 蚕食进攻 / a surprise ~ 奇袭,突然袭击 ②非难,抨击: come under ~ 遭到抨击 ③(疾病)侵袭,发作: a heart ~ 心脏病突发 ④(工作、任务等的)开始 ⑤起唱的准确性 ‖~er n. 攻击者

attain [ə'tein] ❶ vt. ①达到;完成;获得: ~ one's goal 达到目的 ② 到达: He has ~ed the age of ninety. 他已达九十高龄. / ~ the top of a hill 到达山顶 ❷ vi. 到达 (to): ~ to manhood 到达成年时期 ‖~able a. 可达到的

attainment [ə'teinmənt] n. ① 达到,到达: the ~ of one's object 达到目的 ② 【常用复】成就,造诣: scientific ~s 科学上的造诣

attempt [ə'tempt] **I** vt. ①尝试,试图: ~ a difficult task 试图完成一项艰难的工作 / ~ to carry out a plan 试图执行某一计划 ②试图夺取(要塞等) ③【古】企图杀害: ~ sb.'s life 企图杀害某人 **II** n. ①企图,试图: make an ~ to do sth. 试图做某事 ②试图夺取: make an ~ on a fortress 试图夺取某一要塞 ③【律】未遂行为,未遂罪 ‖~able a. 可以尝试的

attend [ə'tend] ❶ vt. ①出席,参加: ~ a meeting 参加会议 / ~ school 上学 ②照顾,护理;侍侯 ③陪伴;伴随: Treatment with medicinal herbs is ~ed with good results. 用草药治疗效果良好. ❷ vi. ①专心;注意 (to): ~ to one's work 安心(好)自己的工作 / carefully ~ to the advice and criticisms of customers 倾听顾客的意见 ②照顾,护理 (to): ~ to the wounded day and night 日夜护理伤员 ③伴随;侍侯 (upon)

attendance [ə'tendəns] n. ① 到场;出席: The ~ (rate) is high. 出勤率高. / Attendance was large: There was a large ~ at the meeting. 到会人数很多. ③护理: a doctor in ~ 护理医生 ‖dance ~ on (或 upon) sb. 奉承某人,向某人献媚

attendant [ə'tendənt] **I** n. ①侍者;服务员 ②出席者 ③随从 ④伴随物 **II** a. ①在场的 ②护理的 ③伴随的;附随的

attention [ə'tenʃən] n. ① 注意,留心;关心: pay ~ to state affairs 关心国家大事 / listen with ~ 专心听 / I was all ~. 我十分留意. / ~ to orders 【军】注意命令 / Your application will

have ~. 你们的申请将得到考虑. ② 注意力: undivided ~ 一心一意 ③ [复]殷勤: pay one's ~s to sb. 向某人献殷勤 ④【军】立正姿态;(口令)立正: *Attention!* 立正! ‖*attract* (或 *draw*) *sb.'s ~* 引起某人的注意 / *bring sth. to sb.'s ~* 使某人注意某事 / *call sb.'s ~ to sth.* 叫某人注意某事 / *come to ~* 【军】采取立正姿势 / *devote one's ~ to* 专心于 / *give one's ~ to* 注意 / *stand at ~* 【军】立正 ‖~al a.

attentive [ə'tentiv] a. ①注意的,当心的: an ~ audience 聚精会神的听众(或观众) / lend an ear to 倾听… ②有礼貌的;关心的;殷勤的 (to) ‖~ly ad. / ~ness n.

attest [ə'test] ❶ vt. ①证实,证明: ~ the truth of a writing 证实一个文件的真实性 ②作为…的证明;表明 ③使宣誓 ❷ vi. 证实,证明 (to): I can ~ to the absolute truth of his statement. 我可以证实他的话是千真万确的. ‖~ed a. (家畜等)经检验证明为无病的 / ~or n. 证明者;证人

attic ['ætik] n. 顶楼;屋顶室

attire [ə'taiə] **I** vt. 使穿衣;装饰,打扮 (in): ~ oneself in 穿上…服装 / be neatly ~d 穿着整洁的服装 **II** n. 服装,衣着;盛装

attitude ['ætitju:d] n. ①姿势 ②态度;看法 (to, towards): What's your ~ towards this question? 你对这个问题有什么看法? ③【空】飞行姿态 (= ~ of flight): ~ control 飞行姿态控制装置 ④ (芭蕾舞中的)鹤立式 ‖strike ~ 装腔作势

attorney [ə'tə:ni] n. ① (业务或法律事务中的)代理人: a letter of ~ 委任状 / a power of ~ 委托书;代理权 ② [美] 律师 (英国称 solicitor) ‖~ship n. 代理人的职务;代理权 ‖at'torney=at-'law n. [美]律师 / Attorney General [英]检察总长;[美]司法部长 / at'torney-in-'fact n. 代理人

attract [ə'trækt] ❶ vt. ① 吸引: Like ~s like. 物以类聚. / A magnet ~s iron. 磁石吸铁. / Cathode rays are ~ed by a positive charge. 阴极射线被阳电荷所吸引. ② 引起(注意、兴趣、赞赏等);诱惑: ~ sb.'s attention 引起某人的注意 / ~ moths with lamps 点灯诱蛾 ❷ vi. 有吸引力 ‖~or n. 引人注意的人;有吸引力的人(或物)

attraction [ə'trækʃən] n. ① 吸引: ~ sphere 【生】吸引球 ②吸引力;诱惑力 ③吸引物;喜闻乐见的事物: The display of fireworks offers many ~s. 焰火很吸引人. ④【物】引力: The ~ of the moon for the earth causes the tides. 月亮对地球的引力引起潮汐. / ~ of gravity 重力 / magnetic ~ 磁力 / molecular ~ 分子吸引力 ⑤【语】形态同化

attractive [ə'træktiv] a. 有吸引力的,引起注意的,引起兴趣的,有迷惑力的: goods ~ in price and quality 价廉物美的货物 ‖~ly ad. / ~ness n.

attributable [ə'tribjutəbl] a. 可归因的,可归属的 (to): be ~ to 可归因于…

attribute I [ə'tribju(ː)t] *vt.* ① 把…归因于; 把…归咎于 (to) ② 认为…是某人做的; 认为…是某人创造(to): ~ an invention *to* sb. 认为是某人的发明 II ['ætribjuːt] *n.* ①属性, 品质, 特征 ② (人物、职务等的)标志, 象征 ③【语】定语

attribution [,ætri'bjuːʃən] *n.* ①归因; 归属 ②归属物; 属性

attributive [ə'tribjutiv] I *a.* ①归属的; 属性的 ②定语的: an ~ adjective 定语形容词 II *n.*【语】定语 ‖**~ly** *ad.*

auburn ['ɔːbən] *n. & a.* 金棕色(的), 茶褐色(的)

auction ['ɔːkʃən] I *n.* ①拍卖: sell sth. by (或[美] at) ~ 拍卖某物 / a Dutch ~ 削价拍卖 ②拍卖式桥牌(桥牌的一种, ＝ ~ bridge) ③(某些纸牌游戏的)叫牌 II *vt.* 拍卖: ~ *off* 拍卖掉 / *put up at* ~ [美]把…交付拍卖 / *put up to* (或 *for*) ~ 把…交付拍卖

audacious [ɔː'deiʃəs] *a.* ①大胆的, 有冒险精神的: an ~ explorer 大胆的探险家 ②鲁莽的, 放肆的; 蛮横无礼的; 厚颜无耻的 ‖**~ly** *ad.* / **~ness** *n.*

audible ['ɔːdəbl] *a.* 听得见的: an ~ signal 音响信号, 音频信号 / an ~ whisper 听得见的低语 ‖**audibility** [,ɔːdi'biliti] *n.*【物】可闻度 / **~ness** *n.* / **audibly** *ad.*

audience ['ɔːdjəns] *n.* ①听众; 观众; 读者: a large (small) ~ 人数多(少)的听众(或观众、读者) ②倾听; 意见等被听取的机会: be given an ~ 得到发表意见的机会 ③ (国家领导人等对外国使节等的)正式会见, 接见: grant sb. an ~ 接见(或召见)某人 / have an ~ with (或 have an ~ of) 拜会… / be received (或 admitted) in ~ 被接见 / request (或 seek) an ~ (with) 要求(为…所)接见 / an ~ chamber (或 room) 接见室, 会见室 ‖*give* ~ (*to*) 听, 倾听

audio-visual ['ɔːdiou'vizjuəl] *a.* 听觉视觉的: ~ aids 直观教具

audit ['ɔːdit] I *n.* ①审计, 查帐 ②决算 II ❶ *vt.* ①查(帐) ②[美](大学生)旁听(课程) ❷ *vi.* 审计, 查帐

audition [ɔː'diʃən] I *n.* ①听; 听觉, 听能 ②(演员等发声的)试听: give an ~ to sb. 试听某人的发声 II ❶ *vt.* 试听(演员等)的发声 ❷ *vi.* 试演 (尤指发声)

auditor ['ɔːditə] *n.* ①审计员, 查帐人 ②听者; 听众之一 ③[美](大学)旁听生

auditorium [,ɔːdi'tɔːriəm] *n.* ①听众席, 观众席; 旁听席 ②[美]讲堂, 礼堂

aught [ɔːt] I *n.* ①任何事物, 任何一部分 ②零 (naught 的转讹): read .01 as point ~ one 把 .01 读为点零一 II *ad.* [古]不管怎样, 到任何程度 ‖*for* ~ *I care* 我才不管呢(表示不在意) / *for* ~ *I know* 也未可知, 也许

augment I [ɔːg'ment] ❶ *vt.* ①扩大, 增加, 增长; 【军】扩编 ②【语】在…上增音 ③【音】在…上增音; 延长 ❷ *vi.* 扩大, 增加 II ['ɔːgmənt] *n.* ①增加 ②【语】增音

augur ['ɔːgə] I *n.* ① (古罗马用观察飞鸟等方法的)占卜官 ②预言者, 卜者 II ❶ *vt.* ①预言 ②预示, 成为…的预兆: ~ well (ill) 主吉(凶) ❷ *vi.* ①作预言 ②成为预兆

augury ['ɔːgjuri] *n.* ① (古罗马的)占卜术, 占卜仪式; 预言术 ②预兆, 征兆

August ['ɔːgəst] *n.* 八月(略作 Aug.)

august [ɔː'gʌst] *a.* 尊严的, 可敬的; 庄严的, 威严的, 雄伟的 ‖**~ly** *ad.* / **~ness** *n.*

auld lang syne ['ɔːld læŋ 'sain] [苏格兰]昔日; 美好的往日

aunt [ɑːnt] *n.* ①姨母; 姑母; 伯母; 婶母; 舅母 ②大娘, 大妈, 阿姨(对年长妇女的尊称) ‖*go and see one's* ~ [俚]上厕所, 去大便

aura ['ɔːrə] ([复] aurae ['ɔːriː] 或 auras) *n.* ① (人或物发出的)气味(或香味) ②【电】电风; 辉光: blue ~ 蓝辉, 电子管中的辉光 ③【医】先兆, 预感

auspice ['ɔːspis] *n.* ①预兆, 前兆, 吉兆 ②(根据飞鸟行动的)占卜 ③[复]保护, 赞助, 主办: under the ~*s* of 在…的保护(或赞助、领导)下, 由…主办(或主持)

auspicious [ɔːs'piʃəs] *a.* ①吉利的, 吉祥的 ②顺利的; 繁荣昌盛的 ‖**~ly** *ad.* / **~ness** *n.*

austere [ɔs'tiə] *a.* ①严峻的; 严厉的 ②严正的, 严肃的; 稳重的: the most ~ of critics 最严肃的批评家 ③简朴的, 朴素的: an ~ style 简朴的风格 ④紧缩的, 节制的 ⑤酸苦的, 涩味的 ‖**~ly** *ad.* / **~ness** *n.*

authentic [ɔː'θentik] *a.* ①可靠的, 可信的; 权威性的; 有根据的: an ~ report 可靠的报道 ②真的, 真正的: an ~ manuscript 一部真正的原稿 ③【律】确证了的, 正式的 ‖**~ally** *ad.*

authenticate [ɔː'θentikeit] *vt.* 证实; 鉴定; 使生效: ~ a date by documentary proof 用文件来证实日期 ‖**authentication** [ɔː,θenti'keiʃən] *n.* 证明 / **authenticator** *n.* 证明者

author ['ɔːθə] I *n.* ①著者; 作家 ②创造者; 创始人; 发起人 ③某作家的全部著作 II *vt.* ①著(书), 写作 ②创造, 创始 ‖**~ess** ['ɔːθəris] *n.* 女作家(通常仍用 author) / **~ial** [ɔː'θɔːriəl] *a.* 著者的; 作家的 / **~ship** *n.* ①著作(活动) ②原作者; 根源 ③原创造者; 根源

authorise ['ɔːθəraiz] *vt.* ＝authorize

authority [ɔː'θɔːriti] *n.* ①权, 权力: have (exercise) ~ over 对…有(行使)权力 / an organ of ~ 权力机关 / supreme in ~ 权力无上的 ②权威, 威信; 许可: by the ~ of 蒙…的许可 / On whose ~? 得到谁的许可? ③[复]当局, 官方: the *authorities* concerned 有关当局 / the military *authorities* 军事当局 ④根据; 典据: on the ~ of a book (person) 根据某书(某人) / have good ~ for stating that … 有足够的证据说… ⑤权威; 有权威性的典籍: an academic ~ 学术权威 / a great ~ *on* phonetics 语音学权威 ⑥代理权; to purchase 委托购买证

authorizable [ˈɔːθəraizəbl] *a.* ① 可授权的 ② 可批准的,可认定的

authorize [ˈɔːθəraiz] *vt.* ① 授权;委任,委托: be ~d to issue the following statement 受权发表下列声明 ② 批准,允许,认可 ‖**authorization** [ˌɔːθəraiˈzeiʃən] *n.* ① 授权;委任 ②核准,认可 / ~d *a.*委任的;核准的,许可的;公认的: an ~d agent 指定的代理人 / an ~d translation 经 (原作者)同意的译本 / the *Authorized* Version (基督教《圣经》的)钦定英译本

autobiography [ˌɔːtoubaiˈɔɡrəfi] *n.* 自传;自传文学

autocracy [ɔːˈtɔkrəsi] *n.* ① 独裁;专制制度 ② 独裁政府;独裁统治的国家

autocrat [ˈɔːtəkræt] *n.* ① 独裁者;专制君主 ② 独断独行的人

autograph [ˈɔːtəɡrɑːf] **I** *n.* ① 亲笔;亲笔签名: an ~ album (签名)纪念册 ②手稿 ③亲笔(或手稿等)的石版复制品 **II** *vt.* ①亲笔书写 ②在…上亲笔签名 ③以石版术复制

automatic [ˌɔːtəˈmætik] **I** *a.* ① 自动的 ② 无意识的;机械的 ‖an ~ *control system* 自动控制系统 / an ~ *digital calculator* 自动数字计算机 / ~ *direction finding*【自】自动测向 / *following*【军】自动跟踪 / an ~ *lubricating device* 自动润滑装置 / ~ *navigation*【军】自动导航 / an ~ *numbering machine* 自动号码机 / ~ *pilot*【空】自动驾驶仪 / an ~ *spotter*【军】自动弹着发信机 / ~ *stoking*【工】自动加煤 / ~ *transmission*【机】自动变速(装置),自动换档 / ~ *tuning*【无】自动调谐,自动调整 **II** *n.* ① 自动机;自动装置 ②自动枪(或炮) ‖**-ally** *ad.* / ~**ity** [ˌɔːtəˈtisiti] *n.* ① 自动性;自动化程度 ② 无意识性;机械性

automation [ˌɔːtəˈmeiʃən] *n.* ① 自动,自动化: process ~ (生产)过程自动化 ②自动学

automobile [ˈɔːtəməbiːl, ˌɔːtəməˈbiːl] **I** *n.* [美] 汽车,机动车: the ~ industry 汽车制造业 / an armoured ~ 装甲汽车 **II** *vi.* 驾驶汽车;乘汽车 **III** *a.* ①自动的 ②汽车的

autonomous [ɔːˈtɔnəməs] *a.* ①自治的;自治权的;自主的: an ~ region 自治区 ②【生】独立存在的 ③【植】自发的

autonomy [ɔːˈtɔnəmi] *n.* ①自治;自治权;自主 ②人身自由 ③【哲】自律,意志自由 ④ 有自主权的国家;自治的团体 ⑤【医】自主性

autumn [ˈɔːtəm] *n.* ①秋,秋季(美国一般用 fall): in ~ 在秋天 / in (the) late ~ 在晚秋 / in the ~ of 1973 在一九七三年的秋天 / ~ crops 秋季作物 / ~ harvesting (sowing, ploughing) 秋收(种,耕) ②成熟期;渐衰期: the ~ of one's life 中年(接近晚年)

auxiliary [ɔːɡˈziljəri] **I** *a.* ①辅助的,补助的 ②附属的,从属的 ‖an ~ *agent* (染料的)助剂 / an ~ *airdrome*【军】辅助机场 / an ~ *engine* 备用发动机,辅助发动机 / an ~ *fuel tank* (飞机的)副油箱 / ~ *service*【军】辅助勤务 / an ~ *ship*

(或 *vessel*)【军】辅助舰,勤务舰 / an ~ *shop* 辅助车间 / ~ *troops*【军】辅助部队;援军 / ~ *valence*【化】副(原子)价 / an ~ *verb*【语】助动词 **II** *n.* ①辅助者,补助者 ②【语】助动词 ③[复]【军】(来自外国的)援军;辅助部队 ④附属人员(或团体)

avail [əˈveil] **I** ❶ *vi.* 有利,有益,有助: His eloquence did not ~ against the facts. 他的雄辩在事实面前不起什么作用。 ❷ *vt.* 有利于,有益于,有助于: I am afraid my help didn't ~ you much. 恐怕我的帮助对你用处不大。 **II** *n.* 效用,帮助;利益 ‖~ *of* [美] =~ oneself of / ~ *oneself of* 利用: We ~ *ourselves of* this opportunity to express our heartfelt gratitude to you. 我们就此机会向你们表示衷心的感谢。 / to little ~ 没有什么用处 / to no ~ 完全无用 / without ~ 无益,无效,徒劳地

available [əˈveiləbl] *a.* ①可用的,合用的;可得到的,可达到的: employ all ~ means 用尽所有办法,千方百计 / ~ power【物】可用功率 / ~ fertilizer【农】有效肥料 / Chinese commodities ~ *for* export 供出口的中国商品 / If I am not ~ when you phone, ask for my brother. 你打电话来时如果我不在,可叫我兄弟代接。 ②通用的,有效的: The ticket is ~ on (the) day of issue only. 此票仅(发售)当天有效。 ③(因政治背景等原因)有当选希望的;愿接受提名(或参加选举)的 ‖**availability** [əˌveiləˈbiliti] *n.* ①可用性;有效性;效力 ②可得性;可得到的东西(或人员) / ~**ness** *n.* / **availably** *ad.*

avalanche [ˈævəlɑːnʃ] **I** *n.* ①(冰雪、土块等的)崩落: with the momentum (或 force) of an ~ 以排山倒海之势 ②(雪崩似的)压下: an ~ of letters 似雪片般飞来的大批信件 / an ~ of questions 连珠炮似的大量问题 ③【物】离子雪崩: electron ~ 电子雪崩 **II** ❶ *vi.* 雪崩;雪崩似地倒下;以排山倒海之势涌现 ❷ *vt.* 大量投入(市场等),大量涌进

avarice [ˈævəris] *n.* 贪婪

avenge [əˈvendʒ] *vt.* 替…报仇;为…雪耻: be ~d 得以雪耻 ‖~**r** *n.* 报仇者

avenue [ˈævinjuː] *n.* ① 林荫道;道路 ②[英](通往乡村住宅、两旁栽树的)小路 ③ [美](城市中的)大街 ④[喻]途径,手段: an ~ to prosperity 通向繁荣的途径 / an ~ of research 研究的途径

aver [əˈvəː] (averred; averring [əˈvəːriŋ]) *vt.* ①断言,主张 (that) ②【律】证明,确证 ‖~**ment** *n.*

average [ˈævəridʒ] **I** *n.* ①平均;平均数: The ~ of 4, 5 and 9 is 6. 四、五、九的平均数是六。 / take (或 strike) an ~ 算出平均数 ②一般水平,平均标准: above (below) the ~ 在一般水平以上(以下) / be well up to the ~ 完全达到一般水平 / His opinion is the ~. 他持一般人的意见。 ③【商】海损 **II** *a.* ①平均的: the ~ age 平均年龄 / the ~ rate of increase (或 growth) 平均增长率 ②通常的,正常的,平常的: the ~ man 普通人 / an article of ~ quality 普通产品,大路货

③【商】按海损估价的 **III** ❶ *vi.* (为得到更有利的平均价格而)买进; 卖出 ❷ *vt.* ①从…得出平均数, 均分: If you ~ 9 and 5, you get 7. 把九加五的和均分, 得七。② 平均为: The rainfall ~s 800 mm. a year. 每年雨量平均为八百毫米。③使趋向平衡 ❹ 按比例分配 ‖~ *out* ①达到平均数: The gain ~d out to 20 percent. 利润平均为百分之二十。② 最终得到平衡 / *on an* (或 *the*) ~ 作为平均数, 按平均数计算: On an (或 the) ~, there are 1,000 visitors a day. 平均每天有一千名参观者(或来访者)。‖~**ly** *ad.*

averse [ə'və:s] *a.* ①反对的, 不乐意的, 不情愿的: He is ~ *to* (或 *from*) flattery. 他不喜欢听恭维话。/ be ~ *to* coming (或 come) 不愿意来, 不想来 ②【植】(叶子等)与茎方向相反的 ‖~**ly** *ad.* / ~**ness** *n.*

aversion [ə'və:ʃən] *n.* ①厌恶, 反感: have (或 take) an ~ *to* (或 *from, for*) 对…抱反感 ②讨厌的人(或东西): one's pet ~ 某人最不喜欢的东西

avert [ə'və:t] *vt.* ①转移(目光、思想等)(*from*) ②挡开(灾难等); 防止(危险等): Preparedness ~s peril. 有备无患。‖~**ible** *a.* 可避免的; 可防止的

aviary ['eivjəri] *n.* 鸟舍; 鸟类饲养场 ‖**aviarist** *n.* 鸟类饲养家

aviation [,eivi'eiʃən] *n.* ①航空; 航空学, 飞行术: civil ~ 民航 / an ~ corps 飞行队 / an ~ ground 飞机场 ②飞机制造业 ③[总称]军用飞机: artillery reconnaissance ~ 炮兵侦察机

aviator ['eivieitə] *n.* 飞行员, 飞机驾驶员

avid ['ævid] *a.* ①渴望的; 贪婪的 (*for, of*) ②做起(某事)来劲头足的: an ~ reader 读起书来废寝忘食的人 ‖~**ly** *ad.*

avidity [ə'viditi] *n.* ①热望; 热情; 贪婪 ②【化】亲合力, 活动性

avocation [,ævou'keiʃən] *n.* ①(个人)副业; 业余爱好 ②[罕]正业, 本职

avoid [ə'vɔid] *vt.* ①避免; 回避, 躲开: learn from past mistakes and ~ future ones 惩前毖后 / ~ sb.'s company 避免和某人来往 / I cannot ~ meeting him. 我无法避而不见他。(或: 我免不了要碰见他。) ②【律】使无效; 撤销; 废止 ‖~**able** *a.* ①可避免的; 可回避的 ②可作为无效的

avoidance [ə'vɔidəns] *n.* ①回避; 躲避 ②【律】无效; 废止 ③(职位等的)空缺

avoirdupois [,ævədə'pɔiz] *n.* ①常衡(以 16 盎司为 1 磅): an ~ pound 常衡磅 / the ~ weight 常衡制 ②[美口]肥胖; 体重

avow [ə'vau] *vt.* 公开宣称, 声明; 坦率承认: ~ one's fault (guilt) 认错(罪) / ~ oneself (to be) a writer 自称为作家 ‖~**able** *a.* 可明言的; 可承认的 / ~**al** [ə'vau-əl] *n.* 公开宣布, 声明; 供认

await [ə'weit] *vt.* ①等候, 期待: I ~ your answer. 我等你的答复。②(事件等)等待着: A warm welcome ~s you. 热烈的欢迎等待着你。

awake [ə'weik] **I** (过去式 awoke [ə'wouk], 过去分词 awoke 或 awaked) ❶ *vt.* ①唤醒, 使醒: The sound of the doorbell *awoke* the baby. 门铃声把婴孩吵醒了。②唤起; 使觉悟; 使奋发 ❷ *vi.* ①醒: I ~ at six every morning. 我每天早上六点醒。/ ~ to find ... 醒来发觉… ②觉醒, 觉悟; 奋起 ③意识, 醒悟 (*to*): ~ *to* the fact that ... 认识到…的事实 / ~ *to* the danger 认识到危险 **II** *a.* [用作表语] ①醒着的: Is he ~ or asleep? 他醒着还是睡着? / I lay ~ all night. 我一夜未曾睡眠。②警觉的; 意识到的: be ~ *to* ... 意识到…, 意识到…

awaken [ə'weikən] ❶ *vt.* 使觉醒, 唤醒 ❷ *vi.* 醒; 醒悟: ~ *to* the importance of ... 认识到…的重要性 ‖~**ing** *n.* 觉醒, 醒悟 *a.* 觉醒中的; 唤醒的; 惊醒的

award [ə'wɔ:d] **I** *vt.* 授予, 给与; 判给: ~ a prize to sb. 授奖与某人 / He was ~ed his damages by the court. 法院判给他损失赔偿费。**II** *n.* ①判定, 判决; 裁决书 ②奖; 奖品: the first (second) ~ 一(二)等奖 ‖~**ee** [ə,wɔ:'di:] *n.* 受奖者

aware [ə'wɛə] *a.* [用作表语]意识到的, 知道的, 认识的: be ~ *of* 知道, 意识到 / become ~ *of* 发觉, 开始意识到 ‖~**ness** *n.*

awash [ə'wɔʃ] *a.* [常用表语] ①被浪潮冲打的: The ship's deck was ~. 船上的甲板被浪潮冲打。②被水覆盖的: rocks ~ at high tide 涨潮时被淹没的岩石

away [ə'wei] **I** *ad.* ①离, 远离: He is ~ in the countryside. 他下乡去了。/ The place is two li ~ from here. 那个地方离这儿有两里路。/ The sports are two weeks ~. 离运动会还有两星期。/ ~ back 很久以前 ②…去, …掉: The snow melted ~. 雪融化了。/ wash the dirt ~ 洗掉污垢 / explain ~ the matter in a few words 几句话就把那事解释过去了 / He was phoned for and ~ he went. 有电话叫他去, 他就走了。③[用于无动词感叹句的句首]走开: *Away with you!* [口]滚开! 去你的吧! ④不断…下去: Don't just work ~. You must sum up experience from time to time. 不要一味埋头干下去, 你们必须随时总结经验。⑤立刻: right ~ 立刻, 马上 **II** *a.* 在外的: home and ~ games 在本单位中与在外单位中进行的比赛 ‖**do** ~ **with** 见 **do**¹ / **make** ~ **with** 见 **make**

awe [ɔ:] **I** *n.* 畏惧; 敬畏; 怕: be struck with ~ 肃然敬畏 / stand (或 be) in ~ of 敬畏; 怕 / hold (或 keep) sb. in ~ 使某人敬畏 **II** *vt.* 威吓; 使敬畏: No difficulty could ~ us. 任何困难都吓不倒我们。‖~**less** *a.* 无畏惧的, 大胆的 / ~**some** [mes'ɔ:me] *a.* ①使人敬畏的; 可畏的 ②感到畏惧(或敬畏)的 ‖'~-**in,spiring** *a.* 使人畏惧的; 使人敬畏的 / '~-,**stricken**, '~-**struck** *a.* 敬畏的; 畏惧的

awful ['ɔ:ful] *a.* ①令人畏惧的, 可怕的; 令人敬畏的 ②威严的; 庄重的; 令人崇敬的 ③['ɔ:fl] [口]

极度的,非常的; 极坏的: What ~ weather! 天气糟透了! ‖~ly ad. ①令人畏惧地; 令人敬畏地 ②['ɔːfli] [口]非常,很,了不得: Thanks ~ly for your help. 十分感谢你的帮助。/ an ~ly hard rain 极大的雨 / ~ness n. 令人畏惧; 威严

awkward ['ɔːkwəd] a. ①笨拙的; 不熟练的: The child is still ~ with his chopsticks. 那孩子用筷子还不太熟练。②使用不便的: an ~ tool 使用不便的工具 ③尴尬的: in an ~ situation 处境尴尬 ④难应付的,难处理的; 棘手的: an ~ corner to turn 难拐弯的转角 / an ~ question 棘手的问题 ‖an ~ customer [口]难对付的家伙 / the ~ age 未成熟的青春期 ‖~ly ad. / ~ness n.

awl [ɔːl] n. 钻子; 鞋钻

awning ['ɔːniŋ] n. ①遮篷 ②【船】天篷

awoke [ə'wouk] awake 的过去式和过去分词

awry [ə'rai] a. [常作表语] & ad. ①曲; 歪; 斜: look ~ 斜视 ②错: go (或 run, tread) ~ 出差错; 失败

ax(e) [æks] I ([复] axes ['æksiz]) n. ①斧 ②(经费、人员等的)削减 II vt. ①用斧砍 ②大刀阔斧地削减(经费、人员等) ‖get the ~ [俚]被解雇,被开除 / give sb. the ~ 解雇某人; 开除某人 / hang up one's ~ 停止无用的计划; 洗手不干; 退休 / have an ~ to grind 另有企图; 有个人打算 / lay the ~ to the root of 着手根除,着手消灭 / put the ~ in the helve 解决难题,解谜 / send the ~ after the helve 坚持做没有指望的事 / set the ~ to 着手砍倒; 着手破坏 ‖'ax,hammer n. 斧槌

axiom ['æksiəm] n. ①公理; 自明之理 ②原理,原则,规律 ③格言

axiomatic(al) [ˌæksiə'mætik(əb)] a. ①公理的; 自明的 ②格言的; 充满格言的 ‖**axiomatically** ad.

axis ['æksis] ([复] axes ['æksiːz]) n. ①轴; 轴线: the visual ~ 视轴 / the earth's ~ 地轴 / major (minor) ~ 【数】(椭圆的)长(短)轴 / guidance ~ 【空】瞄准轴; 导引轴,导向轴 ②中心线; 中枢: the canal ~ 运河中心线 / an ~ of communication 通信干线; 交通轴线 ③轴心(国家或集团之间的联盟): the Axis 轴心国(指第二次世界大战中德、意、日三国联盟) ④【解】枢椎,第二颈椎 ⑤【植】茎轴 ⑥【化】晶轴

axle ['æksl] n. (轮)轴; 车轴; 轴干: an ~ journal 轴颈 / an ~ bearing 轴承 / an ~ seat 轴座 / an ~ sleeve 轴套 / wheel and ~ 差动滑车 ‖~ box 轴箱 / ~ pin 轴销,销 / '~tree n. 轴干

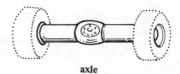

axle

ay(e)[1] [ai] I ad. & int. 是; 当然 II n. 赞成票; 投赞成票者: The ~s have it. 赞成的占多数。

ay(e)[2] [ei] ad. [古]常常; 永远 ‖for ~ 永远

azure ['æʒə] I a. ①天蓝色的,蔚蓝的 ②[喻]无云的, 晴空的 II n. ①天蓝色, 蔚蓝色, 天青色 ②[诗]苍天,碧空 III vt. 使成天蓝色

B

babble ['bæbl] I ❶ vi. ①(婴孩或婴孩般)咿哑学语 ②喋喋不休,唠叨 ③吐露秘密 ④(流水)潺潺作声 ❷ vt. ①唠唠叨叨地讲 ②吐露(秘密等) (out) II n. ①婴孩咿哑学语声 ②胡言乱语 ③潺潺声 ‖~r n. ①说话不清楚的人 ②胡说乱道的人 ③吐露秘密的人

babe [beib] n. ①婴儿 ②缺乏经验、容易上当的人 ③[美俚]姑娘 ‖~s and sucklings 天真的孩子们; 天真而单纯的人们; 毫无经验的人们

Babel ['beibəl] n. ①(基督教《圣经》中)没有建成的通天塔 ②[b-]空想的计划 ③[a b-]喧哗,混乱声

baby ['beibi] I n. ①婴儿; 幼畜 ②孩子气的人; 胆怯的人 ③[常作定语]小型物: a ~ grand (piano) 小型钢琴 / a ~ car 小型汽车 ④[美俚]姑娘 ⑤一个家庭(或团体)中年龄最小的人 II vt. 把…当作婴孩对待,娇养 ‖hold (或 carry) the ~ [口]做不愿做的事情,干苦差使 ‖~hood n. 婴孩期 / ~ish a. 孩子气的 / ~ blue 淡蓝色 / ~ carriage 童车 / ~ carrier 轻航空母舰 / ~ kisser [美俚]为竞选而到处笼络人心的政客 / '~-sit vi. (代人临时)照看婴孩 / '~-sitter n. (代人临时)照看婴孩者

bachelor ['bætʃələ] n. ①未婚男子,单身汉 ②学士: a Bachelor of Arts (Science) 文(理)学士 ③未交配的雄兽(尤指海狗) ④[史]青年骑士; 最低一级的爵士 ‖~dom, ~hood n. (男子)独身,独身身分 / ~ism ['bætʃələrizəm] n. (男子)独身,独身主义 / ~ship n. ①(男子)独身 ②学士学位 ‖~ girl 经济上独立的未婚女子 / ~'s button 【植】矢车菊 ②小的果味饼干 / ~'s hall 单身男子的住处: keep ~'s hall (男子)过独身生活

bacillus [bə'siləs] ([复] bacilli [bə'silai]) n. 【微】

芽孢杆菌, 杆菌 ‖**Bacillus Calmette-Guérin** [kæl'metgei'rẽ:n]【药】卡介苗 / ~ **carrier** 杆菌载体

back [bæk] **I** *n.* ①背, 背部; 背脊: lie (fall) on one's ~ 朝天躺着(摔倒) / give sb. a ~ (或 make a ~ for sb.) 弯着腰让某人从自己背上跳过(或攀登) / the ~ of a horse (chair) 马(椅)背 / the ~ of a hill 山脊 / the ~ of a ship 船的龙骨
②背面, (纺织品等的)反面: the ~ of the hand 手背 / the ~ of a piece of cloth 一块布的反面
③后面, 后部: a child-care centre *at* the ~ of the factory 工厂后面的托儿站 / a room *in* the ~ of the house 房屋的后间
④(足球等的)卫(可指球员或其位置): a full (half) ~ 后(前)卫球员
II *a.* [无比较级; 最高级用 backmost] ①[表示位置]后面的; 背后的: the ~ wheels of a truck 卡车后轮 / ~ teeth 臼齿
②离开中心区的, 偏僻的: a ~ street 后街 / the ~ slums 贫民窟
③倒的, 反向的; 往回去的: a ~ current 倒流 / ~ cargo (船只等载运的)归程货物 / a ~ answer 顶撞的回话
④【语】舌后的; 软颚的; 口腔后部的: a ~ vowel (舌)后元音
⑤过期的; 拖欠的: a ~ issue 过期期刊 / a ~ file 过期报刊杂志(或过期文件)的合订本 / ~ pay 欠薪
III *ad.* ①在后; 向后; 后仰着: The house stands way ~ from the highway. 那所房屋远离公路。 / Stand ~! 往后站!
②回; 回原处(或原状); 回复过来: Put the tools ~ on the shelf. 把工具放回到架子上。 / hold (或 keep) ~ one's tears 忍住眼泪 / I'll be ~ in a minute. 我一会儿就回来。 / nurse sb. ~ to health 护理某人使其恢复健康
③作为回答; 作为报复: answer ~ 回嘴 / hit ~ 反击
④以前: three years ~ 三年前
IV ❶ *vt.* ①使后退; 倒(车): ~ a tractor *into* (*out of*) the shed 把拖拉机倒开进(出)停车棚
②[美]位于…的背后, 背靠着
③支持(论点、行动、企业等): ~ sb. *up* 撑某人腰
④给…装上背衬, 裱(画): ~ sth. (*up*) with stainless steel 用不锈钢作某物的背衬
⑤背书(支票等)(指在票据背面签字担保)
⑥下赌注在…上
❷ *vi.* ①倒退; (风)逆转: He ~ed *up* three steps. 他往后退了三步。 / ~ *off* a little in preparation for the jump 起跳前稍稍后退一点
②[美]背靠; 坐落
‖*at* sb.'s ~ 支持某人, 给某人撑腰 / ~ *and belly* 背与腹, [喻]衣食 / ~ *and edge* 完全地; 全力地 / ~ *and fill* ①使风帆时张时缩地前进以避开障碍 ②忽而这样忽而那样, 拿不定主意 /

~ *and forth* 来来往往地, (前后)来回 / ~ *away* 逐渐后退 / ~ *down* 放弃要求, 让步; 声明取消前言 / ~ *of* [美] ①在…的后面: a stream ~ *of* the house 屋后的溪流 / the motives ~ *of* the action 行动背后的动机 ②在…以前: five years ~ *of* this 五年前以上 / ~ *out* (*of*) 收回(诺言、承担的责任等); 停止不干(某事): He agreed to come, but ~ed out. 他说好来的, 可是变卦了。 / ~ *out of* the treaty obligations 背弃条约义务 / ~ *to* ~ ①背靠背 ②一前一后 / ~ *up* ①支持 ②(使)倒退 ③(使)阻塞, (使)积滞 / *behind* sb.'s ~ 在某人背后, 背着某人 / *be on one*'s ~ ①仰卧 ②[口]生着病 / *be on* sb.'s ~ [美俚]嘲笑(或指责)某人; 打扰(或惹恼)某人 / *break* sb.'s ~ (工作等)把某人压得喘不过气来 / *break the* ~ *of* sth. 完成某事中最困难(或最大量)的工作 / *cast* sth. *behind one*'s ~ 把某事置之脑后 / *get off* sb.'s ~ [美俚]不再嘲笑(或打扰)某人 / *get* (或 *have*) one's *own* ~ 报仇, 报复 / *get* (或 *put, set*) sb.'s ~ *up* 使某人发怒 / *go* ~ *on* (或 *upon, from*) ①丢弃(朋友等) ②食(言), 违(约) / *in* ~ *of* [美] = ~ of / *on the* ~ 在…以外(常用以表示接二连三的灾祸) / *pat* (或 *slap*) sb. *on the* ~ 对某人表示赞许(或鼓励等) / *put one*'s ~ *into* sth. 发奋做某事, 埋头干某事 / *rip up the* ~ 背后攻击, 背后说人坏话 / *see the* ~ *of* sb. 摆脱某人: I should be glad to *see the* ~ *of* him. 我真巴不得他快点走开。 / *talk through the* ~ *of one*'s *neck* 吹牛, 讲蠢话 / *turn one*'s ~ *on* (或 *upon*) ①对过脸去不理(以表示轻视、怠怒等) ②背弃, 抛弃; 违背 / *with one*'s ~ *to the wall* 处于绝境, 作困兽斗
‖~**less** *a.* 无(靠)背的 / ~**most** *a.* back 的最高级

‖~**ache** *n.* 背痛, 腰痛 / ~**bencher** *n.* 后座议员(指英国下院的普通议员) / ~ **benches** 后座议员席(英国下院中普通议员坐的席位) / '~**bite** *vt. & vi.* 背后说(人)坏话; 背后说坏话 / '~**biter** *n.* 背后中伤别人的人 / '~**blocks** [复] *n.* [澳]边远地区, 人烟稀少之地(尤指远离海岸、河道等) / '~**board** *n.* 后部挡板; (篮球架上的)篮板 / '~**breaking** *a.* 使人劳累至极的 / '~**chat** *n.* ①闲扯, 聊天 ②机智的对答, 反唇相讥 / ~**cloth** [英] = ~drop / '~**country** *n.* [美]偏僻的农村地区; 边远地区 / '~**cross** *vt. & vi.* 【生】(使)回交, (使)逆代杂交 *n.* 回交, 逆代杂交; 逆代杂交的产物 / '~**date** *vt.* 回溯: The wage increases are to be ~*dated* to January. 工资提高从一月份算起。 / ~ **door** ①后门 ②秘密途径, 非法手段 / '~**door** *a.* 秘密(进行)的; 非法(的)途径的 / '~**down** *n.* 原先态度(或主张等)的改变 / '~**drop** *n.* (舞台后部的)彩画幕布; 背景 / ~ **end** ①后端 ②[英]晚秋 / '~**fill** *vt.* 把(挖出的洞穴等)重新填没 *n.* 用来重新填没洞穴(或壕沟等)的东西 / '~'**fire** *n.* ①迎火(把草原

或森林中的一块地带先纵火烧光，以阻止野火或林火蔓延） ②(内燃机等的)逆火，回火 *vi.* ①回火；逆火；迎火 ②[喻]发生意外，产生事与愿违的恶果: These measures ~*fired*. 这些措施产生了适得其反的结果。 / '~-**for**'**mation** *n.* 【语】逆序造词，倒back构词(指脱落一词的后缀以构成新词的方法；如从 television 逆构新词 televise)；由逆序造词法造成的词 / '~**hand** *n.* ①左向书法，向左倾斜的手写体 ②反手一击；反手击球 (法) *vt.* 用反手击 *a. & ad.* = ~handed / '~'**handed** *a.* ①反手的；反向的: a ~*handed* stroke 反手击球 ②间接的，转弯抹角的；迟疑不决的: a ~-*handed* compliment 讽刺挖苦的恭维话 *ad.* 反手地 / '~,**hander** *n.* 反手一击；间接攻击 / '~**lash** *n.* ①后冲；后座 ②(在政治和社会发展上)强烈和不利的反应 ③【机】轮齿隙，齿隙游移 *vi.* 发生后冲 / '~,**lining** *n.* ①【印】(加固书脊的)背衬料 ②【建】背衬 / '~**list** *n.* 出版商多年来一直在重版的书目 *vt.* 把(书)列入多年重版书目 / '~**log** *n.* ①(营火等用的)巨木 ②[英]积压的工作；积压而未交付的订货 ③[美]紧急时可依靠的东西 ④储备 *vt. & vi.* (把…)积压起来 / ~**matter** 书本正文后面的附加资料(包括附录、索引、参考书目等) / '~-'**page** *a.* 登在报纸最后几页上的，不太有新闻价值的 / '~,**pedal** *vi.* 使自行车踏脚板倒转 ② 变卦: *pedal on an earlier promise* 背弃早先的诺言 ③(拳击中)猛地后退 / '~**rest** *n.* 靠背 / ~ **room** 里屋；密室(尤指政客等密谋策划的场所) / '~**room** *a.* 在密室中(工作)的: a ~*room* boy [英俚]从事秘密研究工作的人；智囊人物 / '~'**seat** *n.* (大厅、车辆等的)后座；[口]等级低(或次要)的位置: a ~*seat* driver 坐在汽车后座对驾驶员指手划脚的人；干涉与自己职责无关的事情的人 / take a ~*seat* 处于次要地位；做出自卑的样子，知趣靠边 / '~**set** *n.* ①倒流 ②倒退；挫折; (疾病等)的复发；涡流 / '~'**side** *vi.* 后退; [常用复]屁股: *get off one's* ~*sides and translate words into action* (停止空谈)起而行动 / '~**sight** *n.* ①[测]后视 ②[军]反视，(靠近枪托等的)瞄准孔(或口)，表尺缺口 / ~ **slang** 倒读隐语(如用 nam 代man) / '~**slap** *vt. & vi.* 拍(某人)的背以示亲密；(对某人)表示特别友好 / '~**slide** *vi. & n.* 退步，倒退；没落 / '~**space** *vi.* 使打字机逆行一位 / '~'**stage** *ad.* 在(或往)后台; 在(或往)幕后；私下，秘密地: retire ~*stage* 退居幕后 *a.* ①后台的；关于戏剧界人物私生活的 ②幕后的，秘而不宣的: ~*stage* deals 幕后(秘密)交易 / '~'**stair(s)** *a.* 用后楼梯的，肮脏的 / '~**stay** *n.* ①[海]后牵索 ②后撑条 / '~**stitch** *n.* (缝纫中的)扣针(脚) *vt. & vi.* 用扣针脚倒缝 / '~**stop** *n.* ①(靶场中用沙土、沙包等筑成的)后障 ②(球场等的)后部挡board(如铁丝网、篱笆等)；(棒球)击球手后面的接球手 ③【机】(防齿轮倒转的)棘爪 *vt.* ①挡住 ②支持，为…撑腰 / '~**stroke** *n. & vi.* ①反手击球 ②仰泳 *vt.* 用反手击 / '~**sword** *n.* ①单刃刀 ②(击剑中用

的)木剑 / ~ **talk** 回嘴(尤指下属或下辈的顶撞) / '~**track** *vi.* 走回头路；后退；放弃(或改变)过去的立场(或态度、意见等) / '~**up** *a.* ①候补的，替代的 ②支持性的 *n.* ①支持 ②阻塞，积滞 / '~**wash** *n.* (水流、气流等的)回流，倒流；[喻]反响，余波 / '~,**water** *n.* ①回水，回流 ②死水; [喻]死气沉沉的状态(或地方) / '~**woodsman** ['bækwudz-mən] *n.* ①林区(或边远地区)的人 ②[英]不(或很少)参加上议院活动的贵族 / ~**woodsy** ['bæk,wudzi] *a.* [美]乡土气的，粗野的 / '~-'**yard** 后院: a "~*yard*" blast furnace 土高炉

backbone ['bækboun] *n.* ①脊骨，脊柱 ②主要山脉 ③支柱，主要成分，骨干: the ~ of agriculture 主要农产品 / They are the ~ of the football team. 他们是这个足球队的骨干。④骨气，勇气；坚定的品质 ⑤书脊 ‖*to the* ~ 彻底地

background ['bækgraund] *n.* ①背景；后景；经历: the ~ of a scene 舞台的后景 / the historical (social) ~ of the event 这件事的历史(社会)背景 / Tell me your ~. 把你的经历和情况告诉我。②背景情况: a ~ briefing (或 session) 背景情况介绍会 ③隐蔽的地位，幕后: stay in the ~ 处于隐蔽地位 ④(纺织品等的)底(子): cloth with red spots on a white ~ 白底红点的布 ⑤(广播、电影等的)衬托音乐，配乐，伴音 ⑥干扰收听电子讯号的外来杂音 ‖*recede into the* ~ ①(人)失势 ②(问题等)不再突出，不再重要

backing ['bækiŋ] *n.* ①支持，后援，后盾: a firm ~ for a just struggle 对正义斗争的坚决支持 / (一群)支持者: have a large ~ 有一大批支持者 ③衬垫物 ④【建】背衬，里壁；回填土 ⑤倒退 ⑥(行政官或法官对)令状的签署认可

backward[1] ['bækwəd], **backwards** ['bækwədz] *ad.* ①向后: lean ~ 往后靠 ②倒，逆: count from ten to one 从十倒数到一 / walk ~ 后退着走 / go ~ 倒退，退步 ③回向原处: flow (roll) ~ 流(滚)回 ‖*backward(s) and forward(s)* 来回地，忽前忽后 / *spell* ~ 倒拼；误解，曲解

backward[2] ['bækwəd] *a.* ①向后的 ②倒的，相反的: a ~ movement of the truck 卡车的倒驶 / a ~ process 相反的程序 ③落后的，(进展)缓慢的: The rainy season is ~ this year. 今年雨季来得晚。④迟疑的，畏缩的: He is never ~ in giving his views. 他从来不怕发表自己的意见。⑤智力差的 ‖*~ly ad.* / ~**ness** *n.*

bacon ['beikən] *n.* 咸猪肉，熏猪肉(背部或肋部的肉) ‖*bring home the* ~ [俚]①成功 ②谋生 / *save sb.'s (one's)* ~ [口]使某人(自己)免遭死亡(或伤害、失败等)

bacteria [bæk'tiəriə] [复] *n.* [bacterium 的复数] 细菌: iron ~ 铁细菌 / pathogenic ~ 病原细菌 / root nodule ~ 根瘤细菌 ‖*~l a.* 细菌的: ~*l* fertilizer 细菌肥料 / the ~*l* degumming method 微生物脱胶法 ‖**bac'teria-'free** *a.* 无菌的

bad [bæd] **I** (worse [wə:s], worst [wə:st]) *a.* ①坏的;恶的,不道德的: In given conditions, a ~ thing can be turned into a good one. 在一定条件下,坏事可以变为好事。/ used in a ~ sense 用作贬义的 ②(质量等)低劣的;(能力等)拙劣的: a ~ cyclist 不大会骑自行车的人 / be ~ at translation 不善于翻译 ③有害的;不利的: ~ for the stomach 伤胃 / have a ~ time 日子不好过 ④严重的,厉害的: a ~ blunder 大错 / a ~ cold 重伤风 / a ~ storm 猛烈的暴风雨 ⑤病的,痛的,不舒服的: a ~ finger 痛的(或受伤的)手指 / He isn't worse today, is he? 今天他的病没有恶化吧? ⑥(食物等)腐败的;(气味等)臭的: a ~ egg (变质的)臭蛋; [喻]坏蛋 / The meat has gone ~. 肉坏掉了。⑦错误的;不适当的: ~ grammar 不通的语法 ⁄ a ~ example 不恰当的例子; 坏样 / That's not a ~ idea. 那个主意倒不错。⑧使人不愉快的,(伙伴等)讨厌的; [美口]懊恼的: feel ~ about sth. 因为某事而感到不愉快 ⑨[律]不成立的;空名的 **II** *n.* 坏;恶;不幸 **III** *ad.* =badly ‖*a* ~ *lot* [俚](一个或一帮)坏家伙 / ~ *blood* 恨,恶感 / ~ *debts* 坏帐,倒帐 / ~ *language* 骂人的话 / *be in a* ~ *way* 病情严重;处于困境 / *be taken* ~ 起病 / *feel* ~ 感到不愉快;有病 / *go from* ~ *to worse*(病情、处境、行为等)越来越坏,每况愈下 / *go to the* ~ [口]①变坏,堕落 ②得病 ③弄得毫无办法 / *in* ~ [美口]①倒霉 ②失宠(*with*): *in* ~ *with* sb. 失宠于某人 / *not* ~ (或 *not so* ~, *not half* ~) [口]不坏,不错 / *take the* ~ *with the good* 幸与不幸都得忍受 / *the* ~ [总称]坏人,恶人 / *too* ~ [美口]可惜,糟糕,不幸: *Too* ~ (或 It's *too* ~) I missed that film. 真可惜,我错过了那部电影。/ *to the* ~ 亏损: John was sixty dollars *to the* ~. 约翰亏损了六十元。/ *with* (*a*) ~ *grace* 不情愿地,勉强地 ‖~-ness *n.* 坏,恶劣;严重 ‖'~-land *n.* [美][常用复]荒原,崎岖地 / '~-man *n.* 偷牲口贼;不法之徒;(旧时美国西部)受人雇用的刺客

badge [bædʒ] *n.* ①徽章,像章 ②标志;象征

badger¹ ['bædʒə] *n.* ①獾 ②獾皮,獾毛 ③[美][B-]威斯康星州人 ‖~ **game** [美俚]美人计 / '~-legged *a.* 两腿长短不一的

badger

badger² ['bædʒə] *vt.* 纠缠,使困恼: ~ sb. *with* questions 对某人问个不休 / ~ sb. *for* sth. 纠缠某人要求某事物 / ~ sb. *to do* (或 *into doing*) sth. 纠缠某人做某事

badly ['bædli] (worse [wə:s], worst [wə:st]) *ad.* ①坏,恶劣地 ②有害地 ③有缺点地,拙劣地 ④严重地; [口]非常: The car is ~ in need of repair. 汽车急需修理。/ She went on working though her arm ached ~. 虽然她的手臂痛得厉害,她仍坚持工作。/ be ~ beaten 被打得焦头烂额 ‖~ *off* ①穷的 ②(感到)缺少的: The school was then ~ *off* for teachers. 当时学校缺少教师。

badminton ['bædmintən] *n.* ①羽毛球 ②一种夏季饮料(甜味葡萄酒汽水)

baffle ['bæfl] **I** ❶ *vt.* ①使挫折,阻碍: ~ the enemy 挫败敌人 / ~ sb.'s plans 挫败某人的计划 / ~ description 难以形容 / ~ definition 难下定义 ②使困惑 ③用隔音板隔(音) ❷ *vi.* 徒作挣扎 **II** *n.* ①迷惑: ~ painting 【军】涂保护色;迷彩 ②挡板;折流板;缓冲板;栅极;反射板;阻遏器;遮护物;障板 ‖**baffling** *a.* 令人迷惑的,莫名其妙的;起阻碍作用的: a *baffling* problem 令人迷惑的问题 ‖'~-board *n.* (扬声器的)反射板;隔音板 / '~-gab *n.* 冗长而难解的谈话(或文章)

bag [bæg] **I** *n.* ①袋,包;钱包;手提皮包(尤指妇女用的): a tool ~ 工具袋 / a travelling ~ 旅行袋 / a field ~ 军用挂包 / a vanity ~ 妇女随身携带、盛放化妆品的小手提包 ②[复]财富 ③猎囊;(猎囊内的)全部猎物;(空战中)被击落的敌机总数: make a good ~ 猎获大批猎物 / count the ~ 清查战果 ④袋状物;(棒球的)垒囊;松垂的眼泡皮;衣服的鼓胀处;牛的乳房 ⑤[复][英口]裤子 ⑥[美俚]个人的兴趣范围;个人的环境 ⑦[美俚]无吸引力的女子,丑姑娘;妓女 ⑧[俚]啤酒壶 **II** (bagged; bagging) ❶ *vt.* ①把…装进袋里; [口]把…占为己有,获得;偷窃 ②捕杀(鸟、兽等);击落(敌机等);一网打尽… ③使成袋状,使鼓胀 ④[俚]解雇 ⑤[美俚]逃(学) ❷ *vi.* ①(衣、裤等象布袋那样地)膨大(或垂挂) ②怀孕 ‖*a* ~ *of bones* 骨瘦如柴的人(或动物) / *a* ~ *of wind* 夸夸其谈的人 / *a green* (或 *blue*) ~ (英国)律师的公事包 / ~ *and baggage* [口]①连同全部财物 ②完全地,彻底地 / ~*s of* [俚]许多 / *empty the* ~ [口]和盘托出,尽所欲言 / *give sb. the* ~ [口]解雇某人 / *have* (或 *get, tie*) *a* ~ *on* [美俚]狂饮作乐 / *have sth. in the bottom of the* ~ 留下某物作为最后手段 / *hold the* ~ ①两手空空;在分配物中只得到最差的一份 ②独自承担本应与他人共同承担的全部责任 / *in the* ~ ①[口]十拿九稳的 ②[俚]喝醉了的 / *leave* (或 *give*) *sb. the* ~ *to hold* 危难中抛弃某人,自己拔脚溜走而叫某人背黑锅 / *let the cat out of the* ~ 见 cat / *put sb. in a* ~ 占某人上风 / *set one's* ~ *for* 对…有野心,设计

谋取… / *the (whole)* ~ *of tricks* 各种方法,种种策略 ‖**~ful** *n.* 满满一袋,一袋 ‖**~ fox** 用袋子带往猎场使狗追捕的狐狸 / **'~-play** *n.* [美俚]巴结,拍马屁;在上司面前显本事 / **'~wig** *n.* 丝袋假发(头部后的假发盛于一丝袋中,故名)

baggage ['bægidʒ] *n.* ①[美]行李(英国一般用luggage): a piece of ~ 一件行李 ②【军】辎重 ③精神包袱 ④多余的东西;过时货 ⑤坏女人;妓女 ⑥女子,姑娘 ‖**excess** ~ 超重行李;[美俚]不必要的东西(或人),累赘,负担 ‖ **~ car** 行李车厢;【军】辎重车 / **'~man** *n.* 行李收发员 / **'~master** *n.* (火车站,行李车等)行李负责人 / **~ office** 行李房

bah [bɑ(:)] *int.* 呸! [表示轻蔑]

bail¹ [beil] I *n.* 【律】保释金;保释人;保释: go ~ for sb. 为某人作保释人 / be out on ~ 在保释中 / accept (refuse) ~ 准许(不准许)保释 / hold sb. to ~ 拘留某人直至交保 / forfeit one's ~ 保释后不如期出庭 / save (或 surrender) one's ~ 保释后如期出庭 II *vt.* ①准许保释;为…作保释人: ~ sb. *out* 准许保释某人;把某人保释出 ②将(财物)委托于人 ③帮助…摆脱困境 ‖*give* (或 *take*) *leg* ~ [口]逃走 / *I'll go* ~ *that* …. [口]我肯定… / *skip* (或 *jump*) ~ 保释中逃跑 ‖**~able** *a.* 可保释的 / **~ee** [bei'li:] *n.* (财物的)受委托人 / **~ment** *n.* 保释 (财物的)委托 / **~or** *n.* (财物的)委托人 / **~ bond** 保释保证书 / **~sman** ['beilzmən] *n.* 保释人

bail² [beil] I *n.* 戽斗,桶(用来舀出船舱里的水) II ❶ *vt.* 舀(水);从(船)中戽水(out): ~ (out) the boat 戽出船舱里的水 / ~ water out of a boat 舀出船舱里的水 ❷ *vi.* 中途跳伞(out)(从飞机上)跳伞(out) ‖**~er** *n.* ①舀船舱水的人 ②戽斗

bail³ [beil] I *n.* ①[史]城堡的外层防卫桩;城堡中的院子 ②马厩里的栅栏;关隔性出口的装置 ③(板球)三柱门上的横木 II *vt.* ①[古]把…禁锢起来 ②(澳)拦截(up)

bail⁴ [beil] *n.* ①(篷帐的)半圆形的支撑箍 ②(壶、桶等的)半圆形拎环 ③(打字机上)把纸张顶压在圆筒上的夹紧箍

bairn [bɛən] *n.* [苏格兰]小孩(英格兰北部也用)

bait [beit] I *n.* ①饵 ②[喻]引诱物 ③中途休息(或吃东西) II ❶ *vt.* ①装饵于;引诱: ~ a hook 把饵装在钩上 ②(在中途)喂(马等) ③欺负,折磨(人) ❷ *vi.* 中途休息,吃食(在中途吃东西) ‖*fish or cut* ~ 要么全力以赴要么索性放弃 / *jump at the* ~ 轻易上当 / *rise to a* ~ (鱼)上钩;(人)入圈套,上当 / *swallow the* ~ 吞饵而上钩;入圈套

baize [beiz] *n.* 台面呢(粗纺,缩绒)

bake [beik] I ❶ *vt.* ①烤,烘,焙(面包等) ②烧硬,焙干(砖头等) ❷ *vi.* ①烘面包(或饼等) ②(面包等)在烘焙中;(砖头等)在焙干中 II *n.* ①烤,烘,焙 ②吃烤面包(或其他烘烤食物)的聚餐会 ‖**~house, '~shop** *n.* ①面包店 ②面包烘房

bakery ['beikəri] *n.* ①面包烘房 ②面包店

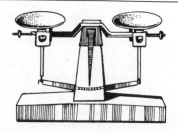

balance

balance ['bæləns] I *n.* ①天平,秤: weigh sth. in the ~ 用天平称某物 / analytical ~ 【化】分析天平 / dial ~ 【化】刻度盘天平 ②平衡,均势: be out of ~ 不平衡 ③收付平衡;收付差额,余额:a ~ of financial revenue and expenditure 财政收支的平衡 / a favourable (an unfavourable) ~ of trade 顺(逆)差,贸易出(入)超 / a ~ of (international) payments (一国、一地的)国际收支差额 / a ~ of power (国与国之间的)力量均势 ④结余;结欠;找头: a ~ at the bank 银行结余 / the ~ due 结欠金额 / You may keep the ~. 找头你留着吧。⑤(钟、表等的)平衡轮,摆轮 ⑥平衡块;平衡力 ⑦[B-]【天】天秤宫,天秤座 ⑧(艺术作品中)布局和比例的协调 ⑨(情绪的)稳定 ⑩[the ~][口]剩余部分: The ~ of the day was devoted to the discussion of the report. 那天剩下来的时间全用来讨论报告了。II ❶ *vt.* ①(用天平等)称 ②权衡,斟酌;对比,比较(计划等): ~ the two plans 把两个计划比较一下 ③使平衡;使(力量等)均等: Can you ~ yourself on skates? 你穿了溜冰鞋能保持身体平衡吗? / ~ a budget 平衡预算 / ~ one side *with* (或 *by, against*) another 使一方与另一方成均势 / a ~d diet (或 ration) 均衡饮食 / a ~d reaction 【化】平衡反应 / a ~d sentence 均衡句 / *balancing plane* 【空】安定翼面;平衡翼 ④结算,清(帐): ~ accounts 结帐;使收支平衡 ⑤抵销,跟…相抵;(在重量,数目或比重上)跟…相等: The expenses ~ the receipts. 支出跟收入相抵。❷ *vi.* ①平衡: The scales ~. 秤打平了。/ He can ~ on one foot. 他能独脚站着保持平衡。②(价值、重量、力量等)均等: ~ in power 势均力敌 ③收支平衡: The account ~s. 帐上收支平衡。④摇摆;踌躇 ‖*be* (或 *hang*) *in the* ~ 安危(或成败)未定 / *hold the* ~ 举足轻重 / *keep one's* ~ 保持(身体)平衡;保持镇静 / *lose one's* ~ 失去平衡;心慌意乱 / *on* ~ 总的说来: His suggestion has, *on* ~, proved useful. 总的说来,他的建议已被证明为有用的。/ *redress the* ~ 作公平的处理 / *strike a* ~ 结帐;作出被认为公平的处理(或调整): *strike a proper* ~ between work and leisure 劳逸结合 / *throw sb. off his* ~ 使某人摔倒;使某人心慌 / *tremble in the* ~ 到达紧要关头;处于极度危险中 ‖**~ beam** 【体】平衡木 /

~ bridge 开启桥 / **~ sheet** 【会计】资产负债表 / **~ wheel** (钟、表等的)平衡轮,摆轮

balcony ['bælkəni] ***n.*** ①阳台 ②(戏院的)楼厅 ‖**balconied** ***a.*** 有阳台的

bald [bɔ:ld] ***a.*** ①秃头的;(头)秃的 ②无毛的,无叶的,无树的;光秃的 ③(文章体裁等)单调的;不加虚饰的 ④毫不掩饰的,赤裸裸的: a ~ lie 明目张胆的谎言 ‖**~ly** ***ad.*** 不加虚饰地: put it *~ly* 直截了当地说 / **~ness** ***n.*** ‖'**~-'faced** ***a.*** ①(动物)脸上有白斑的 ②厚颜无耻的 / '**~head** ***n.*** ①秃头的人 ②一种家鸽 / '**~-'headed** ***a.*** 秃头的,秃顶的 / '**~pate** ***n.*** 秃头的人

bale[1] [beil] **I** ***n.*** 大包,大捆: a ~ of cotton 一包棉花 **II** ***vt.*** 把…打包: a *baling* press 打包机

bale[2] [beil] ***n.*** [古]灾祸,不幸;痛苦 ‖**~ful** ***a.*** 不吉的;邪恶的;有害的

bale[3] [beil] ***n., vt.*** & ***vi.*** = bail[2]

balk [bɔ:k] **I** ***n.*** ①阻碍,障碍 ②错误;挫折 ③田埂 ④【建】大木;梁 ⑤【矿】煤层中的岩石包裹体 **II** ❶ ***vt.*** 阻碍;使受挫折: ~ sb.'s plans 使某人的计划受到挫折 / be *~ed* in one's purpose 达不到目的 ❷ ***vi.*** ①(马等)逡巡不前 ②畏缩不前;回避

ball[1] [bɔ:l] **I** ***n.*** ①球;球状物: The ~ is with you. 该你发球了。(或:该轮到你了。) / a ~ of string 一团绳 ②星球(特指地球) ③(人体上的)圆形突出部分: the ~ of the foot (the thumb) 拇趾(拇指)球 ④弹丸: ~ ammunition【军】[总称]实心弹 ⑤[美]球类活动(尤指棒球) ⑥眼球 ⑦(棒球投手投出的)坏球 ⑧[the ~](企业等的)管理大权 ⑨[俚]人,家伙: an odd ~ 怪人 ⑩[复]胡说八道 **II** ***vt.*** & ***vi.*** 捏(或绕)(…)成球形 ‖***a ~ of fire*** ①一团火球;[美俚]精力充沛的实干家 ②[美俚]特快列车 / ***a ~ of fortune*** 受命运摆弄的人 / ***be ~ed up*** [美俚]被弄糊涂;被弄得乱糟糟 / ***be on the ~*** [美俚]在精力充沛地行动;知情;内行 / ***carry the ~*** [口]负起责任;担当起领导职务 / ***catch the ~ before the bound*** 先期发动;事先下手 / ***Get on the ~!*** [美俚]机灵些!敏捷些! / ***have something (nothing) on the ~*** [美俚]颇有(毫无)本领 / ***have the ~ at one's feet*** 有机会获得成功 / ***keep one's eye on the ~*** [美俚]警惕 / ***keep the ~ rolling*** 不使谈话(或其他活动)中断 / ***make a ~s of*** 把…弄糟 / ***no ~*** (板球)犯规的球 / ***on the ~*** [美俚]警惕;活跃 / ***play ~*** 开始(或继续)赛球;开始(或继续)某项活动 / ***play ~ with sb.*** [口]与某人合作 / ***put*** (或 ***leave***) ***the ~ in sb.'s court*** 把球踢到某人的场地上(指轮到某人作出反应、采取行动等) / ***set*** (或 ***start***) ***the ~ rolling*** 开始活动(特指谈话) / ***take up the ~*** 接着讲(或做);值班,接替 ‖**~ and chain** ①[美](系有金属圆球的)禁锢犯人用的锁链 ②[美俚]妻子 / **~ and socket** 杵臼关节,球窝 / **~ bearing** 滚珠轴承 / **~ cartridge** 实弹 / **~ cock** 浮球旋塞,浮球阀 / **~ firing** 实弹射击 / '**~-,flower** ***n.***【建】圆球饰 / **~ park** 棒球场 / **~ pen**, '**~-point**, '**~-point pen** 圆珠笔 / '**~proof** ***a.*** 防弹的 / **~ turret** 飞机机身下部的球形炮塔

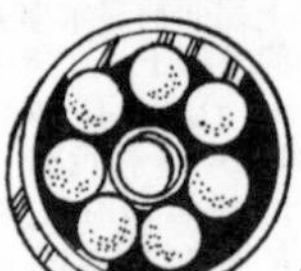

ball bearing

ball[2] [bɔ:l] ***n.*** ①跳舞会 ②[俚]狂欢作乐的聚会;狂欢作乐 ‖***have a ~*** [美俚]尽情作乐 / ***open the ~*** [口]开始 ‖'**~room** ***n.*** 舞厅

ballad ['bæləd] ***n.*** ①【音】叙事曲 ②民歌,民谣 ‖**~eer, ~ier** [,bælə'diə] ***n.*** 民谣歌手 ‖'**~-,monger** ***n.*** ①民谣歌本零售商(尤指沿街叫卖者) ②蹩脚诗人

ballast ['bæləst] **I** ***n.*** ①【船】压载,压舱物,镇重物 ②使(性格等)沉着的因素;稳定因素,镇定物;[喻]安定,沉着 ③【交】石碴,道碴 ④【电】镇流电阻,镇流器 ⑤(气球、飞艇等的)沙囊 **II** ***vt.*** ①使稳定,在…上放镇重物 ②为(铁路等)铺道碴 ‖***be in ~*** (船只)只装着沙石等压舱物 ‖**~ing** ***n.*** ①压舱材料 ②道碴材料

ballet ['bælei; 美 bæ'lei] ***n.*** ①芭蕾舞,舞剧 ②芭蕾舞蹈音乐 ③芭蕾舞剧团 ‖'**~-,dancer** ***n.*** 芭蕾舞演员,舞剧演员

ballistic [bə'listik] ***a.*** 弹道(学)的,衡量冲击强度的,发射的: a ~ missile 弹道导弹 / a ~ rocket 弹道火箭 ‖**~s** [复] ***n.*** [用作单或复] ①弹道学,发射学: rocket *~s* 火箭弹道学,导弹弹道学 ②(火器、弹药等的)发射特性

balloon [bə'lu:n] **I** ***n.*** ①气球;玩具气球: a ~ barrage 气球阻塞网(一种防御敌机空袭的设施) / a barrage ~ 阻塞气球 ②(蒸馏时用的)球形玻璃容器 ③漫画中圈出人物讲话的线条 **II** ❶ ***vi.*** ①膨胀如气球 ②坐气球上升(或旅行) ③激增 ❷ ***vt.*** 使膨胀成气球状 **III** ***a.*** ①气球状的 ②(一笔货物)分量轻而体积大的 ③(分期付款中)最后一笔数目特大的 ‖**~ing** ***n.*** ①气球的操纵(或乘坐、升空) ②【军】飞机拉飘 / **~ist** ***n.*** 驾驶(或操纵)气球的人 ‖**bal'loonfish** ***n.*** 河豚 / **~ tire** 低压大轮胎

ballot ['bælət] **I** ***n.*** ①选票;无记名投票用纸: cast (或 take) a ~ 投票 / vote by ~ 投票选举(或表决) ②投票总数 ③投票权 ④抽签 ⑤候选人名单: place sb. on the ~ 推某人为候选人 **II** ❶ ***vi.*** ①无记名投票: ~ for (against) 投票赞成(反对)… ②抽签: ~ for sth. 为某事进行抽签 ❷ ***vt.*** ①向…拉票 ②通过投票(或抽签)选出 ‖**~age** ['bælətidʒ] ***n.*** 决选投票(在各候选人得票均未能达法定多数时对其中得票最多的二、三候选人再次投票决选) ‖**~ box** 投票箱 / **~ paper** 投票用纸

balm [bɑ:m] ***n.*** ①香油,香脂,香膏 ②止痛药膏 ③[喻]安慰物 ④香味,芳香 ‖**~ cricket** 蝉

balsam ['bɔ:lsəm] *n.* ①香油,香脂,香膏 ②缓和物;安慰物;[喻]安慰 ③凤仙花属植物;凤仙花(=garden ~) ‖-**ic** [bɔ:l'sæmik] *a.* ①香脂的,香油的 ②安慰的;止痛的 ‖ **pear** 苦瓜 / ~ **fir** 胶枞;胶冷杉

bamboo [bæm'bu:] *n.* 竹 ‖~**shoot** 笋,竹笋

ban [bæn] **I** *n.* ①禁止;禁令: be put (或 placed) under a ~ 被禁止 / lift the ~ on 对…开禁 ②【宗】诅咒,革出教门 ③(封建时代的)动员令 ④ 谴责(尤指舆论方面的) **II** (banned; banning) ❶ *vt.* 禁止,取缔: Swimming in this river is banned. 此河禁止游泳。 ❷ *vi.* 诅咒

banal [bə'nɑ:l] *a.* 平庸的;陈腐的 ‖-**ity** [bə'næliti] *n.* ①平庸,陈腐 ②陈词滥调

banana [bə'nɑ:nə] *n.* ①香蕉;芭蕉属植物: a hand of ~s 一串香蕉 ②[美俚]喜剧演员 ③[美俚]大鼻子 ‖~ **oil** 【化】香蕉油,醋酸戊酯 / ~ **republic** "香蕉国"(常指由外资控制的、只有单一经济作物的拉丁美洲小国)

band [bænd] **I** *n.* ①带;带形物;箍带: a rubber ~ 橡皮筋,橡皮圈 / iron ~s round a bucket 水桶的铁箍 ②镶边,嵌条【建】扁带饰;带条 ④【矿】夹层,夹石 ⑤(收音机)波段,频带(wave ~ 的简称): 25-metre ~ 二十五米波段 ⑥一帮,一伙(人) ⑦乐队(尤指管乐队): a military ~ 军乐队 / a brass ~ 铜管乐队 **II** ❶ *vt.* ①带绑扎 ②加条饰于;镶边于 ③团结,联合 ❷ *vi.* 团结,联合(with) ‖**to beat the ~** [美俚][作状语用]又快又猛地 ‖'~**master** *n.* (管)乐队指挥 / ~ **saw** 带锯 / ~ **shell** (在后方装有壳形响板的)(室外)音乐台 / ~**sman** ['bændzmən] *n.* (管)乐队队员 / '~**stand** *n.* (室外)音乐台 / ~ **switching** 【无】波段转换 / '~**wag(g)on** *n.* [美](游行队伍前面的)乐队车;[喻]潮流,浪头;因时兴新鲜而吸引人的党派: jump (或 climb) on the ~wag(g)on [口]看风使舵;赶浪头 / ~ **wheel** 【机】带轮 / '~**width** 【讯】(频)带宽度,通带宽度

bandage ['bændidʒ] **I** *n.* 绷带: a first-aid ~ 急救绷带 **II** *vt.* 用绷带包扎: ~ (up) sb.'s leg 用绷带把某人的腿包扎起来

bandit ['bændit] ([复] banditti [bæn'diti(:)] 或 bandits) *n.* ①土匪,盗匪;歹徒: a ~ gang 匪帮 ②[军俚]敌机 ‖~**ry** *n.* 盗匪活动

bandy¹ ['bændi] **I** ❶ *vt.* ①把(球)打来打去,来回掷;左右摆弄: This apparatus is no toy to be bandied about. 这部仪器不是玩具,不可能随意摆弄。 ②来回传递,互换: ~ words with sb. 与某人顶嘴(或辩论) ③(轻率、嘲弄地)谈论;散布(谣言等): ~ sth. about 到处乱传某事 ❷ *vi.* [古]联合,混合 **II** *n.* 一种曲棍球

bandy² ['bændi] *a.* 膝向外曲的 ‖'~-**legged** *a.* 两腿向外弯曲的

bane [bein] *n.* ①毒物(现只用于复合词中, 如 ratsbane) ②祸根 ③死亡,毁灭

bang¹ [bæŋ] **I** ❶ *vt.* ①猛敲;猛撞; 砰地把(门、

盖等)关上: ~ one's fist on a desk 砰地在桌上捶一拳 / ~ sth. into sb. (或 sb.'s head) 硬把某事灌输进某人头脑 ②(粗手粗脚地)把…扔来扔去 ③[俚]超过,胜过 ❷ *vi.* ①猛敲;猛撞;猛地关上: ~ on (或 at) a door 砰地打门 / ~ against a wall 砰地撞在墙上 / The door ~ed shut. 门砰地碰上了。 ②砰砰作响: The children ~ed down the stairs. 孩子们砰砰啪啪地奔下楼梯。 **II** *n.* ①猛击;猛撞 ②砰砰的声音 ③热情,精力 ④[美俚]刺激,快感; 麻醉品的服用 **III** *ad.* ①砰地: Bang went the fireworks. 焰火砰地爆开了。 ②猛地,突然 ‖~ **up** ①砰地撞上;接好一个 ~ **receiver** *up* 砰地撞上(电话)听筒 ②弄伤;弄坏 / **with a** ~ ①砰地一声 ②成功地: The performance went over with a ~. 演出极为成功。 ③热气腾腾地;剧烈而突然地 ‖'~-~ *n.* 砰砰的枪声,射击;[喻]暴烈行为

bang² [bæŋ] **I** *vt.* 把(前额头发)剪成刘海式 **II** *n.* 前刘海 ‖'~-**tail** *n.* [美俚]比赛用的马

banish ['bæniʃ] *vt.* ①流放,放逐 ②消除,排除(顾虑、恐惧等): ~ all superstitions 大破迷信 ‖~**ment** *n.* 流放

banister ['bænistə] *n.* ①栏杆小柱 ②[复]楼梯的扶手;栏杆

banjo ['bændʒou] ([复] banjo(e)s) *n.* 班卓琴(一种类似吉他的弦乐器)

banjo

bank¹ [bæŋk] **I** *n.* ①(河、海或湖的)岸,堤;(隧道、坑等的)边: a ~ pier 桥台,岸墩 / a snow protection ~ 防雪障 ②埂,垄;堆,层: a ~ of earth between paddy fields 稻田之间的田埂 / a ~ of snow 雪堆 / a coal ~ (劣质)煤堆 ③向上斜坡 ④(海中水面下的)浅滩,沙洲 ⑤(飞机、车辆等转弯时的)倾斜状态,倾斜 ⑥【矿】采煤工作面地区(或通道),井口区: a pit ~ 井口出车台 / a front ~ 挖泥船工作面 **II** ❶ *vt.* ①在…旁边筑堤: ~ up a river 筑河堤(挡水) ②堆积: ~ up the hay 堆干草 ③封(炉、炉火): ~ up a furnace 封炉 ④使倾斜 ⑤把…排成一行 ⑥使(路的弯曲部分)外侧比内侧超高: a ~ed curve 超高曲线 ❷ *vi.* ①堆积起来(up) ②【空】(飞机)倾斜着飞行,倾斜;(汽车等)倾斜行驶: ~ing flight 倾斜飞行

bank² [bæŋk] **I** *n.* ①银行；银行办公处(或大楼) ②库(指血清、骨头等的贮藏所): a blood ~ 血库 ③赌场主；(赌博的)庄家；庄家的赌本 **II ❶** *vi.* ① 把钱存入银行；与银行往来: ~ with 与…(银行)有往来 ②开办银行 ③(赌博中)做庄家 ❷ *vt.* 把(钱)存入银行 ‖~ **on** (或 **upon**) 指望；信赖: ~ on (或 upon) sb.'s help 指望某人的帮助 / *break the* ~ 耗尽资源 ‖~ **acceptance** 银行承兑汇票 / ~ **account** 银行往来帐 / ~ **annuities** 英国统一公债 / ~ **bill** ①[英]银行与银行之间的汇票 ②[美]钞票 / '~**book** *n.* 银行存折 / ~ **clearing** 银行票据交换 / ~ **credit** 银行信贷 / ~ **deposit** 银行存款 / ~ **discount** 银行贴现 / ~ **draft** 银行汇票 / ~ **holiday** (美国的)星期日以外的银行假日;(英国的)公假日 / ~ **money** [总称]银行票据(支票、汇票等) / ~ **note** 钞票 / ~ **paper** [总称] ①(流通的)钞票 ② 银行承兑的票据 / ~ **rate** (银行规定的)贴现率

bank³ [bæŋk] **I** *n.* ①(一)排，(一)系列: a ~ of oars (古代有桨帆船上的)一排桨 ②(风琴或打字机等的)键排: a four-~ typewriter 四键排打字机 ③[美]一排电梯 ④[电]组合: a ~ of capacitors 电容器组 ⑤报纸小标题 **II** *vt.* 把…排成一排

banker ['bæŋkə] *n.* ①银行家: Let me be your ~. 你需要钱，我可以借给你。②(赌博的)庄家 ③(某些赌博中的)发牌人 ④一种(赌博性)纸牌戏 ‖~'s **bill** 银行对外国银行开出的汇票

bankroll ['bæŋkroul] **I** *n.* 资金 **II** *vt.* 提供资金给，资助(人、企业、戏剧的演出、电影的摄制等) ‖~**er** *n.* 提供资金者,资助者

bankrupt ['bæŋkrəpt] **I** *n.* 破产者；无力还债的人 ②丧失了(名誉、智力等)的人 **I** *a.* ①破产的；无力还债的 ② 垮了的; 枯竭的 ③ 丧失了…的 (*of, in*): be ~ in reputation 名誉扫地 **III** *vt.* 使破产

bankruptcy ['bæŋkrəptsi] *n.* ①破产；无偿付能力: declare ~ 宣告破产

banner ['bænə] **I** *n.* ①旗；旗帜；(写有标语等的)横幅[注意: 与 flag 比，banner 常作"旗帜"解，带有抽象的意义，而 flag 则指具体的"旗子"] ②[美] 头号标题 (=~ headline) ③旗 **II** *a.* ① 杰出的，第一流的: a ~ year for wheat crops 小麦收成最好的一年 ② 突出地支持某一政党的 ‖*carry the* ~ [美俚] (由于没有地方睡)在街上走一夜 / *join* (或 *follow*) *the* ~ *of* 投到…的旗帜之下 ‖~**et(te)** [,bænə'ret] *n.* 小旗

banns [bænz] [复] *n.* 结婚预告: ask (或 call, publish) the ~ 在教堂中于婚礼前将结婚者姓名公布以征求意见 / forbid the ~ 对公布之婚事提出异议

banquet ['bæŋkwit] **I** *n.* 宴会, 盛宴: a state ~ 国宴 **II ❶** *vt.* 宴请, 设宴招待 ❷ *vi.* 饮宴, 大吃大喝 ‖~**er** *n.* 赴宴的客人 ‖~**ing hall** 宴会厅

bantam ['bæntəm] **I** *n.* ① [B-] [动]矮脚鸡 ②矮小而好斗的人 ③ =~weight (*n.*) **II** *a.* 矮小而好斗的 ‖'~**weight** *n. & a.* (拳击或摔角)最轻量级选手(的)

banter ['bæntə] **I** *n.* 善意的取笑, 逗弄 **II ❶** *vt.* 取笑, 逗弄 ❷ *vi.* 开玩笑

baptism ['bæptizəm] *n.* ①(基督教)洗礼, 浸礼 ②[喻]洗礼 ③(轮船等的)命名礼 ‖**baptist** *n.* 施洗礼者: the *Baptist* Church (或 the *Baptists*)(基督教新教)浸礼会

baptize, baptise [bæp'taiz] *vt.* ①给…施洗礼(基督教的一种仪式) ②洗炼, 使纯化 ③命名

bar [bɑ:] **I** *n.* ①(铁、木等)条, 杆, 棒: a steel ~ 钢条 / a ~ of soap 一条肥皂 / arch (slide) ~ [机]拱(滑)杆 / parallel ~s [体]双杠 ②栅, 栏；障碍物: the ~s of a gate (grate) 门(炉)栅 ③(光、颜色等的)线, 条, 带；[音]小节(纵)线: a ~ of light 一条光线 ④(港口、河口的)沙洲 ⑤ [物]巴(压力单位) ⑥法庭的围栏；[常作 the B-]法庭(指审判席、律师席或被告席): a prisoner *at* the ~ (或 *Bar*) (刑事)被告 ⑦停止诉讼(或权利要求)的申请 ⑧[常作 the B-] 律师的职业, 律师界: be called to the *Bar* 取得律师资格 ⑨[喻]审判台；制裁, 谴责 ⑩表示军阶的肩章(或领章)上的线(或条)；彩色勋带 ⑪(旅馆、饭店的)酒吧间；餐柜: a quick-lunch (cold-drink) ~ 快餐(冷饮)柜台 ⑫(专售某一商品的)柜台 ⑬ [美]蚊帐 **II** (barred; barring ['bɑ:riŋ]) *vt.* ① 闩上 ②阻挡, 拦住: ~ sb. *in* 把某人关在里面 ③妨碍；排挤, 排斥；[口]不准: We ~ smoking here. (我们这里)禁止吸烟。 **III** *prep.* [口]除…外 (=barring): ~ one 除了一个之外 / We'll come on time ~ (或 *barring*) traffic delay. 除非路上发生耽搁, 我们将准时到达。 ‖*behind* ~s (或 *behind bolt and* ~) 关在监牢里 / (*be tried*) *at the* ~ (或 *Bar*) 受到公开审问 / *cross the* ~ (或 *Bar*) 死, 去世 / *go to the* ~ (或 *Bar*) 当律师 / *prisoners'* ~s 儿童捕人游戏 / *the colo(u)r* ~ 对有色人种(在法律上与社会上)的歧视 / '~**bell** *n.* [体]杠铃 / ~ **chart, graph** 条线图(一种统计表) / '~**fly** *n.* [美俚]老是泡在酒吧间里酗酒的人 / ~ **iron** 条形铁 / '~**keeper** *n.* [美]酒吧间老板 (或招待员) / ~ **magnet** [电]条形磁铁 / '~**maid** *n.* 酒吧间女招待员 / '~**man** *n.* 酒吧间男招待员 / '~**room** *n.* 酒吧间 / '~**tender** *n.* 酒吧间招待员

barb [bɑ:b] **I** *n.* ①(箭、鱼钩等的)倒钩 ②[喻]刺人的话 ③[动]羽支；倒刺；(触)须 ④[美俚]不加入学生会的大学生 **II** *vt.* 装倒刺于: ~*ed* wire entanglements [军]有刺铁丝网

barbed wire

barbarian [bɑ:'bɛəriən] **I** *a.* 野蛮人的,不文明的, 未开化的 **II** *n.* ①野蛮人;原始人 ②粗鲁无礼的 人 ③残暴的人

barbaric [bɑ:'bærik] *a.* 野蛮(人)的;粗野的;肆无 忌惮的 ‖**~ally** *ad.*

barbarism ['bɑ:bərizəm] *n.* ①(语言、文体等的) 不规范,不纯;不规范的语句(或文字) ②野蛮状 态 ③原始风尚

barbarity [bɑ:'bæriti] *n.* ①残暴;暴行 ②=bar- barism

barbarous ['bɑ:bərəs] *a.* ①野蛮的;粗俗的 ②残 暴的 ③(语言等)不规范的 ‖**~ly** *ad.* / **~ness** *n.*

barbecue ['bɑ:bikju:] **I** *n.* ①烤烧的整只猪(或牛 等) ②(吃烤肉的)野外宴会 ③可携带的烤肉架 ④晒咖啡豆的场地 **II** *vt.* ①烤烧(整只猪、牛等) ②用叉架烤烧(肉、鱼等)

barber ['bɑ:bə] **I** *n.* ①理发师 ②话多的人 **II** *vt.* 为…理发剃须 ‖*do a ~* [美俚]讲话讲得很多 ‖**'~shop** *n.* [美]理发店 *a.* [美口](尤指伤感歌 曲)男声重唱的 / **~'s itch** 须癣 / **~('s) pole** 理 发店红白两色的旋转招牌 / **~'s shop** [英]理发 店

bard [bɑ:d] *n.* ①古代的吟游诗人 ②(史诗等的) 作者;吟唱(或朗诵)者 ‖**~ic** *a.*

bare [bɛə] **I** *a.* ①赤裸的,光秃的: with one's head ~ 光着头 / walk in ~ feet 赤着脚走 / be ~ *to* the waist 赤膊 ②无遮蔽的,无掩护的: a ~ hill 无草木的山 / ~ floors 不铺地毯的地 板 / a ~ sword (拔)出鞘的剑 ③(几乎)空的, 缺乏的;无装饰的: a room ~ *of* furniture 没有 (或很少)家具的房间 / sleep on ~ boards 睡在 没有垫褥的床板上 / be ~ *of* credit 缺乏信用 ④稀少的,微小的;仅有的,勉强的: a ~ possi- bility 一点点可能性 / a ~ majority 勉强过半 数 / make a ~ mention of... 仅仅提一下… / the ~ necessities of life 最低限度的生活必需品 ⑤不掩饰的,直率的: ~ facts 简单明了的事实 / speak the ~ truth 讲直话 ⑥(织物)磨损了 的,穿得已无毛头的 **II** *vt.* ①露出,暴露: ~ one's thoughts 暴露思想 / ~ one's heart 讲 心里话 / ~ the end of a wire 剥开电线头 ②拔出(刀、剑等) ‖*at the ~ idea* (或 *thought*) *of* 一想起…(就) / ~ *navy* [美俚](美海军)只 发罐头食品的严格配给 / *believe sb.'s ~ word* (或 *believe sb. on his ~ word*) 轻信某人的毫 无根据的话 / *escape with ~ life* 见 **life** / *lay ~* 暴露,揭发;摊开: lay ~ an issue (或 a problem) 把问题展开(或摊开) ‖**~ness** *n.* ‖**'~- back** *ad.* & *a.* 无马鞍(的) / **'~backed** *a.* 祖 背的,无马鞍的 / **~ bones** 梗概 / **~ contract** 【律】不附担保的契约 / **'~faced** *a.* ①不戴面具 的 ②露骨的,无耻的: tell a ~*faced* lie 无耻 地说谎,当面撒谎 / **'~facedly** *ad.* 露骨地,无 耻地 / **'~facedness** *n.* 露骨,无耻 / **'~foot** *ad.* & *a.* ①赤脚(的): run ~*foot* 赤脚奔跑 ②

[美俚](火车或引擎)没有刹车(的) / **'~-'footed** *a.* 赤脚的 / **'~-'handed** *ad.* & *a.* ①不戴手套 (的) ②赤手空拳(的),手无寸铁(的) ③[美口]确 实有罪(的) / **'~-'headed** *ad.* & *a.* 光着头的(的), 不戴帽(的) / **'~sark** *n.* =berserker *ad.* 不披 挂甲胄的

barely ['bɛəli] *ad.* ①赤裸裸地,无遮蔽地 ②公开 地,露骨地 ③仅仅,勉强,几乎没有: ~ enough 勉强够 / be ~ of age 刚成年 / I ~ know her 我只是有点认识她。/ She had ~ time to catch the bus. 她几乎来不及赶上公共汽车。

bargain ['bɑ:gin] **I** *n.* ①买卖合同;成交条件;交 易: make (或 strike) a ~ with sb. 与某人成交 / drive a hard ~ over sth. 为某事拼命讨价还价 / a good (bad) ~ 赚钱(蚀本)生意 ②(经讨价还 后)成交的商品;廉价货: It's a real ~. [口]真 便宜。/ buy at a ~ price 廉价买进 / a ~ sale 廉价出售 / a ~ hunter 到处找便宜货买的人 **II** *vi.* ①议价,讨价还价 ②成交,商定: ~ on doing sth. 商定做某事 **❷** *vt.* ①议(价);提出条 件(或要求) (that) ②把…议价卖掉;通过讲价钱 去掉: try to ~ out obstacles 企图通过讨价还价 扫除障碍 ‖*A ~'s a* . 达成的协议决不可撕 毁。/ ~ *away* 论价出售,卖脱;(为获取某物而) 廉价出售 / ~ *for* ①想廉价把…弄到手 ②指望; 预期: That's more than I ~*ed for*. 这个 我可没料到。/ ~ *into the* 此外还,再者 / *make the best of a bargain* 见 **best** ‖**~ee** [,bɑ:gi'ni:] *n.* 买主 / **~er** *n.* 议价者,讨价还价 者 / **~or** *n.* 【律】卖主 ‖**~ basement** 廉价部 (一般都设在百货大楼的地下室) / **~ counter** [美]廉价货品柜

barge [bɑ:dʒ] **I** *n.* ①驳船 ②大型游艇 ③(美海 军旗舰上将官用的)专用汽艇 ④[俚]粗笨大船 **II** **❶** *vt.* 用驳船运载 **❷** *vi.* ①蹒跚 ②[口]闯入 (*in*, *into*) ③[口]相撞 (*against*) ‖~ *in* ①闯入 ②[美俚]插嘴;干涉 / ~ *into* ①闯入 ②与…相 撞 ‖**bargee** [bɑ:'dʒi:] *n.* [英] =~man ‖**'~man** *n.* 驳船(或游艇)上的船员 / **~ pole** (驳船上用 的)撑篙: I wouldn't touch it with a ~ *pole*. 我 很讨厌它。

baritone ['bæritoun] 【音】**I** *n.* ①男中音;男中音 歌手 ②萨克斯号 **II** *a.* 男中音的

bark[1] [bɑ:k] **I** *n.* ①茎皮,树皮 **II** *vt.* ①用某种树皮 鞣(革) ②剥去(树)的皮 ③擦破(指节、膝盖等 处)的皮 ‖~ *a man with the* ~ *on* 粗鲁的人 ‖**~ beetle** 一种棘胫小蠹科的甲虫 / **~ borer** 蛀树 皮虫 / **'~-bound** *a.* 被树皮紧箍因而生长受阻 的

bark[2] [bɑ:k] **I** **❶** *vi.* ①(狗、狐等)吠,叫;(枪、引擎 等)发出声响: The dog ~*ed* furiously *at* him. 狗朝着他凶恶地吠叫。②(人)叫骂,咆哮 ③[俚] 咳嗽 **❷** *vt.* ①大声叫嚷,怒气冲冲地喊出 (*out*): ~ *out* a string of dirty words 用粗话连声叫 骂 ②大叫大嚷地推销 **II** *n.* ①吠叫声;狗吠似的 声响(如枪击声、咳嗽声等) ②叫喊 ‖~ *at the* moon (狂犬)吠月/空嚷,徒劳/ ~ *up the wrong tree* 见 **tree** / *His ~ is worse than his bite.* [谚]他急躁易怒,但无恶意。

bark³ [ba:k] *n.* ①三桅帆船 ②[诗]小船

barley ['ba:li] *n.* 大麦 ‖~ **broth** 烈性啤酒 / '~**corn** *n.* ①大麦粒 ②古时尺度名 ③烈性酒 (尤指威士忌) / '~-**mow** *n.* 麦堆 / ~ **sugar** 麦芽糖 / ~ **water** (供病人饮用的)大麦茶

barn [ba:n] *n.* ①谷仓 ②[美]牲口棚;电车(或公共汽车)的车库 ③[蔑]没有装饰的大房子 ④靶(恩)(核反应的截面单位,等于 10^{-24} 厘米²/核) ‖~ **dance** 美国传统谷仓舞 / ~ **door** ①仓库大门 ②[喻]不会打不中的目标 ③【无】挡光板 / '~**yard** *n.* 仓前空场: ~*yard* grass (或 millet) 稗 / ~*yard* manure 厩肥

barnacle ['ba:nəkl] *n.* ①一种北极鹅 ②[动]藤壶 (附在岩石、船底上的甲壳动物) ③[口]纠缠不休难以摆脱的人

barometer [bə'rɔmitə] *n.* ①气压计,气压表;晴雨计: The ~ rises (falls). 气压上升(下降)了。 (或: 天要放晴(下雨)了。) ②[喻]标记

baron ['bærən] *n.* ①男爵 ②贵族 ③[美]巨商: an oil ~ 石油大王 ‖~**age** ['bærənidʒ] *n.* [总称] 男爵;贵族 / ~**ess** *n.* 男爵夫人;女男爵 / ~**ial** [bə'rounjəl] *a.* ①男爵的,适合男爵身分的;男爵领有的 ②豪华的 / ~**y** *n.* 男爵领地;男爵爵位

baronet ['bærənit] *n.* 从男爵

baroque [bə'rouk] I *a.* ①【建】过分雕琢和怪涎的 (特指十七世纪欧洲的一种建筑风格) ② 在音乐上表现奇异风格的 ③在文学作品上结构复杂、形象奇特而又模糊的 ④奇异的,怪样的 II *n.* 巴罗克艺术风格;巴罗克建筑形式

barque [ba:k] *n.* =bark³

barrack ['bærək] I *n.* ①[常作 a ~s][用作单]兵营,营房 ②(工地等的)棚屋,临时工房 ③简陋的房子 II ❶ *vt.* ①使驻兵营内;使住棚屋内 ② [澳]嘲弄,辱骂 ❷ *vi.* [澳]①嘲笑(at),喝倒采 ②声援,助威 ‖~s **bag** (用以盛放装备和个人物品的)士兵背囊

barrage ['bæra:ʒ; 'bæra:ʒ] I *n.* ①火网;掩护炮火;[军]弹幕射击,拦阻射击: an umbrella ~ 防空火网 / lift the ~ 延伸弹幕射击 ②[喻]接二连三的猛击,倾泻: a ~ of questions 连珠炮似的问题 ③['ba:ridʒ] 堰,拦河坝 II *vt.* 以密集火力进攻(或阻击);向…倾泻 ‖~ **balloon** (阻御敌机空袭用的)阻塞气球 / ~ **fire** 弹幕射击 / ~ **jamming** 【无】全波段干扰,阻塞干扰 / ~ **plan** 弹幕射击计划

barred [ba:d] *a.* ①上了闩的 ②被禁止的;受阻的 ③划(出)线条的

barrel ['bærəl] I *n.* ①桶,琵琶桶 ②一桶(一种容量单位,在美国一般等于 31 ½ 加仑,在英国一般于 36 法定加仑) ③圆筒 ④[军]枪膛 ⑤炮筒 ⑥照相机的镜头筒;自来水笔的吸水管 ⑦[口]许多: a ~ of fun 很有趣 ⑧马(或牛)的躯体 II (barrel(l)ed; barrel(l)ing) ❶ *vt.* 把…装

桶 ❷ *vi.* [俚](汽车等) 高速行进 ‖*have sb. over a* ~ [美俚]完全支配某人(尤指在经济方面) / *scrape the bottom of the (pickle)* ~ 见 **bottom** ‖**barrel(l)ed** *a.* 装了桶的 ‖~ **bulk** 五立方呎容积 / '~-'**chested** *a.* 胸部宽得同身高不相称的 / ~ **drain** 筒形排水渠 / ~ **house** ①廉价小酒店 ②疯狂乱奏的爵士音乐 / ~ **organ** 手摇风琴 / ~ **roll** 【空】(特技飞行中的)横滚;桶滚

barrel

barren ['bærən] I *a.* ①(土地等)贫瘠的,荒芜的,不毛的: turn the ~ hill into an orchard 把荒山变成果园 ②(植物等)不结果实的 ③不生育的,不妊的 ④(思想等)贫乏的,无聊的; (计划等)无结果的: a ~ subject 枯燥的题目 ⑤没有…的 (*of*): ~ *of* practical value 无实际价值的 II *n.* 土地贫瘠的地区;[复]荒地 ‖~**ness** *n.* ‖'~**wort** *n.* 淫羊藿属植物;高山淫羊藿

barricade [,bæri'keid] I *n.* 路障,街垒;挡墙 II *vt.* 阻塞;设路障于

barrier ['bæriə] *n.* ①栅栏;屏障 ②海关关卡 ③障碍,妨碍因素;障碍物: a ~ light 海岸探照灯 / a ~ breaker 障碍突破船 / a tank ~ 防坦克障碍物 / set up (remove) a ~ between 在…中间设置(拆除)障碍 / the language ~ 语言上的隔阂 ④扩伸到海洋中的南极洲冰层 ‖~ **reef** 堤礁

barring ['ba:riŋ] *prep.* 除…外,不包括…

barrister ['bæristə] *n.* (在英国有资格出席高等法庭的)律师(指不是被告所聘的一般辩护律师) / ~-at-law)

barrow¹ ['bærou] *n.* ①(独轮或两轮)手推车 ②担架 ‖~ **boy** (水果、蔬菜等的)叫卖小贩 / ~**man** ['bæroumən] *n.* =~ boy / ~ **pit** 采石坑;手车运输的露天矿

barrow² ['bærou] *n.* ①冢,古墓 ②(只用于英国的山名前)山

barrow³ ['bærou] *n.* 阉猪

barter ['ba:tə] I ❶ *vi.* 进行易货贸易,作物品交换: ~ *with* . . . *for* sth. 跟…通过物物交换以得到某物 ❷ *vt.* ①以…作易货贸易,拿…作物物交换: ~ rice *for* textiles 用大米换取纺织品 ②[喻]出卖(权利、荣誉等) II *n.* ①物物交换,易货: on a ~ basis 以易货(贸易)方式 ②进行易货贸易的商品 ‖~**er** ['ba:tərə] *n.* 进行易货贸易者

base¹ [beis] **I** *n.* ①基础,底部;底层(底子): the ~ of a column 柱脚 ②根据地;【军】基地: a cotton ~ 产棉区 / a missile ~ 导弹基地 / a naval ~ 海军基地 / a ~ hospital 后方医院 ③【化】碱、(染色)固色剂 ④【数】底;基线,基点,基面 ⑤【语】词根;词干 ⑥【体】(棒球)垒;起点,目标: get to (或 reach) first ~ (棒球击球手)跑到第一垒;[美俚]取得成功的开端 **II** *vt.* 把…基于;把(飞机等)的基地设在 (on, upon): carrier-~d aircraft 舰载机 ‖ **off** ~ ① 大错特错的 ②冷不防地: This question caught me off ~. 这问题一下子把我给难住了。③[美俚]傲慢的 / ~ prison (或 prisoner's) ~ 儿童捕人游戏 ‖'~band *n.*【无】基(本频)带 / '~board *n.*【建】踢脚板 / '~'fertilizer *n.* 基肥 / '~,level *n.*【地】基准面 / ~ line 基线;(网球场等的)底线 / ~ map (地质工作者用的)工作草图 / ~ oil 粗石油,原油 / ~ paper 原纸 / ~ pay (津贴等除外的)基本工资 / '~plate *n.*【机】底板,支承板;【医】(装假牙齿的)底板

base² [beis] **I** *a.* ①卑鄙的: a ~ act (motive) 卑鄙的行为(动机) ②低级的,劣等的: a ~ metal 贱金属(指铁、铅等) / a ~ coin (含有贱金属的)假硬币 ③【语】(语言)不纯的,讹误的 ④【音】低音的 **II** *n.*【音】低音;低音部 ‖**~ly** *ad.* / **~ness** *n.* ‖**~born** *a.* ①出身低微的 ②私生的 / '~-court *n.* (城堡)外院;(农庄)后院 / '~-'minded *a.* 卑鄙的;品质恶劣的

baseball ['beisbɔ:l] *n.* ①【体】棒球运动 ②棒球

basement ['beismənt] *n.* ①建筑物的底部 ②【建】地下室;地窖;底层 ‖~ complex【地】基底杂岩

bash [bæʃ] **I** ❶ *vt.* [口] 猛击,猛撞: ~ sb. on the head 猛击某人的头部 ②打坏(in): ~ in a roof 把屋顶打坏 ❷ *vi.* 猛击撞毁 **II** *n.* [英] 猛击: have a ~ at sth. [俚]试做某事 ②[俚]狂欢;狂欢会

bashful ['bæʃful] *a.* 害羞的,忸怩的 ‖~ly *ad.* / ~ness *n.*

basic ['beisik] **I** *a.* ①基本的,基础的 ②【化】碱的;碱性的;碱式的: ~ dyes 碱性染料 / ~ process【冶】碱性法 / ~ slag【冶】碱性(转炉)渣 ③【矿】基性的;含少量硅酸的 **II** *n.* [常用复]基础,基本 ②基础训练 ‖**~ally** *ad.* 基本地 ‖**Basic English** 基本英语 (二十世纪二十年代一些英国学者人为地搞出的一种所谓简化的"国际交际语",由八百五十个英语基本词汇构成) / ~ private (美)陆军三等兵

basin ['beisn] *n.* ①盆,水盆;洗脸(或洗手)盆 ②一盆的(容)量 ③水坞,【船】系船池;水洼;内湾 ④盆地;流域: an ocean ~ 海洋盆地 ⑤【矿】煤田 ‖**~ful** *n.* 一满盆

basis ['beisis] ([复] bases ['beisi:z]) *n.* ① 基础;根据: factories working on a two-shift ~ 实行两班制的工厂 / provide a sound ~ for further research 为进一步研究提供可靠的根据 / the ~ of an argument 论据 ②主要成分 ③军事基地

bask [bɑ:sk] *vi.* ①(舒适地)取暖: ~ in the sun 晒太阳取暖 ②[喻]感到舒适,得乐趣

basket ['bɑ:skit] **I** *n.* ①篮;篓;筐: a wastepaper ~ 废纸篓 ②一篮(或一篓、一筐)的量: a ~ of apples 一筐苹果 ③气球的吊篮 ④(篮球运动中的)篮;(一次)投篮得分 **II** *vt.* 把…装入(或投入)篮(或篓、筐)内 ‖be left in the ~ 被剔除在篮底;被忽略 / sneeze into a ~ [委婉语]上断头台,被斩首 / the pick of the ~ 一批中最好的,精华 ‖**~ful** *n.* 一满篮、一满篓;一满筐 / **~ry** *n.* ①(篮、篓、筐等的)编织术 ②[总称](篮子等)编织物 ‖~ chair 柳条椅 / ~ fish, ~ star 筐鱼 / '~,handle arch【建】三心拱 / ~ hilt (剑等)带有篮状护手的柄 / '~work *n.* [总称](篮子等)编织物

basketball ['bɑ:skitbɔ:l] *n.* ① 篮球运动: play ~ 打篮球 ②篮球 ‖**~er** *n.* 篮球运动员

bass [beis] 【音】**I** *n.* ①男低音;男低音的音调 ②男低音歌手 ③ 低音部 ④ 低音乐器(尤指低音提琴) **II** *a.* 低音的: a ~ drum (horn) 大鼓(号) / a ~ viol 低音提琴 ‖**~ist** *n.* 低音提琴手

bassoon [bə'su:n, bə'zu:n] *n.*【音】巴松管,大管,低音管 ‖**~ist** *n.* 巴松管吹奏者

bassoon

bastard ['bæstəd] **I** *n.* ①私生子 ②杂种;假冒品;劣等货 ③[俚]坏种,讨厌鬼 ④[俚]家伙(用于亲昵的开玩笑场合) **II** *a.* ①私生的;杂交的: a ~ dog 杂种狗 ②奇形怪状的;尺码异常的 ③不合标准的,劣质的: ~ sugar 粗劣的食糖 ④假的;非权威的 ‖**~ly** *a.* 私生子(似)的;假冒的 / **~y** *n.* ①私生子身份 ②生私生子 ‖**~ file** 粗齿锉 / ~ wing (鸟类的)小翼羽

bastion ['bæstiən; 美 'bæstʃən] *n.* ①棱堡 ②设防地区;阵地工事 ③ [喻]堡垒: a ~ of iron 铜墙铁壁

bat¹ [bæt] **I** *n.* ①短棍 ②(棒球、板球等的)球棒;(网球、乒乓球等的)球拍;赛马师的短鞭: carry one's ~ (板球赛中)在一局结束时未被判令出局 ③(棒球等的)击球;(板球等的)击球手 ④(粘土等的)一块,一团 ⑤[常用复]棉花胎 ⑥[口]打击,猛击 ⑦[英俚]步子,速度: go off at a rare ~ 飞快地跑掉 ⑧[美俚]闹饮,狂欢: go on a ~ 酗酒胡闹 ⑨[美俚]美元 **II** (batted; batting) ❶ *vt.*

① 用球棒打(球); 用球拍打打(球) ②挥打 ③详细讨论, 反复考虑 ❷ *vi.* 用球棒(或球拍)打球; 轮到击球 ‖*at* ~ (在棒球等比赛中)正在击球; 轮到击球 / ~ *around* [美俚] ① 在…到处游荡 ② 详细讨论, 反复考虑(计划等) / ~ *hides* [美俚] [总称]钞票 / ~ *out* 粗制滥造(作品或) / *go to for sb.* [美俚]替某人辩护, 为某人出力 / *off one's own* — 全凭自己的力量, 独立地 / (*right*) *off the* ~ 一下子, 马上

bat² [bæt] *n.* ① 蝙蝠: as blind as a ~ 瞎得跟蝙蝠一样; 有眼无珠 ②[俚]妓女 ‖*have* ~*s in the belfry* ① 发痴 ② 异想天开 ‖'~-*blind*, '~-*eyed a.* (象蝙蝠一样)半瞎的; 愚蠢的

bat³ [bæt] (batted; batting) *vt.* [口] 眨(眼睛)(尤指因惊奇等而眨眼) ‖*not* ~ *an eyelid* 不眨眼; 不为所动; 处之泰然

bat⁴ [bɑ:t, bæt] *n.* [the ~] 外国语中的口语 ‖*sling the* ~ [军俚]说外国话[注意: 在这习语中 ~ 一般发 [bɑ:t] 音]

batch [bætʃ] *n.* ①(面包等的)一炉 ②一次操作所需的原料量; 一次生产量: the ~ number (产品或原料的)批号 ③一批: a fresh ~ of visitors (letters) 新到的一批来访者(信件) ‖*in* ~*es* 分批地; 成批地

bate [beit] ❶ *vt.* ① [古]减少, 降低 ②压低, 抑制: with ~d breath 屏息地 ③减去: He would not ~ a jot of it. 他一点不肯减让了。 ❷ *vi.* [方]减退, 变弱

bath [bɑ:θ] I ([复] baths [bɑ:ðz]) *n.* ①浴, (洗)澡: have (或 take) a cold (hot) ~ 洗一个冷水(热水)澡 ②浴水: draw sb. a ~ 给某人放(一盆)浴水 / Your ~ is ready. 洗澡水给你准备好了。 ③浴缸; 澡盆 ④浴室; (公共)澡堂 ⑤[常用复]洗澡处; 温泉浴场: sea-water ~s 海水浴场 ⑥浸没: a ~ of blood 血洗, 大屠杀 ⑦[化]浴; 浴器, 浴锅; 电镀槽 ⑧[冶]池铁浆(指反射炉中之铁) ⑨[摄]定影液 ‖*an air* ~ 空气浴 / *a mud* ~ 泥浴(疗法) / *an oil* ~ 油浴 / *a salt* ~ 盐浴 / *a sand* ~ 沙浴 / *a shower* ~ 淋浴 / *a sitz* (或 *hip*) ~ 坐浴(器) / *a steam* (或 *vapour*) ~ 蒸汽浴 / *a sun* ~ 日光浴 II *vt. & vi.* [英](给…)洗澡 ‖'~*house n.* ① (公共)澡堂 ②海滨更衣处 / ~ *mat* 浴室防滑垫 / '~*robe n.* [美]浴衣, 睡衣 / '~*room n.* 浴室; 盥洗室 / '~*tub n.* ①浴缸; 澡盆 ②[美俚]摩托车的边车

bathe [beið] I ❶ *vt.* ① 把…浸没在液体中; 给…洗澡: be ~d in sweat 浑身大汗 ②弄湿, 洗, (用药水等)冲洗(伤口等): ~ one's feet 洗脚 / The doctor told him to ~ his eyes twice a day. 医生叫他每天洗眼两次。 ③ (日光等)沐浴, 笼罩: a city ~d in a festive atmosphere 沉浸在节日气氛中的城市 ❷ *vi.* ①洗澡 ②游泳 ③沉浸, 沐浴 (*in*) II *n.* [英]游泳; 洗澡: go for a ~ 去游泳; 去洗海(或河, 湖)水澡 ‖~*r n.* 洗澡的人 [英]游泳者

bathos ['beiθɔs] *n.* ①[语]突降法(指在文章或讲话中由庄重突转平庸) ②(虎头蛇尾的)下降

平淡, 陈腐乏味 ④ 做作出来的悲哀, 过分的感伤

batman ['bætmən] ([复] batmen) *n.* (英国军队中的)传令兵, 勤务兵

baton ['bætən] I *n.* ①棍, 棒; 警棍 ②官杖(某些国家用以表示官职, 军衔等的短杖) ③(交响乐队, 军乐队等的)指挥棒: wield a good ~ 指挥熟练 / dance to sb.'s ~ 跟着某人的指挥棒转 ④ (接力赛中的)接力棒 II *vt.* 用短棍打 ‖*ist n.* 指挥者

battalion [bə'tæljən] *n.* ①[军]营; 营部 ②[复]部队, 军队: recruit new ~s 征集新部队 ③大队(的人)

batten¹ ['bætn] I *n.* ①(船)压条; 条板 ②[建]板条; 挂瓦条; 压缝条 II *vt.* 用板条钉住: ~ *down the hatches* 封舱

batten² ['bætn] ❶ *vi.* 贪吃; 养肥自己 ❷ *vt.* 养肥(猪, 羊等)

batter¹ ['bætə] ❶ *vt.* ① 连续猛击; 炮击; 打烂: ~ sb. *about* 痛打某人 ②磨损(家具等), 把…用旧: a ~ed raincoat 一件破旧的雨衣 ❷ *vi.* 作连续猛击: ~ *at the door* 擂门 ‖~*ing artillery* [总称]攻城炮 / ~*ing charge* [军]最大装(弹)药量 / ~*ing ram* 攻城槌(一种古代兵器): ~*ing ram* tactics 冲撞战术 / ~*ing train* 攻城炮列

batter² ['bætə] I *n.* (墙壁等的)内倾, 倾度 II *vt. & vi.* (使)内倾

battery ['bætəri] *n.* ①[律]殴打: assault and ~ 殴打(已遂) ; 人身攻击 ②炮兵连; 兵器群; (一艘舰艇上的)炮组 ③(炮的)待发射状态: put the cannons in ~ 准备开炮 ④[电]电池(组): dry ~ 干电池(组) / storage ~ 蓄电池(组) / charger 电池充电器 ⑤(器具等的)一套, 一组: a ~ of lenses (prisms) 透镜(棱镜)组 ⑥(乐队的)一组打击乐器 ⑦(棒球队的)投手和接手 ⑧孵蛋箱组 ‖*turn sb.'s* ~ *against himself* (在辩论中)以子之矛攻子之盾

battle ['bætl] I *n.* ① 战役, 会战; 战斗 ②斗争: a ~ of words 舌战 ③[美]竞赛 ④胜利, 成功: The ~ is to the just. 胜利属于正义的人们。 ‖*an air* ~ 空战 / *a close* ~ 近战, 肉搏 / *a decisive* ~ 决战 / *a drawn* ~ 不分胜负的战斗 / *a fierce* ~ 激战 / *a land* ~ 陆战 / *a naval* (或 *sea*) ~ 海战 / *a pitched* ~ 列阵的大战; 难分难解的酣战 / *a sham* ~ 模拟战, 军事演习 / *a street* ~ 巷战 II ❶ *vi.* ①战斗: ~ *against* heavy odds 以寡敌众 ②斗争; 搏斗 ❷ *vt.* [美]与…作战; 与…斗争: ~ one's way through the crowd 从人丛中挤过去 ‖*accept* ~ 应战 / *a general's* ~ 战略和战术的较量 / *a soldier's* ~ 勇气和力量的较量 / *do* ~ 作战 / *fall* (或 *be killed*) *in* ~ 阵亡 / *fight one's* ~ *over again* 回忆过去经历过的战役(或斗争) / *give* ~ 挑战 / *give the* ~ 认输 / *go into* ~ 投入战斗 / *half the* ~ 成功一半 / *have* (或 *gain, win*) *the* ~ 战胜 / *join* ~ 参战 / *offer* ~ 挑战 / *refuse* ~ 拒绝应战 ‖'~-*ax(e) n.* ①(中世纪的)战斧 ②[口]悍妇 / ~ *bill* 战斗配置表 / ~ *bowler* [俚]

钢盔 / '~-clad *a.* 全副武装的 / ~ **cruiser** 战
列巡洋舰 / ~ **cry** ①(作战时的) 呐喊 ②战斗口
号 / ~ **disposition** 战斗部署 / ~ **dress** 战地服
装 / '~**field** *n.* 战
场 / '~**front** *n.* 作战正面;前线 / '~**ground**
n. ①战场 ②斗争的舞台 / ~ **group** 战斗群 /
'~-,**ready** *a.* 作好战斗准备的 / ~ **royal** ①混
战,格斗 ②激烈的争论 / '~**ship** *n.* 战列舰 /
~ **sky** 作战空域 / '~,**wag(g)on** *n.* [俚]战列舰

battlement ['bætlmənt] *n.* [常用复]雉堞,城垛;
【建】雉堞墙

bauble ['bɔ:bl] *n.* ① 小玩意,小摆设 ② 华而不实
的东西

baulk [bɔ:k, bɔ:lk] *n., vt. & vi.* =balk

bauxite ['bɔ:ksait] *n.* 【矿】铝土矿,矾土

bawl [bɔ:l] **I** ❶ *vi.* ① 高声叫喊 (*at, against*): ~
at sb. 对某人吆喝 ②[口] 大哭 ❷ *vt.* ① 大声
喊 ② 责骂 **II** *n.* ① 高声叫喊 ②[口]大哭 ‖~
about 叫卖 / ~ *out* ①喊叫 ②[美俚]痛骂

bay[1] [bei] *n.* ①海湾,湾 ②山脉中的凹处 ‖~ **salt**
海盐,粗粒盐 / **Bay Stater** (美国)马萨诸塞州人

bay[2] [bei] **I** *n.* ①(猎犬等的)吠声(尤指追捕猎物
时的连续吠声) ②走投无路的处境,绝境 **II** ❶
vi. (猎犬追猎物时连续地)吠 ❷ *vt.* ①向…
吠叫;吠叫着追赶 ②使陷入绝境,使走投无路 ③
用深沉拖长的声调说出 ‖~ *the moon* (狂犬)
吠月;空嚷,徒劳 / *be* (或 *stand*) *at* ~ 陷入
绝境;作困兽斗 / *bring* (或 *drive*) *to* ~ 使陷入
绝境;迫使…作困兽斗 / *keep* (或 *hold, have*)
at ~ 牵制 / *turn* (或 *come*) *to* ~
陷入绝境;作困兽斗

bay[3] [bei] *n.* ①月桂树 ②[常用复] (古时给诗人,
英雄等的)桂冠; [喻]荣誉 ‖'~,**berry** *n.* ① 月
桂果 ②杨梅属植物 / ~ **rum** 一种香水 / '~**tree**
n. 月桂树

bay[4] [bei] *n.* ①【建】架间,柱、檩、搁栅等之间的部
位;壁洞; ~ **window** 凸窗 ②[军]飞机的机舱;
浮桥桥节 ③(谷仓中)堆放干草(或粮食)处 ④底
板,台,机架,支柱,座

bay[5] [bei] **I** *a.* 栗色的 **II** *n.* 栗色马

bayonet ['beiənit] **I** *n.* (枪上的)刺刀: a ~ assault
(或 charge) 白刃战 / ~ drill (或 practice) 劈刺
训练 / Charge (或 Fix) ~s! 上刺刀! / by ~
(或 the ~) 用武力 / at the point of the ~ 在武
力威逼下 **II** *vt.* 用刺刀刺;用武力(或压力)迫使
(*into*)

bayonet

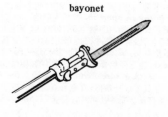

baza(a)r [bə'zɑ:] *n.* ①(东方国家的)市场,集市 ②
(英、美等国的)廉价商店;百货商店 ③义卖市场

be [强 bi:; 弱 bi] *v.* (现在式 am, are, is; 过去式 was,
were; 过去分词 been; 现在分词 being) ❶ *vi.*
①是: Unity *is* power. 团结就是力量. / That
being the case, we have to take new measures.
情况既然是这样,我们必须采取新的措施.
②[表示时间、度、量、价值等]是;值;等于: Today
is Sunday. 今天是星期日. / Two and two *is* (或
are) four. 二加二等于四.
③[常用命令语气或不定式]做,成为: Be thrifty.
要节约.
④在;存在: There *are* four textile mills in the
city. 城里有四家纺织厂.
⑤逗留,(继续)呆: I won't ~ long. 我一会儿就
回来.
⑥到达: Has anyone *been* here? 有人到这儿来
过吗? / The doctor has *been* to see the patient.
医生来(或去)看过病人了.
⑦发生,产生: When will the mass meeting ~?
(或 When is the mass meeting to ~?) 群众大会
什么时候举行?
❷ *v. aux.* ①[与动词的现在分词连用,构成
各种进行时态]: We shall ~ working in the
same workshop soon. 咱们很快就要在同一个车
间干活了.
②[与及物动词的过去分词连用,构成被动语态]:
The letter *was* written yesterday. 这封信是昨
天写的. / Chemical fertilizer *is being* produced
on a large scale. 化肥正在大量生产.
③[与动词不定式连用,表示职责、义务、意图、
约定、可能性等]: *We are* to meet at the school
gate. 我们约定在校门口碰头.
④[与不及物动词 come, go 等的过去分词连用,
构成完成时]: He *is* come. 他已经来了. (=He
has come.)
[注意:下列各句中 be 和 were 表示虚拟语气:
If I *were* you, ... 假如我是你的话,…
‖*Be it so*! 就这样吧! / ~ *it that* . . . 即使… /
~ *it true or not* 不管是否如此 / ~ *that as it
may* 即使如此,尽管这样 / *have been* (and
gone) *and done it* 干下了蠢事 / *Let him* ~.
[口]随他去.(或:由他去.) / *the . . . to* ~ 未来
的…: the team-leader *to* ~ 未来的队长
‖'~-**all** *n.* 全部: the ~-*all* and the end-all 最
高目标(或理想);主要成分(或因素);全部内容

beach [bi:tʃ] **I** *n.* 海滩;湖滩;河滩 **II** *vt.* 使(船)
冲上岸滩 ‖*on the* ~ 失业的;贫穷潦倒的 ‖'~-**y**
a. 岸边浅滩的;近岸的 ‖'~-,**comber** *n.* ①(冲
打海滩的)巨浪 ② 流浪者(尤指流浪在南太平洋
海滩、码头的白人) / '~**head** *n.* 滩头堡,登陆
场 / ~-**la-mar** ['bi:tʃlə'mɑ:] *n.* 西太平洋岛屿上
流行的一种混杂着土语的英语 / '~,**master** *n.*
【军】海滩勤务队队长 / '~-,**rescue** *n.* 海滨浴场
救生员

beacon ['bi:kən] **I** *n.* ①灯塔;信标(指示或引导飞

机或舰船航行方向的火光、灯塔或无线电发射机等); 指向标: a responder ~ 响应器信标 / a light 信标灯; 信标灯光 / an air ~ 航空信标 / a runway localizing ~ 跑道定位信标 ②(旧时作信号用的)烽火, 篝火 ③[英](标示行人可以穿越马路之处的)指路灯 ④[美]定向无线电波 **II** ❶ *vt.* 照亮; 为…设置信标; 信标导航 ❷ *vi.* 象灯塔般照耀

bead [bi:d] **I** *n.* ①(装饰用)有孔小珠; 念珠: tell one's ~s (数念珠)祷告 ②水珠; 空泡: ~s of sweat 汗珠 ③枪的准星: draw a ~ on 向…瞄准 ④[建]凸圆线脚, 串珠线脚 ⑤[机]卷边; 车轮圆缘 **II** ❶ *vt.* 用珠装饰; 把…象串珠子一样连起来 ❷ *vi.* 形成珠; 起泡 ‖**~ing** *n.* ①串珠状雕饰 ②玻璃熔接 ③起泡; [总称](啤酒等的)泡沫 / **~y** *a.* ①珠子般的; (眼睛)小而亮的 ②饰以珠子(或珠状物)的 ③有泡沫的, 多泡沫的 ‖**~roll** *n.* ①名单, 名册; 目录 ②一串念珠

beadle [bi:dl] *n.* ①(英国旧时教区的)牧师助理 ②(英国大学举行典礼时的)执礼杖者 ③(法院等处的)差役 ④小官吏 ‖**~dom** *n.* (小官吏式的)洋洋自得; 鼍掌; 小官僚习气

beak [bi:k] *n.* ①(猛禽、龟鱼等的)嘴 ②(茶壶等器皿的)鸟嘴形口子; (古代战舰的)鸟嘴形船头 ③钩形鼻 ④[建]鸟嘴形 ⑤[英俚]治安官; 法官; 教师 ‖**~ed** *a.* 有钩形嘴的; 钩形的

beaker ['bi:kə] *n.* ①大酒杯; 一大酒杯的量 ②(实验室、药房等处用的)烧杯

beam [bi:m] **I** *n.* ①梁, 桁条 ②[船]横梁; (舰船船身等的)最大宽度 ③(秤)杆; (犁)柄; 卷轴; 横杆; 杠杆 ④(鹿角的)主干 ⑤(灯光, 日光、月光等的)束, 道, 柱: a ~ of light 一道光 / a ~ of hope 一线希望 ⑥[喻]笑容, 喜色 ⑦[无]射线, 射束; 电子注; 波束; (扩音器的)最大有效范围: ~ system 定向制 / ~ antenna 定向天线 / ~ rider (missile) 驾束(导弹) **II** ❶ *vi.* ①发光; 发热 ②[喻]微笑: ~ with satisfaction 满意地微笑 / He ~ed on his friends. 他对着他的朋友们微笑。 ❷ *vt.* ①为…上梁, 上梁于 ②发射(光、热、无线电信号等) ③定向发出(无线电信号、广播节目等): This programme is ~ed to Australia and New Zealand at 12:00 daily 这节目每天十二点钟向澳大利亚和新西兰播送。 ④(用波束)导航(飞机等) ⑤[用雷达]探测(飞机、船只等) ‖*a ~ in sb.'s eye* 某人本身的大缺点 / *~ sea* 横浪 / *fly the ~* 按照无线电射束飞行 / *kick the ~* 过轻; 不足抗衡, 输 / *off the ~* ①未按无线电射束飞行, 脱离航向 ②[俚]不对头, 做错 / *on the ~* ①[船]正横地; 与龙骨垂直地 ②航向正确 ③[俚]对头, 做对 / *on the starboard (port)* ~ 在右(左)舷 / *ride the ~* =fly the ~ ‖ **compass** 长臂圆规

bean [bi:n] **I** *n.* ①豆; 蚕豆 (=broad ~); 菜豆属植物, 豆科植物 ②豆形果实(如咖啡豆); 结豆形果实的植物 ③无价值的东西; [复]少量: I haven't heard ~s about the matter. 关于这件事我一点儿也没听说过。 ④[俚]硬币 ⑤[美俚]

头, 脑袋 **II** *vt.* [美俚]打…的头部 ‖*Every ~ has its black.* [谚]凡人各有其短处。 / *full of ~s* ①精神旺盛, 兴高采烈 ②弄错的 / *give sb. ~s* [俚]惩罚(或责骂)某人 / *haven't a ~* 身无分文 / *know how many ~s make five* 精明, 不易上当 / *old ~* [俚](熟人间的称呼)老兄 / *spill the ~s* [美俚]说漏嘴, 不慎泄密 ‖**~ery** *n.* 廉价小饭馆 / **~ie, ~y** *n.* (学生戴在头顶的)小帽 ‖**'~ball** *n.* [美俚]擦过(或打中)棒球击球员头部的猛球 / **~ cake** 豆饼: ~ *cake fertilizer* 饼肥 / **~ curd** 豆腐 / **'~feast** *n.* [英俚]①每年一次雇主"请"雇工的宴会 ②闹宴, 狂欢 / **'~pod** *n.* 豆荚 / **~ pole** ①豆架 ②[美俚]瘦长个子 / **'~stalk** *n.* 豆茎

bear[1] [beə] (过去式 bore [bɔ:], 过去分词 borne 或 born [bɔ:n]) ❶ *vt.* ①负担, 负荷; 承担: ~ a heavy burden 负重荷 / ~ the responsibility of 担负着…的责任 / ~ expenses 负担费用 ②佩, 带; 带有, 具有: ~ a badge 佩戴徽章 / ~ arms 带着武器 / ~ scars 带有伤疤 / ~ a message 带(口)信 ③忍受, 容忍: ~ pain 忍受痛苦 / He is always the first to ~ hardships. 他总是吃苦在别人前头。 / cannot ~ for sb. to do sth. 不能容忍某人做某事 / 承受; 经得起, 耐(得住): The thin ice cannot ~ truckloads. 薄冰承受不了卡车重量。 / ~ing capacity 承载力 / Polyester ~s washing. 涤纶耐洗。 ⑤生育, 养(孩子); 结(果实); 产生: She has borne two children. 她已生了两个孩子。 ⑥怀有, 抱有, 心怀(感情、爱憎等): ~ in mind that … 把…牢记于心 / ~ oneself 举止; 表现: ~ oneself well 举止大方 ⑦推动; 挤压 ⑧提供: ~ witness 作证 ❷ *vi.* ①忍受, 忍耐; 承受: Will the wooden bridge ~? 木桥能经得住吗? ②结果实: The peach trees ~ well. 桃树结果很多。 ③开动, 运动; 指向; 转向: The ship bore south. 船向南开。 / ~ left 朝左边转 ‖*~ a hand* 见 hand / *~ and forbear* 一忍再忍 / *~ a part in* 见 part / *~ away* ①夺得, 夺取; 赢得(奖品、战利品等) ②(船只)改变航道, 避开逆风 / *~ down* 压倒, 击败 / *~ down on* 冲向, 袭击; 【海】(船)迎向, 逼近(上风来船): ~ in with 驶向, 驶近 / *~ off* ①赢得 ②使离开; 驶离 / ~ on (或 upon) ①卡(人), 对…施加压力 ②有关, 对…有影响: What he has said ~s on an important problem. 他讲的话同一个重要问题有关。 ③对准, 瞄准 / *~ out* 证实, 证明 / *~ up* ①支持, 拥护 ②不失望, 不气馁 ③驶向下风 / *~ up for* (向下风)驶向 / *~ with* 宽容; 耐心等待; 忍受 / *be borne in upon sb.* 被某人确信

bear[2] [beə] **I** *n.* ①熊 ②粗鲁的人; 笨拙的人 ③【机】打孔器; 小型冲机 ④卖空的证券交易投机商(俗称空头) **II** *vt.* 使跌价 ‖*be a ~ for punishment* 能忍受粗暴待遇的; 顽强的, 倔强的 / *like a ~ with a sore head* 脾气暴躁 / *loaded for ~* ①具备成功条件; 有充分准备 ②[美俚]发怒; 准备打架; 准备毁坏对方名誉 / *Sell the ~'s* *skin before one has caught the ~.* [谚]熊未到手先卖皮。(或: 过早乐观。) / *the Great (Little) Bear* 【天】大(小)熊座 ‖**~ cat** ①力大勇猛的汉子 ②熊猫 / '**~,garden** *n.* 嘈杂的场所;喧闹的景象 / **~ leader** 陪伴少年旅行的私人教师 / '**~-pit** *n.* (动物园)展出熊的凹坑 / '**~'s-breech** *n.* 老鼠簕属植物 / '**~'s-foot** *n.* 舟形乌头;斗篷草 / '**~skin** *n.* 熊皮;熊皮制品;像熊皮般的毛织品

beard [biəd] **I** *n.* ①(下巴上的)胡须;络腮胡子: grow (或 cultivate) a ~ 蓄须 ②(动物的)颌毛 ③(植物的)芒,髯毛 ④(牡蛎的)鳃 ⑤倒刺,钩刺 ⑥[美俚]广播中的读错字 ⑦先锋派人物;颓废派人物 **II** *vt.* ①使长胡须;使长颌毛(或芒刺) ②抓住…的胡须;[喻]公然反对,公然蔑视 ‖**~ the lion in his den** 太岁头上动土 / *in spite of sb.'s* 公然反对某人,故意蔑视某人 / *laugh in one's* 偷偷嘲笑 / *singe sb.'s* 侮辱某人 / *speak in one's* 咕噜着含糊地说 / *to sb.'s* 当着某人的面 ‖**~ed** *a.* ①有胡须的: a heavily ~ed man 胡须很长的人 ②有颌毛的;有芒刺的 / **~less** *a.* ①无胡须的;年轻无知的 ②无颌毛的;无芒刺的

bearer ['bɛərə] *n.* ①负荷者;运载工具: a litter (或 stretcher) ~ 担架兵 / an ammunition ~ 弹药兵 / a ~ company 担架连 ②带信人,持信人;持票(指支票、票据等)人 ③结果实的植物: a good (poor) ~ 高产(低产)的植物 ④抬棺人;抬轿人 ⑤[机]托架;支座

bearing ['bɛəriŋ] *n.* ①支承;【机】轴承: miniature ~ 微型轴承 / ball ~ 滚珠轴承 ②忍耐,忍受: beyond (all) ~ 忍无可忍 ③关系,联系;方面 ④[常用复]方位,方向: lose one's ~s 迷失方向;不知所措 / the correct ~s for advance 前进的正确方向 / a target ~ 【军】目标方位 ⑤生育;结果实: an apple tree coming into ~ 即将结果的苹果树 ⑥举止,姿态

bearish ['bɛəriʃ] *a.* ①像熊一样的;粗鲁的;笨拙的 ②(在证券交易等方面)引起跌风的 ‖**~ly** *ad.* 粗鲁地;笨拙地 / **~ness** *n.* 粗鲁;笨拙

beast [bi:st] *n.* ①(四足)兽: wild ~s 野兽 / a ~ of prey 食肉兽,猛兽 ②牲畜;[英]菜牛: a ~ of burden 驮畜 / man and ~ 人畜 ③[喻]凶残的人;举止粗鲁的人 ④[the ~] 兽性 ⑤[the B-]【基督教】反对基督的人

beastly ['bi:stli] **I** *a.* ①野兽(般)的 ②残忍的;卑鄙下流的 ③[口]令人厌恶的,糟透的: ~ weather 恶劣的天气 **II** *ad.* [英俚]非常;极糟地: It's ~ bad. 糟透了! ‖**beastliness** *n.* ①兽性;残暴;淫猥;粗鲁 ②贪食;酩酊大醉

beat [bi:t] **I** (beat, beaten ['bi:tn]) ❶ *vt.* ①(接连地)打,敲;冲击: ~ waist drums 打腰鼓 / Waves ~ the shore. 波浪冲击岸边。②打败,战胜;超越: ~ (a) drought 战胜旱灾 / the world record in the high jump 打破跳高世界纪录 ③踏出,走出(道路);挤进,挤出: ~ a new path 开辟新道路(或途径) / ~ one's way through the

crowd 挤入人群 ④ 在…里搜索: ~ the woods *for* medicinal herbs 在树林里搜寻草药 ⑤锤薄,敲平: ~ *out* metal with a hammer 用锤头把金属锤薄(或锤平) ⑥打,搅拌(蛋、奶油、面粉等)使起泡(成糊) ⑦振(翼),扑打(翅膀) ⑧[音]打(拍子) ⑨[口]使迷惑,使感困难;使吃惊: Your question has *beaten* me. 你的问题把我难住了。⑩[口]欺骗 ❷ *vi.* ①(接连地)打,敲;(日)晒,(雨)打;(风)吹打: ~ *at* (或 *upon*) the door 大声敲门 / We kept working as the hot sun was ~*ing* down on us. 烈日直晒在我们身上,我们照样继续干活。/ The rain was ~*ing against* (或 *on*) the window. 雨打在窗户上。②(心脏等)跳动 ③在树林(或灌木等)中搜索 ④(蛋、奶油等)打出泡沫: These eggs ~ well. 这些蛋能打出很多泡沫。⑤[口]获胜,赢 ⑥[海](帆船)逆风换抢驶行 **II** *n.* ①(接连的)敲打;敲击声: ~s of a drum 击鼓声 ②(心脏等)跳动(声): normal heart ~s 正常的心脏跳动(声) ③节拍,拍子;(用手、指挥棒)打拍子 ④常走的道路;经常巡逻的路线: a patrol's ~ 巡逻兵的巡逻路线 ⑤抢先发表新闻 ⑥[俚]欺骗 ⑦ =beatnik **III** *a.* ①[俚]疲劳的: be quite (或 dead) ~ 筋疲力尽的 ②颓废的;属于"垮了的一代"(或类似其思想、行动)的 ‖**~ about** 搜索 / **~ around** (或 [美] *around*) *the bush* 见 **bush** / **~ a retreat** 见 **retreat** / **~ away** 打掉,打走 / [矿]用楔锤破地 / **~ down** ①打倒,推翻;镇压 ②[口]杀(价);杀(某人)的价 / **~ it** [美俚]走,滚 / **~ off** 击退,打退(进攻) / **~ one's brains** 见 **brain** / **~ out** ①锤薄,敲平(金属等) ②弄清(真相),搞懂(内容等) / **~ up** ①(帆船)迎风换抢 ②热切地到处寻找 ③惊扰 ④召集,集拢 ⑤搅(蛋等) ⑥[俚]痛殴,毒打 / **~ up and down** 来回奔走 / (be) *off* (或 *out of*) *one's* ~ 做自己不熟悉的事;超出自己熟悉的领域(或范围) / *off the* ~ 不合拍子 / *on the* ~ 合拍子 / ~ *generation* (美国)"垮了的一代"(二十世纪五十年代末出现于美国知识阶层中的一个颓废流派;以蓄长发、穿奇装异服、吸毒、反对世俗陈规、排斥温情、强调"个性自我表达"等为特征) / '~-'up *a.* 年久失修的,残破的;褴褛的

beaten ['bi:tn] **I** beat 的过去分词 **II** *a.* ①(接连地)被打击的;被鞭挞的;被击败的: a ~ zone 【军】被弹区,落弹地带 ②锤薄的,敲平的: silver (gold) ~ 银(金)箔 ③踏平的,走出来的;[喻]陈旧的: go off the ~ track 打破常规 ④筋疲力尽的;精神沮丧的 ‖'~-up *a.* 破旧的: a ~-up car 一辆破旧的车

beater ['bi:tə] *n.* ①打击者 ②拍打器;搅拌器;(造纸等用的)打浆机,浆缸 ③(帮助赶出禽兽的)猎人助手 ④[纺]打手,翼板

beating ['bi:tiŋ] *n.* ①打,敲;鞭打;搅拌 ②(心脏等)跳动 ③失败,溃败 ④(造纸工艺中的)打浆 ⑤(鸟的)鼓翼 ‖**take a ~** 挨打;受到打击,受到谴责

beatnik ['bi:tnik] *n.* (美国)"垮了的一代"派成员 (参见 **beat** 条下的 **beat generation**)

beau [bou] ([复] beaus 或 beaux [bouz]) *n.* ①花花公子 ②(女子的)情人; 向女子献殷勤的男人

beautiful ['bju:təful] *a.* ① 美的, 美好的, 优美的: ~ flowers 美丽的花朵 / ~ weather 美好的天气 / the true, the good, and the ~ 真善美 ② [口]极好的, 绝妙的 ‖~**ly** *ad.* / ~**ness** *n.*

beautify ['bju:tifai] ❶ *vt.* 使美丽, 美化; 装饰 ❷ *vi.* 变美 ‖**beautification** [,bju:tifi'keiʃən] *n.* 美化; 装饰 / **beautifier** *n.* 美化者; 装饰者

beauty ['bju:ti] *n.* ① 美, 美丽 ② 美人; 美的东西; 美好的事物 ③ 妙处, 美点: That's the ~ of it. 妙就妙在这一点上。‖*Beauty is but skin deep.* [谚]美丽只是外表罢了。(指不能以貌取人) ‖~ **culture** 美容业; 美容术 / ~ **parlo(u)r**, ~ **shop** 美容院 / ~ **sleep** [口]午夜前的酣睡 / ~ **spot** ①痣; 小疵瑕 ②妇女搽饰在脸部等处的黑斑 ③ 风景区

beaver¹ ['bi:və] *n.* ①【动】河狸(旧译作海狸, 现仍沿用); 象河狸的某些啮齿兽 ②河狸的毛皮; 用海狸皮做的帽子 ③【纺】海狸呢, 水獭呢; 海狸绒布(双层双面) (= ~ cloth) ④[美俚](下巴上的)大把胡须; 蓄胡须的人 ⑤工作勤奋而认真的人 ‖~ **board** 一种人造纤维板

beaver² ['bi:və] *n.* 头盔的下半部护面具

becalm [bi'ka:m] *vt.* ①使平静(或安静) ②[常用被动语态]因无风而使(帆船)停止不动

became [bi'keim] become 的过去式

because [bi'kɔz, bə'kɔz, bikəz] Ⅰ *conj.* 因为: A: Why didn't you phone me last night? B: *Because* (或 It is ~) I didn't want to disturb you. 甲: 你昨晚为什么不打电话给我? 乙: 因为我不想打扰你。/ Don't scamp your work ~ you are pressed for time. 不要因为时间仓促而马马虎虎。[注意: 与 for 相比, because 引起的从句表示的是更直接而不是推断的原因, 语气更强, 有时且可置于主句之前。试比较下列两句: *Because* he is ill, he is absent today. 因为他病了, 所以他今天缺席。/ He must be ill, *for* he is absent today. 他今天缺席, 看来一定是生病了。] Ⅱ *ad.* 因为 (of): The football match was cancelled ~ of rain. 因为下雨足球赛取消了。

beckon ['bekən] Ⅰ ❶ *vt.* (用点头、招手等方式)召唤: He ~ed me in. 他招手(或点头)要我进去。❷ *vi.* 表示召唤: He ~ed to me to come nearer. 他示意要我走近些。Ⅱ *n.* 召唤的表示

become [bi'kʌm] (became [bi'keim], become) ❶ *vi.* 成为; 变得: This unit has ~ more advanced than before. 这个单位比过去更为先进了。❷ *vt.* 适合; 同⋯相称: This coat ~s him very well. 这件上衣他穿着很合适。‖*What has* (或 *will*) ~ *of sb.* (*sth.*)? 某人(某事物)情况怎样?

becoming [bi'kʌmiŋ] Ⅰ *a.* 合适的, 相称的: a ~ cap 一顶合适的帽子 Ⅱ *n.* 【哲】【心】 (变化过程的)形成, 发生 ‖~**ly** *ad.* / ~**ness** *n.*

bed [bed] Ⅰ *n.* ①床; 床铺, 垫褥; 床位: a single (double) ~ 单人(双人)床 / twin ~s 两只一式的单人床 / a straw ~ 草垫 / a 200-~ hospital 有两百几床位的医院 / be confined to one's ~ 卧病在床 ②底座; 【建】底盘; 路基, 地基: ~ of concrete 混凝土底座 / railroad ~ 铁路路基 ③ (河)床, (湖、海的)底; 矿床 ④一层; 一堆(常指树叶、木屑等); 【地】层, 底: ~ vein 层状脉 ⑤(苗)床, 圃; (花)坛: seed ~ preparation 苗床整地 ⑥坟墓 Ⅱ (bedded; bedding) ❶ *vt.* ①使睡; [美]供⋯住宿 ②栽, 种: ~ (out) the rice seedlings 插稻秧 ③安装, 固定: Bricks are *bedded in* cement. 用水泥砌牢砖头。④把⋯分层; 铺平; 给(牲畜)铺草: *bedded* ore 层状矿 / ~ down an ox 给牛铺草 ❷ *vi.* ①上床; 铺床睡下 (down) ②分层 ‖a ~ of down (或 roses, flowers) 称心如意的境遇; 安乐窝 / a ~ of hono(u)r 阵亡将士的墓 / be brought to ~ 临产: be brought to ~ of a boy 生了一个男孩子 / ~ and board ①膳宿 ②夫妇关系 ③[美]家 / die in (one's) ~ 因病(或因年老)而死去 / get out of ~ on the wrong side 见 side / go to ~ ① 上床, 去睡 ②[俚]住嘴 / go to ~ in one's boots 酩酊大醉 / keep the ~ (因病)卧床 / lie in (或 on) the ~ one has made 自作自受 / lie on a ~ of thorns 如坐针毡, 坐立不安 / make the ~(s) 铺床(准备睡) / put to ~ ①使(孩子等)上床去睡 ②[美]把(铅字等)排好放到印刷机上 ③[美俚]编辑(报纸等)直到可以付印 / put to ~ with a shovel ①把⋯葬入坟墓 ②[美俚]把(喝醉的)扶上床 / take to one's ~ (生病)上床 / the narrow ~ 墓 ‖'~**bug** *n.* 臭虫 / '~,**chamber** *n.* [古]卧室; 英国王室的寝室 / '~**clothes** [复] *n.* 床上用品(指被、褥等) / '~,**cover** *n.* 床罩 / '~**fast** *a.* (年老、病弱)卧床不起的 / '~,**fellow** *n.* ①同床者 ②[喻]伙伴, 同伙; 同事; 同盟者: Misery acquaints men with strange ~*fellows.* [谚]落难时不择伙伴。/ '~**gown** *n.* (妇女的)睡衣 / '~**key** *n.* 装(或拆)床架用的扳钳 / '~-**lift** *n.* 床靠(使伤、病员能坐起的病床活动装置) / '~,**maker** *n.* [英] ①[古]做床的工匠 ②(牛津与剑桥大学中)打扫宿舍的人 / '~**pan** *n.* (尤指病人在床上用的)便盆 / '~,**piece**, '~**plate** *n.* (安置机器或火炉的)底板, 座板 / '~**post** *n.* 床架杆: in the twinkling of a ~*post* 尽快地, 立即 / between you and me and the ~*post* 私下地, 秘密地 / '~**rock** *n.* ①基岩 ②(作为理论等根据的)基本事实(或原则) ③ 最低点, 最少量 / '~**roll** *n.* 铺盖 / '~**room** *n.* 卧室。~ **room** 供白天在附近大城市工作的人们居住的: ~*room* suburbs 城郊宿舍区 ②卧室的 / '~**side** *n.* 床边(尤指病床边) *a.* 床边(用)的; 护理的: a good ~*side* manner (尤指医生)对病人关心体贴的态度 / '~,**sitter** *n.* [口]卧室兼起居室 / '~-'**sitting-room** *n.* [英]卧室兼起居室 / '~**sore** *n.* 【医】褥疮 / '~**spread** *n.* 床罩 / '~**stead** *n.* 床架 / '~**straw** *n.* 【植】猪殃

袂; 砧草(可作草垫): lady's ~*straw* 莲子菜 / '~**tick** *n*. (垫)褥套 / '~**time** *n*. 就寝时间: a ~*time* story 给孩子上床时讲的故事; [喻] 动听但不可信的解释 / '~-**wetting** *n*. 溺褥

bedding ['bediŋ] *n*. ①被褥; 床上用品: protective ~【军】防毒被单 ②(家畜的)垫草 ③基础, 底层 ④【建】基坑 ⑤【地】层理

bedlam ['bedləm] *n*. ①精神病院, 疯人院 ②喧闹, 喧闹声 ‖~**ite** *n*. 精神病病人; 疯子, 狂人

bedraggle [bi'drægl] *vt*. (在泥水中)拖湿, 拖脏(衣服等)

bee [bi:] *n*. ①蜂; 蜜蜂 ~ 蜂王 / a working (或 worker) ~ 工蜂 / keep ~*s* 养蜂 ②忙碌的人 ③诗人 ④(邻居、朋友等为娱乐或一起工作而举行的)聚会: a sewing ~ 缝纫会 (指妇女们聚在一起做针线活) / a spelling ~ (小学生的)拼音比赛会 ⑤奇思怪想, 怪念头 ‖*as busy as a ~* 极忙碌 / *have a ~ in one's bonnet* (或 *head*) ①想得入了迷; 苦思 ②胡思乱想; 神经有点失常 / *put the ~ on* [美俚]向…借钱; 从…弄到钱 ‖'~**bread** *n*. 蜜蜂的食料 / **eater** 蜂虎 (一种食蜂的鸟) / '~**hive** *n*. ①蜂房, 蜂箱 ②[口]熙熙攘攘的地方 / '~**house** *n*. 养蜂场 / '~**keeper** *n*. 养蜂人 / '~**line** *n*. (两点之间的)直线; (两地之间的)直路: make a ~*line* for a place 径直朝某地而去

beech [bi:tʃ] *n*. 【植】山毛榉 ‖~**en** *a*. ‖'~**mast**, '~**nut** *n*. 山毛榉坚果

beef [bi:f] I ([复] beeves [bi:vz] 或 beefs) *n*. ①牛肉: ~ broth 牛肉汤 / ~ extract 牛肉汁 ②[常用复]菜牛 ③(男子的)肌肉; 体力; 力量: Put your ~ into it! 使劲儿干! ④([复] beefs) [美俚]抱怨, 牢骚; 吵架 II ❶ *vt*. [美俚]加强, 充实(*up*): ~ *up* military forces 加强军事力量 ❷ *vi*. [美俚] ①抱怨, 找岔子 ②告发, 密告 ③争吵 ‖~ **cattle** [总称]菜牛 / '~**eater** *n*. ①吃牛肉的人 ②身体强壮的人, 大力士 ③英王卫士 ④伦敦塔的守卫人 ⑤[美俚]英国人 / '~-'**squad** *n*. [美俚]大力士打手队 / '~'**steak** *n*. 牛排 / '~**tea** 牛肉茶, 牛肉汁 / '~-'**witted** *a*. 愚笨的

been [bi:n, bin] be 的过去分词

beer [biə] *n*. ①啤酒: ~ on draught (或 draught ~) 生啤酒 / dark ~ 黑啤酒 ②由植物根酿造的饮料 (或淡酒) ‖~ *and skittles* 吃喝玩乐 / *small* ~ ①淡啤酒 ②[总称]琐细的事情, 微不足道的东西: chronicle *small* ~ 记载无足轻重的事 / *think no small* ~ *of oneself* 自命不凡 ‖~ **belly** 大肚子; 大腹便便的人 / '~**house** *n*. [英]啤酒店 / '~-**money** *n*. 酒钱, 小帐

beet [bi:t] *n*. 【植】①恭菜, 甜菜, 糖萝卜 ②[美] =~**root** ‖'~**root** *n*. 甜菜根

beetle[1] ['bi:tl] I *n*. ①甲虫 ②近视眼的人 II *vi*. (甲虫般地)急促来回; 乱撞; 瞎撞 ‖~ *off* [英俚]离开 / *blind as a* ~ 十分近视 ‖'~-**crusher** *n*. 大靴子; 大脚

beetle[2] ['bi:tl] I *n*. 槌, 木夯; 杵; 捶布机 II *vt*. 用大槌捶打; 用杵捣; 捶(布) ‖*between the* ~ *and*

the block 上下交迫; 陷于困境; 岌岌可危 ‖'~-**brain** *n*. 傻瓜 / '~-'**headed** *a*. 呆头呆脑的

beetle[3] ['bi:tl] I *vi*. 突出; 凸出; 伸出: *beetling* cliffs 悬崖 II *a*. 突出的; 外伸的 ‖~-**browed** *a*. ①眉毛浓而突出的 ②皱眉头的: 怒目而视的

befall [bi'fɔ:l] (befell [bi'fel], befallen [bi'fɔ:lən]) ❶ *vt*. 临到…; 发生于: What *befell* them? 他们出了什么事? ❷ *vi*. 降临, 发生: A misfortune has ~**en**. 发生了一件不幸的事.

before [bi'fɔ:] I *prep*. ①[表示时间] 在…以前: the day ~ yesterday 前天 / the year ~ last 前年 / We'll see that film ~ long. 我们不久将要看看那部电影了. ②[表示位置] 在…前面; 当着…的面; ~ one's eyes 就在眼前 / one's mind 在脑子里 (或心目中) / Harder tasks are ~ us. 我们面前还有更艰巨的任务. / put a proposal ~ the meeting 向会议提出建议 / appear ~ the court 到法庭 ③[表示次序] 在…之前, 先于: Those with babies got into the tram ~ (the) others. 带小孩的人比别人先上电车. ④与其… II *ad*. ①[表示时间]以前: We've seen that film *long* ~. 我们早就看过那部电影了. / Education has been popularized as never ~. 教育空前普及. ②[表示位置, 方向]在前面; 向前: look ~ and after 瞻前顾后 III *conj*. ①[表示时间]在…前: Be a pupil ~ you become a teacher. 先做学生, 再做先生. / I'll do it now ~ I forget it. 我趁着还没有忘记的时候就做吧. / We had scarcely left our school ~ it began to rain. 我们刚离开学校, 天就下雨了. ②与其…(宁愿…) ‖~ *Christ* 公元前(略作 B.C.) / (*sail*) ~ *the mast* 见 **mast**[1] / *sail* ~ *the wind* 见 **wind**[1] ‖**be'fore-,mentioned** *a*. 上述的

beforehand [bi'fɔ:hænd] *ad*. ①预先, 事先: prepared (或 ready) ~ 事先准备好 / be ~ *with* one's packing 预先打行李 ②提前地; 超前地: be ~ *with* one's payment (准备) 提前付款 ‖*be* ~ *with the world* 见 **world**

befriend [bi'frend] *vt*. 以朋友态度对待, 亲近; 帮助

beg [beg] (begged; begging) ❶ *vt*. ①乞讨, 乞求: ~ one's bread 乞食, 乞饭 ②请求, 恳求: ~ a favour *of* sb. 请某人帮个忙 / ~ sb. to do sth. 请求某人做某事 / He *begged* a week off. 他请了一星期的假. ③(用于正式的、有礼貌的场合)请(原谅); 请(允许): ~ leave to ... 请允许… ❷ *vi*. ①乞求 (*for*) ②请求, 恳求: I ~ to disagree. 对不起, 我不同意. / I ~ to inform you that .... (旧式商业书信用语) 谨通知您… / ~ *of* sb. to do sth. 请求某人做某事 ③乞讨; 靠乞讨生活 ‖~ *off* 请求免除(责任、罚责等): He promised to come and help but has since *begged off*. 他答应来帮忙的, 但后来请求原谅不能来. / ~ *sb. off* 替某人请求原谅, 为某人说情; 辞退某人 / ~ *the question* 见 **question** / *go begging* ①去乞讨 ②(商品等)销路极坏,

没人要 / I ~ your pardon. (或 Beg your pardon.) 见 **pardon**

began [bi'gæn] begin 的过去式

beget [bi'get] (过去式 begot [bi'gɔt], 过去分词 begotten [bi'gɔtn] 或 begot; 现在分词 begetting) *vt.* ① (指父亲)生(子女) ② 产生,引起,招致

beggar ['begə] I *n.* ① 乞丐;穷人 ②募捐者 ③[口]家伙: What a fine little ~! 多可爱的小家伙! II *vt.* ① 使沦为乞丐; 使贫穷 ②使成为无用; 难以作…: The beautiful scene ~s description. 这个美景难以用笔墨形容。‖*Beggars must not* (或 *cannot*) *be choosers.* [谚] 要饭的那能挑肥拣瘦。(或:饥不择食。) / *Let us match with ~s.* [谚]龙配龙,凤配凤。/ *Set a ~ on horseback and he'll ride to the devil.* [谚]叫化子发财忘乎所以。

begin [bi'gin] (began [bi'gæn], begun [bi'gʌn]; beginning) ❶ *vi.* 开始: ~ on (或 upon) a technical innovation 着手搞一项技术革新 / ~ at page 4 从第四页开始 / The match will ~ at nine o'clock. 比赛将在九点钟开始。 ❷ *vt.* ①开始,着手: I *began* English last year. 我去年开始学英语。/ ~ a new book 开始读(或写)一本新书 / ~ building (或 to build) a dam 着手建造堤坝 / We shall ~ the meeting at eight o'clock. 我们将在八点钟开会。②创建 ‖~ *the world* 见 **world** / *not* ~ *to* … [口]毫不…: They *don't* ~ *to* compare. 它们根本不能比。/ *to* ~ *with* 首先,第一: *To* ~ *with, we* must consider the problem all-sidedly. 首先,我们必须全面地考虑这个问题。/ *Well begun is half done.* [谚]开头有好的等于一半成功。

beginner [bi'ginə] *n.* ①初学者,生手 ②创始人

beginning [bi'giniŋ] *n.* ①开始,开端: at the ~ of the month (在)月初 / He has made a good ~. 他做出了一个良好的开端。② 起源: have its ~(s) in … 起源于… ③(书等的)开头部分 ④[常用复]早期阶段 ‖*from ~ to end* 从头到尾,自始至终 / *the ~ of the end* 预示结果的先兆

begone [bi'gɔn] *vi.* [常用于命令句] 去: *Begone*! 去! 滚! / order sb. to ~ 勒令某人走开

begotten [bi'gɔtn] beget 的过去分词

begrudge [bi'grʌdʒ] *vt.* ① 为(某事)发牢骚,对(某事)抱怨 ② 妒忌: ~ others their achievements (或 the achievements of others) 妒忌别人的成就 ③ 勉强给,吝惜: They never ~d (us) what we needed. 我们需要的东西,他们总是毫不吝惜地给我们。‖**begrudgingly** *ad.* 不乐意地,勉强地

beguile [bi'gail] *vt.* ① 欺骗,欺诈: ~ sb. of (或 out of) sth. 诈骗某人的某物 / ~ sb. into doing sth. 诱骗某人干某事 ② 消磨(时间等) ③ 使高兴,娱(人): ~ the children with games 做游戏以哄孩子 ‖~**ment** *n.*

behalf [bi'hɑ:f] *n.* [用于 on ~ of, in ~ of 等习语中]利益,方面,支持 ‖*in* ~ *of* [现罕用]为…的利益 / *on* ~ *of* 代表…;为了…: *on sb.'s* ~ 代表某人;为了某人: Don't trouble to do it *on my* ~. 不要为了我去麻烦了。

behave [bi'heiv] ❶ *vi.* ① 举动,举止;表现: ~ well (badly) 行为好(坏) ② 开动,运转: How is the new engine *behaving*? 新发动机运转得怎样? ③ 举止端正,循规蹈矩: Do ~! 规矩点!(对孩子等的用语) ❷ *vt.* [~ oneself] ①使举动好,使举止规矩: *Behave yourself*! 规矩点!(对孩子等的用语) ②使运转正常

behavio(u)r [bi'heivjə] *n.* ① 举止,行为;(待人的)态度 ②机器(或物质等)发生作用的情况: the ~ of tin under heat 锡在受热情况下发生的变化 ‖*be on one's good* (或 *best*) ~ 举动规矩,行为检点 / *put sb. on his best* ~ 规劝(或警告)某人要规规矩矩 ‖~**al** [bi'heivjərəl] *a.* 关于行为的

behead [bi'hed] *vt.* 砍…的头,斩…的首: ~ a tree 截去树木的顶端 / ~ed river【地】夺流河,被夺河

beheld [bi'held] behold 的过去式和过去分词

behest [bi'hest] *n.* [书面语] ① 命令;训诲 ② 紧急指示

behind [bi'haind] I *prep.* ① 在…后面,在…背后: leave sth. ~ one (离开后)遗落某物; (死后)遗留某物 ② 落后于; 不如: ~ the times 落后于时代; 不合时宜 ③ 迟: The train was not ~ (its) time. 火车没有误点。④ 作…的后盾,支持 II *ad.* ① 在后,向后: stay (或 remain) ~ (别人走后)留下来 / help those who lag (或 fall) ~ 帮助落后的人们 / He is never ~ *with* (或 *in*) his work. 他工作从不拖拉。② 在背后(幕后): There is more ~. 背后(或其中)还有文章。③迟,过期: My watch runs ~. 我的表慢了。/ be ~ *in* one's payment 逾期付款 III *n.* [口]屁股 ‖*put* ~ *one* 拒绝考虑(某事) ‖**be'hindhand** *a.* [常作表语] & *ad.* ① 在后(的);落后(的) ② 迟(的),慢(的);过期(的) / **be'hind-the-'scene(s)** *a.* 幕后的

behold [bi'hould] I (beheld [bi'held]) ❶ *vt.* [书面语] ①见到 ②注视,看 ❷ *vi.* 看 II *int.* 看哪 ‖~**er** *n.* 观看者

beholden [bi'houldən] *a.* [常作表语]受惠的;铭感的: be ~ *to* sb. *for* … 因…而感激某人

beige [beiʒ] I *n.* ①原色呢叽;混色线呢;薄斜纹呢 ②米色 II *a.* 米色的

being ['bi:iŋ] I be 的现在分词 II *n.* ①存在,生存: It is man's social ~ that determines his thinking. 人们的社会存在,决定人们的思想。②生命: respond with one's whole ~ 全力响应 ③ 存在物;生物;人: inanimate ~s 无生物 / a human ~ 人 / a social ~ 社会的人 ④ 本质,特质 ⑤ [the B-]【宗】上帝: the Supreme *Being* 上帝 ‖~ *as* (或 *that*) [方][口]既然;因为 / *bring* (或 *call*) *into* ~ 使形成,使产生 / *come into*

~ (事物、局面等)形成,产生;成立: *for the time* ~ 暂时,眼下 / *in* ~ 现有的: the forces *in* ~ 现有部队

belabo(u)r [bi'leibə] *vt.* ①痛打;痛斥 ②对…作过多的说明: the obvious 对十分明显的事物作不必要的反复说明

belated [bi'leitid] *a.* ① 延误的,来迟的: a ~ report 一份来得太迟的报告 ② 迟迟未去的,遗留下来的 ③(旅客等)天色已晚还在行路的: a ~ traveller 一个天黑了还在赶路的旅客

belch [beltʃ] **I** ① *vi.* ①打嗝 ②(炮、火山等)猛烈地喷射,爆发;一阵阵冒出 ② *vt.* ①(炮、火山等)猛烈地喷射,爆发出(烟、焰等) ②猛烈发出 **II** *n.* ①打嗝 ②(烟、焰等的)爆发;(炮、火山等的)爆发声

belie [bi'lai] (belying) *vt.* ① 给人以…的假象,使被误解: His appearance ~s him. 他的外貌给人以假象。② 与…不符合,与…不相等: What he does ~s his commitments. 他言行不一。③未能实现(诺言等);使(希望等)落空

belief [bi'li:f] *n.* ①相信;信心;信念: It is my ~ that .... 我相信… ②信仰;信条: religious ~s 宗教信仰 ‖*beyond* ~ 难以置信 / *to the best of my* ~ 在我看来

believe [bi'li:v] ① *vt.* ①相信 ②认为: I ~ him (to be) right. 我认为他是对的。② *vi.* 相信 ②信任: We ~ *in* him. 我们信任他。[比较: We ~ him. 我们相信他的话。] ③信奉,信仰 (in) ‖~ *it or not* [口]信不信由你 / ~ *me* [口]真的 / *make* ~ 假装 ‖**believable** *a.* 可相信的;可信任的 / ~**r** *n.* 信仰者;信徒

belittle [bi'litl] *vt.* ①轻视,小看,贬低 ②使相形之下显得微小

bell [bel] **I** *n.* ①钟;铃;门铃: an electric ~ 电铃 ②钟声;【海】船钟;雾钟;轮班钟: rise at the ~ 听到钟声起床 / eight ~s【海】八击钟 ③钟状物 ④[复](上瘦下肥的)喇叭裤 **II** *vt.* ①系铃于 ②使成铃状 ‖*bear* (或 *carry away*) *the* ~ 得第一,得胜 / *lose the* ~ 战败 / *ring the* ~ ①敲钟;摇铃 ②[美俚]成功;得到赞许 / *That rings a* ~. [口]那使人回想起某事了。‖'~-,bottom **trousers** (上瘦下肥的)喇叭裤 / '~**boy** *n.* [美]旅馆服务员,旅馆侍者 / ~ **buoy** 【海】装钟浮标 / '~**button** ①铃的按钮 ②铃按钮式的钮扣 / '~,flower *n.*【植】风铃草属植物: Chinese ~*flower* 桔梗 / ~ **founder** 铸钟工人 / ~ **founding** 铸钟术 / ~ **foundry** 铸钟厂 / '~-**hop** *n.* =~boy / '~**man** *n.* ①敲钟者 ②在街上敲钟向公众报事的人 ③ =~boy / ~ **metal** 钟铜(青铜) / '~**pull** 铃扣;门铃的拉索 / ~ **push** 电铃按钮 / '~,**wether** *n.* ①带头羊 ②(一群人的)首领

bellicose ['belikous] *a.* 好战的;好斗的 ‖**bellicosity** [,beli'kɔsiti] *n.*

bellied ['belid] *a.* ①有腹的;大肚皮的;鼓起的,凸

起的,张满的: a ~ sail 张得鼓鼓的帆 ②[用以构成复合词]腹…的: big-~ 大肚皮的;怀孕的

belligerent [bi'lidʒərənt, be'lidʒərənt] **I** *a.* ① 交战中的 ② 好战的,挑起战争的 **II** *n.* 交战的一方(指国家、集团或个人)

bellow ['belou] **I** ① *vi.* ①(公牛、象等)吼叫 ②(人、海等)怒吼;吼叫;(雷、炮等)轰鸣 ② *vt.* 大声喊出: ~ (*out* 或 *forth*) a song 高唱歌曲 **II** *n.* ①(公牛、象等的)吼声 ②怒吼声

bellows ['belouz] [单复同] *n.* ①风箱,手用吹风器(俗称皮老虎): a pair of ~ (有时用 a ~) (一副)手用吹风器 ②【机】波纹管;真空膜盒: spring-opposed ~ 弹簧承力波纹管 ③(管风琴等的)风箱 ④(照相机的)皮腔 ⑤肺部

bellows

belly ['beli] **I** *n.* ①(人或动物的)肚,腹部;腹腔;胃;子宫 ②胃口,食欲 ③(物件的)凸部(或凹部,内部): the ~ of a plane (ship) 飞机(轮船)的内部 **II** ① *vt.* 使张满,使鼓起: The wind *bellied* (*out*) the sails. 风把帆张得鼓鼓的。② *vi.* ① 张满,鼓起: The sails *bellied* (*out*). 帆张满风。②以腹贴地而前行 ‖~**ful** *n.* ①饱腹,餍足 ②[俚]满腹,过分,过量: We have had a ~*ful* of it. 我们已受够了。/ ~**ing** *a.* 张满的,鼓起的 ‖'~-**ache** *n.* 腹痛 *vi.* 无端抱怨 / '~**band** *n.* (马的)腹带 / ~ **flop** [口] ①肚子先着水的笨拙跳水动作 ②(滑雪时)肚子贴着雪橇的下滑 / '~-**land** *vi.* (飞机)以机腹着陆 / ~ **landing** 机腹着陆 / ~ **laugh** ①捧腹大笑 ②[俚]逗人发笑的东西(如剧本中的某句台词) / '~-**pinched** *a.* 挨饿的 / ~ **tank** 机腹副油箱 / '~-,**timber** *n.* [开玩笑用语]食物 / '~-,**worship** *n.* 大吃大喝

belong [bi'lɔŋ] *vi.* ①属,附属 ②是(社团、家族等的)一员 ③[常与 *in, with, under* 等连用]应归入(类别、派别、范畴等): Put it where it ~s. 把它放在应放的地方。/ ~ *in* a different classification 属于不同的类别 ④住: I ~ here. 我住在这里。⑤如鱼水地处于某一环境中: Anybody could see that he didn't ~. 谁都看得出来他觉得自己无所归属,格格不入。⑥[俚]拥有 (*to*): Who ~s *to* this toothbrush? 这支牙刷是谁的?

belonging [bi'lɔŋiŋ] *n.* ①[常用复]所有物; 行李: It didn't take me long to arrange my ~s; for I had brought little. 整理行李没花去我多少时间, 因为我本来就带得不多。②[复]附属物 ③[复]亲属 ④(团体成员间的)亲密忠诚关系

beloved [bi'lʌvd, bi'lʌvid] **I** *a.* ① [bi'lʌvd] [用作表语]为…所爱的(by, of) ②[用作定语]被热爱的 **II** *n.* 被心爱的人, 爱人

below [bi'lou] **I** *prep.* ①[表示位置、职位等]在…下面: 100 metres ~ sea level 海平面下一百米 / the caption ~ the picture 图画下面的说明 ②[表示数量、程度、年龄等]在…以下: ten degrees ~ zero 零下十度 ③在…的下方: the boat ~ the bridge 位于桥的下游那边的船 ④[表示能力等]低于 ⑤有失…的身分, 不值得(通常用 beneath) **II** *ad.* ①在下面; 向下: *Below* there! 下面当心! ②在下方 ③在下级 ④在(书的)一页的下端; 在下文 **III** *a.* ①下列的; 下文的: the ~ form 下面的表格 ②零下的: five ~ 零下五度 ‖*be* ~【海】在舱内 / *one's breath* 见 **breath** / *down* ~ 见 **down**[1] / *from* ~ 从下面: material coming *from* ~ 下面反映上来的材料 / *go* ~【海】下舱内去 / *here* ~ 见 **here**

belt [belt] **I** *n.* ①带; 腰带; 肩带; 带状物 ②[机]皮带: V-~ 三角皮带 ③地带; 区: a cotton (wheat, coal) ~ 产棉(小麦, 煤)区 / a green ~ of a city 城市的绿化地带 ④[军]子弹带, 腰皮带; 单层铁丝网; (舰船)吃水线以下的装甲带 ⑤[美]环行线电车路; 环行铁路 ⑥[美俚]打击 ⑦[美俚]大口一饮(尤指烈酒); 快感, 刺激 **II** ❶ *vt.* ①在…上系腰带 ②用带绑住 ③用皮带打; [俚]重打 ④[美俚]饮(酒)(down); 狂饮 ❷ *vi.* (有力地)快速移动 ‖*hit below the* ~ ①用不正当手段打人(原指拳击中打对方的下身) ②暗箭伤人 / *hold the* ~ (在拳击等体育运动中)夺得锦标 / *pull in one's* ~ =tighten one's ~ / *the Black Belt* ①美国南方(土地肥沃的)黑土区 ②美国南方黑人多于白人的地区 ③美国城市中黑人多于白人的地区 / *the Great* (*Little*) *Belt* (由北海通至波罗的海的)大(小)海峡 / *tighten one's* ~ ①束紧腰带, 忍饥受寒 ②节约度日 / *under one's* ~ ①在胃中 ②在已往经历中 ‖~ed *a.* 束了腰带的 / ~*ing n.* ①带料; 带类 ②[机]传动带装置 ③[俚]鞭打 ‖'~-,tighten *vi.* 实行紧缩政策, 勒紧裤带

bemoan [bi'moun] *vt.* ①悲叹; 哀泣; 痛哭 ②惋惜; 不满于

bench [bentʃ] **I** *n.* ①长凳; 横在船中的坐板 ②(木工等的)工作台 ③法官席; [总称]法官; 法官的职位; 法院: the King's (或 Queen's) *Bench* 英国高等法院 ④(英国议会的)议员席: front ~es 前座议员席 (英国下院中执政党议会党团领袖和其他重要议员的席位) / back ~es 后座议员席 (英国下院中普通议员的席位) / cross ~es 中立议员席 (英国下院中两大政党以外中立政党的议员坐的席位) ⑤[地]阶地; 【矿】(煤矿的)台阶,

(矿的)梯段: a ~ terrace 阶式梯田 ⑥[美]狗展览会: a ~ show 家畜(尤指狗)比赛展览会 ⑦[美]平而狭的高地 ⑧运动员等候比赛坐位席; 坐在场外的全体候补运动员 **II** ❶ *vt.* ①在…放木凳 ②使坐在席位上 ③展览(狗) ④使退出比赛 ❷ *vi.* 【地】形成阶地 ‖*be on the* ~ ①当法官 ②当主教 ③坐在比赛场外的候补运动员席位上, 坐冷板凳 / *be raised to the* ~ ①被任为法官 ②被任为主教 / *the Upper Bench* 【英史】皇家高等法庭 ‖~er *n.* 英国律师协会的主管委员 ‖~ **board** 【无】台式配电盘; 操纵台, 控制盘 / ~ **jockey** 坐在比赛场外嘲笑对方运动员和裁判员的运动员 / ~ **man** 收音机和电视机修理工 / ~ **mark** 【测】水准基点, 水准标点 / ~ **warrant** 【律】法院拘票

bend [bend] **I** (过去式 bent [bent], 过去分词 bent 或[罕] bended) ❶ *vt.* ①使弯曲: ~ a bow 弯弓 / ~ one's brows 皱眉头 ②使屈从 ③把(目光、精力等)集中于: All eyes were *bent on* me. 大家都瞧着我。/ ~ one's mind to one's work 专心工作 ④把(脚步等)转变方向: ~ one's steps towards 转向…走去 ⑤【海】系 ❷ *vi.* ①弯曲; 屈身: The river ~s *to* the east. 这条河折向东流。/ ~ down to pick up an axe 俯身拾起斧头 ②屈从 ③集中全力: ~ *to the* oars 拚命划(船) **II** *n.* ①弯曲; 弯曲处 ②【海】索结; [复](木船的)外部舷板 ‖*above sb.'s* ~ [美]为某人力所不及 / ~ *over backwards* (to do sth.) [贬]拚命(做某事) / *on* ~ed *knees* 着(哀求) / *the* ~s 【医】潜函病, 沉箱病; 高空病 ‖~er *n.* ①弯曲物; 弯曲者; 折弯机: a pipe-~-er 弯管机 ②[美口]狂饮: go on a ~er 闹饮

beneath [bi'ni:θ] **I** *prep.* ①在…(正)下方; 在(或紧靠着)…底下; 低于 ②有失…的身分; 有损于(尊严等); 不值得: ~ notice 不值得注意的 / contempt 卑鄙到极点的 **II** *ad.* 在下方; 在底下

benediction [,beni'dikʃən] *n.* ①【基督教】礼拜末尾的祈福; 祝福; 感谢 ②[B-]【天主教】祝福式

benefaction [,beni'fækʃən] *n.* ①善行 ②捐助物; 捐款

benefactor ['benifæktə] *n.* 捐助人; 恩人 ‖**benefactress** ['benifæktris] *n.* 女捐助人; 女恩人

beneficence [bi'nefisəns] *n.* ①慈善 ②善行 ③捐助物; 捐款

beneficial [,beni'fiʃəl] *a.* ①有利的, 有益的, 有助的: ~ *to* (the) health 有益于健康的 / ~ *to* rheumatism 有利于治疗风湿病的 ②【律】可享利益的, 有使用权的 ‖~ly *ad.*

beneficiary [,beni'fiʃəri] **I** *a.* (封建法律中)受封的, 臣服的 **II** *n.* ①【律】(遗嘱、保险等的)受益人 ②(封建社会的)封臣 ③受俸牧师

benefit ['benifit] **I** *n.* ①利益, 好处 ②恩惠 ③津贴; 救济金; 保险赔偿费: disability ~ 残废抚恤金 ④义演; 义赛: a ~ concert 义演音乐会 **II** ❶ *vt.* 有益于: ~ the people 有益于人民 / This medicine will ~ you. 这种药对你有好处。

❷ *vi.* 受益: We ~ *by* daily exercises. 每天做操对我们有益. ‖*for the ~ of* 为…; 为…的利益 / *give sb. the ~ of the doubt* (在证据不足的情况下)假定某人是无辜的 ‖~ *society* 互济会

benevolence [bi'nevələns] *n.* ①仁慈 ②善行 ③捐助物; 捐款

benevolent [bi'nevələnt] *a.* 仁慈的; 慈善的; 乐善好施的 ‖~*ly ad.*

benighted [bi'naitid] *a.* ①(常指天色已晚还在赶路的人)不觉天黑了的 ②愚昧的, 无知的

benign [bi'nain] *a.* ①慈祥的, 宽厚的 ②(气候等)温和的, 有益于健康的 ③【医】(瘤等)良性的 ‖~*ly ad.*

bent[1] [bent] bend 的过去式和过去分词

bent[2] [bent] **I** *a.* ①弯的 ②决心的, 一心的 **II** *n.* ①爱好; 癖好: have a ~ *for* painting 爱好绘画 ②【建】排架; 横向构架 ‖*follow one's* ~ 凭爱好办事 / *to the top of one's* ~ 尽情地

benumb [bi'nʌm] *vt.* ①使麻木, 使失去感觉: My feet were ~ed with cold. 我的脚冻得麻木了. ②使僵化; 使瘫痪

bequeath [bi'kwi:ð] *vt.* ①(按遗嘱)遗赠(个人动产等) ②把…给予后代, 把…传下 ‖~*al n.* ①遗赠 ②遗产, 遗物

bequest [bi'kwest] *n.* ①遗赠 ②遗产, 遗物

bereave [bi'ri:v] (bereaved 或 bereft [bi'reft]) *vt.* ①[过去式和过去分词一般用 bereft]使失去 (*of*): Indignation *bereft* him *of* speech. 他愤怒得说不出话来. / a man *bereft of* reason 丧失理性的人 ②[过去式和过去分词一般用 bereaved](死亡等)使丧失(亲人等) (*of*): the ~d husband 丧失妻子的人 ‖~*ment n.* (亲人等的)丧失; 居丧

beret ['berei] *n.* 贝雷帽(一种扁圆的无沿帽): the Green *Berets* 绿色贝雷帽(指美国的"特种部队")

berry ['beri] **I** *n.* ①浆果(如草莓、葡萄、西红柿等) ②(某些植物的)干果仁, 干种子(如咖啡豆等) ③(龙虾等的)卵 ④[美俚]一元钱 **II** *vi.* ①结出浆果 ②采集浆果: Let's go ~*ing.* 咱们去采浆果吧. ‖*the berries* [美俚]绝妙的人(或物) ‖*berried a.* ①结浆果的 ②(龙虾等)有卵的

berserk ['bə:sə:k] **I** *n.* 狂暴的人 **II** *a.* 狂暴的: go ~ 突然变得狂暴 / ~ fury 暴怒 **III** *ad.* 狂暴地

berth [bə:θ] **I** *n.* ①(船与灯塔、沙滩等之间留出的)回旋(或操作)余地, 安全距离: keep a clear ~ of the shoals (船为避免搁浅而)远离着沙滩 ②停泊处, 锚位 ③【船】船台(=building ~) ④(船、车、飞机等的)座位; 卧铺: book (或 reserve) a ~ 订购卧铺票 ⑤(轮船上的)住舱 ⑥职位; 球员(在球赛中)的位置 **II** *vt.* ❶ *vt.* ①使停泊 ②(给旅客等)提供铺位 ❷ *vi.* ①停泊 ②占铺位 ‖*give a wide ~ to* (为安全或谨慎起见)远离; 对…敬而远之 ‖~*age* ['bə:θidʒ] *n.* 【海】停泊费; 泊位

beseech [bi'si:tʃ] (besought [bi'sɔ:t] 或 beseeched) *vt. & vi.* 恳求, 哀求

beset [bi'set] (beset; besetting) *vt.* ①镶, 嵌(珠宝饰物等) ②困扰; 围攻: be ~ *with* difficulties 困难重重 / be ~ *by* doubts 为疑问所困扰 ③包围住: a town ~ *with* towering mountains 高山环抱的城镇 ‖~*ment n.* ①(被)包围; (被)围攻; (被)困扰 ②烦心事, 烦恼 ‖*besetting a.* ①不断侵袭的: a *besetting* sin 常常容易重犯的恶习 ②(念头等)老是缠着人的

beside [bi'said] *prep.* ①在…旁边; 在…附近: keep sentry ~ a bridge 在桥旁站岗 ②与…相比; 比…上: *Beside* yours our achievement counts for little. 与你们的成就比较起来, 我们的算不了什么. / The products of this factory can be ranked ~ the best of their kind in our country. 这家工厂的产品比得上国内最好的同类产品. ③在…之外; 与…无关: ~ the point (或 question, mark) 离题, 不中肯 ‖~ *oneself* 若狂, 发狂: ~ *oneself* with joy 欣喜若狂

besides [bi'saidz] **I** *prep.* ①除…之外(尚有…): This design has many other advantages ~ lower cost. 这个设计除费用低外, 还有许多其他优点. ②除…之外(不再有…): We have no other tools ~ these. 除这些工具外, 我们没有别的工具了. **II** *ad.* 而且; 还有: The task is very difficult; ~, time presses. 任务艰巨, 而且时间紧迫. / It's too late to go to the football match now; ~, it's beginning to snow. 现在去看足球比赛已经太晚了, 何况, 又开始下雪了.

besiege [bi'si:dʒ] *vt.* ①包围, 围困; 围攻 ②拥在…周围: be ~d with inquiries 被一大堆查询弄得应接不暇 ‖~*ment n.* (被)围困; (被)围攻 / ~*r n.* 围攻者

besought [bi'sɔ:t] beseech 的过去式和过去分词

best [best] **I** *a.* [good, well 的最高级] ①最好的: This machine is the very ~ of its kind. 这部机器确是同类机器中最好的. / What is the ~ thing to do? 该怎么干才对好呢? / We are the ~ of friends. 我们是最好的朋友. ②最大的, 最适合的: handle a problem with the ~ of care 以最大的谨慎处理问题 / the ~ person for the job 最适合做这项工作的人 ③大半的: the ~ part of an hour 大半个钟头 **II** *ad.* ①[well 的最高级]最好地: Do as you think ~. 你认为怎么最好就怎么做吧. ②最 **III** *n.* 最好的人; 最好的东西: Strive for the ~, prepare for the worst. 作最好的打算, 争取最好的结果. **IV** *vt.* [口]打败; 胜过 ‖*(all)* (完全)出于好意 / *as ~ one can* 尽最大努力 / *at ~* 充其量, 至多: He can't get here before two *at ~*. 他最早也要两点钟才能到这儿. / *at one's ~* 处在最好状态 / *(be) all for the ~* 结果总会好的 / *for the ~* 最好 / *do one's ~* 尽力 / *do one's level ~* 全力以赴 / *(even) at the ~ of times* (即使)在最有利的情况下 / *get* (或 *have) the ~ of* 胜过… / *give sb.* ~ [英口]承认不如某人, 向某人认输 / *had ~* 最好, 顶好:

We *had* ~ do it at once. 我们最好马上就干。/ *hope for the* ~ 抱乐观的希望 / *in one's (Sunday)* ~ 穿着节日的服装 / *make the* ~ *of* 充分利用(时间、机会等) / *make the* ~ *of a bad business* (或 *job, bargain*) (在遭到失败或不幸时)尽力把损失减到最小 / *make the* ~ *of both worlds* 见 **world** / *make the* ~ *of one's way* 尽快走 / *make the* ~ *of things* 随遇而安 / *The* ~ *is the enemy of the good.* [谚]要求过高反难成功。/ *the* ~ *of it* (或 *the joke*) 最令人发笑的一点 / *to the* ~ *of my belief* 在我看来 / *to the* ~ *of one's ability* (或 *power*) 尽全力 / *to the* ~ *of one's knowledge* (*recollection*) 就自己所能知道(记起)的 / *try one's* ~ 尽力 / *with the* ~ 跟任何人一样好,不比任何人差: Old as he is, he can play table tennis *with the* ~. 他虽然年纪大了,可打起乒乓来不比任何人差。‖~ **bet** 最安全可靠的办法,最好的措施 / ~ **man** 男傧相 / ~ **seller** 畅销书(或唱片等) ②畅销书作者,畅销唱片制作者 / '~-'**selling** *a.* 畅销的

bestial ['bestjəl] *a.* ①野兽的; 野兽般的 ②兽性的; 残忍的; 无理性的 ‖~**ly** *ad.*

bestir [bi'stə:] (bestirred; bestirring [bi'stə:riŋ]) *vt.* [常接 oneself] 使(自己)发奋, 激励

bestow [bi'stou] *vt.* ①把…赠与, 把…给与: ~ praises *on* (或 *upon*) sb. 对某人大加赞扬 ②使用,花费: ~ much time (energy) *on* one's work 把大量时间(精力)花在工作上 ③放置,安置;贮藏 ④留宿,为…供宿: ~ sb. *for* the night 留某人住一夜 ‖~**al** [bi'stouəl] *n.* ①赠与;赠品 ②贮藏,收藏

bestride [bi'straid] (过去式 bestrode [bi'stroud], 过去分词 bestridden [bi'stridn] 或 bestrid [bi-'strid] 或 bestrode) *vt.* ①跨骑着(马、自行车等); 横跨在…之上: a bridge *bestriding* the torrential river 横跨在激流之上的桥梁 ②高踞…之上, 控制

bet [bet] I [bet 或 betted; betting) ❶ *vt.* ①用(钱或物)打赌;与(某人)打赌: He ~ me ten dollars that John would come (或 on John's coming). 他认为约翰会来,与我打赌十元。②敢断定: I ~ he won't come. 我敢断定他不会来。❷ *vi.* 打赌: ~ *on* sth. 对某事打赌 / ~ *against* sth. 打赌某事不可能发生 II *n.* ①打赌: accept (或 take up) a ~ 同意打赌 / make a ~ *with* sb. 与某人打赌 ②打赌的钱(或物), 赌注 ③被打赌的对象 ‖~ *one's bottom dollar on* 对…孤注一掷 / *you* ~ [口]你可确信的, 的确, 当然

betake [bi'teik] (betook [bi'tuk], betaken [bi'teikən]) *vt.* [~ oneself] ①使用 (to): ~ oneself *to* certain measures 使用某些手段 ②去, 往 (to): ~ oneself *to* one's native place 到故乡去

betide [bi'taid] ❶ *vi.* 发生: whate'er ~ (或 whatever may ~) 无论发生什么事情 ❷ *vt.* (祸)降临

betimes [bi'taimz] *ad.* ①早 ②准时, 及时 ③不久以后

betray [bi'trei] *vt.* ①背叛, 出卖 ②辜负 ③泄漏(秘密等) ④暴露; 表现: His accent ~ed his nationality. 从他的口音可以知道他的国籍。/ ~ oneself 暴露本来面目, 原形毕露 ⑤把…引入歧途; 玩弄, 诱奸(妇女): be ~ed *into* error 受蒙骗而犯错误 ‖~**al** [bi'treiəl] *n.* / ~**er** *n.* 背叛者; 背信者; 告密者; 诱惑者

betroth [bi'trouθ] *vt.* [常用被动语态](女子)同…订婚 (to) ‖~**al** *n.* 订婚 / ~**ed** *a.* 订了婚的. *n.* 订婚者

better¹ ['betə] I *a.* [good, well 的比较级] ①较好的, 更好的: Fewer but ~. 少而精。/ Well, nothing is ~ than that. 呵, 那再好不过了。②(健康状况)有所好转的: Is he ~ today? 他今天好些了吗? ③大半的: the ~ part of a month 大半个月 II *ad.* [well 的比较级] ①更好地: sum up experience so as to do still ~ 总结经验, 再接再厉 ②更; 更多: This pair of shoes fit(s) you ~. 这双鞋子对你更合适。/ The ~ I know him, the more do I learn from him. 我越是了解他, 从他学到的东西就越多。III ❶ *vt.* 改善; 超过: ~ the life of the people 改善人民生活 / ~ a record 刷新纪录 ❷ *vi.* 改善 IV *n.* ①较好的事物: a change for the ~ 好转 ②较优者; [常用复]上司: He's my ~. 他比我高明。‖*all the* ~ 更加好 / *be* ~ *off* 境况(尤指经济境况)较好 / *be the* ~ *for it* 因此(反)而更好: Make stricter demands on him. He'll be the ~ for it. 要求严格些, 对他反而有好处。/ *Better late than never.* [谚]迟做总比不做好。/ ~ oneself 改善自己地位(或经济状况等) / ~ *than one's word* 做得比答应的还要好 / *for* ~ *for worse* (或 *for* ~ *or worse*) 不论好坏, 不管怎么样 / *get the* ~ *of* 打败; 智胜 / *go* (*sb.*) *one* ~ [美俚]胜过(某人) / *had* ~ 最好还是…: You *had* ~ set off at once. (或 *Better* set off at once.) 你还是马上动身的好。/ *know* ~ (*than*) 见 **know** / *no* ~ *than* 几乎等于 / *no* ~ *than one should be* 行为不规矩 / *none the* ~ *for it* 不因此而好些 / *not* ~ *than* 并不比…好; 顶多不过是 / *one's* ~ *half* [谑]妻子 / *so much the* ~. 这样就更好了。/ *think* ~ *of* 见 **think** ‖~-**off** ['betə'ɔ(:)f] *a.* 境况(尤指经济境况)较好的 / '~-to-'**do** *a.* 较为富裕的. *n.* [单复同]较为富裕的人

better² ['betə] *n.* 打赌者 (=bettor)

between [bi'twi:n] I *prep.* ①在(两者)之间; 在…中间: ~ is something ~ a cup and a bowl. 这东西既象杯子又象碗。②联系着…: after all there has been ~ us 在我们共同经历了这一段(友谊、患难等)之后… ③(来往于)…之间 ④为…所共有 ⑤由于…共同作用的结果: *Between* astonishment and joy, she could hardly say a word. 她惊喜交集, 一句话也说不出来。II *ad.*

当中，中间: a meeting with a short break ～ 中间有短暂休息的会议 ‖～ **ourselves** (或 ～ **you and me**) 只限于咱俩之间(不得外传) / (**few and**) **far** ～ 稀少: The malaria cases in this region have become *few and far* ～. 疟疾病例在这一地区已极为罕见。/ **in** ～ 在中间；每间隔；在…期间: trees planted with the space of 10 metres *in* ～ 每间隔十米种一棵的树木 ‖～ **decks** 【船】甲板间 / **be'tweenmaid** *n.* [英]家庭助理女佣 / **be'tweentimes, be'tweenwhiles** *ad.* 有时，间或

betwixt [bi'twikst] *prep.* & *ad.* [诗][古] =between ‖～ **and between** 两可之间的

bevel ['bevəl] I *n.* ①【数】斜截；斜角；斜面 ②【机】斜角规 II *a.* 倾斜的；斜角的 III (bevel(l)ed; bevel(l)ing) ❶ *vt.* 使成斜角，斜截，斜切 ❷ *vi.* 成斜角，斜 ‖～ **gear** 【机】伞(形)齿轮 / ～ **wheel** 【机】斜齿轮

beverage ['bevəridʒ] *n.* 饮料(如汽水、茶、酒等)

bevy ['bevi] *n.* ①(女孩、妇女的)(一)群 ②(鸟等，尤指鹌鹑的)(一)群

bewail [bi'weil] *vt.* & *vi.* 悲悼；哀悼；痛哭

beware [bi'wɛə] *vt.* & *vi.* [用于祈使句，或与 must, should 等连用]谨防，当心: Beware (of) dangers! 提防危险!

bewilder [bi'wildə] *vt.* 迷惑；使为难；把…弄糊涂 ‖～**ment** *n.*

bewitch [bi'witʃ] *vt.* ①施魔力于，蛊惑 ②使着迷，使心醉 ‖～**ing** *a.* / ～**ment** *n.* 中妖术；(被)迷惑；妖术，魔力

beyond [bi'jɔnd] I *prep.* ①[表示位置]在(或向)…的那边，远于: peak ～ peak of tea plantations 重重茶林/go ～ the mountains 到山的那边去 / from ～ the seas 来自海外 ②[表示时间]迟于: Some shops keep open ～ midnight. 有些商店营业到半夜以后。③[表示范围、限度]超出: ～ compare 无与伦比 / ～ sb.'s power 是某人力所不及的 / ～ praise 夸不胜夸的 ④[常用于否定句和疑问句]除…以外: I know nothing of it ～ what he told me. 除了他告诉我的以外，别的我都不知道。II *ad.* 在远处；向远处；更远地: look ～ 往远处看 / stretch as far as the horizon and ～ 一直伸展到地平线以外 III *n.* 远处: the back of ～ 极远的地方；天涯海角 / the (great) ～ 【宗】来世

bezel ['bezl] *n.* ①凿子的刃角 ②宝石的斜面 ③(钟、表等)嵌玻璃的沟缘

Bi 【化】元素铋 (bismuth) 的符号

biannual [bai'ænjuəl] *a.* 一年两次的，半年一次的 ‖～**ly** *ad.*

bias ['baiəs] I *n.* ①(成衣等的)斜线: cut on the ～ 斜裁 ②偏见，倾向性，癖好: have a ～ against sth. (sb.) 对某事(某人)有偏见 / have a ～ towards sth. (sb.) 对某事(某人)有偏心 ③【电】偏压 II *a.* & *ad.* 斜 III (bias(s)ed; bias(s)ing) *vt.* [常用被动语态] ①使有偏见；使有倾向性:

be *bias(s)ed against* 对…有偏见 / be *bias(s)ed towards* 偏心于 ②【无】加偏压到… ‖**bias(s)ed** *a.* 有偏见的

bib¹ [bib] *n.* (小孩的)围涎；(大人的)围裙的上部 ‖**one's best ～ and tucker** 最好的衣服 ‖～**cock** 弯管旋塞(龙头)

bib² [bib] (bibbed; bibbing) *vt.* & *vi.* 常常喝(酒)；过多地喝(酒)；一点点地喝(酒) ‖**bibber** *n.* 酒鬼，贪酒的人 / **bibbing** *n.*

Bible ['baibl] *n.* [the ～] ①基督教《圣经》 ②犹太教《圣经》 ③圣经: The Koran is the Moslem ～. 古兰经是穆斯林圣经。‖**King James's** ～ 钦译《圣经》(即基督教《圣经》的钦定英译本) / the **Wicked** (或 **Adulterous**) ～ 一六三一年版基督教《圣经》(指印漏 Thou shalt not commit adultery 句中的 not 一词的那种版本) ‖**Biblical, biblical** ['biblikəl] *a.* 《圣经》的；出于(或符合)《圣经》的 / ～ **Belt** 基督教《圣经》地带(美国南部严格信奉《圣经》的地带) / ～ **class** 读经班 / ～ **clerk** (牛津大学一些学院的)礼拜堂读经生 / ～ **college** 设置宗教课程、训练宗教工作者的基督教大学 / ～ **oath** 吻经的立誓；庄严的誓言 / ～ **paper** 圣经纸(薄型不透明而坚韧的印刷纸) / '～-,pounder, '～-,puncher *n.* [俚]牧师(尤指过分热忱的) / ～ **punching** [俚]讲经传道 / '～-,reader *n.* 读经人(被雇去挨家讲解《圣经》的人) / ～ **society** 《圣经》出版协会，圣经会

bibliography [,bibli'ɔɡrəfi] *n.* ①书目提要；文献目录 ②目录学；文献学 ‖**bibliographic(al)** [,bibliou'ɡræfik(əl)] *a.*

bicarbonate [bai'kɑ:bənit] *n.* 【化】碳酸氢盐: ～ of soda 小苏打，碳酸氢钠

bicentenary [,bai-sen'ti:nəri] *n.* & *a.* 二百年(的)；二百周年纪念(的)

biceps ['baiseps] *n.* 【解】二头肌

bicker ['bikə] I *vi.* ① (为小事与人)口角，争吵 ② (雨等)淅沥淅沥地下；(溪流)潺潺地流 ③ (火焰、光等)闪烁 II *n.* ① (小的)口角(或争吵)；争吵声 ②潺潺的流水声

bicycle ['baisikl] I *n.* ①自行车，脚踏车: ride (on) a ～ 骑自行车 / go by ～ 骑自行车去 ②[美俚]学生作弊时的夹带 II *vi.* 骑自行车 ‖**bicyclist** *n.* 骑自行车的人

bid [bid] I ❶(过去式 bade [beid, bæd] 或 bid, 过去分词 bidden ['bidn] 或 bid; 现在分词 bidding) *vt.* ①[过去式一般用 bade] 祝；表示: ～ sb. good morning 祝某人早安 / ～ farewell to sb. 向某人告别 / ～ welcome to the visitors (或 ～ the visitors welcome) 向来宾表示欢迎 ②[过去式一般用 bade] 命令；吩咐: Do as you are ～ (或 bidden). 照吩咐你的去做吧。/ He bade me (to) go in. 他叫我进去。[注意: 句中的 "to" 一般均略去] ③[过去式一般用 bid] 邀请 ④[过去式和过去分词一般用 bid] (拍卖中)喊(价)，出(价) ⑤[过去式和过去分词一般用 bid] (打桥牌时)叫(牌) ⑥[过去式一般用 bade] 公开宣布 ⑦[过

式和过去分词一般用 bid) [美口] 接纳…为成员
❷ (bid; bidding) vi. 出价; 叫牌; [美]投标: ~
against each other on (或 for) a new project (资
本主义国家营造公司等)投标相互竞争 以取得一
项新工程的营造权 Ⅱ n. ①出价, 喊价; [美]投
标;出价(或投标)数目 ②出价 (或投标) 的机会
③邀请 ④(桥牌中的)叫牌; 够叫牌资格的一手牌
⑤企图 ‖~ defiance to 见 defiance / ~ fair
to 有…的希望, 有…的可能: The effort ~s fair
to succeed. 这番努力可望成功。/ ~ in sth. (拍
卖人)故意出最高价使某(拍卖)物落到自己手里 /
~ up 哄抬(拍卖物)的价钱; 哄抬(价钱) / make
a ~ for ①(拍卖中)出价买; 投标争取…的营造
权 ②企图获得

bidding ['bidiŋ] n. ①命令, 吩咐 ②(拍卖时的)出
价, 喊价 ③邀请 ④叫牌 ‖at sb.'s ~ 根据某人
的命令 / do sb.'s ~ 照某人的意旨办事

bide [baid] (过去式 bode [boud] 或 bided, 过去分
词 bided) ❶ vi. [古][诗]持续; 住; 等侯 ❷ vt.
①忍耐 ②等待 (只用于习语 ~ one's time 中)
‖~ one's time 等待时机

biennial [bai'eniəl] Ⅰ a. ①两年一次的 ②持续两
年的 ③【植】二年生的 Ⅱ n. ①两年发生一次的
事物 ②【植】二年生植物 ‖~ly ad.

bier [biə] n. ①棺材架;尸体架 ②棺材

big [big] (bigger, biggest) Ⅰ a. ①大, 巨大; 长大
了的: a ~ city 大城市 / Develop agriculture in a ~ way. 大办农业。②怀着…的;充满
着…的 (with): be ~ with child (a young) 怀
孕 / be ~ with rage 怒气填膺 / a year ~ with
successes 不断胜利的一年 ③重要的, 重大的;
出名的; (演出等) 极成功的, 极受欢迎的: a ~
man 大人物 ④自大的, 傲慢的: ~ talk (或
words) 大话 / a ~ talker 说大话的人 / ~ looks
自大的神气 ⑤宽宏的, 大度的 Ⅱ ad. ①大量
地, 大大地 ②[口]自大地 ③宽宏地, 大度地 ④
宽广地 ⑤成功地 ‖as ~ as life 与原物一般大
小 / be too ~ for one's boots (或 breeches,
trousers) 妄自尊大, 摆架子 / go over ~ [美国]
(演出等)大受欢迎; (演员等) 走红 / make ~
[美国]飞黄腾达 / talk ~ 说大话, 吹牛, 自吹自
播 ‖~ness n. 大, 巨大 ‖'~-'bellied a. 大肚
皮的; 怀孕的 / Big Ben 伦敦英国议院塔上的大
钟 / Big Bertha ①大炮 ②大型客机 / Big
Board [美]纽约证券交易所行情牌; 纽约证券交
易所 / '~-'boned a. 骨骼大的 / ~ boy [俚] ①
大型野炮 ②大人物 ③百元钞票 / ~ brother
①老大哥 ②[B-B-]专制国家(或组织)的领导
者;专制国家(或组织) / Big Brotherism "老大
哥"主义 / ~ bug [俚]要人, 名人 / ~ business
巨大的企业 / ~ butter-and-egg man [美俚]
头脑简单的乡下富翁, 土财主 / '~-'character
poster 大字报 / ~ cheese [美俚]大人物 ②
粗鲁愚蠢的男子 / Big Ditch [美俚][the B-D-]
①大西洋 ②巴拿马运河 / ~ drink [美俚]
①大西洋(或太平洋) ②密西西比河 / ~ end

大端(指环绕曲柄销的连杆端) / ~ friend [军
俚]己方轰炸机 / ~ game ①(为娱乐消遣而
猎取的)大猎物(如狮、虎等) ②(有危险性的)重
大的目的物 / ~ gun [俚]要人, 名人 / '~head
n. 自高自大; 自高自大的人 / '~-'headed a. 自
负的, 自高自大的 / ~ house ①宽宏大量
的 / ~ house [美俚]州监狱; 联邦监狱 /
'~-'hearted a. 宽宏大量的 / ~ jeep [口]巨型轰炸机 / ~ John [俚]新兵 /
'~-league a. [口](在某一行中)水平最高的 /
~ mouth [美俚]多话的人, 喋喋不休的人 /
~ name [美俚]名士 / '~-name a. [美俚]
大名鼎鼎的 / ~ noise [俚] ①耸人听闻的声
明(或事实) ②有影响的人物;有势力的人物 /
重磅炸弹 / ~ one [美俚] ①千元钞票 ②大便
③ [the b-o-]重要的娱乐节目 / ~ pond [the b-
p-]大西洋 / ~ shot 大人物, 大亨, 有权势的
人 / ~ stick ①显示武力, 显示实力: a ~ stick
policy 大棒政策 ②[美俚]救火云梯 ③[复]海军
大片森林地区 / ~ stink [美俚]唠叨得没完没
了的怨言 / '~-ticket a. 高价的 / ~ time ①
[美俚](一种职业中收入或地位方面)最高的一级
②[口]欢乐的时刻(尤指跳舞、唱歌等) / '~-time
a. [美俚]有名的, 杰出的; 第一流的; 重要的, 主
要的 / ~ top [美口] ①马戏团的主要帐篷 ②
马戏团生活 / ~ wheel [美俚]要人, 大亨 /
'~-wig n. 要人, 名人

bigamy ['bigəmi] n. 重婚(罪)

bigot ['bigət] n. 执拗的人;抱偏见的人 ‖~ed a.
偏执的; 顽固的: follow one's ~ed course 固执
己见, 一意孤行

bike [baik] n. & vi. [口] ①(骑)自行车 ②(骑)
摩托车 ‖~r n. 骑自行车(或摩托车)的人

bilateral [bai'lætərəl] a. ①两边的; 在两边的; 有
两边的 ②存在于双方间的, 双边的: a ~
agreement 双边协定 / ~ talks 双边会谈 ③左
右对称的 ‖~ism n. 互惠主义(特指两国贸易) /
~ly ad.

bile [bail] n. ①胆汁: ~ acid 【化】胆汁酸 ②坏
脾气;暴躁

bilge [bildʒ] Ⅰ n. ① (桶等的)腹部, 膨出部分 ②
(船)舭(船底和船侧间的弯曲部分) ③ 船底污水
④ [俚]废话, 无聊话(或文章) Ⅱ ❶ vt. 把(船)
的舭部凿破; 使(船)舭部灌水 ❷ vi. ①(船)舭
部破漏 ②(船)停靠在舭部 ③鼓胀, 凸出 ④[美
俚]考试不及格 ‖bilgy a. 有船底污水臭味的 ‖~
keel [船]舭龙骨 / '~-pump n. 船底污水泵 /
~ water 舱水, 船底污水

bilingual [bai'liŋgwəl] Ⅰ a. ①两种语言的;用两种
语言写(或印)的 ②(能)使用两种语言的 Ⅱ n.
能使用两种语言的人 ‖~ism n. 使用两种语言 /
~ly ad.

bilious ['biljəs] a. ①胆汁的;胆汁过多的;肝气不
和的 ②暴躁的, 易怒的

bill¹ [bil] Ⅰ n. ①帐单: a hotel ~ 旅馆帐单 / pay
a ~ 付帐 ②单子;清单;(人员、职称等的)表:
a theatre ~ 剧目单 / a ~ of fare 菜单;节目

单 / a ～ of quantities 建筑工程清单 / a ～ of health (船只的)检疫证书 / a clean ～ of health (船只的)无疫证书 ③(影剧等的)招贴, 广告, 传单: Post no ～s! 禁止招贴! ④议案, 法案 ⑤票据; 汇票; 凭单: ～s payable 应付票据 / ～s receivable 应收票据 / a ～ of exchange 汇票 / a ～ of lading (略作 B/L) 提(货)单 / a clean ～ 光票 / a documentary ～ 跟单汇票 / a ～ of sale 卖契 ⑥[美]钞票, 纸币; [美国]百元钞票 ⑦【律】起诉书, 诉状: find a true ～ (陪审团认为)诉状应予受理 / ignore the ～ (陪审团认为)诉状不予受理 **II** *vt.* ①给…开帐单 ②(用招贴、传单等)通告; 宣布: He was ～ed to appear as …. 据宣布, 他扮演… ③把…列成表 ‖*a Bill of Oblivion* 大赦令 / *a ～ of privilege* 贵族要求贵族阶级审判的申请书 / *fill the ～* ①出类拔萃/(演员等)领衔演出, 挂头牌 ②[美口]满足需要, 解决问题, 会钞 / *sell (sb.) a ～ of goods* [美口]以噱头骗得(某人)相信(或同意) / *the Bill of Rights* ①《权利法案》(一六八九年颁布的英国资产阶级确立君主立宪制的宪法性文件之一) ②《人权法案》(美国宪法的第一次修正案, 一七八九年通过) ‖*～board n.* ①张贴广告、传单的木板(或墙、篱笆等) ②【船】锚床 / ～ **broker** 证券经纪人 / *'～fold n.* 钱夹 / *'～head n.* (印有企业名称、地址的)空白单据 / *～,poster, '～,sticker n.* 张贴广告的人

bill² [bil] **I** *n.* ①(鸟类、鸭嘴兽等细长而扁平的)嘴 ②狭窄的岬; (锚)爪尖; 形似鸟嘴的东西 **II** *vi.* ①(鸽)接嘴 ②抚爱 ‖*～ and coo* 互相接吻, 抚爱和低声交谈 ‖*～hook n.* (砍树、修枝等用的)钩刀

billet¹ ['bilit] **I** *n.* ①【军】宿舍分配令(军事当局发出的招待军人住宿的书面命令) ②(军营以外的)部队宿舍 ③职位, 工作 **II** *vt.* ①分配(士兵)宿舍; 安顿 ②把宿舍分配令送达(户主) ③给…职位 ❷ *vi.* 宿营, 住屯 ‖*Every bullet has its ～.* 见 **bullet**

billet² ['bilit] *n.* ①木柴块 ②(金属的)短条; (金属的)坯段; 钢坯: a steel ～ 钢坯 / a ～ mill 钢坯轧机 ③【建】错齿饰

billiard ['biljəd] **I** *a.* [只作定语]台球的, 弹子戏的: a ～ room 弹子房 **II** *n.* 连撞两球的得分 ‖*～s* [复] *n.* [用作单]台球(俗称"弹子")戏

billiard

billion ['biljən] *num.* ①(英国、德国)万亿 ②(美国、法国)十亿 ‖*～th num.* ①(英、德)第一万亿(个); 一万亿分之一 ②(美、法)第十亿(个); 十亿分之一

billionaire [,biljə'nɛə] *n.* 亿万富翁

billow ['bilou] **I** *n.* ①巨浪; 波涛 ②波浪般滚滚向前的东西(如烟火、声音、军队等) ③(波浪似地)翻腾: ～*ing* smoke and flames 滚滚的烟火 ❷ *vt.* 使翻腾 ‖*～y a.* 巨浪的; 巨浪般的; 波涛汹涌的 ‖*～ cloud* 波状云

bin [bin] *n.* ①(贮藏食物、煤等的)箱子 ②垃圾箱

bind [baind] **I** (bound [baund]) ❶ *vt.* ①捆, 绑: ～ rice stalks 捆稻草 / ～ the cut wheat into sheaves 把割下的小麦扎成一捆一捆 ②包扎; 裹围: ～ up a wound 包扎伤口 ③装订(书); (缝纫时)给…滚边: ～ up two books into one volume 把两本书合订成一册 ④使凝固; 使结合: Severe frost ～s the soil. 严寒使土壤冻结。/ an ice-bound lake 封冻的湖泊 ⑤使便秘: ～ the bowels 引起便秘 ⑥使受法律(或合同、道义)约束: ～ sb. to secrecy 使某人保证不泄密 / ～ sb. to fulfil a contract 责令某人履行合同 ⑦使(协议等)确定不变 ❷ *vi.* ①变硬, 凝固 ②(紧身衣裤等)使人活动不方便; (门窗等)开关不灵便 ③具有约束力: an obligation that ～s 必须履行的义务 **II** *n.* ①捆扎物; 捆绑 ②【矿】煤系中的页岩(或泥岩) ③【音】连结线(即‿) ‖*～ oneself to do sth.* 保证(或立誓)做某事 / *～ sb. over to (do) sth.* 使某人具结保证(做)某事: ～ sb. over to keep the peace 勒令某人守法, 否则将再次受审 / ～ *sb. over to good behaviour* 勒令某人规规矩矩, 否则将再次受审 / *in a ～* 处于困境 / *Safe ～, safe find.* 见 **safe¹**

binder ['baində] *n.* ①包扎者; 装订工 ②包扎工具; 绳索, 带子 ③【建】粘结料; 系梁; 【冶】粘合剂 ④【医】结合剂; (产妇用的)腹带; 绷带 ⑤收割扎束机; (缝纫机上的)滚边器 ⑥活页封面 ⑦临时契约; 购买不动产时的定金(或定金收据) ⑧装订机

binding ['baindiŋ] **I** *a.* ①捆绑的 ②粘合的; (食物)引起便秘的 ③有约束力的, 附有义务的: This treaty is ～ on (或 upon) all parties. 本条约对缔约各方都具有约束力。**II** *n.* ①捆绑 ②绷带; 滚条 ③(书)的装订; 装帧; 封皮 ④粘合剂 ‖*～ energy* 【物】结合能 / *～ post* 【物】接线柱

bingo ['biŋgou] **I** *n.* 一种用纸牌搭成方块的赌博 **II** *int.* 瞧!

binocular [bi'nɔkjulə, bai'nɔkjulə] **I** *a.* 双目的。双筒的 **II** *n.* 双目镜; [复](双筒)望远镜

biographer [bai'ɔgrəfə] *n.* 传记作者: sb.'s ～ 为某人写传记的人

biography [bai'ɔgrəfi] **I** *n.* ①个人经历; 传记 ②传记文学 ③事物发展过程的记述 **II** *vt.* 为…作传记

biological [,baiə'lɔdʒikəl] *a.* 生物学(上)的: a ～ laboratory 生物实验室 ‖*～ly ad.*

biology [bai'ɔlədʒi] *n.* ①生物学 ②生态学 ③[总称]一个地区的生物 ‖**biologist** *n.* 生物学者,生物学家

bipartisan, bipartizan [bai,pɑ:'ti'zæn, bai'pɑ:tizən] *a.* 由两党成员组成的;代表两党的;被两党支持的 ‖**~ship** *n.* 两党关系(特指两大政党在对外政策上达成的协议)

biped ['baiped] I *n.* 二足动物 II *a.* 二足的,有二足的 ‖**~al** ['bai,pedl] *a.* 有二足的

birch [bə:tʃ] I *n.* ①桦,白桦 ②桦木 ③(鞭打用的)桦条(或桦条束) II *vt.* 用桦条打 III *a.* 桦木的;桦木制成的 ‖**~en** *a.* 桦木的;桦木制成的

bird [bə:d] I *n.* ①鸟,禽: a useful (pernicious) ~ 益(害)鸟 / a ~ of prey 猛禽(尤指鹰类) / a game ~ 供猎食的鸟 / a song ~ 鸣禽 ②[美口]火箭,导弹 ③羽毛球 ④[俚]人,家伙;姑娘;[常作讽刺语]非凡人物: an old ~ 老家伙;精明鬼 / What a queer ~! 真是个怪人! ⑤[俚](轰赶某人时的)嘘声;解雇 II *vi.* ① 在野外观察辨认野鸟 ②打鸟,捕鸟 ‖*a ~ in the bush* 未到手的东西;未定局的事情 / *a ~ in the hand* 已到手的东西;已定局的事情 / *A ~ in the hand is worth two in the bush.* [谚]双鸟在林不如一鸟在手。/ *a ~ of ill omen* ①凶鸟(如乌鸦、猫头鹰等) ②报凶讯的人 / *a ~ of Jove* 鹰 / *a ~ of Juno* ['dʒu:nou] 孔雀 / *a ~ of paradise* 风鸟,极乐鸟 / *a ~ of passage* ①候鸟 ②漂泊不定的人 / *a ~ of peace* 鸽 / *a ~ of wonder* 凤凰 / *a jail ~* [美口]囚犯 / *A little ~ told (或 whispered to) me.* 有人私下告诉我。/ *an early ~* ①早起的人 ②早到者 / *~s of a feather* 一丘之貉 / *Birds of a feather flock together.* [谚]物以类聚,人以群分。/ *eat like a ~* 吃得极少 / *for the ~s* [美俚作表语]毫无意义;荒唐可笑 / *get the ~* 被嘘,被喝倒采;被解雇 / *give sb. the ~* 嘘某人;解雇某人 / *hear a ~ sing* 私下听人说 / *It's an ill ~ that fouls its own nest.* [谚]家丑不可外扬。/ *kill two ~s with one stone* 一箭双雕 / *The ~ is (或 has) flown.* 要捉的人(或囚徒)逃跑了。/ *the ~s and the bees* [口]关于两性关系的基本常识 / *The early ~ gets (或 catches) the worm.* [谚]捷足先登。/ *the secular ~* 不死鸟,凤凰 ‖**~brain** *n.* [美]笨蛋,轻浮而没头脑的人 / **~cage** *n.* 鸟笼;类似鸟笼的场所(如牢房等) / **~call** *n.* 鸟语;摹仿鸟叫的声音;摹仿鸟叫声的器具 / **~ colonel** [美俚]陆军上校 / **~ dog** ①捕鸟猎犬 ②挖掘人才(如球员等)的人;兜揽生意的人 ③[美][军俚]战斗机,歼击机 / **~ fancier** 玩鸟的人 / **~house** *n.* 鸟房 / **~lime** *n.* 粘鸟胶(涂在树上捕鸟用的胶);陷捕鸟 *vt.* 在…上涂粘鸟胶;用粘鸟胶捕捉;陷捕 / **~man** *n.* 鸟类学家 ②飞行员;飞机乘客 / **~seed** *n.* 鸟食 / **~'s-eye** *n.* ①一种有鲜艳小花的植物(如粉报春等) ②【纺】鸟眼花纹(织物) ③(木材上的)椭圆形鸟眼纹理 *a.* ① 俯视的,概观的;鸟瞰的: a

~'s-eye view 鸟瞰图;概观 ②有鸟眼花纹的;鸟眼纹材的,械木(制)的 / **~'s-foot** *n.* ①叶(或花)象鸟足的植物(尤指某些豆科植物);三叶草 ②象鸟足的动物,海盘车 / **~ shot** 鸟枪子弹 / **~'s nest** ①鸟巢;燕窝 ②胡萝卜 【船】桅上了望台 / **~-nest** *vi.* 掏鸟巢,摸鸟蛋 / **~-witted** *a.* 轻浮的;心思不专一的

birth [bə:θ] *n.* ①分娩;出生,诞生: Pigs often have twelve or thirteen young at a ~. 猪每胎通常产仔十二三只。②出身,血统: of no ~ 出身低微的 / of (good 或 high) ~ 出身高贵的 ③起源,开始 ‖*a second ~* 再生,重生,新生: *by ~* 在血统上;生来,天生地: He is British *by ~* although he was born in France. 他虽然生在法国,但父母是英国人。/ She is French *by ~* and British by marriage. 她原是法国人,但嫁了英国人。/ *give ~ (to)* 生;产生: She gave ~ *to* a girl last night. 她昨晚生了一个女孩。‖**~ control** 节育 / **~day** *n.* 生日,诞生的日期 ②开始 / **~mark** *n.* ①胎记,胎痣 ②某人的特征 / **~place** *n.* 出生地,故乡;发源地 / **~rate** *n.* 出生率 / **~right** *n.* 生来就有的权利;长子继承权

biscuit ['biskit] *n.* ①[英]饼干(美国称 cracker) ②[美]软饼 ③淡褐色 ④本色陶器(或瓷器),素坯: ~ kiln 坯窑

bisect [bai'sekt] ❶ *vt.* 把…分为二;把…二等分 ❷ *vi.* 分开;相交,交叉 ‖**~ion** [bai'sekʃən] *n.* ①平分,二等分 ②平分点;平分线 ③平分的两部分之一 / **~or** *n.* ①二等分物 ②【数】平分线

bisegment [bai'segmənt] *n.* 线的平分部分之一

bishop ['biʃəp] *n.* ①(基督教的)主教 ②(国际象棋中的)象 ③加有香料的果子酒

bison ['baisn] *n.*【动】(北美洲的)骠犇

bison

bit¹ [bit] *n.* ①一点,一些;[常用复]吃剩的食物;小片: a ~ of water 一点儿水 / know a ~ of Spanish 懂点儿西班牙语 / a ~ of good advice 一点宝贵的意见 / make a supper from the ~s 用吃剩的食物做一顿晚饭 / a few ~s of wood 少量木片 ②[口]一会儿: Wait a ~. 等一会儿。③辅币;[美口]一角二分半 ④(戏中的)只

有三两句台词的小角色 ⑤[美俚]小妮子 ⑥[美俚]刑期 ‖*a ~ and a sup* 少量的饮食物 / *a ~ of a...* 一点儿…的味道: He is *a ~ of a humorist.* 他有点儿风趣。 / *a ~ of muslin* [俚]女子 / *a dainty ~* 少量可口的食物 / *a (little)* ~ [作状语用]少许: feel *a ~* cold 觉得有点儿冷 / *a nice ~ of (money)* 相当多的(钱) / ~ *by ~* 一点一点地, 渐渐 / *~s and pieces* [口]零碎东西 / *do one's ~* 尽自己的一分力量 / *every ~* 每一点; 完全, 全部: Their design is *every ~* as good as ours. 他们的设计方案同我们的相比毫无逊色。 / *give sb. a ~ of one's mind* 对某人直言不讳 / *like a ~ of skirt* 见 skirt / *not a ~ (of it)* 一点儿也不: A: Sorry to have bothered you. B: *Not a ~ (of it).* 甲:对不起,打扰你啦。乙:哪儿的话! / *pull to ~s* ①把…撕成碎片 ②把…攻击得一钱不值 / *quite a ~* 相当多 / *tear (smash) sth. to ~s* 把某物撕(砸)得粉碎

bit² [bit] **I** *n.* ①(马)嚼子 ②[喻]制约物 ③(工具上的)钻、切部分, 刀片, 刀头; 钻头; 钳子嘴; 钥匙齿 **II** (bitted; bitting) *vt.* ①给(马)上嚼子; 训练(马)使其习惯于嚼子 ②控制, 抑制 ③给(钥匙)做牙齿 ‖*draw ~* 勒马; 放慢速度 / *take (get) the ~ between the teeth* (马)不服控制; (人)放荡不羁,不服管束

bit³ [bit] *n.* 【自】(二进制数)位(有时音译作"彼特"): ~ of information 信息单位 / ~ traffic 位传送

bitch [bitʃ] **I** *n.* ①母狗(或母狼、母狐等) ②[贬]脾气坏的妇女; 坏女人, 淫妇 ③怨言, 牢骚 ④难事; 使人不愉快的事 **II** [俚] ❶ *vt.* ①弄脏, 弄污 ②对…埋怨 ③欺骗 ❷ *vi.* 埋怨 ‖*~y a.*

bite [bait] **I** (过去式 bit [bit], 过去分词 bitten ['bitn] 或 bit) ❶ *vt.* ①咬, 叮, 螫: He was *bitten* in the leg. 他腿上被咬(或叮)了一口。 / She *bit* the thread in two. 她把线咬断了。 / A piece has been *bitten* from the apple. 这只苹果已被咬掉一块。 ②(利器等)刺穿; (寒风等)刺痛: The sword *bit* him to the bone. 剑刺到了他的骨头。 / This mustard is hot enough to ~ your tongue. 这种芥末很辣,你的舌头会吃不消的。 / be *bitten* by frost 被冻伤 ③(锚等)咬住; [喻]紧紧攫住: The vice *bit* the iron bar. 台钳钳住了铁条。 / be completely *bitten with* angling mania 钓鱼成癖 ④(酸等)腐蚀 ⑤诓骗; 使亏 ❷ *vi.* ①咬; (狗等)爱咬人 ②(武器、工具等)穿透, 弄穿: a drill that can ~ through steel plates 能穿透钢板的钻子 ③刺痛 ④腐蚀 ⑤(鱼)上钩; (人)上当: The fish were *biting* well yesterday. 昨天钓不到少鱼。 ⑥咬得住, 钉牢: Car wheels don't ~ on ice-clad roads. 车轮在结冰的路面上容易打滑。 **II** *n.* ①咬, 叮; (鱼的)上钩 一口(食物)(食物):[口]随便作成的一顿饭: He is so absorbed in the work that he hasn't had a ~ since morning. 他工作得这样专心, 从早晨到现在还

没吃过一口东西。 ③ 被咬的伤口; 伤痛; [喻]刺痛: a snake ~ 蛇咬的伤口 / There is a ~ *to* his words. 他话里带刺。④紧咬; 穿透力: a file with plenty of ~ 一把锋利的锉刀 ⑤(锯、锉等的)齿 ⑥【医】上下齿的咬合情况 ⑦腐蚀 ⑧(一次收取的)一笔数目(如捐税) ‖~ *at* ①向…咬去 ②冲着 / ~ *in* 咬入 / ~ *off* ①咬掉, 啃去: Giant shovels are *biting off* big chunks from the hill. 巨型铲土机正把小山头一大口一大口地啃去。②(在广播过程中)截断(节目等) / ~ *off more than one can chew* 贪多嚼不烂; 承担力所不及的事 / ~ *the dust* (或 *ground*) 倒下死去; 大败 / *make two ~s at* (或 *of*) *a cherry* ①把原来一次可以完成的事分作两次做 ②匀分微不足道的东西 ③踌躇; 过分小心, 拘谨 / *Once bit* (或 *bitten*) *twice shy.* [谚]一次被咬,下次胆小。(或: 从经验取得教训。) / *put the ~ on* [美俚]向…借钱; 从…弄到钱 ‖~r *n.* ①咬人的动物 ②骗子: The ~r bit (或 bitten). 骗人者反受人骗了。

bitten ['bitn] bite 的过去分词

bitter ['bitə] **I** *a.* ① 有苦味的 ② 辛酸的, 痛苦的; 厉害的, 剧烈的: ~ fighting 苦战, 奋战 / a ~ experience 惨痛的经验 ③严寒的, 刺骨的: a ~ wind 刺骨的风 ④怨恨的, 抱怨的: ~ words 怨言 / a ~ enemy 死敌 **II** *n.* ①苦; 苦味; 苦味物 ②苦啤酒 ③[复]苦味药酒: gin and ~s 杜松子药酒 **III** *ad.* 苦苦地; 悲痛地; 厉害地 **IV** ❶ *vt.* 使变苦 ❷ *vi.* 变苦 ‖*Bitter pills may have wholesome effects.* [谚]良药苦口。 / *take the ~ with the sweet* 接受顺境也接受逆境 ‖~*ish* ['bitəriʃ] *a.* 带苦味的 / ~*ly ad.* 苦苦地; 悲痛地; 厉害地 / ~*ness n.* 苦味; 辛酸; 苦难 ‖~ *end* [船]索端; 锚链在船内的一端: to the ~ *end* 到底, 拼到死 / ~*-ender* ['bitər'endə] *n.* [口]顽抗到底的人; 坚持到底的人 / ~*sweet* n. ①又苦又甜的; 又苦又乐的 n. ①【植】美洲南蛇藤 ②又苦又甜的东西

bitumen ['bitjumin; 美 bi'tju:min] *n.* 【矿】沥青

bivouac ['bivuæk] **I** *n.* 露营; 一夜的露营, 临时宿营地: a ~ site 露营地 **II** (bivouacked; bivouacking) *vi.* 露营

bizarre [bi'zɑ:] *a.* 希奇古怪的, 异乎寻常的

black [blæk] **I** *a.* ①黑的; 漆黑的: ~ beer 黑啤酒 / ~ as coal 象煤一般黑的 / the *Black* Sea 黑海[欧亚之间]
②黑肤色的; 黑人的; 有关黑人的
③暗淡的; 阴郁的; 怒气冲冲的: a ~ future 暗淡的前途 / be in a ~ mood 情绪低落 / be ~ *with* anger 怒气冲冲 / give sb. a ~ look 恶狠狠地瞪某人一眼
④邪恶的; 不吉利的: the ~ art 妖术 / ~ tidings 坏消息 / Things look ~. 事情不妙。
⑤极度的: ~ despair 绝望 / a ~ stranger 完全陌生的人
⑥弄脏的; 丢脸的: a ~ mark 污点
⑦(教士等)穿黑衣的

⑧ 黑市的,非法交易的: the ~ market 黑市,非法市场 / ~ gasoline 黑市汽油
⑨ [英] 被(罢工工人)抵制装卸的: a ~ ship 被抵制装卸的船
II n. ①黑色;黑漆;黑颜料;黑墨水: be written in ~ 用黑墨水写的
②黑人: the American ~s 美国黑人
③黑斑;污点;煤炱
④黑衣: wear (或 be dressed in) ~ 穿丧服
⑤(小麦的)黑穗病;黑穗病霉菌
III ❶ vt. ①弄黑;弄脏
②用黑鞋油擦
❷ vi. 变黑
‖as ~ as night 昏黑,漆黑 / at ~ as one's hat 墨黑的 / ~ and blue 遍体鳞伤: be beaten ~ and blue 被打得青一块紫一块 / ~ and white ①白纸黑字: put sth down in ~ and white 把某事印出(或写出)来 ②钢笔画 ③黑白影片 / ~ in the face (因发怒或用力)脸色发紫 / ~ out ①用墨涂掉;使停刊;封锁(新闻) ②(幕间或剧终时)熄灭灯光;对…实行灯火管制 ③晕过去;(眼前短时)发黑 / call white ~ (或 call ~ white) 颠倒黑白 / in the ~ 赢利 / look ~ (at) (对…)怒视 / paint sb. ~ 把某人描写成坏人
‖~ly ad. ~ness n.
‖~-and-'tan a. ①身体黑色、脸脚等处深褐色的(指一种狗) ②[常作 Black-and-Tan] [美]主张(或实行)黑人、白人按比例选举代表的 ③黑人和白人常去的 n. 黑人和白人都去的夜总会 / '~-a-vised a. 面色黝黑的 / '~-ball n. (表示反对的)黑票;秘密反对票 vt. 投票反对;排斥 / '~'beetle n. 蟑螂 / ~ belt ①黑人聚居地带 ②黑土带 / ~berry ['blækbəri] n. 黑莓: plentiful as ~berries 遍地皆是,多得很 vi. 采黑莓: go ~berrying 采黑莓去 / ~bird n. ①乌鸫,黑鸟 ②被殖民主义者劫持到贩奴船上去的黑人 / ~,birding n. (殖民主义者的)贩奴活动 / '~,board n. 黑板: a ~board bulletin 黑板报 / '~,body n. 黑体(指能全部吸收外来电磁辐射而毫无反射和透射的理想物体) / ~ book 记有黑名单的书;记人罪过的书;记过簿: be (deep) in sb.'s ~ books 不得某人之宠 / 失某人之宠 / ~ box [美俚]"黑箱"(指结构复杂的电子仪器) / '~-browed a. 愁眉苦脸的;绷着脸的 / '~cap n. 莺 / '~coat n. ①[贬]牧师 ②[英]职员: the ~coat workers 职员阶层 / ~ coffee (不加牛奶或糖的)浓咖啡 / Black Country 黑乡(英格兰中部的工矿区) / ~ damp n. 矿内缺氧空气,二氧化碳,窒息性空气 / ~ death 黑死病 / ~ diamonds 煤 / ~ dog 沮丧: be under the ~ dog 在沮丧中 / ~ draught 一种泻药 / ~ eye 黑眼睛; 被打得发青的眼圈; [口]丑事 / '~face n. ①黑面羊 ②[美]演黑人角色的化装 ③[印]粗黑体字 / 'Blackfeet [复] n. 北美印第安人的一族 / '~fellow n. 澳洲土人 / '~fish n. 小黑鲸; 刚产完卵的鲑鱼 / ~ flag 海盗旗

/ ~ frost 严霜 / ~ gang [总称]船上的火夫; 船上轮机人员 / Black Hand ①黑手党(二十世纪初纽约的一个由意大利移民组织的诈骗集团) ②从事诈骗等的秘密团体 / '~'hearted a. 黑心的 / ~ hole (军营中的)牢房 / '~jack n. ①外涂柏油的革制盛酒容器 ②海盗旗 ③包着皮的铅头棍棒 vt. 用包着皮的铅头棍棒殴打 / '~lead n. [矿]石墨;笔铅 vt. 用铅粉擦(或涂) / '~leg n. [英](破坏罢工的)工贼;骗子;[植]胫病;甜菜蛇眼病;[动]气肿疽 vi. 当工贼 vt. 出卖(罢工同伴) / '~-'letter a. 倒霉的: a ~-letter day 倒霉的一天 n. [印]黑体活字 / ~ light 黑线(指看不见的紫外线或红外线) / '~list n. 黑名单 vt. 把…列入黑名单 / Black Maria [口]囚车; 巡警车 / '~-'market vi. 做黑市买卖 vt. 在黑市上卖(或买) / '~-,marke'teer n. 黑市商人 vi. 做黑市交易 / '~out n. ①(幕间或剧终时的)灯光熄灭 ②灯火管制(期) ③(因供电问题引起的)灯光熄灭 ④临时的眩晕(或失明、记忆缺失) ⑤删除;(新闻)封锁 / ~ pudding (用猪、羊血、大麦等制成的)黑香肠 / Black Rod 黑棍侍卫(英国上议院中引导议员入席的官吏,因黑棍故名) / ~ rot [植]黑斑病 / ~ rust [植]黑锈病 / ~ sheep 害群之马; 败家子 / 'Black-shirt n. (前意大利法西斯组织)黑衫党党员 / '~smith n. 铁匠; 锻工 / '~strap n. ①一种普通红葡萄酒 ②一种掺糖蜜的甘蔗酒 ③赤糖糊(精炼糖时的副产品,用于制酒精) (=~strap mollasses) ④[美俚]咖啡 / ~ tea 红茶 / '~thorn n. [植]黑刺李 / ~ widow (吃掉雄蜘蛛的)一种美洲有毒雌蜘蛛 / '~wood n. 黑木相思树;黑檀

blacken ['blækən] ❶ vt. ①使…变黑 ②诽谤 ❷ vi. 变黑 ‖~ing n. 致黑;发黑度

blackguard ['blægɑːd] I n. ①恶棍 ②滥骂人的人,出言不逊的人 II a. 庸俗低级的; 滥骂人的 III vt. 滥骂; 用下流话骂 ‖~ism n. 恶棍行为 / ~ly a. & ad.

blackmail ['blækmeil] I n. 敲诈; 勒索: nuclear ~ 核讹诈 II vt. 敲诈; 向…勒索 ‖~er n. 敲诈者; 勒索者

bladder ['blædə] n. ①[解]膀胱; 囊 ②气泡 ③囊状物; 球胆 ④ 空话连篇的人 ‖'~wort n. [植]狸藻属植物, 狸藻

blade [bleid] n. ①刀身,刀片; 刀刃,刀口 ②草片,(谷类等的)叶片; 桨片; (舌、骨等的)扁平部分; 肩胛骨 ③剑 ④击剑人 ⑤浮荡少年,恶少 ⑥[语]舌面 ‖in the ~ 尚未结果 ‖~d a. ‖'~bone n. [解]肩胛骨 / '~smith n. 刀匠

blame [bleim] I vt. ①责备,谴责; 找…的差错: have only oneself to ~ 只能怪自己 / Blame it! [美]该死! / Blame me if I do (don't). 我要是(要是不)这样做,随你怎么办好了。 ②[口]把…归咎,推诿 (on, upon): Don't ~ it on him, but on me. 别怪他,该怪我。 II n. ①责备,责怪: incur ~ for 因为…受责备 ②(过错、失败等的)

责任: bear the ~ 负责,受过 / lay (或 put) the ~ on (或 upon) sb. *for sth.* 把某事的责任加在某人身上;把某事归罪于某人 ‖*and small ~ to him* 而这也不能多怪他 / *Bad workmen often ~ their tools.* [谚]拙匠常怪工具差。/ *be to ~* 该受责备,应负责: I am to ~. 是我不好。/ In this matter he seems to *be* in no way to ~. 在这件事情上,看来他没有什么责任。/ *lay the ~ on the right* (*wrong*) *shoulders* 责备应(不应)受责备的人;使应该(不应该)负责的人负责 / *shift the ~* (*on*) *to other shoulders* 把责任推到别人身上

blanch [blɑ:ntʃ] ❶ *vt.* ①【化】漂白;使变白 ②(惧怕、寒冷等)使(面部)苍白 ③使(植物)不见日光而变白 ④【冶】在…上镀锡 ⑤用沸水去(杏仁等)的皮 ❷ *vi.* 发白,变苍白 ‖~**ing** *a.* 漂白的;使变白的

bland [blænd] *a.* ①温和的,和蔼的: a ~ manner 和蔼的态度 ②无动于衷似的 ③乏味的,平淡无奇的 ④(药、食品、饮料、气候等)刺激性少的,温和的 ‖~**ly** *ad.* / ~**ness** *n.*

blandish ['blændiʃ] *vt. & vi.* 奉承,讨好 ‖~**ment** *n.* [常用复]奉承,讨好

blank [blæŋk] Ⅰ *a.* ①空白的,空着的: a ~ cartridge【军】空包弹 / a ~ form 空白表格 / a ~ sheet of paper 一张白纸 / a ~ wall 没有窗(或门)的墙 ②空虚的,单调的,茫然的: a ~ silence 一片沉寂 / His memory was completely ~. 他什么都记不起了。③完全的,无限的: a ~ denial 完全否认 / a ~ impossibility 完全不可能的事 ④失色的,没有表情的: a ~ expression 茫然若失的神情 ⑤没有韵的: ~ verse 无韵诗 ⑥饥荒的: a ~ year 荒年 Ⅱ *n.* ①空白,空地;[美]空白表格: leave a ~ 留出一个空白 / fill certain ~s in science 填补科学上的一些空白 / an application ~ 空白申请书 ②靶子中心的白点; 瞄准的对象 ③(没有中奖的)签,票 ④【机】坯件 ⑤省略号 (一) 的读法;诅咒语(如 damn, damned 等)的代用语 ⑥【军】空包弹 Ⅲ ❶ *vt.* ①使无效,取消,作废 (*out*) 封锁一个空白 使(对方)得零分 ③使不能通行,封锁 (*off*) ④成为空白: His memory often ~s out when he gets excited. 他一兴奋就什么也不记得了。‖*a ~ cheque* ①空白支票 ②开支票人签过名由收款人自填款项数目的支票 ③ 自由行动的权力 / *draw a ~* ①抽空签 ②[口]终于失败 / *in ~* 有空白待填写的 ‖~**ly** *ad.* / ~**ness** *n.* ‖'~**book** *n.* 空白簿 / ~ **endorsement** (票据的)不记名背书

blanket ['blæŋkit] Ⅰ *n.* 羊毛毯,毯子,毛毡;象毛毯似的东西: a ~ of snow 一片白雪 Ⅱ *a.* [美]总括的;共通的,一揽子的: a ~ policy 总括保险单 / ~ rules 适用于各种情况(包括各种偶然性)的规则 Ⅲ *vt.* ①(用毯子)盖,覆 ②(规章、税率等)普遍地适用于 ③掩盖(丑事等);扑灭;妨碍 ④(帆船)抢…的上风 ‖*a wet ~* 扫兴的人;败兴

的事(或物) / *throw a wet ~ on* (或 *over*) 对…泼冷水 ‖~ **roll**【军】背包

blare [bleə] Ⅰ ❶ *vi.* (象喇叭似般)发嘟嘟声;吼叫: The trumpets ~d (forth). 喇叭发出嘟嘟声。❷ *vt.* 高声发出(或奏出);大声宣布: ~ out a warning 高声发出警告 Ⅱ *n.* ①(喇叭等的)嘟嘟声;高声: the ~ of a brass band 铜管乐队的吹奏声 ②(颜色等的)光泽

blaspheme [blæs'fi:m] *vt. & vi.* 亵渎;辱骂 ‖~**r** *n.* 渎神者;辱骂者

blast [blɑ:st] Ⅰ *n.* ①一阵(风);一股(强而突然的气流);疾风,狂风: a ~ of wind 一阵大风 / When the window was opened an icy ~ rushed into the room. 窗一打开,一股冷气冲进屋来。②【冶】鼓风;送风 ③爆炸,爆破;爆炸气浪,冲击波: an H-bomb ~ 氢弹爆炸 / ~ protection 防冲击波 / a ~ wave 冲击波 ④突然的毁灭性的影响;枯萎病: ~ of rice【农】稻瘟病 / a ~ area【军】焦灼区 ⑤管乐器(或汽笛)的声音 ⑥一次用的炸药量 ⑦[美俚]口头攻击 Ⅱ ❶ *vt.* ①(用炸药)炸 ②摧毁;使枯萎;毁灭: Frost ~ed the blossoms. 霜把花打掉了。The tree had been ~ed by lightning. 那棵树被闪电击倒了。③口头攻击(他人) ❷ *vi.* ①发出尖响的声音 ②使用炸药 ③猛烈攻击 ④枯萎 ⑤公开批评;发牢骚;广播 ‖*Blast it* (或 *him*)! 活该! 该死! / ~ *off* (火箭、导弹)发射升空;使发火起飞 / *full* ~ 【冶】(高炉)全风 ②[俚]完全的;大规模的;强烈的 ③[口]飞快地;最有效率地;最强烈地 / *in* (*out of*) ~ 正在(不在)鼓风 ‖~**ed** *a.* ①被摧毁的;枯萎的 ②该死的 ‖~ **furnace**【冶】鼓风炉;高炉 / '~-**off** *n.* (火箭、导弹的)发射 / ~ **pipe** 风管

blatant ['bleitənt] *a.* ①吵嚷的,喧哗的;大喊大叫的 ②炫耀的,显眼的 ‖~**ly** *ad.* clamour ~*ly* 公然叫器

blaze[1] [bleiz] Ⅰ *n.* ①火;火焰;熊熊燃烧: It took the firemen two hours to put the ~ out. 消防队花了两小时才把火扑灭。/ The fire burst into a ~. 火烧得旺起来了。②直射的强光;光辉;闪耀: the ~ of noon 中午的强光 ③(感情等的)迸发,爆发: a ~ of rage 大怒 ④[复]地狱: Go to ~s! (或 What the ~s!) 该死! Ⅱ ❶ *vi.* ①燃烧;冒火焰 ②发(强)光;放光彩;闪耀 ③激发: ~ with anger 发怒 ❷ *vt.* ①使燃烧;使冒火焰 ②用光照耀;发出…的光彩 ‖~ *away* ①连续射击 ②连续发射完(子弹等) ②热烈急促地讲;使劲干 / ~ *up* ①燃烧起来 ②(人)发起怒来 / *like* ~s 猛烈地,激烈地

blaze[2] [bleiz] *vt.* 传播;宣布: ~ sth. abroad (或 about) 宣扬某事,传播某事

blaze[3] [bleiz] Ⅰ *n.* ①(牛、马等脸上的)白斑 ②(刮去树皮后)树身上留下的痕迹 Ⅱ *vt.* ①在(树)上刮去树皮留痕 ②在树皮上刻痕指示(道路等): ~ a new trail through brambles 在荆棘丛中闯出新路

blazer ['bleizə] *n.* ①传播者 ②(颜色鲜艳的)运动茄克, 运动上衣

blazon ['bleizn] I *n.* ①纹章 ②纹章的确切说明 ③夸示 II *vt.* ①绘制(纹章) ②用专业语言描述(纹章) ③用纹章装饰 ④宣布; 宣扬; 夸示 (*forth, out, abroad*) ‖**~ment** *n.* / **~ry** *n.* ①解释(或绘制)纹章的艺术 ②纹章 ③炫示

bleach [bli:tʃ] I ❶ *vt.* 漂白, 晒白; 使脱色 ❷ *vi.* 变白; 脱色 II *n.* ①漂白; 漂白法 ②漂白剂 ③漂白度

bleak [bli:k] *a.* ①苍白的; 惨淡的, 暗淡的 ②凄凉的; 萧瑟的 ③无遮蔽的, 风吹雨打的; 荒凉的, 光秃秃的 ④阴冷的 ‖**~ly** *ad.* / **~ness** *n.*

blear [bliə] I *a.* ①眼花的; 烂的: a ~ eye 烂眼睛, 睑缘炎 ②轮廓模糊的, 朦胧的 II *vt.* 使(眼、头脑)迷糊; 使轮廓模糊 ‖**~-eyed** ['bliər'aid] *a.* ①泪眼模糊的; 烂眼睛的 ②迟钝的; 目光短浅的

bleat [bli:t] I ❶ *vi.* ①(羊、小牛等)叫 ②咩咩地叫 ③讲蠢话; 哀声哭诉 ❷ *vt.* 轻声颤抖地说 II *n.* 羊(或小牛)的叫声; 咩咩的叫声

bleed [bli:d] I (bled [bled]) ❶ *vi.* ①出血, 流血: a wound that ~s freely (或 profusely) 大量出血的伤口 ②(在战斗中)洒热血 ③悲痛, 同情: Our hearts ~ for you. 我们为你感到悲痛。④渗出, 流出 ⑤(植物)伤流, 流出液汁 ⑤(印染、油漆等)渗开, 渗色 ⑥[印]被印成出血版 (*off*) (图片的边超出开本而被切去, 叫做出血版) ⑦出钱; 被敲诈 ❷ *vt.* ①使出血; [医]给…放血 ②榨取(某人)的血汗 ③榨取(树木)的液汁 ④从…中抽干)水; 从…抽气减压 ⑤放(气) ⑥放出(液、浆等) ⑥[印]把…印成出血版; 切裁(超出开本的纸页) II *n.* 出血版 ‖**~ white** ①流尽鲜血; [喻]被榨尽血汗 ② 使流尽鲜血; [喻]榨尽(某人)的血汗 ‖**~er** *n.* ①放血者 ②易出血者; 出血者 ③敲诈钱财的人 ④【电】分压器 ⑤[船]泄水孔 ‖**~ing** *a.* 流血的; (心情)悲痛的; (印染、油漆等)渗色的 *n.* ①出血; 放血 ②(沥青路面)泛油; (水泥混凝土表面)泛出水泥浮浆

blemish ['blemiʃ] I *vt.* 有损…的完美; 玷污 II *n.* 瑕疵, (小)缺点; 污点

blench [blentʃ] ❶ *vi.* 退缩, 畏缩 ❷ *vt.* [古]无视, 回避(事实等)

blend [blend] I (blended 或 blent [blent]) ❶ *vt.* ①混和, 把…混成一体: ~ flour *with* broth 加面粉把汤弄稠 / be good at ~*ing* pigments 善于调色 ②把(不同种茶叶或酒类或烟丝等)掺在一起 ③染(毛皮) ❷ *vi.* ①混和, 交融, 混成一体 ②调和, 相称: How well the voices of the two ~! 这两人的嗓子配在一起多好啊! II *n.* ①混合, 融合 ②混合物, 混成品(如掺了酒精的威士忌酒等) ③合成词 (=~ word, 系由一词的首部分, 接合另一词的尾部分而构成的新词, 如英语中由 *motorist* 的首部分及 *hotel* 的尾部分构成的新词 motel) ‖**~er** *n.* 掺和者; 家用搅拌(或液化)食物的电器 ‖**~ing inheritance** 【生】融合遗传

bless [bles] (blessed 或 blest [blest]) *vt.* ①(用宗教仪式等)使神圣化, 使(食物等)净化 ②[~ oneself] 在(自己)胸前划十字 ③为…祈神赐福; 为…祝福 ④赞美(上帝), 对(上帝)感恩: God be ~ed! (基督教徒常用的感叹语)感谢主! ⑤(上帝)保佑, 赐福于; 使幸福 ⑥使有幸得到, 使具有: You are certainly ~ed *with* a glib tongue. 你倒真会说话! ⑦[过去式和过去分词一般用 blest] [口]诅咒; 使倒霉: I'll be *blest* if I go. 我才不去呢! ⑧保护…使免于 (*from*) ‖**Bless me!** (或 **Bless my soul!** 或 **Well, I'm blest!**) (表示惊愕、愤慨等)哎呀! 我的天哪!

blessed ['blesid] *a.* ①神圣的 ②[宗]在天国享福的, 有福的: the ~ 有福的人(们)【天主教】被教会宣布死后已升天的人(们) ③使人有福的, 愉快(或满足)的: a ~ event [谑]福事(指孩子诞生) ④该死的: Will this ~ rain never stop? 这该死的雨怎么老下个没完呢? ⑤[作加强气用]: Not a ~ drop of rain throughout the month. 整整一个月没下一滴雨。‖**~ly** *ad.* / **~ness** *n.* single ~*ness* [谑]独身

blessing ['blesin] *n.* ①(上帝的)赐福; 祈神赐福; 祝福 ②(教徒在饭前后的)感恩祷告: ask a ~ 饭前(或饭后)祷告 ③同意, 允准: have the ~ of 得到…的同意 ④幸事: a ~ in disguise 貌似灾祸实际使人得福的事(或经历等) / The storm is over, what a ~! 这场暴风雨过去了, 真是幸事!

blew [blu:] blow 的过去式

blight [blait] I *n.* ①(植物的)雕枯病, 枯萎病; 使枯萎的气候(或土壤)条件; 虫害: a late ~ of potato 马铃薯晚疫病 ②挫折(别人的希望、计划等)的因素(或人); 扼杀, 毁损: a ~ *upon* sb.'s hopes 使某人的希望化为泡影的因素 ③受挫; 遭毁损状态 II ❶ *vt.* ①使(植物)染上枯萎病, 使枯萎 ②挫折; 毁损; 摧残: a life ~*ed* by illness 受疾病折磨的一生 ❷ *vi.* 枯萎

blind [blaind] I *a.* ①眼睛失明的, 瞎的; 盲人的: He is ~ in one eye (或 of an eye). 他一只眼睛失明。/ go ~ (人)变瞎 / a ~ angle 【军】盲角, 遮蔽角 ②视而不见的; 盲目的, 无识别能力的 ③未经目击的; 【空】单凭仪表操纵的: a ~ purchase 不看样品(或实物)的购买(或买下的东西) / a ~ flying (landing) 【空】盲目飞行(着陆) ④轻率的, 鲁莽的; 无目的的 ⑤[俚]醉的: be ~ to the world 烂醉 ⑥无结果的; (植物)不开花的: a ~ shell 未炸哑弹, 失效弹 ⑦难解的, 不易识别的; 隐蔽的: a ~ letter 死信(指地址写得无法辨认因而难以投递的信) / a ~ ditch 暗沟 ⑧堵死的, 一端不通的: a ~ wall 无窗的墙 / a ~ alley 死胡同 [书籍装订] 不烫金的, 不着色的 II *vt.* ①使失明, 把…的眼睛弄花 ②遮暗; 使相形之下暗淡失色 ③蒙蔽, 使失去判断力: be ~ed by the lust for gain 利令智昏 ④给(新造道路)铺路面, 填塞 III *n.* ①遮光物; 遮帘; 百叶窗; 窗帘: draw up (pull down) the ~s 拉上(放下)窗帘(或遮帘) ②(狩猎时的)埋伏处 ③障眼物; 挡箭牌; 诱饵 IV *ad.* ①盲目地, 胡乱地: go it ~ 盲干 ②

【空】单凭仪表操纵地 ‖~ *as a mole* 瞎的 / *turn a* (或 *one's*) ~ *eye to* 见 eye ‖~ly *ad.* / ~ness *n.* night ~ness 夜盲 ‖~ **baggage** 铁路的铁闷子车 / ~ **coal** 无烟煤 / ~ **date** [俚] (由第三者安排的)男女双方的初次会面 / ~ **lift** 窗帘的升落开关 / ~ **P** 表示段落的符号(即‖) / ~ **pig** =~ tiger / '~·**reader** *n.* [英] (邮局的)辨字员 / ~ **side** 未加防备的一面 / ~ **spot** ①【物】盲点 ②【无】静区 / ~ **stitch** (缝纫中的)暗针 / '~·**stor(e)y** *n.* 【建】暗楼 / ~ **tiger** [俚] 违法秘密售酒的小店 / ~ **transmission** 盲目发送 / '~·**worm** *n.* 【动】蛇蜥 / ~ **zone** 盲区(雷达达波探测不到的地区)

blindfold ['blaindfould] I *vt.* ①蒙住…的眼睛; 蒙住(眼睛) ②遮住…的视线 ③蒙骗,使不理解 II *a.* ①被蒙住眼的;看不清的 ②盲目的 III *ad.* 盲目地;胡乱地 IV *n.* ①遮眼的蒙布(或带) ②障眼物;蒙蔽人的事物(或言行等)

blink [bliŋk] I ❶ *vi.* ①眨眼睛 ②闪亮,闪烁;微微闪光 ③对…眼开眼闭;惊愕地看 (*at*) ❷ *vt.* ①(眼睛);眨着眼挤掉(眼泪等) ②使闪烁,使闪亮: ~ one's flashlight 一明一暗地打着手电筒 ③闭眼不看,不睬,不顾(事实等): There is no ~ing the fact that .... 不能否认…的事实。④以闪光信号表示 II *n.* ①眨眼睛;一瞥 ②一瞬间 ③闪光 ④冰映光(指因海上大片冰带反射所引起的地平线处的白白) ⑤水照云光(指地平线上空因海水颜色反射而呈现的暗黑色,表示前面有大片海水) ‖on the ~ [俚] ①(机器、工具等)坏了,不能用 ②(人)不舒服 ‖~ing *a.* [英俚]可恶的,该死的

bliss [blis] *n.* ①巨大的幸福,狂喜 ②福,极乐 ③天堂

blister ['blistə] I *n.* ①水疱,疱 ②(植物的)疱状突起;疱病 ③【药】发疱药;引起发疱的东西: a ~ gas 糜烂性毒气 ④(金属上的)砂眼,疱疤;(漆器等上的)气泡 ⑤【无】(雷达的)天线罩 ⑥(飞机上的)固定枪座 ⑦(船)附加外壳;(军舰的)防雷隔堵 II ❶ *vt.* ①使(手、脚等)起疱;使(漆器等)起泡 ②狠揍;狠狠责骂,辱骂 ❷ *vi.* 起水疱;起泡 ‖~ **beetle** 【动】斑蝥 / ~ **copper** 粗铜

blitz [blits] I *n.* ①闪电战,闪击战;猛烈的空袭: ~ tactics 闪电战术 / ~ units 闪击部队 ②(非军事性的)突袭,闪电式行动: make a ~ tour of Western Europe 对西欧作一次闪电式访问 II *vt.* 用闪电战(或猛烈的空袭)攻击(或摧毁): ~ed areas 遭猛烈空袭的地区

blizzard ['blizəd] *n.* 暴风雪;夹雪的暴风

bloat [blout] I *vt. & vi.* ①(使)肿起;(使)膨胀 ②(使)得意忘形 II *n.* ①肿胀病人 ②[俚]醉鬼 ③(家畜的)气胀病 ‖~ed *a.* ①肿胀的 ②得意忘形的 ③(因多食而)病态地发胖的 ④[俚]喝醉的

bloc [blɔk] *n.* ①(立法机构中)临时性政党集团; (美国会及州议会的)跨党派议员集团 ②集团: the sterling ~ 英镑集团

block [blɔk] I *n.* ①大块;大块木料(或石料、金属);【建】块料,砌块;【军】炸药包: a ~ of ice 一大块冰 / children's building ~s 儿童玩的积木 ②砧座;铁砧 ③拍卖台 ④木(或金属)印版;帽模,帽楦;(橱窗陈列帽、假发用的)木制假头;[俚]头 ⑤滑轮;滑轮组,滑车: ~ and tackle 滑轮组; [美]牵制自己行动的人(指妻子、老板等) ⑥一排房屋;街区;街区各街道当中的地区);[美]街段(两条平行街道之间的街的距离): The bank is just two ~s away. 过两条横马路就是银行。⑦[英]大厦,大楼: a ~ of offices 办公室大楼 ⑧【交】铁路区段,区截;(戏院等的)座位划区: the ~ system (铁路)区截制 ⑨一组;一批: an experimental ~ of trees 一个试验林 ⑩【无】部件 ⑪大宗股票 ⑫集团 ⑬阻塞;障碍物;炮闩; 【体】阻挡: a traffic ~ 交通堵塞 / a road ~ 路障 / a stumbling ~ 绊脚石 ⑭[英]阻止议案通过的声明 ⑮【无】停振;【医】(心传导)阻滞 ⑯傻瓜;硬心肠的人 II *vt.* ①阻塞;拦阻: Blocked! (路标)此路不通!②封锁 ③使(帽等)成形 ④使成块状 ⑤用区截制管理(铁路的车辆) ⑥[英]宣布反对(议案) ⑦限制使用(货币、财产等): ~ed currency 使用范围受限制的货币,不能兑换外汇的货币 ⑧(~ in (或 out) 草拟(大纲等);画出…的略图 ‖~ up 堵塞;阻碍 ②垫高: ~ up the rear wheel 把后轮垫高 / cut ~s with a razor 剃刀砍木头(指用非其当)/ do the ~ 在街上蹓跶 / go to the ~ ①上断头台 ②被提出拍卖 / knock sb.'s ~ off 给某人吃苦头,痛打某人 / on the ~ 出售中的;拍卖中的 / send sb. to the ~ 把某人送上断头台 ‖'~·**buster** *n.* [俚]巨型炸弹 / ~ **chain** (自行车等的)车链 / ~ **charge** 方形炸药包 / ~ **effect** 【无】体效应 / '~·**head** *n.* 傻瓜;(橱窗陈列帽、假发用的)木制假头 / '~·**house** *n.* 碉堡;地堡: ~house warfare 堡垒战 / ~ **letter** 印刷体字母: Write in ~ letters. 用印刷体书写。/ ~ **printing** 刻版印刷 / '~·**ship** *n.* 沉没的障碍船(或舰);仓库船 / ~ **signal** 【交】区截信号 / ~ **tin** (提炼过的)锡块,锡锭

blockade [blɔ'keid] I *n.* ①封锁;封锁行动: enforce a ~ 实行封锁 / raise a ~ 解除封锁;迫使解除封锁 / run a ~ 偷越封锁 / a paper ~ 纸上封锁,有名无实的封锁 ②实施封锁的部队 ③堵塞;(交通的)阻断 II *vt.* ①封锁;闭塞;挡住 ‖~r *n.* 封锁者;执行封锁的船 ‖**block'ade-,runner** *n.* 偷越封锁的人(或船)

blockage ['blɔkidʒ] *n.* ①封锁状态 ②障碍: a ~ in the drainpipe 排水管阻塞

blond(e) [blɔnd] I *a.* ①(头发)亚麻色的,淡黄色的 ②(皮肤)白皙的;白里透红的 ③(人)白肤金发碧眼的 ④淡金色的;经漂染成浅色的 II *n.* ①白肤金发碧眼的人(指女人时一般只作作 blonde) ②原色丝花边 (=~ lace)

blood [blʌd] I *n.* ①血,血液;生命液(指无脊动物体中一种与血液相似的液体,植物的液、汁、浆

等）：give one's ~ to sb. 把自己的血输给某人 ②杀人；流血：a man of ~ 杀人成性的人 / demand ~ for 要求以血还血 ③血气；气质；脾气：His ~ was up. 他情绪激昂（或很气愤）。④血统；家世；种族；家族；家族关系；门第；贵族门第：be of the same ~ 是同一（家）族的 ⑤生命；活力；元气 ⑥纯种马 ⑦纨袴子弟，浪子；[美俚]大学生交际圈子里的红人 ⑧[总称]人员：We need new ~ here. 我们这里需要新的人员。II vt. ①[古] 放…的血 ②用血染；用血弄湿 ③使（猎狗）先尝到被猎取的猎物的血（或试闻猎物的气味等）；让（新手等）取得经验 ‖bad ~ 恨，恶感：make bad ~ between the two 使两人互相仇恨 / ~ and iron【史】(德国俾斯麦的)铁血政策；滥用武力 / ~ and thunder 流血和喧闹 / Blood is thicker than water. [谚]血浓于水。(指：亲人总比外人亲。) / blue ~ 贵族血统 / freeze sb.'s ~ (或 make sb.'s ~ freeze) 使某人极度恐惧 / fresh ~ [总称](社团或家庭的)新成员 / have sb.'s ~ on one's head 对某人的死亡（或灾难）应负责任 / in cold ~ 蓄意地(指并非一时的感情冲动)；残忍地 / in sb.'s ~ (或 in the ~) 遗传下来的，生来就有的 / let ~ 放血 / make sb.'s ~ boil 使某人愤怒 / make sb.'s ~ run cold 使某人不寒而栗，使某人毛骨悚然 / of the (royal) ~ (或 of the ~ royal) 王族的 / out for sb.'s ~ 要某人的命 / penny ~ [英俚](描写惊险情节、鬼怪、凶杀等的)廉价小说（或刊物）/ shed ~ ① 流血(指受伤而死) ②屠杀，杀人 / spill ~ 犯伤人（或杀人）的罪 / spill the ~ of 杀死… / stir sb.'s ~ 激起某人的热情(或欲望等) / sweat ~ 累死累活地干；万分忧虑 / young ~ [总称] ①新成员 ②纨袴子弟 ‖~ed a. ①(牛等)纯种的 ②[用以构成复合词]…血的：warm-~ed 热血的；热情的；易激动的 ‖'~-and-'thunder a. (小说或戏剧)充满喧闹的；充满了刺激性情节的 / ~ bank 血库 / '~bath n. 血洗，大屠杀 / ~ brother 亲兄弟 / ~ brotherhood 歃血为盟的兄弟间的情谊 / '~-ce'mented a. 鲜血凝成的：~ corpuscle【医】血球 / ~ count【医】血球计算；从血球计算得出的数字 / '~,curdling a. 使人吓得连血也冻起来的，令人毛骨悚然的 / ~ donor 供血者，献血者 / ~ feud 氏族（或家族）之间的仇杀 / ~ fluke【医】血吸虫，住血吸虫 / ~ group 血型 / '~,guilty a. 犯杀人罪的 / ~ heat 人体血液的正常温度 / ~ horse 纯种马 / '~hound n. ①一种猎狗；一种警犬 ②机警凶猛的追捕者，侦探 / '~,letting n. ①放血 ②流血 / ~ line n. 血统；世系 / '~lust n. 杀戮欲 / ~mobile ['blʌdməbi:l] n. [美]流动收血车，血液车 / ~ money ① 血腥钱(如受雇杀人所得的钱)；损人而得到的利益（或报酬）②偿付给被杀者亲属的钱 / ~ parasite 血液寄生虫 / ~ platelet 血小板 / ~ poisoning 血中毒 / ~ pressure 血压 / ~ purge 血腥的清洗 / '~'red a. ①被血染红的 ②血红的 / ~

bloodless ['blʌdlis] a. ①无血的 ②(手术、斗争、胜利等)不流血的 ③ 贫血的，无血色的，苍白的 ④无生气的，没精神的 ⑤冷酷的 ‖~ly ad.

bloody ['blʌdi] I a. ①有血的；由血做成的 ②出血的 ③血污的 ④血红的，血色的 ⑤流血的，血淋淋的 ⑥[英俚]该死的 (有时仅用来加强语气而没有什么意义)：a ~ rascal 大流氓 / not a ~ one 一个也没有 II ad. [英俚]很，非常：a ~ good lot 多得要命 III vt. 血污，血染 ‖~ mary ['mæri] 由番茄汁加伏特加酒而成的一种饮料 / '~-'minded a. 残忍的，狠心的 / ~ murder 血腥的谋杀：yell (或 scream) ~ murder 高声呼救 ②[美俚]大败 / ~ shirt 被谋杀者的血衣

bloom [blu:m] I n. ①花(尤指观赏植物的花)，(一棵树或一季内开出的)全部花朵 ②开花；开花期：come into ~ 开花 / pass out of ~ 过了开花期，花谢 ③[只用单]青春，兴旺时期；完美：the ~ of life 青年时代，兴旺时期 ④(面颊的)红润，(外观的)清新 ⑤(水果包皮、植物叶面等的)粉衣，粉霜 ⑥(因反射过强在电视上引起的)刺目的闪光 II ❶ vi. ①开花 ②进入青春时代，焕发青春 ③繁盛，突然激增 ④发亮 ❷ vt. 使繁盛；使艳丽 ‖in (full) ~ (盛)开着花；正在(充分)发挥中 / take the ~ off 把…弄得不美（或不新鲜）

blossom ['blɔsəm] I n. ①花(指果树的花)，(一棵树或一季内开出的)全部花朵：apple ~s 苹果花 / The tree has an excellent ~ this year. 今年这棵树开得很好。 ②开花；开花期：be in ~ 开着花 ③兴旺时期 II vi. ①开花；(降落伞)展开 ②繁盛，兴旺 ③发展，长成 (into)：~ (out) into an expert 成长为专门家 ‖nip in the ~ 把…消灭于萌芽状态

blot [blɔt] I n. ①墨水渍；污渍 ②不雅观的事物，看上去有损整体美的东西：a ~ on the landscape 损害风景的东西(如与风景气氛不协调的建筑等) ③(道德上的)污点 II (blotted; blotting) ❶ vt. ①涂污(信纸等) ②把…弄模糊，遮暗 ③[古]污损(名誉等)；使蒙耻 ④(用吸墨水纸等)吸干；吸去：~ up the gravy with a towel 用毛巾擦吸渍出的肉汁 ❷ vi. ①弄上墨渍；弄上污渍：This pen ~s badly. 这支笔墨水漏得厉害。 ②

(信纸等) 吸墨水; 被弄上污渍 ‖*a* ~ *on one's escutcheon* 名誉上的污点 / ~ *one's copybook* 弄坏自己的名声, 失足 / ~ *out* ①涂去, 抹掉 (记忆等) ②把…弄模糊, 遮暗 ③消灭; 杀掉 ‖**blotting pad** 吸墨水纸滚台 / **blotting paper** 吸墨水纸

blotch [blɔtʃ] **I** *n.* ①(皮肤上的) 斑; 小脓疱 ②(墨水、颜料等的) 大滴污渍, 大片污渍 **II** *vt.* 弄脏, 涂污 ‖**~y** *a.* 斑似的; 布满污渍的

blouse [blauz] *n.* ①(工人、水手、妇女等的) 宽大的短外套; 罩衫 ②(美国陆军的) 军上装; 制服上衣

blow¹ [blou] **I** (blew [blu:], blown [bloun]) **❶** *vi.* ①(风) 吹: It was ~*ing* hard. 风刮得很大。/ The door *blew* open. 门吹开了。②(喇叭、口哨等) 吹响: Do you hear the bugle ~*ing*? 你听到军号在响吗? ③吹气; 呼吸困难急促, 喘气: puff and ~ 直喘气 ④喷水; 喷气 ⑤(轮胎等) 爆炸; (保险丝) 烧断; ⑥[口] 吹牛 ⑦(苍蝇) 产卵 ⑧[俚] 跑掉 (*away*) ⑨[美俚] 吸麻醉品 **❷** *vt.* ①吹, 吹动, 使(成功的希望等)告吹 ②吹响(乐器、号角等) ③吹(火等); 使通气: ~ (*up*) the fire 吹火(使旺盛) / ~ the bellows 扇风箱 / one's nose 擤鼻子 ④使充气; 使爆炸 ⑤吹制: glass 吹制玻璃器皿 ⑥发布(或传播)(新闻) ⑦使发怒 ⑧使(保险丝)烧断: A short circuit will ~ (*out*) the fuse. 短路会烧坏保险丝。⑨[常用被动语态]使(马)喘息: The horse was badly ~ *n.* 马跑得直喘。⑩(昆虫)产卵于 ⑪[口]挥霍: ~ money on 在…方面挥霍 ⑫[俚]离开 ⑬[美俚]吸(大麻等)毒品 **II** *n.* ①吹风: go for (或 get) a ~ 出外吹吹风, 出去呼吸新鲜空气 ②疾风 ③吹(指吹笛等) ④擤: Give your nose a good ~, sonny. 小家伙, 把你的鼻子好好擤一下。⑤吹牛; 吹牛者 ⑥(保险丝的)烧断 ⑦[冶]吹炼 ‖~ *hot and cold* 摇摆不定 / ~ *in* ①[俚]突然来到; 突然来访 ②一下子花光(所有的钱) / ~ *off* ①吹掉 ②将(热水、蒸气等)放掉 ③[口](以高声或长谈等)说出自己的思想(或感情) / ~ *off steam* 见 **steam** / ~ *one's own horn* 见 **horn** / ~ *one's own trumpet* 见 **trumpet** / ~ *out* ①吹熄(灯火等) ②(轮胎)突然爆裂(空气、蒸气等)突然冒出 ③(保险丝)烧断 / ~ *over* ①经过, 走过 ②(云等)吹散 ③被淡忘: The impression is so deep that it can hardly ever ~ *over.* 印象这么深刻, 不可能忘掉的。/ ~ *the expense* 见 **expense** / ~ *the gaff* 见 **gaff** / ~ *the lid off* 见 **lid** / ~ *the whistle* (*on*) 见 **whistle** / ~ *up* ①使充气, 给(轮胎等)打气: I have to get my front tyre ~*n* up. 我得把前胎打一下气。②爆炸, 裂开 ③爆炸掉 ④[口]严责 ⑤[口]发脾气 ⑥放大(照片、地图等) / ~ *upon* ①使走味 ②使名誉扫地, 搞臭 ③告发, 告密 / *I'll be ~ed* 真使…我就不是人: *I'll be ~ed if it is so.* 绝不会有这回事。/ *see sb. ~ed first* 见 **see¹** ‖'~**ball** *n.* (蒲公英等类植物的) 种子球状 / '~**by** *n.* 漏气 / '~**cock** *n.* 放泄旋塞 / '~**fish** *n.* 河豚; (美南部的) 黄

麻鲈 / '~**fly** *n.* 绿头苍蝇 / '~**hard** *n.* [美俚]吹牛者 / '~**hole** *n.* ①(鲸鱼等的)鼻孔 ②(坑道中的)气孔 ③(铸件的)气泡 ④鲸鱼(或海豹等)从中呼吸空气的冰孔 / ~**ing cat** [美俚]爵士乐师 / ~ **job** [美俚]喷气机 / '~**lamp** *n.* 喷灯 / '~**off** *n.* ①喷出; 喷出器 ②[俚]大言不惭的人 ③高潮; 结局 ④争吵 / '~**out** *n.* ①(突然)漏气, 喷气 ②车胎爆裂 ③保险丝烧断 ④[俗]盛宴, 丰富的一餐 ⑤熄火; 停炉 ⑥[俚]大事件 / '~**pipe** *n.* 吹管, 吹焊器: an oxyhydrogen ~*pipe* 氢氧吹管 / '~**torch** *n.* ①喷灯: a multidirection oxyacetylene ~*torch* 多向氧炔切割器 ②[美俚]喷气战斗机 / '~**up** *n.* ①爆炸; (脾气等的)爆发 ②[摄]放大; 放大了的照片 ③崩溃, 破裂

blow² [blou] *n.* ①打, 一击; 打击 ②(精神上的)打击; 灾祸 ‖*at a* (*single*) ~ (或 *at one* ~) 一下子: *come to* ~*s* 动手互殴 / *exchange* ~*s* 互殴 / *get a* ~ *in* 打着 / *stop a* ~ *with one's head* [谑]头上挨到一拳 / *strike a* ~ *against* 反对, 企图阻止 / *strike a* ~ *for* 为…而战斗; 拥护 / *without striking a* ~ 不费一兵一卒; 毫不费力

blow³ [blou] **I** (blew [blu:], blown [bloun]) **❶** *vi.* (花)开 **❷** *vt.* ①使开花 ②开(花) **II** *n.* 花; 开花: in full ~ (花)盛开

blower [ˈblouə] *n.* ①吹制(玻璃等的)工人 ②风箱; 鼓风机 ③增压器, 压缩机: an axial-flow ~ 轴向式压缩机 / a high ~ 高增压器 / a three-stage ~ 三级增压器, 三级压缩机

blown¹ [bloun] **I** blow¹ 的过去分词 **II** *a.* ①吹胀的; 吹制的: hand ~ glass 人工吹制成的玻璃器皿 ②喘气的 ③被炸毁的 ④(食物等)有蝇卵(或蝇蛆)附着的

blubber¹ [ˈblʌbə] **I** **❶** *vi.* 又哭又闹 **❷** *vt.* ①哭着说, 哭诉: ~ sth. out 哭诉某事 ②哭肿(脸) **II** *n.* 哭泣; 哭泣声

blubber² [ˈblʌbə] *n.* ①鲸脂, 鲸油; 海兽脂 ②多余脂肪

blue [blu:] **I** *a.* ①蓝色的, 天蓝色的 ②(人的脸色等)发灰的; (动物的毛皮)青灰色的: turn ~ with fear (人)吓得脸发青 / His face was ~ with cold. 他脸冻得发紫。③沮丧的, 忧郁的; 使沮丧的: He looks ~. 他看上去情绪低落。/ Things are looking ~*r* than ever for them. 对他们那帮子人说来, 情况越来越糟了。④穿蓝色服装的; 以蓝色为标志的, (英国)保守党的 ⑤(女人)有学问的 ⑥清教徒的, 禁律严的 ⑦下流的, 淫猥的: ~ films 色情影片 **II** *n.* ①蓝色 ②蓝色(染料); 【纺】上蓝剂 ③蓝布; 蓝色服装; [复](美国)海军蓝制服 ④穿蓝制服的人; 佩戴蓝色标志的人: the light (dark) ~*s* [英]剑桥(牛津)大学校运动代表队(或啦啦队)(因该两校分别以浅蓝、深蓝两色为标志而得名) ⑤[英]大学运动代表队队员; 大学校队队员资格: win one's ~ 被选拔为(大学)校队队员 ⑥蓝色物(如箭靶上的蓝色环等) ⑦女学者 ⑧[the ~] 蓝天; 海洋 ⑨[the ~*s*]

忧郁, 烦闷: be in (或 have) the ~s 闷闷不乐 ⑩ [the ~s] 一种伤感的美国黑人民歌; 慢四步爵士舞曲 Ⅲ ❶ vt. ①把…染成蓝色, 上蓝于 ②[英俚]乱花(钱) ❷ vi. 变蓝, 呈蓝色 ‖a true ~ (政党等) 忠实的成员 (尤指英国的顽固保守党人) / be ~ in the face (因大怒或过分费力) 弄得脸上突然变色 / about the gills 见 gill[1] / once in a ~ moon 千载难逢(地) / out of the ~ 骤地, 突然地: a bolt out of the ~ 晴天霹雳 / sing the ~s 垂头丧气 / till all is ~ 直到酩酊大醉 ②到极点, 到末了; 无限期地 ‖~ness n. ‖~ alert (预备警报后的)空袭警报; 台风警报 / 'Bluebeard (法国民间故事中) 连续杀掉六个妻子的人; 乱娶妻妾的男子 / ~bell n.【植】①(圆叶)风铃草 ②开蓝色铃状花的植物(如风信子等) / ~berry ['blu:bəri] n.【植】乌饭树; 乌饭树的紫黑浆果 / '~bird n. (北美产的)蓝色鸣鸟 / '~'black a. 深黑色的, 蓝黑色的 / ~blood 贵族(或王族)出身, 一个贵族(或王族)出身的人 / ~book n. [B- B-] 蓝皮书(英美等国政府就某一专题发表的封皮为蓝色的正式报告书或外交文书) ②名人录 ③(大学的)笔试用蓝面簿; 笔试 / '~bottle n. ①【植】麦仙翁; 矢车菊; 麝香兰 ②绿头大苍蝇 / ~ chip 热门的股票 / '~-chip a. (股票等)热门的, 靠得住的 / ~ 一流的; (在同行业中)最赚钱的 / ~coat n. 穿蓝制服的人; 警察 / '~-collar a. 穿蓝领子工装的, 体力劳动的 / ~ devils ①忧愁; 沮丧; 忧郁病 ②(酒醉后的)震战性谵妄 / '~-eyed a. ①蓝眼睛的 ②心爱的 ③[美俚]易受骗的 / '~fish n. 北美大西洋沿岸的一种蓝色食用鱼(类似竹笑鱼) ②深蓝色的鱼(如绿鳕) / ~ funk ①[英]不能控制的恐惧 ②[美俚]孤哀, 沮丧 / gag[美俚]端不上台面的低级下流笑话 / ~ gum 桉树 / '~jacket n. 水兵; 水手 / ~ jeans 蓝布工装裤 / ~ john [矿]萤石, 氟石 / ~ law ①(殖民初期新英格兰的)清教徒法规 ②禁止星期日饮酒、娱乐等的法规 / ~ man [俚]穿制服的警察 / ~ murder 恐怖的喊声 / '~nose n. 清教徒式的人; 鼓吹清规戒律的道德家 / '~-'pencil vt. 用蓝铅笔校订(或删改) / ~ peter (蓝底方白格的)开船旗 / ~ pill [药]蓝丸, 汞丸 / '~print n. 蓝图; 行动计划 vt. 为…制蓝图; 详细制订(规划等) / ~ ribbon ①(竞赛中第一名得的)蓝绶带 ②最高荣誉 ③(英美等国)一些禁酒组织的蓝色标志 / '~-'ribbon a. 第一流的;(陪审团等)特别选出的 / ~ ruin ①劣酒 ②灾难; 大失败, 大丢丑 / '~-'sky a. (股票等)价值极微的, 不保险的 / '~-'sky law 股票买卖控制法 / '~stocking n. 女学者, 女才子 / ~ stone ①[矿]①胆矾 ②蓝灰沙岩 ③硬粘土 / ~ streak ①一闪而过的东西 ②连珠炮似的一席话 / '~throat n.【动】蓝喉鸲 / ~ water 大海

bluff[1] [blʌf] Ⅰ a. ①(船头等)前面垂直而平阔的; (河岸等)壁立的, 陡的 ②坦率的; 粗率的 Ⅱ n. 陡岸, 悬崖, 峭壁 ‖~ly ad. / ~ness n.

bluff[2] [blʌf] Ⅰ ❶ vt. ①(用假象)吓唬, 吓住:

sb. out of doing sth. 吓住某人使他不敢做某事 ②欺骗; 假装 ❷ vi. 吓唬人 Ⅱ n. ①吓唬: put on a good ~ 大事讹诈 ②吓唬人的人 ‖call sb.'s ~ 诱使某人摊牌 ‖~er n. 吓唬人的人

blunder ['blʌndə] Ⅰ ❶ vi. ①跌跌撞撞, 绊跌; 慌乱地走(或跑): ~ into (或 against) a wall 慌手慌脚地撞上一堵墙 ②(因无知、慌乱或疏忽)犯错误, 犯大错 ❷ vt. ①(在慌乱中竟愚蠢地)说出, 漏出 (out) ②做错, 办错(事情) Ⅱ n. 大错 ‖~ away 因无知(或管理不善)而挥霍掉; 愚蠢地抛弃 / ~ upon (或 on) sth. 偶然发现某物 ‖~er ['blʌndərə] n. 犯大错的人 ‖'~head n. 傻瓜, 笨蛋

blunt [blʌnt] Ⅰ a. ①(刀子等)不锋利的, 钝的 ②(感觉、理解力等)迟钝的 ③(人、人的言谈举止等)生硬的; 率直的, 不转弯抹角的: a ~ refusal 干脆的拒绝 / That's the ~ fact. 事实的的确确就是这样。/ to be ~ (with you) [作插入语]老实(跟你)说 Ⅱ ❶ vt. ①把…弄钝; 把…弄迟钝 ②减弱, 挫折 ❷ vi. 变钝 Ⅲ n. ①钝器 ②短粗的针 ③[俚]现钞 ‖~ly ad. to put it ~ly [作插入语]直截了当地说 / ~ness n.

blur [blə:] Ⅰ (blurred; blurring ['blə:riŋ]) ❶ vt. ①涂污, 弄脏; 污损(名声等) ②把(界线、视线等)弄得模糊不清: ~ out distinctions between right and wrong 抹煞是非界线 / Tears of joy blurred our eyes. 喜悦的眼泪把我们的眼睛弄糊了。❷ vi. ①弄上污迹 ②变得模糊起来 Ⅱ n. ①污迹 (道德等方面的)污点 ②模糊不清的东西; 模糊一片

blurt [blə:t] Ⅰ vt. 突然说出, 脱口说出 (out): ~ out a secret 漏出秘密 Ⅱ n. 无意之中漏出的话

blush [blʌʃ] Ⅰ ❶ vi. ①脸红; 羞愧: ~ for (或 with) shyness 因害羞而脸红 / ~ at the thought of 一想到…就脸红 / ~ for sb. 替某人害臊 / I ~ to own my mistake. 我抱愧认错。②(花等)呈现红色 ❷ vt. 把…弄成红色 Ⅱ n. ①脸红: Spare my ~es. 别出我洋相! ②红色; 红光 ③[古]一瞥 ‖at (the) first ~ 乍一看(之下) / put sb. to the ~ 使某人受窘脸红 ‖~ful a. 脸红的; 使人脸红的

bluster ['blʌstə] Ⅰ ❶ vi. ①(风)呼啸狂吹; (浪等)汹涌 ②(人)咆哮, 恐吓 ❷ vt. ①怒气冲冲地说; 蛮横地喊: ~ out (或 forth) threats 大声威吓 ②恐吓, 胁迫 Ⅱ n. ①狂风声; 巨浪声 ②大吵大嚷: work without ~ and ostentation 不声不响踏踏实实地工作 ③空洞的大话; 大声的威吓 ‖~ oneself into anger 勃然大怒 ‖~er ['blʌstərə] n. 咆哮的人, 吓唬人的人

boar [bɔ:] n. ①(未阉的)公猪 ②公野猪

board [bɔ:d] Ⅰ n. ①木板, 板; 纸板: a bulletin ~ 布告栏 / His name is on the ~ of honour. 他的名字上了光荣榜。/ bound in cloth ~s (书)布面精装的 / tongue and groove ~【建】企口板 / 船舷 on ~ 在船(或车、飞机)上 ③边; 海岸 ④餐桌; 伙食: ~ and lodging 膳宿 ⑤会议桌; 全

体委员;委员会;(政府机关或商业)部门: a ～ of directors 董事会 / the *Board* of Trade (英国) 商务部 / a ～ of trade [美] 商会 / on the ～ 将在会上讨论 ⑥[复]舞台: on the ～s 做演员 **II ❶** *vt.* ①用板铺;用板堵: ～ the floor 铺地板 / ～ up a window 用木板把窗堵住 ②(收费)供～膳食 ③上(船、车、飞机): ～ a train 上火车 (为攻击等而)靠拢(船);强行登(船) **❷** *vi.* 搭伙: ～ in 在住宿处搭伙 / ～ out 在外搭伙 / ～ with a poor-peasant family 在一家贫农家里搭伙 ||*free on ～* 【商】船上交货,离岸价格(略作 FOB 或 f.o.b.) / *go by the ～* (桅杆等)落水,(计划等)落空;失败 ②被丢到海里;被丢开 / *sweep the ～* 赢得全部赌注;全胜 / *tread the ～s* 上舞台,做演员 / *walk the ～s* 做演员 ||～**foot** 板呎(木材的计量单位,等于厚一吋、面积一平方呎的木材) / '～-'money *n.* (给付人的)伙食钱(= ～ wages) / '～-**room** *n.* (董事会等的)会议室 / '～-**walk** *n.* [美]木板路(尤指海滨的)

boarding ['bɔːdiŋ] **I** *n.* ①铺木板;木板;大木板(由几块木板拼成) ③上船(或车、飞机) ④攻击(或占领)敌船 **II** *a.* 供膳的;供膳宿的 ||～-**card** *n.* (民航班机等的)搭载客货单 / '～-**house** *n.* 供膳的寄宿处 / '～-'**out** *n.* 在外面搭伙 / ～ **school** 寄宿学校 / '～-'**ship** *n.* 检查中立国船舶有无违禁品的船

boast [boust] **I** *n.* ①自夸的话: It has never been her ～ that she alone could accomplish the work. 她从来没有夸口说只有她能够完成那项工作。②可以夸耀(或自豪)的事物: make a ～ of 自豪地说到 **II ❶** *vi.* 夸,自夸(*of, about*): Nobody should ～ of his learning. 谁也不应当夸耀自己的学识。**❷** *vt.* ①夸口说: He ～ that he is an authority. 他自称是权威。/ He ～ed himself (to be) an all-round man. 他自称是多面手。② 以…而自豪;自恃有: The town ～s a beautiful lake. 这个镇上有一个美丽的湖。||～**er** *n.* 自夸的人,大言不惭的人

boastful ['boustful] *a.* ①(人)好夸口的,自负的 ②(言语等)自夸的 ||～**ly** *ad.* / ～**ness** *n.*

boat [bout] **I** *n.* ①(用桨、帆或引擎的)小船,艇: a sailing ～ 帆船 / a harbour ～ 港务船 / 渔船;小汽船;大轮船 ③船形器皿: a gravy ～ 酱(或卤汁)碟 **II ❶** *vi.* 乘船(游玩),划船(游玩): go ～ing 划船(游玩) **❷** *vt.* ①把…放在船上 ②用船装运;～ *it* 乘小艇航行 / *the oars* 停划并把桨收到船内 / *burn one's ～s* 破釜沉舟;背水布阵 / *have an oar in everyman's ～* 多管闲事 / *in the same ～* 处境相同,面临同样的危险 / *miss the ～* 错过机会,坐失时机 / *rock the ～* 捣乱 / *take ～* 上船 / *take to the ～s* (船沉时)乘船上的救生艇以求脱险 ||～**ful** *n.* 一船所载的量 / ～**ing** *n.* 划船(游玩) / ～**drill** 救生演习 / '～-**hook** *n.* 有钩的篙子 / ～-**house** *n.* 水边停放游艇的场所(常附设俱乐部) / ～ **line** (大船)系小艇的索 / ～**man** ['boutmen] *n.* 船工。②出租(或出售)小艇的人 / ～ **race** 划艇竞赛,赛船 / ～ **train** 为方便旅客按时与船衔接的列车

boater ['boutə] *n.* ①船工 ②[英]硬草帽

boatswain ['bousn, 'boutswein] *n.* 水手长 ||～'s **chair** 【船】高空操作坐板,工作吊板

bob[1] [bob] **I** *n.* ①短鬈发,发髻;女子的短发式 ②剪短的(马)尾 ③歌曲的短迭句;诗节末尾的短行 ④微不足道的东西 **II** (bobbed; bobbing) *vt.* 剪短(发、尾等) ||**bobbed** *a.* 剪短的 ||～ **wig** (英国法院中法官所戴的)短而鬈的假发

bob[2] [bob] **I** *n.* ①[口]一束(或一串)叶子(或花、葡萄等) ②悬挂的装饰品(如耳环) ③浮动,摆动 ④(钓鱼丝上的)浮子 ⑤【物】摆锤,振子坠 ⑥屈膝(礼) ⑦轻敲,轻打 ⑧[俚]步兵 **II** (bobbed; bobbing) **❶** *vi.* ①上下跳动;[喻]再度浮起 ②(一种游戏)试图咬住悬挂的水果(*for, at*) ③行屈膝礼 **❷** *vt.* ①敲;轻敲;使敲(或撞) ②急速拉动 ||～ **up** 突然出现: This question has *bobbed* up again. 这个问题又出现了。/ ～ **up like a cork** 恢复元气;东山再起 ||**bobbed** *a.* 形成束的,形成串的

bobbin ['bɔbin] *n.* ①【纺】筒管;筒子,木管;亚麻捆 ②【电】绕线管,线圈架;点火线圈

bobby ['bɔbi] *n.* [俚]警察

bode [boud] *vt. & vi.* 预兆;预示 ||～ **well** (**ill**) 主吉(凶);预兆吉(凶兆)的;凶兆的 / ～**ment** *n.* 预兆;凶兆;预言;预示

bodice ['bɔdis] *n.* ①(妇女的)紧身围腰 ②(妇女罩在衬衫等外面的)宽大的背心

bodily ['bɔdili] **I** *a.* 身体的,肉体的: in ～ fear 怕身体受伤 **II** *ad.* ①亲自 ②全部,整体: The building was transported ～ to another place. 整幢房屋不拆好地被迁到另一个地方。

body ['bɔdi] **I** *n.* ①身体,躯体,(植物等的)躯干;车身;船身: the ～ of a ship 船身 ②尸体,尸首 ③主体,主要部分;正文。④团体;机关 ⑤人[常用以构成复合词,如 anybody, everybody 等] ⑥物体: a heavenly ～ 天体 ⑦质地;(液体的)稠度;(酒等的)强度 ⑧(一)群;(一)批;(一)片: a large ～ of men (facts) 一大批人(事实) ⑨上衣的主要部分(除衣领、衣袖外);女紧身衣 ⑩【数】立体 ⑪[印]铅字身 **II** *vt.* 赋…以形体 ||～ **forth** 给…以形象;象征 / *in a ～* 全体,一块儿 / *keep ～ and soul together* 仅能维持生活 ||'～-,**builder** *n.* ①车身制造者 ②滋补的食物 ③锻炼肌肉使之发达的器械 / ～-**centred** *a.* 【物】体心的: ～-*centred lattice* 体心点阵 / ～-**colo(u)r** 不透明的颜色(或颜料等) / ～ **corporate** 【律】法人团体 / '～-**guard** *n.* ①警卫员 ②保镖 / ～ **plan** (船)横剖型线图 / ～ **politic** 国家 / ～ **shirt** [美]紧身衬衫;紧身背心 / ～ **snatcher** 盗尸人

bog [bɔg] **I** *n.* 泥塘,沼泽 **II** (bogged; bogging) *vt. & vi.* [常用被动语态](使)陷入泥沼,(使)沉入泥沼 (*down*) ||～ **down** (使)陷于困境;(使)停

顿: be *bogged down* deeper and deeper in political and economic crises 在政治和经济危机中越陷越深 / How did the work ~ *down*? 工作怎样会停下来的? ‖~**-berry** ['bɔg,beri] *n.*【植】酸果蔓属植物; 大果酸果蔓 / ~ **oak** 长期埋于泥炭田中的变黑的橡树

bogus ['bougəs] *a.* 伪造的, 伪的: a ~ certificate 伪造的证件

Bohemian [bou'hi:mjən] I *a.* ①波希米亚的 ②波希米亚人的 ③波希米亚语的 ④生活豪放不羁的 (尤指艺术家等) II *n.* ①波希米亚人 ②波希米亚语 ③生活豪放不羁的艺术家

boil [bɔil] I ❶ *vi.* ①达到沸点 ②汽化 ③象沸水一样滚泡 ④(人、感情等)激动; (海)翻腾: ~ with fury 激怒 ❷ *vt.* ①煮 ②在沸水中煮 ③用煮沸方法制造 (或分出) (盐、糖等) ④使(人、感情等)激动 II *n.* ①煮沸; 沸点; 沸腾: come to the ~ 开始沸腾 / bring to the ~ 使沸腾 / at (或on) the ~ 沸腾着, 滚着 ②【医】疖 ‖~ *away* 不断沸腾; 汽化; 煮干 / ~ *down* ①熬浓: ~ *down* syrup 熬浓糖浆 ②[喻]压缩: ~ a story *down* to five hundred words 把故事压缩到五百个字 ③(糖浆等)被熬浓 ④(文章等)宜于压缩 / ~ *down to* 归结起来是… / ~ *over* ①沸溢 ②发怒; 激动 ‖~ed *a.* ①煮沸的, 烧滚的: ~*ed*-off silk【纺】熟丝; 熟绸 / ~*ed* oil 清油, 熟油 ②[俚]喝醉的

boiler ['bɔilə] *n.* ①煮器 (壶、锅、釜的泛称) ②锅炉: a once through ~ 贯流锅炉, 直流锅炉 ③热水贮槽 ④熬煮东西的人 ‖~ **iron** 锅炉钢板 / '~,**maker** *n.* 锅炉制造工 (或装配工、修理工) / ~ **plate** 锅炉钢板 / ~ **room** 锅炉房 / ~ **scale** (锅炉的)水垢 / ~ **suit** 连衫裤工作服 / ~ **tube** 锅炉管

boisterous ['bɔistərəs] *a.* ①(风、海水、行动、言词等)狂暴的, 汹涌的 ②(人或行动)吵吵嚷嚷的; 兴高采烈的 ‖~**ly** *ad.* ~**ness** *n.*

bold [bould] *a.* ①大胆的, 勇敢的: a ~ resolve 雄心壮志 ②冒失的, 鲁莽的; 无耻的; 无礼的 ③醒目的, 粗大的: ~ lines 粗线 / in ~ outline 轮廓鲜明的 (地) / write a ~ hand 写字粗大醒目 ④险峻的, 陡直的: a ~ cliff 绝壁 ‖(as) ~ *as brass* 极其无耻的 / *make* ~ *to* (或 *make so* ~ *as to*) 冒昧地…, 擅自… ‖~**ly** *ad.* ①大胆地 ②冒失地 / ~**ness** *n.* ‖'~**face** *n.* 【印】黑体, 粗体 / '~**faced** *a.* ①冒失的, 鲁莽的 ②【印】黑体的, 粗体的

bole [boul] *n.* 树干, 树身

boll [boul] *n.* 【植】(棉、亚麻的)圆荚, 铃: a cotton ~ 棉桃, 棉铃 ‖~ **stainer** 【动】棉椿象, 污棉虫 / '~**worm** *n.* 【动】蟛蛉

bollard ['bɔləd] *n.* ①【海】(码头或船甲板上的)双系缆柱, 系缆柱 ②(行人安全岛顶端的)护柱

bolster ['boulstə] I *n.* ①长枕, 垫枕 ②垫枕状的支撑物; 【机】软垫, 垫木; 车架承梁; 【建】托木, 雀替 II *vt.* ①(用支撑物)支撑, 垫 ②费力支持 (*up*) ‖~**ing** ['boulstəriŋ] *n.* 支撑, 支持

bolt[1] [boult] I *n.* ①[古]弩箭 ②意外(或不幸)事件 ③闪电, 雷电 ④(门、窗的)插销(和 U 形钉); 锁簧 ⑤螺栓; 栓: an eye ~ 有眼螺栓 / a stud ~ 双头螺栓, 柱螺栓 ⑥(棉布的)匹; (纸等的)卷 ⑦【军】枪栓; 枪机 ⑧马的脱缰; 快跑; 逃走 II ❶ *vt.* ①发射(箭等) ②脱口说出 (*out*) ③囫囵吞下 ④闩(门), 拴住: ~ sb. in (out) 把某人关在室内 (室外) ⑤[美]拒绝支持 (自己党派的政策、提名等); 退出(党派或团体) ❷ *vi.* ①射; 窜 ②(马)脱缰; 逃跑 ③囫囵吞下 ④[美]拒绝支持自己党派的政策 (或提名等); 退出党派(或团体) III *ad.* 象箭似地; 突然 ‖~ *from the blue* ①晴天霹雳 ②意外(或不幸)事件 / A fool's ~ *is soon shot*. ①蠢人一下子把箭射完。(指不善于弯弓待发) ②蠢人易于智穷力竭。③蠢人很快花掉钱。/ ~ *upright* 笔笔直直 / *make a* ~ *for it* 赶快逃走 / *shoot one's* (*last*) ~ 尽其所能, 竭尽全力 ‖~**ing** *n.* ①栓位 ②吞下 ③逃走 ‖~ **head** 【机】螺栓头; 【化】(蒸馏用)长颈烧瓶; 【军】(枪)机头 / '~**hole** *n.* ①动物防险洞 ②[喻]躲避处, 安全的地方 / '~**rope** *n.* 缝在帆边的粗缆

bolt[2] [boult] I *vt.* ①筛(粉、谷等) ②[古]细查 ③筛选 II *n.* 筛子

bomb [bɔm] I *n.* ①炸弹: a fragmentation ~ 杀伤弹 / a tear-gas ~ 催泪弹 ②高压弹(内含高压气体的容器) ③【地】火山弹(指火山喷出的球状熔岩) ④用铅衬里的放置放射性物质的容器(如钴炮) ⑤意外发生的不愉快事件 ⑥[美俚](演出等的)显著失败 ⑦治疗用放射源 II ❶ *vt.* 投弹于, 轰炸 ❷ *vi.* [美俚]失败 ‖~ *out* ①把(地方等)炸毁 ②把(人)炸得无家可归 / ~(*s*) *away* 投弹完毕(轰炸员向驾驶员及机上其他人员表明炸弹已经投下时的信号) / ~ *up* 给(飞机)装上炸弹 ‖~ **bay** (飞机上的)炸弹舱 / ~ **carrier** 轰炸机 / ~ **cluster** 集束炸弹; 集束燃烧弹 / ~ **damage**【军】轰炸效果 / '~-**dis'posal** *n.* 未爆弹处理 / '~-'**dropping** *n.* 投弹 / '~ed-out *a.* ①空袭时被炸毁的 ②(人)因住屋被炸毁而无家可归的 / '~-**hatch** *n.* 炸弹舱门 / ~ **load** 载弹量 / '~-'**proof** *a.* 防空的, 防弹的 *n.* 防空洞 / ~ **release** 投弹器; 投弹 / '~**shell** *n.* ①炸弹 ②[喻]出人意料之外的事件 ③突然引起注目的人物(或事物) / ~ **shelter** 防空洞 / '~**sight** *n.* 轰炸瞄准具 / ~ **site** 被炸后的废墟 / ~ **thrower** 投弹手

bombard[1] ['bɔmbɑ:d] *n.* 射石炮(中世纪的臼炮)

bombard[2] [bɔm'bɑ:d] *vt.* ①炮击; 轰炸 ②[喻]攻击, 痛斥, 向(某人)发出连珠炮似的问题 ③【原】轰击; 碰撞; 粒子辐射: ~ uranium with neutrons 用中子轰击铀 ‖~**ment** *n.*

bombast ['bɔmbæst] *n.* 装腔作势故意夸大的语言(或文章)

bomber ['bɔmə] *n.* ①轰炸机: a jet ~ 喷气式轰炸机 / a strategic ~ 战略轰炸机 ②投弹手

bona fide ['bounə 'faidi] [拉]真正的(地); 真诚的(地)

bond [bond] **I** *n.* ①契约; 契约所规定的义务 ②公债; 债券: Premium *Bonds* [英]政府有奖债券 ③(付款)保证书; 保证人 ④结合物; 粘结剂; 结合力; 联结 ⑤[复]镣, 铐; 监禁, 下牢 ⑥[化]键; 【建】砌合; 【交】接续线 ⑦证券纸 ⑧[商]关栈保留 **II ❶** *vt.* ①把(进口货物)存入关栈 ②使成为用债券保证的债 ③砌合(砖); 粘着(水泥等) **❷** *vi.* 结合在一起; 团结 ‖*burst one's ~s* 赢得自由 / *enter into a ~ with sb.* 与某人订契约 / *in ~* (货物)在关栈中, 尚未完税 / *in ~s* 在拘留中; 被奴役 / *take out of ~* (完税后)由关栈提出(货物) ‖*~ed a.* (货物)扣存关栈以待完税的 / *~er n.* [无]联接器, 接合器 / *~ing n.* ①结合; 搭接 ②[电]电缆铠甲或铅壳的连接, 加固和接地, 屏蔽接地 ③压焊 ‖*~,holder n.* 债券持有者 / *~man* ['bondmən] *n.* 奴隶; 农奴 / *~ paper* 证券纸 / *~ servant* 奴隶, 奴役的人 / *~ service* 奴役 / *'~slave n.* 奴隶 / *~sman* ['bondzmən] *n.* ①奴隶 ②[律]保证人 / *'~stone n.* 【建】束石 / *~(s),woman n.* 女奴隶

bondage ['bondidʒ] *n.* 奴役; 束缚: in ~ to 被…所奴役

bone [boun] **I** *n.* ①骨; 身体中的硬组织: skin and ~(s) 瘦得皮包骨(的状态) ②[复]骨骼; 死尸; 身体 ③骨状物(象牙等); 骨制品 ④[复][音]响板 ⑤[复][口]骰子 ⑥[俚]用功的学生 ⑦[美][复]在黑人(一般由白人扮作黑人)乐团演唱中站在演唱者两端作滑稽问答的人 **II ❶** *vt.* ①剔去…的骨: ~ a fish 剔鱼骨 ②施骨肥于 ③用鲸骨撑大(妇女上衣) ④[俚]偷 ⑤测量…的高度: a *boning* rod 测高杆 **❷** *vi.* [俚]专心致志(up): ~ up on a subject 专攻一门学问 ‖*a ~ of contention* 争论的原因 / *bred in the ~* 根除不了的 / *carry a ~ in the mouth* (或 *teeth*) [海](船只)破浪前进 / *cast (in) a ~ between* 使…之间起争端, 离间 / *cut to the ~* 彻底取消; 削减: *cut costs to the ~* 把成本减到最低程度 / *devil's ~s* 骰子 / *feel in one's ~s* 确信 / *have a ~ in one's leg (throat)* 难于行走(启齿) / *have a ~ to pick with sb.* 同某人有争论 / *lay one's ~s* 埋葬, 死 / *make no ~s about (it, to)* 对…毫不犹豫 / *roll the ~s* 吹牛, 夸张; 闲谈 / *to the ~* 深入骨髓的, 透骨; 到极点 / *will not (或 never) make old ~s* 活得长久 ‖*~less a.* 无骨的 / *boning n.* 去(鱼)骨 ‖*~ ash* 骨灰 / *~ bed* 【地】骨层 / *~ black* 骨炭 / *~ china* 一种含有骨灰(或磷酸钙)的瓷器 / *'~-deep a.* 刻骨的 / *'~-dry a.* 十分干燥的 / *~ dust* 骨粉(作肥料用) / *'~head n.* [俚]笨蛋, 傻瓜 / *'~,idle a.* 懒极的 / *~ meal* 骨粉 / *'~set n.* 【植】泽兰属植物; 贯叶泽兰 / *'~,setter n.* [医]正骨者 / *'~,setting n.* 正骨法 / *'~-,shaker n.* [俚]破旧摇晃的车辆 / *'~yard n.* [俚]墓地; 动物尸骨堆放地

bonfire ['bɔn,faiə] *n.* 大篝火; 营火: make a ~ of 烧掉…

bonnet ['bonit] **I** *n.* ①(无边有带的)女帽; 童帽 ②烟囱帽; 机器罩; 阀门帽 ③[俚](赌场、拍卖场中的)同谋者, 诱骗他人上当者 **II** *vt.* ①给…戴帽子 ②拉下(某人)的帽子使遮住其眼睛 ③[俚](合伙)诱骗

bonny, bonnie ['boni] *a.* ①美丽的 ②健康的; 强壮的 ③快活的; 好的 ‖*bonnily ad.*

bonus ['bounəs] *n.* ①额外津贴 ②奖金 ③红利 ④政府发给退伍军人的钱: an army discharge ~ 退役费

bony ['bouni] *a.* ①骨的; 像骨的 ②多骨的: a fish 多骨的鱼 ③骨胳大的 ④瘦的, 憔悴的

boo [bu:] **I** *int.* 呸[表示嫌恶或轻蔑] **II** *n.* 呸的一声 **III ❶** *vi.* 发出呸的声音 **❷** *vt.* 讥笑

booby ['bu:bi] *n.* ①笨蛋, 呆子 ②【动】鲣鸟 ③(球队等)得分最少者; (歌舞剧等)演出最差者: the ~ prize 末名奖 ‖~ hatch ①[海]活盖小舱口, 便道小舱口 ②精神病院 / ~ mine 【军】饵雷, 诡雷 / ~ trap 【军】饵雷; 陷阱 / *'~-trap vt.* 在…设饵雷; 在…设陷阱

book [buk] **I** *n.* ①书, 书籍, 书本: a ~ of reference 参考书 / the ~ of time 历史 ②[the B-]基督教《圣经》 ③(书的)卷, 篇 ④(象书一样装订成册或连接的)支票(或戏票等) ⑤[常用复]帐簿; 登记簿; 名册: enter in the ~s 把…记入帐簿 / the visitors'. ~ 来客登记簿 / enter sb.'s name on the ~s 把某人的姓名载入名册 / take sb.'s name off the ~s 把某人的姓名从名册上除去 ⑥(歌剧的)歌词 ⑦(赛马赌博等)的登记簿, 赌帐 **II ❶** *vt.* ①把…记载入册 ②预定, 定(戏票、车位等) **❷** *vi.* ①预定 ②[英](旅客在旅馆里)登记姓名 ‖*an open ~* 尽人皆知的事物; 毫无秘密(或隐瞒)的事 / *a sealed ~* ①天书 ②高深莫测的事: It's a *sealed* ~. 我对这一窍不通。 / *be ~ed* 被捉住, 逃不了 / *be in sb.'s good (bad 或 black) ~s* 得(失)某人的好感, 得(失)宠于某人 / *be written in the ~ of life* 【宗】列于死后必将获救者名单中 / *bring sb. to ~ (for sth.)* (为某事)盘问(或责问)某人; (为某事)严责(或申斥)某人 / *by the ~* 按常规 / *hit the (或 one's) ~s* [美]用功 / *hold ~* (演出时)当提词人 / *keep ~s* 上帐, 记帐 / *kiss the ~* 吻基督教《圣经》宣誓 / *know like a ~* 熟悉; 通晓 / *make ~* ①(在赛马等中)接受不同数目的赌注; 打赌 ②以接受打赌为业 / *one for the ~s* 出乎意料的事, 惊人的事 / *on the ~s* 载入名册 / *set ~s* 考试规定所需阅读的书 / *shut the ~s* 停止交易(来往) / *speak by the ~* 说话确切 / *speak like a ~* 用正式语句讲话, 咬文嚼字 / *suit sb.'s ~* 适合于某人, 对某人便利 / *take a leaf out of sb.'s ~* 学某人的样子 / *the devil's ~s* 纸牌 / *throw the ~ at* [俚] ①尽量加罪名于…身上 ②给…以最大限度的惩罚 / *without ~* 凭记忆; 无根据 ‖*~ed a.* 记载入册的; 登记了的 / *~let* ['buklit] *n.* 小册子 ‖*~ account* 往来帐户 /

'**~,binder** *n.* 装订工人 / '**~,bindery** *n.* 装订厂，装订场所 / '**~,binding** *n.* 装订 / '**~case** *n.* 书橱；书箱 / **~ concern** [美]出版社 / **~ credit** 帐面信用 / **~ debt** 帐面负债 / '**~end** *n.* 书立，书挡 / '**~,hunter** *n.* 珍本书收购者，猎书者 / '**~,keeper** *n.* 簿记员；记帐人 / '**~,keeping** *n.* 簿记 / '**~-,learned** *a.* 迷信书本的 / **~ learning, '~lore** *n.* ①书本知识 ②[口]正规教育 / '**~,maker** *n.* ①编纂者(尤指编书谋利者) ②(赛马等的)登记赌注者 / '**~,making** *n.* 编书；赛马赌博等的登记簿 / '**~man** ['bukmən] *n.* ①文人；学者 ②书商 / '**~mark** *n.* 书签 / **~mobile** ['bukmə,bi:l] *n.* 车上图书馆，流动图书馆 / '**~-phrase** *n.* 只言片语 / '**~plate** *n.* (贴在书上的)藏书者的印记 / **~ post** [英](取费低廉的)书籍邮寄 / **~ review** 书评 / '**~,seller** *n.* 书商 / '**~shelf** *n.* 书架 / '**~shop,** '**~store** *n.* 书店 / '**~stall** *n.* 书摊，书亭 / '**~-stand** *n.* ①书柜 ②书摊，书亭 ③书架 / **~ structure** 【矿】页状构造(岩) / '**~-,token** *n.* (定额的)书籍预约证 / **~ value** 帐面价值 / '**~work** *n.* 书本钻研 / '**~worm** *n.* ①蠹鱼，蛀书虫 ②书呆子；极爱读书者

booking ['bukiŋ] *n.* (讲演，演出等的)预约 ‖**~ clerk** 售票员 / **~ office** 售票处

bookish ['bukiʃ], **booky** ['buki] *a.* ①书籍的；书上的 ②只有书本知识的，书生气的 ③咬文嚼字的

boom[1] [bu:m] **I** *n.* ①(炮、雷、风、风琴等的)隆隆(或轰轰、嗡嗡等)声，有回响的声音 ②(大蛙等的)叫声 **II** ❶ *vi.* 发出隆隆声 ❷ *vt.* 用隆隆声表达(*out*): The clock ~ed out three. 大钟沉重地敲了三下。‖*lower the* ~ *on* 惩罚，对…采取严厉措施 ‖~**ing** *n. & a.*

boom[2] [bu:m] **I** *vi.* ①突然增加，迅速发展 ②兴旺；出名 ❷ *vt.* ①使迅速发展；使兴旺；使出名 ②吹捧；支持 **II** *n.* ①(商业等的)景气，繁荣；(政治形势等的)突然好转 ②激增；暴涨 ‖~**ing** *n. & a.* ‖'**~town** *n.* [美]新兴城市

boom[3] [bu:m] *n.* ①吊杆；帆的下桁，帆杠: a heavy (或jumbo) ~ 重吊杆 ②栅栏，水栅，横江铁索，河中标柱: ~ defence 【军】栅栏防御 / ~ **nets** 【军】栅栏网(设在港口和航道的水底铁丝网) ③连接飞机主支架与尾部的梁(或支架)

boomerang ['bu:məræŋ] **I** *n.* ①飞镖(澳大利亚土著的武器，用曲形坚木制成，投出后可飞回原处) ②[喻]自食其果的言行 **II** *vi.* 使人自食其果

boon [bu:n] **I** *n.* ①恩惠；福利；神益；方便: Do you find this dictionary a ~? 你觉得这本词典有用吗? ②[古]请求: ask a ~ of sb. 请求某人 **II** *a.* [古][诗]温和的；愉快的，欢乐的: a ~ companion 酒友；好友

boost [bu:st] **I** *vt.* ①升，提；推 ②提高，促进；支援 ③(用广告等)吹捧 ④【电】升压 ⑤助爆 **II** *n.* ①升 ②提高，增加 ③帮助 ④宣传；吹捧 ‖~**er** *n.* ①提(或推)的人 ②支援者 ③【电】升降压机，调压机；升压电阻；(火箭的)助推器 ④多级火箭

的第一级 ⑤(收音机、电视接收机的)放大器 ⑥【军】助爆药 ⑦【药】辅助药剂(尤指增强免疫力的辅助剂)

boot[1] [bu:t] **I** *n.* ①[美](皮或橡胶制的)长统靴 ②筒状刑具(夹足、腿用) ③[英](汽车的)行李箱 ④【机】保护罩 ⑤踢 ⑥解雇 ⑦[美]海军(或海军陆战队)新兵 **II** *vt.* ①穿(靴) ②用刑具夹(足、腿) ③踢 ④[俚]解雇 ‖*bet your ~s* 有把握，必定 / ~ *and saddle* 骑兵上马的信号 / *die in one's ~s* 不死在床上，横死，暴死 / *get the ~* [俚]解雇 / *give sb. the ~* [俚]把某人解雇 / *go to bed in one's ~s* 酩酊大醉 / *have one's heart in one's ~s* 见 heart / *I'll eat my ~s if ....* 见 eat / *in seven-league ~s* 极快 / *lick the ~s of* 奉承，拍…马屁 / *like old ~s* 可怕地，惊人地 / *over shoes over ~s* 见 shoe / *put the ~ on the wrong leg* 错骂；错怪 / *The ~ is on the other leg.* ①事实正与此相反。②应由其他方面负责。/ *wipe one's ~s on sb.* 侮辱某人 ‖~**ed** *a.* ①穿着靴的 ②被踢的 ③[俚]被解雇的 ‖'**~black** *n.* 以擦皮鞋为业的人 / ~ **camp** 海军(或海军陆战队)新兵训练中心 / '**~jack** *n.* 脱靴器 / '**~lace** *n.* 鞋带；[英]鞋带 ~ **last** 靴(或鞋)的楦头 / '**~leg** *vt. & vi.* 非法地酿(或卖、运)(酒) *n.* 违禁私卖的酒 / '**~lick** *vt. & vi.* [美俚]巴结，奉承 / '**~,licker** *n.* [美俚]拍马者，奉承者 / '**~,maker** *n.* 制靴工人 / '**~strap** *n.* 靴襻 *a.* 依靠自己力量的 *vt.* [*~strap oneself*] 依靠自己的努力成功 / '**~topping** 【船】水线间船壳 / '**~tree** *n.* 靴(或鞋)的楦头

boot[2] [bu:t] [古] **I** *vt.* [常与 it 连用]有利，有用: It ~s (me) not. (对我)毫无益处。/ What ~s it to weep? 哭有何用? **II** *n.* 效用 ‖*to* ~ 除此以外，再者

booth [bu:ð] *n.* ①(有篷的)货摊 ②[美]公用电话间 ③(隔开的)小间；(餐厅中的)火车座 ④(选举时的)投票站 (= polling ~)

boots [bu:ts] [单复同] *n.* [英]旅馆中擦皮鞋和搬行李等的人

booty ['bu:ti] *n.* ①战利品: war ~ 缴获品 ②掠夺物，赃物 ‖*play* ~ 勾结，朋比为奸

borax ['bɔ:ræks] *n.* 【化】硼砂；月石

border ['bɔ:də] **I** *n.* ①边，缘；边沿；(女服的)滚边 ②边界，边境，国界，国境；边境地区: ~ disputes 边境争端 / ~ incidents 边境事件 ③(花园里沿边的或走道两边的)花坛 **II** ❶ *vi.* ①接界(*on, upon*): The two villages ~ on each other. 这两个村互相接界。②近似(*on, upon*) ❷ *vt.* ①在(衣服等)上镶边 ②接近: The new airport ~s the city on the south. 新机场靠近城市的南面。‖**~er** ['bɔ:dərə] *n.* 边境(尤指英格兰和苏格兰之间的边境)居民 / **~ing** ['bɔ:dəriŋ] *n.* 边界标志物 ‖'**~land** *n.* ①边疆 ②[喻]模糊不清的境界 / **~ line** 边界，国界；分界线 / '**~line** *a.* ①边界上的 ②不明确的，两可的；可疑的: a ~line case 难以确定的两可情况 ③迹近淫秽的

bore¹ [bɔ:] **I** *vt. & vi.* ①钻(孔);挖(洞);【机】镗(孔) ②挤入(人群) **II** *n.* ①孔,洞;枪膛,炮膛;【机】膛 ②内径,(枪、炮等的)口径 ③钻孔器 ‖~ *from within* 从内部动摇一党派(或国家)的基础进而破坏之 ‖~**r** ['bɔ:rə] *n.* ①【机】镗床;镗孔刀具 ②【动】凿船虫;钻蛀虫/ *rice* ~*r* 稻螟虫

bore² [bɔ:] **I** *vt.* 使厌烦: be ~*d* to death (tears) 厌烦得要死(哭出来) **II** *n.* 惹人厌烦的人(或物)

bore³ [bɔ:] *n.* (涨潮时的)激浪

bore⁴ [bɔ:] bear 的过去式

boric ['bɔ:rik] *a.*【化】硼的;含硼的: ~ acid 硼酸

born [bɔ:n] **I** bear¹ 的过去分词 **II** *a.* ①出身于…的 ②天生的,生来的 ‖~ *again* 再生 / ~ *of* 源于 / ~ *with a silver spoon in one's mouth* 见 **spoon** / *in all one's* ~ *days* 一生,生平

borne [bɔ:n] bear¹ 的过去分词

borough ['bʌrə] *n.* ①[英]享有特权的自治城市;有权派议员到议会去的城市 ②[美]自治村镇 ③[美]纽约市行政区 ‖ *a pocket* ~ ①【英史】由一人(或一家)控制的议员选区 ②由一人(或一个集团)控制的政治团体

borrow ['bɔrou] ❶ *vt.* ①借: May I ~ your pen? 可以借用一下你的钢笔吗? / ~ money *from* (或 *of*) sb. 向某人借钱 ②借用: words ~*ed from* French 从法语中借用的词 / The whole thing is a "hotchpotch", ~*ing* his metaphor. 用他的譬喻来说,这真是个"大杂烩"。③(演算减法时)向某数借(一位) ❷ *vi.* 借;借位 ‖~*ed plumes* 见 **plume** / ~ *trouble* 自找麻烦 / *not on* ~*ing terms* 见 **term** ‖~**er** *n.* 借东西的人;借用者 / ~*ing* *n.* 借;借用的东西(或词);向其他民族仿效的风俗习惯 ‖~ *pit*【建】取土坑

bosom ['buzəm] **I** *n.* ①胸;(衣服的)胸部;胸状物: the ~ of a hill 山腹 ②内心,胸怀: a ~ *friend* 知心朋友 ③内部;中间,当中: live in the ~ of one's family 和家属生活在一起 **II** *vt.* ①怀抱 ②把…藏在心中

boss¹ [bɔs] **I** *n.* ①[口]工头,领班;老板;上司 ②(政治机构中的)头子,首领 **II** *vt.* ①当…的首领 ②指挥,把…差来遣去 **III** *a.* ①主要的;首领的 ②[俚]好的,第一流的 ‖ *a straw* ~ 工头助手,领班助手

boss² [bɔs] **I** *n.* ①瘤;节疤;突出部 ②盾上的浮雕 ③【建】凸饰 ④【地】岩瘤 ⑤【机】铸锻件表面凸起部;轮毂 **II** *vt.* ①浮雕 ②用饰钮装饰 ‖~*ed a.* 有凸饰的

botanical [bə'tænikəl] **I** *a.* 植物(学)的: a ~ garden 植物园 **II** *n.* 植物性药材

botany ['bɔtəni] *n.* ①植物学 ②[总称](某地区的)植物 ③植物的生态 ④植物学书;植物学论著

botch [bɔtʃ] **I** *vt. & vi.* ①拙劣地修补 ②笨手笨脚地弄坏 **II** *n.* ①拙劣的补钉(或修补部分) ②粗劣的工作 ‖~**er** *n.* 笨手笨脚地工作的人,拙劣的工作者(尤指写作拙劣者) / ~**y** *a.*

both [bouθ] **I** *a.* 两,双: I want ~ (the) baskets (或 ~ these baskets). 这两个篮子我都要。/ *Both*

(the) windows are *not* open. (或 The windows are *not* ~ open.) 两扇窗子并不都开着。[比较: *Neither* window is open. 两扇窗子都没开。] **II** *pron.* 两者;两人,双方: *Both* (of them) are doctors. 他们两人都是医生。**III** *ad.* [与 and 连用]两个都;既…又…,不但…而且…:

bother ['bɔðə] ❶ *vt.* ①烦扰,打扰: ~ one's head (或 brains) (*about*) (为…)费脑筋 / Don't ~ yourself *about* me. 别为我操心。②迷惑,使糊涂: That doesn't ~ me, though it's rather complicated. 那个虽然比较复杂,还不至于把我弄糊涂。③[表示不耐烦的感叹]: *Bother* it! 讨厌! / *Bother* the drizzling rain! 毛毛雨真讨厌! ❷ *vi.* ①烦恼;操心: Don't ~ *about* answering (或 ~ *to* answer) this. 此信不必费心回复。②[表示不耐烦的感叹]讨厌 **II** *n.* ①麻烦;纠纷,吵闹: It's too much ~ going there by a roundabout route. 绕道去那里太麻烦了。/ We had (a lot of) ~ (*in*) repairing it. 我们修理这个很费事。/ What is all this ~ *about*? 吵闹些什么呀? ②讨厌的人;麻烦的事物: His absence is quite a ~ to us. 他不到场真是一件使我们十分伤脑筋的事。

bottle ['bɔtl] **I** *n.* ①瓶;酒瓶;(盛放酒等的)皮袋 ②一瓶(的量): a ~ of ink (milk) 一瓶墨水(牛奶) / drink a whole ~ 喝一满瓶 ③[the ~] 酒;喝酒: [the ~] 奶瓶;奶瓶里的奶: raise (或 bring up) a child on the ~ 用牛奶喂大孩子 **II** *vt.* ①把(酒等)装瓶,把(水果等)装瓶贮藏 ②抑制(怒气、怨气等) (*up*) ③ 把…逼入不能逃脱(或不能自由活动)的境地 (*up*) ‖ *crack a* ~ 打开酒瓶喝酒 / *hit the* ~ [俚]酗酒 / *keep to the* ~ 嗜酒 / *over a* ~ 喝酒(一面…): talk merrily *over a* ~ 对酒畅谈 / *use old* ~*s for new wine* 用旧瓶装新酒 ‖~*d a.* ①瓶装的: ~*d gas* 瓶装液态丁烷(供照明、烹饪、取暖等用),瓶装煤气 ②[俚]喝醉的,醉醺醺的 / **bottling** *n.* 装瓶: a *bottling machine* 装瓶机 ‖'~**brush** *n.* ①洗瓶刷 ②【植】红千层属植物;问荆 / '~-**fed** *a.* 人工喂养的 / ~ *glass* (深绿色粗制)瓶玻璃 / '~**gourd**【植】葫芦 / '~-**green** 深绿色 / '~**neck** *n.* 瓶颈口;[喻](交通容易阻塞的)狭口,隘道;妨碍生产流程的一环 *vt.* 梗塞,阻塞 *a.* (港口等)狭隘拥挤的 / ~ *nose* 酒糟鼻 / ~ **washer** 洗瓶工人;杂务工

bottom ['bɔtəm] **I** *n.* ①底部,底: the ~ of a trunk 箱底 / There is some deposit in the ~ of the flask. 这只烧瓶的底部是些沉淀物。②尽头;末端: at the ~ of the garden 在花园的尽头 / the ~ of a mountain 山脚 / at the ~ of page 10 在第十页的下端 ③(会议桌等的)末席;(名单等的)末尾 ④船底,舱底;货船 ⑤【纺】(织物的)地,底色;底色 ⑥原因,原由: What's at the ~ of it? 到底是什么原因? ⑦椅背 ⑧[口]屁股 ⑨[常用复]河边低地 ⑩(马等的)持久力,耐久力 **II** *a.* ①最底的;最低的;最后的 ②根

本的: the ~ cause 根本原因 **III ❶** *vt.* ①给…装底; 装椅面子 ②查明…的真相(或原因等) ③测量(海底等)的深浅 ④建立…的基础 (*upon, on*) **❷** *vi.* ①到达(或停在)底部 ②建立基础 (*upon, on*) ‖*at* ~ 本质上; 实际上 / *be at the* ~ 是…的起因,引起 / *Bottoms up!* 干杯! / ~ *up* 颠倒 / *from the* ~ *of one's heart* 衷心地,真诚地 / *get to the* ~ *of* 弄清…的真相 / *go to the* ~ 沉没 / *knock the* ~ *out of* 证明…无价值 / *scrape the* ~ *of the* (*pickle*) *barrel* [美俚]利用最后一招 / *send to the* ~ 弄沉,打沉 / *smell the* ~ (*ground*) (船)因水浅而失速; [海]擦底过 / *stand on one's own* 自立 / *swim to the* ~ [谑]沉下去 / *touch* ~ ①达到最低点 ②查核事实 ‖**~less** *a.* 无底的; 没有根据的; 深不可测的; 无限的 ‖**'~land** *n.* 河边低地,洼地

boudoir ['bu:dwɑ:] *n.* [法]闺房

bough [bau] *n.* 树枝(尤指大树枝) ‖**'~pot** *n.* ①大花瓶 ②花束

bought [bɔ:t] **I** buy 的过去式和过去分词 **II** *a.* 买来的; 现成的(指非定制的)

boulder ['bouldə] *n.* 巨砾; 漂砾; 圆石: ~ clay. 泥砾,冰砾泥 / a ~ pavement 砾石地 / a ~ dam 顽石坝

boulevard ['bu:livɑ:d] *n.* ①宽阔的大路; 林荫大道 ②[美]干道,大街

bounce [bauns] **I ❶** *vi.* ①(球)反跳,弹起 ②(人)跳(起); 匆促地动: ~ *about* 蹦蹦跳跳 / ~ *off* (或 *out of*) one's chair 从椅子上跳起来 / He ~d into the room. 他猛然冲进房来。③[俚](支票)被拒付而退还给开票人 ④[英]吹牛; 虚张声势 **❷** *vt.* ①拍(球),使跳回 ②使撞击 ③[口]骂(人) ④[英]强迫; 诈骗: ~ sb. *into* (*out of*) *doing* sth. 强迫某人做(不做)某事 / ~ sb. *out of* sth. 从某人处骗取某物 ⑤[俚]撵走; 把…解雇 **II** *n.* ①弹(力) ②跳跃,跳动: give a ~ 跳起 ③[俚]活力 ④[英]吹牛,虚张声势 ⑤[俚]驱逐,解雇: give sb. the (grand) ~ 把某人解雇 / get the (grand) ~ 被解雇 ⑥猛击; [军](在较高的高度上对敌机)突然袭击 **III** *ad.* 砰地一下子; 突然: come ~ *against* 跟…砰地相撞 ‖**'~-back** *n.* 反冲,反联

bound¹ [baund] **I** bind 的过去式和过去分词 **II** *a.* ①被束缚的: ~ *by* ice 冰封的 ②密切关联的 ③一定的,必定的 ④(道德上或法律上)受到约束的,有义务的: be ~ *to* carry out the plan 有执行这个计划的义务 ⑤[口]下了决心的 ⑥装订的 ⑦便秘的 ⑧(在化学或物理)结合中的: Some vitamins occur in ~ forms. 有几种维生素存在于结合形式中。‖*be* ~ *up in* 热心于; 忙于 / *be* ~ *up with* 与…有密切关系 / *I'll be* ~ [用作插入语]我敢肯定

bound² [baund] *a.* 准备(或正在)到…去的; (船等)开往…的 (*for*): Where are you ~ (*for*)? 你上哪儿去? / be outward (homeward) ~ 开往国外(本国)的

bound³ [baund] **I** *n.* [常用复]边界; 界限; 范围: The place is out of ~s to the school children. 此地小学生不准入内。/ beyond the ~s of possibility 超出可能范围的,不可能的 **II** *vt.* ①限止 ②形成…的边界,邻接 ③说出…的疆界: The teacher asked the class to ~ their country. 教师要求班上学生讲出本国的边界。‖break ~s 超出界限; [军]擅自进入禁止军人进入的场所

bound⁴ [baund] **I** *n.* (向上或向前的)跳动: He cleared the hedge at one (或 a) ~. 他一跃跳过篱笆。/ advance by leaps and ~s 飞跃前进; hit the ball on the ~ 在球弹起时打它 **II ❶** *vi.* 跳跃; (球等)弹起; 跳着跑: His heart ~ed with joy. 他高兴得心头砰砰直跳。/ The dog ~ed towards the gate. 这狗向大门跳奔过去。**❷** *vt.* 使跳

boundary ['baundəri] *n.* 分界线,边界 ‖ ~ **layer** 边界层 / ~ **light** 机场界限灯 / ~ **marker** 机场界限信标

bounden ['baundən] *a.* 有责任的,必须担负的

bounder ['baundə] *n.* [口]喧闹鲁莽的人

boundless ['baundlis] *a.* 无边际的; 无限的 ‖**~ly** *ad.* / **~ness** *n.*

bounteous ['baunties] *a.* [书面语]①慷慨的 ②丰裕的,充足的 ‖**~ly** *ad.* / **~ness** *n.*

bountiful ['bauntiful] *a.* ①慷慨的 ②丰裕的,充足的: a ~ supply of food 充足的食品供应 ‖**~ly** *ad.* / **~ness** *n.*

bounty ['baunti] *n.* ①慷慨; 恩惠 ②赠物,赠礼 ③奖励金; 补助金 ‖~ **hunter** 为获得赏金而追捕野兽(或歹徒)的人 / ~ **jumper** (美国南北战争时)入伍后领取了津贴而开小差的人

bouquet ['bu(:)kei, bu'kei] *n.* ①花束; 一大串烟火 ②恭维话 ③(酒等的)香味; (文学、艺术作品等的)特殊风格

bourgeois ['buəʒwɑ:] **I** [单复同] *n.* ①中世纪城镇中的自由民 ②店主,商人 ③资产阶级分子; 具有资产阶级观点(或特性)的人 ④[复]资产阶级 **II** *a.* 资产阶级的; 中产阶级的; 平庸的

bourgeoisie [,buəʒwɑ:'zi:] *n.* 资产阶级; 中产阶级

bout [baut] **I** *n.* ①一回,一场,一阵(可指战斗、工作、闹饮、疾病等); 一个来回(指耕地等): this ~ 这一回 (=on this occasion) ②回合,较量,比赛 **II** *vt.* 来回耕(田)

bow¹ [bou] **I** *n.* ①弓: bend (或 draw) the ~ 拉弓 ②琴弓 ③弓形(部分); 弓形物,虹 ④蝴蝶结; 蝴蝶结领结 (=~ tie): tie one's shoelaces in a ~ 把鞋带打成一个蝴蝶结 ⑤凸肚窗 (=~ window) ⑥弓手 ⑦眼镜框; 眼镜脚 **II ❶** *vt.* ①用弓拉(琴) ②把…弯成弓形 **❷** *vi.* ①用弓拉琴 ②弯成弓形 ‖*Cupid's* ~ ①爱神丘比特之弓 ②弓形的上嘴唇 / *draw* (或 *pull*) *the long* ~ 吹牛 / *have two* (或 *many*) *strings to one's* ~ 多备一手,以防万一 ‖**~ed** *a.* 弯曲的,弓形的 / **~ing** *n.* [音]弓法 ‖**'~-backed** *a.* 驼背的,弯

腰屈背的 / ~ **compass**(es) 两脚规,圆规;外卡
钳 / ~ **drill** 弓钻 / ~ **instrument** 擦奏乐器,
弓弦乐器 / '~**leg** *n.* 弓形腿 / ~**line** ['boulin,
'boulain] *n.* 帆角索 / ~ 单套结(=~line knot)
/ ~**man** ['boumən] *n.* 弓手 / ~ **pen** 小圆规 /
~ **saw** 弓锯 / '~**shot** *n.* 箭的射程 / ~**string**
n. ①弓弦 ②绞索 *vt.* 绞死 / ~ **tie** 蝴蝶结领
结 / ~ **wave** ①弹道波;冲击波 ②涡流 / ~
window ①【建】凸肚窗 ②【俚】罗汉肚,大肚皮
bow² [bau] **I ❶** *vi.* ①鞠躬;点头(以示招呼、感谢、
同意等): a ~ing acquaintance 点头之交 ②屈
服,服从 (*to*): ~ *to* sb.'s command (opinion) 屈
从某人的指挥(意见) **❷** *vt.* ①点(头),弯(身
等)(以示尊敬、同意或服从): ~ the neck to 向
…低头屈服 ②点头(或鞠躬)表示(感谢、同意
等): ~ one's thanks 鞠躬致谢 ③压弯 (*down*):
be ~ed (*down*) with age 因年老而腰弯 **II** *n.* 鞠
躬;点头;屈从,低头 ‖~ *and scrape* 打躬作揖,
过分恭敬 / ~ *sb. in* (*out*) 恭敬地接进(送走)
某人 / *make a* ~ 鞠躬 / *make one's* ~ ①
正式进入 ②正式引退(如退出舞台或社会生活) /
scrape a ~ (深深欠身)鞠躬;打躬作揖 / *take
a* ~ 鞠躬答礼;答谢(如对人们的鼓掌等)
bow³ [bau] *n.* ①[常用复]艏,船头,舰首,飞艇的前
缘部分: the port (starboard) ~ 左(右)舷的船
头 ②前桨手 / ~s on 头向前 / ~s under 困难
地(行进);(船头)被淹没 / *in* ~s 命令前桨手起
桨开船,准备靠岸(或靠近大船) / *on the* ~ 在艏
方向(左右45°范围内) ‖~ **chaser** 舰首炮 / ~
gun 前枪(舰艇、坦克等前方的机枪) / ~**man**
['baumən] *n.* 前桨手 / ~ **oar** ①前桨 ②前桨
手 / '~**sprit** *n.* 第一斜桅;牙樯
bowel ['bauəl] *n.* ①[除医学上和作过语用外,常用
复]肠(脏人肠): bind the ~s 造成便秘 /
loosen (或 move) the ~s 大便 / have loose ~s
腹泻 / keep one's ~s open 保持大便通畅 ②[复]
同情心: have no ~s 无情,没有心肝 ③[复]内
部: in the ~s of the earth 在地壳底下 ‖*relax
the* ~s 通便 / *relieve the* ~s 大便,小便
bowl¹ [boul] *n.* ①碗,钵;一碗(一钵)的量: a rice
~ 一只饭碗 / a ~ of rice 一碗饭 ②大酒杯;烈
酒;狂饮: over the ~ 在酒席上;一边喝着酒(一
边…) ③碗状物,(匙)的盛物部分,(烟斗的)斗;一
匙(或一烟斗)的量: fish ~s 鱼缸 ④[美]圆形竞
技场 ⑤深的盆地 ‖~**ful** *n.* 一满碗(或钵、匙等)
bowl² [boul] **I** *n.* ①(成斜线行进的)滚木球;[复]
滚木球戏 ②(滚木球戏中的)投球 ③【机】滚筒,
滚子 **II ❶** *vi.* ①玩滚木球戏;(在滚木球戏中)
投球 ②稳而快地行驶: Buses ~ along over
the smooth road. 公共汽车在平坦的大道上疾
驰。/ We were ~ing along the highway in a
car. 我们正乘着一辆汽车在公路上轻快地行驶
着。③(在板球戏中)投球给击球员 **❷** *vt.* ①滚
(球、铁环等);使快而稳地行驶 ②(在滚木球戏
中)完成(规定的回数);得到…分: ~ 150 (在滚
木球戏中)得到一百五十分 ③(板球戏中)因击中
三柱门或击落柱上横木而迫使(击球员)退场 (*out*)

‖*at long* ~s 远距离地(尤指军舰远距离炮轰) /
~ *over* ①用急行的东西击倒 ②[口]使大吃一
惊: I was completely ~ed over by the news. 这
消息使我完全不知所措。‖~**ing** *n.* 滚木球
戏: a ~ing green 玩滚木球戏的草坪
bowler ['boulə] *n.* ①玩滚木球戏者;(板球的)投球
手 ②(通常为黑色的)圆顶硬礼帽 (=~ hat)
box¹ [bɔks] **I** *n.* ①箱,盒;箱(或盒)状物: casting
~【机】砂箱,型箱 / feeding ~【机】进刀箱 ②一
箱(或一盒)的容量;一箱(或一盒)的内容;[英]一
盒礼物 ③专座;(法庭里的)陪审席,证人席;[马车
等的)驾驶员座位 ④(戏院的)包厢: a press ~ 记
者席 ④岗亭;信号所 ⑤[美]邮箱,信箱 ⑥(报刊
上的)花边文字 **II** *vt.* ①把…装箱(或盒) ②给
…装上罩壳箱 ③使(帆船)顺风转向;改变(桅横
杆)方向 ‖*a* ~ *and needle* (一副)罗盘 / *an
eternity* ~ [俚]棺材 / *in* ①=~ *up* ②拦
阻(另一匹赛马) 使它不能跑在前头 / ~ *the
compass* ①依次列举罗盘的三十二方位 ②(在
辩论等中)兜了一个圈子(又回到原处) / ~ *up*
①把…装起箱来;把…装入箱内 ②把…困住;把
…困在狭小的地方,监禁;使处于困境 / *in a* ~
[口]处于困境,进退维谷 / *in the same* ~ 处在
同样的困境 / *in the wrong* ~ 处于窘境,不得
其所 / *Pandora's* ~ 见 Pandora ‖~**ful** *n.* 一
满箱,一满盒 ‖~ **barrage** 【军】缘边射击 /
'~**board** *n.* (制箱、盒用的)硬纸板 / ~ **calf**
(有小方格花纹的)小牛皮 / '~**car** *n.* [美]棚车
(英国称 box waggon) / ~ **cloth** 缩绒厚呢 /
'~,**keeper** *n.* (戏院的)包厢侍者 / ~ **kite**
【气】(测气象用的)箱形风筝 / ~ **number** 信箱
号 / ~ **office** ①(戏院等的)票房,售票处 ②卖
座力;提高卖座力的东西: (be) good (或 big) ~
office [俚]卖座好 / '~-,**office** *a.* 票房的 /
~ **pleat** [纺]箱形折缝 / ~ **seat** ①(马车上的)驾
驶员座位 ②(戏院中)包厢的座位;(运动场等)
正面看台的座位 ③利于观看的地位 / ~ **stall**
(牛、马等)单个动物的方形舍栏
box² [bɔks] **I ❶** *vt.* ①用手打(某人的)耳光: ~
sb.'s ear(s) 打某人耳光 ②和…拳击 **❷** *vi.* 拳
击,打拳 **II** *n.* 一巴掌,一拳: give sb. a ~ on
the ear(s) 打某人一记耳光
box³ [bɔks] *n.* ①[植]黄杨(尤指锦熟黄杨) ②黄杨
木 (=~wood)
boxer¹ ['bɔksə] *n.* 制箱者,制盒者;装箱者,装盒者
boxer² ['bɔksə] *n.* ①拳击家;拳击员;拳术师 ②
[B-] 义和团(现译为 Yi Ho Tuan)的一员 ‖*the
Boxer Indemnity* 庚子赔款 / *the Boxers* 义和
团
boxing ['bɔksiŋ] *n.* 拳击,拳术,打拳: hexagram
(或 shadow) ~ 太极拳 ‖~ **glove** 拳击手套 /
~ **match** 拳击比赛 / ~ **weights** 拳击等级
boy [bɔi] *n.* ①男孩,少年 ②家伙(对任何年龄的男
子的昵称);也用于感叹的俚语中): He's quite a
~. 他是个好家伙。/ Cheer up, old ~! 振作起
来,好朋友! / Oh, ~! [俚]好家伙!(表示欢欣或
惊奇的感叹语) ③儿子: Both are my ~s. 两人

都是我的儿子。④勤杂人员；练习生；(旅馆、饭店等的)服务员，男仆: an office ～ (办公室里的)勤杂人员；练习生 ‖a ～ in buttons 侍役 / a slip of a ～ 瘦长的年轻男子 ‖~hood n. ①男孩时代；少年时代 ②男孩们，少年们 ‖'~friend n. [口]男朋友 / ～ scout ①童子军的成员 ②[俚][贬]极天真(或不切实际)的男子

boycott ['boikot] I vt. 联合抵制；联合拒绝购买(或经售、使用)；联合起来拒绝跟…来往: ～ schools (或 classes) 罢课 II n. 联合抵制；联合起来拒绝购买(或经售、使用)；联合起来拒绝来往(旧音译"杯葛")

Br 【化】元素溴 (bromine) 的符号

brace [breis] I n. ①支柱；【医】支架；【矿】支撑；井口 ②一双，一对(指狗、猎物等；也贬指人): several ～(s) of partridge 几对鹧鸪 ③【机】拉条；撑臂: a ～ and bit 手摇曲柄钻(包括曲柄及钻头) ④大括号(即 { }) ⑤【海】转帆索 ⑥[英][复](裤子的)背带(美国称 suspenders): a pair of ～s 一副背带 ⑦[口](新兵等)过分僵直的立正姿势 II ❶ vt. ①拉紧，系紧 ②支住，撑牢 ③激励，振奋 ④[俚]向…借钱 ⑤【海】用转帆索转(帆) ❷ vi. ①[口]打起精神；下定决心 ②迅速作好(进攻的)准备 ‖~ oneself up 打起精神 / ～ up [口]打起精神；下定决心 / in a ～ of shakes 马上，立刻 / splice the main ～ [俚]喝酒 ‖~r n. ①(击剑等时带在臂或腕上的)保护套 ②[俚]兴奋饮料

bracelet ['breislit] n. ①手镯 ②[俚]手铐

bracing ['breisiŋ] I a. 振奋精神的；爽快的，凉爽的: a ～ lecture 振奋人心的报告 / a ～ wind 一阵凉风 II n. ①【建】联结系，联系 ②背带 ③支柱，支撑物

bracken ['brækən] n. 【植】欧洲蕨

bracket ['brækit] I n. ①托架；【建】隅撑；托座: ～ light 【建】壁灯 / ～ bracing 【建】托座联条 ②[复]括号(指 [ ], ⟨ ⟩, ( ), { }): an explanatory note between (或 in) ～s 括号中的一个注解 ③(收入额等的)等级；阶层，一类人: the high (low) income ～ 高(低)额收入等级 / the lower paid ～ 较低的工资等级 / the 31 to 40 age ～ 从三十一岁到四十岁这一档 ④【军】夹叉射击 II vt. ①给…装上托架 ②把…括在括号内 ③把…分类 ④【军】夹叉射击

brackish ['brækiʃ] a. ①(水)含盐的；稍咸的 ②味道不好的；引起恶心的

brad [bræd] n. 角钉，土钉 ‖'~awl n. 锥钻，打眼钻

brag [bræg] I (bragged; bragging) ❶ vi. 吹牛，自夸 (of, about) ❷ vt. 夸说 (that) II n. 自大；大话；自夸的人 III (bragger, braggest) a. 第一流的，极好的

braid [breid] I n. ①编带；缏；辫子: a straw ～ 草帽缏 ②(衣服上的)镶边 II vt. ①把(草等)编成缏；把(头发)编成辫子 ②给(衣服等)镶边 ‖~er n. 编打的人；打缏机

braille [breil] I n. 布莱叶盲字；点字法(法国人Louis Braille 创制的用凸点符号供盲人书写、摸读的文字符号体系) II vt. 用盲字印(或写)

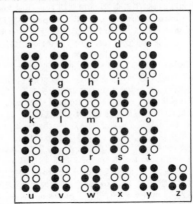

braille

brain [brein] I n. ①脑(子)；[复]脑髓 ②[常用复]脑力，智能；智囊 II vt. ①打碎…的脑袋: ～ an ox 打碎一头牛的脑袋 ②打…的头部 ‖beat (或 cudgel, rack) one's ～s 绞脑汁: rack one's ～s to find ways and means 动脑筋，想办法 / blow out sb.'s ～s (用枪等)把某人打得脑袋开花 / coin one's ～s 动脑筋挣钱 / have sth. on the ～ 一心想着某事；热中于某事 / pick (或suck) sb.'s ～s 窃取某人脑力劳动的成果 / turn sb.'s ～ 冲昏某人头脑，使某人得意忘形 ‖~less a. 没有头脑的，愚蠢的 ‖'~case n. 脑壳，头颅 / '~child n. [口]脑力劳动的产物(如计划、作品等) / ～ drain 智囊流失(指有些国家的科技人员等流向国外的情况) / ～ fag 脑衰竭，脑疲惫 / ～ fever 脑(脊髓)膜炎 / ～man ['breinmən] n. 谋士，参谋 / '~pan n. 脑壳，头颅 / '~power n. ①智能 ②智囊 / '~power drain =～ drain / '~sick a. 疯狂的 / '~storm n. ①【医】脑猝变，脑猝病 ②[美][谑]妙主意 / ～ trust ①智囊团；专家顾问团 ②[英][B- T-]在广播电台即席选答听众问题的小组 / ～truster 智囊团的一员，参谋 / ～ wave ①脑波 ②[口]灵机；妙想 / '~work 脑力劳动 / '~,worker n. 脑力劳动者

brainwash ['breinwɔʃ] I vt. ①对(人)实行洗脑；把某种思想强加于(人) ②通过宣传(或推销)说服 II n. 洗脑；强行灌输思想 ‖~ing n.

braise, braize [breiz] vt. (用文火)炖，蒸

brake [breik] I n. ①制动器，刹车；闸: an emergency ～ 紧急制动器 / take off the ～ 开闸 / ～ horsepower 【机】制动马力 ②[喻]阻碍 ③大耙；麻梳；剥(柳条)皮器 ④【植】欧洲蕨；丛林，矮树林 ⑤(金属板的)压弯成形机 II ❶ vt. ①制动，刹(车) ②捣碎(麻等) ❷ vi. 制动，刹车

‖*ride the* ~ 半制动(指刹车或离合器不踏到底) ‖~(s)man ['breik(ə)mən] *n.* 司闸员,制动手 / ~ van【交】司闸车,缓急车

bramble ['bræmbl] *n.*【植】悬钩子属植物(尤指欧洲黑莓);荆棘 ‖**brambly** *a.* ① 长满悬钩子属植物的;多荆棘的 ② 象荆棘的;多刺的

bran [bræn] *n.* 麸,糠: a ~ cake 糠饼 / ~ pie 摸彩袋

branch [brɑ:ntʃ] I *n.* ①枝,分枝 ②支流,支脉;支线 ③(学科)分科;部门: a ~ of science 一门科学 ④支部;分部;分行;分店: a ~ office 分局,分店 / a combined ~【军】多种兵合成兵团 II *vi.* ①出枝 ②分岔;分门: The road ~es here. 这条路在这里岔开。 ❷ *vt.* ①使分支;分割 ②用枝叶装饰 ‖~ off 分叉;岔开 / ~ out ①长出枝条 ②(在业务等方面)扩充范围

brand [brænd] I *n.* ①燃烧着的木头 ②打印用的烙铁;烙印,火印,(古时烙在犯人身上的)印记;[喻]犯罪(或耻辱)的标记;(标示所有权的)标记: the ~ of a class 阶级烙印 ③商标,牌子 ④[诗]火炬;剑 II *vt.* ①在…上打烙印 ②在…上打标记 ②铭刻;铭记: be ~ed on sb.'s memory 铭刻在某人记忆中 ③污辱;给…抹黑 ‖a ~ from the burning 因忏悔而得救的人;大难得救的人 / the ~ of Cain 杀人罪 ‖~er *n.* 打烙印(或火印)的人;烙器 ‖~ iron 烙铁 (=branding iron) / '~-'new *a.* 崭新的,新制的

brandish ['brændiʃ] *vt. & n.* 挥舞

brandy ['brændi] I *n.* 白兰地酒 II *vt.* 在…中加白兰地酒;把…浸泡在白兰地酒中 ‖'~-ball *n.* 带白兰地酒味的糖果 / '~-'pawnee *n.* 掺水的白兰地酒 / ~ snap 带白兰地酒味的姜饼

brass [brɑ:s] I *n.* ①黄铜 ②[复]黄铜器,黄铜制品;[总称]铜管乐器 ③[俚]钱 ④[俚]厚脸皮 ⑤[美俚][总称]高级军官;高级官员 ⑥[机]黄铜轴承衬 II *a.* ①黄铜制的;含黄铜的 ②(天空等)黄铜色的 ③(声音)洪亮回响的 ④铜管乐器的 III *vt. & vi.* [俚]缴纳,支付 (up) ‖(be) ~ed off [英俚]厌烦的,牢骚满腹的 / *double in* ~ [俚] ①(在爵士乐队中)能使用一种以上的乐器 ②本行外还兼长其他的 / '~-'bound *a.* ①包黄铜的 ②顽固守旧的 ③不妥协的 ④厚脸皮的 / ~ check [美]大财团给报界人士的贿赂 / ~ farthing 小钱;微乎其微的数量: not care a ~ farthing 毫不在乎 / ~ founder 黄铜铸工 / ~ foundry 黄铜铸造厂 / ~ hat [俚]高级将领;高级官员 / ~ knuckles 指节铜套(套在四指关节上的铜套,握拳时铜套向外,用于打人可致人于死命) / ~ plate (钉在门上或棺材上的)黄铜名牌 / ~ rags [英]水手用的揩布: part ~ rags with sb. [俚]不再同某人保持亲密关系 / ~ ring [俚]得发财的机会 / '~-smith *n.* 黄铜匠 / ~ tacks [俚]黄铜平头钉 / ②[口]事实真相;重要事情: get (或 come) down to ~ tacks 讨论实质问题;讨论重要事情 / '~-'visaged *a.* 厚脸的 /

wind ①铜管乐器 ②[复](管弦乐队)铜管乐部分

brassiere ['bræsiə] *n.* [法]奶罩

brat [bræt] *n.* [贬]小鬼,小家伙

bravado [brə'vɑ:dou] ([复] bravado(e)s) *n.* [西]虚张声势

brave [breiv] I *a.* ①勇敢的 ②华丽的;盛装的 ③很好的 II *n.* ①勇敢的人 ②北美印第安战士 III *vt.* ①冒(风雨,危险等);敢于做(某事): ~ the storm 冒风雨 ‖~ it out 拼着干到底 ‖~ly *ad.* / ~ness *n.* / ~ry ['breivəri] *n.* ①大胆,勇敢 ②华丽;盛装

bravo¹ ['brɑ:vou] ([复] bravo(e)s) *n.* 坏蛋,亡命之徒(尤指被人雇用的刺客)

bravo² [brɑ:'vou] [意] I *n.* 喝采声,叫好声 II *int.* 好啊! 妙啊! III *vt.* 向…喝采叫好

brawl [brɔ:l] I *n.* ①吵架,喧嚷 ②[美俚]喧闹的舞会(或宴会) II *vi.* ①吵架;对骂 ②(水)哗哗地流 ‖~er *n.* 争吵者;喧闹者

brawn [brɔ:n] *n.* ①肌肉 ②膂力,体力 ③腌的野猪肉

bray¹ [brei] I *n.* 驴叫声;似驴叫声;(喇叭的)嘟嘟声 II ❶ *vi.* (驴)叫;(喇叭)发嘟嘟声 ❷ *vt.* 粗声粗气地说;哄乱地演奏

bray² [brei] *vt.* ①捣碎,研碎 ②薄薄地涂(油墨等)

braze [breiz] *vt.* ①用黄铜(或似黄铜的材料)制造(或镶饰) ②用黄铜镀,使成黄铜色;使坚如黄铜

brazen ['breizn] I *a.* ①黄铜制的;黄铜色的;坚如黄铜的 ②声音响亮而刺耳的 ③厚颜无耻的: ~ lies 无耻谎言 II *vt.* 厚着脸皮对待 (out, through): ~ it out (做错事后)厚着脸皮干下去(或混下去) ‖~ly *ad.* 厚颜无耻地 / ~ness *n.* 厚颜无耻 [喻]猖狂 ‖**Brazen Age** (希腊)黄铜时代 / '~-faced *a.* 厚脸皮的,无耻的

brazier ['breizjə] *n.* 铜匠 ‖~y ['breizjəri] *n.* 黄铜细工

breach [bri:tʃ] I *n.* ①破坏;违反;不履行: a ~ of arrest【军】违反约束规定 / a ~ of discipline 违反纪律;违犯军纪 / a ~ of faith 失信,不忠行为,出卖行为 / a ~ of the peace 扰乱治安的行为,闹事 / a ~ of close 非法侵入他人地界的行为 / a ~ of privilege 对议会等权利的侵害 / a ~ of promise 毁约(尤指赖婚) ②【军】突破;突破口 ③缺口,裂口: open a ~ 打开缺口 / the ~ between the subjective and the objective 主观和客观的分裂 / (友好关系的)破裂(或中断);不和 ⑤ 波浪的碎溅;冲击船(或防波堤等)的波浪: a clean ~ 冲走甲板上所有物件的浪头 / a clear ~ 冲过甲板的大浪 ⑥(鲸的)跳出水面 II ❶ *vt.* 攻破,突破;使有缺口: ~ the line of encirclement 突破包围圈 ❷ *vi.* (鲸)跳出水面 ‖*slip one's* ~ 断气,死 / *stand in the* ~ 承受最厉害的攻击,首当其冲 / *throw* (或 *fling*) *oneself into the* ~ 挺身担当重任(或危局)

bread [bred] **I** *n.* ①面包: a loaf (piece, slice) of ~ 一只(一块,一片)面包 / brown ~ 黑面包 / steamed ~ 馒头 ②食物,粮食; [喻]生计: make (或 earn) one's ~ 糊口,谋生 ③[宗]一块(或一份)面包 ④[美俚]钱 **II** *vt.* 在⋯外裹上面包粉末 ‖*~ and butter* ①涂黄油的面包 ②[喻]生计 / *~ and cheese* 普通食品; 生计 / *~ and milk* 浸泡在沸牛奶中的面包块 / *~ and scrape* 黄油涂得不足的面包 / *~ and wine* 【宗】圣餐 / *~ buttered on both sides* 安适的境遇 / *break ~* 进餐; 【宗】进圣餐 / *break ~ with* 受到⋯的款待 / *cast* (或 *throw*) *one's ~ upon the water(s)* 不期望报答地做好事; 行善 / *eat the ~ of affliction* 遭受痛苦,遭受折磨 / *eat the ~ of idleness* 坐食,游手好闲 / *know which side one's ~ is buttered* (on) 知道自己的利益所在 / *out of ~* 失业 / *quarrel with one's ~ and butter* 做对自己饭碗不利的蠢事; 与自己作对 / *ship's ~* 【海】硬饼干 / *take the ~ out of sb.'s mouth* 敲掉某人的饭碗 ‖*~-and-'butter a.* ①[主英]年轻的,不成熟的,女学生派头的 ②关于生计的; 日常生活的 ③象固定收入一样可靠的 ④对所受款待表示感谢的: a *~-and-butter* letter 客人走后给主人的感谢信 / *'~,basket n.* [俚]胃 ②产谷物的地区 / *~ board* ①揉面粉板; 切面包板 ②手提式电子实验线路板 / *'~crumb n.* 面包屑 / *'~fruit, ~ tree n.* 【植】(生长在南太平洋诸岛的)面包果 / *'~line n.* [美]领救济(或施舍)食物的穷人队伍 / *'~stuffs* [复] *n.* 做面包的原料(即谷物、面粉等) / *~ ticket* 面包券,饭票 / *'~,winner n.* 养家活口的人(或手艺、职业、工具等)

breadth [bredθ] *n.* ①宽度; 广度: develop in ~ and depth 向广度和深度发展 / spread in ~ 全面铺开 ②(布的)幅面; (船)幅: three ~s of cloth 三幅布 ③(胸襟等的)宽广,大量,宽容: ~ of view 见识的广阔 ④(艺术品等的)雄浑 ‖*by a hair's ~* 间不容发,险些儿 / *to a hair's ~* 精确地,丝毫不爽

break[1] [breik] **I** (broke [brouk], broken['broukən]) **❶** *vt.* ①打破; 折断; 冲破: The boy *broke* the teapot. 这男孩把茶壶打破了。 / ~ one's head 撞破(或擦破)头 / ~ one's leg 折断腿骨 ②损坏: Be careful not to ~ the instruments. 小心别损坏仪器。 ③打开; 开垦, 翻(土); 开创: ~ new ground in science 开辟科学的新天地 / ~ a fresh path 开创新路 ④破坏; 违反; 破除; 通过法律手续使(遗嘱)失效: ~ an agreement 破坏协定 / ~ a promise 违反诺言 / ~ an appointment 失约 / ~ the law 违反法律 ⑤使(突然)中止, 打断: ~ a deadlock 打开僵局 / ~ sb.'s sleep 打扰某人的睡眠 / ~ an electric circuit 切断电路 ⑥越出: ~ prison 越狱 / ~ surface (潜水艇)浮出水面

⑦弄垮; 制服, 使屈服 ⑧超过, 打破(纪录): ~ a speed record 打破速度纪录 ⑨削弱, 减弱: The shelter belt ~s the force of the wind. 防风林带减弱了风力。 ⑩降(军官)的职; 革(军官)的职 ⑪(谨慎小心地)透露(坏消息等) ⑫训练; 驯(马等) ⑬破获(案件); 识破(密码) ⑭兑开(大额钞票等): ~ a five-yuan note 把一张五元钞票兑开 ⑮【律】闯入(房屋等) ⑯解开(链条等) ⑰使破产; 使耗尽资金; 使前途无望 ⑱证明(辩解)的虚伪 ⑲使(证券等)的价格急剧下降 ⑳拆开(整体); 拉开(扭打的人等): ~ a dinner set 把一套餐具拆散 / ~ formation 【军】(士兵等)离开编队 ㉑使放弃习惯 (of); 放弃(习惯): ~ sb. of smoking 使某人戒烟 ㉒打开(枪)的装弹和发射部件 **❷** *vi.* ①破, 破碎; 断裂; 坏掉: The stick *broke* in two. 棍棒断裂成两段。 / The toy *broke*. 玩具坏了。 ②决裂 ③(天)破晓: He got up as soon as day *broke*. 天一亮他就起身。 ④(嗓音、天气等)变, 突变: The boy's voice is beginning to ~. 这个男孩的嗓音在开始变了。(指在变成成年人) / The cold wave *broke*. 寒流突然过去了。 / After an hour of heavy rain the storm *broke*. 下了一小时大雨后, 暴风雨停止了。 ⑤(在健康、体力、抵抗力等方面)垮掉, 变弱: The suspect *broke* under questioning. 嫌疑分子连进行追问竟垮了下来。 ⑥(暴风雨、事件等)突然发生: The storm *broke*. 暴风雨突然来了。 ⑦(事情)传开: The news soon *broke*. 消息不久就传开了。 ⑧(浪)冲击: The sea waves were ~*ing over* (或 *on, against*) the rocks. 海浪冲击着岩石。 ⑨(军队等)溃散 ⑩破产; (银行等)倒闭 ⑪(潜望镜、鱼等)突然出现于水面 ⑫突然奔起来: ~ for cover 突然奔向掩护处 ⑬(脓肿、水泡等)自内部破裂 ⑭[方](天气)转晴 ⑮(证券等)突然显著跌价 ⑯突然转向 ⑰暂停工作(或活动): At noon we ~ for lunch. 中午我们暂停工作去吃午饭。 ⑱折拢, 弯起, 拆开: a bed that ~s 一张可折拢的床 ⑲(奶酥)在制造黄油时分成流汁和脂肪; (乳剂)永久分成油质层和水质层 ⑳(事情)发生, 发展: Things are ~*ing right for* us. 情况正朝着有利于我们的方向发展。

II n. ①破裂；破裂处: a ~ in the hedge 篱笆的破裂处

②决裂；绝交: a ~ between the two countries 两国的绝交

③破晓: at (the) ~ of day 在黎明时

④中止，停顿；【电】断路；断路器: a ~ in the circuit 电路的中断 / a ~ in production for retooling 为改装机器设备而暂停生产

⑤(工作或勤奋的)休息时间: Now let's have a ~. 现在我们休息一下吧。/ during ~s from cotton picking 在摘棉花休息时

⑥突变: a ~ in the weather 天气的骤变

⑦(物价等的)下降: tax ~s 减税

⑧[口]改过自新的机会

⑨[口]不恰当的行动(或言论)

⑩[俚]运气: a lucky (bad) ~ 好(坏)运气 / get a ~ 碰到好运气

⑪闯进；冲出；奔: a jail ~ 越狱 / The deer made a ~ for the thicket. 鹿奔向树丛。

⑫赛跑(或赛马)的开始

⑬【矿】断裂；断层

⑭船楼端部

‖ ~ *a butterfly on the wheel* 见 **butterfly** / ~ *away* ①突然离开 ②(柄等)脱下 ③(被抓住的人等)脱逃，脱身 脱离(教会、政党等)(*from*) ⑤放弃(习惯等)，打破(陈套)(*from*) / ~ *cover* 见 **cover** / ~ *down* ①打破，毁掉，破除: ~ *down* a door 把门打掉 ②制服，压倒: ~ *down* all resistance 压倒一切阻力；粉碎一切抵抗 ③坍塌；毁掉: The bridge *broke down*. 桥坍塌了。/ The car *broke down* on the way. 车子在路上抛锚了。④(计划等)失败，不成功 ⑤(健康、精神)垮下来，(人)在健康(或精神)方面垮下来; 情不自禁地痛哭起来 ⑥中止，停顿: How did the talks ~ *down*? 谈判怎么会中止的? / She suddenly *broke down* as she was singing. 她在唱歌时突然停住了。⑦把(化合物等)分解; 把(机器等)拆散(以便贮藏或运输); 把(成本、总数等)分成细目 ⑧(化合物等)分解; 易于分成若干部分: The chronicle ~s *down* into three major parts. 这部编年史分成三大部分。/ ~ *even²* / ~ *faith* 见 **faith** / ~ *forth* ①喷发 ②(欢呼、愤怒等)突然发出: Cheers *broke forth* from the crowd. 欢呼声突然从人群中发出。③忽然滔滔不绝地讲起话来 (或呼喊起来): The crowd *broke forth* in cheers. 群众突然欢呼起来。/ ~ *ground* 见 **ground¹** / ~ *in* ①训练; 使驯服: ~ a horse *in* 驯马 ②使(新物件)逐渐合用: ~ *in* a new pair of shoes 穿用新鞋使逐渐合脚 ③破门而入，闯入 ④打断: Don't ~ *in* when he is telling the story. 他讲故事的时候，别打断他。⑤开始活动，开始工作: He *broke in* with us last year. 他去年开始和我们一道工作。/ ~ *in on* (或 *upon*) 打扰; 打断: Don't ~ *in on* their conversation. 别打断他们的谈话。/ ~ *into* 破门而入(锁着的房子等) ②突然…起来:

~ *into* cheers 突然欢呼起来 / ~ *into* a run 突然奔跑起来 ③侵占(某人的时间等) / ~ *into* (或 *to*) *pieces* (使)成为碎片 / ~ *loose* 见 **loose** / ~ *off* ①(使)折断: The mast *broke* (或 was *broken*) *off*. 桅杆折断了。②突然停止讲话: I don't know why he *broke off* in the middle of a sentence. 我不知道他为什么一句话没说完忽然停住不说了。③突然停止(讲话等) ④(使)脱落 ⑤断绝，结束；解除(婚约): ~ *off* diplomatic relations with 与…断绝外交关系 ⑥暂停工作，休息一下: Let's ~ *off* for fifteen minutes and do exercises. 我们休息十五分钟做体操吧。⑦【军】突然改变航向 / ~ *one's word* / ~ *open* 见 **open** / ~ *out* ①(战争、火灾、疫病等)突然发生，爆发 ②叫嚷: ~ *out into* curses 大声叫骂起来 ③突然发生: ~ *out into* a cold sweat (*into* pimples) 发了一身冷汗(发疹) ④逃出 ⑤倒空(容器);卸下(船舱)的货 ⑥从贮藏处取出来准备使用;使处于准备状态 ⑦开始起(锚) ⑧悬(旗) ⑨起出，取出: ~ *out* a sled from the ice 从冰中起出雪橇 / ~ *sb.* (*oneself*) *of a habit* 见 **habit** / ~ *sb. on the wheel* 见 **wheel** / ~ *sb.'s heart* 使某人很伤心 / ~ *short* 使突然终止 / ~ *step* / ~ *the back of sth.* 见 **back** / ~ *the bank* 见 **bank²** / ~ *the ice* 见 **ice** / ~ *the neck of* 见 **neck¹** / ~ (*the*) *ranks* 见 **rank¹** / ~ *through* ①突围 ②突破，冲垮: ~ *through* all obstacles 冲垮一切障碍 / ~ *up* ①打碎，拆散；破碎，破掉: ~ *up* the whole into parts 化整为零 / ~ *up* an old ship 把旧船拆开 / *Break* it *up*! 别打(或别吵架)啦! ②分裂；分解: ~ *up* a word into syllables 把一个字分成音节 ③驱散 ④(集会)结束; (学校等)期末分散: The meeting didn't ~ *up* until noon. 集会到中午才结束。/ When do you ~ *up*? 你们什么时候放假? ⑤分类 (*into*) ⑥(体力)衰退; (人)衰老; (人)意志动摇起来，慌乱起来; (军队)士气衰落下去 ⑦(天气)变坏 ⑧[口]使苦恼 / ~ *wind* 见 **wind¹** / ~ *with* ①与…绝交 ②破除，结束: ~ *with* a bad habit 去掉坏习惯 / *make* a ~ *of* (台球戏中)连续得(分) / *without* a ~ 不断地，不停顿地

‖ '~*away* n. ①脱离; 【军】脱离队形: a ~*away from* the old traditional ideas 摆脱旧的传统观念 ② 故意制造得一碰就碎的东西(例如演戏用的椅子、刀枪等) a. [英]脱离组织的; [美俚]一碰就散开(或脱落)的 / '~**bone fever** 【医】断骨热，登革热 / '~**down** n. ①(机械等的)损坏; 故障，倒塌: a ~*down* gang (van) (火车等出事时的)抢修队(抢修车) ②(身体、精神等方面的)垮，衰竭: a nervous ~*down* 精神崩溃 ③【化】破裂，断裂; 【电】击穿: ~*down* voltage 击穿电压，破坏电压 ④失败，崩溃: the ~*down* of negotiations 谈判的破裂 ⑤分类; 分类，(成本等的)分成细目; 分类细帐: a statistical ~*down* of data 数据的统计性分类 ⑥美国黑人首创的一种舞蹈 / '~-'**even** *a.* 得失相当的，不盈不亏的: a ~-*even* point 【商】

损益两平点 / '~**head** n. 船头破冰用的装置 / '~**in** n. ①闯入 ②【军】突破 / '~**neck** a. 危险的: at (a) ~neck speed 以危险的高速 / a ~neck road 危险的(尤指极陡的)路 / '~**out** n. ①爆发 ②【军】突围 ③越狱 / '~**over** n. (报刊文章)转页刊登的部分 / '~**point** n. ①【化】转效点 ②【电】断点,停止点 / '~**point order** (射流技术中的)返回指令 / '~**through** n. ①突破,突破点;【军】突破,突贯: make a ~through at some single point 突破一点 / a ~through point 突破点 ②(科技等方面)惊人的进展,关键问题的解决: ~throughs in medical science 医学上的惊人进步 ③(物价、价值的)突然增涨 / '~**up** n. ①分裂,解散,崩溃: ~up value 破产企业的财产清理价值 ②解体,腐朽 ③停止,完结 / '~,**water** n. 防浪堤: a floating ~water 防浪木排 / ~**wind** ['breikwind] n. [英]幕;防风篱,挡风墙;防风林

break² [breik] n. 四轮大马车

breakage ['breikidʒ] n. ①破损, 毁损 ②破损处;破损量: a ~ in the water mains 自来水管的破损处 ③[常用复]破损物; 损耗 ④抵销损耗的款项;对于损耗的赔款

breaker¹ ['breikə] n. ①碎浪;激浪 ②破碎装置;轧碎机: a rock ~ 碎石机 ③打破者;开拓者;破坏者 ④驯服者: a horse~ 驯马者 ⑤【电】电流断路器 ⑥(汽车的)护胎带

breaker² ['breikə] n. 小水桶

breakfast ['brekfəst] I n. 早餐: At what time do you have ~? 你什么时候吃早点? / at ~ 早餐时;正在进早餐 II ❶ vi. 进早餐 ❷ vt. 给(请)(某人)吃早餐

breast [brest] I n. ①乳房; [喻]营养的来源: a child at the ~ 乳儿 / give a baby the ~ 给孩子喂奶 / past the ~ 断了奶的 ②胸(脯),胸腔;(衣服的)胸部 ③胸怀,心绪: a troubled ~ 心烦意乱 ④(器物的)侧面;窗腰;(山)腹;墙裙;炉胸;【矿】工作面;(无烟煤矿)煤房 II vt. ①把胸部对着… ②对付; 毅然对抗;逆…而进: ~ it out 硬挺到底 / ~ the waves 破浪前进 ||make a clean ~ and plate to: make a clean ~ of one's guilt 坦白认罪 / '~**bone** n. 胸骨 / '~-'**deep** a. 齐胸深的 / ~ **drill** 胸压手摇钻 / '~-'**high** a. 齐胸高的 / '~**hook** n. 【船】尖蹼板,船首甲板撑材 / '~**pin** n. 领带夹针; [美]胸口饰针 / '~,**plate** n. 胸铠; 使用胸压工具时工人胸前的护垫 ②(乌龟等的)肚甲 ③马鞍 ④(古时)犹太教高僧镶有十二颗宝石的法衣 / ~ **pump** 吸奶器 / '~**rail** n. 【船】船楼横栏杆 / '~**stroke** n. 【体】俯泳(如蛙式、蝶式等) / ~ **wall** 挡土墙 / '~**work** n. ①【军】胸墙 ②前后两甲板的栏杆

breath [breθ] n. ①气息,呼吸;呼吸能力: draw a (deep)~ 吸(深)呼 ②一口气 / a ~ sound 【语】气息音 ②气味,香气: a ~ of fresh air 一阵新鲜空气 ③空气的轻微流动: There isn't a ~ of air

(或 wind). 一点风也没有. ④声息,低语: Not a ~ was heard. 任何声息也听不到. ⑤一瞬间; 短暂的休息 ⑥生命,精神 ⑦示意,迹象: not a ~ of suspicion 毫无可疑之处 ||**above one's** ~ 高声地 / a ~ **of life** (或 one's nostrils) 必不可少的东西 / **below** (或 **under**) one's ~ 低声悄语地,低声地 / **catch one's** ~ ①喘息 ②歇口气 / **draw one's** ~ 呼吸正常 ③屏息 / **get one's** ~ (**again**) 恢复正常状态 / **hold one's** ~ (由于激动、害怕等原因)不出声,屏息 / **in a** ~ 一口气,一举 / **in one** ~ 一口气,一举;同时 / **in the same** ~ 同时: The two cannot be mentioned **in the same** ~. 两者不能相提并论. / **keep** (或 **save**) **one's** ~ **to cool one's porridge** 省点力气别开口 (指说了也没用) / **lose one's** ~ 喘不过气来,呼吸困难 / **out of** ~ 上气不接下气 / **save one's** ~ 不作声,沉默 / **short of** ~ 呼吸短促: He is sometimes **short of** ~. 他有时候要气喘. / **stop sb.'s** ~ 把某人闷死 / **take** ~ 歇口气,歇会儿 / **take sb.'s** ~ **away** (或 **knock the** ~ **out of sb.**) 使某人大吃一惊 / **waste** (或 **spend**) **one's** ~ 白费口舌 / **with bated** ~ 屏息地 ||~**ed** a. ①[常用以构成复合词]有…气味的 ②【语】气息音的

breathe [briːð] ❶ vi. ①呼吸: ~ in 吸入 / ~ out 呼出 / ~ hard (或 with difficulty) 呼吸困难 ②生存: be still breathing 还活着 ③歇口气; 停一下 ④ 低语; (风等)发出轻微的声音 ❷ vt. ①呼吸: ~ wholesome air 呼吸新鲜空气 ②使喘息;使疲乏 ③发散;表示出(感情等):吐露: not ~ a word (about) (关于…)秘而不宣 ④使休息,使歇口气 ⑤低声说,低声唱;【语】发(气息音) ⑥注入,灌输: ~ new life **into** 向…注入新的生命 ||~ **again** (或 **freely**) (在紧张等以后)安下心来,宽心 / ~ **one's last** 断气,死 / ~ **upon** ①使失去光泽 ②损毁(名誉等)

breathless ['breθlis] a. ①屏息的,不出声的: with ~ attention 全神贯注地 ②气喘吁吁的: in a ~ hurry 匆促得气也透不过来 ③无风的; 闷热的 ④气绝的,死了的 ||~**ly** ad. / ~**ness** n.

bred [bred] breed 的过去式和过去分词

breech [briːtʃ] n. ①屁股,臀部 ②炮尾 ||'~**block** n. 枪闩,炮闩,闭锁机 / '~**cloth**, '~**clout** n. 腰布 / '~,**loader** n. 后膛炮 / '~,**loading** a. 后膛装填的

breed [briːd] I (bred [bred]) ❶ vi. ①(动物)生产; 孕育 ②繁殖,育种: Rabbits ~ quickly. 兔子繁殖很快. ③滋生,产生 ❷ vt. ①(动物)产(仔),孵(卵) ②使繁殖,饲养: ~ cattle 饲养家畜 ③养育;培育;教养: well bred 教养良好的 ④引起,惹起;产生: Dirt ~s disease. 脏东西会引起疾病. ⑤【原】再生,增殖 II n. 品种,种类: a new ~ of sheep 新品种的羊 ||~ **in and in** 近亲繁殖;近亲结婚 / ~ **out** 在人工繁殖过程中消除(品种的特性) / ~ **out and out** 异种繁殖 / **What's bred in the bone will come out in the flesh**. [谚]本

性总要表现出来。‖**~er** *n.* ①繁殖的动物(或植物) ②饲养员; 养育员 ③起因, 起源者 ④【原】增殖反应堆: ~er reactor 增殖反应堆, 扩大再生核燃料反应堆 / **~ing** *n.* ①(动物的)生育, 繁殖 ②饲养: livestock ~ing 畜牧业 育种: cross ~ing 杂交育种 / close ~ing 近亲繁殖 ④ 教养, 熏陶

breeze[1] [briːz] **I** *n.* ①微风: spring ~s 春风 / a land (sea) ~ 陆(海)风 ②[口] 发脾气; 小争吵: kick up a ~ 引起小风波 ③ [美俚] 容易的事情 **II** *vi.* ①吹微风 ②[俚]迅速、轻快地前进(或进行) ③[美俚](快速)离去; 逃走, 逃出监狱 ‖~ in ① 象一阵风似地来到, 突然出现; 闲逛着走进 ②(比赛中)轻而易举地取胜 / ~ off [美俚] ① 住嘴不说 ②离去, 走开 / in a ~ [口]毫不费力地 / shoot the ~ ①吹牛, 说大话 ②闲聊; (指讲话或写文章)空谈 ‖**~less** *a.* 无风的, 平静的 ‖**~way** *n.* 房屋之间有顶的过道(或走廊)

breeze[2] [briːz] *n.* 焦炭渣, 煤屑, 煤渣: a ~ block 煤渣砌块 / a ~ brick 煤渣砖

breeze[3] [briːz] *n.* [英方]虻, 牛虻

breezy ['briːzi] *a.* ①有微风的; 通风的 ②活泼轻快的; 快活的; 爱谈笑的: He has a ~ manner. 他举止活泼轻松。 ③ 漠然的, 傲慢的 ‖**breezily** *ad.* 活泼地, 轻快地 / **breeziness** *n.* 活泼, 轻快

brethren ['breðrin] [复] *n.* [古] =brothers

brevet ['brevit] **I** *n.* 【军】名誉晋级(令) **II** (brevet-(t)ed; brevet(t)ing) *vt.* 名誉晋升

breviary ['briːvjəri] *n.* ①摘要, 缩略 ②【天主教】每日祈祷书

brevity ['breviti] *n.* ①(陈述等的)简短, 简洁 ②(生命等的)短暂, 短促 ‖*Brevity is the soul of wit.* 言以简洁为贵。

brew [bruː] **I** ❶ *vt.* ①酿造(啤酒等); 调制(饮料): ~ a liquid preparation with medicinal herbs 煎药 ②图谋, 策划(叛乱、恶作剧等) ❷ *vi.* ①酿酒 ②(风暴等)酝酿: A storm is ~ing. 风暴即将来临。 **II** *n.* 酿造; 酿造出来的饮料; (酒、茶等的)品味; (一次)酿造量 ‖*As you ~, so you must drink.* [谚]自作自受。(或: 自食其果。) ‖**~er** *n.* 酿(啤)酒的人; 酿(啤)酒商 / **~ing** *n.* ①(酿酒等的)准备工作 ②(啤酒等的)酿造; (暴风雨等的)酝酿 ③(一次)酿造量

brewery ['bruəri], **brewhouse** ['bruːhaus] *n.* 啤酒厂, 酿酒厂

briar ['braiə] *n.* =brier

bribe [braib] **I** *n.* 贿赂; 行贿物, 诱饵: give (或 offer, hand out) ~s to sb. 向某人行贿 / take ~s 受贿 **II** ❶ *vt.* 向…行贿; 收买: be ~d into secrecy 受了贿赂替人保密 ❷ *vi.* 行贿 ‖**bribee** [brai'biː] *n.* 受贿者 / **briber** *n.* 行贿者

bribery ['braibəri] *n.* 行贿; 受贿: commit ~ 行贿; 受贿

bric-a-brac ['brikəbræk] *n.* 古玩; 小摆设(如瓷器、花瓶、扇子等)

brick [brik] **I** *n.* ① 砖; 砖块: lay ~s 砌砖 /

refractory ~s 耐火砖 ②砖状物(如茶砖、砖形面包等): a ~ of ice cream 一块冰砖 ③积木 ④ [俚]心肠好的人; 好汉 **II** *a.* ①用砖砌造(或铺)的: a ~ wall 砖墙 ②砖似的: ~ red 砖红色 / ~ tea 茶砖 **III** *vt.* ①用砖建造; 用砖铺 ②用砖围砌; 用砖填补(洞等)(up): be togged to the ~s [美俚]穿戴得十分漂亮 / drop a ~ [口] 失言; 出错, 出丑 / have a ~ in one's hat 有醉意 / hit the ~s [美俚] ①走上街头 ②罢工; 在纠察线上巡行 ③被从监狱中释放出来 / like a ~ (或 like ~s) [口]活泼地, 勇猛地 / like a hundred (或 a ton) of ~s [口] 以压倒的威力; 来势猛烈地 / make ~s without straw 无米之炊, 做劳而无功的工作 ‖**~y** *a.* 砖头造的; 散满砖头的; 似砖的 (尤指砖颜色) ‖'**~bat** *n.* ①碎砖, 砖片(尤指以扔人的) ②贬责的话 / ~ clay (制砖的)粘土 / ~ dust 砖粉, 砖屑 / '**~field** *n.* 制砖工场, 砖厂 / '**~kiln** *n.* 砖窑 / '**~layer** *n.* 砌砖工人 / ~ nogging 【建】木架砖壁 / '**~work** *n.* 砖房; 砖坊工 / '**~yard** *n.* 制造(或出售)砖头的地方

bridal ['braidl] **I** *a.* ①新娘的: the ~ veil 新娘披的纱 ②婚礼的 **II** *n.* 婚宴; 结婚仪式

bride [braid] *n.* 新娘 ‖'**~-cake** *n.* 喜饼, 礼饼 / '**~-price** *n.* (成婚前)男方给女方的聘金(或礼)

bridegroom ['braidgrum] *n.* 新郎

bridesmaid ['braidzmeid] *n.* 女傧相

bridesman ['braidzmən] ([复] bridesmen) *n.* 男傧相

bridge [bridʒ] **I** *n.* ①桥, 桥梁: a ~ of boats 船桥 / a ~ team (或 party)【军】架桥队 / ~ parts 架桥器材 / the role of a ~ 桥梁作用 / build a trade ~ with 与…建立贸易联系 ②(船上的)驾驶台, 桥楼 ③(提琴等的)琴马 ④鼻梁; (眼镜上的)鼻架; (假牙上的)齿桥 ⑤[电]电桥 ⑥桥牌(一种纸牌游戏): auction ~ 拍卖式桥牌 / contract ~ 合约桥牌 **II** *vt.* ①架桥于; 用桥连接 ②[喻]越过, 跨过(障碍等): ~ over the difficulties 克服困难, 渡过难关 ‖a ~ of gold (或 a golden ~) 敌败的退路, 逃路 / burn one's ~s 破釜沉舟, 背水作阵 / Don't cross the ~ until you come to it. [谚]不要杞人忧天。(或: 莫自寻烦恼。) ‖'**~board** *n.* 【建】短梯基, 楼梯梁 / ~ crane 桥式起重机 / '**~head** *n.* 【军】桥头堡 / ~ house 【船】驾驶室, 桥楼室 / tower 桥塔 / ~ train 【军】①舟桥纵列 ②[总称]架浮桥用具 / '**~work** *n.* ①桥梁工事 ②(假牙的)桥

bridle ['braidl] **I** *n.* ①马勒(缰、辔、口衔等的总称), 缰绳 ②约束(物) ③【机】束带, 限动物 ④【海】系船索(链) ⑤【解】系带 **II** ❶ *vt.* ①给(马)上辔头 ②约束, 控制: ~ one's temper 抑制脾气 ❷ *vi.* 昂首表示轻蔑(或发怒): ~ at sb.'s remarks 听了某人的话发起怒来 ‖*give the ~ to* 松缰使(马)自由前进; [喻]放纵 / go well up to ~ 勇往直前 / *lay the* ~ *on the neck of* 放松, 放纵 ‖~ **bridge** 通马不通车的狭桥 / **hand** 执缰绳的手(通常指左手) / ~ **path**, **road**, ~ **way** 通马不通车的路, 马道 / ~ **rein** 马缰 / '~**wise** *a.* (马)听骑者指挥的

brief [bri:f] **I** *a.* ①短暂的: a ~ **stay** 稍稍呆几天, 小住 ②简短的, 简洁的: a ~ note 便条 / *To be* ~ (*with you*), I disagree. 简单地(对你)说, 我不同意。/ be ~ *of speech* 说话简短 / a cold and ~ welcome 冷淡而简短的欢迎 **II** *n.* ①(罗马教皇的)敕书 ②概要, 摘要; 短文 ③【律】诉讼要点摘录; (律师的)辩护状: file a ~ (律师向法院)提出辩护 / have plenty of ~*s* (律师)生意很忙 ④[常用复]三角裤 ⑤=briefing **III** *vt.* ①作...的摘要, 节录 ②[英]向(辩护律师)作指示; 聘请(律师) ③向(飞行员等)作出发前的最后指示; 向...下达简令; 在事先向...作简要指点: ~ sb. *in* (或 *on*)sth. 事先对某人作某事方面的指点 ④向...作简要介绍(或汇报) ‖hold a ~ (诉讼中)当辩护律师 / hold a ~ *for* 为...辩护; 主张 / *in* ~ 简言之; 以简洁的形式 / *take a* ~ 【律】接手承办案件 ‖~**ly** *ad.* / ~**ness** *n.*

briefing ['bri:fiŋ] *n.* ①下达简令; 情况的简要介绍(或汇报); 简况介绍(或汇报)会: a (news) ~ officer [美]新闻发布官 ②简令; 简要情况 ‖**chart** 任务简要讲解图 / ~ **room** 简令下达室

brier ['braiə] *n.* 多刺的木质茎植物(如蔷薇属植物等); 多刺的木质植物丛 ‖~**y** ['braiəri] *a.* 荆棘丛生的, 多刺的

brig[1] [brig] *n.* 方帆双桅船

brig[2] [brig] *n.* [美俚]①(美国军舰上的)禁闭室 ②监狱 ③警卫室

brigade [bri'geid] **I** *n.* ①【军】旅: a mixed ~ 混成旅 ②(执行一定任务的)队: a fire ~ 消防队 / a shock ~ 突击队 **II** *vt.* ①把...编成旅 ②把...编成队

brigadier [,brigə'diə] *n.* ①旅长 ②(英)陆军(或海军陆战队)准将 ‖~ **general** (美)陆军(或空军、海军陆战队)准将

brigand ['brigənd] *n.* 土匪, 强盗(尤指流窜匪帮中的一员) ‖~**age** ['brigəndidʒ], ~**ism** *n.* 土匪行为, 掠夺 / ~**ish** *a.* 土匪般的

brigantine ['brigəntain] *n.* (前桅为横帆, 主桅为纵帆的)双桅帆船

bright [brait] **I** *a.* ①明亮的, 辉煌的; [喻]光辉灿烂的: a ~ sky 晴空 / The garden is ~ with flowers. 鲜花满园。/ a ~ future 美好的未来 / see the ~ side of things 看到事物的光明面 ②(颜色)鲜明的: a ~ red 鲜红色 ③(酒等)晶莹的 ④欢快的, 生气勃勃的: be in a ~ humour 兴高采烈 / speak in a ~ voice 喜气洋洋地说话 ⑤聪明的, 伶俐的: a ~ idea 巧主意 ⑥(名声等)显赫的 **II** *ad.* 光亮地; 鲜明地; 欢快地: The sun shines ~. 阳光灿烂。‖*be* ~ *in the eye* 见 eye / ~ *and early* 一大早 ‖~**ly** *ad.* / ~**ness** *n.* ‖'~**-eyed** *a.* 眼睛晶莹的 / '~**work** *n.* (船、

车、机械等上面)镀(或擦)得发光的金属部分

brighten ['braitn] **①** *vt.* ①使发光, 使发亮 ②使快活, 使活跃: Their presence greatly ~ed up the evening party. 他们(的)在场使晚会大为活跃。**②** *vi.* ①发光, 发亮: His face ~ed up. 他脸上露出了喜色。②快活起来, 活跃

brilliance ['briljəns] *n.* ①光辉; 辉煌 ②(色彩)鲜明 ③(才华等放出的)异彩

brilliant ['briljənt] **I** *a.* ①光辉的; 辉煌的: a ~ light 耀眼的光 / a ~ example 光辉的榜样 ②卓越的, 英明的; 才华横溢的: ~ leadership (guidance) 英明的领导(指导) / Never think "How ~ I am!" 千万不要认为"我多么高明!" ③(色彩)鲜明的 **II** *n.* 宝石(尤指多角形的钻石); 把宝石切成多角形的琢磨法【印】3½点铅字(一般使用中最小号的铅字) ‖~**ly** *ad.* a ~*ly* lit hall 灯火辉煌的大厅

brim [brim] **I** *n.* ①(杯、碗、漏斗等的)边, 缘: full to the ~ 满到边 ②帽边 **II** (brimmed; brimming) **①** *vt.* 注满(容器等) **②** *vi.* 满溢 ‖~**ful** *a.* 满到边的; 洋溢着...的 (*of*) / ~**less** *a.* 无边缘的 / **brimmer** *n.* 满杯

brimstone ['brimstən] *n.* 硫黄(石) ‖**brimstony** *a.* 硫黄质(或色)的

brindle ['brindl] **I** *n.* ①斑, 斑纹(点) ②有斑纹的动物 **II** *a.* 有斑纹的 ‖~**d** *a.* 有斑纹的

brine [brain] **I** *n.* ①盐水; 咸水; 近乎饱和的盐水 ②海水; 海 ③[诗]泪水 **II** *vt.* 用盐水浸(或泡); 用盐水处理 ‖~**pan** 蒸发海水以取盐的铁锅

bring [briŋ] (brought [brɔ:t]) **①** *vt.* ①带来, 拿来: *Bring* the basket to me, please. (或 *Bring* me the basket, please.)请把篮子带给我。/ *Take* the axe to the next room, and ~ the file here. 把斧头拿到隔壁房间去, 把锉刀拿到这儿来。[take 指从说话人处带到另一处去, bring 则指从他处带到说话人处, 或从说话人处带给对方] ②使(人)来到: What ~*s* you here today? 今天是什么风把你吹来了? / Why don't you ~ him *along*? 你为什么不带他一块儿来呢? ③产生, 引起, 导致 ④促使; 劝使: She couldn't ~ herself to believe the news. 她不能(使自己)相信这个消息。⑤使处于某种状态: ~ the car to a stop 使车子停下来 / ~ the kettle to boil furiously 使壶水沸腾 ⑥(货品)卖得(多少钱) ⑦提出(诉讼、论据等): ~ a charge against sb. 对某人提出控诉(指责) ⑧[方]陪, 护送: May I ~ you home? 我可以陪你回家吗? **②** *vi.* (船等)停下, (船等)到终点 (*to, up*) ‖~ *about* ①带来, 造成: ~ *about* great changes 带来巨大的变化 / What *brought about* his illness? 他怎么得病的? ②使(船)掉过头来 / ~ *around* (或 *round*) ①使改变思想; 使信服; 劝使: ~ sb. *around* to the correct way of thinking 使某人的思想方法步入正轨 ②[口]使恢复知觉(或健康): The new acupuncture-therapy will ~ you *around* in no time. 新针疗法将很快使你恢复健康。③[口]使来访 / ~ *back* ①带回来, 拿回来: Please ~

(me) *back* the saw. 请把锯子带回来(给我)。② 使回忆起来 ③使恢复: ~ sb. *back* to health 使某人恢复健康 / ~ *down* ①使倒下; 打倒 ② 击落 ③打伤, 打死 ④降低(温度、物价等): I'm sure the injection of penicillin will ~ your fever *down.* 我确信注射青霉素会使你的热度降下来。 / ~ *down* the prices of medicines 降低药价 ⑤把(记录)写到(某时为止)(to) / ~ *down on oneself* 招致(他人的愤恨、惩罚等) / ~ *down the house* 见 **house** / ~ *forth* 使产生; 生(孩子); 开(花), 结(果): weed through the old to ~ *forth* the new 推陈出新 / ~ *forward* ①提出(建议、论据等): ~ *forward* a new design 提出一项新的设计 ②把…提前: ~ *forward* a meeting from Wednesday to Monday 把会议从星期三提前到星期一 ③使涌现出; 显示 ④(在帐目上)把(数字等)过到次页 / ~ *home to* sb. 使某人深切地感到(或清楚地认识到) ②确实证明是某人所犯的: ~ a fraud *home to* sb. 确实证明某人犯诈骗罪 / ~ *in* ① 收(庄稼等): We have brought *in* a good cotton harvest. 我们获得了棉花丰收。 ② 生产, 产出: How much does the fishery ~ (them) *in*? 渔业(使他们)增加多少收入? ③挣得 ④引来, 引进(风尚、话题等): ~ *in* new customs and new habits 带来新风俗、新习惯 ⑤(陪审团) 宣读(判决案): ~ (sb.) *in* guilty (not guilty) 宣判(某人) 有罪(无罪) / ~ *low* 见 low[1] / ~ *off* ①救出(尤指从出事的船上) ②使成功; 完成: It was a difficult task but we brought it *off*. 那是一项困难的工作, 但我们终于完成了任务。 / ~ *off* a technical innovation 完成一项技术革新 / ~ *on* ①引起, 导致: ~ *on* fresh attack of rheumatism 引起风湿病的复发 ②使发展(或前进): The use of chemical fertilizer is ~*ing* the crops on nicely. 使用化肥使庄稼长得好极了。 ③提出(论点等)供讨论 / ~ *out* ①使显出; 使(意义等)明白表示出来: ~ *out* the facts and reason things out 摆事实, 讲道理 / ~ *out* the meaning of a passage 阐明一段文字的意义 ②出版; 生产: ~ *out* a new type of transistor radio 生产一种新型的晶体管收音机 ③使(女子)初次参加社交 ④说出: He was so excited that he could hardly ~ *out* a thank-you. 他激动得进一声"谢谢你"也说不出来。 / ~ *over* ①把…带来 ②使某人转变 / ~ *through* ①救活; 使渡过困难: ~ all the newly transplanted seedlings *through* 使新移植的秧苗都存活 / ~ *to* ①使恢复知觉 ②使(船等)停下: ~ a ship *to* by dropping the anchor 下锚停船 ③(船等)停下 / ~ *to bear* ① 施加(压力、影响等) ② 运用, 竭尽(全力) / ~ all one's strength in getting the log *upon* the waggon 竭尽全力把木头弄上货车 ③完成, 实现, 使成功: He has a way of his own in ~*ing* his views *to bear*. 他有自己独特的方式促别人接受他的意见。 ④瞄准 / ~ *to pass* 使发生; 使实现; 完成; 实行 / ~ *under* 镇压, 压制; 使就范 / ~ *up* ①教育, 培养; 使成长 ②提

出(供讨论或促使注意): ~ a matter *up* for consideration 提出一件事供人考虑 ③使(车辆等)忽然停住 ④(船等)停下; (船等)到终点 ⑤把(某人)带上法庭并对他进行控告 ⑥呕出

brink [briŋk] *n.* 边; (河流等的)边沿; [喻]边缘: on the ~ of bankruptcy 濒临破产

brisk [brisk] **I** *a.* ① 活泼的, 活跃的; 轻快的: at a ~ pace 以轻快的步伐 ②(天气等)令人爽快的, 清新的: ~ winter morning air 冬天早晨的清新空气 ③兴旺的, 生气勃勃的: Our market is ~ and the prices are stable. 我们的市场繁荣, 物价稳定。 ④(酒等)起泡的; 味浓的 ⑤(在语气或态度方面)尖刻的 **II ①** *vt.* 使活泼, 使活跃; 使兴旺 **②** *vi.* 活泼起来; 兴旺起来 (up) ‖~ly *ad.* / ~ness *n.*

bristle ['brisl] **I** *n.* ①(动、植物的) 短而硬的毛; (猪等的)鬃毛 ②(刷子等的)毛 ③(人的) 须茬儿 **II ①** *vi.* ① (毛发等)直立 ② 发怒; 准备格斗: ~ with anger 怒得毛发倒竖 ③密密地覆盖; 充满 (with): a harbour *bristling with* masts 桅樯林立的港口 / solve a problem *bristling with* difficulties 解决一个困难重重的问题 **②** *vt.* ①使(毛发等)直立; 把…弄粗糙 ②给(刷子等)安鬃毛 ‖set up sb.'s ~s 激怒某人 ‖**bristly** *a.* ①(硬而短的)毛发丛生的; 粗糙的 ②(毛发等) 短而硬的 ‖'~-**tail** *n.* (双尾目和缨尾目中的)无翅昆虫

British ['britiʃ] **I** *a.* ①不列颠的, 英国的; 不列颠人的, 英国人的 ②英联邦的; 英联邦人的 ‖the ~ Commonwealth of Nations 英联邦 / the ~ Empire 英帝国 / ~ English 英国英语(区别于美国、澳大利亚等地使用的英语) / the ~ House of Lords (Commons) 英国上(下)议院 / the ~ Isles 不列颠群岛 / the ~ Museum 不列颠博物馆(旧称大英博物馆) / the ~ thermal unit 英国热单位(略作 Btu, B.t.u.) / a ~ warm (英国军官穿的)双排钮扣的短大衣 **II** *n.* ①古不列颠人的语言 ② 英国英语 ③ [the ~] [总称]英国人; 英联邦人 ‖~er *n.* [美]英国人 / ~ism *n.* =Briticism

brittle ['britl] **I** *a.* ①易碎的, 脆弱的; 易爆的: He has a ~ temper. 他动不动就要发脾气。 ②易损坏的; 不永久的: outwardly strong but inwardly ~ 外强中干的 / a ~ promise 靠不住的诺言 ③(声音等)尖利的 ④冷淡的; 专为自己打算的 **II** *n.* [美]松脆花生薄片糖 ‖~ness *n.*

broach[1] [broutʃ] **I** *n.* ①锥形尖头工具(如钻头、剥刀、石匠用的凿子等); 扩孔器 ②(烤肉用的)铁叉 ③(教堂的)尖塔 ④(女子服装上的)饰针 **II ①** *vt.* ①在(桶)上打眼子 ②钻开(矿脉等) ③用凿子开(洞); 把(眼子)弄大 ④【机】拉削 ⑤首次宣布; 把(题目等)提出讨论(或辩论) **②** *vi.* (鲸鱼、鱼雷等)冒出水面 ‖~er *n.* ①剥孔机; 绞孔机; 拉床(=broaching machine) ②剥孔机(或绞孔机等)的操作工人

broach[2] [broutʃ] *vt. & vi.* (使船)横转侧面受到风浪(而有倾覆危险)

broad [brɔːd] **I** *a.* ①宽的,广阔的;辽阔的 ②广大的;广泛上的,非限制的: use a word in its ~ sense 在广义上使用一个词 ③完全明朗的;明白显著的: in ~ daylight 在光天化日之下 / a ~ hint 明白的暗示 ④主要的;概括性的: achieve ~ agreement on an issue 就一个问题的主要方面达成协议 / He gave his views in ~ outline. 他概略地谈了自己的看法。⑤宽宏的: a man of ~ views 宽宏大量的人 ⑥粗俗的: a ~ joke 下流的笑话 ⑦(在发音等方面)方言性的;口音重的: a ~ accent 土腔 ⑧(元音)开放的,形成开音节的 **II** *ad.* 宽阔地: be ~ awake 完全醒着 **III** *n.* ①(手掌等的)宽阔部分;[美俚](男子的)肩宽 ②[英][复]江河的开阔部分 ③[复][美俚]纸牌 ④[美俚]女人;下流女人 ‖as ~ as (it is) long ①(房间等)长宽相等 ②没有区别,半斤八两: It is as ~ as (it is) long whether we go by tram or by bus. 我们坐电车去还是坐公共汽车去,是完全一样的。‖**~ly** *ad.* ~ly speaking [作插入语]广义地说 / **~ness** *n.* / **~way(s)**, **~wise** *ad.* 宽面朝前地,横着 ‖**~ax(e)** *n.* 钺 / **~ bean** 蚕豆 / '**~brim** *n.* ①一种宽边帽(尤指贵格派教徒戴的) ②[贵格派教徒,公谊会会员] / '**~cloth** *n.* ①各色细平布 ②绒面呢 / ~ ga(u)ge ①宽轨距(指四呎八时半以上的轨距) ②宽轨铁路;在宽轨铁路上行驶的火车 / '**~ga(u)ge** *a.* ①宽轨距的 ②[口]气量大的 / ~ jump [美]跳远 / '**~leaf**, '**~leafed**, '**~leaved** *a.* 阔叶的 / **~loom** *a.* 用阔幅织布机织成的 / **~loom** *n.* 阔幅绸缎;阔幅地毯 / '**~'minded** *a.* 容得下不同意见的,宽宏大量的 / '**~sheet** *n.* 单面(或双面)印刷的大幅纸张;单面(或双面)印刷品 / '**~side** *n.* ①(水面以上的)舷侧 ②全部舷炮;舷炮的齐射 ③连珠炮似的攻讦(或谴责) ④宽面 ⑤=~sheet *ad.* ①舷侧着: a ship ~side on to the lighthouse 一边面向灯塔的船只 ②齐射地 ③无目标地,胡乱地 / '**~sword** *n.* 大刀,大砍刀

broadcast['brɔːdkɑːst]**I** (broadcast 或 broadcasted) ❶ *vt.* ①(用无线电或电视)广播 ②乱传(消息等) ③撒播(种子) ❷ *vi.* ①广播 ②在广播节目中讲话(或演出) **II** *a.* (经由无线电或电视)广播的: a ~ message 广播稿 ②被撒播的;散布在四处的 **III** *n.* ①广播,播音: the ~ of world news 国际新闻的广播 ②广播节目: an evening ~ of world news 晚上播送的国际新闻节目 ③撒播 **IV** *ad.* ①经广播 ②四散地: sow seed ~ 撒种 / **~er** *n.* ①播种机 ②广播电台;广播机构 ③广播装置 ④广播员

brocade [brə'keid] **I** *n.* (织有金银丝浮花的)锦缎,花缎;织锦: more flowers on the ~ 锦上添花 **II** *vt.* 在(织物)上织出花纹;把(花纹)织入织物 ‖**~d** *a.* ①锦缎似的 ②用锦缎装饰的

brochure ['brəuʃjuə] *n.* 小册子

brogue[brəug] *n.* ①粗革厚底皮鞋;半统工作靴 ②有装饰性小孔的皮鞋,拷花皮鞋

brogue[2] [brəug] *n.* 土腔,土音(尤指爱尔兰人讲英语时的土腔)

broke [brəuk] **I** break[1] 的过去式 **II** *a.* [俚][作表语用]一个钱也没有的;破了产的 ‖*be ~ to the wide* (或 *world*) [俚]一个钱也没有,穷到极点 / *go ~* 破产 / *go for ~* 全力以赴

broken ['brəukən] **I** break[1] 的过去分词 **II** *a.* ①被打碎的,破碎的: ~ bits of china 瓷器碎片 ②(腿、臂等)骨折的 ③零碎的,不完整的: ~ meat 肉屑 / ~ tea 茶叶末子 / ~ time 零星时间 ④(地面等)起伏不平的;断续的;(天气)晴不定的: a ~ sleep 时醒时睡 ⑤被破坏的,遭违背的: a ~ home 破裂的家庭(尤指夫妇分居或离婚,其子女缺少照顾的家庭) / a ~ promise 背弃的诺言 ⑥【植】(花)有不规则斑纹的,患杂锦病的 ⑦衰弱的;沮丧的,低沉的: a ~ constitution 虚弱的体质 / a ~ man (在精神等方面)潦倒的人 / a ~ spirit 消沉的意志,心灰意懒 ⑧破了产的,倒闭了的 ⑨[口]降了级的 ⑩蹩脚的: ~ English 不标准的英语 ⑪养驯了的 ‖**~ly** *ad.* / **~ness** *n.* ‖'**~-'down** *a.* (在健康等方面)衰弱之极的,快垮掉的 / '**~-'hearted** *a.* 心碎的,悲伤过度的 / **~ line** ①虚线(即……) ②【数】折线 / **~ lot** (一百股以下的)零星股份 / ~ **reed** 难以依靠的人(或物) / '**~-winded** ['brəukən'windid] *a.* (马)喘息的,呼吸急促的

broker ['brəukə] *n.* ①(股票、公债等的)经纪人,掮客,(买卖)中间人,代理人 ②[英](官方批准的)对债务人财物的估价(或出售)人 ③[英]旧货商

brokerage ['brəukəridʒ] *n.* ①经纪业,中间人业务 ②付给经纪人的经手费,佣金,回扣

bromide ['brəumaid] *n.* 【化】溴化物;溴化物乳剂: potassium ~ 溴化钾 / ~ paper 溴素纸,印相(或放大)纸 ②[美俚]庸俗讨厌的人;庸俗讨厌的话(或想法)

bronchitis [brɔŋ'kaitis] *n.* 【医】支气管炎

bronze [brɔnz] **I** *n.* ①青铜,古铜: the *Bronze* Age 青铜时代 / a ~ statue 铜像 ②青铜制(艺术)品 ③青铜色 **II** *vt.* 镀青铜于;上青铜色于 ❷ *vi.* 变成青铜色;被晒黑 ‖**bronzy** *a.* 带青铜色的

brooch [brəutʃ] *n.* 胸针,饰针

brood [bruːd] **I** *n.* ①(鸡等)一窝;同窝幼鸟;(昆虫等)一次产出的卵; 一次孵化的幼生: a ~ of chickens 一窝小鸡 / Some insects produce seven or eight ~s a year. 有些昆虫一年产七、八次卵。②(同种或同类的)事物;一组(事物);[贬](同父母的)孩子们: a ~ of ideas 类似的一组想法 **II** ❶ *vt.* ①孵(蛋);孵出 ②(母鸡等)翅膀掩护(小鸡等) ③盘算,细想 ❷ *vi.* ①孵蛋;伏窝似地静坐 ②(云等)低覆,黑压压地笼罩: amidst ~ing twilight 在暮色苍茫之中 / A tower ~s over the valley. 塔楼俯瞰着山谷。③郁闷地沉思;沮丧 ‖**~er** *n.* ①孵卵的动物;(鸡等)孵房;孵卵器 ②沉思的人 / **~y** *a.* ①(母鸡等)要孵卵的;有繁殖力的 ②郁郁沉思的

brook[1] [bruk] *vt.* [常用在否定句中]容忍,忍受: ~ no delay 刻不容缓

brook² [bruk] *n.* 小河,溪

brooklet ['bruklit] *n.* 小溪,涧

broom [bru:m] **I** *n.* ①金雀花,金雀花属植物 ②扫帚 **II** *vt.* 用扫帚扫,扫除 ‖*A new ~ sweeps clean.* [谚]新官上任三把火。 / *jump the ~* [方]结婚 ‖**~y** *a.* 金雀花属的,多金雀花的 ‖'**~corn** *n.* 高粱,蜀黍(可制扫帚) / '**~stick** *n.* 扫帚柄

broth [brɔ(:)θ] *n.* 肉汤;清汤

brothel ['brɔθl] *n.* 妓院,窑子

brother ['brʌðə] **I** *n.* ①兄弟: my elder (younger) ~ 我的哥哥(弟弟) / the Li ~s (或 the ~s Li) 李氏弟兄 ②同事; officers 同事军官 ③[复]常用 brethren ['breðrin] 同行业(或教会、社团)的人 **II** *vt.* 以兄弟相称;兄弟般地对待: He used to ~ me. 他把我视同兄弟。 ‖**~hood** *n.* ①兄弟(般的)关系 ②兄弟会 / **~less** *a.* 无弟兄的 ‖**~-in-law** ['brʌðərinlɔ:] ([复]~s-in-law) *n.* ①姐夫,妹夫 ②内兄,内弟 ③大伯,小叔

brotherly ['brʌðəli] *a.* 弟兄的;兄弟般的: ~ relations 兄弟般的关系 ‖**brotherliness** *n.* 兄弟的情谊;友情,友爱

brought [brɔ:t] bring 的过去式和过去分词

brow¹ [brau] *n.* ①[常用复]眉,眉毛: Knit the ~s and you will hit upon a stratagem. 眉头一皱,计上心来。②额 ③悬崖;山顶,坡顶;陡坡 ④容貌,表情: an angry ~ 怒容 ‖**~ed** *a.* [常用以构成复合词]眉毛…的: dark-~ed 眉毛浓的 ‖**~ague, ~ ache** [医]额部神经痛

brow² [brau] *n.* [船]滑轮跳板

browbeat ['braubi:t] (browbeat, browbeaten ['braubi:tn]) *vt.* ①吹胡子瞪眼睛,吓唬;欺侮: ~ sb. *into* doirg sth. 威逼某人做某事

brown [braun] **I** *a.* 褐色的,棕色的;皮肤黝黑的: ~ bread 黑面包 / ~ coal 褐煤 / ~ paper 牛皮纸 / ~ rice 糙米 / ~ sugar 红糖 / ~ ware 陶器 **II** *n.* ①褐色,棕色;褐(或棕)色颜料 ②[英俚]铜币 **III** *vt. & vi.* (使)变成褐色(或棕色)(尤指由于日晒或烘烤) ‖*be in a study* 沉思默想,空想,幻想 / **~ off** [美俚]出大错 / **~ out** (为防备空袭或节约用电)把(城市等)的灯火弄暗淡 / *do sb.* ~ [英俚]使某人上当 / *do up* ~ [美俚]把…彻底搞好 / *the* ~ 黑压压的一群飞鸟: fire into the ~ 向鸟群打枪 / [喻]向机群开炮(或发火箭等) ‖**~ness** *n.* / **~ish, ~y** *a.* 带褐色的 / **Betty** 用苹果、面包屑等烘制的布丁 / '**~ed-'off** *a.* [俚]厌烦透了的;因失意而发怒的 / '**~nose** *vt.* [美俚]拍…马屁 / '**~out** *n.* 灯火暗淡(尤指剧院的灯光效果) / '**Brownshirt** *n.* 德国褐衫党党员,纳粹党党员 / '**~stone** *n.* (建筑用的)褐色沙石: a ~stone district 富人住宅区

browse [brauz] **I** *n.* ①(牲畜吃的)嫩草(或嫩叶等) ②放牧;吃草: the sheep *at* ~ 在吃草的羊 ③浏览 **II** ❶ *vt.* ①(牲畜)吃(嫩草等) ②放牧: ~ cattle *on* grass 放牛吃草 ③浏览(书刊),(尤

指为了挑书而)随便翻阅 ❷ *vi.* ①(牲畜)吃草;吃(on): cattle *browsing* in the meadow 在草地上吃草的牛 / ~ on grass (牛羊等)吃草 ②浏览: ~ among books in a library 在图书馆里浏览图书

bruise [bru:z] **I** *n.* ①(人体或水果、植物等碰撞后产生的)青肿,伤痕 ②擦伤;[喻](感情等方面的)挫伤 **II** ❶ *vt.* ①使(皮肉)青肿;碰伤(水果、植物等): He fell and ~d his leg. 他摔了下来,腿上起了紫血块。 / Pack the pears carefully so that they won't get ~d. 把梨子小心装箱,使勿受损伤。②使(木料、金属)产生凹痕 ③研碎,捣烂(水果等) ④挫伤(感情等) ❷ *vi.* 变成青肿;产生伤痕: Tomatoes ~ easily. 西红柿很容易碰伤。‖**~r** *n.* ①职业拳击家 ②彪形大汉;气力大、爱打架的人

brunette [bru:'net] *a. & n.* (白种人中)浅黑型的(女人)

brunt [brʌnt] *n.* 正面的冲击;主要的压力 ‖*bear the* ~ 首当其冲: bear the ~ of an attack 在进攻面前首当其冲

brush [brʌʃ] **I** *n.* ①刷子,毛刷;【电】电刷;[美俚]一把大胡子: a laundry ~ (洗衣用的)板刷 ②画笔: a writing ~ 毛笔 ③粗大的尾巴(尤指狐狸尾巴) ④[美]灌丛;灌木地带;柴 ⑤(一)刷: Give the clothes a good ~. 把衣服好好刷一刷。⑥遭遇战,激烈的小接触;争吵: a narrow ~ with death 差一点丢掉性命的遭遇 **II** ❶ *vt.* ①刷;擦;揩;拂: ~ a door 给门刷上油漆 ❷ *vi.* ①擦过,掠过(by, past, through): He ~ed past (或 by) me in the street. 他和我在街上擦肩而过。②(马奔时)两脚相擦受伤 ‖*be tarred with the same* ~ 是一路货色,是一丘之貉 / ~ *aside* ❶扫除(障碍等) ②漠视(事实等),不顾(困难等) / ~ *away* ①刷去;揩去;拂去 ②= aside / ~ *off* ①刷去;揩去;拂去 ②由于擦刷而脱落: Dried mud on one's shoes ~es off easily. 鞋上的烂泥干后一刷就脱落。③把…打发走;丢弃;毫不客气地拒绝 ④[俚]逃走;[美俚][常用于祈使句]走开,离去 / ~ *up* ①擦亮;刷新(房屋等);把…打扮整洁 ②重新学习(以免荒疏),复习: ~ up(on) one's English 复习英语 ③提高(技巧等),使完善 / *give sb. the* (或 *a*) ~ 把某人打发开;根本不理睬某人 / *the* ~ ①绘画艺术;画家的风格 ②画家: a painting from the same ~ 同一画家画的一幅画 ③[美俚]丛林(地带);不开化的地区 ‖**~ing** *n.* [复]刷拢来的东西 / **~y** *a.* ①多灌丛的 ②毛刷一样的;蓬松的 ‖~ burn 擦伤 / ~ cut 一种刷形短发的发式 / ~ *discharge* 【电】刷形放电,电晕放电 / '~-fire war 小规模(或局部地区)的战争,灌木林火式战争 / '~-'off *n.* 打发走;丢弃;毫不客气的拒绝: give sb. the ~-off 把某人打发开;根本不理睬某人 / ~ *pencil* 画笔 / '~'up *n.* ①擦亮;刷新;打扮整洁: Go and have a ~up. 去把自己弄弄整洁。②重新学习,复习;

give one's French a ～*up* 重新学习一下法语 ③ (技巧等的) 提高，改进 / ～**wheel**【机】刷轮 / '～**wood** *n.* ①灌丛 ②柴 / '～**work** *n.* 绘画; 画法，画家的风格

brusque [brusk] *a.* 粗暴的，鲁莽的，唐突的 ‖～**ly** *ad.* / ～**ness** *n.*

brutal ['bru:tl] *a.* ①兽性的，残忍的; 蛮横的 ②(天气等) 令人难受的: a ～ winter 严冬 / ～ heat 酷热 / the ～ facts 严峻的事实 ‖～**ism** ['bru:təlizəm] *n.* 兽性，残忍 / ～**ity** [bru(:)'tæliti] *n.* 残忍，暴行，野蛮行为 / ～**ly** ['bru:təli] *ad.* 残忍地，蛮横地

brute [bru:t] **I** *n.* ①兽，畜生 ②人面兽心的人，残忍的人 ③[the ～] 兽性 **II** *a.* ①畜生的; 畜生般的 ②残忍的，蛮横的 ③没有理性的: by ～ force (一味)凭着蛮力

bubble ['bʌbl] **I** *n.* ①泡，水泡，气泡 ②泡影，妄想: a ～ company (为行骗而)虚设的公司 ③冒泡(声); 沸腾(声): The kettle is *at the ～*. 壶里的水在开了。 **II ❶** *vi.* ①冒泡，沸腾; (水等)往上冒: Water ～*d up* through the sand. 水渗过泥沙冒了出来。 ②(水)汩汩地流; 发嘻嘻声: ～ *with laughter* 格格地笑 **❷** *vt.* ①使冒泡 ②滔滔不绝地说(话): He ～*d* questions. 他接二连三地提问题。 ③[古]哄骗 ‖～ *and squeak* 油煎土豆卷心菜，油煎菜肉 / ～ *over* ①冒着泡溢出 ②抑制不住地激动起来: ～ *over* with joy (wrath) 抑制不住内心的喜悦(愤怒) / *prick a* ～ 戳破肥皂泡; 揭穿真面目 / *South Sea Bubble* 【史】南海泡沫(十八世纪初英国殖民公司南海公司在南美进行股票投机的骗局) ‖～**r** *n.* ①喷泉饮水口 ②【化】起泡器 ‖～ **chamber** 【原】泡沫室，起泡室 / ～ **gum** 可吹成泡泡的口香糖 / '～**head** *n.* [美俚]笨蛋 / '～**top** *n.* (汽车后部等的)透明防弹罩

buccaneer [ˌbʌkə'niə] **I** *n.* ①海盗(尤指十七、十八世纪出没于中美洲、南美洲沿海一带的海盗) ②肆无忌惮的冒险家 **II** *vi.* 作海盗 ‖～**ish** [ˌbʌkə-'niərif] *a.* 海盗似的

buck¹ [bʌk] **I** *n.* ①([复] buck(s)) 雄鹿; 公羊; 牡兔 ②纨袴子弟，花花公子; [美]男人(尤指黑人和印第安人) ③[美]跳木架; 【体】鞍马 ④[美俚]元: ten ～*s* 十块钱 / [英]捕鳝鱼的竹笼 **II** *vi.* ①(马等)猛然弯背跃起 ②[美](山羊等)低着头撞过去 ③[美口]强烈反抗，反对 (*at, against*) ④[美口](车辆)颠簸; (引擎等)颤动 **❷** *vt.* ①(马等)猛然弯背跃起把(骑者)摔下来 (*off*) ②[美]低着头撞; [美](足球运动中)冲入(对方阵地) ③[美口]强烈反抗，反对 ④[美]传递: ～ the bricks down the line 列队递砖 **III** *a.* ①雄的; [美俚]男的 ②[美俚]某一军衔等级中最低一级的: a ～ private 列兵 / a ～ general 准将 ‖～ *for* [美俚]千方百计谋求(官职等) / ～ *up* [口](使)精神振作起来; [用于祈使句]快点: The good news ～*ed* us all *up*. 这个好消息使我们大家欢欣鼓舞。 / *in the* ～*s* [美俚]手头有钱 / *old* ～ (熟人间的)

称呼语)老朋友 ‖'～**eye** *n.* ①【植】七叶树(或其果实) ②[B-][口]美国俄亥俄州人 / ～ **fever** 无经验的猎人见到猎物时的紧张激动 / '～**horn** *n.* 鹿角 / '～**hound** *n.* 猎鹿用的小猎狗 / '～**jump** *vi. & vt.* (马等)猛然弯背跃起(把骑者摔下来) / '～**,jumper** *n.* 烈马，劣马 / '～**saw** *n.* 木锯 / '～**shot** *n.* 大号铅弹 / '～**skin** *n.* ①鹿皮 ②[复]鹿皮马裤 / '～**thorn** *n.* 【植】①鼠李 ②(美国南部产)一种山榄科植物 / '～**tooth** *n.* 龅牙，獠牙 / '～**wheat** *n.* 荞麦

buck² [bʌk] *n.* (打扑克时用的)庄家标志 ‖*cut the* ～ ①很有效地(或很快地)做 ②干得出色，不负所望 / *pass the* ～ *to* [口] 推卸责任给 ‖～ **passer** 老是推卸责任者 / '～**,passing** *n.* 推卸责任 / ～ **slip** [美俚]为把事情推给别人而写的便条

buck³ [bʌk] [古][方] **I** *n.* ①洗衣服的碱水，起泡的肥皂水 ②用碱水(或肥皂水)浸洗过的衣服 **II** *vt.* 用碱水(或起泡的肥皂水)浸(或洗) ‖～ **basket** [古]洗衣筐

buck⁴ [bʌk] **I** *n.* ①谈话 ②自吹自擂 **II** *vi.* 闲谈; 吹牛 (*about*) ‖'～**stick** *n.* [俚]吹牛的人

buck⁵ [bʌk] *ad.* [美方]完全地: ～ naked 一丝不挂

bucket¹ ['bʌkit] **I** *n.* ①水桶，吊桶，提桶: a fire ～ 灭火水桶 ②(挖土机等的)铲斗，勺斗; (往复泵的)活塞; (水轮、汽轮机等的)叶片: a dredging ～ 挖泥船的挖斗 / a skip ～ 翻斗，箕斗 / a turbine ～ 涡轮叶片 ③(一)桶，满桶; 大量: The rain was coming down in ～*s*. 天下着倾盆大雨。 ④[俚]破旧的大船; 破旧的大汽车 ⑤[俚]屁股 **II** *vt.* ①用桶打(水); 用桶装运 ②利用(顾客的资金)买空卖空 ‖*a drop in the* ～ 沧海一粟 / *give sb. the* ～ [口]解雇某人 / *kick the* ～ [俚]死掉 ‖～**ful** *n.* (一)桶，满桶 ‖～ **brigade** 救火时排成一行传递水桶的队列 / ～ **seat** (汽车、飞机上)座板可翻起的凹背单人座位 / ～ **shop** 利用顾客的资金买空卖空的投机商号

bucket² ['bʌkit] **❶** *vt.* [口]催(马)拚命跑; 急急忙忙地(或横冲直撞地)驾驶(汽车等) **❷** *vi.* ①[口]催马拚命跑 ②[口]急速行进; 急忙地干; [英]冒命划桨: a boat ～*ing through* the heavy sea 冒着海上汹涌的波涛飞速前进的一只船 / ～ *into* one's work 忙着干起活来 ③颠簸着行进: The jeep ～*ed* over the rocky road. 吉普车颠簸着开过石子很多的道路。 ④ 游荡，踏踱

buckle ['bʌkl] **I** *n.* 扣子，带扣; (鞋子、服装等的)扣形装饰品 **II ❶** *vt.* ①把…扣住(或扣紧) (*on, up*): ～ the harness *up* 把挽具扣紧 ②使弯曲; 使翘棱; 使起伏不平 **❷** *vi.* ①扣住，扣紧: This belt won't ～. 这根腰带扣不上。 ②(由于压力或热力)变成弯曲; 翘棱; 变成起伏不平; 变形; 坍塌 (*up*) ③屈服; 屈从 ‖～ (*down*) *to* (使)认真地干起来: Let's ～ *to*! 咱们干起来吧! / ～ (*down*) *to* a job 认真地开始工作 / ～ oneself *to* a task 全力以赴地对待一项任务 / *make* ～ *and tongue* *meet* 使收支相抵,量入为出 ‖~**d** *a.* ①(鞋等)有扣的 ②弯曲的;翘棱的

buckler ['bʌklə] I *n.* ①圆盾 ②防御物;庇护者 ③[船]锚链孔盖 II *vt.* 防御,防护

bucolic [bju(:)'kɔlik] I *a.* 农村风味的;田园生活的;牧民生活的 II *n.* ①[常用复]牧歌;田园诗 ②农民

bud[1] [bʌd] I *n.* ①芽,萌芽 ②[动]芽体 ②蓓蕾 ③未成熟的人(或东西) II (budded; budding) ❶ *vt.* ①使发芽 ②[植]使芽接 ❷ *vi.* ①发芽,萌芽 ②开始生长(或发育、发展) ③[植]芽接 ④未成熟 / *in* ~ 发芽;含苞未放 / *nip in the* ~ 把…消灭于萌芽状态,防…于未然 ‖**budded** *a.* 发了芽的,有着蓓蕾的,接了芽的

bud[2] [bʌd] *n.* 伙伴,弟兄 (buddy 的缩略)

budge[1] [bʌdʒ] [用于否定句] ❶ *vi.* 微微移动: It won't ~ an inch. 它一动也不动。 ❷ *vt.* 推动: I can't ~ him. 我推不动他。

budge[2] [bʌdʒ] *n.* 羔皮

budget ['bʌdʒit] I *n.* ①预算,预算案: a ~ estimate 概算 / making 预算编制 / ~ control 预算控制 / introduce (或 open) the ~ (向英国下议院)提出预算案 / a ~ deficit 预算赤字 / a family ~ 家庭收支预算 ②[方] 皮包; 皮包中的东西 [喻]一束,一组(新闻、信件等);(报纸的)要闻集成 II ❶ *vt.* ①把…编入预算;按照预算来计划(或安排) ②安排,预定: ~ one's time 安排自己的时间 ❷ *vi.* 编预算: ~ for the coming year 为下一年度编造预算 III *a.* 合算的,廉价的: a ~ dress 便宜的服装 ‖~**ary** *a.* 预算上的 / ~**eer** [,bʌdʒi'tiə], ~**er** *n.* 编预算的人

buff [bʌf] I *n.* ①(水牛或黄牛皮制的坚韧而柔软的)浅黄色皮革 ②浅黄牛皮革制的制服(或军外衣) ③人的皮肤 : in ~ 裸着身子 ④浅黄色,米色 ⑤[美]爱好者,迷;热心者: a football ~ 足球爱好者,足球迷 II *vt.* ①用软皮擦亮(或擦净) ②使(皮革)柔软 III *a.* ①浅黄牛皮制的 ②浅黄色的

buffalo ['bʌfələu] I ([复] buffalo(es)) *n.* ①水牛 ②[美]野牛 ③水陆坦克 II *vt.* ①压迫,威吓 ②哄骗,愚弄

buffer[1] ['bʌfə] I *n.* ①[机]缓冲器,缓冲垫,减震器 ②缓冲的人(或物): a ~ state 缓冲国 / a ~ zone 缓冲地带 ③[化]缓冲;缓冲剂: ~ solution 缓冲溶液 II *vt.* ①缓冲 ②用缓冲液处理

buffer[2] ['bʌfə] *n.* [俚] (常用 old ~) 老朽;低能的家伙 ②[海]水手长的副手

buffet[1] ['bʌfit] I *n.* ①殴打,打击 ②冲击,折磨 II ❶ *vt.* ①用手打中;连续地打 ②冲击: be ~ed by the storms of the economic crisis 受到经济危机的冲击 ③与…搏斗: ~ the waves 与浪搏斗 ❷ *vi.* ①奋斗 ②打开一条路(尤指在困难条件下);搏斗

buffet[2] *n.* ①['bʌfit] 碗橱,餐具架 ②['bufei](车站、火车内的)餐室,简便食堂;供应便餐的柜台;小卖部: cold ~ 冷食肉 / a ~ supper (lunch)

自助晚餐(午餐)(就餐者自己取食,或站或坐,无固定餐桌) ‖~ **car** ['bufei kɑ:] 餐车

buffoon [bʌ'fu:n] *n.* 演滑稽戏的人,小丑 ‖~**ery** *n.* 打诨,滑稽

bug [bʌg] I *n.* ①臭虫 ②[美口]虫子(尤指蟑螂等害虫) ③病菌;由病菌引起的疾病 ④(机器等上的)缺陷,瑕疵 ⑤(暗设的)防盗报警器 ⑥窃听器 ⑦癖好,狂热;有癖好者,…迷: have a ~ about sth. 热衷于某事 / a ~ at languages 热衷于钻研各种语言的人 / a camera ~ 摄影迷 ⑧双座小型汽车 ⑨要人,名人: a big ~ [贬]大亨,大好佬 II (bugged; bugging) ❶ *vt.* ①在…设防盗报警器 ②在(房间或电话等处)装窃听器;通过窃听器窃听 ③烦扰,激怒 ④使(眼球)暴突 ❷ *vi.* ①捉臭虫 ②(眼球)暴突 ‖~ **off** [俚]停止打扰走开 / ~ **out** ①(眼球)暴突 ②撤退;逃窜 ③兴味索然地离开 / ~ **up** [俚]激动起来;被弄得稀里糊涂 / *put a* ~ *in sb.'s ear* 事先给某人暗示(或警告) / ~ **doctor** [美俚][监狱等处的]精神病医师;心理学专家 / ~**-eyed** *a.* ①暴眼的 ②惊讶得瞠目结舌的 / '~**house** [美俚] *n.* 疯人院 *a.* 疯狂的,发疯的 / '~,**hunter** *n.* [口]昆虫学者 / '~,**hunting** *n.* [口]昆虫采集 / ~ **test** [美俚]智力测验;心理测验

bugaboo ['bʌgəbu:], **bugbear** ['bʌgbɛə] *n.* ①吓唬人的东西;鬼怪 ②无端的恐惧 ③令人头痛的事

bugger ['bʌgə] I *n.* ①鸡奸者 ②(常用作亲热或幽默的说法)没用的家伙 II *vt.* ①鸡奸 ②诅咒,使遭神罚 ③使极度疲乏 ‖~**y** ['bʌgəri] *n.* 鸡奸

bugle[1] ['bju:gl] I *n.* 军号,喇叭: a ~ call 号声,集合号 / a ~ horn 号角 II ❶ *vi.* 吹号 ❷ *vt.* 吹号召集; 吹号表示(冲锋、撤退等) ‖~**r** *n.* 号手;司号兵

bugle[2] ['bju:gl] *n.* 筋骨草属植物;匍匐筋骨草

bugle[3] ['bju:gl] *n.* (女服上装饰用的)喇叭形玻璃(或塑料)珠子

build [bild] I (built [bilt]) ❶ *vt.* ①建筑,造: ~ railways 筑铁路 / ~ positions 建筑工事 / ~ a nest (鸟)筑巢 / The house is *built* of wood. 这房子是木造的。②建设,建立①创立,构成④抬高…的身分,把(演员)捧出名;扩大 (up) ❷ *vi.* ①建造;从事营造业 ②到达最高峰;向最高峰发展: The wind began to ~. 风力开始增大。/ Then the song began to ~ to a climax. 接着,歌曲便开始向高潮发展。 II *n.* ①构造,造型 ②体格: a man of strong ~ 体格强壮的人 ‖~ **on** (或 **upon**) ①依赖,指望: Don't ~ on his promise. 不要依赖他的诺言。 ② 把…建立于: ~ one's hopes *on* sb.'s promise 把希望寄托在某人的诺言上 / ~ **up** ①树立; 逐步建立: ~ *up* one's reputation 使自己逐渐出名 ②增进(健康),锻炼(体质等) ③(用砖)砌塞(门、窗等) ④逐步集结: The tension is ~*ing up*. 张力逐步增大。(或: 形势逐步紧张起来。) ⑤[美俚]用好话逐步赢得…的好感(以便最后利用) ‖'~**up** *n.* ①组

合, 集结: a military ~*up* 军事集结 ②[美口]造
舆论: give sb. the ~*up* 为某人造舆论

building ['bildiŋ] *n.* ① 建筑物, 营造物, 房屋
② 营造, 建筑; 建筑术: ~ materials 建筑材料
‖~ **berth** 造船台 / ~ **code** 建筑条例 / ~
land 建筑地 / ~ **lease** 租地造屋权 / ~ **line**
建筑界线, 房基线 / '~-**so,ciety** *n.* [英]房屋互助
协会(负责从会员中筹款并贷款给需造屋、买屋的
会员的组织)

bulb [bʌlb] I *n.* ①【植】鳞茎, 球茎 ②球状物; 电
灯泡;(寒暑表的)水银球 ③【解】球, 延髓 ④毛
根 ⑤(照相机的)快门 II *vi.* ①生球茎 ②肿成
球状 ‖~**ed** *a.* 有球根的; 球状的, 圆的

onion bulb

electric bulb

bulb

bulge [bʌldʒ] I *n.* ①膨胀; 肿胀 ②(体积、数字等
的)暂时增大; 暴增 ③凸出部分,(桶等的)鼓胀部
分;(身体上)容易发胖的部位 ④[船]底边 ⑤优
势: have (或 get) the ~ on 胜过 II ❶ *vi.* ①膨
胀 ②上涨 ③凸出: His pocket was *bulging* with
apples. 他的口袋由于装了苹果而鼓起来。 ❷ *vt.*
使膨胀

bulk [bʌlk] I *n.* ① 容积, 体积; 大块 ② 大批, 大
量: ~ buying 大量购买 ③货舱; 船舱载货: break
~ 开始卸货 ④ 大部分, 大多数: the ~ of the
population 人口的大多数 ⑤肥胖的人 II ❶ *vi.*
①显得大(或重要): ~ large (或 larger) 显得
大; 显得重要 ②胀; 形成大块: ~ up 形成大块;
形成大数目; 胀大 ③(重要性、尺寸等)增加 ❷
vt. 使成大量; 使成大块; 将(鱼)堆积如山 ‖*in*
① 散装: load grain *in* ~ 把谷物散装入船 ②大
批, 大量: sell *in* ~ 整批(或大量)出售, 逛售, 批
发 ‖'~-**head** *n.* ①(船、飞机的)舱壁 ②[建]挡
土墙; 堤岸; 堵壁

bulky ['bʌlki] *a.* 庞大的, 笨大的 ‖**bulkiness** *n.*

bull[1] [bul] I *n.* ① 公牛; 雄的象(或鲸等大动物)
② 买空的证券投机商(俗称多头) ③ 象公牛一样
的人, 粗壮的人; [美俚]工头(尤指大农场监工)
④[B-]【天】金牛宫; 金牛座 ⑤[美俚]警察; 侦探
⑥[美俚]火车头 ⑦[俚]空话, 大话, 胡说八道
II *a.* 公牛般的; 公牛的 ②雄的 ③哄抬价格
的: ~ operations (证券投机中)哄抬价格的活动
III ❶ *vi.* ①哄抬行市 ②[俚]夸口, 吹牛

闲谈: Come in and ~ a while. 进来随便谈一
会儿吧。 ❷ *vt.* ①企图抬高(证券、市场等)的价
格: ~ the market 哄抬市场价格 ②强行实现
③[俚]以说大话来欺骗; 威吓 ‖*a ~ in a china
shop* 鲁莽闯祸的人 / *a ~ of the bog* 【动】麻
鹬 / *like a ~ at a (five-barred) gate* 狂怒地;
猛烈地; 凶猛地 / *milk the ~* 作徒劳无益的事 /
shoot (the) ~ ①吹牛, 说大话 ②闲聊; 空谈 /
take the ~ by the horns 不畏艰险 / *throw the
~* [美俚]胡说八道 ‖'~**boat** *n.* 牛皮浅水船 /
'~**calf** *n.* 小公牛; [口]笨蛋 / '~**dog** *n.* ①叭
喇狗(一种颈粗性猛的狗) ②[俗]手枪; 大炮 ③
[冶](搅炼炉的)补炉底材料 ④(英国大学的)舍
监随从 ⑤晨报(或星期日报)的第一次版 *vt.* (抓
住牛角)摔(小公牛) / '~**doze** *vt.* ①强迫; 威胁;
压倒 ②用推土机清除(或挖出、削平) / '~,**dozer**
n. ①恐吓者, 威胁者 ②推土机, 开土机 / '~-
fight *n.* 斗牛(戏) / '~**fighter** *n.* 斗牛士 /
'~**finch** *n.* 【动】红腹灰雀 ②(旁边有沟的)
树篱 / '~**frog** *n.* 【动】牛蛙, 喧蛙 / '~**head** *n.*
①头大的鱼(尤指杜父鱼、美洲鲵鱼) ② 顽固的
人 / '~**horn** *n.* 手提式电子扩音器 / '~**necked**
a. 有短而粗的颈项的 / '~**nose** *n.* 【建】外圆
角 / '~**pen** *n.* ①牛栏 ②(法庭等的)犯人候审
大房间 ②[美俚]拳击比赛场子 / '~**ring** *n.* 斗
牛场 / ~ **session** [美俚]自由讨论; 闲谈 /
'~'**s-eye** *n.* ① 靶的中心 /【军】十环: make (或
score) the ~'*s-eye* [喻]取得巨大成功 ②打中靶心
的一击 ③【海】(舷侧)圆窗; 单眼木制滑车 ④圆
天窗 ⑤牛眼灯; 凸透镜 ⑥圆形硬糖 / '~**shit**
n. 胡说, 废话 / '~**terrier** *n.* 一种猛犬 / '~
tongue 牛舌形犁片 / ~ **trout** ①[英]鳟鱼 ②
红点鲑 / '~**whack** *n.* [美]牛鞭 *vt. & vi.* 用
牛鞭打 / '~,**whacker** *n.* 赶牛者 / '~**whip** *n.*
长的牛鞭 / '~**work** *n.* 牛马活, 苦活

bull[2] [bul] *n.* 教皇训令; 训令

bull[3] [bul] *n.* 自相矛盾的话; 矛盾可笑的错误
(=Irish ~)

bullet ['bulit] *n.* ① 枪弹, 子弹 ②[美俚]豆; 钱 ‖*a
spent* ~ 冲力已尽的子弹; 强弩之末 / *Every ~
has its billet.* [谚]每颗子弹都有归宿。(意指战
场上中弹与否, 全是所谓天命) / '~ **bait** [美俚]
招枪弹的无经验新兵(尤指海军陆战队士兵); 炮
灰 / '~-**head** *n.* 圆头的人; [俚]顽固的人; 傻
瓜 / '~-'**headed** *a.* 圆头的; 固执的; 愚笨的 /
'~**proof** *a.* 防弹的, 枪弹打不穿的

bulletin ['bulitin] I *n.* ① 公报, 公告 ②(医生发表
的知名人士的)病情报告书 ③ 新闻简报 II *vt.*
用公报发表

bullion ['buljən] *n.* ① (造货币等用的)条金, 条
银; 块金, 块银; 锭形金属: large quantities of ~
大量的条金 / lead ~ 锭形铅 ②金银丝的花边
(或饰带)

bullock ['bulək] *n.* ①小公牛 ②阉牛

bully[1] ['buli] I *n.* ①恶霸, 暴徒; 恃强欺弱的学生:
a local ~ 土豪 / play the ~ 横行霸道, 恃强欺弱
②妓院的拉客者, 拉皮条者; 靠妓女过活的人 II

❶ *vt.* ①威吓: ~ sb. into doing sth. 威胁某人做某事 ②欺侮 **❷** *vi.* 充当恶霸(或恃强欺弱者等) **III** *a.* ①好的, 第一流的 ②象恶霸的, **IV** *ad.* 十分, 突出地 **V** *int.* 好!妙 ‖*Bully for you!* 干得好! / *come the ~ over sb.* 对某人装出盛气凌人的样子 ‖**~boy** *n.* 架子十足的恶棍(尤指与某一政治派别有勾结或充当其代理人者);受人雇用的流氓

bully² ['buli] *n.* 罐头牛肉 (=~ beef)

bulwark ['bulwə(ː)k] **I** *n.* ①堡垒;防御物;保障 ②防波堤 ③[常用复]【船】舷墙 **II** *vt.* 用堡垒防护,防御,保护

bump¹ [bʌmp] **I** **❶** *vt.* ①撞伤(头等);撞击 ②把…从职位上排挤掉 ③[美俚]杀死,谋杀 **❷** *vi.* ①碰,撞,冲撞 (*against, into*): ~ into sb. on the road 路上偶然遇到某人 / ~ up *against* difficulties 碰到困难 ②(笨重车辆)颠簸地行驶 (*along*): The truck ~*ed along* the rough mountain road. 卡车在崎岖的山路上颠簸地行驶。 **II** *ad.* 突然地;猛烈地: run ~ *against* the wall 突然撞上墙上 **III** *n.* ①碰,撞,撞击 ②(因碰撞而起的)肿块 ③头盖骨上的隆起部分(脑相家认为是才能的象征);[口]能力,才能: the ~ of locality 善于记住地点(或辨认地方)的能力 / have no ~ of music 无音乐才能 ④(车的)颠簸 ⑤[空]飞机因气流突变而感受的颠簸 ‖~ **off** [俚] ①用力推开 ②杀死

bump² [bʌmp] **I** *n.* 鹭鸶的叫声 **II** *vi.* 作鹭鸶叫

bumper¹ ['bʌmpə] *n.*【机】减震器, 缓冲器,(汽车)保险杠: Cars are parked ~ to ~. 汽车一辆接一辆地停着。

bumper² ['bʌmpə] **I** *n.* ①(干杯时的)满杯 ②同类中特大者 ③[俚]丰收,满场,满座 **II** *a.* 丰盛的,大胜利的: a ~ harvest (或 crop) 丰收 / a ~ year 丰年 / a ~ book 一本内容空洞的大书

bumpkin ['bʌmpkin] *n.* [贬]乡下人,土佬儿‖**~ly** *a.*

bumptious ['bʌmpʃəs] *a.* [口]自以为是的, 傲慢的,自负的 ‖**~ly** *ad.* / **~ness** *n.*

bun¹ [bʌn] *n.* ①小(圆)果子面包,小(圆)面包 ②小面包式的卷发 ‖*take* (或 *yank*) *the* ~ [口]得第一名

bun² [bʌn] *n.* [俚]闹饮 ‖*get a* ~ *on* [俚]喝醉

bunch [bʌntʃ] **I** *n.* ①(一)球,束,串: a ~ of grapes (keys) 一串葡萄(钥匙) / a ~ of flowers 一束花 ②[俚]一群,一帮,一伙 ③[矿]小矿巢;管状矿脉膨大部分: an ore ~ 矿囊,矿巢 **II** **❶** *vi.* ①捆成一束,穿成一串 ②凸出,隆起 ③打褶 **❷** *vt.* ①使成一束(或一捆等) ②打(褶) ‖*a* ~ *of fives* 手;拳头 / *the best* (或 *pick*) *of the* ~ 一批中最好的,精华 ‖**~y** *a.* 成束的,成球的 ‖'**~backed** *a.* 驼背的 / '**~grass** *n.* (美国西部的)丛生的草类(如硷地鼠尾粟、密集野麦等)

bundle ['bʌndl] **I** *n.* ①包袱,包裹 ②捆,束,包: a ~ of firewood 一捆柴 ③.(相当大的)一堆 ④[俚](数目可观的)一笔款项 ⑤【植】维管束;【解】

(神经的)束 **II** **❶** *vt.* ①包,捆,扎 ②把…乱七八糟地塞进 (*in, into*) ③把…匆忙撵走 (*away, off, out*) **❷** *vi.* 匆忙离开 (*off, out, away*) ‖*a ~ of nerves* 神经极度紧张不安和敏感的人 / **~ up** ①把…捆扎起来 ②使穿得暖和: *Bundle* yourself *up* warmly. 你要穿得暖些。

bung [bʌŋ] **I** *n.* ①(桶等的)塞子 ②桶孔 ③家畜的盲肠(或肛门) **II** *vt.* ①(用塞子)塞(桶口) ②塞住 ③[俚]扔(石子等),丢 ④使膨胀 ‖~ **off** ～ **up** ①逃走 ②[美]打伤,把…打成青紫 ②打坏,打瘪 ③塞满 ‖**~hole** *n.* 桶孔,桶口

bungalow ['bʌŋgəlou] *n.* 有游廊的平房,平房

bungle ['bʌŋgl] **I** **❶** *vt.* 粗制滥造;搞坏,贻误 **❷** *vi.* 拙劣地工作 **II** *n.* 拙劣的工作 ‖**~r** *n.* 工作笨拙的人 / **bungling** *a.* 笨拙的,粗劣的

bunk¹ [bʌŋk] **I** *n.* ①(车上或船上倚壁而设的)床铺,铺位 ②睡铺 ③牲口的食槽 **II** **❶** *vi.* ①睡在铺位上 ②[口]去睡 **❷** *vt.* 为…提供睡铺 ‖~ **bed** 附有梯子的双层床

bunk² [bʌŋk] [俚] **I** *vi.* 逃去,逃跑 (*off*) **II** *n.* 逃走: do a ~ 逃去

bunk³ [bʌŋk] *n.* [口]空话,废话;(欺骗选民的)演说

bunker ['bʌŋkə] **I** *n.* ①煤箱;(船上的)燃料舱,煤舱 ②(高尔夫球场上的)洞,障碍 ③【军】(地下)钢骨水泥掩体,地堡 **II** *vt.* ①把(煤)堆进煤舱;把(油)注入燃料舱 ②把(高尔夫球)打入洞内,[喻]使陷入困境

bunny ['bʌni] *n.* 小兔子(儿童对兔的爱称) ‖~ **hug** 一种美国交际舞

Bunsen ['bʌnsn] *n.* ‖~ **burner** 本生灯(一种煤气灯)

bunting ['bʌntiŋ] *n.* ①旗布;(节日用来装饰街道、房屋等的)旗帜 ②【动】鹀;黄胸鹀

buoy [bɔi] **I** *n.* ①浮标 ②救生圈 **II** *vt.* ①使浮起;使…浮到水面上 (*up*) ②用浮标指示(水道、礁等) (*out*) ③鼓励,支持 (*up*): ~ up one's spirits 振作精神

buoy

buoyance ['bɔiəns], **buoyancy** ['bɔiənsi] *n.* ①浮力;弹性: Salt water has more ~ than fresh water. 咸水的浮力比淡水大。 / centre of ~ 【物】浮力的中心,浮心 ②快活,轻快 ③(股票市场、物价等的)保持高价

buoyant ['bɔiənt] *a.* ①有浮力的: ~ force 浮力 / a ~ mine 浮雷 ②轻快的,精神活泼的: a ~ step 轻快的步伐 ③(物价等)降而复升的;保持高价的 ‖**~ly** *ad.*

burden ['bə:dn] I *n.* ① 担子; 负担, 艰难; 负重: a beast of ～ 驮兽 / a ship of ～ 货船 ②(船的)装载量, 吨位: a ship of 10,000 tons ～ 万吨轮 ③(诗歌、发言等的)重点, 要点 ④ 歌曲收尾的叠句, 重复句, 复唱词 ⑤ 责任, 义务: The ～ is mine, not yours. 这个责任是我的, 不是你的。/ (the) ～ of proof 【律】举证责任 II *vt.* ①装货上(船、车等) ②使负重担(如债务、捐税等), 麻烦, 劳累 (*with*) ‖**～some** ['bə:dnsəm] *a.* 难于负担的; 压抑的; 忧虑的; 累赘的

bureau [bjuə'rou, 'bjuərou] ([复] bureaux [bjuə-'rouz] 或 bureaus) *n.* ①局; 司; 处; 办公署 ②社, 所: a travel ～ 旅行社 ③[英]有抽屉的办公桌, 写字枱 ④[美](装有镜子的)衣柜, 镜枱

bureaucracy [bjuə'rokrəsi] *n.* ① 官僚政治; 官僚主义: overcome ～ 克服官僚主义 ②[总称]官僚

bureaucrat ['bjuəroukræt] *n.* 官僚: ～ capital 官僚资本 ‖**～-'capitalist** *n.* 官僚资本家

bureaucratic [,bjuərou'krætik] *a.* 官僚政治的; 官僚主义的 ‖**～ally** *ad.*

burglar ['bə:glə] *n.* 夜盗, 窃贼 ‖a belly ～ [美俚] 伙食采购员, 膳务员 / a cat ～ 惯从屋顶侵入的窃贼

burial ['beriəl] *n.* 埋葬, 葬; 埋藏: a ～ case 棺材 / a ～ ground 葬地 / a ～ service 葬礼

burlesque [bə:'lesk] I *n.* ① 滑稽剧(或诗、文等); 讽刺画; 滑稽; 讽刺 ②[美]杂耍表演; 粗俗的歌舞表演(包括滑稽短剧、脱衣舞等) II *a.* 滑稽的, 讽刺的, 嘲弄的 III *vt. & vi.* 装滑稽来取笑, 讽刺, 嘲弄 ‖**～ly** *ad.* / **～r** *n.* 杂耍表演者; 粗俗歌舞表演者

burly ['bə:li] *a.* ①粗壮的, 强壮的, 结实的 ②直截了当的 ‖**burliness** *n.*

burn [bə:n] I (burnt [bə:nt] 或 burned) ❶ *vt.* ①烧; 点(烛、灯等): ～ gas (coal) 烧煤气(煤) / pine torches 点松树明子 ②烧毁; 烧焦; 烧伤; 烫痛: be severely ～t 被严重烧伤 / Be careful not to ～ your mouth. 小心别烫痛嘴。③烧灼; 烙 ④烧制; 烧成: ～ bricks 烧砖 / ～ a hole 烧成一个洞 ⑤晒: a sun-～t face 晒黑了的脸 ⑥使(喉咙等)辣得难受: ～ the tongue with pepper 舌头被辣椒辣得发烧 ⑦激起…的愤怒(或欲望等) ⑧[俚]用电刑处死 ⑨【化】使燃烧; 利用(铀等)的核能 ⑩消耗; 浪费, 挥霍: money to ～ 供挥霍的钱 ⑪[俚]使恼怒: What ～t him, after all? 到底是什么激怒了他? ⑫[俚]欺骗: Harry ～t Henry over that deal. 在那件交易上哈里欺骗了亨利。❷ *vi.* ①燃烧; 点着: The charcoal is ～ing. 炭在烧。/ The stove is ～ing. 炉火在燃烧。/ All the lights were ～ing. 灯全点着。②发热; 放光: The patient was ～ing with fever. 病人在发热。/ ～ blue 烧得发蓝光 ③烧毁; 烧焦; 烫伤; 烫痛: The rice is ～ing. 饭烧焦了。④晒黑 ⑤激动, 激怒; 渴望 ⑥[俚]被电刑处死 II *n.* ①烧伤, 灼伤; 火(或高温等)毁伤处: flash ～ 【医】闪光灼伤, 爆伤 / X-ray ～ 【医】X

射线灼伤 ②烙印 ③[美](森林等中故意或偶然)烧成的空地 ④ 宇宙飞行火箭发动机在飞行中的起动 ‖**～ away** ①继续燃烧 ②烧掉, 烧毁; (逐渐)消灭: The haze has ～t away. 雾消散了。/ The sunlight has ～t away the haze. 日光使雾消散了。/ ～ daylight 白日点灯, [喻]徒劳无益 / ～ down ①(把…)烧成平地 ②(蜡烛等)渐渐烧完; 火力减弱 / ～ in 留下不可磨灭的印象: What he heard ～t in. 他听到的话给他留下不可磨灭的印象。/ ～ into ①烧进 ②给…留下不可磨灭的印象: His words ～t into my mind. 他的话在我脑中留下不可磨灭的印象。③使…成为不可磨灭的印象; 使深印于: That day is ～t into my memory. 那一天在我记忆中留下不可磨灭的印象。/ ～ itself out (燃烧物)烧尽 / ～ low 烧力减弱 / ～ one's boats (或 bridges) 破釜沉舟, 背水布阵 / ～ oneself out (因过劳等而)筋疲力尽 / ～ one's fingers 由于管闲事(或鲁莽)而吃苦头 / ～ out ①烧坏: ～ out an electric light bulb 烧坏电灯泡 ②烧掉(某人)的家(或店、财产等); 烧火把…赶出 ③烧尽, 烧光(炉等)因燃料缺乏而自停烧 / ～ the candle at both ends 过分地耗费精力 / ～ the midnight oil 工作到深更半夜, 开夜车 / ～ up ①(炉火等)烧起来, 旺起来 ②烧掉 ③[美俚](使)发怒 ④[美俚]臭骂 / have money (time) to ～ 有用不完的钱(时间) / Money ～s a hole in his pocket. 见 money ‖**～t out** *n.* ①烧尽, 大火灾 ②(喷气发动机或火箭发动机的)熄火; 熄火时间 ③烧坏

burning ['bə:niŋ] I *a.* ①燃烧的; 高热的: a ～ fever 高烧 ②(欲望等)炽烈的 ③ 极端恶劣的: a ～ shame (或 disgrace) 奇耻大辱 ④ 热烈争论的; 紧要的: a ～ question 热烈争论的问题; 紧要的问题 II *n.* 燃烧 ‖**～ glass** 取火镜, 凸透镜 / **～ point** 燃(烧)点

burnish ['bə:niʃ] I ❶ *vt.* 擦亮(金属等) ❷ *vi.* 因受擦而发亮: This metal ～es well. 这种金属容易擦亮。II *n.* 光泽, 光亮 ‖**～er** *n.* 把东西磨光(或擦亮)的人; 摩擦抛光器 / **～ing** *n.* 【机】摩擦抛光

burrow ['bʌrou] I *n.* ①(狐、兔等的)地洞, 穴 ②(地下)躲藏处 II ❶ *vt.* ①打(地洞), 掘(穴); 掘成: ～ a dwelling in the side of a hill 在山坡上掘成一个住所 ②在(地)下打洞 ③把…藏在洞里; 把…藏起来 ❷ *vi.* ①钻进地洞躲藏起来, 潜伏 ②打地洞 ③探查, 密查 (*into*)

bursar ['bə:sə] *n.* ①(大学的)掌管财务者 ②(苏格兰大学中)一种奖学金; 得奖学金的学生

burst [bə:st] I (burst) ❶ *vi.* ①爆裂, 炸破; 胀破; 冲破; 溃决: The sun ～ through the clouds and shone over the earth. 太阳冲破乌云, 阳光普照大地。/ ～ing strength 【纺】(织物)破裂强度 ②突然发生, 突然出现: The entire hall ～ into thunderous cheers. 全场发出雷鸣般的欢呼。/ ～ with laughing 捧腹大笑 / ～ with anger 勃然大怒 ③忽然出现: ～ into the room 闯入房间 ④(芽、蕾等)绽开: The cotton bolls are ～ing.

棉花铃子正在绽开。⑤充满 ❷ *vt.* ①冲破 ②遭受…破裂: He ~ a blood vessel. 他爆了一根血管。(或:[口]他很激动。) ③充满: Grain is ~ing the granary. 谷堆满仓。Ⅱ *n.* ①突然破裂;爆炸 ②突发;一阵迸发;【军】点射;连发射击: a ~ of gunfire 一阵炮火 / a ~ of speed 速度的突然增加 ‖*be ~ing to* 急着要: He is ~ing to tell us the good news. 他急着要告诉我们这个好消息。/ ~ *forth* ①突发;爆发 ②突然说起话来 ③飞出,喷出;忽然出现 / ~ *in* ①闯进来 ②猛烈把(门等)向内推开 ③打断 (*upon, on*): ~ *in upon* a conversation 打断谈话 ④突然出现;突然来到: ~ *in upon* sb. 突然出现在某人面前 / ~ *into* ①闯入 ②突然发作;突然…起来 : ~ *into* flame(s) 突然燃烧起来 / ~ *into* laughter (tears) 突然笑(哭)起来 ③开出: ~ *into* blossom 开花 / ~ *open* ① (门等)猛然被推开 ② 猛然打开(门等) / ~ *out* ①闯出来 ②大声叫喊 ③突然…起来: ~ *out* laughing (crying) 突然笑 (哭) 起来 ④(战争、疾病等)突然发生;突然出现 / ~ *up* [口] ①爆炸 ②失败;垮台 ③突然发怒(或激动等) ④使失败;使垮台 / ~ *upon* (或 *on*) 突然来到 / *go* ~ [口]失败;破产 ‖*~-up n.* [口]垮台

bury ['beri] *vt.* ①埋葬: be *buried* beneath the waves 遭灭顶 ②埋藏,遮盖,掩蔽: be *buried* in thought 出神深思 / ~ oneself in study 埋头研究 ③死去(家属): He has *buried* both parents. 他父母都死了。④为…举行葬礼 ⑤把(友谊等)从记忆中除去 ‖*be buried alive* ①被活埋 ②隐居(不与外界接触) ‖*~ing n.* 埋葬,葬;埋藏

bus [bʌs] Ⅰ *n.* ①公共汽车 ②[俚]飞机;汽车;机器脚踏车 ③【电】汇流条,母线 Ⅱ (bussed; bussing) ❶ *vi.* ①乘公共汽车去 ②[美]当餐馆里的服务员助手 ❷ *vt.* 用公共汽车运送 ‖*miss the* ~ ①失掉机会 ②事业失败 ‖*bus(s)ing n.* 公共汽车接送;[美]用校车接送学生(指为调整学生中的种族比例把非本区学生接来读书) ‖*~ bar* 汇流排 / '*~boy n.* [美]餐馆里的服务员助手 / '*~girl* [美]餐馆里的服务员女助手 / '*~man n.* 公共汽车的驾驶员(或乘务员):a *~man's* holiday 照常工作的假日 / ~ *stop* 公共汽车站

bush [buʃ] Ⅰ *n.* ①灌木,矮树;灌木丛,矮树丛: ~-fire war 灌木林火式战争 ② [the ~] (澳大利亚等地)未开垦的(丛林)地 ③蓬头,蓬松的毛发;蓬松的尾巴 ④(从前酒店用来做标记的)长春藤 ⑤【机】衬套;轴衬;轴瓦 Ⅱ ❶ *vi.* ①丛生 ②成灌木形 ❷ *vt.* ①用灌木支撑(或标志、保护、装饰) ②【机】加(金属)衬套(或轴套)于… ‖*beat about* (或[美] *around*) *the* ~ 旁敲侧击 / *Good wine needs no* ~. [谚]酒好客自来。‖*~ing n.* 轴套;轴衬;衬圈;套管;轴瓦;【电】塞孔的套管 / '*~buck n.* 南非羚羊 / '*~,fighter n.* 丛林游击队员,丛林(地)战士 / '*~,fighting n.* 灌木地战;丛林游击战 / '*~,hammer n.* ①凿石锤 ②(处理混凝土路面过

滑用的)气动凿毛机 / ~ *harrow* (耙草或覆盖种子用的)耙 / ~ *hook* (剪割灌木用的)长柄大镰刀 / *~man* ['buʃmən] *n.* ① [B-] 南非卡拉哈里沙漠地区一个游牧部落的成员 ②澳洲丛林中的居民(或农民,旅行者) / ~ *pilot* 在无人区飞行的飞行员 / '*~,ranger n.* ① (澳大利亚的)丛林土匪 ②居住在丛林中的流浪者 / ~ *telegraph* 情报(或谣言)的迅速传播 / '*~whack vi.* ①开伐丛林;在丛林中开路 ②丛林伏击 *vt.* 在丛林中伏击 / '*~,whacker n.* ①在丛林中开路者,丛林开伐者;林中居民 ②(美国南北战争中的)游击队员 ③(砍丛林的)大镰刀

bushel[1] ['buʃl] *n.* ①蒲式耳(计量谷物等的容量单位,在英国等于 36.368 升,在美国等于 35.238 升):a Chinese ~ 一斗 ②容量为一蒲式耳的容器 ③相当于容量为一蒲式耳的东西的重量 ④大量 ‖*hide one's light* (或 *candle*) *under a* ~ 不露锋芒 / *measure others' corn by one's own* ~ 拿自己作标准来衡量别人,以己度人

bushel[2] ['buʃl] *vt. & vi.* 修补(或翻新)(衣服)

bushy ['buʃi] *a.* ①灌木茂盛的 ②灌木似的 ③浓密的: ~ eyebrows 浓眉 ‖*bushily ad.* / *bushiness n.*

business ['biznis] *n.* ①商业,生意;营业: do ~ with many countries 和许多国家做生意 / ~ hours (或 hours of ~) 营业时间 / *Business* as usual. 照常营业。②商店,商行 ③职责;事务,事: a public (private) ~ 公(私)事 / the ~ of the meeting 会议的议程 ④有权利(或无权利)做(或 no ~ doing) sth. 没有权利做某事 ⑤难事(讨厌的)事;(无价值的)事物(或设计等) ⑥【戏】(演员的)动作(或表情等)(区别于"对白") ‖*a man of* ~ (商业或法律上的)代理人 / *Business is* ~. 公事公办。/ *do sb.'s* ~ (或 *do the* ~ *for sb.*) [口]要某人的命 / *get* (或 *come*) *to* ~ 开始干正事;言归正传 / *give* (*get*) *the* ~ [美俚]给予(受到)粗暴对待;加以(被人)作弄 / *go into* ~ 从事商业 / *go out of* ~ 停业,歇业;停止做原来的工作 / *know one's* ~ 精通自己所干的一行 / *mean* ~ 是当真的: I mean ~. 我可不是开玩笑。/ *Mind your own* ~. 不要你管(我的事)。/ *monkey* ~ [美俚]胡闹;欺骗;恶作剧 / *on* ~ 因事,因公: No admittance except *on* ~. 非公莫入。/ *send sb. about his* ~ 把某人赶走 / *the ~ end* (工具、武器等)使用的一头;锐利的一头: *the ~ end* of a chisel 凿子尖的一头 ‖*~like a.* 事务式的;有条理的 / '*~man n.* ①商人 ②办理实务的人 / '*~ unionism* 工联主义

bust[1] [bʌst] *n.* ①半身雕塑像 ②胸部(尤指妇女的);(妇女的)胸围

bust[2] [bʌst] Ⅰ (bust(ed)) ❶ *vt.* ①使破裂,使爆发;击破 ②使破产;使失败: Johnson's business (Johnson) went ~. 约翰逊的企业(约翰逊)失败了。③使降级 ④驯服(马等) ⑤殴打 ⑥逮捕 ❷ *vi.* ①爆裂,爆炸 ②破产;失败 (*up*) ③被降级 Ⅱ *n.* [俚]①失败;商业上的大不利 ②

殴打 ③欢闹(尤指闹饮): go on the ~ 欢闹,痛
饮 ④逮捕 ‖**~ed** *a.* [美口]破产了的;失败了
的;被降级的;被逮捕的 ‖'**~-up** *n.* [美俚] ①
失败,破产 ②争吵,(婚姻等的)破裂

bustle¹ ['bʌsl] I ❶ *vi.* 喧闹;活跃;奔忙;忙乱:
about (或 ~ *in and out*) 东奔西跑,非常忙碌 /
Tell him to ~ *up*. 告诉他赶快点。/ The work
site *~d* with activity. 工地上一片繁忙景象。❷
vt. 使活跃,催促;使忙乱: She *~d* the children
off to school. 她催促孩子们上学去。II *n.* 喧闹,
熙嚷;活跃;奔忙;忙乱: without hurry or ~ 不
慌不忙 / be in a ~ (人)吵吵闹闹的;(地方)乱
哄哄的 / joyful ~ 兴高采烈 ‖**bustling** *a.* 忙
碌碌的,熙嚷的;活跃的

bustle² ['bʌsl] *n.* (妇女撑背后裙褶的)腰垫,裙撑

busy ['bizi] I *a.* ① 忙的; 繁忙的; 热闹的: the ~
farming season 农忙季节 / be ~ *at* (或 *with*,
over, *about*) one's work 忙着工作 / people ~
fighting drought 忙着抗旱的人们 / one of the
busiest seaports in the world 世界上最繁忙的海
港之一 ②占用着;没空的: The line is ~! (或
Line's ~!) (电话)线没空! ③爱管闲事的 ④(图
案等)复杂的,使人眼花缭乱的 II ❶ *vt.* 使忙:
They are *~ing* themselves (*in*) packing up. 他
们正忙着整理行装。❷ *vi.* 忙碌,奔忙 ~ (*about*,
around) III *n.* [俚]侦探 ‖~ *as a bee* 极忙
碌 / *get* ~ 开始工作,干起来 ‖**~ness** *n.* 忙碌
‖'**~,body** *n.* 爱管闲事的人 / '**~work** *n.* 为免
学生空闲而布置的作业

but [强 bʌt; 弱 bət] I *conj.* ① 但是,可是;而
(是): I'm sorry, ~ I won't be able to come
tonight. 很抱歉,我今天晚上不能来了。/ a glorious ~ arduous task 光荣而艰巨的任务 / *Not
that* I don't want to go, ~ *that* I have no
time. 不是我不想去,而是我没空。
② 而不;若不;除非: It never rains ~ it pours.
[谚]不雨则已,一雨倾盆。(指事情不发生则已,
一旦发生便接踵而来)
③[用于否定词或疑问词之后,表示否定意义,相
当于 that not]: No task is so difficult ~ (或 ~
that, ~ *what*) we can accomplish it. 不管任务
怎样困难,我们都能完成。/ Who knows ~ (或
~ *that*, ~ *what*) it may be so? 谁能说不会这
样呢?
④[用于否定词加 doubt, deny, question 等词之
后,无实义,相当于连接词 that]: There is no
question ~ (或 ~ *that*) he will succeed. 他会成
功,这是没有问题的。
⑤[表示可能性,无实义,相当于连接词 that]: It
is ten to one ~ we'll overfulfil our production
quota. 我们十之八九能超额完成生产任务。
II *pron.* [关系代词,意义相当于 who not, that
not]: There is no one of us ~ wishes to go. 我
们人人都想去。
III *prep.* 除了: Nobody knew it ~ me (或 I).
除了我以外,没有人知道这件事。[注意:用 I 时,
but 是连接词] / It is *anything* ~ bad. 这完全

不是什么坏事。/ Last evening I did nothing ~
repair my farm tools. 昨天晚上我除了修理农
具外,没有做其他的事情。/ last ~ one (two) 倒
数第二(三)
IV *ad.* 只,仅仅: He left ~ an hour ago. 他一
小时前刚走。
V *vt. & n.* (见习语 But me no ~s.)
‖*all* ~见 *all*/~ *for* 要不是 / *But me no ~s.*
别老跟我说"但是,但是"了。[本句中前面的 But
是及物动词,后面的 buts 是复数名词] / ~ *then*
但另一方面: The method is good, ~ *then* it will
take too much time. 方法虽好,但太费时间了。/ ~
cannot — 见 *can*¹ / *cannot choose* — 见
choose / *cannot help* — 见 *help* / *not* ~ *that*
(或 *not* ~ *what*) 见 *not*

butcher ['butʃə] I *n.* ①[英]屠夫;卖肉者 ②屠杀
者,残杀者 ③拙劣的工作者 ④[美](火车或剧
场里兜售糖果、报纸等的)小贩 ⑤[美俚][贬]军
医 II *vt.* ① 屠宰,宰割 ②屠杀,残杀 ③(因注
释、编辑不好或粗暴批评而)弄糟,搞坏 ‖*the ~,
the baker, the candlestick maker* 各行各业的
人 ‖**~ly** *a.* ①屠夫般的 ②残忍的 ③笨手笨脚
的 ‖'**~-bird** *n.* 【动】百劳科的鸟;百劳 /
knife 屠刀 / ~ *shop* ①肉店 ②[美俚][贬]医
院 / *~'s meat* ①(猪、牛、羊等的)鲜肉 ②[俚]
赊帐的肉食

butler ['bʌtlə] *n.* 男管家;主管酒类、膳食的男仆
‖*~'s pantry* (厨房至餐室间的)配膳室

butt¹ [bʌt] *n.* ①(容量 108—140 英制加仑的)大酒
桶;桶 ②108—140 英制加仑的容量 ③(制革中)
背部和胁部的皮

butt² [bʌt] *n.* ①粗端;(工具)柄;枪托: a ~ buffer
【军】枪托缓冲器 / a ~ stroke 【军】枪托冲击 ②
(树木的)残株,根端;残余(部分) ③[美俚]烟蒂;
香烟 ④[美俚]屁股 ⑤【动】鲽类的鱼;大西洋
庸鲽

butt³ [bʌt] *n.* ① 靶垛 ②[复]射击场 ③ 靶,射击
目标 ④ 目的,目标 ⑤ 笑柄,抨击的对象: a ~ of
ridicule 嘲笑的对象 / make a ~ of sb. 嘲弄某
人 ⑥[古]界限: ~s and bounds 【律】地界

butt⁴ [bʌt] I ❶ *vt.* ① 抵触,顶撞 ② 碰撞 ③ 紧
靠,靠着 ④使邻接 (*on, upon, against*) ❷ *vi.* ①
顶撞,冲撞 ② 伸出,突出,凸出 ③ 邻接,毗连 II
① 顶撞,冲撞;碰撞: come (full) ~ against
和…对面相撞 ②(击中的)突刺 【机】平接
(合);对接: ~ joint 对接(头) / ~ welding 对
(头)焊接 ④【建】铰链 ‖~ *and* ~ 一头接一头,
一端接一端 / ~ *in* [美俚] ①插手;干涉;插嘴
②闯入 / ~ *into* 插手于

butter ['bʌtə] I *n.* ①黄油(旧称白脱油) ②似黄
油的东西;(植物)脂;脂样的物质: peanut ~ 花
生酱 / cocoa ~ 可可脂 / ~ of tin 【化】氯化锡
③[口]奉承话,巴结话 II *vt.* ①涂黄油于…上;
用黄油煮(菜);涂黄油似的东西于…上 ②[口]巴
结,讨好 (*up*) ‖*Butter to ~ is no relish.* 千篇
一律的东西令人生厌。/ *Fine words ~ no
parsnips.* 花言巧语是不中用的。/ *know which*

side one's bread is ~ed (on) 知道自己的利益所在 / *look as if ~ would not melt in one's mouth* ① 看来一本正经 ② 装得老老实实 ‖~**bean** 肾形豆；利马豆；棉豆 / '~**boat** n. (船形)黄油碟 / ~**cooler** 内盛冷水防止黄油融化的器皿 / '~**cup** n. 毛茛属植物 / '~**fat** n. 乳脂 / '~ˌ**fingered** a. [口]拿不稳东西的；容易失球的 / ~ˌ**fingers** [复] n. [用作单][口]拿不稳东西的人 / '~**nut** n. 灰胡桃树；灰胡桃 / '~**scotch** n. 黄油硬糖 / '~**wort** n. 捕虫堇属植物

butterfly ['bʌtəflai] n. ① 蝴蝶：a ~ bomb 【军】蝶形炸弹 / ~ valve 【机】蝶形阀 / a ~ nut 蝶形螺母 / a ~ stroke 蝶式游泳，蝶泳 ②[喻]轻浮的人(尤指妇女)；追求享乐的人 ‖*break a ~ on the wheel* 小题大作；杀鸡用牛刀 / *butterflies in the stomach* (或 *tummy*) 因害怕而起的发抖，神经质的发抖

buttock ['bʌtək] I n. ① 半边屁股，臀部 ②[复]屁股，臀部 ③[船]艉型，船艉 ④(摔角中的)揹撺 II vt. (摔角中)揹撺 ‖~ **line** [船]船体纵剖线

button ['bʌtn] I n. ① 钮扣 ②(电铃等的)按钮(开关)；(门等的)球形捏手：press (或 push, touch) the ~ 揿(电铃等的)按钮 / a control ~ 调整按钮 ③ 钮扣似的东西；圆形小徽章 ④ 没有价值的小东西：not care a ~ 毫不介意 ⑤[复][英口]服务员，僮仆：服务员的制服：send for the ~s 请别人(或打铃)叫服务员来 ⑥【植】芽，苞；未熟的小蘑菇 ⑦[冶]金属小珠 ⑧[俚]颊尖 ⑨[复][俚]神经的健全 II ❶ vt. ① 钉钮扣于；用钮扣装饰 ②扣，扣紧(up)：~ (up) one's coat 把外衣钮扣扣紧 / ~ up one's lip [俚]住嘴，闭口；不露风声 ❷ vi. 扣上钮子(up)；装有钮子：My collar won't ~. 我的衣领扣不起来。/ This jacket ~s at the side. 这件上衣钮子钉在身腰上。‖*a boy in ~s* 侍役 / *have a ~* (或 *a few ~s) missing* [俚]神经失常，行为古怪 / *have all (one's) ~s* [俚]神经正常 / *on the ~* [美俚]①击中下颌 ②准确，确切 ③准时 / *push* (或 *press) the panic* ~ [俚]惊慌失措，慌乱行事而铸成大错 / *take by the* ~ 强留；拖住(某人)谈话 ‖~**ed** a. 用钮扣装饰的；扣紧的 / ~**less** a. 没有钮扣的 / ~**y** a. ①钮扣的；象钮扣的 ②钮扣多的，用许多钮扣装饰的 ‖'~**hold** vt. [古]强留(客人)长谈 / '~**hole** n. ①钮孔，钮眼 ②强留客人长谈 vt. ①在…上开钮眼 ②抓住(某人)的衣钮；强留(客人)长谈 / '~**hook** n. 钮扣钩 / ~ **stick** (擦亮金属钮扣时用以防止沾污制服的)条形垫物 / '~**wood** n. 悬铃木属(篠悬木属)的植物

buttress ['bʌtris] I n. ①【建】扶垛，扶壁；【矿】支壁 ②象扶壁的东西；山的扶壁状凸出部；马蹄后跟的角质凸出部；(树干基部的)根脚 ③支柱；支持；支持者 II vt. ① 用扶壁支住(或加固) ② 支撑；支持(up)：an argument ~ed (up) by solid facts 以确凿的事实为依据的论点

buxom ['bʌksəm] a. (妇女)丰满的，有健康美的 ‖~**ly** ad. / ~**ness** n.

buy [bai] I (bought [bɔ:t]) ❶ vt. ① 买：~ing power 购买力 ② 获得；赢得 ③(用贿赂等)收买 ④[俚]同意；赞成；相信 ❷ vi. 买 II n. ①购买：make a ~ of wheat 购买小麦 ②买卖，交易；买得上算的货物：a good (bad) ~ 一件合算(不合算)的买卖 ‖~ *in* 大宗买进 / ~ *into* [美俚]买进…的股份；成为(某公司)股东；付钱获得(某会)成员资格 / ~ *it* [俚]①(回答问题或谜语时用)放弃：I'll ~ it. 我答不出。(或：我不晓得。) ②被杀，死于非命 / ~ *off* ①出钱使摆脱服役(或勒索等) ②收买 / ~ *out* 出钱使(某人)放弃地位(或财产)；买下…的全部产权 / ~ *over* 收买，贿赂 / ~ *up* 全买；尽可能买进 ‖~**able** a. 可买的；可收买的 / ~**er** n. ①买者 ②进货员

buzz [bʌz] I ❶ vi. ①(蜂等)嗡嗡叫，(机器等)营营响 ②用蜂音器传信 ③[口]匆忙行走：~ about (或 around) 闹哄哄地跑来跑去 / ~ along 匆忙走过 / ~ off 匆忙离去 / ~ 喊喊喳喳 ⑤(谣言等)流传 ❷ vt. ① 使嗡嗡叫，使营营响 ②用蜂音器传呼 ③异口同声地说：~ applause 同声赞扬 ④散布(谣言) ⑤猛扔(石子等) ⑥(飞机)低飞掠过,俯冲；飞近(另一飞机)进行骚扰 ⑦[口]打电话给 ⑧[英方]喝完(一瓶酒) II n. ①嗡嗡声，蜂音 ②喊喊喳喳，嘈杂声 ③流言,谣言 ④蜂音器传出的信号 ⑤[俚]电话：give sb. a ~ 给某人打电话 ⑥[美]圆锯(= ~ saw) III int. (指消息)早过时了！ ‖~**er** n. 蜂音器；(工厂等用的)汽笛 / ~**ing** a. 嗡嗡响的，营营响的 n. ①嗡嗡声 ②[军]低飞掠过，俯冲 ‖~ **bomb** [口]【军】"V"型飞弹，嗡嗡弹，飞机型飞弹

by [bai] I prep. ①在…旁，靠近：There is a pumping station ~ the river. 河边有一个抽水站。②在…身边,在…手头：I've got a medical handbook ~ me. 我手头有一本医药手册。③(方向)偏于：The ship sailed north ~ east. 船向北偏东的方向驶去。④ 沿；经，由：come ~ the highway 由公路来 / come ~ the fields 经过田野来 ⑤ 经过…旁边 ⑥在(白天、夜晚等的)情况下：march ~ night 夜晚行军 ⑦不迟于；到…(为止)：finish the task ~ the end of the month 在月底前完成这任务 ⑧[表示方法、手段]靠，用，通过：travel ~ air (land, sea) 航空(陆路,航海)旅行 / go ~ train (boat, bus) 乘火车(船,公共汽车)去 / shake sb. ~ the hand 和某人握手 / What do you mean ~ that? 你这样讲(或做)是什么意思? / multiply (divide) 9 ~ 3 用三乘(除)九 / a son ~ sb.'s former wife 某人前妻生的儿子 ⑨由于：~ mistake 由于差错 ⑩ 根据,按：~ Article 3 of the Treaty 根据条约第三条 / sell ~ the catty 论斤出售 / freight charged ~ weight (volume) 按重量(体积)计算的运费 / It is 3 o'clock ~ my watch. 我表上是三点钟。⑪ 被，由 ⑫相差：increase ~ 30% 增加百分之三十 / miss the train ~ ten minutes 晚了十分钟没赶上火车 / too many ~ one 多了

一个 ⑬[表示面积]: a room 5 m. ~ 4 m. 一间长五米宽四米的房间 ⑭逐一 ⑮[表示关系]就…来说: a doctor ~ profession 以医生为职业的人 / an Englishman ~ birth 祖籍英国的人 ⑯对, 对待: He did well ~ me. 他待我好。⑰对着…(发誓): swear ~ God 对着上帝起誓(英美等国家常用) **II** *ad.* ①在近旁: live close ~ 住在很近的地方 ②经过: The parade has passed ~. 游行队伍已走过去了。③(搁)在一边; 存放: lay (或 put) sth. ~ 把某物搁在一边; 把某物贮存起来 ‖ ~ *and* ~ 不久以后 / ~ *and large* ①总的说来, 大体上, 基本上: The quality is good ~ *and large.* 总的讲, 质量是好的。/ *By and large* he gave us a lot of help. 总的说来他给了我们很多帮助。②无论吃风不吃风(指帆船照样能行动) / ~ *far* 见 **far** / ~ *half* 见 **half** / ~ *oneself* ①单独 ②独力, 自行 / ~ *the by(e)* 顺便说到 / ~ *the way* 见 **way** ‖'~-and-'~ *n.* 将来

by(e)-by(e)[1] ['bai bai] *n.* [儿语]睡觉; 床: go to ~ 睡觉去

by(e)-by(e)[2] ['bai'bai] *int.* [口][儿语]再会, 回头见

by(e)-election ['bai-i,lek∫ən] *n.* 补缺选举

by-end ['baiend] *n.* 附带目的; 私下的目的

bygone ['baigɔn] **I** *a.* 过去的, 以往的; 过时的: in ~ days 往日 **II** *n.* [复]过去的事情, 往事: Let ~s be ~s. 过去的事让它过去吧!

bypass ['bai-pɑ:s] **I** *n.* (通常为避免车辆拥挤而筑的)迂回的旁道, 旁路; 【机】旁通管; 【电】分路迂回: ~ capacitor (或 condenser)【电】旁路电容器 **II** *vt.* ①绕过, 绕…走 ②为…加设旁道; 使(液体、气体)通过旁道 ③忽视; 回避; 越过: These problems cannot be ~ed. 这些问题不能回避。/ ~ the immediate leadership 越级

bypath ['bai-pɑ:θ] *n.* 小道, 僻径: ~s of history 稗史

by-product ['bai,prɔdəkt] *n.* 副产品

byre ['baiə] *n.* 牛棚, 牛栏

byroad ['bairoud] *n.* 小路; 支路

bystander ['bai,stændə] *n.* 旁观者

byword ['baiwə:d] *n.* ①谚语, 俗话 ②笑柄 ③绰号

C

cab [kæb] **I** *n.* ①出租马车; 出租汽车 (=taxicab): take a ~ 乘出租马车(或汽车) ②(机车、卡车等的)司机室 **II** (cabbed; cabbing) *vi.* 乘出租马车(或汽车)(常作 ~ it) ‖~**man** ['kæbmən] *n.* 出租马车(或汽车)驾驶人 / ~ **rank** [英] ①等候出租的马车(或汽车)行列 ②出租汽车停车处 / '~**stand** *n.* 出租马车(或汽车)停车处

cabaret ['kæbərei] *n.* ①有歌舞表演的餐馆(或酒吧间)(有时音译作"卡巴莱") ②"卡巴莱"餐馆(或酒吧间)中的歌舞表演(也称 ~ show)

cabbage ['kæbidʒ] **I** *n.* ①【植】甘蓝, 卷心菜, 洋白菜 ②[美俚]纸币, 钱 ③[美俚]少女 ④[英](裁缝据为己有的)裁剪时多余的衣料 **II** *vt. & vi.* 偷 ‖'~,head *n.* [美]笨蛋

cabby ['kæbi] *n.* [口]出租马车(或汽车)驾驶人

cabin ['kæbin] **I** *n.* ①(简陋的)小屋 ②船舱; 机舱: a passenger ~ 客舱 / a captain's ~ 船长室 ③(铁路的)信号室 **II** ❶ *vi.* 住在小屋里 ❷ *vt.* 把…关在小屋里; 使拘束 ‖~ **boy** 船舱服务员 / ~ **class** (客轮)二等舱 / ~ **cruiser** (有住宿设备的)汽艇 / ~ **passenger** 房舱旅客

cabinet ['kæbinit] **I** *n.* ①(存放或陈列用的)橱, 柜: a filing ~ 公文柜 ②内阁; 全体阁员; [英]内阁会议; 美国州长(或市长)的顾问团: a ~ council 内阁会议 / a *Cabinet* Minister 内阁大臣, 阁员 / a ~ member (or officer) 阁员, 部长 / a shadow ~ 影子内阁, 在野内阁 / a ~ crisis 内阁危机 ③[古]私人小房间, 密室; 博物馆的小陈列室 ④矿物标本组 ⑤生物标本培育箱 **II** *a.* ①内阁的 ②细木工做的 ③小房间用的; 小巧的 ‖'~,maker *n.* ①家具木工, 细木工 ②组阁者 / '~,making *n.* ①家具制造, 细木工艺 ②组阁 / ~ **photograph** 六时照片 / '~**work** *n.* 细木工; 细木工做的家具

cable ['keibl] **I** *n.* ①(周长十时或十时以上的)缆, 索; 钢丝绳 ②【电】电缆; 多心导线, 被覆线 ③ =~('s) length ④【船】锚链; 左搓三根三股索 ⑤ =~gram **II** ❶ *vt.* ①通过海底电报(或电报等); 给…发海底电报 ②(用缆索等)缚住 ❷ *vi.* 发海底电报 ‖cut (或 slip) one's (或 the) ~ (水手用语)死 ‖~gram *n.* 海底电报 ‖~ address 电报挂号 / ~ car 缆车 / '~-laid *a.*【船】(索)左搓三根三股的 / ~ railway 缆车铁道 / ~ ship 海底电缆敷设船 / ~('s) length 链(海上测距单位, 相当于1/10 浬) / '~way *n.* 索道

cacao [kə'kɑ:ou, kə'keiou] *n.*【植】①可可(树) ②可可豆

cache [kæ∫] **I** *n.* ①(勘探人员等贮藏粮食、器材等的)地窖, 藏物处 ②(地窖等处的)贮藏物 **II** *vt.* 贮藏, 窖藏

cackle ['kækl] **I** *vi.* ①(鸡等下蛋后)咯咯叫 ②咯咯地笑; 嘀嘀咕咕地讲 **II** *n.* ①咯咯的叫 ②咯咯的笑 ③嘀嘀咕咕的讲话; 废话 ‖~r *n.* 嘀嘀咕咕地讲话的人

cactus ['kæktəs] ([复] cacti ['kæktai] 或 cactuses) *n.*【植】仙人掌,仙人球; [C-] 仙人掌科(或属)

cad [kæd] *n.* 举止粗俗、行为不端的人,无赖

caddie ['kædi] I *n.* ①受雇为打高尔夫球者的人背球棒的人,球童 ②[苏格兰]杂役 ③有轮子的小型运送工具 II *vi.* 当球童

caddy ['kædi] *n.* ①茶叶盒,茶叶罐 ②[美](存放常用物品的)盒(或箱等)

cadence ['keidəns] *n.* ①调子 ②声音的抑扬(顿挫) ③节奏,拍子 ④【音】收束 ‖~d *a.* 音调抑扬的

cadet [kə'det] *n.* ①军校学员;军官候补生: a ~ corps [英]学生军训队 ②练习生 ③少子,幼子;弟弟 ‖~ship *n.* 军校学员(或军官候补生等)的地位(或级别、学习期等)

cadge [kædʒ] ❶ *vt.* [口]乞得,乞讨到 ❷ *vi.* ①[英方]贩卖,叫卖 ②[口]以乞讨为生 ‖~r *n.* ①小贩 ②乞丐;游手好闲的人

café ['kæfei; 美 kə'fei] *n.* ①咖啡 ②咖啡馆;餐馆;露天餐馆;酒吧 ‖*café au lait* ['kæfei ou 'lei] [法]牛奶咖啡 / *café noir* [法 kafe nwa:r] [法](不加牛奶的)浓咖啡

cafeteria [,kæfi'tiəriə] *n.* [美]顾客自取饭菜的食堂(或餐馆),自助食堂

cage [keidʒ] I *n.* ①笼;鸟笼;囚笼,车房 ②【矿】罐笼;【机】盒,罩;升降机箱 ③骨架构造 ④战俘营 ⑤篮球的球篮;冰球的球门;室内练习场 II *vt.* 把…关入笼中;把(冰球等)击入球门

cairn [kɛən] *n.* (用作纪念或路标等的)圆锥形石堆

cajole [kə'dʒoul] *vt.* 哄骗,勾引,引诱: ~ sb. into (out of) doing sth. 哄骗某人做(不做)某事 / ~ sth. out of (或 from) sb. 从某人处骗得某物 ‖~ment *n.* / ~r *n.* 骗子 / **cajolingly** *ad.*

cake [keik] I *n.* ①饼,糕,蛋糕 ②[苏格兰]燕麦饼: a sponge ~ 蛋糕 / a potato ~ 土豆饼 ②块;饼状物: a ~ of soap 一块肥皂 ③(硬或脆的)块结物 ④[美俚]妖媚女子 II ❶ *vt.* ①加块结物于…上: shoes ~d with mud 粘着泥块的鞋 ②使块结;使胶着 ❷ *vi.* 块结;胶着: Mud ~d on his shoes. 泥块粘在他的鞋上。 ‖*a piece of* ~ [口]轻松(或愉快)的事情 / *~s and ale* 欢乐,物质享受 / *sell like hot ~s* 销售得很快 / *take the* ~ [俚]得奖;优胜 / *the land o'* (或 *of*) *~s* 见 land / *You cannot eat your ~ and have it.* 两者不可兼得。 ‖'~,eater *n.* [美俚]花花公子 / '~walk *n.* 步态竞赛(美国黑人的一种娱乐);步态舞

calabash ['kæləbæʃ] *n.* 葫芦

calamitous [kə'læmitəs] *a.* 造成灾难的;灾难的;不幸的 ‖~ly *ad.* / ~ness *n.*

calamity [kə'læmiti] *n.* 灾难,灾害,祸患,不幸事件: struggle against natural *calamities* 与自然灾害作斗争 ‖~ howler [美]悲观论者

calcium ['kælsiəm] *n.*【化】钙: ~ carbide 碳化钙;电石 / ~ chloride 氯化钙

calculate ['kælkjuleit] ❶ *vt.* ①计算,核算: ~ the cost of production 计算生产成本 / It is ~d that more than thirty thousand people have visited the exhibition. 据计算有三万多人参观了这个展览会。 ②预测,推测: ~ an eclipse 预测日(或月)食 ③[常用被动语态]计划,打算: The new assembly hall is ~d to hold about a thousand people. 这个新会堂计划容纳约一千人。 ④[美口]以为,认为: I ~ we'll be in time. 我认为我们是来得及的。 ⑤[美]想要 ❷ *vi.* ①计算,核算 ②预告;打算: ~ on a long-term basis 作长期打算 ③[美]以为,认为 ‖~ on (或 upon) 指望着,期待着

calculated ['kælkjuleitid] *a.* ①被计算(出来)的;被预测(出来)的 ②特意计划的;故意作出的: a ~ insult 有意的侮辱 ③适合的,适当的 ④很可能…的 ⑤专为自己打算的

calculating ['kælkjuleitiŋ] *a.* ①计算的: a ~ machine 计算机 ②专为自己打算的

calculation [,kælkju'leiʃən] *n.* ①计算;计算出来的结果 ②仔细的分析(或打算),深谋熟虑 ③预测 ④自私的打算;算计

calculator ['kælkjuleitə] *n.* ①计算者 ②计算表 ③计算机;操纵计算机的人

calendar ['kælində] I *n.* ①历法: ~ month【天】历月 / ~ year【天】历年 / the lunar (solar) ~ 阴(阳)历 ②历,日历,月历 ③日程表;一览表;【律】案件日程表 II *vt.* ①把…列入表中 ②为(文件等)作排列、分类和索引

calender ['kælində] I *n.* ①【机】砑光机,轮压机;压延机 ②【纺】轧光机 II *vt.* 用砑光机砑光,把…上轮压机

calf [kɑ:f] ([复] calves [kɑ:vz]) *n.* ①小牛;(鲸、象等大哺乳动物的)仔 ②小牛皮: tree ~ 染成树木似的花纹、做书壳用的小牛皮 ③冰山(或冰川)上崩落漂流的冰块 ④[口]呆头呆脑的年轻人 ⑤大岛附近的小岛 ⑥腓,小腿 ‖*a cow in* (或 *with*) ~ 怀孕的母牛 / *golden* ~ 金犊(古代以色列人崇拜的偶象); (作为崇拜对象的)金钱 / *kill the fatted* ~ 设宴欢迎 / *slip her* ~ (牛)流产 ‖~hood *n.* 幼犊期(或状态) ‖~bound *a.* 小牛皮装订的 / '~,dozer *n.* 小型推土机 / knee【医】膝内翻 / ~ love 童年时的恋爱 / '~skin *n.* 小牛皮 / ~'s teeth 乳齿

calibrate ['kælibreit] *vt.* ①校准 ②使标准化,使合标准 ③标定,分度 ④测量…的口径

calibre ['kælibə] *n.* ①口径;(枪、炮的)口径,(子弹、炮弹的)直径: a medium-~ atomic bomb [军]中型原子炸弹 ②圆柱径 ③【机】轧辊型径 ④能力,器量;质量: a man of large (small) ~ 能力大(小)的人 ‖~d *a.* [常用以构成复合词]口径…的;直径…的

calico ['kælikou] I ([复] calico(e)s) *n.* ①[英]白布;[美]印花布 ②有斑点的兽 ③[美俚]女人;姑娘 II *a.* ①[英]白布制成的;[美]花布制成的;(似印花布般)有斑点的 ‖~ printing【纺】棉布印花

caliph ['kælif] *n.* 哈里发(伊斯兰教国家政教合一的领袖的称号)

call [kɔ:l] **I ❶** *vt.* ①大声读(或说)出; 叫, 叫唤; 叫醒: ~ the roll 点名 / ~ a halt 叫停 / ~ a doctor 请医生 / *Call* me if I don't wake up in time. 到时我不醒, 就叫醒我。
②把…叫做, 称呼: We ~ him Iron Ox. 我们管他叫"铁牛"。/ ~ black white 指黑为白, 混淆黑白
③认为, 估计为: Nothing can be ~ed unknowable. 没有什么事物可以认为是不可知的。/ You may ~ it ten km from here to the seaside. 从这里到海边的路程不妨算作十公里。
④(宣布)召开, 召集: A meeting was ~ed for August 15. 定于八月十五日开会。
⑤下令举行(罢工等)
⑥召, 征; 招聘; 传讯: be ~ed to active duty in the army 被征召服兵役 / be ~ed to testify 被传去作证
⑦打电话给…; 用电话传递; (在广播、电讯中)呼唤: *Call* me (*up*) this afternoon. 今天下午打个电话给我。/ The destroyer is ~*ing* the base. 驱逐舰在呼叫基地。
⑧要求偿还(贷款等); 收兑(债券等)
⑨(因天雨等)停止(棒球赛等); 暂停计算(比赛时间)
⑩(桥牌中)叫(某一花色的牌); 吊(牌); 叫(对方)摊牌
⑪要求(某人)实践他的声明
⑫责备, 申斥: He deserved to be ~ed on his mistake. 他犯了错误, 应受责备。
⑬模仿(鸟兽)的叫声以引诱
⑭(棒球赛中)裁定(球员)跑到某垒是否安全
⑮正确地预测(或猜测)到
❷ *vi.* ①叫, 喊; (动物)鸣, 叫: Do you hear someone ~*ing* in the distance? 你听见远处有人在喊叫吗?
②要求: When duty ~s, ... 当义务(或任务)要求这样做的时候…
③访问, 拜访 (*on, at*): He ~ed on you (at your office) yesterday. 昨天他曾(到你办公室)来看过你。/ The teacher has ~ed to know if we have any difficulties. 教师来过, 问我们有没有困难。
④(车、船等)停靠 (*at*): This train ~s at every station. 这次列车每站都停靠。
⑤打电话; (在广播、电讯中)呼唤: This is ... ~*ing*. 这是…电台在广播(或发讯)。
⑥(在纸牌戏中)叫牌; 吊牌; 叫对方摊牌
II *n.* ①叫, 喊; 号召; 号令: a ~ to arms 战斗的号令
②召集; 召唤: The committee met at the ~ of the chairman. 委员会应(该会)主席的召集而开会。/ accept a ~ (to a post) 应召(任某职)
③号声: blare (或 sound) the ~ to charge 吹响冲锋号 / the ~ to quarters 回营号

④访问, 拜访; (车、船等的)停靠: make (或 pay) a formal (courtesy, brief) ~ 进行一次正式(礼节性, 短时间)访问 / return sb.'s ~ 回访某人 / a place of ~ 经常访问的地方; (船只)停靠地点
⑤(一次)电话, 通话; 呼叫: make (或 give) sb. (telephone) ~ 打电话给某人 / get (或 receive) a ~ from sb. 接到某人的电话 / a trunk ~ [英] 一次长途电话 (=[美] a long-distance ~) / a local ~ 一次本地通话
⑥(广播、电讯中的)信号: ~ letters (或 a ~ sign, a ~ signal) 呼号
⑦付款要求(或通知); 要求; 邀请; 请求: He has many ~s on his time. 他有许多事要办。(直译作: 许多事要占用他的时间。) / respond to three curtain ~s 谢幕三次
⑧[主要用于否定或疑问句] 必要, 需要, 理由: There is no ~ to be anxious (或 for anxiety). 没有焦急的必要。
⑨(神等的)感召; 由神感召而得的圣职; (自然界等的)吸引(力): the ~ of the sea 海洋(生活)的吸引力
⑩(动物的)叫声, 鸣声, (以引诱动物为目的的)模仿动物的叫声, 鸣声; 哨子: a duck ~ (用来呼鸭的)鸭声哨子
⑪对演员们排演的召集: The ~ is for two o'clock. 演员们被召集在两点钟排演。
⑫律师资格的准给
⑬在特定期间内规定入伍人数的命令
⑭按照一定价格(或在一定时期内)买进一定数量的股票(或粮食等)的权利
⑮点名
⑯被喊出(或指出)的名字(或东西): His ~ was heads; my ~ was tails. (掷钱币猜正反面时)他说正, 我说反。
⑰(纸牌戏中的)叫花色; 吊牌; 叫对方摊牌
⑱网球比赛中的得分记录
⑲运动比赛中的裁决
‖*a ~ of nature* 要大便(或小便)的感觉 / *a close ~* [口]侥幸的脱险 / *a duty* ~ 礼节上的访问 / *at ~* =on ~ / *at sb.'s beck and ~* 唯某人之命是从 ①追在…的后面叫喊: They ~ed after the departing truck. 他们在开动的卡车后叫喊。②以(某人)的名字为…命名: They ~ed the baby John *after* his grandfather. 他们以他祖父的名字约翰来命名这个婴孩。/ ~ *a spade a spade* 是啥说啥, 直言不讳 / ~ *away* ①叫走, 把…叫开去 ②把(思想、注意力等)转移开 / ~ *back* ①叫回来, 收回(说错的话等) ②(在对方打电话来以后)打回电去 / ~ *down* ①祈求到; 招来, 招惹 ②[美俚]责骂: ~ sb. *down for* 为…责骂某人 / ~ *for* ①要求, 需要; 提倡, 号召: problems that ~ *for* immediate solution 迫切需要解决的问题 / What he said didn't seem to be ~ed *for*. 他说的话似乎不适当。/ ~ *for* economy 提倡节约 ②邀约; (到某处)拿取: Let's go to the meeting together, and I'll ~ *for* you.

开会时咱们一起去吧, 到时候我来叫你。③ 为争取⋯而叫喊; 叫喊 / ~ *for* help 叫人来帮忙; 呼救 / *forth* ①唤起, 引起 ②振作起, 鼓起(勇气、精神等); ~ *forth* all one's energy 使出全部精力, 全力以赴 / ~ *in* ①召集; 召集; 招请: ~ *in* a doctor 请医生 ②使停止流通, 收回(出借图书、债款、旧币等) ③来访: *Call in*, or ring us up. 你可以亲自来访, 也可以打电话来。/ ~ *off* ①叫走, 叫⋯叫开去 ②使(思想、注意力等)转移开 ③放弃, 取消: The football match was ~ed *off* on account of the weather. 因天气不好而取消了足球赛。④依次唱(名), 报告(数字) / ~ *on* (或 *upon*) ①号召; 呼吁; 请求 ②约请, 指派: be ~ed *on* (或 *upon*) to speak at the banquet 应邀在宴会上讲话 / I feel ~ed *on* to warn you that ⋯⋯我觉得我应该警告你⋯ ③访问, 拜访 / ~ *out* ①出动(军队等) ②唤起, 引起 (= ~ forth) ③(工会等)命令(工人们)罢工 ④要求与⋯进行决斗 ⑤大声叫唤; 大声叫出来 / ~ *over* 点(名) / ~ *sb.'s attention to sth.* 叫某人注意某事 / ~ *the tune* (或 *shots, turn*) 定调子; 发号施令; 操纵 / ~ *to account* 叫⋯account / ~ *together* 召集 / ~ *up* ①征召(服役); 召唤, 传(讯) ②使人想起 ③提出(议案等) ④打电话给⋯; 【讯】呼唤 / *have the* ~ 处于主要地位; 需要量最大 / *on* ~ 随叫随到的; 【军】待命的; 随时可支取, 随时可收回 / *within* ~ 在附近的; 随叫随到的 ||~-*back* *n.* [美] ①收回(指收回产品进行修理等)②(对暂时停雇职工的)招回 ③加班 / ~ *bell* 叫人(或报警)的铃 / '~-*board* *n.* (车站等处的)公告板 / ~ *box* ①[英]公用电话亭 (= [美] public telephone booth) ②由用户到局领取邮件的邮政信箱 / '~-*boy* *n.* ①旅馆男服务员 ②戏院中招呼演员准备上台的人 / ~ *girl* 用电话召唤的妓女 / '~-*ing card* [美] 名片 / ~ *loan* 【商】短期同业拆借 / ~ *market* 【商】短期同业拆借市场 / ~ *money* 【商】拆款 / ~ *number* 图书的书架号码 / '~-,*over* *n.* 点名 (= roll~) / '~-*up* *n.* (服兵役的)征集令, 征集令: ~-*up age* 征集年龄

caller[1] ['kɔ:lə] *n.* ①呼唤者 ②召集者 ③访问者 ④打电话者

caller[2] ['kælə] *a.* [苏格兰] ①(鱼等)新鲜的, 未变质的 ②(天气等)凉爽的

calligraphy [kə'ligrəfi] *n.* ①书法 ②笔迹 ||**calligrapher** [kə'ligrəfə], **calligraphist** *n.* 书法家

calling ['kɔ:liŋ] *n.* ①(神的)感召; (从事某种工作的)内心倾向; 冲动 ②职业, 行业: What ~ does he follow? 他是干什么的? ③雌猫的叫春(期)

calliper ['kælipə] *n.* & *vt.* =caliper

callous ['kæləs] I *a.* ①硬结的; 起老茧的 ②无情的, 冷淡的; 无感觉的 (*to*); 无同情心的 (*to*) II *vt.* ①使硬结 ②使无感觉; 使麻木不仁 ||~-*ly* *ad.* / ~-*ness* *n.*

callow ['kælou] I *a.* ①(鸟)羽毛未生的, 幼小的 ②[喻]乳臭未干的, 没有经验的 ③[爱尔兰](草地)低湿的 II *n.* [爱尔兰]低湿的草地

calm [kɑ:m] I *a.* ①(天气、海洋等)静的, 平静的: a ~ sea 风平浪静的海洋 / ~ weather 无风的天气 ②(人)镇静的, 沉着的 ③厚颜无耻的 II *n.* ①平静, (几乎)无风: a ~ before the storm 暴风雨前的平静 ②镇定 III ❶ *vt.* 使平静; 使镇定: ~ oneself 使自己镇静下来 ❷ *vi.* 平静下来; 镇定下来 (*down*): The sea ~ed *down*. 海上风平浪静了。/ ~-*ly* *ad.* / ~-*ness* *n.* ||~ *belt* 无风地带

calorie ['kæləri] *n.* ①卡(热量单位): ~ value 【物】热值 / a small ~ 小卡 / a large (或 great) ~ 大卡, 千卡 ②[C-] 大卡, 千卡 ③产生一千卡热量的食物量

calumniate [kə'lʌmnieit] *vt.* 诬蔑, 诽谤, 中伤 ||**calumniation** [kə,lʌmni'eiʃən] *n.* / **calumniator** *n.* 诬蔑者, 诽谤者 / **calumniatory** [kə'lʌmniətəri] *a.*

calve [kɑ:v] ❶ *vi.* ①生小牛(或小鹿等) ②(冰河等)崩解 ❷ *vt.* ①生(小牛、小鹿等) ②使(冰块)崩解

camber ['kæmbə] I *n.* ①(道路、木梁、甲板等的)中凸形, 上挠度, 反挠度 ②小船坞 ③【空】弧, 弧高(翼型)/ ~-*line* 【船】梁拱, 拱高 II ❶ *vt.* 把(道路、甲板等)造成弧形(或中凸形) ❷ *vi.* (道路、梁等)向上拱 ||~ *beam* 【建】弓背梁

cambric ['keimbrik] *n.* 细薄布, 麻纱, 细纺(棉织物)

came[1] [keim] come 的过去式

came[2] [keim] *n.* (固定花格窗玻璃等用的)有槽铅条

camel ['kæməl] *n.* ①骆驼: an Arabian (a Bactrian ['bæktriən]) ~ 单(双)峰驼 ②【船】起重浮箱, 打捞浮筒 ||*strain at a gnat and swallow a* ~ 见 gnat / *swallow a* ~ 默忍难于置信(或难于容忍)的事 ||'~-*back* *n.* ①骆驼的背 ②司机室设在锅炉上方的蒸汽机车 ③轮胎表面的补胎料 ④【交】驼峰 / ~('*s*) *hair* 骆驼毛, 驼绒毛; 骆驼绒

camel

cameo ['kæmiou] *n.* ①浮雕宝石 (或贝壳、玉石) ②有侧面浮雕像的小徽章

camera ['kæmərə] *n.* ①照相机, 摄影机; (电视)摄像机; 暗箱: a cine ~ 电影摄影机 / a colour television ~ 彩色电视摄像机 / a pickup ~ 摄像机 / a streak ~ 扫描照相机 ②审判员密谈室 ③罗马教廷的财政部 ‖in ~ ①禁止旁听地 ②秘密地 / on ~ 被电视机摄取,出现在电视上 ‖~ gun【军】空中照相枪 / '~man n. 摄影师,照相师;摄影记者 / ~ plane 摄影飞机 / '~-shy a. 不愿照相的 / ~work 摄影技巧

camouflage ['kæmuflɑːʒ] **I** n. ①伪装: ~ works 【军】伪装工事 / peace ~ 和平伪装 ②隐瞒,欺瞒 ③[喻]幌子 **II** vt. 伪装,掩饰: ~ the anti-aircraft guns with boughs of trees 用树枝把高射炮伪装起来

camp [kæmp] **I** n. ①营,野营;临时(或半永久性)兵营;野营地,设营地;帐篷: a summer ~ 夏令营 / a concentration ~ 集中营 / a prisoner-of-war ~ 战俘营 / pitch a ~ 扎营 / strike ~ 撤营,拔营 ②采木区的新兴市镇 ③扎营的一群人 ④阵营 ⑤军队生活 ⑥[美俚](搞同性关系者的)庸俗下流,忸怩作态 **II ❶** vi. ①设营;宿营,露宿 ②住宿 **❷** vt. ①使扎营住宿: The herdsmen ~ed themselves on the grasslands. 牧民们在草原上扎营住宿。②临时安顿: ~ the soldiers in new quarters 把战士们安顿在新营地 ‖~ out 野营 / go ~ing 进行野营 / in the same ~ 志同道合的 ‖~er n. ①野营者,露营者 ②野营用的车辆 / ~ing n. 野营,露营 / ~y a. [美俚](在搞同性关系方面)一副下流相的,忸怩作态的 ‖~bed 行军床 / ~chair 轻便折椅 / Camp David 戴维营[美国] / '~fire n. ①营火 ②营火会 ‖'~fire girl 美国营火少女团团员(从七岁到十八岁) / ~ follower 随营人员;随军谋生者;营妓 ②依附于某一团体(或派别)者 / ~ meeting【宗】野营布道会 / '~site n. 营地 / '~stool n. 轻便折凳

campaign [kæm'pein] **I** n. ①战役: a plan of ~ 作战计划 ②运动: a ~ to increase production and practise economy 增产节约运动 ③竞选运动 **II** vi. ①参加运动;搞运动 ②作战,出征 ③竞选

campaigner [kæm'peinə] n. ①参加运动的人 ②参加多次战役的军人 ③竞选者 ‖an old ~ 老练的人

camphor ['kæmfə] n. 樟脑;【化】莰酮-[2]: a ~ ball 樟脑丸 ‖~ ice 樟脑冰(樟脑、白蜡、鲸蜡和蓖麻油制成的油膏) / ~ tree【植】樟树 / '~wood n. 樟木

campus ['kæmpəs] n. [美]校园,学校场地;大学: ~ activities 校内活动 / ~ buildings 学校建筑物 / on the ~ of ... University 在 … 大学(的校园)内 ‖on (the) ~ 在校内

can[1] [强 kæn; 弱 kən](过去式 could [强 kud; 弱 kəd]; 否定式 cannot [强 'kænɔt; 弱 'kænət], cannot, can't [kɑːnt]) v. aux. ①[表示能力]能,会: Can you drive a tractor? 你会开拖拉机吗? ②[表示可能性]可能,会得: Difficulties ~ and must be overcome. 困难能够而且必须克服。/

Can the news be true? 这消息会是真的吗? / How ~ (或 could) you be so careless! 你怎么会这么粗心! (用 could 语气较婉转) ③[句首有疑问词而 can 又重读,表示惊异、迷惑、不耐烦等]究竟能,到底可能: What ~ he mean? 他究竟是什么意思? / Where ~ it be? 这东西究竟放到哪里去了呢? ④[口][表示许可或请求,代替 may, might]可以: Can (或 Could) I borrow two books at a time? 我可以一次借两本书吗? / Stop, you can't play ball on the street! 停下来,街道上不准玩球! ⑤[和感觉动词连用,代替现在或过去时态]: It was so dark that I could see (=I saw) nothing. 天太暗了,我什么都看不见。/ I ~ smell (=I smell) something burning. 我闻到有东西烧焦的气味。⑥[表示偶尔发生的事情]有时会: The writer ~ be (=is sometimes) quite sarcastic. 这个作家有时也很会挖苦的。‖as ... as (...) ~ be … 得不能再… / as good as (good) ~ be 好得不能再好 / as far as (far) ~ be 远得不能再远 / ~ but 只得;充其量不过: I ~ but hurry back. 我只得赶紧回来。/ cannot but ①不得不: He cannot but agree. 他不得不同意。②不会不,必然: One's world outlook cannot but come through in what one says and does. 一个人的世界观必然在他的言行中表现出来。③不能不: One cannot but be struck by his enthusiasm. 人们不能不被他的热情所感动。/ cannot help 不得不: I cannot help thinking so. 我不得不这样想。/ cannot help but [美]不得不[后接原形动词] / cannot ... too (或 over)... …总不嫌过分,越…越好: You cannot be too (或 over) careful. 你越仔细越好。(直译应为: 你无论怎样仔细,总不嫌过分的。) / I cannot recommend the film too strongly. 无论我怎样竭力推荐这部影片,也不嫌过头。/ This point cannot be overemphasized. 这一点无论怎样强调也不嫌过分。/ ~ only =~ but

can[2] [kæn] **I** n. ①(盛液体等的)容器(如罐、壶、桶等): a watering ~ (浇花等用的)喷水壶 / ash ~ [美]垃圾筒 ②[美](保藏食物的)罐头,听头(=[英]tin); 罐头中的食品: a ~ of meat 一听肉 / a ~ opener 开罐刀具 ③[俚]监牢;厕所 ④[军俚]深水炸弹;驱逐舰 (=tin ~) ⑤臀部 **II** (canned; canning) vt. ①把(食品等)装罐;给(机件)装上罩子 ②[俚]把…灌制唱片;把…录音 ③[美俚]开除(学生);解雇(职工);监禁;停止;停用 ‖carry the ~ [俚]代人受过 / in the ~ [美] (影片)已经拍好(准备上映的) ‖'~ful n. 一罐

canal [kə'næl] **I** n. ①运河 ②沟渠,水道 ③【解】管: auditory ~ 听管,耳道 / alimentary ~ 消化道 **II** (canal(l)ed; canal(l)ing) vt. 在…开运河,在…开沟渠

canary [kə'nɛəri] n. ①【动】金丝雀 ②加那利群岛的一种葡萄酒 ③[美俚]告密者 ④一种鲜黄色 ⑤[美俚]姑娘;女歌手 ‖~ bird 金丝雀 / ~ grass【植】蕲草

cancel ['kænsəl] I (cancel(l)ed; cancel(l)ing) ❶ *vt.*
①删去;省略;划掉: ~ a word (figure) 把字(数
字)划掉 ②取消,把…作废: The meeting (trip,
football match) has been *cancel(l)ed*. 会议(旅行,
足球赛)取消了。/ ~ an order for goods 取消
定货单 ③(用邮戳等)盖销(邮票等) ④抵销 ⑤
【数】约去(约数);消去(方程式或帐目两面的相等
部分): 9 and 12 can be *cancel(l)ed* (*out*) by 3. 九
和十二可以用三来通约。 ❷ *vi.* 相互抵销力量
(或效果) II *n.* ①删去;省略;【数】(相)约
(相)消 ③盖销 ④[常用复]轧票机 ‖**cancel-
(l)er** *n.* [无]消除器,补偿设备

cancellation [ˌkænsəˈleiʃən] *n.* ①删去;省略;划掉
②取消,作废 ③【数】(相)约,(相)消 ④(邮票等
的)盖销;盖销记号

cancer ['kænsə] *n.* ①癌(瘤);癌症;肿瘤(症): ~
of the lung (stomach, liver) 肺(胃,肝)癌症 /
~ cells 癌细胞 ②弊端;社会恶习 ③[C-]【天】巨
蟹宫;巨蟹座: the Tropic of *Cancer* 北回归线,
夏至线 ‖**~ed** *a.* 得了癌症的

candid ['kændid] *a.* ①公正的, 无偏见的 ②正直
的, 耿直的, 坦率的;直言相告的: a ~ opinion 直
言 / To be ~ (with you), I don't agree. 老实
(同你)说,我不同意。③趁人不备时拍摄的: a ~
picture 趁人不备时拍的照片 ④ (光等)白色的
‖**~ly** *ad.* / **~ness** *n.* ‖**~ camera** 一种趁人
不备时拍照的袖珍照相机

candidate ['kændidit, 'kændideit] *n.* ① 候选人;
候补者: a ~ *for* the position 某职位的候选人
②投考者

candidature ['kændiditʃə] *n.* [英]=candidacy

candle ['kændl] I *n.* ①蜡烛;烛形物 ②【物】烛光
(光强度单位,指国际烛光或新烛光) II *vt.* 对着
光检查(蛋等) ‖*burn the ~ at both ends* 过分
地耗费精力 / *can't* (或 *be not fit to*) *hold a ~
to* 与…不能相比 / *hide one's ~ under a
bushel* 不露锋芒 / *hold a ~ to the sun* 徒劳,
白费 / *not worth the ~* 得不偿失的,不上算的
‖**bomb** 照明弹 / '**~light** *n.* ①烛光;一种
柔和的人工光 ②上灯时间,黄昏 / '**~,power** *n.*
【物】① 用烛光表示的光强度 ② 烛光 (光强度单
位) / '**~stick** *n.* 烛台 / '**~wick** *n.* 烛心

cando(u)r ['kændə] *n.* ①坦率,爽直 ②公正, 正直
③白色;光明

candy ['kændi] I *n.* ①[美]糖果(=[英] sweets):
a ~ store [美]糖果店 / a bag of ~ (或 *candies*)
一袋糖果 / two pieces of ~ 两颗糖 ②砂糖结晶:
冰糖(=[英] sugar ~; [美] rock ~) ③[美]毒品
可卡因 II ❶ *vt.* ①糖煮,蜜饯 ②使结晶成为砂
糖 ❷ *vi.* 结晶成为砂糖 III *a.* [美俚](服饰)花
哨时髦的 ‖*He'd take a ~from a baby.* [美
口]他是个贪得无厌的下流坏。‖~ **stripe** (织物
的)条纹图案,条子花

cane [kein] I *n.* ①(藤、竹等的)茎 ②藤料,竹料 ③
手杖;笞杖; [美]棍,棒 ④甘蔗 II *vt.* ①用藤制

作(椅背等) ②用笞杖打 ‖'**~brake** *n.* 藤丛 /
~ **chair** 藤椅 / ~ **sugar** 甘蔗糖

canine ['keinain] I *a.* ①犬的; 似犬的 ②犬属的
③['kænain] 犬齿的 II *n.* ①犬 ②['kænain] 犬
齿,犬牙 ‖~ **madness** 【医】狂犬病 / ~ **tooth**
犬齿,犬牙

canister ['kænistə] *n.* ①(放茶叶、咖啡等的)罐 ②
【军】(榴)霰弹; (榴)霰弹筒 ③【军】滤毒罐(防毒
面具内用) ‖~ **shot** 【军】(榴)霰弹

canker ['kæŋkə] I *n.* ①【医】口溃疡,口疮;马蹄癌
②【植】溃疡(由霉菌、细菌或有毒物质引起的植物
萎缩、脱叶等病症) ③【动】尺蠖;伤害植物芽和叶
的害虫 ④[喻]腐败的原由 II ❶ *vt.* ①[古]使
(患)溃疡 ②使腐败,腐蚀 ❷ *vi.* ①传染着溃疡
②受到腐蚀 ‖'**~worm** *n.* 尺蠖;伤害植物芽和
叶的害虫

canna ['kænə] *n.* 【植】美人蕉; [C-] 美人蕉属

cannery ['kænəri] *n.* ①罐头食品厂 ②[俚]监狱

cannibal ['kænibəl] *n.* & *a.* ①吃人的人(的) ②吃
同类的动物(的)

canning ['kæniŋ] *n.* 罐头食品的制造: a ~ factory
罐头食品制造厂

cannon ['kænən] I ([复] cannon(s)) *n.* ①大炮,
火炮,加农炮(现通常用 gun) ②榴弹炮;(飞机上
的)机关炮 ③【机】空心轴;【动】炮骨 ④[美俚]手
枪;枪 ⑤[美俚]盗贼;扒手 II ❶ *vi.* 开炮,炮轰
❷ *vt.* [美俚]对…进行偷盗(或扒窃)
‖'**~ball** *n.* ①炮弹(现通常用 shell) ②快车 ③
(网球)炮弹式发球 ④[美俚] 囚犯之间传递的秘
密消息 *vi.* (炮弹般地)疾驶 / ~ **bit** 圆镳 / '**~-
bone** 【动】炮骨 / ~ **fodder** 炮灰 / '**~-shot** *n.*
炮弹(旧称);射程

cannon

cannot [强 'kænɔt; 弱 'kænət] can[1] 的否定式(在
美国往往分写为 can not; 在英国除需强调否定
词 not 外,一般连写)

canny ['kæni] *a.* ① 精明的,机警的 ②谨慎的 ③
狡猾的 ④节俭的(尤指苏格兰人) ⑤[苏格兰]温
和的,安静的 ⑥[苏格兰] 幸运的 ⑦[英方]悦目
的

canoe [kəˈnu:] I *n.* 独木舟;皮舟;划子 II ❶ *vi.*
①划独木舟 ②乘独木舟 ❷ *vt.* 用独木舟载运
‖*paddle one's own ~* 专靠自己,独立进行

canon ['kænən] *n.* ① (基督教或天主教的) 教规,
宗教法规 ②准则,标准,原则 ③基督教《圣经》的

正经; [总称]某作家的真作 ④天主教中的圣徒名单 ⑤【音】两重轮唱 ⑥【印】一种大型铅字 ⑦天主教弥撒的主要部分 ⑧ 大教堂牧师会的一员 ‖~ law 教会法规

canopy ['kænəpi] I n. ①华盖; 天篷 ②天盖: the ~ of the heavens (或 sky) 天空, 苍穹 ③【空】(飞机的) 座舱罩; (降落伞的) 伞盖 ④【建】挑棚; 雨篷 ⑤【植】冠; 覆盖; 冠层(古代种子) II vt. 用天篷遮盖 ‖**canopied** a. 遮有天篷的

cant[1] [kænt] I n. [总称] ①假话; 伪善的话 ②行业术语, 行话 ③(小偷等的)黑话, 切口 ④哀诉声 ⑤无意义的时髦话 II vi. ①说伪善的话, 侈谈 ②讲行话; 说黑话 ③哀诉 ‖~ing a. 伪善的

cant[2] [kænt] I n. ① (结晶体、岸等的)斜面 ②【建】(建筑物的)外角; 四角木材 ③引起倾斜的突然的动作(如推、掷等) ④【船】斜肋骨(=~ frame) II vt. ①把…的棱角切除 ②使(船、桶等)倾斜 ③使(网等)倒转 ④投, 掷(球等) ⑤突然改变…的方向 ❷ vi. ①倾斜 ②倒转 ③(船)改变方向 ‖~ed a. 有角的; 倾斜的 ‖~ hook 活动铁钩

cant[3] [kænt] a. [英方]活泼有力的

can't [kɑːnt; 美 kænt] =cannot

cantankerous [kən'kærəs] a. 脾气不好的; 爱争吵的 ‖~ly ad. / ~ness n.

cantata [kæn'tɑːtə] n. [意]【音】大合唱

canteen [kæn'tiːn] n. ① (兵营、工厂等的)小卖部: a dry (wet) ~ 食品(酒类)小卖部 ② 私人经营的士兵俱乐部 ③临时(流动)餐室 ④水壶; 饭盒; 炊具箱 ⑤家用餐具箱

canter[1] ['kæntə] n. ①流浪汉 ②讲话者; 说伪善话的人

canter[2] ['kæntə] I n. (马的)慢跑 II ❶ vt. 使(马)慢跑 ❷ vi. (马)慢跑; 骑着马慢跑 ‖**win in a** ~ 很容易地获胜

canto ['kæntou] n. ①长诗的篇章(相当于书的"章") ②【音】旋律 ③[俚]比赛的一段

canton I ['kænton] n. ①一些国家的行政区(如瑞士的州、法国的县或乡) ②纹章右上角的方形部分 ③旗上端靠近杆的部分 II vt. ① [kæn'ton] 把…分成若干行政区 (out) ② [kən'tuːn]【军】分配营房给(军队等); 驻扎 ‖~al ['kæntənl] a. 州的, 县的

canvas, canvass ['kænvəs] n. ①粗帆布 ②(一套)风帆 ③(一套)篷帐(特指马戏团的) ④一块油画布; 一幅油画 ⑤供刺绣等用的网形粗布 ⑥拳击(或角力)场的地板 ‖**kiss the** ~ [美俚](在职业性拳击赛中)被击倒 / **under** ~ ①(士兵等)过篷帐生活的 ②(船)扯着风帆的 ‖~**back** n. 一种北美野鸭 / ~ **shoe** 帆布鞋

canvass, canvas ['kænvəs] I ❶ vt. ①详细检查: ~ the votes cast 检查选票 ②讨论, 详细讨论: ~ all the items on the agenda 详细讨论议程上所有项目 ③在(或向)…游说(或运动投票, 征求意见、订户等): ~ a district for votes 为争取选

票在选举区进行游说 ❷ vi. 游说: ~ for a candidate 为候选人活动 / ~ for insurance 兜揽保险 II n. (只用 canvass) ①(选票等的)详细检查 ②讨论 ③游说 ‖**canvasser** n. ①检票员 ②游说者 ③兜揽生意的人, 推销员

canyon ['kænjən] n. 峡谷: the Grand Canyon 科罗拉多大峡谷[美国]

cap [kæp] I n. ①便帽; 制服帽; 军帽; 天主教红衣主教的法冠; 大学方帽: a service ~ 军帽 / a steel ~ 钢盔 / ~ insignia 帽徽 / a ~ of liberty 自由帽(法国革命时一种标志自由的锥形软帽) ②盖, 罩, 套: a gas tank ~ 储气罐盖 / the ~ of a pen 笔套 ③【建】帽盖; 【船】桅帽; 【植】根冠; (蘑菇的)菌盖 ④【军】火帽, 雷管 ⑤【矿】顶板岩石; 焰晕: a rock ~ 覆盖岩层 II (capped; capping) ❶ vt. ①给…戴帽; 覆盖: Snow capped the mountains. 雪覆盖了山顶。②(苏格兰大学中)授学位给… ③装雷管在…上 ④…脱帽致意 ⑤胜过; 凌驾: ~ the climax 超过限度; 出乎意料 ⑥接引(诗句等)(除第一人外, 每人引句的首字母必须跟前一人引句的首首或末字母相同) ❷ vi. 脱帽致意 (to) ‖a ~ of maintenance ①旧时表示官爵的一种帽子 ②(旧时英王加冕时捧行其前的)国王冠 / ~ and bells 滑稽演员戴的系铃帽 / ~ and gown (大学师生穿戴、表示学位的)方帽长袍 / ~ in hand 恭敬地, 谦恭地 / fuddle one's ~ 酩酊, 泥醉 / pull ~s 口角, 扭打 / put on one's thinking ~ 动脑筋想 / set one's ~ at (女子)向(男子)挑逗 / The ~ fits. 言之中肯。(或: 恰如其分。) ‖~ful n. 少许, 少量: a ~ful of wind 一阵轻风 / ~ piece 帽木

capability [ˌkeipə'biliti] n. ①能力, 才能: the ~ to do sth. 做某事的能力 / the ~ of solving practical problems 解决实际问题的能力 ②性能; 容量; 接受力: the ~ of a metal to be (或 for being) fused 金属的可熔性 ③[复]潜在能力: national defence capabilities 国防力量

capable ['keipəbl] a. 有能力的, 有才能的, 有技能的: a very ~ pilot 技能熟练的飞行员 / a ~ group leader 能干的小组长 ‖~ of ①有…能力的, 有…本领的 ②能…的; 可以…的: This machine is ~ of improvement (或 being improved). 这台机器是可以改进的。③有做出(坏事)的倾向的, 做得出(坏事)的: ~ of misspelling longer words 易于拼错较长的词 ‖**capably** ad.

capacious [kə'peiʃəs] a. 宽敞的, 容积大的 ‖~ness n.

capacity [kə'pæsiti] n. ①容量, 容积, 吸收力: The assembly hall was filled to ~. 大会堂里挤满了人。 / breathing (或 vital) ~ 肺活量 / ~ tonnage 载重量 / a seating ~ of 1,000 一千人的座位 / a ~ audience 满座的听(或观)众 ②能量; 生产力: The cotton mill is running at full ~. 这座棉纺厂全力进行生产。/ fighting ~ 战斗力 / generating ~ 发电量 ③能力; 接受

力，智能：a ~ to learn (或 for learning, of learning) languages 学语言的能力 / He has a mind of great ~. 他接受力很强。 ④ 职位，资格：in the ~ of 以…的资格 / 【电】电容；负载量：discharge ~ 放电容量 ⑥【律】权力

cape[1] [keip] n. 披肩，斗篷 ‖**~d** a. 披斗篷的

cape[2] [keip] n. 海角，岬：the *Cape* 好望角[非洲](阿扎尼亚) (=the *Cape* of Good Hope) ‖**Cape Cod** [kɔd] 科德角[美国]：a *Cape Cod* cottage 一种长方形的低矮海滨别墅(屋顶呈三角形，中央有烟囱) / ~ **doctor** 南非的一阵强烈东南风 / ~ **Dutch** =Afrikaans / **Cape Horn** 合恩角[智利] / ~ **smoke** 南非的一种白兰地酒

caper ['keipə] I vi. 跳跃，雀跃 II n. ① 跳跃，雀跃 ② 把戏，开玩笑 ‖*cut a* ~ (或 *cut* ~*s*) ① 跳跳蹦蹦 ② 搞把戏，开玩笑

capillarity [,kæpi'læriti] n. 【物】毛细作用，毛细现象

capillary [kə'piləri] I a. ① 毛状的 ② 毛细作用的，毛细现象的 ③ 表面张力的 II n. 【物】毛细管：~ action 毛细管作用 / blood ~ 【医】毛细血管

capillary

capital ['kæpitl] I n. ① 资本；资方：invest much ~ in the enterprise 在企业中投入许多资本 / a foreign company with a ~ of two million U. S. dollars 一家拥有两百万美元资本的外国公司 / the antagonism between labour and ~ 劳资对抗 ② 首都；首府；省会 ③ 大写字母：write in ~s 用大写字母写 / speak in ~s 强调地说 ④【建】柱头，柱顶 ‖*constant* (*variable*) ~ 不变(可变)资本 / *current* ~ / *fixed* ~ 固定资本 / *monopoly* ~ 垄断资本 / *production* ~ 生产资本 / *special* ~ 专用资本 / *working* ~ 周转资本 II a. ① 资本的：~ goods 资本货物(生产工业品所需的生产资料) ② 首位的；重要的，基本的：a ~ city 首都；首府；省会 / a ~ error 大错 / a ~ letter 大写字母 / a ~ ship 主力舰 / ~ construction 基本建设 / ~ works 基本建设工程 ③ 可处死刑的，致死的：a ~ crime 死罪 / ~ punishment 死刑 ④【口】顶好的，第一流的：A: What do you think of the performance? B: *Capital*! 甲：演出怎么样？乙：好极了！ / What a ~ idea! 好主意! ‖*make* ~ (*out*) *of* 利用 ‖**~ly** ad. 极好，极妙：He speaks French ~*ly*. 他法语讲得极好了。 ‖~ **account** 资本帐；股本帐 / ~ **assets** 资本资产(固定资产和专利权等) / ~ **expenditure** 基本建设费用 / ~ **levy** 资本课税 (指资本主义国家对私人及工商业在所得税以外所征的财产税) / ~ **stock** 股本

capitalism ['kæpitəlizəm] n. 资本主义，资本主义

制度：*laissez-faire* ~ 自由资本主义 / monopoly ~ 垄断资本主义 / under ~ 在资本主义制度下

capitalist ['kæpitəlist] I n. ①资本家；富豪 ②资本主义者 II a. ① 有资本的 ② 资本主义的：the ~ system (road) 资本主义制度(道路) / ~ society 资本主义社会 / a ~ country (或 state) 资本主义国家 ‖**~-im'perialism** n. 资本帝国主义

capitalize, capitalise [kə'pitəlaiz] ❶ vt. ① 用大写字母写(或印)；用大写字母作为开头写(或印) ② 投资于；提供资本给 ③ 使变为资本；使作为资本使用 ④ 计算 (某一时期内收益等)的现在价值 ❷ vi. 利用 (on, upon) ‖**capitalization** [kə,-pitəlai'zeiʃən] n.

Capitol ['kæpitl] n. ① [the ~] 美国国会大厦 ② [c-] 美国州议会大厦 ‖~ **Hill** 美国国会

capitulate [kə'pitjuleit] vi. ①(有条件)投降 ②停止抵抗

capitulation [kə,pitju'leiʃən] n. ① (有条件的)投降 ② 投降条约 ③ [复]投降条约内的全部条款 ④(文件、声明等的)摘要

caprice [kə'pri:s] n. ①不能解释的怪想(或行为)；突变：the large and small ~s of the weather 天气的大小突变 ②反复无常，任性：at the ~ of 由于…的任性 ③空想的艺术(尤指音乐)作品；随想曲

capricious [kə'priʃəs] a. 反复无常的，任性的；无定见的；变幻莫测的：a ~ climate 变幻莫测的气候 ‖**~ly** ad. / **~ness** n.

capsize [kæp'saiz] I ❶ vi. (船等)倾覆，翻身 ❷ vt. 使(船等)倾覆 II n. (船的)倾覆

capstan ['kæpstən] n. 绞盘，起锚机 ‖~ **bar** 绞盘棒

capsule ['kæpsju:l] I n. ①【医】囊，被膜；荚膜；胶囊 ②【植】蒴果；孢蒴(苔藓) ③【化】小皿；小盖皿 ④【空】气密小座舱，容器；封壳：space ~ 【宇】宇宙密闭小舱，宇宙容器 ⑤(金属或橡皮等制成的)瓶盖，管盖 ⑥ 摘要 II a. ① 简略的：a ~ biography 简历,简略的传记 / in ~ form 以简略形式 ② 小而结实的：a ~ submarine 小而结实的潜水艇 III vt. 压缩，节略

captain ['kæptin] I n. ①首领，队长：the ~ of a football team (fire brigade) 足球(消防)队长 / a ~ of industry 工业界头子 ②船长 ③(英)陆军(或海军陆战队)上尉，(美)陆军(或空军、海军陆战队)上尉 ④(英、美)海军上校 ⑤名将;战略家 ⑥【军】舰长，(飞机)机长 II vt. 做…的首领，指挥 ‖*a copper* ~ 冒充有地位的人 ‖**~cy**, **~ship** ①舰长(或上尉等)的职位 ②大将的才略

caption ['kæpʃən] n. ①(章、节、文章、文件等的)标题：under the ~ of 在…的标题下；以…为标题 ②(图片等的)解说词 ③(电影)的字幕 ④【律】附在诉讼卷宗文件上的说明部分 ⑤[英]逮捕 II vt. 在…上加标题；在(电影)上加字幕

captious ['kæpʃəs] a. 吹毛求疵的；强词夺理的 ‖**~ly** ad.

captivate ['kæptiveit] *vt.* 迷住，强烈感染 ‖**captivation** [ˌkæpti'veiʃən] *n.* 魅力，吸引力 / **captivator** *n.* 有吸引力的人(或物)

captive ['kæptiv] **I** *n.* ①俘虏；被监禁的人 ②着迷的人 **II** *a.* ①被俘虏的；被监禁的；被控制的；被拴住的：a ~ balloon 被拴住的气球 ②为另一企业所控制并为它的需要而经营的 ③被迷住的 ‖*take*(或 *hold, lead*) ~ 活捉，俘虏

captivity [kæp'tiviti] *n.* 监禁；被俘；束缚

capture ['kæptʃə] **I** *n.* ①捕获，夺得；【原】俘获 ②俘虏；战利品 **II** *vt.* ①捕获，俘获 ②夺得，占领：~ a prize 获得奖品 / a fortress 占领堡垒 ③赢得，引起(注意)：~ the attention of the listeners 引起听众的注意 / The event ~d the headlines of all newspapers. 这件事各报都用大标题登出。‖~**r** ['kæptʃərə] *n.* 捕获者，俘获者

car [kɑ:] *n.* ① 车，车辆：an air cushion ~ 气垫车 / an armoured ~ 装甲车 / a mail ~ 邮车 ②汽车，小汽车；电车：an open ~ 敞篷汽车 / a baby ~ 微型汽车 / by ~ 乘汽车(或电车) ③ (火车)车厢：the ~s [美]列车 / a baggage ~ 行李车 / a freight ~ 货车 / a dining ~ 餐车 / a sleeping ~ 卧车 ④ 电梯 ⑤ (飞艇、气球等的)吊舱 ⑥[诗]战车 ‖~ **coat** 短大衣 / ~**fare** *n.* [美]电车(或火车)费 / ~ **ferry** 火车(或汽车)渡口 / '~**hop** *n.* [美]把饭菜端给汽车乘客的服务员 / '~**load** *n.* 【交】车辆荷载；满载一节货车的货物；整车 / '~**loading** *n.* [常用复]以铁路货车数计算的货物运入(或运出)量 / ~**man** ['kɑ:mən] *n.* ①电车(或汽车)驾驶员 ②(车辆上货物的)搬运工人 ③火车的检修工人，制造车辆的工人 / ~ **park** [英]停车场 / ~ **pool** 汽车的合伙使用(指一群有汽车的人轮流合用他们汽车的安排) / '~**port** *n.* [美]没有门户的敞开的汽车间 / '~**sick** *a.* 晕车的 / ~ **sickness** 晕车 / ~ **wash** 汽车洗擦处

caramel ['kærəmel] *n.* ①焦糖；酱色 ②(牛奶等制的)小块坚硬糖果 ‖~**ize** *vt.* 使成焦糖

carat¹ ['kærət] *n.* =karat

carat² ['kærət] *n.* 克拉(宝石的重量单位；等于二百毫克)

caravan ['kærəvæn] *n.* ① (往返于沙漠等地带的)商队，旅行队 ②结队成列的车马 ③有蓬的车辆；马戏团(或吉卜赛人)旅行用的大篷车

carbide ['kɑ:baid] *n.* 【化】①碳化物 ②碳化钙

carbolic [kɑ:'bɔlik] *a.* ‖~ **acid** 【化】石炭酸，(苯)酚

carbon ['kɑ:bən] *n.* ①【化】碳：~ black 炭黑 / ~ dioxide 二氧化碳 / ~ monoxide 一氧化碳 / ~ tetrachloride 四氯化碳 / decolourizing ~ 脱色炭 (=decolourizing charcoal) ②【电】碳精棒，碳精片，碳精粉；碳精电极 ③ (一张)复写纸 ④复写的副本 ‖~ **copy** 复写的副本；[口]极相像的人(或物) / ~ **paper** 复写纸

carbonic [kɑ:'bɔnik] *a.* ①(含)碳的：~ acid 碳酸 ②自碳中提取的

carbuncle ['kɑ:bʌŋkl] *n.* ①【矿】红玉，红宝玉 ②【医】癰 ‖~**d** *a.* 镶红(宝)玉的；有癰的

carburet(t)er, carburet(t)or ['kɑ:bjuretə] *n.* ①【机】汽化器 ②【化】增碳器

carcass, carcase ['kɑ:kəs] *n.* ① (动物的)尸体 ②[蔑]人的死尸，身躯 ③(牲畜屠宰后的)躯体：~ meat 生肉 ④(船舶、房屋等的)架子，骨架 ⑤(废船等的)遗骸

card¹ [kɑ:d] **I** *n.* ①卡，卡片；名片；请帖；入场券：a record ~ 记录卡 / a membership ~ 组织成员卡 / a visiting(或[美]calling) ~ 名片 / a punched ~ 穿孔卡片 / a New-Year ~ 贺年片 / a ~ of buttons 一板钮扣 ②明信片 ③纸牌；[喻]办法，措施，计划；[复]牌戏：a pack of ~s 一副纸牌 / a sure(safe, doubtful) ~ 有把握(稳妥，靠不住)的办法 ④ (赛马会、运动会等的)节目单 ⑤[口]引人发笑的人，怪人 ⑥罗盘标度板 (=compass ~) ⑦[美俚](供吸毒者一次服用的)一服麻醉剂 **II** *vt.* ①在…上附加卡片 ②把…制成卡片；把(得分等)记入卡片 ③把…列入时间表 ‖*a house of ~s* 见 house / *a knowing ~* 精明鬼 / *a leading ~* 先例，榜样；论述中最强有力的论点 / *count on one's ~* 预盼成功，指望自己的一着能奏效 / *have a ~ up one's sleeve* 心中有个打算，有一个秘而不宣的计划；胸有成竹 / *have*(或 *hold*) *the ~s in one's hands* 有成功的把握 / *in the ~s* [美]=on the ~s / *leave a*(或 *one's*) ~ *on sb.* 在某人处留下名片(以代替面谒) / *make a ~* 一牌而赢一墩 / *on the ~s* 可能的，有可能实现的 / *play one's best ~* 拿出绝招 / *play one's ~s well* 办事高明，做事有心计 / *play one's trump ~* 打出王牌 / *show one's ~s*(或 *put one's ~s on the table, lay one's ~s on the table*) 摊牌，公布自己的打算 / *shuffle the ~s* 进行角色大调动；改变方针政策 / *speak by the ~* 说话精确(或有把握) / *stack the ~s* 洗牌作弊；暗中布局舞弊 / *the ~* 合适的措施(或对策等)；意想中的事物：That's the ~ for it. (对那事)就该这么办。/ *The ~s are in sb.'s hands.* 某人有成功的把握。(或：某人必操胜券。) ‖~**='carrying** *a.* ①持会员(或党员)证的 ②[口]彻底的，真正的 / ~ **index** 卡片索引 / ~ **shark** [口] ①玩纸牌老手 ②=sharp(er) / ~ **sharp(er)** *n.* 打牌时经常作弊的人 / ~ **vote** 凭卡投票(用于某些欧洲工会，卡上记明所代表的人数)

card² [kɑ:d] **I** *n.* 【纺】①梳棉(或梳毛、梳麻)机；钢丝卡 ②纹板 **II** *vt.* ①在(梳棉机等)梳理：~*ing* machine 梳棉(或毛、麻)机

cardboard ['kɑ:dbɔ:d] *n.* 卡(片)纸板，卡纸

cardigan ['kɑ:digən] *n.* 羊毛衫，羊毛背心，开襟绒线衫

cardinal¹ ['kɑ:dinl] **I** *a.* ①主要的，基本的：~ numbers 基数 / a ~ principle 一条基本原理 / ~ points of the compass 指南针上的基本方位

(东、南、西、北) / ~ winds【气】主要风向 ②深红的 **II** *n.* ①深红色 ②一种女子短外套 ③基数 ‖~ **flower**【植】红花半边莲

cardinal[2] ['kɑ:dinl] *n.*【天主教】红衣主教, 枢机主教 ‖~**ship** *n.* =cardinalate

care [kɛə] **I** *n.* ① 小心, 谨慎, 注意: Take ~ (或 Have a ~)! 留神! / Handle with ~! (货运包装用语) 小心轻放! / Take ~ there's no mistake. 当心不要弄错。② 关怀, 爱护 ③照管, 管理; 负责照管的事情: That will be your ~. 那件事由你负责。④忧虑, 烦恼; [常用复]心事, 牵累: be free from ~ 无忧无虑 **II ❶** *vi.* ①关心; 担心; 介意, 计较 (*for*, *about*): ~ *for* sb.'s safety 为某人的安全担心 / He doesn't ~ *about* his clothes 他不讲究衣着。/ I don't much ~ *about* going. 我不太想去。/ not ~ a pin (或 a damn, a farthing, a rap, a fig) 毫不关心; 毫不在意 / A: Would you like to come along with us? B: I don't ~ if I do. 甲: 跟我们一起去好吗? 乙: 也好。(直译为: 假使我这样做, 我也不在乎。) ②关怀, 照顾 (*for*): ~ *for* the younger generation 关怀年青的一代 ③ 喜欢, 愿意, 想望 (*for* 或接不定式): Would you ~ *for* a game of table tennis? 来打一盘乒乓球, 好吗? / I don't ~ *to* go there. 我不愿到那里去。/ I don't (或 shouldn't) ~ *for* him to read this letter. 我不愿让他看这封信。**❷** *vt.* 介意, 计较: I don't ~ how far I'll have to go. 无论走多远, 我都不在乎。‖***Care killed a cat.*** [谚]忧虑伤身。/ *for all I* ~ 与我无关 / (*in*) ~ *of* 由…转交 / *leave in* sb.'s ~ 把…交由某人照管 / *take* ~ *of* 照顾, 照料; 满足…的需要: have children to *take* ~ *of* 有孩子要照顾 / *take* good ~ *of* state property 爱护国家财产 / Here, let me *take* ~ *of* the cleaning. 来, 让我来打扫吧。/ Rafts *take* ~ *of* transportation on that river. 在那条河上, 用木筏进行运输。②处理; 清除: devices that *take* ~ *of* the waste from the factory 处理工厂废料的装置 ‖~-**free** *a.* 无忧无虑的 / '~-,**laden** *a.* 忧心忡忡的 / '~,**taker** *n.* (空屋等的)看管人; 暂时行使职权者: a ~*taker* government 看守政府 / '~**worn** *a.* 受忧虑折磨的

career [kə'riə] **I** *n.* ①生涯, 经历: follow (enter upon) a diplomatic ~ 从事外交生涯 ②历程, 发展 ③职业, 专业: a ~ open to women 妇女可从事的职业 ④全速 **II** *vi.* 猛冲, 飞跑 (*about*) **III** *a.* 职业性的, 把一般人短期从事的活动作为终身职业的: a ~ soldier 职业军人 ‖***carve (out)*** *a* ~ 谋求发迹 / *in full* ~ 开足马力地, 全速地 / *make a* ~ (或 ~s) 向上爬, 追求个人名利 ‖~ **woman** [口] 职业妇女 (常指为追求女性解放而不结婚者)

careful ['kɛəful] *a.* ① 仔细的; 小心的: be ~ *with* (或 *in* doing) one's work 过细做工作 / be ~ *of* public property 爱护公共财物 / Be ~ not

to misuse this word. 注意不要用错这个词。/ He was ~ enough to check up every detail. 他非常仔细, 把每一个细节都核对过了。/ Be ~ how you start the machine. 怎样开动这部机器, 须加注意。② 细致的, 精心的: ~ reading 细心阅读 ‖~**ly** *ad.* / ~**ness** *n.*

careless ['kɛəlis] *a.* ①粗心的, 疏忽的, 粗枝大叶的 ②由于粗心而引起的: a ~ mistake 由于疏忽而引起的错误 ③ 漫不经心的, 不介意的: be ~ *about* one's speech 讲话随便 / be ~ *of* the consequences 不顾及后果 ④ 无忧无虑的 ⑤出于自然的 ‖~**ly** *ad.* / ~**ness** *n.*

caress [kə'res] **I** *n.* 爱抚, 拥抱 **II** *vt.* ① 抚爱, 抚摸 ② 奉承; 哄骗

caressing [kə'resiŋ] *a.* 爱抚的 ‖~**ly** *ad.*

caret ['kærət] *n.* 脱字号(即 "∧")

cargo ['kɑ:gou] ([复] cargo(e)s) *n.* 船货, 货物: ship (discharge) the ~ 装(卸)货 / ~ capacity 载货容积 / a ~ hold 货舱 / a ~ liner 定期货轮; 运货班机 / a ~ ship (或 vessel) 货船 / a ~ transport plane 货运飞机; 运输机

caricature [,kærikə'tjuə] **I** *n.* ①漫画, 讽刺画; 讽刺文 ② 对别人声音、姿态等的滑稽模仿, 歪曲的模仿; 笨拙的模仿 ③ 漫画艺术, 漫画手法 **II** *vt.* 用漫画(或讽刺画)表现; 使滑稽化 ‖***make a*** ~ *of* 作…的漫画; 使滑稽化 ‖***caricaturable*** [,kærikə-'tjuərəbl] *a.* 适于被讽刺的; 具有被讽刺的形态的 / **caricatural** [,kærikə'tjuərəl] *a.* 讽刺画的, 讽刺文的, 滑稽的

carillon [kə'riljən] *n.* ①钟琴; 电子钟琴 ②供钟琴演奏的乐曲

carmine ['kɑ:main] **I** *n.* ①洋红色 ②胭脂红; 洋红; 卡红 **II** *a.* 洋红色的

carnage ['kɑ:nidʒ] *n.* ① 残杀, 大屠杀 ② [总称] 被屠杀的人(或动物)的尸体, 成堆的尸体

carnal ['kɑ:nl] *a.* ① 肉体的, 物质的 ② 性欲的, 好色的 ③世俗的: ~ ambition 名利心 ‖~**ly** *ad.*

carnation [kɑ:'neiʃən] *n.* ①石竹属植物; 麝香石竹 ② 淡红色, 肉色 ③[复] (绘画上的)肉色部分

carnival ['kɑ:nivəl] *n.*【宗】(四旬节前持续半周或一周的) 嘉年华会, 狂欢节 ② 狂欢, 庆祝, 欢宴 ③在各地巡回流动的游艺团; 有组织的联欢节目

carol ['kærəl] **I** *n.* 颂歌; 欢乐之歌; 鸟啭声: a Christmas ~【宗】圣诞颂歌 **II** (carol(l)ed; carol(l)ing) **❶** *vi.* ①愉快地唱歌 ②唱圣诞颂歌 **❷** *vt.* ①(愉快地)歌唱 ②歌颂 ‖**carol(l)er** *n.* 欢唱颂歌的人

carp[1] [kɑ:p] ([复] carp(s)) *n.* 鲤鱼; 鲤科的鱼: silver ~ 白鲢

carp[2] [kɑ:p] *vi.* 找岔子, 挑剔, 吹毛求疵: ~ at sb. 对某人挑剔 / ~ on (或 about) sth. 对某事挑剔 ‖~ **er** *n.* 吹毛求疵的人 / ~**ing** *a.* 吹毛求疵的, 爱挑剔的: ~*ing* criticism 苛刻的批评 / a ~*ing* tongue 尖嘴

carpenter ['kɑ:pintə] **I** n. 木工, 木匠 **II ❶** vi. 做木工活 **❷** vt. 以木工手艺造作 (或修理) (房屋、器物等) ‖the ～'s son 木匠之子 (耶稣的别名) ‖～('s) scene (换布景、道具时安插的) 幕间小节目 / ～'s square 木工角尺, 曲尺

carpentry ['kɑ:pintri] n. ① 木工业 ②[总称]木作, 木器

carpet ['kɑ:pit] **I** n. ①地毯, 毛毯, 毡毯, 梯毯 ②【建】磨耗层 ③似地毯一样的覆盖物: a ～ of grass 一片绿茵 **II** vt. ①铺地毯在…上; 把花草铺布…上; (花草等) 铺在…上 ②[主英]把…叫入室内训斥 ‖on the ～ ①在被考虑中; 在被审议中 ②[口]受训斥 / roll out the red ～ for sb. 展开红地毯隆重地欢迎某人 / shove sth. under the ～ 把某事掩盖起来 / ～ing n. 地毯料; [总称]地毯 / ～less a. 没有铺地毯的 ‖～bag n. 毛毡制的手提包 (或旅行袋) / ～bagger n. ①[美]南北战争后 (只带一只旅行袋) 去南方投机谋利的北方人 ②[英]不属本选区的但想参加竞选的人 ③[英]非本地区的政客 / ～ bomb【军】对…进行面积轰炸, 对…进行地毯式轰炸 / ～ bombing【军】面积轰炸, 地毯式轰炸 / ～ knight 游手好闲、只图享受的骑士 / ～ rod 扣住梯毯的金属条 / ～ sweeper 扫地毯器 / ～weed n.【植】粟米草属植物; 轮生粟米草

carriage ['kæridʒ] n. ①四轮马车: a ～ and pair 双马车 ②(火车)客车厢 (=[美] car) ③(站立时等的) 姿势, 仪态 ④运输; 运费: ～ paid (forward, free) 运费已付 (未付, 免付) ⑤车架; 炮架; 飞机起落架 ⑥【机】(机床的) 拖板; (打字机等的) 滑动架; (电传打字机的) 托架 ⑦(议会中提案的) 通过 ⑧[古]经营; 管理 ‖～able a. ①手提的 ②可通行马车的 / ～ful n. 整整一(马)车 ‖～ clock 正斜放置都会走动的时钟 / ～ drive (公园等中的) 行车道 / ～ trade 自备马车阶级, 上层阶级 / ～way n. 车行道: a dual ～way 复式车行道, 有中央分隔带的车行道

carrier ['kæriə] n. ①搬运人; 递送人; [美]邮递员; 送报人: a mail ～ [美]邮递员 (=[英] postman) ②从事运输业的人 (或公司); 两个邮局中间运输邮件的交通工具; 运输业者 (指铁路及轮船公司等) ③载重架 (如自行车的衣架等);【机】托架, 承载器; 传导管, 转运工具 ④运载工具; 航空母舰: an aircraft ～ 航空母舰 / a troop ～ 部队运输机 (或船) ⑤【化】载体 ⑥【无】载流; 载波 ⑦【医】带菌者, 带虫者; 媒介物 ‖aircraft ～ ①舰载机 ②运送物资 (或邮件、乘客) 的飞机 ③母机 / ～ bag 装载物品的手提厚纸袋 / ～-based a. 以航空母舰为基地的, 舰载的: ～-based aircraft 舰载机 / ～-borne a. 舰载的 / ～-'nation n. 为别国代理海外贸易的国家 / ～ pigeon 信鸽 / ～ rocket 运载火箭 / ～ ship 航空母舰 / ～ wave【无】载波

carrion ['kæriən] **I** n. ①动物尸体的腐肉 ②腐朽、污秽的东西 **II** a. 腐肉的; 食腐肉的; 腐朽的; 污秽的 ‖～ crow 食腐肉的乌鸦

carrot ['kærət] n. ①胡萝卜 ②[复][俚]红头发 (的人) ③政治诱骗, 不能兑现的允诺 ‖the stick and the ～ (或 stick and ～) 见 stick ‖～top n. [俚]红发人

carry ['kæri] **I ❶** vt. ①运送, 运载; 手提, 肩挑; 担负: This freighter can ～ a 12,600-ton cargo direct to any port in Asia. 这艘货轮能够装载一万二千六百吨货物直接航行到亚洲的任何一个港口。/ a baby in one's arms (on one's back) 抱(背)着一个孩子 / be eager to ～ heavy loads 争挑重担 ②把…带(到) (to): ～ the news to sb. 把消息告诉某人 / How far do you think the fuel will ～ us? 你看这些燃料能使我们行驶多远? ③携带, 佩带; 怀有: How many kilogrammes of luggage can I ～ with me? 我可以随身携带多少公斤行李? / a watch (an umbrella) 带表(伞) / a lot of figures in one's head 记住一大串数字 ④传送; 传播: That pipe carries water. 那管子是送水(用)的。/ Air carries sounds. 空气(能)传声音。/ The important statement was soon carried all over the world by radio. 那篇重要声明通过无线电广播迅速传遍全世界。⑤刊登: newspapers that ～ weather reports 登有天气预报的报纸 ⑥带有, 具有; 包含: an article that carries conviction (much weight) 一篇有说服力 (很有分量) 的文章 / Does the loan ～ any interest? 这笔贷款是否带利息? / The charge carries a possible sentence of three years. 根据这项控告他可能被判三年徒刑。⑦支撑, 支持: These pillars are too thin to ～ the roof. 这些柱子太细, 支撑不住屋顶。⑧推进, 使延伸; 把 (帐目等) 转到下页 (或下栏等): ～ sth. to a new stage in its development 把某事物推进到一个新的发展阶段 / a fence across a stream 把篱笆筑过小溪 ⑨攻占, 攻克 ⑩使获得赞同 (或通过); 获得…的赞同 (或通过): He carried his point. (他使)他的观点获得赞同。/ The resolution was carried. 决议获得通过。/ The bill carried the Senate. (或 The bill was carried by the Senate.) 议案获得参议院通过。/ The speaker carried the audience with him. 演讲者赢得听众的赞同。/ ～ an election 选举获胜 ⑪使保持一定的姿势: ～ one's head on one side 头侧向一边 / ～ oneself like a soldier 举止象军人 ⑫有 (某种商品) 出售; (出资或亲自) 办理: Do you ～ stationery? 你们有文具出售吗? / ～ a weekly with the help of 在…帮助下办一个周刊 ⑬(土地等) 出产, 生产; 供养 (牲畜): This pasture carries three hundred head of cattle. 这块草地供养三百头牛。⑭(音调相当准地) 唱; 奏 ⑮[方]陪同, 护送 ⑯把…留在帐册上; 把…作为负债人记入帐册 ⑰(猎狗) 尾随 (踪迹) ⑱扯 (帆) ⑲故意放松对方而使 (对方) 得胜 ⑳由于持有 (或占有) …而承担费用 **❷** vi. ①被携带: These bags ～ easily. 这些袋子便于携带。②(枪炮、火箭、声音等) 能

达到, 能传到: How far does this gun ~?
这炮(或枪)能射多远? / My voice doesn't ~
well. 我的声音传不远。③(议案等)获得通过
④(文学、戏剧等)具有感染力 ⑤(猎狗)追踪
II *n.* ①(枪、炮等的)射程 ②运载; 携带; 运载
(或携带)方法 ③(船只或货物从一河道到另一河
道的)陆上搬运 ④旗手持旗行进的姿势 ⑤持枪
(或剑)礼 ⑥[美俚]需用救护车(或担架)运送的
病人 ‖~ **all** (或 *everything*) *before one* (或
it) 势如破竹; 获得全面胜利 / ~ *away* ①运走,
拿走 ②使失去自制力; 冲昏…的头脑: not to be
carried away by success 不被胜利冲昏头脑 / ~
back ①运回, 拿回 ②使回想起 / ~ *forward*
①推进, 发扬: ~ *forward* one's achievements 发
扬成绩 ②结转, 将(帐目)转入次栏(或页、册) /
~ *into effect* 实行, 实现, 实施 / ~ *it* 获胜 /
~ *off* ①夺去…的生命 ②获得(奖品等) ③(成
功地)对付; 若无其事地应付: ~ *it off* (well) 装
作若无其事地应付过去 ④使成为过得去 / ~ *on*
①继续开展 ②坚持下去: They *carried on* in
spite of the extremely difficult conditions. 尽
管条件极端困难, 他们仍然坚持下去。③[口]举
止幼稚愚蠢; 行动失常; 吵吵闹闹; 歇斯底里发作
④[口](与…) 调情 (*with*) / ~ *out* ①进行(到
底), 开展, 实现 ②贯彻, 执行, 落实: ~ *out* a plan
to the full 不折不扣地执行计划 / ~ *over* ①贮
存(货物等)供下一季节供应 ②将(帐目)结转次
页; [英](在交易所中)将…转期交割 ③(从前
一阶段或先前的活动领域)继续下去, 遗留下来
④延期 / ~ *sth.* *too far* 把某事做得过分 /
~ *through* ①进行(到底); 贯彻 ②维持, 使
渡过困难 / ~ *with one* 记得 ‖~*all n.* ①一
种四轮运货马车 ②一种载客汽车(两边座位相对); 军
用大轿车 ③大提包(或箱) ④[矿]轮式铲运机,
一种搬运泥土、碎石的自载式输送机 / ~*ing
capacity* 承载能力; 【海】载货量; 【电】容许负荷
量, 载流容量 / ~*ing charge* ①持有(或租用)财
产所带来的费用(如税款等) ②(分期付款购货
的)附加价格 / '~*ings-'on* [复] *n.* 愚蠢的行为;
轻率的行为 / ~*ing trade* 运输业 / '~*out* *a.*
酒菜供顾客带出外吃的 / '~-,*over n.* 遗留(下
来); 遗留物
cart [kɑːt] **I** *n.* ①二轮运货马(或牛)车 ②二轮轻
便马车 ③手推车 **II** ❶ *vt.* 用车运送: ~ the
grain 运谷 ❷ *vi.* 驾驶运货马车 ‖*in the* ~ [俚]
处于困境 / *put the* ~ *before the horse* 本末
倒置 ‖~*age* ['kɑːtidʒ] *n.* 货车运货; 货车运费 /
~*er n.* 驾驶货车的人 ‖~ *ladder* (在货车上为
增加容量装的)货架子 / '~*load n.* 一满车(的装
货量) / '~*wheel n.* ①一种银币 ②横翻筋斗
cartel [kɑː'tel] *n.* ①挑战书, 决斗书 ②交战国间
交换俘虏的协议 ③【经】卡特尔 ④为采取共同行
动而组成的政治联盟 ‖~ *ship* 交换俘虏用的船
cartilage ['kɑːtilidʒ] *n.* 【解】软骨: ~ bone 软骨
性骨 / fibrous ~ 纤维软骨 / calcareous ~ 钙化
软骨

cartography [kɑː'tɔgrəfi] *n.* 制图学, 制图法
‖**cartographer** [kɑː'tɔgrəfə] *n.* 制图员 / **car-
tographic(al)** [,kɑːtə'græfik(əb)] *a.*
carton ['kɑːtən] *n.* ①纸板箱(或盒); 纸板 ②靶子
中心的白点; 射中白点的子弹
cartoon [kɑː'tuːn] **I** *n.* ① 草图, 底图 ②(尤指政
治性)漫画; 连环漫画 ③卡通, 动画片 (=animated
~) **II** *vt.* & *vi.* (为…)画漫画, (为…)画草图;
(使)漫画化 ‖~*ist* *n.* 漫画家; 动画片画家
cartridge ['kɑːtridʒ] **I** *n.* ①【军】弹药筒; 子弹 ②
[美]软片, 胶卷 ③【无】拾音器心座 ‖~ *bag* 弹
药包 / ~ *belt* 子弹带 / ~ *box* (串在皮带上的)
子弹盒 / ~ *case* ①药筒 ②弹壳 / ~ *chamber*
①药室 ②弹膛 / ~ *clip* 弹夹 / ~ *paper* ①弹
壳纸, 弹药纸 ②图画纸 / ~ *pouch* 弹药盒
carve [kɑːv] ❶ *vt.* 刻, 雕刻: This statue was
~d out of marble. 这个像是用大理石雕成的。/
~ one's name on a fountain pen 把名字刻在钢
笔上 ②切开; 切(熟肉、鸡等) ❷ *vi.* ①做雕刻工
作 ②切开熟肉 ‖~ (*out*) *a career* 谋求发迹 /
~ *out one's* (或 *a*) *way* 开辟道路 / ~ *up* 瓜
分, 划分 ‖~*n a.* [古][诗]雕刻的 / ~*r n.* ①
雕刻师, 雕刻工 ②切肉人; 切肉刀; [复]切肉用
具 / **carving** *n.* 雕刻, 雕刻术; 雕刻品
cascade [kæs'keid] **I** *n.* ①小瀑布(尤指连续数级
瀑布中的一级) ② 瀑布状物 (如下坠的波浪形花
边、布匹等) ③【化】阶式蒸发器 ④【物】串联, 级,
级联: ~ shower (宇宙射线中的)级联簇射 ⑤
【无】格, 栅, 格状物 ⑥【空】叶栅 **II** *vi.* & *vt.* ①
(使)瀑布似地落下 ②(使)阶式地连接
case[1] [keis] *n.* ①情况, 状况: in good (evil) ~ (在
健康、处境等方面)状况良好(不好的) ②事实, 实
情: A: Is that the ~? B: No, that's not the ~.
甲: 事实是那样吗?乙:不, 事实并非如此。/ That
is often the ~ *with* him. 他走往往是这样的。③
事例, 实例: a ~ in point 恰当的例子, 例证 / a
typical ~ 典型 / in nine ~s out of ten 十之八
九 ④ 病症, 病例; 患者: an emergency (或
urgent) ~ 急症病例 / a stretcher ~ 必须用担
架抬的重病员 / a walking ~ 可自己步行看门诊
的轻病员 / a burn ~ 烧伤病例 / a ~ of cholera
霍乱病例(或患者) ⑤诉讼, 案件, 判例; 论辩: a
civil (criminal) ~ 民事(刑事)案 / try a ~ 审
案 / a leading ~ 判例 / state one's ~ 陈述自己
的情况和理由 / He has no ~. 他无话可辩。
⑥[美俚]怪僻的人 ⑦[美俚]一百元 ⑧【语】格:
the nominative (possessive, objective) ~ 主(所
有, 宾)格 ‖*a gone* ~ 不可救药的人 / *a hard* ~
不可救药的人; 难对付的人; 处于困境的人 / *as
the* ~ *may be* 看情况, 根据具体情况 / *as the*
~ *stands* 事实上 / *give the* ~ *for* (*against*)
sb. 作出对某人有利(不利)的判决 / *in any* ~
无论如何, 总之 / *in* ~ ①假使: *In* ~ he comes,
let me know. 如果他来的话, 告诉我一声。②免
得, 以防(万一): Please remind me of it again
tomorrow *in* ~. 请你明天再提醒我一

下，免得我忘记。/ It may rain; you'd better take an umbrella (just) in ~ (=in ~ it rains). 可能下雨，拿把伞吧，以防万一。/ in ~ of 假使…，如果发生…，万一…: In ~ of fire, ring the alarm bell. 如遇火警，即按警铃。/ in no ~ 决不 / in the ~ of 就…来说；至于…/ in this (that) ~ 既然是这(那)样，假使这(那)样的话 / make a Federal ~ out of sth. [美俚] 过分强调某事的重要性，过分夸大某事 / make out one's ~ 证明自己有理由 / put (the) ~ that 假定… / such (或 that) being the ~ 事实既然如此 ‖~ history ①病历 ②个人历史 / ~ law 【律】判例法(以判决例为根据的法律) / ~ load (法庭等的)承办案件数；(保健站等的)病例数 / '~work n. 对于申请户等情况的个别调查工作

case² [keis] **I** n. ①箱(子)，盒(子)；套(子)，壳(子)；容器: three ~s of eggs 三箱蛋 / a cigarette ~ 一只香烟盒 / the ~ of a watch 表壳 ②框子，架子: a window ~ 窗框 ③【印】活字分格盘: the upper (lower) ~ 大写(小写)字盘 / work at ~ 排字 **II** vt. ①把…装入箱(或盒等)内: The goods have been ~d up for transport. 货物已经装箱待运。②包，包围 (with, up, over) ③[美俚]探察，查看(尤指企图盗窃时) ‖~ bay 【建】梁间；桁间 / ~ harden ①[冶]使(铁合金)表面硬化 ②使定形；使麻木不仁 / '~, hardened a. ①[冶]表面硬化的 ②(思想等方面)已定型的；无感觉的；无情的 / ~ knife ①餐刀 ②有鞘小刀

casein ['keisi:in] n. 【生化】酪蛋白

casement ['keismənt] n. ①【建】窗扉 ②[诗]窗 ‖~ cloth 一种薄窗帘布 / ~ window 竖铰链窗

cash [kæʃ] **I** n. ①现金，现款: be in (out of) ~ 有(无)现款 / be short of ~ 缺少现款，支付不足 / ~ down [商]即期付款 / on delivery 【商】货到付款 (略作 C. O. D.) ②[单复同](中国过去的)小铜钱 **II** vt. 把…兑现: ~ a cheque 兑支票 ‖~ in ①兑现 ②收到…的货款 ③结清帐目而停业 ④[俚]发财 ⑤[口]死亡 / ~ in on 靠…赚钱 / ~ in 乘机利用 ‖~ account 现金帐 / '~= and-'carry n. & a. [商]现购自运(的) / '~ book n. 现金帐 / '~boy n. (往来于货柜和出纳柜之间的)送款员 / ~ carrier 送款机 / ~ payment 现金付款 / ~ price 现金付款的最低价格/ ~ register 现金收入记录机

cashier¹ [kæˈʃiə] n. ①出纳员 ②[美]银行(或信托公司)内负责财务的高级职员 ‖~'s cheque 银行本票

cashier² [kəˈʃiə] vt. ①撤职 ②废除，抛弃

cashmere [kæʃˈmiə] n. ①开士米(一种细毛料)，山羊绒 ②开士米织物，精纺细毛织

casing ['keisiŋ] n. ①包装(箱、袋、筒、框等的总称) ②【油】套管；套，罩 ③汽车外胎 ④门窗外框 ⑤(做香肠用的)肠衣 ⑥[船](机舱的)棚 ‖'~head

gas【油】井口气体，套管头气体

casino [kəˈsi:nou] n. ①娱乐场；赌场 ②(公园等处的)凉棚 ③一种纸牌戏

cask [ka:sk] n. 木桶；一满桶

casket ['ka:skit] n. ①(精美的)小匣子，首饰盒 ②[美]棺材

cassava [kəˈsɑ:və] n. 木薯；木薯粉

casserole ['kæsəroul] n. ①【化】勺皿 ②(烧菜和上菜用的)焙盘；蒸锅

cassock ['kæsək] n. ①教士穿的黑色长袍 ②教士职位 ③教士

cassowary ['kæsəwɛəri] n. 【动】食火鸡

cast [ka:st] **I** (cast) ❶ vt. ①投，扔，抛，撒，掷: ~ a vote (或 ballot) 投票 / ~ anchor 抛锚 / ~ a net 撒网 / ~ seed 播种 / ~ the lead 【海】投锤(测水的深浅) ②投射(光、影、视线等)；加…于 (on, at): His words ~ (a) new light on the problem. 他的话使人们对这个问题有了新的认识。/ ~ a glance (或 a look, an eye) at (或 over, on) 向…瞧了瞧 / ~ the blame on (或 upon) sb. 归咎于某人 / ~ doubt on 引起对…的怀疑，使人们不相信… / ~ a spell on sb. (用魔力)迷住某人 ③脱落；早产，早落(果实): Snakes ~ their skins. 蛇蜕皮。/ The horse ~ a shoe. 马掉了铁掌。/ The cow ~ a calf. 这头母牛早产了。④铸(造): ~ a stainless steel bust 铸一座不锈钢的胸像 ⑤计算，加起来: ~ accounts 算帐 / ~ (up) a column of figures 把一栏数字加起来 ⑥选派，扮演角色；为(戏剧、角色)选派演员: The part ~ to him. 这个角色分派给他演。⑦使弯曲，使歪: a beam ~ by age 年久已歪的横梁 ⑧解雇，辞退；剔除(牲畜等) ⑨[律]使败诉: be ~ in a lawsuit 败诉 ⑩安排，分类整理 ❷ vi. ①投；抛垂钓鱼钩(或钓饵) ②把几个数字加起来；计算；预测，估计 ③图谋，筹划，打算；思索 ④帆船顺风换抢 **II** n. ①一掷，一撒，一举；撒网，抛垂鱼钩 【海】锤测；投(射)程: stake everything on a single ~ of the dice 孤注一掷 / the last ~ 最后一举 / a bow's ~ 箭的射程 ②铸型，铸件；模子，模型；模压品: His leg was in a plaster ~. 他的腿上了石膏。③加起来；计算；预测 ④演员名表；派角色；班底: choose the ~ 选派演员 ⑤型，性质；色调，特色；倾向，歪斜: a ~ of features 面容 / a ~ of mind 气质 / a ~ of character 性格 / a greenish ~ 带绿的颜色 / a ~ in the eye 斜视 ‖~ about 搜索，寻觅 (for)；想方设法，计划: ~ about for an opportunity 寻找机会 / ~ about (how) to solve the problem 设法解决问题 / ~ aside 消除，抛弃；废除 / ~ away ①丢掉，抛弃: ~ away illusions 丢掉幻想 ②使(船)失事；使漂流 / ~ back 回想，追溯: You may remember, if you ~ back for a few years. 你只要把几年前的事回想一下，或许还记得起。/ ~ down 使沮丧 ②使下降；推翻，毁灭 / ~ (in) one's lot with 与…共命运 / ~ into the shade 使逊色

使相形见绌 / ~ *loose*【海】解开(缆绳等);解缆放(船);使脱离 / ~ *off* ①抛弃 ②释放,使自由 ③解缆放(船);解(缆) ④(编织毛线等时)收(针) ⑤【印】估计(印刷项目)的排版篇幅 ⑥解缆,开航 / ~ *on* 披上(衣服等);(编织毛线等时)起(针) / ~ *oneself on* (或 *upon*) 委身于,指望 / ~ *out* 驱逐,逐出 / ~ *sth. behind one's back* 把某事置之脑后 / ~ *sth. in sb.'s teeth* 用事来直斥(或嘲骂)某人 / ~ *up* ①计算,把…加起来 ②呕吐出 ③使从深处扬起来 ④[方]说…来作为责备的理由:He ~ *up to me that I had not done my best.* 他责备我,说我没有尽力。 ‖**~er** *n.* ①投掷的人 ②翻砂工人,铸工 ③ =castor² ‖**'~away** *n.* ①乘船遭难的人 ②被抛弃的人(或物) ③无赖汉 *a.* ①(人)乘船遇难的 ②被人摈弃的;堕落的 / **~ charge** (火箭发动机的)浇注火药柱 / **~ing vote** (赞成票数和反对票数相等时主持会议者所投的)决定性一票 / '**~-iron** *a.* ①用铸铁制的 ②铁一般的,顽强不屈的;不可变动的 / **~ iron** 铸铁: nodular ~ *iron*【冶】球墨铸铁 / **'~off** *a.* 被抛弃的;(衣服)穿旧的,无用的 *n.* ①对印刷项目所需篇幅的估计 ②被抛弃的人(或物) / **~ steel**【冶】铸钢

castanets [,kæstə'nets] [复] *n.*【音】响板(一副木或象牙制的圆形凹板,用手指拍合,作为音乐或舞蹈的伴奏器)

caste [ka:st] *n.* ①(印度的)社会等级,种姓: the ~ system 种姓等级制度 ②特权阶级 ③等级制度;社会地位: lose ~ 失去社会上的地位

castellated ['kæsteleitid] *a.* ①造成城堡形的 ②建有城堡的

castigate ['kæstigeit] *vt.* ①惩罚;鞭打 ②申斥,严厉批评 ③修订(书等) ‖**castigation** [,kæsti-'geiʃən] *n.* / **castigator** *n.* 鞭打者;申斥者;修订者 / **castigatory** *a.* 鞭打的;申斥的;修订的

casting ['ka:stiŋ] *n.* ①投,掷,扔 ②【机】浇铸;铸件: ~s and forgings 铸件和锻件 / centrifugal ~ 离心浇铸 / investment (或 lost wax) ~ 失腊浇铸 / permanent mould ~ 硬模浇铸 / sand ~ 砂型浇铸 / die ~ 压铸;压铸件 ③【动】脱落物(如毛、皮等)

castle ['ka:sl] I *n.* ①城堡 ②巨大建筑物 ③船楼 ④(国际象棋的)车 ⑤ 不受侵扰的退避所 II *vt.* ①置…于城堡中;筑城堡防御 ②(国际象棋)用车

castle

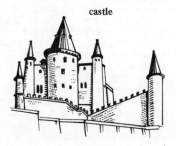

护(王) ‖*a ~ in the air* (或 *in Spain*) 空中楼阁;白日梦 ‖'**~-,builder** *n.* 空想家

Castor ['ka:stə] *n.*【天】北河二(双子座 α 星)

castor¹ ['ka:stə] *n.* ①海狸 ②【医】海狸香 ③海狸皮;海狸皮(或其他皮)帽 ④[俚]帽 ④一种制男大衣的厚毛料

castor² ['ka:stə] *n.* ①调味瓶;调味瓶架: ~ sugar 细白砂糖 ②(家具、机器等的)小脚轮

castor³ ['ka:stə] *n.*【植】蓖麻(系 ~-oil plant 的简称) ‖**~ bean** 蓖麻籽 / **~ oil** 蓖麻(籽)油: a ~ *oil* artist (或 merchant) [美俚]医生

castrate [kæs'treit] *vt.* ①阉割 ②使丧失精力 ③删改(书籍) ④【植】去雄 ‖**castration** [kæs-'treiʃən] *n.* ①阉割 ②删改 ③【植】去雄

casual ['kæʒjuəl, 'kæʒuəl] I *a.* ①偶然的,碰巧的: a ~ meeting 巧遇 / a ~ visitor 不速之客 ②临时的,不定期的: ~ expenses 临时费用 / a ~ labourer 临时工 ③漫不经心的,随便的: a ~ attitude 不够郑重的态度 / put in a ~ remark 临时随便插一句话 ④不拘礼的,非正式的: clothes for ~ wear 便服 II *n.* ①临时工;[英]不定期接受救济金的人 ②【军】待命士兵,待运士兵 ‖*the ~ poor* [英]不定期接受救济金的人们 ‖**~ly** *ad.* / **~ness** *n.* ‖**~ ward** [英](济贫院的)临时收容所

casualty ['kæʒjuəlti, 'kæʒuəlti] *n.* ①严重伤亡事故 ②[常用复]【军】伤亡人员(包括被俘、失踪、患病等人员);伤亡: a ~ clearing station (英军)伤员医疗站(略作: C.C.S.) ③(事故中)伤亡的人员(或损失的物品);受害者: ~ insurance 灾害保险

casuist ['kæzjuist] *n.* 决疑者;诡辩家

cat [kæt] I *n.* ①猫;猫科(包括狮、虎、山猫等);猫皮 ②心地恶毒的女人;爱(用指甲)抓人的孩子 ③【船】起锚滑车;锚架 ④【船】独桅艇 ⑤一种有九条皮条的鞭子 ⑥【军俚】履带式拖拉机 ⑦鲇科的鱼,鲇鱼;鮰鱼 ⑧(无论怎样安放都能三脚站立的)有三对活动脚的六脚器 ⑨[美俚]爵士音乐演奏者(或爱好者);家伙 II ① *vt.* ①【海】把(锚)吊放在锚架上 ②用九尾鞭打 ❷ *vi.* [口]呕吐 ‖*a barber's ~* 面现病容和饥色的人 / *A ~ has nine lives.* [谚]猫有九命。(指生命力强) / *a ~ in the pan* 叛徒,变节者 / *A ~ may look at a king.* [谚]猫也有权看国王。(意指: 小人物也该有些权利。) / *bell the ~* 为大家的利益承担危险的事,为别人冒险 / *~s and dogs* [美俚]价值低的股票;杂物,杂货 / *fight like Kilkenny* [kil'keni] *~s* 死拼到两败俱伤 / *grin like a Cheshire ~* 常常无缘无故地傻笑 / *let the ~ out of the bag* 泄露秘密 / *not* (或 *no*) *room to swing a ~ in* 没有活动的余地,地方狭窄 / *rain ~s and dogs* 下倾盆大雨 / *see which way the ~ jumps* 观望形势后再作决策 / *shoot* (或 *jerk*) *the ~* [俚]呕吐 / *skin the ~* 以两手悬于单杠上,以身体及两脚由两臂间穿过向后翻转 / *That ~ won't jump.*

[口]这一手行不通。/ *wait for the* ~ *to jump* =see which way the ~ jumps ‖ *~like* a. 象猫一样的,偷偷摸摸的 ‖ '*~bird* n. (北美洲产的)一种鸣禽(鸣声如猫叫) / '*~-blend* n.【化】催化裂化残油与直馏残油混合物 / ~ *block*【船】大型起锚滑车 / *~boat* n.【船】独桅艇 / *burglar* 惯从屋顶侵入的窃贼 / ~ *call* n. (会议或剧场中)表示不赞成的嘘声 *vt.* 用嘘声反对 *vi.* 发出嘘声 / ~ *cracker* (石油)催化裂化器 / ~ *davit*【船】有档锚吊杆 / '*~-eyed* a. 黑暗中能见物的 / '*~fall* n.【船】吊锚索 / '*~fish* n. ①鲇科的鱼,鲇鱼 ②鲴鱼(产于美洲) / '*~gut* n. 羊肠线 / '*~head* n.【船】锚架 / ~ *hole*【船】锚链孔,船尾缆孔 / ~ *hook*【船】起锚滑车上的钩子 / ~ *ice* (水面下降后与水面有一定空间的)乳白色薄冰 / '*~lap* n. [美俚]非浓缩的饮料(如茶等) / '*~nap* n. 瞌睡 / '*~nip* n.【植】假荆芥 / '*~-o'-nine-tails* [ˈkætə'nain-teilz] [单复同] n. 一种有九条皮条的鞭子 / *~'s cradle* 挑绷子游戏 / *~'s eye*【地】猫眼石 ②(汽车等处的)小型反光装置 / '*~-sleep* n. =~nap / '*~'s-paw* n. ①被人利用的人 ②【气】猫掌风(一种小区域微风) / *~'s pyjamas* [俚]了不起的东西 / *~('s) whisker* [无]触须,晶须 / *~'s whiskers* [俚] =~'s pyjamas / '*~tail* n. 香蒲属植物 / '*~walk* n. 狭窄的人行道;狭窄的过道

cataclysm [ˈkætəklizəm] n. ①洪水 ②【地】灾变 ③(政治和社会的)大变动 ‖*~al* [ˌkætə'klizməl], *~ic* [ˌkætə'klizmik] a.

catacomb [ˈkætəkoum] n. ①[常用复]地下墓穴,坟窟,陵寝 ②酒窖

catalog(ue) [ˈkætələɡ] I n. ①(图书或商品等)目录,目录册: a card ~ 卡片目录 ②[美]大学学年中行事一览表 II *vt.* 为…编目录;把…编入目录;按目录分类 ‖catalog(u)er n. 编目人 ‖*catalogue raisonné* [ˌreizə'nei] [法]分科排列(附有解释)的目录

catalyst [ˈkætəlist] n.【化】催化剂,接触剂(旧译触媒) / [喻]刺激(或促进)因素

catapult [ˈkætəpʌlt] I n. ①弹弓,弹皮弓 ②古代的石弩 ③【军】(导弹或飞机的)弹射器 II ❶ *vt.* 用弹弓射;用弹射器发射;一下子把…抛到高处 ❷ *vi.* ①被发射 ②行动迅猛(指好象有发射器推动着) ‖~ *passage*【军】飞机弹射道

cataract [ˈkætərækt] n. ①大瀑布 ②奔流;大水,大雨 ③【医】内障,白内障

catarrh [kə'tɑː] n.【医】卡他,粘膜炎: intestinal ~ 肠卡他 ‖*~al* [kə'tɑːrəl] a.

catastrophe [kə'tæstrəfi] n. ①戏剧(尤指悲剧)的结局 ②大灾难,大祸;大败 ③大变动 ④【地】灾祸 ⑤【物】灾变 ‖**catastrophic** [ˌkætə'strɔfik] a. / **catastrophism** n.【地】灾变说

catch [kætʃ] I (caught [kɔːt]) ❶ *vt.* ①捉(住),抓住,逮住,捕获;钩住,截住,接住;【机】挡住,接收: ~ sb. *by* the arm 抓住某人的手臂 /

He *caught* his foot on a tree stub. 他的脚给树根绊了一下。/ I was *caught in* the downpour. 我被大雨淋着了。②赶上: ~ a train (bus) 赶上火车(公共汽车) / ~ the post 赶邮班 ③偶然(或突然)撞见,发觉: Let me ~ you at it again! 要是我再撞见你干这种事,你可要吃苦头了! (或: 别再干这种事!) / *Catch* me (或 You won't ~ me *doing* that again)! 我可不会再干那种事了! ④感染;着(火): ~ (a) cold 伤风 / ~ a fever 发热 ⑤打(中) ⑥听到,听清楚: 领会,理解: I didn't ~ the last two words. 最后两个字我没听清楚。/ Did you ~ my idea? 你懂得我的意思吗? ⑦引起(注意等): ~ sb.'s eye 引起某人的注意 ⑧突然制住(或中止): ~ one's breath 屏息 / ~ oneself (发觉自己讲错而)突然住嘴 ❷ *vi.* ①接,抓(住);锁住;(水)结(薄)冰: The lock won't ~. 这锁锁不上。/ This pond seldom ~*es*. 这池塘难得结冰。②被抓住;被钩住: His foot *caught* on a tree stub. 他的脚被树根绊了一下。③燃着: The match won't ~. 火柴擦不着。④(庄稼)茁壮起来 ⑤当棒球接手 II n. ①抓,接球;【化】(接)受器 ②捕获物(或量),(值得)获得的物(或人): That's no ~. 那是无足轻重的东西。(或: 那是得不偿失的东西。) ③窗钩,门扣;拉手 ④欺骗,诡计;难人的问题(或办法): There is a ~ in it (somewhere). 这里面有跷蹊。/ out-of-the-way and ~ questions 偏题和怪题 ⑤(声息等的)梗塞,噎 ⑥轮唱 ⑦(歌曲等的)片段 ⑧(庄稼的)茁壮 ‖ *~ as ~ can* 能抓到什么就抓什么,(用一切办法) / ~ *at* 想抓住;死命抓住;渴望取得: a drowning man ~*ing at* a straw 死命想抓住稻草的快溺死者 / ~ *it* [口]受责,受罚 / ~ *on* [口]①理解(*to*): I don't quite ~ *on* (*to* what he is saying). 我不很理解(他正在讲什么)。②变得流行 / ~ *sb. napping* 见 nap[1] / ~ *sb. out* 发现某人的错误: He was *caught out*. 他的错误被发觉了。/ ~ *sb. red-handed* 当场捉住某人 / ~ *up* ①赶上 (*to, with*): Go on in front; I'll soon ~ you *up*(或 ~ *up with* you). 你先走,我就会赶上你的。②握住,吸住,把…卷入: be *caught up* in the wave of 被卷入…的浪潮中 ③很快地拾合(或拿)起来 ④打断…的话 ⑤指出…出了差错 ⑥急忙采用(新词、新语等) ‖*~er* n. 捕捉者;捕捉器;棒球接手 ‖*~all* n. ①装杂物的容器(或地方) ②【化】截流器;分沫器;总受器 / '*~-as-* '*~-can* a. 用一切方法的;没有计划的,没有系统的 n. 兰开夏式摔角 ~ *basin* 放在阴沟口的滤污器 / ~ *crop*【农】填闲作物 / '*~cry* n. 吸引人们注意(或争取人们支持)的话(或口号) / ~ *drain* 截水沟,集水沟 / '*~fly* n.【植】捕虫瞿麦,捕蝇草 / '*~,penny* a. ①(商品)只为赚钱而制造的;不值钱的 ②起招徕作用的,不值钱的商品 / '*~phrase* n. 吸引人们注意的话(或字句) / '*~weed* n.【植】猪殃殃 / '*~word* n. ①(印在一页右下角)和下页第一个词相同的词 ②(词典等的)眉题(=guide word) ③戏剧说白的接头语 ④流行语,时髦话;标语,口号

catching ['kætʃiŋ] *a.* ①(疾病)传染性的 ②动人的,有感染力的

catchment ['kætʃmənt] *n.* ①集水 ②集水处 ③集水量 ‖~ **area** 汇水面积 / ~ **basin** 集水盆地

catchy ['kætʃi] *a.* ①吸引人的 ②(曲调等)易记的 ③使人上当的;难人的: a ~ question 难人的问题 ④时断时续的

catechism ['kætikizəm] *n.* ①问答教学法 ②【宗】教义问答手册 ③口试用的一系列提问 ‖put sb. through a ~ 严格盘问某人 ‖catechist *n.* 问答式教学者

catechize ['kætikaiz] *vt.* ①(常指宗教上)用问答法教学 ②盘问

categorical [,kæti'gɔrikəl] *a.* ①无条件的,绝对的 ② 明白的,明确的,断言的 ③范畴的 ‖~ly *ad.*

category ['kætigəri] *n.* ①种类,部属;类目 ②【数】范畴,类型 ③【哲】范畴

cater ['keitə] ❶ *vi.* ①供应伙食;提供娱乐节目(for, to): ~ for a banquet (wedding) 为宴会(婚礼)备办宴席 / a restaurant ~ing only to the Muslims 专供回教徒就餐的饭店,清真馆子 ②迎合,投合(for, to): ~ to the need of ... 迎合…的需要 ❷ *vt.* 为(宴会等)供应酒菜 ‖~er ['keitərə] *n.* 包办伙食的人;筹备文娱节目的人

caterpillar ['kætəpilə] *n.* ①【动】毛虫;蠋(一般指鳞翅目幼虫) ②履带拖拉机(或牵引车) (=~ tractor)

cathedral [kə'θi:drəl] Ⅰ *n.* (一个教区内的)总教堂;大教堂 Ⅱ *a.* ①大教堂的;象大教堂的 ②权威的

cathode ['kæθoud] *n.* 【电】阴极,负极(电源、电子管或电表等工作时电位较低的一个电极) ‖~ray【物】①(阴极发射出的)高速电子 ②阴极射线

Catholic ['kæθəlik] Ⅰ *a.* 天主教的 Ⅱ *n.* 天主教徒 ‖~ism [kə'θɔlisizəm], ~ity [,kæθə'lisiti] *n.* 天主教;天主教的教义(或信条等)

catholic ['kæθəlik] *a.* ①一般的,普遍的,广泛的: ~ tastes 广泛的兴趣 ②宽容的,气量大的 ‖~ally *ad.* / ~ity [,kæθə'lisiti] *n.*

cattle ['kætl] *n.* [总称] ①牛: Our team has five head of ~. 我们一队有五头牛。②牲口,家畜 ③卑鄙的人们 ‖kittle ~ 难以应付的人(或事物) ‖~ leader (牛)鼻环 / '~-lifter *n.* 偷牛(或家畜)的人 / ~-man 牧牛人,养牛人 / ~ pen 牛栏,牛圈,畜槛 / ~ plague 牛疫 / ~ rustler [美] 偷牛的人

caught [kɔ:t] catch 的过去式和过去分词

cauldron ['kɔ:ldrən] *n.* 大锅【化】煮皂锅

cauliflower ['kɔliflauə] *n.* ①【植】花椰菜(甘蓝的变种) ②花椰菜的头部(可供食用)

caulk [kɔ:k] *vt.* ①堵…的缝 ②【船】捻(船)的缝(用旧麻絮等填塞船板空隙);【机】敛…的缝(锤打铆打的钢板,使铆缝不漏水,不漏气) ‖~er *n.* 捻船缝的人;堵塞工具 / ~ing 堵缝,捻缝,敛缝

cause [kɔ:z] Ⅰ *n.* ①原因,起因: an internal (external) ~ 内(外)因 / ~ and effect 因果 ②理由,缘故;动机: There is no ~ for anxiety. 不必焦虑。/ without reason or ~ 无缘无故 ③事业,(奋斗的)目标: a just ~ 正义的事业 / the final ~ 最终目标 ④【律】诉因;案件 Ⅱ *vt.* ①使产生,使发生,引起: What ~d the accident? 是什么引起这个事故的? ②使遭受,给…带来: I'm afraid that I am causing you much trouble. 我怕我给你增添很多麻烦了。③使,促使: ~ sb. to do sth. 使某人做某事 / ~ sth. to be done 使某事做成 ‖make common ~ with 与…联合起来,与…合作 / the First Cause 【哲】第一推动力;【宗】上帝,造物主 ‖~less *a.* 无原因的;无正当(或明显)理由的 / ~r *n.* 引起者;根由

causeway ['kɔ:zwei], **causey** ['kɔ:zi] Ⅰ *n.* ①(穿越湿地的)堤道 ②高于路面的人行道 ③公路 Ⅱ *vt.* 在…上(或通过…)筑堤道(或人行道等)

caustic ['kɔ:stik] Ⅰ *a.* ①【化】苛性的,腐蚀(性)的 ②【物】焦散的 ③刻薄的,挖苦的,讽刺的 Ⅱ *n.* ①【医】腐蚀剂,苛性药;【化】苛性碱 ②【物】焦散曲线;焦散面 ‖~ally *ad.* 刻薄地,挖苦地 / ~ity [kɔ:s'tisiti] *n.* ①【化】苛性(度),腐蚀性 ②刻薄,挖苦 ‖~ curve 【物】焦散曲线 / ~ potash 苛性钾,氢氧化钾 / ~ soda 苛性钠,氢氧化钠 / ~ surface 【物】焦散面

cauterize ['kɔ:təraiz] *vt.* ①【医】烧灼,烙,腐蚀 ②使麻木不仁 ‖cauterization [,kɔ:tərai'zeiʃən] *n.*

caution ['kɔ:ʃən] Ⅰ *n.* ①小心,谨慎: When operating a machine, we must use ~. 在操纵机器时,我们必须谨慎。/ for ~'s sake 为慎重起见 / with ~ 小心翼翼地 ②告诫,警告: give sb. a ~ 给某人警告 ③[口]与众不同的人(或物) Ⅱ *vt.* 警告,告诫 (against, to, not to): I ~ed him against being late. 我告诫他不要迟到。/ The veteran worker ~ed me not to inspect the machine without first turning off power. 老工人告诫我不要在关断电源前就去检查机器。‖fling ~ to the winds 不顾一切;行事鲁莽 ‖~ary *a.* 告诫的,警告的 / ~ money 英国大学的入学保证金;英国法学协会入会的保证金

cautious ['kɔ:ʃəs] *a.* 细心的,谨慎的: The students are ~ not to make any mistakes in spelling. 学生们在拼写时非常小心,以避免发生错误。/ be ~ of 留心…,谨防… ‖~ly *ad.* / ~ness *n.*

cavalcade [,kævəl'keid] *n.* ①骑马队伍;车队;船队 ②游行行列

cavalier [,kævə'liə] Ⅰ *n.* ①骑士 ②对女人献殷勤的男子 ③[C-] 英国查理一世时代的保皇党党员 Ⅱ *a.* ①自由自在的;豪强的 ②献殷勤的 ③傲慢的

cavalry ['kævəlri] *n.* ①[总称]骑兵 ②【军】高度机动的地面部队(包括骑兵部队、机械化部队和摩托化部队) ‖'~man *n.* 骑兵

cave[1] [keiv] Ⅰ *n.* ①山洞,窑洞 ②地窖 ③[英]脱

党; 一群脱党者 **II** ❶ *vt.* ①在…挖(窑)洞 ②使
陷下; 使倒坍, 使崩溃 ③暗中破坏 ❷ *vi.* ①陷下,
倒坍 ②投降, 停止抵抗 ‖~ *in* ①(使)下陷, 坍
陷 ②[口]屈服, 投降; 垮掉 ‖~ **dweller** (史前
的)穴居人 / ~ **dwelling** 窑洞 / '~-**house** *n.*
窑洞 / '~-**in** *n.* 塌方(矿井、地道等的坍陷) /
'~**man** *n.* (石器时代的)穴居人; 行动与感情象
原始人的人

cave² ['keivi] *int.* [英][学俚]当心(老师来了)!

cavern ['kævən] **I** *n.* 大洞穴, 大山洞 **II** *vt.* ①
置…于山洞中 ②挖空 (*out*) ‖~**ed** *a.* 洞穴状的,
在洞穴中的, 有洞穴的

cavil ['kævil] **I** (cavil(l)ed; cavil(l)ing) ❶ *vi.* 挑
剔, 吹毛求疵, 找岔子 (*at, about*) ❷ *vt.* 对…挑
剔, 找…的岔子 **II** *n.* 吹毛求疵 ‖**cavil(l)er** *n.*
吹毛求疵的人

cavity ['kæviti] *n.* ①洞; 中空 ②[解]腔, 窝:
abdominal ~ 腹腔

cayenne [kei'en] *n.* 辣椒, 辣椒粉 ‖~ **pepper**
['keien 'pepə] 辣椒粉, 辣椒

cease [si:s] **I** ❶ *vi.* 停, 息: The rain has ~d. 雨
停了。/ ~ *from* quarrelling 停止吵架 ❷ *vt.*
停止, 结束: Cease fire! 【军】停火! / ~ talking
停止谈话 / ~ to exist 灭亡, 不再存在 **II** *n.* 停
息: They worked on without ~. 他们不停地工
作下去。‖'~-'**fire** *n.* 停火命令; 停火

ceaseless ['si:slis] *a.* 不停的, 不绝的: make ~
efforts to improve the quality of the products 不
断努力提高产品质量 ‖~**ly** *ad.* / ~**ness** *n.*

cedar ['si:də] *n.* 【植】①雪松 ②类似雪松的树(如
铅笔柏、杉等) ③雪松(或铅笔柏等)的木材 ‖~**n**
a. [诗]雪松(制)的, 杉木(制)的

cede [si:d] *vt.* 割让, 让与, 放弃

ceiling ['si:liŋ] *n.* ①天花板; 顶篷 ②(规定价格、
工资等的)最高限度 ③[空]升限, 上升限度; 云幕
高度; 绝对升限 ④[船]舱底垫板; 舱室内覆板
‖*hit the* ~ [美俚]①(大学里)考试失败(尤指
由于紧张而考不及格) ② 勃然大怒; 极度激动
‖~ **capacity** [空]上升能力 / ~ **height** 【空】
升限, 上升限度; 云幕高度

celebrate ['selibreit] ❶ *vt.* ①庆祝: ~ a victory
庆祝胜利 ②歌颂, 赞美 ③举行(仪式) ❷ *vi.* ①庆
祝 ②举行宗教仪式 ③[口]欢宴作乐 ‖~**d** *a.*
著名的, 驰名的 / **celebrator** *n.* 庆祝的人

celebration [ˌseli'breiʃən] *n.* ①庆祝, 庆祝会; 典
礼: in ~ of 为庆祝… / hold a ~ 举行庆祝(会)
②公共的宗教仪式

celebrity [si'lebriti] *n.* ①著名, 名声 ②著名人士

celerity [si'leriti] *n.* 迅速, 敏捷

celery ['seləri] *n.* 【植】芹菜; [C-]芹属

celery

celestial [si'lestjəl; 美 si'lestʃəl] **I** *a.* ①天的; 天
空的; 天上的: a ~ body 天体 / a ~ globe 天
球仪 / the ~ latitude (longitude) 黄纬(经) / ~
navigation 天体导航法 / ~ photography 天体
照相学 / the Celestial City 【宗】天国 / the
Celestial Empire 天朝(指封建时代的中国) ②神
圣的 ③[C-] (指封建时代的)中国的 **II** *n.* ①天
上的人, 神仙 ② [C-] (指封建时代的)中国人
‖~**ly** *ad.*

celibacy ['selibəsi] *n.* ①独身生活; 独身 ②禁欲

celibate ['selibit] **I** *n.* 独身生活的人 **II** *a.* 独身的

cell [sel] *n.* ①小房间; 单人牢房; [诗]村舍; 隐居
者所住的小屋; (大修道院的)附属修道院, (修道
院中的)密室: a condemned ~ 死刑犯监禁室 ②
【生】细胞 ③盒, 槽; 蜂房的巢室; (昆虫的)翅室
④【植】子房室; 花粉囊 ⑤【电】(原)电池 ⑥【无】
元件, 单元 ⑦[空]机翼构架; (气球等的)气囊 ⑧
【原】晶胞, 晶格 ⑨【气】单体, 环型 ⑩(政治运动
和党派的)基层组织 ‖*a dry* ~ 干电池 / *fuel* ~
【化】燃料箱; 【物】热元件, 燃料电池 /*photoelectric*
~ 【物】光电管 / *thermoelectric* ~ 【物】温差电
偶; 热电元件 ‖*the narrow* ~ 墓 ‖'~**block** *n.*
(若干监房组成的)监狱分区 / ~ **division** 细胞
分裂

cellar ['selə] **I** *n.* ①地窖, 地下室 ②酒窖; 藏酒量
II *vt.* 把…藏入地窖(或酒窖) ‖*from ~ to rafter*
整幢房子, 上上下下 / *keep a good* ~ 藏有大
量的酒 / *the* ~ [口]象牙 ②[美]最低点 ‖~**er** ['selərə]
n. 管地窖的人

cello, 'cello ['tʃelou] *n.* 大提琴 (violoncello 的简
称) ‖**cellist** ['tʃelist] *n.* 大提琴手; 大提琴家

cellophane ['seləfein] *n.* 玻璃纸, 赛璐玢

celluloid ['seljuloid] **I** *a.* 细胞状的 **II** *n.* 【化】
赛璐珞; 假象牙; 硝纤(假)象牙 ②[美]电影胶片

cellulose ['seljulous] *n.* 植物纤维质素; 【化】纤维
素: ~ acetate 醋酸纤维素

cement [si'ment] **I** *n.* ①水泥: ~ flour 水泥粉 /
~ grit 水泥烧粒 / ~ mortar 水泥灰浆 ②胶
泥; 胶黏剂, 结合剂; (牙科等用的)粘固粉 ③【解】
牙骨质 **II** ❶ *vt.* ①用水泥抹 ②用水泥涂 ③粘
接, 胶合 ③【冶】对…进行渗碳处理: ~ed steel
渗碳钢 ④巩固, 加强; 凝成, 把…结合在一起 ❷
vi. 粘紧, 粘牢: Snow is ~ing. 雪正在凝结。

cemetery ['semitri] *n.* 公墓; 墓地

cenotaph ['senətɑ:f] *n.* 衣冠墓; (为葬于别处的死
者所立的)纪念碑

censor ['sensə] **I** *n.* ①(古罗马调查户口、检查社会
风纪等的)监察官 ②(新闻、电影、书刊等的)审查
员, (信件、电报等的)检查员; 【军】保密检查; 保密
检查员 ③[英]大学学监 ④[心]潜意识压抑力
II *vt.* ①审查(新闻、书刊、电影等), 检查(信件、
电报等) ②删改 ‖~**ial** [sen'sɔ:riəl] *a.* 监察官
的; 审查员的, 检查员的

censorship ['sensəʃip] *n.* ①审查(制度), 检查(制
度); 【军】保密检查 ②检查员(或审查员)的职位
③古罗马监察官的职位 ④【心】潜意识压抑力

censure ['senʃə] I *vt.* 指责,非难,苛评 II *n.* ①指责,非难: a vote of ~ on sb. 对某人的不信任投票 ②训斥

census ['sensəs] I *n.* ① 人口调查,人口普查: take a ~ 调查人口 ②(调查得来的)统计数字 II *vt.* 调查(地区等)的人口数字;统计…的数字 || ~ **paper** 人口(或户口)调查表

cent [sent] *n.* ①分(货币单位) ②分币 ③百: five per ~ 百分之五 (5%) || *not care a* ~ 毫不在乎 / *put in one's two* ~s (*worth*) 发表意见;发言

centenarian [ˌsenti'neəriən] I *n.* 百岁(或百岁以上)的老人 II *a.* 百岁(或百岁以上)的;一百周年的

centenary [sen'ti:nəri] I *a.* 一百年的,一世纪的;一百周年的 II *n.* ①一百年,一世纪 ②一百周年纪念

centennial [sen'tenjəl] I *a.* ①(每)一百年的;一百周年纪念的 ②一百岁的;继续了一百年的 II *n.* ①一百(周)年 ②一百周年纪念

centigrade ['sentigreid] *a.* ①百分度的 ②摄氏温度计的 || ~ **thermometer** 摄氏温度计

centigram(me) ['sentigræm] *n.* 厘克 (=1/100 克,略作 cg.)

centimetre, centimeter ['senti,mi:tə] *n.* 公分,厘米 (=1/100 米,略作 cm.)

centipede ['sentipi:d] *n.* 【动】蜈蚣

central ['sentrəl] I *a.* ①中心的: ~ heating (大厦中的)集中供暖(法) ②主要的: a ~ figure 主要人物 / the ~ idea of an article 文章的主题思想 / an argument ~ to a question 对某一问题极为重要的论据 ③中枢的; 中枢神经系统的: ~ nervous system 【解】中枢神经系统 ④走中间道路的 ⑤【语】(中)央的: a ~ vowel (中)央元音 II *n.* 【美】电话总机; 电话接线员 || ~ly *ad.* / ~ness *n.* || ~ **torce** 【物】辏力,有心力 / ~ **staging** 观众围着舞台四周坐的剧场(布置)

centralize ['sentrəlaiz] ❶ *vi.* 形成中心,集中 ❷ *vt.* ① 成为…的中心;把…集中起来 ② 把(权力等)集中在中央组织;使(国家等)实行中央集权制 || **centralization** [ˌsentrəlai'zeiʃən] *n.*

centre ['sentə] I *n.* ①中心;中央: the ~ of a circle 圆心 / the ~ of attraction 引力中心;惹眼的人(或物) / the ~ of gravity 重心 ②中心区: the shopping ~ of a town 城镇的商业区 ③中枢,核心; 神经中枢 ④中心站: a health ~ 医疗站 / a control ~ 调度中心,调度所;(导弹发射等的)控制中心 ⑤[有时作 C-] (政党等的)中间派;中间派的意见 ⑥(球队的)中锋;(军队或舞台的)中部 ⑦【建】拱架; 中心点 ⑧【机】中心;顶针;顶尖: dead ~ (冲程的)死点,静点;(车床的)死顶针 II ❶ *vt.* ①集中,使聚集在一点: ~ attention (efforts) *on* 把注意力(精力)集中在…上 ②把…放在中部: ~ a picture on the wall 把画挂在墙壁的中部 ③定…的中心;矫

正(透镜等)的中心 ④传(球)给中锋 ❷ *vi.* 居中,有中心,被置于中心: The discussion ~s on (或 *round*) the most important question. 讨论集中在最重要的问题上。|| ~**less** *a.* 无中心的 / ~**most** *a.* 在最中心的 || ~ **bit**, ~ **drill** 【机】中心钻 / '~**board** *n.* ①船底中心垂直升降板(遇大风时,可降入水中,以免船身倾斜) ② 装有升降板的小船 / '~**fold** *n.* 一期报纸中最中间的一张 / ~ **forward** (足球等的)中锋 / '~**piece** *n.* 在中央的东西;放在餐桌中央的装饰品

centrifugal [sen'trifjugəl] I *a.* ①离心的;利用离心力的: ~ force 【物】离心力 / ~ inflorescence 【植】离心花序 / ~ machine 【机】离心机 / ~ pump 【机】离心泵 ②【生】输出的,排泄的 II *n.* 离心机 || ~**ly** *ad.*

centripetal [sen'tripitl] *a.* ①向心的: ~ force 【物】向心力 / ~ inflorescence 【植】向心花序 / ~ pump 【机】向心泵 ②【生】输入的 || ~**ly** *ad.*

centurion [sen'tjuəriən] *n.* (古罗马军团的)百人队队长

century ['sentʃuri] *n.* ①世纪;百年: in the eighties of the twentieth ~ (或 in the 80's of the 20th ~) 在二十世纪八十年代 ②百个;板球中的一百分: a ~ of poems 一百首诗 ③百元(钞票);百镑(钞票) ④古罗马军团中的百人队;古罗马选民单位 || **centuries-'old** *a.* 历史悠久的 / ~ **plant** 【植】龙舌兰(世纪树)

ceramic [si'ræmik] I *a.* 陶器的,陶瓷的;制陶的: the ~ industry 陶瓷工业 / ~ cutting tools 【机】陶瓷合金刀具 II *n.* ①一件陶瓷制品; [复][总称]陶瓷制品: refractory ~s 高温陶瓷 / artistic ~s 美术陶瓷 ②[~s] [用作单]制陶术; 陶瓷学

cereal ['siəriəl] I *a.* 谷类的;谷类植物的;谷类制成的 II *n.* ①[常用复]谷类;谷类植物 ②(加工过的)谷类食物(如麦片等)

cerebral ['seribrəl] *a.* ①脑的;大脑的: ~ cortex 【解】大脑皮层, 大脑皮质 / ~ haemorrhage (anaemia) 脑溢血(贫血) / ~ hemispheres 大脑(两)半球 ②(文学、音乐等)触动理智的;理智方面的(指非感情的)

ceremonial [ˌseri'mounjəl] I *a.* 礼仪的,仪式的;正式的: ~ dress 礼服 / ~ usage 礼节上的惯例 II *n.* 礼仪,仪式 || ~**ly** *ad.*

ceremonious [ˌseri'mounjəs] *a.* ①仪式隆重的: a ~ welcome 盛大的欢迎 ②(过分)讲究礼节的: a ~ person (过分)讲究礼节的人 ③客套的;死板的 || ~**ly** *ad.* / ~**ness** *n.*

ceremony ['seriməni; 美 'seri,mouni] *n.* ①典礼,仪式: perform the opening (closing) ~ 举行开幕(闭幕)式 / the launching ~ of a new ocean liner 一艘新的远洋轮船的下水典礼 / elaborate *ceremonies* (包括多项的)隆重典礼 / a master of (the) *ceremonies* 典礼官;司仪 ②礼节,礼仪 ③虚礼,客气 || *stand on* (或 *upon*) ~ 讲究客套(而不亲切);客气: Please don't *stand on* ~. 请不要拘礼。/ *without* ~ 不拘礼节地

certain ['sə:tən] **I** *a.* ①确凿的，无疑的: The evidence is ~. 证据确凿。 ②可靠的: a ~ remedy for ... 治疗…有效的药/纠正…的可靠方法 ③[只作表语]一定的，必然的；确信的，有把握的: I am ~ (that) .... 我确信…/ I am not ~ whether .... 我不能确定是否… ④[只作定语]某，某一，某种，一定的: a ~ unit 某单位；某部队/ a ~ Smith 一个姓史密斯的人/ on ~ conditions 在某些条件下，在某种情况下/ to a ~ extent 在一定程度上 ⑤[只作表语]一些: have a ~ hesitation 有点儿犹豫不决 **II** *pron.* 某几个; 某些: ~ of his friends 他的某些朋友 ‖for ~ 肯定地；确凿地: I cannot say for ~. 我说不准。/ I don't know for ~. 我不确切知道。/ **make** ~ (把…)弄确实，弄清楚: make ~ when the train leaves 弄清楚火车什么时候开 / make ~ of the date of the meeting 把开会日期弄清楚

certainly ['sə:tənli] *ad.* ① 一定，必定: Victory ~ belongs to the people! 胜利一定属于人民! ②[口]当然; 当然可以: A: Are you going with us? B: Certainly! 甲:你跟我们一起去吗? 乙:当然! / A: May I borrow your pen? B: Certainly! 甲:我可以借用你的笔吗? 乙:当然可以!

certainty ['sə:tənti] *n.* 必然的事,毫无疑问的事;必然,确实,肯定: It can be said with ~ that .... 可以断言… ‖for a ~ 确实无疑地: know for a ~ that ... 确实知道… / to a ~ 必然,一定

certificate **I** [sə'tifikit] *n.* ①证(明)书,执照: a birth (marriage) ~ 出生(结婚)证书/ a health ~ 健康证明书/ a medical ~ 诊断书 ②证券,单据: a ~ of deposit 存款单 ③证明 **II** [sə'tifikeit] *vt.* 发证书给…;用证书证明 ‖~d [sə'tifikeitid] *a.* 有(授权)证书的

certify ['sə:tifai] ❶ *vt.* ①(用保证书或许可证等)证明: This is to ~ that .... 兹证明… / The accounts were certified (as) correct. 帐目被证明为正确无误。 ②(医生)诊断(某人)是疯子 ③[美](银行)担保(支票)的可靠性 ❷ *vi.* 用书面形式证明 (to) ‖certifier *n.* 证明者

certitude ['sə:titju:d] *n.* ①确信 ②必然性,确实性

cessation [se'seiʃən] *n.* 停止,休止: ~ of hostilities 停战;休战/ without ~ 无休止地

cession ['seʃən] *n.* (领土的)割让;(权利、财产等的)让与或转让

cesspool ['sespu:l] *n.* ①污水渗井;污水池 ②[喻]污秽场所;藏垢纳污之地

chafe [tʃeif] **I** ❶ *vt.* ①擦热(双手或皮肤) ②擦破,擦伤,擦痛 ③惹怒;使急躁: The loud noise ~d him. 吵闹声使他烦躁。 ❷ *vi.* ①(动物)用身体擦(铁笼等) ②(河流)冲洗(崖岸等) (against, on) ③发怒,焦躁: ~ at the delay 因拖延而感到焦躁/ ~ under restraint (insults) 因受到约束(侮辱)而感到恼怒 **II** *n.* ①摩擦;擦伤(处) ②焦躁,发怒: in a ~ 愤怒,焦躁

chaff [tʃɑ:f] **I** *n.* ①[总称]谷壳 ②秕,切细的稻草(作饲料用) ③无价值的东西 ④诙谐;打趣 **II** *vt. & vi.* (对…)打趣,(跟…)开玩笑 ‖be caught with ~ 上当,受欺骗 ‖~·cutter *n.* 切草(作饲料)机

chagrin **I** ['ʃægrin; 美 ʃə'grin] *n.* 懊恼,悔恨,委屈: to sb.'s ~ 使某人懊恼的是 **II** ['ʃægrin, ʃə'gri:n; 美 ʃə'grin] *vt.* 使懊恼,使悔恨: be (或 feel) ~ed at (或 by) 因…而懊恼

chain [tʃein] **I** *n.* ①链,链条;项链;表链: a bicycle ~ 自行车链条/ an anchor ~ 锚链 ②[用复]枷锁,镣铐;囚禁;束缚: in ~s 上着镣铐; 在囚禁中/ a ~ on sb.'s mind 某人思想上的束缚 ③一连串,一系列;连锁: a ~ of events 一串的事件/ a ~ of mountains 山脉,山系 ④【测】测链 (=20.1168 米) ⑤【纺】经纱 ⑥【电】电路 (=circuit) ⑦【化】链 ⑧(一个公司下属的)联号 **II** *vt.* ①用链条拴住; 拘禁; 束缚: ~ a gate 用链条把大门锁住/ ~ a boat to a tree 用链条把船拴在树上/ ~ed to one's work 工作忙得难以脱身 ②【测】用测链测量 ‖A (或 The) ~ is no stronger than its weakest link. [谚]一环薄弱,全局必垮。 (常指一个破绽便使整个一论点站不住脚) ‖~less *a.* 无链的;无束缚的/ ~let ['tʃeinlit] *n.* 小链子 ‖~ armo(u)r =~ mail / ~ belt 链带/ ~ brake 链闸;链刹车/ ~ bridge 链式吊桥/ ~ cable 锚链/ ~ coupling 【机】链形联接器/ ~ gang 用链拴在一起的囚犯队/ ~ letter 连锁信(要求收信人看过信后复写成一定份数,再分寄给其他人,如此不断持续以扩大收信人范围)/ ~ locker 锚链舱/ ~ mail 锁子甲/ ~man *n.* ['tʃeinmən] *n.* 测链员/ ~ mo(u)lding 【建】链饰,链条花边/ ~ plate 【海】系链钮;系索钮/ ~ pump 链泵/ '~-re'act *vi.* 发生连锁反应/ ~ reaction 连锁反应/ ~ riveting 并列铆,并列铆接/ ~ rule 【数】连锁法/ ~ saw 链锯/ ~ shot 链弹/ '~-smoke *vi.* 一支接一支地抽(烟)/ ~ smoker 一支接一支抽烟的人/ ~ stitch 【纺】链状针迹;链状线圈;绞花组织/ ~ store [美]联号(同一公司下属的商店)/ ~ timber 【建】系木;木圈梁/ '~wale *n.* 【海】护桅索承扣板/ ~ wheel 链轮,滑轮

chair [tʃeə] **I** *n.* ①椅子,单人靠背椅,单人扶手椅: Won't you take a ~? 你请坐好吗? / sit on a ~ 坐在椅子上/ sit in a ~ 坐在扶手椅子里/ an easy ~ 安乐椅/ a double ~ 双人椅/ a folding ~ 折椅 ②(会议的)主席;议长;会长;主席席位(或职位): Chair! Chair! 主席! 主席! (表示要求维持会场秩序)/ address the ~ (开会时)向主席讲话(表示要求发言)/ appeal to the ~ (开会时)请主席裁决/ in the ~ (开会时)担任主席;处在主席地位/ leave the ~ (开会时的主席)结束会议/ take the ~ (担任会议主席)开始会议/ The ~ is calling for order. [美](开会时)主席在叫大家遵守秩序。 ③大学教授的

职位(或讲座): hold a ～ of Chinese literature 当中国文学教授 ④(铁路)轨座 ⑤[美]电椅: go to (或 get) the ～ 被处(上电椅的)死刑 / send sb. to the ～ 把某人处(上电椅的)死刑 ⑥轿子 ⑦[美]证人席 ⑧单马轻便马车 Ⅱ vt. ①使人座 ②使就任要职(或名誉职) ③任(会议)的主席 ④[英]把(比赛、选举等中的得胜者)用椅子高抬着走 ‖'～bed n. 坐卧两用的椅子 / '～borne a. [美俚]坐办公室的(尤指不参加战斗的军官) / ～ car ①有活动座椅的(铁路)客车 ②有舒适的单人座椅的豪华客车 / ～ rail【建】护墙板; 靠椅栏 / '～,warmer n. [美俚]闲荡汉, 懒汉

chairman ['tʃɛəmən] Ⅰ ([复] chairmen) n. ①主席 ②议长; 委员长 ③抬轿人 Ⅱ (chairman(n)ed; chairman(n)ing) vt. 当(会议等)的主席(或议长等) ‖～ship n. 主席(或议长等)的职位(或身分)

chaise [ʃeiz] n. 两轮(或四轮)轻便马车

chalet ['ʃælei] n. ①瑞士的木造农舍; 阿尔卑斯山区的牧人小屋 ②农舍式的房屋; 避暑处(或休假地)的小屋

chalice ['tʃælis] n. ①(高脚)酒杯; 圣餐杯 ②【植】杯状花

chalk [tʃɔːk] Ⅰ n. ①白垩 ②粉笔; 颜色粉笔: a piece of ～ 一枝粉笔 / some coloured ～s 几枝颜色粉笔 / a ～ drawing 粉笔画 ③用粉笔划的记号 ④[英]比赛的得分 Ⅱ vt. ①用粉笔写(或画) ②用白垩粉擦 ③打…的图样 ④用粉笔记下(货帐等) ⑤[英]往(田里)施白垩 ‖as like as ～ and (或 to) cheese 外貌相似而实质不同的 / by a long ～ (或 by long ～s) [英]相差很大 / ～ it up ①把它宣布出去 ②把它记在帐上 / ～ out 打…的图样; 计划 / ～ up ①记下(分数、货帐等) ②达到, 得到 / not know ～ from cheese 不辨黑白 / stump one's ～s 跑开; 逃走 / walk the ～(s) ①在粉笔线中间直线行走(以证明并未喝醉) ② 遵守规矩 ‖～ bed 【地】白垩层 / '～stone n. 石灰岩; 【医】痛风石 / '～-talk n. 用粉笔在黑板上(作图)说明的讲话

challenge ['tʃælindʒ] Ⅰ n. ①挑战; 要求决斗; 邀请比赛: give (accept) a ～ 挑(应)战 / a letter of ～ 挑战书 / a ～ tennis match 网球邀请赛 ②要求, 需要; 鞭策: look upon . . . as a ～ to greater exertions 把…看作进一步努力的鞭策 ③(对某一表决票或某人投票资格表示的)异议; 质问; 怀疑 ④【军】查问时用的口令: A sentry gave the ～, "Who goes there?" 哨兵喝问: "谁?" ⑤【律】(对某陪审员出庭等表示的)反对 ⑥要求船只(或飞机等)回答的信号 ⑦用接触致病性传染物所进行的免疫性试验 Ⅱ ❶ vt. ①要求; 挑动: ～ sb. to a contest 向某人提出挑战要求比赛 / He ～d me to try again. 他挑战似地要我再试一下。②要求, 需要; 引起: ～ attention (admiration) 使人们非注意(赞扬)不可 / ～ sb.'s interest 引起某人的兴趣 ③ 对…表示异议; 非难; 怀疑:

～ sb.'s right to vote 对某人的投票权表示异议 ④【军】向…发出查问的口令 ⑤【律】宣布反对(某陪审员等) ❷ vi. ①提出挑战 ②表示异议; 反对 ③(猎犬在嗅到兽迹时)吠 ‖beyond ～ 无与伦比; 无可非难 / rise to the ～ ①接受挑战, 迎战 ②(善于)应付某种复杂局面 / take a ～ lying down 对挑战俯首屈服 / ‖～r n. 挑战者; 反对者; 查问口令者 / challenging a. 挑战的; 引起争论的 ‖～ cup 优胜杯 / ～ flag 优胜旗

chamber ['tʃeimbə] Ⅰ n. ①房间, 寝室; [英][复]单人的套间 ②议院: the lower (upper) ～ 下(上)议院 ③(立法或司法机关的)会议室, 会议厅; 会所: a ～ of commerce 商会 ④[复]法官的议事室; 高级官员的接待室 ⑤(枪的)弹膛, 药室 ⑥(动植物体内的)腔, 室 ⑦便壶, 夜壶 Ⅱ a. ①(音乐)室内的, 小规模的: ～ music 室内乐(少数人演奏的音乐, 例如四重奏等) / a ～ orchestra 小型管弦乐队 / a ～ organ 小型风琴 ②私人的, 秘密的: a ruler's ～ council 统治者的私人顾问团 Ⅲ vt. ①把…关在房间里; 禁闭: be ～ed in a narrow cave 被关在狭窄的洞穴里 ②使备有房间: a ～ed corridor 旁边有房间的走廊 ③装(弹药) ‖'～maid n. (旅馆或寝室的)女服务员, 侍女 / ～ pot 便壶, 夜壶

chamberlain ['tʃeimbəlin] n. ①国王的内侍; 贵族的管家: Lord Chamberlain (of the Household) (英国的)宫廷大臣 / Lord Great Chamberlain (of England) (英国的)掌礼大臣 ②财务管理人

chameleon [kə'miːljən] n. ①【动】变色蜥蜴, 变色龙 ②反复无常的人 ③ [C-]【天】蝘蜓座 ‖～ic [kə,miːli'ɔnik] a. 象变色龙的; 反复无常的

chamois ['ʃæmwa:] ([复] chamois ['ʃæmwa:z]) n. ①【动】(产于欧洲和高加索地区的)山羊般的小羚羊 ②羚羊皮, 麂皮, 油鞣革

champ¹ [tʃæmp] Ⅰ ❶ vt. ①(马等)大声地嚼(或咬) ②捣烂 ❷ vi. ①(马等)大声咀嚼, 发出咬牙响声 ②不耐烦, 焦急 Ⅱ n. 嚼, 嚼声

champ² [tʃæmp] n. [口]冠军 (=champion)

champagne [ʃæm'pein] n. ①香槟酒 ②香槟酒(似)的颜色(指淡橙黄色、浅灰褐色)

champaign ['tʃæmpein] n. 平原, 原野

champion ['tʃæmpjən] Ⅰ n. ①战士, 斗士; (主义等)的拥护者 ②得胜者; 冠军: table tennis world ～s in men's and women's singles 男女乒乓球单打世界冠军 / a boxing ～ 拳击冠军 ③提倡者: a ～ of mass physical culture 群众体育运动的提倡者 Ⅱ a. [俗]优胜的, 第一流的: the ～ team 冠军队 / a ～ idiot 大傻瓜 Ⅲ vt. 拥护, 支持: ～ a just cause 支持正义事业 ‖～less a. 无冠军的

championship ['tʃæmpjənʃip] n. ①冠军的地位, 冠军称号: He won four ～s in five years. 他五年内四次获得冠军称号。②锦标赛: the World Table Tennis Championships 世界乒乓球锦标赛 ③拥护, 支持; 提倡: sb.'s ～ of the new theory 某人对于新学说的拥护 ④ 保持冠军称号的期间

chance [tʃɑːns] **I** *n.* ①机会: It's the ~ of a lifetime. 这是一生难得的机会。②[常用复]可能性; 或然性: There is a ~ that.... 有可能… / Chances (或 The ~s) are (that) the new machine will arrive tomorrow. 新机器明天可能运到。/ The ~s are ten to one that we will win. 我们十之八九会胜。③偶然性, 运气: leave it to ~ 听任命运, 任其自然 **II** *a.* 偶然的: a ~ meeting 偶然的相遇 / a ~ acquaintance 偶然相识的人 **III** ❶ *vi.* 碰巧; 偶然发生: I ~d to see your father in the street. 我碰巧在街上看到了你的父亲。/ It (so) ~d that I was in the countryside at the time. 那时我恰巧在乡下。❷ *vt.* 冒…的险: ~ it [口] 碰碰运气看 ‖ *a fat* ~ 见 **fat** / *a game of* ~ 见 **game** / *an off* ~ 万一的希望; 很小的可能: There is an off ~ of finding him at home. 很少有希望在他家里找到他。/ *as it may* ~ 要看当时情况 (不能预料) / *by any* ~ 万一; 碰巧: If, by any ~, he fails to come, we'll ask Hsiao Li to work the machine. 万一他不来, 我们就叫小李开机器。/ *by* ~ 偶然; 意外地 / ~ *on* (或 *upon*) 碰巧遇见; 偶然发现 / ~ *one's arm* [英口] 冒险一试 / *not* (*even*) *a dog's* ~ 一点机会也没有 / *on the* ~ *of* 怀着…的希望, 期望… / *a good* (*stand no*) ~ 很有 (没有) 可能, 大有 (没有) 希望: He stands a good ~ of succeeding in the experiment. 他的实验很有成功的希望。/ *take a* ~ (或 *take* ~*s*) 冒险; 投机: take a ~ with the weather 怀着天气可能会好的侥幸心情 (而冒险出游等) / *take one's* ~ 碰运气, 听任命运 / *the main* ~ 发财的机会, 得意的机会 ‖ '~-'**medley** *n.* 【律】①非有意的杀人, 过失杀人 ②偶然的行动; 偶然性

chancellor ['tʃɑːnsələ] *n.* ① [英] 大臣, 司法官: the Lord Chancellor (或 the Chancellor of England, the Lord High Chancellor) 大法官 (阁员之一, 兼任上议院议长) / the Chancellor of the Exchequer 财政大臣 ② [英] 大使馆 (或领事馆) 的一等秘书 ③ (英国某些大学的) 名誉校长; (美国某些大学的) 校长 ④ (奥地利等国的) 总理 (或首相) ⑤ (美国某些州) 平衡法院的法官 ‖~-**ship** *n.* 大臣 (或大法官、总理等) 的职位

chancery ['tʃɑːnsəri] *n.* ① [C-] 英国大法官法庭 (今属英格兰高等法院一部) ② [美] 平衡法院 (美国平衡法院的法律和诉讼事务 ③ 档案馆 ④ 大臣 (或总理、大使馆等) 的办事处

chandelier [ˌʃændi'liə] *n.* 枝形吊灯

chandelier

chandler ['tʃɑːndlə] *n.* ①蜡烛 (或肥皂等) 商人; 蜡烛 (或肥皂等) 制造人 ②杂货零售商: a ship ~ 出售船用杂货 (如绳索、帆布等) 的商人

change [tʃeindʒ] **I** ❶ *vt.* ① 改变, 变革, 改造: ~ reality 变革现实 / ~ the world 改造世界 / ~ one's mind 改变主意 / ~ one's name (address) 改名字 (地址) ② 换去; 交换; 以…换; 兑换: ~ one's clothes 换衣服 / ~ the subject 换话题 / ~ seats with sb. 与某人调换座位 / ~ A for B 用 A 去换 B ❷ *vi.* ①变, 改变, 变化 ②换衣; 换车 (船等): Wait, it won't take me long to ~. 等一下, 我很快就可以换好衣服。/ ~ into one's working clothes 换上工作服 / Where do we ~? 我们在哪里换车? / ~ to a local train 换乘区间车 / All ~! (火车等到达终点站时招呼乘客用语)全部下车! **II** *n.* ① 改变, 变化, 转变: a ~ for the better (worse) 好转 (变坏) / a ~ from cold to hot 从冷变热 / a ~ in one's world outlook 世界观的转变 ② 更换, 调换; 替换物: make a ~ in the plan 对计划作一点更动 / a ~ of air 换换空气 (尤指易地疗养) / Take a ~ of clothes with you. 把你替换的衣服带去吧。③找头; 零钱; 辅币: Here is your ~. 这是你的找头。/ I have no ~ about me. 我身边没有零钱。/ loose (或 small) ~ 零钱 / ② 交易所 (常作 'change) ⑤ [音] 转调, 换调 ‖*a* ~ *of heart* ①改变主意 ②变心; 变节 ③弃邪归正 / *a* ~ *of scene* 改换环境 (尤指通过旅行) / ~ *about* 见异思迁; 变节 / ~ *down* (*up*) (汽车) 把变速器换到低 (高) 档, 开慢 (快) / ~ *foot* 见 **foot** / ~ *of life* 月经停止 / *for a* ~ 为了改变一下 / *get no* ~ *out of sb.* 不能胜过某人 (指辩论、商业竞争等) / *give sb.* ~ 给某人以相应的报答 (含有讽刺之意) / *put the* ~ *on sb.* 欺骗某人; 对某人隐瞒 / *ring the* ~*s* 敲奏各种钟调; 用种种方法说 (或做) / *take the* (或 *one's*) ~ *out of sb.* 对某人报复 / ~ *gear,* ~ *wheel* 【机】变速轮 / '~'**over** *n.* ①改变, 转变; 变更, 转换 ② (电影影片切割时) 换机映 / '**changing-room** *n.* 更衣室

changeable ['tʃeindʒəbl] *a.* 可变的; 易变的; 不定的 ‖**changeability** [ˌtʃeindʒə'biliti], ~**ness** *n.* / **changeably** *ad.*

channel ['tʃænl] **I** *n.* ① 海峡, 水道; 航道: the (English) Channel 英吉利海峡 ②河床, 河底 ③沟渠 ④槽; 【机】槽铁, 凹形铁 (=~ iron) ⑤[喻]路线, 途径: through diplomatic ~s 通过外交途径 / an intelligence ~ 【军】情报系统 ⑥【电】电路; (电缆的) 管道, 【讯】信道, 波道, 【自】通道, 通路 **II** (channel(l)ed; channel(l)ing) *vt.* ① 在 (某地) 开辟 (或形成) 水道; 在…上开槽 ②开辟 (道路): The river has channel(l)ed its way through the soft rock. 这条河流已在松软的岩石中冲成一条水道。③ 为…开辟途径; 引导 ‖~**ize** *vt.* =channel (*vt.*)

chant [tʃɑːnt] **I** *n.* ①歌; 单调的歌 ② [宗] 赞美诗, 圣歌 ③唱歌 (或唱赞美诗) 时的语调; 单调的语调

II ❶ *vi.* ①唱 ②单调重复地唱歌(或说话) ❷ *vt.* ①唱;单调地唱(或说) ②歌颂,颂扬: ~ the praises of 绝口称赞 / ~ horses 用欺诈手段贩卖马

chantey, chanty ['tʃɑːnti] *n.* 水手(起锚时)的劳动号子

chaos ['keiɒs] *n.* ① [常用 C-] 浑沌 ②混乱,无秩序

chaotic [kei'ɒtik] *a.* ① 浑沌的 ② 混乱的,无秩序的 ||~ally *ad.*

chap¹ [tʃæp] *n.* ①[口]家伙,小伙子: Hullo, old ~! 喂,老朋友! ②[英方]买者

chap² [tʃæp] *n.* ① [复](动物的)颚;(人的)面颊 ②猪头肉的颚颊部分 ||lick one's ~s 馋涎欲滴地等待着

chap³ [tʃæp] I (chapped; chapping) *vt. & vi.* (使皮肤等)皲裂,龟裂,变粗糙 II *n.* 龟裂(处),皲裂(处)

chapel ['tʃæpəl] *n.* ①小教堂;(医院、学校等的)附属教堂: a ~ of ease 为便利远处教徒做礼拜而设的英国国教附属教堂 ② 教堂内的私人祈祷处 ③(学校等的)礼拜仪式: keep a ~ 做礼拜 / cut ~ 逃避做礼拜 ④英国国教以外的教堂: Are you church or ~? 你是(英国)国教教徒还是非国教教徒? ⑤印刷厂工人的工会: hold a ~ 开印刷工会会议 ⑥殡仪馆;殡仪馆的礼堂

chaperon(e) ['ʃæpərəun] I *n.* 在社交场所陪伴未婚少女的年长妇女 II *vt.* ①陪伴,伴随(未婚少女) ②护送

chaplain ['tʃæplin] *n.* (学校、医院、军队、监狱等的)牧师

chaplet ['tʃæplit] *n.* ①花冠;项圈;串珠 ②[建]串珠饰 ③[动](昆虫的)刺冠 ||~ed *a.* 戴花冠的

chapter ['tʃæptə] *n.* ①(书的)章,回;章节: the first ~ of a book 书的第一章 ②[喻](历史或人生的)重要章节 ③【宗】牧师会;牧师会的例行会议 ④(俱乐部、社团等的)支部,分会 ||a ~ of accidents 接踵而来的灾祸;一连串未预见到的事情 / give ~ and verse for 注明(引用资料等)的出处,指明…的确切依据 / to the end of the ~ 见 end ||~ house ①牧师会礼堂 ②(俱乐部、会社等的)分会会所

char¹ [tʃɑː] I *n.* ①[常用复]家庭杂务 ②[英口]打杂女工 II (charred; charring ['tʃɑːriŋ]) *vi.* 打杂,做家庭杂务: go out charring 出去给人家干杂活 ||'~,woman *n.* [英]打杂女工

char² [tʃɑː] I (charred; charring ['tʃɑːriŋ]) *vt. & vi.* (把…)烧成炭,(把…)烧焦,(把…)烧黑 II *n.* 炭,木炭 ||charring ['tʃɑːriŋ] *n.*【化】炭化: charring in heaps 堆烧法

char³ [tʃɑː] ([复] char(s)) *n.*【动】红点鲑属的鱼;红点鲑,白点鲑

char⁴ [tʃɑː] *n.* [英俚]茶(是汉语"茶"的音译)

character ['kæriktə] I *n.* ①(事物的)特性,性质,特征(的总和): the general (individual) ~ 共(个)性 / be different in ~ 有着不同的性质 /

acquired ~【医】后天特性,后天性 ②性格,品质;骨气;名声: of a firm ~ 性格坚强的 / a man of ~ 有个性的人;有骨气的人 / get a good (bad) ~ 得好(坏)名声 ③(小说、戏剧等)人物,角色;知名人物;[口]怪人: a leading ~ 主角 / a positive (negative) ~ 正(反)面人物 / a historical ~ 历史人物 / He is quite a ~. 他真有点与众不同。④书写符号;印刷符号(如 "A", "a", "4", "÷", "£" 等);(汉)字;字体: a Chinese ~ 一个汉字 / in italic ~s 用斜体字 (=in italics) ⑤ 身分,资格: in one's ~ as ambassador 以大使身分 ⑥品德评语,鉴定;(雇主给雇员的)品德证明书: give sb. a good ~ 给某人好评;推荐某人 ⑦人物素描 II *vt.* ①[写]印;刻 ②使具有特性;表示…的特性 ||in ~ (与自己的个性或习惯或所演的角色)适合,相称,符合 / in the ~ of 以…的资格;扮演 / out of ~ (与自己的个性或习惯或所演的角色)不适合,不相称,不符合 / ~less *a.* 无特征的,平凡的 ||~ actor 性格演员 / ~ assassination (对知名人士等的)人格毁损

characteristic [,kæriktə'ristik] I *a.* 特有的,独特的;表示特性的: the ~ flavour of bananas 香蕉所特有的味道 / ~ function 【数】特征函数,示性函数 II *n.* 特性,特征,特色: the ~s of the present situation 目前形势的特点 / airplane ~s 飞机性能 ||~ally *ad.*

characterize, characterise ['kæriktəraiz] ❶ *vt.* 表示…的特性,刻划…的性格;成为…的特性: be ~d as a man of principle 被描绘成一个有原则的人 ❷ *vi.* (在文艺作品中)塑造人物,描绘性格: be good at characterizing 善于塑造人物 ||characterization [,kæriktərai'zeiʃən] *n.*

charade [ʃə'rɑːd; 美 ʃə'reid] *n.* ①(用诗、画、动作等凑成一个字的)一种字谜(游戏) ②几乎没有掩饰的伪装

charcoal ['tʃɑːkoul] *n.* ①炭,木炭 ②炭笔 ③木炭画 ||~ burner 烧炭人;炭炉

charge [tʃɑːdʒ] I ❶ *vt.* ①装(满),使充满,使饱含: a blast furnace with ore 为高炉装料 / ~ a gun (with powder) 为火炮装火药 / ~ a battery (或 an accumulator) 为蓄电池充电 / The air is ~d with vapour (odours). 空气中饱含水汽(各种气味)。/ ~ a brush with pigment 使画笔蘸满颜料 / ~d water 苏打水,汽水 / one's memory with facts 记住大量事实 ②使承担(任务、责任): ~ oneself (或 ~d) with a task 承担一项任务 ③责令,告诫,指示: ~ sb. to do sth. 责令某人做某事 ④控告,指控(with);把…归罪为 (to, on, upon): be ~d with murder and arson 被控杀人放火 / ~ sb. with negligence 指责某人疏忽 / ~ the failure to self-conceit 把失败归因于自满 / ~ a fault upon sb. 把过失归咎于某人 ⑤ 要(价),收(费);要(人)支付(多少钱): ~ (sb.) fifty cents for mending a pair of shoes (为某人)修理一双皮鞋索价五角 ⑥把…记

入(帐册等)，在(帐册等)上记入…：～ the purchases *to* sb.'s account (或 ～ sb.'s account *with* the purchases) 把所购货物记在某人帐上 / ～ a library book *to* a borrower 把图书馆出借的书记在借书人名下 ⑦袭击 ❷ *vi.* ①冲锋，向前冲：*Charge!* 冲锋! ②收费,要价: Do they ～ for the use of the telephone? 打电话收不收费？/ high (low) 要价高(低) Ⅱ *n.* ①负载；电荷；(容器的)定量装载物；(一发子弹所装的)炸药量(一定量的)炸药: the ～ of chemicals in a fire extinguisher 一具灭火器中所装的化学药剂 / a shell with a large powder ～ 装药量大的炮弹 / a dynamite ～ 一料炸药;炸药包 / a satchel ～ 炸药包 / a blasting ～ 爆破装药 ②充电;充气;装料 ③主管,掌管；看管,看守: have ～ of 主管着… ④被托管的人(或事物)；靠人赡养的人 (on): The nurse took her ～s to help in gleaning. 保育员带领她照管的孩子们去帮助拾麦穗(或稻穗)。⑤费用,价钱；应付项目,借项;借款(如书)项目: hotel ～s 旅馆费 / free of ～ 免费 / at one's own ～ 自费 / a ～ *to* a customer's account (记入)客户帐目中的一笔借项 / an amortization ～ 折旧提成 ⑥控告,指控,指责: bring a ～ *of* treason *against* sb. 指控某人叛国 / arrest sb. *on* a ～ *of* ... 以…罪拘捕某人 ⑦训令,指示,嘱咐 ⑧突然猛攻；冲锋；冲锋号 / sound the ～ 吹冲锋号 ⑨[美俚]快感, 刺激 ‖*Charge bayonet!* 上刺刀! (冲锋前的号令) / ～ *off* ① 把…当作损耗处理,对…扣除损耗费 ②把…归于某一项 / ～ *of quarters* 在值班时间外被派在其单位所在区域内维持秩序的军人 / ～s *forward* 运费等货到后由收货人自付 / *give sb. in* ～ [英]把某人送交警察 / *in* ～ ① 主管,掌管,看管: An experienced worker is *in* ～ of the project. 一位有经验的工人负责这项工程。/ the person *in* (overall) ～ (总)负责人 ② 在…掌管(或看管)之下 / *in full* ～ ① 负全责 ② 勇猛向前 / *lay sth. to* sb.'s ～ 指控某人犯某事,归责某人犯某种错误 / *take* ～ ① 掌管,负责;看管: *take* ～ of a task 负责一项任务 / *take* ～ of sb.'s children 照管某人的孩子 / be sent to a shop to *take* ～ 被派到一家商店去负责工作 ② (指物)不受控制: The driving belt *took* ～ and ran out. 传动带不受控制,脱了出来。/ *under the* ～ *of* 在…掌管(或看管)之下 ‖～**d** *a.* ①充满强烈感情的；(气氛等)紧张的 ②【物】带电的: ～d particles 带电粒子 / ～**r** *n.* ①装料人；装料机 ②装弹机 ③充电器 ④冲锋者 ⑤战马 ⑥委托者 ⑦控诉者 ‖～ **account** [美](客户购货的)赊购帐 (=credit account) / '～**-a-,plate**, ～ **plate** *n.* 赊货牌(顾客赊购货物时用的一种金属小牌) / ～ **sheet** (警察局中的)案件记录

chargeable ['tʃɑːdʒəbl] *a.* ①可能被控的: be ～ *with* libel 可能被控犯诽谤罪 ②应课税的,应付费的 ③应由某人负责的;可记在某人帐上的: expense ～ *on* sb. 应由某人负担的费用 / expense

～ *to* sb.'s account 可记在某人帐上的费用 ‖**chargeability** [,tʃɑːdʒə'biliti] *n.*

chargé d'affaires ['ʃɑːʒei dæ'fɛə] ([复] chargés d'affaires ['ʃɑːʒei dæ'fɛəz]) [法]代办: a *chargé d'affaires ad interim* 临时代办

chariot ['tʃæriət] Ⅰ *n.* ①古代双轮马拉战车;战车 ②轻便四轮马车 ③[诗]漂亮的车,凯旋车 Ⅱ ❶ *vt.* 用马车(或战车)载 ❷ *vi.* 乘马车(或战车) ‖～**eer** [,tʃæriə'tiə] *n.* 驾驶马车(或战车)者

chariot

charitable ['tʃæritəbl] *a.* ① 大慈大悲的; 慈善的 ②宽厚的 ‖～**ness** *n.* / **charitably** *ad.*

charity ['tʃæriti] *n.* ①【宗】上帝之爱;基督教徒间的兄弟之爱 ②施舍(行为): a ～ performance 义演 / live on ～ 靠赈济过活 ③慈善事业,慈善团体;赈济(物): a Brother (Sister) of *Charity* 【宗】慈善团体的教士(女教士) ④(对别人的)宽大,宽容,宽厚 ‖*be cold as* ～ 象慈善机关对穷人那样冷冰冰的 / *Charity begins at home.* [谚]施舍先及亲友。(常作不捐款的借口) ‖～ **school** 慈善学校

charlatan ['ʃɑːlətən] Ⅰ *n.* ①庸医 ②骗子;假充内行的人 Ⅱ *a.* 假充内行的 ‖～**ish** *a.* 庸医般的;骗子般的

charm [tʃɑːm] Ⅰ *n.* ①魅力,魔力 ②[常用复]妩媚;诱人之处,可爱之处 ③咒文,符咒;随身护符 ④链条(或镯子)上的小饰物 Ⅱ ❶ *vt.* ①施符魔法;用魔法(或符咒)保护;(用魔力)控制,要(蛇等): ～ sb. asleep 用魔法对某人施催眠术 / a ～ed life 似有魔法保护的生命 ②迷住;使陶醉: A: I'll bring my father to see you Sunday. B: Oh, I shall be ～ed. 甲: 星期日我带我父亲来看你。乙: 噢,那可太好啦。(或: 那可太荣幸啦。) ③(用魔法)使具有神力 ④(用魔法、魅力等)治愈(疾病、悲伤等) (*away*, *off*);诱出: ～ *away* sb.'s sorrow 驱走了某人的悲伤 / ～ consent out of sb. 哄诱某人许诺 ❷ *vi.* ①行魔法 ②有魔力,令人陶醉 ‖*like a* ～ 效验如神地 ‖～**er** *n.* ①魔术师 ②耍蛇的人 ③使人着魔的人(或物)

charming ['tʃɑːmiŋ] *a.* ①媚人的;可爱的;极好的: a ～ smile 可爱的微笑 / It is very ～ of you to come. 你能来,那太好了。② 施展魔力的,使用魔法的 ‖～**ly** *ad.*

chart [tʃɑːt] Ⅰ *n.* ①海图,航(线)图: a nautical ～ 航海地图 / a flight ～ 航空地图 ②图,图表;

曲线(标绘)图: a physical ~ 地势图 / a statistical ~ 统计图 / a target ~【军】轰炸目标图 / a weather ~ 天气图 ③(仪器中用的)有刻度的记录纸 II *vt.* ①制…的海(或地)图;把(航线等)绘入海图;[喻]指引 ②用图表表示③制订…的计划 ‖~ist *n.* 制图者 / ~less *a.* ①图籍未载的,尚未绘入地图(或海图)的 ②没有图籍可凭的 ‖~ house, ~ room (船上的)海图室

charter ['tʃɑːtə] I *n.* ①(君主或立法机构对成立自治市、公司等的) 特许状,凭证;(社团对成立分会等的)许可证 ② 宪章: the *Charter* of the United Nations 联合国宪章 / the "Eight-Point *Charter*" for agriculture 农业的"八字宪法" / the Great *Charter* (英国)大宪章 (=the Magna Charta) ③特权,豁免权 ④契据,证书 ⑤(船只、飞机、公共汽车等的)租赁 ⑥ 租船契约 (=~ party): a time ~ 定期租船契约 II *vt.* ①特许(成立公司等),发执照给…:a ~ed accountant (英国)会计师(持有皇家特许状,为会计师协会会员) / a ~ed bank 特许银行 ②租,包(船、飞机、车辆等): a ~ed plane 包机 ‖~er ['tʃɑːtərə] *n.* 租船人;租用者 ‖~ member (社团、公司等的)创始成员 / ~ party 租船契约,租船合同

chary ['tʃɛəri] *a.* ①谨慎小心的: be ~ of catching cold 小心感冒 ②节俭的;吝啬的 ③有戒心的;怕陌生的: be ~ of strangers 怕生

chase¹ [tʃeis] I ❶ *vt.* ①追逐,追赶;追击,追猎 ②驱逐 ③寻觅,找寻: The librarians are busy *chasing* books called for by readers. 图书馆工作人员正忙于寻找读者要借的书。/ ~ *down* all possible clues 寻找一切可能的线索 ❷ *vi.* ①追逐,追赶,跟踪 (*after*) ②匆忙地走,奔跑: ~ all over (或 around) town looking for sth. 为找寻東西而满城奔跑 II *n.* ①追逐,追赶;追击,追猎;追求: in ~ of sb. (sth.) 追求某人(某物) ②[the ~] 打猎 ③被追猎的动物;被追逐的人(或物)(如船等) ④[总称]追猎者 ⑤[英] 狩猎地;(允许在一定区域打猎或饲养猎物的)狩猎权 ⑥[美俚]紧张而忙乱的活动 ⑦(网球的)一种击球法 ‖ a wild-goose ~ 徒劳的搜索,无益的举动 / ~ oneself [俚]走开: Go ~ yourself! 走开! 别来捣乱! / give ~ (*to*) 追赶(…);追击(…) / lead sb. a ~ 诱使某人徒劳追逐而陷于困境 ‖~ gun, ~ piece (追击时用的)舰首(或船尾)炮 / ~ port 船首(或船尾)炮门

chase² [tʃeis] *vt.* ①雕镂,镂刻: ~d silver 雕花银器 / be ~d with stars 刻有星形 ②在…上镶嵌宝石 ③ 在…上开槽,把…刻成锯齿形 ④用螺纹梳刀刻(螺纹)

chase³ [tʃeis] *n.* ① 炮前身(炮耳至炮口部分) ②【印】盛放已排活字的长方形金属框,活版架 ③槽,凹沟;【建】管子槽

chaser¹ ['tʃeisə] *n.* ①追杀者;追赶者;追猎者 ②(追击时用的)舰首(或船尾)炮: a bow ~ 舰首炮 ③追击飞机;追击舰艇,猎潜舰艇 ④(越野)障碍

赛参加者 ⑤ [口]喝烈性酒后紧接着再喝的少量清水; 喝咖啡后紧接着再喝的小杯酒 ‖*an ambulance* ~ [美口]专办交通伤人案件的律师

chaser² ['tʃeisə] *n.* ①镂刻者 ②【机】螺纹梳刀;梳刀盘

chasm ['kæzəm] *n.* ①【地】(地壳的)陷窟,断层,裂口;峡谷,深渊 ②(意见、感情、兴趣等的)大差别,大分歧: the political ~ between 在…之间政治上的大分歧 ③空隙,空白,中断处: a ~ in the narrative 叙述中的脱节处

chassis ['ʃæsi] ([复] chassis ['ʃæsiz]) *n.* ①(汽车等的)底盘;(飞机等的)机架;【机】底架;【无】机壳,底架;【军】炮底架 ②[俚]身体,体形

chaste [tʃeist] *a.* ①贞洁的 ②纯洁的,高雅的 ③(文风等)简洁朴实的 ‖~ly *ad.* / ~ness *n.*

chasten ['tʃeisn] *vt.* ①惩戒,责罚 ②遏制,使缓和 ③磨炼,纯洁(思想等);精练(文章) ‖~er *n.* 惩戒者,责罚者

chastise [tʃæs'taiz] *vt.* 惩戒,严惩;责打 ‖~ment ['tʃæstizmənt]; 美 tʃæs'taizmənt] *n.* / ~r *n.* 惩罚者;责打者

chastity ['tʃæstiti] *n.* ①贞洁 ②纯洁,高雅 ③(文风等的)简洁朴实

chat [tʃæt] I *n.* ①闲谈,聊天;非正式的谈话: have a ~ with 与· 闲谈 / a column devoted to ~ about popular science 大众科学讲话专栏 ②鸣禽 II (chatted; chatting) *vi.* 闲谈,聊天

chattel ['tʃætl] *n.* ①(一件)动产: sb.'s goods and ~s 某人个人所有的杂物用品 / a ~ mortgage 用动产作抵的抵押 / a ~ personal 动产 / a ~ real (租借地权等)准不动产 ②奴隶

chatter ['tʃætə] I ❶ *vi.* ①喋喋不休,饶舌 ②(鸟)啁啾;(鼠等)吱吱叫;(溪流)潺潺作声;(机器)震颤,颤动 ③(牙齿)打战 ❷ *vt.* ①喋喋地说 ②[英方] 撕碎 II *n.* 喋喋不休;啁啾;震颤声 ‖~er ['tʃætərə] *n.* ①喋喋不休的人 ②燕雀类的鸟 ‖~box *n.* 唠唠叨叨的人,饶舌者(常指小孩)

chauffeur ['ʃoufə] I *n.* (汽车)司机 II ❶ *vi.* 做汽车司机工作 ❷ *vt.* ①开汽车运送 ②开(汽车等)

cheap [tʃiːp] I *a.* ①便宜的,廉价的: dirt ~ 极便宜的 ②低劣的,劣质的;可鄙的: ~ and nasty 质量低劣的 / hold sth. ~ 轻视某事物 / make oneself ~ 干出降低自己声誉的事 ③虚伪的,低级的: ~ flattery 虚伪的奉承 / journalism 低级的报刊 ④贬了值的: ~ dollars (money) 贬了值的美元(钱) ⑤(商店等)取价低廉的;[英]特别减价的: a ~ trip (指车票、船票等降低价格的)减价旅行 ⑥容易得到的 II *ad.* 便宜地,廉价地: get sth. ~ 廉价买到某物 ‖*feel* ~ [口]①觉得身体不舒服 ②感到惭愧 / *on the* ~ 便宜地: Don't try to get things on the ~. 不要贪便宜。‖~ly *ad.* / ~ness *n.* ‖~Jack, '~-John *n.* ①(流动)小贩 ②廉价(或劣质)商品经售者

cheapen ['tʃiːpən] ❶ *vt.* ①减低…的价钱 ②降低…的威信,降低…的地位 ③使变得粗俗,使变得低级 ❷ *vi.* 减价,跌价

cheat [tʃiːt] I *n.* ①欺诈,欺骗行为;骗取 ②骗子 ③雀麦 ④[美国]汽车上的反光镜 II ❶ *vt.* ①骗取,诈取: ~ sb. (*out*) *of* sth. (money) 骗取某人的某物(钱) ②哄,骗: ~ sb. *into* the belief that ... 哄骗别人相信… ③消磨(时间),消除(疲劳) ④用智谋挫败(对方);逃脱: ~ death 逃脱死亡 ❷ *vi.* 欺诈;作弊: ~ at cards 打牌时作弊 ‖~ *the journey* 消磨旅途的寂聊 ‖~**er** *n.* ①骗子 ②[复][俚]眼镜

check [tʃek] I *n.* ①制止,控制;制止人(或物);【军】挫折,牵制 ②受到挫折(或阻挡、牵制) ③突然停止 ④检查,检验,核对;查对无误的记号(通常用√): an on-the-spot ~ 现场检验,现场调查 ④寄存物的凭证;号牌;行李票 ⑤[美]支票(=[英] cheque);(餐馆的)帐单;(赌博的)筹码 ⑥(象棋中)被"将军"的局面 ⑦(木材或钢铁等的)细裂缝,罅缝;【建】幅裂;槽口,半糟边 ⑧方格图案,方格图案中的一个小方格;格子织物,格纹 II ❶ *vt.* ①制止,控制;妨碍;停止: ~ oneself 克制自己 / ~ fire 【军】暂停射击 ②检查,检验,核对;在…上作经查对无误的记号: ~ the drawings *against* actual conditions 根据实际情况检查图纸 / ~ the accounts 查对帐目 ③[美]寄存: Have you ~ed your baggage? 你已将行李托运(或寄存)了吗? ④(象棋中)将(对方的"王")一军 ⑤使产生裂缝 ⑥在…上画(或印)方格图案 ⑦[农]条播,方形栽植 ❷ *vi.* ①逐项相符: The accounts ~. 帐目核对无误。 ②[美]开支票 ③裂成小方格 ④(象棋中)将一军 III *int.* ①[口]行! 对! ②(象棋用语)将! ‖*cash* (*hand, pass*) *in one's* ~ ①把筹码兑成现钱 ②[俚]死 ‖~ *in* 登记,报到: ~ *in* at a hotel 到旅馆办理登记手续 / ~ *in* at a congress 向大会报到 ②[美俚]死 / ~ *off* ①经查对无误而在…上作记号 ②认为…决不可能因而不再考虑 / ~ *out* 办清手续后离开;付帐后离开 ②[美俚]死 ③检验;被认为无误 ④合格,通过: The trainees ~ed *out* all right. 实习生顺利地通过了考试。 / ~ *up* 核对;检验: ~ *up* (*on*) the work 检查工作 / ~ (*up*) *with* 与…相符合 / *discover* ~ (象棋中)移动一子以将对方军 / *hold* (或 *keep*) *in* ~ 制止,控制,牵制 / *put a* ~ *on* 制止,禁止 / *shepherd*('s) ~ 见 shepherd ‖~**ed** *a.* 有格子花的 / ‖'~**book** *n.* [美]支票簿 (=[英] chequebook) / '~**list** *n.* ①(核对用的)清单 ②[美]选举人名单 / '~**mate** *vt.* ①(象棋中)将死(对方的"王") ②打败,使受挫折 *n.* ①(象棋中"王"的)将死 ②大败,垮台 / ~**nut** *n.*【机】防松螺母 / '~**out** *n.* ①(旅馆规定旅客)结清帐目后必须离去的时间 ②(购货时的)结帐 / '~**point** *n.* (过路车辆)检查站 /【军】试射点;检验点 / '~**post** *n.* 检查哨所 / '~**rein** *n.* ①马缰绳 ②控制 *vt.* 控制 / '~**room** *n.* [美]衣帽间 (=[英] cloakroom); 行李寄存处 / ~**string** (要驾驶员停车的)拉铃绳索 / ~ **taker** (戏院、车站等的)收票员 / '~**-up** *n.* ①检查,查对: the three ~-*ups* (on class origin, performance of duty and will to fight) 三查(查阶级、查工作、查斗志) ②[美]体格检查: a general ~-*up* 全身(体格)检查 / ~ **valve** 【机】止回阀

cheek [tʃiːk] *n.* ①面颊,脸蛋: rosy ~s 红润的双颊 ②厚脸皮,没礼貌(或冒失)的话(或行为): have the ~ *to* (do) 厚着脸皮去(做) / No more (或 None) of your ~! 别无礼! ③[复]【机械】(或器具)上两侧成对的部件;【机】颊板;中型箱: the ~s of a vice 老虎钳的一对钳嘴 ‖~ *by jowl* (*with*) (和…)紧紧靠着,(和…)亲密地 / *sour one's* ~s 不高兴 / *to one's own* ~ 不与人共享的 / *with one's tongue in one's* ~ 见 tongue ‖'~**bone** *n.* 颊骨,颧骨 / ~ **tooth** 臼齿

cheer [tʃiə] I ❶ *vt.* ①使振奋,使高兴,使快慰: The good news ~ed (*up*) everybody who heard it. 喜讯使每一个听到的人感到高兴。 ②欢呼,高呼: ~ the victory 为胜利而欢呼 ③以欢呼声激励: ~ sb. *on* (以欢呼)激励某人 ④为…喝采,向…欢呼 ❷ *vi.* ①感到振奋,感到高兴 (*up*) ②欢呼;喝采 II *n.* ①振奋,高兴: words of ~ 鼓励人的话 / with good ~ 欣然地 ②欢呼,喝采: three ~s for 为…欢呼三声(英语中通常指呼三声 hurrah) ③心情: What ~? 你感到怎样? ④款待,欢迎 ⑤菜肴,酒菜: good ~ 好酒菜 ‖*be of good* ~ ①高兴,兴致勃勃;充满希望 ②奋勇,勇敢 / ~ *oneself hoarse* 欢呼叫喊哑嗓子 ‖~**ing** ['tʃiəriŋ] *n.* 欢呼,喝采 *a.* 令人振奋的,令人高兴的 / ~**less** *a.* 缺乏欢乐的,阴暗的,惨淡的 / ‖'~**leader** *n.* 啦啦队队长

cheerful ['tʃiəful] *a.* ①快乐的;高兴的: a ~ look 高兴的神情 ②乐意的,心甘情愿的 ③使人感到愉快的;使人振奋的: a sunny, ~ room 阳光充足,令人愉快的房间 ‖~**ly** *ad.* / ~**ness** *n.*

cheerily ['tʃiərili] *ad.* ①高兴地,活泼地 ②爽快地

cheery ['tʃiəri] *a.* ①喜气洋洋的,兴高采烈的,活泼的 ②(天气等)爽快的

cheese[1] [tʃiːz] *n.* ①乳酪,干酪: two cream ~s 两块干乳酪 ②(形状、质地或气味)象干酪的东西 ‖*as like as chalk and* (或 *to*) ~ 见 chalk / *bread and* ~ 普通食品;生计 / *get the* ~ 碰钉子,失望 / *hard* ~ 倒霉,受苦 / *quite the* ~ [俚]很对头,十分得体 ‖'~**cake** *n.* 乳酪饼 / '~**cloth** *n.* 干酪包布(一种粗布) / ~ **cutter** 切干酪的阔面刀 / '~**monger** *n.* 乳酪商 / '~**paring** *n.* & *a.* 吝啬的),小气(的) / '~**-plate** *n.* (直径 5-6 吋的)乳饼盘

cheese[2] [tʃiːz] *n.* [美俚] ①出色(或高级)的东西 ②重要人物: He is the big ~. 他是个要人。

cheese[3] [tʃiːz] *vt.* [俚]停止 ‖*Cheese it!* ①停止! 当心! 静一点! ②快跑掉!

chef [ʃef] *n.* [法] ①男厨师长 ②厨师

chemical ['kemikəl] **I** *a.* 化学的, 化学上用的, 用化学方法得到的: ～ change 化学变化 / ～ combination 化合(作用) / ～ composition 化学成分, 化学组成 / a ～ compound 化合物 / ～ equilibrium 化学平衡 / a ～ equivalent 化学当量 / ～ fertilizer 化肥 / a ～ formula 化学式 / ～ reaction 化学反应 / ～ warfare 化学战争 / ～ weapons 化学武器 **II** *n.* [常用复]化学制品;化学药品: heavy ～s 大量生产的化学药品 (如硫酸、烧碱等) / an organic ～ 有机药品 ‖～**ly** *ad.*

chemist ['kemist] *n.* ① 化学家, 化学师 ② [英] 药剂师; 药品商: a ～'s shop [英] 药房

chemistry ['kemistri] *n.* ① 化学: applied (practical) ～ 应用(实用)化学 / organic (inorganic) ～ 有机(无机)化学 ② 物质的组成和化学性质: the ～ of iron 铁的组成和化学性质 ③ 化学过程和现象 ④[喻]神秘的变化(过程)

cheque [tʃek] *n.* 支票(=[美] check): a bearer ～ 不记名支票/a certified ～ 保付支票 / a crossed ～ 划线支票 ‖ *a blank* ～ ① 空白支票 ② 开支票人签过名由收款人自填款项数目的支票 ③ 自由行动的权力 ‖～**book** *n.* 支票簿

chequer ['tʃekə] **I** *n.* ①(一粒) 棋子; [复]西洋跳棋 (=draughts) ② 方格图案; 格子花 **【植】**花楸果 ④[复]**【建】**排列成方格式的石头 **II** *vt.* ① 把…画(或制)成方格图案形 ②(常用被动语态)交替变换(常指生活上的波折或情绪变化等)

cherish ['tʃeriʃ] *vt.* ① 爱护: Support the army and ～ the people. 拥军爱民。② 抚育, 珍爱 ③ 抱有(希望), 怀有(感情等)

cherry ['tʃeri] **I** *n.* ① 李属的植物, 樱桃 ② 樱桃树; 樱桃木 ③ 樱桃色, 鲜红色 ④[俚]处女膜; 处女状态 **II** *a.* ① 樱桃色的, 鲜红色的 ② 樱桃木制的 ③ 樱桃制的; 有樱桃味的 ‖ *make two bites at* (或 *of*) *a* ～ 见 **bite** ‖～ **bomb** 球形红色烟火 / ～ **brandy** 樱桃白兰地 / ～ **picker** [俚]车载升降台(用于修理高空电线、发射台上的宇宙飞船等) / ～ **pie** ① 包有樱桃酱的馅饼 ②【植】缬草; 香水草(天芥菜) ③【植】柳叶菜 / '～**stone** *n.* ① 樱桃核 ②(北美产的)小蛤蜊 / ～ **tree** 樱桃树

cherub ['tʃerəb] *n.* ① 小天使, (绘画中)有翅膀的孩子 ② 可爱的天真无邪的人(尤指孩子); 胖娃娃 ③([复] cherubim ['tʃerəbim])【宗】(九级天使中第二级司知识的)天使 ‖～**ic** [tʃe'ru:bik] *a.* 小天使(似)的; 天真可爱的, (脸)胖胖的

chess[1] [tʃes] *n.* 国际象棋: have a game of ～ 下一盘象棋 / play (at) ～ 下象棋 ‖'～**board** *n.* 棋盘 / '～**man** *n.* 棋子

chess[2] [tʃes] *n.*【植】雀麦

chess[3] [tʃes] *n.* 浮桥的踏板

chest [tʃest] *n.* ① 箱子, 柜子, 盒子: an ammunition ～ 弹药箱 / a carpenter's ～ 木匠的工具箱 / a ～ of drawers 五斗橱, 衣柜 / a ～ of tea 一箱茶叶 / a medicine ～ 药箱 ② 金库, 钱库; 公款, 资金: the community ～ 团体公款 ③胸腔,

chest of drawers

胸腔: ～ trouble 肺病 ‖ *get sth. off one's* ～ [口]把某事(指要讲的话)讲完(才舒服) / *throw a* ～ [俚]挺胸直立 ‖～**ed** *a.* [用以构成复合词]有…胸腔的: pigeon-～ed【医】鸡胸的 ‖～ **note**, ～ **voice** 最低的歌声(或说话声) / ～ **protector** (绒布制的)护胸

chestnut ['tʃesnʌt] **I** *n.* ①栗子 ②栗树; 栗木 ③栗色; 栗色马 ④[口]陈腐的笑话(或故事等) ⑤马前腿部内侧的胼胝 **II** *a.* 栗子(似)的; 栗色的 ‖ *drop sth. like a hot* ～ 忙不迭地摔脱某物 / *pull sb.'s* ～*s out of the fire* 为某人火中取栗

chevron ['ʃevrən] *n.* ①(纹章) 人字形的标识 ②【军】V 形臂章 ③【建】锯齿形花饰

chew [tʃu:] **I ❶** *vt.* 嚼(烟), 咀嚼, 嚼碎 **❷** *vi.* ① 咀嚼 ② 嚼烟 ③深思, 细想 (*over, upon*) **II** *n.* ① 咀嚼 ② 嚼物(例如嚼烟) ‖～ *the cud* ①(牛等)反刍 ②深思, 细想 / ～ *the fat* 见 **fat** / ～ *the rag* 见 **rag**[1] ‖～**ing gum** 橡皮糖, 口香糖

chic [ʃi:k] *n. & a.* [法]漂亮(的); 时式的; 潇洒(的)

chicanery [ʃi'keinəri] *n.* ① 诡计; 诈骗 ② 诡辩

chick[1] [tʃik] *n.* ① 小鸡; 小鸟 ② 小孩 ③[俚]少妇 ‖'～-**pea** *n.*【植】鹰嘴豆 / '～**weed** *n.*【植】繁缕

chick[2] [tʃik] *n.* (印度和东南亚的)一种竹帘

chicken ['tʃikin] **I** *n.* ① 小鸡; 小鸟; [美]鸡, 家禽: a Mother Carey's ['kɛəriz] ～ 海燕 ② 鸡肉 ③ 年轻人; 没有经验的人; [美俚]年轻的女子: She is no ～. 她不是没有经验的小丫头。④胆怯的人, 懦夫 ⑤[美俚](军队)纪律的细节 **II** *a.* ① 鸡肉制的 ②(海虾等)小而嫩的 ③[美俚]胆怯的; 软弱的 ④ [美俚]拘泥于 (军队) 纪律的细节的 **III** *vi.* [美俚]害怕, 丧胆, 逃跑 (*out*) ‖ *count one's* ～*s before they are hatched* 蛋尚未孵先数鸡; 过早乐观 / *play* ～ [美俚](为吓倒对方)互相挑战和威胁 / ～ **broth** 鸡汤 / ～ **cholera** 鸡瘟 / ～ **colonel** [美][军俚]陆军上校 / ～ **feed** ①鸡食 ②[俚]小额钱币; 零钱; 为数甚微的款项 / ～ **head** 笨蛋, 蠢人 / '～**hearted** *a.* 胆怯的; 软弱的 / '～**livered** *a.* 胆怯的 / ～ **pox**【医】水痘

chicory ['tʃikəri] *n.* ① 菊苣属植物 ② 菊苣(根可充作咖啡用)

chide [tʃaid] (过去式 chid [tʃid] 或 chided, 过去分词 chid 或 chidden ['tʃidn] 或 chided) **❶** *vt.* 责

骂, 责备 ❷ vi. ①责骂, 责备 ②[喻](风等)怒号, (猎犬等)吼叫

chief [tʃi:f] **I** n. ①首领, 领袖: a ~ (或 head) of state 国家元首 / the ~ of a tribe 部落酋长 ②主任, 首长; [作称呼用]长官: a department ~ 部(门)主任 / a ~ of staff 参谋长 ③头目, 头子 ④主要部分, 最有价值的部分 **II** a. ①主要的, 首要的: ~ (或 ~est) of all 其中最主要的是… / *Chief* among the country's exports are copper and coal. 铜和煤是该国出口商品中主要的两项。②首席的, 主任的: a ~ delegate 首席代表 / a ~ engineer 总工程师;【海】轮机长 / a ~ justice 审判长, 首席法官; 法院院长 / a ~ executive 主管人(在美国常作 Chief Executive, 指总统、州长、市长等) / a ~ mate (或 officer)【海】大副 / a ~ petty officer (美) 海军军士长; (英) 海军上士 / a ~ warrant officer (美) 陆军(或空军)一级准尉 ‖ ~ *itch and rub* [美俚]头子 / *in* ~ ①主要地, 尤其: We did so for many reasons, and this one *in* ~. 我们这样做的理由有很多, 而主要的是这个。②在首席地位, 总…: an editor *in* ~ 总编辑 ‖ ~ dom n. ①首领的地位 ②酋长领地; 酋长领地所辖居民 / ~ less a. 没有首领的 / ~ ship n. 首领的地位

chiefly ['tʃi:fli] **I** ad. 主要地; 首要地, 尤其 **II** a. 首领的; 首领般的

chieftain ['tʃi:ftən] n. ①(强盗、土匪等的)首领, 头子 ②(苏格兰高地的)族长; 酋长 ③[诗]指挥官, 队长 ‖ ~ cy, ~ ship n. 首领(或头子、族长等)的地位

chiffon ['ʃifɔn] [法] **I** n. ①雪纺绸, 薄绸 ②[常用复]女子服装装饰品 **II** a. ①用薄绸制成的 ②象薄绸般透明(或柔软)的 ③(馅)因加入起沫蛋白等而松软的

chilblain ['tʃilblein] n. 冻疮: have ~s 生冻疮 ‖ ~ ed a. 生冻疮的

child [tʃaild] ([复] children ['tʃildrən]) n. ①胎儿, 婴儿 ②小孩(可指男孩或女孩): a spoilt ~ 受溺爱的孩子 / a *children's* court [美]少年法庭 / *Children's* Day 儿童节 ③儿子, 女儿: a natural ~ 私生子(子孙, 后裔 ⑤有孩子气的人), 幼稚的人 ⑥某时代的人物 ⑦(头脑、空想等的)产物: a ~ of the imagination 想象的产物 / fancy's ~ 想象中的产物, 空想 ⑧追随者, 依附者: *children* of Izaak Walton ['aizək 'wɔːltən] 爱钓鱼的人们 ‖ *A burnt ~ dreads the fire.* [谚]一次被火烧, 见火就害怕。/ a ~ of nature 自然的宠儿; 天真的人 / a ~ of fortune 幸运儿 / a ~ of sb.'s loins 某人亲生的孩子 / ~'s play ①容易干的事 ②不重要的行为 / drag up a ~ [口]胡乱把孩子养大 / from a ~ 自幼 / (heavy) with ~ 怀孕 / own a ~ 承认自己是孩子的父亲 / *The ~ is father of (或 to) the man.* [谚]三岁定到老。/ this ~ [口][谑]我, 我自己, 鄙人 ‖ ~ hood n. 幼年(时代), 童年; 早期: second ~ hood 老年的智力衰退时期 / ~ less a. 无子女的 / ~ like, ~ ly a. 孩子般天真的, 诚实的 ‖ ~, bearing n. 分娩; 生小孩 / '~ bed n. 分娩(状态) / '~ birth n. 分娩; 生小孩 / ~ bride ①年轻的新娘 ②童养媳 / ~ labo(u)r [总称]童工 / ~ wife 年轻的妻子

childish ['tʃaildiʃ] a. ①孩子的, 孩子所特有的: a ~ game 儿童游戏 ②幼稚的, 傻气的: a ~ idea (answer) 幼稚的想法(答复) ‖ ~ ly ad. / ~ ness n.

chill [tʃil] **I** n. ①寒冷, 寒气: There is a ~ in the air this evening. 今晚有些冷飕飕。/ take the ~ off the wine 烫一烫酒 ②寒战, 风寒: feel a ~ both in hands and feet 手足发冷 / catch a ~ 着凉 ③扫兴, 寒心: cast a ~ over sb. (坏消息等)使某人感到寒心; 使人扫兴 ④(态度的)冷淡 ⑤【冶】冷模; 激冷部分: ~ casting 冷铸 **II** a. ①凉飕飕的, 冷的 ②冷淡的; 使人寒心的 **III** ❶ vt. ①使变冷; 使感到冷: be ~ ed to the bone (或 the marrow) 感到寒气刺骨 ②使(轻度)冷冻: ~ ed beef 冷冻牛肉 ③使扫兴, 使寒心, 使沮丧 ④使冷淬 ⑤[英方]把(饮料)暖一暖 ❷ vi. ①变冷; 感到寒冷, 发冷 ②冷淬 ‖ ~ er n. ①惊险小说 ②冰箱内的食物冷冻格 ③脱蜡冷结晶器 ④冷却装置 ⑤冷冻工人 / ~ ness n.

chilli ['tʃili] n. (干)辣椒

chilly ['tʃili] **I** a. ①寒冷的 ②感到寒冷的: I'm rather ~. 我感觉有些冷。③冷淡的, 不友好的 ④易于引起恐惧的 **II** ad. [罕]冷淡地

chime[1] [tʃaim] **I** n. ①(音调谐和的)一套钟和敲钟的装置 ②[常用复](一套钟的)谐和钟声 ③谐音, 韵律; 和谐 ④单调 **II** ❶ vi. ①(乐器、钟等)奏出谐和的乐声 ②协调, 一致 ❷ vt. ①在(钟)上敲击出谐和的乐声; (钟)敲出(谐和的乐声) ②用钟响报(时); 打钟召集(人) ③单调而重复地讲(话等) ‖ ~ *in* ①插话; 插话表示赞成 ②插(话) / ~ *in with* 与…协调, 与…一致

chime[2] [tʃaim] n. (桶两端的)凸边

chimney ['tʃimni] n. ①烟囱, 烟筒 ②(煤油、汽油灯的)玻璃罩 ③(登山时)仅容一人攀登的岩石裂口 ④烟囱状的东西; (火山等的)喷烟口 ⑤[美方]壁炉 ⑥[英俚]烟瘾极大的人 ‖ *smoke like a* ~ 烟瘾极大 ‖ ~ cap 烟囱帽 / ~ corner 壁炉边 / ~ jack 旋转式烟囱帽 / '~ piece n. 壁炉架 / ~ pot ①烟囱帽管 ② = ~ -pot hat / '~ -pot hat [英俚]高顶礼帽 / ~ stack 丛烟囱(一个有几个顶管的烟囱) / ~ stalk [英] ①工厂的高烟囱 ②丛烟囱 / ~ swallow 在烟囱上(或旁边)作巢的燕子 / ~ sweep(er) 扫烟囱工人 / ~ swift = ~ swallow / ~ top 烟囱顶部

chimpanzee [,tʃimpən'zi:] n. 黑猩猩

chin [tʃin] **I** n. ①颏, 下巴 ②(单杠的)引体向上动作 **I** ❶ vt. (chinned; chinning) ❶ vt. ①用下巴夹住 (提琴等) ② ~ oneself (拉单杠时)引体向上 ❷ vi. [俚]聊天; 唠叨 ‖ *have a* ~ 闲谈, 聊天 / *keep one's* ~ *up* [口]不气馁, 不灰心 / *stick one's* ~ *out* 暴露自己; 招致麻烦(或攻

击等);冒风险 / *take it on the* ~ [俚]输;忍受责罚(或痛苦等) / *up to the* ~ ①直到下巴 ②深陷 / *wag* (*one's*) ~ [俚]闲谈;唠叨 ‖'~-'bone *n.* 颏骨 / '~-'deep *a.* 深陷的;深到下巴的 / ~ music [俚]闲谈,空谈: jerk ~ music 闲谈 / '~-wag *n. & vi.* 闲谈,聊天

china ['tʃainə] *n.* 瓷器;瓷料: a piece of ~ 一件瓷器 / blue ~ 青瓷 ‖ ~ clay 瓷土,高岭土 / ~ closet 瓷器(陈列)橱 / ~ shop 瓷器店 / ~ stone 做瓷器的石料 / '~ware *n.* [总称]瓷器

chink[1] [tʃiŋk] I *n.* ①裂缝,裂口 ②漏洞,弱点,空子 II *vt.* 堵塞…的裂缝

chink[2] [tʃiŋk] I *n.* ①(金属、玻璃器等的)丁当声 ②[俚]现钱,现钱 II *vi. & vt.* (使)丁当响

chintz [tʃints] *n. & a.* 擦光印花布(的)

chip[1] [tʃip] I *n.* ①(削木或凿石所留下的)片屑;(金属等的)切屑;(玻璃、瓷器等的)碎片 ②(土豆、水果等的)薄片;[复]油煎土豆片 ③(碎裂的)凹口,缺口: a ~ on the edge of a bowl 碗边上的缺口 ④(编帽或篮子等用的)木片条,棕榈叶片: a ~ basket (作水果篮等用的)木片条篮子 ⑤[Chips][海俚]船上的木匠 ⑥(作赌注用的)筹码;[复][俚]钱: The ~s are down. 赌注已下。(或:情况危急。) ⑦微小的东西,无价值的东西: not care a ~ for 对…毫不在意 ⑧(作燃料用的)干粪块 ⑨集成电路块 II (chipped; chipping) ❶ *vt.* ①削,凿,铲: ~ old paint off a container 铲掉容器上的旧漆 ②在(瓷器等)上造成缺口;把…切成薄片: The plate has a chipped edge. 盘子上边有凹口。/ ~ potatoes 把土豆切成片 ③削成,凿成(某种形状);刻(题词等) ④(用话语)逗弄,挖苦 ⑤(小鸡等)啄碎(蛋壳) ❷ *vi.* 形成缺口;碎裂 ‖*a* ~ *in porridge* (或 *pottage, broth*) 无关紧要之物,可有可无之物 / *a* ~ *of* (或 *off*) *the old block* 与父亲一模一样的儿子 / (*as*) *dry as a* ~ 枯燥无味的 / *cash in one's* ~*s* ①把筹码兑成现钱 ②[俚]死 / ~ *in* [口] ①插嘴,打断别人的话 ②捐助;提供帮助 ③下赌注 / *have a* ~ *on one's shoulder* 好斗;易被激怒 / *in the* ~*s* [俚]有钱,富有 / *let the* ~*s fall where they may* 不管后果如何 ‖chippings [复] *n.* (削下或凿下的)片屑 / '~-board *n.* 废纸制成的纸板

chip[2] [tʃip] I *n.* (摔角时)使人摔倒的一种技巧 II (chipped; chipping) *vt.* 使摔倒

chiropodist [ki'rɔpədist] *n.* 手足病医生(尤指足病医生)

chiropody [ki'rɔpədi] *n.* 手足病治疗

chirp [tʃə:p] I *n.* 鸟叫声;虫鸣声 II ❶ *vi.* ①(鸟等)吱吱地叫;(草虫等)唧唧地叫 ②(人)喊喊喳喳 ❷ *vt.* 喊喊喳喳地讲出(或唱出)

chirpy ['tʃə:pi] *a.* 快活的,活泼的

chirrup ['tʃirəp] I *n.* (鸟、虫等的)反复不断的吱吱唧唧叫声;(哄孩子和催马的)啧啧声 II *vi.* 发出唧唧叫声;发出啧啧声

chisel ['tʃizl] I *n.* ①凿子,錾子: a chipping ~ 平錾 / a cold ~ 冷錾子 / a pneumatic ~ 气錾 ②[俚]欺骗,诈骗 II (chisel(l)ed; chisel(l)ing) ❶ *vt.* ①凿,镂,雕 ②[口]欺骗,诈骗;骗取;争夺 ❷ *vi.* ①凿,镂,雕 ②[俚]欺骗,诈骗 ③钻进 (*in*) ‖*full* ~ [美俚]飞快地;猛冲地 / *the* ~ 雕刻师的凿刀;雕刻术

chivalry ['ʃivəlri] *n.* ①(中世纪的)骑士制度;骑士气概(或品质) ②骑士团 ③对女子献殷勤的绅士们

chloride ['klɔ:raid] *n.* 【化】氯化物: sodium ~ 氯化钠(食盐) / ~ of lime 漂白粉

chlorine ['klɔ:ri:n] *n.* 【化】氯,氯气

chloroform ['klɔ(:)rəfɔ:m] I *n.* 【化】氯仿,三氯甲烷 II *vt.* 用氯仿处理;用氯仿麻醉;用氯仿杀死

chock [tʃɔk] I *n.* ①(用以防止转动、滑动等的)楔子,垫木 ②【机】塞块 ②【海】导缆钩,导缆器 II *vt.* 用楔子垫阻;把(船)放在垫木上 III *ad.* 紧密地,满满地 ‖~ *up* ①用楔子牢牢垫稳 ②把(房间等)塞满: a room ~ed *up* with furniture 塞满家具的房间 ‖'~-a'block *a. & ad.* 塞满的(地),挤得满满的(地) / '~-'full *a.* (塞)满了的,挤得满满的

chocolate ['tʃɔkəlit] I *n.* ①巧克力,朱古力 ②巧克力糖: a bar of ~ 一条巧克力糖 / a box of ~s 一盒巧克力糖 ③巧克力饮料 ④赭色 II *a.* 巧克力制的;含有巧克力的;赭色的 ‖~ cream 奶油夹心巧克力 / ~ drop [贬]黑人

choice [tʃɔis] I *n.* ①选择,抉择: a ~ between going and staying 去和留的抉择 / the ~ of words 词的选用 / He made a careful ~. 他作了谨慎的选择。②选择机会;选择权;选择能力: offer a ~ 提供选择机会 ③被选中的东西;入选者:精华:Which is your ~? 你选哪一个? ④供选择的种类: This shop has a large (or great) ~ of hats and shoes. 这家商店有很多种类鞋帽可供购。⑤审慎: pick words with ~ 用词审慎 II *a.* ①值得选用的 ②精选的,上等的: ~ goods 上等品 ③挑三拣四的: be ~ of one's food 挑食,吃东西挑挑拣拣 ④[美]宠爱的,爱惜的 ‖*at* ~ 可随意选择 / *by* ~ 出于自择 / *for* ~ ①出于自择 ②要选就选…: I should take this one *for* ~. 要挑我就挑这个。/ *have no* ~ ①不特别偏爱那个,不在乎那个 ②不能选择 / *have no* ~ *but to* (do) 除(做)…外别无他法,非(做)…不可 / *have one's* ~ 有选择权,可以挑选 / *Hobson's* ~ 无选择余地 / *make* ~ *of* 选定… / *of* ~ 精选的,特别的 / *take one's* ~ 选择 ‖~ly *ad.* / ~ness *n.*

choir ['kwaiə] I *n.* ①(教会的)歌唱队,唱诗班 ②歌唱队(或教士)的席位 ③(歌手、舞者等的)队,组;(鸟等的)群 ④一组同类的乐器 II *vt. & vi.* 合唱

choke [tʃouk] I ❶ *vt.* ①闷塞,闷死;掐死;噎塞: The smoke almost ~d me. 烟呛得我几乎透不过气来。②阻塞,堵塞,塞满: The chimney is almost ~d (up) with soot. 烟囱几乎被烟垢堵住了。/ ~ the flow of electric current 阻止电流 ③ 抑制,压住: Anger ~d his words. 他气得话也说不出来。/ ~ down one's anger 抑制愤怒 ④闷住,阻止,扑灭(火等);干死(植物) ⑤【机】阻塞…的气门(以得到更浓缩的燃料混合物) ⑥(棒球中)握着(球棒)的中段 ❷ vi. ①窒息;噎住;说不出话来: ~ with anger 气得说不出话来 ②(管子、渠道等)塞住: The channel ~s. 这条水道塞住了。**II** n. ①窒息;噎 ②【机】阻塞门,阻气门;【无】扼流圈(=choking coil) ‖~ **back** 抑制(怒气、眼泪等) / ~ **down** 硬咽(食物);强抑(感情等) / ~ **sb. off** 使某人放弃(做某事) ②除掉某人 / ~ **up** ①阻住,噎住 ②(由于强烈的感情而)说不出话来 ③阻塞,填塞 ④塞得太满 ‖~ **damp** n. (煤矿、深井中的)碳酸气 / ~ **pear** 味涩的梨;[喻]难以忍受的责备(或事实)

cholera ['kɔlərə] n. 【医】霍乱: epidemic ~ 流行性霍乱 ‖~**ic** [,kɔlə'reiik] a.

choose [tʃuːz] (chose [tʃouz], chosen ['tʃouzn]) ❶ vt. ①选择,挑选: ~ three *from* (或 *among, out of*) these books 从这些书中挑三本 / ~ A before B 挑甲不挑乙 / There is nothing (not much) to ~ *between* the two. 两者一样(差不多),没有什么可挑的。/ Choose me a good hoe. 替我挑一把好锄头。/ Whom shall we ~ *for* (或 *as*) our team leader? 我们选谁当队长? ②[后接不定式]选定;愿意 ❷ vi. ①选择: These samples are for you to ~ *from*. 这些样品是供你挑选的。②喜欢: You may take all if you ~. 你合意的话,可都拿去。/ Do just as you ~. 你喜欢怎么办,就怎么办。‖**cannot** ~ **but** [后接原形动词]只得 / ~ **up** [口](在临时性非正式比赛中)对阵双方的球员 / pick and ~ 挑挑拣拣;挑剔 ‖~**r** n. 选择者

chop[1] [tʃɔp] **I** (chopped; chopping) ❶ vt. ①砍,劈,斩: ~ down a tree 砍下一棵树 / ~ off a finger 砍掉手指 / ~ wood 劈木柴 ②切细,剁碎: ~ the meat up 把肉剁碎 ③劈路前进: a way through the undergrowth 在矮树林中劈出一条路来 ④[喻]割断(up): ~ up history 割断历史 ❷ vi. 砍,猛击: ~ at sth. 朝某物猛砍 **II** n. ①砍,劈,剁 ②一块排骨 ③砍(或劈)的痕迹 ④被风吹皱的水面 ‖~ **back** 突然掉转方向,急忙掉头逃跑 / ~ **in** [口]插嘴,多嘴 / ~ **out** (或 **up**) (地层)露现 / lick one's ~s 馋涎欲滴 / ~ [美俚]幸灾乐祸 ‖'~**house** n. 小饭馆 / '~**stick** n. [常用复]筷子 / ~ **suey** ['suːi] (中国菜)炒杂碎

chop[2] [tʃɔp] n. =chap[2]

chop[3] [tʃɔp] **I** (chopped; chopping) vi. (风等)突然转向(about, round) **II** n. 交换 ‖~ **and change** 变化无常,摇摆不定 / ~ logic 强词夺理地争辩

chop[4] [tʃɔp] n. ①戳记,官印;护照,许可证 ②商标;货物品质: the first ~ 一级,头等

chopper ['tʃɔpə] n. ①伐木者 ②斧头;屠刀,大砍

刀 ③【电】断路器;断续器;【无】振动换流器;限器,斩波器;【原】中子选择器 ④[美俚]直升飞机 ⑤[美俚]验票员 ⑥[美俚]机关枪;机枪手;带机枪的匪徒

choppy[1] ['tʃɔpi] a. ①波浪滔滔的 ②裂缝多的;有皱纹的 ③不连贯的

choppy[2] ['tʃɔpi] a. (风)方向常变的

choral ['kɔːrəl] a. 合唱队的;合唱的 ‖~**ly** ad.

choral(e) [kɔ'raːl] n. (合唱的)赞美诗

chord [kɔːd] **I** n. ①(乐器的)弦;[喻]心弦: touch the right ~ 触动心弦 ②【音】和弦,和音: common ~ 大调(或小调)三和弦 ③【解】索,带: vocal ~s 声带 ④【空】翼弦,翼长 ⑤【数】弦 ⑥【建】弦材,桁弦 **II** ❶ vi. ①协调,和谐 ②弹奏 ❷ vt. ①上…的弦;调…的弦 ②使和谐

chore [tʃɔː] n. [美] ①[复]家庭杂务 ②日常零星工作 ③困难的(或不合意的)工作

choreography [,kɔ(ː)ri'ɔgrəfi] n. ①用符号来表示舞蹈动作的艺术 ②舞蹈(表演) ③舞蹈设计(尤指芭蕾舞)

chorister ['kɔristə] n. ①(教堂内的)唱诗班歌手(尤指男孩) ②唱诗班的领唱人

chorus ['kɔːrəs] **I** n. ①合唱;合唱队;歌舞团: a female (male) ~ 女声(男声)合唱 / a mixed ~ 男女合唱,混声合唱 ②合唱曲;歌舞剧中的合唱台词 ③齐声,一齐: a ~ of protest 一片抗议声 / read in ~ 齐声朗读 ④(歌的)迭句;合唱段 ⑤作配角的合唱者与舞蹈者 ⑥(英国古代剧)宣读开场白和收场白的角色 **II** vt. & vi. 齐声背诵;合唱;异口同声地说 ‖'~ **girl** 歌剧合唱队女演员 / ~ **master** 合唱队指挥

chose[1] [tʃouz] choose 的过去式

chose[2] [ʃouz] n. 【律】动产 ‖a ~ in action 可依法赢得(尚未实际占有的)动产;对某件尚未实际占有的动产的权利 / a ~ in possession 实际占有的动产,占有物

chosen ['tʃouzn] **I** choose 的过去分词 **II** a. ①挑选出来的;精选的 ②【宗】上帝所选的: the ~ people 上帝的特选子民(指犹太人)

Christ [kraist] n. 【基督教】救世主(特指耶稣基督): before ~ 公元前(略作 B. C.) ‖~**hood** n. 基督的品格(或身分) / ~**like**, ~**ly** a. 具有基督精神(或德性)的;象基督一样的

christen ['krisn] vt. ①【宗】为…施洗礼;洗礼时命名: be ~ed John 洗礼时被命名为约翰 ②(举行仪式)命名(船舶等) ③(隆重地)首次使用(汽车、船舶等) ‖~**ing** n. 洗礼仪式;命名仪式

Christendom ['krisndəm] n. 基督教世界;[总称]基督教徒

Christian ['kristjən] **I** n. 基督教徒;信徒 **II** a. ①基督教的;信基督教的: the ~ era 公元,基督纪元 / a ~ name 教名 / the Young Men's (Women's) ~ Association 基督教青年(女青年)会 / ~ Science【宗】基督教科学派(主张信仰疗法的基督教派别) ②基督的 ③[口]合礼俗常规的 ‖~**ism** n. 基督教徒的教义和仪式

Christianity [ˌkristiˈæniti] *n.* ① [总称]基督教徒 ②基督教 ③基督教徒的身分;基督教徒的品性

Christmas [ˈkrisməs] *n.* ①【基督教】圣诞节: ~ Day 耶稣生日, 圣诞 (12月25日) / ~ Eve 圣诞前夜(12月24日) / at ~ 在圣诞节 / a ~ present 圣诞节礼物 / A merry ~ (to you)! 恭贺圣诞! ② 圣诞节节期 (= ~tide) ‖'~-box *n.* [英](给邮递员等的)圣诞赏钱 / ~ card 圣诞贺片 / ~ carol 圣诞节颂歌 / '~tide *n.* 圣诞节节期 (12月24日至1月6日) / ~ tree 圣诞树

chrome [kroum] Ⅰ *n.* ①【化】铬; 铬黄: ~ steel 铬钢 / ~ red 铬铅红 ②镀有铬合金的东西 Ⅱ *vt.* 用铬的化合物来印染

chromium [ˈkroumjəm] *n.*【化】铬

chronic [ˈkrɔnik] Ⅰ *a.* ①长期的, 慢性的: a ~ disease 慢性病 ②惯常的, 经常的 ③ [英]剧烈的, 顽固的 Ⅱ *n.* 患慢性病的人 ‖~ally *ad.*

chronicle [ˈkrɔnikl] Ⅰ *n.* ①年代记, 编年史 ②历史, 记事 Ⅱ *vt.* 把…载入编年史; 记述 ‖~r *n.* 年代史编者; 记录者

chronologic(al) [ˌkrɔnəˈlɔdʒik(əl)] *a.* 年代学的; 按照年月顺序的: a *chronological* table 年表 ‖chronologically *ad.*

chronology [krəˈnɔlədʒi] *n.* ①年代学 ②(资料等)按年月次序的排列 ③年表

chronometer [krəˈnɔmitə] *n.* 精密记时计; 航行表;天文钟

chrysalis [ˈkrisəlis] ([复] chrysalides [kriˈsælidiːz] 或 chrysalises) *n.* ①【动】蝶蛹 ②[喻]处于预备(或转化)状态的东西

chrysanthemum [kriˈsænθəmem] *n.*【植】①菊(花): the land of the ~ 菊花之乡(日本的别称) ② [C-] 菊属

chubby [ˈtʃʌbi] *a.* 圆脸的; 丰满的: a ~ boy 圆脸蛋的男孩 / ~ cheeks 丰满的脸颊 ‖chubbiness *n.*

chuck[1] [tʃʌk] Ⅰ *vi.* ①(母鸡等)咯咯地叫 ②咯咯地唤鸡; 咂咂地催马前进 Ⅱ *int.* & *n.* ①咯咯(声); 咂咂(声) ②宝贝儿(表示亲热的用语)

chuck[2] [tʃʌk] Ⅰ *vt.* ①轻拍, 抚弄: ~ the child under the chin 抚弄孩子的下巴 ②扔, 抛: ~ away rubbish 扔掉垃圾 ③赶走, 驱逐: ~…out of a place 把…赶出某处 ④丢弃, 放弃: Chuck it! [英俚]停下来! 别干下去了! / ~ up the sponge 认输, 放弃竞争 / ~ up one's job 丢弃自己的工作,离职不干 Ⅱ *n.* ①抚弄 ②扔掉; 丢弃 ③赶走,撵出 ‖~ away 扔掉; 浪费; 失去(机会等) / get the ~ [俚]被解雇 / give sb. the ~ [英俚]把某人解雇 / '~-er-out ['tʃʌkər'aut] *n.* [英](戏院、旅馆、会议场所等雇来)撵走捣乱分子的人

chuck[3] [tʃʌk] *n.* ①(牛等的)颈肉 ②[俚]食物 ‖~ wag(g)on [美](拓荒、伐木等时用的)流动炊事车

chuck[4] [tʃʌk] Ⅰ *n.*【机】(车床等的)夹盘, 夹头, 卡盘: universal ~ 万能夹头 Ⅱ *vt.* 用夹头夹住:把…装进夹头

chuckle [ˈtʃʌkl] Ⅰ *vi.* ①抿着嘴轻声地笑, (高兴地)暗自笑: ~ to oneself 暗喜, 自笑 / ~ over (或 at) sth. 为某事十分开心 ②(母鸡)咯咯地叫 Ⅱ *n.* 轻声笑, 暗自笑 ‖~head *n.* [口]傻瓜, 笨蛋 / '~,headed *a.* [口]愚蠢的,呆笨的

chug [tʃʌg] Ⅰ *n.* (机器等的)嘎嘎声 Ⅱ (chugged; chugging) *vi.* 嘎嘎嘎嘎地响

chum[1] [tʃʌm] Ⅰ *n.* 好朋友; [美]同房间的人: a new ~ [澳]新来的移民, 生手 Ⅱ (chummed; chumming) *vi.* ①同室居住 ②成为好朋友: ~ up with sb. 与某人成好朋友 ‖split ~s 绝交

chum[2] [tʃʌm] *n.* 鱼饵(尤指切成小块的鱼)

chunk [tʃʌŋk] *n.* ①(厚)块: a ~ of bread 一块(厚)面包 ②相当大的数量(或部分) ③结实的马;矮胖的(男)人

church [tʃəːtʃ] Ⅰ *n.* ①教堂, 礼拜堂 ②教会, 教派; 教会全体成员: the Eastern *Church* 东正教会 / the Western *Church* 天主教会, 罗马公教 / the *Church* of England (或 English *Church*, Anglican *Church*) 英国国教, 圣公会 / the High (Low) *Church* 高(低)教会派(注重(不注重)教会礼仪等的圣公会中的一派) / the Methodist *Church* 美以美教会 / the World Council of *Churches* 世界基督教协进会 ③【宗】礼拜: They are in (或 at) ~. 他们在做礼拜。/ go to (或 attend) ~ 去做礼拜 / ~ service 礼拜 ④ 神职, 牧师的职位: enter (或 go into) the ~ 就神职, 做牧师 ⑤全体基督教徒: *Church* militant 【宗】与邪恶作战的世间基督教徒 Ⅱ *vt.* 把(某人)带到教堂接受宗教仪式 Ⅲ *a.* 教会的; [英]国教的 ‖(*as*) *poor as a ~ mouse* 赤贫的 / ~ing *n.* (妇女)平安生产后的教堂礼拜 / ~ism *n.* 墨守教会仪式 / ~ly *a.* ①教堂的; 符合教会的 ②虔诚的 ‖'~,goer *n.* 常去做礼拜的教徒 / ~man ['tʃəːtʃmən] *n.* 教士, 牧师; 国教教徒 / ~ text 墓碑上的黑体字[印]黑体字 / '~,warden *n.* ①(具有教徒身分的)教区委员, 教会执事 ②[英]陶土制的长烟斗 / '~yard *n.* 教堂院子; (教堂的)墓地: a ~yard cough [英]临死前的干咳 / a fat ~yard 葬有很多死人的墓地

churl [tʃəːl] *n.* ①[英史]下层自由民; 出身低贱的人 ②(中世纪的)农民; 乡下人 ③粗暴的人 ④吝啬鬼, 守财奴

churn [tʃəːn] Ⅰ *n.* (炼制黄油用的)搅乳器; [英]大的盛奶罐; 【机】摇转搅拌筒 Ⅱ ❶ *vt.* ①用搅乳器搅拌(牛奶等); 制造(黄油) ②剧烈搅拌 ❷ *vi.* ①用搅乳器搅拌 ②剧烈搅动 ③(波浪)翻腾 ‖~ out 靠机械力产生;艰苦地做出 ‖~ing *n.* ①搅乳; 搅拌 ②一次炼出的黄油量 ‖~ dasher, ~ staff 搅乳装置, 搅乳棒

chute [ʃuːt] *n.* ①急流; 瀑布 ②斜道, 滑运道;【机】斜槽 ③ [口]降落伞 (parachute 的缩略)

chutney [ˈtʃʌtni] *n.* 一种酸辣调味品(用水果、洋葱和辣椒等制成)

cicada [siˈkaːdə, siˈkeidə] ([复] cicadae [siˈkaːdiː, siˈkeidiː] 或 cicadas) *n.*【动】蝉

cider ['saidə] *n.* 苹果汁; 苹果酒: a ~ press 苹果汁榨取器

cigar [si'gɑ:] *n.* 雪茄烟, 叶卷烟 ‖~ **holder** 雪茄烟烟嘴 / **ci'gar-shaped** *a.* 雪茄烟状的

cigaret(te) [,sigə'ret] *n.* 纸烟, 香烟, 卷烟 ‖~ **case** 香烟盒 / ~ **holder** 香烟烟嘴 / ~ **paper** 卷烟纸

cinder ['sində] *n.* ①炉渣, 矿渣, 煤渣; 未燃尽的煤 (或木炭等) ②[复]灰烬 ③【地】火山渣 ‖~ **path** 煤渣路 (或跑道) / ~ **sifter** 煤渣筛 / ~ **track** 煤渣跑道

cinema ['sinimə] *n.* ①电影院 ②电影, 影片 ③电影工业; 电影制片(技)术

cinnamon ['sinəmən] *n.* ①樟属植物; 樟属中几种树的芳香内皮: Chinese ~ 肉桂 / ~ oil 桂皮油 ②黄棕色 ‖~**ic** [,sinə'mɔnik] *a.*

cipher ['saifə] I *n.* ①零(即 0) ②不重要的人, 无价值的东西 ③密码, 暗号; 密码电报: a ~ key 密码索引, 暗号注解 / a ~ officer 译电员 / a ~ telegram 密码电报 / in ~ 用密码, 用暗号 ④阿拉伯数字: a number of four ~s 四位数 ⑤(尤指姓名首字母等的)拼合文字, 花押字 ⑥[音](风琴的阀出毛病时的)连响 II *vt. & vi.* ①计算; 算出 (out) ②用密码书写 ‖~ **in algorism** 零; 傻偶

circa ['sə:kə] *prep.* [拉]大约(通常略作 c., ca., cir., circ. 或 C., 用在年代前面): born ~ 250 B. C. 生于公元前约二百五十年

circle ['sə:kl] I *n.* ①圆, 圆周; 圈; 环状物: the great (small) ~ of a sphere【数】球的大(小)圆 / sit (dance) in a ~ 围成一圈坐着(跳舞) / the Arctic Circle 北极圈 / ~ of declination【天】赤纬圈 / ~ of longitude【天】黄经圈 / vertical ~【天】平经圈 ②(天体运转的)轨道 ③(具有共同兴趣、利益的人们所形成的)圈子; 集团: have a large ~ of friends 交游很广 / cultural (academic, theatrical, business) ~s 文化(学术, 戏剧, 商)界 / fashionable ~ 讲究时髦的人士; (资产阶级的)上流社会 ④周期, 循环; 完整的一系列: the ~ of the seasons 四季的循环 / a ~ of sciences 一系列有关的科学 ⑤【逻】循环论证(一种逻辑错误: 以乙来论证甲, 而乙的真实性又是以甲来论证的) ⑥(活动、势力、影响等的)范围, 领域: The article touches a wide ~ of subjects. 这篇文章涉及多方面的问题。 ⑦楼厅(剧场的二楼厅座); 马戏场 ⑧铁路的环形交叉口; 圆形场地 II ❶ *vt.* 环绕; 绕过; 围: a man-made satellite that ~s the earth 环绕地球运转的人造卫星 / The ship has ~d the cape. 船绕过了地角。 / a stock farm ~d with a fence 四周围着篱笆的饲养场 ❷ *vi.* ① 盘旋, 旋转; 环行: The aircraft ~d (round or around) over the landing strip. 飞机在着陆跑道上空盘旋。 / ~ back towards home (绕圈)折返 ②流传: The happy news soon ~d round (或 around). 喜讯很快就传开了。 ‖*argue in a* ~ 用循环论证来辩论 / *a swing around* (或 *round*) *the* ~ (指政客)发表政见的巡回旅行 /

a vicious ~ ①恶性循环 ②【逻】循环论证 / *come full* ~ 兜了一圈, 回到原位 / *run round in* ~*s* [口]忙得团团转 / *square the* ~ 做办不到的事情 ‖~**wise** *ad.* 围成一圈地, 环形地

circlet ['sə:klit] *n.* ①小圈 ②(手镯等)环形饰物

circuit ['sə:kit] I *n.* ①环行; 周线; 范围: make (或 fetch) a ~ (of the school campus) (绕校园)兜一个圈子 / the periodic ~ of the earth round (或 around) the sun 地球绕太阳周期性的环行 / 巡回审判(或传道); 巡回区 ③同业性的联合组织; 轮回上演(或上映)的若干戏院(或电影院) ④事物变化的顺序 ⑤【电】[无]电路; 回路; 线路: closed (open) ~ 闭(开)路 / integrated ~ 集成电路 / printed ~ 印刷电路 / return ~ 回路 / short ~ 短路 II *vt. & vi.* (绕…)环行 ‖*ride* ‖*ride* ❘~ **binding** 软皮面、圆角、有护边的书籍装订形式 / ~ **breaker** 【电】断路器 / ~ **rider** (基督教卫理公会的)巡回牧师

circuitous [sə(:)'kju(:)itəs] *a.* ①迂回的, 绕行的: take a ~ route 绕着走 ②间接进行的 ‖~**ly** *ad.* / ~**ness** *n.*

circular ['sə:kjulə] I *a.* ①圆形的, 环形的: a ~ saw 圆锯 ②循环的; 环绕一圈的: ~ motion 圆周运动 / a ~ tour 环程旅行 / a ~ ticket 环程客票 ③迂回的: a ~ treatment of the problem 对问题所作的非直截了当的处理 ④【逻】循环论证的 ⑤供流传的: a ~ letter 通函; 通知 II *n.* 通知, 通告; 通函 ‖~**ly** *ad.*

circularize ['sə:kjuləraiz] *vt.* ①发通知给…; 发意见征询书给… ②(用通知等)宣传; 公布 ③使成圆形

circulate ['sə:kjuleit] ❶ *vi.* ①(血液等)循环, 环流: Blood ~s through the body. 血液在全身循环。 ②(货币、书刊等)流通, 通用: a *circulating* library 流通图书馆 ③(消息、名声等)流传, 传播 ④【数】(小数点后数字)循: *circulating* decimal 循环小数 ❷ *vt.* ①使(血液等)循环, 使环流 ②使(货币等)流通, 使周转 ③散布, 传播(消息等)

circulation [,sə:kju'leiʃən] *n.* ①循环, 环流; 运行: He has a good (bad) ~. 他血液循环良好(不好)。 ②(货币、消息等的)流通, 传播; (报刊等的)发行: in ~ 在传播中, 流通中 / put the new coins into ~ 发行新硬币 / withdraw the book from ~ 停止发行(或流通)这本书 ③发行额, 流通额; 销路: a newspaper with a daily ~ of five million 一张日销五百万份的报纸 / have a large (small) ~ 销路大(小) ④通货, 货币

circumcise ['sə:kəmsaiz] *vt.* ①【医】割除…的包皮(或阴蒂); 对…进行环切术 ②【宗】净(心等)

circumference [sə'kʌmfərəns] *n.* 圆周, 周围; 周线, 圆周线: The lake is thirty *li* in ~. 这湖周围三十里。

circumflex ['sə:kəmfleks] I *n.* 附加在元音字母上的声调符号, 音调符号; 长音符号(如希腊语中的 ～ 和 ～, 法语中的 ∧) II *vt.* 标声调符号(或长

音符号)于 **III** *a.* 有升降调特点的,有声调符号的;弯曲的

circumfluence [sə(:)'kʌmfluəns] *n.* 环流,周流

circumlocution [ˌsə:kəmlə'kju:ʃən] *n.* 迂回说法;累赘的话;遁辞: the *Circumlocution* Office 办事拖拉的官僚机关 ‖**circumlocutory** [ˌsə:kəm-'lɔkjutəri] *a.*

circumnavigate [ˌsə:kəm'nævigeit] *vt.* 环航(世界) ‖**circumnavigation** ['sə:kəmˌnævi'geiʃən] *n.* 环球航行 / **circumnavigator** *n.* 环球航行者

circumscribe ['sə:kəmskraib] *vt.* ①在…周围画线,立界限于 ②限制,约束 ③给…下定义 ④【数】使外接,使外切

circumspect ['sə:kəmspekt] *a.* 谨慎小心的,周到的,慎重的 ‖**~ion** [ˌsə:kəm'spekʃən] *n.* / **~ly** *ad.* / **~ness** *n.*

circumstance ['sə:kəmstəns] *n.* ①[复]情况,形势,环境: act according to ~s 随机应变 / in (或 under) present (或 the prevailing) ~s 在当前情况下 / in (或 under) certain (any) ~s 在某种(任何)情况下 / the whole ~s 全部情况 ②(事情的)详情,细节: without omitting a single ~ 详详细细地,毫无遗漏地 ③事件,事实;(有关)事项: a grave ~ 严重事件 / time, place, or other ~s 时间、地点或其他事项 ④[复]境况,境遇: in favourable (adverse) ~s 在顺(逆)境中 / in easy ~s 在富裕的生活环境中 / in bad (good) ~s 境况不好(好) / in reduced ~s 在境况较差的情况下,在穷困中 / in straitened ~s 在穷困中 ⑤仪式,形式: pomp and ~ 排场 / without ~ 不讲仪式地 ⑥命运,机会 ‖*in* (或 *under*) *no* ~*s* 无论如何不,决不 / *in* (或 *under*) *the* ~*s* (情况)既然这样 ‖**~d** *a.* 在(某种)环境(或境况)下: differently ~d 处境不同的 / well ~d 境况优裕的

circumstantial [ˌsə:kəm'stænʃəl] *a.* ①按照情况的 ②偶然的,有关而非主要的 ③详细的,详尽的 ④仪式隆重的 ‖**~ity** ['sə:kəmˌstænʃi'æliti] *n.* ①详尽 ②偶然性 / **~ly** *ad.*

circumvent [ˌsə:kəm'vent] *vt.* ①围绕;包围 ②对…用计取胜,智胜 ③用陷阱捉住 ④防止…发生 ‖**~ion** [ˌsə:kəm'venʃən] *n.*

circus ['sə:kəs] *n.* ①(圆形的)马戏场,杂技场;(古罗马的)竞技场 ②马戏(或杂技等)的表演 ③马戏团(包括人、马、道具等): a travelling ~ 流动马戏团 ④[军]飞行表演(=flying ~) ⑤[英]十字路口的圆形广场

cirrus ['sirəs] ([复] cirri ['sirai]) *n.* 【动】触毛,触须;【植】卷须 ②【气】卷云

cistern ['sistən] *n.* ①蓄水池(或箱),贮水器;【化】槽,桶 ②水塘,水池 ③【解】淋巴间隙

citadel ['sitədl] *n.* ①城堡;堡垒,要塞 ②避难所

cite [sait] *vt.* ①引用,引证;举(例) ②~ a line of verse 引用一行诗 ③【律】传讯 ④【军】传令嘉奖

citied ['sitid] *a.* ①有城市的 ②似城市的

citify ['sitifai] *vt.* 使城市化 ‖**citified** *a.* [常贬]

有城市风的

citizen ['sitizn] *n.* ①公民 ②市民,(城市)居民 ③[美]平民,老百姓 ‖**~hood** *n.* ①公民(或市民)身分;公民权 ②国籍 / **~ry** *n.* [总称]公民;[美]平民(别于军人等) / **~ship** *n.* ①公民(或市民)身分;公民的权利和义务 ②国籍 ③个人的品德表现: a pupil's ~*ship* in his school 学生在学校的表现 ‖**~'s arrest** (根据不成文法)公民自行对犯罪者的逮捕

citron ['sitrən] *n.* 【植】枸橼(香橼)

citrus ['sitrəs] ([复] citrus(es)) *n.* 【植】①[C-]柑橘属 ②柠檬,柑橘

city ['siti] *n.* ①城市,都市,市 ②全市居民 ③城邦 ‖*the City of God* (基督教中的)天堂 / *the City* (*of London*) 英国伦敦的商业区 / *the City of* (*the*) *Seven Hills* 罗马的别称 / *the Eternal City* 罗马的别称 / *the Holy City* ①圣城(基督教中指耶路撒冷城;天主教中指罗马;伊斯兰教中指麦加) ②天堂 ‖**~ward(s)** *ad.* 向城市 ‖**City article** 商业经济新闻摘要 / '**~bred** *a.* 在城市里长大的 / **City Company** 伦敦市行会 / **~ council** 市议会 / **City editor** ①[英]商业金融栏编辑 ②[美][c- e-]本地新闻编辑主任 / **~ father** 市政府的主要成员(如市参议员等) / **~ hall** ①市政厅 ②市政府 / **City man** (英国的)金融家,实业家 / **~ manager**(美国市参议会任命的)市行政官 / '**~scape** *n.* 城市景象(画) / **~ slicker** [口](农民眼中的)城市滑头 / **~-state** *n.* (古代希腊的)城邦

civic ['sivik] *a.* ①城市的: a ~ centre 市中心 ②市民的;公民的: ~ duties 公民的义务 / ~ rights 公民权

civil ['sivl] *a.* ①公民的,市民的,国民的;民用的: a bureau of ~ administration 民政局 / ~ defence 民防系统(尤指防空) / ~ rights 公民权 / ~ death 褫夺公权 / ~ disobedience (以拒绝遵守政府法令,拒绝纳税等方式进行的)非暴力反抗 / ~ aviation 民用航空 / ~ engineering 土木工程(学) ②国内的,国民间的: a ~ war 内战,国内战争 / the *Civil* War [美]南北战争(1861—1865);[英]查理一世与议会的战争 (1642—1649) ③文明的;有礼貌的,客气的: ~ society 文明社会 / a ~ answer 有礼貌的回答 / keep a ~ tongue 说话很有礼貌 ④【律】民事的,根据民法的;法律规定的: a ~ code 民法典 / *Civil Law* 罗马法 / a ~ case (suit) 民事案件(诉讼) ⑤非军职的,文职的,文官的: return to ~ life 退役 / a ~ servant 文职人员;公务员 / the ~ service [总称]文职人员;(军队以外的全部) 行政机构 / the ~ list 英国等议会批给王室的年俸 ⑥非神职的,非宗教的: a ~ marriage (西方国家中不采用宗教仪式的)世俗结婚 ⑦历法规定的: a ~ year (day) 民用年(日)(区别于天文年、天文日) ‖**~ly** *ad.* ①彬彬有礼地 ②从公民权利角度说;根据民法

civilian [si'viljən] **I** *n.* ①平民,老百姓(与军、警相

对而言) ②民法专家;罗马法专家 **II** *a.* 平民的,民间的;民用的: ~ clothes 便服(区别于军警制服) / a ~ worker 民工 / a ~ internee 被拘留敌侨 / ~ supplies 民用补给品 ‖**~ize** *vt.* 使从军人转为平民,把(军职)转为文职;使转为民用

civilization, civilisation [ˌsivilaiˈzeiʃən] *n.* ① 文明;文化: (The) Chinese ~ is one of the oldest in the world. 中国文化是世界上最古老的文化之一。②开化,教化 ③文明世界

civilize, civilise [ˈsivilaiz] ❶ *vt.* ①使文明;开化 ②教育 ❷ *vi.* 变成文明(社会)

Cl [化]元素氯 (chlorine) 的符号

clack [klæk] **I** ❶ *vi.* ①作噼啪声,作咔嗒声 ②喋喋不休,唠叨 ③(家禽)咯咯地叫 ❷ *vt.* ①使作噼啪声,使作咔嗒声 ②喋喋地讲,唠叨地说 **II** *n.* ①噼啪声,咔嗒声 ②唠叨;喋喋不休的舌头 ③ [机]瓣,瓣阀

clad [klæd] **I** clothe 的过去式和过去分词 **II** *a.* 穿衣的;被覆盖的 **III** (clad; cladding) *vt.* 在(金属)外包上另一种金属 ‖**cladding** *n.* 【物】包层

claim [kleim] **I** *vt.* ①(根据权利)要求;认领;索取: ~ compensation (或 to be compensated, that one should be compensated) for the losses 要求赔偿损失 / ~ payment from (或 of) sb. 要某人付款 / Has anyone ~ed this watch? 有人来认领这只表吗? ②自称,声称;主张: Don't ~ to know what you don't know. 不要强不知以为知。/ It is ~ed that.... 有人主张…(或: 据说…) ③值得,需要: This matter ~s our attention. 这事需要我们予以注意。**II** *n.* ①(根据权利而提出的)要求: a ~ for damages 赔偿损害的要求 / territorial ~s 领土要求 / make a ~ to sth. 提出要得到某物;认领某物 / I have many ~s on my time. 我很忙。(或: 有很多事要占去我的时间。) ②(对某事物的)权利;要求权;所有权: have no ~ on sb. (to sth.) 没有对某人(某事物)提出要求的权利 ③主张;断定 ④要求(而得到)的东西;要求(而得到)的矿区土地 ‖*hold down a ~* 留居一地以便得到对土地的所有权 / *jump a ~* [美]强占别人得到的(矿区)土地 / *lay ~ to* (根据权利)要求;主张;自以为: lay no ~ to being perfect (或 to perfection) 自称不甚完善 / *put in a ~ for sth.* 提出有权得到某物;认领某物 / *set up a ~ to sth.* 提出对某事物的要求;表明对某事物的主张 / *stake out* (或 *off*) *a ~* 立界标以表明(土地等的)所有权;坚持要求 (获得某物) ‖**~ jumper** [美]强占别人得到的(矿区)土地者

claimant [ˈkleimənt], **claimer** [ˈkleimə] *n.* (根据权利)提出要求者 (to)

clairvoyance [kleəˈvɔiəns] *n.* ①超人的视力 ②洞察力

clam [klæm] **I** *n.* ①[动]蛤;蛤肉 ②夹钳;夹子 ③[美俚]嘴紧的人,沉默寡言者 ④[美俚]美元 ⑤ =clamshell ⑥[美俚]错误 **II** (clammed; clamming) *vi.* 捞蛤 ‖**~ up** [俚]嘴紧,拒不开口

‖**~bake** *n.* [美]①海滨野餐会 ②喧嚣的社交集会(尤指政治集会) ③[俚]乱糟糟的广播(或电视)节目 / **~shell** *n.* ①蛤壳 ②蛤壳状挖泥器

clamber [ˈklæmbə] *vi., vt. & n.* 攀登,爬

clammy [ˈklæmi] *a.* ①冷湿的,滑腻的,粘糊糊的 ②造成冷湿的 ③冷淡的 ‖**clammily** *ad.* / **clamminess** *n.*

clamo(u)r [ˈklæmə] **I** *n.* 吵闹,喧嚷;(表示支持或抗议的)叫喊: make war ~s 发出战争叫嚣 ❶ *vi.* 吵闹,喧嚷;叫喊: ~ against 吵吵闹闹地反对 / ~ for 吵吵闹闹地要求 / ~ to (do) 叫嚷要(做) ❷ *vt.* ①用喧嚷迫使: ~ sb. down 对某人叫喊不使他讲下去 / ~ sb. into (out of) 吵吵闹闹地迫使某人做(停止做)… ②用喧嚷发出(或表示)

clamp[1] [klæmp] **I** *n.* 夹钳,夹子 **II** *vt.* ①(用夹钳)夹住,夹紧 ②强加(任务等) ‖**~ down** ①强制执行(宵禁、灯火管制等) ②施加压力;箝制,取缔 (on): ~ down on improper activities 取缔不正当活动 ‖**~-down** *n.* 压制;取缔

clamp[2] [klæmp] **I** *n.* (砖等的)堆 **II** *vt.* 堆(砖等) (up)

clamp[3] [klæmp] *n. & vi.* 重踏

clan [klæn] *n.* ①苏格兰高地人的氏族(或部落) ②氏族,部族,克兰 ③宗派,小集团,一伙人 ④[口]家族 ‖**~ship** *n.* ①氏族(或部族)制度 ②氏族(或部族)状态 ③小集团精神

clandestine [klænˈdestin] *a.* 秘密的,暗中的,私下的 ‖**~ly** *ad.* / **~ness** *n.*

clang [klæŋ] **I** ❶ *vi.* ①发铿锵声 ②(鹤等)鸣叫 ❷ *vt.* 使发铿锵声 **II** *n.* 铿锵声;(鹤等的)鸣叫声

clank [klæŋk] **I** *vi. & vt.* (使)发当啷声,(使)发铿锵声 **II** *n.* 当啷声,铿锵声

clap[1] [klæp] **I** (clapped; clapping) ❶ *vt.* ①拍,轻拍: ~ hands 拍手(呼人) / ~ one's hands 拍手(喝采) / ~ sb. on the back 用手轻拍某人背部(表示友好) ②振(翼),拍(翅膀): ~ wings 鼓翅 ③撞击…砰然出声 ④急速(或用力)地放;急忙处理: ~ spurs to a horse 急忙地踢马飞跑 / ~ up a bargain 匆忙成交 ❷ *vi.* ①拍手 ②砰然出声 **II** *n.* ①拍手喝采(声) ②霹雳声;破裂声: a ~ of thunder 雷鸣 ③轻轻的拍 ④发出碰撞声的装置 ‖*in two ~s of a lamb's tail* 立即 ‖**~board** *n.* 楔形板;护墙板;隔板 / **~net** *n.* 捕鸟(或捕虫)的网

clap[2] [klæp] *n.* [the ~]【医】淋病

claret [ˈklærət] **I** *n.* ①红葡萄酒,红酒(尤指法国波尔多产的) ②紫红色 ③[俚]血 **II** *a.* 紫红色的 ‖*tap sb.'s ~* [俚]把某人打得鼻子出血 ‖**colo(u)r** 紫红色 / **~-,colo(u)red** *a.* 紫红色的

clarify [ˈklærifai] ❶ *vt.* ①澄清,讲清楚,阐明: ~ matters 澄清真相 / ~ one's stand 阐明自己的立场 ②[化]澄清(液体等) ③使(头脑)清楚 ❷ *vi.* (液体等)澄清 ②变成易懂 ‖**clarification** [ˌklærifiˈkeiʃən] *n.*

clarinet [,klæri'net], **clarionet** [,klæriə'net] *n.* 【音】单簧管

clarion ['klæriən] **I** *n.* ①号角 ②号角声 **II** *a.* 响亮清晰的: a ~ call 嘹亮的号角声

clarity ['klæriti] *n.* 清澈; 透明; 明晰

clash [klæʃ] **I** ❶ *vi.* ①(铃铛、刀剑等)碰撞作声 ②猛撞, 冲突: ~ *into* sb. 蓦地撞在某人身上 ③(意见、利益、颜色等)抵触, 不调和(*with*) ❷ *vt.* 使(铃铛、刀剑等)碰撞作声 **II** *n.* ①(刀剑等的金属)碰撞声: It came down with a ~. 这东西当的一声掉落在地。 ②抵触, 冲突; 不调和: a ~ of opinions 意见的冲突 / a ~ of colours 色彩的不调和

clasp [klɑːsp] **I** *n.* ①扣子, 钩子, 扣紧物(如书夹子等) ②(挂奖章等用的)银质棒状扣; 别针 ③拥抱, 紧握, 握手 **II** ❶ *vt.* ①扣住, 扣紧, 钩住 ②拥抱, 抱紧 ③紧握: ~ hands with sb. (或 ~ sb. by the hand) 与某人紧紧握手 / ~ one's hands 交叉紧握十指 ④(藤等)紧紧缠绕 ❷ *vi.* 扣住, 扣紧, 钩紧: The button won't ~. 扣子扣不上。 ‖~**er** *n.* ①扣子, 钩子 ②缠绕物(如藤须等) ③【动】交合突, 鳍脚 ‖~ **knife** 折刀

class [klɑːs] **I** *n.* ①阶级: the working ~ 工人阶级 / the peasant ~ 农民阶级 ②社会等级: the upper (lower) ~es 上(下)层社会 ③班级; 年级: [美](某年)毕业班: the first-year (second-year) ~ 一(二)年级 / the ~ of 1970 一九七〇届毕业班 ④(一节)课: an on-the-spot ~ 一节现场教学课 / We have four ~es today. 我们今天有四节课。 / take ~es in politics 上政治课 / a physics ~ (或 a ~ *in* physics) 物理课 / in ~ 在上课; 在课堂上 / out of ~ 在课外 / Class is at eight. 八点钟上课。 / attend ~ 上课 ⑤(高低、优劣的)等级; 种类: travel third ~ 乘三等车(或舱)旅行 / He is doing first ~. 他干得非常好。 / various ~es of readers 各种读者 ⑥【生】(动植物分类)纲; 【矿】晶族: the ~ of mammals 哺乳动物纲 ⑦[口]优越, 出众; 风度: He is a ~ table tennis player. 他是一个优秀的乒乓球员。 ⑧[英](大学考试)优: take a ~ 大学考试得优等 / a ~ list 优等生名单 ⑨同年应征士兵 **II** *vt.* 把…分类(或分等级); 把…归入某类(或某等级) ‖*in a* ~ *by itself* (或 *oneself*) 独一无二, 独具一格 / *no* ~ [俚]低劣的 / *the* ~*es* 上层社会 / '~**book** *n.* [美]①记录学生缺勤、分数等的班级记录簿 ②班级纪念刊 / '~**fellow** *n.* 同班同学 / '~-**for-it'self** *n.* 自为的阶级 / '~-**in-it'self** *n.* 自在的阶级 / '~**mate** *n.* 同班同学 / '~**room** *n.* 教室, 课堂

classic ['klæsik] **I** *a.* ①(文学、艺术等)最优秀的, 第一流的 ②传统的; 不朽的: the ~ races (英国传统的)五大赛马 ③古典(指古罗马或古希腊文艺)的; 古典派的: a ~ myth 古希腊(或古罗马)神话 / a ~ style 古典流派的风格 ④历史上值得纪念的; 与著名文学作品(或作家)有关的: a ~ ground 文艺胜地 ⑤确实的, 可靠的, 典型的: a

~ case of pneumonia 典型的肺炎病例 **II** *n.* ①文豪, 大艺术家; 杰作, 名著 ②[复]经典(著作); (古罗马或古希腊的)古典著作: the Chinese ~s 中国的古典作品 / the *Classics* (希腊、罗马的)古典文学 ③古典(指古罗马或古希腊的)作家, 古典学者 ④传统的事件; 典型的事例; 可靠的出典 ⑤[俚]妇女的传统服装

classical ['klæsikəl] *a.* ①(文学、艺术等)标准的, 第一流的; 经典的 ②古典(派)的; 古典文学(古希腊、古罗马)的; 古典派作家的: ~ architecture 古典(式)建筑 / ~ music 古典派音乐 / the ~ school 古典学派 / ~ studies 古典文学研究 / a ~ education 古典文学教育 ③精通古典的 ④传统的, 权威的 ⑤人文科学的, 文科的: a ~ curriculum 人文科课程 ‖~**ly** *ad.* 古典派地

classification [,klæsifi'keiʃən] *n.* ①分类; 分级 ②分类法 ③类别; 等级; (文件等的)密级

classify ['klæsifai] *vt.* ①把…分类; 把(货物等)分等级 ②把…归入一类(或同一等级) ‖**classified** *a.* ①分成类的; 被归入一类的 ②机密的, 保密的: *classified* information (material, documents) 秘密情报(材料, 文件) / **classifier** *n.* ①分类者 ②【矿】分级机 ③【化】分粒器 ④(汉语等中的)量词

clause [klɔːz] *n.* ①条款, 款项: an additional ~ 附加条款 / a saving ~ 对例外情况作规定的附加条款 ②【语】分句, 从句: coordinate ~s 等立分句 / an attributive ~ 定语从句 / a noun ~ 名词从句 / a principal ~ 主句

claw [klɔː] **I** *n.* ①(动物的)爪, 脚爪; (蟹、虾等的)钳, 螯 ②[贬]手; 魔爪: put the ~ on sb. [美俚]逮捕某人; 向某人借钱 / in sb.'s ~s 在某人掌握中 ③爪形器具(如拔钉锤等) ④被抓的伤口 **II** ❶ *vt.* ①用爪子抓(或挖、掘、撕); [苏格兰]搔 ②抓爬(路): They ~ed their way to the mountain top. 他们奋力爬上山顶。 ③[美俚]逮捕, 抓 ❷ *vi.* 用爪子抓(或挖) ‖~ *hold of* 抓住 / *Claw me and I'll* ~ *thee.* [谚]你捧我, 我就捧你。 / ~ *off* ①【海】把船头转朝上风 ②[俚]狠狠地打击(或击败); 责骂 / *get one's* ~*s into* sb. 恶意攻击某人 / *pare* (*cut*) *the* ~*s of* 斩断…的魔爪; 解除…的武装 ‖~**ed** *a.* 有爪(或螯)的 ‖~ **bar** (拔铁道枕木钉等用的)爪杆; 撬棒 / ~ **hammer** ①拔钉锤, 羊角榔头 ②[俚]燕尾服

claw

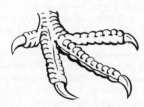

clay [klei] *n.* ①粘土;泥土: porcelain ～ 瓷土 ②肉体,人体: a man of common ～ 平常人 ③似粘土的物质 ④陶土制的烟斗 ‖*a yard of* ～ 陶制长烟管 / *dead and turned to* ～ 死了 / *moisten* (或 *wet*) *one's* ～ 饮酒 ‖*～-cold a.* 土一样冷的(常指死人) / ～ **pigeon** ①(泥制的)靶子 ②[美俚]易被捉弄的人;容易的工作 / ～ **pipe** 陶土制的烟斗 / ～ **slate**【地】粘板岩 / ～ **stone**【地】变朽粘土岩

clean [kli:n] I *a.* ①清洁的, 干净的; 整洁的: ～ clothes 清洁的衣服 / wash the sheets ～ 把被单洗干净 / a ～ sheet of paper 一张未用过的纸 / a ～ copy 誊清稿 / a ～ proof【印】清样 ②纯洁的;清白的;不淫猥的: have a ～ record 经历清白 / keep a ～ tongue 不说下流话 ③未沾染(疾病)的: keep ～ of infection 使不受传染 ④彻底的,完全的: a ～ sweep 大胜,全胜 / make a ～ sweep of 彻底扫除…,扫尽… / make a ～ break with one's bad habits 彻底去除恶习 ⑤干净利落的,巧妙的: a ～ stroke (或 blow) (打球等)干净利落的一击 ⑥整齐的,光洁的: A sharp knife makes a ～ cut. 快刀切得整齐。 / a ～ edge 整齐的边缘 / ～ timber 无疤节的木材 ⑦匀称的,美好的: a ship with ～ lines 造型优美的船 ⑧爱清洁的,有洁癖的 ⑨不长杂草及其他野生植物的 ⑩(原子弹、氢弹等)爆炸时无(或很少)放射性尘埃的 ⑪(船舱等)出空了的;[美俚]分文没有的,身上没有一个钱的;[美俚]不带暗藏枪枝(或走私品、毒物等)的 ⑫(肉类等)可供食用的 II *ad.* ①干净地;纯洁地 ②彻底地,完全地: I ～ forgot about it. 我把它完全忘掉了。 / My view is ～ contrary. 我的看法完全相反。 / ～ gone (消逝得)无影无踪 / ～ mad 完全疯狂 / ～ wrong 完全错误 III ❶ *vt.* ①把…弄干净,为…去除污垢;使净化: ～ one's shoes 擦掉鞋上的尘土 / ～ one's clothes ～*ed* 把衣服弄干净(常指送洗衣店干洗) ②出空,剥光: ～ one's plate 吃尽盘中菜肴 / ～ a chicken 把鸡去毛开膛(以备烹饪) ③[俚]使得得精光,使成为一无所有 ❷ *vi.* ①被弄干净: Enamel wares ～ easily. 搪瓷器皿容易弄干净。 ②做清洁工作 IV *n.* 去垢,刷净: give it a ～ 把它弄干净 ‖～ *down* 刷干净(墙壁、马匹等) / ～ *out* ①把…打扫干净 ②把…清除出去;除掉 ③[俚]使…失去钱财,使…耗尽资源 / ～ *up* ①(把…)收拾整洁 ②除掉;清理: ～ *up* past-due bills 清理逾期票据 ③使净化,使…清除不良现象 ④[口]净赚…;发财 / ～ *up on* 击败…,胜过… / *come* ～ 全盘招供 / *show a* ～ *pair of heels* 见 **pair** ‖～*er n.* ①打扫清洁的人; 清洁工人; 干洗商: a dry ～*er* 干洗商; 干洗工 / take sb. to the ～*ers* [俚](在赌博等中)赢去某人所有的钱 ②清洁器;除垢剂: a vacuum ～*er* 吸尘器 / ～*ness n.* ‖*'～-bred a.* 纯种的 / *'～-cut a.* ①轮廓分明的 ②形态优美的 ③清楚的,明晰的 ④整洁好看的 / *'～-'fingered a.* ①未受贿的 ②手巧的 / *'～-'handed a.* 清白的,没有做过坏事的 / *'～-'limbed a.* 四肢长得匀称优美的 / *'～-,living a.* 生活严谨的,不淫猥的 / *'～out n.* 清除 / ～ **room** 绝对清洁室(见于宇宙飞船装配工序及医院等中) / *'～-'shaven a.* 脸刮得光光的 / *'～-'up n.* ①清除,扫除 ②[口]获利,赚钱

cleanliness ['klenlinis] *n.* 清洁

cleanly[1] ['klenli] *a.* 清洁的; 爱清洁的; 一直很清洁的

cleanly[2] ['kli:nli] *ad.* 清洁地,干净地

cleanse [klenz] *vt.* ①使清洁;清洗 ②使纯洁,净化 ‖～*r n.* ①做清洁工作的人 ②清洁剂(如去污粉等)

clear [kliə] I *a.* ①清澈的;光亮的;无污垢的: the ～ water of a lake 清澈的湖水 / ～ glass 明净的玻璃 / a light 明亮的(灯)光 / ～ blue (red) 净蓝(红) / have a ～ conscience 问心无愧 ②晴【气】碧(空): a ～ day (night) 晴天(夜) / a ～ sky 晴空 ③清晰的;分明的;条理清楚的: a ～ photograph 一张清晰的照片 / draw a ～ line of demarcation (between . . .) (在…之间)划一条清楚的界线 / a ～ mind 清楚的头脑 / Have I made myself ～? 我讲清楚了没有? ④(理解)清楚的,明确的: I want to be quite ～ on this point. 在这一点上我希望搞清楚。 / Are you ～ about what you should do next? 你对下一步的工作明确么? ⑤(声音)嘹亮的 ⑥畅通的;无阻的;清除了…的(of): The road is ～. 道路畅通。 / Are the rivers ～ of ice yet? 河上的冰融尽了没有? / be ～ of debt (suspicion) 还清了债(解除了嫌疑) ⑦(木材)无节疤等毛病的; 没有桠枝的 ⑧(船只)已卸完货的 ⑨净得的;十足的;整整的: a ～ profit 净利 / five ～ days 整整五天 II *ad.* ①清楚地,清晰地: He speaks loud and ～. 他说话响亮清楚。 ②[加重语气用]完全;一直;整整: ～ outstrip sb. 远远超过某人 / ～ on to the end 一直到底 / three feet ～ 实足三呎 ③离开,不接触(of): Stand ～ of the rails. 站得离轨道远些。 / steer ～ of the reef 避开暗礁 III ❶ *vt.* ①使清澈;使清楚: ～ the river water 使河水变清 / ～ one's mind about sth. 弄清楚某事 ②扫清;清除;结清;使(计数器)归零: ～ the table 收拾桌子 / ～ one's throat (咳一声)清清嗓子 / ～ a gun 退弹 / ～ snow from the street (或 ～ the street *of* snow) 扫清路上的积雪 / ～ an account 清账 / This post office ～*s* 5,000 pieces of mail an hour. 这邮局每小时处理五千份邮件。 ③开拓,开垦: ～ land 开垦土地 ④穿过;越过: The truck only just ～*ed* the gate. 卡车刚好从大门中间穿过。 ⑤为(船或船货)结关;(船只)结关后离开 ⑥宣布…无罪;开释 ⑦净得 ⑧交换(单据);把(支票)兑现;出售(商品) ⑨(议案等)通过;批准,准许: The bill ～*ed* the legislature. 这项议案经立法机关通过了。 / ～ a plane for landing 准许一架

飞机降落 ❷ vi. ①变清澈; 变清楚; 变明朗: The weather has ~ed up. 天放晴了。②(船只)结关; 结关后离港 (from) ③办妥票据、消失; [俚] 溜走 ⑤(文件等)送交审批: The plan must ~ through a higher body. 这项计划必须送交上一级机关审批。Ⅳ n. 【机】间隙, 余隙 ‖all ~ (空袭)解除警报 / (as) ~ as a bell 很健全; 很清楚 / (as) ~ as day (或 daylight, noonday) 一清二楚 / ~ away ① 把…清除掉: ~ away obstacles 排除障碍 ②(云、雾等)消失 / ~ off ① 清除, 摆脱(负担、烦恼等); 清偿(债务) ② 走开; 溜掉 ③(云、雾等)消散 / ~ out ①结关后离港 ② 离开; 逃走 ③ 把…清出(或出空); 使(人)把钱用光 / ~ up ① 整理, 收拾: ~ up the desk 整理书桌 ~ up the mess 收拾一堆乱七八糟的东西 ②消除, 解除(误会、疑点等) ③(天气)放晴 / in ~ 用一般文字(指不用明码或密码) / in the ~ ①不受到阻碍(或限制) ②无嫌疑, 无罪 ③以(两边之间的)内宽计算: The corridor is 2 metres in the ~. 走廊内宽为两米。④ =in ~ / keep ~ of 不接触…; 避开… ‖~ly ad. ①明白地; 清晰地: see (hear) ~ly 看(听)清楚 ②显然: Clearly you are right. 显然你是对的。/ ~ness n. ‖'~-'cut a. 轮廓清晰的; 明确的, 鲜明的 / ~-eyed ['kliər'aid] a. 目光锐利的; 能明辨是非的 / '~-'headed a. 头脑清楚的 / '~-'sighted a. 目光锐利的 / '~starch vt. & vi. 用无色淀粉浆水(给衣服)上浆 / '~way n. 超速道路

clearance ['kliərəns] n. ① 清除, 清理; 出清, 出空; 排除障碍: a ~ sale 减价出售存货 ② 【建】净空(如车辆通过隧道时两侧或上面所留下的空隙); 【机】余隙, 间隙; (公差中的)公隙 ③ (船只的)结关; 出(入)港证 (= ~ papers); 离开, 通过 ④(军事、飞行等方面的)许可(证), 批准 ⑤ 票据交换 ⑥辞职照准

clearing ['kliəriŋ] n. ①(森林中的)空旷地 ②(林业用语)集材 ③ 票据交换, (银行之间的)汇划结算; [复]汇划结算的款项总额 ‖~ bank 交换银行 / ~ hospital 【军】前方医院 / '~house n. ①票据交换所 ②(技术)情报交换所 / ~ station 【军】医疗后送站, 师救护所

cleavage ['kli:vidʒ] n. ① 劈开, 分裂; 劈开处 ②【物】【矿】解理, 劈理 ③【生】卵裂

cleave[1] [kli:v] (过去式 cleaved 或 cleft [kleft] 或 clove [klouv], 过去分词 cleaved 或 cleft 或 cloven ['klouvn]) ❶ vt. ①劈, 劈开: ~ (down) a tree 砍倒一棵树 / ~ sth. in two 把某物劈成两半 / 把…分成几个小部分(或小派别等) ③开(路); 穿过(波浪等): ~ a path through the jungle 在密林中开路前进 ❷ vi. ①(木头等顺着纹路)被劈开, 裂开: This wood ~s easily. 这种木头容易劈开。②(船等)破浪前进; (鸟等)掠过空中; 穿过: The ship is cleaving through the water. 船正在破浪前进。‖~r n. 劈东西的人(或器具); 屠夫的切肉刀

cleave[2] [kli:v] (过去式 cleaved 或 clave [kleiv], 过去分词 cleaved) vi. ①粘着, 粘住 (to) ② 依恋; 坚持 (to)

clef [klef] n. 【音】谱号: F ~ 低音谱号 / G ~ 高音谱号

cleft[1] [kleft] n. ① 裂缝, 裂口 ② "V" 字形凹刻

cleft[2] [kleft] Ⅰ cleave[1] 的过去式和过去分词 Ⅱ a. ①劈开的, 裂开的: ~ palate 【医】裂腭 ②【植】半裂的: ~ grafting 【植】劈接, 割接 ‖in a ~ stick 在进退两难中

clemency ['klemənsi] n. ① (气候等的)温暖, 温和 ② 仁慈, 宽厚

clement ['klemənt] a. ①温暖的, 温和的 ② 仁慈的, 宽厚的

clench [klentʃ] Ⅰ ❶ vt. ①敲弯, 敲平(钉子等); 敲弯(钉头)以钉牢 ② 握紧(拳头等); 咬紧(牙关): with ~ed fists 握紧着拳头 / ~ one's jaws 咬紧牙关 ③捏紧, 抓牢: ~ sth. in (或 with) one's hand(s) 用手紧握某物 ④确定, 决定(论据、交易等) ❷ vi. ① (钉、铆钉等)钉牢 ② 握紧; 咬紧 Ⅱ n. ①敲弯的钉头 ②握紧, 捏紧; 咬紧

clergy ['klə:dʒi] n. [集合名词] (基督教的)牧师; (其他宗教的)教士(可指总体或一群教士)

clerical ['klerikəl] Ⅰ a. ①牧师的; 教士的 ②办事员(式)的; 办公室工作的: a ~ error 誊抄工作中的笔误 / a ~ staff 全体办事人员 / ~ work 办公室工作(指誊抄、归档等) Ⅱ n. ① 牧师 ②[贬]主张扩张教士政治势力者 ③[复]牧师的服装 ‖~ism n. 教权主义 / ~ist n. 教权主义者 / ~ly ad.

clerk [klɑ:k; 美 klə:k] Ⅰ n. ① 职员, 办事员; 书记员, 秘书: a bank ~ 银行办事员 / a correspondence ~ 文书 ② 管理员: a ~ of the works 工程建筑管理员 ③[美]店员 ④教会文书, 执事 Ⅱ vi. [美]当店员 ‖in holy orders (正式用语)牧师, 教士 / St. Nicholas's [snt 'nikələsiz] Clerks 盗贼们 / the Clerk of the Weather 风伯雨师 ‖~ly a. & ad. / ~ship n. 职员(或办事员、店员等)的职位

clever ['klevə] a. ① 聪明的, 伶俐的, 灵巧的: be ~ at painting 擅长绘画 / ~ fingers 灵巧的手指 / a ~ horse 擅长跳越障碍物的马 ②机敏的, 精巧的: a ~ speech 机敏的谈话 / Quite a ~ book, isn't it? 这本书挺不错, 是吗? ③ [俚]英俊的; 壮健的 ④[美]善良的, 性情温和的, 热情的 ‖~ish ['klevəriʃ] a. 有点小聪明的 / ~ly ad. ①聪明地, 巧妙地 ②[方]完全, 全然 / ~ness n.

click [klik] Ⅰ n. ①卡嗒一声(常指上锁、扣板机等时发出的声音) ②【机】爪, 掣子 ③(某些非洲语言中的)倒吸气音 Ⅱ ❶ vi. ① 发出卡嗒一声: The door ~ed shut. 门卡嗒一声关上了。②恰好吻合, 配对; (两人)一见如故, 一拍即合。③进行顺利; 成功, 受观众欢迎 ❷ vt. 使发出卡嗒声; 卡嗒卡嗒地敲: ~ one's heels 喀嚓一声立正 / ~ out an article on a typewriter 在打字机上劈劈啪啪地打出一篇文章

client ['klaiənt] *n.* ① 委托人; (律师的) 当事人; (私人医生的) 病人, 病家 ②(商店等的) 顾客 ③ (古罗马) 贵族保护下的平民; [古] 受人庇护者, 依附于他人者 ‖**~less** *a.* (律师等) 没有人委托办事的; (商店等) 没有顾客的

cliff [klif] *n.* 悬崖, 峭壁 (尤指海边的) ‖**~ dweller** ① 住公寓大厦的人 ②[常作 C- D-] 在美国西南部居住崖洞中的古代印第安人 ③ 悬崖居民 / '**~-,hanger** *n.* ①(分期连载的) 惊险故事; (有续集的) 惊险电影 (或戏剧) ②扣人心弦的紧张比赛 / **~sman** ['klifsmən] *n.* 擅长爬悬崖的人

climate ['klaimit] *n.* ① 气候: a mild (vile) ~ 温和 (恶劣) 的气候 / a relaxing ~ 使人懒洋洋的气候 ②风土; 地带: a dry ~ 干燥地带 ③一般 (社会) 趋势, (社会) 风气: the ~ of opinion 舆论

climax ['klaimæks] I *n.* ①[语] 逐渐增强达到顶点 (指一种修辞手法) ② (兴趣等的) 顶点, 极点; (小说, 戏剧等的) 高潮: The heat of summer has reached (或 come to) its ~. 已经是夏季最热的天气了。 ③【植】演替顶极 II *vi. & vt.* (使) 达到顶点, (使) 达到高潮

climb [klaim] I ❶ *vi.* ①(攀) 登, 爬: ~ up a mountain 登山 / ~ over a wall 翻过墙 / ~ aboard a car 上车 ~ into (out of) one's overalls 匆匆穿上 (脱下) 工装裤 ②(太阳, 炊烟等) 徐徐上升; (物价等) 逐渐上涨; (飞机) 爬升 ③ (植物) 攀缘向上; (道路, 楼梯等) 倾斜向上 ④(在社会地位等方面) 向上爬, 钻营: ~ to power 捞到大权, 上台 ❷ *vt.* ①爬, 攀登: ~ a ladder 爬梯子 / make the water ~ the hills 引水上山 / ~ the peaks of science and technology 攀登科学技术高峰 ②使 (飞机) 爬升 ③(植物) 在…上攀缘而上 II *n.* ①攀登; 【空】爬升 ② 需攀登的地方; 山坡: a steep and toilsome ~ 爬起来很费力的陡坡·‖~ **down** ①(从…上) 爬下 ② 退让, 屈服, 认错 / ~ **the rigging** [俚] 发脾气 ‖'**~-down** *n.* ① 往下的爬行 ② 退让, 屈服, 认错

clime [klaim] *n.* [诗] 地方, 风土

clinch [klintʃ] I ❶ *vt.* ① 敲弯, 钉住 ② 确定, 决定 (论据, 交易等): ~ an argument 使一个论据成为确定无疑 / The experiment ~ed his suspicions. 实验结果证明他的猜测是对的。 ③[俚] 拥抱 ❷ *vi.* ① 敲弯, 钉牢 ② (摔跤等时) 扭住对手 ③[俚] 拥抱 II *n.* ①绳索一端的活结圈套 ②(钉、铆钉等的) 敲弯部分; 敲弯的钉; 钉牢 ③扭住对手: get into a ~ 扭成一团 ④[俚] 拥抱

cling [kliŋ] (clung [klʌŋ]) *vi.* ①粘着; 缠着, 紧紧握着: ~ing clothes 紧身的衣服 / The odour clung to the room. 那气味充斥着房间, 散不出去。 ②依附, 依靠, 依恋 (to): He is of a ~ing sort. 他是那种老是依靠人家的人。 ③坚持, 墨守 (to): ~ to the hope that ... 始终抱着…的希望 / ~ to one's own view 坚持己见 ‖**~y** *a.* ‖**~ing vine** 依赖男子的女子 / '**~stone** *n.* 粘核桃

clinic ['klinik] *n.* ①诊所, 门诊所: the factory ~

工厂医务室 ②临床 (或临诊) 讲授; 临床 (或临诊) 课 ③特殊病例的分析、处理讨论课 ④会诊

clinical ['klinikəl] *a.* ① 临床的, 临诊的: ~ diagnosis 临床诊断 / a ~ thermometer 体温表 ②(感情、态度、判断等) 冷静的, 不偏不倚的; 分析的 ‖**~ly** *ad.*

clink [kliŋk] I ❶ *vi.* 丁当作响 ❷ *vt.* 使丁当作响: ~ glasses (干杯时) 碰杯 II *n.* ① 丁当声: the ~ of keys (glasses) 钥匙 (玻璃杯) 的丁当碰撞声 ②[英俚] 钱, 硬币 ③[英方] 猛烈的一击 ④[方] 瞬间: in a ~ 在一瞬间 ⑤[俚] 监狱, 牢房: be in ~ 在狱中 ‖~ **off** [英方] 突然匆匆离去 ‖'**~stone** *n.* 【地】响岩

clinker ['kliŋkə] I *n.* ① 炼砖, 缸砖 ②【冶】渣块; (炼铝时的) 烧结块 ③[英] 头等货 ④[俚] 大错误; 大失败 II ❶ *vt.* ①使烧成渣块 ②从…清除熔渣 ❷ *vi.* 烧成渣块 ‖'**~-built** *a.* 【船】迭接的, 重迭搭造的

clip[1] [klip] I *n.* ① 夹, 钳; 回形针; 钢夹 ②【军】弹夹 ③【无】接线柱 II (clipped; clipping) *vt.* ①夹住, 钳牢: ~ papers together 把文件夹住 ② 捏紧; 束紧 ③ (美式足球中) 在 (对方球员) 身后冲撞 (或下绊) 使不能前进 (或跌倒) ‖'**~board** *n.* 上有夹紧纸张装置的书写板 / '**~-'on** *n.* 用夹子夹上去的 / '**~sheet** *n.* (为剪贴方便) 只在单面排印的新闻 (或通告等)

clip[2] [klip] (clipped; clipping) ❶ *vt.* ① 剪, 剪短 ②剪取 (羊等) 的毛; 修剪: ~ a hedge 修剪篱笆 ③ 剪 (或削) 取…的边端 ④ 剪辑 (报纸、杂志等); (从报刊上) 剪取: ~ an article from a newspaper 从报上剪下一篇文章 ⑤ (在拼法、发音方面) 省略: a clipped word 缩略词 (如 ad 就是 advertisement 的缩略词) ⑥轧 (车票等) ⑦删去; 削减 (权力、影响等) ⑧[俚] 痛打, 猛击 ⑨ [俚] 骗取…的钱财, 敲…的竹杠 ❷ *vi.* ①剪; 剪辑报刊 ②疾飞而过 II *n.* ① 剪, 剪短; 修剪 ②羊毛一次 (或一季) 的剪下量; 剪下来的东西 (如胶片的一段) ③猛击 ④快步 ⑤指甲刀; [苏格兰] [复] 大剪刀 ‖~ **sb.'s wings** 使某人无所施其技; 扼杀某人的雄心 ‖~ **joint** [美俚] 索价特别高昂的咖啡馆 (或夜总会等); 专敲顾客竹杠的场所

clipper ['klipə] *n.* ① 剪剪者; 剪取者 (如剪羊毛工人等) ② [常用复] (理发、修指甲等用的) 轧刀, (剪树枝或羊毛用的) 大剪刀: the barber's ~s 理发推子 / nail-~s 指甲钳, 指甲刀 ③快速帆船; 快速飞机 (尤指巨型远程民航班机); 快马: a China ~ 快速运茶帆船 ④【无】削波器, 限制器, 限幅器 ⑤[俚] 出色的东西

clipping ['klipiŋ] I *n.* 剪下物; [美] (报纸、杂志等的) 剪辑, 剪报: sweep up the hair ~s 扫掉剪下的头发 / a newspaper ~ 剪报 / a ~ bureau (或 service) [美] 剪报公司 (专替顾客剪辑有关某一专题报刊资料的商业机构) II *a.* ①快速的 ②[俚] 第一流的, 出色的

clique [kli:k] I *n.* 派系, 小集团: a renegade ~ 叛徒集团 II *vi.* [口] 结党

cloak [klouk] **I** *n.* ① 斗篷, 大氅 ② 覆盖(物): a ~ of snow 一层覆盖着的积雪 / a ~ of secrecy 一层笼罩着的神秘气氛 ③伪装,借口 **II** *vt.* ① 给…披斗篷 ②覆盖; 包藏,掩盖 ‖*under the ~ of* ①在…覆盖下: *under the ~ of* darkness 趁着黑夜 ② 披着…的外衣, 以…为借口 ‖'~-and-**'dagger** *a.* ①(作品、作家等)描写间谍密探的 ②阴谋的; 间谍的、搞特务活动的 / '~*room n.* ①衣帽间; 行李寄放处 ② 议院的休息室 ③ [英] [委婉语]厕所

clock¹ [klɔk] **I** *n.* ① (时)钟: wind up a ~ 开钟 / set a ~ by the time signal on the radio 按照收音机报时信号拨准钟 / put a ~ fast 把钟拨快 / The ~ gains (loses). 钟快(慢)了。 ② (附在机件上的)仪表(或钟)(如速度表、里程计等) ③特制的上下班记时钟,生产记录钟 (=time ~) ④[口](比赛时用的)记录钟; 秒表 ⑤[英俚] (人的)面孔 ⑥ 蒲公英的短茸毛头 ‖*an alarm ~* 闹钟 / *an atomic ~* 原子钟 / *an electric ~* 电钟 / *a program(me) ~* 程序钟 / *a turret ~* 塔钟 **II ❶** *vt.* ①为(比赛等)记时,为(运动员)掐秒表; (运动员)花…跑(或游)完: The winner ~*ed* ten minutes for the whole distance. 得胜者跑完全程用了十分钟。 ②(用机械)记录(速度、距离、次数等): The exhibition ~*ed* an average of 4,000 visitors a day. 据统计,展览会参观人数平均每日四千人。 **❷** *vi.* (用把名牌等投入自动记时计等方式)记下(上下班)时间: ~ *in* (或 *on*) and *out* (或 *off*) (雇员本人投名牌入自动记时) 记下上班到达及下班离开时间 ‖*the ~ round* (或 *round the ~*) 连续一整天(或一昼夜): work *the ~ round* 连续工作一昼夜(或一整天) / *turn* (或 *put*) *back the ~* ①把钟拨慢 ②[喻] 向后倒退, 开倒车, 守旧规 / *when one's ~ strikes* 临终 / *work against the ~* 抢着在某一时刻前做完工作 ‖~*er n.* (比赛、交通情况等的)计时员 / ~*wise a. & ad.* 顺时针方向的 (地) / '~*face n.* 钟面 / '~,*maker n.* 制造 (或修理)时钟的工人 / '~ *radio* 自动定时开关的收音机 / '~ *watcher* 老是看钟等下班的人 / '~*work n.* 时钟机构;类似时钟机构的装置(如玩具、炸弹中的发条和齿轮): a ~*work* toy 有发条装置的玩具 / with ~*work* precision 极精确地 / like ~*work* 有规律地;自动地

clock² [klɔk] **I** *n.* 袜子跟部(或旁边)织绣的花样 **II** *vt.* 在…上织绣花样

clod [klɔd] **I** *n.* ①土块,泥块 ② [the ~] 泥土、土壤; [喻](指与精神相对而言的)肉体 ③ 呆子; 乡下佬 ④牛的颈肉 ⑤【矿】煤层的软泥土顶板(煤层顶底板页岩 **II** (clodded; clodding) *vt.* 对…掷泥块

clog [klɔg] **I** *n.* ①(绑在人或动物腿上以阻碍行动的)重物,坠子 ②障碍,障碍物 ③ 木底鞋 **II** (clogged; clogging) **❶** *vt.* ①阻碍, 妨碍 ②塞满,填满(管子、道路等): The pipes were *clogged* with dirty matter. 管子里塞满了脏物。 **❷** *vi.*

①阻塞,填塞 ② 粘成(或凝成)一块 ③ 跳木鞋舞 ‖~ *dance* 木鞋舞

cloister ['klɔistə] **I** *n.* ①修道院; 修道院的生活; 隐居地 ②(修道院、教堂、学院等处的)回廊, 走廊 **II** *vt.* ①使居于修道院中; 使与尘世隔绝 ②设回廊于 ‖~*ed a.* ①居于修道院内的; 隐居的 ②有回廊的

close¹ [klous] **I** *a.* ① 近的, 接近的; 紧密的, 稠密的: fire at ~ range 近距离射击 / a ~ combat 近战, 白刃战, 肉搏战 / leave sb. ~ to tears 使某人快要掉眼泪了 / ~ planting 密植 / fly in ~ formation 以密集队形飞行 ② 紧贴的; 齐根的: a ~ coat 紧身上衣 / cut the hair ~ 把头发剪得极短 ③亲密的,(关系)密切的: be as ~ as lips to teeth 唇齿相依 ④严密的, 周密的; 仔细的; 准确的 keep a ~ watch 严密监视 / pay ~ attention to the development of the situation 密切注意形势的发展 / ~ reading 仔细的研读 / a ~ translation 紧扣原文的翻译 ⑤ 势均力敌的; 几乎相等的: a ~ match 一场不相上下的比赛 ⑥关闭的,封闭的; 狭窄的; 狭隘的: a ~ vowel 【语】闭元音 / a ~ alley 狭弄堂,小胡同 ⑦只限于少数特权人物的: a ~ corporation 由少数人控制,股票不上市的公司 ⑧ 闷人的,不通风的;闷热的; 潮湿的: a ~ day 闷热的日子 ⑨ 秘密的,隐藏的; 嘴紧的,沉默的: ~ terrain (或 ground, country) 【军】隐蔽地 / keep sth. ~ 保守某事的秘密 ⑩ 吝啬的,小气的 ⑪(钱等)得来不易的 **II** *ad.* 接近; 紧, 紧密; 秘密地: sit ~ against the wall 紧靠墙壁坐着 / The door is ~ shut. 门紧闭着。 ‖*a ~ call* (或 *thing*) [口]侥幸的脱险 / *a ~ shave* ①剃光头头发(或胡须) ②侥幸的脱险 / *be packed as ~ as herrings* 见 herring / *at hand* 就在眼前; 就在旁边 / *by* 在(…)附近 / *on* (或 *upon*)接近,差不多: He is ~ *on* forty. 他快四十岁了。 / It was ~ *upon* midnight. 时近午夜。 / ~ *to* ①接近于: *Close to* a hundred experiments have been made. 已进行了近一百次试验。②在附近, 在左近: The villagers reported that the tiger was still lurking ~ *to*. 村民们报告说那只老虎还躲藏在附近一带。 / *keep* (或 *lie*) ~ 躲避 / *press sb.* ~ 紧逼某人 / *run sb.* ~ (赛跑中)紧紧钉住某人 / *sail ~ to the wind* 见 wind¹ ‖~*ly ad.* / ~*ness n.* ‖'~-cropped, '~-cut *a.* (头发、草等)剪得短短的; 头发(或毛发)剪短了的 / '~-'fisted *a.* 吝啬的,小气的 / '~-'fitting *a.* 紧身的; 贴切的 / '~-'grained *a.* ①木理细密的 ②有条不紊的 / '~-'hauled *a.* 迎风驶行的 / '~-in *a.* ①近战的: a ~*in* weapon 近战武器 / ~*-in* defence 近距离防御 ②接近(城市)中心的 / '~-'knit *a.* ①紧紧结合在一起的 ②(论据等)严谨的 / '~-'mouthed, '~-'lipped *a.* 嘴紧的 / ~ *quarters* 近距离: fight at ~ *quarters* 近战, 肉搏 / ~ *season* 禁猎期 (= [美] closed season) / '~-'set *a.* (眼睛或牙齿)

等) 长得紧靠在一起的 / ~ **shot** (电影等的) 近景 / '~**stool** *n.* 马桶 / '~-**up** *n.* ①(电影等的) 特写镜头 ②仔细的观察 ③小传

close² [klouz] **I** ❶ *vt.* ①关,闭;封闭: Please ~ the windows before leaving. 离开前请将窗子关上。/ ~ one's eyes *to* the fact that 无视…的事实 / The shop is ~d for a week. 这家商店停止营业一个星期。/ This road is ~d *to* heavy motor traffic. 此路禁止载重机动车辆通行。②终止,结束;结清(帐目);商定(交易): He ~d his speech with "Thank you, Mr. Chairman." 他讲了声 "谢谢主席先生" 后就结束了他的讲话。/ ~ a meeting (discussion) 结束会议(讨论) / ~ a bargain 讲好价钱成交 ③ 使靠拢,使接近;靠拢(其他船只等);接通(电流): ~ (the) ranks 使队伍靠拢; [喻]紧密团结 / ~ an electric current (或 a circuit) 接通电流 ❷ *vi.* ①关,闭;结束,停止: The door won't ~. 这门关不上。/ The park ~s at 7 p.m. 这公园下午七时关门。②靠拢,接近;会合: Left (Right) ~! [军]向左(右)靠拢! ③扭打,搏斗 ④同意 (on, upon, with) **II** *n.* ①结束,终止: at the ~ of the year 在年底 ②[古]扭打,搏斗 ③ [klous] (四周围住的) 场地,院子; [英] (从街道通入院子的) 通道,入口 ‖**break sb.'s ~** 侵入某人的土地 / **bring to a ~** 结束…,终止…: bring a chapter *to* a ~ 结束一章 / ~ **about** 围住,包围 / ~ **down** ①关闭,停歇;封闭 ②(电台)停止播音 / ~ **in** ①包围;封闭;迫近: The evening ~d *in.* 夜幕降临。/ 渐短: The days are closing *in.* 日渐短。/ ~ **off** ①结(帐) ②隔离,封锁;阻塞: ~ *off* the area *to* all traffic 断绝该地区一切交通 / ~ **out** ①抛售 ②停止,停闭 / ~ **over** 淹没;封盖;遮蔽: Midsummer heat ~d *over* the city. 这城市处于盛夏的炎热之中。/ ~ **round** 包围 / ~ **up** ①靠近,靠紧 ②关闭,停歇 ③停止,堵塞 ④(伤口)愈合 ⑤(排球、网球等运动中)封网 / ~ **upon** ①(手、指)握紧(某物) ②(眼睛在入睡或死亡前)最后看见的是… / ~ **with** ①靠近,逼近 ②接受,答应: ~ *with* an offer 【商】接受减价 / **come to a ~** 结束;终止 / *draw* to a ~ 渐近结束 ‖~**r** *n.* 关闭者;关闭器,【电】闭合器 / '~**down** *n.* ① 关闭;封闭 ②(夜的)降临 ③(电台的)停止播音

closed [klouzd] *a.* ①关闭的,闭合的,封闭(性)的;排外的: a ~ syllable 【语】闭音节 / a ~ cabin 密闭舱 / a ~ port (暂时禁止进入的) 封闭港 / the ~ hand (桥牌中)叫了牌正在做局的玩牌人 / a ~ economy 闭关自守的经济 ②保密的: a ~ ballot 秘密投票 ③已定了的: a ~ issue 已议决的事情 ‖~ **chain** 【化】闭链 / ~ **circuit** 【无】闭路式;闭路式电视 / '~-'**circuit** *a.* 闭路式的 / '~-'**door** *a.* 关着门的;秘密的 / '~-'**doorism** *n.* 关门主义 / ~ **primary** 仅由某一政党成员参加的预选 / ~ **rule** 议会禁止对某一议案再提修正意见的规定 / ~ **shop** (根据工会与资方协议)只雇用某一工会会员的商店(或工厂);只雇用某一工会会员的制度

closet ['klɔzit] **I** *n.* ①私室,小房间 ②(国王、官吏等的)议事室,密室 ③壁橱,碗橱,衣橱 ④盥洗室,厕所;抽水马桶 **II** *a.* ①关起门来的;秘密的: a ~ consultation 密商 ②闭门造车的,空谈的: ~ strategist 纸上谈兵的战略家 **III** *vt.* 把…关在小室中; 把…引进密室会谈: be ~ed with ·sb. 与某人在密室中商谈 ‖~ **drama** 只能作为阅读用而不适合演出的剧本

closing ['klouziŋ] **I** *a.* 结束的,末了的;闭会的: ~ time 停止营业(或打烊)时间; 截止时间;下班时间 / the ~ years of the century 这个世纪的最后几年 / a ~ address 闭幕词 **II** *n.* 结束;封闭,封闭口;结帐: an annual ~ (of accounts) 一年一度的结帐

closure ['klouʒə] **I** *n.* ①关闭;【电】闭合;【机】锁合 ②结束,截止;末尾 ③关闭物;围墙;罩子;隔板;【建】填塞砖 ④(议会中的)终止辩论(以进行投票) **II** *vt.* 使(辩论)终止(以进行投票);使(发言者)终止辩论

clot [klɔt] **I** *n.* ①(血等的)凝块;(粘土等的)块: a blood ~ 血块 ②(人、动物等的)群 ③[俚]呆子,蠢人 **II** ❶ *vi.* (血等)凝块;凝集 ❷ *vt.* 使凝块;使结团;使拥塞: Perspiration clotted his hair. 汗水使他的头发粘在一起。/ a street clotted with traffic 交通拥塞的街道

cloth [klɔ(:)θ] ([复] cloths [klɔ(:)θs, klɔ:ðz]) *n.* ①布;(棉、毛、丝、麻、合成纤维等)织物;衣料: a piece of ~ 一块布(或衣料等)/ woolen ~ 呢绒 / ~ of gold (silver) 金(银)线织品 / the ~ of state (国王宝座等的)华盖布 ②布块;桌布: American ~ [英]上光油布 ③(某一职业的标识性)服装(尤指教士的服装); [the ~] [集合名词] 教士 【海】帆 ‖**cut from the same ~** 从同一块布上裁出;一路货色 / **cut one's coat according to one's** ~ 量入为出 / **lay the** ~ 预备开席 / **made out of whole** ~ 纯属虚构,凭空捏造 / **remove the** ~ 食后撤席 ‖'~-'**binding** *n.* (书的)布面装订,布封面 / ~ **yard** ①布码(一般为 37 吋)②一种长箭

clothe [klouð] (clothed 或 clad [klæd]) *vt.* ①给…穿衣;为…提供衣服: be ~d (或 clad) in khaki (red) 穿着卡其(红色)衣服 / feed and ~ sb. 为某人提供衣食 ②覆盖,使披上: a mountain ~d in (或 with) magnificent trees 长满参天大树的山 / be ~d with shame 蒙受耻辱 ③表达: ~ an idea *in* unmistakable language 用明白无误的语言表达一个想法 ④赋予,使具有权力(或特性)

clothes [klouðz] [复] *n.* ① 衣服: a suit of ~ 一套衣服 / put on one's ~ 穿衣 / take off one's ~ 脱衣 / hang out one's ~ 晒衣服 ②[总称]被褥 ③各种衣物;待洗的衣物: ~ in long 在裸裎中 ‖'~-**bag** *n.* 放待洗(或洗净)的衣物的袋 / '~-**basket** 放待洗(或洗净)的衣物的篮 / '~-**brush** *n.* 衣刷 / '~-**horse** *n.* 晒衣架 / '~-**line** *n.* ① 晒衣绳 ②[美俚]私人事情;家丑 / ~ **moth** (蛀蚀衣物的)蛀虫 / '~-**peg** *n.* [英](晒衣用的)衣夹 / '~-**pin** *n.* =~-peg / '~-**press** *n.* 衣

橱,衣柜 / ～ **prop** [英] 晒衣绳支架 / ～ **tree** 柱式衣架,衣帽架

clothing ['klouðiŋ] *n.* ①[总称]衣服；被褥: articles of ～ 各种服装和衣着用品 (如衣服、帽子、手套等) ②[海]帆装 ‖～ **wool**【纺】粗梳羊毛

cloud [klaud] I *n.* ①云: a sky without a speck of ～ 万里晴空 / a white ～ 一朵白云 ②云状物(如尘雾等): a mushroom ～ (核爆炸形成的)蘑菇云 ③(鸟、虫、飞机等)飞掠过的一大群(或一大队): a ～ of arrows 箭如飞蝗 ④ 遮暗物；阴影；模糊: under the ～ of night 夜色朦胧中 / the war ～s 战云 / with a ～ on one's brow 双眉紧锁地 / a ～ of words 暧昧的话 ⑤(镜子等上面的)朦胧的影斑,(大理石等的)黑斑 ⑥轻柔的羊毛围巾 II ❶ *vt.* ①使布满着云 ②把…弄得朦胧不清;把…弄暗 ③使黯然 ④诽谤(名誉等);毁损(友谊等) ❷ *vi.* ① 云层密布; (镜面等)布满模糊斑点: The sky ～ed over. 天空云层密布。②(脸色等)阴沉下来 ‖*blow a* ～ (或 *blow the* ～*s*) [谑]吞云吐雾(指抽烟) / *Every* ～ *has a silver lining.* [谚]黑暗之中总有一线光明。/ *in the* ～*s* ①在云层中; [喻]虚无飘渺 ②(人)空想着;心不在焉 / *kick the* ～*s* [俚]被绞死 / *under a* ～ ①失宠;受嫌疑 ②不悦,有心事 / *wait till the* ～*s roll by* 等到乌云消散; 等到有利时机再干 ‖～**ed** *a.* ①布满着云的,模糊的,含糊的; (人)头脑糊涂的 ③斑驳的 / ～**let** ['klaudlit] *n.* 微云,小朵云 ‖'～,**berry** *n.*【植】云莓 / '～-**built** *a.* 空想的,虚无飘渺的 / '～**burst** *n.* 大暴雨 / '～-**capped** *a.* (山峰等)高耸入云的 / ～ **castle** 空想 / ～ **chamber**【物】云室 / '～-,**cuckoo-** 'land *n.* 虚无飘渺的幻梦;理想国 / ～ **drift** ①浮云,飞云 ②(杀虫药等的)飞机喷雾 / '～-,**hopping** *n.* (尤指以隐蔽为目的)云中飞行 / '～-,**kissing** *a.* (建筑物)高耸入云的,摩天的 / '～**land** *n.* ①云区,云层 ②幻境;仙境 / ～ **nine** [俚]狂喜状态,极乐的心境 / ～ **rack** 浮云,飞云 / '～**scape** *n.* 云景,云的图画 / ～ **seeding**【气】(人工降雨时)云的催化 / '～**world** *n.* =～land

cloudless ['klaudlis] *a.* 无云的,晴朗的 ‖～**ly** *ad.* / ～**ness** *n.*

cloudy ['klaudi] *a.* ①云的;云一般的 ②多云的;被云遮住的;阴天的: a ～ moon 被云遮住的月亮 / a ～ day 阴天 ③(情绪等)阴郁的,烦恼的 ④(在意义等方面)模糊的,不明了的: ～ ideas 模糊的观念 ⑤(液体、水晶等)浑浊的; (大理石等)有云纹的: a ～ mirror 模糊不清的镜子

clout [klaut] I *n.* ①[英方](作补钉用的)破布,碎布;碎皮 ②作家务用的布片(尤指擦碗布等揩布) ③(婴孩等的)衣服 ④(用手的)一击 ⑤(箭的)靶心;中靶的一箭: In the ～! 射中! ⑥神通;影响 ⑦鞋底的铁掌;鞋底大头钉 II *vt.* ①给…打补钉;给(鞋靴)敲铁掌 ②[口](用手)猛击 ‖～**ed** *a.* 有补钉的;(鞋等)打着铁掌的 ‖～ **nail** 鞋底大头钉

clove[1] [klouv] cleave[1] 的过去式

clove[2] [klouv] *n.*【植】丁香;丁香树: oil of ～*s* 丁香油 ‖～ **hitch**【海】丁香结

clove[3] [klouv] *n.*【植】小鳞茎

clover ['klouvə] *n.*【植】三叶草,苜蓿属植物 ‖*live* (或 *be*) *in* ～ (或 *live like pigs in* ～) 生活优裕,养尊处优 ‖'～**leaf** *n.* 苜蓿叶式(立体)交叉的公路

clown [klaun] I *n.* ①(马戏、喜剧等的)小丑,丑角 ②乡下佬;粗人 II *vi.* 扮小丑

cloy [klɔi] ❶ *vt.* 使吃饱,使吃腻: ～ the appetite with too much sweet food 因吃甜食太多而倒胃口 / be ～ed with pleasure 享乐过度 ❷ *vi.* 过饱,吃腻; (乐趣等)因过度而使人发腻

club [klʌb] I *n.* ①棍棒(通常指一端较粗的木棒): Indian ～s 体操用的棍棒 ②(高尔夫球等的)球棒 ③俱乐部;夜总会;会,社;俱乐部(或夜总会等)的会所: a country ～ [美]野外体育俱乐部 / the International Seamen's *Club* 国际海员俱乐部 ④(纸牌中的)梅花; (一张)梅花纸牌 ⑤[动]锤节,(昆虫触角中的)棒 II (clubbed; clubbing) ❶ *vt.* ①用棍棒打;象用棍棒一样地打: ～ a mad dog to death 用棍子打死疯狗 ②把…当棍棒用;把…象棍棒似地握着: ～ a rifle 把枪倒拿着当棍棒用 / ～ one's newspapers 把报纸卷成棍棒样子握着 ③把(头发)撮集成棍棒状 ④凑,贡献: ～ resources 凑集资金 / ～ ideas and exertions 群策群力 ⑤[主英]使乱作一团 ❷ *vi.* ①组成俱乐部;协作;结合 (together, with) ②摊付费用 III *a.* ①俱乐部的 ②(一顿饭)按规定菜单的(指不自行点菜) ‖**clubby** *a.* ①俱乐部似的; 爱社交的 ②只对少数人开放的 ‖'～'**foot** *n.* (先天)畸形足 / '～'**footed** *a.* 畸形足的 / '～**haul** *vt.* 用一种紧急措施把(船)掉向 / '～**house** *n.* ①俱乐部会所 ②运动员的更衣室 / ～ **law** 暴力统治 / '～**man** ['klʌbmən] *n.* 俱乐部会员; 交际家 / ～ **moss**【植】石松 / '～'**room** *n.* 俱乐部聚会室 / '～**root** *n.* (植物的)根肿病 / ～ **sandwich** 一种多层(一般为三层)鸡肉夹心面包,多层鸡肉三明治 / ～ **steak** (腰顶端部的)小牛排

cluck [klʌk] I *vi. & vt.* ①咯咯地叫唤 ②(人用舌)发咯咯声 II *n.* ①(母鸡唤小鸡时的)咯咯声 ②孵蛋鸡 ③[俚]笨蛋

clue [klu:] I *n.* ①(为调查、猜谜等提供的)线索,暗示: give (find) a ～ to sth. 提供(找到)关于某事的线索 ②(故事的)线索;思路 II *vt.* 为…提供线索,提示: ～ sb. to what happened 就已发生的情况给某人提供一点线索 / ～ sb. on how the machine works 告知某人机器如何运转

clump [klʌmp] I *n.* ①(树、灌木等的)丛,簇; (人、建筑物等的)群: a ～ of bushes 灌木丛 / people standing around in little ～s 三五个一堆站在附近的人们 ②(密密的)一团;一块: a ～ of earth (wood) 土(木)块 ③重踏的脚步声 ④特厚的(皮)鞋底 (=～-sole) ⑤[微]细菌凝块 II ❶ *vi.*

①用沉重的脚步行走 ②丛生; 成群; 结块, 结团 ❷ vt. ①把…栽成一丛; 使成群; 使结块(或结团) ②给(靴子)上厚皮底 ‖~ block 【机】粗笨滑车

clumsy ['klʌmzi] a. ① 笨拙的; 手脚不灵活的, 姿势不雅观的: ~ fingers 笨拙的手指 / a ~ man 手脚笨拙的人 ② 愚笨的, 不圆滑的: ~ tactics 拙劣的伎俩 / a ~ apology 愚蠢的道歉(指不看对象、场合, 或不讲方式等) ③制作粗陋的; (文体等)臃肿的 ‖**clumsily** ad. / **clumsiness** n.

cluster ['klʌstə] I n. ①(同类事物或人的)一串, 一束, 一簇, 一群, 一组: a ~ of grapes 一串葡萄 / a ~ of flowers 一束鲜花 / a ~ of bees 一群蜜蜂 / a ~ of characteristics 一组特征 / Here and there in the suburbs are newly built houses in ~s. 郊区到处都有新造的住宅区。/ a ~ bomb unit 集束炸弹 ②【语】辅音群; 元音群 II ❶ vt. ①使成群, 把…集成一束(或一簇、一组) ②群集在 ❷ vi. 群集; 丛生: ~ round sb. 围绕着某人 ‖~ed a. 成群的; 集束的: ~ed column 【建】集柱, 束柱 ‖~ college(综合性大学内的)专科学院

clutch[1] [klʌtʃ] I ❶ vt. 抓住, 攫住 ❷ vi. 抓, 攫: ~ at a straw 捞救命稻草 ‖ ❶ n. 【常用复】爪子; 手; 毒手; 掌握, 控制: be in sb.'s ~es 在某人掌握下 / get into (out of) the ~es of 遭(逃脱)…的毒手; 陷入(摆脱)…的控制 / (一把)抓住, 攫住: within the gravitational ~ of the earth 在地心吸力范围之内 / make a ~ at sth. 拼命想攫取某物 ③【机】离合器; 离合器踏板; 离合器杆; 起重机的钩爪: ride the ~ (驾驶时)脚一直踩在离合器踏板上 ④紧要关头

clutch[2] [klʌtʃ] n. 一次所孵的卵; (刚孵出的)一窝鸡

clutter ['klʌtə] I n. ①[方]喧闹, 喧嚷 ②杂乱, 零乱: in a ~ 杂乱, 不整齐 ③(房屋、商店等)拥挤而杂乱的一群 II ❶ vt. 乱糟糟地堆满, 把…弄得杂乱: a ~ed room 东西堆得乱七八糟的房间 / The desk is ~ed up with books and papers. 桌上乱糟糟地堆满书报纸张。❷ vi. [方]喧闹; 吵吵闹闹地乱跑

Co 【化】元素钴(cobalt)的符号

Co., co. [缩] ① company ② county

coach [kəutʃ] I n. ①(旧时的)四轮大马车, 公共马车 ②长途公共汽车 ③(铁路上的)客车 ④汽车拖着的活动房子 ⑤汽车车身(尤指轿车车身) ⑥客机的二等票 ⑦[船]军舰后甲板上的舱房(通常供舰长用) ⑧私人教师, 辅导者; (体育运动等的)指导, 教练员 II ❶ vt. ①训练, 指导; 辅导: ~ a basketball team 训练并指导一个篮球队 ②充当…的私人辅导员(或教练员) ❷ vi. ①乘马车旅行 ②作指导(或辅导), 作指点; 接受辅导 ‖drive a ~ and six through an Act of Parliament [英] 把国会决议说得荒谬异常以使它无效 ‖~er n. ①拉马车的马 ②辅导员; 教练员; (棒球运动中)指点垒及击球的球员 ‖~-and-'four n. 四驾马车 / ~ box 赶马车人的座位 / '~₁building n. [英] 汽车车身的设计和制造 /

'~-built a. (汽车车身)木制的 / ~ house 马车房 / ~man ['kəutʃmən] n. ①赶马车人 ②钓鱼用的假蝇饵 / '~work n. 汽车车身的设计、制造和装配

coagulate [kəu'æɡjuleit] I vt. & vi. (使)凝结; (使)合成一体 II a. 凝结的 ‖**coagulation** [kəu₁æɡju-'leiʃən] n. 凝结 / **coagulative** a. 凝结的; 引起凝结的 / **coagulator** n. 【化】凝结器; 凝结剂

coal [kəul] I n. ①煤; 煤块: cut (或 mine) ~ 采煤 / a hot (或 live) ~ 烧红的煤块 ②木炭 |brown ~ 褐煤 / coking ~ 炼焦煤, 焦性煤 / hard ~ 无烟煤 / raw ~ 原煤 / small ~s 煤屑, 末煤 / soft ~ 烟煤 II ❶ vt. ①给…上煤, 给…加煤: ~ a steamer 给轮船上煤 ②把…烧成炭 ❷ vi. 上煤, 加煤: ~ at a port (船)在港口上煤 ‖blow the ~ 调唆, 煽动 / call (或 haul) over the ~s 责备, 申斥: call sb. over the ~s for sth. 为某事责备某人 / carry (或 send) ~s to Newcastle 做徒劳而多余的事 (Newcastle 为英国产煤地) / heap ~s of fire on sb.'s head 以德报怨使某人感到后悔惭愧 ‖~ bed 煤层 / '~-'black a. 漆黑的, 墨黑的 ‖~ breaker, ~ cracker 碎煤机 / ~ bunker 煤仓 / ~ cutter 采煤机, 截煤机 / ~ cutting 掘煤, 采煤 / ~ drop 卸煤机 / ~ dust 煤粉, 煤屑 / ~ face (正在开采的)煤层截面, 采煤工作面 / '~field n. 煤田; 产煤区 / '~fish n. 【动】鳕鱼 / ~ gas 煤气 / ~ house 煤库 / '~ing station 煤港, 装煤站 / ~ measures 【地】煤系 / mine 煤矿 / ~ miner 煤矿工人 / ~ oil 煤馏油; 煤油 / '~pit n. 煤坑; 竖井 / '~sack n. 【天】煤袋(银河中的黑斑, 尤指近南十字座的黑斑) / ~ screen 煤筛 / ~ scuttle 煤斗; 【船】煤舱口 / ~ seam 煤层 / ~ series 【地】煤系 / ~ tar 煤焦油 / '~-₁whipper n. [英]卸煤工人; 卸煤机

coalesce [₁kəuə'les] vi. ①(断骨等)接合; (创口)愈合 ②结合; (政党等)携手联合

coalition [₁kəuə'liʃən] n. 结合; 联合; 结合体; (政党、个人或国家间临时性的)联盟: a ~ government 联合政府

coarse [kɔːs] a. ①粗的; 粗糙的; 粗劣的: ~ powder (cloth) 粗粉(布) / a ~ imitation 粗糙的仿制品 / ~ fare 粗食 ②(工具等)供做粗活用的; 粗线条的; 约略的 ③粗鲁的, 粗暴的, 粗俗的: ~ manners 粗暴的态度 / a ~ joke 粗俗的笑话 ④(言语等)猥亵的 ⑤粗声粗气的, 沙声的 ‖~ly ad. / ~ness n. ‖'~-₁fibred a. ①粗纤维的 ②[喻]粗鲁的 / '~-₁grained a. ①(木材)纹理粗的 ②[喻]粗鲁的

coast [kəust] I n. ①海岸; 海滨(地区); [the C-] [美]美国太平洋沿岸: sail along the ~沿海岸航行 ②[美]适宜滑雪的山坡; (骑自行车或乘橇的)滑行(下坡) ③[美俚](吸毒者、爵士音乐迷等过瘾后的)飘飘然状态 II ❶ vt. 在…作沿海航行 ❷ vi. ①沿岸航行; 在同海岸港口间作贸易: ~ing trade 沿海贸易（尤指一国内部沿海港口间的贸易）②(靠惯性)滑行(下坡) ③(人)随波逐流;毫不费力地做 (along) ④[美俚]处于飘飘然状态 ‖*skirt the* ~ 沿海岸航行;[喻]谨慎行事 / *The* ~ *is clear.* 道路已畅通无阻。(原走私贩用语,指沿途无危险或障碍) ‖~**ward** *a.* & *ad.* 朝着海岸(的) / ~**wards** *ad.* 朝着海岸 / ~**wise** *a.* & *ad.* 沿着海岸(的) ‖~ **artillery** [集合名词]海岸炮; 海岸炮兵 / ~ **guard** ①[总称]海岸警卫(或缉私、救生)队 ②海岸警卫(或缉私、救生)队队员 (=~guardsman) / '~**land** *n.* 沿海地区 / '~**line** *n.* 海岸线 / '~,**waiter** *n.* [英]监督沿岸货运的海关官员

coastal ['koustl] *a.* 海岸的;沿海岸的: a ~ plain 海岸平原 / the ~ waters of a country 一个国家的近海水域 ‖ **Coastal Eastern** [美](美国)东北部大西洋沿岸(尤指新英格兰地区)使用的美国英语

coat [kout] I *n.* ①外套,上衣;女式上装:a ~ and skirt (妇女的)一套上装和裙子 / the red ~ 红外套(英军的传统服装) ②类似外套的东西: A thick ~ of gloom enveloped the valley. 山谷笼罩在深沉的阴暗中。③皮毛; 表皮;【解】层,膜;(漆等的)涂层。这件木器已涂完最后一道漆。④[方]衬裙,裙子 II *vt.* 给…穿上外套; 在…上涂(或盖、包): pills ~ed with sugar (或 sugar-~ed pills) 外包糖衣的药丸 / Your tongue is ~ed. 你舌苔发厚。‖ *a* ~ *of arms* 盾形纹章 / *a* ~ *of mail* 锁子铠甲 / *cut one's* ~ *according to one's cloth* 量入为出 / *dust sb.'s* ~ 殴打某人 / *lace sb.'s* ~ [俚]鞭打某人 / *smoke sb.'s* ~ 打得某人灰尘满身;殴打某人 / *take off one's* ~ ①脱掉上衣 ②准备打架,挑衅 / *The* ~ *fits.* ①衣服正合身。②说中了!(或:想对了!) / *trail one's* ~ 故意引起争吵,故意挑衅 / *turn one's* ~ 背叛,变节 / *wear the king's* (或 *the queen's*) ~ [英]当兵 ‖~**ee** ['kouti:] *n.* 紧身短上衣 / ~**ing** *n.* ①涂层 ②上衣衣料 / ~ **card** (纸牌中的)人头牌(指 J, Q, K) / ~ **hanger** (普通)衣架 / ~ **holder** 替别人(尤指竞技人、殴斗者)拿上衣的人 / '~**tail** *n.* 男上衣后摆;[复]女子长外衣的下摆:trail one's ~*tails* 故意引起争吵,故意挑衅 / on sb.'s ~*tails* 依靠某人,叨某人的光

coax [kouks] I ❶ *vt.* ①用好话劝;诱(出),哄(出): ~ a child to stop crying 哄小孩止哭 / ~ sb. into (out of) doing sth. 哄某人做 (不做)某事 / ~ sb. away 把某人骗走 / ~ consent out of sb. 连哄带骗地得到某人同意 ②耐心地处理,慢慢把…弄好: ~ a fire to light 把火慢慢弄旺 / ~ a cold engine to start (费好多手脚)使冷却的引擎发动起来 ❷ *vi.* 哄骗 II *n.* 哄骗的话语(或行动) ‖~**ing** *n.* & *a.* 哄骗(的)

cob[1] [kɔb] *n.* ①(煤、石头、矿石等的)圆块;(面包等的)小圆块 ②玉米棒子 ③【动】雄鹄 ④结实的

矮脚马 ⑤ =~nut ⑥[英方]大人物 ‖~ **coal** 圆煤块 / '~**nut** *n.* 大榛子; 欧洲榛

cob[2] [kɔb] *n.* [英](混有稻草的)糊墙泥

cobalt [kə'bɔ:lt, 'koubɔ:lt] *n.* 【化】钴;钴类颜料 ‖~**ic** [kou'bɔ:ltik] *a.* 钴的; 高钴的,三价钴的 / ~ **blue** 钴蓝 / ~ **green** 钴绿

cobble[1] ['kɔbl] I *n.* ①(铺路等用的)大鹅卵石,圆石块;【地】中砾 ②[英][复]圆煤块 II *vt.* 用圆石砌(路) ‖'~**stone** *n.* 圆石块,大鹅卵石

cobble[2] ['kɔbl] *vt.* ①修,补(鞋等);粗粗地补(破洞等) ②粗制滥造 (up)

cobbler ['kɔblə] *n.* ①皮匠,补鞋匠 ②[古]手脚笨拙的工匠 ③一种厚的水果馅饼 ④(由酒、糖、柠檬等制成的)一种冷饮品 ‖~'s wax 鞋线蜡

cobra ['koubrə] *n.* 【动】眼镜蛇

cobweb ['kɔbweb] I *n.* ①蜘蛛网;蜘蛛丝 ②蜘蛛网状的东西(指轻薄细软的织物,经年积累的陈腐物): clear away the ~s from the mind 克服思想上的紊乱状态 II (cobwebbed; cobwebbing) *vt.* 蛛网(或蛛网状的东西)布满于 ‖*blow away the* ~*s* 出外透透空气 / *have a* ~ *in the throat* 口渴 ‖ **cobwebbed** *a.* 蛛网(或蛛网状东西)密布的 / **cobwebby** *a.* (似)蛛网的;蛛网(或蛛网状东西)密布的

cocaine [kə'kein] *n.* 【药】可卡因,古柯碱

cock[1] [kɔk] I *n.* ①公鸡 ②雄禽(有时也与其他动物连用指雄性): a ~ lobster 雄的大螯虾 ③山鹬 (=woodcock) ④[古]鸡叫; 黎明 (=~crow) ⑤风信鸡,风标 ⑥(水管、煤气管等的)旋塞,龙头,开关: turn the ~ on (off) 开(关)龙头 / a three way ~ 三通旋塞 ⑦(枪的)击铁;击铁待发位置,准备发射 ⑧(天平的)指针 ⑨首领,头目;神气十足的人 ⑩(帽边、眼梢等的)翘起,向上翘;歪戴,歪着:a knowing ~ of the eye 心领神会的眼色 II ❶ *vt.* ①使翘起,使竖起;歪戴(帽子): ~ one's ears 竖起耳朵 / ~ one's nose 翘起鼻子(表示轻蔑) / ~ one's hat 歪戴帽子; 卷起帽边 ②扳起(枪枝)的击铁 ❷ *vi.* ①大摇大摆地走;摆架子 ②翘起,竖起 ③(扳起击铁)准备发射 ‖*a* ~ *of the loft* (或 *dunghill*) 在小天地中称王称霸的人 / *a* ~ *of the walk* (或 *school*) 称王称霸的人 / *at full* (*half*) ~ 处于全(半)击发状态: go off at half ~ 操之过急,仓卒行事 / ~ *of the north* 【动】花鸡 / *live like fighting* ~*s* 吃得好,吃最好的东西 / *Old* ~! (旧时表示亲暱的称呼)老兄! / *red* ~ 纵火引起的火灾 / *set* (*the*) ~ *on* (*the*) *hoop* ①放荡;放纵;放纵 / *That* ~ *won't fight.* 那一手行不通。(或: 这话讲不通。) / *the* ~ *of the wood* 北美产的一种啄木鸟 ‖~**-a-doodle-doo** ['kɔkədu:dl'du:] ①喔喔啼(鸡鸣声) ②[儿语]公鸡 / ~**-a-hoop** ['kɔkə'hu:p] *a.* & *ad.* 得意洋洋的(地),自鸣得意的(地) / '~**-and-'bull story** 荒诞的故事,无稽之谈 / ~**crow**(**ing**) *n.* 黎明 / '~,**fighting** *n.* 斗鸡: This beats ~*fighting*. 这实在有趣。/ '~**pit** *n.* ①斗鸡场;多次发生过战争的地方 ②

船尾舵手座 ③(下级军官及伤员用的)下层后舱 ④飞机座舱;赛车的车舱 / **~scomb** ['kɔkskoum] *n.* ①鸡冠 ②鸡冠花 ③小丑的帽子 / '**~shot**, '**~shy** *n.* ①掷棒(或石等)的靶子 ②(向靶子的)一掷 / **~ sparrow** *n.* ①公麻雀 ②矮小而强悍的人 / '**~spur** *n.* ①公鸡的距 ②鸡距形的煤气喷灯 ③【植】稗属植物: **~spur** hawthorn 鸡距山楂 / **[印]**(篇首或段落开头处及所用的)特高大写字母;附在字母右肩上的字(如 5^n 中的 n) ②前端翘起的帽子 *a.* ①(大写字母)特高的 ②附在字母右肩上的

cock² [kɔk] **I** *n.* (田中)锥形的小干草堆 **II** *vt.* 把(干草等)堆成锥形小堆

cockade [kɔ'keid] *n.* 帽章,帽上的花结

cockatoo [kɔkə'tu:] *n.*【动】白鹦

cockerel ['kɔkərəl] *n.* ①(未满一年的)小公鸡 ②好斗的年轻人

cockney ['kɔkni] **I** *n.* [贬] ①伦敦佬(尤指住东区的人);伦敦方言 ②柔弱的都市人 ③装腔作势的女人 **II** *a.* [贬]伦敦佬的;(似)伦敦佬派头的;伦敦方言的: a **~** accent 伦敦腔 ‖**~dom** *n.* ①[总称]伦敦佬 ②伦敦佬聚居处 / **~fy** *vt.* 使带上伦敦佬派头(或腔调);把…弄得花哨庸俗 / **~ish** *a.* 带点伦敦佬派头的;有点儿伦敦腔的 / **~ism** *n.* 伦敦佬派头;伦敦方言中的语言现象: Dropping one's *h*s is a distinct **~ism** 把 [h] 音略去不发是标准的伦敦腔。

cockroach ['kɔkrəutʃ] *n.* 蟑螂

cocktail ['kɔkteil] **I** *n.* ①鸡尾酒 ②西餐中头道进食的开胃品(如茄汁等) ③截短尾巴的马;非纯种的(赛跑)马 ④门第低而地位高的人 ⑤一种甲虫 **II** *a.* ①鸡尾酒的: a **~** party 鸡尾酒会,酒会 / the **~** hour [美]通常喝鸡尾酒的时间(指下午五时前后) ②(女服)在半正式场合穿的 ‖**~ed** *a.* 截短了尾巴的

cocoa ['koukou] *n.* ①可可粉;可可茶 ②可可树 ③可可色 ‖**~ bean** 可可豆,可可子 / **~ nib** 可可子的子叶 / **~ powder** 一种褐色火药

coco(a)nut ['koukənʌt] *n.* ①椰子(果) ②[俚]头,脑袋 ‖ *That accounts for the milk in the* **~**. [谑]啊,原来如此。 ‖**~ butter, ~ oil** 椰子油 / **~ matting** 椰毛编织的垫子 / **~ milk, ~ water** 椰子汁 / **~ palm, ~ tree** 椰子树

cocoon [kə'ku:n] **I** *n.* ①茧;(昆虫的)卵袋 ②茧状物;(军用物品等的)塑料保护喷层 **II** ❶ *vt.* ①作茧包藏 ②以茧状物(或喷层)包: a gun 在大炮上喷上一层喷层 / be **~ed** in several layers of shawls 包在好几条大围巾之中 ❷ *vi.* 作茧;成茧状

cod¹ [kɔd] ([复] cod(s)) *n.*【动】鳕 ‖'**~fish** *n.* 鳕 / '**~-liver oil** 鱼肝油

cod² [kɔd] *n.* [方]荚,壳

cod³ [kɔd] (codded; codding) *vt. & vi.* [俚]哄骗,愚弄

coda ['koudə] *n.*【音】结尾;符尾

coddle ['kɔdl] **I** *vt.* ①煮(蛋等) ②悉心照料;娇养,溺爱 **II** *n.* 娇生惯养的人

code [koud] **I** *n.* ①法典,法规: a civil **~** 民法典 / a penal (或 criminal) **~** 刑法典 ②规则,准则;礼教习俗: a moral **~** 道德准则 ③代号,代码;电码;密码: a **~** telegram 密码电报;电码电报 / the International *Code* 国际电码 **II** *vt.* …译成电码 ‖**~ book** 电码本 / **~ flag** 信号旗

codicil ['kɔdisil] *n.* ①【律】遗嘱的附录(尤指对遗嘱所作的删改) ②补遗,附录 ‖**codicillary** [ˌkɔdi'siləri] *a.*

codify ['kɔdifai] *vt.* ①把(法律)编集成典 ②编纂;整理 ‖ **codification** [ˌkɔdifi'keiʃən] *n.*

coerce [kou'ə:s] *vt.* ①强制,胁迫,迫使: **~** sb. *into* doing sth. 强迫某人做某事 ②强制地取得(一致等): a **~**d consent 硬逼出来的同意

coeval [kou'i:vəl] **I** *a.* 同时代的;同年代的;同时期的;同年龄的 **II** *n.* 同时代的人;同年代的东西 ‖**~ly** *ad.*

coffee ['kɔfi] *n.* ①咖啡,咖啡茶,咖啡粉,咖啡豆,咖啡树: three black **~**s 三杯(不加牛奶的)清咖啡 / white **~** 牛奶咖啡 ②咖啡色 ‖'**~-and** *n.* [俚]一杯咖啡加一两个面包卷的简单餐点 / **~ bean,** '**~ berry** *n.* 咖啡豆 / **~ cake** (用面粉、牛奶、蛋、奶油、糖等做的)早餐点心 / **~ cooler** 专挑轻活的人 / **~ cup** 咖啡杯 / **~ grinder** ①咖啡豆的磨具 ②[美俚]飞机引擎 / **~ grounds** 咖啡渣 / '**~house** *n.* 咖啡馆 / **~ mill** 咖啡豆的磨具 / **~ palace** =**~**house / '**~pot** *n.* ①咖啡壶 ②午餐柜;小饭店 / **~ room** 咖啡室,旅馆的餐厅 / **~ shop** 咖啡店,小餐馆 / **~ stall** 卖咖啡、点心等的流动摊 / **~ table** 咖啡茶几: a **~** table book 供咖啡茶几上摆设用的书(常指内容贫乏但装璜精美的画册) / **~ tavern** 不卖酒的小餐馆 / **~ tree** 咖啡树

coffer ['kɔfə] **I** *n.* ①(放金钱或贵重物品的)保险箱 ②[复]资产,财源;国库;金库: the **~**s of a bank 银行的金库 ③围堰;(桥梁工程等用的)潜水箱,沉箱;浮船坞;【船】隔离舱;【建】平顶的镶板 **II** *vt.* ①把…装入箱中;把…放存金库内;珍藏 ②用平顶镶板装饰 ‖**~ing** ['kɔfəriŋ] *n.*【建】格子平顶 ‖**~dam** *n.* 围堰;潜水箱;【船】隔离舱

coffin ['kɔfin] **I** *n.* ①棺材,棺木,柩 ②(马的)蹄槽 ③不适于航海的破旧船 (=**~** ship) ④运送放射性物质的重屏蔽容器 **II** *vt.* 把…装入棺材,收殓;严密收藏 ‖*drive a nail into* sb.'*s* **~** (忧愁、烟酒等)促某人早死 ‖ **~ bone** [动]蹄骨 / **~ joint** [动]蹄关节 / **~ nail** [美俚]香烟 / **~ plate** 棺盖上的金属牌(用以记死者名字及生卒年月日等) / **~ varnish** [美俚]蹩脚的威士忌酒

cog¹ [kɔg] **I** *n.* ①【机】嵌齿;(齿轮的)轮牙;(爬坡机车齿轮的)大齿;(木工的)雄榫,凸榫: hunting **~**s 【机】追逐齿 ②[口]从属但不可缺少的人(或物) **II** (cogged; cogging) *vt.* 在…上装齿轮(或装榫) ‖*have a* **~** *loose* (头脑等)有点不正常,有些毛病 / *slip a* **~** 出差错 ‖**~ railway** (火车爬

坡时)有嵌齿的铁轨 / **'~wheel** *n.* 嵌齿轮

cog² [kɔg] (cogged; cogging) ❶ *vi.* 〔古〕(掷骰子时)诈骗;欺骗;行贿 ❷ *vt.* ①用骗人手段掷(骰子) ②〔古〕诈骗

cog³ [kɔg] *n.* 小船,附属于大船的供应船

cogent ['koudʒənt] *a.* 有说服力的;无法反驳的 ‖**~ly** *ad.*

cogitate ['kɔdʒiteit] ❶ *vt.* (慎重)考虑;谋划 ❷ *vi.* 深思熟虑: ~ *upon* sth. 对某事慎重考虑 ‖ **cogitation** [,kɔdʒi'teiʃən] *n.* ①考虑,深思 ②〔复〕思想

cognac ['kounjæk] *n.* 法国科涅克(Cognac)地方产的白兰地酒;法国白兰地酒

cognate ['kɔgneit] Ⅰ *a.* ①同族的;母族的 ②〔语〕同词源的;同语族的: ~ languages 同语族的语言 / a ~ object 同源宾语(如 "live a life" 中的 "life") ③同性质的,同种的,同类的 Ⅱ *n.* ①亲族 ②同词源的词;同语系的语言 ③同性质的东西,同源物 ‖ **cognation** [kɔg'neiʃən] *n.* ①〔语〕同词源,同语系 ②亲族;同族

cognizance ['kɔgnizəns] *n.* ①认识,认知;认识范围 ②观察,注意 ③〔律〕审理;审理权,裁判权 ④特殊的标志(如纹章上的图案等) ⑤监视,支配 ‖ *fall* (或 *be*) *within* (*beyond*) *sb.'s* ~ 在某人认识(或注意)范围之内(外);在某人管辖(或审理权)范围之内(外) / *have* ~ *of* 认识到,注意到;对…有审理权 / *take* ~ *of* 认识到,注意到;承担对…的审理权

cognovit [kɔg'nouvit] *n.* 〔拉〕〔律〕(被告承认原告诉讼为正当时所具结的)被告承认书,具结

cohere [kou'hiə] *vi.* ①粘着;粘合;可粘合 ②(论据等)紧凑,连贯;符合: The adornments do not ~ *with* the basic design. 装饰物与设计的基调不协调。 ③团结一致

coherence [kou'hiərəns], **coherency** [kou'hiərənsi] *n.* ①粘着;粘合性 ②(逻辑上的)紧凑,连贯,一致性 ③〔物〕相干性: *coherence* effects 相干效应 ④〔化〕内聚现象;内聚力

coherent [kou'hiərənt] *a.* ①粘着的,粘附的 ②紧凑的,连贯的,首尾一致的;表达清楚的: a ~ thinker 思想很有条理的人 ③〔物〕相干的,相参的 ‖**~ly** *ad.*

coil¹ [kɔil] Ⅰ ❶ *vt.* 卷,盘绕;把…卷成圈: ~ a rope 卷绳 / The snake ~ed itself round the branch. 蛇盘绕在树枝上。 ❷ *vi.* 成圈状;盘绕 Ⅱ *n.* ①(一)卷;(一)圈;(河流等)的弯绕,环形:wind up a rope in a ~ 把绳子卷起来 ②〔无〕线圈,绕组: primary (secondary) ~ 初级(次级)线圈 / choke (或 choking) ~ 扼流圈,阻流圈 / ~ former 线圈架 ③蛇管,盘管,旋管

coil² [kɔil] *n.* 〔古〕〔诗〕纷乱 ‖*shuffle off this mortal* ~ 摆脱尘世的烦恼(指死去)

coin [kɔin] Ⅰ *n.* ①硬币: a subsidiary ~ 辅币 / a silver ~ 银币 / a small heap of ~(s) 一小堆硬币 ②〔俚〕金钱 ③〔古〕角;隅石;楔形物 Ⅱ *vt.* ①铸造(硬币);把(金属)铸成硬币 ②创造,杜撰

(新词、新语等) ‖(a) *false* ~ 伪币;〔喻〕假造的东西 / ~ *money* 暴发,获大利 / ~ *one's brains* 动脑筋挣钱 / *pay* sb. *back in his own* ~ 以其人之道还治其人之身 ‖*~er* *n.* ①造币者;〔英〕伪造货币者 ②(新词等的)创造者,杜撰者 ‖**~-op** ['kɔi,nop] *n.* (投入硬币,机器即自行开动的)自动洗衣店

coincide [,kouin'said] *vi.* ①(在空间、时间方面)恰好相合,恰好重合 ②一致,相符: They do not ~ *in* opinion. 他们的意见不合。 / My free time doesn't ~ *with* yours. 我和你不是同时有空。

coincidence [kou'insidəns] *n.* 符合,一致;巧合;巧合的事物: by a curious ~ 由于奇怪的巧合 / What a happy ~! 多巧啊!

coincident [kou'insidənt] *a.* 同时发生的,重合的;一致的,符合的 (*with*) ‖**~ly** *ad.*

coke¹ [kouk] Ⅰ *n.* 焦,焦炭: a ~ oven 炼焦炉 Ⅱ *vt.* & *vi.* (使)成焦炭 ‖**coking** *n.* 炼焦;焦化 *a.* 炼焦的,粘结的

coke² [kouk] *n.* 〔美俚〕=cocaine ‖*d* *a.* 〔美俚〕受麻醉品刺激的

coke³ [kouk] *n.* =coca-cola

colander ['kʌləndə, 'kɔləndə] *n.* 滤器,滤锅

cold [kould] Ⅰ *a.* ①冷,寒: a ~ day 一个寒冷的日子 / feel ~ 觉得冷 / sweat a ~ sweat 出一身冷汗 / a ~ current 寒流 ②冷淡的,不热情的: a ~ reception (response) 冷淡的接待(反应) ③使人战栗的,使人丧心的;使人扫兴的;无趣味的: ~ news 使人扫兴的消息;过时消息 / ~ counsel 逆耳的忠告 ④冷静的,客观的;经过周密考虑的;冷酷的,无情的: ~ facts 冷酷的事实 ⑤已死的;失去知觉的: lie ~ (in death) 直挺挺地死了 / pass out ~ 昏过去 / be knocked ~ 被打昏 ⑥勉强忍住的;未到爆发程度的: with ~ fury in one's heart 心中憋着一股怒火 ⑦(土壤)粘而湿的;(肥料)腐烂得慢的 ⑧(颜色)使人生冷感的(指青、绿、灰等) ⑨没有准备的,贸然的 ⑩(钱数)确定无疑的,十足的 ⑪(猎物的遗臭等)已变淡的 Ⅱ *ad.* ①完全地: The actor had his lines down ~. 这演员把台词背得滚瓜烂熟了。②〔常与动词构成复合词〕冷门 Ⅲ *n.* 寒冷: *Cold* and heat succeed each other. 寒来暑往。/ stand in the ~ 在冷空气里站着 / shiver with ~ 冷得发抖 ②伤风,感冒: catch (a) ~ 伤风,感冒 / get (have) a ~ 得(患着)感冒 / easily take ~(s) 容易伤风 / take a bad (或 heavy) ~ 患了重伤风 / a diplomatic ~ "外交病"(指托病不出面等) ③〔物〕零下温度: five degrees of ~ 零下五度 ‖*Feed a ~ and starve a fever.* 〔谚〕伤风时宜吃,发热时宜饿。/ *have* ~ *feet* 害怕,胆寒;临阵畏缩 / *have* (或 *get*) sb. ~ 把某人置于自己的掌握之下;任意摆布某人 / *in* ~ *blood* 蓄意地(指非一时感情冲动);残忍地 / *leave* sb. ~ 没有打动某人 / *leave* sb. (*out*) *in the* ~ 不理睬某人;把某人撇在一边以示冷落 / *make* sb.'s *blood run* ~ 使某人不寒而栗,使某人毛骨悚

然 / *throw* ~ *water on* 对…泼冷水 ‖~ly *ad.*
冷淡地 / ~ness *n.* ‖'~-'blooded *a.* 冷血的;
无情的; 残酷的 / '~-'bloodedly *ad.* 无情地;
残酷地 / '~-'bloodedness *n.* 无情; 残酷 / ~
chisel 冷凿 / '~'cock *vt.* 把…打昏 / ~ coil
冷却旋管(俗称盘香管) / ~ cream 冷霜, 润肤
膏 / '~-draw *vt.* 冷拉(金属丝等) / ~ frame
植物防寒(玻璃)温室 / ~ front 【气】冷锋 /
'~-,hammer *vt.* 冷锤(铁条等) / '~-
'hearted *a.* 冷淡的; 冷心肠的 / '~'heartedly
ad. 冷淡地; 无情地 / '~'heartedness *n.* 冷淡;
冷心肠 / '~-'livered *a.* 不动肝火的, 冷静的 /
~ pig [英俚]泼醒人所用的冷水 / '~-'pig *vt.*
[英俚]用冷水泼醒 / '~proof *a.* 抗寒的; 耐寒
的 / '~-roll *vt.* 冷轧(钢材等) / '~-'short *a.*
【冶】冷脆的 / ~ shoulder ①冷淡 ②冷冻的烤
羊肉(前腿部分) / '~-'shoulder *vt.* 冷待 / ~
snap 寒汛 / ~ sore (伤风发热时)嘴边的疱疹,
唇疱疹 / ~ steel 冷武器(指刀、剑等) / ~
storage ①冷藏; 冷藏库 ②搁置, 停顿 ③[美俚]
坟墓 / ~ turkey ①必定无疑的牺牲品; 必败无
疑者 ② 冷漠孤高的人 ③ 突然完全戒除吸毒瘾
④ 直截了当, 如实 ⑤[作状语用]无事先准备地,
单刀直入地 / ~ war 冷战 / ~ warrior 冷战
分子, 冷战大王 / ~ wave 气温的突然大降; 寒潮
colic ['kɔlik] I *n.* 绞痛, 疝痛, 腹痛 II *a.* ①绞痛
的 ②结肠的
collaborate [kə'læbəreit] *vi.* ①协作, 合作(尤指在
文艺、科学等方面): ~ *on* a book *with* sb. 同某
人合著一部书 ②勾结 (*with*) ‖ collaborator *n.*
协作者, 合作者; 勾结者
collaboration [kə,læbə'reiʃən] *n.* ①合作, 协作:
lend one's cheerful ~ to a task 愉快地在一件工
作中贡献自己的力量 ②勾结 ‖ *in* ~ *with* 与…
合作; 与…勾结在一起 ‖~ism *n.* 鼓吹与敌人合
作; 通敌(行为) / ~ist *n.* 通敌者
collapse [kə'læps] I ❶ *vi.* ①倒坍: The roof ~d
under the weight of the snow. 屋顶被雪压坍了。
②崩溃, 瓦解; (价格等)暴跌 ③(健康、精神等方
面的)衰退, 垮下 ④(椅子等)折迭起来 ❷ *vt.* ①倒坍;
使倒坍; 使崩溃; 使衰萎 ②折迭 II *n.* ①倒坍;
崩溃; 衰弱 ②(价格等的)暴跌 ③【医】虚脱; 萎陷
collar ['kɔlə] I *n.* ①衣领, 硬领: seize (或 take)
sb. by the ~ 抓住某人领口 / a stand-up ~ 竖
领 ②项圈; 护领 ③(马等的)轭; (狗等的)脖圈,
颈圈 ④环状物; 【机】环; 轴环; 【建】柱环 ⑤(猪肉
等的)肉卷 ⑥[美俚]逮捕: make a ~ on sb. 逮
捕某人 II *vt.* ①扭住…的领口 (或头颈) ②给
(衣服)上领子; 给…加轭(或颈圈) ③捕, 抓; 占
取; 窃取: Who has ~ed my matches? 谁拿了我
的火柴? ④[口]硬拉住…说话 ⑤做(肉)卷
‖ *against the* ~ (马上坡时)轭具擦疼肩膀;
[喻]冒着困难; 下死劲 / *be hot under the* ~
[俚]发怒 / *in the* ~ 受到约束 / *slip the* ~
(狗等)挣脱颈圈; 逃脱 ‖~ed *a.* 有领圈的; 上了
轭(或颈圈)的; (肉)成卷的 / ~less *a.* 无领的;

无轭(或颈圈)的 ‖ ~ beam 【建】系梁, 系杆 /
'~bone *n.* 【解】锁骨 / ~ harness 颈部马轭 /
~ stud 把领子扣在衬衫上的领扣 / ~ work
[喻]艰巨的工作
collate [kɔ'leit] *vt.* ① 对照; (详细地)核对; 校对
②(装订)整理 ③【宗】委任(牧师)职务 ‖ collator
n. 校对者; 整理者
colleague ['kɔli:g] *n.* 同事, 同僚
collect¹ [kə'lekt] I ❶ *vt.* ①收集, 搜集, 采集
(租、税、帐等); 募集(捐款): ~ manure 积肥 /
~ stamps 集邮 ②集中(思想等); 使镇定: ~
oneself 使自己镇定下来 ③ 推断出, 认定 ④领取
(信件等); 接走: I'll come round to ~ my child
one of these days. 日内我将来接回我的孩子。❷
vi. ①聚集, 堆积: Clouds are ~ing. 云集拢来
了。②收款, 收帐; 搜集 II *a.* 由收到者付款的,
送到即付现款的: a ~ telephone call 向受话者
收费的电话 III *ad.* 由收到者付款地, 送到即付
现款地: send a package ~ 以由收包裹者付款的
方式寄包裹 ‖~ing post 【军】①伤病员收容所
②[英]战俘收容所 / ~ing station 【军】①伤病
员收容站 ②废弃物资收集站 ③难民收容站
collect² ['kɔlekt] *n.* 【宗】短祷告
collected [kə'lektid] *a.* ① 收集成的 ② 泰然自若
的, 镇定的 ‖~ly *ad.* 镇定地 / ~ness *n.* 镇定
collection [kə'lekʃən] *n.* ① 收集, 采集, 搜集; 集
成: a motley ~ of things 大杂烩 / a ~ of snow
积雪 ②收藏品, 收集物 ③收款; 募捐; 捐
来的款子: make (或 take up) a ~ for 为…募
捐 ④[英][复](牛津大学等各学院的)学期考试
collective [kə'lektiv] I *a.* ① 集合的; 聚合性的:
~ fruit 【植】聚花果 / a ~ noun 【语】集合名
词 ② 共同的, 集体的, 集团的; 集体主义的: the
~ wishes of the people 人民的共同愿望 / the ~
economy 集体经济 / ~ ownership 集体所有制 /
a ~ farm 集体农庄 / ~ security 集体安全 / ~
bargaining 由工会代表劳方集体进行的劳资谈
判 II *n.* ①集体; 集体事业; 全体人员 ②【语】集
合名词 ‖~ly *ad.*
collector [kə'lektə] *n.* ①收集人; 收藏家; 采集者:
a stamp ~ 集邮者 ②收税员, 收款员; 募捐人;
(印度的)税务兼地方行政长官 ③收集物; 收集
器: a dust ~ 招积灰尘的东西 ④【电】集电器;
集电极; 【机】集合器 ‖~ship *n.* 收税员的职权
(或管辖区)
college ['kɔlidʒ] *n.* ①(综合大学中的)学院 ②(独
立的)学院, 高等专科学校; [美]大学: a teachers
~ 师范学院 / ~ of agriculture 农学院 ③大
学预科 / [英]公学, 书院(专指若干中学程度的公
立学校) ④职业学校, 技术学校 ⑤学院(或学校)
的建筑物 ⑥学会; 社团: the *College* of Cardinals
【天主教】红衣主教团(罗马教皇的枢密院) ⑦
[俚]监狱; 感化院 ‖~-'bred *a.* 受过大学教育
的 / ~ pudding 一人一份的葡萄干布丁
collide [kə'laid] *vi.* ①(车、船等)猛撞 ②冲突, 抵
触(*with*)

collier ['kɔliə] *n.* ① (煤矿) 矿工 ② 运煤船; 煤船船员 ③ 烧炭人

colliery ['kɔljəri] *n.* 煤矿 (包括建筑物和设备等在内)

collision [kə'liʒən] *n.* ① (车、船等的) 碰撞 ② (利益、意见等的) 冲突 ③ (辅音的) 不和谐组合 ‖come into ~ (with) (跟···) 相撞; (同···) 冲突起来 / in ~ 相撞; 在冲突中 ‖~ mat【海】防漏毡, 堵漏毯

colloquial [kə'loukwiəl] *a.* 口语的, 会话的; 用通俗口语的 ‖~ly *ad.*

colloquy ['kɔləkwi] *n.* ① (正式) 谈话; 会谈 ② 用对话体写的著作

collusion [kə'lju:ʒən] *n.* 共谋, 勾结, 串通 ‖in ~ with 与···勾结

colon[1] ['koulən] ([复] cola ['koulə] 或 colons) *n.*【解】结肠

colon[2] ['koulən] *n.* 冒号 (即:)

colon[3] [kou'loun] ([复] colones [kou'louneis]) *n.* 科朗 (哥斯达黎加和萨尔瓦多的货币单位)

colonel ['kə:nl] *n.* ① (英) 陆军 (或海军陆战队) 上校; (美) 陆军 (或空军、海军陆战队) 上校 ②中校 (=lieutenant ~)

colonial [kə'lounjəl] I *a.* ① 殖民地的; 关于殖民地的: a ~ country 殖民地国家 / the Colonial Office (英国的) 殖民部 (一九六六年八月与联邦关系部合并成联邦部; 一九六八年十月联邦部又与外交部合并) ②[C-] (美国独立时) 十三州时代的, 美国初期的 ③拥有殖民地的; 由殖民地构成的 ④【生】集群的; 群体的 II *n.* 殖民地居民

colonialism [kə'lounjəlizəm] *n.* ①殖民主义 ②殖民地的地位 (或特征) ③殖民政策 ‖colonialist *n. & a.* 殖民主义者 (的)

colonist ['kɔlənist] *n.* ①殖民地开拓者; 移住民 ②殖民地居民

colonize ['kɔlənaiz] ❶ *vt.* ①开拓殖民地于 (某地区) ②移 (民) 于殖民地 ③[美] (为扩充一党的势力) 从别地非法把选民移入 (某地区) ④ (为政治企图派人) 打入, 混进 (部门等) ❷ *vi.* ①开拓殖民地 ②移居于殖民地 ‖colonization [ˌkɔlənai'zeifən] *n.* / ~r *n.* 殖民地开拓者; 殖民者

colony ['kɔləni] *n.* ①殖民地 ②移民队, 殖民队 ③ (住在外国大都市一区域的) 侨民团 ④ (艺术家、外交家等的) 一群; 同类人的聚居地: a ~ of artists 聚居的艺术家们; 艺术家的聚居地 ⑤【生】集群; 群体; 菌落: a ~ of termites 一群白蚁 ⑥[史] (希腊的) 殖民都市; (罗马人) 在征服地区的驻防地

colossal [kə'lɔsl] *a.* ①巨像的, 巨像似的; 庞大的 ②[口]异常的, 非常的

colossus [kə'lɔsəs] ([复] colossi [kə'lɔsai] 或 colossuses) *n.* 巨像; 巨人; 巨物: a ~ with feet of clay 泥足巨人

colo(u)r ['kʌlə] I *n.* ①颜色; 色彩; 彩色: primary (或 fundamental, simple) ~s 原色 (指红、黄、

蓝等) / secondary ~s 次色, 混合色, 调和色 (由两种原色调成的颜色) / local ~ 地方色彩 / a ~ scheme 色彩设计 ② 脸色, 血色; 红晕: He has very little ~. 他脸色苍白。③肤色; 有色人种的肤色: a person of ~ 有色人种的人, 非白种人 / people of all ~s 各色人种的人 (包括白种人) / a ~ question 种族问题 ④颜料; 染料: an oil ~ 油画颜料; 油溶性染料 / an acid (a basic) ~ 酸性 (盐基性) 染料 ⑤[常用复]旗帜; [复] (作为所属团体色彩标志的) 绶带, 徽章, 衣帽; [复]立场, 观点: salute the ~s 向军旗敬礼 ⑥外貌; (表面的) 真实性; 幌子: His story has some ~ of truth. 他的一番叙述听来似乎是真的。 ⑦ 生动, 多采: add ~ to an article 使一篇文章生色 ⑧[音]音色 II ❶ *vt.* ①给···着色; 染; 改变···的颜色 ②使带上色彩; 渲染, 伪装, 歪曲: a highly ~ed version of facts 对事实大肆渲染 (或歪曲) 的叙述 ❷ *vi.* 获得颜色; (果实成熟时等) 变色; 脸红 (up): The leaves have begun to ~. 叶子已经开始发黄 (或红紫)。‖all the ~s of rainbow 五颜六色 / change ~ (因感情原因) 变脸色 / gain (或 gather) ~ 脸色变得红润 / get (或 win) one's ~s [英]被选入运动队 (尤指校队等) / give a false ~ to 歪曲 / give (或 lend) ~ to 使显得可信 / give sb. his ~s [英]把某人选入运动队 / haul down one's ~s 投降 / have a high ~ 脸色红润 / join (be called to) the ~s (被征)入伍 / lay on the ~s (too thickly) 过分渲染, 夸大 / lose ~ 脸色变得苍白 / lower one's ~s 放弃要求 (或主张); 投降 / nail one's ~s to the mast 明白宣布并坚持自己的主张 / off ~ [口]身体不舒服; 精神不好 / paint sth. in bright (dark) ~s 用鲜艳 (晦暗) 的颜色来画某物; 把某事物描述得很光明 (阴暗) / put false ~s upon 歪曲 / Queen's ~ [英]英国军队的团旗 / sail under false ~s (船只) 挂着假冒的旗帜航行 ② 欺世盗名, 冒充, 欺骗 / see sth. in its true ~s 看清某事物的真相 / see the ~ of sb.'s money 接受某人的钱 / (serve) with the ~s 在军队中服役 / show one's ~s ①露出真面目 ②表明立场观点 / show oneself (或 be exposed, be revealed) in one's true ~s 暴露真面目, 现原形 / stick to one's ~s 坚持自己的立场观点 / strike the ~s 降旗投降 / turn ~ ①改变颜色 ②脸变红; 脸变白 / under ~ of 在···的幌子下 / with flying ~s 出色地, 成功地: come off with flying ~s 结果大获全胜 ‖~ bar 对有色人种的歧视、隔离 / ~ blind *a.* 色盲的 / ~ blindness 色盲 / ~ box 颜料盒 / '~-breed *vt.* 饲养 (鸟类) 使有某种彩色 / ~ camera 彩色摄影机 / '~-cast *n.* 彩色电视放送 *vt. & vi.* 通过彩色电视放送 / '~-fast *a.* 不褪色的 / ~ film ①彩色胶片 ②彩色影片 / ~ filter 滤色器; 滤色镜 / ~ guard 护旗队 / ~ line (种族歧视制度下的) 种族分界线 / '~-man *n.* ①颜料商 ②染色物 / photography 彩色摄影 / '~-plate *n.* (套色彩印用的) 彩色版; 套色彩印图片 / ~ printing 彩

印 / ～**sergeant**(英)海军陆战队上士 / ～ **wash** 白色(或彩色)的涂料,刷色

colo(u)red ['kʌləd] I *a.* ①有色的; [常用以构成复合词]有…色的: cream-～ 奶油色的 / flesh-～ 肉色的 ②经过渲染的,有色彩的;伪装的 ③有色人种的(尤指黑人的) ④混血种的(尤指非纯白色的) II *n.* 有色人种的人(尤指黑人);混血人 ‖～ **pencil** 颜色笔,颜色铅笔

colo(u)ring ['kʌləriŋ] *n.* ①着色(法) ② 色彩, 色调 ③面色;外貌;伪装: under the ～ of 在…的外貌下 ④ 颜料 ⑤(新闻报道等的)倾向性 ⑥ 特质 ‖～ **matter** (食物等的)着色剂, 染料, 色素

colt [koult] I *n.* ①小马(尤指小雄马), 驹(子) ②生手,新手 ③笞绳 II *vt.* 用笞绳抽打 ‖～**'s tail** 卷云

column ['kɔləm] *n.* ① 柱,支柱, 圆柱; 柱状物: a ～ of mercury 水银柱 / a ～ of smoke 烟柱 ②【军】纵队; 小分(遣)队; (舰队的)纵阵: a single ～ (或 a ～ of files) 一路纵队 / a ～ of threes (fours) 三路(四路)纵队 / a fifth ～ 第五纵队 (现泛指敌人派入的间谍和资敌的内奸) ③(报刊中的)专栏: literary ～s 文艺栏 / advertisement ～s 广告栏 ④【数】列;柱 ⑤【化】柱,塔: ～ still 柱馏器 ‖～**ar** [kə'lʌmnə] *a.* ①圆柱的;圆柱形的 ②印成栏的;排成栏的: a ～ar book 多栏式帐簿 / ～**ed** *a.* 有圆柱的; 圆柱形的 / ～**iation** [kə,lʌmni'eiʃən] *n.* 【建】列柱;列柱法 / ～**iform** [kə'lʌmnifɔ:m] *a.* 圆柱形的 / ～**ist** ['kɔləmnist] *n.* 报刊专栏作者

column

coma[1] ['koumə] *n.* ①【医】昏迷 ②惰怠;麻木

coma[2] ['koumə] ([复] comae ['koumi:]) *n.* ①【天】彗发 ②【物】彗形像差 ③【植】种缨;序缨;树冠

comb [koum] I *n.* ①梳, 马梳 ②【纺】精梳机 ③【动】蜂房(=honeycomb) ④【动】肉冠; 鸡冠状的东西 ⑤【动】栉 ⑥山顶;浪峰 II ❶ *vt.* ①梳(发);用马梳梳(马) ②【纺】精梳 ③彻底搜查(某处): a ～*ing* operation 扫荡 ❷ *vi.* (浪)涌起,卷起 ‖～ **out** ①在…中去除不需要的人(或物): ～ *out* a department 在一个部门中裁减人员 ②彻底查出 ③搜罗 / *cut the* ～ *of* 使屈辱 ‖～**er** *n.* ①梳刷者 ②【纺】精梳机 ③卷浪 ‖～**-out** *n.* ①去除不需要的人(或物) ②彻底查出 ③搜罗

combat ['kɔmbət] I *n.* ① 战斗; 格斗; 反对: ～ effectiveness 战斗力 / ～ disposition 战斗部署 / a ～ task 战斗任务 / a ～ hero 战斗英雄 / (a) single ～ 两人决斗 ②竞争,争论 II (combat(t)ed; combat(t)ing) ❶ *vt.* 跟…战斗;反对: ～ diseases 与疾病作斗争 / ～ liberalism 反对自由主义 ❷ *vi.* 战斗,搏斗: ～ *with* (或 *against*) wind and waves 与风浪搏斗 / ～ *for* 为…而奋斗 ‖～ **car** 轻型装甲车;轻型坦克 / ～ **fatigue** 战斗疲劳症 / '～-'ready *a.* 作好战斗准备的 / '～-'worthy *a.* 有战斗力的

combatant ['kɔmbətənt] I *a.* 战斗的 II *n.* ①战斗员 ②格斗者

combination [,kɔmbi'neiʃən] *n.* ① 结合, 联合, 合并; 结合体, 联合体 ②附有旁座的摩托车 ③[复]连裤内衣 ④【化】化合 ⑤【数】组合;配合 ⑥ =～ lock ⑦一物两用(或多用)的工具 ‖*in* ～ *with* 与…联合,与…结合 ‖～ **cracking** 【化】(液相和汽相)联合裂化 / ～ **lock** 字码(或号码)锁

combine[1] [kəm'bain] ❶ *vt.* ①使结合; 使联合: ～ theory *with* practice 把理论和实践结合起来 / a ～*d* operation 联合作战 ②兼有,兼备(各种性质等): a ～*d* bridge 铁路公路两用桥 ③使化合: ～ hydrogen *with* oxygen 使氢氧化合 ❷ *vi.* ①结合;联合 ②化合

combine[2] ['kɔmbain, kəm'bain] I *n.* ① (为某种目的而结成的)集团; (以操纵物价为目的的)联合企业 ② 联合收割机 (=～ harvester) II *vt.* 用联合收割机收割

combustible [kəm'bʌstəbl] I *a.* ①易燃的; 可燃的 ② 易于激动的 II *n.* [常用复]易燃物; 可燃物 ‖**combustibility** [kəm,bʌstə'biliti] *n.* 易燃性; 可燃性

combustion [kəm'bʌstʃən] *n.* ①燃烧: an internal ～ engine 内燃机 / spontaneous ～ 自燃 ②(有机体的)氧化 ③骚动

come [kʌm] I (came [keim], come) *vi.* ①来,来临: He *is* ～. 他已来了。(着重"已来"的状态) / Shall I ～ with you? 我跟你一起走好吗? / When his turn ～s (或 When it ～s to his turn), ... 当轮到他时, … / National Day is *coming*. 国庆节快到了。/ She will be 21 ～ May. [口]到五月份她将满二十一足岁。(句中 ～ May=when May ～s) ②(事物)来到, 落到; 产生: I am determined to…whatever may ～ to me. 不管我遭到什么, 我决心… / A new idea has ～ to my mind. 我想出了一个新主意。/ What has ～ *of* his scheme? 他的计划结果怎样? ③来(自); 出生(于) (*from, of*): Strength ～s *from* unity, and wisdom *from* work. 团结出力量,劳动出智慧。④出现(于), 位(于): This quotation ～s *on* p. 104. 这段语录在一○四页上。/ Iron ～s between manganese and cobalt in atomic weight. 铁的原子量在锰与钴之间。

⑤达(到)，伸展(到)：The bus line ~s to the hotel. 公共汽车路线直达旅馆门前。
⑥到达(某一点)，谈到：Now we ~ to Chapter III. 现在我们讲第三章。
⑦[后接不定式]终于…，开始…：Walking tractors have ~ to be widely used. 手扶拖拉机已被广泛使用。/ You will ~ to realize that someday. 你总有一天会认识到那一点的。
⑧[与 how 连用，构成问句；时常不用助动词 do，而将主谓语颠倒](怎么)会的：How did you ~ (或 How came you) to know him so well? 你怎么会跟他那么熟的? / How ~s it that (或[美口] How ~) you finished your work so soon? 你怎么会那么快就搞完了你的工作?
⑨[作联系动词] 是；成为是：The screw has ~ loose. 螺丝钉松了。/ ~ apart 分开，分裂 / ~ untied (结头)松开 / ~ unstitched 脱线
⑩成熟起来；渐趋完成：The wheat is coming nicely. 小麦成熟情况良好。
⑪日子过得…：How are you coming these days? 你最近(过得)怎样?
⑫成形：The butter will not ~. 黄油做不成。(指不能凝结成形)
⑬需要(某种)代价：~ high (商品等)售价高
⑭[口]摆出…：~ the bully (the virtuous) over sb. 对某人装出盛气凌人(道貌岸然)的样子
⑮(货物等)被供应：This sweater ~s in six sizes. 这种球衫有六种尺码供应。
⑯满…足岁：My sister is coming seventeen. 我妹妹即将满十七足岁。
⑰[美俚]极为激动，极受刺激
II int. [表示促使注意、鼓励、不耐烦、责备等]喂! 嗨!得啦!：Come, tell me all about it. 喂,把这件事全告诉我吧。/ Come, we must hurry. 喂,我们得赶紧啦。/ Come, ~, no time for such trifles now. 得啦,得啦,没有时间谈这些琐事了。
‖~ about ①发生：How did it ~ about? 那事是怎么发生的? ②(风等)改变方向；转帆(指转变船帆的吃风方向) / ~ across ①(越过…而)来到；过来 ②(偶然)遇见；(偶然)发现：~ across a friend in (或 on) the street 在街上碰到一位朋友 / ~ across some source materials in the library 在图书馆里发现一些资料 ③[俚]付欠款,捐款;照做,照干;吐露所知的情况 / ~ after (…)后面 / ~ again [美俚]再说一遍,重复一遍 / ~ alive ①活跃起来; 觉悟起来 ②显得象真的似的 / ~ along ①一起来,一道走：She came along with us. 她是和我们一起来的。/ Come along! 快来! ②进展,进步 ③出现 / Come and get it! [美口]饭准备好了,来吃吧! / ~ and go ①来来往往 ②作短暂的过访;忽来忽去 / ~ around ① round / ~ away 脱开：The handle came away. 柄脱掉了。/ ~ back ①回来 ②(旧事等)在记忆中重现 ③恢复原有地位;复辟 ④(健康)恢复 ⑤(风尚等)又流行起来 ⑥[美俚]回嘴; 回击 / ~ before ①在…之前来 ②(地位等方面)在…之上 ③被交由…处理 / ~ between ①在…中间 ②离间; 使分开 / ~ by ①从旁走过 ②得到,获得：How did you ~ by this spanner? 你怎样弄到这把扳手的? ③[美方]来串门 / ~ clean 全盘招供 / ~ down ①下来; 降下 ②(树)倒下;(屋)倒塌 ③败落,没落：~ down in the world 社会地位降低,失势,败落 ④垂下 ⑤流传下来：folk tales that have ~ down to us 流传下来的民间故事 ⑥出钱,捐钱 ⑦病倒：~ down with pneumonia 患肺炎(而病倒) / ~ down on (或 upon) ①申斥;惩罚 ②向…索取(钱等)(for) ③袭击：~ down heavy on sb. 向某人猛烈袭击 / ~ for 来接(人); 来取(物)：He came for me. 他来邀我。(或:他找到我头上来的。) / ~ forth ①出来;涌现：Many new things are coming forth. 许多新事物正在涌现。②被公布 / ~ forward 站出来(要求做某事); 主动响应 / ~ home ①回家 ②打中;~ home to sb. 打入某人的心中;被某人所理解 ③[海](锚)脱掉 / ~ in ①进来：Come in, please! 请进来! ②(潮水)升涨 ③到达;(火车)进站 ④到成熟季节,当令 ⑤流行起来 ⑥(比赛时)获得…名：~ in second 获得第二名 ⑦当选,就任;(党派等)上台 ⑧(钱)到手,被收入 ⑨用起来：This pocket dictionary may ~ in handy (或 useful) now and then. 这本袖珍词典有时候倒可能挺合用的。⑩起作用;有份儿：Where do I ~ in? 我该做什么? (或: 哪儿是我的份儿?) / Where does the joke ~ in? 好笑在什么地方? ⑪[讯]对对方的呼唤进行)回话,回复 / ~ in for 接受(份儿,遗产等);受到(批评、处分等) / ~ into ①进入;~ into the world 出生 / The tree has ~ into leaf (bud, blossom). 树长出叶(发芽,开花)。②得到：~ into power 当权 / ~ into one's own 得到自己名下应得的东西;进入繁荣期,盛行起来 ③继承(财产等) / ~ it strong [俚]做得过分;过于夸大 / ~ near ①走近 ②接近,不亚于,赶得上：~ near the world standard 赶得上世界水平 ③[后接…ing] 几乎,险些儿：~ near being run over 几乎被(车辆)压死 / ~ of ①出身于 ②由…引起 / ~ off ①(从…)离开：~ off work 下班 / A button has ~ off (my coat). (我的上衣)掉了一个扣子。②举行,进行：The table-tennis finals ~ off tomorrow. 乒乓球决赛明日举行。③(计划等)实现,成功：Did the experiment ~ off? 试验成功没有? ④结果是,成为：~ off well (badly) in a match 在比赛中成绩优良(不良) / ~ off victorious (或 ~ off a victor) 获得胜利 / ~ off with flying colours 获得大胜 / The day came off fine. 后来天放晴了。/ ~ off it [口]不胡诌;不胡闹 / ~ off one's perch (或 one's high horse) 不再骄傲自大 / ~ on ① = ~ upon ②跟着来：You go first. I'll ~ on immediately. 你先走,我马上跟着来。③进步,进展;成长：The corn is coming on splendidly. 玉米长势好极了。

④开始(…起来); 袭来: It *came on* dark. 天黑下来了。/ Rain *came on* (或 It *came on* to rain) just before daybreak. 天快亮时开始下起雨来。/ He felt a cold *coming on*. 他觉得开始有点儿感冒了。⑤(问题、案件等)被提出来: The case will soon ~ *on* for trial. 这案件很快就要开审。⑥(演员)出台 ⑦(戏剧等)上演 / **Come on!** [表示劝说、激励、不耐烦等]来! 快! 得啦! / ~ *out* ①出来; 由…出来,由…产生 (of) ②长出; (花)开: The buds are *coming out*. 出芽了。③传出,被获知; (本性、秘密等)露出: When the news *came out*, ... 消息传出来时,…④被刊行,被出版 ⑤罢工⑥结果是; 显现: ~ *out* victorious 获胜 / ~ *out* first 得第一名 / He *came out* well in that photograph. 那张照片中他照得很好。⑦(污点)被去掉; (颜色)褪去: These ink stains won't ~ *out*. 这些墨水渍去不掉。⑧(题目等)被解出: The equation has ~ *out*. 方程式已解出了。⑨(总数、平均数等)计, 总计 ⑩(商品等)被展出,被供应 ⑪初次进入社交界; 初次登台 / **Come out of that!** [俚]走开! / ~ *out with* ①发表,公布 ②说出,提供: In the article he *came out with* a series of convincing arguments. 在这篇文章中, 他提出了一系列具有说服力的论据。③展出,供应 / ~ *over* ①过来; 从远方来: Come *over* here and give me a hand. 过来帮我一下。/ They *came over* from the North to see us. 他们从北方远道来看望我们。②顺便来访 ③转到…方面来 (to): ~ *over* to our side (敌人)向我方投诚; (在辩论中)站到我们方面来 ④(感觉、影响等)支配,攫住: A fit of dizziness *came over* the patient. 病人忽然感到一阵头晕。/ ~ *over queer* (或 *funny, dizzy*) [口]感觉眩晕 / ~ *round* ①来,前来; (非正式地)访 访: Yesterday he *came round* with some problems about his work. 昨天他来谈有关他工作上的一些问题。/ Come *round* when you have time. 有空来玩。②绕道而来: ~ *round* along the bank of the lake 绕湖岸过来 ③重又来到: May Day will soon ~ *round*. 五一节就要到了。④(风向等)转变 ⑤改变主意; 回心转意 ⑥苏醒过来; (病人)复元 ⑦笼络,诱骗: ~ *round sb.* by cajoling 用花言巧语诱骗某人 / ~ *through* ①经历(困难等); 经历…而活着: ~ *through* a war (a serious illness) 经历了一场战争(严重的疾病) ②脱险 ③获得成功 ④(消息)传出 ⑤[美俚]出力,资助,捐助 ⑥[美俚]招认,招供 / ~ *to* ①共计,达到: The monthly steel output of our plant ~*s to*...tons. 我厂每月钢产量达到…吨。②达到…地步; 得到…结果; 归结为…: If it ~*s to* that, ... 假使事情真的到那种地步的话,…/ ~ *to little* 没有什么结果 / What you say ~*s (down) to* this. 你所说的话归结起来无非是这个意思。③达成: ~ *to* a decision 作出决定 / ~ *to* an understanding 取得谅解 ④继承(财产) ⑤苏醒;复苏,恢复生机 ⑥停止;停泊; [海]使船头

顶风 / ~ *to light* 见 **light**[1] / ~ *to oneself* (或 *to one's senses*) ①(昏迷后)苏醒过来 ②醒悟过来 / ~ *to pass* 见 **pass** / ~ *to stay* ①来住;来定居 ②成为永久性的东西: These new customs have ~ *to stay*. 这些新风尚已经固定下来。/ ~ *under* ①编入,归入(某一项目) ②受到(影响、支配等): ~ *under* sb.'s notice 受到某人的注意 / ~ *under* the influence of 受到…的影响 / ~ *under* fire 遭到射击 / ~ *up* ①走近 ②上来,上楼 ③(从土中)长出,发芽: The seeds haven't ~ *up* yet. (种子的)芽还没有长出土来。④发生; 被提出: The question hasn't ~ *up* yet. 这个问题还没有被提出来。⑤流行起来 ⑥[英]进大学 / ~ *up against* 碰到(困难、反对等): ~ *up against* a series of problems 碰到一系列的问题 / ~ *upon* (或 on) ①(灾难、恐惧等)突然向…袭来; (想法等)突然产生: An idea *came upon* him. 他想起了一个主意。②要求: ~ *upon* sb. for sth. 向某人要求某物 ③成为…的负担 ④(偶然)遇见,(偶然)发现 / ~ *up to* 达到; 符合: The water *came up to* his waist. 水齐他的腰。/ ~ *up to* standard 合乎标准 / ~ *up with* ①赶上 ②提出,提供: ~ *up with* a proposal 提出建议 / ~ *up with* a response 作出反应 / ~ *what may* (或 *will*) 不管发生什么事, 不管怎样 / ~ *within* (包括)在…的范围之内 / **see sb. coming** 使某人上当,欺骗某人 / **to** ~ [用作名词]未来 / [用在名词后作定语] 未来的,将到来的: in (the) years to ~ 在未来的岁月里 / for some time to ~ 在将来的一段时间内 / books to ~ 将出版的书
‖'~-and-'go *n.* ①来往 ②伸缩 *a.* ①大约的 ②易变的, 不定的 / ~-at-able [kʌm'ætəbl] *a.* [口]可接近的, 易到手的 / '~-back *n.* ①复原; 复辟: stage a ~*back* 搞复辟, 卷土重来 ②尖刻的对答 ③抱怨的原因 / '~-down *n.* ① 败落 ②屈辱, 倒霉 / ,~-'hither *a.* & *n.* 勾引(的) / '~-on *n.* ①吸引; 引诱; 诱惑(物) ②骗子 ③受骗的人. 有吸引力的 / ~-'outer *n.* [美]退会分子; 要求取代现有组织的分子, 急进分子

comedian [kə'mi:djən] *n.* ① 喜剧演员 ② 喜剧作家 ③丑角式人物

comedy ['kɔmidi] *n.* ①喜剧; 喜剧因素 ② 喜剧场面; 喜剧性事件 ③喜剧作品 ‖**cut the** ~ [俚]停止开玩笑; 不再胡闹

comet ['kɔmit] *n.* 【天】彗星: a ~ finder 寻彗镜 ‖~ary, ~ic [kə'metik] *a.* 彗星的; 彗星似的

comet

comfort ['kʌmfət] I *n.* ①安慰: take (seek) ~ in 在…中得到(寻求)安慰 / Be of good ~. 振作起来! ②舒适,安逸 ③安慰者;给予安慰的东西 ④[常用复]使生活舒适的事物 ⑤[美]盖被 II *vt.* 安慰;使舒适 ‖**cold** ~ 简直不起作用的安慰 / **creature** ~**s** 衣食(指物质生活舒适的东西) ‖**~er** *n.* ①安慰者; [the C-]【宗】圣灵 ②羊毛围巾 ③[英]橡皮奶头 ④[美]盖被 ‖**~less** *a.* ①无安慰的 ②不舒适的 ‖**~ station** [美]公共厕所

comfortable ['kʌmfətəbl] I *a.* ①安慰的 ②舒适的,惬意的;轻松自在的: a ~ income 相当不错的收入 / Please make yourself ~. 别客气! (招待客人用语) ③[美俚]喝醉了的 II *n.* [美]盖被 ‖**~ness** *n.* / **comfortably** *ad.*

comic ['kɔmik] I *a.* ①喜剧的: ~ opera 喜歌剧 / a ~ strip (报刊上的)连环漫画 ②滑稽的,好笑的 II *n.* ①喜剧演员 ②喜剧成分,喜剧因素 ③连环漫画;连环漫画杂志; [复](报刊上的)连环画页

comical ['kɔmikəl] *a.* 好笑的,滑稽的;怪里怪气的 ‖**~ity** [ˌkɔmi'kæliti] *n.* / **~ly** *ad.*

coming ['kʌmiŋ] I *a.* ①正在来到的,即将来到的: the ~ Friday 即将来到的星期五(在星期五以前说,指的是本星期五;在星期五以后说,指的是下星期五) / the ~ week 下周 ②(人或事物)有指望成功的: the ~ thing [美]即将变得时髦的东西;即将具有重要性的东西 ③应得的: have it ~ (受奖或受罚等)是应得的 II *n.* 来到,到达 ‖**~ in** ([复] ~**s in**) ①进入;开始 ②[常用复]收入

comity ['kɔmiti] *n.* 礼让,礼貌: the ~ of nations 国际礼让(指互相尊重对方法律、习俗等)

comma ['kɔmə] *n.* ①逗号(即,): put a ~ 加逗号 / inverted ~**s** 引号(即'或"") ②小停顿 ‖**~ bacillus** 【微】弧杆菌

command [kə'mɑːnd] I ❶ *vt.* ①指挥,统帅;命令 ②控制;对…有支配权: ~ oneself 控制自己 ③俯临,俯瞰: a fortress ~*ing* the entrance to the valley 俯临山谷入口的要塞 ④应得;博得: ~ respect 使人不得不肃然起敬 / ~ a ready sale in the market 在市场上博得畅销 ❷ *vi.* 指挥;控制: Who ~**s** here? 这里是谁在指挥? II *n.* ①统帅(地位);指挥(权): put (或 place) sb. *in* ~ of a company 让某人指挥一个连队 ②命令,口令;【自】指令: give a ~ 下一个命令 / a preparatory ~ (口令的)预令 / a ~ of execution (口令的)动令 ③司令部,指挥部 ④部队;军区,防御区(在一个指挥官统率或管辖下的全部部队或地区的总称) ⑤控制(权);掌握;运用能力: the ~ of the air (sea) 制空(海)权 / He has a good ~ of the English language. 他精通英语。 ⑥【军】瞰制 ‖a ~ car 指挥车 / a ~ channel 指挥系统;指挥用波道 / a ~ echelon (或 element) [军]指挥机构;指挥组 / a ~ guidance system 指令制导系统,指令式导引系统(一种控制导弹的系

统) / a ~ module (宇宙飞船等的)指令舱,指挥舱 / a ~ pilot [美]特级驾驶员(美空军中技术等级最高的驾驶员) / a ~ post 指挥所 (装在飞机上的)指挥用无线电台 III *a.* (演出、研究等)根据命令(或要求)而作的 ‖**at** (*one's*) ~ 可以自由使用(或支配): He has a large vocabulary at ~. 他掌握大量词汇。 / They helped us by every means at their ~. 他们用一切可能办法帮助我们。 / **be at sb.'s** ~ 听候某人吩咐 / **do sth. at** (或 **by**) **sb.'s** ~ 奉某人命做某事 / **get** ~ **of** 控制 / **take** ~ **of** 开始担任…的指挥 / **under** (**the**) ~ **of** 由…指挥 ‖**~ism** *n.* 命令主义 / **~ist** *a.* 命令主义的

commandant [ˌkɔmən'dænt] *n.* ①指挥官,司令(尤指要塞或防区司令) ②军事学校校长

commandeer [ˌkɔmən'diə] *vt.* ①征用(粮食、马匹、房屋等);强征…入伍 ②[美口]强占

commander [kə'mɑːndə] *n.* ①指挥员,司令员;指挥官;司令官: a company ~ 连长 / a ~ of the guard 卫队长,卫兵长 ②海军中校: a lieutenant ~ 海军少校 ③大木槌 ‖**~ship** *n.* 指挥员(或指挥官)的职位(或身分) ‖**~ in chief** 总司令

commandment [kə'mɑːndmənt] *n.* 戒律;【宗】诫,圣训: taboos and ~**s** 清规戒律 / the ten ~**s**【基督教】十诫

commando [kə'mɑːndou] ([复] commando(e)s) *n.* 突击队;突击队员: a ~ vessel (或 ship) 登陆艇

commemorate [kə'meməreit] *vt.* 纪念

commemoration [kəˌmemə'reiʃən] *n.* ①纪念 ②纪念会,纪念仪式;纪念物

commence [kə'mens] ❶ *vt.* 开始; (正式)倡导: ~ doing (或 to do) sth. 开始做某事 ❷ *vi.* ①开始 ②[英]得学位: ~ doctor 得博士学位 ‖**~ment** *n.* ①开始,开端 ②学位授予典礼(日),毕业典礼(日)

commend [kə'mend] *vt.* ①把…交托给 (*to*): ~ sth. *to* sb.'s care 把某物交托给某人保管 ②称赞,表扬,嘉奖: ~ sb. *upon* his diligence 表扬某人勤奋 / ~ good people and good deeds 表扬好人好事 ③推荐 ‖~ *itself* (或 *oneself*) *to* sb. 给某人好印象;会被某人接受: This book does not ~ *itself to* me. 这本书给我的印象不好。/ *Commend me to....* 请代我向…致意。

commendation [ˌkɔmen'deiʃən] *n.* ①称赞,表扬 ②推荐

commensurate [kə'menʃərit] *a.* ①同量的,同大的 (*with*) ②相称的,相当的 (*to, with*) ‖**~ly** *ad.* / **~ness** *n.* / **commensuration** [kəˌmenʃə'reiʃən]

comment ['kɔment] I *n.* ①注释;评注 ②评论: make ~**s** on (或 upon) sth. 评论某事 II *vi.* ①注释 ②评论;评头品足 (on, upon)

commentary ['kɔmentəri] *n.* ①评论 ②注解(本);评注 ③解说词 ‖a running ~ ①(对某一著作的)连续、系统的注解 ②当场连续不断的评述;实况广播报道

commentator ['kɔmenteitə] *n.* ① 评论员; 时事评论员 ②注释者 ③实况广播员

commerce ['kɔmə(:)s] *n.* ①商业, 贸易: a chamber of ～ 商会 ②社交; (意见等的)交流 ③性交

commercial [kə'mə:ʃəl] **I** *a.* ①商业的, 商业上的; 商务的: a ～ college 商学院, 商业学校 / a ～ traveller [英]旅行推销员 / a ～ counsellor (attaché) 商务参赞(专员) ②商品化的; 以获利为目的的, 质量低劣的: ～ lead 商品铅 ③由广告商付费的 **II** *n.* 无线电(或电视)中的广告节目 ‖～**ism** *n.* ①商业主义; 商业精神; 利润第一主义 ②商业习惯 ③商业用语 / ～**ist** *n.* 商业家; 商业主义者; 营利主义者 / ～**ity** [kə,mə:ʃi'æliti] *n.* 商业性 / ～**ly** *ad.*

commiserate [kə'mizəreit] *vt.* & *vi.* 怜悯; 同情: ～ (*with*) sb. *on* his misfortune 对某人的不幸表示同情 ‖**commiseration** [kə,mizə'reiʃən] *n.*

commissar [,kɔmi'sɑ:] *n.* ① 政委 (=political ～) ②人民委员(苏联政府部长的旧称)

commissariat [,kɔmi'sɛəriət] *n.* ① 军粮部门; 军粮供应 ②(人民)委员部(苏联政府各部的旧称)

commission [kə'miʃən] **I** *n.* ①委任; 委托; 代办; 代理; 委托事项: go beyond one's ～ 越权 ②委任状; 【军】任职令; 授衔令; 委任权; 所受军衔: get one's ～ 取得军官资格 ③委员会; a Royal *Commission* (英国)皇家专门调查委员会 [注意: commission 一般指处理专门事务的委员会] ④犯(罪): the ～ of an illegal act 犯法 ⑤佣金: draw a ～ of ten percent on each sale 在每笔生意中抽取百分之十的佣金 **II** *vt.* ①委任, 任命; 委托; 委托制作(画像等): be ～ed to negotiate with sb. 被授权与某人谈判 ②把(船舰等)编入现役 ③(军官)受命指挥(舰只) ‖*in* ～ 服现役中 ②可使用: put an old car back *in* ～ 修好旧汽车以供使用 / *on* ～ ①被授权; 被委托 ②取佣 / *out of* ～ ① 退出现役 ② 不能使用; 损坏: The telephone station was put *out of* ～ by the storm. 风暴使电话局的工作中断了。 ‖～**ed** *a.* 受委任的, 受任命的: a ～ed officer 军官(指少尉以上军官) ②现役的 ‖～ **day** [英] 大审开审日 / ～ **merchant** (取佣金的)代理商 / ～ **plan** 委员市政制(以五、六人的委员会统一行使市的立法和行政职务, 以代替市长和市参议会)

commissionaire [kə,miʃə'nɛə] *n.* [主英](剧院、旅馆、大商店等处)穿制服的看门人

commissioner [kə'miʃənə] *n.* ①专员; 委员; 政府特派员: High *Commissioner* (英联邦成员国与英国之间互派的)高级专员 ②地方长官 ③(政府公益部门的)长官 ④ 职业运动队的行政管理人 ‖～**ship** *n.* 专员(或委员等)的职位

commit [kə'mit] (committed; committing) *vt.* ① 犯(错误、罪行), 干(坏事、傻事): ～ a mistake (或 an error) 犯错误 / ～ murder (suicide) 凶(自)杀 ②把…交托给; 把…提交给(to): ～ a child *to* the care of a nursery 把孩子交托给托儿所 / ～ a matter *to* a committee 把一件事提

交委员会(讨论) ③把…押交; 把…判处: ～ sb. *to* prison 把某人送进监狱 / ～ a prisoner *for* trial 把犯人交付审判 / ～ sb. *to* five years' imprisonment 判处某人五年徒刑 ④使承担义务, 使作出保证; 使表态: ～ sb. *to* do sth. 责成某人做某事 ⑤调配…供使用, 指定…用于 ⑥把(部队)投入战斗 ⑦约束; 连累 ‖～ *sth. to memory* 把某事记住 / ～ *sth. to paper* (或 *writing*) 把某事写下来 / ～ *sth. to the flames* 把某物烧掉 ‖**committable** *a.* (罪犯或罪行)可以拘禁的, 可以判处的; 可能犯的

commitment [kə'mitmənt] *n.* ①交托(看管或保管); 提交 ②关禁, 关押; 入狱执行书 ③承担义务, 所承担的义务; 许诺, (商业上的)约定: a treaty ～ 按条约所承担的义务 ④信奉, 赞成, 赞助: ～ *to* a doctrine 信奉(或支持)某一学说 ⑤投入(战斗)

committee [kə'miti] *n.* 委员会: be (或 sit) *on* a ～ 任委员会委员 / The bill is now *in* ～. 议案正由委员会审议中。/ a ～ *of the whole* (*house*) 议员全体委员会 (指议会议决某些特殊事项时采用的一种议事方式, 由全体议员参加, 以程序规则的灵活 随便为特征) / a ～ *on* ～s (或 a ～ *of selection*)议会内的委员指派委员会 / an executive ～ 执行委员会 / a Party ～ 党委 / a standing ～ 常务委员会 ‖**committeeman** *n.* ① 委员会成员, 委员 ②选区的政党头子 / **com'mittee-,woman** *n.* 女委员

commix [kɔ'miks] *vt.* & *vi.* [古][诗]混合 ‖～**ture** *n.* 混合; 混合物

commode [kə'moud] *n.* ①洗脸台 ②小衣橱, 五斗橱 ③便桶

commodious [kə'moudjəs] *a.* ①宽敞的 ②使用方便的 ‖～**ly** *ad.* / ～**ness** *n.*

commodity [kə'mɔditi] *n.* ① 日用品; 商品: a *commodities* fair 商品展览会 ②农产品; 矿产品

commodore ['kɔmədɔ:] *n.* ①海军准将; (英)分遣舰队指挥官 ②商船队队长 ③游艇总会会长 ‖*an air* ～ (英)空军准将

common ['kɔmən] **I** *a.* ①公共的, 共有的; 共用的; 共同的: a ～ cup 公用杯子 / a property ～ *to* all metals 金属的一种共性 / seek ～ ground 求同/ pass *by* ～ consent 以一致同意通过 ②普通的, 一般的; 通常的; 平常的: the ～ people 老百姓 / become ～ knowledge 成为众所周知的事情 / a ～ saying 俗话 / a grammatical mistake ～ *among* beginners in English 初学英语的人常犯的语法错误 ③粗俗的; 低劣的 ④[数]共通的 ⑤【语】通(性)的; 通(格)的 **II** *n.* ①[复][总称]平民 ②[常作 Commons] (英国)下议院 ③[复]共餐食物; (英国一些大学的)定额食宿; 公共食堂 ④公地 ⑤对别人土地的使用权 (=right of ～) ‖*be on short* ～*s* 吃不饱 / *or garden* 平凡的, 普通的 / *in* ～ 共用, 公有; 共同: The two have nothing *in* ～. 两者没有共同之处。/ *In* ～ *with* everyone else I hold that* .... 同大家

一样,我也认为… / **out of (the)** ~ 不平常,非凡
‖**~ly** *ad.* / **~ness** *n.* ‖**~ carrier** 【律】运输
业者 / **~ cold** 感冒 / **~ denominator** ①【数】
公分母 ②共同特色 / **~ divisor, ~ factor** 【数】
公因子,公因数 / **~ law** 习惯法,不成文法 /
'**~-law** *a.* ①根据习惯法的: a **~**-*law* marriage
未行正式仪式(或未经法律批准)的婚姻,同居 ②
按习惯法同居的;(子女等)由同居男女所生的 /
~ logarithm 【数】常用对数 / **Common Market**
(欧洲)共同市场("欧洲经济共同体"的俗称) / **~
measure** ① = **~** time ② = **~** metre / **~ metre**
普通韵律(四行成一节,音节数为八、六、八、六) /
~ multiple 【数】公倍(数) / **~ nuisance** 妨
害治安的行为 / **~ pleas** (美国某些州的) 中级
法院 / **Common Prayer** 英国国教的祈祷书 /
~ room ① 公共休息室 ② 教员公用室 / **~
school** 免费公立学校;公费小学 / **~ sense** 常
识 / '**~'sense** *a.* 有常识的;明明白白的,一望而
知的 / **~ stock** 【经】普通股 / **~ time** 普通拍
子(每一小节二或四拍) / **~ touch** 能打动一般
普通人的本领 / **~ year** 【天】平年
commoner ['kɔmənə] *n.* ①平民(指个人) ②[罕]
英国下议院议员 ③[英](牛津大学的)自费生 ④
对他人土地有使用权的人
commonplace ['kɔmənpleis] I *a.* 平凡的; 陈腐的
II *n.* ①平常话 ②平凡的事物; 毫无疑义的事物
‖**~ness** *n.* ‖**~ book** 摘句簿
commonwealth ['kɔmənwelθ] *n.* ①全体国民 ②
国家;共和国;民主国 ③联邦: the British *Commonwealth* of Nations 英联邦 / *the Commonwealth* of Australia 澳大利亚联邦 ④[美]州(只
用于 Kentucky 肯塔基、Massachusetts 马萨诸
塞、Pennsylvania 宾夕法尼亚、Virginia 弗吉尼
亚等四州) ‖*the Commonwealth* 【英史】共和政
体(指一六四九年克伦威尔处死英王查理一世后
开始到一六六○年封建王朝复辟时止的英共和
政体)
commotion [kə'mouʃən] *n.* 混乱; 动乱, 骚动:
produce (或 cause) a ~ 引起一场骚动
communal ['kɔmjunl] *a.* ①公社的; 公社制的:
the primitive ~ system 原始公社制度 ②巴黎公
社的 ③公共的, 公有的: ~ land 公地 / ~
marriage 杂婚;群交 ④对立宗教(或种族)间的
‖**~ity** [,kɔmju'næliti] *n.* ① 公社性 ②集体性,
团结
commune[1] ['kɔmju:n] *n.* ①公社 ② (法国等国
家的)最小行政区 ③[美](嬉皮士等的)群居村
commune[2] [kə'mju:n] *vi.* ①亲密地交谈; 谈心
(*with*): ~ *with* oneself (或 one's own heart) 沉
思 ②[美]【宗】接受圣餐
communicable [kə'mju:nikəbl] *a.* ①(思想等)可
以传授的 ②(疾病)传染性的 ‖**~ness** *n.* / **com-
municably** *ad.*
communicant [kə'mju:nikənt] *a.* & *n.* 【宗】受
圣餐的(人) ②传达消息的(人),报道情况的(人)
communicate [kə'mju:nikeit] ❶ *vt.* ①传达,传送

(热、感情、消息等) ②传染(疾病) ❷ *vi.* ①通讯;
通话: ~ *with* sb. by letter (telegraph) 与某人通
信(通电报) ②(房间、道路等)互通 ③【宗】受圣
餐
communication [kə,mju:ni'keiʃən] *n.* ①通信,通
讯;传达; (意见等的)交换,交流,交往: air-to-air
~ 空对空通讯联络 ②(疾病的)传染 ③传达的信
息;信: Your ~ is under consideration. 你方
来信正予以考虑中。④[复]通讯系统 ⑤交通;交
通工具: a ~ trench 【军】交通壕 / the Ministry
of *Communications* 交通部 ‖*privileged* ~ 【律】
① 法律上特许不予泄露的内情 ② 作为举证而泄
露的内情(法律上不构成诽谤罪) ‖**~ cord** (火车
内的)警报索
communicative [kə'mju:nikətiv] *a.* ①爱说话的;
爱传话的 ②通讯联络的 ‖**~ly** *ad.* / **~ness** *n.*
communion [kə'mju:njən] *n.* ①共享,共有 ②(思
想、感情等的)交流 ③宗教教派 ④【宗】圣餐 (=
Holy Communion)
communiqué [kə'mju:nikei] *n.* [法]公报: a joint
~ 联合公报 / a press ~ 新闻公报
communism ['kɔmjunizəm] *n.* 共产主义
communist ['kɔmjunist] I *n.* ①[也作 C-] 共产主
义者;[常作 C-] 共产党员 ②[C-] =Communard
II *a.* 共产主义的;共产党的; 共产主义者的;信仰
共产主义的 ‖**~ic** [,kɔmju'nistik] *a.* 共产主义
的;共产主义者的 ‖'**~-led** *a.* 共产党领导的
community [kə'mju:niti] *n.* ①公社;团体;社会;
(政治)共同体: a village ~ 村社 / the European
Community 欧洲共同体 ②同一地区的全体居民;
公众: a ~-run workshop 街道工厂 ③共有; 共
同性,一致 ④【生】群落 ‖**~ centre** 公共会堂 /
~ chest 募集的救济基金 / **~ property** 夫妻共
有的财产 / **~ singing** (在场的人一起参加的)大
合唱
commutation [,kɔmju(:)'teiʃən] *n.* ①交换; 代偿
②代偿的钱 ③减刑 ④【电】交换, 转换, 变换; 换
向, 整流 ⑤(持有长期车票者在两地间的)经常来
往 ‖**~ ticket** (一定时间内在固定线路上使用
的)长期车票
commute [kə'mju:t] ❶ *vt.* ①用…交换; 兑去; 变
换: ~ foreign money to domestic 把外币兑成本
国货币 ②改变(付款)的方式 ③减轻(刑罚等)
④ =commutate ❷ *vi.* ①补偿 ②购买和使用长
期车票; 经常来往 ‖**~r** *n.* 长期车票使用者;经
常往来于某两地间(如郊外住所与市内办公处)的
人: **~r** time 上下班时间
compact[1] ['kɔmpækt] *n.* 契约;合同
compact[2] [kəm'pækt] I *a.* ①紧密的; 坚实的; 结
实的: ~ òrganization 严密的组织 ②(文体)简
洁的; 紧凑的 II ❶ *vt.* ①使紧密;使结实 ②使
简洁 ③组成 ❷ *vi.* 变成紧实 III ['kɔmpækt] *n.*
①连镜小粉盒 ②小型汽车 ‖**~ly** *ad.* / **~ness**
n. 紧密,坚实,简洁;【物】紧密度
companion[1] [kəm'pænjən] I *n.* ①同伴; 同事; 同
忧乐的人;志趣相同的人: **~s** in arms 战友 / ~

cells 【植】伴(细)胞 ②成对(或成副、成双等)物之一：Here's the glove for my left hand, but where's the ~? 这里是我左手的手套，可是右手的在哪里呢？/ the ~ volume 成套书中的一卷；姐妹篇 ③受雇服侍病人(或老人)者 ④[作书名用]指南，参考书 ⑤【天】伴星 (=~ star) Ⅱ *vt.* 陪伴 ‖~**ship** *n.* ①伴侣关系；友谊 ②[英]排字的伙伴们 ③一群同伴

companion[2] [kəm'pænjən] *n.* 【船】升降口；升降口罩 ‖~ **hatch** 升降口罩 / ~ **ladder** 升降口梯 / com'panionway *n.* 升降口

company ['kʌmpəni] Ⅰ *n.* ①交际，交往；陪伴：~ manners 客套，虚礼 / in the ~ of 在…陪同下 / I'm glad of your ~. 有你作陪我很高兴。②客人；同伴，朋友：I have ~ this evening. 今晚我有客。/ receive a great deal of ~ 接待许多客人 / judge sb. by the ~ he keeps 从某人所交的朋友来判断他的为人 ③(一)群，(一)队；一伙：a ~ of students 一群学生 / a theatrical ~ 剧团 / a ship's ~ 全体船员 ④公司，商号：Smith & *Company*, Limited 史密斯有限公司(常略作 Smith & Co., Ltd.)/ a ship ~ 轮船公司 ⑤【军】连；连队 Ⅱ ❶ *vt.* 陪伴 ❷ *vi.* 交往 ‖*be good* ~ 是有趣的伙伴 / *fall into* ~ *with* 偶然结识… / *for* ~ 陪着：He'll go with us to the docks *for* ~. 他将陪我们去码头。/ *in* ~ (*with*) (和…)一起：We went *in* ~ (*with* a group of students). 我们是(和一群学生)一起去的。/ This is as far as we two go *in* ~. 我们两人一致的地方到此为止。/ *inflict one's* ~ *upon sb.* 打扰某人 / *keep* ~ *with* sb.…结交；和…亲热 / *keep* (或 *bear*) *sb.* ~ 陪伴某人；陪某人片刻：I'll keep you ~ as far as the station. 我将一直陪你到车站。/ *part* ~ (*with*) ①(和…)分离；不再(和…)交往：part ~ halfway 半途分手；半途拆伙 ②(目标、方向、政策、意见等方面)(同…)有分歧：On this point I'm afraid I must *part* ~ *with* you. 在这一点上，我不能同意你的意见。/ *present* ~ *excepted* 在场(或在座)者除外 / *Two's* ~, *three's none*. [谚]两人成伴，三人不欢。‖~ **man** 忠于公司的雇员，公司资方的狗腿子 / ~ **officer** 【军】尉官 / ~ **union** [美]公司工会(一种资本家控制的御用工会)

comparable ['kɔmpərəbl] *a.* ①可比较的 (*with*)；比得上的 (*to*) ②类似的 ‖**comparably** *ad.*

comparative [kəm'pærətiv] Ⅰ *a.* ①比较的，比较上的：~ linguistics 比较语言学 / the ~ degree 【语】比较级 ②相当的：a ~ stranger 相当陌生的人 Ⅱ *n.* ①匹敌者；比拟物 ②[the ~]【语】比较级："Better" is the ~ of "good" "better" 是 "good" 的比较级。‖~**ly** *ad.* ~*ly* speaking [常作插入语]比较地说来 / **comparativist** *n.* =comparatist

compare [kəm'pεə] Ⅰ ❶ *vt.* ①比较，对照：The results have been carefully checked and ~d. 这些结果已经过仔细核对和比较。/ ~ the present *with* the past 对比今昔 / not to be ~d *with* (或

to) 不能与…相比 ②比喻，比作 ③把(形容词或副词)变成比较级(或最高级) ❷ *vi.* 比得上；相比：Cast iron cannot ~ *with* steel *in* tensile strength. 铸铁在抗张强度方面比不上钢。Ⅱ *n.* 比较 ‖(*as*) ~*d with* 与…比较 / *beyond* (或 *past*, *without*) ~ 无与伦比 / ~ *notes* 对笔记；交换意见

comparison [kəm'pærisn] *n.* ①比较，对照：make a ~ between the two designs 将这两种设计进行比较 / There is no ~ between the two. 两者根本不能相比。/ degrees of ~ 【语】(形容词或副词)的各比较等级(包括 the positive degree 原级、the comparative degree 比较级、the superlative degree 最高级三级) ②比喻 ‖*bear* (或 *stand*) ~ *with* 比得上，不亚于 / *beyond* (或 *out of all*, *without*) ~ 无与伦比 / *by* ~ 比较起来：The old method suffers *by* ~. 老方法相形见绌。/ *Comparisons are odious.* [谚]人比人气死人。/ *gain by* ~ 比较之下显出其长处 / *in* ~ *with* 与…比较：Advanced and backward only exist *in* ~ *with* each other. 先进和落后只在相互比较中才存在。

compartment [kəm'pɑ:tmənt] *n.* ①分隔空间：a ~ ceiling 格子平顶 ②分隔间；列车车厢的分隔间：a smoking ~(火车中的)吸烟室 ③水密舱，防水船舱(=watertight ~) ④(英国议院中在政府规定期限内讨论的)特殊协议事项 ‖~**al** [,kɔmpɑ:t'mentəl] *a.*

compass ['kʌmpəs] Ⅰ *n.* ①罗盘，指南针：a mariner's ~ 航海罗盘 / a radio ~ 无线电罗盘 / a radio ~ station 无线电定向台 / a ~ course (或 heading) 罗盘航向 / a ~ bearing 罗盘方位 ②[常用复]圆规：a pair of ~es 一只圆规 ③界限，范围：beyond the ~ of 越出…的范围 ④【音】音域 ⑤迂回的路：fetch (或 go) a ~ 迂回，绕道 Ⅱ *vt.* ①围绕…而行；包围 ②了解，领会 ③图谋，计划 ④达到(目的)；获得 ‖*box the* ~ ①依次列举罗盘的三十二方位 ②(在辩论等中)兜了一个圈子又回到原处 ‖~**able** *a.* 能达到的；能围绕的；能了解的 / ~**ing** *a.* 围绕的；达到的 ‖~ **card** 罗盘的盘面 / ~ **plane** 凹刨 / ~ **saw** 斜形绕圆锯 / ~ **window** 圆肚窗，半圆形凸窗

compassion [kəm'pæʃən] *n.* 同情；怜悯：We will never take ~ on snake-like scoundrels. 我们决不怜惜蛇一样的恶人。‖*fling oneself on* (或 *upon*) *sb.'s* ~ 乞求某人怜悯(或同情)

compassionate [kəm'pæʃənit] Ⅰ *a.* 有同情心的 Ⅱ [kəm'pæʃəneit] *vt.* 同情，怜悯 ‖~**ly** *ad.* / ~**ness** *n.*

compatible [kəm'pætəbl] *a.* ①可和谐共存的；适合的，一致的 (*with*) ②[无]兼容制的：~ colour TV system 【无】兼容制彩色电视系统 ‖**compatibility** [kəm,pætə'biliti] *n.* / **compatibly** *ad.*

compatriot [kəm'pætriət] Ⅰ *n.* 同国人，同胞 Ⅱ *a.* 同国的 ‖~**ic** [kəm,pætri'ɔtik] *a.* 同国人的，同胞的

compel [kəm'pel] (compelled; compelling) **vt.** ①
强迫,使不得不;迫使屈服: ～ sb. to do sth. 强
迫某人做某事 ②强制获得(反应、同意、服从等)
‖**compellable** *a.* 可强迫的的 / **compelling** *a.* 激
发兴趣(或爱慕等)的;使人非相信不可的
compendious [kəm'pendiəs] *a.* 扼要的, 简明的
‖～**ly** *ad.* / ～**ness** *n.*
compendium [kəm'pendiəm] (〔复〕compendiums
或 compendia [kəm'pendiə]) *n.* 概要,概略,纲要,
简编
compensable [kəm'pensəbl] *a.* 应予以补偿(或酬
报)的;可补偿(或酬报)的
compensate ['kɔmpenseit] ❶ **vt.** ①补偿,赔偿;酬
报: ～ sb. *for* 因为…向某人赔偿 ②【机】补整,
补偿: ～d pendulum【物】补偿摆 ❷ **vi.** 补偿,赔
偿 (*for*) ‖**compensator** *n.* ①赔偿者; 赔偿物
②【机】补偿器, 补助器
compensation [,kɔmpen'seiʃən] *n.* ①补偿, 赔偿;
补偿物,赔偿费: make ～ *for* sb.'s losses 补偿某
人的损失 ②【机】补整 ‖～**al** *a.*
compete [kəm'piːt] **vi.** ①比赛: ～ in a race 参加
赛跑 ②竞争;对抗: ～ with (或 against) sb. for
sth. 与某人竞争以得到某物
competence ['kɔmpitəns] *n.* ①能力;胜任: one's
～ *for* (或 to do) the task 对某一任务的胜任 ②
权能,权限: exceed one's ～ 越权 ③ =compe-
tency
competency ['kɔmpitənsi] *n.* ①足以使人过舒适
生活的富裕收入;充裕的生活条件: have a ～ 收
入富裕 / live in … 生活富裕 ② =competence
competent ['kɔmpitənt] *a.* ①有能力的,能胜任的
(*for*) ②应该做的, 被许可的: It was ～ to him
to refuse. 他拒绝是对的。 ③ 足够的: ～ knowledge 足够的知识 ④ 有权能的; 有法定资格的:
the ～ authorities 主管当局 ‖～**ly** *ad.*
competition [,kɔmpi'tiʃən] *n.* ①比赛: chess ～s
棋类比赛 ②竞争: keen trade ～ between 在…
之间剧烈的贸易竞争 ③竞争者
competitive [kəm'petitiv] *a.* 竞争的; 比赛的
‖～**ly** *ad.* / ～**ness** *n.*
competitor [kəm'petitə] *n.* 竞争者;比赛者; 敌手
compile [kəm'pail] **vt.** 编辑,编制(书籍、索引、报
告等); 搜集, 汇编 (资料等): ～ a budget 编制
预算 ‖**compilation** [,kɔmpi'leiʃən] *n.* 编辑;汇编;
编辑物 / **compilatory** [kəm'pailətəri] *a.* 编辑
的;汇编的 / ～**r** *n.* 编辑者;汇编者
complacence [kəm'pleisns], **complacency** [kəm-
'pleisnsi] *n.* 自满(情绪);自鸣得意
complacent [kəm'pleisnt] *a.* 自满的; 自鸣得意的
‖～**ly** *ad.*
complain [kəm'plein] ❶ **vi.** ①抱怨, 叫屈; 诉苦;
抗议 (*of, about*): She ～ed *of* his carelessness.
她抱怨说他根枝大叶。 ②说自己有病痛 (*of*) ③
申诉; 控告: ～ *to* sb. *of* sth. 向某人控诉某事
❷ **vt.** 抱怨; 控诉: She ～ed that he did not work
hard. 她抱怨他工作不努力。 ‖～**ant** [kəm-
'pleinənt] *n.* ①抱怨者; 抗议者 ②控诉人; 原告

complaint [kəm'pleint] *n.* ①抱怨, 叫屈; 诉说; 抱
怨(或痛苦)的缘由 ②控告;[美](民事诉讼中)原
告方面的控诉: make (或 lodge, lay) a ～ against
控告…③疾病
complaisance [kəm'pleizəns] *n.* 殷勤; 恳切; 讨好
complement I ['kɔmplimənt] *n.* ①补足物;【语】
补(足)语 ②船上的定员;【军】编制人数, 定额装
备 ③【数】余数; 余角;余弧 ④(血清中的)补体,
防御素 II ['kɔmpliment, ,kɔmpli'ment] *vt.* 补
充;补足
complemental [,kɔmpli'mentl] *a.* 补足的;补充的
complementary [,kɔmpli'mentəri] *a.* 补足的;补
充的;互补的: ～ colours 互补色 / ～ angle
【数】余角 / ～ function【数】余函数 ‖**comple-
mentarity** [,kɔmplimen'tæriti] *n.* 【物】互补性,
并协性
complete [kəm'pliːt] I *a.* ①完整的,完全的;圆满
的;十足的: a ～ stranger 素不相识的人 / ～
success 完满的成功 ②完成的; 结束的: When
will the work be ～? 这个工作将在什么时候完
成? II *vt.* 完成,结束; 使完满: The work is not
～d yet. 这个工作尚未完成。 ‖～**ly** *ad.* /
～**ness** *n.*
completion [kəm'pliːʃən] *n.* 完成, 结束; 完满:
bring sth. to ～ 把某事完成,使某事趋向完善
complex ['kɔmpleks] I *a.* ①合成的;复杂的,综合
的: a ～ sentence【语】复合句 / ～ number【数】
复数 ②【化】络合的: ～ compound 络合物 / ～
ion 络离子 II *n.* ①复杂;合成物 ②综合企业: an
iron and steel ～ 钢铁联合企业 / a laboratory
～ 综合实验室 ③【生】染色体组 ④【心】情结;复
合;[喻]强烈情绪: the inferiority (superiority)
～ 自卑(优越)情结(指心理上的一种病态) ⑤
【数】复数;复合形;线丛 ‖～**ly** *ad.*
complexion [kəm'plekʃən] *n.* ①肤色(尤指面部肤
色) ②情况, 局面; 样子: put a false ～ on sb.'s
remarks 曲解某人的话 ③(人的)气质, 脾性
‖～**al** *a.* / ～**ed** *a.* [常用以构成复合词](脸部)
肤色…的: fair-～ed 肤色白的 / ～**less** *a.* 苍
白的
complexity [kəm'pleksiti] *n.* 复杂(性); 复杂的
事物
compliance [kəm'plaiəns] *n.* ①依从 ②屈从 ‖*in*
～ *with* 依从…,按照…
compliant [kəm'plaiənt] *a.* ①依从的 ②屈从的
‖～**ly** *ad.*
complicate I ['kɔmplikeit] ❶ **vt.** ①使复杂;使麻
烦, 使难弄: a headache ～d by an eye trouble
因眼病并发而加剧的头痛病 ②使陷入: get ～d
in a matter 被卷入一个事件 ❷ **vi.** 变复杂 II
['kɔmplikit] *a.* ①复杂的; 麻烦的 ②【动】(昆虫
翅膀)纵折的
complicated ['kɔmplikeitid] *a.* 结构复杂的; 难懂
的,难解的 ‖～**ly** *ad.* / ～**ness** *n.*
complication [,kɔmpli'keiʃən] *n.* ①复杂;混乱;纠
纷;复杂的情况 ②【医】并发病,并发症

complicity [kəm'plisiti] *n.* 同谋关系，共犯关系 (*in*)

compliment I ['kɔmplimənt] *n.* ①赞美的话(或行为)；敬意: give (或 present) a ~ to sb. 赞扬某人 ②[复]问候，道贺，贺词: With the ~s of the season 谨致佳节贺词(西方人在圣诞、新年互相祝贺时的用语) / With the ~s of the author 作者敬赠 II ['kɔmpliment, ˌkɔmpli'ment] *vt.* ① 赞美；向…致意；祝贺: ~ sb. *on* his courage 夸奖某人的勇敢 ②向…送礼以表敬意 ‖ ~ *away* 赠送，把…作为赠品散发 / ~ *sb. into* 用恭维话使某人… / ~ *sb. out of sth.* 恭维某人以骗取某物

complimentary [ˌkɔmpli'mentəri] *a.* ①赞美的；表敬意的；问候的: ~ remarks 赞美话 / a ~ closing 信件结尾表示敬意的俗套 (如 Yours sincerely 等) ②免费赠送的: a ~ ticket 赠券 ‖ **complimentarily** [ˌkɔmpli'mentərili; 美ˌkɔm-plimen'tærili] *ad.*

comply [kəm'plai] *vi.* 照做 (*with*): You must ~ *with* the library rules. 你必须遵守图书馆的规则。/ ~ in public but oppose in private 阳奉阴违

component [kəm'pounent] I *a.* 组成的，合成的: a ~ part 组成部分 / ~ velocity 【物】分速度 II *n.* 组成部分，成分；【物】分；部分；组元；分(向)量；【自】元件，组件，部件

comport [kəm'pɔ:t] ❶ *vt.* [~ oneself] 举动，表现: ~ *oneself* decently 举止大方 ❷ *vi.* (举动、行为等)适合，一致 (*with*) ‖ **~ment** *n.* 举动，行为

compose [kəm'pouz] ❶ *vt.* ①组成，构成: be ~*d* of 由…组成 ②创作(乐曲、诗歌等)；为(歌词等)作曲 ③[印]排(字)，排(版)；排(稿) ④使安定，使平静；把(思想等)理出头绪: ~ a patient 使病人镇静下来 / ~ one's features 使脸色平静下来 / ~ one's thoughts for action 在行动前打定主意 ⑤调停(纠纷等) ❷ *vi.* ①创作；作曲 ②排字 ‖ ~ *oneself* 镇静，安心 ‖ **~r** *n.* 作曲者；创作者

composite ['kɔmpəzit] I *a.* 合成的，混成的，复合的: a ~ formation 【军】混合编队 II *n.* ①合成物，混合物，混合式 ②菊科植物 ‖ **~ly** *ad.* / **~ness** *n.*

composition [ˌkɔmpə'ziʃən] *n.* ①写作；作曲 ②作品；作文；(大型)乐曲 ③构成，组成；构图；成分；合成物，混合物(尤指人造的): the class ~ of the membership 成员的阶级组成(情况) / the ~ of the soil 土壤的成分 / ~ billiard balls 人造台球 ④气质，脾性 ⑤妥协 ⑥[印]排字 ⑦偿还部分欠款而了结债务的协议 ‖ ~**al** *a.*

compost ['kɔmpɔst] I *n.* ①堆肥，混合肥料: store ~ 积肥 ②混合，合成 II *vt.* 把…做成堆肥；施堆肥于

composure [kəm'pouʒə] *n.* 镇静，沉着

compote ['kɔmpout] *n.* ①水果糖浆 ②果盘，果碟

compound¹ ['kɔmpaund] I *n.* ①混合物；化合物 ②复合词 II *a.* 混合的；化合的；复合的: a ~ steam engine 复式蒸汽机 / ~ eye 【动】复眼 / ~ flower 【植】复合花 / ~ fracture 【医】哆开骨折，有创骨折 / ~ pendulum 【物】复摆 / ~ ratio 【数】复比 III [kɔm'paund] ❶ *vt.* ①使复合；使混合；使化合；使合成 ②(由互让而)解决(争端、债务等) ③【电】复激；复卷 ❷ *vi.* 和解，妥协 ‖ ~**able** [kəm'paundəbl] *a.* 能混合的，能化合的；能和解的 / ~**er** [kəm'paundə] *n.* 复合者，混合者

compound² ['kɔmpaund] *n.* ①用围墙圈起的建筑物及场地；院子 ②用篱笆(或围墙)圈起的场地(如战俘临时集中营等)

comprehend [ˌkɔmpri'hend] *vt.* ①了解，领会 ②包含，包括

comprehensible [ˌkɔmpri'hensəbl] *a.* 能理解的 ‖ **comprehensibility** ['kɔmpriˌhensə'biliti] *n.* / **comprehensibly** *ad.*

comprehension [ˌkɔmpri'henʃən] *n.* ①理解，理解力: above (或 beyond) ~ 难以理解的，不可理解的 / achieve a better ~ 进一步领会 / be slow of ~ 理解力迟钝 ②包含，包含力: a term of wide ~ 含义广泛的名词

comprehensive [ˌkɔmpri'hensiv] *a.* ①包含内容多的，综合的: ~ planning 全面规划 / a ~ review of the work 对工作的全面检查 / take a ~ view of the situation 通观全局 ②理解的，有理解力的 ‖ **~ly** *ad.* / **~ness** *n.*

compress [kəm'pres] I ❶ *vt.* 压缩，浓缩，使(语言等)简练 ❷ *vi.* 经受压缩 II ['kɔmpres] *n.* ①(止血、消炎用的)敷布；压布: cold ~ 冷敷布；冷敷法 ②(棉花等的)打包机 ‖ ~**ed** *a.* ~ed air 压缩空气 / ~**or** *n.* ①【医】压迫器；压肌 ②压缩机，压气机

compression [kəm'preʃən] *n.* 压缩，浓缩，凝缩: ~ of ideas 思想、意见的简括 / a ~ pump 压气泵

comprise [kəm'praiz] *vt.* ①包含，包括 ②由…组成: The committee ~s seven persons. 委员会由七人组成。③构成: Nineteen articles ~ Book One. 十九篇文章构成了第一卷。‖ **comprisable** *a.* 能被包含的 / **comprisal** *n.* ①包含 ②概要

compromise ['kɔmprəmaiz] I *n.* ①妥协，和解；互让了结 ②妥协方案，折衷办法，和解契约 ③折衷物，中间物 ④遭到损害: a ~ of one's good name 好名声的遭损 II ❶ *vi.* 妥协，让步: ~ *with* sb. on sth. 在某事上和某人妥协 ❷ *vt.* ①互让解决(分歧、争端等) ②危及，使遭致损害: ~ one's reputation (或 oneself) 有损自己的名誉 ③放弃(利益、原则等)；泄露(秘密材料等)

comptroller [kən'troulə] *n.* (政府或某一单位账目等的)审计员

compulsion [kəm'pʌlʃən] *n.* 强制，强迫: by ~ 强迫地 / under (或 upon, on) ~ 被迫地

compulsive [kəm'pʌlsiv] *a.* 强迫的，有强迫力的 ‖ **~ly** *ad.* / **~ness** *n.*

compulsory [kəm'pʌlsəri] *a.* 强迫的, 强制的; 义务的: a ~ subject 必修科目 / a ~ service system 义务兵役制 ||**compulsorily** *ad.*

compunction [kəm'pʌŋkʃən] *n.* 内疚, 良心的责备; 后悔, 懊悔: without ~ 不在乎地, 无动于衷地

computation [ˌkɔmpju(:)'teiʃən] *n.* ①计算, 估计 ②计算法 ③计算的结果; 计算出来的数(或量) ||~al *a.* 计算(上)的: ~al mathematics 计算数学

computator ['kɔmpju(:)teitə] *n.* 计算机

compute [kəm'pju:t] I ❶ *vt.* 计算; 估计: The losses are ~d at £20. 估计损失二十镑。❷ *vi.* 计算; 估计 II *n.* 计算; 估计: beyond ~ 不可计量

computer [kəm'pju:tə] *n.* ①计算机, 电子计算机: a control ~ 控制计算机 / a giant general-purpose transistorized digital ~ 晶体管大型通用数字计算机 ②计算者 ||~ism [kəm'pju:tərizəm] *n.* 电子计算机主义 (指认为计算机万能的观点等)

computerize [kəm'pju:təraiz] *vt.* ①给 … 装备电子计算机 ② 使电子计算机化; 用电子计算机计算: with ~d precision 以计算机般的精确 ||**computerization** [kəmˌpju:tərai'zeiʃən] *n.*

comrade ['kɔmrid] *n.* 同志; 亲密的同伴, 朋友, 同事 ||~ly *a.* 同志式的, 同志般的 / ~ry *n.* 同志情谊 / ~ship *n.* 同志关系; 友谊 ||'~-in-'arms *n.* 战友

COMSAT [缩] Communications Satellite Corporation 通信卫星公司(美国)

con¹ [kɔn] (conned; conning) *vt.* 研究; 精读; 默记 (over)

con² [kɔn] I *ad.* 从反面 II *n.* 反对的论点; 反对者; 投反对票者; 反对票: the pros and ~s 赞成者和反对者; 赞成和反对的票数; 正面和反面的理由

con³ [kɔn] =conn

con⁴ [kɔn] I *a.* 骗取信任的: a ~ game (或 job) 骗局 / a ~ man 骗子 II (conned; conning) *vt.* 骗; 哄骗

con [kɔn; 意 kon] *prep.* [意][音]带着, 以 ||~ amore [ə'mɔ:ri] 热情地; 亲切地 / ~ brio ['bri:-ou] 活泼地, 精神饱满地 / ~ espressione [意 ˌespres'jo:ne] 带表情地, 富于表情地, 鲜明有力地 / ~ fuoco [意 'fwo:ko] 热忱地, 热烈地

concave ['kɔn'keiv] I *a.* 凹的, 凹面的: a ~ lens 凹透镜 / a ~ mirror 凹面镜 II *n.* 凹面; 凹面物 (尤指天穹) ||~ly *ad.* / ~ness *n.*

conceal [kən'si:l] *vt.* 把 … 隐藏起来; 隐蔽; 隐瞒: a ~ed firing position 隐蔽的发射阵地 / ~ sth. from sb. 对某人隐瞒某事 ||~ment *n.* ①隐藏, 隐蔽: ~ment from the air 对空隐蔽 ②隐蔽处; 隐藏物

concede [kən'si:d] ❶ *vt.* ①(退一步)承认; 给与, 让与: ~ a point in an argument 在辩论中承认对方某一点 / ~ a right to sb. 给某人权利 / ~ that the statement is true 承认报告属实 ②

[俚](运动中)失(局): ~ a game 失一局 ❷ *vi.* 让步: ~ to sb. 对某人让步 ||~dly *ad.* 无可争辩地, 明白地

conceit [kən'si:t] I *n.* ①自负, 自高自大, 骄傲自满: guard against ~ 防止骄傲自满 ②想法; 个人的意见 ③奇想, 幻想; 牵强附会的比喻; (作品风格上的)做作 ④外形花哨而不切实用的东西 II *vt.* ①[方]想像 ②[英方]喜欢, 中意于 ||in one's own ~ 自以为 / out of ~ with 不再喜欢…

conceited [kən'si:tid] *a.* ①自负的, 自高自大的, 骄傲自满的 ②充满奇想的; 花哨的 ||~ly *ad.* / ~ness *n.*

conceivable [kən'si:vəbl] *a.* 可想象的, 想得到的; 可相信的: every ~ means 一切办法, 一切手段 / It is hardly ~ that .... 简直难以想像… ||**conceivability** [kənˌsi:və'biliti] *n.* / ~ness *n.* / **conceivably** *ad.*

conceive [kən'si:v] ❶ *vt.* ①构想出(主意、计划等) 想象, 设想: I simply can't ~ why .... 我实在想象不出为什么… ②开始怀(胎儿); 抱有(想法等): ~ a child 开始怀孕 / ~ a prejudice 抱有偏见 ③[常用被动语态] 表达: be ~d in plain words 用简明的文字表达出来 ❷ *vi.* ①怀孕 ②想, 想象 (of)

concenfrate ['kɔnsentreit] I ❶ *vt.* ①集中, 使集中于一点: ~ troops 集结军队 / ~ one's attention on sth. 把注意力集中在某事上 ②浓缩, 蒸浓, 提浓 ❷ *vi.* ①集中; 全神贯注 (on, upon): ~ on one's work 倾全力于工作 ②浓缩 II *n.* 浓缩物; [矿]精矿, 精练 ||~d *a.* 集中起来的; 经浓缩的: a ~d attack 集中攻击 / a ~d fertilizer 浓缩肥料, 高效肥料

concentration [ˌkɔnsen'treiʃən] *n.* ①集中; 专心: ~ of fire 火力集中 / a boy with little power of ~ 注意力不易集中的男孩 ②浓缩; 浓度: a ~ cell 浓差电池 ||~ camp 集中营

concentric [kɔn'sentrik] *a.* 同一中心的; 同轴的: ~ circles [数]同心圆 / be ~ with 与 … 同中心 ||~ally *ad.*

concept ['kɔnsept] *n.* 概念; 观念, 思想: the fundamental strategic ~ 根本战略思想

conception [kən'sepʃən] *n.* ①概念的形成; 思想的构成; 概念, 观念, 想法: a clear (vague) ~ 清楚(模糊)的概念 / the materialist ~ of history 唯物史观 / have no ~ of 对…完全不懂 ②开始怀孕; 胚胎, 胎儿 ||~al *a.*

concern [kən'sə:n] I *vt.* ①涉及, 对…有关系, 影响: This ~s us deeply. 这事对我们关系极大。/ be ~ed in sth. 和某事有牵连 ②使关心; 使挂念, 使担心: ~ oneself with state affairs 关心国家大事 / be ~ed about the growth of the younger generation 关心年青一代的成长 / be extremely ~ed over (或 at) sth. 为某事而忧虑重重 II *n.* ①关系; 所关切的事; [口]事物: have no ~ with sth. 同某事没有关系 / a matter of the utmost ~ 头等要事 / an important ~ 要事 ②关心,关怀;担心,忧虑,挂念: show ~ for sb. 对某人表示关心 / feel ~ over sb.'s failing health 对某人日益恶化的健康情况感到忧虑 / with ~ 关切地,放心不下地 ③【经】康采恩 (= [德] konzern); 商行,企业 ④小东西,小玩意儿 ‖as ~s 关于:' As ~s that matter, I should like to say .... 关于那件事,我想说…

concerned [kən'sə:nd] a. ①有关的: all parties ~ 有关各方 / Present at the meeting were leading members of the departments ~. 出席会议的有各有关部门的领导人。②关切的,担心的: with a ~ air 带着关切的神情 ‖~ly [kən'sə:nidli] ad.

concerning [kən'sə:niŋ] prep. 关于: Please inform me ~ this matter. 请把关于这件事的情况告诉我。

concert ['kɔnsət] I n. ①音乐会,演奏会;【音】协奏曲: a ~ grand (piano) 音乐会用的大型钢琴 / a ~ hall 音乐厅 ②一致,协作; 和谐 II [kən'sə:t] ❶ vt. 商议;共同议定; 安排 ❷ vi. 协力 ‖in ~ 一致,一齐 ‖'~,master, ~meister ['kɔnsət-,maistə] n. 首席小提琴手(通常兼司管弦乐队副指挥) / ~ pitch ①音乐会的音高标准 (较通常标准略高) ②高效能;充分准备就绪状态

concerted [kən'sə:tid] a. ①商定的; 一致的: take ~ action 采取一致行动 / make ~ efforts 齐心协力 ②【音】协调的 ‖~ly ad. fight ~ly against the enemy 共同对敌

concertina [,kɔnsə'ti:nə] n. ①六角手风琴 ②【军】蛇腹形铁丝网 (= ~ wire)

concerto [kən'tʃə:tou] ([复] concerti [kən'tʃə:ti] 或 concertos) n. 【音】协奏曲: a piano ~ 钢琴协奏曲 ‖~ grosso ['grousou] [复]大协奏曲

concession [kən'seʃən] n. ①让步;(退一步)承认; 让与物: make a ~ to 对 …让步 ②(政府对采矿权、土地使用权等的)特许; 特许权 ③租界, 租借地

conciliate [kən'silieit] vt. ①安抚,劝慰;博得…的好感(或欢心等) ②调和,调停 ③赢得(支持,好感等) ‖conciliator n. 安抚者,劝慰者;调停者

conciliation [kən,sili'eiʃən] n. ①调解,调和; 和解: a ~ board 调解委员会 / a court of ~ 调解法庭 ②抚慰 ③(好感等的)赢得,争得 ‖~ism n. 调和主义 / ~ist n. 调和主义者 a. 调和主义的

conciliatory [kən'siliətəri] a. 抚慰的;调解的,调和的

concise [kən'sais] a. 简明的,简洁的,简要的 ‖~ly ad. / ~ness n.

conclave ['kɔnkleiv] n. ①秘密会议,私人会议: sit in ~ 举行秘密会议 ②(天主教)红衣主教选举教皇的秘密会议(或会场)

conclude [kən'klu:d] ❶ vt. ①结束: ~ a speech (an argument) 结束演说(辩论) / To be ~d. (长篇连载时用语)下期(或下次)登完。②缔结,议定: ~ a treaty with 和…订立条约 / ~ business after viewing samples 看样后成交 ③推断出,断

定: From what you say I ~ that .... 从你所说的我推断出… ④决定: We ~d not to go. 我们决定不去。❷ vi. ①结束;终了 ②断定,决定; 达成协定 ‖concluding a. 结束的,最后的: a concluding speech 结束演说,闭幕词

conclusion [kən'klu:ʒən] n. ①结束,终了;结尾,结局: at the ~ of the ceremony 在仪式终了时 / bring the matter to an early ~ 把事情早日了结 / come to a ~ 告终 ②(条约等的)缔结;(买卖等的)议定 ③结论,推论: They came to the ~ that .... 他们得到的结论是… / You should not jump at ~s. 你不应当武断地乱下结论。/ draw a ~ from 由…得出结论 ‖a foregone ~ 未经商议即已决定的结论;预料中必然的结局 / in ~ 在结束时,最后: I will in ~ say a few words about discipline. 最后我简单谈一下纪律问题。/ try ~s with (在竞争、辩论等中)和…决胜负

conclusive [kən'klu:siv] a. 最后的;结论性的,确定性的: ~ evidence 确证,真凭实据 ‖~ly ad. / ~ness n.

concoct [kən'kɔkt] vt. ①调合,调制(汤、饮料、肥皂等),混合 ②编造(借口、谎话、小说情节等);策划 ‖~er, ~or n. 调制者;策划者 / ~ion [kən'kɔkʃən] n. ①调合,调制,混合;调制品,混合物 ②编造,策划;阴谋

concord ['kɔŋkɔ:d] n. ①和谐,一致,协调;(国际间)和平友好: in ~ 和谐地 ②(国际间的)协定,协约 ③【语】(人称、性、数、格的)一致,呼应 ④【音】和声,谐声

concordance [kən'kɔ:dəns] n. ①和谐,一致,协调 ②(某作家或书籍中所用的)重要语词索引 (to)

concordant [kən'kɔ:dənt] a. 一致的,协调的 (with) ‖~ly ad.

concourse ['kɔŋkɔ:s] n. ①集合,汇合;合流,总汇 ②群集 ③群集场所; [美](公园或车站内的)中央广场;中央大厅

concrete ['kɔnkri:t] I a. ①具体的; 有形的: make a ~ analysis of ~ problems 对具体问题作具体分析 / ~ action 具体行动 / in the ~ 具体地,实际上 / ~ number 【数】名数 / a ~ noun 【语】具体名词 ②固结成的;混凝土制的 II n. ①具体物 ②混凝土;凝结物: ~ works 混凝土工事 / reinforced ~ 钢筋混凝土 / a ~ mixer 混凝土拌和机 III [kən'kri:t] ❶ vt. ①使凝固,使固结 ②[喻]使结合 ③ ['kɔnkri:t] 用混凝土修筑;浇混凝土于 ❷ vi. ①凝固,固结 ②浇筑混凝土 ‖~ly ad. / ~ness n.

concubine ['kɔŋkjubain] n. ①小老婆,妾 ②情妇

concur [kən'kə:] (concurred; concurring [kən'kə:riŋ]) vi. ①同时发生; 共同起作用: Several circumstances concurred to bring about this result. 几种情况凑合在一起产生了这个结果。②同意,一致,赞成: ~ with sb. (an opinion) 同意某人(某个意见) / ~ in a statement 赞成某个陈述

concurrence [kən'kʌrəns] *n.* ① 同时发生; 凑合, 相helped, 协力 ②同意, 一致: with the ~ of 在…的同意下 ③法律上的同样有权(或有效)状态

concurrent [kən'kʌrənt] **I** *a.* ① 同时发生的; 共存的, 并存的 ②合作的 ③同意的, 一致的 ④(权力等)由两个负责当局行使的: a ~ resolution (美国国会两院的)共同决议 ⑤【数】共点的: ~ lines 共点线 ⑥【机】相合的, 顺流的 **II** *n.* 同时发生的事件; 共同起作用的因素; 共存物 ‖~ly *ad.* hold a post ~ly 兼任某职

concussion [kən'kʌʃən] *n.* ① 冲击, 震动: a ~ charge【军】震荡装药 / a ~ fuze【军】激发引信 ②【医】震荡; 脑震荡

condemn [kən'dem] *vt.* ①谴责: strongly. ~ the crimes of imperialist aggression 强烈谴责帝国主义的侵略罪行 ② 宣告(某人)有罪; 判 (某人)刑; 证明(某人)有罪: ~ sb. to death (imprisonment) 判某人死刑(徒刑) ③宣告…不适用 ④宣告没收(或征用)(财产等) ⑤ 宣告(病人)患不治之症 ‖~able [kən'demnəbl] *a.* 应受谴责的; 应定罪的 ‖~ed *a.* 已被定罪的; 定了罪的人用的: a ~ed cell (或 ward) 死刑囚犯的监房 / ~er, ~or [kən'demnə] *n.* 谴责者; 宣判者

condemnation [ˌkɔndem'neiʃən] *n.* ① 谴责 ②定罪, 宣告有罪 ③谴责(或定罪)的理由 ④(关于某事物)不适用的宣告 ⑤征用; 没收

condensation [ˌkɔnden'seiʃən] *n.* ①【物】冷凝(作用), 凝聚(作用)【化】缩合(作用): ~ polymerization 缩聚(作用) ③(文章等)的压缩; 经节缩的作品

condense [kən'dens] ❶ *vt.* ① 使冷凝, 使凝结, 缩合; 压缩, 浓缩: ~d milk 炼乳 ② 缩短, 精简 (文章等): ~ a news story 压缩一则新闻报道 ③加强(电气): a ~d spark 高电容火花 ④聚集(光线): condensing lens【物】聚光透镜 ❷ *vi.* ① 浓缩; 凝结 ②(气体)变成液体(或固体) ‖~r *n.* 冷凝器, 凝结器; 聚光器; 电容器

condescend [ˌkɔndi'send] *vi.* ①俯就, 屈尊: ~ to ask for advice 屈尊求教 ②带着优越感表示关心, 用恩赐态度相待: hate to be ~ed to 不喜欢别人用恩赐的态度对待自己 ③堕落, 丢丑: ~ to take bribes 堕落到受贿 / ~ to trickery 堕落到采用欺骗手段 ‖~ upon〔苏格兰〕对…详加说明

condiment ['kɔndimənt] *n.* 调味品 (例如胡椒) ‖~al [ˌkɔndi'mentl] *a.*

condition [kən'diʃən] **I** *n.* ① 条件: subjective (objective) ~ 主观(客观)条件 ②(人、事物本身的)状况, 状态; [复]环境; 形势: The patient was in a critical ~. 病人的情况十分危急。/ The cargo has been delivered in good ~. 货物已完好无损地到达。/ The ship is not in a ~ to make a long voyage. 这条船的情况不宜于远程航行。/ in (或 under) war ~s 在战争环境中 / in (或 under) favourable ~ 在有利形势下 ③(社会)地位, 身分: people of every ~ (或 of all ~s) 各种身分的人 / be low in ~ 社会地位低下

④【语】条件从句 ⑤[美] (有补考资格的)不及格分数 (通常用 "E" 作为评分符号) **II** *vt.* ①决定, 规定; 为…的条件; 制约: The pairs of opposites ~ one another for their existence. 对立面的双方互为存在的条件。/ He never ~ed his going upon the weather. 他从不因天气不好而不去。② 使处于正常(或良好)状态: ~ the air of the workshop 调节车间空气 / ~ livestock 把牲畜养壮 ③使适应, 使习惯于环境: ~ the plant to the northern climate 使作物适应北方的气候 ④检验(生丝、棉纱等) ⑤[美]要求(学生)补考: be ~ed in mathematics 须补考数学 ⑥引起(人、动物)的条件反射 ‖change one's ~ 结婚 / in an interesting ~ 〔英〕怀孕 / in (out of) ~ ① 健康状况好(不好), 身体条件适合(不适合): Athletes must train to be in ~. 运动员必须锻炼以保持良好的竞技状态。② 保存得好(不好), 保养得好(不好) / make it a ~ that... 以…为条件 / on (或 upon) ~ that... 如果…, 在…条件下: He can use the bicycle on ~ that he return(s) it tomorrow. 自行车可以借给他, 条件是明天必须归还。/ on this (that) ~ 在这个(那个)条件下 ‖~er n. ①【机】调节器 ②【农】土壤团粒结构促进剂 / ~ing n. ①(空气等的)调节; ②【冶】整修(礼) ②【心】条件作用

conditional [kən'diʃənl] **I** *a.* ①附条件的; 视…而定的 (on, upon): a ~ contract 有条件的契约, 暂行契约 / This is ~ on the overall plan. 这决定于总的计划。②【语】条件的: a ~ clause 条件从句 **II** *n.* 【语】条件词; 条件从句 ‖~ity [kənˌdiʃə'næliti] *n.* 条件性; 制约性; 条件限制 / ~ly *ad.*

condole [kən'doul] *vi.* 吊唁, 哀悼; 慰问: ~ with sb. upon (或 on) a misfortune 就某一不幸向某人表示慰问 ‖~ment *n.* =condolence

condolence [kən'doulens] *n.* [常用复]吊唁, 吊慰; 慰问: a letter of ~ 吊唁信 / present one's ~s to 向…吊唁 / express ~s on the death of 哀悼…的去世

condone [kən'doun] *vt.* ① 宽恕, 不咎(罪过) ② (行为等)抵消(过失等) ‖**condonation** [ˌkɔndou'neiʃən] *n.*

condor ['kɔndɔː] *n.* 【动】(南美产)神鹰, 秃鹰

conduce [kən'djuːs] *vi.* 导(致), 有助(于) (to): Heart-to-heart chats ~ to the solution of ideological problems. 谈心活动有助于解决思想问题。

conducive [kən'djuːsiv] *a.* 有助于…的, 有益于…的, 助长的 (to): a method ~ to quick results 易于迅速收到效果的方法 ‖~ness *n.*

conduct I ['kɔndʌkt] *n.* ①行为, 品行, 举动: good (bad) ~ 好(坏)品行 ②指导; 引导: under the ~ of 在…的引导下 ③实施, 处理, 经营, 进行: the ~ of state affairs 国家的处理 ④(艺术上的)处理方法 **II** [kən'dʌkt] ❶ *vt.* ①引导, 带领, 陪伴(游客等); 指导; 指挥(军队、乐队等): ~ sb. over a school 引导某人参观学校 / ~ water uphill 引

水上山 ②实施,处理,经营,进行: ~ mobile warfare 打运动战 / ~ investigations (propaganda) 进行调查(宣传) ③[~ oneself]为人,表现 ④ 传导,传(热、电等) ❷ vi. ①引导,带领;指导;指挥乐队 ②(路)通(至) (to) ③传导

conductivity [ˌkɔndʌk'tiviti] **n.** 传导率;传导性: electrical ~ 导电性;电导率 / ionic ~ 离子导电性;离子电导率 / magnetic ~ 导磁率;磁导率 / thermal ~ 导热性;热导率

conductor [kən'dʌktə] **n.** ① 指导者;响导者;管理人 ②(电车等)的售票员;[美]列车员 ③ (乐队、合唱队)的指挥 ④【电】导体;导线 ⑤避雷针 (= lightning ~) ‖~ial [ˌkɔndʌk'tɔːriəl] a.

conduit ['kɔndit] **n.** ① 管道,导管;水道,水管 ②【电】导线管,管道(电缆): ~ system (电车的)地下管道系统;(电灯的)暗线装置系统

cone ['koun] **I n.** ①锥形物;【数】【物】锥面,锥体: ~ bearing 锥形轴承 / a ~ of fire 束束弹道 / ~ of silence 【无】静寂区,圆锥形静区 ②【植】(松树的)球果;球花 ③【地】锥状地形;火山锥 ④风暴信号 ⑤蛋卷冰淇淋 **II ❶ vt.** ① 使成锥形 ②[用被动语态>]集中探照(敌机) ❷ vi. (松树)结球果 ‖'~-shaped a. 锥形的

cone shaped   pine cone

cone

confection [kən'fekʃən] **I n.** ①糖果;蜜饯 ②混合,调制 ③【医】糖果剂 ④精巧的工艺品;时髦的女服 **II vt.** [古]调制 ‖~ary a. ① 糖果的;蜜饯的 ②糖果商的;糖果业的 n. ①糖果店 ②糖果;蜜饯

confederacy [kən'fedərəsi] **n.** ①同盟,联盟,邦联;同盟(或联盟,邦联)的全体成员: the (Southern) *Confederacy* 【美史】(一八六〇至一八六一年间南部十一州的)南部邦联 (=the Confederate States of America) ②共谋,违法的结社

confederate [kən'fedərit] **I a.** ①同盟的,联合的 ②[C-]【美史】南部邦联的 **II n.** ①同盟者,联合者;同盟国 ②共谋者,同伙,党羽 ③ [C-]【美史】南部邦联的支持者 **III** [kən'fedəreit] **vt. & vi.** (使)结成同盟,(使)联合;(使)结党

confer [kən'fəː] (conferred; conferring [kən'fəːriŋ]) ❶ vt. 授与(称号、学位等): ~ a title on (或 upon) sb. 授与某人一个称号 ❷ vi. 交换意见,协商: ~ with sb. on (或 about) sth. 与某人商议某事 ‖~ment n. 授与

conference ['kɔnfərəns] **n.** ①讨论,会谈: be in ~ 正在开会 ②会议,讨论会,协商会:a fact-finding ~ 调查会 / a press (或 news) ~ 记者招待会 / a ~ on educational work 教育工作会议 / have a ~ with 和…协议 / hold a ~ 举行会议 ③[美](运动、宗教团体、学校等的)联合会

confess [kən'fes] ❶ vt. ① 供认,坦白(罪行、过失、隐私等);承认: ~ one's guilt (或 ~ that one is guilty, ~ oneself guilty, ~ oneself to be guilty) 认罪 ②表明信仰… ③向上帝(或神父)忏悔(罪恶等);(神父)听取…的忏悔 ④证明 ❷ vi. ①供认,交代;承认: ~ to a weakness 承认缺点 / ~ to having done (或 doing) sth. 承认干了某事 ②忏悔;(神父)听取忏悔 ‖~ and avoid 【律】承认所控告的事实而又主张法律上不能成立诉讼 ‖~or n. ① 供认者;忏悔者 ②忏悔神父 ③在遭迫害时声明坚守信仰的教徒

confessed [kən'fest] a. ①众所周知的,无可疑余地的,明白的,有定论的: a ~ fact 公认的事实,已明白的事实 ②已认罪的,罪状明白的 ③已向牧师忏悔(而得到赦免)的 ④被人公开信仰的 ‖stand ~ as 被揭露为…;被认为… ‖~ly [kən'fesidli] ad. 公开表明地;确定无疑地

confession [kən'feʃən] **n.** ① 招供,供认;交代,坦白: make a ~ 招供;坦白 ②(自)供状;自白书 ③(表明信仰等的)声明;表白 ④(尤指天主教;向神父作的)忏悔,告解 ⑤ (成员具有共同信条的)基督教团体(或教派) ‖~al a. ①坦白的;忏悔的 ②公开声明的 n. ① (神父听取忏悔的)忏悔室,告解所 ②(向神父所作的)忏悔 / ~ary a. & n. [罕] =~al

confetti [kən'feti(ː)] [复] **n.** [用作单] ①糖果 ②(婚礼等中投掷的)五彩纸屑

confidant [ˌkɔnfi'dænt] **n.** (常指可与谈有关恋爱事情的)密友,知己

confide [kən'faid] ❶ vt. ① 吐露(秘密等): ~ sth. to sb. 向某人吐露某事 / ~ to sb. that ... 向某人吐露… ②信托,交托,委托: ~ a task to sb. 把任务交给某人 ❷ vi. 信任(in);吐露秘密: ~ in sb. 信任某人;向某人吐露秘密 / ~ in sb.'s honesty 相信某人的诚实

confidence ['kɔnfidəns] **I n.** ①信任: a vote of ~ 信任票 / enjoy (或 have) sb.'s ~ 得到某人的信任 / be in sb.'s ~ 被某人信任;参与某人的机密 / have (或 place) ~ in sb. 信任某人 / take sb. into one's ~ 把某人当作知心人 ②信心,自信,把握: We have full ~ (that) we shall succeed. 我们完全有把握取得成功。③大胆;过于自信;狂妄 ④(向知心人)吐露的秘密;私房话: exchange ~s 交谈知心话 **II a.** 骗得信任(或信托)的;欺诈的: a ~ game (或 trick) (骗取财物等的)骗局 / a ~ man (或 trickster) (欺诈钱财等的)骗子

confident ['kɔnfidənt] **I a.** ①确信的;有信心的,自信的: a ~ manner 满怀信心的态度 / be ~ of success 确信成功 / We are ~ that we can overcome (或 ~ *of* overcom*ing*) the difficulties. 我们相信能克服困难。②过于自信的,自负的;大胆的;狂妄的 **II** *n.* [古]知心人 ‖**~ly** *ad.*

confidential [͵kɔnfi'denʃəl] *a.* ①极受信任的,心腹的,参与机密的: a ~ secretary 机要秘书 ②秘密的,机密的: *Confidential* (文件等封套上用语) 机密 / a ~ order 密令 / ~ information 机密情报 ③(语气等)表示信任的 ④易于信任他人的 ‖**~ly** *ad.*

configuration [kən͵figju'reiʃən] *n.* 构造,结构;形状,外形;【化】构型

confine [kən'fain] **I** *vt.* ① 限制: She ~*s* her remarks *to* scientific management. 她所讲的仅限于科学管理问题。② 禁闭;使闭门不出: He is ~*d to* the house by illness. 他因病不出门。③ [用被动语态]分娩,坐月子 **II** ['kɔnfain] *n.* [常用复]境界,边缘;区域,范围 ‖**~d** *a.* ①有限的,狭窄的 ②在分娩中的,坐月子的 / **~ment** *n.*

confirm [kən'fəːm] *vt.* ①使(权力等)更巩固;使(意见等)更有力; 使更坚定 (指在信念等方面) (*in*): ~ sb. *in* his dislike of sth. 使得某人更不喜爱某物 ②使有效,批准: ~ a title *to* sb. 批准授与某人一个称号 ③进一步证实,进一步确定: ~ a report 证实一个报道 / ~ a telephone message by letter (打电话后)写信进一步肯定电话中所说的内容 ④坚持说 (*that*) ⑤(基督教中)给…行按手礼,给…行坚信礼 ‖**~able** *a.* ①可进一步确定(或证实)的 ②可批准的 / **~ed** *a.* ①坚定的 ②确定的,证实了的 ③成习惯的,根深蒂固的: a ~ed criminal 惯犯 / a ~ed habit 积习 / a ~ed disease 痼疾

confirmation [͵kɔnfə'meiʃən] *n.* ①证实,确定;证据: in ~ of 以证实… ②确认;批准 ③(基督教中的)按手礼,坚信礼

confiscate ['kɔnfiskeit] **I** *vt.* 没收,把…充公,征用 **II** *a.* 财产被没收的,被充公的,被征用的 ‖**confiscation** [͵kɔnfis'keiʃən] *n.* / **confiscator** *n.* 没收人

conflagration [͵kɔnflə'greiʃən] *n.* 大火,大火灾;(战争等的)爆发

conflict **I** ['kɔnflikt] *n.* ①斗争,战斗;倾轧 ②抵触;冲突;争论,论战: in ~ with 和…冲突 / an inner ~ 内心冲突 / an armed ~ 武装冲突 / a ~ of opinions (ideas) 意见(思想)上的冲突 / a ~ of interest [美]违背公众利益的行为 / a wordy ~ 文字论战 **II** [kən'flikt] *vi.* ①斗争,战斗;倾轧 (*with*) ②抵触,冲突 (*with*) ‖**~ing** [kən'fliktiŋ] *a.* 抵触的,冲突的

confluence ['kɔnfluəns] *n.* ①合流,汇合;合流点,汇合处;汇流而成的河 ②集合,聚集 ③人群

conform [kən'fɔːm] **I** ❶ *vt.* 使一致,使符合;使遵照,使适合: ~ oneself *to* the new customs 使自己适应新风俗 ❷ *vi.* ①一致,符合; 遵照,适合: ~ *to* rules 遵守规则 / ~ *to* (或 *with*) the interests of the people 符合人民利益 ② 适应环境 ③【英史】遵奉国教 **II** *a.* =conformable

‖**~ist** *n.* ①遵奉者 ②英国国教徒

conformation [͵kɔnfɔː'meiʃən] *n.* ①符合,一致 ②构造,形态

conformity [kən'fɔːmiti] *n.* ① 依照,遵照,遵奉;适合,一致: in ~ with (或 *to*) 依照,和…相一致;遵奉 ②一致点 ③【英史】遵奉国教 ④【地】(地层的)整合

confound [kən'faund] *vt.* ① 混淆,使(思想等)混乱: ~ right *and* (或 *with*) wrong 混淆是非 ②使惊惶(失措): be ~ed at (或 *by*) the sight of (或 *to see*) ... 一见到…就惊惶(失措) ③挫败 ④把…毁灭掉(用在诅咒语中): Confound it! 该死的! / Confound you! 混蛋! 去你的!

confront [kən'frʌnt] *vt.* ① 使面对,使面临,使遭遇: be ~ed *with* (或 *by*) 面临… ②(困难等)临到(人)头上 ③勇敢地(或镇定地)面对(危险等),正视; 对抗: ~ the vital questions of 正视…的重大问题 ④使对质,使对证: ~ the accused *with* his accuser 使被告和原告对质 ⑤比较,使对照 ⑥ 同…相对 (指房屋等) ‖**~ation** [͵kɔnfrʌn'teiʃən] *n.* (尤指敌对国家的)对抗

confuse [kən'fjuːz] *vt.* ①使混乱;混淆,把…混同;弄错: ~ black and white 混淆黑白 / A is not to be ~*d with* B. 不可将甲误作乙。②把…弄糊涂;使慌乱 ‖**confusable** *a.* ① 可能被混淆的 ②可能被弄糊涂的 / **~dly** [kən'fjuːzidli] *ad.* 混乱地; 慌乱地 / **~dness** [kən'fjuːzidnis] *n.* 混乱,慌乱

confusion [kən'fjuːʒən] *n.* ① 混乱;混乱状态;骚乱: in ~ 在混乱中 / be thrown into ~ 陷入混乱状态 ②混淆 ③慌乱: be covered with ~ 很窘;十分慌乱 ④ 失败,毁灭,倒霉(用作诅咒语): *Confusion* on (或 *to*) ...! …该死! ⑤见鬼去吧! / drink ~ to sb. 举杯诅咒某人 ‖**worse confounded** 比以前更加混乱;非常混乱,一团糟

confute [kən'fjuːt] *vt.* 驳倒(人、论据等) ‖**confutation** [͵kɔnfjuː'teiʃən] *n.*

congeal [kən'dʒiːl] *vt.* & *vi.* (使)冻结,(使)凝结 ‖**~able** *a.* 可冻结的,可凝结的 / **~er** *n.* 冷却器;冷藏箱 / **~ment** *n.*

congenial [kən'dʒiːnjəl] *a.* ①同族的,同类的: 性情相似的,志趣相投的: be ~ *to* (或 *with*) sb. 和某人志趣相合 ②(气候、水土、职位等)相宜的;惬意的 ‖**~ity** [kən͵dʒiːni'æliti] *n.* / **~ly** *ad.*

congenital [kən'dʒenitl] *a.* (疾病、缺陷等)先天的,天生的 ‖**~ly** *ad.*

congest [kən'dʒest] ❶ *vt.* ①[常用被动语态]充满;拥挤: The street is much ~*ed.* 街上非常拥挤。②使(人口等)拥塞,使密集 ③【医】使充血 ❷ *vi.* 拥挤;【医】充血 ‖**~ion** [kən'dʒestʃən] *n.* / **~ive** *a.* 充血的,充血性的

conglomerate [kən'glɔmərit] **I** *a.* ①聚成球形的,成团的 ②密集的;由不同种类的部分组成的: a ~ language 由各种语种组成的语言 ③【地】砾岩的 **II** *n.* ①密集体(如人群、房屋等);团;混合

物 ②【地】砾岩 ③(多种行业、企业的)联合大企业 **III** [kən'gloməreit] *vt.* & *vi.* (使)成球形; (使)成团 ‖~**r** [kən'gloməreitə] *n.* 联合大企业的经营者 / **conglomeration** [kən,glomə'reiʃən] *n.*

congratulate [kən'grætjuleit] *vt.* 祝贺,向…致祝贺词: ~ sb. *on* (或 *upon*) sth. 为某事向某人祝贺 / ~ oneself *that* . . . 因…而自己庆幸 ‖**congratulator** *n.* 祝贺者

congratulation [kən,grætju'leiʃən] *n.* ①祝贺,庆贺 ②[常用复]祝贺词: *Congratulations (on* . . .)! 祝贺(…)! / Convey my ~s to him. (请)代我向他祝贺。

congratulatory [kən'grætjulətəri] *a.* 祝贺的: a ~ telegram (letter) 贺电(信)

congregate ['kongrigeit] **I** *vt.* & *vi.* (使)集合 **II** *a.* ①集合在一起的 ②集体的

congregation [,kongri'geiʃən] *n.* ①集合;集会;人群 ②(教堂中的)会众;(某地区的)全体教徒 ③【天主教】红衣主教会议(罗马教廷所辖的一种行政机构) ④(基督教《圣经》典故)在旷野中的全体以色列人,全体以色列人的大会 ⑤[英]大学教职员全体会议

congress ['kongres] *n.* ①(代表)大会;专业人员代表会议 ②(美国等国的)国会,议会;国会(或议会)会议(期) ③聚会;社交: the *Congress of Vienna* 维也纳会议(1814—1815;英、普、俄、奥等国为结束反拿破仑战争,恢复封建王朝统治而召开的会议;会后建立反动的神圣同盟) ‖**Congressite** ['kongresait] *n.* (印度)国大党党员 ‖**Congress gaiter, Congress shoe, Congress boot** 两侧有松紧布的半统靴

congruence ['kongruəns], **congruency** ['kongruənsi] *n.* ① 适合,一致;和谐 ②【语】(语法上的)一致 ②【数】迭合,全等,相合;同余(式)线汇,汇

conic ['konik] **I** *a.* 圆锥形的;圆锥的: ~ section 【数】圆锥曲线,二次曲线 **II** *n.* 【数】圆锥曲线,二次曲线; [~s]【用作单】锥线法(论)

conical ['konikəl] *a.* 圆锥形的;圆锥的 ‖~**ly** *ad.* / ~**ness** *n.*

conifer ['kounifə] *n.* 【植】针叶树(如松、枞等)

conjectural [kən'dʒektʃərəl] *a.* 推测的,猜想的;爱猜想的 ‖~**ly** *ad.*

conjecture [kən'dʒektʃə] **I** *n.* ① 推测,猜想;假设,猜测而得的结论: It's mere ~. 这纯属猜测。 / venture a ~ 姑且猜猜看 ② (校阅时的)揣摩 **II** ❶ *vt.* ① 猜测;假设,猜想出 ②(校阅时)揣摩出 ❷ *vi.* 猜测;假设

conjugal ['kondʒugəl] *a.* 婚姻的;夫妇关系上的,夫妇之间的 ‖~**ity** [,kondʒu'gæliti] *n.* / ~**ly** *ad.*

conjugate I ['kondʒugeit] ❶ *vt.* ①结合,联合;连接;使成对 ②【语】列举(动词)的变化形式 ❷ *vi.* ①成婚 ②【生】配合;成对 ③【语】列举动词的变化形式;(动词)变化 **II** ['kondʒugit] *a.* ①结合的,配合的;对生的 ②【语】同

根的,同源的 ③【数】【物】共轭的;缀合的 **III** ['kondʒugit] *n.* 【语】同根词

conjugation [,kondʒu'geiʃən] *n.* ①结合,联合;配对 ②【语】(动词的)各个变化形式;变化形式相似的一组动词 ③【生】(两个生殖细胞的)接合

conjunction [kən'dʒʌŋkʃən] *n.* ①结合,联合;连接;并合;关联 ②(事件的)同时发生,同处发生 ③【语】连接词 ④【天】(天体的)会合 ‖in ~ *with* 与…协力;与…连接: This section should be studied *in* ~ *with* the preceding three. 这一节应连同前面三节一起研读。‖~**al** *a.*

conjunctive [kən'dʒʌŋktiv] **I** *a.* 连接的;联合的; 【语】连接的;联系的 **II** *n.* 【语】连接词;连接法 ‖~**ly** *ad.*

conjure ['kʌndʒə] ❶ *vt.* ① [kən'dʒuə] 祈求,恳求 ②召(鬼),念咒召唤 ③用戏法变出,用魔术作成(或驱走);用魔术影响 ④ 想象;用幻想作出 ❷ *vi.* ①念咒召鬼,施魔法 ②变戏法 ‖~ *away* 用魔法驱除(烦恼、疾病等) / ~ *up* ①用魔法召(鬼) ②凭幻想(或用魔法)作出 ‖~**r, conjuror** ['kʌndʒərə] *n.* ① [kən'dʒuərə] 恳求者 ②施魔术者,念咒的人;变戏法的人 ③[喻]非常聪明的人

connect [kə'nekt] ❶ *vt.* ①连接,连结: The two cities are ~ed by a railway. 这两个城市有铁路相连。/ ~ a hose to the faucet 把软管接在水龙头上 ②把…联系起来;给…接通电话 ③联想 ❷ *vi.* ①连接;相通;衔接: The two trains ~ here. 这两次列车在这里衔接。/ The trolleybus ~s here *with* a bus for the airfield. 这辆无轨电车在这里衔接去机场的公共汽车。②击中 ‖~**er, ~or** *n.* ①连接器;联系者 ②连接物 ③**ing rod** 接器,插塞和塞孔 ③**ing rod** 【机】连杆

connected [kə'nektid] *a.* ①连接的,连结的 ②关联的;有联系的 ③连贯的 ‖~**ly** *ad.* / ~**ness** *n.*

connective [kə'nektiv] **I** *a.* 连接的,连结的: ~ tissue 【解】结缔组织 **II** *n.* ①连接物 ②【语】起连接作用的词(或词组) ③【植】药隔 ‖~**ly** *ad.*

connexion [kə'nekʃən] *n.* ①联系;联结 ②联系关系: parallel (series) ~ 【电】并(串)联 / one's social ~s 社会关系 ②连贯性,上下文关系;方面: in this (that) ~ 在这(那)一点上 ③连接物体;(通讯、交通等的)联系手段;(火车、轮船等的)联运: a rubber ~ 橡皮接头 / a ~ ticket 联运票 ④[常用复]亲戚(尤指近亲) ⑤(政治、宗教等的)团体,教派 ⑥[总称]顾客;(贸易上的)往来关系: a firm with a good ~ 有很多顾客的商号 ⑦(电报、电话)通讯线: You are in ~. (电话)给你接通了。⑧性交: criminal ~ (男女间的)私通 ⑨[美俚]毒品贩子 ‖*cut the* ~ 把东西拆开;割断联系 / *in* ~ *with* ①与…有关系;与…连起 ②关于 ‖~**al** *a.*

connive [kə'naiv] *vi.* ①默许;纵容 (*at*) ②共谋;取得默契 (*with*)

connoisseur [,koni'sə:] *n.* 鉴赏家,鉴定家;行家,内行 (*in, of*) ‖~**ship** *n.* 鉴赏的能力;行家的地位

connotation [ˌkɔnouˈteiʃən] *n.* ①含蓄; (词等的) 涵义 ②【逻】内涵

connote [kəˈnout] *vt.* ①(词、词组等) 含蓄着, 意味着: The word "tropics" ~s heat. "热带"这个词意味着热。②【逻】内涵着

conquer [ˈkɔŋkə] ❶ *vt.* ①征服, 攻克, 战胜; (经过奋战后) 占领: Man can ~ nature. 人定胜天。②克服(困难等), 破除(坏习惯等) ③抑制(情欲等) ❷ *vi.* 得胜, 胜利 ‖~able [ˈkɔŋkərəbl] *a.* 可征服的 / ~or [ˈkɔŋkərə] *n.* 征服者, 胜利者: (William) the *Conqueror*【英史】征服者(威廉)(指英王威廉一世)

conquest [ˈkɔŋkwest] *n.* ①征服; 赢得, 获得 ②掠取物; 征服地 ③(在爱情等方面)被俘虏(或魅惑)的人 ④ [the C-]【英史】(一〇六六年)威廉的征服英国(常作 the Norman Conquest) ‖*make a ~ of* ①征服… ②赢得…的爱情

consanguinity [ˌkɔnsænˈgwiniti] *n.* ①同宗; 同血缘, 亲族关系: lineal ~ 直系亲属 / collateral ~ 旁系亲属 ②亲密关系

conscience [ˈkɔnʃəns] *n.* 良心, 道德心: have a good (或 clear) ~ 问心无愧 / have a bad (或 guilty) ~ 感到内疚; 心里有鬼 ‖*for ~('s) sake* 为了问心无愧 / *have sth. on one's ~* 因为某事而内疚 / *have the ~ to* (do) (竟)厚着脸皮(做) / *in all ~* (口) 当然, 一定, 的确 ②凭良心说; 公平地说 ‖*~less a.* 没良心的, 没道德心的 ‖*~ money* 为求得心安而付的钱(如补缴所逃避的捐税等) / *'~-'smitten a.* 受良心责备的

conscientious [ˌkɔnʃiˈenʃəs] *a.* 认真的; 诚心诚意的; 谨慎的; 凭良心做的 ‖*~ly ad.* ~ly remould one's world outlook 认真改造世界观 / ~ness *n.* ‖*~ objector* (为了道德或宗教上的原因而)拒服兵役者

conscious [ˈkɔnʃəs] *a.* ①有意识的, 意识到的, 自觉的; 被意识到的: I was ~ that I had made a mistake. 我意识到自己犯了一个错误。/ ~ activity自觉行为; 能动性 / with ~ superiority 抱着优越感 ② 神志清醒的: The patient was perfectly ~. 病人神智非常清楚。③ =self-conscious ④ [常用以构成复合词] 有…意识的: class-~ 有阶级意识(或觉悟)的 ‖*~ly ad.*

consciousness [ˈkɔnʃəsnis] *n.* 意识, 知觉; 觉悟, 自决定意识。/ from matter to ~ 由物质到精神 / lose (recover) ~ 失去(恢复)知觉

conscript I [kənˈskript] *vt.* 征募, 征(兵); 征召…服役 **II** [ˈkɔnskript] *n.* 应征士兵 **III** [ˈkɔnskript] *a.* 被征募入伍的 ‖*~ fathers* (古罗马的)元老院议员们

conscription [kənˈskripʃən] *n.* 征兵, 征募; 征集

consecrate [ˈkɔnsikreit] **I** *vt.* ①献祭 ②奉献 ③使神圣不可侵犯: rules ~d by time 年深月久固定下来的规则 ④使献圣职 **II** *a.* 献祭的; 奉献的 ‖*consecration* [ˌkɔnsiˈkreiʃən] *n.* ①献

祭 ②奉献 ③任圣职的仪式

consecutive [kənˈsekjutiv] *a.* 连续的; 连贯的; 顺序的: five ~ days 连续五天 / ~ numbers 连续数 ‖*~ly ad.* / ~ness *n.*

consensus [kənˈsensəs] *n.* ① (意见等的) 一致, 合意; 舆论 ②【生】同感, 交感

consent [kənˈsent] **I** *vi.* 同意, 赞成; 答应(to): ~ to a proposal (plan) 同意一个提议(计划) / ~ to (do) 同意(做) **II** *n.* 同意, 赞成; 答应: with the ~ of 经…同意 / with one ~ (或 by common ~) 经一致同意 / the age of ~ 【律】承诺年龄 ‖*Silence gives ~.* [谚]沉默即同意。‖*~er n.* 同意者, 赞成者 / ~ingly *ad.* 赞同地

consequence [ˈkɔnsikwəns] *n.* ①结果, 后果 ②【逻】推论, 推断 ③重要(性), 重大; 重要的样子: a person of ~ 举足轻重的人 / It's of no ~. 这是无足轻重的。‖*in ~* 结果是, 因此 / *in ~ of* 由于…的缘故 / *take the ~s* 承担后果

consequent [ˈkɔnsikwənt] **I** *a.* ①作为结果的, 随之发生的: sb.'s long illness and ~ absence from school 某人长期以来的疾病与由此而造成的缺课 ②合乎逻辑的; 必然的 **II** *n.* ①当然的结果; 推论 ②【语】(条件从句的)结论句 ③【数】后项; 【逻】后件 ‖*~ly ad.* 因而, 所以

consequential [ˌkɔnsiˈkwenʃəl] *a.* ①作为结果的, 随之发生的 ②推论的; 间接的 ③引出重要结果的, 重大的 ④自大的, 趾高气扬的 ‖*~ity* [ˌkɔnsiˌkwenʃiˈæliti] *n.* / ~ly *ad.* / ~ness *n.*

conservation [ˌkɔnsə(ː)ˈveiʃən] *n.* ①保存; (森林等自然资源的)保护; 资源保护区: the ~ of soil and water 水土保持 ②【物】守恒, 不灭: ~ of energy (mass) 能量(质量)守恒 ‖*~al a.* / ~ist *n.* 自然资源保护论者

conservatism [kənˈsəːvətizəm] *n.* ①保守主义; 守旧性 ②[C-] (英国)保守党的主张和政策; (英国)保守党

conservative [kənˈsəːvətiv] **I** *a.* ①保存的, 防腐的 ②保守的, 守旧的: get rid of rightist ~ ideas 克服右倾保守思想 ③[C-] (英国)保守党的; (加拿大)进步保守党的 ④有节制的; 稳健的: according to a ~ estimate 按照保守的估计 **II** *n.* ①保守主义者, 因循守旧的人 ②[C-] (英国等的)保守党人 ③稳健派 ④防腐剂, 保存物 ‖*~ly ad.* / ~ness *n.*

conservator *n.* ①[ˈkɔnsə(ː)veitə] 保护者, 管理人 ②[kənˈsəːvətə] (公共福利的)监督官

conservatory [kənˈsəːvətri] *n.* (培养植物的)暖房, 温室

conserve [kənˈsəːv] **I** *vt.* ①保存, 保藏, 保养: ~ one's strength 养精蓄锐 ②用糖渍保存: ~ fruit 制果子酱 **II** *n.* [常用复]蜜饯, 果酱; 【医】糖果剂

consider [kənˈsidə] ❶ *vt.* ①考虑, 细想: ~ a proposal (suggestion) 考虑一个提议(建议) / We are ~ing reorganizing (或 how to reorganize) the production process. 我们正在考虑改革生产过程。②认为, 把…看作: We ~ that he is not to blame. 我们认为这不是他的过错。/ ~ it necessary to do sth. 认为有必要做某事 ③考虑到;照顾,体谅: ~ sb.'s age (ill health) 照顾某人年老(体弱) ④看重 ⑤凝视,端详 ❷ *vi.* 考虑,细想: Let me ~. 让我考虑一下。‖*all things* ~*ed* 考虑到所有情况,全面地考虑: *All things* ~*ed, it is a good plan.* 从全面考虑,这个计划是好的。‖~*ed a.* ①经过深思熟虑的 ②被尊敬的,被看重的

considerable [kən'sidərəbl] *a.* ①值得考虑的 ②值得重视的,重要的 ③相当大(或多)的,很大(或多)的: a ~ distance (number) 相当大的距离(数目) ‖~**ness** *n.* / **considerably** *ad.* 相当大地;…得多: *considerably* better 好得多

considerate [kən'sidərit] *a.* ①考虑周到的 ②体谅的,体贴的,替(人)着想的 (*of*): be ~ *of* others 能体谅别人 ‖~**ly** *ad.* / ~**ness** *n.*

consideration [kən,sidə'reiʃən] *n.* ①考虑,思考: give a problem careful ~ 仔细考虑问题 / Your suggestion is *under* ~. 你的建议正在考虑中。②需要考虑的事;所考虑的事 ③体谅,照顾 ④尊敬 ⑤报酬;补偿 ⑥[罕]重要性 ‖*in* ~ *of* 考虑到,由于;作为对…的酬报 / *leave sth. out of* ~ 对某事不加考虑;忽视某事 / *on* (或 *under*) *no* ~ 决不: *On no* ~ can we agree to this. 我们绝对不能同意这一点。/ *take into* ~ 考虑到,顾及

considering [kən'sidəriŋ] *prep.* 就…而论,考虑到: He is strong ~ his age. 就他的年龄而论,他可算得上强壮的。/ The boy did quite well ~ the circumstances. 考虑到具体情况,可以说那孩子干得很不错了。

consign [kən'sain] *vt.* ①把…委托给,把…交付与 (*to*): ~ an orphan to sb.'s care 委托某人抚养一个孤儿 / ~ a task *to* sb. 把任务交给某人 / ~ a letter *to* the flames (*to* the wastepaper basket) 把一封信烧掉(丢进废纸篓) ②寄存,寄售;托运(货物等): ~ money in a bank 把钱存在银行里 / ~ goods by rail 把货物交火车运送 ‖~**ee** [,kɔnsai'ni:] *n.* 受托人;承销人,代售人;收货人 / ~**or, ~er** *n.* 委托人;发货人;寄售人

consignment [kən'sainmənt] *n.* 交付,托付;托付物(尤指一次寄存或寄售的货物): a new ~ of goods 新到的一批货物 / a ~ sale 寄售 / ~ merchandise 寄售品 ‖*on* ~ 以托销方式: goods shipped *on* ~ 发出(或运出)的托销货

consist [kən'sist] *vi.* ①由…组成,由…构成 (*of*): Water ~*s of* hydrogen and oxygen. 水由氢和氧组成。/ a committee ~*ing of* nine members 由九名委员组成的委员会 ②在于,存在于 (*in*): Happiness ~*s in* struggle. 幸福存在于斗争中。③并存,一致 (*with*): Theory should ~ *with* practice. 理论应与实践相一致。

consistence [kən'sistəns] *n.* 坚固性;浓度,密度,稠度

consistency [kən'sistənsi] *n.* ①坚固性;浓度,密

度,稠度 ②(性格上的)坚韧 ③一致性,连贯性;言行一致: These accounts show no ~. 这些报道前后不一。

consistent [kən'sistənt] *a.* ①坚固的,坚实的 ②一致的,连贯的;始终如一的: His action is always ~ *with* his words. 他始终是言行一致的。/ a ~ policy 一贯的政策 ‖~**ly** *ad.*

consolation [,kɔnsə'leiʃən] *n.* ①安慰,慰问: seek ~ in 在…中寻求安慰 / a letter of ~ 慰问信 / a ~ match (prize) 安慰赛(奖) ②起安慰作用的人(或事物)

console[1] [kən'soul] *vt.* 安慰,慰问

console[2] [kən'soul] *n.* ①[建]肘托;带卷涡式的托石 ②【自】控制台;仪表板 ③(收音机、电视机等的)落地式支架 ‖~ **table** (装在墙上的)蜗形腿狭台

consolidate [kən'sɔlideit] ❶ *vt.* ①巩固,加强: ~ the beachhead 巩固滩头阵地 ②把…合成一体,使联合起来: a ~*d* school [美]合并而成的公立学校 (常指农村的小学) / a ~*d* list of sick and wounded 伤病汇报表 / ~*d* annuities (英国政府于一七五一年开始发行的)统一公债 (略作consols) ❷ *vi.* ①巩固,强固: ~ at every step 步步为营 ②合并,联合 ‖**consolidatory** *a.*

consolidation [kən,sɔli'deiʃən] *n.* ①巩固,加强 ②合并,联合 ③[医]坚实,坚实变化

consonance ['kɔnsənəns] *n.* ①调和,一致 ②(字音的)和谐 ③【音】和音;【物】共鸣,谐和 ‖*in* ~ *with* 和…一致

consonant ['kɔnsənənt] **I** *n.* 【语】辅音;辅音字母 **II** *a.* ①符合的,一致的 (*with, to*) ②谐音的;【音】和音的 ③辅音的 ‖~**al** [,kɔnsə'næntl] *a.* 辅音的 / ~**ly** *ad.*

consort I ['kɔnsɔ:t] *n.* ①配偶(尤指帝王的夫或妻);伙伴: the queen ~ 王后 / the king (或 prince) ~ 女王的丈夫 ②协力,联合: in ~ *with* sb. 与某人联合着 ③僚舰,僚艇;供船 ④一组乐师;一组同类乐器 **II** [kən'sɔ:t] ❶ *vi.* ①陪伴 (*with*) ②一致,相称: His words and actions ill ~ together. 他的言行很不一致。/ The illustrations ~ admirably *with* the text. 插图与文字非常相配。❷ *vt.* [常接 oneself] 使结伴,使配对

conspicuous [kən'spikjuəs] *a.* ①明显的,显著的;惹人注目的: be ~ for one's bravery 以勇敢而受人注意 / cut a ~ figure 露头角,惹人注目 / ~ consumption 摆阔性的挥霍浪费 / be ~ by one's absence 因缺席而引人注目 ②(服饰等)过分花哨的,触目的 ‖~**ly** *ad.* / ~**ness** *n.*

conspiracy [kən'spirəsi] *n.* ①阴谋,密谋;阴谋集团: unmask a ~ 揭露阴谋 / form a ~ against 密谋反对… ②同谋,共谋 ③(事态、因素等巧合的)协同作用 ‖a ~ *of silence* (对丑事等)保持缄默的密约

conspirator [kən'spirətə] *n.* 共谋者;阴谋家

conspire [kən'spaiə] ❶ *vi.* ①密谋策划;搞阴谋 ②(巧合地)协力促成: All things ~*d* towards that result (或 ~d to bring about that result). 一切因素都导致了那个结果。❷ *vt.* (共同)图谋

constable ['kʌnstəbl] *n.* ①[英]警察；警官：Chief Constable [英]警察局长 / a special ~ (特殊场合等的)临时警察 ②(中世纪王室或贵族家庭的)总管；古城堡主 ‖*outrun the* ~ 负债

constancy ['kɔnstənsi] *n.* 坚定，坚贞；经久不变：~ of purpose 目标坚定

constant ['kɔnstənt] **I** *a.* ① 坚定的，坚贞的；经久不变的，永恒的：a ~ believer in materialism 坚信唯物主义的人 / a ~ temperature room 恒温室 ② 经常的，不断的：the ~ growth of productivity 生产力的不断发展 **II** *n.* 【数】常数；【物】永定，不变，恒量 ‖~ly *ad.*

constellate ['kɔnstəleit] ❶ *vt.* 使形成星座；使群集；(以星群般的饰物)装饰 ❷ *vi.* 形成星座；群集 ‖**constellation** [,kɔnstə'leiʃən] *n.* ①【天】星座；(注定命运或性格的)星宿 ②(如明星般)灿烂的一群 ③【心】丛

consternation [,kɔnstə(:)'neiʃən] *n.* (极度的)惊愕，惊恐：throw sb. into ~ 使某人惊恐万状 / The enemy troops fled in ~. 敌军狼狈逃窜。

constipate ['kɔnstipeit] *vt.* 使便秘；使(肠道)秘结；使呆滞 ‖**constipation** [,kɔnsti'peiʃən] *n.*

constituency [kən'stitjuensi] *n.* ①全体选民；选区的居民，选举区 ②(一批)顾客；(一批)赞助者；(一批)订户 ‖*nurse a* ~ (候选人或当选人)笼络选区的选民

constituent [kən'stitjuənt] **I** *a.* ① 形成的，组成的：a ~ corporation (组成母公司的)一家子公司 ② 有选举权的；有权制定(或修改)宪法的：a ~ assembly 立宪会议；国民代表大会 **II** *n.* ①(有权选举议员等的)选民，选举人，委托人 ②成分，要素；【语】构成成分，组成要素

constitute ['kɔnstitju:t] *vt.* ① 构成，组成：Three squads ~ a platoon. 三个班组成一排。② 设立(机构、委员会等)；制定(法律等)；使(文件等)通过法律手续：the ~d authorities 合法当局 ③ 指定，任命，派…为：He ~d himself their chief adviser. 他自命为他们的首席顾问。

constitution [,kɔnsti'tju:ʃən] *n.* ① 建立，设立；制定；任命 ②(事物的)构造，组成(方式) ③(人的)体格，体质；性格，素质：build up a strong (或 tough) ~ 练出强健的体格 / a man of delicate ~ 体质很弱的人 ④ 章程，规章；宪法：establish (revise) a ~ 制订(修改)宪法 / an unwritten ~ 不成文宪法 / a draft ~ 宪法草案 ⑥ 政体

constitutional [,kɔnsti'tju:ʃənl] **I** *a.* ①体质上的；气质上的 ②保健的：a ~ walk 增强体质的散步 ③组成的，构成的：a ~ formula (化学上的)结构式 ④符合宪法的；符合规章的；宪法(或规章)所规定的：~ rights (宪法规定的)公民权利 / ~ monarchy 君主立宪制 ⑤宪法(上)的；规章的 ⑥拥护宪法的 **II** *n.* 保健体育活动(尤指散步) ‖~ism *n.* ① 宪政，立宪政体 ② 立宪主义 / ~ist *n.* 立宪主义者，拥护立宪政者 / ~ity [,kɔn-

sti,tju:ʃə'næliti] *n.* 合宪法性 / ~ize *vt.* 使具有宪法；使宪法化 / ~ly *ad.* ①在体质上；在气质上 ②在构造上，在本质上：Despite repeated heatings the material remained ~ly the same. 经多次加热后材料的质地还是没有变。③按宪法

constrain [kən'strein] *vt.* ① 强逼，强使：~ sb. to do sth. 强制某人做某事 / I feel ~ed to apologize to you. 我觉得非向你表示歉意不可。② 硬作出；使(关系等)紧张 ③攫住；紧闭夹住；抑制

constrained [kən'streind] *a.* 被强迫的；强装出来的；紧张的；被约束的：a ~ smile 强作的不自然的笑容 / ~ motion 【物】约束运动 ‖~ly [kən'streinidli] *ad.*

constraint [kən'streint] *n.* ① 强逼，强制；压抑，拘束：act under (或 in) ~ 被迫着行动 / feel (show) ~ in sb.'s presence 在某人面前感到(表现得)局促不安 ② 强制力，压制因素 ③ 紧张感，(关系等的)紧张状态

constrict [kən'strikt] ❶ *vt.* ①压缩，使缩小 ②使枯竭，阻塞 ❷ *vi.* 收缩 ‖~ion [kən'strikʃən] *n.* ①压缩，收缩 ②压抑 ③压缩物，阻塞物

construct [kən'strʌkt] **I** *vt.* ① 建造：~ a new reservoir 造一座新水库 ②构筑；创立(学说等)；构(词)；造(句)：The story is skilfully ~ed. 故事的构思相当巧妙。③作(几何图) **II** ['kɔnstrʌkt] *n.* 构成物；思维的产物 ‖~or *n.* 建造者；造船技师

construction [kən'strʌkʃən] *n.* ① 建造，建筑；建设：under ~ 正在建造中 / a bridge of recent ~ 新近建成的桥 / a ~ site 建筑工地 / capital ~ 基本建设 / China's socialist ~ 中国的社会主义建设 ② 建筑方法，建造术；结构；建筑物，建造物：ships of similar ~ 结构类似的船只 / The new building is a very solid ~. 新建的大楼非常坚固。③【语】句法关系，句法结构 ④【数】作图(法) ⑤建造物；意义：put a good (bad) ~ on (或 upon) 对…作出善(恶)意的解释 / put a wrong ~ on (或 upon) 对…进行曲解 / What he said does not bear such a ~. 他的话不是这样的意思。⑥(构成派别乱搞成的)雕塑品 ‖~al *a.* / ~ist *n.* (对宪法等成文法)作解释的人

constructive [kən'strʌktiv] *a.* ① 建设的；建设性的：a ~ suggestion 建设性建议 ② 推定的；经过解释的：a ~ fraud 【律】推定欺诈(指虽无恶意动机，但侵害他人或公共利益，在法律上应以欺诈论处的行为) ‖~ly *ad.* / ~ness *n.*

construe [kən'stru:] **I** ❶ *vt.* ①对(句子等)作语法分析；把…逐字译出 ②作…注作：His remarks have been wrongly ~d. 他的话被误解了。/ His withdrawal was ~d as a protest. 他的退场被看作是一种抗议的表示。③【语】(习惯上)使连用："Depend" is ~d with "on". 动词"depend"与前置词"on"连用。❷ *vi.* ①作句法分析；(句子)可作语法分析：The sentence won't ~. 这句子读不通。(指语法上站不住脚) ②解释 **II** ['kɔnstru:] *n.* 逐字直译；逐字直译的段落

consul ['kɔnsəl] *n.* ①领事: an acting ～ 代理领事 / a ～ general 总领事 / an honorary ～ 名誉领事 ②【史】(古罗马)执政官; (一七九九至一八〇四年间法国) 三执政官之一 ‖~ship *n.* 领事职位; 领事任期

consular ['kɔnsjulə] *a.* 领事(馆)的, 领事职权的: a ～ court 领事法庭 / ～ jurisdiction 领事裁判权

consulate ['kɔnsjulit] *n.* ①领事馆: a ～ general 总领事馆 ②领事职位; 领事任期 ③[the C-]【史】(一七九九至一八〇四年间法国的) 执政府

consult [kən'sʌlt] **I** ❶ *vi.* ①商量, 磋商; 协商: ～ with the masses 同群众商量 ②会诊 ❷ *vt.* ①向…商量, 请教, 询问; 找(医生)看病: ～ a veteran worker 请教老工人 ②查阅(词典、书籍等) ③考虑: ～ sb.'s convenience (wishes) 考虑到某人的便利(愿望) **II** *n.* =consultation ‖~ one's pillow 通夜思考 ‖~able *a.* 可与之商量的; 可被咨询的 / ~ee [,kɔnsʌl'ti:] *n.* 被商量者, 顾问 / ~er *n.* 向人商量者; 查阅者 / ~ing *a.* 咨询的; 顾问的: a ～ing engineer 顾问工程师 / ~ing room 【医】诊察室

consultant [kən'sʌltənt] *n.* ①请教者; 查阅者; 商议者 ②顾问 ③会诊医生, 顾问医生

consultation [,kɔnsəl'teiʃən] *n.* ①商量, 磋商: democratic ～ 民主协商 ②评议会, (专家等的)会议 ③【医】会诊

consume [kən'sju:m] ❶ *vt.* ①消费; 消耗; 浪费: 吃光, 喝光 ②消灭, 毁灭 ❷ *vi.* 消灭, 毁灭; 消磨; (花、叶等)枯萎 (away) ‖be ～d with 被…所吞噬; 因(忧愁、妒嫉等)而变得憔悴

consumer [kən'sju:mə] *n.* 消费者, 用户: a ～s' cooperative 消费合作社 / ～ credit 对于分期付款的主顾的信用 / ～ goods 消费品, 生活资料 / ～ prices 日用品价格 ‖con'sumer-,city *n.* 消费城市

consummate [kən'sʌmit] **I** *a.* ①完全无缺的, 圆满的 ②极为精通的, 老于此道的 ③尽善尽美的, 无比的 **II** ['kɔnsʌmeit] *vt.* 完成; 使完善, 使(愉快等)达顶点 ‖~ly *ad.* / consummation [,kɔnsʌ'meiʃən] *n.* 完成, 结果; 完美, 极致 / consummator ['kɔnsʌmeitə] *n.* (圆满)完成者

consumption [kən'sʌmpʃən] *n.* ①消费(量); 消耗: the coal ～ of a machine 机器的耗煤量 / ～ goods 消费品, 生活资料 ②【医】肺结核; 结核病

consumptive [kən'sʌmptiv] **I** *a.* ①消费的; 消耗性的 ②肺结核的; 患结核病的 **II** *n.* 肺结核病人 ‖~ly *ad.*

contact ['kɔntækt] **I** *n.* ①接触; 联络, 联系: be in (out of) ～ with 与…在接触中(失去联系) / come into ～ with many new ideas 接触到许多新思想 / The pilot tried to make ～ with his base. 飞行员试图与基地联系。/ first ～ 【天】(日、月食中的)初亏 ②交往, 交际 ③【电】接点, 触点; 接触通电; 接触器: make (break) ～ 通(断)电 ④(从飞机上对地面等的)目力观察: fly by ～ 依靠目力观察而不是依靠仪器来飞行 ⑤【数】相切 ⑥【医】曾与传染病接触者 ⑦熟人(尤指有权有势者); 门路 **II** [kən'tækt] ❶ *vt.* 使接触; 与…接触, 与…联系: For further details, please ～ our local office. 详情请向我们当地的分支机构探询。❷ *vi.* 接触, 联系 **III** *a.* 保持接触的, 有联系的; 由接触而引起的: a ～ battle 遭遇战 / ～ resin 接触成型树脂, 触压树脂 **IV** *ad.* 用目力观察(飞行): The ceiling was so low that the patrol was flown ～. 云层很低, 巡逻机只好进行目视飞行。[kən'tækt] *int.* 开动(叫飞机发动的信号) ‖~or [kən'tæktə] *n.* 【电】接触器, 开关 ‖~ agent ①【化】接触剂 ②【军】卫生联络员 / ～ breaker 【电】接触断路器 / ～ flying 【空】目力飞行, 目视飞行 / ～ lenses ①(直接附在眼球上的)无形眼镜 ②接触透镜 / ～ maker 【电】断续器, 断路器 / ～ officer 联络军官 / ～ potential 【电】接触电位 / ～ twin 【矿】接触双晶

contagion [kən'teidʒən] *n.* ①(接触)传染; 传染病; 传染病毒 ②(学说、思想、感情、谣言等的)蔓延; 感染, 传播 ③毒; 歪风; 腐败势力

contagious [kən'teidʒəs] *a.* ①(接触)传染的; (有)传染性的; 有感染力的: a ～ disease 传染病 / ～ laughter 有感染力的笑声 ②为对付传染病用的: a ～ ward 传染病房 ‖~ly *ad.* / ~ness *n.* ‖~ abortion 造成家畜流产的传染性疾病

contain [kən'tein] ❶ *vt.* ①包含; 容纳: This box ～s soap. 这只箱子装有肥皂。/ Sea water ～s salt. 海水含有盐分。/ The angle is ～ed by the lines AB and AC. 此角由直线 AB 和 AC 构成。②等于; 相当于 ③控制, 抑制, 遏制; 【军】牵制: He couldn't ～ himself for joy. 他高兴得不能自制。/ a ～ing force 牵制部队 ④【数】被…除尽: Ten ～s five and two. 十可被五和二除尽。❷ *vi.* 自制 ‖~er *n.* ①容器 ②【交】集装箱: a ～er ship 集装箱船

contaminate [kən'tæmineit] *vt.* ①弄脏; 沾污, 污染; 传染: a ～d zone 污染地带 ②毒害 ‖contamination [kən,tæmi'neiʃən] *n.* ①污染; 沾染物: radioactive contamination 放射性沾染 ②(文章等的)拼凑 / contaminative *a.* 污染的; (把东西)弄脏的 / contaminator *n.* 污染物, 沾染物

contemplate ['kɔntempleit] ❶ *vt.* ①注视, 凝视 ②沉思 ③期待, 期望; 反复打算: ～ a purchase 打算买某件东西 ❷ *vi.* 冥思苦想, 仔细考虑 ‖contemplator *n.* 沉思者, 冥想者

contemplation [,kɔntem'pleiʃən] *n.* ①注视 ②沉思, 冥想, 仔细考虑: be lost in ～ 想得出了神 ③期望, 打算, 意图: new work under (或 in) ～ 在计划中的新工作 ④【宗】默祷; 感到神之存在

contemplative ['kɔntempleitiv] *a.* ①沉思的; 好沉思的 ②【宗】忏悔祈祷的 ‖~ly *ad.* / ~ness *n.*

contemporaneous [kən,tempə'reinjəs] *a.* 同时期的, 同时代的; 同时发生的 (with) ‖~ly *ad.* / ~ness *n.*

contemporary [kən'tempərəri] I *a.* ① 当代的 ② 同时代的，同年龄的: be ~ *with* 与…同时代 II *n.* ① 同时代(或时期)的人；同年龄的人: He and I were *contemporaries* at school. 他和我是同期同学。② 同时期的东西(如同时期发行的报刊等)

contempt [kən'tempt] *n.* ① 轻视，轻蔑: show ~ for sth. 对某事物表示轻视 / hold sb. in ~ 蔑视某人 / be beneath ~ 不值得一顾 ② 受辱，丢脸: bring sb. into ~ 使某人受辱(或丢脸) ③ 不顾；不尊敬: in ~ of danger 不顾危险 / ~ of court 藐视法庭(罪)

contemptible [kən'temptəbl] *a.* 卑鄙的，不齿的，可轻视的 ‖**contemptibility** [kən,temptə'biliti], **~ness** *n.* / **contemptibly** *ad.*

contemptuous [kən'temptjuəs] *a.* 轻视的，轻蔑的；傲慢的 ‖**~ly** *ad.* / **~ness** *n.*

contend [kən'tend] ❶ *vi.* ① 竞争，斗争: ~ for spheres of influence 争夺势力范围 / ~ with (或 against) difficulties 向困难作斗争 / the ~ing armies 敌对的两军 ② 争论: the two ~ing sides 争论的双方 ❷ *vt.* 坚决主张；为…力争 ‖**~er** *n.* 竞争者，斗争者；争论者

content¹ ['kɔntent] *n.* ① 容量；含量: moisture ~ 含水量；含湿度 / the sugar ~ per *mu* of beet 每亩甜菜的产糖量 ② 内容；[常用复]容纳的东西；(书刊等的)目录: the unity of political ~ and artistic form 政治内容和艺术形式的统一 / the ~s of a room 房间里的东西 / (a table of) ~s 目录，目次 ③ 要旨，要意: the ~ of an article 文章的要旨

content² [kən'tent] I *a.* ① 满足的，满意的；甘愿的: be (或 rest) ~ *with* 以…为满足 / I should be well ~ to do so. 我很愿意这样干。② 赞成[(英国上议院用语) II *vt.* 使满足；[~ oneself]满足: We should never ~ *ourselves with* book knowledge only. 我们切不可满足于仅仅有一点书本知识。III *n.* ① 满足，满意 ② [英]赞成票 ‖*to one's heart's* ~ 尽情地，心满意足地: sing *to one's heart's* ~ 纵情歌唱

contention [kən'tenʃən] *n.* ① 竞争，斗争；争论 ② (争论中的)论点

contentious [kən'tenʃəs] *a.* ① 好争论的 ② 引起争论的: a ~ clause in a treaty 条约中有争议的条款 ‖**~ly** *ad.* / **~ness** *n.*

contentment [kən'tentmənt] *n.* ① 满足，满意 ② 使人满意的事物

contest [kən'test] I ❶ *vt.* ① 争夺(土地，阵地，胜利等): ~ every inch of land 寸土必争 ② 辩驳，争议 ❷ *vi.* 争夺(*with, against*) II ['kɔntest] *n.* ① 争夺 ② 竞赛，比赛: a ~ of strength (speed) 力量(速度)的竞赛 ‖**~able** *a.* 可争论的；可竞争的

contestant [kən'testənt] *n.* 竞争者；参加比赛者

context ['kɔntekst] *n.* ①(文章的)上下文，前后关系: quote a remark out of its ~ 脱离上下文引

用一句话，断章取义 / guess the meaning of a word from the ~ 从上下文猜出一个词的意义 ②(事物等发生的)来龙去脉

contiguity [,kɔnti'gju(ː)iti] *n.* 接触；邻近，接近

contiguous [kən'tigjuəs] *a.* 接触着的；邻近的，接近的: ~ angle 【数】邻角 ‖**~ly** *ad.* / **~ness** *n.*

continence ['kɔntinəns] *n.* ① 自制，克制；节欲 ② 节制行

continent¹ ['kɔntinənt] *a.* 自制的，克制的；节欲的 ‖**~ly** *ad.*

continent² ['kɔntinənt] *n.* ① 大陆，陆地；大洲: the ~ of Asia 亚洲(大陆) ② [the C-] 欧洲大陆

continental [,kɔnti'nentl] I *a.* ① 大陆的；大陆性的: ~ climate 大陆性气候 ② [常作 C-] 欧洲大陆的 ③ [C-] (美国独立战争时期)美洲殖民地的 II *n.* ① 欧洲大陆人 ② [常作 C-] 美国独立战争中的美国士兵 ③ 美国独立战争时期发行的钞票 ④ [C-] [美俚]一种起源于英国后传至欧洲大陆的男子方式 ‖*not care a* ~ [美俚]毫无关系，毫不介意 / *not worth a* ~ [美俚]毫无价值 ‖**~ly** *ad.* ‖~ **code** 【讯】大陆电码(即国际莫尔斯电码) / ~ **drift** 【地】大陆漂移 / ~ **facies** 【地】陆相 / ~ **shelf** 【地】大陆架

contingency [kən'tindʒənsi] *n.* ① 偶然，偶然性；可能，可能性: necessity and ~ 必然性和偶然性 ② 偶然发生的事，意外事故: be prepared for any ~ 准备应付任何意外事故，以防万一 / in case of ~ 万一 ‖~ **fund** 应急费用 / ~ **reserve** 应急储备金

contingent [kən'tindʒənt] I *a.* ① 可能发生的，可能的；偶然的，意外的: a ~ event 意外事件 ② 应急的，应急用的: a ~ fund 应急费用 ③ 因事而变的，有条件的；伴随的: be ~ *on* (或 *upon*) 依…而定 ④ 不是逻辑上必然的 II *n.* ① 意外事情，偶然事故 ② 小分队，分遣部队，分遣舰队；(派遣的)代表团 ‖**~ly** *ad.* ‖~ **fee** 成功酬金(如胜诉后付给律师的酬金)

continual [kən'tinjuəl] *a.* 不断的，连续的；频繁的 ‖**~ly** *ad.*

continuance [kən'tinjuəns] *n.* ① 继续，连续，持续: a ~ of bumper harvests 连年丰收 ② 持续的时间: of long ~ 持续很久的 ③ 逗留，停留 ④【律】诉讼延期

continuation [kən,tinju'eiʃən] *n.* ① 继续，连续，持续: The ~ of the meeting was delayed until the next day. 会议延至第二天继续进行。② 继续部分；延长物；扩建物；增加物: a ~ of a story 故事的续篇 / a ~ *to* a workshop 车间的扩建部分 ‖~ **school** 业余补习学校

continue [kən'tinju(ː)] ❶ *vi.* ① 继续，连续；延伸，延长: They ~d on for a mile. 他们又继续向前行进了一哩路。/ The rain ~d (for) two days. 雨连续下了两天。/ How far does this road ~? 这条路全长多少? (或：这条路通到哪里?) ② 留，依旧: ~ at one's post 留任 / The weather ~d fine. 天气仍然很好。❷ *vt.* ① 使继续，使连续；

使延伸,使延长: ～ doing (或 to do) sth. 继续做某事 / ～ one's subscription to the magazine for another year 续订该杂志一年 / To be ～d. (未完)待续。 / ～d from (on) page 15 上接(下转)第十五页 ②使留下,挽留: be ～d in office 被挽留继续任职 ③【律】使(诉讼)延期

continuing [kən'tinjuiŋ] *a.* 继续的,连续的,持续的 ‖～ **education** [美] (为使受教育者学得最新的知识和技能的)进修教育

continuity [ˌkɔnti'njuːiti] *n.* ①继续(性),连续(性),持续(性) ②电影分镜头剧本; 剧情说明 ③广播节目之间的说明词(或音乐) ④连环画的故事情节和对话

continuous [kən'tinjuəs] *a.* 继续的,连续的,持续的; 延伸的,延长的: ～ development 不断的发展 / ～ escort 【军】全航线护送 / ～ function 【数】连续函数 / ～ spectrum 【物】连续光谱 / ～ current 【电】恒向电流,直流 / the ～ tense 【语】进行时 ‖～**ly** *ad.* / ～**ness** *n.*

contort [kən'tɔ:t] ❶ *vt.* 扭弯,弄歪;曲解: a face ～ed with anger 因气愤而变得异样的脸 / a word out of its ordinary meaning 曲解词义 ❷ *vi.* 扭弯,弄歪 ‖～**ive** *a.*

contortion [kən'tɔ:ʃən] *n.* 扭弯,弄歪;曲解 ‖～**ist** *n.* 善作柔体表演的杂技演员

contour ['kɔntuə] **I** *n.* ①轮廓,外形;轮廓线,周线 ②等高线;恒值线 ③【讯】(电视台服务区的)等场强线 **II** *vt.* ①画…的轮廓,使与轮廓相符 ②循等高线修筑(道路等) **III** *a.* ①使与轮廓相符的 ②(为防止雨水冲蚀)循等高线开沟的 ‖～ **line** 等高线;恒值线;轮廓线 / ～ **map** 等高线(地)图 / ～ **pen** 曲线笔

contra ['kɔntrə] **I** *prep.* & *ad.* 相反(地),反对(地) **II** *n.* ①相反,反对;相反的事物: pros and ～s (常写作 pros and cons) 赞成和反对的论点 ②【会计】对方(尤指贷方)

contraband ['kɔntrəbænd] **I** *n.* ①走私,非法的买卖;非法的运输 ②禁运品,违禁品,走私货: ～ of war 战时禁运品 ③美国南北战争时逃入(或被北军带入)北军战线内的黑人 **II** *a.* 禁运的,非法买卖的 ‖～**ist** *n.* 走私者,违禁品买卖者

contract ['kɔntrækt] **I** *n.* ①契约,合同: make (或 enter into) a ～ with sb. 与某人订立契约 / sign a ～ 签订契约 / a breach of ～ 违约行为 / a bear ～ 【律】无条件契约 / 承包契约: be built by ～ (被)包工建筑 ③婚约 ④【律】契约法 ⑤(桥牌)合约(指约定要打到的副数); 合约桥牌(=～ bridge) ⑥[美俚]小思小惠,贿赂 ⑦[语]缩约词,缩约形式 **II** [kən'trækt] ❶ *vt.* ①缔结;订(约): ～ an alliance 结盟 / ～ a marriage 订婚约 / ～ a friendship (an acquaintance) with sb. 与某人结交(结识) ②承包,承办;把(工程等)包给 (to): ～ a project (out) to a building company 把工程包给一家建筑公司 ③把…许配给,使订婚约 (to) ④得(病),养成(习惯),负(债): ～ pneumonia 得肺炎 ⑤使缩小,使缩短: Low

temperature ～s metals. 低温使金属收缩。 / "I am" is sometimes ～ed to "I'm". "I am" 有时缩略为 "I'm"。 ⑥使蜷起来,使皱起;使变狭: ～ a muscle 使肌肉收缩 / ～ the brows 皱眉头 ⑦限定,限制 ❷ *vi.* ①订契约;承包,承办: ～ with a factory for ten lathes 向一家工厂订购十台车床 / ～ for the supply of raw materials to a factory 承办一家工厂原材料的供应 ②缩小,缩短; 皱起; 变狭 **III** *a.* 收缩了的,缩短了的;【语】缩约的: a ～ word 【语】缩约词 ‖～ (*oneself*) *out of* 约定使自己不受…的约束 / ～ *out* ①立契约把(工程等)包出 ②[主英]退出合约 ‖～**or** [kən'træktə] *n.* ①订约人 ②承包人,承包商,包工头 ③收缩物;收缩肌 ‖～ **bridge** 合约桥牌

contraction [kən'trækʃən] *n.* ①收缩,缩短;【医】挛缩 ②【语】缩约词,缩约形式 ③(病等的)传染;(债等的)招致 ④订约 ⑤营业缩减期,商业收缩期

contradict [ˌkɔntrə'dikt] ❶ *vt.* ①反驳; 否认 ②同…矛盾;同…抵触: ～ oneself 自相矛盾 / a construction directly ～ing basic grammar 直接违反基本语法的语言结构 ❷ *vi.* 反驳 ‖～**able** *a.* 可加以反驳的 / ～**or** *n.* 反驳者;相矛盾的人;抵触因素

contradiction [ˌkɔntrə'dikʃən] *n.* ①矛盾: the universality (absoluteness) of ～ 矛盾的普遍性(绝对性) / the principal ～ 主要矛盾 / an antagonistic ～ 对抗性矛盾 / a thing full of ～s 充满矛盾的事物 ②否认; 反驳; 抵触: a flat ～ 直截了当的反驳 / in ～ with 与…矛盾着, 与…相抵触 ③自相矛盾的说法: a ～ in terms 语词矛盾的说法(如 a round square 一个圆形的正方形)

contradictory [ˌkɔntrə'diktəri] **I** *a.* ①矛盾的,对立的;引起(或构成)矛盾的: ～ elements 相互矛盾着的各种因素 ②爱反驳别人的 **II** *n.* ①矛盾因素,抵触因素;对立物 ②矛盾的说法;【逻】矛盾命题 ‖**contradictorily** *ad.* / **contradictoriness** *n.*

contralto [kən'træltou] **I** *n.* 女低音;女低音歌手;(歌剧中的)女低音角色 **II** *a.* 女低音的

contraption [kən'træpʃən] *n.* [贬][谑]奇妙的装置,新发明的玩意儿

contrarily *ad.* ① ['kɔntrərili] 相反地,相对立地 ② [kən'trɛərili] 故意作对地

contrary ['kɔntrəri] **I** *a.* ①相反的,相对的,对抗的: The result is ～ to expectation. 结果与预料恰好相反。 ②逆行的; 逆的: a ～ wind (current) 逆风(逆流) ③ [kən'trɛəri] 故意作对的 **II** *n.* ① [the ～] 相反;反面,对立面: An examination of the facts proves the ～. 仔细考察事实之后发现情况正好相反。 ②[复]相反事物 ③【逻】反对命题 **III** *ad.* 相反地: go (或 run) ～ to sb.'s interests 违反某人利益 ‖*by contraries* ①和预料相反地 ②相反地: interpret *by contraries* 从反面解释 / *on the* ～ 正相反: A: Are you nearly through? B: *On the ~*, I've only just begun. 甲: 你快干完了吗? 乙: 恰恰相反, 我才刚刚开始呢。/ *quite the ~* 恰恰相反 / *to the ~* 意思相反的(地): I know nothing *to the ~*. 我不知道任何相反的情况。/ Go ahead unless (you are) advised *to the ~*. 如果没有相反的通知, 你们就干起来好了。

contrast I ['kɒntræst] *n.* ①对比, 对照; (对照之下形成的)悬殊差别: There can be no differentiation without ~. 有比较才能鉴别。/ present a striking ~ between A and B 使甲乙两者形成鲜明的对照 ②大不相同的人(或物) ③【物】衬比; 【摄】反差 II [kən'træst] ❶ *vt.* 使对比, 使对照 ❷ *vi.* 形成对照: ~ sharply *with* 与…形成鲜明对照 ‖*gain by* ~ 对比之下显出其长处 / *in* ~ *with* 与…形成对照 ‖*~ive* [kən'træstiv] *a.*

contravene [ˌkɒntrə'viːn] *vt.* ①违反, 触犯(法律等) ②否认; 反驳(建议等) ③抵触, 与…冲突

contravention [ˌkɒntrə'venʃən] *n.* ①违反, 触犯 ②反驳

contretemps ['kɔ̃ːntrətɑ̃ːŋ] ([复] contretemps ['kɔ̃ːntrətɑ̃ːŋz]) *n.* 【法】①来得不巧的事情, 不幸的意外事 ②【音】切分音法

contribute [kən'tribju(ː)t] ❶ *vt.* ①(为集体事情)贡献出: Every one is called on to ~ ideas. 要求人人出主意, 想办法。/ ~ information 自愿提供情况 / ~ one's share 出自己应尽的一份力量 ②捐(款) ③投(稿): ~ a poem to a newspaper 向报社投一篇诗稿 / a ~d article 来稿 ❷ *vi.* ①出一份力; 起一份作用: The exchange of goodwill missions greatly ~s to (或 towards) a better understanding between the two countries. 互派友好代表团大大有助于两国的相互了解。②捐献; 捐钱: ~ much (或 heavily) to a fund 为一笔基金提供大量捐款 ③投稿 ‖**contributing** *a.* ①贡献(或捐献)的; 起一份作用的: a contributing factor in the growth of the city 在城市发展过程中起作用的一个因素 ②经常投稿的: a contributing editor 特约编辑; 特约撰稿者 / **contributor** *n.* 投稿者; 捐助者

contribution [ˌkɒntri'bjuːʃən] *n.* ①贡献; 捐献, 捐助; 贡献物; 捐献物 ②投稿; 投寄的来稿 ③(向占领地人民强迫征收给驻军的)特别税 ‖*lay under* ~ 强迫…付特别税

contributory [kən'tribjutəri] I *a.* ①贡献的; 捐助的 ②应作一份贡献的; 应捐助的 ③起一份作用的; 有助于…的 (*to*): ~ negligence 【律】(车祸案等中)受伤方自己的粗心 II *n.* ①贡献者; 捐助者 ②【律】(企业倒闭时)负连带偿还责任的人 ③起作用的因素

contrite ['kɒntrait] *a.* 悔悟的; 由悔悟引起的 ‖*~ly* *ad.* / *~ness* *n.* / **contrition** [kən'triʃən] *n.* 悔悟, 后悔

contrivance [kən'traivəns] *n.* ①发明; 设计 ②发明(或设计)的能力 ③发明物; 机械装置 ④人为状态; 人为的修饰: tell a story without dramatic

~s 不加渲染地讲一个故事 ⑤诡计

contrive [kən'traiv] ❶ *vt.* ①发明; 设计; 造出; 策划 ②设法做到; 竟然弄到…的地步: Can you ~ to be there by six? 你能设法在六点钟赶到那里吗? / How could you ~ to make such a mess of things? 你怎么会把事情弄得这样糟糕的? ❷ *vi.* ①设计; 图谋 ②设法对付过去: I can ~ without it. 没有这个我也行。‖*~d* *a.* 人造的; 不自然的 / *~r* *n.* 发明者; 设计者; 制造者; 持家人

control [kən'troul] I (controlled; controlling) *vt.* ①控制; 支配: The machine is automatically controlled. 这机器是自动控制的。②管理(物价等) ③抑制(感情等): ~ oneself (或 one's feelings) 抑制自己的感情 ④(用对照物)核实, 检验 II *n.* ①控制; 支配; 调节; 抑制; [常用复]控制的手段(或措施): have (no) ~ over (或 of) 能(不能)控制… / lose ~ of 失去对…的控制 / price ~s 物价管理(的规定) ②[常用复]操纵装置, 控制器; (收音机)调节装置: be at the ~s of 掌握操纵器 / the ~s of an aircraft 飞机的操纵器 ③(实验的)对照, 对照物 ④赛车途中的停车站(供检修车辆等用) ‖*analog(ue)* ~ 模拟控制 / *birth* ~ 节制生育 / *closed (open) loop* ~ 闭(开)环控制 / *a* ~ *board* 控制板; 操纵台 / *a* ~ *column (或 stick)* (飞机的)操纵杆; 驾驶杆 / *a* ~ *experiment* 对照实验 / *a* ~ *figures* 控制数字 / *a* ~ *of light* 灯火管制 / *a* ~ *panel* 控制盘 / *a* ~ *plane* 操纵导弹的飞机 / *a* ~ *tower* 机场指挥塔台 / *digital* ~ 数字控制 / *fire* ~ 【军】火力控制 / *matching* ~ 【自】自动选配装置 / *military* ~ 军事管制 / *(numerical)* ~ *programme* ~ (数字)程序控制 / *quality* ~ 产品质量检查 / *remote* ~ 遥控 / *synchronizing* ~*s* 【无】同步调整装置 / *traffic* ~ 交通管理 ‖*beyond* ~ 无法控制 / *in* ~ *(of)* 控制(住); 管理: be *in* complete ~ *of* the situation 完全控制住局势 / Who is *in* ~ here? 这里谁负责? / *out of* ~ 不受控制: keep ... *under* ~ 对…加以控制 / *under the* ~ *of* 受…的管理; 受…的控制 ‖*~ment* *n.*

controller [kən'troulə] *n.* ①管理员 ②主计员; 审计官 ③操纵器, 控制器, 调节器 ④【船】(锚链的)掣链器

controversial [ˌkɒntrə'vəːʃəl] *a.* ①争论的 ②受争论的 ③引起争论的: a ~ issue (figure) 引起争论的问题(人物) ‖*~ism* *n.* 争论精神; 争论癖 / *~ist* *a.* 争论者 / *~ly* *ad.*

controversy ['kɒntrəvəsi] *n.* 争论, 论战; 争吵: It has evoked (或 given rise to) much ~. 这引起了很多争论。/ a ~ noised about throughout the scientific world 在科学界引起轩然大波的争论 / enter into (a) ~ with sb. over sth. 与某人就某事争论起来 / beyond ~ 无可争议

contumely ['kɒntju(ː)mli] *n.* 傲慢无礼, 谩骂, 侮辱

contuse [kən'tjuːz] *vt.* ①打伤(常指皮肉不破裂的内伤); 撞伤 ②【医】挫伤; 捣碎 ‖**contusion** [kən'tjuːʒən] *n.*

conundrum [kə'nʌndrəm] *n.* 谜；猜不透的难题；难答的问题

convalescent [ˌkɔnvə'lesnt] **I** *a.* 恢复健康的，渐愈的；恢复期的：a ~ hospital (或 home) 疗养院，休养所 **II** *n.* 恢复中的病人

convection [kən'vekʃən] *n.* ① 传送 ② (热、电等的)运流，对流 ③【气】对流

convector [kən'vektə] *n.* 热空气循环对流加热器

convene [kən'vi:n] **❶** *vt.* 召集；召唤；传(被告等) **❷** *vi.* 集合 ‖**~r** *n.* 会议召集人

convenience [kən'vi:njəns] **l** *n.* ①便利，方便；有便的时候，适当的机会：at one's (own) ~ (自己认为)最方便地(或最合适地) / for ~ 为了方便起见 / When will it suit your ~? 什么时候对你方便? / Please reply at your earliest ~. (书信用语)请尽早回信。/ Come whenever it is to your ~. 你什么时候方便，就什么时候来。②便利设施；厕所：Gas is one of the modern ~s the newly-built house provides. 这座新造的房屋装有煤气等现代化设备。**II** *vt.* 为…提供方便 ‖*make a ~ of sb.* 利用某人

convenient [kən'vi:njənt] *a.* ① 便利的，方便的；合适的：if it is ~ to you 如果你方便的话 ② 近便的，附近的 ③适合于一时情况需要的，实用主义的 ‖**~ly** *ad.*

convent ['kɔnvənt] *n.* 女修道院；女修道会：enter a ~ 当修女

convention [kən'venʃən] *n.* ①(政治、宗教、政党等的)会议，大会；全国性大会 ② 召集，集会 ③公约；(换俘、停战等的)协定：the Geneva *Conventions* 日内瓦公约 ④ 惯例，习俗；常规 ⑤(打桥牌等时)叫牌的一套常规

conventional [kən'venʃənl] *a.* ①惯例的，常规的；普通平凡的：a ~ war 常规战争 / ~ weapons 常规武器 ②(艺术等)因袭的，传统的 ③ 协定的 ‖**~ism** *n.* 依从俗例；因袭主义 / **~ist** *n.* 依从俗例的人；因袭主义者 / **~ity** [kənˌvenʃə'næliti] *n.* ① 惯例性；因袭性 ② 习俗，老一套的行为 / **~ize** *vt.* 使照惯例；使习俗化 / **~ly** *ad.*

converge [kən'və:dʒ] **❶** *vi.* ① 会聚，集中；为共同利益而结合在一起 ②【数】【物】收敛 **❷** *vt.* 使集中于一点；使会聚

conversant [kən'və:sənt] *a.* 熟悉的，精通的 (*with*)

conversation [ˌkɔnvə'seiʃən] *n.* ① 会话，谈话；非正式会谈：have (或 hold) a ~ with 与…会谈；与…谈话 / in ~ with 和…谈话 ② 社交；性交：criminal ~ 【律】通奸 ‖**~ piece** ①一种风俗画 ②(尤指室内的)易引起话题的东西

conversational [ˌkɔnvə'seiʃənl] *a.* ①会话的，交谈的 ②健谈的 ‖**~ly** *ad.*

converse[1] ['kɔn'və:s] *vi.* ①交谈，谈话 (*with, on, about*) ②认识，熟识 **II** ['kɔnvə:s] *n.* 交谈

converse[2] ['kɔnvə:s] **I** *a.* 相反的，颠倒的，逆的：~ theorem 【数】逆定理 **II** *n.* ①【逻】反题 ②【数】逆，反 ‖**~ly** *ad.*

conversion [kən'və:ʃən] *n.* ① 变换，转化：the ~ of water into ice 水的变成冰 / ~ training 【军】改装训练；(英军)改装训练班 ② (对教徒的)改依；(宗教、党派、意见、信仰等的)改变 ③兑换，更换 ④【逻】换位法；【数】换算：~ table 换算表 ⑤【心】转变性：~ hysteria 转变性歇斯底里 ⑥(橄榄球的)触地得分；(篮球的)罚球得分

convert I [kən'və:t] **❶** *vt.* ① 转变，变换：~ alkaline land into good fields 把碱地改变为良田 ②使皈依宗教；(在宗教、党派、意见、信仰等方面)使改变 ③兑换 ④【逻】使换位 ⑤强占 ⑥(橄榄球)使触地得分 **❷** *vi.* 皈依；改变信仰 **II** ['kɔnvə:t] *n.* 皈依宗教者；改变信仰者

convertible [kən'və:təbl] **I** *a.* ① 可改变的，可变换的：~ husbandry 【农】轮作 / a ~ vehicle 【军】两用车辆(可从轮胎型转变为履带型的卡车) ②可兑换的 ③车篷可折叠(或取掉)的 **II** *n.* 可改变的事物；篷汽车 ‖**convertibility** [kənˌvə:tə'biliti] *n.* 可改变(性)，可变换(性) / **convertibly** *ad.*

convex ['kɔn'veks] **I** *a.* 凸的，凸面的，凸圆的：a ~ lens 凸透镜 **II** *n.* 凸面，凸圆体，凸状 ‖**~ity** [kɔn'veksiti] *n.* 凸，凸状 / **~ly** *ad.*

convey [kən'vei] *vt.* ①运送(旅客、货物等)；搬运，转运 ② 转达，传达，传送(思想、感情等)：~ one's deepest sympathy to 向…表示深切慰问 / Every word ~s some meaning. 每一个词都有某种意义。③ 传播(声音等) ④【律】转让(财产等) ‖**~able** *a.* 能传达的；可转让的 / **~er, ~or** *n.* ①搬运者；传达者；转让财产者 ② 输送机，输送设备

conveyance [kən'veiəns] *n.* ① 运输，搬运 ② (思想、感情等的)传达，传播 ③运输工具(尤指车辆) ④【律】(财产等的)转让；转让证书

convict I [kən'vikt] **I** *vt.* ① 证明…有罪；宣判…有罪：~ sb. *of* 宣判某人有…罪 ② 使知罪 **II** ['kɔnvikt] *n.* ① 罪犯 ② 囚犯(常指长期被监禁者) ‖**~ive** *a.* 定罪的 / 使人信服的

conviction [kən'vikʃən] *n.* ①定罪，证明有罪 ②深信，确信：be open to ~ 愿意服理 / carry ~ 有说服力 / in the full ~ that 深信… ③服罪

convince [kən'vins] *vt.* ① 使确信，使信服：This ~d me of my honesty 这使我相信他确实是诚实的。② 使认识错误(或罪行)：He was ~d of his error. 他认识了错误。

convincing [kən'vinsiŋ] *a.* 有说服力的，使人信服的：a ~ argument 令人信服的论据 ‖**~ly** *ad.* / **~ness** *n.*

convivial [kən'viviəl] *a.* ① 欢宴的；欢乐的 ② 爱吃喝交际的；乐天的 ‖**~ist** *n.* 爱饮宴作乐的人 / **~ity** [kənˌvivi'æliti] *n.* ① 欢宴 ② 爱交际；乐天派性格 / **~ly** *ad.*

convocation [ˌkɔnvə'keiʃən] *n.* 召集；集会(尤指宗教会议或学校仪式) ‖**~al** *a.*

convoke [kən'vouk] *vt.* 召集…开会，召集(会议)

convoy ['kɔnvɔi] **I** *vt.* 替…护航；护送 **II** *n.* ①护航；护送：under the ~ of troops 在军队护

下 ② 护航队;护送队: a ～ ship 护航军舰 ③ 被
护航的船; 被护送的军队

convulse [kən'vʌls] *vt.* ① 使剧烈震动, 摇动: be
～*d* with laughter 笑得前仰后合 ② 使痉挛, 使
抽搐

convulsion [kən'vʌlʃən] *n.* ① 震动; 骚动;【地】灾
变 ② [复]大笑: He was in (was thrown into)
～*s*. 他(被引得)捧腹大笑。③ [常用复]痉挛,
惊厥: fall into ～*s* 发惊厥 ‖～**ary** *a.*

convulsive [kən'vʌlsiv] *a.* ①震动的; 起痉挛的 ②
(笑)使人前仰后合的 ‖～**ly** *ad.* / ～**ness** *n.*

coo [ku:] I ❶ *vi.* ①(鸽)咕咕地叫 ②谈情话: bill
and ～ 喁喁情话; 喁喁细语 ❷ *vt.* 温柔爱恋地
说; 轻轻地说: ～ one's words 轻轻地说话 II *n.*
鸽子的叫声; 鸽子叫似的轻音

cook [kuk] I ❶ *vt.* ① 烹调, 煮, 烧 ②窜改, 伪造
(帐目等) ③[俚]损坏, 毁坏 ④ [俚]给…上电刑
❷ *vi.* ①(食物)在煮着; 适合烹调 ②烧菜, 做菜
③发生: What's ～*ing*? [美俚]发生了什么事?
④[俚]失败, 完蛋 II *n.* ① 炊事员 厨师: a mess
～ 炊事兵 / a plain ～ 家庭厨师 ②(工业、技术
上的)烧煮过程 ‖*a cold* ～ 做殡仪馆生意的人 /
～ *sb.'s goose* ①干掉某人 ② 彻底挫败某人的
计划(或希望等) / ～ *up* [口]造出; 伪造, 虚构:
～ *up* a story 编造一个故事 / *Too many* ～*s*
spoil the broth. [谚]厨师多毁坏汤。‖～**ed** *a.*
①精疲力竭的; 未达到目的就完蛋的; 被捕得昏厥
的 ②喝醉了的 ‖'～**book** *n.* 食谱 /
'～**house** *n.* 厨房, 船内厨房;【军】野外烧煮场 /
'～**out** *n.* 在外面野餐的郊游 / '～**room** *n.* ＝
～house / '～**shop** *n.* 菜馆,饭店

cooker ['kukə] *n.* ① 炊事用具(尤指炉、锅等) ②
烹饪用水果 ③ 窜改者,伪造者

cookery ['kukəri] *n.* ① 烹调法 ② 烹调的地方
‖'～**book** *n.* 烹调书

cool [ku:l] I *a.* ① 凉的, 凉快的: ～ clothes 凉快
的衣服 ② 冷静的, 沉着的: Keep ～! 镇定! /
keep one's head ～ 保持冷静的头脑 ③ 冷淡的;
give sb. a ～ reception 给某人以冷淡的接待 ④
厚脸皮的 ⑤ (颜色)给人凉感的(如蓝、绿、灰等)
⑥有冷藏设施的; 冷藏着的 ⑦(音乐、绘画等)缺
乏感情的;强调理性的 ⑧(数额等)不折不扣的,整
整的 ⑨[美俚]极妙的 ⑩(动物的嗅迹)已极微弱
的 II ❶ *vi.* ①变凉; 冷却下来 ②(怒气等)平息;
(人)平静下来; 失去热情: Has his anger ～*ed* yet?
他息怒了没有? / He gradually ～*ed on* the
project. 他对那项计划逐渐不热心了。❷ *vt.* ①
使凉快; 使冷却 / ～ an engine with water 用水
使引擎冷却 ②使(怒气等)平息;使平静下来 ③
[美俚]杀掉 ④ [美俚]在(考试等)中失败; 失去
(机会等) III *n.* ① 凉; 凉快的地方(或时候、东
西等): the ～ of a summer evening 夏日夜晚的
凉爽 ②平静, 镇静 ③(二十世纪五十年代美国流
行的) 一种接近古典派的较保守的爵士音乐 ‖*as*
～ *as a cucumber* 泰然自若, 极为冷静 / ～
down (或 *off*) ①(使)变冷; (使)渐渐冷却 ②

(使)平静下来 / ～ *it* 放松(或放慢)下来;平静下
来 / ～ *one's coppers* 喝解酒饮料润喉 / ～
one's heels 见 **heel**¹ / *leave sb.* ～ 引不起某人
兴趣, 不能打动某人 / *play it* ～ [美俚]抑制住
感情;持清高冷漠态度;不表态 ‖～**ing** *n.* & *a.*
冷却(的): double-water internal ～*ing*【机】双水
内冷(的) / ～**ly** *ad.* / ～**ness** *n.* ‖'～-'**headed**
a. 头脑冷静的

cooler ['ku:lə] *n.* ① 冷却器; 冰箱 ②[俚]监狱,单
人监房 ③ 冷饮品; 冷饮酒类 ④【化】冷却剂

coolie ['ku:li] *n.* 苦力

coop [ku:p] I *n.* ① (关家禽的)笼, 棚; 家禽养殖
场 ②[英]捕鱼的笼 ③禁闭地区;[俚]监狱 II *vt.*
① 把(家禽)关进笼子(或棚) ② 把…禁闭(或禁
锢)起来: ～ *up* the mind in 把思想束缚在…之
中 ‖*fly the* ～ [美俚]逃走

cooper ['ku:pə] I *n.* 制桶工人, 修桶工人: a dry
(wet) ～ 干品用(液体用)桶类的制造工 / a white
～ 普通箍匠 II ❶ *vt.* ①制造(桶类), 修(桶) ②
把…装入桶内 (*up*) ③ 挫败; 毁掉 ❷ *vi.* 做桶,
修桶 ‖～**age** ['ku:pəridʒ] *n.* ① 制桶工场 ②制
桶业 ③ 制桶工钱 ④ [总称]桶

cooperate [kou'ɔpəreit] *vi.* ① 合作, 协作: ～
harmoniously with sb. 与某人和谐地合作 / ～
with sb. in working out a plan 与某人合作拟出
一项计划 ②(事物)配合: Everything ～*d* to
make the evening party a success. 各种因素配
合起来使晚会非常成功。‖**cooperator** *n.* (产
销)合作社社员; 合作者

cooperation [kou,ɔpə'reiʃən] *n.* ① 合作, 协作:
agricultural ～ 农业合作化 / in ～ with 与…合
作,与…协同 ②【生】协同作用, 互助 ‖～**ist** *n.*
合作论者

cooperative [kou'ɔpərətiv] I *a.* ① 合作的, 协作
的; 合作化的: ～ efforts 共同努力 / ～ medical
service 合作医疗(制度) ② 抱合作态度的: The
surgeons found the patient very ～. 外科医生
们发现病人与他们合作得很好。③ [美](大学文
科)有关(或包含)各种实习活动的 II *n.* 合作团
体;合作社: a credit ～ 信用合作社 / an advanced
(elementary) agricultural producers' ～ 高级(初
级)农业生产合作社 ‖～**ly** *ad.* / ～**ness** *n.*

co-opt [kou'ɔpt] *vt.* ①(某一组织的原有成员)增
选(某人)为成员 ②指派, 指定…为代表 ③吸收,
把…同化过来; 接收; 占有 ‖～**ation** [,kouɔp-
'teiʃən], ～**ion** [kou'ɔpʃən] *n.* (原有成员对新成员
的)增选 / ～**ative**, ～**ive** *a.* 增选的

coordinate [kou'ɔ:dinit] I *a.* ①同等的;【语】并
列的: a ～ clause 并列子句 ②【数】坐标的
II *n.* ①同等的人(或事物) ②【数】坐标 III [kou-
'ɔ:dineit] *vt.* & *vi.* (使) 成为同等; (使)协调
‖～**ly** *ad.* / **coordinative** [kou'ɔ:dineitiv] *a.* 使
同等的; 使协调的 / **coordinator** [kou'ɔ:dineitə]
n. ① 协调人 ②【语】并列连接词 ③【医】共济器

coordination [kou,ɔ:di'neiʃən] *n.* ①同等 ②调整,
配合;【医】共同调济,共济,共济官能 ③协作,协调

cope[1] [koup] *vi.* (机会均等地)竞争; 对付, 妥善处理 (*with*): know how to ~ *with* a complicated situation 知道如何应付复杂局面 / ~ *with* difficulties (设法)克服困难 / Yes, I can ~. 是的, 我能对付.

cope[2] [koup] I *n.* ①(教士的)斗篷式长袍 ②[喻]笼罩, 遮盖物: the ~ of night 夜幕 / under the ~ of heaven 蓝天之下 ③【建】顶层, 墙帽 ④ 铸模的上型箱 II ❶ *vt.* 加盖于…; 给…盖筑顶层 ❷ *vi.* 如墙帽般突出 (over) 【建】(墙等的)盖顶, 墩檐, 墙帽 ||'~stone *n.* 盖石, 墙帽

copious ['koupjəs] *a.* ① 丰富的, 富饶的; (语言)词汇丰富的 ②(文词)冗长的 ③大量的 ④满腹经纶的 ||~ly *ad.* / ~ness *n.*

copper[1] ['kɔpə] I *n.* ①铜: a ~ furnace 冶铜炉 / ~ sulphate 硫酸铜 ②铜币; 铜容器; 铜制物 ③铜色 II *a.* 铜的; 铜制的; 铜色的: a ~ beech 叶色似铜的山毛榉 III *vt.* ① 涂铜于…; 用铜板包 (船底等) ②[美俚]下赌注于…上 ||a ~ *captain* [英]冒充有地位的人 / *cool one's* ~s 喝解渴饮料润喉 / *have hot* ~s 喝酒后嘴喉干燥 ||~ish ['kɔpəriʃ] *a.* 有点儿含铜的; 有点儿象铜的 / ~ize ['kɔpəraiz] *vt.* 镀铜于…; 用铜处理 / ~y ['kɔpəri] *a.* 含铜的; 象铜的 ||~ bit 铜焊头 / '~bottom *vt.* 用铜板包(船底等) / '~head *n.* 北美一种头呈铜色的毒蛇 / '~plate *n.* 铜板; 铜版 / '~skin *n.* 美洲印第安人 / '~smith *n.* 铜匠 / '~ wire 铜丝

copper[2] ['kɔpə] *n.* [美俚]警察

coppice ['kɔpis] *n.* ① 矮林, 小灌木林 ② 萌生林 ||'~-wood *n.* 小树丛, 矮树丛

copra ['kɔprə] *n.* 椰子仁干, 干椰肉

copse [kɔps] *n.* 矮林, 小灌木林 ||'~-wood *n.* 矮树丛

copy ['kɔpi] I *n.* ①抄本, 副本; 摹本, 复制品; (电影)拷贝: a clean (或 fair) ~ 誊清后的稿子 / a rough (或 foul) ~ 草稿 / make ten *copies* of a document 把文件复制十份 ②(书报等的)一本, 一册, 一份: a book printed in one million *copies* 印数一百万册的一本书 ③ (供排字付印的)稿子 ④ 范本, 字帖 II ❶ *vt.* ① 抄写, 誊写; 复制: ~ out a letter 把一封信全文抄下 ② 模仿; 抄袭 ❷ *vi.* ① 抄写, 誊写; 临摹 ② 模仿; 抄袭 ||hold ~ 当校对助手 / make good ~ 成为(记者等报道的)好材料 ||~ist *n.* ①抄写员; 复制者; (考试时)抄旁座试卷的作弊学生 ②依样画葫芦的人 ||'~book *n.* 习字帖: blot one's ~book 弄坏自己的名声, 失足 / '~cat *n.* 盲目的模仿者 / '~desk *n.* (报馆)编辑部 / '~holder *n.* ①【律】誊本保有权; 登录不动产保有权 ②校对助手 (向校对员读原稿的人) / '~reader *n.* (出版社、报馆的)编辑 / '~right *n.* 版权, 著作权 *vt.* 为(书籍)取得版权; 保护…的版权 *a.* 版权的; 有版权保护的 / '~writer *n.* 撰稿员 (尤指写广告的)

coral ['kɔrəl] I *n.* ① 珊瑚: ~ agate 珊瑚玛瑙 / a ~ island 珊瑚岛 ② 珊瑚玩具 ③ 海虾卵 ④珊瑚色(尤指红色) ⑤ 珊瑚虫 II *a.* 珊瑚的; 珊瑚色的; 珊瑚制的 ||~ rag 珊瑚石灰岩 / ~ reef 珊瑚礁

cord [kɔːd] I *n.* ①细绳,粗线,索: a detonating ~ 火药导线 ②【解】索状组织, 带, 索: spinal ~ 脊髓 / umbilical ~ 脐带 / vocal ~s 声带 ③灯芯绒类(布); [常用复]用灯芯绒做的裤子 ④木柴堆的体积单位 ⑤【电】塞绳,软线 ⑥束缚,约束 ⑦绞刑用的绳 II *vt.* ①捆, 缚, 绑 ②成捆地堆积 ||~ed *a.* ① 用绳索等捆缚的 ②(织品)起凸线的, 起棱纹的 ③(肌肉)紧张的 / ~less *a.* ①无绳的 ②不用电线的; 电池式的; 电池及外来电源两用式的 ||'~wood *n.* 成捆出售的木材(或柴)

cordage ['kɔːdidʒ] *n.* ①[总称]绳索; 船上索具 ②(以一百二十八立方呎为单位测量的)某一指定地区的木材总数

cordial ['kɔːdjəl] I *a.* ①热诚的, 衷心的, 真诚的; 亲切的: a ~ welcome (handshake) 热烈的欢迎(握手) ② 强心的; 刺激的: ~ medicine 兴奋剂 II *n.* ①兴奋剂; 【药】酷剂 ②兴奋饮料 ③加香料的甜酒 ||~ity [,kɔːdi'æliti] *n.* 热诚; 热诚亲切的话语(或举动) / ~ly *ad.* 热诚地, 真诚地: Yours ~ly (或 *Cordially* yours) [美]您的真诚的(信末署名前的客套语) / ~ness *n.*

cordite ['kɔːdait] *n.* 无烟线状火药

cordon ['kɔːdn] I *n.* ①【军】哨兵线; 警戒线; 警戒圈: post (或 place, draw) a ~ 设警戒线 / a sanitary ~ 防疫线, 卫生交通封锁线 ②饰带, 绶章 ③【建】带饰 ④(果园中)修剪成单干形的果树 II *vt.* 用警戒线围住 (*off*) ||*cordon bleu* [法 kordɔ̃ blø] [法] ①法国波旁王朝时代的蓝绶带; [喻]最高勋位 ②(某一行业中的)佼佼者(尤指第一流的厨师) / *cordon sanitaire* [法 kordɔ̃ sanitɛːr] [法] ①防疫线 ②(国与国之间的)封锁线

corduroy ['kɔːdərɔi] I *n.* ①灯芯绒; [常用复]灯芯绒裤子 ② 木排路(指在低湿地上用木头铺成的) II *a.* ①灯芯绒制的, 象灯芯绒条纹的 ②用木头铺成的: a ~ road 木排路 III *vt.* ①在…上筑木排路 ②用木排筑(路)

core [kɔː] I *n.* ①果实的心; 核心; 精髓: get at the ~ of a matter 深入到事情的核心 ②【电】电缆心线束; 盘心; 铁心 ③【矿】岩心 ④【冶】(空心铸件上用的)型芯, (铸造模用)坭芯 ⑤【建】三夹板的心板 ⑥ [美](为各专业学生共修的)基础课程 ⑦ (绵羊体内的)肿瘤 II *vt.* 挖去…的果心 ||*be rotten to the* ~ 腐烂到核心, 腐烂透顶 / *to the* ~ 直到骨子里, 彻底 ||~less *a.* 无(果)心的 / ~r ['kɔːrə] *n.* ①果实的去心器 ②岩心提取器

cork [kɔːk] I *n.* ①软木; 软木塞: burnt ~ (演员化装用的)软木塞炭 ②钓鱼用的浮子 ③ 木栓 II *a.* 软木制的: a ~ jacket 软木救生衣 III *vt.* ①塞住; 抑制: ~ up one's feelings 把感情抑制起来 ②用软木塞炭涂黑(脸) ||*like a* ~ 轻松愉

快的；(沮丧后) 很快恢复过来的: bob up *like a*
~ 恢复元气；东山再起 ‖~ **oak**, ~ **tree** 栓皮
槠 / ~ **opera** [美俚]把脸涂黑的滑稽歌剧
corkscrew ['kɔ:kskru:] I *n.* 开塞钻 II *a.* 塞钻形
的，螺旋状的: a ~ dive (飞机) 螺旋式俯冲
III ❶ *vt.* ① 使盘旋着前进；使成螺旋状 ②(费力
地)探得(消息等) ❷ *vi.* (道路等)盘旋地向前

corkscrew

corn¹ [kɔ:n] I *n.* ①[英]谷物，五谷 (=grain)；
[英]谷类庄稼 ② 谷粒；(胡椒、水果等的)子 ③
[英]小麦；[美、加拿大、澳大利亚]玉蜀黍，玉米
(=Indian ~ 或 maize)；[苏格兰、爱尔兰]燕麦
④[美口]玉米威士忌酒 ⑤ 陈腐、伤感的东西(指
乐曲、思想等) ⑥[美俚]钱 II ❶ *vt.* ① 使成粒
状 ② 腌(肉类等) ③ 给(土地)种上谷物 ④ 以谷
物喂(牲畜) ❷ *vi.* (谷穗等)成熟，结实 ‖**acknowledge the ~** [美]接受指责，认错；认输 /
~ in Egypt 丰饶，(意料不到的)多 / **eat one's
~ in the blade** 寅吃卯粮 / **measure others'
~ by one's own bushel** 拿自己做标准来衡量别
人，以己度人 ‖**~ed** *a.* ① 呈粒状的 ② 腌的 ③
[俚]喝醉的 ‖**~ball** [美俚] *a.* 乡巴佬(似)的；
老派的，陈腐的 *n.* 粗俗陈腐的人；过时货 /
beef 咸牛肉 / **~ belt** 主要种玉米的地带；[C-
B-] 美国中西部种玉米地带 / **~ borer** 玉米螟
虫 / **'~brash** *n.* 粗钙质砂岩 / **~ bread** 玉米
面包 / **~ chandler** [英]粮食零售商 / **'~cob**
n. 玉米棒子的芯，玉米穗轴 / **~ cockle** 【植】麦
仙翁 / **'~crake** 【动】秧鸡 / **~ dodger** [美]玉
米饼；玉米团子 / **'~-ex,change** *n.* 谷物交易
所 / **'~,factor** *n.* 谷物商 / **'~-fed** *a.* ①(牲
畜等)用谷物喂养的 ②吃得得好的；健壮的 ③[俚]
质朴的，乡气的 / **'~field** *n.* [英]小麦田 /
玉米田 / **'~field meet** [美俚]列车的正面相撞 /
~ flag 【植】水仙菖蒲；黄菖蒲 / **'~flakes** [复]
n. 玉米片(玉米粒脱壳、轧扁而成) / **~ flour** ①
[美](精磨)玉米粉 ②[英]谷物磨成的粉(指米粉粉
等) / **'~flower** *n.* 【植】矢车菊 / **'~husk** *n.*
(整只)玉米的壳 / **~ juice** 威士忌酒(尤指玉米
威士忌酒) / **'~land** *n.* 种(或适于种)谷物的土
地(美国指种玉米的土地) / **'~-laws** [复] *n.*
[英史](限制谷物进口的)谷物法 (一八四六年废
除) / **'~loft** *n.* 谷仓 / **'~meal** *n.* (粗磨)玉米
粉 / **~ mill** ①[英]面粉机 ②[美]磨玉米的机器 /
~ pone (手捏)玉米饼 / **'~-rent** *n.* [英]以谷

物交纳 (或按谷价折合) 的地租 / **~ sheller** ①
玉米脱粒机 ②[美俚]连发枪 / **'~stalk** *n.*
玉米杆 ②[澳俚]澳大利亚白人(尤指新南威尔士
人) / **'~starch** *n.* (精磨)玉米粉；玉米淀粉 /
~ sugar 玉米葡糖
corn² [kɔ:n] *n.* 鸡眼，钉胼 ‖**tread on sb.'s ~s**
触犯某人，伤某人的感情 / ‖**~ plaster** 鸡眼膏药
corner ['kɔ:nə] I *n.* ① 角，犄角；(街道)拐角: sit
in the ~ of a room 坐在屋角里 / stand *at* a
street ~ 站在街道拐角处 / The shop is *on* (或
at) the ~. 那铺子就在拐角上。② (书本、箱子
等的)包角 ③ (遥远的)地区；角落，冷僻处: The
delegates came from all ~s of the country. 代
表们来自全国各地。④ 困境，绝路: be in a tight
~ 处于困境 / drive sb. into a ~ 逼得某人走投
无路 ⑤ 囤积(居奇)；垄断: make a ~ in sth. 囤
积某物 / have the ~ on sth. 垄断某物 ⑥(足
球赛)角球 (=~ kick) II ❶ *vt.* ①使走投无路，
把…难住 ② 囤积；垄断: ~ the market 垄断市
场 ❷ *vi.* ①相交成角，形成角 ②(车辆、驾驶员)
转弯 ③囤积 (in) III *a.* ①角上的，转弯处的 ②
(适)用于角隅的: ~ bar 【建】角隅钢筋 ‖**around
the ~** [美] =round the ~ / **a warm ~** 激
战地区 / **cut ~s** (或 a ~) ① (不绕角走)抄近
路 ② 以最简捷、经济的方式做事 / **cut off a ~**
(不绕角走)抄近路 / **in ~s** (或 a ~) ① 在角
落里 ② 偷偷摸摸地，秘密地 / **put sb. in the ~**
罚某人立壁角 / **round the ~** ① 在拐角处；[常与
just 连用]在附近；即将来临: He lives just *round*
the ~. 他就住在拐角处。(或: 他就住在附
近。) / **the four ~s** ① 十字路口: a store at
the four ~s 在十字路口的商店 ② (全部)范围:
the four ~s of the earth 天涯海角 / the four
~s of a document (treaty) 文件(条约)的范围 /
turn the ~ ①(沿街角)拐弯 ② 转危为安，渡过
难关 ‖**~ed** *a.* ①[用以构成复合词]有…角的:
three-~ed (有)三只角的 / sharp-~ed 尖角的
② 被逼入绝境的，被难住的 / **~wise**, **~ways**
ad. ①形成角状地 ②对角地 / **~ boy** 街头的游
手好闲者；流氓 / **~ chisel** 角凿 / **~ kick** (足
球赛)角球 / **~ man** ① 街头的游手好闲者；流
氓 ② 黑人乐队两端的演奏者 / **'~stone** *n.*
①【建】墙角石 ②(奠基典礼上放下的)奠基石 ③
[喻]柱石，基础
cornet ['kɔ:nit] *n.* ① (乐器)短号 ②(放糖果的)
圆锥形纸袋；(盛冰淇淋、奶油等用的)圆锥形蛋卷
③ 慈善修女团团员戴的大白帽 ④[古]英国骑兵
旗手 ‖**~ist** *n.* 吹短号者 / **'~-,player** *n.* 吹短
号者
corollary [kə'rɔləri] *n.* ①【数】系，系定理，推论
②必然的结果
corona [kə'rəunə] ([复] coronas 或 coronae
[kə'rəuni:]) *n.* ①冠，冠状物 ②【植】副(花)冠；根
颈 ③【解】冠；头顶；牙冠 ④【建】檐板；(教堂的)
圆形吊灯 ⑤【天】日冕；【气】日华，月华 ⑥【电】
电晕，电晕放电 ⑦一种哈瓦那雪茄烟的商标名
coronation [,kɔrə'neiʃən] *n.* 加冕典礼

coroner ['kɔrənə] *n.* 验尸官: a ~'s inquest 验尸

coronet ['kɔrənit] *n.* ①（王子或显贵戴的）冠 ②（女子的）冠状头饰品 ③【解】蹄冠, 冠, 小(纤毛)冠

corporal[1] ['kɔ:pərəl] *a.* 肉体的, 身体的: ~ punishment 肉刑(包括鞭打、监禁、处死等); 体罚 ‖**-ity** [ˌkɔ:pəˈræliti] *n.* 肉体性; 物质性 / **~ly** *ad.*

corporal[2] ['kɔ:pərəl] *n.* 【军】下士: a ~ of the guard 警卫班长 / the Little *Corporal* "小伍长"(拿破仑一世的绰号) ‖**~'s guard** ① 一支小分队警卫 ②一小群

corporate ['kɔ:pərit] *a.* ① 社团的, 法人的: a ~ body 法人团体 (=a body ~) ②共同的; 全体的: ~ responsibility 共同责任 ‖**~ly** *ad.*

corporation [ˌkɔ:pəˈreiʃən] *n.* ①【律】社团, 法人: the ~ aggregate 社团法人 / the ~ sole 单独法人 ② 公司, 企业; [美] 有限公司: a ~ lawyer [美]公司法律顾问 / a trading ~ 贸易公司 ③ (市、镇的)自治机关: the municipal ~ 市自治机关 ④[口] 大肚皮

corps [kɔ:] ([复] corps [kɔ:z]) *n.* ①军团; 军(介于师与集团军之间的陆军单位): a ~ commander 军长 ②兵队; 技术兵种, 特殊兵种: the Corps of Engineers (美国)陆军工兵部队 / a dare-to-die ~ 敢死队 / a chemical ~ 化学兵部队 ③ 队, 团: the Peace Corps (美国的)和平队 / a diplomatic ~ 外交使团(指驻在一国的全体外交人员) ④(德国大学的)学生联合会 ‖*de ballet* [法 kɔ:r də balε] [法] 芭蕾舞团 / *the Corps Diplomatique* [法 kɔ:r diplomatik] [法]外交使团 ‖ **~man** ['kɔ:mən] *n.* (美国海军的)看护兵

corpse [kɔ:ps] **I** *n.* 死尸, 尸体; [喻] 被废弃的东西: a political ~ 政治僵尸 **II** *vt.* ①[英方]杀死 ②[美俚](演戏中)使(另一演员)出丑; 破坏(戏剧场面或演员的动作) ‖**~ candle** ① 点在尸体旁的蜡烛 ② (被迷信的人认为预示死亡的) 墓地鬼火, 磷火

corpulent ['kɔ:pjulənt] *a.* 肥胖的

corpuscle ['kɔ:pʌsl], **corpuscule** [kɔ:'pʌskju:l] *n.* ①【医】血球; 细胞, 小体: red (white) ~s of the blood 红 (白) 血球, 红 (白) 细胞 ② 微粒, 粒子 ‖**corpuscular** [kɔ:'pʌskjulə] *a.* 微粒的; 小体的, 细胞的

corral [kɔ:'rɑ:l] **I** *n.* ① 畜栏; 捕捉野兽的栅栏 ② (作防御用的) 车阵 **II** (corralled; corralling) *vt.* ①把…关进畜栏 ②用 (车辆)围成栅栏 ③把…聚集在一起 ④[美口]觅得; 寻找

correct [kə'rekt] **I** *vt.* ① 改正, 纠正; 修改; 矫正, 校正: ~ mistakes 纠正错误 / ~ sb. 纠正某人 / ~ "a" to "the" 把 "a" 改为 "the" / ~ a composition 修改作文 / ~ one's watch 对准表 ②责备; 惩罚 ③ 制止(不良倾向等); 中和 **II** *a.* ①正确的: a ~ answer 正确的回答 ② 恰当的, 符合的; 端正的; 符合一般性准则的: ~ conduct 端正的行为 / It's the ~ thing to do. 对啊, 正应

如此。 ‖*stand ~ed* 承认有错: I stand ~ed. 我承认有错(接在别人的指责、批评后说的话) ‖**~ly** *ad.* / **~ness** *n.* / **~or** *n.* ①校正者; 矫正者; 校对员: a ~or of the press [英]校对员 ②责备者; 处罚者

correction [kə'rekʃən] *n.* ① 改正, 纠正; 修改; 矫正, 校正; 勘误;【数】补值 ② (对罪犯的)教养: a house of ~ 教养院, 改造所 ③ 责备; 惩罚 ④ 制止; 中和 ⑤ (市价上涨后的)回落 ‖*under ~* 有待改正: I am speaking under ~. 我说得不一定对。 ‖**~al** *a.*

corrective [kə'rektiv] **I** *a.* 改正的, 纠正的; 矫正的; 惩治的; 制止的; 中和的: ~ training [英]【律】(对少年犯等的)教养处分 **II** *n.* 矫正药; 起矫正作用的东西(或措施) ‖**~ly** *ad.*

correlate ['kɔrileit] **I** *n.* 互相关联的事物 **II** *vt.* & *vi.* (使)相互关联 (with, to) ‖**correlator** *n.* 【无】相关器

correlation [ˌkɔri'leiʃən] *n.* 相互关系, 伴随关系, 关联(作用)

correlative [kɔ'relətiv] **I** *a.* 相关的; 互相关联的; 相依的 (with, to): ~ conjunctions 【语】关联连词 (如 "either" 和 "or" 就是一组关联连词) / **II** *n.* ① 相关物 ② 关联词 ‖**~ly** *ad.* / **correlativity** [kɔˌrelə'tiviti] *n.* 相关(或相依)性; 相关(或相依)程度

correspond [ˌkɔris'pɔnd] *vi.* ①符合, 一致: ~ to objective reality 符合客观现实 / ~ with sb.'s needs 适合某人的需要 ② 相当, 相应: The American Congress ~s to the British Parliament. 美国的 "Congress" (国会) 相当于英国的 "Parliament" (议会)。 ③ 通信: We ~ regularly. 我们定期通信。

correspondence [ˌkɔris'pɔndəns] *n.* ①符合, 一致: There isn't much ~ between their views and ours. 他们和我们的见解不很一致。 ②相当, 相应;【数】对应 ③ 通信 (联系); 互通的信件: commercial ~ 商业通信 / keep up (drop) (或 a ~) 保持 (停止) 通信 / have a large ~ to answer 有许多回信要写 ‖*bring ... into ~ with* ① 使…与…一致起来 ② 使…与…相互通信 / *by* (或 *through*) ~ 用写信的办法 / *in ~ with* ① 和…相一致 ②与…有通信联系 ‖**~ school** 函授学校

correspondent [ˌkɔris'pɔndənt] **I** *n.* ①对应物 ② 通信者; (新闻)通讯员, 记者: a special ~ 特派记者 / a war ~ 随军记者 / a good (bad) ~ 勤(懒)于写信的人 ③【商】客户 **II** *a.* 符合的, 一致的; 相当的 ‖**~ly** *ad.*

corridor ['kɔridɔ:] *n.* ① 走廊, 回廊; 通路 ② 走廊地带;【军】纵向狭隘地形(或地带); 空中走廊; 指定航路 ‖**~ train** [英]从头到尾有走廊的列车

corroborate [kə'rɔbəreit] *vt.* 使(信仰等)进一步巩固; 确证, 证实 ‖**corroboration** [kəˌrɔbə'reiʃən] *n.* 确证 / **corroborator** *n.* 确证者; 确证物

corrode [kə'roud] **❶** *vt.* 腐蚀; 侵蚀: Salt water ~s iron. 盐水腐蚀铁。 **❷** *vi.* 起腐蚀作用

corrosive [kə'rousiv] **I** *a.* 腐蚀的,腐蚀性的: Rust and acid are ~. 锈和酸都是腐蚀性的。**II** *n.* 腐蚀剂 ‖~**ly** *ad.* / ~**ness** *n.* ‖~ **sublimate** 【化】升汞;氯化汞

corrugate ['kɔrugeit] **I** ❶ *vt.* 弄皱,使起皱,使起波纹: ~*d* iron 波纹铁 / ~*d* paper 瓦楞纸 ❷ *vi.* 起皱,起波纹 **II** ['kɔrugit] *a.* 起皱的,起波纹的,弄皱的 ‖**corrugator** *n.* ①【医】皱(眉)肌 ② 波纹纸制造机;波纹纸制造工

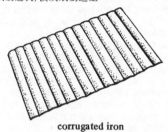

corrugated iron

corrupt [kə'rʌpt] **I** *a.* ① 腐败的;贪污的: ~ officials 贪官污吏 / ~ practices 腐败的行径(尤指行贿受贿) ② (语言、版本等)讹用的;多讹误的: the ~ form of a word 一个词的讹用形式 / a ~ text (因传抄等而)错误百出的文本 ③ 腐烂的;污浊的: ~ air 污浊的空气 **II** ❶ *vt.* ① 使败坏,腐蚀 ② 贿赂,收买 ③ 使腐坏,使污浊 ④ 讹用(语、词等);使(稿本等)搀杂讹误 ❷ *vi.* ① 腐坏;腐烂 ② 腐败,堕落 ‖~**ly** *ad.* / ~**ness** *n.*

corruptible [kə'rʌptəbl] *a.* ①易腐坏的 ② 可收买的,易腐化的 ‖**corruptibility** [kə,rʌptə'biliti] *n.* / **corruptibly** *ad.*

corruption [kə'rʌpʃən] *n.* ① 腐坏;腐化;败坏: ~ of social morals 社会道德的败坏 ②[古]起腐化作用的东西 ③ 贪污;贿赂 ④ (语词的)讹用,讹误 ⑤[美方]脓 ‖~ *of blood* [英]【律】血统玷污(禁止重罪犯享有、继承、传授财产、称号等的法律规定)

corset ['kɔ:sit] **I** *n.* 妇女紧身胸衣 **II** *vt.* 给…穿紧身胸衣

cosmetic [kɔz'metik] **I** *n.* 化妆品 **II** *a.* ①化妆用的;整容的 ② 装饰性的,装门面的: make some ~ concessions 作一些摆样子的让步 ‖~**ian** [,kɔzmə'tiʃən] *n.* 化妆品制造专家;整容专家

cosmopolitan [,kɔzmə'pɔlitən] **I** *a.* ① 世界主义的 ②全世界的,全世界各地都有的;【动】【植】遍生的 **II** *n.* ① 世界主义者 ②【动】【植】世界性

cosmos ['kɔzmɔs] *n.* ①宇宙 ②秩序,和谐 ③【植】大波斯菊;[C-] 大波斯菊属(即秋英属)

cost [kɔst] **I** (cost) ❶ *vt.* ①价值为;(使)花费(金钱、时间等): This work ~ them much labour. 这件工作花去他们很大的劳动。②使失去(生命、健康等): ~ sb. his life 使某人丧失生命 / The patient's dangerous condition ~ the doctors and nurses many a sleepless night. 病人的危险状态使医生和护士们好几夜不曾合眼。③(根据成本)为(产品)估计价格 ❷ *vi.* 花费: How dear the lesson ~s! 这个教训的代价多大啊! **II** *n.* ①成本;费用: reduce the production ~ 降低生产成本 / the ~ of living 生活费用 ②代价 ③[复]诉讼费(尤指判处对胜方的诉讼费用) ‖~ *accounting* 成本会计 / ~ *accounts* 成本账 / ~ *and freight* (略作 C. F.) 离岸加运费价格 / ~, *insurance, and freight* (略作 C. I. F.) 到岸价格 / ~ *price* (或 *prime* ~) 成本价格,原价 ‖*at all* ~*s* 不惜任何代价 / *at the* ~ *of* 以…为代价 / ~ *sb. dear(ly)* 使某人花很多钱;使某人大受损失(或大吃苦头) / *count the* ~ (做事前)权衡利害得失 / *to one's* ~ 吃了苦头之后才…;由于付了代价才…: I know it *to my* ~. 这一点我是吃了苦头才知道的。‖~**ing** *n.* [主英]成本会计 / ~**less** *a.* 没有成本的,不需花钱的 ‖'~=**'plus** *a.* 在实际成本之外加以一定比例费用的

coster ['kɔstə], **costermonger** ['kɔstə,mʌŋgə] *n.* [英]叫卖水果(或蔬菜)的小贩

costly ['kɔstli] *a.* ① 昂贵的;代价高的 ② 价值高的,豪华的 ‖**costliness** *n.*

costume ['kɔstju:m, kɔs'tju:m] **I** *n.* ①服装;服装式样;装束: a riding ~ 骑服 ② 妇女的外套,女服 ③化装服,戏装: a ~ piece (或 play) 古装戏 **II** *vt.* 为…提供服装

cosy ['kouzi] *a., ad. & n.* =cozy

cot[1] [kɔt] **I** *n.* ① 小屋; 槛, (鸽) 笼: a sheep ~ 羊槛 ② 手指(或脚趾)套 ③ [诗] 茅屋, 村舍 **II** (cotted; cotting) *vt.* 把(羊等)关进槛内

cot[2] [kɔt] *n.* 帆布床,吊床;[英]儿童摇床,儿童病床

cot 【数】余切 (cotangent) 的符号

cote [kout] *n.* (畜)槛; (鸽)笼

cottage ['kɔtidʒ] *n.* ① 村舍;小屋 ② (疗养院、学校等内部的)单幢住所 ③ (避暑地等的)小型别墅 ‖~ *hospital* [英]诊疗所 / ~ *industry* 家庭手工业 / ~ *piano* 小型立式钢琴

cotton ['kɔtn] **I** *n.* ① 棉花, 棉, 棉属植物: pick (grow) ~ 采(种)棉花 / prune ~ branches 给棉花整枝 ②棉线: sewing ~ 缝纫用线 ③棉布: ~ clothes 棉布衣服 / ~ goods 棉织品 ④(其他植物所生的)棉状物 ‖*absorbent* ~ [美]脱脂棉,药棉 / *ginned* ~ 皮棉 / *raw* ~ 原棉 / *unginned* ~ 籽棉 / *waste* ~ 废棉 **II** *vi.* ① 和谐,一致 (*together, with*) ② 发生好感;开始交好 (*to, up to, on to*): He rather ~s to the idea. 他很倾向于这个主意。③ [俚]理解,懂得 (*on, on to*) ‖~ *aphid* 棉蚜 / **Cotton Belt** 美国南部的种棉地带 / ~ *boll* 棉桃,棉铃 / ~ *cake* 棉籽饼 / ~ *cloth* 棉布 / ~ *gin* 轧棉机,轧花机 / ~ *grass* 【植】羊蒂禾 / ~ *grower* 棉农,植棉者 ②棉花种植园主 / ~ *mill* 棉纺织厂 / ~ *oil* 棉籽油 / '~='**padded** *a.* 填棉絮的: a ~*-padded* coat (quilt) 棉袄(被) / ～ **picker** ①采棉人 ②摘棉机 / '～-,picking *a.* [美俚]毫无价值的; 糟透的; 该死的 / ～ **plant** 棉株, 棉树 / ～ **powder** 火棉 / ～ **press** 皮棉打包机; 皮棉打包厂(或间) / ～ **print** 印花棉布 / '～**seed** *n.* 棉籽: a ～*seed* cake 棉籽饼 / ～*seed* oil 棉籽油 / ～ **spinner** ①纺纱工人 ②纱厂主 / ～ **stainer** 【动】棉红椿象, 污棉虫 / '～**tail** *n.* 美洲产白尾棕色兔 / ～ **textile** 棉纺织品 / ～ **thread** 棉线 / ～ **tree** 【植】异叶杨, 木棉树 / ～ **waste** ①废棉, 回花 ②丝头, 回丝(揩擦机器等用) / '～**weed** *n.* 鼠曲草属植物 / '～**wood.** 三角叶杨 / ～ **wool** ①原棉, 棉絮 ②[英]脱脂棉, 药棉 / ～ **yarn** 棉纱

couch [kautʃ] **I** *n.* ①睡椅, 长沙发椅 ②休息处; [诗]床, 寝处 ③兽穴 ④麦芽床 ⑤【植】匍匐冰草, 茅根, 麦斛 **II ❶** *vt.* ①[常用被动语态或接 oneself] 使躺下 ②表达, 隐含: a refusal ～*ed in* plain terms 直言拒绝 / ～ a lie *under fair* words 用漂亮的词藻掩饰谎言 ③端着(枪、矛等) 准备攻击 ④贴线缝绣(图样等) ⑤【医】除去(白内障); 除去(人、眼)的白内障 ⑥把(谷物)放在麦芽床上发芽 **❷** *vi.* ①躺下 ②蹲伏; 埋伏 ③(残叶)集堆腐烂

cough [kɔf] **I** *n.* 咳, 咳嗽: a dry ～ 干咳 / have a bad ～ 咳得厉害 **II ❶** *vi.* 咳, 咳嗽; 发出咳嗽似的声音 **❷** *vt.* 咳出 ‖～*down* (听众)用咳嗽声阻挠(演讲者) / ～ *oneself hoarse* 咳得嗓子沙哑 / ～ *out* 咳出; 一边咳嗽一边说出 / ～ *up* ①咳出 ②[俚]勉强说出, 供出; 被迫付出 ‖～ **drop** 咳嗽糖 / ～ **lozenge** 咳嗽片 / ～ **mixture** 咳嗽药水 / ～ **syrup** 咳嗽糖浆

could [强 kud; 弱 kəd] (can 的过去式) *v. aux.* ①[用于虚拟语气][表示与事实相反的设想]能, 可以: If I ～ go with you, I should feel very glad. 假使我能同你们一起去, 我会感到非常高兴。/ If I ～ have gone with you, I should have felt very glad. 当时假使我能同你们一起去, 我会感到多么高兴呀。/ I ～ do it (if I would). (倘若我愿意的话,)我是能办到这一点的。②[表示可能性]能, 可能 ③[用于婉转语气]能: *Could* you do something for me? 你能替我做件事情吗? [注意: 本句因用了 could 语气比之用 can 要婉转、客气得多] / You ～ do with a haircut. 你该理发了。[因为是向别人提出劝告或建议, 句中的 could 不能用 can 代]

couldn't ['kudnt] =could not

council ['kaunsil] *n.* ①政务会; 理事会; 委员会: the State *Council* 国务院 / the *Council* of Ministers 内阁 / the U. N. Security *Council* 联合国安全理事会 ②商议会, 讨论会议; 宗教会议: hold a ～ of war 举行一次军事会议(或非军事性的制订行动计划的会议) ③顾问班子; 立法班子: the Privy *Council* (英国)枢密院 ④地方自治会; 地方议会: a city (town, county) 市(镇, 郡)议会(或议会) ⑤(若干组织的)联合

体; (某一组织的)分支机构; 俱乐部; 社团 ⑥(地方性的)工会代表会议 ⑦议事, 商讨 ‖～ **board** 议事桌; 全体议事者 / ～ **chamber** 会议室 / ～ **estate** (英国市、镇、郡等)地方当局拥有的地产 / ～ **house** ①会场, 会堂 ②(英国市、镇、郡等)地方当局营造的房屋 / ～**man** ['kaunsilmən] *n.* [美]市政会成员, 市议员 / '～-'manager plan [美]由市议会推选市长的市政制度 / ～ **school** (英国)郡办学校

council(l)or ['kaunsilə] *n.* ①地方议会议员 ②顾问, 评议员 ③参赞 ‖～**ship** *n.* 地方议员(或顾问、参赞等)的职位

counsel ['kaunsəl] **I** *n.* ①商议; 评议; 审议: take (或 hold) ～ with sb. 与某人商议 ②劝告, 忠告 ③意见; 计划; [古]意图, 目的 ④律师, 辩护人: a ～ on both sides (原、被告)两造的辩护人 **II** (counsel(l)ed; counsel(l)ing) **❶** *vt.* 劝告, 忠告: ～ sb. *to* go at once (当面)劝某人立刻去 / ～ sb.'s going at once (不当着某人的面)建议某人立刻就去 **❷** *vi.* 商议, 商讨; 劝告 ‖～ *of perfection* ①要别人必须做到十全十美的要求 ②达不到的理想 / *darken* ～ 使更加混乱 / *keep one's own* ～ 不宣布自己的意图(或意见等) / *King's* (或 *Queen's*) *Counsel* 英国王室法律顾问 / *take* ～ *of one's pillow* 通夜思考 ‖**counsel(l)or** *n.* ①顾问 ②(大使馆等的)法律顾问; 参赞 ③律师 ④夏令营管理人

count[1] [kaunt] **I ❶** *vt.* ①点, 数; 从一数到…; 计点: ～ the pages 点页数 / ～ three 从一数到三 / ～ the number of people present 计算出席人数 / ～ one's luggage on arrival 到达时把行李检点一下 ②算(入): Don't ～ (*in*) the broken ones. 别把破的计算在内。/ There are fifty people present, (not) ～*ing* the children. 儿童(不)计算在内, 出席者五十人。/ *Count* me in! 我也算一个! ③认为, 信为; 看作: ～ it an honour (to do sth.) (把做某事)引以为荣 / ～ sth. of no importance 把某事物看得无关紧要 / ～ sb. *as* (或 *for*) dead (lost) 以为某人已死(已无望) **❷** *vi.* ①数, 计数: Can you ～ from one to twenty (或 ～ up to twenty) in English? 你能用英语从一数到二十吗? / ～ on one's fingers 扳着手指数 / ～ by thousands 以千计数 ②算数, 被算进; 有(考虑的)价值; 算得上: That doesn't ～. 那可不算数。(或: 那可不值得考虑。) / Every second ～*s.* 每秒钟都很重要。(或: 分秒必争。) / ～ among the largest in the country 算得上是国内最大者之一 ③共计: They ～*ed* thirty-five. 共有三十五个。**II** *n.* ①计算; 合计数: an accurate ～ 精确的计数 / We may need more ～*s* before we are certain of the total. 我们也许还需要数几遍才能确定总数。②计数: background ～ 【物】本底计数 / blood ～ 【医】血球计数 ③【纺】支, 支数: fine (medium) ～ 细(中)支棉纱 ④【律】(控告的一条)罪状 ⑤争论点, 问题: They agree on this ～. 在这一点上,

他们意见一致。⑥(拳击中的)十秒钟计时(裁判员给与被击倒者的再起机会) ‖*beyond* ~ 数不尽,不计其数 / ~ ... *against* ... 认为…是不利于··的 / ~ *down* ①倒着数 ②(准备发射导弹等以前)用倒数方式计算(秒数) / ~ *for little* 简直无足轻重 / ~ *for much* 关系重大,很有价值 / ~ *for nothing* 毫无价值 / ~ *with* 见 kin / Count off! (口令)报数! / ~ *on* (或 upon) 依靠;期待;指望: ~ on self-reliance 依靠自力更生 / ~ on sb.'s coming (或 ~ on sb. to come) 指望某人会来 / ~ *out* ①点…的数 ②把…不计在内;把(某人)作不参加论 ③(在英国)宣布法定人数不足使(下议院)休会 ④[美口]少报选票使(候选人)落选 ⑤(拳击中)判定(被击倒者)为输 / ~ *up* ①把…加起来: Count up those figures for me. 替我把那些数字加起来。②共计(to) / *lose* ~ *of* 在数…的过程中忘记数到哪儿了 / *out for the* ~ 死的;毁了的 / *out of the* ~ 不计其数,数不尽 / *out of the* ~ 完全失去知觉的;睡得极熟的,吵不醒的 / *take* ~ *of* 计…的数: take ~ of votes 计算票数 / *take much* (*no*) ~ *of* 很(不)重视… / *take the* ~ (拳击者)在被打倒后经裁判数过十秒钟尚未起立;[喻]被判失败,打输;死 ‖~*able a.* 可数的 *n.*【语】可数名词 ‖~*down n.* (准备发射导弹等以前)用倒数方式进行的时间计算 / '~-'*out n.* ①(英国下议院)因不满法定人数而宣布的休会 ②[美口]被故意少报选票而落选的候选人 ③(拳击中)判定(被击倒者)作输

count[2] [kaunt] *n.* (西欧除英国外的)伯爵(英国称 earl) ‖~ *palatine* ①(神圣罗马帝国的)大法官 ②在领地内享有王权的伯爵

countenance ['kauntinəns] **I** *n.* ①面部表情;面容;面目;脸色 : a smiling (sad) ~ 笑(愁)容 ②赞助,赞同;支持;鼓励:·give (或 lend) ~ to sb. (a plan) 赞助某人(某项计划) ③镇定,沉着 **II** *vt.* 支持,鼓励 ‖*change* (*one's*) ~ (因为情绪变化而)变脸色 / *in* ~ 镇定 / *keep one's* ~ 泰然自若;忍住不笑 / *lose* ~ 失色,慌张起来 / *put sb. out of* ~ 使某人难堪

counter[1] ['kauntə] *n.* ①计算者 ②计数器,计算器 ③柜台 ④ 筹码 ⑤(讨价还价的)本钱,资本,有利条件 ‖*over the* ~ (指证券买卖)通过经纪人事务所而不是通过交易所 / *under the* ~ 私下地,通过"后门" ‖~ *cheque* 银行取款单 / '~*,jumper n.* [美口]站柜台的(对店员的蔑称)

counter[2] ['kauntə] **I** *ad.* 反方向地;(与…)相反地 (*to*): run (或 go, act) ~ *to* 违反…,与…背道而驰 **II** *a.* ①相反的;对立的: ~ tides 逆流 ②反对的,敌意的 ③位于对面的 ④收回成命的: a ~ order 收回成命的命令(即宣布取消前一命令的命令) ⑤复本的: a ~ list 副(名)单 **III** *n.* ①相反,反面: believe the ~ of a saying 相信(与此)相反的说法 ②起抵销作用的事物;制止 ③(拳击)还击 ④(马的前胸部;船尾突出部 ④(皮鞋等)鞋帮后部跟部的

坚硬部分 ⑤(拳击等)(受击或挡掉来拳时的)回拳,回击 ⑥铅字笔划间的凹进处 **IV** ❶ *vt.* ①反对;反击 ②抵销 ③引证…来辩驳 ❷ *vi.* 防御;反击

counteract [,kauntə'rækt] *vt.* 抵抗,抵制;阻碍;中和;抵销 ‖~*ion* [,kauntə'rækʃən] *n.* 反作用,对抗作用,抵抗;阻碍;中和

counterattack ['kauntərə,tæk] *n.*, *vt.* & *vi.* 反攻,反击

counterattraction ['kauntərə,trækʃən] *n.* 对抗引力,反引力

counterbalance **I** ['kauntə,bæləns] *n.* ①平衡;平衡力;抗衡 ②【机】平衡块,砝码 **II** [,kauntə'bæləns] *vt.* 使平衡,抵销

counterclaim ['kauntə-kleim] **I** *n.* 反要求;反诉 **II** ❶ *vi.* 反诉;提出反要求 (*for, against*) ❷ *vt.* 提出…作为反诉(或反要求)

counterfeit ['kauntəfit] **I** *a.* ①伪造的,假冒的;仿造的: a ~ note 假钞票 ②虚伪的,虚假的: ~ virtue 假冒为善 **II** *n.* ①伪造物,假冒物;仿造品 ②[古]肖像 ③[古]骗子 **III** ❶ *vt.* ①伪造(货币,手迹等);仿造 ②假装 ③与…极相像 ❷ *vi.* ①假装 ②进行伪造活动 ‖~*er n.* 伪造者(尤指造假货币的人)

counterfoil ['kauntəfɔil] *n.* (支票等的)存根,票根

countermand [,kauntə'mɑ:nd] **I** *vt.* ①取消,撤回(已发出的命令、定货单等) ②(下逆命令)叫回,召回 **II** *n.* ①(命令、定货单等的)撤回,取消 ②逆命令

counterpart ['kauntəpɑ:t] *n.* ①副本,复本 ②配对物;补足物 ③极相似的东西;(在职位、性格、作用 等方面)相对应的人,对手方: The U. S. Congress is the ~ of the British Parliament. 美国的国会相当于英国的议会

countersign ['kauntəsain] **I** *n.* ①副署,连署,会签 ②【军】口令 ③暗号;应信信号 **II** *vt.* 副署,连署(文件等);确认

counting ['kauntiŋ] *n.* 计算 ‖~*house n.* (公司、商店等的)存账室;办公室 / ~ *machine* 计算机 / ~ *room* =~house / ~ *tube* 计数管

countless ['kauntlis] *a.* 无数的,多得不计其数的

countrified ['kʌntrifaid] *a.* 乡下派头的,乡土气的

country ['kʌntri] **I** *n.* ①国家;国土: a Third World ~ 第三世界国家 / the Low *Countries* 低地国家(荷兰、比利时、卢森堡的总称) ②[the ~] [总称]国民;选民 ③家乡,故乡;祖国;国籍所属国家 ④[the ~]乡下,农村 (=the countryside): work (live) in the ~ 在农村工作(生活) ⑤(具有某种地理特点的)区域;地区;知识领域: a vast stretch of wooded (hilly) ~ 一大片林(山)区 / It was unknown (或 strange) ~ to me. 这地区对我说来是陌生的。(或:这是一个我所不熟悉的领域。) ⑥土地: Much ~ was sown to wheat. 许多土地都用来种小麦。⑦ 陪审团: a trial by the ~ 由陪审团进行的审讯 **II** *a.* ①乡下的,农

村的; 乡村风味的; 乡气的: ~ life 农村生活 ②
[方]祖国的; 故乡的 ‖across ~ 越过田野 / go
(或 appeal) to the ~ [英] (于议会投反对政府
的票后) 解散议会重新选举下议院 / put oneself
on one's (或 the) ~ ①诉诸本选区的选民 ②要
求陪审团审判 / the God's ~ ①天赋之国(美国
人对美国的自称) ②远离边疆的文明地区 ③乡
野 ④故乡 / the never-never ~ 幻想中的地方
‖'~·born a. 生在乡村的, 乡村中生长的 / ~
club 城郊俱乐部 (附有高尔夫球场等) / ~
cousin 乡下佬 / '~-dance n. 英国乡村舞 (尤
指排成两排的对舞) / ~ gentleman 乡绅 / ~
house =~seat / ~ jake [美] 乡下佬 / ~man
['kʌntrimən] n. ①同国人, 同胞; 同乡 ②乡下人
③某特定地区的人: a north ~man 北方人 / ~
mile [美口] 极长的一段距离 / ~ note [英] 地
方银行发行的钞票 / ~ party 代表农业利益的
政党, 农民党 / ~ road 乡间道路, 公路旁的泥
路 / ~ rock [地]围岩 / ~'seat n. 乡间宅第(尤
指英国上层人士或乡绅的乡间住宅) / '~side n.
①乡下, 农村: in the ~side 在农村 ②[总称]农
村居民 / '~'wide a. 全国性的, 全国范围的 /
'~,woman n. ①女同胞 ②乡下女人

county ['kaunti] n. ①(英国的)郡: the County of
London 伦敦郡 ②(美国的)县(州以下最大的行政
区) ③(中国等国的)县 ④(中国西藏自治区的)
宗 ⑤[the ~]全郡(或全县)居民; [英]全郡士绅
‖~ agent [美]由州和联邦政府联合雇用的农业
和家政顾问 / ~ palatine 享有王权伯爵的领
地 / ~ seat 县府所在地, 县城 / ~ town (英
国)郡的首府

coup [ku:] ([复] coups [ku:z, ku:]) n. [法] ①
突然的一击, 漂亮的一击 ②突然的行动; 大成功;
妙计 ③(军事) 政变 ‖make (或 pull off) a
great ~ 大获成功, 一鸣惊人 ‖~ de grâce [də
'grɑ:s]([复] ~s de grâce) ①(为使重伤者免受痛
苦而给予的)致命一击, 慈悲的一击 ②[喻]致命
的打击; 给予致命一击的事件 / ~ de main [də
'mẽ:n]([复] ~s de main) 突击, 奇袭 / ~ d'état
[dei'tɑ:]([复] ~s d'état 或 ~ d'états [dei-
'tɑ:z])(军事)政变(有时音译作: "苦迭打")/ ~
de théâtre [də tei'ɑ:tr]([复] ~s de théâtre) ①
(戏剧中)扣人心弦的情节急转 ②戏剧性的事态
急转 / ~ d'oeil [də:j]([复] ~s d'ceil) 一瞥

coupé, coupe ['ku:pei] n. ①双座四轮轿式马车 ②
小轿车 ③[英]铁路客车车尾部的分隔车厢

couple ['kʌpl] I ([复] couple(s)) n. ①(一)对,
(一)双; 夫妇; 未婚夫妻: a ~ of players 一对选
手 / five ~(s) of rabbits 五对兔子 / a newly
wedded ~ 一对新婚夫妇 ②[口]几个, 三两个:
in a ~ of days 在三两天内 ③[物]力偶; 电偶 II
❶ vt. ①连接, 结合; 把…拴在一起; 【电】使耦
合 ②使成夫妇[对]使交配 ③联想; 并提: ~
sb.'s name with sth. 把某人的名字与某事联系
起来 ❷ vi. ①结合, 结婚 ②成对地出现 ②[动]
交尾 ‖in ~s 成双搭对地

couplet ['kʌplit] n. 两行诗; 对句; 对联

coupling ['kʌpliŋ] n. ①联结, 结合; 【动】交尾 ②
连接器, 联轴节; (火车的)车钩; 挂钩 ③【电】耦合

coupon ['ku:pɔn] n. ①(公债、债券等的)息票 ②
联券票 ③(附在商品上的)赠券; (连在广告上的
可定货或索取赠品的)附单 ④(食品、布匹等的)
配给票 ⑤[美俚]政党首领(对参加国会竞选者)
的承认

courage ['kʌridʒ] n. 勇气, 胆量, 英勇 ‖Dutch ~
酒后之勇 / have the ~ of one's convictions
有勇气去做自己认为正确的事 / have the ~ of
one's opinions 敢于提出(或实行)自己的主张 /
lose ~ 丧失勇气 / take (或 pluck up, muster
up) ~ 鼓起勇气, 奋勇 / take one's ~ in both
hands 勇往直前, 敢作敢为

courageous [kə'reidʒəs] a. 勇敢的, 有胆量的, 无
畏的 ‖~ly ad. / ~ness n.

courier ['kuriə] n. ①送急件的人; 信使(尤指外交
信使、秘密情报递送者、军队的传令兵等) ②(作
报刊名用)信使报 ③被雇用照料旅行事务并陪伴
旅客的服务员

course [kɔ:s] I n. ①过程; 经过; 进程: the ~ of
development 发展过程 / the ~ of life 一生 /
the ~ of events 事态的发展 / advance the ~ of
推进…的发展 ②道路; 行动方向, 方针; 路线:
the ~ of a mountain range 山脉走向 /
decide upon a ~ of action 定出行动步骤 ③河
流; 航线; 航向 / ~ (罗盘上的)方位点: The ship's
is due south. 这条船朝着正南方向航行。④习惯
的程序; [复]行为: follow the normal ~ 循常轨 /
evil ~s 放荡的行为 ⑤课程; 学程: a ~ in French
(或 a French ~) 法语课程 / take a science (an
arts) ~ 修一门理 (文) 科课程 / complete one's
college ~ 读完大学 ⑥疗程 ⑦【建】层; 一层砖
石; 一排: lay the ~s 砌砖 ⑧一道菜: a dinner
of five ~s (或 a five-~ dinner) 五道菜的一餐
饭 / a soup (fish, dessert) ~ 一道汤(鱼, 甜点心)
⑨跑道; 跑马场; 高尔夫球场 ⑩追猎(尤指用猎犬
追猎野兔等): the ~ at a hare 追猎野兔 ⑪[船]
下桁大横帆: main (fore, mizzen) ~ 大桅(前桅,
后桅)横帆 ⑫[复]月经 ⑬【军】导航波束 II ❶
vt. ①追, 追逐; (用猎犬)追猎: ~ sb. at the heels
紧追在某人后面 ②使(马等)跑; 使(猎狗)追猎
③越过, 跑过 ❷ vi. ①跑, 追; (用猎犬)追猎 ②
运行; 流动, 流淌: Blood ~s through the veins.
血液在血管中循环流动。III ad. [口](也作 '~)
当然, 自然 (= of ~) ‖a ~ of exchange(外汇)
兑换率 / by ~ of 照…的常例 / hold (或 keep
on) one's ~ 抱定宗旨, 坚持方针 / in ~ [美]
学完正式课程并经过考试 / in ~ of 正在…中:
a highway in ~ of construction 正在修建的公
路 / in due ~ 及时地; 到(一定的)时候, 在适当
的时候: I shall answer your letter in due ~. 到
时候我会写回信给你的。/ in the ~ of 在…的
过程中; 在…期间 / in the ~ of nature (或 in
the ordinary ~ of things) 正常地, 按事物的正

常趋势 / ***in (the) ~ of time*** 最后；经过一定的时间 / ***lay a*** (或 ***one's***) ~ (朝某方向)直驶；[喻]制订计划 / ***of ~*** 当然，自然 / ***on (off) ~*** 在(不在)规定的轨道上 / ***run its (their) ~*** 自然地发展；按常规进行 / ***shape one's ~*** 订定方针，决定某种做法 / ***stay the ~*** 持续到底；不中途放弃 / ***take its (their) ~*** =run its (their) ~ / ***take one's own ~*** 照自己的意思去做；一意孤行 / ***walk over the ~*** 轻而易举地获胜

court [kɔːt] **I** ***n.*** ①庭院，院子 (=~yard) ②(网球等的)球场(常指四面有围墙的) ③院落；大院；[美]汽车游客旅馆 (=motel) ④(展览会、博物馆中某种展出品的)陈列区 ⑤法院；法庭；(开)庭：appear in ~ 出庭，到案 / *Court* is now adjourned.(法庭)现在休庭了。⑥(公司等的)委员会，理事会；(某些社团的)分会 ⑦[总称]委员们，理事们 ⑧[美]立法机关，议会 ⑨官廷；朝廷；(君主)受觐：be presented at ~ 进宫廷觐见 ⑩奉承，殷勤；求爱：pay ~ to 向…献殷勤；向…求爱 ‖*a civil ~* 民事法庭 / *~ circular* [英](报纸上逐日发表的)宫廷活动录 / *~ dress* 朝服 / *a ~ guide* (英国的)士绅录 / *a ~ of appeal* 上诉法院 / *a ~ of claims* 申诉法院 / *a ~ of first instance* 初审法院 / *a ~ of justice* (或 *law*) 法院，法庭 / *a ~ of last resort* 最高上诉法院 / *a ~ of requests* (英国的)小额债权法院 / *a criminal ~* 刑事法庭 / *a police ~* 警察法庭 **II** ❶ ***vt.*** ①招致；企求：~ sb.'s approval (support) 企图获得某人的赞同(支持) / ~ fame 求名 ②引诱，吸引 ③讨好，奉承；向…求爱 ❷ ***vi.*** 求爱 ‖***clear the ~*** 命所有旁听者退出法庭 / ***go to ~*** ①起诉 ②朝见君主 / ***hold a ~*** ①开庭，开审 ②(君主等)举行受觐礼 / ***out of ~*** ①在法庭外面，不经法院：settle a case *out of* ~ 不经法院解决案件 ②【律】被驳回(的)；[喻]不值一顾(的)：His contentions cannot be laughed *out of* ~. 对他的争辩不能一笑置之。/ put (rule) sth. *out of* ~ 认为(判断)某事不值得考虑 / put oneself *out of* ~ 使自己显得荒谬可笑 / ***the Court of St. James's*** 英国宫廷：an ambassador accredited to *the Court of St. James's* 驻英大使 ‖**~ship** ***n.*** 求爱，求婚 ‖**~ card** 花牌(纸牌中的K, Q, J) / **~ day** 开庭日，审判日 / **~ game** 球场运动(常指网球、手球等) / **'~'house** ***n.*** ①法院(指处所) ②[美]县政府办公大楼 ③[美]县政府所在地 / **~ plaster** 橡皮膏(尤指绸底的) / **~ roll** 法庭中的租佃登录册 / **'~room** ***n.*** 审判室 / **~ tennis** (在四面有围墙的场子上打的)硬地网球 / **'~'yard** ***n.*** 庭院，院子

courteous ['kəːtjəs] ***a.*** 有礼貌的；谦恭的；殷勤的 ‖**~ly** ***ad.*** / **~ness** ***n.***

courtesy ['kəːtisi] ***n.*** ①礼貌，谦恭；殷勤；谦恭有礼的言词(或举动)：a ~ call (或 visit) 礼节上的访问 ②好意，优遇：the ~ of the port 本国公民回国抵港时海关给予的优先履行手续的待遇 ③ = curtsey, curtsy (*n.*) ‖***by ~*** [美] 为表示礼貌起见；承蒙好意 / ***by ~ of*** [美] ①蒙…允许：*by ~ of* the author 经作者同意(转载稿件、图片等时的编者用语) ②蒙…好意赠送(或借用) ③经由…的途径 / ***drop a ~*** (西方女子)行屈膝礼 ‖**~ card** 特别优待券 / **~ title** 礼节上的尊称

courtier ['kɔːtjə] ***n.*** ①廷臣，朝臣 ②奉承者，谄媚者

courtly ['kɔːtli] **I** ***a.*** ①适合朝廷气派的；显贵的；优雅的 ②奉承的 ③赞成(或倾向)朝廷政策的 **II** ***ad.*** 有礼貌地 ‖**courtliness** ***n.***

court-martial ['kɔːt'mɑːʃəl] **I** ([复] courts-martial 或 court-martials) ***n.*** ①军事法庭：a drumhead ~ 战地临时军事法庭 / a summary ~ 简易军事法庭(仅能判处士兵以轻刑的法庭) / a general ~ 最高军事法庭 ②军法审判 **II** (court-martial(l)ed; court-martial(l)ing) ***vt.*** 对…进行军法审判

cousin ['kʌzn] ***n.*** ①堂(或表)兄弟；堂(或表)姐妹 ②亲戚；远亲 ③(在地位等方面)同等的人：the rural children and their city ~*s* 农村和城市儿童 ④卿(国王对贵族的尊称) ⑤同民族而国籍不同的人 ⑥[美俚]老朋友 ⑦[美俚]易受骗者 ‖***a first ~*** 堂(或表)兄弟；堂(或表)姐妹 / ***a second ~*** 父母的堂(或表)兄弟姐妹所生的儿子(或女儿) / ***call ~(s) with*** 说自己是…的亲属 ‖**~hood, ~ship** ***n.*** 堂(或表)兄弟姐妹关系；亲戚关系 / **~ly** ***a.*** 堂(或表)兄弟姐妹关系(般)的 ‖**'~-'german** ([复] ~s-german) ***n.*** 堂(或表)兄弟；堂(或表)姐妹

cove[1] [kouv] **I** ***n.*** ①山凹 ②小湾，小海湾；(河)湾 ③【建】凹圆线脚；穹窿，拱；墙壁顶上的藏灯凹处 **II** ***vt.*** & ***vi.*** (使)成穹形，(使)内凹

cove[2] [kouv] ***n.*** [英俚]家伙，汉子

covenant ['kʌvinənt] **I** ***n.*** ①盟约，契约 ②【律】契约；契约条款；违反契约的诉讼 **II** ❶ ***vt.*** 用盟约(或契约)保证 ❷ ***vi.*** 缔结盟约；立契约 ‖***a ~ of salt*** 不可背弃的盟约 ‖**~ed** ***a.*** 立过契约的，有契约上义务的 / **~er** ***n.*** 誓约者，盟约者

cover ['kʌvə] **I** ❶ ***vt.*** ①盖，铺；覆盖，盖设；遮盖；包：Snow ~*ed* the ground. 雪覆盖着地面。/ ~ sb. *with* mud (车辆等)溅得某人满身是泥 / ~ a tree *with* straw 用草把树包起来 ②掩盖，掩饰；隐匿：Lies cannot ~ *up* facts. 谎言掩盖不了事实。/ ~ one's nervousness (embarrassment) 掩饰紧张心情(窘态) / ~ (*up*) one's tracks 隐匿踪迹 ③掩护；掩蔽：~ oneself behind a tree 躲在树后 ④对准；(枪炮等)控制(住) ⑤包括，包含；适用于：The exhibition ~*s* an area of . . . square metres. 展览会展出面积为…平方米。/ The rules ~ all cases. 这些规则普遍适用。⑥行过(路程) ⑦负担支付(开支等)；弥补(损失等)；补进(卖完的商品等)；给(货物等)保险：These expenses are ~*ed* by the state. 这些费用都由国家负担。/ The goods are ~*ed* against fire. 这些货物已保火险。⑧对…进行新闻采访，报道：~ a conference 采访开会情况 ⑨(种马等)和…交配；(鸡等)孵(蛋)

⑩【体】(为夺球)钉住(对手);掩护(本队球员) ⑪ (出同额赌注)接受(对方打赌);出较大的牌来压倒(对方的牌) ❷ vi. ①覆盖;涂 ②把帽子再次戴上 ③代替,顶替 (for) II n. ①盖子;套子: a ~ for a pan 锅盖 ②(书的)封面,封底,封皮;包皮;封袋 ③(自行车的)外胎 ④床罩 ⑤掩护(物),掩蔽(物);掩蔽处: give an operation air (top) ~ 为作战提供空中(高空)掩护 ⑥【军】集中照射 ⑦(一副)餐具;餐席: Covers were laid for eight. 摆好了八副餐具。/ a dinner of twenty ~s 二十客的餐席 ⑧【商】保证金 ⑨覆盖地面的东西(如草木、积雪等) ⑩戴着帽 ②被落满;被盖满;被缀满: The trees are ~ed with fruit. 树上结满果子。/ be ~ed with sweat 浑身是汗 ③充满着: be ~ed with shame (confusion) 羞愧(慌乱)不堪 / break ~ (野兽等)从隐藏处出来 / ~ in 遮盖住;填满 / ~ over 遮没 / ~ up ①掩盖,掩饰;隐匿 ②包庇 (for) ③裹住: It's very cold out; you must ~ yourself up well. 外面很冷,你得穿暖和些。/ from ~ to ~ 从头至尾: He read the magazine from ~ to ~. 他从头至尾地看完了那本杂志。/ take ~ 隐蔽;(利用掩护物)躲避: take ~ from rain 避雨 / under ~ 隐藏着,在遮蔽处 / under ~ (to) 附在(寄给…)的信中 / under separate ~ 在另函(或另包)内 / under (the) ~ of ① 在…掩护下;趁着 ②打着…幌子,以…为借口 / under the same ~ 在同一封信中 ‖~all ['kʌvərɔːl] n. [常用复](衣裤相连的)工作服 / ~ charge 附加费,服务费 / ~ crop 护田、肥田的农作物,覆盖作物 / ~ girl 封面女郎(指其照片被刊作杂志封面的女子) / ~ note 暂保单,保险证明 / ~ story 用作杂志封面图片题材的报道 / ~-up ['kʌvərʌp] n. 掩盖手段,掩盖手法

covering ['kʌvəriŋ] I n. ①覆盖(物);套,罩 ②掩蔽(物),掩护(物) ③【商】(卖空方为了结交易对证券等的)补进 II a. ①掩护的: ~ fire 掩护火力 / a ~ force (party)【军】掩护部队(组) ②附加说明的: a ~ letter 对函内附件的说明信

coverlet ['kʌvəlit], **coverlid** ['kʌvəlid] n. 床罩

covert ['kʌvət] I a. ①隐藏的;偷偷摸摸的,暗地里的: a ~ wrecker 暗藏的破坏分子 / with ~ malice 存心不良地 / in ~ conversation 在暗中谈论 ②【律】受丈夫保护的 II ['kʌvə, 'kʌvət] n. ①(小兽等的)隐蔽处(指森林、树丛等);掩蔽处,掩护物: draw a ~ for 拨开树丛寻觅 / shoot a ~ 在树丛中打猎 / in (或 under) the ~ of 在…的掩护之下 ②【动】覆羽(蔽覆羽翮基部的羽毛) ‖~ly ad. / ~ness n. ‖~ coat (骑马、射击时穿的)轻皮短外套

covet ['kʌvit] ❶ vt. 妄想(别人的东西),觊觎 ❷ vi. 垂涎;渴望 ‖~able a. 值得渴望的

covetous ['kʌvitəs] a. 贪婪的; 妄想占有的 (of) ‖~ly ad. / ~ness n.

cow[1] [kau] n. ①母牛;奶牛: milk a ~ 挤牛奶 ② (象、犀、鲸、海豹等的)母兽 ③ [美]家牛(兼指公

牛、母牛) ④[美俚]牛奶;奶油;牛肉 ⑤[美俚] 肥胖难看的人 ⑥ [美俚]西点军校三年级生 ‖a sacred ~ ①(印度的)圣牛 ②神圣不可侵犯的人(或事物) / till the ~s come home 无限期地;永远不可能地 ‖~like a. 母牛似的 / ~bane n. 【植】毒芹 / '~bell n. ①母牛的颈铃 ②【植】白玉草 / '~,berry n. 【植】牙疙瘩 / '~bird n. 【动】北美产的一种黑色小鸟(常接近牛身旁,并在其它鸟巢中产卵) / '~boy n. ①牧童;(美国西部的)骑马牧者,牛仔 ②[美俚]鲁撞的人(尤指横冲直撞的驾驶者) / '~,catcher n. (装置在火车头等前面的)排障器 / ~ college [美俚]农业学院;小而不出名的大学 / '~-dung n. 牛粪 / '~fish n. 【动】海牛;角鱼;海豚 / '~grass n. 【植】红和蓝翘摇 / '~hand n. =~boy / '~heel n. 牛蹄冻 / '~herd n. 放牛的人 / '~hide n. ①牛皮 ②牛皮鞭 vt. (用牛皮鞭)鞭打 / '~house n. 牛舍 / '~lick n. (牛舐过似的)翘着不易压平的一绺头发 / ~man ['kaumən] n. ①放牛的人 ②牧场主 / '~pea n. 豇豆 / '~poke n. [美俚] =~boy / ~ pony [美]牧牛者骑的矮种马 / '~pox n. 牛痘 / '~,puncher n. [美口] =~boy / '~shed n. 牛棚 / '~skin n. & vt. =~hide / '~slip n. 【植】黄花九轮草,立金花 / '~'s-tail, ~ tail n. 散开的绳头 / ~ tree【植】(南美产的)乳树

cow[2] [kau] vt. 吓唬,威胁: We shall never be ~ed

coward ['kauəd] I n. 懦夫,胆怯者 II a. 懦怯的,胆小的

cowardice ['kauədis] n. 懦弱,胆怯

cowardly ['kauədli] a. & ad. 懦怯的(地),胆小的(地) ‖**cowardliness** n.

cower ['kauə] vi. 畏缩;抖缩: ~ with cold 冷得打哆嗦

cowl[1] [kaul] I n. ①带头巾的僧衣;僧衣的头巾 ②烟囱帽(风筒上的)通风帽 ③罩: a cylinder ~ 汽缸罩 ④【空】整流罩 (=cowling) II vt. 在…上装帽(罩) ‖~ed a. 戴有头巾的;装有帽罩的

cowl[2] [kaul] n. [英方](有两只拎环的)大水桶

cowrie, cowry ['kauri] n. ①【动】宝贝,海蚆 ②(古时在亚非作货币用的)贝壳

cox [kɔks] I n. [口]舵手,艇长(尤指赛艇艇长) II ❶ vi. 做舵手(或艇长) ❷ vt. 做(船、艇)的舵手(或艇长)

coxcomb ['kɔkskoum] n. ①纨袴子,花花公子 ②(古时丑角头戴的)鸡冠帽 ③[古]头 ④ 鸡冠 ⑤鸡冠花

coy [kɔi] a. ①(通常指女子)怕羞的: be ~ of speech 羞于言谈 ②装作害羞的,忸怩的 ③不肯表态的 ④[古](地方)偏僻的,隐蔽的 ‖~ly ad. / ~ness n.

cozen ['kʌzn] ❶ vt. 欺骗,哄骗: ~ sb. (out) of sth. 向某人诈骗某物 / ~ sb. into doing sth. 诱使某人做某事 ❷ vi. 干欺骗的勾当

Cr【化】元素铬 (chromium) 的符号

crab¹ [kræb] **I** *n.* ①蟹;蟹肉: ～ fishery 捕蟹渔业 ②[the C-]【天】巨蟹座 ③【机】起重机,绞车 ④[复](掷骰子)双么;[喻]失利 ⑤【动】毛虱,阴虱 (=～ louse) ⑥【空】侧航;偏斜;空中照相的倾侧误差:～ angle 侧航角;偏斜角 ⑦[俚][无]宽波段雷达干扰台 **II** (crabbed; crabbing) ① *vi.* ①捕蟹 ②蟹似地侧着身体疾走;侧航;偏斜 ② *vt.* ①使侧航;使偏斜 ②(隼)用爪抓,攫,斗 ‖*a case of ～s* 失败 / *catch a ～* 一桨没划好(桨划得过深或未入水中) / *turn out* (或 *come off*) ～s 终于失败 ‖*let* ['kræblit] *n.* 小蟹 / ～*like a.* & *ad.* 蟹似的(地) ‖～ *louse* 【动】毛虱,阴虱 / ～ *pot* 捕蟹笼 / '～,sidle *vi.* (蟹似地)横爬,横行

crab² [kræb] **I** *n.* ①(野生)酸苹果;酸苹果树 (=～ apple) ②脾气乖戾的人,爱发牢骚的人 **II** (crabbed; crabbing) ① *vt.* ①使易发脾气;使不高兴 ②[口]就…发牢骚,抱怨 ③损害,破坏:～ sb.'s act [口]挫败某人的计划 ② *vi.* [口]发牢骚;找岔子,挑剔 (at, about) ‖～ *apple* (野生)酸苹果;酸苹果树 / ～*stick n.* ①酸苹果树制的手杖(或棍子) ②脾气乖戾的人 / ～ *tree* 酸苹果树

crabbed ['kræbid] *a.* ①脾气乖戾的,易怒的 ②(字迹)难辨认的;(文章等)难懂的,晦涩的 ‖～*ly ad.* / ～*ness n.*

crack [kræk] **I** ① *vi.* ①发出爆裂声,劈啪地响: The fireworks ～ed overhead. 烟火在头顶上空劈劈啪啪地爆响。②裂开,爆裂: The bottle will ～ if you pour boiling water into it. 要是你倒开水进去,这瓶子会裂的。/ The ropes ～ed under pressure. 绳索崩断了。③(人或人的健康、精神等)衰退,垮掉 ④(嗓音)变哑,变粗(尤指男孩发育期的变音) ⑤[俚]说笑话,嘲弄,讥刺: Quit ～ing! 别胡说八道了! ⑥[方]吹牛;闲谈 ⑦【化】裂化 ② *vt.* ①使发出爆裂声,使劈啪地响:～ a gun 鸣枪 / ～ a whip 把鞭子在空中抽得劈啪作响 ②使破裂,使爆裂;使开缝:～ a cup across the bottom 使杯底裂开 / ～ a door (window) 使门(窗)霹开一条缝 ③砸开,(砰地一声)打开:～ a nut 打碎坚果 / ～ a bottle 开酒瓶喝酒 / ～ a book 打开书本阅读 ④(砰地一声)打,(用拳、掌等)击:～ sb. over the head 打某人的头 ⑤解开(难题等),揭开(秘密);宣布(价格等):～ a criminal case 破案 / ～ a mystery 揭开奥秘 ⑥突破(障碍);闯进,破门而入(或出) ⑦撞毁;毁损,使(嗓音)变粗,使(嗓音)变哑 ⑧说(笑话) ⑩使发疯,使神经错乱 ⑪突然打断 ⑫【化】使裂化 ⑬[美俚]找开(钞票) **II** *n.* ①破裂声,爆裂声,劈啪声: the ～ of a cannon (rifle) 炮(枪)声 ②[口](砰的)一击 ③裂缝,龟裂,碎裂;缝隙: The dish has a ～ in it. 这只盘子上有条裂纹。/ open the door a ～ 把门打开一条缝 ④弱点,缺点,瑕疵: There is a ～ in your mind. 你精神有点毛病啦。⑤(嗓子的)变音,粗哑 ⑥[俚]尝试: Let me take a ～ at it. 让我来试一

试。⑦[英方]大话,谎言;谈话,闲谈;[复]新闻 ⑧[俚]挖苦话,俏皮话: get off a ～ 说了句俏皮话 ⑨[口]一瞬,片刻: I'll be back in a ～. 我一会儿就回来。/ at the ～ of dawn 在破晓时 ⑩古怪的人;[英俚]出色的人(或东西) ⑪夜盗;夜盗行为 **III** *a.* 第一流的,顶呱呱的:～ troops 精锐部队 / a ～ shot 神枪手 **IV** *ad.* 啪地一声: hit sb. ～ on the back 啪地一声打某人的背 ‖～ *a crib* [俚]闯入人家偷盗 / ～ *a smile* 展颜微笑 / ～ *back* [美俚]回嘴 / ～ *down* (on) (对…)采取严厉措施;制裁;镇压 / ～ *on* 加(速),开足(马力),扯满(所有的帆) / ～*up* ①(飞机、汽车等)撞坏,撞毁 ②使撞毁 ③衰退,垮掉(在感情方面)失去控制 ④吹捧:～ sb. (sth.) up 吹捧某人(某事物) / ～ *wise* [美俚]说俏皮话 / *get ～ing* 开始,开始工作;开始移动: Let's get ～ing. 让我们动手干吧。/ *the ～ of doom* 【宗】世界末日的霹雳 / *walk a* (或 *the*) ～ 沿地板缝笔直走(以证明未喝醉) ‖～*ajack* ['krækədʒæk] *a.* 杰出的,第一流的 *n.* 能手,杰出的人;第一流的东西 / '～-*brained a.* 发疯的;古怪的;愚蠢的 / '～*down n.* 制裁;镇压 / '～*jaw a.* 难发音的,难念的 / '～*pot a.* & *n.* 古怪的(人);发疯的(人) / '～*sman* ['kræksmən] *n.* 夜贼;盗保险箱的贼 / '～-*up n.* ①(飞机、汽车等的)撞坏,撞毁 ②(健康、精神等的)衰退,衰弱;失去控制 ③崩溃,垮台

cracked [krækt] *a.* ①有裂缝的;弄破了的;碎的:～ wheat 碾碎的(小麦)麦粒;(小麦)麦片 ②(嗓音)粗的,哑的 ③发疯的,疯颠的 ④【化】裂化的:～ gasoline 裂化汽油

cracker ['krækə] *n.* ①击破者 ②爆竹;(内装糖果等的)彩包爆竹 ③一种薄脆饼干;[美]饼干 (= biscuit) ④[复]胡桃夹 (=nutcrackers) ⑤崩溃,破产 ⑥[贬](美国南方的)穷苦白人 ⑦[方]吹牛的人;[俚]谎话 ⑧破碎机: a coal ～ 碎煤机 ⑨【化】(石油)裂化设备 ‖'～,barrel *n.* [美口]高谈阔论的;(哲学思想等)不成熟的 / '～*jack a.* & *n.* =crackajack

crackle ['krækl] **I** ① *vi.* ①劈劈啪啪地响 ②生气勃勃;闪耀;发火花 ③龟裂 ② *vt.* 使劈啪爆裂;啪地压碎 **II** *n.* ①劈啪声,爆裂声 ②(瓷器等上的)细裂纹,碎裂花纹;有细裂纹的瓷器 ③闪耀

cradle ['kreidl] **I** *n.* ①摇篮;[喻]策源地,发源地 ②[诗]安息地,安息处 ③婴儿时期: in the ～ 在婴儿时期 / from the ～ 自幼 ④摇篮架(指附在大镰刀上使割下的作物平整均匀的配件;(附有摇篮架的)大镰刀;(雕刻用的)锯齿形凿刀 ⑤【船】支舱架,下水架;救生吊篮 ⑥【医】支架;护架;摇床;【建】(砌拱间等的)支架;吊篮;吊架 ⑦【机】摇架;【军】摇架(承受炮弓后坐力的炮架部分) ⑧【矿】淘金槽;移动式摇动洗矿槽 / (搁电话听筒的)叉簧 ⑨(修制汽车用的)轮脚架 ⑩[美俚]铁路敞车 **II** ① *vt.* ①把…放在摇篮里;把(婴儿)放在摇篮里摇;象放在摇篮里似地兜着:～ a baby to sleep 摇婴儿入睡 / ～ an infant in one's arms 怀抱婴儿 ②抚育 ③用附有摇篮架的大镰刀刈割(作物) ④用架支住,支撑 ⑤淘洗(矿砂) ⑥把…搁在支架上: ～ the telephone receiver 把电话听筒放好 ❷ vi. 用附有摇篮架的大镰刀刈割 ‖*from the ～ to the grave* 从生到死,一生 / *rob the ～* 和比自己年岁小很多的人作伴(或结婚) / *stifle in the ～* 把…扼杀在摇篮里 ‖～song n. 摇篮曲,催眠曲

craft [krɑ:ft] I n. ①工艺;手艺;(需要手艺的)行业,职业: the potter's ～ 陶工的技艺;陶工业 / arts and ～s 工艺美术 ②技巧;[贬]手腕,诡计: a man full of ～ 诡计多端的人 ③行会;行会成员;同行: the ～ of carpenters 木工行会 / the Craft 互济会 ④[单复同]船(尤指小船);航空器(指飞机、飞艇等) II vt. [一般以过去分词形式出现](以手工)精巧地制作 ‖*the gentle ～* 钓鱼;钓鱼者组织的成员 ‖～ **brother** 同行 / ～ **guild** (手工业)行会 / ～ **union** 行业工会,同行工会

craftsman ['krɑ:ftsmən]([复] craftsmen) n. 手艺人,工匠;名匠 ‖～**ship** n. (工匠的)技术,技艺

crafty ['krɑ:fti] a. ①狡猾的,诡计多端的: as ～ as a fox 象狐狸一样狡猾 ②[英方]灵巧的,巧妙的

crag[1] [kræg] n. ①岩,巉崖 ②【地】砂质泥灰岩(英国上新世),岩石碎片

crag[2] [kræg] n. [英方]颈,喉

cram [kræm] I (crammed; cramming) ❶ vt. ①把…塞进;塞满: He crammed the letters into a drawer. 他把信件塞进抽屉。 / ～ a suitcase with clothes 把衣服塞满箱子 / The room was crammed. 房间被塞满了。 ②贪婪地吃(食物) ③[口]填鸭式地教(学生);死记硬背(功课): ～ up history for an exam 死记历史应付考试 ❷ vi. ①贪婪地吃,吃得过多 ②[口]赶功课;临时准备应考 II n. ①[口]填塞;压碎 ②[口]死记硬背;死记住的功课;临时抱佛脚的学生 ③[英俚]谎言 ‖～ *oneself (with food)* 塞饱肚皮 / ～ *sth. down sb.'s throat* 把某物硬塞给某人吃下去;(填鸭式地)反复对某人灌输某事 ‖'～-'full a. 塞满了…的(of)

cramp[1] [kræmp] I n. ①(肌肉)痉挛,痛性痉挛: writer's ～ 指痉挛,书写痉挛 ②肌肉(过分活动后)局部(或暂时)麻痹 ③[常用复]急性腹痛 II vt. 使起痉挛 ‖～**fish** n. 电鳐科的鱼

cramp[2] [kræmp] I n. ①夹,钳;扣钉 ②约束物;约束 II vt. ①用夹子夹紧 ②掌(舵) ③使(车子前轮)向左(或右)转动 ④束缚: Arrogance ～ed his progress. 骄傲阻碍了他的进步。 / We are ～ed for room here. 我们这里很挤。 III a. ①紧缩的,狭窄的 ②难懂的,难读的;字迹难辨认的: a ～ word 难懂的词 ‖～ *sb.'s style* [俚]使某人受拘束而不能正常发挥其平时的才能 ‖～**ness** n. ‖～ **iron** 夹子,钳子;铁钩;扣钉

crane [krein] I n. ①【动】鹤 ②[the C-]【天】天鹤座 ③起重机;摄影升降机;虹吸器;(机车的)给水管 II ❶ vt. ①伸(颈): ～ one's neck to have a look 伸长着脖子张望 ②用起重机起吊(或搬运) ❷ vi. ①(鹤似地)伸着脖子看 ②(起跳等之前)退缩;(行动前)踌躇 (at) ‖～ **fly** 【动】大蚊 / ～**sbill** ['kreinzbil] n. 【植】(斑点)老鹳草

cranium ['kreinjəm]([复] craniums 或 crania ['kreinjə]) n. 头盖,脑壳,头盖骨

crank [kræŋk] I n. ①【机】曲柄 ②[古]弯曲 ③奇怪的说法(或想法、行为);幻想,一时的怪念头 ④[口]怪人;脾气坏的人;狂热者 II ❶ vt. ①使成曲柄状;给…装上曲柄;用曲柄连结;用曲柄开动(汽车等): ～ (up) an engine (用曲柄)开动引擎 ❷ vi. ①转动曲柄 ②曲折行进 III a. ①(机器等)不正常的,有毛病的;摇晃的,不稳的 ②(船)易翻的;易倾斜的 ③[美方]愉快的,精神好的 ④[美方]骄傲的,自负的 ‖～ *out* 制成,作成(尤指机械呆板地) ‖～ **axle** 曲柄轴 / ～**case** n. 曲柄轴箱 / '～**pin** n. 曲柄销(或栓) / '～**shaft** n. 曲轴

cranny ['kræni] n. ①(墙上等的)裂缝,裂口 ②冷僻的角落 ‖**crannied** a. 有裂缝的;裂缝多的

crape [kreip] I n. ①绉丝;绉线;绉纱;绉布;绉绸;绉呢 ②(哀悼时袖上戴的)黑纱;(帽上的)黑丧章 II vt. ①用绉纱(或绉纱似的东西)覆盖 ②使(头发)卷曲 ‖～ **cloth** 绉纱似的毛织品

crash[1] [kræʃ] I ❶ vi. ①(发出猛烈声音地)碰撞,倒入,坠落;(飞机等)坠毁,撞坏: The car ～ed into a tree. 车子猛撞在树上。 / A wall ～ed to the ground. 墙轰地坍了下来。 ②发出撞击声,发出爆裂声: The door ～ed open. 门砰地一声开了。 / Thunder and lightning ～ed. 雷电交加 ③(发出很响声音地)冲,闯 (into, through, down, out) ④失败,垮台,崩溃 ❷ vt. ①(发出猛烈声音地)撞击,砸碎;使(飞机等)坠毁,使(飞机等)撞坏: ～ a bottle against the wall 把瓶猛摔在墙上 / be ～ed to pieces 被砸得粉碎 ②使发出撞击声,使发出爆裂声 ③(发出很响声音地)冲,闯: ～ one's way through brush 闯过灌木丛 ④无票拥入(会场、剧场等),闯入: ～ the gate [俚]擅自入场 ⑤[美俚](突然或轰动一时地)取得在…中出现的地位: The incident ～ed the headlines. 这一事件成了头条新闻。 / ～ television 成为电视新闻人物或(事件) II n. ①(发出猛烈声音的)碰撞;倒下;(飞机等的)坠毁,撞坏: a car ～ 汽车撞车事故 / the cause of the plane ～ 飞机失事的原因 ②撞击声,爆裂声: fall with a ～ 轰隆一声倒下 / a ～ of applause 一阵掌声 ③失败,垮台,崩溃 III a. 应急的;速成的: a ～ programme (或 project) 应急计划 IV ad. 砰地一声: A stone came ～ through the window. 一块石子啪地飞进窗来。 ‖～**ing** n. 撞击声,爆裂声 a. ①碰撞的,发出撞击声的 ②[口]完全的,极度的;倒下,坠落 ‖～ **boat** (援救海上失事飞机的)救生艇 / ～ **dive** (潜水艇遇到紧急情况时的)急速潜

没 / '~-dive vi. (潜水艇)急速潜没 / ~ helmet (飞行员、摩托车运动员等的)防撞头盔 / '~-land vi. & vt. (使)强迫着陆 / ~ pad (装在坦克等里边起保护作用的)防震垫; [美俚]临时睡觉(或居住)处 / ~ truck 失事飞机救援车

crash² [kræʃ] n. (做毛巾、窗帘等用的)粗布: a ~ towel 粗毛巾

crass [kræs] a. ①极度的,非常的: ~ stupidity 愚不可及 ②愚钝的 ③粗糙的,粗厚的 ‖~ly ad.

crate [kreit] I n. ①板条箱, 柳条箱(或篮、篓等) ②[美俚]破旧汽车, 破旧飞机 II vt. 用板条箱(或柳条箱等)装

crater ['kreitə] n. ①火山口 ②弹坑; 陨石坑 ③[the C-] 【天】巨爵座 ‖~iform ['kreitərifɔːm] a. 火山口状的 ‖~ wall 火山口壁

cravat [krə'væt] n. (一种老式的)领带;围巾

crave [kreiv] ❶ vt. ①恳求,请求 ②渴望,热望 ③需要: ~ fresh air 需要新鲜空气 ❷ vi. 渴望,热望 (for)

craven ['kreivən] I n. 懦夫,胆小鬼 II a. 胆小的,怯懦的 ‖cry ~ 叫饶,投降 ‖~ly ad.

crawl¹ [krɔːl] I ❶ vi. ①爬,爬行; 蠕动; 匍匐前进: The snake has ~ed into a hole. 蛇爬到洞里去了。②缓慢地移动;徐徐行进: The hours ~ed by. 时间慢慢地过去。/ A tractor is ~ing up on the highway. 一辆拖拉机在公路上缓慢地开过来。③(为虫、蚁等)爬满,充斥着: The ground is ~ing with caterpillars. 地上爬满了毛虫。④(由于恐惧、厌恶等) 起鸡皮疙瘩,汗毛直竖: make sb.'s flesh ~ 使某人毛发直竖 ⑤(通过谄媚)向上爬; 巴结: ~ into sb.'s favour 拍上了某人马屁 ⑥用自由式游泳 ❷ vt. ①在…上爬 ②[俚]粗暴地责骂,训斥 II n. ①爬,爬行; 蠕动; 匍匐前进 ②缓慢的行进: go at a ~ 慢吞吞地行进 ③自由式游泳 ‖~ space (屋顶、地板等下面)供电线、水管通过的狭小空隙

crawl² [krɔːl] n. (在浅水中圈养鱼 鳖等)的围栏

crayfish ['krei-fiʃ] n.【动】蝲蛄,(产于淡水中的一种)小龙虾

crayon ['kreiən] I n. ①粉笔; 蜡笔; 颜色笔(通称颜色铅笔 =colo(u)red pencil): a picture in ~(s) 粉笔画;蜡笔画 ②粉笔画;蜡笔画 ③(电弧灯的)碳棒 II vt. 用粉笔(或蜡笔等)画

crazy ['kreizi] a. ①疯狂的; 古怪的; 蠢的: You are ~ to do such a thing. 你干这样的事真蠢。②[口]狂热的,热衷的,着迷的: The boy is ~ on (或 about) skating. 那孩子溜冰着了迷。/ be ~ for sth. 渴望某物 / be ~ for sb. 迷恋某人 ③(船、建筑等)破烂的; 摇摇晃晃的, 歪斜的; (道路等)弯弯曲曲的 ④用不规则碎块拼成的: a ~ pavement 碎石人行道 / a ~ quilt 用碎布块拼成的被面 ⑤[美俚]美妙的; 刺激的; 使人感到满意的 ‖like ~ [口]发疯似地 ‖crazily ad. / craziness n. ‖~ bone [美]【医】肱骨内髁(肘部尺骨神经通过处,撞击时有刺痛感) / '~-cat n. [美俚]疯子; 傻瓜

creak [kriːk] I vi. 吱吱嘎嘎地作响 II n. 吱吱嘎嘎的声音: The door opened with a ~. 门嘎地一声开了。‖~y a.

cream [kriːm] I n. ①乳脂; (鲜)奶油: whipped ~ 搅打过的奶油,掼奶油 ②含奶油的食品: chocolate ~ 奶油夹心巧克力 / ice ~ 冰淇淋 ③雪花膏;膏状物: cold ~ 冷霜 / furniture ~ 家具蜡 ④乳状悬浮液: ~ of lime 石灰乳 / ~ of tartar 酒石(即酒石酸氢钾) ⑤精华; 最精采的部分: the ~ of a nation (an army) 国家(军队)的精华 / the ~ of a joke 笑话的妙处 ⑥奶油色,米色 ⑦米色的马;米色的动物 ⑧盛奶油的器皿 II ❶ vt. ①使(牛奶)结成奶油;从(牛奶中)提取奶油 ②从…提取精华 ③加奶油于…;用奶油煮… ④把…打成奶油状;使成奶油状 ⑤用雪花膏擦(脸) ⑥[美俚]啪啪地打; 击败 ❷ vi. 结成奶油; 结成奶油状物 ‖~er n. ①(从牛奶中)分离奶油的器具; 撇奶油用的薄盆子 ②盛奶油的器皿 ③做奶油的人 ‖~,colo(u)red a. 奶油色的,米色的 / ~ laid [主英]米色直纹纸 / ~ puff ①奶油泡夫(一种点心) ②[美俚]软弱的人, 女子气的男人 ③[美俚]保养得很好的汽车(指供出售的旧汽车) / ~ separator 奶油分离器 / '~ware n. [总称]米色的陶器 / ~ wove [主英]米色布纹纸

creamery ['kriːməri] n. ①乳脂(或黄油、乳酪)制造厂 ②奶品商店

creamy ['kriːmi] a. ①含有大量奶油的;含奶油的 ②奶油般的 ③奶油色的,米色的 ‖creaminess n.

crease [kriːs] I n. ①(衣服、纸等的)折缝,折痕;皱痕: ~-resisting cloth 防皱布 / the ~s in a pair of trousers 裤子的折缝,裤腿折痕 ②(板球等投手或打手的)界限线 II ❶ vt. ①使起折痕;弄绉 ②[美](用枪弹)擦伤 ❷ vi. 起折绉,起折痕;起皱: This material ~s easily. 这料子易起皱。‖~d a. / ~r n. 压折缝的器具

create [kri(ː)'eit] ❶ vt. ①创造; 创作: ~ a drama 创作戏剧 ②引起,产生; 造成 ③封授: ~ sb. a peer 封某人为贵族 ❷ vi. [英俚]大惊小怪: You needn't ~ about it. 对此你不必大惊小怪。

creation [kri(ː)'eiʃən] n. ①创造; 创作; (骚动等的)产生; (爵位 职位等的)授予: ~ of peers 增封新贵族(英国政府用以克服上院阻挠的最后手段) ②创造物; 创作物(指文学艺术作品、服装等) ③天地万物; 宇宙 ④ [the C-] (基督教《圣经》)创世 ‖That beats (或 licks) ~! 那简直是闻所未闻,见所未见!

creative [kri(ː)'eitiv] a. ①有创造力的; 创造性的; 创作的: ~ power 创造力 ②产生的,引起的: events ~ of alarm 引起惊慌的事件 ③使增强想象力的: ~ toys 启发儿童想象力的玩具 ‖~ly ad. / ~ evolution 创造进化论(法国柏格森所提出的反科学的哲学学说)

creator [kri(ː)'eitə] n. ①创造者;创作者 ② [the C-]【宗】造物主,上帝

creature ['kriːtʃə] n. ①创造物 ②生物; 动物; [美]

家畜,牛马: dumb ~s 牲畜 ③(含有怜爱或轻蔑的意思)人,家伙: a poor ~ 可怜的人 / What a despicable ~! 可鄙的家伙! ④工具;奴才;奴隶: a ~ of habit 受习惯支配的人,习惯的奴隶 ⑤ [the ~] [方]威士忌酒,烈性饮料 ‖~ **comfort** 物质方面的享受物(指好吃的食物、好看的衣服等)

crèche [kreiʃ] *n.* [法] ①(日间)托儿所 ②育婴堂,弃儿养育院 ③【宗】基督诞生画

credence ['kri:dəns] *n.* ①信任: give (refuse) ~ to the story 相信(不信)所说的情况 ②凭证,证件: a letter of ~ 介绍信,信任状; (大使等的)国书 ③【宗】祭器台,供桌

credential [kri'denʃəl] I *a.* 信任的 II *n.* ①凭证 ②[常用复]信任状,证书; (大使等的)国书

credible ['kredəbl] *a.* 可信的,可靠的 ‖**credibility** [,kredi'biliti] *n.* a *credibility* gap 信用差距(指政府官员参言论与事实的不符) / **credibly** *ad.*

credit ['kredit] I *n.* ①信任,相信: Do you give ~ to what the man said? 你相信那人讲的话吗? ②信誉,声望,荣誉: gain ~ in foreign trade 在对外贸易中赢得信誉 / a man of the highest ~ 一个极有声望的人 ③称赞 ④[a ~](为…)增光的人(或事物)(to) ⑤信用,赊欠;信用贷金: give ~ (银行)提供信用贷款; (商店)允许赊欠 / ~ sales 赊销 / a cooperative 信用合作社 ⑥(银行中的)存款;债权 ⑦【会计】贷;贷方;记入贷方的金额(debit 之对): enter (或 place, put) a sum to sb.'s ~ 把一笔款子记入某人的贷方 ⑧(美国等学校中的)学分 ⑨【商】信用状 (=letter of ~) II *vt.* ①相信: Do you ~ his story? 你相信他所说的情况吗? ②把…记入贷方 ③把…归于(to);认为…有(某种优点或成就等)(with): ~ sb. *with* a principled stand 认为某人有原则立场 / be ~ed *with* some achievement 被认为取得了一些成绩 / *do* ~ *to* 为…带来光荣(或信誉) / *give sb.* ~ *for* ①为某人提供(若干数额)信用贷款 ②为…而称赞某人 ③相信某人有(某种优点等): I did not *give* you ~ *for* such skill. 我没想到你有这样的本领。/ He is more careful than I *gave* him ~ *for.* 他比我原来想的更细心。/ *have* ~ *with sb.* 得到某人的信用 / *reflect* ~ *on* (工作等)使…增光 / *take* ~ *to oneself* 居功 / *to one's* ~ 足以使某人增光,值得赞扬: have great achievements *to one's* ~ 立下了巨大的功劳 / It is greatly *to your* ~ *that* you have overcome such difficulties. 你们克服了这样大的困难,值得大大称赞。‖~ **account** (客户购货的)赊购帐 / ~ **line** ①(电讯、文章、电影等)注明记者(或作者、制片人等)姓名的字行 ②(对某客户的)放款最高限额 / ~ **man** (客户)信用调查员 / ~ **rating** 客户信贷分类 / ~ **squeeze** 信用紧缩,贷款紧缩 / ~ **titles** (影片上、电视中)导演和制片人等的名单 / ~ **union** 存款互助会

creditable ['kreditəbl] *a.* ①可信的 ②值得赞扬的;为…带来荣誉的(to) ③值得给予信用贷款的 ④可归(功)于…的(to) ‖~**ness** *n.* / **creditably** *ad.*

creditor ['kreditə] *n.* ①债权人: a ~ nation 债权国 ②贷方;贷项

credulous ['kredjuləs] *a.* 轻信的,易信的 ‖~**ly** *ad.* / ~**ness** *n.*

creed [kri:d] *n.* ①【宗】信经,信条,教义; [the C-] 使徒信经 ②信念;纲领

creek [kri:k] *n.* ①[英]小湾,小港 ②小河,支流 ③[英方]山间狭道 ‖*up the* ~ 处于困境 ‖~**y** *a.*

creel [kri:l] *n.* ①鱼篮 ②【纺】粗纱架;筒子架;经轴架

creep [kri:p] I (crept [krept]) *vi.* ①(身体凑近或贴着地面)爬行,匍匐而行; (植物)蔓延: ~ forward 匍匐前进 ②潜行,蹑手蹑脚地走动;微微地移动: ~ about on tiptoe 踮着脚尖走动 / Suspicion *crept* into his mind. 不由使他产生怀疑(恐惧)。/ The hours *crept* by. 时间悄悄地过去了。③(由于恐惧、厌恶等)起鸡皮疙瘩,汗毛直竖: make sb.'s flesh ~ 使某人汗毛直竖 ④巴结,奉承: ~ into sb.'s favour 巴结上某人 ⑤【海】用打捞钩探索海底(如找寻电缆等) ⑥(材料)潜伸;蠕变 II *n.* ①爬;蠕动 ②[复][口]毛骨悚然的感觉;战栗: give sb. the ~s 使某人毛骨悚然 ③用有洞篱笆围住的栏圈(仅幼仔能出入) ④[美俚]使人害怕(或厌恶)的人;无足轻重的人 ⑤(材料的)潜伸;蠕变; [无]频率漂移: ~ strength 抗蠕变强度 ‖~**hole** *n.* ①(动物)躲藏的洞穴 ②遁辞,借口 / '~-**mouse** *a.* 胆怯的,易惊的

creeper ['kri:pə] *n.* ①爬行者;爬行动物;爬虫 ②【植】匍匐植物; [C-] 爬山虎属 ③[常用复](绑在鞋下防滑用的)铁齿板 ④[常用复](小孩爬行时穿的)连衫裤 ⑤打捞钩(打捞用的四爪锚) ⑥【机】定速运送器

creepy ['kri:pi] *a.* ①爬行的;蠕动的 ②感到毛骨悚然的 ③令人毛骨悚然的 ‖'~-'**crawly** *a.* (令人)感到毛骨悚然的

cremate [kri'meit] *vt.* 焚毁,把(尸体等)烧成灰 ‖**cremator** *n.* ①烧尸体(或垃圾等)的人 ②焚尸炉;垃圾焚化炉

cremation [kri'meiʃən] *n.* 焚化;火葬

creosote ['kriəsout] *n.* 【化】(杀菌或木材防腐用的)杂酚油,木馏油: ~ oil 【化】杂酚油

crêpe [kreip] *n.* [法] ①【纺】绉丝;绉线;绉布;绉绸;绉呢: a ~ twist 紧拈,绉拈 ②【化】绉(橡)胶 (=~ rubber) ③绉纸 (=~ paper) ④(丧服用的)黑绉纱 ⑤小而极薄的烤饼 ‖~ *de Chine* [də 'ʃi:n] 双绉

crescendo [kri'ʃendou] [意] I *n.* ①【音】渐强 ②逐渐增强, (向高潮)渐进;顶峰 II *a.* & *ad.* 【音】渐强的(地)

crescent ['kresnt] I *n.* ①月牙,蛾眉月;新月 ②新月状(物) ③[C-]旧时土耳其苏丹的标志;

土耳其的威力 ④ 伊斯兰教: the Cross and the Crescent 基督教与伊斯兰教 **II** *a.* ① 新月状的 ②[诗](新月般)渐渐增大的

cress [kres] *n.* 【植】十字花科的植物; 水蓊菜, 水芹

crest [krest] **I** *n.* ①(鸟、禽的)冠, 鸡冠; 冠毛 ②盔上的羽毛饰; 盔 ③顶饰; (盾等的)纹饰; 【建】脊饰 ④顶; 山顶; 浪峰 ⑤(马、狮等的)颈脊, 长于颈脊上的鬃毛 ⑥【解】脊突; 嵴: frontal ~ 额脊突 / neural ~ 神经嵴 **II ❶** *vt.* ①在…上加顶饰; 成为…的顶饰 ②达到…的顶点 **❷** *vi.* 达到顶点; 成浪峰 ‖*on the ~ of the wave* 在最走运的时候 ‖~ed *a.* 有顶饰的; 有冠毛的: ~ed notepaper 印有顶饰的信纸 ‖'~,fallen *a.* 冠毛垂倒的;[喻]垂头丧气的 / ~ table【建】墙帽 / ~ tile【建】屋脊瓦

cretonne [kre'ton] *n.* (做窗帘、家具套等用的)印花(或提花)装饰布

crevasse [kri'væs] **I** *n.* ①(冰河、雪原等的)裂缝, 冰隙 ②[美](堤防的)裂口 **II** *vt.* ①使生裂缝, 使有冰隙 ②使有裂口

crevice ['krevis] *n.* 罅隙, 裂缝

crew[1] [kru:] *n.* ①全体船员; 全体乘务员; (赛艇的)全体队员 ②水手们: officers and ~ 全体船员和水手们 ③同事们, 一起工作的人们: a flying (ground) ~ 空(地)勤人员 / a gun ~ 机枪手(组); 炮手(组) ④[贬]一帮人, 一伙人: a motley ~ 乌合之众 ‖~ cut 平头(指发式) / ~man ['kru:mən] *n.* 船员; 乘务员

crew[2] [kru:] [主英] crow[2] 的过去式

crib [krib] **I** *n.* ①有栏杆的儿童小床 ②牛栏; 秣槽 ③简陋小屋, 小房间 ④[矿]木垛, (铁或木制的)井壁基框;【建】迭木框 ⑤[美](谷物等的)围栏 ⑥[口](文章等的)剽窃 ⑦[口]学生作弊用的外文对照本(或注释本等) ⑧(cribbage 牌戏中)玩牌者丢弃的牌(作为发牌者记分用) ⑨[美俚]低级妓院; 小酒吧间; 小厨房 **II** (cribbed; cribbing) **❶** *vt.* ①把…关进栅栏(或小屋等狭小处);幽闭 ②在…设置栅栏 ③[口]剽窃, 抄袭; 偷窃 **❷** *vi.* ①[口]剽窃, (学生)抄夹带, 作弊 ②(马等漱口水)咬秣槽 ‖*crack a ~*[俚]闯入人家偷盗 ‖'~-,biting *n.* (马)咬秣槽漱口水的习癖

crick [krik] **I** *n.* 【医】(颈或背肌肉的)痛性痉挛, 痛痉 **II** *vt.* 引起(颈、背等)痉挛

cricket[1] ['krikit] *n.* ①蟋蟀 ②木制矮垫脚凳 ③【建】斜坡小屋顶 ‖*as lively (merry) as a ~* 象蟋蟀一样地活泼(愉快)

cricket[2] ['krikit] **I** *n.* ①[体]板球 ②[口]公平的行为, 光明正大的行为: It's not (quite) ~. [英口]这个行为不光明磊落。**II** *vi.* 打板球

crime [kraim] **I** *n.* ①罪, 罪行; 犯罪; 罪恶: a capital ~ 杀头罪, 死罪 / commit a ~ 犯罪 / towering ~s 滔天罪行 / prevent (detect, punish) ~ 防止(侦查, 惩办)犯罪 / Such reckless spending is a ~. 如此挥霍是一种罪恶。②憾事; 羞耻事 **II** *vt.* [英][军俚]指控…违反军纪;

宣告…违反军纪罪 ‖*a ~ against nature* 鸡奸 ‖~less *a.* 无罪的

criminal ['kriminl] **I** *a.* ①犯罪的; 刑事上的; 犯了罪的: a ~ act 犯罪行为 / a ~ action (或 suit) 刑事诉讼 / ~ conversation 通奸 / ~ law 刑法 ②可耻的, 应受谴责的 **II** *n.* 罪犯, 犯人: a war ~ 战犯 ‖~ity [,krimi'næliti] *n.* 有罪; 犯罪行为 / ~ly *ad.*

criminology [,krimi'nolədʒi] *n.* 犯罪学

crimp[1] [krimp] **I** *n.* 诱骗(或迫使)别人去做水手(或当兵)的人; 兵贩子 **II** *vt.* 诱骗(或迫使)…去做水手(或当兵) ‖~er *n.* 兵贩子

crimp[2] [krimp] **I** *vt.* ①使卷曲; 使成波形: ~ the hair 卷曲头发; 烫发 / ~ed yarn 鬈曲弹力纱(一种化学纤维) ②把(鞋面革)弯成鞋形; (玻璃制造中)拉(玻璃)成波形 ④把(鱼肉)划痕使皱缩 ⑤[美俚]妨碍; 束缚 **II** *n.* ①[常用复]卷曲的头发 ②皱缩; 卷曲; 打褶 ③[美俚]障碍; 约束: put a ~ in (或 into) 妨碍…, 束缚… ‖~er *n.* 折皱器 / ~ing iron 卷发器, 烫发铗

crimson ['krimzn] **I** *n.* 深红, 梅红, 绯红 **II** *a.* ①深红色的, 绯红色的 ②[喻]血腥的; 血的 **III ❶** *vt.* 使成绯红色 **❷** *vi.* 变绯红色

cringe [krindʒ] *vi. & n.* ①畏缩 ②卑躬屈膝, 阿谀奉承

crinkle ['krinkl] **I ❶** *vt.* 使皱, 使成波状, 使卷曲: ~d yarn 鬈绉纱, 波曲纱 **❷** *vi.* ①皱, 成波状, 卷曲 ②沙拉沙拉响 **II** *n.* ①皱, 波状, 卷曲 ②[植]皱叶病

crinoline ['krinəli:n] *n.* ①(旧时)制女衬裙的粗布(或马鬃等) ②(旧时支撑女裙的)裙架; 有衬架支撑的女裙 ③(军舰舰身四周的)水雷防御网

cripple ['kripl] **I** *n.* ①跛子; 跛足的动物; 残废的人(或动物) ②残缺(或不完美)的事物 ③(擦洗或油漆窗户等用的)脚手架 **II** *vt.* ①使跛, 使残废 ②使丧失活动能力; 削弱(经济等): ~ the enemy 削弱敌人(战斗力) **❷** *vi.* [苏格兰]一拐一拐地走路, 跛行 (along) **III** *a.* 跛的, 拐的, 残废的 ‖~dom, ~hood *n.* 残废; 无能

crisis ['kraisis] ([复] crises ['kraisi:z]) *n.* ①危机: a political ~ 政治危机 ②危急存亡之际;决定性时刻; 转折点: The matter has been brought to a ~. 事情已到紧要关头。③[医]危象; 临界, 转换期

crisp [krisp] **I** *a.* ①脆的, 松脆的; 易碎的: ~ biscuits 松脆的饼干 ②清新的, 爽快的; 霜冻的: ~ air 清新的空气 ③鲜嫩的: ~ lettuces 鲜嫩的莴苣 ④干脆的, 净利落的; 活跃的, 有生气的: ~ manner 干脆的态度 / a ~ style 劲健的风格 ⑤(头发等)卷缩的, 卷曲的 **II** *n.* ①[英][常用复]油炸马铃薯片(袋装出售) ②松脆物: be burned to a ~ 烧脆 ③[俚]钞票 **III ❶** *vt.* ①使卷曲, 使起皱, 使起波纹 ②使发脆; 把…烘脆 **❷** *vi.* ①卷曲, 起波纹 ②发脆; 冻硬: The ground ~ed with frost. 地面霜冻。‖~ly *ad.* / ~ness *n.*

criterion [krai'tiəriən] ([复] criteria [krai'tiəriə] 或 criterions) *n.* (批评、判断的)标准, 准则, 尺度

critic ['kritik] I *n.* ①批评家, 评论家: ~*s* of art and literature 文艺批评家 ②爱挑剔的人, 爱非议的人 II *a.* =critical

critical ['kritikəl] *a.* ①批评(性)的, 批判(性)的; 评论(性)的: a ~ remark (opinion) 批评性的话(意见) / a man with a ~ eye 具有批判眼光的人 ②对…表示谴责的, 对…感到不满的(of); 苛求的: be ~ *of* sth. 对某事表示谴责 / be ~ in one's choice 选择苛刻 ③紧要的, 关键性的; 危急的: a ~ moment (或 juncture) 紧要关头, 关键时刻 / The patient's condition is ~. 病人情况危急。④应急所必需的: ~ materials 【军】稀有的重要作战物资 ⑤【物】临界的: ~ angle 临界角 / ~ temperature 临界温度 ⑥【原】数量上足够发生链式反应的 ||~**ly** *ad.*

criticism ['kritisizəm] *n.* ①批评, (一个)批判性意见: constructive ~ 建设性批评 / be above (或 beyond) ~ 无可批评 / be beneath ~ 无批评价值 / open to ~ 有可供批评之处 / invite customers' ~*s* 欢迎顾客批评②批判③评论; 评论文: literary and art ~ 文艺批评 ④非难 ⑤批评术, 批评法 ⑥考订: the higher ~ 考据, 考证(尤指用所谓科学历史方法考据《圣经》) / the textual ~ 考订, 校勘

criticize ['kritisaiz] ❶ *vt.* 批评; 批判; 评论; 非难: ~ sb. 批评某人 / ~ a painting 评论一幅画 ❷ *vi.* 批评; 批判; 评论; 非难

croak [krouk] I *n.* (蛙、鸦等的)呱呱叫声 II ❶ *vi.* ①呱呱地叫 ②发牢骚; 鸣冤; 嘶哑着声音说话 ③预示不吉 ④[俚]死 ❷ *vt.* ①用嘶哑的声音说; 用阴惨的声音预报(灾难等) ②[俚]杀死

crochet ['krouʃei] I *n.* 钩针编织品: a ~ hook 编织用的钩针 II *vt. & vi.* 用钩针编织

crock[1] [krɔk] I *n.* ①瓦罐, 瓦壶, 坛子 ②[英方]金属罐, 壶 ③碎瓦片 ④胡说八道; 荒谬行为

crock[2] [krɔk] I *n.* ①[方](炊具等的)烟垢, 煤灰 ②(染色皮革、布等)摩擦下来的有颜色的物质 II ❶ *vt.* [方]用煤烟弄脏 ❷ *vi.* 摩擦脱色: a suede that will not ~ 一种不会摩擦脱色的山羊皮革

crock[3] [krɔk] I *n.* ①破损的东西; 衰竭的人, 病弱者; 残废者 ②疲竭的马, 老马 ③[英俚]老母羊 II ❶ *vt.* [俚]使无用; 使成废物; 使成残废 ❷ *vi.* [俚]衰竭; (房屋等)破损: He is ~*ing* up. 他日趋衰老。

crockery ['krɔkəri] *n.* [总称]陶器, 瓦器

crocodile ['krɔkədail] *n.* ①鳄(鱼) ②鳄(鱼)皮(革) ③[古]假慈悲的人 ④[英口](行走时两人一排)成一字长蛇阵的女学生 ||~ *tears* 鳄鱼的眼泪; 假哭; 假慈悲: shed ~ *tears* 猫哭老鼠假慈悲

crocus[1] ['kroukəs] *n.* ①【植】藏红花 ②桔黄色 ③擦粉(一种红色氧化铁的粉, 供擦光用)

crocus[2] ['kroukəs] *n.* [美俚]庸医

crony ['krouni] *n.* [俚]亲密的朋友; 老朋友 ||~**ism** 任人唯亲

crook [kruk] I *n.* ①(牧羊人或主教用的)弯柄杖 ②钩; 锅钩; 钩形物 ③(道路、河流等的)弯子 ④弯曲; 弯曲部分 ⑤[俚]无赖, 骗子, 窃贼 II ❶ *vt.* ①使弯曲, 使成钩形: ~ one's finger (arm) 弯起手指(手臂) ②[俚]欺骗; 偷窃 ❷ *vi.* 弯曲, 成钩形 III *a.* =crooked ||*by hook or* (*by*) ~ 见 hook / ~ (*one's*) *elbow* (或 *little finger*) [俚]喝威士忌酒 / *on the* ~ [俚]狡诈地, 靠不正当手段 / *shepherd's* ~ 牧羊杖 / *There is a* ~ *in the lot of every one.* [谚]人生总有不如意处。||~**ery** *n.* 不正当行为 ||'~**back** *n.* 驼背 / '~**backed** *a.* 驼背的

crooked ['krukid] *a.* ①弯的; 歪的; 扭曲的: a ~ road 弯弯曲曲的道路 / The map on the wall is a bit ~. 墙上的地图有些歪。②畸形的; (因年老而)弯腰曲背的 ③不正当的, 欺诈的; 不正派的: ~ dealings 不正当交易 ④ [krukt] (手杖)柄弯的 ||~**ly** *ad.* / ~**ness** *n.* ||~ *stick* ①弯柄手杖 ②[口]不诚实的人; 无用的人; 懒散的人

croon [kru:n] I *vi. & vt.* ①低声歌唱, 低吟; 哼唱(尤指哼唱伤感歌曲) ②低声哼唱(催眠曲等使小儿入睡) II *n.* 单调的低唱声; 低哼(或低唱)的伤感流行歌曲 ||~**er** *n.* [美]低声哼唱伤感歌曲的歌手

crop [krɔp] I *n.* ①(谷类、水果、草等的)一熟, 一次收获(量), 收成: reap a good (或 bumper, rich) ~ of rice 水稻丰收 / cotton ~ 棉花收成 / yield two (three) ~*s* a year 一年两(三)熟 / single-~ (double-~) rice 单季(双季)稻 ②作物, 庄稼: the main ~(*s*) of an area 一地区的(各种)主要作物 / be in (或 under) ~ (土地)种着庄稼 / be out of ~ (土地)未种庄稼 / rotate ~*s* 进行轮作 ③(同时产生的)一批, 一群; 大量: a ~ of questions 一大堆问题 / a ~ of promising table-tennis players 一批有希望的乒乓选手 ④(指发式)平头; 剪平头: have a close ~ 把头发剪成平头 ⑤(鸟类的)嗉囊 ⑥鞭柄; 鞭梢有圈的短柄鞭 ⑦整张的鞣革 ⑧耳记(尤指剪掉牲畜耳尖作为记号) ⑨(钢锭等的)末端切下部分 ⑩(食用)脊骨肉 ⑪【建】叶尖饰; 【地】露头 ||a *cash* ~ 专供销售(或立可销售)的农作物 / a *catch* ~ 填闲作物 / a *cover* ~ 覆盖作物 / an *early* (*late*) *autumn* ~ 早(晚)秋作物 / a *food* ~ 粮食作物 / a *green manure* ~ 绿肥作物 / a *high-yielding* ~ 高产作物 / an *industrial* ~ 经济作物 / a *money* ~ =a cash ~ / an *oil-bearing* ~ 油料作物 / a *root* ~ 块根作物 / *standing* ~*s* 未割下的作物 / a *sugar* ~ 糖类作物 / a *white* ~ (指成熟时失去绿色的)谷类作物 II (cropped; cropping) ❶ *vt.* ①在(土地)上播种, 在(土地)上种植; 垦(地); 种②收割, 收获(庄稼、鱼类等) ③剪去; 修剪(树木); 剪短(头发、尾巴、动物的耳尖); 切齐(书边) ④(牛羊等)啮(草等) ❷ *vi.* ①收成, 收获: The cotton *cropped* well this year. 今年棉花收成

好。②咭草 ‖~ **up** (或 **out**) ①(问题等)突然发生,出现: deal with problems that have recently *cropped up* 处理最近产生的新问题 ②(岩石、矿脉等)露头 / **stick in** *sb.'s* ~ ①使某人难以消化 ②使某人难以接受 ‖'~-'**dusting** *n.* 散布农药 / '~-'**eared** *a.* ①(牲畜等)剪去耳朵尖的 ②剪短耳朵发露出耳朵的 / '~-,**over** *n.* (西印度群岛)甘蔗收割结束后的狂欢

cropper ['krɔpə] *n.* ①种植者; [美]分益佃农, 分成制农民 ②(用于形容词后)作物: a good (或 heavy) ~ 高产作物 ③修剪工人, 裁切工人; 修剪机, 裁切机 ④[动]球胸鸽 ⑤[口]栽跟头; 惨败: come (或 get) a ~ 猛摔一交; 遭到惨败

croquet ['krəukei] *n.* 槌球游戏

cross [krɔs] **I** *n.* ①十字形(包括 +、×、丅、キ 等形);十字形记号;十字形的东西(如十字架、十字勋章、十字形装饰物、立有十字架的石碑等): a boundary ~ 十字形界标 / mark the wrongly spelled word with a ~ 在拼错的词上打一个叉 / make one's ~ on a contract 在契约上画押 / the Red Cross (Society) 红十字会 / the Grand Cross (英国)大十字勋章 / the Victoria Cross (英国)维多利亚十字勋章 / the Distinguished Service Cross (英国)服务优异十字勋章 ②[the C-]【基督教】(耶稣被钉死在上面的)十字架;基督教,基督教教义: a follower of the Cross 基督教信徒 ③[喻]磨难,苦难;烦恼: bear (或 take up) one's ~ 忍受苦难 ④(动、植物的)异种交配,杂交;杂种,混血儿;混合物: A mule is a ~ between a horse and an ass. 骡是马和驴交配所生的杂种。⑤[俚]欺诈性的比赛;骗局 ⑥横穿过(舞台等)的动作;(字母等上的)横划 ⑦【讯】绞线,混线;交扰 ⑧[the C-]【天】(南、北)十字座 ‖a Buddhist ~ 卍字 / a ~ of St. Anthony (或 a Tau ~)丅字形十字(丅) / a Geneva ~ 红十字 / a Greek ~ 正十字(+) / a Latin ~ 纵长十字(†) / a Maltese ~ 马尔他十字(✠) / a St. Andrew's ~ 斜十字(×)

II ❶ *vt.* ①越过, 穿过, 渡过: ~ the snow mountains and the marshy grasslands 爬雪山, 过草地 / ~ a river (a bridge, a street, the sea) 过河(桥、街、海) / The idea has just ~ed my mind (或 me). 这个主意是我刚才想到的。②把…运过,把…带过: ~ livestock to the other side of the river 把牲口运过河 ③使交叉,使相交;与…相交(叉): ~ one's arms on one's breast 把双臂交叉在胸前 / Line A ~es line B at right angles. A 线与 B 线成直角相交。④遇到;错过: ~ an acquaintance on the street 在街上碰见一个熟人 / Your letter ~ed mine in the post. 你的信与我的信在邮寄过程中互相错过了。

⑤画横线穿过…; 在…上打叉; 划掉, 勾销 (*off*, *out*): Don't forget to ~ your t's. 写 t 时不要忘记上面那一横。(或: 一言一行都不要马虎草率。) / ~ sb.'s name *off* the list 把某人的名字从名单上划掉 ⑥跨, 骑: The river is ~ed by a stone bridge. 河上架着一座石桥。/ ~ a horse 骑马 ⑦【基督教】(用手)画十字于…: ~ oneself 在自己身上画十字(表示敬意或祈求上帝保佑) ⑧反对, 阻挠; 使受挫折: be ~ed in one's wishes 愿望受挫 / ~ up the whole plan (arrangement) 打乱了整个计划(安排) ⑨使杂交: ~ the apple *with* the pear 使苹果与梨杂交 ⑩[俚]欺骗; 背叛, 出卖 (*up*)

❷ *vi.* ①横穿, 横过, 横渡; 转到另一方, 投诚: ~ *over* a river by wading (in a ferryboat) 涉水(乘渡船)过河 / ~ to the other side of the street by subway 从地道过街 ②交叉, 相交; 错过: Our letters must have ~ed in the post. 我们的信一定是在邮寄过程中交叉(而互相错过)了。③杂交

III *a.* ①交叉的,横穿过的 ②相反的;互相矛盾的 ③脾气坏的, 易恼的; 发怒的: be ~ *with* sb. (*at* sth.) 对某人(为某事)生气 ④相互的 ⑤杂交的;杂种的;涉及许多种类的 ⑥[俚]不老实的, 不正当的; 用不正当手段得来的 ‖as ~ as two sticks 非常生气 / ~ one's fingers 见 finger / ~ one's heart 见 heart / ~ sb.'s palm (或 hand) 见 palm / ~ sb.'s path 见 path / ~ swords 见 sword / ~ the cudgels 见 cudgel / No ~ no crown. [谚]无苦即无乐。(或: 没有困难就没有成功。) / on the ~ ①斜, 对角: be cut on the ~ 被对角切开 ②[俚]不光明正大, 不公正, 不老实: get sth. on the ~ 用不正当手段获得某物 / run ~ to 与…相反 / take a child to Banbury ['bænbəri] Cross 将小孩放在膝盖上颠摇

‖~ly *ad.* 易怒地; 发怒地 / ~ness *n.* 易怒; 发怒 / ~ways *ad.* ①交叉地 ②横斜地 / ~wise *ad.* ①交叉地 ②横斜地 ③与目的相反地; 不对头地 *a.* 横的; 交叉的; 对角的

‖~ action 【律】反诉 / '~bar *n.* ①闩, 横杆 ②球门横木 ③织物的横色条 / '~beam *n.* 横梁, 大梁 / ~ bearings 【海】交叉方位 / '~=bedding *n.* 【地】交错层 / '~belt *n.* 斜挂在肩上的子弹带 / '~bench *n.* 中立议员席(英国下院中两大政党以外的中立政党的议员坐的席位) *a.* 中立的, 不偏不倚的 / '~bones [复] *n.* 交叉的大腿骨(画在骷髅下, 表示死亡、剧毒等, 过去的海盗旗上常画有此图) / '~bow *n.* 弩, 石弓(一种古代武器) / '~bred *a.* 杂种的; 杂交的 *n.* 杂种 / '~breed *vt.* & *vi.* (使)杂交 *n.* 杂种 /

'~-'buttock n. 侧身用臀部顶住对方向前猛扔的一种摔角方法 / '~-'check n. & vt. (从不同角度或根据不同资料)反复核对 / '~-'country a. ①横穿全国的: a ~-country tour 横穿全国的旅行 ②越野的 ad. 越野地 / '~ current n. ①逆流 ②[常用复]矛盾的倾向 / '~cut vt. & vi. 横切,横穿 a. 横切的,横穿的 / '~ 横切,横穿;剖面 ②对角(或横穿)的小路;捷径 ③横切锯 /【矿】石门,横巷 / ~ entry 【会计】抵销记入 / ~-examination ['krɔsig,zæmi'neiʃən] n. 盘问 / ~-examine ['krɔsig'zæmin] vt. & vi. 盘问 / '~-eye n. 【医】内斜视;斗鸡眼 / '~-'fertilize vt. & vi. 【植】(使)异花受精;【动】(使)异体受精;[喻](使)相互补充而得益 / '~-'file vt. & vi. [美]在预选中登记作为一个以上政党的候选人 / ~ fire ①【军】交叉火力 ②【讯】串报,串扰电流 / '~-'firing n. 【物】交射 / '~-'grained a. ①(木材)纹理不规则(或交叉)的 ②脾气倔的;固执的;难相处的 ~ hairs (望远镜、瞄准器等上的)十字丝,十字标线 / '~-hatched a. 用交叉线画成阴影的 / '~head n. ①【机】十字头 ②(插在文章中的)小标题 / ~ heading 【矿】工作区间通道,联络巷道 / '~-'index vt. 给(词典、条目等)设互见索引 vi. 设互见索引 / '~-legged a. 盘着腿的;跷着二郎腿的 / '~-'light n. ①与另一光线交叉的光线 ②有助于理解某事物的侧面材料(或意见等) / '~-link n. 【化】交键 / '~,over n. ①交叉,穿过 ②转到另一方,投诚 ③【物】跨接 /【交】转线轨道;(铁路)渡线;跨路线桥 ⑤【无】电子束相交区最小截面 ⑥【生】交换型,交换体 / '~patch n. [口] 脾气坏的人,爱抱怨的人 / '~piece n. 横档;[船]绞盘横杆 / '~-,polli-'nation n. 【植】异花传粉 / '~-'purposes [复] n. ①相反的目的,自相矛盾的目的;相反的计划: be at ~-purposes 互相误解;有矛盾 ②一种问答游戏 / '~-'question vt. 盘问 n. 盘问时所提的问题 / ~ rate 套汇率 / '~-'reference vt.(对一书或文件等中)使相互参照 n. 相互参照;相互参照条目,互见条目 / '~road n. ①横路,交叉路 ②[复]十字路,十字路口;聚会的中心地点 [复][喻]需作抉择的重要关头: stand at the ~roads 面临抉择;徘徊歧途 / '~ section n. ①横断面,截面;断面图 ②[原](核反应的)有效截面 ③(有代表性的)剖面,典型 / '~-stitch n. 十字缝,十字花形针脚的刺绣 / ~ talk ①【讯】串话,串音;交调失真 ②[口]拌嘴 ③交谈 ④相声 / '~-tie n. [美](铁轨的)枕木;横向拉杆 / '~-trail n. 【军】横偏移 / '~trees [复] n. [船]桅顶横桁 / '~-,under n. 【物】穿接 / ~ voting 投反对自己所属党派的票 / '~walk n. 人行横道,过街人行道 / '~way n. =~road / '~wind n. 侧风 / ~ wires =~ hairs / '~word puzzle 一种纵横填字字谜

crossed [krɔst] a. ①十字形的,交叉的,相交的 ①划掉的,勾销的;划线的: a ~ cheque (只能通过银行收款的)划线支票 ③遭反对的,受挫折的

crossing ['krɔsiŋ] n. ①横渡,横穿: have a good (rough) ~ 横渡时风平浪静(风浪很大) ②交叉;交叉点,十字路口: a level (或 grade) ~ 平面交叉;铁路与公路平交道 ③渡口;(穿过街道等的)横道: a street ~ 人行横道,过街人行道(也叫 a crosswalk, a footway ~, a pedestrian ~ 等) ④杂交 ⑤反对,阻挠(尤指用不正当手段)

crotchet ['krɔtʃit] n. ①小钩;钩状物;【动】趾钩;【建】叉架;叉柱 ②怪念头;怪癖 ③【音】四分音符(♩)

crouch [krautʃ] I ❶ vi. 蹲伏,蜷缩;低头弯腰: ~ down for shelter 蹲下把身子藏起 / a ~ing start 【体】蹲下起跑法 / ~ to sb. 拜倒在某人脚下 ❷ vt. 屈(膝);低(头) II n. 蹲伏(姿势)

crow¹ [krou] n. ①鸦,乌鸦(包括 raven, rook 等) ②铁挺,撬棍,起货钩 (=~bar) ③[the C-]【天】乌鸦座 ‖as the ~ flies 笔直地,按直线地 / a white ~ 稀有的东西 / eat ~ [美口]做使自己丢脸的事(如被迫收回成命) / have a ~ to pull (或 pluck, pick) with sb. 在某事上要同某人争一번; 要就某事向某人提出批评 ‖'~bar n. 铁挺,撬棍,起货钩 / '~,flower n. 【植】毛茛 / '~foot n. ①([复] crowfoots)【植】毛茛,玉柏 ②([复] crowfeet) =~'s-foot / ~ quill ①乌鸦的羽毛管 ②鸦羽管(或金属)制的细笔尖 / '~-foot n. ([复] crow's-feet) ①【植】毛茛 ②([复] crowfeet) =~'s-foot / '~'s-feet) ①[常用复]眼睛外角旁的皱纹 ②(军用)铁蒺藜 ③【海】(船篷等的)吊索 / '~'s nest ①桅上了望台;守望楼 ②指挥交通的岗亭

crow

crow² [krou] I (过去式 crowed 或 crew [kru:],过去分词 crowed) vi. ①(雄鸡)啼 ②(因胜利等)欢呼;(小孩)欢叫 ③得意洋洋,幸灾乐祸 (over) ④吹嘘,自夸 (about, over) II n. ①鸡啼 ②(因胜利等发出的)欢呼声;(小孩的)欢叫声

crowd [kraud] I n. ①群,人群: a ~ of children 一群小孩 / push one's way through the ~ 挤过人群 / a cheering ~ 欢呼的人群 ②大众,老百姓: follow (或 go with) the ~ 随大流 / ~ ideas 大众的想法 / a ~ pleaser 哗众取宠的人(或事物) ③一伙人,一帮人;(有共同兴趣或习惯等的)一群人: a ~ of books 一大堆书 II ❶ vt. ①挤;挤满,使挤满: ~ sb. off the sidewalk 把某人从人行道上挤出去 / Fifty thousand spectators ~ed the stadium. 五万观众挤满了体育场。 / ~ a room with people

(或 ~ people into a room) 使房间挤满人 / The hall was ~ed to the doors. 大厅里挤满了人,一直挤到门口。②塞满,装满,堆满: ~ a room with furniture 把房间塞满家具 / His mind was ~ed with whys. 他脑子里全是问号。/ ~ sb. with questions 向某人提一大堆问题 ③催促;催逼: ~ sb. for an answer 催某人回答 ④逼近: He is ~ing forty. 他快四十岁了。❷ vi. ①挤,拥挤: ~ into a bus 挤进公共汽车 / ~ in through the gate 从大门拥入 / The young pigs ~ed against one another for warmth. 小猪挤在一起取暖。②聚集,群集: They ~ed round the player with congratulations. 他们围着那个运动员,向他祝贺。③急速前进;涌上前: The ship ~ed eastward. 船向东疾驶。/ Please don't ~ so. Stand back. 请不要挤上来,往后退。/ Memories ~ed on (或 upon) my mind. 多少往事涌上心头。/ Darkness of evening ~ed in. 夜幕降临。‖~ (on) sail 张起异常多的风帆 / ~ out 挤出;排挤 / would pass in a ~ 并不坏得显眼,还过得去

crowded ['kraudid] a. ①拥挤的;满座的;塞满的: a ~ city (hall, train) 拥挤的城市(大厅,火车) / a ~ programme 排得满满的节目单;内容繁多的计划(或日程表) ②靠紧的,密集的: the ~ trees in a forest 森林里茂密的树木 ③多事的;经历丰富的: a ~ life 经历丰富的一生

crown [kraun] I n. ①(象征荣誉、胜利等的)花冠;[喻]荣誉;[美]锦标 ②王冠,冕;[the C-] 君王,王权,王国政体 ③王冠状的东西 ④(英国)旧时五先令硬币;[欧洲某些国家货币]克朗 ⑤头顶;头 ⑥顶部;拱顶;树顶;帽顶;顶峰 ⑦齿冠(牙齿露出部分);镶上的齿冠 ⑧锚冠 ⑨【植】冠;根颈;副(花)冠 ⑩【动】冠状部 ⑪【机】(带轮顶部的)隆起 ⑫一种纸张的尺寸‖ a Crown Colony 英国直辖殖民地 / ~ glass 冕牌玻璃(光学仪器用) / ~ land 王家领地; (某些英国自治领和殖民地的)公有土地 / ~ law [英]刑法 / a ~ lawyer [英]刑事律师 / the Crown Office 英国高等法院中央办公室的一个部门; 英国大法官法庭的国玺部 / a ~ prince 王储 / a ~ princess 王储的妻子; 女王储 / a ~ witness [英]刑事案件公诉人方面的证人 / pleas of the ~ [英]刑事诉讼, 公诉 II vt. ①为…加冕; 为…加冕,立…为王 ②(以荣誉等)酬报(with): a name ~ed with glory 一个光荣的称号(或名字) ③为…加顶; 使圆满完成 ④打…的头部 ⑤注满(使表面呈冠状) ⑥为(牙齿)镶嵌齿冠 ‖the ~ of the year 收获季节,秋季 / to ~ all [用作插入语] 更使人高兴的是…;更糟糕的是… / wear the ~ 戴上王冠,做皇帝;做殉道者 ‖~ed a. ①戴王冠的;象戴王冠的 ②[常用以构成复合词]有…帽顶的: high-~ed 有高帽顶的 ‖~-court n. [英]巡回刑事法庭 / ~ piece [英]旧制五先令硬币 / '~-piece n. 构成顶部的东西;马笼头顶部 / ~ wheel【机】冕状齿轮,差动器侧面伞形齿轮

crown

crozier ['krouʒə] n.【宗】(主教或修道院院长的)权杖

crucial ['kru:ʃəl, 'kru:ʃəl] a. ①决定性的,紧要关头的: a ~ test 决定性的试验 / the ~ moment 紧要关头 ②严酷的,极困难的 ③十字形的: a ~ incision (外科手术中的)十字形切开 ‖~ly ad.

crucible ['kru:sibl] n. ①坩埚: a platinum (plumbago) ~ 白金(石墨)坩埚 ②[喻]熔炉,严峻的考验

crucifix ['kru:sifiks] n. ①【宗】耶稣钉在十字架上的图像 ②十字架

crucifixion [,kru:si'fikʃən] n. ①在十字架上钉死的刑罚; [the C-]【宗】耶稣在十字架上钉死(可指其事或图像) ②酷刑;折磨,苦难

crucify ['kru:sifai] vt. ①把…钉死在十字架上 ②抑制(情欲等);消灭(肉体等) ③折磨,使苦恼 ④(反动军队中的一种处地刑罚)把…象钉十字架那样绑起来

crude [kru:d] I a. ①天然的,未加工的,粗制的: ~ oil (或 petroleum) 原油,石油 / ~ materials 原料 / ~ salt 粗制盐 ②(食物等)未煮熟的,生的 ③粗鲁的,粗野的: ~ manners 粗鲁的态度 ④粗糙的,原始的;拙劣的;未修饰的,赤裸裸的: a ~ device 粗糙的装置 / ~ statistics 未经整理分类的统计数字 / ~ ideas 不成熟的意见 / ~ facts 原始的事实,赤裸裸的事实 ⑤【语】无词形变化的 II n. 天然的物质(尤指原油) ‖~ly ad. / ~ness n.

crudity ['kru:diti] n. ①未成熟状态;粗糙 ②[复]粗鲁的举止,粗鲁的言语: crudities of speech and behaviour 粗鲁的言语和行为

cruel [kruəl] I a. ①残忍的,残酷的: a ~ scuffle 一场残酷的搏斗 / be ~ to sb. 对某人残忍凶狠 ②令人痛苦的;存心让别人痛苦的: give sb. ~ disappointment 使某人大失所望 II ad. [方]极,非常 ‖~ly ad. ①残酷地 ②极,非常,厉害地

cruelty ['kruəlti] n. ①残忍,残酷 ②[复]残酷的行为;刻毒伤人的言语

cruet ['kru():it] n. ①(餐桌上的)调味品瓶(如酱油瓶、醋瓶等) ②【宗】(装葡萄酒或水的)祭坛用瓶 ‖~ stand 调味品瓶架

cruise [kru:z] I ❶ vi. ①巡航 ②巡游 ③[口]在街上徘徊 ④(出租汽车)兜客 ⑤(飞机)用巡航速度飞行 ❷ vt. ①巡航于… ②[美]勘查(林区)的木

材产量 **II** *n.* 巡航;巡游: go on a round-the world ~ 进行一次环球航行

cruiser ['kru:zə] *n.* ①巡洋舰: a ~ force 巡洋舰部队 / a heavy ~ 重型巡洋舰 / a missile-carrying ~ 导弹巡洋舰 ②(配备必要生活及娱乐设置的)游艇 (=cabin ~) ③警察巡逻车; 揽客汽车;巡航机;巡航机动船: a ~ tank 巡逻坦克 ④漫游者, 旅行者 ⑤[美]森林地估测者 ⑥[美]森林地估测者穿的长统靴 ‖'**~weight** *n.* [主英]轻重量级(拳击手)

crumb [krʌm] **I** *n.* ①面包屑; 糕饼屑; 碎屑 ②少许, 点滴: a ~ of comfort 少许的安慰 / ~s of knowledge 点滴的知识 ③面包心 (crust 之对) ④[俚]无价值的人; 可厌的人 ⑤[复][美俚]几个小钱 ⑥[美俚]虱子 **II** *vt.* ①捏碎, 弄碎 ②把…裹上面包屑(油煎) ③[美口]抹去…上的碎屑: ~ a table after a meal 餐后抹掉台上的碎屑 ‖**to a ~** 精细地, 精确地 / **~-y** *a.* ①尽是面包屑的 ②柔软的 ③[美俚] =crummy (*a.*)

crumble ['krʌmbl] **I** ❶ *vt.* 弄碎, 把…弄成细屑 ❷ *vi.* ①破碎, 碎裂: ~ to (或 into) dust 碎成粉末, 化为乌有 ②崩溃, 瓦解; 灭亡; (希望等)消失 **II** *n.* ①[方]碎屑; 面包屑 ②碎裂(或瓦解)中的东西

crumple ['krʌmpl] **I** ❶ *vt.* ①把…弄皱; 扭弯: The smile ~d his face. 他笑得满脸起了皱纹。 ②使崩溃, 打垮 ❷ *vi.* ①起皱; 扭弯 ②崩溃 **II** *n.* 折皱, 皱纹 ‖**~ up** ①把…揉皱(或扭弯); 起皱; 扭弯: ~ up paper into a ball 把纸揉成一团 / a hat that has ~d up under a heavy volume 被一本厚书压瘪的帽子 ②压碎, 打垮, 使崩溃; 碎裂, 崩溃 ‖**~d** *a.* ①弄皱了的; 被扭弯的 ②(牛角)弯曲的

crunch [krʌntʃ] **I** *vt. & vi.* ① 嘎吱嘎吱地咬嚼 ②(车轮、皮靴等)嘎吱嘎吱地碾(或踏)过 **II** *n.* ①嘎吱嘎吱的声音 ②嘎吱嘎吱的咬嚼 ③[美俚]摊牌; 危境 ‖**~-y** *a.* 发嘎吱嘎吱声的

crusade [kru:'seid] **I** *n.* ①[史]十字军东侵;宗教战争 ②[喻]讨伐;改革运动: a dry ~ [美]禁酒运动 / a ~ *against* tuberculosis 防痨运动 / a ~ *for* social welfare in Britain 英国国内争取社会福利的运动 **II** *vi.* 开战, 讨伐 (*against*); 征战 (*for*) ‖**~r** *n.* ①十字军参加者 ②某种社会运动的参加者; 战斗者: a consumer ~r (美国)参加保护用户利益运动的人

crush [krʌʃ] **I** ❶ *vt.* ①压碎, 压坏; 碾碎; 榨: Don't sit on the box. You'll ~ it. 不要坐在箱子上, 你会把它压坏的。 / ~ grapes 榨葡萄 ②弄皱, 揉皱 ③压服, 压倒, 压垮: ~ difficulties underfoot 把困难踩在脚下 ④塞; 挤, 使挤入: ~ clothes into a trunk 把衣服塞进皮箱 / ~ one's way through the crowd 挤过人群 / We can't ~ any more people into the hall; it is crowded already. 我们不能再放人进入大厅了, 里面已很挤了。 ⑤紧抱, 拥抱: a baby to one's breast 把婴孩紧紧抱在怀里 ⑥[古]喝(酒) ❷ *vi.* ①(被)压碎; (被)碾碎: Eggs ~ easily. 蛋容易被压碎。

②(衣服等)起皱, 揉皱: This synthetic dress material does not ~. 这种合成纤维衣料不会皱。 ③挤, 挤(向前), 挤(入): ~ towards the door 挤向门口 / ~ into the front seats 挤到前面的座位上 **II** *n.* ①压碎, 毁坏; 压榨; 压皱 ②极度拥挤; (拥挤的)人群; (人数众多的)聚会, 盛大的招待会(或舞会) ③(水果的)汁: orange ~ 桔子汁 ④迷恋; 迷恋的对象: have (或 get) a ~ on sb. 迷恋某人, 爱上某人 ⑤[澳]两旁有篱笆的窄通道(用以使牲畜逐个通过, 以便打印记或注射疫苗等) ‖**~ down** ①碾碎 ②压倒; 镇压 / **~ out** ①榨出(汁水) ②熄灭 ③[美俚]越狱 / **~ up** ①碾碎, 粉碎 ②把…捣成一团 / **~ barrier** (人行道边设置的)防挤栏杆 / '**~-room** *n.* [英](戏院的)休息室

crust [krʌst] **I** *n.* ① 面包皮;干面包片 ② 硬外皮, 外壳: rice ~s 锅巴 ③(附在酒瓶或酒坛里面的)酒垢 ④[地]地壳 ⑤[动]甲壳 ⑥[医]痂, 痂皮 ⑦[美俚]老面皮, 厚颜无耻 **II** ❶ *vt.* 用硬皮(或外壳)覆盖; 在…上结硬皮(或痂): Ice ~ed the pond. 池塘结着一层冰。 ❷ *vi.* 结成硬皮; 覆有外壳: The snow has ~ed over. 雪已结成了冰。 ‖**~ed** *a.* ①有硬皮的; 有外壳的 ②长了酒垢的 ③陈旧的; 古色古香的: a ~ed habit 多年积习

crusty ['krʌsti] *a.* ①有硬皮的, 有外壳的 ②象硬皮(或外壳)一样硬的 ③执拗的, 顽固的; 易发脾气的; 粗鲁的 ‖**crustily** *ad.* / **crustiness** *n.*

crutch [krʌtʃ] **I** *n.* ①(跛子用的)拐杖, 丁字形的拐杖: go on ~s 拄着拐杖行动 / a pair of ~s 一副拐杖 ②支柱; 叉柱; [海]桨叉; 吊杆支架; 船尾肘材 ③人体两腿分叉处 ④[喻]支持 **II** *vt.* 用丁字形拐杖支持; 支撑

crux [krʌks] ([复] cruxes 或 cruces ['kru:si:z]) *n.* ① (纹章上的)十字形, 十字架形 ②难事, 难题; 症结 ③关键, 最重要点: Where does the ~ lie? 关键在那里? ④ [the C-] [天]南十字座

cry [krai] **I** ❶ *vi.* ①叫喊; (鸟兽)叫 ②哭, 流泪: ~ over sth. 为…而哭泣, 为…而悲伤 / ~ for joy 高兴得掉下眼泪 ❷ *vt.* ①叫喊; 大声地说 ②大声报道; 叫卖: ~ the good news all over the village 大声喊着把好消息传遍全村 / ~ one's wares 叫卖货物 ③哭出; 哭得使…: ~ hot tears 掉下热泪 / ~ oneself to sleep 一直哭到睡着 **II** *n.* ①叫喊; 喊声; (鸟兽的)叫声: give (或 utter) a ~ 发出一声叫喊 ②叫卖声 ③(一阵)哭; 哭泣; 哭声: have a good ~ 痛痛快快地哭一场 ④ 呼声, 舆论 ⑤要求, 呼吁 ⑥传说, 谣传 ⑦[美俚]喊的或政党竞选时提出的)口号 ⑧时髦的风尚 ⑨一群猎狗 ‖**a far ~** ①遥远的距离, 一大段距离 ②大不相同的东西 / **~ against** 大声疾呼反对… / **~ back** (杂交品种等)出现返祖现象 / **~ down** ①贬低 ②喝下(演讲者等) / **~ for** ①哭着要; 吵着要求; 恳求 ②迫切需要 / **~ off** ①取消(买卖、契约等) ②[主英]打退堂鼓退出, 撒手 (*from*); 取消前言 / **~ out** ①大声呼喊 ②大声抱怨 / **~ over spilt milk** 作无益的后

悔 / ~ up 称颂, 推崇 / follow in the ~ [贬]
同一伙无名小卒一起跟在后面 / in full ~ (猎
狗群)吠叫着追猎; [喻]全力追击 / lift up a ~
高声叫喊; 大声疾呼 / much ~ and little wool
徒劳, 空忙; 雷声大雨点小 / within ~ 在声音听
得见的地方, 在附近 ‖'~,baby n. 爱哭的孩子;
爱哭(或爱抱怨)的人

crying ['kraiiŋ] a. ①哭的; 叫喊的 ②引人注意的;
急需处理的: a ~ need 迫切的需要 ③臭名昭著
的, 极坏的

crypt [kript] n. ①地窖; 教堂地下室(作墓穴等用)
②【解】小囊; 隐窝, 腺窝

cryptic(al) ['kriptik(əl)] a. ①秘密的, 隐蔽的; 神
秘的 ② 隐义的, 含义模糊的; 使用密码的: a
~ remark 含义隐晦的话 ③【动】隐藏的: ~
colouring 保护色, 隐藏色 ‖**criptically** ad.

crystal ['kristl] I n. ①水晶: as clear as ~ 象水
晶一样明澈; [喻]极其明白 / What he is driving
at is ~ clear. 他想干什么不是一清二楚的吗!
②结晶(体): Salt forms ~s. 盐会结晶。 ③水
晶饰品 ④水晶玻璃; 水晶玻璃制品; [美]钟面(或
表面)玻璃 ⑤【无】晶体(指检波用的矿石) ⑥水
晶般明澈的东西(如水、冰等) ⑦[口](由迷信方
法得到的)预卜, 预言 II a. ①水晶的; 水晶制的
②水晶般的, 清澈的, 透彻的: a ~ stream 清澈
见底的溪流 / the ~ clearness of an argument
一个论创的透彻性 ③晶体的; 用晶体的: a ~
(radio) receiver (或 a ~ set) 晶体收音机, 矿石
收音机 ‖~ detector 晶体检波器 / ~ gazing
水晶球占卜术(凝视水晶球以期借里面所呈现的
图象来占卜未来的迷信活动)

crystalline ['kristəlain] a. ①水晶的; 水晶制的 ②
水晶般的, 清澈透明的, 清晰的 ③结晶(质)的, 结
晶体组成的; 结晶状的 ‖**crystallinity** [,kristə-
'liniti] n. 结晶性; 结晶度 ‖~ lens 【解】(眼球的)
水晶体

crystallize ['kristəlaiz] ❶ vt. ① 使结晶 ②使定
形, 使(计划、思想等)具体化 ③给(水果等)裹上
糖屑: ~d fruit 裹糖屑蜜饯(如冰糖山楂等)
❷ vi. ①结晶 ②具体化, 明朗化 ‖**crystallization**
[,kristəlai'zeiʃən] n.

Cs 【化】元素铯(caesium) 的符号

Cu 【化】元素铜(copper) 的符号, 由拉丁名 cuprum
而来

cub [kʌb] n. ①幼狐; [美]幼兽 ②不懂事的小家
伙; 生手(尤指初出茅庐的新闻记者) ③(八至十
一岁的)幼年童子军 II (cubbed; cubbing) vi.
①(狐等)生仔 ②猎幼兽

cube [kju:b] I n. ①立方形, 立方体: a jin of ~
sugar 一斤方糖 ②【数】立方, 三次幂: The ~ of
5 is 125. 五的三次幂是一百二十五。 / a ~
root 立方根 ③[美俚]骰子 II vt. ①使自乘至三
次幂; 求…的立方(或容积): ~ a number 使一数
自乘三次, 求一数的立方(值) / a solid ~ 求一
个立体的体积 ②使成立方体; 把(土豆等)切成小
方块 ③在…上铺方石

cubic ['kju:bik] I a. ①立方体的, 立方形的: ~
content 容积, 体积 / ~ sugar 方糖 ②【数】三次
的, 立方的: ~ equation 三次方程 II n. 【数】三
次曲线; 三次方程; 三次多项式

cubicle ['kju:bikl] n. ①(宿舍中的)小卧室 ②(以
墙或幕隔成的)小室

cuckoo ['kuku:] I n. ①杜鹃, 布谷鸟 ②杜鹃叫声;
学杜鹃叫的咕咕声 ③[美俚]疯疯癫癫的人; 怪人
II a. ①象杜鹃的 ② 疯狂的, 疯癫的 III ❶ vi.
杜鹃叫; 学杜鹃叫 ❷ vt. 单调地重复叫(或说)
‖a ~ in the nest 夺取他人父母之爱的人; 破
坏他人家庭幸福的人 ‖~ clock 报时似杜鹃叫
声的钟 / '~,flower n. 【植】布谷鸟剪秋罗 /
'~pint n. 【植】斑叶阿若母

cucumber ['kju:kʌmbə] n. 黄瓜 ‖as cool as a ~
泰然自若, 极为冷静

cud [kʌd] n. ①反刍的食物 ②[美](含在嘴里嚼
的)嚼烟; 口香糖 ‖chew the ~ ①(牛等)反刍
②深思, 细想

cuddle ['kʌdl] I ❶ vt. 拥抱, 怀抱 ❷ vi. 紧贴着身
子躺(或睡)(together); 蜷缩着身子躺(或睡)(up)
II n. ①拥抱 ②紧贴身子的躺(或睡) ‖~some a.
可拥抱的; 可爱的 / cuddly a. ①可拥抱的 ②
喜欢拥抱的

cudgel ['kʌdʒəl] I n. (短而重的)棍棒 II (cudgel-
(l)ed; cudgel(l)ing) vt. 用棍棒打 ‖cross the ~s
不参加争论 (或斗争) / ~ one's brains (for)
(为…)绞脑汁 / take up the ~s for 尽力捍卫
…; 努力为…辩护

cue¹ [kju:] I n. ①【戏】尾白, 提示 (指演出时给
同台演员或拉幕、灯光人员作暗示的说白或动作)
②[喻]暗示: take one's ~ from 从…处得到暗
示 / follow sb.'s ~ 按某人指点行事 ③(分配给
自己的)角色 ④[古]意向, 心情 ⑤[音]演奏指示
乐节 II (cu(e)ing) vt. ①给…暗示 ②插入
演出: ~ in sound effects 插入音响效果

cue² [kju:] I n. ① (人或车辆等候着的) 长队,
长蛇阵 ② 发辫 ③ (台球戏中用的) 弹子棒 II
(cu(e)ing) vt. ①把…编成发辫 ②用弹子棒打

cuff¹ [kʌf] I n. ①袖口; 臂腕 ②裤脚的翻边 ③
[复]手铐 II vt. ①装上袖口(或翻边) ②用
手铐铐 ‖off the ~ [美俚]即兴地; 非正式地 /
on the ~ [美俚]以赊账方式; 免费地 ‖~ links
(衬衫袖口的) 链扣

cuff² [kʌf] I n. 掌击, 一巴掌: give sb. a good ~
on the ear 狠狠地搂某人一记耳光 / be at ~s
with sb. 与某人殴斗 II ❶ vt. 用巴掌打… ❷
vi. 殴斗

cul-de-sac ['kuldə'sæk] ([复] culs-de-sac 或 cul-
de-sacs) n. [法] ①死巷, 死胡同 ②[喻]困境, 死
路 ③【解】盲管

culinary ['kʌlinəri] a. 厨房的; 烹饪的; 烹饪用的:
the ~ art 烹饪法

culminate ['kʌlmineit] ❶ vi. ①达到顶点(或高
潮); 告终 (in): ~ in bankruptcy 终致破产 ②
【天】到中天(最高度), 到子午线 ❷ vt. 使达到顶

点，使达到最高点 ‖**culminating** *a.* 达到顶点的，达到最高点的

culmination [ˌkʌlmi'neiʃən] *n.* ①达到顶点，达到极点 ②顶点，极点；最高潮 ③【天】中天

culpable ['kʌlpəbl] *a.* 应受谴责的；应受处罚的；有罪的：hold sb. ～ 认为某人应受责备 / ～ negligence 应受处罚的疏忽行为（指造成事故、损失或灾难等的）‖**culpability** [ˌkʌlpə'biliti], ～**ness** *n.* / **culpably** *ad.*

culprit ['kʌlprit] *n.* ①犯人，罪犯 ②刑事被告，未决犯

cult [kʌlt] *n.* ①【宗】礼拜，祭礼 ②狂热的崇拜，迷信；崇拜对象：～ the personality ～（或 the ～ of personality）个人崇拜，个人迷信 ③【集合名词】一群狂热的崇拜者，一群信徒 ‖～**ism** *n.* ①崇拜，迷信 ②热衷搞迷信崇拜的倾向 / ～**ist** *n.* 热衷搞迷信崇拜的人

cultivate ['kʌltiveit] *vt.* ①耕；耕作：～ the soil 耕地 ②栽培（植物）；养殖（鱼类、软体动物、甲壳动物等）；蓄（胡须等）：～ yeasts 培养酵母 ③培养；修习；磨炼（才能等）：～ the habit of analysis 养成分析的习惯 ④力求与（某人）交往 ‖**cultivable** ['kʌltivəbl], **cultivatable** *a.* ①可耕作的；可栽培的 ②可培养的；可教化的

cultivated ['kʌltiveitid] *a.* ①耕过的；耕作的；栽培的：～ land 耕地 / the ～ area 耕地面积 / a ～ plant 栽培的植物 ②有教养的，有素养的；优雅的

cultivation [ˌkʌlti'veiʃən] *n.* ①耕作：intensive and careful ～ 精耕细作 ②栽培；养殖 ③培养；修习；磨炼 ④教养；修养

cultivator ['kʌltiveitə] *n.* ①耕种者，栽培者 ②修习者 ③【农】中耕机

cultural ['kʌltʃərəl] *a.* ①文化上的，文化的：～ objects and historic monuments 文物古迹 / ～ and educational work 文化教育工作 ②教养的，修养的 ③栽培的；养殖的；培养的：a ～ variety 一个经人工培养的变种 ‖～**ly** *ad.* ‖～ **lag** 文化间滞（指文化某一方面的相对落后，如社会制度对科技发展而言）

culture ['kʌltʃə] **I** *n.* ①文化；精神文明：a man of considerable ～ 文化修养很高的人 ②教养，陶冶；修养：moral (intellectual, physical) ～ 德（智，体）育 ③栽培；养殖，养育；【生】培养：the ～ of cotton（或 cotton ～）棉花的栽培 / silk ～ 养蚕 / the ～ of bacteria 细菌的培养 / a ～ fluid 培养液 ④耕作 **II** *vt.* ①使有教养 ②耕作；栽培；培养（细菌等）

cultured ['kʌltʃəd] *a.* ①有教养的；有修养的 ②耕种了的；人工培养的；人工养殖的：～ fields 耕地 / ～ pearls 人工养殖的珍珠（=culture pearls）

culturist ['kʌltʃərist] *n.* ①栽培者；培养者；养殖者 ②文化主义者

culvert ['kʌlvət] *n.* ①排水渠；阴沟；水道 ②电缆管道 ③【建】涵洞

cumbersome ['kʌmbəsəm] *a.* ①拖累的，麻烦的 ②笨重的，不方便的 ‖～**ly** *ad.* / ～**ness** *n.*

cumbrous ['kʌmbrəs] *a.* =cumbersome

cumulative ['kjuːmjulətiv] *a.* ①累积的，渐增的，累加的：～ knowledge 累积的知识 / ～ interest 累加利息（指逾期不付追加的利息）/ ～ voting 累积投票（指投票人可投每个候选人人数的票，并可将票全部投给一人）②【律】（证据等）与同一事实相重的；加重的；累积的：～ evidence 复证 / a ～ penalty（对累犯的）加重处罚 / a ～ offence 累犯 / a ～ sentence 与前刑合并的判决（或处刑）‖～**ly** *ad.* / ～**ness** *n.*

cumulus ['kjuːmjuləs]（[复] cumuli ['kjuːmjulai]）*n.* ①一堆 ②【气】积云

cuneiform ['kjuːniifɔːm] **I** *a.* ①楔形的：～ bones 楔状骨 / ～ characters 楔形文字 ②楔形文字的 **II** *n.* ①楔形文字；用楔形文字写成的东西 ②【解】楔状骨

cunning ['kʌniŋ] **I** *a.* ①狡猾的，狡诈的 ②精巧的；熟练的：～ workmanship 精巧的制作 ③[美]（小孩、小动物等）可爱的 **II** *n.* ①狡猾，狡诈 ②灵巧；熟练 ‖～**ly** *ad.* / ～**ness** *n.*

cup [kʌp] **I** *n.* ①杯子：a coffee ～ 咖啡杯 / a ～ and saucer 一副杯碟 ②（一）杯；一杯的容量（约半品脱）：Have another ～? 再来一杯怎么样? / half a ～ of water 半杯水 ③优胜杯，奖杯：a challenge（或 prize）～ 优胜杯，奖杯 / win the ～ 得优胜杯 / a ～ event 锦标赛 / the Cup Final 争锦标的决赛 ④【宗】圣餐杯 ⑤酒；饮酒：be too fond of the ～ 贪杯 ⑥经历，遭遇：His ～ of happiness was full. 他幸福之极。/ drink a bitter ～ 饮一杯苦酒，尝一次不幸 ⑦【医】火罐，吸杯 ⑧ 杯状物；【植】花萼；杯状结构；【解】骨臼 ⑨ 酒、糖、冰、香料配成的饮料 **II** (cupped; cupping) *vt.* ①为…拔火罐 ②使成杯状：～ one's hand to one's ear（为了听得清晰）使手成杯状置于耳背 ③把…置于杯内；把…置在杯状物中：～ one's chin in (the hollow of) one's hand 用手掌心托着下巴 ‖a ～ of cold water 施舍的象征 / be a ～ too low 无精神，意气消沉 / between ～ and lip（事情）将成未成之际 / in one's ～s 在喝醉时 / kiss the ～ 呷，饮；饮酒 / Let this ～ pass from me. 但愿能免掉这个苦难。/ sb.'s ～ of tea [口]配某人胃口的东西，使某人感兴趣的东西：Football is not his ～ of tea. 足球可不是他的爱好（或特长）。/ the ～s that cheer but not inebriate 茶 ‖～**ful** *n.*（一）满杯；半品脱之量 ‖～,**bearer** *n.* 斟酒者 / ～,**cake** *n.* 杯形糕饼 / ～,**holder** *n.* 奖杯保持者 / ～ **shake** 木材的环形裂口 / ～ **tie** 优胜赛决赛

cupboard ['kʌbəd] *n.* ①碗碟橱，食橱 ②[英]小橱 ‖a skeleton in the ～ 不为外人所知的家丑 ‖～ **love** 因企图得到某物而表示的亲热（如孩子想从食橱得到些食物而向管理食橱的人所表示的亲热）

cupidity [kjuː(ː)'piditi] *n.* 贪财，贪心：arouse（或 excite）sb.'s ～ 引起某人的贪财心

cupola ['kju:pələ] *n.* ①小圆屋顶; 圆顶; 屋顶钟形小阁 ②化铁炉, 冲天炉 ③装甲炮塔 ④【解】钟形感器

cur [kə:] *n.* ① 杂种狗, 劣种狗; 恶狗 ②坏种, 卑怯的家伙

curable ['kjuərəbl] *a.* 可医好的 ‖**curability** [,kjuərə'biliti] *n.*

curate ['kjuərit] *n.* 副牧师: a ~ in charge 教区的临时代理牧师

curator [kjuə'reitə] *n.* ①管理者, 掌管者 ②(博物馆、图书馆等的)馆长 ③[英]大学董事会的财产管理员, 大学学监 ④(未成年者、疯子等的)监护人, 保护人 ‖**~ship** *n.* 管理者(或馆长等)的职位(或身分)

curb [kə:b] **I** *n.* ① 勒马的链条(或皮带) ②(马后脚生的)硬瘤 ③控制, 约束, 抑制: put (或 place) a ~ on 控制… ④路边; (街道的)路边镶边石; 井栏; (建筑物上的)边饰 ⑤[美]场外证券市场(=~ market) **II** *vt.* ① 给(马)装上勒马链; 勒住(马) ②控制, 抑制, 约束: ~ one's anger 抑制愤怒 ③设路边石于…; 设井栏于… ‖ ~ **bit** 马嚼铁 / ~ **exchange** 场外交易 / ~ **roof**【建】复斜屋顶 / ~ **service** [美] 送食物到人行道边汽车乘客手上的服务 / '**~stone** *n.* [美]侧石, 路边石 (=[英] kerb stone) *a.* ①场外(证券)交易的: a ~*stone* broker (证券交易的)场外经纪人 ②(意见等)偶然有感而发的 ③非专门训练的; 门外汉似的

curd [kə:d] **I** *n.* 凝乳; 凝乳状物: ~*s* and whey 奶油点心; 酥酪 / bean ~ 豆腐 / ~ soap 酪状皂 **II** *vt.* & *vi.* (使)凝结

curdle ['kə:dl] **①** *vt.* ①使凝结: ~ sb.'s blood 吓得某人浑身冰凉 ②使(牛奶等)结块变质; 使变坏 **②** *vi.* ①凝结 ②变质, 变坏

cure¹ [kjuə] **I ①** *vt.* ①治愈: ~ a patient (a disease) 治愈病人(疾病) / ~ sb. *of* his illness 医好某人的疾病 ②纠正, 矫正; 消除(弊病等): ~ a child *of* a bad habit 纠正小孩的不良习惯 ③(用腌、熏、晒、烤等方法)加工处理: ~ meat by salting 腌肉 / ~*d* tobacco 烤烟 ④使(橡胶)硫化 **②** *vi.* ①起治疗作用; 受治疗 ②被加工处理(指腌、熏、晒、烤等) ③(橡胶)被硫化 **II** *n.* ①治愈; 痊愈; effect a ~ by acupuncture treatment 用针刺疗法治愈疾病 / His ~ took only a few weeks. 不过几个星期, 他的病就治好了。/ 60 cases with 56 ~*s* 六十个病例中的五十六个治愈例 ②疗法; (治疗某种疾病的)药; (处理社会问题等的)对策: a new ~ for a disease 一种疾病的新疗法(或新药) ③治疗, 疗程: take a ~ 接受(一个疗程的)治疗 ④矿泉疗养地 ⑤(用腌、熏、晒、烤等方法进行的)加工处理 ⑥【化】硫化, 熟化, 固化 ⑦牧师的职责, 教化; 牧师的职位 ‖**~less** *a.* 无法医治的 ‖**~-all** ['kjuərɔ:l] *n.* 万应灵药

curfew ['kə:fju:] *n.* ① (中世纪人们熄灯睡觉的)晚钟; 晚钟声; 打晚钟的时刻 ②宵禁(时间); 宵禁令: impose a ~ upon a city 在一个城市里实行宵禁 / lift a ~ 撤消宵禁

curio ['kjuəriou] *n.* 古董, 骨董, 古玩, 珍品

curiosity [,kjuəri'ɔsiti] *n.* ① 好奇(心): arouse (gratify) sb.'s ~ about sth. 打动(满足)某人对某事物的好奇心 / I asked out of mere ~. 我只不过是出于好奇问问罢了。②奇品; 珍品, 古玩: a medical ~ 医学上的罕见病例 / a ~ shop 古玩店 ③奇特性

curious ['kjuəriəs] *a.* ① 好奇的; [贬]爱东探西问的: I'm ~ to have a look at it. 我非常想看一看这件东西。/ Don't be too ~ about things you are not supposed to know. 对于不要你知道的事别去打听。②稀奇古怪的, 难以理解的: What a ~ mistake! 多么荒谬的错误! / a ~ coincidence 奇妙的巧合 ③[古]仔细留心的; 精细的 ‖**~ly** *ad.* / **~ness** *n.*

curl [kə:l] **I** *n.* ①卷毛, 卷发 ②卷曲物, 螺旋状物: a ~ of smoke 一缕烟 ③卷曲: a ~ of the lip(s) 嘴唇的上翘(表示轻蔑) / keep the hair in ~ 使头发卷曲着 ④(马铃薯等的)苗叶卷缩病 **II ①** *vt.* 使卷曲, 使成螺旋状 **②** *vi.* ①卷曲, 卷缩; (烟)缭绕 ②作冰上溜石游戏 ‖**~ up** ①卷; 蜷: ~ oneself *up* 把身子蜷作一团 ②[口]崩溃; (使)倒下 / **make sb.'s hair** ~ 使某人战栗, 把某人吓坏 ‖~**er** *n.* ①卷曲者; 卷曲物 ②作冰上溜石游戏者 ‖'~,**paper** *n.* 卷发纸

curly ['kə:li] *a.* ①卷曲的; 卷缩的 ②有卷毛(或卷发)的 ③(木材)有皱状纹理的 ‖'~-**pate** *n.* 头发卷曲的人

currant ['kʌrənt] *n.* ①无核小葡萄干 ②茶蘼子属植物; 茶蘼子属植物的果实

currency ['kʌrənsi] *n.* ① 通货, 货币: a paper ~ 纸币 / foreign *currencies* 外币 ② 通用, 流通; 流传, 传播: a story that enjoys wide ~ 一个到处流传的故事 / The rumour soon gained ~. 谣言不久就传播开来了。/ give ~ to 散布… / find ~ among 在…中间得以流行起来 ③流通时间: Most slang has short ~. 大多数俚语只通用一时。

current ['kʌrənt] **I** *a.* ① 通用的, 流行的: a ~ account 往来帐户; 活期存款帐户 / ~ assets 流动资产 / ~ money 通用的货币 / the ~ thinking 流行的想法 / be ~ in that region 在那个地区很通行 ② 现时的, 当前的, 现行的: ~ English 当代英语 / ~ events 时事 / the ~ month (week) 本月(周) / the 10th ~ 本月十日 / the ~ price 时价, 市价 / the ~ situation 时局, 当前形势 / the ~ standards 现行标准 ⑧草写的: ~ handwriting 草书, 草体 **II** *n.* ①流, 水流, 气流: the main (adverse) ~ 主(逆)流 / a swift (warm) ~ 急(暖)流 / an up-and-down ~ 升降气流 / velocity ~ 流速 ②电流: an alternating ~ 交流(电) / a direct ~ 直流(电) / a pulse ~ 脉冲电流 / ~ intensity (density) 电流强(密)度 / turn on (off) the ~ 接通(关断)电流 ③趋势, 倾向, 潮

流: go *with* (*against*) the ~ of the times 顺应
(违背)时代潮流 / the ~ of thought 思潮 ‖ *pass*
(或 *go, run*) ~ ① (钱币等)有流通价值 ② 通
行,流行: The news *passes* ~ at present that
.... 关于…的消息现在流传很广。‖ ~less *a.*
无电流的,无流的 / ~ly *ad.* ①普通地,通常地
②当前 / ~ness *n.* ‖ '~-'carrying *a.* 载电的,
载流的 / '~-con'ducting *a.* 导电的

curriculum [kəˈrikjuləm] ([复] curriculums 或
curricula [kəˈrikjulə]) *n.* ①学校的全部课程:
The subject is not included in the ~. 这门学科
不包括在课程表内。②(一门)课程

curry[1] [ˈkʌri] I *n.* 咖喱(粉);咖喱食品 II *vt.* 在
…中用咖喱调味 ‖ ~ paste 咖喱酱 / ~ powder
咖喱粉

curry[2] [ˈkʌri] *vt.* ① 梳刷(马匹等) ② 加脂于(皮
革),鞣(皮) ③擦,打 ‖ ~ favo(u)r (*with sb.*) 求
宠(于某人),拍(某人)马屁 ‖ ~comb *n.* 马梳,
马栉 *vt.* 用马梳梳刷

curse [kə:s] I *n.* ① 诅咒,咒骂;咒语,骂人话 ②
祟,灾祸;祸因,祸根: Mosquitoes used to be a ~
in this part of the country. 在过去,蚊子是这
儿的一个大害。③ 被诅咒的事物 ④[宗]逐出教
门 II (cursed 或 curst [kə:st]) ❶ *vt.* ①诅咒,
咒骂,恶骂 ②降祸于;使苦恼: be ~d *with* 被…
所苦,因…而遭殃 ③[宗]逐(某人)出教门 ❷ *vi.*
诅咒,咒骂 ‖ *be under a* ~ 被诅咒;被作祟 /
call down (或 *lay*) a ~ *upon sb.* 诅咒某人 /
Curses come home to roost. 诅咒他人,回头
应验到自己。/ *Curse upon it!* 该死! / *the* ~
[俚]月经(期)

cursed [ˈkə:sid] *a.* ①被咒骂的 ②该咒的;可恶的,
万恶的 ‖ ~ly *ad.* / ~ness *n.*

cursory [ˈkə:səri] *a.* 粗略的,草率的;仓卒的 ‖ cursorily *ad.* / cursoriness *n.*

curt [kə:t] *a.* 简短的,三言两语的;粗率无礼的: a
~ answer 草率的回答 ‖ ~ly *ad.* / ~ness *n.*

curtail [kə:ˈteil] *vt.* ① 截短,缩短(讲话、假期、节
目等);省略(词)的一部分: "Telly" is a ~ed
word. "telly" 是一个缩略词。② 削减(经费
等) ③剥夺(某人)的特权(或官衔等): ~ *sb. of*
his citizenship 褫夺某人公权 ‖ ~ment *n.* /
step [建]起步级

curtain [ˈkə:tn] I *n.* ① 帘;窗帘;门帘: draw the
~ 拉开(或拉上)帘子 / draw the ~ back (或
aside) 拉开帘子 ② (舞台上的)幕; 启幕; 落幕:
The ~ has come down on Act II. 第二幕已结
束。/ *Curtain* is at 7 p. m. 晚上七时开演。
③幕状物: a fire ~ [军]弹幕 / a ~ of smoke
烟幕 ④ (连接两棱堡的)幕墙;间壁 ⑤[复][美
俚]死;完蛋: be ~s for sb. 意味着某人要完蛋了
II *vt.* ① 给…装上帘子 ②遮掉,隔开
(*off*): ~ *off* a corner 用帘子遮掉一角 ‖ a ~
lecture 妻子私下对丈夫的训斥 / *behind the* ~
在幕后;秘密地 / *Curtain!* (叙述者要人注意所
述情景时用语)想象一下这种情景! / *draw the*

~ *on sth.* ①结束某事 ②掩盖某事;停止谈论某
事 / *lift the* ~ *on sth.* ①揭开某事的序幕 ②
揭露某事 / *ring down the* ~ ①响铃落幕 ②把
事情结束 / *the Bamboo Curtain* 竹幕 / *The*
~ *falls.* ①幕落。②故事结束。/ *The* ~ *rises.*
①幕启。②故事开始。/ *the Iron Curtain* 铁幕
‖ ~ *call* 要求谢幕的掌声(或欢呼声);谢幕: take
a ~ *call* 应要求谢幕 / '~fall *n.* 幕落(时) /
'~-fire *n.* [军]弹幕射击,拦阻射击(=barrage) /
~ line 全剧(或一幕)的最后一行台词/ ~ raiser
①(正戏演出前的)开场小戏 ②(主要比赛前的)
小型比赛节目

curtsey, curtsy [ˈkə:tsi] I *n.* (西洋女子的)屈膝
礼: drop (或 bob) a ~ 行屈膝礼 II *vi.* 行屈
膝礼

curvature [ˈkə:vətʃə] *n.* ①弯曲;弯曲部分: point
of ~ [测]曲点 ②[数]曲率: radius of ~ 曲率
半径

curve [kə:v] I *n.* ① 曲线: hyperbolic ~ [数]双
曲线 / normal ~ [数]正规曲线,常态曲线 ②
弯,弯曲;弯曲物;弯曲部分;(统计中的)曲线图
表: a sharp ~ in the road 道路的急转弯 ③
[复](圆)括号(即( )) II ❶ *vt.* 弄弯;使成曲
线,把…扳成弯状 ❷ *vi.* 成曲形;(依)曲线行进

cushion [ˈkuʃən] I *n.* ① 垫子;坐垫,靠垫 ②[机]
软垫;垫层;缓冲器 ③(台球台子的)橡皮边 ④插
针的针扎 ⑤(猪等的)臀部软肉 ⑥(马的)颌叉
⑦[俚](棒球运动的)垒 ⑧起缓冲作用的事物;缓
解病痛的药物(或治疗) ⑨[美]安逸;奢侈: be on
the ~ 景况优裕 II *vt.* ①把…安置在垫子上;
(为使安适)用垫子支撑: The nurses ~ed the
patient's injured shoulder. 护士们用垫子支撑
病人受伤的肩膀。② 给…安上垫子: ~ a chair
给椅子安上垫子 ③使减少震动;缓和…的冲击:
~ing effect [机]缓冲作用,减震作用 ④ 暗中压
制(抗议等);掩盖(丑事等) ⑤使(台球)停靠在台
边 ‖ ~ capital [建]罗曼式柱头;带枕柱头 / ~
tyre 半实心轮胎,垫式轮胎

custard [ˈkʌstəd] *n.* 牛奶蛋糊(或冻) ‖ apple
[植]番荔枝属植物(或其果实)

custodian [kʌsˈtoudjən] *n.* 管理人,保管人;看守人
‖ ~ship *n.* 保管人(或看守人)的资格(或责任)

custody [ˈkʌstədi] *n.* ① 保管,保护,监护 ②拘留,
监禁 ‖ *be in the* ~ *of sb.* 被托交某人保管中;
受某人保护;受某人监管 / *in* ~ 被拘留(或监
禁)中 / *take sb. into* ~ 拘留某人

custom [ˈkʌstəm] *n.* ① 习惯,风俗,惯例;[律]习
惯法: social ~s 社会风俗 / It is the ~ *with*
(或 *of*) certain foreigners to do so. 这样做法是
某些外国人的习惯。② [the Customs] 海关;[复]
关税: How long will it take us to pass the
Customs? 办完海关手续要多少时间? / The
Customs formalities are simple. 海关手续很
简单。③ (顾客对商店等的)惠顾;[总称]顾客:
withdraw one's ~ from a shop 不再去某某商店
买东西 / be glad to have sb.'s ~ 很乐意某人来

购买货物 ‖ a ~s bond 海关罚款；海关保税 / ~s clearance 出口结关 / ~s detention 海关扣留 / ~s duties 关税 / ~s entry 进口报关 / a ~s officer 海关人员 / a ~s seal 海关加封 / a ~s tariff 关税率 **II** a. 定制的，定做的：~ clothes 定做的衣服 ‖ '~-'built, '~-'made a. 定制的，定做的 / '~-(s)house n. 海关 / '~-,tailor vt. 定制，定做

customary ['kʌstəməri] **I** a. ① 通常的，常例的，·习惯的 ② 习惯法的，惯例的：a ~ law 习惯法 **II** n. 惯例书；礼法书 ‖**customarily** ['kʌstəm-ərili; 美 ,kʌstə'merili] ad. / **customariness** n.

customer ['kʌstəmə] n. ① 顾客，主顾 ② [口]家伙：a queer ~ 怪人 / an awkward ~ 难对付的家伙 / a rough ~ 粗暴无礼的家伙

cut [kʌt] **I** (cut; cutting) ❶ vt. ①切；割；剪；截；砍；削：~ a loaf of bread in two 把一只面包一切为二 / ~ wheat (grass) 割麦(割草) / ~ one's finger 割破手指 / ~ sb. free from the ropes 割断绳索使某人自由 / ~ the ribbon for an exhibition 为展览会剪彩 / have one's hair ~ 剪头发，理发(这里 cut 是过去分词) / ~ a hedge 修剪树篱 / ~ the feet to fit the shoes 削足适履 ②刺穿；刺痛；伤害(指感情方面)：The icy wind ~ him to the bone. 他感到寒风刺骨。/ ~ sb. to the heart 使某人极为伤心 ③掘成；凿出；开辟：~ an air-raid shelter in the side of a hill 在山坡上挖防空洞 / ~ steps in a rock 在岩石上开凿步阶 / ~ a path through a thick forest 在密林中开出一条路 ④雕刻；琢磨：~ an inscription on a piece of marble 把题词镌刻在一块大理石上 / ~ a figure in stone 雕刻石像 / ~ a diamond 琢磨钻石 ⑤削减；缩短；删节；剪辑(影片)：~ the prices 降低物价 / ~ the planned time by two months 将预定时间缩短两个月 / The article is too long; it has to be ~. 这篇文章太长了，要加以删节。⑥ 与…相交，与…相切；穿过：the point where AB ~s CD AB 线与 CD 线相交处的那一点 / The path ~s the meadow diagonally. 那条路斜穿过草地。⑦阉割(家畜) ⑧停止，打断；和…绝交；排斥：Cut the nonsense (comedy)! 别胡说(无聊)了！/ plant trees to ~ the wind 植树挡风 / ~ sb. from an organization 把某人从一个组织中排除出去 ⑨关(机器等)；切断(电路)；终止拍摄(电影某一场景) ⑩ 不理睬(某人)，假装不看见(某人)：~ sb. (dead) in the street 在街上遇到某人时假装不看见 ⑪ 显出，给人…的印象：~ a smart figure 出风头 ⑫逃避(上课、开会等)：~ classes 旷课 ⑬溶解，分解；冲淡：~ resin with benzene 用苯溶解树脂 ⑭【机】切削，割削

⑮灌制(唱片)；(用打字机)将…打在蜡纸上 ⑯摊分(利益、赃物等) ⑰急转…的方向 ⑱出(牙齿) ⑲削(球) ⑳签(牌)(指把洗过的牌在分发前分成两迭，上下倒置)；抽(牌) ❷ vi. ①切；割；剪；截；砍；削(可指作出或承受以上各种动作)：This knife ~s well. 这把刀切起来快。/ This metal ~s easily. 这种金属容易切削。②(用鞭)抽，(用刀、剑等)砍，击；刺痛，刺痛，(在感情方面)伤害：a freezing wind that ~s to the marrow 刺骨的寒风 / The coat ~s at the arm-pits. 这件外套腋下处勒得太紧。/ a remark that ~s 刺人的话 ③(议论、分析等)起作用：His analysis ~s quite deep. 他的分析相当深刻。④相交，相切；穿(过)，斜穿；抄近路：The two lines ~ at point A. 这两条线在 A 点相交。/ a tunnel cutting through a hill 穿山隧道 ⑤很快地离开；疾驰：I must ~. 我得赶快走了。/ a torpedo boat cutting through the water 在水面疾驰的鱼雷艇 ⑥(拍摄电影时)停拍；切换电视(或电影)镜头；剪辑影片 ⑦旷课 ⑧摊分，分赃 ⑨急转方向：The car ~ to the left. 车子向左急转。⑩打削球 ⑪签牌；抽牌 ⑫(画成)触目 **II** n. ①(刀、剑、鞭等的)切，割，剪，砍，削，击，抽：give the horse a ~ across the flank 在马腹上横抽一鞭 ②伤口，切口；切面：~s on one's arms 臂上的伤口 / a smooth ~ 光滑的切面 ③某一部位的食肉(如肋条、腿肉)；切下的肉；(同一批)割下的作物；(从一群中)挑选出的一批牲口：a ~ of pork 一刀猪肉 / This year's ~ of wheat is simply splendid. 今年小麦收成简直好极了。④削减；缩短；删节；删掉的部分：Big ~s have been made in the prices of medicine. 药品价格有了大幅度的降低。/ make some ~s in a film 对影片作某些删节 ⑤伤人的话(或行为)；(对某人的)不理睬：That was a ~ at me. 那是对我的攻击。⑥(人工挖凿或自然侵蚀而成的)河道，沟渠 ⑦近路，捷径 ⑧挖土，挖方 ⑨(分摊到的)一份 ⑩(电视或电影镜头的)切换 ⑪【机】切削，割削；割纹：machine ~ 机械切削，机割 / multiple ~ 多刃切削 ⑫【化】馏份；加入每加仑溶剂中的树脂磅数

⑬(服装、头发等的)式样;类型: the ~ of sb.'s face 某人的脸型
⑭等级(尤指社会地位)
⑮插图;雕刻版,版画: illustrate with ~*s* 附图说明
⑯旷课
⑰(乒乓、网球等的)削球;(削球的)旋转: exchange ~*s* 对削
⑱签牌;抽牌
⑲布匹长度单位(自四十码到一百码不等)
III ***a.*** ①经过切割(或裁剪、雕刻等)的: a ~ plane 剖面 / ~ flowers 插花 / ~ glass 雕玻璃,刻花玻璃;刻花玻璃器(如瓶、缸等)
②削减的,缩小的: at ~ prices 廉价地
③阉割过的
④有锯齿边的
⑤喝醉的
‖***a ~ above*** (***below***) [口]高(低)于…一等,胜(次)于: Don't always think you're *a ~ above* others. 不要老以为自己比别人高明。/ ***a short ~*** 近路,捷径 / ***~ about*** ①乱切;乱砍 ②乱跑 / ***~ across*** 抄近路穿过,对直通过 / ***~ adrift*** ①使分开、割断…的联系 ②(使)独自谋生;(被)抛弃 / ***~ after*** 急急忙忙地跟随(某人或某物) / ***~ and carve*** ①乱切;乱砍 ②变更 ③使精练 / ***Cut and come again.*** [口]请尽量吃。/ ***~ and run*** ①砍断锚索立即开船逃走 ②急忙逃走;急忙离开 / ***~ and thrust*** 肉搏战,短兵相接的搏斗 / ***~ at*** ①向…猛砍,向…猛击 ②危害,毁掉(希望等) / ***~ away*** ①切掉;剪掉;砍掉 ②逃走;跑开 / ***~ back*** ①修剪(树枝等);截短 ②削减,缩减(生产等): 中止(契约等) ③【化】稀释 ④急转方向 ⑤(故事、电影等)倒叙 / ***~ both ways*** (议论、行动等)对双方都起作用,两面都说得通;模棱两可,两边倒 / ***~ down*** ①砍倒,砍伤,砍死 ②(疾病等)夺去…的生命,损害…的健康 ③胜过,使逊色 ④削减;缩短;改小;删节: ~ *down* on smoking 减少抽烟 / ***~ in*** ①插嘴: ~ *in* with a few remarks 插嘴讲几句 ②(突然)插入: ~ *in* on a queue 插(入)队(伍) ③超车抢档 ④把…剁入;把…插进;使挨进 ⑤【机】开动;【电】接通 / ***~ into*** ①侵犯(利益等) ②打断(讲话等) / ***~ it*** ①快走开,逃走 ②停止;住口 / ***~ it fat*** 做得过分;炫耀 / ***~ it fine*** 扣得很紧(尤指时间方面),几乎不留余地 / ***~ loose*** 见 **loose** / ***~ no ice*** 见 **ice** / ***~ off*** ①切掉;割掉;剪下;删去: ~ *off* a corner 切掉一只角;(不绕角走)抄近路 ②切断;断绝;使隔绝: be ~ *off* while talking by telephone 通电话时线路被切断 ③(突然)中止,中断 ④关掉(马达等);(马达等)停掉 ⑤(疾病等)使(人)死亡: be ~ *off* in one's prime 壮年时(生病)死掉 ⑥剥夺…的继承权/ ***~ on*** 很快地向前走 / ***~ out*** ①切掉;割掉;删掉 ②裁剪出;排定(工作等) tasks ~ *out* for the week 规定的一周任务 / have one's work ~ *out* for one 工作已经排定;十分忙碌 ③使适合: be ~ *out* for 适合于;天生是…的料子 ④切(或剪、削、掘)成;侵蚀成 ⑤停止;放弃: *Cut* it *out*! 停止! 住嘴! / ~ *out* an engine 关掉发动机 / ~ *out* tobacco (drinking) 戒烟(酒) ⑥取代(对手),把(对手)排挤掉 ⑦使分离出来: ~ *out* a car from a train 把一节车厢从列车脱下 ⑧突然离开,赶快离开 ⑨(超车时)横入对面来车车道 ⑩用插入敌船与海岸之间的战术俘获(敌船) / ***~ round*** 卖弄,故意做给人看(尤指感情方面) / ***~ short*** ①使停止;打断: ~ sb. *short* 打断某人的话 ②缩减;截短: ~ *short* the stay abroad 缩短在国外逗留的时间 / ***~ the*** (***Gordian***) ***knot*** 见 **knot** / ***~ the record*** 见 **record** / ***~ through*** ①抄近路穿过 ②刺穿;凿穿;剪断 / ***~ under*** 卖得比…便宜 / ***~ up*** ①切碎;在…上弄出许多伤口;齐根割掉 ②(牲口等)宰后得肉;(布料等)裁得出: This pig ~*s up* well. 这头猪出肉很多。/ This piece of cloth will ~ *up* into three suits. 这段布可以裁成三套衣服。 ③对…吹毛求疵,抨击 ④歼灭 ⑤使丧气,使消沉;使痛心 ⑥插科打诨,恶作剧,胡闹;[美俚]闲聊: Don't think I'm only *cutting up*. 别以为我在开玩笑。/ ~ *up* a matter with sb. 与某人闲谈某事 ⑦遗下财产: ~ *up* fat (或 well) [谑]留下大笔遗产 / ***~ up rough*** (或 ***nasty, rusty, savage, stiff, ugly***) 发脾气,发怒 / ***draw ~s*** 抽签 / ***give sb. the ~ direct*** 故意不理睬某人 / ***the ~ of sb.'s jib*** 某人的相貌(或仪表)
‖**'~-and-'come-again** ***n.*** 丰富 / **'~-and-'dried, '~-and-'dry** ***a.*** ①早已准备好的;陈套的 ②呆板的,没有生气的 / **'~-and-'try** ***a.*** 试验(性)的 / **'~away** ***a.*** 部分被切(割)掉的;剖面的 ***n.*** ①前下摆向后斜切的燕尾服 ②(切去一角露出内部结构的)剖面图 / **'~back** ***n.*** ①截短;被截短的东西 ②中止;削减 ③【化】稀释产物 ④(踢足球时)带球急转 ⑤(故事或电影的)倒叙 ⑥电视镜头拼合摄影法 / **'~-'in** ***n.*** ①插入的东西(如书报边行缩进处的插图,电影中插入的特写镜头,广播中插入的广告等) ②(分享的)一份 ③【机】切入,割入 ④【电】接通 ***a.*** 插入的 / **'~line** ***n.*** 插图等下面的说明文字;图例 / **'~off** ***n.*** ①切掉;截断;切(或割)下的东西 ②近路;(河流弯曲处)截弯取直的河道 ③中止,停止;截止点 ④【机】停汽,关车;截断装置 / **'~out** ***n.*** ①切下(或删掉)的东西;剪成(或刻成)的东西 ②【电】终止,阻断;断流器 ③(内燃机的)排气装置 / **'~ˌover** ***a.*** 树木被砍光的 ***n.*** ①树木被砍光的一片地 ②【讯】接入,开通;转换 / **'~purse** ***n.*** 小偷,扒手 / **'~-'rate** ***a.*** ①减价的;有减价货出售的 ②次等的 / **'~throat** ***n.*** 凶手,谋杀者 ***a.*** ①杀人的,残酷的,无情的 ②(桥牌等)三人玩的 / **'~up** ***n.*** 插科打诨的人,胡闹的人 / **'~ˌwater** ***n.*** ①(桥等的)分水角,杀水装置 ②【船】首柱分水处,船鼻 / **'~worm** ***n.*** 夜盗蛾

cute [kju:t] ***a.*** [口]①聪明的,伶俐的 ②漂亮的,逗人喜爱的 ③装腔作势的,做作的 ‖**~ly** ***ad.*** / **~ness** ***n.***

cuticle ['kju:tikl] *n.* ① 表皮 ②【解】护膜 ③【植】角质层

cutlas(s) ['kʌtləs] *n.* (从前水手用的)短剑,弯刀

cutler ['kʌtlə] *n.* ① 刀匠,磨刀匠;刃具工人 ②经营刃具的商人

cutlet ['kʌtlit] *n.* (羊、牛、猪等的)肉片;炸肉排

cutter ['kʌtə] *n.* ①用于切割(或剪削等)的器械(如刀具、切草机、截煤机等):a high speed ~ 高速刀具 / a cotton stalk ~ 棉秆切碎机 ②从事切割(或剪削等)工作的人(如服装裁缝师、影片剪辑员、采煤工人等)·③刻纹头,机械式录音头 ④快艇,小汽艇 ⑤【地】倾斜节理 ⑥一种轻便雪橇

cutting ['kʌtiŋ] I *n.* ① 切;割;剪;削;掘 ② 切(或割、剪、削)下的东西 ③(影片)剪辑 ④[英]剪报(=[美] clipping) ⑤[英]路堑;(筑路时排除障碍物的)开挖 ⑥(用来插种的)插枝,插条 ⑦(唱片)录音 II *a.* ①供切(或割等)用的 ②锋利的 ③凛冽的,寒冷刺骨的 ④(话语等)尖刻的,尖锐的 ⑤(声音)刺耳的;(疼痛)剧烈的 ‖~ly *ad.*

cycle ['saikl] I *n.* ① 周期;循环;一转:the business ~ 商业循环,经济循环 / the life ~ of insects 昆虫的生活周期 / lunar (solar) ~【天】太阴(阳)周 / the ~ of the seasons 季节的循环 / on a three-year ~ 按三年一轮转 ②(一段)长时期,(一个)时代 ③(故事等的)始末;(表现同一主题或描写同一人物的)一组小说(或戏剧、诗歌等):a song ~ 组歌 ④ 自行车;三轮脚踏车;机器脚踏车 ⑤天体运转的轨道 ⑥【无】周(波):~s per second 周/秒,赫 ⑦【数】环 ⑧【地】旋回 II ❶ *vi.* ①(周而复始地)循环,轮转 ②骑自行车(或三轮脚踏车、机器脚踏车) ❷ *vt.* 使循环,使轮转 ‖~r,

cyclist *n.* 骑自行车(或机器脚踏车等)的人 / **cycling** *n.* 骑自行车 *a.* 骑自行车用的 ‖'~car *n.* (三轮或四轮的)小型机动车

cyclone ['saikloun] *n.* 气旋;旋风 ‖**cyclonic** [sai'klɔnik] *a.*

cyclop(a)edia [ˌsaiklə'pi:djə] *n.* 百科词典,百科全书 (=encyclop(a)edia)

cygnet ['signit] *n.* 小天鹅

cylinder ['silində] *n.* ①圆筒,圆柱体;【工】机筒;钢瓶,烘筒;量筒 ②【机】汽缸,气缸 ③(印刷机)滚筒 ④【数】柱,柱面 ⑤(左轮手枪的)旋转弹膛 ⑥(刻有楔形文字的)圆柱形陶器 ‖(*work*) *on all* ~*s* [口]竭尽全力地(干) ‖~ **ga(u)ge** 缸径规,圆筒内径测量器 / ~ **head**, ~ **cap** 汽缸盖 / ~ **press** 滚筒印刷机,轮转印刷机

cymbal ['simbəl] *n.* [常用复]【音】铙钹,钹钹,钹 ‖~**ist** *n.* 击钹者

cynic ['sinik] I *n.* ① [C-] 犬儒学派的人 ②玩世不恭的人,好挖苦人的人;愤世嫉俗者 II *a.* ① [C-] 犬儒学派的:the *Cynic* School 犬儒学派 ② =cynical

cynical ['sinikəl] *a.* 愤世嫉俗的;玩世不恭的,冷嘲热讽的 ‖~**ly** *ad.*

cynosure ['sinəzjuə, 'sainəzjuə] *n.* ① [the C-]【天】小熊座 (=Ursa Minor) ② [the C-]【天】北极星 (=the North Star) ③ 指引方向的东西(如指针) ④引起众人注视的人(或事物);赞美的目标:the ~ of all eyes 众人注意的目标

cypher ['saifə] *vt.*, *vi.* & *n.* =cipher

cypress ['saipris] *n.* ①柏属植物 ②柏树 ③柏树枝(作哀悼标志用) ④黑纱(作哀悼标志用)

D

dab[1] [dæb] I (dabbed; dabbing) ❶ *vt.* ① 轻拍,轻敲: ~ a baby in the face 轻拍婴儿的脸(表示爱抚) ②轻敷,轻搽: ~ paint on a picture 给油画敷彩 ❷ *vi.* ①轻拍,轻敲 (at) ②轻敷,轻搽 (on, at) II *n.* ①轻拍,轻敲 ②轻敷,轻搽 ③(轻敷、轻搽、轻涂用的)湿而软的小块(如颜料等) ‖~r *n.* 玩水者;涉猎者,浅尝者

dab[2] [dæb] *n.*【动】比目鱼;孙鲽属的鱼,孙鲽

dab[3] [dæb] *n.* [口]能手,熟手 (at): a ~ at (playing) tennis 网球能手

dabble ['dæbl] ❶ *vt.* 弄湿,溅湿: ~ one's hand in the water 用手玩水 ~d with mud 被泥浆溅湿 ❷ *vi.* ①玩水 ②涉猎;把…高兴爱好尝试一下 (in, at): ~ in (或 at) art 涉猎艺术 ‖~r *n.* 玩水者;涉猎者,浅尝者

dad [dæd], **dada** ['dædə] *n.* [口]爸爸,爹爹

daddy ['dædi] *n.* ①[口] =dad ②[美俚]出钱供养情妇的男子(尤指年老的富人) ‖~ **longlegs** [用作单或复] ① 长脚双翅昆虫 ② 盲蛛,盲蜘(一种长脚蜘蛛)

dagger ['dægə] I *n.* ① 匕首,短剑 ②剑号(即 †): the double ~ 双剑号(即 ‡) ③剑形物 II *vt.* ① 用剑刺 ②用剑号标明 ‖*at* ~*s drawn* 剑拔弩张,势不两立 / *look* ~*s at sb.* 对某人怒目而视 / *speak* ~*s to sb.* 恶言伤害某人

dagger

dahlia ['deiljə] *n.* ① 大丽花属的观赏植物; 大丽花 ②[D-] 大丽花属 ③ 一种红色 ‖*a blue ~* 不可能有的东西

daily ['deili] **I** *a.* 每日的, 日常的: industrial articles for ~ use 日用工业品 / a ~ paper 日报 / ~ life 日常生活 / one's ~ bread 每日食粮; 生计 **II** *ad.* 每日, 天天 **III** *n.* ① 日报 ②[口] 朝来夜去的女佣 ‖~ **double** ①双赌注(指需在两次赛马中赌中才算赢)②[美俚] 同时在两个不同领域中得到成功

dainty ['deinti] **I** *a.* ① 轻巧的, 精致的 ②(食物)美味的, 可口的, 讲究的 ③(人)秀丽的, 优雅的 ④(对食物、服装等)过分讲究的, 挑剔的 **II** *n.* 美味精致的食物 ‖**daintily** *ad.* / **daintiness** *n.*

dairy ['dɛəri] *n.* ① 牛奶房, 制酪场; 牛奶场 ② 牛奶及乳品店 ③ 制酪业: ~ products 乳制品 ‖~**ing** *n.* 乳制品业 ‖~ **breed** 为生产牛奶而培养的牛种 / ~ **cattle** 奶牛 / '~**maid** *n.* 牛奶房(或牛奶场)女工 / '~**man** *n.* ① 牛奶房(或牛奶场)男工 ② 牛奶场主; 牛奶及乳品商人

dais ['deiis] *n.* ①(宴会大厅一端的)台, 高台 ②(教室的)讲台; (广场上的)演奏台, 演出坛

daisy ['deizi] **I** *n.* ① 雏菊属(或菊属)的植物; 雏菊 ②[俚] 上等货; 第一流的人物, 漂亮姑娘 **II** *a.* [俚] 上等的, 极好的 ‖**push (up) daisies** [俚] 葬在地下 ‖~ **ham** 去骨熏腿

dale [deil] *n.* [英方][诗] 谷, 溪谷 ‖*up hill and down* ~ 翻山越岭; 拼命地; 坚持地; 彻底地

dalliance ['dæliəns] *n.* ① 嬉戏; 调戏 ② 放荡度日

dally ['dæli] ❶ *vi.* ① 嬉戏; 调戏 (with) ② 闲荡, 延误 (over): ~ over one's work 延误工作 ❷ *vt.* (在嬉戏中)浪费(时间) (away): ~ time away 蹉跎光阴

dam¹ [dæm] **I** *n.* ① 水坝, 水堤, 水闸: a storage ~ 蓄水坝 ② 拦在堤坝里的水 ③(阻止液体、气体或空气流动的)障碍物, 屏障; 【矿】隔墙, 密封墙 【医】(牙科用的)橡皮障 **II** (dammed; damming) *vt.* ① 筑坝拦(水) (up, out) ② 抑制, 控制 (in, up): ~ up one's feelings 抑制感情

dam

dam² [dæm] *n.* ① 母兽 ②[古][蔑] 母亲

damage ['dæmidʒ] **I** *n.* ① 损害, 毁坏; 破坏; 损失: do ~ to 损害… / the ~ radius 【军】破坏半

径 / the ~ effect 【军】破坏效果 ②[复]【律】损害赔偿金: costs and ~s 讼费和损害费 ③[常用复][口] 费用 **II** *vt.* 损害, 毁坏: ~ fruit trees 损害果树 ‖~**able** *a.* 可损害的 / **damaging** *a.* 有破坏性的

damask ['dæməsk] **I** *n.* ① 缎子, 锦缎 ② 织花台布 ③(作兵刃用的)大马士革钢 (= ~ steel); 大马士革钢上的波形花纹 ④ 红玫瑰色 **II** *a.* ① 大马士革的 ② 缎子的, 锦缎的 ③ 大马士革钢制的 ④ 红玫瑰色的 **III** *vt.* ① 在…上织花纹; 为…饰花纹 ② 使成红玫瑰色 ‖~ **rose** 大马士革蔷薇

dame [deim] *n.* ①[诗][古] 夫人, 贵妇人 ② 老妇人 ③[俚] 女人, 少女

damn [dæm] **I** ❶ *vt.* ①(上帝)罚…入地狱; 诅咒: *Damn* you! (或 God ~ you!) 该死的! / I'll be (或 I am) ~ed if I ... . 要是我…, 我就不是人! ② 指责(作品等), 把…骂得一钱不值 ③ 毁掉(前途等) ❷ *vi.* (诅咒用语): *Damn*! (或 God ~!) 该死! **II** *n.* ① 诅咒 ② 丝毫: not worth a ~ 毫无价值; 根本不值得 / He does not give (或 care) a (tinker's) ~ about it. 他对此根本不在乎。 ‖~**ation** [dæm'neiʃən] *n.* ① 罚入地狱 ②(对作品等的)指责 ③(前途等的)毁掉 *int.* 该死! / ~**atory** ['dæmnətəri] *a.* 指责的. a ~*atory term* 指责性字眼

damnable ['dæmnəbl] *a.* ① 活该的, 该死的 ②[口] 糟透的: ~ weather 糟透的天气 ‖**damnably** *ad.*

damned [dæmd] **I** *a.* ①打入地狱的 ②[口]该死的, 糟透的 **II** *ad.* [口] 非常, 要命地: It is ~ kind of you. 你真好极了。(只用于熟人间) ‖*do one's ~est* [俚] 拼死命干 / *see sb. ~ first* 见 **see¹**

damp [dæmp] **I** *n.* ① 湿气, 潮湿 ②(矿井)瓦斯, 有毒气体 ③ 消沉, 沮丧 **II** *a.* 有湿气的, 潮湿的: a ~ squib [口] 引不起注意(或同情)的事情 **III** ❶ *vt.* ① 使潮湿 ②(用灰等)封(火), 灭火 (down) ③ 阻抑, 抑止 ④【物】阻尼, 使减幅, 使衰减; 【音】制止(弦)的振动: ~ed inductance 阻尼电感 ❷ *vi.* ① 变潮湿 ②【物】减幅, 衰减 ‖*cast* (或 *throw, strike*) a ~ *over* 泼…的冷水, 使沮丧 / ~ *off* (植物根茎等因湿气、细菌等)腐坏, 枯萎 ‖~**ly** *ad.* / ~**ness** *n.* ‖~ **course** 【建】防潮层 / '~**proof** *a.* 防潮的

damper ['dæmpə] *n.* ① 令人扫兴的人(或事物); 起抑制作用的因素: put a ~ on 扫…的兴; 抑制… ②【机】风档, 气流调节器: a ~ of the chimney 烟囱风门 ③【音】制音器 ④【物】阻尼器, 减震器 ⑤[美俚] 现金记录机; 银行

damsel ['dæmzəl] *n.* 年轻女人; 闺女

damson ['dæmzən] *n.* 【植】布拉斯李; 布拉斯李树

dance [dɑːns] **I** ❶ *vi.* ① 跳舞, 舞蹈 ② 手舞足蹈(旗等)飘扬; (树枝等)摇晃: They ~d for joy. 他们快乐得手舞足蹈。 ❷ *vt.* ① 跳(舞): dance a dance 跳一个舞 ② 使摇晃; 上下摆动(小孩) **II** *n.* ① 跳舞, 舞蹈: a social ~ 交谊舞 ② 舞会: give a ~

举行舞会 ③ 舞曲 ④ 舞蹈艺术 ‖*~ attendance on* (或 *upon*) *sb.* 奉承某人，向某人献媚 / *~ away* (或 *off*) ① 跳着舞走开 ② 因跳舞而失去 (机会等) / *~ to another tune* 改弦易辙 / *~ to sb.'s tune* (或 *pipe*) 跟着某人亦步亦趋 / *~ upon* (或 *on*) *nothing* (或 *~ on a rope*) 被绞死 / *lead sb. a* (*pretty*) *~* 给某人造成许多麻烦；使某人疲于奔命 / *St. Vitus's ~* 【医】舞蹈病 ‖*~r n.* 舞蹈演员；跳舞者 ‖*~-band n.* 伴舞乐队 / *drama* 舞蹈剧 / *~ hall* 舞厅 / *Dance of Death* =*danse macabre* / '*~-,orchestra n.* 伴舞乐队

dandelion ['dændilaiən] *n.* 蒲公英；蒲公英属植物

dandle ['dændl] *vt.* ① (上下摆动着) 播弄 (小孩) ② 宠，娇养

dandy ['dændi] **I** *n.* ① 花花公子，纨绔子 ② [口] 第一流的东西 ③ 一种双桅帆船 ④ [英] (送牛奶工人用的) 二轮小车 (=*~-cart*) **II** *a.* ① 服装华丽的 ② [口] 极好的，第一流的 ‖*~ish a.* 花花公子的；花花公子般的 ‖*~ brush* 鲸须马刷 / *~ fever* =dengue / *~ roll* (造纸工业用的) 压胶辊

danger ['deindʒə] *n.* ① 危险 ② 危险物；威胁：*~s to health* 对健康的威胁 ‖*be in ~ of* 有…的危险 / *in ~* 在危险中 / *make ~ of* 对…踌躇不决；认为…难办 / *out of ~* 脱离危险 ‖*~ money* 危险工作的额外报酬 / *~ signal* 危险信号 / *~ zone* 危险地带

dangerous ['deindʒrəs] *a.* 危险的 ‖*~ly ad.*

dangle ['dæŋgl] **I** ❶ *vi.* ① 摇晃地 (或可以自由摆动地) 悬挂着 ② 追求，尾随 (*after*) ❷ *vt.* ① 使摇晃地挂着 ② [喻] 用 (希望等) 眩惑 **II** *n.* 摇晃着的悬挂；被摇晃地悬挂着的东西 ‖*~r n.* ① 吊着摇晃的东西 ② 追逐女人的男子 ‖*dangling participle* [语] 垂悬分词

dank [dæŋk] *a.* 阴湿的：*a ~ and chilly cave* 阴湿寒冷的洞 ‖*~ish a.* / *~ly ad.* / *~ness n.*

dapper ['dæpə] *a.* ① (常指矮小的人) 干净利落的 ② 衣冠楚楚的

dapple ['dæpl] **I** *a.* 有斑点的，有花纹的 **II** *n.* ① 有斑纹的状态 ② 有斑纹的动物 **III** *vt. & vi.* (使) 有斑纹 ‖*~-'grey, '~-'gray a.* 有深灰色斑纹的 *n.* 有深灰色斑纹的马

dare [dɛə] **I** ❶ *v. aux.* [后接不带 to 的不定式；主要用于疑问、否定或条件句] ① 敢：*Dare he swim across?* 他敢游过去吗？ / *Who says he ~ not* (do it)? 谁说他不敢 (做这事)？ ② 竟敢 (过去式 dared 或 [古] durst，过去分词 dared) *vt.* ① 敢 ② 竟敢 ③ 敢于面对，敢于承担 (风险)：*We will ~ any hardship and danger.* 我们敢于承担任何艰险。 ④ 激 (将)，估计…没胆量：*I ~ you to do it!* 量你也不敢！ ❷ (过去式 dared 或 [古] durst，过去分词 dared) *vt.:* *Try it if you ~.* 要是你敢的话，你就试试看。 **II** *n.* ① 大胆；果敢行为 ② 挑战，激将 ‖*I ~ say* [作插入语用] 我想，大概：*There's something

wrong with the radio, I ~ say.* 收音机恐怕有点毛病。

daredevil ['dɛə,devl] *a. & n.* 胆大妄为的(人)，蛮干的(人) ‖*~ry, ~try n.* 胆大妄为，蛮干

daring ['dɛəriŋ] *n. & a.* 大胆(的)，勇敢(的)；鲁莽(的) ‖*~ly ad.* / *~ness n.*

dark [dɑ:k] **I** *a.* ① 黑暗的，暗的：*It is getting ~.* 天黑下来了。 ② (头发、皮肤等) 黑色的；(颜色) 浅黑的，深的：*~ eyes* 黑眼睛 / *~ green* 深绿，墨绿 ③ 隐蔽的，隐秘的：*It is a ~ secret.* 这是十分秘密的事。 / *keep sth. ~* 把某事隐藏起来秘而不宣 / *keep* (oneself) *~* 躲藏着 ④ 隐晦的，模糊的：*a ~ threat* 隐晦的威胁 ⑤ 阴险的；阴暗的 ⑥ 坏的，邪恶的 ⑦ 无知的；蒙昧的：*in the ~est ignorance* 在极端无知之中 / *the Dark Ages* 欧洲中世纪 / *the Dark Continent* 黑暗的大陆 ⑧ [美俚] (戏院等) 已打烊的 **II** *n.* ① 黑暗；暗处 ② 黄昏：*at* (before, after) *~* 在天黑时 (以前，以后) ③ 暗色：*the lights and ~s of a picture* 画面的明暗面 ④ 模糊，隐晦，隐秘 ⑤ 无知 ‖*a ~ horse* 见 **horse** / *as ~ as night* 昏黑，漆黑 / *in the ~* ① 在黑暗中；秘密地：*leap in the ~* 鲁莽从事 ② 不知道：*leave sb. in the ~* 不给某人知道 / *be utterly in the ~ about* (或 *as to*) 对…全然不知 / *whistle in the ~* 给自己壮胆 ‖*~ly ad.* / *~ness n.* 黑暗；势力 / *the prince of ~ness* 撒旦，魔鬼 ‖*~-field microscope* 超显微镜 / *~ lantern* 有遮光装置的提灯 / '*~'room n.* 【摄】暗室

darken ['dɑ:kən] ❶ *vt.* ① 使变暗；遮暗 ② 使变黑 ③ 使 (视力等) 模糊 ④ 使暗淡，使阴沉，使不乐 ❷ *vi.* ① 变黑；转暗；变得阴暗：*It suddenly ~ed up and threatened to rain.* 天突然暗下，快要下雨了。 ② (颜色) 变深 ③ (表情等) 变得阴沉 ④ (记忆等) 变得模糊 ‖*~ counsel* 见 **counsel**

darling ['dɑ:liŋ] **I** *n.* 心爱的人，宠儿：*My ~!* (或 *Darling!*) 亲爱的 (夫妻之间的称呼)；宝宝，乖乖 (父母对儿女的爱称) **II** *a.* ① 心爱的，宠爱的 ② 漂亮的，吸引人的 ‖*~ly ad.* / *~ness n.*

darn[1] [dɑ:n] **I** *vt. & vi.* 织补 **II** *n.* 织补；织补处

darn[2] [dɑ:n] damn 的委婉语

darning ['dɑ:niŋ] *n.* 织补；织补物 ‖*~ ball, ~ egg, ~ last* 球形织补架 / *~ needle* ① 织补针 ② [美] 蜻蜓

dart [dɑ:t] **I** *n.* ① 标枪；镖，箭 ② 突进 ③ 昆虫的刺 ④ [~s] [用作单] 投镖游戏 ⑤ 飞快的一瞥；飞快的动作 ⑥ 突然的刺痛 **II** ❶ *vt.* 投掷 (标枪等) 发射：*The sun ~s* (forth) *its beams.* 太阳光芒四射。 / *~ a glance* 飞快地瞥了一眼 ❷ *vi.* 急冲，突进：*The rocket ~s skyward.* 火箭直冲云霄。 ‖*~er n.* ① 突进者；突进物 ② (类似鸬鹚的) 吃鱼的细颈尖嘴潜水鸟 ③ (美洲产) 河鲈科小淡水鱼

dash [dæʃ] **I** ❶ *vt.* ① 使猛撞；猛砸；击碎：*The ship was ~ed against the rocks.* 船触礁了。 / *~ sth. to bits* (或 *pieces*) 把某物弄得粉碎 ② 泼泼，

溅: ~ water over sth. 用水喷射某物 / clothes ~ed with mud 溅着泥的衣服 ③搀加(with): ~ wine with water 用水搀酒 ④使(希望、计划等)破灭 ⑤使沮丧; 使窘: ~ sb.'s spirits 使某人精神沮丧 ⑥匆忙完成(off): ~ off a letter 匆忙写一封信 ⑦[口] damn 的委婉语 ❷ vi. ①冲撞: The waves ~ed upon (或 against) the rocks. 波浪撞击岩石。②猛冲, 突进: ~ by 掠过去, 冲过去 / The train ~ed through the station. 火车飞快地驶过车站。II n. ①撞击; 溅泼; (水的)撞击声 ②搀和, 注入; 少量搀和物: add a ~ of salt 加少许盐 ③闯劲, 锐气 ④炫耀, 虚饰 ⑤打击, 挫折 ⑥破折号(即——) ⑦[讯](莫尔斯电码的)划, 长划(与 dot 相对) ⑧短跑, 猛冲: make a ~ at 向…猛冲 ⑨仪表板 ‖at a ~ 一鼓作气地, 一气呵成地 / cut a ~ 大出风头, 摆阔 / ~ along 滔滔不绝地说 / ~ in 急画, 急写 / ~ out 冲出; 删去 ‖'~board n. ①(车辆的)挡泥板, (船只的)遮水板 ②仪表板 / ~ light 仪表板灯 / ~ plate 【机】缓冲板 / '~pot n. 【机】减震器; 【无】阻尼延迟器

dashing ['dæʃiŋ] a. ①精神抖擞的, 冲劲很足的 ②打扮漂亮的 ‖~ly ad.

dastard ['dæstəd] I n. 卑怯的人; 懦夫 II a. 卑怯的 ‖~ly a. 卑怯的

data ['deitə] datum 的复数 ‖~ logging 【自】数据记录; 巡回检测 / '~phone n. 【讯】数据送话器; 数据电话机 / ~ processing 【自】数据处理

date¹ [deit] I n. ①日期; 日子: fix the ~ for a meeting 确定开会日期 / the ~ of birth 出生年月日 / What's the ~ today? 今天几号? ②(历史上某一)年代, 时期: sculpture of an early ~ 古代的雕刻 / the ~ of things found in an excavation 出土物的时代 ③[美口]约会(尤指男女间的); 约会对象: make a ~ with sb. 与某人约会 / sb.'s steady ~ 与某人关系相当肯定的异性朋友 II ❶ vt. ①注(明)…的日期 ②确定…的年代; 显示出…的时代(或年龄)特征: a fossil 确定化石的年代 ③[美口]和…约会 ❷ vi. ①注(明)日期; 计算时间 ②属(于某一历史时期); 始(于某一历史时期): These machines are beginning to ~. 这些机器快要过时了。‖a heavy ~ 重要的约会(尤指男女间的) / out of ~ 废弃的; 过时的 / to ~ 到此为止: To ~ we have received more than a hundred applications. 到此刻为止, 我们收到了一百多份申请书。/ up to ~ (或 down to ~) 直到最近的; 现代的, 新式的, 时新的: bring a nuclear physics textbook up to ~ 使原子物理教科书反映最新科学成就 ‖~d a. ①注有日期的 ②过时的 / ~less a. ①无日期的 ②无限期的 ③远古的 ④经住时间考验的 ⑤无伴侣的 / ~r n. 日期戳子 ‖~ bait [美俚]引诱男子与自己约会的女子 / '~line n. ①日期 ②[常作 ~ line]日界线 ③(标明日期和地名的)新闻电讯的电头 vt. 在(新闻电讯)上注电头 / '~mark n. 日戳

date² [deit] n. ①海枣, 枣椰子: a Chinese ~ 枣, 中国枣子 ②[D-]【植】海枣属 ③ =~ palm ‖~ palm 战捷木, 枣椰树

dative ['deitiv] n. & a. 【语】与格(的)

daub [dɔ:b] I vt. & vi. ①涂抹 ②乱涂, 乱画 ③弄脏 II n. ①涂料(如泥灰、油脂等) ②涂抹 ③拙劣的画 ‖~er n. ①涂抹的人; 涂抹工具 ②拙劣的画家 ③涂料

daughter ['dɔ:tə] I n. ①女儿 ②(某国、某地的)妇女 ③【原】子核 II a. ①女儿(似)的 ②第一代所生的 ‖a ~ of Momus 爱嘲弄的人; 滑稽的人 ‖~hood n. 女儿身分, 女儿时期 / ~ly a. 女儿(似)的 / ~ element 【化】子元素 / ~-in-law ['dɔ:tərinlɔ:] ([复] ~s-in-law) n. 媳妇(儿)

daunt [dɔ:nt] vt. 威吓; 使胆怯, 使气馁

dauntless ['dɔ:ntlis] a. 无所畏惧的, 吓不倒的, 大胆的 ‖~ly ad. / ~ness n.

dawdle ['dɔ:dl] ❶ vi. 游荡, 闲混; 偷懒 ❷ vt. 闲混(时间): ~ away one's time 混日子 ‖~r n. 游手好闲的人, 二流子, 懒汉

dawn [dɔ:n] I vi. ①破晓: The day was just ~ing. 天刚亮。②(时代、局面等)开始出现, 渐露端倪 ③渐被理解(或感知)(on, upon): The truth began to ~ on me. 我开始明白真相。/ It has ~ed upon him that .... 他开始认识到… II n. ①黎明, 拂晓: at ~ 拂晓时 / Dawn breaks. 破晓。/ from ~ till dusk 从早到晚 ②[喻]开端, 曙光: the ~ of civilization 文明的开端 / the ~ of victory 胜利的曙光 ‖~ing n. ①黎明 ②开端 ③东, 东方 ‖~ chorus 【无】磁暴时发射出的长波讯号所产生的干扰声(常可在清晨从无线电中听到)

day [dei] n. ①白昼, 白天; 黎明: before ~ 天亮前 / Day breaks (或 dawns). 天亮了。He works ~s and goes to school nights. 他白天工作, 晚上上学。[句中的 ~s 作状语, 是美国用法] ②(一)天, (一)日: What ~ is it? 今天星期几? / in a ~ or two 一两天内 ③工作日: an eight-hour ~ 八小时工作日 / a six-~ week 六个工作日的一周 ④[常用复]时代: at ~ in the present ~ 在现代 ⑤[常用单, by his, their 等物主代词连用]活动时期, 全盛时期; 机会 ⑥[常用复]寿命 ⑦节日; 重要日子: National Day 国庆节 / New Year's Day 元旦 / Old Year's Day 除夕 / the Day of Judgement 【宗】(世界)末日 ⑧竞赛, 战斗; 胜利: win (lose) the ~ 打胜(败) / The ~ is ours. 胜利是属于我们的。‖a ~ off 休息日 / a fine ~ for young ducks 雨天 / against a rainy ~ 未雨绸缪也 / all ~ (long) 一天到晚, 整天地 / All Saints' Day 【宗】万圣节(十一月一日) / all the ~ 整天地 / any ~ ①随便那一天 ②不论怎样 / a rainy ~ ①雨天 ②穷困时 / by the ~ 按日计 / The ~ is ours. 胜利是属于我们的。by (或 during the) ~ 在白天 / by the ~ 按日计 / call it a ~ [口]收工: Let's call it a ~.

今天就做到这里，收工吧。/ *carry the ~* 得胜 / *clear as ~* 一清二楚 / *~ about* 每隔一天地 / *~ after ~* 日复一日地(常表示每天重复) / *~ and night* (或 *night and ~*) 日日夜夜地 / *~ by ~* 一天一天地，逐日(常表示逐渐转变) / *~ in, ~ out* (或 *~ in and ~ out*) 天天(常表示连续不息) / *~s marked with a white stone* 幸福的日子 / *~s of grace* (票据等付款的)宽限日期 / *end one's ~s* 死 / *every other (third) ~* 每隔一(两)天 / *fall on evil ~s* 倒霉 / *(from) ~ to ~* 天天；从一天到另一天(常表示逐渐转变、不固定) / *from this ~ onwards* 从今天起 / *have one's ~* 走运；正在得意的时候 / *have seen better ~s* 曾过过富裕日子 / *if a ~* (岁月等)十足: He is sixty, *if a ~*. 他肯定满六十岁了。/ *in all one's born ~s* 一生，生平 / *in broad ~* 在大白天 / *know the time of ~* 见 time / *make sb.'s ~* 使某人的日子过得快活 / *many a long ~* 好久 / *not to be named on* (或 *in*) *the same ~ with* 与…不可同日而语，比…差得多 / *of a ~* 短命的: stuff *of a ~* 昙花一现的东西 / *of the ~* 当代的；当时的 / *one ~* (过去或将来的)某一天: You'll come to realize it *one ~*. 你总有一天会懂得这一点的。/ *one fine ~* (常用作讲故事时的开场白)有一天，有一次(=once upon a time) / *one of these ~s* 日内；总有一天 / *one of these fine ~s* 总有一天 / *one's ~* 在家见客日 / *on one's ~* 在最兴旺的时候 / *pass the time of ~* (*with sb.*) 见 time / *salad ~s* 见 salad / *some ~* (将来)总有一天，(日后)某一天 / *Sufficient for the ~ is the evil thereof.* [谚]当天的苦恼就够了(别再为未来担心)。/ *the ~ after* (*before*) *the fair* 过迟(早)地 / *(the) ~ after tomorrow* 后天 / *(the) ~ before yesterday* 前天 / *the ~ of reckoning* 算帐的日子；[喻]进行补偿(或报复)的日子；【宗】最后审判日 / *the last ~* 【宗】最后审判日，世界末日 / *the Lord's Day* 【宗】主日(即星期日) / *the other ~* 在不久前某天 / *these ~s* 现在，现时；如今，目前. Everyone is interested in world events *these ~s*. 现在大家都关心世界大事。/ *this ~ week* (*month, year*) 上星期(上月，去年)的今天；下星期(下月，明年)的今天 / *this many a ~* 好久以来 / *those ~s* 那些日子；那个时代 / *to a ~* 一天也不差: It's two years *to a ~*. 恰好两年。/ *to this ~* 至今 / *wear through the ~* 好歹挨过了一天 / *without ~* 不定期，无限期(休会等) / '*~blindness*【医】昼盲，夜视症 / '*~boarder* 寄膳走读学生 / '*~book n.* ①日记簿 ②日记帐 / *~ boy* 走读男生 / '*~break n.* 黎明 / '*~-care center* [美]日托托儿站 / *~ coach* [美](列车的)硬席车厢 / '*~dream vi.* & *n.* 白日做梦，幻想，空想 / '*~dreamer n.* 空想家 / '*~fly n.* 蜉蝣 / *~ girl* 走读女生 / '*~labo(u)r* 散工 ②做散工的人们 / *~ labo(u)rer* 做散工的人 / *~ letter* [美](比一般电报缓发的)日间电报 / '*~long a.*

& *ad.* 整天的(地) / '*~man n.* ①做散工的人 ②做日班的人 / *~ neutral*【植】光期钝感的 / *~ nursery* 日托托儿所 / '*~room n.* (学校等的)休息室；(营房等的)娱乐室 / *~ school* 走读学校；日校 / *~ shift* 日班 / '*~star n.* 晨星；[诗]太阳 / '*~-taler* ['deitələ] *n.* 计日工 / *~ ticket* [英]当天来回火车票 / '*~time n.* 白天，日间 / '*~-to-~ a.* (工作)日常的；(借款)暂时的 / '*~-,tripper n.* 当天结束旅程的旅客

daylight ['deilait] **I** *n.* ①日光；白昼: *by ~* 在白天；在天黑前 / 黎明: *at* (*before*) *~* 黎明时(前) ③公开: The truth has been brought into *~*. 真相大白。④空隙；间隔: No *~*! (敬酒时用语)斟满! ⑤[复][俚]知觉，神智 **II** *vt.* 为(房间等)引进日光 ❷ *vi.* 提供日光 ‖*burn ~* 白日点灯；[喻]徒劳无益 / *darken sb.'s ~* 把某人打瞎，用拳头把某人打得昏天黑地 / *in broad ~* ①在大白天 ②在光天化日之下，公开地 / *let ~ into* ①使(问题等)明朗起来 ②[俚]刺穿；射穿 / *see ~* 看到胜利的曙光 / *throw ~ on sth.* 披露(或阐明)某事 ‖*~ lamp* 日光灯 / *~ saving* (*time*) 经济时(即夏令时间) / *~ signal* 色灯信号

daze [deiz] **I** *vt.* ①使发昏，使迷乱，使茫然 ②使眼花缭乱 **II** *n.* 迷乱，茫然；眼花缭乱

dazzle ['dæzl] **I** *vt.* & *vi.* ①(光等)炫耀；眩(眼) ②眩惑；迷惑 **II** *n.* ①眩惑；炫耀，眩眼 ②使人眼花缭乱的事物 ‖*lamps, ~ lights* (汽车的)强光前灯 / *~ paint* 军舰等所涂的)伪装色彩

deacon ['di:kən] **I** *n.* ①(基督教圣公会、天主教等的)副主祭 ②(浸礼会、长老会等的)执事 **II** *vt.* ①在唱之前高声朗读(赞美诗) ②在(水果、蔬菜等)中挑出好的摆在表面 ③在(货品等)上搞欺骗 ‖*~ess n.* 女执事

dead [ded] **I** *a.* ①死的；无生命的: He has been *~* (*for*) *three years.* 他已死了三年了。/ *~ leaves* 枯叶 / *~ matter* 无机物 / *~ labour* 无生命的劳动力(指机器等；与工人相对而言) ②无感觉的，麻木的；死一般的: *~ fingers* 麻木的手指 / *in a ~ faint* 昏死过去 ③[美口]精疲力竭的 ④呆板的；(聚会等)死气沉沉的: *a ~ description* 呆板无趣的描写 ⑤无动静的；不流动的；(商品、资金等)呆滞的: *a ~ calm* 死寂 / *in the ~ hours of the night* 在夜深人静时 / *~ air* 不流动的空气 / *a ~ season* 淡季 ⑥熄灭了的；用完了的，不发挥作用的；失灵的: *a ~ volcano* 死火山 / *a ~ match* 擦过的火柴 / *a ~ oil well* 废油井 / The microphone has gone *~*. 话筒坏了。⑦(语言、习惯等)废弃了的；(法律等)名存实亡的，已失去重要性的: Latin is a *~ language*. 拉丁语是一门已死亡的语言。/ *a ~ issue* 已被人们忘怀的事 ⑧(球等)无弹性的 ⑨贫瘠的，不毛的；非生产的: *~ soil* 贫瘠的土壤

⑩(声音)闷住的
⑪(色彩)灰暗的; (金属)无光泽的
⑫(饮料)走了味的
⑬突然的; 完全的, 绝对的: The car came to a ~ stop. 汽车蓦地刹住。/ in ~ earnest 十分认真地 / a ~ loss 全部亏损
⑭准的; 丝毫不差的: a ~ shot 神枪手 / hit the ~ centre of the target 正中靶心 / runners on a ~ level (赛跑时)跑得完全一样快而肩并肩的运动员
⑮【电】不通电的, 无电压的, 断开的;【讯】无信号的, 静的: The line is ~. (电话)线路断了。
II *ad.* ①完全地, 绝对地: be ~ asleep 沉睡着 / be ~ sure 绝对肯定
②突然地: stop sb. ~ 突然拦住某人
③直接地, 正对地
III *n.* ①死者
②最冷的时刻; 最寂静的时刻: in the ~ of winter 在隆冬 / at ~ of night 在深夜
③[俚]无法投递的邮件, 死信
‖*a ~ one* [俚]①已退出流浪生活的人 ②吝啬鬼 ③没用的人, 笨人 / *be (as) ~ as mutton* (或 *a doornail, a dodo*) 确已僵死了的; 被彻底废弃(或遗忘)的 / *be ~ against* 直接针对着; 死命反对: The wind *was ~ against* us. 风迎面刮来。/ *be ~ beat* 精疲力竭的; 彻底垮了的 / *be ~ on the target* 正中目标; 正对着目标 / *be ~ to* 对…无感觉的, 对…无反应的: a man ~ *to shame* 恬不知耻的人 / *be ~ to the world* 对世事不闻不问; 烂醉; 熟睡 / *be stone ~* 死得硬邦邦的 / *Dead men tell no tales.* 死人不会告密的。/ *~ to rights* [作状语或表语用]肯定无疑(地); 当场 / *drop ~* 倒毙 / *Seek ~!* 去找! (叫猎狗去找打死的猎物)
‖**~ness** *n.*
‖**'~-air space** 【建】(空心墙的)闭塞空间 / **~-a'live, '~-and-a'live** *a.* 没精打彩的; (职业等)单调的 / **~ angle** 【军】死角 / **'~-beat** *a.* 【无】①速示的, 不摆的, 不振荡的 ②非周期的, 非调谐的 *n.* (仪表指针的)速示, 不摆; 无差拍 / **~ beat** [美俚]手头拮据的人; 赖账的人 / **~ block** (火车的)缓冲板 / **~ cat** 猛烈的指责, 讥嘲的攻击 / **~ centre** 【机】(冲程的)死点, 静点; (车床的)死顶尖 / **~ colo(u)r** ①暗色 ②(画的)底色 / **~ duck** 必然要完蛋的人(或物) / **~ end** ①(街道、管道等)闭塞不通的一头 ②[无]闲端, 空端 ③死胡同 / **~-'end** *a.* ①(街道)一头不通的; [喻]没出路的 ②贫民区的 *vi.* 到达尽头, 终止 / **'~-eye** *n.* ①【船】(接索用的)穿孔木滑车, 三眼滑轮 ②神枪手 / **'~-fall** *n.* [美]①捕兽陷阱(野兽跌入即被落下重物砸死) ②一堆倒下的树木 ③[口]黑酒店; 下等赌场 / **~ freight** 空舱费 / **~ ground** 【军】射击死角 / **~ hand** ①永远管业(土地等归法人所有而不能变卖)②过去对现今的影响 / **'~-head** *n.* ①免票(搭车、看戏等)的人 ②空车 ③光吃粮不干事的

人 *vi.* ①免票搭车(或看戏等)②(卡车等)空车而回 / **~ heat** 胜负不分的赛跑 / **~ horse** ①预付的工资 ②旧债 / **'~-house** *n.* [古]停尸所 / **~ letter** ①形同虚设的规定 ②(无法投递的)死信 / **~ lift** ①不靠机械单凭气力的一举 ②[口]需全力以赴的难事 / **'~-light** *n.* 【船】舷窗外盖; 舷窗玻璃 ②关死的天窗 ③[复][俚]眼睛 / **'~-line** *n.* ①监牢周围的死线; 不可逾越的界限 ②最后限期(*for*) / **~ load** 静负荷, 固定负载; 静重 / **'~-lock** *n.* 僵持, 僵局 *vt. & vi.* (使)僵持, (使)陷入僵局 / **'~-man** *n.* 【海】叉杆; 锚定桩; 锤回绳 / **~ march** 哀乐 / **~ marines, ~ men** [口]空酒瓶 / **'~-pan** [美俚] *n.* 无表情的脸; 无表情 *a. & ad.* 无表情的; 不带感情色彩的(地) *vi. & vt.* 无表情地说; 不带感情色采地说(或写) / **~ pigeon** =~ duck / **~ point** = ~ centre / **~ reckoning** ①航位推测法 ②测, 猜想 / **~ rise** 【船】船底横向斜度 / **~ soldiers** = ~ marines / **~ stock** ①呆滞商品(或资金) ②农具, 农业机械(与 livestock 相对)/ **~ water** ①死水 ②船舷侧旋涡 ③【军】水面射击死角 / **'~-weight** *n.* ①重负 ②静负荷, 固定负载; (车辆的)自重 ③【船】(总)载重量 / **'~-wood** *n.* ①枯枝, 枯木 ②没有用处的东西, 累赘的人(或物) ③【船】船首(或船尾)鳍 ④[美俚]优势: have (或 get) the ~*wood* on sb. 占某人上风

deaden ['dedn] ❶ *vt.* ①抑制(声音等); 使(冲动力等)缓和: drugs to ~ the pain 止痛药物 ②使失去光泽 ③使失去感觉, 使麻木 ④(使(酒等)走味 ⑤使(墙等)具有隔音性能 ❷ *vi.* ①减弱; 缓和 ②失去光泽 ‖**~ing** *n.* 隔音材料; 去光泽的材料

deadly ['dedli] **I** *a.* ①致命的; (揭露等)击中要害的; (植物)毒性的 ②死一般的: ~ pallor 死白的脸色 ③不共戴天的; 殊死的 ④[口](社交活动等)死气沉沉的, 令人受不了的 ⑤非常的, 极度的: in ~ haste 火急地 **II** *ad.* ①死一般地: He (或 His face) turned ~ pale. 他脸如土色。②非常, 极: ~ tired 累极了 ‖**deadliness** *n.* ‖**~ sins** [宗]该罚入地狱的七大重罪

deaf [def] *a.* ①聋的: ~ and dumb 又聋又哑的 / ~ as an adder (或 a post) 全聋 / be ~ of an (或 in one) ear 聋了一只耳朵 ②不听; 不愿听, 对…充耳不闻: be ~ to advice 不听劝告 / turn a ~ ear to 对…充耳不闻 ‖**~ness** *n.* ‖**'~-aid** *n.* 助听器 / **'~-mute** *n.* 聋哑者: a hospital for ~-mutes 聋哑医院 *a.* 聋哑的 / **'~-,muteness** *n.* 聋哑 / **'~-,mutism** *n.* 聋哑状态

deafen ['defn] ❶ *vt.* ①使聋; 使听不见: be ~ed with cheers 被欢呼声震得耳朵发聋 ②【建】使隔音 ❷ *vi.* 变聋, 震聋 ‖**~ing** *a.* 震耳欲聋的, 非常吵闹的 *n.* 【建】止响物

deal[1] [di:l] **I** (dealt [delt]) ❶ *vt.* ①分配, 分给 (*out*): ~ *out* two apples apiece 分给每人两个苹果 ②发(纸牌) ③给予 ④做买卖(*with*); 经营 (*in*): ~ *in* furs 经营皮货 ②对付, 应付, 处理, 安排(*with*): ~ properly *with* all kinds of complicated situations 恰当地应付各种复杂局面 / *Deal with* a man as he ~*s with* you. 以其人之道，还治其人之身。/ That man is easy to ~ *with*. 那人容易打交道。③论述，涉及 (*with*): a book ~*ing with* Asian problems 一本论述亚洲问题的书 ④发(纸)牌 **II** *n.* ①[口]买卖，交易;[美口]协议，(政治上的)密约: a package ~ 一揽子交易 / a dirty ~ 肮脏交易 ②待遇: a square (raw) ~ [口]公平的(不公平的)待遇 ③[美]政策;实行政策的时期: a new ~ 新政 ④发(纸)牌;轮到发牌 ‖*a big* ~ [美口]要人;重要事物 / *a* ~ [口] =a great ~ / *a great* (或 *good*) ~ ①大量: *A great* ~ of work awaits us. 大量工作等着我们去做。②[常接比较级]~得多: She is a great ~ better today. 她今天(身体)好多了。/ *Big* ~! (假装赞叹、惊奇等的感叹语)妙极! / ~ *well* (*badly*) *by sb.* 待某人好(坏) / *Good* ~! [美俚]很好! / *make a big* ~ *out of* [美口]把…视为极其重要;就…小题大作 / *make* (或 *do*) *a* ~ *with* 与…做买卖;与…订密约;和…妥协 ‖~**er** *n.* ①商人 ②发(纸)牌者 ③以某种特殊方式待人的人: a plain ~*er* 率直的人，坦白无诈的人 / ~**ing** *n.* ①分配，分给 ②对待，处理: fair ~*ing* 公正待人 ③[常用复]买卖，交易;交往: have (no) ~*ings with* 和…(无)交往

deal² [di:l] *n.* 松木(板),冷杉木(板);松(或冷杉)木材

dealt [delt] deal¹ 的过去式和过去分词

dean [di:n] *n.* ①(大学、学院的)院长;系主任;教务长;学监 ②(基督教的)教长: *Dean* of Canterbury 坎特伯雷教长 ③(一个团体中的)老前辈，长者 ‖~**ery** *n.* 教长的职权(或宅邸) / ‖~**'s list** (定期公布的)成绩优秀学生名单

dear [diə] **I** *a.* ①亲爱的(常用于称呼前，表示亲切、客套等): *Dear* Sir 亲爱的先生(用于书信中) ②可爱的，被爱的;可贵的: a ~ child 可爱的孩子 ③热切的: sb.'s ~*est* hope 某人心底的愿望 ④(价)贵的;索价高的: It is too ~. 这价钱太贵了。/ a ~ shop 售价贵的商店 **II** *n.* 亲爱的人,可爱的人(常用作称呼,表示亲爱): my ~ 亲爱的 **III** *ad.* ①深爱地 ②高价地 **IV** *int.* 呵!哎呀! [表示伤心、焦急、惊奇等]: *Dear*, ~! (或 *Dear* me! 或 Oh, ~!) 哎呀! ‖*for* ~ (或 *dear*) *life* / *hold sth.* (*sb.*) ~ 重视 (或宠爱) 某物(某人) / *That's* (或 *There's*) *a* ~! 这才乖呢! 这才是好孩子! ‖~*ly* *ad.* ①深爱地 ②高价地 ③热切地 / ~**ness** *n.* ①亲爱 ②价贵: ~*ness* allowance 物价津贴 ‖**Dear John** [美口]女友给男方的绝交信;绝交信 / ~ **money** 高利贷(款)

dearth [də:θ] *n.* ①缺乏,供应不足 ②饥馑

deary ['diəri] *n.* [口]亲爱的,宝贝儿(用作表示亲爱的称呼,有时也含有讽刺或幽默的意思)

death [deθ] *n.* ①死,死亡: die a hero's ~ 英勇牺牲 / a ~ ray weapon 【军】死光武器 ②灭亡,毁灭: the ~ of a language 一种语言的消亡 ③致死的原因: This insecticide is the ~ of locusts.

这种杀虫剂能杀死蝗虫。④[D-] 死神(西方常画作手持大镰刀、身穿黑袍的骷髅) ⑤屠杀,谋杀 ⑥褫夺公权 ‖*as sure as* ~ 见 **sure** / *at* ~'s *door* 见 **door** / *be* ~ *on* [俚] ①善于,是…的能手 ②对…极为不满(或反对) / *be in at the* ~ ①(打猎时)亲见猎物被弄死 ②于事件结束时在场 / *be the* ~ *of sb.* ①把某人笑死(指笑话) ②害死某人,要某人的命;伤透某人的心 / *catch one's* ~ (*of cold*) 得致命的感冒 / *civil* ~ 【律】褫夺公权 / ~ *in the pot* 暗藏的危险 / *Death pays all debts* (或 *scores*). [谚]一死百了。/ ~ *under shield* 战死,阵亡,马革裹尸 / *die a dog's* ~ 悲惨地死去;可耻地死去 / *do to* ~ ①杀死 ②重复得使…发腻 / *hold on like grim* ~ 死不放手 / *meet* (*with*) *one's* ~ 死去 / *put to* ~ 置…于死地,杀死,处死 / *ride to* ~ 见 **ride** / *talk to* ~ 以无限制讨论使(议案等)不得通过 / *to* (或 *unto*) ~ 极度: be sick *to* ~ 病得很厉害,病危 / be sick *to* ~ *of* 对…极厌倦,对…腻得要命 / *to the* ~ 至死;到底 ‖~**ful** *a.* ①致命的;谋杀的 ②死(一样)的 ③不死的,永恒的 / ~**like** *a.* 死了似的 / ~**ly** *a.* ①致死的 ②死(一样)的 *ad.* ①死了似地 ②非常地 ‖~ **agony** 临死时的痛苦 / '~**bed** *n.* ①死亡时睡的床 ②临终 *a.* 临终时做的: a ~*bed* will 临终时的愿望,遗嘱 / a ~*bed* struggle 垂死挣扎 / '~**blow** *n.* ①致命的一击 ②致死的打击 / ~ **chamber** ①死了人的房间 ②死囚行刑室 / ~ **cup** 【植】鬼笔鹅膏 (一种有毒蘑菇) / ~ **duty** [英]遗产税 / ~ **house** 死囚行刑前的监房 / ~ **knell** 丧钟(声) / ~ **penalty** 死刑 / ~ **point** 【生】死点 (生物所能生存的温度的最高和最低点) / ~ **rate** 死亡率 / ~ **rattle** 死前的喉鸣,临终的痰声 / ~ **report** 【军】死亡报告 / ~ **sand** 一种以含有放射性粒子的沙制成的大规模杀人武器 / '~'s-**head** *n.* 象征死亡的骷髅头 / '~'s-**head moth** 【动】骷髅蛾 / ~ **struggle** 垂死挣扎 / ~ **tax** [美] =~ duty / ~ **throe** 死的痛苦 / '~**trap** *n.* ①不安全的建筑物 ②非常危险的场所(或境遇) / ~ **warrant** ①死刑执行令 ② (对幸福、希望等的) 致命打击 / '~**watch** *n.* ①临终的看护;死囚的监守人 ②【动】(窃蠹科的)蛀木器的小甲虫

debar [di'bɑ:] (debarred; debarring [di'bɑ:riŋ]) *vt.* 阻拦,阻止; 排除; 禁止: ~ sb. *from* a place 不许某人进入某处 ‖~**ment** *n.*

debase [di'beis] *vt.* ①降低,贬低; 使低劣 ② 降低(硬币)的成色;降低(货币)的交换价值 ‖~**ment** *n.*

debatable [di'beitəbl] *a.* ①可争辩的,可争论的; 会产生争论的 ②争论中的,未决定的

debate [di'beit] **I** ❶ *vi.* ①争论,辩论; 讨论: ~ about sth. 争论某事 ②参加辩论,参加讨论 ③思考: ~ with oneself 心中盘算 ❷ *vt.* ①争论,辩论;讨论: The subject was hotly ~*d*. 这个题目曾经过热烈的辩论。②与…辩论: ~ sb. 与某人辩论 ③思考: ~ a matter in one's mind 心中

盘算一件事 **Ⅱ** *n.* 争论,辩论; 讨论: Truth develops through ~ between different views. 各种不同意见辩论的结果,就能使真理发展。/ a ~ with sb. 与某人的一场辩论 / the point in ~ 争论点 / open the ~ 在辩论时首先发言 ‖**~r** *n.* 辩论家;争论者;讨论者

debauch [di'bɔ:tʃ] **Ⅰ ❶** *vt.* 使堕落,使道德败坏;诱奸 **❷** *vi.* 放荡,淫逸 **Ⅱ** *n.* ①放荡,淫逸 ②狂饮暴食 ‖**~ee** [,debɔ:'tʃi:] *n.* 放荡的人,纵欲者 / **~ery** *n.* 放荡,淫逸;狂饮暴食

debenture [di'bentʃə] *n.* ①债券 ②(海关)退税凭单

debilitate [di'biliteit] *vt.* 使衰弱 ‖**debilitating** *a.* / **debilitation** [di,bili'teiʃən] *n.*

debility [di'biliti] *n.* 衰弱,虚弱

debit ['debit] **Ⅰ** *n.* ①【会计】借方 ②记入借方的款项 **Ⅱ** *vt.* 将…记入借方: ~ £5 against (或 to) sb. (或 ~ sb. with £5) 把一笔五镑的帐记入某人的借方

debonair [,debə'neə] *a.* ①殷勤的,有礼的 ②高兴的,快活的,轻松的

debris ['debri:] ([复] debris ['debri:z]) *n.* ①(破坏物的)碎片;瓦砾堆;废墟 ②【地】岩屑,碎石;【矿】尾矿,废石;(登山中遇到的)积聚的冰块

debt [det] *n.* ①债;欠款 ②【宗】罪 ‖*a ~ of hono(u)r* 法律上不承认的借款;赌债 / *bad ~s* 坏帐,倒帐 / *get* (或 *run*) *into* ~ 借债,负债 / *in* ~ *to sb.* (或 *in sb.'s* ~) 欠某人的债;受某人的恩惠 / *out of* ~ 不欠债 / *pay the* ~ *of nature* (或 *pay one's* ~ *to nature*) 死 ‖**~ collector** 收债人

debtor ['detə] *n.* ①债务人,欠债的人 ②【会计】借方

début ['deibu:] *n.* [法] ①初进社交界 ②(演员的)首次演出;首次露面

decade ['dekeid] *n.* ①十;十个合成的一组: a ~ of suggestions 十条建议 ②十年,十年期: several ~s 数十年 / the first ~ of the twentieth century 二十世纪第一个十年 (指从 1901 到 1910)

decadence ['dekədəns] *n.* 颓废,堕落;衰微

decadent ['dekədənt] **Ⅰ** *a.* 颓废的 **Ⅱ** *n.* 颓废者;颓废派艺术家(或作家)

decamp [di'kæmp] *vi.* ①撤营 ②逃走,逃亡 ‖**~ment** *n.*

decant [di'kænt] *vt.* ①移注,倾注(酒等) ②轻轻倒出(上面清的液体),滗;【化】倾析 ‖**~ation** [,di:kæn'teiʃən] *n.* ①移注,倾注 ②滗;【化】倾析

decapitate [di'kæpiteit] *vt.* ①将…斩首,杀…的头 ②[美](因政治理由)立即免…的职 ‖**decapitation** [di,kæpi'teiʃən] *n.* / **decapitator** *n.* ①刽子手;断头机 ②[美]免别人职的人

decarbonize, decarbonise [di:'kɑ:bənaiz] *vt.* 【化】使脱碳,除去…的碳 ‖**decarbonization** [di:-kɑ:bənai'zeiʃən] *n.*

decay [di'kei] **Ⅰ ❶** *vi.* ①腐朽,腐烂 ②衰败,衰微

(精力等)衰退 **❷** *vt.* 使腐朽,使腐烂: a ~ed tooth 蛀牙,龋齿 **Ⅱ** *n.* ①腐朽,腐烂 ②衰败,衰微;衰退: fall into ~ 衰败; 塌坏,损坏 ③【原】(放射性物质的)衰变,蜕变;【无】(荧光屏的)余辉;(电荷存储管的)电荷减少: plasma ~ 等离子体衰变

decease [di'si:s] **Ⅰ** *n.*【律】死亡 **Ⅱ** *vi.* 亡故

deceit [di'si:t] *n.* 欺骗,欺诈;虚假;欺骗行为

deceitful [di'si:tful] *a.* 欺诈的,骗人的,不老实的 ‖**~ly** *ad.* / **~ness** *n.*

deceive [di'si:v] **❶** *vt.* 欺骗,诓骗;使弄错;使失望: ~ sb. *into* doing sth. 骗某人去做某事 / ~*d in* sb. 看错了某人(指受其蒙骗) / be ~*d in* one's hopes 失望 / ~ oneself 自欺;想错 **❷** *vi.* 欺诈,行骗 ‖**~r** *n.* 欺骗者,骗子

decelerate [di:'seləreit] **❶** *vt.* 使减速,降低…的速度 **❷** *vi.* 降低速度;减速运转(或行驶) ‖**deceleration** ['di:,selə'reiʃən] *n.* 减速(度) / **decelerator** *n.* 减速器;减速者

December [di'sembə] *n.* 十二月(略作 Dec.)

decency ['di:snsi] *n.* ①正派;(行为、举止等的)合乎礼仪;体面: for the sake of ~ 为了面子 ②[复]礼仪 ③[复]过象样的生活所需要的东西

decent ['di:snt] *a.* ①正派的;(言语、举止等)合乎礼仪的 ②体面的;象样的,还不错的: live in ~ conditions 生活过得还不错 / It's quite a ~ day. 天气很不错。 ③公平的;大方的 ④[英俚](学生用语)和气的,不严格的 ‖**~ly** *ad.*

decentralize, decentralise [di:'sentrəlaiz] *vt.* ①分散(行政权等) ②使撤离中心点(或集中地) ‖**decentralization** [di:,sentrəlai'zeiʃən] *n.*

deception [di'sepʃən] *n.* ①欺骗,诓骗,蒙蔽: practise ~ on sb. 向某人进行欺骗 ②受骗 ③诡计,骗术;骗人的东西

deceptive [di'septiv] *a.* ①骗人的 ②靠不住的;容易使人误解的 ‖**~ly** *ad.* / **~ness** *n.*

decide [di'said] **❶** *vt.* ①决定,决意: ~ policies 决定政策 / ~ (not) to go 决定(不)去 / It has been ~d that the meeting shall be postponed. 已决定会议延期举行。 ②解决;裁决,判决: The question has been ~d. 问题已解决。 ③使下决心,使决断: That ~s me. 那使我下了决心。 **❷** *vi.* 决定,下决心;判定: ~ against doing so 决定不这样干

decided [di'saidid] *a.* ①决定了的;坚决的,果断的: a ~ attitude 坚决的态度 / be quite ~ 抱定了决心 ②明显的,明确的: a ~ difference 明显的不同 ‖**~ly** *ad.* / **~ness** *n.*

deciduous [di'sidjuəs] *a.* ① (在成熟期或一定季节)脱落的: ~ leaves 落叶 / ~ antlers of deer 脱落的鹿角,自解的鹿角 / ~ teeth 乳齿 ②每年落叶的: a ~ tree 落叶树 ③非永久的,暂时的

decimal ['desiməl] **Ⅰ** *a.* 十进法的,小数的;以十为基础的: ~ point【数】小数点 / a ~ system (重、量、衡等的)十进制 **Ⅱ** *n.*【数】小数(十进小数): to 3 places of ~s 至小数第三位 ‖**~ism** *n.* 十进

法; 十进制 / ~**ist** n. 主张十进制者 / ~**ly** ad.

decimate ['desimeit] vt. ①选杀…的十分之一 ②大批杀死(或毁坏) ③取…的十分之一; 对…征 收什一税

decipher [di'saifə] Ⅰ vt. ①译解(密码等) ②解释 (难以理解的事物, 古代文字等) ③辨认(潦草的 字迹) Ⅱ n. 密电(或密信)的译文 ‖~**ment** n. ①译解, 解释, 辨认 ②译文

decision [di'siʒən] n. ①决定, 决心: come to (或 arrive at) a ~ 决定下来 / make a ~ 作出决定 ②果断, 坚定: a man of ~ 果断的人 ③决议; 结 果: a draft ~ 决议草案 / pass a ~ 通过一项 决议

decisive [di'saisiv] a. ①决定性的: a ~ battle 决 战 / a ~ blow 决定性的打击 / a ~ factor 决定 因素 ②明确的; 果断的: a ~ tone of voice 明确 果断的语气 / ~ evidence 确证 ‖~**ly** ad. / ~**ness** n.

deck [dek] Ⅰ n. ①甲板, 舱面: the upper (lower) ~ 上(下)甲板 / ~ composition 【船】甲板敷料 ②桥面; 层面: the top ~ of a double-~ bus (train) 双层汽车(火车)的上层 / a ~ roof 平台 式屋顶 ③【美俚】盛海洛因等毒品的袋子 Ⅱ vt. ①给 (船)装甲板 ② 装饰: well-~ed canned food 装璜 美观的罐头食品 ③[美俚]击倒 ‖**clear the ~s** ①(战舰)准备战斗 ② 准备行动 / ~ **out (with)** (用…)装饰(或打扮) / **hit the ~** [美俚]①被打 倒; 躺倒在地 ②起床, 下床 准备行动 / **on** ~ ①在甲板上 ②准备齐全; 在手边 ③(运动、游戏 时)下一个轮到 / **sweep the** ~ ①(大浪等)将甲 板上所有东西扫光 ②(打牌时)通吃, 把赌桌上所 有的赌注全赢来 ‖~**er** n. ①装饰者 ②[用以构 成复合词]有…层的东西; 有…层甲板的船: a double-~**er** bus 双层公共汽车 / triple-~**er** sand-wiches 三层夹心面包, 三层三明治 / a three-~**er** 三层甲板的船 / ~**ing** n. ①装饰 ②【建】铺面, 盖 板 ③桥面板, 桥梁车行道 ‖ ~ **bridge** 上承桥 / ~ **cabin** 甲板船室 / ~ **chair** (甲板上的)躺椅, 折迭式躺椅 / '~**hand** n. 舱面水手 / '~**house** n. 甲板室, 甲板室 / '~**mounting** n. 上甲板 装备 / ~ **officer** 驾驶员, 舱面船员 (指舵长、大 副、二副等, 以别于轮机员) /【军】舱面军官 / '~**plate** n. 铁甲板 / '~-**tube** n. 上甲板水雷发射 管 / ~ **watchman** 停泊值班水手

deckle ['dekl] n. ①(造纸用的使纸浆定型的)制模 框 ②(造纸用的)框梢 ③~e edge = **edge** 纸 的毛边 / '~-**edged** a. 有毛边的, 未裁齐的

declaim [di'kleim] ❶ vi. ①作慷慨激昂的演说, 雄辩 ② 朗诵, 朗读 ③ (用激动的语气) 攻击 (**against**) ❷ vt. 朗诵, 朗读 ‖~**er** n. 演讲者; 朗 诵者

declamation [,deklə'meiʃən] n. ①慷慨激昂的演 说, 雄辩; 雄辩术 ②正式演说 ③朗诵, 朗读

declaration [,deklə'reiʃən] n. ①宣布, 宣言; 宣言, 声明: a ~ of war 宣战文告 / a joint ~ 联合声

明 / the *Declaration* of Independence (美国)独 立宣言 (一七七六年七月四日) / the *Declaration* of Rights (一六八九年规定英国宪法基本原则的) 民权宣言 【律】(原告的) 申诉; (证人的) 陈述, 证言 ③(纳税品等的)申报: a customs ~ 报关单 ④(桥牌的)叫牌

declare [di'klɛə] ❶ vt. ①宣布, 宣告; 声明: ~ war on (或 against) the old world 向旧世界宣战 / ~ sb. (to be) innocent 宣布某人无罪 ②表明; 显 露 ③断言; 宣称: He ~d that it was true (或 ~d it to be true). 他断言那是真实的。④申报 (纳税品等): Anything to ~? 有东西要报税 吗? ⑤(桥牌)叫(王牌) ❷ vi. 声明; (公开)表明 态度: ~ for (against) sth. 表态支持(反对)某事 ‖~ off 宣布作罢; 取消(约定等): The match was ~d off. 比赛取消了。/ ~ oneself 发表 意见, 表明态度; 显露身分(或真实面目等): He ~d himself (to be) satisfied. 他表示满意。/ *Well, I* ~! 嗐! 怪了! ‖~**r** [di'klɛərə] n. 宣告 者; (桥牌中)叫定王牌的人

declared [di'klɛəd] a. 公然宣称 (或承认) 的: ~ objectives, ~ and covert 公开宣称的和隐蔽的目 的 ‖~**ly** [di'klɛəridli] ad. 公然地 ‖ ~ **value** 申 报价格

declination [,dekli'neiʃən] n. ①倾斜, 下倾; 偏斜 ②衰微 ③【物】偏角; 磁偏角 ④【天】赤纬 ⑤谢 绝, 拒绝 ‖~**al** a.

decline [di'klain] Ⅰ ❶ vi. ①下倾, 下降, 下垂: The prices are *declining*. 价格下降。②偏斜 ③衰 退, 衰落: His health is *declining*. 他的健康越来 越差。④将近结束: The day is *declining*. 时近 黄昏。/ *declining* years 晚年 ⑤谢绝, 拒绝 ❷ vt. ①使下倾, 使下降, 使下垂 ②谢绝, 拒绝: ~ an invitation 谢绝邀请 / ~ to answer a ques-tion 拒绝回答问题 ③【语】使变格, 按变格规则 处理 Ⅱ n. ①下倾, 下降; 下垂: a ~ in prices 物价的下跌 ②衰退, 衰落 ③最后部分, 结束部 分: the ~ of life 晚年 ④消耗体力的疾病 (如 肺结核) ⑤斜面, 山坡 ‖**fall into a** ~ 衰弱; 生 肺病

declivity [di'kliviti] n. 斜坡; 倾斜

declutch ['di:'klʌtʃ] ❶ vi. 分开离合器 ❷ vt. (分 开离合器) 使停止运转

decode ['di:'koud] vt. 译(电报等), 【自】译(码) ‖~**r** n. ①译电员 ②【自】译码器

decompose [,di:-kəm'pouz] vt. & vi. ①【化】分解 ②(使)腐败, (使)腐烂 ‖**decomposability** [,di:-kəm,pouzə'biliti] n. 分解性 / **decomposable** a. 可分解的

decomposition [,di:-kɔmpə'ziʃən] n. ①【化】分解 (作用): double ~ 双分解, 复分解 ②腐败; 解体

decontaminate ['di:-kən'tæmineit] vt. 清除… 的污垢; 清除…的毒气; 去除…的放射性污染 ‖**decontamination** ['di:-kən,tæmi'neiʃən] n.

decorate ['dekəreit] ❶ vt. ①装饰, 装璜, 修饰: The hall is ~d with flags. 礼堂里悬挂着

旗。② 授勋(章)给… ❷ vi. 装饰,布置 ‖**decorator** n. (室内)装饰家;制景人员 a. 适宜于室内装饰的: a *decorator* fabric 室内装饰用的织物

decoration [,dekə'reiʃən] n. ①装饰,装璜,装帧 ②[复]装饰品: festival ~s 节日的装饰物 ③勋章,奖章

decorative ['dekərətiv] a. 装饰的,装璜的;可作装饰的: ~ art 装饰艺术

decorous ['dekərəs] a. 有礼貌的;正派的;有教养的 ‖~ly ad. / ~ness n.

decorticate [di'kɔ:tikeit] vt. 剥去…的皮(或壳、荚等) ‖**decortication** [di,kɔ:ti'keiʃən] n. / **decorticator** 剥皮器

decorum [di'kɔ:rəm] n. ①礼貌;正派;体面;得体 ②[复]礼节,礼仪

decoy [di'kɔi] I n. ①诱擒鸟兽的场所,圈套 ②(诱擒鸟兽用的)引诱物,囮子 ③诱骗者;诱人入圈套的东西 ④[军]假目标: a ~ airdrome 假飞机场 II vt. 诱骗: ~ wild ducks into a net 引诱野鸭落网 / ~ duck 野鸭囮子

decrease [di:'kri:s] I ❶ vi. 减少,减小: ~ in number 数目减少 / ~ to 减少到… ❷ vt. 减少,减小: ~ the number to 把数目减少到… II ['di:kri:s] n. ①减少,减小: a ~ in temperature 温度的降低 ②减少额,减小量 ‖**on the ~** 在减少中 ‖**decreasingly** ad. 渐减地

decree [di'kri:] I n. ①法令,政令 ②[宗]教令;天命,天意 ③[律]判决 II ❶ vt. ①颁布(法令、政令): ~ an amnesty 颁布大赦 ②注定 ③判决: ~ a punishment 判刑 ❷ vi. 发布命令,规定 ‖~ nisi ['naisai] [英]离婚判决书(六星期内无异议即生效)

decrepit [di'krepit] a. 老弱的,衰老的,老朽的

decrepitude [di'krepitju:d] n. 老弱,衰老,老朽

decry [di'krai] vt. ①诋毁 ②大声反对 ③贬低(货币)价值

dedicate ['dedikeit] vt. ①奉献,供奉 ②献(身);把(时间、力量等)用在… (to) ③题献(著作): *Dedicated* to sb. (谨以本书)献给某人 / ~ to (建筑物等)举行落成式 ‖**dedicatee** [,dedikə'ti:] n. 被献呈者 / **dedicator** 供献者;题献者

dedication [,dedi'keiʃən] n. ①供献;献身 ②献题,献辞

deduce [di'dju:s] vt. 演绎,推演,推断: ~ a conclusion *from* premises 从前提推出结论 ‖**deducible** a. 可推断的

deduct [di'dʌkt] vt. ①扣除,减去: ~ losses *from* the total receipts 从总收入中减去损失 ②演绎

deduction [di'dʌkʃən] n. ①扣除;扣除额 ②演绎,演绎法 ③推演出来的结论,推论

deductive [di'dʌktiv] a. 演绎的, 推论的: the ~ method 演绎法 / ~ reasoning 演绎推理 ‖~ly ad.

deed [di:d] I n. ①行为, 行动 ②实际 ②功绩,事迹: achieve new ~s of merit 立新功 ③[律]

契约 II vt. [美]立契转让(私人财产) ‖**do the ~** 产生效果: That medicine will *do the* ~. 那种药会见效。/ *in (very)* ~ (或 *in* ~ *and not in name* 或 *in word and* ~) 真正,不只是口头上 ‖~**less** a. 没有行动的; 没有功绩的; 不活动的 ‖~**box** n. 文件箱,契约箱 / ~ **poll** [律]单方执行的契约

deem [di:m] ❶ vt. 认为,相信: ~ it (或 ~ that it is) one's duty to do sth. 认为做某事是自己的责任 ❷ vi. 想,相信: ~ highly of . . . 对…给予高度的评价

deep [di:p] I a. ①深的: ~ ploughing 深耕 / ~ breathing 深呼吸 ②纵深的: be drawn up six ~ 排成六列横队 ③远离中心的: 球场边边线的: a ~ closet 里间 ④(声音)深沉的;(颜色)深浓的: a ~ red 深红 ⑤深刻的: ~ insight 深刻的洞察力 / a ~ thinker 思想深刻的人 ⑥深奥的,奥妙的: a ~ book (question) 深奥的书(问题) / a ~ one 十分狡猾、叫人莫测高深的人 ⑦(感情)深切的,深厚的 ⑧(人)埋头的(于);深陷(于)(in): be ~ in work 埋头工作 / be ~ in a map 专心查阅地图 / be ~ in thought 沉思着 / ~ in debt 债台高筑 ⑨非常的,极度的: ~ disgrace 奇耻大辱 / a ~ drinker 酒量极大的人 II ad. 深;迟: dig ~ 深挖 / drink ~ 痛饮 III n. ①深处;深渊: the ~ [诗]海 / in the ~ of night 在深夜 ②[常用复]海的深处 ‖**go (in) off the ~ end** 见 end / *in* ~ *water(s)* 陷入困境的(或 *Still waters run* ~. (或 *Smooth water runs* ~.) 见 water ‖~**ly** ad. / ~**most** a. [古]最深的 / ~**ness** n. ‖~ **drawing** [机]板材的深冲(成形) / '~-**drawn** a. (叹息、呼吸等)深长的 / '~-**dyed** a. 深染的;顽固不化的 / '~-**freeze** n. ①(以极低温度快速)冷藏箱; 以极低温度冷藏 ②(活动等)的暂时中止 vt.(以极低温度快速)冷藏 / ~ **fry** 炸(指烹饪)/ '~**going** a. 深入的,深刻的 / '~-**laid** a. 秘密策划的,处心积虑的 / '~-**read** [di:p'red] a. 熟读的,通晓的 / '~-**rooted** a. 根深的;(习惯、偏见等)根深蒂固的 / '~-**rooted** loyalty 极大的忠诚 / '~ **sea** 海洋的深水部分 / '~-**sea** a. 深海的;远洋的: ~-*sea* fishes 深海鱼类 / ~-*sea* fishing 远洋捕鱼 / '~-**seated** a. (感情、原因、疾病等)由来已久的,根深蒂固的: a ~-*seated* disease 痼疾 / '~-**set** a. (眼睛等)深陷的 / ~ **space** 外层空间 / '~**water** a. / ~-**sea**

deepen ['di:pən] ❶ vt. 加深: ~ a well 把井挖深 / ~ the movement to increase production and practise economy 深入开展增产节约运动 ❷ vi. 深化,变得更深: the ~ing crisis 日益严重的危机 / The night ~s. 夜深了。

deer [diə] ([复] deer(s)) n. 鹿: a white-lipped ~ 白唇鹿 ‖**small** ~ [总称]无足轻重的动物(或东西) / ~ **forest** (无树木的)猎鹿的旷地 / ~ **hound** n. 一种大猎狗 / ~ **lick** 含盐的泉水(或沼泽地)(鹿常去舐食盐分) / ~ **neck** 鹿颈(指獐

长马颈) / '~-**skin** *n.* 鹿皮；鹿皮服装 / '~-,**stalker** *n.* ①猎鹿的人 ②一种前后翘起的布帽 / '~-,**stalking** *n.* 猎鹿

deface [di'feis] *vt.* ①损伤…外观；使失面子 ②磨灭(碑文等) ‖~**ment** *n.* ①毁损 ②毁损物

defame [di'feim] *vt.* 破坏…的名誉，诽谤 ‖**defamation** [,defə'meiʃən] *n.* / **defamatory** [di-'fæmətəri] *a.*

default [di'fɔ:lt] I *n.* ①不履行，违约，拖欠，不参加(比赛) ②【律】缺席：judgement by ~ 缺席判决 ③欠缺 II ❶ *vi.* ①不履行，拖欠 ②不到案；不出场；不参加(或不终场)，由于不参加比赛(或不终场)而输球 ❷ *vt.* ①不履行，拖欠 ②对…处以缺席裁判 ③不参加(比赛)，在(比赛)中不终场；由于不参加(或不终场)而输掉(比赛) ‖*in* ~ *of* 因没有…；在缺少…时 / *make* ~ 【律】缺席 ‖~**er** *n.* ①缺席者；拖欠者；违约者 ②盗用公款者 ③[英]违反军规者

defeat [di'fi:t] I *vt.* ①战胜，击败：~ the aggressors 打败侵略者 ②使(希望、计划等)失败，挫折 ③(计划)无效，废弃 II *n.* ①战胜，击败 ②战败，失败；挫折

defect [di'fekt] I *n.* 缺点；欠缺；不足之处 II *vi.* 逃跑，开小差；背叛 ‖**have the** ~**s of one's qualities** 有随优点而来的缺点 / *in* ~ *of* 假如没有…时 ‖~**or** *n.* 开小差者，逃兵；背叛者 ‖~ **detector** 【机】探伤仪

defection [di'fekʃən] *n.* ①背信，(义务等的)不履行 ②背叛，变节

defective [di'fektiv] I *a.* 有缺点的；有缺陷的，不完全的：physically ~ 生理上有缺陷的 / a ~ verb 【语】不完全变化动词 (如 ought 等) II *n.* ①身心有缺陷的人 ②【语】不完全变化词 ‖~**ly** *ad.* / ~**ness** *n.*

defence [di'fens] *n.* ①防御，保卫，防护：a ~ area 防区 / air ~ 防空 / ~ in depth 纵深防御 / frontier ~ 边防 / united army-and-civilian ~ 军民联防 / the science (或 art) of ~ 防务术(指拳击、剑术) ②防务，防御物；[复]防御工事：coast ~s 海防工事 ③【律】辩护，答辩；被告方(包括被告及其辩护律师) ④ (比赛中的) 守方 ‖~ **mechanism**, ~ **reaction** 【生】防御反应

defenceless [di'fenslis] *a.* 无防御的，无防备的；无助的，没有保护的 ‖~**ly** *ad.* / ~**ness** *n.*

defend [di'fend] *vt.* ① 防御，保卫 ~ oneself *against* the enemy 防御敌人 / ~ sb. *from* harm 保护某人使其不受伤害 ② 为…辩护，为…答辩 ‖~**er** *n.* ①防御者；保护人；辩护人 ②【体】保持锦标者

defendant [di'fendənt] I *n.* 【律】被告 II *a.* 处于被告地位的

defensible [di'fensəbl] *a.* ①能防御的 ②能辩护的 ‖**defensibility** [di,fensi'biliti] *n.* / **defensibly** *ad.*

defensive [di'fensiv] I *a.* 防御的，防卫的；守势的：~ warfare 防御战 / ~ works 防御工事 / a ~

position 防御阵地 / ~ arms 防御武器 II *n.* 防御，守势：assume the ~ 采取守势 / be (或 act) on the ~ 进行防御，采取守势 ‖~**ly** *ad.*

defer[1] [di'fə:] (deferred; deferring [di'fə:riŋ]) *vt.* & *vi.* 推迟，(使)延期，(使)迟延 ‖~**able** [di'fə:rəbl] *a.* & *n.* =deferrable / ~**ment** *n.* 延期，迟延；【军】缓役 / **deferred** *a.* 推迟的，迟延的：a *deferred* telegram 迟发电报 / payment on *deferred* terms 分期付款 / **deferrer** *n.* 推迟者，延期者

defer[2] [di'fə:] (deferred; deferring [di'fə:riŋ]) *vi.* 听从，遵从：~ *to* sb.'s opinions 听从某人的意见 **deference** ['defərəns] *n.* ①听从，依从 ②敬重，尊敬：pay (或 show) ~ *to* sb. 对某人表示敬意 ‖*in* ~ *to* 遵从，服从

defiance [di'faiəns] *n.* ①挑战；挑衅 ②蔑视；违抗 ‖*bid* ~ *to* 蔑视；与…对抗 / *in* ~ *of* 无视，不顾：He jumped into the river to save the child *in* ~ *of* the icy water. 他不顾冰冷彻骨的河水跳到河里去救小孩。/ *set sth. at* ~ 蔑视某事物，与某事物相对抗

defiant [di'faiənt] *a.* 挑战的；对抗的 ‖~**ly** *ad.*

deficiency [di'fiʃənsi] *n.* ①缺乏，缺少，不足：~ disease 【医】营养缺乏症 ②[复]不足之数；不足之处，缺陷

deficient [di'fiʃənt] I *a.* 缺乏的，不足的，欠缺的：~ *in* judgement 判断力不强的 II *n.* 有缺陷的人(或东西) ‖~**ly** *ad.*

deficit ['defisit] *n.* 亏空(额)；赤字 ‖~ **financing** 赤字财政 (政府为刺激生产大量增加开支和发行公债的做法) / ~ **spending** 赤字开支

defile[1] I [di'fail] *vi.* 纵列行军，单列前进，鱼贯而行 II ['di:fail] *n.* 隘路(只容单人独骑通过的狭道)；峡谷

defile[2] [di'fail] *vt.* ①污损，弄脏 ②玷污，亵渎 ③败坏，使腐败 ‖~**ment** *n.* 污损；玷污；脏东西 / ~**r** *n.* 弄脏者，亵渎者

definable [di'fainəbl] *a.* ①可限定的，有界限的 ②可下定义的

define [di'fain] *vt.* ①解释；给…下定义 ②立(界限)，限定，规定：~ sb.'s duties 规定某人的任务 ③明确表示：~ one's position 表明立场

definite ['definit] *a.* ①明确的，确切的：a ~ answer 明确的答复 / be ~ in answer 回答得明确 ② 一定的，肯定的：It's ~ that he'll come. 他肯定要来的。③ 限定的，有定数的：the ~ article 【语】定冠词 / ~ integral 【数】定积分 ‖~**ly** *ad.* / ~**ness** *n.*

definition [,defi'niʃən] *n.* ①定义，解说：give a ~ 下定义 ②划界，限界，限定 ③明确性，鲜明性 ④【物】清晰度，分辨力 ‖~**al** *a.*

definitive [di'finitiv] I *a.* ①决定的，最后的；确定的：a ~ answer (sentence) 最后正式的答复(判决) / a ~ victory 最后的胜利 ②权威性的 ③限定的，明确的 ④【生】发育完全的，定形的：~ organ 定形器官 ⑤【生】定局的：~ host (寄生

动植物的)定局宿主 **II** *n.*【语】限定词(或语)(= ~ word, 如 this, that, some, any) ‖**~ly** *ad.* / **~ness** *n.*

deflate [di'feit] ❶ *vt.* ①(抽掉、排去空气等)使缩小; 使瘪下去: ~ a tire 放掉轮胎的气 ②降低…的地位(或重要性), 使泄气 ③紧缩(通货) ❷ *vi.* 缩小, 瘪掉 ‖**deflatable** *a.* 可放气的; 可紧缩的

deflect [di'flekt] *vt. & vi.* (使)偏斜, (使)转向, (使)弯曲

deform [di'fɔːm] ❶ *vt.* ①损坏…的形状, 使变丑 ②【物】使变形 ❷ *vi.* 变形 ‖**~ed** *a.* ①形状损坏的, 丑的, 破相的; 变了形的 ②【动】畸形的

deformity [di'fɔːmiti] *n.* ①畸形, 残废, 丑恶 ②(道德、智力等方面的)缺陷 ③畸形的人(或物); 残废的人; 残缺的东西

defraud [di'frɔːd] *vt.* 欺骗; 骗取, 诈取: ~ sb. of sth. 骗取某人的某物 ‖**~er** *n.* 诈骗者, 骗子

defray [di'frei] *vt.* 支付(经费、费用等) ‖**able** *a.* 可支付的 / **~al** *n.* 支付, 支出 / **~ment** *n.* =~al

defrost [di(:)'frɔ(:)st] ❶ *vt.* ①除去…的冰霜 使不结冰 ③对…解除冻结 ❷ *vi.* 解冻 ‖**~er** *n.* 【空】除霜器

deft [deft] *a.* 灵巧的, 熟练的: a ~ hand 能手 ‖**~ly** *ad.* / **~ness** *n.*

defunct [di'fʌŋkt] **I** *a.* ①已死的 ②不再存在的, 已消灭的: a ~ journal 已停刊的刊物 **II** *n.* [the ~] 死者

defy [di'fai] **I** *vt.* ①公然反抗; 蔑视; 对…满不在乎: ~ severe cold 不畏严寒 ②使不能, 使落空: Things like these ~ enumeration. 诸如此类, 不胜枚举。/ The door *defied* all attempts to open it. 这扇门怎么样都开不开。③向…挑战; 激; 惹: I ~ you to do that. 我看你不敢这么干。**II** *n.* [美俚]挑战, 对抗

degenerate [di'dʒenərit] **I** *a.* ①退化的 ②堕落的, 颓废的 ③【医】变质的, 变性的 **II** *n.* ①堕落者 ②智力衰退者 ③【生】退化生物 ④【医】性欲倒错者 **III** [di'dʒenəreit] ❶ *vi.* ①堕落; 蜕化; 退化 (into) ②【医】变质, 变性 ❷ *vt.* 使蜕变质; 使退化

degeneration [di,dʒenə'reiʃən] *n.* ①退化; 衰退; 堕落 ②【生】退化(作用); 【医】变质, 变性 ③【物】简并化; 【无】衰减; 负反馈

degrade [di'greid] ❶ *vt.* ①使降级; 贬黜 ②使堕落; 使卑微; (价值、品质等)低落 ③【生】使退化 ④【地】使陵削, 使受剥蚀 ⑤【化】使降解 ⑥【物】使衰变 ❷ *vi.* ①(地位、身分等)下降 ②退化; 堕落; (价值、品质等)低落 ‖**~d** *a.* ①降了级的 ②退化了的; 堕落了的; (价值、品质等)低下的 / **degrading** *a.* 品质低劣的; 卑劣的; 退化的

degree [di'griː] *n.* ①度, 度数: at ten ~s centigrade 在摄氏十度(写作: at 10℃.) / at minus ten ~s centigrade 在摄氏零下十度 (写作: at -10℃.) / 5 ~s of frost 零下五度 / an angle of sixty ~s 六十度的角 / twelve ~s east longitude 东经十二度 ②程度: Each is useful in its ~. 各有程度不同的用处。/ He is not in the slightest ~ injured. 他一点也没受伤。/ a third-~ burn (或 a burn of the third ~) 三度烧伤 / differ in ~ and in kind 在程度上和性质上都不同 ③【律】(罪行的)轻重: murder in the first ~ 蓄意谋杀 / murder in the second ~ 误杀 ④地位, 身分; 阶层 ⑤学位, 学衔 ⑥亲等: a cousin in the first ~ 一个嫡堂(或嫡表)兄弟(或姐妹) / prohibited ~s (of marriage)【律】禁止通婚的亲等 ⑦【数】次(数): a term of the third ~ 三次项 ⑧【语】(形容词和副词的): 级: the positive (comparative, superlative) ~ 原(比较, 最高)级 ⑨【音】度, 音阶 ‖**by ~s** 逐渐地 / **the third ~** [美]拷问 / **to a ~** ①[口]极度地 ②[美]稍微, 有些 / **to the last ~** 极度地 / **to the nth ~** 极度地, 无穷地 ‖**de'gree-'day** *n.*【气】度-日

dehydrate [diː'haidreit] ❶ *vt.* ①使脱去水分, 【化】使脱水: ~d vegetables 脱水蔬菜 ②把…弄得没有力量(或味道) ❷ *vi.* 脱去水分, 【化】脱水 ‖**dehydration** [,diːhai'dreiʃən] *n.*

deice ['diː'ais] *vt.* 除去 … 的冰(如附在飞机机翼上的冰); 防止…上结冰 ‖**~r** *n.*【空】除冰设备

deify ['diːifai] *vt.* 把…神化; 把…奉若神明; 崇拜

deign [dein] ❶ *vi.* 降低自己的身分; 屈尊; 垂顾: ~ to ask sb. below oneself 屈尊下问 / ~ not to do sth. 不屑做某事 ❷ *vt.* 俯准; 赐予: Will you ~ no answer? 您不给回答吗?

deject [di'dʒekt] *vt.* 使沮丧, 使气馁 ‖**~ed** *a.* 沮丧的, 情绪低落的

delay [di'lei] **I** ❶ *vt.* 耽搁, 延误, 推迟: The ship was ~ed two hours. 船迟了两小时。/ I ~ed answering your letter owing to pressure of work. 我因工作忙而没有及时答复你。❷ *vi.* 耽搁, 延误 **II** *n.* 耽搁, 延误, 延迟: without ~ 毫不迟延地, 立即 / admit of no ~ 刻不容缓 ‖**~(ed)-'action** *a.* 延迟动作的; 【军】定时的, 延期的: a ~ed-action bomb 定时(延期)炸弹 / a ~ed-action fuse 定时(延期)信管 / **~ed action** 照相机的自拍装置 / **~ing action**【军】阻滞战斗 / **~ing force**【军】阻滞部队

delectable [di'lektəbl] *a.* ①使人愉快的 ②美味的 ‖**delectably** *ad.*

delectation [,diːlek'teiʃən] *n.* 欢娱, 享乐

delegate **I** ['deligit] *n.* ①代表: a walking ~ [美]工会的交涉代表 ②美国众议院有发言权而无投票权的州代表; 美国 Virginia, West Virginia, Maryland 三州州众院 (the House of Delegates) 的议员 **II** ['deligeit] *vt.* ① 派遣…为代表 ② 授 (权); 把…委托给 (to): ~ authority to an agent 授权给代理人 ③【律】把(自己的债务人)转给自己的债权人

delegation [,deli'geiʃən] *n.* ①(代表的)委派, 派遣 ②代表团

delete [di'li:t] *vt.* ①删除(文字等) ②擦掉(字迹等)

deletion [di'li:ʃən] *n.* ①删除 ②删除部分 ③【生】(染色体的) 缺失, 中间缺失

deliberate [di'libərit] I *a.* ①深思熟虑的, 蓄意的, 故意的: ~ murder 谋杀 ②审慎的, 不慌不忙的: take ~ aim 不慌不忙地瞄准 / ~ reconnaissance 周密的侦察 II [di'libəreit] ❶ *vi.* ①仔细考虑: ~ on a question 考虑问题 ②商议: ~ with sb. over a question 与某人商议问题 ❷ *vt.* ①仔细考虑: ~ what to do 考虑该做什么 ②商议: The committee ~d the matter. 委员会商议了这个问题。 ‖~ly *ad.* 审慎地; 故意地, 蓄意地 / **~ness** *n.* 审慎; 故意, 蓄意

deliberation [di,libə'reiʃən] *n.* ① 考虑, 细想: after long ~ 深思熟虑之后 / a question under ~ 考虑中的问题 ②审议, 评议: be taken into ~ 被审议 / budget ~ 预算审议 / What's the result of all your ~(s)? 你们评议的结果怎么样? ③谨慎, 审慎: with ~ 慎重地 ④故意

delicacy ['delikəsi] *n.* ①细软, 娇嫩 ②精美, 精致; 雅致 ③娇气, 病弱; 脆弱 ④微妙, 棘手: a matter of great ~ 很微妙(或棘手)的问题 ⑤(色、光的) 柔和, 微弱 ⑥(感觉、仪器等的) 灵敏, 精密 ⑦体贴 ⑧灵巧 ⑨精美的食物: the *delicacies* of the season 时鲜 ‖*feel a ~ about* (或 *in*) 对…感到棘手

delicate ['delikit] *a.* ①细软的, 娇嫩的, 纤细的: as ~ as silk 绸缎般地柔软 / the ~ skin of a baby 婴孩娇嫩的皮肤 ②精美的, 精致的; 雅致的, 不庸俗的: porcelains of ~ workmanship 工艺精致的瓷器 ③娇气的, 奢侈的: ~ upbringing (或 nurture) 娇生惯养 / ~ living 奢侈的生活 ④病弱的; 脆弱的; 碰不起的: be in ~ health 身体虚弱 / a ~ stomach 容易吃坏的胃 / a ~ vase 容易碰碎的花瓶 ⑤微妙的, 难以处理的, 棘手的: a ~ diplomatic question 微妙的外交问题 / a ~ difference 讲不大清楚的差别 / a ~ surgical operation 很难做的外科手术 ⑥(色、光) 柔和的, 淡的, 微弱的: with a ~ shade of red 带点淡红色 ⑦(感觉、仪器等) 灵敏的: He has a ~ ear for music. 他对音乐很有鉴赏力。 / a ~ sense of smell 灵敏的嗅觉 / a ~ balance 精密的天平 ⑧体贴的, 顾到别人情绪的 ⑨灵巧的: a ~ touch 生花的妙笔; 神妙的弹奏 ⑩美味的, 鲜美的: ~ food 美味的食物 / a ~ flavour 鲜味 ‖~ly *ad.*

delicious [di'liʃəs] I *a.* ①美味的, 可口的; 芬芳的 ②妙的, 有趣味的: a ~ joke 很妙的笑话 II *n.* [美] [D-] 一种红苹果 ‖~ly *ad.* / **~ness** *n.*

delight [di'lait] I ❶ *vt.* 使高兴, 使欣喜; 悦(目): be ~ed at the news 听到这消息而高兴 / I've read your article and am ~ed with it. 我读过你的文章了, 很喜欢。 ❷ *vi.* ①喜爱; 取乐: He ~s to contradict me (或 in contradicting me) 他老爱跟我抬杠 ②给人愉快 II *n.* ①快乐, 高兴: take (或 find) ~ in 以…为乐 / To our ~ 使

the newly designed machine works very well. 使我们高兴的是, 新设计的机器运转良好。 / *with* ~ 高兴地, 乐意地 ②乐事, 乐处: Singing is one of her ~s. 唱歌是她的爱好之一。 / The scene is a perfect ~ to the eye. 这景象真是好看极了。

delighted [di'laitid] *a.* 高兴的, 快乐的: a ~ look 高兴的神气 ‖~ly *ad.*

delightful [di'laitful] *a.* ①(事物)令人高兴的; 使人快乐的: ~ weather 爽快的天气 ②(人)讨人喜欢的, 可爱的 ‖~ly *ad.* / **~ness** *n.*

delineate [di'linieit] *vt.* ①描出…的外形, 画出…的轮廓 ②用线条画画, 描绘 ③叙述, 描写

delinquency [di'liŋkwənsi] *n.* ①懈怠, 失职 ②过失;【律】少年犯罪: the problem of juvenile ~ 少年犯罪问题 ③拖欠的债务

delinquent [di'liŋkwənt] I *a.* ① 懈怠的, 失职的 ②拖欠(税款, 债务)的 ③有过失的; 违法的 II *n.* ①懈怠者, 失职者 ②有过失者; 违法者(特指少年犯罪者)

delirious [di'liriəs] *a.* ①谵妄(性)的, 神志昏迷的, 说胡话的 ② 极度兴奋的, 发狂的: be ~ with delight 狂喜

delirium [di'liriəm] ([复] deliriums 或 deliria [di'liriə]) *n.* ① 谵妄, 神志昏迷, 说胡话: lapse into ~ 陷入谵妄状态, 说胡话 ②极度兴奋, 发狂 ‖ ~ **tremens** ['tri:menz]【医】(因酒精中毒引起的)震颤性谵妄

deliver [di'livə] *vt.* ①放, 释放, 解救: ~ sb. from danger 救某人出险 / ~ sb. from pains 解除某人的疼痛 ②交付: ~ sth. (over) to sb. 把某物交付给某人 ③移交, 引渡 ④投递, 传送(信件、邮包、口信等): ~ a message 带信; 传话 ⑤提供, 供给: The well ~s much water. 这口井水源充足。 ⑥ (使)发表; (使)表达: ~ a speech at a meeting 在会上讲话 / ~ oneself *of* an opinion 发表意见 ⑦给(产妇)接生, 使分娩; 帮助产下(婴儿): The obstetrician ~ed the child. 产科医生接生。 ⑧拉(选票), 拉(支持者) ⑨给予(打击); 抛(球), (棒球等中)投(球): ~ battle 发动攻击 ‖*be ~ed of* 生下(孩子); 作出(诗) / ~(笑话) / *~ a gaol* (或 *jail*) 把监狱中的犯人全部提出来审讯 / ~ *oneself* (*to the police*) (向警察局)自首 / *~ the goods* 交货; [喻]履行诺言, 不负所望 ‖~ed *a.* 【商】包括交货费用在内的: the ~ed price 包括交货费用在内的价格 / **~er** [di'livərə] *n.* 救助者; 交付者; 递送者

deliverance [di'livərəns] *n.* ①解救; 释放 ②投递, 传送 ③正式意见, 判决

delivery [di'livəri] *n.* ①交付, 交货: cash on ~ 【商】货到付款(略作 C.O.D.) / take ~ of 提取 ②投递, 传送: There are three *deliveries* every day. 每天送信三次。 / general ~ (邮件的)存局待领 ③一次交付(或投递)的货物(或邮件) ④转让; 引渡 ⑤分娩: a difficult ~ 难产 / an easy ~ 顺产 ⑥陈述, 讲演; 讲课(或唱歌)的

腔调: a clear ～ 口齿清晰 / a telling ～ 动人的口才 ⑦发出; 投掷; (棒球等的)的投球法 ⑧释放; 解救 ‖a ～ book【商】交货簿, 送货簿 / a ～ order【商】交货单, 出货单, 栈单 / a ～ port【商】交货港, 到货港 / a ～ receipt【商】送货(或送件)回单 ‖~man [di'livərimən] n. 送货人

dell [del] n. 小山谷

delta ['deltə] I n. ①希腊语的第四个字母 (Δ, δ) ②三角形物; (河流的)三角洲: the (Nile) Delta 尼罗河三角洲 ③【数】变数的增量 II a.【化】(有机化合物分子中离特定基团或原子)第四位的, δ 位的 ‖~ ray【物】反冲粒子, δ 粒子 / ～ wing 三角形机翼

delude [di'lu:d] vt. 欺骗, 哄骗: ～ oneself 自欺, 弄错

deluge ['delju:dʒ] I n. ①洪水 ②大雨, 暴雨: a ～ of rain 一场大雨 ③洪水般的泛滥 II vt. 使泛滥, 使满溢, 淹浸: be ～d with letters 接到纷至沓来的信件 ‖After me the Deluge! 身后之事与我何干!

delusive [di'lu:siv] a. 欺骗的; 妄想的; 虚妄的 ‖~ly ad. / ~ness n.

delve [delv] I ❶ vt. ①[英方]挖, 掘, 刨 ②探究, 钻研 ❷ vi. ①[英方]挖, 掘, 刨 ②探究, 钻研: ～ into a subject 钻研某一题目 ③(路面等)凹陷 II n. 穴, 凹, 坑

demagog(ue) ['deməgɔg] n. ①煽动者, 蛊惑民心的政客 ②[史]古代民众领袖

demand [di'mɑ:nd] I ❶ vt. ①要求: ～ an immediate answer of (或 from) sb. 要求某人立即答复 ②需要: This work ～s care and patience. 这工作需要细心和耐心。③要求知道, 查问: The guard ～ed his business. 警卫问他来干什么。④要求(某人)到场 ❷ vi. 要求; 查问 II n. ①要求; 所要求的事物: make strict ～s on oneself 严格要求自己 / I have many ～s upon my time. 我有许多工作要花时间去做。/ a bill 见票即付的汇票, 即期汇票 (=a bill payable on ～) ②需要; 需求(量): supply and ～ 供与求 / There is a great ～ for these goods. 这些商品需要量很大。/ The pamphlet is in great ～. 这本小册子需要量很大。‖~er n. 要求者

demarcate ['di:mɑ:keit] vt. ①给…划界, 勘定…的界线 ②区别; 分开

demarcation [,di:mɑ:'keiʃən] n. ①分界, 定界: the ～ line between two countries 国界线 / a military ～ line 军事分界线 ②划分, 区分, 界限

demean[1] [di'mi:n] vt. [～ oneself]行为, 举止: ～ oneself well (ill) 表现好(不好)

demean[2] [di'mi:n] vt. 使降低身分, 使卑下: ～ oneself to do sth. 降低身分去做某事

demerit [di:'merit] n. 缺点, 过失, 过: merits and ～s 优点和缺点, 功过

demise [di'maiz] I n. ①不动产的转让, 遗赠 ②逊

位, 让位 ③帝王死亡; 崩, 薨; 死亡 II vt. ①转让, 遗赠(不动产) ②逊(位), 传(位)

demist [di:'mist] vt. 除去(汽车挡风玻璃等上)的雾 ‖~er n. 除雾器

demobilize, demobilise [di:'moubilaiz] vt. 使复员; 遣散: a ～d soldier 复员军人 ‖demobilization ['di:,moubilai'zeiʃən] n.

democracy [di'mɔkrəsi] n. ①民主, 民主主义; 民主政治, 民主政体: socialist ～ 社会主义民主 ②民主国 ③[the ～] 平民阶级 ④[D-] (美国)民主党 (=the Democratic Party of the United States)

democrat ['deməkræt] n. ①民主主义者; 民主人士: a non-Party ～ 党外民主人士 ②[D-] (美国)民主党党员

democratic [,deməˈkrætik] a. ①民主的, 民主主义的; 民主政体的: ～ centralism 民主集中制 / ～ consultation 民主协商 / the people's ～ dictatorship 人民民主专政 ②平民的 ③[D-] (美国)民主党的 ‖~ally ad. ‖,Demoˈcratic-Reˈpublican a. (美国)民主党和共和党的

demolish [di'mɔliʃ] vt. ①拆毁(建筑物); 破坏(组织); 推翻(计划、制度) ②[口]吃完, 吃光

demolition [,deməˈliʃən] n. 拆毁, 破坏;【军】爆破: a ～ bomb 爆破弹 ‖~ derby [美]撞车比赛(参加者各驾破车互撞, 最后剩下未撞毁的车获冠军)

demon ['di:mən] n. ①【宗】精灵; 守护神 ②【宗】恶魔 ③恶棍; 凶猛的动物 ④精力(或技巧)过人的人 ‖a ～ for work 工作起来精力过人的人

demonstrate ['demənstreit] ❶ vt. ①论证, 证实 ②(用实例、实验等)说明, 表演 ③表明, 表示(感情) ❷ vi. 示威: ～ against sb. (sth.) 示威反对某人(某物)

demonstration [,deməns'treiʃən] n. ①论证, 证明 ②示范, 表演: teach by ～ 进行示范教学 ③表明, 表示(感情): make a ～ of gratitude 作感谢的表示 ④示威(运动) ⑤【军】示威行动; 佯动: a ～ crossing【军】佯渡 ‖~al a. / ~ist n. 示威运动参加者

demonstrative [di'mɔnstrətiv] I a. ①论证的 ②感情外露的 ③【语】指示的: a ～ pronoun 指示代词 II n. 【语】指示词 (指指示代词、指示形容词) ‖~ly ad. / ~ness n.

demonstrator ['demənstreitə] n. ①证明者; 示范者 ②示威者 ③用来向顾客作示范表演的产品

demoralize, demoralise [di'mɔrəlaiz] vt. ①使道德败坏 ②使士气低落; 使丧失功能 ③使陷入混乱 ‖demoralization [di,mɔrəlai'zeiʃən] n.

demote [di'mout] vt. [美]使降级

demotion [di'mouʃən] n. 降级

demur [di'mə:] I (demurred; demurring [di'mə:riŋ]) vi. ①表示异议, 反对 (to, at) ②迟疑, 犹豫 ③【律】抗辩 II n. 异议, 反对: without ～ 无异议

demure [di'mjuə] a. ①娴静的, 拘谨的, 严肃的 ②假正经的 ‖~ly ad. / ~ness n.

den [den] **I** *n.* ①兽穴,窝 ②(动物园的)兽笼 ③ 匪窟,贼窝 ④简陋污秽的小室 ⑤私室,书斋 **II** (denned; denning) ❶ *vi.* ①穴居 ②入洞,进窝 (冬眠)(*up*) ❷ *vt.* 把…赶入洞穴

denationalize, denationalise [di:'næʃnəlaiz] *vt.* ①使失去独立民族资格 ②开除…的国籍;剥夺… 的国民权利 ③使国有化,使恢复为私营 ‖**denationalization** ['di:,næʃnəlaizeiʃən] *n.*

denial [di'naiəl] *n.* ①否定;否认: make a ~ of sth. 否定(或否认)某事 ②拒绝相信;拒绝接受; 拒绝给予 ③克制自己

denim ['denim] *n.* ①斜纹粗棉布(经纱为蓝或褐色,纬纱为白色) ②[复](蓝色斜纹粗布制成的)工作服,工装裤

denizen ['denizn] **I** *n.* ①居民 ②(享有某些或全部公民权的)外籍居民 ③外来语;外来动物(或植物) ④常客(常去某地的人) **II** *vt.* ①给…居住权及某些公民权 ②移植

denomination [di,nɔmi'neiʃən] *n.* ①命名,名称 ②种类;宗派,派别 ③(度量衡、货币等的)单位: money of small ~s 小额货币,零钱 / reduce fractions to the same ~ 把分数化为同分母

denominator [di'nɔmineitə] *n.* ①【数】分母: least common ~ 最小公分母 ②命名者 ③共同特性 ④标准,一般水准

denote [di'nout] *vt.* ①指示,表示;意味着: The sign *x* ~s an unknown number. *x* 符号表示一个未知数。②[逻]概指 ‖**~ment** *n.*

denounce [di'nauns] *vt.* ①谴责,痛斥,斥责 ②告发: ~ sb. to the authorities 向当局告发某人 ③通告废除(条约、协定等)‖**~ment** *n.* / **~r** *n.* 斥责者;告发者

dense [dens] *a.* ①密集的;稠密的: a ~ forest 密林 / a ~ crowd 密集的人群 ②(烟、雾等)浓厚的 ③愚钝的 ④极度的 ⑤【摄】(底片)厚的,反差强的 ‖**~ly** *ad.* / **~ness** *n.*

densify ['densifai] *vt.* 使增加密度

density ['densiti] *n.* ①密集(度),稠密(度)②【物】【化】密度: current ~ 电流密度 ③愚钝 ④【摄】厚度,不透明度

dent [dent] **I** *n.* ①凹部,凹痕 ②【机】(齿轮的)齿 【纺】筘齿 ③[英方]打,击 ④压缩,削减 **II** ❶ *vt.* ①使凹,使出现凹痕 ②削弱: ~ sb.'s influence 削弱某人的影响 ❷ *vi.* 凹进 ‖**make a ~ in** 对…产生不利的影响,削弱

dental ['dentl] **I** *a.* ①牙齿的;牙科的: ~ surgery 牙科;口腔外科 ②[语]齿音的: ~ consonants 齿音字母 **II** *n.* 【语】齿音,齿音字母(如 d, t, th 等) ‖**~ize** *vt.* 使齿音化

dentist ['dentist] *n.* 牙医生 ‖**~ry** *n.* 牙科学;牙科

denture ['dentʃə] *n.* ①一副牙齿 ②假牙,托牙;(尤指)全口假牙

denude [di'nju:d] *vt.* ①剥光,使赤裸;滥伐…上的树木: Most trees are ~d of leaves in winter. 多

数树木在冬季都要落叶。②剥夺,夺去: ~ sb. *of* a right (possession, hope) 剥夺某人的权利(财产,希望) ③【地】使剥蚀,使岩石裸露

denunciate [di'nʌnsieit] *vt.* =denounce

denunciation [di,nʌnsi'eiʃən] *n.* ①斥责,痛斥;谴责 ②告发 ③[古]恐吓,警告 ④宣告(条约等)无效

deny [di'nai] ❶ *vt.* ①否定,否认: To ~ contradiction is to ~ everything. 否认事物的矛盾就是否认了一切。/ knowing the plan 否认知道这个计划 / There is no ~ing the fact that .... …这一事实是不容否认的。②拒绝相信;拒绝接受;拒绝给予: ~ sb. admission 拒绝某人入场 ③克制 ❷ *vi.* 否定;拒绝 ‖**~ oneself** 节制;戒绝,摒弃 / **~ oneself to** 不会见(客人)

deodorize, deodorise [di:'oudəraiz] *vt.* 除去…的臭味,防止…的臭味 ‖**deodorization** [di:,oudərai'zeiʃən] *n.* / **deodorizer** *n.* 除臭剂,解臭剂,防臭剂

depart [di'pa:t] ❶ *vi.* ①(人)离开,起程 ②(火车)开出: The train ~s at 6:30 a.m. 列车上午六点三十分开出。(时刻表中常略作: dep. 6:30 a.m.) ③违反,不合 ④去世: ~ *from* life 去世 ❷ *vt.* [古][诗]离去(现只用于去世): ~ this life 去世 ‖**~ed** *a.* [古][诗]过去的,以往的;去世的: the ~ed [单复同]死者

department [di'pa:tmənt] *n.* ①(行政、企业等机构的)部,司,局,处,科;部门: the business ~ 营业部(或科等)/ the *Department* of Defense (美国)国防部 / the Statistics *Department* (英国)统计局 / the State *Department* (美国)国务院 / the propaganda ~s 宣传部门 / a ~ store 百货商店 / the women's clothing ~ (大商店中的)女子服装部 ②(学校、学术机构的)系;学部,研究室: the *Department* of Antibiotics 抗菌素研究室 ③(工厂的)车间;工段: the assembling (或 fitting) ~ 装配车间 ④(法国等的)县,行政区 ⑤知识范围,活动范围: Literature is his ~. 他从事文学工作。

departure [di'pa:tʃə] *n.* ①启程;离开;出发: a ~ platform (火车)出发站台 / take one's ~ 出发,动身 / a new ~ 新发展,新方针 ②违背,背离(*from*) ③[古]去世,死 ④[测]横距,东西距 ⑤【讯】偏离,偏移;发射,飞出: frequency ~ 频率漂移 ⑥【海】航迹推算起点

depend [di'pend] *vi.* [一般与 on, upon 连用] ①靠,依靠;依赖: All living things ~ *on* the sun *for* their growth. 万物生长靠太阳。②相信;信赖: We can ~ *on* his arriving here on time. 我们可以相信他会准时到来。/ He is a man to be ~ed *upon*. 他这人靠得住。③依…而定: The development of things ~s fundamentally *on* internal causes. 事物的发展根本上是由内因决定的。/ That ~s *on* how you tackle the problem. 这要看你如何处理那个问题。④悬而未决: The matter is ~ing. 事情尚未解决。⑤[古]悬挂,下垂 ‖**~ upon it** [口]毫无疑问,没

错: Our work will be finished this week, ~ *upon it*! 我们的工作这星期肯定可以完成。/ *that* ~*s* (或 *it all* ~*s*)[口]要看情况而定: I may go there, but *that* ~*s*. 我可能去，但那要看情况。

dependable [di'pendəbl] *a.* 可靠的 ‖**dependability** [di,pendə'biliti] *n.* / **dependably** *ad.*

dependant [di'pendənt] *n.* ①受赡养者 ②随从，侍从

dependence [di'pendəns] *n.* ①依靠，依赖；相依性: the ~ of theory *on* practice 理论对于实践的依赖关系 ②信任，信赖 ③从属；隶属

dependency [di'pendənsi] *n.* ①从属；依赖 ②从属物 ③属地，属国

dependent [di'pendənt] **I** *a.* ①依靠的；依赖的 (*on, upon*) ②由…决定的，随…而定的 (*on, upon*) ③从属的；隶属的: a ~ clause【语】从句 / a ~ territory 属地 ④下垂的: a lamp ~ from the ceiling 从天花板悬吊下来的灯 **II** *n.* =dependant

depict [di'pikt] *vt.* ①描绘；雕出: a series of pictures ~*ing* the life story of the hero 描绘这位英雄的一生的一组图画 ②描写，描述 ‖~**er**, ~**or** *n.* / ~**ion** [di'pikʃən] *n.* ①描绘 ②图画；雕刻的图 ③描写 / ~**ive** *a.* 描绘的；描写的

deplete [di'pli:t] *vt.* ①(部分或全部地)弄空，使空虚；耗尽…的精力(或资源等): ~ a lake *of* fish 捉完湖里的鱼 ②【医】减少…的体液；放去…的血

deplore [di'plɔ:] *vt.* ①哀叹，悲叹；哀悼 ②痛惜，悔恨 ‖**deploringly** [di'plɔ:riŋli] *ad.*

deploy [di'plɔi] *vt. & vi.*【军】展开，调度，部署 ‖~**ment** *n.*

depopulate [di:'pɔpjuleit] **I** ❶ *vt.* (战争、疫病等)使(某地)人口减少；灭绝(某地)的人口 ❷ *vi.* 人口减少 **II** *a.* [古]人口减少的 ‖**depopulation** [di:,pɔpju'leiʃən] *n.*

deport [di'pɔ:t] *vt.* ①[~ oneself]举止: ~ oneself properly 举止恰如其分 ②驱逐…出国，放逐 ‖~**ation** [,di:pɔ:'teiʃən] *n.* 放逐 / ~**ee** [,di:pɔ:'ti:] *n.* 被驱逐出国者；被判处放逐者

depose [di'pouz] ❶ *vt.* ①废黜；免…的职，罢…的官 ②【律】宣誓证实 ③置放 ❷ *vi.* 宣誓作证 ‖**deposable** *a.* 可废黜的，可免职的 / **deposal** *n.* 废黜，免职

deposit [di'pɔzit] **I** ❶ *vt.* ①存放，寄存: ~ sth. *with* sb. 把某物寄放在某人处 ②储蓄；付(保证金): ~ money in a bank 把钱存在银行里 ③产(卵)，下(蛋) ④使沉淀，使淤积: When the river rises, it ~*s* a layer of mud on the land. 河流泛滥时在陆地上积了一层泥土。/ ~ concrete【建】浇注混凝土 ❷ *vi.* 沉淀，淤积 **II** *n.* ①存放；寄存物 ②存款；保证金，押金: a current (fixed) ~ 活期(定期)存款 / a savings ~ 储蓄(金) ③沉淀，沉积物；【矿】沉积；矿床: oil ~ 油田；石油藏量 ④保藏处，仓库 ‖~**or** *n.* ①存放者；储户 ②【化】淀积器

depository [di'pɔzitəri] *n.* ①受托人 ②保藏处 ‖~

library [美]指定出借政府出版物的图书馆

depot ['depou] *n.* ①仓库 ②【军】兵站，(补给品)仓库 ③['di:pou][美]车站，航空站 ‖~ **ship** (随舰队同行的)补给修理船

deprave [di'preiv] *vt.* 使堕落，使腐败 ‖**depravation** [,deprə'veiʃən] *n.* / ~**d** *a.* 堕落的，腐化的

depravity [di'præviti] *n.* ①堕落，腐败 ②腐败堕落的行为

deprecate ['deprikeit] *vt.* ①对…表示不赞成，反对 ②[古]祈求免去 ‖**deprecatingly** *ad.* / **deprecation** [,depri'keiʃən] *n.*

depreciate [di'pri:ʃieit] ❶ *vt.* ①降低…的价值，降低…的价格，使(货币)贬值 ②蔑视，贬低: We must not ~ their achievements. 我们决不可贬低他们的成就。❷ *vi.* 跌价，贬值 ‖**depreciatingly** *ad.* 蔑视地，贬低地

depreciation [di,pri:ʃi'eiʃən] *n.* ①价值低落，跌价，贬值 ②折旧: ~ funds 折旧费 / ~ of machinery 机器折旧 ③蔑视，贬低

depredation [,depri'deiʃən] *n.* [常用复]劫掠；毁坏

depress [di'pres] *vt.* ①降低，压低；抑制 ②使沮丧，使消沉 ③使萧条，使不景气；使衰落 ④使减值，使跌价

depressing [di'presiŋ] *a.* ①抑压的 ②沉闷的，使人沮丧的 ‖~**ly** *ad.* / ~**ness** *n.*

depression [di'preʃən] *n.* ①降低，压低 ②凹地，洼地；凹陷 ③沮丧，意气消沉 ④不景气，萧条(期) ⑤【气】低(气)压；(显示气压降低的)气压计水银柱的下降 ⑥【医】抑郁症；机能降低 ⑦【天】地平线以下星体的角距离；【测】俯角

depressive [di'presiv] *a.* ①抑压的，压下的 ②抑郁的，令人沮丧的

deprive [di'praiv] *vt.* ①夺去，剥夺；使丧失: be ~*d of* one's rights 被剥夺权利 ②免去…的职务(尤指圣职) ‖~**d** *a.* 被剥夺生活必需品的；丧失了受良好教育权利的

depth [depθ] *n.* ①深，深度，厚度，(色泽)浓度: What is the ~ of the well? 这口井有多深？/ The snow fell to a ~ of three feet. 雪下了三呎深。/ the ~ of attack (defence)【军】进攻(防御)纵深 / ~ of engagement【机】衔接深度，啮合深度 / the ~ of colour 颜色的浓度 / the ~ of the sound 声音的低沉 / ~ of field【摄】景深 ②深处，深渊；正中: from the ~ of one's mind 从心底里，真心 / in the ~ of night 在深夜 / in the ~ of the country 在穷乡僻壤 ③深奥，深刻，深沉: an article that shows ~ of thought 表现(作者)思想深刻的文章 / a man of great ~ 深沉的人 ‖*out of* (或 *beyond*) sb.'s (one's) ~ ①深得要淹没某人(自己): If you can't swim, don't go *out of your* ~. 你若不会游泳，别走入水深过头的地方。②非某人(自己)所能理解，为某人(自己)力所不及 ‖~ **bomb**, ~ **charge** 深水炸弹 / '~-**bomb**, '~-**charge** *vt.* 用深水炸弹攻击(或炸毁) / ~ **finder** 回音测深仪 / ~

ga(u)ge 深度计 / ～ **perception**【心】深度知觉 / ～ **psychology** 精神分析学

deputation [,depju(:)'teiʃən] *n.* ①委派代表 ②代表团: a ～ *to* the conference 参加大会的代表团

depute [di'pju:t] *vt.* ①将(工作、权力等)委托(给…): ～ one's authority *to* a substitute 授权给代理人 ②派…为代表

deputize, deputise ['depjutaiz] ❶ *vt.* 委…为代表,授权…为代表 ❷ *vi.* 担任代表 (*for*)

deputy ['depjuti] *n.* ①代理人: act as a ～ *for* sb. 做某人的代理人 ②代表: (法国等)下院议员: the Chamber of *Deputies* (法国等的) 国民议会,下院 ③[用作定语]副; 代理: a ～ chairman 代理主席(或议长),副主席(或议长) / a ～ mayor 副市长 / a ～ commander in chief 副总司令 / the *Deputy* Assistant Secretary (美国)助理国务卿帮办,助理部长帮办 ④[英]小客栈的经理

derail [di'reil] Ⅰ ❶ *vt.* [常用被动语态]使(火车等)出轨;使离开原定进程: be (或 get) ～ed 出轨 ❷ *vi.* 出轨 Ⅱ *n.*【交】脱轨(器) ‖～ment *n.*

derange [di'reindʒ] *vt.* ①捣乱,扰乱(秩序等);打乱(计划等) ②使精神错乱,使发狂: be (mentally) ～d 精神错乱 ‖～ment *n.* ①搅乱,混乱 ②精神错乱

derelict ['derilikt] Ⅰ *a.* ①被抛弃的,遗弃的;无主的(尤指海上弃船) ②[美]玩忽职守的,不负责的: be ～ *of* (或 *in* one's duty) 玩忽职责 Ⅱ *n.* ①遗弃物,无主物(尤指海上弃船) ②被社会抛弃的人;乞丐 ③[美]失职的人 ④海水退去露出的新陆地

deride [di'raid] *vt.* 嘲笑,嘲弄 ‖～r *n.* 嘲笑者,嘲弄者 / **deridingly** *ad.*

derision [di'riʒən] *n.* ①嘲笑,嘲弄: be in ～ 被嘲弄 / hold (或 have) sb. in ～ 嘲笑某人 ②嘲笑目标,笑柄: be the ～ *of* 是…的笑柄

derisive [di'raisiv] *a.* ①嘲笑的,嘲弄的 ②幼稚可笑的 ‖～ly *ad.* / ～ness *n.*

derisory [di'raisəri] *a.* =derisive

derivation [,deri'veiʃən] *n.* ①引出,诱导 ②衍生,衍生物 ③起源,由来 ④【语】派生;派生关系;词源: the ～ of words 词的派生 / words of Latin ～ 拉丁语词源的词 ⑤【数】求导(数)

derivative [di'rivətiv] Ⅰ *a.* ①被引出的,被诱导的;衍生的 ②派生的 Ⅱ *n.* ①引出物,派生物 ②【语】派生词 ③【数】导数,微商 ④【化】衍生物 ‖～ly *ad.*

derive [di'raiv] ❶ *vt.* ①取得,得到: ～ knowledge *from* practice 从实践得到知识 ②派生出,导出,衍生出: words ～d *from* Latin 从拉丁语派生的词 ③引申出,推知: ～ itself *from* 由…而来,源出… ❷ *vi.* ①起源,由来 (*from*) ②衍生,导出

derogate ['derəgeit] ❶ *vt.* 贬损,贬低 ❷ *vi.* ①减损,贬低,毁损 (*from*) ②堕落;背离 (*from*) ‖**derogation** [,derə'geiʃən] *n.* ①减损,贬低,毁损 ②(法律、合同、条约等的)部分废除 (*of, to*) ③堕落;背离

derogatory [di'rɔgətəri]· *a.* ①毁损的,贬抑的,减损的: be ～ *to* sb.'s reputation 有损某人的名誉 ②【语】贬义的: a ～ term 贬义词 ‖**derogatorily** [di'rɔgətərili; 美 di,rɔgə'tɔrili] *ad.*

derrick ['derik] *n.* ①【机】人字起重机;(船上起重用的)摇臂吊杆 ②【矿】钻塔;(油井的)井架 ③[美俚]偷贵重物品的人,小偷

derringer ['derindʒə] *n.* 一种大口径短筒小手枪

derringer

descant Ⅰ ['deskænt] *n.* ①【音】童高音 ②曲调,歌曲,旋律 ③评论;详谈 Ⅱ [dis'kænt] *vi.* ①评论;详谈 (*on, upon*) ②唱歌

descend [di'send] ❶ *vi.* ①下来,下降: ～ from a hill 从山上下到平地 / ～ from a carriage 下车 ②下倾,下斜: The road ～s to the river. 这条路向下倾斜通到河边。③传下,遗传: ～ from an ancient family 是一个古老家族的后裔 ④袭击;突然去访问(*on, upon*): Letters of congratulation ～ed *upon* us like snowflakes.贺信雪片似地飞来。⑤屈尊,降低身分 ⑥由远而近;由大而小 ⑦转而说到 (*to*): ～ to particulars (或 details) (在介绍过总的情况后)转谈到细目 ⑧【天】移向南方,移向地平线 ❷ *vt.* 下,降: ～ the stairs 下楼梯 ‖～**able**, ～**ible** *a.* 能遗传的,能相传的 / ～**er** *n.* ①下降者,下降物 ②下行字母 (g, p, y 等);下行字母伸至基线以下的部分 / ～**ing** *a.* 下降的,下行的,递降的: a ～*ing* arc【军】弹道降弧 / a ～*ing* scale【音】下行音阶 / a ～*ing* letter (伸至基线以下的)下行字母 (g, p, y 等)

descendant, descendent [di'sendənt] Ⅰ *n.* ①子孙,后裔 ②从某一来源派生(或传下)的东西 Ⅱ *a.* ①从一个祖先(或来源)传下的 ②下降的

descent [di'sent] *n.* ①下降,降下: a ～ *of* temperature 温度的下降 / The balloon made a slow ～. 气球慢慢地降下。②斜坡;坡道: The land slopes to the sea by a gradual ～. 陆地(呈斜坡状)逐渐向海边倾斜。③血统;遗传: He is of Irish ～. 他祖籍爱尔兰。④袭击 (*on, upon*): make a ～ *upon* 袭击…⑤屈尊,降格

describe [dis'kraib] *vt.* ①描写,描绘,叙述: ～ a scene 描绘一个情景 / Words cannot ～ my joy. 言语不能形容我的快乐。②形容,把…说成 (*as*) ③画(图形),制(图): ～ a circle 画一个圆 ‖**describable** *a.* 可描述的,可描绘的;可画的 / ～**r** *n.* 叙述者,描写者;制图者

description [dis'kripʃən] *n.* ①描写,描述,形容,叙述: give a ～ *of* the battle 描述战况 / answer (to) the ～ 与描述的相符(常指人的容貌、特征

等) / beyond ~ 难以形容 ②(物品)说明书;货名;图说 ③ 种类: persons of that ~ 那一类人 / of all ~s (或 of every ~) 形形色色的,各式各样的 ④作图;绘制: the ~ of a triangle 三角形的绘制 ‖**warm ~s** 色情的描述

descriptive [dis'kriptiv] *a.* 描述的,描写的;说明的: a ~ catalog(ue) 附有说明的分类目录 / geometry 画法几何(学) / ~ linguistics 描写语言学 / a ~ style 叙事体 ‖**~ly** *ad.*

descry [dis'krai] *vt.* ①望见,看到,辨别出 ②发现

desecrate ['desikreit] *vt.* 把(神物)供俗用;亵渎;污辱 ‖**desecration** [,desi'kreiʃən] *n.*

desert[1] ['dezət] **I** *n.* ①沙漠;不毛之地 ②[喻]荒凉的境地;枯燥无味的事物;历史上的荒芜时代 **II** *a.* ①沙漠的 ②荒芜的,不毛的;无人居住的

desert[2] [di'zə:t] ❶ *vt.* ①丢弃,舍弃;抛弃,遗弃: His presence of mind never ~ed him. 他从不失去镇静。②擅离(职守等) ❷ *vi.* 逃跑掉,开小差 ‖**~ed** *a.* ①被舍弃的,荒废的,无人(居住)的 ②被抛弃的,被遗弃的 / **~er** *n.* 背离者;叛离者;逃兵

desert[3] [di'zə:t] *n.* ①功过,功罪 ②[常用复]应得的赏(或罚): treat people according to their ~s 给人们以应有的赏罚 / obtain (或 meet) one's ~s 得到应有的赏罚 ③美德

deserve [di'zə:v] ❶ *vt.* 应受,值得: ~ punishment (a reward) 应受处罚(奖赏) / ~ to be mentioned 值得提起 ❷ *vi.* 应受报答,值得受赏: ~ well (ill) *of* 有受…奖赏(处罚)的价值;有功(罪)于…

deserving [di'zə:viŋ] **I** *a.* ①该受的,值得…的 (*of*): a problem ~ *of* public attention 一个值得大家注意的问题 ②[用作定语]有功的 **II** *n.* 功过,赏罚 ‖**~ly** *ad.*

desiccate ['desikeit] ❶ *vt.* ①使干燥,使脱水;用干燥法保存(食物): ~d milk 奶粉 ②使…的感情(或智力等)枯竭 ❷ *vi.* 变成干燥 ‖**desiccation** [,desi'keiʃən] *n.* 干燥(作用),脱水 / **desiccator** *n.* ①干燥器,保干器;防潮砂 ②干货制造者

design [di'zain] **I** ❶ *vt.* ①计划,谋划: ~ an attack 计划进攻 / ~ doing (或 to do) sth. 打算做某事 / Was this ~ed, or did it just happen? 这是预先计划的呢,还是偶然发生的? ②设计,构思,绘制: ~ an engine 设计一台发动机 / ~ a musical composition 构思一支乐曲 ③预定,指定: ~ sth. for some purpose 派定某物作某种用途 / ~ sb. for some profession 打算要某人从事某种职业 ❷ *vi.* ①计划,谋划 ②设计,构思,制图 **II** *n.* ①计划;企图,图谋: carry out a ~ 实行一项计划 / cherish evil ~s 心怀叵测 ②设计;图样;图案: engrave a ~ on metal 在金属上刻花样 / make ~s for a monument 设计一座纪念碑 / of the latest ~ 最新设计的,最新式的 ③(小说等的)构思,纲要 ‖**by ~** 故意地,蓄意地

have ~s on (或 against) 对…抱不良企图;企图加害于(某人);企图盗窃(某物) ‖**~er** *n.* 设计者,制图者;谋划者 / **~ing** *a.* ①有事先计划的 ②阴谋的,诡诈的 *n.* ①设计(工作) ②计划

designate ['dezigneit] **I** *vt.* ①指明,指出,标示: ~ boundaries 标明疆界 ②指定,选派 (*to, as, for*): ~ sb. to an office 任命某人任某职 ③把…叫做,称呼: be ~d by the name of 被称为… **II** ['dezignit] *a.* [用于被修饰的名词后]指派好而尚未上任的;选出而尚未上任的: the president ~ 当选总统。‖**designative** *a.* 指定的;指明的 / **designator** *n.* 指示者,指定者;指示物 / **designatory** ['dezignətəri] *a.* =designative

designation [,dezig'neiʃən] *n.* ①指明,标示 ②指定,选派,任命 ③名称,称号;牌号;【军】番号

designed [di'zaind] *a.* 事先计划好的,故意的 ‖**~ly** [di'zainidli] *ad.*

desirable [di'zaiərəbl] **I** *a.* ①称心的,合意的;吸引人的 ②值得想望的,值得弄到手的 ③合乎需要的 **II** *n.* 称心合意的东西;值得弄到手的东西;合乎需要的东西 ‖**desirability** [di,zaiərə'biliti] *n.* / **~ness** *n.* **desirably** *ad.*

desire [di'zaiə] **I** *n.* ①愿望,心愿;欲望;情欲: ~ *for* independence 要求独立的愿望 / have a strong ~ *to* do sth. 迫切想做某事 / a subjective ~ 主观愿望 ②要求,请求: do sth. *at* sb.'s ~ 应某人要求做某事 ③想望的东西,想望的事物 **II** ❶ *vt.* ①想望,期望,希望: I ~ to see you. 我很想见你。/ leave much to be ~d 还有许多有待改进之处 / leave nothing to be ~d 完美无缺 / be (not) all that could be ~d 令人(并不令人)满意 ②要求,请求: He ~d me to wait. 他要我等着。/ ~ an immediate answer 要求立即答复 ❷ *vi.* 愿望,期望

desirous [di'zaiərəs] *a.* [用作表语]想望的,想望的,渴望的: be ~ *to* do (或 *of doing*) sth. 想干某事 / be ~ *of* sth. 想得到某物 ‖**~ly** *ad.* / **~ness** *n.*

desist [di'zist] *vi.* 停止;断念: ~ *from* discussing 停止讨论

desk [desk] *n.* ①书桌,写字台,办公桌: be (或 sit) at the (或 one's) ~ 在读书(或写文章);在办公 / a rolltop ~ 有活动盖板的办公桌 ②【宗】读经台,[美]讲道台 ③[the ~] 文书(或办事员等)职业;[美](报馆)编辑部 ④值勤人员的工作台: Leave your key at the ~ when you are out of the hotel. 离开旅馆时请把钥匙交到服务员的台子上。⑤乐谱架 ⑥(在一机构中专门负责某方面事务的)部,司,组 ‖**~man** *n.* 办公室工作人员;报馆编辑人员

desolate ['desəlit] **I** *a.* ①荒芜的,荒凉的,无人居住的 ②孤寂的,凄凉的 **II** ['desəleit] *vt.* ①使荒芜,使荒凉,破坏 ②使孤寂,使凄凉 ‖**~ly** *ad.* / **~ness** *n.*

desolation [,desə'leiʃən] *n.* ①荒芜,荒凉,渺无人烟 ②颓败;废墟,荒地 ③孤寂,凄凉

despair [dis'pɛə] I n. ①绝望: drive sb. to ~ 使某人陷于绝望 ②令人绝望的人(或事物) ③(使竞争者)望尘莫及的人(或事物) II vi. 绝望,丧失信心

despairing [dis'pɛəriŋ] a. 绝望的 ||~ly ad.

despatch [dis'pætʃ] vt., vi. & n. =dispatch

desperado [ˌdespə'rɑːdou] ([复] desperado(e)s) n. ①亡命之徒;暴徒(尤指美国西部的土匪) ②[美俚]无赖(指借了债或赌输了钱不打算偿付的人);不量入为出的生活奢侈者

desperate ['despərit] a. ①令人绝望的;危急的: in a ~ state 在绝境中 / a ~ illness 重病 ②(因绝望而)不顾一切的,拚死的,铤而走险的,孤注一掷的: conduct a ~ struggle 作拚死的斗争 / a ~ remedy 孤注一掷的措施 ③极度渴望的: be ~ for a drink of water 极想喝一些水 ④极端的;(气候)险恶的: a ~ fool 大傻瓜 / a ~ night 狂风暴雨之夜 ||~ly ad. / ~ness n.

desperation [ˌdespə'reiʃən] n. 绝望;拚命: rise in ~ 在绝望中奋起 / drive sb. to ~ 逼得某人走投无路

despicable ['despikəbl] a. 可鄙的,卑鄙的 ||~ness n. / despicably ad.

despise [dis'paiz] vt. 鄙视,藐视;看不起 ||despisingly ad.

despite [dis'pait] I n. ①憎恨,怨恨 ②恶意,侮辱 ③轻蔑,轻视 II prep. 不管,尽管,任凭: remain modest ~ one's achievements 尽管有成绩仍然保持谦虚 ||(in) ~ of 不管,尽管,任凭 (=in spite of)

despoil [dis'poil] vt. 抢劫,掠夺;剥夺: ~ a town 抢劫一个市镇 / ~ sb. of his right 剥夺某人的权利 ||~ment n.

despond [dis'pond] vi. 沮丧,泄气,失望 (of) ||~ence n., ~ency n.

despot ['despot] n. 专制君主,暴君: a local ~ 恶霸

dessert [di'zəːt] n. ①[美]甜点心(如水果、布丁、冰淇淋等,作为正餐的最后一道) ②[英](作为正餐最后一道的)水果(或甜食等) ||des'sertspoon n. 点心匙

destination [ˌdesti'neiʃən] n. ①[罕]指定,预定 ②目的地,终点: the port of ~ 【海】目的港 ③目标,目的

destine ['destin] vt. ①[常用被动语态]命定;注定 ②预定,指定 (for, to): a room ~d for the reception of foreign visitors 用以接待外宾用的房间 / John was originally ~d to the bar. 约翰的父亲起初想叫他去学当律师。

destiny ['destini] n. ①命运: grasp one's ~ in one's own hands 掌握自己的命运 ②[Destinies]【希神】命运三女神

destitute ['destitjuːt] a. ①没有的,缺乏的: be ~ of shame 无耻 ②贫困的,赤贫的 ||the ~ 贫民们 / the less ~ 次贫的人们 / the utterly ~ 赤贫的人们 ||destitution [ˌdesti'tjuːʃən] n.

destroy [dis'troi] vt. ①破坏,摧毁,毁坏 ②打破(希望、计划),使失败 ③消灭,除灭,歼灭

destroyer ['dis'troiə] n. ①破坏者,消灭者;起破坏作用的东西 ②驱逐舰: a ~ escort 护航驱逐舰 / a ~ flotilla 驱逐舰纵队 / a ~ screen 驱逐舰警戒网 / a ~ tender 驱逐舰供应船

destruct [dis'trʌkt] I n. (火箭、导弹等失灵后的)自毁 II vi. 自毁

destructible [dis'trʌktəbl] a. 可破坏的,可消灭的 ||destructibility [dis,trʌkti'biliti] n.

destruction [dis'trʌkʃən] n. ①破坏,毁灭,消灭 ②毁灭的原因 ||~ist n. 好破坏者;鼓吹毁灭者

destructive [dis'trʌktiv] a. 破坏(性)的,毁灭(性)的;危害的 (of) ||~ly ad. / ~ness n. ||~ distillation 【化】毁馏,分解蒸馏

desultory ['desəltəri] a. ①散漫的,杂乱的,随意的: a ~ talk 漫谈 / ~ reading (随意)阅读 / a ~ collection 杂乱的一堆 ②不连贯的,无条理的 ||desultorily ['desəltərili; 美 ,desəl'tɔrili] ad. / desultoriness n.

detach [di'tætʃ] vt. ①分开,拆开,分离: ~ a gear from a machine 从机器上拆下齿轮 ②分遣,派遣(军队、军舰) ||~able a. 可分开的,可拆开的

detached [di'tætʃt] a. ①分离的,孤立的,独立的: a ~ building 一所独立的建筑物 / the ~ works 【军】前哨工事 ②超然的,公正的: assume a ~ air 装出超然的样子 / a ~ view 不偏不倚的见解 ③分遣的,派遣的: a ~ force 分遣队,别动队 / ~ service 【军】派遣性任务 ||~ly ad. / ~ness n.

detachment [di'tætʃmənt] n. ①分开,拆开,分离 ②分遣;分遣队,支队;特遣舰队: an advanced ~ 先遣队 ③独立,超然,不偏不倚

detail ['diːteil, di'teil] I n. ①细目,细节,详情: discuss the ~s of a plan 讨论计划的细目 ②逐一处理;详细: explain in ~ 详细解释 / go (或 enter) into ~s 详细叙述,逐一说明 ③零件,元件;详图: an engine ~ 发动机详图 ④枝节;琐碎: There is too much ~ in his speech. 他的讲话太琐碎了。 ⑤【军】分遣,分遣队;行动指令: a guard ~ 【军】值日卫兵 ⑥【摄】影象的细节,清晰度 II ● vt. ①详述,细说 ②【军】分遣,选派: Ten soldiers were ~ed to guard the bridge. 十名战士被派去保卫那座桥梁。 ● vi. 画详图 ||for further ~s 为了知道详细情况(请询问、参看等) ||~ed a. 详细的,明细的: a ~ed report (analysis) 详细的报告(分析) ||~ drawing 详图,明细图 / ~ man (药品制造商的)新药推销员

detain [di'tein] vt. ①拘留,扣押 ②留住,阻住: I was ~ed by an unexpected caller that afternoon. 那天下午我被一个突然的来访者缠住了。 ||~ee [ˌdiːtei'niː] n. (因政治等原因)被拘留者 / ~er n. ①【律】他人物件的扣押 ②拘留,扣押 ③继续拘留状

detect [di'tekt] vt. ①察觉,发觉,发现: The decay

of food can usually be ~ed by the sense of smell. 食物的腐坏一般可由嗅觉察出。/ ~ sb. in (doing) a dishonest act 察觉某人在作不正当的事 ②侦查；探测，检测 ③【无】对…检波 ‖~able a. 可察觉的，易发现的

detection [di'tekʃən] n. ①察觉，发觉 ②侦查；探测，检测 ③【无】检波

detective [di'tektiv] I a. 侦探的，探测的；侦探用的: a ~ story 侦探小说 II n. 侦探: a private ~ 私家侦探

detention [di'tenʃən] n. ①拘留，扣押；【军】禁闭: be under ~ 在拘留中 / ~ barracks 军事监狱 / a house of ~ 拘留所 / a ~ home 青少年罪犯的临时拘留所 ②阻留，滞留: a ~ basin 拦洪水库 ③(罚学生的)课后留校，关晚学

deter [di'tə:] (deterred; deterring [di'tə:riŋ]) vt. 使不敢，威慑，吓住；拦住，阻止: No difficulty can ~ us from trying it again. 任何困难阻挡不住我们再进行试验。/ paint sth. to ~ rust 在某物上涂上涂料以防锈

detergency [di'tə:dʒənsi] n. 去垢性；去垢力

detergent [di'tə:dʒənt] I a. 使干净的，使清洁的，净化的 II n. 清洁剂，去垢剂: a synthetic ~ 合成洗涤剂

deteriorate [di'tiəriəreit] ❶ vt. ①使恶化 ②败坏；使变坏 ③使退化 ❷ vi. ①恶化 ②变质，变坏；堕落 ③退化 ‖**deterioration** [di,tiəriə'reiʃən] n. / **deteriorative** a.

determinant [di'tə:minənt] I a. 决定性的；限定性的 II n. ①决定因素 ②【数】行列式 ③【生】定子，决定体；因子

determinate [di'tə:minit] a. ①确定的，明确的；限定的 ②【植】(花序)有限的 ③【动】(卵裂)定型的 ④【数】有定数的，有定值的 ‖~ly ad. ‖~ cleavage【动】定(型卵)裂

determination [di,tə:mi'neiʃən] n. ①决定；确定；测定；限定: a matter for ~ by the departments concerned 应由有关部门决定的事情 / the ~ of the meaning of a word 词义的确定 ②决心: a written statement of ~ 决心书 / a man of ~ 有决断力的人 ③(血液等向某一点)涌集的倾向 ④【律】诉讼的终止；判决；产权的终止

determinative [di'tə:minətiv] I a. 有决定(或限定)作用的 II n. ①有决定(或限定)作用的东西 ②【语】限定词 ‖~ly ad. / ~ness n.

determine [di'tə:min] ❶ vt. ①决定；确定；测定；限定: ~ the velocity 测定速度 ②使决意: His advice ~d me to delay no more (或 ~d me against further delay). 他的劝告使我决定不再拖延。③【律】使终止 ❷ vi. ①决定；决心: We ~d on an early start. 我们决定尽早出发。②【律】终止

determined [di'tə:mind] a. ①决意的；已决定了的 ②坚决的: a ~ look 坚决的表情 ‖~ly ad. / ~ness n.

deterrent [di'terənt] I a. 制止的，威慑的 II n. 制止物，威慑物；制止因素，威慑因素: the "nuclear ~" "核威慑力量" ‖~ly ad.

detest [di'test] vt. 嫌恶，憎恶，痛恨

detestable [di'testəbl] a. 可恶的，可憎的 ‖~ness n. / **detestably** ad.

detestation [,di:tes'teiʃən] n. ①嫌恶，憎恶 ②憎恶的东西，极讨厌的东西 ‖be in ~ 被厌恶，被讨厌 / have (或 hold) in ~ 厌恶…，讨厌…

dethrone [di'θroun] vt. ①废黜 ②使(某人)从重要位置下台 ‖~ment n.

detonate ['detouneit] ❶ vi. 爆炸，起爆 ❷vt. 使爆炸 ‖a detonating cap 雷管，起爆帽 / a detonating cord (或 fuse) 导爆索，火药导线 / detonating powder 起爆药 / a detonating slab (为保护工事使弹提早爆炸的) 防弹墙 ‖**detonation** [,detou'neiʃən] n. 爆炸；(爆炸的)巨响；【机】(内燃机的)爆燃，爆鸣: detonation by influence【军】感应炸 / **detonative** ['detəneitiv] a.

detonator ['detouneitə] n. ①雷管，起爆管；起爆剂；炸药 ②【交】(浓雾时铁道上作信号用的)爆鸣器

detour, détour ['deituə] I n. 弯路，迂回路；迂回: make a ~ 迂回，绕道 / avoid ~s 避免走弯路 II ❶ vi. 迂回，绕道 ❷ vt. ①使绕道 ②绕过，兜过

detract [di'trækt] ❶ vt. ①[古]毁损，贬低，减损 (价值、名誉等) ②转移: ~ attention 转移注意力 ❷ vi. 毁损，贬低，减损 (from): That does not ~ from his merit. 那并没有贬低他的功绩。‖~ion [di'trækʃən] n. 减损，毁损，贬低 / ~ive a. 减损的，毁损的，贬低的 / ~or n. 毁损者

detriment ['detrimənt] n. ①损害，伤害: to the ~ of 有损于…，对…不利 / without ~ to 无损于… ②损害物；造成损害的根源

detrimental [,detri'mentl] I a. 有害的，不利的 (to) II n. ①有害的人 (或物) ②[俚]不受欢迎的求婚者 ‖~ly ad.

devastate ['devəsteit] vt. ①使荒芜，破坏，劫掠，蹂躏 ②压倒 ‖**devastation** [,devəs'teiʃən] n. / **dèvastative** a. / **devastator** n. 破坏者，蹂躏者，劫掠者

develop [di'veləp] ❶ vt. ①(逐步)展开(情节、音乐主题、方程式等): ~ an argument point by point 逐步展开论点 ②发展，发扬；发挥 ③开发(资源、矿山等)；开辟利用(土地等) ④使成长(或生长)；使发达: Warm rains and summer suns ~ the plants. 和暖的雨水和夏日的阳光促使植物生长。⑤使(颜色等)显现；【摄】显(影)，冲洗 ⑥(逐步)显现出；产生: the symptoms of consumption 出现肺病的症状 / Don't let your children ~ a tendency to an easy life. 别让你的孩子养成好逸恶劳的习惯。❷ vi. ①发展: Things ~ ceaselessly. 事物总是发展的。/ a ~ing country 发展中的国家 ②生长，发育；产生 ③(逐步)显现出来 ‖~able a. 可发展的；可开发的；可显(影)的 / ~er n. ①开发者 ②【摄】显影剂；【化】显色剂 ‖~ed dye【化】显色染料 / de'veloping-'out paper【摄】显象纸

development [di'veləpmənt] *n.* ①展开;【音】展开(部) ②发展;进展: the latest ~s in foreign affairs 外交上最近的发展 ③开发,开辟: a ~ area [英]失业严重地区;政府鼓励工业投资的地区 ④生长,成长;进化;发达 ⑤【摄】显影

deviate ['di:vieit] I ❶ *vi.* 背离,偏离: ~ *from* the right path (main theme) 离开正路(主题) / ~ *from* the principle (rule) 违背原则(规则) / Take care not to ~. 当心不要出偏差。❷ *vt.* 使背离,使偏离 II *a.* 脱离社会常轨的 III *n.* 脱离(社会)常轨的人 ||**deviator** *n.* 偏离正路的人

deviation [,di:vi'eiʃən] *n.* ①背离,偏离;偏向,偏差: guard against "Left" and Right ~s 防止"左"倾和右倾的偏向 ②【数】偏差数,离差: mean square ~ 均方差 ③【海】(故意而且不必要的)绕航;罗盘偏差,自差 ④(仪表上指针的)漂移 ⑤【生】(个体发育的变异中的)离差

device [di'vais] *n.* ①设计,计划;方法,手段: try various ~s to do sth. 多方设法做某事 ②谋略,策略;诡计: employ all kinds of base ~s 采用各种卑劣手段 ③[复]意志,心愿 ④发明物(特定用处的)器械,装置,设备,仪表,器件: a safety ~ 安全装置 / a nuclear ~ 核装置(如原子弹) / a pick-up ~ 拾音器,拾波器; 电视摄象管 / a rocket-propelled ~ 火箭推进器 ⑤(装饰性)图案,纹章;(纹章等上面的)题铭 ||**leave sb. to his own** ~s 听任某人自行其是,对某人不加干涉

devil ['devl] I *n.* ①魔鬼,恶魔 ②[the D-] 魔王,撒旦 (=Satan) ③恶棍 ④精力旺盛的人;无所顾忌的人 ⑤可怜的家伙(常与 poor 连用) ⑥恶兽,猛兽 ⑦(贪欲等邪恶的)化身: the ~ of greed 十足的贪婪鬼 ⑧(受律师、作家等雇用的)助手: a printer's ~ 印刷所学徒 ⑨[纺](破布等的)扯碎机;打稻纱头机 ⑩加有辛辣调味品的菜肴 ⑪难事; 难以操纵(或控制)的东西 ⑫[气]小尘暴,尘旋风 (=dust ~) ⑬ [the ~] [口]究竟(同who, how, why, where, what 等连用): Who the ~ is he? 他究竟是谁? II (devil(l)ed; devil(l)ing) ❶ *vt.* ①折磨,嘲弄,激怒 ②用辛辣调味品烤(肉等) ③(用扯碎机)扯碎(破布) ❷ *vi.* 做律师(或作家等)的助手 ||a ~'s 讨厌的…,异常的…,有趣的…: a ~'s darning needle 蜻蜓 / be in a ~ of a hole 处境很困难 / be the ~ 极度困难; 是讨厌(或麻烦)的事物 / between the ~ and the deep sea 进退维谷 / ~ a one 一个也没有 / give the ~ his due 公平对待,一视同仁;平心而论 / go to the ~ ①堕落,毁灭 ②滚开,见鬼去 / He that sups with the ~ must have a long spoon. [谚]和坏人打交道必须提高警惕。/ like the ~ 象什么似地,猛烈地: He is running like the ~. 他拚命地奔跑。/ Needs must when the ~ drives. 情势所迫,只好如此。/ paint the ~ blacker than he is (说到自己所不喜欢的人或物时)过甚其词 / play the ~ with 弄糟…,有害于…;使失败 / Pull ~, pull baker! (拔河等时鼓励双方的用语)大

家加油,加油! / raise the ~ ①兴妖作怪 ②起骚动;弄得非常热闹 / say the ~'s paternoster 发牢骚,嘀咕 / see the ~ [俚]喝醉 / serve the ~ 做坏事 / Talk of the ~ and he will appear. [谚]说到某人,某人就到。/ the ~ among the tailors ①吵闹,乱哄哄 ②一种烟火 / the ~ and all 一切坏事 / the ~ on two sticks 扯铃,空竹 / the ~'s advocate 见 advocate / the ~'s book(s) (或 picture book) 纸牌 / the ~'s tattoo 手指(或脚)的不停的敲响 / The ~ take the hindmost. [谚]落在后头,只好吃亏。/ the ~ to pay 今后的麻烦,可怕的后果 / to beat the ~ [美俚][作状语用]又快又猛地 / when the ~ is blind 当魔鬼变瞎时(指永不可能) / whip the ~ round the stump (或 post) 规避,取巧;自欺欺人 / Young saints, old ~s. 见 saint ||~dom *n.* 魔界;魔鬼的支配力(或地位、身分等) ||~'-box *n.* [口]电子计算机 / ~-,dodger *n.* [俚]牧师,教士(尤指随军牧师) / ~ dog [美]海军陆战队人员 / ~fish *n.* ①蝠鲼属鱼,蝠鲼(一种大型的虹鱼) ②头足类动物;章鱼 ③鮟鱇鱼 / ~-may-care *n.* 不顾一切的,无法无天的 ②怡然自得的 ③轻率的,漫不经心的 / ~'s-bones [复] *n.* [俚]骰子 / water【化】废液 / ~wood *n.* [植]美洲木犀

devilish ['devliʃ] I *a.* ①魔鬼似的,凶暴的;穷凶极恶的 ②精力旺盛的 ③可恶的,该咒骂的 ④异常的,非常的;过分的: in a ~ hurry 匆促之极 II *ad.* [口]非常,极;过分地 ||~ly *ad.* / ~ness *n.*

devious ['di:vjəs] *a.* ①远离大路的,僻远的,偏僻的 ②迂回的,曲折的 ③不定向移动的: a ~ breeze 方向不定的微风 ④离开正道的,误入歧途的,错误的 ⑤不光明正大的,不正当的; 狡猾的 ||~ly *ad.* / ~ness *n.*

devise [di'vaiz] I *vt.* ①设计,发明;想出计划: a new machine 发明新机器 / ~ how to do sth. 计划如何做某事 ②图谋 ③【律】遗嘱赠与(不动产) II *n.* 遗赠;遗赠的财产;遗赠财产的遗嘱(或条款) ||**devisable** *a.* ①能设想的, 能计划的 ②能遗赠的 / **devisee** [,devi'zi:, divai'zi:] n. 【律】受遗赠者 / ~r *n.* 设计者,发明者,计划者 / **devisor** [,devi'zɔ:, di'vaizɔ:] *n.* 【律】遗赠者

devitalize, devitalise [di:'vaitəlaiz] *vt.* ①使失去生命,使失去生命力 ②使伤元气,使衰弱 ||**devitalization** [di:,vaitəlai'zeiʃən] *n.*

devoid [di'vɔid] *a.* [常作表语]缺乏,没有 (of): be ~ of common sense 缺乏常识

devolution [,di:və'lju:ʃən] *n.* ①(责任、权利等的)转移; 授权代理;(中央对地方)权力下放 ②【生】退化

devolve [di'vɔlv] ❶ *vt.* 转移,移交 ❷ *vi.* ①被移交 ②流(或滚)向前(或向下)

devote [di'vəut] *vt.* 把…专用(to): ~ every effort to finding the principal contradiction 用全力找出主要矛盾 ||~ oneself to 献身于;致力于

devoted [di'voutid] *a.* ①献身…的;专心于…的;专用于…的 (to): a magazine ~ to children's literature 儿童文学刊物 ②虔诚的;热心的;忠诚的,忠实的: a ~ friend 忠实的朋友 ③慈爱的;恩爱的 ‖~ly *ad.* / ~ness *n.*

devotee [,devou'ti:] *n.* ①信徒(尤指宗教信徒) ②热心之士;爱好者: a ~ of music 爱好音乐者

devotion [di'vouʃən] *n.* ①献身;忠诚,忠实;热心,专心: ~ to duty 忠于职守 ②热爱 ③【宗】信仰,虔诚;礼拜;[复]祈祷

devour [di'vauə] *vt.* ① 狼吞虎咽似地吃 ② 吞没;毁灭: The fire ~ed the forest. 大火烧毁了森林。③挥霍,耗尽(财产等) ④贪看,贪听;盯着看: ~ a book 贪婪地读一本书 ⑤吸引,吸住: be ~ed by curiosity 心中充满好奇 ‖~ the way [诗](马等)兼程急进 ‖~ingly [di'vauəriŋli] *ad.* 吞灭似地;贪婪地

devout [di'vaut] *a.* ①虔诚的,虔敬的 ② 诚恳的: ~ thanks 恳切的感谢 ‖~ly *ad.* / ~ness *n.*

dew [dju:] I *n.* ①露,露水: The grass is wet with ~. 草为露水沾湿。②露水一样的东西(如泪水、汗等) ③[总称]植物在蒸腾作用中生成的小水珠 ④(象露水一样的)纯洁,清新;清新的气氛: a lad in the ~ of his youth 朝气蓬勃的小伙子 II ❶ *vt.* (露水等)弄湿 ❷ *vi.* 结露水: It is beginning to ~. 在结露水了。‖'~berry *n.* 悬钩子属植物,悬钩子;悬钩子属植物的果实 / '~claw *n.* 【动】(狗等脚上不与地面接触的无机能的)残留趾;悬蹄 / '~drop *n.* 露珠 / '~fall *n.* 结露;(黄昏)起露的时候 / '~lap *n.* (牛等动物颈部)下垂的皮肉 / ~ point【物】露点 / pond [英](山丘上天然或人造的)露池 / '~ret *vt.* 把(麻等)放在露水下湿润 / ~ worm (适于作鱼饵用的)蚯蚓

dewy ['dju:i] *a.* ① 带露水的;露水的;似露的 ②[诗]纯洁的;清新的: a ~ slumber 甜睡 ‖'~-eyed *a.* 显示天真和信任的

dexterity [deks'teriti] *n.* ①灵巧,敏捷(指身、手) ②聪明,伶俐 ③惯用右手

dexterous ['dekstərəs] *a.* ①(身、手)灵巧的,敏捷的 ②聪明的,伶俐的,机警的 ③用右手的 ‖~ly *ad.* / ~ness *n.*

diabolic(al) [,daiə'bolik(əl)] *a.* 恶魔的;恶魔似的;凶暴的 ‖diabolically *ad.*

diagnose ['daiəgnouz] ❶ *vt.* ①诊断(疾病): The doctor ~d the illness as pneumonia. 医生诊断这病为肺炎。② 断定…的原因(或性质);断定: ~ the pupil's reading difficulties 找出学生阅读上困难的原因 ❷ *vi.* 诊断;判断

diagnosis [,daiəg'nousis] ([复] diagnoses [,daiəg-'nousi:z]) *n.* ①【医】诊断(法): make a ~ 作出诊断 / an erroneous ~ 误诊 / differential ~ 鉴别诊断 ②[生](分类学上的)特征简述 ③调查分析,判断: according to sb.'s ~ of the circumstances 按照某人对情况的判断

diagonal [dai'ægənl] I *a.* ① 对角线的; 对顶的 ②斜的;斜纹的: ~ cloth 斜纹织物 II *n.* 【数】对角线,对顶线 ②斜纹符号(表示"或"、"每";如 A and/or B "A和B"或"A或B",又如 100 *li*/hour 每小时一百里) ③斜行,斜列 ④斜行物;斜纹织物 ‖~ly *ad.*

diagram ['daiəgræm] I *n.* 图解;图表;简图;(曲)线图;示图: draw a ~ 绘图表,作图解 II (dia-gram(m)ed; diagram(m)ing) *vt.* 用图解法表示

dial ['daiəl] I *n.* ①日晷 ②表面,钟面;罗盘面板;(仪表等)的标度盘,刻度盘 ③转盘;(自动电话机的)拨号盘。~ tone【讯】拨号音 ④(收音机的)调谐度盘;(机器的)调节控制盘 ⑤[矿]矿用罗盘 ⑥[俚]脸 II (dial(l)ed; dial(l)ing) *vt. & vi.* ①用日晷测量;用标度盘测量 ②拨(电话号码),打电话(给…) ③调(收音机电台) ④转动调节控制盘来控制(机器) ‖~ plate 表面,钟面;罗盘面板 / ~ telephone 自动电话

dialect ['daiəlekt] *n.* ①地方话,方言,土语: the Shanghai ~ 上海话 / a ~ ballad 方言民谣 ②[语]语支: English is a West Germanic ~. 英语是西日耳曼语的一支。③某一职业(或集团)人员的用语: the ~ of atomic physicists 原子物理学家的通用语 ④(某人的)语调;惯用语

dialog(ue) ['daiələg] I *n.* ①对话体(作品): a philosophical essay written in ~ 用对话体写的哲学论文 ②对话;交换意见: a ~ between two states 两国对话 ③(小说、戏剧中的)对白 II (dialogued; dialoguing) ❶ *vi.* 对话 ❷ *vt.* 用对话表达 ‖dialogic [,daiə'lodʒik] *a.* 对话(体)的 / dialogist [dai'ælədʒist] *n.* 对话者;对话体文章的作者

diameter [dai'æmitə] *n.* ① 直径, 对径, 径: the inside (outside) ~ 内(外)径 ②透镜放大的倍数: a microscope magnifying 2,000 ~s 放大二千倍的显微镜

diamond ['daiəmənd] I *n.* ①金刚石,金刚钻,钻石: black ~ 黑金刚石,墨玉;[喻]煤 / ~ spar【矿】刚玉 ②人造金刚石;象金刚石的物质 ③划玻璃用的钻刀 ④菱形;(纸牌)方块,一张方块牌 ⑤(垒球、棒球的)内场;球场 ⑥[印]钻石体活字(4¹/₂点的活字) II *vt.* 饰钻石于;好象用钻石把…装饰起来 ‖a rough ~ (或 a ~ in the rough) ①未经加工的天然金刚石 ②浑金璞玉;外粗内秀的人 / ~ cut 棋逢敌手;以智胜智 ‖~ anniversary =~ jubilee ①.具有菱纹的 *n.* ①衲脊蛇(一种背部有菱纹斑的北美大毒蛇) ②菱纹背泥龟 ③菱纹背蛾 / ~ field 石产地 / ~ jubilee 六十周年(有时指七十五周年)纪念 / ~ point ①钻石刻刀 ②[交]铁轨菱形交叉处 / ~ wedding 结婚六十年 (有时指七十五年)纪念

diaphanous [dai'æfənəs] *a.* ①(织物等)透明的 ②精致的,轻妙的 ‖~ly *ad.* / ~ness *n.*

diaphragm ['daiəfræm] *n.* ①【解】膈,隔膜;隔膜 ③【动】(无脊椎动物的)横隔板;【植】(茎内的)横

隔膜　④【物】光阑，光圈　⑤【讯】(电话机等的)膜片；振动膜　‖~atic [,daiəfræg'mætik] a.

diarrh(o)ea [,daiə'riə] n. 【医】腹泻: have ~ 泻肚 / dysenteric ~ 痢疾性腹泻‖**diarrh(o)eic** [,daiə'ri:ik], **diarrh(o)etic** [,daiə'retik], **~l** a. 腹泻的

diary ['daiəri] n. 日记；日记簿: keep a ~ 记日记(指有此习惯) / a pocket ~ 袖珍日记簿 / a ~ for instruction 教学日记

diatribe ['daiətraib] n. 谩骂；讽刺

dice [dais] I die² 的复数 II ([复] dice(s) n. ①骰子；掷骰赌博: play ~ 掷骰子 ②(骰子形)小方块 III ❶ vt. ①将(菜等)切成小方块，将…切成丁: ~d chicken 鸡丁 ②用骰子形花纹装饰: ~d leather 有小方块花纹的皮 ③掷骰子输掉(away); 因掷骰子使(某人)处于(into): John ~d himself into debt. 约翰因掷骰子而负了债。❷ vi. 掷骰子‖**load the** ~ (**against sb.**) (对某人)使用灌铅骰子；[喻]用不正当手段占(某人)便宜 / no ~ 没有用‖**~y** a. [英口]冒险的，投机的

dice

dicky ['diki] a. [英俚]站不稳的，软弱的；靠不住的

dictaphone ['diktəfoun] n. ①(供速记员用的)口述录音机 ②录音电话机

dictate I [dik'teit] ❶ vt. ①口述，使听写: ~ a letter to a typist 向打字员口授信稿 ②命令；支配 ❷ vi. ①口述，口授: The teacher ~d to a class. 教师给一班学生做听写。②命令；支配: refuse to be ~d to 拒绝按别人意旨行事 II ['dikteit] n. [常用复]命令；支配

dictation [dik'teiʃən] n. ①口述，听写: write at sb.'s ~ 照某人的口述写 / take the ~ of 记录…的口授 / take down from ~ 按口授笔录 / We have ~ today. 我们今天要听写了。/ Hand in your ~s, please. 请把你们的听写交来。②命令；支配

dictator [dik'teitə] n. ①独裁者；专政者 ②口述者，口授者

dictatorial [,diktə'tɔ:riəl] a. ①独裁的；专政的 ②专横傲慢的‖**~ly** ad.

dictatorship [dik'teitəʃip] n. 专政

diction ['dikʃən] n. ①措词，用词风格；词令 ②(歌唱中的)发音；发音法

dictionary ['dikʃənəri] n. 词典，字典: consult a ~ 查词典 / Look up (for) the word in the ~. 这个词查一查词典吧。/ a style 学究气的文体 / ~ English 学究气的英语‖ a **walking** (或 living) ~ 活词典；知识广博的人

did [did] do¹ 的过去式

didactic(al) [di'dæktik(əl), dai'dæktik(əl)] a. 教训的，教导的，说教的‖**didactically** ad.

didn't ['didnt] =did not

die¹ [dai] (died; dying) ❶ vi. ①死: To ~ for the people is a glorious death! 为人民而死，虽死犹荣 / ~ a martyr at one's post 以身殉职 / ~ young 夭折 / ~ of illness (hunger, cold) 病(饿，冻)死 / ~ by violence 横死 / ~ through neglect 因无人照顾抚养而死 / Oh, I'm dying of laughing. (夸张用语)啊，笑死我啦! ②(草木)枯萎，雕谢(back, down) ③[喻]灭亡 ④变弱；平息；消失；熄灭(away, down, out) ⑤漠然不受影响(to): ~ to shame 恬不知耻 ⑥[用进行时态]渴望，切望: I'm dying for (或 to have) a drink. 我口渴得要命。❷ vt. [后接同源名词]死: ~ a glorious death 光荣死去‖ by one's own hand 自杀 / ~ game 至死不屈 / ~ hard ①难断气 ②顽固得很 / ~ in harness 工作时死去 / ~ in (one's) bed 因病(或因年老)而死去 / ~ in one's boots (或 shoes) 不死在床上，横死，暴死 / ~ off 相继死去直至死光 / ~ on the vine (计划等)未能实现，中途夭折 / Never say ~! 不要气馁! ‖**~-a,way** a. 消沉的，颓丧的，憔悴的 n. (声音等的)逐渐消逝 / '**~hard** n. 顽固分子，死硬分子: the ~hards 顽固派，死硬派 / '**~-hard** a. 顽固的，死硬的 / '**~hardism** n. 顽固

die² [dai] ([复] dice [dais]) n. 骰子；骰子状物‖ as straight (或 true) as a ~ ①绝对真实；绝对可靠 ②非常老实 / The ~ is cast. [谚]木已成舟。(指事情已经决定，再也不能改变) / upon the ~ 在危急存亡的关头

die³ [dai] n. ①冲垫 ②钢型；印模；冲模；铆头模 ③螺丝钢板 ④[建]底座的墩身‖ ~ **casting** 压铸法 / '**~,sinker** n. 制模工；刻模机 / '**~stock** n. 【机】板牙铰手

diesel ['di:zəl] n. [常作 D-] ①内燃机(旧译狄赛尔内燃机)，柴油机 (=~ engine) ② 内燃机推动的车辆(或船只)‖**~-e'lectric** a. 柴油发电机的 / ~ **oil**, ~ **fuel** 柴油

diet¹ ['daiət] I n. 饮食，食物; (适合某种疾病的)特种饮食: a liquid ~ 流质饮食 / be on a ~ 进规定的饮食 / The doctor put the patient on a special ~. 医生给这个病人规定特别饮食。/ have a light ~ 吃容易消化的东西 II ❶ vt. 给(病人)指定饮食: The doctor has ~ed the patient strictly. 医生严格规定病人的饮食。❷ vi. 进规定的饮食，忌食，忌口

diet² ['daiət] n. (丹麦、日本等的)议会，国会‖**~al** a.

differ ['difə] vi. ①不同，相异(from): Chinese ~s greatly from English in pronunciation. 华语发音跟英语大不相同。②意见不同(或不一致): I'm afraid we shall have to ~. 恐怕我们只好保留不同的意见了。/ We ~ from (或 with) him on(或 about, upon) that question. 我们在那个问题上跟他意见不同。/ We ~ with you as to the precise meaning of this phrase. 对于这个短语的确切释义我们跟你看法不一致。‖**agree to ~** 各自保留不同意见(不再说服对方) / **beg to ~** 恕不同意

difference ['difrəns] **I** n. ①差异,差别: The ~s between manual labour and mental labour are diminishing. 体力劳动和脑力劳动的差别正在缩小。/ a quantitative ~ 数量上的差别 / a qualitative ~ 质量上的差别 / a ~ in character 性格上的差别 / make a world of ~ 有天壤之别 ② 不和,争论: eliminate ~s of opinion 消除意见分歧 ③【数】差,差额;差分: a ~ of two catties 两斤之差 / The ~ between 6 and 3 is 3. 六和三的差是三。/ ~ equation 差分方程 **II** vt. 区别 ‖**make a ~ between** 区别对待 / **make some (no)** ~ 有些 (没有) 关系,有些 (没有)影响: It makes no ~. 那没有关系。/ That makes no ~ to me. 那对我没有影响。/ **split the ~** 妥协,折中

different ['difrənt] a. ①差异的,不同的: qualitatively ~ contradictions 不同质的矛盾 / be ~ from (或 than, 或[英] to) 与…不同 ②各别,各种: A department store sells many ~ things. 百货公司出售各种各样的东西。/ Different trees bear ~ fruits. 什么样的树结什么样的果。③ [美][常作表语]异常的 ‖~**ly** ad.

differential [ˌdifə'renʃəl] **I** a. ①差别的,区别的: ~ diagnosis【医】鉴别诊断 ②特异的 ③微分的: ~ calculus【数】微分 (学) / ~ circuit【无】微分电路 / ~ equation【数】微分方程 ④【机】【物】差动的,差示的: ~ gear train 差动(或差速)齿轮系 / ~ thermometer 差示温度计 **II** n. ①[数]微分: partial (total) ~ 偏(全)微分 ②[机]差动;差速器,分速器 ③(铁路的)运费率差 ④差别,差异 ⑤(同一行业中熟练工和非熟练工的)工资级差 ‖~**ly** ad. ‖~ **rent** 级差地租

differentiate [ˌdifə'renʃieit] **❶** vt. ①区分,区别: ~ one variety from another 区别品种 ②使变异 ③使分化 ④【数】求…的微分 **❷** vi. ①区分,区别 ②变异,分化

difficult ['difikəlt] a. ①难的,困难的,艰难的: Nothing is ~ to a man who wills. 世上无难事,只怕有心人。/ The place is ~ of access. 这地方很难进去。/ bear the ~ days of the past in mind 牢记过去艰难的岁月 ②(人)难弄的: He is a ~ man to get on with. 他是个不易相处的人。‖~**ly** ad.

difficulty ['difikəlti] n. ①困难,艰难: Do you have (或 find) any ~ in understanding spoken English? 你听懂英语有困难吗? / in times of ~ 在遇困难时 / with ~ 困难地,艰难地 / without ~ 容易地,毫不费力地 ②难点,(一种具体的)困难 ③[常用复]困境(尤指经济拮据): the difficulties of English grammar 英语语法的难点 / overcome

difficulties (或 every ~) 克服种种困难 / be in (financial) difficulties 手头拮据 ③异议,反对 ‖**make difficulties** 留难;表示异议 (或反对) / **make no ~** (或 **make no difficulties**) 不留难;表示无异议(或不反对)

diffidence ['difidəns] n. ①缺乏自信 ②羞怯,胆怯 ③踌躇(指不敢申述自己的意见)

diffident ['difidənt] a. ①缺乏自信的 ②羞怯的,胆怯的 ③踌躇的 ‖~**ly** ad.

diffract [di'frækt] vt.【物】使衍射,使绕射: ~ed ray 衍射线 / ~ed wave 衍射波 ‖~**ion** [di'frækʃən] n.【物】衍射,绕射: ~ion grating 衍射光栅 / ~ion optics 衍射光学

diffuse[1] [di'fju:z] **❶** vt. ①使(热,气体等)散发;使扩散;使渗出 ②传播(知识等);散布(谣言等);普及 ③【物】使(光线)漫射: ~d light 漫射光 **❷** vi. ①散开,扩散;渗出 ②传播;散布 ③【物】漫射 ‖~**r** n. ①【物】漫射体 ②【机】扩散器;喷雾器 ③【化】浸提器;洗料池 ④【无】扬声器纸盆 ⑤传播者,散布者

diffuse[2] [di'fju:s] a. ①弥漫的,散开的,扩散的 ②(文章等)冗长的,噜苏的 ③漫射的 ④向各个方向移动的 ‖~**ly** ad. / ~**ness** n.

diffusion [di'fju:ʒən] n. ①散开,扩散,弥漫 ②(知识等)传布 ③冗长,噜苏 ④【化】渗滤 ⑤【物】漫射;光线在半透明物质中的传布 ⑥【摄】照片影象轮廓线的逐渐变淡

dig [dig] (dug [dʌg] 或[古] digged; digging) **❶** vt. ①掘(土),挖(洞,沟等): ~ a field for planting 翻土备种 / ~ a tunnel 掘地道 ②掘取(甘薯等),采掘(矿物) ③发掘,探究: ~ facts from historical documents 从历史文献中寻找事实 / ~ out the truth 发现真相 ④ 把(指尖等)戳进,插入; 戳: ~ one's spurs in (或 into) the horse's flanks 用靴刺刺马的侧腹(使马快跑) / ~ one's feet into the mud 把脚伸进烂泥 / ~ sb. in ribs 用肘碰碰某人胸口(暗示要他注意) ⑤[美俚]理解 ⑥[美俚]喜欢 ⑦[美俚]看,看到 **❷** vi. ①挖掘;发掘: ~ through a hill to make a tunnel 凿山筑隧道 / ~ for scientific data 搜集科学资料 ②[口]苦干,苦学 (at): ~ at a subject 钻研一门学科 ③[俚]居住,住宿 **II** n. ①挖掘;[口](考古)挖掘的地点;出土物 ②刺,戳 ③[口]挖苦: That was meant to be a ~ at me. 那是对我的挖苦。④ [美]刻苦钻研的学生 ⑤[美俚]私货among 匿处 ⑥[复][英口]宿处,住地 ‖~ **down** ①挖下去 ②掘倒 ③掏腰包 / ~ **in** ①掘土以掺进(肥料等) ②[口]专心致志地干起来 / ~ **into** ①挖到…里面去;钻研 ②用…的大部分;[口]吃去…的大部分 / ~ (**oneself**) **in** ①挖壕固守 ②[口]使自己站住脚 / ~ **out** ①掘出;挖掉: ~ oneself (或 one's way) out 掘出一条路使自己出来 ②发掘,发现 ③[美俚]逃跑;匆匆走掉 / ~ **up** ①掘起;挖出: ~ up river (pond) silt 挖河 (塘) 泥 ②(经调查研究)发现 ③开垦(荒地等)

digest [di'dʒest, dai'dʒest] **I** **❶** vt. ①消化(食物),

助消化 ②领会,领悟,融会贯通: ~ a book 领会一本书 / ~ the important points in the book 领会书中要点 ③整理(资料、材料等),做…的摘要 ④忍受(侮辱等) ⑤【化】蒸煮(某物),煮解(某物);加热浸提(某物)(指用加热法从…中抽提出可溶性部分) ❷ vi. 消化: This food ~s well. 这食物容易消化。 II ['daidʒest] n. ①摘要;文摘 ②(法规等的)汇集;[the D-]《学说汇纂》(公元六世纪东罗马皇帝查士丁尼命令汇编的法学家学说摘录,共五十卷) ‖~er n. ①做摘要者 ②蒸煮器,蒸煮锅;加热浸漫器

digestion [di'dʒestʃən, dai'dʒestʃən] n. ①消化(作用);消化力: food that is easy (difficult) to ~ 易(难)消化的食物 / have a good (poor) ~ 消化力强(弱) ②领悟 ③【化】蒸煮(作用),煮解;加热浸提 ④【微】菌致分解(污水处理中, 由厌氧细菌分解有机物并释放出可燃性气体) ‖**have the ~ of an ostrich** 消化力强

digestive [di'dʒestiv, dai'dʒestiv] I a. 消化的, 有消化力的;助消化的: the ~ system 消化系统 II n. 助消化药, 消化促进剂;化脓药膏

digger ['digə] n. ①挖掘者;挖掘机;挖掘器, 挖掘机;(挖掘机上的)挖斗 ②矿工(尤指采矿矿工): coal ~s 采煤工 ③[D-] 挖植物根作食物的美国印第安人 ④[俚]澳洲人 ⑤[美俚]扒手 ⑥[美俚]为金钱而与男人交友谈情(或结婚)的女人 ⑦地蜂,穴蜂 (=~ wasp)

digging ['digiŋ] n. ①挖掘, 采掘 ②[复]矿区, 矿山(尤指金矿) ③[复]发掘物 ④[复][俚]房屋, 寓所, 住处(原指金矿工人的宿营地)

digit ['didʒit] n. ①手指, 足趾 ②一指宽的长度单位(相当于 3/4 吋) ③数字(0 到 9 中的任一数字);位(数): The number 1970 contains four ~s. 1970 这个数目是四位数。 / binary ~ 【数】二进制数字;二进制数位 ④【天】太阳(或月亮)直径的 1/12 (作为测定日食、月食的食分的单位)

dignify ['dignifai] vt. ①使有尊严, 授…以荣誉, 使高贵 ②把…夸大为

dignitary ['digniteri] n. 职位高的人(尤指宗教方面的)

dignity ['digniti] n. ①尊贵, 高贵 ②(举止、态度的)庄严, 尊严, 端庄 ③高位, 显职 ④职位高的人(尤指宗教方面的) ‖**beneath sb.'s ~** 不合某人的身分(或地位) / **stand upon (或 on) one's ~** 坚持受到应有的礼遇;保持尊严(拒绝做有失身分的事)

digress [dai'gres] vi. 扯开, 离开主题 (from): ~ from the main subject 说(或写)到主题以外

digression [dai'greʃən] n. 离题; 枝节话: return from the ~ 言归正传

dike[1] [daik] I n. ①堤, 堤防, 坝 ②沟, 渠, 排水道 ③防护栏, 障碍物 ④【地】岩墙, 岩脉 II vt. ①筑堤防护, 用堤围绕 ②开沟泄(水) ③[美]使穿得漂漂亮亮 (out, up)

dike[2] [daik] n. [美俚]搞同性关系的女人

dilapidate [di'læpideit] ❶ vt. ①使(部分)损毁 ②[古]浪费, 乱花(钱财等) ❷ vi. (部分)损毁 ‖~d a. (房屋等)坍坏了的,(器具、衣服等)破旧了的

dilate [dai'leit] ❶ vt. 使膨胀, 使扩大: with ~d eyes 张大了眼睛 ❷ vi. ①膨胀, 扩大 ②详述, 铺张 (upon): ~ upon a subject 详述某题目

dilatory ['dilətəri] a. 拖拉的, ‖**dilatorily** ['dilətərili; 美 ‚dilə'tɔ:rili] ad. / **dilatoriness** n.

dilemma [di'lemə] n. ①【逻】二难推理, 两刀论法 ②窘境, 困境, 进退两难: be in a ~ 处在进退两难的境地 ‖**on the horns of a ~** 见 horn ‖~**tic** [‚dilə'mætik] a.

dilettante [‚dili'tænti] I ([复] dilettantes 或 dilettanti [‚dili'tænti:]) n. ①艺术爱好者 ②(艺术或科学方面)半瓶醋的业余爱好者, 浅薄的涉猎者 II a. 外行的;浅薄的 ‖**dilettantish** a. (在艺术或科学方面) 只是弄着玩的; 作浅薄涉猎的

diligence[1] ['dilidʒəns] n. 勤勉, 勤奋, 用功, 努力

diligence[2] ['diliʒɑ̃:ns] n. 公共马车, 驿车

diligent ['dilidʒənt] a. 勤勉的, 勤奋的, 用功的, 孜孜不倦的: be ~ in one's work 工作勤奋 ‖~**ly** ad.

dillydally ['dilidæli] vi. [口]磨蹭, 吊儿郎当地磨时间

dilute [dai'lju:t] I vt. ①冲淡, 稀释: ~ wine with water 用水把酒冲淡 ②(用搀杂的方法)削弱 II a. 稀释的, 淡的: a ~ acid 稀酸, 淡酸 ‖**dilutee** [‚dailju'ti:] n. 担负熟练工人一部分工序的非熟练工人 / ~**r** n. 稀释剂

dilution [dai'lju:ʃən] n. ①冲淡, 稀释 ②冲淡物, 稀释物 ③【化】稀度; 浓度

dim [dim] I (dimmer, dimmest) a. ①不明亮的, 微暗的;暗淡的: the ~ light of an oil lamp 暗淡的油灯光 ②模糊的, 朦胧的, 不清楚的: the ~ outline of a ship 轮船的模糊的轮廓 / ~ sounds of a distant bell 远处隐约的钟声 / ~ memories of one's childhood 对于童年时代的模糊记忆 / His eyesight is getting ~. 他的视力开始模糊。 ③无光泽的 ④[口]迟钝的 ⑤悲观的, 怀疑的: take a ~ view of 对…抱悲观的看法 II (dimmed; dimming) vt. & vi. (使)变暗淡; (使)变模糊; (使)失去光泽 III n. ①汽车停车时用的小灯 ②车辆前灯的短焦距光束 ‖~**ly** ad. / ~**ness** n. ‖~**out** n. (防止敌方空袭等的)半对火管制 / '~**wit** n. [美俚]笨蛋, 傻子 / '~-'**witted** a. 笨的, 傻的

dime [daim] n. (美国和加拿大的)一角银币;数目极小的钱: a ~ store [美]出售五分、一角小商品的小店; 出售廉价商品的小店 / a ~ museum [美]廉价低级的展览馆 ‖**a ~ a dozen** [口]一角一个;多得很

dimension [di'menʃən] I n. ①尺寸; 尺度, 线度 ②【数】维(数), 度(数), 元: of one ~ 一度的; 线性的 / of two ~s 二度的;平面的 / of three ~s

（长、宽、高）三度的；立体的 ③【物】量纲，因次 ④ [复]面积；容积；大小：take the ~s of a field 丈量一块田地 / a building of great ~s 巨大的建筑物 ⑤范围；方面：uncover a new ~ of actuality 揭示出现实中新的一面 **II** *vt.* ①使形成所需的尺寸 ②在…上标出尺寸 ‖~**al** *a.*

diminish [di'miniʃ] **❶** *vt.* ①减少，减小，缩减：the law of ~ing returns 报酬递减律 ②削弱…的权势；降低…的声誉 ③【音】把(音程)减半音：~ed fifth 减五度 / ~ed seventh 减七和弦 ④【建】使成尖顶 **❷** *vi.* ①变少，缩小 ②【建】成尖顶 ‖~**able** *a.* 可缩减的；可削弱的

diminutive [di'minjutiv] **I** *a.* ①小的，小型的 ②【语】指小的 ③昵称的，爱称的 **II** *n.* ①【语】指小词(如 booklet 为 book 的指小词) ②微小的东西(或人) ③昵称，爱称 ‖~**ly** *ad.* / ~**ness** *n.*

dimple ['dimpl] **I** *n.* ①酒窝，笑窝，靥 ②微凹；涟漪，波纹 **II** **❶** *vt.* 使起微凹；使起涟漪 **❷** *vi.* 现酒窝；起涟漪 ‖**dimply** *a.*

din [din] **I** *n.* 闹音，喧声，嘈扰声 **II** (dinned; dinning) **❶** *vt.* ①以喧声扰(人) ②絮絮不休地说：~ sth. into sb.'s ears 对某人絮絮不休地说某事 **❷** *vi.* ①喧闹 ②絮絮不休

dine [dain] **❶** *vi.* 吃饭，进餐，就餐：~ on (或 upon, off) fish and eggs 吃鱼和蛋 **❷** *vt.* ①招待…吃饭，宴请 ②(房间、桌子)可容…吃饭：A square table usually ~s eight persons. 一张方桌通常容八人就餐。‖~ *and wine* (款待…) 吃喝 / ~ *out* 外出吃饭 / ~ *with Duke Humphrey* 不吃饭，枵腹 ‖~**r** *n.* ①吃饭的(客)人，就餐者 ②(火车的)餐车 ③餐车式的饭店

dingdong ['diŋ'dɔŋ] **I** *n.* ①丁当(声)，丁冬(声)(尤指钟、铃、开饭铜锣声) **II** *a.* ①丁当作响的 ②[口](比赛等)双方不相上下的，交错领先的 **III** *ad.* ①丁当作响地 ②起劲地：fall to work ~ 起劲地干了起来 **IV** **❶** *vi.* ①发丁当声 ②令人厌烦地重复一种声音(或动作)；唠叨 **❷** *vt.* 多次重复给…加深印象

dingey, dinghy ['diŋgi] *n.* ①东印度的小船 ②军舰上的小艇；救生橡皮筏;(附属大船的)供应小船

dingey[1] ['diŋgi] *n.* =dingey, dinghy

dingy[2] ['diŋdʒi] *a.* ①暗黑的 ②脏的；失去光泽的 ③褴褛的，邋遢的

dining ['dainiŋ] *n.* 吃饭，进(正)餐 ‖~ **car** 餐车 / ~ **hall** 餐厅 / ~ **room** 餐室，食堂 / ~ **table** 餐桌

dinner ['dinə] *n.* ①正餐：early ~ 午时的正餐 / late ~ 晚上的正餐 / Have you had ~ yet? 你吃过饭吗? / be at ~ 在吃饭 / ask sb. to ~ 请人吃饭 / It's time for ~. 是吃饭的时候了。②宴会：a state ~ 国宴 / give a ~ for (或 in honour of) 设宴招待某人 ‖*eat one's ~s* [英]学法律 ‖~ **bell** 吃饭铃(或钟) / ~ **hour** 吃饭(指午餐或晚餐)时间 / ~ **jacket** (没有燕尾的)晚礼服 / ~ **pail** (工人用的)饭盒子 /

party 宴会；聚餐会 / ~ **set**, ~ **service** (一套)餐具 / ~ **table** 餐桌 / ~ **time** = ~ **hour** / **wag(g)on** (有脚轮的)食品输送架

dinosaur ['dainəsɔ:] *n.* 恐龙(古生物) ‖~**ian** [,dainə'sɔ:riən] *n.* 恐龙 *a.* 恐龙的；像恐龙的

dinosaur

dint [dint] **I** *n.* ①陷痕，凹痕 ②[古]打，击 **II** *vt.* 把…打出凹痕 ‖*by ~ of* 由于；凭借：They overfulfilled their task *by ~ of* hard and skilful work. 他们苦干加巧干，超额完成了任务。

diocese ['daiəsis] *n.* 主教管区

dip [dip] **I** (dipped; dipping) **❶** *vt.* ①浸；蘸；…浸入又取出：~ a pen into the ink 拿钢笔蘸墨水 / ~ a bucket into the well 把吊桶放入井内(吊水) / ~ one's hand into the bag 把手伸进袋里(掏东西) ②浸染；(浸烛芯于融蜡中)制造(蜡烛) ③汲出，舀取：~ out (或 up) congee with a ladle 用勺舀粥 ④把…下降后即行升起：~ the flag in salute (对另一船舰)扬旗致敬,行点旗礼 ⑤【宗】为…施浸礼 ⑥把…放在杀虫液里浸洗 ⑦[口][常用被动语态]使欠款：be slightly *dipped* 负少量的债 ⑧[美俚]扒窃 **❷** *vi.* ①浸一浸 ②下沉，下降；【空】(飞机在上升前)骤降 ③倾斜 ④汲取，舀，掏：~ into one's pocket *for* sth. 往衣袋里掏某物 ⑤翻阅一下，浏览；稍加探究(into)：~ *into* a book 浏览一本书 / ~ *into* a problem 对某一问题稍加探究 **II** *n.* ①浸渍，蘸湿；泡(一泡)：have (或 take) a ~ in the sea 洗一场海水浴 ②舀取 ③(浸物体的)液体，溶液；洗羊的消毒水 ④倾斜，偏倾；下沉，下降：a ~ in price 价格下降 ⑤【空】飞机上升前的急降 ⑥蜡烛 ⑦【物】磁倾角 (=magnetic ~);【测】俯角 ⑧(双杠上的)双臂屈伸 ⑨[美俚]扒手 ‖~ *into one's purse* 乱花钱 ‖'~-**dye** *vt.* 浸染(针织物) / ~ **needle** 【物】磁倾针；磁倾仪 / ~ **net** 小捞网，捞鱼网

diphtheria [dif'θiəriə] *n.* 【医】白喉(症) ‖~**l** *a.* 白喉的

diphthong ['difθɔŋ] *n.* 【语】①双元音，复合元音(如 oil 中的 [ɔi] 等) ②双元音的词(如 oil, doubt) ③元音连字(如 œ, æ) ‖~**al** [dif'θɔŋgəl] *a.* / ~**ize** ['difθɔŋgaiz] *vt.* 使双元音化

diploma [di'pləumə] *n.* ①（[复] diplomas 或 diplomata [di'pləumətə]）公文,文书 ②执照,特许证 ③毕业文凭;学位证书 ④奖状 ‖~ **mill** [美]滥发文凭的大学

diplomacy [di'pləuməsi] *n.* ①外交;外交手腕: shuttle ~ 穿梭外交 ②交际手段

diplomat ['dipləmæt] *n.* 外交家,外交官

diplomatic [,diplə'mætik] *a.* ①外交上的: establish ~ relations at the ambassadorial rank 建立大使级外交关系 / resume (sever) ~ relations 恢复(断绝)外交关系 / ~ immunity 外交豁免权 ②外交工作的: a ~ body (或 corps) 外交使团 / a ~ agent 外交代理人 ③外交手腕的;老练的,有策略的: a ~ way of dealing with a problem 处理问题的圆滑手段 ④古抄本的;不改真本原样的: a ~ edition 仿真本 / ~ evidence 文献上的证据

diplomatist [di'pləumətist] *n.* ①外交家,外交官 ②有外交手腕的人

dipper ['dipə] *n.* ①长柄勺;戽斗;(挖土机等的)铲斗 ②浸渍工人,浸制工人 ③【摄】显影液槽 ④【动】善于潜水的鸟(尤指河乌等) ⑤ [the D-] 【天】(大熊星座的)北斗七星(=the Big Dipper): the Little *Dipper* 小北斗(小熊星座的七颗主星) ⑥[宗]浸礼会会友

dire ['daiə] *a.* ①可怕的;悲惨的;灾难的,不幸的 ②极端的;急迫的: in ~ need of 极需… ‖~**ly** *ad.* / ~**ness** *n.*

direct¹ [di'rekt, dai'rekt] I *a.* ①径直的;直接的: be in ~ contact with sb. 与某人有直接联系 / ~ discourse【语】直接引语 ②直系的: a ~ ancestor 直系祖先(例如曾祖) / a ~ relative 直系亲属(例如父亲、儿子) ③直截了当的,直率的: a ~ way of speaking 直截了当的说话方式 ④正好的: the ~ opposite (或 contrary) 正好相反的东西 ⑤【天】自西向东运行的,顺行的: ~ motion 顺行 ⑥ (不用媒染剂)直接染色的 II *ad.* 径直地;直接地: translate ~ from the original 直接从原文译出 ‖~**ness** *n.* ‖~ **action** 直接行动(指罢工、商品抵制行动等) / ~ **current** 直流电(略作 D. C. 或 d. c.) / ~ **dye**【印染】直接染料 / ~ **method** (语言教学中的) 直接教学法 / ~ **primary** (**election**) (美国)由选民直接投票的预选 / ~ **proportion**【数】正比例 / ~ **tax** 直接税

direct² [di'rekt, dai'rekt] ❶ *vt.* ①指引 ②指导;导演: One's thinking ~s one's actions. 思想指导行动。③指挥;命令 ④把…对准某一目标(或方向): ~ one's eyes downward 使眼睛向下看 ⑤把(邮件等)寄至 (to): Please ~ the letter *to* my home address when I am away. 我不在时请把信寄到我家里。❷ *vi.* 指导;指挥

direction [di'rekʃən, dai'rekʃən] *n.* ①方向;方位;方面;范围: in all ~s (或 in every ~) 向四面八方;向各方面 / Those with book learning must develop in the ~ of practice. 有书本知识的人应该向实践方面发展。②趋向,倾向: the ~ of

popular sentiment 人心所向 / a new ~ in language teaching 语言教学的新倾向 ③指导;指挥;管理: work under the ~ of sb. 在某人指导下工作 ④[常用复]指示;用法说明: give ~s 发出指示 / ~s for use 用法说明 / Full ~s inside. 内附详细说明书。⑤ [古]（收件人的)姓名住址 (=address) ‖~ **finder**【无】测向器,无线电罗盘 / ~ **indicator**【空】方向指示器

directive [di'rektiv, dai'rektiv] I *n.* ①命令,指令,指示 ②[无]指挥仪,指挥机 II *a.* ①指示的,起指导作用的,管理的: ~ rules 规程 ②[无]有方向性的,定向的,指向的

directly [di'rektli, dai'rektli] I *ad.* ①径直地;直接地 ②直截了当地,直率地 ③正好地: ~ in the centre of the room 正好在房间的中心 ④马上,立即: I'll be there ~. 我马上就去。II [有时也读作 'drektli] *conj.* [英口]一当,一…(就…): He made for the door ~ he heard the knock. 一听到敲门声他就跑去开门了。

director [di'rektə, dai'rektə] *n.* ①指导者;处长,署长,局长,主任,总监: the ~ of a research institute 研究所所长 / the *Director* of the CIA (美国)中央情报局局长 ②理事;董事: a board of ~s 理事会;董事会 ③(戏剧、电影等的)导演;(乐队等的)指挥 ④【机】司动部分 ⑤【无】(天线)导向偶极子;引向器,导向器 ⑥[军]炮兵射击指挥仪: a ~ crew 瞄准手 ‖a ghostly ~ 听忏悔的神父 ‖~**ship** *n.* 指导者(或处长、董事等)的职位(或任期)

directorate [di'rektərit, dai'rektərit] *n.* ①指导者(或处长、董事、导演等)的职位 ②理事会;董事会

directory [di'rektəri, dai'rektəri] I *n.* ①姓名住址录;工商行名录: a telephone ~ 电话号码簿 ②[美]董事会 ③[宗]教堂的礼拜规则书 II *a.* 指导(性)的

dirge [də:dʒ] *n.* 挽歌,哀悼歌;庄重悲哀的乐曲

dirk [də:k] I *n.* 短剑,匕首 II *vt.* 用短剑刺

dirt [də:t] *n.* ①污物,污垢(如烂泥、灰尘等) ②泥土,松土;【矿】含金土(或沙): a ~ road [美]泥路 ③[古]没有价值的东西 ④肮脏;卑鄙;下流话,下流黄色的东西(如黄色小说、电影等) ⑤恶毒价伤的闲话 ⑥[美]秘密情报,真相 ⑦[美俚]钱 ‖as cheap as ~ 便宜透顶的 / dig ~ about sb. [美俚]讲某人的坏话 / do sb. ~ [美俚]用卑劣的手段中伤某人 / eat ~ 含垢忍辱 / fling (或 throw) ~ at sb. 谩骂某人,毁谤某人 / hit the ~ [美俚]①下火车;从开动的货车上跳下 ②(为躲避炸弹等)迅速卧倒,闪入邻近掩体 / pay ~ [美俚]想望的事物,有利可图的东西 / treat sb. like ~ 把某人看得一钱不值 / yellow ~ [蔑]黄金 ‖~ **bed**【建】泥土层 / ~ **cheap** 便宜透顶的(地) / '~-,**eating** *n.* 食土病 / ~ **farmer** [美口]自己动手种地的小农(别于 gentleman farmer) / ~ **track** *n.* 煤渣跑道(供摩托车比赛等用) / ~ **wag(g)on** [美]垃圾车

dirty ['də:ti] I *a.* ①脏的;弄脏的: ~ clothes 脏衣服 / a ~ copy【印】修改甚多的校样;涂改很多

(或字迹潦草、难以辨认)的原稿 / a ~ job 脏活 ②(伤口)感染的, 化脓的 ③卑鄙的: What a ~ business! 真卑鄙! / You ~ dog! 你这个卑鄙家伙! ④下流的, 黄色的 ⑤(气候)恶劣的; 暴风雨的; 雾深的: a ~ night 暴风雨之夜 ⑥(颜色)灰褐的; 不清的 ⑦(声音)沙哑的, 嘎嘎的 ⑧(原子弹、氢弹)含有大量放射性尘埃的 **II ❶** *vt.* ①弄脏, 沾污 ②毁谤, 中伤 **❷** *vi.* 变脏 ‖*~ work* ① 苦活; 吃力不讨好的工作 ② 卑鄙的勾当 / *do the ~ on sb.* [俚]用卑劣的手段中伤某人 / *give sb. a ~ look* 对某人瞪一眼 ‖*dirtily ad.* / *dirtiness n.* / *~ish a.* 有点儿脏的

disability [ˌdisəˈbiliti] *n.* ①无能, 无力; 伤残 ②【律】无资格

disable [disˈeibl] *vt.* ①使无能; 使伤残; 使失去斗力 ②【律】使无资格 ‖*~d a.* 残废的; 失去战斗力的: a ~d soldier 残废军人 / a ~d ship (plane) 不堪使用的军舰(飞机) / *~ment n.*

disabuse [ˌdisəˈbju:z] *vt.* 去除…的错误想法, 使省悟, 纠正: ~ sb. of a prejudice 去掉某人的偏见

disadvantage [ˌdisədˈva:ntidʒ] **I** *n.* ①不利; 条件 ②损害, 损失(指在名誉、信用、经济等方面) **II** *vt.* 使不利 ‖*at a ~* 处于不利地位 / *be taken at a ~* 被人乘隙攻击 / *to the ~ of* 对…不利

disadvantaged [ˌdisədˈva:ntidʒd] *a.* 社会地位低下的; 被剥夺了基本权利的; 生活条件差的

disadvantageous [ˌdisædva:nˈteidʒəs] *a.* ① 不利的 (to) ② 贬损的, 诽谤的 ‖*~ly ad.* / *~ness n.*

disaffected [ˌdisəˈfektid] *a.* (对政府等)不满的; 不忠的

disaffection [ˌdisəˈfekʃən] *n.* 不满; 不忠(尤指政治上的)

disagree [ˌdisəˈgri:] *vi.* ①意见不同, 不同意; 争执: I ~ with you about this. 对于这件事我跟你意见不同。②不一致, 不符: His conduct ~s with his words. 他言行不一。③(食物、天气等)不适合, 有害 (with) ‖*~ment n.*

disagreeable [ˌdisəˈgriəbl] **I** *a.* ①不合意的, 不爽快的, 讨厌的 ②难相处的, 脾气坏的 **II** *n.* [常用复]不愉快的事, 麻烦事 ‖*~ness n.* / *disagreeably ad.*

disallow [ˈdisəˈlau] *vt.* ①拒绝承认 ②不允许; 否决 ‖*~ance* [ˌdisəˈlauəns] *n.*

disappear [ˌdisəˈpiə] *vi.* ①不见, 失踪 ②消失, 消散 ‖*~ance* [ˌdisəˈpiərəns] *n.*

disappoint [ˌdisəˈpoint] *vt.* 使失望; 使(计划等)受挫折, 使(希望等)落空: be ~ed at hearing that . . . 听到…感到失望 / be ~ed in sb. (sth.) 对某人(某事)失望 / be ~ed of one's purpose (hopes) 没有达到目的(实现希望) / be agreeably ~ed 高兴地发现原来的忧虑没有根据 ‖*~edly ad.* 失望地

disappointment [ˌdisəˈpointmənt] *n.* ①失望, 失

意; 扫兴, 沮丧 ②使失望的人; 令人扫兴的事情 ‖*to sb.'s ~* 令某人失望的是: To my ~, you didn't come that day. 使我失望的是, 你那天没有来。

disapprobation [ˌdisæprouˈbeiʃən] *n.* 不认可, 不赞成; 非难, 不满

disapprove [ˈdisəˈpru:v] *vt.* & *vi.* 不赞成; 不许可, 不同意; 非难: He ~d (of) my plan. 他不同意我的计划。‖*disapproval* [ˌdisəˈpru:vəl] *n.* / *disapprovingly ad.*

disarm [disˈa:m] **❶** *vt.* ①缴…的械, 解除(城市、船只等)的攻防装备; 弄去(动物、昆虫等)的防卫器官 ②消除(怒气、敌意、怀疑等); 消除…的防气(或敌意、怀疑) **❷** *vi.* ①放下武器 ②裁军

disarmament [disˈa:məmənt] *n.* ①放下武器; 解除武装 ②裁军: a ~ conference 裁军会议

disarrange [ˈdisəˈreindʒ] *vt.* 使混乱, 扰乱 ‖*~ment* [ˌdisəˈreindʒmənt] *n.* 混乱, 紊乱

disaster [diˈza:stə] *n.* 灾难, 祸患; 天灾 ‖*di'saster-'ridden a.* 灾难深重的

disastrous [diˈza:strəs] *a.* 灾难性的; 造成惨重损失的: struggle against ~ floods 与特大洪水搏斗 ‖*~ly ad.*

disavow [ˈdisəˈvau] *vt.* 不承认; 抵赖; 拒绝对…承担责任 ‖*~al n.*

disband [disˈbænd] *vt.* & *vi.* 解散; 遣散 ‖*~ment n.*

disbelief [ˈdisbiˈli:f] *n.* 不信, 怀疑

disbelieve [ˈdisbiˈli:v] **❶** *vt.* 不相信, 怀疑 **❷** *vi.* 不信, 怀疑 (in) ‖*~r n.* 不信(宗教)的人

disburse [disˈbə:s] *vt.* ① 支出; 支付 ② 分配 ‖*~ment n.* 支付, 支出; 付出款, 支出额

disc [disk] *n.* ①圆盘; 圆板; 盘状物; 圆面: cam ~ [机]凸轮盘 / the sun's (moon's) ~ 日(月)轮②[动]盘 [植]花盘: sunflower ~ 向日葵花盘 ③唱片 ④【农】(圆盘耙凹圆形的)耙片 **II** *vt.* ①用圆盘耙耕作(土地) ②把…灌成唱片 ‖*~a.* 圆盘形的 ‖*~ harrow* 圆盘耙 / *~ jockey* [美俚]无线电唱片音乐节目广播员

discard I [disˈka:d] **❶** *vt.* ①(纸牌戏中)垫(牌); 打出(无用的牌) ②丢弃, 抛弃; 遗弃: ~ the dross and select the essential 去粗取精 ③解雇 **❷** *vi.* (纸牌戏中)垫牌 **II** [ˈdiska:d] *n.* ①垫牌; 垫出的牌 ②抛弃, 丢弃; 被弃的物(或人)

discern [diˈsə:n] **❶** *vt.* ①看出; 辨出: ~ a distant object 看出远处的东西 / ~ a strange odo(u)r 闻出一股怪味 ②觉察, 了解 ③辨别, 识别: ~ the false from the genuine 辨别真伪 **❷** *vi.* 辨明, 分清: ~ between right and wrong 分清是非 ‖*~ing a.* 有眼力的, 有洞察力的: those with ~ing eyes 明眼人 / *~ment n.*

discharge [disˈtʃa:dʒ] **I** **❶** *vt.* ①卸(货物等); 卸下(船)上的货物: ~ cargo (from a ship) 起货上岸 / ~ a ship (of her cargo) 卸下船上货物 ②射出; 开(炮等): ~ (a shot from) a gun 开炮 ③排出(液体气体等); 【电】放(电): The sore is still *discharging* pus. 疮还在流脓。④ 允许… 离开；释放；解雇: be ~d from hospital (prison) 出院 (狱) ⑤ 使免除，使卸脱: ~ sb. *from* an obligation 免除某人的义务 ⑥ 履行；清偿 ⑦ 【律】撤销(法院的命令) ⑧ 拔销，除去(染料、颜色) ❷ *vi.* ①(船等)卸货 ②排出液体(或气体等)；(江河)流注: The water pipe ~*s* freely. 水管排水畅通。③(枪炮等)发射 ④(染料、墨水等)渗开 **II** *n.* ①卸货 ②发射 ③流出，排出，放出；【电】放电: a ~ pump 排出泵，排气泵 ④流出物；排泄物；流量: a purulent ~ *from* a wound 创伤的脓水 / a ~ regulator 流量调节器 ⑤解除；释放；退役；解雇 ⑥退伍(或解职、释放)证明书 ⑦履行；清偿: be active in the ~ of one's duties 积极执行任务 ⑧(印染中的)拔染；拔染剂 ‖~**r** *n.* ①卸货者；卸货工具 ② 发射者；发射装置；排出装置 ③履行者 ④【电】放电器，避雷器；火花间隙 ‖~ lamp 放电灯，放电管

disciple [di'saipl] *n.* 门徒，信徒，追随者；【宗】耶稣十二门徒之一 ‖*a* ~ *of Momus* 爱嘲弄的人，滑稽的人 ‖~**ship** *n.* 门徒的地位；做门徒的一段时期

disciplinarian [ˌdisipli'nɛəriən] **I** *n.* 实施纪律者 **II** *a.* 有关纪律的；惩戒性的；训练上的

disciplinary ['disiplinəri] *a.* ①纪律的；惩戒性的: ~ measures 纪律措施 / take ~ action 进行处分 ②训练上的

discipline ['disiplin] **I** *n.* ①纪律；风纪: labo(u)r ~ 劳动纪律 / military ~ 军纪 / be strict in ~ 纪律严明 ②训练: be under perfect ~ 受着很好的训练 / In learning a foreign language, various forms of practice are good ~*s*. 在学习外语时各种方式的实践活动是很好的训练方法。③惩戒，惩罚 ④【宗】教规，戒律；修行 ⑤[古]学科 **II** *vt.* ①训练，训导 ②使有纪律 ③惩戒 ‖**disciplinable** *a.* 可以训练的；应惩罚的

disclaim [dis'kleim] *vt. & vi.* ①放弃；不认领；不索取 ②否认；不承认 ‖~**er** *n.* 放弃；不承认

disclose [dis'klouz] *vt.* ①揭开；揭发: ~ illegal activities 揭露非法活动 ②透露，泄露(秘密等)

disclosure [dis'klouʒə] *n.* ①揭发；泄露 ②被揭发(或泄露)出来的事物

discolo(u)r [dis'kʌlə] *vt. & vi.* (使)变色；(使)褪色；(使)污染 ‖~**ation** [disˌkʌlə'reiʃən] *n.*

discomfit [dis'kʌmfit] *vt.* ①[古](在战场上)打败，击溃 ②打乱…的计划；挫败 ③使为难，使狼狈 ‖~**ure** [dis'kʌmfitʃə] *n.* ①失败，败北；挫败 ②困窘，狼狈

discomfort [dis'kʌmfət] **I** *n.* ①不舒适，不自在；不安 ② 使不舒适(或不自在)的事物；不便；困难 **II** *vt.* 使不舒适；使不自在；使不安

discompose [ˌdiskəm'pouz] *vt.* ①使不安；使烦恼，使失常 ②使混乱；扰乱 ‖~**dly** [ˌdiskəm'pouzidli] *ad.* 不安地，心绪不宁地 / **discomposingly** *ad.* 使人不安地，使人心绪不宁地 / **discomposure** [ˌdiskəm'pouʒə] *n.* 不安，烦乱，失常

disconcert [ˌdiskən'sə:t] *vt.* ①使仓皇失措，使窘，使为难 ②挫败，破坏(计划等) ‖~**ingly** *ad.* / ~**ment** *n.*

disconnect ['diskə'nekt] *vt.* 拆开，分离，断开: ~ one thing *from* (或 *with*) another 把一物和另一物分开

disconnected ['diskə'nektid] *a.* ①分离的，断开的，不连接的 ②(讲话、写作等)不连贯的，支离破碎的；无条理的 ‖~**ness** *n.*

disconsolate [dis'kɔnsəlit] *a.* ①忧郁的，郁郁不乐的 ②令人不快的

discontent ['diskən'tent] **I** *n.* ①不满意 ②不满的人 **II** *a.* 不满的 (*with*) **III** *vt.* [常用被动语态] 令(人)不满: be ~*ed with* sb. (sth.). 对某人(某事)不满 ‖~**ment** *n.*

discontented ['diskən'tentid] *a.* 不满的 ‖~**ly** *ad.* / ~**ness** *n.*

discontinue ['diskən'tinju(:)] ❶ *vt.* ①中止，中断，停止；停止使用，停止出版(或订阅) ②【律】撤销(诉讼) ❷ *vi.* 中止，中断，停止；停чий

discord ['diskɔ:d] **I** *n.* ①不和，倾轧 ②不一致，不调和 ③【音】不谐和(音) ④嘈杂声 **II** [dis'kɔ:d] *vi.* 不一致，不调和；不和，倾轧 (*with, from*)

discordant [dis'kɔ:dənt] *a.* ①不一致的，不调和的；不和的 ②【地】不整合的 ‖~**ly** *ad.*

discothèque ['diskətek] *n.* 放送流行歌曲唱片供人跳舞的夜总会

discount ['diskaunt] **I** *n.* ①折扣: allow (或 give, make) ten per cent ~ *off* (或 *on*) the prices of goods 按货价打九折 / accept a statement with some ~ 不全信一种说法 ②【商】贴现；贴现率 **II** ['diskaunt, dis'kaunt] ❶ *vt.* ①打去(若干)折扣；打折扣卖: ~ twenty per cent 打八折 ②【商】(持票人或受票人)把(票据)贴现 ③不全信，对…持怀疑态度: ~ a statement 怀疑一个说法 ④看轻，把…不当一回事: His rich experience is not to be ~*ed*. 他的丰富经验不可小看。⑤预料到 ❷ *vi.* 贴现 ‖*at a* ~ ①低于正常价格(或票面价值)；打折扣 ②(货物)没有销路，容易到手；不受欢迎，不被重视 ‖~**able** *a.* ①可打折扣的 ②【商】可贴现的 ③不可全信的 ‖~ **broker** 【商】贴现掮客 / ~ **rate** 【商】贴现率

discourage [dis'kʌridʒ] *vt.* ①使泄气，使失去信心，使沮丧: not ~*d* by difficulties 没有因为困难而泄气 ②阻拦，留难；(试图)劝阻: ~ sb. *from* smoking 劝阻某人吸烟 ‖~**ment** *n.*

discourse [dis'kɔ:s] **I** *n.* ①讲话，演说；【宗】讲道 ②[古]会话，谈话 ③论述，论说；论文 ④[古]推理能力 **II** ❶ *vi.* ①谈论，谈话 ②演讲；论述 (*upon, of*) ❷ *vt.* [古]说，讲；说出

discourteous [dis'kə:tjəs] *a.* 不礼貌的，失礼的 ‖~**ly** *ad.* / ~**ness** *n.*

discover [dis'kʌvə] ❶ *vt.* ①发现，发见，看出: ~ new coal mines 发现新煤矿 / We have ~*ed* that he is quite careful in his work. 我们发现他工作很仔细。②暴露；显示: ~ oneself 显露自

己的身分 ❷ *vi.* 有所发现 ‖~ *check* (象棋中) 移动一子以将对方军 ‖~**able** [dis'kʌvərəbl] *a.*

discoverer [dis'kʌvərə] *n.* 发现者

discovery [dis'kʌvəri] *n.* ①发现: the ~ of new chemical elements 新化学元素的发现 ②被发现的事物: make new *discoveries* in science 在科学上作出新发现 ③[古]暴露, 显露

discredit [dis'kredit] **I** *n.* ①丧失名誉, 丧失信用: bring ~ on (或 upon) oneself 使自己丧失信誉 / things to the ~ of sb. 使某人丧失信誉的事情 ②(一种)耻辱: Don't be a ~ to the collective. 别给集体丢脸。③不信, 怀疑: throw (或 cast) ~ on 使人怀疑… **II** *vt.* ①不信, 怀疑; 使成为不可信: His theories were ~ed by scientists. 他的理论受到科学家们的怀疑。/ Later researches ~ed the earlier conclusions. 后来的研究推翻了早先的结论。②使丧失信誉; 使丢脸: ~ sb. completely *with* the public 使某人在公众面前信誉扫地

discreet [dis'kri:t] *a.* (在行动、说话等方面)谨慎的, 考虑周到的 ‖~**ly** *ad.*

discrepancy [dis'krepənsi] *n.* 差异; 不一致, 不符合: a ~ between theory and practice 理论和实际的脱节

discretion [dis'kreʃən] *n.* ①[古]离散, 分立; 不连续 ②[罕]辨别(力); 判断(力): the age of ~ 懂事年龄, 责任年龄(英国法律规定为十四岁) ③谨慎 ④斟酌决定的自由; 处理权(限): Use your own ~. 你自己斟酌决定吧。‖*at* ~ 随意, 任意 / *at the* ~ *of* 随…的意见, 凭…自行处理 / *be within sb.'s* ~ (to do) (做…)是某人的自由 / *Discretion is the better part of valo(u)r.* [谚][谑]小心即大勇。(常作为胆怯者解嘲的借口) / *surrender at* ~ 无条件投降 / *with* ~ 慎重地, 审慎地 ‖~**al** *a.* 自由决定的, 任意的

discriminate [dis'krimineit] ❶ *vt.* ①区别, 辨别: ~ one thing *from* another 把一事物与另一事物区别开来 ②区分出, 辨出 ❷ *vi.* ①区别, 辨别: ~ *between* two things 区别两事物 ②有差别地对待: ~ *against* 歧视… / ~ *in favour of* 特别优待…

discriminating [dis'krimineitiŋ] *a.* ①形成区别的, 识别性的: The ~ mark of this species is its varicoloured plumage. 杂色羽毛是这类禽鸟独特的标识。② 有辨别力的, 有识别力的 ③ 区别对待的, 有差别的: ~ duties (或 tariffs) 差别关税 ‖~**ly** *ad.*

discrimination [dis,krimi'neiʃən] *n.* ①辨别, 区别 ②识别力, 辨别力: target ~ 【军】分辨目标的能力 ③不公平待遇, 差别待遇, 歧视: racial ~ 种族歧视

discursive [dis'kə:siv] *a.* ①东拉西扯的, 散漫的, 离题的 ②【哲】推论的 ‖~**ly** *ad.* / ~**ness** *n.*

discus ['diskəs] *n.* ①【体】铁饼: the ~ throw 掷铁饼 ②【动】盘; 【植】花盘

discuss [dis'kʌs] *vt.* ①讨论, 商议; 辩论: They put their heads together to ~ what to do next. 他们聚在一起讨论下一步干什么。/ ~ business with sb. 与某人谈生意(或正经事) ②论述, 详述: What does the book ~? 这本书讲的是什么? ③[口]津津有味地吃(或喝) ‖~**ible** *a.* 可讨论的, 可商议的

discussion [dis'kʌʃən] *n.* ①讨论, 商议; 辩论: a heated (或 hot) ~ 热烈的讨论 / The incident caused much ~. 这事件引起议论纷纷。/ Your suggestion is still *under* ~. 你的意见还在讨论中。/ a bill down for ~ 已提交讨论的议案 / a stormy ~ *about* (或 on) sth. 围绕某事的一场激烈争论 ②论述, 详述 ③津津有味的吃(或喝) (of)

disdain [dis'dein] **I** *vt.* ①轻视, 蔑视; 以傲慢的态度对待 ②不屑, 鄙弃: ~ to reply (或 replying) 不屑答复 **II** *n.* 轻蔑, 蔑视

disease [di'zi:z] *n.* ①病, 疾病; 【植】病害: an acute (a chronic) ~ 急性(慢性)病 / catch (suffer from) a ~ 得(害着)病 ②(精神、道德、社会制度等的)不健全状态; 弊病

diseased [di'zi:zd] *a.* 害了病的; 不健全的; 【植】有病害的

disembark ['disim'bɑ:k] *vt.* & *vi.* (使)上岸, (使)起岸, (使)登陆 ‖~**ation** [,disembɑ:'keiʃən] *n.*

disembody ['disim'bodi] *vt.* ① [主要以过去分词形式作定语用]使脱离肉体; 使脱离现实: a *disembodied* spirit 游魂 / a *disembodied* ideal 脱离现实的理想 ②[古]遣散(军队) ‖**disembodiment** *n.*

disenchant [,disin'tʃɑ:nt] *vt.* 使从着魔状态解脱出来, 使清醒, 使不再着迷; 使不抱幻想 ‖~**ment** *n.*

disengage ['disin'geidʒ] ❶ *vt.* ①解开, 解除; 使脱离(或脱身): ~ sb. *from* a contract 使某人不再负契约义务 ②【军】使脱离接触 ③【化】使分离, 使离析 ❷ *vi.* 脱出, 松开

disengagement ['disin'geidʒmənt] *n.* ①解开, 脱身 ②【化】分离; 离析 ③解约; 解除婚约 ④自由自在 ⑤【军】脱离战斗, 脱离敌人

disestablish ['disis'tæbliʃ] *vt.* ①废除…的既成状态 ②使(教会)与政府分离 ③解除…的官职 ‖~**ment** *n.*

disfavo(u)r ['dis'feivə] **I** *n.* ①不赞成, 不喜欢; 冷待, 疏远 ②受冷待, 失宠 ③不利 **II** *vt.* 不赞成; 冷待, 疏远 ‖*be in* ~ 受冷遇 / *fall into* ~ 失宠

disfigure [dis'figə] *vt.* ①毁损…的外形(或容貌) ②损害, 玷污 ‖~**ment** *n.*

disfranchise ['dis'fræntʃaiz] *vt.* ①剥夺…的公民权, 剥夺…的公权(尤指选举权) ②[英]剥夺(某地)选派议会议员的权利 ‖~**ment** *n.*

disgorge [dis'gɔ:dʒ] ❶ *vt.* ①吐出, 呕吐 ②被迫交出, 吐出(赃物) ③(江河等)流出 ❷ *vi.* ①呕吐 ②(河水等)流出

disgrace [dis'greis] **I** *n.* ①丢脸, 耻辱, 不光彩; 失宠: bring ~ on sb. 给某人带来耻辱 / be in ~ 失宠;蒙受耻辱,丢脸 ②丢脸的事,丢脸的人: be a ~ to... 对…说来是一大耻辱 **II** *vt.* ①使丢脸,使受耻辱 ②使失宠; 贬黜

disgraceful [dis'greisful] *a.* 不名誉的, 丢脸的, 不光彩的 ‖ ~ly *ad.* / ~ness *n.*

disgruntle [dis'grʌntl] *vt.* 使不满,使不高兴 ‖ ~d *a.* 不满的,不高兴的 (at, with) / ~ment *n.*

disguise [dis'gaiz] **I** *vt.* ①把…假扮起来,把…假装起来: ~ one's voice 伪装自己的声音 ②隐瞒, 隐蔽, 掩饰(思想、感情、愿望等) **II** *n.* ①伪装衣,伪装物;伪装的行为;借口 ②假装,伪装: in ~ 乔装着 / make no ~ of one's feelings 不掩饰自己的情感,真情毕露 ‖ ~dly [dis'gaizidli] *ad.* 假装地;匿名地 / ~ment *n.* / ~r *n.* 伪装者,假装者

disgust [dis'gʌst] **I** *n.* ①发呕 ②厌恶,憎恶 (at, for, towards, against) **II** ❶ *vt.* ①使作呕: This smell ~s me. 这气味使我作呕。②使厌恶, 使讨厌: be ~ed at (或 by, with) sth. 厌恶某物 ❷ *vi.* 令人作呕;令人厌恶 ‖ ~edly *ad.* 厌恶地 / ~ful *a.* ①令人作呕的;令人厌恶的 ②因厌恶而产生的

disgusting [dis'gʌstiŋ] *a.* 令人作呕的;可憎恶的,讨厌的 ‖ ~ly *ad.*

dish [diʃ] **I** *n.* ①盘,碟 ②盘装菜,盘装食品,一道菜: a cold ~ 冷盘 / a made ~ 拼盘 / a standing ~ 每日例菜; [喻]炒冷饭,老生常谈 ③盘形物,盘形 ④一盘的容量,满满的一盘 ⑤[美俚]漂亮女子 ⑥[美俚]爱好;心爱物 **II** ❶ *vt.* ①把(食物)放在盘中 ②使成盘形;把…挖空 ③[英俚]挫败(对手) ❷ *vi.* ①成盘形 ②[俚]闲谈 ‖ a ~ of gossip (一次)闲谈 / ~ out ① 把(菜肴等)盛在盘中端上;(用餐时)分(饭菜) ② [喻]托出;抛出;提供,发布(消息等);施加(打骂等): ~ it out [美俚]出钱; 施以惩罚; 严加责骂 ③ 把…挖空成盘状 ④ 滔滔不绝地讲出 / ~ up ①上菜;把(菜肴等)盛在盘中端上 ②把(论点等)发挥得娓娓动听 ‖ ~ed *a.* ① 盘形凹陷的; (房屋)有圆屋顶的,穹窿形的 ②[英俚]被挫败了的;完蛋了的 / ~ful *n.* (一)满盘;一盘的容量 ‖ ~antenna【无】截抛物面天线 / '~cloth, '~rag *n.* 洗碟布 / '~clout *n.* [英]①洗碟布 ②软弱而愚蠢的人 / ~ towel 擦干(碗)碟的布 / '~washer *n.* ①洗碟子的人 ②洗碟机 / '~water *n.* ①洗碟子的水 ②[美俚]味道蹩脚的汤(或茶、咖啡)

dishearten [dis'hɑ:tn] *vt.* 使失去勇气,使沮丧,使失去信心: feel ~ed at 因…感到泄气 / a ~ing remark 使人失望的话 ‖ ~ment *n.*

dishevel [di'ʃevəl] (dishevel(l)ed; dishevel(l)ing) *vt.* 使(头发、衣服等)松散杂乱 ‖ dishevel(l)ed *a.* 散乱的,乱蓬蓬的

dishonest [dis'ɔnist] *a.* 不老实的,不诚实的,不正直的: a ~ man 不诚实的人 / ~ conduct 不正直的行为 / ~ profits 不正当的收益 ‖ ~ly *ad.*

dishono(u)r [dis'ɔnə] **I** *n.* ①不名誉,不光彩,耻辱: live in ~ 过可耻的生活 ②丢脸的人(或事) ③[商](票据的)拒收;拒付;无法偿付 **II** *vt.* ①使丧失名誉,使丢脸,使受耻辱 ②奸污 ③拒收;拒付(票据): a ~ed cheque 空头支票 ‖ ~able [dis'ɔnərəbl] *a.* 不名誉的,不光彩的,耻辱的,无耻的

disillusion [,disi'lu:ʒən] **I** *vt.* 使醒悟;使幻想破灭,使幻灭 **II** *n.* 醒悟;幻灭 ‖ ~ment *n.*

disinclination [,disinkli'neiʃən] *n.* 不愿;厌恶: have a ~ for sth. (或 to do sth.) 不愿做某事

disincline ['disin'klain] *vt.* 使不愿,使无意于: be ~d to go out 不愿出去 / feel ~d for any more sleep 不想再睡下去

disinfect [,disin'fekt] *vt.* ①杀死…的细菌,给…消毒;使洗净: ~ drinking water with bleaching powder 用漂白粉消毒饮水 ②清除,去掉 ‖ ~ion [,disin'fekʃən] *n.* 灭菌(法),消毒(法)

disingenuous [,disin'dʒenjuəs] *a.* 不真诚的,不坦率的;假装坦率的,诡诈的 ‖ ~ly *ad.* / ~ness *n.*

disinherit ['disin'herit] *vt.* 剥夺…的继承权

disintegrate [dis'intigreit] ❶ *vt.* ①使崩溃,使溃散,使瓦解 ②使分裂,使分解;使崩解 ❷ *vi.* ①崩溃,溃散,瓦解 ②分裂,分解;崩解 ③【原】蜕变,衰变

disintegration [dis,inti'greiʃən] *n.* ①崩溃,溃散,瓦解 ②分裂,分解;崩解 ③【原】蜕变,衰变 ④[地]剥蚀

disinterest [dis'intrist] **I** *vt.* 使兴味索然; 使不再有利害关系 **II** *n.* ①无兴趣 ②无私利 ③漠不关心

disinterested [dis'intristid] *a.* ①无私的,公平的,无偏见的: ~ assistance 无私的援助 ②[口]不关心的,不感兴趣的 ‖ ~ly *ad.* / ~ness *n.*

disjoint [dis'dʒɔint] ❶ *vt.* ①使关节脱位,使脱臼 ②使脱离,使断离,拆散 ③破坏…的连贯性 ❷ *vi.* 关节脱位,脱臼

disjointed [dis'dʒɔintid] *a.* ①关节脱位的,脱臼的 ②不连贯的,支离的 ③次序混乱的,没有条理的 ‖ ~ly *ad.* / ~ness *n.*

disk [disk] *n. & vt.* =disc

dislike [dis'laik] **I** *vt.* 不喜欢,厌恶 **II** *n.* 不喜爱,厌恶: likes and ~s 爱好和厌恶 / have a ~ to (或 for, of) 厌恶…,不喜爱…

dislocate ['disləkeit] *vt.* ①使离开原来位置;使(骨头)关节脱位,使脱臼 ②打乱…的正常秩序: Traffic was temporarily ~d by the snowstorm. 暴风雪使交通暂时混乱。

dislocation [,dislə'keiʃən] *n.* ①离开原位;关节脱位,脱臼 ②[地]断层,断错;[物]位错 ③混乱,打乱

dislodge [dis'lɔdʒ] ❶ *vt.* ①把…赶出住处(或占有的地方,有利的地位等),把…驱逐出 ②取出,移动: A sharp blow ~d the lid. 猛力一击敲

开了盖子。❷ *vi.* 离开住处（或占有的地方等）‖**dislodg(e)ment** *n.*

disloyal [dis'lɔiəl] *a.* 不忠诚的 (*to*) ‖~**ist** *n.* 不忠的人 / ~**ly** *ad.* / ~**ty** *n.* 不忠

dismal ['dizməl] **I** *a.* ①忧郁的; 凄凉的, 阴沉的: ~ weather 阴沉的天气 ②沉闷无趣的: the ~ science 沉闷的科学 **II** *n.* ①[the ~s]低落的情绪 ②[美]沼泽 ‖~**ly** *ad.*

dismantle [dis'mæntl] *vt.* ①脱掉…的衣服; 去掉…的覆盖物: ~ a gun *of* its covering 卸下炮衣 ②拆除…的设备（或装备、防御工事等）: ~ a military base 撤除军事基地 ③拆卸(机器) ④粉碎, 夷平

dismay [dis'mei] **I** *vt.* 使灰心, 使沮丧; 使惊愕: be ~ed to learn that … 获悉…感到震惊（或沮丧）**II** *n.* 灰心, 沮丧; 惊愕: be struck with ~ *at* the news 听到这消息感到惊慌

dismember [dis'membə] *vt.* ①割下(动物)的肢, 肢解 ②割裂; 把…撕成碎片; 拆卸 ③瓜分(国家等)

dismiss [dis'mis] ❶ *vt.* ①让…离开; 打发 ②免…的职; 解雇; 开除(工人、学生等): ~ sb. *from* his post 撤销某人的职务 ③遣散, 解散: The squad leader ~ed the meeting. 班长宣布散会。/ The class is ~ed. 现在下课。④消除(顾虑等);不考虑: ~ doubts *from* one's mind 消除疑虑 / an idea lightly as no good 轻率地说一个主意不行而不予考虑 ⑤[律]驳回, 对…不予受理 ❷ *vi.* 解散: Dismiss! (口令)解散!

dismissal [dis'misəl] *n.* ①打发 ②免职; 解雇;开除: a disciplinary ~ 惩罚性撤职 ③遣散, 解散 ④不予考虑 ⑤[律]驳回

dismount ['dis'maunt] **I** ❶ *vi.* 下马; 下车: ~ *from* horseback 下马 ❷ *vt.* ①[古]下（马）;下(车) ②使下车; 使掉下 ③(从座子上)取下, 卸下: ~ a statue from its pedestal 从台架上取下雕像 / ~ a gun (from the gun carriage) (从炮架上)卸下大炮 ④拆卸(机器等) **II** *n.* ①下马;下车 ②[体]跳下动作

disobedience [ˌdisə'bi:djəns] *n.* 不服从, 不顺从 (*to*)

disobedient [ˌdisə'bi:djənt] *a.* 不服从的,不顺从的 (*to*) ‖~**ly** *ad.*

disobey ['disə'bei] *vt.* & *vi.* 不服从, 不顺从

disoblige ['disə'blaidʒ] *vt.* ①不满足…的愿望, 对…不通融 ②得罪 ③使遭受不便 ‖**disobliging** *a.* 不亲切的, 不通融的

disorder [dis'ɔːdə] **I** *n.* ①混乱, 杂乱;【物】无序 ②骚动, 骚扰: be thrown into ~ 被卷入动乱 ③(身心、机能的)失调, 轻病: a nervous ~ 神经错乱 **II** *vt.* ①使混乱, 扰乱 ②使错乱, 使失调 ‖~**ed** *a.* ①混乱的, 杂乱的 ②(身心)失调的, 不正常的

disorderly [dis'ɔːdəli] **I** *a.* ①混乱的, 杂乱的, 无秩序的 ②目无法纪的, 暴乱的, 骚动的 ③【律】妨害治安的: ~ conduct 妨害治安行为 **II** *ad.*

无秩序地, 杂乱地 ‖**disorderliness** *n.* ‖~ **house** ①赌场 ②妓院

disorganize [dis'ɔːgənaiz] *vt.* 瓦解;打乱 ‖**disorganization** [disˌɔːgənai'zeiʃən] *n.*

disown [dis'oun] *vt.* ①否认…是自己的; 否认…同自己有关系; 声明同（子女等)脱离关系: ~ a letter 不承认是自己写的信 ②否认…的权威性; 否认…的正确性

disparage [dis'pæridʒ] *vt.* ①轻视, 轻蔑, 贬低 ②毁谤, 说…坏话 ‖~**ment** *n.*

disparity [dis'pæriti] *n.* 不同;不等;悬殊;不一致: ~ *in* age 年龄的不同

dispassionate [dis'pæʃənit] *a.* 不动情感的, 平心静气的;不带偏见的 ‖~**ly** *ad.* / ~**ness** *n.*

dispatch [dis'pætʃ] **I** ❶ *vt.* ①(迅速地)派遣, 派出; (迅速地)发送(信件、电报等): ~ a fleet 派出舰队 ②调遣: ~ buses at a terminal 在终点站调度公共汽车 / production ~ing work 生产调度工作 ③迅速办理, 迅速了结; 匆匆吃完: anxious to ~ the matter in hand 急于了结手头的事情 / ~ one's lunch 匆匆吃完午饭 ④杀死; 处决 ❷ *vi.* [古]赶快 **II** *n.* ①(迅速)派遣, (迅速)发送: request the ~ of two companies to the front 请求派遣两个连到前线去 / send sth. by ~ 作快件发送某物 ②急件, 公文急报;快信; (新闻)电讯 ③迅速(办理); 敏捷: do sth. with ~ 从速办理某事 ④调度 (日本式)切腹自杀 ‖**happy ~** (日本式)切腹自杀 ‖~**er** *n.* ①发送者 ②调度员; 交通调度员 ‖~ **boat** 递送公文的船 / ~ **box**, ~ **case** 公文递送箱 / ~ **rider** 【军】(骑马或摩托车的)通信员

dispel [dis'pel] (dispelled; dispelling) *vt.* ① 驱散, 赶跑: The sun soon *dispelled* the thick fog. 太阳很快就驱散了浓雾。② 消除, 消释: ~ sb.'s doubts 消除某人的疑虑

dispensable [dis'pensəbl] *a.* 非必需的, 省得了的 ‖**dispensability** [disˌpensə'biliti] *n.*

dispensary [dis'pensəri] *n.* ①药房, 配药处 ②施药处, 施药所 ③诊疗所, 门诊部: a travelling ~ 巡回医疗队

dispensation [ˌdispen'seiʃən] *n.* ① 分配, 分与; 分配物 ②施与; 施与物 ③执行, 施行 ④【医】配方 ⑤管理方法; 体制; 制度 ⑥【宗】(天)命, (天)道 ⑦【宗】特许; 豁免 ⑧省却, 免除 (*with*)

dispense [dis'pens] ❶ *vt.* ①分配, 分发(施舍物品等) ②施与(恩惠等) ③执行, 施行(法律等) ④配(药), 配(方); 发(药) ⑤免除, 豁免 ❷ *vi.* [古]豁免 ‖~ *with* ①省却, 免除: Machinery ~ with much labour. 机器节省了大量劳动力。②无需, 没有…也行 ‖~**r** *n.* ①施与者; 分配者 ②配药者, 药剂师 ③分配器, 配出器 ④自动售货机

dispersal [dis'pəːsəl] *n.* ①疏开; 分散; 散布 ②消散; 驱散

disperse [dis'pəːs] **I** ❶ *vt.* ①使疏开;使分散; 解散(集会等): ~ sb.'s attention 使某人注意力分散 ②击溃(敌人等); 驱散(云、雾等) ③散布, 传播

(消息、知识等) ④【物】使(光线)色散; 使弥散 ❷ *vi.* ①分散; 散开; 散去 ②(云雾等) 消散 Ⅱ *a.* 分散的, 弥散的 ‖~r *n.* ①分散剂 ②(蒸馏塔中的)泡罩 ‖~ **system**【化】分散体系

dispirit [di'spirit] *vt.* 使气馁, 使沮丧

displace [dis'pleis] *vt.* ①移置, 转移 ②迫使(某人)离家(或祖国) ③取代(某人)的职位, 顶换; 【化】取代(某物), 置换(某物) ④撤换, 把…免职 ⑤【海】排出…量的水, 有…的排水量: The ship ~s 20,000 tons. 这艘船的排水量为两万吨。⑥使过滤 ‖~**able** *a.* 可移置的; 可取代(或替换)的 / ~r *n.* ①【化】取代剂, 置换剂 ②过滤器 ‖~d **person** 由于战争(或迫害)而逃离原居住地(或本国)的人(略作 DP)

displacement [dis'pleismənt] *n.* ①移置, 转移; 取代, 置换 ②撤换, 免职; (被)逐出状态 ③【化】取代(作用), 置换(作用) ④【物】位移;【医】移位 ⑤【海】排水量;【机】排出量 ⑥过滤

display [dis'plei] Ⅰ *vt.* ①展开; 陈列, 展览: ~ a map on the table 把地图展开在桌上 / ~ a flag 悬旗 / The peacock ~ed its fine tail feathers. 孔雀开屏。②表现; 发扬 ③炫耀, 夸耀 ④【印】(用大字等)醒目地排印 Ⅱ *n.* ①陈列, 展览; 显示, 表现: the exhibits on ~ 陈列的展览品 ②炫耀, 夸耀: make a ~ of 把…炫耀一下 ③【印】醒目排印 ④【动】(雄性动物在繁殖期的)求偶夸耀行为

displease [dis'pli:z] ❶ *vt.* 使不愉快, 使不高兴; 使生气; 惹怒: be ~d with sb. *for* doing sth. 因某人做某事而对他生气 / be ~d *at* sb.'s conduct 对某人的行为不满 ❷ *vi.* 使人不快; 使人生气

displeasure [dis'pleʒə] Ⅰ *n.* ①不愉快 ②不满, 生气 Ⅱ *vt.* [古]使不快; 使生气

disport [dis'pɔ:t] Ⅰ ❶ *vt.* [~ oneself] 娱乐, 玩耍 ❷ *vi.* 娱乐, 嬉戏 Ⅱ *n.* 娱乐, 游戏

disposal [dis'pouzəl] *n.* ①配置, 布置, 排列: the ~ of troops 兵力的部署; 军队住宿的安排 ②处理, 处置: the ~ of property (rubbish) 财产(垃圾)的处理 / the lenient (severe) ~ of a criminal 对罪犯的从宽(从严)处理 ③卖掉; 让与 ④控制; (自由)处置权 ‖**at** sb.'s ~ 由某人作主, 听某人之便; 供某人之用, 由某人支配: put (或 leave) sth. *at* sb.'s ~ 把某事交某人自由处理 / try every means *at* one's ~ 尽自己的一切力量

dispose [dis'pouz] ❶ *vt.* ①配置, 布置, 安排: ~ troops along a river 沿河部署兵力 / ~ these tools within reach 把这些工具安放在伸手可以取到的地方 ②处理, 处置; 整理 ③使做倾向于, 使有意于: ~ sb. *for* (或 *to*) sth. 使某人有意于(做)某事 / I am ~d to agree with you. 我倾向于你的观点。④[古]赋与 ❷ *vi.* 处置, 处理 ‖~ *of* ①处理, 处置; 安排 ②转让, 卖掉: ~ *of* a batch of goods 卖掉一批货物 ③吃掉, 喝光 ④解决, 办妥: ~ *of* a job 办妥一件事 / *Man proposes, God* ~*s.* 见 **man**

disposition [,dispə'ziʃən] *n.* ①布置, 配置, 安排;【军】部署: the ~ of furniture in a room 房内家具的布置 / battle (或 combat) ~【军】战斗部署 ②处理, 处置; 支配, 控制: at sb.'s ~ 随某人支配 ③(财产等的)转让, 出售 ④气质, 性情: of a cheerful ~ 性情开朗的 ⑤倾向, 意向: show a ~ to come again 有意再来(或重复)一次

dispossess ['dispə'zes] *vt.* ①使不再占有, 剥夺: ~ sb. *of* sth. 夺去某人的某物 ②撵走, 逐出: ~ sb. from his home 把某人撵出家门 ‖~**ion** ['dispə'zeʃən] *n.* 夺取, 剥夺; 驱逐 / ~**or** *n.* 夺取(他人土地、财物)者

disproportion ['disprə'pɔ:ʃən] Ⅰ *n.* 不相称, 不均衡 Ⅱ *vt.* 使不相称, 使不均衡 ‖~**al** *a.* =disproportionate

disprove [dis'pru:v] *vt.* ①证明…不成立 ②反驳, 驳斥 ‖**disproval** [dis'pru:vəl] *n.* 反证; 反驳

disputable [dis'pju:təbl] *a.* 可争论的, 可质疑的, 不一定的

disputant [dis'pju:tənt] Ⅰ *n.* 争论者, 辩论者; 争执者 Ⅱ *a.* 从事争论的

dispute [dis'pju:t] Ⅰ ❶ *vi.* 争论, 辩论; 争执: ~ with (或 against) sb. on (或 about) sth. 同某人争论某事 ❷ *vt.* ①争论, 辩论; 争执: They ~d how to get the best results. 他们争论如何才能取得最好的效果。/ a ~d area (所属权)有争议的地区 ②对…提出质疑: Your bravery has never been ~d. 没有人怀疑过你的勇敢。/ ~ the soundness of a judgement 对一个判断的正确性表示怀疑 ③阻止, 抵抗 ④争夺(土地、胜利等) Ⅱ *n.* 争论, 辩论; 争执, 争端: settle (adjust) a ~ 解决(调解)争端 ‖**beyond** (或 **past, without**) ~ ①没有争论余地的 ②无疑地 / **in** ~ (问题等)在争论中; 尚未解决 ‖~r *n.* 争论者, 争辩者

disqualify [dis'kwɔlifai] *vt.* 取消…的资格, 使不合格, 使不能: ~ sb. *from* participation in an organization 取消某人参加一个组织的资格 / be *disqualified for* 没有…的资格 ‖**disqualification** [dis,kwɔlifi'keiʃən] *n.* 无资格, 取消资格; 使取消资格的事物

disquiet [dis'kwaiət] Ⅰ *vt.* 打搅, 使不安; 使忧虑, 使烦恼 Ⅱ *n.* 不安, 不平静; 焦虑 ‖~**ing** *a.* 使不安的, 使不平静的; 使焦虑的 / ~**ly** *ad.*

disquietude [dis'kwaiitju:d] *n.* 不安; 焦虑

disquisition [,diskwi'ziʃən] *n.* ①专题论文; 学术讲演 (on) ②[古]研究, 探究 ‖~**al** *a.*

disregard ['disri'gɑ:d] Ⅰ *vt.* 不理, 不顾, 漠视, 无视 Ⅱ *n.* 漠视, 忽视 (of, for) ‖~**ful** *a.* 漠视的, 无视的

disrepair ['disri'pɛə] *n.* 失修, 破损: be in (a state of) ~ (房屋、器具等)年久失修, 破损

disreputable [dis'repjutəbl] *a.* ①名誉不好的, 声名狼藉的; 不体面的 ②破烂不堪的; 极脏的 ‖~**ness** *n.* / **disreputably** *ad.*

disrepute ['disri'pju:t] *n.* 坏名声, 声名狼藉: incur ~ 招致丑名 / fall into ~ 声名扫地

disrespect ['disris'pekt] I *n.* 无礼，失礼 II *vt.* 不尊敬，不尊重

disrobe ['dis'roub] ❶ *vt.* 脱去…的衣服；[喻]剥去…的外衣 ❷ *vi.* 脱衣服

disrupt [dis'rʌpt] *vt.* ①使崩裂；分裂，瓦解：~ a state 分裂一个国家 ②使混乱，破坏：~ traffic 引起交通混乱 / . ~ public order 破坏治安 ‖~ion [dis'rʌpʃən] *n.* / ~ive *a.* 分裂的；破坏(性)的：~ive voltage 击穿电压 / ~or, ~er *n.* 分裂者；破坏者

dissatisfaction ['dis,sætis'fækʃən] *n.* ①不满，不平 (with, at) ②令人不满的事物

dissatisfy ['dis'sætisfai] *vt.* 使不满，使不平：be *dissatisfied with* (或 at) 对…不满(或不平) / a ~ing dinner 使人不满意的一餐饭 ‖**dissatisfied** *a.* 不满的；显出不满的：There was a *dissatisfied* look in his eyes. 他眼睛里露出不满的神色。

dissect [di'sekt] ❶ *vt.* ①把…分成碎片；分割；解剖(动、植物等)：a ~ing knife (room) 解剖刀(室) / ~ a sparrow 解剖麻雀 ②仔细分析(问题、理论、报告等) ❷ *vi.* 进行解剖；进行分析 ‖~ed *a.* ①分成部分的 ②[地]受沟、谷等)切割的 ③【植】(叶等)多裂的 / ~ion [di'sekʃən] *n.* ①解剖；分析 ②解剖标本 / ~or *n.* ①解剖者；解剖学家 ②解剖器具 ③分析者

dissemble [di'sembl] ❶ *vt.* ①掩饰(思想、感情等) ②假装不见，佯作不知 ❷ *vi.* 掩饰；作伪，伪装 ‖~r *n.* 假好人，伪君子

disseminate [di'semineit] ❶ *vt.* ①播(种)，散播(种子) ②散布；传播(思想、理论等) ❷ *vi.* 广为传播 ‖**dissemination** [di,semi'neiʃən] *n.* / **disseminator** *n.* 播种者；传播者

dissension [di'senʃən] *n.* 意见分歧，争论(尤指党派纷争)；不和，纠纷：sow ~ 离间 / internal ~s 内部纷争

dissent [di'sent] I *vi.* ①不同意，持异议：~ from sb.'s view 不同意某人的意见 / He and I ~ed from each other. 他和我意见不一致。②[英]不信奉国教 II *n.* ①不同意，异议 ②[英]不信奉国教；[总称]不信奉国教者 ‖~er *n.* ①持异议(尤指不同政见)者，反对者；老是唱反调的人 ②[英][D-]不信奉国教者

dissertation [,disə(:)'teiʃən] *n.* (专题)论述；(学位)论文；学术演讲

disservice ['dis'sə:vis] *n.* 危害，损害：do sb. a ~ 危害某人 ‖~able *a.* 危害性的，起损害作用的

dissimilar ['di'similə] *a.* 不一样的，不同的 (to, from, with) ‖~ly *ad.* 不同地

dissimulate [di'simjuleit] *vt. & vi.* ①掩饰 ②假装不见，佯作不知 ‖**dissimulation** [di,simju'leiʃən] *n.* 掩饰 / **dissimulator** *n.* 假好人，伪君子

dissipate ['disipeit] ❶ *vt.* ①驱散，使(云、雾、疑虑等)消散：~ sb.'s interest in sth. 使某人对某事变得无兴趣 ②浪费，挥霍 ❷ *vi.* ①消散 ②放荡；酗酒 ‖~d *a.* ①驱散了的 ②浪费掉的 ③放荡的 / ~r, **dissipator** *n.* 浪荡子

dissipation [,disi'peiʃən] *n.* ①驱散，消散：~ of the clouds 乌云的消散 ②浪费；消耗：plate ~ 【无】屏极耗散 ③放荡(尤指狂饮)；胡闹

dissociate [di'souʃieit] ❶ *vt.* ①使分离；使游离出(from) ②【化】使离解 ③【心】分裂：~d personality 分裂人格 ❷ *vi.* ①分离；游离 ②离解 ‖~ oneself from 割断与…的关系

dissolute ['disəlju:t] *a.* 无节制的；放荡的 ‖~ly *ad.* / ~ness *n.*

dissolution [,disə'lju:ʃən] *n.* ①溶解；融化；液化；分解 ②(婚约、契约等的)解除 ③(议会、公司等的)解散 ④死亡；消亡 ⑤结束；结清

dissolve [di'zɔlv] I ❶ *vt.* ①分解 ②使溶解；使融化；使液化：~ sugar in water 把糖溶解在水里 / Heat ~d the candle into a pool of wax. 热使蜡烛融化成一摊蜡。③使感动，软化：be ~d in tears 感动得眼泪汪汪 ④解散；使终结：~ partnership 散伙 ⑤驱散，使消失 ⑥使(电影、电视画面)渐隐，使溶暗：~ a picture into another 使一画面渐化入另一画面 ⑦弄明白，解(谜)：~ a mystery 使真相大白 ⑧废除，使无效 ❷ *vi.* ①分解 ②溶解；融化；液化：Salt ~s in water. 盐溶于水。③感动，软化：~ in grief 悲痛过度不能自拔 ④(议会等)解散；(婚约等)取消 ⑤消失；(电影、电视画面)溶暗：The view ~d in mist. 那景色在雾中消失了。/ ~ in (out) (电影、电视画面)溶入(出) II *n.* (电影、电视画面的)溶暗：a lap ~ 淡出；淡入

dissonance ['disənəns] *n.* ①不和谐；不协调；不一致 ②【音】不谐和音

dissonant ['disənənt] *a.* ①不和谐的；不协调的，不一致的 ②【音】不谐和的，刺耳的 ‖~ly *ad.*

dissuade [di'sweid] *vt.* 劝阻，劝止：~ sb. from going 劝某人勿去

distaff ['dista:f] I *n.* ①【纺】手工纺纱杆，撵杆，绕线杆 ②妇女们干的事情 ③女子；女性 ④母系 (=~ side) II *a.* ①女子的 ②母系的

distance ['distəns] I *n.* ①距离：Keep a safe ~ between cars! 保持(适当)车距! / It's *some* (*no*) ~ to the station. 到车站相当远(近)。/ My house is within walking ~ of the factory. 我家离厂很近，走走过去就行了。/ go a long ~ in doing sth. 在做某事方面有很大进展 ②远隔，远离 ③远处，远方：The picture looks better (或 to advantage) at a ~. 这幅画远看更好一些。/ We saw a light in the ~. 我们看到远处有灯光。④一长段时间；(时间上的)间隔：look back over a ~ of a century 回顾过去漫长的一个世纪 / At this ~ (of time) it is difficult to date the fossil. 时间隔得这么久了，很难确定化石的年代。⑤冷淡，疏远 ⑥【音】音程 II *vt.* ①把…放在一定的距离之外；使看上去显得遥远 ②(竞争中)把…远远甩在后面 ‖*at a respectful* ~ 敬而远之 / *keep one's* ~ 保持疏远 / *keep (sb.) at a* ~ (对某人)保持疏远 / *know one's* ~ 对自己的地位身分有自知之明

distant ['distənt] *a.* ①远的；久远的；远隔的，稀疏的：a ~ relative 远房亲戚 / ~ control 遥控 / a ~ look 茫然的表情 / in the not too ~ future 在不远的将来 / a grove of ~ trees 稀疏的树林 ②疏远的，冷淡的：be ~ towards sb. 对某人冷淡 ③隐约的：a ~ resemblance 约略的相像 ‖**~ly** *ad.*

distaste ['dis'teist] *n.* 不喜欢，厌恶 (*for*)

distasteful [dis'teistful] *a.* ①令人厌恶的；不合口味的：Smoking is ~ to me. 我不喜欢抽烟。②表示厌恶的 ‖**~ly** *ad.* / **~ness** *n.*

distemper[1] [dis'tempə] **I** *n.* ①坏脾气；愠怒 ②疾病(尤指犬类疾病)；犬瘟热；马腺疫；兽类传染性卡他 ③(政治上或社会上的)混乱，动乱 **II** *vt.* ①在…中造成动乱 ②[常用被动语态]使不正常，使失调

distemper[2] [dis'tempə] **I** *n.* ①胶画颜料(用蛋黄、胶水等调和颜料而成的涂料) ②胶画法；胶画 ③水浆涂料 **II** *vt.* ①把(各种材料)调制成胶画颜料；用胶状物调制(颜料) ②用胶画颜料画；用胶画颜料涂(壁等)

distend [dis'tend] *vt. & vi.* (使)扩张；(使)膨胀；(使)肿胀

distil(l) [dis'til] (distilled; distilling) **❶** *vt.* ①蒸馏；用蒸馏法提取：~ useful solvents from waste water 从废水中蒸馏出各种有用的溶剂 / distilled water 蒸馏水 ②提取…的精华 ③使滴下 **❷** *vi.* ①滴下，滴出

distinct [dis'tiŋkt] *a.* ①与其他不同的，独特的，性质截然不同的：things similar in form but ~ in kind 样子相似实质不同的东西 / Silk is ~ from rayon. 丝跟人造丝截然不同。②明显的，清楚的；确定无误的：There is a ~ improvement in your work. 你的工作有显著的进步。/ a ~ conservative 确定无疑的保守分子 ③难得的 ④[诗]修饰的；变化多端的 ‖**~ly** *ad.* 清楚地；显然：speak ~ly 说话清晰 / **~ness** *n.*

distinction [dis'tiŋkʃən] *n.* ①区分，区别；差别；级别：a line of ~ (区别的)界限 / draw a clear ~ between right and wrong 分清是非 / A should be made *between* the primary and secondary tasks. 要区分主要和次要任务。/ without ~ of (或 as to) sex and age 不分男女老幼 ②个性，特性 ③卓著；盛名：fight with ~ 作战中表现杰出 / people of ~ 知名人士 / gain (或 win) ~ 出名荣誉；荣誉称号；勋章：confer a ~ upon sb. 授与某人称号(或勋章) / win a ~ 荣获勋章(或称号) ‖**a ~ without a difference** 名义上的区别，人为的区别(指实际上并没有什么区别)

distinctive [dis'tiŋktiv] *a.* ①区别性的，鉴别性的 ②有特色的，与众不同的 ‖**~ly** *ad.* / **~ness** *n.*

distinguish [dis'tiŋgwiʃ] **❶** *vt.* ①区别；辨别；识别 ②(凭感觉器官)辨认出：In spite of the haze he can ~ the hills fairly well. 虽然有雾气，他还能辨认出那些小山。③把…区分类：

things *into* classes 把东西分成类 ④[~ one-self] 使杰出；使显出特色 **❷** *vi.* 区别；辨别；识别：~ *between* right and wrong 分清是非 ‖**~able** *a.* 区别得出的；可辨别的；(凭感觉器官)辨认得出的

distinguished [dis'tiŋgwiʃt] *a.* ①以…著名的 ②卓越的，卓著的，杰出的；高贵的：~ services 功勋 / a ~ writer 杰出的作家 / a ~ guest 贵宾 ③(饰物等)符合显贵身分的

distort [dis'tɔ:t] *vt.* ①弄歪(嘴、脸等)：~ the features 使容貌变形 ②歪曲；曲解 ③把…弄得很不正常：a ~ed pattern of behaviour 反常行为 ‖**~edly** *ad.* 被歪曲地

distortion [dis'tɔ:ʃən] *n.* ①弄歪；歪曲；曲解 ②变形 ③[物](透镜成像产生的)畸变；【无】(信号等的)失真：~ of image 像畸变 / frequency ~ 频率失真 ‖**~al** *a.*

distract [dis'trækt] *vt.* ①分散(注意、心思等)；使(人)分心：The noise ~ed me *from* my reading. 喧闹声使我不能专心读书。②[常用被动语态]弄昏，迷惑；使发狂：be ~ed between different opinions 被不同的意见弄得糊里糊涂(无所适从) / be ~ed *with* (或 *by*) anxiety 为忧虑所烦扰

distraction [dis'trækʃən] *n.* ①精神涣散，心神烦乱；精神错乱，发狂：drive sb. to ~ 使某人发狂 ②消遣，娱乐

distraught [dis'trɔ:t] *a.* 异常激动的；心神错乱的；发狂的

distress [dis'tres] **I** *n.* ①悲痛，苦恼，忧伤：suffer excessive ~ 无限悲伤 ②贫困，穷苦 ③危难，不幸：a ship in ~ 遭难船只 / a radio ~ signal 无线电求救信号 ④【律】扣押财物；被扣押的财物 **II** *vt.* ①使悲痛，使苦恼，使忧伤：be ~ed about sth. 为某事而苦恼 / be ~ed at some sad news 因听到某个不幸消息而悲痛 / ~ oneself 担忧，担心 ②使贫困：~ed areas 贫苦地区(尤指失业严重的地区) **III** *a.* ①亏本出售的：~ merchandise 亏本出售的商品 ②扣押物的：a ~ sale 扣押物的出售 ‖**~ call** 遇险信号 / **~ gun** 遇险信号炮 / **~ rocket** 遇险信号用火箭 / **~ warrant** 【律】扣押令

distribute [dis'tribju(:)t] *vt.* ①分发；分配：~ pictures among children 把图片分给孩子们 / ~ magazines to subscribers 把杂志发送给订阅者 ②散布，分布：~ manure over a field 把肥料撒在田里 ③把…分类，区分 ④[印]拆(版) ⑤【逻】周延 ⑥【电】配(电) ‖**~r** *n.* =distributor

distribution [,distri'bju:ʃən] *n.* ①分发；分配；配给物：the mail-order ~ of books 邮订发书 ②法院对无遗嘱死亡者财产的分配 ③销售 ④分布；分布状态；(生物的)地理分布范围；【无】频率分布 ⑤分配装置；分配系统 ⑥区分，分类 ⑦[印]拆版 ⑧【逻】周延，周延性 ⑨【电】配电 ‖**~al** *a.*

distributive [dis'tribjutiv] *a.* ①分发的；分配的；分布的：~ law 【数】分配律 ②【语】个体的，个别的 ③【逻】周延的 **II** *n.* 【语】个体词(如 each, every 等) ‖~ly *ad.* ‖~ **education** [常作 D-E-] (学校与企业主合办的) 课堂教学与职业训练相结合的教育

district ['distrikt] **I** *n.* ①区,管区,行政区: the *District* of Columbia 哥伦比亚特区 (美国首都华盛顿所在的行政区域) ②地区,区域: a mountainous ~ 山区 / a residential ~ 住宅区 ③(美国各州的)众议员选区: an election ~ (美国)基层选区 ④英国教区中的分区 **II** *vt.* 把…划分成区 ‖~ **attorney** (美国)地方检察官 / ~ **council** 英国(市或乡的)区自治会 / ~ **court** 美国地方初审法院 / ~ **judge** 美国地方初审法院法官 / ~ **leader** 美国议会议员选区的政党领导人 / ~ **school** 美国的乡村学校 / ~ **visitor** 英国教区的牧师助理

distrust [dis'trʌst] **I** *n.* 不信任,怀疑: have a ~ *of* sb. (sth.) 对某人(某事)怀疑 **II** *vt.* 不信任,怀疑. ~ one's own eyes 不相信自己的眼睛

disturb [dis'tə:b] *vt.* ①打扰(某人),扰乱(人心等),妨碍(安眠、安静): I'm sorry to ~ you. 对不起,打扰你了. ~ the peace [律]扰乱治安 ②弄乱(计划等): Don't ~ my things. 别弄乱我的东西。③激荡(水面) ‖~**er** *n.* 打扰者 ‖~**ing force** [天]摄动力

disturbance [dis'tə:bəns] *n.* ①骚动,动乱: make a ~ 扰乱,闹乱子 ②打扰,干扰; (情绪等的)纷乱; (身心等方面的)障碍,失调: atmospheric ~ [气]大气扰动; [无]天电干扰 ③[律](权利的)侵犯, (治安的)妨害

disuse I ['dis'ju:z] *vt.* [常以过去分词的形式出现]不用,废弃: a ~d well 废井 **II** ['dis'ju:s] *n.* 不用,废弃: become rusty *from* ~ 因不用而生锈 / The word has fallen *into* ~. 这个词已废而不用了

ditch [ditʃ] **I** *n.* ①(明)沟,沟渠: a drainage ~ 排水沟 ②[英][the D-](空军俚语)英吉利海峡;北海 **II** ❶ *vt.* ①在…上开沟,在…上筑渠 ②用沟渠围住: a pasture hedged and ~ed 周围有篱笆和沟渠的牧场 ③把(汽车)开入沟内;被迫使(飞机)降落在水面上;[美]使(火车)出轨: a ~ing device (无人驾驶飞机的)强迫降落装置 ④抛弃 ❷ *vi.* ①开沟,筑渠;修渠 ②被迫把飞机降落水面上 ‖*be driven to the last* ~ 陷入绝境 / *die in the last* ~ 奋战马死 / *the Big Ditch* [美俚]①大西洋 ②巴拿马运河 ‖'~,water *n.* 沟中死水: as dull as ~*water* 非常单调乏味的

ditto ['ditou] **I** *n.* ①同上,同前(略作 d° 或 do.) ②同样的东西,复制品;极相似的人(或物): a suit (或 a suit of ~s) 同一料子的一套衣服 ③用来表示"同上"、"同前"的符号(即 〃) **II** *ad.* 和以上所说一样地;同样地: We shall act ~. 我们将同样办理。 **III** *vt.* 重复: The next speaker ~ed his argument. 下一个发言的人重复了他的论点。‖*say* ~ *to* 对…表示同意

ditty ['diti] *n.* 小调,小曲 ‖~ **bag** (水手、渔民等)装零星杂物的袋子 / ~ **box** (水手、渔民等)装零星杂物的提箱

divan [di'væn] *n.* ①(土耳其等的)国务会议;会议室;接见室;法院 ②['daivæn](可作床用的)长沙发 ③吸烟室;烟店 ④波斯语诗集,阿拉伯语诗集 ‖~-bed ['daivænbed] *n.* 可作床用的长沙发

dive [daiv] **I** (过去式 dived 或 dove [douv], 过去分词 dived) ❶ *vi.* ①(头先入水地)跳水 ②(潜艇、潜泳者等)潜水 ③(飞机)俯冲: The mercury ~d to ten below zero. 温度突然下降到零下十度。④猛冲;突然从视野中消失: He ~ into his foxhole. 他跳入散兵坑。/ ~ for cover 迅速隐蔽 / ~ down an alley 窜入一条小巷 ⑤把手伸入(*into*): ~ *into* a bag 把手伸入提包 ⑥钻研,探究(*into*): ~ *into* the heart of the matter 探究事情的实质 ❷ *vt.* ①把(头、手等)伸入,插进(*into*) ②使(飞机、潜艇等)突然下降 **II** *n.* ①跳水,潜水,(飞机)俯冲,(潜艇)下潜;突然下降: a fancy ~ 花式跳水 ②猛冲;突然隐去 ③埋头探究 ④[英]设在地下室的饮食店: an oyster ~ 专售牡蛎的地下食品店 ⑤[美]下等酒吧间;下等娱乐场所;盗贼等的隐匿处 ⑥[俚](拳击中)假装被打倒 ‖'~-bomb *vt. & vi.* 俯冲轰炸 / ~ bomber 俯冲轰炸机

diver ['daivə] *n.* ①跳水者;潜水员;潜水采珠员 ②潜水鸟(尤指䴙䴘)

diverge [dai'və:dʒ] ❶ *vi.* ①(道路、路线等)分叉,岔开 ②(意见等)分歧,背驰(*from*) ③离题: ~ *to* another topic 离开本题谈另一问题 ❷ *vt.* 使岔开,使转向: ~ a compass needle 使罗盘的指针偏斜

divergence [dai'və:dʒəns] *n.* ①分叉,岔开;歧异,背驰;离题;偏差 ②[物]发散;[数]散度,发散量 ③[生]趋异

divergent [dai'və:dʒənt], **diverging** [dai'və:dʒin] *a.* ①分叉的,岔开的;歧异的,背道而驰的 ②[物][数]发散的: *diverging* lens 发散透镜 / *divergent* infinite series 发散的无穷级数 ‖**divergently** *ad.*

divers ['daivə(:)z] **I** *a.* ①若干个,好几个: ~ styles of art 好几种艺术风格 ②[古]各种各样的 **II** *pron.* 若干个,好几个

diverse [dai'və:s] *a.* ①(和…)不一样的(*from*) ②多种多样的;形形色色的: offer ~ suggestions 提出各种各样的建议 ③多变化的;有各种不同形式(或性质)的 ‖~**ly** *ad.*

diversified [dai'və:sifaid] *a.* ①多样化的 ②多种经营的: develop a ~ economy 发展多种经营

diversify [dai'və:sifai] ❶ *vt.* ①使不同;使多样化: ~ a course of study 使学习内容多样化 ②把(资金)用来购买多种的证券;把(资金等)分投在好几家公司内 ③增加(工、农业生产)的品种: ~ agriculture 使农产品多样化 ❷ *vi.* 从事多种经营

diversion [dai'və:ʃən] *n.* ①转向,转移: a flood ~ project 分洪工程 / ~ of attention *from* 注意力从…的转移 ②航线(或航行目的地)的改变;[英]

绕道: traffic ~s (由于修路等原因的)交通改道 ③【军】牵制;佯攻: create (或 make) a ~ 进行牵制 ④消遣,娱乐 ‖~ist n. ①政治上的异端分子 ②进行牵制活动者

diversity [dai'və:siti] n. ①差异: ~ of opinion 意见的不同 ②多样性;变化: a great ~ of methods 多种多样的方法 / qualitative ~ 质的多样性

divert [dai'və:t] ❶ vt. ①转移;使转向: ~ the course of a river 使河流改道 / ~ sb.'s interest from sth. 转移某人对某事的兴趣 / ~ the funds to some other purpose 把资金拨充其他用途 ②【军】牵制(敌人) ③使娱乐,使高兴 ❷ vi. 转移;转向: Traffic was ordered to ~ to another road. 命令车辆改道行驶。‖~ing a. 有趣的

divest [dai'vest] vt. 脱去…的衣服;剥夺: ~ a child of his clothes 脱去小孩的衣服 / ~ sb. of power 剥夺某人的权力 ‖ ~ oneself of 脱(衣);放弃,抛弃: He simply cannot ~ himself of the idea. 他硬是不能抛弃这个想法。‖~ment n.

divide [di'vaid] Ⅰ ❶ vt. ①分,划分: Let's ~ ourselves into two groups. 我们分成两个小组吧。/ ~ a thing in two 把东西分成两半 ②分开;隔开,隔离: ~ the patients with hepatitis from the others 隔离肝炎病人 ③分配;分享,分担: ~ sth. among 在(三个或三个以上)之间分配某物 / How shall we ~ up the work? 我们怎样分工? / ~ one's time between work and study 把时间分别用在工作和学习上 / ~ the blame with sb. 和某人共同承担过错 ④分裂;使对立,使(意见)分歧;使踌躇【化】分离: Opinions are ~d on the question. 对这问题,意见有分歧。/ On this point his mind was ~d at first. 起初,他对这点在思想上感到无所适从。⑤在…上刻度: ~ a sextant 在六分仪上表明度数 ⑥【数】除(尽): Divide seven by two (或 Divide two into seven) and you get three and a half. 用二除七得三又二分之一。/ Three ~s nine. 三能除尽九。⑦要求(议会等)对问题进行表决 ❷ vi. ①分,分开: All things invariably ~ into two. 事物都是一分为二的。/ The railway ~s here into two lines. 铁道在这里分成两条支线。②分裂;意见分歧: On some minor points he and I ~d. 在一些细节问题上,他与我意见不同。③【数】(被)除(尽): Six ~s by two. 六能被二除尽。/ Three will not ~ into seven. 三除不尽七。④(议会等)表决 Ⅱ n. ①分;分配 ②分水界,分水岭;分界线 ‖be ~d against itself (团体等)发生内讧 / ~ and rule 分而治之 / the Great Divide ①主要分水岭;[美]落矶山脉分水岭 ②重大危机;生死关头: cross the Great Divide 死

divided [di'vaidid] a. ①分开的;分离的;分裂的 ②【植】(叶)分裂的,全裂的

dividend [dividend] n. ①红利,股息;债息;被分成几股的一笔资金 ②【数】被除数 ‖ ~ warrant 领取股息通知书,股息单

divider [di'vaidə] n. ①划分者;分割者;分裂者;间隔物 ②分配器;分隔器;【电】分压器: current ~ 分流器 ③【数】除数;除法器 ④[复]两脚规,分线规

divination [ˌdivi'neiʃən] n. ①占卜 ②预言;预见;预测

divine [di'vain] Ⅰ a. ①神的,神性的 ②敬神的;神圣的 ③神学的 ④神授的,天赐的 ⑤非凡的,天才的 ⑥[口]好透了的: What ~ weather! 真是好天气! Ⅱ n. 神学学者;牧师 Ⅲ vt. & vi. 占卜;预言;(凭直觉)推测 ‖~ly ad. ‖diving rod "魔杖"(一种用迷信方法探寻矿脉、水源等所用的木叉式探水杖)

diviner [di'vainə] n. ①占卜者;预言者;推测者 ② =divining rod

diving ['daiviŋ] a. 潜水的,跳水的;潜水用的,跳水用的 ‖ ~ bell 钟型潜水器 / ~ board 跳水板 / ~ dress, ~ suit 潜水服

divinity [di'viniti] n. ①神性,神力,神威,神德 ②神;[the D-]【宗】上帝 ③神学;大学的神学院: a doctor of ~ 神学博士(略作 D. D.) ④令人敬服的人,值得崇拜的人 ‖ ~ calf (神学书籍封面用的)暗褐色、不烫金的小牛皮 / ~ school 神学院

divisible [di'vizəbl] a. ①可分的,可分割的 ②【数】可除尽的: Ten is ~ by five. 十能被五除尽。‖divisibly ad.

division [di'viʒən] n. ①分,分开,分割: the ~ of the day into hours 把一天按若干小时进行的划分 ②分配 ③(意见等)的分裂,不一致 ④间隔物;分界线 ⑤区域;英国的选举区: an administrative ~ 行政区 ⑥部分;部门;(机关的)科,处;【军】师;海军舰船分队;海军航空兵分队(由两个以上同型飞机小队组成的作战单位): a ~ commander 师长 / an air ~ [美]空军师 ⑦【生】部(动、植物分类的单位) ⑧【数】除(法): long (short) ~ 长(短)除法 ⑨(议会表决时为计算票数)赞成和反对的分成两组 ⑩[英](监狱中犯人待遇的)分级 ⑪【农】扦插 ‖Divisionism n. 新印象画派(十九世纪末兴起的一种绘画流派,以把各种颜色点子密密层层地点在画布上,在观者的视网膜上引起色彩效果为特征) ‖~ bell 通知会场外的议员即将进行表决的铃声

divisor [di'vaizə] n. 【数】除数,约数: common ~ 公约数

divorce [di'vo:s] Ⅰ n. ①离婚 ②分离,脱离: put an end to the ~ of theory from practice 克服理论脱离实际的现象 / the ~ between state and religion 政教的分离 Ⅱ vt. ①使离婚: be ~d from 与…离婚 / ~ one's spouse 与配偶离婚 / ~ a pair 使夫妇离婚 ②使分离,使脱离 ‖~ment n.

divulge [dai'vʌldʒ] vt. ①泄漏(秘密等) ②[古]宣布,公布 ‖~nce n.

dizzy ['dizi] Ⅰ a. ①头晕目眩的 ②使人头晕的;过分高(或快)的: a ~ height (speed) 使人发晕的高度(速度) ③被弄糊涂的;愚蠢的,戆的 Ⅱ vt.

①使头昏眼花 ②使茫然;使混乱 ‖**dizzily** *ad.* / **dizziness** *n.*

do¹ **I** [强 du:; 弱 du] (did [did], done [dʌn]; 第三人称单数现在式 does [强 dʌz; 弱 dez]) **❶** *vt.*
①做,干;尽(力): We have *done* sowing. 我们已播种完毕。/ What's to be *done*? 怎么办? / ~ manual labo(u)r 从事体力劳动 / ~ good (evil) 做好(恶)事 / ~ one's shopping (washing) 买(洗)东西 / ~ all one can 竭尽全力 / ~ one's duty 尽本分 / What did you ~ *with* yourself on Sunday? 星期天你是怎么过的? / We did not know what to ~ *with* ourselves for joy. 我们高兴得不知怎样才好。
②给与,予: The tempering in the countryside *did* him a lot of good. 在农村的锻炼对他很有好处。/ Will you ~ me a favo(u)r? 帮我个忙好吗? / The frost *did* no damage to the crops. 霜冻并没有使庄稼受到损害。/ He won't ~ anything to you. 他不会拿你怎么样的。/ What have you *done* to yourself (your hand)? 你(你的手)怎会受伤的?
③制作;产生: ~ a film 摄制影片 / ~ a painting (an article) 作画(文) / ~ ten copies 复制十份 / ~ wonders 产生惊人的效果;创造奇迹
④算出,解答: ~ sums 做算术
⑤翻译: ~ a new folk song *into* English 把一首新民歌译成英语
⑥学习,研究: ~ one's lessons 预(或复)习功课 / ~ physics at a university 在大学里学物理
⑦整理,使整洁: ~ the bed 铺床 / ~ the room 收拾房间 / ~ the dishes 洗碗碟 / ~ one's hair (女子)做头发 / ~ one's nails 修剪指甲 / ~ one's teeth 刷牙
⑧料理,照应;负责报道(事件等),负责写(小说等)的评论: He ~es the fiction for a newspaper. 他负责给报纸写小说评论。
⑨适合,对…合用: Will this spanner ~ you? 这把扳头对你合用吗?
⑩走(完): They *did* the journey in an hour. 他们一小时完成了旅程。/ The car is ~ing 50 kilometres an hour. 汽车正以每小时五十公里的速度前进。
⑪搞垮;弄坏: Now you've *done* it. 这回可给你弄坏了。
⑫演出(戏剧),扮演(角色);充当;[口]做出…的样子: ~ the host 做主人(指招待客人) / ~ the polite 表现得彬彬有礼 / ~ the big 充英雄
⑬[口]游览(城市等),参观(博物馆等)
⑭[口]招待,款待: They ~ you very well at that hotel. 那家旅馆服务很周到。
⑮[口]欺骗: ~ sb. *out of* sth. 从某人处骗取某物
⑯[口]服(若干年月)的徒刑
❷ *vi.* ①做;行动: ~ as sb. says 按某人所说的去做 / It's time to be ~ing. 干起来吧。
②[口]发生: What's ~ing over there? 那边在

干什么? / There is nothing ~ing. 没有发生什么(特殊的)事。
③行;足够: That will ~. 行了。(或:够了。)
④生长;进展: Vegetables ~ well here. 这里蔬菜长得好。/ The new apprentices are ~ing quite well. 新艺徒们(在学习、工作、生活等各方面)进步很快。
❸ *v. substitute* [用来避免动词的重复]: A: Who broke the cup? B: I *did*. 甲: 谁把杯子碎了? 乙: 是我。/ They fulfilled their task ahead of time as we *did* ours. 同我们一样,他们也提前完成了任务。/ Some have books, some *don't*. 一些人有书,一些人没有。[注意:这是美国用法;在英国一般以 haven't 代句中的 don't]
❹ [强 du:; 弱 du, də, d] (did; 第三人称单数现在式 does) *v. aux.* ①[构成疑问句]: *Do* you smoke? 你抽烟吗? / *Does* he study English? 他学英语吗?
②[构成否定句]: She *doesn't* (*didn't*) bow down before difficulties. 她不(没有)向困难低头。
③[用于加强语气;发强音]: He *did* accomplish the task in time. 他的确准时完成了任务。/ *Do* be careful! 一定要仔细!
④[用于倒装句]: Well ~ I remember it. 那个我可记得清清楚楚。/ Not only *did* they promise to help, but .... 他们不仅答应给予帮助,而且…

II [du:] ([复] dos 或 do's [du:z]) *n.* ①要求做到的事: the ~s and don'ts of public hygiene 公共卫生注意事项
②[俚]欺骗,骗局: It's all a ~. 这完全是骗局。
③[英口]欢庆会,宴会
④[英][军俚]交战
⑤[俚]分配: Fair ~'s! 公平分配!
‖**can** (或 **could**) ~ **with** ①将就;能对付: *Can* you ~ *with* cold meat for lunch? 你午餐吃冷肉行吗? / I *can* ~ *with* two more buns. 我还能吃两个小面包。②需要;希望得到: He *could* *with* a haircut. 他需要理发了。/ I'm thirsty and *could* ~ *with* a glass of water. 我口渴,真想喝一杯水。/ *Do as you would be done by*. [谚]你愿意别人如何待你,你就应该如何待人。(源出基督教《圣经》) / ~ *away with* ①废除,去掉: ~ *away with* all fetishes and superstitions and emancipate the mind 破除迷信,解放思想 ②弄死,干掉 / ~ *by* 对待 / ~ *down* ①胜过: If it's a game of skill, you'll ~ me *down*. 要是比技巧,你将胜过我。②欺骗 / ~ *for* ①对于…有效(或行得通等) ②[口]照应;…管家: Her neighbour *did for* her during her illness. 她生病时,由一位邻居照应她。③[口]设法弄到: How will you ~ *for* water while (you're) crossing the desert? 你们越过沙漠时水的问题怎么解决呢? ④代替: Will this screwdriver ~ *for* the one you lost? 这把旋凿能代替你丢失的那把吗? ⑤干掉,使丧失性命;毁掉 /

in ①[俚]杀害;搞垮 ②使极度疲乏 ③欺骗 / ~ *in Rome as Rome does* (或 *as the Romans do*) 入国问禁,入乡随俗 / ~ *it all* [美俚]服无期徒刑 / ~ *one's best* 尽力 / ~ *one's damnedest* [俚]拼死命干 / ~ *oneself well* 生活过得好,养尊处优 / ~ *one's utmost* 见 utmost / ~ *or die* 决一死战 / ~ *out* 打扫,收拾: ~ *out* a room 把房间收拾好 / ~ *over* 重做;重新装饰(房子等) / ~ *right* 做得对 / ~ *sb. brown* [英俚]使某人上当 / ~ *sb. in the eye* 欺骗(或愚弄)某人 / ~ *sb. proud* 使某人感到极为荣幸 / ~ *time* 服徒刑 / ~ *up* ①修缮,整新;使整洁: The house needs ~*ing* (或 to be *done*) up. 这所房子需要修一下。 / ~ *up* one's hair (女子)梳理头发;把头发盘起 ②包扎: ~ *up* the books 把书包扎好 ③扣(好): ~ *up* one's coat 把上衣扣好 / ~ *up brown* [美俚]把…彻底搞好 / ~ *well* ①(病人等)进展情况良好;(植物)长得好 ②做得好,处理得好: You would ~ *well* to take his advice. 你还是接受他的劝告为好。 ③(在考试、竞赛中)取得良好成绩 / ~ *with* ① 与…相处: be difficult to ~ *with* (人)难以相处 ② 忍受: We can't ~ *with* such carelessness. 我们不能容忍这种粗枝大叶的作风。 ③ 对付,处置: find a way to ~ *with* the untamed elephant 找到对付那头象的办法 / ~ *without* 没有…也行: This is something we can very well ~ *without*. 没有这东西我们也完全能行。 / ~ *wrong* 做错;作恶,犯罪 / *Have done!* 停止!(或:结束!) / *have done with* 做完,毕;已和…无关,已和…断绝关系: Let's *have done with* it. 我们快把这事结束了吧。 / *Have you done with* the hammer? 榔头你用好了吗? / *have to* ~ *with* 和…有关;和…打交道: The story *has to* ~ *with* the outstanding deeds of a model worker. 这故事是讲一位劳动模范的先进事迹的。 / *have something* (*nothing, not much, a great deal*) *to* ~ *with* 和…有些关系(没有关系,关系不大,关系很大) / *How* ~ *you* (或 *d'ye*) ~? 您好!(被正式介绍时及招呼时用语,被招呼者一般用同样的话回答) / *make* ~ (*with*) 见 make / *Nothing* ~*ing!* 见 nothing / *to* ~ 必须做: What (is) *to* ~? 怎么办? / *What can I* ~ *for you?* 您有什么事吗?(服务员等的招呼语)您要什么? ‖*~-all* *n.* 经管各种事务的人 / *~-or-'die* *a.* (人)不屈不挠的;(斗争等)殊死的,敢死的

do² [dou] *n.*【音】七个唱名之一(在固定唱名法中相当于音名 C)

docile ['dousail, 'dɔsail; 美 'dɔsil, 'dɔsail] *a.* 容易管教的,驯顺的,驯良的: a ~ horse 驯良的马 ‖*~ly* *ad.* / **docility** [dou'siliti] *n.*

dock¹ [dɔk] **I** *n.* ①船坞;[常用复](连带码头、办公室、仓库等的)一排船坞,船埠 (或 graving) ~ 干坞 / a wet ~ 船坞,系船船坞 / a floating ~ 浮坞 / ~ trials【船】码头试车 ②[美]码头,停泊处 ③飞机检修架;杂役 / *'~-'all*

dock at the harbour

机库 ④[英]【交】(铁路终点站的)站台,月台 ⑤(舞台下面的)布景存放处 **II ❶** *vt.* ①把…引入船坞;把…引入码头 ②在…设置船坞 ③使(宇宙飞行器)在外层空间相接 **❷** *vi.* ①入船坞;靠码头: This freighter can sail for 40 days without ~*ing*. 这艘货轮可不停靠码头持续航行四十天。 ② 与另一宇宙飞行器在外层空间相接 ‖*in dry* ~ [口]失业; *Job's* ~ 医院 / ~ *charge*, ~ *dues* 入坞费;码头费 / *'~hand* *n.* 码头工人 / *'~,master* *n.* 船坞长 / *'~,walloper* *n.* ①流浪在码头上打短工者 ②码头上货物搬运工 / *'~yard* *n.* ①船舶修造厂 ②海军船坞;[英]军舰修造所

dock² [dɔk] **I** *n.* ①尾巴的骨肉部分(不包括尾上的毛) ②剪短的尾;去毛的尾 **II** *vt.* ①剪短(尾巴);剪短…的尾巴 ②把…的头发剪短 ③削减(薪给、供应、津贴等) ④(惩罚性地)剥夺,扣去…的应得利益 (*of*) ‖*~-tailed* *a.* 截短尾巴的

dock³ [dɔk] *n.* ①酸模属草类;酸模 ②草本植物

dock⁴ [dɔk] *n.* 刑事法庭的被告席: be in the ~ 在受审 ‖~ *brief* [英]【律】律师给无钱被告的免费辩护

dock in a courtroom

docking ['dɔkiŋ] **I** *n.* 入船坞 **II** *a.* 入船坞的: ~ accommodations 入船坞设施

doctor ['dɔktə] **I** *n.* ①博士(缩写为 D. 或 Dr.): *Doctor* of Science (Medicine, Laws) 理学(医学,法学)博士 / Ph D 哲学博士 / Litt D (或 D

Litt) 文学博士 / *Dr*. Brown 布朗博士 ②医生，医师，大夫；兽医：send for a ~ 请医生 ③巫医 ④[古]学者，先生 ⑤[俚]修理师，修理人：a first-rate car ~ 第一流的修汽车师傅 ⑥[俚]船上(或营地)的厨师 ⑦临时应急的工具(或装置) ⑧(钓鱼用)人造彩色苍蝇 ⑨(为增加食物滋味而加的)掺和物，掺料 **II** ❶ *vt*. ①授…以博士衔；称…为博士 ②诊治，医疗 ③修好(机器等) / ~ a lathe back to use 修复车床以供使用 ④修改，挽杂(酒等)；窜改(文件，账目等)：~ statistics 窜改统计数字 ⑤阉割(家畜) ❷ *vi*. ①行医 ②[方]服药 ‖*put the ~ on sb*. 欺骗某人 / *when ~s differ* (或 *disagree*) [谑] 在大学者们意见分歧的情况下 ‖**~ship** *n*. 博士学位

doctorate ['dɔktərit] *n*. 博士衔，博士学位

doctrine ['dɔktrin] *n*. ①教义，教条；主义 ②学说：the ~ of evolution 进化论 ③[口]教训，训诲

document **I** ['dɔkjumənt] *n*. ①公文，文件；文献：classified ~s 保密文件 ②证件；证券：accounting ~s 会计凭证 / shipping ~s 装货单据 ③纪实影片 **II** ['dɔkjument] *vt*. ①用文件(或证书等)证明；为…提供文件(或证书等)：~ sb.'s claims 用文件证明某人的要求(或权利) / ~ a text 为正文提供文件(或旁证等) ②根据大量纪实材料作成(影片、小说等) ‖**~al** [ˌdɔkju'mentl] *a*.

documentary [ˌdɔkju'mentəri] **I** *a*. ①公文的，文件的；证件的：~ proof (evidence) 文件证明 / a ~ bill (或 draft) 跟单汇票 ②纪录的，记实的：a ~ film 纪录影片 / the ~ theatre 记实戏剧(根据文件或纪录片等资料反映历史或当代事件的戏剧) **II** *n*. 纪录影片；记实小说：a full-length ~ 大型纪录片 ‖**documentarily** [ˌdɔkju'mentərili]，美 ˌdɔkju,men'terili] *ad*.

dodge [dɔdʒ] **I** ❶ *vi*. 躲闪，躲开，躲避；推托，搪塞：~ about 东躲西闪 / ~ behind a tree 躲到树后 ❷ *vt*. 闪开，躲开，避开：~ a blow 闪开一击 / ~ difficulties 回避困难 / ~ a duty 逃避职责 **II** *n*. ①躲闪，躲开；推托，搪塞 ②诡计；妙计，窍门 ‖*be up to all ~s* 诡计多端 / *on the ~* [俚]无固定住处以逃避拘捕

doe [dou] *n*. ①雌鹿；雌兔；雌羚羊；雌山羊 ②[美俚](在社交场合)无男伴的女子

does [强 dʌz；弱 dəz] do¹ 的第三人称单现在式

doesn't ['dʌznt] =does not

dog [dɔg] **I** *n*. ①狗，犬；犬科动物：a hunting ~ 猎犬 / a messenger ~ 通信犬 ②雄狗；雄兽(尤指狐、狼等)：a ~ fox 雄狐 ③[英][the ~s] 跑狗(比赛) ④无赖汉，坏蛋；废物 ⑤[口][常加形容词修饰]家伙：You (dirty) ~! 你这个(坏)小子! / a lucky ~ 幸运儿 ⑥[美]浮华，阔气 ⑦[复][美俚](人的)双脚 ⑧[美口]小红肠；小红肠面包卷 ⑨[美俚]蹩脚货；不受喜爱(或欢迎)的人；不成功的事 ⑩[复](炉中的)铁架 ⑪[the D-][天]大(或小)犬座 ⑫[机]轧头，挡块，止动器；铁

钩，搭钩；拔钉钳；【船】(水密门)夹扣 ⑬【气】假日，幻日；雾虹；预示即将下雨的小块云 ⑭[美][D-](任何一支)印第安族 ⑮[美俚]本票，期票 ⑯[美俚]妓女 **II** (dogged; dogging) *vt*. ①尾随，追踪：~ sb.'s steps 跟踪某人 ②(灾难等)缠住 ③【机】用轧头轧住；用钩抓住 ‖*a dead ~* 没用的东西，废物 / *a ~ in a blanket* 葡萄卷饼，布丁 / *a ~ in the manger* 占着毛坑不拉屎的人 / *a ~'s age* [口]好久 / *a jolly ~* [俚]快活人；有趣的伙伴 / *a sad ~* ①放荡的人 ②鲁莽家伙，易闯祸的人 / *a sly ~* 暗中寻欢的人；暗地里偷鸡摸狗的人 / *Barking ~s do not* (或 *seldom*) *bite*. [谚]吠犬不咬人。/ *be top ~* 处于支配地位 / *be under ~* 处于被支配地位 / *call off the ~s* ①停止追逐(或查询) ②打断不愉快的谈话 / *die a ~'s death* (或 *die like a ~*) 悲惨地死去；可耻地死去 / *~ and maggot* [英][军俚]饼干和干酪 / *~ it* [俚] ①打扮起来摆阔 ②偷懒 ③躲开 / *Every ~ has his day*. [谚]凡人皆有得意日。/ *Give a ~ a bad* (或 *an ill*) *name and hang him*. [谚]一旦给人个坏名声，他就永远洗刷不掉。(意指谗言可畏) / *give* (或 *throw*) *sth. to the ~s* ①扔弃某物 ②牺牲某物保护自己 / *go to the ~s* 堕落，毁灭 / *help a lame ~ over a stile* 助人渡过难关 / *He who has a mind to beat his ~ will easily find his stick*. [谚] 欲加之罪，何患无辞。/ *lead* (*sb*.) *a ~'s life* (使某人)过着受折磨的日子 / *Let sleeping ~s lie*. [谚]莫惹是非。/ *Love me, love my ~*. [谚] 爱屋及乌。/ *not* (*even*) *a ~'s chance* 一点机会也没有 / *not have a word to throw at a ~* (因孤僻或高傲而)不和别人说话 / *put on* (*the*) *~* 摆架子 / *shoot over* (或 *to*) *a ~* 打猎时用狗找回猎物 / *teach an old ~ new tricks* 教八十岁姥姥学吹打；使守旧的人接受新事物 / *the ~ before its master* [英俚]暴风前的海浪 / *the ~s of war* 战争造成的破坏，兵燹：let slip the ~s of war [诗]开战 / *try it on the* (或 *a*) *~* 牺牲别人进行试验；电影试演检验效果 / *wake a sleeping ~* 招惹是非 ‖**~hood** *n*. 狗性 / **~like** *a*. 狗一样的；忠于主人的 ‖**'~berry** *n*. 梾木属植物的果实，山茱萸果实；梾木属植物，山茱萸 / **'~-,biscuit** 喂狗的饼干；硬饼干 / **'~-box** *n*. 铁路上运狗的车厢 / **'~cart** *n*. ①狗拖车 ②单匹马拉的马车 / **'~-'cheap** *a*. & *ad*. 极便宜的(地) / **~ days** ①三伏天，大热天 ②无所作为的时期；无精打采的日子 / **'~-ear** *n*. (书页的)折角 *vt*. 把(书页)折角 / **'~-eared** *a*. (书页)折角的，(书)翻旧了的 / **'~-,eat-'~** *n*. & *a*. 狗咬狗(的)，损人利己的(的) / **'~fight** *n*. & *vi*. 狗打架，狗咬狗；[口](飞机等)混战 / **'~fish** *n*. 【动】角鲨，星鲨；弓鳍鱼 / **'~hole** *n*. ①狗洞 ②破旧简陋的房间 ③[俚]不安全的小煤矿 / **~house** *n*. 狗窝；小窝棚：in the ~house [俚] 失宠，受耻辱 / **Latin** 不正规的拉丁语 / **~ lead** 狗链子

'~leg, '~legged a. 象狗的后腿一样折曲的: a ~leg(ged) staircase【建】双壁楼梯 / ~ paddle 狗爬式游泳 / '~-,paddle vi. 狗爬式游泳 / robber 【军俚】军官的传令兵 / '~'s-,body n. ① 豆粉布丁 ② [海俚] 打杂; 级别低的船员 / '~'s-ear n. & vt. =~-ear / '~shore n.【船】(下水滑道的) 抵键, (下水前用的) 斜支柱 / '~-skin n. (做手套等用的) 狗皮 / '~sleep n. 不时惊醒的睡眠 / ~('s) nose 啤酒和杜松子酒混合的饮料 / ~ spike (铁路上的) 钩头道钉 / Dog Star【天】天狼星 (大犬座主星); 南河三 (小犬座主星) / ~'s tooth (男子衣料的) 格子花纹 / ~ tag ① 狗牌, 狗照 ② (战时士兵挂在颈上的) 身分识别牌 / '~-'tired a. 累极了的 / '~tooth n. ① 犬齿 ②【建】犬牙饰, 四叶饰 / '~trot n. & vi. 小步跑 / '~vane n.【船】(桅上) 风向指示器 / '~watch n. ①【海】(下午四点到六点或六点到八点的) 两小时值班 ② 夜班 (尤指额外的一班) / '~wood n. 株木属植物, 山茱萸

dogged ['dɔgid] a. ① 顽强的 ② 顽固的, 固执的: ~ adherence to 对…的死抱不放 ‖*It's ~ (that) does it.* 天下无难事, 只怕有心人。‖~ly ad. / ~ness n.

doggerel ['dɔgərəl] **I** n. 打油诗; 拙劣的诗 **II** a. (诗) 浅薄拙劣的, 嘞头的

dogma ['dɔgmə] ([复] dogmas 或 [罕] dogmata ['dɔgmətə]) n. ① 教义, 教理 ② 武断的意见

dogmatic(al) [dɔg'mætik(əl)] a. ① 教条主义的: a ~ attitude 教条主义的态度 ② 教义的, 教理的 ③ 固执己见的, 武断的: a ~ statement 武断的话 ‖**dogmatically** ad.

dogmatize, dogmatise ['dɔgmətaiz] **❶** vi. ① 教条地说 (或写) ② 武断 **❷** vt. 把…说成教条, 把…作为教条阐述

doing ['du(ː)iŋ] n. ① 做, 干 ② [复] 活动, 举动, 所作所为 ③ [复] [俚] (统指任何) 所需要的东西 ④ [复] [方] 社交活动

doldrums ['dɔldrəmz] [复] n. ① 忧郁, 郁闷; 无生气, 意气消沉: That country's postwar economy has always been in the ~. 战后那个国家的经济一直毫无生气。②【气】赤道无风带; 赤道无风带的微风

dole[1] [doul] **I** n. ① [古] 命运 ② 施舍; 少量的施舍物 ③ [the ~] [英口] 失业者可以申请的救济: be (go) *on* the ~ 接受 (开始接受) 失业救济 **II** vt. 少量地发放 (救济品) (*out*) ‖~sman ['doulzmən] n. 接受施舍物的人; 接受失业救济的人

dole[2] [doul] n. [诗] 悲哀

doleful ['doulful] a. ① 令人悲哀的; 表示悲哀的 ② 感觉悲哀的 ‖~ly ad. / ~ness n.

doll [dɔl] **I** n. ① 玩偶, 娃娃 (指玩具) ② 好看而没有头脑的女子 ③ [美俚] 姑娘, 少女 ④ [俚] (常作称呼) 宝贝儿 **II** [口] vt. & vi. (把…) 打扮得漂漂亮亮 (*up*) ‖*cutting out (paper)* ~s [美俚] 发疯的 ‖'~face n. 长着一张娃娃脸的人 /

'~house n. ① (儿童放娃娃的) 玩具小屋 ② 很小的住屋

dollar ['dɔlə] n. ① 元 (美国、加拿大、澳大利亚、埃塞俄比亚等的货币单位; 符号为 $ 或 $) ② 价值一元的硬币 (或纸币) ③ [英俚] 五先令 ‖*bet one's bottom ~* 孤注一掷 / *It's ~s to buttons.* [口] 这是十拿九稳的。/ *It's ~s to doughnuts.* [俗] 相差悬殊。‖~ area 美元地区 (指货币与美元有联系的地区) / '~-a-'year a. [美] 领象征性薪俸的 / ~ bloc 美元集团 / ~ diplomacy 金元外交 / '~-(s)-and-'cent(s) a. 纯经济的

dolorous ['dɔlərəs] a. (令人) 忧伤的, (令人) 悲哀的 ‖~ly ad.

dolphin ['dɔlfin] n. ①海豚科动物; 海豚, 江猪 ②【动】鲯鳅 ③ [the D-]【天】海豚座 ④ (码头的) 系缆桩, 系缆浮标

dolt [doult] n. 笨蛋, 傻瓜

domain [də'mein, dou'mein] n. ① 领域, 领土, 版图; 领地 ② 产业, 房地产; 产业所有权 ③ (活动、学问、影响等的) 范围, 领域: the ~ of science 科学领域 / Chemistry is · his special ~. 化学是他的专业。/ be out of sb.'s ~ 非某人所长 ④【数】域 (尤指函数的定义域) ‖**eminent ~**【律】(国家对一切产业的) 支配权, 征用权

dome [doum] **I** n. ① 圆屋顶 ② 圆盖; 穹窿;【化】(蒸馏釜的) 拱顶: the ~ of the sky 穹苍 ③【机】汽室; 圆顶帽 ④ [诗] 大厦 ⑤ [美俚] 头, 脑袋 ⑥【地】穹地, 圆丘 ⑦【化】(结晶的) 坡面 **II** ❶ vt. ① 加圆屋顶于…上 ② 使成圆顶 ❷ vi. 成圆顶状, 膨胀成圆顶状 ‖'~d a. (圆) 顶的; 圆盖形的; 半球形的 / ~like a. 穹顶的

domestic [də'mestik] **I** a. ① 家里的, 家庭的: ~ economy 家庭经济 / ~ science 持家学 ② 本国的, 国内的: the full utilization of ~ resources 国内资源的充分利用 / ~ and foreign policies 国内外政策 ③ 国产的, 自己制造的: ~ products 国产, 国货, 土产 ④ 一心只管家务的; 一心追求家庭乐趣的 ⑤ 养在家里的, 驯养的: ~ animals (fowls) 家畜 (禽) **II** n. ① 家仆, 佣人 ② [美] [复] 国货, 本国制造品 ‖~ally ad.

domesticate [də'mestikeit] vt. ① 使归化; 采用 (异族风俗等) ② 使喜家居, 使专注于家务 ③ 驯养 (动物), 驯化 (动植物) ④ 使通俗化 ‖**domestication** [də,mesti'keiʃən] n. / **domesticator** n. ① 驯养者, 驯化者 ② 使归化者

domesticity [,doumes'tisiti] n. ① 家庭生活 ② 对于家庭生活的爱好, 深居简出 ③ [复] 家务, 家事

domicile ['dɔmisail] **I** n. ① 住处 ②【律】户籍 (法律上的长住处): sb.'s ~ of choice (出生地以外) 自己选择的 (出生地的) 户籍 ③ [商] 期票支付场所 **II** ❶ vt. ① 使 (某人) 定居下来: ~ oneself in (或 at) a place 落户于某地 ② 指定 (期票) 在某地支付 ❷ vi. 定居, 安家

dominance ['dɔminəns] n. ① 优势, 支配, 控制, 统治: gain ~ *over* 对…取得优势, 支配… ②【生】显性; 优势度

dominant ['dɔminənt] **I** ***a.*** ①支配的，统治的；占优势的：a ~ position 统治地位 ②居高临下的，高耸的：a ~ peak 最高峰，主峰 ③【生】显性的；优势的：~ character 显性性状 / ~ mutant 显性突变型；显性突变体 ④【音】第五音的 **II** ***n.*** ①主因，要素；主要的人（或物）②【生】显性性状；显性基因；优势种 ③【音】全阶第五音 ‖**~ly** ***ad.***

dominate ['dɔmineit] ❶ ***vt.*** ①支配，统治，控制：~ the situation 控制局势 ②（山、塔等）高出于，俯视 ❷ ***vi.*** ①处于支配地位，拥有压倒势力：At one time this view was *dominating* over the academic circles. 这种观点一度在学术界占着支配地位。②超出在上，高耸 ‖**domination** [ˌdɔmi'neiʃən] ***n.*** / **dominator** ***n.*** 支配者，统治者；占优势者

domineer [ˌdɔmi'niə] ❶ ***vi.*** ①跋扈，作威作福 (*over*) ②高耸 (*over*) ❷ ***vt.*** 对…飞扬跋扈，盛气凌人地对待 ‖**~ing** [ˌdɔmi'niəriŋ] ***a.*** 盛气凌人的

dominion [də'minjən] ***n.*** ①统治，管辖，支配；统治权：exercise ~ over 对…行使统治（或管辖）权 ②疆土，领土，版图；（封建地主的）领地 ③[D-]（英帝国的）自治领 ④【律】所有权 ‖***Old Dominion*** [美] 弗吉尼亚州的别名 ‖**Dominion Day** 自治领日（七月一日，加拿大的法定假日，纪念一八六七年加拿大获得英帝国自治领的地位）

domino ['dɔminou] ([复] domino(e)s) ***n.*** ①（化装跳舞会上穿的带有面具、头巾的）化装外衣；穿化装外衣的人 ②（遮住眼睛和部分面孔的）黑色小蒙面具 ③[~(e)s] [用作单] 西洋骨牌（游戏）：the ~ theory（或 the theory of falling ~*(e)s*）多米诺（骨牌）理论（政治用语；指一个倒，全部倒；牵一发而动全身）④[复][美俚]牙齿 ‖***It is ~ with ....*** …完蛋了。

don[1] [dɔn] ***n.*** ①[D-] 先生（西班牙人用在人名前的尊称）②西班牙贵族，绅士 ③[古]名人，名家，（某方面的）专家 (*at*) ④英国牛津大学（或剑桥大学）学院的学监；大学教师

don[2] [dɔn] (donned; donning) ***vt.*** 披上，穿上，戴上：He *donned* work clothes and a wicker helmet. 他穿上工作服，戴上柳条帽。/ ~ the cloak of [喻]披上…的外衣

donate [dou'neit; 美 'douneit] ❶ ***vt.*** 捐赠，赠送：~ blood 献血 ❷ ***vi.*** 捐赠，赠送 (*towards*)

donation [dou'neiʃən] ***n.*** ①捐赠，赠送 ②捐赠物，赠品，捐款

done [dʌn] **I** do[1] 的过去分词 **II** ***a.*** ①完毕了的：One more question and I'm ~. 我再提一个问题就完了。/ Will you never get ~ with that noise? 你吵得还有个完没有？/ get sth. ~ as quick as possible 尽快把某事干完 ②注定要完蛋的 ③煮熟了的：The meat is ~. 肉煮熟了。④精疲力竭的：The horse was too ~ to go any farther. 马疲乏得不能再走了。⑤合乎礼俗的：It isn't ~. 那样做是失礼的。**III** ***ad.*** [美俚] 已经（=already）‖***be ~ for***（人、物）不中用了，完蛋了：These shoes *are ~ for*. 这些鞋子完蛋了。/ ***be ~ in***（或 ***up***）精疲力竭 / ***Done!*** 好！行！赞成！得！（=Agreed!）/ ***Easier said than ~.*** 见 **easy** / ***No sooner said than ~.*** 说到做到。/ ***Well ~!*** 干得好！/ ***What's ~ cannot be undone.*** [谚]事已定局，无可挽回。（或：覆水难收。）

donkey ['dɔŋki] ***n.*** ①驴 ②笨蛋，蠢驴 ③固执的人；顽固的人：as stubborn as a ~ 非常固执 ④【机】辅助发动机；辅助机车；辅助锅炉；辅助泵 ‖**~ act** [美俚]蠢举，失策 / **~ boiler** 辅助锅炉 / **~ engine** 【机】辅助发动机；辅助机车 / **~man** ['dɔŋkimən] ***n.*** 辅机操作工 / **~ pump** 辅助泵 / **~'s breakfast** [美俚]草垫 / **~'s years** [美俚]很久，多年：I met him *~'s years* back. 我在好久好久以前遇见过他。/ **'~work** ***n.*** 呆板的例行工作；恼人的苦活

donor ['dounə] ***n.*** ①赠与人，捐献者 ②【医】供血（或输血）者（=blood ~）；（移植术中）皮肤（或组织）的供给者；移植体：the ~ area in skin grafting 植皮中的移植区 ③【物】施主（指能给出电子的半导体杂质）；【化】给予体，供体

don't [dount] **I** =do not **II** ***n.*** 要他人别做某事的要求；禁止的事

doom [du:m] **I** ***n.*** ①厄运；死亡：go to one's ~ 灭亡 ②【史】法律，法令；[古]判决，定罪；【宗】末日审判：the day of ~ 【宗】最后审判日，世界末日（=doomsday）**II** ***vt.*** 注定，命定；判决

door [dɔ:, dɔə] ***n.*** ①门；通道：the front (back) ~ 前（后）门 ②家，户 ‖***at death's ~*** 生命危在旦夕 / ***behind closed ~s*** ①与外界隔绝地 ②秘密地 / ***close***（或 ***shut***）***the ~ on***（或 ***upon, against***）①把…拒于门外 ②把（谈判等）的门堵死 / ***darken the ~*** 闯入 / ***from ~ to ~*** 挨家挨户地 / ***in ~s*** 在屋内 / ***keep open ~s*** 款待来客；好客 / ***lay sth. at sb.'s ~*** 把某事归咎于某人 / ***lie at sb.'s ~***（过失、罪责）归于某人 / ***lock***（或 ***shut***）***the stable ~ when***（或 ***after***）***the horse is stolen*** 贼去关门 / ***next ~*** 隔壁的；在隔壁：the family *next ~* 隔壁邻居 / go *next ~* 到隔壁那一家去 / ***next ~ to*** ①与…相邻 ②几乎：It's *next ~ to* impossible. 这简直不可能。/ ***not darken sb.'s ~*** 不再登某人家门 / ***open the ~s to*** 向…开门 / ***out of ~s*** 在户外 / ***show sb. the ~*** 把某人撵走 / ***slam the ~*** ①关门；无礼排斥，摈弃 ②拒绝讨论（或考虑）/ ***slam the ~ in sb.'s face*** 拒绝某人进入；拒绝听取某人意见 / ***sweep before one's own ~*** 正人先正己 / ***within ~s*** 在屋内 / ***without ~s*** 在户外 ‖**'~bell** ***n.*** 门铃 / **~ buster** 商店为招揽顾客而四出大做广告的商品 / **'~case, '~frame** ***n.*** 门框 / **'~-hinge** ***n.*** 门上的铰链 / **'~ˌkeeper** ***n.*** 看门人 / **'~knob** ***n.*** 门上的球形捏手 / **'~man** ***n.*** 门口仆役 / **'~mat** ***n.*** ①门前的擦鞋棕垫 ②[喻]逆来顺受的可怜虫 / **~ money** 入场费 / **'~nail** ***n.***（供装饰用的）缀在

门上的大钉子 / '~**plate** *n.* 门牌 / '~**post** *n.*
门柱 / '~**sill** *n.* 门槛 / '~**step** *n.* 门前的石
阶 / '~**stone** *n.* 门口铺石 / '~**stop** *n.* 制门器
(指用于使门开至一定宽度或不致猛然碰上的弹
簧等) / '~**way** *n.* 门口;[喻]入门 / '~**yard**
n. [美]门前庭院

dope [doup] I *n.* ①粘稠物, 胶状物 ②【化】(机翼)
涂料, 涂布油;(制炸药等的)吸收剂; 添加剂; 抗爆
剂 ③(给马等服的)兴奋剂 ④[俚]麻醉品, 毒品
(如鸦片等): a ~ habit 吸毒瘾 ⑤[俚]酒; 软饮
料(一种没有酒精成分的饮料,如可口可乐等) ⑥
[俚]吸毒者; 呆子 ⑦[美俚](有关赛马实力的)情
报; 内幕; (可靠的)内部消息 II ❶ *vt.* ①用粘稠
物处理(某物); 给…上涂料; 向…内掺入添加剂
(或抗爆剂): ~*d* fuel 含抗爆剂的燃料; 乙基化
汽油; 含铅汽油 ②给(马)服兴奋剂 ③给(人)服
麻醉品 ④预测出, 解出 ❷ *vi.* 服用麻醉品
‖~ **off** [俚]昏睡; 昏昏沉沉 / ~ **out** ①(根据现
有材料)预测 ②猜出, 解出 ③想出(解决问题的
方法等), 拟出(计划等) ‖~ **fiend** [俚]有吸毒
瘾的人 / '~**sheet** *n.* (赛马等的)内情简报

dormant ['dɔ:mənt] *a.* ①休眠的, 蛰伏的: a ~
plant 休眠植物 / a ~ snake 蛰伏的蛇 ②在眠
态中的; 暂停活动(或作用)的: a ~ volcano 暂死
的火山 / ~ capital 游资 ‖*lie* ~ 蛰伏着; 潜伏着
‖~ **partner** 不参加活动、通常隐名的合伙人 /
~ **window** [方]【建】屋顶窗, 老虎窗

dormitory ['dɔ:mitri] *n.* ①[英]集体寝室; [美]
宿舍 ②(在城市工作的人们的)郊外居住区

dorsal ['dɔ:səl] *a.* ①【动】背面的, 背部的: ~ fin
脊鳍 ②【植】远轴的 ‖~**ly** *ad.*

dose [dous] I *n.* ①(药的)剂量, 用量; 一剂, 一服:
take a ~ 吃一剂药 / an effective (a lethal) ~
有效(致死)剂量 ②一次, 一番: a ~ of punishment 一次惩罚 / a ~ of flattery 一番奉承 ③
一次投入量; 放射能剂量 ④(酒等的)增味剂 ⑤
[美俚]花柳病(尤指淋病) II ❶ *vt.* ①给…服药:
~ oneself with quinine 给自己服奎宁 ②给(药):
~ out aspirin to a patient 给病人服阿斯匹灵
③加增味剂于(酒等) ❷ *vi.* 服药 ‖~ *sb.* **with**
his own physic 以其人之道还治其人之身

dossier ['dɔsiei] *n.* 一宗档案材料(尤指关于个人经
历的)

dost [dʌst] [古] do¹ 的第二人称单数现在式

dot¹ [dɔt] I *n.* ①小点, 圆点 ②一点点大的东西:
a mere ~ of a child 小不点儿, 小家伙 ③【音】符
点(在音符后的一点, 表示延长 1/2); 表示断奏的
记号 ④【数】小数点, 相乘的符号 ⑤句号 II
(dotted; dotting) ❶ *vt.* 打点于; 星罗棋布于:
~ the canvas with specks of paint 用颜料在油
画布上打上许多小点 / Tractors *dotted* the fields.
田野里拖拉机星罗棋布。 / a *dotted* line 虚线 ②
[英俚]打: ~ *sb.* one in the eye 一拳打在某人眼
睛上 ❷ *vi.* 打点 ‖~ *and carry one* (做加法
时)逢十进一 / ~ *and go one* 一瘸一拐 / ~
the (或 *one's*) *i's and cross the* (或 *one's*) *t's*

一丝不苟; 详述, 讲清楚 / *off one's* ~ [俚]傻
头傻脑的; 发疯的 / *on the* ~ 准时地 / *sign on
the dotted line* 在虚线上署名; [喻]全部接受,
毫不迟疑地同意 ‖'~-**and**-'**dash** *a.* ①一点一
划间的: run a ~-*and-dash* line across the sheet
在纸上画一条点划相间 (·—·—·—) 的线 ②莫尔斯
(Morse) 电码的 / '~-**se**₁**quential** *a.* 【无】(彩色
电视的)色顺序制的

dot² [dɔt] *n.* 嫁妆, 妆奁 ‖~**al** ['doutl] *a.*

dotage ['doutidʒ] *n.* ①老年昏愦, 老年糊涂 ②溺爱,
过度的偏爱

dote [dout] *vi.* ①昏愦, (因年老)智力衰退 ②溺爱,
过分喜爱 (*upon, on*)

double ['dʌbl] I *a.* ①两倍的; 加倍的: do ~ work
做双份工作 / The material is ~ width. 这块料
子是双幅的。/ The production is now ~ what
it was ten years ago. 目前的产量是十年前的两
倍。/ ~ whisky 双料威士忌 ②双的; 双重的;
【植】重瓣的: ~ cropping rice 双季稻 /
exploitation 双重剥削 / a ~ agent 双重间谍
(指同时为雇佣方及其敌方工作的特务) / a ~
standard (对不同的人所采用的)不同标准 ③供
两者用的: a ~ bed 双人床 / (意义)双关的; 模
棱两可的 ⑤两面派的: play the ~ game 耍两面
派 ⑥(乐器)低八度的 II *ad.* ①双倍地: at ~
the speed 以加倍速度 ②双重地 ③双双地: ride
~ 两人合骑一马 III *n.* ①两倍 ②折迭, 重迭 ③
【军】跑步: advance at (或 on) the ~ 跑步前进
④[复](网球、乒乓球等的)双打: mixed ~ 男女
混合双打 ⑤替代演员, 后备演员(或歌手) ⑥极
相似的人(或物) ⑦幽灵 ⑧(桥牌中的)加倍 ⑨
急转弯, 突然转向;折回 ⑩诡计; 回避 ⑪[印]排
重的字句; 双印(指同一页上由于不慎印了两次)
IV ❶ *vt.* ①是…的两倍; 使…加倍: The output
has been ~*d* in the past five years. 在过去五年中
产量翻了一番。②把…对折; 握紧(拳头) ③替代
(演员); 兼演(两角) / (在译制片中)为…配音 ④
【音】使…高(或低)八度 ⑤【海】绕过(海岬等) ❷
vi. ①变成两倍; 增加一倍; (桥牌中)加倍 ②跑
步 ③往回跑; 曲折迂回: The animal ~*d* on its
tracks. 那野兽急忙折回逃跑。④替演出 (*for*);
兼演两角 (*as*) ⑤兼作: a big dining hall that
~*s as* an auditorium 兼作礼堂用的大饭厅 ⑥兼
奏 (*on*) ‖~ **back** ①把…对折 ②往回跑 / ~ *or
quits* (指打赌等)要末债务加倍要末一笔勾销 /
~ **up** ①把…对折; 可对折 ②弯曲(手脚等), 握
紧(拳头) ③(因大笑或剧痛而)弯着身子; 使把身
子弯曲起来 ④与别人挤住在一起 / *see* ~ 见
see¹ ‖~**ness** *n.* [无]倍压器, 倍频
器 ②【纺】并线机 ③【自】倍增器, 乘 2 装置 ‖
doubly *ad.* ‖~-'**acting** *a.* 【机】双动的 /
'~-₁**barrel** 双管枪 (或炮) / '~-₁**barrel(l)ed**
a. ①双管的 ②(姓氏)双的(如 Fowkes-Fowey)
③意义双关的, 模棱两可的 ④双重目的的 /
'~-₁**bedded** *a.* 备有两只床的; 备有双人床的 /
'~-'**breasted** *a.* (外套等)双排钮扣的 / '~-

'chinned *a.* 双下巴的 / **'~-'cross** *n. & vt.*
[口]欺骗,出卖 / **'~-'crosser** 骗子 / **'~-'dealer**
n. 两面派人物 / **'~-'dealing** *n. & a.* 搞两面派
(的) / **'~-deck(ed)** *a.* 双层结构的: a ~-*deck*
bed 双层床 / a ~-*decked* bridge 铁路公路两用
桥 / **'~-'decker** *n.* 双层结构;双层船;双层电
车;双层桥梁;双层床 / **~ Dutch** 难以理解的东
西(尤指演说) / **'~-'dyed** *a.* ①(印染中)两次染
色的,双染的,双染 ②(在信仰等方面)根深蒂固的;彻
头彻尾的 / **'~-'edged** *a.* ①双刃的 ②双重目
的的 ③意义双关的;两可的 / **'~-'ender** *n.* ①
头尾相似的船 ②两头可开的电车 / **~ entry** 复
式簿记 / **~ exposure【摄】**两次曝光,双重曝光 /
'~-faced *a.* ①两面可用的 ②口是心非的,伪
善的 / **~ feature** (一部)上下两集的电影 / **'~-**
'header *n.* ①双头式列车(指由两辆机车牵引的
列车) ②(棒球)同一对球队一天内的两次比赛 /
'~-'jointed *a.* 双重关节的,前后左右可自由活
动的 / **~-leaded** ['dΔbl'ledid] *a.* (印刷品等)行
距宽的 / **'~-'lock** *vt.* 给…上双锁;特别谨慎地
锁上 / **'~-'minded** *a.* ①思想上动摇的 ②口是
心非的 / **'~-'park** *vt. & vi.* (把车)停在与人
行道平行停靠的车旁 / **'~-'quick** *a.* 很快的
ad. 跑着步 *n.* 跑步 *vt. & vi.* (使)跑步 / **'~=**
re'fine *vt.* 把…两次精炼 / **'~-'space** *vt. &*
vi. (在打字机上)隔行打印 / **~ star【天】**双星 /
~ take 一种开始是征住后来才恍然大悟的反应
(尤指喜剧中这种表演): do a ~ *take* 开始是一
征后来才恍然大悟 / **'~-'talk** *n.* ①不知所云的
话 ②模棱两可的欺人之谈 / **'~-team** *vt.* 用两
名球员拦阻(对方球员) / **'~think** *n.* 矛盾想
法 / **~ time** ①跑步 ②双倍工资 / **'~-time** *vt.*
& vi. =~-quick (*vt. & vi.*) / **'~-'tongued** *a.*
欺骗的 / **'~-'track** *vt.* 使(铁路)成复轨

doublet ['dΔblit] *n.* ① (十四世纪至十六世纪的)
男紧身上衣,马甲 ②成对物,对偶物;[复]骰子成
的成对 ③一对中的一个;[语]一对同源词(如 card
和 chart) 中的一个 ④[印]排重的字句 ⑤(双管
猎枪)一枪打中的双鸟 ⑥[物]双合透镜;(光谱)
双重线;偶极子,对称振子;[无]偶极天线

doubt [daut] **I** *vt.* ❶ *vt.* ①怀疑;不信;拿不准[注意:
后接名词或代词时,疑问句和否定句用连接词 that,
肯定句一般用连接词 whether, if 等]: ~ the cor-
rectness of 怀疑…的正确性 / ~ sb. 怀疑某人 /
We *don't* ~ *that* (或 *but* 或 *but that*) he can do
a 'good job of it. 我们并不怀疑他能把这事干得
很好。 / I ~ *if* it's true. 我看这未必是事实。 /
I ~ very much *whether* I shall be able to come.
我拿不准是否能来。 ②[古]恐怕 ❷ *vi.* 怀疑
(*about, of*): We have never ~*ed* of the success
of our experiment. 我们的实验会成功,对于这
点我们从未怀疑过。 **II** *n.* ①怀疑,疑惑,疑问
②[常用复]疑虑 ‖*beyond* ~ [常作插入语]
毫无疑问的 / *give sb. the benefit of the* ~
(在证据不足的情况下)假定某人是无辜的 / *hang*
in ~ 悬而未决 / *in* ~ ①感到怀疑,拿不准

的: When *in* ~ about the meaning of a word,
consult a dictionary. 拿不准词义时,查查词典。
②被怀疑的: The outcome of the match was *in*
~ then. 当时比赛的结果还看不准。 / *make*
~ (*of*) (对…)毫不怀疑 / *no* ~ 无疑地;[口]很
可能: You have *no* ~ heard the news. 你总会
听到这个消息了吧。 / *throw* (或 *cast*) ~ *upon*
使人对…产生怀疑 / *without* (*a*) ~ 无疑地
‖**~er** *n.* 怀疑者,令人怀疑的人 / **~ing** *a.* 抱
怀疑态度的人;不信宗教的人 / **~ing** *a.* 抱怀疑
态度的: a ~*ing* Thomas ['tɔmɔs] 一贯抱怀疑态
度的人

doubtful ['dautful] *a.* ①怀疑的; 疑惑的: be (或
feel) ~ *of* (或 *about*) sth. 对某事有怀疑 / I am
~ (*as to*) which to choose. 我决不定选择哪一个。
②可疑的;使人产生疑问的: a ~ character 可疑
的人物 / a ~ point of grammar 语法上的疑
点 / It was never ~ that they would come as
promised. (人们)从未怀疑他们将如约前来。 ③
难料的;未定局的: The weather looks ~. 这天
气靠不住。 ④含糊的;不确定的: a ~ expression
含糊的词句 / a ~ syllable (letter) 可读长音或
短音的音节(字母) ⑤未必好的: a ~ taste 低级趣
味 / a person of ~ repute 声誉不大好的人
‖**~ly** *ad.* / **~ness** *n.*

doubtless ['dautlis] **I** *ad.* ①无疑地: This is ~ the
best. 这无疑是最好的。 ②[口]很可能: You are
~ right, but we had better make a further
study of it. 大概你是对的,不过我们最好还是
再研究一下。 **II** *a.* [罕]无疑的 ‖**~ly** *ad.* /
~ness *n.*

dough [dou] *n.* ①(揉捏好的)生面: knead ~ 揉面
②生面团似的一团(如陶土、油灰等) ③[美俚]钱,
现钞 ④[俚]美国步兵 (=~boy) ‖**'~boy** *n.* ①
(油炸的)面团;汤团 ②[俚]美国步兵 / **'~face**
n. (美国内战时) 不反对(或同情)南方黑奴制的
北方人 (或北方议员) / **'~foot** ([复] **~feet** 或
~foots) *n.* [美]步兵 / **'~nut** *n.* ①炸面饼圈
②[美俚]汽车轮胎

doughty ['dauti] *a.* [古][谑]勇猛的; 能干的
‖**doughtily** *ad.* / **doughtiness** *n.*

dour [duɔ] *a.* ①顽强不屈的;严厉的;执拗的 ②阴
郁的,郁郁寡欢的;[苏格兰](天气)阴沉的 ‖**~ly**
ad. / **~ness** *n.*

dove[1] [dΔv] *n.* ① 鸽(一般指小野鸽;家鸽通常称
pigeon);斑鸠(尤指欧斑鸠) ②[宗]圣灵 ③和平
的象征,和平使者;报喜人 ④鸽派人物,主和派人
物 ⑤纯洁温柔的人;[常作亲热称呼]宝贝儿
儿 ‖**~let** ['dΔvlit] *n.* 幼鸽 / **~like** *a.* (鸽子般)
纯洁可爱的,温柔的 ‖**~cot(e)** *n.* 鸽棚,鸽房:
flutter the ~*cot(e)s* 扰乱鸽棚; [喻]使温顺和平
的人们骚动起来 / **'~-eyed** *a.* 双眼温柔无邪的

dove[2] [douv] dive 的过去式

dovetail ['dΔvteil] **I** *n.* ①鸠尾榫,楔形榫 ②鸠尾
接合 (=~ joint) **II** ❶ *vt.* ①用鸠尾榫接合;
把…制成鸠尾榫 ② [喻]和…吻合;使吻合,使相

呼应: Our discoveries ~ those made by others. 我们的发现和他人的发现相吻合。/ ~ one's arguments 使论点前后呼应 ❷ *vi.* 吻合: My plans ~ed with his. 我的打算与他的打算相吻合

dowager ['dauədʒə] *n.* ① 受有亡夫遗产(或称号)的寡妇; 王(或公等)的未亡人: a queen ~ 王太后 ②[口]年长有钱的贵妇

dowdy ['daudi] I *a.* ①不整洁的,邋遢的 ②不漂亮的;过时的 II *n.* 邋遢女人,懒散女人 ‖**dowdily** *ad.* / **dowdiness** *n.* / **~ish** *a.* 有点过时的;

down¹ [daun] I (最高级 downmost) *ad.* ①向下; 在下面: I'll come ~ in a minute. 我马上就下(楼)来。/ Down! [是祈使句 "Lie (Sit, Put 等) ~!" 的省略]卧倒(或坐下,放下等)!/ the fields ~ in the valley 下面山谷里的田野 / The food won't stay ~. 东西吃下去就呕出来。②(物价等)降下: The death rate is ~. 死亡率下降了。③(在情绪、健康状况等方面)处于低落状态: He is badly ~, we'd better have a heart-to-heart talk with him. 他情绪很不好,我们最好跟他谈谈心。/ be ~ in health 身体不好 / be ~ with flu 害了流行性感冒而病倒 ④减退下去; 平息下去: The tide is ~. 潮退了。/ The fire is burning ~. 火快熄灭了。⑤(在体积方面)由大到小; (在数量方面)由多到少: be worn ~ with use 因使用过久而磨损 / One of the tyres is ~. 一只车胎(快)没气了。/ boil a long article ~ to two hundred words 把一篇长文章缩写成二百字的摘要) ⑥(从首都、城市、北方、上游、内地、大学往边远地区、农村、南方、下游、海边等一般被看作下方的地方)往下方;在下方: go ~ to the south 南下 / ~ east (或 East) [美]在(或往)美国东北部沿海地区(尤指缅因州) / south (或 South) [美]在(或往)美国东南部 ⑦往市区 (或市内商业区);在市区 (或市内商业区): Does this bus go ~? 这辆公共汽车是开往市区的吗? ⑧(在时间、顺序、地位等方面)直(到) (to): ~ to page ten 直到第十页 ⑨(记)下,(抄)下: take ~ sb.'s address 记下某人的地址 ⑩(议案、新闻稿等)(发)下: The paper was (或 went) ~ at six yesterday. 昨天报纸六点钟付印。 ⑪现(付): half ~ and half in instalments 一半付现,一半分期付款 ⑫(追)到底: run ~ a spy 穷追而捉到间谍 / run ~ a rumour 把谣言查个水落石出 ⑬停当;认真地: settle ~ in the countryside 在农村安家 / get ~ to work 认真开始工作 ⑭彻底地;完全地: dust ~ the house 彻底扫扫房子 / a truck loaded ~ with boxes 一辆装满了

箱子的卡车
II (最高级 downmost) *a.* ①向下的: a ~ pressure 向下的压力 ②(列车)下行的;下行列车的: a ~ platform 下行列车月台 ③现(付)的: make a ~ payment of ten yuan 现付十元
III *prep.* ①沿着⋯往下;往下进入;通过⋯往下: run ~ a hill 跑下山 / go ~ the shaft of a mine 下矿井 / goods ~ cellar [美]地下室里的货物 ②往(河流)的下游;在(河流)的下游: sail ~ the river 顺流而下 / live ~ the stream 住在小河的下游 ③(由郊区、城市的住宅区)往 (市区、市内商业区);在(市区、市内商业区): He works ~ town. 他在市中心区工作。 ④沿着(街道、海岸等): walk ~ the street 沿街走去 ⑤(在时间方面)⋯以来: ~ the ages 自古以来
IV *vt.* [口] ①击落(敌机等);打倒;把⋯压下去 ②喝下;吞下 ③放下: ~ one's axe and take a short rest 放下斧头坐下休息一会 / ~ tools 放下工具(可指开始罢工或收工)
V *n.* ①[复]下降,衰落 ②(广播剧等中叙事时为了区别于对话用的)较低声调 ③[口]恶感,怨气
‖**be ~ and out** [口] ① (拳击中)被击倒而不能继续比赛 ②穷困潦倒 / **be ~ for** 被列入名单中作⋯事: I see you're ~ for a speech at the rally. 我看到大会上把你列入发言者的名单。/ **be ~ in spirits** 见 spirit / **be ~ on** 对⋯有怨气(或恶感) / **be ~ on one's luck** 见 luck / **come ~ in the world** 见 world / **~ below** 在底下(包括在楼下、甲板下、地面下等;根据上下文可有多种意义);【宗】在地狱中 / **~ in the mouth** 见 mouth / **~ (the) wind** 见 wind¹ / **(~) to the ground** 见 ground¹ / **~ under**(在)对跖地(对欧美人来说,指澳大利亚、新西兰) / **~ with** ①打倒 ②把⋯拿下(或弄下): Down with the blackboard. 把黑板拿下来。/ **have a ~ on** [口] =be ~ on / **money ~** (购物)现款支付 / **ups and ~s** 见 up
‖**'~-and-'out** *a. & n.* 被击垮了的(人) / **'~-and-'outer** *n.* 被击垮了的人 / **'~-beat** *n.* 【音】强拍 ②下降,衰退;低沉 *a.* 悲观的;低沉的 / **'~-cast** *a.* ①(人)垂头丧气的,萎靡不振的 ②(眼)向下看的 *n.* ①【地】下落,陷落 【矿】下风井,通风坑 / **'~country** *a. & ad.* [美]在(或往)沿海地区 / **'~draught** *n.* (烟囱的)倒灌风;向下通风;向下气流 / **'~easter** [美口] ①美国东部沿海地区的人 (尤指缅因州人) ②美国东部沿海地区造的船 (尤指从缅因州开出的帆船) / **'~fall** *n.* ①(雨雪等突然或大量的)下降 ②垮台;(城市的)陷落 ③垮台的原因 / **'~,fallen**

a. 垮了台的 / **'~grade** *n.* (路等的)下坡: be on the ~*grade* 每况愈下 *a.* & *ad.* 下坡的(地); 倾斜的(地) *vt.* ①降低(商品等)的等级; 降低(谈判等)的级别 ②降低(工人或工种)的等级和工资 ③贬低; 不重视 / **'~'hearted** *a.* 消沉的; 沮丧的; 郁郁不乐的: Are we ~-*hearted*? [俚]我们才不泄气哩! / **'~'hill** *n.* ①[古]下坡 ②衰退(阶段): the ~*hill* of life 下半生 *a.* 下坡的; 倾斜的 *ad.* ①往山脚 ②趋向衰退: The U. S. dollar is going ~*hill* more and more. 美元的地位日益低落。/ **'~-lead** *n.* 【无】(天线的)下引线 / **'~'line** *ad.* 沿铁路线 / **'~pipe** *n.* [英]水落管 / **'~pour** *n.* ①倾盆大雨 ②(日光的)照射 / **'~range** *a.* & *ad.* [字]离开发射中心和沿着试验航向的(地) / **'~right** *a.* ①明显不过的; 彻头彻尾的: a ~*right* lie 弥天大谎 ②爽直的; 直截了当的: a ~*right* answer 一个率直的答复 *ad.* ①彻底地; 十分地: feel ~*right* ashamed of one's misconduct 对自己的不良行为感到极羞耻 ②爽直地; 直截了当地: Let's go ~*right* to our task! 我们就干起来吧! / **'~'right-ness** *n.* ①明显 ②彻底 ③率直 / **'~'slide** *n.* (行市的)下跌; (工商业的)下降 / **'~'stair** *a.* = ~stairs (*a.*) / **'~'stairs** *a.* 楼下的: a ~*stairs* room 一间楼下的房间 *ad.* 在楼下; 往楼下: live ~*stairs* 住在楼下 / walk ~*stairs* 走下楼梯 *n.* 楼下 / **'~'state** *n.* 州的最南部地区 *a.* & *ad.* 在(或从、往)州的最南部(的) / **'~'stream** *n.* & *ad.* 顺流的(地); (在)下游的 / **'~swing** *n.* ①(高尔夫球棒等的)朝下挥动 ②下降趋势 / **'~throw** *n.* 【地】下落; 下落地块 ②(声誉等)的低落 / **'~time** *n.* (工厂、机器等由于检修、待料等的)停工期 / **'~-to-earth** *a.* 切实的, 实事求是的: a ~-*to-earth* style of work 实事求是的工作作风 / **'~'town** *ad.* 在(或往)城市的商业区: live (go) ~*town* 住在(去)市商业区 *n.* & *a.* 城市商业区(的): a ~*town* street 一条城市商业区的街道 / **'~ train** (铁路的)下行列车 / **'~trend** *n.* (尤指经济方面的)下降趋势 / **'~,trodden** *a.* 被蹂躏的; 被压制的 / **'~turn** *n.* ①向下, 下转 ②下降趋势 / **'~'wash** *n.* ①(从高处如山上等)冲刷下来的物质 ②【空】下冲气流, 下洗气流; 下冲, 下洗 / **'~wind** *a.* & *ad.* 顺风的(地) ②顺风 ②下降气流

down² [daun] *n.* ①开阔的高地; [常用复]丘陵(作牧场用的)丘陵草原; 砂丘 ②[常作 D-](英国东南部丘陵草原产的)塘种绵羊 ||*the Downs* 英国东南部的丘陵草原; 英国多佛(尔)海峡的一部分(为船只停泊处) || **'~land** *n.* ①山地牧场 ②澳大利亚温带草原 ②【地】丘陵地

down³ [daun] ([复] down(s)) *n.* ①绒毛, 柔毛; 绒羽: duck ~ 鸭绒 ②软毛; 毳毛; 汗毛; (男孩脸上初生的)细软短须 ③【植】茸毛; (蒲公英等的)冠毛

downward ['daunwəd] **I** *a.* ①向下的: give the rope a ~ pull 把绳子向下一拉 ②趋向没落的 **II** *ad.* =downwards

downwards ['daunwədz] *ad.* ①向下; (在年代、位次等方面)往下: lie on the ground face ~ 脸向下躺在地上 / children of six and ~ 六岁和六岁以下的儿童 ②趋向没落: go ~ politically 政治上衰退

downy¹ ['dauni] *a.* ①长绒毛(或茸毛)的②绒毛(或茸毛)状的; 绒羽般柔软的 ③用绒羽制成的: a ~ quilt 鸭绒被 ④[俚]狡猾的; 机警的: a ~ bird 调皮的家伙 ||*do the* ~ [俚]躺在床上睡觉

downy² ['dauni] *a.* 丘陵草原性的; 丘陵起伏的

dowry ['dauəri] *n.* ①嫁妆 ②天赋, 天资 ③[古]寡妇(从亡夫得到的)产业 ④[古]丈夫在婚前给予新娘的财礼

doze¹ [douz] **I** ❶ *vi.* ①打瞌睡, 打盹儿 (*off*): ~ over a book 看书时打瞌睡 ②昏昏沉沉 ❷ *vt.* 在瞌睡中度过(时间) (*away*) **II** *n.* 瞌睡, 打盹: fall (或 go off) into a ~ 打起瞌睡来

doze² [douz] *vt.* 用推土机清除(或挖出、削平)

dozen ['dʌzn] ([复] dozen(s)) *n.* ①[与数词或 many, several 等连用时, 复数不加 "s"] (一)打, 十二个: two (many, several) ~ pencils 两(许多, 几)打铅笔 / I want three ~ of these eggs. 我要三打这种蛋。/ some ~ (of) people 约十二人 ②[~s] 几十; 许多: some ~s of people 几十个人 / for ~s of years 好几十年以来 ||*baker's* (或 *devil's, printer's*) ~ 十三个 / *a long* ~ 十三个 / *be six of one and half a ~ of the other* 半斤八两差不多 / (*pack*) *in* ~ 成打地(包装) / (*sell*) *by the* ~ 论打(出售) / *talk nineteen to the* ~ 喋喋不休

drab¹ [dræb] **I** *n.* ①邋遢女人 ②娼妓 **II** (drabbed; drabbing) *vi.* 嫖妓女

drab² [dræb] **I** *n.* ①褐色斜纹布, 灰色斜纹布; 黄褐色厚呢 ②黄褐色 ③单调, 无生气 **II** *a.* 黄褐色的 ②单调乏味的, 无生气的: ~ language 干巴巴的语言 ||~**ly** *ad.* / ~**ness** *n.*

drachm [dræm] *n.* ① =drachma ② =dram

draff [dræf] *n.* ①渣滓, 糟粕 ②猪食 ||~**y** *a.* 渣滓很多的, 糟粕很多的; 没有价值的

draft [drɑ:ft] **I** *n.* ①草稿, 草案, 草图: a ~ for (或 of) a speech 讲话草稿 / a ~ resolution 决议草案 ②汇票; 支取(款项); 要求: a demand ~ 即期汇票 / make a ~ on sb.'s confidence 要求某人给予信任 ③分遣队(的选拔) ④[美]征兵, 征集: a ~ card 征兵证 ⑤【商】重量损耗扣 ⑥【机】(出模)斜度 ⑦(石工的)凿槽; 琢边 ⑧[美]拉, 牵引, 拖, 曳 ⑨一网(鱼) ⑩(一)饮, (一)吸, (一)阵; 【药】顿服量; 顿服药 ⑪[美](船的)吃水(深度) ⑫通风; 气流; 穿堂风; 通风装置 **II** *vt.* ①起草; 为…打样, 设计: ~ a decision 起草一项决定 ②选派: ~ men from the regiment for a special assignment 从团里选派人员去执行一项特殊任务 ③[美]征集; 征(兵): be ~ed into the army 应征入伍 ④在(石)上凿槽(或琢边) ||~**ee** [drɑ:f'ti:] *n.* [美]应征入伍者 / ~**er** *n.* 起草人 || **'~-age** *n.* [美]应征年龄的 / ~ **board**

[美]征兵局 / ~ **center** [美]征兵站 / ~ **dodger** [美]逃避服兵役的人 / ~ **resister** [美]抵制服兵役的人

draftsman ['drɑ:ftsmən] ([复] draftsmen) *n.* ① 起草人 ②打样人,制图员 ③善于描绘的人(别于善于着色的人) ‖~**ship** 制图术

drag [dræg] **I** (dragged; dragging) ❶ *vt.* ①拖,拉;(船)拖动(原来钩住的锚): ~ a net in fishing 拖网捕鱼 / ~ oneself along 拖着脚步走 / ~ sb. into a mire 把某人拖进泥淖;拖某人下水 ②探(海底等);用拖网捉: ~ a river for a sunken boat 在河底打捞沉船 / ~ the sea 扫海 ③用耙子耙(地) ④[美俚] 陪伴(女子)去参加舞会 ⑤[美俚]深深地吸(香烟) ⑥[美俚]使厌烦得要命 ❷ *vi.* ①拖曳;(原来钩住的锚)被拖动;吃力地,慢吞吞地行进;落在后面 ②拖拉,拖长: The performance *dragged*. 表演不紧凑。/ Time seemed to ~. 时光过得很慢。③用拖网等探寻(或捕捉) (*for*) ④吸: ~ on a cigarette 猛抽香烟 **II** *n.* ①被拖物;大把;橇;高大马车;货运慢车;水底拖捞器,拖网 ②刹车,制动器;海锚 ③障碍物;累赘;极为讨厌的人(或事物);【空】阻力: a ~ on progress 阻碍进步的因素,绊脚石 ④拖曳;迟缓的行动 ⑤深喝一口水(或酒等);深吸一口烟;[美俚]香烟 ⑥野兽的臭迹;(训练猎犬的)人工臭迹;利用人工臭迹的追猎 ⑦[俚]影响: have a big ~ with sb. 与某人很有些交情(意指很得某人照顾) ⑧[美俚]舞会;由男子陪伴到舞会去的女子 ⑨ =~ race ⑩[美俚]街道,道路 ‖~ **in** ①把…拉进去 ②硬扯…拉扯进来: Why ~ me *in*? 干吗把我也拉扯进去? / ~ **it** [美俚]离职;离开;停止谈话';断绝关系 / ~ **on** (或 **out**) 拖延; ~ **out** one's feeble existence 苟延残喘 / ~ **one's freight** [美俚]离开,出发 / ~ **up a child** [口] 胡乱把孩子养大 ‖~ **anchor** [海]海锚,浮锚 / ~ **chain** ①【机】牵引链;刹车链 ②[喻]障碍 / '~**line** *n.* ①牵引绳索 ②[矿]绳斗电铲,索斗铲 / '~**net** *n.* ①拖网,捕捞网 ②法网,天罗地网; catch all in a ~*net* 一网打尽 / ~ **race** [美俚]把汽车拆卸减重后举行的短程高速驾驶比赛 / '~**rope** *n.* 牵引绳索

draggle ['drægl] ❶ *vt.* 拖脏,拖湿 ❷ *vi.* ①拖脏,拖湿;(裙等)拖曳 ②慢吞吞前进,落在后头 ‖~**-tail** *n.* 拖着又脏又湿裙子的(邋遢)女子

dragon ['drægən] *n.* ①龙 ②凶暴的人,严厉的人;凶恶严格的监护人; ③【动】飞龙(一种有翼膜能滑翔的蜥蜴) ④【动】飘鸽(一种善飞的信鸽) ⑤装甲曳引车 ⑥(十七世纪时士兵佩在腰间的)龙骑枪;佩带龙骑枪的士兵 ⑦ [the D-] 【天】天龙座 ‖*the old Dragon* 魔鬼 ‖~**ish** *a.* 似龙的;凶暴的 ‖~**fly** *n.* 蜻蜓 / ~**'s blood** 【化】龙血树脂,麒麟血 / ~**'s teeth** ①排列成多层的楔形反坦克混凝土障碍物 ②相互争斗的根源

dragoon [drə'gu:n] **I** *n.* ①龙骑兵;重骑兵 ②暴徒 ③飘鸽(一种善飞的信鸽) **II** *vt.* (使用军队)迫害,镇压;用暴力使…就范: ~ sb. *into* doing sth. 迫使某人做某事

drain [drein] **I** ❶ *vt.* ①排去(水等液体) (*off, away*);排去…的水(或其他液体): dig trenches to ~ the water *away* 开沟排水 / ~ the water-logged land 排去水涝地的水 ②喝干: ~ (the wine in) a cup 干一杯 ③耗尽: be ~*ed of one's* energy 精力衰竭 ❷ *vi.* ①(水等)流掉,渐渐枯竭 (*away*) ②(土地)排水;(衣服、碗碟等)滴干: Put the umbrella there to ~. 把伞放在那里让它滴干。**II** *n.* ①排水,放干 ②排水沟,排水管,阴沟;[复](建筑物的)排水设备 ③【医】导管,排液管(尤指排浓管);引流,导液 ④(财富等的)不断外流,逐渐流尽: the ~ of gold from that country 那个国家黄金的不断外流 ⑤消耗,负担: a great ~ on sb.'s strength (income) 对某人精力(收入)的极大消耗 ⑥[口]一口,一点儿(指酒等液体): Don't drink it all, leave me a ~! 不要喝光,留一点给我! ‖**go down the ~** ①被抛弃;(资金等)被浪费掉 ②(计划等)失败,破产 ③(人)每况愈下 ‖'~**board** *n.* 滴水板 (=~ing board) / '~**pipe** *n.* 排水管 / '~**pipe trousers** 瘦裤腿裤子

drainage ['dreinidʒ] *n.* ①排水,放水;排水法;逐步流出 ②排水设备;排水系统,下水道 ③排出的水;污水 ④排水区域;(河流的)流域 ⑤【医】导液法,引流法 ‖~ **area** 排水面积;排水区域;(河流的)流域 / ~ **basin** 【地】流域盆地 / ~ **system** 排水系统;【地】水系 / ~ **tube**【医】导液管,引流管

drake[1] [dreik] *n.* ①雄鸭 ②(打水漂用的)浮石片 ‖*play ducks and* ~*s* 玩打水漂游戏 ‖~**stone** *n.* (打水漂用的)浮石片

drake[2] [dreik] *n.* ① (十七、十八世纪的)小型炮 ②(钓鱼用的)蜉蝣

dram [dræm] *n.* ①打兰,英钱(衡量单位;在药衡中 1 打兰为 $\frac{1}{8}$ 啢,合 3.887 克;在常衡中 1 打兰为 $\frac{1}{16}$ 啢,合 1.771 克) ②液量打兰 (=fluidram) ③(酒等的)少量,少许: a ~ drinker 爱浅斟慢饮的人 ‖~**shop** *n.* [古]小酒店

drama ['drɑ:mə] *n.* ①一出戏剧,剧本;戏剧: a problem ~ 一出问题剧(指十九世纪中叶至二十世纪初在欧洲流行的一种社会问题剧) / stage a ~ 上演一出戏 / be interested in Chinese ~ 对中国戏剧有兴趣 ② [the ~] 戏剧艺术;戏剧事业 ③(充满巧合或冲突等的)戏剧性事件;戏剧场面 ④戏剧效果,戏剧性: a news report full of ~ 富有戏剧性的一篇新闻报道

dramatic [drə'mætik] *a.* ①戏剧的;剧本的;演剧的: ~ art (criticism, description, performance) 戏剧艺术(评论,描写,表演) ②戏剧般的,戏剧性的;激动人心的;惹人注目的: a ~ event (scene) 富有戏剧性的事件(场面) ‖~**ally** *ad.* ①从戏剧角度 ②戏剧性地;鲜明地;显著地

dramatics [drə'mætiks] *n.* [复] *n.* [用作单或复] ①演剧活动(尤指业余的): children engaging in extracurricular ~ 从事课外演剧活动的孩子们 ②演剧技术;舞台技术 ③戏剧性的行径

dramatist ['dræmətist] *n.* 剧作家,剧本作者

dramatize, dramatise ['dræmətaiz] ❶ *vt.* ①把(小说,故事等)改编为剧本 ②演戏似地表现;把…戏剧化;使惹人注目 ❷ *vi.* ①具有戏剧性,适于改编成剧本 ②(演戏似地)装假 ‖**dramatization** [,dræmətai'zeiʃən] *n.* ①(小说,故事等的)改编为剧本 ②戏剧式表现,戏剧化 ③(由小说等)改编成的剧本

drank [dræŋk] drink 的过去式

drape [dreip] I ❶ *vt.* ①(松乱随便地)披上(衣服等);披盖: ~ a padded overcoat over the shoulders 把棉大衣披在肩上 / Wild flowers ~*d* the hillside. 野花铺满山坡。②(成褶地)悬挂,装饰: a doorway ~*d* with a heavy curtain 挂着一道厚帷幕的门道 / a banquetting hall ~*d* with the national flags of the two countries 悬挂两国国旗的宴会大厅 ③把(衣服等)制成一定的褶皱状 ❷ *vi.* (衣服等)成褶皱状 II *n.* ①[常用复]窗帘,布帘;手术室里经消毒的挡避帷帘 ②褶皱,裥;服装式样: a suit with an English ~ 一套英国式服装

draper ['dreipə] *n.* [英]布商(出售被单、桌布、衣服等): He has gone to the ~'s. 他到布店去(买衣服)了。

drapery ['dreipəri] *n.* ①[英]布,布匹;织物,服装 ②[英]布和服装业: an establishment (或 store) 卖布和服装的商店 ③[复]帷幕;装饰用褶皱织物 ④(人物画、人像雕刻等上的)衣饰 ‖**draperied** *a.* 悬有(褶形)布帘的

drastic ['dræstik] I *a.* ①激烈的,猛烈的: a ~ remedy 烈性药物 / ~ price cuts on medicines 药品的大幅度减价 ②(法律等)极端的,严厉的: take ~ measures 采取严厉措施 II *n.* 剧泻药;剧药 ‖**~ally** *ad.*

draught [dra:ft] I *n.* ①拉,牵引,拖,曳: a ~ animal(或 a beast of ~)挽畜(指牛、马等) ②(一)网(鱼): a ~ of fish(es) 一网鱼 ③(一)饮,(一)吸,(一)阵;泄出;【药】顿服量;顿服药: have a ~ of water 饮一口水 / have a ~ of joy 开心一阵 / beer on ~ (桶装)生啤酒 ④(船的)吃水(深度): a ship of 5 m. ~(或 a ship with a ~ of 5 m.)一艘吃水五米的船 ⑤通风;气流;穿堂风;通风装置: You'll catch cold if you sit in a ~. 坐在风口会着凉的。/ There is not much ~ up the chimney; that's why the fire doesn't burn well. 烟囱通风不好,所以火不旺。⑥[复]西洋跳棋(相当于美国的 checkers) ⑦[罕]草稿,草案;草图 ⑧[罕]分遣队(的选拨) ⑨[罕]汇票;(款项的)支取;要求 II *vt.* ①选派(分遣队) ②起草;给…打样,设计 ③[罕]征集,征(兵) ‖*at a* ~ 一下子: drink *at a* ~ 一饮而尽 / *feel the* ~ [俚]手头拮据 ‖'~**board** *n.* 西洋跳棋盘

draughtsman ['dra:ftsmən]([复] draughtsmen) *n.* ①起草人 ②打样人,制图员 ③西洋跳棋子 ‖~**ship** *n.* 制图术

draw [drɔ:] I (drew [dru:], drawn [drɔ:n]) ❶ *vt.*

① 拉,拖;拉长,拖长;拉成(丝等): ~ a curtain apart 把幕拉开 / ~ a bow 拉弓 / heat the metal and ~ it into a long wire 把金属加热拉长成丝 / ~ wire (把铜等)拉成丝

② 拔(出);抽(签);(用抽签等方法)决定: ~ a nail (tooth, cork) 拔钉子(牙齿,瓶塞) / ~ a gun *on* sb. 拔出枪来对付某人 / ~ lots 抽签

③ 取出…的内脏;使流出;【医】吸出(脓等): ~ a chicken 取出鸡的内脏 / A blunt knife ~*s* no blood. 钝刀子割肉割不出血来。

④ 汲取;领取,提取;获得;引出: ~ water from a well 从井里打水 / ~ one's salary 领取工资 / ~ a lesson 吸取教训 / ~ a conclusion 引出结论

⑤ 引起;招来: His speech *drew* prolonged applause. 他的讲话博得长时间的鼓掌。/ ~ ruin upon oneself 自取灭亡

⑥ 吸(人);吸引: ~ a deep breath 深深地吸一口气 / Almost all the people were ~*n* into the patriotic health and sanitation campaign. 几乎所有的人都投入了爱国卫生运动。/ The more he reads the story, the more he is ~*n to* it. 那个故事他越读越爱读。

⑦ 逗引…说话: He was not to be ~*n*. (不论怎样启发他)他坚决不开口。

⑧ (船)吃(水): a ship ~*ing* 10 metres of water 吃水十米的船

⑨ 泡(茶)

⑩ 划,画,绘制;描写: ~ a picture 画图 / ~ a parallel (或 comparison) between 指出…之间的相同处,在…之间作一比较

⑪ 开立(票据等);草拟;制订: ~ *up* a document (plan) 草拟文件(计划)

⑫ 把…打成平局: ~ a basketball match 把一场篮球赛打成平局

⑬[常用被动语态]扭歪(脸等): a face ~*n* with pain 因疼痛而扭歪着的脸

⑭ 抽补(纸牌);吊(牌)

❷ *vi.* ①拉,拖: The cart ~*s* easily. 这车子容易拉。

② (牙齿等)被拔出;拔剑,拔刀,拔枪

③ 用抽签(或抽牌等)方法决定

④ 支取;【医】(膏药等)吸脓

⑤吸引人: The play ~*s* well. 这戏很卖座。

⑥(船)吃水

⑦(茶)泡开

⑧划线;制图;画画

⑨ 打成平局,不分胜负: The teams *drew* (3—3). 两队打成平局(三平)。

⑩ (向某一方向)移动: Summer is ~*ing* near (to a close). 夏天快到了(快过去了)。/ We *drew* towards the town. 我们向那个城镇进发。

⑪ 缩,皱: His skin seemed to ~ with the cold. 因为冷,他的皮肤似乎收缩起来。

⑫(烟囱等)通风: The pipe does not ~ well. 这烟斗不太畅通。

⑬(猎狗)追踪(或接近)猎物
II *n.* ①拉,拖;吸
②拔出;抽签
③有吸引力的事物(或人物): The film is a great ~. 这电影很吸引观众。
④平局,不分胜负: The game ended *in a* ~. 比赛结果是平局。
⑤(纸牌游戏中)抽补进的牌
⑥(吊桥的)可吊起部分
‖*a sure* ~ 肯定可以搜出狐狸的地方;一定可以引起评论(或引人谈论)之处 / *beat to the* ~ ①抢在…之前拔出武器 ②抢在…前行动 / *be quick on the* ~ 见 **quick** / ~ *and quarter* ①(古时刑罚)四马分尸 ②(绞死后)取出内脏,肢解尸体 / ~ *away* ①拉开;引开;离开 ②(比赛中)跑到前面与别人拉开距离 / ~ *back* ①收回(已付关税等) ②往回走;退却,缩回 / ~ *forth* 引起;博得(赞美等) / ~ *in* ①收(网、针等) ②引诱,使加入 ③(天)接近黄昏;(白昼)短起来 ④紧缩开支 / ~ *it fine* (区别得)十分精确 / ~ *it mild* 不夸大 / ~ *off* ①脱去(手套等) ②放掉(多余的水等) ③撤退 / ~ *on* ①戴上(手套);穿上(靴子等) ②吸收;利用;凭,靠: *on what is progressive* 吸收进步的东西 / ~ *on* 支取 / ~ *on sb. at 30 days' sight* 见票三十天后向某人支取 / ~ 引诱 ⑤招来 ⑥临近;接近 / *oneself up* ①挺直身体 ②控制自己 / ~ *out* ①拉长,拖长 ②掏出(手帕等);抽出 ③引出;逗引…说话 ④拟订(计划等) ⑤(白昼)长起来 / ~ *round* 围在…的四周 / ~ *together* (使)团结起来,(使)一致 / ~ *up* ①写出;草拟,制订 ②使(车、马等)停住;(车、马等)停住: The car *drew up at the door.* 汽车在门口停了下来。 ③逼近(*to*),追上(*with*) ④【军】整(队): The troops were ~*n up ready for inspection.* 部队整好队准备接受检阅。 / *play off a* ~ 见 **play**
‖'~**back** *n.* ①退税,退款 ②欠缺,弊端: Slow drying is the chief ~*back of this paint.* 这漆最大的缺点是干得慢。③障碍: Complacency is a ~*back to progress.* 自满是进步的障碍。 / '~**bridge** *n.* 吊桥 / '~**down** *n.* ①(水库等的)水位降低 ②消耗;减少 / '~**knife,** '~**shave** *n.* (木工用的)刮刀

drawer [drɔ:] *n.* ①抽屉: a chest of ~s 有抽屉的橱 ②[复]内裤 ③['drɔ:ə] 拖曳者;(酒吧的)汲酒者;制图师;开票人,(汇票)发票人 ‖~**ful** *n.* (一)抽屉

drawing ['drɔ:iŋ] *n.* ①抽签 ②绘图 ③图画;图样;素描 ④提存 ⑤【机】冲压成形;拉拔,拔丝 ⑥【冶】回火,退火 ‖*in* ~ (图画等)画得准确的 / *out of* ~ (图画等)画得不准确的;不协调的 ‖~ **block** 活页画图纸 / ~ **board** 制图板,图板 / ~ **card** 能吸引观众的表演(或演讲、表演者等) / ~ **compasses** 制图圆规 / ~ **knife** (木工用的)刮刀 / ~ **pin** 图钉 / ~ **room** ①客厅,休憩室 ②(宫廷内的)正式接见(室) ③[美]私人的卧铺车室

drawl [drɔ:l] **I** *vt.* & *vi.* 慢吞吞地说(出);拉长声音唱(出) **II** *n.* 慢吞吞地说话的样子;慢吞吞地说出的话(或唱出的调子) ‖~**ingly** *ad.*

drawn [drɔ:n] **I** draw 的过去分词 **II** *a.* ①拔出鞘的;不分胜负的: a ~ game 不分胜负的比赛 ③内脏已挖去的 ④(脸)扭歪的,拉长的 ‖'~**out** *a.* 拉长了的;在时间方面过长的 / '~**work** *n.* 抽花刺绣品;抽绣

dray [drei] **I** *n.* (无围边的)大车,运货马车 **II** ❶ *vt.* 用大车拖运 ❷ *vi.* 赶大车 ‖~ **horse** 运货马车的马 / '~**man** *n.* 运货马车车夫 / '~**plough** *n.* 粘质土犁

dread [dred] **I** *n.* ①畏惧,恐怖;担心: be in ~ of sb. (sth.) 害怕某人(某物) ②引起畏惧的人(或事物);敬畏的对象 **II** *vt.* & *vi.* 惧怕;担心 **III** *a.* 令人畏惧的,使人敬畏的

dreadful ['dredful] **I** *a.* ①可怕的: What a ~ scene! 多么可怕的一幕! ②令人敬畏的 ③令人惊骇的;糟透的: ~ weather 讨厌的天气 ④极端的: a car in ~ disrepair 坏得一塌糊涂的汽车 **II** *n.* 廉价的惊险小说(或刊物)(=penny ~) ‖~**ly** *ad.* I am ~ly tired. 我累坏了。

dream [dri:m] **I** *n.* ①梦: have a ~ (about sth.) 做梦(梦见某事物) ②梦想,空想 ③理想,愿望 ④一般美妙的人(或事物);美景: The landscape is a perfect ~. 这景色太美了。**II** (dreamed [dremt, dri:md] 或 dreamt [dremt]) ❶ *vi.* ①做梦;梦见,梦到 (*of, about*) ②梦想;空想 ③向往,渴望: The boy ~s of becoming a pilot. 那孩子一心想当个飞行员。④[常与 not, little, never 等连用]想(不)到: I little ~t of seeing you here. 真没想到在这儿见到你。❷ *vt.* ①做(梦);梦见,梦到: ~ a dream 做一个梦 ②想象,臆想: I didn't say that, you must have ~t it. 我没讲过这个话,只是你的臆想罢了。③(因空想而)虚度(时间等)(*away, out, through*): Don't ~ away your time! 不要糊里糊涂地虚度光阴! ④[常与 not, little, never 等连用]想(不)到: I never ~t that … 我从没想到… ‖*be beyond sb.'s* ~ 超过某人的期望 / ~ *up* [口](凭想象)虚构,凭空想出: ~ *up a plan* 凭空想出一个计划 / *go to one's* ~s 进入梦乡,入睡 / *read a* ~ 详梦 ‖~**er** *n.* ①做梦的人 ②空想家,梦想家 / ~**ful** *a.* 多梦的,常做梦的 / ~**less** *a.* 无梦的,不做梦的 / ~**like** *a.* 梦一般的,梦幻的 / '~**boat** *n.* [美俚]理想目标;理想人物;爱人 / '~**land** *n.* ①梦境;梦乡 ②幻想世界 / ~ **reader** 详梦的人 / '~**world** *n.* =~land

dreamy ['dri:mi] *a.* ①(人)爱空想的 ②令人喜爱的,理想的;[美俚]刮刮叫的 ③(景色)梦一般的,朦胧的;(神情等)恍惚的 ④[诗]多梦的 ⑤(曲调等)柔和怡神的,轻柔的 ‖**dreamily** *ad.* / **dreaminess** *n.*

dreary ['driəri] *a.* 沉闷的,阴郁的;使人意气消沉的 ‖**drearily** *ad.* / **dreariness** *n.*

dredge[1] [dredʒ] **I** *n.* ①挖泥机,疏浚机;挖泥船;捕捞船 ②(捕鱼等用的)捞网,拖网 **II ①** *vt.* ①疏浚(河道,港湾等);挖掘(泥土等)(*up, away, out*) ②捞取,挖取: ~ something out of context to support one's point 断章取义以证明自己的论点 **②** *vi.* 疏浚,挖泥;挖,捞

dredge[2] [dredʒ] *vt.* 把面粉撒在(食物)上;撒(面粉等)在食物上

dredger[1] ['dredʒə] *n.* ① 挖泥工,疏浚工 ②挖泥机,疏浚机;挖泥船;捕捞船: a mine ~ 扫雷艇 / a scoop-type suction ~ 耙吸式挖泥船 ③捞网,拖网

dredger[2] ['dredʒə] *n.* (盖子上有小孔的)撒面粉(或其他粉末状调味品的)器具

dreg [dreg] *n.* ①[常用复]残渣,糟粕;[喻]渣滓,废物: the ~s of society 社会渣滓 ②少量的残剩物: not a ~ 丝毫没有 ‖*drink*(或 *drain*)*to the* ~s ① 把…喝得一点不剩 ② 享尽(快乐等);吃尽(苦头等) ‖**dreggy** *a.*

drench [drentʃ] **I** *vt.* ①使浸透;使淋透: He was ~ed through (with rain). 他被(雨)淋得浑身湿透。/ be ~ed in sweat 满身大汗 ②使充满,使洋溢: sun-~ed fields 沐浴在阳光里的田地 ③ 给(牲口)灌药 **II** *n.* ①雨淋,弄湿 ②一饮;一服药剂(尤指畜用药水) ③浸液 ‖~**ing** *n.* 湿透: We got a ~ing. 我们湿透了。

dress [dres] **I** *n.* ①[a ~]女服,童装 ②(统指)服装(尤指外衣): He doesn't care much about ~. 他不太注意衣着。③礼服: evening ~ 夜礼服 / full ~ 大礼服 ④覆盖物;外形,形式: birds in their winter ~ 长着冬季羽毛的鸟儿 / a Greek story in English ~ 希腊故事的英译本 **II ①** *vt.* ① 给…穿衣;供衣着给: *Dress* yourself more neatly. 穿得整齐一点。/ be ~ed in blue 穿着蓝衣服 ②整理,修整;装饰: ~ a shopwindow 布置商店的橱窗 / ~ the streets 装饰街道 ③敷裹(伤口);给(伤员)敷裹伤口 ④ 整(队): ~ the ranks 整队 ⑤梳理(头发);给(马等)刷洗: ~ down a horse 梳马 ⑥修剪(树木等);使(织物、石料等)表面光洁: ~ building stones 修琢建筑石材 ⑦做(菜): ~ a salad 拌色拉 ⑧耕种(土地);给(土地,庄稼)施肥 ⑨适当处理;【矿】选(矿石): a ~ed chicken (煺)光(的)鸡 / ~ ore 选矿 **②** *vi.* ①穿衣: Get up and ~ quickly. 快起床穿衣。②穿夜礼服: ~ for dinner 穿上夜礼服去进餐 ③【军】看齐: ~ to the left 向左看齐 / Right (Left)—~! (口令)向右(左)—齐! ④(食用动物)褪光后净重: The duck ~ed two *jin*. 这只光鸭重两斤。 ‖*all ~ed up and nowhere to go* 打扮得整整齐齐却无处可去炫耀 / ~ *sb.* *down* 狠狠地训斥(或揍)某人 / ~ *ship*(为表示庆祝等)给船舰悬挂旗帜 / ~ *up*(给…)穿上盛装 ‖~ **affair** 须穿礼服的场合 / ~ **circle**(剧院的)花楼 / ~ **coat** 燕尾服 / ~ **form** 陈列女服的人体模型 / ~ **goods** 妇孺衣料 / ~ **guard**(女式自行车上的)护衣装置 / ~ **improver** 妇女

托裙腰垫 / '~**make** *vi.* 做女服(或童装)/ '~,**maker** *n.* 做女服(或童装)的(女)裁缝 / ~ **parade** [美]穿正式礼服的阅兵 / ~ **preserver**(妇女腋下的)护衣汗垫 / ~ **rehearsal** 彩排 / ~ **shield** =~ preserver / ~ **shirt** 礼服用白衬衫 / ~ **suit**(一套)大礼服

dresser ['dresə] *n.* ①食具柜;[美]梳妆台 ②(医院的)敷裹员 ③(剧团的)服装员 ④服装讲究的人;[与形容词连用]服装…的人: a careful (careless) ~ 服装讲究(不讲究)的人 ⑤整形器;(树木)枝剪;(石料)打磨机

dressing ['dresiŋ] *n.* ①穿衣;化妆;装饰 ②修饰(铸件等)的修整;(石面等)的修琢 ③【军】整队 ④【医】敷裹;敷料 ⑤ 加味品;调味品 ⑥【农】追肥;肥料 ⑦【矿】选矿 ⑧【纺】整理;上浆;梳棉 ⑨[口]训斥;揍 ‖~ **case** 化妆用品盒 / ~ **down** [口]狠狠训斥;揍: give sb. a ~ *down* 狠狠训斥(或揍)某人一顿 / ~ **gown** 晨衣 / ~ **room** 化妆室 / ~ **station** 【军】绷扎所 / ~ **table** 梳妆台

dressy ['dresi] *a.* [口] ①(人)讲究穿着的,(穿了好衣服后)挺刮刮的 ②(服装)时髦的

drew [druː] draw 的过去式

dribble ['dribl] **I ①** *vt.* ①使点滴流下;使逐渐落下 ②渐次支出(*out*);逐渐消磨(*away*) ③(足、篮、冰球等运动中)运(球),短传(球) **②** *vi.* ①滴;(烟雾、人群等)慢慢流动;逐渐消散: Then the music ~d away. 接着,音乐声慢慢地消失了。②(婴儿、白痴等)口角流涎 ③运球(前进),短传 **II** *n.* ①点滴;细流;少量 ②微雨 ④运球 ‖~**r** *n.* ①流涎的人 ②运球前进的人

drib(b)let ['dribulit] *n.* ①一滴 ②少量;小额: ~s of information 点滴的消息 / withdraw troops by(或 in)~s(每次少量地)渐次撤回军队

drier ['draiə] *n.* ①干燥工 ②干燥器 ③【化】干燥剂;催干剂,干料,燥液

drift [drift] **I** *n.* ①漂流;流速 ②漂流物;吹积物;(漂流或吹积物的)一堆: harbour ~ 港湾里漂流的杂物 / a ~ of snow (sand, leaves) 吹积成的一堆雪(沙,树叶) ③趋势,动向,倾向: the general ~ of affairs 事情的一般趋势,大势 ④ 大意,意旨: Did you get the ~ of the argument? 辩论的中心你明白了吗? ⑤坐观;放任自流: a policy of ~ 观望政策,放任自流的政策 ⑥【海】【空】流,偏航,【无】漂移,偏移,偏差;【宇】(导弹的)航差 ⑦【机】冲头,打孔器;打桩机 ⑧【矿】水平坑道;小平巷 ⑨(南非的)浅滩 ⑩【地】冰碛 **II ①** *vi.* ①漂流;漂泊;游荡: The boat ~ed down the river. 船顺水漂流而下。/ smoke ~ing from the chimney 从烟囱里飘出的烟 / ~ apart (两者)漂离;疏远 ②吹积 ③放任自流: Do not let matters ~. 不要听之任之。④(价格等)缓慢地变动;渐渐趋向(*towards*);不知不觉地陷入(*into*): ~ towards collapse 渐趋崩溃 / ~ into a habit 逐渐陷入一种习惯 **②** *vt.* ①使漂流 ②把…吹积(吹积物等)覆盖: The wind ~ed the snow into high banks. 风把雪吹积成许多大雪堆。/ a path

~ed with leaves 盖满落叶的路 ③【机】在…上打孔 ‖~er *n*.①漂流物;【军】漂流水雷 ②流浪者 ③流网渔船,飘网渔船 ④【矿】架式钻机 ‖~ **anchor** 【海】浮锚 / ~ **angle** 【海】【空】偏航角,漂移角 / '~**bolt** *n*.【机】系栓 / ~ **ice** 漂冰,流冰 / ~ **net** 流网 / '~**sand** 流砂 / '~**weed** *n*.漂浮海草,漂浮海藻 / '~**wood** *n*.①浮木 ②被扔弃的零星东西 ③社会上的寄生虫

drill[1] [dril] **I** *n*.①操练;训练: soldiers at ~ 操练中的兵士 / ~s in grammar 语法训练 ②[英口]规定的步骤 ③钻;钻头;钻孔器;钻床: a bench (hand) ~ 台(手)钻 / a (fluted) twist ~ 麻花钻 ④【动】(一种钻进牡蛎壳破坏牡蛎繁殖的)海蜗牛;荔枝螺 **II** ❶ *vt*.①操练;训练: ~ troops on a parade ground 在演兵场上练兵 / ~ pupils in grammar 在语法方面训练学生 ②钻(孔);在…上钻孔 ③[美俚]用子弹打穿,枪杀 ④使(球等)笔直行进 ❷ *vi*.①操练,训练 ②钻孔,钻通 (through) ③(子弹等)穿过 (through) ‖~ 操练员 / ~ 钻探工 ③钻机;钻床 ‖~ **bit** 钻;钻头 / ~ **ground** 练兵场,操练场 / '~**master** *n*.【军】教官 / ~ **sergeant** 军士级教练员

drill[2] [dril] 【农】 **I** *n*.①(条播的)垄沟;(条播植物的)行 ②播种机(尤指条播机): a field (hill-drop) ~ 台(穴)播机 **II** *vt*.①播种(种子);在…上条播 ②用播种机播(种),用播种机撒(肥料)

drill[3] [dril] *n*.斜纹布,卡其

drill[4] [dril] *n*.【动】(西非的)鬼狒

drink [driŋk] **I** (drank [dræŋk], drunk [drʌŋk]) ❶ *vt*.①饮,喝: a glass of boiled water 喝一杯开水 / ~ sth. off (或 up, down) 把某物一饮而尽 / ~ poison to quench thirst 饮鸩止渴 ②(植物、土壤等)吸收: The plants ~ (up) moisture. 植物吸收水分。/ The soil drank (in) the rain. 土壤吸收了雨水。③[~ oneself]喝酒喝得…: ~ oneself drunk 喝酒喝醉 ④举杯祝贺;向…举杯祝贺: ~ sb.'s health 举杯祝某人健康 / ~ success to sb. (sth.) 举杯祝某人(某事)成功 ⑤把(钱、时间等)花在喝酒上 ❷ *vi*.①饮,喝: ~ like a fish 牛饮,大口喝 ②吸收: ~ deep of what is progressive 大量吸取进步的东西 ③喝酒;酗酒: He doesn't ~. 他没有喝酒的习惯。/ ~ hard (或 heavily) 酗酒 ④干杯: ~ to (the health of) sb. 为某人的健康干杯 **II** *n*.①饮料: bottled ~s 瓶装饮料 / a cooling (hot) ~ 冷(热)饮 ②一些(或一口)饮料: Give me a ~ of water. 给我一些水喝。③酒;喝酒;酗酒: ~ and tobacco 烟酒 ④[the ~][俚] L俚]:The spaceship hit the ~. 宇宙飞船溅落海上。‖*be in* ~ 喝醉了 / *be on the* ~ 常常喝酒,酗酒 / ~ *down* ①以酒消(愁) ②比酒量使(对方)醉倒 / ~ *in* (如饥以渴地)吸取,陶醉于 / *knock over a* ~ [美俚]喝酒 / *the big* ~ [美俚]①大西洋(或太平洋) ②密西西比河 ‖~ *n*. 酒徒 ‖~ **money**, ~ **penny** [古]赏钱,小账

drinkable ['driŋkəbl] **I** *a*.可以喝的 **II** *n*.[常用复]饮料: eatables and ~s 饮食

drip [drip] **I** (dripped; dripping) ❶ *vt*.使滴下: ~ sweat 大汗淋漓 / Everything she said dripped acid. 她的话里字字句句都带着刺。❷ *vi*.①滴下;湿透 ②漏下,撒下 **II** *n*.①流滴;水滴(声);点滴: the ~ technique of painting 绘画的滴色法 / the ~ from a wet umbrella 湿雨伞上滴下的水珠 ②【机】滴水器 ③【建】滴水槽,(屋)檐 ④【医】(向血管注滴用的)慢滴器;滴液 ⑤[俚]使人厌烦的人,讨厌鬼 ⑥[俚]恭维话,甜言蜜语 ⑦[俚]无聊的闲谈 ‖~-~, '~-**drop** *n*.不断的滴水 / ~ **mo(u)ld** 【建】滴水槽 / '~**stone** *n*.①【建】滴水石 ②钟乳石,石笋;已成钟乳石(或石笋)的碳酸钙

dripping ['dripiŋ] **I** *n*.①滴下; 滴下的水声 ②[复]滴下的液体;烤肉上滴下的油汁 **II** *a*.滴水的,湿淋淋的 ‖*be* ~ *wet* 上下里外全部湿透 ‖~ **pan** 烘烤食物时接油滴的盘子

drive [draiv] **I** (drove [drouv], driven ['drivn]) ❶ *vt*.①驱,赶: ~ cows into a cowshed 把母牛赶进牛房 ②驱使;迫使;逼迫 ③驾驶(马车、汽车等);用车送: ~ a tractor 驾驶拖拉机 ④推动,发动(机器等): a machine ~n by waterpower 水力发动的机器 ⑤把(钉、桩等)打入 (into) ⑥挖(隧道等);铺设(铁道等): ~ an oil well 打油井 ⑦努力做(生意);使成交: a roaring trade 生意兴隆 / ~ a hard bargain 讨价还价坚持成交条件 ⑧推迟: Don't ~ it to the last minute. 不要把事情拖到不能再拖的地步。⑨用力击(球),猛力掷(球);抽(球) ❷ *vi*.①赶车;开车;乘车: Drive with caution! 小心驾驶! / ~ in a taxi 搭出租汽车 ②飞跑;猛冲;驱(进): The clouds are driving across the sky. 云在天空中疾驰。/ The rain was driving in our faces. 雨扑面打来。/ ~ straight in 长驱直入 ③用力击球,猛力掷球;抽球 **II** *n*.①驱赶;驱使 ②驾驶;驱车旅行;旅程: go for a ~ 驱车玩一玩 / an hour's ~ (汽车等)的一小时旅程 ③车道(尤指私宅内的汽车道) ④击球,掷球;抽球 ⑤(顺流而下的)木排 ⑥(被驱赶的)畜群 ⑦动力,干劲 ⑧[美]运动;竞赛: a subscription ~ 征求订户运动 ⑨(工作等的)压力,紧张状态 ⑩倾向,趋势 ⑪【机】传动,驱动;传动装置;【无】激励: gear (chain) ~ 齿轮(链)传动 / push-pull ~ 推挽激励 ⑫[军]大规模猛攻 ‖~ *at* 意指: What's he driving at? 他到底什么意思? / ~ *away at* 努力做(工作等) / ~ *down* 压低 / ~ *home* ①用车把…送到家 ②把(钉子等)打入 ③使人理解(或接受): The point was ~n home. 这论点说得被大家理解(或接受)了。/ ~ *hard* 强迫某人拼命工作 / ~ *up* 抬高 / *let* ~ (*at*) (对准…)打(或发射) ‖'~-**in** *n*.[美]服务到车上的路旁餐馆(或银行等);可以坐在车内观看的露天电影院 / '~**way** *n*. 车道

drivel ['drivl] **I** (drivel(l)ed; drivel(l)ing) ❶ *vi*.①说傻话,喋喋不休地胡说 ②淌口水 ❷ *vt*.胡乱而愚蠢地说出 **II** *n*.胡言乱语;胡扯 ‖~ *away* 浪费(时间、精力等) ‖drivel(l)er *n*.胡说八道的人

driven ['drivn] **I** drive 的过去分词 **II** *a.* ①出于不得已的 ②吹积起来的: ~ snow 吹积的雪 ③【机】从动的: ~ gear 从动齿轮

driver ['draivə] *n.* ①驾驶员, 司机; 赶车工 ②赶牲口的人 ③监工, 锤, 夯, 打桩机: a steam pile ~ 蒸汽打桩机 ④【机】传动装置; 主动轮; 策动器 ⑥【无】激励器; 末级前置放大器 ‖*the ~'s seat* 发号施令的地位, 控制地位

driving ['draiviŋ] **I** *a.* ①(力等)推动的;【机】(带等)传动的; (轴等)主动的 ②猛冲的: a ~ rain 瓢泼大雨 ③有干劲的 **II** *n.* 驾驶; 驱车 ‖~ belt 【机】传动带 / ~ box 【机】主机轴箱 / ~ gear 【机】主动齿轮 / ~ licence 驾驶执照 / ~ shaft 【机】主动轴 / ~ test 驾驶考试 / ~ wheel 【机】主动轮

drizzle ['drizl] **I** ❶ *vi.* 下蒙蒙细雨, 下小雨 ❷ *vt.* ①蒙蒙细雨般撒下 ②用细水珠弄湿 **II** *n.* 蒙蒙细雨

droll [droul] **I** *a.* 滑稽可笑的; 古怪离奇的: a ~ story 滑稽故事 **II** *n.* 滑稽的人; 滑稽角色 **III** *vi.* [古]说笑话; 开玩笑 ‖~ness *n.* / ~y *ad.*

dromedary ['drʌmədəri] *n.* 善跑的乘骑用的骆驼;【动】单峰骆驼

drone [droun] **I** *n.* ①雄蜂 ②寄生虫; 懒汉 ③(无线电遥控的)无人驾驶飞机; 飞行靶标 ④深沉的嗡嗡声; 单调沉闷的话; 男低音 ⑤语言无味的人 ⑥风笛的低音管 **II** ❶ *vi.* ①发出嗡嗡声 ②用单调沉闷的声调说话(或唱歌) ③闲荡; 平平淡淡地过去 ❷ *vt.* ①低沉单调地说出(或唱出)(out) ②无所事事地打发 (日子)(away) ‖**droningly** *ad.* ①嗡嗡地, 单调低沉地 ②懒洋洋地; 吊儿郎当地

droop [dru:p] **I** ❶ *vi.* ①(头、树枝等)低垂, 下垂; (眼睛)朝下: the ~ing willows 垂柳 ②(草木)凋萎; (人)衰颓; (精神)萎靡: Don't let your spirits ~. 不要萎靡不振。③[诗](太阳等)西落 ❷ *vt.* 使下垂 **II** *n.* ①低垂; 消沉 ②下降

drop [drop] **I** *n.* ①滴;[复]【药】滴剂: eye ~s 滴眼剂, 眼药水 ②滴状物(如粒糖、耳坠): fruit ~s (球形)水果糖 ③点滴, 微量: a ~ of fever 少许热度 ④一杯(或一口)酒: He has had (或 taken) a ~ too much. 他喝醉了。⑤落下, 下降;【电】电压降: a ~ in temperature 温度下降 ⑥落下物; 下垂物; 树木的落果; 绞刑架下的活动踏板; 耳坠; 舞台的垂幕; 门上的锁孔盖;【建】吊饰;【机】落锤 ⑦下落的距离; 高低平面间相差的距离;【军】弹道降落距离 ⑧空投; 空投的人(或物): a supply ~ 补给品空投 / a ~ zone 空投 (或伞降)地域 ⑨(动物)的产仔(量): the entire ~ of lambs for the year 羊羔的全年总产量 ⑩(邮筒等)的投入口 ⑪【体】踢落地球(=~kick) **II** (dropped) dropping) ❶ *vt.* ①使滴落下 ②使落下, 垂下, 放下, 投下; [美俚]口服(麻醉品): ~ one's eyes 垂下两眼 / an airplane *dropping* its wheels 放下轮子准备着陆的飞机 / ~ anchor 抛锚 / ~ a letter into the pillar-box 把信投进邮筒 / ~ shells 打炮 / ~ bombs 扔炸弹 ③(失手)落下; 丢失: Don't ~ the teapot. 别把茶壶打了。/ ~ one's guard 丧失警惕 ④ 遗漏, 省略: ~ a letter in a word 词里漏了一个字母 / ~ a stitch (编织中)漏了一针 / The relative pronoun "that" is often *dropped* if it is the object. 关系代词"that"在作宾语时常常被省略。⑤降低(声音、速度等) ⑥丢弃, 中断(与…的联系): Let's ~ the subject (matter). 我们别再谈这个问题 (这件事)吧。/ ~ a bad habit 改掉坏习惯 / The truck *dropped* its trailor. 卡车卸掉了拖车。~ an acquaintance 和一熟人停止往来 ⑦[美]开除, 解雇 ⑧击倒; 射落 ⑨(不经意地)说出; (随便地)投寄: ~ a hint 暗示 / ~ a word 露口风 / ~ sb. a postcard 给某人寄张明信片 / ~ sb. a few lines 给某人写封短信 ⑩下(客), 卸(货) ⑪(动物)产(仔) ⑫把(鸡蛋)打入沸水中煮 ⑬[俚]把落地球踢进(球门) ⑮【海】超越 ⑯(纸牌戏中)吊出(王牌等), 迫使(牌)脱手 ❷ *vi.* ①滴下; 落下, 掉下 ②(价格、温度等)下降; (风、声音等)变弱: His voice *dropped* to a whisper. 他放低声音讲话。③停止; 终止: The correspondence *dropped*. 通信中断了。/ let the matter ~ 不再提这件事 ④(因疲劳、受伤等)倒下 ⑤(话等)无意中漏出 ⑥[美](动物)出生 ⑦(猎犬等扑向猎物前)蹲下 ⑧(纸牌戏中)被迫扔下王牌 ‖*a ~ in the bucket* (或 *ocean*) 沧海一粟, 九牛一毛 / *at the ~ of a hat* ①信号一发(就行动) ②立即, 毫不迟疑地 / ~ *a brick* 见 **brick** / ~ *a courtesy* 见 *courtesy* / ~ *courtesy* ① 偶然遇见 (或发现) ②训斥; 惩罚 / ~ *across* ①偶然遇见(或发现) ②训斥; 惩罚 / ~ *asleep* 不觉睡着; 入睡 / ~ *astern* 落在(他船)后面 / ~ *away* (一个一个地)离开, 散去 / ~ *back* ①退后, 后撤 ②恢复 (旧习惯等)(into) / ~ *behind* 落伍, 落后; 落在…之后 / ~ *by* [美]随便访问一下 / ~ *by* ~ 一滴一滴地; 一点一点地 / ~ *dead* 倒毙 / ~ *down* ①卧倒 ②顺着(河流、山坡等)向下移动 / ~ *in (on sb.)* 顺便走访(某人): Would you ~ *in (on us)* tomorrow evening for a chat? 你明晚有便来(和我们一起)谈谈好吗? / ~ *into* ①跌入, 落入 ②偶然进入(某地) ③不知不觉养成(习惯) ④不知不觉进入(某种状态): ~ *into* sleep (conversation) 不觉睡着(谈起来) / ~ *it!* 停止! 别那样了! 别闹了! / ~ *off* ①(一个一个地)离开, 散去 ②逐渐减少 ③睡着 ④死去 / ~ *on* 训斥, 惩罚 / ~ *out* ①掉落, 掉出: One of his teeth had *dropped* out. 他的一只牙齿掉了。②退出; 离队 / ~ *through* 落空, 失败 / *get* (或 *have*) *the* ~ *on (sb.)* [俚] ①抢先拔枪瞄准(某人); 先发制(人) ②胜过(某人) / *a* ~ *in one's eye* 有点醉意 / *in* ~s = ~ *by* ~ / *take a* ~ *of something* 喝一点酒 ‖*let* *n.* 微滴: ~*let* infection 【医】飞沫传染 / **droppage** *n.* [总称]落下来的东西(如树木的落果等) / **dropper** *n.* ①落下的人(或物) ②滴管, 滴瓶

③【矿】分脉，支脉 ‖~ **curtain** (戏院等的) 垂幕 / '~-'**forge** vt. 【冶】落锤锻造 / ~ **hammer** 【机】落锤 / '~**head** n. 使打字机(或缝纫机头)藏在台板下的活动装置 / '~**kick** n.【体】踢落地球 / ~ **leaf** (桌子等的) 活动翻板 / ~ **letter** 由同一邮局局收寄并投递的信件 / '~**light** n. (上下滑动的) 吊灯 / '~-**off** n. 陡坡 / '~**out** n. [美] ①中途退出；退学 ②中途退出的人；退学学生 ③退出习俗社会的人 / ~ **press**【机】模锻压力机；落锤 / ~ **scene** 可升降的布景幕布；[喻] 结局；最后下场 / ~ **shot** (羽毛球等的) 扣球 / ~ **shutter** (旧式照相机上下滑动的) 快门

dropping ['drɔpiŋ] n. ①滴下，落下；【军】空投，空降，伞降 ②点滴；滴下物，落下物: ~s from a candle 烛泪 / ~s from trees 树的落叶 ③[复] (动物的) 粪；【纺】落棉，落毛 ‖~ **electrode**【化】滴液电极 / ~ **fire**【军】零零落落的步枪射击 / a ~ **gear** 空投装置 / a ~ **ground**【军】空投场 / ~ **reaction**【化】点滴反应 / ~ **resistor**【物】降压电阻器

dross [drɔs] n. ①【冶】浮渣 ②废物；渣滓；杂质: discard the ~ and select the essential 去粗取精 ③【矿】劣质细煤 ‖~y a.

drought [draut], **drouth** [drauθ] n. ①干旱(季节)；旱灾: combat ~ 抗旱 / ~ resistance 抗旱(性) ②(长期的) 缺乏: a period of financial ~ 财政枯竭时期 ③[方] 渴 (尤指想喝酒) ‖~y a. ‖ ~ **en'during** a. 耐旱的 / '~-**re'sistant** a. 抗旱的

drove [drouv] I drive 的过去式 II n. ①(被驱赶的或向前走动的) 畜群: a ~ of horses 一群马 ②(一起走动或行动的) 人群 ③石工的平凿；凿平的石面 III ❶ vt. ①赶(牲口) ②用平凿凿(石) ❷ vi. 赶牲口

drown [draun] ❶ vt. ①把…淹死 ②淹没，浸湿: The river used to overflood, ~ing whole villages. 过去这条河常常泛滥，淹没整个整个的村庄。/ Cheers ~ed his voice (或 him). 欢呼声淹没了他的话声。/ ~ oneself in work 埋头工作 / eyes ~ed in tears 泪汪汪的眼睛 ③解(忧愁等): ~ one's worries in drink 借酒浇愁 ❷ vi. 溺死: a ~ing man 溺水的人 ‖ ~ **out** ①淹没，压过(另一声音) ②(水) 把…赶出 / like a ~ed rat (湿得) 象落汤鸡

drowse [drauz] I ❶ vi. ①打瞌睡，打盹儿(off) ②呆滞不动；处于不活动状态 ❷ vt. ①使瞌睡，使发呆 ②昏昏沉沉地消磨掉(away) II n. 瞌睡: fall into a ~ 打起瞌睡来

drowsy ['drauzi] a. ①昏昏欲睡的；瞌睡的 ②催眠的；使人懒洋洋的 ③(村庄、街市等) 沉寂的，没有动静的 ‖**drowsily** ad. / **drowsiness** n.

drudge [drʌdʒ] I n. ①做苦工的人 ②做单调乏味工作的人 ③单调乏味的工作 II ❶ vi. 做苦工；干单调乏味的工作 (at, over) ❷ vt. 强使做苦工 ‖~**ry** n. 苦工；单调乏味的工作 / **drudgingly** ad. 苦役般地；辛劳地；单调乏味地

drug [drʌg] I n. ①药，药物，药材: crude ~s 生药 ②麻醉药品，麻醉剂，成瘾性毒品: the ~ habit 吸毒癖 / a ~ addict (或 user) 吸毒成瘾的人 ③滞销货: a ~ on (或 in) the market 市场上的滞销商品 II (drugged; drugging) ❶ vt. ①使服麻醉药，使麻醉；使服毒品；掺麻醉药于 ②使沉醉；毒化 ❷ vi. 常用麻醉药；吸毒成瘾 ‖~-,**fast** a.【医】抗药性的，耐药性的 / '~-**store** n. 药房 ②[美] 杂货店 (出售药物、糖果、饮料及其他杂物的店铺): a ~store cowboy [美俚] 在杂货店里 (或街头) 闲逛的人；吹牛的人

druggist ['drʌgist] n. ①药商 ②药剂师 ③[美] 杂货店老板

drum [drʌm] I n. ①鼓: beat ~s and gongs 敲锣打鼓 ②鼓状物；圆桶，【机】鼓轮；圆筒；滚筒；(自动枪炮的) 盘形弹匣: magnetic ~【自】磁鼓 ③【解】鼓膜；鼓室；中耳；【动】鼓状共鸣器 ④鼓声；打鼓般的声音 (尤指麻鸻的叫声) ⑤【建】(作石柱用的) 鼓形石块；(支持圆屋顶的) 圆柱形墙壁 ⑥【动】(发鼓鼓声的) 石首鱼科的鱼，石首鱼 (=~ fish) II (drummed; drumming) ❶ vi. ①打鼓；冬冬地敲: ~ at the door 冬冬地敲门 / ~ on the piano 连续猛击钢琴键 ②(鸟、昆虫鼓翅) 发出嗡嗡声 ❷ vt. ①打鼓奏(曲调)；敲出(曲调) ②冬冬地敲: ~ the floor with one's feet 连续用脚蹬地 ‖a drumming in the ears 耳鸣 / beat the (或 a) ~ (for 或 about) 鼓吹(…) / ~ for ①大力招募，招徕 ②鼓吹 / ~ out 轰走；开除 / ~ sth. into sb. (或 sb.'s head) 反复向某人灌输某事物 (使他记住) / ~ up ①大力征集，召集；招徕 ②鼓吹；鼓动(情绪等) / follow the ~ 当兵 ‖'~-**beat** n. 鼓的一击(声) / '~-,**beater** n. 鼓吹者 / '~-,**beating** n. 鼓吹 / '~-**fed gun** 圆盘机关枪 / '~**fire** n. (步兵进攻前) 连续的猛烈炮火 / '~**head** n. ①鼓面 ②【解】鼓膜 ③【机】绞盘头 / '~**head court-martial** 战地军法审判 / ~ **major** 军队的鼓手长；行进军乐队的指挥 / '~**stick** n. ①鼓槌 ②(煮熟的) 家禽腿下部

drummer ['drʌmə] n. ①鼓手 ②[美] 旅行推销员

drunk [drʌŋk] I drink 的过去分词 II a. [常作表语] ①醉的: be dead (half) ~ 烂(半)醉 ②陶醉的，兴奋的: be ~ with joy (success) 陶醉于欢乐(胜利)中 III n. [俚] ①醉汉；酒鬼，酗酒犯 ②酒会，狂饮 ‖as ~ as a lord 酩酊大醉 / as ~ as a sow 烂醉

drunkard ['drʌŋkəd] n. 醉汉；酒鬼: a sentimental ~ 酒醉好哭的人

drunken ['drʌŋkən] a. [常作定语] ①醉的；常醉的: a ~ sot 酒鬼 ②酒醉引起的: a ~ frolic 醉后的胡闹 ③喝醉酒似的，摇摇晃晃的: in a ~ manner 摇摇晃晃地 ‖~**ly** ad. / ~**ness** n.

dry [drai] I a. ①干的；干燥的: ~ firewood 干柴 / a ~ cough 干咳 / Keep ~! 保持干燥！(或: 请勿受潮!) ②干旱的: a ~ summer 干旱的夏天 ③干枯的；枯竭的: a ~ well 枯井 / The cows are ~. 这些奶牛不产奶了。④[口]

(使)口渴的: I feel ~. 我口渴。/ ~ work 使人口渴的活儿 ⑤不用水的, 与液体无关的; 不经滑润的: a ~ shampoo 干洗的洗发(剂) / a ~ death 非溺死; 不流血的死 ⑥(面包等)不涂黄油的 ⑦(酒等)不甜的, 无果味的 ⑧干巴巴的, 枯燥乏味的: a ~ subject 枯燥无味的题目 ⑨冷冰冰的; 不加渲染的; 不带个人偏见(或感情)的: ~ sarcasm 冷嘲 / ~ facts 不加渲染的事实, 铁一般的事实 / view sth. in a ~ light 不带偏见地看某事物 ⑩无预期结果的, 没有收获的: a ~ interview 一无所获的会见 ⑪[口]空弹的; 演习的: ~ firing 空弹射击 ⑫禁酒的: The country has gone ~. 那个国家禁酒了。 II ❶ vt. ①把…弄干; 使干燥: ~ one's hands on (或 with) a towel 用毛巾擦干双手 / ~ clothes by squeezing (in the sun) 把衣服拧干(晒干) ②使(奶牛)停止产奶 ❷ vi. 变干; 干涸: Nylon dries quickly. 尼龙织物干得快。 III n. ①干; 干涸 ②干物; 干旱地区 ③禁酒论者 ‖a ~ eye 不流泪的眼(指不哭的人) / do a ~ (演员)记不起台词 / ~ as a bone 干透的 / ~ straight [口]结果很好; 终于好转 / ~ up ①(使) 干涸 ②[俚]住口; 讲不出话来; (演员)忘记台词 / not ~ behind the ears [美俚]乳臭未干的, 无经验的 / row ~ 不使水花飞溅地划桨 ‖~er n. =drier / ~ish a. 有点儿干的 / ~ly ad. =drily / ~ness n. ‖~ battery 干电池组 / ~ cell 干电池 / '~-boned a. 骨瘦如柴的 / '~-bulb a. 干球的: a ~-bulb thermometer 干球温度计 / ~ camp 无水宿营地 / ~ cell 干电池 / ~-'clean vt. 干洗 / ~ cleaner ①干洗剂 ②干洗商 / '~-'cleanse vt. 干洗 / '~-cure vt. 干腌 / ~ dock 干船坞 / ~-'dock vt. & vi. (使)入干船坞 / ~ farming 【农】旱地农作(法) / ~ fly (钓鱼用的)假虫饵 / ~ goods ①[英]谷类; 干物类 ②[美]织物类 / ~ ice 干冰 / ~ land ①旱地区 ②陆地 / ~ measure 干量 / ~ nurse ①保姆(区别于 wet nurse 奶妈) ②保育人(尤指常给人以必要的指导的人) / '~-nurse vt. 当…的保姆(或保育人) / ~ oil 干性油(如桐油等); 无水石油 / ~ plate 【摄】干片 / '~-point n. (不用酸的)铜版雕刻(术); 铜版雕刻针; 铜版画 vi. 铜版雕刻 / ~ rot 干朽, 干枯; (道德、社会等的)内部腐败 / ~ run ①演习; (飞机)摹拟投弹练习 ②排演, 试演 / '~-salt vt. 干腌 / '~-salter n. 干货商 / '~-,saltery n. 干货店; 干货类, 干货业 / '~-'shod a. & ad. 不湿脚的(地) / ~ wall 清水墙 / ~ walling 墙垣干砌, 无浆砌墙 / ~ weight 干重 /【空】净重

dryad ['draiəd] n. [希神]林中仙女; 树精

dual ['dju(ː)əl] I a. 双的; 二重的; 二元的; 二体的: ~ nature 双重性的妇女 / ~ nationality 双重国籍 / ~ control 双重操纵; 双重管辖; 两国共管;【空】复式操纵(装置) II n. [语]双数 ‖~ly ad. ‖~-'purpose a. ①双重目的的, 两用的 ②【农】(家畜、家禽品种)兼用的: a ~-purpose

hen 卵肉兼用鸡 / a ~-purpose cow 乳肉兼用牛

dub [dʌb] I (dubbed; dubbing) vt. ❶(以某种称号)授与; 给…起绰号: ~ sb. a model stock raiser 授某人以模范饲养员称号 ②用剑拍肩封…为爵士 ③用油脂涂(皮革等) ④把(木板、皮片等)刮光(或锤平) ⑤打击; 戳 ⑥为(电影、广播节目等)配音; 复制(录音、唱片等); 把(对话、音乐等)灌进录音带: ~ Chinese films in English 用英语译配中国影片 ⑦(高尔夫球戏中)很拙劣地打; 笨拙地做(某事) II n. ①鼓的一击(声) ②[美俚]新手; 笨蛋 ③配入影片声带中的对话(或音乐等)

dubious ['djuːbjəs] a. ①(对事物)半信半疑的, 犹豫不决的: be ~ of (或 about) sth. 对某事半信半疑 ②暧昧的, 含糊的: a ~ answer 含糊其词的答复 ③引起怀疑的, 可疑的: a ~ character 可疑分子 ④未定的, 未定局的; 无把握的: The result is still ~. 结局未定。 ‖~ly ad. / ~ness n.

ducal ['djuːkəl] a. 公爵的; 公爵似的; 公爵领地的

duchess ['dʌtʃis] n. ①公爵夫人; 女公爵 ②容貌威严的妇女 ③[英俚]小贩的妻子 ‖a meddling ~ 爱管闲事, 神气活现而一事无成的老太婆

duck¹ [dʌk] n. ①鸭; 雌鸭 (drake 雄鸭之对); 鸭肉; [集合名词]鸭类 ②[口]亲爱的人, 宝贝儿 ③有吸引力的物(或人), 可爱的物 (或人): a ~ of a car 吸引人的汽车 ④[美俚]家伙: a queer ~ 古怪的家伙 ⑤[军俚](登陆用)水陆两用摩托车 ⑥[体]鸭蛋, 零分 (= ~ egg 或 ~'s egg): make a ~ 得零分 ‖a dead ~ (注定要)完蛋的人(或物) / a fine day for young ~s 雨天 / a sitting ~ 易捕获的猎物; 易打中的目标; 易打击的对象 / chance the ~ 好歹要干一下; 不管三七二十一 / ~ soup [美俚]容易做的事情; 好欺侮的人 / in two shakes of a ~'s tail 马上, 立刻 / knee-high to a ~ 很小的; 微不足道的 / like a ~ in a thunderstorm 惊惶失措的 / like a ~ to water (象鸭子入水)很自然地; 毫无疑惧(或困难)地; 如鱼得水 / like water off a ~'s back 不发生作用的, 毫无影响的 / make ~s and drakes of (或 play ~s and drakes with) 浪费; 挥霍 (钱财等) / play ~s and drakes 玩打水漂(掷出扁石使在水上漂跃)游戏 / Will a ~ swim? 那还用问吗! 当然愿意罗! ‖'~-bill n. 【动】鸭嘴兽 ②多齿白鲟, 匙吻白鲟 ③【矿】鸭嘴装载机 / '~-billed a. (嘴巴)象鸭嘴的 / '~-board n. [常用复](战壕或泥地上铺的)狭板道 / ~ hawk 【动】①[美]游隼 ②[英]白头鹞 / '~-legged a. 短腿的 / '~-pin n. 滚球戏; (滚球戏用的)小柱子 / ~ shot 打野鸭的弹丸 / '~weed n. 【植】浮萍

duck² [dʌk] I ❶ vi. ①突然潜入水中 ②迅速低下头(或弯下身) ③闪避; 逃避 ❷ vt. ①把(人等)猛按入水中 ②突然低下(头或身子) ③躲避: ~ the issue 回避问题 II n. 突然的一潜; 闪避

duck³ [dʌk] n. ①帆布; 粗布 ②[复]帆布裤子; 帆布衣服

duckling ['dʌkliŋ] *n.* 小鸭, 幼鸭

ducky ['dʌki] *a.* [俚] ①玲珑的; 可爱的 ②令人满意的

duct [dʌkt] I *n.* ①管, 输送管; 槽, 沟, 渠道: an air ~ 气管, 气道 ②【动】【植】导管: spermatic ~ 输精管 ③(电线、电缆的)管道: wave ~ [无]波道 II *vt.* 通过管道输送(气体) ||**~less** *a.* 无管的: ~less gland 【解】无管腺, 内分泌腺

dud [dʌd] I *n.* ①[复][俚]衣服, 破衣服; 个人的衣物财产 ②未能爆发的炮弹(或炸弹), 哑弹, 闷弹 ③不中用的东西 II *a.* 不中用的, 没有价值的; 假的: a ~ cheque 假支票

dudgeon ['dʌdʒən] *n.* 愤恨, 愤怒: in high ~ 非常愤怒

due [djuː] I *a.* ①适当的; 应有的, 应得的; 正当的: in ~ time 在适当的时候 / in ~ form 按照适当的(或规定的)形式 ②(车、船等)预定到达的; 预期的; 约定的: The train is ~ to leave (arrive) at six. 列车定于六点钟开出(到达)。 ③应支付的; (票据等)到期的: the amount ~ to sb. 应付给(或欠)某人的款项 / fall (或 become) ~ 到期 II *ad.* (罗盘指针)正(南、北等): sail ~ east 向正东方向航行 III *n.* ①应得物; 应得权益: give sb. his ~ 给某人以应得的评价; 公平对待某人 ②[复]应付款: harbo(u)r ~s 入港税 ||**~ to** ①应归于 ②由于: be ~ to internal causes 由于内因 / The flight was cancelled ~ to the fog. 班机因雾停航。 ||**~ bill** [美](以服务抵偿债务的)借约

duel ['dju(ː)əl] I *n.* ①决斗 ②(双方的)斗争: a ~ of wits 斗智 / an artillery ~ 炮战 / a verbal ~ 争辩, 舌战 II (duel(l)ed; duel(l)ing) *vi.* 决斗 ||**duel(l)ist** *n.* 决斗者; 斗争者

duet [djuː'et], **duetto** [djuː'etou] *n.* ①【音】二重唱(曲); 二重奏(曲) ②二重唱(或二重奏)演出小组 ②[喻]对话; 对骂 ③(一)对, (一)双 ||**play a ~** 演双簧 ||**duettist** *n.* 二重唱者; 二重奏者

duffel ['dʌfəl], **duffle** ['dʌfl] *n.* ①粗厚起绒的呢料 ②(野营者、猎人等的)一套用具 ||**duffel bag** 行李袋

duffer ['dʌfə] *n.* ①[俚]卖骗人货的小贩 ②笨蛋; 不中用的人; 糊涂人 ③假货; 不中用的东西

dug[1] [dʌg] dig 的过去式和过去分词

dug[2] [dʌg] *n.* 哺乳动物的乳房(或乳头)

dugout ['dʌgaut] *n.* ①独木舟 ②挖在山坡(或地下)的洞; 防空洞; 地下掩敝部 ③棒球运动员休息处 ④[俚]重新服役的超龄军官; 退休后重新任职者

duke [djuːk] *n.* ①公爵; (欧洲公国的)君主 ②[古](罗马的)省督军 ③[复][美俚]手, 拳头 ④一种樱桃 ||**~dom** *n.* ①公国; 公爵领地 ②公爵的爵位

dull [dʌl] I *a.* ①迟钝的; 呆笨的: be ~ of hearing. 听觉不灵敏 ②阴暗的; 阴郁的; 沉闷的, 单调的: a ~ colo(u)r 暗淡的颜色 / ~ weather 阴沉的天气 / a ~ talk 单调无味的谈话 / a ~ pain 隐痛

③呆滞的, 不活跃的: a ~ market 萧条的市场 / a ~ season 淡季 ④(刀等)钝的; (镜子等)模糊的 II ❶ *vt.* ①弄钝; 使迟钝 ②使阴暗 ③缓和, 减轻(痛苦等); 使不活泼 ❷ *vi.* ①变得迟钝 ②(兴趣、痛苦等)减少, 减轻 ||**~ard** *n.* 蠢人, 笨蛋 / **~ish** *a.* ①有点迟钝的 ②有点沉闷的 / **dul(l)ness** *n.* / **~y** *ad.* ||'**~-witted** *a.* 笨的, 迟钝的

duly ['djuːli] *ad.* ①按时地; 及时地; 正式地: Your letter has been ~ received. 您的信已经按时收到。(商业用语) / The train has ~ arrived. 火车按时到达了。②充分地, 适当地: ~ supply sb. with sth. 以某物充分地供应某人 / ~ solve a problem 适当地解决一个问题

dumb [dʌm] *a.* ①哑的, 不能说话的: a ~ person 哑巴 ②不说话的, 无言的; 沉默寡言的; 没有发言权的: (a) ~ show 哑剧 / strike sb. ~ 使某人楞住 / remain (或 be) ~ 保持沉默 ③无声的, 无声的: a ~ piano (练习运指的)无声钢琴 ④缺乏应有条件的; (船)没有帆(或动力)的 ⑤[美俚]笨的, 愚蠢的: a ~ *Dora* ['dɔːrə] [美俚]傻女人, 幼稚的女人 ||**~ly** *ad.* / **~ness** *n.* ||**'~bell** *n.* ①哑铃: ~bell exercise 哑铃体操 ②[俚]笨蛋, 蠢货 / **dum(b)'found(er)** *vt.* 使惊讶得发呆 / ~ **iron** ①填缝铁条 ②汽车车架与弹簧链条间的连接部分 / ~ **struck** 被吓得发楞的 / '**~'waiter** *n.* [美](用餐时使用的)旋转碗碟架; (楼上楼下之间的)送菜升降机

dummy ['dʌmi] I *n.* ①哑巴; 经常沉默的人; 笨蛋 ②名义代表; 傀儡 ③(牌戏, 尤指桥牌)"明家"(即牌叫定后, 摊牌于桌上的人) ④人形靶; (橱窗中陈列的)假人; 作样品用的假货; 样本 ⑤虚设物; 模仿物; 伪装物 ⑥[英]橡皮奶头 ⑦(有凝汽器的)无机车机 ⑧【印】(书籍印刷前用白纸等制的)样书 II *a.* ①摆样子的, 做幌子的, 假的: a ~ watch (gun) 假表(枪) ②空名的; 虚构的: a ~ director 空名经理(实在并无其人) ③傀儡的, 不能独立行动的 ||a ~ *bomb* 假炸弹, 练习弹 / a ~ *cartridge* 假子弹, 练习弹 / a ~ *horse* 【体】木马 / a ~ *round* (或 *projectile*) 假弹, 练习弹 / ~ *up* [俚]闭口不说, 拒绝泄漏所知情况 / *sell the* ~ (橄榄球赛中)做假动作骗对手; 声东击西

dump[1] [dʌmp] I *n.* ①堆垃圾的地方; 垃圾堆 ②(材料、衣服等)堆存处; 前线军需品临时集结处: an ammunition ~ 弹药集结处 / a petrol ~ 汽油库 ③[俚]丑陋场所(或地方); [俚]破烂, 地方 ④砰(或落)的一声 ⑤【自】(计算机的)清除; 信息转储, 切断电源 II ❶ *vt.* ①倾倒(垃圾); 抛弃(废物、候选人等): ~ sth. on the heap 把某物抛到堆上 ②倾销: ~ surplus goods abroad 向国外倾销过剩货物 ③把…砰的一声抛下 ④[美俚]故意输掉(比赛) ❷ *vi.* ①倒垃圾 ②倾销商品 ③砰地落下 ||~ *car* 【矿】垃圾车; 卸货车, 自动倾卸车 / ~ *clearance* 清洁工人; 倾卸者 ②倾销者 / ~ing *n.* 倾销 ||~ **car** (铁道上的)倾斜车, 自动倾卸车 / '**~cart** *n.* 倒垃圾车 / ~ **truck** 自动卸货卡车

dump² [dʌmp] *n.* ①[英]短而粗的东西 ②[英] [古]矮胖的人 ③[英]造船用螺栓 ④铅制筹码 ⑤球形糖果 ⑥澳大利亚已废货币; [俚]小货币: not worth a ~ 不值一文

dump³ [dʌmp] *n.* ①[常用复]忧郁, 沮丧: (down) in the ~s 神情沮丧的 ②[古]忧郁的曲调

dumpling ['dʌmpliŋ] *n.* ①汤团; 团子; 苹果布丁 ②[口]矮胖的人(或动物)

dun¹ [dʌn] **I** (dunned; dunning) **❶** *vt.* ① 向…催讨 ② 对…纠缠不清; 使烦恼 **❷** *vi.* 催债 **II** *n.* ①催债者; 纠缠不清者 ②催讨, 催债

dun² [dʌn] **I** *a.* ①暗褐色的 ②[诗]阴郁的, 阴暗的 **II** *n.* ①暗褐色 ②暗褐色马 ③[动]蜉蝣的亚成虫; 毛翅目昆虫 ④模仿成蜉蝣亚成虫的钓鱼饵 **III** (dunned; dunning) *vt.* 使成暗褐色

dunce [dʌns] *n.* 笨伯 ‖~('s) cap 旧时学校中给成绩差的学生戴的圆锥形纸帽

dune [djuːn] *n.* (风吹积成的)沙丘

dung [dʌŋ] **I** *n.* ①(牲畜的)粪; 粪肥 ②丑恶的事物 **II** *vt.* 施粪肥于 ‖~ **beetle**【动】粪金龟子 / '~**-cart** *n.* 粪车 / ~ **depot** 粪库 / ~ **fly** 粪蝇 / '~**-fork** *n.* 粪耙

dungaree [ˌdʌŋgə'riː] *n.* ① 粗棉布, 粗蓝斜纹布 ②[复]粗布工作服, 粗蓝斜纹布工作服

dungeon ['dʌndʒən] *n.* ①土牢, 地牢 ②(中世纪的)城堡主塔, 城堡主楼

dupe¹ [djuːp] **I** *vt.* 欺骗, 诈骗, 愚弄: ~ sb. into doing sth. 骗某人去做某事 **II** *n.* 容易受骗的人, 被人愚弄的人 ‖~r 欺骗者, 诈骗者

dupe² [djuːp] *n.* & *vt.* =duplicate (*n.* & *vt.*)

duplicate ['djuːplikit] **I** *a.* 复制的; 完全一样的; 成对的; 副的; 二重的; 二倍的: a ~ copy 副本 **II** *n.* ① 复制品; 副本, 抄件: be done (或 made out) in ~ 制成正副两份 ② 完全相似的对应物 ③当票 (桥牌比赛中的)换手重打 **III** ['djuːplikeit] *vt.* ① 使加倍; 使成双 ② 复写; 打印; 复制 ③使重复

duplication [ˌdjuːpli'keiʃən] *n.* ①成倍; 成双 ②复写; 打印; 复制品 ③重复

duplicity [djuː(ː)'plisiti] *n.* ①口是心非; 表里不一; 奸诈, 欺骗 ②两重性, 重复

durable ['djuərəbl] **I** *a.* ① 耐用的: a ~ pair of shoes 一双耐穿的鞋 ② 持久的: ~ friendship 永恒的友谊 **II** *n.* [常用复]耐久的物品 (=~ goods) ‖**durability** [ˌdjuərə'biliti] *n.* / ~**ness** *n.* / **durably** *ad.* ‖~ **goods** 耐久的物品(指家庭用具, 汽车, 机器等)

duration [djuə'reiʃən] *n.* 持续; 持久; 持续时间, 期间: a meeting of short (long) ~ 短(长)会 / the ~ of flight (飞机的)续航时间 ‖*digit* ~【自】数字脉冲宽度 / ~ *of fire*【军】射击持续时间 / ~ *of runs*【机】运转时间 / ~ *of service* 设备使用年限 / ~ *record*【空】续航纪录 ‖*for the* ~ (指战争等)在整个非常时期内

duress(e) [djuə'res] *n.* ①强迫, 胁迫: Accomplices under ~ shall go unpunished. 胁从不问。②束缚, 监禁 ‖*a plea of* ~【律】以被胁迫承认为理由申请宣告无效

during ['djuəriŋ] *prep.* 在…的期间; 在…的时候: ~ the day (the summer, the last few years) 在白天(夏季, 最近几年间) / He came to see me ~ my illness. 在我生病的时候他来看我。

dusk [dʌsk] **I** *n.* ① 薄暮, 黄昏; 幽暗: in the ~ of the evening 暮色苍茫中 / at ~ 黄昏时刻 / from dawn till ~ 从早到晚 **II** *a.* 微暗的; 微黑的 **III** *vt.* & *vi.* (使)微暗; (使)变微黑 ‖~**ish** *a.*

dust [dʌst] **I** *n.* ① 灰尘, 尘土; [a ~] 一片灰尘: radioactive ~ 放射性尘埃 / What a ~! 好大的灰尘! ② 粉末; 【植】花粉; 【矿】金矿粉末: insecticidal ~ 杀虫药粉 / coal ~ 煤粉 ③[英]垃圾, 灰烬 ④土; 葬身地; 遗骸 ⑤混乱, 骚动 ⑦[俚]钱 **II** **❶** *vt.* ① 去掉…上的灰尘: ~ a room 打扫房间 / ~ a cap 掸掉帽上的灰 ② 把…弄成粉末 ③撒(粉末); (把粉末)撒在…上: ~ sugar on to a cake (或 ~ a cake with sugar) 在饼上撒糖 / mountains ~ed with snow 被雪覆盖的群山 ④[俚]蒙蔽 **❷** *vi.* ①去掉灰尘 ②扬起灰尘 ③(鸟)用沙土洗澡 ‖*be humbled in* (或 *to*) *the* ~ 遭到奇耻大辱 / *bite the* ~ 倒下去; 大败 / *crumble to* ~ ①倒, 垮 ②化为乌有 / *down with one's* (或 *the*) ~ 现款交易, 付款 / ~*'em off* [美俚] ①用功 ②话旧 ③重理旧业 / ~ *sb. off* [美俚]打击(或痛打)某人; 把某人杀掉 / ~ *sb.'s jacket* (或 *coat*) 殴打某人 / ~ *(the eyes of) sb.* 蒙蔽某人 / *eat* ~ 含垢忍辱 / *in* ~ *and ashes* 见 **ash¹** / *in the* ~ 死了 / *kick up* (或 *make*) *a* ~ ①扬起灰尘 ②引起骚动 / *kiss the* ~ ①屈服 ②被杀 / *lick the* ~ ①被打得一败涂地 ②卑躬屈节 / *lie in the* ~ 成废墟; 战死 / *make the* ~ *fly* ①做得卖力 ②动得迅速 / *raise a* ~ ①扬起灰尘 ②引起骚动 / *shake the* ~ *off one's feet* (或 *shake off the* ~ *of one's feet*) 愤然(或轻蔑地)离去 / *the* ~ *and heat* (*of the day*) 战斗(或竞争)的混乱和激烈 / *throw* ~ *in sb.'s eyes* 迷惑(或蒙蔽)某人 ‖~**less** *a.* 没有灰尘的 ‖'~**band** *n.* (表的)防尘圈 / '~**bin** *n.* [英]垃圾箱 (美国称 ash can) / ~ **bowl** 长期遭受干旱和尘暴的地区 / '~**brand** *n.* [英]【植】黑穗病 / **cart** [英]垃圾车 / ~ **cloak** [英](防尘的)罩衣 / '~**coat** *n.* =cloak / '~**-**colo(u)r *n.* 灰褐色 / ~ **cover** ①(家具等的)布罩 ②(书的)护封 / ~ **devil**【气】小尘暴, 尘旋风 / ~ **guard** [英](机器的)防尘板, 防尘罩 / ~ **heap** *n.* 垃圾堆 / ~ **jacket** (书的)护封 / ~ **man** ['dʌstmən] *n.* [英] ① 清除垃圾的人 ②(神话中)使小孩瞌睡的怪物 / '~'**off** *n.* 从战区撤出死伤人员的直升飞机 / '~**pan** *n.* 畚箕 / '~**proof** *a.* 防尘的 / ~ **shot** 最小号的子弹 / ~ **storm**【气】尘暴 / '~**up** *n.* [美] ①争吵, 争论 ②[俚]骚乱, 喧闹

duster ['dʌstə] *n.* ①打扫工 ②揩布; 尘拂, 掸帚

除尘器 ③撒粉器(尤指杀虫剂的喷洒器)；撒(胡椒等的)粉瓶；撒糖器 ④[美]避尘衣，风衣

dusty ['dʌsti] *a.* ①满是灰尘的②灰土一般的；粉末状的③土灰色的④干巴巴的，无聊的⑤含糊的，不明朗的: a ~ answer 含糊的回答 ‖*not so* ~ [英俚]还不错

duty ['dju:ti] *n.* ①责任；义务；本分: strengthen one's sense of ~ 加强责任感 / fail in one's ~ 失职 ②职务；勤务: be on guard (patrol, sentry) ~ 执行警卫(巡逻,放哨)任务 / air (ground) ~ 空(地)勤 / a ~ doctor for emergency cases 急诊值班医生 ③尊敬,敬意: pay (或 send) one's ~ to sb. 对某人表示敬意 ④税: customs (licence) *duties* 关(牌照)税 / *duties on* imported goods 商品进口税 ⑤【机】(机器在给定条件下所做的)功;能率;负载；工作状态: a heavy-~ tractor 一台重型拖拉机 / the ~ of a pump 泵的能率 ⑥【农】(单位土地上某种作物所需要的)灌溉水量,灌溉率 (=~ of water) ‖*a* ~ *call* 礼节上的访问 / *be in* **bound to** (do) 有义务做 / *do* ~ *for* 当…用: make water *do* ~ *for* alcohol as a solvent 用水代替酒精作溶剂 / *do one's* ~ 尽职;尽本分 / *off* ~ 下班: be *off* ~ 下了班 / When do you come *off* ~? 你们什么时候下班? / *on* ~ ①值班: Who is *on* ~ today? 今天谁值班? ②上班: go *on* ~ at 8 a. m. 上午八点钟上班 / take sb.'s ~ 替代某人的工作 ‖'~-'*bound* *a.* 义不容辞的 / '~-'*free* *a.* & *ad.* (货物)免税的(地) / '~-'*paid* *a.* (货物)已缴税的

dwarf [dwɔːf] I *n.* ①矮子；矮小的动物(或植物)②(北欧神话中)巧于金属小工艺的矮神 ③【天】矮星 (= ~ star, 如太阳) II ❶ *vt.* 使矮小;阻碍…的发育;使相形见绌 ❷ *vi.* 变矮小 III *a.* 矮小的 ‖~*ish* *a.* 比较矮小的 / ~*ism* *n.* 矮小;【植】矮态

dwell [dwel] I (dwelt [dwelt] 或 dwelled) *vi.* ①住;留居;寓于 : ~ for years *in* the same town 在同一个城镇里住了多年 ②(马跳障碍物前)踌躇 II *n.* 机器运转中有规则的小停顿 ‖~ *on* (或 *upon*) 细想；详细讲述(或研究)；拖长发…的音: He *dwelt upon* that point for several minutes. 他对那一点详细地讲了好几分钟。‖~*er* *n.* 居住者

dwelling ['dweliŋ] *n.* 住处,寓所 ‖~ *house* 住宅 / ~ *place* 住处

dwindle ['dwindl] ❶ *vi.* ①缩小, 变小；减少: ~ away into nothing 缩小到零,化为乌有 / ~ from one hundred to ten 从一百减少到十 ②衰落, 退化 ❷ *vt.* 使缩小

dye [dai] I *n.* ①染色: take ~ well (badly) 容易(难于)染色 ②染料: acid (basic) ~*s* 酸(碱)性染料 / aniline (azo) ~ 苯胺(偶氮)染料 / reactive ~*s* 活性染料 II ❶ *vt.* 染, 把…染上颜色: ~ a dress in blue 把一件衣服染成蓝色 / ~ sth. in the wool 生染某物；使染物染透 ❷ *vi.* 着色,(染)上色: This cloth ~*s* well (或 readily). 这种布很好染。‖*of (the) deepest* ~ 彻头彻尾的,直到骨子里的 ‖~*r* *n.* 染色工,染色技师,染色工作者 ‖'~-d-in-the-'*wool* *a.* 彻头彻尾的/ '~*house* *n.* 染厂,染坊;染色间/ '~*jigger* *n.* 【纺】卷染机,染缸 / '~*stuff* *n.* 染料,颜料;(橡胶的)着色剂 / ~ *vat* 染缸,染槽 / '~*wood* *n.* 染料木(含染料的植物,如苏木等)/ '~-*works* [复] *n.* [用作单或复]染厂

dying ['daiiŋ] I *die¹* 的现在分词 II *a.* ①快要死的,垂死的②临终的: one's ~ wish 临终心愿 / A man should study till his ~ day. 活到老,学到老。③ 快熄灭的；行将完结的: a ~ fire 快熄灭的火 / the ~ day 快完的一天

dyke [daik] *n.* & *vt.* =dike

dynamic [dai'næmik] I *a.* ①动力的；动力学的；动态的: ~ equilibrium 动态平衡 / a ~ loud-speaker 电动扬声器 / a ~ load 动力荷载,动力载重 ②有生气的；能动的；有力的；精悍的: man's conscious ~ role 人的自觉能动性 ③【医】机能上的(与 organic 相对) ④【哲】物力论的,力本论的 II *n.* ①动力,原动力 ②动态

dynamite ['dainəmait] I *n.* ①达那炸药,甘油炸药②具有爆炸性的事(或物) ③精力充沛的人 II *vt.* ①(用炸药)炸毁 ②使…完全失败 ‖'~-,*laden* *a.* (局势等)充满爆炸性的

dynamo ['dainəmou] *n.* ①【电】发电机(尤指直流发电机): a direct (an alternating) current ~ 直(交)流发电机 ②精力充沛的人

dynasty ['dinəsti, 'dainəsti] *n.* 王朝；朝代: the Ching ~ 清朝 / overthrow a ~ 推翻一个王朝

dysentery ['disəntri] *n.* 痢疾: malignant ~ 恶性痢疾 ‖*dysenteric* [,disən'terik] *a.*

dyspepsia [dis'pepsiə], **dyspepsy** [dis'pepsi] *n.* 消化不良

E

each [iːtʃ] I *a.* 各,各自的；每: There is a line of trees on ~ side of the river. 河的两边各有一行树。 II *pron.* 各,各自；每个: *Each* has his merits. 各有所长。/ Divide the class into two sections of ten students ~. 把班级分成两个小组,每组十个学生。 ‖~ *and every* 每个: *Each and every* difference contains contradiction. 每个差异中无不包含矛盾。/~ *other* [用作宾语]互相

eager ['i:gə] *a.* 渴望的，热切的: be ~ *for*(或 *after*, *about*) sth. 渴求某事物 ‖**~ly** *ad.* / **~ness** *n.* ‖**~ beaver** 做事特别卖力的人(尤指做事过于卖力以取悦上司的人)

eagle ['i:gl] *n.* ①鹰 ②鹰徽;鹰旗 ③[E-]【天】天鹰座 ④(高尔夫球中)比标准少两次的打数 ⑤[美](上校军官肩章上的)银鹰标识;(背面有鹰徽的)十元金币 ⑥[美俚]战斗机老牌驾驶员 ‖**~-'eyed** *a.* 眼力敏锐的,目光炯炯的 / **~ owl**【动】鹛鸮

ear[1] [iə] *n.* ①耳朵;耳状物(指水壶、杯子等的耳形捏把);(鸟的)耳羽;[复]灯花(指灯芯上的积炭) ②听觉;听能: be sweet (harsh) to the ~ 悦 (不悦)耳, 好(不好)听 / have a keen ~ 听觉灵 / have an ~ for music 能欣赏音乐 ③倾听;注意: It has come to my ~ that .... 我听说…(或:我意识到…) ④ 报头左 (或右) 上角的小型广告 (或天气预报)栏 ‖*a flea in one's* (或 *the*) ~ 见 **flea** / *A word in your* ~*s.* (附耳过来)跟你说句私房话。/ *be all* ~*s* 全神贯注地倾听着 / *bend sb.'s* ~ [美俚] ①和感兴趣的某人交谈;和某人谈重要(或秘密,有趣)的事 ②和某人谈个不休,讲得某人厌烦 / *be on one's* ~ [美俚] 在发怒 / *bring a hornets' nest* (或 *a storm*) *about one's* ~*s* 见 **nest** / *close* (或 *stop*) *one's* ~*s* 塞住耳朵;不听 / *fall on deaf* ~*s* 根本不被听取,等于白说;没有被理睬 / *fall together by the* ~*s* 扭打起来 / *for sb.'s private* ~ 对某人私下讲的: This is *for your private* ~. 这是秘密的。(指只能私下对你说) / *get sb. on his* ~ [美俚]使某人发怒 / *give* ~ *to* 听,倾听,注意 / *give one's* ~*s* 不惜任何代价(要): I would *give my* ~*s* for a glimpse of it (或 to have a glimpse of it). 我一定要看一看这个东西。/ *give sb. a thick* ~ 把某人的耳朵打肿 / *have an* (*no*) ~ *for* 对…听觉灵敏(不灵敏) / *have* (或 *keep*) *an* ~ *to the ground* 注意着舆论等的动向; 留心着可能发生的事 / *have itching* ~*s* 爱听新奇的事 / *have* (或 *win, gain*) *sb.'s* ~ (在意见、看法等方面) 得到某人的注意听取和接受: I don't think you can *have his* ~. 我看他不会听你的。/ *in at one* ~ *and out at the other* 一耳进一耳出,听过即忘 / *laugh* (*grin*) *from* ~ *to* ~ 咧着嘴出声 (不出声) 笑 / *lend an* ~ *to* =give ~ to / *Little pitchers have long* (或 *large*)~*s.* 见 **pitcher**[1] / *meet the* ~ 被听到 / *over head and* ~*s* (*in*) 见 **head** / *pin sb.'s* ~*s back* [美俚]收拾某人 / *play* (*sing*) *by* ~ (不看乐谱)凭听觉记忆演奏(唱) / *pound one's* ~ [美俚]睡 / *prick up one's* ~*s* (紧张地、警觉地) 竖起耳朵听 / *Pull in your* ~*s!* [美俚] ①当心! ②住嘴! / *set ... by the* ~*s* 使…争吵不和 / *sleep on both* ~*s* 酣睡 / *talk sb.'s* ~ *off* [俚] 对某人说个不停, 对某人唠叨不休 / *tickle sb.'s* ~*s* (以言词)奉承某人 / *turn a deaf* ~ *to* 对…根本不听, 对…置若罔闻 / *up to the*

(或 *one's*) ~*s* 深陷在 (债务等中) / *Were your* ~*s burning* (*last night*)? (昨天晚上)你耳朵热吗? (指有人在谈起你) / *with open* ~*s* 急切地注意着 ‖**~ache** ['iəreik] *n.* 耳痛 / **'~-cap** *n.* (御寒用的)耳套 / **~-drop** *n.* 耳坠,耳饰 / **'~-drops** [复] *n.* 耳药水 / **【解】**耳鼓 / **'~-flap** *n.* [常用复] (帽上可放下护耳御寒的)耳扇,帽瓣 / **'~-lap** *n.* ① =~flap ② =~-lobe ③ 外耳 / **'~-lobe** *n.* 耳垂 / **'~-mark** *n.* ①(打在牛、羊等耳朵上表示所有权的)耳戳 ②标记,特征 *vt.* ①在(家畜)耳朵上打戳记 ②在…上做标记 ③指定(款项等)的用途 / **'~-muffs** [复] *n.* (御寒用的)耳套 / **'~-phone** *n.* 头带受话器,耳机 / **'~-pick** *n.* 挖耳勺 / **'~-piece** *n.* ①耳机,头戴式耳机 ②耳承 ③眼镜脚 ④(帽的)护耳片 / **'~-,piercing** *a.* (声音等)撕裂耳鼓,刺耳的 / **'~-plug** *n.* (防水或防震聋用的)耳塞 / **'~-reach** *n.* =~shot / **'~-ring** *n.* 耳环,耳饰 / **'~-shot** *n.* 听觉所及的范围: He lives *within* (*out of*) ~*shot* of the factory whistle. 他住在听得见(听不见)工厂汽笛声的地方。/ **'~-,splitting** *a.* 震耳欲聋的 / **'~-tab** *n.* =~flap / **~ trumpet** (半聋人用的)助听器 / **'~-wax** *n.* 耳垢 / **'~-wig** *n.* ①【动】蠼螋;蚰蜒 ②【动】土蚕;土蛇 ③偷听者 *vt.* 通过私下谈话掮掇(或烦扰)某人

ear[2] [iə] I *n.* 穗: Drooping ~*s* of rice promise another good harvest. 沉甸甸的稻穗预示着又一次丰收。II *vi.* 抽穗 ‖ *be in the* ~ 正在抽穗

earl [ə:l] *n.* [英]伯爵

early ['ə:li] I *a.* ①早的;早熟的: an ~ riser 早起的人 / ~ ag(e)ing 【医】早衰 / an ~ maturity of mind 思想的早熟 / ~ rice 早稻 / ~ vegetables 时鲜蔬菜 ②及早的,早日的: We hope for an ~ production of the play. 我们希望剧本早日上演。/ Please reply at your *earliest* convenience. 请尽早回复。③早期的,早先的;古时的: the ~ part of the century 世纪的初期 / ~ tools found in recent excavations 最近发掘出土的古代工具 II *ad.* 早;在初期: ~ to bed and ~ to rise 早睡早起 / This year the peaches bear ~. 今年桃子早熟。/ ~ in the present century 在本世纪初期 / ~ next year 明年初 ‖*an* ~ *bird* 见 **bird** / *earlier on* 在更早一些时候 / ~ *and late* 从早到晚 / ~ *or late* 迟早 / *keep* ~ *hours* 早起早睡 / *The* ~ *bird gets* (或 *catches*) *the worm.* [谚]捷足先登。‖**~ ambulation** (外科手术后)早期下床走动护理法 / **~ door** [英](戏院的)提早入座门 / **Early English style** 【建】早期英国哥特式(指一一八〇到一二五〇年间的英国建筑式样) / **'~-Vic'torian** *a.* (英国)维多利亚女王朝初期的;老式的 / **'~-,warning radar** 预先警报雷达,远程警戒雷达

earn [ə:n] *vt.* ①赚得,挣得: ~ one's living 谋生 ②博得;赢得;使得到

earnest[1] ['ə:nist] I *a.* ①认真的;诚挚的;热切的

②重要的 **II** *n.* 认真,诚挚 ‖*in (real)* ~ 认真地: remould oneself *in (real)* ~ 认真改造自己 / *in sad* ~ 一本正经地,十分严肃地 ‖**~ly** *ad.* / **~ness** *n.*

earnest² ['ə:nist] *n.* ①定钱,保证金: ~ money 定钱 ②预示;保证

earnings ['ə:niŋz] [复] *n.* ①工资,收入 ②利润,收益

earth [ə:θ] **I** *n.* ①地球: The ~ revolves on its axis. 地球绕轴自转。/ an artificial ~ satellite 人造地球卫星 ②陆地;地面,地上: fall to ~ 落地 ③土,泥: till the ~ 耕地 / fuller's ~ 【化】漂白土 ④尘世,人间;一切世俗之事 ⑤地球上的人类;人的躯体 ⑥(狐、貛等的)洞穴: stop an ~ 填塞洞穴 ⑦【电】接地: ~ wire (接)地线 ⑧【化】难以还原的金属氧化物类(如氧化铝、氧化锆) **II** ❶ *vt.* ①把…埋入土中,用土掩盖(根部等)(*up*) ②把(狐等)追赶入洞 ③【电】把…接地 ❷ *vi.* 躲进洞里 ‖*break* ~ 破土动工 / *bring sb. back to* ~ 使某人回到现实中来 / *come back* (或 *down*) *to* ~ 回到现实,不再作幻想 / *move heaven and* ~ 见 **heaven** / *multiply the* ~ 增加人口,生儿育女 / *on* ~ ①在世界上,在人间: men *on* ~ 世人 ②[用于疑问词、否定词或最高级加强语气]究竟,到底;全然: What *on* ~ is the matter there? 那里究竟发生了什么事? / Where *on* ~ can he be? 他到底在哪儿呢? / That is the funniest thing *on* ~. 那是最滑稽的事情了。/ *on God's* ~ 普天之下 / *run* (或 *go*) *to* ~ (狐等)跑入洞内 / *run ... to* ~ 直捣…的洞穴,于人洞内 / *take* ~ ①(狐等)逃入洞内 ②[喻]隐匿 / *the salt of the* ~ 见 **salt** ‖**~ward(s)** *ad.* 向地球;向地面 / **axis** 地(球)轴 / **'~born** *a.* ①从地里出生的 ②人类的,会死的;尘世的 / **'~bound** *a.* ①生牢在土中的,生牢泥土的;只在陆地的;只在地面的 ③行向地球的④世俗的;缺乏想象力的,平凡的 / **~ closet** [主英](用土来覆盖粪便的)厕所 / **'~flow** *n.* 【地】泥流 / **~ inductor** 【电】地磁感应器 / **'~light** *n.* = **~shine** / **'~mover** *n.* 大型挖(或推)土机 / **'~nut** *n.* 落花生: =nut 油 花生油 / **~ oil** [古] 石油 / **~ plate** 【电】接地板 / **'~quake** *n.* ①地震 ②[喻]大震荡,大变动 / **~ scraper** 刮土机 / **'~,shaking**-*a.* 极其重大的,震撼世界的;翻天覆地的 / **'~shine** *n.* 【天】地球反照 / **'~work** *n.* ①土木工事 ②土方工程,土工 / **'~worm** *n.* 蚯蚓

earthen ['ə:θən] *a.* ①泥土做的;陶制的 ②大地的;现世的 ‖**'~ware** *n.* [总称]陶器

earthly ['ə:θli] *a.* ①地球的;尘世的,世俗的;现世的: ~ pleasures 人间乐趣 ②[口][用于否定句或疑问句]可能的,想得出的: no ~ reason 完全无理由 / What ~ purpose can it serve? 这究竟有什么用处呢? ‖*not an* ~ [英俚]完全没有希望: have *not an* ~ to win 根本没有希望得胜 ‖**earthliness** *n.* 世俗,尘缘

earthy ['ə:θi] *a.* ①泥土(似)的 ②粗陋的;朴实的 ③现实的

ease [i:z] **I** *n.* ①舒适;悠闲;安心;自在: at (one's) ~ 舒适;舒坦;自由自在,不拘束 / (stand) at ~ 【军】稍息 / feel (或 be) ill at ~ 感到不安;不自在 / ~ of mind 心情的舒畅 ②容易;不费力: He writes with ~. 他笔墨流畅。 **II** ❶ *vt.* ①减轻(痛苦、负担等);使舒适;使安心: Take this medicine; it will ~ the pain. 把这药吃下去,它会镇痛。/ ~ sb.'s mind 使某人安心,使某人宽慰 / ~ sb. *of* his troubles 消除某人的烦恼 ②放松,放宽(绳索、帆等): ~ (*down*) the speed of a boat 放慢船的速度 / ~ a drawer 松动(轧住的)抽屉 / Ease her (或 the helm, the wheel)! 【海】回舵! ③小心地移置: They ~*d* the piano into place. 他们小心地把钢琴放好。 ❷ *vi.* ①缓和;减轻;放松 (*off, up*) ②灵活地移动 (*along, over*)

easel ['i:zl] *n.* 画架;黑板架

easily ['i:zili] *ad.* ①容易地,不费力地 ②舒适地,适意地 ③流畅地,顺利地: The machine is running ~. 机器运转得很好。④远远,大大地,毫无疑问地: He is ~ the best singer among us. 他无疑是我们中间唱得最好的人。⑤很可能,多半: He may ~ be late today. 今天他很可能迟到。

east [i:st] **I** *n.* ①东,东方: The sun rises in the ~. 大阳在东方升起来。/ ~ by north (方向)东偏北 ②[the E-]东部,东部地区: the Far (Middle, Near) *East* 远(中,近)东 / the *East* 世界的东方;[美]美国东部地区 ③东风 **II** *a.* ①东的;东部的;朝东的 ②从东方来的 **III** *ad.* 在东方;向东方: face ~ 朝东 / sail due ~ 正东航行 ‖*down East* 新英格兰 / *in the* ~ *of* 在…的东部 / *on the* ~ (*of*) 在(…的)东面 / (*to the*) ~ *of* 在…之东,在…的东面: The village lies (*to the*) ~ *of* the woods. 村庄位于树林的东面。

Easter ['i:stə] *n.* 【宗】(耶稣)复活节 (指每年过春分月圆后第一个星期日);从复活节开始的一周 ‖**~ egg** (作礼物用的)复活节彩蛋 / **~ Monday** 复活节后的星期一 / **'~tide** *n.* 复活节季节(可分别指从复活节至升天节之间的四十天,或从复活节至圣灵降临节之间的五十天,或从复活节至三一节之间的五十七天)

easterly ['i:stəli] **I** *a.* ①东的;向东方的 ②从东方来的: an ~ wind 东风 **II** *ad.* ①向东方 ②从东方: The wind blows ~. 风从东方吹来。 **III** *n.* 东风;[复]东风带

eastern ['i:stən] **I** *a.* ①东的,东方的;东部的: the ~ countries 东方国家 / the *Eastern* Hemisphere 东半球 / the *Eastern* Church 东正教 ②朝东的: an ~ window 东窗 ③从东吹来的: an ~ wind 东风 **II** *n.* ①东方人 ②东正教徒 ‖**~er** *n.* ①东方人;居住在东方的人 ②[E-]美国的东部人

eastward ['i:stwəd] **I** *a.* 向东的 **II** *n.* 东向；东部 **III** *ad.* 向东

eastwards ['i:stwədz] *ad.* 向东

easy ['i:zi] **I** *a.* ①容易的，不费力的: be ~ of access (人)容易接近; (物)容易得到; (地方)交通方便 / a situation ~ to handle 容易处理的局面 / guard against any wishful thinking about ~ success through good luck 不行侥幸成功的如意算盘 ②安逸的，安乐的; 宽裕的，小康的: an ~ life 安乐的生活 / be in ~ circumstances 家道小康，生活安逸 ③(在心境等方面)安心的，平静的; (在身体上)适意的: (be) ~ in mind 安心 / Make yourself ~ about the matter. 这事你放心好了。/ The patient is *easier* after the injection. 注射后病人觉得舒服些了。④(衣、鞋、物质条件等)宽适的，舒服的: ~ shoes 宽适的鞋子 / an ~ fit 宽适的衣服 / an ~ arrangement of the hostel 招待所的舒适的布置 ⑤从容的，自在的; 大方的: an ~ pace 从容的步子 / free and ~ 自由自在,毫不拘束 / ~ manners 大方的举止 ⑥宽容的，不苛求的; 易忍受的: be on sb. 对某人宽容 / He is ~ to get along with. 他很平易近人。/ an ~ contract 不难履行的合同 ⑦易懂的，流畅的; (坡度)不陡的: an ~ language 易懂的语言 / an ~ flowing style 流畅的文笔 / The steps rise in ~ flights. 台阶坡度不大地级级上升。⑧随随便便的; 易顺从的: an ~ disposition 懒散的性格 / be of ~ virtue (女子)水性杨花的 / be ~ in one's morals 放荡不羁 ⑨自然而然的: an ~ familiarity with the process 对这一过程的自然而然的熟悉 ⑩(商品)供过于求的; (市价)疲软的,低落的; (银根)松的 ⑪(无主桥牌局中的"A"牌)双方各半分配的 **II** *ad.* ①[口]容易地; 不费力地 ②慢慢地; 当心地: Go ~ here, the road is very rough. 这儿得慢慢地走,路很不平。/ Easy! 慢! 当心! **III** *n.* 短暂的休息: take an ~ 歇一下 ‖*as ~ as pie* [俚]极容易 / *as ~ as rolling* (或 *falling*) *off a log* [美]极其容易 / *Be ~*! (爱尔兰)别忙! (=Don't hurry!) / *Easier said than done.* [谚]说来容易做来难。/ *Easy ahead*! (驶船口令)低速前进! / *Easy all*! (划船口令)停! / *~ as my eye* 易如反掌 / *~ come, ~ go* [谚]来得容易去得快(指钱财) / *Easy does it*! 别着急! (=Take your time!) / *~ on the eyes* 悦目的, 好看的 / *go ~* 从容不迫; 安闲 / *on ~ street* 生活安定,家道小康 / *on ~ street* / *on ~ terms* / *rest ~* 高枕无忧 / *sit ~ on* 见 sit / *Stand ~*! (英军口令)稍息! (比 at ease 可更自由随便些) / *take it* (或 *things*) *~* ①不紧张,从容,不急: Take it ~! 放心好了。(或: 别着急。) ②松懈,懒散: We must not *take things ~*, though we have had good harvests several years running. 虽然连续几年丰收,可是我们决不能松动。③[美俚]再见 ‖*~ chair* 安乐椅 / *~ mark* ①[口]易受欺骗的人,糊涂虫,傻子 ②易达到的目标 / *~ money*

①来得容易的钱(指非正当所得) ②易被榨出钱来的人 / *'~-,money* *a.* 放松银根的; 银根松的 / *~ rider* [美俚]①寄生虫,食客 ②拉皮条的人

easygoing ['i:zi,gouiŋ] *a.* ①(马)行动时平稳自在的 ②(人)懒散的; 随和的; (品德)放荡的,不严肃的 ③悠闲的,轻松的,舒适的 ‖*~ness n.*

eat [i:t] (ate [et; 美 eit], eaten ['i:tn]) **❶** *vt.* ①吃; 喝(汤) ②蛀;腐蚀;销蚀: Acid *ate* holes *in* my coat. 我的外套被酸烂了几个洞。**❷** *vi.* ①吃; 吃饭 ②吃上去有(某种)味道: lt ~*s* well (tender, crisp). 这东西吃上去味道好(嫩,松脆)。③腐蚀,侵蚀: Acids ~ *into* metals. 酸会腐蚀金属。‖*~ away* 继续吃下去; 蚕食掉,侵蚀掉: Eat away, boys. There's enough time yet. 孩子们,继续吃吧。时间还早。/ Rust has ~*en* away the iron hinge. 铁铰链已被锈坏。/ *~ crow* 见 crow[1] / *~ humble pie* 见 pie[1] / *~ into* (或 *in*) 蛀坏,腐蚀; 耗掉: ~ *into* sb.'s pocket too much 使某人花费太多 / ~ *into* 吃…中的一部分,吃一些… / *~ off* 吃掉;腐蚀掉 / *~ one's fill* 见 fill / *~ one's head off* 见 head / *~ one's heart out* 见 heart / *~ one's (own) words* 见 word / *~ one's terms* (或 *dinners*) [英]学法律 / *~ out* ①上馆子吃饭 ②咬断;咬光 ③侵蚀;侵入 ④[美俚]责骂 / *~ sb. out of house and home* 见 house / *~ the wind out of* 见 wind[1] / *~ up* ①吃完,吃光: Eat up your dinner before it gets cold. 把饭吃完,别让它冷了。②耗尽; 吞掉,吞灭: ~ up one's (sb.'s) savings 耗尽自己(某人)的积蓄 / ~ up another three enemy battalions 又吃掉敌人三个营 / be ~en up by flame 被火吞灭 ③[常用被动语态]使沉迷于; 使纠缠于(with): be ~en up with pride 狂妄自大 / be ~en up with disease 疾病缠身 ④对…极为欣赏(或感兴趣); 完全相信 / *I'll ~ my hat* (或 *boots, hands, head*) *if ....* (赌咒语)我决不… (或: 决无…这回事)。/ *Well, don't ~ me*! [谑]唔,别那么凶啊!

eatable ['i:təbl] **I** *a.* 可食用的 **II** *n.* [常用复]食物,食品

eaves [i:vz] [复] *n.* (屋)檐 ‖*~drop vi. & vt.* 偷听 *n.* 檐水 / *'~,dropper n.* 偷听者

ebb [eb] *n. & vi.* ①落潮,退潮 ②[喻]衰落,衰退 ‖*at a low ~* 衰败,不振 / *~ and flow* 涨落; 盛衰;消长 / *on the ~* (潮水等)正在退落 ‖*~ tide* 落潮,退潮

ebony ['ebəni] **I** *n.* ①【植】乌木,乌檀(柿属的一种) ②[E-] 柿属 **II** *a.* ①乌木制的 ②似乌木的,乌木色的,漆黑色的

eccentric [ik'sentrik] **I** *a.* ①(人、行为等)古怪的,偏执的 ②不同圆心的; 【机】偏心的 ③【天】(轨道)不正圆的; (天体)在不正圆轨道上运行的 **II** *n.* ①行为古怪的人 ②偏心圆 ③【机】偏心轮 ‖*~ally ad.* ‖*~ angle* 【数】离心角,偏心角 / *~ anomaly* 【天】偏近点角

eccentricity [ˌeksen'trisiti] *n.* ①古怪; 怪僻 ②【数】离心率, 偏心率, 偏心距, 偏心度

ecclesiastic [iˌkli:zi'æstik] Ⅰ *n.*【基督教】教士, 牧师 Ⅱ *a.* =ecclesiastical

echo ['ekou] Ⅰ ([复] echoes) *n.* ①回声; 反响 ②重复; 仿效 ③附和者; 应声虫 ④共鸣 ⑤[无]回波, 反射波: radar ~ 雷达回波 ⑥(桥牌戏中向搭档报信息的)应答性出牌 Ⅱ ❶ *vi.* ①发出回声; (声音)被传回; 起反响, 起共鸣: The empty room ~ed. 空屋发出回声。/ The sounds of gongs and drums ~ed in the great hall. 大会堂里锣鼓喧天。②重复: a theme which ~es throughout the play 全剧重复着的一个主题 ③(桥牌戏中)打出报信息的应答牌 ❷ *vt.* ①重复, 模仿(别人的话、思想等): ~ sb.'s nonsense 跟着某人瞎说 ②反射(声音等) ‖*cheer sb. (sth.) to the ~* 对某人(某事物)大声喝采 ‖**~gram** *n.* (测肿瘤)超声波回声图; 回声深度记录 / **~graph** *n.* 回声深度记录器 ‖**~ chamber** (为音响效应而设的)回声室, 反响室 / **~ sounder** 回声测深仪

eclipse [i'klips] Ⅰ *n.* ①【天】食: annular ~ 环食 ②被遮蔽; (声名、威望等的)黯然失色 Ⅱ *vt.* ①食, 掩蔽(天体)的光 ②把…遮暗; 使失色

eclipse of the sun

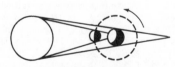

eclipse of the moon

ecliptic [i'kliptik] Ⅰ *n.*【天】黄道: obliquity of the ~【天】黄赤交角 Ⅱ *a.* 黄道的; 日食(或月食)的

eclogue ['eklog] *n.* 牧歌, 田园诗(常以牧童对话形式写成)

economic [ˌi:kə'nɔmik] *a.* 经济(上)的; 经济学的: the ~ base 经济基础 / an ~ blockade 经济封锁 / ~ reckoning 经济核算 / (an) ~ crisis 经济危机

economical [ˌi:kə'nɔmikəl] *a.* ①节俭的, 节约的: an ~ person 节俭的人 / an ~ stove 经济炉 ②经济学的, 经济上的 ‖**~ly** *ad.* 节约地, 节俭地; 在经济(学)上

economics [ˌi:kə'nɔmiks, ˌekə'nɔmiks] [复] *n.* (用作单或复) ①经济学 ②(国家的)经济情况; 经济

economist [i(:)'kɔnəmist] *n.* ①经济学家 ②节俭的人

economize [i(:)'kɔnəmaiz] *vt. & vi.* 节约, 节省: ~ (*in*) raw materials 节省原料 / ~ (*on*) man-

power and material resources 节约人力物力 ‖**economization** [i(:)ˌkɔnəmai'zeiʃən] *n.* / **~r** *n.* 废气预热器

economy [i(:)'kɔnəmi] *n.* ①经济: collective ~ 集体经济 / state-owned ~ 国营经济 / national ~ 国民经济 ②节约, 节省; 节约措施: practise strict ~ 厉行节约 / She has made various little economies. 她在许多小地方节省了。③经济实惠: an ~ sedan 经济实惠的轿车 / It's poor ~. 那是不经济的。④组织, 系统: the ~ of the human body 人体机构

ecstasy ['ekstəsi] *n.* 狂喜; 出神, 入迷: an ~ of delight 欣喜若狂 / be in (go into) ecstasies over sth. 对(开始对)某事物心醉神迷 / He listened to the music with ~. 他听音乐听得出神。

ecstatic [eks'tætik] *a.* 欣喜若狂的; 出神的, 入迷的 ‖**~ally** *ad.*

ecumenical [ˌi:kju(:)'menikəl] *a.* =oecumenical

eczema ['eksimə] *n.*【医】湿疹

eddy ['edi] Ⅰ *n.* (空气、水、烟、雾等的)旋涡; 涡流 Ⅱ *vt. & vi.* (使)起旋涡; (使)旋转

Eden ['i:dn] *n.* ①【基督教】《圣经》中人类始祖居住的)伊甸园 ②[喻]乐园, 安乐土 ‖**~ic** [i:'denik] *a.*

edge [edʒ] Ⅰ *n.* ①刀口; 利刃, 锋; 锐利: The knife has no ~. 这刀子很钝。/ a cutting ~ 切削刃 / the cutting ~ of irony 讽刺的利刃 ②边, 棱; 边界; 界线; (悬崖等的)边缘: the gilt ~s of a book 烫金的书边 / on the water's ~ 在水边 / straight ~【机】直规; 直缘 / built-up ~【机】切削瘤 / The town stands on the ~ of a plain. 这城镇位于平原边沿。/ on the ~ of bankruptcy 濒于破产 / on the ~ of screaming 几乎尖声喊叫起来 ③优势; 优越条件: a decisive ~ in military strength 军事力量上的决定性优势 / Open spaces give the suburbs an ~ over the city. 宽阔空旷是郊区胜过城市之处。④[美俚]微醉状态 Ⅱ ❶ *vt.* ①使(刀、剑等)锋利, 使开刃: ~ the ax 开斧刃 / Resentment ~d his reply. 怨恨使他回答得尖锐。②给…加上边: ~ a blouse with lace 给女衫镶边 / ~ the path with trees 在小路边上树木 / Factories and warehouses ~ the waterfront. 工厂和货栈林立在江边。③使渐进; 徐缓地移动; 挤进 (*in, into*); 挤掉 (*out, off*): ~ oneself through a crowd 挤进人群 / ~ one's way into a hall 挤进大厅 / Edge your chair a little. 把你的椅子稍为挪动一下。❷ *vi.* 徐徐移动; 侧着移动: ~ away from the corner 慢慢地从角落里走开 / ~ away from one's responsibilities 渐渐卸掉责任 / ~ along the wall 沿着墙侧身移动 ‖*at hard ~* (练击剑时)用真剑; 真刀真枪的(地) / *be on a razor's ~* 在锋口上; 处于十分危险的境地, 在危急关头 / *do the inside (outside)* (溜冰时)用冰鞋内(外)棱蹓滑 / *~ down upon (in with)* 斜行接近 / *~ sb. on* 怂恿某人, 煽动某人 / *fall by (或 be put to) the ~ of the sword* 被

杀死 / *give sb. the ~ of one's tongue* 痛骂
某人 / *have the* (或 *an*) *~ on sb.* (*sth.*) [俚]
胜过某人 (某事物): *have the ~ on* top speed 胜
过最高速度 / *not to put too fine an ~ on it*
直截了当地说 / *on ~* ①直立着(放),竖着: set
a book *on ~* 把书竖放 ②紧张不安;易怒: set
sb.'s nerves *on ~* 使某人的神经紧张不安 ③急
切,忍不住,热望: He is all *on ~* to look at it.
他非常想看一看这东西。 / *on the ~ of one's
chair* (或 *seat*) 焦急 (或不安) 地等待着 / *set
sb.'s teeth on ~* 见 **tooth** / *take the ~ off*
①使钝 ②减弱(胃口等);挫…的锐气(或锋芒) /
turn the ~ of 弄钝…的锋芒; 减弱…的锐气
‖**~less** *a.* 没刀刃的,钝的 ‖**~bone** *n.* 牛的
臀骨 / **~(d) tool** 有刃之物,利器: play with *~d
tools* 玩弄利刃; [喻]干危险的事 / **~ runner**
【机】轮转机;碾子 / **'~stone** *n.* ①(道路的)边
缘石 ②(磨机的)立磨轮

edgeways ['edʒweiz], **edgewise** ['edʒwaiz] *ad.*
以刃向外(或向前);以边缘向外(或向前);从旁边,
沿边;边对边地 ‖*get a word in ~* (趁健谈的
人讲话的间隙)插嘴

edging ['edʒiŋ] *n.* ①边缘 ②缘饰 ‖**~ shears** (园
丁用的)修边剪刀

edible ['edibl] **I** *a.* 可以吃的,食用的: ~ oil 食用
油 **II** *n.* [常用复]食品 ‖**edibility** [ˌedi'biliti] *n.*
可食用性 / **~ness** *n.*

edict ['i:dikt] *n.* 法令,敕令,布告 ‖**~al** [i:'diktəl]
a.

edification [ˌedifi'keiʃən] *n.* (尤指道德、精神方面
的)教诲,开导,启发

edifice ['edifis] *n.* 大建筑物,大厦

edify ['edifai] *vt.* 教诲,开导,启发 ‖**edifier** *n.* 教
导者,启发者

edit ['edit] *vt.* ①编辑,校订 ②剪辑(影片、录音磁
带等)‖ **~ out** 在编辑(或剪辑)过程中删除

edition [i'diʃən] *n.* ①版本,版次: a pocket ~
袖珍版 / the first ~ 第一版,初版 / a revised ~
修订版 / an ~ *de luxe* 精装版 ②[喻]很相似的
人(或物),翻版: He is a taller ~ of his elder
brother.　他跟他的哥哥很相像,不过高一些。

editor ['editə] *n.* ①编辑;编者;校订者: a chief ~
(或 an ~ in chief)主编,总编辑 / a contributing
~ 特约编辑 / a managing ~ 编辑主任,主编 /
a city (或 City) ~ [英]商业金融栏编辑;[美]本
地新闻编辑主任 ②社论撰写人 ③影片剪辑装置
‖**~ship** *n.* 编辑的职位;编辑工作

editorial [ˌedi'tɔ:riəl] **I** *a.* ①编辑的;编者的: an
~ staff 编辑部全体人员 / an ~ assistant 编辑
助理 ②社论(性)的 **II** *n.* 社论 ‖**~ist** *n.* 社论
撰写人 / **~ly** *ad.* ①以编者身分 ②以社论形
式,作为社论

educate ['edju(:)keit] *vt.* ①教育: be *~d* at a
technical college 在技术学校受教育 ②培养;训练
③使受学校教育,为…付学费 ‖**~d** *a.* 受过教育
的: *~d* youth (或 young people) 知识青年 /

educator *n.* 教育者,教育工作者

education [ˌedju(:)'keiʃən] *n.* ①教育: elementary,
secondary and higher ~ 初等、中等和高等教
育 / get (或 receive) an ~ 受教育 ②训导;训练;
培养 ③教育学

educational [ˌedju(:)'keiʃənl] *a.* ① 教育的: an
~ system 教育制度 ② 有教育意义的: science
and ~ films 科教片 ‖**~ly** *ad.* 用教育方法; 从
教育的观点 ‖**~ park** 教育园(大城市里一种采
用公园式布局、从幼儿园直到大学的综合性教育
设施) / **~ television** ① (播送有关文化知识和
情况介绍等内容、一般不插播广告的) 大众电视
②教育电视

education(al)ist [ˌedju(:)'keiʃən(ə)list] *n.* ① [英]
教育者 ②教育学家

eel [i:l] *n.* ①鳗鲡;美洲鳗 ②蛇形鱼类(如黄鳝、八
目鳗) ③油滑的人 ‖**~-buck** *n.* [英]捕鳗笼 /
'~-grass *n.* [植]大叶藻 / **'~-spear** *n.* 捕鳗叉 /
'~-worm *n.* 【动】鳗蛔虫;线虫类

eerie, eery ['iəri] *a.* ①[苏格兰](因迷信而)胆怯
的,不安的 ②引起恐惧的;可怕的;怪异的 ‖**eerily**
ad. / **eeriness** *n.*

efface [i'feis] *vt.* 擦掉,抹去; [喻]消除(痕迹等),
使(印象等)被忘却;超越,使黯然失色 ‖*~ oneself*
不露面(以期不被人注意);埋没自己 ‖**~able** *a.*
能擦掉的,可抹去的;会被忘却的 / **~ment** *n.*

effect [i'fekt] **I** *n.* ① 结果: cause and ~ 因果 ②
效果,效力;作用,影响: the unity of motive and
~ 动机和效果的统一 / curative ~s 疗效 / a
great pushing ~ *on* production 对生产的巨大的
推动作用 ③(在视、听觉方面引起的)印象;外表,
外观: This painting gives you a three-dimensional ~. 这张画给人一种立体感。 / sound ~s
音响效果 ④ 要旨, 意义: I don't remember
his precise words, but he did say something to
that ~. 我不记得他确切的原话了, 但他肯定表
示过那样的意思。 / a statement to the following
~ 大意如下的声明 ⑤实行, 实施 ⑥[复]财物,
动产: personal ~s 个人财产(或财物) / no ~s
无存款(银行在空头支票上的批语;略作 N/E) **II**
vt. ① 产生, 招致: ~ a change in temperature
引起温度变化 ② 实现, 达到(目的等)· ~ the
greatest economy 力求节约 / ~ a policy 取得保
险单(指加入某项保险) ‖*be of no ~* 无效 /
bring into (或 *to*) *~* 实行,实现,实施 / *carry*
(或 *put*) *into ~* =bring into (或 to) ~ / *come*
(或 *go*) *into ~* 开始生效;开始实行 / *give ~ to*
使实行起来: *give ~ to* sb.'s suggestions 实行某
人的建议 / *in ~* ①在功效方面;实际上: The
two methods are *in ~* identical.　这两个方法
实际上是一样的。 ②正实行中, 有效: These
regulations continue *in ~*. 这些规章仍然有
效。 / *take ~* (药等)见效; (法规等)生效 / *to
the ~ that …* ①大意是…: He spoke to the
~ *that* we should all go with him.　他说的大意
是我们都应该和他一起去。 / We received a
letter *to the ~ that* he would soon arrive.　我

们收到一封信, 大意是他即将到达。 ② 以便: He started early *to the* ~ *that* he might get there by lunchtime. 他一早就动身了, 以便在午饭前赶到那里。 ‖~**or** *n.* 【生】效应器; 效应基因

effective [i'fektiv] **I** *a.* ①有效的; 生效的: the ~ range of a weapon 一件武器的有效射程 / take ~ measures 采取有效措施 ②有力的, 给人深刻印象的: an ~ speech 打动听众的讲演 ③实在的, 实际的: the number of ~ members 实际成员人数 ④(军队、士兵等)有战斗力的: ~ forces 实有战斗兵力 **II** *n.* [常用复]【军】实际可以作战的部队(或士兵), 有生力量 ‖~**ly** *ad.* / ~**ness** *n.* combat ~**ness** 战斗力

effectual [i'fektjuəl] *a.* 奏效的; 有效的 ‖~**ly** *ad.* / ~**ness** *n.*

effeminacy [i'feminəsi] *n.* 柔弱; 娇气; 女子气

effeminate [i'feminit] *a.* 柔弱的; 娇气的; 女子气的 ‖~**ly** *ad.*

effervesce [,efə'ves] *vi.* ①冒气泡, 起泡沫【化】泡腾 ②(人)兴奋; 生气勃勃

effervescence [,efə'vesns], **effervescency** [,efə'vesnsi] *n.* ①冒泡, 起泡(沫)【化】泡腾 ②生气勃勃, 兴高采烈

effervescent [,efə'vesnt] *a.* ①冒泡的; 泡腾的: ~ granules 【药】泡腾颗粒剂 ②生气勃勃的, 兴高采烈的

effete [e'fi:t] *a.* ①(动植物等)生产力已枯竭的 ②衰老的, 枯竭的; 虚弱的, 无能的: an ~ empire 衰落的帝国 ‖~**ly** *ad.* / ~**ness** *n.*

efficacious [,efi'keiʃəs] *a.* 有效验的, 灵验的: an ~ drug 有效验的药 ‖~**ly** *ad.* / ~**ness** *n.*

efficiency [i'fiʃənsi] *n.* ①效率: raise labo(u)r ~ 提高劳动效率 ②功效; 效能, 实力 ‖~ **apartment** 有小厨房和卫生设备的小套公寓房间 / ~ **expert** (研究如何取得设备、人力最高效率的)效率专家

efficient [i'fiʃənt] *a.* (直接)生效的; 效率高的; 有能力的, 能胜任的: a simple and ~ structure 精简的机构 ‖~**ly** *ad.*

effigy ['efidʒi] *n.* (被憎恨或蔑视的人的)肖像, 雕像, 模拟像: burn (hang) sb. *in* ~ 把某人的模拟像烧掉(绞死)

effort ['efət] *n.* ①努力, 艰难的尝试: make an ~ (或 make ~*s*) 作出努力 / make every ~ 尽一切努力 / spare no ~ 不遗余力, 尽力 / in a common ~ 共同努力 / without ~ 毫不费力地 ②努力的成果; 成就: a fine literary ~ 文学上的精心杰作 ③【机】作用力

effrontery [e'frʌntəri] *n.* 厚颜无耻 (的行为): have the ~ to do sth. 厚着脸皮去做某事

effusion [i'fju:ʒən] *n.* ①流出; 泻出; 喷出;【医】渗出 ②(讲话或文章中思想、感情的) 抒发, 倾泻 ③渗出物

effusive [i'fju:siv] *a.* ①流出的, 喷出的, 溢出的: ~ rocks 【地】喷发岩 ②溢于言表的; 感情奔放的: be ~ in one's gratitude 感激不尽 ‖~**ly** *ad.* / ~**ness** *n.*

egg[1] [eg] **I** *n.* ①(鸟)蛋; 鸡蛋; (鱼、爬行动物等的)卵; 卵细胞: ~ tube 【解】卵巢管 / an ~ white (一个蛋的)蛋白 ②蛋形物 ③[俚]人, 家伙 ④[俚]炸弹; 手榴弹; 鱼雷 **II** *vt.* ① (烹调中)把…用蛋黄(或蛋白)调和(或覆盖) ②[口]向…掷鸡蛋 ‖*a bad* ~ [口]坏家伙, 坏蛋; 失败的计划 / *a good* ~ [俚]好人; 好东西 / *as sure as* ~*s is* ~*s* 见 / *break the* ~(*s*) *in sb.'s pocket* 打破某人计划 / *bring one's* ~*s to a bad* (或 *the wrong*) *market* 失算, 失败 / ~ *and anchor* (或 *dart, tongue*) 【建】卵锚饰 / *from the* ~ *to the apple* 自始至终 / *golden* ~*s* 大利益 / *Good* ~! 真好! 妙极! / *have* ~*s on the spit* 手头有事, 正在忙着 / *in the* ~ 尚在初期的, 未成熟的 / *lay an* ~ ①(鸡等)下蛋 ②[俚](演出等)完全失败 ③[俚]投炸弹 / *put* (或 *have*) *all one's* ~*s in one basket* 孤注一掷 / *teach one's grandmother* (*how*) *to suck* ~*s* 见 grandmother / *tread* (*as*) *on* ~*s* 如履薄冰, 瞻前顾后, 战战兢兢 ‖'~,**beater** *n.* ① 打蛋器 ②[美俚]直升飞机 / '~,**cup** *n.* (吃鸡蛋用的)蛋杯 / ~ **dance** ①蒙着眼睛在散放着鸡蛋的场中跳的舞 ②[喻]错综复杂的工作 / '~**head** *n.* [美俚]知识分子, 有学问的人 / '~**plant** *n.* 茄子 / ~ **roll** 油煎蛋皮肉卷 / '~**-shaped** *a.* 蛋形的 / '~**shell** *n.* 蛋壳; (鸡)蛋壳色; 易碎的东西: ~*shell china* 薄瓷器 / **tooth** 【动】破卵齿 / '~**-whisk** *n.* =~beater

egg[2] [eg] *vt.* 怂恿, 煽动 (*on*): ~ sb. *on* (to do sth.) 怂恿某人(干某事)

egoism ['egouizəm] *n.* ① 自我主义, 利己主义: departmental ~ 本位主义 / national ~ 民族利己主义 ②自私自利, 私心 ‖**egoist** *n.* 自我主义者; 利己主义者; 自私自利的人

egotism ['egoutizəm] *n.* ① 自我中心 (指言必称"我"的习惯); 自我吹嘘; 自高自大 ②利己主义, 自私自利 ‖**egotist** *n.* 言必称"我"者; 自高自大的人; 利己主义者

egress ['i:gres] **I** *n.* ①外出, 出去 ②外出权 ③出口; 出路 ④【天】终切 **II** *vi.* 外出

eider ['aidə] *n.* ①【动】绒鸭 (=~ duck) ②绒鸭的绒毛 ‖'~**down** *n.* 绒鸭的绒毛; 鸭绒被; 鸭绒垫

eight [eit] **I** *num.* 八; 八个(人); 第八(卷、章、页等): *Eight* plus ~ equals sixteen. 八加八等于十六。 *Eight* are on duty. 八个人在值班。 / the ~-hour day 八小时工作制 / ~ of them 他们中间的八个人 / ~ of them 他们八个人 / Volume *Eight* 第八卷, 卷八 / ~ page 第八页 **II** *n.* ① 8 字形(图案、绳结等): a figure of ~ in skating 8字形溜冰花式 ②八个(人或物)一组; 八人的划船队; 八桨划船; [复]八桨划船比赛: the *Eights* 英国牛津和剑桥大学的划船比赛 ③ 八汽缸发动机; 八汽缸汽车 ④八岁: a child of ~ 八岁的孩子 / *It is* ~ *now.* 现在八点钟了。 ⑤八号的衣服(或鞋袜等): wear an ~ 穿八号的衣服(或鞋袜等) ⑦方块八点的纸牌 ‖*have one* *over the* ~ 见 one ‖~**fold** *a.* & *ad.* 八倍；八重 / ~**some** ['eit-səm] *n.* 八个人跳的一种苏格兰舞 (=~some reel) ‖~ **ball** 一种弹子戏中写上 8 字的黑球：behind the ~ *ball* [俚]处于不利地位 ②老实人 / ~**pence** ['eitpəns] *n.* 八便士 / ~**penny** ['eitpəni] *a.* 八便士的 / '~'**score** *n.* & *a.* 一百六十

eighteen ['ei'ti:n] **I** *num.* 十八；十八个(人或物)；第十八(卷、章、页等)(用例参看 **eight**)**II** *n.* ①十八岁 ②十八点钟(即下午六点) ‖~**mo** [ei'ti:nmou] *n.* & *a.* =octodecimo / ~**th** *num.* ①第十八(个) ②十八分之一(的) *n.* (月的)第十八日

eighth [eitθ] **I** *num.* ①第八(个)：the *Eighth Route Army* 八路军 ②八分之一(的)：three ~*s* 八分之三 **II** *n.* (月的)第八日 ‖~**ly** *ad.* 第八(列举条目等时用) ‖~ **note** [音]八分音符

eightieth ['eitiiθ] *num.* ①第八十(个) ②八十分之一(的)

eighty ['eiti] **I** *num.* 八十；八十个(人或物)；第八十(页等) **II** *n.* ①[复](世纪的)八十年代 ②八十岁；[复]八十到八十九岁的时期

either ['aiðə, 'i:ðə] **I** *a.* ①(两者之中)任一的：You may use ~ hoe. 两把锄头中你可以随便用哪一把。 / in ~ case (或 event)(两种情况中)不论发生哪一种情况 / *Either* way, you were wrong. 不管怎么说，你总是错了。 ②(两者之中)每一方的：There is a water pump on ~ bank of the river. 河的两岸各有一台抽水机。**II** *pron.* (两者之中)任何一个：*Either* of them will agree to this arrangement. 他们两人都会同意这样的安排的。 / A: Do you speak German or French? B: I don't speak ~. 甲：你会讲德语或法语吗？乙：我都不会。**III** *ad.* ①[用于否定句或否定词组后加强语气]也，而且；根本：If he doesn't go, I won't ~. 如果他不去，我也不去。 / You don't know ~. 你也不知道呀。 / This new product is of high quality and is not expensive ~. 这种新产品质量非常好，而且也不贵。 / A: Oh, it's raining! B: It isn't ~. 甲：啊，下雨了！乙：根本没有下！②[用于疑问句或条件从句中选择部分后加强语气]：Who will do it for him or for you ~? 谁来为他，或者为你，做这事呢？**IV** *conj.* 或者，要末[一般只用于"~...or..."结构中] ‖~...**or**... 或者…或者…，不论…还是…：*Either* you come in person, *or* you entrust someone with the matter. 你要末自己来，要末就托人办理这件事。 / It is wrong to regard our work ~ as totally good *or* as completely bad. 说我们的工作样样都好或者一无是处，都是错误的。 ‖~-**or** ['aiðər'o:] *n.* ①[哲]"异"；按位加 ②两者择一 *a.* 非此即彼的，两者择一的

ejaculate [i'dʒækjuleit] **I** ❶ *vt.* ①突然喊出(或说出) ②(从生物体中)射出；射(精) ❷ *vi.* 射出液体 ②射(精) (一次射出的)精液 ‖**ejaculation** [i,dʒækju'leiʃən] *n.* ①(尤指精液等的)射出 ②突然的喊出(或讲出) / **ejaculator** *n.* 射出者，射

出器；突然叫喊者

eject[1] [i(:)'dʒekt] *vt.* ①逐出，驱逐；排斥；(通过诉讼)排除(租户等)的占有权；免…的职：~ sb. *from* the meeting 把某人逐出会场 / ~ sb. *from* the office 免某人的职 ②喷射，吐出：The chimney ~*s* smoke. 烟囱吐出烟来。 ‖~**ment** *n.* ①驱逐，赶走；喷吐 ②[律]收回不动产的诉讼

eject[2] ['i:dʒekt] *n.* [心]投射；推断的事物

eke[1] [i:k] *vt.* 增加，增加；放长：~ a few words *for* the occasion 加上几句适时的话 / let out and ~ the sleeves 把衣袖放长 ‖~ **out** ①弥补…的不足；节约使(供应等)持久：~ *out* the coal *with* the cinders 用煤渣来补充煤的不足 / ~ *out* the stores *by* rationing 以定量配给延长储藏物品的供应 ②竭力维持：~ *out* a living 勉强糊口

eke[2] [i:k] *ad.* [古]也(=also)；而且

elaborate [i'læbərit] **I** *a.* ①精心制作的；详尽阐述的；煞费苦心的：an ~ design 精心的设计 / ~ directions 详尽的指示 ②复杂的 ③辛勤的：an ~ collector of stamps 多方设法搜集邮票的人 **II** [i'læbəreit] ❶ *vt.* ①精心制作：~ a system of logic 精心搞出一套逻辑体系 ②详尽阐述，发挥：~ one's proposal 详尽阐述自己的建议 ③从简单成分合成(复杂有机化合物)：Green plants ~ organic compounds from inorganic by means of photosynthesis. 绿色植物通过光合作用从无机化合物合成有机化合物。❷ *vi.* ①成为精细，变成复杂 ②作详细说明 (*on, upon*)：~ *on* a theory (plan) 对理论(计划)作详细说明 ‖~**ly** *ad.* / ~**ness** *n.* / **elaborator** [i'læbəreitə] *n.* 精心制作者；详尽阐述者

elaboration [i,læbə'reiʃən] *n.* ①精心制作；精致；详尽阐述 ②精心完成的作品；详尽的细节；增添的东西

elapse [i'læps] **I** *vi.* (时间)过去，消逝：A little time ~*d*. 一些时间过去了。**II** *n.* (时间的)过去，消逝

elastic [i'læstik, i'lɑ:stik] **I** *a.* ①弹性的；有弹力的 ②灵活的；可伸缩的：~ regulations 灵活的规则 ③易顺应的；(心情)易轻快的：an ~ temperament 开朗的性情 **II** *n.* 橡皮带，松紧带；橡皮圈 ‖~**ally** *ad.* / ~ **deformation** [物]弹性变形

elate [i'leit] **I** *vt.* [常用被动语态]使得意洋洋；使欣欣鼓舞：We are ~*d* at the news. 这个消息使我们欣欣鼓舞。**II** *a.* [诗] =elated

elation [i'leiʃən] *n.* ①得意洋洋；兴高采烈，欢欣鼓舞 ②(病态的)安乐感，自鸣得意

elbow ['elbou] **I** *n.* ①肘；(衣服的)肘部 ②肘状物(如路的转弯等)；[机]弯管；弯头 **II** *vt.* 用肘推，挤进：~ sb. aside 把某人挤在一旁 / ~ one's way through the crowd 在人群中挤过去 ❷ *vi.* ①挤着前进 ②转弯 ‖*at one's* (或 *the*) ~ 近在手边 / bend (或 crook, lift) one's ~ 喝酒太多 / *out at* (*the*) ~*s* (衣衫)露肘的；褴褛的；(人)贫困的 / *rub* ~*s with* 与(名人等)交往 / *shake the* ~*s* 掷骰子，赌博 / *up to* *the* ~*s in* 忙于(工作等) ‖~ **grease** [口] 使劲的擦拭; 苦干; 费(腕)力的工作, 重活 / '~**room** *n.* 活动余地; 行动上的自由, 自由行动的机会

elder[1] ['eldə] I *a.* ① 年龄较大的: an ~ brother (sister) 兄(姐) ② 从前的: ~ times 昔日 ③ 资格老的; 地位高的: an ~ statesman 政界元老(一般指已退休的) II *n.* ① 年龄较大者: He is my ~ by two years. 他比我大两岁。②[复]长者, 前辈: respect the ~s 敬老 ③ 前人, 祖先 ④(教会的)长老 ‖~**ly** *a.* 上了年纪的; 中年以上的 / ~**ship** *n.* (教会中) 长老的地位(或职责); [总称]长老 ‖'~**care** *n.* 六十五岁以上穷苦老人的医疗照顾

elder[2] ['eldə] *n.* 【植】接骨木

eldest ['eldist] *a.* 最年长的; 排行中第一的: sb.'s ~ son (daughter) 某人的长子(女) / sb.'s ~ brother (sister) 某人的大哥(姐)

elect [i'lekt] I ❶ *vt.* ① 选举; 推选: be ~ed to a new leading post 被选到新的领导岗位 / We ~ed him monitor. 我们选他为班长。② 选择, 决定: She has ~ed to become a teacher. 她决定当教师。❷ *vi.* 作出选择; 进行票选 II *a.* [放在所修饰的名词后] ①选定的, 选中的: the bride ~ 选中的未婚妻 ②选出而尚未上任的: the president-~ 当选(但尚未就职的)总统 III *n.* [the ~] 被选定的人(们); 特权集团;【宗】上帝的选民

election [i'lekʃən] *n.* ①选举: conduct general ~s from the lower level upward 实行由下而上的普选 / an ~ campaign 竞选运动 ②当选: ratify sb.'s ~ to chairman of the committee 批准某人当选为委员会的主席 ③ 选择权(利) ④【宗】上帝的选拔 ‖*carry an* ~ 竞选获胜 ‖~ **year** [美] (总统)选举年

elective [i'lektiv] I *a.* ①(职位、权力等)选任的, 由选举产生的 ②有选举权的 ③[美](学校课程)选修的, 可以选择的 ④有选择倾向的;【化】有择的: ~ affinity 有择亲和势 II *n.* [美]选修课程 ‖~**ly** *ad.* / ~**ness** *n.*

elector [i'lektə] *n.* ①有选举权的人 ②[史]选帝侯(德国有权选举神圣罗马帝国皇帝的诸侯) ③(美国)选举团的成员

electorate [i'lektərit] *n.* ①全体选民 ②选民区, 选举区 ③[史]德国有权选举神圣罗马帝国皇帝的诸侯的身分(或领地)

electric [i'lektrik] I *a.* ①电的; 导电的; 发电的; 用电的; 电动的: an ~ arc 电弧 / an ~ current 电流 / an ~ wire 电线 / an ~ generator 发电机 / ~ light 电光 / an ~ light 电灯 / ~ welding 电焊 ②令人震惊的, 惊心动魄的: an ~ performance 惊人的表演 II *n.* ①带电体 ②电动车辆 ‖~ **blanket** 电(热床)毯 / ~ **blue** 铁蓝色 / ~ **capacity** 电容 / ~ **chair** 电椅(指处死的一种刑具) / ~ **engineering** 电机工程; 电工技术 / ~ **eye** ①光电池 ②电眼 / ~ **furnace** 电炉 / ~ **locomotive** 电力机车 / ~ **torch** 电筒

electrical [i'lektrikəl] *a.* 电的; 电气科学的: ~ engineering 电机工程 / an ~ transcription (广播用的)唱片; 唱片广播节目 ‖~**ly** *ad.*

electrician [ilek'triʃən] *n.* 电工; 电学家

electricity [ilek'trisiti] *n.* ①电; 电学 ②电流; 静电, 电荷 ③强烈的紧张情感; 热情

electrify [i'lektrifai] *vt.* ①使充电, 使起电 ②使电气化 ③使触电 ④[喻]使震惊, 使兴奋, 使激动: an ~ audience 使观众震动 ‖**electrification** [i,lektrifi'keiʃən] *n.* ①起电; 起电装置 ②电气化

electrocute [i'lektrəkju:t] *vt.* ①以电刑处死(罪犯) ② 使触电而死 ‖**electrocution** [i,lektrə'kju:ʃən] *n.*

electrode [i'lektroud] *n.* ①电极: deflecting ~【无】致偏电极 / focus(s)ing ~【无】聚焦(电)极 ②电焊条

electrolysis [ilek'trolisis] *n.* ①电解(作用), 电蚀 ②用电针去除毛发

electron [i'lektrɔn] *n.* 电子 ‖~ **accelerator** 电子加速器 / ~ **bomb** 镁壳燃烧弹 / ~ **camera** 电子摄像机 / ~ **gun** 电子枪 / ~ **lens** 电子透镜 / ~ **microscope** 电子显微镜 / ~ **multiplier** 电子倍增器 / ~ **telescope** 电子望远镜 / ~ **tube** 电子管

electronic [ilek'trɔnik] *a.* 电子的: an ~ analog(ue) computer 电子模拟计算机 / ~ control 电子控制 / an ~ digital computer 电子数字计算机 / an ~ image storage device 电子录像设备 ‖**elec'tronic-con'trolled** *a.* 电子控制的 / ~ **media** 电子舆论工具(指广播、电视) / ~ **music** 电子音乐 / ~ **organ** 电子琴

electronics [ilek'trɔniks] [复] *n.* [用作单] 电子学: molecular ~ 分子电子学

elegance ['eligəns], **elegancy** ['eligənsi] *n.* ①(举止、服饰、风格等的)雅致, 漂亮, 优美 ②雅致(或漂亮、优美)的东西

elegant ['eligənt] *a.* ①(举止、服饰、风格等)雅致的, 漂亮的, 优美的 ②讲究的, 精致的 ③[口]上品的, 第一流的 ‖~**ly** *ad.*

elegiac [,eli'dʒaiæk] I *a.* ①哀歌体的, 挽歌体的 ②表示悲哀的 II *n.* ①哀歌(或挽歌)体对句(=~ couplet) ②[复]哀歌, 挽歌

elegy ['elidʒi] *n.* 哀歌, 挽歌

element ['elimənt] *n.* ①要素(古希腊哲学中土、水、气、火四大要素之一) ②组成部分, 成分, 分子: reduce sth. to its ~s 把某物分析出来 ③(人或物的)自然环境, 适应的环境 ④[复] 自然力, 风雨: a war of the ~s 暴风雨 ⑤[复]原理, 基础: the ~s of grammar 语法基础 ⑥【机】单体, 单元; 零件 ⑦【化】元素 ⑧【数】元, 素 ⑨【电】电池; 电极 ⑩【无】元件 ⑪【军】组织; 部队; 小单位, 分队 ‖*in one's* ~ 处于适宜的环境; 在自己的活动范围之内, 内行 / *out of one's* ~ 处于不适宜的环境; 在自己的活动范围之外, 外行

elemental [,eli'mentl] I *a.* ①(古希腊哲学)四大要素(土、水、气、火)的 ②自然力的: ~ forces

自然力 ③基本的 ④初步的 ⑤【化】元素的 **II** *n.*
①(古希腊)四大要素的精灵 ②[常用复]基本原
理 ‖**~ly** *ad.*

elementary [,eli'mentəri] *a.* ①基本的: ~ species
【生】原种 / ~ particle【物】基本粒子 ②初级的,
基础的: an ~ school 小学 / ~ arithmetic 初等
算术 ③【化】元素的 ④自然力的 ‖**elementarily**
[,eli'mentərili; 美 ,elimen'terili] *ad.* / **elemen-
tariness** *n.*

elephant ['elifənt] *n.* 象 ‖*a white ~* [喻]无用
而累赘的东西;沉重的负担 / *see the ~* [美俚]
见世面,长世故 ‖**~ dugout**【军】①大壕沟 ②
大防空洞

elevate ['eliveit] *vt.* ①抬起; 使升高 ②提高(思
想、嗓子等);振奋(情绪等) ③提升…的职位

elevation [,eli'veiʃən] *n.* ①高度: a building of
imposing ~ 雄伟高大的建筑物 ②标高, 仰角,
【军】射角 ③海拔 ④提高;提升, 晋级 ⑤高地,
高处 ⑥(皮肤上的)隆肿 ⑦崇高, 壮严: ~ of
thought 思想的崇高 ⑧(建筑物的)正视图, 立
视图

elevator ['eliveitə] *n.* ①起重工人 ②起卸机 ③
[美]电梯 (= [英] lift) ④升降机: a pneumatic
~ 气压升降机 ⑤【空】升降舵 ⑥(能吊卸、储存、
有时也进行加工的)谷物仓库 ⑦【生】牙挺;起子;
(上)提肌

eleven [i'levn] **I** *num.* 十一; 十一个(人或物);
第十一(卷、章、页等)(用例参看 **eight**) **II** *n.*
①十一个(人或物)一组(尤指十一人的足球队
等): He is in the ~. 他是足球队的一员。
②十一点钟;[复][英口]上午十一点左右的茶点
③十一岁 ‖*the Eleven*【基督教】耶稣的(除犹
大之外的)十一门徒

eleventh [i'levnθ] **I** *num.* ①第十一(个) ②十
一分之一(的) **II** *n.* (月的)第十一日 ‖*at the
hour* 在最后时刻; 在危急之时

elf [elf] ([复] elves [elvz]) *n.* ①(神话中)淘气的
小鬼,小精灵 ②顽皮的小孩 ③矮子 ④恶作剧的
人; 恶人 ‖**~ bolt** 石箭头 / **'~lock** *n.* [常用
复]乱发 / **'~-struck** *a.* 着迷的

elfin ['elfin] **I** *a.* 小精灵的,小精灵般的 **II** *n.*
①小精灵 ②矮子 ③小孩

elicit [i'lisit] *vt.* 得出,引出(真理等); 使发出,
引起,诱出(回答等): ~ the truth from a witness
从证人处得到(或使证人吐露)真实情况 / ~ a
fact 使谈出事实

elide [i'laid] *vt.* ①取消 ②省略(元音、音节等)
③不予考虑 ④削减;删节

eligible ['elidʒəbl] **I** *a.* ①符合被推选的条件
的, 合格的 (*for*) ②适宜的 **II** *n.* 合适的人
‖**eligibility** [,elidʒə'biliti] *n.* / **eligibly** *ad.*

eliminate [i'limineit] *vt.* ①排除, 消除, 消灭: ~
toxins *from* the intestine 从肠中排出毒素 / ~
a possibility 排除一种可能性 / ~ the false and
retain the true 去伪存真 / ~ errors 消灭差错
②【数】消去 ‖**eliminator** *n.* 排除者;【电】消除器

elixir [i'liksə] *n.* ①(中世纪炼金术士所幻想的)
炼金药, 长生不老药 ②万应灵药 ③【药】酏剂,
甘香酊酒剂

ellipse [i'lips] *n.* ①【数】椭圆 ②=ellipsis

elliptic(al) [i'liptik(əb)] *a.* ①椭圆的, 椭圆形的
②省略的 ‖**elliptically** *ad.*

elm [elm] *n.* 【植】①榆 ②榆木

elocution [,elə'kju:ʃən] *n.* ①演说术; 雄辩术 ②朗
诵法 ‖**~ary** *a.* / **~ist** *n.* ①演说术教师 ②朗
诵者;演说家

elongate ['i:lɔŋgeit] **I** *vt. & vi.* 拉长, (使)伸长,
(使)延长 **II** *a.* ①拉长的, 伸长的, 延伸的 ②(树
叶等)细长的 ‖**elongation** [,i:lɔŋ'geiʃən] *n.* ①拉
长, 伸长, 延长; 延伸率 ②(线的)延长部分
③【天】距角

elope [i'loup] *vi.* ①私奔 ②逃走, 出走 ‖**~ment**
n. / **~r** *n.* 私奔者

eloquence ['eləkwəns] *n.* ①雄辩: Facts speak
louder than ~. 事实胜于雄辩。②雄辩术; 口
才; 修辞

eloquent ['eləkwənt] *a.* ①雄辩的, 有说服力的:
Facts are ~ proof. 事实是有力的证明。②富
于表情的, 意味深长的: an ~ gesture 富于表情
的姿势 ‖**~ly** *ad.*

else [els] **I** *a.* [常接在疑问代词、不定代词后]
其他的, 别的: What ~ did he say? 他还说了些
什么? / Who ~'s umbrella can this be? 这还
可能是其他什么人的伞呢? / Anything ~ I can
do for you? 我还能为你做些别的事吗? / Little
~ remains to be done. 没有剩下什么事要做
的了。/ Within our ranks everybody regards
anybody ~'s difficulties as his own. 在我们队
伍里, 人人都把别人的困难当作自己的困难看
待。**II** *ad.* ①[常接在疑问副词后]另外, 其他:
When ~ shall we meet again, if Friday is not
convenient for you? 要是星期五对你不便, 那
么另外什么时候再碰头呢? / We went to the
park and nowhere ~. 我们到公园里去了, 其他
什么地方也没去。/ How ~ could we have
succeeded but for the policy of self-reliance?
要不是自力更生的政策,我们怎能成功呢? ②[前
面常用 or]否则,要不然,要不然, (or) ~ you'll
miss the train. 快走, 否则你要赶不上火车了。/
We must constantly study hard, (or) ~ we'll
lose our bearings. 我们必须不断努力学习, 不
然就会迷失方向。/ He threatened: "Submit
or ~." 他威胁说:"快屈服,不然的话,哼!"

elsewhere ['els'hwɛə] *ad.* 在别处; 向别处

elucidate [i'lju:sideit] *vt.* 阐明;解释 ‖**elucidation**
[i,lju:si'deiʃən] *n.* / **elucidative, elucidatory**
a. / **elucidator** *n.* 阐明者, 解释者

elude [i'lju:d] *vt.* ①(巧妙地)逃避, 躲避(责任、困
难、危险等): ~ observation 避人耳目 ②使困
惑, 难倒: ~ sb.'s understanding (问题等)为某
人所不理解 / It ~s me. 这个我弄不懂。

elusive [i'lju:siv] *a.* ①躲避的; 闪避的 ②难以捉

摸的, 难以理解的, 容易被忘记的 ‖**~ly** *ad.* /
~ness *n.*

elves [elvz] elf 的复数

emaciate [i'meiʃieit] ❶ *vt.* ①使衰弱, 使消瘦
②使(土壤)贫瘠 ❷ *vi.* 消瘦起来 ‖**~d** *a.* 憔悴
的, 消瘦的 / **emaciation** [i,meisi'eiʃən] *n.*

emanate ['eməneit] ❶ *vi.* ①(气体等)发出, 发散;
(光等)放射 (*from*) ②发源 (*from*) ❷ *vt.* [罕]
发散; 放射 ‖**emanation** [,emə'neiʃən] *n.* ①发
出, 发散; 放射 ②发出(或发散、放射)的东西
③[原]射气 / **emanative** *a.* 流出的, 发散的;
放射的

emancipate [i'mænsipeit] *vt.* ①解放; 使不受(政
治、社会、法律等的)束缚: an ~d serf 解
放了的农奴 ②[律]使(孩子、妻子)摆脱家长的管
教而获得合法的权利

emancipation [i,mænsi'peiʃən] *n.* 解放

emasculate I [i'mæskjuleit] *vt.* ①阉割; 使无男
子气, 使柔弱 ②删削(文章等)使无力; 使(语言
等)贫乏 II ['i'mæskjulit] *a.* 阉割了的; 柔弱的
‖**emasculation** [i,mæskju'leiʃən] *n.* / **emascu-
lative** ['i'mæskjuleitiv], **emasculatory** ['i'mæskju-
leitəri] *a.*

embalm [im'bɑ:m] *vt.* ①以香油 (或药料等)涂
(尸)防腐 ②使不朽, 使不被遗忘 ③使充满香气
‖**~ment** *n.*

embank [im'bæŋk] *vt.* 筑堤围拦; 筑堤防护: ~ a
river 筑河堤 ‖**~ment** *n.* ①筑堤 ②(河、海的)
堤岸; (铁路的)路堤

embargo [em'bɑ:gou] I ([复] embargoes) *n.*
①(战时)封港令(指禁止外轮进港, 禁止商船出入
港口) ②禁止贸易令; 禁运(全部或部分物资): a
gold ~ 禁止黄金输出 ③禁止(或限制)买卖
④禁止; 阻止 II *vt.* ①禁止(船只)出入港口; 禁
运(物资) ②征用(船只、物资) ‖**be under an ~**
①在封港中; 在停止贸易中; 在禁运中 ② 被禁止
(或阻止) / **lay** (或 **put, place**) **an ~ on** ①禁
止 (船只) 出入港; 对…实行禁运 ② 对…予以禁止
(或阻止、限制) / **lift** (或 **raise, take off**) **the
~ on** 对…解禁

embark [im'bɑ:k] ❶ *vi.* ① 上船 ② 从事, 开始
搞: ~ **on** (或 *in, upon*) a new undertaking 着
手一项新工作 ❷ *vt.* ①使上船, 使坐飞机,
搭载: ~ passengers and cargo 载客和装货
②使从事, 使着手 ③投(资) ‖**~ation, embarca-
tion** [,embɑ:'keiʃən] *n.* ①乘坐; 装载(物) ②开
始, 从事

embarrass [im'bærəs] *vt.* 使窘迫, 使困恼; 使
为难, 使负债; 使财政困难 ③麻烦, 妨碍 ④使
(问题)复杂化 ‖**~ment** *n.* ①窘迫 ②使人为难
的事物

embarrassing [im'bærəsiŋ] *a.* 令人为难的; 麻烦的
‖**~ly** *ad.*

embassy ['embəsi] *n.* ① 大使的职务 ② 大使
的派遣 ③大使馆, 大使的住宅 ④大使及其随员,
大使馆全体人员 ⑤重任; 差使 ‖**go on an ~** 去
做大使 / **send sb. on an ~** 派遣某人出任大使

embed [im'bed] (embedded; embedding) *vt.* ①栽
种(花等) ②埋置; 把…嵌入; [医]包埋: a bullet
embedded in the flesh 嵌在肉里的子弹 / lie
embedded in sb.'s memory 牢牢印在某人记忆中
‖**~ment** *n.*

embellish [im'beliʃ] *vt.* ①装饰, 修饰 ②给(叙事、
文章)添加细节; 给…润色

ember ['embə] *n.* [常用复]余火, 余烬

embezzle [im'bezl] *vt.* 盗用, 贪污 ‖**~ment** *n.* /
~r *n.* 盗用者, 贪污者

embitter [im'bitə] *vt.* ①加苦味于 ②加重(痛苦
等) ③激怒; 使怨恨 ‖**~ment** *n.*

emblem ['embləm] I *n.* ①象征; 标志 ②符号;
徽章; 纹章图案: a state (或 national) ~ 国徽
③(某种品质的)典型 ④[古]寓意画 II *vt.* 用图
案(或符号)表示, 用象征表示

embody [im'bɔdi] *vt.* ①体现; 使具体化 ②包
含, 收录: The new edition *embodies* many improvements. 新版有许多改进之处。 ③使(精神
等)肉体化

embolden [im'bouldən] *vt.* 给…壮胆, 使更勇敢:
~ sb. to do sth. 鼓励某人去做某事

embrace[1] [im'breis] I ❶ *vt.* ①拥抱, 抱 ②抓住:
~ an opportunity 抓住机会 ③接受, 信奉(主义、
信仰等) ④着手: ~ a new profession 从事新的
职业 ⑤围住, 环绕: a valley ~d by
forests 树林环绕的山谷 ⑥包括, 包含: The
report ~s many important points. 报告中包
括许多要点。⑦看到, 领会 ❷ *vi.* (相互)拥抱:
They ~d. 他们相互拥抱。 II *n.* ①拥抱; 怀抱
②包围; 掌握 ③接受

embrace[2] [im'breis] *vt.* 笼络, 收买(陪审员等)
‖**~r, embraceor** *n.* 笼络(或收买)陪审员的人 /
~ry [im'breisəri] *n.* 笼络(或收买)陪审员的行
为

embrasure [im'breiʒə] *n.* ①[军]炮眼, 枪眼, 射击
孔 ②[建]斜面墙(门窗等漏斗形边墙) ③[医]楔
状隙

embrocate ['embroukeit] *vt.* [医](用洗液等)涂擦
‖**embrocation** [,embrou'keiʃən] *n.* ①擦法 ②
擦剂

embroider [im'brɔidə] ❶ *vt.* ①绣(花纹) ②在(织
物)上绣花纹 ③给(故事等)添油加酱, 对…加以
渲染 ❷ *vi.* 绣花, 刺绣

embroidery [im'brɔidəri] *n.* ①绣花; 刺绣法; 绣
制品 ②润饰; 装演

embroil [im'brɔil] *vt.* ①使(事态等)混乱; 使纠缠
②使卷入纠纷: be ~ed in a quarrel 卷入争吵
‖**~ment** *n.*

embryo ['embriou] I *n.* ①胚, 胚胎; (尤指受孕后
八周内的)胎儿 ②萌芽时期; 萌芽状态的事物
II *a.* 胚胎的; 初期的, 萌芽的, 未发达的 ‖**in ~**
尚未成熟的; 在计划中的, 在酝酿中的

emend [i(:)'mend] *vt.* 校勘, 校订: ~ an author
校订作家的著作 ‖**~able** *a.* 可修正的, 可订
正的

emendation [ˌiːmenˈdeiʃən] *n.* 校勘，校订

emerald [ˈemərəld] I *n.* ①【矿】祖母绿，纯绿柱石 ②绿宝石，绿刚玉 ③艳绿色 ④【印】欧美一种活字(相当于 6.5 点) II *a.* ①艳绿色的 ②纯绿宝石制的 ‖**Emerald Isle** 绿宝石岛(爱尔兰的别名)

emerge [iˈməːdʒ] *vi.* ①浮现；出现；形成：The moon ~d from behind the clouds. 月亮从云后出现。②(问题等)冒出；(事实等)暴露

emergence [iˈməːdʒəns] *n.* ①浮现；出现 ②【植】突出体 ③【动】羽化

emergency [iˈməːdʒənsi] *n.* 紧急情况；突然事件；非常时刻：in case of ~ 若发生紧急情况 / proclaim a state of ~ 宣布处于紧急状态 ‖an ~ act 紧急法令 / an ~ airport 应急机场 / an ~ brake 紧急刹车 / an ~ bridge 便桥 / an ~ call 紧急召集 / an ~ door(或 exit) 太平门,安全门 / ~ measures 紧急措施,应变措施 / an ~ meeting 紧急会议 / an ~ treatment 紧急治疗,急诊

emery [ˈeməri] *n.* 宝砂，刚玉砂，金刚砂 ‖~ **cloth** (金刚)砂布 / ~ **paper** (金刚)砂纸 / ~ **wheel** (金刚)砂轮

emetic [iˈmetik] I *n.*【药】催吐剂 II *a.* 催吐的 ‖~**ally** *ad.*

emigrant [ˈemiɡrənt] I *a.* 移居的；移民的 II *n.* 移居外国的人，移民；迁徙的动物；移植的植物

emigrate [ˈemiɡreit] ❶ *vi.* ①永久移居外国(与 immigrate(从外国)移来相对) ②[英口]迁移 ❷ *vt.* 使移居,移(民)

emigration [ˌemiˈɡreiʃən] *n.* ①移居；移民出境 ②[总称]移民

eminence [ˈeminəns] *n.* ①(地位、造诣等的)卓越，显赫，著名：a man of ~ in the world of learning 学术界有卓越成就者 / a position of ~ 显赫的地位 ②高地,高处 ③地位高的人,名家,大家 ④[E-](天主教中对红衣主教的尊称)阁下 ⑤【解】隆凸，隆起

eminent [ˈeminənt] *a.* ①著名的(指某人在世时的名誉,如死后仍出名,不能用 ~,应用 famous),杰出的：be ~ among one's contemporaries 在同时代的人中是杰出的 ②(品德等)突出的,优良的 ‖~**ly** *ad.* ‖~ **domain**【律】(国家对一切产业的)支配权,征用权

emir [eˈmiə] *n.* ①埃米尔,(穆斯林国家的)酋长(或贵族、王公) ②穆罕默德后裔的称号 ‖~**ate** [eˈmiərit] *n.* 埃米尔的统治；酋长国：the United Arab *Emirates* 阿拉伯联合酋长国[亚洲]

emissary [ˈemisəri] I *n.* ①使者(尤指传递恶耗或秘密者) ②间谍 II *a.* 密使的；间谍的

emission [iˈmiʃən] *n.* ①(光、热、电子、气味等的)散发，发射 ②发出物；发射物 ③【医】泄出；泄精

emit [iˈmit] (emitted; emitting) *vt.* ❶散发，放射(光、热、声音等)：Geysers ~ water. 间歇泉喷出水来。②发表(意见等) ③发行(纸币等) ‖**emitter** *n.*【物】发射体,(晶体管的)发射极

emolument [iˈmɔljumənt] *n.* 报酬；酬金；薪水；津贴

emotion [iˈmouʃən] *n.* ①激动：with ~ 激动地 ②感情；情绪,情感 ‖~**less** *a.* 没有感情的；冷漠的

emotional [iˈmouʃənl] *a.* ①感情(上)的；情绪(上)的 ②(易)激动的；易动感情的 ③激起感情的,激动人的 ‖~**ism** *n.* 唯情论,感情主义,感情表露 / ~**ist** *n.* 唯情论者.容易动感情的人 / ~**ly** *ad.*

emperor [ˈempərə] *n.* 皇帝 ‖~**ship** *n.* 皇帝的身分(或地位、统治)

emphasis [ˈemfəsis] ([复] emphases [ˈemfəsiːz]) *n.* ①强调,重点,重要性：lay (或 put, place) ~ on (或 upon) 把重点放在,着重于 / speak with ~ 强调地说 ②【语】强语气,强调语势,强音 ③显著,突出

emphasize [ˈemfəsaiz] *vt.* ①强调,着重 ②加强…的语气,重读 ③使(事实等)显得突出(或重要)

emphatic [imˈfætik] *a.* ①强调的, 着重的 ②加强语气的 ③有力的；断然的；显著的：an ~ victory 大胜 ‖~**ally** *ad.*

empire [ˈempaiə] *n.* ①帝国 ②帝权；绝对统治(over) ③由一个集团(或个人)控制的地区(或企业)：a publishing ~ 大出版企业 ‖*the Empire* ①英帝国 ②罗马帝国 ③(拿破仑统治下的)法兰西第一帝国 ‖**Empire City** [美]纽约市 / **Empire Day** 英帝国节(五月二十四日,现称 Commonwealth Day 英联邦节) / **Empire State** [美]纽约州

empirical [emˈpirikəl] *a.* 经验主义的；以经验为根据的：~ formula【化】实验式,经验式 ‖~**ly** *ad.*

emplace [imˈpleis] *vt.*【军】放列,使(火炮)进入阵地 ‖~**ment** *n.*【军】①放列动作 ②炮兵掩体,炮位,炮台

employ [imˈplɔi] I *vt.* ①用,使用 ②雇用 ③使忙于,使从事于：~ oneself (或 be ~ed) in 从事于 II *n.* 使用；雇用；职业：in the ~ of sb. (或 in sb.'s ~) 受雇于某人 / be out of ~ 失业

employe(e) [ˌemplɔiˈiː] *n.* 受雇者,雇工,雇员

employer [imˈplɔiə] *n.* ①雇用者,雇主 ②使用者

employment [imˈplɔimənt] *n.* ①使用：the flexible ~ of forces 兵力的灵活使用 ②雇用：in the ~ of 受雇于 ③职业,工作：get (lose) ~ 就(失)业 / be out of ~ 失业 ‖an ~ agency (或 bureau) 职业介绍所 / an ~ agent 经营职业介绍所者 / an ~ certificate 学校发给学龄儿童可参加有酬工作的证明书 / an ~ exchange [英](劳工部等机构设立的)劳工介绍所

emporium [emˈpɔːriəm] ([复] emporiums 或 emporia [emˈpɔːriə]) *n.* ①商场,商业中心 ②大百货商店

empower [imˈpauə] *vt.* ①授权,准许：~ sb. to do sth. 授权(或准许)某人做某事 ②使能够：Science ~s man to control natural forces more effectively. 科学使人类能更有效地制服自然。

empress [ˈempris] *n.* ①女皇；皇后：an ~ dowager 皇太后 ②有极大权力的女人

empty [ˈempti] I *a.* ①空的；(房屋等)未占用的,没

人居住的,无家具设备的; (车、船等) 未载东西的: an ~ box 空匣 / ~ factory space 空着的工厂场地 ②空洞的; 空虚的, 无实在意义的; 缺乏力量 (或效果) 的: an article ~ of matter 内容空洞的文章 / ~ lip service 说得好听的空话 / an ~ pleasure 无谓的乐事 ③无聊的, 愚蠢的, 傻的: an ~ thing 无聊的事 / an ~ idea 愚蠢的想法 ④空闲的; 无用的, 徒劳的: ~ hours 空闲时间 / a certain amount of ~ mileage 一段白走的路程 ⑤杳无人烟的; 空寂的; 缺乏温暖的: ~ land 荒地 / in quiet ~ places 在冷落寂静的地方 ⑥[口] 空着肚子的, 饥饿的: feel ~ 觉得饿了 ⑦(家畜) 未怀孕的: an ~ heifer 未怀孕的小母牛 ⑧【逻】无元的, 无元的: an ~ class 空类, 零类 **II** ❶ **vt.** ①使成为空的: ~ a glass 干杯, 喝干 / ~ a house 搬空房屋 / ~ a city 撤空城市 ②倒, 倒空: ~ the grain from a sack 把粮食从袋中倒空 / ~ grain into a bin 把粮食倒进仓里 / No waste or garbage is to be *emptied* on highways. 废物和垃圾不许倒在公路上。 ③使流入: The stream *empties* itself *into* the river. 这小溪流入大河。 ④ 使失去 (*of*): ~ a phrase *of* all meaning 使一句话变得毫无意义 ❷ **vi.** ①成为空的; 流空: The theatre *emptied* rapidly after the show. 演出结束后, 剧场里的人很快就走空了。 / This sticky liquid *empties* slowly. 这种粘液要好一会儿才能流空。 ②(江河等) 流入: The river *empties into* the ocean. 这条河流入海洋。 **III** **n.** [常用复]空箱; 空桶; 空瓶; 空的货车: returned *empties* 退回的空瓶 (或空箱等) ‖(*be*) ~ *of* 缺乏, 无 ‖**emptily** *ad.* / **emptiness** *n.* ‖'~-'handed *a.* 空手的; 一无所获的 / '~-'headed *a.* 傻而无知的; 浮躁而轻率的 / ~ word 【语】虚词

emulate ['emjuleit] *vt.* ①同 … 竞争; 同 … 竞赛; 努力赶 (或超) ②竭力仿效 ‖**emulator** *n.* 竞争者; 竞赛者; 热心模仿者

emulation [,emju'leiʃən] *n.* ① 竞赛: socialist ~ 社会主义竞赛 / an ~ drive 竞赛运动 ②仿效, 模仿

emulsion [i'mʌlʃən] *n.* ① 乳胶, 乳浊液 ②【医】乳剂; 【摄】感光乳剂

enable [i'neibl] *vt.* ①使能够, 使成为可能, 使实现: ~ every student *to* develop morally, intellectually and physically 使每个学员在德、智、体几方面都能得到发展 / ~ passage of a bill 使议案能够通过 ②授予 … 权力

enact [i'nækt] *vt.* ①制定 (法律); 颁布; 通过 (法案等) ②演出; 扮演 ‖~**ing clause** 说明 (法案) 制定经过的条文

enamel [i'næməl] **I** *n.* ①搪瓷; 珐琅; 釉药 ②搪瓷制品 ③ (牙齿的) 珐琅质 ④ 瓷漆 ⑤指甲油 **II** (enamel(l)ed; enamel(l)ing) *vt.* ①涂釉于 ②给 … 上彩色, 彩饰 ③使成光滑面 ‖**e'namelware** *n.* [总称]搪瓷器

enamo(u)r [i'næmə] *vt.* 使倾心, 使迷恋: be ~ed *of* 倾心于, 恋慕

encamp [in'kæmp] ❶ *vi.* 扎营; 野营 ❷ *vt.* 使扎营; 把 … 安置于营中 ‖~**ment** *n.* ① 设营; 野营 ②营, 营地

encase [in'keis] *vt.* ①把 … 装箱, 把 … 放入套 (或盒、壳) 内 ②包装; 围 ‖~**ment** *n.* ①装箱, 包装 ②包装物; 箱, 套, 鞘

enchant [in'tʃɑ:nt] *vt.* ① 用魔法迷惑 ② 使心醉, 使喜悦: be ~ed *with* (或 *by*) 为 … 所陶醉 ‖~**er** *n.* 巫士; 妖人 / ~**ment** *n.* ①迷惑 ②着迷 ③妖术; 魅力 / ~**ress** *n.* 女巫; 妖妇

enchanting [in'tʃɑ:ntiŋ] *a.* 迷人的; 醉人的 ‖~**ly** *ad.*

encircle [in'sə:kl] *vt.* ①环绕; 包围, 合围 ②绕 … 行一周 ‖~**ment** *n.*

enclose [in'klouz] *vt.* ①围住; 圈起; 关闭住: ~ a yard *with* a fence 用篱笆围住院子 ②把 (公文、票据等) 封入: the ~d 函内附件

enclosure [in'klouʒə] *n.* ①围绕; 圈地 (指把公地圈作私有); 封人 ②围场; 围栏, 围墙 ③附件; 包入物

encore [ɔŋ'kɔ:] **I** *int.* 再来一个! 再演奏 (或演唱) 一次! **II** *vt.* 要求 … 再演奏 (或演唱) 一次, 要求 … 再来一个: The audience ~d the singer. 听众要求歌唱者再演唱一次。 **III** *n.* ① 重演的要求: The pianist got an ~. 钢琴演奏者被听众要求再奏一次。 ② 重演, 重奏, 重唱: The singer gave several ~s. 这位歌唱者应听众要求又唱了几次。

encounter [in'kauntə] **I** ❶ *vt.* ① 遭遇, 遇到: ~ difficulties 遇到困难 ②意外地遇见 ❷ *vi.* 偶然相遇 (或遭遇) **II** *n.* ①遭遇, 冲突; 遭遇战: an ~ action 遭遇战 ②偶然 (或短暂) 的见面 ‖~ **group** "交朋友" 小组 (现代美国的一种所谓精神治疗方式, 受治疗者在组内自由与其他成员交流内心感情)

encourage [in'kʌridʒ] *vt.* ①鼓励; 怂恿; 赞助; 促进: ~ sb. *to* do sth. 鼓励某人去做某事 / energetically ~ the practice of making investigations and studies 大兴调查研究之风 ‖~**ment** *n.* ①鼓励; 赞助 ②鼓励物, 奖品

encroach [in'kroutʃ] *vi.* 侵犯; 侵占; 蚕食 (*upon*, *on*): ~ *upon* sb.'s time (property) 占用某人的时间 (财产) / The sea is ~*ing upon* the land. 海水侵蚀着陆地。 ‖~**ment** *n.* 侵犯; 侵占; 侵占物

encrust [in'krʌst] ❶ *vt.* 包外壳于; (用银、宝石等) 镶饰 ❷ *vi.* 长壳 (或皮) ‖~**ment** *n.*

encumber [in'kʌmbə] *vt.* ①妨害, 阻碍 ②塞满; 阻塞: a passage ~ed *with* lumber 被木料阻塞的通道 ③拖累, 牵累: be ~ed *with* 为 … 所累 ④使负担债务 (或抵押等)

encumbrance [in'kʌmbrəns] *n.* ①妨害, 阻碍, 障碍物 ②累赘: This piece of luggage is an ~ to me. 这件行李是我的累赘。 ③【律】(在不动产上设定的) 债权 (指抵押权等) ‖*without* ~ 无儿女牵累

encyclop(a)edia [en,saiklou'pi:djə] *n.* 百科全书; 某科全书

encyclop(a)edic(al) [en,saiklou'pi:dik(ǝb] *a.* 百科全书的; 广博的; 包含各种学科的

end [end] **I** *n.* ① 末端; 尽头; 梢, 尖: the ~s of a pole 杆的两端 / from beginning to ~ 从头至尾 / the East End (of London) 伦敦东区(劳动人民聚居区) / the West End 伦敦西区(富人聚居区) / the ~ of the railway 铁道的终点 / the ~ carriage of a train 列车的最后一节车厢 / the ~ of a pencil 铅笔尖端 ②完结, 结束; 终止; 限度, 极顶: the ~ of the book 书的结尾 / by the ~ of the year 到年底为止 / That's the ~ (of our transmission). (本次播音)到此结束。 / demand an ~ to all unequal treaties 要求废除一切不平等条约 / There is no ~ to progress. 进步无止境。 / at the ~ of one's forbearance 忍无可忍 ③死亡; 下场 ④目的; 目标: means and ~s 手段和目的 / with a lofty ~ in view 怀着崇高的目标 ⑤ 残片; 残余: a cigarette ~ 香烟头 / odds and ~s 零碎杂物, 残余 ⑥结果, 结局; 最后情况: the ~ of a matter 事情的结局 **II ❶** *vt.* ①结束, 终止; 消灭, 了结 ②为…的结尾: K ~s the word *work*. work 这词以 k 结尾。 / A band ~ed the parade. 游行队伍的末尾是一个乐队。**❷** *vi.* ① 完结, 结束; 终止: for ten days ~ing (on) November 21 到十一月廿一日为止的十天中 ②死 ‖*a rope's ~* ① 两端用线结住的打人用短绳 ② 绞索 / *a shoemaker's ~* 蜡线 / *at a loose ~* 没有事做; 闲着 / *at loose ~s* ①不知做什么好, 无所适从; 不安定 ②处于杂乱状态 / *at one's wit's ~* 智穷计尽; 不知所措 / *at the ~ of one's rope* (或 *tether*) 山穷水尽; 智穷力竭 / *at the ~ of one's row* 山穷水尽; 智穷力竭; 筋疲力尽 / *be at an ~* 结束; 穷尽 / *be at the ~ (of)* 到(…的)尽头, 达(…的)限度 / *begin* (或 *start*) *at the wrong ~* 方法不对头地试干(某事); 开始就错 / *be on the receiving ~* [口] ① 接受别人的礼物(或好意) ② 成为攻击目标 ③【体】是接球的一方 / *bring to an ~* 使结束 / *carry sth. through to the ~* 把某事进行到底 / *come out at* (或 *of*) *the little ~ of the horn* 夸口以后没做到 / *come to an ~* 告终, 结束; 完结 / *come to an untimely ~* 过早死亡, 夭折 / *come to a sticky ~* 落得个不好的下场, 结果不得好死 / *~ for ~* 两端的位置颠倒(或倒转)过来: Turn the table ~ *for ~.* 把桌子转个向。 / *~ in* 以…为结果: ~ in bubbles 终成泡影 / *~ off* 结束: ~ *off* one's talk with a joke 用讲一个笑话结束了谈话 / *~ on* 一端向前地: The two ships collided ~ *on.* 这两条船两端相撞。 / *~ to ~* 头尾相接, 衔接着: put the bricks ~ *to ~* 把砖头排成一长条 / *~ up* ①竖着, 直立着 ②[俚]死 ③结束, 告终 / *from ~ to ~* 从头到尾地: read the article *from ~ to ~* 从头至尾读这文章 / *gain* (或 *achieve, win*) *one's ~(s)* 达到目的 / *get* (或 *have*) *hold of the wrong ~ of the stick* 见 **hold** / *go (in) off the deep ~* ①(游泳时)

投入深水; 冒险; 贸然行事 ② 不必要地十分激动(或惊慌); 发脾气 / *have sth. at one's finger ~s* (或 *fingers' ~s*) 熟练掌握某事, 对某事十分熟练: He has English at his finger ~s. 他英语非常熟练。 / *in the ~* 最后; 终于 / *keep one's ~ up* (或 *keep up one's ~*) (在困难面前)保持愉快和战斗的情绪; 精神饱满地对付 / *make an ~ of* ①终止; 把…结束: *make an ~ of* the trouble 使麻烦的事情结束 ②干掉(人); 除去(物) / *make (both) ~s meet* 使收支相抵, 量入为出; 靠微薄收入为生 / *meet one's ~* 死, 送命 / *most an ~* 见 **most** / *no ~* [口]无餍地; 非常: We enjoyed his kindness no ~. 我们对他的好意感激不尽。 / *be no ~ fine* 好极了 / *no ~ of* 无数, 很多, 非常: be confronted with no ~ of trouble 面临很多麻烦 / *no ~ of a fellow (a fool)* 极好(极傻)的人 / *on ~* ①竖着: put a thing *on ~* 把东西竖着放 / set sb.'s hair *on ~* 使某人毛骨悚然 ②连续地: four hours *on ~* 连续四小时 / *play both ~s against the middle* ①为了有所得而脚踏两头船 ② 使敌对双方相争而从中渔利 / *put an ~ to* 结束, 终止; 废除, 除去 / *step off the deep ~* 见 **step** / *the business ~* (工具、武器等的)使用的一头; 锐利的一头 / *The ~ justifies* (或 *sanctifies*) *the means.* [谚]只要目的正当, 可以不择手段。 / *the ~s of the earth* 最远的地方, 天涯海角 / *the journey's ~* 旅行目的地 / *the short (dirty) ~ of the stick* 不公平的待遇; 不利的环境 / *the supreme ~* 最重要的目的, 最高目的; 至善 / *the thin ~ of the wedge* 得寸进尺的开端; 可能有重大后果的小事 / *the world's ~* 见 **world** / *the wrong ~ of the stick* 见 **stick** / *think no ~ of* 极端看重(人或事物) / *to the (bitter* 或 *very) ~* 到底, 直到死: fight *to the ~* 战斗到底 / *to the ~ of the chapter* 到最后, 到底; 至死 / *to the ~ of time* 永远 / *to the ~ that . . .* 为…起见, 以便: criticize sb.'s mistakes *to the ~ that* they may not be repeated 批评别人的错误以免重犯 / *without ~* 无尽的, 无穷的 / *world without ~* 永远, 永久 ‖*'~-'all n.* 结尾, 终结; 最终目标 / *~ ga(u)ge* 【机】端(面)规(块) / *~ man* ①在一排末端的人 ②(专门化装演黑人戏的剧团在演出时)站在一排演员的末端与对话者作巧辩的演员 / *'~-,paper n.* 衬页(书籍卷首和卷尾的空白页) / *'~ point* 终点 / *product* 最后产物; 最终结果 / *'~-'result n.* 最终结果; 归宿 / *~ run* [美] ① (橄榄球中)在自己一端抱球向左或右兜圈前冲的动作 ② 规避的伎俩 / *~ table* (放在沙发旁的)茶几

endanger [in'deindʒǝ] *vt.* 危害, 危及, 使遭到危险: ~ sb.'s life (property, reputation, security) 危及某人的生命(财产, 名誉, 安全) ‖**~ment** *n.*

endear [in'diǝ] *vt.* 使受喜爱, 使受钟爱: ~ *oneself to* one's friends 使自己为朋友们喜爱 ‖**~ment** *n.* 亲爱; 亲爱的表示, 爱抚: a term of ~ment 表示亲爱的称呼

endearing [in'diəriŋ] *a.* 可亲可爱的, 惹人喜爱的: ～ qualities 讨人喜欢的品质 ‖～ly *ad.*

endeavo(u)r [in'devə] **I** *n.* 努力, 尽力 **II** *vi.* 努力, 尽力, 力图: ～ to compose oneself 努力使自己镇定下来 ‖*do one's* ～(*s*) 尽力, 竭力 / *make every* ～ 尽一切努力 / *make one's best* ～*s* 尽最大努力

endemic [en'demik] **I** *a.* ①某地(或某种人)特有的 ②(疾病等)地方性的 ③(动、植物)某地特产的 **II** *n.* 地方性流行病 ‖～ally *ad.*

ending ['endiŋ] *n.* ①结尾; 结局 ②死亡 ③【语】词尾

endless ['endlis] *a.* ①无止境的, 无穷的 ②太长久的, 没完的: an ～ speech 冗长的讲话 ③两端接连的, 环状的: an ～ chain (自行车等的)循环链 ‖～ly *ad.* / ～ness *n.*

endorse [in'dɔ:s] *vt.* ①【商】在(支票等)背面签名, 背书; 签署(姓名); 签名表示收到(若干款项) ②签(注); 批注(公文等): have one's licence ～d [英](驾驶员等)执照被注上违章记录 ③赞同; 认可: 担保: The application was ～d by the committee. 申请书已由委员会批准。‖～ *over* 【商】背书…转让权利: ～ *over* a bill to another person 背书票据把权利转让给别人

endorsement [in'dɔ:smənt] *n.* ①背书; 签名; 签注; 赞同; 认可; 保证: ～ in blank 无记名式背书 / ～ in full 记名背书 ②保险单上所加的变更保险范围的条款

endow [in'dau] *vt.* ①捐赠基金给(人、组织等), 资助 ②赋予(*with*): be ～ed *with* courage (ability, power, the spirit of sacrifice) 有勇气(能力, 力量, 牺牲精神)

endowment [in'daumənt] *n.* ①捐赠; 捐款; 捐赠的基金: an ～ fund 捐赠的基金 / ～ insurance 人寿定期保险 ②才能, 天资: men of great ～*s* 很有才能的人们

endurance [in'djuərəns] *n.* ①忍耐, 耐劳, 忍耐力: beyond (或 past) ～ 忍无可忍的(地) ②持久(力), 耐久(性): cold ～ 耐寒性 / ～ flight 【空】持久飞行 / ～ limit 【机】疲劳极限 / an ～ test 耐久试验

endure [in'djuə] ❶ *vt.* ①忍受, 耐: ～ pain (suffering, hardship, cold) 忍受痛苦(苦难, 艰苦, 寒冷) ②[常与 cannot 等否定词语连用] 容忍: I *can't* ～ his unreasonable action. 我不能容忍他的无理行为。❷ *vi.* ①忍受, 忍耐: ～ to the end 忍耐到底 ②持久, 持续

enduring [in'djuəriŋ] *a.* 持久的; 不朽的 ‖～ly *ad.*

endways ['endweiz], **endwise** ['endwaiz] *ad.* ①末端向前地 ②末端朝上地; 竖着 ③两端接地 ④向着两端 ⑤在末端

enemy ['enimi] **I** *n.* ①敌人, 仇敌, 仇人: a public ～ (社会或国家的)公敌; (公众协助查缉的)要犯 ②[集合名词]敌兵, 敌军 ③ 敌国; 敌舰; 敌机 ④[喻]大敌; 危害物, 大害: Conceit is the ～ *of*

(或 *to*) progress. 骄傲自大是进步的大敌。/ be one's own ～ 害自己 **II** *a.* 敌人的; 敌方的: an ～ plane (ship) 敌机(舰) / an ～ agent 敌特 ‖*an* ～ *worthy of sb.'s steel* (值得某人与之一斗的)劲敌, 强敌 / *How goes the* ～? 现在是几点钟? / *our ghostly* ～ 恶魔 ‖▲ **alien** 敌国人(指两国交战时居住或被拘留在一交战国的敌国公民), 敌侨

energetic [,enə'dʒetik] *a.* 有力的; 精力旺盛的; 精神饱满的: conduct an ～ struggle against 对…进行有力的斗争 / The more he worked, the more ～ he became. 他越干越有劲。‖～ally *ad.*

energy ['enədʒi] *n.* ①活力, 劲; (语言、文笔等)生动: What he writes is full of ～. 他写的文章生气勃勃。②[复]精力, 能力 ③【物】能, 能量: atomic ～ 原子能 / kinetic ～ 动能 / potential (或 latent) ～ 势能 / conservation of ～ 能量守恒, 能量不灭/～ sources(或 the sources of ～) 能源 / an ～ crisis 能源危机

enervate **I** ['enə:veit] *vt.* 使衰弱, 削弱: an ～d style 软弱无力的文体 **II** *a.* 无力的, 衰弱的 ‖**enervation** [,enə:'veiʃən] *n.*

enfeeble [in'fi:bl] *vt.* 使衰弱 ‖～ment *n.*

enfold [in'fould] *vt.* ①包, 把…包进 (*in, with*) ②拥抱 ③折迭

enforce [in'fɔ:s] *vt.* ①实施, 执行: ～ discipline 执行纪律 ②强制, 强迫: ～ obedience to an order 强迫服从命令 / ～ obedience *upon* (或 on, from) sb. 强迫某人服从 ③加强; 坚持, 主张等): ～ an argument by analogies 用种种比方来加强论点 / ～ a demand 坚持要求 ‖▲**able** *a.* 可实施的; 可行的 / ～dly [in'fɔ:sidli] *ad.* / ～ment *n.* 实施, 执行; 厉行; 强迫: the strict ～ment of a new law 新法律的严格执行 / a law ～ment agency (officer) 执法机构(官吏) / ～r *n.* ①实施(或强制等)者 ② 流氓集团内为维护黑纪律而设的执法人

enfranchise [in'fræntʃaiz] *vt.* ①给与…公民权(或选举权) ②给(城、镇等)以政治权利(在英国指选派议员) ③释放(奴隶等) ‖～ment *n.*

engage [in'geidʒ] ❶ *vt.* ①[常用被动语态] 使从事于(*in*);使忙着: The line is ～d.(电话)线没空。②[～ oneself 或用被动语态]约束, 使订婚 (*to*): She ～*s herself* to do the work. 她自愿承担这项工作。/ I was otherwise ～d that evening. 那天晚上我另外有约(或有事)。/ Tom is ～d to Anne. 汤姆已与安妮订婚。③保证: Can you ～ *that* ...? 你能担保…吗? ④雇用, 聘; 预定(铺位等): ～ a nurse 雇一保姆 / ～ sb. as technical adviser 聘某人为技术顾问 / ～ a hotel room 预定旅馆房间 ⑤使参加, 使卷在其中; 与…交战: We tried to ～ him in conversation, but in vain. 我们设法使他跟我们谈话, 但没成功。/ ～ the enemy fleet 与敌人舰队交战 ⑥吸引住(注意力等) ⑦占去(时间等): Reading ～*s* all my

spare time.　阅读占去了我所有的空余时间。⑧
【机】使(齿轮等)接合,啮合　⑨【建】使(柱)附墙:
an ~d column 附墙柱,半身柱　❷ vi. ①应允;
保证: That's all I can ~ for.　我所能担保的
仅此而已。②从事于,参加 (in) ③交战 (with) ④
【机】接合,啮合

engagement [in'geidʒmənt] n. ①约束;保证;婚
约,订婚: enter into an ~ with 与…订约 /
fulfil (break) one's ~ 践(毁)约 / an ~ ring 订婚
戒指　②约会;约定: a previous ~ 前约,预先的
约会 / He has a speaking ~ for next week.
有人约他下星期去做报告。③ 交战,(打)仗: a
meeting ~ 遭遇战 / a minor ~ 小规模交火 /
fight several ~s 打几仗 ④【常用复】【商】(金钱)
债务: meet one's ~s 还债 ⑤雇用;雇用期 ⑥
【机】(齿轮等)的接合,啮合

engaging [in'geidʒiŋ] a. 有吸引力的,迷人的;可爱
的: an ~ manner 吸引人的风度 ||~ly ad.

engender [in'dʒendə] ❶ vt. 产生;造成;引起:
~ tension (respect, a response) 引起紧张(尊敬,
反应) ❷ vi. 发生;(逐渐)形成

engine ['endʒin] I n. ①引擎,发动机: a jet ~ 喷
气发动机 / a gasoline ~ 汽油机 / a steam ~
蒸汽机　②机车,火车头　③机械,工具,器械: a
fire ~ 灭火机;救火车 / a dental ~ 钻牙机 / an
~ of warfare 兵器,武器 / an ~ of torture 刑
具　④【古】方法,手段 II vt. 在…上安装发动机
||~ **driver** [英]火车司机 / ~ **lathe** 普通车床 /
~ **room** 发动机房;轮机舱

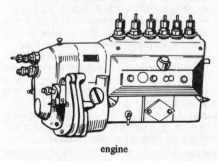

engine

engineer [ˌendʒi'niə] I n. ①工程师;技师: a civil
~ 土木工程师 ②火车司机;轮机员: a locomotive
~ 火车司机 / a first ~ 大管轮,二轨(俗称)
③轮机制造人　④精明的管理员　⑤【军】工兵: a
corps of ~s 工兵部队 II vt. ①设计;建造;监
督…的施工: ~ a bridge 设计桥梁 ②指导,操
纵,管理: ~ a campaign 指导运动 ③策划:
~ an incident 制造事故(或事变) ||~**ship** n. 工
程师职务(或地位)

engineering [ˌendʒi'niəriŋ] n. ①工程,工程学:
civil (electrical, mechanical, mining) ~ 土木(电
机,机械,采矿)工程 / a key ~ project 关键工
程 / ~ geology 工程地质 / ~ science 技术科

学 / the Engineering Corps 工兵部队 ②操纵,
管理 ||**Nature's** ~ 天工

English ['iŋgliʃ] I a. ①英格兰的 ②英国的;英语
的: ~ history 英国史 / the ~ language 英语
II n. ①英语: Old (Middle, Modern) ~ 古代
(中世纪,近代)英语(分别指公元五世纪至约一一
五〇年间、约一一五〇年至一五〇〇年间及一五
〇〇年以来的英语) / the Queen's (或 King's)
~ (英国"上流社会"所谓的)标准英语 / current
(或 present-day) ~ 当代英语 / American ~ 美
国英语,美国语 / spoken ~ 英语口语 / He speaks
correct ~. 他说一口正确的英语。② [the ~]
[总称]英吉利人,英国人 III vt. ①把…译成英语
② [e-] 使(球)旋转 ||~ **as she is spoke** 英语口
语;英语语音 / **in plain** ~ 用浅显的英语;直率
地说,坦白地说 ||~**er** n. ①英国人 ②翻译英语
的人 / ~**ism** n. ①英国方式;英国人的特点 ②
英国人特有的英语习惯用法 / ~ **Channel** 英吉
利海峡 / ~ **horn** (管乐器)英国管 / ~ **man**
['iŋgliʃmən] n. ①英吉利人,英国人;英国男子
② 英国船只 / ~ **sonnet** 英国十四行诗(由三
节四行诗与两行对句组成的诗) / ~**woman**
['iŋgliʃwumən] n. 英国女人

engrave [in'greiv] vt. ①雕上,刻上: ~ a design
on a metal plate 在金属板上刻上图案 ②在(石、
木等)上雕刻 ③铭记,牢记(在心头): be ~d upon
(或 upon) sb.'s memory 在某人记忆中留下深刻
印象 / be ~d in sb.'s heart 被铭刻在某人的心上
④ 镂(版);用镂版印;照相制(版) ||~**r** n. 雕刻
师,雕刻工人;镂版工人

engraving [in'greiviŋ] n. ①雕刻;雕刻术 ②雕版;
图版;版画;雕版印刷品

engross [in'grous] vt. ①用大字体书写(正式文
件等) ②正式写成(议案,决议,条约等) ③(以垄
断方式)大量(或全部)收买;独占: ~ the conversation 只管自己讲(不让别人开口) ④占用(精力);
吸引(注意);使全神贯注: be ~ed in thought
深思着 ||~**ing** a. 引人入胜的;很有趣味的;非
常引人注意的: an ~ing story 引人入胜的故事 /
~**ment** n.

engulf [in'gʌlf] vt. ①吞没;席卷 ②狼吞虎咽;
吞食

enhance [in'hɑ:ns] vt. ①提高,增加(价值,吸引力
等);增强,增进: ~ combat readiness 加强战斗准
备 ②提高…的价值;美化 ||~**ment** n.

enigma [i'nigmə] n. ①谜;暧昧不明的话(或文章)
②不可思议的人(或物)

enjoin [in'dʒɔin] vt. ①嘱咐,责成,命令: ~ a duty
on sb. 命令某人一项责任 / ~ sb. to obey the
rules 命令某人遵守规则 / ~ that sth. (should)
be done 责成完成某事 ②[主美]禁止: ~ sth.
禁止某事 / ~ sb. from doing sth. 禁止某人干
某事

enjoy [in'dʒɔi] vt. ①享受,享有(利益,权利,声誉
等): ~ free medical care 享受公费医疗 /
~ prestige 享有威望 ②享受…的乐趣;欣赏;喜

爱 ‖~ *oneself* 过得快活

enjoyable [in'dʒɔiəbl] *a.* 愉快的;快乐的;有趣的 ‖**enjoyably** *ad.*

enjoyment [in'dʒɔimənt] *n.* ①享受;享有: We are in the ~ of a happy life. 我们享受着幸福的生活。 ②享乐;欢乐;愉快: take ~ in music 欣赏音乐 ③乐趣;乐事

enlarge [in'la:dʒ] ❶ *vt.* ①扩大,扩展(胸襟、思想等): an ~d edition 增订版 / an ~d meeting 扩大会议 ②放大(照片) ③[美]释放 ❷ *vi.* ①扩大 ②详述 (*on, upon*): ~ *on* (或 *upon*) one's opinions 详述己见 ‖~**r** *n.*【摄】放大机

enlargement [in'la:dʒmənt] *n.* ①扩大;扩展: the ~ of one's mind 胸襟的开扩 ②增补物;扩建部分: The index is an ~ to the book. 索引是这本书的附录。 / an ~ to (或 *on*) a building 大厦的扩建部分 ③(照相的)放大;放大的照片 ④【医】增大,肥大,肿大: the ~ of the liver 肝肿

enlighten [in'laitn] *vt.* ①启发,开导;教导: ~ sb. *on* sth. 就某事对某人作启发 ②使摆脱偏见(或迷信): Listen to both sides and you will be ~ed. 兼听则明。③[古]照耀,照明 ‖~**ed** *a.* 开明的,进步的,有知识的: the ~ed gentry 开明士绅 / an ~ed judgement 有见识的判断 / ~**ing** *a.* ①有启发作用的;使人领悟的 ②[古]照耀的,照明的 / ~**ment** *n.* 启蒙,启发: the *Enlightenment* (尤指十八世纪欧洲的)启蒙运动 / the Age of *Enlightenment* 启蒙时代

enlist [in'list] ❶ *vt.* ①征募,使服兵役: ~ men *for* the air force 征召空军 ②谋取;赢取(或支持);罗致;谋取(赞助、支持等): ~ the help (support) of sb. 谋取某人的赞助(支持) / ~ sb. *in* a cause 在某事业中谋取某人的赞助 ❷ *vi.* ①入伍,应募: ~ *as* a volunteer 入伍当志愿兵 / ~ *for* military service 入伍服兵役 / ~ *in* the army 参军 ②赞助,支持,加入 ‖~**ed** *a.* 应募入伍的: an ~ed man [美]士兵 / ~**ment** *n.* ①征募;应募入伍 ②服(兵)役期

enliven [in'laivn] *vt.* ①使有生气,使活跃 ②使快活

enmesh [in'meʃ] *vt.* ①网捕,使陷入网中 ②绊缠住 ‖~**ment** *n.*

enmity ['enmiti] *n.* 敌意,仇恨;不和,敌对: be at ~ with 与…不和 / have an ~ against 对…有敌意

ennoble [i'noubl] *vt.* ①封…为贵族 ②使崇高 ‖~**ment** *n.*

ennui [ɑ:'nwi:] *n.* 厌倦;无聊

enormity [i'nɔ:miti] *n.* ①穷凶极恶: the ~ of the crime 罪大恶极 ②无法无天的行为 ③巨大,庞大

enormous [i'nɔ:məs] *a.* ①巨大的,庞大的 ②[古]极恶的,凶暴的 ‖~**ly** *ad.*

enough [i'nʌf] I *a.* 足够的,充足的: have ~ time (或 time ~) *to* do the work 有足够时间做这件工作 / be fool ~ *to* try it 蠢到竟想试做这件

事 II *n.* 足够,充分: We have ~ *to* do to finish the job on time. 要准时完成这件事,我们得使大大努力。/ I have had ~ *of* him. 他那一套我已受够了。/ You have done *more than* ~. 你已做得太多了。III *ad.* ①足够地,充分地: It is light ~ *to* read. 看书光线还是够亮的。/ The egg isn't boiled ~. 蛋没有煮透。/ This book is easy ~ *for* me to read. 这本书很容易,我足可读懂。/ Be good (或 kind) ~ *to* reply early. 请早日答复。②十分: He is always ready ~ *to* help us. 他总是很自愿帮助我们的。③相当地,尚: This coat is good ~. 这件外衣还好。IV *int.* 够了: *Enough!* 够了! (或:别再说了!) ‖**cry** "~" 认输,服输 / ~ **and to spare** 绰绰有余: There is room ~ *and to spare* for another ten people in the bus. 这辆公共汽车即使再上十个人,也不会怎么挤的。/ *Enough is as good as a feast.* [谚]足食犹如筵席。(或:不过分就是好,知足则常乐。) / **not** ~ **to swear by** 仅仅一点点 / **oddly** (或 **strangely, curiously**) ~ [用作插入语]说也奇怪,够奇怪的 / **sure** ~ [用作插入语]无疑,果真,确实 / **well** ~ ①[常贬]还好,还可以: He swims *well* ~. 他游泳游得还好。②很,相当: You know *well* ~ what I mean. 你当然懂得我的意思啦。

enquire [in'kwaiə] *vi. & vt.* =inquire

enrage [in'reidʒ] *vt.* 激怒: be ~d at (或 *by*) sb.'s conduct 对某人的行为极为愤怒 / be ~d with sb. 对某人勃然大怒

enrapture [in'ræptʃə] *vt.* 使狂喜

enrich [in'ritʃ] *vt.* ①使富裕 ②使丰富: ~ the power of expression 丰富表达力 / ~ one's experience *with* practice 通过实践来丰富经验 ③使(土壤)肥沃 ④装饰,增美 ⑤加料于,增进(食品)的营养价值(或滋味) ⑥浓缩: an ~ed mixture 浓缩混合物 / ~ed uranium【原】浓缩铀 ‖~**ment** *n.* ①发财致富;丰富;加肥;增添装饰 ②浓缩,加浓 ③【矿】富集

enrol(l) [in'roul] (enrolled; enrolling) ❶ *vt.* ①登记,把…编入;招收 ②使入伍;使入会;使入学: ~ *oneself in* the army 参军 / ~ sb. *as* a member of 吸收某人为…会员 ③卷,包 ④最后誊清(议会通过的议案) ❷ *vi.* 登记;成为会员 ‖**enrollee** [in,rou'li:] *n.* 被征入伍者;入学者;入会者 / ~**ment** *n.* ①登记,注册;入伍,入会,入学 ②注册人数;入学人数: a school with an ~*ment* of 500 students 一所有五百人注册入学的学校

ensign ['ensain] *n.* ①旗;军旗,团旗,军舰旗: a national ~ 表示国籍的旗 / the blue ~ 英国海军预备舰队旗 / the red ~ 英国商船旗 / the white ~ 英国皇家海军旗 ②(表示职位、等级、权力等的)徽章,标志 ③(美)海军少尉

enslave [in'sleiv] *vt.* ①使做奴隶,奴役 ②征服,制服;使受制 (*to*): be ~d *to* a bad habit 改不掉坏习惯 ‖~**ment** *n.* 奴役;束缚

ensue [in'sju:] ❶ *vi.* ①接着发生; 接着而来: A warm debate ~*d.* 接着是一场热烈的辩论。/ the ensuing year 下一年 / the months *ensuing* 以后几个月 ②结果产生, 结果是: What will ~ *from* (或 *on*) such an action? 这种行动会产生什么结果呢? ❷ *vt.* (基督教《圣经》用语)追求

ensure [in'ʃuə] *vt.* ①保证, 担保: ~ success (safety, supplies) 保证成功(安全,供应) / We can ~ *that* the work shall be done in the right way. 我们可以保证把工作做好。②保护, 使安全: ~ sb. *against* (或 *from*) danger 保护某人免受危险 ③保证给, 赋予 (*to, for*): This provision ~*s to* (或 *for*) us a voice in the matter. 这个规定使我们对这件事有发言权。

entail [in'teil] **I** *vt.* ①必需; 使承担: The work ~*s* precision. 这工作需要精确性。/ great expense *on* sb. 使某人承担一笔费用 ②把(疾病等)遗传给; 把…遗留给 (*on, upon*) ③【律】限定(地产等)的继承人; 把(某物)永远赠送 (*on*) **II** *n.* ①【律】(地产等的)限定继承权; 限定继承人的地产 ②(品质、信仰等的)不可动摇的继承; 永远继承的事物 ‖*dock the* ~ 【律】撤销限定继承权 ‖~**ment** *n.*

entangle [in'tæŋgl] *vt.* ①缠住, 套住; 使纠缠; 使混乱: The birds got ~*d* in the nets. 鸟被网缠住了。/ The ropes were ~*d.* 绳子缠在一起了。/ an ~*d* affair 纠缠不清的事情 ②使卷入; 使陷入; 牵连, 连累: get ~*d with* sb. 与某人有牵连 ‖~**ment** *n.* ①纠缠; 纠纷; 牵连 ②缠住物, 纠缠物; 障碍物: barbed wire ~*ments* 带刺的铁丝网

enter ['entə] ❶ *vt.* ①进, 入: ~ a house 走进房屋 / Rivers ~ the sea. 江河流入海洋。/ ~ a spare-time school 进业余学校 / A new idea ~*ed* his mind. 他想出了一个新主意。/ A bullet ~*ed* his body. 枪弹穿入他的身体。②把…放入: ~ a key in the door 把钥匙插进门里 ③加入, 参加: ~ the army 参军 / ~ a war 参战 / ~ a discussion 参加讨论 ④使进入; 使加入; 使参加; 报(名)参加: ~ a baby *at* a nursery 把孩子送进托儿所 / ~ oneself *for* a philosophy study group 参加哲学学习小组 / ~ a horse *in* a race 使马参加比赛 / ~ one's name *for* a contest 报名参加比赛 ⑤把…记上; 登录; (书面)提出: ~ an item in an account 把一笔帐记入帐户 / ~ up an account (a ledger) 把一批帐目登入帐户(帐簿) / ~ a book in a catalog(ue) 把书登入图书目录 / ~ a protest 提出抗议 ‖提出抗议(会议等的)记录; 提出抗议 / ~ a bid 投标 ⑥开始从事; 开始进入; 开始研讨: ~ a profession 开始从事某一职业 ⑦【律】在法庭上正式提出 ⑧把(船或货)申报海关 ⑨占有(土地)⑩使(马、狗等)首次上场(或出猎); 训练(马、狗等) ❷ *vi.* ①入; 进去; 进来;【戏】登场, 上场, 上: Knock on the door before you ~. 进入之前先敲门。/ *Enter*, please. 请进来。②参加

③刺进去, 穿进去: The bayonet ~*ed* deep. 一刺刀戳得很深。‖~ *an appearance* 见 *appearance* / ~ *into* 进入; 参加; 受…约束; 开始从事: ~ *into* combat readiness 进入战备状态 / ~ *into* conversation 开始谈话 / ~ *into* business 开始经商 / ~ *into* society 参加社交 ②成为…的一部分: ~ *into* the composition of 成为…的组成部分 / Flour has largely ~*ed into* their diet. 面粉已成为他们的主食之一。/ A tone of menace ~*ed into* his voice. 他的声音带上威胁的口气。③讨论, 研讨: We'll ~ *into* details next time. 关于细节问题我们下次再讨论。/ We had barely ~*ed into* the matter when he came in. 我们刚开始讨论此事, 他就进来了。④体谅, 分享(感情等): ~ *into* sb.'s views 同意某人的意见 / ~ *upon* (或 *on*) 开始; 着手: ~ *upon* one's new duties 开始担任新职 / The book is ~*ing upon* its third edition. 这书正在出第三版。②开始研讨: ~ *upon* a question 开始讨论问题 ③占有(土地、财产等) ‖~**able** ['entərəbl] *a.* 可进入的; 可参加的

enterprise ['entəpraiz] *n.* ①(艰巨、复杂或冒险的)事业, 计划; 事业单位, 企业单位: undertake (或 build) an ~ 创办事业 ②办企业; 干事业: free ~ (企业的)自由经营 ③事业心, 进取心; 冒险精神, 胆量: a man of ~ 有事业进取心的人 ‖~**r** *n.* 干事业的人; 企业家; 创业者

enterprising ['entəpraiziŋ] *a.* 有事业心的, 有进取心的; 有魄力的, 有胆量的 ‖~**ly** *ad.*

entertain [,entə'tein] ❶ *vt.* ①招待, 款待: ~ friends *at* (或[英] *to*) dinner 请朋友们吃饭 / ~ guests *with* refreshments 以茶点招待客人 ②使欢乐, 使娱乐 ③抱着, 怀着; 持有(信心、意见等): ~ hopes 抱着希望 / ~ doubts 心中存有怀疑 ④容纳, 接受, 准备考虑: ~ a proposal 准备考虑一个建议 ❷ *vi.* 款待, 请客 ‖~**er** *n.* ①款待者 ②供人娱乐者; 表演者

entertaining [,entə'teiniŋ] **I** *a.* 有趣的, 使人娱乐的: an ~ tale 引人入胜的故事 **II** *n.* 招待, 款待 ‖~**ly** *ad.*

entertainment [,entə'teinmənt] *n.* ①招待, 款待; 招待会: give a farewell ~ to sb. 为某人举行送行 / give an ~ to sb. 招待某人 / the ~ of a guest 对于宾客的招待 ②娱乐物; 乐趣, 欢乐: This is a serious novel, not an ~. 这是一本严肃的小说, 不是供消遣的。/ find ~ *in* 以…为乐 ③表演会, 文娱节目 ④抱有, 怀有(指希望、怀疑等) ⑤(对建议等的)采纳 ‖~ *tax* 娱乐税

enthral(l) [in'θrɔ:l] (enthralled; enthralling) *vt.* ①迷住, 吸引住 ②使做奴隶, 奴役 ‖**enthralling** *a.* 迷人的; 吸引人的 / ~**ment** *n.*

enthrone [in'θroun] *vt.* ①使(国王、主教等)登位, 立…为王(或主教等); 使占最高地位 ②[喻]推崇, 崇拜 ‖~**ment** *n.*

enthusiasm [in'θju:ziæzəm] *n.* ①热情; 热心; 热忱; 积极性: an outburst of ~ 热情奔放 / The performance moved the audience to ~. 演出使观众极为感动。/ ~ for labour 劳动积极性 ②激发热情的事物；热心研究的对象：Astronomy is his ~. 天文学是他热心研究的学科。③[古]宗教狂；神秘的灵感 ‖**enthusiast** [in'θju:ziæst] *n.* 热心人，热情者；热中者：an *enthusiast about* public health 热心于公共卫生的人 / an *enthusiast for* table tennis 爱打乒乓球的人（或爱看乒乓比赛的人）/ a chess *enthusiast* 棋迷

enthusiastic [in,θju:zi'æstik] *a.* 热情的，热心的，热烈的：~ support 热情的支持 / be ~ *about*（或 *for*）sth. 对某事热心 / an ~ discussion 热烈的讨论 ‖**ally** *ad.*

entice [in'tais] *vt.* 诱惑，怂恿：~ sb. *to do*（或 *into doing*）sth. 诱使某人去做某事 ‖**～ment** *n.*

entire [in'taiə] **I** *a.* ①完全的，整个的；全部的，完整的：enjoy sb.'s ~ confidence 得到某人的完全信任 ②纯粹的 ③【植】全缘的：~ leaf 全缘叶 ④（马等）未经阉割的 **II** *n.* ①全部，整体 ②种马 ‖**-ly** *ad.* 完全地；彻底地 / **～ness** *n.*

entitle [in'taitl] *vt.* ①给（书、文章等）题名；给…称号（或尊称）：The editorial is ~d "...". 这篇社论的题目是《…》。/ be ~d "Your Excellency" 被尊称为"阁下" ②给…权利（或资格）：~ sb. to do sth. 给某人做某事的权利 / be ~d to high praise 值得高度赞扬 ‖**～ment** *n.* 权利

entity ['entiti] *n.* ①存在，实体；统一体：the opposites of a single ~ 一个统一体中的对立面 / The whole country is a single ~. 全国一盘棋。②（与属性等区别的）本质

entomology [,entə'mɔlədʒi] *n.* 昆虫学

entrails ['entreilz] [复] *n.* ①内脏；肠 ②（物体的）内部

entrain[1] [in'trein] ❶ *vt.* 使上火车：~ the party and their luggage 使一行人和他们的行李上火车 ❷ *vi.* 上火车（动身）

entrain[2] [in'trein] *vt.* ①拖，拽；带走（人或物）②产生，导致：This invention ~s changes in several branches of science. 这个发明给好几个科学部门带来了变化。③【化】带走；使（空气）以气泡状存在于混凝土中：~ed oil 带走的油 ‖**-er** *n.*【化】夹带剂

entrance[1] ['entrəns] *n.* ①进入：make（或 effect）one's ~ 进入 / allow free ~ to 允许自由进入… / force an ~ into 闯进… ②入口，进口，门口：the ~ to the building (city, harbour) 大厦（城市，海港）的入口 / the front (back) ~ 前(后)门 ③入场；入会；入学；入港，入场权（或费）：~ free 免费入场 / an ~ examination 入学考试 / an ~ channel 进口航道 / No ~. (车辆等)不准入内。/ the ~ fee 入会（或入学）费 ④开始，着手 ⑤就任：~ *into*（或 *upon*）(one's) office 就职 ⑥（演员的）登场；(合唱或合奏中歌声或乐器的)起点 ⑦【海】（水线下）船首尖部

entrance[2] [in'tra:ns] *vt.* 使出神；使神志恍惚；使狂喜；使入迷：be ~d in thought 想得出神 /

stand ~d at the grand sight 站着出神地看着壮丽的景象 / be ~d with fear 吓得魂不附体 / be ~d with the performance 完全被演出吸引住了 ‖**～ment** *n.*

entrancing [in'tra:nsiŋ] *a.* 令人出神的；令人神志恍惚的；使人喜悦的；迷人的 ‖**～ly** *ad.*

entrant ['entrənt] *n.* ①进入者 ②新加入者，新会员，新学员；刚就业者 ③参加竞赛者：~s for a race (competition) 参加赛跑(竞赛)者

entreat [in'tri:t] ❶ *vt.* ①恳求，请求：~ sb. to do sth. 恳求某人做某事 / a favo(u)r of sb. 向某人求情 ②[古] 对待，对付 ❷ *vi.* 恳求 ‖**～ingly** *ad.* 恳求地，哀求地 / **～ment** *n.*

entreaty [in'tri:ti] *n.* 恳求，请求：a look of ~ 恳求的神情 / listen to sb.'s *entreaties* 倾听某人的恳求

entrench [in'trentʃ] ❶ *vt.* ①用壕沟围，用壕沟防御；置…于壕沟中：The troops were ~ed near the hill. 部队在山边以壕沟防卫自己。②掘，深挖(尤指壕沟) ③牢固地树立；使处于牢固地位；使盘踞：the position *in* which one is ~ed 牢固地占有的地位 / ~ oneself *in* a place 扎根于一个地方 ❷ *vi.* ①掘壕；占据壕沟 ②侵占，侵犯(*on*, *upon*) ‖**～ment** *n.* ①掘壕沟 ②堑壕；堡垒，防御设施

entrust [in'trʌst] *vt.* 委托，信托；托管(物件等)：~ power *to* sb. 把权力委托给某人 / ~ sb. *with* a task 把任务交给某人 / ~ one's books *to* sb. while one is away 离开(某处)时托某人代管书籍 ‖**～ment** *n.*

entry ['entri] *n.* ①进入；入场(权)；入场(或入城等)典礼；入会权：obtain ~ 得到入场(或入会等)权 ②入口；门口；河口；通道 ③登记，记载；条目，项目；词条；帐目：make an ~ in a journal (list) 记入日记帐(名单)中 / a vocabulary ~ 词条 / a dictionary ~ 词典的词目 / pass ~ 转帐 / bookkeeping by single (double) ~ 单(复)式簿记 ④参加比赛的人(或物)的名单 ⑤【商】报关手续；报单：an ~ for consumption 进口货物报单 / an ~ for free goods 免税货物报单 ⑥【律】对土地的侵占，对房屋的侵入 ‖**～ word** (章、节、词条、项目中)开头的词

entwine [in'twain] ❶ *vt.* ①使缠绕，使盘绕；[喻] 使纠缠：a pillar ~d *with* ivy 常春藤缠绕的柱子 / ~ ivy *round*（或 *about*）a pillar 使常春藤缠绕柱子 ②拥抱 ❷ *vi.* 缠绕；纠缠

enumerate [i'nju:məreit] *vt.* ①数，点：We found more people than we could ~. 我们见到数不清的人。/ The census ~s persons over eighty years old. 根据人口调查共有…个八十岁以上的人。②列举，枚举：~ the items on a list 列举表上项目 ‖**enumeration** [i,nju:mə'reiʃən] *n.* 计数；列举；细目；详表：defy *enumeration* 不胜枚举 / the *enumeration* method 查点法 / **enumerative** [i'nju:mərətiv] *a.* 点数的；列举的

enunciate [i'nʌnsieit] ❶ *vt.* ①确切地说明，阐明

(理论、原则等) ②宣布, 发表: ~ the aims of a programme 宣布方案的目的 ③(清晰地)发…的音 ❷ vi. (清晰地)发音 ‖**enunciation** [i,nʌnsi'eiʃən] n. ①阐明 ②发表; 宣告, 公告 ③清晰的发音 / **enunciative** [i'nʌnʃiətiv] a. ①阐明的; 宣告的 ②发音清晰的 / **enunciator** n. ①阐明者; 宣告者 ②发音清晰的人

envelop [in'veləp] I vt. ①包, 裹; 封: be ~ed in a shawl (blanket) 用围巾(毯子)裹住 ②围绕; 包围: The peak was ~ed in clouds. 峰顶被云遮蔽。/ be ~ed in mystery 神秘莫测 II n. =envelope ‖**~ment** n. ①包, 裹; 封 ②封皮, 封套 ③包围: close ~ment 近距离包围

envelope ['enviloup] n. ①包裹物; 封皮, 封套; 信封 ②壳层, 外壳 ③(气艇、气球等的)气囊; 蒙皮: an airship hull ~ 气艇艇身蒙布; 气艇气囊 ④【天】包层; air ~ 大气层 ⑤【数】包迹; 包(络)线 ⑥【生】包膜, 包被

enviable ['enviəbl] a. 值得羡慕的; 引起妒忌的 ‖**~ness** n. / **enviably** ad.

envious ['enviəs] a. 妒忌的; 羡慕的: be ~ of sb.'s success 羡慕(或妒忌)某人的成功 ‖**~ly** ad.

environment [in'vaiərənmənt] n. ①围绕, 周围; 围绕物 ②环境, 四周, 外界: natural ~ 自然环境 / a story of man's struggle with his ~ 人类同环境斗争的故事

envisage [in'vizidʒ] vt. ①正视, 面对: ~ realities 正视现实 ②想象, 设想: reach heights never before ~d by man 达到前人从未想象过的高度 / targets ~d in the programme 计划中设想的指标·/ ~ the international situation 展望国际形势 ‖**~ment** n.

envoy ['envɔi] n. ①使者, 代表; 使节; (全权)公使: diplomatic ~s 外交使节 / a special ~ 特使 / an ~ extraordinary and minister plenipotentiary 特命全权公使 / an imperial ~ 钦差大臣 ②[古](诗、散文、文集的)跋(或献词); (作为结语或献词的)结尾诗节 ‖**~ship** n. 使节身分

envy ['envi] I n. ①妒忌; 羡慕: feel ~ at 对…感到妒忌(或羡慕) / out of ~ 出于妒忌 ②妒忌对象; 羡慕目标: become the ~ of others 成为他人羡慕的目标 II vt. 妒忌; 羡慕: How I ~ you! 我真羡慕你!

epaulet(te) ['epoulet] n. ①【军】肩章 ②(妇女外衣等上的)肩章形饰物 ‖**win one's ~s** (士兵)升为军官

ephemeral [i'femərəl] I a. ①(昆虫等)朝生暮死的, 短命的; (花等)短生的; (疾病)一天即愈的: an ~ plant 短生植物 ②短暂的, 一时的: glory 短暂的荣华 II n. 短命的东西(尤指短生植物) ‖**~ly** ad. ‖**~ fever** (牛)发三日烧的病

epic ['epik] I n. ①史诗, 叙事诗: a national ~ 民族史诗 ②史诗般的文艺作品 ③可写成史诗的事迹(或传说等) II a. ①史诗的, 叙事诗的

②英雄的, 壮丽的; 庄严的: an ~ deed 英雄事迹, 壮举 ③有重大历史(或传奇)意义的 ④特别长的; 宏大的, 大规模的: of ~ proportions 体积惊人地巨大的

epicure ['epikjuə] n. ①讲究饮食的人 ②[古]享乐主义者

epidemic [,epi'demik] I a. 流行性的, 传染的: ~ disease 流行病 / ~ encephalitis 流行性脑炎 II n. ①流行病, 时疫: an ~ preventive worker 防疫员 ②(流行或传)播: an influenza ~ 流行性感冒的传播 ③(风尚等)的流行

epigram ['epigræm] n. ①机智的短诗, 讽刺短诗 ②警句, 警辞语

epigrammatic [,epigrə'mætik] a. 警句(式)的; 讽刺短诗的; 简练的, 机智的 ‖**~ally** ad.

epilepsy ['epilepsi] n. 【医】癫痫, 羊痫疯

epilog(ue) ['epilɔg] n. ①(文艺作品的)结尾部分, 尾声; 后记, 跋 ②[戏]闭幕词, 收场白(常用韵文) ③(英国广播公司某些节目结束时的)宗教仪式

Episcopalian [i,piskə'peiljən] I a. 主教派教会的, 圣公会的 II n. ①主教统治制的鼓吹者 ②主教派教会成员, 圣公会成员

episode ['episoud] n. ①(文艺作品中的)一段情节; (几部曲中的)一部曲; 插曲 ②(一系列事件中的)一个事件 ③【音】插曲, 间调 ④【地】插段 ‖**episodic(al)** [,epi'sɔdik(əl)] a.

epistle [i'pisl] n. ①[the Epistles] (基督教《圣经·新约》中的)使徒书 ②书信(尤指写得很华丽的正式信件) ③书信体诗文

epistolary [i'pistələri] a. ①书信的 ②书信体的: an ~ novel 书信体小说 ③用书信进行的

epitaph ['epitɑ:f] n. ①墓志铭 ②纪念死者(或往事)的诗文 ‖**~ial** [,epi'tæfiəl], **~ic** [,epi'tæfik] a.

epithet ['epiθet] n. ①表示性质、特征的形容词(或名词、短语等) ②称号 ③【动】【植】(一属中的)亚类名称 ‖**~ic(al)** [,epi'θetik(əl)] a. (用)性质形容词的

epitome [i'pitəmi] n. ①梗概, 概括; 节录: This handbook is a neat ~ of everyday hygiene. 这本手册概括了日常卫生的要点。②缩影, 集中体现

epoch ['i:pɔk] n. ①(新)纪元; (新)时代: mark an ~ in science 开辟科学上的新纪元 / an entire historical ~ 整个历史时代 ②值得纪念的事件(或日期) ③【天】历元 ④【地】世: Eocene ~ 始新世 ⑤【电】(信号)出现时间; 恒定相位延迟 ‖**~-,making**, **'~-,marking** a. 划时代的, 开新纪元的: an ~-making (或 ~-marking) event 划时代的大事

equable ['ekwəbl] a. ①平稳的, (相当)稳定的: an ~ temperature 无甚变化的温度 ②平静的: an ~ temper 平静的性情 ‖**equably** ad.

equal ['i:kwəl] I a. ①相等的, 均等的; 相同的: He speaks English and Russian with ~ ease. 他讲英语和俄语同样流利。/ divide sth. into four ~ parts 把某物四等分 / It is ~ to me whether he comes or not. 他来不来对我都一样。②平等的: put sb. on an ~ footing 以平等地位对待某人 ③胜任的, 经得起的 (to); 不相上下的: He is ~ to (doing) this task. 他能胜任这项任务。/ be ~ to any trial 经得起任何考验 / be ~ to anything 事事能干 / I don't feel ~ to a cup of wine just now. 现在我喝不下酒。/ an ~ contest 势均力敌的竞赛 ④合适的 (to): make a quick decision ~ to the occasion 当机立断 ⑤(性情等)平静的; 平稳的: keep an ~ mind 保持平静 / speak in an ~ tone 用平稳的声调讲话 **II** *n.* ①相等的事物(或数量); (地位等)相同的人: Let x be the ~ of y. 设 x 等于 y。/ mix with one's ~s 和同等的人交往 ②匹敌者; 堪与比拟的东西: Is he your ~ in swimming? 他游泳跟你一样好吗? / I never saw its ~. 我从来没见过比这更好的了。**III** (equal(l)ed; equal(l)ing) *vt.* ①等于: Three times three ~s nine. 三乘三等于九。②比得上; 敌得过: Industrial liquid waste, when properly treated, can ~ fertilizers in usefulness. 经过适当处理的工业废液在效用方面抵得上肥料。③完全补偿(或酬报) ④[古]使相等; 使平均 ‖*be the ~ of one's word* 说到做到 / *be without* ~ 无比, 无敌 ‖**~ly** *ad.* 相等地, 相同地; 公平地; 平均地 ‖**opportunity employer** [美]标榜在招工方面不搞肤色、性别、种族歧视的雇主

equality [i(ː)'kwɔliti] *n.* ①同等; 平等, 均等: ~ in quality 质量相同 / racial ~ 种族平等 / ~ between the sexes 男女平等 / the principle of ~ and mutual benefit 平等互利的原则 【数】相等; 等式: the sign of ~ 等号 ‖*be on an ~ with* 与…平等

equalize ['iːkwəlaiz] ❶ *vt.* ①使相等; 使均等, 使平均; 使平等 ②补偿, 补足 ❷ *vi.* 相等; [主英](在比赛中)与对方拉平比分 ‖**equalization** [ˌiːkwəlai'zeiʃən] *n.* 相等; 均等, 平均: *equalization* of landownership 平均地权 / ~**r** *n.* ①使相等者; 使平均者 ②平衡器, 均衡器; 【电】均压线; 【自】补偿器

equanimity [ˌiːkwə'nimiti] *n.* 沉着, 平静, 镇定: bear (regard) sth. with ~ 对某事处之泰然(安之若素)

equate [i'kweit] ❶ *vt.* ①使相等, 使等同 (to, with) ②同等对待 ③【数】表示…相等, 把…作成等式 ❷ *vi.* 等同

equation [i'kweiʃən] *n.* ①(对供应等的)平衡, 均衡; 平均; 相等 ②(个别或综合的)因素 【数】方程(式); 等式: differential ~ 微分方程 ④【化】反应式 ⑤【天】(时)差: ~ of time 时差 / ~ of light 光行时差 ‖*personal* ~ ①【天】人差 ②个人在观察上的误差 ‖**~al** *a.* ①方程式的; 相等的 ②【语】省略谓语动词的

equator [i'kweitə] *n.* ①赤道; 【天】天球赤道: celestial (magnetic) ~ 天球(地磁)赤道 ②(平分球形物体的面的)圆 ③(任何)大圆

equator

equatorial [ˌekwə'tɔːriəl] **I** *a.* 赤道的; 赤道附近的: ~ bulge 赤道隆起带 / ~ low 赤道低压 **II** *n.* 赤道仪 (=~ telescope) ‖**~ly** *ad.*

equerry [i'kweri] *n.* ①马厩总管 ②(英国)王室侍从

equestrian [i'kwestriən] **I** *a.* 马的; 骑马的; 马术的; 骑士的: an ~ statue 骑马者的雕塑像 **II** *n.* 骑马者; 骑手, 马术家

equidistant ['iːkwi'distənt] *a.* ① 等距离的 ②(地图上所有方向的距离)同比例的 ‖**~ly** *ad.*

equilateral ['iːkwi'lætərəl] **I** *a.* ①【数】等边的; 等面的: ~ triangle 等边三角形 / ~ hyperbola 等轴双曲线, 直角双曲线 ②两侧对称的 **II** *n.* 等边形; 等边

equilibrium [ˌiːkwi'libriəm] ([复] equilibria [ˌiːkwi'libriə] 或 equilibriums) *n.* ①平衡, 均衡; 平均; 相称: scales *in* ~ 平衡的天平 / indifferent ~【物】随遇平衡 / ~ constant【化】平衡常数 / the ~ of supply and demand 供求均衡 / the theory of ~【哲】均衡论 ②均势: political ~ 政治均势 ③(心情的)平静 ④(判断上的)不偏不倚

equine ['iːkwain] 【动】 **I** *a.* (似)马的; 马科的 **II** *n.* 马; 马科动物

equinoctial [ˌiːkwi'nɔkʃəl] 【天】 **I** *a.* ①二分点的; 昼夜平分(时)的 ②春分(或秋分)的 ③赤道的 **II** *n.* ① =~ line 二分圈 ② =~ gales 春分(或秋分)时的暴风雨 / ~ **line**, ~ **circle** 天球赤道, 昼夜平分线 / ~ **year** 分至年

equinox ['iːkwinɔks] *n.* 【天】① 昼夜平分时 ②二分点: vernal ~ 春分; 春分点 / autumnal ~ 秋分; 秋分点 / precession of the ~es (分点)岁差

equip [i'kwip] (equipped; equipping) *vt.* 装备, 配备: ~ a ship *for* a voyage 装备船只准备出航 / be *equipped with* modern machines 配备着现代化机械 / ~ oneself *for* (或 to go on) a long journey 为长途旅行准备行装 ②(智力上)准备; 训练: be well *equipped for* a new task 对新任务有充分准备

equipment [i'kwipmənt] *n.* ①装备, 配备; 设备, 器材, 装置: speed up the ~ of a laboratory 加速配备实验室 / a machinery ~ plant 机械装配厂 / military ~s 军事装备 / voice recording ~ 录音设备; 通话记录器 ②铁道车辆; (汽车等)运输配备 ③(一企业除房地产外的)固定资产 ④[总称](智力或感情的)特征; 资质

equitable ['ekwitəbl] *a.* ①公平的, 公正的 ②【律】衡平法的; 衡平法上有效的 ‖**~ness** *n.* / **equitably** *ad.*

equity ['ekwiti] *n.* ①公平, 公道; 公平的事物 ②【律】衡平法; 衡平法上的权利: ~ of redemption 衡平法上关于赎回担保物的权利 ③[英][E-]演员协会 ④(押款金额之外的)财产价值 ⑤[英][复](无固定利息的)股票, 证券 ‖~ **capital** 投资于新企业的资本

equivalence [i'kwivələns], **equivalency** [i'kwivələnsi] *n.* ①(力量等的)均等, 相等; 相当 ②等价, 等值; 等量 ③【化】等价, 化合价相等 ④(语词的)同义; 同类(指同属正确或同属错误等)

equivalent [i'kwivələnt] **I** *a.* ① (在力量等上)相等的, 相当的, 相同的: be ~ *to* 等于, 相当于 ②等价的, 等值的; 等量的; 等效的: ~ focal length 【物】等值焦距 / an ~ circuit 等效电路 ③同意义的 ④【化】等价的: ~ weight 当量 ⑤【数】等面积的, 等体积的: a square ~ *to* a triangle 同三角形等积的正方形 **II** *n.* ①相等物; 等价物, 等值物; 等量物 ②等值; 等量 ③对应词(或语): a Chinese ~ *of* (或 *for*) that word 与那个词相等的汉词 ④【化】当量, 克当量: electrochemical ~ 电化当量 ‖**~ly** *ad.*

equivocal [i'kwivəkəl] *a.* ①多义的, 歧义的; 模棱两可的, 含糊的: an ~ reply 模棱两可的回答 ②暧昧的, 可疑的: ~ behaviour 可疑的行为 ③不明确的, 不肯定的: an ~ outcome 未定的结局 ‖**~ly** *ad.* / **~ness** *n.*

era ['iərə] *n.* ①时代; 年代 ②纪元: before the Christian ~ 公元前 ③阶段;【地】代: Eozoic ~ 始生代

eradicate [i'rædikeit] *vt.* ①连根拔除, 使断根: ~ weeds from a garden 除去园中杂草 ②根除, 消灭, 歼灭: ~ cholera 消灭霍乱 ‖**eradication** [i,rædi'keiʃən] *n.* / **eradicator** *n.* 根除者; 根除器; [复]去墨水液, 褪色灵

erase [i'reiz] *vt.* ①擦掉, 抹掉; 除去; 删去: ~ the pencil marks 擦掉铅笔痕迹 / The recording can be ~d and the tape used again. 录音可以抹去, 磁带可以再用。/ ~ a name *from* a list 从名单上划掉一个名字 ②擦(净), 擦(净): ~ the blackboard 揩黑板 ③消灭; 击毁; [美俚]杀死

eraser [i'reizə] *n.* ①擦除器(如黑板擦、橡皮、挖字刀等): an ink ~ 擦墨水橡皮(或药水) ②【无】消磁器; 抹音器 ③[美](拳击用语)击倒对手的一击

erasure [i'reiʒə] *n.* ①擦掉; 删去; 消除 ②擦掉处; 删去处; 擦掉(或删去)的字(或记号等)

ere [εə] [古][诗] **I** *conj.* ①在…以前: Go ahead ~ it is too late. 及早赶去。②(与其…)毋宁: He will die, ~ he will yield. 他宁死不屈。**II** *prep.* 在…之前: ~ daybreak 黎明之前 / ~ long 不久以后

erect [i'rekt] **I** *a.* ①直立的, 垂直的, 竖直的: an ~ bearing 挺直的体态 / stand ~ 直立 / hold

oneself ~ 保持姿势挺直 ②竖起的: with every hair ~ 毛发悚然 ③[古]向上的 ④[古]不屈的, 坚毅的; 警惕的 ⑤【医】勃起的 **II** ❶ *vt.* ①使竖立, 使竖直: ~ a flagstaff 竖旗杆 / ~ oneself 挺直身子 ②树立; 建立, 设立: ~ a bridge 架桥 / ~ a monument 立纪念碑 / ~ trade barriers 设置贸易障碍 ③安装; 装配: ~ an engine 安装发动机 / an ~ing shop 装配车间 ④把(原理等)上升为体系 (*into*); 提升 ⑤【数】作(垂直线等) ⑥【医】使勃起 ❷ *vi.*【医】勃起 ‖**~ly** *ad.* / **~ness** *n.*

erection [i'rekʃən] *n.* ①直立, 竖立, 竖直 ②建立, 建造; 安装; 装配: an ~ diagram 装配图 ③建筑物, 建筑物 ④【医】勃起

ermine ['ə:min] *n.* ①【动】貂; 扫雪鼬 ②貂皮 ③(标志法官职位或贵族身分的)貂皮长袍: He has worn the ~ for ten years. 他任法官已有十年了。‖**~d** *a.* ①饰有貂皮的 ②穿着貂皮袍的

erode [i'roud] ❶ *vt.* ①腐蚀, 侵蚀: Acid ~s metal. 酸腐蚀金属。②腐蚀成; 侵蚀成: The running water ~d a gulley. 流水冲蚀出一条沟渠。❷ *vi.* 受腐蚀; 遭侵蚀 ‖**erodible** *a.* 会被腐蚀的; 受到腐蚀的

erosion [i'rouʒən] *n.* ①腐蚀, 侵蚀; 侵害: plant trees to prevent soil ~ 植树预防土壤侵蚀 ②【医】糜烂; 齿质腐损

erotic [i'rɔtik] **I** *a.* ①(引起)性爱的; (引起)性欲的; 色情的 ②强烈地受性欲影响的 **II** *n.* 好色的人; 情诗 ‖**~ally** *ad.*

err [ə:] *vi.* ①犯错误; 弄错; (陈述、仪器等)不正确: ~ *from* the truth (right path) 背离真理(正路) / ~ *in* observation (one's judg(e)ment) 观察 (判断)方面出错 / ~ *on the side of* mercy 失之宽大 / a gauge that must not ~ by more than 0.01 mm. 误差不超过 0.01 毫米的量规 ②作恶 ③[古]入歧途; 漫游

errand ['erənd] *n.* ①差使(如送信、买东西等): run (或 go) (on) ~s for sb. 为某人跑腿, 为某人去办事 / send sb. *on* an ~ 派某人去干一件事 ②[古]使命 ③[古]口信 ‖*a fool's ~* 见 **fool**[1] ‖**~-boy** *n.* 供差遣的僮仆

errant ['erənt] *a.* ①周游的; 漂泊的: an ~ knight 游侠 ②错误的; 迷路的; 走入歧途的: an ~ sheep 迷途的羔羊 ③无定的: an ~ breeze 飘忽不定的微风

erratic [i'rætik] **I** *a.* ①飘忽不定的; 不稳定的; 无规律的: an ~ star 游星 ②(人或其行为、习惯、意见等)古怪的; 乖僻的; 反复无常的 ③[古]流浪的, 漂泊的 ④【地】移动的, 漂移性的: ~ block 漂砾, 漂块 ⑤【医】游走的; 不规则的 **II** *n.* ①古怪的人; 乖僻的人; 乖僻者; 反复无常的人 ②【地】漂砾 ‖**~ally** *ad.*

erratum [e'rɑ:təm] ([复] errata [e'rɑ:tə]) *n.* ①(书写或印刷中的)错误 ②[复]勘误表

erroneous [i'rounjəs] *a.* 错误的, 不正确的: an ~ tendency 错误的倾向 ‖**~ly** *ad.* / **~ness** *n.*

error ['erə] *n.* ①谬误；错误: Carelessness often leads to ~s. 粗枝大叶往往造成错误。/ an ~ in (或 of) judgement 判断上的错误 / commit (或 make) an ~ 犯错误 / a typographical (spelling, grammatical) ~ 印刷(拼法,语法)错误 ②谬见；错误思想 ③罪过；违犯(行为)；邪恶；行为不正: fall into ~ 入歧途 ④差错，误差: the ~ of a planet 行星观测上位置与计算上位置间的误差 ⑤(棒球中的)错打 ‖*a writ of* ~ 见 **writ¹** / *by* ~ 错误地 / *in* ~ ①弄错了的: I'm afraid he is *in* ~ (in saying that). 我恐怕他(说那句话)是弄错了的。② 错误地: He has sent the book to you *in* ~. 他错把书寄给你了。‖**~less** *a.* 无错误的,正确的

erudite ['eru(ː)dait] **I** *a.* 博学的,有学问的 **II** *n.* 博学者，有学问的人 ‖**~ly** *ad.* / **erudition** [,eru(ː)'diʃən] *n.* 博学,博识

erupt [i'rʌpt] ❶ *vi.* ①(火山、喷泉等)喷发；喷出；爆发,迸发 ②(疹)发出；(牙齿)冒出 ❷ *vt.* 喷出；喷射出

eruption [i'rʌpʃən] *n.*【地】喷发: The volcano is *in* ~. 火山正在喷发。②(战争、情感等的)爆发,迸发 ③【医】发疹；疹；(牙齿的)冒出 ④喷出物

escalate ['eskəleit] ❶ *vi.* (象自动楼梯式传送带似地)逐步上升；(战争等)逐步升级 ❷ *vt.* 使逐步上升；使逐步升级 ‖**escalation** [,eskə'leiʃən] *n.* 逐步上升；逐步升级

escalator ['eskəleitə] **I** *n.* ①【建】自动楼梯 ②规定(工资等)定期按生活费用作出上下调整的条款 **II** *a.* 规定(价格、工资等)定期按比例作出上下调整的

escapade [,eskə'peid] *n.* ① 越轨行动；恶作剧 ②[古]逃走,逃避

escape [is'keip] **I** ❶ *vi.* ①逃跑；逃脱；逃亡；避免: ~ *from* prison 越狱 / ~ *from* the net 漏网 ②漏出；流出: The gas is *escaping* somewhere. 什么地方在漏(煤)气了。/ Water ~d rapidly from the drainpipe. 水从排水管中迅速流出。❷ *vt.* ① 逃避；逃脱；避免: None of the criminals ~d punishment (或 being punished). 罪犯一个也没有逃脱惩罚。/ ~ observation (或 being seen) 不被人看到 / There is no *escaping* him. 怎么也避不开他。② 没有被…注意到；被…忘掉: The misprint ~d the proofreader. 这个印刷错误没有被校对者看出。/ The exact date has ~d me. 我记不起确切日期了。③从…处冒出；被…禁不住地说出: A moan ~d the patient. 那病人不禁呻吟了一声。**II** *n.* ①逃跑；逃脱；逃逸；排泄；漏出: make one's ~ 逃跑 / a narrow (或 near, hairbreadth) ~ 九死一生 / the rocket's ~ *from* the gravitational pull 火箭的飞出地心吸力 / ~ canal【建】排水沟渠 ②逃避(现实) ③逃路；出口；逃的工具: a fire ~ (火警时使用的)太平梯,安全梯；安全出口 ④【植】野化植物,退化植物 ‖**escapee** [,eskei'piː] *n.* 逃脱者；逃亡者；逃犯；逃俘 ‖**~ artist** ①有脱身术的人

(尤指魔术师或杂技演员) ②善于越狱的罪犯 / ~ **clause** (贸易等)例外条款 / ~ **hatch** (危急时的)出口；(摆脱困境等的)出路；(解决困难等的)办法 / ~ **pipe** 放出管 / **~-proof** *a.* 防逃脱的 / ~ **shaft**【矿】(发生事故时撤退人员用的)太平竖井,安全竖井 / ~ **velocity**【字】逃逸速度,克服地球吸力的速度,第二宇宙速度

escapement [is'keipmənt] *n.* ①擒纵机；(钟、表等的)司行轮,摆轮；棘轮装置(尤指打字机上控制间隔的装置) ②[罕]逃跑；[古]逃路；出口

escapement

eschew [is'tʃuː] *vt.* 避免(某种行为、食物等)；避开(危害、恶事等)

escort **I** ['eskɔːt] *n.* ①警卫队,护卫队；护航部队；护航舰；护航飞机: a convoy ~ 车运警卫部队 / an ~ carrier 护航航空母舰 / an ~ of jet fighters 喷气战斗机护航队 ②护卫者，护送者；陪同者 ③护卫,护送；护航；陪同: *under* the ~ *of* 在…的护送下 / conduct ~ operations 护航 **II** [is'kɔːt] *vt.* 护卫, 护送；陪同: ~ sb. home 陪某人回家

escutcheon [is'kʌtʃən] *n.* ①饰有纹章的盾 ②【动】(鞘翅目昆虫的)小盾片；盾纹面 ③孔罩；锁眼盖 ④【船】船尾楯部(标志船名处) ‖*a blot on one's* ~ 见 **blot**

esophagus [iː(ː)'sɔfəgəs] *n.*【解】食管

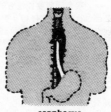

esophagus

especial [is'peʃəl] *a.* 特别的,特殊的: a matter of ~ importance 一件特别重要的事 ‖*in* ~ 尤其,格外

especially [is'peʃəli] *ad.* 特别,尤其，格外；主要: It has been ~ hot this week. 这个星期天气特别热。/ Cotton is growing fine, ~ in that area. 棉花长势很好,尤其是在那个地区。

espionage [,espiə'nɑːʒ] *n.* 谍报；间谍活动,刺探: electronic ~ equipment 电子侦察设备

espouse [is'pauz] *vt.* ①娶(妻);嫁(女) ②拥护,信奉,支持;采纳

esprit ['espri:; 法 espri] *n.* [法]精神;机智 ‖~ *de corps* [法 d kɔ:r] 团结精神,集体精神 / ~ *fort* [法 fɔ:r] 意志坚强的人;不信宗教权威的人

espy [is'pai] *vt.* ①窥探;窥见,(偶然)看见 ②发现(缺点等)

esquire [is'kwaiə] *n.* [英] ①[E-]…先生(略作 Esq.): Henry Barker, *Esq.* 亨利·巴克先生(信封等用的尊称) ②(地位次于骑士的)绅士 ③[古]地主,乡绅 ④[古]骑士的随从,持盾者,候补骑士

essay ['esei, 'esi] **I** *n.* ①小品文,随笔;文章: an "eight-legged ~" 八股文 ②尝试;企图: make an ~ to assist sb. 试图帮助某人 ③尝试结果;试验 ④(邮票或纸币的)未接受的图案印刷样张 **II** [e'sei, 'esei] *vt.* 试做,试图: ~ a dramatic role 试演某一角色 / ~ to do sth. 试图做某事 ‖~**ist** *n.* 小品文作者,随笔作者 ‖~ **question** 问答题(与填充题、是非题相对而言)

essence ['esns] *n.* ①本质,实质;本体,实体: the ~ of dialectics 辩证法的本质 / see the ~ through the phenomena 透过现象看本质 / be different (the same) *in* ~ 实质上不同(一样) / "Left" in form but Right *in* ~ 形"左"实右 ②精华,精髓;要素;精粹,香精,香料;香油;香气: ~ of beef 牛肉精(或汁) / ~ of resin 松香精 / ~ of peppermint 薄荷精(或油) ‖~**d** *a.* 香料的;香气的

essential [i'senʃəl] **I** *a.* ①本质的,实质的;基本的: ~ differences 本质的区别 / an ~ part 基本部分 ②必要的 ③提炼的,精华的: discard the dross and select the ~ 去粗取精 / an ~ oil (香)精油,香料油 ④[医]特发的;自发的,原发的: ~ anemia 原发性贫血 **II** *n.* [常用复] ①本质,实质: In considering a problem, one must grasp its ~s. 观察问题要抓住它的本质。②要素,要点;必需品: *Essentials of Physics* «物理学纲要» / ~s of life 生活必需品 ‖~**ly** *ad.* 本质上,实质上;基本上 ‖~ **character** 【生】种特征

establish [is'tæbliʃ] ❶ *vt.* ①建立;设立(公司等);创办(学校、医院等): ~ the socialist system 建立社会主义制度 / ~ diplomatic relations with 同…建立外交关系 ②制定;规定: ~ new rules and regulations 制定新的规章 / be ~ed by law 为法律所规定 ③派,委任;安置;使定居: ~ sb. *as* 委派某人为… / ~ oneself in the countryside 在农村安家落户 ④使开业,使营业;使立足于 (*in*): be ~ed in New York *as* a physician 在纽约开业行医 / ~ sb. *in* business 使某人立足于商界 ⑤确立;证实: ~ one's credit 确立信誉 / ~ a scientific law 证实科学定律 ⑥使固定;使(信仰等)坚定 ⑦使(风俗、先例等)被永久性地接受: ~ a claim to sth. 使(自己)对某物的要求权得到承认 ⑧定…为国教 ⑨(纸牌戏中)使(某花色)剩下

的牌都能赢(俗称"把(某花色的牌)打大") ❷ *vi.* (植物等)移植生长

established [is'tæbliʃt] *a.* ①(被)建立的;(被)设立的;(被)制定的: a newly ~ institution 一个新设的机构 ②确立的;确认的;确定的,既定的: the ~ principles of international law 公认的国际法准则 / an ~ fact 既成事实 / an ~ rule 规 / an ~ custom 常规 ③国定的: (the) *Established* Church 英国国教 ④(植物等)移植生长的

establishment [is'tæbliʃmənt] *n.* ①建立;设立;确立;确定;创办,开设 ②建立的机构(或组织);行政机关;军队;企业,公司;(仆人众多的)家庭,(大)住宅: industrial and mining ~s 工矿企业 / service ~s 服务性企业 / an ammunition ~ 弹药库 ③[常作 the E-] 既成权力机构(或体制) 幕后统治集团: the *Establishment* newspapers 代表既成体制的报纸,代表官方的报纸 ④固定收入(或职务);定员;编制: a war (peace) ~ 战时(平时)编制 ⑤法典,法规 ⑥(植物等的)移植生长 ⑦[古]固定收入 ‖*Church Establishment* (或 *the Establishment*) 国教(尤指英国国教) / ~ *of the port* 标准潮讯,潮候时差

estate [is'teit] *n.* ①房地产: an industrial ~ 工业用地,工业区 / a housing ~ [英]住宅区 / an ~ agent [英]房地产中间商(或掮客) ②[总称]财产,产业;遗产;【律】个人的全部资产;地产等所有权;地产等的性质(或范围): real ~ 不动产 / personal ~ 动产 / landed ~ 地产 ③庄园,种植园: a tea ~ 茶树种植园 ‖~ **duty** 财产税;遗产税

esteem [is'ti:m] **I** *vt.* ①尊重,尊敬;珍重 ②认为,感到: I ~ it (as) an honour (或 a privilege) to attend this meeting. 我能参加这个大会,感到十分荣幸。/ We shall ~ it (as) a favour if you will inform us soon. (商业信件等用语)如蒙早日通知,不胜感谢。/ ~ a proposal worthless 认为一个建议没有价值 ③[古]估价,评价 **II** *n.* ①尊重,尊敬: as a mark (或 token) of ~ 以表示尊敬意 / gain (或 get) the ~ of sb. 受到某人的尊敬 / have a great ~ for 对…十分敬佩 ②[古]价值;评价;判断;意见 ‖*hold sb. (sth.) in* ~ 尊重某人(某事物): The veteran worker is held in high (或 great) ~. 那位老工人深受尊敬。

estimate ['estimeit] **I** ❶ *vt.* ①估计;估量;预算: the ~d cost 估计成本 ②评价;判断 ❷ *vi.* 估计;估价: ~ for the repair of a bridge 估计修桥的费用 **II** ['estimit, 'estimeit] *n.* ①估计;估价,估计数,预算: by rough ~ 据粗略的估计 / make an ~ of the height of a mountain 估计一座山的高度 / The time and labo(u)r required may be less than the ~s. 需要的时间和人工也许比估计的要少些。/ the *Estimates* 英国财政大臣每年提交议会的国家支出预算 ②(承包人的)估价单;估计成本单 ③(从典型统计得出的)数值(指人口参数等) ④评价;判断: form an ~

of sb.'s abilities 评价某人的才能 / an intelligence ~ 情报(或敌情)判断 ‖**estimator** *n.* (对所需人力、物力等的)估计者

estimation [ˌesti'meiʃən] *n.* ①估计；估价；预算：the ~ of atmospheric pressure 对于气压的估计 ②评价；判断；意见。参见：form a true ~ of sb. 对某人作出正确的评价 / sink in sb.'s ~ 在某人眼中评价降低 / *in my* ~ 照我看来，照我的估计 ③尊重，尊敬：hold sb. *in* (high) ~ 尊重(十分尊重)某人 ④【化】估定；测定

estrange [is'treindʒ] *vt.* ①使疏远，使隔离；离间：~ oneself *from* sb. 跟某人疏远 / ~ sb. *from* his friends 使某人跟朋友们疏远 / be ~d *from* each other 互相疏远 ②使离开(惯常的环境等)；使远离 (*from*) ‖**~ment** *n.*

estuary ['estjuəri] *n.* 港湾，河口湾，三角湾，江口湾：an ~ deposit 港湾沉积

etcetera [it'setrə] *n.* 附加的人(或物)；[复]附加项目；零星杂物

et cetera [it'setrə] [拉]等等，以及其他等等(略作 etc. 或 &c.) [注意：对于人名不宜用 etc.，宜用 and others]

etch [etʃ] **I** ❶ *vt.* ①蚀刻(图案等)；浸蚀(金属版等)；腐蚀 ②把…铭刻(在心灵或记忆中)；刻划，描述：The place was ~ed deeply in his mind. 这个地方给他留下了深刻的印象。/ a sharply ~ed character in a novel 小说中一个被刻划得很鲜明的人物 ❷ *vi.* 施行蚀刻法，使用蚀镂术 **II** *n.* 腐蚀(剂)，蚀刻(剂)：mass ~ (晶体的)粗蚀 ‖**~er** *n.* 蚀刻者；蚀刻器

etching ['etʃiŋ] *n.* ①蚀刻；浸蚀；蚀刻法，蚀镂术：close ~ (晶体的)精蚀 / electrochemical ~ 电化浸蚀，电抛光 ②蚀刻画；蚀刻版；蚀刻版印刷品

eternal [i(ː)'təːnl] *a.* ①永久的，永恒的；无穷的 ②永存的，不朽的 ③[口](闲谈、争吵等)不停的，无休止的 ④[the E-]【宗】上帝 ‖*the Eternal City* 不朽城(罗马的别称) ‖**~ly** [i(ː)'təːnəli] *ad.* / **~ness** *n.*

eternity [i(ː)'təːniti] *n.* ①永恒；无穷；世世代代 ②不朽，永生；未来；来生 ③[复]永恒的真理；无限的时间；永远不变的事物 ④(似乎)无终止的一段时期：an ~ of waiting 无尽期的等待 ‖*an ~ box* [俚]棺材 / *send sb. to ~* 使某人死去 / *through all eternities* 永远

ether ['iːθə] *n.* ①【化】醚；乙醚 ②【物】以太，能媒：~ wave 以太波 ③[诗][古]太空，苍天 ④气氛

ethereal, etherial [i(ː)'θiəriəl] *a.* ①轻飘的，飘渺的；稀薄的 ②天上的；太空的；非人间的 ③微妙的，精微的；幽邃的 ④【物】以太的 ⑤【化】用醚制的；似醚的(有高度挥发性的)：~ oil 香精油 ‖**~ity** [i(ː),θiəri'æliti] *n.* / **~ly** *ad.*

ethic ['eθik] *a.* = ethical (*a.*)

ethical ['eθikəl] **I** *a.* ①伦理学的；伦理的；道德的：an ~ principle 道德原则 ②合乎道德的(尤指合

乎职业道德或规矩的) ③(药品)合乎规格的；凭处方出售的 **II** *n.* 凭处方出售的药品 (= ~ drug) ‖**~ly** *ad.* ‖ ~ **dative** 【语】泛指的人称的与格 / ~ **genitive** 【语】泛指的第二人称的所有格

ethics ['eθiks] [复] *n.* ①[用作单]伦理学；道德学 ②[用作单]伦理学论文(或书籍) ③伦理观，道德观；道德标准；(某种职业的)规矩：press ~ 新闻界的规矩，新闻道德

ethnic ['eθnik] **I** *a.* = ethnical **II** *n.* 少数民族的成员；种族集团的成员

ethnography [eθ'nɔgrəfi] *n.* 人种史，人种论

ethnologist [eθ'nɔlədʒist] *n.* ①人种学者，民族学者 ②人类文化学者

ethnology [eθ'nɔlədʒi] *n.* ①人种学，民族学 ②人类文化学

etiquette [ˌeti'ket] *n.* ①礼节；礼仪：diplomatic ~ 外交礼节 / a breach of ~ 失礼行为 ②[总称](同业间的)规矩；成规；格式：medical ~ 医务界的成规 / be against the ~ of the game 违反比赛规则

etymologic(al) [ˌetimə'lɔdʒik(əl)] *a.* ①词源学的，语源学的 ②词源的，语源的 ‖**etymologically** *ad.*

etymology [ˌeti'mɔlədʒi] *n.* ①词源学，语源学 ②词源，语源

eucalyptus [ˌjuːkə'liptəs] ([复] eucalypti [ˌjuːkə'liptai] 或 eucalyptuses) *n.* 【植】①桉树属植物：~ oil 桉树油 ②[E-]桉树属

Eucharist ['juːkərist] *n.* 【宗】圣餐；圣餐中用的面包和酒 ‖**~ic(al)** [ˌjuːkə'ristik(əl)] *a.*

eugenic [juː'dʒenik] *a.* 优生学的 ‖**~ist** [juː'dʒenisist] *n.* 优生学家 / **~s** [复] *n.* [用作单或复]优生学

eulogize ['juːlədʒaiz] *vt.* 颂扬；赞颂

eulogy ['juːlədʒi] *n.* ①颂扬，赞颂 ②颂词；颂文：pronounce a ~ on sb. 向某人致颂词

eunuch ['juːnək] *n.* 宦官，太监，阉人

euphemism ['juːfimizəm] *n.* 【语】委婉法；委婉语；婉词："*Pass away*" is a ~ for "*die*"。"去世"是"死"的委婉语。

euphemistic(al) [ˌjuːfi'mistik(əl)] *a.* 委婉的；婉言的：a *euphemistic* way of speaking 委婉的说法 ‖**euphemistically** *ad.*

euphony ['juːfəni] *n.* 声音的悦耳，声音的和谐；悦耳的声音，和谐的声音

evacuate [i'vækjueit] ❶ *vt.* ①【军】后送(部队等)；遣送，疏散(居民)；撤离：~ the sick and wounded from a combat area 把伤病员从战斗地域撤走 / ~ a town 撤离城镇 ②搬空，腾出(房子等)：~ a building 撤空大楼 ③(用泵)抽出：~ water from a pond 抽干池水 ④排泄；排清(肠胃等内的东西) ❷ *vi.* ①(有组织地)撤走；撤离；疏散 ②小便；大便 ‖**evacuative** *a.*

evacuation [iˌvækju'eiʃən] *n.* ①后送；疏散；撤离 ②(房屋等的)撤空；抽空，排空 ③排泄，泻出；排泄物：~ of bowels 大便 ‖ ~ **hospital** 后送医院

evacuee [i,vækju(ː)'iː] *n.* 被后送的人员; 被疏散的人员

evade [i'veid] ❶ *vt.* 逃避; 躲避; 回避; 规避: ~ an attack 躲避攻击 / ~ *doing* a duty 逃避职责 / ~ (*paying*) taxes 逃税 / ~ (*paying*) one's debts 逃避债务 / ~ difficulties 回避困难 / ~ a question 回避问题 / ~ an answer 避不作答 ❷ *vi.* 避掉; 逃避; 规避

evaluate [i'væljueit] *vt.* ①把⋯定值; 估⋯的价, 评价 ②【数】求⋯的值; 以数目表示 ‖**evaluation** [i,vælju'eiʃən] *n.* ①估价, 评价 ②【数】赋值, 值的计算

evanescent [,iːvə'nesnt] *a.* ①(印象等) 很快消失的; 短暂的, 瞬息的 ②纤细的; 轻盈的 ③【植】(叶脉) 隐失的

evangelic(al) [,iːvæn'dʒelik(ə)l] 【宗】Ⅰ *a.* ①福音的; 合乎福音的 ②福音派新教会的 ③[E-] 英国低教会派的 ④热衷于传道的 Ⅱ *n.* 福音派的信徒 ‖**evangelicalism** *n.* 福音派教义(的信仰) / **evangelically** *ad.* 按照福音; 福音传道士般地

evaporate [i'væpəreit] ❶ *vt.* ①使蒸发; 通过升华使(金属等) 沉淀: Heat ~*s* water. 热使水蒸发。②使脱水, 去除⋯的水分 ③发射(电子) ④使消失, 消灭 ❷ *vi.* ①蒸发; 挥发; 发散蒸气 ②[口]消失; (人) 失踪; 死亡 ‖~**d** *a.* 浓缩的; 脱水的, 蒸发干燥的: ~*d* milk 炼乳 / ~*d* vegetables 脱水蔬菜 / ~*d* apple 苹果干 / **evaporating** *a.* 蒸发用的; 蒸发作用的: *evaporating* dish 【化】蒸发皿 / *evaporating* column 【化】浓缩柱, 蒸浓柱 / **evaporator** *n.* (食物干燥用的) 蒸发器

evaporation [i,væpə'reiʃən] *n.* ①蒸发(作用); 发散; 升华沉淀作用: ~ cooling 蒸发冷却 / an ~ gum test (石油) 蒸发胶质试验 / ~ nucleon 【原】蒸发核子 ②脱水; 脱水法 ③(电子的) 发射

evasion [i'veiʒən] *n.* ①逃避; 规避; 回避; (捐税等的) 偷漏: ~ of responsibility 逃避责任 / tactics 【军】规避战术 ②遁词, 借口, 推诿

evasive [i'veisiv] *a.* ①逃避的; 躲避的; 偷漏(捐税等)的: an ~ action 【军】规避动作 ②托词的, 推诿的 ③闪避的, 难以捉摸的; 含糊其词的: an ~ talk 躲躲闪闪、含糊其词的谈话 ‖~**ly** *ad.* / ~**ness** *n.*

Eve [iːv] *n.* 夏娃 (基督教《圣经》中的人物, 亚当之妻)

eve [iːv] *n.* ①(节日等的) 前夜, 前夕: New Year's Eve 除夕 (十二月卅一日) / Christmas Eve 【基督教】圣诞节前夕; 圣诞节前一天 (十二月二十四日) ②(重大事件发生的) 前一刻, 前夕: on the ~ of victory 在胜利前夕 ③[诗] 傍晚

even[1] ['iːvən] *ad.* ①[加强语气]甚至(⋯也), 连(⋯都): He doubts ~ the facts. 他甚至怀疑事实。/ I haven't ~ thought of it. 这个我连想都没想过。②[后接比较级]甚至(比⋯)更, 还 ‖~ *as* ①恰恰在⋯的时候 ②正如: It happened ~ *as* we expected. 事情正如我们预料的

那样发生了。/ ~ *if* (或 ~ *though*) 即使, 纵然: Even if we achieve great success in our work, we should not be conceited. 即使我们在工作中取得了巨大的成绩, 也不应该自满。/ ~ *now* (*then*) 即使在现在 (那时); 尽管这样 (那样): Difficulties were increasing. Even *then* he did not lose heart. 尽管困难增加了, 他也毫不灰心。/ ~ *so* 虽然如此: The new method is not perfect; ~ *so*, it's much better than the old one. 新方法并不完美, 虽然如此, 它比老方法好得多。/ *never* ~ 连⋯也不: She *never* ~ tasted the food. 她对这食物连尝也没尝一下。

even[2] ['iːvən] Ⅰ *a.* ①平的, 平坦的; 平滑的: the ~ ground at the top of a mountain 山顶的平地 / ~ country 平坦的原野 ②不曲折的; 无凹陷的; 连贯的: an ~ coastline 不曲折的海岸线 / ~ breathing 均匀的呼吸 / an ~ tempo 均匀的节拍 / ~ grain 【植】均匀纹理 / be of ~ quality 质量稳定 ④一致的, 同样的; 齐的: of ~ date 【律】【商】同一日期的 / The two horses ran ~. 两匹马并驾齐驱。/ The water was ~ *with* the rim. 水齐到边上了。/ The typhoon laid the trees ~ *with* the ground. 台风把树木刮倒在地。⑤对等的, 均等的: We are now ~. 我们现在扯平了。/ stand an ~ chance of winning 胜负的可能性各半 / ~ money 同额的赌注 ⑥公平的; 平均的; 平衡的: an ~ exchange (bargain) 公平的交换 (交易) / ~ shares 平均的份儿 / The scales hang ~. 天平平衡着。(或: 势均力敌。) ⑦(性情等) 平静的: speak in an ~ tone 心平气和地讲 ⑧双数的, 【数】偶(数)的: an ~ page 双(数书)页 / an ~ committee 人数成双的委员会 / evenly ~ 能再平分的偶数的 (指四除得尽) / unevenly (或 oddly) ~ 不能再平分的偶数的 (指二除得尽, 四除不尽) ⑨恰好的, 整整的: an ~ li 整整一里 Ⅱ ❶ *vt.* 使平坦; 使平; 使相等: ~ out the soil with a spade 把土铲平 / ~ up scores *with* 与⋯拉平比分 / ~ up accounts *with* 与⋯结清账目 / ~ up blood debts *with* sb. 向某人清算血债 ❷ *vi.* 变平; 成为相等 ‖*be* ~ *with* sb. 与某人扯平 / *break* ~ 打成平手; 得失相当; 不盈不亏: Avoid battles of attrition that ends in *breaking* ~. 避免打那种得失相当的消耗战。/ ~ *odds* 见 **odds** / ~ *Steven* (或 *Stephen*) ['stiːvn] [美俚] 比分相等的(地); 半斤八两; 各半地 / *up on* sb. [美口]向某人报复(或报怨) / *get* *with* sb. 与某人扯平; 跟某人算账, 向某人报复 / *make* ~ (排字中)使最后一行排足 ‖~**ly** *ad.* / ~**ness** *n.* ‖~**-'handed** *a.* 不偏不倚的, 公正的 / ~**-'tempered** *a.* 性情平和的

even[3] ['iːvən] *n.* [古][诗][方]黄昏, 傍晚 (=evening) ‖~**fall** *n.* [诗]黄昏, 傍晚 / ~**song** *n.* ①(英国国教的)晚祷 ②黄昏时唱的歌; [诗]黄昏 / ~**tide** *n.* [诗]薄暮, 黄昏

evening ['iːvniŋ] *n.* ①傍晚, 黄昏, 晚上(从日落至就寝): Good ~! 晚上好! (晚上分别时也可

用，表示"再见") / this (yesterday 或 last) ~ [用作状语]今天(昨天)晚上 / in the ~ 在晚上 / on Wednesday ~ 在星期三晚上 / on (或 in) the ~ of April 15 在四月十五日晚上 / one cold winter ~ [用作状语]在一个寒冷的冬夜 / an ~ paper 晚报 ②(联欢性的)晚会;晚上娱乐时间: a musical ~ 音乐晚会 / an ~ of bridge 桥牌晚会③后期;末期,衰落期: in the ~ of life 在晚年 ④[方]下午(至黄昏) ‖of an ~ 往往在晚上(指动作的习惯性) ‖~s ad. [美]每晚;在任何晚上 ‖~ dress, ~ clothes 夜礼服 / ~ gown (女子)夜礼服 / Evening Prayer【宗】晚祷 / ~ primrose【植】月见草,待宵草 / ~ school 夜校 / ~ star 晚星 (指木星、水星等,尤指金星) / ~ student 夜校学生

event ['i'vent] n. ①事件; 大事; 事变; 事情: current ~s 时事 / It was quite an ~. 这的确是件大事。/ The new book was the cultural ~ of the year. 这本新书的(出版)是今年文化界的大事。/ the day's ~s 当天发生的事情 / in the natural course of ~s 按照事情的自然发展 ②偶然事件,可能发生的事情 ③活动; 经历: the theatre of human ~ 人类活动的领域 ④(运动会等的)比赛项目: a team ~ 团体赛 / a target ~ 射靶比赛 / field and track ~s 田径赛 / enter for an ~ 参加一项比赛 ⑤[律]诉讼(或判决)的结果; [古]结局 ‖at all ~s 不论怎样,无论如何: At all ~s, we will carry the struggle through to the end. 我们无论如何要把斗争进行到底。/ Coming ~s cast their shadows before. [谚]未来之事先有朕兆。/ in any ~ =at all ~s / in either ~ 两种情况中不论哪一种发生,无论是这样还是那样 / in that ~ 如果那种情况发生,如果那样 / in the ~ ①结果,到头来: Those who play with fire will get burned in the ~. 玩火者到头来必自焚。②[美]如果: In the ~ (that) she has not been informed, I will tell her. 如果她还不知道,我会告诉她的。/ in the ~ of 如果…发生: Rich harvests are guaranteed even in the ~ of drought. 即使天旱也保证能丰收。/ pull off the ~ 比赛获胜(或得奖) / wise after the ~ 事后聪明的 ‖~less a. 无大事的,平静无事的 ‖~ counter 信号计数器,转换计数器 / ~ magnet【讯】步调磁铁

eventful ['i'ventful, i'ventfəl] a. ①多事的,充满大事的,多变故的: an ~ year 多事的年头,多事之秋 / an ~ life 经历丰富的一生 ②重大的: an ~ affair 重大的事件 / an ~ conversation 重要的谈话 ‖~ly ad. / ~ness n.

eventual [i'ventjuəl] a. ①最后的, 结局的: ~ success (failure) 最后的成功(失败) ②可能发生的,万一的 ‖~ly ad. 终于,最后

eventuality [i,ventju'æliti] n. 可能发生的事, 不测事件: possible eventualities 可能的突然事变 / be ready for any eventualities 以防万一

ever ['evə] ad. ①永远: ~ go hand in hand 永远在一起,总是不可分的 ②不断地,老是: He is ~ repeating the same old story. 他老是老调重弹。③[用于一般疑问句、否定句以及表示条件和比较的从句]在任何时候: This is the profoundest lesson I (have) ~ had. 这是我有生以来最深刻的一课。/ None of us will ~ forget that exciting scene. 我们大家都永远不会忘记那激动的场面。/ be it ~ so hard 无论这样艰难 / Work as hard as ~ you can. 尽最大努力干吧。④[与形容词的比较级、最高级连用,加强语气]比以往任何时候都: the biggest crop ~ 空前的大丰收 ⑤[用于特殊疑问句,加强语气]究竟,到底: Which ~ do you want? 你究竟要哪一个? / When (Where, How) ~ did you drop it? 你究竟什么时候(在哪儿,怎样)丢失这个东西的? / How could you ~ have succeeded in such a difficult task? 这么困难的任务,你们到底是怎么完成的? ⑥[美口]用在动词 "to be" 作谓语的倒装句中, 加强语气]非常, 极: Was he ~ delighted! 他高兴极了! ‖ **Did you ~?** 这种(怪)事你听(或看)到过吗? / ~ after (或 afterwards) 从那时以后,以后一直: We repaired the machine and it worked well ~ after. 我们修好了机器,从那以后它一直转得很好。/ ~ and again 时时,不时地 / ~ and anon [古] = ~ and again / ~ so [口][俚]非常[旧时用 never so]: Thank you ~ so much. 多谢你。/ He is ~ so diligent. 他勤奋极了。/ Everybody enjoyed himself ~ so at the evening party. 在联欢晚会上大家都非常愉快。/ ~ such [口][俚]很…的: It is ~ such a useful tool. 这工具非常有用。/ Ever yours (或 Yours ~) 永远属于你的(熟人之间通信时,用于信末署名前的客套语) / for ~ (and a day) ① 永远 ②老是: He is for ~ asking whys. 他老是问这问那没个完。/ for ~ and ~ 永远 (语气比 for ~ 强) ‖~-vic'torious a. 常胜的,战无不胜的

evergreen ['evəgri:n] I a. ①常绿的,常青的: an ~ tree 常绿树 ②[喻]永葆青春的,永久的 II n. ①常绿树;常绿植物;冬青;万年青 ②[复]装饰用的常绿树树枝

everlasting [,evə'lɑ:stiŋ] I a. ①永久的,不朽的;持续不尽的,无穷尽的: the zone of ~ snow 常年积雪带 ②持久的;耐久性的: ~ cloth【纺】永固缎纹织物 / cotton homespun 耐用的手工棉织物 ③冗长的,使人厌烦的: ~ talk 喋喋不休的话 ④【植】干后形状颜色不变的 II n. ①永久,永恒,无穷 ②干后花的形状和颜色不变的植物;【植】蜡菊,蝶须,鼠曲草 ③一种牢固结实的缎纹(或斜纹)毛呢 ‖from ~ to ~ 永远地,无穷地 / the Everlasting【宗】上帝,神 ‖~ly ad. 永久地;无穷地;持续不尽地

evermore ['evə'mɔ:] ad. ①永远,始终 ②将来,今后 ‖for ~ 永远地

every ['evri] a. ①每一的, 每个的: ~ year 每一

年 / ～ person 每个人 / She enjoyed ～ minute of the performance. 她自始至终很欣赏这场演出。/ Not ～ lathe can (或 Every lathe cannot) work such high-precision tools. 不是每一部车床都能加工这种精密工具的。②一切的，全部的，完全的：We went there, ～ one of us. 我们大家都到那儿去了。[注意: ～ 和 each 都解释"每一"、"每个"，但 ～ 更强调全体或全部，each 更强调个人或各别；例如: She knows ～ pupil of the class. 意为"她认识班级中所有的学生。" 若在这句中用 each 代替 ～，则意为"她认识班级中每一个学生。" 又，～ 只作形容词，each 可作形容词和代词] ③ 每隔…的；每…中的: receive an injection ～ three days (或 ～ third day) 每三天打一针 / choose one out of ～ ten boys 每十个男孩中选一个 / one car to ～ twenty people 每二十人乘一辆车 ④ 一切可能的；充分的: He was given ～ chance to try the job. 他得到一切可能的机会去试做这件事。/ have ～ reason to say 有充分的理由说 ‖～ bit 每一点；完全，全部: What you said is true, ～ bit of it. 你说得对，完全对。/ ～ now and then 常常，不时地 / ～ once in a while 偶尔，间或 / ～ other ① 每隔: ～ other week 每隔一星期 / write on ～ other line 隔行写 ②所有其他: He was absent, but ～ other man was present. 只有他缺席，所有其他的人都到了。/ ～ so often [口]时常，不时 / ～ time 见 time / ～ which way [口] ①四面八方 ②非常混乱地 ‖～-way ad. 在每一方面，从各方面说来: This plan is ～-way better than that one. 这个计划在每一方面都比那个计划更好。

everybody ['evribɔdi, 'evribədi] *pron.* 每人，人人: Is ～ here? 大家都到了吗？/ *Everybody* has expressed his determination. 每个人都表过决心了。[注意:句中的 his 现常可用 their 代替] / I stayed, ～ *else* went. 我留下，别人都去了。[注意: ～ 与 everyone 同义，但口语中常用 ～]

everyday ['evridei] *a.* ①每日的: ～ routine 每日的例行公事，日常工作 ②日常的；平常的；普通的: ～ life 日常生活 / ～ English 日常用英语 / an ～ occurrence 日常之事 / ～ clothes 便服 / ～ people 普通人

everyone ['evriwʌn] *pron.* =everybody

everything ['evriθiŋ] *pron.* ①每件事，事事，凡事: do ～ carefully 细心地做每件事 / be careful in ～ 事事细心 / have nothing to lose but ～ to gain 有百利而无一弊 ②(有关的)一切;最重要(或优秀)的事物: *Everything* depends on .... 一切都靠 ～ (或: 一切要看 … 而定。) / be ～ to sb. 在某人看来是最重要(或宝贵)的 / In learning English, grammar is not ～. 学英语时，单学语法是不行的。‖take ～ bar the **kitchen sink** (出门旅行的人)差不多把家里的东西全带出来了，带着许多多多东西

everywhere ['evriʰwɛə] **I** *ad.* 处处，到处；无论那里: *Everywhere* are scenes of prosperity. 到处是繁荣的景象。/ He has looked ～ for you. 他到处都找过你了。/ *Everywhere* they went, they were warmly welcomed. 他们每到一处都受到了热烈的欢迎。**II** *n.* 处处，到处: People come from ～ to celebrate the victory. 人们从各处来庆祝胜利。

evict [i(ː)'vikt] *vt.* ①驱逐，赶出(佃户、房客等) ②收回(租地、租屋等) ‖～**ion** [i(ː)'vikʃən] *n.* ①逐出 ②收回 / ～**or** *n.* ①驱逐者 ②收回者

evidence ['evidəns] **I** *n.* ①明显，显著，明白 ②形迹，迹象: give (或 bear, show) ～(s) of 有…的迹象 / give no ～ of 没有…的迹象 ③根据，证据: ～ for (或 of) a conclusion 结论的根据 / external (internal) ～ 外来的(内在的)证据 ④【律】证据；证人；证词: call sb. in ～ 叫某人来作证 / give ～ 作证，提供证据 ‖*circumstantial* ～ 情况证据 / *collateral* ～ 旁证 / *conclusive* ～ 确证 / *documentary* ～ 书面证据 / *material* ～ 物证 / *oral* (或 *parol*) ～ 口头证据 / *verbal* ～ 证言 **II** *vt.* ①使明显；显示 ②证明 ‖*in* ～ 明显的，显而易见的 / *turn Queen's* (或 *King's* 或 [美] *State's*) ～ 供出对同犯不利的证据

evident ['evidənt] *a.* 明显的，明白的: an ～ mistake 明显的错误 / It is (quite) ～ that .... (很)显然… / with ～ pride 得意扬扬地 ‖～**ly** *ad.* 明显地，显然

evil ['iːvl] **I** (evil(b)er, evil(b)est) *a.* ①坏的，邪恶的，罪恶的: an ～ man 坏人 / of ～ repute 名声坏的 / ～ thoughts 邪念 ②有害的；中伤的；恶毒的: ～ speaking 中伤，诽谤 / an ～ tongue 谗言；谗言者 ③不幸的；不吉的；不祥的: ～ news (或 tidings) 噩耗，凶讯 / in an ～ hour 在不幸的时刻 / an ～ sign 不祥的征兆 ④可厌的；不愉快的;[古]低劣的: an ～ smell 讨厌的气味 / an ～ tree 无价值的树 / ～ weather 不舒服的天气 ⑤[美俚]失望的；发怒的 ⑥[美俚](表演等)极有刺激性的 **II** *n.* ①邪恶，罪恶；恶行；弊病: do no ～ 不干坏事，不作恶 ②不幸，不吉；祸害，灾难；苦痛: famine, pestilence and other ～s 饥荒、疫病及其他灾难 ③诽谤，恶言 ④【医】瘰疬(=king's ～) **III** *ad.* [古]恶劣地，邪恶地 ‖*an* ～ *eye* 见 **eye** / *Of two* ～s *choose the less.* 两害中择其较小者。/ *speak* ～ *of sb.* 诽谤某人 / *Sufficient for the day is the* ～ *thereof.* [谚]当天的苦恼就够人受了。(意指别再为未来担心。) / *the Evil One* 【宗】魔鬼 / *the social* ～ ①社会邪恶(指贩毒、盗窃活动等) ②卖淫 ‖～**ly** *ad.* ‖～'**doer** *n.* 坏人，作恶的人 / ～'**doing** *n.* 坏事，恶劣行为 / ～'**minded** *a.* 狠心的；恶毒的

evince [i'vins] *vt.* 表示，表明，显示(感情、性质等): His conversation ～d great courage. 他的谈话显示了很大的勇气。

evoke [i'vouk] *vt.* ①引起；唤起；召(魂)：~ warm acclamations 博得热烈的喝采 / ~ great indignation 引起强烈的愤慨 / ~ memories of the past 唤起对过去的回忆 ②[英][律]把(案子)吊到上级法院

evolution [ˌiːvəˈljuːʃən, ˌevəˈljuːʃən] *n.* ①进展，发展；渐进；演变；展开：the ~ of the aeroplane 飞机(构造)的发展 / a social and economic ~ 社会和经济的发展 / the ~ of the seasons 季节的变换 ②(气体等的)放出，散出；放出物，散出物 ③【生】进化，演化：the Theory of *Evolution* 进化论 ④【生】种族发生，系统发育；个体发生，个体发育：the ~ of a plant from a seed 植物之由种子而发育 ⑤【数】开方 ⑥【天】(天体的)形成，演化：~ of star 星体演化 ⑦【军】(按计划的)队形变换；位置变换：an ~ unit【军】机动单位 ⑧(舞蹈者等的)规定动作 ‖~al, ~ary *a.* 展开的；发展的；进化的；进化论的 / ~ism *n.* 进化论，进化主义：vulgar ~ism 庸俗进化论

evolve [i'volv] ❶ *vt.* ①使发展，使逐渐形成；使进化，使演进，使演化：~ a theory (plan) 发展一种理论(一个计划) ②引伸出；推论，推定(事实等)：~ the truth *from* a mass of confused evidence 由大量庞杂的证据中推断事实 ③放出，发出(气体、热等) ❷ *vi.* ①进展，发展；展开 ②进化；渐进，演化；发育：Man has ~d *from* the ape. 人是从类人猿进化来的。‖~ment *n.* 展开；进展；发展；进化

ewe [juː] *n.* 母羊 ‖one's ~ lamb 最珍贵的东西 ‖'~-'necked *a.* (马、狗等)颈似母羊的

ewer ['juː(ː)ə] *n.* 大口水壶，水罐

ex¹ [eks] *n.* ①(英语字母) X, x ② X 形状的东西

ex² [eks] *n.* [口]已离婚的配偶

ex [eks] *prep.* [拉] ①从，自；依据 ②[商]无，不，未；无权获得 ③[商]在…交货 ‖~ *animo* ['ænimou] 衷心的(地) / ~ *bond* (纳税后)关栈交货 / ~ *dividend* 不包括下期红利，红利未付 / ~ *interest* 无利息(不论到期与否) / ~ *libris* ['laibris] (贴在书本封里的)藏书者签条 / ~ *new* [英]无权要求新股 / ~ *officio* [əˈfiʃiou] 依据职权的(地)；职权上：an ~ *officio* member 当然成员 / ~ *pier* (或 *quay, wharf*) 码头交货 / ~ *rail* 铁路旁交货 / ~ *rights* 无权认购新股 / ~ *ship* 船上交货 / ~ *warehouse* (或 *store*) 仓库交货，货栈交货

exact [ig'zækt] **I** *a.* ①确切的，正确的：What are his ~ words? 他的原话是怎么说的？ / The urgent work was completed in less than one day — six hours, to be (more) ~. 这件紧急工作在不到一天的时间里——(更)确切地说，只花了六个小时——就完成了。②精确无误的；精密的：be ~ in one's statement (or words) 说话严谨 / an ~ science 一门精密的科学 ③严格的：an ~ order 一个严厉的命令 **II** *vt.* ①强要，强求：~ payment of sb. 逼某人付款 / ~ obedience from sb. 强使某人服从 ②急需，需要：The task

~s the utmost effort on our part. 这个任务需要我们全力以赴。‖~ing *a.* ①苛求的；严格的：on ~ing terms 以苛刻的条件 / an ~ing microbe 对生存条件要求极高的微生物 ②(工作等)需付出极大努力的,艰难的 / ~ness *n.* =exactitude / ~or, ~er *n.* 强征(捐税等)的人

exactly [ig'zæktli] *ad.* ①确切地，精确地：carry out an order to the letter 不折不扣地执行命令 / What ~ is he up to? 他究竟想干什么？ / A: Do you mean to say that he will possibly consent? B: Not ~. 甲：你的意思是不是说他可能会同意的？ 乙：不完全如此。②恰恰正是：That's ~ what I want. 那正是我需要的东西。③(表示赞同地回答)确实如此：A: The boy is quite clever. B: *Exactly*. 甲：这孩子很聪明。乙：一点不错。

exaggerate [ig'zædʒəreit] ❶ *vt.* ①夸张，夸大，把…言过其实：The importance of this matter has been ~d. 这件事的重要性被夸大了。②使增大，使过大，使渲染 ❷ *vi.* 夸张，夸大，言过其实：People will not believe a man who always ~s. 人们不会相信老是夸大的人。‖**exaggerator** *n.* 夸张者，言过其实的人

exaggerated [ig'zædʒəreitid] *a.* ①(被)夸张的，(被)夸大的，言过其实的：an ~ report 夸大的报告 / an ~ sense of one's importance 自高自大 ②过大的，逾常的：the ~ crests of certain fowls 某些禽类的过大的冠 ‖~ly *ad.*

exaggeration [igˌzædʒəˈreiʃən] *n.* ①夸张，夸大；浮夸 ②夸张的言语(或比喻) ③(艺术等的)夸张手法

exalt [ig'zɔːlt, eg'zɔːlt] ❶ *vt.* ①使高，高举，升起 ②提升，提拔；提高…的地位(或荣誉等)：be ~ed to the position of … 被提升任…之职 ③赞扬；吹捧：~ sb. to the skies 把某人捧上天 ④使喜悦；使得意；使昂扬 ⑤加浓(色彩等)；加强(想象力等) ❷ *vi.* 使人欢欣，令人得意 ‖~ation [ˌegzɔːˈteiʃən] *n.* ①升高，高举 ②提拔；晋升；提高 ③兴奋；得意；意气风发 ④【化】炼浓 / ~ed *a.* ①高贵的；崇高的：a person of ~ed rank (或 position) 地位高的人 ②兴奋的，得意扬扬的

examination [igˌzæmiˈneiʃən] *n.* ①检查，细查：a physical ~ 体格检查 / an ~ *into* the why and how of an accident 对事故的起因和经过所作的周密调查 / On closest ~ no serious flaws were found. 经严密检查后未发现重大缺陷。②审查；查问：put sb. (sb.'s conduct) under ~ 审查某人(某人的行为) / the ~ of a witness 对证人的询问 ③考试：an open-book ~ *in* political economy 政治经济学的开卷考试 / take a written (an oral) ~ 参加笔(口)试 / a driver's ~ 驾驶员技术及格测验 / pass an ~ 考试及格 / fail (in) an ~ 考试不及格 / an ~ paper 考卷 ‖~al *a.* 检查的；审查的；考试的

examine [ig'zæmin] ❶ *vt.* ①检查；细查；诊察：

example   284   excess

~ to what extent the proposal is workable 仔细考虑这个建议可行的程度如何 ②对…进行审查；查问 ③对…进行考试：~ sb. *in* chemistry 考某人的化学 ❷ *vi.* 检查；细查；调查：~ *into* a rumour 调查谣言的来龙去脉 ‖**examinee** [ig-,zæmi'ni:] *n.* 受审查者；受试人

example [ig'za:mpl] **I** *n.* ①例子，实例；例题：cite an ~ in point 举出一个适当的例子 ②范例，样本：This building is an ~ of early Chinese architecture. 这座建筑物代表着中国早期的建筑式样。③ 模范，榜样 ④ 儆戒：Let this be an ~ to you. 让这件事成为你今后的儆戒吧。**II** *vt.* [常用被动语态]代表(着)，作为…的示范 ‖*beyond* ~ 没有先例 / *Example is better than precept.* [谚] 以身作则胜于口头训诲。/ *for* ~ 例如 / *make an* ~ *of sb.* 惩罚某人以儆他人，惩一儆百 / *set* (或 *give*) *a good* ~ *to sb.* 为某人树立好榜样 / *take* ~ *by* 临摹 / *without* ~ 没有先例

exasperate I [ig'za:spəreit] *vt.* ①激怒，触怒；使气恼：~ sb. to do sth. 激怒某人使做某事 / We were ~d at (或 *by*) his ill behaviour. 我们对他的不良行为非常恼怒。/ be ~d *with* (或 *against*) sb. 生某人的气 ②使(疾病、痛苦等)加剧，使恶化 **II** [ig'za:spərit] *a.* ①被激怒的，恼怒的 ②【生】具硬突起的，(表面)粗糙的

exasperation [ig,za:spə'reiʃən] *n.* ①恼怒；激怒；愤激 ②加剧，恶化；激化

excavate ['ekskəveit] ❶ *vt.* ①开凿；挖掘(壕沟等)；在…挖掘：~ a tunnel 挖掘隧道 / ~ the side of a hill 在山坡上挖掘 ②挖出(矿砂、泥土等)；发掘(古物等) ❷ *vi.* 凿，掘开；变成空洞 ‖**excavation** [,ekskə'veiʃən] *n.* ①开凿；挖掘；挖七；发掘 ②洞，穴；坑道；开凿成的山路 ③发掘物；出土文物 / **excavator** *n.* ①开掘者；发掘者 ②挖掘器；挖土机；电铲

exceed [ik'si:d] ❶ *vt.* ①超过；胜过：This month's output ~s last month's *by* ten percent. 本月的产量超过上月百分之十。/ The concert ~ed our expectations. 音乐会比我们预料的好。②越出：~ conventional rules 越出常规 / ~ one's authority (或 instructions) 越权 ❷ *vi.* (在数量或质量方面)超过其他，突出：~ *in* number (size) 在数目(规模)方面领先

exceeding [ik'si:diŋ] **I** *a.* 超越的，胜过的；非常的，极度的 **II** *ad.* [古] =~ly ‖**~ly** *ad.* 极端地，非常：an ~ly exciting scene 一个非常激动人心的场面

excel [ik'sel] (excelled; excelling) ❶ *vt.* 胜过，优于：The new lathe vastly ~s the old one *in* performance. 这部新车床在性能上大大超过旧的。❷ *vi.* 胜过别的；杰出：~ *in* (或 *at*) chess 擅长下棋 / He ~s *as* a long-distance swimmer. 他是个出色的长距离游泳运动员。

excellence ['eksələns] *n.* ①优秀，杰出，卓越：~ *at* (或 *in*) many forms of sport 对各种的擅长

②[常用复]优点；美德：with many ~s 具有许多优点 / a moral ~ 道德上的优点 ③[E-]阁下 (=Excellency)

excellency ['eksələnsi] *n.* ①[E-] 阁下(对大使、总督、主教等的尊称)：Your *Excellency* 阁下(直接称呼时用) / His (或 Her) *Excellency* 阁下(间接提及时用) ②[常用复]优点；美德 (=excellence)

excellent ['eksələnt] *a.* 优秀的，卓越的，杰出的，极好的：an ~ harvest 大丰收 ‖**~ly** *ad.*

except [ik'sept] **I** *prep.* 除…之外：Every one of us, ~ him, went to see the exhibition. 除他以外，我们都去参观了展览会。/ He usually goes to work on his bike ~ when it rains (或 ~ on rainy days). 除了雨天，他一般都骑自行车上班。/ His account is correct ~ *that* some details are omitted. 除了有些细节未提到之外，他的叙述是正确的。[注意：except 与 besides 不同。试比较：We all went ~ him. 除他以外，我们都去了。We all went *besides* him. 除他之外，我们大家也都去了。] **II** ❶ *vt.* 把…除外；不计：All of us, nobody ~ed, agree to his suggestion. 我们大家，无人例外，都赞同他的建议。❷ *vi.* 反对 (to, against) **III** *conj.* ①[古] 除非 (= unless) ②只是；要不是：I would go ~ it's too late. 要不是时间太晚的话我就去。‖*~ for* 除…外；若无：His composition is good ~ for some spelling mistakes. 他的这篇作文写得很好，只是有几处拼写错误。

excepting [ik'septiŋ] **I** *prep.* 除…外[用在句首或 not, without, always 等后面] **II** *conj.* ①[古] 除非 ②只是，要不是

exception [ik'sepʃən] *n.* ①例外，除外：There is an ~ to this grammatical rule. 这条语法规则有个例外。/ without (any) ~ 无(毫无)例外地 / Everyone should keep discipline, and you are no ~. 每个人都应该遵守纪律，你也不能例外。②反对，异议；【律】(口头或书面的)抗议 ‖*by way of* ~ 作为例外 / *make an* ~ 把…作为例外 / *make no* ~s 不容许有例外，一律办理 / *take* ~ ①反对，表示异议 ②有反感；感到被触犯 (*take* ~ *to* (或 *against*) 对…表示反对或抗议) / *The* ~ *proves the rule.* 例外能反证规律。/ *with the* ~ *of* 除…外

exceptional [ik'sepʃənl] *a.* ①例外的；异常的，罕见的，特殊的：~ circumstances 特殊情况 ②超优的，出众的：~ skill 卓越的技巧 ‖**~ism** *n.* 例外论 / **~ity** [ik,sepʃə'næliti] *n.* / **~ly** *ad.*

excerpt I ['eksə:pt] *n.* 摘录，选录，节录：~s from a diary 日记摘抄 **II** [ek'sə:pt] *vt.* 摘，选；引用 (*from*)：~ passages *from* a book (an article) 从一本书(一篇文章)中摘录几段 ‖**~ion** [ek'sə:pʃən] *n.* ①摘，选；引用 ②摘录，选录

excess [ik'ses] **I** *n.* ①超越，超过：an ~ of supply *over* demand 供过于求 ②超额量：an ~ of ten jin 十斤的超额量 ③ 过量，过剩：an ~ of rain 雨量过多 ④(饮食等的)过度，无节制 ⑤[复]过

度行为; 暴行 **II** *a.* 过量的; 额外的; 附加的: ~ sleep 过度的睡眠 / ~ fare 补票费 / ~ luggage 超重行李 ‖*in ~ of* 超过: a population *in ~ of* two million 两百万以上的人口 / *to ~* 过度, 过分: Don't carry your grief *to ~*. 不要过分悲哀。/ be serious *to ~* 过于严肃

excessive [ik'sesiv] *a.* 过多的, 过分的; 极度的: ~ rainfall 过多的雨水 ‖~**ly** *ad.* / ~**ness** *n.*

exchange [iks'tʃeindʒ] **I ❶** *vt.* ①交换; 调换: ~ a horse *for* a cow 用一匹马交换一头牛 / You may ~ the shirt but not return it for a refund. 你可调换这件衬衫, 但不能退货。②互换; 交流; 交易(货物): ~ greetings 相互问好 / ~ ambassadors 互派大使 / May I ~ seats *with* you? 我和你调一个座位好吗? ③兑换; 把…换成 **❷** *vi.* ①(货币)交换; 兑换: This currency ~s at par. 这货币平价兑换。②调换岗位, 调换任务 ③交易 **II** *n.* ①交换, 互换; 交流; 交易; 调换: ~ value (value in ~) 交换价值 / Let's have an ~ of views on the matter. 我们对这件事交换一下意见吧。/ an ~ of war prisoners 交换战俘 / an ~ of goods between the city and the countryside 城乡物资交流 ②(外币)兑换; (新旧货币)调换; 汇划; 汇票; 贴水, 汇水; 兑换率; [复] (银行在票据交换所中提出的)交换票据: foreign ~ 外汇 / ~ quotations 外汇行情 / a bill of ~ 汇票 / first (second, third) of ~ 第一(第二, 第三)联汇票 / the rate (或 course) of ~ 汇兑率 / ~ control 外汇管理 ③交易所: a stock ~ 证券交易所 ④交换机构; 电话局: a labour ~ [英]劳工介绍所 / the central (telephone) ~ 中央电话局 ⑤[美]经售和修理某类商品的店铺; 合作商店, 合作社: a post ~ (美国)陆军消费合作社(略作 PX) ⑥交换刊物; 从报纸翻印的文件 ‖*Exchange is no robbery.* [谑] 交换并非霸夺。(作不公平交换时的辩解) / *in ~ for* 交换 ‖~**r** *n.* 交换器 ‖~ **student** (两国之间)交换的留学生

exchequer [iks'tʃekə] *n.* ①国库; 金库 ②资金; 经济来源; (个人的)资财 ③[E-] 英国财政部: the Chancellor of the *Exchequer* (英国)财政大臣 ④[E-] 英国高等法院的一个部门 ⑤ [E-] 【英史】(中世纪)财务署, 税务署 ‖~ **bond** 英国国库债券

excise[1] [ek'saiz] **I** *n.* ①(国内)货物税 ②领许可证税, 执照税 **II** *vt.* ①向…强征货物税 ②[英]向…索高价 ‖**ex'ciseman** *n.* 英国的收税官

excise[2] [ek'saiz] *vt.* ①割去, 切除; 删去 ②【植】【动】在…上切切口, 将…开槽

excision [ek'siʒən] *n.* ①切除; 删除 ②【医】切除(术) ③[宗] 逐出教会

excitable [ik'saitəbl] *a.* 能被激动的; 易兴奋的, 易激动的; 过敏的 ‖**excitability** [ik,saitə'biliti] *n.* ①【物】可激发性 ②【医】兴奋性

excite [ik'sait] **❶** *vt.* ①刺激; 使兴奋, 使激动: ~ a nerve 刺激神经 ②激发, 激励; 唤起; 引起: ~

attention (interest, jealousy) 引起注意(兴趣, 妒忌) ③【物】激起(电流); 使励磁; 激发(原子等) ④【摄】使感光 **❷** *vi.* [口]兴奋, 激动: Don't ~! 别激动! ‖~**ment** *n.* ①刺激; 兴奋, 激动; 骚动: speak *in* ~*ment* 发言激昂 / a high pitch of ~*ment* 极度兴奋 ②激动的事物 ‖~**r** *n.* ①刺激者; 激励者; 刺激物, 兴奋剂 ②【无】激励器; 主控振荡器; 辐射器; 主控振荡槽路 ③【物】励磁机

excited [ik'saitid] *a.* ①兴奋的; 激昂的 ②【物】已激发的; 已励磁的 ‖~**ly** *ad.*

exciting [ik'saitiŋ] *a.* 令人兴奋的, 使人激动的: ~ news 振奋人心的消息 ‖~**ly** *ad.*

exclaim [iks'kleim] *vi. & vt.* (由于惊讶、痛苦、愤怒、高兴等而)呼喊; 惊叫; 大声说

exclamation [,eksklə'meiʃən] *n.* ①呼喊, 惊叫 ②感叹; 惊叹; 感叹词; 惊叹语 ‖~ **mark**, ~ **point** 感情号, 感叹号, 惊叹号(即!)

exclamatory [eks'klæmətəri] *a.* 叫喊的; 感叹的, 惊叹的 ‖~ **sentence** 感叹句

exclude [iks'klu:d] *vt.* ①拒绝接纳(或考虑), 把…排除在外; 排斥(可能性等): ~ sb. *from* membership (the school) 拒绝某人入会(校) / ~ sb. (*from*) getting in 不准某人入内 / The train has twenty cars, the baggage and mail ones ~d (或 *excluding* the baggage and mail ones). 这列火车, 除行李车和邮车外, 有二十节车厢。~ the possibility of danger 排除危险的可能性 / the law of ~d middle 【逻】排中律 ② 逐出

exclusion [iks'klu:ʒən] *n.* ①排斥, 排除在外: an attitude of ~ 排斥态度 ② 被排除在外的事物 ‖*to the ~ of* 排斥着: Never concentrate all your attention on one or two problems, *to the ~ of* others. 别把全部注意力集中在一两个问题上而不顾其他问题。‖~**ary** *a.* 排斥的 / ~**ism** *n.* 排外主义 / ~**ist** *a.* 排外主义的 *n.* 排外主义者 ‖~ **principle** 【物】(泡利)不相容原理

exclusive [iks'klu:siv] **I** *a.* ①除外的; 排外的, 排他的 ②孤傲的(尤指不愿与社会地位、教育程度等较低的人相处的): an ~ attitude 孤傲的态度 ③专有的, 独占的; 唯一的: an ~ right to sell sth. 某物的专卖权 / an ~ privilege 独有的特权 / ~ jurisdiction 唯一的管辖权 ④全部的: give a question one's ~ attention 把全部注意力放在某一问题上 ⑤[美] 时式的, 时髦的 ⑥(商店、商品等)索价高昂的, 高级的; 别处没有的 ⑦(社团、俱乐部等)不愿吸收新成员的 ⑧势利的, 不大众化的 **II** *n.* ①独家新闻; 专有权 ②孤傲的人 ‖*~ of* 除; 不计算…在内: ~ *of* Sundays 星期日除外 ‖~**ly** *ad.* / ~**ness** *n.* / **exclusivism** *n.* 排他主义; 排外主义: "Left" *exclusivism* "左"倾的排外主义

excommunicate **I** [,ekskə'mju:nikeit] *vt.* 【宗】开除…的教籍; 把…逐出教会 **II** [,ekskə'mju:nikit] *a. & n.* 被开除教籍的(人), 被逐出教会的(人) ‖**excommunication** ['ekskə,mju:ni'keiʃən] *n.* 开除教籍, 逐出教会; 开除教籍的公告

excrement ['ekskrimənt] *n.* [常用复]粪便; 排泄物 ||**~al** [ˌekskri'mentl], **~itious** [ˌekskrimen'tiʃəs] *a.*

excrescence [iks'kresns], **excrescency** [iks'kresnsi] *n.* 赘生物; 赘疣, 瘤

excrescent [iks'kresnt] *a.* 赘生的; 多余的, 无用的;【语】赘音的

excrete [eks'kri:t] *vt.* 排泄; 分泌: The skin ~*s* sweat. 皮肤出汗。

excruciate [iks'kru:ʃieit] *vt.* ①[古]使受酷刑, 拷打 ②折磨; 使苦恼 ||**excruciating** *a.* ① 造成剧痛的; 极痛苦的; 使苦恼的; 难忍受的 ②剧烈的, 极度的: *excruciating* delight (pain) 非凡的高兴(痛苦) / **excruciation** [iksˌkru:ʃi'eiʃən] *n.* ①酷刑, 拷问 ②剧痛; 苦恼, 苦楚

exculpate ['ekskʌlpeit] *vt.* 开脱, 使无罪, 申明(某人)无罪: ~ sb. *from* a charge 开脱某人的罪责 ||**exculpation** [ˌekskʌl'peiʃən] *n.* 开脱; 申明无罪 / **exculpatory** [eks'kʌlpətəri] *a.* 开脱罪责的; 申明无罪的

excursion [iks'kə:ʃən] *n.* ① 远足; 短途旅行; (集体)游览: go on (或 make) an ~ to 到…去旅行 / an ~ train 游览火车 / ~ rates 游览收费率 ②远足队; 游览团体 ③离题 ④【医】肺的一个完全的呼吸动作 ⑤【物】偏移, 漂移: amplitude ~ 振幅偏移 ||**~al, ~ary** *a.* / **~ist** *n.* 远足者; 短途旅行者; 游览者

excuse I [iks'kju:z] *vt.* ① 原谅: *Excuse* me *for* interrupting you (或 *Excuse* my interruption). 请原谅, 打扰你(们)了。/ *Excuse* me, but could you tell me the time? 对不起, 请问现在几点钟? [注意: 作"对不起"时, "Excuse me" 是客套语, 常用于要走开、插话、表示异议等场合; 而 "I am sorry" 常表示确已犯某种过失] ② 为…辩解; 成为…的理由: ~ oneself *for* one's mistake 为自己的错误辩护 / Nothing can ~ such irresponsible behaviour. 这种不负责任的行为是完全没有理由可言的。③给…免去: ~ sb. *from* attendance at the meeting 同意某人不参加会议 / This ~*d* him another trip. 这就省了他再跑一趟了。**II** [iks'kju:s] *n.* ①原谅, 饶恕: an ~ for some fault 对某种过失的原谅 ②[复]歉意, 道歉: Please make my ~*s* to your friend. 请代我向你的朋友表示歉意。③借口; 辩解; 理由: Too much work is no ~ for not studying. 工作太忙不能成为不学习的理由。/ be absent without ~ 无故缺席 / make (或 invent, cook up) a lame ~ 捏造一个站不住脚的借口 ④请假条 ⑤免去; 免除的借口(或请求) ||**~ oneself** ① 替自己辩解 ② 说声"请原谅"就走开, 表示要走开: He ~*d* himself to us. 他向我们说了一声"请原谅", 就离开了。/ ~ oneself *from* 借口推托; 婉言拒绝 / *in* ~ *of* 作为…的辩解: You should not plead inexperience *in* ~ *of* your mistake. 你不应该借口缺乏经验来为你的错误辩解。

execrable ['eksikrəbl] *a.* ①该咒骂的; 可憎恶的,

讨厌的 ②恶劣的, 坏透的: ~ weather 恶劣的天气 ||**execrably** *ad.*

execrate ['eksikreit] **❶** *vt.* ①痛骂; 咒骂;[古]诅咒 ②憎恶, 嫌恶 **❷** *vi.* 咒骂 ||**execration** [ˌeksi-'kreiʃən] *n.* ①诅咒; 咒骂; 诅咒话; 憎恶, 嫌恶 ②被咒骂的人(或物) / **execrative, execratory** *a.*

executant [ig'zekjutənt] *n.* 执行者; 实行者;【音】演奏者

execute ['eksikju:t] *vt.* ① 实行; 实施; 执行; 履行; 贯彻; 完成: ~ a command 执行命令 / ~ fire 【军】开火 / ~ one's duties 尽职 ②处…处死 ③作成; 制成(艺术品等); 演奏(乐曲等): a statue ~*d* in bronze 铜像 / ~ a piece of music 演奏一曲 ④【律】经签名盖章等手续使(证书、契约等)生效, 使合法; [英]让渡(财产): ~ a deed 签名使契据生效

execution [ˌeksi'kju:ʃən] *n.* ①实行, 实施; 执行; 履行; 完成: forcible ~ 强制执行 ②处死刑: ~ by shooting 枪决 ③制作; 演奏; 技巧; 手法: the ~ of a carving 雕刻品的制作 / marvellous ~ 惊人的技巧 ④ (武器等的) 破坏效果, 杀伤力 ⑤【律】(经签名盖章等)法律文件的生效, 合法; (授权将判决付诸实施的)执行令状 ||**carry** (或 **put**) **into** ~ 实行, 实现, 实施 / **do** ~ 奏效, 见效; [喻](姿容等)惑人; 杀伤 ||**~er** *n.* 刽子手; 死刑执行人

executive [ig'zekjutiv] **I** *a.* ①执行的; 善于执行的; 实施的; 行政上的: an ~ committee 执行委员会 / ~ authorities 行政当局 / an ~ branch 行政部门 ②行政官的; 总经理的 **II** *n.* ① [the ~] 行政官[员]; (工会、党派等的)执行委员会 ②执行者; 行政官; 高级官员: the (chief) ~[美]最高行政官, 行政长官(指总统或州长) ③[美]总经理; 董事 ||**~ agreement** [美]行政协定(总统未经咨询参议院而与外国所订的协定) / ~ **council** 咨询会议; 行政会议; 最高行政会议 / **Executive Mansion** [美]总统官邸; 州长官邸 / ~ **officer** 【军】①主任参谋 ②副舰长 / ~ **order** 美国总统的行政命令 / ~ **park** [美]远离市中心的商业机构办公区 / ~ **session** 内部会议(尤指立法机构的)

executor *n.* ① ['eksikju:tə] 执行者; 实行者 ② [ig'zekjutə] 指定的遗嘱执行人 ||**~ial** [igˌzekju-'tɔ:riəl] *a.* / **~ship** [ig'zekjutəʃip] *n.* (遗嘱)执行人的职务

exemplary [ig'zempləri] *a.* ①模范的, 值得效法的: ~ behaviour (或conduct) 模范的行为 / play an ~ role in work 在工作中作出榜样 ②警戒性的; 惩戒性的: ~ damages【律】(惩罚性的)超过实际损失的赔偿 ③作样板的, 示范的; 作例证的; 典型的 ||**exemplarily** [ig'zempləri1i]; 美 [ˌegzəm'plerili] *ad.* / **exemplariness** *n.*

exemplify [ig'zemplifai] *vt.* ①举例说明; 作为…的例子(或榜样) ②【律】制定(文件等)的经公章证明的誊本 ||**exemplification** [igˌzemplifi'keiʃən] *n.* ①举例, 例证; 范例 ②【律】经公章证明的誊本, 正本

exempt [ig'zempt, eg'zempt] **I** *vt.* 免除，豁免 (*from*): ~ sb. *from* taxation 免除某人纳税 **II** *a.* 被免除的；被豁免的 (*from*): goods ~ *from* taxes 免税货物 / be ~ *from* military service 免服兵役 **III** *n.* 被免除者；被豁免(义务等)的人；免税人 ∥~**ible** *a.* 可享豁免权的 / ~**ion** [ig'zempʃən] *n.* 免除；豁免；免税(尤指部分所得税)；免除的原因

exercise ['eksəsaiz] **I** *n.* ① 行使，运用；实行，履行: ~ of collective wisdom 集体智慧的运用 / ~ of local initiative 地方积极性的发挥 / ~ of one's duties 执行任务 ②训练；锻炼；[常用复]体操，运动: lack of ~ 缺乏锻炼 / vocal ~s 练声 / You'd better take more ~。你最好多锻炼身体。/ gymnastic ~s 体操 ③练习，习题，功课: spelling ~s 拼写练习 / an ~ in English grammar 英语语法习题 / do one's ~ 做练习(或功课) ④ 【军】演习；操练: a field ~ 野外演习 / an ~ ground 演兵场 ⑤[美][复]典礼；仪式；答辩(为取得学位的考试形式)；传统做法: graduation ~s 毕业典礼 / an ~ of devotion 拜神仪式 / an ~ older than recorded history 比历史记载更悠久的习惯做法 **II** ❶ *vt.* ①实行，行使(权力等)；履行；运用；施加 ~ a function 执行某种职责 / ~ influence (pressure) *on* sb. 给某人施加影响(压力) / ~ strict control *over* 严格控制… ②训练，锻炼: ~ troops 练兵 / ~ the voice 练嗓子 / ~ oneself in bayoneting 练刺杀本领 ③[常用被动语态]使扰忧；使烦恼；使生气 (*about*): be ~d about sth. 为某事而担忧 ❷ *vi.* 练习；锻炼: You don't ~ enough. 你锻炼不够。∥~**r** *n.* ①行使(职权等)的人 ②锻炼者；受训练者 ③锻炼肌肉用的器械

exert [ig'zəːt, eg'zəːt] *vt.* 用(力)；发挥(威力等)；施加(压力等)；产生(影响等)；行使(职权等): ~ all one's strength 尽全力 / ~ every effort 尽一切力量 / ~ one's utmost 尽最大努力 / ~ pressure (influence) *on* sb. 对某人施加压力(影响) / ~ direct control of 对…加以直接控制 ∥~**oneself** 努力，尽力: ~ oneself to fulfil the task 努力完成任务

exertion [ig'zəːʃən, eg'zəːʃən] *n.* ①尽力，努力，费力: make (或 use) ~ 尽力 / with all one's ~s 尽最大的努力 / combine ~ and rest 劳逸结合 / be able to stand the ~ of travelling 经得起旅途劳顿 ②行使；发挥: the ~ of power (或 authority) 权力的行使

exeunt ['eksiʌnt] *vi.* [拉](舞台指示)(某几个角色)退场，下: ~ omnes ['omniːz] (演员)全体退场

exhale [eks'heil, eg'zeil] ❶ *vt.* ①呼出，呼(气)；发散出(蒸汽、气味等): ~ air *from* the lungs 从肺里呼气 ②[古]使蒸发 ❷ *vi.* (气味等)蒸发，发散；呼气 ∥**exhalation** [ˌekshə'leiʃən, ˌegzə'leiʃən] *n.* ①蒸发；发出；呼气(怒气等的)发作 ②发散物(如气体、蒸气、光)；薄雾

exhaust [ig'zɔːst] **I** ❶ *vt.* ①抽完，汲干；把…的内容抽空: ~ the air *from* a tube (或 ~ a tube *of* air) 抽光管中空气 / ~ (the water of) a well 把井水汲干 / ~ed tea 泡得无味的茶叶 ②用完，花光，耗尽；竭尽；试尽: ~ the funds in a week 一周内用完资金 / ~ sb.'s patience 使某人忍无可忍 / ~ the possibilities 试尽一切可能 ③[~ oneself, 或用被动语态]使筋疲力尽 ④ 详尽地论述: ~ a subject 对一个题目作详尽无遗的论述 ❷ *vi.* ①排出气体 ②(气体等)被排出 **II** *n.* ①排出；排气(或水等): steam heating 废汽供暖 ②排出的气 ③排气装置；排气管 ∥~**er** *n.* 排气器 / ~**less** *a.* 用不完的；不会枯竭的 ∥~ **gas** 废气 / ~ **pipe** 排气管

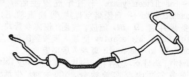

exhaust pipe

exhausting [ig'zɔːstiŋ] *a.* 使耗尽的；使人筋疲力尽的 ∥~**ly** *ad.*

exhaustion [ig'zɔːstʃən] *n.* ①耗尽；枯竭 ②(气体等的)排出 ③筋疲力尽 ④详尽无遗的论述

exhaustive [ig'zɔːstiv] *a.* ①会耗尽的，使耗尽的 ②(论述等)彻底的，详尽无遗的: ~ research 彻底的研究工作 / I don't claim to be ~ on this subject. 我并不认为自己把这个问题讲透了。 ∥~**ly** *ad.* / ~**ness** *n.*

exhibit [ig'zibit] **I** ❶ *vt.* ①展览，展出，陈列: ~ unearthed cultural relics 展览出土文物 ②表示，显出，显示: ~ great courage 表现出极大的勇气 / ~ no fear 毫无惧色 ③【律】正式提交(证据等) ④【医】用(药)；给(药) ❷ *vi.* 开展览会，展出产品(或作品等) **II** *n.* ①展出，展览(会): On ~ are new products of industry and agriculture. 展出的是工农业新产品。②展览品，陈列品: Please do not touch the ~s. 请勿触摸展览品。③显示，呈现【律】证据，证件，物证 ∥~**or, ~er** *n.* (展览会等的)参加者，展出者；电影放映者；电影院老板(或经理)

exhibition [ˌeksi'biʃən] *n.* ①展览；(体育运动等的)表演，显示: place artistic handicrafts *on* ~ 展出手工艺品 / an ~ match 表演赛 / an ~ flight 【空】表演飞行 ②展览会；展览品，陈列品；(学生的)成绩展览 ∥*make an ~ of oneself* 出洋相，当众出丑 ∥~**er** *n.* 展出者

exhilarate [ig'ziləreit] *vt.* 使高兴；使活跃；使振奋 ∥**exhilaration** [igˌzilə'reiʃən] *n.*

exhort [ig'zɔːt] ❶ *vt.* ①规劝；激励；告诫: ~ sb. to be careful 劝告某人要细心 / ~ sb. to diligence and thrift 劝某人勤奋 ②提倡，主张(改革等) ❷ *vi.* 规劝；告诫 ∥**exhortation** [ˌegzɔː'teiʃən, ˌeksɔː'teiʃən] *n.* / **exhortative, exhortatory** *a.* / ~**er** *n.* 劝勉者；告诫者；提倡者

exhume [eks'hju:m] *vt.* ① (从墓内等) 掘出 (尸体等) ② [喻] 发掘 (旧剧目等) ‖**exhumation** [ˌekshju:'meiʃən] *n.*

exigence ['eksidʒəns], **exigency** ['eksidʒənsi] *n.* ①紧急(状态), 危急(关头); 事变: take measures to meet any possible ~ 采取措施以应付任何可能的事变 ② [复]急事; 迫切的需要; 苛求, (很高的) 要求: meet the *exigencies* of the hard times 适应艰苦时期的要求

exile ['eksail] **I** *n.* ① 流放, 放逐, 充军; 离开本国, 离乡背井: live in ~ 过流放生活; 过离乡背井的生活 / send sb. into ~ 流放某人 / an ~ of fifteen years 十五年流放生活 / send oneself into ~ 自愿离乡背井 ② 被流放者; 离乡背井者 **II** *vt.* 流放, 放逐; 使离乡背井: ~ sb. from his country 把某人流放到国外 / oneself to the south 离乡远居南方

exist [ig'zist] *vi.* ①存在: Salt ~s in many things. 许多东西中存在着盐分。 ②生存; 生活; 继续存在: ~ on vegetable food 靠植物性食物生存 / One cannot ~ without air. 人没有空气就不能生存。

existence [ig'zistəns] *n.* ①存在; 实在 ②生存; 继续存在; 存在状态; 生活(方式): the ~ of a state of war 战争状态的延续 / lead a frugal ~ 过俭朴的生活 ③存在物; 实在物, 实体 ‖*bring* (或 *call*) *into* ~ 使产生; 使成立 / *come into* ~ 开始存在; 产生; 成立 / *in* ~ 存在的, 现有的: There is nothing *in* ~ that is unchanging. 一切存在的事物没有不变化的。 / the most magnificent bridge *in* ~ 现有的最雄伟的大桥 / *lead a Jekyll and Hyde* ~ 过双重人格的生活 / *put out of* ~ 消灭, 灭绝; 杀死

existent [ig'zistənt] **I** *a.* 存在的, 实在的; 现存的; 目前的 **II** *n.* 存在的事物; 生存者

existing [ig'zistiŋ] *a.* 存在的; 现存的; 目前的: the ~ order 现存的社会秩序(或制度) / equipment 现有(或原有)设备 / ~ circumstances 现状 / the ~ situation 当前形势

exit ['eksit] **I** *n.* ① (演员的) 退场, 退出; 退出权 ②出口, 通道; 安全门, 太平门: an ~ from an airfield 飞机场的出口 / an emergency ~ 安全门, 太平门 ③去世, 死亡 **II** *vi.* 退出, 离去; 去世 ‖*make one's* ~ ①退出, 离去 ②死, 去世

exit ['eksit] *vi.* [拉](舞台指示)(某一个角色)退场, 下: *Exit* John. 约翰下。

exodus ['eksədəs] *n.* [只用单] ① (成群的) 出去, 退出, 离去(尤指大批移民的出国) ② [the E-] (古代以色列人)出埃及; [E-] (基督教《圣经》中的)《出埃及记》

exonerate [ig'zɔnəreit] *vt.* ① 使免(罪) (*from*): ~ sb. *from* accusation 宣布某人无罪 ② 免除, 解除(*from*): ~ sb. *from* responsibility 免除某人的责任 ‖**exoneration** [igˌzɔnə'reiʃən] *n.* 免罪, 免除 / **exonerative** *a.* 免罪的; 免除的

exorbitant [ig'zɔ:bitənt] *a.* (要求、取费等)过度

的, 过高的, 昂贵的 ‖~**ly** *ad.*

exorcize, exorcise ['eksɔ:saiz] *vt.* 祓除, 驱除(妖魔等); 从…驱除妖魔

exotic [eg'zɔtik, ek'sɔtik] **I** *a.* ① 外(国)来的; 外国产的, 外国种的: an ~ word 外来词 ②异国情调的; 异乎寻常的, 奇异的; 吸引人的 **II** *n.* 外来物; 舶来品; 外来植物; 外来词 ‖~**ally** *ad.* ‖~ **dancer** 跳脱衣舞(或其他黄色舞)的人

expand [iks'pænd] ❶ *vt.* ①张开, 展开(帆、叶、瓣等): The eagle ~ed his wings. 鹰展翅。 ②使膨胀; 使扩张; 使伸展: Heat ~s metals. 热使金属膨胀。 / ~ the chest by inspiration 吸气使胸腔扩张 ③扩大, 扩充; 推广; 发展; 【军】扩编: ~ reproduction 扩大再生产 / ~ the double cropping rice area 扩大双季稻种植面积 / ~ the people's medical and health services 发展人民的医药卫生事业 ④阐述; 详谈; 完全写出: ~ one's view 阐述自己的观点 ⑤【数】展开(代数式等) ❷ *vi.* ①张开, 展开 ②扩张; 发展; 增长, 推广开来: This factory ~s to the riverside. 这个厂的地界扩展到河边。 / The shipbuilding industry is rapidly ~ing. 造船工业正在迅速发展。 / an ~ing bullet 裂开弹 ③膨胀: Metals ~ *with* heat. 金属遇热膨胀。 ④阐述; 详谈 (*on, upon*) ⑤变得和蔼可亲(或心情舒畅); 热情洋溢

expanse [iks'pæns] *n.* ①广阔(的区域); 太空, 苍天; 浩瀚: the blue ~ (of the sky) 蔚蓝的天空 / the boundless ~ of the ocean (或 a wide ~ of waters) 浩瀚的海洋 ②膨胀; 扩张

expansion [iks'pænʃən] *n.* ①张开, 伸展: the ~ of a bird's wings 鸟翼的展开 ②扩张; 膨胀: ~ of territory (或 territorial) 领土扩张 / Heat causes the ~ of gases. 热使气体膨胀。 / ~ and contraction 伸缩 / the ~ of the currency 通货膨胀 ③扩大, 扩充; 发展: a rapid ~ of foreign trade 对外贸易的迅速发展 ④扩展物; 扩大部分 ⑤辽阔; 浩瀚 ⑥(讲题等的)详述, 阐述 ⑦【数】展开(式); 【物】膨胀: the ~ of a determinant 行列式的展开 / ~ in series 展成级数 ‖~**ism** *n.* 扩张主义 / ~**ist** *n.* 扩张主义者 *a.* 扩张主义的 ‖~ **joint** 【建】伸缩(接)缝

expansive [iks'pænsiv] *a.* ① 使扩张的; 扩张(性)的; 膨胀(性)的; 开展(性)的 ②广阔的, 辽阔的; 广泛的; 浩瀚的 ③豪爽的, 开朗的; 兴高采烈的; (言语)滔滔不绝的: an ~ person 胸襟开阔的人 ④豪华的: ~ living 奢华的生活 ⑤ [心]自大狂的; (病态地)感到舒畅的 ‖~**ly** *ad.* / ~**ness** *n.*

expatiate [eks'peiʃieit] *vi.* ①细说; 详述, 阐述: ~ *on* (或 *upon*) a subject 详述一个题目 ②漫游, 漫步 ‖**expatiation** [eksˌpeiʃi'eiʃən] *n.* / **expatiatory** *a.*

expatriate I [eks'pætrieit] ❶ *vt.* ①把…逐出国外, 流放 ② [~ oneself] 移居国外; 放弃原国籍 ❷ *vi.* 移居国外; 放弃原国籍 **II** [eks'pætriit] *a.*

移居国外的; 被流放(国外)的 **III** [eks'pætriit] *n.* 移居国外的人; 放弃原国籍的人; 被流放(国外)的人 ‖**expatriation** [eks,pætri'eiʃən] *n.*

expect [iks'pekt] *vt.* ①期待; 预期; 盼望: He is ~*ing* a letter. 他正在等信。/ I ~ to be back next Monday. 我预计下星期一回来。/ You will be ~*ed* this afternoon. 盼望你今天下午来。/ I had not ~*ed that* things should turn out like this. 我没料到事情的结果竟是这样。/ The work was finished sooner than ~*ed*. 工作比预期的完成得快。②期望, 嘱望; 指望, 要求: We ~ much of him. 我们对他寄予很大希望。/ You are ~*ed* to finish it in time. 望你及时把它完成。/ ~ every man to do his duty 要求人人尽责 ③[口](料)想, 认为: A: Is she going to sing at the evening party? B: I ~ so. 甲: 晚会上有她的演唱节目吗? 乙: 我想有吧。/ I ~ not (或 I don't ~ so). 我认为不会。‖*be* ~*ing* [口]怀孕: His wife *was* ~*ing*. 他的妻子当时正怀孕。

expectant [iks'pektənt] **I** *a.* ①期待的; 预期的; 期望的: an ~ attitude 观望态度 / an ~ mother 待产妇 / ~ treatment (或 method)【医】期待疗法 ②【律】(有继承权而)期待占有的 **II** *n.* 期待者(如谋求职位者) ‖~**ly** *ad.*

expectation [,ekspek'teiʃən] *n.* ①期待; 预期: patient ~ 耐心的期待 / a general ~ of success 普遍预期成功 / ~ of life (根据概率统计求得的)估计寿命 ②期望; 嘱望: fall short of (或 not live up to) sb.'s ~*s* 辜负某人的期望 / meet (或 answer, come up to) sb.'s ~*s* 不负某人所望 / according to ~ 如所预料 / beyond (或 contrary to) ~ 出乎意料, 预料不到地 ③[复]前程(尤指晋升、继承遗产等的希望): great ~*s* 继承大宗遗产(或晋升高位)的前景 ④[常用复]期望的事物 ⑤【数】期望(值) ‖*in* ~ 在指望中的; 期望着: money *in* ~ 指望中的钱 / wait *in* ~ 期待着

expedience [iks'piːdjəns], **expediency** [iks'piːdjənsi] *n.* ①得计, 得策; 便利, 方便, 有(私)利 ②(出于私利的)权术; 权宜之计

expedient [iks'piːdjənt] **I** *a.* ①得策的, 得计的; 便利的, 方便的, 有(私)利的: It is ~ that he should go away at once. 他最好还是立刻走掉。/ do whatever is ~ 怎么便利就怎么办 ②权宜之计的; 出于私利的: an ~ measure to meet an emergency 应急的权宜措施 **II** *n.* 紧急的手段(或办法); 权宜之计: a temporary ~ 权宜手段 / go to every ~ 不择手段

expedite ['ekspidait] **I** *vt.* ①加快(进程等); 促进(措施等); 迅速处理(事务等): That will ~ matters. 那将加速事情的进展。②发出, 派出 **II** *a.* ①无阻碍的, 畅通的 ②迅速的, 敏捷的; 机智的 ③便利的

expedition [,ekspi'diʃən] *n.* ①远征(队); 探险(队); 考察(队): go *on* an ~ 去远征(或探险、考察) / make an ~ *to* the North Pole 去北极探险 / a scientific ~ *to* Mt. Jolmo Lungma 赴珠穆朗玛峰的科学考察(团) / a shopping ~ 上街购物; 一同上街购物的一群人 / a mountaineering ~ 登山队 / a punitive ~ 讨伐 ②迅速, 敏捷: use ~ 从速, 迅速; with ~ 迅速地 ③派遣 ‖*go on a fishing* ~ [美]试探一下, 摸底 ‖~**ary** *a.* 远征的; 探险的: ~*ary* forces 远征军; 派遣军

expel [iks'pel] (expelled; expelling) *vt.* ①驱逐, 赶出; 开除: be *expelled from* (the) school (或 be *expelled* the school) 被学校开除 ②排出(空气等); 发射(子弹等): ~ air *from* the lungs 排出肺里的空气 ‖**expeller** *n.* 驱逐者; 开除者

expend [iks'pend] *vt.* ①消费, 花费(时间、精力、金钱等); 用光, 耗尽: ~ much care *in* writing 用心写作 / ~ a large sum *on* sth. 在某物上用一大笔款子 [注意: 表示花钱时, expend 不及 spend 常用] ②【海】把(暂时不用的绳)绕在桅杆上

expenditure [iks'penditʃə] *n.* ①(时间、金钱等的)支出, 消费, 花费, 使用: administrative ~ 行政管理支出 / ~ *on* national defence 国防支出 / revenue and ~ 收入和岁出, 收支 / limit one's ~(*s*) to what is necessary 把消费限制在必需品上 ②支出额, 消费额; 经费, 费用: military ~*s* 军费 / current ~ 经(常)费

expense [iks'pens] *n.* ①花费, 消费, 支出; (精力、时间等的)消耗: spare no ~ 不惜费用 / at the public (one's own) ~ 公(自)费 ②[常用复]开支; 经费: travel(l)ing ~*s* 旅费 / selling ~*s* 销售费用 / constant (variable) ~*s* 固定(变动)费用 / ~*s in* the trial manufacture of new products 新产品试制费 / cut down one's ~*s* 节省开支 ③费钱之物: A motorcycle can be a great ~. (买)一辆摩托车可能要花很多钱。‖*at sb.'s* ~ ①归某人付费(或负担) ②在使某人受损害的情况下: have a laugh *at sb.'s* ~ 以某人为笑柄, 取笑某人 / *at the* ~ *of* ①归…付费(或负担) ②在损害…的情况下, 以…为牺牲: Those who try to profit *at the* ~ *of* others will come to no good end. 企图损人利己的人不会有好下场。/ *at the* ~ *of* one's health 在损害健康的条件下 / *blow the* ~ [俚]挥霍, 尽量花钱 / *go to the* ~ *of* 为…的目的花钱, 为…的目的付费 / *out-of-pocket* ~*s* 见 pocket / *put sb. to* ~ 使某人负担费用, 使某人花钱 ‖~ **account** 支出帐, 报销单

expensive [iks'pensiv] *a.* 花费的, 花钱多的; 高价的, 昂贵的; 奢华的 ‖~**ly** *ad.* / ~**ness** *n.*

experience [iks'piəriəns] **I** *n.* ①经验, 体验; 经历, 阅历: All genuine knowledge originates in direct ~. 一切真知都是从直接经验发源的。/ sum up ~ 总结经验 / learn *by* (或 *from, through*) ~ 从经验中学到(或懂得) / a meeting to exchange ~ 经验交流会 / a man of (rich 或 much) ~ 经验丰富的人 / with an ~ of forty years at sea 有四十年航海经验 / gain ~ in teaching 获得教学经验 / a common ~ 共同的经历(或遭遇) / undergo an ~ 经历,体验 / What was your ~ with the task? 你对这项任务有什么体会? ②[常用复](宗教上)灵性的感受 Ⅱ vt. 经历,体验;感受;遭受: He has ~d what hardships mean. 他体验过艰苦的生活。/ ~ pleasure (pain) 感到愉快(痛苦) / ~ difficulties (setbacks) 遭到困难(挫折) ||~ religion 见 religion / Experience teaches· (或 Experience does it.) 经验给人教训。(或:经验给人智慧。)||~d a. 有经验的,经验丰富的,熟练的,老练的: an ~d driver 熟练的驾驶员 / have an ~d eye (由于经验丰富而)看得准,目光锐利 ||~ meeting [美]【宗】灵性交流会;祈祷会 / ~ table (根据人寿保险公司统计资料制成的)寿命估计表

experiment [iks'perimənt] Ⅰ n. 实验;试验: scientific ~ 科学实验 / make (或 carry out) an ~ in physics 进行物理实验 / an ~ with new teaching methods 新教学方法的试验 Ⅱ [iks-'periment] vi. 进行实验(或试验): ~ on (或 upon) frogs 用青蛙做实验 / ~ with medicinal herbs 试验草药 / ~ in selected units 在试点单位进行试验 ||~er [iks'perimentə] n. 实验者;试验者 ||~ station (农业等)试验站

experimental [eks,peri'mentl] a. 实验(性)的;试验(性)的;实验上的;经验上的;根据实验的,根据试验的: ~ evidence 实验证据 / an ~ plot 试验田 / an ~ farm 实验农场 / an ~ class 试点班 / ~ work in selected spots 试点(工作) / ~ knowledge 经验知识 ||~ism n. 实验主义;实验论;经验论 ||~ist n. ①实验主义者;经验主义者 ②(科学)实验者;试验者 ||~ly ad.

expert ['ekspə:t] Ⅰ n. ①专家;能手;熟练者;有经验者: a civil engineering ~ 土木工程专家 / an ~ in electronics 电子学专家 / an ~ on international trade 国际贸易专家 / an ~ with the needle 针线能手 ②[军]特等射手;特等射手级 Ⅱ a. ①熟练的,老练的;有经验的: ~ acting 熟练的演技 / the ~ hands of a shoemaker 制鞋工人灵巧的双手 / become ~ at (calculating) figures 成为计算数字的能手 / be ~ in piloting ships 能熟练地领航 / an ~ marksman 特等射手 ②专家的,内行的;专门的: an ~ in capacity 以专家的身分 / an ~ opinion 内行的意见 / ~ evidence 【律】鉴定人证明 / ~ knowledge (skill) 专门知识(技能) / ③(制作品)精巧的,巧妙的 Ⅲ ❶ vt. 在…中当专家: ~ an enterprise 在一个企业中当专家 ❷ vi. 当专家 ||~ly ad. / ~ness n.

expiate ['ekspieit] ❶ vt. 抵偿,补偿;赎;为(作恶、犯罪等)而受罚: ~ sin (或 a crime) 赎罪 ❷ vi. 抵罪;赎罪 ||**expiation** [,ekspi'eiʃən] n. 抵罪;赎罪 / **expiator** n. 抵罪者;赎罪者 / **expiatory** ['ekspiətəri] a. 抵罪的;赎罪的

expiration [,ekspaiə'reiʃən] n. ①满期,届期;截止,告终: at the ~ of one's term of office (service) 在任职(服役)期满时 / at the ~ of a year (a truce) 在一年(休战)期满时 ②呼气;呼出物,嘘出的声音 ③[古]最后一息;断气,死亡

expire [iks'paiə] ❶ vi. ①满期;(期限等)终止;开始无效: My passport ~s in a month. 我的护照再过一个月就满期了。②呼气,吐气 ③咽气,死亡;熄灭 ❷ vt. 呼出;[古]发出(气味等)

expiry [iks'paiəri] n. ①(期限、协定等的)满期,终止 ②呼气 ③[古]断气,死亡

explain [iks'plein] ❶ vt. ①解释,说明;阐明: ~ a difficult problem 解释难题 / Will you please ~ this point to us? 请你把这一点对我们解释一下好吗? ②为…辩解;说明…的理由(或原因): Can you ~ such conduct? 你能为这种行为辩解吗? / That ~s his hesitation. 原来那就是他犹豫不决的原因。❷ vi. 解释,说明;辩解 ||~ away 把…解释过去: ~ away the use of offensive language 为讲过无礼的话而辩解 / ~ oneself 说明自己的意思(或动机);为自己的行为辩解 ||~able a. 可说明的,可解释的;可辩解的

explanation [,eksplə'neiʃən] n. ①解释,说明: give a clear ~ 解释明白 / repeated ~s 反复的解释 / notes in ~ 注解 ②辩解,辩明: Have you anything to say in ~ of your conduct? 你有什么话要为自己的行为辩解吗? ③(为消除误会或分歧等的)交谈,互相讲明: come to an ~ with sb. 同某人交谈后消除了彼此间的误会

explanatory [iks'plænətəri] a. 解释的,说明的,辩明的: ~ notes 注释 / an ~ title (电影中的)说明字幕 / find sb. ~ and reasonable 发现某人愿意讲清道理 ||**explanatorily** [iks'plænə-tərili; 美 iks,plænə'tɔ:rili] ad. / **explanatoriness** n.

expletive [eks'pli:tiv] Ⅰ a. 填补的,补足的;附加的;多余的 Ⅱ n. ①语助词,虚词(如 "It is easy to say so." 中的 It, 或 "make it clear what you mean" 中的 it) ②惊叹语(如 My goodness!);赌咒语(如 Damn it!) ③填补物;附加物

explicit [iks'plisit] a. ①明晰的,清楚的;明确的;详述的: ~ directions (views) 明确的指示(意见) / be ~ about an affair 对一件事情态度鲜明 ②明率的,不含糊的: ~ in terms 直截了当地 ③显然可见的 ④(租金等)须直接付款的: ~ costs 直接以货币支付的成本 ||~ly ad. / ~ness n. ||~ faith (由于彻底理解而对教义或主义的)明确的信仰 / ~ function 【数】显函数

explode [iks'ploud] ❶ vt. ①使爆炸;使爆发;使破裂: ~ an atom (a hydrogen) bomb 爆炸一颗原子(氢)弹 ②破除(迷信等);戳穿,驳倒(理论等): ~ all fetishes and liberate the mind 破除迷信,解放思想 / ~ the myth of 穿…的神话 ③【语】发(b, p, t 等)爆破音 ④[古]

把(演员)轰下台 ❷ *vi.* 爆炸；爆发；突变: The shell (boiler) ~*d*. 炮弹(锅炉)爆炸了。/ ~ *with* anger 勃然大怒 / ~ *with* laughter 哄然大笑 / an *exploding* population 激增的人口 ‖~**d** *a.* 爆炸了的；被戳穿的；被破除的；分解的: an ~*d* view (机器、飞机等的)部件分解图 / ~**r** *n.* ①爆炸物 ②爆炸装置；爆炸剂；放炮器；雷管

exploit¹ ['eksploit] *n.* 功绩，功勋；辉煌的成就；英勇的行为: military ~*s* 战绩

exploit² [iks'ploit] *vt.* ①开拓，开发；开采: ~ the virgin lands (或 soil) 开垦荒地 / ~ an oil field 开发油田 / ~ a coal mine 开采煤矿 ②利用；利用…而自肥: ~ every possibility 利用一切可能性 / ~ one's office 利用职权(营私舞弊) ③剥削: the ~*ing* classes 剥削阶级 / the ~*ed* [总称]被剥削者 ‖~**er** *n.* 剥削者

exploitation [,eksploi'teiʃən] *n.* ①开拓，开发；开采: the ~ of natural resources 自然资源的开发 ②剥削；出于私利的利用 ③利用 ④宣传，广告: a new film's ~ campaign 为新影片所作的宣传运动

exploration [,eksplɔ:'reiʃən] *n.* ①探究，探索；钻研；考察: make further ~*s* 进一步探索(或考察) / space ~ 宇宙空间探索，星际探索 ②勘探，勘查；探测，测定；探险: mineral ~ 矿藏的勘探 / pressure (velocity) ~ 压力(速度)分布测定 ③【医】(伤处等的)探查；探察术

explore [iks'plɔ:] ❶ *vt.* ①探究，探索，钻研；考察: ~ ways and means of solving the question 寻求解决问题的方式方法 / latent possibilities 挖掘潜力 / ~ archives 查档案 / ~ social and economic conditions 考察社会和经济状况 ②勘探；探测；在…探险: ~ a trackless wilderness 勘探无人迹的荒野 ③【医】探察(伤处等) ❷ *vi.* (有系统地)探索，考察，勘探；探险: ~ *for* oil 勘探石油 / an *exploring* team 勘探队，考察队 ‖**explorative** [eks'plɔ:rətiv], **exploratory** [eks'plɔ:rətəri] *a.* / ~**r** [iks'plɔ:rə] *n.* ①探索者；勘探者；探险者；考察者: an Arctic ~*r* 北极探险考察者 ②勘探器，探测器，探测线圈 ③【医】探察器；探针

explosion [iks'plouʒən] *n.* ①爆炸，炸裂；爆发: nuclear ~ 核爆炸 / thermal ~ 热爆炸 / ~ of firedamp 【矿】煤气爆炸 / an ~ chamber (发动机的)燃烧室 ②(大规模的、迅猛的)扩张，激增；剧变: a population ~ 人口激增 ③(感情、笑声等的)爆发，迸发: an ~ of rage 大发雷霆 ④【语】爆破

explosive [iks'plousiv] I *a.* ①爆炸(性)的；爆发(性)的: an ~ bullet 炸裂弹 / ~ forming 【工】爆炸成型 / an ~ engine 爆发内燃机 / an ~ situation 爆发性局势 ②【语】爆破音的 ③暴躁的: an ~ person 脾气暴躁的人 II *n.* ①爆炸物，炸药；[复]爆破器材: ~ D "D"型炸药 / high ~ 高爆炸药 / detonating ~ 高级炸药 / plastic ~ 可塑炸药 / packages of ~*s* 炸药包 / an ~ compartment 炸药室 ②【语】爆破音(如 p, t, k 等) ‖~**ly** *ad.* / ~**ness** *n.* ‖~ **train** 导火索；分段装药；传爆系统

exponent [eks'pounənt] I *a.* 阐述的；说明的，讲解的 II *n.* ①(原理、方法等的)阐述者；说明者，讲解者 ②(理论、观点等的)倡导者；代表者；拥护者 ③(音乐的)演奏者 ④典型；标本；例子；样品 ⑤【数】指数，幂: positive (negative) ~ 正(负)指数，正(负)幂 / fractional ~ 分数指数

export [eks'pɔ:t] I ❶ *vt.* ①输出(物资、思想、信仰等) ②运走，带走，排出: The blood ~*s* waste products from the tissues. 血液把身体组织里的废物排出。❷ *vi.* 输出物资 II ['ekspɔ:t] *n.* ①输出品: an excess of ~*s* 出超 / invisible ~*s* 无形输出(指一国在国际收支中不是因商品输出而带来的各项收入，如运费、保险费、国际旅游费等) ②输出，出口: the ~ of tea 茶叶的出口 / the ~ of capital 资本输出 III ['ekspɔ:t] *a.* 出口的；准备出口的；出口物的: the ~ trade 出口贸易 / an ~ duty (或 tax) 出口税 / an ~ crop 专供出口的农作物 / an ~ surplus 出超 ‖~**able** *a.* 可输出的 / ~**ation** [,ekspɔ:'teiʃən] *n.* ①输出，出口 ②输出品，输出物 / ~**er** *n.* 出口商；输出者

expose [iks'pouz] *vt.* ①使曝露；使暴露；使面临: be ~*d* to all kinds of weather 经受风吹雨打 / ~ sb. *to* danger 使某人面临危险 / ~ oneself *to* sb.'s influence 使自己受某人的影响 / a student who has been ~*d* to English for some years 接触英语达六年左右的学生 ②揭露，揭发 ③陈列(商品等)，摆出 ④遗弃(婴孩) ⑤使曝光；使露光

exposé [eks'pouzei] *n.* [法] ①(事实等的)陈述 ②(丑事、罪恶等的)暴露，揭露: a devastating ~ of 对…的彻底揭露

exposed [iks'pouzd] *a.* 暴露的；无掩蔽的: leave the head ~ 让头露出在外面 / an ~ frontier 无掩护的边界 / an ~ electric wire 裸(电)线 ‖~**ness** *n.*

exposition [,ekspə'ziʃən] *n.* ①(理论、计划等的)说明，讲解；评注；说明性讲话(或文章等) ②展览会，博览会；陈列: an agricultural ~ 农业(产品)展览会 ③曝露，显露；露光；曝光 ④(对婴儿等的)遗弃 ⑤【戏】展示部分(阐明情节、人物等) ⑥【音】呈示部

expostulate [iks'pɔstjuleit] *vi.* 规劝，忠告: ~ *with* sb. *about* (或 *for, on*) sth. 为了某事劝戒某人 ‖**expostulation** [iks,pɔstju'leiʃən] *n.* / **expostulatory** [iks'pɔstjulətəri] *a.*

exposure [iks'pouʒə] *n.* ①曝露；暴露；揭露，揭发: "literature of ~" "暴露文学" ②曝光；曝光时间；(照相)软片: an ~ meter 曝光表，曝光计 / How many ~*s* have you made? 你底片拍掉几张了？③位向，方向，方位: a house with a southern ~ 一座朝南的房子 ④(商品等的)陈列 ⑤(婴孩等的)遗弃

expound [iks'paund] ❶ *vt.* ①详述(理论、观点等);陈述(意见等);为…辩护 ②解释,说明(《圣经》等) ❷ *vi.* 阐述;解释,说明

express [iks'pres] **I** *vt.* ①表达;表示;表白: No words can ~ the grandeur of that scene. 那场面的宏伟无法用语言表达。/ ~ an opinion 发表一个意见 / ~ one's views 表达自己的观点 / His face ~ed great joy. 他脸上显出很高兴的样子。/ a conviction generally ~ed among those present 在场的人当中的一种普遍信念 ②(记号或符号)表示: The sign "=" ~es equality. 符号 "=" 表示相等。③把…作快递邮件寄去: ~ a package 作快包裹 / 榨,从…榨出东西来;压出(汁水等): ~ apples for cider 榨苹果制酒 / ~ juice *from* (或 *out of*) oranges 榨柑橘汁 **II** *a.* ①明白的,明确的;确切的: an ~ provision 明文条款 / He is the ~ image of his father. 他酷似他的父亲。②特殊的: for the ~ purpose of 为了…的特殊目的 ③特快的;快速的: an ~ train 快车 / ~ mail 快邮 **III** *ad.* 乘快车;以快递方式 **IV** *n.* ①[英]专差;专差急送的文件 ②快递邮件;快运;快汇;快递: send goods *by* ~ (由铁路等)快运货物 ③快车; 快运之物;快汇的钱 ④[美]捷运公司 ‖ ~ **oneself** ①表达自己的意思 ②(在艺术创作活动中)表达自己的感情(或想象等) ‖ ~**ly** *ad.* ①明显地;明确地 ②特意地,特地 ‖ ~ **delivery** [英]快递(美国称 special delivery) / **ex'pressway** *n.* 快速公路,高速公路

expression [iks'preʃən] *n.* ①表达;表示: ~ of ideas 思想的表达 ②表情;脸色;声调,腔调: read with ~ 有表情地朗读 / There is an ~ of happiness (或 a happy ~) on every face. 每人脸上都喜气洋洋。③表达方式;词句;措词: an idiomatic ~ in English 英语的习惯表达方式 / a colloquial ~ 口语 ④榨出: the ~ of juice out of oranges 榨出柑橘汁 ⑤【数】式;符号;【生】表现度 ‖ *beyond* (或 *past*) ~ 无法表达,形容不出 / *find* ~ *in* 在…中表现出来 / *give* ~ *to* 表达出,反映 ‖ ~**al** *a.* ①表情的 ②表现的: ~ arts 表现艺术 / ~**less** *a.* 没有表情的,呆板的 ‖ ~ **mark** 【音】表示感情色彩的符号

expressive [iks'presiv] *a.* ①表现的;表达…的 (*of*) ②富于表情的;富有意味的: an ~ nod 富有意味的点头 ‖ ~**ly** *ad.* / ~**ness** *n.*

expulsion [iks'pʌlʃən] *n.* ①驱逐: an ~ order 驱逐出境的命令 ②开除;开除: the ~ of sb. *from* school 某人的被开除出校

expunge [eks'pʌndʒ] *vt.* ①除去;删去;省略;勾销: ~ a name *from* a list 把一个名字从名单上除去 / ~ a passage *from* a book 删去书中的一段 ②擦去,拭去 ③消灭,歼灭

expurgate ['ekspə:geit] *vt.* 删除(书籍等)中的不妥部分,使纯洁;修订: an ~d edition 修订版;洁本 ‖ **expurgation** [,ekspə:'geiʃən] *n.* 删改,订正 / **expurgator** *n.* (书的)删改者,修订者

exquisite ['ekskwizit] **I** *a.* ①优美的;高雅的;巧妙的,精致的: an ~ portrait 精美的画像 / ~ craftsmanship 精湛的技艺 / ~ lace (chinaware) 精致的花边(瓷器) ②剧烈的,异常的: ~ pleasure (pain) 极度的愉快(痛苦) / ~ stupidity 极度的愚蠢 ③敏锐的,微妙的: an ~ observer (critic) 敏锐的观察者(批评家) / have an ~ sense of hearing (或 have an ~ ear) 听觉灵敏 ④精选的 **II** *n.* 爱修饰的人,花花公子 ‖ ~**ly** *ad.* / ~**ness** *n.*

extant [eks'tænt] *a.* ①(书籍、文件等)现存的,尚存的;未逸失的;未废的;未毁的 ②[古]突出的,显著的

extemporary [iks'tempərəri] *a.* =extemporaneous ‖ **extemporarily** [iks'tempərərili; 美 iks,tempe'rerili] *ad.*

extend [iks'tend] ❶ *vt.* ① 伸,伸出;拉开: ~ed his arms in front of him. 他向前伸出双臂。/ ~ one's leg 伸直腿 / He fell asleep with his body ~ed on the grass. 他伸展着身子躺在草地上睡着了。②延长,延伸: ~ a railway 延长一条铁路线 / ~ the deadline until the end of the month 展期到月底截止 / ~ one's visit for a few days longer 把访问时间延长几天 ③扩充,扩展: ~ the area of double and triple cropping 扩大二熟作物和三熟作物的种植面积 / ~ a building 扩建一座建筑物 / ~ the sense of a word 扩大一个词的涵义 / ~ the book to three volumes 把书扩充到三卷 ④【军】使疏开 ⑤致;给予,提供: ~ warm greetings to 向…热烈祝贺 / ~ an invitation to sb. 邀请某人 ⑥演化出(速记等)的全文 ⑦[英]【律】对(地产等)估价;没收,扣押 ⑧[常用被动语态]使(比赛者或马等)竭尽全力: The horse was fully ~ed. 这马尽了全力驱策。⑨把…搀杂,(搀入东西)增加(食品等)的数量(或效能等): ~ ground meat with flour 把面粉搀入肉糜中 ⑩【会计】把(数字)转入另一栏;算出…的总金额;写出…的金额: ~ the credit balance 结出贷方余额 ❷ *vi.* ①伸展;扩大;延续: The factory compound ~s eastward as far as the railway. 这个工厂的场地向东一直延伸到铁路边。/ ~ into many fields 发展到很多领域中 / The chapter ~s to a hundred pages. 这一章长达一百页。/ ~ from Monday to Thursday 从星期一持续到星期四 / The celebrations ~ed over three hours. 庆祝活动延续了三小时。②【军】疏开,散开

extended [iks'tendid] *a.* ①伸出的;伸展的: an ~ hand 伸出的手 ②延长的;持久的: an ~ play (每分钟四十五转,可放六到八分钟的)慢速唱片,密纹唱片 / ~ active duty 超期服役 / ~ bonds 延期偿付的债券 ③扩大的,扩展的;广大的: the ~ application of sb.'s experience 某人经验的推广运用 / an ~ formation (或 order)【军】疏开队形 / an ~ type 阔身活字

extension [iks'tenʃən] *n.* ①伸长;伸展;扩大;(可)

扩展的范围: the ~ of multiple cropping areas 复种面积的扩大 / the ~ of knowledge (influence) 知识(影响)的扩大 ②延长; 延期; (可)延长的程度; 延长的日期: the ~ of a railway 铁路的延长 (部分) / the ~ of a treaty (loan) 条约有效期(贷款偿还期)的延长 ③延长部分; 扩大部分; 附加部分; 增设部分: a pedal ~ 踏板的接长节 / an ~ to a factory 工厂的扩建部分 / a house with two ~s 有两个添造部分(如棚等)的房子 / a university ~ 大学的附设部分(如夜校、函授班等) ④电话分机 ⑤【逻】外延 ⑥【医】伸直; 牵伸(术) ⑦【物】广延(性) ⑧【军】延伸 ⑨【会计】(从另一栏)转来的金额; 算出的金额(如发票上所示单价与数量相乘而得的总金额) ‖~al a. ①【逻】外延的 ②客观现实的; 具体的, 事实的 ‖~ ladder 伸缩梯 / ~ spring 牵簧 / ~ table (可加装活动板的)伸缩桌

extensive [iks'tensiv] a. ①广大的; 广阔的; 广泛的; 广博的: ~ reading 泛读 / an ~ report 一个广泛详尽的报告 / an ~ order 大批定货 ②【农】粗放的, 大面积(耕种)的 ③【逻】外延的 ④【物】广延的 ‖~ly ad. / ~ness n.

extent [iks'tent] n. ①广度, 宽度; 长度: a farm of considerable ~ 一个相当大的农场 / a racing track 1,000 metres in ~ 一千米长的跑道 ②范围: within the ~ of human knowledge 在人类知识范围内 ③程度, 限度: to some (a great, a certain) ~ 在某种(很大, 一定)程度上 / to the ~ of 到…的程度(或程度) / to such an ~ that … 竟然到…的地步 / to the full ~ of one's power 竭尽全力地 ④一大片(地区): a vast ~ of woodland 一大片森林地带 ⑤【律】[英]扣押令; 扣押; [美]临时所有权令(均指债权人对债务人的财产) ⑥[英][古](对土地等的)估价

extenuate [eks'tenjueit] vt. ①(用偏袒的辩解或借口)减轻: Nothing can ~ his crime. 他的罪行无法(用任何辩解)减轻。②低估; 藐视 ③[古]使细; 使瘦薄 ④[古]减少; 减弱; 使衰弱 ‖**extenuating** a. 使减轻的; 情有可原的: extenuating circumstances 【律】可使罪行减轻的情况 / **extenuation** [eks,tenju'ei∫ən] n. ①减轻; 偏袒的辩解 ②[古]细; 瘦削; 稀薄; 衰弱 / **extenuatory** [eks'tenjuətəri] a. ①使减轻的 ②[古]使细(或瘦)的; 使弱的; 使薄的

exterior [eks'tiəriə] I a. ①外部的; 外面的; 外表的; 外来的: ~ angle 【数】外角 / ~ lines 【军】外线 / ~ forces 外力 ②对外的, 外交上的: an ~ policy 对外政策 ③【建】(适合)外用的: an ~ paint 屋外油漆 II n. ①外部; 外表; 表面: the ~ of a house 房子的外部 / a murderous heart under a smiling ~ 笑里藏刀 ②(戏剧的)户外布景; (电影、电视的)外景 ‖~ly ad. 在外部; 从外表上看

exterminate [eks'tə:mineit] vt. 根除, 灭绝; 消灭, 扑灭 ‖**extermination** [eks,tə:mi'nei∫ən] n. an extermination camp (德国纳粹)灭绝人的集中营 / **exterminator** n. ①根绝者; 扑灭者(尤指消灭害虫者) ②根绝物(尤指杀虫剂等) / **exterminatory** [eks'tə:minətəri] a.

external [eks'tə:nl] I a. ①外(面)的, 外部的, 在外的: an ~ cause 外因 / ~ secretion 外分泌 ②外界的; 客观的, 物质的: the ~ world 客观世界 / ~ reality 客观现实 ③【医】外用的: ~ application 外用 / ~ remedy 外用药 / for ~ use only 只供外用 ④外表的, 外观的 ⑤表面的, 形式(上)的; 肤浅的: the ~ signs of a disease 疾病的表面征状 ⑥对外的; 外国的; 外来的: ~ trade 对外贸易 / ~ intervention 外来(或外国)的干涉 II n. ①外部, 外面 ②[复]外形, 外观; 形式; 外部情况: judge people by ~s 从外表(或表面)判断人 ‖~ly ad. 在(或从)外部; 在(或从)外面; 外表上 ‖**ex'ternal-com'bustion engine** 外燃机 / ~ **examination** 由校外人士(或机构)主持的考试 / ~ **respiration** 外呼吸(指血液与外界空气之间的气体交换过程, 即一般所称的呼吸) / ~ **student** 校外学生(获准入学并可参加学位考试但不到校学习的学生)

externalism [eks'tə:nəlizəm] n. ①外在性, 外在化; 客观性 ②【哲】现象论 ③讲究外表; 拘泥形式(或虚礼)

extinct [iks'tiŋkt] I a. ①(火、希望等)熄灭了的; 消灭了的: an ~ volcano 死火山 ②绝种的, 灭绝的: an ~ family 已绝嗣的家族 / an ~ animal 已灭种的动物 ③(职位等)废除了的; (贵族称号等)无合法继承人的 ④(法令等)过时的, 失效的 II vt. [古]使熄灭; 消灭 ‖~ive a. 使熄灭的; 使消灭的

extinction [iks'tiŋk∫ən] n. ①熄灭, 消灭, 灭绝; 废除: the ~ of a species 一个物种的灭绝 ②【物】消光

extinguish [iks'tiŋgwi∫] vt. ①熄灭(火、希望、热情等), 扑灭 ②消灭, 灭绝 ③压制, 压抑; 迫使…沉默 ④使黯然失色; 使相形见绌 ⑤使无效; 取消, 清偿 ⑥偿清(债务等) ‖~able a. 可熄灭的, 可扑灭的; 可灭绝的 / ~er n. ①熄灭者; 消灭者②熄灯(或烛)器; 灭火器 / ~ment n.

extirpate ['ekstə:peit] vt. ①根除(杂草、恶习等); 灭绝, 消灭 ②破除(异端、邪说等) ③【医】摘除(肿瘤 等) ‖**extirpation** [,ekstə:'pei∫ən] n. / **extirpator** n. 根除者; 扑灭者

extol(l) [iks'tol] (extolled; extolling) vt. ①赞美, 颂扬: ~ sb.'s bravery 赞美某人勇敢 / ~ sb. as a brave man 称赞某人是个勇敢的人 ②吹捧: ~ sb. to the skies 把某人捧上天, 对某人大肆吹捧 ‖**extoller** n. 赞美者; 吹捧者 / ~**ment** n.

extort [iks'to:t] vt. 敲诈; 勒索; 强取, 逼取: ~ money from sb. 向某人勒索钱财 / ~ a confession (promise) from sb. 逼某人招供(允诺) / ~ a meaning from a word 曲解一个词的意义

extortion [iks'to:∫ən] n. ①敲诈; 勒索; 强求; 逼取 ②被勒索的财物 ‖~**ary** a. [古]=~ate /

~ate *a.* ①敲诈的; 强求的 ②过分的; 昂贵的 / ~er *n.* 敲诈者; 勒索者; 强求者

extra ['ekstrə] **I** *a.* ①额外的, 外加的; 另外收费的: do ~ work 做额外工作; 加班 / run ~ trains on holidays 在假日增开列车 / In our hotels room service is not ~. 在我们的旅馆里不另收房间服务费。②特大的; 特佳的: ~ quality 特优质量 **II** *ad.* ①特别地, 格外地; 非常: work ~ hard 工作特别努力 / an ~special edition [英](晚报的)最新号外 / He was ~ glad to see us. 他见到我们高兴极了。②另外: Price 5 yuan, packing and postage ~. 包装和邮费在外, 价格五元。**III** *n.* ①额外人手; 额外的东西 ②另收费用的项目; [常用复]外加费用 ③(报纸的)号外 ④质量特别好的东西: a real ~ (广告常用语)上等产品 ⑤(拍摄电影群众场面时雇来的)临时演员 ⑥(板球中的)额外得分, 非击球所得之分

extract I [iks'trækt] *vt.* ①(用力)取出, (使劲)拔出, 抽出: ~ a tooth 拔牙 / ~ a bullet *from* a wound 从伤口中取出子弹 / ~ a promise *from* sb. 迫使某人作出诺言 ②榨出(油质等); 提取(蜜等); 萃取; 蒸馏(出): ~ cottonseed oil 榨棉籽油 / ~ juice *from* sugarcanes 榨甘蔗汁 / ~ coal *from* seams 从矿层中采煤 ③引出, 推断出(原理等); 吸取, 得到(乐趣等) ④摘录, 选录; 选取(精华); 引用: ~ a passage *from* a book 从书中摘录一段 ⑤【数】开(方), 求(根): ~ the root 开方, 求根 ⑥【军】退(弹) **II** ['ekstrækt] *n.* ①摘录, 选录; 摘~s *from* press reports 报纸新闻摘录 ②抽出物; 蒸馏品; 精华, 汁: lemon ~ 柠檬精 / beef ~ (或 ~ of beef) 牛肉汁 ③【化】提取物; 萃取物 ④【药】浸膏

extractable, extractible [iks'træktəbl] *a.* ①可抽出的; 可拔出的 ②可榨出的; 可榨取的 ③【化】可提取的 ④可推断出的; 可摘录的

extraction [iks'trækʃən] *n.* ①抽出; (牙等的)拔出; 榨取; 取出 ②【化】提取(法); 萃取(法); 开采: ~ rate 提取率 / ~ column 提取塔 / the ~ of oil 石油汲取, 石油采出 ③抽出物; 拔出物; 提取物; 采出物 ④摘录; 摘要; 精选 ⑤血统; 出身: She is of Spanish ~. 她有西班牙血统。/ a student of peasant ~ 农民家庭出身的学生 ⑥【数】求根(法), 开方(法)

extradite ['ekstrədait] *vt.* 引渡(逃犯、战俘等); 使(逃犯等)被引渡 ‖**extradition** [ˌekstrə'diʃən] *n.* (根据条约或法令对逃犯等的)引渡

extraneous [eks'treinjəs] *a.* ①体外的, 外部的; 外来的, 新异的: protect the contents of the box from ~ moisture 保护箱内物不受外面潮气的侵袭 / ~ cracking 【化】外部裂化(轻质碳氢化合物的裂化) / an ~ interference 外来干扰 / reflex 【心】新异反射 / ~ stimulus 【心】新异刺激 ②无关的, 不重要的, 支节的: a matter ~ *to* the question 与问题无关的事 ‖~**ly** *ad.* / ~**ness** *n.*

extraordinary [iks'trɔ:dnri, iks'trɔ:dinəri] *a.* ① 非常的; 特别的, 破例的; 非凡的: an ~ sight 特别的景象; 奇景 / an ~ expenditure 特别(或临时)支出 / an ~ weather 反常的天气 / an ~ session 临时会议 / make ~ progress in science and technology 在科学技术方面取得极其巨大的进步 ②离奇的, 使人惊奇的: How very ~ that you should have never heard of the matter! 真怪啊, 你竟然没听说过这件事! ③ [ˌekstrə'ɔ:dneri] 特命的, 特派的: an ambassador ~ and plenipotentiary 特命全权大使 ‖**extraordinarily** [iks'trɔ:dnrili; 美 iks,trɔ:di'nerili] *ad.* / **extraordinariness** *n.*

extravagance [iks'trævigəns], **extravagancy** [iks'trævigənsi] *n.* ①奢侈, 铺张; 浪费: oppose *extravagance* and waste 反对铺张浪费 ②过度, 无节制 ③放肆; 放肆的话(或行动)

extravagant [iks'trævigənt] *a.* ①奢侈的; 浪费的: ~ *in* dress 衣服奢华的 ②过度的, 过分的, 过高的: ~ claims 过分的要求 / an ~ price 过高的价格 ③(言行等)放肆的, 越轨的: ~ acts 放肆的行为 ④[古]游荡的 ‖~**ly** *ad.*

extreme [iks'tri:m] **I** *a.* ①末端的, 尽头的: the ~ borders of a country 国家最远的边疆 / stand at the ~ edge of the bank 站在河岸的极边缘 / an ~ outpost 最前哨 ②极度的, 极端的; 最大的; 过分的: the ~ penalty 极刑, 死刑 / an ~ case 极端的例子, 极罕见的例子 / be in danger 在极度危险中 / an ~ descent 急剧的下降; 极陡的下坡 ③ 急进的; 激烈的; 严厉的; 狂热的: quite ~ in one's views 观点很急进 / take ~ measures 采取激烈措施 / the most ~ fashion in decoration 最新式的装饰 ④[古]最后的, 最终的: in one's ~ moments 在临终时刻 **II** *n.* ①在末端的事物; 极端; [复]极端不同的性质(或事物等); 【数】(比例或级数的)首项(或末项); 【逻】主项(或谓项); (三段论法中的)大项(或小项): carry sth. to (或 into) ~s 把某事引向极端 / the ~s of heat and cold 冷热的悬殊 ②极度(状态); 最大程度: an ~ of distress 极度痛苦 / enthusiasm carried to an ~ 过分的热情 / prejudice at its ~ 最大的偏见 ③急进行为, 极端措施, 激烈手段(或步骤等): be forced to an unpleasant ~ 被迫采取不愉快的激烈措施 ‖*Extremes meet.* [谚]两极相通。/ ~s *of fortune* 盛衰荣枯 / go to ~s 走极端 / in the ~ 极端, 非常 / run to an ~ 走极端 ‖~**ly** *ad.* 极端, 极其, 非常 / ~**ness** *n.* ‖~ **term** 【数】外项 / ~ **unction** (天主教)牧师对临终人涂油的礼节 / ~ **value** 【数】极值

extremity [iks'tremiti] *n.* ①末端; 终极; 尽头: The factory is situated at the eastern ~ of the city. 这所工厂位于城市的东端。/ at the ~ of a small path 在小径尽头处 ②极度, 极端: in an ~ of pain (joy) 在极度痛苦(喜悦)中 ③极困(或危险)的境地; 绝境: be driven to ~ 陷于困窘困(或危险)的境地 ④临死; 覆灭时刻: be at ~ 临终 / to the last ~ 临终之时; 濒于毁灭 ⑤[常

用复] 非常手段; 激烈措施: resort (或 proceed, go) to *extremities* 采取非常手段 ⑥(身体的)一肢; (人的)手, 足: the *extremities* 四肢, 手足 ‖*expect the* ～ 准备万一, 准备一死

extricate ['ekstrikeit] *vt.* ①使解脱, 使脱出; 解救: ～ sb. *from* difficulties 使某人摆脱困难 / ～ an animal *from* a net 把动物从网中解脱出来 ②使(气体)游离; 放出, 化散(热气等) ‖**extrication** [ˌekstri'keiʃən] *n.* / **extricator** *n.* 解脱者; 救出者

extrinsic [eks'trinsik] *a.* ①外在的; 非固有的; 非本质的: ～ *to* sth. 非某物所固有的 ②外来的; 外部的; 外表的; 体外的: look for ～ aid 寻求外来援助 / the ～ feature of a new building 新厦的外貌 ‖～**ally** *ad.*

extubate [eks'tju:beit] *vt.*【医】从(喉等)处除管

exuberance [ig'zju:bərəns] *n.* ①繁茂; 充溢; 充沛; 丰富: an ～ of vegetation 草木繁茂 / an ～ of feeling 情感洋溢 ②生气勃勃的行动; 丰富有力的言语

exuberant [ig'zju:bərənt] *a.* ①繁茂的, 茂盛的: ～ crops 茂盛的农作物 / an ～ growth of hair 毛发的丰茂丛生 ②丰富的, 多产的; an ～ imagination 丰富的想象 ③(人、行动等)活力充沛的, 精神旺盛的;(情感等)充溢的: an ～ capacity for work 十足的干劲 / children in ～ spirits 兴高采烈的孩子们 ④(语言等)华而不实的, 浮夸的; 冗长的: heap ～ praise on sb. 大肆夸奖某人 ⑤极度的, 非凡的: ～ zeal 极大的热忱 / mountains of ～ bulk 非常大的山脉 ‖～**ly** *ad.*

exude [ig'zju:d] ❶ *vt.* ①使渗出; 使流出 使发散, 使散布: ～ an odour 使气味发散 ❷ *vi.* ①(汗等)渗出; 流出 ②发散开来

exult [ig'zʌlt] *vi.* 狂喜; 欢跃: ～ *in* (或 *at*) a victory 为胜利而欢欣鼓舞 / ～ *over* the success of the experiment 因实验成功而欢跃 / ～ *to* find that ... 了解到⋯而感到喜悦

eye [ai] **I** *n.* ①眼睛; 眼圈: open (close) one's ～*s* 睁开(闭上)眼睛 / shortsighted ～*s* 近视眼 / see *with* one's own (或 very) ～*s* 亲眼目睹 / give sb. a black ～ 把某人的眼眶打青 / the apple of the ～ 瞳人, 眼珠; [喻]宝贵的事物 ②眼光; 视力; 观察力: Their ～*s* met. 他们的眼光相遇了。 / a good ～ *for* distances 能望到远处的好眼力 / have a sharp (或 discerning) ～ 有敏锐的目光 / view sth. *with* a friendly ～ 用友好的眼光(或态度)看待某事物 ③看; 注目, 注意: be in the public ～ 公开露面; 为公众所注目; 著名 ④[常用复]见解, 观点, 判断: In my ～*s*, that will do. 我看那样行。 ⑤眼子, 孔; 眼状物(如针眼、靶心、孔雀翎斑等); 索眼, 圈, 环: a hook and ～ (扣住衣领的)一副风纪扣, 一副领钩 ⑥风吹来的方向,【气】风眼 ⑦【植】(马铃薯等的)芽眼; 花心;(菊科的)花盘;

【微】眼点;【物】光电池, 光电管 ⑧[美俚]侦探 **II** *vt.* ①看, 注视: ～ sb. narrowly 端详某人 ②在⋯上打孔眼 ‖*a beam in sb.'s* ～ 见 **beam** / *a dry* ～ 不流泪的眼(指不哭的人) / *all my* ～ (*and Betty Martin*) [俚] 胡说八道, 鬼话; 欺骗 / *a mote in sb.'s* ～ 见 **mote** / *an evil* ～ 狠毒的眼光(按照迷信说法会造成伤害) / *an* ～ *for an* ～ (或 ～ *for* ～) 以眼还眼, 报复 / *an* ～ *in the sky* [美俚]侦察卫星 / *a straight* ～ 能看出(某物)是否直(或正)的眼力 / *be all* ～*s* 极注意地看着, 非常留神 / *be bright in the* ～ [口]喝醉 / *before* (或 *under*) *sb.'s very* ～*s* 在某人面前公开地 / *cast an* ～ *at* (或 *over*) sth. 看某物 / *cast sheep's* ～*s at* sb. 对某人做媚眼 / *catch sb.'s* ～ 引某人注目; 注视 / *cry one's* ～*s out* 哭肿眼睛, 痛哭流涕 / *do sb. in the* ～ 欺骗(或愚弄)某人 / *dust the* ～*s of* 欺骗, 蒙蔽 / *easy as my* ～ 易如反掌 / *easy on the* ～*s* 悦目的, 好看的 / *Eyes front!* (口令)向前看! / *Eyes right* (*left*)! (口令) ①向右(左)看! ②向右(左)看齐! / *feast one's* ～*s on* 看着⋯以饱眼福 / *get one's* ～*s in* (球类运动)由于练习而能用眼跟上球的动向 / *give sb. the* (*glad*) ～ [美俚]向某人做媚眼 / *have an* ～ *for* 很能看出; 很能鉴赏: *have an* ～ *for* proportion (beauty) 很懂得匀称(审美) / *have an* ～ *to* ①照看, 照顾 ②觊觎, 对⋯有所企图 / *have an* ～ *to the main chance* 谋私利, 只顾自身利益 / *have* ～*s bigger than the belly* 嘴馋 / *if you had half an* ～ 如果你不是完全瞎了(或糊涂透顶)的话 / *in a* (或 *the*) *pig's* ～ [美俚]永不, 决不 / *in sb.'s mind's* ～ 在某人心目中, 在某人想象中: reappear *in her mind's* ～ 又重现在她的眼前 / *in the* ～*s of* 在⋯心目中; 在(或从)⋯看来: *in the* ～*s of* history 从历史角度来看(或判断) / *in the wind's* ～ (或 *in the* ～ *of the wind*)【海】逆着风 / *keep an* ～ *on* ①照看: Will you *keep an* ～ *on* my children for a while? 替我照看一下孩子好吗? ②密切注视着 / *keep one's* ～*s open* 留心看着; 注意; 保持警惕 / *keep one's* ～*s peeled* [俚]擦亮眼睛, 提高警惕; 谨慎小心 / *look sb. in the* ～ 无愧于心(或无所畏惧)地正视某人 / *lose an* ～ 瞎掉一只眼 / *make* ～*s at* sb. 向某人送秋波 / *make sb. open his* ～*s* 使某人瞠目吃惊 / *Mind your* ～! [口]当心! 留神! / *My* ～(*s*)! [俚](表示惊讶或反对)天哪! 呀! / *never take one's* ～*s off* 始终注视(或注意)着 / *One's* ～*s draw* (或 *gather, pick*) *straws.* 昏昏欲睡。 / *pipe one's* ～ (嘲笑语)哭, 流泪 / *put one's* ～*s together* 入睡 / *run one's* ～(*s*) *over* (或 *through*) 扫视, 浏览 / *see* ～ *to* ～ (*with sb.*) (与某人)看法完全一致 / *see with half an* ～ 一望而知 / *set* ～*s on* 看到, 望见 / *shut* (或

close) one's ~s to 闭眼不(愿)看; 假装不看见 / spit in the ~ of 藐视, 蔑视 / strike the ~ 引人注目, 醒目 / the ~ of day (或 heaven, the morning) 太阳 / the ~ of the typhoon (或 hurricane) ①台风眼 ②公众注意的事物(或地区)/ the ~s of the blind 盲人用的手杖 / throw dust in sb.'s ~s 见 dust / to the ~ ①从表面上看来 ②当面, 公然(指违抗等)/ turn a (或 one's) blind ~ to 对…熟视无睹(或假装不见) / up to the (或 one's) ~s 深深陷在, 埋头于: be up to the ~s in work 工作极忙 / wet the other ~ 再喝一杯酒 / wipe sb.'s ~ ①比某人先下手, 先发制人(尤指捕杀另一猎人的猎物) ②使某人看到自己的狂妄 / with an ~ to (或 on) ①着眼于: plan the work with an ~ to the interests of the whole 从全局利益出发安排工作 ②对…有企图, 打…的主意 / with one's ~s open ①注意地, 警惕地 ②明知(故犯)地 / with the naked ~ 用肉眼(不借助望远镜等)/ worth a Jew's ~ [古]极为贵重
‖~less a. 无眼的; 瞎的 / ~let ['ailit] n. ①(供穿线、挂钩等用的)针眼, 小孔; (镶小孔用的)金属圈, 金属环 ②监视孔; 枪眼; 孔眼 vt. 在…上打小孔
‖'~ball n. 眼球 vt. [美俚]打量 / ~ bank 【医】眼库 / ~ bath [英]洗眼杯 / '~bolt n. 【机】有眼螺栓, 吊环螺栓 / '~bright n. 【植】小米草(旧时用以治眼疾) / '~brow n. ①眉毛; 眉: The miraculous effect of medicinal herbs has raised some conservative ~brows. 草药的奇效简直使一些思想保守的人瞠目吃惊。②【建】窗头线(饰); 滴水; 波形老虎窗(或屋顶窗) ③【纺】回丝; 飞花 / '~-,catcher n. 引人注目的

事物 / '~-,catching a. 引人注目的 / '~cup n. 洗眼杯 / '~glass n. ①镜片 ②[复]眼镜, 夹鼻眼镜 ③洗眼杯 ④(望远镜等装置中的)(接)目镜 / '~hole n. ①眼窝 ②~let (n.) / '~lash n. 睫毛 / '~lid n. 眼睑: hang on by the ~lids 千钧一发 / not stir (或 bat) an ~lid 不眨眼; 不为所动; 处之泰然 / '~-,opener n. ①使人十分惊奇(或恍然大悟)的事物(尤指新闻、新发现等) ②很有启发的事物(如书籍) ③迷人的事物(或人) ④[美俚]晨起喝的清醒神志的酒 / '~-,opening a. 令人十分惊奇的; 很有启发性的 / '~piece n. (望远镜等装置中的)(接)目镜 / '~-'popping a. [美]使人瞠目(吃惊)的: an ~-popping record 惊人的纪录 / '~reach n. =~shot / '~-,servant n. 在(雇主等)监视下才尽职的佣人 / '~-,service n. ①在(雇主等)监视下的尽职 ②爱慕的眼光 / '~shade n. 眼罩 / ~ shadow 眼睑膏 / '~shot n. 视界, 视野: out of (或 beyond) ~shot 在视界之外 / within (或 in) the ~shot of 在…视界之内 / '~sight n. 视力, 目力 / '~sore n. 丑的东西, 刺眼的东西(或人) / '~spot n. 【动】眼点(退化的单眼) ②(眼状)颜色斑点 / '~strain n. 眼疲劳 / '~strings [复] n. 眼筋肉; 眼神经 / '~tooth n. 上颚犬牙: draw sb.'s ~-teeth 杀其人威风; 无情地剥削某人; 使某人在不知不觉中受到损失 / '~wash n. ①眼药水; 洗眼剂 ②[俚]胡说, 吹牛; 拍马; 把戏, 骗局; 表面文章 / '~,water n. ①眼分泌液 ②眼药水; 洗眼水 / '~wink n. 一眨眼; 瞬息 / '~,winker n. ①睫毛 ②(引起眨眼的)落入眼中的微粒 / '~'witness n. 目击者; 见证人: give an ~witness account of the incident 对事件作亲眼所见的第一手叙述

F

fable ['feibl] I n. ①寓言: Aesop's Fables 《伊索寓言》②虚构的故事; 传说 ③无稽之谈 ④[古](史诗、戏剧等的)情节 ⑤大众闲谈的题材: He became the chief ~ of the village. 他成了村中的中心话题。II ❶ vi. 讲寓言; 编寓言 ❷ vt. 煞有介事地讲述: It is ~d that .... 据说… ‖~d a. 寓言中的; 虚构的 / ~r n. 编寓言者; 虚构情节者
fabric ['fæbrik] n. ①织物, 织品; 布: cotton (linen, silk, woollen) ~s 棉(亚麻, 丝, 毛)织品 / synthetic ~s 合成纤维织物 / aeroplane ~【空】飞机蒙布 ②构造, 结构, 组织: soil ~ 土壤结构 / the ~ of society 社会的组织 ③建筑物; 构造物 ④【地】组构 ⑤工厂
fabricate ['fæbrikeit] vt. ①制作; 装配; 组合: a

~d building 装配式房屋 / a ~d ship 组合船 ②捏造; 伪造 ‖ fabrication [,fæbri'keiʃən] n. / fabricator n. 捏造者; 装配工; 修整工; 金属加工厂
fabulous ['fæbjuləs] a. ①寓言般的 ②寓言中的, 传说上的 ③惊人的, 难以置信的, 非常的, 巨大的 ④编写寓言的: a ~ writer 寓言作家 ⑤[口]极好的 ‖~ly ad. / ~ness n.
facade, façade [fə'sɑ:d] n. ①【建】(房屋的)正面, 立面 ②表面, 外观; (掩饰真相的)门面
face [feis] I n. ①脸, 面孔; 面貌; 面容, 表情: a smiling ~ 笑脸 / with a smile on one's ~ 面带笑容地 ②面子, 威信; 厚颜: save one's ~ 保全面子 / a loss of ~ 丢面子, 丢脸的事 / have the ~ to do sth. 居然有脸做某事 ③(硬币、纸

币等的)正面,票面,表面;(有文字、图案或加工装饰的)面: the ~ of a building 建筑物的正面 / the ~ of a watch (clock) 表(钟)面 / the ~ of cloth (leather)布(皮革)的正面 / the ~ of the earth 地球表面 ④外观,外表;局面 ⑤地形;【矿】采掘面,工作面;(矿石等的)晶面;【机】(刀具的)切削面: coal (gravel) ~ 采煤(砂矿)工作面 / cutting ~【机】(刀具的)切削面 / incident ~【原】(原子)轰击面 ⑥【印】(铅字字模的)面;(版)面 ⑦【军】(队伍的)面(尤指方形队伍的任何一面) II ❶ vt. ①面向,面对 ②朝…(面)向…: buildings facing the river 面向着河的建筑物 ③正视;蔑视;对付 ④(困难、死亡、毁灭等)面临: be ~d with two alternatives 面临两种抉择 ⑤(用石灰、水泥等)抹盖; 给(衣服等)加贴边;给(饮料等)搀色: a wall with concrete 混凝土抹墙 / a woollen blanket ~d with cloth 用布料镶边的毛毯 ⑥使(石料等)的表面平滑 (off, up) ⑦【军】命令(队伍)改变方向: The captain ~d the column to the left. 队长命令纵队向左转。 ⑧ 翻出(纸牌)的正面 ❷ vi. 向,朝: new buildings that ~ (to the) south 朝南的新建筑物 / a workers' sanitorium facing on the lake 临湖的工人疗养院 / Left (Right) ~!【军】(口令)向左(右)转! / About ~!【军】(口令)向后转! ‖accept the ~ of 偏爱…,偏袒… / a ~ as long as a fiddle 阴郁的脸孔 / a smooth ~ ①没胡子的脸 ②一副讨好面孔 / ~ about (或 round) 转过身来;[喻]改变主意: As I came near him he ~d round. 我走近时,他转过身来。 / ~ down ①(用目光)压倒 ②(勇敢、坚定地)降服,挫败 / ~ sth. out 把某事坚持到底 / ~ the music 见 music / ~ up to 勇敢地对付 / fall (lie) on one's ~ 脸朝下倒下(躺着) / feed one's ~ [美俚]吃饭 / fly in the ~ of 悍然不顾; 公然违抗 / grind the ~s of the poor 压榨贫民 / hide one's ~ from 羞于见(某人) / in (the) ~ of 面对; 纵然, 即使: step to the fore in ~ of difficulties 迎着困难上 / bumper harvests achieved in ~ of unfavourable weather conditions 在气候不利的情况下所取得的大丰收 / in the ~ of day 公开地, 在光天化日之下 / keep a straight ~ 不露笑容 / laugh in sb.'s ~ 当面嘲笑某人, 公然蔑视某人 / Let's ~ it. [美口]面对现实吧! (或: 鼓起勇气来!) / lift sb.'s ~ 用手术消除某人面部的皱纹, 为某人整容 / look sb. in the ~ 直视某人: be unable to look sb. in the ~ (因差惭等)不敢正视某人 / make a ~ (或 ~s)(表示厌恶、轻蔑、嘲笑等)做鬼脸: He made a ~ at the taste of the medicine. 尝到药的味道, 他做出一副苦相。 / on the ~ of it 从表面判断; 乍看起来 / pull a ~ =make a ~ / pull a long ~ 牵拉着脸, 愁眉苦脸 / put a bold ~ on sth. 对某事装作满不在乎(或很有信心) / put a good ~ on sth. ①掩饰某事 ②对某事持乐

观(或顺从)态度 / put a new ~ on sth. 使某事物改观 / put on a long ~ =pull a long ~ / set one's ~ against 坚决反对, 抵制 / show one's ~ 露面, 到场 / slap sb. in the ~ 打某人一耳光;[喻]侮辱某人 / stare sb. in the ~ 盯着某人的脸看;(物)就在某人眼前;(事)迫在眉睫 / straighten one's ~ 板起面孔 / to sb.'s ~ 当着某人的面; 坦白地, 公开地, 勇敢地: criticize sb. to his ~ 当面直率地批评某人 / wear a long ~ =pull a long ~ ‖~d a. (常用以构成复合词)有…面容的; 有…表面的; 有…贴边的: straight-~d 板着面孔的,不露笑容的 / a marble-~d brick building 大理石面的砖房 / satin-~d lapels 镶有缎边的翻领 / a neatly ~d terrace 表面整齐的地坛 / ~less a. 姓名不详的; 不露面的 ‖~-ache n.【医】面神经痛 / ~ brick【建】面砖 / ~ card (纸牌中的)人头牌(指 K, Q, J 三种) / '~-,centred a.【物】(原子)面心的: ~-centred crystal 面心晶体 / ~-centred cubic alloy steel【冶】面心立方系合金钢 / '~-cream n. 润肤香脂 / '~'down ad. 面朝地下 / ~ guard (厂矿、击剑等用的)护面具,面罩 / ~-,harden vt. 使…的表面硬化 / '~-lift(ing) n. ①(除去面部皱纹等的)整容外科术; 整容 ②(建筑物、汽车等的)改建, 翻新 / '~off n. ①(冰球赛等中的)开球 ②对峙, 敌对 ③面对面的会议 / '~plate n.【机】面板; 花盘 / '~-,saving n. & a. 保全面子(的) / '~-to-~ ad. 面对面地: I went into the room and found myself ~-to-~ with him. 我走进房间, 面对面地碰上了他。 / ~ value ①票面价值 ②表面价值

facet ['fæsit] I n. ①(多面体的)面,(宝石等的)刻面, 小(平)面 ②(题目、性格、思想等的)某一方面 ③【建】柱槽筋, 凸线 ④(动)(昆虫的)小眼面 II (facet(t)ed; facet(t)ing) vt. 在…上刻面

facetious [fə'si:ʃəs] a. ①滑稽的: a ~ story 滑稽故事 ②爱开玩笑的 ‖~ly ad. / ~ness n.

facile ['fæsail, 'fæsil] a. ①易做到的, 易得到的; 不花力气的 ②敏捷的; 流畅的: a man with a ~ pen (tongue) 笔头快(能说会道)的人 / a ~ liar 随口撒谎的人 / a ~ style 流畅的文体 ③(性格)柔顺的, 温和的 ‖~ly ad. / ~ness n.

facilitate [fə'siliteit] vt. [不以人作主语] ①使容易, 使便利: Tractors ~ farming. 拖拉机使耕作便利。②推进, 促进: Friendly contacts between different peoples ~ the cultural interchange. 各国人民的友好接触促进文化交流。 ‖ **facilitation** [fə,sili'teiʃən] n.

facility [fə'siliti] n. ①容易, 简易 ②熟练, 灵巧, 敏捷: play the piano with ~ 熟练地弹钢琴 / have great ~ in doing sth. 很有做某事的能力 ③[常用复]设备, 工具; 方便, 便利: transport facilities 交通工具(如船、车等) / facilities for study 学习上的便利(指图书馆、实验室等) / a new ~ for outpatient treatment 新设的门诊所(或门诊间) ④柔顺

facing ['feisiŋ] *n.* ①(衣服等的)贴边, 镶边; 贴(或镶)边材料 ②【建】(保护或装饰建筑物的)面层, 覆盖层; 饰面 ③[复]军装上的领章、袖章及其他装饰 ④【机】衬片; 刮面; 刮面法 ⑤【军】转法, 方向变换 ‖*go through one's ~s* 受考验, 被考查 / *put sb. through his ~s* 考验某人的才能

facsimile [fæk'simili] **I** *n.* ①摹写; 摹真本: reproduced in ~ 复制得一模一样的 ②(讯)传真(通信): ~ telegraph 传真电报 / ~ transmission 传真发送 / ~ paper 传真感光纸 **II** *vt.* ①摹写 ②是…的摹真本

fact [fækt] *n.* ①事实: an indisputable ~ 无可争辩的事实 / Facts speak louder than eloquence. 事实胜于雄辩。/ I know it for a ~. 我知道这是确实的。②实际, 实情, 真相: This report is based entirely on ~. 这篇报告是完全根据实际情况写成的。③(犯罪)行为: before (after) the ~ 作案前(后) / an accessory after the ~ 事后从犯 ④论据: His ~s are open to question. 他的论据大有问题。‖*as a matter of ~* 事实上, 其实 / *in ~* 其实, 实际上 / *in point of ~* 实际上, 就事实而论 / *the ~s of life* 生活(尤指性生活)方面的基本知识 ②生活中的严酷现实 ‖*~-finding a.* 进行实地调查的: hold a ~-finding meeting 开调查会

faction ['fækʃən] *n.* ①派别, 宗派, 小集团 ②派系斗争, 内讧 ‖*~al a.*

factor ['fæktə] **I** *n.* ①因素, 要素: the key ~ 关键 / a positive ~ 积极因素 ②【数】因子, 因数; 【物】系数; 【化】当量换算因素; 【生】遗传因子, 基因; 【摄】曝光系数: amplification ~ (电子管的)放大系数 / common ~ 公因子, 公因素 / engagement ~ 【机】接触比, 重迭系数 / space ~ 【无】方向性系数; 占空因素 ③代理商; 依法指定的管理被没收(或被扣押)财产的人; [苏格兰]地产管理人, 管家 **II** *vt.* ①【数】将…分解因子 ②代理经营; 代管(产业) ‖*~age* ['fæktəridʒ] *n.* ①代理业 ②代理商的佣金

factory ['fæktəri] *n.* ①制造厂, 工厂 ②商行在国外的代理处 ‖ ~ **farm** 工厂化农场 / ~ **ship** 加工船(指设有鱼类加工厂的船)

faculty ['fækəlti] *n.* ①才能, 本领; 官能: have a ~ *for* painting 擅长绘画 / the ~ of hearing 听的官能 ②(从事某一专门职业的)全体人员; (高等院校或系的)全体教员及有学衔的行政人员; [美](任何学校的)全体教员: the medical ~ 医务界 / a ~ meeting 教员会议 ③(大学的)系, 科, 学院: the Faculty of Medicine 医学院 ④(授予的)权力 ‖*collect one's faculties* 镇定下来

fad [fæd] *n.* 一时的风尚; 一时的爱好 ‖**faddish, faddy a.** 一时流行的; 喜爱时尚的 / **faddism** *n.* 一时的狂热性, 追随时尚 / **faddist** *n.* 追随时尚的人

fade [feid] **I** ❶ *vi.* ①雕谢, 枯萎: The flowers in the vase have ~d. 瓶中的花已经雕谢。②(颜色)褪去: The colour in this material will not ~

这料子不会褪色。③(声音等)衰弱下去, 消失 ❷ *vt.* 使褪色 **II** *n.* (电影、电视中的)淡入; 淡出 ‖~ *in* (使)淡入, (使)渐显(指电影、电视中的画面); (使)渐强(指电影、广播中的声音) / ~ *out* (使)淡出, (使)渐隐(指电影、电视中的画面); (使)渐弱(指电影、广播中的声音) ‖~**r** *n.* 【无】①音量(或光量)控制器 ②混频电位器 ③增益节节器 ‖*~a,way* *n.* 逐渐消失 / '*~-in n.* (电影、电视中画面的)淡入, 渐显; (电影、广播中声音的)渐强 / '*~-out n.* (电影、电视中画面的)淡出, 渐隐; (电影、广播中声音的)渐弱

fag [fæg] **I** *n.* ①累人的活儿; 疲劳 ②(英国学校中)受高年级学生使唤的低年级生; 奴仆; 做苦工的 ③[俚]香烟(有时指低级香烟) ④[美俚]男性同性关系的人 **II** (fagged; fagging) ❶ *vi.* ①辛苦地工作: ~ *(away)* at sth. (或 at doing sth.) 辛苦地做某事 ②替高年级生跑腿 ❷ *vt.* ①使疲劳: be fagged out 累极 ②强迫(低年级生)跑腿 ③磨损, 拆散(绳索的末端) ‖~ **end** 绳索的散端; 零头布 ②末端; 残渣, 废渣

fag(g)ot ['fægət] **I** *n.* ①柴把, 柴捆; (林业用语)束枝条 ②【冶】成束熟铁块, 束铁 ③长条抽板; 束芯装饰针迹 ④[英]加调味品的烤肝片 **II** *vt.* 束, 捆: ~ed sticks 捆在一起的柴 / He ~ed the pamphlets together. 他把小册子捆在一起。②用花式针迹接缝

Fahrenheit ['færənhait] **I** *a.* 华氏温度计的, 华氏的: a ~ thermometer 华氏温度计 / the ~ scale 华氏温标 / Water freezes at 32°~. 水在华氏三十二度结冰。**II** *n.* 华氏温度计; 华氏温标

fail [feil] **I** ❶ *vi.* ①失败; 不及格: ~ in an examination 考试不及格 ②[后接不定式]不, 不能; 忘记 ③缺乏, 不足; (作物)歉收: The hot water supply ~ed last night. 昨晚热水供应中断。/ He is full of vigour, but ~s in carefulness. 他劲头十足, 但还不够过细。④(健康、体力、视力等)衰退; 减弱; 消失: His eyesight is ~ing. 他的视力在衰退。/ ~ in health 健康衰退 / The wind ~ed. 风停了。⑤停止作用: The patient's heart ~ed. 病人的心脏停止了跳动。/ One of the plane's engines ~ed. 飞机的一个发动机停止转动。⑥破产; 失去支付能力 ❷ *vt.* ①使失望; 弃: My memory ~s me at this moment. 我一时想不起来了。/ Words (或 My tongue) ~ed me. 我激动得讲不出话来。/ His heart ~ed him. 他失去了勇气。/ Time ~ed me to finish my talk. 我想把话讲完, 但时间不够了。②评(学生等)不及格; 没有通过(考试); 没有通过(某一学科)的考试: ~ sb. in mathematics 使某人数学不及格 / He ~ed (a test) in chemistry. 他化学(测验)不及格。**II** *n.* (考试)不及格; 不及格者 ‖*without* ~ 必定, 务必: The chief criminals shall be punished *without* ~. 首恶必办。‖*~ed a.* 已失败的 ‖*~-safe a.* (携核弹的飞机等)具有自动防止故障特性的

failing ['feiliŋ] **I** *n.* 缺点,弱点;失败 **II** *prep.* 如果没有…,若无…时: *Failing* specific instructions, use your own judgement. 如无具体指示,请自行酌办。**III** *a.* 失败的;衰退(或减弱)中的

failure ['feiljə] *n.* ①失败: *Failure* is the mother of success. 失败为成功之母。②失败的人;失败的尝试(或经验): He is a ~ as an artist. 他是一不成功的艺术家。/ Success came after many ~s. 经过多次失败获得了成功。③缺乏,不足;失灵,故障: a crop ~ 粮食歉收 / engine ~s 引擎故障 ④衰退: the ~ of memory (eyesight) 记忆力(视力)衰退 ⑤破产,无支付能化 ⑥疏忽;不履行,没做到: ~ to keep a promise 失约,不守诺言 ⑦[美]不及格;不及格等级(符号"F") ⑧【机】断裂;变钝

faint [feint] **I** *a.* ①虚弱的,衰弱的: His strength grew ~. 他的体力渐渐衰退了。②懦怯的;(行动等)软弱无力的 ③微弱的;不明显的,不清楚的: I haven't the ~est idea of what you mean. 我一点也不懂你的意思。④[只作表语]将昏晕似的;萎顿不堪的: She looks ~ 看来她象要晕倒了。**II** *n.* 昏厥: go off in a ~ 昏过去 / fall in a dead ~ 昏倒 **III** *vi.* ①昏厥,晕倒 ②变得没气力 ③变得微弱;变得不鲜明: The aroma soon ~ed. 香气很快就消失了。‖~ing *n.* 昏厥 / ~ish *a.* 较弱的;有些昏晕的 / ~ly *ad.* / ~ness *n.*

faintheart ['feinthɑ:t] **I** *n.* 懦夫;无决断的人 **II** *a.* 懦怯的;无决断的

fainthearted ['feint'hɑ:tid] *a.* 懦怯的;无决断的 ‖~ly *ad.* / ~ness *n.*

fair[1] [fɛə] **I** *a.* ①美丽的;女性的: ~ landscape 美丽的景色 / the ~ (sex) 女性 / a ~ companion 女伴 ②(肤色)白皙的; (头发)金色的: a ~ complexion 白皙的肤色 ③干净的,清楚的;无污点的: a sheet of ~ white paper 一张洁白的纸 / make a ~ copy of a composition 誊写一篇作文的清稿 / a ~ name (或 reputation) 清白的名声 ④(天气)晴朗的;(风向)顺利的,有希望的: ~ weather 晴朗的天气 / a ~ wind 顺风 / in a ~ way to succeed 有成功的希望 ⑤公平的,合理的: be ~ in buying and selling 买卖公平 / do sth. by ~ means 用正当方法做某事 / a ~ valuation 合理的估价 / a ~ referee 公正的裁判员 ⑥按法律允许的狩猎的;可据理加以攻击的: ~ game [总称]准予捕猎的鸟兽 / be ~ game for ridicule 活该成为嘲笑的对象 ⑦(财产等)丰富的: ~ cultural heritages 丰富的文化遗产 ⑧相当的;尚好的;中等的: a ~ proportion of the students 相当一部分的学生 / He has a ~ knowledge of English. 他英语尚好。/ His performance is merely ~. 他的演出只不过一般。/ ~ average quality (略作 FAQ) 【商】中等品 ⑨(言论)说得好听的,花言巧语的 ⑩(船的外表线条)平顺的 ⑪十足的,整整的,完全的: A ~ month has passed. 足足一

个月过去了。/ It's a ~ miracle! 这真是奇迹! **II** *ad.* ①公平地,公正地: play ~ 公平地比赛,光明正大地比赛; [喻]公平办理,行为光明磊落 ②正面地,直接地: strike sb. ~ in the face 正打在某人的脸上 ③清楚地: copy (或 write out) ~ 抄写清楚 ④[古]有礼貌地: speak sb. ~ 对某人讲话彬彬有礼 **III** *n.* [古] ①美;美人 ②美(好)的事物 **IV** ❶ *vi.* (天气)转晴 ❷ *vt.* ①把…誊清 ②使表面平顺 ‖bid ~ to 见 bid / ~ and softly (针对粗暴态度等用语)慢点,别急;郑重点,态度好点 / ~ and square 正大光明的(地) / ~ play 见 play / ~ to middling [口]过得去,还算好 / for ~ [美口]完全地;肯定地 / see ~ (play) 公平裁判;公平对待,公平处理 / through ~ and foul (或 through foul and ~) 在任何情况下,不管顺利或困难 ‖~ness *n.* ‖'~'haired *a.* ①金发的 ②[口]被宠爱的 / '~light *n.* [英]门顶窗,气窗 / '~'minded *a.* 公正的,无偏见的: a ~-minded man 公正的人 / '~-'spoken *a.* (谈吐等)有礼貌的;温和的;婉转的;嘴甜的 / ~ trade 公平贸易 / '~-'trade *vt.* 按公平贸易约定买卖 / '~-'trade agreement 公平贸易约定(厂商规定代理商不得低于规定价格抛售的约定) / '~-way *n.* ①(河流、海港)航道 ②【空】水上飞机升降用水面跑道 / '~-,weather *a.* 只适宜于好天气的; [喻]只能同安乐不能共患难的: ~-weather friends 不能共患难的朋友

fair[2] [fɛə] *n.* ①定期集市 ②商品展览会,商品交易会: China's Spring (Autumn) Export Commodities *Fair* 中国春季(秋季)出口商品交易会 / a world's ~ 世界博览会 ③义卖市场 ‖'~ground *n.* 集市场所

fairly ['fɛəli] *ad.* ①公正地;正当地: treat sb. ~ 公平对待某人 / come by sth. ~ 正当地取得某物 ②完全;简直: He was ~ beside himself with joy. 他欣喜若狂。/ It may be ~ asserted that…. 简直可以断定说… ③相当;还算: ~ good 还好,尚好 ④清楚地: w⒉ite ~ 清楚地书写

fairy ['fɛəri] **I** *n.* ①小妖精;仙女 ②[美俚]漂亮姑娘 ③[美俚]男性同性恋爱者;女子般的男子 **II** *a.* ①小妖精(似)的;仙女(似)的 ②优雅的;小巧玲珑的 ③幻想中的,虚构的 ‖~like *a.* 小妖精似的;仙女般的 / ~ godmother (危难时提供及时帮助的)慷慨朋友,恩人 / ~ lamp 彩色小灯 / '~land *n.* 仙境;奇境 / ~ light 彩色小灯 / ~ ring ①蕈圈,仙人圈(蕈类在草地上形成的环状斑纹,从前迷信说法称系由仙女跳舞而成) ②(产生蕈圈的)蕈,食用小皮伞蕈 / ~ tale ①神话故事,童话 ②谎言

faith [feiθ] *n.* ①信任;信念 ②信仰;宗教信仰;信条: the Christian and Jewish ~s 基督教和犹太教 / the ~ (或 *Faith*) 正统的宗教(如基督教徒称基督教) / state one's artistic ~ 说出自己的艺术信条 ③信义;诚意;忠诚: in good ~ 真诚地 / in bad ~ 欺诈地 ④保证,诺言;约定: give

(或 pledge) one's ~ to sb. 向某人保证 ‖by (或 upon) my ~ 我担保 / in ~ 确实,的确 / keep (break) ~ ①忠于(背弃)信仰 ②守(背)信: keep (break) ~ with sb. 对某人守(背)信 / lose ~ in 失去对…的信念;不再信任… / on ~ 单凭信仰(指不经考虑地): accept sb.'s statement on ~ 盲目地相信某人的话 / on the ~ of 在…的保证下 / pin one's ~ on (或 upon, to) 把全部信心寄托于… / Punic ~ 背信弃义 ‖~ cure, ~ healing (靠祈祷等治病的)信仰疗法

faithful ['feiθful] **I** a. ①守信的;忠实的,忠诚的: a ~ friend 忠诚的朋友 / be ~ in word and deed 言行忠实 ②如实的,正确的;可靠的: a ~ translation 忠实于原文的译文 ③(诺言等)切实遵守的 **II** ([复] faithful(s)) n. ①[the ~] [总称]虔诚的宗教徒(尤指伊斯兰教徒) ②信徒 ‖~ly ad. 忠诚地;切实地;切实遵守地: Yours ~ly (或 Faithfully yours) 您的忠实的(正式或商业信件等信末署名前的客套语) / promise ~ly 切实遵守地允诺 / ~ness n.

faithless ['feiθlis] a. ①背信弃义的;不忠的 ②不可靠的;不老实的;奸诈的 ③[罕]无(宗教)信仰的 ‖~ly ad. / ~ness n.

fake[1] [feik] **I** ❶ vt. ①伪造,赝造;捏造: ~ a painting 赝造一幅图画 / ~ (up) a report 捏造一份报告 ②伪装: ~ illness 装病 ③[俚]即席奏出: ~ an accompaniment 即席伴奏 ❷ vi. 伪装 **II** n. ①假货,赝品;捏造的报道,虚构的故事: The antique is a ~. 那古董是一件赝品。 ②魔术用具 ③冒充者,骗子: a medical ~ 冒牌医生 **III** a. 假的,赝造的;冒充的: ~ diamonds 赝造的钻石 ‖~ sb. out [口]以欺骗、讹诈手法胜过某人 ‖~ment n. ①欺骗 ②假货,赝品 / ~r n. ①伪造者,捏造者 ②骗子;卖滑头货的小贩 / ~ry ['feikəri] n. ①伪造,捏造;伪装 ②假货,赝品

fake[2] [feik] **I** n. 【海】一卷绳索 **II** vt. 卷(绳索)

falcon ['fɔ:lkən, 'fɔ:kən] n. ①【动】隼,游隼 ②(猎鸟用的)猎鹰(术语上专指雌鹰) ③(十五到十七世纪用的)小炮 ‖~er n. 养猎鹰者;鹰猎者 / ~ry n. 猎鹰训练术;鹰猎

falcon

fall [fɔ:l] **I** (fell [fel], fallen ['fɔ:lən]) ❶ vi. ①落下;降落;跌落;跌倒: Leaves ~ in autumn. 秋天树叶落下。 / The rain is ~ing. 正在下雨。 / ~ into a river 跌入河中 ②(温度、价格等)下降,跌(落);(风势、声音等)减退,减弱;(情绪等)低落: The temperature is ~ing. 温度在下降。 / The storm fell towards evening. 傍晚时暴风雨减弱了。 / a voice ~ing to a whisper 逐渐微弱得象耳语一样的语声 ③下垂;降临: The curtain ~s. 幕落。 / Two plaits ~ over her shoulders. 两条辫子垂在她的肩上。 / Night ~s. 夜晚来临。 ④(地面等)倾斜;(河流)(向)下流,注(入);(潮汐)退落: an apple orchard ~ing to the river 向河边倾斜的苹果园 ⑤(羊羔等)出生 ⑥(房屋)坍倒;(城市、阵地等)陷落,被攻克;(政府、政权等)垮台,被推翻: The wall has fallen. 墙倒了。 ⑦阵亡,战死;死亡: ~ to sb.'s gun 被某人击毙 ⑧(地位、声誉、威信等)降低 ⑨(目光)向下;(脸色)变阴沉: His eyes (或 glance) fell. 他目光朝下。 / His face (或 jaw) fell. 他的脸沉下来了。 ⑩堕落;陷入罪恶 ⑪(日期)适逢: National Day ~s on a Monday this year. 今年国庆日是星期一。 ⑫落(到),轮(到): The accent ~s on the first syllable. 重音在第一音节。 / It ~s to our lot to do this. 该我们来做这事。 ⑬(光线等)射;(声音等)传: The shot fell wide of (its) mark. 那一枪没有打中目标。 / His eye fell upon me. 他的目光落到了我身上。 / A cry fell on our ears. 我们听到一声叫喊。 ⑭变成,成为: The child fell asleep (ill). 那孩子睡着了(病了)。 / ~ due (帐单等)到期 ⑮被说出: Not a word fell from her lips. 她一声也不吭。 ⑯属(于): ~ within the country's jurisdiction 属于国家管辖之下 ❷ vt. [美][英方]击倒,砍倒(树木)

II n. ①落下;跌倒;下垂;(房屋等)坍倒: A ~ into the pit, a gain in your wit. 吃一堑,长一智。 ②(雨、雪等的)降落;降落量: a heavy ~ of rain (snow) 一场大雨(雪) ③(树木的)伐倒;(木材的)采伐量 ④下降;向下倾斜;落差;(情绪等的)低落: a sharp ~ in temperature 温度的剧降 / a ~ in prices 价格的下跌 / a canal (field) with a ~ of two metres in a hundred metres 每一百米落差为二米的一条运河(一块田地) ⑤下崽;(一)胎(主要指一次所生的羊羔) ⑥(城市、要塞等的)陷落;(政府、政权等的)垮台,崩溃;衰亡;失败: Pride will have a ~. 骄必败。 ⑦(地位、声望、威信等的)降低

⑧堕落

⑨[常用复]瀑布: the ~s of Niagara 尼亚加拉瀑布[美国]

⑩[主美]秋天,秋季: in the ~ of 1970 在一九七〇年秋天

⑪【机】起重机绳;【海】辘绳

⑫向下飘荡的服装;领子的翻下部分;(外衣的)宽下摆;大裤脚

⑬【语】降调;【音】(乐曲的)终止

⑭(摔角中)把对手摔输;一局摔角

III a. 秋季的: ~ clothes 秋令服装

‖~ *across* 碰见,遇到 / ~ *afoul of* 见 afoul / ~ *among* 偶然遇到(坏人们等),偶然陷入…之中 / ~ *apart* 崩溃,土崩瓦解 / ~ *away* ①背离;离开 ②消失 ③消瘦 ④(地势)倾斜 / ~ *back* 后退,退却 / ~ *back on*(或 *upon*)①求…的支持,求助于;转而依靠 ②退到 ③回过来再谈 / ~ *behind* ①落在(…的)后面,跟不上: ~ *behind* with one's studies 学习跟不上 ②拖欠 / ~ *down (on)* [口](在…方面)失败 / ~ *flat* 达不到预想效果;完全失败: His joke *fell flat*. 他的笑话没有使人感到好笑。 / ~ *for* [俚]①爱上,迷恋 ②受…骗,上…的当: We must not ~ *for* such nonsense. 我们决不能听信这种胡说八道。 / ~ *foul of* 见 foul / ~ *home*(木材或船侧上部)向里弯 / ~ *in* ①(房屋等)坍下,往里坍塌 ②【军】集合 ③同意 ④(债务等)到期;(租约等)满期,失效 / ~ *in* ①落入 ②陷入(混乱、错误等);进入(某种状态) / ~ *into* a stupor 陷入昏迷状态 / ~ *into* a rage 勃然大怒 ③(河流)注入: This river ~s *into* the sea. 这条河流入海洋。 ④(可)分成: The story ~s *into* three parts. 这故事分成三部分。 ⑤ 属于: ~ *into* the same category 属于同一范畴 ⑥开始: ~ *into* conversation with sb. 和某人交谈起来 / ~ *in with* ①偶尔遇到 ②同意…,赞成…: ~ *in with* sb.'s views 同意某人的看法 / ~ *off* ①下降,跌落;【军】(飞机)侧降 ②减少;缩小 ③变坏;衰退 ④【海】偏向下风,(船只)不易驾驶,不受控制 ⑤离开;叛离 / ~ *on*(或 *upon*)①扑到;袭击 ②袭击,进攻 / ~ *out* ①争吵,吵架;闹翻 ②结果: It (so) *fell out* that they were late for the train. 他们终于没有赶上火车。/ The experiment *fell out* as we had expected. 试验结果同我们预料的一样。 ③离队;【军】原地解散 / ~ *out of* 放弃(习惯)等 / ~ *over each other* 争夺;竞争 / ~ *over oneself* ①(因匆忙、动作不灵而)跌跤 ②热衷,渴望 *(for)* / ~ *short (of)* ①不足,缺乏 ②达不到;不符合: The arrow *fell short (of)* the target). 箭没有射到(目标)。 / ~ *to* ①着手: ~ *to* reaping the wheat 开始割起小麦来 / ~ *to* argument 辩论起来 ②开始攻击 ③开始吃 ④自动合上 / ~ *under* ①受到(影响)等 ②被列为;归入…类: These goods ~ *under* class A. 这些货物列为甲级。/ *nod to its* ~ 摇摇欲坠 / *ride for a* ~

①乱骑马 ②行动莽撞; 招致失败(或危险) / *the Fall (of man)* 【基督教】人类的堕落(指亚当受诱惑吃禁果后堕落人间) / *the* ~ *of the leaf* 秋天 / *try a* ~ *(with)* (与…)比一下摔角; (与…)较量一番

‖~*a,way* n.【宇】(火箭各级的)分开,散开,排出 / '~**back** n. ①可依靠的东西 ②退却 / ~**guy** [美俚] ①(阴谋等失败后的)替罪羊,替死鬼 ②容易上当受骗的人 / ~ **line** ①【地】瀑布线 ②(滑雪的)直接下滑线 / '~**off** n. ①下降,减退 ②【宇】(火箭各级的)分开,散开,排出 / '~**out** n. ①【原】微粒回降;回降物,放射性尘埃: radioactive ~ 放射性微粒回降 ②附带结果 / '~**pipe** n. 水落管 / '~**trap** n. 陷阱 / '~**up** n. 放射性尘埃对海洋地区的污染 / ~ **wind** 【气】下降风,下吹风

fallacious [fə'leiʃəs] a. ①谬误的 ②靠不住的,虚妄的;令人失望的 ‖~**ly** ad. / ~**ness** n.

fallacy ['fæləsi] n. ①谬误: a ~ of the eye 视觉上的谬误 ②谬论,谬见

fallen ['fɔ:lən] **I** fall 的过去分词 **II** a. ①落下的;倒下的;伐倒的;伏地的: ~ leaves 落叶 / ~ trees 伐倒的树木 ②摧毁的;倒塌的 ③陷落的,被攻克的;被推翻的: a ~ fortress 被攻克的堡垒 ④堕落的 ⑤死去的: the ~ [总称]阵亡者,战死者

fallible ['fæləbl] a. 易犯错误的;难免有错误的 ‖**fallibility** [,fæli'biliti] n. / **fallibly** ad.

falling ['fɔ:liŋ] **I** n. ①下降,落下,坠落;落下物: the ~ of commodity prices 物价的下落 ②陷落,凹陷;(岩石等的)崩塌: risings and ~s in the ground 地面的凸起和凹陷 ③堕落 **II** a. ①下降的,落下的: a ~ tide 落潮 / a ~ intonation (或 tone) 降语调 ②(家畜等)变衰弱的,衰退的 ‖~'**out** ([复] fallings-out 或 falling-outs) n. 吵架,争吵 / ~ **sickness** 癫痫;(家畜的)癫痫发作 / ~ **star** 流星

fallow[1] ['fæləu] **I** a. ①(耕地)休闲的: a ~ field 休闲地,休耕地 / a ~ crop 休闲作物 ②未孕的: a ~ sow 未孕的母猪 ③潜伏的,不活跃的 **II** n. 【农】休闲地,休耕地;休闲 **III** vt. 使(土地)休闲 ‖~ **lie** — ①休闲;休整 ②潜伏(指潜在的特征等);尚未被利用: a skill *lying* ~ 尚未发挥的技能 ‖~**ness** n.

fallow[2] ['fæləu] a. 淡棕色的 ‖~ **deer** (欧洲产)鹿

false [fɔ:ls] **I** a. ①假的,虚伪的,不真实的: give a ~ impression 给人以假象 / see through a ~ appearance 识破假象 / eliminate the ~ and retain the true 去伪存真 / make a ~ attack 佯攻 / ~ pride 妄自尊大,虚荣心 ②谬误的,不正确的: a ~ argument (verdict) 错误的论点(判决) / ~ weights 不准的砝码 ③无信义的,欺诈的,不老实的: be ~ to one's word 背信,不守诺言 / be ~ of heart 不忠实,无信义 / bear (或 give) ~ witness 作假见证 / a ~

charge (或 accusation) 诬告 ④ 伪造的; 人造的, 人工的: a ~ coin 伪币 / ~ teeth 假牙 ⑤(常用于植物名称)似乎象(其实不同)的: ~ eggplant 【植】假茄子 ⑥临时的, 非基本的; (为了保护、加固或伪装)装上去的 ⑦不合调的; sing a ~ note 唱出一个走调的音 ⑧鲁莽的, 不智的: a ~ start 犯规的起跑; 冒失的开端 / make a ~ turn in one's boat 鲁莽地使船掉头 ⑨违反意图的, 违反原则的; 有损害的; 尴尬的: put sb. in a ~ position 使某人处于违反原则行事的地位; 使某人被误解 **II** *ad.* 欺诈地; 叛卖地[只用于以下短语]: play sb. ~ 欺骗某人; 叛卖某人 ‖*run* 见 **run**[1] / *sail under ~ colo(u)rs* 见 **colo(u)r** / *take* (或 *make*) *a ~ step* 见 **step** ‖**~ly** *ad.* **~ness** *n.* ‖~ **alarm** ①骗人的警报 ②昙花一现的人物 / ~ **arrest** 【律】(个人对个人的)非法强行拘留 / ~ **attic** 【建】假(屋)顶层 / ~ **bottom** (船只、箱子、抽屉等隔开夹层的)假底, 活底 / '**~-card** *n.* 为迷惑对方而出的牌 / ~ **face** 假面具 / '**~'hearted** *a.* 不忠实的; 欺诈的 / ~ **imprisonment** 非法监察 / ~ **keel** 【船】副龙骨, 保护龙骨 / ~ **papers** (船只携带的关于所运货物和目的地等的)假证件 / ~ **pretences** 诈骗 / ~ **smut** 【农】稻麴病 / '**~work** *n.* 【建】脚手架,工作架,临时支撑

falsehood ['fɔ:lshud] *n.* ①谬误, 不真实: the struggle between truth and ~ 真理和谬误的斗争; 正确与错误的斗争 ②说谎; 欺骗 ③谎言: tell a ~ 撒谎 ④错误的信仰(或理论、思想等)

falsetto [fɔ:l'setou] [意] **I** *n.* 【音】假声: in ~ 用假声 ②用假声唱的人 **II** *a.* 用假声(唱)的 **III** *ad.* 用假声

falsify ['fɔ:lsifai] ❶ *vt.* ① 窜改(文件等); 伪造: ~ a record 窜改记录 ② 歪曲: ~ sb.'s motives 歪曲某人的动机 ③ 证明…是假的, 证明…是无根据的: The new discoveries have *falsified* that hypothesis. 新的发现已证明那个假定是无根据的。/ His expectations have been *falsified*. 他的期望落空了。④ 搞错, 误用 ❷ *vi.* 说谎 ‖**falsification** ['fɔ:lsifi'keiʃən] *n.* 窜改; 伪造; 窜改; 歪曲 ② 证明为假, 证明为无根据 / **falsifier** *n.* 弄虚作假者; 说谎者; 伪造者; 窜改者

falter ['fɔ:ltə] **I** *vi.* ①蹒跚, 踉跄; 摇晃, 摇摆 ②(声音)颤抖; 支吾: His voice began to ~. 他的声音开始发颤。③踌躇, 犹豫, 畏缩: He never ~s in his determination. 他的决心从不动摇。❷ *vt.* 支吾地说, 结巴地讲出: ~ *out* a reply 结结巴巴地回答 **II** *n.* 颤抖; 支吾; 踌躇, 犹豫, 畏缩

fame [feim] **I** *n.* ①名声; 名望: come to ~ 成名 / ill ~ 坏名声 ②[古]传闻 **II** *vt.* ①[常用被动语态]使闻名, 使有名望 ②盛传; 称道 ‖**~d** *a.* 有名的, 著名的: a ~d summer resort 著名的避暑胜地

familiar [fə'miljə] **I** *a.* ①熟悉的; 通晓的: a ~ voice 熟悉的声音 / things ~ *to* sb. 某人所熟悉的事物 / He is ~ *with* English. 他通晓英语。

②亲近的: a ~ friend 熟不拘礼的朋友 / be on ~ terms with 与…亲密, 交情很好 ③无拘束的, 随便的; 放肆的, 冒昧的: a ~ essay 小品文, 随笔 / a ~ conversation 随便的交谈 / His manner is too ~. 他的态度太放肆了。④(男女间)亲昵的 ⑤家族的; (胜地等)供人们携家游憩的 ⑥(野生动物)较驯服的 **II** *n.* ①熟友; 伴侣 ②常客 ③高级官吏的家属 ④ (天主教)修道院(或主教等)的仆人 ⑤ 传说中供女巫使唤的妖精 (= ~ spirit) ‖**~ly** *ad.*

familiarity [fə,mili'æriti] *n.* ①熟悉; 通晓: ~ *with* standard pronunciation 对于标准发音的通晓 ② 亲近; 亲昵; 随便; 放肆 ③[常用复]放肆的言行; 爱抚 ‖*Familiarity breeds contempt.* [谚]熟悉了就会觉得没有什么了不起。(或: 家曙生狎侮。)

familiarize, familiarise [fə'miljəraiz] *vt.* ① 使熟悉; 使通晓: ~ oneself *with* one's job 使自己熟悉工作 ② 使家喻户晓: a ~d technical term 已为人所熟知的术语 ‖**familiarization** [fə,miljərai-'zeiʃən] *n.*

family ['fæmili] **I** *n.* ①家, 家庭; 家属; 亲属: My ~ are all fond of playing table tennis. 我全家都爱打乒乓。② 子女: He has a ~ of three. 他有三个子女。/ He is the eldest of the ~. 他是最大的孩子。③氏族, 家族 ④僚属; (宗教、哲学信念等方面的)派, 派别: (the President's) official ~ [美](总统的)内阁 ⑤门第; 名门 ⑥【动】【植】科;【化】【数】【天】族;【语】语族: animals of the cat ~ 猫科动物 / the Germanic ~ of languages 日耳曼语族 **II** *a.* 家庭的; 家族的: a ~ likeness 亲属之间的相似; 隐约的相似 / ~ ties 亲属关系 / a ~ butcher 供应家庭的肉商(区别于供应军队等) ‖*a happy ~* ① 快乐家庭 ② 同处一个牢笼的不同类动物 / *in a ~ way* ①象一家人一样地, 不拘礼节地 ②[美]怀孕 / *in the ~ way* [英]怀孕 / *of* (*good*) ~ 出身门第高的 / *run in the ~* (性格特征等)为一家人所共有, 世代相传 ‖**~ allowance** (工资外的)家庭津贴 / ~ **Bible** 家庭用大型《圣经》(附有空白页, 供记载家庭生死、结婚事项用) / ~ **circle** ①家庭圈子 ②(剧场中廉价的)家庭席 / ~ **farm** 个体农场(主要由一家人从事农业劳动的农场) / ~ **man** ① 有妻子女的人, 有家累的人 ② 爱好家庭生活的人 / ~ **name** 姓 / ~ **planning** 计划生育 / ~ **tree** 系谱; 系谱图

famine ['fæmin] *n.* ①饥荒 ②[古]饥饿 ③严重的缺乏: a coal (water) ~ 煤(水)荒 ‖~ **prices** 缺货时的高价

famish ['fæmiʃ] ❶ *vt.* ①[常用被动语态]使挨饿 ②[古]使饿死 ❷ *vi.* ①挨饿; 饥饿: be ~*ing* [口]感到很饿 ②[古]饿死

famous ['feiməs] *a.* ①著名的, 出名的: a place ~ *for* its hot springs 以温泉出名的地方 ②[口]好的, 非常令人满意的: He has a ~ appetite. 他的胃口很好。/ a ~ dinner 一顿非常令人满意的饭 ‖**~ly** *ad.* [口]极好, 非常令人满意地

He is doing ~*ly* at his new job. 他在新的工作岗位上干得很出色。

fan¹ [fæn] **I** *n.* ①扇子；风扇；鼓风机: an electric ~ 电风扇 / a folding ~ 折扇 / a draft ~ 通风风扇, 吸风机 / an exhaust ~ 抽气扇, 排气风扇 ②扇形物(如孔雀尾、棕榈树叶等) ③簸箕; 扬谷机 ④螺旋桨; 螺旋桨叶片 **II** (fanned; fanning) ❶ *vt.* ①扇: ~ oneself 给自己扇扇子 / ~ a stove 扇炉子 ②扇动; 激起: ~ the flame 扇动情绪 ③(用扇子等)驱走 (*away*) ④簸(谷); 扬去(糠等) ⑤(微风)吹拂 ⑥把…展成扇形 (*out*) ⑦[美俚]拍打; 殴打, 鞭打; 搜查 ❷ *vi.* ①飘动; 拍翅 ②成扇形展开 ‖~**like** *a.* ①象扇的; 象风扇般转动的 ②折迭的 / **fanner** *n.* ①扇风者; 鼓风机; 扬谷器 / **fannings** [复] *n.* 簸出物; 筛出的粗茶叶 ‖~**-jet** *n.* [空]鼓风式喷气发动机; 鼓风式喷气飞机 / '~**light** *n.* [建]楣窗, 扇形气窗 / '~**-shaped** *a.* 扇状的 / '~**-tail** *n.* ①扇形尾端 ②[动]扇尾鸽 ③[建]扇形尾饰 / ~ **tracery** [建]扇形(花)格架 / ~ **truss** [建]扇形桁架

fan² [fæn] *n.* ①(运动、电影等的)狂热爱好者: a movie ~ 影迷 ②狂慕者(通常指对演员等) ‖~ **mail** [总称](影迷、球迷等)向明星表示崇拜的信件

fanatic [fə'nætik] **I** *a.* 狂热的, 盲信的; 盲目热中的 **II** *n.* 狂热者, 盲信者, 入迷者

fanatical [fə'nætikəl] *a.* =fanatic (*a.*) ‖~**ly** *ad.*

fanciful ['fænsiful] *a.* ①爱空想的; 沉湎于空想的 ②存在于空想中的, 想象出来的: a ~ tale 想象出来的故事 ③奇异的, 怪诞的: ~ costumes 奇装异服 ‖~**ly** *ad.* / ~**ness** *n.*

fancy ['fænsi] **I** *n.* ①想象力; 幻想力: Children usually have a lively ~. 儿童们往往有丰富的幻想力。 ②设想; 幻想, 空想: go off into wild flights of ~ 无根据地胡思乱想 ③(一时的)爱好; 迷恋 (*for*): have a ~ for bicycling (chess) 热中于骑自行车(下棋) / a passing ~ 一时的爱好 ④(在艺术、穿着等方面的)鉴赏力, 审美观点 ⑤时新的纺织品; 杂色的花朵(或植物) ⑥培育珍贵动物的技能 ⑦[the ~](在艺术、娱乐等方面)有特殊癖好的人们, …迷(尤指拳击迷们) ⑧癖好(尤指拳击) **II** *a.* ①根据想象的, 空想出来的: a portrait 想象的肖像画(非真实人物的肖像) ②(衣着、食品等)花式的: ~ goods 花哨的小商品 / ~ cakes 花式糕点 / ~ diving 花式跳水 / a ~ fair [英]小商品商场 ③奇特的, 异样的; 品种珍贵的; 杂色的: ~ dress (化装舞会等的)化装服饰 / ~ birds (goldfish) 珍种禽鸟(金鱼) / ~ chrysanthemums 杂色菊花 ④ (价格等)太高的; 供应高价的: sell at a ~ price 以十分昂贵的价格出售 ⑤[美](商品, 特指食品)特级的, 最高档的: ~ fresh fruits 特级鲜果 **III** ❶ *vt.* ①想象, 设想: *Fancy* meeting so many old friends here! 真想不到在这里遇到这么多的老朋友! / *Fancy* that! 那真想不到! ②(无根据地)相信, (自负地)认为: I ~ he will act quickly. 我想

他会迅速行动的。/ He *fancied* himself (to be) an authority. 他自以为是个权威。 ③喜爱, 爱好: Don't you ~ anything? (问病人等)你想吃点什么东西吗? ④饲养, 培育(品种奇特的动植物) ❷ *vi.* 想象; 幻想: Just ~! 你想想看! (或: 好不奇怪!) ‖*after sb.'s* ~ 中某人意的, 合某人意的 / *take a* ~ *to* 喜欢…起来, 爱上… / *take* (或 *catch*) *the* ~ *of* 使…喜爱; 吸引: The exhibits *took the* ~ *of* the visitors. 展出品深受参观者的喜爱。‖~**-free** *a.* ①不受拘束地进行想象的 ②没有恋爱对象的; 未婚的 / ~ **house** [俚]妓院 / ~ **man** ①情夫 ②靠妓女过活的男人 / ~ **woman** ①情妇 ②妓女 / '~**work** *n.* 刺绣品, 钩编织品

fang [fæŋ] **I** *n.* ①(犬、狼等的)尖牙; 犬齿; (毒蛇的)毒牙 ②牙根 ③尖端; (工具等的)齿; 爪 **II** *vt.* 灌水引动(水泵) ‖~**ed** *a.* 有尖牙的; 有毒牙的

fantastic [fæn'tæstik] *a.* ①幻想的, 异想天开的 ②奇异的, 古怪的: ~ shapes 奇形怪状 ③极大的, 大得难以相信的 **II** *n.* [古]古怪的人 ‖*trip the light* ~ [美]跳舞 ‖~**ality** [fæn,tæsti'kæliti] *n.* ①奇异, 荒谬 ②奇谈; 怪事 / ~**ally** *ad.* / ~**alness** *n.*

fantasy ['fæntəsi, 'fæntəzi] **I** *n.* ①幻想 ②怪念头 ③幻想曲; 幻想作品 ④想象力的产物; 离奇的图案; 奇妙的发明 ⑤想入非非 **II** ❶ *vt.* 想象 ❷ *vi.* ①空想, 作白日梦 ②奏幻想曲

far [fɑː] **I** (farther ['fɑːðə] 或 further ['fəːðə], farthest ['fɑːðist] 或 furthest ['fəːðist]) *ad.* ①(表示空间或时间上的距离)远, 遥远地; 久远地: stand high and see ~ 站得高, 看得远 / ~ back in the past 在遥远的过去 / study (work) ~ *into* the night 学习(工作)到深夜 ②(常用于比较, 强调程度、性质)大大…; …得多 **II** (farther 或 further, farthest 或 furthest) *a.* ①(常用于书面语)遥远的, 远方的; 久远的: a man of ~ sight 目光远大的人 ②(用于地名)远的: the *Far* East 远东 / the *Far* West (太平洋沿岸的)美国西部地区 ③较远的 (=farther)的: at the ~ end of the street 在街道的那一头 **III** *n.* 远处, 远方: Has he come from ~? 他是从远方来的么? ‖*a* ~ *cry* 见 **cry** / *as* (或 *so*) ~ *as* ①…那么远, 远到, 直到 ②(表示程度、范围)就…; 尽…; 至于: as ~ as possible 尽可能, 尽量 / *as* ~ *as in me lies* 尽我的力量 / *as* ~ *back as* (表示时间)远在…: *as* ~ *back as* the 18th century 远在十八世纪 / *be* ~ *gone* 见 **gone** / *by* ~ (修饰比较级、最高级, 强调数量、程度等) …得多; 最…: He is *by* ~ the tallest among us. 他在我们这些人中间个子最高。/ *His explanation is clearer by* ~. 他的解释清楚得多。/ *carry sth. too* ~ 见 **carry** / ~ *and away* 大大…; 无疑地, 肯定地: This is ~ *and away* the best book on the subject. 这无疑是论述这一问题的最好的一本书。/ ~ *and near* 远近, 到处, 四面八方 / ~ *be it from me* 我决不会(认为…, 想要

…等) / ~ *from* ①远离 ②远远不, 完全不; 非但不 / (*few and*) ~ *between* 见 **between** / *go* ~ 见 **go** / *go too* ~ 见 **go** / *how* ~ (离…)多远: *How* ~ is it to the station? 到车站有多远? ②到什么程度 (或范围): Practice will prove *how* ~ the plan works. 实践将证明这个计划的可行性如何。/ *in so* ~ *as* (表示程度、范围) 就…; 尽…; 至于 (=as (或 so) ~ as) / *so* 迄今为止; 就此范围说来 / *So* ~, *so good*. 到目前为止, 一切顺利。/ *thus* ~ =so ~ ‖**~away** ['fɑ:rəwei] *a.* 【无】(时间、距离、程度等) 遥远的, 远远的 ②(表情) 心不在焉的, 恍惚的, 出神的: a ~*away* look 恍惚的神色 / **~-end** ['fɑ:rend] *n.* 【无】(线路或电路的) 远端 / '~='famed *a.* 名声远扬的 / '**~'fetched** *a.* 牵强的; 不自然的: a ~*fetched* comparison 牵强的比较 / '**~'flung** *a.* 蔓延的, 漫长的; 辽阔的 ②遥远的 / **~-off** ['fɑ:r'(ɔ)f] *a.* 遥远的 / **~-(-)out** ['fɑ:r'aut] *a.* [美俚] ①最新颖的(特指爵士乐的); (艺术上) 先锋派的 ②远离现实的 ③(因埋头干事、一心思索等而) 出神的 ④极端的; 不寻常的 / '**~'seeing** *a.* 看得远的, 目光远的; 有先见的, 深谋远虑的 / '**~'sighted** *a.* 远视的; 有远见的 / '**~sightedness** *n.* 远视; 远见

farce [fɑ:s] **I** *n.* ①笑剧, 滑稽戏 ②滑稽; 可笑的事物; 冒充的东西 ③馅儿 **II** *vt.* ①[古]填塞 ②为(演说、作品等)加穿插

fare [feə] **I** *vi.* ①过活; 遭遇; 进展: How did you ~ there? 你在那里过得怎样? ②吃, 进食: They ~*d* plainly. 他们吃得很简单。③[古]行走, 旅行: ~ forth 出发 **II** *n.* ①车费; 船费: bus (taxi) ~ 公共汽车(出租汽车)费 / a uniform ~ of ten cents for any distance 不论远近一律一角的车费 / All ~*s*, please! (公共车辆售票员用语) 请买票! ②乘客 ③伙食: good (simple) ~ 良好的(简单的)伙食 / a bill of ~ 菜单 ④精神粮食(尤指文艺、娱乐方面的) ⑤(渔船的) 捕获量 ‖*You may go farther and ~ worse.* [谚] (劝人安于现状) 走得更远可能情形更坏。(或: 知足常乐。)

farewell ['feə'wel] **I** *int.* 再会! 别了! (常含有永别了或不容易再见面的意思): ~ *to* 对…永别了; 不会再… **II** *n.* ①告别话; 告别: make one's ~*s* 道别, 告辞 / take one's ~ of sb. 向某人告别 ②送别会; (欢送退休艺人的) 送别演出 **III** *a.* 告别的: a ~ speech 告别词

farm [fɑ:m] **I** *n.* ①农场, 农庄: a state ~ 国营农场 / work *on* a ~ 在农场工作 ②饲养场, 畜牧场; 培养水产的)塘: a chicken ~ 养鸡场 / a fish ~ 鱼塘 ③(儿童等的) 寄养场所 ④包出税收; 包税区 ⑤[美](棒球联合总会所属的) 棒球分会 / ~ *and sideline products* 农副产品 / ~ *crops* 农作物 / ~ *implements* (或 *tools*) 农具 / ~ *machinery* 农业机械 **II** ① *vt.* ①耕(田); 耕种 ②在…上经营农场 ③寄养(小孩等): ~ *out* one's baby *with* sb. 把婴儿托给某人 ④承包(企业等)的收入 ⑤佃出, 出租(土地、企业); 把

(囚犯等) 作为劳动力出租 (*out*) ⑥包出(工件、活计、税收) (*out*) ⑦把(土地)种乏; 使(地)力耗尽 (*out*) ② *vi.* 种田, 务农; 从事畜牧 ‖**~ing** *n.* 农业, 农事, 耕作; 畜牧: learn ~*ing* 学农 / spring ~*ing* 春耕 / take the road of collective ~*ing* 走农业集体化道路 / be engaged in sheep-~*ing* 从事牧羊 ‖'**~hand** *n.* 农业工人, 农场工人; 雇农 / '**~house** *n.* 农场里的住房(尤指主要住房) / ~ **labo(u)rer** =~hand / '**~land** *n.* 农场的农田和建筑物; 农庄 / '**~stead** *n.* 农场建筑物周围(或圈内)的空地(尤指盖前空地)

farmer ['fɑ:mə] *n.* ①农民, 农夫 ②农场主 ③畜牧者; 牧场主 ④承包者; 包税人 ‖a dirt ~ [美口] 自耕农, 小农 / an afternoon ~ [俚]拖延的人

farther ['fɑ:ðə] [far 的两种比较级形式之一, 另一形式为 further; farther 常用于本义"更远的", further 常用于引申意义"进一步"] **I** *ad.* ①(距离、时间上) 更远地, 更往前地: Can you go any ~? 你还走得动吗? / go ~ north 继续向北 ②进一步地; 而且; 此外 (现代英语多用 further) **II** *a.* (距离、时间上)更远的, 再往前的: on the ~ side of the road 在路的那一边 / at the ~ end of the street 在街道的那一头 ‖~ 更远(些), 再往前(些): The station is about two li ~ on. 到火车站大约还有两里路。②(书中说明等)在后面, 在下面 / I'll see you ~ (或 further) first. [口]我决不干。(或: 我才不干哩。) / No ~! 别再向前走啦! (或: 别再说啦!)

farthest ['fɑ:ðist] [far 的两种最高级形式之一, 另一形式为 furthest] **I** *a.* (距离、时间上)最远的: The news soon spread to the ~ corner. 那消息很快就传播到最远的地方。**II** *ad.* ①(距离、时间上)最远地: choose the seat ~ from the door 选择离门最远的座位 ②最大程度地; 最大限度地 ‖(*the*) ~ 至多; 最远(也不过…); 最迟(也不过…): The village is two kilometres from here at ~. 那村庄离这里至多两公里。/ We shall be ready in a few days or a week at ~. 我们过几天, 多过一星期, 就准备就绪。

farthing ['fɑ:ðiŋ] *n.* ①[英]四分之一旧便士(的硬币) ②极少量, 一点儿: not care a ~ 一点也不在乎 / not worth a ~ 一文不值, 毫无价值

fascinate ['fæsineit] ❶ *vt.* ①迷住, 使神魂颠倒 ②强烈地吸引住 ③使呆住; 蛊惑: The serpent ~*d* its prey. 蛇(用目光)吓住了它要捕食的动物。❷ *vi.* 迷人, 极度吸引人 ‖**fascinator** *n.* ①迷人者 ②网眼毛披巾

fascinating ['fæsineitiŋ] *a.* 迷人的, 消魂夺魄的 ‖**~ly** *ad.*

fascination [,fæsi'neiʃən] *n.* ①迷惑力, 魅力 ②迷恋, 强烈爱好: the child's ~ with transistor radios 那孩子对半导体收音机的强烈爱好

fashion ['fæʃən] **I** *n.* ①样子; 方式: act after sb.'s ~ 照某人的样子去做 ②流行式样; (言论、行为等的)风尚, 风气: the latest ~*s* (服装等的)最

新式样 / come into ~ 开始风行 / go out of ~ 不再风行 ③[the ~] 风行一时的事物; 红人, 名流 ④ 上流社会 ⑤[古] 种类 II vt. ①形成; 制作; 把…塑造成 (into): a canoe from a tree-trunk 用树干削成独木舟 / ~ the clay into bricks 把泥土制成砖头 / ~ sb. into a fine sports-man 把某人培养成优秀运动员 ②使适合, 使适应 ③改变, 改革 ||after (或 in) a ~ 勉强; 马马虎虎: He can speak French after a ~. 他马马虎虎能讲一点法语。/ after the ~ of 照…的样子; 模仿… / be all the ~ (服装等) 极时髦, 风行一时 / be in (the) ~ (人、物) 合于时尚 / be out of (the) ~ (人、物) 不合于时尚 / follow the ~ 赶时髦 / pit a bit on one's plate to make ~ 拨一点儿到盘子里作作样子(指实际上并没有吃) / set the ~ 创立新式样; 开创新风尚 ||~,monger n. 讲究时髦的人, 赶时髦的人 / ~ plate ①时装样片 ②穿着时髦的人 / ~ plate stem [船] (钢板) 组成船首柱

fashionable ['fæʃənəbl] I a. ①流行的, 时髦的 ② 赶时髦的; 上流社会的; 为上流社会的人们所欢迎的 II n. 时髦的人 ||~ness n. / fashionably ad.

fast[1] [fɑːst] I a. ①紧的, 牢的: The telegraph-poles are ~ in the ground. 电线杆牢牢地树在地上。/ make the boat ~ 把船拴牢 / make the door ~ 把门关紧 / take (a) ~ hold of sth. 紧紧抓住某物 ②忠实的, 可靠的: a ~ friend 可靠的朋友 ③不褪的 ④酣畅的: fall into a ~ sleep 酣睡起来 ⑤ 快的, 迅速的; 短暂的: a ~ train (horse) 快车(马) / ~ work 迅速完成的工作; 很快就能完成的工作 ⑥(钟表) 偏快的; (衡器) 偏重的, 所示分量超过实际分量的; 夏令时间的 (指将钟表拨快一小时的时间制度): My watch is five minutes ~. 我的表快五分钟。/ ~ time 夏令时间 (= daylight saving time) ⑦适于进行快速行动的: a ~ highway 快速公路 ⑧放荡的: lead a ~ life 过放荡生活 ⑨[摄] 感光快的; 曝光时间短的 ⑩ (细菌等) 抗…的: acid-~ 抗酸的 II ad. ①紧紧地, 牢固地: The door was ~ shut. 门紧闭着。/ hold ~ to the handle 握紧手柄 ②酣畅地: be ~ asleep 熟睡 ③快, 迅速地: Don't read so ~. 不要读得这样快。/ It's raining ~. 雨下得很大。④放荡地 ⑤[古] 贴近, 靠近: ~ by the hill 就在山边 ||a ~ one 见 one / as ~ as one's legs could carry (one) 拚命跑 / Fast bind, ~ find. [谚]藏得牢, 丢不了。/ ~ play ~ and loose 见 play / stand ~ 不后退, 屹立不动; 不让步 ||~ buck [美俚] 轻易得来的钱; 不择手段得来的钱 / ~ counter [美] 伪报选举票数者; 诡计多端的人; 骗子 / '~-fingered a. [美俚] ①不合法的, 非法的 ②聪明的, 巧妙的 ③狡猾的 / '~-'food a. (餐馆等) 专门提供快餐服务的 / '~-'talk vt. 花言巧语地企图说服 (或影响)

fast[2] [fɑːst] I vi. 禁食; 斋戒; 绝食 ② 节制饮食; 忌食某些食物 II n. 禁食; 斋戒; 绝食; 节食; 禁食期; 绝食期; 节食期: a ~ of three days 三天的禁食期 ||break one's ~ ①开斋, 开戒 ②吃早饭 ||~ day 斋戒日

fasten ['fɑːsn] ❶ vt. ①扎牢; 扣住; 闩住; 钉牢: a parcel 扎包 / ~ the door (the bolt) 把门(插销)销上 / ~ an ox to the tree 把牛拴在树上 / ~ the sheets of paper together 把纸张钉在一起 ② 把(目光、注意力、思想等)集中于 (on, upon): ~ one's eyes on sb. 盯住某人 / ~ one's attention upon a problem 把注意力集中在某一问题上 ③ 把(绰号、罪名等)强加于 (on, upon): ~ a crime on sb. 加罪于某人 ④[~ oneself] 纠缠 (on, upon): ~ oneself on sb. 缠住某人不放 ❷ vi. ①扣紧; 闩住: The door will not ~. 门闩不上。②抓住; 钉住不放地进行攻击 (on, upon): ~ upon a pretext 抓住某种借口 / ~ upon an idea 坚持一种想法

fastener ['fɑːsnə] n. ①扣件; 钮扣; 揿钮; 钩扣; (钉纸张的) 扣钉: a zip (或 slide) ~ 拉链 ②结扎者; 结扎工

fastening ['fɑːsniŋ] n. ①扣紧, 扎牢 ②扣件, 扣拴物(如锁、闩、钩、扣、钉等)

fastidious [fæs'tidiəs] a. ① 爱挑剔的, 难讨好的; 过分讲究的: be ~ about one's dress 过分讲究衣着 ②(微生物等)需要复杂营养的 ||~ly ad. / ~ness n.

fasting ['fɑːstiŋ] I n. 禁食 II a. 禁食的: the ~ blood-sugar level 空腹时的血糖水平 / a ~ cure 禁食疗法

fastness ['fɑːstnis] n. ①牢固, 固定(性) ②快速, 迅速 ③不褪色(性); [纺] 坚牢度: ~ to acids (washing) 耐酸(耐洗)坚牢度 ④放荡 ⑤要塞; 僻静的处所 ⑥抗(毒)性

fat [fæt] I (fatter, fattest) a. ①肥胖的; 肥大的; 丰满的; 饱满的: a ~ little baby 肥胖的婴孩 / ~ fingers 粗大的手指 / The pods of the beans are getting ~. 豆荚饱满起来了。②(肉)肥的; 多油脂的, 多脂肪的 ③(牛、羊等)养肥了供食用(或销售、展览)的 ④肥沃的; 富的; (职务等)收益多的;(薪给等)优厚的: ~ soil 肥沃的土壤 ⑤厚的; (费用、银行存款等)大的: a ~ letter 厚厚的一封信 / a ~ price 很大的代价 ⑥(嗓音)圆润的; (香味)浓郁的 ⑦丰富的; 塞得满满的: This book is ~ with firsthand information. 这本书第一手材料很丰富。⑧[印](铅字)比标准笔划粗的 ⑨迟钝的, 呆笨的 ⑩(某物质)含量高的; (煤)含高挥发物的; (木材)含树脂多的: ~ coal 肥煤, 烟煤 / ~ wood 多树脂木材 / ~ lime 脂石灰, 浓石灰 II n. ①肥肉, 脂肪; 油脂: put on ~ 发胖 ②最优美的文艺作品; 最好的部分 ③(演员所任角色中)能够发挥演技的部分 ④肥胖: a person somewhat inclined to ~ 一个略微显得肥胖的人 ⑤[常用复]已经养肥可供销售的食用动物 ⑥多余额; 积余; 储备; [俚] 钱: skim away personnel 裁减冗员 / fry the ~ out of sb. 向某人勒索金钱, 向某人诈取油水 III (fatted;

fatting ❶ *vt.* ①养肥 (*up, out*) ②用油脂处理 (皮革) ③在…中加入脂肪 ❷ *vi.* 长肥 ‖a ~ **chance** (作反语用;字面上说"多的"而实际上指) 微小的机会 / *a ~ lot* (作反语用;字面上说"多的"而实际上指) 很少: *A ~ lot* of good it did him. 这对他一点好处也没有。 / *chew the ~* [俚]聚谈,闲聊 / *cut it ~* 做得过分;炫耀 / *cut up ~* [谑]留下大笔遗产 / *live on one's own ~* (经济或知识方面) 吃老本 / *live on the ~ of the land* 生活奢侈 / *The ~ is in the fire.* 事情搞糟了。(或: 闯祸了。) ‖**~less** *a.* 无脂肪的 / **~ly** *ad.* ①富饶地,丰富地 ②象胖子般地 / **~ness** *n.* ‖**~ cat** ①[美俚]政治运动的出资人 (尤指本人别为竞选人) ②[美俚]富有和有权势的人,大亨 ③自满而懒惰的人 / **~-guts** [复] *n.* 肥胖的人 / **'~head** *n.* [口]笨蛋,呆子 / **'~-'headed** *a.* [口]愚笨的 / **'~-'witted** *a.* 愚笨的,傻的

fatal ['feitl] *a.* ①命运的;决定命运的 ②命中注定的;致命的 ③致命的;毁灭性的;不幸的: a ~ blow 致命的打击 / a ~ wound 致命伤 / be ~ to 对…是致命的 ‖*the ~ sisters*【希神】【罗神】命运三女神 ‖**~ly** *ad.* / **~ness** *n.*

fatalism ['feitəlizəm] *n.* 宿命论 ‖**fatalist** *n.* 宿命论者

fatalistic [,feitə'listik] *a.* 宿命的;宿命论的 ‖**ally** *ad.*

fatality [fə'tæliti] *n.* ①命运决定的事物 ②天数,命运;厄运;宿命论 ③灾祸,灾难 ④死亡(事故): The accident caused several *fatalities*. 事故使数人死亡。 ⑤致命性: the degree of ~ of certain diseases 某些疾病的致命程度

fate [feit] Ⅰ *n.* ①命运,天数: decide (或 fix, seal) sb.'s ~ 决定某人的命运 ②毁灭;灾难;死亡: go to one's ~ 赴死 ③结局 ④[the Fates]【希神】【罗神】命运三女神 Ⅱ *vt.* [常用被动语态]命定,注定 ‖*as sure as ~* 见 *sure* / *meet one's ~* 死,送命 / *tempt ~* 蔑视命运;冒险 ‖**~d** *n.* ①命运决定的 ②注定要毁灭的

fateful ['feitful] *a.* ① 命中注定的 ② 与命运有关的,重大的: a ~ decision 重大的决定 ③致命的;带来灾难的 ④ 预言性的 ‖**~ly** *ad.* / **~ness** *n.*

father ['fɑːðə] Ⅰ *n.* ①父亲; 岳父, 公(丈夫的父亲) (=~-in-law); 继父 (=step~); 养父 (= adoptive ~) ②[常用复]祖先; 前辈; 长辈 ③创始人,奠基人; 创造者,发明者; 根源,源泉: the *Father* of English poetry 英国诗歌之父(指 Chaucer 乔叟) / the ~ of radio 无线电的发明者 ④ [常用复](城市、团体等的)长老,长者;(议会的)元老;(古罗马)元老院议员: the City *Fathers* 市议会议员们 / the *Father* of the House of Commons [英]下议院中任期最久的议员 ⑤ [F-]上帝,(三位一体中的)圣父;[常作 F-](阐明教义的)早期基督教著作家; 修道院长; 神父,教士: the Holy *Father* 教皇 (=the Pope) ⑥ [F-](称呼)老爹,大爷;…老人: *Father* Time 时间老

人 / *Father* Christmas【基督教】圣诞老人 Ⅱ *vt.* ①(指父亲而言)生(孩子);当…的父亲;承认自己为…的父亲 ②(象父亲般)对待,保护;治理 ③创立;制订(计划等);创作,发明;培养: ~ a proposal 创议 ④确定(孩子)的生父;确定(作品)的作者;确定(罪行等)的责任 (*on, upon*): ~ an article *on* sb. 认为文章是某人所写 / ~ a crime *upon* sb. 认为是某人作的案 ⑤把…强加于 (*on, upon*) ‖a *ghostly ~* 听忏悔的神父 / *be gathered to one's ~* 见老祖宗去,死 / *Father Thames* 泰晤士河 / *Is your ~ a glazier?* [俗][谑](当一个人的视线被另一人挡住时说)你父亲是玻璃工人吗? (或: 你以为我能透过你看东西吗?) / *Like ~, like son.* [谚]有其父必有其子。 / *The child is ~ of* (或 to) *the man.* 见 *child* / *the Father of lies* 撒谎的始祖 (指 Satan 魔鬼) / *the Father of Lights* 上帝 / *the ~ of one's country* 国父(指一国的缔造者) / *the Father of Waters* 江河之父 (指伊洛瓦底江或密西西比河或尼罗河) / *The wish is ~ to the thought.* 见 *wish* ‖**~hood** *n.* 父亲的身分(或资格);父性;父权 / **~less** *a.* 没有父亲的 ②生父不明的 / **~like** *a.* & *ad.* 父亲般的(地) / **~ship** *n.* ①父亲的身分;父性 ②最老成员的身分(如指英国下议院中任期最久的议员) ‖**~ figure** 父亲般的人物;长者;领袖 / **~-in-law** ['fɑːðərinlɔː] ([复]**~s-ín-law**) *n.* ①岳父;公(丈夫的父亲) ②继父 / **~land** *n.* 祖国 / **~ right** *n.* ①父权 ②父系继承权

fatherly ['fɑːðəli] Ⅰ *a.* ①父亲的: ~ duties 做父亲的职责 ②父亲般的;爱护的;慈祥的 Ⅱ *ad.* 父亲般地 ‖**fatherliness** *n.*

fathom ['fæðəm] Ⅰ ([复]fathom(s)) *n.* ①吋(长度单位,合 6 呎或 1.829 米,主要用于测量水深): The harbour is five ~(s) deep. 港深五吋。 ②[英]剖面为一平方吋的木材量(长度不论) Ⅱ *vt.* ①测…的深度 ②推测;揣摩;了解: ~ sb.'s motives 探测某人的动机 ❷ *vi.* 测深;进行探索 ‖**~able** *a.* ①深度可测明的 ②可以了解的

fatigue [fə'tiːg] Ⅰ *n.* ①疲劳,劳累: physical (mental) ~ 体力(精神)上的疲劳 ②【物】(金属材料等的)疲劳: ~ strength 疲劳强度 ③【医】疲劳(指组织、器官等暂时失去对刺激的反应能力): auditory ~ 听觉疲劳 ④累活;【军】杂役,劳动 ⑤[复](士兵担任杂役时穿的)劳动服装,工作服 Ⅱ ❶ *vt.* ①使疲劳: feel ~d 感到疲劳 ②使(金属材料等)疲劳 ❷ *vi.* ①疲劳: The patient ~s easily. 病人容易疲劳。 ②(金属材料等)疲劳 ③(士兵)担任杂役 ‖**~less** *a.* 不知疲劳的 ‖**~ clothes, ~ dress**【军】劳动服装,工作服 / **~ duty**【军】杂役,劳动(如打扫兵营) / **~ party**【军】杂役队,劳动队

fatten ['fætn] ❶ *vt.* ①养肥 (*up*) ②使肥沃 ③使充实 ❷ *vi.* ①长肥 ②(靠…)发财,致富 (*on*)

fatty ['fæti] Ⅰ *a.* ①脂肪的; 油脂的; 油腻的:

acid 【化】脂肪酸 / ~ compound 【化】脂肪族化合物 ②肥胖的 ③【医】脂肪过多的: ~ liver 脂肪肝 / ~ degeneration 脂肪变性 Ⅱ **n.** 胖子 ‖**fattiness** n.

fatuous ['fætjuəs] **a.** 愚昧的, 昏庸的; 蠢的 ‖**~ly ad.** / **~ness** n.

fault [fɔ:lt] Ⅰ **n.** ①缺点, 毛病: merits and ~s 优缺点 / a ~ in a bolt of cloth 一匹布中的疵点 / ~ detection 【机】探伤 ②错误: acknowledge one's ~s 承认错误 / commit a ~ 犯错误 ③[只用单](承担错误的)责任; 过失: A: Whose ~ is it? B: The ~ is mine. (或 That's my ~.) 甲: 这是谁的责任? 乙: 这是我的过错。/ The ~ lies with me, not with you. 是我的责任, 不是你的责任。④【地】断层 ⑤故障; 误差: a ~ in the electrical circuit 电路故障 / image ~ 【物】象差, 影像失真 / numerical ~s 数值误差 ⑥(网球等的)发球失误 Ⅱ ❶ **vt.** ①找…的缺点; 挑剔: His argument is logical and hard to ~. 他的论点逻辑严密, 无懈可击。②[方]弄错 ❷ **vi.** ①产生断层 ❷ **vi.** ①弄错, 出差错 ②【地】产生断层 ‖**a ~ on the right side** 因祸得福 / **at ~** ①(猎犬追踪猎物等时)失去嗅觉, 停滞不前; [喻]感到困惑, 不知所措 ②出毛病, 有故障: The loudspeaker is at ~. 扩音器出毛病了。/ My memory is at ~. 我想不起来了。③ =in ~ / **Faults are thick where love is thin.** [谚]一朝情义淡, 样样不顺眼。/ **find ~ (with)** 挑剔, 找(…的)岔子 / **in ~** 有过错, 有责任: Who's in ~? 是谁的过错? / **to a ~** 过分, 过度: meticulous to a ~ 过分小心, 谨小慎微 / **whip a ~ out of sb.** 鞭打某人矫正其缺点 / **with all ~s** [商]不保证商品没有瑕疵 ‖**'~,finder** n. 喜欢挑剔的人, 吹毛求疵的人 / **'~,finding** n. 找岔子, 挑剔 **a.** 喜欢挑剔的, 吹毛求疵的

faultless ['fɔ:ltlis] **a.** 无错误的; 无缺点的, 完美无缺的; 无可指责的 ‖**~ly ad.** / **~ness** n.

faulty ['fɔ:lti] **a.** 有错误的, 有缺点的, 不完善的: a ~ pronunciation 不很正确的发音 ‖**faultily ad.** / **faultiness** n.

faun [fɔ:n] **n.** (古罗马传说中半人半羊的)农牧之神

fauna ['fɔ:nə] ([复] **faunae** ['fɔ:ni:] 或 **faunas**) **n.** ①动物群(尤指某一地区或某一时期的动物群, 与 flora 植物群相对) ②动物区系 ③动物志 ‖**~lly ad.** 动物群方面; 动物区系方面; 动物志上

favo(u)r ['feivə] Ⅰ **n.** ①好感, 喜爱; 欢心, 宠爱 ②偏袒, 偏爱: show ~ towards neither party 对双方都不偏袒 ③赞成, 赞同: look with ~ on 赞同地看待 …; 赞成 … ④恩惠, 善意的行为: do sb. a ~ (或 do a ~ for sb.) 给某人以恩惠; 帮某人一个忙 / May I ask a ~ of you? 请您帮个忙行吗? ⑤庇护: under ~ of night 在黑夜的掩护下 ⑥[古]信, 函件 ⑦纪念品, 礼物(尤指小礼物); 徽章 ⑧特许的权利 Ⅱ **vt.** ①喜爱, 喜爱; 支持, 赞成: We ~ your proposal. 我们赞成你的提议。②赐与, 给与 (with): Kindly ~ us with an early reply. (常用于商业书信)请早日复信。③有利于, 有助于: The weather ~ed the harvesting. 天气有利于收割工作。④偏爱, 偏袒: A mother should not ~ any of her children. 母亲不应偏爱她的任何子女。⑤像: The child ~s his mother. 这孩子像妈妈。⑥体恤: walk on without ~ing one's blistered feet 尽管脚上起泡照样继续前进 ‖**by ~ of** (或 **~ed by**) (信封上用语)烦请…面交 / **by your ~** [古]如果您允许我这样说的话 / **curry ~ (with sb.)** 求宠(于某人), 拍(某人)马屁 / **find ~ with sb.** (或 **in sb.'s eyes**) 得宠于某人, 受某人青睐 / **in ~ of** ①赞同…, 支持…: be in ~ of sb.'s suggestion 赞同某人的建议 ②有利于…: The score was 2 to 1 in ~ of the guest team. 比分为二比一, 客队获胜。③(签票据等)以…为受款人: draw a cheque in ~ of sb. 开一张付款给某人的支票 / **in sb.'s ~** ①得某人欢心; 受某人欢迎 ② 对某人有利: The situation both at home and abroad is in our ~. 国内外形势都对我们有利。③(签票据等)以某人为受款人 / **out of ~ (with)** 失宠(于…); 不受(…的)欢迎 / **under ~** [古]如果您允许我这样说的话 ‖**~er** ['feivərə] n. 宠爱者; 支持者, 赞成者

favo(u)rable ['feivərəbl] **a.** ①赞成的; 称赞的: He is ~ to our plan. 他赞成我们的计划。/ a ~ comment 好评 ②有利的, 顺利的: a ~ situation 有利的形势 / a ~ balance of trade 贸易顺差 ③讨人喜欢的; 赢得赞同的: make a ~ impression on sb. 给某人以好的印象 ④起促进作用的: a ~ wind 顺风 ‖**~ness** n. / **favo(u)rably ad.**

favo(u)red ['feivəd] **a.** ①受到优待的; 有天赋的 ②受优惠的; 优惠的: the most-~-nation clause 最惠国条款(给予某国以最低进口关税待遇的贸易条款) / ~ rates of credit 优惠的贷款率 ③[常用以构成复合词]有…容貌的, 有…外貌的: ill-~ 容貌难看的

favo(u)rite ['feivərit] Ⅰ **n.** ①特别喜爱的人(或物) ②受宠的人, 亲信, 心腹 ③最有希望获胜者(尤指马) Ⅱ **a.** 特别喜爱的: a ~ song 最喜爱的歌 ‖**be a ~ with sb.** 是某人的宠儿, 为某人所特别喜欢 ‖**~ son** ①受宠爱的儿子 ② 在故乡被称赞的人 ③[美]党派全国代表大会上为本州代表所拥护为总统候选人的人

favo(u)ritism ['feivəritizm] **n.** 偏爱, 偏袒; 得宠: appoint people by ~ 任人唯亲

fawn[1] [fɔ:n] **vi.** ①(狗等)摇尾乞怜 ②奉承, 讨好 (on, upon) ‖**~er** n. 乞怜者; 奉承者 / **~ing a.** 乞怜的; 奉承的

fawn[2] [fɔ:n] Ⅰ **n.** ①(未满一岁的)幼鹿: be in ~ (母鹿)怀孕 ②小山羊; 小动物 ③鹿毛色, 浅黄褐色 Ⅱ **vt. & vi.** 生(小鹿、小山羊或小动物) Ⅲ **a.** 浅黄褐色的

fear [fiə] **I ❶** *vt.* ①害怕，畏惧 ②为…担心，为…忧虑: I ~ (that) he must have gone. 我怕他已经走了。/ ~ the worst 担心会发生(或已经发生)最坏的情况 ③敬畏(神等) **❷** *vi.* ①害怕; 感到顾虑: Never ~! 不用怕! (或: 别担心!) / not ~ to speak one's mind 敢于说出自己的想法 ②恐怕; 担心，担忧: A: Is the injury very serious? B: I ~ so. 甲:伤势很重吗? 乙:恐怕是的。/ ~ for sb.'s safety 为某人的安全担忧 **II** *n.* ①害怕，恐惧: without ~ of hardship or death 不怕苦，不怕死 ②担心，忧虑; 值得忧虑之处: I have a ~ that we will be late. 我怕我们要迟到了。/ There is no ~ of his losing his way. 他不会迷路的。③(对神等的)敬畏 ‖*be in ~ (of)* (为…而)提心吊胆 / *be overcome with* (或 *by*) ~ 感到十分害怕 / *for ~* ①由于害怕 ②生怕，以免 (*of, that, lest*): walk on tiptoe *for ~ of* waking the patient 踮着脚走以免惊醒病人 / He handled the instrument with care *for ~* (*that*) it should be damaged. 他小心地弄那仪器,生怕把它弄坏。/ *in ~ and trembling* 惶恐战栗, 忐忑不安 / *No ~!* [口]当然不! 不会的! / *strike ~ into* 使…感到害怕 / *without ~ or favo(u)r* 公正地; 公平地

fearful ['fiəful] *a.* ①可怕的, 吓人的 ②害怕的; 担心的; 胆怯的: be ~ of falling 怕摔倒 / be ~ that (或 lest) the patient should get worse 担心病人的情况恶化 / be ~ to do sth. 对于做某事感到胆怯 ③[口]非常的; 极坏的; 极大的: in a ~ mess 非常混乱 / a ~ liar 大骗子 ④敬畏的 ‖~ly *ad.* / ~ness *n.*

fearless ['fiəlis] *a.* 不怕的, 大胆的, 无畏的 ‖~ly *ad.* / ~ness *n.*

feasible ['fi:zəbl] *a.* ①可行的, 行得通的, 可实行的: a ~ scheme 可行的计划 ②[口]似真的, 可能的; 有理的: an explanation that seems ~ enough 理由似乎很充足的解释 ③可用的, 适宜的: land ~ for cultivation 可耕的地 ‖**feasibility** [,fi:zə'biliti] *n.* / **feasibly** *ad.*

feast [fi:st] **I** *n.* ①盛宴, 筵席: a festival ~ 节日宴会 ②节日, 节期(尤指宗教节日): a movable (an immovable) ~ 非固定日期(固定日期)的节日 ③[喻](感官、精神等方面的)享受, 使人极感愉快的东西: a ~ for the eyes 极为好看的东西 / an intellectual ~ 智力的享受 / a ~ of reason 富有教益的谈话 **II ❶** *vt.* ①盛宴款待 ②使(感官等)得到享受: ~ one's eyes on the wonderful performance 尽情欣赏精采表演 **❷** *vi.* ①参加宴会 ②享受, 感到异常愉快 ‖*a death's head* (或 *a skeleton*) *at the ~* 令人扫兴的人(或事物) / *a Dutch ~* 主人先醉的酒宴 / *a ~ for the gods* 极其精美的饮食;使人很愉快的事物 / *a ~ of reason and a flow of soul* 富有教益的谈话;非常美妙的谈话 / *~ away* 在欢宴中度过… / *the Feast of Tabernacles* 见 **tabernacle** /

the ~ of trumpets 犹太人的新年

feat[1] [fi:t] *n.* ①功绩: ~s in arms 武功 ②武艺, 技艺: ~s of horsemanship 骑马的绝技

feat[2] [fi:t] *a.* [古] ①灵巧的 ②漂亮的; 整洁的 ③合适的 ‖~ly *ad.*

feather ['feðə] **I** *n.* ①羽毛; 翎毛: lighter than a ~ 轻于鸿毛的 ②(箭、帽的)羽饰 ③禽类(指猎物): fur and ~ (作为狩猎对象的)兽类与禽类 ④种类;本质: birds of a ~ [喻]同类 ⑤状态; 心情 ⑥服装,服饰 ⑦羽状物; 轻的东西; (狗等腿上的)丛毛 ⑧[机]滑键; (铸件的)周缘翅片(或加强肋等) ⑨(潜水艇上潜望镜引起的)微波, 羽状water波 ⑩(收回划桨时)使桨与水面平行 ⑪(玻璃、宝石等)羽状斑疵 **II ❶** *vt.* ①(箭上翻毛)用羽毛覆盖; 用羽毛装饰 ②射掉(飞禽)的羽毛 ③(用楔形部件)使连接 ④(收回划桨时)使(桨)与水面平行;【空】使(螺桨)顺流变距; 使(旋翼)周期变距 **❷** *vi.* ①长羽毛 ②象羽毛般地飘动(或展开、生长等) ③看来象羽毛 ④使桨与水面平行;【空】(螺桨)顺流变距;(旋翼)周期变距 ‖*~ in one's cap* 可以夸耀的事物; 卓越的成就; 荣誉的标志 / *Birds of a ~ flock together* 见 **bird** / *crop sb.'s ~s* 杀某人的威风; 使某人丢脸 / *cut a ~* (船)破浪前进 / *~ one's nest* 见 **nest** / *Fine ~s make fine birds.* [谚]好的衣装只能打扮出个好外表。/ *in fine* (或 *high, good, full*) *~* 身强力壮; 精神饱满; 情绪很好 / *knock sb. down with a ~* 使某人十分惊奇 / *make the ~s fly* 引起争吵(或争斗) / *not a ~ to fly with* 一贫如洗;破产;垮台 / *rise at a ~* [美口]一碰就跳起来, 一碰就冒火 / *ruffle one's ~s* 发怒 / *ruffle sb.'s ~s* 激怒某人 / *show the white ~* 显示惧弱,胆怯 / *singe one's ~s* ①损害自己的名誉 ②(由于某举动而)使自己遭受损失 / *wag the ~* 炫耀自己的身分 ‖~ed *a.* ①有羽毛的 ②用羽毛(或羽状物)覆盖的 ③有羽翼的;羽状的;飞速的: ~ed tin 羽状锡(锡的羽状结晶) ④边沿削薄的: a ~ed board 边沿削薄的木板 / ~less *a.* 无羽毛的 / ~ bed ①羽毛褥垫;安有羽毛褥垫的床 ②舒适的处境;闲职 ③因轮藻丛生而形成的羽毛状池底(或湖底) / '~bed *vi.* ①要求资方雇用超过工作需要的人员 ②担任闲职 *vt.* ①给(某一工种)配备多余的人手; 使成为闲职 ②以政府津贴资助 *a.* 要求(或同意)雇用超过工作需要的人员的; (工作等)因雇用超过工作需要的人员而闲空的: a ~bed soldier 职务闲散的士兵; 放荡的人, 嫖客 / '~'bedding *n.* 超过工作需要的人员雇用(指工会为防止失业等向资方提出的招雇多余人手的要求) / '~brain, '~head, '~pate *n.* 愚蠢的人;轻浮的人 / '~brained, '~headed, '~pated *a.* 愚蠢的; 轻浮的 / ~ duster 羽毛掸子 / ~edge ['feðəredʒ] *n.* (木板、剃刀等的)薄边: ~edge section 【建】薄边断面 *vt.* 削薄(木板等)的边 / '~'footed *a.* 脚步很轻的 / ~ star 【动】毛头星 / '~stitch *n.* 羽状绣花针

迹 / '～**weight** n. ①体重较轻的人；轻微的东西 ②不重要的人(或物) ③(拳击、摔跤等的)次轻级运动员 a. ①轻的 ②次轻级的 ③轻微的；琐细的

feature ['fi:tʃə] I n. ①面貌的一部分(眼、口、鼻等) ②[复]面貌，相貌: a man with Oriental ～s 东方脸型的男子 ③特征，特色 ④特写，特辑；正片；号召物: a two-～ programme 连映两部正片的一场电影 / a ～ film 故事片，艺术片 II ❶ vt. ① 是…的特色: Round-the-clock service ～s this store. 日夜服务是这家商店的特色。② 以…为特色: a lathe featuring a new electronic control device 以一种新型电子控制器为特色的车床 ③特写；特载；以…作为号召物；(电影)由…主演；放映: The solemn statement was ～d in full in the newspapers. 各报全文刊登了这一庄严声明。④描绘…的特征 ⑤[俚]想象 ⑥[方]与…容貌相似 ❷ vi. 起重要作用；作重要角色 ‖make a ～ of 以…为特色；以…为号召物: a magazine that makes a ～ of children's stories 一种以儿童故事为特色的杂志 ‖**～less** a. 无特色的，平凡的 ‖**～-length** a. (电影)达到正片应有长度的

February ['februəri] n. 二月(略作 Feb.) ‖**～ fill-dike** 多雨雪的二月，沟渠满溢的二月

fed[1] [fed] feed 的过去式和过去分词

fed[2] [fed] n. [常作 F-] [美俚] (美)联邦调查局调查员；联邦政府工作人员 ‖**the Fed** [美]联邦储备制

federal ['fedərəl] I a. ①联盟的；联合的 ②联邦的；联邦制的 ③[F-] 美国联邦政府的 ④[F-] 【美史】(南北战争时期)北部联邦同盟的；亲联邦政府(或军队)的 ‖the Federal Bureau of Investigation 联邦调查局(美国)(略作 FBI) / a ～ district 联邦政府所在地区 / the Federal Reserve Bank 联邦储备银行(美国)(略作 FRB) / the Federal Reserve Board 联邦储备委员会，联邦储备银行董事会(美国)(略作 FRB, 1935 年改名为 Board of Governors of the Federal Reserve System)[美国] / the Federal Trade Commission 联邦贸易委员会(美国) II n. [F-] [美史](南北战争时期)北部联邦同盟盟员；联邦军队战士；联邦政府支持者 ②联邦政府工作人员 ‖**make a Federal case out of sth.** [美俚]过分强调某事的重要性，过分夸大某事 ‖**～ism** n. ①联邦的 ②[F-]【美史】联邦主义 ‖**～ist** n. ①联邦制拥护者 ②[F-]联邦党成员 ❶[F-]【美史】北部联邦同盟盟员 ‖**～ly** ad. 在全联邦范围内；在联邦政府一级

federate I ['fedərit] a. 同盟的；联合的 II ['fedəreit] vt. & vi. (使)结成同盟(或联邦)

federation [,fedə'reiʃən] n. 同盟，联盟；联合会；联邦，联邦政府 ‖**～ist** n. 联合主义者

fee [fi:] I n. ①费(如会费、学费、入场费、手续费等)；酬金: a membership ～ 会费 / a tuition

学费 / vehicle and shipping licence ～s 车船使用牌照税 / a lawyer's ～ 律师聘金 ②赏金，赏钱 ③[史]采邑，封地；封地所有权 ④[律]世袭土地；祖传土地 ‖**～ simple**【律】不限制具有一定身分的人才能继承的土地 / **～ tail**【律】具有一定身分的人才能继承的土地 II vt. ①付费(或小帐)给 ②[英]雇用；聘请 ‖**hold in ～ (simple)**【律】享有不限制具有一定身分的人才能继承的土地 / **not to set (或 to value) sth. at a pin's** 把某事物看得毫无价值；毫不重视某事物 ‖**～-TV** ['fi:,ti:'vi:] n. 收费电视，投币电视

feeble ['fi:bl] a. ①虚弱的，无力的: a ～ old man 虚弱的老人 ②微弱的；薄弱的: a ～ light 微弱的光线 / a ～ barrier 易摧毁的障碍物 ‖**～ness** n. / **feeblish** a. 有点弱的 / **feebly** ad. ‖**～-'minded** a. 低能的；意志薄弱的，无决断的

feed [fi:d] [fed [fed]] I ❶ vt. ① 喂(养)；饲(养): ～ a baby at the breast 喂奶，哺乳 / ～ the chickens 喂养小鸡 / What do you ～ the poultry on? 你们用什么饲养家禽？/ The patient cannot ～ himself yet. 病人还不能自己进食。② 供应(饲料)给，用(某物)喂 (to): ～ oats to the horses 用燕麦喂马 ③ 向…供给 (with)；加进(原料等) (to): ～ a spinning machine with rove 给纺纱机加粗纱 / plants with fertilizer 给植物施肥 / ～ coal to a furnace 给炉子加煤 ④[无]馈给(信号)；通过线路向电台传送；以供广播 ⑤放牧(牲畜)；使用(土地)作牧场 ⑥满足(欲望等)；加深(恶感等)，助长(某种情绪) ⑦为(演员)提台词；传球给 ❷ vi. ①(牛、马等)吃东西: the cattle ～ing in the meadows 在草地上吃草的牛 ②用餐 ③以…为食物 (on, upon): Sheep ～ chiefly on grass. 羊主要以草为食物。/ The gas turbine ～s on the fuel it pumps. 这台燃气轮机以它所抽入的燃料为能源。④ 流入，进入 【无】馈入: The river ～s into a lake. 这条河注入一个湖泊。/ Oil ～s into an engine. 油流入发动机。 II n. ①(动物或婴儿的)一餐，一顿；喂食；进食: Let the horse have a ～. 让马吃一顿食。/ two biscuits at one ～ 一次喂两块饼干 / out at ～ (牛、马等)在外吃草 ②饲料；牧草；一次喂给的饲料 ③【机】进给；进料；给水；进料器；进刀；【电】馈电，供电 ④[口]一餐；丰盛的一餐 ‖automatic ～【机】自动进给 / ～ belt【机】进料皮带 / ～ cable【电】馈电电缆，电源电缆 / ～ pipe【机】进料管；给水管 / hydraulic ～【机】水力进给；水力进刀，液压输送 / jump ～【机】(仿形切削的)快速进程；中间越程 / shunt ～【电】并联馈电 / ～ work【机】工件进程 ‖**be fed up** 吃得过饱 ❷(对…)极其厌恶 / **Feed a cold and starve a fever.** [谚]伤风时宜宽，发热时宜饿。/ ～ **high** (或 **well**) (使)吃得又多又好 / ～ **one's face** [美俚]吃饭 / ～ **up** 供给…营养(或额外)食物 / ～ **off one's** (牛、马等)厌食；[口](人)有病，不想吃东西 / **on the** ～ (鱼)在进食；在寻食 / **Well fed, well bred.** [谚]吃得饱，懂礼貌。‖**～back** n. ①【无】回授，

反馈: positive (negative) ~*back* 正(负)反馈 ②回复;反应 / ~ **bag** (吊在马嘴下的)饲料袋; [俚]一餐: put on the ~ *bag* [俚]开始吃 / '~-**in** 【电】馈入 *a.* 【机】进给的;进料的 / ~ **pump** 给水泵,进水泵;进料泵 / '~**stock** *n.* (送入机器或加工厂的)原料 / '~**stuff** *n.* 饲料;饲料中的营养成分 / '~-**tank** *n.* 给水箱 / '~,**water** *n.* (经过预热或净化的锅炉的)给水

feeder ['fi:də] *n.* ①饲养员; 给食的人; 加料工人 ②奶瓶; [英]围涎 ③吃(得多或快)的人(或动物等): That man is a prodigious ~. 那人是个大肚汉. / This plant is a gross ~. 这植物需要大量肥料. ④进料器; 给水器; 加油器; 加煤器; (机床的)进刀装置 ⑦【电】馈电电线 ⑥(河流的)支流 ⑦【矿】支脉 ⑦铁路支线 (= ~ line); 航空支线 (= ~ airline) ⑧[适于]养肥的牲畜 ⑨(主要剧情的)陪衬情节; 配角 ⑩煽动者; 鼓励者

feel [fi:l] **I** (felt [felt]) ❶ *vt.* ①摸,触;试探: ~ sb.'s pulse 为某人诊脉; 试探某人的意图 / ~ one's way forward 摸索着前进; 谨慎行事 ②感觉, 觉得, 感知, 身受: ~ hunger 觉得饿 / ~ great joy at the good news 听到好消息感到非常高兴 / ~ a little stone in one's shoe 觉得鞋里有块小石子 ③以为, 认为: He *felt* it his duty to save state property. 他认为抢救国家财产是自己的责任. / He has done his best. 在我看来他已尽了最大努力. ④【军】侦察(敌情、地形等) ❷ *vi.* ①有知觉; (人)有某种感觉: How are you ~*ing* today? 你今天(身体)觉得怎么样? / ~ happy (cold) 感到高兴(冷) / We ~ full of energy and confidence. 我们浑身是劲,信心百倍. / I ~ as if it were going to rain. 我觉得好象要下雨了. / I ~ the same. 我有同感. ②(东西)摸上去有某种感觉;给人某种感觉: Cotton ~s soft. 棉花摸上去很柔软. / It ~s cold outside. 外面很冷. ③摸索; 摸索着寻找 (*for*): ~ *for* a few screws in a tool box 在工具箱里摸着找几个螺丝钉 / ~ *about* in the dark 在暗中摸索着走 ④同情 (*for*): We ~ keenly *for* you. 我们非常同情你. **II** *n.* [只用单] ①触,摸; 触觉; 感觉: Let me have a ~. 让我摸一下. / I can tell he is quite ill by the ~ of his forehead. 一摸他的前额,我就知道他病得不轻. / a surface rough to the ~ 摸上去很粗糙的表面 ②(事物给人的)感受: a festive ~ 节日气氛 / get the ~ of the dockers' life 体验码头工人的生活 ‖~ **bad** 见 **bad** / ~ **like** ①摸上去如同 ②[口]想要: Do you ~ *like* having a walk with me (或 ~ *like* a walk with me)? 跟我一道去散散步怎么样? / ~ (*like* 或 *quite*) *oneself* ①觉得身体情况正常 ②沉着,镇定 / ~ **out** 试探出,摸清 / ~ sb. **out** 试探出某人的态度(或意向等) / ~ **small** 见 **small** / ~ **up** (或 *equal*) **to** [口]觉得能担当: He doesn't ~ *up to* a long walk. 他觉得不能走远路. ‖~**er** *n.* ①触角; 触须 ②试探手段; 试探者; 试探器, 探针: put forth (或 throw out) a ~*er* (用话或动作)试探

他人的反应 ③【军】侦察兵 ④【机】测隙规, 厚薄规 ⑤[无]灵敏元件 ⑥[美俚]手指

feeling ['fi:liŋ] **I** *n.* ①触觉; 知觉; 感觉: have no ~ in one's injured finger 受伤的手指没有感觉 / a ~ of cold (comfort) 冷(舒服)的感觉 ②感情: improve the ~ between the two peoples 增进两国人民之间的感情 / good (ill) ~ 好(恶)感 ③[复](与理智相对而言的)感情, 情绪: hurt sb.'s ~s 伤某人的感情 ④同情; 体谅: show much (no) ~ for... 对…深表(毫无)同情 / a person of ~ 善于体谅的人 ⑤恶感, 反感, 气愤 ⑥看法; 感想; 预感: It is my ~ that things are not so simple. 我感觉事情并不这么简单. / The ~ of the meeting was for his proposal. 与会的多数人同意他的提议. ⑦气氛; (艺术品的)情调 ⑧(对艺术等的)感受, 敏感, 鉴赏力: have a ~ for music 对音乐有感受力 / a ~ for words 富有语感 **II** *a.* ①富于感情的; 富于同情心的 ②衷心的 ‖*one's better* ~*s* 良心,天良 / *relieve ons's* ~*s* 发泄感情; 泄愤 / ~**ly** *ad.* 富于感情地 / ~**ness** *n.*

feet [fi:t] foot 的复数

feign [fein] ❶ *vt.* ①假装, 佯作: ~ agreement 假装同意 / ~ (oneself) to be asleep (或 ~ oneself asleep 或 ~ that one is asleep) 佯作睡着 ②捏造, 杜撰; 伪造: ~ an excuse 捏造借口 ③[古]想象 ❷ *vi.* 做假

felicitate [fi'lisiteit] *vt.* ①祝贺 ②把(某人)看有福, 庆幸: ~ oneself *on* 因…而自我庆幸 ‖**felicitation** [fi,lisi'teiʃən] *n.* [常用复]祝贺; 祝词

felicitous [fi'lisitəs] *a.* ①(措词等)恰当的, 巧妙的 ②善于措词的 ③[罕]幸福的, 快乐的 ‖~**ness** *n.*

felicity [fi'lisiti] *n.* ①幸福, 福气; 幸运 ②(措词等的)恰当, 巧妙 ③恰当(或巧妙)的语句: express oneself with ~ 措词恰当(或巧妙) ③恰当(或巧妙)的语句

feline ['fi:lain] **I** *a.* ①猫的; 猫科的 ②象猫一样的; 狡猾的, 奸诈的; 偷偷摸摸的: ~ amenities 笑里藏刀 **II** *n.* 猫; 猫科动物

fell[1] [fel] fall 的过去式

fell[2] [fel] **I** *vt.* ①击倒,打倒; (疾病等)致…于死地 ②砍倒; 砍伐: ~ a tree 砍倒一棵树 ③(缝纫时)以平式接缝缝… **II** *n.* ①一季所伐的木材 ②(衣服等的)平缝

fell[3] [fel] *n.* ①兽皮, 生皮 ②人的皮肤 ③毛丛; 羊毛: a ~ of hair 蓬松的头发 ‖~,**monger** *n.* [英]生皮煺毛商(或工匠)

fell[4] [fel] *n.* [英] ① [F-] (与专有名词连用, 作地名)…山, …岗 ②(英国北部的)沼泽地, 荒野

fell[5] [fel] *a.* ①凶猛的, 残暴的; 可怕的; 致命的: a ~ disease 致命的病 ②[苏格兰]尖锐的; 辛辣的 ‖~**ness** *n.*

fellow ['felou] **I** *n.* ①[常用复]伙伴; 同事; 同辈; 同(时)代人: ~s at school 同学 / ~s in arms 战友 ②[常用复]同伙, 同谋者: ~s in crime 同案犯 ③对等者; 对手: pass all one's ~s 超过所有的对手 ④ ['felou, 'fele] [口]人; 家伙, 小伙

子; 某个人; 我: a young ~ 小伙子 / a queer (lazy) ~ 怪人(懒汉) / Poor ~! 可怜的人! / the ~ [蔑]这个家伙 / What a ~! (表示赞叹) 好家伙! (表示谴责)这个家伙! / my dear (或 good) ~ (用于称呼)亲爱的朋友,老朋友 / old ~ (用于称呼)老朋友,老兄 / You look at a ~ in a queer way. 你用异乎寻常的样子看着人(或看着我)。 ⑤[美口]男朋友; 求婚者 ⑥配对物, 一对中之一: Here's one of my shoes, where's its ~? 我的一只鞋在这儿,还有一只在哪儿呢? ⑦(大学中的)研究员 ⑧(学术团体的)会员: *Fellow of the Royal Society* (英国)皇家学会会员 (略作 F. R. S.) **II** *a.* 同伴的; 同事的; 同类的: a ~ student 同学 / a ~ worker 一起工作的人 / a ~ countryman 同国人, 同胞 / a ~ passenger 同车(或船等)的旅伴 / ~ creatures 同类(动物); 人类 ‖~ **commoner** ①(英国牛津大学等中)可与研究员同桌吃饭的大学生 ②同桌吃饭的人 / ~ **feeling** 同情; 相互了解 / '~'**man** *n.* (同属人类的)人; 同胞 / ~ **travel(l)er** ①旅伴 ②(政治上的)同路人, 同情者 / '~-'**travel(l)ing** *a.* (政治上)同路的

fellowship ['felouʃip] *n.* ①伙伴关系; 交情; 友谊: promote good ~ with 增进与…的友谊 ②(经历、活动、利害关系等方面的)共同参与, 合伙关系: ~ in crime 共同犯罪 ③(在共同的宗旨下组织的)团体, 会; 联谊会; 【基督教】团契 ④(常指学术团体的)会员资格: be admitted to ~ 获准入会 ⑤(大学中的)研究员职位; 研究员薪金; 研究员基金 ⑥(英国某些大学中的)评议员职位 ‖*offer* (或 *give*) *sb. the right hand of* ~ 见 **hand**

felon[1] ['felən] **I** *n.* 重罪人, 重罪犯 **II** *a.* [古]凶恶的; 邪恶的; 残忍的

felon[2] ['felən] *n.* 【医】瘰疽; 甲沟炎

felt[1] [felt] feel 的过去式和过去分词

felt[2] [felt] **I** *n.* ①毡; 毡制品 ②(造纸用)毛布 ③油毛毡 **II** *a.* 毡制的: a ~ cap (rug) 毡帽(地毯) **III** ❶ *vt.* ①把…制成毡 ②使粘结 ③用毡覆盖… ❷ *vi.* 粘结起来 (*up*) ‖~**ed** *a.* 毡制的; 制成毡的 ②用毡覆盖的 ③粘结起来的 / ~**ing** *n.* ①制毡(过程) ②制毡材料 ③毡 / ~**y** *a.* ①毡状的 ② =~ed

female ['fi:meil] **I** *a.* ①女(性)的; 妇女的: the ~ population (全体)女居民; 女子人口 / a ~ pilot 女飞行员 / a song composed for ~ voices 为女声谱的歌 / the ~ sex 女性 ②雌的, 【植】雌性的; 雌蕊: a ~ dog 雌狗 / a ~ flower 雌花 ③【机】阴的, 内的: ~ screw 阴螺纹, 内螺丝 ④柔弱的; (声、色)柔和的; (音调)高的: a ~ sapphire 淡色蓝宝石 **II** *n.* ①女子: Over 30 percent of the teachers are ~. 教师中女子三分之一以上是女的。 ②牝兽; 雌鸟 ③【植】雌性植物, 雌株 / ~ **fern** 【植】①蹄盖蕨 ②欧洲蕨 / ~ **impersonator** 男扮女的演员 / ~ **suffrage** 妇女选举权(或参政权)

feminine ['feminin] **I** *a.* ①女性的; 妇女的: the ~ members of society 社会中的全体女性 ②娇柔的; 女子气的 ③【语】阴性的: a ~ noun 阴性名词 / the ~ gender 阴性 ‖~ *caesura* 不是紧接着重音的诗行中断 / ~ *ending* 最后一个重音在倒数第二音节的诗行结尾 / ~ *rhyme* 第二音节无重音的双音节韵(如 motion, ocean) **II** *n.* [语]阴性; 阴性词 ‖~**ly** *ad.* / ~**ness** *n.*

feminism ['feminizəm] *n.* ①男女平等主义 ②争取女权运动 ‖**feminist** *n.* 男女平等主义者

fen [fen] **I** *n.* ①沼泽 ② [the Fens] 英国 Cambridgeshire 及 Lincolnshire 等地的沼泽地带 **II** *vt.* & *vi.* [方] =fend ‖~ **fire** 沼地磷火 / '~**land** *n.* 沼泽地 / ~ **man** ['fenmən] *n.* 沼泽居民(尤指英国沼泽地带的居民) / ~ **pole** 跳沟竿(尤指英国沼泽地带居民所用)

fence [fens] **I** *n.* ①栅栏; 围栏; 篱笆: erect a bamboo ~ 筑竹篱 / a Virginia (或 snake, worm) ~ 弯弯曲曲的栅栏 / an electronic ~ 【军】电子对空搜索仪 ②击剑(术): a master of ~ 精于剑术的人 ③遮拦; 剑令 ④买卖赃物的人(或场所) ⑤[美][常用复](公职人员)争取政治支持的途径; 政治利益: build one's ~s for election as senator 设法争取对自己竞选参议员的支持 ⑥[古]防护 **II** ❶ *vt.* ①把…用栅(或篱)围起来 (*about, in, round, up*): ~ (*up*) the yard with bamboo sticks 用竹栅把场地围起来 / The farm is ~d in (或 round) with elms. 农场周围榆树成篱。 ②(筑栅)防护; 保卫 (*from, against*): ~ the seedbeds *from* the north wind 为苗床筑篱挡住北风 ③(用篱)拦开, 隔开 (*off, out*): ~ off a piece of ground 用栅篱把一块地隔开 / The cattle are well ~d out. 牛群被妥善地隔在篱之外。 ❷ *vi.* ①击剑 ②搪塞, 回避正面答复问题 ③买卖赃物 ④(马等)跳越栅栏 ‖*come down on one side or the other of the* ~ 见 **side** / *come down on the right side of the* ~ 见 **side** / *with* 搪塞, 回避: ~ *with* a question (或 a questioner) 避免作正面答复 / *make* (或 *walk*) *a Virginia* ~ 摇摇晃晃地走 / *mend* (或 *look after*) *one's* ~s 修补篱笆(指从政治利益出发, 与有关方面调整关系, 争取支持) / *on the* ~ 抱骑墙态度; 抱观斗态度 / *ride (the)* ~ [美]①检修牧场的栅篱 ②采取骑墙态度 / *rush one's* ~s [口]鲁莽; 过于匆忙 / *sit on the* ~ (在辩论、争论中)采取骑墙态度, 保持中立 ‖~**less** *a.* ①无围栏的 ②[诗]无设防的 / ~**r** *n.* ①击剑者 ②修筑栅篱的人 ③善于跳栅篱的马匹 ‖'~-**hanger** *n.* 未打定主意的人, 犹豫不定者 / ~ **month,** ~ **season,** ~ **time** 禁猎期; 禁止捕鱼期 / ~ **rider** [美]牧场中检修栅篱的工人; 骑墙派 / '~-**sitter** *n.* 骑墙派

fencing ['fensiŋ] *n.* ①栅栏; 围栏; 篱笆 ②筑栅栏的材料 ③击剑(术) ④辩论的回避 ⑤买卖赃物 ‖~ **cully** [英]窝藏赃物者 / ~ **ken** [英]窝藏赃物的场所

fend [fend] ❶ *vt.* ①[古][诗]保护 ②挡开: ~ off

a blow 挡开一击 / He raised his arm to ~
branches *from* his eyes. 他举起手臂挡开树枝,使
不致触到眼睛。③[英方]供养 ❷ *vi.* ①[英方]努
力;力争 ②供养;照料: ~ for oneself 自己谋生;
照料自己 / He had two children to ~ for. 他要
扶养两个孩子

fender ['fendə] *n.* ①防御物,防护板,防撞物 ②火
炉围栏 ③(车辆的)挡泥板,(船只的)碰垫,护
舷材 ⑥ (机车、电车的) 缓冲装置, 救护装置
‖**~less** *a.* 无防撞物的;无挡板的

ferment I ['fə:ment] *n.* ①酶,酵素 ②发酵 ③激动;
骚动: be in a ~ 在骚动中 II [fə(:)'ment] *vt.* &
vi. ① (使)发酵 ② (使)激动, (使)骚动 ‖**~able**
[fə(:)'mentəbl] *a.* 可发酵的,发酵性的 ‖**~ation**
[,fə:men'teiʃən] *n.* amino acid ~*ation* 氨基酸发
酵 / a ~*ation* tun (或 tank) 发酵槽 / **~ative**
[fə'mentətiv] *a.* 发酵的

fern [fə:n] *n.* 【植】蕨,蕨类植物: royal ~ 王紫萁
(一种蕨类植物) ‖**~y** *a.* 蕨的; 象蕨的; 多蕨的

fern

ferocious [fə'rouʃəs] *a.* ①凶恶的,凶猛的,残忍的:
a ~ tiger 猛虎 ② [口]十分强烈的, 极度的:
a ~ appetite 特大的胃口 / ~ heat 酷热 ‖**~ly**
ad. / **~ness** *n.*

ferret¹ ['ferit] I *n.* ①白鼬,雪貂 ②搜索者,侦查者
③[军]电磁探测飞机(或车辆、船只) II ❶ *vi.* ①
用雪貂狩猎: go ~*ing* 带雪貂去狩猎 ②搜索:
~ about for sb. (sth.) 到处搜寻某人(某物) ❷ *vt.*
①用雪貂猎取;追赶;把(猎物等)逐出 ②搜出,查
获(秘密、罪犯等): ~ *out* military secrets 刺探
出军事秘密 ③使苦恼 ‖**~y** *a.* 雪貂似的;搜索
者般的;爱窥探的

ferret² ['ferit], **ferreting** ['feritiŋ] *n.* (棉、毛、丝
的)细带

ferroconcrete ['ferou'kɔŋkri:t] *n.* 【建】铁筋混凝
土,钢筋混凝土

ferrous ['ferəs] *a.* ①铁的,含铁的: ~ and non-~
metals 黑色及有色金属 ②【化】亚铁的, 二价铁
的: ~ oxide 氧化亚铁 / ~ nitrate 硝酸亚铁

ferry ['feri] I *n.* ① 摆渡; 经营摆渡的特许权 ②渡
口, 渡船场 ③ 渡船: a railway ~ operating on
the cross-channel route 行驶在横渡海峡航线
上的火车渡轮 ④飞机渡运(指把飞机从接收地飞
送至使用地,或从一基地飞送至另一基地);飞机

渡运航线: a ~ pilot 飞机渡运驾驶员 II ❶ *vt.*
① 渡运; (乘渡船)渡过: ~ goods across a river
把货物摆渡过河 / a river 乘渡船过河 ② 运
送: Official cars *ferried* the delegates to the
reception. 官方汽车把代表们送到招待会。③ 把
(飞机)飞送指定的交付地; 把(飞机)由一个基地
飞送另一个基地 ④(越海)空运 ❷ *vi.* 摆渡; (船)
来往行驶: ~ across to the opposite bank 渡到对
岸 ‖**~boat** *n.* 渡船 / **~ bridge** (上下渡船
用的)浮桥;列车轮渡 / **~man** ['ferimən] *n.* 渡
船工人 / **~ steamer** 渡轮

fertile ['fə:tail; 美 'fə:til] *a.* ①肥沃的,富饶的;利
于丰产的: ~ land (soil) 肥沃的土地(土壤) /
a ~ shower 时雨 / the sun's ~ warmth 带来丰
产的阳光 ② 多产的,丰产的 ③(创造力或想象力)
丰富的: a ~ imagination 丰富的想象力 / ~ *in*
expedients 很会随机应变的 ④【生】可繁殖的, 能
(生)育的: ~ pollen 能育花粉 / ~ egg 受精卵
⑤[原]可变成裂变物质的: ~ material 燃料, 原
料,增殖性物质,变成核燃料的中子吸收剂 ‖**~ly**
ad. / **~ness** *n.*

fertility [fə'tiliti] *n.* ①肥沃, 肥力; 丰产, 多产:
the ~ of soil 土壤的肥力 ②【生】能育性,繁殖力
③(思想等的)丰富: the ~ of imagination 想象
力的丰富 ④人口出生率

fertilize, fertilise ['fə:tilaiz] *vt.* ①使肥沃, 施肥
于; 使多产; 使丰富: ~ the soil 给土壤施肥 ②
【生】使受精: Bees can ~ flowers. 蜜蜂能使花受
精。/ ~*d* egg 受精卵 ‖**fertilizable** *a.* 可施肥
的; 可受精的 / **fertilization** [,fə:tilai'zeiʃən] *n.*
adequate *fertilization* 合理施肥 / artificial
fertilization 人工受精

fertilizer ['fə:tilaizə] *n.* ① 肥料(尤指化学肥料):
(a) chemical ~ (一种)化学肥料 / accumulate ~
积肥 ②【植】传播花粉的媒介(如虫、鸟、风、水等)

fervent ['fə:vənt] *a.* ①炽热的 ②热情的;热烈的,
强烈的 ‖**~ly** *ad.*

fervid ['fə:vid] *a.* ① [诗]炽热的 ②热情的;热烈
的; 激烈的: ~ enthusiasm 高度的热情 / a ~
orator 激昂的演说家 ‖**~ly** *ad.* / **~ness** *n.*

fervo(u)r ['fə:və] *n.* ①炽热 ②热烈;热情

festal ['festl] *a.* ①节日的 ②喜庆的,欢乐的 ‖**~ly**
ad.

fester ['festə] I *n.* 脓疮 II ❶ *vi.* ① 溃烂, 化脓:
The wound did not ~. 伤口并未化脓。②(怨恨
等)郁积,变得愈来愈恼人;恶化 ❷ *vt.* ①使溃烂,
使化脓 ②使愈来愈恼人;使恶化

festival ['festəvəl] I *n.* ①节日,喜庆日: the Spring
Festival 春节 ② (定期举行的)音乐节, 戏剧节
③欢乐,喜庆 II *a.* 节日的,喜庆的: a ~ atmosphere 节日的气氛

festive ['festiv] *a.* ①节日的, 节日似的; 欢宴的:
on ~ occasions 在节日场合; 在节日 / the ~
board 筵席 ②欢乐的,欢庆的,欢快的 ‖**~ly** *ad.*

festivity [fes'tiviti] *n.* ①节日,喜庆日 ②欢庆, 欢
乐 ③[常用复]庆祝,庆祝活动: the *festivities* on
May Day 五一节的庆祝活动

festoon [fes'tu:n] **I** *n.* ① (两端挂住中间下垂的) 花彩; ~ lighting (电)灯彩 ②【建】垂花饰 ③花彩装饰物; 缀边被套(或窗帘) **II** *vt.* ① 给…饰花彩, 结彩于: a hall ~ed with electric lights 结着灯彩的大厅 ②使成为花彩形 ‖~ery *n.* 花彩装饰, 彩饰

fetch[1] [fetʃ] **I** ❶ *vt.* ① (去)拿来, (来)拿去; 请求, 接去: ~ (sb.) a dictionary from the library (替某人)到图书馆去取一本词典来 / ~ a doctor 去请医生 / I will come over and ~ you. 我会来接你。② 推导出, 演绎出: an argument ~ed from afar 牵强附会地得出的论据 ③吸(一口气);发出(叹声、呻吟等): ~ a sigh 叹一口气 ④使得;引出,使发出: ~ the discussion to a close 结束讨论 / His words ~ed a laugh from all present. 他的话使在场的人都笑了。 ⑤ [主方] 做成 ⑥售得, 卖得: a good price 卖得好价 ⑦ 给以(一拳、一击等); 杀死: ~ sb. a blow 打某人一拳 / The second shot ~ed him. 第二发子弹结果了他。⑧吸引, 使发生兴趣; 激恼 ⑨到达;(船顶着风浪)抵达: ~ the harbour 抵港 ⑩ [口]使信服 (round): His argument ~ed her round. 他的论据使她信服了。⑪[主方]使苏醒 (round, to) ❷ *vi.* ①取物; (猎狗)衔回猎获物 ②绕道而行 (about, round) ③【海】航行, 前进;转航 **II** *n.* ①拿, 取; 衔回猎获物 ②计谋, 诡计 ③【气】风浪区 ④【海】两点间的连线;对岸距离;(海湾)的全长 ‖*a far* (或 *long*) ~ 一段远距离 / ~ *and carry* 做杂务, 打杂; 当听差 / ~ *away* ①(因船只颠簸而)滑离原处 / ~ *down* ①打落(飞鸟等) ②减轻(刑罚等) ③使(物价等)下跌 / ~ *in* 引进; 招徕 / ~ *off* ①使摆脱困境 ②杀死 ③把…一饮而尽 / ~ *out* ①拿出 ②引出 ③使显现出 / ~ *up* ①引起, 产生 ②回想起; 拿出 ③弥补(失去的时间等) ④使停止; 站停, 停止;到达 ⑤呕吐 ⑥[主方]扶养, 养大 ⑦[方]恢复过来;苏醒 / ~ *way* =~ *away* ‖~*er n.* 取物(或请人等)的人 ‖*~-up n.* 突然的停止

fetch[2] [fetʃ] *n.* 活人的魂;鬼

fete, fête [feit] **I** *n.* ①节日, 喜庆日 ②游园会 ③盛大的招待会;盛宴 ④祝名日, 生日(在天主教国家中, 某圣徒之名为名的人, 把该圣徒节日视作本人生日庆祝) **II** *vt.* ① 款待, 盛宴招待; (通过举行宴会等)纪念 ②给以…巨大荣誉 ‖*fête champêtre* [fɑ̃:m'peitr] 游园会

fetid ['fetid] *a.* 恶臭的 ‖~*ly ad.* / ~*ness n.*

fetish ['fi:tiʃ] *n.* ①原始人认为赋有神力而加以崇拜的物品, 物神 ②偶像;迷恋(物), 迷信(物) ③【心】物恋对象 ④ 物神崇拜的仪式 ‖~*ism n.* ①拜物教, 物神崇拜 ②盲目崇拜 ③【心】物恋 / ~*ist n.* 拜物教徒;盲目崇拜者;【心】恋物欲者

fetter ['fetə] **I** *n.* ①[常用复]脚镣: be in ~*s* 上着脚镣, 被羁锢着 ②[喻]桎梏;束缚, 羁绊 **II** *vt.* ①为…上脚镣 ②束缚, 羁绊

fettle ['fetl] **I** ❶ *vt.* ①[英方]修补, 整顿 ②殴打 ③【冶】用矿渣等涂(炉床) ❷ *vi.* [英方]准备好 ②纷扰, 小题大做 **II** *n.* ①状况;情绪: in pretty good ~ 情况极佳; 身强力壮 / The good news put him in fine ~. 这个好消息使他兴高采烈。②涂涂炉床材料 / ~*r n.* 修理工;保养工 / *fettling n.*【冶】涂炉床材料

feud[1] [fju:d] **I** *n.* 长期不和; (部落或家族间的)世仇: be at ~ (with) (与…)长期不和 / sink a ~ 捐弃旧怨 **II** *vi.* 长期争斗;世代结仇

feud[2] [fju:d] *n.* (封建制度下的)封地, 采邑

feudal[1] ['fju:dl] *a.* 世仇的

feudal[2] ['fju:dl] *a.* ①封建的;封建制度的: the ~ age 封建时代 / a ~ lord 封建主 / the ~ system 封建制度 ②封地的, 采邑的 ‖~*ly ad.* 以封建方式

feudalism ['fju:dəlizəm] *n.* 封建主义;封建制度 ‖*feudalist n.* ①封建主义者 ②研究中古封建制的学者

fever ['fi:və] *n.* ①发热, 发烧; 热度: be in a ~ 在发烧, 有寒热 / have a high ~ 发高烧 / have not much ~ 热度不很高 ②热病: ~ and ague 疟疾 / scarlet ~ 猩红热 / quartan ~ 间三日疟, 四日疟 / typhoid ~ 伤寒 / yellow ~ 黄热病 ③狂热, 高度兴奋: send sb. into a ~ of excitement 使某人激动若狂 / be in a ~ of impatience 极度急躁 **II** *vt.* & *vi.* ①(使)发烧, (使)患热病 ②(使)狂热, (使)高度兴奋 ‖*run a* ~ 发烧 ‖~*ed a.* 发烧的; 高度兴奋的 ‖~ *blister*【医】唇疱疹 / ~ *heat* ①发热(指发烧时的体温) ②高度兴奋, 狂热 / ~ *pitch* 高度兴奋, 狂热 / ~ *tree*【植】蓝桉 / *~weed n.* 刺芹属植物 / *'~wort n.* 泽兰属植物

feverish ['fi:vəriʃ] *a.* ①发烧的, 有热病症状的: Your hands feel ~. 你的手摸上去有些发烧。②热病的 ③ 容易引起热病的; (地区等)热病蔓延的: ~ swamps 产生热病的湿地 ④ 狂热的;兴奋的;动荡的: ~ excitement 极度的兴奋 / a burst of ~ activity 一阵兴奋的活动 ‖~*ly ad.* / ~*ness n.*

few [fju:] **I** *a.* ①少数的, 不多的: every ~ weeks (minutes) 每隔几星期(几分钟) / try to make ~*er* mistakes 尽量少错 ②[表示否定]很少的, 几乎没有的; [a ~] [表示肯定]有些, 几个: *Few* people know it. 几乎没有什么人知道这一点。/ A ~ people know it. 有几个人知道这一点。/ a man of ~ words 沉默寡言的人 / Such instances are ~. 这样的事例不多。/ in a ~ days 几天以后 **II** *n.* [用复数] ①[表示否定]很少数, 几乎没有; [a ~] [表示肯定]少数, 几个: *Few* of my friends were there. 我的朋友中几乎没有人在那里。/ A ~ of us speak French. 我们中间有几个人能讲法语。/ to name (only) a ~ [用作插入语](仅)举几个(指人名、例子等) / [the ~]少数人: the privileged ~ 少数特权阶级分子 ‖*a good* ~ (或 *quite a* ~, *not a* ~, *some* ~) 相当多, 不少: *quite a* ~ illustrations 相当数量的插图 / *at the ~est* 至少 / (~ *and*) *far between*

见 **between** / *no ~er than* 不少于: The project requires *no ~er than* a thousand workers. 这项工程需要的工人不下一千。‖**~ness** *n.*

fiancé [fi'ɑ:nsei; 美 ,fi:ɑn'sei] *n.* [法] 未婚夫

fiancée [fi'ɑ:nsei; 美 ,fi:ɑn'sei] *n.* [法] 未婚妻

fiasco [fi'æskou] ([复] fiasco(e)s) *n.* 大败, 惨败; 可耻的下场

fiat ['faiæt] *n.* ① 命令, 法令 ② 许可, 批准 ‖**~ money** [美] (根据政府法令作为法币发行的) 不兑现纸币

fib¹ [fib] I *n.* 无伤大雅的谎言, 小谎 II (fibbed; fibbing) *vi.* 撒小谎 ‖**fibber** *n.* 惯撒小谎的人

fib² [fib] [英] I (fibbed; fibbing) *vt.* 击, 打 II *n.* (一) 拳, (一) 击

fibre ['faibə] *n.* ① 纤维, 纤维质: artificial ~ 人造纤维 / synthetic ~ 合成纤维 / bast 【植】韧皮纤维 / nerve ~ 【解】神经纤维 ② 纤维制品; 硬板纸 ③结构, 质地; 力量; 性格: a fabric of coarse (fine) ~ 质地粗(细)的织物 / His close reasoning gave ~ to his argument. 他的严密的逻辑使他的论点有力。/ a man of strong moral ~ 品性坚强的人 ④【植】须根 ‖**~d** *a.* 有纤维的, 纤维质的 / **~less** *a.* 无纤维的 / **~board** *n.* 纤维板 / '**~fill** *n.* (被褥等用的) 纤维填塞物 / **~ glass** 玻璃纤维 / **~ optics** 纤维光学

fibrous ['faibrəs] *a.* ① 含纤维的; 纤维状的; 纤维构成的: ~ cartilage 【解】纤维软骨 / ~ glass 玻璃纤维, 玻璃丝 / ~ root 【植】纤维根; 须根 ② 能分成纤维的 ③坚韧的, 有筋骨的 ‖**~ly** *ad.* / **~ness** *n.*

fickle ['fikl] *a.* (在感情等方面) 易变的, 无常的 ‖**~ness** *n.*

fiction ['fikʃən] *n.* ① 虚构, 杜撰; 捏造 ② 小说: a (work of) ~ 一篇小说 ③ 明知不符事实而习惯上仍采用的假设 ‖**~eer** [,fikʃə'ni(:)ə] *n.* (尤指粗制滥造的) 小说作家 / **~ist** *n.* 小说家(尤指长篇小说作家)

fictitious [fik'tiʃəs] *a.* ① 虚构的, 杜撰的; 非真实的: a ~ character 虚构的人物 / under a ~ name 以假名 ②习惯上假定的; 假设的 ③假装的 ④小说的; 小说中的 ‖**~ly** *ad.* / **~ness** *n.*

fiddle ['fidl] I *n.* ① 小提琴(非正式名称); 正式名称为 violin); 提琴类乐器 ②(船上防止碗、碟等自桌上滑落的) 桌面框 ③ 欺骗行为 II ❶ *vi.* ①拉提琴 ②瞎搞, 乱动 (with): ~ with a clock 把钟乱摆弄一通 ③无意识而不停地拨弄 (with): ~ about *with* a pencil 用手不停地拨弄铅笔 ④游荡; 不经意地干活 ❷ *vt.* ①用提琴奏 (曲调等) ②浪费 (时间等) (away) ③[俚] 欺骗; 伪造 (帐目等) III *int.* 胡说! ‖*a face as long as a ~* 阴郁的脸孔 / *while Rome is burning* 大难临头依然歌舞升平 / *fit as a ~* 非常健康; 精神很好 / *hang up one's ~ when one comes home* 在外谈笑风生在家死气沉沉 / *play first ~* 担任第一小提琴手; 居首要职位, 当第一把手 / *play second ~ (to)* 充当 (…的) 副手 ‖'**~back** *n.*

[常作定语] 小提琴形状的东西 / **~ bow** 提琴弓 / **~deedee** ['fidldi'di:] *int.* 胡说! *n.* 无聊话 / **~faddle** ['fidl,fædl] *vi.* 瞎搞; 闹着玩儿 *n.* 无聊话; 琐碎小事; 游荡者 *int.* 胡说! *a.* 为琐事操心的 / **~head** *n.* 提琴头状船首 / **~ pattern** 提琴形 (指刀、叉等的柄部顶端) / '**~stick** *n.* ①提琴弓 ②无价值的东西 / '**~sticks** *int.* 胡说!

fiddle

fidelity [fi'deliti, fai'deliti] *n.* ①忠诚, 忠实 (*to*): ~ *to* one's cause 对事业的忠诚 ②逼真; 精确: be translated with the greatest ~ 翻译得非常精确 ③(收音、录音设备等的) 逼真度, 保真度, 重现精度: a high ~ amplifier 高保真度放大器

fidget ['fidʒit] I ❶ *vi.* ①坐立不安, 烦躁: The boy kept ~*ing*. 这男孩动个不停。/ She is always ~*ing* about her mother's health. 她老是为她母亲的健康担忧。②(不安地或心不在焉地) 弄, 玩弄 (*with*): ~ *with* one's tie 不安地玩弄自己的领带 ❷ *vt.* 使坐立不安; 使烦躁: What's ~*ing* you? 什么事使你烦躁不安? II *n.* ①[常用复] 坐立不安, 不安定; 烦躁: in a terrible ~ 极度不安 / suffer from the ~s (或 have the ~s) 感到烦躁 / give sb. the ~s 使某人烦躁不安 ②烦躁不安的人

fidgety ['fidʒiti] *a.* ①坐立不安的, 不安定的; 烦躁的: a ~ child 不安定的小孩 ②为琐事操心的; 过分注意细节的 ‖**fidgetiness** *n.*

field [fi:ld] I *n.* ①原野, 旷野 ②(一块)田; 牧场: a paddy ~ 一块水稻田 / work in the ~ 在田间干活 / terraced ~s 梯田 / a ~ of cattle 一牧场的牲口 ③广阔的一大片: ~ of ice 茫茫一大片冰 ④战场; 战地; 作战训练(或演习)场地: a ~ of battle 战场 / hold the ~ 守住阵地 / lose the ~ 败阵 ⑤战斗, 战役: a hard-fought ~ 血战 / a stricken ~ 阵地战(场) ⑥运动场; 场(地); (棒球)外场: a baseball (cricket) ~ 棒(板)球场 / a flying ~ 飞行场(地) / a landing ~ (户外比赛的)全体出场的运动员; 全体上场的球员; 除名选手外的全体出场的运动员; (在棒球、板球运动中)非击球手一方的队: a good ~ 坚强的选手阵容 ⑧矿区, 产地, 井田: a coal ~ 煤田, 煤矿区 / a gas ~ 天然气产地 / a maiden (或 virgin) ~ 未采的井田, 未采的矿区 ⑨实地; 野外: technical personnel working in the ～ 在实地(或野外)进行工作的技术人员 ⑩领域,方面 ⑪【物】场;【数】域;体. gravitational ～ 重力场 / magnetic ～ 磁场 / real number ～ 实数域 / root ～ 根域 ⑫(望远镜等的)视野: the ～ of a microscope 显微镜的视野 / the visual ～ 视界;(雷达等的)可见区 / a wide ～ of vision 广阔的视野 ⑬(旗、画、钱币等的)底子,底色 ⑭影响人们行为的各种因素的综合 **II ❶** *vt.* ①把(谷物等)曝露于场上 ②使(球队或球员等)上场;把…投入战场: ～ a new team 使新队上场参加比赛 ③(棒球、板球运动中)接(或截)(球);守(球) ④圆满地答复: ～ a tough question 圆满地答复一个棘手的问题 **❷** *vi.* (棒球、板球运动中)担任外场手(或守队队员) **III** *a.* ①田间的;野生的: ～ crops 大田作物 / ～ care 田间管理 / ～ flowers 野生的花 ②野外的,实地的: ～ operations 野外作业 / a ～ worker 实地工作者 ③【体】田赛的 ||*a fair ～ and no favo(u)r* 平等的比赛条件 / *a ～ of hono(u)r* 决斗场 / *in the ～* ①在战地,在作战 ②参加比赛: Are you *in the ～* for the relay race? 你参加接力赛跑吗? / *keep the ～* 继续作战;继续比赛 / *play the ～* 东搞搞西搞搞(指做事、恋爱等方面不专一) / *take the ～* 上阵;开始作战;开始比赛 / *win the ～* [古]获胜,胜利 / **～er** *n.* (棒球、板球)外场员;守队队员 / **～ward(s)** *ad.* 向原野,向田野 ||～ **ambulance** 战地救护车;野战救护队 / **～ army** 野战军 / **～ artillery** [总称]野战炮;野战炮兵 / **～ battery** 野战炮兵连 / **～ book** 野外工作记录本 / **～ day** ①野营演习日 ②户外集会 ③体育比赛日 ④野外科学活动日 ⑤特别愉快的时刻;获得意外成功的时刻 ⑥有重要活动(如辩论等)的日子 / **～ event** 【体】田赛 / **～ exercise** 野外演习 / **～ glasses** 双筒望远镜 / **～ grade** 【军】校级 / **～ gun** 野战炮 / **～ hand** ①田间农业劳动者 ②[美]干农活的黑奴 / **～ hospital** 野战医院 / **～ house** (运动场的)贮藏室;更衣室 / 运动场周围的房屋 / **～ ice** [地]冰原水 / **～ lens** ①向场(透)镜 ②(显微镜等的)物镜 / **～ magnet** 【物】场磁体;场磁铁 / **～ marshal** (英)陆军元帅;最高级的陆军将官 / **～ mouse** 野鼠,田鼠 / **～ night** 有重要活动(如辩论等)的夜晚 / **～ note** (一项)野外记录 / **～ officer** 【军】校官 / **～ pea** 【植】紫花豌豆 / **～piece** n. 野战炮 / **'～-se'quential** a. [无](彩色电视)场序制的,帧序制的 / **～ service** 野战勤务 / **'～s-man** ['fi:ldzmən] *n.* =～er / **～ sports** ①野外运动(打猎、赛马、射击等) ②田赛 / **'～-strip** *vt.* 对(枪炮)作拆卸检修 / **～ telegraph** 野战电报机 / **'～-test** *vt.* 对…作现场试验 / **～ theory** 【物】场论 / **～ trial** 猎狗的现场追猎试验 / **～ winding** 【物】磁场绕阻 / **～work** *n.* ①野战工事 ②野外测量;野外考察,实地调查;现场工作

fiend [fi:nd] *n.* ①魔鬼;[the F-] 魔王;撒旦 ②恶魔般的人,极邪恶的人 ③[口]…迷,…狂;对…嗜

好成癖者: a film ～ 电影迷 / a cigarette ～ 烟鬼 ④(某一方面的)能手,神手: a ～ at tennis 网球能手 ||～**like** *a.* 魔鬼似的

fierce [fiəs] *a.* ①凶猛的;残忍的: a ～ tiger 猛虎 ②猛烈的: a ～ storm 狂风暴雨 ③狂热的 ④[美]极讨厌的;难受的: a ～ pain 剧痛 / a ～ light 刺眼的强烈光线 / a ～ silence 令人难受的死一般的寂静 ⑤[英方]精力旺盛的 ||～**ly** *ad.* / ～**ness** *n.*

fiery ['faiəri] *a.* ①火的;火焰的; 燃烧着的;火一般的,如火似荼的 ②火热的;红肿的: 火红的: a ～ sore 红肿的溃疡 / a ～ sky 火红的天空 ③激烈的: a ～ speech 激烈的演说 ④易怒的,暴躁的: a ～ temper 暴躁的脾气 / a ～ steed 烈马 ⑤(眼)炯炯有神的 ⑥易燃的,易爆炸的 ||**fierily** *ad.* / **fieriness** *n.*

fife [faif] **I** *n.* (军乐中与鼓同奏友尖音的)横笛 **II ❶** *vi.* 吹横笛 **❷** *vt.* 用横笛吹奏(曲子) ||～**r** *n.* 吹横笛的人 ||～ **rail** 【海】桅杆栅栏,桅边系索杆

fifteen ['fif'ti:n] **I** *num.* 十五;十五个(人或物);第十五(卷、章、页等)(用例参看 **eight**) **II** *n.* ①十五个(人或物)一组;[英]橄榄球队 ②(网球)赢得第一球的得分,一分 ③十五岁 ④十五点钟(即下午三点): at ～thirty 在十五点三十分 ||～**th** *num.* ①第十五(个) ②十五分之一(的) *n.* (月的)第十五日

fifth [fifθ] **I** *num.* ①第五(个) ②五分之一(的): one (或 a) ～ 五分之一 / two ～s 五分之二 **II** *n.* ①[美]五分之一加仑(瓶) ②【音】五度音程;五度和音;第五音,属音 ③[F-]第五次修订的美国宪法 ④[复](商品)五等品 ⑤(月的)第五日 ||～**ly** *ad.* 第五(列举条目等时用) ||**Fifth Avenue** 纽约第五街(以讲究时髦、阔绰著称) / ～ **column** 第五纵队(现文指敌人派入的间谍和资敌的内奸) / ～ **columnism** 第五纵队战术,利用内奸 / ～ **columnist** 第五纵队队员 / **Fifth Monarchy** 【宗】基督的王国 / ～ **monarchy man** 【英史】十七世纪狂热盼望基督第二次降临的基督教徒 / **Fifth Republic** (法兰西)第五共和国 (1958—) / ～ **wheel** ①半拖车接轮;转向轮;试验(汽车停车距离等的)专用轮 ②备用轮 ③多余的人(或物)

fiftieth ['fiftiiθ] *num.* ①第五十(个) ②五十分之一(的)

fifty ['fifti] **I** *num.* 五十;五十个(人或物);第五十(卷、章、页等)(用例参看 **eight**) **II** *n.* ①五十个(人或物)一组 ②[复](世纪的)五十年代 ③五十岁;[复]五十到五十九岁的时期 **III** *a.* 许多的: I have ～ things to tell you. 我有许多话要告诉你。 ||**'～-'** *a.* ①各半的,对半的: on a ～-～ basis 平分,对等地 ②利弊各半的 *ad.* ①各半,对半 . go ～-～ 平分 ②利弊各半地

fig¹ [fig] *n.* ①【植】无花果;无花果树;无花果属植物 ②无价值的东西;不足道的事;少许,一点儿: A ～ for this! 这算得什么! / not care (或

fig 316 **file**

give) a ～ (*for*) (对…)毫不介意 / not worth a ～ 毫不足取 ③侮辱人的手势(把大拇指夹在两指间或塞入口中) ‖～ **leaf** ①无花果树叶 ②裸体塑像上遮蔽阴部的叶形物; 遮羞布 / ～ **tree** 无花果树

fig[2] [fig] **I** *n.* ①服装: be in full ～ 穿着盛装 ②健康状况: be in fine ～ 精神抖擞 **II** (figged; figging) *vt.* ①给…穿上盛装, 打扮 (*out, up*) ②(把生姜或胡椒塞入马的肛门或阴道)使(马)跑得快 (*out, up*)

fight [fait] **I** (fought [fɔːt]) ❶ *vi.* ①打仗; 搏斗; 打架: ～ at close quarters (或 range) 近距离搏斗; 短兵相接 / ～ back in self-defence 自卫还击 ②奋斗 ③当职业拳击手 ❷ *vt.* ①与…战斗; 与…斗争; 打(仗): ～ a battle 打一仗 ②指挥(士兵、军舰)战斗; 操纵(船只)与风暴搏斗 ③为(事业、诉讼等)进行斗争; 对(问题)进行争辩 ④逗引(鸡、犬等)相斗 ⑤反对(提案等) ⑥与…进行拳击; 参加(拳击赛等) ⑦毛手毛脚地操纵(变速器等) **II** *n.* ①战斗; 斗争: put up a ～ against waste 开展反浪费斗争 / a running ～【军】追击战 / a hand-to-hand ～ 肉搏战, 格斗 / a sham ～ 假打; [英]军事演习 / a stand-up ～ 光明正大的战斗 ②战斗精神; 战斗力: The retired workers still have plenty of ～ in them. 退休工人仍然斗志旺盛。 ③拳击赛 ④争吵 ‖*a straight* ～ 一对一的两人竞选 / ～ *down* 努力抑制, 克服 / ～ *off* 击退; 排斥; 竭力避免; ～ *shy of* 见 **shy**[1] / ～ *tooth and nail* 猛烈作战; 拼命打 / *show* ～ 显示斗志, 不示弱

fighter ['faitə] *n.* ①兵士; 斗争者②战斗机, 歼击机: a jet ～ 喷气式战斗机 / an escort ～ 护航战斗机 ③好斗的人 ④(职业)拳击手 ‖～**-bomber** *n.* 战斗轰炸机 / ～**-inter**'**ceptor** *n.* 战斗截击机 / ～ **plane** 战斗机, 歼击机

fighting ['faitiŋ] **I** *a.* ①战斗的; 搏斗的; 斗争的: ～ tasks 战斗任务 ②好战的; 好斗的 ③适于格斗的 ④容易引起争斗的: ～ words 容易引起争端的话 **II** *n.* 战斗, 搏斗; 斗争: air ～ 空战 ‖～ **chance** 经过努力奋斗可能获得成功的机会 / ～ **cock** ①斗鸡 ②好斗的人 / ～ **top** 军舰桅顶上的(高射)炮台

figment ['figmənt] *n.* 臆造的事物, 虚构的事

figurative ['figjurətiv] *a.* ①比喻的, 借喻的; 象征的: in a ～ sense 在比喻的意义上 ②用修辞手段的, 多文采的 ③用图形表现的 ‖～**ly** *ad.* / ～**ness** *n.*

figure ['figə] **I** *n.* ①外形, 轮廓; 体形; 隐约可见的人影(或物影): have a well-developed ～ 体态壮健 / the ～ of a ship on the horizon 地平线上的船形 ②图形; 图案; (书本中的)插图, 图表: a square (round) ～ 方(圆)形 / a geometrical (plane, solid) ～ 几何(平面, 立体)图形 ③画像; 塑像 ④形象; 人物; 身分, 地位: a person of ～ 地位高的人 ⑤数字(指数目字 0 到 9 或统计数字等); 位数; 符号(字母、数字符号、密码

等); have a head for ～s 数字概念强 / double ～s 两位数 / reach five ～s 达五位数 / complete (incomplete) ～s 完全的(不完全的)统计数字 ⑥[复]计算; 算术: She is very good at ～s. 她很会计算。 ⑦价格: sell sth. at a low (high) ～ 以低(高)价出售某物 ⑧【语】修辞手段, 修辞格 (= ～ of speech) ⑨【逻】(三段论法中按中项的不同位置而构成的)格 ⑩(溜冰、飞行的)花式; 特技: skating ～ 花式溜冰 ⑪【音】音型; (舞蹈中的)舞步型 **II** ❶ *vt.* ①描绘; 塑造; 想象: ～ sth. to oneself 想象某事物 ②用图案(或花纹等)装饰 ③用数字表示(数目等) ④[美]计算(开支): ～ expenses 计算开支 ⑤相信, 估计, 揣测: I ～ he'll be back soon. 我估计他很快会回来。 / I ～ it like this. 关于这点, 我是这样想的。 ⑥表示, 象征 ❷ *vi.* ①出现; 露头角; 扮演角色 (*as*): ～ in history (a battle) 在历史上(某一战役中)赫赫有名 ②计算, 做算术 ③考虑; 估计 ④跳某种舞的步型 ‖*cut* (或 *make*) *a* ～ 露头角: *cut a fine* ～ 崭然露头角 / *cut a poor* (或 *sorry*) ～ 出丑 / *cut a foolish* ～ 成为笑柄, 闹笑话 / *cut no* ～ 不显赫, 无足轻重 / *do sth. on the big* ～ [美]大规模地干某事 / ～ *for* 谋取, 企图获得 / ～ *in* 包括进, 算进(某项开支等) / ～ *on* ①把…估计在内 ②指望: We ～ *on* your coming early. 我们指望你会早些来。③计划: I ～ *on* going there on Monday. 我打算星期一到那儿去。/ ～ *out* ①合计 ②计算出; 解决: ～ *out* the amount of moisture in the soil 计算出土壤的湿度 / ～ *out a problem* 解决一道算题 ③领会到, 断定: I couldn't ～ *out* who he was. 我想不出他是谁。/ ～ *up* 计算…, 把…总加起来: ～ *up an account* 算出帐目的总数 / *go* (或 *come*) *the big* ～ [美]彻底地干, 干到底 / *in round* ～s ①(舍弃零数)以整数表示; 以约数表示 ②[喻]大概; 总而言之 ‖～**d** *a.* 有形状的; 用图画(或图表)表示的; 有图案的 ‖ **eight** 8 字形(如绳结、溜冰式、飞行式等) / '～**head** *n.* ①船头雕饰 ②挂名首脑, 傀儡

filament ['filəmənt] *n.* ①细丝; 丝状体 ②【纺】长丝; 单纤维 ③【植】花丝 ④(电灯泡、电子管的)灯丝; 丝极: tungsten ～s 钨丝 / a ～ current 灯丝电流 ‖～**ary** [ˌfilə'mentəri] *a.* / ～**ed** *a.* 有细丝的 / ～**ous** [ˌfilə'mentəs] *a.*

filch [filtʃ] *vt.* 偷(不贵重的东西) ‖～**er** *n.* 小偷子

file[1] [fail] **I** *n.* ①文件夹 ②汇订的文件(或卡片等); 档案, 案卷, 卷宗 ③纵列 ④(国际象棋盘上的)格子纵列 **II** ❶ *vt.* ①把…归档: Please ～ (away) these letters. 请把这些信件归档。②提出(申请等); 呈请把…备案: ～ an application with the authorities 向当局提出申请书 / a ～ suit against sb. 对某人提出控告 ③用电话(或电报)向通讯社发送(稿子) ④命令(士兵)排成纵队行进 ❷ *vi.* ①排成纵队行进: They ～*d* out of the room. 他们从房里鱼贯而出。/ ～ *off* (或 *away*)

排成纵队出发 ②(在预选中)备案作候选人 ‖a ~ of men 被派出执行任务的二人小分队 / ~ 13 [俚]字纸篓 / in ~ 成二列纵队；依次，鱼贯地 / in single (或 Indian) ~ 成一路纵队，成单行 / on ~ 存档: place a document on ~ 把文件归档 / the rank and ~ 见 rank¹

file² [fail] **I** *n.* ①锉(刀): a flat ~ 扁锉 / a round ~ 圆锉 / a square ~ 方锉 / a triangular ~ 三角锉 ②狡猾的人: an old (或 a deep) ~ 老奸巨猾的家伙 / a close ~ 吝啬鬼 **II ❶** *vt.* ①锉；把…锉平，把…锉光: ~ sth. smooth 把某物锉光 / ~ away the rough edges 把粗糙的边缘锉平 ❷ *vi.* 琢磨 ❷ *vi.* 用锉刀工作 ‖bite (或 gnaw) a ~ 做不可能成功的事情，白费力气

filial ['filjəl] *a.* ①子女的；孝顺的 ②【生】子代的，后代的: ~ generation 子代，杂交后代 ‖**-ly** *ad.*

filigree ['filigri:] **I** *n.* ①金丝(或银丝、铜丝)的细工饰品 ②精致华丽而不很坚固的物品 **II** *vt.* ①用金丝(或银丝、铜丝)饰品装饰 ②用精致华丽但不坚固的饰品装饰

filing ['failiŋ] *n.* ①锉；琢磨 ②[常用复]锉屑: iron ~s 铁锉屑

fill [fil] **I ❶** *vt.* ①装满，盛满，注满，充满: ~ a glass with water 往玻璃杯里注满水 / Sounds of drums and gongs ~ed the air. 锣鼓声响彻天空。/ ~ed with boiling anger 满腔怒火 ②全部占据；占满，坐满: A big audience ~ed the hall. 观众济济一堂。/ All the streets were ~ed with rejoicing people on that gala day. 在那个节日里，所有街道都挤满了欢乐的人们。③堵塞，填塞；填充；填补；(用土等)填满: ~ a hole with mud 用泥土填洞 / ~ (in) a form 填表 / ~ (out) a cheque 开支票 / ~ (up) the blanks 填空白 / ~ a hollow tooth (或 the cavity of a tooth)镶补龋齿 ④饱；供给…: ~ the guests with nice food 用佳肴款待客人 ⑤担任(职务): The vacancy has been ~ed. 空缺已有人补上。⑥满足: ~ an urgent need 满足急需 ⑦供应(定货)；配(药方): ~ an order 供应定货 / ~ a doctor's prescription 照医生所开药方配药 ⑧【海】(风)张满(帆)；调整(帆)使帆背吃风: The wind ~ed the sails. 风张满了帆。❷ *vi.* 充满: The gymnasium soon ~ed with people. 体育馆里很快就挤满了人。/ The sails ~ed with wind. 帆被风张满。**II** *n.* ①饱；满足；充分 ②足以填满某物之量；装填物: the ~ for a trench 填沟物 ③(铁路的)路堤；填方，填土 ‖eat one's ~ 吃个饱 / drink one's ~ 喝个够 / ~ away 转帆向风；乘风前进 / ~ in ①填充；填写: ~ in an application form 填写申请表格 ②填满: ~ in sunken places with stones 用石块填洼处 ③临时补缺，暂代 / ~ out 填写，填好 ②使长大 变大；长胖 / ~ up 填；填补；装满: ~ up the tank with petrol 给油箱装满汽油 / ~ up a vacancy 填补空缺 ②淤积: The

ditch has ~ed up with mud. 沟渠已积满了泥土。‖**~er** *n.* ①装填者 ②装填物；挽入物(如挽入肥料的土等)；(油漆前堵塞罅隙的)填料 ③作雪茄烟烟心的烟草 ④(报纸等的)补白 ⑤活页簿纸 ⑥漏斗；注入器；装罐机 / **~ing** *n.* ①装填；充填；填满；装填物(尤指牙医生用来补牙的材料)；(糕点里面的)馅子 ②【美】【纺】纬纱；浆料 ‖**~-in** *n.* ①临时填补空缺的人，替工；临时填补物 ②[口](事实等的)简明摘要 *a.* 临时填补性的 / **~ing station** [美]汽车加油站；[美俚]小城市

fillet ['filit] **I** *n.* ①头带；束发带 ②带子；带状物；(书面等上的)饰线，轮廓线 ③【建】平缘；木摺；突出横饰线 ④肉片；鱼片 ⑤【解】襻，丘系；[复](牛、马等的)腰部 ⑥【机】嵌条、(内)圆角: light ~ 浅角焊缝 **II** *vt.* ①用带缚；用饰带(或饰线等)装饰 ②把(肉、鱼)切成片

film [film] **I** *n.* ①薄层；膜，薄膜: a ~ of oil on water 水面上薄薄的一层油 / a ~ of a plastic 一块塑料薄膜 / carbon resistance ~【电】炭膜电阻 ②薄雾；轻烟；细丝状物 ③胶卷；软片: a roll of ~ 一卷软片 / a negative (positive) ~ (照片的)底(正)片 ④影片，电影: go to the ~s 去看电影 / a colour ~ 彩色影片 / a documentary ~ 纪录片 / a wide-screen ~ 宽银幕电影 / a three-dimensional ~ 立体电影 ⑤【医】(眼的)薄翳 **II ❶** *vt.* ①在…上覆以薄膜 ②拍摄；把…摄成电影: ~ a scene 拍摄一个场景 / ~ a novel 把一部小说摄制成电影 ❷ *vi.* ①生薄膜；变成朦胧 ②摄制电影 ③适于拍摄(或摄成电影): He ~s well. 他很上照。/ The story won't ~ well. 这小说不适于摄制成电影。‖**~dom** *n.* 电影界；电影业 ‖**~-fan** *n.* 电影迷 / **~,goer** *n.* 上电影院的人；爱看电影的人 / **~graph** *n.* 电影摄片录音设备 / ~ **pack** (供荧光下装入照相机的)盒装胶片 / ~ **star** 电影明星 / **~-strip** *n.* (教学用的)电影胶片；幻灯片 / ~ **studio** 电影制片厂

filter ['filtə] **I** *n.* ①滤器；滤纸: ~ press【化】压滤机 / bacterial ~ 细菌滤器 ②过滤用多孔物质(如砂、炭、纸、布等) ③【物】滤光器，滤色镜；【无】滤波器: infrared ~ 红外线滤光器 / band ~ 带通滤波器 **II ❶** *vt.* ①过滤 ②用过滤法除去 ❷ *vi.* ①滤过 ②[喻]透过；渗入；(消息等)走漏，慢慢传开: daylight ~ing through thick clouds 透过浓云的日光 / The news ~ed through. 消息走漏了。③(车辆等在十字路口)进入另一交通行列 ‖ ~ **bed** 滤垫；滤水池 / ~ **paper** 滤纸(尤指定量滤纸) / ~ **tip** 香烟头上的过滤嘴；有过滤嘴的香烟 / **~-tipped** *a.* 有过滤嘴的

filth [filθ] *n.* ①污秽，污物 ②淫猥；猥亵语 ‖**~ disease** 由于水、土污染引起的疾病，由于环境不洁(或缺乏卫生习惯)引起的疾病

fin [fin] *n.* ①鳍；鳍状物: a caudal (ventral) ~ 尾(腹)鳍 ②【机】翅(片)；(铸件的)周缘翅片；散热片: damping ~ 阻尼片 ③【空】垂直(或水平

安平面; 直尾翅: rear ～ 尾翼 ④【船】(潜艇的)鳍板; (游艇的) 鳍状龙骨 ⑤【军】弹尾; (火箭的)舵 ⑥ 汽车尾部的突起状装饰物 ⑦ (潜水时缚在脚上的) 鸭脚板, 橡皮脚掌 ⑧【俚】手; 臂: Tip us your ～. 让我们握手。⑨【美俚】(人的) 头 **II** (finned; finning) **❶** *vi.* 猛烈地挥动鳍; 露鳍于水面上 **❷** *vt.* ①给 … 装上鳍(片)(或鳍板等) ②切除…的鳍 ‖～ **keel** (游艇等的) 鳍状龙骨

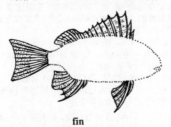

fin

final ['fainl] **I** *a.* 最后的; 最终的; 决定性的: the ～ day of a school term 一学期的最后一天 / in the ～ analysis 归根到底 / a ～ decision 最后决定, 不可更改的决定 / a ～ judgement 最后判决 **II** *n.* ①[常用复]期终考试; 最后一次考试; 决赛: prepare for the ～s 准备参加期终考试 / take one's ～ 参加最后一次考试 / be qualified to play in the ～s 有资格参加决赛 ②[口]报纸(在一天中的) 最晚版 ‖～**ist** *n.* 决赛选手 / ～**ly** *ad.* ①最后; 最终 ②不可更改地; 决定性地 ‖～ **thrill** [美俚]死亡

finale [fi'nɑ:li] *n.* ①(戏剧的)最后一场; 最后一幕 ②结尾, 结局 ③【音】终曲

finance [fai'næns] **I** *n.* ① 财政; 金融; 财政学: the Minister of *Finance* 财政部长 ②[常用复]财源; 资金 **II** *vt.* ①供资金给; 为…筹措资金 ②赊货给 *vi.* 筹措资金 ‖**financing** *n.* ①筹措资金; 理财 ②筹集的资金 ‖～ **company** 信贷公司

financial [fai'nænʃəl, fi'nænʃəl] *a.* 财政的; 金融的: ～ affairs 财务 / the ～ condition (或 situation) 财政状况 / a ～ statement 财务报表; 决算表(指资产负债表、损益计算书等) ‖～**ly** *ad.* ‖～ **year** [英]财政年度, 会计年度(美国称 fiscal year)

financier [fai'nænsiə, fi'nænsiə] **I** *n.* 财政家; 金融家 **II** *vi.* ① (以欺诈等手段) 从事金融活动 ② 骗取; 欺骗

find [faind] **I** (found [faund]) **❶** *vt.* ①找到: I looked for it for several days but haven't *found* it yet. 这东西我找了好几天了, 可是至今仍未找到。/ Will you ～ me a spade (或 ～ a spade for me)? 你替我找一把铲子来好吗? / ～ ways and means to overcome difficulties 找到克服困难的各种方法 ②发现; 发觉; 感到: I *found* him in (out) when I called. 我去看他时发现他正在(不在)家。/ You have to take it as you ～ it.

对它你只得将就些算了。/ ～ it necessary to get a map 感到必须搞到一张地图才行 / Do you ～ it pays (或 to pay, 或 pay)? 你认为这样做合算吗? ③找出; 查明: ～ (*out*) the principal contradiction 找出主要矛盾 ④得到: ～ great satisfaction in 在…中得到很大满足 / An unjust cause ～s little support. 失道寡助。/ ～ enough courage to do sth. 获得足够的勇气去做某事 / ～ currency 开始流通 ⑤知道是有的, 见到…的存在: This precious mineral is *found* in many provinces. 许多省都有这种珍贵的矿物。⑥ 裁决; 作出(裁决): ～ sb. guilty 裁决某人有罪 / ～ a verdict 作出裁决 ⑦(自然地)形成; 达到: Rivers ～ their way to the sea. 江河流入大海。/ The shell *found* its mark. 炮弹击中目标。⑧ 供给, 供应; 筹集(经费等): ～ sb. *in* food and clothing 供给某人衣食 / They are *found in* everything. 他们一切都得到供应。**❷** *vi.* 裁决, 判决: ～ for (against) the plaintiff 作出有利(不利)于原告的裁决 **II** *n.* 发现; 发现物(尤指猎物、矿藏等); 被发觉有惊人能力的人: an important archaeological ～ 考古学上的一项重要发现 / a sure ～ 必能发现(狐狸等)的地方;[俚]一定能找到的人(或物) ‖**all** (或 **everything**) **found** (工资以外)膳宿等全部供给 / ～ **oneself** ①发觉自己的处境: ～ *oneself* in a dilemma 发觉自己陷入进退两难的困境 ②(在健康等方面)自我感觉: How do you ～ *yourself* today? 今天你觉得(身体)怎样? ③发现自己的特长并加以发挥; 发现自己所能胜任的工作 ④(在衣食等方面)自理 / ～ **out** ①找出, 发现; 查明(真相等) ②想出; 认识到(*that*) ③把(坏人、罪犯等)揭发出来; 使受应得的惩罚(或报应)

finding ['faindiŋ] *n.* ①发现; 发现物: The humo(u)r of it takes ～. 其中的幽默要好好体味才能发现。②[常用复]调查(或研究)的结果;【律】裁决, 判决 ③[美][复]零碎的工具用品(如缝纫用的针线等)

fine[1] [fain] **I** *a.* ① 美好的; 优良的; 优秀的; 杰出的 ② 精制的: ～ sugar (salt) 精制糖(盐) ③(金银等)纯净的, 含量高的; 精炼的: ～ silver (aluminium) 纯银(铝) / a kettle of ～ copper 纯铜水壶 / gold 18 carats ～ 十八开金 ④细的; 纤细的; 纤巧的; 细微难察的: ～ rain 细雨 / ～ ore【矿】细矿粉 / ～ linen (thread, china) 细麻布(纱线, 瓷器) / a ～ pen 笔尖细的钢笔 / ～ workmanship 精巧的制作 / a ～ distinction 细微的差别 ⑤(刀刃等)快的, 锋利的; (感觉等)敏锐的, 灵敏的: have a ～ ear for 对 … 听觉灵敏 / a ～ measuring instrument 精密量具 ⑥好看的, 漂亮的; 硕大的: a ～ view 壮丽的景色 / people in their ～ festival attire 身穿节日盛装的人们 / ～ apples (potatoes) 硕大的苹果(土豆) ⑦(天气)晴朗的: *Fine* weather, isn't it? 天气真好, 是不是? ⑧(运动员等)锻炼得体格健全的, 能适应大运动量的 ⑨(讲话、写作等)假作恭维的; 委婉的; 过分夸饰的; 炫耀的: say ～ things about sb. 恭维某人 /

~ words 漂亮话 / call things by ~ names 用好听的名称称呼事物 (常指用生僻的词代替通俗的词以炫耀自己; 或避而不用带不愉快色彩的词) **II ad.** ①[口]很好; 妙: That'll suit me ~. 那对我太合适了。/ talk ~ 说得好听 ②[常用以构成复合词]细微地; 精巧地: cut it ~ 扣得很紧(尤指时间方面), 几乎不留余地 / a ~-toothed comb 细齿梳子 **III n.** 好天气: in rain or ~ 不管天晴下雨 **IV ❶ vt.** 使纯, 澄清; 精炼, 使精细; (在线条、比例等方面)使细(小) (away, down): ~ down beer 澄清啤酒 ❷ vi. ①变纯, (液体)澄清; 变得精细; (天气)转晴: The ale will ~. 啤酒会澄清的。/ The weather gradually ~d. 天气逐渐转晴。②(在线条、比例等方面)变细(小), 缩小 (away, down) ‖one ~ day (常用作讲故事时的开场白)有一天, 有一次 (=once upon a time) / one of these ~ days 总有一天 / the ~st [美俚](纽约的)警察 / train ~ (把…)锻炼得处于良好的状态 ‖~ly ad. / ~ness n. ‖~ arts 美术(指诗歌、音乐、绘画、雕塑、建筑等) / '~'comb vt. 仔细搜查 / ~ cut 细切的烟草 / '~-'draw vt. ①细(密)缝 ②拉细(铁丝等) ③[喻]细致推(理) / '~-'drawn a. ①细(密)缝的 ②拉细的 ③(推理、论证等)过于琐细的, 微妙的 / '~'spun a. ①细纺的, 拉细的; 脆弱的 ②微妙的, 过分琐碎的: a ~spun theory 琐细得不切实际的理论 / '~-tooth-'comb vt. 仔细搜查

fine² [fain] **I n.** ①罚金, 罚款: impose a ~ on sb. 处某人以罚金 / a ~ for delaying payment 滞纳罚金 ②结尾, 终结(现只用于习语 in ~ 中) **II vt.** 处…以罚金 ‖in ~ 最后; 总而言之

fine ['fi:ne] **n.** [意][音]末尾: Al Fine 到末尾

finery¹ ['fainəri] **n.** ① 华丽的服饰 ② [罕]漂亮, 时髦

finery² ['fainəri] **n.**[冶]精炼炉

finesse [fi'nes] **I n.** ①手腕, 手段; 策略; 技巧 ②(桥牌中)先出较小的牌保留好牌以赢牌的手法 **II ❶ vt.** ①用巧计实现; 用巧计战胜 ②出(较小的牌) ❷ vi. ①施展巧计 ②出较小的牌

finger ['fiŋgə] **I n.** ①手指(尤指大拇指以外的手指): the index ~ 食指 / the middle (或 long) ~ 中指 / the ring ~ 无名指 / the little(或small) ~ 小指 ②指状物; (手套的)每一手指部分; 【机】指; 指针: a setting ~ 定位指 / the ~ of a clock 钟的指针 ③一指之阔 (3/4—1 吋); 一中指之长(约 4¹⁄₂ 吋) ④[美俚]警察; 告密者 **II ❶ vt.** ①用指触碰, 拨弄, 抚摸 ②用指弹奏(乐器、曲调); 给(乐谱)标明指法符号 ③指出 ④(象手指般)伸入: The beams of the searchlights ~ed the sky. 一道道探照灯光刺破天空。⑤受(贿) [美俚]尾随, 监视; 指责; 告发 ❷ vi. ①用指触碰, 拨弄 ②用指弹奏 ③(象手指般)伸出: The docks ~ out into the water. 码头伸向水面。‖(a) ~ on the wall 灾难的预兆 / burn one's ~s 由于管闲事(或鲁莽)而吃苦头 / by a ~'s breadth

差一点 / by the ~ of God 靠神力 / crook one's little ~ [俚]喝酒 / cross one's ~s 把一手指交叉放在同一只手的另一手指上(迷信的人认为这样会带来好运气或减轻说谎的罪过) / give sb. the ~ [美俚]恶意对待某人, 亏待某人; 让某人倒霉 / have a ~ in the pie 染指, 参与其事 / lay (或 put) a ~ on 触碰; 动一根毫毛 / lay (或 put) one's ~ on 正确地指出(错误、症结等); put one's ~ on sb.'s weak spot 指出某人(性格上)的弱点 / look through one's ~s at 对…假装没看见 / My little ~ told me. 我自然知道罗。/ not lift (或 stir, turn) a ~ 不尽一举手之劳; 一点忙都不帮 / One's ~s are all thumbs. 某人笨手笨脚。/ One's ~s itch to do sth. 某人急于想干某事。/ put one's ~ in another's pie 多管闲事 / put one's ~ in one's eye 哭泣 / shake one's ~ at sb. 用食指点某人(表示责备、警告等) / slip through sb.'s ~s 从某人的手缝中溜掉; 被某人错过 / snap one's ~s at 向…捻指(表示轻蔑、不在乎等) / stick to (或 in) sb.'s ~s (钱)被某人侵吞 / turn (或 twist, wind, wrap) sb. round (或 around) one's (little) ~ 左右某人; 任意摆布某人 / with a wet ~ 不费力地 ‖~ed a. ①有指的; 指状的, 掌状的 ②[用以构成复合词]有…指的; 手指…的: light-~ed 手指轻巧的; 善于扒窃的 ③ 被手指污染的 / ~less a. 无指的; 失去指的 ‖~ alphabet 手势语 / '~board n. ① (提琴等的)指板; (钢琴等的)键盘 ② =~post / ~ bowl 餐桌上供人餐后洗手指用的小盆 / '~fish n. [动]海盘车 / ~ language 手势语 / ~ man [美俚](盗贼等的)眼线 / ~ mark 指迹 / '~nail n. 指甲 / ~ painting 指画法(一种用手指蘸颜料洒在湿纸上的画法); 指画法作品 / ~ plate (门等表面上)防止被手指污染的防护板(层) / '~post n. ①指路牌; 指向柱 ②指南 / '~print n. 指纹印, 手印 vt. 打下…的指纹印 / '~stall n. (皮或橡皮制的)护指套 / ~ wave 手指烫发法(指仅用手指、梳子等卷发, 与电烫相别)

fingering¹ ['fiŋgəriŋ] **n.** ①用手指拨弄 ②用指弹奏; 【音】指法; [总称]指法符号

fingering² ['fiŋgəriŋ] **n.** 细绒线 (=~ yarn)

fingertip ['fiŋgətip] **n.** ①指尖 ②(射箭等用的)指尖套 ‖have sth. at one's ~s ①手头有某物随时可供应用: After repeated experiments we have all the data at our ~s. 经多次实验我们掌握了所有的数据。②精通某事物; 熟知某事物 / to one's (或 the) ~s 完全地, 地道地

finicky ['finiki], **finical** ['finikəl], **finicking** ['finikiŋ] **a.** 过分讲究(吃、穿等)的; 难以讨好的; 过分讲究细节的: finicky airs 娇气 ‖**finicality** [ˌfini'kæliti] **n.** / **finically ad.** / **finicalness n.**

finish ['finiʃ] **I ❶ vt.** ①结束, 完毕; 完成: Have you ~ed that book? 那本书你看完了吗? / ~ reading a periodical 读完一本期刊 / ~ school

毕业 / The workers ~ed the dyke with remarkable speed. 工人们以惊人的速度筑成了堤坝。 ②给…抛光;给…最后加工;使完美,润饰 ③用完;吃完;耗尽: The boy ~ed the cake just in a few bites. 这孩子几口就把糕吃下去了。④[口]消灭;杀掉;使完蛋: That shock almost ~ed him. 那一惊几乎把他吓死。⑤结束对…的学业培养 ❷ vi. 结束,终结;停止,终止: Have you ~ed with. the dictionary? 这本词典你已经用完了吗? / He ~ed third in the contest. 他在竞赛中得了第三名。 II n. [只用单] ① 结束;最后阶段: the ~ of a race 赛跑的最后一段距离 ② 致使完蛋的原因: That was his ~. 这就是他完蛋的原因。③完美;(举止、谈吐、姿态等的)优雅: give the last ~ to sth. 对某物进行最后的精细加工 / add a ~ to a poem 对一首诗歌作最后润饰 ④(家具等表面的)抛光(剂);罩面漆;末道漆;漆;【建】终饰;用作饰面的高级木材 ‖be in at the ~ 最后猎获猎物时亲自在场;[喻](在比赛、斗争等的)最后阶段亲自在场 / ~ off [结束;完成;对…进行最后加工 ②用光,耗尽 / ~ up with 以…结束;最后有…: We had a celebration, with a new film to ~ up with. 我们开了个庆祝会,最后放映了一部新电影。 / ~ with ① 完成;结束: We've ~ed with the present tense and now let's pass on to the past tense. 我们已学完了现在时态,现在开始学过去时态。②与…断绝关系

finished ['finiʃt] a. ① 完结了的,结束了的;完成了的: a ~ product 成品 ② 精致完美的;绝顶的 ③(家具等)处理光洁的 ④[口]完蛋了的

finite ['fainait] a. ① 有限的 ②【数】有穷的, 有限的;有尽的: ~ decimal 有限小数 / ~ progression (或 series) 有限级数 /【语】限定的: a ~ verb 限定动词 / the ~ forms of a verb 动词的限定形式(例如: am, is, are, was, were) ‖~ly ad. / ~ness n.

fiord [fjɔːd, fiˈɔːd] n. 峡湾(尤指挪威海岸边的)

fir [fəː] n. ①【植】冷杉,枞;松科常绿树(如黄杉等) ② 冷杉木, 枞木 ‖'~-,apple, '~-ball, '~-cone n. 冷杉球果 / '~-,needle n. 冷杉针叶,枞叶

fire ['faiə] I n. ①火: Keep away from ~! 切勿近火! / Cotton catches ~ easily. 棉花易燃。②炉火: Warm yourself at the ~. 来烤烤火吧。③ 火灾, 失火: Fire! 着火啦! / a forest ~ 森林火灾 ④发光(或炽热)体;闪光: St. Elmo's ~ 桅顶(或飞机翼梢、塔尖等)的电光 / the ~ of lightning 闪电光 ⑤发烧: St. Anthony's ~ 丹毒 ⑥炮火;[喻]猛烈的批评: open (cease) ~ 开(停)火 / ground ~ 地面火力 ⑦热情;激情; 生动的想象; 生气: His eyes were full of ~. 他的眼中充满怒火。/ the force and ~ of a speech 一篇讲话的力量和激情

⑧火刑;(火刑)拷问
⑨磨难,苦难
II ❶ vt. ① 烧; 点燃: ~ a house 放火烧屋 / ~ dry leaves 烧(或点燃)干树叶 / ~ (up) a cigar 点燃雪茄烟
②烧制(砖等);焙,烘制(茶叶等): ~ pottery 烧制陶器
③ 给(炉子等)加燃料,给…烧火: ~ a furnace 给炉子生火
④使发光;使发红;使发亮
⑤ 放(枪、炮等),射出(子弹);使爆炸: ~ a gun (torpedo) at 向…开枪(放鱼雷) / ~ a salute 放礼炮 / ~ a shot 射出一发(子弹)
⑥激起, 激动, 使充满热情
⑦(兽医等)烧灼
⑧[美口]猛地发出;猛力投掷: ~ questions 提出一连串问题
⑨ [口]解雇,开除
❷ vi. ① 着火;烧火,司炉: Damp wood will not ~. 潮湿的木头不会着火。/ There was no one to ~ for them. 没有人替他们烧火。
②激动;突然发怒
③开火;(枪等)射击: ~ back in self-defence 自卫还击 / Fire! 开火!
④ 由于燃烧而发生变化: This clay ~s to a reddish colour. 这种粘土烧后变成淡红色。
‖a running ~ ①连发,连射 ②一连串的批评指责 / between two ~s 遭两面夹攻 / by ~ and sword 大肆烧杀破坏[作状语用] / carry ~ in one hand and water in the other 口不应心, 施展两面手法 / ~ away ①[口]开始并象连珠炮似地接下去(特指谈话或提问) ② 不住地射击 / ~ out [美]解雇,开除 / ~s of heaven (或 heavenly ~s) [诗]星星 / ~ up ①生火 ②突然发怒 / go through ~ and water 赴汤蹈火 / hang ~ (枪、炮)发射不出;迟缓发射;(行动或事情的发生)延误;犹豫不决 / hold ~ 忍着不表态(或不采取行动) / Kentish ~ 长时间的鼓掌;一片反对、捣乱声 / lay a ~ (把燃料放入炉中)准备生火 / lift ~ [军] ① 延伸射击 ② 中止射击 / make a ~ 生火 / miss ~ ①(枪、炮)不发火,打不响 ② 得不到预想的效果 / nurse a ~ ① 看管着火使不熄灭 ② 烤火 / on ~ ① 起火,着火;[喻]非常激动,充满热情 / on the ~ [美俚]在予以考虑(或审议)中 / open ~ ①开火 ②开始 / play with ~ 玩火: He who plays with ~ gets burned. 玩火者必自焚。/ pull out of the ~ 使转败为胜 / rapid ~ 速射(指轻兵器或自动兵器的射速,在 slow ~ 和 quick ~ 之间) / sacred ~ ① 真挚的爱; 神圣的爱 ② 天才 / set ~ to 使燃烧;点燃 / set ... on ~ 使燃烧,放火烧 / show sth. ~ 把某物稍稍稍一下 / Soft ~ makes sweet malt. [谚]文火煮出好麦芽糖。(意指: 慢工出细活。) / strike ~ (用火石等)打火 / take ~ 着火, 开始燃烧, 激动起来 / under ~ 遭到炮火射击;受到攻击

(或批评、责难等)

‖ **~less** a. 无火的

‖ **~ action** 【军】火战(使用各种武器的对敌战斗) / **~ alarm** 火警,报火机,警钟 / **~arm** ['faiərɑ:m] n. 火器(在美国一般仅指步枪、手枪等) / **'~ball** n. ①火球(指原子武器或热核武器爆炸后在空中出现的圆球体)②流星 ③【军】(旧式)燃烧弹 ④[美口]工作起来劲儿十足的人 / **~ balloon** (下部点火,因热气膨胀而浮起的)火气球 / **'~bird** n. 美洲产的色彩鲜艳的小鸟(如金莺) / **~ blast, ~ blight** (植物病理)火疫 / **'~boat** n. 消防艇 / **~ bomb** 【军】燃烧弹 / **'~box** n. ①[机]机车锅炉炉膛,燃烧室 ②盛放火警报警器的箱子 / **~brand** n. ①燃烧的木头 ②煽动叛乱者,挑动争执者 / **'~break** n. 防火线(指森林等处伐去树木以防野火蔓延的一条地带) / **'~brick** n. (耐)火砖 / **~ brigade** 消防队 / **'~bug** n. [口]纵火者;放火狂者 / **'~clay** n. (耐)火泥,耐火(粘土) / **~ company** ①[美]消防队 ②[英]火灾保险公司 / **~ control** ①【军】实施射击;射击指挥;火力控制(用电子仪器等进行的)射击控制 ②消防 / **'~cracker** n. 爆竹,鞭炮 / **'~damp** n. 【化】沼气 / **'~dog** n. (壁炉的)薪架 / **~ drake** n. (神话中的)喷火龙 / **~ drill** 消防演习 / **'~eater** n. ①吞火魔术师 ②易发火打架的人,脾气暴躁的人 / **'~eating** a. 强暴的;咄咄逼人的;好战的 / **~ engine** 救火车 / **~ escape** 太平梯;安全出口 / **~ extinguisher** 灭火器 / **~ fighter** 消防人员 / **'~fly** n. 萤火虫 / **~ grate** 炉篦 / **'~guard** n. ①火炉栏 ②=~break ③(森林)防火员 / **~ hose** 救火皮带 / **'~house** n. 消防站(=~ station) / **~ hydrant** 消防栓,消防龙头,灭火龙头 / **~ insurance** 火(灾保)险 / **~ irons** 火炉用具(如火钳、通条、火铲) / **~ lane** =~break / **'~light** n. (炉)火光 / **~ line** ①=~break ②[常用复]火灾现场的警察线(或拦路绳)③(草原、森林等的)火灾最前线 / **~man** ['faiəmən] n. ①司炉工,烧火工人 ②消防队员 ③[矿]爆破工;瓦斯检验员,通风员 / **~ marshal** [美]防火部门主管人 / **'~-new** a. 全新的(=brand-new) / **~ office** [英]火灾保险公司 / **pan** 火盆 / **'~place** n. 壁炉 / **'~plug** n. 灭火塞(指设在路边或屋内的消防龙头) / **~ policy** 火(灾)险单 / **'~,power** n. 【军】火力:a close-knit network of ~power 严密的火力网 / **'~proof** n. 防火的;耐火的 vt. 使防火;使耐火 / **'~,proofing** n. 防火;耐火;耐火装置(材料) / **'~-,raising** n. [英]纵火罪 / **'~room** n. 锅炉间,火室 / **~ sale** [美]火灾中损坏物品的减价出售 / **~ screen** 火炉栏 / **~ ship** (旧时装有易燃品驶向敌船的)火攻船 / **'~side** n. ①炉边 ②家 ③[古]家庭 a. 炉边的;亲切的,不拘束的 / **~ station** 消防站 / **'~stone** n. 耐火岩石;耐火粘土;燧石;黄铁矿 / **'~storm** n. (原子爆炸等引起的)风暴性大火 / **~ tower** (森林等处的)火

警观察塔 / **'~trap** n. 无太平门等设施的建筑物;易引起火灾的废物堆 / **~ trench** 【军】散兵壕 / **~ truck** [美]救火车 / **~ wall** 防火墙,隔火墙 / **'~,water** n. [口]烈酒 / **'~weed** n. 在火烧过(或开拓出来)的土地上生长极快的野草(如曼陀罗) / **'~wood** n. 木柴,柴火 / **'~work** n. ①烟火具(爆竹、花炮等)②【军】烟火信号弹 ③[复]激情(如暴躁、紧张、热情等)的表现 / **~ worship** 拜火;拜火教

firing ['faiəriŋ] n. ①生火,点火 ②烧窑;烘烤 ③(锅炉等的)司炉,添煤 ④(炉火的)燃料 ⑤射击 ⑥[口]解雇 ‖ **~ line** ①【军】射击线;射击线上的部队 ②[喻]第一线(尤用于 on the ~ 这一词中) / **~ party, ~ squad** ①(对军事法庭判处死刑的犯人执行枪决的)行刑队 ②(举行军人葬礼时的)鸣枪队 / **~ point** 射击位置(指打靶时发射的位置)

firm¹ [fə:m] **I** a. ①结实的;坚硬的:~ muscles 结实的肌肉 / ~ ground 陆地 ②牢固的,稳固的:as ~ as a rock 稳如磐石 ③坚定的;坚决的;有力的:严格的 ~ in (或 of) purpose 意志坚定 / take measures 采取坚决的措施 / a ~ handshake 紧紧的握手 / be ~ with children 严格对待孩子 ④(行市等)坚挺的 ⑤【商】确定的:a ~ offer 确盘 **II** ad. 稳固地;坚定地:hold ~ 固守 / stand ~ 站稳立场 **III** ❶ vt. ①使牢固,使稳固;使稳定;使坚定 ②确认(契约等) ❷ vi. ①变牢固,变稳固;变稳定 ②变坚实 ‖ **~ly** ad. / **~ness** n.

firm² [fə:m] n. (合伙)商号,商行 ‖ a long ~ [英](骗取货物而不付钱的)滑头商号

firmament ['fə:məmənt] n. 天空,太空 ‖ **~al** [,fə:mə'mentl] a.

first [fə:st] **I** num. 第一(个):the ~ lesson 第一课 / the ~ round of competition (voting) 第一轮比赛(投票) / learn sth. (at) ~ hand from sb. 直接从某人处得知某事 **II** n. ①开始;开端:from the (very) ~ 从开始起 ②第一(等);[复](商品)一等品:These are all ~s. 这些都是一等品。③(比赛)冠军(考试)第一名(优,等生;分数)优等:take (或 get) a ~ 得第一名(或冠军) ④【音】(合唱或合奏的)高音部;领唱者;主奏的(弦)乐器 ⑤[...the F-](帝王称号)…一世 ⑥(特定时代或统治时期的)第一年 ⑦(月的)第一日:The ~ of May (或 May (the) ~) is International Labour Day. 五月一日是国际劳动节。**III** a. ①第一位的,首要的;第一流的:the ~ grade 头等 ②首先的,最初的,开始的:the ~ snow 初雪 / the ~ two (间或也用 the two ~)开头两个 ③基本的,概要的:the ~ principles 基本原理(或原则)④【音】高音(调)的;唱(或演奏)高音部的:the ~ violin 第一提琴手;弦乐四重奏的领奏者 **IV** ad. ①首先,最初:Friendship ~, competition second. 友谊第一,比赛第二。/ come in ~ (在赛跑等中)最先到达终点,得第一 ②第一次,首次:When did you ~ go to the countryside? 你是什么时候第一次下乡的? ③第一(列举条目等时用): First, ...; second, ... 第一点, ...; 第二点, ... ④宁愿 ‖*at* ~ 起先, 开始时候 / *at* ~ *sight* 见 sight /*at* (*the*) ~ *blush* 见 blush / ~ *and foremost* 首要地, 首先 / ~ *and last* 总的说来 / *First come*, ~ *served.* 先到先招待。/ ~, *midst*, *and last* 彻头彻尾, 始终, 一贯 / ~ *of all* 首先, 第一 / ~ *or last* 迟早, 早晚 / *from* ~ *to last* 自始至终, 一贯 / *in the* ~ *place* 见 place / (*the*) ~ *thing* 见 thing¹ ‖~*ly ad.* 第一, 首先(列举条目时用) ‖~ **aid** (对病人的)急救 / '~-**aid** *a.* 急救的: a ~-*aid* kit 急救药箱 / '~-**born** *a.* & *n.* 头生的(子女), 最长的(子女) / **First Cause** 造物主, 上帝 / '~-'**class** *a.* ①头等的, 第一流的: *~-class* cabins (carriages) 头等舱(车) ② 第一类的: ~-*class* mail 第一类邮件, (不受检查、邮资最贵的)密封邮件 ③[口]极好的 *ad.* ①乘头等车(或舱等): travel ~-*class* 乘头等车(或舱等)旅行 ②作为第一类邮件(或密封邮件) ③[口]极好 / '~ **coat** (油漆等的)底涂, 底层 / **First Commoner** (英国)下议院议员 / ~ **cost** (利息等未计入的)原始成本 / ~ **day** (一周的第一天)星期日 / '~-de,**gree** *a.* ①最低级的; 最轻度的,【医】第一度的: ~-*degree* burn 第一度灼伤 ②最高级的, 一级的;最严重的: ~-*degree* combat readiness 一级战备状态 / **First Empire** (法兰西)第一帝国 (1804—1815) / ~ **floor** ①[英]二(层)楼 ②[美]底层, 一楼(有时也指旅馆等的二楼) / ~ **form** [英](中等学校)一年级 / '~-**fruits** [复] *n.* ①(谷物、瓜果等)一个季节中最早的收获(常指用以供神的祭品) ②[喻](工作)最初的成果 / '~-'**hand** *a.* (来源、资料等)第一手的, 原始的;直接的: ~*hand* material (或 data) 第一手(原始)材料 / ~*hand* experience 直接经验, 切身体会 / ~*hand* investigation 直接调查, 实地考察 *ad.* 第一手地; 直接地: study a situation ~*hand* 直接研究情况 / **First International** 第一国际 (1864—1876) / ~ **lady, First Lady** 第一夫人, 总统夫人(或元首夫人等) ②(文化艺术界的)女领袖人物 / '~-'**line** *a* 【军】第一线的: ~-*line* aircraft (troops, ships) 第一线飞机(战斗部队, 舰只) ②头等的, 最重要的: ~-*line* industrial centres 最重要的工业中心 / ~ **name** 西方人名的第一个字, 教名(如 Anna Louis Strong 中的 Anna) / ~ **night** (戏剧、歌剧等)初次上演的夜场 / ~ **offender** 初次犯罪者, 初犯 / ~ **officer** 【海】大副 / ~ **papers** 要求加入某一国国籍的初步申请书 / ~ **person** ①[语]第一人称 ②用第一人称叙述的文体 / ~ **quarter** 【天】(月的)上弦 / '~-'**rate** *a.* 第一流的, 优秀的;[口]极好的: [口]很好: feel ~-*rate* 感到精神很好 / get on ~-*rate* 搞得很好;相处得很好 / ~-*rate* **reading** 议案交付审议时的正式初读 / **First Republic** (法兰西)第一共和国 (1792—1804) / '~-'**run** *a.*

[美](电影)初次放映的;(电影院)首先放映新片的, 头轮的 / '~-'**runner** *n.* 头轮 (电影院) / '~-'**strike** *a.* 先打击(或进攻)的, 先下手的: ~-*strike* capability 先发制人的能力 / '~-**string** *a.* 正式的(别于"代替的"而言);第一流的 / ~ **water** (钻石、珠宝)第一水, 头等(光泽最佳) ②[喻]第一流, 最优秀: music of the ~ *water* 第一流的音乐 ③[贬]极端: a fool of the ~ *water* 大傻瓜

firth [fə:θ] *n.* 河口湾, 港湾

fiscal ['fiskəl] I *a.* ①国库的; 国库岁入的 ②[美]财政的: a ~ year 财政年度, 会计年度 (=[英] financial year) II *n.* ①(苏格兰和欧洲某些国家的)检察官 ②印花税票 ‖~*ly ad.* 在国库方面, 在国库岁入方面;财政上 ‖~ **agent** 财务代理银行(或商行) / ~ **stamp** 印花税票 (=revenue stamp)

fish¹ [fiʃ] I ([复] fish(es)) *n.* ①鱼; 鱼肉: catch a lot of ~*es* 捕到许多种鱼 / stewed ~ 清燉鱼 ② [常用以构成复合词]水生动物: cuttle~ 墨鱼, 乌贼 ③[贬]家伙, 人: a queer ~ 怪人 / a poor ~ 可怜虫, 倒霉的家伙 ④[美俚]容易受骗的人, 笨蛋;生手;新囚犯 ⑤[美俚][谑]天主教徒 ⑥[美俚]美元 ⑦[美][军俚]鱼雷(也作 tin) ⑧ [the Fish(es)] 【天】双鱼宫 ⑨【海】吊锚器 II ❶ *vt.* ①捕, 钓(鱼等);采集(珊瑚); 在…中捕鱼: ~ a river 在河里捕鱼 ②捞取; 掏出; 摸索出: ~ up sunk ammunition 捞起沉在水底的军火 ③用吊锚器吊起(锚) ❷ *vi.* ①捕鱼;钓鱼: ~ in the sea 在海上捕鱼 / go ~*ing* 去钓(或捕)鱼 ②用钩等捞取;摸索寻找; 转弯抹角地引出; 间接探听: ~ *for information* 探听消息 ‖*All's ~ that comes to his net.* 凡是到手的他都要。(表示来者不拒) / *a loose* ~ (道德上)放荡不羁者 / *a (pretty) kettle of* ~ 见 kettle / *big* ~ *in a little pond* 矮子里头的长子 / *cry stinking* ~ 叫卖臭鱼; 暴露自己的缺点, 拆自己台 / *drink like a* ~ 大喝, 牛饮 / *feed the* ~*es* 葬身鱼腹; 晕船 / *Fish begins to stink at the head.* [谚]鱼要腐烂头先臭。(意指: 上梁不正下梁歪。) / *in troubled waters* 见 water / ~ *or cut bait* 要么全力以赴要么索性放弃 / ~ *out* ①捞出; 摸出;摸索出 ②把…中的鱼捕尽 / *have other* ~ *to fry* 另有他图; 另有更重要的事情要干 / *like a* ~ *out of water* 如鱼离水, 感到生疏, 不适应 / *neither* ~, *flesh, nor fowl* (或 *nor good red herring*) 非驴非马, 不伦不类 / *Never offer to teach* ~ *to swim.* [谚]不要班门弄斧。/ *The best* ~ *smell when they are three days old* [谚] 再好的鱼三天也要变臭。(意指: 久住招人嫌。) / *The best* ~ *swim* (或 *are*) *near the bottom.* [谚]好鱼居水底。(意指: 有价值的东西不能轻易得到。) / *There's as good* ~ *in the sea as ever came out of it.* [谚]海里的好鱼是取之不尽的。(指纵然失去一个机会还会

没有其他机会等) ‖'~-and-'chips [复] n. 油煎鱼加炸土豆 / ~ ball 炸鱼圆; 鱼饼 / '~bone n. 鱼骨 / ~ cake 鱼饼 / ~ culture 渔业; 养鱼法 / ~ farm 养鱼场 / '~-,farming n. 养鱼 / ~ fry ①炸鱼 ②吃炸鱼的野餐 ③鱼秧 / globe 金鱼缸 / ~ glue 鱼胶 / ~ hawk 鹗 / '~hook n. 鱼钩, 钓钩 / 有柄的椭圆形煮鱼锅 (用作肥料或饲料的)鱼粉 / '~,monger n. [主英]鱼贩子 / '~net n. ①鱼网 ②[军]伪装网 / ~ paper 青绿纸, 鱼膏纸 / '~-pond n. 养鱼塘; [谑]海 / ~ pot 鱼笼 / sound 鱼鳔 / ~ stick (涂面包粉的)炸鱼排 / story 不可靠的夸张故事, 吹牛 / ~ tail n. 鱼尾状的 vi. 摆尾飞行(指摇摆机尾使飞机减速着陆) / ~tail wind (扰乱步枪弹道的)不定风 / ~ torpedo 鱼雷 / '~wife, '~,woman n. ①卖鱼妇 ②骂街的泼妇 / '~works [复] n. [用作单或复]鱼类制品厂

ish² [fiʃ] I n. ①[建]接合板, 夹片, 鱼尾板; 悬鱼饰 ②[海]桅杆的加强夹箍 II vt. 用接合板连接(或加固) ‖~ joint 夹板接合 / ~plate n. 接合板

isher ['fiʃə] n. ①捕鱼人; 捞取者 ②捕鱼船 ③[复] fisher(s) 食鱼貂 ‖the great ~ of souls 撒旦, 魔鬼 ‖~man ['fiʃəmən] n. 捕鱼人; 捕鱼船

ishery ['fiʃəri] n. ①渔业, 水产业 ②渔场; 养鱼场 (兼指养鱼场的工人) ③(在一定水域内的)捕鱼权 ④(在一定水域内的)捕鱼术, 捕鱼术

ishing ['fiʃiŋ] n. ①钓鱼, 捕鱼 ②渔场 ③捕鱼权 ‖~ expedition ①审前盘问(或调查) ②(为诬陷人或搜集新闻材料而进行的)非法调查, 巧立名目、手段不当的调查 / ~ ground 渔场 / ~ line 钓丝 / ~ net 渔网 / ~ population 渔民 / ~ rod 钓竿 / ~ season 渔汛期 / ~ tackle 钓具

ishy ['fiʃi] a. ①鱼的; 多鱼的 ②(在味道等方面)象鱼的 ③(目光等)呆滞的, 无表情的; 冷冰冰的; 无光彩的: a ~ stare 两眼发呆的凝视 / a ~ handclasp 冷冰冰的握手 ④[俚]可疑的, 靠不住的: a ~ story 可疑的故事(或说法) / There's something ~ about it. 这里面有鬼。‖fishily ad. / fishiness n.

ission ['fiʃən] I n. ①分裂, 裂开 ②[生]分裂生殖 ③[原]裂变: nuclear ~ 核裂变 / a ~ bomb (裂变式)原子弹 / ~ products 裂变产物 II vt. & vi. [原](使)裂变

issure ['fiʃə] I n. ①裂缝, 裂隙 ②(思想、观点等的)分歧 ③[解](脑等的)裂纹, 沟 ④[医]裂伤: anal ~ 肛裂 II vt. & vi. (使)裂开

ist [fist] I n. ①拳(头): clench one's ~ 握拳 抓住, 抓牢: get one's ~ on sth. (sb.) 抓住某事物(某人) ③[口]手; 手迹, 笔迹: Give me your ~ 让我们握握手。/ write a good ~ 字写得好 ④[印]指标; 参见号(即 ☞) II vt. ①拳打 ②把(手)握成拳头 ③紧紧把住; [海]操纵(帆、桨等) ‖grease sb.'s ~ (或 grease the ~ of sb.) 向某人行贿 / make a good (poor) ~ at (或 of) 把…做得很成功(不成功) / the mailed ~ 暴

力; 武力威胁 ‖~ed a. 有拳头的; 握成拳头的 / ~ful n. ①一把: a ~ful of sand 一把沙子 ②相当大的数量

fit¹ [fit] I (fit(ted); fitting) ❶ vt. ①(使)适合; (使)符合; (使)配合: ~ one's deeds (或 actions) to one's words 言行一致 / Does the key ~ the lock? 这个钥匙能开这把锁吗? / ~ a stopper into a bottle 配瓶塞 ②使(服装等)合身, (服装等)合…的身: ~ the dress to the figure 量体裁衣 / This coat ~s you well. 你穿这件上衣很合身。③使适应: ~ one's thinking to the new conditions 使自己的思想适应新的情况 ④使合格; 使胜任; 训练: ~ oneself to a new task 使自己能担当新任务 ⑤耕(地) ⑥对…提供设备; 对…安装配备: ~ (up) a laboratory with the latest equipment 给实验室配备最新设备 ❷ vi. ①适合, 符合; 配合: The door ~s well. 这门好关。②(服装等)合身, 合式 ③适应 II (fitter, fittest) a. ①适合的, 恰当的; 正当的, 合理的: be ~ for the standard 合乎标准 / The dried grain is ~ to store (或 to be stored). 晒干的谷物可以贮藏。/ Do as you think (或 see) ~. 你认为怎么恰当就怎么办。②健康的, 健全的: keep ~ 保持健康 / feel ~ 感觉到身体很好 ③相称的; 合格的; 能胜任的: She is ~ for the job. 她能胜任这项工作。④[口][常用作状语]就要…, 几乎要…: laugh ~ to burst oneself 捧腹大笑 III n. ①[常用单, 前加不定冠词和形容词]适合; 合身(的衣服): This garment is a tight (good) ~. 这件衣服很贴(合)身。②[机]配合 ‖~ in with ... 适合, 符合; 适应: ~ in with the needs of the new society 适应新社会的需要 / like a glove 完全相合, 恰恰正好 / ~ on ①装上: ~ a handle on 装上把手 ②试穿: have a new shirt fitted on 试穿新衬衫 / ~ out 装备, 配备; 为(旅行等)作准备: ~ out a ship with necessary equipment for a voyage 为船只配备必需的设备准备出航 / ~ to be tied 十分恼火的 / ~ to kill 极度地; 大大地 / the survival of the fittest 见 survival ‖~ly ad. 适合地, 恰当地; 适时地 / ~ness n. ①适合, 恰当; 合理: the ~ness of things 事物的合情合理 ②健康: a ~ness test (军队等的)健康合格检查 / a ~ness campaign 增进健康的运动 / fitter n. ①裁剪和试样的服装工人 ②装配工, 钳工 ‖~-up n. [英] ①临时搭成的戏台; 可携带的舞台装置 ②携带活动舞台装置的小型流动剧团 (=~-up company)

fit² [fit] n. ①(病的)发作; 痉挛: ~s of coughing 一阵阵咳嗽 / fall (down) in a ~ 昏倒 ②(感情等的)突发: a ~ of fury 勃然大怒 / burst into a ~ of laughter 哈哈大笑起来 ‖beat sb. into (或 give sb.) ~s 轻易地打败某人 / by ~s (and starts) 一阵一阵地, 间歇地: We must never do anything by ~s and starts. 我们干任何工作都决不可冷忽热。/ give sb. a ~ [口]使某人大吃一惊; 使某人大发脾气 / have (或 throw) a

~[口]大发脾气; 大为烦恼 / *when the* ~ *is on sb.* (*for sth.*) 当某人(对某事)兴之所至的时候

fitting ['fitiŋ] I *a.* 适合的, 恰当的; 相称的 II *n.* ①试穿, 试衣: be ready for a ~ 准备试衣 ②[英](服装、鞋袜等的)尺寸, 尺码 ③装配; 修整: a ~ shop 装配车间; 装配厂 ④[常用复]装置, 设备; 器材; 家具: gas (electric light) ~s 煤气(电灯)装置 ⑤[常用复]【机】(接头)配件, 附件, 零件 ‖~**ly** *ad.* / ~**ness** *n.*

five [faiv] I *num.* 五; 五个(人或物); 第五(卷、章、页等)(用例参看 **eight**): a *Five*-Year Plan 五年计划 II *n.* ①五个(人或物)一组; ②[复] [口]五厘息金的证券 (= ~-percents) ③篮球队 ④[~s][用作单]一种类似手球的球戏 ⑤五岁 ⑥五点钟 ⑦五号的衣服(或鞋袜等) ‖*a bunch of* ~*s* 手; 拳头 ‖~**fold** *a.* & *ad.* 五倍; 五重 / ~**r** *n.* [英俚]票面为五镑的钞票; [美俚]票面为五元的钞票 ‖'~-**and**-'**dime** *n.* [美口] = ~-and-ten(-cent store) / '~-**and**-'**ten**(-**cent store**) [美]五分一角商店; 出售低价小商品的杂货商店 / '~-**case note** [美俚]票面为五元的钞票 / **Five Civilized Nations** 【史】北美克利克等五个印第安部落(其区域在今美国俄克拉何马州东部) / '~-,**finger** *n.* ①【植】委陵菜; 牛角花 ②【动】海盘车, 海星 ③[美俚]贼 *a.* 运用五个手指的: ~-*finger* exercises for the piano 弹钢琴五指练习 / ~ **hundred** 五百分牌戏; 任何一种以得五百分为胜局的游戏 / **Five Nations** 【史】(北美易洛魁印第安人几个部落组成的)易洛魁联盟 / '~-**ouncers** [复] *n.* [美俚]拳; 一拳 / '~**pence** *n.* 五便士 / '~,**penny** *a.* 五便士的 / ~ **senses** 五官感觉(指视、听、触、嗅、味五种感觉) / '~-**spot** *n.* 五点的纸牌; [美俚]票面为五元的钞票 / '~-**star** *a.* ①五颗星的: the *Five-Star* Red Flag 五星红旗 ②五星级(美国最高级军衔)的: a ~-*star* general 五星上将 ③第一流的

fix [fiks] I ❶ *vt.* ①使固定; 装置; 安装: ~ a lid on a box 在盒子上装盖子 / ~ a microphone in the hall 在大厅里安装扩音器 / ~ a big-character poster to the wall 把大字报张贴在墙上 / *Fix* bayonets!【军】(口令)上刺刀! / ~ one's wavering opinion 打定主意 ②用(眼睛等)盯住, 凝视; 倾注(感情等); 吸引(注意): ~ sb. with a stare 瞪眼看某人 / ~ one's attention *on* (或 *upon*) 集中注意力于… / The exhibited new machines ~ed our attention. 展出的新机器把我们吸引住了。③牢记: ~ the facts in one's mind 把事实牢牢记住 ④确定: ~ the date of an excavation (a linguistic change)确定出土文物(语言演变)的时代 / ~ a date for the meeting 确定会期 ⑤归(咎), 归(罪): Don't ~ all the blame on other people. 不要一切过失推给别人。⑥修理: ~ a watch (bicycle) 修表(自行车) ⑦整理: ~ one's bed (room) 整理床铺(房间) / ~ one's hair 梳头 ⑧安排; 准备(饭食等): ~ lunches for the children 给孩子们准备中饭 ⑨烧(火); 封(火) ⑩[口]向

…报仇; 惩罚, 收拾 ⑪[口]用不正当手段操纵(选举、陪审团等) ⑫【化】使凝固; 使不挥发: bacteria that ~ nitrogen 固氮菌 ⑬使(颜色)固着, 使(颜色)经久不褪; 【摄】定(影) ⑭阉割(家畜等) ⑮【生】(为显微镜检查等目的而)固定(机体、组织等) ❷ *vi.* ①固定 ②(目光等)注视 ③确定, 决定; 选定 (*on*, *upon*): ~ on the date for a march 确定行军日期 / ~ *upon* a person to do a certain work 选定担任一件工作的人 ④[美口]准备, 打算: I'm ~*ing* to go hunting. 我准备去打猎。⑤【化】凝固, 不挥发 II *n.* ①困境, 窘境: (be) in a ~ 陷入困境, 进退维谷 ②(船只、飞机等的)方位; 定位: radio (radar) ~ 无线电(雷达)定位 ③概略, 串谋; 受操纵的局面(如选举等) ④[俚]吸毒者的自我毒品注射 ‖~ *up* ①修补, 修理好 ②解决; 商妥: ~ *up* a dispute 解决争端 ③治愈(病人) ④ 安顿, 照应: We were ~*ed up* for the night in a hostel. 我们被安顿在招待所过夜。打扮

fixation [fik'seiʃən] *n.* ①固定; 【摄】(底片、相片等的)定影, 定象: ~ of tissues 【生】组织固定法 ②[心]注视; 固结; 固恋

fixed [fikst] *a.* ①固定的: a ~ deposit 定期存款 / the ~ par of exchange 汇兑的法定平价 / a ~ rate of exchange 固定汇率 / a ~ gun 【军】固定机枪 ②确定的; 不变的; 固执的: a ~ colo(u)r 不变的颜色 / a ~ stare 凝视的目光 / a ~ idea 固执的观念(或想法) ③ 不易挥发的: a ~ oil 固定油 ④[美口](在经济上)处境…的: be well ~ 生活宽裕 ⑤[美俚](比赛等)已通过作弊预先安排好结果的 ‖~**ly** ['fiksidli] *ad.* / ~**ness** ['fiksidnis] *n.* ‖~ **capital** 固定资本 / ~ **charge** 固定支出

fixing ['fiksiŋ] *n.* ①固定, 固着; 安装; 修理; 【摄】定影: a ~ agent 固定剂 / ~ solution 【摄】定影液 ②[美][复]设备; 装饰; (菜)的配料, 调味品

fixture ['fikstʃə] *n.* ①固定, 固定状态 ②固定物; [常用复](房屋内的)固定装置; (土地上的)附着物: the electric ~s of a room 室内电气装置 / bathroom ~s 浴室附属装置 ③运动项目(或庆祝活动)的预定举行日; 预定的运动项目(或庆祝活动) ④固定于某地(或某项工作)的人: He seems to be a ~ in the school. 他似乎固定在这个学校里工作。⑤【机】装置器; 工件夹具

fizz [fiz] I *vi.* ①嘶嘶地响 ②兴奋; 高兴 II *n.* ①嘶嘶声 ②活跃 ③起泡和发嘶嘶声的饮料(如香槟酒等)

fizzle ['fizl] I *vi.* ①嘶嘶地响 ②[口](在开始时有成功希望的计划等)终于失败 (*out*) II *n.* ①嘶嘶音 ②[口]失败

fjord [fjɔ:d] *n.* = fiord

flabbergast ['flæbəgɑ:st] *vt.* [口]使大吃一惊, 使目瞪口呆

flabby ['flæbi] *a.* ①(肌肉等)不结实的, 松弛的: muscles ~ from lack of physical labo(u)r 由于缺乏体力劳动而松软的肌肉 ②优柔寡断的, 软

软弱的: a ~ character 优柔寡断的性格(或人)
‖**flabbily** *ad.* / **flabbiness** *n.*

flaccid ['flæksid] *a.* ① (肌肉等)不结实的，松弛的
② 软弱的: a ~ opinion 软弱无力的意见 ‖**~ity**
[flæk'siditi] *n.* / **~ness** *n.*

flag[1] [flæg] I *n.* ①旗: the national ~ 国旗
②舰旗，旗子；旗舰 ③鹿尾；(猎狗等的)茸
尾 ④[复](猎鹰等的)腿上长羽；(鸟的)次级飞
羽 ‖*a black* ~ 黑旗(海盗旗或升在监狱外宣布执
行死刑的旗帜) / *a* ~ *of convenience*【海】方便
旗(指为与外国商船竞争而在外国登记取得的船
籍) / *a* ~ *of truce* 休战旗 / *a white* ~ 白
旗(表示投降、休战、求和) / *a yellow* ~ 黄旗(传
染病船旗、隔离病船旗或救护船旗) II (flagged;
flagging) *vt.* ①悬旗于…: ~ the streets for a
festival 在街道悬旗庆祝节日 ②打旗号表示;打
旗号(或用其他信号)使(火车等)停下 (down): ~
an order 打旗号传达命令 / ~ a train down 打
旗号(或举灯等)使火车停止 / He *flagged* me a
taxi. 他为我招呼来一辆出租汽车。‖*dip the*
~ 【海】降旗后旋即升起以示敬意 / *drop the*
~ 【体】发出竞赛开始(或结束)的信号 / *haul down*
one's ~ 投降 / *hoist a* ~ *half-mast high* 下
半旗致哀 / *hoist one's* ~ (舰队司令等)升旗开
始行使指挥权 / *lower* (或 *strike*) *the* (或
one's) ~ 降旗表示投降(或致敬);(舰队司令等)
降旗离开指挥岗位 ‖*~boat n.* (作水上比赛目标
的)旗艇 / ~ **captain** 旗舰舰长 / ~ **day** [英]
公益事业基金的募捐日，旗日(捐者得一小旗，故
名) / **Flag Day** [美]六月十四日(美国国旗制定
纪念日) / ~ **lieutenant** 海军将官的副官 / ~
list 海军将官名册 / ~**man** ['flægmən] *n.* 信号
兵; 信号旗手; (铁道等的)扳道工 / ~ **officer** (能
在舰上悬旗表示职位的)海军将官 / '~**pole** *n.*
旗杆 / ~ **rank** 海军将级军衔 / '~**ship** *n.* 旗
舰 / '~**staff** *n.* 旗杆 / ~ **station** (铁道上的)
旗站，信号停车站 / ~ **stop** [美](公共汽车、
火车等的)招呼站 / '~**wagger** *n.* [主澳]
=~waver / '~**waver** *n.* ①摇旗者 ②沙
文主义者 ③(某一政党、宗派的)摇旗呐喊
者 ④ 激起沙文主义情绪的东西(如歌曲等) /
'~**waving** *n.* 沙文主义情绪(或宗派意识)的
强烈表现(或扇动)

flag[2] [flæg] I *n.* ①(铺路用的)石板，扁石 ②[复]
石板路 II (flagged; flagging) *vt.* 用石板铺(路
等) ‖~**stone** *n.* (铺路用的)石板，扁石

flag[3] [flæg] *n.* ①【植】菖蒲; 鸢尾; 香蒲 ②菖蒲叶
(或花)

flag[4] [flæg] (flagged; flagging) *vi.* ①无力地下垂;
(草木等)萎垂 ②(力气、兴趣、热情等)衰退，减
退，低落 ③失去吸引力

flagon ['flægən] *n.* 酒壶; 大肚酒瓶

flagrant ['fleigrənt] *a.* 罪恶昭彰的; 臭名远扬的;
公然的: a ~ encroachment on another nation's
sovereignty 对于别国主权的公然侵犯 ‖~**ly** *ad.*

flail [fleil] I *n.* ①连枷 ②扫雷装置 II *vt. & vi.*

用连枷打(谷等); 鞭打; 抽打 ‖~ **tank** 扫雷
坦克

flair [fleə] *n.* 鉴别力，眼光; 资质: have a ~ for
对…有鉴别力; 有…的资质

flake[1] [fleik] I *n.* ①薄片: ~s of snow 雪片 /
wheat ~s 麦片 / fall in ~s 一片一片地落
下，纷纷落下 ②火星，火花 ③【动】肌隔 ④【植】
花瓣带条纹的石竹 II ❶ *vt.* ①使成薄片: ~ a
fish 切鱼片 ②象雪花般覆盖: Shavings ~c the
floor. 刨花撒满了地。❷ *vi.* ① 剥落 (away,
off): The paint has ~d. 油漆剥落了。②霏
霏落下;雪片似地降落: Petals ~d down in the
breeze. 花瓣随风纷纷落下。‖~ **white** 铅白，
碳酸铅白(绘画用白色颜料)

flake[2] [fleik] *n.* ①晒鱼(或其他食物)的架子 ②贮
藏食品的搁板 ③(修船等用的)舷侧踏板

flake[3] [fleik] *n. & vt.* =fake[2] ‖~ **out** [俚] ①入
睡 ②昏过去

flamboyant [flæm'bɔiənt] I *a.* ①【建】火焰式的:
~ architecture 火焰式建筑 ②火焰似的; 火红色
的 ③艳丽的: ~ in attire 穿着艳丽的服装 ④浮
夸的: ~ speech 浮夸的言语 II *n.* 火焰色的红花

flame [fleim] I *n.* ①火焰; 火舌 ②光辉，光芒
③热情; 激情 ④[谑]情人 II ❶ *vi.* ①发火焰，
燃烧: The fire ~d in the brazier. 火盆中升起
火舌。The bonfire ~d away all the evening.
整个晚上篝火都在燃烧。②强烈地,激情地)爆
发: He ~d with rage. 他勃然大怒。③闪耀;
发光: The sun's rays ~d in the window. 窗上
闪耀着阳光。/ eyes *flaming* furiously 冒着怒火
的眼 ❷ *vt.* ①用火焰(或烽火)传送: The message
was ~d by signal fires from one village to
another. 消息用烽火从一个村子传送到另一个村
子。②点燃; 激起 ③用火焰烧; 加热于: ~ the
lip of each culture tube 把每一培养管的翻口烧
一下(以灭菌) ④照亮; 使成火红色 ‖*commit*
sth. to the ~*s* 把某物烧掉 / ~ *forth* (或 *up*)
(激情)爆发: His anger ~d up at the sight. 见
此情景他勃然大怒。/ ~ *out* 突然冒火焰:
They poured oil on the fire and it ~d out. 他
们把油倒在火上，于是腾起熊熊烈火。/ ~ **bomb**
火焰炸弹 / '~**out** *n.* (喷气发动机)燃烧中断,熄
火 / ~ **projector** =~thrower / '~**thrower**
n. 喷火器 / ~ **tracer** 曳光弹

flaming ['fleimiŋ] *a.* ①燃烧的; 熊熊的; 灼热的
②火焰般的; 火红的, 烂漫的 ③热情的; 激情的
④夸张的: a ~ description 夸张的描写 ⑤惊人
的;荒诞的 ‖~ **onions** [俚](在空中爆炸时的)高
射炮弹(或球状曳光弹)的火光

flamingo [flə'miŋgou] ([复] flamingo(e)s) *n.* 【动】
火烈鸟(体形似鹤，趾间有蹼，有粉红色、深红色
和黑色羽毛的涉禽)

flange [flændʒ] I *n.* ①【机】凸缘，法兰(盘); 凸缘(制
造)机: ~ wheel 轮缘 / ~ of bush 衬套凸缘
②(铁路)轨底; 【建】(梁)翼缘 II *vt.* 给…装凸缘

flank [flæŋk] I *n.* ①胁; 胁腹 ②侧面; 【建】厢房:

the ～ of a hill 山的侧面 / ～ of thread【机】螺纹面 ③【军】翼侧,侧翼: the left (right) ～ 左(右)翼 / a ～ attack 翼侧攻击 / ～ fire 侧射,侧射火力 / a ～ movement 向翼侧运动 II ❶ vt. ① 位于…的侧面; 经过…的侧面 ② 掩护…的翼侧; 攻击…的翼侧 ❷ vi. 侧面与…相接 (on, upon): The fort ～ed on a swamp. 堡垒侧面靠着沼泽。‖by the left (right) ～ 向左(右)转的预令: By the left (right) ～, march! 向左(右)转走! / turn the ～ of ① 从翼侧包抄(敌军) ② 智取…; 驳倒…

flannel ['flænl] I n. ① 法兰绒; 绒布, 棉法兰绒 ② [复] 法兰绒衣服(如内衣、男子长裤等) ③ [英] (洗、擦用) 法兰绒布块: a face ～ 洗面用法兰绒布块 ④ 法兰绒的 III (flannelled; flannel(l)ing) vt. ① 用法兰绒包(或裹) ② 给…穿上法兰绒衣服 ③ 用法兰绒擦擦 ‖～ly a. ① 法兰绒似的 ② (声音) 透过法兰绒似地闷声的 ‖～board 法兰绒板(一种教学用具, 示教用的图例等经按压可粘附在其上面) / ～cake [美] 烤饼 / '～mouth n. [美] ① 花言巧语的人 ② 乡土音很重的人 / '～mouthed a. [美] ① 花言巧语的 ② 乡土音很重的

flannelet(te) [,flænl'et] n. 绒布, 棉法兰绒

flap [flæp] I (flapped; flapping) ❶ vt. ① 拍打, 拍击: ～ the flies away (或 off) 拍掉苍蝇 / The scarf flapped her face. 围巾拂着她的脸。② 使 (上下、前后地) 拍动, 摆动, 飘动(翅、翼): The wind flapped the sails. 风吹帆飘。/ an eagle flapping its wings 振翅飞行的鹰 ③ 拉下(帽)的边 ④ 扔, 掷: ～ a book down hastily 急忙把书扔下 ⑤ 唤起…注意, 鼓动 ❷ vi. ① 拍动, 摆动; 飘动 (鸟翼等) 振动, 扑动 ② 拍翅飞行 ③ (帽边等) 垂下 (down) ④ 讲蠢话; 乱吹 ⑤ [俚] 激动起来; 被搞糊涂 II n. ① 拍打, 拍动; (鸟的) 振翅 ② [口] 激动; 慌乱(状态): be in a ～ 在激动中(或慌作一团) / get into a ～ 激动(或慌乱) 起来 ③ 垂下物; (袋) 盖; (帽) 边; 信封口盖 ④ [空] 襟翼, 阻力板: landing ～ 着陆襟翼, 着陆阻力板 ⑤ [医] (切肢手术后遗下的或移植用的) 瓣, 片 ⑥【机】(整流罩、散热器等的) 风门片; 鱼鳞片; 瓣 ⑦ (折迭式桌子的) 折板, 铰链板 (活板门) 的活板 ⑧ (鱼鳃) 盖 ‖～door n. 吊门, 活板门 / '～eared a. (人) 有大耳朵的; (动物) 有垂耳的 / '～jack n. ① 煎饼; 烤饼 ② (化妆用) 粉盒 / '～seat n. 折椅

flare [flεə] I ❶ vi. ① (火焰) 闪耀; 突然烧起来; 闪亮; [喻] 突然发怒 (out, up): The fire ～d out brightly. 火光闪亮。② (衣裙等) 张开: His overcoat ～d behind him as he ran. 当他奔跑的时候, 他的大衣向后张开。③ 船舷外倾 ❷ vt. ① 使闪闪地燃烧, 使闪亮 ② 使 (衣裙等) 张开 ③ 使 (船侧) 外倾 II n. ① 摇曳的火焰; 闪耀, 闪烁: the sudden ～ of a flashlight in the darkness 手电筒在黑暗中的突然闪出亮光 ② (衣裙等的) 张开; (船) 【船】 (水线以上) 船侧外倾 ③ (声、激情、怒气

等的) 爆发: a ～ of trumpets 一阵喇叭声 / a ～ of temper 大发雷霆 ④ 招摇, 炫耀 ⑤ 照明弹; 照明灯: landing ～s 着落照明弹; 机场着陆照明灯火 ⑥【物】物镜反射光斑; 【摄】(底片的) 翳雾斑 ⑦ (太阳的) 耀斑, 色球爆发 ‖～back n. 火舌回闪; 炮尾焰 / ～ path (使飞机在夜间安全降陆和起飞的) 照明跑道 / ～ point 【化】 燃烧点, 着火点 / ～-up ['flεər'ʌp] n. ① 突然起燃 ② 怒气(或疾病) 的发作(或加剧) ③ 昙花一现式的出名 ④ 短时期的炫耀 ⑤ 喧笑, 欢闹

flash [flæʃ] I n. ① 闪光; 闪亮物: a ～ of lightning 闪电 / ～es of fireworks 烟火的闪光 ② (弹药等的) 突然燃烧; (信号旗的) 挥动: a muzzle ～ 枪口焰 (思想等的) 闪现: a ～ of hope 一线希望 ④ 刹那, 转瞬间: in a ～ 一刹那间 ⑤ (简短的) 电讯 ⑥ = ～back ⑦ (掺入酒中含焦糖的) 色料 ⑧ (为帮助行船而开闸) 灌注的水; 堰闸 【军】徽章, 肩章 ⑩ (服装、外表等的) 浮华, 虚饰; (人、行为等的) 浮夸, 华而不实 ⑪为人注目者 (尤指优秀运动员); 惹人注目的东西 ⑫ [总称] (盗贼等的) 黑话, 隐语 ⑬手电筒 【摄】闪光; 闪光灯下摄成的照片 II ❶ vt. ① 使闪光; 使 (火光) 闪烁; 闪烁着显出: ～ one's bayonet 闪晃一下亮出刺刀 / ～ sb. a meaning look 给某人使一个眼色 ② 反照, 反射 ③ (火速地) 发出(电讯、电报等); 使迅速传遍: ～ a danger signal 发出危险信号 / The good news was ～ed across (或 over) the country. 好消息闪电般传遍全国。④ 用水突然灌注(或灌满); 灌水使 (船) 浮过障碍 ⑤ [口] 亮出 (财物等) 炫耀 ⑥ 把 (玻璃) 制成薄片; 给 (玻璃) 镶色; 在…上覆以有色玻璃膜: ～ed glass 镶色玻璃 ⑦ (用防护物) 覆盖 (屋顶等) ❷ vi. ① (火焰等) 一闪, 闪现; (弹药等) 突然燃烧: Sickles ～ed in the sunlight. 镰刀在阳光中闪亮。/ A lighthouse was ～ing afar. 灯塔在远处闪光。② (眼光等) 闪耀; (思想等) 闪现; (感情等) 爆发: His eyes ～ with anger. 他眼中冒出怒火。/ An idea ～ed into (或 through) his mind. 他脑子里闪过一个念头。/ It ～ed upon me that ... 我忽然想到… ③ 反射, 反照 (back) ④ 飞驰, 掠过: A jet plane ～ed by (或 past). 一架喷气式飞机在空中掠过。/ ～ing fingers on a piano 在钢琴上来回轻捷跳动的手指 ⑤ (河水等) 冲泻, 泛滥, 暴涨 III a. ① 闪光的, 闪耀的; 一闪而过的 ② (服装、外表等) 浮华的; (人、行为等) 浮夸的, 华而不实的 ③ 盗贼的, 社会败类的 ④ (洪水等) 暴涨的 ⑤ 火速的: a ～ message 火急文电 ⑥ 带有闪光(照相) 设备的 ‖a ～ in the pan 昙花一现(的人) / ～ it away [俚] 炫耀, 招摇 ‖'～back n. (小说等的) 倒叙; (电影的) 闪回(指穿插倒叙往事的镜头) / ～ card n. 火速回闪 / '～board n. (坝正调节水位的) 闸板 / '～ bomb 闪光炸弹 / '～bulb n. 【摄】闪光灯(泡) / ～ burn (原子弹子弹等的) 闪光烧伤 / '～-'dry vt. 使风干(如放在上升的热空气气流中) / ～ flood 暴雨等造成的) 骤发洪水 / '～-'forward n. (小说、电影

等中的) 提前叙述未来事件 / **～ gun**【摄】(与闪光灯配合的) 闪光操纵装置; 闪光粉点燃器 / **～ lamp**【摄】闪光灯 / **'～light** *n.* (灯塔、机场等的)闪光信号灯 ②手电筒 ③【摄】闪光; 闪光灯; 闪光灯下摄成的照片 / **'～,over** *n.*【电】飞弧, 闪络, 跳火 / **～ point** ①【化】闪(燃)点 ②[喻](战争等的)爆发点 / **'～tube** *n.* 闪光管

flashing ['flæʃiŋ] *n.* ①闪光; 炫耀 ②(开坝闸)灌水(以利驶船); (河水等)暴涨 ③(防屋顶等漏水的)金属盖片, 防雨板 ④【化】急骤蒸发; 玻璃镶色

flashy ['flæʃi] *a.* ①闪光的, 闪烁的; 昙花一现的 ②浮华的; 华而不实的; 恶俗的: **～ clothes** 奇装异服 / **the gabblers who are ～ without substance** 华而不实的空谈家 ③(脾气等)暴烈的 ‖**flashily** *ad.* / **flashiness** *n.*

flask [flɑːsk] *n.* ①瓶, 长颈瓶;【化】烧瓶: **volumetric** (或 **measuring**) **～** 量筒瓶 ②(旅行者携带的)水瓶(或酒瓶) ③【机】(翻砂用)砂箱 ④(打猎者带在身边的)火药筒

flat[1] [flæt] **I** *a.* ①平的, 平坦的; 扁平的: **～ land** 平地 / **a ～ plateau** 平坦的高原 / **a ～ nose** 扁鼻子 / **a ～ peach** 蟠桃 / **a ～ tyre** 瘪了的车胎 ②平伸的, 平展的: **crops ～ after a storm** 暴风雨后倒伏的庄稼 ③浅的: **a ～ pan (dish, plate)** 浅锅(碟、盘) ④【军】(弹道等)低平的: **a ～ arrow** 平射的箭 / **～ fire** 平射 ⑤断然的, 干脆的; 直截了当的: **a ～ refusal (denial)** 断然拒绝(否认) / **That's ～!** [口]绝对如此! (或: 断无二话!) / **a ～ lie** 弥天大谎 ⑥(人物、生活、精神状态等)无聊的; 单调的; 不起伏的 ⑦(谈吐等)走了气(或味)的: **The beer tastes ～.** 啤酒走气了。/ **a ～ drink** 淡而无味的饮料 ⑧(市场等)萧条的, 不景气的; (价格等)无涨落的, 一律的: **a ～ rate** 统售价格; 统一收费率 ⑨[美口]一贫如洗的, 不名一文的 ⑩(图画等)平板的, 无景深的; (颜色等)单调的, 不鲜明的 ⑪【摄】无深浅反差的; (灯光安排)无明暗的, 轮廓不清楚的 ⑫【音】降音的; 降半音的: **D ～** 比 D 调低半音的音调 ⑫【语】(元音)平舌的(如 [ɑ] 等); (辅音)浊音的, 带声的 ⑬【海】(风帆)绷紧的 **II** *ad.* ①平直地, 仰卧地: **fall ～ on the floor** 直挺挺地倒在地板上 ②断然地, 干脆地, 直截了当地: **Tell him ～ that . . . .** 直截了当地告诉他… ③恰恰, 正好: **He ran the 100-metre dash in 10 seconds ～.** 他一百米跑十秒正。④【音】以降调 ⑤无(利)息地: **a loan given ～ to sb.** 给某人的无息贷款 **III** *n.* ①平面, 平坦部分: **the ～ of the hand** 手掌 ②平地; 低洼沼泽地; 沙洲, 浅滩 ③扁平物; 平底船; 平板车; 浅苗床; 平面布景片; 漏气车胎 ④[复]平底(拖)鞋 ⑤[俚]傻子, 愚人 ⑤【音】降半音; 降号: **sharps and ～s** 升半音和降半音; 钢琴上的黑键 **IV** (flatted; flatting) *vt. & vi.* ①(使)变平 ②(使)降半音 ‖**fall ～** 见 **fail** / **～ out** 竭尽全力, 用全速 ②疲惫的 / **join the ～s** 使成为连贯的一体; 装出始终如一的样子 ‖**～ly** *ad.* 断然, 毅然, 直截了当地: **refuse ～ly** 断然拒绝 / **～ness** *n.*

～ways, ～wise *ad.* 平面向下; 平面与另一物接触着 ‖**'～boat** *n.* (浅水)平底船 / **'～car** *n.* (铁路)无顶平板货车, 平板车 / **～ file** 扁锉 / **'～fish** *n.* 比目鱼 / **～ foot** *n.* ①[复]扁脚; 平脚; 有平脚缺陷的人 ②([复])～foots) [美俚]穿制服的巡警 / **'～-'footed** *a.* ①平脚的; 拖着脚步走的 ②脚跟站稳的 ③果断的 ④无准备的: **catch sb. ～-footed** 乘其不备抓住某人 *ad.* 直截了当地, 决意地 / **'～-'hat** *vi.* 不顾死活地低飞 / **'～head** *n.* ①[F-]北美印第安人 ②[美俚]傻瓜, 易受骗者 ③(铆钉等的)扁平头 / **'～iron** *n.* 熨斗 / **～ race** (无障碍物的)平地赛跑 / **'～-'roofed** *a.* (建筑物等)平顶的 / **～ silver** [总称]银制刀、叉、匙等餐具(别于银制盘、碟等) / **～ spin** ①(飞机的)水平螺旋 ②[美俚]精神错乱 / **'～top** *n.* ①平顶建筑物 ②[美俚]航空母舰 / **'～ware** *n.* [总称]扁平餐具(尤指刀、叉、匙等) / **'～worm** *n.* 扁平无环节的寄生虫(如肝蛭、绦虫等); 扁虫

flat[2] [flæt] *n.* ①(楼房的)一层 ②[主英](在同一层楼上的)一套房间(通常指包括起坐室、卧室、浴室、厨房等的公寓房间) ③[常用复]公寓 ④[船]平台(甲板) ‖**～let** ['flætlit] *n.* [英]只有一个房间而附有浴室、厨房的套间

flatten ['flætn] **❶** *vt.* ①把…弄平: **～ crumpled paper** 把皱拢的纸弄平 ②击倒; 使倒伏: **～ one's opponent** 击倒对手 / **crops ～ed by a storm** 被暴风雨吹倒的庄稼 ③使(漆等)失去光泽 **❷** *vi.* ①变成(更)平 ②倒伏 / **～ out** ①展平; (经延压等)变平 ②【空】(俯冲或爬高后)拉平(飞机); 转为水平飞行 ‖**～er** *n.* 【冶】压延工; 压延机 ‖**～ing oven**【化】平板(玻璃)炉

flatter[1] ['flætə] *vt.* ①谄媚, 阿谀, 奉承 ②使高兴, 使满意: **The music ～ed his ears.** 这音乐使他听得很满意。/ **I feel greatly ～ed by your invitation.** 承蒙邀请, 不胜荣幸。/ **Oh, you ～ me.** 啊, 过奖了。③(画、肖像等上的形象)胜过(真人或实物): **His portrait ～s him.** 他的肖像比本人漂亮。‖**～ oneself** 自以为: **He ～ed himself that he would win.** 他自以为必胜。

flatter[2] ['flætə] *n.* ①【机】平面锤; 扁条拉模 ②敲平者

flatulence ['flætjuləns], **flatulency** ['flætjulənsi] *n.* ①【医】肠胃气胀 ②空虚; 浮夸; 自负

flaunt [flɔːnt] **I** **❶** *vi.* ①(旗等炫耀地)飘扬, 招展 ②招摇 **❷** *vt.* ①(炫耀地)挥动, 夸耀, 夸示 ②[美]藐视 **II** *n.* ①(旗等的)飘扬, 招展 ②招摇, 夸耀, 夸示

flavo(u)r ['fleivə] **I** *n.* ①味: **Condiments impart ～ to food.** 调味品使食品有味道。/ **a pungent bitter ～** 一股辛辣味 ②风味, 风韵, 情味: **a local ～** 地方风味 / **the acrid ～ of an essay** 文章的泼辣风格 ③[古]气味, 香味 **II** *vt.* ①给…调味, 加味于: **～ the soup with onions** 在汤里加洋葱调味 ②给…增添风趣 ‖**～less** *a.* 无味的; 无风趣的, 乏味的

flavo(u)ring ['fleivəriŋ] *n.* 调味品, 调味香料:

There is too much ～ in the dish. 这只菜调味品加得太多了。 / Some ～s have little food value. 有些调味品很少营养价值。

flaw¹ [flɔ:] **I** *n.* ①裂隙，裂缝 ②缺点；瑕疵 ③(使证件、程序等无效的)缺陷 **II** ❶ *vt.* ①使破裂 ②使有缺陷；使无效 ❷ *vi.* ①生裂缝 ②变得有缺陷

flaw² [flɔ:] *n.* 一阵狂风；短暂的风暴

flawless ['flɔ:lis] *a.* 无裂隙的；无缺点的；无瑕的 ‖～**ly** *ad.* /

flax [flæks] *n.* ①【植】亚麻 ②亚麻纤维；亚麻布 ③象亚麻的植物 ‖*quench smoking* ～ 使有希望的事情中途夭折 ‖～ **brake, ～ breaker** 剥麻机，亚麻碎茎机 / '～**seed** *n.* 亚麻籽，亚麻仁

flaxen ['flæksən] *a.* ①亚麻的；亚麻制的 ②(头发)亚麻色的，淡黄色的

flay [flei] *vt.* ①剥…的皮：～ an ox 剥牛皮 ②掠夺…的东西，抢劫…的财物 ③严厉批评；痛责 ‖～**er** *n.* 剥皮者；抢劫者；痛责者 ‖'～**flint** *n.* [古]吝啬鬼；敲诈者

flea [fli:] *n.* ①蚤；蚤目的昆虫: a sand (water) ～ 沙(水)蚤 ②(伤害植物叶和芽的)叶甲科的甲虫(=～ beetle) ‖*a ～ in one's (或 the) ear* 刺耳话，尖刻的责难，讥讽；send sb. away with *a ～ in his ear* 用讥诮话气走某人 / *skin a ～ for its hide* 爱财如命，非常贪小 ‖'～**bag** *n.* ①床；睡(眠)袋(=sleeping bag) ②低廉的旅馆 ③生蚤的动物 ④邋遢的老妇人 / ～ **beetle** 叶甲科的甲虫 / '～**-borne** *a.* 蚤传播的 / ～ **market** 欧洲街道上的廉价品和旧货市场 / '～**-pit** *n.* [俚]被认为有跳蚤(或臭虫等)的公共场所(如电影院等) / '～**wort** *n.*【植】①亚麻籽车前 ②旋复花(用作驱蚤剂)

fleck [flek] **I** *n.* ①(皮肤的)斑点，雀斑 ②(色、光的)斑点: ～s of colour on a bird's breast 鸟胸部的色斑 / ～s of sunlight on the ground under a tree 树荫下的斑驳日光 ③微粒；小片: a ～ of dust 微粒尘土 / a ～ of snow 微小的雪片 **II** *vt.* 使有斑点；使斑驳: a sky ～ed with clouds 有着点点云朵的天空 ‖～**er** *vt.* 使有斑点；使斑驳 / ～**less** *a.* 无斑点的；无缺点的

fled [fled] flee 的过去式和过去分词

fledge [fledʒ] ❶ *vi.* 长飞羽；(幼虫)长翅(变为成虫) ❷ *vt.* ①喂养(小鸟)到羽毛丰盛 ②用羽毛盖；在…上装羽毛: ～ an arrow 在箭上装羽毛 ‖～**d** *a.* 羽毛已长成的 / ～**less** *a.* 羽毛未丰的

flee [fli:] (fled [fled]) ❶ *vi.* ①逃，逃走 ②消失；消散: Mists *fled* before the rising sun. 日出雾散。 ❷ *vt.* 逃离；逃避

fleece [fli:s] **I** *n.* ①羊毛(尤指未剪得的全部羊毛 ②羊身上一次剪得的全部羊毛 ③羊毛状物(如白云、白雪、头发等) ④【纺】绒头织物；长毛大衣呢；粗梳回丝 **II** *vt.* ①剪下(羊)的毛 ②诈取: ～ sb. *of* his money 诈取某人的钱 ③(羊毛般)盖满，点缀: a sky ～d with white clouds 白云朵朵的天空 ‖～**d** *a.*【纺】(针织物)布面起绒的

fleet¹ [fli:t] *n.* ①舰队(尤指有固定活动地区的舰队)；[the ～] 海军: a ～ fighter 海军战斗机 / an admiral of the ～ (英)海军元帅 ②(统一指挥下或同属某行业、单位的)船队；机群: 汽车队: a whaling ～ 捕鲸队 / a ～ of trucks (taxis) 一队卡车(出租汽车) / a ～ of the desert 沙漠旅行队，商队 / an aerial ～【军】大机群 / a ～ of clouds overhead 空中成堆的云朵 ③ [英]成一排的捕鱼网(具)；有一百只钩子的钓索 ‖～ **admiral** (美)海军五星上将 / ～ **air arm** [总称]海军航空兵部队

fleet² [fli:t] *n.* [英]①小河，河浜；小海湾 ② [the F-] (伦敦)弗利特河(流入泰晤士河，现已成阴沟)；弗利特河畔的债案犯监狱 ‖**Fleet marriage** 在弗利特河一带由声名极坏的教士主持的秘密结婚 / **Fleet Street** (伦敦)舰队街(以报馆集中著称，这街名是从河名来的，跟"舰队"实在没有关系)；伦敦报业，伦敦新闻界

fleet³ [fli:t] **I** ❶ *vi.* ①疾飞；掠过: planes ～*ing* across the sky 掠过天空的飞机 ②飞逝，消逝 ③【海】(船员)变换位置 ❷ *vt.* ①消磨(时间) ②【海】变换(船员)的位置: ～ aft the crew 把船员调到船尾 ③放下(绞盘的索、缆等) **II** *a.* ①快速的；敏捷的: ～ of foot 捷足的，走路快的 ②转瞬即逝的 ‖～**ly** *ad.* / ～**ness** *n.* ‖～**-'foot(ed)** *a.* 走路快的，快腿的

fleet⁴ [fli:t] [方] **I** *a.* 浅的: a ～ soil 浅土，薄土 **II** *ad.* 浅，不深地: plough (sow) ～ 浅耕(种)

fleeting ['fli:tiŋ] *a.* 疾驰的；飞逝的，短暂的: a ～ target【军】瞬间目标

flesh [fleʃ] *n.* ①肉(指人或脊椎动物身体的肌肉组织) ②(供食用的)兽肉(与鱼、禽的肉相区别) ③果肉(指水果、蔬菜的可食部分) ④肉体(与灵魂、精神相对而言) ⑤人性；情欲 ⑥亲骨肉；亲属[主要用于短语 one's (own) ～ and blood ⑦人类 ⑧众生(指一切生物) ⑨人体；肌肤: sun-tanned ～ 太阳晒黑的皮肤 ⑩有色肉 **II** ❶ *vt.* ①以肉喂(猎犬等) ②用猎物的血肉训练(鹰、犬等)，使(鹰、犬等)闻惯猎物味 ③把(刀剑等)刺入肉体；用(笔等)伤人 ④赋…以血肉 ⑤使肥，使长肉(up) ⑥(制革时)从(兽皮)上去肉 ⑦[古]使满足 ❷ *vi.* [口]长肉，发胖(up, out) ‖*after the ～* 世俗地；粗鄙地 / *a pound of ～* 见 pound¹ / *a thorn in sb.'s ～* 见 thorn (become) one ～ (成为)一体；(结为)夫妇 / ～ *and blood* ①肉体；人性；情欲 ②人类 ③ [常用作定语]现实；现世 / ～ *and fell* ①全身 ②完全地 / *gain* (或 *put on*) ～ 长肉发胖 / *go the way of all* ～ 见 way / *in the* ～ 以肉体形式 ②活着的 ③亲自，本人 / *lose* ～ 消瘦，变瘦 / *make sb.'s* ～ *creep* (神奇恐怖的事等)使某人战栗 / *neither fish, ～, nor fowl* (或 *nor good red herring*) 非驴非马，不伦不类 / *one's* (*own*) ～ *and blood* 亲骨肉；亲属 / *pick up* ～ 病愈长胖 / *proud* ～【医】(创口长出的)浮肉 / *th* *arm of* ~ 人力, 人的努力 ‖**~less** *a.* ①瘦弱的 ②无肉体的; 非物质形体的 ‖**'~-and-'blood** *a.* 血肉般的 / **'~-,colo(u)red** *a.* 肉色的 / **'~-,eating** *a.* 食肉的 / **'~-fly**【动】麻蝇 / **peddler** [美俚](戏院的)经理人 / **~pots** [复] *n.* ①奢侈的生活 ②寻欢作乐的场所 / **~side** 兽皮贴肉的一面 / ~ **tights** (杂技演员等穿的)肉色紧身衣 / ~ **wound** 皮肉之伤, 轻伤

fleshy ['fleʃi] *a.* ①多肉的, 肥胖的 ②肉的, 似肉的 ③【植】肉质的: ~ fruit 肉果

flew [flu:] fly¹ 的过去式

flex [fleks] I **①** *vt.* ①屈曲(四肢): He stretched and ~ed his knees. 他伸屈膝关节。②折曲(地层等) **②** *vi.* 屈曲; 折曲 II *n.* ①屈曲; 折曲 ②[主英]【电】花线, 皮线

flexible ['fleksəbl] *a.* ①柔韧的, 易弯曲的; 挠性的: ~ cord【电】花线, 皮线 / ~ coupling【机】弹性联轴节; 活动耦合 ②柔顺的: a ~ character 柔顺的性格 ③可变通的, 灵活的: ~ strategy and tactics 灵活机动的战略战术 ‖**flexibility** [,fleksə'biliti] *n.* 挠性, 揉曲性, 柔(韧)性; 机动性, 灵活性 / **flexibly** *ad.*

flick [flik] I **①** *n.* ①(用鞭)轻打; (用指)轻弹; (用布、手帕)轻拂: test the glass with the ~ of a finger 用手指轻弹来试验玻璃(的质量) ②(击球时手腕等的)急速、突然的动作, 抽动 ③轻弹声, (鞭等的)轻击声: the busy ~ and chatter of typewriter keys 打字机键不住的轻快敲击声 ④(溅到泥等的)污点, 斑点 ⑤[俚]电影: the ~s 电影院; 电影的放映; [总称]电影 ⑥【军】照见瞬间(指探照灯照见空中飞机的瞬间), 照见(指探照灯照见空中飞机) 【军】(口令)集中照射 II **①** *vt.* ①(用鞭等急速地)轻打, 轻拍: ~ a horse with a whip 用鞭在马身上轻轻一抽 ②(用指等轻轻)弹去, 拂去 (*away, off, from*): He ~ed the ashes *from* his cigar. 他弹去雪茄烟烟灰。/ ~ the dust *from* a desk with a handkerchief 用手帕轻轻拂去桌上的灰尘 ③急速地轻抽(鞭子); 轻弹: ~ a whip at a horse 用鞭轻抽马匹 / He ~ed the knife open. 他(用手腕)轻轻一振亮出刀刃。**②** *vi.* ①(急速地)轻击, 轻弹, 轻拂 (*at*) ②(翅)拍动; (旗)飘扬 ‖**'~-knife** *n.* 一种轻振手腕刀刃即可从柄中伸出的小刀(常用作武器)

flicker ['flikə] I **①** *vi.* ①(鸟)扑动翅膀 ②闪烁; 摇曳; 忽隐忽现: The candle ~ed in the wind. 蜡烛在风中闪烁不定。/ shadows ~ing on the wall 墙上摇曳不定的影子 ③[美俚]昏倒; 假装昏倒 **②** *vt.* 使摇曳; 使闪烁不定; 使忽隐忽现 II *n.* ①扑动; 闪烁; 摇曳; 忽隐忽现: a ~ of hope 一线希望的闪现 ②[美俚]假装昏倒的乞丐 ③[常用复][美俚]电影 ④[~s][美俚][用作单或复]电影制片业 ‖**~y** ['flikəri] *a.*

flickering ['flikəriŋ] *a.* 扑动的; 闪烁的; 摇曳的; 忽隐忽现的: ~ leaves 颤动着的树叶 / the tongue of a snake 一伸一吐的蛇舌 ‖**~ly** *ad.*

flier ['flaiə] *n.* = flyer

flight¹ [flait] I *n.* ①飞翔, 飞行: a bird *in* ~ 飞行中的鸟儿 / take a ~ (或 take one's ~, wing one's ~) 飞行 / the ~ of a spaceship 宇宙飞船的飞行 ②飞翔的一群; 飞行的一队; (箭等的)齐发, 连发: a ~ of sparrows 一群飞雀 / a ~ of arrows (rockets) 齐发的箭(火箭) ③飞机的航程; (有特定航线的)定期客机, 班机; 搭机旅行: a long-distance (round-the-world) ~ 长距离(环球)飞行 ④(鸟的)能飞的距离; 射程, 经路; (射箭等的)射远比赛 ⑤空军小队; (四架以上飞机的)飞行编队 ⑥楼梯(或阶梯)的一段; (赛跑等用的)一组跨栏: climb four ~s of stairs 走四段楼梯 / My room is two ~s up. 我的房间要上两段楼梯。⑦(鹰、隼对猎物的)追逐; (候鸟等的)迁徙: the autumn ~s of swallows to the south 燕子的秋天南飞 ⑧(时间的)飞逝; (才智、想象力等的)焕发, 奔放: a ~ of fancy 奇想, 异想天开 ‖**aerial** ~ 空中飞行 / *air patrol* ~ 空中巡逻飞行 / *a circular* (或 *circuitous*) ~ 圆圈飞行 / *cosmic* (或 *space*) ~ 宇宙飞行 / *a horizontal* (或 *level*) ~ 水平飞行 / *an inverted* ~ 倒飞 / *a reconnaissance* (或 *recon*) ~ 侦察飞行 / *a soaring* ~ 滑翔飞行 II **①** *vi.* (鸟等)成群飞行; (候鸟)迁徙 **②** *vt.* 射击(飞禽)/ 使(鸟)惊起 ‖*in the first* (或 *highest*) ~ 占主要地位; 领先 ‖~ **chart** 航空地图 / ~ **control** ① 飞行控制, 飞行指挥 ② (地面的)飞行控制站 / ~ **course** 航线 / ~ **crew** [总称]飞行人员 / ~ **deck** ① (航空母舰上的)飞行甲板 ②驾驶舱 / ~ **engineer** 机上机械员 / ~ **feather** (鸟翼的)拨风羽 / ~ **formation** 空军小队; (泛指)飞行编队 / ~ **indicator** 陀螺地平仪 / ~ **lieutenant** (英)空军上尉 / ~ **line** ①飞行路线 ②机场保养工作地区 / ~ **log** 飞行记录簿 / ~ **map** 航空照相用地图 / ~ **nurse** 机上护士 / ~ **path** (飞机、导弹等的)飞行经路, 航迹 / ~ **pay** 飞行津贴 / ~ **personnel** [总称]飞行人员 / ~ **recorder** 飞行自动记录仪 / ~ **refuel(l)ing** 空中加油 / ~ **route** 飞行路线 / ~ **sergeant** (英)空军上士 / ~ **shooting** 射远比赛 / ~ **simulator** (地面上训练飞行人员用的)飞行摹拟装置 / ~ **skins** =~ pay / ~ **status** 飞行资格 / ~ **strip** 简易机场, 着陆场 / **'~-test** 航空军医 / '~-test *vt.* 试飞(飞机) / ~ **time** 飞行时间

flight² [flait] *n.* ①逃跑, 溃退: seek safety *in* ~ 溜之大吉 ②(资金等的)抽逃; 外逃: ~ of capital (或 capital ~) 资本的抽逃

flighty ['flaiti] *a.* ①忽发奇想的 ②反复无常的; 轻浮的 ③(马等)易惊的 ④痴呆的, 有些疯癫的 ‖**flightily** *ad.* / **flightiness** *n.*

flimsy ['flimzi] I *a.* ①轻而薄的; 脆弱的; 易损坏的 ②没价值的; 不足信的: a ~ excuse 站不住脚的借口 ③(人)浮夸的 II *n.* ①薄纸(尤指复写用的) ②(新闻社提供的)薄纸稿件; 新闻电稿的薄纸副本 ③电报 ④[英俚]钞票 ‖**flimsily** *ad.* / **flimsiness** *n.*

flinch [flintʃ] **I** *vi.* 退缩; 畏缩 (*from*) **II** *n.* 退缩; 畏缩

fling [fliŋ] **I** (flung [flʌŋ]) ❶ *vt.* ①(用力地)扔, 抛, 掷, 丢: The storm *flung* the ship *upon* the rocks. 暴风雨把船抛到岩石上。/ ～ *off* one's pursuers 甩掉(或避开)追踪者 / ～ *aside* all cares 丢开一切忧虑(或顾虑) ②使突然陷入; 把…粗暴推入: ～ sb. *into* prison 把某人关进监狱 ③ [～ oneself] (蓦地)投入; (突然)跳入: The little girl *flung herself into* her mother's arms. 小女孩一头栽进母亲的怀里。④急伸, 挥动(手臂): ～ one's arms about 左右上下猛挥双臂 ⑤扫视; 用(眼光)扫视: ～ sb. an angry look (或 ～ an angry look upon sb.) 怒冲冲地看某人一眼 ⑥(猛烈地)推(门、窗等): ～ a door *open* (*to*) 砰地打开(关上)门 ⑦(匆忙地)披上(衣服): ～ one's coat *on* 匆匆披上上衣 ⑧急派(军队等) ⑨发出(声音、气味、怒骂等): ～ *off* a merry tune 哼出愉快的调子 / The sun ～*s* bright rays *on* the fields. 灿烂的阳光普照田野。/ ～ a sharp reply 尖锐地回答 ⑩ (在摔角中)打翻(对手); 使(骑者)摔倒 (*off*) ❷ *vi.* ①猛冲, 直冲; 急行: ～ *out of* (*into*) a room 突然奔出(冲进)房间 / ～ *away* (或 *off*) in a rage 怒气冲冲地跑掉 ② (马等)乱踢 (*out*) ③ 破口大骂 ④[苏格兰]跳来跳去 **II** *n.* ① 扔, 抛, 掷 ② 讽刺, 嘲弄; 攻击 ③ [口](随意的)尝试 ④(一时的)放肆, 放纵 ⑤ 奔放的舞蹈: the Highland ～ 苏格兰高地流行的一种奔放的舞蹈 ‖***at one*** ～ 一举, 一鼓作气地 / ～ ***caution to the winds*** 见 **caution** / ～ ***sth. in sb.'s teeth*** 见 **tooth** / ～ . . . ***to the winds*** 见 **wind**[1] / ***have*** (或 ***take***) ***a*** ～ ***at*** ①试做(某事) ②嘲弄(某人) / ***have one's*** ～ 恣意行乐 / (***in***) ***full*** ～ 莽撞地

flint [flint] *n.* ① 燧石, 打火石; (打火机用的)电石 ② 坚硬物: a heart of ～ 硬心肠 / set one's face like a ～ 打定主意, 决不变更 ‖***fix sb.'s*** ～ ***for him*** 惩罚某人 / ***flay a*** ～ 贪得无厌 / ***skin a*** ～ 一钱如命 / ***wring*** (或 ***get***) ***water from a*** ～ 见 **water** ‖～ **glass** 燧石玻璃 / '～**lock** *n.* 燧发机; 燧发枪 / '～**stone** *n.* 燧石, 打火石

flip [flip] **I** (flipped; flipping) ❶ *vt.* ① 把…往上一抛使在空中翻转; 掷: ～ (up) a coin 往上抛硬币(按其落下时的正反面作出抉择) ② 用指轻弹; 轻击: ～ the dust from one's boots 弹去靴上的尘土 ③(用鞭等)抽打; 急速地挥(扇、鞭等); 急拉(鱼饵) ④翻(纸牌等) ⑤[美俚]跳上(驰行着的车辆) ❷ *vi.* ①用指轻弹; (用鞭等)抽打 (*at*): ～ *at* an ass with a whip 用鞭抽驴 ② 一蹦一蹦地跳跃; (用鳍状肢)啪嗒啪嗒地走动: He saw a seal *flipping* over the rocks. 他见一只海豹在岩石上啪嗒啪嗒走动。③翻动书页(或纸张) ④[美俚]起强烈(或热烈)的反应 (*over*) **II** *n.* ①抛; 弹; 轻击; 抽打 ② 筋斗(尤指在空中的) ③(足球)短距离快速传球 ④加有香料(有时还加牛奶和鸡蛋)的热甜啤酒(或苹果酒等饮料) ⑤[美俚](飞机的)一次飞行 **III** (flipper, flippest) *a.* [美俚]无礼的; 冒失的; 轻率的 ‖'～**-flap** *n.* ① 啪嗒啪嗒的响声(或动作) ② 向后翻的筋斗 ③ 一种爆竹, 一种烟火 ④(游乐场所内平面旋转着的横档端部装有游者坐椅的) 旋转器 / '～**-flop** *n.* ① 啪嗒啪嗒的响声(或动作) ②向后翻的筋斗 ③突然转向反方向; (观点、态度等的)突然改变 ④【电】双稳态多谐振荡器, 触发器; 触发电路 *vi.* ①啪嗒啪嗒地动 ② 向后翻筋斗 ③ 突然转向反方向; (在观点、态度等方面)突然改变 / ～ **side** [美口]唱片的反面(常录有较不出名的乐曲)

flippant ['flipənt] *a.* ①[古]能说会道的 ②无礼的, 轻率的: a ～ answer (remark) 无礼的回答(话) ‖～**ly** *ad.*

flirt [flə:t] **I** ❶ *vt.* ① 倏地扔掉; 用指弹掉 ② 摆动, 挥动(尾巴、折扇等) ❷ *vi.* ① 摇摇晃晃地移动, 飘动 ②调情, 卖俏 (*with*) ③不认真地考虑(或对待)(*with*) **II** *n.* ①急扔; 急掸; (尾巴等的)摆动 ②调情者, 卖俏者 ‖～**ation** [flə:'teiʃən] *n.* 调情 / ～**atious** [flə:'teiʃəs] *a.* 轻佻的, 爱调情的

flit [flit] **I** (flitted; flitting) *vi.* ① 掠过; 迅速飞过: The clouds *flitted* across the sky. 云朵掠过天空。② 迁移; 离开 ③ (鸟、蝙蝠等)飞来飞去 (*about*) **II** *n.* ① 掠过; 飞来飞去 ② 迁移

float [flout] **I** ❶ *vi.* ① 漂浮, 浮动; 飘动: Rafts ～*ed* down the river. 木筏顺流而下。② (计划等)付诸实行 ③(票据等)在流通中 ④(谣言等)在传播中 (*about*) ⑤ 摇摆, 动摇 (*between*) ⑥【经】(货币)浮动 ❷ *vt.* ① 使漂浮; (水面、水域等)容纳; 承受; 载: ～ timber down a stream 使木材顺流漂浮而下 / There is enough water in the harbour to ～ a fleet. 海港里的水域足够容纳一个舰队。② 用水注满; 淹没 ③ 发行(公债、债券等); 筹(款): ～ bonds (securities) 发行债券(证券) / ～ a loan (用发行债券等方式)募集贷款 ④ (通过发行债券等方式)筹资开办(公司、商号等) ⑤实行(计划等); 赢得对…的支持: ～ a scheme 赢得支持而将计划付诸实行 ⑥ (用镘刀)抹平(水泥、灰泥等): a ～*ed* surface 镘平面 ⑦(在水中)研磨, 浮选(颜料) ⑧ [俚](为减轻社会压力)迫使(流浪汉等)外流 ⑨【经】使(货币)浮动 **II** *n.* ① 漂浮 ② 漂浮物, 浮游物; 木筏; 浮标; (动植物的)浮囊; 浮冰; 浮萍; (钓鱼用的)浮子; 水箱浮球; 救生圈; 【机】浮体: ball ～ 球状浮体 ③浮筒; 浮码头; 浮坞; (水车的)蹼板, 承水板 ④(游行时用的)彩车; 装载展品模型的车辆; 活动模型: colo(u)rful ～*s* with industrial and agricultural exhibits 装载工农业展品的彩车 ⑤ (泥水工用的)镘刀; 单纹锉刀 ⑥(流通在市面上应收而未收的)商业票据 ⑦(向政府报领得来的)土地许可证 ⑧[常用复](舞台的)脚灯 ⑨【纺】(织物上的)浮纱, 织疵, 跳花 ⑩ 上面浮有冰淇淋的饮料 ⑪【经】浮动: a joint currency ～ 货币共同浮动 ‖'～**board** *n.* (水车的)蹼板, 承水板; (轮船等的)轮翼 / ～ **bridge** 浮桥; (铁路轮渡的)固定浮坞 / ～ **finish**【建】镘修整; 浮镘出面 / ～ **grass**

水草 / '**~plane** *n.* 水上飞机,浮筒飞机 / '**~- stone** *n.* 浮石,轻石;(泥水工用来磨光砖石等的)磨石 / **valve** 浮阀

floatation [flou'teiʃən] *n.* ①漂浮;(船的)下水: the centre of ~ 浮体重心 / a ~ balance 浮力秤 ②(企业等的)筹资开办,创立;(为创立企业的)筹款 ③【矿】浮选(法): ~ oil 浮选油 / oil ~ 浮油选矿

floating ['floutiŋ] *a.* ①漂浮的;(货币等)浮动的;浮置的: a ~ body 浮体 / 【机】浮动刀具 / ~ algae 【植】浮游藻类 ②流动的,不固定的: the ~ population 流动人口 / ~ capital 游资,流动资本 / a ~ debt 流动债务,短期债务 / the ~ vote 流动票(指不依附于某一政党的人们所投的总票数) ③【医】浮动的,游离的;不在正常位置的: ~ kidney 浮游肾 【船】在水运中的,未到的;在海上的: ~ cargo 路货 / ~ aero- drome 航空母舰 / ~ anchor 浮锚,海锚 / ~ axle 浮轴 / ~ battery ①浮动蓄电池;浮置(或浮充)电池组 ②(设于船或筏上的)流动炮台 / ~ bridge 浮桥 / ~ crane 水上起重机 / ~ dock 浮坞 / ~ island ①蛋白浇蛋的蛋糕 ②漂浮在水面上的大片植物 ③(墨西哥城等处在湖中的筏上铺土建成的)浮动花园 (=~ garden) / ~ light 桅顶灯(如搁浅船只发出的危险信号);灯船;浮标灯 / ~ policy 总保(险)单 / ~ rate 【经】浮动汇率 / ~ rib 浮动肋骨

flock¹ [flɔk] **I** *n.* ①(飞禽、牲畜等的)群;羊群 ②(某一人管理或领导下的)群,同属一个牧师管辖的全体教徒;一家的子女: a teacher and his ~ 教师和他的学生 ③ 大量,众多: People came in ~s to see the new dam. 人们成群结队地来参观新建的水坝。 **II** *vi.* 聚集,群集;成群结伙去(或来): ~ around sb. 聚集在某人周围 / ~ to the square 成群结队地走向广场 ‖*fire into the wrong* 打错目标,失误 / *~s and herds* 羊和牛 ‖'**,master** *n.* (尤指羊群的)牧主;牧群管理人

flock² [flɔk] **I** *n.* ①毛束;棉束 ②(填塞被、椅等用的)毛屑;棉屑 ③(供植绒用的)细绒 ④絮状沉淀 **II** *vt.* ①用毛(或棉)屑填塞 ②为…植绒 ‖~ing 植绒花纹 ‖~ bed 毛(或棉)屑垫子的床

floe [flou] *n.* 大片浮冰;浮冰块

flog [flɔg] (flogged; flogging) *vt.* ①(用鞭、棍等)鞭打,鞭挞,抽打: ~ a horse along 鞭马前进 ②驱使;迫使: ~ oneself into a rage 使自己的脾气发作起来 / ~ ... into sb. 把…强行灌输给某人 ③严厉批评 ④[俚]打败,胜过 ⑤[英俚]出售(尤指非法地) ‖**flogging** *n.* 鞭打

flood [flʌd] **I** *n.* ①洪水;水灾: battle against the mountain ~ 与山洪搏斗 / a ~ diversion area 分洪区 / a ~ detention dam 拦洪坝 ②(因雨)涨潮,涨水;潮水最高点: The river was in ~. 河水泛滥。 / The tide is nearly at the ~. 潮水几乎已涨到最高点了。 ③[诗]水: go through fire

and ~ 赴汤蹈火 ④(流出或发出的)一大阵,一大批,大量;滔滔不绝: What a ~ of rain! 好一阵大雨! / a ~ of light 一片强光 / a ~ of words 滔滔不绝的一席话 ⑤[口]泛光灯 (=~ light) **II** ❶ *vt.* ①淹没;使泛滥: Heavy rainfalls ~ed the lowlands. 大雨淹没了低地。 / transform ~ed areas into fertile land 把洪泛区改造成良田 / irrigate by ~ing the fields 用引水盖没农田 / rivers ~ed by rainstorms 因大雨而泛滥的河流 ②涌到,涌进;充满,充斥: a room ~ed with sunlight 充满阳光的房间 / Warmth ~ed my heart. 我心里热呼呼的。 ❷ *vi.* ①为水所淹;溢出;(潮水)涨: Wine ~ed from the glass. 酒从杯中溢出。 ②(大量地)涌进;涌出,喷出;充斥: Letters of congratulation ~ed in. 大批祝贺信潮水般地涌来。 / A troop of harvesters are ~ing into the fields. 大队收割人员涌到田间。 ③【医】患子宫出血 ‖*at the ~* 在方便而有利的时机 / *the Flood* (或 *Noah's Flood*) 【宗】(基督教《圣经》中所说的)大洪水 ‖'**~gate** *n.* ①(河流、运河的)水闸,水闸门;防洪闸门 ②(怒气等的)制约: open the ~gate of wrath 大发雷霆 ③大量: a ~gate of facts 大量事实 / '**~light** *n.* 泛光灯;泛光照明,强力照明 *vt.* 泛光照明;用泛光灯照明 / '**~mark** *n.* 高潮线 / '**~plain** *n.* 涝原,泛滥平原,漫滩 / ~ tide ①涨潮 (ebb tide "落潮" 之对) ②高峰;巨量 / '**~water** *n.* 洪水 / '**~way** *n.* 分洪河道 / '**~wood** *n.* [美]漂流木,浮木

flooding ['flʌdiŋ] *n.* ①泛滥;灌溉 ②【化】溢流;(分馏时的)液阻现象;(油漆干燥时或加热时的)变色 ③【医】血崩

floor [flɔː] **I** *n.* ①(房间、门廊等的)地面;地板: a wood ~ 木地板 / sweep the ~ 扫地 / a moulding ~ 翻砂车间 ②(室内场)地: a competi- tion ~ 竞技场 ③(船的)肋舱 ④(海洋、山洞等的)底 ⑤(楼房的)层(常略作fl.): the ground ~ [英]底层,一楼(相当于美国说法 the first ~) / the first (second) ~ [英]二(三)楼;[美]一(二)楼 / the top ~ 顶楼 / On which ~ do you live? 你住在几楼? [注意: 说建筑物共有若干层时不用 floor,而用 storey; 如 a five-storeyed building 五层楼的房子] ⑥(物价、工资等的)最低额: establish ~s 规定底价 ⑦(议会的)议员席;(证券交易所等的)经纪人席 ⑧(在会上的)发言权: have (get 或 obtain) the ~ 有(取得)发言权 / take the ~ 发言(尤指在辩论中发言) / The chairman gave him the ~. 主席允许他发言。 **II** *vt.* ①在…上铺设地板(或基面) / a bridge with concrete plates 用水泥板铺桥面 ②把…打翻在地;击败;克服: ~ sb. with one blow 一拳把某人打翻在地 / ~ the paper (或 ~ an examination paper) 把试卷上的问题全部解答掉 ③[口]难倒: This mathematical problem ~ed him. 这道数学题目把他难住了。 ④[美口]把(汽车的加速器等)压到底 ‖*get in on the*

ground ~ 以享有与发起人同样优先权的资格
入股; 取得有利地位 / **mop** (或 **wipe**) **the ~
with sb.** [俚]击倒某人, 把某人打得大败
‖**~less** a. 无地板的 ‖**~board** n. ①[总称]
适合做地板用的木料 ②一块地板(常指可掀起的
活动地板) ③汽车底部板 / **~ broker** (交易所
内代客买卖的)场内经纪人 / '**~cloth** n. ①铺
地板厚漆布 ②揩地板布 / **~ knob** (装在地板上
的)门碰头 / **~ lamp** (放在地板上可移动的)落地
灯, 落地灯 / **~ leader** (资产阶级议会中的)党
派头目 / **~ plan** [建]楼面布置图 / **~ show** 夜
总会的节目表演 / **~ slab** (铺设水泥楼面、地面
的)水泥板 / **~ trader** (交易所内自行买卖自负
盈亏的)场内商人 / '**~,walker** n. ①[美](百货商
店的)巡视员,招待员 / **~ wax** 地板蜡

flop [flɒp] I (flopped; flopping) ❶ vi. ①扑拍; 跳
动; 脚步沉重地走: The fish were still *flopping*
about on the bank. 鱼还在岸上扑扑地跳动着。
②猛然躺下(或坐下、跪下等): ~ into an armchair 蓦地坐在扶手椅中 ③[美俚]上床: It's time
to ~. 该上床了。④(行径等)突然转变 ⑤(作
品、戏剧等)彻底失败, 不受欢迎 ❷ vt. 噗地一声
放下; 啪啪地翻动: He *flopped* down the bag and
ran to help us. 他噗地一声放下袋子, 赶来帮助
我们。/ ~ the pages of a book 啪啪作响地翻书
页 II n. ①拍击(声); 重坠(声) ②(书、戏剧
等)大失败 ③[美俚]睡觉的地方; 睡一夜,
过夜 III a. 噗地一声; 恰巧 / '**~house** n. 廉价
住所;低级旅馆/'**~,over** n.电视图象的上下跳动

flora ['flɔːrə] ([复] floras 或 florae ['flɔːriː]) n. ①
植物群 (尤指某一地区或某一时期的植物群, 与
fauna 动物群相对): the ~ and fauna of Africa
非洲的动植物 ②[植]植物区系 ③植物志

floral ['flɔːrəl] a. ①植物群的; 植物区系的 ②花的;
象花的: ~ designs 花卉图案 ③[F-] 花神的
‖**~ly** ad. ‖**~ leaf** [植]花叶; 苞片

florid ['flɒrid] a. ①(文体等)绚丽的, 华丽的 ②炫
耀的 ③红润的,血色好的 ④[罕]用花装饰的;象
花一样的 ‖**~ity** [flɔ'riditi] n. / **~ly** ad. /
~ness n.

florist ['flɒrist] n. ①花商 ②种花者 ③花卉研究者

floss [flɒs] n. ①(蚕茧外的)乱丝,绪丝 ②绣花丝
线 ③细场线 ④絮状物;木棉: candy ~ 棉花糖
⑤[植]绒毛;(玉米的)黍须 ⑥[冶](浮于熔化金
属表面的)浮渣 ‖**~ silk** 乱丝,绪丝;绣花丝线

flotilla [flou'tilə] n. ①小舰队 ②[美](海军)纵队
(下辖二个以上中队) ③船队

flotsam ['flɒtsəm] n. ①(遇难船只的)飘浮的残骸
(或其货物)(区别于 jetsam) ②[总称]流离失所
者, 流浪者 ③[总称]零碎物 ‖**~ and jetsam**
①(飘浮于水面或冲到岸上的)船只残骸(或其货
物) ②[总称]流离失所者, 流浪者; 被毁掉的人
③[总称]零碎物,无价值的东西

flounce[1] [flauns] I n. (衣裙上的)荷叶边 II vt. 镶
荷叶边在…上 ‖**flouncing** n. ①做荷叶边的料子
②荷叶边

flounce[2] [flauns] I vi. ①跳动;暴跳 ②肢体乱动,
挣扎: The horse ~d on the slippery ice. 马在滑
溜的冰上挣扎。③毅然离开;猝然离开(out, off)
II n. 跳动, 骤动: He moved with a ~ to open
the door. 他跳起身来去开门。

flounder[1] ['flaundə] I vi. ①(站不稳时)挣扎, 肢体
乱动; 跟跄 ②错乱地做事(或说话): ~ through
a song 错误百出地唱完一只歌 II n. 挣扎; 跟跄
前进

flounder[2] ['flaundə] n. [动]比目鱼, 鲽形目的鱼
(尤指鲽、鲆)

flour ['flauə] I n. ①面粉;(任何谷类磨成的)粉 ②
粉状物质 II vt. ①撒粉于… ②把…做成粉
③使碎成粉 ‖**~y** ['flauəri] a. 面粉的;粉状
的;撒满粉的

flourish ['flʌriʃ] I ❶ vi. ①茂盛; 繁荣; 兴旺
②(作家、哲学家等)处于活跃状态, 处于旺盛时
期: The painter ~ed around 1250. 那画家于一
二五〇年左右处于全盛时期。③手舞足蹈 ④奏
华丽的乐段; 响亮地吹奏喇叭 ⑤用华丽的词藻;
(写字时)加花饰 ❷ vt. ①挥舞: ~ a sword 挥舞
剑 ②盛饰;炫耀,夸耀 II n. ①茂盛; 繁华; 兴旺:
in full ~ 在全盛期 ②华丽的词藻 ③(手写花式
字上的)花饰 ④挥舞 ⑤装饰性乐段; 响亮的喇叭
吹奏 ⑥戏剧性动作 / a ~ of trumpets (重要事
情开始前的)大肆宣扬 / with a ~ of trumpets
自吹自擂地, 耀武扬威地 ‖**~ing** a. 茂盛的, 欣
欣向荣的, 蒸蒸日上的

flout [flaut] I ❶ vt. 蔑视, 轻视; 嘲笑: ~ sb.'
advice 轻视某人的劝告 ❷ vi. 表示轻蔑(at) II n.
①表示轻蔑的言行;侮辱 ②嘲笑

flow [flou] I ❶ vi. ①(河水等)流动; (潮)涨:
Rivers ~ into the sea. 江河流入海中。/ *Flowing*
water does not get stale. 流水不腐。/ Time ~s
away. 光阴流逝。②涌出: The river ~ed over
its banks. 河水泛滥。③来自, 是…的结果
④川流不息: Trucks and cars ~ed along the
highway. 卡车和汽车在公路上川流不息。⑤(谈
话、文体等)流畅: a ~ing speech 滔滔不绝的讲
话 / The lines in this painting ~. 这幅画的线条
很流畅。⑥(衣服、头发等)飘垂,飘拂; (旗)飘扬:
⑦(国家等)富有; (酒等)斟满: with one's heart
~ing with gratitude 内心充满感激地 ⑧[医]月
经来, 行经(尤指过多) ❷ vt. ①溢过, 淹没 ②
[古]使流动 II n. ①流动;流动物: a steady ~
of news of victories 频传的捷报 / the ~ of goods
between town and country 城乡物资交流 / soil
~ [地]流砂 ②流量, 流速, 流率: the volume of
~ 流量 / the total ~ 总流量 / a good ~ of milk
充足的出奶量 / a ~ of 500 litres a second 每秒
五百升的流率 ③涌出, 洋溢;(资源、供应等)的丰
富: a ~ of spirits 精神焕发, 喜气洋洋 / a ~ of
distant melodies 远处荡漾的音乐声 ④(潮)涨;
泛滥 (尤指尼罗河的周期泛滥): The tide is on
the ~. 涨潮了。⑤(人、车等的)川流不息; (谈
话等的)流畅: a ~ of traffic 车辆行人等的来往

不绝 / a ~ of eloquence 口才流利 ⑥ (衣服、头发等的) 飘垂 ⑦【医】月经 (=menstrual ~) ‖*a land ~ing with milk and honey* [古] 富饶的地方，鱼米之乡 / *ebb and ~* 见 **ebb** / *the ~ of soul* 融洽的交谈，推心置腹 ‖~ **chart** 流程图，作业图；生产过程图解 / '~**,meter** *n.* 流量表；流量计；流速计 / ~ **sheet** =~ **chart** (尤指用于冶金和化学工业的)

flower ['flauə] *n.* ① 花；开花植物；花卉: The ~s are out. 花开了。花开了。② 精华: the ~ of the country's youth 国家的优秀青年们 ③ 开花；盛时: The roses are in ~. 玫瑰正在开花。/ in the ~ of one's age (或 life) 年轻力壮时期 ④ [复]【化】华: ~s of sulphur 硫华 Ⅱ ❶ *vi.* ① 开花 ② 发育，成熟；繁荣 ❷ *vt.* 使开花；用花 (或花纹) 装饰 ② *vt.* of speech 华丽的词藻 (常含讽刺意味) ‖~**ed** *a.* ① 开花的，有花的 ② 用花 (或花纹) 装饰的 / ~**less** *a.* 无花的 / ~**like** *a.* 象花似的 ‖~ **child** [美] 鼓吹爱情与和平的嬉皮士 / ~ **girl** ① 卖花女 ② 在新娘前撒花的女孩 / ~ **piece** 花卉画；花朵装饰 / '~**pot** *n.* 花盆 / ~ **show** 花展 / ~ **stalk** 花柄

flowing ['flouiŋ] *a.* ① 流动的 ② (文章等) 流畅的，通顺的; (线条、轮廓等) 平滑的 ‖~**ly** *ad.*

flown [floun] **fly**¹ 的过去分词

flu [flu:] *n.* [口]【医】流行性感冒 (=influenza)

fluctuate ['flʌktjueit] ❶ *vi.* ① 波动，涨落. 起伏 ② 动摇，不定 ❷ *vt.* 使波动，使起伏 ‖**fluctuation** [,flʌktju'eiʃən] *n.*

flue¹ [flu:] *n.* ① 烟道；暖气管: ~-cured tobacco 烤烟 ② (管风琴的) 唇管；唇管口 ③ [俚] (当铺中用来传送抵押品至收藏处的) 滑槽，斜槽 ‖*in* (或 *up, upon) the* ~ ① 当掉了，进当铺了 ② 死了; (身体或精神上) 垮掉了 ‖~ **pipe** (管风琴的) 唇管

flue² [flu:] *n.* 蓬松的东西

flue³ [flu:] *n.* 渔网 (尤指拖网)

fluency ['flu(:)ənsi] *n.* 流利，流畅: speak with ~ 说话流利

fluent ['flu(:)ənt] *a.* ① 流利的，流畅的: a ~ speaker 说话流利的演说家 / speak ~ English 讲流利的英语 ② (河水等) 畅流的; a ~ metal in a crucible 坩埚中的液态金属 ‖~**ly** *ad.*

fluff [flʌf] Ⅰ *n.* ① (织物上的) 绒毛，蓬松毛; (唇和颊上的) 汗毛 ② 蓬松物 (如一团头发、尘团等) ③ 无价值的东西; 没有内容的趣剧 ④ 失误，错误; 念错台词 ⑤ [俚] 年轻妇女: a bit of ~ 一个年轻妇女 Ⅱ ❶ *vi.* ① 起毛; 变松 ② 出错; (演员) 忘记台词，念错台词 ❷ *vt.* ① 使起毛; 抖松 (羽毛等) ② 把…搞糟 ③ 念错 (台词)，忘记 (台词)

fluffy ['flʌfi] *a.* ① 绒毛状的; 有绒毛的，蓬松的: a ~ cotton boll 蓬松的棉桃 ② 轻软酥松的: a ~ omelette 松软的炒蛋 ③ 愚昧的，蠢的 ‖**fluffiness** *n.*

fluid ['flu(:)id] Ⅰ *a.* ① 流动的; 流体的; 液体的: ~ mechanics 流体力学 / a ~ analogue computer 射

流模拟计算机 ② 不固定的; 易变的: ~ battle lines 非固定作战线 ③ ~ population of large cities 大城市中的流动人口 ③ 可另派用处的; 易转化现金的: ~ capital 流动资本 / ~ assets 流动资产 ④ 流畅的· a ~ style 流畅的文体 Ⅱ *n.* 流体 (液体与气体的总称); 液: cooling ~ 冷却液 / body ~s 体液 ‖~**ic** [flu(:)'idik] *a.* 流体性的 / ~**ity** [flu(:)'iditi] *n.* 流动性; 流度 / ~**ly** *ad.* / ~**ness** *n.* ‖~ **dram**, ~ **drachm** 液量打兰 (= 1/8 ~ounce) / ~ **drive** 【机】液压传动 / '~**'extract** *n.* 【药】流浸膏剂 / '~**'ounce** *n.* 液量咖，液量盎司[美] =1/16 品脱，合 29.6 毫升; [英] =1/20 品脱，合 28.4 毫升)

fluke¹ [flu:k] Ⅰ *n.* ① (台球) 侥幸的击中 ② 侥幸，侥幸成功; 倒霉，意外挫折: The failure was a ~. 那失败是偶然的。Ⅱ ❶ *vt.* 侥幸获得，侥幸做成 ❷ *vi.* 侥幸成功; 意外受挫 ‖**fluk(e)y** *a.* ① 凭运气的 ② 变化无常的 (尤指风)

flummox ['flʌməks] Ⅰ *vt.* [俚] 使惶惑，使慌乱; 打乱 Ⅱ *n.* 失败

flung [flʌŋ] **fling** 的过去式和过去分词

flunk(e)y ['flʌŋki] *n.* ① [贬] (穿号衣的) 仆从; 奴才; 走狗 ② 奉承者，势利小人 ‖**flunkyism** *n.* 奴才相，奴才主义

fluorescent [fluə'resnt] *a.* 荧光的; 发荧光的: a ~ lamp 荧光灯，日光灯 / a ~ screen 荧光屏

flurry ['flʌri] Ⅰ *n.* ① 阵风，疾风 ② 小雪; 小雨 ③ 慌张，仓皇: in a ~ 慌慌张张 ④ (股票市场短暂的) 波动 Ⅱ ❶ *vt.* 使激动; 使慌张: in a *flurried* manner 慌慌张张地 ❷ *vi.* 激动; 慌张

flush¹ [flʌʃ] Ⅰ ❶ *vi.* ① 奔流，涌: The tide ~ed through the narrow inlet. 潮水涌过小海。② (脸) 发红; (人) 脸红: His face ~ed (red) with anger. 他气得满脸通红。/ She ~ed (up) to the roots of her hair. 她的脸红到脖子根了。③ 突然发红，发亮: The aurora ~ed into the sky. 曙光映红天空。④ (植物) 绽出新芽 ❷ *vt.* ① (用水) 冲洗: ~ the toilet (the drains) 冲洗厕所(阴沟) ② 使注满; 淹没: The river ~ed the meadow. 河水淹没了草地。③ 使 (脸等) 涨红; 使脸上发红: ~ sb.'s cheeks with shame 使某人羞愧得两颊通红 / be ~ed with exercise 因体育锻炼而脸上发红 ④ 使兴奋; 使激动; 使得意: ~ed with success 因成功而满脸喜色 ⑤ 使(植物) 绽出新芽: The rain ~ed the plants. 雨后植物绽出新芽。⑥ 用特殊方法喂 (羊) 以备繁殖 Ⅱ *n.* ① 奔流; 涌: a great ~ of water 水的奔泻 ② 冲洗: Give the pot a ~. 把壶冲洗一下。③ 水车排出的水 ④ 萌发，茂盛; 活力: the first ~ of spring 春天草木的初次茂盛 / in the ~ of youth 在精力旺盛的青春时期 ⑤ 兴奋; 激动; 得意: a ~ of joy (anger) 一阵喜悦(愤怒) ⑥ 红光; 红晕: in the first ~ of dawn 在曙光初照时 / the healthy ~ of a child's face 小孩健康的红润脸色 ⑦ 发烧，升火 ‖~ **toilet** 有抽水设备的厕所; 抽水马桶

flush² [flʌʃ] Ⅰ *a.* ① 注满的; 泛滥的: The streams

are ~ *with* the spring runoff. 溪涧涨满春水。
②大量的; 富裕的; (金钱)充足的: be ~ *of* (或
with) money 很有钱, 很富裕 ③挥霍的: be ~
with one's money 挥霍钱财 ④齐平的, 贴合成一
个平面的; 紧接的; 【印】左边每行排齐的, 没有缩
排的: The river is ~ *with* its banks. 河水齐岸。/
The door is ~ *with* the casing. 门与门框齐平无
缝。⑤ 直接的: a blow ~ in the face 正中脸部
的一击 ⑥生气勃勃的; 血色红润的 **II** *ad.* ①齐平
地; 贴合无缝地: a line set ~ 切边(或与其他行)排
齐的一行 / a book cut ~ 切齐的书 ② 直接地:
He went ~ from school into agricultural production. 他从学校毕业后就参加农业生产。**III** *vt.*
使齐平; 嵌平: The mason ~ed the joint with
mortar. 泥工用灰浆把接缝处嵌平。‖~ **deck**
【船】平甲板 / **~,decker** *n.* 【船】平甲板船

flush³ [flʌʃ] **I** ❶ *vi.* ①(鸟等)惊起, 惊飞 ②(人)赶
鸟 ❷ *vt.* 使(鸟等)惊飞 **II** *n.* ①一下子飞起的鸟
群 ②赶鸟

flush⁴ [flʌʃ] *n.* (纸牌戏中)一手同花的五张牌: a
royal ~ 以 A 打头的同花顺次五张牌(最强的一
手牌) / a straight ~ 同花顺次的五张牌(次强的
一手牌)

fluster ['flʌstə] **I** ❶ *vt.* ①使醉醺醺 ②使慌张; 使
激动 ❷ *vi.* 慌慌张张地行动 **II** *n.* 慌张; 激动:
all in a ~ 惊慌失措

flute [flu:t] **I** *n.* ①【音】长笛; (管风琴的)长笛音
栓: play the ~ 吹长笛 ②笛形物(如细长形面包
卷等) ③(柱子等)凹槽; 凹槽形 【纺】【机】沟槽 ④
【机】(刀具的)出屑槽: spiral ~ 螺槽 / straight
~ 直槽 **II** ❶ *vi.* 吹长笛 ②发出长笛般的声音
❷ *vt.* ①用长笛奏(乐曲); 用长笛般的声音唱(或
说) ②在…上做出凹槽(或沟槽) ‖**~d** *a.* ①(声
音)长笛般的 ②有凹槽(或沟槽)的 / **~like** *a.*
象长笛的 / **~r** *n.* ①[古]吹长笛的人 ②做
凹槽(或沟槽)的人; 做凹槽(或沟槽)的器具 /
fluting *n.* ①有沟槽的衣料; 凹槽装饰 ②凹槽;
沟槽 ③做出凹槽(或沟槽) ④吹长笛; 发长笛音 /
flutist *n.* 吹长笛的人

flutter ['flʌtə] **I** ❶ *vi.* ① (鸟)振翼, 拍翅 ②(旗帜
等)飘动, 飘扬 ③ 颤动; (脉搏、心脏)不规则
跳动; 心绪不宁; 发抖 ④焦急地乱动, 坐立不
安: ~ about the room nervously 焦急地在屋
里走来走去 ❷ *vt.* ①振(翼), 拍(翅): The bird
~ed its wings. 鸟拍翅。②使焦急, 使不安 **II** *n.*
①振翼; 飘动, 飘扬 ②不安, 焦急; (情绪、市场等
的)波动: put sb. in a ~ 使某人焦急不安 ③(身
体部分的)病态阵跳 ④电视图象的颤动; 【无】放
音失真 ⑤ 颤振: aileron ~ 【空】副翼颤振 ⑥
[英俚]小赌; 投机

flux [flʌks] **I** *n.* ①流, 流出; 流动 ②涨潮: ~ and
reflux 涨潮落潮; [喻]不断消长 ③ 不断的变动;
波动: be in (a state of) ~ 处于不断的变化中;
动荡不定 【物】流量; 通量; 电通量; 磁通量:
luminous ~ 光通量 / radiant ~ 辐射通量 ⑤熔
解, 熔融; 助熔剂; 焊剂 ⑥【医】(血液、体液的)异

常流出; 肚泻 **II** ❶ *vt.* ①使熔融 ②用焊剂处理
❷ *vi.* ①熔融 ②大量地流出 ‖**'~,meter** *n.* 【物】
磁通(量)计

fly¹ [flai] **I** (flew [flu:], flown [floun]) ❶ *vi.* ①飞;
飞行; 驾驶飞机; 乘飞机旅行: a rocket ~*ing* up to
the sky 飞上天空的火箭 / a new bridge ~*ing*
over the river 架在江上的一座新桥
②(旗帜等)飘扬, 飘荡, 飞舞
③飞跑, 飞奔; (时间)飞逝: Time *flies* (like an
arrow). 光阴似箭。
④ (门、窗等)突然打开; 飞散, 碎: The door *flew*
open. 门突然打开了。/ This glass easily *flies*.
这玻璃容易碎裂。
⑤ [过去式和过去分词一般用 fled] 逃跑, 逃避
(=flee)
⑥ (钱财等)很快用完: make the money ~ 挥霍
金钱
⑦ 消失: mists ~*ing* before the morning sun
在朝阳中消失的雾霭
⑧ [过去式和过去分词用 flied] (棒球)打飞球
⑨放鹰打猎
❷ *vt.* ①飞; 驾驶(飞机); 空运(乘客、货物等):
~ a flight 作一次飞行 / The flier *flew* a
new-type jet plane. 飞行员驾驶一架新式喷气
机。/ ~ emergency medical supplies 空运急救
医疗用品
②飞越; 乘…的飞机旅行: ~ the Pacific 飞越太
平洋
③ 执行(飞行任务): ~ several sorties a day 每
天飞行出击若干次
④使(旗等)飘扬; 插, 挂(旗): What flag is the
ship ~*ing*? 这条船挂的是什么旗?
⑤ 放(风筝、信鸽等); (打猎时) 放(鹰): ~ a
kite 放风筝
⑥ [过去式和过去分词一般用 fled] 逃避; 逃出,
从…逃开: The dethroned king has *fled* the
country. 被推翻的国王逃到国外去了。/ The
bird has *flown* its cage. 鸟已从笼子里飞掉了。
II *n.* ①飞, 飞行; 飞行距离: have a ~ in an
aeroplane 乘飞机飞行
②(衣服等的)钮扣遮布; (帐篷的)门帘(或外层帆
布帐顶); 旗的外端(或幅顶)
③【机】飞轮; 【纺】(手织机用的)滑轮梭子; 锭壳,
锭壳
④【纺】落棉, 飞花; 飞毛
⑤【印】(印刷机上的)拨纸器; (书籍前后的)空白
页, 衬页
⑥ [复]舞台上面悬吊布景的地位
⑦公共马车; 运货马车; [主英]轻便旅行马车
⑧(棒球)飞球
‖**~ at** 猛烈攻击, 扑向; 向…发怒 / **~ blind** 进
行盲目飞行, 进行仪表飞行 / **~ high** 有雄心大
志; 情绪高昂; 野心勃勃 / **~ into** 突发, 忽发:
~ *into* a passion (或 rage) 勃然大怒 / ~ *into*
raptures 欣喜若狂 / **~ low** ①谦卑 ②销声匿
迹 / **~ off** 飞速(或突然)地跑掉; (轮子等)甩

脱,飞出 / ~ (或 *go*) *off at a tangent* (说话时)突然扯出题外;突然背离原来的途径,突然改变行径 / ~ *out* 冲出;突然怒骂(或动武) / ~ *right* [美俚]守道德,为人正直 / ~ *short of* 未达到…的水平 / ~ *up* 突然发怒 / ~ *upon* 猛烈攻击 / *let* ~ 发射,投射 / *let* ~ *at* ① 向…发射;向…射击,向…投击: *let* ~ a stone *at* sb. 向某人投掷一块石头 / He picked up a stone and *let* ~ *at* me. 他捡起一块石头朝我扔来。②驾 / *on the* ~ ①在飞行中 ②[美俚]匆忙地 ③不工作;在街头游荡;作乐 ④狡猾地;诡诈地 / *send* ... ~*ing* ①四处乱抛 ②驱逐(某人) ‖~ **ash** 飞灰,飘尘 / '~**away** *a.* ①(人)轻浮的,轻率的 ②(衣服)过于宽大的,不合身的 ③尖形的,翘状的 ④(飞机制造厂中造好的飞机)随时可交付出厂的;(供本部队使用的补给品)包装好准备空运的 *n.* ①轻浮的人 ②宽大不合身的衣服 ③海市蜃楼 ④(单杠运动中的)翻筋斗跳下 ⑤直接飞离飞机制造厂的新飞机 / ~ **ball** (棒球)飞球 / '~-**bar** *n.* (造纸用具)飞刀 / '~**boat** *n.* ①航行在荷兰沿岸的平底船 ②快艇 / ~ **bomb** 飞弹 / '~-**boy** *n.* [美俚]空军人员;飞机驾驶员 / '~-**by** *n.* (一架或几架飞机)在低空下指定地点,飞越 / 宇宙飞船飞近天体(如火星)的探测;飞近天体进行探测的宇宙飞船 ②绕月球轨道所作的不足一圈的飞行 / '~-**by-**night *n.* 喜欢夜间外出的人;[美俚]夜逃的负债者;无信用的借债人 *a.* 无信用的,不可靠的 / ~ **ladder** 云梯的顶部 / '~**leaf** *n.* 书籍前后的空白页,衬页 / '~**man** ['flaimən] *n.* ①马车驾驶人 ②舞台上方拉绳调换布景的工作人员 / '~**over** *n.* ① [英]有旱桥横跨在上面的道路交叉点;跨线桥 ② [军](指阅兵等的项目)飞机编队低空飞行 / '~-**past** *n.* [英] =~by / ~ **sheet** (广告)传单;[美]小册子 / '~-**tipping** *n.* [英]向街上乱倒垃圾废物 / '~**way** *n.* 候鸟飞行的固定路线 / '~**wheel** *n.* [机]飞轮

fly² [flai] *n.* ①蝇;苍蝇;(作钓饵用的)假蝇: flap (或 swat) *flies* 拍苍蝇 ②(蝇类等对植物的)虫害 ‖*a* ~ *in amber* 保存得很好的珍贵遗物 / *a* ~ *in the ointment* 美中不足之处;使人扫兴的小事 / *a* ~ *on the wheel* 自高自大的人 / *break a* ~ *on the wheel* 浪费精力,杀鸡用牛刀 / *Don't let flies stick to your heels.* [口]赶快,别拖拉。/ *Let that* ~ *stick in* (或 *to*) *the wall.* [苏格兰]对这件事(或这个问题)不要再谈了。/ *rise to the* ~ (鱼)上钩;(人)入圈套,上当 / *There are no flies on him.* [俚]他很能干(或不会上当等)。 ‖'~**blow** *n.* 蝇卵,麻蝇的幼蛆 *vt.* ①产蝇卵于… ②玷污(声誉等) / '~**blown** *a.* ①沾满蝇卵的;满是蝇屎的 ②(声誉等)被玷污了的 / '~**catcher** *n.* ①[动]鹟科食虫鸟 ②[植]捕蝇草 / '~**fish** *vi.* 用假蝇钓鱼 / '~**flap** *n.* 蝇拍 *vi.* (用蝇拍)拍苍蝇 / ~ **net** 防虫网 / '~**paper** *n.* 粘蝇纸,毒蝇纸 / '~**speck** *n.* ①蝇屎污点 ②小点,小团 / '~-

'**swat(ter)** *n.* 蝇拍 / '~**trap** *n.* ①捕蝇器 ②[植]捕蝇草 / '~**weight** *n.* ①体重五十公斤以下的拳击选手 ②小东西,无足轻重的东西

fly

fly³ [flai] *a.* [俚]机敏的; 敏捷的 ‖~ **cop** 便衣侦探

flyer ['flai-ə] *n.* ①飞鸟;飞行物;航空器 ②飞行员 ③(火车、公共汽车等的)快车 ④能飞跑的动物 ⑤(广告)传单 ⑥[建]梯级 ⑦[纺]锭翼,锭壳 ⑧[口]野心勃勃的人 ⑨飞跳,跃起 ⑩[美俚]孤注一掷;投机 ‖*take a* ~ (滑雪赛中)从跳板上飞跳;[喻]冒险行事,贸然尝试

flying ['flaiiŋ] **I** *a.* ①飞的;飞行(员)的: a ~ formation 飞行队形 / a ~ suit 飞行服 / ~ time (飞行员的)飞行时间 ②(旗帜等)飘扬的,飞舞的 ③飞似的,飞速的;飞速机动的: speed on ~ feet 飞跑 / a ~ squad of police (备有车辆等的)机动警察分遣队 ④匆匆的;短暂的: a ~ visit 仓促的短暂访问 / a ~ impression 瞬息即逝的印象 ⑤(谣言等)到处流传中的 **II** *n.* ①飞行 ②[复][纺]飞花;飞毛 ‖~ **blowtorch** [美俚]喷气式战斗机 / ~ **boat** 水上飞机,飞船 / ~ **bomb** [军]飞弹(爆炸性的无人驾驶飞机、导弹和火箭的统称) / ~ **bridge** ①船上的驾驶台 ②浮桥 / ~ **buttress** [建]飞(扶)拱,扶拱垛 / ~ **coffin** [美俚]飞机;滑翔机 / ~ **colo(u)rs** 完全胜利,大成功: They came off *with* ~ colo(u)rs. 他们的结果大获全胜。/ ~ **column** [军]快速突击部队,别动队 / **Flying Dutchman** ①(传说中)注定在海上飘流直到上帝最后审判日的荷兰水手 ②鬼船(被认为一种不祥之兆) / ~ **ferry** 滑帆渡,系留渡(指由钢索控制借水流推动往返于两岸的渡船) / ~ **field** 飞行场(常指私人飞机起落的场地) / ~ **fish** [动]文鳐鱼,飞鱼 / ~ **fox** [动]狐蝠 / ~ **jib** [船]船首斜桅帆,三角帆 / ~ **lemur** [动]猫猴 / ~ **machine** 航空机(指飞机、飞船等) / ~ **officer** (英)空军中尉 / ~ **rings** 吊环 / ~ **school** 飞行学校,航空学校 / ~ **squadron** ①机动舰队 ②(由受过专门训练的工人组成的)机动工组 / ~ **squirrel** [动]鼯鼠 / ~ **windmill** [美俚]直升飞机

foal [foul] **I** *n.* 驹(尤指一岁以下的马、驴、骡): in ~ 怀驹 **II** *vt. & vi.* 产(驹)

foam [foum] **I** *n.* ①泡沫; (马等的) 涎沫(或大汗) ②泡沫材料; 泡沫状物; 泡沫橡皮; 泡沫塑料 ③ [诗]海 **II ❶** *vi.* ①起泡沫; 冒汗水: ~*ing* beer 起泡沫的啤酒 / Waves ~*ed*. 波浪泡沫泛溅。②吐白沫; (发怒时)唾沫四溅; 发怒: The man ~*ed* and stormed. 那人大发脾气, 暴跳如雷。③起着泡沫流动: milk ~*ing* into the pails 起着泡沫注入桶中的牛奶 **❷** *vt.* 使起泡沫; 使成泡沫状物 ‖~ *at the mouth* 见 **mouth** ‖~**less** *a.* 无泡沫的 ‖~**ed concrete** 【建】泡沫混凝土 / ~**ed plastics** 泡沫塑料, 多孔塑料 / ~ **rubber** 泡沫橡皮, 海棉橡皮

fob¹ [fɔb] (fobbed; fobbing) *vt.* [古]欺骗 ‖~ *off* ①(用诡计、借口等)把…对付掉, 搪塞: ~ sb. *off* with empty promises 用空洞的诺言搪塞某人 ②把(冒充品)当真品推销 (on) ③摈弃

fob² [fɔb] *n.* ①(男裤上的)表袋 ②(怀表上的)短链及饰物

focal ['foukəl] *a.* ①焦点的, 在焦点上的; 有焦点的: a ~ point 焦点 ②【医】病灶的, 病灶性的 ‖~ **distance, ~ length** 焦距

focus ['foukəs] **I** ([复] focuses 或 foci ['fousai]) *n.* ①焦点: principal ~【物】主焦点 / real (或 true) ~【物】实焦点 / virtual ~【物】虚焦点 ②焦距; 对焦点, 聚焦 ③(活动、兴趣等的)中心, 集中点: the ~ of the world's attention 世界注意的中心 / the ~ of the struggle 斗争的焦点 ④【医】病灶 ⑤【地】(地震的)震源 **II** (focus(s)ed; focus(s)ing) **❶** *vt.* ①使聚焦; 使(眼睛)注视; 集中: ~ one's attention on the main problems 集中注意力于主要问题 ②调节…的焦距: ~ the lens of a microscope 调节显微镜的焦距 **❷** *vi.* 聚焦; 注视 ③调焦距 ‖*in* ~ 焦点对准; 清晰 / *out of* ~ 焦点没有对准; 模糊 ‖~**ing glass, ~ing screen** (照相机背部)调焦距用的毛玻璃

fodder ['fɔdə] **I** *n.* ①饲料(尤指粗饲料) ②(创作的)素材 ③[美俚]弹药 **II** *vt.* (用饲料)喂 ‖**cannon** ~ 炮灰 / **cut one's own** ~ [美]管自己的事; 自己谋生 ‖~**less** *a.* 没有饲料的

foe [fou] *n.* ①敌人; 敌军 ②反对者 ③危害物: a ~ to health 危害健康的东西 ‖*a* ~ *worthy of sb.'s steel* (值得某人与之一斗的)劲敌, 强敌 / *our* (或 *the arch*) ~【宗】魔鬼

fog¹ [fɔg] **I** *n.* ①雾; a dense ~ 大雾, 浓雾 ②烟雾; 尘雾: a dust ~ 一片尘雾 ③迷惑, 困惑: be lost in a ~ 困惑不解 ④[摄](底片的)雾翳 ⑤(影象的)模糊 ⑤(灭火机喷出的)泡沫, 喷雾 **II** (fogged; fogging) **❶** *vt.* ①以雾笼罩 ②使困惑, 使迷惘; 使模糊 ③[摄]使(底片)形成雾翳 **❷** *vi.* ①被雾笼罩; (因蒙上雾)变得模糊 ②[英][交]沿线设立浓雾信号 ③(植物)由于潮湿而烂死(off) ‖~**less** *a.* 无雾的 / ‖'~**bank** *n.* 雾堤(指海上浓雾) / '~**bound** *a.* ①被雾笼罩的: a ~*bound* coast 浓雾弥漫的海岸 ②被浓雾所阻不能航行的 / '~**bow, '~dog** *n.* 雾虹 / '~,**eater** *n.* (=~bow) ②雾中升起的满月 / '~**horn** *n.* ①雾

角(浓雾信号) ②粗而响的噪音 / ~ **signal** (在火车驶过时发出爆炸声以警告司机的)浓雾信号

fog² [fɔg] *n.* [方]①割后再生的草 ②(地上未割的)过冬草 ③苔藓

fogey ['fougi] *n.* = fogy

foggy ['fɔgi] *a.* ①有雾的, 多雾的: a ~ morning 浓雾的早晨 ②雾蒙蒙的; (玻璃窗等)不明净的 ③模糊的, 朦胧的: I have only a ~ idea of the matter. 我对那事情只有一个模糊的概念。‖**foggily** *ad.* / **fogginess** *n.* ‖**Foggy Bottom** 雾谷(指美国国务院)

fogy ['fougi] *n.* [常作 old ~] 守旧者, 老保守 ‖~**ish** *a.* 有些老保守似的 / ~**ism** *n.* 守旧

foible ['fɔibl] *n.* ①(性格上的)小缺点, 弱点; 怪癖, 癖好 ②(刀剑)自中部至尖端的部分

foil¹ [fɔil] **I** *n.* ①箔, 金属薄片: aluminium ~ 铝箔 ②【建】叶形饰 ③(镜底的)银箔; (宝石等的)衬底 ④陪衬物; 陪衬的角色: serve as a ~ 作陪衬 **II** *vt.* ①在…上贴箔; 以箔为…衬底 ②为…加上叶形饰 ③衬托

foil² [fɔil] **I** *vt.* ①挫败, 使成泡影: He was ~*ed* in his attempt. 他的企图成为泡影了。/ ~ sb.'s scheme 使某人的阴谋不能得逞 ②(打猎时)搞乱(嗅迹或足迹) **II** *n.* ①野兽的嗅迹(或足迹) ②(练剑术用的)钝头剑 ③[复]钝头剑术 ‖*break her* ~ (猎物)奔回原路后从另一条路逃掉 / *run the* ~ (猎物)再在原路上奔跑(使猎犬迷惑); [喻]使迷惑, 使迷失

foist [fɔist] *vt.* ①私自添加, 塞进 (*into, in*) ②骗售(假货、劣货) (*on, upon*): ~ sth. (off) on sb. 把某物骗售给某人 ③把…强加(于), 把…塞(给) (*on, upon*)

fold¹ [fould] **I ❶** *vt.* ①折迭; 对折: ~ a letter 将信折起来 ②合拢, 交迭: ~ one's hands 使十指交叉 / ~ one's arms 交臂(而无所行动) / ~ one's arms *about* (或 *round*) 用双臂抱着… ③抱住: ~ sb. (sth.) in one's arms 抱住某人(某物) ④包; 笼罩: ~ sth. (up) in paper 用纸把某物包起来 / a mountain village ~*ed* in morning haze 朝雾笼罩着的山村 ⑤调入, 拌进(食物作料) ⑥结束掉, 关掉(企业等) **❷** *vi.* ①折迭起来; 对折起来: The map ~s up into a booklet. 这地图可折成小册子。②彻底失败 **II** *n.* ①折, 折迭②褶, 褶痕; 褶层; 褶页 ③(盘起来而成的)团: a ~ of rope 一团绳索 ④[主英](地形的)起伏; 【地】褶皱 ⑤【动】(腕足类的)中隆 ⑥【解】褶: brain ~ 脑褶 ‖~ *up* ①塌下, 垮掉: The frame ~*ed up* under the heavy weight. 架子在重压下垮掉了。②放弃, 撒手 ③倒闭 ‖~**er** *n.* ①折迭者; 折迭机 ②文件夹 ③折迭式印刷品(传单等) ‖'~**away** *a.* 能折拢藏起的, 可折叠一边的: a ~*away* bed 可折拢藏起的床 / '~**out** *n.* (书册中的)褶页

fold² [fould] **I** *n.* ①羊栏 ②羊群 ③[集合名词](具有共同信仰的)信徒 **II** *vt.* 把…关进羊栏 ‖*return to the* ~ 回到信徒行列中; 浪子回头

olding ['fouldiŋ] *a.* 可折迭的 ‖ ~ **bed** 折迭床 / ~ **bridge** 开合桥 / ~ **chair** 折迭椅 / ~ **door** 折门 / ~ **fan** 折扇 / ~ **money** 纸币; (相当数目的)现款 / ~ **rule** 折尺 / ~ **screen** 折迭屏风 / ~ **stair** 折梯 / ~ **stool** 折凳 / ~ **top** (汽车的)折迭式车顶

oliage ['fouliidʒ] *n.* ①[总称]叶子,簇叶 ②【建】叶饰 ‖ ~**d** *a.* 有簇叶的;叶饰的 ‖ ~ **leaf** 营养叶 / ~ **plant** 观叶植物

olk [fouk] **I** ([复] folk(s)) *n.* ① 人们(现常用 people): *Folk(s)* say that .... 人们说… / old ~(s) 老人们 / country ~(s) 乡下人 / town ~(s) 城里人 ②[口]家属,亲属: How are all your ~s? 你家里人都好吗? / the old ~s at home 家里的老人们(指父母等) ③[古]民族,种族 **II** *a.* 民间的: ~ music 民间音乐 / a ~ remedy 民间验方 ‖~ **custom** 民间习俗 / ~ **dance** 民间舞蹈 / ~ **etymology** 通俗词源(指通过长期使用而使一个词变成通俗的形式,如 bridegome 变为 bridegroom) / '~**lore** *n.* ①民间传说 ②民俗学 / '~**lorist** *n.* 民间传说研究者;民俗学者 / ~ **medicine** 民间传统医术(尤指用草药等) / '~**-rock** *n.* 带民歌色彩的摇摆舞乐曲 / ~ **song** 民歌 / ~ **story** = ~tale / '~**tale** *n.* 民间故事 / '~**way** *n.* 社会习俗

ollow ['folou] **I ❶** *vt.* ①跟随;(表示时间、次序等)接着: I ~ed him up the hill. 我跟着他上山。/ ~ the hounds 随着猎狗追猎 / Spring ~s winter. 冬去春来。②追赶;追逐;追求: ~ truth 追求真理 ③沿着…前进: ~ our own road in developing industry 走自己发展工业的道路 ④听从,追随(某人);遵循;信奉;仿效: ~ a policy 按照一种政策办事 ⑤注视;倾听;注意 (运动、发展的事物): He ~ed the ball over the fence. 他看着球越篱飞去。/ We shall ~ closely the development of the situation. 我们将密切注意形势的发展。⑥领会;听清楚: Do you ~ me? 你听懂我的话了吗? / a speech 领会讲话的内容(或精神) ⑦从事(职业等),以…为业: ~ the sea 当水手 / ~ the law 做律师 ⑧因…而起, 是…的必然结果: Houses ~ed factories. 随着工厂的建立也造起来了。/ Trade ~s the flag. 国旗所到之处贸易随之而来。/ The flag ~s trade. 贸易所到之处国旗随之而来。⑨做…的后继人 **❷** *vi.* ①跟随;随着;接着,继: You go first and I'll ~. 你先走,我跟着就来。②结果产生: From different stands there ~ different attitudes. 不同的立场就有不同的态度。/ We've made great achievements, but it doesn't ~ that there're no short-comings. 我们已经取得了很大的成绩,但不能因此说我们就没有缺点了。**II** *n.* ①跟随;追随 ②(台球中)使竿击的球在击中目的球后继续滚动的一击 ③(在餐馆里)添加的半份菜 ‖**as ~s** 如下: The full text reads as ~s. 全文如下:… / ~ **after** 追求;力求达到(或取得) / ~ **on** ①继续下去;经过一段时间再继续: I'll be back soon. Meanwhile ~ on. 我马上就回来。你继续干下去好了。②(板球戏的一方)得分不足以继续攻击 / ~ **out** ①把…探究到底: ~ out all the cross references 查阅所有的互见条目 ②贯彻,执行: ~ out the doctor's directions 完全遵照医生的嘱咐 / ~ **through** ①完成球棒(或球拍)击球后的弧形动作 ②坚持到底 / ~ **up** ①穷追(猎物等)②把…探究到底 / ~ **up** with another question 追问 ③用继续行动来加强…的效果 ④在诊断(或治疗)后与(病人)保持联系 ⑤(足球队员)靠近(盘球人)作为后援 ‖'~'**up** *a.* 作为重复(或补充)的;继续的;接着的: a ~-up letter 接着而来的信(常指推销员连续兜售商品的信) / a ~-up instruction 补充指示 / the ~-up survey of the results of surgery 外科手术后的继续观察 / ~-up units 【军】后续部队 *n.* ①连续广告(或推销)法 ②诊断(或治疗)后与病人保持联系(或对病人的定期复查) ③(对已刊登或播送的报道的)补充报道

follower ['folouə] *n.* ①追随者;信徒;拥护者 ②侍从 ③追求女仆的人 ④(契据的)附页 ⑤【机】从动件,随动件

following ['folouiŋ] **I** *a.* ①接着的,其次的: the ~ day (year) 第二天(年) ②下列的,下述的 ③[the ~]下面: The ~ are (is) noteworthy. 下面几点(一点)值得注意。④[美](潮)顺船向方向吹的(风)顺船向而吹的 **II** *n.* 一批追随者(或拥护者,部下等) **III** *prep.* 在…以后: *Following* the lecture, a discussion was held. 讲课后开了讨论会。

folly ['foli] *n.* ①愚笨,愚蠢: It is ~ to do so. 这样干是愚蠢的。②蠢事;愚行;傻念头;傻话: commit a ~ 干蠢事 ③[古]放荡,罪恶 ④耗费巨大而又无益的事;工程浩大导致破产而常不能完成的建筑物(常与设计者的名字连用, 如 George's *Folly*) ⑤[复]时事讽刺剧,活报剧

foment [fou'ment] *vt.* ①【医】热敷,热罨 ②激起,扇动: ~ dissension 挑拨离间 ‖~**ation** [,foumen'teiʃən] *n.* ~.激起者,扇动者 / ~**er** *n.* 激起者,扇动者

fond [fond] *a.* ①[只作表语]喜爱的,爱好的 (of): be ~ of music 爱好音乐 ②溺爱的;多情的 ③(愿望等)不大可能实现的: a ~ dream 迷梦,黄梁美梦 ‖~**ly** *ad.* ①亲爱地 ②天真地,盲目轻信地: The result was not what he ~ly hoped. 结果并不象他天真地希望的那样。/ ~**ness** *n.*

fondle ['fondl] **❶** *vt.* 爱抚;抚弄 **❷** *vi.* 爱抚 (with)

font¹ [font] *n.* ①【宗】洗礼盘,圣水器 ②[诗]泉;源,始

font² [font] *n.* 【印】(同样大小和式样的)一副铅字,全副活字 ‖**wrong ~** 非同一式样(或大小)的活字(略作 w. f.)

food [fuːd] *n.* 食物;养料: ~ and drink 饮食 / canned ~ 罐头食品 / a staple ~ 主食品 / subsidiary ~ 副食品 / ~ for thought (或 meditation) 思考的材料 / mental (或 intellectual) ~ 精神食粮(如书籍、报刊等) / be ~ for fishes 葬身鱼腹 ‖*be ~ for worms* 死 / *~ for powder* 炮灰,[蔑]兵士 ‖~*less a.* 缺乏食物的 ‖~ **chain**, ~ **cycle**【动】食物链 / '~**stuff** *n.* 食料;粮食: a basket of ~*stuffs* 一篮食物

fool[1] [fu:l] **I** *n.* ①蠢人,傻子;白痴;莽汉: Don't be (such) a ~! 别傻了! / He's no ~. 他决不是傻瓜。(意为: 他是精明能干的。) / We are not ~ enough to believe in such trash. 我们不是傻瓜,不会相信这种鬼话的。②受愚弄(或欺骗)的人: be nobody's ~ 不受人愚弄(或欺骗) / make a ~ of sb. 愚弄(或欺骗)某人 ③(中世纪封建宫廷内或贵族家中供人娱乐的)弄臣, 小丑 ④有癖好(或特长)的人: a chess-playing ~ 棋迷 **II ❶** *vt.* ①愚弄,欺骗;诈取: ~ sb. *into* doing sth. 哄骗某人干某事 / ~ sb. *out of* his money 诈骗某人钱财 ②浪费;虚度: ~ *away* one's money (time) [口]浪费钱(时间) **❷** *vi.* ①成为傻瓜,干蠢事 ②演滑稽角色;开玩笑: I was only ~*ing*. 我只是开开玩笑而已。③游荡, 游手好闲;虚度: ~ *about* (或[美口] ~ *around*) 闲荡;干蠢事(或无用的、琐屑的事) ④瞎弄: Don't ~ *with* that knife. 别玩弄那把小刀。**III** *a.* [美口]愚蠢的,傻的 ‖*A ~'s bolt is soon shot.* ①蠢人一下子把箭射完。(指不善于弯弓待发) ②蠢人易于智穷力竭。③蠢人很快花掉自己。/ go a ~'s *errand* 徒劳(或无效)的任务(或使命): go (be sent) *on* a ~'s *errand* 去(被派去)白白地奔走一场 / *a ~'s paradise* 见 **paradise** / *All* (或 *April*) *Fools' Day* (西方风俗)愚人节(四月一日, 在此日可以任意愚弄他人) / *April* ~ 愚人节中的受愚弄者(或愚弄的行为) / *be a ~ for one's pains* 白费力气,徒劳无功 / *be a ~ to* … 不能同…相比, 与…不可同日而语 / *Fool's haste is no speed.* [谚]欲速则不达。/ *play* (或 *act*) *the* ~ ①做傻瓜,干蠢事;装傻相 ②扮丑角,演滑稽角色,逗人笑 ‖'~**hardy** *a.* 莽撞的, 蛮干的 / '~**proof** *a.* ①(笨人也会干、也能懂的)十分简单明了的 ②十分安全的;极坚固的;有防备的;有安全装置的 ‖~**'s cap** =foolscap / ~**'s gold**【矿】黄铁矿;黄铜矿

fool[2] [fu:l] *n.* 奶油(或牛奶)拌水果(汁)

foolery ['fu:ləri] *n.* ①愚蠢的行为 ②[复]愚蠢的思想(或谈吐、行动)

foolish ['fu:liʃ] *a.* ①愚蠢的,傻的,笨的 ②鲁莽的;荒谬的,可笑的 ‖~ *powder* [美俚]海洛因 / *make* (或 *cut*) *a ~ figure* 成为笑柄,闹笑话 ‖~**ly** *ad.* / ~**ness** *n.*

foolscap *n.* ①['fu:lskæp]大页书写纸②['fu:lzkæp] (宫廷弄臣或丑角戴的)滑稽帽;(处罚学生用的)圆锥形纸帽

foot [fut] **I** ([复] feet [fi:t]) *n.* ①脚,足 ②步;脚步;步调: be swift of ~ 脚步轻快 / have a light ~ 脚步轻快 ③(床等)放置的一头(长袜等)的脚部 ④最下部,底部;底座;(行列等的)末尾: at the ~ of a page 在一页的下端 / at the ~ of a

mountain在山脚处⑤英尺,呎(=12 吋,略作 ft.): a cubic (square) ~ 一立(平)方呎 ⑥([复] foots) 沉淀物, 渣滓;油渣;粗糖 ⑦(缝纫机的)压脚板 ⑧[总称]步兵: horse, ~ and artillery 骑兵、步兵和炮兵 ⑨(诗的)音步 ⑩【动】附节 ⑪【植】花梗;发状根 ⑫【船】帆的下缘 **II ❶** *vt.* ①走在…上,踏在…上,踏在…上;(某种舞)换底(袜子等)换底 ③结算: ~ *up* an account 结算帐目 ④[口]付: ~ a bill 付帐 **❷** *vi.* ①跳舞;步行 ③(船等)行驶,行进 ④总计 ‖*at sb.'s feet* 在某人的脚下(或门下、支配下): lay sth. at *sb.'s feet* 向某人进献某物 / sit at *sb.'s feet* 拜某人为师,追随某人 / *be carried out with one's feet foremost* 被抬着去葬掉 / *change* ~ (或 *feet*) 换步 / *drag one's feet* ①拖着脚步走②迟缓误事; 故意拖拉;不合作 / *fall on one's feet* 安然脱离危难; 运气好 / *feet of clay* 泥足: a colossus with *feet of clay* 泥足巨人 / *find one's feet* ①(小孩等)开始能走路 ②能独立行动 / *find* (或 *know*) *the length of sb.'s* ~ 了解某人的弱点以便加以控制 / ~ *it* [口]步行;跑;跳舞 / *have a ~ in the dish* 获得立足点;占一份 / *have cold feet* 害怕,胆寒;临阵畏缩 / *have one ~ in the grave* 已是风烛残年;离死不远 / *have the ball at one's feet* 见 **ball**[1] / *have two left feet* 极其笨拙 / *in one's stocking feet* 见 **stocking** / *keep one's feet* 站住脚跟 / *kiss the hare's* ~ 迟到 / *measure another's* ~ *by one's own last* 以己度人 / *My* (或 *Me*) ~! [口]怪啦! (或: 胡说! 去你的吧!) / *off one's feet* ①躺着; 坐着: The doctor told the patient to stay *off his feet*. 医生叫病人不要站着。②控制不住自己: carry sb. *off his feet* 使某人极度兴奋,迫使某人无暇考虑而仓卒行事 / *on* ~ ①步行: go home *on* ~ 步行回家 ②在进行中: set a plan *on* ~ 实施计划 / *on one's feet* 站着;[喻](病后)恢复健康;经济上自立: stand *on one's own feet* 独立自主,自立 / *pull* ~ [口]飞速走(或跑);[喻]全力以赴 / *put one's feet up* [口]双腿平搁起来休息 / *put one's* ~ *down* [口]坚决,坚定,行动果断;坚决反对: *put one's* ~ *down* on sth. 坚决不容许某事 / *put one's* ~ *in* (或 *into*) *it* (或 *in one's mouth*) [口]说错话;做错事 / *regain one's feet* 跌倒的人又)重新站起来 / *rise* (spring, struggle) *to one's feet* 站(跳, 挣扎着站)起来 / *rush sb. off his feet* 迫使某人仓促行动 / *set* (*have*, *put*) *one's* ~ *on the neck of sb.* 完全制服某人 / *set sb.* (*sth.*) *on his* (*its*) *feet* 使某人(某物)独立生存(存在)下去 / *show the cloven* ~ (魔鬼)露出爪趾; 现原形,露马脚 / *sling a nasty* ~ [俚]跳舞跳得好 / *sweep sb. off his feet* 使某人大为激动 / *under* ~ ①在脚底: tread *under* ~ 踩在脚下, 踩踏,压迫②在地面: wet *under* ~ 地上湿 / *with both* *feet* 强烈地, 坚决地: He came down *with both feet* against the proposal. 他坚决反对这个建议。‖**~age** ['futidʒ] *n.* 以呎表示的长度, 呎长 (尤指电影胶片的总长度);【矿】进呎 / **~ed** *a.* [常用以构成复合词] ①有脚的; 有⋯脚的: a four-~ed animal 四脚动物 ②脚步⋯的: soft-~ed 脚步轻的 / **~er** *n.* ①[常用以构成复合词]高⋯呎的人; 长⋯呎的东西 ②步行者 ③[英]足球赛 / **~less** *a.* ①无脚的 ②无基础的, 无支撑的 ③[口]笨拙的, 无能的; 无益的 ‖**~-and-'mouth disease** (牛羊等的)口蹄疫 / **'~ball** *n.* ①足球; 足球运动; 橄榄球(运动) ②被踢来踢去的悬案(或难题) / **'~baller** *n.* 足球运动员 / **'~bath** *n.* ①洗脚 ②脚盆 / **'~board** *n.* (马车、汽车等的)踏脚板 / **'~boy** *n.* 穿制服的男仆 / **'~bridge** *n.* (只供行人通过的)小桥 / **'~candle** *n.*【物】呎烛光(照度单位) / **'~fall** *n.* 脚步; 脚步声 / **~ fault** (网球)发球踏线; (排球)脚过中线 / **'~gear** *n.* [总称]鞋袜 / **'~hill** *n.* 山麓小丘; [复]山脉的丘陵地带 / **'~hold** *n.* ①立足点: get a firm ~*hold* 站稳脚跟 ②[军]据点 / **'~light** *n.* [常用复]①[戏]脚光: get across the ~*lights* (演技)受到观众欣赏 / appear before the ~*lights* 登场, 上台 ②舞台生涯: smell of the ~*lights* 象在做戏似的, 装模作样 / **'~loose** *a.* 到处走动的, 自由自在的 / **'~man** ['futmen] *n.* ①男仆 ②步兵 / **'~mark** *n.* =~print / **'~note** *n.* 脚注 *vt.* 给⋯作脚注 / **'~pace** *n.* 一般的步行速度;【建】步测; 梯台 / **'~pad** *n.* (徒步的)拦路强盗 / **~ page** 男仆 / **~ passenger** 步行者, 行人 / **'~path** *n.* 小路; [英]人行道 / **'~-pound** *n.*【物】呎磅(功的单位) / **'~-pound-'second** *n.*【物】呎磅秒单位制的 / **'~print** *n.* ①脚印, 足迹 ②宇宙飞船的预定着陆点 / **~ pump** 脚踏泵 / **'~race** *n.* 竞走 / **'~rest** *n.* 搁脚板 / **'~rope** *n.*【海】脚缆; 踏脚索; 帆的下缘索 / **'~slog** *vi.* 在泥泞中费力地行进 / **'~slogger** *n.* [英俚]长途步行者; 步兵 / **~ soldier** 步兵 / **'~sore** *a.* 走痛了脚的 / **'~step** *n.* ①脚步; 一步跨出去的距离; 脚步声 ②足迹: follow in sb.'s ~*steps* 步某人的后尘 / **'~stone** *n.* 基石 / **'~stool** *n.* 脚凳 / **'~sure** *a.* 脚步稳的 / **~ warmer** 暖脚物(如汤婆子等) / **'~way** *n.* =~path / **'~wear** *n.* 鞋类 / **'~work** *n.* ①【体】步法 ②要跑腿的工作 / **'~worn** *a.* ①走得脚累的 ②被脚踏坏了的

footing ['futiŋ] *n.* ①立足处, 立足点: Keep your ~! 站稳! / lose(或 miss) one's ~ 跌跤 ②地位; 基础;【建】底脚: on a sound ~ 在牢固的基础上 / gain(或 get) a ~ 取得地位 ③关系: on a completely equal ~ 完全平等地 / be on a friendly ~ with sb. 同某人有友好的关系 ④合计, 总额 ⑤[军]编制: on a peace(war) ~ (军队)按平时(战时)编制 / (跑道等的)场地情况 ‖**pay (for) one's ~** 缴入会费; 纳费参加某种行业(或职业)

fop [fɔp] *n.* 纨袴子弟, 花花公子 ‖**~ling** *n.* [古] =fop

for [强 fɔː; 弱 fə] **I** *prep.* ①[表示目的]为了: store up coal ~ the winter 储煤供冬天使用 ②[表示对象、用途等]为; 对于; 供; 适合于: an instrument ~ measuring speed 测量速度用的仪器 / He is the man ~ the job. 他是做此事的恰当人选。/ Not For Sale (常用于商品标签)非卖品 / That will be bad ~ your health. 那将有损于你的健康。/ herbs good ~ cancer 治癌草药 / It's time ~ class. 上课时间到了。③[表示目标、去向]往, 向: leave ~ the countryside 动身下乡 / He is getting on ~ fifty. 他快五十岁了。④代, 替; 代表: teach ~ sb. 为某人代课 / Facts speak ~ themselves. 事实本身就说明问题。/ the member ~ Coventry (英国)考文垂市的议员 ⑤[表示等值或比例关系]换: He answered my argument point ~ point. 他逐点答复了我的议论。⑥[表示愿望、爱好、特长等]对于: He has an eye ~ colour. 他有审辨色彩的目力。/ The veteran worker has a sharp ear ~ any queer sound in the machine. 这位老工人能听出机器中任何不正常的声音。⑦赞成, 拥护; 有利于: I am ~ the slogan "fear neither hardship nor death". 我赞成这样的口号, 叫做"一不怕苦, 二不怕死"。/ We are ~ principled unity. 我们主张有原则的团结。/ Which candidate are you ~? 你赞成哪一位候选人? / Are you ~ or against the proposal? 你赞成还是反对这一提议? ⑧由于, 因为: jump ~ joy 高兴得跳起来 ⑨虽然, 尽管: For all your explanations, I understand no better than before. 尽管你作了解释, 我还是不懂。⑩当作, 作为: take sb. ~ a fool 把某人看成傻瓜 / give sth. up ~ lost 认定某物已失落而不再寻找 / I hold it ~ certain. 我以为那是确实的。/ I know ~ a fact that .... 我确切地知道⋯ ⑪至于, 就⋯而言: So much ~ today. 今天就讲(或做)这么多。/ The day is warm ~ April. 在四月份, 这样的天气算是暖和的了。/ He is tall ~ his age. 就他的年龄而言, 他算是个子高的了。/ The landscape is too beautiful ~ words. 景色美得无法言传。/ That is good enough ~ me. 对我来说, 那是十分好了。⑫[表示时间、距离、数量]达, 计: get rich harvests (~) several years running 连续好几年获得丰收 / I won't be here ~ long. 我不打算在这儿作长期逗留。/ ~ life 终身 ⑬[表示约定的时间]在: an appointment ~ Monday 星期一的约会 ⑭[用于插入语, 表示列举]: Many people want to buy it because, ～ one thing, the price is low. 许多人想买它，原因之一就是价格便宜。/ I ～ one will go. 至少我要去。(不管别人去不去) ⑮[与名词或代词连用，后接动词不定式，构成名词短语]: Here are some books ～ them to read. 这儿有几本给他们看的书。/ There is no need ～ anyone to know. 没有必要让任何人知道。/ The tool-rack is too high ～ me to reach. 这工具架太高了，我够不到。**II** conj. 因为(不用于句首; 较 because 为正式，少用于口语中，但语气比 because 弱; 回答 why 时应用 because): We must get rid of carelessness, ～ it often leads to errors. 我们一定要克服粗枝大叶，因为粗枝大叶常常引起差错。‖**be ～ it** ① 赞成 ② 一定要受到 / **be in ～** 见 **in** / **be in ～ it** 见 **in** / ～ **all** 见 **all** / ～ **all that** 见 **that** / **For crying out loud!** [美俚]唉! (常用于对他人的愚蠢表示诧异) / ～ **oneself** 独自，独力地: I can do it ～ **myself**. 我自己能做这件事。/ **Now ～ it!** 干起来吧! 开始吧! / **O ～ ...!** 要是能有…多好啊! O ～ a glass of water! 要是能有一杯水多好啊! / **what ～** 见 **what**

forage ['fɔridʒ] **I** n. ①(尤指军马用的)草料，饲料: ～ crops 饲料作物 ②搜索粮秣: on the ～ 正在搜寻饲料 **II** ❶ vt. ①向…征集粮秣 ②搜索(粮秣等) ③给(马)吃草料 ④[古]洗劫; 劫掠 ❷ vi. ①搜索粮秣; 征集粮秣 ②掠夺，抢劫 ③搜，抄(for, about) ‖～**r** n. ①粮秣征收员 ②[复]成散开横队的骑兵 ‖～ **cap** 军便帽

foray ['fɔrei] **I** ❶ vt. [古]劫掠 ❷ vi. 袭击 **II** n. (为了战争或掠夺而进行的)突然侵袭，袭击: make (或 go on) a ～ 进行袭击

forbear[1] [fɔː'bɛə] (forebore [fɔː'bɔː], forborne [fɔː'bɔːn]) ❶ vt. 克制，自制; 避免: I ～ to go into details. 我不准备详细说。/ He could not ～ crying out. 他禁不住叫喊起来。❷ vi. ①克制，自制: I cannot ～ from expressing my opinion. 我不能不表示我的意见。②容忍，忍耐: ～ with sb. (sth.) 容忍某人(某事) ‖ **bear and ～** 一忍再忍

forbear[2] ['fɔːbɛə] n. [常用复]祖先

forbearance [fɔː'bɛərəns] n. ①忍耐，克制: exercise the utmost ～ 采取极大的克制态度 / at the end of one's ～ 忍无可忍 ②[律]债务偿还期的延展 ‖**Forbearance is no acquittance.** [谚]缓期不等于作罢。(或: 延展期限不等于免除债务。)

forbearing [fɔː'bɛəriŋ] a. 宽容的; 能忍耐的 ‖～**ly** ad.

forbid [fə'bid] (过去式 forbade [fə'beid] 或 forbad [fə'bæd], 过去分词 forbidden [fə'bidn]; 现在分词 forbidding) vt. ①禁止，不许: The doctor ～s him to smoke. 医生不准他抽烟。/ They ～ him wine. 他们不准他喝酒。/ He ～s me the use of this word. 他不许我使用这个字眼。/

The regulations ～ smoking in this room. 此室内规定禁止吸烟。/ Cameras are forbidden. 禁止拍照。/ Parking forbidden! 禁止停车! ②阻止，妨碍: The rain ～s us to go out. 雨天使我们不能外出。‖**God ～!** 但愿此事不曾发生!

forbidden [fə'bidn] **I** forbid 的过去分词 **II** a. 禁止的 ‖**Forbidden City** 紫禁城 / ～ **fruit** [基督教]禁果 ② 因被禁止反而更想弄到手的东西 / ～ **zone** 禁区

forbidding [fə'bidiŋ] a. 可怕的，令人生畏的; 险恶的: a ～ appearance 严峻的面容 / a ～ coast 险恶的海岸 ‖～**ly** ad. / ～**ness** n.

forbore [fɔː'bɔː] forbear[1] 的过去式

forborne [fɔː'bɔːn] forbear[1] 的过去分词

forby(e) [fɔː'bai] [苏格兰] **I** prep. & ad. 此外，除(…)之外 **II** a. 不同寻常的，极好的

force[1] [fɔːs] **I** n. ①力，力量 ②力气，精力; 魄力 ③势力; 威力: develop the progressive ～s 发展进步力量 / the ～ of habit 习惯势力 / the ～ of mass criticism 大批判的威力 ④[常用复]军队，部队，队伍; 兵力: the (armed) ～s 军队(陆海空军的总称) / the ～ [总称]警察 / join the ～s 参军 / concentrate a superior ～ 集中优势兵力 / a small ～ of infantry 一小队步兵 ⑤(从事某种活动的)队，组，人员: In our factory twenty percent of the labo(u)r (或 work) ～ are women. 我厂劳动力中百分之二十是妇女。/ a sales ～ 推销人员小组 ⑥武力，暴力; 压力: resort to ～ 诉诸武力 / the ～ of public opinion 舆论的压力 ⑦推动力; 控制力; 说服力: There is ～ in what he said. 他的话有说服力。⑧[物]力: constant (magnetic) ～ 恒(磁)力 / interatomic ～ 原子间力 ⑨(法律、条约、规章等的)效力，约束力: old regulations no longer in ～ 已经无效的旧规章 ⑩(文字、言语等的)确切意义; (精神)实质; 要点; 生动性: explain the ～ of a phrase 解释一个短语的确切意义 / a scene described with much ～ 描写得栩栩如生的景象 ‖**the air ～** 空军 / an assault ～ [军]突击队 / centrifugal (centripetal) ～ [物]离心(向心)力 / **the land ～** 陆军 / **the naval ～** 海军 **II** vt. ①强迫，迫使，逼 ②强行…; 强加: ～ a (或 one's) way in (out) 强行闯入(挤出) / ～ (open) a door 用力打开门 / ～ a smile 强作笑颜 / Don't ～ your idea upon others. 不要把自己的想法强加于人。③(用强力)夺取，攻克; 强渡 ④推动 ⑤(竭力)提高; 抬高; 加快: ～ the bidding (拍卖时)抬价 / ～ the pace (或 running) (赛跑时)加快速度使对手很快疲劳 ⑥(通过温室栽培等)促成(植物)早熟; [喻](通过增加作业等)加速(学生)的学业 ⑦迫使(对手)出某张牌; 迫出(某张牌) ⑧勒索; 强奸 ‖**by ～** 凭借暴力; 强迫地 / **by ～ of** 由于; 迫于; 通过，用…的手段: by ～ of arms 用武力 / by ～ of habit 由于习惯 / by ～ of circumstances 由于环境; 迫于形势 / by ～ of contrast 通过对比(来强调) / **by main ～** 全靠力气 / **come (或 enter) into ～** 开始有效; 开始实行: The agreement shall enter *into* ~ upon signature. 协定于签字后立即生效。 / ~ *sb.'s hand* 见 **hand** / ~ *the game* 见 **game** / *in* ~ ①(法律等)有效的 ②大批地; 大举, 大规模地: attack *in* ~ 大举进攻 / turn out *in* ~ 大批出动 / *in great* ~ ①(军队等)大批地, 大举 ②活跃的(尤指在谈话方面) / *join* ~*s* (*with*) ①(军队)会师 ②(同…)联合, (同…)通力合作 / *put . . . in* (或 *into*) ~ 实施…; 使…生效 ‖~**less** *a.* 无力的, 软弱的 ‖~**-'feed** *vt.* ①给…强行喂食 ②强使…接受; 强使(工业等)发展 / ~ **feed** 压油润滑(法) / '~**-land** *vi.* ①强迫降落 ②强行登陆 / ~ **pump** 压力泵; 压力水泵

force² [fɔːs] *n.* [英方]瀑布

forced [fɔːst] *a.* ①强迫的; 被迫的: a ~ sale (商店等倒闭前为偿债等的) 拍卖 / ~ vibration (oscillation)【物】受迫振动(振荡) ②用力的, 竭力的: a ~ march 急行军 / a ~ draught (锅炉等的)鼓风, 压力通风, 强迫的, 不自然的: a ~ laugh 勉强的笑声 / a ~ style (写作等)生硬的风格 ‖~**ly** ['fɔːsidli] *ad.* ‖~ **landing** ①强迫降落 ②强行登陆

forceful ['fɔːsful] *a.* ① 强有力的; 坚强的: a ~ character 坚强的性格 ②有说服力的: a ~ argument 有说服力的论证 ‖~**ly** *ad.* ‖~**ness** *n.*

forceps ['fɔːseps] [单复同] *n.* ①镊子, 钳子 ②【动】(昆虫的)尾铗 ③【解】钳状体

forcible ['fɔːsəbl] *a.* ①强迫的, 用暴力的: a ~ entry 闯入; (非法)侵入 ② 强有力的; 有说服力的: a ~ speech 令人信服的讲话 ‖**forcibility** [,fɔːsə'biliti] *n.* / ~**ness** *n.* / **forcibly** *ad.* ‖~**-'feeble** *a.* 外强中干的, 色厉内荏的

forcing ['fɔːsiŋ] I *n.* ①强迫, 施加压力; 夺取 ②(促成植物早熟的)培育 II *a.* ①强迫的, 施加压力的: a ~ pump (=a force pump) 压力泵; 压力水泵 ②促成(植物早熟)的: ~ culture (crops)【农】促成栽培(作物) / a ~ bed 温床 ‖~ **house** ①(促成植物早熟的)温室, 暖房 ② [喻](产生罪恶等)的温床

ford [fɔːd] I *vt. & vi.* 徒涉 II *n.* 可涉水而过的地方, 津 ‖~**able** *a.* 可涉水而过的 / ~**less** *a.* 无涉水处的, 不能涉过的

fore [fɔː, foə] I *ad.* 在前面; 在船头: ~ and aft 从船头到船尾; 在(或向)船头及船尾 II *a.* ①先时的, 先前的: during the ~ years of the last decade 在前十年的最初几年里 ②在前部的: the ~ part of the train 列车的前部 / the ~ draft 艏吃水 / the ~ hold 前舱 III *n.* 前部; 船头; 前桅; (马等的)前腿 IV *int.* (打高尔夫球者的叫声)让开! ‖*at the* ~ ①(信号旗)悬在前桅上 ②居首, 在前面: stand *at the* ~ 站在前面 / *to the* ~ ①在近处, 在场; 尚活着 ②(钱等)在手头的, 备好的, 立即可得到的 ③在显要的地位; 在前面 ‖~ **edge** 书的前页边(与书脊相对) / ~**-edge** ['fɔːredʒ] **painting** 页边画饰(印在书的前页边上, 书页成扇形展开时才可见到)

forearm¹ ['fɔːrɑːm] *n.* 前臂

forearm² [fɔːr'ɑːm] *vt.* 预先武装; 使预作准备

forebode [fɔː'boud] ❶ *vt.* ① 预示: The black clouds ~ a storm. 乌云预示大风暴将临。 ② 预感(灾祸等) ❷ *vi.* ①预言 ②有预感

forecast ['fɔː-kɑːst] I (forecast(ed)) *vt.* ①预测, 预报: ~ the weather 预报天气 ②预示: This ~*s* a change in the situation. 这预示形势将有所变化。 II *n.* 预测, 预报: a weather ~ 天气预报

forecastle ['fouksl] *n.* 【船】① 艏楼 ②前甲板 ‖*a* ~ *lawyer* [美俚](水手用语)经常要争论(或抱怨、议论)的人 ‖~ **deck** 艏楼甲板

forefather ['fɔː,fɑːðə] *n.* [常用复]祖先, 祖宗; 前人

forefinger ['fɔː,fiŋɡə] *n.* 食指

forefront ['fɔː-frʌnt] *n.* 最前线, 最前方

forego¹ [fɔː'gou] (forewent [fɔː'went], foregone [fɔː'ɡɔn]) *vt.* [罕]走在…之前; 发生在…之前 ‖~**er** *n.* ① 前驱者 ② 祖先 / ~**ing** *a.* 在前的; 前述的: the ~*ing* statement 前面所述 / the ~*ing* 前述事项, 前文

forego² [fɔː'gou] (forewent [fɔː'went], foregone [fɔː'ɡɔn]) *vt.* =forgo

foregone [fɔː'ɡɔn] I forego¹ 和 forego² 的过去分词 II *a.* ① 以前的, 过去的 ② 预先决定的; 预知的; 无可避免的: a ~ conclusion 未经商议即已决定的结论; 预料中必然的结局

foreground ['fɔːɡraund] *n.* ①(图画等的)前景 ②突出的地位

forehead ['fɔrid] *n.* ①额 ②前部

foreign ['fɔrin] *a.* ①外国的; 在外国的: a ~ accent 外国口音 / a ~ country 外国 / a ~ language 外国语 ②外国来的; 外国产的: ~ goods 外国货 / ~ capital 外资 / a ~ visitor 国外来客, 外宾 ③外地的; 外省的; [美]别州的 ④无关的, 不相干的 (*to*): What you say is ~ to the main issue of our discussion. 你讲的跟我们讨论的中心问题无关。 ⑤[医]外来的; 异质的: ~ body (或 substance) 异物 / ~ protein 异体蛋白, 异性蛋白 ‖~ *affairs* 外交事务 / ~ *aid* 外援 / ~ *and home trade* 国际和国内贸易 / a ~ *dogma* 洋教条 / ~ *exchange* 外汇 / ~ *letter paper* (用以减少邮资的)薄信纸 / a ~ *loan* 外债 / *the Foreign Office* (英国等的)外交部 / ~ *parts* 外国 / ~ *policy* 外交政策, 对外政策 / ~ *relations* 外交关系 / a ~ *settlement* 外国人留居区 / a ~ *word* 外国词; 外来语 / *incoming* ~ *mail* 来自国外的邮件 / *the Minister of* (或 *for*) *Foreign Affairs* 外交部长(简称 *the Foreign Minister*) / *the Ministry of Foreign Affairs* 外交部 / *outgoing* ~ *mail* 寄往国外的邮件 / *Secretary of State for Foreign Affairs* (英国)外交大臣(简称 *Foreign Secretary*) ‖~**ism** *n.* ①外国风俗习惯 ②外国语中的语言现象(如习语、发音、语法结构等) / ~**ize** *vt. & vi.* (使)外国化 ‖~**-born** *a.* 出生在外国的

foreigner ['fɔrinə] *n.* ①外国人 ②[方]外人;陌生人 ③外来的东西(特指外国船); 进口货;进口动物

foreman ['fɔ:mən] ([复] foremen) *n.* ①工头,领班 ②陪审长,陪审团发言人

foremost ['fɔ:moust] **I** *a.* ① 最初的; 最前面的 ②第一流的,最重要的 **II** *ad.* 在最前; 最重要地 ∥*first and ~* 首要地,首先 / *head ~* 见 head

forenamed ['fɔ:neimd] *a.* 上述的

forenoon ['fɔ:nu:n] *n.* 午前,上午

forerunner ['fɔ:,rʌnə] *n.* ① 先驱者;滑雪比赛的先导者;预报者 ②(疾病等的)前征,前兆 ③祖先

foresee [fɔ:'si:] (foresaw [fɔ:'sɔ:], foreseen [fɔ:'si:n]) *vt.* 预见,预知: Things turned out to be exactly as he had *foreseen*. 事情正如他所预见的那样。∥*~able a.* 可预见到的: in the *~able* future 在可以预见到的将来 / *~ingly ad.* 有预见地 / *~r n.* 预见者

foreshadow [fɔ:'ʃædou] *vt.* 预示,预兆

foreshore ['fɔ:-ʃɔ:] *n.* ①前滨, 涨滩(高潮线和低潮线中间的海岸) ②岸坡,海滩

foreshorten [fɔ:'ʃɔ:tn] *vt.* (绘画中)按照透视法缩短

foresight ['fɔ:-sait] *n.* ① 先见, 预见; 预见的能力 ②深谋; 远虑 ③[测]前视 ④(枪炮的)准星 ∥*~ed a.* 深谋远虑的;有先见之明的

forest ['fɔrist] **I** *n.* ①森林地带;森林;(森林般的)丛立: cut down a ~ 砍林伐木 / a ~ of chimneys 林立的烟囱 ②英国御猎场 **II** *vt.* 在…植满树木,使成为森林 ∥~ **fire** 森林火灾 / ~ **fly** 虻蝇 / ~ **ranger** 林警,森林保护员

forestall [fɔ:'stɔ:l] *vt.* ①抢在…的前面行动,比…先采取行动 ②(用先发制人的办法)排斥,阻碍,防止: ~ a competitor 用先发制人的办法使竞争者受挫 ③(用囤积、抬高价格等办法)垄断(市场)

foretell [fɔ:'tel] (foretold [fɔ:'tould]) *vt.* 预言;预示: Timely snow ~s a bumper harvest. 瑞雪兆丰年。

forethought ['fɔ:-θɔ:t] **I** *n.* ①预谋;事先的考虑 ②深谋远虑 **II** *a.* 预先计划好的;预谋的 ∥*~ful a.* 深谋远虑的

forever [fə'revə] *ad.* [美]永远; 常常 (=[英] for ever) ∥*~ and a day* ① 极长久地 ② 永久 / *~ and ever* 永远,永久

foreword ['fɔ:wə:d] *n.* 序,序言,前言

forfeit ['fɔ:fit] **I** *n.* ①(因犯罪、失职、违约等)丧失的东西;没收物;罚金 ②(公民权等的)丧失: the ~ of one's civil rights 公民权的被剥夺 ③[~s]用作单罚物游戏: play ~s 玩罚物游戏 ④玩罚物游戏时的抵押物(可由被罚者做一种可笑的动作来赎回) **II** *vt.* 丧失(权利、名誉、生命等);(作为惩罚被没收或被剥夺而)失去: the esteem of one's friends 失去朋友们的尊敬 / ~ one's health 丧失健康 / ~ one's property by one's crime 因犯罪而财产被没收 **III** *a.* 丧失了的, 被

没收的 ∥*~able a.* 可没收的 / *~er n.* 丧失者;受没收处分者

forgather [fɔ:'gæðə] *vi.* ① 聚会 ② 偶遇 (with) ③交往 (with)

forgave [fə'geiv] forgive 的过去式

forge¹ [fɔ:dʒ] **I** *n.* ①锻工车间; 铁匠店 ②锻炉: Everything new comes from the ~ of hard and bitter struggle. 一切新的东西都是从艰苦斗争中锻炼出来的。**II** ❶ *vt.* ① 打(铁等); 锻造: an anchor 锻造铁锚 ②锻炼 ③伪造: ~ a signature 伪造签名 ❷ *vi.* ①锻造;做锻工,做铁匠 ②伪造;犯伪造罪 ∥*~able a.* 可锻造的 / *~ r n.* ①锻工 ②伪造者 / *forging n.* 锻;锻件

forge² [fɔ:dʒ] *vi.* 稳步前进;突然加速前进 (ahead)

forgery ['fɔ:dʒəri] *n.* ① (签字、文件等的)伪造;造罪 ②伪造品,赝品

forget [fə'get] (过去式 forgot [fə'gɔt], 现在分词 forgotten [fə'gɔtn] 或 forgot; 现在分词 forgetting) ❶ *vt.* ①忘,忘记: I quite ~ his name. 我完全记不起他的名字了。/ I *forgot* to tell me about it. 我忘记告诉她这件事。/ I *forgot* telling her about it. 我忘记了曾把这事告诉过她。/ I'm *forgetting* my Latin. 我渐渐忘拉丁文了。/ Don't ~ me to your brother. 别忘记代我问候你的兄弟。②轻忽,忽略: Don't ~ your duties. 别玩忽职责。❷ *vi.* 忘记: I have *forgotten* about it. 我已忘了这事。∥~ *oneself* ①为他人而忘我 ②忘乎所以 ③失去知觉 / *forgive and* ~ 不念旧恶 ∥**forgetter** *n.* 健忘者

forgetful [fə'getful] *a.* ①健忘的 ②不注意的,疏忽的: be ~ of one's sleep and meals 废寝忘食 ∥*~ly ad.* / *~ness n.*

forgive [fə'giv] (forgave [fə'geiv], forgiven [fə-'givn]) *vt.* ①原谅,饶恕,宽恕: He was *forgiven* his offences.(或 His offences were *forgiven* him.) 他的过错受到宽恕。/ ~ sb. *for* being rude 原谅某人的卤莽 / You are *forgiven*. 你得到宽恕了。②豁免: ~ sb. his debt 豁免某人的债务 / ~ a debt 免偿债务 ∥~ *and forget* 见 **forget** ∥*~ness n.* 饶恕,宽恕

forgo [fɔ:'gou] (forwent [fɔ:'went], forgone [fɔ:'gɔn]) *vt.* 摒绝; 放弃: ~ pleasures 摒绝享乐 / ~ an opportunity 放弃机会

forgot [fə'gɔt] forget 的过去式和过去分词

forgotten [fə'gɔtn] forget 的过去分词

fork [fɔ:k] **I** *n.* ① 叉; 耙;(藤等的)叉状支撑物: a hay ~ 干草叉 ②餐叉: a knife and ~ 一副刀叉 ③(路、河、树木等的)分岔;分岔点,岔口;岔路,岔流: a ~ in a road 路的分岔口 / Take the left ~ at the crossroads. 到路口取左边的岔道。④叉状电光 ⑤[物]音叉 (=tuning ~) ⑥ (象棋中)以一棋子同时攻两棋子 ⑦两者间的一种选择 **II** ❶ *vi.* 分歧,分叉: The road ~s here. 路在这里分叉。❷ *vt.* ①使成叉状: ~ one's fingers 开手指 ② 叉;叉起;耙: ~ hay 用叉叉干草 / ~ the ground over 耙地 ③ (象棋中用马等)同时

攻(两棋子) ‖~ **out** (或 **over, up**) [口]支付,交付;放弃 / **play (a good) knife and** ~ (胃口很好地)饱餐一顿,痛痛快快地吃 ‖~**ed** a. 叉状的;有叉的: ~**ed** lightning 叉状闪电 / three-~**ed** 三叉的 ‖~**lift** n.【机】铲车,叉式升降机 / ~ **luncheon**, ~ **dinner** 叉餐(尤指人多席位不够时为方便起见供应仅用叉的食物的聚餐)

forlorn [fə'lɔ:n] a. ①被遗弃的;孤寂凄凉的 ②可怜的,悲惨的 ③几乎无望的: one final ~ attempt 最后一次几乎无望的努力 ④丧失了…的(of) ‖(a) ~ **hope** 见 hope ‖~**ly** ad. / ~**ness** n.

form [fɔ:m] I n. ①形状;形态: take a ~ 成形 / ideological ~s 观念形态 ②(人、动物的)外形;体型: see a ~ in the dark 在暗处看见一个人影 / the well-proportioned ~ of an athlete 运动员的匀称的体型 ③形式;方式: take (或 assume) the ~ of armed struggle 采取武装斗争的形式 / the unity of content and ~ 内容和形式的统一 / various ~s of transport 各种运输方式(或工具) ④结构;类型: the lower ~s of animal (plant) 低等动(植)物 ⑤(组织等的)体制;(文艺等的)体裁,样式: a ~ of government 政体 / a literary ~ 文学体裁 ⑥格式;表格(纸);(大量发出的)打印信件 (=~ letter): a telegraph ~ 电报纸 / an arrival ~ 来客登记表 / fill in (或 out) an application ~ 填写申请书 ⑦【语】词形,形式 ⑧仪式;礼节,礼貌: It is good (bad) ~ to do so. 这样做有礼貌(有失体统)。 ⑨(运动员等的)竞技状态: be in (good) ~ 竞技状态良好 ⑩【物】(晶)面式;【机】【建】型;模壳;[印]印版 ⑪(中等学校的)年级: the first (sixth) ~ 一(六)年级 ⑫长板凳⑬(野兔等的)窟,穴 II ❶ vt. ①形成;构成;【语】构(词),造(句): coal deposits ~ed in prehistoric times 史前期形成的煤层 / a sentence *after* (或 *by, from, upon*) a pattern 按照句型造句 ②塑造 ③(使)组成,建立;养成: ~ a cabinet 组成内阁 / ~ an alliance with sb. 同某人结盟 / ~ good health habits 养成良好的卫生习惯 ④(使)排列,编(队伍): ~ twos (fours) 【军】(排)成两(四)列 / ~ the paraders *into* columns 把游行的人编成纵队 ⑤想出(意见等);作出: ~ a conclusion (judgement) 作出结论(判断) ❷ vi. ①形成,产生: Ice ~s at 0℃. 摄氏零度时结冰。②排(队),列(队): ~ *into* line (*in two ranks*) 排(成两列横)队 ‖a ~ **of address** 称呼 / **in due** ~ 照规定的格式 / **in great** ~ 兴高采烈 / **lose one's** ~ (或 **be out of** ~) (运动员等)竞技状态不好 / (**run**) **true to** ~ 一如往常(的性格、作风等),一如其本性,一贯 ‖~**less** a. 无形状的,无定形的 ‖~**fitting** a. 贴身的: a ~**fitting** sweater 紧身运动衫

formal ['fɔ:məl] I a. ①外形的,形态的;形式(上)的: a ~ resemblance 外形上的相似 / ~ logic【哲】形式逻辑 ②正式的: a ~ call 正式访问 / reach a ~ agreement 达成正式协议 / ~ dress 礼服 ③拘泥形式的,拘谨的,刻板的 ④布置得很整齐的,匀称的,有条理的 ⑤合乎格式的;正规的;正式的: ~ education 正规教育 / a ~ contract 正式契约 ⑥【语】规范的: ~ grammar 规范语法 II n. ①正式的社交活动 ②[口]夜礼服 ‖**go** ~ [口]穿着夜礼服 ‖~**ly** ad. 形式上;正式地

formality [fɔ:'mæliti] n. ①拘泥形式,拘谨: without ~ 不拘形式地 / become a mere ~ 流于形式的 ②[常用复]正式手续: the legal (customs) *formalities* 法律(海关)手续 / go through due *formalities* 经过正式手续 ③礼节;俗套

formalize ['fɔ:məlaiz] ❶ vt. ①使具有形式,使定形 ②使成正式 ❷ vi. 拘泥形式(或仪式、礼节等) ‖**formalization** [ˌfɔ:məlai'zeiʃən] n. 定形;正式化;形式化

format ['fɔ:mæt] n. ①(出版物的)版式,开本;【自】(数据安排的)形式 ②(电视播送或硬币设计等的)组织(或安排、布局)的总计划

formation [fɔ:'meiʃən] n. ①形成;构成;组成;塑造: heat of ~【化】形成热,生成热 ②形成物;结构 ③【军】队形;编队;兵团: close (dispersed) ~ 密集(疏开)队形 / field army (gunboats) *in* battle ~ 列成战斗队形的野战军(炮艇) / ~ flight (或 flying)【空】编队飞行 / break ~ (士兵等)离开编队 / skirmish ~ 散兵线 / large (regional) ~s 大(地方)兵团 ④【语】(词的)构成 ⑤【地】地(岩)层

formative ['fɔ:mətiv] I a. ①形成的;构成的: ~ years 形成性格的时期 / ~ cell【动】形成细胞;毛原细胞 ②【语】构词的 ③造型的 II n. ①构词因素(如前缀、后缀等) ②用构词因素构成的词

former[1] ['fɔ:mə] n. ①形成者,构成者;创造者 ②【机】样板,模型;成形设备: a wood(en) ~ 木模 ③【无】线圈架 ④中等学校一至六年级的学生: sixth ~s 六年级学生

former[2] ['fɔ:mə] a. ①以前的,从前的: sb.'s ~ colleagues 某人从前的同事 / in ~ times 从前 ②在前的: in the ~ case 在前一情况下 / the ~ 前者(与 the latter 相对) ‖~**ly** ad. 以前,从前

formidable ['fɔ:midəbl] a. ①可怕的,令人生畏的: a man with a ~ appearance 样子可怕的人 ②难对付的,难克服的: a ~ task 非常艰难的任务 ‖~**ness** n. / **formidably** ad.

formula ['fɔ:mjulə] ([复] formulas 或 formulae ['fɔ:mjuli:]) n. ①(日常礼节、法律文件或宗教仪式等的)惯用语句,俗套话(如见面时讲的 How do you do? 及信尾的 Very truly yours 等) ②公式,程式;(作为讨论、协商或行动的基本原则的)准则,方案: They proposed a third ~. 他们提出第三种方案。③处方;(婴儿食物等的)配方;用牛奶等配制成的婴儿食物: a ~ for making soap 肥皂配方 ④【数】公式;【化】式: ~ of integration 积分公式 / molecular ~ 分子式 / structural ~ 结构式 ⑤【宗】信仰表白书

formulate ['fɔ:mjuleit] vt. ①用公式表示;把…化成公式 ②系统地阐述(或提出) ③制定(肥皂、

塑料等)的配方; 按配方制造(或制)||**formulation** [ˌfɔ:mju'leiʃən] *n.*

forsake [fə'seik] (forsook [fə'suk], forsaken [fə'seikən]) *vt.* 遗弃, 抛弃; 摒绝: ~ one's wife and children 遗弃妻儿 / ~ bad habits 抛弃坏习惯

forswear [fɔ:'swɛə] (forswore [fɔ:'swɔ:], forsworn [fɔ:'swɔ:n]) ❶ *vt.* ①发誓抛弃; 断然放弃: ~ smoking 立誓戒烟 ②发誓否认 ❷ *vi.* 发伪誓; 作伪证 ||~ oneself 发伪誓; 作伪证

fort [fɔ:t] **I** *n.* ①堡垒,要塞 ②边界上的贸易站(原设有堡垒) **II** ❶ *vt.* 设要塞保卫 ❷ *vi.* 设要塞 ||*hold the* ~ ①守堡垒 ②(对反对者)坚决不让步 ③处理日常事务

forth [fɔ:θ] **I** *ad.* ①向前方; 向前: sway back and ~ 前后摇动 / from that day ~ 从那天起 ②向外, 由隐而显: a spring issuing ~ from the hill 山中涌出的泉水 / burst ~ (芽、蕾)绽开; (火山等)爆发 / put ~ leaves 发芽 **II** *prep.* [古]出于, 来自 ||*and so* ~ 见 **and**

forthcoming [fɔ:'θʌmiŋ, 用作定语时也作 'fɔ:θ-ˌkʌmiŋ] **I** *a.* ①即将到来的, 即将出现的: the ~ holidays 即将到来的假日 ②[只作表语]现有的, (需要时)唾手可得的: The funds are not ~. 资金尚未就绪。③[口]愿意帮助的, 乐于供给消息的 **II** *n.* 来临, 临近

forthright ['fɔ:θrait] **I** *a.* ①笔直前进的 ②直率的; 直截了当的 **II** [fɔ:'θrait] *ad.* ①直率地 ②[古]立刻; 径直地 **III** *n.* [古]直路

forthwith [fɔ:'θ'wiθ] **I** *ad.* 即刻 **II** *n.* [美俚]必须立即执行的命令

fortieth ['fɔ:tiiθ] *num.* ①第四十(个) ②四十分之一(的)

fortify ['fɔ:tifai] ❶ *vt.* ①增强(体力、结构等) ②筑堡于, 设防于: ~ a city 筑工事以巩固城防 / a fortified port 军港 / a fortified zone 筑垒地带 / ~ oneself against cold (用多穿衣或喝酒等办法)御寒 ③使坚强: ~ one's argument with statistics 用统计数字支持自己的论点 / one's confidence 坚定自己的信心 ④增加(酒)的酒精含量: a fortified wine 掺了酒精的饭后酒 ⑤在(食物)中增加(或加入)维生素(或矿物质等) ❷ *vi.* 筑防御工事

fortitude ['fɔ:titju:d] *n.* 坚忍, 刚毅: intestinal ~ 坚韧不拔的精神

fortnight ['fɔ:tnait] *n.* 十四日, 两星期: go away for a ~ 离开两周 / Monday ~ 两星期后(或前)的星期一

fortnightly ['fɔ:tˌnaitli] **I** *a. & ad.* 两星期一次的(地); 每两周的(地) **II** *n.* 双周刊

fortress ['fɔ:tris] **I** *n.* 堡垒, 要塞 **II** *vt.* [诗]为⋯设置要塞; 用要塞保卫

fortuitous [fɔ:'tju(:)itəs] *a.* ①偶然的, 偶然发生的 ②幸运的 ||~**ly** *ad.* / ~**ness** *n.*

fortunate ['fɔ:tʃənit] *a.* ①幸运的; 侥幸的: I was ~ to catch the train at the last minute. 我在

最后一分钟赶上了火车, 真是幸运。/ be ~ in 在⋯方面很幸运, 为有⋯而幸福 ②带来幸运的: a ~ event 幸事 ||~**ly** *ad. Fortunately* the rain stopped before we started. 幸亏在我们动身前雨停止了。

fortune ['fɔ:tʃən] **I** *n.* ①命运, 运气; 好运 ②[F-]司命运的女神 ③财产,大量财产 **II** ❶ *vi.* [古]偶然发生 ❷ *vt.* [古]给⋯以大宗财富 ||**come into a** ~ 继承一笔财产 / **marry a** ~ 跟有钱的女人婚 / **push one's** ~ 设法抬高自己的社会地位; 图发迹 / **seek one's** ~ 寻出路; [喻]去淘金 / **spend a small** ~ [口]化一笔巨款 / **tell sb.'s** ~ 给某人算命 / **tempt** ~ 蔑视命运; 冒险 / **try one's** ~ 碰运气 ||~**less** *a.* 不幸的; 无财产的 ||~ **hunter** 追求有钱女子的男子 / '~-ˌ**hunting** *n.* 为了财产而追求有钱女子 / '~-ˌ**teller** *n.* 给人算命的人 / '~-ˌ**telling** *n.* 算命

forty ['fɔ:ti] **I** *num.* 四十; 四十个(人或物); 第四十(章、页等)(用例参看 **eight**) **II** *n.* ①[复](世纪的)四十年代 ②四十岁; [复]四十到四十九岁的时期 ③(网球)赢得第三球的得分, 三分: ~-all 三平 / ~ love 三比零 ||~ **winks** 见 **wink** / **like** ~ [美口]非常; 猛烈地 / **roaring forties** 【地】大西洋的南纬 30°—50° 之间风浪特大的海域 / **the Forties**【地】苏格兰东北岸和挪威西南岸之间的海域(因该地海深四十呎以上而得名) ||~**ish** *a.* 近四十岁的; 四十岁左右的 / ~-'**eightmo** *n.* 四十八开(本), 四十八开的纸张(或页面) / '~-'**five** *n.* ① 45 口径的手枪(常写作 0.45) ②每分钟四十五次转速的唱片(常写作 45) ③ [the Forty-five]【英史】詹姆士二世党徒的一七四五年的政变 / '~-'**leven** *a.* [美俚]许多的, 数不清的 / '~-'**niner** *n.* (美国)一八四九年争往加利福尼亚州淘金的人

forum ['fɔ:rəm] ([复] forums 或 fora ['fɔ:rə]) *n.* ①古罗马城镇的广场(或市场) ②论坛; 讨论会; (广播、电视)专题讲话(或座谈)节目 ③法庭 ||**the Forum** 古罗马广场(遗址)

forward ['fɔ:wəd] **I** *a.* ①在前部的; 向前的: the ~ ranks of the paraders 游行队伍的前列 / be well ~ with one's work 在工作方面很有进展 ②进步的; 急进的, 过激的: a firm ~ policy 坚定的进步政策 ③(庄稼、季节、儿童等)早的, 早熟的: a ~ spring 来得早的春天 / The child is very ~ at walking. 这孩子很早就会走路了。④热心的; 易于⋯的, 动辄就⋯的: He is always ~ to help others. 他一贯热心帮助别人。/ be ~ to criticize others 动辄批评别人 ⑤唐突的, 鲁莽的; 孟浪的 ⑥[商]期货的, 预约的: ~ prices 期货价格 / payment ~ 预付货款 / ~ delivery 远期交货 ⑦[海](船身)前部的 **II** *ad.* ①向前, 前进: *Forward* march! 【军】开步走! ②将来, 今后 ③出来,(现)出: put ~ a proposal 提出建议 **III** *n.* [体](足球、篮球等的)前锋: the centre ~ 中锋 **IV** *vt.* ①促进; 促使(植物等)生长: ~ production plans 推进生产计

划 ② 发送, 寄发 (货物等): a ~ing agent 运输行, 运输商 / These packages will be ~ed immediately. 这些包裹将立刻发送。/ We are ~ing you our new samples. 现寄上我们的新样品。③ 转递, 转交 (信件等): Please ~! 请转交! / ~ sb.'s mail to his new address 把某人的邮件转送到他的新地址 ‖*backward(s) and ~(s)* 来回地, 忽前忽后 ‖~**ly** *ad.* 在前部; 向前地; 急切地, 热心地; 唐突地, 鲁莽地 / ~**ness** *n.* 急切, 热心; 早熟; 唐突, 鲁莽 / ~ **echelon** [美]【军】先头部队; 先遣指挥部 / '~-,**looking** *a.* 向前看的, 有远见的

forwards ['fɔ:wədz] *ad.* =forward (*ad.*)

fossil ['fɔsl] **I** *n.* ①化石; 地下采掘出的石块 (或矿物): hunt for ~s 寻找化石 ②僵死的事物; 习语中保持的旧词 (如 to and fro 中的 fro) ③老顽固, 守旧者 **II** *a.* ①化石的; 从地下采掘出的: ~ fuels 矿物燃料 / ~ botany 古植物学; 植物化石学 / ~ oil 矿油 (石油的旧称) ②陈旧的, 顽固的

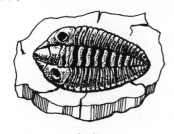

fossil

fossilize ['fɔsilaiz] ❶ *vt.* ①使成化石 ②使 (思想等) 陈旧, 使僵化 ❷ *vi.* ①变成化石 ②[罕]搜集 (或发掘) 化石标本 ‖**fossilization** [,fɔsilai'zeiʃən] *n.* 化石作用

foster ['fɔstə] *vt.* ①养育, 抚养 ②培养, 鼓励, 促进 ③抱 (希望等): ~ hopes for success 抱成功的希望 ‖~**er** ['fɔstərə] *n.* 养育者; 鼓励者 ‖~ **brother** 奶兄弟 / ~ **child** 养子; 养女 / ~ **daughter** 养女 / ~ **father** 养父 / ~ **home** 照顾孤儿 (或犯罪儿童, 精神病者) 的家庭 / ~ **mother** 养母 / '~-'**mother** *vt.* 收养, 抚养; ~-**mother** three children 收养三个小孩 *n.* [英]孵蛋的暖室 / ~ **parent** 养父; 养母 / ~ **sister** 奶姐妹 / ~ **son** 养子

fosterling ['fɔstəliŋ] *n.* 养子; 养女

fought [fɔ:t] fight 的过去式和过去分词

foul [faul] **I** *a.* ①(味道) 难闻的, 恶臭的; (食物等) 腐败的, 恶烂发臭的: a ~ smell (taste) 恶臭的气味 (味道) / fish 臭鱼 ②肮脏的, 污浊的; 泥泞的: a ~ drain 污浊的下水道 ③罪恶的, 邪恶的, 可恶的 ④下流的; 恶语咒骂的: ~ language 下流话 ⑤(天气等) 恶劣的, 暴风雨的; (风) 逆的: ~ weather 坏天气 / in the teeth of

a ~ wind 迎着逆风 ⑥不利于航行的: ~ ground 多暗礁的危险海底 / a ~ coast 多暗礁的海岸 ⑦犯规的; 不正当的: a ~ stroke (kick) 犯规的击球 (踢球) ⑧(管道、通路等) 壅塞的, 淤塞的; (船) 底部粘满了海藻、贝壳的: ~ pipes 壅塞的管子 / The chimney is ~. 烟囱不通了。/ a ship with a ~ bottom 底部粘着海藻、贝壳的船 ⑨(绳索等) 被缠住的 ⑩【印】修改得面目全非的, 错误百出的: a ~ manuscript 改得一塌糊涂的原稿 / a ~ proof 毛校样 (a clean proof 清样之对) ⑪[口]讨厌的; 令人作呕的 ⑫[英方]丑陋的, 不好看的 **II** *ad.* 违反规则地; 不正当地: hit a ball ~ 击球犯规 / play sb. ~ 用卑鄙手段对付某人 **III** *n.* ①(在比赛中) 犯规: a personal (technical) ~ 侵人 (技术) 犯规 / claim a ~ 指出对方犯规 ②缠绕 ③碰撞 **IV** ❶ *vt.* ①弄脏, 污染; 玷污: Soot ~s the air. 烟屑污染空气。/ ~ one's name 玷污名声 ②使壅塞 ③缠住: The rope ~ed the pulley. 绳把滑轮缠住了。④碰撞: This boat ~ed the other. 这只船撞了另一只船。⑤(比赛中) 对…犯规 ❷ *vi.* ①腐败, 腐烂 ②(管道等) 壅塞 (*up*) ③(绳索、链条等) 缠结 ④(船只等) 碰撞 ⑤(比赛中) 犯规 ‖*by fair means or* ~ 用正当或不正当的手段, 不择手段地 / *fall* (或 *run, go*) ~ *of* ①(船只) 与…相撞; 与…缠绕在一起 ②同…冲突 (或抵触); 与…发生麻烦 (或纠葛): *fall* ~ *of* the law 违法 / ~ *out* [美](比赛中) 犯规过限定次数而被罚退场 / ~ *play* 见 **play** / ~ *up* [口]搞糟; 弄乱; 做错, 做坏 / *through fair and* ~ (或 *through* ~ *and fair*) 在任何情况下, 不管顺利或困难 ‖~**ing** *n.* (水管、枪筒等中的) 污垢 / ~**ly** *ad.* 下流地; 卑鄙地; 粗鄙地 / ~**ness** *n.* ‖'~-**mouthed**, '~-**spoken**, '~-'**tongued** *a.* 讲话下流的, 恶语咒骂的 / '~-**up** *n.* 混乱; 故障

found[1] [faund] find 的过去式和过去分词

found[2] [faund] *vt.* ①为 (房屋等) 打基础; 建立; 缔造: When was the new city ~ed? 这座新城市是什么时候兴建的? ②创立 (学说等); (用基金) 创办: ~ a hospital (university) 创办一所医院 (大学) ③使有根据 (*on, upon*): a story ~ed on fact 根据事实写成的故事

found[3] [faund] *vt.* 铸; 铸造; 熔; 熔制 (玻璃等): a ~ing furnace 铸造炉; 熔炉 / metal ~ing 金属铸造

foundation [faun'deiʃən] *n.* ①(城市、学校等的) 建立, 创办: a ~ member [英](团体等的) 创办人, 发起人; 基本成员 ②地基, 地脚; (机器的) 底座: the ~(s) of a building (dam) 房 (坝) 基 / a ~ plate 基础板, 底板 / a frame ~ 架座, 机架地脚 ③基础, 根本; 基本原则; 根据: the ~ of the national economy 国民经济的基础 ④基金; 靠基金建立 (或维持) 的机构: the Ford (Carnegie, Rockefeller) *Foundation* (美国) 福特 (卡内基, 洛克菲勒) 基金会 ⑤(衣服等的) 衬底; 妇女胸衣 (=~ garment) ‖*on the* ~ [英]属于由基金维持

的机构的；领取基金会提供的奖学金(或薪金)的 ‖~al a. 基础的，基本的 / ~er n. [英]领取基金会提供的奖学金(或薪金)的人 ‖~ cream 粉底霜(涂敷其他化妆品前打底用) / ~ muslin (上胶的)硬衬里细纱 / ~ net (上胶的)粗网眼纱 / ~ school 靠基金维持的学校 / ~ stone ①(特指建筑物等的开工典礼上放置的)基石 ②基础；根源

founder¹ ['faundə] n. 奠基者；创立者；缔造者 ‖~-'member n. (团体等的)创办人，发起人 / ~s' shares [英] (公司等的)发起人股份

founder² ['faundə] I ❶ vi. ①(马或骑马者因奔驰过度而)摔倒，变跛；(在泥淖中等中)动弹不得 ②(房屋等)坍倒；(土地等)陷落；(船)沉没 ③垮掉；失败 ④(马)患蹄叶炎 ❷ vt. ①使(马等)摔倒；使跛；(喂动物过饱)使动弹不得 ②使(船)沉没 ③破坏；损害 II n. ①(马的)蹄叶炎 ②(马的)胸肌风湿 (=chest ~)

founder³ ['faundə] n. 铸(造)工，翻砂工；铸字工

foundling ['faundliŋ] n. 弃儿: a ~ hospital 育婴堂

foundry ['faundri] n. ①铸造，翻砂: a ~ worker 铸造工人，翻砂工人 / ~ goods 铸件 ②铸工车间，铸工厂；玻璃(制造)厂 ‖~ iron, ~ pig (适于铸造用的)生铁 / ~ proof [印](打纸型制电版前的)最后校样

fount¹ [faunt] n. ①[诗]泉；源泉 ②(灯的)贮油器；墨水缸

fount² [faunt, fɒnt] n. =font²

fountain ['fauntin] n. ①泉水，喷泉 ②人造喷泉；人造喷泉装置；饮用喷泉 (=drinking ~) ③源泉；根源 ④液体贮藏器(如灯的贮油器、墨水缸) ⑤ =soda fountain ‖~'head n. 源泉；根源，本源 / ~ pen 自来水笔

four [fɔː] I num. 四；四个(人或物)；第四(卷、章、页等)(用例参看 eight) II n. ①四个(人或物)一组；[复][军]四路纵队: arrange by ~s 把…排成四个一组 / a column of ~s 四路纵队 / Make ~s! 成四路纵队集合! ②[复][机]四汽缸发动机；四汽缸汽车 ③四个人的划船队；四桨划船；[复]四桨划船比赛 ④四岁 ⑤四点钟 ‖on all ~s ①匍匐，爬着 ②[喻]完全相似的；完全一致的: The simile is on all ~s with the thing illustrated. 这个譬喻完全贴合。/ the ~ corners 见 corner ‖~fold a. & ad. 四倍；四重 / ~some ['fɔːsəm] n. ①四人一组 ②(游戏中，特指高尔夫球中的)双打: a mixed ~some 混合双打 ③参加双打者 ‖~-by-'two n. 擦枪布 / '~-cornered a. 四边形的；有四人参加的 / '~-coupled a. 有两对轮子的 / '~-course a. (农作物)四年轮作的 / '~-di'mensional a. [数]四维的 / '~-flush vi. [美俚]吹牛；吓唬 / '~-flusher n. [美俚]骗子；吹牛的人 / '~-'footed a. 四足的 / '~-'handed a. 有四只手的；(游戏)四人玩的；[音]二人合奏的 / Four Horsemen (基督教《圣经》中的)四骑士(指战争、饥馑、时疫、

死亡四大害) / Four Hundred (一地区、一社会的)名流，上层 / '~-in-hand ['fɔːrin'hænd] n. ①一人驾驭的四马；四马马车 ②一种活结领带；'~-'letter n. [美]庸俗的，下流的，黄色的: '~-letter words 具有四个字母的庸俗下流词语 / '~-o'clock n. [植]紫茉莉；[动]食蜜虫 / '~-part a. [音]四部合唱的 / ~pence ['fɔːpəns] n. 四便士 / ~penny ['fɔːpəni] a. 四便士的 / '~-ply a. (羊毛等)四股的；(木材等)四层的 / '~-'poster n. 有四根帐杆的卧床 / '~-'pounder n. [军]发射四磅炮弹的火炮 / '~-score n. & a. 八十 / '~-star a. [美]①极好的，优良的 ②(美军)四星(上将)级的 / '~-stroke cycle [机]四冲程循环 / '~-way a. 四面全通的；由四人参加的 / '~-'wheeler n. 四轮出租马车

fourteen ['fɔː'tiːn] I num. 十四；十四个(人或物)；第十四(卷、章、页等)(用例参看 eight) II n. ①十四岁 ②十四点钟(即下午两点) ‖~th num. ①第十四(个) ②十四分之一(的) n. (月的)第十四日

fourth [fɔːθ] I num. ①第四(个): ~ dimension 【物】第四维(相对论中指时间) ②四分之一(的): one (或 a) ~ 四分之一 / three ~s 四分之三 II n. ①[复](商品)四等品 ②[音]四度音程；四度和音；第四音 ③(月的)第四日 ‖the Fourth of July 美国独立纪念日 / the (glorious) Fourth [美] =the Fourth of July ‖~ly ad. 第四(列举条目等时用) ‖~ estate, Fourth Estate 新闻界 / Fourth Republic (法兰西)第四共和国 (1947—1958)

fowl [faul] I n. ([复] fowl(s)) ①禽；家禽(鸡、鸭、鹅；尤指长大成的鸡) ②禽肉 ‖barn-door (或 barnyard) ~ 鸡 / cholera 鸡霍乱，家禽的霍乱症 / ~ pest (或 plague) 家禽的瘟症 / variola 家禽痘疮，家禽疱疹 / game ~ 斗禽(如雄鸡) / guinea ~ 珍珠鸡 II vi. 打(或捕)野禽 ‖~er n. 捕野禽者 ‖~ run [英]养鸡场

fox [fɒks] I n. ①狐 ②狐皮 ③狡猾的人: an old ~ 老狐狸精 ④[海](多根绳子搓成的)绳索 ⑤[美俚]大学一年级生 ⑥[F-](以前住在美国威斯康星州的)印第安人 II ❶ vt. ①使(啤酒等)发酵变酸 ②[常用过去分词]使(书页等)生褐色、黄色斑点 ③为(皮鞋)换新鞋面 ④[俚]欺骗 ❷ vi. ①(啤酒等)变酸 ②(书页等)生斑变色 ③行为狡猾，用狡计 ‖play (the) ~ 行为狡猾 ‖'~-brush n. 狐尾 / ~ earth 狐穴 / '~-glove n. 【植】毛地黄 / '~-hole n. 【军】散兵坑(可容一、二人的小型掩体): a one-man (a two-man) ~hole 单人(双人)散兵坑 / '~-hound n. 猎狐(捕狐的大猎狗) / ~ hunt vi. (用猎狗)猎狐 / ~ hunt (用猎狗)猎狐 / '~-hunter n. 猎狐者 / ~'s sleep 假睡；假装的漠不关心 / ~ tail n. ①狐尾 ②【植】狐尾状植物(尤指看麦娘、狗尾草等)；石松 / '~-tail millet 【植】小米，谷子，粟 / '~-trot n. ①狐步舞 ②(骑马的)小快步 vi. 跳狐步舞

foxed [fɔkst] *a.* ①(书页等)生褐斑的, 变了色的 ②(皮鞋)修过面的 ③(啤酒等)变酸了的 ④ 受骗的

fraction ['frækʃən] *n.* ①小部分; 片断; 碎片: crumble into ~*s* 碎成小片 ②一点儿, 一些: a ~ closer 稍微近一点 ③【数】分数: a common (或 vulgar) ~ 普通分数 / a complex (或 compound) ~ 繁分数 / a proper (improper) ~ 真(假)分数 ④【化】(分)馏(部)分; 级分

fractional ['frækʃənl] *a.* ①部分的; 碎片的 ②分数的, 小数的; (有)零数的; 【商】不足买卖单位的 (如证券交易) ③【化】分馏的, 分级的 ‖*a* column 分馏塔, 分馏柱 / ~ currency [总称]辅币 / ~ distillation 分馏 ‖not by a ~ 一点也不 / to a ~ 完全地, 百分之百地

fractious ['frækʃəs] *a.* ①倔强的, 反抗的 ②暴躁的; 易怒的 ‖~ly *ad.* ~ness *n.*

fracture ['fræktʃə] **I** *n.* ①破裂; 断裂; 折断 ②裂缝; 裂面; 裂痕 ③【医】骨折: comminuted ~ 粉碎骨折 / compound ~ 复合骨折 ④【矿】断口; 断面 **II** *vt. & vi.* (使)破裂; (使)断裂; (使)折断

fragile ['frædʒail] *a.* ①脆的; 易碎的, 易损坏的 ②脆弱的; 虚弱的; 体质弱的: a ~ constitution 虚弱的体质

fragment I ['frægmənt] *n.* ①碎片, 破片, 碎块 ②断片: a shell ~ 弹片 / reduce to ~*s* 弄碎 ③(文艺作品等的)未完成部分: This poem is only a ~. 这仅是一个未完成的诗篇。 **II** ['frægment] *vi. & vt.* (使)成碎片; (使)分裂

fragmentary ['frægməntəri] *a.* ①碎片的, 碎块的; 断片的 ②不完全的, 不连续的: ~ experience 局部经验 ③【地】碎屑的: ~ ejecta 喷屑

fragrant ['freigrənt] *a.* 香的, 芬芳的: ~ flowers 香花 / ~ memories 甜蜜的回忆 ‖~ly *ad.*

frail¹ [freil] **I** *a.* ①脆弱的, 易损的; 虚弱的 ②意志薄弱的, 易被引诱的 **II** *n.* [美俚]少女; 少妇 ‖~ly *ad.* ~ness *n.*

frail² [freil] *n.* ①(盛葡萄干等用的)灯心草篓 ②灯心草篓的容量

frailty ['freilti] *n.* ①脆弱; 虚弱 ②意志薄弱 ③因意志薄弱而犯的错误; 弱点

frame [freim] **I** *n.* ①构架, 骨架; 结构; 【机】架; 座: the ~ of a building 建筑物的构架 / the ~ of an umbrella 伞骨 / a missile ~【军】导弹弹体 / a pea ~ 豌豆架 ②框架, 框子: a window (door) ~ 窗(门)框 / backing ~【摄】安片框 ③(人或动物的)骨胳; 身躯: a man of massive ~ 身躯魁伟的人 ④心情, 精神状态: in a cheerful ~ of mind 心情愉快 ⑤(社会、政府等的)组织, 机构: the ~ of society 社会组织 / the ~ of a government 政府机构 ⑥(电影的)画面, 镜头, (电视图像的)帧 ⑦【船】肋骨: square (斜)直肋骨 ⑧【农】(可搬动的)轻便玻璃温室 ⑨【印】活字架, 排字台 ⑩[美俚]诬陷 ⑪[美俚]职业拳击赛的一个回合; 棒球的一局 **II ❶** *vt.* ①构造; 建造; 塑造: ~ a shelter for bicycles 搭一个

自行车棚 / houses ~*d* to resist storms 造得足以抵御暴风雨的房子 / young people ~*d for* hard struggle 能够进行艰苦奋斗的青年人 ②制定, 拟出(计划等); 设计; 想象: ~ a plan 订计划 ③给…装框子(或框架): ~ a photograph 给相片装框子 / a landscape ~*d* in an archway 从拱门中望出去的景色 ④使适合 ⑤[俚]陷害, 诬害; 捏造(up): be ~*d* 遭到陷害 / ~ a case against sb. 捏造案情陷害某人 ⑥说出, 讲出, 发出: His lips ~*d* a few words. 他讲出了几个字。 **❷** *vi.* [英方]有成功希望 ‖~ of reference 【物】参照系, 参考系统 ②观点; 理论 / sheriff's picture ~ 绞索 ‖~r *n.* ①制订者, 创作者 ②构架(或框架等)的制造者(或装配者) ‖~ aerial, ~ antenna【无】框形天线 / ~ house 木屋; 木板房子 / '~-up *n.* [美俚]诬害; 阴谋 / '~work *n.* ①构架(工程); 框架; 结构: a bridge with a steel ~*work* 钢结构桥梁 ②机构, 结构

franchise ['fræntʃaiz] **I** *n.* ①公民权(尤指选举权) ②[美](政府给予个人、公司或社团经营某种事业的)特权, 特许 ③保险契约规定的免赔限度, 免赔额 **II** *vt.* 给…以特权

frank [fræŋk] **I** *a.* ①坦白的, 直率的; 真诚的: to be ~ with you [用作插入语]老实对你说 / a ~ reply 坦率的回答 ②【医】症状明显的 **II** *vt.* ①免费邮寄 ②盖免费递寄邮戳于(邮件); 用自动邮资盖印机盖印于(邮件) ③在…上盖"邮资已付"戳 ④使(人)便于通行; 准许免费通过 ⑤ 释放; 豁免 **III** *n.* ①免费邮寄权利 ②免费邮寄戳(或签字) ③免费邮寄的信(或其他邮件) ‖~ly *ad.* 免费地; 直率地; 真诚地: ~ly speaking 老实说, 坦率地说 / ~ness *n.* ‖'~ing-ma'chine *n.* 加盖"邮资已付"印记的自动邮资盖印机

frankincense ['fræŋkin,sens] *n.* 乳香 ‖~ oil【化】蓝丹油

frantic ['fræntik] *a.* ①(因忿怒、痛苦、悲哀或快乐等而)激动得发狂似的: ~ applause at the end of the opera 歌剧终了时的狂热掌声 ②狂暴的, 狂乱的 ‖~(al)ly *ad.* / ~ness *n.*

fraternal [frə'tə:nl] *a.* ①兄弟的; 兄弟般的, 友好的: ~ parties (countries) 兄弟党(国家) / ~ relations (solidarity) 兄弟般的关系(团结) ②[美]兄弟会的, 互助会的 ‖~ly *ad.* ‖~ association, ~ order, ~ society [美]兄弟会, 互助会

fraternity [frə'tə:niti] *n.* ①兄弟关系; 友爱; 博爱: ~ between our two peoples 我们两国人民之间的兄弟友谊 ②(美国)大学生联谊会(常以希腊字母命名, 并有秘密仪式); 兄弟会, 互助会 ③一群同职业(或同兴趣、同信仰)的人: the medical ~ 医务界 ④ (动物)一次交配所生的全部幼畜

fraternize, fraternise ['frætənaiz] **❶** *vi.* ①亲如兄弟; 亲善; 友爱 ②与敌兵(或占领区人民)亲善, 与敌对集团的人友善; [口] 与敌国女性发生性关系 **❷** *vt.* [罕]使亲如兄弟, 使亲善 ‖fraternization [,frætənai'zeifən] *n.*

fraud [frɔ:d] *n.* ①欺骗, 欺诈; 欺诈行为; 诡计:

expose a ~ 揭穿骗局 ②骗子;假货 ‖*in* ~ *of* (或 *to the* ~ *of*)【律】为了诈骗…

fraught [froːt] *a.* [只作表语]充满…的: an event ~ *with* significance 一件意义重大的事

fray[1] [frei] **I** *n.* ①吵架;打架;冲突 ②争议;辩论 **II** ❶ *vt.* [古]使惊吓;把…吓唬走 ❷ *vi.* [古]吵架;打架

fray[2] [frei] **I** ❶ *vt.* ①磨损(织物的边缘);摩擦(绳子的末端)以致纤维散开: ~ed cuffs 磨破的袖口 ②使(关系、神经等)紧张 ❷ *vi.* 被磨损,被擦碎 **II** *n.* (织物等的)磨损处 ‖~ing *n.* [总称]织物磨损后落下的碎片;摩擦后落下的东西

freak [friːk] **I** *n.* ①任性的举动,怪诞的行为;怪念头 ②[古]任性;异想天开: out of mere ~ 全出于想入非非 ③畸形的人(或动植物)(= ~ of nature);反常现象: ~s of weather 天气的种种反常现象 ④[美俚]吸毒成瘾者;颓废派一员 **II** *a.* 反常的;奇特的: ~ shapes 奇形怪状 **III** *vt.* 在…上形成奇特的斑纹(或条纹) ‖~ out [俚] ①因服毒品(或受声、像影响)产生幻觉;通过吸毒逃避现实 ②成为颓废派 ③使处于极度兴奋中 ④行动反常 ‖~ed *a.* 有奇特的斑纹(或条纹)的 ‖~-out *n.* ①吸毒引起的幻觉;逃避现实(尤指通过吸毒);通过吸毒逃避现实的人 ②颓废派的聚会 ③反常的行动

freckle ['frekl] **I** *n.* 雀斑;(皮肤上因日晒而生的)斑点 **II** *vt.* & *vi.* (使)生雀斑;(使)生斑点

free [friː] **I** *a.* ①自由的;无约束的: ~ style【体】(游泳,滑冰等的)自由式 / ~ translation 意译 / This screw has worked ~. 这只螺丝松了。
②空闲的;(空间、房屋等)空余的: When will you be ~? 你什么时候有空? / I have two ~ evenings this week. 我本星期两个晚上有空。/ the ~ floor space of the workshop 车间里空余的地方 / Are there any ~ rooms (beds) in your hostel? 你们招待所里还有空房间(床位)吗?
③无…的: an ice-~ harbour 不冻港 / an interest-~ loan 无息贷款 / a nuclear-weapon-~ zone 无核武器区
④免费的;免税的: Admission ~. 免费入场。/ We enjoy ~ medical care. 我们享受公费医疗。/ ~ goods 免征进口税的货物
⑤(用钱)大手大脚的,滥用浪费的;(言论、生活等)随便的,不严肃的,不检点的: *Free* spending of public money is not to be tolerated. 决不能容忍滥用公款的现象。/ be ~ in one's talk 讲话太随便 / be rather too ~ with sb. 对某人在态度上过于随便
⑥丰富的,大量的;(用钱)慷慨的;(讲话等)直爽的,坦白的(*with*): He is ~ *with* his suggestions and criticisms. 他提批评建议很爽快。/ a ~ bloomer 开花多的植物
⑦【化】游离的,自由的: ~ state 游离状态 / ~ oxygen 游离氧
⑧轻快的,从容的: a ~ gait 从容的步伐
⑨(道路等)畅通无阻的;(港口、城市等)自由开放的: a ~ road ahead 前路畅通 / a ~ port (market) 自由港(市场)
⑩【海】(风向)顺风的: a ~ wind 顺风
⑪【语】(重音)自由的,不固定的
II *ad.* ①自由地,无阻碍地;【海】(行船)顺风地: a ship sailing ~ over the sea 在海上顺风行驶的船
②免费地: A special show was arranged to admit ~ the family members of the workers. 安排了一个专场来免费招待工人家属。
III *vt.* 使自由,解放;免除;解除,使摆脱(*of*, *from*): This area is ~d of malaria. 这个地区已消灭了疟疾。/ ~ one's mind *of* the influence of idealism 清除思想中的唯心主义影响 ‖a ~ *hand* 见 *hand* / *for* ~ 免费: get (give) sth. *for* ~ 免费得到(赠送)某物 / ~ *alongside ship*【商】船边交货(略作 FAS 或 f. a. s.) / ~ *and easy* ①不拘形式的,随便的 ②[用作名词]可以吸烟的音乐会;聚餐(尤指在酒吧间的);下流音乐厅(或酒馆) / ~ *from* 不受…影响的;没有…的: be ~ *from* arrogance and rashness 不骄不躁 / ~ *of* ①无…的;摆脱了…的: a house ~ *of* mice 一所消灭了老鼠的房屋 / ~ *of* charge 免费 ②离开;在…外面: The ship was ~ *of* the harbour. 船离开了港口。/ ~ *on board*【商】船上交货,离岸价格(略作 FOB 或 f. o. b.) / ~ *on rail*【商】火车上交货(略作 FOR 或 f. o. r.)/ *have* one's *hands* ~ 见 *hand* / *make* ~ *with* ①擅用 ②对…放肆 / *make* sb. ~ *of* 给予某人分享…的权利;让某人任意利用(图书室等) / *of* one's (own) ~ *will* 出于自愿 / *set* ~ 使获得自由;释放: *set* the war prisoners ~ 释放战俘 / *with a* ~ *hand* 见 *hand* ‖~board *n.* (船)干舷高度,干舷 / ~booter *n.* 海盗;强盗 / ~born *a.* 生来是自由的 / ~-choice *a.* 由牲口任意选择饲料的 / *Free Churches* (由英国国教分离出来的)独立教会 / ~-drop *n.* (不用降落伞的)自由空投(物) *vt.* 自由空投 / ~ energy【物】自由能 / ~ fall ①(跳伞等的)自由降落;降落伞张开前的降落 ②(火箭等的)惯性运动 / ~ flight【宇】自由飞行 / ~-for-all *n.* 任何人可以参加的竞赛(或赛跑);可以自由发表意见的争论;大吵大闹,打群架 对任何人开放的 / ~hand *a.* (不用器械)徒手画的 / ~-handed *a.* 慷慨的;(用钱)大方的 / ~-hearted *a.* 坦白的;慷慨的;冲动的 / ~hold *n.* 地产(或职位等)的完全保有;完全保有的地产 / ~ house 可卖各种牌子的酒的酒店 / ~labo(u)r ①自由人的劳动(与奴隶劳动相对而言) ②[总称]不属于工会的工人 / ~ lance ①(中世纪的)自由骑士;雇佣游勇 ②(不按照团体的路线)自由行动的人 ③(无固定职业,以卖文、卖艺为生的)自由作家(或演员) / ~-lance *vi.* 自由作家(或演员) / ~ list ①免收进出口税的货物单 ②免费入场名单 / ~-living *a.* ①沉溺于吃喝玩乐的 ②【生】独立生存的;非寄生的,非共生的 / ~loader *n.* [美口]老是利用别人家

慨占便宜的人 / **~ love** 未经合法结婚的自由同居 / **'~man** *n.* 自由民; 享有市民特权的人; 荣誉市民 / **~ market** 自由市场 / **'Free₌mason** *n.* 共济会 (Free & Accepted Masons) 成员 / **'Free₌masonry** *n.* 共济会的纲领; 共济会仪式; [集合名词]共济会成员 / **'~,minded** *a.* 无精神负担的 / **~ radical** 【化】游离基 / 无奴隶制的地方;【美史】(南北战争前禁止蓄奴的)自由地区, 自由土地 / **~ speech** 言论自由 / **'~-'spoken** *a.* 直言的; 讲话坦率的 / **'~'standing** *a.*【建】独立式的 / **Free State** ①[常用复]【美史】(南北战争前)自由州; 不使用奴隶地区 ②【史】爱尔兰自由邦 (=Irish Free State) / **'~stone** *n.* ①软性石; 易切石 ②容易与核分开的果实 *a.* (果实等)容易与核分开的 / **'~-'swinging** *a.* 大胆的, 直率的; 不考虑个人的 / **'~'thinker** *n.* (尤指宗教上的)自由思想家; 理性主义者, 唯理论者 / **'~'thinking** *a.* 自由思想的 (尤指宗教上) / **~ thought** (十八世纪尤不受传统宗教思想束缚的)自由思想 / **~ trade** 自由贸易 / **~ trader** 自由贸易主义者 / **~ verse** (不受格律约束的)自由诗 / **~ vibration**【物】自由振动 / **'~way** *n.* 快车道; 超速干道 / **~ wheel**【机】滑轮(自行车的)飞轮 / **'~'wheel** *vi.* ①不踩踏脚让自行车靠惯性滑行 (汽车等)惯性滑行: **~wheel** down a slope (车辆或驾驶者)滑行下坡 ②随心所欲(或放任自流)地行动(或生活) / **'~'wheeling** *n.* (机动车、自行车等)惯性滑行 *a.* 惯性滑行的; 随心所欲的, 放任自流的 / **~ will** 自愿; 自由意志;【哲】自由意志论 / **'~will** *a.* 自愿的, 非强迫的; 自由意志论的 / **~ zone** (海港或机场附近)收受(或转运、堆放)货物不需付关税的地区

freedom ['fri:dəm] *n.* ①自由; 自主: **~** of speech among the people 人民内部的言论自由 / necessity and **~**【哲】必然和自由 ②(行动、使用等)自由权 ③直率, 坦率 ④放肆, 过分亲密 ⑤【物】自由度 ⑥免除, 解脱 (*from*): **~** from taxation 免税 ⑦(城市、公司等的)特权: **~** of the city (授与贵宾的)荣誉市民权 ‖the Four Freedoms 四大自由 (一九四一年美国总统罗斯福提出, 指所谓"言论自由、信仰自由、免于匮乏、免于恐惧") / **~** of the air【军】空战主动权 / **~** of the press 新闻自由, 出版自由 / **~** of the seas 商船在公海上的自由航行权; (国际法)战时中立国船只不受交战国军舰干涉的自由航行权 ‖take (或 use) **~s** with sb. 对某人放肆 / with **~** 自由地 ‖'~-₌fighter *n.* 争取自由的战士 / **Freedom Rider** [美]为争取公民权利去南方各州乘坐实行种族隔离的交通车辆的示威者

freely ['fri:li] *ad.* ①自由地; 无拘束地, 随意地 ②直率地, 坦白地 ③慷慨地, 大量地 ④免费地

freeze [fri:z] **I** (froze [frouz], frozen ['frouzn]) **❶** *vi.* ①结冰; 凝固: Fresh water **~**s at 0°C. 淡水在摄氏零度结冰。②大冷起来; 感到冷极: 冻僵: It is *freezing*. 天气冷极。/ I'm *freezing*.

我感到冷极了。③冻牢, 凝住: The piston *froze* in the cylinder. 活塞冻牢在汽缸里。/ The two metal surfaces *froze* together. 两块金属表面凝在一起了。④愣住, 变呆板(或僵硬); 变得冷淡: Smiles *froze* on their faces. 笑容在他们脸上不自然地僵住了。⑤[美口]站住不动: He yelled **~**. 他大喝一声: 不许动! **❷** *vt.* ①使结冰; 使凝固; 使冻住: The road is *frozen* hard. 路上的冰结得很硬。②用冷冻保藏(食物) ③使冻僵(或冻伤、冻死) ④使呆住; 用非常冷淡的态度对待 ⑤冻结(工资、物价等) **II** *n.* ①结冰; 凝固; (工资、物价等的)冻结 ②严寒期 ‖**~** (on) to sth. [口]紧紧抓住某物 / **~** over 全面结冰 / **~ sb. out** [口](用冷淡态度、竞争等)逐出某人, 逼走某人 / **~ sb.'s blood** (或 **make sb.'s blood ~**) 使某人极度恐惧 / **~** (或 be frozen) to death 冻死 / **~ up** ①(使)冻结 ②变呆板(或僵硬); (态度方面)变得非常冷淡 ‖**~r** *n.* ①制冰淇淋者; 冷藏工人 ②冷冻器, 冷藏箱; 冰箱 ③冷藏车; 冷藏库 ‖**'~-'dry** *vt.* 冻干

freezing ['fri:ziŋ] *a.* ①冻结的; 致冷的, 凝固的: a **~** machine 冷冻机 ②极冷的: What **~** weather! 好冷的天气! ③(态度)非常冷淡的 ‖**mixture** 冷却剂, 冷冻混合物 / **~ point**【物】冰点, 凝固点

freight [freit] **I** *n.* ①[英](船运的)货物; [美](水上、陆上、空中运输的)货物: an aeroplane carrying a heavy **~** 载有大量货物的飞机 / **~** paid 运费付讫 / **~** to be collected 运费待收 ③货运 ④[美]货运列车 (=**~** train) ⑤负担, 重担 **II** *vt.* ①装货于: **~** a ship with wheat 把小麦装上船 ②使充满: Every word he said was **~**ed with meaning. 他说的每句话都意味深长。③运输(货物) ④租(船等)运货; 出租(船等)运货 ‖by **~** 用普通货车运送(区别于 by express 用快车运送) / **dead ~** 空舱费 / **drag** (或 **pull**) **one's ~** [美俚]离开, 出发 / **~ forward** 运费由提货人支付 ‖**~ car** [美](一节)货车 / **~ train** [美]货运列车

freighter ['freitə] *n.* ①租船人 ②(货物的)托运人; 承运人 ③货船; 运输机: an air **~** 运货飞机

French [frentʃ] **I** *a.* ①法国的, 法兰西的 ②法国人的 ③法语的 ④法国式的 **II** *n.* ①[the **~**][总称]法国人 ②法语 ‖pedlar's **~** 窃贼的行话 / take **~ leave** 不告而别; 擅自离开; 擅自行动 ‖**~less** *a.* 不懂法语的 / **~ bean** [英]菜豆 (=kidney bean) / **~ chalk** 滑石粉 / **~ curve** 曲线板, 曲线规 / **~ grey**, **~ gray** 浅灰色 / **~ horn** 法国号(一种涡旋形铜管乐器) / **~ letter** [英俚]避孕套 / **~man** ['frentʃmən] *n.* 法国人, 法兰西人 / **~ window** 落地长窗 / **~woman** ['frentʃ,wumən] *n.* 法国女人, 法兰西女人

frenzy ['frenzi] **I** *n.* 狂乱, 疯狂似的激动: be in a **~** of rage 暴跳如雷 / a **~** of delight 狂喜 **II** *vt.* [常用被动语态]使狂乱

frequency ['fri:kwənsi] *n.* ①屡次，频繁 ②次数，出现率 ③【物】频率，周率: audio ~ 音频 / ~ modulation 调频，频率调制 / medium (或 mean) ~ 中频 / resonance (或 resonant) ~ 谐振频率，共振频率 / ultrahigh ~ 超高频 / ultra-low ~ 超低频 / very high ~ 甚高频 / very low ~ 甚低频

frequent[1] ['fri:kwənt] *a.* ①时常发生的，频繁的; 屡次的: Rains are ~ here in spring. 这儿春季常下雨。 ②经常的; 习以为常的，常见的: a ~ caller (或 visitor) 常客 / a ~ practice 经常的做法 ③(脉搏)快的，急的 ‖**~ly** *ad.*

frequent[2] [fri(:)'kwent] *vt.* 常到，常去，时常出入于: Tourists ~ the place. 游客常去该地。 / Many ships ~ the port. 许多船只常来此港。 ‖**~er** *n.* 常去某处的人; 常客

fresco ['freskou] I ([复] fresco(e)s) *n.* ①壁画法: paint in ~ 作壁画 ②壁画 II *vt.* 在…上作壁画; 用壁画法画出

fresh[1] [freʃ] I *a.* ①新的; 新近的; 新到的: ~ troops 生力军 / ~ news (或 information) 新消息 / ~ paint 未干的油漆 / young workers ~ from school 刚从学校中出来的青年工人 / get rid of the stale and take in the ~ 吐故纳新 ②新鲜的; 未经腌熏的; (水)淡的: ~ fruit (eggs, milk) 新鲜的水果(蛋，牛奶) / ~ meat (fish) 鲜肉(鱼) / ~ water 淡水 ③另外的; 外加的: take a ~ sheet of paper 再拿一张纸 / make a ~ start 重新开始 ④无经验的; 不熟练的: a ~ hand 新手 ⑤(空气，气候)清新的; 凉爽的; (风)强劲的: go out for ~ air 出去呼吸新鲜空气 / a ~ spring morning 清新的春天早晨 ⑥(颜色)鲜艳的; 明朗的; 有生气的; 气色好的: ~ colours 鲜艳的色彩 / a ~ complexion 气色好的脸容 ⑦精神饱满的: We felt ~ even after a long march. 长途行军后，我们还是感到精力充沛。 ⑧(谈话等)有创见的; 生动的; 有启发性的 ⑨(母牛)刚开始产奶的; 新近产犊的 II *ad.* 刚，才: a ~ laid egg 刚生的蛋 III *n.* ①(一天，一年等的)开始: in the ~ of the morning 在清晨 ②河水的暴涨; 泛滥 ③(注入咸水中的)淡水流 ‖**as ~ as paint** 精神饱满的 / **break ~ ground** 见 ground[1] / **~ out of** [美俚] 刚卖掉…; 刚用完… ‖**~er** *n.* [英俚]大学一年级生 / **~ness** *n.* ‖~ **breeze** 五级风(每小时 29—38 公里) / '**~-'caught** *a.* 刚捕获的 / '**~-'coined** *a.* (硬币)新铸造的 / ~ **gale** 八级风，大风(每小时 62—74 公里) / **~man** ['freʃmən] *n.* ①新手，生手 ②大学一年级学生; [美]中学一年级学生 / '**~-run** *a.* (鲑鱼等)刚从海里游到淡水中的 / '**~,water** *a.* ①淡水的: ~water fishery 淡水养鱼业 ②惯于内河航行的 ③无经验的; 不熟练的 ④内地的; 地方的; 不知名的: a ~water college 内地的大学(或学院)

fresh[2] [freʃ] *a.* [美俚] ①冒失的，无礼的; 放肆的 (尤指对异性) ②醉醺醺的

fret[1] [fret] I (fretted; fretting) ❶ *vt.* ①使烦恼; 使烦躁; 使发愁: ~ oneself with regret 因悔恨而烦恼 / Don't ~ yourself ill. 不要愁出病来。 ②侵蚀; 腐蚀; 使销损; 使磨损: a knife *fretted* by rust 锈掉的刀子 / *fretted* rope 磨损了的绳子 / The horse is *fretting* its bit. 马在咬嚼子。 ③(经侵蚀而)形成: The stream *fretted* a channel through the soft earth. 溪流侵袭松软的土地，形成了一条渠道。 ④使(水面)起波纹: The wind *fretted* the surface of the lake. 风吹皱湖面。 ❷ *vi.* ①烦恼; 烦躁; 发愁: What are you *fretting* about? 你为什么事烦恼? / ~ over one's illness 因有病而发愁 / ~ at a teasing remark 因听到嘲弄的话而着恼 ②侵蚀; (对精神等)起折磨作用 ③销损; 磨损; 被腐蚀 ④(水面)起波纹 II *n.* ①烦恼; 烦躁: in a ~ (或 on the ~) 处于烦躁状态 ②侵蚀 ③被侵蚀之处 ‖**~ and fume** 恼火 / **~ away** (或 **out**) 在烦恼中度过

fret[2] [fret] I *n.* ①【建】回纹饰 ②【音】(吉他等弦乐器指板上定音的)档子 ③网状饰物 II (fretted; fretting) *vt.* 用回纹装饰(天花板等) ‖'**~saw** *n.* 线锯 / '**~work** *n.* 【建】浮雕细工

fretful ['fretful] *a.* ①烦恼的; 烦躁的: a ~ baby 躁动不安的婴孩 ②(水面)起波纹的 ③(风)一阵阵的 ‖**~ly** *ad.* / **~ness** *n.*

friar ['fraiə] *n.* 男修道士; 行乞修道士 ‖~'s **lantern** 鬼火

friction ['frikʃən] *n.* ①摩擦; 摩擦力 ②擦热皮肤; moist ~ 【医】湿擦 ③不和，摩擦，倾轧: (a) family ~ 家庭的不和 ‖~ **ball** 摩擦球 / ~ **brake** 摩擦制动器，摩擦闸 / ~ **clutch** 摩擦离合器 / ~ **cone** 摩擦(锥)轮 / ~ **drive** 摩擦传动 / ~ **gear(ing)** 摩擦传动装置 / '~-,**monger** *n.* 扇动不和者 / ~ **tape** 摩擦带; 绝缘胶布

frictional ['frikʃənl] *a.* 摩擦的; 由摩擦而生的

Friday ['fraidi] *n.* ①星期五 ②忠仆(源于英国小说《鲁滨逊飘流记》中鲁滨逊的仆人的名字) ‖*Good* ~ 【基督教】耶稣受难日(复活节前的星期五) ‖~s *ad.* [美]每星期五; 在任何星期五

fridge [fridʒ] *n.* [英口] =refrigerator

friend [frend] I *n.* ①朋友; 友人 ~ 知心朋友 / distinguish between ~ and foe 分清敌友 ②赞助者，支持者，同情者; 助手 ③相识者; [称呼语，用在姓或名前]朋友(如 ~ Dick, ~ Jones 等): my honourable ~ 英国下议院议员间的称呼 / my learned ~ 英国法院律师间的称呼 ④[苏格兰][复]家属 ⑤有帮助的事物(或品质) ⑥[F-] 【基督教】公谊会教友: the Society of *Friends* 公谊会 II *vt.* [罕]与…为友，帮助 ‖**a ~ in** (或 **at**) **court** 有势力的朋友 / **A ~ in need is a ~ indeed.** [谚]患难时朋友才是真朋友。 / **be ~s with** 与…交友 / **keep ~s with** 与…保持友好 / **make ~s again** 言归于好，重修旧好 / **make ~s with** 与…交朋友，与…友好 / **part ~s** 不伤感情地分手

friendly ['frendli] I *a.* ①友好的; 友谊的: be ~ with sb. 与某人友好 / ~ troops 友军 / The talks proceeded in a ~ atmosphere. 会谈在友好的气氛中进行。/ a ~ match (或 game) 友谊赛 ② 赞助的,支持的 (to): be ~ to a cause 赞助某事业 ③(事物)便利的,顺适的: a ~ shower 及时雨 **II** *ad.* 友好地; 朋友般地 ‖**friendlily** *ad.* / **friendliness** *n.*

friendship ['frendʃip] *n.* 友谊;友好; 表现友谊的事例: *Friendship* first, competition second. 友谊第一,比赛第二。/ a ~ visit 友好访问 / a ~ of twenty years 二十年的友谊

frieze[1] [fri:z] **I** *n.* 起绒粗呢 **II** *vt.* 使起绒毛

frieze[2] [fri:z] *n.* 【建】(柱的)中楣 ‖**~ panel** 束腰板 / **~ rail** 上腰板

frigate ['frigit] *n.* ①(十八世纪到十九世纪)装有大炮的快速帆船 ② 驱逐领舰 ③ 护卫舰;护航舰

frig(e) [fridʒ] *n.* [英口] =refrigerator

fright [frait] **I** *n.* ① 惊吓,恐怖: get (或 have) a ~ 吃一惊 / give sb. a ~ 使某人吃一惊 / take ~ (at sth.) (因某事)受惊 ②[口]奇形怪状的人(或物) **II** *vt.* [诗]使惊恐,吓唬

frighten ['fraitn] **①** *vt.* 使惊恐, 吓唬: ~ the birds away 把鸟吓走 / be ~ed out of one's life 吓得要命 / be ~ed out of one's wits 被吓呆,被吓得魂不附体 **②** *vi.* 惊恐,害怕: You'll find that I don't ~ easily. 你会发现我不是轻易就害怕的。‖ ~ **sb. into (out of) doing sth.** 使某人吓得做(不做)某事 ‖**~ed** *a.* ①受惊吓的: a ~ed child 受惊的孩子 ②[口]害怕…的 (of): be ~ed of sb. (sth.) 害怕某人(某事)

frightful ['fraitful] *a.* ① 可怕的: A ~ traffic disaster was avoided. 一次可怕的交通事故避免了。②[口]非常的;丑的,讨厌的: a ~ bore 一个讨厌得要命的家伙(或事物) ‖**~ly** *ad.* 可怕地;[口]非常地 / **~ness** *n.* ①可怕;丑恶,讨厌 ②战争中对敌方平民使用恐怖手段的政策(或行动)

frigid ['fridʒid] *a.* ① 寒冷的: ~ weather 寒冷的天气 / a ~ climate 寒冷的气候 / the ~ zones 寒带 ② 冷淡的;索然无味的: a ~ manner 冷淡的态度 / a ~ conversation 冷淡的谈话 ③(妇女)缺乏性感的 ‖**~ly** *ad.* / **~ness** *n.*

frigidity [fri'dʒiditi] *n.* ① 寒冷; 冷淡;索然无味 ②【医】性感缺失

frill [fril] **I** *n.* ①(服装的)褶边,饰边 ②【动】壳皱 ③[摄]胶片边缘的皱褶 ④复[口]不必要的装饰,虚饰; 臭架子: put on ~s 摆架子,装腔作势;大事渲染 ⑤[美俚]女孩,妇女 **II ①** *vt.* 在…上镶褶边(或饰边) **②** *vi.* (胶片边缘)起皱褶 ‖**~ed** *a.* 有饰边的 / **~ery** *n.* 衣褶边

fringe [frindʒ] **I** *n.* ①穗, 缘饰, 流苏; 毛边, 蓬边 ②边缘; [喻](学问的)初步, 皮毛: on the ~(s) of a forest 在森林的边缘 ③一群略知皮毛(或见解偏激)的人 ④(妇女头发的)前刘海 ⑤[动]伞;缘缨 ⑥[物](光学中的)条纹: diffraction ~s 衍射条纹,绕射条纹 / interference ~s 干涉条纹 ⑦ =~ benefit **II** *vt.* ① 加穗于, 在…上装以

缘饰: a road ~d with willows 两旁柳树成行的道路 ②是…的边缘: Willows ~d the lawn. 草坪周围长着柳树。**III** *a.* ①边缘的 ②附加的 ③较次要的: ~ industries 次要工业部门 ‖**~less** *a.* 无穗的,无缘饰的 ‖**~ area**【无】线条区,电视接收边缘区;散乱边纹区;干扰区域 / **~ benefit** 小额优惠

frisk [frisk] **I ①** *vi.* 欢跃; 轻快活泼地跳跃, 跳跳蹦蹦: Lambs ~ed about in the pastures. 小羊在牧场上跳来跳去。**②** *vt.* ① 轻快地摇动: The puppy ~ed its tail. 小狗轻摇尾巴。②[俚]搜(某人)的身 ③[俚]扒窃 **II** *n.* ①欢跃;快活的时刻 ②搜身

frisky ['friski] *a.* 好欢跃的, 活泼的: as ~ as a kitten 象小猫那样的活泼蹦跳 ‖**friskily** *ad.* / **friskiness** *n.*

fritter[1] ['fritə] **I** *vt.* ①消耗, 浪费 (away): ~ away time (energy, money) 浪费时间(精力, 金钱) ②[罕]弄碎;切细;把…撕成小片 **II** *n.* [罕]碎片;小块

fritter[2] ['fritə] *n.* (果馅或肉馅)油煎饼

frivol ['frivəl] (frivol(l)ed; frivol(l)ing) **①** *vi.* 做无聊事;混日子 **②** *vt.* 浪费, 乱花(金钱、时间等) (away)

frivolous ['frivələs] *a.* ① 轻薄的, 轻浮的: ~ behaviour 轻浮的举动 ②琐屑的,无意义的 ‖**~ly** *ad.* / **~ness** *n.*

fro[1] [frou] *ad.* 往,去; 回, 向后(只用于 to and ~ 一语中): walk to and ~ 来回地走,来来去去

fro[2] [frə, frou] *prep.* [英方] =from

frock [frɔk] **I** *n.* ①(女)上衣;(儿童)外衣 ②工装 ③水手穿的羊毛紧身衣 ④僧袍 ⑤(男子的)礼服大衣 (=~ coat) ⑥(英国军队中)便装军大衣 **II** *vt.* ①使穿工装(或礼服大衣等) ②[宗]授…圣职

frog [frɔg] **I** *n.* ①蛙 ②【动】(马蹄底中部的)蹄楔 ③盘花钮扣 ④(附在腰带上的)挂剑圈,挂武器环 ⑤(铁路)辙叉 ⑥[俚][贬]法国人 **II** (frogged; frogging) *vi.* 捕蛙 ‖**a ~ in the throat** 轻度喉哑 ‖**froggy** *n.* & *a.* 似蛙(的); 多蛙(的) ‖**'~-eater** 食蛙者 / **[F-]** [贬]法国人 / **'~-fish** *n.* 鼍鱼科的鱼; 鮟鱇 / **[宗]**圣职 / **'~-hopping tactics** 跳进战术,越岛战术 / **~man** ['frɔgmən] *n.* 蛙人(穿戴蛙式潜水配备的人) / **'~-march** *vt.* & *n.* 使(犯人)面朝下而由四人执其四肢行走 / **~ spawn**【植】红藻

frolic ['frɔlik] **I** *n.* ①嬉戏;欢乐;闹玩儿 ②欢乐的聚会 **II** (frolicked; frolicking) *vi.* 嬉戏; 闹着玩 **III** *a.* 嬉戏的,欢乐的;闹着玩的 ‖**~ pad** [美俚]夜总会;舞厅

from [强 frɔm; 弱 frəm, frm] *prep.* ①[表示起点]从;从…起: ~ now on 从现在起, 今后 / 1921 to 1949 从一九二一年到一九四九年 ②[表示来源]从…;从, 由: ~ the masses, to the masses 从群众中来, 到群众中去 / Tell him ~ me that he mustn't be late. 请告诉他, 叫他不要迟到。 ③[表示根据]据, 从: Judging ~

the information we have received,.... 从我们所得到的情报来判断，… / paint ~ nature (绘画)写生 ④[表示原因、动机]由于，出于: suffer ~ a bad cold 患重伤风 / act ~ necessity 为需要所迫而采取行动 ⑤[表示原料]由: Steel is made ~ iron. 钢是由铁炼成的。[比较: This bed is made of iron. 这只床是用铁做的。] ⑥[表示情况、状态的转变]: ~ matter to consciousness 从物质到精神 / recover ~ illness 病愈 ⑦[表示脱离、离开]: never divorce oneself ~ the masses 从不脱离群众 / Why was he absent ~ school yesterday? 他昨天为什么不上学? / take five ~ ten 十减五 / apart ~ 除了…之外 ⑧[表示去除、免掉、阻止等]: be free ~ arrogance and rashness 不骄不躁 / protect seedlings ~ frost 保护秧苗使不受霜冻的影响 / What prevented you ~ coming? 什么事使你不能来? ⑨[表示识别、区别]: know right ~ wrong 分清是非 ⑩[后接副词或前置词]: ~ long ago 从很久以前起 / a sound ~ behind the door 从门后传出的声音 / The word has been in use ~ before World War II. 这词从第二次世界大战以前起就通用了。/ ~ under a table 从桌子下面(出来) / ~ out (of) 从…中出来

frond [frɔnd] *n.* ① 蕨类(或棕榈类、苏铁类)的叶 ②植物体(指藻类、苔藓) ③[诗]叶; 棕榈复叶

front [frʌnt] **I** *n.* ①前面, 正面; …前; 前部: the ~ of a building 建筑物的正面 / the east ~ of that building 那栋建筑物东的一面 / the ~ of attack (defence, penetration)【军】进攻(防御, 突破)正面 / sit in the ~ of the auditorium 坐在礼堂前座 ② 前线, 前方; 战线: go (或 be off) to the ~ 上前线 / the home ~ 后方战线(指战时军工生产、民防、治安等活动) ③(政治上的)阵线: a united ~ 统一战线 ④[诗]前额; 脸 ⑤(企业、团体等的)挂名负责人, 出面人物; 掩护物; 门面 ⑥外表; 装腔作势; 厚颜无耻 ⑦态度, 看法: change ~ 改变态度(或看法) ⑧[the ~](海滨避暑地的)滨海人行道; 海边(或湖边等)的土地: walk along the ~ 沿着滨海人行道行走 / a house on the ~ 临海的房屋 ⑨【气】锋(冷热空气的分界处): cold (warm) ~ 冷(热)锋 ⑩(妇女的)额前假发 ⑪(男子衬衫的)硬衬胸 ⑫(旅馆职员呼唤侍者时用语)前面的一个 **II** ❶ *vt.* ①面对, 朝向: ~ the audience 面对听众 / a house ~ing the sea (street) 正面临海(街)的房屋 ②面临于…的前面: a lawn ~ing a house 房屋前面的草地 ③对付; 反对, 对抗; 藐视 ④装饰…的正面: a building ~ed with marble 正面装饰着大理石的建筑物 ⑤【语】把…的发音部位移前; 把…发成舌前音 ❷ *vi.* 朝, 朝向 (on, upon, to, towards): windows ~ing east 朝东的窗子 / a sanatorium ~ing towards the lake 临湖的疗养院 **III** *a.* ①前面的, 前部的;(位置)在前的: a two-pair ~ (room) 三楼前室 ②【语】舌前的; (口腔)前部的: ~ vowels (舌)前元音 **IV** *ad.* 向前, 朝前; 在前面:

Eyes ~!【军】(口令)向前看! / be beset ~ and rear 腹背受敌 ‖**come to the ~** 引人注目; 变得明显; 出名 / ~ **to** ~ 面对面 / **get in ~ of** oneself [美口]着慌; 被搞糊涂 / **have the ~ to** (do) 居然有脸(做…), 竟好意思(做…) / **head and** ~ 见 head ‖**in** ~ 在前面: Please go in ~. 请前面走。/ **in** ~ **of** 在…前面: There is a pond in ~ of the house. 房屋前面有个池塘。/ **out** ~ 在观众(座)中 / **present** (或 **show, put on**) **a bold** ~ 装出大胆不怕的样子 / **put a bold** ~ **on** 勇敢地对付 / **put a bold** ~ **on the matter** 勇敢地对付那事 / **up** ~ ①在前面②预先 ‖**~less** *a.* ①无前部的; 无正面的 ②[军][古]无耻的 / **~ward(s)** *ad.* 向前 ‖**~ bencher** (英国下议院的)前座议员 / **~ line** 前线, 第一线 / **'~-'line** *a.* 前线的, 第一线的 / **~ man** (企业、团体等)的挂名负责人, 出面人物 / **~ matter** 书籍正文前的材料 / **~ office** (机关、机构中的)全体决策人员 / **~ page** ①(书的)标题页 ②(报纸)头版 / **'~-'page** *a.* (消息、新闻等)头版的, 重要的; 轰动的 *vt.* 把…登在头版: **~-page** an editorial 把一篇社论登在头版 / **'~-'runner** *n.* ①赛跑中跑在前头的人 ②竞争中的领先者

frontage ['frʌntidʒ] *n.* ① (建筑物等的)正面; 前方;方向 ②临街(或河、湖等)的土地 ③(临街的)屋前空地; (临街的)地界 ④(军队的)扎营地; 阅兵场地 ‖**~r** *n.* 临街(或临河等)空地的所有者

frontal ['frʌntl] **I** *a.* 前面的,正面的: a ~ attack 正面攻击 / ~ fog【气】锋面雾 ②额前的: ~ bone 【解】额骨 **II** *n.* ①额骨 ②额前的装饰物 ③(建筑物的)正面 ④【建】(门、窗上面的)人字形小墙(檐), 三角楣 ‖**~ly** *ad.*

frontier ['frʌntjə] *n.* ①国境, 边境; 边疆: the Italian ~ of France 法国的毗连意大利一面的边界 / a town on the ~ 边境城市 ‖~ guards 边防战士 ②(靠近未开发地带的)边远地区 ③(未经充分研究或利用的科学、文化等方面的)尖端, 新领域: the ~s of medicine (science) 医学(科学)尖端

frontispiece ['frʌntispi:s] **I** *n.* ① (书籍等的)卷首插画 ②【建】(房屋的)主立面; (有装饰的)正门; (门、窗上面的)人字形小墙(檐), 三角楣 **II** *vt.* 为…加进卷首插画

frost [frɔst] **I** *n.* ①冰冻, 严寒; 冰点以下的温度: There is still ~ in the ground. 土地还冻着。/ ten degrees of ~ [英]冰点下十度(即华氏二十二度) / black ~ 使草木发黑的严寒, 无霜的酷寒 / hard (或 sharp) ~ 酷寒 / early ~s 早寒, 秋寒 / late ~s 晚寒, 春寒 ②霜: There is ~ on the ground. 地上有霜。/ white (或 hoar) ~ 白霜(即普通的霜, 是 black ~ 之对) / a heavy ~ 厚霜 ③(态度、感情等的)冷淡: He has a ~ in his manner. 他的态度是冷冰冰的。④[俚]演出、旅行、宴会等的)失败; 扫兴, 乏味: His wordy and empty speech was a ~. 他的冗长空洞的话不受人欢迎。 **II** ❶ *vt.* ① 结霜于…上; 冻坏

（植物等）②在（糕饼等）上加糖霜混合物 ③使（玻璃、金属等）具有无光泽的霜状表面 ④使（头发等）变霜白 ⑤在（马蹄铁）上加钉 ❷ *vi.* ①受冻; 起霜 ②（油漆等）干成霜状 ‖*a dead ~* [俚]彻底的失败 / *Jack Frost* 霜精; 严寒 ‖*~ed a.* ①结霜的; 冻伤的 ②（糕饼）盖有糖霜混合物的 ③（玻璃、金属等）霜状表面的, 无光泽的, 磨砂的: *~ed glass* 毛玻璃 / *a ~ed bulb* 磨砂灯泡 ④（须、发等）因年老而变白的 ⑤（态度等）冷淡的 ⑥（蔬菜）经过快速冰冻的 / *~ing n.* ①结霜; 冻坏 ②（盖在糕饼上的）糖霜混合物 ③（玻璃、金属等的）无光泽的霜状表面, 磨砂粉, 清漆与胶水的混合物（供美化装饰用） / *~less a.* 无霜（冻）的 ‖*~bite n.* 霜害; 冻伤 *vt.* 使遭冻害; 冻伤 / *'~,bitten a.* 受霜害的; 冻伤的 / *'~-bound a.* (土地等)冰冻的 / *~ heave* (道路等)冻胀, 冰冻隆胀 / *'~work n.* (窗上冻结的)霜花; (银器等的)霜花纹装饰

frosty ['frɔsti] *a.* ①霜冻的, 结霜的; 严寒的: a ~ morning 严寒的早晨 ②霜状的; 闪烁的 ③冷若冰霜的, 冷淡的: a ~ smile 冷淡的笑 / give sb. a ~ stare 冷冷地盯着某人 ④（头发等）白的, 灰白的; [喻]年老的 ‖*frostily ad.* / *frostiness n.*

froth [frɔθ] I *n.* ①泡, 泡沫; (由于激动或患病而生的)口边白沫 ②渣滓, 废物 ③空谈 II ❶ *vi.* 起泡沫 ❷ *vt.* 使（啤酒等）起泡沫

frothy ['frɔθi] *a.* ①起泡沫的; 多泡沫的 ②空洞的, 浅薄的: a ~ exposition 一篇空洞的论述 ③质料轻薄的 ‖*frothily ad.* / *frothiness n.*

frown [fraun] I ❶ *vi.* 皱眉, 蹙额; 表示不满, 不赞许 (at, on, upon) ❷ *vt.* ①用皱眉蹙额对…表示不满: ~ *down* sb.'s opposition 用不悦的表情使某人不敢再反对 / ~ sb. *into* silence 皱眉蹙额使某人不敢再作声 ②用皱眉蹙额表示(不满等) II *n.* 皱眉, 蹙额

frowzy ['frauzi] *a.* ①邋遢的, 肮脏的; 不整洁的 ②难闻的; 闷热的; 霉臭的

froze [frouz] freeze 的过去式

frozen ['frouzn] I freeze 的过去分词 II *a.* ①冰冻的, 冻伤的: ~ food 冷冻食品 / ~ bean curd 冻豆腐 / a ~ sucker 棒冰, 冰棍 / ~ plants 冻伤的植物 ②严寒的 ③冻结的: ~ assets 冻结资产 / ~ credits 冻结债务 ④冷淡的; 呆的

frugal ['fru:gəl] *a.* 节约的, 俭朴的; 花钱少的: be ~ *of* food 节省食物 / a ~ meal 一餐节约饭 ‖*~ity* [fru(:)'gæliti] *n.* build up the country through diligence and ~ity 勤俭建国/*~ly ad.*

fruit [fru:t] I *n.* ①水果: a rich harvest of ~ 水果的丰收 / What ~s are in season now? 现在是哪些水果上市? ②[常用复](蔬菜、谷、麻等的)产物: the ~s of the earth 大地的产物 ③【植】果实: fresh ~ 鲜果 / dry (或 dried) ~ 干果 ④成果, 结果;产物: reap the first ~ of one's research 得到研究的初步成果 / eat the bitter ~ of one's own making 自食其果 ⑤[复]收入, 收益; 报酬: the ~s of industry 勤劳的收获 ⑥(基督教《圣经》用语)子女 ⑦[美俚]下流坯;搞同性关系的男子 ⑧[美俚]邂逅、古怪的人 ⑨[美俚]易受骗上当的人 II ❶ *vt.* 使结果实: ~ seedlings 使树苗长大结果 ❷ *vi.* 结果实: These trees ~ annually. 这些树每年结果实。‖*a ~ of sb.'s loins* 某人生的孩子 / *bear ~* 结出果实; [喻]取得成果; 奏效 / *Forbidden ~ is sweet.* [谚]禁果分外甜。(指不让得到的东西格外有诱惑力) / *the ~ of the womb* 子女; 儿童 ‖*~ed a.* 结有果实的; 加水果(调味)的 ‖*~cake n.* 水果蛋糕 / *~ fly* 【动】①实蝇科的小蝇 ②果蝇 / *~ knife* 水果刀 / *~ sugar* 果糖 / *~ tree* 果树

fruitful ['fru:tful] *a.* ①果实结得多的, 多产的; 收效很多的, 富有成效的: a ~ plan 富有成效的计划 / a congress ~ of (或 in) great measures 制定了许多重大措施的大会 ②肥沃的; 丰饶的: a ~ soil 沃土 ‖*~ly ad.* / *~ness n.*

fruition [fru(:)'iʃən] *n.* ①享用; 享受 ②结果实 ③实现; 完成: bring one's hopes to ~ 实现自己的希望

fruitless ['fru:tlis] *a.* ①不结果实的 ②无效的; 无益的: ~ efforts 徒劳 ‖*~ly ad.* / *~ness n.*

fruity ['fru:ti] *a.* ①果味的; (酒)有葡萄味的 ②(声音)圆润的; 洪亮的 ③[口]富有风趣的: a ~ story 有风趣的故事 ④[美俚]古怪的; 发疯的 ⑤[美俚](男子)带娘娘腔的; 搞男性同性关系的

frustrate [frʌs'treit] I *vt.* ①挫败; 阻挠; 使感到灰心: ~ the enemy in his plans 挫败敌人的计划 / be ~d in an attempt 企图遭到失败 / feel ~d 感到灰心丧气 ②使无效 II *a.* ①受挫的 ②无益的, 无效的

frustration [frʌs'treiʃən] *n.* 挫败; 挫折; 受挫: A series of great ~s awaits the enemy. 一连串的巨大挫折在等待着敌人。/ a sense of ~ 失望

fry[1] [frai] I ❶ *vt.* ①油煎, 油炒, 油炸 ②[美俚]处…以电刑 ❷ *vi.* ①在油里煎 (或炒、炸) ②[美俚]被处电刑 II *n.* ①油煎食品; 炒杂碎(指动物内脏) ②油煎品聚餐(或野餐)会 ③激动: in an awful ~ 极其激动 ‖ *in one's own grease* 见 **grease** ‖*~ing pan* 煎锅, 长柄平锅: out of the ~ing pan into the fire 跳出油锅又入火坑, 逃脱小难更遭大难 / *'~pan n.* [美] =~ing pan

fry[2] [frai] *n.* [总称] ①鱼秧, 鱼苗 ②成群的小鱼 ③群生的幼动物(如蜂等) ‖*small ~* ①孩群 ②小人物; 小东西

fuddle ['fʌdl] I ❶ *vt.* ①使醉 ②使迷糊 ❷ *vi.* 参加饮宴; 常常喝酒; 狂饮 II *n.* ①醉; 泥醉: on the ~ 大醉 ②混乱的一堆 ‖ *one's nose* (或 *cap*) 见 **nose**

fuel [fjuel] I *n.* 燃料: atomic ~ 原子燃料 / nuclear ~ 核燃料 / gaseous (solid) ~ 气体(固体)燃料 / liquid (或 wet) ~ 液体燃料 / jet ~ 喷气式发动机燃料 / ~ oil 燃料油 / a ~ pump 燃油泵 II *vt.* (fuel(l)ed; fuel(l)ing) ❶ *vt.* ①对…供给燃料, 给…加油(或其他燃料): ~ an aeroplane 给飞机加油 / an electric power station fuel(l)ed by uranium 用铀作燃料的发电站 ②支持; 刺激

❷ *vi.* 得到燃料,加油(或煤等) ‖*add ~ to the flames* 火上加油 ‖**fuel(l)ing** *n.*加燃料,加油: a *fuel(l)ing* station 加油站,燃料供应站

fugitive ['fju:dʒitiv] **I** *n.* ①逃亡者,亡命者: a ~ from justice 逃犯 ②难以捉摸的东西 **II** *a.* ①逃亡的;躲避的: ~ sorties【军】避战飞行(飞离基地以躲避敌机攻击) ②短暂的;变动的;易消失的: a ~ colour 易褪之色 ③即兴的,偶成的: ~ verses 即兴诗 ④流浪的,飘泊的

fulcrum ['fʌlkrəm] ([复] fulcrums 或 fulcra ['fʌlkrə]) *n.* ①支点;支轴: a ~ bearing 支点承座;刀口承 ②【植】叶附属物 ③【动】喙基骨;转节;舌骨;鳞状鳞

fulfil(l) [ful'fil] (fulfilled; fulfilling) *vt.* ① 履行(诺言、责任等);把…付诸实现: ~ a promise to the letter 不折不扣地履行诺言 ②完成(任务、计划等) ③达到(目的);满足(愿望、要求等);执行(命令、法律等) ④使完备;结束(工作、时期等): These illustrations ~ the text. 这些插图便使正文臻于完备。‖~ **oneself** 完全实现自己的抱负;彻底发挥自己的才能 ‖~**ment** *n.* 履行;实现;完成;结束

full¹ [ful] **I** *a.* ①满的,充满: plum trees in ~ blossom 盛开着花的李树 / a ~ life 经历丰富的一生 / be ~ of contradictions 充满矛盾 ②(装、盛)满的;(挤)满(人)的: The bucket is ~ to the brim (to overflowing). 水桶满到边(满得溢出来) / an assembly hall ~ of people 挤满人的会堂 ③(供应、资源等)充足的,丰富的;饱的,(喝酒)尽量的: a ~ harvest 丰收 / a ~ meal 丰盛的一餐 / I'm ~ (up). 我吃饱了。 ④完全的,十足的: a ~ dozen (hour) 整整一打(一小时) / a ~ load 满载 ⑤ daylight 大白天 / ~ maturity 完全成熟;壮年 / march at ~ speed 全速行进 / a ~ view 全景;全视图 / a ~ moon 满月,望月 ⑤完美的,最高度的;(资格等)正式的 ⑥(指思想、精神面貌等)富于…的,充满…的 (of):be ~ of vigo(u)r and vitality 朝气蓬勃 / It is despicable to be ~ of oneself. 老是只想到自己是可鄙的。/ My heart is too ~ for words. 我激动得说不出话来。⑦又胖又圆的;丰满的: a ~ figure 又胖又圆的身材 / The seedlings are coming up, ~ and green. 苗长得茁壮碧绿。⑧(衣服、裙子等)宽大的,松散的;多皱褶的: Please make the shirt ~er. 请把衬衫做得宽大些。⑨详尽的,完备的: a ~ report 详尽的报道 / He was very ~ on that point. 他对那一点讲得很详细。⑩强烈的;洪亮的;深色的: the ~ glare of a flash 强烈的闪光 / a ~ tone 洪亮的声调 ⑪同父同母的: They are ~ brothers. 他们是亲兄弟。‖~ *age* 成年(期) / ~ *charge*【军】全装(弹)药 / a ~ *face* 正面的脸;圆肸的脸 / a ~ *general* (admiral)【美】四星上将(海军上将) / a ~ *house* 满座(=house ~); (会议等)多数人出席; (纸牌)三张同点与两张同点的一组牌 / ~ *marks* 满分 / the ~ *name*

(连名带姓、不用缩写的)全名 / ~ *pay* 全薪 / ~ *professor*【美】(正)教授 / the ~ *score*【音】总谱 / ~ *step*【军】大步 / a ~ *stop* (或 point) 句号,句点 / ~ *strength* 全力;【军】满员 / the ~ *text* 全文 / the ~ *yield* 全部(出)产量 **II** *n.* ①全部;整个: Let me tell you the ~ of it. 让我把全部情况告诉你。②顶点: Summer is past the ~. 盛夏已经过去。**III** *ad.* ①十分,极其: We know ~ well that it's a good idea. 我们非常清楚这是个好主意。②完全地,充分地[可用以构成复合词]: be ~ as useful as 同…一样有用 / ~-fashioned 按照体形(或足形)织成的(指衣、袜等) ③恰恰,直接地: look sb. ~ in the face 直盯着某人 **IV** ❶ *vt.* 把(衣服)缝得宽大;把(裙子)缝出皱褶 ❷ *vi.* (月)圆 ‖*as ~ of ... as an egg is of meat* (头脑等)充满了…,尽是… / *at ~ length* 见 **length** / *at the ~* 在充满的时候;在圆满的状态中 / ~ *and by* 【海】扯满篷 / ~ *blast* 见 **blast** / ~ *chisel* 见 **chisel** / ~ *out* 最快地;以最大能量 / *Full speed* (或 *steam*) *ahead!*【海】全速前进! / ~ *up* [俚] ①全满 ②吃饱 ③(激动得)几乎要流泪 / *in* ~ ①充足,十足: pay *in* ~ 全部付清 ②以全文;用完整的词(不缩写): The statement reads *in* ~ as follows: .... 声明全文如下:… / *in* ~ *swing* 见 **swing** / *to the* ~ 完全地,充分地;彻底地: carry out a plan *to the* ~ 全面实现计划 / develop the strong points *to the* ~ 充分发扬优点 ‖'~-**back** *n.* (足球)后卫;后卫的位置 / ~ **binding** (书等的)全皮装订 / '~-'**blooded** *a.* ①血气旺盛的;精力充沛的;热烈的 ②情欲强烈的 ③非混血的;(动物)纯种的 ④内容充实的;(议论等)有力的 ⑤真正的;十足的 / '~-'**blown** *a.* ①(花)盛开的;(帆)张满的: ~-*blown* dignity 神气活现 ②成熟的;充分发展的: a ~-*blown* power plant 大型配套发电厂 / '~-'**bodied** *a.* ①体积大的;肥胖的 ②(酒)浓的;(墨水等)浓的 ③意义重大的 ④(作品等)规模大的;内容充实的 / '~-'**bottomed** *a.* ①(船)底部宽阔的,容量大的 ②(假发)长的,垂到肩背的 / ~-**dress** ①礼服 ②(船、舰等的)挂满旗 / '~-'**dress** *a.* ①礼服的,(正式宴会等)须穿礼服的 ②正式的: a ~-*dress* rehearsal (戏剧)正式排演,彩排 / a ~-*dress* debate [英] 议会的正式辩论 / ~-*dress* talks 正式会谈 ③大规模的: a ~-*dress* operation 大规模作战 / '~-'**fledged** *a.* ①(鸟)羽毛丰满的,能飞的 ②(喻)成熟的,经过充分训练(或培养)的 ③正式的,完全有资格的: a ~-*fledged* worker 正式工人,熟练工人 / '~-'**grown** *a.* 长足的,成熟的 / '~-'**hearted** *a.* ①满腔热情的;十分激动的 ②充满信心的;勇敢的 / '~-'**length** *a.* ①全长的;全身的: a ~-*length* portrait 全身像 ②标准长度(不缩减)的;(作品等)未删节的 ③大型的: a ~-*length* coloured documentary 大型彩色纪录片 / ~**mouthed** ['ful'mauðd] *a.* ①(牛等)口牙长齐的 ②(狗等)大声叫的 ③(演讲等)声音响亮

的 ④(文体等)刚劲的 / **'~-page** *a.* 全页的;整版的: a ~*-page* article in a newspaper 报上登载的占整版幅的文章 / **'~-scale** *a.* ①(图样等)实比的,与原物一样大小的,足尺的 ②全部的; 全面的: a ~*-scale* offensive 全面(大举)进攻 ③(作品等)完整的,未删节的 / **~ throat** [美口]全面的声援 / **'~-'time** *a.* 全部(规定)工作时间(或时期)的; 全部工作日的; 专职的: ~*-time* labour [总称]全劳动力 / ~*-time* service 专任职务;[英]正规军的现役 / **'~-'timer** *n.* [英]全日班小学生

full² [ful] *vt.* [纺]漂洗,浆洗;缩(绒),缩(呢): a ~*ing* mill 漂洗机 / ~*ing* clay 漂土,漂泥

fullness ['fulnis] *n.* ①(充)满,充分; 全部,完全 ②(供应、储藏、资源等的)丰富; 充实 ③(体形等的)圆胖;丰满 ④成熟: in the ~ of time 在适当的时候; 在预定的时候 ⑤(光的)强烈; (声的)洪亮; (颜色的)深度,浓度;【物】丰满度 ‖*in the ~ of one's heart* 真诚地; 激动地

fully ['fuli] *ad.* ①完全地,充分地; 彻底地: be ~ paid (up) 被全部付清 / ~ refined wax 精制石蜡 / It ~ proves that .... 这充分证明… ②足足,至少: I've waited ~ two hours. 我已经等了足足两小时了。/ There were ~ 200 people present. 足足有二百人出席。

fulminate ['fʌlmineit] **I** ❶ *vt.* ①使爆炸 ②大声发出(斥责等) ❷ *vi.* ①爆炸 ②怒喝,大声呵斥,谴责 ③[罕]电闪雷鸣 ④(疾病)暴发 **II** *n.* 【化】雷酸盐;雷汞: mercury ~ 雷酸汞 / silver ~ 雷酸银 ‖**fulmination** [,fʌlmi'neiʃən] *n.*

fulsome ['fulsəm] *a.* 可厌恶的; (恭维等)过分的,虚伪的; 令人作呕的: ~ flattery 令人作呕的奉承 ‖**~ly** *ad.* / **~ness** *n.*

fumble ['fʌmbl] **I** ❶ *vi.* ①乱摸,摸索: ~ in one's pocket for a key 在口袋里摸索钥匙 / ~ along the dark path 摸黑路 ②笨手笨脚地做: ~ with a shoestring 笨手笨脚地解(或绑)鞋带 ③犯大错 (球戏中)漏接,失球 ❷ *vt.* ①摸索,笨拙地做; 笨拙地处理: He ~*d* the door open. 他笨拙地(或摸索着)把门打开。②(球戏中)失(球),漏(球) **II** *n.* ①摸索,乱摸; 笨拙的处理 ②(球戏中的)漏接,失球 ‖**~r** *n.* 摸索者; 粗手笨脚的人 / **fumbling** *a.*

fume [fju:m] **I** *n.* ①(浓烈或难闻的)烟,气,汽: the ~*s* of mosquito incense 蚊香的烟 / the ~*s* of wine 酒气 / The ground was hidden by a white ~. 地上盖着一层白色的水汽。②激动,发怒: in a ~ 怒气冲冲 **II** ❶ *vt.* ①(用香)熏;熏(木材等)使表面呈深色 ②冒(烟或汽): The freighter was *fuming* thick black smoke. 货轮冒出浓烟。❷ *vi.* ①冒烟,出汽; (烟)冒出,(汽)发出 ②发怒;怒斥: ~ at one's opponent 怒斥对方 / ~ over (或 about) trifles 因小事而发怒

fun [fʌn] **I** *n.* ①玩笑,嬉戏; 娱乐,乐趣: He's too fond of ~. 他太喜欢闹着玩了。/ The children were having a lot of ~ with the building blocks. 儿童们搭房子的积木玩得很

开心。/ What ~! 多么有趣! ②有趣的人(或事物): Her baby is great ~. 她的婴儿非常好玩。/ Skating is good ~. 滑冰很有趣。③(使人感觉有趣的)紧张场面 **II** (funned; funning) *vi.* [口]开玩笑; 说笑 **III** *a.* 供娱乐用的; 只为玩玩用的 ‖*for* (或 *in*) ~ 开玩笑地,不是认真地: I am not saying it in ~. 我讲这话不是开玩笑的。/ **~ and games** [口]欢乐,开玩笑 / *like* ~ ①旺盛地,很快地; 大量地: The new products sell *like* ~. 这些新产品销路好得不得了。②[俚]决不 / **make ~ of** (或 **poke ~ at**) *sb.* 取笑某人

function ['fʌŋkʃən] **I** *n.* ①官能,功能,机能,作用: the ~ of the heart 心脏的功能 / organic ~*s* 器官的功能 / perform an important ~ 起重大作用 ②职务,职责 ③盛大的集会(或宴会,宗教仪式): speak at a ~ 在盛大的集会(或宴会等)上讲话 ④【数】函数 **II** *vi.* ①(器官等)活动; (机器等)运行; 起作用: The machine does not ~ properly. 这台机器有点毛病。/ The telephone was not ~*ing*. 这架电话坏了。②行使职责 ‖**~ word**【语】(主要表示语法关系的)虚词

functional ['fʌŋkʃənl] *a.* ①官能的,机能的: a ~ disease 官能病 / a ~ disorder 机能错乱 ②职务上的; (感官等)有功能的,(人)在起作用的 ③(建筑等)从使用的观点设计(或构成)的: ~ architecture 实用建筑(以实用为主,传统、美观等为次的建筑) ④【数】函数的 ‖**~ly** *ad.* ‖ **~ illiterate** 半文盲 / **~ shift**【语】词性转换

functionary ['fʌŋkʃənəri] *n.* (机关等的)工作人员; 官员

fund [fʌnd] **I** *n.* ①资金; 基金,专款: national investment ~*s* 国家投资资金 / a sinking ~ (公司等拨出的)偿债基金 / build up the ~*s* 筹集资金 ②[复](银行)存款: no ~*s* 存款不足 (银行退票时用语,指出票人帐户中存款不足支付支票金额) ③[复]现款: be in (out of) ~*s* 手头有(没)钱 ④[英][the ~*s*](被看作投资对象的)公债 ⑤(物质资源的)储备; (非物质的东西的)蕴藏: a large ~ of land for agricultural use 可供耕作的大量土地 / a ~ of labour 劳动力的储备 / a ~ of knowledge (wit) 丰富的知识(机智) ⑥特别基金管理机构 **II** *vt.* ①把(短期借款)转为有固定利息的长期借款 ②提供资金备付(债款等)的本息; 为…提供资金: ~ workers' pensions 拨出专款备付工人退休金 ③积累 ④[英]投(资金)于公债 ‖**~ed** *a.* 成为有固定利息的长期借款的: a ~*ed* debt (或 liability) 公债(在一年以上的)长期借款 ‖**~,holder** *n.* ①[英]公债持有人 / ~ 证券持有人 / **~ raising** 资金筹措

fundamental [,fʌndə'mentl] **I** *a.* ①基础的; 根本的,基本的,十分重要的: be ~ to a true understanding of the book 对真正理解这本书十分重要 / ~ star【天】基本星 ②原始的; 主要的: the ~ purpose 主要目的 ③【物】基频的

基谐波的 ④【音】基音的 II *n.* ①[常用复]基本原则(或原理),根本法则(或规律);纲要: the ~s of dialectical materialism 辩证唯物论的基本原理 ②【物】基频; 基谐波 ③【音】基音 ‖~ly *ad.* ‖~ particle【物】基本粒子

funeral ['fju:nərəl] I *n.* ①丧葬,葬礼; 出殡的行列: attend a ~ 参加葬(或丧)礼 ②[口]不愉快的事; 需要操心的事: That's your ~. 那是你需要操心的事。/ None of your ~. 与你无关。II *a.* 丧葬的,葬礼的,出殡的: a ~ service (或 ceremony) 葬礼; 丧礼 / a ~ procession 送葬行列 / a ~ oration 悼词 / a ~ march 丧礼进行曲 / a ~ pile (或 pyre) 火葬柴堆 / an urn 骨灰瓮 ‖ ~ home, ~ parlor [美]殡仪馆

funereal [fju(:)'niəriəl] *a.* ①丧葬似的 ②悲哀而严肃的 ③阴森的,幽暗的

fungus ['fʌŋgəs] ([复] funguses 或 fungi ['fʌŋgai]) *n.* ①真菌(包括霉菌、酵母菌和伞菌等) ②突然发生而迅速生长的东西 ③【医】海绵肿

funk[1] [fʌŋk] [口] I *n.* ①恐怖,惊惶: be in a ~ 大为惊恐 ②懦夫 II *vi.* 惊恐; 畏缩 ❷ *vt.* ①害怕; 逃避(工作、战斗等): ~ water 怕水 / ~ riding a horse 怕骑马 ②吓唬 ‖in a blue ~ ①惊恐万状 ②[美俚]意志消沉 ‖~ hole 防空壕; 逃避所 / ~ money 为获取高利(或保障币值)而由一国转移到另一国的流动资金

funk[2] [fʌŋk] I *n.* ①刺鼻的臭味; 霉味 ②早期爵士乐 II ❶ *vt.* 使闻到刺鼻臭味 ❷ *vi.* 发出刺鼻臭味

funnel ['fʌnl] I *n.* ①漏斗 ②漏斗形物: an air ~ 通风筒;【矿】通风井 ③(火车、轮船等的)烟囱 ④[美俚]酒鬼 II (funnel(l)ed; funnel(l)ing) ❶ *vi.* ①成漏斗形; 逐渐变狭(或变) ②经过漏斗 ③汇集 ❷ *vt.* ①使成漏斗形 ②使汇集 ‖funnel(l)ed *a.* ①有漏斗的; 漏斗形的 ②[用以构成复合词]有…个烟囱的: a two-funnel(l)ed steamer 双烟囱轮船 ‖'~-shaped *a.* 漏斗形的

funnel

funny[1] ['fʌni] I *a.* ①滑稽可笑的; 有趣的; 爱开玩笑的, 不严肃的: a ~ story 好笑的故事 / Don't be ~. 别开玩笑。②[口]古怪的, 希奇的: There is something ~ about the matter. 事情有点希奇。③不舒服的, 有病的: He told the doctor that he felt ~ all over. 他对医生

说, 他浑身不舒服。 ④狡猾的; 欺骗性的 II *n.* ①滑稽人物 ②[常用复](报纸或期刊的)滑稽连环漫画栏 ‖get ~ with [口]对…十分不敬 ‖funnily *ad.* / funniness *n.* ‖~ bone 肘部尺骨端(尺骨神经在此接近表面, 受触击时发麻) / '~man *n.* 幽默者; 滑稽演员 / '~-,money *n.* 膨胀的通货(尤指为了政治目的等滥发的货币) / ~ paper 报纸的滑稽栏

funny[2] ['fʌni] *n.* [英]单人双桨小船(狭长形, 接式构造)

fur [fə:] I *n.* ①(兽类的)软毛 ②毛皮; 皮子: a fine fox ~ 一张好的狐皮 / a ~ coat 皮外衣 ③[复]皮衣, 裘; 毛皮围颈物(或手套等): wear ~s 穿皮衣, 穿裘戴皮 ④[总称]软毛兽 ⑤[总称]毛皮兽与禽类 / hunt ~ 猎野兔 ⑤舌苔 ⑥(锅、壶中生的)锅垢, 水锈 (furred; furring ['fə:riŋ]) ❶ *vt.* ①用毛皮覆盖; 用毛皮衬, 用毛皮镶; 使穿毛皮服装 ②使生苔, 使积垢: a furred tongue 生了苔的舌 ③使(锅、壶等)生垢, 使生水锈 ④清除(锅)中的水垢 ⑤【建】钉板条于 ❷ *vi.* 生苔; 积起一层锅垢 ‖make the ~ fly 引起骚乱(或争吵、动武) / stroke the ~ the wrong way 讨好某人而结果适得其反 ‖~ seal【动】海狗

furbish ['fə:biʃ] *vt.* ①磨光, 擦亮 (up) ②刷新; 复 (up): I wish to ~ up the French I learnt at college. 我要重温一下我在大学里学过的法语。

furious ['fjuəriəs] *a.* ①狂怒的: be ~ with sb. (at sth.) 对某人(对某事)大发雷霆 ②狂暴的, 猛烈的; 强烈的: a ~ storm 狂风骤雨 / a ~ attack 猛烈的攻击 / run at a ~ pace 飞跑 / a ~ spring 春意正浓的春天 ③喧闹的, 热烈兴奋的: fast and ~ fun 狂欢 ‖~ly *ad.* / ~ness *n.*

furl [fə:l] I ❶ *vt.* 卷起, 卷紧(帆、旗等); 折拢(扇子); 收拢(伞); 拉拢(帷): ~ the sails 卷帆 ❷ *vi.* (帆、旗等)卷起, 卷紧; (扇子)折拢; (伞)收拢 II *n.* ①卷; 折; 收拢 ②一卷东西

furlong ['fə:lɔŋ] *n.* 弗隆, 浪(英国长度单位, =1/8 哩或 201.167米)

furlough ['fə:lou] I *n.* ①(尤指军人、在国外的官员等)休假: be on ~ 在休假中 ②准假的证件 II *vt.* ①准…休假 ②强迫…休假; 暂时解雇

furnace ['fə:nis] I *n.* ①炉子; 熔炉: blast ~【冶】鼓风炉(炼有色金属用); 高炉(炼铁用) / open-hearth ~【冶】平炉 / electric-arc ~【冶】电弧炉 / induction ~【冶】感应炉 ②极热的地方 ③严峻的考验, 磨炼 II *vt.* 在炉中烧热

furnish ['fə:niʃ] *vt.* ①供应; 提供 ②装备; (用家具等)布置(房间、公寓): a ~ed house 备有家具的出租房子

furnishing ['fə:niʃiŋ] *n.* [常用复]家具, 设备, 陈设品; 服饰品

furniture ['fə:nitʃə] *n.* [总称] ①家具: a piece (a set) of ~ 一件(一套)家具 ②(机器、轮船等的)装置, 设备 ③贮藏物; 内容: the ~ of a bookshelf 书架上的书籍 / the ~ of sb.'s mind 某人的学问 / the ~ of a constitution 章程的内容 ④[印] 空铅，填充材料(用来填塞行距或字距空间的材料，高度略低于铅字) ‖**remove** ~ 替人搬家(指一种行业)

furrow ['fʌrou] **I** n. ①沟；犁沟；垄沟 ②耕地，农田 ③航迹；车辙；面部(或前额)的皱纹 **II ❶** vt. ①犁(地)，破(浪) ②使…起皱纹: a brow ~ed with sorrows 愁容紧锁着的眉梢 **❷** vi. ①[古]犁地 ②起皱纹 ‖**draw a straight** ~ 处世方正 / **plough a lonely** ~ 孤独行动 ‖**~less** a.无沟的；无皱纹的 / **~y** a. 有沟的；皱的

further ['fə:ðə] (far 的两种比较级形式之一，另一形式为 farther；farther 常用于本义"更远"，further 常用于引申意义"进一步") **I** ad. ①(距离、时间上)更远地，再往前地 ②进一步地，深一层地: raise the yields still ~ 进一步提高产量 ③而且，此外 (=~more): We must do our work faster, and ~ better. 我们要把工作做得快一些，而且要做得好一些。**II** a. ①更远的，较远的 ②更多的；进一步的；深一层的: investigation 进一步的调查 / ~ volumes 后续各卷 / strive for ~ progress 继续求进步 / make no ~ delay 不再拖延 **III** vt. 促进，推动: ~ the patriotic public health campaign 推进爱国卫生运动 / ~ one's personal ends 追求个人目的 ‖**for ~ details** 见 **detail** / **I'll see him (或 you** 等) ~ **first.** 让他(或你等)见鬼去。(表示坚决拒绝或不同意。这里 ~ 为"在地狱中"的婉转说法) / **till (或 until)** ~ **notice** 见 **notice** ‖**-ance** ['fə:ðərəns] n. 促进，推动

furthermore ['fə:ðə'mɔ:] ad. 而且，此外

furthermost ['fə:ðəmoust] a. 最远的 (=furthest)

furthest ['fə:ðist] (far 的两种最高级形式之一，另一形式为 farthest) **I** a. (距离、时间上)最远的 **II** ad. ①(距离、时间上)最远地 ②最大程度地；最大限度地

furtive ['fə:tiv] a. ①偷偷摸摸的，鬼鬼祟祟的；狡猾的: take a ~ glance 偷瞧 / a ~ manner 鬼鬼祟祟的态度 / be ~ in one's movements 行动诡秘 ②偷来的 ‖**~ly** ad. / **~ness** n.

fury ['fjuəri] n. ①暴怒，狂怒: be filled with ~ 怒火满腔 / fly into a ~ 勃然大怒 ②猛烈，剧烈: the ~ of the elements 狂风暴雨 ③泼妇 ④[F-] [希神]司复仇的三女神之一 ‖**like** ~ 猛烈地，剧烈地: rain like ~ 下暴雨 / work like ~ 猛干

furze [fə:z] n. [植]荆豆属植物；荆豆 ‖**furzy** a. 荆豆属植物丛生的；像荆豆属植物的

fuse¹ [fju:z] **I ❶** vt. ①熔(化) ②熔合: ~ two pieces of wire together 熔合两根金属丝 **❷** vi. ①熔(化) ②熔合 ③由于保险丝烧断而电路不通: All the lights in the house have ~d. 保险丝烧断，室内电灯都不亮了。**II** n. [电]保险丝，熔丝 ‖**blow a** ~ ①使保险丝熔断 ②[口]勃然大

怒 ‖**'~-wire** n. [总称]作保险丝用的各种金属丝

fuse² [fju:z] **I** n. ①导火线，导火索，导爆线: a safety ~ 安全导火线，缓燃导火索 ② =fuze (n.) **II** vt. =fuze (vt.)

fuselage ['fju:zila:ʒ, 'fju:zilidʒ] n. ①[空](飞机)机身 ②[字]壳体，外壳；弹体

fusion ['fju:ʒən] n. ①熔化，熔解 ②熔化状态，熔解状态 ③熔合，熔接 ④[原]合成，(核)聚变: atomic (或 nuclear) ~ 核聚变，核合成 ⑤(政党等的)联合 ‖**-ist** n. (政党等方面的)联合论者；参加联合的人 ‖**~ bomb** 热核弹(尤指氢弹) / ~ **frequency** (电视中的)(视觉)闪闪频率 / **point** [物]熔点 / ~ **welding** 熔融焊，熔焊(接)

fuss [fʌs] **I** n. ①忙乱；大惊小怪；(神经质的)激动: Don't make (such) a ~. 不要(这么)大惊小怪。/ get into (或 raise) a great ~ about trifles 小题大做 / kick up a ~ 大吵大闹，起哄；滋事 ②过分表面化的赞扬；过度体贴: make a great ~ over sb.'s calligraphy 对某人的书法大肆吹捧 / Don't make so much ~ of the children. 不要这样婆婆妈妈地对待孩子们。③大惊小怪的人；做起事来老是手忙脚乱的人 ④抗议；异议 ⑤(激烈的)争吵 **II ❶** vi.①忙乱；小题大做，大惊小怪: Stop ~ing! 别大惊小怪的! / What is she ~ing about? 她在瞎忙些什么? ②过分体贴关心；奉承 ③过分讲究: ~ with one's clothes 过分讲究衣着 ④烦恼 ⑤抱怨，唠叨；争辩: I don't like to be ~ed at. 我不愿听人唠唠叨叨地训我。⑥[美俚]追求女性；与女子约会 **❷** vt. ①使激动，使烦躁: Don't ~ me, please! 请别来烦我。②[美俚]追求；与(女子)约会 ‖**~ and feathers** 大吹大擂 / ~ **up and down** 瞎忙得团团转 ‖**~,budget** n. [美俚]大惊小怪的人(尤指年老的悍妇) / **'~pot** n. [口]老是大惊小怪的人

fussy ['fʌsi] a. ①大惊小怪的；瞎忙的 ②过分注意细节的，为琐事烦闹的 ③(服装等)过分装饰的；(文体等)浮华而烦琐的 ‖(as) ~ **as a hen with one chick** 在无谓的小事上瞎操心 ‖**fussily** ad. / **fussiness** n.

fusty ['fʌsti] a. ①发霉的；霉臭的 ②守旧的，古板的: a ~ old man 古板守旧的老头 ‖**fustily** ad. / **fustiness** n.

futile ['fju:tail; 美 'fju:til] a. ①无益的，无效的，无用的: The enemy's attempts proved ~. 敌人的企图证明是枉费心机的。②(人)没出息的；轻浮的 ‖**~ly** ad. / **~ness** n.

future ['fju:tʃə] **I** n. ①将来，未来，今后: in (the) ~ 将来，今后(带 the 常指全部的将来，无 the 常指将来某一时间) ②前途；远景 ③[语]将来时；(动词的)将来式 ④[复][商]期货交易: deal in ~s 做期货生意 ⑤[美俚]未婚夫；未婚妻 **II** a. 将来的，未来的: ~ generations 后代 / in ~ ages 在后世 / the ~ tense [语]将来时 / learn from past mistakes to avoid ~ ones 惩前毖后 ‖**for the** ~ 从今以后，在今后: For the ~, try to be more careful. 今后你应该更细心(或留心)些。 ‖**~less** *a.* 无前途的，无希望的

futurity [fju(:)'tjueriti] *n.* ①将来，未来 ②未来性 ③[复]未来的事；远景

fuzz [fʌz] Ⅰ *n.* ①(织物或果实等表面上的)微毛，绒毛；茸毛：the ~ on a peach 桃子上的毛 ②[美俚]警察；侦探 Ⅱ ❶ *vi.* 成绒毛状 ❷ *vt.* ①使成绒毛状 ②使模糊 (*up*) ‖**~ball** *n.* 【植】一种马勃科菌

fuzzy ['fʌzi] *a.* ①有微毛的，有绒毛的；绒毛状的 ②模糊的；(录音等)失真的：a ~ photo 模糊的照片 ‖**fuzzily** *ad.* / **fuzziness** *n.*

G

gabble ['gæbl] Ⅰ ❶ *vi.* 急促不清地说话；喋喋，咕噜：Speak more slowly—don't ~. 讲得慢一点，别说得那么急。 ❷ *vt.* ①上气不接下气地说 ②急促朗读 (*over*, *out*) Ⅱ *n.* 急促不清的话

gable ['geibl] *n.* 【建】①山墙，三角墙 ②三角形的建筑部分(或器具) ‖**~d** *a.* 有山墙的 ‖**~ roof** 人字屋顶，三角屋顶 (=ridge roof) / **~ window** 山墙窗

gable

gad¹ [gæd] Ⅰ (gadded; gadding) *vi.* ①游荡，闲荡 (*about*, *abroad*, *out*) ②追求刺激 ③蔓延，蔓生 Ⅱ *n.* 游荡，闲荡 ‖**~about** *n.* 游荡者，游手好闲的人；寻欢作乐的人 *a.* 游荡的，游手好闲的

gad² [gæd] Ⅰ *n.* ①[方]刺棒，棍 ②【矿】钢楔，小钢凿 Ⅱ (gadded; gadding) *vt.* ①用刺棒刺 ②【矿】用钢楔劈裂(矿石)

gad³, Gad [gæd] *int.* 噢，天哪[表示惊异] ‖**By ~!** 天哪！哎呀！

gadget ['gædʒit] *n.* [口]①(机器等上的)小配件；(小)机件；(小)装置 ②小玩意儿；新发明 ③[喻]诡计，圈套

gaff [gæf] Ⅰ *n.* ①(弯齿)鱼叉，(把大鱼拉上岸用的)手钩，挽钩 ②(爬电杆用的)攀钩；(肉铺的)挂钩 ③【海】桅上斜杆 ④[英俚]低级娱乐场所，杂耍场 ⑤欺骗，愚弄；花招；暗中设下的机关 ⑥滥用 ⑦=gaffe Ⅱ *vt.* ①用鱼叉叉(鱼)，用手钩拉(鱼) ②欺骗，诈骗；在(赌具)上暗设机关进行欺骗 ‖**blow the ~** [俚]泄露秘密 / **stand the ~** [俚]忍受任何困境；有胆量

gag [gæg] Ⅰ *n.* ①塞口物；(牲畜的)口衔；【医】张口器 ②言论自由的压制；(议会)限制辩论时间，停止辩论 ③插科打诨；笑话 ④哄骗；[俚]欺诈 (gagged; gagging) ❶ *vt.* ①塞住…的口，使窒息；【医】用张口器使张开口 ②压制(某人)言论自由；限制(某人)发言 ③在(表演等)中插科打诨 ④欺骗 ⑤关闭(阀门等) ❷ *vi.* ①窒息；作呕 ②插科打诨 ③欺骗 ‖**~ bit** 马衔 / **~ law** 限制言论(或出版)自由的法令 (尤指限制立法机关继续辩论的规定) / **~ man** *n.* ①笑话作者 ②插科打诨的演员 / **~ rein** 马缰 / **~ rule** =~ law

gage¹ [geidʒ] Ⅰ *n.* ①抵押品，担保品 ②挑战；征挑战而扔下的手套(或帽子等) Ⅱ *vt.* 以…为担保；以…为赌注 ‖**throw down the ~** 挑战；寻衅

gage² [geidʒ] *n. & vt.* =gauge

gaiety ['geiəti] *n.* ①快乐，高兴 ②[常用复]狂欢；娱乐；喜庆 ③(服装的)华丽

gain¹ [gein] Ⅰ ❶ *vt.* ①获得；博得；使…获得：~ still greater successes 获得更大的成功 / ~ land from the sea 围垦海滩获得土地 / ~ the audience's attention 吸引住听众(或观众) ②赢得；挣得：~ a battle 打胜仗 / ~ one's living 谋生 ③增加；(钟、表等)快：The car is ~ing speed. 车子越开越快了。 / ~ six kg. in weight 体重增加六公斤 / My watch ~s two minutes a day. 我的表一天快两分钟。 ④(经过努力)到达(某地) ❷ *vi.* ①获得利益 ②增加；增进：~ in influence 影响增长 / The patient ~ed daily. 病人一天天好起来。 ③(钟、表等)走快 Ⅱ *n.* ①营利，获利：regardless of personal ~ or loss 不顾个人得失 / be blinded by the love of ~ 利令智昏 ②[复]获得；得益；利益 ③[复]收益，利润 ④增加，增进；【无】增益，放大：A fall into the pit, a ~ in your wit. 吃一堑，长一智。 / a ~ to knowledge 知识的增进 / ~ control 【无】增益调整 ‖**~ by comparison (contrast)** 比较(对比)之下显出其长处 / **~ on** (或 **upon**) ①跑得比…快；逼近；超过：~ on the runner ahead 快追上跑在前面的人 / ~ on one's pursuers 把追的人抛在后面 ②赢得…的好感 ③(海)侵蚀(陆地) / **~ sb. over** 把某人争取过来 / **~ time** ①(钟、表等)走得快

② (用拖延等办法) 赢得时间 / *No ~s without pains.* [谚] 不劳则无获。‖**~er** *n.* ①获得者;得胜者: come off a **~er** 结果得胜 ②后滚翻花式跳水 / **~ings** [复] *n.* 收入;收益;赢得的东西 / **~less** *a.* 无利可图的;一无所获的

gain² [gein] 【建】**I** *n.* ① (木料上或墙上的) 腰槽 ② 雄榫上的斜肩 **II** *vt.* 在…上开腰槽;用腰槽联接

gainful ['geinful] *a.* ①有利益的,有收益的 ②唯利是图的 ‖**~ly** *ad.* / **~ness** *n.*

gainsay [gein'sei] (gainsaid [gein'seid]) *vt.* [主要用于否定句和疑问句] ①否认,否定: There is no **~ing** his progress. 他的进步是无可置疑的。②反驳;反对: **~** sb. 反驳某人

gait¹ [geit] **I** *n.* ①步态,步法 ②(走、跑、生产等的)速度 **II** *vt.* 训练(马)的步法 ‖*gang one's ain ~* [苏格兰] 走自己的路; 我行我素

gait² [geit] *n.* 【纺】穿经;[英]花纹循环

gaiter ['geitə] *n.* ①鞋罩,绑腿套 ②高帮松紧鞋,有绑腿的高统靴

gala ['gɑːlə, 'geilə] *n.* ①节日;庆祝;盛会: a night 欢乐之夜(如戏院中有特别节目之夜等) ②[古]盛装

galaxy ['gæləksi] *n.* ①【天】星系;[G-]银河系;银河 ②一群出色(或著名)的人物;一堆光采夺目的东西

gale¹ [geil] *n.* ①大风(尤指八级风);[诗]微风: It is blowing a **~**. 刮大风了。②(突发的)一阵: a **~** of wind 一阵大风 / **~s** of laughter 阵阵笑声 ③[口]高兴,欢乐

gale² [geil] *n.* [英] 定期交付的租金: a hanging **~** 欠交租金

gale³ [geil] *n.* 【植】香杨梅

gall¹ [gɔːl] *n.* ①胆汁;胆;胆囊: as bitter as **~** 味苦如胆汁,极苦 ②苦味 ③怨恨;刻薄,恶毒 ④[美口]厚颜无耻;大胆,莽撞: have the **~** to do sth. 竟有脸皮做某事 ‖**~ and wormwood** 极苦恼的事 ‖**~,bladder** *n.* 【解】胆囊 / **'~-stone** *n.* 【医】胆石

gall² [gɔːl] **I** *n.* ①肿痛,擦伤;(马的)鞍伤 ②磨损处;瑕疵;弱点 ③(田野或树丛的)光秃处 ④恼怒,烦恼;懊恼(或烦恼的)事物 **II** ❶ *vt.* ①擦伤,擦损;磨损 ②激怒,烦扰;羞辱 ❷ *vi.* ①(被)擦伤,(被)擦痛;(被)磨损 ②【机】(因摩擦过度而)咬住 ‖**~ing** *a.* ①擦伤的,擦损的 ②激怒的;烦恼的

gall³ [gɔːl] *n.* 【植】瘿;虫瘿;五倍子 ‖**'~fly** *n.* 【动】五倍子虫

gallant ['gælənt] **I** *a.* ①(服装)华丽的;堂皇的,雄伟的 ②勇敢的;骑士风度的,豪侠的 ③[gə'lænt](对女子)献殷勤的;色情的 **II** ['gælənt, gə'lænt] *n.* ①豪侠 ②时髦人物;对女子献殷勤的人;求爱者;情夫 **III** [gə'lænt] ❶ *vt.* ①向…求爱 ②伴送(女子) ❷ *vi.* 调情,求爱(*with*) ‖*the honourable and ~ member* (英国议会)军人身分的议员 ‖**~ly** *ad.*

galleon ['gæliən] *n.* (十五至十八世纪作军舰或商船用的)西班牙大帆船

galleon

gallery ['gæləri] **I** *n.* ①长廊,游廊,门廊,柱廊,走廊;眺台,阳台 ②(剧场中票价最低的)顶层楼座;(教堂、议院等的)边座,楼座: the press **~** 记者席 ③[the **~**][总称]顶层楼座的观众;(网球等的)观众 ④画廊,美术陈列室,美术室;(美术馆等展出或收藏的全部)美术品 ⑤狭长的房间;摄影室,照相馆;室内靶场 ⑥地下通道,地道;【矿】水平巷道,横坑道 ⑦【船】尾部了望台;炮台 **II** ❶ *vt.* 在…建筑长廊(或游廊等);在…挖地道 ❷ *vi.* 建筑长廊(或游廊);挖地道 ‖*a ~ hit* (或 *shot, stroke*) 见 *hit* / *bring down the ~* 博得全场喝采 / *play to the ~* 迎合低级趣味;讨好观众 / *the rogues' ~* (警察部门等的)案犯照片栏 ‖**~ite** *n.* (剧场)顶层楼座观众之一 ‖**~ god** =**~ite**

galley ['gæli] *n.* ①(古代用奴隶等划桨的)单层板大帆船;(古希腊、罗马的)军舰 ②舰长用的大划艇 ③船上的厨房 ④【印】长方形的活字盘;长条校样: proof in **~** 长条校样 ‖**~ proof** 【印】长条校样 / **~ range** 【船】厨房炉灶 / **~ slave** ①划船的奴隶(或犯人);[喻]苦工 ②[美俚]出版商 / **,~'west** *ad.* [美口]彻底地,毁灭性地;混乱地: knock **~-west** 彻底打败… / **'~worm** *n.* 【动】倍足纲的多足昆虫

gallivant ['gæli'vænt] *vi.* [常用现在分词和动名词形式]闲荡,闲逛;与异性游荡;寻欢作乐

gallon ['gælən] *n.* ①加仑(液量单位, =4 quarts): the imperial **~** 英制加仑 (=4.546 升) / the wine **~** 美制加仑 (=3.785 升) ②加仑(干量单位, =1/8 bushel) ③一加仑的容器

gallop ['gæləp] **I** *n.* ①(马等的)飞跑,疾驰: at a full **~** 飞奔;用最大速度 ②骑马奔驰: go for a **~** 去骑马奔驰一阵 ③[口]快步;敏捷动作;迅速发展 **II** ❶ *vi.* ①(马等)飞跑,疾驰 ②匆匆地读(或说): **~** through (或 over) a book 匆匆地读完一本书 ③急速进行,迅速发展: **~ing** consumption 【医】奔马痨 ❷ *vt.* ①使飞跑,使疾驰 ②迅速运输,迅速运送 ‖**~ing dominoes** [美俚]骰子

gallows ['gæləuz] ([复] gallows(es)) *n.* ①绞刑架,绞台: send sb. to the **~** 将某人处以绞刑 / come to the **~** 被处以绞刑 ②(类似绞刑架的)

架状物,挂架;【海】吊杆 ③绞刑;该受绞刑的人 ④[复][方](裤子的)背带,吊带 ‖**have the ～ in one's face** 有犯死罪的面相 ‖**～ bird** 应受绞刑的人 / **～ bitt** [海]双柱吊架 / **humo(u)r** [美]面临大难时的幽默 / **'-ripe** a. 应处绞刑的面相 / **～ look** 犯死罪的面相 / **～ tree** 绞刑架,绞台

galore [gə'lɔː] **I** ad. 许多,丰富,丰盛: a meal with beef and beer ～ 酒肉丰盛的一餐 **II** n. [罕]许多,丰富,丰盛: in ～ 丰盛

galosh [gə'lɔʃ] n. [常用复](高统橡皮)套鞋 ‖**～ed** a. 穿(高统橡皮)套鞋的

galvanic [gæl'vænik] a. ①(电池)电流的: ～ electricity【电】动电 ②突然而勉强的: a ～ smile 不自然的笑 ③触电似的;激励的

galvanism ['gælvənizəm] n. ①由原电池产生的电 ②流电学【电】③[医]流电疗法 ④有力,有劲 ‖**galvanist** n. 流电学家

galvanize ['gælvənaiz] vt. ①通电流于 ②电镀;给…镀锌: ～d iron 镀锌铁皮,马口铁 ③刺激,惊起,激励,使兴奋: be ～d into life 受激励而活跃起来 ‖**galvanization** [ˌgælvənai'zeiʃən] n. / **～r** n. ①电镀工 ②激励者

gambit ['gæmbit] n. ①开局让棋法(国际象棋中开局时牺牲一、二子以取得优势的下棋法) ②开场白;话题 ③精心策划的一着;策略

gamble ['gæmbl] **I ❶** vi. ①赌博;打赌: ～ at cards 赌纸牌 / ～ on horse races 买跑马票进行赌博 ②投机;冒险: ～ on the stock exchange 进行股票投机 ❷ vt. ①赌掉,赌光 (away) ②以…打赌,冒…的险 **II** n. 赌博;投机;冒险 ‖**～r** n. 赌博者,赌徒

gambling ['gæmbliŋ] n. 赌博;投机;冒险 ‖**～-den** n. 赌场,赌窟 / **～ house** 赌场

gambol ['gæmbəl] **I** n. (小孩、小羊等的)跳跃;嬉戏,玩笑 **II** (gambol(l)ed; gambol(l)ing) vi. 蹦跳;嬉戏

game¹ [geim] **I** n. ①游戏,运动;玩耍,娱乐;玩笑: play ～s 做游戏 / have a ～ of bridge 打一会桥牌 ②(体育、棋类等的)比赛;[复]运动会,比赛会: a football ～ 足球比赛 / the Olympic Games 奥林匹克运动会 ③(比赛中的)一局,一盘,一场 ④比分;(获胜所需的)得分;得胜,赢: The ～ is 6 to 5. 比分是六比五。/ a close ～ 接近的比分 / ～ all (或 ～ and ～) 各赢一次 ⑤(棋,纸牌类的)游戏器具,比赛用具 ⑥比赛规则;比赛方式(或技巧): play a good ～ at chess 下一手好棋 ⑦策略;把戏,花招: play a double ～ 耍两面派 / None of your (little) ～s! 别耍花招吧! ⑧[美俚]行业,职业;(冒险性的)行当 ⑨(对勇气、耐心等的)考验 ⑩[总称]猎物;野味 ⑪[总称]追求物,目的物;嘲弄(或攻击)的对象 ⑫(饲养天鹅的)一群 **II ❶** vi. (打牌等时)赌博 ❷ vt. [古]赌掉 (away) **III** a. ①关于野味的,关于猎物的 ②[口]雄壮纠纠的;兴致勃勃的 ‖**a ～**

not worth the candle 不值得做的事情 / **a ～ of chance** 靠碰运气取胜的游戏 / **a ～ of skill** 靠技艺取胜的游戏 / **ahead of the ～** [美口]处于赢家地位(尤指在赌博中) / **be off one's ～** 竞技状态不佳 / **be on one's ～** 竞技状态好 / **big ～** ①[总称](象、狮等)大的猎物 ②[美俚]冒风险(或难以)获得的东西 / **die ～** 至死不屈 / **fair ～** ①[总称]准予捕猎的鸟兽 ②可据理加以攻击的人(或事物);有懈可击的对象 / **fly at higher ～** 怀有更高的理想 / **force the ～** (板球等中)冒险快速得分 / **have a ～ with sb.** (企图)作弄某人;(企图)欺骗某人 / **have the ～ in one's hands** 有必胜把握;有支配力 / **make of** 同…开玩笑;嘲笑,捉弄 / **play a deep ～** 背地里搞鬼 / **play sb.'s ～** 做使某人获利的事,帮某人的大忙 / **play the ～** ①遵守比赛规则 ②行动光明正大 / **That's a ～ two people can play.** 这一套你会我也会。/ **The ～ is up.** 一切都完了。(或: 没有希望了。) / **What a ～!** ①多么精采的比赛啊! ②多有趣啊! ‖**～ly** ad. 雄纠纠地;兴致勃勃地 / **～ness** n. 勇气;兴致勃勃 ‖**acts** 狩猎的行动 / **～-bag** n. 狩猎袋 / **ball** (网球等一局中)决胜负的一球 / **～ bird** 可捕猎的鸟 / **'-cock** n. (雄的)斗鸡;好斗的人 / **fowl** 斗鸡的种鸡 / **'-,keeper** n. 猎场看守人 / **～ laws** 狩猎规则 / **'-,license** n. 狩猎许可(证);买卖野味许可(证) / **～smanship** ['geimzmənʃip] n. (用以取胜而又不犯规的)小动作 / **～s master** [英](学校里)教游戏的老师 / **tenant** 狩猎场(或渔场)承租人

game

game² [geim] a. (腿等)跛的;残废的

gamut ['gæmət] n. ①[音]音阶,全音域 ②[喻]全范围,全部: run the ～ of emotions 百感交集 / the complete ～ of the spectrum 光谱波长的全区域

gander ['gændə] Ⅰ n. ①雄鹅 ②糊涂虫,傻瓜 ③[俚]一看,一眼: take a ～ 看一看 Ⅱ vi. [方]漫步,闲逛 ‖**see how the ～ hops** [美口]观望,察看风使舵 / **What is sauce for the goose is sauce for the ～.** 见 sauce

gang [gæŋ] **I** n. ①(劳动者的)一队,一组: work in ～s 分班组劳动 ②(囚犯等的)一群;(歹徒等的)一帮 ③[口][贬](青少年等的)一伙 ④(工具

等的)一套 ⑤[英方]路,路程 ⑥[美俚]大量 **II ❶**
vi. ①成群结队;合伙行动 ②[苏格兰]走,去 ❷
vt. ①使分成班组 ②[美口]合伙袭击 ③使成套
排列;使成套运转 ‖~ **agley** [苏格兰]失败,出
差错 / ~ **one's ain**(或 **own**)**gait** [苏格兰]走
自己的路;我行我素 / ~ **up** [美]①聚集,会合
②合伙袭击 ③联合施加压力 / ~ **up on**(或
against)[美俚]联合起来反对(或攻击)/ ~ **up
with** [美俚]与…联合起来一致行动 ‖~,**master
n.** 工长 / ~ **mill** 框锯制材厂 / '~**plough
n.**[农]多铧犁,联犁 / ~ **saw** 框锯,直锯 / ~
shag [美俚]淫乱的聚会;爵士乐即席演奏会 /
~ **war**(歹徒帮派间的)打群架

gangrene ['gæŋgri:n] **I n.** ①【医】坏疽:tongue~
舌坏疽 ②[喻]道德败坏 **II vt. & vi.** (使)生
坏疽

gangster ['gæŋstə] **n.**(一帮中的一名)匪徒,歹徒;
暴徒: ~'s **double talk**(匪帮的)黑话 ‖~**ism
** ['gæŋstərizəm] **n.** 强盗行为(或行径)

gangway ['gæŋwei] **I n.** ①通路;出入口 ②[船]
舷门;舷梯;跳板 ③(剧场等)座位间的过道 ④[英]
下议院中划分前后座的过道; 下议院中划分内阁
与反对派席位的过道 ⑤[矿]主运输平巷; 木桥
⑥(木材从水上输送到锯木厂的)倾斜道 **II int.**
避开,让路 ‖**members above**(**below**)**the** ~
见 **member**

gantry ['gæntri] **n.** ①桶架 ②[机](起重架的)构
台(门架);龙门起重架(=~ **crane**);横移桥形台
③(铁路上的)跨轨信号架 ④【字】导弹拖车

gaol [dʒeil] [注意:英国文件中用 gaol,一般文字中
gaol 与 jail 通用;美国用 jail] **I n.** 监狱;监禁:
be sent to ~(被送)入狱 / in ~ 在押,关在监狱
中 / ~ sentences 徒刑 **II vt.** 监禁,把…关进监
狱 ‖**deliver a** ~ 把监狱中的犯人全部提出来审
讯 ‖~**bird n.** 囚犯;惯犯;流氓 / ~ **delivery**
①越狱;劫狱 ②[英]【律】提审囚犯出清监狱 / ~
fever(从前监狱中流行的一种)恶性伤寒

gaoler ['dʒeilə] **n.** 监狱看守 ‖~**ess** ['dʒeiləris] **n.**
监狱女看守

gap [gæp] **I n.** ①豁缝,裂口,缺口;【军】突破口
②山峡,隘口 ③间隙 ④【机】火花隙 ⑤【空】(双翼
机的)翼隔 ④ 中断,(文章等中的)脱漏;(知识等
的)空白 ⑤ 分歧,隔阂;差距: the ~ between
imports and exports 进出口的差额 **II** (gapped;
gapping) ❶ **vt.** 使豁裂,使成缺口 ❷ **vi.** 豁开
‖**stand in the** ~ 身当其冲,挺身阻挡 / **supply**
(或 **fill, stop**) **a** ~ 填补空白;弥补缺陷 ‖**gapped
a.** 豁裂的;有缺口的 / **gappy a.** 有裂口的,破裂
的;脱节的 ‖'~,**filler n.**【无】雷达辅助天线 /
'~-'**toothed a.** 两齿间隙缝很大的(如由于掉落
一齿所致)

gape [geip] **I vi.** ①张口;打呵欠 ②目瞪口呆地
凝视(**at**) ③张开;裂开 **II n.** ①张口;呵欠 ②目
瞪口呆 ③豁口 ④口张时的阔度;【动】嘴裂,喙裂
‖~ **after**(或 **for**)渴望得到 / **the** ~**s** ①(家禽
的)张口病 ②[谑]一阵呵欠 ‖~**seed n.** [英方]

[谑]注目;引人注目的事物

garage ['gærɑ:ʒ] **I n.** ①汽车间(或库);飞机库
②汽车修理厂 **II vt.** 把(汽车等)送入汽车库(或
修理厂)‖'~**man n.** 汽车库工人; 汽车修理厂
工人 / ~ **sale**(在卖主家当场进行的)现场旧货
出售

garb [gɑ:b] **I n.** ①服装;装束;制服 ②外表,外衣
II vt. [常用被动语态或接 oneself] 穿; 装扮:
~ed **in** motley 穿花色衣服的 / ~ **oneself as a**
peasant 打扮成农民模样

garbage ['gɑ:bidʒ] **n.** ①废料;垃圾,污物 ②
食物下脚;[美俚]食物 ③下流(或无聊)的读物(或
话)

garble ['gɑ:bl] **vt.** ① 对(文章、报告等) 断章取义;
窜改,歪曲: a ~d text 经窜改的文章 ②(非有意
地)混淆(或歪曲) ③[罕]筛去…的杂质; 精选,
挑拣

garden ['gɑ:dn] **I n.** ① (花、菜、果)园, 庭园:
a kitchen ~ 菜园 / a nursery ~ 苗圃 ②[常用
复]公园,(动、植物)园: botanical(zoological)
~s 植(动)物园 ③土地特别肥沃的地区 ④[英]
[复](用于一列或数列房屋的命名中)…(花)园
⑤露天饮食店 ⑥[the G-]古希腊伊壁鸠鲁(哲
学)学派 **II ❶ vi.** 从事园艺 ❷ **vt.** …开辟为
花园(或菜园、果园) **III a.** ①(花、菜、果)园的;在
园中生长的,在露天生长的 ②普通的,平凡的,老
一套的 ‖**common or** ~ 见 **common** / **Everything is nice in your** ~. [讽]你家的东西那
有不好的!(或:你家的狗屎都是香的!)/ **lead sb.
up the** ~(**path**)引诱某人,把某人引入歧途 /
the Garden of England(指 Kent
和 Worcestershire 等郡)‖~ed **a.** 有花园的 /
~**ing n.** 园艺(学) ‖~ **apartment** 花园公寓
(有大块草地或花园的公寓式住宅)/ ~ **city** 花
园城市(有计划地辟有花园和绿化区的住宅区)/
~ **cress**【植】独行菜 / ~ **frame** 栽培植物用的
框架 / ~ **glass** 罩植物用的钟形玻璃罩 / ~
party 游园会 / ~ **plot** 园地 / ~ **stuff** [英]
[总称]蔬菜; 水果 / '~-**va'riety** a. 普通的,平
凡的,老一套的

gargle ['gɑ:gl] **I ❶ vt.** ①漱(喉) ②从喉底发出(咕
噜声 ❷ **vi.** ① 漱口,含漱 ②[美俚]喝酒,酗酒
II n. ① 含漱剂 ② 漱口声,喉头发出的咕噜声
③[美俚]酒

gargoyle ['gɑ:goil] **n.** ①【建】滴水嘴(常作怪形生
物状); 象滴水嘴的装饰 ② 奇形怪状的雕刻像
③面貌古怪的人

garish ['gɛəriʃ] **a.** (衣物等)鲜艳夺目的;花花绿绿
的;打扮(或装饰)得俗不可耐的 ‖~**ly ad.** / ~-
ness n.

garland ['gɑ:lənd] **I n.** ① 花环,花冠;金属制的花
环 ②胜利和荣誉的象征 ③[古]诗(文)集 ④【海】
索环;食物网袋 ⑤【建】华饰 **II vt.** ①把…做成
花环 ②给…戴上花环,用花环装饰

garlic ['gɑ:lik] **n.** 大蒜 ‖**be** ~ **for dessert** [俚]
是最不受欢迎的东西 ‖~**ky a.** 有大蒜气味的

garment ['gɑ:mənt] **I** *n.* ①(一件)衣服(尤指长袍、外套) ②[复]服装,衣着 ③ 外表;外衣 **II** *vt.* 给…穿衣服

garner ['gɑ:nə] **I** *n.* ① 谷仓 ②贮备物;积蓄物,积累物 **II** *vt.* ①把…储入谷仓;收集;积蓄 ②[美口]得到

garnish ['gɑ:niʃ] **I** *vt.* ①装璜,修饰: a ~ed net 【军】伪装网 ②(烹饪)加配菜于 ③ =~ee (*vt.*) ④(因甲乙双方诉讼)传讯(有关的第三者) **II** *n.* ①装饰品;(文章的)修饰;华丽的词藻 ②为色香味而添饰的配菜 ||*swept and ~ed* 打扫干净并布置一新的 ||**~ee** [,gɑ:ni'ʃi:] 【律】*n.* 第三债务人(即根据法院扣押令扣押债务人财产者) *vt.* ①通知(受托人)扣押债务人的财产,向(第三债务人)下达扣押令 ②扣押(债务人的财产);扣发(债务人的工资) ‖**~ment** *n.* ① 装饰;装饰品 【律】对第三者的出庭命令;扣押被告财产的通知;对债务人工资的部分扣发;扣押

garret[1] ['gærət] *n.* ① 屋顶间,顶楼;搁楼: from cellar to ~ (或 from ~ to kitchen) 从上到下,整幢房子 ②[俚]头 ‖**~eer** [,gærə'tiə] *n.* ①住顶层小间的人 ② 贫苦的作家

garret[2] ['gærət] *vt.* 【建】用小石块填塞(粗石建筑物)的缝隙

garrison ['gærisn] **I** *n.* 驻军,卫戍部队,警备部队;驻地,要塞 **II** *vt.* 守卫(都市、要塞等);驻防(某地);派(兵)驻防

garrulous ['gæruləs] *a.* ① 饶舌的,喋喋不休的 ②(鸟声)叽叽喳喳的;(水声)潺潺的 ‖**~ly** *ad.* ‖**~ness** *n.*

garter ['gɑ:tə] **I** *n.* ① 吊袜带 ②[英] [the G-] 嘉德勋位(英国的最高勋位),嘉德勋章 ③[英] [G-] 勋章院的五个主管中的第一人 (=Garter King of Arms) **II** *vt.* ① 用吊袜带吊住(袜子),在(腿)上带上吊袜带 ② 授给…最高勋位(或勋章)

gas [gæs] **I** *n.* ①气态,气体 ②可燃气;煤气;沼气;【矿】瓦斯: light the ~ 点亮沼气灯;点燃煤气灶 / marsh ~ 沼气 ③(笑气等)麻醉剂: laughing ~ 笑气(即一氧化二氮) ④毒气 (=poison): nerve ~ 神经毒气 / tear ~ 催泪性毒气 / a ~ projectile 毒气弹 / a ~ barrier 撒毒气地区 ⑤[美口]汽油;(汽车等的)油门 ⑥[俚]空谈,废话;夸大的话,吹牛 ⑦[美俚]成功,令人非常满意的事 **II** (gassed; gassing) ❶ *vt.* ①向…供应气体(如煤气等),给…充气;给(汽车等)加汽油 (*up*) ②用气体处理;【纺】烧(布、线等)的毛 ③向(某处)放毒气;用毒气杀伤(人) ④[美俚]使得到极大快感 ❷ *vi.* ①放出气体 ②(给汽车等)加油 (*up*) ③[口]空谈,吹牛 ‖*step on the ~* 踩油门,加速,加快 / *turn on the ~* ①开煤气 ②[俚]打开话匣子,开始吹牛 / *turn out* (或 *off*) *the ~* ①关掉煤气 ②[俚]关掉话匣子,停止吹牛 ‖**~less** *a.* 无气体的;不用气体的 ‖**~bag** *n.* ① 气囊 ② 闲扯的人 / ~ **bomb** 毒气弹 bracket (墙上有灯头的)煤气灯管 / ~ **burner** ① 煤气灶;煤气灯 ② 煤气喷嘴;煤气火焰 /

chamber ①死刑毒气室 ②(苹果等的)贮藏室 / ~ **coal** (适于提炼煤气、焦炭的)气煤 / ~ **coke** 煤气焦炭 / ~ **constant** 气体常数 / ~ **engine** 燃气发动机 / ~ **fire** 煤气取暖器 / ~ **fitter** 煤气装修工 / ~ **fittings** 煤气设备(包括灯、灶、管道等) / ~ **fixture** (煤气管与喷嘴之间的)煤气装置 / ~ **furnace** 煤气发生炉;煤气炉 / ~ **helmet** =~ mask / '~,**holder** *n.* 煤气库,煤气柜 / '~,**house** *n.* ① [美]煤气厂 ②[喻]贫民区 / ~ **jet** ① 煤气喷嘴;煤气火焰 / ~ **light** *n.* 煤气灯;煤气灯光 / '~-**main** *n.* 煤气总管 / ~-**man** *n.* 煤气厂的工人,煤气收费员;【矿】瓦斯检查员,通风员 / ~ **mask** 防毒面具 / ~ **meter** 煤气表;气量计: lie like a ~ *meter* 一味撒谎 / ~ **oil** 瓦斯油;粗柴油,气油 / '~-,**oven** *n.* ① 煤气灶 ②毒气室 / '~,**pipe** *n.* 煤气管 / '~,**poker** *n.* 煤气点火棒 / ~ **proof** *a.* 防毒气的;不透气的 / ~ **ring** (有环形喷火头的)煤气灶 / ~ **shell** =~ bomb / ~ **station** [美](汽油)加油站 / ~ **stove** 煤气炉 / '~-**tar** *n.* 煤焦油 / ~ **turbine** 燃气轮机 / '~**works** [复] *n.* [用作单]煤气厂

gas mask

gaseous ['geizjəs] *a.* ①气体的,气态的: ~ density 气体密度 / a ~ mixture 气体混合物 ②过热的: ~ steam 过热蒸汽 ③ 空虚的,无实质的 ‖**~ness** *n.*

gash[1] [gæʃ] **I** *n.* ①(深长的)切口(或伤口) ②面等的)裂缝 ③划开 **II** *vt. & vi.* (在…上)划深长切口,划开

gash[2] [gæʃ] *a.* [英俚]【海】多余的;备用的

gash[3] [gæʃ] *a.* [苏格兰]伶俐的;穿着整齐的

gasoline, gasolene ['gæsəli:n] *n.* [美]汽油([英] petrol): a ~ bomb 汽油弹 / jellied ~ 固汽油 (=napalm)

gasometer [gæ'sɔmitə] *n.* ①贮气器 ②煤气表,气量计

gasp [gɑ:sp] **I** ❶ *vi.* ①气喘,喘息;透不过气: ~ for breath (或 air) 气喘 ②热望,渴望 (*for*, *after*) ❷ *vt.* 气呼呼地说 (*out*): ~ out a few words 气呼呼地说了几句话 **II** *n.* 气喘,喘息;透不过气 ‖*at one's last* ~ 在奄奄一息时 / *at the last* ~ ①在奄奄一息时 ②在最后关头,最后 / ~ *one's life away* (或 *out*) 断气,死去 ‖**~er** *n.* ①气喘者 ② [俚]廉价香烟

gasping ['gɑ:spiŋ] *a.* 气喘的;痉挛的;阵发性的 ‖**~ly** *ad.*

gastric ['gæstrik] *a.* 胃的: ~ juice 胃液 / a ~ ulcer 胃溃疡

gate¹ [geit] **I** *n.* ①大门,篱笆门,城门: a folding ~ 活栅门,折迭门 ②出入口,洞口 ③狭长通道;峡谷;隘口: a turnpike ~ 收递行税的关卡 ④门扇,阀门,闸门 ⑤锯架 ⑥(运动会、展览会等的) 观众(数);门票收入: There was a ~ of thousands. 观众成千上万。⑦[冶]浇注道,浇口 ⑧[无]门电路;选通电路;选通脉冲 ⑨[俚]解雇;扔弃 **II** *vt.* ①给…装门 ②[英](大学的一种处分) 不准(学生)外出 ③用门控制 ‖*crash the ~* [俚] 擅自入场 / *get the ~* [美俚]被赶走,被解雇 / *give sb. the ~* [美] 赶走某人; 将某人解雇 / *open a ~ to* (或 *for*) 给…以便利(或机会) / *the ~ of horn (ivory)* 角(牙)门,应验(不应验)的梦兆 (据神话称, 应验的梦自角门进入, 不应验的梦自牙门进入) ‖*~less a.* 无门的 ‖*'~crash vi. & vt.* [俚]擅自进入,无票进入 / '*~crasher n.* [俚]擅自进入者,无票入场者 / '*~fold n.* 折迭插页 / '*~house n.* ①城门上面(或旁边)的房屋 (过去常用来监禁犯人或供守门人使用); (公园等供看门人用的)门房 ②水电站闸门上面的控制室 / *~keeper n.* 看门人 / '*~leg(ged) table* 折迭式桌子 / *~man* ['geitmən] *n.* =~keeper / *~ meeting* 收费的运动会 / *~ money* [总称]入场费,门票费 / '*~post n.* [建]门柱: between you and me and the ~post 只在咱俩私下说说 / '*~way n.* 门口,入口;途径;方法,手段

gate² [geit] *n.* ①[古]街道,路 ②[方]方式,方法

gather ['gæðə] **I ❶** *vt.* ①使聚集,使集拢: The kindergartener ~ed the children round her. 幼儿园阿姨把孩子们聚集在她周围。②搜集;采集;收(庄稼等): ~ data (information) 搜集资料(情报) / ~ mulberry leaves 采桑叶 / ~ (in) a wheat crop 收小麦 ③渐增;积累;恢复: The invalid is ~ing strength. 病人的体力渐渐复原了。 / ~ breath 喘过气来 ④鼓足(劲头等);[~ oneself] 使振作 ⑤得出(印象、想法等);推测: I ~ (that) he will come. 我猜想他会来的。⑥皱拢(眉头等);给(衣裙等)打折裥 ❷ *vi.* ①聚集,聚拢: ~ round a bonfire 围着篝火 ②积聚 ③化脓;(脓疮)出头 ④(眉头等)皱起来 **II** *n.* 折裥 ‖*be ~ed to one's fathers* 见老祖宗去,死 / ~ *head* 见 head / ~ *up* ①拾拢,集拢 ②蜷缩(肢体等) ③概括,集中 / ~ *way* 见 way

gathering ['gæðəriŋ] *n.* ① 聚集(或搜集、采集等) ②集会: a public ~ 公共集会 ③捐款 ④脓肿 ‖*~ coal* (封炉用的)大煤块

gaud [gɔːd] *n.* ①华丽而俗气的东西 (如首饰等);好看而不值钱的小玩意儿 ②[复]排场

gaudy¹ ['gɔːdi] *a.* (衣服、装饰、文风等)华丽而俗气的,炫丽的;华而不实的 ‖*gaudily ad.* / *gaudiness n.*

gaudy² ['gɔːdi] *n.* [英]盛大招待会;盛大宴会(尤指大学中的校友年宴)

ga(u)ge [geidʒ] **I** *n.* ①标准尺寸,标准规格;(铁板等的)厚度;(枪、炮的)口径; (电线等的) 直径 ②规,量规,量器,量计,表: an altitude ~ 高度计,测高仪 / a level ~ 水准仪 / a pressure ~ 压力计 / a rain ~ 雨量器 / a screw pitch ~ 螺距规 / a go ~ 通过规 / a no-go ~ 不通过规 ③[交](铁道)轨距;(汽车等两侧车轮间的)轮距: broad (narrow) ~ 宽(窄)轨 / standard ~ 标准轨距(=1.435 米) ④ 容量,范围 ⑤[海](船只)满载吃水深度;(船只对风或其他船只的)相对位置 ⑥(估计、判断等的)方法,手段,标准 ⑦[建](铺于屋顶上的瓦、石板、木瓦等的)露出部分,茸脚;(掺和于石灰膏中的)熟石膏用量 ⑧[纺]隔距;(针织品) 1½ 时中的针圈数 **II** *vt.* ①(用量具)量;测量,测定 ②使(石块等)成为标准尺寸;使符合标准 ③[建](按适当比例)掺和(石膏) ④估计,评价(人物等) ‖*get the ~ of* 探测…的意向 / *have the weather ~ of* 在…的上风;占…的便宜,处于比…优越的地位 / *take the ~* 估计,测量 ‖*~able a.* 可计量的,可测量的 / *~r n.* ①计量者;零件检验员;量器检查员 ②计量器 ③(国内货物税的)征税员 ‖*~ cock* 试水位旋塞 / *~ glass* (锅炉)水位玻璃管 / *~ lath* [建]挂瓦条 / *~ lathe* [机]样板车床

gaunt [gɔːnt] *a.* ①瘦削的;憔悴的 ②贫瘠的,荒凉的 ‖*~ly ad.* / *~ness n.*

gauntlet¹ ['gɔːntlit] *n.* ①(中世纪武士用的)金属护手;臂铠 ②长手套;防护手套 ‖*fling* (或 *throw*) *down the ~* 挑战 / *pick* (或 *take*) *up the ~* ①应战 ②护卫 ‖*~ed a.* 带金属护手的;带长手套的

gauntlet

gauntlet² ['gɔːntlit] *n.* ①夹道鞭笞的刑罚 ②交叉射击,交叉火网 ‖*run the ~* 受夹道鞭打; [喻]受严厉批评

gauze [gɔːz] *n.* ①(棉、丝等织成的)薄纱;罗;纱布; (金属、塑料等的)网纱 ②薄雾

gave [geiv] give 的过去式

gawk [gɔːk] **I** *n.* 呆子,笨人;腼腆的人 **II** *vi.* 呆呆地看着 ‖*~er n.* 伸长脖子呆看的人

gay [gei] **I** *a.* ①快乐的;愉快的;轻快的: a ~ dance 快乐的舞蹈 ②鲜明的;鲜艳的;装饰华丽的: ~ colours 鲜艳的色彩 ③寻欢作乐的;淫荡的,放荡的;同性恋爱的: lead a ~ life 过放荡的生活 ④[美俚]脸皮厚的;冒失的 **II** *n.* 同性恋爱者 ‖*go ~* 过放荡生活 ‖*~ly ad.* / *~ness n.*

gaze [geiz] I *vi.* 凝视,注视,盯 (*at, on, upon*
等): ~ *out at* the golden rice in the distance 眺
望着远方金黄色的水稻 / ~ *into* the sky 凝视
天空 / *stand high and* ~ *far* 站得高看得远 /
~ *after* sb. 目送某人 II *n.* 凝视,注视: attract
the ~ *of* people 引人注目 / *stand at* ~ 站着呆
呆地钉着看 ‖**~r** *n.* 凝视者

gazelle [gə'zel] ([复] gazelle(s)) *n.* 【动】瞪羚

gazette [gə'zet] I *n.* ①报纸; (G-] (用于报刊名)
…报 ②[英] (政府、大学等的)公报 II *vt.* [英]
在公报上公布,在公报上刊载 ‖*be named in the*
~ 被宣告破产

gazetteer [ˌgæzi'tiə] *n.* 地名词典,地名索引

gear [giə] I *n.* ①【机】齿轮; (齿轮)传动装置; (汽
车等的)排档: bevel ~ 伞形齿轮 / helical ~
斜齿轮 / steering ~ 转向装置 / top ~ 高速
(档),末档 / bottom ~ 低速(档),头挡 / reverse
~ 倒车档;反向齿轮 ②工具;用具;马具 ③【海】索
具,船具: hunting ~ 打猎用具 ③衣服;(士兵
等的)装备 ④动产; 货物 ⑤[英口]胡说 ⑥[英
口]行为;事件 II ❶ *vt.* ①将齿轮装上(机器等);
用齿轮连接; 使接上齿轮; 使(机器)开动: ~
down (up, level) a car 使汽车换慢(快,中)档 ②
装备;(马等)套上马具 (*up*) ③使适合 (*to*)
❷ *vi.* ①(齿轮)连接上 (*into*); (机器)开动
②适合, 一致 (*with*) ‖~ *up* 促进,增加: ~ *up*
production to meet the people's needs 增加生产
以适应人民的需要 / *high* ~ ①【机】高速档 ②
[口]高速度: The work was finished at *high* ~.
这项工作已经以高速度完成了. / *in* ~ ①【机】
齿轮已与机器联接 ②正常 / *low* ~ ①【机】低
速档 ②[口]低速度 / *out of* ~ ①【机】齿轮脱
开 ②失常,有毛病 / *shift* ~*s* 【机】变速,调
档 ② 改变方式(或办法、速度等): *shift* ~*s in*
one's speech 讲话中改变调子 ‖**~ing** ['giəriŋ]
n. 【机】齿轮装置;传动装置 / **~less** *a.* 无齿轮
的 / '~**box** *n.* ①= case ②(汽车等的)变速
箱 / ~ **case** 齿轮箱 / '~-**driven** *a.* 齿轮传
动的 / ~ **shaper** 插齿机;刨齿机 / '~**shift**
n.【机】变速,调档;变速装置 / ~ **wheel** 齿轮

gear

geese [gi:s] *n.* ① goose 的复数 ② [the G-] [俚]
葡萄牙兵

gelatin ['dʒelətin], **gelatine** [ˌdʒelə'ti:n] *n.* ① 明
胶;动物胶;(食用或药用的)胶: vegetable ~ 植

物胶 / blasting ~ 【化】爆炸胶 / ~ paper 照
相软片片基 ② 凝胶体;果子冻 ③ (舞台灯光用)
彩色透明滤光板

gem [dʒem] I *n.* ①宝石,美玉 ②珍宝; 珍品 ③
被人喜欢(或尊敬)的人 ④一种松饼 II (gemmed;
gemming) *vt.* 用宝石装饰(或镶嵌)

gender[1] ['dʒendə] *n.* ①【语】性: the common ~
通性 / the masculine (feminine, neuter) ~ 阳
(阴,中)性 ②[口][谑] (生理上的)性 ‖**less** *a.*
【语】无性的

gender[2] ['dʒendə] *vt.* [诗]产生,发生

gene [dʒi:n] *n.* 【生】基因: dominant ~ 显性基因

genealogical [ˌdʒi:njə'lɔdʒikəl] *a.* 家系的,家谱的;
系统的: a ~ tree 家系图; (动物等进化发育的)
系统树 ‖**ly** *ad.*

genealogy [ˌdʒi:ni'æledʒi] *n.* ①家系,家谱,血统;
(动植物、语言的)系统 ②家谱, 系谱图; 系统图
③家系学, 系谱学

genera ['dʒenərə] genus 的复数

general ['dʒenərəl] I *a.* ①一般的;普通的;综合的:
the ~ opinion 一般的舆论 / a ~ hospital 综合
性(军)医院 / the ~ pronunciation of a word 词
的通常读音 ②普遍的;全体的: a matter of ~
interest 普遍感兴趣的事 ③总的;全面的: the ~
program(me) 总纲 / a ~ offensive 全面进攻
④大体的; 笼统的: a ~ outline 大纲 / He spoke
in ~ terms. 他笼统地谈了一谈. ⑤ (用于职位)
总…,…长: a ~ secretary (或 secretary-~) 总
书记; 秘书长 / the Attorney *General* (美国的)
司法部长; (英国的)检察总长 / a consul ~ 总领
事 / *the General Assembly* (美国某些州的)州议
会; 联合国大会 / ~ *average* (海上保险)共同海
损 / *General Court* (美国)新罕布什尔、马萨诸塞
两州州议会的正式名称 / a ~ *dealer* [英]杂货
商 / ~ *delivery* 邮件的存局候领 / a ~ *delivery*
邮局的存局候领处 / a ~ *election* 普选 / ~
knowledge 一般知识,常识 / a ~ *line* 总路线 / a
~ *officer* 将级军官 / a ~ *order* 【军】一般命令;
卫兵守则 / the *General Post Office* 邮政总局(英
国) / a ~ *practitioner* 普通医生(通看各科的开
业医生) / a ~ *reader* 阅读各种书刊的人,一般
读者(与专业读者相对而言) / a ~ *servant* 做杂
务的仆人 / ~ *staff* 总参谋部 (全体人员) / a ~
store (或 *shop*) 百货店 / a ~ *strike* 总罢工 / a
~ *war* 全面战争 II *n.* ①普通(或一般、普遍)
的事(或物) ②[古]大众 ③将军; (英、美)陆军
(或海军陆战队)上将; (美)空军上将; 军事家:
General of the Army (美)陆军五星上将 / *General of the Air Force* (美)空军五星上将 / [英
口]做杂务的仆人 ⑤【天主教】耶稣会(或多明我
会等)的会长;【基督教】救世军的最高司令 ‖*in* ~
一般地,大体上: *In* ~, your plan is good. 你们
的方案总的来看是好的. ‖~ *post* [主英] ①(邮
件的)上午第一次发送 ② 位置的大变动 / '~-
'**purpose** *a.* 多种用途的

generalissimo [ˌdʒenərə'lisimou] *n.* 大元帅,总司

令,最高统帅

generality [ˌdʒenəˈræliti] *n.* ①一般(性); 一般原则; 普遍(性); 通则 ②概括性); 概念; 笼统 [the ~] 主要部分; 大多数: the ~ of readers 大多数读者

generalization [ˌdʒenərəlaiˈzeiʃən] *n.* ①一般化; 普遍化 ②概括; [贬]判断: Don't make hasty ~s. 不要匆匆下判断。

generalize [ˈdʒenərəlaiz] ❶ *vt.* ①使一般化 ②归纳出, 概括出; 从…引出一般性结论: ~ a conclusion from facts 从事实中引出结论 ③(绘画等中)表达出…的基本特征 ④推广; 使广义化: ~ the use of a new insecticide 推广新杀虫剂 ❷ *vi.* ①形成概念 ②笼统地讲(或写) ③延及全身

generally [ˈdʒenərəli] *ad.* ①一般地: ~ speaking 一般地说来 ②通常地: He ~ gets up very early. 他通常很早起身。 ③广泛地, 普遍地: It is ~ believed that .... 普遍认为…

generate [ˈdʒenəreit] *vt.* ①生殖, 生育 ②发生, 产生(光、热、电等): ~ electricity 发电 / These new boilers ~ more heat than the old ones. 这些新锅炉产生的热量比旧锅炉多。 ③引起; 导致 ④【数】形成, 生成(线、面、体等) ‖**generating** *a.* 产生的, 生成的: a *generating* station (plant) 发电站(厂)

generation [ˌdʒenəˈreiʃən] *n.* ①生殖, 生育; 产生, 发生: the ~ of heat by friction 摩擦生热 ②代, 一代 (约三十年); 世代: the coming ~ 下一代 / the past (或 last) ~ 上一代, 前辈人 / ~ after (或 from ~ to ~) 一代一代, 世世代 / a ~ gap 不合世代; 世代隔阂 / alternation of ~s 【生】世代交替 / a ~ ago 大约三十年前 ③【数】(线、面、体的)形成 ‖**~al** *a.* ①生殖的, 生育的 ②一代的; 代与代之间的, 世代的

generator [ˈdʒenəreitə] *n.* ①生殖者; 发生者; 创始者 ②发电机; 发生器: an electric ~ 发电机 / a gas ~ 煤气发生器 / a steam ~ 蒸气发生器 / a shunt ~ 分(或并)激发电机

generic [dʒiˈnerik] *a.* ①一般的, 普通的 ②(商品名)不注册的(例如 aspirin) ③【生】属的: ~ name 属名 ④【语】全称的,总称的: the ~ singular (plural) 全称单(复)数 ‖**~ally** *ad.*

generosity [ˌdʒenəˈrɔsiti] *n.* ①宽宏大量; 慷慨, 大方 ②宽大的行为; 慷慨的行为 ③丰饶

generous [ˈdʒenərəs] *a.* ①宽宏大量的; 慷慨的, 大方的: a ~ contributor 慷慨的捐助者 / be ~ with one's money 用钱大方 / be ~ in giving help 乐于助人 ②丰富的; 丰盛的: a ~ harvest 丰收 / a ~ amount 大量的 ③肥沃的 ④(酒、色彩等)浓的 ‖**~ly** *ad.*

genesis [ˈdʒenisis] (复 geneses [ˈdʒenisiːz]) *n.* ①起源; 发生; 创始: the ~ of a disease 病的起源 / say a little about the ~ of the statement 稍稍讲一点关于声明的产生经过 ②[G-]《创世纪》(基督教《圣经》中《旧约全书》的第一卷)

genetic [dʒiˈnetik] *a.* ①创始的; 发生的 ②遗传学的: ~ code 【生】遗传密码 / ~ material 【生】遗传物质 ‖**~ally** *ad.*

genetics [dʒiˈnetiks] [复] *n.* [用作单]遗传学

genial[1] [ˈdʒiːnjəl] *a.* ①亲切的, 和蔼的, 友好的 ②适宜于动植物生长的; 宜人的; 温和的, 温暖的: a ~ climate 宜人的气候 / ~ sunshine 温暖的阳光 ③显示天才的 ‖**~ity** [ˌdʒiːniˈæliti] *n.* ①亲切, 和蔼, 友好 ②亲切(或和蔼)的神情(或行动、言语等) ③温和, 温暖 ‖**~ize** *vt.* 使适宜于动植物的生长; 使宜人; 使温暖 ‖**~ly** *ad.*

genial[2] [ˈdʒiːnaiəl] *a.* 【解】颏的

genie [ˈdʒiːni] ([复] genies 或 genii [ˈdʒiːniai]) *n.* (阿拉伯神话中的)神怪, 妖怪

genitive [ˈdʒenitiv] **I** *a.* 【语】生格的; 所有格的: the ~ case 生格;所有格 **II** *n.* 生格;所有格; 属于生格(或所有格)的词(或词组)

genius [ˈdʒiːnjəs] [复] geniuses 或 genii [ˈdʒiːniai]) *n.* ①[只用单]天才, 天资, 天赋; 才华, 创造能力: have a ~ for 有…的天才 ②([复] geniuses) 天才人物 ③(语言、制度等的)全部特征, 本质; (民族、时代等的)精神, 思潮; 倾向, 风气 ④([复] genii) [常作 G-] 守护神 ⑤([复] genii) 神仙; 恶魔; 对别人有好(或坏)影响的人 ‖*sb.'s evil* ~ 附在某人身上的恶魔; 给某人很坏影响的人 / *sb.'s good* ~ 某人的守护神; 给某人良好影响的人 ‖**~ loci** 一地方的风气; 一地方的守护神

genteel [dʒenˈtiːl] *a.* ①上流社会的; 绅士风度的 ②有教养的, 斯文的; 彬彬有礼的 ③时髦的 ④[讽]装绅士派头的; 装体面的; 假斯文的; 赶时髦的 ‖*live in* ~ *poverty* 见 **poverty** ‖**~ism** *n.* 雅语(例如代替 go to bed 而用的 retire for the night) / **~ly** *ad.*

gentile [ˈdʒentail] **I** *n.* ①[常作 G-] 非犹太人, 不信犹太教的人; 非摩门 (Mormon) 教徒 ②异教徒 ③【语】说明国籍(或民族)的词 **II** *a.* ①[常作 G-] 非犹太人的, 不信犹太教的; 非摩门教徒的 ②异教徒的 ③氏族的, 部落的; 民族的 ④【语】说明国籍(或民族)的

gentility [dʒenˈtiliti] *n.* ①出身高贵; 上流阶层, 绅士们 ②斯文; 文雅; 彬彬有礼; 有教养 ③[讽]装体面; 假斯文: shabby ~ 装出来的体面

gentle [ˈdʒentl] **I** *a.* ①出身高贵的, 上流阶层的 ②有礼貌的, 文雅的; 优美的: ~ manners 文雅的举止 ③慷慨的; 好心的; [古]豪侠的 ④(动物等)驯服的 ⑤从容的; 耐心的; 温柔的 ⑥柔和的; 轻度的; 和缓的, 不猛烈的: a ~ slope 不很陡的斜坡 **II** *n.* ①[常用复]出身高贵的人; 绅士 ②蛆 **III** *vt.* ①使驯良; 使驯顺; 使柔和; 使某和 ②驯服(马等); 抚弄, 轻拍 ‖**~ and simple** 贵与贱; 贵人与庶民; 各阶层 ‖**~ness** *n.* ‖**~ breeze** 微风(即三级风) / **~-folk(s)** [复] *n.* 出身高贵的人; 上流人士

gentleman [ˈdʒentlmən] ([复] gentlemen) *n.* ①出身高贵的人; 有身分的人; 绅士 ②有教养的人; 彬彬有礼的人 ③[常用复]男子,(尊称)阁下, 先生;

Gentlemen (商业信等中的称呼)先生们(= Sirs) / Ladies and *gentlemen* (对听众的称呼)女士们、先生们 / my ~ (刚刚我讲到的)那个人 [英][gentlemen] [用作单]男厕所 ⑤ (王室、贵族的)侍从,男仆 (=~ in waiting) ⑥ 有收入而不从事任何职业的人 ⑦[美](众议院的)议员: the ~ from New York 纽约州(选出)的众议员 || *a ~ at large* (依附朝廷的)有闲阶级的人; 无职业者 / *a ~ of fortune* 冒险家; 海盗 / *a ~ of the press* 新闻记者 / *a ~'s* (或 *gentlemen's*) *agreement* 君子协定 / *a ~'s ~* 侍从,男仆 / *gentlemen of the robe* 律师们 / *the ~ in black* 恶魔 / *the old ~* [谑]恶魔 ||~like *a.* 绅士的; 绅士派头的 / ~ly *a.* & *ad.* ||'~-at-'arms *n.* [英]国王的卫士 / ~ farmer (有土地而不劳动的)乡绅

gentlewoman ['dʒentl,wumən] ([复] gentlewomen ['dʒentl,wimin]) *n.* ①贵妇人; 女士; 淑女 ②(王室、贵族的)侍女,女仆 ||~like *a.* 贵妇人的,淑女似的

gently ['dʒentli] *ad.* ①有礼貌地,文雅地; 温柔地 ②柔和地; 轻轻地,渐渐地: *Gently!* 慢一些! (或: 轻一些!) / The hill sloped ~. 山坡渐渐斜下。③出身高贵地; 有教养地

gentry ['dʒentri] *n.* ①贵族们,绅士们; [英](地位、出身低于贵族的)中上阶层 ②[贬][谑]人们; 一类人,一批人: these ~ 这些家伙 ||*the flash* ~ 盗贼们,流氓们 / *the light= fingered* ~ 扒手们

genuine ['dʒenjuin] *a.* ① 真正的, 名副其实的 ② 真诚的, 坦率的 ③ 纯血统的: a ~ breed 纯种 ||~ly *ad.* / ~ness *n.*

genus ['dʒi:nəs] [复] genera ['dʒenərə] 或 [罕] genuses) *n.* ① 类, 种类 [生]属: the ~ Homo 人类 ②[逻]种

geographic(al) [dʒiə'græfik(əb)] *a.* 地理(学)的; 地区(性)的: ~ distribution 地理分布 / ~ latitude 地理纬度 / a ~ mile 地理英里(赤道上经度一分的长度) ||**geographically** *ad.*

geography [dʒi'ɔgrəfi] *n.* ① 地理学: physical ~ 自然地理学 ② 地形; 地势 ③ 地理书, 地志 ④ (生产、建设等的)布局,配置

geologic(al) [dʒiə'lɔdʒik(əb)] *a.* 地质(学)的: a ~ survey 地质调查 / ~ section 【地】地质剖面 ||**geologically** *ad.*

geology [dʒi'ɔlədʒi] *n.* ①地质学: structural ~ 构造地质学 ② (某地方的)地质 ③ 地质学书(或论著) ||**geologist** *n.* 地质学者,地质学家

geometric(al) [dʒiə'metrik(əb)] *a.* ①几何学的: ~ progression 几何级数,等比级数 / ~ projection 几何投影 ②几何图形的: ~ ornament 几何形装饰 / ~ stairs 弯曲楼梯 ||**geometrically** *ad.*

geometry [dʒi'ɔmitri] *n.* ①几何学: plane ~ 平面几何 / solid ~ 立体几何 / analytical ~ 解析几何 / descriptive ~ 画法几何 ②几何形状 ③几

何学书(或论著) ||**geometrize** [dʒi'ɔmitraiz] ❶ *vi.* 研究几何学 ❷ *vt.* 用几何图形表示; 使符合几何学原理和定律

geranium [dʒi'reinjəm] *n.* 【植】老鹳草属植物; 天竺葵; [G-] 老鹳草属: ~ oil 草叶油

germ [dʒə:m] **I** *n.* ①微生物; 细菌; 病菌 ②[生]幼芽,胚芽; 胚原基 ③萌芽; 起源: be in ~ 处于萌芽状态, 处在不发达阶段 **II** *vi.* [喻]萌芽; 发生 ||~ carrier 带菌者 / ~ cell 生殖细胞 / ~ layer [生]胚层 / ~ plasm [生]种质 / ~ theory 【生】生源说 / ~ warfare 细菌战争 / ~ weapon 细菌武器

germicide ['dʒə:misaid] *n.* 杀菌剂 ||**germicidal** [,dʒə:mi'saidl] *a.* 杀菌(剂)的

germinate ['dʒə:mineit] ❶ *vt.* 使发芽; 使发生,使发展 ❷ *vi.* 发芽,开始生长 ||**germination** [dʒə:mi'neiʃən] *n.* 萌芽,发生 / **germinative** *a.* 发芽的,有发芽力的 / **germinator** *n.* 使发芽的物(或人); 种子发芽力测定器

gerund ['dʒerənd] *n.* 【语】动名词 ||~ial [dʒi'rʌndiəl] *a.* 动名词的 ||~-,grinder *n.* 拉丁语法教师; 学究式的教师

gesticulate [dʒes'tikjuleit] ❶ *vi.* (讲话时等)做手势; 用姿势(或动作)示意 ❷ *vt.* 用手势表达 ||**gesticulation** [dʒes,tikju'leiʃən] *n.* 做手势; 示意的动作(或姿势) / **gesticulative** *a.* 做手势的 / **gesticulator** *n.* 做手势的人 / **gesticulatory** [dʒes'tikjulətəri] *a.* 用手势的

gesture ['dʒestʃə] **I** *n.* ①姿势; 手势: ~ language 手势语 ②(外交等方面的)姿态; 表示: make a friendly ~ to sb. 对某人作友好的表示 **II** *vi.* & *vt.* =gesticulate

get [get] **I** (过去式 got [gɔt], 过去分词 got 或[古][美] gotten ['gɔtn]; 现在分词 getting) ❶ *vt.* ①获得,得到: ~ credit for one's work 工作上获得好评 / ~ information 获得消息 / Multiplying 3 by 2 we ~ 6. 二乘三得六。② 挣得; 买: ~ a living 谋生 ③ 收获; 捕获; 赢得: ~ a good crop 获得丰收 ④ 收到; 受到(罚、打击等): ~ a letter 收到信 / ~ a blow on the head 头上被打了一下 ⑤ (电话通话时)接通: 打电话 ⑥ 搞到; 拿: *Get* me some paste. 给我弄点浆糊。/ Go ~ your notebook. 去把你的笔记本拿来。⑦ [口] 理解; 记住; 学得; 听到: Do you ~ me? 你明白我的意思吗? / ~ by heart (或 by rote) 把…背熟 ⑧ 抓住; 打击; 击中; 杀死; 使受伤 ⑨ 感染上(疾病); (毒品等)使上瘾: ~ a cold 患感冒 ⑩[口]难住: Ah! I've *got* you there! 啊,这下我可难倒你啦。⑪[口]吃; 准备(饭): Go and ~ your lunch. 你去吃午饭吧。

⑫[俚]注意到: Did you ~ the look on his face? 你注意到他脸上的神情吗?
⑬[用完成时态]有: Have you got a light? 有火吗?
⑭[用完成时态,后接不定式]必须
⑮[后接复合宾语]使得;把…弄得;使被弄得: Get everything *ready*! 把一切准备好! / ~ one's leg *broken* 把腿弄断 / ~ things *moving* 使事情开始进行 / ~ one's bicycle *repaired* 把自行车送去修好(或把自行车修好) / ~ one's hair *cut* 理发
⑯ 说服,劝说: Get him *to see* a doctor. 劝他去看医生。
⑰[俚]触动…的感情;使高兴;使激动;使恼火
⑱(主要指雄性动物)生(仔)
❷ vi. ① 到达
② 变得;成为
③(开始)…起来;逐渐…起来: ~ talking 谈了起来 / ~ to know (like) 对…逐渐了解(喜爱)起来
④[加过去分词构成被动式]被,受: ~ caught in the rain 遇上雨
⑤[俚]立即走开: tell sb. to ~ 叫某人立刻走开
⑥获得财产
II n. [动]生殖; [总称]幼兽;种
‖~ **about** ①(走动);旅行: He is *getting about* again. 他(病后)又开始走动了。②参加社会活动 ③(消息等)传开来: The news soon *got about*. 消息马上传了开来。/ ~ **above oneself** 变得自高自大 / ~ **abroad** (消息等)传开来 / ~ **across** ①(使)通过: ~ the children *across* the street 带孩子们过马路 ②[口](使)被理解,(把…)讲清楚: ~ one's idea *across* to sb. 使自己的想法被某人理解 / ~ **after** 训诫;攻击 / ~ **ahead** ①进步: ~ *ahead* with one's work 工作取得进展 / Get *ahead* and do it. [美]大胆干吧! ②胜过,超过(*of*) ③获得成功 / ~ **along** ①过活,生活: How are you *getting along* (or *on*)? 你近来过得好吗? ②相处融洽: They are *getting along* (or *on*) quite well. 他们相处得很好。③进展;老起来(指年纪): ~ *along* (or *on*) well *with* one's studies 学习上取得进步 ④[口]走开: Get *along* with you! 滚开! 去你的! 胡说! / ~ **around** [美] =~ round / ~ **at** ①到达;够着: I can't ~ at the tool on the shelf. 我够不着搁板上的工具。②了解,掌握;查明: ~ at the reason 了解原因 ③意指: What is he *getting at*? 他讲这话是啥意思? ④[俚]攻击,逗弄 ⑤[俚]贿赂,腐蚀 / ~ **away** ①逃脱;离开;出发: I'm too busy to ~ away. 我忙得脱不开身。/ Get *away* (with you)! [口]滚开! ②把…送走 / ~ **away with** 侥幸做成;侥幸取走: ~ *away* with it 做了坏事(或错事)而不被发觉(或处分) / ~ **back** ①回来 ②恢复;取回: ~ *back* one's wristwatch from the lost and found 从失物招领处找回手表 ③送回,带回 ④[俚]报复: ~ *back* one's own *on* sb. (或 ~ *back at* sb.) 对某人进行报复 / ~ **behind** ①

落后 ②识破 ③支持 / ~ **by** ①通过;走过: The parade has *got by*. 游行队伍走过去了。②勉强混过 / ~ **done with (sth.)** 结束掉(某事) / ~ **down** ①(从…)下来;下车 ②咽下,吞下: ~ the pill *down* 把药片吞下 ③写下: ~ a message *down* 把口信记下来 ④使沮丧;使抑郁 ⑤开始认真对待,开始认真考虑(*to*): ~ *down to* work 认真着手工作 / ~ **down on** 对…产生恶感,开始不喜欢… / ~ **going** 见 **going** / ~ **home** ①到家里;把…送到家里 ②(言语等)被充分理解;(言论等)中肯 / ~ **in** ①进入;抵达: The train *got in* on time. 火车准时到站。② 收获;收(税等): ~ *in* the crops (或 harvest) 把庄稼收进来 ③请…来(做): ~ *in* a mechanic to repair the tractor 请技工来修拖拉机 ④ 插(话);把…安排进日常工作 ⑤熟识起来(*with*); (使)卷入,(使)陷入 / ~ **into** ①进入: ~ *into* positions 【军】进入阵地 / The wine *got into* his head. 酒力发作了。② 陷入;染上(习惯): ~ *into* trouble 陷入麻烦 ③ 穿上(衣、鞋等) / ~ **it** [口] ①懂得 ②受到处分,挨骂 / ~ **nowhere** (使)无进展;(使)一事无成: It will ~ you *nowhere*. 这样是行不通的。/ ~ **off** ①(从…)下来,下车; 脱下(衣服等) ②(使)动身,(使)开始; (飞机)起飞;离开; 发出(电报等): ~ (sb.) *off* to sleep (使某人)入睡 ③(使)逃脱处分;被容忍 ④[口](和异性)结识(*with*) ⑤[口]说(笑话等) / ~ **on** ①过活,生活(=~ along) ② 相处融洽(=~ along) ③进展;老起来(指年纪)(=~ along) ④(使)上(车等);穿上;安上 接近(*for*): She is *getting on for* fifty. 她年近五十了。/ It's *getting on for* midnight. 快到半夜了。⑥使前进,使进步 ⑦[口]识破(*to*): ~ *on to* sb. (the trick) 识破某人(诡计) / ~ **out** ①(使)出去;离开: Get out! 滚出去! (或: 胡说!) / ~ *out of* bed 下床 ②逃脱;摆脱: ~ *out of* a bad habit 去掉坏习惯 ③(消息等)泄漏 ④发出(声音);说出;公布,出版 ⑤弄出;探听出: ~ a cork *out of* a bottle 从瓶内把塞子弄出来 / ~ sth. *out of* sb. 从某人那里弄到某物(或探听出某事) / ~ **outside of** [俚] [谑] 吃;喝: The snake *got outside of* a frog. 蛇吞吃蛙。/ ~ **over** ①爬过(墙等); 克服(困难、偏见等) ②熬过,做完(不愉快的事等); 走完(一段路程) ③从(病、损失等)中恢复过来;忘却 ④[俚]智胜(某人) ⑤ =~ across / ~ **round** ①规避(法律等) ②说服,争取(某人);智胜(某人) ③花时间和精力去做(*to*) ④ =~ about / ~ **somewhere** (使)有所进展;(使)有些成效(≠ ~ nowhere) / ~ **there** ①到达那里 ②[口]成功 / ~ **through** ①到达: The message *got through* (to us) at last. 这信息终于送到了(我们这儿)。②办完;花光(钱、时间等): ~ *through* (with) one's work 完成工作 ③(使)通过;捱过: ~ a bill *through* Congress 使议案在国会通过 / She *got through* (the examination). 她考试及格了。④ (打电话时)打通 /

~ to ①到达;接触到: ~ *to* the essence of things 触及事物的本质 ②开始: ~ *to* business (talking) 开始做事(谈起来) ③对…产生影响 / **~ together** ①聚集,相聚一处 ②收集,积累 ③[口]取得一致意见 (*n*) / **~ under** 控制,镇压: ~ the fire *under* 控制火势 / **~ up** ①(使)起床;(使)起立 ②爬上,登上;上马 ③(风浪等)猛烈起来 ④赶上: ~ *up to* the others 赶上其他人 ⑤达到;到达: We *got up to* page 12 last lesson. 上一课我们学到第十二页。⑥修整…的外表;打扮: have one's coat *got up* well 把上衣浆洗烫好 / The book is well *got up*. 这本书印刷、装订都很好。⑦安排;组织;筹备 ⑧钻研;致力于;温习 ⑨玩弄 ⑩产生(某种感情) ⑪(命令马)往前跑,快跑 / **~ up and** ~ / [口]离开 / **~ up early** 早起 / **~ with it** [美俚]赶上时髦,不落伍

‖**~-away** *n.* ①[口]逃走: make one's ~*away* 逃跑 ②起步: a car with a good ~*away* 一辆起动快的汽车 / '**~-off** *n.* (飞机的)起飞 / '**~-out** *n.* 脱身;脱逃: all ~*out* [美口]极顶,最大程度 / '**~-rich-'quick** *a.* 企图暴发致富的 / **~-together** ['getə,geðə] *n.* (非正式的)聚会;联欢会 / **~-'tough** *a.* 强硬的: a ~*tough* policy 强硬政策 / '**~up** *n.* ①式样;格式 ②装束,打扮 ③起床,起床时间 ④(书籍)装订式样,版式 ⑤[美]劲头;勇气 (= ~-up-and-go, ~-up-and-~)

getatable [get'ætəbl] *a.* 可到达的;可接近的;能懂的;能获得的

geyser *n.* ① ['gaizə] 间歇(喷)泉 ② ['gi:zə] [英]水的(蒸汽)加热器,(浴室等的)热水锅炉

ghastly ['gɑ:stli] I *a.* ①可怕的,恐怖的 ②死人般的;鬼一样的;苍白的 ③[口]极坏的,糟透的;令人不快的 ④极大的: a ~ mistake 极大的错误 ⑤(微笑等)勉强的 II *ad.* 可怕地;死人般地 ‖**ghastliness** *n.*

ghetto ['getou] I ([复] ghetto(e)s) *n.* [意] ①(城市中的)犹太人区 ②(城市中)少数民族的集中居住区: the Black ~s in Washington 华盛顿的黑人区 II *vt.* =ghettoize ‖**~logist** [ge'tɔlədʒist] *n.* 研究城市少数民族居住区情况的专家

ghost [goust] I *n.* ①鬼;幽灵 ②灵魂 ③幻影,阴影;微量,一点儿 ~ cell [动]血影细胞 / have not the ~ of a chance 毫无机会 ④(光学和电视上的)重象,散乱的光辉 ⑤[口]受雇代为作文(或作画)的人,捉刀人 II ❶ *vt.* ①象鬼似地出没于(某处),幽灵似地缠住(某人) ②受雇而代(某人)作文(或作画) ❷ *vi.* ①象鬼似地游荡 ②受雇而代为作文(或作画) (*for*) / **give up the** ~ 死,断气 / **lay a** ~ 使鬼魂消失,镇鬼 / **raise a** ~ 使鬼魂出现,召鬼 / **the Holy Ghost** 【宗】圣灵 / **when the** ~ **walks** [俚](剧院)发薪水的时候 ‖**~like** *a.* 象鬼样的 ‖**~ dance** [美](十九世纪)北美印第安人的鬼神舞 / **~ town** [美]被遗弃城市的遗迹 / **~ word** (因误读等而)造出来的词;别字

ghostly ['goustli] *a.* ①鬼的,幽灵的;鬼一样的 ②灵魂的,精神的;神灵的;宗教上的 ③受雇而代人作文(或作画)的 ‖ *a* ~ **father** (或 **adviser**, **director**) 听忏悔的神父 / **our** ~ **enemy** 恶魔 ‖**ghostliness** *n.*

giant ['dʒaiənt] I *n.* ①(童话中的)巨人(常喻指身材、能力、力量等特别大的人) ②巨物;巨大的动(或植)物 II *a.* ①巨大的: take ~ strides forward 用巨人般的步伐前进 / ~ star 【天】巨星 ②(动植物名前的)大…: a ~ kangaroo 大袋鼠 / a ~ panda 大熊猫 ‖**~ess** *n.* 女巨人 / **~like** *a.* 巨人般的 ‖**~ killer** 能打败强大对手者 / **~('s) stride** (公园里的)旋转秋千

gibber ['dʒibə] I *vi.* 急促而不清楚地说话;发无意义的声音 II *n.* =gibberish ‖**~ish** ['gibəriʃ] 急促而不清楚的话;莫名其妙的话;无意义的声音

gibbet ['dʒibit] I *n.* ①绞刑架;示众架 ②绞刑 ③(起重机的)臂 II *vt.* ①处…绞刑;把(某人)悬在示众架上 ②使当众出丑

gibe [dʒaib] *vt., vi. & n.* 嘲笑,嘲弄 ‖**~r** *n.* 嘲笑者,嘲弄者 / **gibingly** *ad.* 嘲弄地

giblet ['dʒiblit] *n.* [常用复](鸡、鸭等的)内脏杂件,四件

giddy ['gidi] I *a.* ①头晕的;眼花缭乱的 ②使人眩晕的;使人眼花缭乱的: a ~ height 令人眩晕的高度 ③轻率的;轻浮的,轻佻的 ④急速旋转的 II *vi. & vt.* (使)眩晕;(使)急速旋转 ‖**giddily** *ad.* / **giddiness** *n.* ‖'**~-brained** *a.* 轻率的;轻浮的 / '**~-go-round** *n.* [英]旋转木马

gift [gift] I *n.* ①赠品,礼物: birthday ~s 生日礼物 ②天赋,天资;才能: have a ~ for 对…有天赋 / a man of many ~s 多才多艺的人 ③赠予,授予;赠予权 II *vt.* ①[主英]赠送: ~ with sth. (或 ~ sth. to sb.) 赠送某物给某人 ②(宗教迷信用语)(天)以权力(或才能等)授予 ‖*a* **Greek** ~ 图谋害人的礼物 / **by free** ~ 作为免费赠品 / **have the** ~ **of (the) gab** 有流利的口才,能说会道 / **look a** ~ **horse in the mouth** 见 **horse** / **the** ~ **of tongues** 说外语的能力 ‖**~ed** *a.* 有天赋的;有才华的 ‖'**~book** *n.* 作为赠品的书 / ~ **coupon** (商品中所附的可换赠品的)赠券 / ~ **wrap** (为供顾客作礼物用)以缎带(或花纸等)包装(商品)

gig[1] [gig] I *n.* ①旋转物 ②轻便双轮马车 ③轻快艇;赛艇 ④[纺]刺果起绒机 (= ~ mill) ⑤怪人 II [主英] (gigged; gigging) *vt.* ①乘轻便双轮马车 ②乘轻便快艇 / ~ **lamps** [俚]眼镜 / ~ **mill** 【纺】刺果起绒机;起绒厂,拉毛厂

gig[2] [gig] I *n.* 鱼叉 II (gigged; gigging) ❶ *vt.* ①用鱼叉叉(鱼) ②[美]戳;刺激;激励 ❷ *vi.* 用鱼叉叉鱼

gig[3] [gig] [俚] I *n.* (军队、学校等的)记过 II (gigged; gigging) *vt.* 给(某人)记过;记过处分

gig[4] [gig] *n.* [美俚] ①爵士乐演奏会 ②演奏(或演唱)爵士乐的职业 ③活儿

gigantic [dʒai'gæntik] *a.* 巨人似的; 巨大的, 庞大的: a ~ leap 飞跃 / a ~ struggle 大搏斗 / a ~ net 天罗地网 ‖**~ally** *ad.*

giggle ['gigl] **I** ❶ *vi.* 咯咯地笑, 傻笑 ❷ *vt.* 咯咯地笑着说 **II** *n.* 咯咯笑, 傻笑: a fit of the ~s 一阵傻笑 ‖~ **water** [美俚]酒

gild[1] [gild] (gilded 或 gilt [gilt]) *vt.* ①把…镀金; 给…涂上金色: The morning sun ~s the sky. 朝阳把旭天空染成金色。②使有光彩 ③装饰; 虚饰 ④使有钱; 使阔气 ‖~ *the lily* 见 lily / ~ *the pill* 见pill[1] ‖**~er** *n.* 镀金工人

gild[2] [gild] *n.* =guild

gilding ['gildiŋ] *n.* ①镀金, 涂金 ②镀金材料 ③虚饰的外观, 假象

gill[1] [gil] **I** *n.* ①(鱼的)鳃; (水生动物的)呼吸器 ②(鸡等下颌的)垂肉 ③[常用复](人的)腮; [美俚]嘴巴 ④[植]层, 褶片; 菌褶 **II** ❶ *vt.* 用刺网捕鱼(鱼); 取除(鱼)的内脏 ❷ *vi.* (鱼)被刺网捕住 ‖*blue about the* ~s 垂头丧气; 脸色阴郁 / *rosy about the* ~s 气色好; (酒后)两腮红润 / *turn red in the* ~s 发怒 / *white about the* ~s (吓得或病得)脸色发白 ‖~ **net** 刺网

gill[2] [gil] *n.* 峡谷; 峡流

gill[3] [dʒil] *n.* 及耳(液量单位, =¼ pint)

gill[4] [dʒil] *n.* [常作 G-] 少女; 情人(指女子)

gilt[1] [gilt] **I** gild[1] 的过去式和过去分词 **II** *a.* 镀金的; 金色的 **III** *n.* ①镀金材料, 金色涂层 ②炫目的外表 ③[俚]金钱 ‖*take the* ~ *off gingerbread* 剥去诱人的外衣 / *The* ~ *is off.* 幻想破灭。‖**~-edged** *a.* ① (纸、书籍等)金边的: ~-*edged* shares 金边股票(尤指有政府担保的股票) ②上等的

gilt[2] [gilt] *n.* 小母猪

gimlet ['gimlit] **I** *n.* 手钻 **II** *a.* ① 有钻孔能力的; 锐利的 ② 有钻劲的 **III** *vt.* 用手钻钻; 穿透 ‖**~-eyed** *a.* 目光锐利的

gimmick ['gimik] **I** *n.* [俚] ①(赌博器具中的)暗机关 ②骗人的玩意儿; 别致的玩意儿 ③鬼把戏; 诀窍 **II** *vt.* [口]在…中使用暗机关; 加小发明于 ‖**~y** *a.*

gin[1] [dʒin] **I** *n.* ①(捕猎用的)陷阱; 网, 鱼网 ②三脚起重机, 起重装置 ③轧棉机, 轧花机 **II** (ginned; ginning) *vt.* ①轧(棉): *ginned* cotton 皮棉 / a cotton *ginning* factory 轧棉厂 ②用陷阱(或网)捕捉

gin[2] [dʒin] *n.* 杜松子酒; 荷兰酒 ‖~ *and it* 一种由杜松子酒和苦艾酒混合而成的饮料 ‖~ *mill* [美俚](廉价的)酒店间, 酒馆 / '~-,palace *n.* [英]豪华的酒店

ginger ['dʒindʒə] **I** *n.* ①生姜, 姜: ~ ale (beer) 姜汁酒(啤酒) ②[口]精神, 活力: full of ~ 充满活力 ③姜黄色 **II** *vt.* ①使有姜味 ②使有活力; 鼓舞 ‖a ~ *group* 见 group ‖'~**bread** *n.* ①姜饼 ②华而不实的东西, 俗丽的装饰 *a.* 俗丽的; 华而不实的 / ~ **nut** 姜汁饼干 / '~-**race**, '~**root** *n.* 姜根 / '~**snap** *n.* =~ nut

gingerly ['dʒindʒəli] *ad.* & *a.* 小心谨慎地(的), 战战兢兢地(的) ‖**gingerliness** *n.*

giraffe [dʒi'rɑ:f] ([复] giraffe(s)) *n.* ①长颈鹿 ②[G-][天]鹿豹座

gird[1] [gə:d] (girded 或 girt [gə:t]) ❶ *vt.* ①束, 缚; 束紧(衣服等), 缠上(绳子等): ~ sb. (或 sb.'s waist) with a sash 给某人束上腰带 ②佩带; 给…佩带; 赋予: ~ a sword on 佩上宝剑 / ~ sb. with . . . 给某人佩上…; 赋予某人… ③围绕; 包围: an island ~ed by the sea 四周环海的岛屿 ④(~ oneself) 准备 (for): ~ oneself for a new fight 准备新的战斗 ❷ *vi.* 准备

gird[2] [gə:d] *vi., vt. & n.* 嘲弄, 嘲笑

girder ['gə:də] *n.* [建](大)梁: ~ truss 梁构桁架

girdle[1] ['gə:dl] **I** *n.* ①带; 腰带 ②环形物, 围绕物 ③[美](女子的)紧身褡 ④(剥去一圈树皮而形成的)环形带; [植]成带现象 ⑤宝石与镶嵌底板接触处的边缘 ⑥[解](支持四肢的)带: pelvic ~ 骨盆带 / shoulder ~ 上肢带 ⑦[建](抱)柱带 **II** *vt.* ① 束, 缚, 绕 ② 围绕; 包围: a lake ~d with trees 树木围绕的湖泊 ③剥去(树木)的一圈皮 ‖**~r** *n.* ①做腰带的人 ②束(或缚、绕、围)的人(或物) ③把树咬成环structform的甲虫

girdle[2] ['gə:dl] *n.* [苏格兰](烘饼用的)圆形铁板

girl [gə:l] *n.* ①女孩子, 姑娘, 少女; 未婚女子 ②女儿: the ~s (一家中包括已婚和未婚的)女儿们 ③ 女仆; 保姆 ④ (商店等的)女工作人员: shop (office) ~s 青年女店(职)员 / factory ~s 青年女工 ⑤[用作定语]女…: a ~ guide (或[美] scout) 女童子军 / ~ friend 女朋友, 情人(常作 best ~) ‖*a slip of a* ~ 瘦长的姑娘 / *old* ~ 老太婆, 老伴儿(对女子、妻子等的爱称, 有时作蔑称, 不论年纪大小) ‖**~hood** *n.* ①少女时期 ②[总称]少女 ‖~ **Friday** [美俚]能干的女助手 / ~ **friend** ❶ 女性朋友; 女性伴侣 ❷ 情妇

girt [gə:t] **I** gird[1] 的过去式和过去分词 **II** *n.* =girth (*n.*) **III** ❶ *vt.* ①用带束(或缚) ②给…佩带; 赋予 ③围绕; 包围 ④ 量…的围长: ~ a tree 量树的围长 ❷ *vi.* 围长为

girth [gə:θ] **I** *n.* ①(马等的)肚带 ②(树干、圆筒、腰身等)围长; [船]船壳围长(由甲板一边绕船底至甲板另一边): a funnel 6 metres in ~ 周长六米的烟囱 ③大小; 尺寸 **II** ❶ *vt.* ①围绕; 包围 ②用肚带束(或缚); 给…缚上肚带 ③量…的围长 ❷ *vi.* 围长为

gist [dʒist] *n.* ①(诉讼的)依据 ②要旨: the ~ of a question 问题的要点

give [giv] **I** (gave [geiv], given ['givn]) ❶ *vt.* ①送给, 给: He *gave* me a medical handbook. (或 He *gave* a medical handbook to me.) 他送给我一本医药手册。/ A hoe was ~n (to) him. (或 He was ~n a hoe.) 给了他一把锄头。/ You'd better ~ yourself an hour to get there. 要到那里去的话, 你得准备路上花一个小时。/ *Give* our best regards to him. 代我们向他问好。

②授予; 赐予; 施舍; 捐赠: be ~n the title of 被授予…的称号
③供给; (给病人)服用(药物); 传给: This power station ~s light and power to the whole region. 这座发电站供给这整个地区照明和动力用电。/ ~ sb. one's cold 把感冒传染给某人
④付出; 出售: I would ~ anything to get it. (假如可能的话,)我怎么也要弄到它。
⑤献出; [~ oneself, 或用被动语态] 使沉湎于 (to)
⑥交给; 托付; 嫁出: Give me your bag. 把包让我来拿吧。
⑦产生; 引起: make saline land ~ rich crops 向盐碱地要高产 / Sorry to have ~n you trouble. 对不起,打扰了。/ 4 divided by 2 ~s 2. 二除四得二。
⑧[表示做一次动作]: ~ a shrug of the shoulders 耸一耸肩 / ~ sb. a kick (push) 踢(推)某人一下 / ~ a loud laugh 大笑一声
⑨作出; 举出; 表示出; 提出(建议等): ~ one's pledge 作出保证 / ~ orders 发出命令 / ~ examples 举例 / The thermometer ~s 20°C. 温度计上是摄氏二十度。
⑩举行(音乐会、宴会等); 演出
⑪让出: not ~ an inch 寸步不让
⑫对…施行(责罚等)
❷ vi. ①赠送; 捐助
②让步; 陷下; 塌下; 弯下, 支撑不住: prevent the foundations from giving 防止地基下陷
③(气候)转暖; (冰霜)融化
④(用му等)有弹性: This motorcycle saddle ~s comfortably. 这部摩托车的座垫弹性好,坐起来舒服。
❸ n. 弹性; 可让性; 可弯性: a springboard with a lot of ~ 弹性足的跳水板
‖~ and take 平等交换; 互让; 交换意见 / ~ as good as one gets 回敬,以牙还牙 / ~ away ①送я; 分发(奖品等) ②放弃(机会等) ③泄露 (秘密等); 出卖: His accent ~s him away as a southerner. 他的口音让人听出他是南方人。④ 在婚礼上把(新娘)交给新郎(一种西方习俗) ⑤[美]让步; 陷下, 塌下 / ~ back ①(归)还; 使(声音等)返回; 恢复 ②后退, 往后站 / ~ forth 发出(气味、声音等); 发表 / ~ in ①屈服, 让步 (to): He has ~n in to my views. 他已(放弃自己的主张)接受我的看法。② 交上(考卷等); 呈上(文件等) ③ 宣布: ~ in one's adherence to a principle 宣布坚守原则 / ~ into (过道等)通向 / ~ it sb. hot [口]痛打某人, 痛骂某人; 让某人尝尝厉害 / ~ off 发出(蒸气、光等) / ~ on (门、窗等)面着(街、园等) / ~ or take 增减…而无大变化; 允许有…的小误差 / ~ out ①分发; 发出(气味、热等): ~ out pamphlets 分发小册子 ②发表,公布: ~ out information 发布消息 / ~ oneself out to be a good swimmer 自称是一个游泳能手 ③用完, 耗尽; 精疲力竭:

The horse gave out. 马跑不动了。/ ~ over ①(使)停止; 放弃: Give over that shouting! 别再叫啦! / The rain gave over. 雨停了。②交,托 (to) / ~ oneself (或 be ~n) over 使沉湎于; 使纵情于 (to): ~ oneself (或 be ~n) over to drinking 纵酒 / ~ sb. to understand (或 know) that 使某人理解到…; 告知某人… / ~ sb. what for [口]责骂某人; 痛打某人 / ~ up ①让 (to): ~ up one's seat to an old man 把座位让给老人 ②放弃 ③停止; 抛弃: ~ up smoking 戒烟 ④把…送交; 使(自己)投案 ⑤宣告无法治好(病人); 表示…没有希望; 认输: Give him up! 投降吧! / It was so late that we had ~n him up. 已经很晚了,我们认为他不会来了。⑥ 泄露(秘密等) ⑦ [~ oneself up, 或用被动语态]使埋头于 (to) / ~ upon = ~ on
‖~r n. 给予者: an alms ~r 施舍者 / '~-and-'take n. & a. 平等交换 (的); 互让 (的); 交换意见 (的) / '~away n. ①[口](秘密等的)无意中泄漏(或暴露) ②(用来吸引顾客的)赠品; (电台中的)有奖问答节目

given ['givn] I give 的过去分词 II a. ①给予的; 赠送的 ②特定的; 一定的: in ~ conditions 在一定条件下 ③假设的; 【数】已知的: Given health, this can be done. 假使身体健康,这是能做得到的。④癖好的; 喜爱的; 习惯的: be not ~ to swaggering 不妄自尊大 ⑤(正式文书于某一日期)签订的: Given under my hand this 10th day of May, 1800. 亲笔签名订立于一八〇〇年五月十日。‖~ name [美] ① (不包括姓的)名字 ②教名,受洗礼时的名字

giving ['givin] n. 给予物; 礼物

gizzard ['gizəd] n. ①(鸟等的)砂囊, 胗 ②[口] [谑]胃 ③内脏 ‖fret one's ~ 忧虑 / stick in sb.'s ~ ① 难以被某人消化 ② 难以为某人接受

glacial ['gleisjəl] a. ① 冰的; 冰状(结晶)的: ~ acetic acid 冰醋酸 ② 冰河的; 冰河时期的: the ~ epoch (或 era, period) 冰河时期 ③冰冷的; 冷淡的 ④象冰河运动般缓缓的 ‖~ist n. 冰河学家; 冰河学者

glacier ['glæsjə] n. 冰河, 冰川: a ~ plain 冰川平原 / ~ avalanche 【地】冰崩 ‖~et [,glæsjə'ret] n. 小冰川

glad [glæd] (gladder, gladdest) a. ①[用作表语]高兴的, 乐意的: Glad (或 I am ~) to see you. 见到你很高兴。(常用于初次见面时) / We are ~ that you have succeeded. (或 We are ~ of your success.) 我们为你们的成功高兴。/ be ~ about the results 对结果满意 / I'm ~ of it. (我认为)那好极了。② 令人高兴的, 使人愉快的: a ~ event 大喜事 / ~ news 好消息 ③ 充满欢乐的, 兴高采烈的: ~ looks 喜气洋洋的神情 / ~ (自然景色等)明媚的 ‖~ly ad. / ~ness n. ‖~ eye [俚]挑逗的眼色; 欢乐的眼色 / ~ hand (带有某种动机的)热情欢迎 / '~-hand vt. & vi. 欢迎, 招呼 / '~-,hander n. 欢迎者,打招呼的人

glade [gleid] *n.* ①林间空地(或通道) ②沼泽地

gladiator ['glædieitə] *n.* ①(古罗马的)斗剑士,斗士 ②论争者,辩论家 ③格斗者(尤指职业拳击者) ‖~**ial** [,glædiə'tɔ:riəl] *a.* 斗剑的,格斗的; 论争的

glamo(u)r ['glæmə] I *n.* 魔力; 魅力 II *vt.* 迷惑,迷住 ‖*cast a ~ over sb.* 迷住某人 / ‖~**ize** ['glæməraiz] *vt.* ①使有迷惑力,使有魅力 ②美化 / ‖~**ous** ['glæmərəs] *a.* 富有迷惑力的,有魅力的 ‖~ **girl** [美俚]妖娆女子(尤指电影明星、歌星等)

glance¹ [glɑ:ns] I ❶ *vi.* ①(粗略地)看一下,一瞥; 扫视: ~ *at* one's watch 看一下表 / ~ *over* (或 *through*) a manuscript 把稿子粗看一遍 ②掠过 (*off, aside*) ③(简单或间接地)提到,影射 (*at*) 快而简略地谈: ~ *a* subject 快而简略地谈某个话题 / ~ *off* (或 *from*) sth. 快而简略地将某事一带而过 ④闪光,闪耀 ❷ *vt.* ①用(眼睛)扫视; 瞥见: ~ one's eyes *down* (或 *over*) the page 粗略地把眼睛扫过一页 ②使擦过表面; 使掠过 II *n.* ①一瞥; 眼光: at (the) first ~ 第一眼就… / exchange ~s 互相使眼色 / take (或 give) a ~ *at* 对…粗略看一下 ②闪光

glance² [glɑ:ns] *n.* 【矿】辉矿类: ~ copper 辉铜矿

gland¹ [glænd] *n.* 【解】腺: sweat ~s 汗腺 / thyroid ~ 甲状腺 / lacrimal ~s 泪腺 【植】(分泌蜜等的)腺

gland² [glænd] *n.* 【机】密封压盖; 填料盖; 密封套: packing ~ 压垫盖,填料盖

glandular ['glændjulə] *a.* ①腺的,含腺的; 有腺的特征(或功能)的: ~ cancer 【医】腺癌 ②天生的,固有的 ③肉体的

glare [glɛə] I ❶ *vi.* ①眩目地照射,闪耀; 炫耀 ②瞪眼; 怒目注视 (*at, on*) ❷ *vt.* 瞪着眼表示(敌意等) II *n.* ①眩目的光; 强烈的阳光: the ~ of the sun on the water 水面上耀眼的阳光 ②炫耀的陈设; 显眼: in the full ~ of publicity 在众目睽睽下 ③瞪眼; 愤怒的目光 ④(冰等)光滑明亮的表面

glaring ['glɛəriŋ] *a.* ①耀眼的,闪光的: a ~ white 耀眼的白色 ②瞪眼的,怒目而视的 ③炫耀的,显眼的; 突出的: ~ errors 大错 ④(色彩等)粗俗的,庸丽的,俗丽的 ‖~**ly** *ad.* / ~**ness** *n.*

glass [glɑ:s] I *n.* ①玻璃; 玻璃状物: a piece of ~ 一块玻璃 / blow ~ 吹玻璃 (以制成瓶子或仪器等) / be made of ~ 玻璃制的 ②[总称]玻璃制品,料器; 玻璃暖房 (=~houses); 窗玻璃: ~ and china 器皿和瓷器 / table (或 dinner) ~ 玻璃餐具 / under ~ 在暖房中 ③玻璃杯; 一杯(的容量); 酒: a ~ of water 一玻璃杯水 / be fond of one's (或 a) ~ 喜欢喝酒,爱杯中物 / have had a ~ too much 多喝了一些,喝醉了 ④镜子 (= looking ~): look in the ~ 照镜子 ⑤透镜; 望远镜; 显微镜; [复]眼镜; 双筒镜: The sailor looked through his ~. 水手用望远镜了望。/ wear ~es 戴眼镜 ⑥气压计,晴雨表; 沙漏: The ~ is rising (falling). 气压计的水银柱在上升(下降)。‖*crown* ~ 冕玻璃(硬性光学玻璃) / *cut* ~ 雕玻璃 / *flint* ~ 燧石玻璃(软性光学玻璃) / *frosted* ~ 磨沙玻璃,霜花玻璃 / *ground* ~ 毛玻璃,磨口玻璃 / *optical* ~ 光学玻璃 / *organic* ~ 有机玻璃 / *plate* ~ 板玻璃 / *pyrex* ~ 派热克斯玻璃(原商品名,一种耐热玻璃) / *spun* ~ 玻璃丝 / *stained* ~ 彩画玻璃 / *toughened* ~ 钢化玻璃,淬火玻璃 / *wire(d)* ~ 嵌丝玻璃 II ❶ *vt.* ①给…装上玻璃: a ~ed-in veranda 围着玻璃的游廊 ②把…装入玻璃器内 ③反映; [~ oneself] 映照: The trees are ~ed by the lake. 树木映在湖上。/ The trees ~ themselves in the lake. 树木(的倒影)映照在湖上。③(为寻找猎物等)用望远镜了望: ~ the country from a hill 从山上用望远镜了望乡野 ❷ *vi.* ①成玻璃状;(目光)变得无神迟钝 ②用望远镜了望(寻找)猎物 ‖*look through blue ~es* 悲观地看事物 / *look through green ~es* 妒忌 (或羡慕)地看事物 / *look through rose-colo(u)red ~es* 乐观地看事物 ‖~**less** *a.* 没有玻璃的,未装上玻璃的 ‖~ **arm** 容易发酸(或僵硬)的手臂 / '~,**blower** *n.* 吹玻璃工人 / ~ **case** 玻璃橱柜 / ~ **cloth** ①揩玻璃的布 ②玻璃纤维织物 ③涂玻璃粉织物(擦光用),玻璃沙布 / ~ **culture** 【植】暖房栽培 / ~ **cutter** 雕刻 (或割)玻璃工; 玻璃割刀 (或雕刀) / ~ **dust** 玻璃粉 / ~ **eye** ①玻璃制的假眼睛 ②马的一种盲症 / ~ **fibre** 玻璃纤维 / '~-**glazed** *a.* 浓釉的 / '~**house** *n.* ①玻璃房子,暖房; 装有玻璃天棚的摄影室: Those who live in ~houses should not throw stones. [谚]自己有短处,不要去揭别人的短处。②玻璃工场 ③[英俚]军事监狱 / ~ **jaw** [美俚]拳击选手的经不起打击的下颌 / '~,**making** *n.* 玻璃制造工艺 (或工业) / ~**man** ['glɑ:smən] *n.* ①卖玻璃制品的人 ②装玻璃的工人 ③玻璃制造者 / ~ **paper** 玻璃沙纸,(俗称沙皮) / ~ **snake** 产于美国南部的一种尾巴易断的蜥蜴 / ~ **ware** *n.* [总称]玻璃制品,料器 / ~ **wool** 玻璃棉,玻璃绒 / '~-**work** *n.* ① [~works] [用作单或复]玻璃厂 ②玻璃(制品)工艺(或装饰) ③ [总称]玻璃制品 / '~**wort** *n.* 【植】欧洲海蓬子; 钾猪毛菜

glassy ['glɑ:si] *a.* ①象玻璃的 ②(眼睛等)没有神采的,呆滞的 ③(水等)明净的,平静如镜的 ‖**glassily** *ad.* / **glassiness** *n.* ‖'~-'**eyed** *a.* 眼睛无神的,目光呆滞的

glaze [gleiz] I ❶ *vt.* ①配窗玻璃于; 装玻璃于: ~ a window 配窗玻璃 / ~ *in* a porch 用玻璃围成门廊 ②上釉于; 上光于: ~ pottery (porcelain) 给陶(瓷)器上釉 / ~*d* horse 亮马皮 / ~*d* printing paper 道林纸 / ~*d* tiles 琉璃瓦 ③打光; 擦亮 ④浇糖浆于(食物)的表面 ⑤使(眼睛)蒙上薄翳 ❷ *vi.* ①变成光滑; 变成明亮; 变成薄膜状 ②(眼)变呆滞; 变模糊 II *n.* ①釉料; 釉面 ②光滑面; 光滑层; 光滑的薄冰层 ③上釉; 打光,上光(如油漆、皮革制品等表面) ④(熟肉表面的)冻胶层 ⑤【气】雨凇 (=~d frost) ⑥薄膜(如眼

睛的翳子) ‖~r n. ①上釉工人；打光工人 ②轧
光机；上光机 ‖~ wheel 研磨轮

glazier ['gleizjə] n. 装玻璃工人；釉工：a ~'s
diamond 割玻璃用的金刚钻，玻璃刀 ‖ *Your
father was a bad ~.* (谑)你父亲是个糟糕的
玻璃装配工。(意即:你怎么挡住我的光线呢？)

glazing ['gleiziŋ] n. ①玻璃装配(业)；玻璃装配工
作 ②窗用玻璃；窗框玻璃窗 ③【总称】玻璃窗 ④上釉；上光，磨
光：~ calender【纺】轧光机，擦光机 ④釉料

gleam [gli:m] I n. ①微光，闪光：the first ~s of
day 曙光 ②[喻]短暂微弱的显现；微量：a ~ of
hope 一线希望 II ❶ vi. ①发微光；闪烁 ②短暂
微弱地显现；突然露出 ❷ vt. 使发微光，使闪
烁；显露出 ‖~y a. 发微光的；发闪光的

glean [gli:n] ❶ vt. ①拾(落穗)；拾取(田)里的落
穗：~ the grain that is left in the field 拾起掉
在田里的谷粒 ②搜集(新闻、资料等) ③发现，找
到；探明 ❷ vi. ①拾落穗 ②搜集新闻(或资料
等) ‖~er n. 拾落穗的人；搜集者

glee [gli:] n. ①高兴，快乐，欢欣：in high ~ 欢天
喜地 ②【音】无伴奏的三部以上的重唱曲(尤指男
声) ‖~ club 合唱队 / '~man n. 吟游诗人

gleeful ['gli:ful] a. 极高兴的，欢乐的；令人高兴
的：~ news 喜讯 / in ~ mood 高高兴兴 ‖~ly
ad.

glen [glen] n. 峡谷；幽谷

glib [glib] (glibber, glibbest) a. ①随便的；圆滑
的，油嘴滑舌的：~ excuses 圆滑的借口 ②流利
的，善辩的：a ~ tongue 三寸不烂之舌 ‖~ly
ad. / ~ness n.

glide [glaid] I ❶ vi. ①滑动，滑行：A boat ~d
past. 小船轻轻地驶过。②悄悄地走；(时间等)消
逝；(事情)渐变：Time ~s on. 时间悄悄过去。
③【空】滑翔，下滑 ④【语】(从一个音向另一个音)
滑变 ❷ vt. 使滑动，使滑行 II n. ①滑动，滑
行 ②【空】滑翔，下滑 ③【语】滑移；滑音 ④【音】
滑音，延音 ‖'~-bomb vt. & vi. 下滑轰炸 /
bomb 滑降式炸弹

glider ['glaidə] n. ①滑动者(或物)；滑行者(或物)
②滑翔机；滑翔者(或物)：a winged rocket-
assisted ~ 火箭加速的滑翔机 / a ~ bomb 滑翔
式炸弹 / ~ troops 滑翔部队 ③【宇】滑翔导弹；
可回收的卫星 ④摆动式沙发椅

glider

gliding ['glaidiŋ] a. 滑动的，滑行的；滑翔的：~
angle【空】下滑角 ‖~ly ad.

glimmer ['glimə] I n. ①微光；微弱的闪光 ②模
糊的感觉；少许，微量：a ~ of hope 一线希望
③【矿】云母 (=mica) ④一瞥，一看 ⑤【复】[俚]
眼睛 II vi. ①发出微光；发出闪烁的微光 ②隐
约出现

glimpse [glimps] I n. ①一瞥，一看：catch a ~ of
②隐约的闪现；微微的感觉 ③微光；闪光
II ❶ vt. 瞥见 ❷ vi. ①看一看，瞥见 (at) ②[诗]
隐约出现；露出曙光 ‖*the ~s of the moon* 夜
间世界；世事，俗事

glint [glint] I ❶ vi. ①发微光；闪烁；(光线)反射
②迅速移动，掠过 ③窥视 ④隐约地闪现 ❷ vt.
使发光；使反射 II n. ①闪光；微光
反光 ②隐约的闪现

glisten ['glisn] I vi. 闪耀；反光 II n. 光辉；闪
光；反光

glitter ['glitə] I vi. ①闪闪发光，闪烁 ②(服装)
华丽夺目；炫耀 II n. ①闪光；灿烂的光辉 ②[总
称](装饰用的)小发光物 ‖*All is not gold that
~s.* 见 all / '~ing ['glitəriŋ] a. ①闪闪发光的，
光辉灿烂的 ②华丽的；炫耀的

gloaming ['gloumiŋ] n. 黄昏；薄暮

gloat [glout] I vi. ①爱慕地凝视；贪婪地盯着
(*over, on, upon*) ②心满意足地注视(或沉思)
③幸灾乐祸地注视(或考虑) II n. ①爱慕的凝
视，贪婪的盯视 ②心满意足的注视(或沉思) ③
扬扬得意；幸灾乐祸 ‖~ingly ad.

global ['gloubəl] a. ①球形的，球面的 ②全球的，
世界的：a nonstop ~ flight 环绕地球的不着
陆飞行 ③总括的，综合的；完全的；普遍的：
the ~ sum 总计 (=total sum) ‖~ism n. [美]
(政策或观点等的)全球性 / ~ly ad.

globe [gloub] I n. ①球；球状物 ②[the ~]地
球，世界 ③天体；行星：太阳 ④地球仪
(=terrestrial ~)；天球仪 (=celestial ~) ⑤球
状玻璃器皿；球形金鱼缸；球形玻璃灯罩；
灯泡 ⑥【解】眼球 ⑦(标志君主权力的)小金球
II vi. & vt. (使)成球状 ‖~ amaranth【植】
千日红 / '~fish n.【动】河豚 / '~,flower n.
【植】金莲花 / ~ lightning【气】球状闪电 / '~-
,trotter n. 环球游览者 / '~-,trotting n. 环
球游览 / ~ valve【机】球(形)阀

globular ['glɔbjulə] a. ①球状的；地球状的 ②世
界范围的 ③有小球的 ‖~ity [,glɔbju'læriti] n.
球状，球形 / ~ly ad. / ~ projection 球状投
影(常用于绘制地图) / ~ sailing【海】球面航行
(计算时考虑到地球的球面形状的航海法)

globule ['glɔbju:l] n. ①小球 ②液滴；药丸；血球

gloom [glu:m] I n. ①黑暗；阴暗；朦胧 ②黑暗
处；阴暗处 ③阴郁；忧愁；情绪低落：chase one's
~ away 解闷，消愁 II ❶ vi. ①(天色等)变阴
暗，变阴暗，变朦胧 ②变郁闷，变忧伤，现愁容
❷ vt. ①使黑暗；使朦胧 ②使忧郁，使郁闷 ③
忧伤地说

gloomy ['glu:mi] *a.* ①黑暗的; 阴暗的; 朦胧的 ②令人沮丧的 ③阴郁的, 忧闷的; 悲观的, 无望的: feel ~ 感到忧闷 ‖**gloomily** *ad.* / **gloominess** *n.*

glorify ['glɔ:rifai] *vt.* ①颂扬, 夸赞; 给···以荣耀: ~ labour 歌颂劳动 / ~ oneself 自夸 ②赞美 (上帝), 崇拜 ③使增光; 美化 ④使辉煌, 使光采夺目 ‖**glorification** [,glɔ:rifi'keiʃən] *n.* ①颂扬; 赞美 ②[口]庆祝; 欢庆的事 ③美化

glorious ['glɔ:riəs] *a.* ①光荣的: ~ traditions 光荣传统 ②辉煌的, 灿烂的; 壮丽的: a ~ view 壮观 ③[口]令人愉快的, 非常高兴的: What ~ weather! 多么好的天气! / ~ fun 非常有趣 ④[讽]可怕的: a ~ muddle (或 mess) 一团糟 ⑤[口]酒后狂乐的 ‖**~ly** *ad.*

glory ['glɔ:ri] I *n.* ①光荣, 荣誉 ②荣耀的事, 可赞颂的事物; 可夸耀的事 ③壮观; 壮观; 天上的光辉; 灿烂 ④繁荣; 昌盛; 全盛: be in one's ~ 得意之极; 处于全盛时期 ⑤[宗](对上帝的)赞美, 赞颂, 崇拜 ⑥[宗]天国的荣誉, 天福 ⑦(神像后的)光轮 II *vi.* 自豪, 得意 (in): ~ in one's victory 因胜利而得意扬扬 / ~ in doing sth. (或 to do sth.) 为做某事而自豪 ‖*Glory (be)!* [口]多奇妙啊! 多美啊! / go to ~ 死 / send sb. to ~ [谑]送某人上西天, 杀死某人 / the Old Glory [美]美国国旗的别称 ‖~ hole 火焰窥孔; 乱堆杂物的橱 (或抽屉、房间)

gloss¹ [glɔs] I *n.* ①光泽, 光彩: the ~ of metal 金属的光泽 / put (或 set) a ~ on 使···具有光泽, 润饰··· ②虚饰, 假象 II ❶ *vt.* ①使具有光泽; 上光于 ②掩盖, 掩饰 (over): ~ over one's mistakes 掩盖错误 / ~ things over 含糊敷衍 ❷ *vi.* 发光

gloss² [glɔs] I *n.* ①(书中行间和书边的)注解, 注释; 评注 ②词汇表; 集注; 行间的意译 ③曲解 II ❶ *vt.* ①注解, 注释; 评注 ②曲解; 把···搪塞过去 ❷ *vi.* 作注解(或注释), 写评注; 写不利于原著的评语

glossary ['glɔsəri] *n.* 词汇表; 术语(或特殊用语)汇编

glossy ['glɔsi] *a.* ①有光泽的; 光滑的: a ~ surface 光滑的表面 ②虚饰的; 貌似有理的, 似是而非的: ~ deceit 圆滑的欺骗 ‖**glossily** *ad.* / **glossiness** *n.*

glove [glʌv] I *n.* ①手套(一般指五指分开的; 不分五指的称 mitten): a pair of ~s 一副手套 / with ~s on 戴着手套 / Excuse my ~s. 对不起没脱手套。(握手时未脱手套的客套话) ②拳击手套 (=boxing ~); 棒球手套 II *vt.* ①供给(某人)手套 ②给(手)戴上手套 ‖a (或 the) velvet ~ 内里强硬表面温和的东西, 表面的温和: an iron hand in the velvet ~ 内硬外软 / fit like a ~ 完全相合, 恰恰正好 / go for the ~s 冒险赌博(输了拿不出钱) / hand in (或 and) ~ 见 hand / handle (或 treat) with (kid) ~s 温和灵巧地对待(或处理) / handle

without ~s 严厉对待; 大刀阔斧地处理 / put on the ~s [口]拳击 / take off the ~s (to sb.) (争论中)不饶(某人) / take up the ~ 应战 / throw down the ~ 挑战 ‖~less *a.* 不戴手套的 / ~r *n.* 做(或卖)手套的人 ‖~ compartment 汽车仪表板上的小贮藏柜 (戴着手套进行的)拳击 / ~ money 贿赂 / ~ sponge 一种形似手套的劣质海绵

glow [glou] I *vi.* ①发白热光, 灼热; 发光, 发热: The metal ~ed in the furnace. 金属在熔炉里发出灼热白光。/ Coloured lights ~ed on the festival night. 节日之夜灯火辉煌。②(因运动或激动等而)发热, 发红, 发光; 容光焕发: His face ~ed with delight. 他高兴得满面通红。/ The children's eyes ~ with happiness. 孩子们眼睛里闪耀着幸福的光芒。/ ~ with health 容光焕发 ③洋溢(指感情); 燃烧(指怒火等) ④鲜艳夺目; 呈现红、橙、黄一类色彩: Maple leaves ~ed red in the sunlight. 枫叶在阳光里闪耀着红光。II *n.* ①白热光; 光辉 ②激情; 热烈; 兴高采烈: feel the ~ of happiness 感到幸福的喜悦 ③色彩鲜艳; 红光: the evening ~ 晚霞 / the ~ of health in the cheeks 面颊的红润 ‖all of a ~ (或 in a ~) 红通通; 热烘烘 ‖~ lamp 【电】辉光灯; 辉光放电管 / '~worm *n.* 萤火虫

glower¹ ['glouə] *n.* 【电】炽热体; 灯丝

glower² ['glauə] I *vi.* 怒视; 凝视 (at) II *n.* 怒视; 凝视 ‖~ingly ['glauərinli] *ad.*

glowing ['glouiŋ] *a.* ①发白热光的; 灼热的 ②热情的, 热烈的: ~ praise 热烈的赞扬 ③(色彩)鲜明的, 光辉的; 容光焕发的 ‖~ly *ad.*

glucose ['glu:kous] *n.* 【化】葡萄糖, 右旋糖

glue [glu:] I *n.* ①胶; 胶水(由动物的皮、蹄、骨等熬制而成): stick like ~ to sb. 同某人形影不离 ②各种胶粘物 II *vt.* 胶合, 粘贴; 粘牢; 使如胶似漆地紧附: remain ~d to sb. 老是缠在某人身边 / with one's eyes ~d to sth. 盯着某物 ‖~y *a.* 胶的; 胶质的; 粘着的 ‖~ pot 胶锅 / '~water *n.* 胶水

glum [glʌm] *a.* 闷闷不乐的; 阴郁的, 愁闷的 ‖~ly *ad.* / ~ness *n.*

glut [glʌt] I (glutted; glutting) ❶ *vt.* ①使吃得过饱; 使满足; 使厌腻: ~ oneself with food 食物吃得过饱 / ~ one's eyes 看够 / be glutted with pleasure 享乐过分 ②使(市场)充斥: ~ the market with fruit 使市场上充斥水果 ❷ *vi.* 狼吞虎咽, 暴食 II *n.* ①吃饱, 食厌 ②充斥; 供过于求: a ~ of cotton goods 棉织品的供应过剩

glutinous ['glu:tinəs] *a.* 粘的, 粘质的; 【植】有粘液的: ~ rice 糯米

glutton ['glʌtn] *n.* ①贪食者, 好食者, 饕餮 ②酷爱···的人, 对···入迷的人: a ~ of books 手不释卷的人 / a ~ for work 酷爱工作的人 ③【动】狼獾 ‖~ize ['glʌtənaiz] *vt.* 大吃 *vi.* 吃得过度 / ~y *n.* 暴食, 暴饮

glycerin ['glisərin], **glycerine** [,glisə'ri:n], 'glisərin], **glycerol** ['glisərɔl] *n.* 【化】甘油; 丙三醇

gnarl[1] [nɑ:l] *vi.* (狗等)猖,吼,咆哮

gnarl[2] [nɑ:l] **I** *n.* 木节, 木瘤 **II** ❶ *vt.* ①扭, 拗 ②使有节 ❷ *vi.* 生节 ‖~ed, ~y *a.* ①多节的, 多瘤的; 扭曲的 ②(性情)乖僻的, 乖戾的

gnash [næʃ] **I** ❶ *vt.* 咬(牙); ~ one's teeth 咬牙(切齿) ❷ *vi.* (由于愤怒或痛苦时)咬牙; (牙)喈咬 **II** *n.* 咬

gnat [næt] *n.* ①(咬或叮人的)小昆虫; [英]蚊子 ②小烦扰; 琐碎事情 ‖*strain at a ~ and swallow a camel* 小事拘谨大事糊涂; 见小不见大

gnaw [nɔ:] (过去式 gnawed, 过去分词 gnawed 或 gnawn [nɔ:n]) ❶ *vt.* ①咬, 啮, 啃; 咬断; 咬成: ~ sth. *off* (或 *away*) 咬去某物 / Rats have ~ed a hole. 老鼠咬了个洞。 ②消耗; 腐蚀; 侵蚀: Rust ~s *away* steel. 铁锈腐蚀钢材。 ③折磨 使烦恼 ❷ *vi.* ①啮, 啃 (*at, into*): The dog ~ed at a bone. 狗啃骨头。 ②消耗, 侵蚀 (*at, into*) ③折磨; 烦恼: Anxiety ~ed at his heart. 他忧心如焚。 ‖~er *n.* 咬者; 腐蚀者; 啃齿类动物

gnawing ['nɔ:iŋ] **I** *n.* ①咬; 持续的剧痛 ②[复] (因饥饿等引起的)痛苦 **II** *a.* ①咬的: a ~ animal 啮齿动物 ②令人痛苦的: the ~ pains of hunger 饥肠绞痛 ‖~ly *ad.*

gnome[1] ['noumi] *n.* 格言, 箴言, 警句

gnome[2] [noum] *n.* ①(民间传说中地下矿藏和财宝的)守护神, 土地神; 妖魔 ②矮子, 侏儒

gnu [nu:, nju:] ([复] gnu⒮) *n.* 【动】牛羚(俗名角马)(非洲产)

go [gou] **I** (went [went], gone [gɔn]) ❶ *vi.* ①去; 离去: ~ swimming (camping) 游泳(野营)去 / ~ (on) a journey 去旅行 / Go get a doctor. 去叫医生来! / ~ to school (work) 上学(班) / I must be ~ing now. 我得走了。 / Go! (赛跑口令) 跑! / Can it ~ as printed matter? 这可以作为印刷品寄吗? ②走; 驶: ~ one's own way in developing science and technology 在发展科学技术方面走自己的路 / Who ~es there? (哨兵喝问用语)谁? / The truck can ~ 80 km. an hour. 这卡车每小时能行驶八十公里。 ③通到, 达到: We ~ thus far today. 今天我们就讲(或 做)到这里。 / The child is ~ing three. 这孩子快满三足岁了。 ④归, 属: The women's team championship *went* to the Japanese players. 日本选手获得女子团体冠军。 ⑤诉诸, 求助(于); 查阅 (*to*): ~ to law 诉诸法律 / ~ to a dictionary for a word 到词典中去查一个词 ⑥(机器等)运转; 行动, 进行; 起作用; 行得通: get the motor to ~ 把马达发动起来 / a clock that ~es a month without winding 可连续走一个月

的钟 / Don't ~ to any trouble for me. 别为我麻烦啦! / Go like this with your right hand. 你的右手应这样动作。 / Our conference has *gone* very well. 我们的会议开得很好。 / How ~es it with you? 你近来情况如何? / Never allow such tendencies ~ unchecked. 决不让这些倾向自由发展下去。 / This truth ~es everywhere. 这个真理是到处适用的。 / Whatever he says ~es. 他说到做到。 (或: 他说的都行得通。) / Any other night ~es, but not this night. 其它晚上都可以, 今晚却不行。 ⑦消失; 衰退; (时间)过去: The pain has *gone*. 疼痛消失了。 / His hearing is ~ing. 他的听觉在衰退。 ⑧完结, 垮; 断开; 死: This trust may ~ any day. 这家托拉斯随时都可能垮台。 / The mast *went* in the storm. 风暴中桅杆折断了。 ⑨废弃; 放弃 ⑩花费; 售出: Only five percent of my wages ~es in rent. 房租仅花去我工资的百分之五。 / That used bicycle *went* cheap. 那辆旧自行车廉价卖掉了。 ⑪变为, 成为: ~ mad 发狂 ⑫处于…的状态; 处于一般的状况: often ~ hungry 经常挨饿 / as things ~ 从一般情况来看 ⑬流传; 表达; (货币等)流通: as the saying ~es 俗话说 / He ~es by the name of Little Black Horse. 大家叫他"小黑马"。 ⑭相配; (诗、歌词)有节奏; (与曲调)相配 (*to*) ⑮发出声音; (钟)报时: The bell *went* "dingdong". 钟声"丁当"响。 / The clock *went* nine. 钟敲九点。 ⑯合起来构成; 有助(于); 趋向(于): 1,000 metres ~ *to* the kilometre. 一千米构成一公里。 / Our investigations ~ to prove that.... 我们调查的结果证明… ⑰放置; 被容得下: These tools ~ on the bottom shelf. 这些工具放在架子的底层。 / Will my sweater ~ in your knapsack? 你的背包里还装得下我的球衣吗? ⑱【数】(除)得整数商: Five into sixty ~es twelve times. (或 Five ~es into sixty twelve times.) 五除六十得十二。 ⑲[用进行时态, 后接不定式]将要; 打算: It's ~ing to rain. 快要下雨了。 / We're ~ing to call a meeting to discuss it. 我们打算开个会来讨论一下。 ⑳[用不定式,作定语]剩下: There are six minutes to ~. 还有六分钟。 ㉑[美方]想: I didn't ~ to do it. 我没有想去做这事。 ❷ *vt.* ①以…打赌; (桥牌中)叫(牌); 出(价): ~ 5 dollars on sth. 对某事打赌五元 / ~ 7 dollars for sth. 对某物出价七元 ②承担…的责任 ③忍受; 买得起[常用于否定句]; 享受: I simply

can't ~ such behaviour. 对这种行为我实在忍
受不了。/ I can't ~ the price. 我出不起这
价钱。

④生产,产: ~ 15 bushels to the acre 每英亩(作
物)产十五蒲式耳

II *n.* ①去; 进行: the busy come and ~ of
handcarts 手推车的来回奔忙

②[口]劲道, 精力: full of ~ 劲道十足

③[口]事情(尤指棘手的事): Here is a pretty
~! (或 What a ~!) 这事真难办! (或:这事真
糟。)/ a rum ~ 一个难题

④[the ~][口]时髦

⑤[口]试一下, 干一下: Don't try to solve all
these problems *in* (或 *at*) one ~. 别想一下子
解决所有这些问题。/ itch to have a ~ at it 跃
跃欲试

⑥[口]成功: *Make a ~ of it!* 干得出色些!

⑦[口]机会: give . . . *an open* ~ 给…以顺利进
行的机会

⑧[美口]约定: It's a ~. 就这样约定了。

⑨[英口]一杯(酒); 一份(食物)

⑩拳击比赛; 比赛

III *a.* [美俚] ①一切正常的, 可以开始的
②好的, 行的

‖*a near* ~ 极侥幸的逃脱 / *as* (或 *so*) *far as
it* ~*es* 就现状来说, 就其本身而言: What he
says is true *as far as it* ~*es.* 他的话就其本身而
言是对的(但不能推而广之)。/ *from the word*
~ 从一开始 / ~ *about* ①从事, 干: How shall
we ~ *about* the job? 我们该怎样着手干这件工
作? / ~ *about* to do sth. 设法做某事 ②走动;(消
息等)流传 ③【海】(船)逆风换抢 / ~ *after* 追
逐; 追求 / ~ *against* ①违反; 反对 ②不利于:
The contest is ~*ing against* the blue team. 比
赛中蓝队越来越不利了。/ ~ *ahead* 前进: Go
ahead! 干吧!(或:说吧!) / ~ *full steam ahead*
with technical innovation 大搞技术革新 / ~
all out 全力以赴; 鼓足干劲: ~ *all out* to fulfil
the task 全力以赴地去完成任务 / ~ *aloft* 去
世 / ~ *along* ①前进; 进行 ②(陪…)一起去
(*with*) ③赞同; 附和 (*with*) / ~ *a long way*
with ④(陪…)一起去见
way「Go along *with* you! [口]去你的! /
~ *around* [美] =~ *round* / ~ *at* 扑向;
进攻: They *went at* each other furiously. 他们
两人拚命斯打。②着手干: ~ *at* it hammer and
tongs 大干特干 / ~ *back* ①回去 (*to*) ②追溯
(*to*): The friendly contacts between our two
peoples ~ *back* to the 2nd century. 我们两国人
民之间的友好往来一直可以追溯到公元二世纪。/
~ *back of* [美口] =~ behind / ~ *back on*
(或 *upon, from*) ①违背, 毁(约): Don't ~
back on your word. 可别说了不算数啊! ②背
叛 / ~ *behind* ①寻究: ~ *behind* sb.'s words
推敲某人话中的含义 ②进一步斟酌: ~ *behind*
a decision 对决定再斟酌一下 / ~ *below* 见
below / ~ *beyond* 超出, 越出 / ~ *by* ①走过;
过去 ②依据;按照…判断 ③顺便走访: He was

in when I *went by* yesterday. 我昨天顺便去看
他时他在家。/ ~ *down* ①下去: ~ *down* in
turn to do manual labour 轮流下去参加体力劳
动 ②(船等)下沉;(飞机等)坠落;(日、月等)落下
③(食物等)被咽下; 被接受; 受欢迎 (*well*): His
explanation won't ~ *down with* me. 他的解释
我接受不了。④(风、海面等)平静下来;(价格、数
量等)下降, 减低 ⑤[英]离开大学 ⑥倒下; 垮台;
病倒: ~ *down* on one's knees 跪下 / ~ *down* in
defeat 以失败告终 ⑦延续(至) (*to*): This *World
History* ~*es down* to 1945. 这部《世界史》记述
到一九四五年为止。⑧被载入; 传下去: Their
heroic exploits will ~ *down* in history. 他们的
英雄业绩将被载入史册。/ ~ *downhill* (*uphill*)
走下(上)坡路 / ~ *easy* 轻松一点干;不过分紧
张; 慢慢来 / ~ *far* ①(人)大有前途 ②成功 /
~ *far toward*(s) 大有助于 / ~ *flat out* 全力
out / ~ *for* ①去;去请,去找; 努力获取:
~ *for* a walk 去散步 / ~ *for* a doctor 去请医生
②[口]袭击; 抨击: The presidential candidates
went for each other in the papers. 总统候选
人在报上相互攻讦。③被认为: ~ *for* nothing
(little) 被认为没有(不大有)用处 ④对…适用:
What he said about you ~*es for* me too. 他关
于你的一席话对我也适用。⑤主张; 拥护; 欢喜 /
~ *forth* ①向前去 ②被发表;(命令等)被发布:
The order *went forth* that . . . . 命令宣布说
… / ~ *forward* ①前进: The work is ~*ing*
forward well. 工作进展顺利。②发生: What's
~*ing forward* over there? 那边发生了什么? / ~
fut (或 *phut*) [俚](车胎等)破裂, 泄气;[喻]成
泡影, 告吹 / ~ *glimmering* [口]逐渐消灭, 化
为乌有 / ~ *hang* 不再被关心, 被忘却 / ~ *hard*
with sb. 使某人为难(或痛苦) / ~ *home* ①回
家 ②击中: a criticism that ~*es home* 击中要害
的批评 / ~ *ill* (事态)恶化 / ~ *ill with* 对…
不利 / ~ *in* ①进去; 放进去: This screw's too
big; it won't ~ *in.* 这颗螺丝钉太大, 放不进
去。②放得进…去: This screw's too big; it
won't ~ *in* the hole. 这颗螺丝钉太大,放不进
这个洞。③(钱)用于 ④参加;参加比赛;(纸牌赌
博中)开价 ⑤(天体)被云掩盖 / ~ *in at* [口]痛
打; 猛烈攻击 / ~ *in for* ①从事于 ②酷爱;
追求: ~ *in for* swimming 热爱游泳 ③参加:
~ *in for* an examination 参加考试 ④主张; 赞
成 / *Going! Going! Gone!* (拍卖用语)要卖了!
要卖了! 卖掉了! / ~ *into* ①进入;(门等)
通向: ~ deep *into* sb.'s heart 深入某人之心 ②
加入; 投入: ~ *into* the army 参军 / ~ *into*
production 投入生产 / ~ *into* action 行动起来
③探究: ~ *into* the whys of everything 对每件
事情问个为什么 / ~ *into* details 深入细节 ④进
入…状态: ~ *into* a rage 大发雷霆 / ~ *into*
mourning 戴孝 / ~ [俚](命令)干; 莽撞 /
~ *it* blind 盲目地干 ②放荡; 挥霍 / ~ *it alone*
单干 / ~ *it strong on* sth. 热烈赞许某事物 /
~ *near to* (do sth.) 几乎(做某事) / ~ *off* ①

离去;走掉;(剧本用语)(角色)下 ②去世;消失 ③爆炸;(枪、炮)被发射;响起: The signal pistol *went off* with a bang. 信号枪砰的一声响了。④ 爆发出;开始: ~ *off into* a fit of laughter 爆发出一阵大笑 / ~ *off into* wild flights of fancy 开始胡思乱想起来 ⑤(食物等)变坏: Her voice is ~*ing off*. 她的嗓子坏了。⑥进行: The performance *went off* splendidly. 演出非常成功。⑦ 昏去;睡去: ~ *off into* a faint 昏过去 ⑧(商品)卖掉 / ~ *off with* 拿去;抢走;拐走 / ~ *on* ① 继续下去;继续某种行为: Let's ~ *on*! 让我们继续做(或走、读等)下去! / ~ *on* with one's work 继续自己的工作 / ~ *on* advancing 不停地前进 / Then he *went on* to say that .... 接着他又继续说道… / *Go on*! 说(或做)下去! (也作反义: 看你再胡说!) / If you ~ *on*. like this, you'll make big mistakes some day. 如果你继续这样下去, 势必会有一天要犯大错误。②(时间等)过去 ③发生,进行: What's ~*ing on* here? 这儿发生什么事啦? ④[常用进行时态]接近: It's ~*ing on* for lunchtime. 快吃中饭了。⑤(剧本用语)(角色)上;(运动员)上场 ⑥责骂 (*at*) ⑦依靠(救济等)过活 ⑧依据: What data have you to ~ *on* 或 *upon*)? 你有什么材料作依据? / ~ *out* ①出去;出国去 ②(常指妇女)离家外出工作 ③(灯火等)熄灭 (衣着式样等)过时;(年、月等)过完 ③(某一届政府)辞职,下台;[美]倒塌,垮下 ④罢工 ⑤参加社交活动;[美]参加选拔 ⑥(心)向往;(对…)充满同情(*to*)/ ~ *over* ①走到另一边去;改变立场,转变;(车)翻倒 / ~ *over from* the defensive to the offensive 由防御转为进攻 ②仔细检查;润色(文稿);从头至尾温习;再读一遍: ~ *over* an important article 把重要文章仔细地再读一遍 ③[美口]受欢迎;成功: ~ *over* big 大获成功 ④(提案等)延期讨论 / ~ *round* ①四处走动;绕道走 ②顺便去,非正式去: I *went round* to see him yesterday. 昨天我顺便去看了他。③(消息等)流传 ④(带子)长得足够绕一圈;足够分配: There aren't enough tools to ~ *round*. 工具不够用。/ ~ (*sb.*) *one better* 见 better¹ / ~ *shares* 见 share¹ / ~ *sick* 见 sick¹ / ~ *slow* ①慢慢走 ②怠工 / *so far as* (to do) 竟然到(做…)的地步 / ~ *some* [美口]做(或得)了不少 / ~ *steady* 见 steady / ~ *through* ①经历;经受;通过(考试等) ②仔细检查;全面考虑(或研究);搜查: ~ *through* the items one by one 逐条研究 ③参加;做完(工作等);履行 ④(提案等)被通过;(生意)成交 ⑤用光(钱等) ⑥(书)发行(第几版) / ~ *through with* 做完,完成 / *Go to*! [古] 去你的! / ~ *together* ①相配 ②[口]恋爱 / ~ *too far* 走得太远;做(或说)得过火 / ~ *under* ①沉没;死 ②失败;屈服;破产 / ~ *up* ①上升;攀登;增长: Production keeps ~*ing up*. 生产正在不断上升。/ ~ *up* a hill 上山 / ②被建造起来: New factories are ~*ing up* everywhere. 到处盖起新工厂。③ 被烧毁,被炸毁;[美]破产 ④进大学,上(城市)去(*to*) / ~ *west* 上西天,死 / ~ *with*

①陪…一起去,伴随 ②与…持同一看法 ③与…相配: I want a pair of tights to ~ *with* this sweater. 我要一条与这件运动衫相配的运动裤。④跟…谈恋爱 / ~ *without* 在缺少…的情况下勉强对付过去;没有也行: No ready technical data were available, but we managed to ~ *without*. 我们没有现成的技术资料,但也设法这样干下去了。/ ~ *wrong* ①走错路;行为变坏,走入歧途 ②不对头,出毛病;失败: Something has *gone wrong with* the radio. 收音机出毛病了。/ *Here* ~*es*! (招呼别人注意时用)瞧, 开始了! / *leave* (或 *let* ~ *of*) 松手放开 / *on the* ~ [口]①忙个不停;活跃: He is *on the* ~ all day long. 他整天忙个不停。②衰败 / *the great* ~ [英俚]剑桥大学文学士学位考试 / *There you* ~ *again*. 你这一套又来了。/ *What* ~*es*? [美俚]发生了什么事? / *You may* ~ *farther and fare worse*. [谚]走得更远可能情形更坏。(劝人安于现状) ∥'~-ahead *a.* ①前进着的 ②[口]有进取心的 *n.* ①进取心 ②许可;放行信号: give ... a ~-ahead for (或 to do) sth. 准许…进行某事 / '~-around *n.* 回合;激烈争论 / '~-as-you-'please *a.* 不受拘束的;随意的 / '~-be.tween *n.* 中间人;掮客;媒人 / '~-by *n.* 不理睬;忽视: give ... the ~-by 对…冷淡 / '~-cart *n.* ①(小孩的)学步车;小人车 ②手推车 ③轻便马车 / ~ condition【字】待飞;待发 / '~-.devil *n.* ①拖木橇;运石车 ②刮管器;冲模 ③油井爆破器;坠撞器 / '~-.getter *n.* 聪明而有进取心的人 ②火箭自动制导的控制装置 / '~-'~ *a.* ①摇摆的;跳摇摆舞的小舞场的 ②最时髦的 ③活跃的;乱窜的;无节制的 / '~-kart *n.* 微型竞赛汽车 / '~-off *n.* ①开始,着手;出发: at the first ~-off 一开始 / at one ~-off 一举,一下子 ②爆炸 / ~ side 【机】通(过)端 / '~-'slow *n. & a.* 怠工的 / '~-to-'meeting *a.* 节日穿的;(举止等)最恰当不过的,最好的

goad [goud] **I** *n.* ①(赶家畜用的)刺棒 ②刺痛物,刺激物 **II** *vt.* ①用刺棒驱赶(家畜) ②刺激,驱使,扇动,唆使: ~ sb. *to do* (或 *into* doing) sth. 唆使某人做某事 / ~ sb. *to* (或 *into*) fury 使某人发怒

goal [goul] **I** *n.* ①(赛跑等的)终点,(旅行的)目的地 ②目的,目标: fight for one common ~ 为一个共同目标而奋斗 ③(球戏等的)得分,赢分: get (或 make, score) a ~ 得一分 ④(足球等运动的)球门;守门员 **II** *vi.* 得分 ∥'~-di'rected *a.* 有目的的,有意的 / ~-.keeper *n.* (足球等运动的)守门员 / ~ line (足球等运动的)门线 / '~-post *n.* (足球等运动的)门柱 / '~-post mast [船]龙门架桅

goat [gout] *n.* ①山羊 ②色鬼 ③[俚]替罪羊,牺牲品 ④[the G-]【天】摩羯宫 ‖*act* (或 *play*) *the giddy* ~ 胡闹 / *get sb.'s* ~ [俚]惹某人发火 / *ride the* ~ 加入秘密团体 ‖~*ish*, ~*y a.* ①山羊似的 ②好色的,淫荡的 ‖'~-herd *n.* 看羊的

人 / **～sbeard** ['goutsbiəd] *n.*【植】假升麻; 婆罗门参 / **'～skin.** *n.* 山羊皮(革); 山羊皮衣; (装酒或水的)羊皮囊 / **'～,sucker.** *n.*【动】夜鹰 / **～'s wool** 不存在的东西

goatee [gou'ti:] *n.* 山羊胡子

goatee

gobble ['gɔbl] **I** *n.* 火鸡的叫声 **II** ❶ *vt.* ① 狼吞虎咽 ②[美俚]急急抓住 ❷ *vi.* ①贪食; 吞并 (*up*) ②发出火鸡般的咯咯叫声 / **～r** *n.* 公火鸡

goblet ['gɔblit] *n.* (无柄)酒杯; 高脚杯

goblin ['gɔblin] *n.* 妖怪

god [gɔd] **I** *n.* ① 神; (泥塑或木雕的)神像; 偶像 ②[G-]【宗】上帝 ③ 神化的人(或物), 被极度崇拜的人(或物) ④[the ～s] 剧院中顶层楼座的观众 **II** (godded; godding) *vt.* 使神化,崇拜… 为神 ‖ **～ it** 做神, 俨然以神自居 ‖ *a* (*little*) *tin* **～** 受到不应得的过分尊敬的人; 自命不凡的人 / *a sight* (或 *feast*) *for the ～s* 见 *sight* / *by God* 老天爷作证, 确实(表示发誓) / *God!* (或 *Oh, God!* 或 *My God!* 或 *Good God!*) 天啊! 啊呀! (表示痛苦、悲哀或愤怒等) / *God bless* (*help, damn*) *you* (*him*)! 愿上帝保祐(帮助, 惩罚)你(他)! / *God bless me* (或 *my life, my soul, you* 等)! 天哪! 喔唷! 啊呀! (表示惊讶) / *God forbid!* 苍天不容! 绝对不行! / *God forfend!* 上天不容! 决无此事! / *God grant ...!* 但愿…! / *God helps those who help themselves.* [谚]自助者天助。 / *God knows* ①天晓得, 谁也不知道: *God knows* how high this mountain is. 天知道这山有多高。 / He has gone *God knows* where. 谁知他上哪里去了。②老天爷知道, 确确实实: *God knows* that he is a good runner. 他确确实实是个赛跑好手。 / *God willing* 如果情况许可的话 / *Great God!* 天哪! 啊呀! / *He that serves God for money will serve the devil for better wages.* [谚]为金钱侍奉上帝的人, 为了更多的报酬也会给魔鬼卖力。 / *make a ～ of one's belly* 一味追求吃喝 / *please God* [用作插入语]如果上帝愿意; 如果幸运 / *so help me God* 老天爷作证, 确确实实 / *thank God* [用作插入语]谢天谢地, 幸亏 / *the blind ～* (或 *the ～ of love*) 爱神 (=Cupid) / *the ～ of day* 太阳; 太阳神 (=Phoebus, Apollo) / *the God of Hosts* (基督教《圣经》中的)万军之主

(指耶和华) / *the ～ of this world* 魔王 (=Satan) / *the ～ of war* 战神 (=Mars) / *under God* (除上帝之外)就人间而言 / *with God* 死了的, 【宗】与主同在的 / *wrestle with God* 热忱祈祷 ‖ **～head** *n.* ①神性 ②[the G-]上帝 / **～hood** *n.* 神性 / **～ship** *n.* 神性; 神 / **～ward** *ad.* & *a.* 向上帝的 / **～wards** *ad.* 向上帝; 关于上帝 ‖ **'～,awful** *a.* 非常可怕的, 可憎的 / **'～,child** *n.* 教子(或女) / **'～,daughter** *n.* 教女 / **'～,father** *n.* ①教父 ②名字被用以命名某人(或物)的人 *vt.* 做(某人)的教父 / **'～-,fearing** *a.* 敬神的, 虔诚的 / **'～-for,saken** *a.* 被上帝抛弃的; 堕落的, 邪恶的; 倒霉的; 凄凉的 / **'God-'man** *n.* 基督 / **'～,mother** *n.* 教母 / **'～,parent** *n.* 教父(或母) / **God's acre** (教堂的)墓地 / **'～send** *n.* 意外地来得正好的事物; 天赐 / **'～son** *n.* 教子 / **'～'speed** *n.* (祝愿用语)成功, 平安: bid sb. ～*speed* 祝某人成功(或一路平安)

goddess ['gɔdis] *n.* ① 女神 ② 美人; 非常善良的女子

godless ['gɔdlis] *a.* ①没有神的 ② 不信神的; 不虔诚的 ③邪恶的 ‖ **～ly** *ad.* / **～ness** *n.*

godly ['gɔdli] *a.* ①神的; 神圣的 ② 虔诚的 ‖ **godliness** *n.*

godown ['goudaun] *n.* (亚洲某些地方的)仓库, 货栈

goggle ['gɔgl] **I** ❶ *vi.* ①瞪眼看, 斜眼看 (*at*) ②转动眼珠 ❷ *vt.* 转动(眼珠) **II** *n.* ①瞪眼, 转眼 ②[复]护目镜, 风镜; 【俚】(圆镜片)眼镜: a pair of ～*s* 一副护目镜 **III** *a.* (眼珠)突出的, 转动的, 瞪住的 ‖ **～eyed** *a.* 瞪眼的, 转动眼睛的, 眼珠突出的

going ['gouiŋ] **I** *n.* ①去, 离去 ②地面(或道路)的状况 ③进行情况; 工作条件 ④[复]行为; 行动 **II** *a.* ①进行中的;运转中的: in ～ order 正常运转着 ②营业中的; 营业发达的: a ～ concern 营业发达的商行 ③现行的, 流行的: the ～ rate 现行率 / the ～ prices 时价 ④现存的;活着的 ‖ *get* (或 *set*) ～ ①出发 ②开展,实行 ③使开动 / *～ and coming* 没有出路, 逃脱不了: get sb. ～ *and coming* 使某人无路可退 / *go while the ～'s good* 及时离开; 及时行动 ‖ **'～-'over** *n.* ①彻底审查 ②痛打; 痛骂 / **'～s-'on** [复] *n.* ①举动, 行为 ②发生的事情

gold [gould] **I** *n.* ①金, 黄金; 金币: overlay sth. with ～ 给某物镀金 / on a ～ basis【经】用金本位 / a hundred pounds in ～ 一百英镑金币 ②钱财; 财富 ③宝贵的东西; 宝贵, 优美: a voice of ～ 金嗓子 ④金色, 金黄色: old ～ 古金色 / the red and ～ of the woods in autumn 秋天树林的一片火红 ⑤包金(或镀金)材料(如金箔、金粉、金线): cloth of ～ 金线织物 ⑥金色靶心: make a ～ 射中金心 **II** *a.* ①金(制)的; 含金的: a ～ coin 金币 / a ～ watch 金表 ②(货币等)可以兑换黄金的; 用黄金作储备的; 金本位的: a ～ currency 金本位货币 ③金(黄)色的; 黄金般的

(现常用 golden) ‖*as good as* ~ (小孩)很乖 ‖~ **amalgam** 金汞膏 / ~ **bar** 金条 / '~**beater** *n.* 金箔工 / ~ **bloc** 金本位国家集团 / '~**brick** *n.* ①[口]假金砖; 赝品; 虚有其表的东西 ②[军俚]逃避工作的人, 懒汉 *vi.* 逃避工作, 拈轻怕重, 吊儿郎当 *vt.* 欺骗 / '~**bug** *n.* ①金色甲虫 ②[美俚]主张金本位的人 / ~ **bullion** 金块 / ~ **certificate** 金券 / **Gold Coast** ①黄金海岸 (Ghana 加纳的旧称)[非洲] ②[美口]有钱人聚居区(尤指湖滨等地) / '~**crest** *n.* 【动】戴菊(名) / ~ **digger** ①淘金者 ②[俚]以美色骗取男人钱财的女人 / ~ **dust** 砂金; 金泥; 金粉 / ~ **fever** 淘金热 / '~**field** *n.* 采金地 / '~**finch** *n.* 金翅雀 / '~**fish** *n.* 金鱼 / ~ **foil** 金箔 / ~ **leaf** (比金箔薄, 用于贴饰器物的)金叶 / ~ **mine** ①金矿, 金山 ②[口]财源 / ~ **plate** [总称]金制餐具 / ~ **reserve** 黄金储备 / ~ **rush** 涌往新金矿(或有利可图的地方); 淘金热 / '~**size** (用于在器物上贴饰金叶的)胶粘剂 / '~**smith** *n.* 金(饰)工, 金首饰商 / ~ **standard** 金本位 / **star** [美](表示阵亡官兵的)金星

golden ['gouldən] *a.* ①金(黄)色的; 黄金般的: the ~ waves of wheat 金黄色的麦浪 ②贵重的, 绝好的, 重要的: a ~ saying 金玉良言 / a ~ opportunity 绝好机会 / a ~ remedy 灵药 / ~ opinions 极高评价 / ~ hours 幸福的时刻 ③繁荣的, 昌盛的 ④朝气蓬勃的; 朝日出的 ⑤(声音)洪亮的 ⑥含金的; 产金的: the *Golden State* 美国加利福尼亚州的别名 ⑦金(制)的(现常用 gold) ‖~**ly** *ad.* / ~**ness** *n.* ‖**Golden Age** ①(古代神话中的)黄金时代; [g- a-] [喻]黄金时代 ②[也作 g- a-] [用作定语]六十五岁以上的退休人的 / ~**ager** [也作 G- A-]六十五岁以上的退休人; 年长者 / ~ **apple** ①金【希神】(导致众女神争夺的)金苹果 ②西红柿, 番茄 ③(英王加冕等时用的、象征王权的)宝珠 / ~ **balls** 当铺的标志 (=three balls) / ~ **calf** 金犊(古代以色列人崇拜的偶像); (作为崇拜对象的)金钱 / ~ **eagle** 鹫 (产于北半球的一种山鹰) / '~**eye** *n.* 【动】鹊鸭, 白秋鸭 / **Golden Fleece** ①【希神】金羊毛(历尽千辛万苦而觅取的宝物) ②昔时奥地利和西班牙的最高勋位(或勋章) / **Golden Gate** 金门(美国圣弗兰西斯科湾口的湾口) / ~ **goose** 金鹅(据希腊寓言, 该鹅每天产一金蛋, 其主人欲一次得到全部金蛋, 将鹅杀掉, 结果一无所获) / ~ **key** 贿赂 / '~**knop** *n.* [英]瓢虫 / ~ **mean** 中庸(之道) / '~**mouthed** *a.* 雄辩的 / ~ **number** 【天】金数 / '~**rod** *n.* 【植】(北美产的多年生)菊科植物, 黄花 / '~**seal** *n.* 【植】白毛茛 / ~ **wedding** 金婚纪念(西俗结婚五十周年纪念)

golf [gɔlf] **I** *n.* 高尔夫球 **II** *vi.* 打高尔夫球 ‖~**er** *n.* 打高尔夫球的人 ‖~ **club** ①高尔夫球棍 ②高尔夫球俱乐部 / ~ **links** 高尔夫球场 / ~ **widow** 丈夫老呆在高尔夫球场上的女人

golliwog(g) ['gɔliwɔg] *n.* ①奇形怪状的黑面木偶 ②奇形怪状的人

golosh(e) [gə'lɔʃ] *n.* =galosh

gondola ['gɔndələ] *n.* ①(意大利威尼斯的)一种狭长的平底船 ②大型平底船 ③(铁路上的)敞篷货车 (=~ car) ④(飞艇或飞船的)吊舱, 吊篮 ⑤设在商店中央的商品陈列台 ⑥(运输混凝土的)有漏斗状容器的卡车(或拖车)

gondola

gondolier [,gɔndə'liə] *n.* 平底船的船夫

gone [gɔn] **I** go 的过去分词 **II** *a.* ①已去的; 过去的: The summer is ~. 夏天已过去了。 / past and ~ 过去了的, 一去不复返的 ②遗失了的; 无可挽回的: a ~ case 无可挽回的事(或人) ③深重的; 入迷的 ④怀孕的: She is seven months ~. 她已怀孕七个月了。 ⑤垂死的; 死了的: dead and ~ 死了 ⑥虚弱无力的; 发晕的: a ~ feeling 发晕的感觉 ⑦用光了的 ⑧[美俚]了不起的 ‖~ **far** ~ (病、债、夜等)到了很深的程度; 极度倦: be far ~ in a crisis 深陷危机之中 / The night was far ~. 夜深了。 / *Be ~!* 走开! / *be ~ on sb.* [口]倾心爱某人 ‖~**ness** *n.* / ~**r** *n.* 无可挽救的人(或物)

gong [gɔŋ] **I** *n.* ①锣, 铜锣 ②皿形钟, 铃 ③[俚]奖章, 勋章, 纪念章 **II** *vt.* (交通警)鸣锣令(驾驶汽车者)停驶

good [gud] **I** (better ['betə], best [best]) *a.* ①好的: ~ news 好消息 / ~ points 优点 / a ~ year 好年成 / That's ~! 好! ②愉快的: We had a ~ time together watching the display of fireworks. 我们在一起看烟火, 非常愉快。 / in ~ spirits 兴高采烈 ③健全的; 新鲜的: Meat does not keep ~ in hot weather. 热天肉容易坏。 ④有益的; 有效的; 适合的 ⑤可靠的; 真的: ~ debts 有把握收回的债款 / ~ money 真的货币, 非伪造的货币 ⑥大大的; 充分的; 十足的: a ~ beating 狠狠的一顿打 / We've come a ~ way. 我们走了好多路来到这里。 / have a ~ night 晚上睡得好 / a ~ match 劲敌 / a ~ week's march 整整一星期的行军 ⑦好心的; 乐于助人的; 慈善的: How ~ of you to come and help us! 谢谢你们好意来帮助。 / *Be ~ enough* (或 *Be so ~ as*) *to* give us an early reply. 请尽早回复。 ⑧有教养的; 虔诚的; 诚实的 ⑨[用于祝愿或问好]好的, 平安的: A ~ journey! 一路平安! / *Good morning* (afternoon, evening)! 早上

(下午、晚上)好! / *Good* night! (晚上与人分别时说)再见! / My ~ sirs! (讽)(我的)先生们 **II** (better ['betə], best [best]) *ad.* =well² (*ad.*) **III** *n.* ①好;好事;慷慨的行为: do ~ all one's life 一生做好事情 ②利益;好处,用处: What's the ~ of the haste? 急有什么用? / It's no ~ doing that. 那样做是没有用的。③[集合名词]好人 ||*a* ~ 'un 见 'un / *as* ~ *as* 和…几乎一样,实际上等于: The old machine is well maintained and looks *as* ~ *as* new. 这台旧机器维修得很好,看上去象新的一样。/ What he said has *as* ~ *as* shown his attitude. 他的话实际上已表明了他的态度。/ *as* ~ *as a play* (象戏剧那样)有趣味的 / *as* ~ *as gold* (小孩)很乖 / *Be* ~! [口]好好的! (或: 别淘气!) / *come to* (no) ~ 有(没有)好结果 / *for* ~ (*and all*) 永久地,一劳永逸地 / *for* ~ *or for evil* 不论好歹 / ~ *and . . .* [口]非常;完全: I'm ~ *and* ready. 我都准备好了。/ ~ *at* 善于 / ~ *for* ①值…;有支付…能力的 ②有效的;对…有用的 / *Good for you!* [美口]干得好! 真运气! / *hold* ~ (*for*) (对…)适用 / *It is a* ~ *thing that . . . .* 见 thing¹ / *make* ~ ①成功;发达 ②补偿,赔偿;偿付: make ~ on defective wares 对次货负责退换(或退款) / *make* ~ *a loss* 赔偿损失 ③实现(意图、诺言等) ④证实(控告等) ⑤获得并保持(地位等) / *Much* ~ *may it do you!* [常作反语]这对你好处多着哩! / *not* ~ *enough* [口]不值得做(或接受等) / *Not so* ~! 糟透了! / *say* (或 *put in*) *a* ~ *word for sb.* 见 word / *see* ~ (to do) 认为(做某事)适当: Do as you see ~. 你看着办吧。/ *too* ~ *to be true* 哪有这么好的(事) / *to the* ~ ①有好处: To such a patient some physical exercise is all *to the* ~. 对这样的病人来说,一定的体育活动只会有好处。/ Every cartful removed is one cartful *to the* ~. 装掉一车少一车。②净赚;赢得;多出来 / *up to* (或 *after*) *no* ~ 不怀好意,想作弄人;做坏事 ||*Good Book* (基督教)《圣经》 / ~ *fellow* 热诚而令人感到亲切的人 / '~-'fellowship *n.* 亲密,融洽;善于交际 / '~-for-,nothing, '~-for-naught *a.* 没有用处的,无价值的 人. 无用的人,饭桶 / '~= 'hearted *a.* 好心肠的 / *Good Hope* 好望角[南非(阿扎尼亚)] / '~-'humo(u)red *a.* 心情好的;脾气好的;愉快的 / '~-'looking *a.* (外貌)好看的 / '~man *n.* [古] ①家长, 户主; 丈夫 ②先生 (=mister) / '~-'natured *a.* 脾气好的;温厚的 / '~= neighbo(u)r policy 睦邻政策 / '~-'neighbo(u)r-hood, '~-'neighbo(u)rliness, '~-'neighbo(u)r-ship *n.* 友好行为; 睦邻关系 / ~ *people* 仙女们 / ~ *sense* 判断力强; 机智 / '~-'sized *a.* 大号的;相当大(或多)的 / '~-'tempered *a.* 脾气好的;和气的 / '~-time Charlie [口]乐天派,无忧无虑、寻欢作乐的人 / '~'wife *n.* [苏格兰]主妇 / '~'will *n.* 友好, 亲善; 好意: be on a ~*will* mission 担负着友好亲善的使命 / feel ~-

will towards 对…表示友好 ②(商店、企业等的)信誉,商誉

good-by(e) **I** ['gud'bai] *int.* 再见! **II** [gud'bai] *n.* 告别: wave ~ 挥手告别 / say ~ to sb. 向某人告别 / I still have several ~*s* to say before leaving. 在动身前我还要到好几处去告别。||*kiss sb.* ~ 见 kiss / *kiss sth.* ~ 见 kiss

goodly ['gudli] *a.* ①漂亮的; 讨人喜欢的 ②好的, 不错的 ③颇大的: a ~ crowd 一大群人 ||**good-liness** *n.*

goodness ['gudnis] *n.* ①优良; 德性; 善行; 仁慈 ②精华; 真髓 ||*For* ~' *sake!* 看在老天爷面上! / *Goodness knows* ①(感叹句)天晓得 ②(后接从句)老天作证 / *Goodness me!* 天啊! / *have the* ~ *to* 请…; 有…的好意: Have the ~ to show me the way. 请告诉我怎么走。/ *I wish to* ~ *that . . . .* 我非常想…(或: 但愿…) / *Thank* ~! 谢天谢地

goods [gudz] [复] *n.* ①商品; 货物: consumer ~ 消费品 / printed ~ 印花布 / dry ~ [美]纺织品; [英]谷物 ②动产: ~ and chattels 【律】私人财物,全部动产 ③ [the] ~ [美口]本领; 正要寻找的人(或物); 好人 ||*a piece of* ~ [贬]女人; 人 / *by* ~ 用货车装运 / *deliver the* ~ 交货; [喻]履行诺言,不负所望 / *get the* ~ *on sb.* [美俚]在某人身上发现罪证 / *have all one's* ~ *in the window* 肤浅; 华而不实; 虚有其表 / *know one's* ~ [俚]对本分的工作很内行, 精通自己的业务 / *straight* ~ [美]真相,事实 ||*~= train n.* [英]货物列车

goose [gu:s] **I** ([复] geese [gi:s] 或[罕] gooses) *n.* ①鹅, 雌鹅; 鹅肉 ②呆头鹅, 傻瓜 ③([复] gooses) 长柄熨斗 **II** *vt.* ①突然开大(汽车等)的油门 ②[俚]作嘘嘘声反对(某人), 嘘骂 ||*All his geese are swans.* 他老是言过其实。②敝帚自珍; / *a wild-*~ *chase* 徒劳的搜索, 无益的举动 / *be sound on the* ~ [美]抱正统观点 / *cannot* (或 *be unable to*) *say boh to a* ~ 见 boh / *cook sb.'s* ~ ①干掉某人 ②彻底挫败某人的计划(或希望等) / *get the* ~ [俚]遭听众(或观众)嘘骂 / *give* (. . .) *the* ~ [美俚]加快(…的)速度 / *kill the* ~ *that lays the golden eggs* 杀鸡取蛋 / *make a* ~ *of sb.* 愚弄(或欺骗)某人 / *shoe the* ~ 徒劳无益 / *swim like a tailor's* ~ [谑]沉下去 / *The* ~ *hangs high.* [美口]前景(或形势)好。/ *The old woman is plucking her geese.* [儿语]下雪了。/ *What is sauce for the* ~ *is sauce for the gander.* 见 sauce ||~ *egg* ①鹅蛋; [美俚]零分 ②[俚]青肿块 / '~-flesh *n.* 鸡皮疙瘩: be ~*flesh* all over 浑身起鸡皮疙瘩 / '~-foot ([复] ~foots) *n.* 【植】藜 / ~gog ['gu:sgog] *n.* [英俚] =gooseberry / ~ grass 【植】蟋蟀草, 牛筋草 / '~-herd *n.* 牧鹅人 / '~neck *n.* 鹅头颈; [机]鹅颈钩, 鹅颈管 / ~ quill 鹅毛管; 鹅毛笔 / '~skin *n.* =~flesh / ~ step 鹅步, 正步 / '~-step *vi.* 正步走

gooseberry ['guzbəri] *n.* ①【植】醋栗, 鹅莓; 茶藨子 ②醋栗果实, 醋栗酒 ‖*play ~* 硬夹在两个想单独在一起的人(如情侣)之间 / *play old ~ with* 破坏

gore[1] [gɔ:] *n.* (流出的)血; 成块的血

gore[2] [gɔ:] **I** *n.* 三角形布条; 三角形地带 **II** *vt.* ①使成三角形狭条 ②给…镶上三角形狭条

gore[3] [gɔ:] *vt.* ①(牛、羊等以角)抵破, 抵伤 ②[罕](岩石)划破(船只)

gorge [gɔ:dʒ] **I** *n.* ①咽喉 ②胃: a full ~ 满腹 ③暴食; 饱食; 贪吃 ④(胃中的)食物 ⑤山峡, 峡谷 ⑥(堡垒等后部的)出入口 ⑦(阻塞通道的)障碍物;(用作鱼饵的)硬块状物 **II** ❶ *vt.* ①塞饱: ~ oneself with 大吃… ②狼吞虎咽地吃 ❷ *vi.* 狼吞虎咽 ‖*heave the ~* 作呕 / *make sb.'s ~ rise* 使某人作呕, 惹某人嫌

gorgeous ['gɔ:dʒəs] *a.* ①灿烂的, 华丽的, 豪华的 ②[俚]美丽的; 极好的; 可喜的 ‖*~ly ad.* / *~ness n.*

gorilla [gə'rilə] *n.* ①大猩猩 ②[美俚]貌似大猩猩的人 ③[美俚]暴徒,打手

gormand ['gɔ:mənd] *n.* =gourmand

gorse [gɔ:s] *n.*【植】荆豆; 荆豆属植物 ‖*gorsy a.*

gosling ['gɔzliŋ] *n.* ①小鹅 ②笨人, 傻瓜; 没有经验的人 ‖*shoe the ~* 徒劳无益

gospel ['gɔspəl] **I** *n.* ①[常作 G-]【基督教】福音, 喜讯;《新约》四部福音之一 ②真理, 真实: take sth. as (或 for) ~ 认为某事真实 ③(行动的)准则, 信条, 主义 **II** *a.* 福音的; 传播福音的; 福音赞美诗的 ‖*gospel(l)er n.* ①福音传道师 ②(做礼拜时)诵读福音书者

gossamer ['gɔsəmə] **I** *n.* ①蛛丝, 游丝: A few ~s are spread on the grass. 草上布着几根蜘蛛丝. / Gossamer is floating in calm air. 空中飘浮着游丝. ②纤细的东西 ③薄纱 ④薄雨衣(或织物) **II** *a.* 轻而薄的; 薄弱的; 虚无飘渺的: a ~ justification 站不住脚的辩解 ‖*~ed a.* / *~y* ['gɔsəməri] *a.*

gossip ['gɔsip] **I** *n.* ①闲谈, 聊天; 流言蜚语: have a ~ with 与…闲聊 / be fond of ~ 喜欢说人闲话 ②爱讲闲话的人; 爱传流言蜚语的人 ③(报刊上有关社会新闻或个人隐私的)闲话: the ~ column 闲话栏 ④[英方]朋友, 同伴 **II** *vi.* 闲聊; 传播流言蜚语 ‖*~er n.* 爱闲聊的人; 搬弄是非者 / *~ist n.* 闲话栏作者 / *~y a.* 爱闲聊的; 流言蜚语的 / *'~-monger n.* 传播流言蜚语的人

got [gɔt] get 的过去式和过去分词 ‖*'~-up a.* 假的, 硬装(或做)出来的

gouge [gaudʒ] **I** *n.* ①半圆凿, 弧口凿 ②[美口]凿槽, 凿孔; 凿出的槽(或孔) ③[美口]欺骗, 诈取; 榨取; 骗子 ④【地】断层泥 **II** *vt.* ①(用半圆凿)凿 ②用拇指挖(某人的)眼睛(out); 用拇指挖(某人)的眼睛(out) ③[美口]诈取; 榨取

gourd [guəd] *n.* ①葫芦属植物; 葫芦 ②葫芦制成的容器 ‖*~ful n.* 一葫芦的量

gourmand ['guəmənd] *n.* ①贪吃的人 ②美食家,

讲究饮食的人 ‖*~ism n.* 美食主义

gourmet ['guəmei] *n.* 食物品尝家 ‖*~ powder* 味精

gout [gaut] *n.* ①【医】痛风: rich (poor) man's ~ 由饮食过多(营养不足)引起的痛风 ②(液体等的)一滴; 一块, 一团 ‖*~ fly*【动】麦秆蝇

gouty ['gauti] *a.* 患痛风病的; 象痛风病的; 因痛风而肿胀的 ‖*goutily ad.* / *goutiness n.*

govern ['gʌvən] ❶ *vt.* ①统治, 管理: ~ a country 管理国家 / the ~ing body 理事会, 董事会 ②指导, 支配, 决定, 影响: a ~ing principle 指导原则 ③抑制, 控制(感情等): ~ one's temper 捺住性子 / ~ oneself 克制 ④调节(车速) ⑤【语】支配(在英语中指动词或前置词与其所跟的宾格名词的关系) ❷ *vi.* 统治, 管理

governess ['gʌvənis] *n.* ①家庭女教师; 保育员; 女保姆 ②女统治者, 女管理者; 总督(或州长)的夫人

government ['gʌvənmənt] *n.* ①政府; [英]内阁 ②政治, 政体: democratic ~ 民主政治 ③行政管理; 管理机构 ④行政管理区域 ⑤【语】支配(关系) ‖*~al* [,gʌvən'mentl] *a.* 政府的; 管辖的 ‖**Government house** (英国殖民地等的)政府大厦(或总督官邸) / *'~-in-'exile n.* 流亡政府 / ~ issue (装备、衣着等)由美国政府发给军人的(略作 GI) / *~ man* ①官员, 公务员; 支持政府者 ② =G-man / ~ paper [总称]政府发行的有价证券 / ~ security 政府发行的有价证券

governmentalism [,gʌvən'mentəlizəm] *n.* 政府至上主义(指主张扩大政府职能和权限的理论或扩大政府作用的倾向)

governor ['gʌvənə] *n.* ①统治者, 管辖者 ②地方长官(如省长); (英国殖民地)总督; (美国)州长; (要塞或卫戍区的)司令官; [英]狱长 ③(组织、机构的)主管人员(如学校董事、银行总裁等) ④【机】节速器, 调节器; 【电】调节用变阻器, 控制器: pendulum ~【机】摆调节器 / throttling ~【电】节流调速器 ⑤[英口]老板; 先生; 爸爸 ‖*~ship n.* 统治者(或地方长官等)的职位(或任期) / *'Governor-'General n.* 英国领地(或殖民地)的总督

gown [gaun] **I** *n.* ①长袍, 长外衣(尤指教士、法官、教授等的礼服或妇女的睡衣等) ②[集合名词]大学全体师生: town and ~ (英国牛津和剑桥的)城镇居民和大学里的人 **II** *vt.* [主要用过去分词]使穿长袍, 使穿礼服 ‖*wear the ~* 穿上律师的长袍, 做律师

grab [græb] **I** (grabbed; grabbing) ❶ *vt.* ①攫取; 抓取: Monopoly capitalists ~ super-profits. 垄断资本家攫取超额利润. ②强夺, 霸占 ③(急速地)抓住, 抓牢 ❷ *vi.* ①攫取; 抓取; 强夺: ~ at an opportunity 抢机会 ②(马)后蹄踢着前蹄 **II** *n.* ①掠夺; 攫取; (急速)抓住: a policy of ~ 掠夺政策 / make a ~ at sth. 向某物抓去 ②【机】抓扬机, 挖掘机: bucket ~ 抓斗 ‖*up for ~s* [俚]供人竞购(以售给出价最高者) ‖*grabber n.* 攫取者; 贪财者, 唯利是图的人 ‖*'~-all n.*

心人;[口]杂物袋 ②(海岸附近的)固定鱼网 / **bag, ~ box** [美]摸彩袋,摸彩袋; [喻]百宝囊 / **~ sample**【化】定时取集的样品

grace [greis] **I** *n.* ①优美,雅致: The gymnast performed on the balance beam with an easy ~. 体操运动员在平衡木上表演得优美自如。/ a building of unusual ~ 异常优美的建筑物 / give an added ~ to what is already beautiful 锦上添花 ②[常用复]风度;魅力 ③体面(感);情理: cannot with any ~ ask sb. 难以向某人启齿 / have the ~ to apologize 通情达理地道歉 ④恩惠,恩赐;宽厚,仁慈;赦免;[复]恩遇: an act of ~ 恩赦令 / an Act of Grace 大赦令(尤指经议会通过的) / be in sb.'s good (bad) ~s 受(不受)某人恩宠,得(不得)某人欢心 ⑤[宗](神的)恩典,感化;(对神的)皈依 ⑥(票据等到期后的)宽限: days of ~ 宽限日期 / give sb. a week's ~ 给某人一星期的宽限 ⑦[宗](饭前或饭后的)感恩祷告: say (a) ~ 做感恩祷告 ⑧【音】装饰音 ⑨[the Graces]【希神】赐人美丽和欢乐的三女神 ⑩[His (或 Her, Your) Grace] (对公爵、公爵夫人或大主教的尊称) 大人;夫人 **II** *vt.* ①使优美;使增光: Will you ~ the occasion by your presence? 如蒙光临,不胜荣幸。②【音】缀~以装饰音 ‖*airs and ~s* 做作的姿态,装腔作势 / *a saving ~* 可以弥补缺点的(唯一)优点,可取之处 / *be in a state of ~* [宗]蒙受天恩 / *fall from ~* 【宗】失去天恩;堕落,犯罪 / *the year of ~ ...* (或 *the ...th year of ~*) 耶稣纪元…年,公元…年 / *with (a) bad* (或 (*an*) *ill*) ~ 不情愿地,勉强地 / *with (a) good* ~ 欣然地 / ~ *cup* (感恩祷告后用的)祝酒杯;祝酒 / ~ *note* 【音】装饰音

graceful ['greisful] *a.* 优美的,雅致的 ‖*~ly ad.* / *~ness n.*

graceless ['greislis] *a.* ①不优美的,不雅致的 ②无礼貌的,不知情理的: ~ behaviour 粗野的行为 ③堕落的,道德败坏的 ‖*~ly ad.* / *~ness n.*

gracious ['greiʃəs] **I** *a.* ①有礼貌的;通情达理的,谦和的: It was ~ *of* you to come. 承蒙你光临。②宽厚的,仁慈的 ③优美的,雅致的 **II** *int.* [表示惊异等]: Gracious! (或 Good ~! 或 Gracious Heaven! 或 Gracious me! 或 My ~!) 天哪! 啊呀! ‖*~ly ad.* / *~ness n.*

gradation [grə'deiʃən] *n.* ①分等,分级 ②[常用复]等级,阶段 ③渐变;(颜色等的)层次 ④[语]元音交替

grade [greid] **I** *n.* ①等级;级别; 阶段: ~ A milk 甲级牛奶 / high-~ steel 优质钢 / the ~s of growing up 成长的各阶段 ②程度: a school of collegiate ~ 大专程度的学校 / organic glass with a high ~ of transparency 高透明度的有机玻璃 ③[美](中小学的)年级;某一年级的全体学生; [the ~s] 小学 (=~ school): a pupil in the third ~ 三年级学生 / teach in the ~s 在小学里教书 ④ [美](学校的)评分等级 ⑤ [美]坡度;

斜坡: an ascending (a descending) ~ 升(降)坡 ⑥[动](与良种杂交产生的)改良杂种 ⑦[语]元音交替 **II** ❶ *vt.* ①给…分等级;给…分类: ~ the cotton 把棉花分等 ②[美]给…评分: ~ papers 评试卷(分数) ③把(路面等)筑平(或筑成小坡度)【地】均夷: the ~*d* section of a highway 公路的坡度路段 ④[动]通过与良种杂交改良 (up)⑤使(各种颜色等)渐次变化 ❷ *vi.* ①属于某种等级: This tea ~*s* A. 这是一级茶叶。②(各种颜色等)渐次变化,渐次调和 ‖*at ~* 【交】(铁路等交叉)在同一平面上 / *make the ~* 爬上陡坡;成功;达到理想标准: The trial flight has *made the* ~. 试飞成功。/ *on the up (down)* ~ 在走上(下)坡路 / *up to* ~ 合格 / ~ *crossing* [美](铁路、公路等的)平面交叉 / ~ *label(l)ing* [美]商品质量的标签说明 / ~ *school* [美]小学

gradient ['greidjənt] **I** *n.* ①(道路等的)斜坡,坡道;坡度,斜度 ②【物】梯度,陡度;(温度、气压等的)变化率;梯度变化曲线 **II** *a.* ①倾斜的 ②【动】步行的;适于步行的 ‖*~er n.* 坡度计;水平仪

gradual[1] ['grædjuəl, 'grædʒuəl] *a.* ①逐渐的,逐步的 ②渐进的,顺序变化的;逐渐上升(或下降)的: a ~ slope 缓坡 ‖*~ism n.* 渐进主义 / *~ist n.* 渐进主义者 *a.* 渐进主义的 / *~ly ad.* / *~ness n.*

gradual[2] ['grædjuəl, 'grædʒuəl] *n.*【天主教】(弥撒中圣餐后会众与传道者)对答吟唱的赞美诗;对答吟唱赞美诗集

graduate ['grædjuit, 'grædʒuit] **I** *n.* ①大学毕业生;[美]毕业生: college and secondary school ~*s* 大、中学校毕业生 / a ~ in medicine 医科毕业生 ②【化】量筒,量杯 **II** ['grædjueit, 'grædʒueit] ❶ *vt.* ①[主美]准予…毕业; 授予…学位(或资格等)标上刻度 ②把…分等级 ③蒸发浓缩(溶液等) ❷ *vi.* ①大学毕业,得学位;[美]毕业 ②取得资格: He ~*d as* a seaman. (经过训练)他能当海员了。③渐渐变为 (into);逐步消逝 (away) **III** *a.* ①毕了业的 ②研究生的: a ~ course [美]研究生课程 / a ~ student [美]研究生 / a ~ school [美](大学中的)研究院 ④分等级的 ‖*~d* ['grædjueitid, 'grædʒueitid] *a.* ①毕业了的 ②刻度的;分度的: a ~*d* glass 刻度杯,量杯 ③分等级的: ~*d* taxation 分级课税

graduation [,grædju'eiʃən, ,grædʒu'eiʃən] *n.* ①(大学毕业时的)授学位,获学位; [美]毕业 ②[美]毕业典礼,授学位典礼 ③刻度;分度 ④分等级 ⑤蒸浓

graft[1] [grɑːft] **I** *n.* ①【农】嫁接;接穗;接穗接合处;嫁接植物 ②【医】移植物,移植片;移植 ③[美]贪污,受贿;不义之财: take ~ 贪污 **II** *vt. & vi.* ①嫁接 (*in, into, on, upon*) ②用嫁接法种植(水果、花等)③【医】移植(皮、肉) ④[美]贪污,受贿 ‖*~er n.* ①嫁接者;移植者 ②[美]贪污者,受贿者 / *~ing n.* 嫁接法;移植法

graft[2] [grɑːft] *n.* [英] ①可一铲掘起的土的深度 ②弯口铁铲

grain [grein] **I** *n.* ① 谷物,谷类,谷类植物(英国一般称 corn): public ~ 公粮 / seed ~ 谷种 / refined ~ 细粮 ②谷粒;颗果: Bring in every single ~. 颗粒还仓。③粒子,细粒;晶粒;[喻]些微,一点儿: ~s of sand 沙子 / without a ~ of common sense 一点常识也没有 / with some ~s of allowance 有保留地,不全信地 ④谷(英美最小的重量单位,等于 64.8 毫克,原为小麦谷粒的平均重量;略作 gr., G. 或 g.) ⑤(木材或大理石的)纹理;[喻]性格,本质: woods of fine (coarse) ~ 纹理细(粗)的木材 / across the ~ 与纹理垂直,横着纹 ⑥皮革的正面,粒面 ⑦胭脂虫;(用胭脂虫制的)红色染料;不褪色染料 ⑧[复]麦芽渣,(酒)槽 **II** ❶ *vt.* ①使成颗粒状;使起粒;使结晶 ②把(某物)的表面漆(或画)成木纹(或大理石纹) ③把(生皮)去毛;对(皮革)粒面进行处理 ❷ *vi.* 形成粒状 ‖*against the* (或 *sb.'s*) ~ (跟某人的性格、感情或愿望)格格不入,违拗的 / *a* ~ *of mustard seed* 有极大发展前途的小东西 / *in* ~ 彻底的,真正的;本性的,根深蒂固的 / *with a* ~ *of salt* 有保留地,不全信地: We take his predictions *with a* ~ *of salt.* 我们对他的预测不全相信。 ‖*~less a.* 没有谷粒的; 没有纹理的 ‖*~ elevator* [美]高粮仓 / *'~field n.* 种粮食的田 / ~ **leather** 粒面向外的皮革 / ~ **rust** 谷物锈病 / '~**sick** *n.* (牛的) 瘤胃扩张症 / ~ **side** 皮革粒面 / ~ **sorghum** 高粱

gram[1] [græm] *n.* 【植】① 鹰嘴豆(常用作牲畜饲料) ②绿豆

gram[2] [græm] *n.* 克(重量单位) ‖~ **atom** 【化】克原子 / ~ **equivalent** 【化】克当量 / ~ **molecule** 【化】克分子

grammar ['græmə] *n.* ①语法(学),文法(学);语法规则: English ~ 英语语法 ②语法书 ③(某人的)语法知识;(符合语法规则的)文理: good (bad) ~ 通顺(不通)的文理 ④语法现象 ⑤(艺术、科学、技术等的)基本原理;入门书 ‖~**ian** [grə'mɛəriən] *n.* 语法学家 / ~ **school** ①[英](十六世纪以拉丁语等为主课的)中等学校;普通中学 ②[美]初级中学;小学

grammatical [grə'mætikəl] *a.* ①语法(上)的: ~ analysis 语法分析 / a ~ subject 语法上的主语 ② 符合语法规则的: The construction is not ~. 这种结构不符合语法。 ‖*~ly ad.* / *~ness n.*

gramme [græm] *n.* =gram[2]

gramophone ['græməfoun] *n.* 留声机: a ~ record 唱片

granary ['grænəri] *n.* 谷仓,粮仓;产粮区: a natural ~ 天然粮仓;鱼米之乡

grand [grænd] **I** *a.* ①(最)重大的, 主要的;(同一官衔、爵位中)最高的: the ~ entrance 正门 ②雄伟的;宏大的;盛大的: a ~ view of sunrise 日出的壮丽景色 / a ~ mountain 巍巍高山 / a ~ banquet given in hono(u)r of foreign friends 招待外国朋友的盛大宴会 ③ 豪华的; 华丽的: live in ~ style 过豪华生活 ④自负的,傲慢的: be too

~ to do sth. 高傲得不屑做某事 ⑤[口]极好的,美妙的: What ~ weather! 多好的天气! / have a ~ time 过得很愉快 ⑥ 全部的, 总的: the ~ total 总计数 ⑦庄重的; 崇高的; 显要的: a ~ style 庄重的文体 / a ~ character 崇高的性格 / a ~ air 堂堂仪表 ⑧(亲属关系中)(外)祖…;(外)孙…‖a ~ *hotel* (常指接待各国顾客的)大旅馆 / *the Grand National* (英国)利物浦一年一度的障碍赛马 / *the Grand Old Man* 【英史】英国首相格莱斯顿(Gladstone)的尊称 / *the Grand Old Party* (美国) 共和党的别称 (略作 GOP) / *a ~ orchestra* 大型管弦乐队, 交响乐队 / *a ~ piano* 大钢琴 / *the ~ slam* [美俚](桥牌等的)满贯;(运动比赛等的)全胜 / *a ~ tour* 大旅游(指到欧洲各大城市的旅游; 旧时英国贵族子弟教育的最后一个阶段) **II** *n.* ① 大钢琴 (= ~ piano) ②[单复同][美俚]一千美元: ten ~ 一万美元 ‖*the ~* 摆架子 ‖*~ly ad.* / *~ness n.* ‖'~**aunt** *n.* 叔(或伯)祖母; 姑婆; 舅婆; 姨婆 / *~*baby ['grænd,beibi] *n.* 小孙 (女) 儿 (即婴孩期的 child) / ~**child** ['græn-tʃaild] *n.* 孙 (女); 外孙 (女) / ~**dad**, ~**ad** ['grændæd] *n.* =~pa / ~**daddy** ['grænd,dædi] *n.* =grandfather / ~**daughter** ['grænd,dɔːtə] *n.* (外)孙女 / ~ **duchess** ①大公夫人; 大公爵夫人 ②女大公爵 / ~ **duchy** (大公辖下的)公国; 大公辖领地 / ~ **duke** 大公; 大公爵 / ~ **finale** (戏剧、运动会等的) 高潮性结尾 / ~ **jury** (由十二至二十三人组成的)大陪审团 / ~**ma** ['grænmɑː], ~**ma(m)ma** ['grænmə,mɑː] *n.* [口]奶奶; 外婆 / ~ **mal** [mɑː] 重癫痫病 / ~**nephew** ['grænd,nevju:] *n.* 侄(外)孙; 甥(外)孙 / ~**niece** ['grændni:s] *n.* 侄(外)孙女; 甥(外)孙女 / ~ **opera** (全剧只用唱不用说白的)大歌剧 / ~**pa** ['grænpɑ:], ~**papa** ['grænpə,pɑ:] *n.* [口]爷爷; 外公 / ~**parent** ['grænd,pɛərənt] *n.* (外)祖父 (或母) / ~**sire** ['grænd,saiə] *n.* [方](外)祖父;[古]祖人; 祖先 / ~**son** ['grændsʌn] *n.* (外)孙 / '~**uncle** *n.* 叔(或伯)祖父; 舅公; 姑公

grandeur ['grændʒə] *n.* ① 宏伟, 壮观, 庄严: with ~ 隆重地 / full of power and ~ 威武雄壮 ②富丽堂皇, 豪华 ③ 伟大, 崇高

grandfather ['grænd,fɑ:ðə] *n.* ①(外)祖父 ②大爷 ③祖先 ‖~**ly** *a.* 老祖父 (似) 的; 慈祥的 ‖~**clause** ① 老祖父条款 (指旧时美国南部某些法律中保护白人利益的条款, 按此条款规定, 南北战争前享有选举权的白人的后代, 即使没有文化也有选举权) ②(某些法律中的)不追溯条款 / ~('s) **clock** 有摆的落地大座钟

grandiloquent [græn'diləkwənt] *a.* 夸张的, 夸大的 ‖~**ly** *ad.*

grandiose ['grændiəus] *a.* ① 宏大的; 雄伟的, 壮观的 ② 铺张的; 浮夸的, 夸大的; 沾沾自喜的; 自以为是的 ‖~**ly** *ad.* / **grandiosity** [,grændi'ɔsiti] *n.*

grandmother ['grænd,mʌðə] **I** *n.* ①(外)祖母 ②老奶奶 ③(女性)祖先 **II** *vt.* 悉心照料; 溺爱

‖**teach one's ~** (*how*) **to suck eggs** 教训长辈; 班门弄斧 ‖**~ly** *a.* 老祖母(似)的; 慈祥的; 溺爱的; 唠叨的

grandstand ['grændstænd] **I** *n.* ①(运动场等的) 正面看台 ②全体观众 **II** *vi.* [口](比球等时)做花式动作(以博取观众喝采) ‖**~ play** [口] ①(比球等时为博取观众喝采的)花式动作 ②[喻] 哗众取宠(的言行)

grange [greindʒ] *n.* ①田庄, 农庄 ②[美][G-]格兰其(一八六七年成立的美国全国性保护农民利益的田庄农民秘密组织, 正式名为"保护农业社") ③[古]谷仓 ‖**~r** *n.* ①田庄里的人; 农民 ②[美] [G-]格兰其成员(即"保护农业社"社员)

granite ['grænit] *n.* ①花岗岩, 花岗石: hard as ~ 象岩石一样坚硬 / gneissic ~ [地]片麻状花岗岩 ②坚如磐石, 坚忍不拔 ‖**bite on** ~ 白费力气, 徒劳无功 ‖**granitic** [græ'nitik] *a.* 花岗岩的 ‖**Granite City** 苏格兰阿伯丁市 (Aberdeen) 的别名 / **'~ware** *n.* [总称]①有花岗石斑纹的陶器 ②涂有花岗石色珐琅的铁器

granny, grannie ['græni] *n.* [口] ①奶奶; 外婆 ②老婆婆, 老奶奶 ③婆婆妈妈的人, 唠叨挑剔的人 ④[美]接生婆 ⑤(绳子等)打错的平结 (=~ knot) ‖**teach one's** ~ (*how*) **to suck eggs** 教训长辈; 班门弄斧

grant [grɑːnt] **I** *vt.* ①同意, 准予(补助等); 授予(权利等) ②(sb.) a request 同意(某人的)请求 / ~ a sum of money for collective undertakings 批准(或拨给)一笔用于集体事业的款子 / ~ sb. permission to do sth. 准许某人做某事 ②让渡, 转让(财产等) ③假定…(正确), (姑且)承认: I ~ you. 就算你对。/ ~ the truth of what sb. says 姑且承认某人所说的是真话 / The difficulty is great, I ~, but it is by no means insuperable. 我承认困难是大的, 但决不是无法克服的。**II** *n.* ①同意, 准许; 授予; 转让; 容让 ②授给物(如补助、拨款、授地等); 转让物; 转让证书: make a ~ towards the cost of education 给以助学金 ‖**~ed** (或 **~ing**) *that* ... 假定…, 就算…: Granted *that* you've made some progress, you should not be conceited. 即使你有了一些进步, 你也不应该骄傲自大。/ **take sth. for ~ed** 认为某事当然: We must not *take* (it) *for* ~*ed that* .... 我们决不可想当然地认为… ‖**~able** *a.* 可同意的; 可授与的可转让的 ‖**'~.aided** *a.* 受补助的: ~.aided student 领取助学金的学生 / **'~-in-'aid** *n.* ①(中央给地方的)拨款 ②补助金, 助学金

granulate ['grænjuleit] ❶ *vt.* ①使成颗粒, 使成粒状: ~d fertilizer [农]颗粒肥料 / ~d sugar 砂糖 ②使(皮革等)表面成粒面, 使表面粗糙 ❷ *vi.* ①形成颗粒; 表面变粗糙 ②[医](伤口愈合时)长出肉芽 ‖**granulation** [ˌgrænju'leiʃən] *n.* ①形成颗粒; 形成粒面 ②表面粗糙 ③[医]肉芽; 肉芽形成 / **granulator** *n.* 使形成颗粒(或粒面)的人(或物); 砂糖成粒器

granule ['grænjuːl] *n.* ①颗粒, 细粒: carbon ~s 碳粒 ②粒状斑点 ③[天](日面的)米粒

grape [greip] *n.* ①葡萄; 葡萄藤: a bunch (或 cluster) of ~s 一串葡萄 ②葡萄色, 深紫色 ③[the ~]葡萄酒 ④[军]葡萄弹 ⑤[复](马脚上的)葡萄疮; (牛的)结核病 ‖**sour ~s** 酸葡萄(指把得不到的东西说成是不好的, 聊以自慰) ‖**'~fruit** *n.* 葡萄柚(热带产物) / **'~-shot** *n.* [军]葡萄弹 / **'~stone** *n.* 葡萄核, 葡萄种子 / **~ sugar** 葡萄糖 / **'~vine** *n.* ①葡萄藤 ②谣言, 传闻, 小道新闻 ③(小道新闻等的)流传; 消息的秘密来源: ~vine telegraph 秘密传递消息的途径

graph¹ [græf, grɑːf] **I** *n.* ①[数](曲线)图, 标绘图; 图表, 图形; 图解 ②(统计上的)曲线 **II** *vt.* 用图表表示; 把…绘入图表

graph² [græf, grɑːf] *n.* [语] ①词的拼法 ②独立字母以任何形式的一次出现 ③表示音素的最小字母单位(如字母 a 或字母组合 ph 等)

graph³ [græf, grɑːf] [口][印] **I** *n.* 胶版印刷 **II** *vt.* 用胶版印刷

graphic ['græfik] **I** *a.* ①图的, 图解的, 图示的: the ~ method 图解法 ②书写的, 书法的; 绘画的; 雕刻的; 印刷的: the ~ arts 书画刻印艺术 ③生动的; (轮廓)鲜明的 **II** *n.* ①书画刻印作品 ②(说明性的)图画(或地图、图表)

graphite ['græfait] *n.* [化]石墨: colloidal ~ 胶体石墨 / ~ electrode [电]石墨电极 / ~ moderated reactor [原]石墨减速反应堆

grapnel ['græpnəl] *n.* ①(四爪或五爪的)小锚 ②(用于钩住敌船等的)铁爪篙

grapple ['græpl] **I** ❶ *vt.* ①抓住, 捉牢, 握紧 ②与…扭打, 与…格斗 ③缚紧 ❷ *vi.* ①用铁锚将船只固定 ②抓住; 扭打, 格斗 (with): ~ with nature 战天斗地 / ~ with difficulties 与困难作斗争 / ~ with a problem 尽力解决问题 **II** *n.* ① = grapnel ②抓住; 扭打, 格斗: come to ~s with 和…打起来; 尽力从事(或对付)… ③[机]抓机; 抓斗 ‖**~r** *n.* ①抓钩器; 抓钩者 ②格斗者 ③[俚]手

grasp [grɑːsp] **I** ❶ *vt.* ①抓住, 抱住: ~ sb. by the wrist 抓住某人的手腕 ②掌握; 领会: ~ sb.'s meaning 懂某人的意思 ❷ *vi.* [常用单] ①抓, 紧握; 抱 ②控制 ③(对知识等的)掌握, 了解: have a profound ~ of the practical movement 对于实际运动情况有深刻了解 ④柄; (船的)锚钩: the ~ of an oar 桨柄 ‖**beyond sb.'s** ~ 为某人所抓不到的, 为某人力所不及的; 为某人所不能理解的 / **Grasp all, lose all.** [谚]样样都要, 全数失掉。(意指: 贪多必失。) / ~ **at** 向…抓去, 想抓住; 攫取: ~ at a straw 捞救命稻草 / ~ at an opportunity 抓机会 / ~ **the nettle** 迎着艰险上; 大胆抓起棘手问题 / **within sb.'s** ~ 为某人所抓得到的, 为某人力所能及的; 为某人所能理解的: Success is within our ~ now. 现在成功已经在望。‖**~able** *a.* 能理解的, 可以懂的

grasping ['grɑːspiŋ] *a.* ①抓的, 想抓住的 ②攫取的, 贪婪的 ‖**~ly** *ad.* / **~ness** *n.*

grass [grɑ:s] **I** n. ① (青)草: a blade (或 leaf) of ~ 一根草 / hardy ~ in the storm 疾风劲草 ② 【植】禾本科植物: Cereals, reeds and bamboos are all classed as ~es in botany. 谷类、芦苇、竹在植物学中都列为禾本科植物。③ 草地,牧场;放牧: cut the ~ 修轧草坪 ④[俚]芦笋,龙须菜;莴苣; (色拉中的)生菜 ⑤【矿】矿山地面,矿井地面 ⑥【无】噪音细条,(雷达屏上的)"毛草" ⑦(北美产的)大麻(一种毒品) ⑧闲居(处) **II** ❶ vt. ①使吃草,放牧 ②使长草;给…铺上草皮 ③把(织物、亚麻等)摊在草上晒白 ④把(鱼)弄上岸;把(鸟)打落地 ⑤打倒,摔倒 ❷ vi. 长草 ‖be at ~ 在放牧中; [喻]闲着(如失业、休假等) / between ~ and hay [美]处于未成年与成年之间,将近成年 / cut the ~ from under sb.'s feet 妨碍某人,挫败某人 / go to ~ ①去吃草;去放牧 ②消衰;恶化 ③死去,被埋葬: Go to ~! 去你的! 见你的鬼! ④休假 ⑤被击倒 / hear the ~ grow 特别敏锐 / hunt ~ [口]一败涂地 / keep off the ~ 不践踏草地 / 谨慎小心 / not let the ~ grow under one's feet 抓紧时间行动,不失时机 / put (或 send 或 turn out) . . . to ~ ①放牧 ②使闲居;解雇,开除 ‖~less a. 不长草的,没有草的 / ~y a. ①盖满草的,长满草的 ②像草的,青草味的 ③(动物)食草的 ‖~-blade n. (一片)草叶 / ~ character (汉语的)草字 / ~ cloth 苧麻布,夏布;草编物 / ~ cutter 割草机 / ~ green 草绿色 / '~,hopper n. 蚱蜢;蝗虫 / ~轻型单翼机 / '~land n. 牧场;草地;草原 / '~'plot n. (小块)草地 / ~ roots ① [总称]农业区(与城市和工业区相对而言) ② 基层,基层群众: ~ roots unit基层单位 ③基础,根本 ④浮面的土,地面 / ~ snake 青草蛇(无毒小蛇) / ~ widow ①离了婚(或分居)的女子;丈夫暂时离开的女子 ②被遗弃的女子;有私生子的女子 / ~ widower 离了婚(或分居)的男子;妻子暂时离开的男子 / '~work n. 【矿】坑外作业

grate[1] [greit] **I** n. ①炉栅,炉箅,炉篦 ②火炉,壁炉 ③(门、窗等的)格栅 ④【矿】篦条筛,固定筛 **II** vt. 装炉格于;装格栅于 ‖~d a. 有格栅的;有炉格的 / ~less a. 无格栅的;无炉格的

grate[2] [greit] ❶ vt. ①摩擦,磨碎,轧 ②擦响,磨(牙): ~ the teeth 磨牙,咬牙 ③使焦急;激怒;刺激 ❷ vi. ①摩擦 ②擦响;发出嘎嘎声 ③使人烦躁;触怒;刺激 (on, upon): Such expressions rather ~ on me. 这种说法对我很刺耳。‖~r n. ①摩擦者 ②擦菜板;粗齿木锉;磨光机

grateful ['greitful] a. ① 感激的,感谢的: I am very ~ to you for your help. 我非常感谢你的帮助。/ a ~ letter 表示谢意的信 ② 令人愉快的,可喜的: a ~ rain 一场喜雨 ‖~ly ad. / ~ness n.

gratification [,grætifi'keiʃən] n. ① 满足;满意;喜悦 ②使人满意的事;可喜的事 ③奖金;报酬

gratify ['grætifai] vt. ① 使满足: ~ sb.'s wishes 满足某人的愿望 ② 使满意,使高兴: be gratified with (或 at) the results 对结果感到满意 / be gratified to know . . . 知道…很高兴

gratifying ['grætifaiiŋ] a. 令人满足的;令人满意的;使人愉快的,可喜的: It is very ~ to learn that . . . . 听说…,不胜高兴。‖~ly ad.

grating[1] ['greitiŋ] n. ①(门、窗等的)格栅 ②【物】光栅: diffraction ~ 衍射光栅,绕射栅

grating[2] ['greitiŋ] **I** a. 刺耳的,刺激的: a ~ noise 刺耳的噪音 **II** n. 摩擦;摩擦声 ‖~ly ad.

gratis ['greitis] **I** ad. 免费地,无偿地: render assistance ~ 无偿地提供援助 / aid given ~ 无偿援助 **II** a. [常作表语]免费的,无偿的: Entrance is ~. 免费入场。

gratitude ['grætitju:d] n. 感激,感谢,感恩: out of ~ 出于感激 / express one's ~ to sb. for sth. 为某事对某人表示感谢

gratuitous [grə'tju(:)itəs] a. ①免费的,无偿的: service 免费服务 / a ~ contract 单方面受益的契约 ②无缘无故的,没有理由的: a ~ insult 无理的侮辱 ‖~ly ad. / ~ness n.

gratuity [grə'tju(:)iti] n. ①赏金,小帐: We don't accept gratuities. 我们不收小帐。②退职金;【军】退伍金

grave[1] [greiv] n. ①墓穴,坟墓;墓碑 ②死;阴间: not fear the ~ 不怕死 ③ (名誉等的)葬送处 ④ (储藏土豆等的)地窖 ‖have one foot in the ~ 已是风烛残年;离死不远 / his ~ turn in his ~ / secret as the ~ 守口如瓶 / silent as the ~ 象坟墓那样寂静; 没有一点声音; 一言不发 / someone walking on my ~ 有人在我坟头走动着 (无故突然噤颤时的迷信说法) ‖~less a. ① 没有坟墓的;未葬的 ② 不需坟墓的,不死的 / ~ward ad. & a. 向着坟墓的 / '~clothes [复]n. 尸衣 / '~,digger n. 掘墓人; 【动】埋葬虫 / '~stone n. 墓碑 / '~yard n. 墓地,坟场

grave[2] [greiv] (过去式 graved, 过去分词 graven 或 graved) vt. ①雕刻 ②[喻]铭刻,牢记 ‖~r n. ①雕刻工,雕刻家 ②雕刻工具,刻刀

grave[3] [greiv] **I** a. ①严重的,重大的: ~ consequences 严重的后果 / ~ news 重大消息 ②严肃的;庄重的: ~ as a judge 非常严肃 ③ 沉重的,阴沉的;(颜色)黯淡的 ④ (声音)低沉的;【语】抑音的 **II** n. 【语】抑音(=~ accent) ‖~ly ad. / ~ness n.

grave[4] [greiv] vt. 【海】清除(船底)并涂上沥青等涂料

grave ['grɑːvei] a. & ad. [意]【音】沉重,庄重;极慢

gravel ['grævəl] **I** n. ①[总称]砾,砂砾,砂石: a ~ road 砾石路 ②【矿】砂砾层(尤指含有金砂的): auriferous ~ 含金砾,金砂 / pay ~ 有开采价值的砂金 ③【医】尿砂 **II** (gravel(l)ed; gravel(l)ing) vt. ①以砾石铺(路) ②使(船)搁浅在沙滩上 ③使困惑;使窘困;惹怒,刺激: be gravel(l)ed for sth. 为某事感到为难 ④把蹄夹以石子等使(马)跛

‖**scratch** ~ [美口] ①飞跑,急奔;匆匆离开 ② 为生活奔忙 ‖~**ly** a. 充满砾石的;含有砾石的; 象砾石的;砾石铺筑的 ‖'~-**blind** a. 快瞎的,几 乎盲目的 / '~-**voiced** a. 声音粗哑的 / ~ **walk** (公园中的)砂砾小路

graven ['greivən] I grave² 的过去分词 II a. 雕刻 的; 铭记在心上的; 不可磨灭的: ~ **on** (或 *in*) sb.'s mind 被牢记在心间 ‖~ **image** 木(或 石)雕的偶像

gravitate ['græviteit] ❶ *vi.* ①受重力作用;受引 力作用,受吸引; 倾向 (*to, towards*): The earth ~s *towards* the sun. 地球受太阳吸引。②沉下, 下降 ❷ *vt.* 使受重力吸引而移动,吸引

gravitation [,græviteiʃən] n. ①【物】万有引力,地 心吸力: the law of universal ~ 万有引力定律 ② 引力作用;吸引力;倾向,趋势 ‖~**al** a.

gravity ['græviti] n. ①严肃,庄重;认真: keep one's ~ 保持严肃 ② 严重性;危险性;重要性: the ~ of the situation 情况的严重性 ③ 【物】重 力,引力;地球引力: acceleration of ~ 重力加 速度 / specific ~ 比重 ④重量: the centre of ~ 重心;重点 ⑤【音】(音调的)低沉

gravy ['greivi] n. ① 肉汁,肉卤 ② [美俚]轻松的 工作(或课程); 容易赚得的利润; 非法所得 ‖*By* ~! [美俚]哎呀! 好家伙! / *dip in the* ~ [美 俚]分肥;接公家的油 ‖~ **train** [美俚]不费劲而 赚大钱的机会;轻松的活儿

gray [grei] a., n., vt. & vi. [美] =grey ‖~ **diplomat** [美俚]"灰色外交家"(指军舰) / '~= '**flanneled** a. [美俚]广告商的; 广告业的 / **Gray Lady** [美]红十字会的义务女医士 / '~= **legs** [复] [美俚][总称]西点军官学校学员 / ~ **matter** [美俚][人脑];智力

graze¹ [greiz] I ❶ vi. 喂草;放牧;(牲畜)吃草 ❷ vt. ① 吃(田野)里的草;在田野里吃(草等) ② 用牧草喂;放牧 II n. ① 吃草;放牧: have a ~ on grass 吃一次草 ②牧草

graze² [greiz] I ❶ vt. ①擦过,掠过 ②擦伤,抓破 ❷ vi. ① 轻擦;擦伤,抓破 ② 擦破处 ③[军]瞬发

grazing ['greiziŋ] n. ①放牧;放牧法 ②牧场;牧草 ‖'~-**land** n. 畜牧场;放牧地

grease [gri:s] I n. ① 动物脂,脂肪;润滑脂(俗称 牛油); 油脂状物: axle ~ 轴用(润滑)脂 / silicon ~ 硅脂,硅润滑油 ②羊毛所含的脂;未脱 脂的原毛(或毛皮): wool in the ~ 含脂羊毛 ③ 马踵炎 ④[美俚]贿赂 ⑤[美俚]黄油 ⑥[美俚] 硝化甘油,甘油炸药 II [gri:z, gri:s] vt. ①涂油 脂于;用油脂润滑;使油污 ②使(马)患踵炎症 ③ [美俚]贿赂 ‖*fry in one's own* ~ 自作自受 / ~ *it in* [美俚]使飞机顺利着陆 / ~ *the hand* (或 *palm*) *of* ~ 买通… / ~ *the wheels* 见 **wheel** / *in* ~ (猎物)正肥,适宜于狩猎 / *in prime* (或 *pride*) *of* ~ =in ~ / *stew in one's own* ~ 自作自受 ‖'~-**box** n. (装在火车车轮 上的)润滑油箱 / '~-,**burner** n. [美俚]厨司(尤

指油煎食品的厨司) / '~**bush** n. =~wood / ~ **cup** [机]油杯,滑脂杯 / ~ **gun** ①[机]滑 脂枪,注油枪 ②[美俚]快速发射自动手枪 ③ M3 式手提机关枪 / ~ **heel** 马踵炎 / ~ **monkey** [美俚]机械工人(尤指汽车或飞机的检修工) / '~**paint** n. (演员化装用的)油彩 / '~**proof** a. 防(或抗)油脂的,不透油的 / '~**wood** n.【植】 肉叶刺荃藜;黑肉叶刺荃藜

greasy ['gri:zi, 'gri:si] a. ① 沾有油脂的,油污的; 油脂过多的;(羊毛)未脱脂的 ② 象油脂的;油腻 的;滑(腻)的;(言行等)谄媚的 ③ (马)患踵炎症 的 ④(天气等)阴湿的 ‖**greasily** ad. / **greasi- ness** n. / ~ **grind** [美俚]埋头苦读的学生 / ~ **spoon** [美俚]邋遢的小饭馆

great [greit] I a. ① 伟大的;大的 ②(极)重大的; 超乎寻常的;强烈的: a ~ occasion 盛大的场合 / a handicraft product of ~ beauty 非常优美的 工艺品 / in ~ detail 极详细地 / ~ pain 剧烈 的疼痛 ③(数量)极大的;(时间)久的: a ~ number of people 许多人 / a ~ while ago 好久 以前 / live to a ~ age 活到很大年纪 ④[用在 名词前面]十足的,名副其实的: a ~ elf 十足的 小淘气 / a ~ reader 酷爱看书的人 / They are ~ friends. 他们是真正的好朋友。⑤[口][用在 其他形容词前面]多么…: What a ~ big cabbage! 好大的一棵大白菜! ⑥ [口] 美妙的: That's ~! 好极了! / Wouldn't it be ~ if we could go there! 要是我们能到那儿去多好啊! ⑦崇高的; 显贵的 ⑧(字母)大写的 ⑨(用在由 grand 构成 的表示亲属关系的复合词前, 表示更远一辈的亲 属关系)曾祖(或孙);外曾祖(或孙): a ~- grandfather 曾祖;外曾祖 / a ~-granddaughter 曾孙女;外曾孙女 ‖*the Great Bear* 【天】大熊座 / *Great Britain* 大不列颠 / *the* ~ *cats* 狮(或虎、豹 等) / *the Great Charter* 【英史】大宪章 / *the Great Day* (或 *Assize, Inquest*)【宗】世界末日大 审判 / ~*est common divisor*【数】最大公约数 / a ~ *family* 名门 / *the Great Wall* 长城 / *the Great War* 第一次世界大战 / *the Great White Way* 不夜街(纽约百老汇大街的别院区) / *the* ~ *world* 上流社会 II ad. [口]很好地,成功地: Things are going ~. 事情进展顺利。III n. ① 全部,整体 ② [the ~(s)] 大人物们; 伟大 的事物 ③ [美俚](文艺、体育等方面的)大师,名 家 ④[复][英俚]牛津大学文学士学位考试 ‖a ~ *deal* 见 **deal**¹ / a ~ *many* 见 **many** / ~ *and small* 大人物们和小人物们 / ~ *at* [口]精 于…的,…熟练的: He's ~ at swimming. 他游 泳游得很好。/ *Great God* (或 *Caesar, Scott*)! 天哪! 啊呀! / ~ *on* [口] ①很熟悉…的: The speaker is ~ on international affairs. 做报告 的人对国际事务非常熟悉。②热中于…的 / ~ *with* ① 为(某种感情)所激动的: ~ *with* anger 怒火 ② [英][古]怀孕的: ~ *with* child 怀孕 / *the* ~ *go* [英俚]剑桥大学文学士学位考试 ‖~- **en** vt. 使更伟大(或重大) vi. 变得更加伟大

(或重大) / **~ly** *ad.* ①大大地，非常: **~ly esteemed** 极受尊敬的 ②崇高地 / **~ness** *n.* ‖'~-'**aunt** *n.* =grandaunt / **~ calorie** (热量单位)大卡 / **~ circle** (球面或地球面上通过球心的平面切成的)大圆，大圈 / '~'**coat** *n.* 厚大衣 / **~ divide** ①大分水岭: the *Great Divide* 落基山脉(北美洲主要河流的分水岭) ②(截然相反的两者之间的)分界线: cross the *divide* 死 / **~'hearted** *a.* 慷慨的；不自私的；勇敢的 / **~ hundred** [英] 一百二十 / '~'**nephew** *n.* =grandnephew / '~'**niece** *n.* =grandniece / **~ power** 强国，大国 / '~-'**power** *a.* 强国的，大国的 / **~ pox** [美俚] 梅毒 / **~ primer** [印] 18 点活字 / **~ seal** 国玺: the *Great Seal* 英国的国玺大臣 / '~-'**uncle** *n.* =granduncle

greed [griːd] *n.* 贪心，贪婪 (*for*)

greedy ['griːdi] *a.* ①贪吃的，嘴馋的 ②贪婪的: be ~ of (或 for) gain 贪得无厌 / This typewriter is too ~ on desk space. 这架打字机在书桌上占去的地方太多。③渴望的；(兴趣等)强烈的: be ~ for knowledge 渴求知识 / be ~ to do sth. 急切要做某事 / with ~ interest 以强烈的兴趣 ‖**greedily** *ad.* / **greediness** *n.*

green [griːn] **I** *a.* ①绿的，青的: ~ manure 绿肥 ②青葱的；温暖的，无雪的；妩媚的: ~ hills 青山 / a ~ December 温暖无雪的十二月 ③新鲜的；新近的；(伤口)未愈合的: a young man ~ from school 刚出学校的小伙子 ④精力旺盛的；青春的: remain for ever ~ like the pine tree 永远象松树一样青葱茁壮 / a ~ old age 老当益壮 ⑤未熟的；生的，嫩的: a ~ apple 未熟的苹果 / ~ corn 嫩玉米 ⑥无经验的；没有受过训练的；幼稚的；易受欺骗的: He is still ~ at this job. 他对这件工作还是生疏的。⑦未干的；未经处理过的；尚未能用的；(酒)不陈的；(鱼)未到排卵期的；(蟹等)未到蜕壳期的: ~ timber 没干的木材 / ~ hides 未经处理过的皮革 ⑧(脸色等)发青的；苍白的；[喻]妒忌的: be scared ~ 吓得脸色发青 **II** *n.* ①绿色，青色 ②绿色颜料，绿色染料 ③绿色的东西(尤指衣、布等): be dressed in ~ 穿着绿色衣服 ④[复](装饰用的)青枝，绿叶 ⑤蔬菜；植物 ⑥青春，生气: in the ~ 在青春时期 ⑦(公共)草地；草坪 ⑧[美俚]纸币: long (或 folding) ~ 纸币 **III** ❶ *vt.* ①使变绿；把…染成绿色 ②[俚]耍弄；哄骗 ❷ *vi.* 变成绿色 ‖*Do you see any* (或 *anything*) ~ *in my eye?* 你以为我幼稚可欺吗? / ~ *as grass* 幼稚；无经验 / *with envy* 十分妒忌 / *in the* ~ *tree* (或 *wood*) 处于佳境 ‖**~ly** *ad.* / **~ness** *n.* ‖'~**back** *n.* 美钞 / '~**belt** *n.* 绿化地带 / '~-'**blind** *a.* 绿色盲 / **~ book** (英、意等国政府的)绿皮书 / **~ cross** [军]窒息剂(绿十字毒气) / **~ drake** [动]蜉蝣 / '~-'**eyed** *a.* ①绿眼睛的 ②妒忌的 / '~**finch** *n.* [动](欧洲产的)绿黄色雀科鸣鸟 / **~ fingers** [英口]园艺技能 / '~**fly** *n.* [动](绿色)蚜虫 / '~**gage** *n.* 【植】青梅子，青李子 /

'~**grocer** *n.* [主英]蔬菜水果商 / '~**grocery** *n.* [主英] ①蔬菜水果商店 ②[总称]蔬菜水果类商品 / **~ hand** ①生手；没有经验的人 ②[方]园艺技能 / '~**heart** *n.* 【植】产于热带美洲的心材硬木 / '~**horn** *n.* ①生手；没有经验的人 ②[口]新到的移民 / '~**house** *n.* ①玻璃暖房，温室 ②[军俚]周围有玻璃的座舱；轰炸员舱 / **~ light** ①绿(色交通信号)灯 ②许可；准许: give the ~ *light* to sb. 给某人开绿灯，纵容某人 / **~ line** [军]轰炸线；敌我分界线 / **~ peak** 【动】绿色啄木鸟 / **~ power** [美]金钱的力量 / **~ room** *n.* 演员休息室 / **~ sand** ①[地]海绿石砂 ②(铸造用的)湿砂；新取砂 / '~**shank** *n.* 【动】青足鹬 / '~**sick** *a.* 【医】患萎黄病的；【植】患缺绿病的 / '~**sickness** *n.* 【医】萎黄病，绿色贫血；【植】缺绿病 / '~**stick** *n.* 【医】旁弯骨折 / ~ **stone** [地]绿岩；软玉 / '~**stuff** *n.* 蔬菜；草木 / '~**sward** *n.* 草地；草皮 / '~**tail** *n.* 【动】步鱼 / **~ tea** 绿茶 / **~ thumb** 园艺技能 / **~ vitriol** 【化】绿矾 / '~**weed** *n.* 【植】染料木 / '~**wood** *n.* 绿林；生材: go to the ~*wood* 落草；去当绿林好汉

greenery ['griːnəri] *n.* ① 草木；[总称]绿叶；(装饰用的)青枝绿叶；葱翠 ②暖房

greenish ['griːniʃ] *a.* 略呈绿色的

greet[1] [griːt] *vt.* ① 迎接，欢迎；向…致敬，向…致意: ~ the new year with greater achievements 以更大的成就迎接新年 ② 被(耳、鼻、眼)觉察；呈现在(某人)前: Music ~s the ear. 乐声为耳。/ A beautiful view ~ed us. 美景呈现在我们面前。

greet[2] [griːt] (grat [græt], grutten ['grʌtn]) *vi.* [苏格兰]哭泣，悲泣

greeting ['griːtiŋ] *n.* 问候；致敬；祝贺；贺辞；欢迎辞: offer ~s to sb. 向某人致意 / extend fraternal ~s to sb. 向某人致以兄弟般的敬礼

gregarious [gre'gɛəriəs] *a.* ① 群集的；群居的 ②爱群居的；爱交际的 ③【植】聚生的 ‖**~ly** *ad.* / **~ness** *n.*

grenade [gri'neid] *n.* ①[军]手榴弹，枪榴弹: throw a ~ at 向…投手榴弹 / a ~ discharger 掷弹筒 / a tear gas ~ 催泪性毒气手榴弹 ②灭火弹

grew [gruː] grow 的过去式

grey [grei] **I** *a.* ①灰色的；灰白的: He has ~ hair. 他头发灰白。/ ~ hairs [喻]老人 ②灰暗的；阴暗的；阴郁的: a ~ day 阴天 / ~ prospects 暗淡的前景 ③灰白头发的；老的；老练的，成熟的: He is growing ~. 他头发灰白起来了。/ ~ experience 老练 ④ 古代的，太古的 ⑤(某些教派的教士)穿灰色衣服的: a ~ friar (sister) 方济各会 (Franciscan) 的修道士(修女) ⑥半黑市的: the ~ market 半黑市 **II** *n.* ①灰色；灰淡(光): the ~ of the morning 黎明前的灰白色 ②灰色颜料；灰色衣服；灰色动物(尤指马): be dressed in ~ 穿着灰色衣服 ③未经漂白的

态;坯布,本色布 (=~ cloth): in the ~ (布)未
经漂白 III vt. & vi. (使)变成灰色 ‖~ish a.
淡灰色的 / ~ly ad. / ~ness n. ‖'~back n.
灰色的动物(如灰鲸、斑背潜鸭、雪鲦等) /
'~beard n. ①(白胡子)老人 ②石制大酒壶 ③
[英]一种地衣,本色布 / ~ cloth 坯布,本色布 / '~coat
n. [英] ① 穿灰色衣服的人 ②(英国)昆布兰郡
的义勇骑兵 / ~ collar 灰领工职工(指服务性行
业职工) / '~fish n. 【动】绿鳕;星鲨 / ~ goose
【动】灰雁 / '~-'headed a. ①灰白头发的;老的
②长期服务于…的 (in) ③古老的,陈旧的 / ~
hen 【动】雌黑松鸡 / ~hound n. ①灵猩(一种
身体细长、善于赛跑的狗) / ~hound racing 跑狗
(一种赌博) ②远洋快轮 / '~lag n. =~ goose /
~ mare 比丈夫强的妻子,雌老虎 / ~ matter
【医】(脑的)灰白质; [俚]人脑;智力 / ~ mullet
【动】鲻鱼 / '~wacke n.【地】杂砂岩,硬砂岩
grid [grid] n. ①格子,格网 ②【电】蓄电池的铅板
③【无】栅极: ~ bias 栅偏压 / ~ current 栅流 /
~ leak 栅漏 ④ 地图的坐标方格 ⑤(电力、铁路
的)网 ⑥(烘烤面包等用的)铁笸子
griddle ['gridl] I n. ① (烘烤糕饼等用的)铁盘
②【矿】筛子,大孔筛 II vt. ① 用铁盘烘(或烤)
②筛 ‖~ cake 烙饼,烤饼 / '~-'hot a. 刚出笼
的;刚做成的
grief [gri:f] n. ①悲痛,悲伤: turn ~ into strength
化悲痛为力量 ② 不幸;灾难;伤心事: bring sb.
to ~ 使某人遭受不幸,使某人遭难;使某人失败 /
come to ~ 遭到不幸;遭难;失败 / smile at ~
不过度悲伤
grievance ['gri:vəns] n. ①不满,不平: have a ~
against sb. 抱怨某人 / nurse a ~ 心怀不满
②冤情;苦情: pour out one's ~s against the old
social order 诉旧社会的苦
grieve[1] [gri:v] ❶ vt. 使悲痛,使伤心: be deeply
~d by sth. 因某事而感到非常悲痛 ❷ vi. 悲痛,
伤心; 哀悼 (at, about, for, over): ~ over sb.'s
death 哀悼某人的去世
grieve[2] [gri:v] n. [方]农场管理者,监工
grievous ['gri:vəs] a. ①令人悲痛的,使人伤心的:
~ news 噩耗 ② 表示悲痛的: a ~ cry 痛哭
③ 难忍受的;剧烈的,严重的: ~ pain 剧痛 / a
~ fault 严重的错误 ④(罪恶等)极大的,惨无人
道的: a ~ crime 大罪 ‖~ly ad.
griffin[1] ['grifin] n. ①(印度用英语)新到的白人;
新手,未经世故的人 ②[美] =griffe[1]
griffin[2] ['grifin] n.【希神】鹰头狮身带有翅膀的怪
兽(有时用于纹章)
grill[1] [gril] I n. ① (炙烤肉等用的)烤架,铁笸子
② 炙烤的肉类食物: mixed ~ 炙什锦 ③ =
~room II vt. ①在烤架上炙烤 ②加酷热于;
用酷热对…行刑 ③炙烤般地拷问 ❷ vi. ①在
烤架上炙烤 ②受酷热 ③严厉盘问 ‖'~room n. 专营炙烤肉食的饭店(或餐室)
grill[2] [gril] n. =grille
grille [gril] n. ①格栅,铁格子 ②【建】铁花格;格

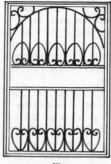

grille

子窗;(邮局或银行等)柜台上的铁栅 ③(养鱼的)
孵卵器
grim [grim] (grimmer, grimmest) a. ① 严厉的,
冷酷无情的,残忍的: a ~ struggle 你死我活的
斗争 ② 坚强的,不屈的: ~ courage 坚韧不拔的
勇气 ③ 讨厌的,可憎的;可怖的: a ~ smile
(或 laugh) 狞笑 ④不祥的,邪恶的 ‖~ly ad. /
~ness n.
grimace [gri'meis] I n. (表示痛苦、厌恶、不以为
然、自鸣得意等的)怪相,鬼脸: make ~s 作怪相
II vi. 作怪相,装鬼脸 ‖~r n. 作怪相的人
grime [graim] I n. 尘垢,烟灰;污垢(尤指皮肤等
表面上的积垢) II vt. 使肮脏;使积垢
grin [grin] I (grinned; grinning) ❶ vi. ①露齿而
笑: ~ with delight 高兴地咧开嘴笑 ②(因痛
苦)咧嘴;(因愤恨)龇牙咧嘴 ❷ vt. 露齿笑着表
示: ~ one's approval 以一笑表示同意 II n. ①
(表示愤怒、痛苦、轻蔑等的)咧嘴 ②露齿的笑:on
the broad ~ 露齿而笑,笑嘻嘻 / ~ and bear it
默默忍受,逆来顺受 ‖grinner n. 露齿而笑的
人;龇牙咧嘴的人 / grinningly ad. 露齿而笑
地;龇牙咧嘴地
grind [graind] I (ground [graund]) ❶ vt. ①磨
(碎);碾(碎): ~ sth. into dust 把某物磨得粉碎
②磨快;磨光;磨薄;磨成…形: ~ a lens 磨镜片 /
~ a knife 磨刀 / ~ balls for bearings 磨轴承
滚珠 ③(用手摇风琴)奏出;苦苦地写出 ④推,摇
(石磨等);摇奏(手摇风琴) ⑤嘎嘎出声地挤压;
咬(牙) ⑥折磨;压榨(出) ⑦苦苦教授,灌输:
~ sb. in mathematics 使某人苦学数学 / ~
Latin into sb.'s head 费很大劲教某人拉丁文 ❷
vi. ①磨,碾;磨碎;磨光;磨快: This wheat ~s
well. 这种麦子很好磨。 ②摩擦得嘎嘎响: The
truck ground to a stop. 卡车嘎的一声刹住。 ③
苦学;苦干: ~ away at one's studies 苦学不倦
④(跳黄色舞蹈时)扭摆 II n. ①磨;摩擦声;磨细
的程度 ②苦差使;枯燥乏味的活;专心的学习 ③
[美]埋头读书的人,书呆子 ④[英]步行锻炼;越
野障碍赛马(或赛跑) ⑤(黄色舞蹈中的)扭摆 ‖a

greasy ~ [美俚]埋头苦读的学生 / **~ out** 苦心用功地做出 / **~ the faces of the poor** 压榨贫民 / **have an ax(e) to ~** 见 **ax(e)** / **the daily ~** [口]日常工作

grinder ['graində] *n.* ①磨工: a knife ~ 磨刀工人 ②研磨机; 磨床: a high-precision ~ 高精度磨床 ③上磨扇 ④臼齿; [复][美口]牙齿 ⑤[美方]夹心面包

grindstone ['graindstoun] *n.* ①磨石 ②【机】砂轮 ‖**keep one's (sb.'s) nose to the ~** 见 **nose**

grip¹ [grip] **I** *n.* ①紧握; 紧咬; 紧夹· ②握力; 握法; (秘密社团人员之间)作为暗号的一种握手: a penholder ~ player 直握板乒乓运动员 / a tennis ~ player 横握板乒乓运动员 ③掌握; 支配; 控制: have a good ~ on an audience 很能吸引住观众 / lose ~ of an audience 失去对观众的吸引 ④理解(力): have a sound (feeble) ~ of a problem 对问题有较深(肤浅)的理解 ⑤【机】柄, 夹: vice ~ 虎钳夹口 / cable ~ 电缆扣 ⑥[美]手提包, 旅行包 ⑦突然的剧痛 ⑧[美俚](电影摄影棚中)管理道具(或灯光等)的工作人员 **II** (gripped 或[古] gript; gripping) ❶ *vt.* ①握(或咬, 夹)牢 ②掌握; 支配; 控制; 抓住(注意力等) ③把(某物)接牢 (to) ④(秘密社团人员之间作为暗号)与(某人)握手 ❷ *vi.* 握(或咬, 夹)得牢: The brake doesn't ~ properly. 刹车不灵。 ‖**be at ~s** 博斗; 勉力对付 (with) / **come** (或 **get**) **to ~s** 博斗起来; 开始勉力对付 (with): come to ~s with a problem 千方百计解决问题 ‖**gripper** *n.* ①握者 ②夹子;【机】抓器, 抓爪 / **gripping** *a.* ①抓的; 夹的: gripping device 【机】夹具; 固定器 ②扣人心弦的: a gripping story 扣人心弦的故事 ‖**~ brake** 手刹车 / **'~sack** *n.* [美]手提包, 旅行包

grip² [grip] *n.* =grippe

grip³ [grip] *n.* [英]小阳沟

gripe [graip] **I** ❶ *vt.* ①握紧; 抓住 ②使苦恼; 压抑; 折磨 ③[美俚]惹烦, 激怒 ④使肠痛 ❷ *vi.* ①肠痛 ②[美俚]诉苦; 抱怨; 发牢骚 ③[古]抓牢 ④[海](帆船)有顶风的倾向 **II** *n.* ①紧握; 抓牢 ②控制, 掌握: in the ~ of 在…的控制下 ③苦恼; 压抑 ④[复][口]腹绞痛, 肠绞痛: have the ~s 闹肚子痛 ⑤抱怨; 牢骚 ⑥柄, 把手 ⑦【机】制动器 ⑧[船]船首添材; [复](把救生艇系于支架的)绊带

grisly ['grizli] *a.* 可怖的, 吓人的

grist [grist] *n.* ①制粉用谷物; 磨碎的谷物; 酿造用的压碎的麦芽 ②[美口]大量, 许多 ③有利的东西 ‖**All is ~ that comes to his mill.** 到他磨里都成粉。(意指: 他能利用一切机会。) / **bring ~ to the mill** 生利, 使有利可图 ‖**'~mill** *n.* 磨坊

gristle ['grisl] *n.* 软骨 ‖**in the ~** 未长成的, 未成熟的 ‖**gristly** *a.* 软骨的; 软骨般的

grit [grit] **I** *n.* ①粗砂, 砂砾; 磨料; (妨害机器运转的)砂粒, 硬渣 ②粗砂岩 ③磨刀石的石质:

hone of good ~ 优质磨石 ④ [~s][用作单或复]去壳谷类; 经去壳但未碾制的粗燕麦粉 ⑤坚忍, 刚毅, 勇气 **II** (gritted; gritting) ❶ *vi.* 摩擦作声 ❷ *vt.* ①在…上铺(或撒)砂砾; 用磨料磨(大理石) ②摩擦, 摩擦(牙齿等)作声; 愤怒(或坚决)地咬(牙): ~ the teeth 咬牙 ‖**hit the ~** [美俚]走路, 跋涉 / **put ~ in the machine** 使事情发生障碍, 阻挠计划的实现 ‖**~stone** *n.* 粗砂岩

gritty ['griti] *a.* ①有砂的; 砂砾般的 ②勇敢的; 坚韧不拔的 ‖**grittiness** *n.*

grizzle¹ ['grizl] **I** *n.* ①灰白头发; 灰色假发 ②灰色; 有灰白花斑的色调 ③灰色(或有灰白花斑的)图案(或动物) ④含硫次焦 ⑤烧得不透的砖, 灰色次砖 **II** *vt.* & *vi.* (使)成灰色 **III** *a.* 灰色的 ‖**~d** *a.* ①灰色的; 灰白的; 有灰斑的 ②灰白头发的

grizzle² ['grizl] *vi.* [英]①焦虑, 烦躁; 抱怨 ②[口](小孩)号哭; 啜泣

grizzly ['grizli] **I** *a.* 灰色的; 灰白的; 有灰斑的 **II** *n.* ①(北美产的)灰熊 (=~ bear) ②【矿】格筛

groan [groun] **I** ❶ *vi.* ①哼, 呻吟, 发呻吟声 ②渴望 (for) ③受压迫, 受虐待 (beneath, under) 承受重压而作声: The shelf ~s with books. 架上堆满了书而嘎吱作声。 / a ~ing board 摆满菜肴的桌子 ❷ *vt.* ①呻吟着(out): ~ out a reply 呻吟着做答复 ②发哼声阻止…讲话 (down) **II** *n.* 呻吟; 呻吟声; 哼声 ‖**~ingly** *ad.*

grocer ['grouse] *n.* 食品商; 杂货商

grocery ['grouseri] *n.* ①[美用复, 英常用单]食品; 杂货 ②[美]食品杂货店 ③食品杂货业

grog [grog] **I** *n.* ①掺水烈酒(酒精和水的混合物) ②(饮掺水烈酒的)饮酒会 ③【冶】(制坩锅等用的)耐火材料, 熟料, 陶渣: ~ brick 耐火砖 **II** (grogged; grogging) ❶ *vi.* 饮掺水烈酒 ❷ *vt.* 用热水从(空酒桶)中浸出一点酒 ‖**groggery** *n.* 小酒馆, 酒店 / **groggy** *a.* ①喝醉酒的 ②头晕眼花的; 脚步踉跄的 ‖**~ blossom** (因饮酒过多形成的)鼻赘疣

groin [groin] **I** *n.* ①【解】腹股沟 ②【建】交叉拱穿棱, 拱肋 **II** *vt.* 使成穿棱, 盖拱肋于

groom [grum] **I** *n.* ①马夫 ②新郎 ③英国宫廷的侍从官 ④[古]男仆; 男人, 家伙 **II** ❶ *vt.* ①饲养(马等); 豢养 ②使整洁, 修饰: be badly (well) ~ed 修饰得不好(好) ③准备, 推荐 ❷ *vi.* 修饰 ‖**~sman** ['grumzmən] *n.* 陪伴新郎者, 男傧相

groove [gru:v] **I** *n.* ①槽, 沟; (车)辙; (录音带、唱片等的)纹(道);【解】(器官、骨的)沟;【印】(铅字尾端的)槽;【建】企口: oil ~【机】(润滑)油槽 nail ~【解】甲沟 ②常规, 习惯: get (或 fall) into a ~ 成习惯, 开始习惯于老一套 ③适合能力和兴趣的职位, 适当的位置 ④最佳状态; 得心应手的状态 **II** *vt.* 开槽于; 做企口于 ‖**in the ~** ①处于最佳状态; 得心应手 ②(歌曲等)流行的 ‖**~r** *n.* 挖槽器; 挖槽工具, 挖槽机

grope [group] I ❶ *vi.* ①(暗中)摸索 ②探索 (*for, after*): ~ about *for* information 到处搜集 情报 ❷ *vt.* 摸索: ~ one's way 摸索着走 II *n.* 摸索 ‖*gropingly ad.* (暗中)摸索着

gross [grous] I *a.* ①总的; 毛的: ~ industrial output value 工业总产值 / ~ national product 国民生产总值 / ~ sales 销售总额 / ~ weight 毛重 / ~ profit 毛利 ②显著的, 十足的; 严重的; 恶劣的: a ~ bookworm 十足的书呆子 / a ~ error 严重错误 ③(语言、举止)粗俗的, 粗野的, 下流的: ~ language 粗俗的话 ④(食物)粗的, 油腻的; 喜欢吃粗(或油腻)食物的 ⑤(感觉)迟钝 的 ⑥(人、身体)臃肿的, 粗壮的 ⑦世俗的, 肉体的 ⑧(不用显微镜)肉眼能够看到的 ⑨稠厚的; 浓密 的; 茂盛的: a ~ fog 浓雾 / ~ vegetation 茂盛 的草木 II *n.* ①总额; 大体 ②[单复同][商]罗 (=12 打): a great ~ 十二罗 III *vt.* [口](在扣 除费用等之前)计得(若干数额) ‖*in (the)* ~ ① 逐批的; 大量的 ②大体上, 总的说来 ‖*~ly ad.* / *~ness n.* ‖*~ feeder* ①滥吃的人 ②大量耗用 肥料的植物 / *~ ton* 长吨 (=long ton)

grotesque [grou'tesk] I *a.* ①奇形怪状的, 奇异 的; 怪诞的, 荒唐的 ②(绘画或雕刻)风格奇异的 II *n.* ①奇形怪状的人(或物、图形等) ②(绘画 或雕刻上的)奇异风格(指将人、动物、植物的图案 奇怪地凑在一起); 风格奇异的作品 ③[英][印] 哥特体字, 粗黑体字 ‖*~ly ad.* / *~ness n.*

ground[1] [graund] I *n.* ①地, 地面: a high ~ 高 地 / Hit the ~! 【军】卧倒! / ~ troops 地面部 队 ②土地; 地产, 田产: till the ~ 种地 ③场所, …场: a parade ~ 练兵场, 阅兵场 / fishing ~s 渔场 / grazing ~s 牧场 / a football ~ 足球 场 / a parking ~ 停车场 / weapons testing (或 proving) ~s 武器试验场 / [复](附属于厂房、 校舍等周围的)场地; 庭园: in the well-kept factory ~s 在整洁的工厂场地上 ⑤(问题所涉及 的)范围, 领域; 研究的科目, 话题: dare to tread on the surgical "forbidden ~" 敢闯外科"禁区" ⑥底色; (绘画等的)底色, 底子 / ~ fertilizer [农] 基肥 / prepare the ~ *for* sth. 为某事准备条 件 / golden characters on a red ~ 红底金字 ⑦ 阵地 ⑧[常用复]根据, 理由, 原因: There is no ~ *for* anxiety. 不必担心。/ I have much (或 many ~s) *for* believing the information. 我有充分根据相信这个消息。⑨底, 海底 ⑩【电】 接地 (=earth); 地线 ⑪[复]渣滓; 沉淀物: coffee ~s 咖啡渣 ⑫(蚀刻)涂在版面上的防蚀剂 ⑬ 【矿】脉石 II ❶ *vt.* ①把…放在地上; 使落地 ②【海】使搁浅; 使触海底 ③使停飞 ④把 …建立在牢固的基础上; 把(论点等)基于(on): ~ one's conclusions *on* 根据… / His ar- guments are well (ill) ~ed (*in* facts). 他的说法 (事实)根据充(不)足。⑤给…以基础训练: ~ the trainees *in* shooting 给学员进行射击基础训练 / be well ~ed in English 在英语方面受过良好的 基础训练 ⑥给(画面等)上底色 ⑦【电】使接地 ❷ *vi.* ①具有基础; 依靠 (*on, upon*) ②落地;

着陆 ③(船)搁浅; 登滩 ‖*above* ~ 在世 / *be dashed to the* ~ (希望、计划等)破灭 / *below* ~ 死了, 埋葬了 / *bite the* ~ 倒下死去; 大败 / *break fresh* (或 *new*) ~ 开垦处女地; 开辟新天 地; 开始新的工作 / *break* ~ ①破土, 动工; 创 办: break ~ *for* a new exhibition hall 动工建造 一座新的展览馆 ②犁田 ③【海】起锚; (锚)被起 / *classic* ~ 文艺胜地 / *common* ~ 一致点, 共同 点: seek *common* ~ on major questions and preserve differences on minor ones 求大同, 存小 异 / *cover* (*the*) ~ ①很快地穿过(或横过、通过、 跑过)一段路; 旅行: The bulldozer *covered* the ~ well. 这台推土机工作效率不错。(指开得很 快) / We have *covered* a great deal of ~ today. 我们今天走了不少路。②(尤指彻底而有效地)处 理一个题目, 完成一项作业 ③包含, 涉及: The research *covered* much ~. 这项研究涉及面很 广。/ *cut the* ~ *from under sb.'s feet* 使某 人论点站不住脚; 使某人失利 / (*down*) *to the* ~ [口]在一切方面; 彻底地: This arrangement suits us (*down*) *to the* ~. 这个安排对我们很适 合。/ *fall to the* ~ ①坠地 ②(计划)失败; (希 望)落空 / *from the* ~ *up* 从头开始: learn sth. *from the* ~ *up* 从头开始学某事 ②彻底 / *gain* ~ ①进展; 发展, 壮大: The patient *gained* ~ daily. 病人健康日益恢复。②普及: Acu- puncture anaesthesia is rapidly *gaining* ~ in surgical operations. 针刺麻醉正在外科手术上得 到广泛使用。/ *gain* ~ *on* (或 *upon*) 逼近, 接近 (追赶或追寻之人或物) / *get off the* ~ ①飞起 ②进行顺利 ③(报刊等)开始发行: a newspaper just *getting off the* ~ 刚发行的报纸 ④(使)开 始 / *give* (或 *lose*) ~ ①退却; 让步 ②失利; 衰 落 / *hold* (或 *keep, maintain, stand*) *one's* ~ ①坚守阵地 ②坚持立场(或论点、要求等) / *kiss the* ~ ①俯伏在地 ②屈辱 / *mop* (或 *wipe*) *the* ~ *with sb.* [俚]击倒某人, 把某人打得大败 / *on delicate* ~ 处境微妙 / *on firm* ~ 处于安全地 位 / *on one's own* ~ 在自己熟悉的领域里; 在 行 / *on the* ~ ①在地上 ②当场; 在手边 ③在 决斗中 / *on the* ~ *of* 以…为理由; 以…为借口 / (*the*) ~*s of* (=on the ~ of / *raze to the* ~ 把 …夷为平地 / *run into the* ~ 把…做过头; 把 …弄糟: Caution is necessary in this work, but don't *run it into the* ~. 这工作需要谨慎, 但也 不要太过分了。/ *shift one's* ~ 改变立场(或主 张等) / *smell the* ~ (船)因水浅而失速; 【海】擦 底过 / *take the* ~ 搁浅; 登滩 / *to* ~ 入洞穴; 躲 起来 / *touch* ~ (船等)碰到水底; (空谈后)触 到实质性的问题 / *worship the* ~ *sb. treads on* 十分钦慕某人, 拜倒在某人脚下 ‖'*-'air a.* 陆空的: ~*-air* communication 陆空通讯联络 / ~ **alert** 【空】地面待机 / ~ **ash** 【植】白蜡树幼 树; 白蜡树手杖 / ~ **bait** 引鱼用的水底诱饵 / **bass** 【音】基础低音 / ~ **box** 【植】矮脚黄杨(常 用作篱围) / ~ **control** 【空】地面控制(站); 地面 制导设备: ~ *control* approach 地面控制进场 /

~ **cover**【植】① 地被; 地被植物的种植; 地被植物 ②(森林中幼树以外的)矮小植物 / ~ **crew** [总称]【空】地勤人员 / ~ **fire** 地面(对空)火力 / '~**fish** *n.* 底栖鱼类 / ~ **floor** ①［英］(楼房的)底层(=［美］first floor) ②有利地位; 优先机会: get in on the ~ *floor* 以享有与发起人同样优先权的资格入股; 取得有利地位 / ~ **game** [总称]地面猎物(如野兔等) / ~ **gripper** [美俚]地勤人员 / ~ **hog**【动】美国土拨鼠 / ~*hog day* [美] 二月二日圣烛节 (传说土拨鼠于该日结束冬眠出洞, 如天晴见到自己影子, 即退入洞中继续冬眠) / ~ **ivy**【植】欧亚活血丹 / ~ **level** ①地平面 ② =~ state / ~ **link-up**【军】空降部队与地面部队的会合 / ~ **loop**【空】地转(飞机滑行时因失去控制而引起的猛烈旋转) / ~ **mine** 海底水雷 / ~ **net** 曳网, 拖网 / ~ **note**【音】基音, 基础低音 / '~**nut** *n.*【植】①有可食块茎的植物(如北美野豆) ② 可食块茎 ③ 落花生 / ~ **observer**【军】地面观察员; 对空监视哨 / ~ **pea** 落花生 / ~ **pine**【植】扁叶石松; 石松 / ~ **plan** 大体方案; 【建】平面图; 底层平面图 / ~ **plane** (透视画中的)地平面 / ~ **plate**【电】接地板 / '~**rent** *n.* 地租 / ~ **return**【电】地回路; 地面反射 / ~ **rule** 程序 / ~ **sea** (飓风和地震引起的)海啸 / '~**sheet** *n.* 铺在地上的防潮布 / ~(**s**)**man** ['graund(z)mən] *n.* 球场管理员 / **speed** 地速 (按地面距离算出的飞机速度) / **staff** = ~ crew ②(板球俱乐部的)全体职业板球运动员 / ~ **state**【原】基态 / ~ **swell** = ~ sea ②【地】地隆 / ~ **tackle**【海】锚泊装置 / '~**-to-**'**air** *ad. & a.* 地对空: a ~*-to-air* missile 地对空导弹 / '~**-to-**'~ *ad. & a.* 地对地 / ~ **torpedo** 海底水雷 / ~,**water** *n.* 地下水 / ~ **wave**【电】地波 / ~ **wire**【电】地线 / '~**work** *n.* 基础; 基本成分 / ~ **zero**【军】(核)爆心投影点

ground² [graund] **I** grind 的过去式和过去分词 **II** *a.* 磨过的, 磨碎的: ~ glass 毛玻璃; 玻璃粉 / ~ rice 米粉

grounding ['graundiŋ] *n.* ①基础训练: a good ~ *in* pronunciation 良好的基础发音训练 ②【纺】(染色)打底

groundless ['graundlis] *a.* 无根据的, 无理由的 ||~**ly** *ad.* / ~**ness** *n.*

group [gru:p] **I** *n.* ①群, 批, 簇 ②(小)组, 团体: hold ~ discussions 分组讨论 / the small ~ mentality 小团体主义 ③【化】基, 团; 组; (周期表的)属, 族 ④【地】界 ⑤(英、美的)空军大队 ⑥群像(指雕塑): a ~ wood carving 群像木雕 **II** ❶ *vt.* ①把…分组(或分类); 聚集: The data can be ~ed under three heads. 这些资料可以分为三大类。/ Factories are ~ed in the south of the city. 工厂都集中在城市的南部。②把… 安排成和谐的构图: ~ the children for a photograph 把孩子们排好拍照 ❷ *vi.* ①聚集; 类同 (*with*): ~ *about* (或 *round*) 围在…的周围 ②组

合起来形成和谐的构图 ||a *ginger* ~ [英](议会中)促使政府采取更积极行动的一群议员; (政党内部)起推动作用的的骨干小组 / ~ *by* ~ 分批地: enter the exhibition hall ~ *by* ~ 分批进入展览会大厅 ||~**let** ['gru:plit] *n.* [美]小群 / ~**ment** *n.*【军】炮兵临时编组 || ~ **captain** (英)空军上校 / ~ **commander** 空军大队长 / ~ **formation**【军】大队编队(飞行) / ~ **leader** 小组长 / ~ **mind**【心】团体心理 / ~ **therapy** 小组治疗(现代美国的一种精神治疗法, 病人由医生带领在组内相互诉说自己的若恼和问题) / '~**think** *n.* 小集团思想 (指集团内成员在思想、观点上的一致) / ~ **work** 团体福利工作

grouping ['gru:piŋ] *n.* ①集团; 派别: political ~s 政治集团 ②编组: tactical ~【军】战斗编组

grouse¹ [graus] [单复同] *n.*【动】①松鸡: black ~ 黑琴鸡 / hazel ~ 榛鸡 / red ~ 红松鸡

grouse² [graus] [俚] **I** *vi.* 抱怨, 发牢骚 **II** *n.* ①怨言, 牢骚 ②惯出怨言的人, 老是发牢骚的人

grove [grouv] *n.* 小树林, 树丛; 园林: a coco(a)nut ~ 一片椰林 ||~**less** *a.* 无树林的

grovel ['grovl] (grovel(l)ed; grovel(l)ing) *vi.* ①趴, 匍匐 ②卑躬屈节, 奴颜婢膝 ||**grovel(l)er** *n.* ①趴着的人 ②卑躬屈节的人

grow [grou] (grew [gru:], grown [groun]) ❶ *vi.* ①生长, 成长; 发育 ②发展; 增长 ③渐渐变得: He has ~n to like volleyball. 他渐渐喜爱起排球来了。④(风俗等)形成 (*up*); 产生 ❷ *vt.* ①植, 栽: Wheat is ~n in this field. 这块地种的是麦子。②[常用被动语态]使长满: a trellis ~n over with grapevines 长满葡萄藤的架子 ③养; 成: ~ a beard 留胡子, 蓄须 ||~ *downwards* 缩小; 减少 / ~ *on* ①(习惯、感觉等)加深对…的影响: Stammering began to ~ *on* him. 他的口吃越来越厉害了。②(书、画等)引起…爱好: a book that ~s *on* sb. 一本某人所喜欢的书 / ~ *out of* ①产生自…: The mistake *grew out of* his carelessness. 这错误是由于他的粗心造成的。②长大得与…不再相称; 变得不适合于: ~ *out of* one's clothes 长大得穿不下原来的衣服 / ~ *out of* usefulness 变得没用了 ③停止, 戒除(恶习等) / ~ *up* ①成熟; 成年; 长成 ②逐渐形成, 发展; 兴起 / ~ *upon* =~ on ||~**able** *a.* 可种的

grower ['grouə] *n.* ①种植者, 栽培者; 饲养者: fruit ~ 种植果树的人 / a cotton ~ 棉农 / livestock ~ 饲养员 ②[前加形容词]…植物: fast (slow) ~ 长得快(慢)的植物

growing ['grouiŋ] *a.* ①生长的; 成长中的 ②增长的; 不断增长的 ③适于生长的: the ~ season for rice 水稻生长季节 ||~**ly** *ad.* / ~ **pains** 发育性病痛, 发身期痛 ②(企业等)早期发展过程中经历的困难

growl [graul] **I** ❶ *vi.* ①(狗等)嗥叫 (*at*); (雷, 炮等)轰鸣 ②(人)咆哮 ❷ *vt.* 咆哮着说 (*out*) **II** *n.* ①(狗等)的嗥叫(声); (人的)咆哮; 轰鸣(声)

growler ['graulə] *n.* ①嗥叫的动物; 咆哮的人; 轰鸣的东西 ②小冰山 ③【电】短路线圈测试仪; 电机转子试验装置 ④ [英]四轮马车 ⑤ [美俚](到酒店打酒用的)大壶(或罐、桶等) ‖*rush the ~* [美俚] 带着酒壶(或罐、桶等)到酒店打酒 ②大量喝酒

grown [groun] I grow 的过去分词 II *a.* ①长成了的; 成熟的: a ~ man 成年人 ②被…长满的: a cress-~ stream 长满水芹的小河 ‖*~-up n.* 成年人 *a.* ①成人的; 成熟的 ②供成年人用的: ~-up clothes 供成年人穿的衣服

growth [grouθ] *n.* ①生长, 成长; 发育: reach full ~ 充分发育; 成熟 ②增长; 增大; 发展: the ~ of production 生产的发展 ③种植, 栽: Have an apple of our own ~. 尝一尝我们自己种的苹果吧。/ of home (foreign) ~ 本国(外国)种出来的 ④生长物; 产物: Moss is the only ~ on the top of this high mountain. 苔藓是这座高山顶上的唯一的生长物。/ a thick ~ of reeds 一片丛生的芦苇 ⑤ 【医】瘤, 赘生物 ‖*~ factor* 【生】生长因素 / *~ industry* 发展特快的新行业 / *~ rate* 生长率; 增长率

grub [grʌb] I *n.* ① 【动】蛴螬 ②做苦工的人; 穷苦文人 ③邋遢人 ④(板球中的)滚球 ⑤ [俚]食物 II (grubbed; grubbing) ❶ *vi.* ①掘地, 刨地 ②搜寻 ③做苦工 (on, along, away) ④ [俚]吃 ❷ *vt.* ①掘除(地)上的残根; 掘出: ~ up weeds 根除杂草 ②(从书本等中)找出 (up, out) ③ [俚]养活; 供给(住宿者等)伙食 ‖*ax(e)* 鹤嘴锄 / *'~stake* n. ①(以分得部分发现物为条件)供给探矿者的贷款(或物品) ②贷款 vt. 供给(探矿者等)贷款(或物品) / *'~,staker* n. 贷款者

grudge [grʌdʒ] I *vt.* ①妒忌: ~ sb. his success 妒忌某人的成功 ②吝惜, 不愿给; 不愿: ~ going 不愿去 II *n.* 妒忌; 怨恨; 恶意: bear(或 owe) sb. a ~ 对某人怀恨在心 / have a ~ against sb. 对…怀恨

grudging ['grʌdʒiŋ] *a.* 不愿的; 勉强的; 吝啬的 ‖*~ly ad.*

gruel [gruəl] I *n.* 粥, 薄糊: millet ~ 小米粥 II (gruel(l)ed; gruel(l)ing) *vt.* 使极度紧张; (用重罚或逼口供等)使精疲力尽 ‖*give sb. his one's ~* 重罚某人; 挫败某人; 杀死某人 / *have (或 get) one's ~* 被责罚; 大败; 被杀 ‖*gruel(l)ing a*: 折磨的; 使精疲力尽的 *n.* 痛打; 惩罚

gruesome ['gru:səm] *a.* 可怕的, 可憎的, 令人厌恶的 ‖*~ly ad. / ~ness n.*

ruff [grʌf] *a.* ①(说话、态度等)粗暴的, 生硬的; 脾气坏的 ②(声音)粗哑的 ‖*~ly ad. / ~ness n.*

rumble ['grʌmbl] I ❶ *vi.* ①抱怨, 发牢骚 (at, about, over) ②咕哝, 嘟囔 ③隆隆响 ❷ *vt.* ①抱怨地表示 (out) ②嘟囔着说 II *n.* ①怨言, 牢骚; 咕哝 ②隆隆声 ‖*~r n.* 爱抱怨的人, 爱发牢骚的人 / *grumblingly ad.*

rumpy ['grʌmpi], **grumpish** ['grʌmpiʃ] *a.* 脾气坏的; 粗暴的 ‖*grumpily ad. / grumpiness n.*

grunt [grʌnt] I ❶ *vi.* ①(猪等)作呼噜声, 喉鸣 ②(表示烦恼、反对、疲劳、轻蔑等)发哼声, 咕哝 ❷ *vt.* 咕哝着说出(或表示) II *n.* ①(猪等的)呼噜声 ②哼哼声, 咕哝 ③ [美俚](电气)线路工的助手 ④ [美俚]猪肉 ⑤ =~er ‖*~er n.* ①作呼噜声的动物(尤指猪) ②哼的人, 咕哝的人 ③ 【动】石鲈 ④ [美俚]摔角运动员

guano ['gwɑ:nou] I *n.* ①(海)鸟粪 ②人造(或天然)肥料(尤指鱼肥) II *vt.* 在…上施鸟粪(或鱼肥)

guarantee [,gærən'ti:] I *n.* ①保证; 保证书: Goods are sold with money-back ~. 售出商品质量不符保证退款。②保证人(法律上用 guarantor): stand ~ for sb. 替某人作保 ③接受保证的人 ④担保物, 抵押品 ⑤迹象 II *vt.* ①保证; 担保: This watch is ~d for two years. 保修期两年。/ ~ the payment of the debts 保证偿还债务 ②[口]包, 管保: I ~ that he'll go. 我保险他会去。‖*~ against (或 from)* 保证…不…: ~ sb. *against* (或 *from*) loss 保证某人不受损失 / ~ sth. *against* breakage 保证某物不破损 ‖*~ fund* 保证基金

guarantor [,gærən'tɔ:] *n.* 【律】保证人

guaranty ['gærənti] I *n.* 【律】①保证; 保证书 ②担保物, 抵押品 ③ =guarantor II *vt.* =guarantee (*vt.*)

guard [gɑ:d] I *n.* ①守卫; 警戒; 看守 ②卫兵(队); 哨兵; 警卫员; 看守员: the ~s company 警卫连 / [the Guards] (英国的)皇家禁卫军: inspect (或 review) a ~ of hono(u)r 检阅仪仗队 ④ [英]列车员 (= [美] conductor); (列车上的)制动手, 司门员 ⑤(篮球等)卫: the right (left) ~ 右(左)卫 ⑥防护装置: a belt ~ 【机】皮带护档 / a welder's ~ 焊接工人的面罩 / a trigger ~ (枪上的)扳机护圈 ⑦(击剑、拳击的)防御; 防御姿势 II ❶ *vt.* ①守卫; 守护; 警卫 ②看守; 监视: ~ a prisoner 看守犯人 ③谨慎使用(言词等): ~ one's tongue 说话谨慎 ④给…安防护装置; 对…进行校正检查 ⑤【医】对…配用矫正剂 ❷ *vi.* ①防止, 警惕; 防范: ~ *against* diseases 预防疾病 ②警卫 ③(击剑中)取守势 ‖*drop (或 lower) one's ~* 丧失警惕 / *mount ~* 上岗 / *off (one's)* 不提防, 不警惕: catch sb. *off* ~ 乘某人不备 / *on ~* 在岗上 / *(on (one's) ~* 警戒, 警惕: The flattery of the bad egg instantly put me *on* ~. 这个坏蛋的奉承立刻使我警惕起来。/ *stand (或 keep)* ~ 站岗 / *the old ~* [总称]某一事业(或主张)的老一辈的维护者(尤指政党内当权的保守派) ‖*~er n.* 守卫者 / *~less a.* 无警戒的; 无保护的 ‖*~ boat* 警戒艇 / *~ flag* 【军】(警戒舰的)值班旗 / *'~house n.* 警卫室, 卫兵室; 禁闭室 / *~ mount* 卫兵换班礼节(或号音) / *'~rail n.* 护栏; (铁路)护轨 / *~ ring* 护圈 / *'~room n.* =~house / *~ ship* 警戒舰 / *~ tent* 岗篷

guarded ['gɑ:did] *a.* ①被保卫着的 ②被看守着的; 被监视着的: a closely ~ secret 严守的秘密 ③谨慎的: a ~ speech 小心谨慎的讲话 ‖**~ly** *ad.* / **~ness** *n.*

guardian ['gɑ:djən] I *n.* ①护卫者; 保护人; 管理员 ②【律】监护人 ③【宗】方济各会教派的修道院院长 ④ [G-] (用于报刊名)卫报 II *a.* 守护的 ‖**~ship** *n.* 守护; 保护; 监护人的职责(或身分) ‖**~ angel** 守护神

guer(r)illa [gə'rilə] *n.* ①[古]游击战(现通常用 ~ war) ②游击队员 ‖*a ~ area* 游击区 / *a ~ detachment* 游击支队 / *~ forces* 游击队 / *a ~ strike* 不经工会同意的罢工 / *a ~ theatre* 流动剧团; 街头活报演出(队) / *~ war* (或 *warfare*) 游击战 ‖**~ism** *n.* ①游击主义 ②游击(战)

guess [ges] I ❶ *vt.* ①猜测; 推测: Just ~ what is in the parcel. 猜猜看这包裹里是什么东西。/ I ~ed it from his remarks. 我是从他的话中推测出这一点的。②猜中, 猜对: ~ a riddle 猜中一个谜语 ③[口]想, 认为: I ~ he'll come soon. 我想他就要来了。❷ *vi.* 猜; 推测: I can't even ~ at what he means. 他什么意思, 我连猜也猜不出。/ I ~ so. 我认为是这样的。II *n.* 猜测; 推测 ‖*at a ~* 猜测起来 / *by ~* 凭猜测 / *by ~ and by god* (或 *by ~ and by gosh*) 凭瞎猜; 凭粗粗估计 / *It's anybody's ~.* 这是大家都拿不准的事。/ *keep sb. ~ing* 让某人捉摸不定 / *One man's ~ is as good as another's.* 猜测终究是猜测而已。‖**~ stick** [俚]尺; 计算尺 / **'~work** *n.* 猜测; 推测

guest [gest] I *n.* ①客人, 宾客: a state ~ 国宾 / a distinguished ~ 贵宾 / the ~ of honour 主宾 / a ~ speaker 邀请来的演讲人 ②旅客, 宿客; 顾客: a paying ~ 搭伙房客 ③客串演员, 特约演员 ④【动】客虫; 【植】寄生植物 II ❶ *vt.* 招待, 款待 ❷ *vi.* 作客; 寄宿 ‖**~ship** *n.* 客人身分 ‖**'~,chamber** *n.* 客房 / **'~house** *n.* 宾馆, 招待所; 高级寄宿舍 / **~ room** =~chamber / **~ rope** [海] ①(用来稳定拖船的)辅助缆索 ②扶手绳

guffaw [gʌ'fɔ:] I *n.* 哄笑, 狂笑 II ❶ *vi.* 哄笑, 狂笑 ❷ *vt.* 大笑着说

guidance ['gaidəns] *n.* ①指引; 指导; 领导: a book for the ~ of beginners in English 指导初学英语者的书 ②[字]制导: ~ system 制导系统

guide [gaid] I *n.* ①领路人, 导游者, 向导; 指导者 ②【军】基准兵; 向导船 ③指南; 指导 ④入门书, 手册; (旅行、游览)指南; 路标; 指引卡: a ~ to farm-tool manufacturing 农具制造手册 / a ~ to a museum 博物馆参观指南 ⑤【机】导引物, 导轨; 【自】波导; 导向装置 ⑥【医】导子, 标: ~ bar (或 rod) 导杆 ⑥[英]女童子军 II ❶ *vt.* ①为…领路; 带领 ②引导, 指引; 指导: a *guiding* principle 指导方针 / ~ sb.'s studies 指导某人学习 ③管理; 操纵; 支配: ~ a plough

扶犁 ❷ *vi.* 任向导 ‖**guidable** *a.* 可引导的 / **~less** *a.* 无向导的; 无指导的; 无管理的 ‖**'~board** *n.* 路牌 / **'~book** *n.* 旅行指南; 参考手册 / **~d missile** 导弹: a ~d missile launcher 导弹发射器 / a ~d missile system 导弹系统 / **~ flag** 【军】旗标, 指示旗 / **'~line** *n.* ①指导路线, 方针; 准则; 指标: lay out economic ~lines 制订经济方针 / a price ~line 价格指标 ②指路绳; 【印】样张, 样行; 标线 / **'~post** *n.* 路标 / **~ rope** 导绳 / **'~way** *n.* 【机】导沟, 导向槽 / **~ word** [印]眉题

g(u)ild [gild] *n.* ①(中世纪的)行会; 同业公会; (互助性质的)协会: the ~ outlook 行会主义 / a ~-master 行会师傅 ②【植】依赖植物集团

guile [gail] *n.* 狡诈; 诡计: achieve one's end by ~ 用诡计达到目的 ‖**~less** *a.* 不狡诈的; 坦率的, 正直的

guillotine [ˌgilə'ti:n] I *n.* ①断头台 ②【机】剪断机; (切纸的)闸刀 ③【医】铡刀, 环状刀: tonsil ~ 扁桃体铡除刀 ④截止审议的方法(指议会中采用的在预定时间内对议案等进行表决的一种方法) II *vt.* ①在断头台上斩决 ②(用剪断机等)剪断 ③截止审议(议案等)

guillotine

guilt [gilt] *n.* ①有罪: confess one's ~ 坦白认罪 ②内疚 ‖**~less** *a.* ①无罪的, 无辜的 ②没有经验的, 不熟悉…的; 没有…的 (*of*)

guilty ['gilti] *a.* ①犯罪的, 有罪的: be ~ of crime 犯了罪的 ②自觉有罪的, 内疚的: have a ~ conscience 问心有愧; 做贼心虚 / ~ looks 内疚的神色 / *plead ~* 服罪 / *plead not ~* 不服罪 ‖**guiltily** *ad.* / **guiltiness** *n.*

guinea ['gini] *n.* ①畿尼(旧英国金币) ② =~ fowl ‖**Guinea corn** 【植】高粱, 蜀黍 / **~ fowl** 【动】珍珠鸡 / **~ grains** 【植】药用卡满龙的种子 / **~ grass** 【植】羊草 / **~ hen** ①雌珍珠鸡 ②=~ fowl / **~ pig** 【动】豚鼠, 天竺鼠 ②供进行医学(或其他科学)实验的人(或物) / **Guinea worm** 【动】麦地那龙线虫(热带的皮下寄生虫)

guise [gaiz] I *n.* ①外观, 姿态; 装束 ②伪装; 借口: in (或 under) the ~ of 在…的幌子下; 假作…/ promote one's private interests under the

~ of serving the public 假公济私 **II** *vt.* & *vi.*
[英方]伪装

guitar [gi'tɑː] **I** *n.* 【音】吉他,六弦琴 **II** *vi.* 弹吉
他 ‖~**ist** [gi'tɑːrist] *n.* 弹吉他的人,善弹吉他
的人

gulf [gʌlf] **I** *n.* ① 海湾(一般比 bay 大): the
Persian *Gulf* 波斯湾(即阿拉伯湾)[亚洲] ②深
渊,深坑;悬崖,鸿沟③旋涡;吞没一切的东西④[诗]
海 ⑤[英][学俚]授予参加荣誉学位考试不及格
者的学位 **II** *vt.* ①吞没;使深深卷入 ②[英][学
俚]使(参加荣誉学位考试不及格者)获得学位 ‖*a
great ~ fixed* 鸿沟; 不可逾越的障碍; 歧异: I
don't think there's *a great ~ fixed* between
them. 我认为他们之间没有根本的分歧。/ *the
~ below* 地狱 ‖~**y** *a.* 多深坑的; 多旋涡的
‖**Gulf States** (美国)墨西哥湾沿岸的各州 /
Gulf Stream 墨西哥湾湾流(由墨西哥湾向北流至
大西洋的水流) / ~**weed** *n.* 【植】果囊马尾藻

gull¹ [gʌl] *n.* 【动】鸥

gull² [gʌl] **I** *n.* 易受骗的人, 笨人 **II** *vt.* 欺骗, 使
上当: ~ sb. out of sth. 骗取某人的某物 ‖~**ish**
a. 笨的, 呆的

gullet ['gʌlit] *n.* ①[解]食管; 咽喉; 咽 ② 水道; 峡
谷 ③锯齿间空隙 ④[建]水落管, 水槽

gullible ['gʌləbl] *a.* 易受骗的, 易上当的; 轻信的
‖**gullibility** [,gʌli'biliti] *n.* / **gullibly** *ad.*

gully¹ ['gʌli] **I** *n.* ①冲沟, 溪谷 ②【建】集水沟; 雨
水口; 檐槽 **II** *vt.* 在…上开沟(或槽); 水流冲成
(沟渠) ‖~ **drain** 【建】下水道 / ~ **hole** 【建】
(沟渠)集水孔

gully² ['gʌli] *n.* [英方]大刀

gulp [gʌlp] **I ❶** *vt.* ① 吞, 一口吞(下); 狼吞虎咽
地吃: ~ *down* a cup of tea 把一杯茶一饮而尽
② 忍住, 抑制: ~ *down* sobs 吞声饮泣 **❷** *vi.*
① 吞咽; 狼吞虎咽 ② 喘不过气来; 哽塞 **II** *n.* 吞
咽; 一口吞下的量, 一大口: empty a glass of
water at one ~ 把一杯水一饮而尽 ‖~**ingly**
ad. 一口地

gum¹ [gʌm] **I** *n.* ① 树胶; 胶浆(用以粘贴或上浆
等); 树脂: sweet ~ 【植】胶糖香树 ②橡皮糖,
口香糖 (=chewing ~); 软糖 (=~drop) ③ 产
树胶的树; 桉树 (=~ tree) ④橡胶; [美][复]高
统橡皮套鞋 (=~ boots) ⑤ 眼屎; 病树的分泌物
II (gummed; gumming) **❶** *vt.* ①(用树胶)粘合
(*down, together, up*); 在…上面涂树胶 ②[美俚]
欺骗 **❷** *vi.* ①分泌树胶; 结胶 ②发粘: The axle
has *gummed* up. 轴上发粘不(润滑)了。‖~ **up**
[美俚]搞乱, 使出毛病 / *up a ~ tree* 进退两
难, 骑虎难下 ‖~ **arabic** 阿拉伯树胶 / ~
dragon [化]龙胶, 黄蓍胶 / ~ **elastic** 弹性胶
(生橡胶的别名) / ~ **foot** [美俚](便衣)警察 /
~ **resin** 树胶脂 / ~ **tragacanth** 【化】黄蓍胶 /
'~**water** *n.* 阿拉伯胶溶液, 胶水 / ~**wood**
n. 产树脂的树的木材

gum² [gʌm] **I** *n.* [常用复]齿龈; 牙床: The dog
bared its ~s at the stranger. 那条狗对陌生人

龇牙咧嘴。 **II** (gummed; gumming) *vt.* ① 锉深
(锯)齿 ② 用牙床咀嚼 ‖*beat* (或 *bump*) one's
~s [美俚]唠叨, 饶舌 ‖~**boil** *n.* 齿龈脓肿

gum³ [gʌm] *n.* [英][俗]上帝 (=God) ‖*by* ~ 老
天爷作证, 确实(表示发誓) / *My* ~! 天啊! 啊
呀! (表示痛苦、悲哀或愤怒等)

gummy ['gʌmi] *a.* ①胶粘的; 粘性的 ②含有树胶
的, 多胶的; 涂有树胶的; 分泌树胶的, 生胶的 ③
(脚踝或腿)肿的, 浮肿的 ④[美俚]拙劣的; 讨厌的
‖**gumminess** *n.* 树胶状, 树胶质; 粘性 / ~ **tu-
mo(u)r** [医]梅毒瘤; (梅毒的)树胶状肿

gun [gʌn] **I** *n.* ①炮; 枪; [美]手枪: a machine ~ 机关枪 ②(信号枪、礼炮)鸣放: a
salute of 21 ~s 二十一响礼炮 ③枪状物; (杀虫
剂等的)喷雾器: spray ~ 【机】喷枪 / electron
~ 【无】电子枪 ④(引擎的)油门, 风门 ⑤ 猎枪
手 ⑥[美俚]扒手; 带枪的暴徒 ⑦[美俚]毒品注
射针 ⑧[美]烟斗 **II** (gunned; gunning) **❶** *vi.*
①用枪射击; 用枪打猎 ②加大油门快速前进 **❷**
vt. ① 向…开枪 ② 开大(引擎、汽车)的油门: ~
a car up a steep grade 开足马力把汽车驶上陡
坡 ‖*a big* (或 *great*) ~ [俚]①大人物 ②高级
军官 / *a son of a* ~ 见 son / *as sure as a
~* [俚] 千真万确 / *beat* (或 *jump*) *the ~* [俚](赛跑
时)发令枪未响即起跑, 偷跑; 信号未发前就开始
行动; [喻]过早地行动 / *blow great ~s* (风)刮
得猛: It *blows great ~s*. 刮大风。/ *give it the
~* 开动; 加速 / *go great ~s* 高速度高效率地
干 / ~ *for* ①用枪搜索捕杀 ②[美俚]追求, 寻
求 / *spike sb.'s ~s* 挫败某人 / *stick* (或 *stand*)
to (或 *by*) one's ~s 坚守阵地; 固执己见 /
under the ~(s) 在严密监视之下 ‖~ **barrel** 炮
筒; 枪筒 / '~**boat** *n.* 炮舰, 炮艇 / ~*boat* diplomacy 炮舰外交 / ~ **car** 铁道运炮车 / ~ **carriage**
炮架 / '~**cotton** *n.* 【军】强棉药 / ~ **crew**
[总称]炮手; 机枪手 / '~**fight** *n.* & *vi.* (两人之
间的)用枪格斗 / '~**fighter** *n.* 用枪格斗出名
的人 / '~**fire** *n.* 炮火; [军]号炮 / ~ **harpoon**
用捕鲸炮发射的鱼叉 / '~-**howitzer** *n.* 加农榴
弹炮 / '~**layer** *n.* 瞄准手 / '~**lock** *n.* 枪机 /
'~**man** ['gʌnmən] *n.* ①带枪的歹徒 ②枪炮工
人 / '~**metal** *n.* 炮铜(铜锡锌合金): ~*metal*
grey 铁灰色 / ~ **moll** [俚]带枪歹徒的情妇
(或女帮凶) / ~ **pit** 火炮掩体 / '~**point** *n.* 枪
口: at ~*point* 在枪口威胁下 / ~ **pointer** 方向
瞄准手 / '~**port** *n.* 炮眼, 炮门 / '~**powder**
n. ① 黑色火药, 有烟火药 ② 中国珠茶 (=~
powder tea) / ~ **room** ①枪炮陈列室 ②(英国
军舰上的)下级军官住所 / '~**runner** *n.* 军火
走私贩 / ~ **running** *n.* 军火走私 / ~ **ship**
[美][军俚]武装直升飞机 / '~**shot** *n.* ①火炮
的单发射击 ②射程 / '~-**shy** *a.* 怕听炮声的;
风声鹤唳的 / '~**sight** *n.* 瞄准器, 标尺 / '~-
smith *n.* 军械工人 / '~**stock** *n.* 枪托

gunner ['gʌnə] *n.* ①炮手; 枪手; 火炮瞄准手; 猎枪
手 ②管理军械(库)的准尉

gunnery ['gʌnəri] *n.* ①[总称]重炮 ②射击 ③射击学, 射击技术; 枪炮操作 ‖~ **jack** [英俚]炮术训练舰的射击检查官 (=~-lieutenant) / ~ **ship** 炮术训练舰

gunny ['gʌni] *n.* ①粗黄麻布 ②黄麻袋 (=~sack, ~-bag)

gunwale ['gʌnəl] *n.* 【船】船舷的上缘 ‖~ **to** (或 **down**) 舷边和水面相平 / ~ **under** 舷边没入水面以下

gurgle [‘gəːgl] **I** *vi.* ①(流水)作汩汩声; (人)发咯咯声 ②汩汩地流 **II** *n.* (流水的)汩汩声; (欢乐的)咯咯声: ~s of delight 咯咯的笑声

gush [gʌʃ] **I** *vi.* ①涌出, 喷出, 进出: Clear water ~ed into the irrigational channel. 清澈的水涌进了灌溉渠道。 / The cut ~ed out (或 forth) *with* blood. 伤口大量出血 ②滔滔不绝地说; 洋洋洒洒地写作; 表现出过分的热情(或感情): ~ *over* one's baby 滔滔不绝地谈论自己的婴儿 **❷** *vt.* ①涌出, 喷出, 进出 ②滔滔不绝地说; 洋洋洒洒地写 **❶** *n.* ①涌出, 喷出, 进出: gas ~ (油)汽喷 ②感情的进发; 过分的热情: a ~ of enthusiasm 热情进发 ③滔滔不绝的讲话; 洋洋洒洒的文章 ‖~**er** *n.* ①喷油井; 自喷井 ②迸发出的东西 ③易动感情的人

gust[1] [gʌst] *n.* ①阵风; 一阵狂风 ②(雨、雹、烟、火、声音等的)突然一阵; (感情的)迸发, 汹涌: a ~ of rain 一阵暴雨 / a ~ of rage 一阵勃然大怒

gust[2] [gʌst] **I** *n.* [古][诗] ①味, 味觉; 美味 ②嗜好, 爱好 ③享受; 欣赏 **II** *vt.* [苏格兰]尝尝; 享受

gusto ['gʌstou] *n.* ①爱好, 嗜好; 趣味 ②兴致勃勃; 热忱; 生气勃勃 ③[古]滋味 ④[古]艺术风格

gusty ['gʌsti] *a.* ①阵风的; 多阵风的; 起大风的 ②迸发的

gut [gʌt] **I** *n.* ①[复]内脏 ②(幽门到直肠间的)肠子; [常用复][口]肚子: the blind ~ 盲肠 / ~ache 肚子痛 ③[常用复]内容, 内部的主要部分; 本质, 实质: have no ~s in it 内容空洞, 毫无力量 / get down to the ~s of a matter 触及问题的实质 / a ~ issue (或 question) 关键问题 ④ [复][俚]勇气; 毅力; 力量, 效力; 莽撞, 无礼: a man of plenty of ~s 很有胆量的人 / ~ language 粗话 ⑤(提琴、网球拍等的)肠线: surgical ~ 外科缝合用的羊肠线 ⑥将钓钩系到约丝上用的一种丝线 ⑦狭水道; 海岬, 海峡; (牛津、剑桥大学)赛船河道的弯头; 狭巷, 狭道 ⑧[美俚]香肠 [美俚] 容易的课程 (=~ course) **II** (gutted; gutting) *vt.* ①取出(鱼等)的内脏 ②损毁(房屋等)的内部装置; 抽去(书籍等)的主要内容 ③ [口]贪婪地吃 ‖*hate sb.'s* ~s [俚]对某人恨之入骨 / *not fit to carry* ~s *to a bear* ①太不中用, 没有价值 ②不能作为人的食物 / *run sb. through the* ~s 折磨某人, 虐待某人 / *spill one's* ~s [美俚]把自己知道的一切原原本本地说出去; 告密 ‖~**less** *n.* 没有勇气的; 没有生气的

gutter ['gʌtə] **I** *n.* ①水槽; 檐槽 ②沟; 边沟, 街沟, 明沟: caves ~ 【建】天沟 ③[印]排版上的隔缝; (装钉)左右两页间的空白 ④贫民区, 贫民窟 **II** **❶** *vt.* 开沟于…; 装檐槽于… **❷** *vi.* 流; (蜡烛)淌蜡; (烛火)风中摇晃 ‖~ **out** ①逐渐变弱而终于熄灭 ②默默无闻地结束 / *lap the* ~ [俚]酩酊大醉 ‖'~-**bird** *n.* ①麻雀 ②声名狼藉的人 / ~ **child** 街头流浪儿 / ~ **film** 迎合低级趣味的电影 / ~ **language** [美俚]脏话 / ~**man** ['gʌtəmən] *n.* 摊贩, 货郎 / ~ **press** [总称]迎合低级趣味的报纸 / '~**snipe** *n.* [贬]街头流浪儿; 穷途末路的人

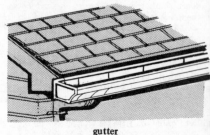

gutter

guttural ['gʌtərəl] **I** *a.* ①喉的, 咽喉的 ②【语】颚音的, 喉音的 ③发出不愉快(或奇怪、不悦耳)声音的 **II** *n.* 【语】颚音(如 [g], [k] 等); 颚音字母(或符号) ‖~**ism** *n.* 颚音的性质(或倾向) / ~**ize** *vt.* 使发颚音; 使颚音化 / ~**ly** *ad.*

guy[1] [gai] **I** *n.* 牵索(或链), 稳索; 拉杆; [无]天线拉线 **II** *vt.* (用牵索等)使稳定, 加固

guy[2] [gai] **I** *n.* ①[英]衣着古怪的人; 怪丑的人 ②[美俚]家伙, 人; 小伙子; 朋友 ③[俚]逃亡, 出奔: give the ~ to 从…逃出; 摆脱…而溜走 **II** **❶** *vt.* 取笑, 嘲弄; 用蜡像对(某人)进行嘲弄 **❷** *vi.* [俚]逃走, 逃亡 ‖*a right* ~ 可靠的人 / *a smart* ~ 自作聪明的人; 精明的家伙 / *a tough* ~ 硬汉 / *do a* ~ [俚]逃走, 逃亡

guzzle ['gʌzl] **❶** *vi.* 滥饮; 大吃大喝 **❷** *vt.* ①狂饮; 滥吃 ②大吃大喝地乱花(钞票等)(away) ‖~**r** *n.* 酒鬼; 大吃大喝的人

gymkhana [dʒim'kɑːnə] *n.* 运动会

gymnasium [dʒim'neizjəm] ([复]gymnasia [dʒim'neizjə] 或 gymnasiums) *n.* ①体育馆, 健身房 ②(德国或欧洲某些其他国家的)大学预科

gymnast ['dʒimnæst] *n.* 体操家; 体育家

gymnastic [dʒim'næstik] **I** *a.* 体操的; 体育的: ~ apparatus 体操用具 **II** *n.* ①训练课程 ②[~s][用作单]体操; 体育 ‖~**ally** *ad.*

gypsy ['dʒipsi] **I** *n.* ①[常作 G-]吉普赛人 ②[G-]吉普赛语 ③象吉普赛人的人; [谑]动人(或顽皮)的姑娘; 黑脸妇女 ④[船](锚机或绞车上的)绞绳筒: ~ **wheel** 锚链轮 **II** *a.* (象)吉普赛人的 **III** *vi.* 吉普赛人似地生活(或流浪) ‖~**fy** *vt.* 使吉普赛化 / ~**ish** *a.* 吉普赛人似的 / ~**ism**

n. 吉普赛人的生活方式 (或状况) ‖~ **bonnet** 宽边女帽 / ~ **cab** [美俚]流动兜客的出租汽车 / ~ **leave** [英俚]不告而别 / ~ **moth**【动】舞毒蛾

gyrate I [,dʒaiə'reit] *vi.* 旋转,回旋; 螺旋形地运转 **II** ['dʒaiərit] *a.* 旋转的; 螺旋状的 ‖**gyration** [,dʒaiə'reiʃən] *n.* 旋转,回旋;【动】螺层 / **gyratory** ['dʒaiərətəri] *a.* 旋转的

gyroscope ['gaiərəskoup, 'dʒaiərəskoup] *n.* 陀螺仪, 回转仪 ‖**gyroscopic** [,gaiərəs'kɔpik, ,dʒaiərəs'kɔpik] *a.*

H

ha [hɑ:] **I** *int.* 哈! [表示惊异、愉快、怀疑、胜利等] **II** *vi.* "哈!" 地叫一声 **III** *n.* "哈!" 的一声

haberdasher ['hæbədæʃə] *n.* ①[美]男子服饰用品商 ②[英]缝纫用品商 ‖~**y** ['hæbədæʃəri] *n.* ①[总称]男子服饰用品;缝纫用品 ②男子服饰用品店;缝纫用品店

habit ['hæbit] **I** *n.* ①习惯: cultivate (或 form, acquire) the ~ of analysis 养成分析的习惯 / change customs and ~s 移风易俗 / Habit is second nature. [谚]习惯成自然。/ force of ~ 习惯势力 ②习性,脾性;特性: You'll not be afraid of snakes if you understand their ~s. 你如果知道蛇的习性,就不会怕它们了。/ a ~ of mind 习性,脾性 / a plant of trailing ~ 一种有蔓延特性的植物 ③体质,体格 ④举止,行为 ⑤表示宗教级别的衣着; 妇女的骑装; [古]衣服 ⑥毒瘾: a ~-forming drug 会使人上瘾的麻醉毒品 **II** *vt.* ①使穿衣 ②[英古]居住在 ‖**be in the** (或 **a**) ~ **of** 有…的习惯(或脾气) / **be off the** ~ [美俚] ①已戒去毒瘾 ②(指吸毒上瘾者)清醒着, 未处于麻醉毒品的影响下 / **break sb.** (**oneself**) **of a** ~ 使某人(自己)去掉某一习惯 / **fall** (或 **get**) **into the** (或 **a**) ~ **of** 沾染…的习惯 / **get out of a** ~ 戒除一种习惯 / **have the** (或 **a**) ~ **of** =be in the (或 a) ~ of / **kick the** ~ [美俚]戒掉嗜好(尤指毒瘾) / **out of** ~ 出于习惯

habitable ['hæbitəbl] *a.* 可居住的; 适于居住的 ‖**habitability** [,hæbitə'biliti], ~**ness** *n.* 可居住性; 适于居住 / **habitably** *ad.*

habitat ['hæbitæt] *n.* ①(动物的)栖息地,(植物的)产地 ②住处 ③聚集处;(某事物)经常发生的地方

habitation [,hæbi'teiʃən] *n.* ①居住: a place fit for ~ 适宜居住的地方 ②[书面语]住处, 住宅 ③聚居地

habitual [hə'bitjuəl] *a.* ①习惯(性)的;习以为常的 ②惯常的,已成规则的: ~ practice 经常的做法,惯技 / sb.'s ~ seat in the dining hall 某人在食堂用餐时惯常坐的位子 ‖~**ly** *ad.* / ~**ness** *n.*

habituate [hə'bitjueit] *vt.* ① [~ oneself] 使习惯于 (to): ~ oneself to the style of plain living and hard struggle 使自己养成艰苦奋斗的作风 /

~ oneself to getting up early 习惯于早起 ②[古]常去; 常出入于 ‖**habituation** [hə,bitju'eiʃən] *n.* ①成为习惯 ②(对麻醉品等的)适应;毒瘾

hack¹ [hæk] **I** ❶ *vt.* ①劈, 砍; 辟出: ~ a way through the jungle 在丛林中辟出一条路 ②耙(地), 平(地), 翻(地); 碎土播(种): ~ in wheat 碎土播下小麦 ③(橄榄球中)踢(对方)的外胫 ④[美方]对付; 宽容: How can you ~ this kind of thing? 你怎能容忍这种事情? ❷ *vi.* ①劈, 砍; 乱劈, 乱砍 (at) ②断续地干咳: a ~ing cough 猛烈的干咳 ③(橄榄球中)故意踢对方的外胫; (篮球中)拉(或打)对方手犯规 ④[英方]结巴着说 ⑤[俚]游荡,闲逛 (around) **II** *n.* ①劈(或砍)的工具; 鹤嘴锄 ②砍痕, 伤痕; (橄榄球中的)踢胫 ③干咳 ④[英方]结巴 ⑤[美方]窘迫,困窘: put sb. under ~ 使某人张口结舌 ⑥(对海军军官的)营房拘禁: have sb. under ~ 把某人拘禁在营房内 ‖**take a** ~ **at** 尝试… ‖'~**saw** *n.*【机】弓锯, 钢锯

hack² [hæk] **I** *n.* ①出租的马; 骑用马; 役用马; 鞍子马; 驽马, 老而无用的马 ②出租马车; 出租汽车; 出租马车赶车人; 出租汽车司机 ③雇佣文人 ④[美俚]监狱看守 ⑤[俚](运货列车后面的)管理员车 ⑥[美]唯命是从的政党工作人员 **II** ❶ *vt.* ①出租(马等) ②雇…当文章 ③用旧, 使变陈腐 ❷ *vi.* ①用普通速度骑走 (尤指骑着出租的马) (along) ②[口]驾驶出租汽车(或出租马车) **III** *a.* ①出租的; 被雇作文人的; 雇佣文人做的: a ~ writer 雇佣文人 ②陈腐的; 平凡的 ‖'~**man** *n.* 出租汽车司机; 出租马车赶车人 / '~**stand** *n.* [美]出租汽车(或马车)停车处 / '~**work** *n.* (职业性的)卖文工作

hack³ [hæk] **I** *n.* ①饲鹰板 ②晒架; 晒砖架;(未烧过的)晒出的砖堆 ③饲草架 ④【机】格架 **II** *vt.* 把…放在架上晒 ‖**be at** ~ 在饲养训练中(指不让小鹰自己外出寻食)

hackney ['hækni] **I** *n.* ①普通乘用的马 ②出租马车; 出租汽车 ③[古]被雇用干苦活的人 **II** *a.* ①出租的 ②陈腐的; 平凡的 **III** *vt.* ①出租 ②[常用被动语态];役使;用旧,使变陈腐 ‖~**ed** *a.* 陈腐的; 平常的: a ~ed tune (phrase) 陈腐的曲调(语句) ‖~ **coach** 出租马车

had [强 hæd; 弱 həd, əd] have 的过去式和过去分

词 ‖~ *best* 见 **best** / ~ *better* 见 **better**¹ /
~ *rather . . . than . . .* 与其…不如…,宁愿…
不愿…

haddock ['hædək] ([复] haddock(s)) *n.*【动】(产
于北大西洋的)黑线鳕

hadn't ['hædnt] =had not

hag [hæg] *n.* ①女巫; (尤指做坏事的)老丑妇;
[古] 母夜叉, 妖怪 ②【动】八目鳗类鱼 ‖**~born**
a. 女巫所生的 / '~**,ridden** *a.* 为恶梦所扰的 /
'~**seed** *n.* 女巫的子女们

haggard ['hægəd] I *a.* ①憔悴的,形容枯槁的 ②
样子凶暴的 ③(鹰)成年被捕的;不驯服的 II *n.*
不驯服的鹰,悍鹰 ‖**~ly** *ad.* / **~ness** *n.*

haggle ['hægl] I ❶ *vi.* (在价格、条件等方面)争论
不休 (*about, over, for, with*): We never ~ *about*
principles. 我们绝不拿原则做交易。 ❷ *vt.*
①乱砍, 乱劈 ②[古](因争论)使烦恼, 使疲惫
II *n.* 争论; 论价, 讨价还价

ha-ha¹ [hɑ(:)'hɑ:] I *int.* 哈哈! ‖ [表示嘲笑等] II *n.*
哈哈的笑声 ‖*give sb. the merry ~* [美俚]嘲
笑某人

ha-ha² ['hɑ:hɑ:] *n.* (造于花园界沟中不遮挡视线
的)矮篱, 矮墙

hail¹ [heil] I ❶ *vt.* ①向…欢呼;为…欢呼: ~ sb.
(as) leader 欢呼拥立某人为领袖 ②招呼, 打信号
招呼 (尤指招呼过路船只) II *n.* 欢呼; 招呼 III
int. 好啊! [表示欢呼、祝贺等] ‖~ *from* 来
自: ~ *from* all corners of the country 来自五
湖四海 / *Hail Mary!*【天主教】万福马利亚! /
within ~ (尤指招呼船只)在听得到招呼的距离
内; 在近处 ‖~*er* *n.* 欢呼的人; 打招呼的人
‖'~-,**fellow**, '~-,**fellow-'well-'met** *a.* 友好的
n. 好友;友好,友情

hail² [heil] I *n.* ①雹子,冰雹;[古]下雹,雹暴 ②
(雹子般的)一阵 II ❶ *vi.* ①下雹: It's ~*ing*.
正在下雹。 ②雹子般地落下 ❷ *vt.* 使象雹子
般落下: ~ blows (curses) down *on* sb. 把某人乱
打(骂)一通 ‖'~**stone** *n.* 雹子,冰雹 / '~**storm**
n. 雹暴

hair [hɛə] *n.* ①头发;毛发,汗毛: I'll have my ~
cut. 我要理发。 / grey ~ 白发[比较: a few
grey ~s 几根白发] ②(动、植物的)毛, 茸毛:
a horse with a fine coat of ~ 长着一身细毛的
马 / root ~s of a plant 植物的根毛 ③毛状物;
粗毛交织物 ④些微, 一点儿: miss the target by
a ~ 差一点儿射中目标 ‖*against the* ~ [古]
违反本性 / *a* ~ *of the dog that bit one* [口]
以毒攻毒(如以酒解酒)的治疗方式 / *comb sb.'s*
~ *for him* 申斥某人 / *do one's* ~ (女子)做头
发 / *do up one's* ~ (女子)梳理头发; 把头发盘
起 / *get in* (*out of*) *sb.'s* ~ [美俚]惹恼(停止
惹恼)某人 / *get sb. by the short* ~s [俚]任意
摆布某人;完全操纵某人 / *hang by a* ~ 千钧一
发;岌岌可危; 摇摇欲坠 / *in the* ~ ①毛向外的
②(兽皮)有毛的 / *keep one's* ~ *on* [俚]保持

冷静, 不发脾气 / *let one's* (*back*) ~ *down* ①
(女子)把头发散开放下来 ②[口]不拘礼节; 态度
随便 / *lose one's* ~ ①脱发 ②发脾气 / *make*
sb.'s ~ *stand on end* 使某人毛骨悚然 / *not*
turn a ~ 不动声色 / *put* (或 *turn*) *up one's*
~ (女孩因成年)束起妇女状的头发 / *smooth*
sb.'s ~ *the wrong way* 使某人恼怒 / *split* ~*s*
(*over sth.*) (对琐事)作无益的、琐细的分析 /
tear one's ~ 撕扯自己的头发(表示愤怒、焦急、
悲伤等) / *to a* ~ (或 *to the turn of a* ~) 丝毫
不差地: This arrangement suits him *to a* ~.
这样的安排对他完全合适。 / *wear one's own* ~
不戴假发 ‖~ed *a.* 有毛发的; [常用以构成复合
词]长着…头发的: *The White-Haired Girl*《白毛
女》/ ~**less** *a.* 秃头的;无毛的 / ~**like** *a.* 毛
发似的 ‖'~**breadth** *n.* 一发之差, 极微小的距
离: have a ~*breadth* escape 死里逃生 / '~**brush**
n. 发刷 / '~**,clippers** [复] *n.* (理发用的)轧
刀 / '~**cloth** *n.* ①马毛(或驼毛等)与绒布的织
物(室内装璜用) ②(苦行者用的)粗毛织衬衣 /
'~**cut** *n.* 理发 / '~**do** *n.* [口](女子)头发式
样;(女子)理发 / '~**,dresser** *n.* ①理发师(在
指为子服务的) ②[英]=barber (*n.*) /
'~,**dressing** *n.* (女子)理发;理发业 *a.* (女子)理
发用的 / '~**dye** *n.* 染发药水 / '~**line** *n.* ①
细缝; 细微的区别 ②【印】向上的一细勾 ③【纺】
细线条;线条精细呢 ④头型轮廓, 发型轮廓 /
【军】瞄准镜上的十字线;光学仪器上的叉线 / '~
net *n.* 发网 / '~**oil** 发油 / '~**pencil** 画笔 /
'~**pin** *n.* ①发夹,夹叉 ②发夹状的东西;(道路
的)急转弯: a ~*pin* bend (陆路上的)U字形转
弯 ③[美俚]女人 / '~-**raiser** *n.* 使人毛发竖起
的东西(或事情) / '~-,**raising** *a.* [口]使人毛发
竖起的,恐怖的 / '~**sbreadth** *n.* =~breadth /
~ **side** 【机】(皮带的)毛面 / ~ **slide** 角质(或玳
瑁)的发夹 / ~ **space** 【印】字间最小间隔 / '~
splitter *n.* 专作无谓分析的人; 好为小事与人争
辩的人 / '~,**splitting** *n. & a.* 作无益而琐细的
分析(的) / '~**spring** *n.*【机】细弹簧;游丝 / '~
stroke 【印】向上纤细的一勾 / '~**tail** *n.* 带鱼
/ '~-**thin** *a.* 细如毛发的 / ~ -*thin* majority 以极微弱多数上台 /
~ -*thin* majority 以极微弱多数 II ❶ *a.* ①一触即
trigger 微火触发器 / '~-,**trigger** *a.* ①一触即
发的; 即时的 ②一碰就坏的 / '~-,**weaving** *n.*
(尼龙)假发植入(术)

hairy ['hɛəri] *a.* ①毛的;多毛的;有茸毛的 ②毛
状的 ③[美俚]粗鲁的, 使人不快的 ④[美俚]
(笑话等)陈腐得发了霉的‖**hairily** *ad.* / **hairiness**
n. ‖'~-'**chested** *a.* 粗壮的 / '~-'**heeled** *a.*
[俚]没教养的, 没礼貌的

hake [heik] *n.*【动】狗鳕, 无须鳕

halcyon ['hælsiən] I *n.* ①【动】翠鸟, 鱼狗 ②传
说中的鸟(巢居海上, 冬至产卵时能使海波平静)
II *a.* ①翠鸟的; 翠鸟产卵期的 ②平静的: ~
days 冬至前后十四天的日子; 海上平静的日子
③愉快的, 美好的 ④富饶的

ale¹ [heil] *a.* (尤指老人)强壮的,矍铄的 ‖*~ and hearty* 矍铄,健壮 ‖*~ness n.*

ale² [heil] *vt.* 强拉;硬拖

alf [hɑːf] **I** [复] **halves** [hɑːvz] *n.* ①半,一半: It is ~ past six. 现在是六点半。(句中的 ~ past 连读作 ['hɑːpast]) / A year and a ~ (或 One and a ~ years) *has* passed. 一年半的时间过去了。/ *Half* (of) our work *is* done. 我们的工作已完成一半。/ *Half of the books are* novels. 这些书有一半是小说书。/ cut sth. in ~ (或 into *halves*) 把某物切成两半 ②(球赛的)半场 ③[英]半学年,学期 ④[美俚](足球)中卫 **II** *a.* ①一半的: ~ an hour (或 a ~ hour) 半小时 / He works ~ shift. 他上半班。②不完全的,部分的: ~ knowledge 一知半解 **III** *ad.* ①一半地: Don't leave the work ~ done. 工作不要做了一半就丢了。②相当地: We were ~ convinced. 我们有点信服了。 ‖*better ~* [谑]妻子 / *by halves* 不完全地;不完善地: We do nothing *by halves*. 我们干什么都是彻底的。/ *cry halves* 要求平分 / *go halves (with sb. in sth.)* (与某人)平分(某物) / *~ as much (或 many) again* 加半倍,一倍半 / *~ the battle* 成功一半 / *not* ~ ①少于一半地;一点儿也不: *not* ~ bad 很不错,挺好 ②[英俚]多于一半地;非常: A: Would you like to come? B: *Not* ~! 甲:你愿来吗? 乙:我非常愿意。[注意:上句中的 half 常与读作 'alf]

‖*~-and-'~ n.* 两种成分各半的东西(如由淡,烈两种酒搀成的酒) *a.* 两种成分各半的 *ad.* 各半 / '~-'back *n.* (足球)中卫 / '~-'baked *a.* [口]烤得半生不熟的;[喻](想法等)肤浅的;(人)无见识的,象半瓶醋似的 / ~ binding 半精装 / ~ blood 同父异母(或同母异父)关系;同父异母(或同母异父)的兄弟(或姐妹) / ~ boot 半高统靴 / '~-'bound *a.* 半精装的 / '~-'bred *a.* 混血的;(动植物)杂种的 / '~-'breed *n. & a.* 混血(的);(动植物)杂种(的) / '~-,brother *n.* 异父(或异母)兄弟 / ~ cell *n.* [化]半电池 / '~-'cocked *a.* ①(枪)处于半击发状态的,机头半张开的 ②事前未充分准备好的,仓促行事的 / '~-'cracked *a.* (人)迟钝的;~ crown 英国银币名(合英旧币二先令六便士) / ~ deck 商船上见习生的宿舍 / '~-'hardy *a.* (植物等)尚能经得起一般寒冷的,在冬季需防霜雪的 / '~-'hearted *a.* 半心半意的: be ~-*hearted about* sth. 对某事半心半意敷衍塞责 / ~ hitch (易解开的)简单结子 / '~-'hourly *a. & ad.* 每半小时的(地) / '~-'length *n.* 半身像 *a.* 半身的 / '~-life *n.* 半排出期(放射性同位素从生物有机体中排出一半量的时间) / ~ line [数]半直线 / '~-'long *a.* [语]半长音的 / '~-'mast *n.* (表示哀悼)半旗: hang (或 hoist, fly) a flag at ~-*mast* 下半旗 *vt.* 下半(旗) /

~ measure 折衷办法 / ~ moon 半月(形) / ~ nelson (摔角)扼颈 / '~-'round *a.* 半圆形的 / '~-seas-'over, '~-'shot *a.* [俚]半醉的 / '~-,sister *n.* 异父(或异母)姐妹 / ~ sole (鞋的)前掌 / '~-'sole *vt.* 给(鞋)打前掌: have one's shoes *~-soled* 给鞋子打前掌 / '~-staff *n. & vt.* =~-mast / ~ step ①小步,快步 ②[音]半音 / ~ stuff (造纸用的)半料料 / ~ timber [建](房屋等)半露木的 / ~-'time *n.* ①半工半薪: be on *~-time* 做半工支半薪 ②(比赛中上下半场间的)休息时间: What's the score at *~-time?* 上半场比分多少? / '~-'timer *n.* [英]以一半时间上课一半时间做工糊口的学龄儿童 / ~ tint 中间色调;(绘画等中的)中间色调部分 / ~ title ① 印在书籍扉页前(或后)面一页上的书名(常以缩略形式出现) ② 印在书籍篇章页上的篇章名 / '~-tone *n.* ①[印]照相铜版,网目铜版: ~*tone* ink 照相铜版印刷油墨 / ~*tone* news 照相铜版印刷用报纸 ②(摄影形象的)中间色调 ③[音]半音 / '~-'track *n.* 半履带;半履带式车辆 / '~-'truth *n.* 只有部分真实性的欺人的报导(或陈述等) / ~-'way *ad.* ①半途 ②几乎,快要: I have ~*way* decided to go. 我已差不多决定要去了。*a.* 半途中的: a ~*way* house 两城镇当中的旅店; [喻]妥协方案,折衷办法; (为长期监禁或住院治疗者等而设的)重返社会训练所;吸毒者的戒瘾治疗中心 / '~-wit *n.* 笨蛋 / '~-witted *a.* 愚笨的,智力上有缺陷的 / '~-'yearly *a. & ad.* 每半年的(地)

hall [hɔːl] *n.* ①会堂,礼堂,大厅: the Town(或 City) *Hall* 市政府,市府大礼堂 / a banquet ~ 宴会厅 ②娱乐厅 ③门厅; (大厦的)过道;走廊 ④(大学的)学院;讲堂;学生宿舍 ⑤[英](大学中的)公共食堂;公共食堂里的一餐: dine in ~ 在食堂里用膳 / *Hall* is at six. 食堂六时开饭。⑥(协会、工会等的)办公大楼,会所 ⑦[英]地主庄园 ⑧(中世纪王公贵族的)府第,邸宅 ‖*a Hall of fame* ① 名人遗物收藏馆 ② [总称](体育运动等方面的)佼佼者 / *Hall of ivy* [美]高等学校 ‖'~'mark *n.* (伦敦金业公会证明金银纯度的)检验印记;品质证明 ②标志,特点 *vt.* 在…上盖检验印记 / '~stand *n.* 衣帽架 / '~way *n.* [美]门厅;过道

hallelujah, halleluiah [ˌhæliˈluːjə] *n. & int.* =alleluia

hallo(a) [həˈlou] **I** *int.* ①喂! ②啊呀! **II** *n.* "喂"的一声;"啊呀"的一声 **III** *vt. & vi.* (向…)"喂"地叫一声

halloo [həˈluː] **I** *int.* 喂! 嗨! [嗾狗声和引人注意的喊声] **II** *n.* "喂"的一声;"嗨"的一声 **III** *vt. & vi.* 嗾(狗); 呼喊(人) ‖*Do not ~ until you are out of the wood(s).* [谚]未出危险境,切莫先高兴。

hallow¹ [ˈhælou] **I** *n.* 圣徒 **II** *vt.* [常用被动语态] ①使成神圣;把…视为神圣: a ~*ed* ground 圣地 ②崇敬

hallow² [həˈlou] *int., n., vt. & vi.* =halloo

hallucinate [hə'lu:sineit] *vt.* 使生幻觉 ‖**hallucination** [hə,lu:si'neiʃən] *n.* 幻觉; 幻觉象 / **hallucinatory** [hə'lu:sinətəri] *a.* 幻觉的, 引起幻觉的

halo ['heilou] **I** ([复] halo(e)s) *n.* ①(环绕日月等的)晕, 晕圈 ②(绘于神像头上的)光环 ③(赋予理想化人物或事物的)光辉, 光荣 ④【解】乳晕, 乳头轮 **II ❶** *vt.* 使成晕圈; 以光圈围绕 **❷** *vi.* 成晕圈

halt[1] [hɔ:lt] **I** *n.* ①(行进间的)暂停前进; 止步 ②停住, 停止: The car came to a sudden ~. 汽车突然停了下来。③[英](铁路)招呼站, 旗站 **II ❶** *vi.* ①(军队等口令)立定, 站住: *Halt!* Who goes there? 站住! 谁? ②停止前进; 停止: The soldiers ~ed for a short rest. 士兵们停下来休息一会儿。/ The leakage ~ed. 渗漏停止了。**❷** *vt.* 使停止前进; 使停止, 使终止: The shelter belt ~ed the soil erosion. 防护林带防止了水土流失。‖*bring to a ~* 使停止 / *call* (或 *cry*) *a ~* (命令)停止: *call a ~ to attacks* 停止进攻

halt[2] [hɔ:lt] **I** *vi.* ①蹒跚, 跛行 ②踌躇, 犹豫: ~ *between two opinions* 拿不定主意 ③(论点, 诗的格律等)有缺点; 不完全 **II** *n.* & *a.* [古]跛(的)

halter ['hɔ:ltə] **I** *n.* ①(马等的)笼头, 缰绳 ②绞索; 绞刑 ③(女用)三角背心 **II** *vt.* ①给…套上笼头 (*up*) ②绞死(某人) ③束缚, 抑制 ‖'~**break** *vt.* 使(马)带惯笼头

halting ['hɔ:ltiŋ] *a.* ①跛的, 蹒跚的 ②踌躇的, 迟疑不决的: speak in a ~ way 说话吞吞吐吐 ‖~**ly** *ad.*

halve [hɑ:v] *vt.* ①把…分为相等的两部分: ~ a match (高尔夫球等比赛中)打成平手 ②平均分担: ~ expenses with sb. 与某人平摊费用 ③将…减半: The new method has ~d the production cost. 新方法使生产成本减少一半。④【建】把开半对搭

halves [hɑ:vz] half 的复数

halyard ['hæljəd] *n.* 升降索; 旗绳; 扬帆索

ham[1] [hæm] **I** *n.* ①火腿: a ~ 一只火腿 / a slice of ~ 一片火腿 / a ~ and egg 一客火腿蛋 ②膝胭; (兽类的)后踝; [常用复]腿臀: squat on one's ~s 蹲下 ③[俚]拙劣的表演者(尤指演得过火的拙劣演员) (hamfatter 的缩略) ④无线电收发报业余爱好者 ⑤[俚]做作的人 **II** *a.* ①过火的, 做作的; [俚]整脚的 ②业余搞无线电收发报的 **III** (hammed; hamming) *vt.* & *vi.* (把剧中角色等)演得过火 ‖'~-**and**-'**egger** *n.* [俚]①普通人 ②不出众的拳击师 / '~-**and**-'**eggery** *n.* [俚]小饭店; 简易餐柜 / '~-'**fisted** *a.* [主英] = ~-handed / '~-**handed** *a.* 笨手笨脚的

ham[2] [hæm] *n.* (旧时的)小镇, 村庄

hamlet ['hæmlit] *n.* 村庄(尤指没有教堂的小村子)

hammer ['hæmə] **I** *n.* ①锤, 榔头: a soldering 烙铁 / a ~ and sickle 锤子和镰刀图案 ②(电铃的)小锤子; 锣锤; (钢琴等的)音锤 ③(会议主席或拍卖人等用的)小木锤, 杵锤 ④【机】落锤, 杵锤 ⑤【军】(用以击动撞针或击发火帽的)击铁 ⑥【体】链球: throw the ~ 掷链球 ⑦【解】(中耳的)锤骨 **II ❶** *vt.* ①锤击; 锤成; (反复)锤打: ~ *in a na* (或 ~ a nail *in*) 把一枚钉子敲进去 / ~ *an into* sb.'s head 把一种思想硬灌给某人 ②[英](交易所)击锤宣布(某人)无力偿债 ③[口](在竞争或比赛中)使惨败 **❷** *vi.* 接连锤打 ‖*a knigh of the ~* 见 knight / *be* (或 *go*) *at it* ~ *an tongs* 闹哄哄地激烈殴斗(或辩论) / *between* (*the*) ~ *and* (*the*) *anvil* 腹背受敌, 被两面夹攻 / *be* (或 *come*) *under the* ~ 被拍卖 / *bring sth under the* ~ 把某物拿去拍卖 / ~ *and tongs* 全力以赴地; 大刀阔斧地: work ~ *and tongs t raise* productivity 全力提高生产率 / ~ *at* ①(接连)敲打: ~ *at* the gate 砰砰地敲打大门 ②(不断)致力于, 埋头于: ~ *at* a problem 努研究一个问题 ③不断强调, 重复论及: ~ *awa at* the same point 老是强调着同一论点 / ~ *out* ①锤成, 锤出: ~ *out* a metal pattern 锤出金属模 ②锤炼出, 设计出: ~ *out* a plan 经过仔细琢酌订出计划 ③在琴上弹出(曲调) ④锤平; [喻调整, 消除: ~ *out* differences in discussion 讨论中消除分歧 / *up to the ~* 第一流的, 极好的 ‖~**less** *a.* ①无锤的 ②【军】内击铁的(指铁在枪的内部) / **~ beam** 【建】橡尾(小)梁 '~**blow** *n.* 锤打 / '~**cloth** *n.* 赶马车人座位上的布篷 / '~**head** *n.* ①锤头 ②愚笨的人 ③【动】双髻鲨 / '~**headed** *a.* 有锤状头的; 愚笨的 / '~**lock** *n.* (摔跤中)将对方的手臂扭到背后 / **~man** ['hæməmən], '~**smith** *n.* 锻工 / '~**toe** *n.* 【医】锤状趾

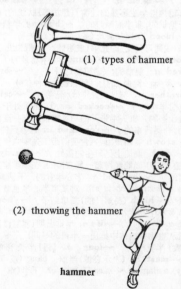

(1) types of hammer

(2) throwing the hammer

hammer

hammock[1] ['hæmɘk] *n.* (帆布或网状的)吊床: a ～ chair 帆布椅

hammock[2] ['hæmɘk] *n.* ①圆丘，小丘；(冰原上的)冰丘 ②(美国南部)产硬木地区

hamper[1] ['hæmpɘ] I *vt.* 妨碍，阻碍；牵制: be ～ed by a heavy load 为重担所拖累 II *n.* ①阻碍物 ②【海】平时不可少而在风浪中反成累赘的船具

hamper[2] ['hæmpɘ] *n.* (装送食物等用的)有盖大篮

hamstring ['hæm-strin] I *n.* 【解】腘旁腱；【动】(兽类的)后腿腱 II (hamstringed 或 hamstrung [hæm-strʌŋ]) *vt.* 割断…的腿腱；使残废

hand [hænd] I *n.* ①手: Ample food and clothing by working with our own ～s. 自己动手 丰衣足食 / stretch out the ～ of friendship to sb. 向某人伸出友谊之手 / a show of ～s 举手(表决)
②(猴子的)脚；(四足兽的)前脚
③(钟表等的)指针: the hour (minute, second) ～ 时(分,秒)针
④人手，雇员(指工人、船员等): Many ～s provide great strength. 人多力量大。/ be short of ～s 缺少人手 / All ～s on deck! 【海】全体船员到甲板上集合!
⑤作某种工作的人，有某种经验的人: a good ～ (或 quite a ～) at pig breeding 养猪能手 / a new (an old, a green) ～ 新(老,生)手 / a picture by the same ～ 同一人画的画
⑥手艺，才能: try one's ～ at chess 试着下棋 / His ～ is out. 他的技能荒疏了。
⑦字迹，手迹: write a good (legible) ～ 字写得好(清楚) / a small ～ 一般书写体
⑧[公文用语]签字: set one's ～ to a document 在文件上签字
⑨支配,掌管;照管: The child is in good ～s. 这孩子由人好好地照看着。
⑩插手; 经手,一手造成: have a ～ in sth. 插手某事
⑪帮助(尤指动手帮助)
⑫方面，面: on every ～ (或 on all ～s) 在各方面 / at (又 on) sb.'s left ～ 在某人左边
⑬[与序数词连用,表示事物的来源,指经过…个人的手]第…手: learn sth. (at) first ～ from sb. 直接从某人处得知某事 / material at second ～ 第二手材料
⑭答允；允婚: Give me your ～ on that. 在那一点上请答应我。(含握手表示赞同之意) / give one's ～ on a bargain 握手成交 / ask for a girl's ～ 向女子求婚
⑮像手的东西；(香蕉的)一串；(烟草、麻等的)一束: a ～ of bananas 一串香蕉
⑯(纸牌游戏中)手中的牌；打牌的人；牌戏的一盘
⑰一手之宽(约四吋,用量马的高度等)
⑱[口]鼓掌: give a performer a big ～ 向演员热烈鼓掌
⑲(织物、皮革等摸上去的)手感

II *vt.* ① 交出；传递，给: Hand me the hammer, please. 请把榔头递给我。/ ～ sb. a blow 给某人一击
②挽扶: ～ sb. into (out of) the car 扶某人上(下)车
③【海】收卷(风帆)
‖*a cool* ～ 大胆而厚脸皮的人 / *a free* ～ 放手处理的权力 / *a light* ～ 熟练(的手艺): play the piano with *a light* ～ 熟练地弹钢琴 / *all* ～*s to the pump(s)* 大家都来帮忙 / *a nap* ～ 见 *nap*[3] / *at* ～ ①近在手边,在附近: I haven't my book *at* ～, but I'll show it to you later. 我的书不在手边,以后再给你看吧。/ live close *at* ～ 住在附近 ②即将到来: The autumn harvest is *at* ～. 秋收即将到来。/ *at sb.'s* ～(s) (或 *at the* ～(s) *of sb.*) 在某人手下 / *bear a* ～ 出一把力,帮助;参加(*in*) / *be prepared to put one's* ～ *in one's pocket* 见 *pocket* / *bite the* ～ *that feeds one* 恩将仇报 / *by* ～ 用手;made *by* ～ 手制的 / The letter was delivered *by* ～. 此信由专人递送。(指不由邮寄) / *by the left* ～ ①贵族男子娶非贵族女子所生的;门第不相称的婚姻所生的 ②私生的 / *by the strong* ～ 强制地 / *change* ～*s* 转手,易手 / *come to* ～ Your letter has just *come to* ～. 刚收到你的信。/ *cross sb.'s* ～ (用钱币)在某人手心中划一个十字(指把钱币付给算命者);[喻]贿赂某人 / *die by one's own* ～ 自杀 / *eat* (或 *feed*) *out of sb.'s* ～ 完全顺从某人,完全受某人控制 / *force one's* ～ (在某人尚未准备好时)迫某人行动(或表态) / *from* ～ *to* ～ 从一人之手转到他人之手 / *from* ～ *to mouth* 现挣现吃地;仅够糊口地 / *get one's* ～ *in* 使自己熟习技能(或熟悉工作) / *get sth. off one's* ～*s* 摆脱掉某事物;摆脱对某事的责任: I have *got it off my* ～*s*. 我已经把这件事了结了。/ *give one's* ～ *to sb.* (女子)答应和某人结婚 / *give sb. a* (或 *the*) *glad* ～ [俚]欢迎某人 / *give (sb.) a* ～ 给予(某人)帮助 / *grease the* ～ *of* 买通…,向…行贿 / ～ *and foot* ①手脚一起;完全地: bind sb. ～ *and foot* 把某人完全捆住(或束缚住) ②勤勉而周到地: serve (或 wait on) sb. ～ *and foot* 辛勤服侍某人 / ～ *down* ①把…传下来 ②宣布(判词等) / ～ *in* 交进,交上 / ～ *in* (或 *and*) *glove* ①亲密地 ②勾结着: have all along worked ～ *in glove* with 一直和…狼狈为奸 / ～ *in* ～ ①手拉手 ②联合;连在一起地: act ～ *in* ～ 联合行动 / ～ *it to sb.* [美俚]赞扬某人,承认某人的长处 / ～ *on* 把…传(给)下去 / ～ *out* ①把…拿出来 ②分派 ③施舍 / ～ *over* 移交; 交出 / ～ *over fist* ①不费力地,大量地 ②=～ over / ～ *over* ～ ①(爬绳等时)节节往上地 ②[喻]稳而快地(前进): overtake sb. ～ *over* ～ 稳而快地追过某人 / ～*s down* 容易地,不费力地: win the game ～ *down* 不费力地在比赛中获胜 / 无疑地 / *Hands off*! 请勿动手!不许碰! / *Hands off . . .*! 不许干涉…! /

Hands up! 举起手来! (要对方不抵抗的命令)/ ~ *to fist* [口]亲密的(地);齐心协力的(地)/ ~ *to* ~ 逼近地: fight ~ *to* ~ 短兵相接,肉搏/ *have an open* ~ 慷慨/ *have one's* ~*s free* ①空着手;没有事情干 ②可以自由地干/ *have one's* ~*s full* 手头工作很忙/ *heavy in* (或 *on*)~ 难以驾驭;[喻](人)难对付,难取悦/ *hold* ~*s* 手挽手/ *hold one's* ~ 迟疑不下手/ *in* ~ ①现有在手头: have enough data *in* ~ 手头有足够的资料 ②(工作等)在进行中: put sth. *in* ~ 开始做某事/ The work is *in* ~, and will soon be completed. 工作在进行中,很快就要完成。③掌握住,控制住: have the situation well *in* ~ 完全掌握着局势/ *join* ~*s* (*with*) ①(同…)携手联合 ②(同…)合伙开店 ③(同…)做夫妻/ *keep a firm* ~ *on* (或 *keep one's* ~*s on*) (紧紧)控制…/ *keep a slack* ~ 放松缰绳;[喻]漫不经心地管理,懈怠/ *keep* (或 *have*) *one's* ~ *in* 使技能不荒疏/ *kiss* ~*s* (或 *the* ~) 吻君王的手(一种礼仪)/ *kiss one's* ~ *to* 向…飞吻/ *lay* ~*s on* ①得到,抓到 ②对…动武,攻击;伤害 ③找到 ④【宗】(为祝福、授牧师职等)对…行按手礼/ *lay one's* ~ *on the table* =show one's ~/ *lay* (*violent*) ~*s on oneself* 对自己下毒手(指自杀)/ *lend a* ~ 帮助: Please lend me a ~ to shift this bookshelf. 请帮我把书架移动一下。 *lend a* ~ *in doing sth.* 帮忙做某事/ *lie on sb.'s* ~(*s*) ①(商品)滞留在某人手中未卖出;(物件)尚在某人手中未用掉 ②(时间)使某人感到无聊/ *lift a* ~ (*to do sth.*) 费举手之劳 (去做某事)/ *lift one's* ~ 举手宣誓/ *lift* (或 *raise*) *one's* (或 *a*)~ *against* 打;威胁/ *light in* ~ (马等)易于驾驭/ *marry with the left* ~ 与门第比自己低的人结婚/ *not lift a* ~ (或 *not do a* ~*'s turn*) 不动手;不帮忙/ *offer one's* ~ ①伸出手来(准备握手) ②向女子求婚/ *offer* (或 *give*) *sb. the right* ~ *of fellowship* ①同某人结交 ②同意某人入伙合作/ *off* ~ 立即,当下;事先无准备地: We cannot give you a reply *off* ~. 我们不能马上给你回音。/ *off sb.'s* ~*s* 已不由某人掌管;不再由某人负责/ *one's* (或 *the*) *right* ~ ①右手;得力助手: put *one's right* ~ *to the work* 尽全力工作 ②右手,右方/ *on* ~ ①现有在手头: have a large stock *on* ~ 手头有大批存货 ②[美]即将发生 ③[美]在场,到场/ *on sb.'s* ~*s* 由某人负责照管: She has a large family *on* her ~*s*. 她有许多子女要由她照顾。/ *on the mending* ~ (病情或事态)在好转中/ *on* (*the*) *one* ~, ... *on the other* (~) 一方面…,另一方面…/ *out of* ~ ①无法控制,不可收拾: His wrath got *out of* ~. 他怒不可遏。②脱手;告终 ③立即: deal with sth. *out of* ~ 立即处理某事/ *play a lone* ~ 单枪匹马地干/ *play for one's own* ~ 为自己的利益而做/ *play into the* ~*s of* (或 *sb.'s* ~*s*) 为某人利益而做;干对某人有利的事/ *put* (或 *set*) *one's* ~ *to the plough* 着手一项工作/ (*ready*) *to one's*

~ 就在手边;就可用/ *set one's* ~ *to* ①着手从事于 ②在…上签字;批准,承认/ *shake sb.'s* ~ (或 *shake* ~*s with sb.* 或 *shake sb. by the* ~) 同某人握手/ *show one's* ~ 摊牌,表明自己的真实目的/ *sit on one's* ~*s* [美俚] ①(观众等)不予鼓掌 ②(应采取行动时)坐守不前/ *stay one's* (*sb.'s*) ~ (使某人)住手不作某事/ *strengthen sb.'s* ~ 增加某人的资本,增强某人的实力/ *strengthen sb.'s* ~*s* 使某人得以采取强有力的行动/ *take in* ~ ①承担 ②处理 ③尝试/ *the upper* ~ 优势: get (或 gain) *the upper* ~ *of* 占…的上风/ have (lose) *the upper* ~ 占(丧失)优势/ *throw in one's* ~ 放弃;退出竞争/ *throw up one's* ~*s* 绝望/ *tip one's* ~ 宣布自己的意图,摊牌/ *to* ~ 在手头/ *turn* (或 *put*) *one's* (或 *a, the*) ~ *to* 承担,着手做/ *wash one's* ~*s* ①洗手 ②解手/ *wash one's* ~*s of* 洗手不干(某事);不再管(某事或某人)/ *wash one's* ~*s with invisible soap and imperceptible water* (由于扭怩、紧张等)搓手/ *with a bold* ~ 大胆地/ *with a firm* ~ 坚决地/ *with a free* ~ ①慷慨地,不吝惜地 ②浪费地,无节制地/ *with a heavy* ~ ①粗手粗脚地,粗枝大叶地 ②高压地;严厉地/ *with a high* ~ 用高压手段;傲慢地/ *with an iron* ~ 以铁腕,苛严地/ *with an iron* ~ *in a velvet glove* 外柔内刚地;口蜜腹剑地/ *with a strong* ~ 断然,强硬地/ *with clean* ~*s* 清白无罪地;廉洁地/ *wring one's* ~*s* (*over sth.*) (为某事)苦恼(或悲痛、绝望)地绞扭着手
‖~*less a.* ①无手的 ②手笨拙的
‖'~*arm n.* (手)枪/ '~*bag n.* ① (女用)手提包 ②旅行包/ '~*ball n.* 手球;手球游戏/ '~*barrow n.* ① 两边有手柄的抬物架 ② 手推小车/ '~*bell n.* 手摇铃(尤指音乐演奏时所用)/ '~*bill n.* 传单/ '~*book n.* 手册/ '~*brake n.* 手煞车/ '~*breadth n.* 一手之宽(从 2½ 吋到 4 吋)/ '~*car n.* 铁路上所用手摇(或马达开动)的四轮小车/ '~*cart n.* 手推(或手拉)小车/ '~*clap n.* 拍手: a slow ~*clap* 慢而有节奏的拍手(表示不耐烦或不满)/ '~*craft n.* =handicraft/ '~*cuff vt.* 用手工造/ '~*cuff n.* [常用复]手铐 *vt.* 给…上手铐/ '~*drill n.* 手摇钻/ '~*glass n.* ①有柄的小镜子 ②(手拿的)放大镜/ '~*grenade n.* 手榴弹/ '~*grip n.* ①紧握 ②柄 ③[复]肉搏: come to ~*grips* 搏斗起来/ '~*gun n.* =~arm/ ~*hold n.* ① 紧握 ② (攀登时)能用手抓住的东西/ '~*-in-'~ a.* ①手牵手的;亲密的 ②并进的/ '~ *language* (聋哑人用的)手势语/ '~ *level n.* 【测】手持水平仪/ '~*line n.* (不用钓鱼杆的)手钓丝/ '~*loom n.* 手织机/ '~ '*luggage n.* 手提行李: a piece of ~*luggage* 一件手提行李/ '~*made a.* 手工制的 *n.* 手工制品(尤指手工品、手制服装)/ '~*maid, '~maiden n.* 侍女,女仆;[喻]起陪衬(或侍奉)作用的东西/ '~*down a.* [口] ①现成的(常指廉价而劣等的) ②用旧的 *n.* [口] ①现成的衣服;旧衣服 ②旧用

物 / ~ **organ** 手摇风琴 / '~**out** n. ①施舍物; 救济品 ②免费发给的新闻通报(或广告单等) ③送给报界刊登的声明 / '~-**over** a. 移交的: complete ~-*over* procedure 完成交接手续 / '~-'**picked** a. ①用手挑选出的 ②精选的 / '~**play** n. 互殴, 扭打 / ~ **pump** 手力唧筒 / '~**rail** n. 扶手, 栏杆 / '~-'**reared** a. 一手养大的 / '~**saw** n. 手锯 / '~**s-down** a. ①唾手可得的, 轻而易举的 ②无疑的 / '~**set** n. 【讯】送受话器, 手机 / '~**shake** n. 握手 / '~**s-off** a. 不干涉的; 不插手的: a ~*s-off* policy 不干涉政策 / '~-**sort** vt. 手拣, 用手工把…分类 / '~**spike** n. 杠, 推杆 / '~**spring** n. 双手, 双脚先后轮流着地向前(或向后)的翻翻 / '~**stand** n. 倒立 / '~-**taut**, '~-**tight** a. 【海】用手劲尽量拉紧的 / '~-**to**-'~ a. 逼近的: a ~*-to-*~ combat【军】白刃战, 肉搏 ② 一个一个传过去的 / '~-**to**-'**mouth** a. 勉强糊口的 / ~ **vice** 手钳 / ~ **vote** 举手选举 / '~**work** n. 手工 / '~'**worked**, '~-'**wrought** a. 手工制成的 / '~'**woven** a. 手织的: ~*woven* cloth 土布

handed ['hændid] a. ①有手的 ②[用以构成复合词]有…手的; 用…手的: two-~ 有两只手的 / left-~ 惯用左手的 ③[用以构成复合词]…个人玩的: a three-~ game 三人玩的游戏 ‖'~-**down** a. 传下来的

handful ['hændful] n. ①一把: a ~ of rice 一把米 ②少数, 一小撮 ③[口]难控制的人; 麻烦的事

handicap ['hændikæp] I n. ①障碍, 不利条件: clear away all ~s on one's way of advance 扫除前进道路上的一切障碍 ②给优者不利条件、给劣者有利条件以使得胜的机会均等的一种赛跑(或竞赛) ③给优者的不利条件(或给劣者的有利条件) II (handicapped; handicapping) vt. ①妨碍, 使不利: Though *handicapped* by poor health, he persisted in working. 他虽然身体不好, 还是坚持工作。/ a *handicapped* child 残废的儿童 ②给(竞赛者)不利条件(或有利条件)

handicraft ['hændikrɑ:ft] n. ①手艺 ②手工业, 手工艺 ③[总称]手工艺品 ‖~**sman** ['hændikrɑ:ftsmən] n. 手工业者; 手工艺人

handiwork ['hændiwə:k] n. ①手工; [总称]手工制品 ②(某人)亲自做的事情

handkerchief ['hæŋkətʃif] ([复] handkerchiefs 或 handkerchieves ['hæŋkətʃi:vz]) n. ①手帕 ②围巾, 头巾 ‖*throw the ~ to sb.* (游戏时)丢手帕给某人使他追赶自己; [喻]看中某人

handl['hændl] I n. ①柄, 把手: a hammer (hoe) ~ 榔头(锄头)柄 ②[喻]把柄; 可乘之机: give sb. a ~ (*against* oneself) 给人拿住把柄(来反对自己) ③[口]称号, 头衔 ④(织物等褾上去的)手感 ⑤(对赛马等所投下的)赌金总额 II ❶ vt. ①触, 摸, 拿; 弄: Wash your hands before *handling* the forceps. 洗手后再拿镊子。②运用; 操纵; 驾驭(马): ~ a gun with precision 打枪打得准 / ~

a machine 开机器 ③处理; 管理, 对待(人) ④经营, 买卖 ❷ vi. ①(用手)搬运: *Handle* with care! 小心轻放! ②易于操纵: This car ~s well. 这车很好驾驶。‖*fly off the ~* [美俚]冒火, 勃然大怒 ‖~**r** n. ①处理者, 管理者; [美](拳击选手的)训练者 ②【自】(信息)处理机 / **handling** n. 处理; 管理; 操纵; 装卸 ‖~-**bar** n. (自行车等的)把手

handsome ['hænsəm] a. ①相当大的, 可观的: a ~ sum 一笔可观的金额 ②慷慨的, 大方的, 气量大的: ~ treatment 优待 / It is very ~ of you to say so. 你这么说真太好了。③漂亮的, 清秀的(一般指男子); 端庄的, 温雅的(指女子) ④堂皇的; 美观的: a ~ building 堂皇的建筑 ⑤熟练的, 灵敏的; [方]操纵起来灵便的; 近便的 ⑥[方]合适的 ‖*Handsome is that ~ does.* [谚] 行为漂亮才是漂亮。‖~**ly** ad. ①漂亮地, 美观地; 慷慨地, 优厚地: He came down ~*ly.* 他慷慨解囊。②[海]慢慢地, 当心地; 整齐地 / ~**ness** n.

handwriting ['hænd,raitiŋ] n. ①笔迹 ②手写物, 手写稿 ‖*the ~ on the wall* 凶事的预兆

handy ['hændi] a. ①手边的, 近便的: Have you got your ticket ~? 你是不是已把票子取出放在手边了? ②便于使用的; 方便的 ③(船等)驾驶起来灵便的 ④手灵巧的: be ~ with a paintbrush 善于用画笔 ‖*come in ~* 迟早有用 ‖~-'**dandy** n. [英](儿童玩的)猜别人哪一只手里握有物件的游戏 / '~**man** n. ①干零碎杂活的人 ②手巧的人

hang [hæŋ] I (hung [hʌŋ] 或 hanged) ❶ vt. ①悬挂 ②(用悬挂的东西)装饰 ③贴(糊墙纸等) ④垂下: ~ one's head and admit one's guilt 低头认罪 ⑤安装(活动的东西): ~ a door on its hinges 把门装到铰链上 ⑥[过去式和过去分词用hanged]绞死; 吊死 ⑦[用于诅咒语中]: *Hang* it! 该死! / *Hang* you! 该死! (指人) ⑧[美]使(陪审团)不能作出决定: The trial ended with a *hung* jury. 审判因陪审团不能作出一致的决定而悬而不决。⑨悬挂展出(画作等) ❷ vi. ①悬挂, 吊着 ②垂下, 披下 ③被绞死; 被吊死 ④悬而不决: The decision is still ~*ing.* 尚未作出决定。⑤逗留; 紧紧缠住: The notion *hung* in his mind for days. 几天来他老是在转这个念头。II n. [只用单] ①悬挂方式 ②[口]做法; 用法; 诀窍: get the ~ of driving a tractor 得知开拖拉机的窍门 ③[口]大意, 要点: I don't quite get the ~ of the discourse. 我不十分了解谈话的要点。④(动作的)暂停: ~ go ~ 不再被关心, 被忘却: let things *go* ~ 听之任之 / ~ *about* ①闲荡 ②聚在…临近 / ~ *around* = ~ about / ~ *back* 犹豫; 畏缩不前 / ~ *behind* 落在后面 / ~ *by a hair* 见 hair / ~ *fire* 见 fire / ~ *in doubt* 见 doubt / ~ *in (the) balance* 见 balance / ~ *it out* 急工, 拖延工作 / ~ *off* = ~ back / ~ *on* ①紧握着不撒手 ②坚持下去 ③赖着不走; (疾病等)继续存在 ④(打电话时用语)不

挂断 ⑤倚，靠：～ *on* sb.'s arm 靠在某人臂上 ⑥渴望：～ *on* (或 *upon*) sb.'s answers 渴望某人的回答 ⑦有赖于，视…而定 / ～ *one on* [俚] 向…猛击一拳 ②大醉／～ *on to* 紧紧握住／*out* ①把…挂出：～ the washing *out* in the courtyard 把洗好的衣服挂在院子里 ②挂出 ③上身伸出(窗外) ④[俚]居住 ⑤[美俚]闲荡 ⑥[口](为等较好的条件而)拖延 (*for*) / ～ *out the laundry* 见 **laundry** / ～ *over* ①挂在…上; 靠近在…上 ②突出，伸出 ③笼罩;威胁 ④被遗留下来 / ～ *round* =～ about / ～ *together* ① 结合在一起 ② 符合：Their accounts do not ～ *together*. 他们的叙述不相符合。/ ～ *up* ①把 …挂起来 ② 挂断(电话)：～ *up* (或 ～ *up the receiver*) 挂断电话 ③延迟，拖延 ④(使)搁住;使受旧框框限制: The fishing boat *hung up* (或 was *hung up*) on a sandbar. 这条渔船在沙滩上搁浅了。/ *hung over* [美俚]因宿醉而感觉不适的／*hung up (on)* [美俚] ①(因…而)精神不安的；(因…而)神经质的 ②(因…而)失意的 ③(嗜…)成瘾;入迷(于…)的 / *I'll be ～ed if ....* 决不,决不会: *I'll be ～ed if* I do so. 我决不会干那种事的。/ *I'll be ～ed if* that's true. 那决不会是真的。/ *not care* (或 *give*) *a ～ (about sth.)* (对某事)一点也不在乎 / *Time ～s heavy on sb.'s hands*. 见 time ‖'~dog n. 卑鄙的人 *a.* 卑鄙的; 惭愧的,自觉有罪的 / ~man ['hæn-mən] *n.* 执行绞刑者; 刽子手 \ ~nail *n.* 手指头上的倒刺 / ~out *n.* [俚] 常去的地方; 聚集处 / '~,over *n.* ① 遗留物(尤指习惯等) ②[俚]宿醉 / '~tag *n.* (商品上的)使用保养说明标签 / '~-up *n.* ①(滑道上的)障碍物; 障碍 ②大难题(尤指个人感情方面的) / '~wire *n.* 炸弹保险丝

hangar ['hæŋə] **I** *n.* 飞机棚,飞机库 **II** *vt.* 把(飞机)放入机库中 ‖*a ～ pilot* [美俚]好胡吹而实不会驾驶飞机的人 ‖~ **deck** (航空母舰上的)(飞)机库甲板

hanger ['hæŋə] *n.* ①挂东西的人; 糊墙的人: a paper ～ 裱糊匠 ②挂物的东西; 挂钩;【机】吊架,吊承: a clothes ～ 衣架 ③挂着的东西(尤指挂在皮带上的短剑) ④执行绞刑者 ⑤钩状笔划 ⑥[主英]陡坡上的丛林 ‖~-on ['hæŋər'ɔn] ([复] ~s-on ['hæŋəz'ɔn]) *n.* 食客;奉承者

hanging ['hæŋiŋ] *n.* ①[常用复]挂在墙上的东西(尤指帘帷等) ②绞死: a ～ matter 可能导致绞刑的事情 ③斜坡,倾斜

hank [hæŋk] **I** *n.* ① (一)绞,(一)束(长度单位; 在棉线中为八百四十码，在毛线中为五百六十码) ②【海】帆环(用以滑动支索扣紧支索帆) ③[方]优势,控制 **II** *vt.* 使成一绞一绞 ‖*get a ～ over sb.* 控制某人 / ～ *for* 【海】两船平排着(指一同改变航向并同等速度行驶); [喻]平等地 / *in a ～* 在困难中

hanker ['hæŋkə] *vi.* 渴望,追求: ～ *for* (或 *after*) knowledge 渴望获得知识 ‖~**ing** ['hæŋkəriŋ] *n.*

hanky-panky ['hæŋki'pæŋki] *n.* ① 阴谋诡计,欺骗; (变戏法所耍的)障眼法,花招: play ～ with sb. 欺骗某人 ②无意义(或愚蠢)的言行

hansom ['hænsəm] *n.* (赶车人坐在乘客座后驾驭的)双轮双座马车

haphazard ['hæp'hæzəd] **I** *n.* 偶然性；任意性: by ～ 偶然地;任意地 **II** *a.* 没有计划的; 杂乱的; 任意的 **III** *ad.* 杂乱无章地; 任意地 ‖~*ly ad.* / ~**ness** *n.*

ha'p'orth ['heipəθ] *n.* [英口]半便士的价值 (= halfpennyworth)

happen ['hæpən] *vi.* ① (偶然) 发生: What has ～ed over there? 那儿发生了什么事? / If anything ～s (或 should ～) to the machine, please let us know. 如果机器出了什么毛病,请通知我们。/ no matter what ～s (或 whatever ～s) 不管发生什么事; 不管出现什么情况 ②[后接不定式] 碰巧: I ～ed to be at the station when he arrived. 他到达时我恰好在车站上。/ Do you ～ to know his address? 你可知道他的地址吗? ③巧遇;偶然发现 (*on, upon*): ～ *upon* sb. in the street 在街上偶然碰见某人 ‖*as it ～s* 碰巧;偶然. *As it ～s*, I have brought the editorial with me. 我碰巧把这篇社论带来了。‖~**ing** *n.* ① [常用复]事件,偶然发生的事 ②目的使观众感到惊奇和意外的无意义的舞台演出

happily ['hæpili] *ad.* ① 幸福地; 幸运地 ②愉快地 ③恰当地;巧妙地: The report is ～ phrased. 报告措词恰恰当。④幸而

happiness ['hæpinis] *n.* ① 幸福: recall past bitterness in contrast with today's ～ 忆苦思甜 ②愉快 ③适当,合适: It's a great ～ to us to welcome you here. 在这儿欢迎您对我们是极大的愉快。

happy ['hæpi] *a.* ① 幸福的; 幸运的 ② 愉快的,快乐的: Happy New Year! 祝新年快乐! ③(感到)愉快的,乐意的: I shall be (或 feel) very ～ to help. 我将非常乐于给以帮助。/ be ～ about (或 over) sth. 因某事而高兴 ④恰当的;妙的: make a few ～ remarks at a send-off party 在送别会上说一些很得体的话 / That's a ～ thought of yours. 你这个想法真妙! ⑤[常用以构成复合词]陶醉于…的,老是喜欢…的: power-～ 权迷心窍的 ‖~-go-,lucky *a.* 逍遥自在的,无忧无虑的

harangue [hə'ræŋ] **I** *n.* ① 高谈阔论的长篇演说,夸夸其谈的文章 ② 训斥性的讲话 **II** ❶ *vi.* 高谈阔论地演说 ❷ *vt.* 向…夸夸其谈地演讲

harass ['hærəs] *vt.* ①使烦恼; 折磨 ②【军】扰乱,骚扰 ‖~**ment** *n.* ①折磨; 骚扰 ②折磨人的东西

harbinger ['ha:bindʒə] **I** *n.* ①[古](军队或王室一行的)先行官 ② 通报者 ③ 预言者;先驱;兆头: The crowing of the cock is a ～ of dawn. 鸡鸣报晓。**II** *vt.* 充作…的前驱;预告,预示

harbo(u)r ['ha:bə] **I** *n.* ① (海)港,港口;港湾: an air ～ 航空港 / coastal ～s 沿海港口 / a ～ pilot

领港员 ②[喻]避难所;退避所 **II ❶** *vt.* ① 隐匿,窝藏;包庇(罪犯等) ②聚藏;包含: a cave ~*ing* bats 蝙蝠洞 ③ 怀着,怀有: ~ ulterior motives 别有用心 ❷ *vi.* ① 入港停泊 ②躲藏;(动物等)聚集 ‖*make* ~ 进港停泊 ‖**~age** ['hɑ:bridʒ] *n.* 停泊处;躲藏处 ‖**~ dues** 港务费 / **~ master** 港务长

hard [hɑ:d] **I** *a.* ① 硬的,坚固的: a ~ nut 坚果; [喻]难题 / be ~ to the touch 摸上去硬邦邦的 ② (问题、工作等)困难的;(人)难对付的;使劲费力的: a ~ knot 死结 / combine ~ work with ingenuity 苦干加巧干 / a hill ~ to climb 很难爬的一座山 / be ~ to get along with (人)很难(与之)打交道 ③艰难的,难以忍受的: a ~ life 艰难的生活 ④ 强烈的,猛烈的,剧烈的 ⑤冷酷无情的;严格的,不妥协的: a ~ heart 铁石心肠 / a ~ customer 挑剔的顾客 / a ~ bargain 大肆讨价还价的交易 ⑥ 确实的;不容怀疑的: a ~ evidence 铁证 / *Hard* facts prove that .... 铁一般的事实证明… ⑦身体(方面)结实的: be in ~ condition 身体很棒 ⑧(钱币)金属制的,硬的 ⑨ (币制)可兑换成金子的;稳定的 ⑩(物价等)高而不下降的 ⑪(颜色等)刺目的;(声音等)刺耳的 ⑫ 含无机盐的: ~ water 硬水 ⑬(底片等)反差强的 ⑭[语]发硬音的(指字母 c 发 [k]音;字母 g 发 [g]音) ⑮(酒)烈性的,酒精成分高的 **II** *ad.* ① 硬: boil eggs ~ 把蛋煮老了 ② 努力地;艰苦地: We must be self-reliant and work ~. 我们必须自力更生,艰苦奋斗。 / be ~ at work 勤奋工作 ③ 困难地;困苦地: Old conventions die ~. 旧的习惯势力是不会轻易消亡的。 ④猛烈地;重重地: rain ~ 下大雨 ⑤牢固地,紧紧地: hold on ~ 紧握;坚持 / look ~ at sb. 紧紧盯着某人 ⑥ 接近地;立即地: follow ~ after sb. 紧跟着某人 **III** *n.* ① [主英]硬海滩,登陆处 ② [英俚](囚犯的)强迫苦役 ‖*as ~ as a brick* 极硬 / *as ~ as nails* ① 身体结实 ②冷酷无情 / *as ~ as the nether millstone* 铁石心肠 / *be ~ hit* (常指感情方面)受到沉重打击,很伤心 / *be ~ on* (或 *upon*) *sb.* 过分严厉地对待某人;使某人极为难堪 / *be ~ pressed* 被紧紧追赶(或催逼) / *be ~ put to it* 见 **put**¹ / *be ~ up* [口] 短缺,在急需中: *be ~ up for money* 手头拮据 / *be ~ with sb.* 使某人为难(或痛苦): It shall *go ~ with* me, but I will find them. 尽管不容易,我总能找到他们的。 / *~ and fast* ①严格的,不容变通的: In our workshop there is a ~ and fast rule against smoking. 我们车间严禁吸烟。 ② (船)搁浅的 / *Hard aport!* [海]左满舵! / *Hard astarboard!* [海]右满舵! / *~ by* 在近旁;在…的近旁 / *~ upon* 接近于;紧跟着: He's ~ upon sixty. 他已快六十岁了。 / He came in ~ *upon* my heels. 他紧跟着我进来了。 / *learn sth. the ~ way* 通过艰难困苦而学到某事 / *run sb. ~* 紧追某人 / *take sth. ~* 心里因某事而不快,对某事非常耿耿于怀 ‖**~ness** *n.* ‖**~back** *a.* & *n.* 硬书皮

的(书) / '**~-'bitten** *a.* ①咬起来凶狠的 ②在战争中得到锻炼的;顽强的 / **~board** *n.* 硬质纤维板 / **~'boiled** *a.* ① (鸡蛋)煮得老的 ②(衣服等)浆硬的,挺直的 ③不动感情的;强硬的 / **~'bound** *a.* 硬书皮装订的 / **~ cash** ①硬币 ②现金 / **~ coal** 煤炭,无烟煤 / **~ core** [总称] ①[英](筑路基等的)碎砖石 ②(组织或运动中)斗志最坚定的核心;铁杆分子 ③到哪儿都需救济的难民(或失业者) / '**~-'core** *a.* ①长期失业需救济的 ②(黄色作品)赤裸裸描写的 / '**~-'cover** *a.* =~bound / **~ currency** 硬通货,硬币 / '**~-'drawn** *a.* 【机】冷拉的 / '**~-'earned** *a.* 辛苦挣得的 / '**~-'favo(u)red**, '**~-'featured** *a.* 面貌凶恶的;其貌不扬的 / '**~-'fisted** *a.* ① (因劳动而)双手坚硬有力的 ②吝啬的 ③强硬的 / **~ goods** 经久耐用(或耐藏)的货物 / '**~'handed** *a.* ①(因劳动而)双手坚硬有力的 ②用高压手段的 / **~ hat** ①(建筑工人等戴的)保护帽;持保守观点的建筑工人(或矿工) ②[英]礼帽 / **~ head** *n.* ⑦精明而讲实际的人 ②鲕 ③一种头上多刺和多骨头的鱼(尤指锯鲉,步鱼等) / '**~'headed** *a.* ①冷静的,精明而讲实际的 ②固执的 / '**~-'hearted** *a.* 无同情心的,冷酷的 / **~ labo(u)r** (囚犯的)强迫苦役 / '**~-'land** *vi.* & *vt.* (使)硬着陆 / **~ landing** 硬着陆 / **~ line** 强硬路线: take a ~ *line* on sth. 就某事采取强硬路线 / '**~-,liner** *n.* 主张强硬路线者 / **~ lines** [英]坏运气: It's really ~ *lines* to lose your spectacles. 你把眼镜弄丢了,可真倒霉! / '**~'mouthed** *a.* ①(马)难以驾驭的 ②顽固的,倔强的 / '**~-'nosed** *a.* ①(猎犬等)嗅觉不灵的 ②顽固的 ③丑陋的 / '**~-of-'hearing** *a.* (人)有点儿聋的 / **~ palate** 硬腭 / **~ pan** *n.* ①硬质地层 ②硬地;坚固的基础 ③隐藏着的真实情况: get down to the ~*pan* of a question 彻底弄清一个问题 / **~ sauce** 甜奶油汁 / '**~,scrabble** *a.* 通过辛苦劳动(使人能) 勉强维持生活的 / **~ sell** 硬行推销 / '**~-'sell** *a.* 硬行推销的,硬挝的 / '**~-'set** *a.* ①面临困难的 ②固定的;坚决的,顽固的 ③(鸡蛋)将要孵化的 ④(人)饥饿的 / '**~-'shell(ed)** *a.* ①有硬壳的 ②僵硬的,不妥协的: a ~*shell* conservative 不妥协的保守派 / '**~-'stand** *n.* 停机坪 / '**~-,surface** *vt.* 给…铺硬质路面 / '**~-'tack** *n.* [总称](供船上食用的)硬饼干 / '**~tail** *n.* 骡子 / '**~-'top** *n.* 有金属顶盖的汽车 / '**~-'top** *n.* 有硬质路面的区域(或道路) *vt.* 给…铺硬质路面 / '**~ware** *n.* [总称] ①金属器具: a ~*ware* store 五金店 ②[美俚]重武器 ③(计算机的)硬部件;导弹构件;机器;计算机 / '**~wareman** ['hɑ:dwæmən] *n.* 五金工人;五金商人 / '**~ wheat** 硬粒小麦,硬质小麦 / '**~-'won** *a.* 辛苦得来的,来之不易的: a ~-*won* victory 得来不易的胜利 / '**~wood** *n.* ①坚硬的木材 ②产坚硬木材的树 *a.* 坚硬木材的 / '**~'working** *a.* 努力工作的,勤勉的

harden ['hɑ:dn] **❶** *vt.* ① 使变硬: ~ steel 【冶】淬火 ②使锻炼得结实坚强,使进一步巩固: a ~*ed* fisherman 饱经风霜的渔民 ③[常用被动语态]使变得冷酷,使麻木: be ~ed to 对…变得无动于衷 ④(用水泥或泥土加固或设在地下以)使不受爆炸(或热辐射)之害 ❷ vi. ①变硬;变坚固 ②变得冷酷(或麻木): His face ~ed. 他的脸色沉下来了。③(价格等)涨定 ‖~ off (使)(幼苗)锻炼得耐寒

hardening ['hɑ:dəniŋ] n. ① 硬化;【冶】淬火: the ~ of arteries 动脉硬化 / ~ by cooling 冷却硬化 ②硬化剂

hardihood ['hɑ:dihud] n. ①大胆,刚毅 ②鲁莽;傲慢 ③强壮

hardly ['hɑ:dli] ad. ①几乎不,简直不(常用作"不"的委婉语): What he said was ~ true. 他所说的不象是真实的。/ You can ~ imagine how enthusiastic these young workers are. 你简直想象不到这些青年工人的热情有多高。/ This is ~ the time to discuss such matters. 在现在讨论这些事根本不合适。②不十分;仅,才: We ~ know him. 我们不大认识他。/ You're ~ well enough to sit up yet. 你身体还不十分好,不能起床。/ Little Wang is ~ twenty. 小王还不到二十岁。③严厉地,粗鲁地 ④艰辛地,费力地 ‖~ any 几乎没有 / ~ anybody (anything, anywhere) 简直没有什么人(什么东西,什么地方) / ~ ever 几乎从不;很少: I ~ ever see him nowadays. 近来我很少见到他。/ ~ ... when ... 刚…就…。We had ~ (或 Hardly had we) gathered in the wheat when it began to rain. 我们刚把小麦收完,就开始下起雨来了。

hardship ['hɑ:dʃip] n. ①受苦,吃苦: fear neither ~ nor death 一不怕苦,二不怕死 ②苦难,困苦

hardy[1] ['hɑ:di] a. ①勇敢的; 果断的 ②鲁莽的;厚脸皮的 ③耐劳的,能吃苦的;强壮的 ④(植物)耐寒的 ‖~ annual ①耐寒的一年生植物 ②[喻]每年总要提出的老问题

hardy[2] ['hɑ:di] n. (锻工用的)一种方柄凿

hare [heə] I [复] hare(s)) a. ①野兔 ②[英俚]坐车不买票的人 II vi. 飞跑 ‖(as) mad as a March ~ 象三月(交尾期)时的野兔一样疯野 / First catch your ~ (then cook him). [谚]勿谋之过早。/ hold (或 run) with the ~ and run (或 hunt) with the hounds 两面讨好 / make a ~ of sb. 愚弄某人 / start a ~ 在讨论中提出枝节问题 ‖~ and hounds (一些人假扮兔子在前撒纸屑,另一些人假扮猎犬的)追逐游戏 / '~bell n. 【植】钓钟柳 / '~brained a. 轻率的;浮躁的 / '~,hearted a. 易受惊的,胆小的 / '~lip n. 【医】兔唇,唇裂

harem ['heərem] n. (伊斯兰教国家中的)闺阁;后宫;[集合名词]妻妾,女眷们

hark [hɑ:k] vi. [主要用于祈使句]听 (to) ‖~ back ①(猎犬)折回寻觅嗅迹 ②回到原题

harlequin ['hɑ:likwin] I n. ①[H-] (意大利,英国等喜剧或哑剧中的)头戴面具和身穿五颜六色衣服的角色 ②丑角,滑稽角色 ③五颜六色 II a. ①滑稽的 ②五颜六色的 ‖~ade [,hɑ:likwi'neid]

n. 以丑角为主的戏;丑角表演

harlot ['hɑ:lət] n. 妓女 ‖~ry n. 卖淫

harm [hɑ:m] I n. 损害,伤害;危害: He meant no ~. 他并没有恶意。/ There is no ~ in trying. 不妨一试。/ Where's the ~ in trying? 试试又何妨? II vt. 损害,伤害;危害 ‖come to ~ 遭不幸 / do sb. ~ 损害某人 / Harm set, ~ get. (或 Harm watch, ~ catch.) 害人反害己。/ out of ~'s way 在安全的地方

harmful ['hɑ:mful] a. 有害的 (to) ‖~ly ad. / ~ness n.

harmless ['hɑ:mlis] a. ①无害的;无恶意的 ②[罕]未受损害的 ‖~ly ad. / ~ness n.

harmonic [hɑ:'mɔnik] I a. ① 和睦的, 融洽的 ②【数】调和的: ~ function 调和函数, 谐函数 ③【音】和声的,悦耳的 ④【物】谐波的 II n. ①【音】泛音;和声 ②【物】谐波;谐音 ‖~ally ad.

harmonica [hɑ:'mɔnikə] n. 口琴 (=mouth organ); (用沾湿的手指弹奏的)由一系列半圆形玻璃键组成的琴;一种打击乐器

harmonious [hɑ:'mounjəs] a. ①协调的, 相称的, 和谐的 ②和睦的,融洽的 ③悦耳的 ‖~ly ad. / ~ness n.

harmonium [hɑ:'mounjəm] n. 簧风琴

harmonize ['hɑ:mənaiz] ❶ vi. ①协调,相称 (with) ②以和声唱(或演奏) ❷ vt. ①使协调,使调和,使一致 ②使(曲调)和谐 ‖**harmonization** [,hɑ:mənai'zeiʃən] n. / ~r n. 使和谐协调的人

harmony ['hɑ:məni] n. ①协调,融洽,和谐: The article lacks ~. 这篇文章里的论点不协调。②融洽,一致 ③(内心的)平静 ④【音】和声;和声学 ‖be in (out of) ~ with 与…是(不是)协调一致的

harness ['hɑ:nis] I n. ①[古]铠甲 ②马具,挽具 ③【纺】综统; (提花机上的)通丝 ④降落伞背带 ⑤[美俚]警察制服;摩托车驾驶员的全套衣帽装备 II vt. ①给…上挽具,套上(马等): ~ a horse 套马 / ~ a horse to a carriage 把马套到车上 ②治理;利用: ~ a river 治河 / ~ the limitless power of the sun 利用无穷尽的太阳能 ‖die in ~ 工作时死去 / in double ~ 已婚的 / in ~ ①[喻]在执行(日常)职责中 ②受约束 / work (或 run) in double ~ (两匹马或牛)同时拉车(或犁);[喻]两人共同工作,(夫妇)双双工作 ‖~ bull, ~ cop, ~ dick [美俚]穿制服的警察,外勤巡警 / ~ horse ①(赛马中)拖两轮车比赛的马 ②挽马

harp [hɑ:p] I n. ①竖琴 ②竖琴状的东西 ③[the H-]【天】天琴座 ④[美俚]爱尔兰人 II vi. ①弹竖琴 ②唠唠叨叨地反复讲 (on, upon) ‖~er, ~ist n. 弹竖琴的人,竖琴师

harpoon [hɑ:'pu:n] I n. (捕鲸等的)鱼叉,标枪 II vt. 用鱼叉叉 ‖~ gun 发射鱼叉的炮,捕鲸炮

harpsichord ['hɑ:psikɔ:d] n. 拨弦古钢琴,羽管键琴

harpy ['hɑ:pi] n. ①[H-]【希神】【罗神】鸟身女妖

②残忍贪婪的坏人 ③恶妇人 ‖~ **eagle** 头部有脊突的大鹰(产于中、南美洲)

harrow ['hærou] **I** n. 耙: a disc ~ 圆盘耙 **II** ❶ vt. ①耙(地): ~ (up) a field 耙地松土 ②弄伤,抓伤;使痛苦,折磨 ❷ vi. (地)被耙松 ‖under the ~ 在困苦中;为难

harry ['hæri] vt. ①掠夺,蹂躏 ②折磨,骚扰: be *harried* by phone calls 被接二连三的电话弄得大为头疼 ③驱走

harsh [hɑːʃ] a. ①粗糙的 ②(声音)刺耳的;(味道)涩口的; (光)刺目的: ~ to the ear 刺耳的 ③严厉的; 苛刻的: ~ terms 苛刻的条件 ‖~ly ad. / ~ness n.

harum-scarum ['hɛərəm'skɛərəm] **I** a. & ad. 轻率的(地),冒失的(地) **II** n. 冒失鬼;轻举妄动

harvest ['hɑːvist] **I** n. ①收获,收割: The summer ~ is about to start. 夏收即将开始。②收成,产量: Rich (或 Good, Bumper) ~s have been gathered in for several years running. 连续几年获得了丰收。/ the ~ of the sea 捕获的总海产量 ③收获季节,收获期: at the cotton (oyster) ~ 在收棉花(捕牡蛎)的季节 ④结果;后果;成果: reap the ~ of one's hard work 获得辛勤劳动的成果 **II** ❶ vt. ①收割(农作物); 收获; 获得(成果等): ~ rice with combines 用联合收割机割稻 ②上收割物 ❷ vi. 收割 ‖~er n. ①收割庄稼人;收获者;收割机 ‖~ **bug** 【动】恙螨 / ~ **fly** 收获期鸣叫的蝉,秋蝉 / ~ **home** ①(庄稼等)的全部收进归仓;收获期 ②收获期结束时所唱的歌 ③庆祝收获完成的节日(如酒宴等) / ~ **louse** =~ bug / '~**man** n. ①收割庄稼的人;收获季节的雇工 ②【动】盲蛛 / ~ **mite** =~ bug / ~ **moon** 收获季节的满月(指九月廿二、廿三日后两周内的第一次满月) / ~ **mouse** (筑巢于谷秆丛中的)一种欧洲田鼠 / ~ **tick** =~ bug

has [强 hæz; 弱 həz, əz] have 的第三人称单数现在式

has-been ['hæzbiːn] n. [口]过时的人物;不再时行的东西

hash [hæʃ] **I** vt. ①切细(肉、蔬菜等) (up) ②[口]把…搞糟, 把…弄乱 ③反复推敲, 仔细考虑 (over) **II** n. ①肉丁烤菜 ②用旧材料拼成的东西;乱七八糟的杂烩 ③复述,重申 ④[美俚]传闻 ‖~ **out** [美口]通过长时间讨论后解决 / **make a** ~ **of** [口]把…弄糟,把…搞坏 ②击败,干掉 / **settle sb.'s** ~ 征服某人;收拾某人 / **house** [美俚]廉价饭馆,经济餐馆 / ~ **mark** (表示士兵已服役年数的)军役袖章;军役袖章上的斜条(每条表示服役三或四年) / '~,**slinger** n. [美俚](尤指小饭馆中的)侍者,女招待

hasheesh, hashish ['hæʃiːʃ] n. 印度大麻的茎和叶制成的麻醉品

hasn't ['hæznt] =has not

hasp [hɑːsp] **I** n. ①门 (或窗、盖等)的搭扣 ②【纺】亚麻(或黄麻)纱绞 **II** vt. 用搭扣扣上

hassock ['hæsək] n. ①草丛 ②跪垫,膝垫 ③[美俚](棒球的)垒

haste [heist] **I** n. ①急速,紧迫;仓促: Make ~! 赶紧! / Make ~ to come. (或 Make ~ and come.) 快来! / Why all this ~? 为什么这么匆忙? ②草率 **II** ❶ vi. 赶紧;匆忙 ❷ vt. [古]催促 ‖in ~ 急速地,匆忙地;草率地: arrive *in* hot ~ 火急地赶到 / *Marry in* ~ *and repent at leisure.* [谚]草率结婚后悔多。/ *More* ~, *less speed.* [谚]欲速不达。

hasten ['heisn] ❶ vt. ①催促: ~ sb. to do sth. 催促某人做某事 ②促进,加速 ❷ vi. 赶紧,赶快: ~ home 急忙回家 / ~ to the destination 赶到目的地去 / ~ to sb.'s assistance 赶去救助某人 / Then he ~ed to add that …. 接着他又赶忙补充说…

hasty ['heisti] a. ①急速的 ②仓促的,草率的;急速赶制成的: avoid ~ conclusions 避免草草作出结论 / a ~ road (trench) 简易公路(堑壕) ③性急的,急躁的;动辄要发火的: I'm sorry I've been ~. 真抱歉,我太性急了。‖**hastily** ad. / **hastiness** n. ‖~ **pudding** ①(放沸水中速煮的)麦片糊;玉米粉糊 ②泥泞的路 ③私生子

hat [hæt] **I** n. ①帽子[注意: hat 一般指有边的帽子,无边的帽子是 cap]: a bowler ~ 礼帽 / a leaf ~ 斗笠 / a gypsy ~ (妇女、儿童戴的)宽边帽 ②【天主教】红衣主教帽;红衣主教职位 **II** (hatted; hatting) vt. 给…戴上帽子 ‖a **bad** ~ [俚]不道德的人,坏蛋 / a **black** ~ [澳][俚]新来的移民 / **as black as one's** ~ 墨黑的 / **bet one's** ~ 把自己的一切拿出来打赌 / **hang up one's** ~ (in another's house) (在别人家里)久留不去, 长期居住 / **in hand** 卑躬屈节地;十分恭敬地 / **I'll eat my** ~ **if** …. 见 eat / **knock into a cocked** ~ 把…打得不成样子;驳得…体无完肤 / **My** ~! [俚]啊! (表示惊讶等) / **pass** (round) **the** ~ 募捐 / **raise** (或 take off) **one's** ~ **to** 向…(脱帽)致敬 / **send round the** ~ 募捐 / **talk through one's** ~ [俚]吹牛,胡说八道 / **throw** (或 have, toss) **one's** ~ **in the ring** 宣布(准备)加入战斗(或竞赛、竞选) / **touch one's** ~ **to** 向…碰帽边致敬 / **under one's** ~ 秘密的,不许对外人说的 ‖~**ful** n. ①一帽子的容量 ②许多 / ~**less** a. 不戴帽子的 / '~**band** n. 帽圈(指帽边上的一圈丝带) / '~-**peg** n. 供挂帽用的钉 / ~ **rack** 一排帽钩 ②瘦弱的动物 / '~-**stand** n. (可移动的)帽架 / ~ **trick** ①魔术师用帽子变的把戏 ②巧妙的一着 ③(一些球类运动中)一人连得三分

hatch[1] [hætʃ] **I** ❶ vt. ①孵出;孵: ~ chickens 孵出小鸡 / ~ eggs 孵蛋 ②内心怀着;图谋,策划: ~ a plot 心怀阴谋 / ~ **up** a plot 策划出阴谋 ❷ vi. (蛋)孵化;(小鸡等)出壳: When will the eggs ~? 蛋什么时候孵化呢? **II** n. ①孵化 ②(小鸡等的) 一孵,一窝 ③结果 ‖**count one's chickens before they are** ~**ed** [谚]蛋尚未孵

先数鸡；过早乐观 / **~es, catches, matches and dispatches** (报纸上的) 出生、订婚、结婚和死亡栏 ‖**~er** *n.* ①孵卵器 ②出谋划策的人

hatch[2] [hætʃ] *n.* ①(飞机等的) 短门，小门；下半扇门；出口；天窗，格子门；开口：an escape ~ 应急出口 ②升降口；舱口；舱盖；舱：~ cover 舱口盖 ③闸门 ④鱼栏 ‖**a booby ~** [美俚] ①囚车；监牢 ②疯人院 / **Down the ~!** [口] 干杯！ / **under ~es** ①在甲板下；被关在船舱内 ②被埋着 ‖'**~way** *n.* 升降口；舱口

hatch[3] [hætʃ] **I** *vt.* 在…上画影线 **II** *n.* 影线 ‖**~ing** *n.* 【机】影线，晕滃

hatchel ['hætʃəl] **I** *n.* 【纺】梳麻针排 **II** (hatchel(l)ed; hatchel(l)ing) *vt.* 用梳麻针排梳理

hatchet ['hætʃit] *n.* 短柄小斧 ‖**bury the ~** 休战；和解 / **dig** (或 **take**) **up the ~** 开战；宣战 / **throw** (或 **fling, sling**) **the ~** 瞎谈，吹牛 / **throw the helve after the ~** ①接二连三地受损失 ②完全放弃 ③孤注一掷，绝望地挣扎 ‖**~ face** 瘦长尖削的脸；面孔瘦削的人 / **~ job** 恶毒的诽谤(或攻击) / **~ man** ①被雇的杀人凶手；打手 ②受雇写谩骂文章的人；走狗

hate [heit] **I** ❶ *vt.* ①恨，憎恨 ②嫌恶 ③[俗]不愿，不喜欢：I ~ troubling (或 to trouble) him. 我真不想去麻烦他。❷ *vi.* 仇恨 **II** *n.* ①怨恨，憎恶；嫉恨 ②憎恨的东西 ‖**~less** *a.* 不憎恨的 / **~r** *n.* 怀恨者 ‖'**~,monger** *n.* (尤指对少数民族等) 煽动仇恨者

hateful ['heitful] *a.* ①可恨的；可恶的，讨厌的 ②[罕]有敌意的 ‖**~ly** *ad.* / **~ness** *n.*

haughty ['hɔːti] *a.* ①傲慢的，目中无人的；轻蔑的 ②[古]崇高的，高贵的 ‖**haughtily** *ad.* / **haughtiness** *n.*

haul [hɔːl] **I** ❶ *vt.* ①拖曳，用力拖(或拉)；把(鱼等)用网拖上来：~ in an anchor 起锚 / ~ timber (a boat) 拖木材(船) ②拖运 ③【海】使(船)改变航向(尤指为了迎风行驶) ④硬拖，硬拉；拘捕：~ sb. to a football match 硬拉某人去看一场足球赛 ❷ *vi.* ①拖，拉：~ *at* (或 *upon*) a rope 拉绳子 ②(风)改变方向 ③改变主意 ④【海】改变船的航向；(船)改变航向 **II** *n.* ①拖，拉 ②捕获物；一网捕得的鱼：a bumper ~ of fish 一大网鱼 ③拖运的距离：long ~*s* by rail 长距离铁路运输 ④运输量 ‖**~ down one's flag** (或 **colo(u)rs**) 投降 / **~ off** ①改变船的航向以避开 ②退却，撤退 ③[口]挥拳打人前先缩回手臂 / **~ over the coals** 见 **coal** / **~ up** ①把…拖上来 ②停下 ③把…拉出来责问(或受审) ④(船)迎风行驶 / **~ upon the wind** 见 **wind**[1]

haunch [hɔːntʃ] *n.* ①(人的)腿臀部 ②(动物的)腰腿；大片的鹿肉(或羊肉等)：a dog sitting on its ~*es* 蹲着的狗 ③【建】梁腋；拱腋

haunt [hɔːnt] **I** ❶ *vt.* ①常去，常到(某地)；缠住(某人) ②(鬼魂等)常出没于；老是附在…身上 ③(思想、回忆等)萦绕；(疾病等)缠住：be ~*ed* by fear of discovery 怕被发觉而老是提心吊胆 ❷ *vi.* ①经常出没，逗留：~ *about* a place *with* sb. 经常同某人一起出没于某一地方 / a smell that ~*s round* for hours 好几个小时不消散的气味 ②(鬼魂等)作祟 **II** *n.* ①常去的地方：the ~*s* of sb.'s schooldays 某人在求学时代常去的地方 / a favourite holiday ~ for Londoners 伦敦人爱在那儿度假期的地方 ②(动物的)生息地 ③(罪犯等的)巢穴 ④[主方]鬼 ‖**~ed** *a.* 常出现鬼的，闹鬼的

have [强 hæv; 弱 həv, əv, v] **I** (过去式和过去分词 had [强 hæd; 弱 həd, əd]; 第三人称单数现在式 has [强 hæz; 弱 həz, əz]) ❶ *vt.* ①有：I ~ no (或 I *don't* ~ a) French dictionary. 我没有法语词典。[注意：在口语中，英国用法常与 got 连用，如 I've got = I have] / The town *has* many large buildings. 镇上有许多大楼。②怀有，持有：*Have* you (或 *Do* you ~) any idea where he works? 你知道他在哪儿工作吗？/ Please ~ the kindness (或 goodness) to write me soon. 请早日给我来信。③拿；得到，取得：May I ~ one? 我可以拿一个吗？/ I've *had* two letters from him. 我已收到他两封信。/ The ayes (noes) ~ it. 赞成的(反对的)占多数。④吃；喝：Would you ~ a cup of tea? 您要喝杯茶吗？⑤进行，从事(某事)：Let's ~ a talk (try). 让咱们谈一谈(试一试)。/ ~ a meeting 开会 / ~ a class 上课 / ~ English lessons 上英语课 ⑥享有；经历；遭受：We've never *had* it so good. 我们以前从未有过这样好的生活。/ We'll ~ a good holiday. 我们将过一个快乐的假日。/ ~ a bad toothache 牙痛得厉害 ⑦[用于否定句中]容忍；允许：We won't ~ any breach of discipline. 我们不允许任何破坏纪律的现象。/ I won't ~ you say such things. 我可不许你说这样的话。⑧使，让；招致：We *had* the machine *repaired*. 我们请人把机器修好了。[比较：We *had repaired* the machine before you came. 你来以前，我们(自己)已把机器修好了。] / ~ everything *ready* for action 做好行动的一切准备 ⑨要；叫；使：I would ~ him wait for me. 我要他等我。/ *Have* him do it. 叫他去做吧。⑩[接不定式]必须，不得不 ⑪表明，坚持说 ⑫明白，懂得：You ~ me, *haven't* you? 你明白我的意思了，对不对？⑬[口]击败，胜过：He *had* John completely in the first game. 在第一局中，他完全击败了约翰。/ That's where you ~ me. 这就是你胜过我的地方。⑭[英俚]哄骗，欺骗：You were *had*! 你受骗啦！⑮生(子) ❷ *v. aux.* ①[加过去分词，构成完成时态]已经；曾经：We *had* already *reaped* the crops when the storm came. 暴风雨来时，我们已经收割完了。②[用于虚拟语气] **II** *n.* ①[常用复][口]有钱人；富国 ②[英俚]诈骗，欺诈 ‖**~ a good time** 过得快乐，过得愉快 / **~ at** 打击，攻击 / **Have done!** 见 **do**[1] / **~ had it** [俚] ①吃够了苦头，受到致命打击 ②(人)已过时 ③无希望，命

运已注定 / ～ *it* (*all*) *over sb.* 胜过某人 / ～ *it in for sb.* [口]对某人怀有仇恨;伺机想害某人 / ～ *it on sb.* 胜过某人,占某人的上风 / ～ *it out* (*with sb.*) (与某人)斗一场解决争端,(与某人)决一雌雄;(同某人)讲个明白 / ～ *on* ①穿着;戴着 ②有(事)在手头;～ nothing *on* this evening 今天晚上没有约会(或没有事) ③(尤指为了欺骗)引起…的兴趣(或同情等),使上钩 / ～ *one's own way* 见 **way** / ～ *one's sleep out* 见 **sleep** / ～ *only to . . . to . . .* 只要…就能…; You ～ *only to* read it over once more to see the misprint. 你只要整个再读一遍就可看出那印错的地方。 / ～ *sb. down* 把某人请来作客[注意: 从城市请到乡下,或从山脉、河流等的上方请到下方一般用 down,反之用 up] / ～ *sb. in* 把某人叫进来,请某人到屋里 / ～ *sb. up* ①把某人请来作客(参见 ～ sb. down) ②对某人起诉,控告某人 / ～ *sth. back* 把某物要回去,收回某物 / ～ *sth. in* 在屋里备有某物 / ～ *sth. out* 把某物弄出来:～ a tooth *out* 拔掉一颗牙齿 / ～ *to do with* 见 **do**¹ / *let sb.* ～ *it* [美俚]让某人吃顿苦头

haven ['heivn] **n.** ①港口;船舶抛锚处 ②避难所,(有掩护的)安全地方: a ～ of rest 避难所 **II** *vt.* ①开(船)入港 ②为…提供避难所,掩护 ‖～**er** *n.* 港务长

have-not ['hævnɒt] **n.** [常用复][口]穷人;穷国

haven't ['hævnt] = have not

haversack ['hævəsæk] **n.** (行军或旅行时用的)帆布背包,干粮袋

haversack

having ['hæviŋ] **n.** [常用复]财产;所有物

havoc ['hævək] **I** *n.* ①大破坏,浩劫: ～ caused (或 wrought, created) by an earthquake 由地震造成的破坏 ②大混乱,大杂乱 **II** (havocked; havocking) *vt.* 严重破坏 ‖*cry* ～ (对军队)下抢劫令 ②发出警呼声(表示灾难将临) / *play* (或 *raise*) ～ *with* 对…造成严重破坏;使陷入大混乱

haw¹ [hɔ:] **n.** 【植】山楂;山楂的果实

haw² [hɔ:] **I** *n.* 吆喝牲畜左转声 **II** *vt. & vi.* (使)向左转

haw³ [hɔ:] **I** *n.* (表示踌躇、疑问或支吾的语声)呃,嗯 **II** *vi.* 发出呃(或嗯)声;(说话时)踌躇,支吾 ‖*hem* (或 *hum*) *and* ～ 嗯嗯呃呃(表示踌躇或支吾等)

haw⁴ [hɔ:] **n.** ①(马、狗等的)第三眼睑,瞬膜 ②[常用复]瞬膜炎

hawk¹ [hɔ:k] **I** *n.* ①鹰,隼 ②(似鹰般)贪婪的家伙;骗子 ③鹰派成员,主战派成员 **II** ❶ *vi.* ①带鹰打猎 ②(象鹰般)猛扑 (*at*);(象鹰般)翱翔(燕等)追捕昆虫 ❷ *vt.* (象鹰般)捕捉 ‖*know a* ～ *from a handsaw* 有常识,尚有见解 ‖'～**-eyed** *a.* 目光锐利的 / '～**-nosed** *a.* 长着鹰钩鼻的 / '～**sbill** *n.* 玳瑁

hawk² [hɔ:k] *vt.* ①叫卖; 兜售: ～ one's wares from door to door 挨户叫卖货色 ②散播(谣言等)

hawk³ [hɔ:k] ❶ *vi.* 清嗓;咳嗽 ❷ *vt.* 咳出: ～ *up* phlegm 把痰咳出

hawk⁴ [hɔ:k] **n.** (泥水匠用的)带柄方形灰浆板

hawker ['hɔ:kə] **n.** 叫卖的小贩

hawser ['hɔ:zə] **n.** [海]粗绳(供系船、下锚用)

hawthorn ['hɔ:θɔ:n] **n.** 【植】山楂

hay [hei] **I** *n.* ①(作牲口饲料用的)干草: dry grass for ～ 把草晒成干草 / make ～ 翻晒干草 ②成果,酬答 ③小额款项 ④[美俚]床 **II** ❶ *vi.* 割草晒干 ❷ *vt.* ①用干草喂 ②将(草)晒成干草 ③在…上植草供制干草用 ‖*hit the* ～ [美俚]上床睡觉 / *look for a needle in a bottle* (或 *bundle*) *of* ～ 大海捞针 / *make* ～ 使混乱 / *make* ～ *out of* 使对己有利 / *make* ～ *while the sun shines* [谚]晒草要趁太阳好;抓紧时机 / *not* ～ [美俚]为数不小的一笔钱,相当大的数目 ‖'～**box** *n.* (保暖等用的)干草箱 / '～**burner** *n.* [俚]马(尤指第二流的赛马) / '～**cock** *n.* 尖顶干草小堆 / *fever* 【医】枯草热,花粉热 / '～**field** *n.* 干草地 / '～**fork** *n.* 干草叉 / ～ *knife* 割干草用的长刀 / '～**loft** *n.* (马厩等处)储藏草料的顶棚 / '～**maker** *n.* ①翻晒干草的人 ②干草机 ③[俚]把人打昏的猛烈的一拳;致命一击 / '～**making** *n.* ①翻晒干草 ②对现成机会的充分利用 / '～**mow** *n.* ①(仓中的)干草堆,草料顶棚 / '～**rack** *n.* ①草料槽 ②装运干草的大车上的装草架 / '～**rick** *n.* =stack / '～**seed** *n.* ①散落的干草种;干草屑 ②[美俚]乡下佬 / '～**stack** *n.* 干草堆: search for a needle in a ～ 大海捞针 / '～**wire** *n.* 捆干草用的铁丝 *a.* ①乱七八糟的;疯狂的: go ～wire 杂乱不堪;变得疯疯癫癫 ②匆忙做成的,拼凑而成的;蹩脚的

hazard ['hæzəd] **I** *n.* ①一种骰子游戏 ②机会;偶然的事 ③危险;公害(指工业废气、废水等的危害) ④(网球场中)可得分区域 ⑤(高尔夫球球场障碍 ⑥[英方]马车停车场 **II** *vt.* ①使遭危险 ②冒险作出: ～ a guess 作无把握的猜测,贸猜一下 ‖*a losing* ～ (台球戏中)打出的球和他球相撞后落入袋中 / *at all* ～**s** 冒着一切危险;不

管怎么样 / *at* ~ ①在危险之中 ②胡乱地,随便地 / *a winning* ~ (台球戏中)打出的球和他球相撞后使他球落入袋中

hazardous ['hæzədəs] *a.* ①碰运气的 ②危险的,冒险的: a ~ climb 冒险的攀登 / ~ chemicals 危险的化学药品 ‖~**ly** *ad.* / ~**ness** *n.*

haze[1] [heiz] **I** *n.* ①霾,烟雾 ②头脑糊涂 **II** *vt.* & *vi.* ①(使)变朦胧; (使)变糊涂

haze[2] [heiz] *vt.* ①使劳累,用劳役折磨 ②[美]欺侮,戏弄; (为折服对方)对(新学生等)行恶作剧 ③[美方]骑马放牧(或驱赶)

hazel ['heizl] **I** *n.* ①【植】榛;榛子,榛实;榛木 ②淡褐色(尤指眼睛的颜色) **II** *a.* ①榛树的;榛木的 ②榛子色的,淡褐色的

he [hi:; 弱 i:, hi, i] **I** *pron.* [主格] ①他 ②某人,任何人: *He* who plays with fire gets burnt. 玩火者必自焚。 **II** [hi:] ([复] hes [hi:z]) *n.* 男;雄: Is it a ~ or a she? 婴儿是男的还是女的? (这句也可用以问动物的雌雄) / a ~-goat 一头公山羊 ‖'~-'**man** *n.* [美] ①专横的大汉 ②具有男性魅力的人

head [hed] **I** *n.* ①头;头像: from ~ to foot 从头到脚,全身 / be taller by a ~ 高过一头 ②头状物体; (植物茎梗顶端的)头状叶丛,头状花序;谷穗: the ~ of a walking stick 手杖柄的头 / the ~ of an arrow 箭头 / two ~s of cabbage 两棵卷心菜 ③首脑,首长: a ~ of state 国家元首 / the ~ of a delegation 代表团团长 / a department ~ 部门主任 ④头脑,才智: Use your ~. 动动脑筋。 ⑤脑袋,生命 ⑥人;个人: count ~s 点人数 ⑦猎物群; [单复同](牛羊等的)头数: one hundred ~ of sheep 一百头羊 ⑧(队伍、名单等的)最前面的部分; (书页等的)上端,天头; (楼梯等的)顶端; (桌位的)首席;船头;弹头: the ~ of a bed 床的搁头的那一端 ⑨(河流的)源头 ⑩(疮、疖等的)脓头 ⑪头痛 (=~ache) ⑫[常用复](印有头像的硬币的)正面: Heads or tails? 正面还是反面? (用硬币打赌时说) ⑬标题;项目,方面: discuss a question under five ~s 分五个题目来讨论问题 ⑭鹿角: a deer of the first ~ 初生角的鹿 ⑮酒沫; [英]牛奶上的一层油: the ~ on a glass of beer 一杯啤酒上的泡沫 ⑯顶点;危机 ⑰(水站等的)蓄水高度,水位差,水头,压力: thirty metres ~ of water 三十米的水头 ⑱海角,岬 ⑲【矿】水平巷道,煤层中开拓的巷道 ⑳[俚]厕所(尤指船舶上的): Where is the ~? 厕所在哪里? ㉑[机]盖

II ❶ *vt.* ①作为⋯的首脑;率领;站在⋯的前头: ~ a delegation 率领一个代表团 / His name ~s the list. 他是名单上的第一名。 ②用头顶(球): The centre forward ~ed the ball into goal. 中锋用头把球顶入球门。 ③砍⋯的头;伐(或修整)⋯的顶枝;收割(庄稼): ~ down peach trees in the first year of their growth 桃树生长第一年时在树顶进行截枝 ④对着: ~ the waves 迎着波浪 ⑤绕水源而过(小溪、湖泊等) ⑥使(车等)对着某处行驶: ~ a ship northward 使船向北行驶 ⑦拦截(羊群等); [喻]阻止,使转移方向 (*off*): ~ (*off*) a flock of sheep 拦截一群羊 / ~ *off* a quarrel 阻止一场争吵 ⑧为(箭等)装头;构成⋯的顶部 ⑨在⋯上加标题 ⑩(在赛跑等中)先于⋯,超过 ❷ *vi.* ①成头状物(指果结实、麦成穗等): The cabbages are ~*ing up* nicely. 卷心菜长势很好。 ②(向特定方向)出发,动身,(船)驶往: ~ eastward 向东去 / be ~*ing for* collapse 走向崩溃 ③(疮、疖等)出脓头 ④(河流等)发源 **III** *a.* ①头的;头部的 ②主要的,首席的 ‖*above the ~s of* 深奥得使(听众等)不能理解 / *an old ~ on young shoulders* 少年老成 / *at the* ~ *of* 居⋯的首位;在⋯的最前面 / *beat sb.'s* ~ *off* 彻底胜过某人 / *be ~ed for* 朝⋯而去 (=~ for) / *be light in the* ~ ①头晕 ②头脑简单,愚蠢 / *be off* (或 *out of*) *one's* ~ 神经错乱;神志不清 / *Better be the ~ than the tail of a horse.* [谚]宁为鸡口,毋为牛后。 / *be weak in the* ~ 不大聪明 / *break Priscian's* ['priʃiənz] ~ 犯语法错误 / *bury one's* ~ *in the sand* 闭眼不看即将来临的危险 / *by (the)* ~ *and shoulders* ①蛮横地;勉强地 ②相当(高)地(指身材、气度): taller *by the* ~ *and shoulders* 高出一个头 / *come to a* ~ ①(疮、疖等)出脓 ②(时机、事情等)成熟;达到危急的关头: Affairs *came to a* ~ then. 当时事情已到了严重关头。 / *(down) by the* ~ 船头较船尾吃水深 / *drag by (the)* ~ *and ears* ①蛮横地拖 ②把⋯勉强地扯进: *drag* the story *by the* ~ *and ears* into one's conversation 硬把那个故事扯到谈话里去 / *eat one's* ~ *off* (家畜等)吃得多而又不肯干活,不值一养; (人)好吃懒做; (人)失业;无所事事 / *gather* ~ ①(疮、疖等)化脓 ②(时机、事情等)成熟 ③(风等)增强 / *get sth. out of one's* ~ 把某事忘掉(或抛诸脑后): Do *get* this idea *out of your* ~. 切勿有这种想法。 / *give . . . its* (或 *his, her*) ~ 让⋯(原指马)自由行动 / *give one's* ~ *for the washing* 俯首受辱 / *go to sb.'s* ~ ①(酒)冲

上某人的头脑 ②使某人兴奋，冲昏某人的头脑: It's fine to have made some achievements, but we mustn't let them *go to* our ~s. 有点成就是好事，但我们不能因此冲昏头脑。/ *hang (hide) one's* ~ (因感羞耻) 把头垂下 [藏起来] / *have a cool* ~ 有冷静的头脑 / *have a good* ~ *for* 有…的才能 / *have a (good)* ~ *on one's shoulders* 有见识 (或能力) / *have a hard* ~ ①有注重实际的头脑 ②头脑顽固 / *have a* ~ [美俚] 头痛 (尤指由宿醉引起的) / *have a* ~ *like a sieve* 记忆力极差，什么也记不住 / *have a long* ~ 有远见 / *have one's* ~ *in a tar barrel* [美] 陷入困境 / *have one's* ~ *screwed on the right way* 头脑清醒明智，有判断力 / *have swelled* ~ 自负 / ~ *and ears* [口] 全身，完完全全 / ~ *and front* 主要部分 (或项目) / ~ *and shoulders above* 远远高出; 大大胜过; stand ~ *and shoulders above* the others 大大胜过其他人，鹤立鸡群 / ~ *first* (或 *foremost*) ①头向前跑 ②冒冒失失地: plunge ~ *first* into another person's room 冒冒失失一头冲进别人的房间 / ~ *on* 迎面地: The two cars crashed ~ *on*. 这两辆车子面对面地相撞。/ ~ *over heels* (或 *heels over* ~) ①头朝下，倒栽 ②完全地，深深地: be ~ *over heels* in debt 背了一身债 / *Heads I win, tails you lose*. (掷钱币打赌时说) 正面我赢，反面你输。(意指无论怎样，总不吃亏) / *Heads up!* [口] 注意! 小心! / ~ *to* ~ 头对头，交头接耳地 / ~ *up* 在…上加盖子 / *hide one's diminished* ~ 失势退隐 / *hold one's* ~ *high* 趾高气扬; 扬眉吐气 / *I'll eat my* ~ *if* … 见 **eat** / *keep one's* ~ 保持镇静 / *keep one's* ~ *above water* ①免遭灭顶 ②不背债 / *knock* ~ 叩头 / *knock* … *on* (或 *in*) *the* ~ 打…的头部; 杀掉; 消灭 / *knock sb.'s* ~ *off* 轻易胜过某人 / *knock their* ~s *together* 拿着两人的头撞; 用武力制止两人争吵 / *laugh (run, scream* 等) *one's* ~ *off* 狂笑 (奔，呼等) 不已 / *lay* (或 *put*) *our* (或 *their, your*) ~s *together* 聚在一起商量 / *lift (up) our* ~ 振作起来，欣喜 / *lose one's* ~ ①被砍头; 丧命 ②慌乱，不知所措 / *make* ~ ①向前进 (尤指遇阻力): *make* ~ with sth. 使某事有进展 ②武装起来反抗 / *make* ~ *against* all difficulties 战胜一切困难 / *make neither* ~ *nor tail of sth.* 对某事一点摸不着头脑 / *on sb.'s* (或 *one's*) ~ ①四脚朝天地: stand facts *on* their ~s 颠倒事实 ②归罪于某人; 报应在某人身上: On his ~ be it! 愿他倒霉吧! ③ [俚] 易如反掌地: Anyone can do it *on his* ~. 这事不论谁做起来都是不费吹灰之力的。/ *over* ~ *and ears* (或 ~ *over ears*) (*in*) 深陷在 (债务等) 中: He couldn't come as he was ~ *over ears in* work. 他工作忙极了，因此不能来。/ *over sb.'s* ~ ①使某人不能理解: They talked *over* our ~s. 他们讲得我们莫名其妙。②(危险) 迫在眉睫地威胁某人 ③不与某人商量

(而越级上告等) ④ (不合理地提升别人) 至某人之上 / *put a* ~ *on sb.* 击败某人 / *put one's* ~ *in a noose* 自己把头套在绞索里，自陷危境 / *put sth. into* (*out of*) *sb.'s* ~ 使某人想起 (忘掉) 某事 / *put sth. out of one's* ~ 不再想某事 / *ram sth. into sb.'s* ~ (填鸭式地) 反复对某人灌输某事 / *raw* ~ *and bloody bones* [口] 骷髅头和交叉骨 (死亡的象征); 用来吓唬小孩的妖怪 / *run one's* ~ *against a wall* 试图干不可能的事，碰壁 / *scratch one's* ~ 搔头皮; (对某事) 迷惑不解 (*over*) / *show one's* ~ 到场，出现 / *take (it) into one's* ~ 突然想到要; 心血来潮地认为 / *talk sb.'s* ~ *off* [俚] 对某人说个不停，对某人唠叨不休 / *turn sb.'s* ~ 使某人感到骄傲，使某人头脑发热: Don't let success *turn* your ~. 别让胜利冲昏你的头脑。/ *Two* ~s *are better than one.* [谚] 两人智慧胜一人。/ *win by a* ~ (赛马时) 以一个马头的距离获胜 ‖ **~ed** a. ①有头的 ②列有标题的: a ~ed paragraph 列有标题的段落 (植物等) 结成头的 / **~less** a. ①无头的 ②无头衔的 ③没头脑的，愚笨的 / **~most** a. 最前面的; 领头的: a ~most ship 先头舰 / **~ship** n. 领导者的地位 (或身分)

‖ **~ache** n. ①头痛 ②头痛的事 ③ [美俚] 妻 / **~achy** a. 头痛的; 使头痛的 / **~band** n. ①扎在头上的带子，束发带 ②印于书页顶端的花饰 ③嵌在书脊上下两端的布片 / **~chair** n. (理发店等的) 有头靠的椅子 / **~cheese** n. 猪头、脚、舌等部位的熟碎肉冻 / ~ *doctor* [俚] 精神病医师 / **~dress** n. 头巾，头饰 / **~fast** 船头上的系缆 / **~frame** n. [矿] 井架: a concrete ~frame 钢筋混凝土井架 / **~gate** n. ①运河的水闸门 ②总水闸门 / **~gear** n. ①头饰; 帽子，安全帽 ②马首的挽具 / **~hunter** n. ①割取敌人的头作为战利品的人 ②物色人材的人 / **~-lamp, ~light** n. (汽车等的) 前灯; 枪灯; (矿工头上的) 照明灯 / **~land** ['hedlənd] n. ①岬 ②畦头 (或篱边) 的未耕地 / **~long** ad. ①头向前地 ②轻率地: rush ~long into danger 轻率冒险 a. ①头向前的 ②轻率的 ③ [古] 险峻的 / **~man** n. ①工头，监工 ②刽子手 / **~master** n. 校长 / **~mistress** n. 女校长 / **~money** n. ①人头税 ②(旧时) 为捕获人犯 (或斩人首级) 所付的赏金 / **~note** n. (判决书等前面的) 批注 / **~office** 总机构 (如总店等) / **~-on** a. 迎头的，正面的 / **~-page** n. 扉页 / **~phone** n. 头戴受话器，耳机 / **~piece** n. ①盔，帽子; 头巾 ②头戴受话器，耳机 ③ [印] (书的) 扉页; (章节开头的) 花饰 ④头脑，才智: have a good ~piece 头脑清楚 / **~rest** n. (牙医诊所、理发店坐椅的) 头靠 / **~room** n. [建] 净空，净空高度; (汽车等内部的) 头上空间 / **~sea** 逆浪 / **~set** n. ①头戴送受话器 ②耳机 / **~shrinker** n. ①割取敌人头颅干缩保存作为战利品者 ②[美俚] 精神病医师 / **~spring** n. ①水源 ②起源 / **~stall** n. 马笼头 / ~ *start* ①

【体】起跑时的让步; 时间上的占先(指比别人早开始或早出发): have (或 get) a ~ *start* on sb. 比某人在时间上占先 / give sb. a ~ *start of three days* 让某人先走(或先做)三天 良好的开端 / '~**stock** *n.* 车头箱, 车床头 / '~**stone** *n.* ① 基石 ② 墙基石 / '~**strong** *a.* 不受管束的, 任性的, 刚愎自用的 / ~ **voice**【音】头声 / '~**water** *n.* 河源 / '~**way** *n.* ① 前进 ② 前进的速度 ③【建】净空, 净空高度 ④(同一路线上两车的)时间间隔: The buses are running on a three-minute ~*way.* 公共汽车每三分钟开出一辆。/ ~ **wind** 逆风 / '~**word** *n.* ①(书的章节前的)标题 ②【语】复合词的主要部分 / '~**work** *n.* ①脑力劳动; 思想灵敏 ②拱顶石饰

header ['hedə] *n.* ①收割台 ②制造钉头(或工具头)的人(或机械) ③【建】半端梁搁栅 ④【建】露头砖, 露头石 ⑤【机】集管, (锅炉的)联管箱 ⑥【口】头朝下的一跳(或跌落): take a ~ off a ladder 从梯子上倒栽下来

heading ['hediŋ] *n.* ①【空】【海】航向: magnetic ~ 【海】磁向 ②题词; 题词; 题名; 信头, 信笺上端所印文字 ③(足球中的)顶球 ④【矿】平巷 ⑤【复】【矿】精矿, 选矿所得重质部分

headline ['hedlain] Ⅰ *n.* ①(报刊的)大字标题; (书籍的)页头标题: banner ~*s* 通栏大字标题 / go into ~*s* 用大字标题登出 / The arrival of the table-tennis team *hit* (或 *made*) the ~*s* in the local press. 乒乓球队的到达成为当地报纸的头条新闻。②【复】新闻广播的摘要 Ⅱ *vt.* ①给…加标题 ②大肆宣传 ‖~**r** *n.* (戏单上用大字刊登其姓名的)红角, 明星

headquarter ['hed'kwɔ:tə] ❶ *vi.* 设总部 ❷ *vt.* ①将…的总部设在 (*in*) ②把…放在总部里

headquarters ['hed'kwɔ:təz] [复] *n.* [用作单或复] ①司令部; 指挥部: general ~ 统帅部, 总司令部 / at the division ~ 在师部 ②(机构、企业等的)总部, 总店

heady ['hedi] *a.* ①卤莽的, 轻率的; 任性的; 暴躁的: a ~ opinion 轻率的意见 ②猛烈的: a ~ tempest 狂风暴雨 ③(酒类等)易使人陶醉的; [喻]令人兴奋的 ④精明的 ‖**headily** *ad.* / **headiness** *n.*

heal [hi:l] ❶ *vt.* ①治愈(尤指伤口); 使恢复健康: The wound has been ~*ed.* 创伤已治好了。/ sb. *of* a disease 治愈某人的疾病 ②使和解, 消停: ~ a quarrel 平息一场争吵 ❷ *vi.* (伤口)愈合, 痊愈: The wound soon ~*ed up* (或 *over*). 伤口不久就愈合了。‖~**er** *n.* 医治者(尤指用宗教迷信方式治病的人); 治疗物: Time is a great ~*er.* [谚]时间能够治好(感情上的)创伤。/ ~**ing** *a.* ①治愈的, 恢复健康的 ②医治用的 / '~**all** *n.* 可医治多种疾病的植物; 万能药

health [helθ] *n.* ①健康; 健康状况: Promote physical culture and build up the people's ~. 发展体育运动, 增强人民体质 / be in good ~ 健康 / be in bad (或 poor) ~ 不健康 / the Ministry of *Health* 卫生部 / a bill of ~【海】【健】康证书 / not for one's ~ [美]不是干着玩的, 另有目的 ②兴旺 ③祝健康的干杯: drink a ~ to sb. 举杯祝某人健康 / Here's to your ~! (敬酒时说)祝你健康! ‖~-**giving** *a.* 有益于健康的 / ~ **physicist** 有害辐射防护学家 / ~ **physics** 有害辐射防护学

healthy ['helθi] *a.* ①健康的, 健壮的; 有益于健康的 ②旺盛的; 相当大的 ‖**healthily** *ad.* / **healthiness** *n.*

heap [hi:p] Ⅰ *n.* ①(一)堆: a big ~ of manure 一大堆肥料 / pile hay in ~*s* 把干草聚成一堆一堆 ②[口]大量, 许多: We have ~*s* of (或 a ~ of) work to do. 我们有许多工作要做。③[美俚]汽车(尤指破旧的) Ⅱ *vt.* ①堆积, 堆起 (*up, together*) ②装满; 大量地给, 倾泻: The barn was ~*ed with* grain. 谷仓里堆满了粮食。/ ~ burning satire and freezing irony *upon* sb. 对某人大加冷嘲热讽 ‖be struck (或 *knocked*) all of a ~ [口]被压倒; 被弄得昏头昏脑 / ~*s of times* [作状语用]无数次地

hear [hiə] (heard [hə:d]) ❶ *vt.* ①听见; 听: I listened but couldn't ~ anything. 我注意听, 但什么也没听到。②听说, 得知 ③注意听, 听取: Let's ~ him *through*. 让我们听完他的话。/ We must ~ opinions contrary to ours. 我们必须听取相反的意见。④ 审理; 听(证人)陈述: ~ a case 审理案件 / ~ witnesses 听取证词 ⑤同意, 允准: ~ sb.'s entreaty 答应某人的请求 ❷ *vi.* ①听见; 听 ②听到 (*of, about*): I heard *of* (或 *about*) it long ago. 我好久以前就听人说起过这件事了。/ You will ~ *about* this later. 关于这件事以后会让你知道的。[注意: 此句在特定上下文中也可译作: 等着瞧吧!] ‖*Hear and tremble*! 好好听着, 牢牢记住! / ~ *from* ①接到…的信(或电报等): Do you often ~ *from* your brother? 你常接到你兄弟的来信吗? ②受到…的批评(或谴责) / *Hear! Hear!* 对啊! 听啊! (或: 说得对! 说得对!)(常用作表示同意或引人注意的喊声; 有时带讽刺意) / ~ *say* (或 *tell*) 听人说起: Have you ever *heard tell* of such things? 你有没有听人说起过这种事情? / ~ sb. *out* 听某人把话讲完: Don't make hasty conclusion; ~ him *out* first. 不要匆匆下结论; 先让他把话讲完。/ *not* (或 *never*) ~ *of* (通常与 will 或 would 连用) 拒绝考虑, 不同意, 不允许 / *not* (或 *never*) ~ *to* [美口] =not ~ *of* ‖~**able** ['hiərəbl] *a.* 听得见的 / ~**er** ['hiərə] *n.* ①听的人 ②旁听者

heard [hə:d] hear 的过去式和过去分词

hearing ['hiəriŋ] *n.* ①听(指动作或过程) ②听力: His ~ is very sharp (bad). 他听觉灵敏(不好)。/ be hard of ~ (人)耳朵有点儿聋 ③听力所及的距离: Her voice is beyond (或 out of) ~. 她的声音听不见。/ Please stay within ~. 请不要跑到(我们相互)叫得应的距离以外去。④倾听: give sb. a ~ 听某人讲; 听某人申诉 /

gain a ～ 获得发言(尤指申诉)的机会 ⑤ 审讯: condemn without a ～ 不加审讯即行宣判 ⑥[美]意见听取会: hold a ～ *into* sth. 就某事举行意见听取会 ‖～ **aid** 助听器 / ～ **examiner**, ～ **officer** [美](组织意见听取会的)政府特派调查员

hearken ['hɑːkən] *vi.* 倾听; 给予注意

hearsay ['hiəsei] **I** *n.* 风闻, 传闻: It's merely ～. 那仅是谣传罢了。**II** *a.* 传闻的; 道听途说得来的: ～ evidence 【律】传闻证据(指证人旁人传说所提供的证据)

hearse [həːs] **I** *n.* ①枢车; [古]棺材 ②(饰有悼文等的)棺架, 基架 **II** *vt.* ①用枢车装运 ②埋葬

heart [hɑːt] **I** *n.* ①心脏; 胸: a smoker's ～ 吸烟者的心脏失调(病) / She hugged the child to her ～. 她把孩子搂在怀里。② 内心; 心地, 心肠: I thank you *from the bottom of my* ～. 我衷心感谢你。/ I hope *from my very* ～ that .... 我从心底里希望…… / have a kind ～ 有一副好心肠 ③感情; 爱好; 爱情: have one's ～ in one's work 热爱自己的工作 / have no ～ for sth. 不喜欢某事物, 无意于做某事 / sing to one's ～'s content 尽情地唱 ④精神, 勇气 ⑤情感: This book appeals more to the ～ than to the head. 这本书更多打动读者的情感, 而不太打动读者的理智。⑥心情, 心境: with a light ～ (心情)轻松愉快地 / with a heavy ～ (心情)沉重地, 忧愁地 ⑦(表示亲爱的称呼)宝贝儿: dear ～ 亲爱的宝贝 / poor ～ 可怜的人儿 ⑧中心; 要点, 实质: the ～ of a city 城市的中心 / the ～ of a cabbage 卷心菜的菜心 / the ～ of a matter 事情的实质 ⑨[主英](土地的)肥沃程度 ⑩心形的东西; (纸牌的)红桃; [复]一组红桃花样的纸牌 **II** *vt.* ① 把…安放在中心部 ② [古]使振作 ‖*a change of* ～ ①改变主意 ②变心; 变节 ③弃邪归正 / *after one's (own)* ～ 完全符合自己的心意 / *a ～ of gold* 道德高尚的人 / *a ～ of oak* 刚强勇敢的人, 果断的人 / *at ～* 在内心里, 本质上 / *break sb.'s* ～ 使某人很伤心 / *cross one's* ～ 在胸口画十字(表示说的是真话) / *cry one's* ～ *out* 痛哭欲绝(尤指暗自悲伤) / *do sb.'s* ～ *good* 使某人高兴 / *eat one's* ～ *out* 因忧患而消瘦, 伤心过度 / *find it in one's* ～ *to* (do) [常用于否定句中]意欲(做…), 忍心(做…): I cannot *find it in my* ～ *to* refuse him. 我不忍拒绝他。/ *give one's* ～ *to sb.* 爱上某人 / *go to sb.'s* ～ 使某人伤心 / *have a* ～ 发发慈悲, 做做好事 / *have one's* ～ *in one's boots* (因害怕而)沮丧, 绝望 / *have one's* ～ *in one's mouth* 非常吃惊 / *have one's* ～ *in the right place* 好心好意; 真心实意 / *have sth. at* ～ 对某事深切关心 / *have the* ～ *to* (do) [常用于否定句中]忍心(做…) / ～ *and hand* 热心地 / ～ *and soul* 全心全意地 / ～ *to* ～ 贴心地; 坦率地, 诚恳地 / *in* ～ ①[主英](土地)肥沃的 ②情绪高昂的 / *in one's* ～ *of* ～s 在内心深处 / *lay sth. to* ～ 认真考虑某事, 把某事铭刻在心 / *learn* (或 *get*) *by* ～ 记住, 背下 / *lie near sb.'s* ～ 为某人所深切关心 / *lose* ～ 丧失勇气(或信心) / *lose one's* ～ *to* 心被…俘去, 爱上… / *near* (*nearest*) *one's* ～ ① 为自己所亲爱(最亲爱)的 ②被自己认为重要(最重要)的 / *One's* ～ *sinks within one.* 某人消沉泄气了。/ *out of* ～ ①[主英](土地)贫瘠的 ②沮丧的, 垂头丧气的 / *pluck up* (*one's*) ～ =take ～ / *set one's* ～ *at rest* 安心, 放心 / *set one's* (*sb.'s*) ～ *on sth.* (或 *on doing sth.*) 使自己(某人)下决心做某事 / *take* ～ 鼓起勇气(或信心), 振作起来 / *take* ～ *of grace* 鼓起勇气 / *take* ～. *to* 对某事耿耿于怀; 为某事忧虑(或伤心) / *wear one's* ～ *on* (或 *upon*) *one's sleeve* 心直, 十分坦率; 过于直率; 感情容易激动 / *wear sb.* (*sth.*) *in one's* ～ 忠于某人(某事) / *weep one's* ～ *out* 哭得死去活来 / *with all one's* ～ (或 *with one's* ～ *and soul*) ①真心诚意地, 全心全意地 ②十分愿意地 / *with half a* ～ 半心半意地 ‖～**ed** *a.* [用以构成复合词]有…心(肠)的: warm-～ed 热心的 ‖～**ache** *n.* 痛心, 伤心 / ～**attack** 心力衰竭; 心脏病发作 / '～**beat** *n.* ①心搏 ②中心; 动力 / '～**break** *n.* 极度伤心; 令人心碎的事情 *vt.* 使心碎 / '～**breaking** *a.* 使心碎的 / '～**broken** *a.* 极度伤心的 / '～**burn** *n.* 【医】胃灼热, 心口灼热 ②妒忌; 不满 / ～**burning** *n.* 妒忌, 不满 / ～ **disease** 心脏病 / ～ **failure** ①心力衰竭 ②心脏停跳 / '～**felt** *a.* 衷心的: ～*felt* thanks 衷心的感谢 / '～**land** *n.* 心脏地带, 中心地带 / '～-**lung machine** (用于心脏手术的)人工心肺机 / '～-**rending** *a.* 使伤心的, 使断肠的 / ～('*s*) **blood** 心血; 生命 / '～-**searching** *n.* 内心的反省 / ～**sease** ['hɑːtsiːz] *n.* ①内心平静 ②【植】三色堇 / '～**sick** *a.* 沮丧的, 闷闷不乐的 / '～**sore** *a.* 悲伤的, 痛心的 / '～-**stirring** *a.* 振奋人心的: ～-*stirring* news 振奋人心的消息 / '～-**stricken**, '～-**struck** *a.* 伤心的, 痛心的 / '～**string** *n.* [常用复]心弦; 深情: touch the ～*strings* of the audience 打动观众的心弦 / '～**throb** *n.* ①心脏的跳动 ②[常用复]热情; 柔情 ③[美俚]情人 / '～-**to**-'～ *a.* 贴心的; 坦率的, 诚恳的: a ～-*to*-～ talk 一次谈心 / '～**warming** *a.* 暖人心房的 / '～-**whole** *a.* ①真诚的; 全心全意的 ②勇敢的 ③还不懂爱情的, 情窦未开的 / '～-**wood** *n.* 【植】心材

hearten ['hɑːtn] ❶ *vt.* 振作; 鼓励, 激励 ❷ *vi.* 振作起来 (*up*)

hearth [hɑːθ] *n.* ①壁炉地面 ②炉边; [喻]家庭 ③【冶】(平炉的)炉床; (高炉的)炉膛, 炉缸: open ～ 平炉 ‖'～**rug** *n.* 炉前地毯 / '～**stone** *n.* ①炉石, 磨石 ②炉边; [喻]家庭

heartily ['hɑːtili] *ad.* ①衷心地; 亲切地; 热心地; 尽情地 ②精神饱满地: throw oneself ～ *into* one's work 精神饱满地投入工作 ③胃口大地: He ate ～. 他吃得很多。④ 非常, 完全: be ～ sick of idle talk 对说空话厌烦得要死

heartless ['hɑ:tlis] *a.* 无情的; 残忍的 ‖**~ly** *ad.* / **~ness** *n.*

hearty ['hɑ:ti] I *a.* ① 衷心的; 亲切的; 热诚的; 尽情的: ~ applause 热烈的掌声 / a ~ welcome 由衷的欢迎 / a ~ burst of laughter 一阵尽情的 欢笑 ②精神饱满的; 健壮的: Old as he is, he is *hale and* ~. 他虽年老, 身体却很强健。③ 丰盛的; [主英]丰饶的, 肥沃的: a ~ meal 丰盛的一餐 / ~ land 丰饶的土地 ④ 强烈的, 猛烈的: a ~ dislike 强烈的反感 / a ~ pull 猛烈的一拉 ⑤胃口好的; ~ eater 胃口大的人 II *n.* ①(水手用语)伙伴: My *hearties*! 伙伴们! ②[常用复]水手 ③(英国大学的)运动员 ‖**heartiness** *n.*

heat [hi:t] I *n.* ①热; 暑热; 热度; 热辐射: a ~ of five hundred degrees 五百度的高温 / the intense ~ of midsummer 仲夏的酷热 / This will relieve the ~ of the fever. 这会减轻发烧的热度。/ latent (radiant, specific) ~ 潜(辐射,比)热 ②热烈; 激烈; 激怒: get into a white ~ 白热化 ③(赛跑中的一次)竞赛, 预赛; (一番)努力: trial (preliminary) ~s 预(初)赛 ④[冶]熔炼的炉次; (每炉)熔炼量: turn out ~ after ~ of high-grade steel 炼出一炉又一炉的好钢 ⑤(芥末等的)辣味 (母兽交尾期的)性欲冲动 ⑦压力, 强迫: turn the ~ on sb. 对某人施加压力 ⑧[美俚](警察对罪犯的)穷追, 大肆侦查; 侦查活动的地区: The ~'s on. 警察正在穷追。⑨[美俚]炮火; 枪弹射击: give sb. the ~ 用枪把某人打死 ⑩[美俚]手枪 ⑪[美俚]喝醉: have a ~ on 喝醉酒 II ❶ *vt.* ①把…加热: ~ the furnace to one thousand eight hundred degrees 把熔炉加热到一千八百度 ②使激动; 刺激 ❷ *vi.* 变热, 发热; 激动; 发怒 ‖a dead ~ 不分胜负的赛跑 / *at a* ~ 一(口)气地: set down the outline of an article *at a* single ~ 一口气写下文章的提纲 / *in the* ~ *of* 在(辩论等)最激烈的时候 / *put the* ~ *on sb.* [美俚]逼使某人付款(或干活等); 使某人为难; 对某人采取强硬措施; 要求某人拼命出力 / *turn on the* ~ [美俚]①出死劲儿; 努力完成 ②激起热情 ③穷追罪犯 ④责备, 申斥 ⑤开枪射击 ‖**~ed** *a.* ①加了热的 ②热烈的; 激到的 / **~er** *n.* ①加热者; 发热器, 加热器; 灯丝: a gas ~er 煤气炉 ②[美俚]手枪 ③[美俚]雪茄烟 ‖ **engine** [物]热机 / ~ **flash** 强热(如原子爆炸时所发生的) / ~ **lightning** 闪电(尤指夏夜无雷声的热闪) / '**~proof** *a.* 抗热的 / ~ **rash** 痱子 / ~ **resisting alloy** 耐热合金 / '~-'**set** *vt.* 对(塑料、织物上的皱褶等)进行热定形 / ~ **spot** *n.* ①雀斑 ②热觉点(皮肤上感觉发热处) / '**~-stroke** *n.* 中暑 / '**~-treat** *vt.* 对…进行热处理 / ~ **treatment** 热处理 / ~ **unit** 热(量)单位 / ~ **wave** ①[气]热浪 ②[物]热(辐射)波

heath [hi:θ] *n.* ①欧石南属植物 ②[英]石南丛生的荒地 ‖**one's native** ~ 出生地; 幼年生长的地方

heathen ['hi:ðən] I *n.* ①异教徒(指基督教徒、犹太教徒、伊斯兰教徒以外的人); 多神教信仰者 ②不信教的人; 野蛮的人, 未开化的人 II *a.* ①异教的 ②不信教的; 未开化的 ‖**~dom** *n.* [总称]异教; 异教国; 异教徒; 异教的风俗信仰 / **~ism** *n.* 异教; 异教教义; 野蛮 / **~ize** *vt.* & *vi.* (使)信奉异教; (使)变野蛮

heather ['heðə] I *n.* 石南属植物 II *a.* 似石南的; 杂色的: ~ mixture 混色毛纱 ‖**set the** ~ **on fire** 煽起骚动 / **take to the** ~ [苏格兰]落草做强盗

heave [hi:v] I (heaved 或 hove [houv]) ❶ *vt.* ①(用力地)举起: ~ an axe 举起斧头 ②使胀起, 使鼓起: The storm ~d the sea into mountainous waves. 风暴中海面上波涛万丈。/ ~ one's chest (或 bosom, breast) 使胸部剧烈起伏 ③(费劲地)发出(叹息、呻吟等): ~ a long sigh 长叹一声 ④[口]投掷; 扔: Don't ~ your things around. 别把你的东西到处乱扔。⑤[海]曳(绳缆等); 使(船)开动: ~ the anchor 起锚 / a ship ahead 拉(或开)船前进 ⑥[地]使平错, 使隆起 ❷ *vi.* ①胀起, 鼓起 ②起伏· The billows ~. 波涛翻腾。③喘息; 呕吐 ④[海]曳, 卷 (*at, on*) ⑤(船)移动前进: A steamer hove in sight. 一艘轮船驶入视线。II *n.* ①举; 拉; 扔: with a mighty ~ 猛拉(或猛扔、猛举)一下 ②胀起, 鼓起; (有节奏的)起伏; 船体在水中的升沉: the ~ of the sea 海水的翻腾 ③[地]平错, 隆起 ④[~s][用作单或复]马喘息病 ‖*Heave away*! (或 *Heave ho*!) (水手在起锚等时的呼声)用力拉啊! / ~ *down* 使(船)倾倒一边以进行维修 / ~ *out* ①使(船的龙骨)露出水面以进行维修 ②扯(帆) / ~ *to* [海]使(船)顶风而停; 顶风停船 ‖**~r** *n.* ①举起(或移动)重物的人(或工具) ②[海](卷绳的)杠杆 ‖'**~-'ho** *n.* [美口]免职; 开除: give . . . the ~-ho 免…的职; 开除…· / get the (old) ~-ho 被免职; 被开除

heaven ['hevn] *n.* ①[常用复]天, 天空: sail the blue ~s 在蓝天中翱翔 / the starry ~s 星空 ②[常作 H-][宗]天国; 上帝: go to ~ 死去, 进天国 ③极乐; 极乐之地: When I was a small child, it was ~ to go nesting. 幼年时, 出去摸鸟蛋总是把我乐得什么似的。‖*By Heaven*! (赌咒时用语)老天在上! / *Good Heavens*! (或 *Heavens*!) 天哪! / *Heaven forbid* (或 *forfend*)! 上天不容! (或:决无此事!) / *Heaven knows* ①天知道 ②[用以加强语气]确实无疑地 / *in* ~ ①已死 ②[用以加强语气]究竟, 到底: Where *in* ~ were you? 你当时究竟在哪里? / *move* ~ *and earth* 竭尽全力 / *the seventh* ~ (或 *the* ~ *of* ~s)①[宗]七重天(指上帝和天使居住的天国最高层) ②极乐; 极乐之地 / *to* ~(*s*) 极度地 / *under* ~ [用以加强语气]究竟, 到底 ‖**~ward** *ad.* & *a.* 向天空的 / **~wards** *ad.* 向天空 ‖**~-dust** *n.* [美俚][药]可卡因 / '**~-sent** *a.* 天赐的; 极巧的

heavenly ['hevnli] **I** *a.* ①天的, 天空的: The sun is a ~ body. 太阳是一个天体。/ *Heavenly Twins* 【天】双子星座 ②天国的, 超凡的; 神圣的: the *Heavenly City* 【宗】天堂 ③[口]极好的, 逗人爱的: What ~ cotton bolls! 多好的棉桃! **II** *ad.* ①极, 无比地 ②借天神之力 ‖**heavenliness** *n.* ‖'~-'minded *a.* 虔诚的

heavily ['hevili] *ad.* ① 重重地; 沉重地: a ~ guarded city 戒备森严的城市 ② 沉闷地 ③ 缓慢地; 吃力地 ④ 大量地: a ~ foliaged tree 叶子浓密的树 ⑤暴虐地

heaviness ['hevinis] *n.* ①重 ②沉闷 ③忧伤, 情绪低落: ~ of heart 心情沉重 ④迟钝; 笨拙

heavy ['hevi] **I** *a.* ①重的; 重型的; 繁重的: shoulder ~ loads 挑重担 / a ~ bomber 重轰炸机 ②装备着重武器的 ③沉重的, 有力的 ④大的; 大量的, 多的: a man with ~ features 粗眉大眼的人 / a ~ crop 大丰收 / a ~ rain (snow) 大雨(雪)/ What ~ traffic! 交通多拥挤啊! / a ~ smoker 烟抽得多的人 ⑤ 狂暴的; 猛烈的: a ~ sea 波涛汹涌的海面 / ~ applause 热烈的鼓掌 ⑥令人忧郁的; (心情)沉重的: ~ news 令人忧愁的消息 / a ~ heart 沉重的心情 ⑦(眼皮等) 重垂着的; 昏昏欲睡的: eyes ~ from prolonged reading 因长时间阅读而疲倦的眼睛 / He was still ~ with sleep. 他(刚被弄醒)仍然昏昏欲睡。⑧ 笨重的, 迟钝的 ⑨(天空等)低压的, 阴沉的 ⑩ ~ weather 阴沉的坏天气 ⑪(作品风格等)冗长乏味的 ⑫(道路)泥泞难走的; (土地)难以耕作的 ⑬(食物等)难消化的; (面包等)发酵没发好的 ⑭(剧中角色)严肃的, 庄重的 ⑮[美俚]深沉的, 含义深的 ⑯[美俚]极好的 ⑰[美俚]老于世故的; 时髦的 **II** *ad.* ①沉重地; 笨重地 ②大量地 **III** *n.* ①[复]重炮(尤指重炮、重装炸机等) ②庄重角色;演技重角色的演员 ③[美俚]强盗; 恶棍 ‖*hang* ~ (时间)过得慢而沉闷无聊: Time *hangs* ~ on his hands. 他觉得时间过得慢而无聊。/ ~ *in* (或 *on*) *hand* 见 **hand** / ~ *with child* 怀孕, 大肚子 / *sit* ~ *on* 见 **sit** ‖'~-'armed *a.* 带有重武器的 / '~-'buying *a.* 大量买进的 / '~-'duty *a.* ①重型的; 经得起损耗的: a ~-*duty* truck 重型卡车 ② 关税重的 / '~-'footed *a.* ①动作迟钝的 ② 冗长沉闷的 / '~-'handed *a.* ①笨手笨脚的 ②严厉的; 手辣的 / '~-'headed *a.* ① 头部大而沉重的: ~-*headed* wheat 沉甸甸的麦穗 ②迟钝的, 愚蠢的 / '~-'hearted *a.* 心情沉重的 / ~ *hydrogen* 【化】重氢 / '~-'laden *a.* ①负担沉重的 (*with*) ②心情沉重的 / '~'set *a.* 身材矮胖的 / ~ *spar* 【化】重晶石 / ~ *water* 【化】重水 / '~weight *n.* ①特别重的人(或物) ②重量级拳击(或摔角)运动员 ③[俚]有影响的要人

heckle ['hekl] **I** *vt.* ①【纺】栉梳(麻) ②诘问(当众演说者等), 诘难 **II** *n.* 【纺】针排 ‖-*r n.* 诘问者

hectare ['hekta:] *n.* 公顷(等于 100 公亩或 2.471 英亩, 合 15 市亩; 略作 ha.)

hectic ['hektik] **I** *a.* ① 肺病的, 消耗热的: a ~ fever 消耗热, 肺病热 ②(因患病)发热的; 潮热升火的 ③ 兴奋的, 激动的, 闹哄哄的: have a ~ time 非常激动; 闹哄哄地乱了一场 **II** *n.* ①肺病热, 消耗热; 肺病热患者 ②(肺病患者脸上的)潮红 ‖~ally *ad.*

hectograph ['hektougra:f] **I** *n.* 【印】胶版誊写版 **II** *vt.* 用胶版誊写版印刷

hector ['hektə] **I** *n.* 威吓者, 虚张声势的人 **II** *vt.* & *vi.* ①(向…)说大话; 吓唬 ②折磨; 愚弄

he'd [hi:d] =he had; he would

hedge [hedʒ] **I** *n.* ①(矮树)树篱: a dead ~ 用树枝编成的围篱 / a quickset 由活树围成的树篱 ②障碍(物) ③【商】套头交易(指为避免损失而买进现货卖出期货或反之) ④(赌博中的)两面下注 ⑤模棱两可的话 **II** ❶ *vt.* ①用树篱围住(或隔开) ② 设障碍于…; 妨碍; 包围: ~ sb. *about* (或 *round, in*) with rules 以清规戒律束缚某人的手脚 / ~ sb.'s path with difficulties 在某人的道路上设置障碍 ③ 两面下注以避免(赌博、冒险等损失) ❷ *vi.* ①筑树篱; 修整树篱 ②躲闪, 规避, 推诿 ③两面下注以防损失 **III** *a.* ①树篱的; 树篱之下(或旁边)的 ②偷偷摸摸的, 名声不好的 ‖*be* (或 *sit*) *on the* ~ 骑墙, 要两面派 / ~ *off* ①用树篱(或其他障碍物)把…遮隔掉 ②两面下注 / ~ *out* 用树篱(或其他障碍物)把…隔开 / *not grow on every* ~ 稀少, 稀有 / ~ *in* ①植(或修整)树篱的人 ②两面下注的人 ‖~**hog** ['hedʒhɔg] *n.* 【动】猬; [美]豪猪 ②【军】棱形筑垒; 刺猬弹(指一种反潜用的深水炸弹); 环形筑垒阵地 ③【植】野毛茛 ④易怒的人, 难对付的人 / ~**hop** *vi.* 掠地飞行, 极低空飞行; [俚]跳栏飞行 / '~hopper *n.* 掠地飞行的飞机(或驾驶员) / ~**priest** *n.* [英]低级而无知识的教士 / '~row *n.* 栽成树篱的一排灌木 / ~ **school** (爱尔兰等地的)露天学校, 野外学校 / ~ **sparrow** 篱雀(一种英国和欧洲常见的鸣鸟, 多栖于篱上)

heed [hi:d] **I** *vt.* & *vi.* 注意, 留意 **II** *n.* 注意, 留意: give (或 pay) much ~ to sb.'s advice 很重视某人的劝告 / He took no ~ of what I said. 他完全把我的话当作耳边风。‖~**ful** *a.* 注意的, 留心的 (*of*) / ~**less** *a.* 不注意的, 掉以轻心的 (*of*)

heel[1] [hi:l] **I** *n.* ①脚后跟, 踵; (马等)后я)的后跟; 蹄的后部; [复](四脚兽的)后脚 ②(鞋、袜等)的后跟 ③踵状物; 桅杆的下端; 梯子的底脚; (植物的)节瘤; (提琴的)弓把; (枪托的)托踵 ④(酒瓶中剩下的)酒脚; 干酪皮; 面包头 ⑤[美俚]卑鄙的家伙; 小偷 ⑥[美俚]越狱; 从犯罪地点逃跑 **II** ❶ *vt.* ① 给…钉后掌: sole and ~ a pair of shoes 给一双鞋打前后掌 ②紧跟; 追赶: ~ sb. upstairs 紧随某人上楼 ③用脚后跟践踏: ~ a cigarette butt out 踩灭烟头 ④[俚]供钱给; 武装 ⑤用脚后跟向后传送 (球); 用高尔夫球棍末端击(球) ❷ *vi.* ① 在后紧随; 快跑 ②(足球)用脚后跟向

后传球 (out) ③用脚后跟跳舞 ‖at ~ 跟在后面;
close at ~ 紧跟在后 / at (或 on, upon) sb.'s
~s 紧跟在某人后面;紧追着某人 / betake oneself to one's ~s 溜之大吉 / bring sb. to ~
①使某人紧跟 ②使某人就范 / clap (或 lay)
sb. by the ~s ①给某人钉脚镣,监禁某人 ②制
服某人;使某人受挫折 / come to ~ ①(狗)紧
随在主人后面 ②服从,附和 / cool one's ~s 久
等,空等 / cop a ~ [美俚]逃跑;越狱 / down
at (the) ~ ①(鞋子)穿得把后跟磨掉 ②褴褛
的;十分邋遢的 / drag one's ~s ①拖着脚步走
②迟缓误事;故意拖拉;不合作 / follow on (或
upon) the ~s of 紧跟在…的后面 / have the
~s of 追过… / Heel! (或 Keep to ~!) (唤狗
的用语)跟着! / ~ in 定植前在(树木等)的根
部壅土暂栽 / ~s over head (或 head over
~s) 见 head / kick one's ~s 久等,空等 / kick
up its ~s (马) 溜腿 / kick up one's ~s ①高
兴得跳起来 ②活跃一阵 ③[俚]死 / lay in by
the ~s = in / lay sb. (fast) by the ~s 把
某人逮捕下狱;束缚某人的手脚 / out at the ~s
①鞋跟(或袜后跟)有洞的 ②褴褛的 / over head
and ~s 见 head / set by the ~s ①给…上脚
镣,监禁,束缚 ②推翻,使倾覆 / show a clean
pair of ~s (或 show one's ~s, 或 take
to one's ~s) 逃走,滑脚溜走,逃之夭夭 /
the ~ of Achilles 唯一致命的弱点 / to
~ 紧跟着,追随着: follow sb. to ~ 亦步亦趋
地跟着某人 / tread on the ~s of 紧随…之后 /
turn on one's ~ 急向后转 / under the ~ of
[喻]被…践踏,被…蹂躏 ‖~ed a. ①有鞋后
跟的 ②[美俚]有钱的 ③(尤指用枪)武装了的 /
~er n. ①绱鞋后跟的人 ②[美口]政客的追随
者,地区内为政党办事的小喽罗;可鄙的人 ③用
脚跟奔走的斗鸡 / ~less a. 没有后跟的
‖~-and-'toe a. 竞走(步法)的: ~-and-toe
walking 竞走 / '~ball n. (鞋匠用来上光的)硬
蜡和煤烟的混合物 / '~piece n. ①鞋后跟 ②
踵状物 / '~plate n. 钉于鞋后跟防磨损的金属
片 / '~post n. 柱脚 / '~tap n. ①用来加高
鞋后跟的皮 ②杯中喝剩的酒: No ~taps! 一
饮而尽!

heel² [hi:l] **I** n. (船的)倾侧 **II ❶** vt. 使(船)倾
侧 **❷** vi. (船)倾侧 (over): ~ to port (starboard)
船向左(右)舷倾侧 ‖~ing n. (船的)倾侧: ~ing
error 【海】倾斜自差

hefty ['hefti] **I** a. [美口] ①很重的: a ~ blow 重
重的一击 ②有力的;健壮的: a ~ man 魁梧的大
汉 ③异常大的: a ~ majority 压倒多数 / a ~
sum 一笔巨款 **II** n. [美俚]魁梧大汉 ‖**heftily**
ad. / **heftiness** n.

heifer ['hefə] n. ①(未生过牛犊的)小母牛 ②
[美俚]漂亮姑娘

height [hait] n. ①高;高度;海拔: take sb.'s ~ 量
某人的身高 ②「常用复]高处,高地: climb the
~s of science and technology 攀登科学技术高

峰 / hold *Height 101* 坚守一〇一高地 ③顶高,
绝顶: The tide was at its ~. 潮水涨到最高点
了。/ in the ~ of summer 在盛夏 / be the ~
of absurdity 荒谬绝伦 ‖**~-to-'paper** n. 【印】
铅字的标准高度

heighten ['haitn] **❶** vt. ①加高;提高 ②增加,增大;
加强: ~ one's speed 加快速度 / ~ one's confidence 增强信心 ③加深(颜色等),使显著;使出
色 **❷** vi. ①变大;(颜色等)变深,变显著 ②[古]
升高,长高,变高

heinous ['heinəs] a. 极可恨的;极凶残的: ~ crimes
滔天罪行 ‖**~ly** ad. / **~ness** n.

heir [ɛə] n. 后嗣;继承人: the right ~ 【律】合
法继承人 ‖*cut off one's ~ with a shilling*
(用象征性的一先令)取消继承者的继承权 ‖**~ess**
['ɛəris] n. 嗣女;女继承人 / **~less** a. 无后
嗣的 / **~ship** n. 继承权 ‖**~ apparent** 【律】有
确定继承权的人 / **~ at law** 【律】法定继承
人 / **~ presumptive** 【律】假定继承人

heirloom ['ɛəlu:m] n. ①【律】相传动产(指随不动
产一起转移产权的动产) ②传家宝

held [held] hold 的过去式和过去分词

helicopter ['helikɔptə] **I** n. 直升飞机 **II ❶** vt.
用直升飞机载送: ~ sb. aboard the ship 用
直升飞机把某人送到船上 **❷** vi. 乘直升飞机
‖**~ carrier** 直升飞机母舰 / **~manship** ['heli-
kɔptəmənʃip] n. 驾驶(或乘坐)直升飞机来往

helicopter

helium ['hi:ljəm] n. 【化】氦

hell [hel] **I** n. ①地狱,阴间 ②极大的痛苦;苦境:
a ~ on earth (或 a living ~) 人间地狱 ③[常
用于加强语气或咒骂]: cold as ~ 冷得要命 /
Where the ~ have you been hiding? 你究竟躲
到哪里去了? / Go to ~! 滚开! 见鬼去吧!/
Hell! 混蛋! ④大混乱,毁坏: play ~ with sth.
把某物(或某事)弄得一塌糊涂 ⑤训斥,大骂: get
~ from sb. for being late 因晚到而被某人大骂
一顿 ⑥胡闹;蠢态 ⑦[俚](印刷所的)坏铅字箱;
[古]裁缝作坊的废料角 ⑧赌窟 **II** vi. ①放荡地
欢饮;闹饮 ②(车辆)疾驰 ‖*a ~ of a ...* 极度
的;难以容忍的,糟糕的;极好的: a ~ *of a mess*

一场糊涂 / a ~ of an actor 一个糟糕的(或极好的)演员 / be ~ for 对…极度关心;竭力坚持… / be ~ on [美俚] ①使…十分痛苦 ②对…十分严格 ③对…极端有害 / catch ~ [美俚]挨训斥,受惩罚 / give sb. ~ 使某人受不了 / ~ and gone [美俚] ①极远的: He would be the ~ and gone away from here by now. 此时他一定已去得相当远了。 ② 不可挽回的 / ~ and (或 or) high water 任何困难 / Hell and Tommy [俚]彻底毁灭,堕落 / ~ around [美俚]混日子;经常出没下等酒吧间 / Hell breaks loose. 喧闹起来。(或: 大乱起来。) / ~ to pay 严厉惩罚,痛责 / in ~ [用于加强语气]究竟,到底: What in ~ are you doing? 你到底在做什么? / just for the ~ of it [美俚]只是为了捣乱;只是为了好玩 / like ~ 拼命地,极猛地: run like ~ 拼命地跑 / raise ~ [俚]喧闹;怒斥 / (ride) ~ for leather 拼命地(骑),尽全力(骑) / The ~ of it is .... [美俚]妙就妙在…;麻烦就在于…: The ~ of it was that nobody recognized him. 糟就糟在没有人认出他。 / to beat ~ [美俚][作状语用]又快又猛地 / what the ~ ①[用于加强语气或咒骂]: What the ~ do you want? 你到底要什么? ②[表示无所谓、不在乎]: What the ~, I may as well go. 行,我去也可以。 ‖~ward ad. & a. 向着地狱(的) ‖'~-bent a. ①固执的,死心塌地的: be ~-bent on having one's own way 一意孤行 ②不顾一切的,拼命的 / '~box n. [俚](印刷所的)坏铅字箱 / ~ buggy [美][军俚]坦克 / '~cat n. 老丑妇;泼妇 / ~dive [军俚]俯冲轰炸 / '~fire n. 地狱火(迷信说法所称的上帝惩罚罪人之火);[喻]苦苦折磨人的东西 / '~-fired ad. & a. 极度地(的) / '~=for-'leather a. & ad. 拼命的(地);极快极猛的(地) n. 不顾一切,慌忙 / '~hole n. 地狱般的地方;下流(或罪恶)场所 / '~hound n. ①(神话中的)地狱看门狗 ②恶魔;恶魔般的人 / ~'s bells [作惊叹语用] ①[表示惊诧]喔唷! ②[表示愤慨、不耐烦等]见鬼! / ~ ship 地狱船(指对水手进行残酷虐待的船只)

he'll [hi:l] =he will; he shall

hello ['he'lou] I int. 喂![表示问候、惊奇等或用以唤起注意] II n. 表示问候(或惊奇,或唤起注意时)的叫声: Say ~ to him for me.(或 Tell him "~" for me.) 代我问候他。 III ① vi. 发"喂"声 ②vt. 向…发"喂"声 ‖~ girl 女电话接线员

helm¹ [helm] I n. ①舵,舵柄,舵轮;转舵装置: Down (with the) ~! 转舵使船背风! / Up (with the) ~! 转舵使船向风! ②(组织、企业等的)领导: take the ~ of 开始掌管… / the man at the ~ 掌舵人,舵手 / at the ~ of a state 掌握着政权 II vt. 给…掌舵;指挥 ‖~sman ['helmzmən] n. 舵手

helm² [helm] [古][诗] I n. 头盔 II vt. 给…戴上(或配备)头盔 ‖~ cloud [英方](暴风雨来临时笼罩山头的)山头云

helmet ['helmit] I n. ①头盔;钢盔 ②软木遮阳帽;(救火员、运动员等的)防护帽;保护头部的盔状物: a safety ~ (建筑工人等戴的)安全帽 / a gas ~ 防毒面具 ③盔状花冠(或花萼) ④[美俚]警察 II vt. 给…戴上(或配备)头盔 ‖~ed a. ①戴头盔的 ②头盔状的

help [help] I ① vt. ①帮助: May I ~ you with your luggage? 我帮你拿行李好吗? / We ~ed him to mend his bicycle. 我们帮他修理自行车。 / Customers' criticisms ~ (to) improve the service work of our shops. 顾客的批评意见帮助我们的商店改进服务工作。②援助;助长,促进(成长等): ~ digestion 帮助消化 ③治疗;补救: This medicinal herb ~s a cough. 这种草药可治咳嗽。④使进食,款待 ⑤[与 can, could 连用]避免,阻止: I'll not give you any trouble if I can ~ it. 我要是想得出办法,就不会来给你添麻烦了。② vi. ①有帮助;有用: This medical handbook ~s a lot. 这本医药手册很有用。②[呼救用语]: Help! Help! A boy is drowning. 救人啊! 救人啊! 一个男孩子要淹死了。③ (宴会时)招待,伺候 II n. ①帮助: Thank you for your kind ~. 谢谢您好意相助。 / Your advice was a great ~ to me. 你的劝告对我大有帮助。②帮手,助手 ③治疗;挽救办法: be past ~ 无法挽救 ④[美]佣工: the ~ wanted column (西方报纸上的)招工栏 ⑤[口](食物的)一份 ‖~ of some (no, much) ~ to sb. 对某人有些(没有,很有)帮助 / cannot ~ but [美][后接原形动词]不得不… / ~ a lame dog over a stile 见 dog / ~ ... on (或 forward) 使…获得进步(或进展) / ~ oneself (to) ①自用(食物等): Help yourself. (招待客人用语)请随便吃! / Help yourself to the cigarettes. 请抽烟! ②擅自取用(…) / ~ sb. down 把某人挽扶下来 / ~ sb. into (out of) 挽扶某人进入(走出): The medical orderly ~ed the granny into the inner room. 卫生员将老大娘搀进内屋。 / ~ sb. off (on) with 帮某人脱去(穿上)…: Please ~ him off with the damp clothes. 请帮他把湿衣服脱掉。 / ~ sb. out 帮助某人解决难题(或摆脱困境);帮助某人完成工作: I don't know how to translate this passage. Please ~ me out. 我不知道这一段怎么翻译,请帮我一下。 / ~ sb. over ①帮某人越过… ②帮某人度过… / ~ sb. to ①给某人进(食)(尤指夹菜、斟酒等): What shall I ~ you to then? 您还要吃点什么? ②帮助某人得到,帮助某人发现: This clue ~ed us to the solution. 这一线索帮助我们解决了问题。 / ~ sb. up ①把某人扶起 ②扶某人攀登(斜坡等) / It can't be ~ed. (或 There is no ~ for it.) 实在没法儿。 / so ~ me (或 so ~ me God) (赌咒时用语)我敢断言,千真万确 / with the ~ of …的帮助下 ‖~er n. ①帮手,助手;佣工 ②起帮助作用的东西

helpful ['helpful] a. 有帮助的,有用的;有益的:

publish more new books ~ *to* teen-agers 出版更多对青少年有益的新书 ‖**~ly** *ad.* / **~ness** *n.*

helping ['helpiŋ] **I** *n.* (食物的)一份: Give me another ~, please. 请再给我一份. **II** *a.* ①帮助人的: be ready to lend a ~ hand 乐意助人 ②辅助的: a ~ verb 助动词

helpless ['helplis] *a.* ①无助的, 未受到帮助的 ②不能自助的, 孤弱的: a ~ orphan 无依无靠的孤儿 ③无能的, 没用的; 无效的 ‖**~ly** *ad.* / **~ness** *n.*

helpmate ['helpmeit], **helpmeet** ['helpmi:t] *n.* 良伴; 配偶

helter-skelter ['heltə'skeltə] **I** *ad.* 手忙脚乱地, 慌慌张张地, 狼狈地: flee ~ 狼狈逃窜, 作鸟兽散 **II** *a.* 手忙脚乱的, 慌张的, 狼狈的 **III** *n.* 手忙脚乱, 慌张

hem[1] [hem] **I** *n.* ①(衣服等的)折边 ②(钢板、塑料板等的)卷边 ②边, 缘 **II** (hemmed; hemming) ❶ *vt.* ①给…缝边, 给…镶边 ②包围; 禁闭 (*in, around, about*) ~ sb. *out* 把某人逐出 ❷ *vi.* 做折边

hem[2] [hem] **I** [m̩m, hm] *int.* 哼! (踌躇、疑问或唤起注意、清嗓等时发出的声音) **II** *n.* 哼声, 清嗓声 **III** (hemmed; hemming) *vi.* ①发哼声, 哼一声 ②结结巴巴地说 ‖~ *and* haw 嗯嗯呃呃 (表示踌躇或支吾等)

hemisphere ['hemisfiə] *n.* ①(地球或天球的)半球: the Eastern (Western) *Hemisphere* 东(西)半球 / the Southern (Northern) *Hemisphere* 南(北)半球 / Magdeburg ['mægdəbə:g] ~*s* 【物】马德堡半球(气压实验用具) ②半球地图, 半球模型 ③半球上所有的国家(或居民) ④(活动、知识等的)范围, 领域 ⑤大脑半球 (=cerebral ~) ‖**hemispheric(al)** [,hemi'sferik(ə)l] *a.*

hemp [hemp] *n.* ①大麻; 大麻纤维; 纤维; 长纤维的植物 ② [the ~] (由大麻制成的)麻醉药 ④ [谑]绞索 ‖**~en** *a.* 大麻的; 似大麻的; 大麻制的 ‖~ palm 【植】棕榈

hen [hen] **I** *n.* ①母鸡 ②雌禽; 雌虾(或鱼、蟹等) ③(鸟、虾等的)雌性: a ~ bird 雌鸟 / a ~ crab 雌蟹 ④[美俚]女人(尤指爱唠叨的或爱管闲事的中年妇女) **II** (henned; henning) *vi.* [美俚](女人)聊天; 传播流言蜚语 ‖*a* ~ *on* 策划中的阴谋, 图谋: He suspected that there was *a* ~ *on*. 他怀疑其中有阴谋. / (*as*) *mad as a wet* ~ [美俚]非常生气 / *a wet* ~ (或 *an old* ~) [美俚]讨厌的人; 泼妇 / *like a* ~ *on a hot girdle* 极不安静, 极不舒服 / *like a* ~ *with one chicken* 大惊小怪, 唠唠叨叨 / *sell one's* ~*s on a rainy day* 亏本出售 ‖~ *and* chickens 【植】屋顶长生花 / '~**bane** *n.* 【植】天仙子 / '~**coop** *n.* ①鸡棚, 家禽的笼舍 ②[美俚](大学)女生宿舍 / ~ fruit [俚]鸡蛋 / ~ harrier 【动】鸡鵟 / '~-,hearted *a.* 懦弱的, 胆小的 / '~**house** *n.* 家禽的笼舍 ②[美俚]军官俱乐部 / ~ party [俗]妇女聚会 / '~**pecked** *a.* 受老婆虐待的;

怕老婆的 / '~**roost** *n.* 鸡窝 / ~ track 写得叫人看不懂的字

hence [hens] **I** *ad.* ①从此地; 从今世; [古]从此以后; 今后: go ~ 走开; [喻]死 / *Hence with*! 走开! 带走! / five years ~ 五年以后 ②因此; 由此: *Hence* these songs. 因而有了这些歌曲. **II** *int.* [诗]去: *Hence*! 出去! 走开!

henceforth ['hens'fɔ:θ] **henceforward** ['hens-'fɔ:wəd] *ad.* 从今以后, 今后

henchman ['hent∫mən] ([复] henchmen) *n.* ①亲信, 心腹 ②(政治上的)顺从者, 仆从

her [hə:; 弱 ə:, hə, ə] *pron.* ① [she 的宾格]她: Give ~ the sickle. She wants one. 把这把镰刀给她, 她要. / a letter for ~ 一封给她的信 ② [口][用作表语]她 (=she): It's ~. 是她. (=It's she.) ③[口][用于 than 后面]她 (=she): He's taller than ~. 他比她高. ④[古]她自己 (=herself): She leaned ~ against the tree. 她靠在树上. ⑤ [she 的所有格]她的: ~ paintings 她画的画; 属她所有的画 / That's ~ pen, not yours. 那是她的笔, 不是你的.

herald ['herəld] **I** *n.* ①(旧时)传令官 ②(英国的)司宗谱纹章的官 ③(常用作报纸的名称)通报者; 使者; 预言者; 先驱 **II** *vt.* ①宣布; 通报 ②预示…的来临: The first buds ~ spring. 嫩枝报春到. ③欢呼

herb [hə:b] *n.* ①草本植物 ②香草; 药草: medicinal ~*s* 药草 / a ~ prescription 草药方 ‖**~less** *a.* 缺乏草本植物的 ‖~ beer 草药制的饮料 / ~ tea, ~ water (草药煎成的)汤药

herbaceous [hə:'beiʃəs] *a.* ① 草本的; 草质的: a ~ border (花园沿边)种多年生草本植物的花坛 ②(在纹理、颜色、形状等方面)似绿叶的

herbage ['hə:bidʒ] *n.* ①[总称]草本植物(尤指牧草) ②草本植物的浆汁部分 ③【律】(在别人土地上的)放牧权

herbal ['hə:bəl] **I** *a.* 草本植物的; 草本植物制的 **II** *n.* ①草药书 ②[古]植物标本集, 草本集 ‖**~ist** *n.* ①草本植物学家 ②草药采集者; 种药的人 ③草药商 ④草药医生

herculean [,hə:kju'li(:)ən] *a.* ① [H-]【希神】[罗神]海格立斯的, 大力神的 ②(在力量等方面)大无比的: a man of ~ build 巨人(指体格魁梧) ③费力的, 艰巨的: a ~ task 艰巨的任务 / make ~ efforts 作极其巨大的努力

herd [hə:d] **I** *n.* ① 兽群; 牧群(尤指牛群) ② [常用以构成复合词]放牧人: a cow~ 放牛的人 ③ [贬]民众, 百姓 **II** ❶ *vt.* ①使集在一起; 把…赶在一起 ②放牧 ❷ *vi.* 成群 (*together, with*) ‖*ride* ~ ①骑在马上看管牛群 ②监督; 管理 ‖~**er** *n.* ①牧人 ② [美俚]监狱看守

herdsman ['hə:dzmən] ([复] herdsmen) *n.* ①牧人 ②牧主 ③ [the H-]【天】牧夫座

here [hiə] *ad.* ①在这里, 在这里: *Here* we are. (抵达目的地时的用语)到了. ②向这里, 到这里: come ~ 到这里来 / *Here* comes the bus! 公共

汽车来了! ③ 在这点上; 这时: *Here* the speaker paused for a while. 讲到这里, 作报告的人停了一会儿。④[用在名词后, 以引起注意或加强语气] ⑤【宗】在这个世界上, 在尘世间 **Ⅱ** *n.* ①这里: from ~ 从这里 ②【宗】今世 / *Here!* (点名时的回答)到! 有! / ~ *and now* 此时此地: Let's start the experiment ~ *and now*. 我们此时此地就开始做实验吧。/ ~ *and there* 各处 / *below* 【宗】在尘世间 / *Here goes!* 见 **go** / *Here's to . . .!* (敬酒时说)向…敬一杯! / *Here's to your health!* (敬酒时说)祝你健康! / ~, *there and everywhere* 到处 / *Here you are.* [口] ①你已在这里了。(或: 你已到了。) ②这就是你所要的东西。: A: Where is my pen? B: *Here you are.* 甲: 我的钢笔到哪儿去了? 乙: 喏, 这不就是! / *neither* ~ *nor there* [口] 不中肯; 与题目不相干; 不重要 ‖**~about(s)** ['hiərə,baut(s)] *ad.* 在这里附近 / **~after** [hiər'ɑ:ftə] *ad.* 从此以后, 今后 *n.* 未来; 【宗】来世 / **~at** [hiər'æt] *ad.* [古] 因此; 因此 / **~away(s)** ['hiərə'wei(z)] *ad.* =~about(s) / **~by** *ad.* (用于公文等中)以此, 特此: Notice is ~*by* given that . . . . …特此布告。/ **~'from** *ad.* 由此 / **~in** ['hiər'in] *ad.* 此中, 于此: *Herein* lies the answer. 这里就包含着答案。/ **~inabove** ['hiərinə'bʌv] *ad.* 在上文 / **~inafter** ['hiərin-'ɑ:ftə] *ad.* 在下文 / **~inbefore** ['hiərinbi'fɔ:] *ad.* 在上文 / **~inbelow** ['hiərinbi'lou] *ad.* 在下文 / **~into** ['hiər'intu] *ad.* 到这里面 / **~of** [hiər'ɔv] *ad.* ①关于这个 ②在本文(件)中 / **~on** [hiər'ɔn] *ad.* =~upon / '~'**to** *ad.* ①到这里, 到此 ②对于这个 / **~tofore** ['hiətu'fɔ:] *ad.* 到现在为止; 在此以前 / **~under** [hiər'ʌndə] *ad.* (书、文件等中)在下面 / **~upon** ['hiərə'pɔn] *ad.* ①于是 ②关于这个 / '~'**with** *ad.* ①与此一道: A set of samples is enclosed ~*with.* 随信附上一套样品。②用此方法

hereditary [hi'reditəri] *a.* ①世袭的; ~ property 世袭财产 ②遗传的: a ~ disease 遗传病 / a ~ feud (祖上传下的)宿怨 ‖**hereditarily** *ad.*

heredity [hi'rediti] *n.* ①遗传 ②遗传特征 ③继承 ④传统

here's [hiəz] =here is

heresy ['herəsi] *n.* ①【宗】异教; 异端; 信奉异教 ②左道邪说; 信奉邪说

heritage ['heritidʒ] *n.* ①世袭财产 ②继承物; 传统; 遗产 ③(长子)继承权

hermetic(al) [hə:'metik(əb] *a.* ①炼金术的; 奥妙的 ②密封的; 与外界隔绝的: a ~ seal 密封 ‖**hermetically** *ad.*

hermit ['hə:mit] *n.* ①隐士 ②用胡桃和葡萄干做的一种小甜饼 ③【动】热带森林里的蜂鸟 ‖~ **crab** 寄居蟹

~ro ['hiərou] *n.* ①古代神话中半神式的英雄 ②英雄, 英雄人物; 勇士: a combat (或 battle) ~ 战斗英雄 / an unsung ~ 无名英雄 ③(戏剧、小

说中的)男主角, 男主人公 ④ (某一事件或时期的)中心人物 ‖**~ism** ['herouizəm] *n.* ①英雄行为; 英雄品质 ②英雄主义 ‖~ **worship** ①英雄崇拜 ②对个人的盲目崇拜 / '~-,worship *vt.* 把…当作英雄崇拜 / '~-,worshipper *n.* 英雄崇拜者

heroic [hi'rouik] **Ⅰ** *a.* ①古代神话中的英雄的, 神异的: the ~ age 英雄时代(尤指特洛伊战争终了以前古希腊的"英雄时代") / a ~ legend 神异的传说 ②英雄的; 英勇的; 崇高的: ~ deeds 英雄的事迹 ③歌颂英雄的; 史诗的; (诗剧等)属于英国王政复辟时期的: ~ poetry 英雄诗; 史诗 ④(语言)夸大的, 堂皇的; (声音等)洪大的; (塑像等)大于实物的: a statue of ~ size (或 on a ~ scale) 大于真人的塑像 ⑤(措施等)冒险一试的; (药物)猛烈的; (剂量)大的: ~ measures 孤注一掷的措施 / a ~ drug 烈性的麻醉品 **Ⅱ** *n.* ①英雄诗; 史诗; 英雄诗体 ②[复]英勇的行为; 夸大(或过火)的语言(或动作作势) ‖~ **couplet** 英雄偶句诗体(互相押韵的含有五个抑扬音步的两行诗, 多用于长篇史诗中) / ~ **verse,** ~ **line,** ~ **metre** 英雄诗体

heroin ['herouin] *n.* 【药】海洛因, 二乙酰吗啡

heron ['herən] ([复] heron(s)) *n.* 【动】苍鹭 ‖**~ry** *n.* 苍鹭的巢穴

herring ['heriŋ] ([复] herring(s)) *n.* 鲱鱼: ~ oil 鲱油 ‖*be packed as close as* ~*s* 挤得象罐头里的鲱鱼 / *draw a red* ~ *across the track* (或 *trail*) 扯些不相干的东西来分散谈话的中心 ‖~ **pond** (海)洋 / [谑]北大西洋

hers [hə:z] *pron.* [物主代词]她的(东西); 她的家属(或有关的人): Is this his or ~? 这是他的还是她的? / My eyesight is good; ~ is even better (than mine). 我的视力好, 她的视力更好。/ Give my greetings to her and ~. 请向她和她的家人问好。[注意: 句中 hers 一词亦可读作"她的爱人"、"她的朋友"等, 视上下文而定]

herself [hə:'self] *pron.* ①[反身代词]她自己: She hurt ~ while rescuing the child. 她在救孩子时自己受伤了。②[用以加强语气]她亲自, 她本人: She ~ told me the news. 她亲自告诉了我这个消息。③[用于 be, become, come to 等之后]她的正常情况(指健康、情绪等): She *is* not quite ~ today. 她今天不大舒服。(或: 她今天情绪有些反常。) / After treatment she *became* ~ again (*came to* ~). 经过治疗后她复原了(苏醒过来了)。‖*(all) by* ~ ①她独自地 ②她独立地

he's [hi:z; 弱 hiz, iz] [口] ① =he is ② =he has

hesitant ['hezitənt] *a.* 踌躇的; 犹豫的 ‖~**ly** *ad.*

hesitate ['heziteit] *vi.* ①踌躇; 犹豫: ~ at nothing 对什么事都毫不迟疑 / ~ to do (或 about doing) sth. 对做某事犹豫不决 ②含糊, 支吾: ~ in speaking 说话吞吞吐吐 ③口吃

hesitatingly ['heziteitiŋli] *ad.* 踌躇地; 犹豫地; 含糊地

hesitation [ˌheziˈteiʃən] *n.* ①踌躇;犹豫: march forward without ~ 勇往直前 / feel some ~ in accepting the invitation 对接受邀请有点犹豫不决 ②含糊 ③口吃 ‖**hesitative** [ˈheziteitiv] *a.*

heterodox [ˈhetərədɔks] *a.* ①不合于公认标准的 ②异教的;异端的 ‖**~y** *n.* ①违反公认标准 ②异教;异端;违反公认标准的意见

heterogeneous [ˌhetərouˈdʒiːnjəs] *a.* ①异类的,异族的 ②由不同成分组成的,异质的,不纯的 ③【数】非齐次的,非齐性的,不纯一的;参差的 ④【化】不均匀的;多相的

hew [hjuː] (过去式 hewed, 过去分词 hewn [hjuːn] 或 hewed) ❶ *vt.* ①(用斧、刀等)砍;劈: ~ off a large limb of the tree 砍去一根大树枝 ②砍倒: ~ trees 砍倒树木 ③砍成;劈出;开辟: ~ one's way 开出一条路; 排除障碍前进 / ~ out paths up a mountain 开辟山路 ❷ *vi.* ①砍;劈 ②坚持;遵守 (*to*) ‖**~er** *n.* 砍伐者;采煤工人: ~*ers* of wood and drawers of water 砍柴挑水的人; [喻]干苦力活者

hexagon [ˈheksəgən] *n.* 六角形,六边形 ‖**~al** [hekˈsægənəl] *a.* ~*al* system 【矿】六方晶系

hexameter [hekˈsæmitə] I *n.* 六韵步组成的诗行 II *a.* 六韵步的

hey [hei] *int.* 嗨[表示惊讶、疑问、喜悦或用以唤起注意等] ‖*Hey for . . .!* ···好啊! (赞美某人或某物) / *Hey presto!* (魔术师用语)说变就变!

heyday¹ [ˈheidei] *int.* [古]嗨[表示喜悦、惊奇等]

heyday² [ˈheidei] *n.* ①全盛期: in the ~ of youth 在青春时期 ②[古]高兴

hiatus [haiˈeitəs] ([复] hiatus(es)) *n.* ①裂缝;空隙 ②(稿件等的)脱字;漏句 ③拖宕;中断;(时间的)间歇 ④(语音的)元音连续(如 he enters 中的 e)

hibernate [ˈhaibəːneit] *vi.* ①(动物)越冬;冬眠 ②(人)避寒 ‖**hibernation** [ˌhaibəːˈneiʃən] *n.*

hiccup [ˈhikʌp] I *n.* 打嗝儿,打呃;打呃声 II (hiccup(p)ed; hiccup(p)ing) ❶ *vi.* 打呃; 作打呃声 ❷ *vt.* 打着呃说出 (*out*)

hidden [ˈhidn] I hide¹ 的过去分词 II *a.* 隐藏的;秘密的;神秘的: ~ property 埋藏的财物,地财 / a ~ microphone 窃听器

hide¹ [haid] I (过去式 hid [hid], 过去分词 hidden [ˈhidn] 或 hid) ❶ *vt.* ①把···藏起来,隐藏: A fox cannot ~ its tail. 狐狸尾巴是藏不住的。/ ~ one's head (因自觉有罪或害臊)把脸藏起来 ②隐瞒: ~ sth. *from* sb. 把某事瞒着某人 / ~ one's feelings 掩饰感情 ③遮掩掉,掩蔽: Sugar coating ~*s* the taste of pills. 糖衣掩盖了药片的药味。❷ *vi.* 躲藏,隐藏 II *n.* (观察野兽活动的)躲藏处 ‖**~ out** [美口]躲藏(尤指躲避警察的耳目) / ~ *up* [俚]包庇(坏人) ‖**'~-and-'seek** *n.* 捉迷藏; [喻]与躲闪的人(或事物)打交道: play (at) ~*-and-seek* (*with*) (与···)捉迷藏; (与···)打躲躲闪闪的交道 / **'~away** *n.* 隐藏处 ②偏僻的小餐馆(或娱乐处) / **'~out** *n.*

躲藏处(尤指盗匪的秘密藏身处) / **hiding power** (油漆等的)遮盖力,覆盖力,盖底力

hide² [haid] I *n.* ①兽皮;皮革 ②[口](人的)皮肤; [俚]厚脸皮 II *vt.* ①剥···的皮 ②痛打 ‖*bat ~s* [美俚][总称]钞票 / *have a thick ~* 脸皮厚 / *have the ~ to do sth.* (竟)厚颜无耻地做某事 / ~ *and hair* 连皮带毛; 完全 / *~ or hair* [用于否定句]影踪: I haven't seen ~ or hair of him. 我连他的影子也没有看到。/ *save one's ~* 使自己免于被打(或被罚);使自己免于丧命 / *tan sb.'s ~* 把某人打一顿

hiding¹ [ˈhaidiŋ] *n.* 躲藏(指动作或情况);躲藏处 ‖*be in ~* 躲藏着 / *come out of ~* 从躲藏处出来 / *go into ~* 躲藏起来 ‖**~-place** *n.* 躲藏处;储藏处

hiding² [ˈhaidiŋ] *n.* 痛打;鞭打

hierarchy [ˈhaiəraːki] *n.* ①分成等级的僧侣统治集团;僧侣统治 ②统治集团 ③等级制度: a rigid ~ of power 森严的权力等级 / a sense of ~ 等级观念

hieroglyph [ˈhaiərəglif] *n.* 象形文字

higgledy-piggledy [ˈhigldiˈpigldi] *ad., a. & n.* 杂乱无章,乱七八糟

high [hai] I *a.* ①高的: a ~ mountain 高山 / It's two metres ~. 这东西有两米高。[注意:指人的身材高一般多用 tall] / a ~ dive 从高处往水里的一跳 / ~ flying 高空飞行 ②高原的: High Asia 亚洲高原 ③(指程度、数量、大小等)高度的;强烈的;很大的;非常的: a ~ explosive 高爆炸药 / a food ~ in vitamin C 富于维生素 C 的食物 / in ~ spirits 兴高采烈 ④(指等级、质量等)高级的,高等的: a ~ commander 高级指挥员 / a ~*er* leading body (或 organ) 高级领导机关 / ~*er* education 高等教育 / an institution of ~*er* learning 高等学校 / leather goods of ~ quality 高质量的皮革制品 ⑤高尚的: a man of ~ character 品格高尚的人 ⑥高音调的,尖声的: ~ notes 高音符 / speak in a ~ voice 尖声讲话 / ~ words 怒气冲冲的话 ⑦(时间、季节等)正盛的;(时机)成熟的: ~ noon 正午 / ~ summer 盛夏 / It is ~ time for us to start. (或 It is ~ time that we started.) 现在该是我们出发的时候了。⑧昂贵的;奢侈的: ~ living 奢侈的生活 ⑨傲慢的;夸口的: a ~ manner 傲慢的态度 / talk in ~ language 说大话 ⑩(肉类)开始变质的: ~ game 略微变质的野味 ⑪偏激的;严正的 ⑫严重的;重大的: a ~ insult 严重的侮辱 / ~ treason 重大叛国罪 / at this ~ hour of that country's history 在该国历史上的这个关键时刻 ⑬久远的: ~ antiquity 远古 ⑭[俚]醉了的;被麻醉品麻醉了的: He is a bit ~. 他有点儿醉了。

⑮【地】高纬度的,离赤道较远的: ~ latitude 高纬度

⑯【机】(齿轮)以最高速转动的

⑰【语】(舌位)高的: a ~ vowel 高元音

II *ad.* ①高: aim ~ 力争上游

②高价地;高额地: pay ~ 付高价 / play ~ 大赌;出大牌

③奢侈地: live ~ 过奢侈生活

III *n.* ①高峰;高水准: hit an all-time ~ 创历史上最高的纪录

②高地;高处

③天上,天空

④(齿轮的)高速度转动

⑤高(气)压;高气压地带: barometric ~【气】高气压

⑥[美]中学

⑦(纸牌中的)王牌

‖ ~ *and dry* ①搁浅 ②孤立无援 ③落在时代潮流的后面 / ~ *and low* ①高低贵贱(的人们) ②到处: search ~ *and low* 到处搜寻 / ~ *and mighty* [口]趾高气扬,神气活现 / ~ *on* 热心于,热衷于 / ~, *wide, and handsome* [美口]无忧无虑,充满自信地 / *How is that for* ~? [俚]好不奇怪! / *on* ~ ①在高处 ②在天空;在天堂 / *ride the* ~ *horse* 见 **horse** / *the Most High*【宗】上帝

‖ ~-,altitude *a.* 高空的: a pilotless ~-*altitude* military reconnaisance plane 军用无人驾驶高空侦察机 / ~-*altitude* sickness 高山症 / ~-analysis [作定语用](肥料)高成分的(指含有百分之二十以上的植物养料) / ~-,angle *a.*【军】高角的;高射界的 / ~ball *n.* [美](铁路)指示火车全速前进的信号 ②速度很快的火车 ③掺了姜汁啤酒(或苏打水)的威士忌(或白兰地)*vi.* [俚]高速前进 / ~ beam 车前灯的远距离光束,高光束,上方光束 / ~,binder *n.* [美俚]①恶棍;暴徒 ②骗子 ③腐败的(或搞阴谋的)政客 / ~-blown *a.* 浮夸的 / ~-born *a.* 出身高贵的 / ~boy *n.* 高脚柜 / ~bred *a.* ①良种的 ②出身高贵的 ③有教养的 / ~brow *n.* (自以为)有高度文化修养的人 *a.* [贬]高级趣味的,有高度文化修养的 / ~-browed *a.* ①额头高的 ②=~brow (a.) / ~browism *n.* 自以为有学问,炫耀学问 / ~ chair 幼童坐的高脚椅(前有挡板围住) / High Church【宗】高教会派(英国教会中注重仪式等的一派) / ~-'class *a.* 高级的,上等的,第一流的 / ~ cockalorum ①[英](孩子玩的)跳背游戏 ②自命不凡的人;大亨,要人 / ~ command ①统帅部,最高指挥部 ②(机关中的)最高领导班子 / ~ commissioner 高级专员(尤指英联邦各国相互派驻的大使级代表) / ~ day 节日;假日 / ~er-up ['haiər'ʌp] *n.* [美口]上级;长官,首长 / ~falutin ['hai-fə-'lu:tin], ~faluting ['hai-fə-'lu:tiŋ] *n.* 大话,夸张的言词 *a.* ①(言词等)夸大的 ②自大的,傲慢的 / ~ fidelity (收音、录音设备等的)高保真

度 / ~'flier, ~'flyer *n.* ①高飞的人(或物) ②有很大野心的人;好高骛远者 ③(政治上或宗教上)极端保守的人 / ~-flown *a.* ①野心勃勃的 ②(思想等)高超的 ③(言语等)夸张的 / ~-,flying *a.* ①高飞的 ②自负的;野心勃勃的 / ~ frequency【无】高频的(略作 H.F.) / High German 高地德语(原为德意志南部和中部使用的德语,现为标准德语) / ~-'grade *a.* 品质优良的: ~-*grade* steel 优质钢 / ~-'grown *a.* 长满高大植物的 / ~-'handed *a.* 高压的;专横的 / ~ hat 高帽,礼帽 / ~-'hat [俚]*n.* 自以为了不起的人;势利鬼 *a.* ①傲慢的;势利的 ②华贵的,时髦的 *vt.* 盛气凌人地对待,冷待 / ~-jack *vt.* [口] =hijack / ~-jacker *n.* [口] =hijacker / ~ jinks, ~ jinx ①喧闹的玩乐 ②(苏格兰旧时流行的)在喝酒时的罚金游戏 / ~ jump 跳高 / ~-'keyed *a.* ①音调高的 ②=~-strung / ~-land ['hailənd] *n.* ①高地,高原 ②[the Highlands] 苏格兰高地 / ~ 'high *a.* ①高原的 ②[H-]苏格兰高地的 / ~lander ['hailəndə] *n.* ①住在高原的人 ②[H-]苏格兰高地的人;苏格兰高地联队士兵 / ~-'level *a.* ①高级的 ②在高级阶层中进行(或作出)的 / ~light *n.* ①(图画、照片等中)光线最强处 ②最精采的场面,最重要的部分 *vt.* ①以强烈光线照射 ②集中注意力于,着重 / ~-liver 生活奢侈者 / ~-'minded *a.* 品格高尚的 / ~-muck-a-'muck, ~-muckety-'muck *n.* [俚]大人物;神气活现的人 / ~-'octane *a.*【化】高辛烷的 / ~-'pitched *a.* ①音调高的,尖声的 ②[喻]调子高的;紧张的 ③(屋顶等)坡度陡的 / ~ polymer【化】高分子 / ~-'power(ed) *a.* ①力量大的;精力充沛的 ②大功率的 ③(职业等)使人极度紧张的 / ~-'pre'cision *a.* 高精(密)度的,高准确度的 / ~-'pressure *a.* ①高压的;高气压的 ②强行推销的 ③(职业等)使人极度紧张的 *vt.* 用高压手段影响;向…强行推销 / ~-'priced *a.* 高价的,昂贵的 / ~-'proof *a.* 含酒精度高的 / ~-,ranking *a.* 高级的: a ~-*ranking* official 高级官员 / ~-'rise *a.* 有多层楼房并装有电梯的 *n.* 多层高楼 / ~ road ①[主英]大路,公路 ②最容易(或最好)的途径 / ~ roller ①肆意挥霍的人 ②狂赌的人 / ~ school ①[美]中学: a junior (senior) ~ *school* 初(高)中 ②[英]大学预科 / ~ seas 公海 / ~ sign (通过手势、眼色传递的)暗号 / ~-,sounding *a.* 夸大的,浮夸的 / ~-'speed *a.* 高速的: ~-*speed* photography 快速照相术 / ~-*speed* steel【冶】高速钢,锋钢 / ~-'spirited *a.* ①勇敢的;高尚的 ②兴奋的;易怒的 / ~-,stepping *a.* ①(马)抬高脚步的 ②生活奢华的,放荡的 / ~-strung *a.* 十分敏感的;易激动的;紧张的 / ~-tail *vi.* 迅速撤走: *tail it* off with another man 同另一个人一起迅速逃走 / ~ tea [英](下午五至六时之间、有肉食冷盆的)正式茶点 / ~-'tension *a.* 高(电)压的 / ~-'test *a.* ①经过严峻考验的 ②有高度挥发性的: ~-*test*

gasoline 高度挥发性汽油 / ~ **tide** 高潮 / '~=
'**toned** *a.* ①声调高的 ②[谑][讽]高贵的,高尚
的 ③[口]时髦的,漂亮的 ④[口]优良的,优秀的
⑤自负的; 夸大的 / ~ **water** 高潮 / '~-'**water**
a. ①水达到最高点的: a ~-*water* mark (或 line)
高水位线,高潮线; [喻]顶点 ②(裤子等)特别短
的/ '~**way** *n.* ① 公路;大路 ② (水陆)交通干
线 ③达到目的的途径 / '~**wayman** ['haiweimən]
n. 拦路的强盗 / '~-'**wrought** *a.* 极度紧张的;
极激动的

highly ['haili] *ad.* ①高(指地位、等级等) ②高度
地;很,非常: a ~ scientific approach 高度科学性
的方法 / a ~ skilled worker 高度熟练的技工 /
be ~ pleased 非常高兴 ④ 赞许地: speak ~ of
sb. 称赞某人 / think ~ of sb. 对某人评价很
高 ④高贵地;庄严地 ⑤按高额 ‖'~-'**strung** *a.*
=high-strung

highness ['hainis] *n.* ①高;高度 ②高尚;高贵
[H-] (对王室成员的尊称)殿下: His (或 Her)
Highness 殿下(间接提及时用) / Your *Highness*
殿下(直接称呼时用)

hike [haik] **I** ❶ *vi.* ① 作长途徒步旅行;步行:
You have to park your car and ~ in. 你必须把
车停在外面,步行进去。②飞起,扬起,飘起 (*up*)
③[美俚]在高空检修电线 ❷ *vt.* ①拉起,使升起
②急遽抬高(价格等);[美俚]涂改(支票)(指提高
支票上开的金额) **II** *n.* ①徒步旅行: go on a ~
作徒步旅行 ②提高,增加: a wage ~ 工资的增
加 ‖~**r** *n.* ① 徒步旅行者 ②[美俚]高空电线
检修工

hilarious [hi'leəriəs] *a.* 欢闹的,狂欢的 ‖**ly** *ad.*
/ ~**ness** *n.*

hill [hil] **I** *n.* ①小山;丘陵;斜坡;【军】高地: *Hill*
1001 一〇〇一高地 ②(植物根部的)土堆; 小堆
③成堆种植的作物 ④[美] [H-] 美国国会 (=
Capitol Hill) **II** *vt.* ①把…堆成土堆 (*up*) ②堆
土于…的根部 ‖*a ~ of beans* [口]少量; 小事 /
go over the ~ [美俚]越狱; [军俚]开小差 /
over the ~ [美口]开小差 ②在衰退中 / *up
~ and down dale* 翻山越谷; 拼命地; 坚持地;
彻底地 ‖'~**,billy** *n.* [美俚]居住在美国南部山
区的农民;乡下人 / '~**man** *n.* 住在山区的人 /
'~**side** *n.* (小山)山腰,山坡 / ~ **station** (印
度等地的)山中避暑地 / '~**top** *n.* (小山)山顶

hilt [hilt] **I** *n.* (刀、剑、工具等的)柄 **II** *vt.* 装柄
于 ‖(*up*) *to the ~* 完全地,彻底地: be proved
to the ~ 被完全证明

him [him; 弱 im] *pron.* [he 的宾格] ①[用作宾
语]他: We hastened to help ~. 我们赶紧去帮
助他。/ Listen to ~. 听他讲。②[口][用作表
语]他 (=he): That's ~. 正是他。③[口][用
于 than 后面]他 (=he): You're stronger than
~. 你比他强壮。④[古]他自己 (=himself): He
bethought ~ of it. 他想起了这回事。

himself [him'self] *pron.* ①[反身代词] 他自己:
An educator must first educate ~. 教育者必须

自己先受教育。②[用以加强语气]他亲自,他本人:
He ~ told me so. 他亲口这样对我说的。③[用于
be, become, come to 等之后]他的正常情况(指健
康、情绪等): He's not quite ~ today. 他今天
不大舒服。(或: 他今天情绪有些反常。) / The
patient has *come to* ~. 病人苏醒过来了。‖(*all*)
by ~ ①他独自地 ②他独力地: The boy can
now swim across the river *by* ~. 这个男孩子现
在能独自游过河了。

hind[1] [haind] (比较级 hinder, 最高级 hindmost
['haindmoust] 或 hindermost ['haindəmoust]) *a.*
后面的,后部的; 在后的: a ~ leg 后腿 / a ~
wheel 后轮 ‖'~**brain** 【解】后脑 / '~**gut** *n.*
【解】后肠 / '~**quarter** *n.* ① (牛、羊、猪等的)
后腿肉 ②[复](四腿动物的)两条后腿 / '~**sight**
n. ① (来福枪的)照尺 ② 事后的认识: realize
with ~*sight* 在事后认识到…

hind[2] [haind] *n.* (三岁以上的)红色雌鹿

hind[3] [haind] *n.* [英] ①(英格兰北部和苏格兰的)
农场熟练雇工 ②农场管家 ③[古]农民

hinder[1] ['hində] ❶ *vt.* 阻止,阻碍; 妨碍: That
~*ed* him *from* going further. 这使他不能再继
续向前了。/ Don't ~ him in his work. 不要
妨碍他的工作。❷ *vi.* 阻碍(或妨碍)行动

hinder[2] ['haində] *a.* 后面的,后部的; 在后的

hinge [hind3] **I** *n.* ①铰链;折叶 ②(蚌等的)铰合
部; 蝶铰 ③关键,转折点 ④(在集邮簿上粘贴邮票
用的)透明胶水纸 ⑤[美俚]一瞥,一看: take (或
get) a ~ 看一看 **II** ❶ *vt.* 给…装上铰链;用
铰链接合 ❷ *vi.* ① 靠铰链转动 (或附着) (*on*,
upon) ② 随…而定,以…为转移 (*on*, *upon*)
‖*off the* ~ ① 脱开铰链的: The window
is (或 has gone) *off the* ~s. 这扇窗子的铰链脱落
了。②健康失调的;精神错乱的 ‖~**d** *a.* 有铰链
的 / ~**less** *a.* 无铰链的 ‖~ **joint** ①【解】屈戌
关节 ②【机】铰链接合

hint [hint] **I** *n.* ①暗示: drop (或 give) a ~ 给
人暗示,露口风 / take a ~ 接受别人的暗示,领
会 ②提示;(建议或指导性的)线索: Hints for
Beginners (作书名或标题)初学者须知 ③点滴;
微量: with a ~ of suspicion 多少带点怀疑的
❶ *vt.* 暗示: He ~s broadly (vaguely) that ...
他清楚地(隐约地)暗示说… ❷ *vi.* 暗示: ~ at
one's anxiety 暗示别人自己很着急

hinterland ['hintəlænd] *n.* ①内地 ②穷乡僻壤;
远离城镇的地方 ③港口可供起卸的内地贸易区
④物资供应地区

hip[1] [hip] **I** *n.* ①臀部;【解】髋,髋部: a ~ pocke
(裤子的)臀部口袋 / ~ fire 【军】坐射 / ~ join
【解】髋关节 ②【动】(昆虫的)基节 ③【建】屋椎
④[复][美俚]不成功的结局 **II** (hipped; hipping
vt. 给(屋顶)造屋脊 ‖*on* (或 *upon*) *the* ~ 处
于不利地位 / *shoot from the* ~ 鲁莽地行事
(或讲话) / *smite* ~ *and thigh* 不留情地痛打
彻底压倒 ‖~ **bath** 坐浴;坐浴浴盆 / '~**bone**
【解】髋骨,无名骨 / ~ **disease** 【医】髋关节疾病

~ **gout** 坐骨神经痛 / ~ **roof**【建】四坡屋顶 / '~**shot** *a.* 髋骨位置不正的

hip² [hip] *n.*【植】蔷薇果

hip³ [hip] *a.* [美俚]①熟悉内情的,市面灵通的;赶时新的: be ~ *to* the current happenings 非常熟悉目前正发生的事件 ②聪明的;机灵的 ③(美国)颓废派的,"希比派"的 ‖*I'm* ~. [美俚]别噜苏了! 我懂了! ‖ ~ **chick** [美俚]对计新的东西很有见解的女学生

hip⁴ [hip] **I** *n.* 病态的忧郁;情绪低沉 **II** (hipped; hipping) *vt.* 使忧郁

hip⁵ [hip] *int.* 集体的喝采(或欢呼)声[一般仅用于欢呼语 "Hip, ~, hurrah!"]

hippodrome ['hipədroum] *n.* ①(古希腊战车和马的)竞技场 ②马戏场

hippopotamus [,hipə'potəməs] ([复] hippopotami [,hipə'potəmai] 或 hippopotamuses) *n.*【动】河马

hire ['haiə] **I** ❶ *vt.* ①租;雇: ~ a hall for an evening 租借礼堂使用一个晚上[注意:租赁土地、房屋一般用 rent, 若系暂时租借也可用 ~] / ~ *out* boats by the day 按日计算出租船只 / a ~*d* farmhand 雇农 ②为(已做好的工作)付钱: He ~*d* the mowing done. 他为已完毕的割草工作付了钱。 ❷ *vi.* 接受雇佣 (*on, out*) **II** *n.* ①租用,雇用: let out sth. *on* ~ 出租某物 / bicycles *on* (或 *for*) ~ 供出租的自行车 / work *for* ~ 当雇工 / be in the ~ of sb. 受雇于某人 ②租金;工钱 ‖~ **oneself** (*out*) *to* 受雇于 ‖~**r** ['haiərə] *n.* 雇主,租借者 ‖ ~ **purchase**,~ **system** [英]分期付款购买法 / **hiring hall** [美](航运业等工会举办的)职业介绍所(挨次介绍登记者就业)

hireling ['haiəliŋ] **I** *n.* 佣工;单纯为金钱而听人使唤的人 **II** *a.* 被雇用的;为了金钱而工作的

hirsute ['hə:sju:t] *a.* 多毛的;(尤指动物到达发情期时)有粗毛的 ‖~**ness** *n.*

his [hiz; 弱 iz] *pron.* ① [he 的所有格]他的: ~ hoe 他的锄头 ② [he 的物主代词]他的(东西);他的家属(或与他有关的人): This hoe is ~, not mine. 这把锄头是他的,不是我的。 / a friend of ~ 他的一个朋友 / *His* is (或 are) better than yours. 他的(东西)比你的好。[所指的东西是单数时用 is, 是复数时用 are]

hiss [his] **I** ❶ *vi.* ①(蛇、沸水等)嘶嘶作声 ②用嘘声表示反对 ❷ *vt.* ①发嘶嘶声表示;嘶嘶地说出 ②用嘘声责骂(或轰赶): ~ sb. off (或 from) the stage 把某人嘘下台 **II** *n.* 嘶嘶声;拖长的 [s] 声

historian [his'tɔ:riən] *n.* ①年代史编者,编史家 ②历史学家

historic [his'tɔrik] *a.* ①历史上有名的,有历史意义的: a ~ city 历史名城 / a ~ spot 古迹 ②历史的: ~ times 有史时期 (与史前时期相对) / the ~ (或 historical) present【语】历史现在时态(指为描写生动起见,用现在时态叙述过去事件)

historical [his'tɔrikəl] *a.* ①历史的,历史上的: a ~ event 历史事件 / a ~ personage 历史人物 ②有关历史的: ~ studies (根据或关于)历史的研究 ③(时态)写过去事件所用的 ④根据历史上的发展(或演变)叙述的: ~ linguistics 历史语言学 ‖~**ly** *ad.* 在历史上

history ['histəri] *n.* ①历史,历史学: the ~ of social development 社会发展史 / unprecedented in ~ 史无前例的 ②过去事情的记载,沿革;来历: one's personal ~ 个人履历 ③过去的事;过时了的事物: That is all ~ now. 那都是过去的事了。 ‖*make* ~ 做出永垂史册的事情

histrionic [,histri'ɔnik] **I** *a.* ①戏剧的;演员的;表演的;舞台的: ~ muscles【解】表情肌 ②演戏似的;有意做作的 **II** *n.* ①演员 ②[~s][用作单或复]戏剧表演;舞台艺术 ③[~s][用作单或复]装模作样

hit [hit] **I** (hit; hitting) ❶ *vt.* ①打,打击;击中: ~ sb. on the head 打某人的头 / ~ the target (或 mark) 打中目标 ②碰撞;使碰撞: The truck ~ a rock and tumbled over. 卡车撞在一块岩石上,翻倒了。 / The child ~ his forehead against the corner of a desk. 孩子的额角在书桌的角上碰了一下。 / *Hit* the ground! 卧倒! / ~ a snag 遇到意外困难 ③表击;使遭受 ④(精神上)打击;伤…的感情: be hard ~ (常指感情方面)受到沉重打击,很伤心 ⑤达到,到达: ~ an all-time high in total grain output 粮食总产量达到历史上最高记录 ⑥偶然碰上;找到: The ship ~ fog on its voyage. 船在航行时碰上了雾。 ⑦探到;说中: You have ~ it! 你猜对了! (或:你说中了!) ⑧投合: ~ sb.'s fancy 投合某人爱好 ⑨(板球等中)得(分) ⑩[美俚]走上: ~ the right path 走上正路 ⑪[美俚]沉溺于(喝酒等恶习): ~ the bottle 酗酒 ❷ *vi.* ①打,打击;击中: ~ back in self-defence 进行自卫还击 ② *hitting* accuracy 命中率 ②碰撞 (*against*) ③偶然碰上;找到: ~ *upon* (或 *on*) an idea 想出一个主意 ④(在内燃机汽缸内)点火 **II** *n.* ①一击;击中: score a ~ 命中 / eight ~*s* and two misses 八次击中,两次未中 ②碰撞 ③讽刺,抨击;俏皮话: a ~ at sb. 对某人的讽刺 / That's a clever ~. 这是一句巧妙的俏皮话。 ④好运气 ⑤风行一时的作品(或电影、歌曲、演出等);轰动一时的成功人物(或事物) ⑥(板球等的)得分 ‖*a gallery* ~ (或 *shot, stroke*)(赛球或演戏时)卖弄技巧的表演,为博得喝采的表演 / ~ *below the belt* 见 **belt** / ~ *it off* 相处得好,合得来: They ~ *it off* well (with the natives). 他们(和本地人)相处得很好。 / ~ *off* ①把…打掉 ②逼真地模仿;简明、恰当地描绘 ③即席作(诗等) ④(板球等中)得(分) ⑤适合: That ~*s off* well with our plan. 那跟我们的计划很合得上。 / ~ *or miss* 不论成功与否;漫无目的地 / ~ *out* 猛打: ~ *out at* sb. 向某人打去;(猛烈)抨击某人 / ~ *sb. when he's down*

乘某人之危打击他 / ~ *the* (或 *one's*) *books*
[美]用功 / ~ *the* (*right*) *nail on the head* 见
nail / ~ *up* ①请求: ~ sb. *up for* a loan (*for*
work) 请求某人借款(介绍工作) ②(板球等中)
得(分) / *make a* ~ (演出等)获得成功,受欢迎
‖**~-and-'miss** *a.* 有时打中有时打不中的; 碰
巧的 / '**~-and-'run** *a.*①(汽车驾驶员等)闯了
祸逃走的 ②打了就跑的: *~-and-run tactics* 打
了就跑的战术 / '**~-or-'miss** *a.*①不定的, 偶
然的 ②(地毯等)没有固定花样的 / ~ **parade**
(歌曲等的)最流行的一批

hitch [hitʃ] I ❶ *vi.* ①蹒跚 ②被钩住,被拴住,被
套住 ③[美俚] =~hike (*vi.*) ④[口]和谐, 和好
❷ *vt.* ①急拉;急推 ②(用环、钩、结等)钩住,拴
住,套住: ~ a horse to a wag(g)on 把马套上车
③[美俚][常用被动语态]使结婚 ④[美俚] =~
hike (*vt.*) Ⅱ *n.* ①急拉;急推 ②故障,障碍
碍: The discussion passed *without a* ~. 讨
论顺利地结束了。④【海】索结 ⑤钩住,拴住,套
住 ⑥[美][军俚]士兵的服役期 ⑦[美俚]搭便车
旅行 ‖~ **up** ①拉起;把…系上,拴上 ②[美俚]
使结婚 ‖'**~hike** *vi.* 沿途免费搭乘他人便车旅
行 *vt.* 要求(免费搭车);得(免费搭车)的机会

hither ['hiðə] I *ad.* 这里;向这里;到这里 这
边的;附近的,邻近的 ‖~ *and thither* 到处;向
各处;忽此忽彼 / *on the* ~ *side of* 见 **side**

hive [haiv] I *n.* ①蜂房;蜂箱 ②蜂群 ③熙攘的人
群 ④喧闹而繁忙的场所: The construction site
was a ~ of activity. 建筑工地上是一片繁忙
紧张的活动。Ⅱ ❶ *vt.* ①使(蜂)入蜂箱 ②贮
(蜜)于蜂箱中 ③贮备 ❷ *vi.* ①(蜂)进入蜂箱
②聚居 ‖~ **off** (蜜蜂)分封;[喻]从团体中分出
(如总公司以一部分商品分派给分公司生产)

hives [haivz] [复] *n.* [用作单或复]【医】荨麻疹

hiya ['haijə] *int.* [美口]您好! (=How are you?)

hoard [hɔ:d] I *n.* ①窖藏的钱财 ②秘藏的东西 Ⅱ
❶ *vt.* ①贮藏,积聚 (财宝、物品等) (*up*) ②把…
珍藏在心中;心怀 ❷ *vi.* 贮藏,囤积 ‖~**er** *n.* 贮
藏者;囤积者

hoarding¹ ['hɔ:diŋ] *n.* 窖藏; 囤积; [常用复]贮藏
(或囤积)物

hoarding² ['hɔ:diŋ] *n.* ①(修建房屋时的)临时围
篱,板围 ②[英]招贴板(利用板围张贴广告之处)

hoarse [hɔ:s] *a.* (声音)嘶哑的,嘶哑的;嘎哑的
(或 roar) oneself ~ 把嗓子喊哑 ‖~**ly** *ad.* /
~**n** *vt.* & *vi.* (使)变哑 / ~**ness** *n.*

hoary ['hɔ:ri] *a.* ①灰白的 ②(因年老)头发灰白
的 ③古老的;久远的: ~ platitude 陈词滥调 /
~ antiquity 远古 ④(植物)有灰白色茸毛的
‖**hoariness** *n.*

hoax [houks] I *n.* 欺骗,骗局;戏弄 Ⅱ *vt.* 欺
骗;戏弄: ~ sb. into believing a falsehood 骗某
人相信谎话 ‖~**er** *n.* 欺骗者

hob¹ [hɔb] I *n.* ①炉旁的铁架(可放锅子等) ②(投
环戏的)标桩 ③【机】元阳模;滚铣刀 Ⅱ (hobbed;
hobbing) *vt.* ①给…钉平头钉 ②【机】滚铣

hob² [hɔb] *n.* [英方]①顽皮的小妖精 ②乡下佬
‖*play* (或 *raise*) ~ ①恶作剧;捣乱 ②任意歪
曲: *play* (或 *raise*) ~ *with* historical facts 大肆
歪曲历史事实

hobble ['hɔbl] I ❶ *vi.* 跛行,蹒跚 ❷ *vt.* ①使跛
行 ②把(马)的脚拴住 ③阻碍 Ⅱ *n.* ①跛行 ②
绊住马腿的绳子(或器械等) ③[古]困境 ‖*get*
into a ~ 陷于窘境,为难 ‖**hobblingly** *ad.*

hobby ['hɔbi] *n.* 形成癖好的业余消遣 ‖*ride a* ~
沉溺在业余癖好中; 反复说(或做)自己喜欢的事
‖~**ist** *n.* 有业余癖好者 ‖~**horse** *n.* ①(用于
玩具的)竹马;走马台上的木马;摇动木马 ②乡村
舞会中系于跳舞者腰间用柳条编成的马; 系着柳
条马跳舞的人 ③反复爱讲的话题: Now he's
started on his ~*horse*. 现在他又开始老调重弹
了。④癖好

hobgoblin ['hɔb,ɡɔblin] *n.* ①淘气的妖精 ②吓人
(或令人厌恶)的东西,怪物

hobnail ['hɔbneil] I *n.* ①(钉在靴底上的)平头钉
②穿钉有平头钉靴子的人; 乡下人 Ⅱ *vt.* 钉平头
钉于 ‖~**ed** *a.* 钉有平头鞋钉的;土里土气的 ‖~
liver, ~ed liver 【医】(肝硬变引起的)鞋钉肝;
门静脉性硬变

hobnob ['hɔbnɔb] I (hobnobbed; hobnobbing) *vi.*
①共饮; 亲切地交谈 (*with, together*) ②亲密,亲
近 (*with*) Ⅱ *n.* 聚会,交谈

hock¹ [hɔk] I *n.* ①【动】(有蹄类的)跗关节(=~
joint) ②(指家畜)腿肉: pork ~s (猪的)腿肉 Ⅱ
vt. 割断蹄筋使废废

hock² [hɔk] I *n.* ①典当,抵押 ②[美俚]监牢 Ⅱ
vt. 典当,抵押 ‖*in* ~ ①在典当中 ②在坐牢 ③
负着债 ‖~**er** *n.* 典当者 ‖~ **shop** [美俚]当铺

hockey ['hɔki] *n.* 曲棍球: ice ~ 冰上曲棍球,冰
球 / field ~ 曲棍球

hocus-pocus ['houkəs'poukəs] I (hocus-pocus(s)ed;
hocus-pocus(s)ing) *vt.* & *vi.* [俗]哄骗,戏弄 Ⅱ *n.*
①变戏法者用的咒语(或手法) ②转移注意力的
言语(或行动) ③欺骗

hod [hɔd] *n.* ①(搬运灰泥、砖瓦等用的)灰浆桶,
砖斗 ②煤斗 ‖~ **carrier** 帮助搬运灰泥、砖瓦等
的杂务工

hoe [hou] I *n.* 锄头 Ⅱ *vt.* & *vi.* 锄 ‖*a hard* (或
long) *row to* ~ 见 **row**¹ / ~ *one's own row*
见 **row**¹ ‖~ *n.* 锄者 ‖'**~cake** *n.* [美]玉米
饼 / '**~down** *n.* [美俚]①一种乡村舞;喧闹的
舞会(或宴会) ②大声争辩,怒气冲冲的争论 ③
吵闹;闹事;打群架

hog [hɔg] I ([复] hog(s)) *n.* ①猪(尤指供食用的
重一百二十磅以上者);阉过的公猪;猪科动物
raise ~s 养猪 ②野猪 ②[常拼作f
hogg] [英]尚未剪毛的小羊;从小羊身上剪下
的毛 ③【海】扫底部船壳的帚状工具 ④[口]自私
(或贪婪、贪吃、粗鄙、肮脏)的人 ⑤鲁莽的骑车者
(或驾车者) ⑥[美俚]火车头 ⑦【机】弯拱
(hogged; hogging) ❶ *vt.* ①(象猪一样)拱起
(背);使(船、船底等)中部拱起 ②修剪(马鬃)

用帚状工具清扫(船底) ④[美俚]贪心攫取,过多地拿取 ❷ vi. ①(指船底或龙骨)中部拱起 ②[口]横冲直撞 ‖a ~ in armo(u)r 穿了考究衣服感到局促不安的人;举止笨拙的人 / bring one's ~s to the wrong market [口]找错了门路,向不适当的人(或在不适当的场合)提出要求 / go the whole ~ [俚]彻底地干,干到底;完全接受: If we start it, we shall go the whole ~. 要是着手干的话,我们就干脆干个彻底。/ high on (或 off) the ~ [美口]花钱很多地,奢侈地 / on the ~ [美俚]没钱,破产 ‖'~back n. ①拱起的背 ②象猪背一样拱起的东西;陡峻的拱地,陡峻的山脊 / ~ cholera 猪霍乱 / '~-,killing n. [美方]喧闹的聚会 / '~leg n. [美方]左轮手枪 / ~man ['hogmen] [美方]猪倌人 / ~pen n. 猪圈 / ~'s-back n. =~back / ~'s fennel 前胡属植物 / '~skin n. 猪皮;猪皮做的东西 / ~ still 【化】蒸馏塔 / '~-tie vt. ①把…的脚缚住 ②使不能行动;使陷于困境 / '~wash n. ①猪食,泔脚 ②无聊的话,废话;空洞的作品 / '~wild a. 无约束的,混乱的;过于兴奋而狂乱的

hoist [hoist] I ❶ vt. 升起,扯起,绞起 ❷ vi. 扯起来,绞起来 II n. ①升起,扯起,绞起 ②【机】起重机,吊车;卷扬机;升降机 ③[海]一挂旗;一面旗(或一张帆)升起后的高度;桅杆的中部 ‖~er n. ①起重机;卷扬机 ②起重机司机 ‖'~way n. 提升间(例如矿井井筒内的)

hold [hould] I (held [held]) ❶ vt. ①拿着,握住 ②抓住,夹住: ~ a baby in one's arms 抱着孩子 / ~ sth. between the jaws of a spanner 用扳钳的钳口夹住某物 ③托住,支持: ~ a platform by pillars 用柱子支撑平台 ④掌握(权力等);担任(职务): ~ power 掌权 / ~ a leading post 担任领导工作 ⑤占据,守住;吸住(注意力等): ~ a position 守住阵地 / ~ the attention of the audience 吸引住听众 ⑥抑制,止住,约束: ~ one's breath 屏息,屏住气 / Hold your tongue! 住嘴! / There's no ~ing him. 他这人是管不住的。 ⑦认为,认…为 ⑧包含有,持有(见解等): ~ much promise of a bumper harvest 很有丰收的希望 / ~ the view that ... 持有…的见解 ⑨拥有(财产、股票等) ⑩举行: ~ a meeting (a debate, talks) 举行会议(辩论,会谈) ⑪court【律】开庭 ⑪容纳,装得下;包含: The old barn cannot ~ the grain we have produced. 旧的谷仓已装不下我们生产的粮食了。 ⑫[美]扣留,拘留 ⑬使保持某种状态: ~ the enemy at bay 不使敌人迫近 / ~ one's head high 趾高气扬;扬眉吐气 ⑭使受约束;使遵守: ~ sb. responsible 要某人负责 / ~ sb. to his word 要某人遵守诺言 ⑮【律】裁定;用契约约束;依法占有 ⑯[音]延长发音(音) ❷ vi. ①顶住,持: Will the rope ~? 绳子吃得住(能不断)吗? ②持续,保持: We hope the fine weather will ~ throughout the week. 我们希望这个星期天气一直能这样好。 ③有效,适用: The contract still ~s. 契约仍然有效。 ④[常用于命令式]停止

II n. ①抓;掌握: take a firm ~ of sth. 把某物紧抓在手 / have a firm ~ over sb. 牢牢控制住某人 ②可手攀(或可脚踏)的东西,支撑点 ③货舱,底层舱 ④监禁;监牢 ⑤保留(或延误)的通知: put a ~ on the hotel rooms still unoccupied 向旅馆预订尚未租出的空房间 / announce a ~ on all take-offs until the weather clears 宣布班机等天好再起飞 ⑥(拳击、摔角等中的)擒拿法 ⑦【音】延长号;延音 ‖catch (或 claw, seize) ~ of 抓住 / get ~ of 抓住 / get (或 have) ~ of the wrong end of the stick 完全误解 / ~ aloof (或 ~ oneself aloof) 不接近别人,做出清高超然的样子 / ~ back ①踌躇;退缩不前 ②阻止: No one can ~ back the wheel of history. 谁也无法阻止历史车轮的前进。 / ~ sb. back from doing sth. 阻止某人做某事 ③抑制(眼泪等) ④扣住,隐瞒(消息等): You are ~ing it back from me. 你在故意瞒我。/ ~ by 坚持(意见、目的等) / ~ down ①压制,镇压 ②抑制(热情等) ③压低;缩减 ④牵制 ⑤垂下(头部等) ⑥[口]保住(职位等) / ~ forth ①[贬]滔滔地演讲 ②给予,提供: ~ forth hopes of recovery 有复原的希望 / ~ good (for) 见 good / ~ hard [用于命令式]停止 / ~ in 约束,抑制: ~ oneself in 抑制自己的感情 / ~ off ①不接近;拖延: We hope the rain will ~ off till evening. 我们希望这场雨能拖到晚上再下。 ②不使…接近: ~ off the enemy 阻住敌人 / ~ on ①继续: The speaker held on for a full hour. 演讲的人讲了整整一小时。/ ~ on one's way 继续前进 ②抓住…不放;坚持 (to): ~ on to the bar (在公共车辆上)拉住横杠 ③(打电话时用语)不挂上 ④[口][常用于命令式]停止 / ~ one's ground 见 ground¹ / ~ one's own 见 own¹ / ~ out ①伸出;端出 ②提出,提供: ~ out a promise 作出诺言 / ~ out unlimited prospects 有无限的前途 ③坚持 ④支持,维持 / ~ over ①将…延迟: ~ the matter over till the next meeting 将这件事延迟到下次会上讨论 ②期满后继任;续雇 ③以…威胁: ~ sth. over sb.'s head 以某事威胁某人 / ~ to ①坚持(原则、方向等) ②紧握 / ~ together ①连在一起不破;使结合在一起不破 ②(使)团结一致 / ~ true 见 true / ~ up ①举起(或拿起)…展示;举出…表示: ~ sb. up to sharp ridicule 举出某人当众加以尖刻的嘲笑 ②支撑 ③继续下去,支持下去;仍然有效 ④阻挡,使停顿;停止下来: It held up at midnight. 午夜时雨止了。 ⑤拦截,抢劫 ⑥[口]向…索高价 / ~ water 见 water / ~ with ①赞同,赞成 ②[常用于否定句]容忍 / lay ~ of (或 on)①握住,抓住 ②控制住;占有 / let go (或 leave, lose) ~ of 撒手放开 / no ~s barred [口]无清规戒律约束 / take ~ of =lay ~ of (或 on) ‖~all n. (旅行时放衣物杂物的)手提包,手提箱 / '~back n. ①阻碍物 ②暂时停顿;被暂时扣下的东西(如工资等) / '~down n. (费用等的)缩减 / '~fast n. ①紧紧扣住的东西

(如钩子、钉子、夹钳等) ②【植】固着器 ③【动】吸附器官 / **~man** ['houldmən] *n.* 舱内装卸工人 / '**~out** *n.* ①(谈判等场合中的)坚持,不让步 ②坚持者,不让步的人/ [美俚]坚持不合作者 / '**~,over** *n.* [口] ①遗留下来的人(或物) ②任期满后继任的人员 ③(一次比赛后)继续参加比赛的运动员;(一次演出后)继续参加演出的演员 ④留级生 / '**~up** *n.* ①停顿,阻碍 ②拦劫,抢劫 ③[口]索高价

holder ['houldə] *n.* ①持有者;占有者;(支票、汇票等)持票人: a feudal estate-~ 封建领主 / a ~ of a table-tennis championship 乒乓球冠军保持者 ②托(或夹)的东西(如架、柄等): a ciga-rette ~ 烟嘴 / a mirror ~ 镜架 / a lamp ~ 灯座‖**~-on** ['houldər'ɔn] *n.* (船上的)铆工

holding ['houldiŋ] *n.* ①占有物;所有物;占有的土地;租入的土地 ②[常用复]拥有的财产(尤指股票、债券): gold ~s 黄金储备 ③支持物,托住物 ④(法院的)裁定 ⑤【体】持球;非法抱人(或撞人) ‖**~ company** 控股公司(指以控制股权为目的的投资公司) / **~ pattern** (飞机在机场上空等待腾出着陆跑道时所作的)椭圆形盘旋

hole [houl] I *n.* ①洞: drill a ~ in the ground 在地上钻洞 ②孔眼;破洞,裂开处: a bullet ~ 弹孔 / blind ~【机】盲孔,未穿孔 / centre ~【机】中心孔,顶针孔 ③(动物的)洞穴,窝 ④水流深凹处 ⑤[常与地名连用]水湾,海湾 ⑥狭小、阴暗、肮脏的地方(或房间) ⑦牢房 ⑧躲藏处 ⑨漏洞;缺陷,缺点: find ~s in sb.'s argument 在某人论据中找出漏洞 ⑩[口]为难的处境,困境 ⑪高尔夫球的穴;高尔夫球得分 ⑫【物】空穴;空子 ⑬铁路的支线 II ❶ *vt.* ①凿洞于,穿孔于 ②把…放入(或打入,赶入)洞中 ③筑,挖(矿井、隧道等): ~ a tunnel through the mountain 穿山筑隧道 ❷ *vi.* ①(高尔夫球等)进入穴中 ②凿洞;挖通矿井 ‖**a square peg in a round ~** 见 peg / **be in a devil of a ~** 处境很困难 / **be in a ~** 处于困境,为难: He *is in* rather *a ~*. 他处境极为困难. / **be in the ~** ①[口](经济上)短少,亏空: Jack *is* fifty dollars *in the* ~ this month. 杰克本月亏空五十美元. ②(纸牌戏用语)得一负点 / **every ~ and corner** 每个角落,到处 / **~ out** 将(高尔夫球)打入穴中;击高尔夫球入穴 / **~ (out) in one** 一击就把高尔夫球打入穴中 / **~ up** ①(常指在洞中)蛰居 ②躲藏 ③把…安置在避难处(或躲藏处) ④把…监禁 / **like a rat in a ~** 见 rat / **make a ~ in** 在…凿洞 ②在…中花费了一大笔钱 / **make ~** 钻油井 / **Money burns a ~ .n his pocket.** 见 money / **pick a ~** (或 **~s**) **in** 在…中找碴子 / **pick a ~ in sb.'s coat** 找某人的碴子 / **the nineteenth ~** [谑]高尔夫球俱乐部的酒吧间 / **~ up** 挖洞者 ②(常与数字连用)有(若干)洞穴的场所(指高尔夫球场等) / **~y** *a.* 有洞的;多洞的 ‖'**~-and-'corner** *a.* [口]秘密的,偷偷摸摸的

holiday ['hɔlədi] I *n.* ①假日;节日: ~ clothes 节日的盛装 ②[主英][常用复]假期: the school

~s 学校的假期 II *vi.* 出外度假 ‖*blind man's* ~ 黄昏 / *make* ~ 度假 / *on* ~ 在休假中,在度假 / *take a* ~ 休假 ‖**~er** *n.* 度假者 / **~-,maker** *n.* 度假者 / **~ task** [英]学生的假期作业

holiness ['houlinis] *n.* ①【宗】神圣 ②[H-](对罗马教皇的尊称,常与 His 或 Your 连用)陛下

hollow ['hɔlou] I *a.* ①空的;中空的: a ~ pipe 空心管子 / a ~ square·【军】空方阵 ②凹的,凹陷的: ~ cheeks 深陷的双颊 ③空虚的;虚假的: ~ words 空话 / ~ promises 虚伪的诺言 ④空腹的,饿的: a ~ feeling in the stomach 空腹的感觉 ⑤(声音)空洞的;沉重的: a ~ voice 空洞的声音 II *ad.* [俗]完全: beat sb. (all) ~ 把某人完全打败;完全胜过某人 III *n.* ①洼地;洞,穴;坑: a ~ in the road 路上的一个坑 / in the ~ of a tree 在树穴中 ②山谷: a wooded ~ 多树木的山谷 IV ❶ *vt.* 挖空 (out) ❷ *vi.* 变空 ‖*hollow ~* 耗损成空壳: That tooth of mine is nearly wearing ~. 我的那只牙齿几乎蛀空了. ‖**~ly** *ad.* / **~ness** *n.* ‖'**~-drill steel**【冶】空心钻钢 / '**~-eyed** *a.* 眼睛凹陷的 / '**~-'hearted** *a.* 不真诚的,虚伪的 / '**~ware** [总称](玻璃、金属等制成的)凹形器皿

holly ['hɔli] *n.* 冬青属植物

hollyhock ['hɔlihɔk] *n.* 【植】蜀葵

holocaust ['hɔləkɔ:st] *n.* ①燔祭(指烧全兽祭神) ②大屠杀(尤指大量烧杀人命或牲畜) ③大破坏

holster ['houlstə] *n.* 手枪皮套

holy ['houli] I *a.* ①神圣的;神的;供神用的 ②献身于宗教的 ③圣洁的;至善的 ④唤起敬仰的 ⑤[俚]非常的,极其的: a ~ terror 可怕的人;淘气的孩子 II *n.* 神圣的东西;圣堂: the *Holy of Holies* 犹太神殿中的至圣所;神圣的地方 ‖**Holy Alliance** 【史】(1815—1816 俄、普、奥三国君主所订的)神圣同盟 / **Holy Bible** 【宗】圣经 / **Holy City** 【宗】圣城(如耶路撒冷、麦加、罗马) / **Holy Communion** 【宗】圣餐礼 / **Holy Father** 罗马教皇;教皇的称号 / **Holy Ghost** 【宗】圣灵 / **Holy Land** 【宗】圣地(指耶稣的故乡巴勒斯坦) / **Holy Office** (天主教的)宗教法庭 / **Holy Roman Empire** 【史】神圣罗马帝国 (962—1806) / **Holy Spirit** 【宗】圣灵 / **Holy Thursday** 【宗】①耶稣升天节(复活节后四十天后的星期四) ②洗足木曜日(复活节前的星期四) / **Holy Week** 【宗】复活节前的一周 / **Holy Writ** 基督教《圣经》

holystone ['houlstoun] I *n.* 【海】磨甲板沙石 II *vt.* 用沙石磨

homage ['hɔmidʒ] *n.* ①(封建制度下封臣对封主的)效忠;效忠的仪式 ②封建主与封臣的关系 ③尊敬;敬意 ‖*pay* (或 *do*) ~ *to* 向…表示敬意

home [houm] *n.* ①家;[美]住宅 ②家乡 ③家庭 ④疗养所;养育院;收容所: a nursing ~ 疗养所 / a ~ for the aged 敬老院 ⑤产地;发源地 ⑥(活动的)中心地,根据地: The pilot is heading for ~. 那个飞行员正向基地返航. ⑦【体】(径赛

的)终点; (棒球的)本垒 **II** *a.* ①家庭的: ～ life家庭生活②家乡的;本地的: a ～ game 在本地举行的比赛 ③本国的;国内的;总的: ～ products 国产品 / ～ and foreign affairs 内政外交 / the ～ trade 国内贸易 / the *Home* Office [英]内政部 / the ～ office 总机构 (如总公司、总店等) ④中要害的: a ～ thrust (用武器或语言)击中要害的一戳 / a ～ question 中要害的质问 **III** *ad.* ①在家;回家,到家: He will be ～ in half an hour. 他将在半小时内到家。/ on one's way ～ 在回家的路上 ②在家乡;回家乡 ③在本国;回本国: call an ambassador ～ 召大使回国 ④中要害;深入地: hit (或 strike) ～ 打中要害 / The thrust went ～. (指钢刀或讽刺等)这一击深深刺中了。/ drive a nail ～ 把钉子深深敲入 / He drove the point ～ with that apt quotation. 他这句恰当的引语说中了要害。 **IV** ❶ *vi.* ①回家: The plane ～d to its carrier. 飞机飞回航空母舰。②安家; 设总部(或总公司) ③【军】寻的 ("的"指目标): a *homing* air-to-ground missile 自动导的空对地导弹 ❷ *vt.* ①把…送回家 ②给…住处 ‖a ～ from ～ 象家里一样安适和自在的地方 / a ～ *truth* 见 **truth** / at ～ ①在家;在家乡;在本地: The next match will be held at ～. 下次比赛在本地举行。②(在规定时间)在家接待客人: Mrs. Smith will be at ～, Monday, May 20, 5 p.m. 史密斯夫人定于五月二十日(星期一)下午五时在家会客。(英美请帖用语) / not at ～ to visitors 不接待客人 ③象在家里一样舒适、自在: be (或 feel) at ～ 感觉安适,无拘束 / Please sit down and make yourself at ～. 请坐下,别拘束。④熟悉的(with, on, in): He is at ～ in French. 他法语很好。/ *bring* ～ *to sb.* 见 **bring** / *come* ～ 见 **come** / ～ *free* [美俚]稳成功的,肯定得胜的 / *one's long* (或 *last*) ～ 坟墓 / *pay* ～ 见 **pay**[1] ‖～**less** *a.* 无家可归的 / ～**like** *a.* ①象一样舒适、亲切的 ②(饭菜等)简单而有益于健康的 / ～**ward** *a.* & *ad.* 向家(的);回家乡(的) / ～**wards** *ad.* 向家(乡);向本国 ‖～**-bird** *n.* 喜欢呆在家里不爱外出的人 / ～,**body** *n.* 以家庭为生活中心的人 / ～**'born** *a.* 土生土长的 / ～**bound** *a.* 回家(乡)的;回本国的: a ～*bound* traveller 正在(或准备)回家(或回乡、回国)的旅客 / a ～*bound* ship 返航的船只 / ～**'bred** *a.* ①家里饲养的;国内生产的 ②粗野的 / ～ **brew** ① 家酿的酒 (尤指啤酒) ② 当地培育的人(或东西) / ～**-'brewed** *a.* & *n.* 家酿的(酒) / ～**-,coming** *n.* ①回到家(乡);回到本国 ②[美]返校节 / ～**-ec** ['houm'ek] *n.* (美国学生用语) = economics / ～ **economics** 家政学 / ～**-farm** *n.* 所с供应大庄园(或企业等)自用的农场 / ～ **front** ①大后方 ②作为一国战争力量组成部分的民用工业 / ～**'grown** *a.* 本国产的;土生的: a ～*grown* expert 土专家 / **Home** Guard (一九四〇年组织的)英国国民军(成员) / ～ **help** 家务女佣 / ～,**keeping** *a.* 家居不外出的 /

land *n.* 祖国 / '～'**made** *a.* 家里做的;本国制的 / '～,**maker** *n.* 持家的妇女;主妇 / ～ **plate** (棒球)本垒 / ～ **range** 动物活动的范围 / ～ **run** (棒球)本垒打 / ～ **sick** *a.* 想家的;患怀乡病的 / '～,**sickness** *n.* 思家病,怀乡病 / '～**spun** *a.* ①家里纺的;家里做的 ②简朴的,粗陋的 ③朴实的,不做作的 *n.* 土布;手工纺织呢,手织大衣呢 / '～**stead** *n.* ① 家宅(包括房屋及其周围的田地),宅基 ②(在美国与某些英国领地)分给定居的移民耕种的土地 / '～**steader** *n.* ①占有宅地的人 ②分得土地的定居移民 / '～**stretch** *n.* ①(赛马)跑道的末一转弯和得胜标之间的一段距离 ②(任何工作的)最后一部分 / '～**town** *n.* 故乡,家乡 / '～**work** *n.* ①(学生的)家庭作业,课外作业 ②家里做的工作 ③(讨论等之前的)准备工作

homely ['houmli] *a.* ①家常的,简朴的: a ～ meal 简陋的一餐饭,家常便饭 ②朴实的,不做作的 ③如在家里的,不拘束的,亲切的: a ～ atmosphere 象家里那样的亲切气氛 ④[美](人或其容貌)不好看的 ‖**homeliness** *n.*

homicide ['homisaid] *n.* 杀人;杀人者

homogeneous [,homə'dʒi:njəs] *a.* ①同类的;同族的;相似的 ②均匀的;同质的;均一的: a ～ degree 均匀度 / a ～ ray 单色射线 ③【数】齐性的;齐次的: ～ integral equation 齐次积分方程

homonym ['hɔmənim] *n.* ①同音异义词;同形异义词;同形同音异义词 ②同名的人(或物) ③【生】异物同名 ‖～**ic** [,hɔmə'nimik] *a.* = homonymous

homonymous [hɔ'mɔniməs] *a.* ①同音(或同形)异义的;(词义)模棱两可的 ②同名的

hone[1] [houn] **I** *n.* (细)磨石;磨孔器 **II** *vt.* 把…放在磨石上磨

hone[2] [houn] *vi.* [方] ①咕噜,抱怨 ②想念,怀念

honest ['ɔnist] *a.* ①诚实的,正直的;[古]贞节的: an ～ attitude 老实态度 / an ～ face 诚实坦率的脸 ②有声誉的 ③[主英]可信任的,可靠的 ④用正当手段获得的: ～ gain 正当的收益 ⑤真正的,纯正的: ～ wool 真羊毛 / ～ milk 纯牛奶 ⑥简单的;普通的: This cafeteria serves good ～ food. 这家食堂供应很好的普通饭菜。‖*be quite ～ about it* [常作插入语]老实说 ‖～**ly** *ad.* ‖～ **Injun** [俚][作状语用]真的,说真的 / '～**-to-'God**, '～**-to-'goodness** *a.* 真正的,道地的

honesty ['ɔnisti] *n.* ①诚实,老实;正直;[古]贞节: ～ in politics 政治上的诚实 ②缎花属植物 ‖*Honesty is the best policy.* [谚]诚实才是上策。

honey ['hʌni] **I** ([复] honeys 或 honies) *n.* ①蜂蜜,蜜 ②甜;甜蜜: have ～ on one's lips and murder in one's heart 口蜜腹剑 ③宝贝儿(常用作称呼) ④极出色的东西;妙品 **II** (honeyed 或 honied) ❶ *vt.* ①(加蜜)使甜 ②对…说甜言蜜语;奉承 ❷ *vi.* 说甜言蜜语;奉承 **III** *a.* ①(似)蜂蜜的 ②[古]心爱的 ‖～**ed** *a.* ①加了蜜

的;多蜜的 ②甜如蜜的: ~ed words 甜言蜜语 ‖~ bag (蜜蜂体中的)蜜囊 / '~bee n. 蜜蜂 / '~bunch,~bun n. [美口]亲爱的人(常用作称呼) / '~comb n. 蜜蜂窝;蜂窝状的东西 vt. ①使成蜂窝状 ②把…弄成千疮百孔; 充斥 vi. 满是洞孔 / '~,cooler n. [美俚](对女子的)奉承; 用奉承赢得女子信任的男子 / '~dew n. ①甘汁,蜜露 ②加甜味的烟草 / '~lipped a. 嘴甜的,甜言蜜语的 / ~ locust 【植】美洲皂荚 / ~man [美俚]靠女子生活的情夫 / '~moon n. 蜜月 vi. 度蜜月 / '~,mooner n. 度蜜月的人 / ~mouthed ['hʌnimauðd] a. =~lipped / 'Honey,suckle n. 【植】忍冬属 / '~-sweet a. 如蜜一样甜的 / '~-'tongued a. =~lipped / ~ wag(g)on [美俚]垃圾车

honorarium [,ɔnə'rɛəriəm] ([复] honorariums 或 honoraria [,ɔnə'rɛəriə]) n. (对习俗上不应取酬的服务的)酬金,谢礼

honorary ['ɔnərəri] I a. ①荣誉的,光荣的 ②名誉的;义务的: an ~ member of the association 协会的名誉会员 ③纪念性的: an ~ ode 赞歌 ④(债务等)道义上的,信用的 II n. ①名誉团体 ②名誉学位;获名誉学位的人 ③[古]=honorarium

hono(u)r ['ɔnə] I n. ①荣誉,光荣: leave ~ to others and reserve difficulties for oneself 把荣誉让给别人,把困难留给自己 ②尊敬,敬意:show ~ to sb. 向某人表示敬意 / hold sb. in ~ 尊敬某人 ③名誉,面子;自尊心,廉耻: pledge one's ~ 用自己的名誉担保 / a sense of ~ 廉耻心 ④道义 ⑤(妇女的)贞操 ⑥(用于客套语中)荣幸: I have the ~ to inform you that .... (用于正式场合或书信中)我荣幸地通知您,… / We request the ~ of your company at dinner. (请帖用语)道备便酌,敬请光临。 ⑦[H-](对法官或某些高级官员的尊称,与 Your, His 或 Her 连用)阁下;先生: Your Hono(u)r (直接称呼时用)阁下;先生 / His Hono(u)r the Mayor (间接提及时用)市长先生 ⑧[与不定冠词连用]光荣的人;光荣的事: prove to be an ~ to the collective 成为替集体增光的人(或因素) ⑨徽章,勋章 ⑩[复]表示敬意的仪式;葬典: military ~s 军葬礼;(向总统或贵宾致敬的)军礼 / the funeral (或 last) ~s 葬礼 ⑪[商]信用: for the ~ of 了…的信用 / a debt of ~ (法律上不能追索的)信用借款 ⑫[复](大学中的)优等成绩;给予优等生的荣誉;[英]优等成绩奖金: graduate with ~s 以优等成绩毕业 ⑬(纸牌中)价值最高的牌(指王牌中的 10, J, Q, K, A);[常用复]点子 ⑭(高尔夫球的)先打权 ‖an affair of ~ (为争名誉而进行的)决斗 / a guard of ~ 仪仗队 / a point of ~ 为维持面子必须做的事(尤指为了面子必须决斗) II vt. ①尊敬: an ~ed guest 贵宾 ②使增光;给…以荣誉: feel ~ed to do sth. 因做某事感到荣幸 / Will you ~ me with a visit? 可否请您光临? ③[商]承兑,承认并如期支付;[喻]实践,允准: ~ a cheque 承

兑支票 / ~ sb.'s signature 承认某人的签字而付款 / ~ a debt in advance 提前还债 / ~ one's promise 实践诺言 / ~ an application 批准申请 ‖be bound in ~ (或 be in ~ bound) to do sth. 道义上必须做某事 / be on one's ~ to do sth. 道义上有责任做某事 / do ~ to ①向…表示敬意 ②给…带来荣誉 / do the ~s (of)(在…场合)尽主人之谊 / give one's word of ~ 用名誉担保 / ~ bright [俚]=on one's / in ~ of 为向…表示敬意;为纪念…: give a banquet in ~ of the delegation 设宴招待代团 / on (或 upon) one's ~ (或 on one's word of ~) 以名誉担保 / pay (或 give) ~ to 向…致敬 / put sb. on his ~ 信任某人(指相信他为了自己的名誉不会食言等) / the ~s of war 给予战败者的恩典(如允其持本国军旗行军等) ‖~ roll 荣誉名册 / ~ system ①无监视的考试制度 ②信任犯人因而不加监视的制度

hono(u)rable ['ɔnərəbl] a. ①荣誉的,光荣的: an ~ discharge 荣誉退役 / an ~ duty 名誉职位 / ~ mention 褒奖 / win ~ distinctions 立下光辉的功勋 ②可尊敬的,高尚的 ③正直的 ④名誉好的 ⑤[H-]尊敬的(英国议员、伯爵以下的贵族子弟及高级官员的名字前用的尊称; 美国国会议员及高级官员的名字前用的尊称; 略作 Hon.) ‖Most Honourable [英]用于侯爵 (或 Bath 勋爵、枢密院)名字前的尊称(略作 Most Hon.) / Right Honourable [英]用于侯爵以下的贵族(或枢密顾问官、伦敦市长)的名字前的尊称(略作 Rt. Hon.) ‖hono(u)rably ad.

hood[1] [hud] I n. ①兜帽,头巾 ②(大学制服外以其颜色表示学位的)垂布 ②(马、鹰的)头罩 ③【机】(发动机)罩;(烟囱等的)帽盖;车篷 ④【建】帽盖;出檐 ⑤【动】羽冠 II vt. 用头巾包;给…戴头罩,加罩‖~ed a. ①戴头兜的,有头兜的;头兜状的 ②(眼镜蛇等)颈部因胁骨运动而膨胀的 ③头部颜色与身体其他部分截然不同的 ④ 顶饰羽冠状的

hood[2] [hud] n. [美俚]强盗;行凶的年轻无赖,恶棍

hoodwink ['hudwiŋk] vt. ①[古]蒙住…的眼睛 ②欺骗,蒙蔽: be ~ed for the moment 一时受了蒙蔽

hoof [hu:f] I ([复] hoofs 或 hooves [hu:vz]) n. ①蹄;(马等的)足 ②[俚]人足 II ❶ vt. ①走 ② 踢; 踏;用蹄踏 ❷ vi. ①走 ②踢; 踏;跳舞 ‖beat (或 pad) the ~ [俚]走,拖着脚步走 / it [美俚]①步行 ②(学生用语)逃走,跑掉 ③手演跳舞 / ~ out 踢出,逐出 / on the ~ (马、牛等)活着的;尚未屠宰的 / show the (cloven) ~ (魔鬼)露出爪脚;显原形,露马脚 / under the ~ 被践踏,被蹂躏 ‖~ed a. 有蹄的 / ~er n. ①步行者 ②[美俚]舞蹈演员;跳舞女郎 ③[美俚]黑人 ‖'~-beat n. 蹄声 / '~-pad n. (防止两蹄相击的)蹄垫 / '~-pick n. (剔去蹄下石片等用的)蹄签

hook [huk] I n. ①钩,挂钩;针钩 ②钩状物

③镰刀 ④[俚]锚 ⑤钩状岬;河湾 ⑥[喻]陷阱,圈套 ⑦[美俚]妓女 ⑧[复][美俚]手;手指 ⑨[美俚]麻醉药(尤指海洛因) ⑩(拳击中的)肘弯击;(高尔夫球中的)左曲球 ⑪[音]钩符 **II** *vt.* ①用钩连结;钩住 ②用钩钩(鱼) ③引(人)上钩,欺骗 ④偷,扒 ⑤(牛等)用角尖挑刺 ⑥使成钩状 ⑦[纺]用钩针编结 ⑧(拳击中)用肘弯击;(高尔夫球中)使(球)向左弯 ❷ *vi.* ①弯成钩状;弯曲 ②钩住;钩紧 ‖*by* ～ *or* (*by*) *crook* 不择手段地,用种种方法 / *drop* (或 *slip*) *off the* ～*s* [英]死 / *get* (*sb.*) *off the* ～ [美俚](使某人)摆脱危境 / *get the* ～ [美俚]被解雇 / *go off the* ～*s* ①发狂 ②死 / *go on the* ～ *for* ① 为(某人,某事)而负债(或借钱) ②为(某人)冒险 / ～ *in* 以钩钩住 / ～ 勾引上;强力拉拢 / ～ *it* [美俚](常用作叫人逃跑的报警语)逃走,快逃 / ～, *line, and sinker* [美口]完全地,全部地 / ～ *on to* 钩住,挂在…上;依附于,追随 / ～ *up* 用钩钩住;用钩钩起: be ～*ed up* with 与…挂上钩 / *on one's own* ～ [美口]独自地;自做自当地;自担风险地 / *on the* ～ 陷入圈套,难以摆脱 / *sling one's* ～ [俚]逃走,离开 / *take one's* ～ = it / *with a* ～ *at the end* (在同意的同时)心中尚有保留地 ‖～*let* ['huklit] *n.* 小钩子 / ～ *and eye* 风纪扣 / '～*nose n.* ①钩鼻 ②[美俚][蔑]犹太人;守财奴 / '～*shop n.* [美俚]妓院 / '～*up n.* ①[无]试验线路;把…勾引上 ②[美俚]电路耦合;接续图 ②联播电台 ③ 联合,同盟(常指敌对分子或团体的结合) / '～*worm n.* 【动】钩虫 / ～ *wrench* 【机】钩形扳手.

hooka(h) ['hukə] *n.* 水烟筒

hooka(h)

hooked [hukt] *a.* ①钩状的 ②有钩的 ③用钩针做的: a ～ rug 钩针编结地毯 ④[美俚]吸毒成瘾的;入了迷的(on) ⑤[俚]已婚的 ‖～*ness n.*

hooligan ['hu:ligən] *n.* 小流氓,街头恶棍 ‖～*ism n.* 流氓行为

hoop[1] [hu:p] **I** *n.* ①箍 ②箍状物;(孩子玩的)铁环;(马戏团中供表演者穿过用的)大铁圈 ③[常用复](旧时妇女撑开裙子下摆用的)裙环,鲸骨圈 ④戒指 ⑤(篮球的)篮,篮圈 ⑥(槌球戏中的)弓形小铁门 **II** *vt.* 加箍于;用箍把…围住 ‖*go through the* ～(*s*) 经受磨炼 / *roll one's* ～ ①顺

利向前 ②稳妥办事 ③[美俚]只管自己的事 ‖～*er n.* 箍桶人 / ～ *iron* 铁箍 / ～*man* ['hu:pmən] *n.* 篮球运动员 / '～*skirt. n.* 有裙环的女裙

hoop[2] [hu:p] **I** *vi.* 发呼呼声(尤指作百日咳患者的咳嗽声) **II** *n.* (百日咳患者的)咳嗽声 ‖～*ing cough* 百日咳

hoot [hu:t] **I** ❶ *vi.* ①作猫头鹰叫声 ②作汽笛响声;作汽车喇叭响声 ③ 作表示蔑视不满的叫喊: ～ *at* sb. 呵斥某人 ❷ *vt.* ①用呵斥声表示(轻蔑等) ②轰赶: ～ sb. *out of the room* 把某人轰出房间 / ～ a speaker *down* 把演讲者轰下去 **II** *n.* ① 猫头鹰叫声 ② 汽笛响声;汽车喇叭声 ③ 表示蔑视不满的叫声 ④ 极少量 ‖*not care a* ～ (或 *two* ～*s*) 毫不在乎 / *not worth a* ～ (或 *two* ～*s*) 毫无价值 ‖～*er n.* 汽笛

hooves [hu:vz] hoof 的复数

hop[1] [hop] **I** (hopped; hopping) ❶ *vi.* ①(人)单足跳;(蛙、鸟等)齐足跳 ②[口]跳舞 ③[俚]去 ④ 作短途旅行(尤指飞行) ❷ *vt.* ① 跳过;[口]飞过: ～ the hedge 跳过篱笆 ②使(球)跳③跳上(火车等);免费搭乘;得到(免费乘坐)的机会: ～ a ride 免费搭乘 **II** *n.* ① 单足跳;弹跳 ② 跳舞会 ③[俚](长距离飞行中的)一段航程 ④ 短途旅行 ⑤免费搭乘 ‖*be hopping mad* [美口]怒不可遏,气得跳起来 / *catch on the* ～ [英]趁人不备时抓住… / ～ *it* [俚]走开 / ～ *off* [口](飞机)起飞 / ～ *on* (或 *all over*)[俚]责骂 / ～, *skip* (或 *step*) *and jump* 三级跳 / ～ *to it* 开始做事 / *on the* ～ [口]到处奔忙 ‖'～-o'-my-'thumb *n.* 矮子 / '～scotch *n.* 小孩独脚跳踢石子的游戏,"造房子"游戏 ①[主方]=toad ②[美俚]痛饮

hop[2] [hop] **I** *n.* ①[植]蛇麻草,忽布 ②[复]蛇麻子(用以使啤酒等带苦味) ③[美俚]一种麻醉药(尤指鸦片);有毒瘾的人 **II** (hopped; hopping) ❶ *vt.* ①加蛇麻子于;加味 ②加…于;加味 ②加…服麻醉药;用麻醉药刺激 (up) ③ 超额增大(发动机)的功率,超额增大(车辆)的发动机功率(up) ❷ *vi.* 长蛇麻子;采蛇麻子 ‖*be hopped up* [美俚]兴奋的;抽鸦片烟抽得昏昏沉沉的 / *full of* ～s [美俚](似因麻醉品药性未过而)瞎讲着,胡说着 ‖～*bind*, / ～*bine n.* 蛇麻草蔓 / ～ *field* 蛇麻草田 / ～ *fiend* [美俚]吸毒鬼 / ～ *fly* 蛇麻草蚜虫 / ～ *garden* [英]蛇麻草园 / '～*head n.* [美俚]吸毒鬼 / '～*joint n.* [美俚]①低级酒店 ②鸦片馆 / ～ *picker* 采蛇麻草的人;采蛇麻草机 / ～ *pillow* 蛇麻草做芯子的枕头(传说可促进睡眠) / ～ *pocket* 计量蛇麻草的袋 / ～ *pole* 蛇麻草的支柱

hope [houp] **I** *n.* ①希望: There is much ～ of further improvement. 大有进一步改进的希望。②被寄托希望的人(或物) **II** ❶ *vt.* 希望: It is sincerely ～*d* that .... 恳切希望… ❷ *vi.* ①希望,期待: ～ for the best 抱乐观的希望;作最好的打算 / A: He is annoyed with me, isn't he?

B: I ~ not. 甲:他大概生我气了吧? 乙:我希望不是这么一回事。②[古]信任(in) ‖(a) forlorn ~ ①微乎其微的希望;孤注一掷的举动 ②敢死队 / beyond ~ 没有希望 / ~ against ~ 抱一线希望 / in ~s of (或 in the ~ that) 怀着…的希望: We are sending out samples in ~s of gaining comments. 我们正在寄送样品,征求批评意见。/ pin (或 lay) one's ~(s) on 把希望寄托在…上 ‖~r n. 希望者 ‖~ chest 女子的嫁妆;装嫁妆的箱子

hopeful ['houpful] I a. ①怀有希望的: be (或 feel) ~ about the future 对未来抱有希望 / be (或 feel) ~ of success 对成功抱有希望 ②有希望的: a ~ outlook 有希望的前途 II n. 有希望成功的人;有希望被选上的人: a presidential ~ 可望当上总统的人 ‖~ly ad. / ~ness n.

hopeless ['houplis] a. 没有希望的;绝望的; 医治不好的: a ~ case 绝症;绝望病人;无希望造就的人 ‖~ly ad. / ~ness n.

hopper[1] ['hopə] n. ①单足跳者;跳虫(尤指跳蚤、干酪蛆等) ②(磨粉机等的)漏斗,送料斗,加料斗;(即除垃圾及粪用的)底卸式船 (或斗);贮水槽 ③投放要求立法机关讨论的议案的箱子 ④钢琴琴键后抬举小木槌的机件 ‖~grass n. [方]蚱蜢;蝗虫

hopper[2] ['hopə] n. 采摘蛇麻子的人(或机械)

horde [hɔːd] I n. ①蒙古游牧部落 ②游牧部落;游牧民族 ③[贬]人群;群: a ~ of locusts 一群蝗虫 II vi. 形成游牧部落聚居;成群结队

horizon [hə'raizn] n. ①地平,地平线;地平圈: apparent ~ [气]视地平 / celestial ~ [气]天球地平 / true ~ [气]真地平 / visible ~ [气]可见地平 ②水平 ③[喻]眼界;见识: widen one's ~ 开阔眼界 ④[地]层位 ‖on the ~ 刚冒出地平线;在地平线上

horizontal [,hɔri'zɔntl] I a. ①地平的,地平线的 ②水平的;卧式的: a ~ plane 水平面 / a ~ bar 单杠 / a ~ engine 卧式发动机 ③由同一级别的人所组成的 II n. 水平线;水平面;水平物 ‖~ity [,horizon'tæliti] n. 水平状态 / ~ly ad. ‖~ union 不同工业内各行业的职工工会(与 vertical union 同一工业内跨行业的职工工会相对)

horn [hɔːn] I n. ①(牛、羊、鹿等动物的)角,触角; (动物头上的)角状羽毛,触须 ②魔鬼头上的角 ③角质;角质物;角制物;角状物;角状容器: a shoe ~ 角质鞋拔 / a drinking ~ 角制杯 / a powder ~ 古代装火药的角 ④半岛;岬,海角;河流的支流;海湾的分叉 ⑤(新月的)钩尖;(铁砧的)尖角;(马鞍的)鞍头 ⑥(角制的)号角;(管乐器)喇叭,号,管: a French ~ 法国号 / an English ~ 英国管 ⑦角状扩声器,扬声器;警报器 ⑧[地]角峰 ⑨[喻]防卫武器;力量;光荣 ⑩[美俚]鼻子 ⑪[空]操纵杆 II vt. ①装角于 ②把…做成角状 ③(动物)用角抵触(或挑) ④把(牛角)截去;截短(牛角) ⑤[船]使(船的框架)与其龙骨成直角 ‖a ~ of plenty 丰饶角;丰饶的象征 / blow

(或 *toot*) one's own ~ 自吹自擂 / come out at (或 of) the little end of the ~ 见 end / draw (或 haul, pull) in one's ~s ①退缩;撤退 ②克制自己,软化下去 / ~ in [美俚]闯入;侵入,干涉 / lift up one's ~ 趾高气扬;盛气凌人 / lock ~s ①(牛等)角纠缠在一起相斗 ②难分难解地搏斗 / on the ~s of a dilemma 进退维谷 / show one's ~s 露出凶相 / take a ~ 饮酒,喝一杯酒 / take the bull by the ~s 不畏艰险 ‖~er n. ①制角器者 ②吹号角者 ③[俚]服海洛因的人 / ~ful n. 满满一角杯 / ~less a. 无角的 / ~like a. 似角的 ‖~ antenna 喇叭形天线 / '~bar n. 马车的横木 / '~beam n. 【植】鹅耳枥属树 / '~bill n. 【动】犀鸟科鸟;犀鸟 / '~blende [矿]角闪石 / '~book n. [矿]旧时蒙有透明角片的儿童识字书;初级论文 / '~-'mad a. 狂怒的 / '~pipe n. ①号笛(一种单簧管乐器) ②号笛舞(英国水手跳的一种活泼民间舞); 号笛舞曲 / '~'rimmed a. (眼镜)有角质架的 / '~stone n. [矿]角岩 / ~swoggle ['hɔːn,swɔgl] vt. [美俚]欺骗,瞒 / '~work n. (防御用的)角堡

horned [hɔːnd] a. ①有角的: ~ cattle 有角的牛 ②角状的: the ~ ['hɔːnid] moon [诗]半月 ‖~ bladderwort 【植】具角狸藻 / ~ grebe 【动】角鸊鷉 / ~ puffin 【动】角目鸟 / ~ toad 【动】角蟾 / ~ violet 【植】簇生堇菜 / ~ viper 【动】角蛙

hornet ['hɔːnit] n. 【动】大黄蜂 ‖bring (或 raise, arouse) a ~s' nest about one's ears 见 nest / stir up (或 arouse) a nest of ~s 见 nest

horny ['hɔːni] a. ①角制的;角的 ②角状的;有角的 ③似角一样坚硬的;粗硬起老茧的 ④[美俚]好色的,猥亵的 ‖horniness n. ‖'~-handed a. 手上长有老茧的

horoscope ['hɔrəskoup] n. 星占;算命天宫图 ‖cast a ~ 以占星术算命

horrible ['hɔrəbl] I a. ①令人毛骨悚然的,可怕的,恐怖的: ~ crimes 令人发指的罪行 ②[口]极讨厌的;糟透的: What ~ weather! 这鬼天气! II n. [常用复]穿得奇异古怪的人 ‖~ness n. / horribly ad.

horrid ['hɔrid] a. ①[古]粗糙的,粗硬的 ②可怕的 ③[口]引起反感的,令人厌恶的: a ~ bore 讨厌透顶的人(或物) ‖~ly ad. / ~ness n.

horrify ['hɔrifai] vt. ①使恐怖,使毛骨悚然;(表情等)显出恐怖的样子: a horrified stare 神色恐怖的凝视 ②[口]使震惊,使极度厌恶 ‖horrification [,hɔrifi'keiʃən] n. / ~ing a.

horror ['hɔrə] n. ①恐怖,战栗: strike ~ into sb. 使某人毛骨悚然 / give sb. the ~s 使某人吓得发抖 ②极端厌恶: have a ~ of sth. 极讨厌某事 ③引起恐怖(或厌恶)的事物 ‖~ fiction 恐怖小说 / '~-,stricken, '~struck a. 受惊吓的

hors [hɔː] ad. & prep. [法](在…)之外 ‖~ concours [kɔ̃:ŋ'kuːr] (展览品)参加展览但不是

为了得奖的 / ~ de combat [də 'kɔ̃:mbɑ:] 失去战斗力的 / ~ d'oeuvre ['də:vr] 餐前的小吃

horse [hɔ:s] **I** n. ① 马(尤指成长的公马);马科动物: mount (dismount) a ~ 上(下)马 / ride a ~ 骑马 / rein in one's ~ at the edge of the cliff 悬崖勒马 ② [总称]骑兵: three hundred light ~ 三百名轻骑兵 / a regiment of ~ 一团骑兵 ③ 象马的东西; 有脚的木架 (如锯木架、烘衣架等);【体】木马 ④ [口] (棋中的)马 ⑤ 【矿】夹块, 夹石 ⑥ 【海】(作系帆或其他用途的)绳索, 铁杆 ⑦ 马力 ⑧ [美俚]碎牛肉 ⑨ [美俚](考试作弊时用的)夹带 ⑩ [美俚]粗鲁的家伙; 笨蛋 ⑪ [美俚]一千美元 ⑫ [美俚]恶作剧 **II** ❶ vt. ① 使骑上马;为…备(或套)马 ② 把…放在人背(或木马)上加以鞭挞;鞭打 ③ 背(人) ④ [俚]作弄 ⑤ 猛推, 粗暴地拉 ❷ vi. ① 骑马 ② 作弄人;胡闹 **III** a. ① 马的 ② 马拉的; 骑(或套)着马的 ③ (同类中)大而粗硬的 ‖ a dark ~ ① 实力难测的赛马 ② [喻]实力难测的竞争者, 竞争中出人意料的获胜者 / a ~ of another (或 different) colo(u)r 完全另外一回事 / a ~ on sb. [俚]针对某人的一个恶作剧 / back the wrong ~ (赛马中)下错赌注; [喻]支持失败的一方 / be on one's high ~ 趾高气扬 / change ~s 换马, 调换主持人, 换班子 / come off one's high ~ 不再骄傲自大 / eat like a ~ 吃得很多 / flog a dead ~ 白费力, 徒劳; 事后再作无益的议论 / from the ~'s mouth 见 mouth / hitch ~s (together) [古]同心协力; 情投意合 / hold one's ~s [俚]忍耐 / ~ and foot ① [常用作状语]骑兵和步兵; 全军 ② 全力以赴地 / ~ around [俚]哄闹, 胡闹 / look a gift ~ in the mouth 对礼物吹毛求疵 / mount (或 ride) the high ~ 趾高气扬, 耀武扬威 / Never swap (或 swop) ~s while crossing the stream. [谚]行到河中不换马。(意指危难时不宜作大变动) / outside of a ~ [口]骑在马上 / put the cart before the ~ 本末倒置 / spur a willing ~ 无故加鞭; 给予不必要的刺激 / talk ~ 吹牛, 说大话 / To ~! (口令)上马! / work for a dead ~ 从事不可能再得到报酬的工作 / work like a ~ 辛苦地干活 / You may take a ~ to the water, but you cannot make him drink. [谚]带马到河边容易, 逼马饮水难。(意指不要逼人做他不愿做的事) ‖ '~-and-'buggy n. [美]过时的, 老式的 / '~back n. 马背: go on ~back 骑马去 ② 隆起的呈状地带 ad. 在马背上 / '~bean豆 / ~ box 运马的有篷货车 / '~breaker n. 驯马师 / ~ chestnut 七叶树属植物; 欧洲七叶树 / '~cloth n. (盖在马身上或装饰马用的)马衣, 马被 / ~ collar 马颈圈: grin through a ~ collar (古时一种游戏)把头从马颈圈伸出来作作鬼脸; [喻]硬充滑稽 / ~ coper, ~ dealer 马贩子 / ~ doctor ① 马医 ② 蹩脚医生 / '~faced a. 马脸的, 脸长而难看的 / '~,feathers [复] n. [俚]胡说, 梦话 / '~flesh n. ① 作食用的马肉

② [总称]马: a good judge of ~flesh 善于鉴别马的人 / '~fly n. 虻 / ~ gear 马具 / '~hair n. 马毛; 马鬃 / '~hide n. ① 马皮; 马皮革 ② 棒球 / ~ latitudes 【气】回归线无风带 (约南北纬30° 一带) / '~laugh n. 纵声大笑, 哄笑 / '~leech n. ① (一种欧洲产的)黄蛭 ② 贪心的人: daughters of the ~leech 贪得无厌的人们 (源出基督教《圣经》) / mackerel 【动】竹筴鱼 / ~man ['hɔ:smən] n. ① 骑兵 ② 骑手, 骑师 ③ 养马人 / '~manship n. (骑)马术 / '~-ma,rines [复] n. 水上骑兵 (指不存在的东西): Tell that to the ~-marines! 谁相信这话! / ~ opera [美俚]西部"牛仔"影片中(或广播剧,电视剧) / '~play n. & vi. (作)粗鄙而喧闹的游戏; 胡闹 / '~,power [机]马力 / ~ race, ~ racing 赛马 / '~,radish n. 【植】辣根 / ~ sense [口]起码常识 / '~shit n. ① 马粪 ② [俚]胡说 / '~shoe n. ① 马蹄铁 ② 马蹄形(即 U 形)的东西 vt. 给(马)钉掌 / '~tail n. 马尾 / 【植】木贼属的一种 / ~ trade ① 马的买卖 ② 双方在大事讨价还价后互相让步的交易 / ~ trader 做马生意的人 / '~whip n. 马鞭 vt. 用马鞭抽打 / '~,woman n. ① 女骑手, 女骑师 ② 女养马人

horticulture ['hɔ:tikʌltʃə] n. 园艺(学) ‖ **horticultural** [,hɔ:ti'kʌltʃərəl] a. 园艺的 / **horticulturist** [,hɔ:ti'kʌltʃərist] n. 园艺家

hose [houz] **I** ([复] hose(s)) n. ① ([复] hose) [复]长统袜; 短统袜(商品名) ② (旧时)男子穿的紧身裤; 短裤 ③ (用于救火、浇水等的)软管: six fire ~(s) 六根水龙软管 **II** vt. ① 用水龙管浇(或洗、喷) ② [美俚]拍…马屁; 欺骗 ‖ ~ cart (消防队的)水管车 / ~ man ['houzmən] n. 消防人员 / ~ pipe n. 水龙软管

hosier ['houʒə] n. 内衣类经售商

hospice ['hɔspis] n. ① 旅客招待所(尤指教会办的) ② 收容贫、病者的机构, 济贫院

hospitable ['hɔspitəbl] a. ① 好客的; 殷勤的, 招待周到的: a ~ reception 热情的接待 ② (气候、环境等)宜人的; 适宜的 ③ 易接受的: be ~ to new ideas 易接受新思想 ‖ ~ness n. / hospitably ad.

hospital ['hɔspitl] n. ① 医院: be taken (或 sent) to a ~ 被送进医院 / be in ~ 在住院 ② [用于机构名称中]慈善收容院 ③ [古]旅客招待所 ④ (钢笔等小东西的)修理商店 ‖ a field ~ 野战医院 / an infectious ~ 传染病院 / an isolation ~ 隔离病院 / a maternity (或 lying-in) ~ 产科医院 / a mental ~ 精神病医院 ‖ a Hospital Saturday (Sunday) 医院的星期六(星期日)募捐日(一般星期六指在街头募捐; 星期日指在教堂内募捐) / walk the ~s 当实习医生 ‖ ~ism n. ① 医院制度 ② 医院制度中有损病员健康的种种缺陷; 长期孤儿院生活的影响

hospitality [,hɔspi'tæliti] n. ① 好客; 殷勤 ② (气候、环境等的)宜人; 适宜

host¹ [houst] **I** n. ① 主人: a ~ country 东道国 /

act as ~ at a dinner party 在宴会上作主人 ② 旅馆老板 ③ (广播、电视的) 节目主持人 ④ 【生】寄主; 宿主 ⑤【物】基质 II vt. 作主人招待; 在…上作主人: ~ the visitors 招待来客 / ~ a garden party 作游园会的主人 / The conference was ~ed by that committee. 该委员会充当这个会议的东道主。‖play ~ to 在…上作主人; 招待… / reckon without one's ~ 未经考虑重要因素 (或未与主要有关人员磋商) 而作决定; 无视困难

host² [houst] n. ①[古] 军队 ②一大群; 许多 ‖be a ~ in oneself 能以一当十; 能高人一等 / the ~(s) of heaven ①日月星辰 ②天使军 / the Lord (或 God) of Hosts (基督教《圣经》中的) 万军之主 (指耶和华)

host³ [houst] n. [常作 H-]【宗】圣饼

hostage ['hɔstidʒ] n. 人质; 抵押品: be held as a ~ 被扣作人质 / Three persons were taken ~. 三人被扣作人质。‖~s to fortune 可能失去的人 (或物) ‖~ship n. 充当人质, 被抵押状态

hostel ['hɔstəl] n. ①旅店 ②寄宿舍, (在校外的) 学生宿舍; (有关当局为徒步或骑自行车旅行的青年所设的) 招待所 (=youth ~) ‖~er n. ①招待所 (尤指教会设立的招待所) 管理员; [古] 旅馆老板 ②投宿招待所的骑车 (或徒步) 旅行者 / ~ry n. 旅店; 旅馆

hostess ['houstis] n. ①女主人 ②旅馆的女老板 ③(客机上的) 女服务员; [美] (列车、公共汽车上的) 女服务员 ④[美] (舞厅里的) 舞女

hostile ['hɔstail] I a. ①敌方的; 敌意的, 敌对的: a ~ country 敌国 / be ~ to 对…有敌意 ②不友善的 II n. [美] ①反对白种人的印第安人 ②敌对分子 ‖~ly ad.

hostility [hɔs'tiliti] n. ①敌意, 敌视: arouse sb.'s ~ 引起某人的敌意 / feel no ~ towards sb. 对某人不怀敌意 ②敌对 (状态); 敌对行动; [复] 战争行动: the outbreak (suspension) of hostilities 战事的爆发 (停止)

hostler ['ɔslə] n. ①旅店中料理马 (或骡) 的人 ②机车 (或机器) 的维修人

hot [hɔt] I (hotter, hottest) a. ①热的: ~ weather 热天气 / like a cat on ~ bricks 象热锅上的蚂蚁 / a ~ forehead 发烫的前额 / a ~ bath 热水浴 / The days are getting hotter. 天渐渐热起来了。②热情的; 热切的: a ~ patriot 热烈的爱国者 / be ~ on playing table tennis 热衷于打乒乓球 / be ~ for reform 迫切要求改革 ③激动的; 急躁的, 发火的; 激烈的, 猛烈的: a ~ temper 急躁的脾气 / the ~ blood of youth (青年时代的) 血气方刚 / Hot words were exchanged between them. 他们之间相互激烈争吵起来。/ a ~ debate 一场激烈的辩论 / a ~ fight 激战 ④刚做好的; 刚到达的; (公债等) 刚发行的; (消息等) 最新的; 热门的: a ~ subject 热烈讨论中的题目 / ~ news [口] 最新消息 ⑤[美俚] 有生气的, 活跃繁忙的: This is a ~ city. 这是一座充满活力的

城市。/ The news kept the wire ~. 新闻使这条电信线路忙极了。⑥(味道) 刺激的, 辣的; (打猎时野兽留下的气味) 强烈的: I don't like mustard; it's too ~. 我不爱吃芥末, 这东西太辣了。⑦(颜色) 给人热感的 (如红、黄等) ⑧紧随的; 紧迫的 ⑨(爵士音乐) 速度快、节奏强的 ⑩通高压电的 ⑪[原] 强放射性的: a ~ laboratory 强放射性物质研究实验室, "热"实验室 ⑫杰出的, 极好的: He is ~ in mathematics. 他数学极好。⑬极其走运的; 极有利的 ⑭(在体育比赛中) 一时能作出非凡表演的 ⑮(车辆等) 快的 ⑯违禁的, 非法的 ⑰被警察通缉的; (被窃物品) 刚被偷盗的, 正被警察大肆搜查中的 ⑱[俚] (被窃的珠宝等) 因易于识别而难以出手的 ⑲[口] 荒诞的, 不可信的 ⑳淫秽的; 性欲强的 II (hotter, hottest) ad. ①热 ②热切地, 紧迫地: come ~ on sb.'s heels 紧接某人而来 ③愤怒地 III (hotted; hotting) ❶ vi. [主英] 变热; 变得激动 (或骚动) 起来 (up) ❷ vt. [主英] ①使热, 把…加温: There's some dumplings left; I can ~ them up in a minute. 还有一些团子剩着, 我马上就可以加热。②使激动起来; 使骚动 ‖(all) ~ and bothered [俚] 骚动中的 / at its (或 the) hottest 在最激烈的一点上 / be ~ on sb.'s trail 见 trail / be ~ under the collar 见 collar / blow ~ and cold 摇摆不定 / get ~ ①变热; 变得兴奋, 激动起来: get ~ over an argument 争辩得激动起来 ②[俚] 使劲儿干 ③接近: Guess again, you're getting hotter. 再猜一下, 你差不多快猜着了。/ give it sb. ~ 见 give / go ~ and cold 发烧; 害臊 / ~ and ~ [用作状语] (食物) 一出锅就端上来 / ~ and strong 猛烈地, 激烈地 / make it ~ for sb. [口] 弄得某人日子不好过 / make it (或 make a place) ~ for sb. (或 too ~ to hold sb.) (用敌视态度) 弄得某人呆不下去 / not so ~ 不太杰出: Little Bob didn't flunk out, but his record isn't so ~. 小鲍勃没有不及格, 但成绩不太好。/ the ~s [美俚] 爱情; 性欲 ‖~ly ad. / ~ness n. ‖~ air [俚] 空话; 浮夸的文章 / ~·'air artist [俚] 吹牛大王 / ~ blast 【冶】热鼓风 / '~-'blooded a. ①易激动的, 热切的 ②(马) 英国种的; 阿拉伯种的 ③(家畜) 纯种的 / '~box n. (火车的) 车轴 / ~ cake 烤饼: sell like ~ cakes [口] (货物) 很快地卖掉 / ~cha ['hɔtʃə] n. [美俚] 爵士音乐 / ~ charging 【冶】热装料 / ~ corner ①(垒球) 第三垒 ②[美俚] (战场上或政治上的) 关键地方 / ~ dog ①[口] 小红肠; 红肠面包 ②[美俚] (表示高兴、热情、激动的感叹词) 好极了 / '~foot n. [复] (~foots) 暗中将火柴放在别人鞋中加以点燃的恶作剧 ad. 匆忙地 vi. 急匆匆地走 / '~·'galvaniz·ing n. 热镀锌 / '~head n. 急性子的人, 鲁莽的人 / '~·headed a. 急性子的, 鲁莽的人 / ~ house n. 温室: ~house production 温室生产 / Young people should not grow up in ~houses. 青年人不应在温室中成长。/ ~ line "热线"

[喻] 直接联系的途径 / ~ **money** (为获取高利或保障币值而由)一国转移至另一国的流动资金 / ~ **pants** [美俚] (妇女穿在外面的) 冬季短裤 / ~ **pilot** [美俚] 技术好胆子大的飞行员 / ~ **plate** 电炉; 煤气灶 / ~ **pot** 罐焖土豆烧牛(或羊)肉 / ~ **potato** 难题, 棘手的问题: handle a ~ *potato* 处理一件棘手的事 / '~-**press** *vt.* 热压 *n.* 热压机 / ~ **rod** [美俚] 把旧汽车拆卸减重而成的高速汽车 / ~ **rodder** [美俚] 驾驶减重高速汽车者 (一般为青少年) / ~ **seat** [美俚] ①电椅 ②困境 / ~ **shortness** 热脆性 / '~-**shot** *n.* ① (运送易腐败物品等的) 快车; 快船; 快机 ② 大人物; 飞黄腾达的野心家 / ~ **spot** [美俚] ① 麻烦地点; 潜在的危险地区 ②电椅 ③低级下流的夜总会 ④辐射最强处; 过热点 / ~ **spring** 温泉 / '~**spur** *n.* 性急的人 / ~ **stuff** [俚] ① 好手, 专家 ②意志坚强的人 ③脾气暴躁的人 / ~ **tap** 【冶】(钢锭的) 热帽 / ~ **war** 热战 (系 "冷战" 之对) / ~ **water** ①热水 ②困境: get into ~ *water* (尤指由于言行失检等) 陷入困境 / '~-'**water bottle**, '~-'**water bag** 热水瓶 / '~-'**water heating** 暖气设备 / ~ **well** 温泉 / ~ **wire** [美俚] 消息; 好消息 / '~-**wire** *a.* 【电】热线式的; 热电阻线的 / '~-,**working** *n.* 【冶】热加工

hotchpotch ['hɔtʃpɔtʃ] *n.* ①(汤或菜的) 杂烩 ②乱七八糟的混杂物 ③【律】财产混同 (指将各项产业合并, 以便在继承中平分)

hotel [hou'tel] **I** *n.* 旅馆 **II** (hotelled; hotelling) *vt.* 使住旅馆 ‖*the sheriff's* ~ [俚] 监狱 ‖~ **car** 带餐室的卧车

hound¹ [haund] **I** *n.* ①猎狗; 狗; [英] [the ~s] 猎狐的一群猎狗 ②追逐游戏中扮演猎狗的人 ③卑鄙的人 ④【动】角鲨, 星鲨; 弓鳍鱼 ⑤ [常用以构成复合词] 有…瘾的人: an autograph ~ 爱请人在纪念册上签名题字的人 **II** *vt.* ①用猎狗追猎; 追逐; 追逼 ②唆使 (on); 使追猎 (at); ~ sb. *on* 唆使某人, 煽动某人 ‖*a tea* ~ [美俚] ① 爱交际的男子, 爱和女人交际的男子 ②娘娘腔的男子 / *follow the* (或 *ride to*) ~s 骑马纵狗打猎 / ~s *of law* 缉捕吏

hound² [haund] *n.* [复] 【船】桅肩

hour ['auə] *n.* ① 小时: There is half an ~ to go. 还有半小时才开始(或才到达, 才做完)。/ work for ~s at a stretch 一连工作几小时 / combat flying ~s 【军】战斗飞行小时 / Seize the day, seize the ~! 要只争朝夕! (或: 要抓紧每日每时!) ② 时间, 时刻: the lunch ~ 午饭时间 / help in sb.'s ~ of need 在某人困难的时候给予帮助 / What are you doing here at this ~? 这时候你在这儿干什么?(句中的 "这时候" 常有 "极早" 或 "极晚" 的含义) ③目前, 现在: the question of the ~ 当前的问题 ④ [复] 一段时间: the happiest ~s of one's life 一生中最幸福的(一段)时间 ⑤…点钟: What's the ~? 现在几点钟了? / The ~ is 2:30. 两点半了。⑥(二十四小时连续计时制中的)…点钟: 09:00 (或 0900) ~s (读作 o

nine ~s 或 o nine hundred ~s) 早上九点 / 13:45 (或 1345) ~s (读作 thirteen forty-five ~s) 下午一点四十五分 ⑦课时; [复] 工作时间: The office (business) ~s are (from) 8 a.m. to 5 p.m. 办公(营业)时间从上午八点到下午五点。⑧(以正常速度)一小时内所完成的行程; 一小时内所做的工作: It is four ~s from here to that city by rail. 坐火车从这儿到那个城市行程是四小时。⑨【天】赤经十五度 ⑩【宗】每日的七次定时祈祷; [复] 祈祷文 ‖*after* ~s 工作(或学习)完毕后 / *An* ~ *in the morning is worth two in the evening.* [谚] 一日之计在于晨。/ *at all* ~s 在任何时间, 一直不断地 / *at the eleventh* ~ 在最后时刻; 在危急之时 / *by the* ~ 按钟点: hire a bicycle *by the* ~ 按钟点租一辆自行车 / *after* ~ 一小时又一小时, 连续地 / *in a lucky* (或 *good*) ~ 在幸运的时刻 / *in an evil* ~ 在不幸的时刻 / *keep early* ~s 早起早睡 / *keep late* ~s 晚睡晚起 / *off* ~s 业余时间: a friendly game during *off* ~s 业余时间的友谊比赛 / *One's* ~ *has come* (或 *struck*). 某人的死期(或末日)到了。/ *on the* ~ 在某一钟点准точ地: From 8 a.m. to 4 p.m. the suburban trains leave every hour *on the* ~. 从早上八点到下午四点, 近郊火车每小时正开出一列。(指八、九、十等每一点钟准点开出) / *out of* ~s 在上班时间之外 / *serve the* ~ 随波逐流; 趋炎附势 / *The darkest* ~ *is that before the dawn.* [谚] 黎明前的天最黑。/ *the inevitable* ~ 死期 / *the rush* ~s (交通) 拥挤时间, 高峰时间 / *the small* (或 *wee*) ~s 半夜一、二、三点钟 ‖~ **angle** 【天】时角 / ~ **circle** 【天】时圈 / '~**glass** *n.* 沙漏, 水漏 (古代计时器) / ~ **hand** (钟表的) 时针

hourglass

houri ['huəri] *n.* ① 伊斯兰教天堂女神 ② 妖艳的女人

hourly ['auəli] **I** *a.* ① 每小时的; 每小时一次的; 以钟点计算的: the ~ output (outflow of water) 每小时产量(排水量) / There is an ~ train service in the suburbs. 郊外有一小时一班的火车。② 时时刻刻的: in ~ expectation of sb.'s arrival 时刻盼望某人到来 **II** *ad.* ① 每小时一次: The long-distance bus runs ~. 长途汽车一小时开一班。②时时刻刻, 随时: with ~ renewed energy 以时刻增长的充沛精力

house [haus] I ([复] houses ['hauziz]) *n.* ①房子; 住宅: from ~ to ~ 挨家逐户地 ②家庭;家务: manage the ~ 当家 ③库,房 ④(养动物的)棚: a hen-~ 鸡棚 ⑤机构;所,社;商号: a printing ~ 印刷所 / a wholesale ~ 批发商行 ⑥议院;(议院举行会议的)大楼,会议厅;(议院开会时的)法定人数: the *House* of Commons (英国的)下院,下议院 / the *House* of Lords (英国的)上院,上议院 / the *House* of Representatives (美国的)众议院 / the upper (lower) ~ (议会的)上(下)议院 ⑦家族(尤指皇族或贵族);王朝: an ancient ~ 世家,望族 / the *House* of Windsor 英国王室 ⑧剧场;戏剧的一场;(剧场或音乐厅的)观众,听众: a full ~ (戏院)客满 / The second ~ starts at 4 p.m. 第二场下午四点钟开始。⑨宗教团体;宗教团体的会所;教堂;庙,庵 ⑩供膳的寄宿舍;住在寄宿舍里的男学生们 ⑪[美]旅馆 ⑫[美]妓院 ⑬[英][the H-]下议院;上议院;[口]证券交易所;贫民习艺所 II [hauz] ❶ *vt.* ①给…房子住;给…房子用: ~ the immigrants 供给移民住房 ②收藏: farm tools in a shed 把农具放在小屋里 ③覆盖;藏有: Those caves may ~ snakes. 那些洞里也许有蛇。④给(机器、齿轮等)装外罩 ⑤[建]把…嵌入 ⑥[海]安置(炮等);收好(桅木) ❷ *vi.* ①住 ②躲藏 (*up*) ‖a ~ of call ①搬运工人等候生意的地方;零工待雇处 ②常去的场所;常去的酒店 / a ~ of cards 孩子用纸牌搭成的房子;[喻]不牢靠的计划 / a ~ of correction 教养院,改造所 / a ~ of detention 拘留所 / a ~ of God 教堂 / a ~ of ill fame 妓院 / an iron ~ [美俚]监牢 / as safe as a ~ 非常安全 / bow down in the ~ of Rimmon ['rimən] 为求一致而牺牲自己的原则(源出基督教《圣经》) / bring down the ~ [口]博得满场喝采(或鼓掌) / bring the ~ about one's ears 使一家人都与自己为敌 / (burn) like a ~ on fire (燃烧得)猛烈而迅速 / carry the ~ 博得全场喝采 / clean ~ ①打扫、整理房屋 ②去除不需要(或讨厌)的人(或事物),内部清洗 / count the ~ 计算出席(或到场)人数 / eat sb. out of ~ and home 把某人吃穷 / give sb. a lot of ~ [美俚]给某人很多鼓励(或关心、注意) / ~ and home 家(加强语气的说法) / keep a good ~ 待客周到 / keep ~ 管理家务,当家 / keep open ~ 好客 / keep the ~ 家居不外出 / make a House [英]使下议院出席的议员达法定人数(四十人) / move ~ 搬家 / on the ~ 由店家出钱,免费 / play ~ [口]假扮大人做家务(一种儿童游戏) / set (或 put) one's ~ in order ①把屋子整理收拾好 ②[喻]进行内部整顿 / the big ~ (或 the Big House) [美俚](州或联邦的)监狱 / the narrow ~ 墓 / the pudding [俚]胃,肚子 / the third ~ [美](国会的)第三院,院外活动集团 ‖~ful *n.* 满屋,一屋子 / ~less *a.* 无家的 ②无房屋的 / ~let ['hauslit] *n.* 小房子 / ‖~ agent [主英]房地产经纪人 / ~ arrest 准离家的软禁: be under ~ arrest 被软禁在家 / ~boat *n.* ①可供住家的船,水上住家 ②宽敞的游艇 / '~bound *a.* (因病或有事等而)闭居家中的 / '~breaker *n.* ①(为抢劫等而)侵入他人住宅者 ②[英]拆房屋者 / '~breaking *n.* ①(为抢劫等而)侵入住宅 ②[英]拆房子 / ~broke, '~broken *a.* ①(狗、猫等)有家居的卫生习惯的 ②管教好的,有礼貌的 / '~clean *vi.* ①打扫房子和家具 ②去除不需要的人(或东西),清洗 *vt.* ①打扫 ②改革(指去除冗员和恶习) / '~coat *n.* 妇女在家穿的宽大便服 / dog 看家狗 / ~ flag 【海】(商船的)公司旗 / '~fly *n.* 家蝇 / ~keep *vi.* 管理家务(尤指准备膳食) / ~keeper *n.* 管理家务的主妇;女管家: be a bad (good) ~keeper 不会(会)当家 / '~keeping *n.* ①家务管理,家政 ②(企业中)房屋的管理 / '~leek *n.* 长生草属植物 / '~lights [复] *n.* 照亮剧场中观众席座的灯光 / '~maid *n.* 女仆 / ~maid's knee (因多跪着劳动而引起的)膝盖骨囊炎 / '~master *n.* (学生宿舍的)舍监 / '~mate *n.* 住在同一所房子里的人 / moss [美俚]在家具下(或地板上)积聚的灰尘 / '~mother *n.* (青年寄宿舍等的)女管家 / ~ mouse 家鼠 / ~ organ 商号为增进营业而出版的刊物 / ~ party 留客人在别墅等处过夜(或小住)的聚会;参加别墅聚会的全体宾客 / ~ physician 住院内科医生 / ~ place [方]农场住宅中的起居室 / '~-proud *a.* 关心家事的;讲究家庭摆设的 / '~-renter *n.* 租屋者 / '~room *n.* 房子中摆东西(或住人)的地方: not give sth. ~room 不要某物;不接受某礼物 / staff [总称]住院医生 / ~ surgeon 住院外科医生 / '~-to-' *a.* 挨户的 / ~top *n.* 屋顶: cry (或 proclaim) sth. from the ~tops 公开、广泛地宣扬某事 / '~warming *n.* 庆祝迁居的聚会 / '~wife *n.* ①([复]~wives ['hauswaivz])家庭主妇;做家务的妇女 ②['hʌzif]([复]~wifes ['hʌzifs] 或 ~wives ['hʌzivz])针线盒 / '~wifely *a.* ①家庭主妇的;家庭主妇似的 ②持家节俭而井井有条的 / ~wifery ['hauswifəri] *n.* 家务,家政 / '~work *n.* 家务劳动

household ['haushould] I *n.* ①同住在一家的人;家庭,户: a peasant ~ 农户 / the head of a ~ 户主,家长 ②家务 ③[复]次等面粉 II *a.* ①家庭的: ~ duties 家务 / ~ expenses 家庭开支 / ~ wares 家庭用器具 ②家常的,普通的: a ~ remedy 家常药品 ‖a ~ word 家喻户晓的词(或用语) / ~ troops 王室禁卫军 ‖~er *n.* ①占有房子的人,住户 ②户主

housing ['hauziŋ] *n.* ①住房供给;住房建筑: a ~ project 住房建筑计划 / open ~ [美]黑人白人的自由混合居住 ②[总称]房屋,住房 ③遮蔽物;遮盖物 ④【建】柄穴 ⑤【机】套,壳: bearing ~ 轴承箱 / fan ~ 风扇壳 ⑥[海]桅脚

hove [houv] heave 的过去式和过去分词

hovel ['hɔvəl] *n.* ①陋屋; 放杂物的小房屋, 茅舍 ② 棚; 窖的圆锥形外壳

hover ['hɔvə] I ❶ *vi.* ①(鸟等)翱翔, 盘旋 (over, about) ②徘徊, 逗留在附近 (near, about): The mercury ～ed around 35°C. 气温停留在摄氏三十五度左右。③ 彷徨, 犹豫: ～ between the two alternatives 动摇于两种选择之间 ❷ *vt.* 伏窝孵化: a hen ～ing her chicks 正在伏窝的母鸡 II *n.* 翱翔; 徘徊 ‖'～craft *n.* 气垫船 / '～plane *n.* [英]直升飞机

how [hau] I *ad.* ①(指方式、方法)怎样, 怎么: How is it done? 这是怎样做的? / Tell us ～ you fulfilled the heavy task ahead of schedule. 告诉我们, 你们是怎样提前完成这一艰巨任务的。/ Do it ～ you can. 你能怎样做就怎样做好了。/ I don't know ～ to explain it. 我不知道怎样来说明它。②(指数量、程度)多少; 多么: How much baggage am I allowed to take? 我可以带多少行李? / How many students are there in your class? 你班上有多少学生? / How do you like the performance? 你觉得这场演出怎么样? / How old is he? 他(年龄)多大了? / How kind you are! 你多好啊! / How well she sings! 她唱得多么好! ③(指健康等情况)怎样: How are things in your factory? 你们工厂里情况怎样? ④(指价值)多少: How is the U.S. dollar today? 今天美元市价多少? ⑤(指原因或目的)怎么: How is it that you are still here? 你怎么还在这儿? ⑥[用于间接陈述中, 意义及作用和 that 相仿] II *n.* 方式, 方法: explain the ～s and whys of the issue 解释这问题的情况和原由 ‖And ～! 见 and / Here's ～! (祝酒时用)祝您身体健康! / How about ...? (你以为)…怎么样?: How about playing badminton now? 现在来打羽毛球好吗? / How are you? ① 你身体怎样? ②(招呼用语)你好! / How come ...? [美口]怎么会…的? / How do you do? 你好! (见面时用语, 尤用于被正式介绍见面时。说此话时, 对方也用同样的话回答) / How goes it ...? 你的情况怎样?: How goes it in your factory? 你们厂里情况怎么样? / How is that for ...? [口]好不…! 多么…!: How is that for high (或 queer)? 好不奇怪! / How is that for impudent (或impudence)? 多么放肆! / How much? ①(价钱)多少? ②[俚]什么? (要求对方重讲一遍时用; =[英] What? 或[美] How?) / How now? 这是什么意思? / How so? 怎么会这样的? 为什么?: The plan won't work. How so? 这个计划行不通吗? 怎么说的? / How's that? ①怎么会那样呢? ②你怎么看? / How the deuce (或 devil, 或 dickens) ...? …到底是怎么回事? / How then? 这是什么意思? ②后来怎样? 还有什么? ‖～-do-you-do ['haudju:'du:] *n.*, ～-d'ye-do ['hau-di'du:], ～-de-do ['haud'du:] *n.* [口]尴尬的局面 / '～-to *a.* 给以基本知识的: a ～-to book

基础知识书

howdah ['haudə] *n.* 象轿(驮在象或骆驼背上可供几人乘坐的亭子状坐位)

howe'er [hau'εə] *ad. & conj.* =however

however [hau'evə] I *ad.* ①无论如何, 不管怎样: However hard the task (may be), we must fulfil it in time. 不管任务多么艰巨, 我们必须及时完成它。②可是; 仍然: I'd like to go with you: ～, my hands are full. 我很想和你一块儿去, 可是我忙不过来。/ The composition is all right; there is room for improvement, ～. 这篇作文还不错, 不过还可以改进。II *conj.* ① 不管用什么方法: He can go ～ he likes. 他爱怎么去就怎么去好了。②[古]虽然

howl [haul] I *n.* ①(狼、狗等的)嗥叫 ②号叫, 嚎哭 ③(表示蔑视或高兴的)狂笑 ④[美俚]令人发笑的东西, 笑话 ⑤【无】啸鸣, 嗥鸣; 颤噪效应 II ❶ *vi.* ①嗥叫 ②号叫, 嚎哭 ③狂笑; 狂闹, 欢闹 ④(风等)怒吼, 怒号 ❷ *vt.* 狂喊着表示; 喝住: ～ down a speaker 叫喊得使人们听不到讲话者的声音

howler ['haulə] *n.* ①大声叫喊者 ②(南美的一种)吼猴 ③【无】嗥鸣器 ④[口]大错, 大笑话 ‖come a ～ 遭到失败

howling ['hauliŋ] I *a.* ①嗥叫的; 咆哮的 ②荒凉的, 凄凉的 ③[俚]极大的, 极度的, 显眼的: a ～ shame 一桩极为可耻的事情 / a ～ success 极大的成功 II *n.* 【无】啸声, 嗥鸣; 颤噪效应: acoustic ～ 音响啸声

hub [hʌb] *n.* ①【机】(轮)毂; 冲头 ②(兴趣、重要性、活动等的)中心: a ～ of commerce 商业中心 ③(电器面板上的)电线插孔 ‖from ～ to rim [美]完全, 从头至尾 / up to the ～ 深深陷入, 被完全缠住 ‖'～cap *n.* ①【机】毂盖 ②[美俚]骄傲自大的人

huddle ['hʌdl] I ❶ *vi.* ①挤作一团 (together) ②蜷缩 (up) ③聚在一起商量 ❷ *vt.* ① 乱堆, 乱挤 ②把…卷缩一团: ～ oneself up 把身体缩成一团 ③草草编造: ～ up a story 草率地结束一篇故事 / ～ a job through 草率地做完一件工作 ④把…隐藏起来 II *n.* ①(杂乱的)一团, 一堆, 一群 ②混乱 ③[美俚]秘密会议; 足球运动员在比赛过程中的战术磋商: go into a ～ with sb. 与某人秘密商议

hue[1] [hju:] *n.* ①形式, 样子 ② 颜色; 色彩 ‖～d *a.* [常用以构成复合词]有…颜色的: green-～d 绿色的

hue[2] [hju:] *n.* ‖a ～ and cry ① 追捕犯人时的叫喊声; 通缉令 ②嘈杂声; 叫喊声, (表示反对的)叫嚷: raise a ～ and cry against 掀起一阵大叫大嚷反对…

huff [hʌf] I ❶ *vt.* ① 把…吹胀; 提高(股票等)的价格 ②吓唬 ③激怒 ❷ *vi.* ①喷(或吹)气 ②进行恫吓 ③发怒 II *n.* 发怒: in a ～ 怒冲冲地 / take ～ 发怒

hug [hʌg] I (hugged; hugging) *vt.* ①紧抱,紧紧拥抱 ②(熊用前腿)抱住 ③[~ oneself] 使沾沾自喜,使深自庆幸: ~ oneself on (或 for) 因…而沾沾自喜 ④抱有,坚持(观点、信仰、偏见等) ⑤紧靠: The road ~s the river. 道路紧靠河边。II *n.* ① 紧紧拥抱: give sb. a big ~ 紧紧拥抱某人 ②(摔角中的)抱住 ③(熊用前腿的)紧抱 ‖'~-me-tight *n.* (女子的)紧身短马甲

huge [hju:dʒ] *a.* 巨大的,庞大的,其大无比的 ‖~ly *ad.* / ~ness *n.*

hulk [hʌlk] I *n.* ①巨大笨重的船 ②巨大笨重的人(或物) ③废船船体;用作仓库的废船;[常用复]【史】用作监狱的船,囚船 ④(房屋等的)残骸,外壳 II *vi.* ① [英方]笨重地移动(或走动) ②显得巨大 (up) ‖~ing *a.* 庞大的;笨重的

hull [hʌl] I *n.* ①(果、实等的)外壳;豆荚: shrimp ~s 虾壳 ②[海]壳;船壳,船体 ③【空】机身,(飞船的)船身 II *vt.* ①去…的壳 ②(用炮弹、鱼雷等)打穿…的船壳 ‖~ down (船只)远在只见桅杆、看不到船身的地方;(坦克等)藏在能观察到敌人并能向其射击的隐蔽处

hullabaloo [ˌhʌləbə'lu:] *n.* 喧嚣,吵闹: raise (或 make) a ~ 大吵大嚷

hum[1] [hʌm] I (hummed; humming) ❶ *vi.* ①(蜜蜂等)发嗡嗡声 ②发哼哼声;哼曲子: She was humming to herself. 她独自哼着歌。③[口]忙碌,充满活气: make things ~ 使气氛活跃起来 ④[俚]发出难闻的气味 ❷ *vt.* ①哼(歌): ~ a song 哼一首歌 ②哼着歌使…: ~ a child to sleep 哼着歌使孩子入睡 II *n.* ①嗡嗡声;哼哼声;嘈杂声 ②[俚]恶臭 ‖~ and haw (或 ha) 嗯嗯呃呃(表示踌躇或支吾等) / ~s and ha's (说话中踌躇时的)嗯嗯支吾声

hum[2] [hʌm] *int.* ①哼[表示不满、怀疑、轻视、惊奇、高兴等] ②嗯哼(清嗓以引人注意时发出的声音)

hum[3] [hʌm] *n.* [俚]欺骗

human ['hju:mən] I *a.* ①人的;人类的: a ~ being 人 / the ~ race 人类 / ~ history 人类历史 ②凡人皆有的,显示人的特点的 ③有人性的;通人情的 II *n.* 人(= being) ‖~ly *ad.* ①从人的角度①在人力所及范围 ②充满人性地 /~ness *n.* ‖~ engineering ①人事管理 (尤指工业企业内的人事管理) ② 机械设备利用学(指专门研究人类如何充分利用机械设备的科学) / ~ nature 人性

humane [hju(:)'mein] *a.* ①仁慈的, 人道的: ~ treatment 人道的待遇 ②(指学科而言)使人文雅的, 高尚的 ‖~ly *ad.* / ~ness *n.* ‖~ killer 牲口无痛屠宰机 / Humane Society ①[英]拯救溺水者协会 ②慈善协会;保护动物协会

humanism ['hju:mənizəm] *n.* 人文主义,人本主义,人道主义 ‖humanist *n.* 人文主义者,人本主义者,人道主义者

humanistic [ˌhju:mə'nistik] *a.* 人文主义的,人本主义的,人道主义的

humanitarian [hju(:)ˌmæni'tɛəriən] I *n.* ①博爱主义者,慈善家 ②人道主义者 II *a.* ①博爱的,慈善的 ②人道主义的 ‖~ism *n.* ①博爱主义 ②人道主义 ③【宗】基督凡人论

humanity [hju(:)'mæniti] *n.* ① 人性;[复]人的属性(尤指美德) ②人类;(许多)人: a great contribution to ~ 对人类的一大贡献 ③博爱,仁慈;[复]仁慈的行为 ‖the humanities ①希腊、拉丁文学;古典文学 ②人文学科(通常包括语言、文学、哲学等): There are eight departments in the humanities. 文科共有八个系。

humanize ['hju:mənaiz] ❶ *vt.* ①使成为人;使具有人的属性,赋与…人性: ~d milk 经过处理变得似人乳的牛奶 ②使变得仁慈博爱 ❷ *vi.* ①变得仁慈博爱 ②具有(或传播)博爱思想 ‖humanization [ˌhju:mənai'zeiʃən] *n.* 人性化;博爱化

humble ['hʌmbl] I *a.* ①谦卑的;恭顺的: in my ~ opinion 据本人愚见 ②地位低下的;(动、植物等)低级的 II *vt.* ①压低(地位、身分等);使…的威信(或权力)丧失殆尽: ~ sb.'s pride 压下某人气焰 ②使谦卑: ~ oneself 自卑, 低声下气 ‖eat ~ pie 见 pie[1] ‖~ness *n.* / humbly *ad.* ‖'~-bee *n.* 野蜂

humbug ['hʌmbʌg] I *n.* ①欺骗, 欺瞒 ②骗子;吹牛的人 ③空话,骗人的鬼话;用来骗人的东西;骗人之举: Humbug! 胡扯! ④一种薄荷糖果 II (humbugged; humbugging) ❶ *vt.* 欺骗;哄骗: ~ sb. into doing sth. 骗某人做某事 / ~ sb. out of sth. 向某人骗取某物 ❷ *vi.* 行骗

humdrum ['hʌmdrʌm] I *a.* 单调的;平凡的;无聊的 II *n.* ①单调;无聊 ②无聊话 ③无聊的人 III (humdrummed; humdrumming) *vi.* 作单调的动作 ‖~ness *n.*

humid ['hju:mid] *a.* 湿的, 湿气重的: ~ air 湿空气 ‖~ly *ad.* / ~ness *n.*

humiliate [hju(:)'milieit] *vt.* 羞辱, 使丢脸: ~ oneself 丢脸,出丑 ‖humiliating *a.* 丢脸的,羞辱性的 / humiliation [hju(:)ˌmili'eiʃən] *n.* 羞辱,蒙耻: bring humiliation upon sb. 使某人蒙受耻辱 / humiliator *n.* 羞辱者

humility [hju(:)'militi] *n.* ①谦卑 ②[复]谦卑的行为

hummock ['hʌmək] *n.* ①小圆丘,圆岗;波状地 ②(冰原上的)冰丘 ③沼泽中的高地

humorous ['hju:mərəs] *a.* 富于幽默的; 有幽默感的 ‖~ly *ad.* / ~ness *n.*

humo(u)r ['hju:mə] I *n.* ①幽默,诙谐;幽默感: have a (no) sense of ~ 有(缺乏)幽默感 / a man without ~ 没有幽默感的人 ②幽默的东西: a ~ magazine 幽默杂志 / Have you read any ~ recently? 近来读到过什么幽默的东西吗? ③脾性;情绪,心情: in a good (bad) ~ 情绪好(不好) / out of ~ 情绪不好 / in the ~ for sth. 有做某事的心情 / When the ~ takes him, he can . . . 当他有兴致的时候,他能…… ④(动物的)体液(=

物的)汁液: aqueous (vitreous) ~ 【解】水样(玻璃状)液 ⑤古怪念头,想入非非 II vt. ①使满足;迁就: ~ a child 哄孩子 ②使自己适应于 ③(针对特点)用技巧调理(或拨弄): Don't force the lock, you must ~ it. 不要硬去把那锁头搞开,你应想个巧办法才好。‖~ed a. [用以构成复合词]脾气…的: good-~ed 性情好的 / ~less a. 缺乏幽默感的;一本正经的 / ~some ['hju:-məsəm] a. 幽默滑稽的;古怪的

hump [hʌmp] I n. ①(驼)峰;(一些动物背部的)隆肉 ②驼背 ③小圆丘,小丘 ④山脉: the Hump 喜马拉雅山脉(第二次世界大战中美英飞行员用语) ⑤[英]忧郁: give sb. the ~ 使某人垂头丧气 / get (或 have) the ~ 闷闷不乐 ⑥危机 ⑦费力 II ❶ vt. ①使作弓状隆起: The cat ~ed its back. 猫弓起了背。②[~ oneself] [美俚]使努力苦干 ③[英]把…背在背上;搬运 ❷ vi. ①努力,苦干 ②急速移动;飞跑 ③隆起 ‖get a ~ on 赶紧 ②苦干 / get sb. on the ~ 使某人大费力气 / hit the ~ [美俚]越狱;开小差 / over the ~ 已越过最困难(或危险)阶段;(服苦役等)已度过一半时间 ‖~ed a. 驼背的;有隆肉的 / ~less a. 无驼肉的 ‖'~back n. ①驼背,弓背 ②驼背者 ③【动】座头鲸 / '~backed a. 驼背的

humph [mm, hʌmf] I int. 哼! [表示怀疑、不满等] II vi. 发"哼"声 III n. "哼"的一声

humus ['hju:məs] n. 腐殖质, 腐殖土壤: ~ soil 【农】腐殖土

hunch [hʌntʃ] I ❶ vt. ①使(背部等)弯成弓状;使隆起: ~ up one's shoulders 耸起双肩 ② 推: ~ one's chair closer to the table 把椅子推近桌子 ❷ vi. ①向前移动 ②弯成弓状;隆起: ~ over the steering wheel 弯身坐在驾驶盘前 II n. ①肉峰,隆肉 ②厚片,大块 ③推 ④[口]预感· I have a ~ that.... 我总感到…‖'~back n. 驼背;驼背者 / '~backed a. 驼背的

hundred ['hʌndrəd, 'hʌndrid] I num. 百;百个(人或物): a (或 one) ~ men 一百个人 / two ~ and twenty-two items 二百二十二个项目(例中的 and 在美国常略) / several ~(s) of (或 several ~) foreign guests 几百位外宾 / some ~ persons 约一百人 / some ~s of persons 几百人 / born in nineteen ~ 生于一九〇〇年 / in the nineteen ~s 在一九〇〇到一九九九年间 / eight ~ hours (上午)八点(二十四小时连续计时制说法,常写作 0800 hours) / sixteen ~ thirty hours 十六点三十分(常写作 1630 hours, 即下午四点半) II n. ①一百个(人 或 物)一组 ②[复]数以百计;许多: ~s of examples 许许多多例子 ③[英]一百镑;[美]一百美元;一百美元票面的钞票 ④【英史】郡的分区;【美史】县的分区 ⑤百岁: live to (be) a ~ 活到一百岁 III a. 许多: We have a ~ things to do. 我们有许多事情要做。‖a cool ~ [口]百镑巨款;巨款 / a ~ and one 许多: in a ~ and one ways 千方百计 / a ~ percent 百分之百;完全 / by the ~ (或 by ~s) 数以百计;大批大批地 / great (或 long) ~ 一百二十 / ~s

and thousands 撒在糕饼等上面作点缀的蜜饯(或小糖果) / like a ~ of bricks [口]以压倒的势力;来势猛烈地 / ninety-nine out of a ~ 百分之九十九,几乎全部 / the four ~ [美]美国的四百豪富家族 ‖~fold a. & ad. 一百倍;一百重 / ~th num. ① 第一百(个) ② 百分之一(的): five ~ths 百分之五 ‖'~-per'cent a. 百分之百的;完全的 / '~-per'center n. 极端民族主义者 / '~-per'centism n. 极端民族主义 / '~weight n. 英担(衡量名; 在英国等于一百十二磅,也称作 long ~weight; 在美国等于一百磅,也称作 short ~weight; 均略作 cwt.)

hung [hʌŋ] I hang 的过去式和过去分词 II a. [美俚]堕入情网的

hunger ['hʌŋgə] I n. ①饥饿;长期挨饿所造成的虚弱: die of (或 from) ~ 饿死 ②食欲 ③[喻]欲望, 渴望 (for, after) II ❶ vi. ① 挨饿 ② 渴望 (for, after) ❷ vt. 使挨饿 ‖Hunger is the best sauce. [谚]饥者口中尽佳肴。/ ~ march 反饥饿示威游行 / ~ strike 绝食(尤指狱中的抗议行动) / '~-strike vi. 举行绝食抗议

hungry ['hʌŋgri] a. ①饥饿的;显出饥饿样子的: I am (或 feel) ~. 我饿了。/ go ~ 挨饿 / a ~ look (脸上的)饥色 ②[可用以构成复合词]渴望的: be ~ for knowledge 渴望知识 ③[罕]促进食欲的 ④(土壤等)贫瘠的,不毛的 ‖as ~ as a hunter 非常饥饿的 ‖hungrily ad. / hungriness n.

hunk[1] [hʌŋk] n. [口]大块, 大片, 厚块: a ~ of bread (meat) 一大块面包(肉)

hunk[2] [hʌŋk] a. [美俚] ①行的,好的,可以的: He now felt himself all ~. 他现在感到恢复正常了。②相等的,两相抵销的: get ~ on sb. (或 with sb. good) 向某人报复

hunt [hʌnt] I ❶ vt. ①追猎, 猎取: ~ lions 猎狮 ②在…中行猎: ~ the woods 在树林中打猎 ③驱使(或指挥)…行猎: ~ a pack of hounds 带着一群猎狗打猎 ④追赶;搜索; 追获: ~ the cat out of the kitchen 把猫赶出厨房 ❷ vi. ①打猎 ②(兽类等)猎食: Wolves ~ in packs. 狼是成群猎食的。③搜寻 ④【电】摆动,振荡 II n. ①打猎 ②猎队 ③猎区 ④搜索,搜寻 ‖~ down 穷追…直至捕获; 搜寻…直至发现 / ~ for (或 after) 追寻…; 搜寻…; ~ for novelty 猎奇 / ~ out 搜寻出 / ~ up 猎取;搜寻… / still ~ 暗中活动

hunter ['hʌntə] n. ①猎人 ②猎食其他动物的野兽 ③猎犬 ④猎马 ⑤猎用表(=hunting watch) ⑥搜索者;搜寻者 ‖as hungry as a ~ 非常饥饿的 ‖~'s moon 狩猎季节的满月(指紧接收获季节满月后的第一次满月)

hunting ['hʌntiŋ] n. ①打猎 ②搜索, 搜寻: leak ~ 【电】泄漏点寻觅 ③【电】摆动;不规则的振荡;寄生振荡 ‖~ boot 猎靴 / ~ box [主英]猎舍 / ~ cap 猎帽 / ~ case 猎用表的表盒 / ~ crop 猎鞭 / ~ field, ~ ground 猎场 / ~ horn 猎

号 / ~ **knife** 猎刀(一种短尖刀,用以杀死猎物或切割兽肉、切剥兽皮等) / ~ **watch** 猎用表

huntsman ['hʌntsmən] (【复】huntsmen) n. ①猎人 ②管猎犬的人 ‖~**ship** n. 打猎术

hurdle ['hə:dl] I n. ①(用树枝等编成的)临时活动篱笆 ②(赛马用)栏;(赛跑用)跳栏: the high (low) ~s 高(低)栏赛跑 ③【史】旧时英国送犯人到刑场的囚笼 ④障碍: The final ~s have been removed. 最后的障碍已被排除了。 II vt. ①篱笆围 (off) ②跳过(栏);越过 ③克服(障碍) ‖~**r** n. ①跳栏运动员 ②制篱笆者;制栏者 ‖~ **race** 跳栏赛跑

hurl [hə:l] I ❶ vt. ①猛投, 猛掷: ~ a spear at a wild animal 掷矛去刺野兽 ②猛推 ③激烈地叫出(或说出): Insults were ~ed back and forth. 双方口出恶言,互相辱骂。 ❷ vi. ①猛投,猛掷 ②猛冲,猛撞 II n. 猛投,猛掷 ‖~**er** n. 投掷者

hurly-burly ['hə:li,bə:li] n. 骚乱,喧闹

hurrah [hu'rɑː], **hurray** [hu'rei] I int. 哇哇! II n. ①"好哇"的欢呼声 ②激动 ③纷争 III vt. & vi. (向…)高喊"好哇" ‖**hurrah's nest** [美俚]大混乱的场所;乱糟糟的东西

hurricane ['hʌrikən] n. ①飓风,十二级风 ②象飓风般猛烈的东西;(感情等的)爆发: a ~ of blows 一阵猛烈的打击 ‖~ **bird** 军舰鸟 / ~ **deck** 最上层甲板,飓风甲板 / ~ **globe** (灯、烛等的)防风罩 / ~ **lamp** 防风灯

hurried ['hʌrid] a. ①匆促的; 慌忙的: eat a ~ meal 匆匆吃一顿饭 ②急速的 ‖~**ly** ad. / ~**ness** n.

hurry ['hʌri] I n. ①匆忙,仓促;急切: In his ~ he forgot to leave his address. 匆忙间他忘了留下地址。 / Why all this ~? 为什么这样急? ②[用于疑问句及否定句中]必须赶紧的理由: What's the ~? 干吗这么急? / There is no ~ for it. 没有必要这么急急匆匆。 ③混乱,骚动 II ❶ vt. ①使赶紧;使加快;催促: ~ one's pace 加快脚步 / Hurry him, or he'll be late. 催他一下,不然他要迟到了。 ②急派;急运: More people have been hurried to the construction site. 已赶紧派出更多的人到建筑工地去了。 / ~ forward supplies 把供应品赶紧运去 ❷ vi. 赶紧; 匆忙: No need to ~. 不必急急匆匆。 / ~ to sb.'s rescue 赶紧去救援某人 ‖~ away (或 off) ①匆匆离去 ②使赶快离开 / ~ through 匆匆赶完: ~ through a book 匆匆看完一本书 / ~ up ①赶紧: Hurry up, or we'll be late. 快一些,不然咱们要迟到了。 ②使赶快 / in a ~ ①匆忙: be in a tearing ~ to catch the train 性急火燎地去赶火车 ②很快地; 一下子很容易地: The humour of it is not to be absorbed in a ~. 其中的幽默不是一下子能领会的。 ③[口]情愿地 ‖~-'up a. ①匆忙的;(工作等)紧急的,突击性的 ②应付紧急事故的: a ~-up waggon 急修车,抢险车

hurt [hə:t] I (hurt) ❶ vt. ①刺痛; 使受伤痛 ②危害,损害 ③伤…的感情,使痛心; 使(感情)受到创

伤: feel ~ 感到自尊心受了伤害 / It ~s me to think that …. 想到…我感到痛心。 ❷ vi. ①刺痛;伤痛: These new shoes ~. 穿着这双新鞋脚有点痛。②危害;损害: The rain may hold off, but it won't ~ to take an umbrella with you. 雨可能下不下来,不过带把伞去总没有坏处。③[方]需要 II n. 伤痛;伤害;(精神、感情上的)创伤 ‖~**less** a. [古]无害的

hurtle ['hə:tl] I ❶ vi. ①猛烈碰撞; 发出碰撞声 ②猛飞,急飞 ❷ vt. ①猛投,猛掷 ②[古]使猛烈冲撞 II n. 碰撞

husband ['hʌzbənd] I n. ①丈夫 ②[英]管家 ③节俭的管理人 II vt. ①节俭地使用(或经营) ②[罕]做…的丈夫 ③[谑]谨慎使用 ④[古]耕(地); 栽培(植物) ‖~**age** ['hʌzbəndidʒ] n. 船主付给船舶管理人的佣金 / ~**like** a. 善于管理农活的 / ~**ly** a. ①善于管理农活的 ②丈夫(般)的 ‖~**man** ['hʌzbəndmən] n. 农民

husbandry ['hʌzbəndri] n. ①耕作;家畜的科学管理: animal ~ 畜牧业 ②家政;节俭

hush [hʌʃ] I ❶ vt. ①使不作声; 使静下: ~ a baby to sleep 哄使婴儿安静入睡 / listen with ~ed attention 默不作声全神贯注地倾听 ②压下…不作张扬,遮掩: ~ sth. up 把某事包起来秘而不宣 ❷ vi. 静下来, 沉默下来: Hush up! 别作声! II n. 静寂;沉默 ②秘而不宣 III [ʃ:, ʃ:] int. 嘘! 别作声! ‖~ **money** 封住嘴巴的贿赂

hush-hush ['hʌʃ'hʌʃ] I a. 秘密的, 秘而不宣的 II n. 秘密气氛;保密政策: Why all the ~ about it? 为什么这么秘密? III vt. ①勒得…闭嘴不作声 ②压下…不作张扬

husk [hʌsk] I n. ①外皮;壳;荚;外果壳 ②[喻]毫无价值的外表部分 ③支架 ④牛瘟 II vt. 除去…的外壳(或外皮): ~ rice 舂糙米

husky ['hʌski] I a. ①结实的, 强健的; 大个子的 ②庞大的,强大的 II n. 强健结实的人

hussar [hu'zɑː] n. (欧洲)轻骑兵(以军服花哨著称)

hussy ['hʌsi] n. ①轻佻的女子,荡妇 ②鲁莽的少女

hustings ['hʌstiŋz] [复] n. [用作单或复] ①【史】议员竞选演说坛; [喻]发表竞选演说的地方 ②选举程序 ③地方法院

hustle ['hʌsl] I ❶ vt. ①硬挤; 乱推; 乱敲 ②挤道,逼使: ~ sb. into a decision 强使某人作出决定 ③[口]使匆匆做成 ④强卖;强夺(尤指用不正当手段) ❷ vi. ①硬挤过去; 奔忙 ②[口]使赶快做 ③非法经营(尤指诱人赌钱、处女拉客等) II n. ①匆忙; 推 ②[口]努力: Get a ~ on! 快干! 使劲干! ③拉生意的骗局 ‖~**r** n. ①乱挤乱推的人(尤指与扒手合作的同伙等) ②非法挣钱的人(尤指妓女等) ③精力充沛的人

hut [hʌt] I n. ①小屋; 棚屋 ②临时木建营房 ③[美俚]监房 II (hutted; hutting) vt. & vi. (使)住进小屋, (使)住进临时营房

hutch [hʌtʃ] I n. ①(盛物用的)箱, 橱; 碗橱 ②(动物、家禽的)笼, 舍; 兔箱 ③小屋, 棚屋

④【矿】洗矿槽; 跳汰机筛下室; 通过跳汰机筛板的细条 ⑤矿车 II *vt.* ①把…装在箱内 ②【矿】在洗矿槽里洗(矿)

hyacinth ['haiəsinθ] *n.* ①【矿】红锆石 ②【植】风信子 ③紫蓝色 ‖**~ine** [,haiə'sinθain] *a.*

hyaena [hai'i:nə] *n.* =hyena

hybrid ['haibrid] I *n.* ①【生】杂种 ②混血儿; 由两种不同的文化传统教育出来的人 ③混合源物 ④(由不同民族语言中的词组成的)混合词(如 hydroplane, sociology) ⑤【无】混合波导联结; 桥接岔路, 等差作用 II *a.* 混合的; 杂种的 ‖**~ism** *n.* ①杂交; 混血; 杂成 ②杂种性; 混合性; 杂种状态 / **~ity** [hai'briditi] *n.* 杂种性 ‖**~ computer** (模拟、数字)混合型计算机

hydra ['haidrə] ([复] hydras 或 hydrae ['haidri:]) *n.* ①[H-]【希神】九头蛇 ②多源的、难以一举根绝的祸害, 大患 ③ [H-]【天】长蛇座 ④【动】水螅 ‖**~-headed** *a.* 多头的, 多中心的; 多分支的

hydrant ['haidrənt] *n.* 消防龙头; 配水龙头, 给水栓, 取水管

hydraulic [hai'drɔ:lik] *a.* ①水力的; 液力的 ②水力学的 ③水压的; 液压的 ④【建】水硬的: ~ cement (lime) 水硬水泥(石灰) ‖**~ally** *ad.* ‖**~ brake**【机】水力闸; 闸式水力测功器 / **~ press** 水压机 / **~ ram** 水力夯锤; 压力扬吸机

hydro¹ ['haidrou] *n.* [英] ①水疗处 ②接待水疗病人的旅馆

hydro² ['haidrou] *a.* =hydroelectric

hydroelectric ['haidrou-i'lektrik] *a.* 水力发电的: a ~ (power) station 水电站

hydrogen ['haidridʒən, 'haidrədʒən] *n.*【化】氢: ~ peroxide 过氧化氢 / ~ sulphide 硫化氢 ‖**~ bomb** 氢弹(常略作 H-bomb)

hyena [hai'i:nə] *n.* ①【动】鬣狗 ②残酷 (或阴险、贪婪)的人

hygiene ['haidʒi:n] *n.* 卫生学; 卫生术: personal ~ 个人卫生

hygienic(al) [hai'dʒi:nik(əl)] *a.* ①卫生学的 ②卫生的; 促进健康的

hymn [him] I *n.* ①【宗】赞美诗, 圣歌 ②赞歌 II *vt. & vi.* (为…)唱赞美诗 ‖**~al** ['himnəl] *n.* 赞美诗集 *a.* 赞美诗的; 使用赞美诗的 / **~ist** ['himnist] *n.* 赞美诗作者 ‖**~book** *n.* 赞美诗集

hyperbole [hai'pə:bəli] *n.*【语】夸张法

hyphen ['haifən] I *n.* 连字号(即 -) II *vt.* 用连字号连接

hypnosis [hip'nousis] ([复] hypnoses [hip'nousi:z]) *n.* ①催眠; 催眠状态: be under ~ 处于催眠状态 ②催眠术; 催眠术研究

hypnotize ['hipnətaiz] *vt.* ①使进入催眠状态 ②使着迷 ‖**hypnotization** [,hipnətai'zeiʃən] *n.*

hypocrisy [hi'pɔkrəsi] *n.* 伪善, 虚伪

hypocritic(al) [,hipə'kritik(əl)] *a.* 伪善的, 虚伪的 ‖**hypocritically** *ad.*

hypodermic [,haipə'də:mik] I *a.* ①皮下的; 皮下组织的: ~ injection 皮下注射 ②皮下注射用的: a ~ needle 皮下注射针头; 安上针头的皮下注射器 ③刺激性的 II *n.* ①皮下注射 ②皮下注射器 (=~ syringe) ‖**~ally** *ad.*

hypotenuse [hai'pɔtinju:z] *n.*【数】弦, 斜边: ~ of a right triangle 直角三角形的斜边

hypothesis [hai'pɔθisis] ([复] hypotheses [hai'pɔθisi:z]) *n.* ①假设 ②【逻】前提

hysteria [his'tiəriə] *n.* ①【医】癔病 ②歇斯底里: war ~ 战争歇斯底里

hysterical [his'terikəl] *a.* ①癔病的; 歇斯底里的 ②患癔病的 ‖**~ly** *ad.*

I

I [ai] I *pron.* [主格]我: I am very busy. 我很忙。(口语常用 I'm very busy.) / It is I. 是我。(口语常用 It's me.) II ([复] I's 或 Is [aiz]) *n.* ①自我 ②极端自私的人; 说起话来老是"我怎么怎么"的人 ③[the I] 自我意识 ‖**I CAN CATCH** (或 **I Can Catch**) [美国]州际商务委员会(美国)(由该机构的缩略形式 ICC 化出)

ice [ais] I *n.* ①冰; 冰块: artificial ~ 人造冰 / dry ~ 干冰(即固体二氧化碳) / ~ water 冰(冻的)水 ②冰制食品; 冰淇淋; 冰状物: water ~ 冰糕 / two ~s 两客冰淇淋 ③冰状物; 糖衣, 糖霜(指撒在糕饼上的冰糖屑) ④ (态度等的)冷若冰霜 ⑤[俚]钻石 ⑥贿赂; 为弄到好票子私下付给剧院工作人员的钱 II ❶ *vt.* ①冰冻; 使成冰: an ~d melon 冰冻西瓜 / His refusal ~d our enthusiasm. 他的拒绝把我们的热情打消了。②用冰覆盖: The river was ~d over. 河给冰封起来了。 ③在(糕饼等)上面涂上糖霜(或糖衣) ❷ *vi.* 结冰 (up, over): prevent the wings of the aircraft from *icing up* 不使机翼结冰 ‖**break the ~** 打破沉默, 开个头; 使气氛活跃起来 / **cut no ~** 不起作用, 无效 / **on ~** [俚] 在狱中 / **on thin ~** 如履薄冰, 处境极其危险 / **piss on ~** 生活阔绰 / **put ... on ~** ①把…暂时搁起; 把…遗忘 ②杀死… ③有把握地把…握在手中 / **skate over thin ~** 谈论棘手的问题 ‖**~ age** ①【地】冰期 ②冰

ice ax(e)

河时代(略作 I & A) / **~ ax(e)** 破冰斧(爬山砍冰用) / **~ bag** 冰袋 / **'~berg** *n.* ① 冰山；流冰 ② (感情上) 冷冰冰的人 / **'~blink** *n.* 冰原反光 / **'~boat** *n.* ① 在冰上滑行的船 ② =~-breaker / **'~bound** *a.* 冰封住的: the ~bound season 封冻期 / **'~box** *n.* ① 冰箱 ② [俚] 单人牢房 ③ [美俚] 严寒地带 ④ [美俚] 供演员上台前培养感情的后台小房间; 供球员上场前做准备运动的地方 / **'~.breaker** *n.* 冰船; 破冰设备 / **~ cap** *n.* [地] 冰帽 ② 头戴式冰袋 / **~ chest** =~box / **~-'cold** *a.* 冰冷的, 极冷的 / **~ cream** 冰淇淋 / **'~-cream** *a.* 乳白色的 / **'~-fall** *n.* 冰布 (指冰川的陡峭部分); 冰崩 / **~ field** (两极地方的)冰原 / **~ floe** 大浮冰 / **'~-free** *a.* 不冻的: an ~-free harbour 不冻港 / **~ hockey** [体]冰球, 冰上曲棍球 / **'~-house** *n.* 冰窖; 制冰场所 / **'~jam** *n.* ① 流冰壅塞 ② 阻塞, 僵局 / **~khana** ['ais,ka:nə] *n.* 冰上汽车比赛 / **~ machine** 制冰机 / **'~man** *n.* ① 零售冰的人 ② 善于在冰上行走的人 ③ 制冰的人 / **~ pack** ① (飘浮海上的) 大片冰积块群 ② 冰袋 / **~ pick** (餐桌上用的)碎冰锥 / **~ plant** [植]冰叶日中花 / **'~show** 冰上表演 / **'~-skate** *vi.* 溜冰 / **'~-tray** *n.* (冰箱内)制冰块的盘子

icing ['aisiŋ] *n.* ①(糕饼表层的)糖霜, 酥皮 ②[空]结冰

icon ['aikɔn] *n.* ①人像, 画像; 肖像; 雕像 ②[宗]圣像 ③偶像; 崇拜的对象 ‖**~ic** [ai'kɔnik] *a.* ① 人像的; 圣像的; 偶像的; 似偶像的 ②传统的, (人像, 胸像)风格固定的

icy ['aisi] *a.* ① 冰的, 多冰的; 冰覆盖着的: ~ waters 结冰的河水 / ~ roads 覆盖着冰的路 ② 冰似的, 冰冷的: an ~ wind 寒风 ③冷冰冰的, 冷淡的; 不友好的: an ~ welcome 冷淡的欢迎

I'd [aid] [口] =I had; I would; I should

idea [ai'diə] *n.* ①思想; 概念: the general ~ of an article 文章大意 / He has a clear ~ of his responsibility. 他清楚地知道自己的职责是什么。②意见 ③主意, 念头; 打算; 计划: a man full of ~s 主意很多的人 / That's the ~! 是这个意思。(或: 对啦!) / What an ~! (或 The ~ of such a thing!) 多傻的念头啊! / the young ~ 小孩子的想法 ④想象; 模糊的想法: I have no ~ (of) what he said. 你根本想象不到他说了些什么。⑤[哲]理念; 观念: absolute ~ 绝对观

念 ‖*at the bare ~ of* 一想起…就… / *get ~s into one's head* 抱不切实际的想法 / *put ~s in sb.'s head* 使某人存奢望; 使某人得意忘形 / *the big ~* [美][讽] 计划; 建议; 行动: What's the big ~? 有何高见? ‖**~less** *a.* 没思想的; 没主意的 ‖**~ man** 谋士

ideal [ai'diəl] Ⅰ *a.* ① 理想的, 称心如意的, 完美的: an ~ place for camping 野营的理想场所 ② 观念的, 概念的 ③ 空想的, 虚构的, 不切实际的 ④ 唯心论的; 理想主义的 Ⅱ *n.* ① 理想 ②思想, 观念 ③完美的典型, 模范 ④假想中的事物 ⑤最终的目的, 鹄的 ⑥[数]理想子环, 理想子代数, 理想数: ~ point 理想点; 假点, 伪点 ‖**~ism** *n.* ① 唯心主义, 唯心论; 观念论; 理念论: subjective ~ism 主观唯心主义 / objective ~ism 客观唯心主义 / historical ~ism 历史唯心主义 ②理想主义 / **~ist** *n.* ①唯心主义者, 唯心论者 ②理想主义者; 空想家 *a.* ① 唯心主义的, 唯心论的: the ~ist conception of history 唯心(历)史观 ② 理想主义的; 空想家的 / **~ly** *ad.*

idealistic [ai,diə'listik] *a.* ① 唯心主义者的; 理想主义者的; 空想家的 ②唯心论的 ‖**~ally** *ad.*

idealize [ai'diəlaiz] ❶ *vt.* 使理想化; 使观念化 ❷ *vi.* ①形成理想(或观念) ②用唯心的(或理想主义的)方式表现事物; 作理想化的解释, 持理想化的看法 ‖**idealization** [ai,diəlai'zeiʃən] *n.*

identical [ai'dentikəl] *a.* ① 同一的: This is the ~ place where we stopped before. 这就是我们从前停留过的地方。/ the same (或 very) ~ person 就是同一个人 ② 完全相同的, 相等的: We have ~ views on these problems. 在这些问题上我们有完全一致的看法。/ My opinion is ~ with his. 我的意见和他的意见相同。③有同一原因的, 有同一来源的 ④[数]恒等的; [生]同卵的: ~ equation 恒等式 / ~ twins 同卵双生 ‖**~ly** *ad.* 同一; 同样

identification [ai,dentifi'keiʃən] *n.* ①认出, 识别; 鉴定; 验明: the ~ of high yielding seeds 高产量种子的鉴别 / a target ~ bomb [军]目标识别炸弹 ② 身分的证明: He used a letter of introduction as ~. 他用一封介绍信作为身分的证明。/ an ~ tag (记有士兵姓名、军号、血型等的) 身分证明牌 ③[心]自居作用(以理想中的某人自居的一种变态心理)

identify [ai'dentifai] ❶ *vt.* ① 使等同于, 认为…一致 (*with*) ② 认出; 识别; 鉴定, 验明: ~ one's baggage among hundreds of others 在几百件行李中认出自己的行李来 /~ the payee of a cheque 验明支票的受款人 ③[生]确定…在分类学上的位置: ~ a biological specimen 鉴定生物学的标本在分类学上的位置 ❷ *vi.* 一致, 成为一致 ‖**oneself with** ① 和…打成一片 ② 参加到…中去

identity [ai'dentiti] *n.* ① 同一(性); 一致: ~ of thinking and being 思维与存在的同一性 / reach (an) ~ of views 取得一致的看法 / establish the

~ of lost goods 证实失物与失主所报相符合 ② 身分;正身;本体;个性,特性: establish (或 prove) sb.'s ~ 证明某人的身分 / an ~ certificate 身分证明书 / an ~ card 身分证 / because of mistaken ~ 由于被错认了人 ③【数】恒等(式)

ideology [,aidi'ɔledʒi] *n.* ①思想(体系);思想意识: in the realm of politics and ~ 在政治思想领域内 ②思想方式;意识形态,观念形态 ③空想,空论 ④ 观念学 ‖*socialist* ~ 社会主义思想

idiom ['idiəm] *n.* ①习语,成语 ②语言习惯用法;(某一)语言的特性: This expression is against ~. 这一表达方式不合乎语言习惯。③(某一民族、地区或行业的)语言;方言: the ~ of the Middle West 美国中西部地区的方言 ④(某一作家、艺术家等的)风格,特色

idiomatic [,idiə'mætik] *a.* ①符合语言习惯的;成语的: an ~ expression 惯用表达法 / speak ~ English 说一口道地的英语 ②用许多习语的,富于习语的 ③ 富有习语性质的 ④(某一团体或个人)特有的,独特的 ‖**~ally** *ad.* / **~ness** *n.*

idiosyncrasy [,idiə'siŋkrəsi] *n.* ①(人的)特质,特性,癖性 ②(作者)特有的风格 ③【医】特(异反)应性;特异体质 ‖**idiosyncratic** [,idiəsin'krætik] *a.*

idiot ['idiət] *n.* ①白痴 ②[口]傻子,极端愚蠢的人 ‖**~ board, ~ card** [美俚]电视台演员的提词板

idle ['aidl] **I** *a.* ①空闲的,闲着的: ~ machines (capital) 闲置的机器(资本) / lie ~ 被搁置不用 ②[喻]空转的: an ~ wheel 惰轮;空转轮;调紧皮带轮 ③懒散的;无所事事的: an ~ fellow 游手好闲的家伙 ④ 无用的;无效的;无根据的: It would be ~ to argue further. 再辩论下去也不会有什么效果。/ an ~ dream 痴心妄想 / an ~ rumour 毫无根据的谣传 **II** ❶ *vt.* ①虚度,空费: Don't ~ *away* your precious time. 不要把大好时光浪费掉。②使空闲;使闲滞: a strike ~d dock 因罢工而瘫痪的码头 ③使(发动机等)空转 ❷ *vi.* ①懒散;闲逛;无所事事 (*about, along*) ②【机】空转;慢转 ‖**~ness** *n.* live in ~ness 游手好闲 / **~r** *n.* ①游手好闲者;懒汉 ②【机】惰轮;空转轮;调紧皮带轮 ③【机】空载,无效 / **idly** *ad.*

idol ['aidl] *n.* ①偶像: emancipate the mind, topple old ~s 解放思想,破除迷信 ②崇拜的对象,宠物: make an ~ of sb. 崇拜某人 ③ 非正统的受崇拜的神;异教崇拜的神 ④幻象;幽灵 ⑤【逻】谬论,谬见

idyl(l) ['idil, 'aidil] *n.* ①描写田园生活的短诗(或散文);叙事诗 ②适合田园诗文的主题 ③【音】田园乐曲;牧歌 ‖**idyllist** ['aidilist] *n.* 田园诗人;田园乐曲的作者

if [if] **I** *conj.* ①[表示条件]如果: If you demand his presence, warn him in advance. 如果你们要他来,就事先通知他。/ Return If Undelivered 无法投递请退回原处 / If you will wait a minute,

I shall go and find him. 请等一下,让我去把他找来。/ If weather permits, ... 如果天气好的话,…(常略作 I. W. P.) ②[表示假设]要是,假如: If I were you, I would not go. 如果我是你,我就不去。/ If it should rain tomorrow, the rally would be postponed. 要是明天下雨,群众大会就延期举行。/ If it had not been for your help, we would not have succeeded. 要不是有你们的帮助,我们就决不会成功。[注意: 在书面语中可将上述三句中的助动词 were, should, had 移至主语前,省去 if] ③[表示让步]虽然,即使 ④当,无论何时 ⑤是否: I wonder ~ it is the right size. 我不知道尺寸是否合适。[注意: 在这类句子中,if 等于 whether,但 if 一般用在口语中,且不能用于句首] ⑥[表示和事实相反的愿望,用过去时态的虚拟语气]要是…多好: If I had been warned! 要是有人及早提醒我多好!· ⑦[表示惊奇或恼怒,用陈述语气的否定句,意义则是肯定的]: If I haven't repeated the mistake! 我真不该重犯这样的错误! **II** *n.* 条件;设想: Your argument seems to have too many ~s. 你的论据似乎假设太多了一些。‖**as ~** 见 as / **~ and when** (公文用语) ①=if ② =when / **~ only** ①[只要: If only it clears up, we'll go. 只要天一放晴,我们就去。②要是…就好: If only you had worked with greater care! 你要是更过细一些该多好啊! / If only he arrives in time! 但愿他能及时赶到! / **~ so** 要是这样

igloo, iglu ['iglu:] *n.* ①爱斯基摩人的圆顶茅屋 ②圆顶建筑

igloo

igneous ['igniəs] *a.* ①火的,似火的 ②【地】火成的: ~ rock 火成岩 / magma 岩浆

ignite [ig'nait] ❶ *vt.* ① 点燃;点火于;使燃烧 ②使灼热 ③使兴奋;使激动: His speech ~d the audience. 他的讲话激动了听众。❷ *vi.* 着火,发火;变得灼热 ‖**~r, ignitor** *n.* ①点火器;点火剂,点火药;点火者 ②引爆装置

ignition [ig'niʃən] *n.* ①点火;着火;【机】发火;【化】灼热: an ~ charge 点火药 / an ~ point 燃点 ②【机】发火装置

ignoble [ig'noubl] *a.* ①卑鄙的,不体面的;可耻的: an ~ man 卑鄙无耻的人 / an ~ purpose 卑鄙

的目的 ②卑贱的, 低下的; 出身微贱的 ‖**ignobil-ity** [ˌignou'biliti], **~ness** n. / **ignobly** ad.

ignominious [ˌigne'minies] a. 耻辱的; 可鄙的; 不光彩的: an ~ treaty 屈辱性的条约 ‖**~ly** ad. / **~ness** n.

ignorance ['ignerens] n. ①无知; 无学; 愚昧: sheer ~ of sth. 对某事的全然无知 / from ~ 出于无知 ②不知: be in ~ of sth. 不知某事

ignorant ['ignerent] a. ①无知的; 没有学识的; 愚昧的: an ~ person 无知的人 ②由无知(或无经验)引起的: an ~ error 出于无知的错误 ③不知道的: be ~ of conditions at the lower levels 不了解下情 ‖**~ly** ad.

ignore [ig'nɔ:] vt. ①不顾; 不理; 忽视: ~ personal danger 不顾个人安危 ②【律】驳回

iguana [i'gwɑːne] n. 【动】鬣蜥(产于美洲和西印度群岛的一种大蜥蜴)

iguana

ill [il] I (worse [wəːs], worst [wəːst]) a. ①[一般用作表语]有病的, 不健康的; 要呕吐的: fall (或 be taken) ~ 得病 / be mentally ~ 有精神病 / be ideologically ~ 思想上有病 / You look ~ these days. 近来你的气色不好。/ a man seri-ously ~ with TB 患严重结核病的人 ②[用作定语]坏的; 不吉祥的; 邪恶的; 恶意的, 粗暴的: ~ news 坏消息 / ~ luck 不幸 / ~ health 不健康 / be of ~ repute 臭名昭著 / an ~ wind 妖风, 歪风 / ~ blood (或 will) 仇视, 敌意 ③[用作定语]拙劣的, 不完美的; 不良的, 不恰当的: ~ management 管理不善 / ~ breeding 教养不好 ④难以处理的, 麻烦的: It is ~ to be defined. 很难对它下定义。 II (worse, worst) ad. ①坏, 不利地: speak (think) ~ of sb. 把某人说(想)得很坏 / be ~ clad 穿得破破烂烂 / The remark was ~ received. 这句话引起的反应不好。②不完全, 不充分; 几乎不: It ~ becomes you to do so. 你这么做是挺不合适的。/ I'm ~ prepared for it. 对此我没有什么准备。/ I can ~ afford the time. 我匀不出这点时间。③粗暴地; 不友好地 III n. ①坏, 恶: do ~ 作恶 / I don't know whether the outcome will be good or for ~. 我不知道结果是好还是坏。②罪恶 ③[常用复]病害; 灾祸, 不幸 ‖**be ~ off** 贫困; 不幸 / **~ at ease** 不安; 不自在 ‖**'~-**

a'dapted a. 与…不协调的 (to) / **'~-ad'vised** a. 没脑筋的; 鲁莽的 / **'~-'being** n. 不好的境地, 不幸, 贫困 / **'~-'boding** a. 不祥的, 主凶的 / **'~-'bred** a. ①教养不好的; 粗鲁的 ②(动物等)劣种的 / **'~-con'ditioned** a. ①坏心眼的 ②情况糟的 / **'~-dis'posed** a. ①坏心眼的, 存心不良的 ②对…敌视的, 不赞成…的 (towards) / **'~-effect** n. 恶果 / **'~-e'quipped** a. 装备不良的 / **'~-'fated** a. ①注定要倒霉的, 倒运的 ②招致不幸的 / **'~-'favo(u)red** a. ①其貌不扬的, 凶相的 ②使人不快的 / **'~-'feeling** n. 敌意, 仇视 / **'~-,fortune** n. 厄运 / **'~-'founded** a. 无理由的, 站不住脚的 / **'~-'gotten** a. 非法获得的: ~-gotten gains 不义之财 / **'~-'hu-mo(u)red** a. 情绪不好的, 易发火的, 阴郁的 / **'~-'judged** a. 判断失当所引起的, 不智的 / **'~-'mannered** a. 举止粗鲁的 / **'~-'natured** a. 怀着恶意的; 脾气坏的 / **'~-'omened** a. 凶兆的, 不吉的 / **'~-'sorted** a. 不配对的, 不相称的 / **'~-'starred** a. =~-fated / **'~-'suited** a. 与…不适合的 (to) / **'~-'tempered** a. =~-humo(u)red / **'~-'timed** a. 不适时的, 不合时宜的: Your remark is ~-timed. 你这句话说得不是时候。/ **'~-'treat, '~-'use** vt. 虐待; 不友好地对待: We don't ~-treat captives. 我们不虐待俘虏。/ **'~-'treatment, '~-'usage** n. 虐待; 苛待 / **'~-'wisher** n. 希望别人倒霉的人

I'll [ail] [口] =I shall; I will

illegal [i'liːgəl] a. 不合法的, 非法的; 违规的: an ~ act 非法行为 ‖**~ity** [ˌili(ː)'gæliti] n. / **~ly** ad.

illegible [i'ledʒəbl] a. 难以辨认的; 字迹模糊的; 印刷模糊的 ‖**illegibility** [iˌledʒi'biliti] n. / **illegibly** [i'ledʒəbli] ad.

illegitimate [ˌili'dʒitimit] I a. ①非法的, 违法的 ②私生的 ③不合理的, 不合逻辑的 ④不符合惯例的; 【语】不符合习惯用法的 II n. 没有合法身分的人(尤指私生子) III [ˌili'dʒitimeit] vt. 宣布…为非法 ‖**~ly** ad. / **illegitimation** [ˌiliˌdʒiti-'meiʃən] n.

illiberal [i'libərəl] a. ①缺乏教育的, 无教养的; 粗鲁的 ②气量狭窄的, 吝啬的; 思想偏狭的 ‖**~ity** [iˌlibə'ræliti] n. / **~ly** ad.

illicit [i'lisit] a. 违法的, 违禁的; 不正当的: ~ sale 私卖 / ~ intercourse 私通, 通奸

illiteracy [i'litərəsi] n. ①文盲; 未受教育, 无知: wipe out ~ 扫除文盲 ②(语言)错误

illiterate [i'litərit] I a. ①文盲的; 未受教育的, 无知的 ②缺乏语言(或文学等)方面知识的: He is musically ~. 他缺乏音乐方面的知识。③语言错误的: an ~ letter 语言上错误百出的信 II n. 文盲, 无知的人 ‖**~ness** n.

illness ['ilnis] n. 病, 疾病: triumph over ~ 战胜疾病 / suffer from a serious ~ 患重病 / ~es of women 各种妇女病

illuminate [i'ljuːmineit] ❶ vt. ①照亮, 照明

② 阐明，使明白；启发，教导：~ a statement with many examples 用许多实例阐明一个论点 / an *illuminating* lecture 一堂有启发性的讲课 ③ 使显扬；使光辉灿烂 ④ 用灯装饰 (街道、房屋等)：The whole city was ~d in celebration of National Day. 全市灯火辉煌庆祝国庆。⑤ 用鲜明色彩装饰(书、稿的第一个字母) ; 用经过装饰的字、画等装饰(书、稿等) ❷ *vi.* 照亮 ‖~d *a.* ① 被照明的；受启发的；加了灯饰的；加了彩的：a well-~d room 照明很好的房间 ②[美俚] 喝醉了的 ‖**illuminating engineering** 照明工程(学) / **illuminating projectile, illuminating flare**【军】照明弹

illumination [i,lju:mi'neiʃən] *n.* ① 照明，照亮；光亮；照(明)度：stage ~ 舞台照明 / the brilliant ~ of the room 房间的强照明 ② 阐明，解释；启发：find great ~ in sb.'s remark 从某人的话中得到很大的启发 ③[常用复]灯彩，灯饰 ④[复](书稿第一个字母等的)彩饰，画饰

illusion [i'lju:ʒən] *n.* ① 错觉，幻觉：an optical ~ 视错觉 ② 假象 ③ 幻想；错误的观念：be under no ~ about (或 as to) sth. 对某事不存在幻想；cast away ~s 丢掉幻想 ④ 薄纱 ‖~al, ~ary *a.* / ~ism *n.* ① 物质世界幻觉说 ② 引起错觉的艺术手法 / ~ist *n.* 物质世界幻觉论者；幻想家；魔术师

illusive [i'lju:siv] *a.* ① 产生错觉的；因错觉产生的 ② 虚幻的；迷惑人的 ‖~ly *ad.* / ~ness *n.*

illustrate ['iləstreit] ❶ *vt.* ①(用图或例子等)说明，阐明：~ a lesson with pictures 用图画来说明一篇课文 / ~d by charts and diagrams 用图表说明的 ② 用插图等装饰(书、报等)：an ~d magazine 有插图的杂志 ❷ *vi.* 举例 ‖**illustrator** *n.* 插图画家

illustration [,iləs'treiʃən] *n.* ① 说明；图解：He cited instances *in* ~ *of* this theory. 他举例说明这种理论。② 例证，实例；插图

illustrative ['iləstreitiv] *a.* 用作说明的，解说性的；作为例证的：facts ~ *of* a viewpoint 说明一种观点的许多事实 / plenty of ~ material 大量的解说性材料 ‖~ly *ad.*

illustrious [i'lʌstriəs] *a.* ① 辉煌的，卓越的；著名的，杰出的：~ heroes of our era 当代杰出的英雄人物 ② 有光泽的；明亮的 ‖~ly *ad.* / ~ness *n.*

I'm [aim] [口] =I am

image ['imidʒ] **I** *n.* ① 像；肖像；偶像 ② 映象；影象；图象：see one's ~ in the mirror 在镜子里照见自己的像 / television ~s 电视图象 / real (virtual) ~【物】实(虚)像 ③ 相像的人(或物)；翻版：She is the very ~ of her mother. 她活象她的母亲。④ 形象；典型 ⑤ 形象化的描绘：This novel is the ~ of rural life. 这部小说是农村生活的生动写照。⑥【语】形象化的比喻，象喻：~s in a poem 诗歌里的比喻 / speak in ~s 讲话形象化；用比喻讲 ⑦ 印象，概念；思想 ⑧【心】意象；心象 **II** *vt.* ① 作…的像；使…成像 ② 反映：the

clouds ~d in a lake 映入湖中的云影 ③ 想象 ④ 形象地描写；用比喻描写 ⑤ 象征 ⑥ God's ~ 人体 / the spitting ~ of [口] 同…简直一模一样的人(或东西) ‖~less *a.* 缺少形象的 ‖~ converter【无】光电图象变换管 / ~ dissector【无】析象管 / ~ orthicon【无】超正析(摄)象管，移象正析象管

imagery ['imidʒəri] *n.* ① [总称]像；雕刻；雕像；造像术 ② 意象 ③ 形象化的描述；比喻

imaginable [i'mædʒinəbl] *a.* [常与最高级形容词或 all, every, only 等连用，放在被修饰的名词后] 可以想象得到的：This is the only solution ~. 这是唯一想得出的解决办法。/ save the patient by every means ~ 用一切想得出的方法抢救病人 / the best thing ~ 再好没有的东西 ‖**imaginably** *ad.*

imaginary [i'mædʒinəri] *a.* ① 想象中的；假想的，虚构的；幻想的：an ~ character in a tale 故事里的虚构人物 ②【数】虚数的：~ number 虚数 / ~ root 虚根 ‖**imaginarily** [i'mædʒinərili; 美 i,mædʒi'nerili] *ad.* / **imaginariness** *n.*

imagination [i,mædʒi'neiʃən] *n.* ① 想象；想象力；创造力：a writer of rich ~ 想象力丰富的作家 / have a good (poor) ~ 想象力好(差) / be successful beyond (all) ~ 出乎(完全出乎)意料地取得成功 ② 空想；妄想 ③ 想象出来的事物

imaginative [i'mædʒinətiv] *a.* 富于想象力的；唤起想象力的；想象的：an ~ artist 富于想象力的艺术家 / ~ power (或 faculty) 想象力 ‖~ly *ad.* / ~ness *n.*

imagine [i'mædʒin] ❶ *vt.* ① 想象；设想；料想：We cannot ~ life without any contradictions. 我们不能设想没有任何矛盾的生活。/ Our producers should constantly ~ themselves to be in the consumers' position. 我们的生产单位要经常设身处地为用户着想。/ The boy likes to ~ himself a flyer. 那孩子喜欢想象自己是一个飞行员。/ Just ~ how happy he was! 请想一想，他多么幸福啊! ② 捏造 ❷ *vi.* 想象起来；想起来；料想起来

imam, imaum [i'mɑ:m] *n.*【伊斯兰教】阿訇 ②[I-] 伊玛目(某些伊斯兰教国家元首的称号或指伊斯兰教教长)

imbecile ['imbisi:l] **I** *n.* 低能者，低能儿；笨人 **II** *a.* 低能的；愚笨的：an ~ act 愚蠢的行为 ‖~ly *ad.* / **imbecility** [,imbi'siliti] *n.* ① 低能；愚笨 ② 愚蠢的行为

imbue [im'bju:] *vt.* ① 使浸透 ② 染 ③ 使充满；鼓舞(with)

imitate ['imiteit] *vt.* ① 模仿，仿效，摹拟，学样：~ sb.'s intonation 模仿某人的语调 / ~ the strokes of model Chinese calligraphy 临摹中国字帖中的书法 ② 仿制，仿造；伪造：fabrics made to ~ silk 仿丝绸织物 ‖**imitator** *n.* 模仿者；临摹者；仿造者；伪造者

imitation [,imi'teiʃən] *n.* ① 模仿，摹拟；仿造；伪

造: set sb. a good example for ~ 为某人做出仿效的好榜样 / ~ leather (wool) 人造革(毛) ②仿制品; 伪造物, 赝品: Beware of ~s. 谨防假冒。③【生】拟态

imitative ['imitətiv] *a.* ①模仿的, 摹拟的: be ~ of sb. 仿效某人 / ~ words 摹声词(如 hiss, moo) ②爱模仿的 ③仿制的, 仿造的; 伪造的 ‖~ly *ad.* / ~ness *n.*

immaculate [i'mækjulit] *a.* ①纯洁的; 无瑕疵的; 无斑点的: ~ white linen 洁白的亚麻布 ②无缺点的: an ~ text 完全正确的版本 ③无过失的, 清白无辜的 ‖~ly *ad.* / ~ness *n.* ‖**Immaculate Conception** 【宗】(关于圣母玛利亚的)纯洁受胎(说), 圣灵怀胎(说)

immaterial [,imə'tiəriəl] *a.* ①非物质的, 无形的 ②不重要的: ~ points 非要点 / That's quite ~ to me. 那对我无所谓。‖~ism *n.* 非物质论(主要指英国贝克莱的主观唯心主义) / ~ist *n.* 非物质论者 / ~ity ['imə,tiəri'æliti] *n.* 非物质(性); 无形物 / ~ize *vt.* 使无实体, 使无形

immediate [i'mi:djət] *a.* ①直接的; 最接近的: the ~ cause 直接原因, 近因 / one's ~ superior 上一级领导, 顶头上司 / put long-term interests before ~ interests 把长远利益放在眼前利益之上 / in the ~ future 在最近的将来 ②紧靠着的: sb.'s ~ neighbo(u)rs 某人的紧邻 ③立即的; 即时的: give an ~ reply 立即答复 / ~ delivery 【商】即交 / ~ shipment 【商】即装 ④直觉的: ~ knowledge 直觉感知 ‖~ness *n.*

immediately [i'mi:djətli] I *ad.* ①立即, 马上: I got in touch with him ~ after I received the letter. 我接信后立即和他联系。②直接地; 紧密地: two ~ contiguous areas 两个紧密相邻的地区 II *conj.* [主英]一经…(立即): We held a meeting to sum up our experiences ~ we finished the work. 工作一结束, 我们立即开会总结经验。

immemorial [,imi'mɔ:riəl] *a.* 无法追忆的; 古老的, 太古的: from time ~ 远古以来 ‖~ly *ad.*

immense [i'mens] *a.* ①广大的; 巨大的: an ~ ocean 无边的海洋 / an ~ amount 巨额 ②[俚]极好的: The performance was ~. 演出好极了。‖~ly *ad.* ①大大地, 无限地 ②[口]非常, 很: We enjoyed the play ~ly. 我们非常喜爱这出戏。/ ~ness *n.* / **immensity** *n.* ①广大; 巨大; 无限, 无限的空间 ②巨物

immerge [i'mə:dʒ] ❶ *vt.* [古] =immerse ❷ *vi.* ①浸入 ②专心, 埋头: There is no need to ~ further into this topic. 不必再钻在这个题目里了。

immerse [i'mə:s] *vt.* ①沉浸; 【宗】给…施浸礼: ~ sth. in the water 把某物浸在水里 ②使沉浸于; 使陷入 (in): The whole city was ~d in a festival atmosphere. 全城沉浸在节日气氛中。 be ~d in difficulties 陷入困难

immersion [i'mə:ʃən] *n.* ①沉浸, 沉没; 【宗】浸礼: ~ lens 【物】浸没透镜 ②专心; 陷入: ~ in

thought 沉思 ③【天】掩始 ‖~ **heater** 浸没式加热器, 浸入式热水器

immigrant ['imigrənt] I *a.* (从外国)移来的, 移民的, 侨民的 II *n.* ①移民, 侨民 ②从异地移入的动物(或植物)

immigrate ['imigreit] ❶ *vi.* (从外国)移来; 移居入境: ~ into a country 迁入某一国家(作移民) ❷ *vt.* 使移居入境

immigration [,imi'greiʃən] *n.* 移居; 外来的移民: the ~ law 移民法 / the numerous ~s into a certain country 迁入某国的大批侨民

imminence ['iminəns] *n.* 急迫; 迫近的危险(或祸患); 危急

imminent ['iminənt] *a.* 急迫的; 迫近的; 危急的: A storm is ~. 暴风雨即将来临。

immortal [i'mɔ:tl] I *a.* ①不朽的, 流芳百世的: The heroes of the people are ~. 人民英雄永垂不朽。/ ~ deeds 不朽的功勋 ②[口]永久的, 不变的: an ~ enemy 永久的敌人 ③不死的, 永生的 ④神的 II *n.* ①不朽者; 流芳百世的人 ②[常作 Immortals]古代希腊、罗马的诸神 ③[I-]法国科学院院士 ‖~ity [imɔ:'tæliti] *n.* 不朽, 永存; 不灭的声望 / ~ly *ad.*

immortalize [i'mɔ:təlaiz] *vt.* 使不朽, 使不灭 ‖**immortalization** [i,mɔ:təlai'zeiʃən] *n.*

immovable [i'mu:vəbl] I *a.* ①不可移动的; 固定的 ②不动的; 静止的 ③不可改变的; 不屈的; 坚定不移的 ④不激动的; 无感觉的, 冷淡的 ⑤[律]不动的 II *n.* ①不可移动的东西 ②[复]【律】不动产 ‖**immovability** [i,mu:və'biliti] *n.* 不动; 不变; / ~ness *n.* / **immovably** *ad.*

immune [i'mju:n] I *a.* ①免除的: be ~ from taxation 免税 ②不受影响的, 无响应的: be ~ to all pleas 不容申辩; 对所有要求都置之不理 ③有免疫力的; 可避免的 ④【医】免疫的: ~ agglutinin 免疫凝集素 II *n.* 免疫者 ‖**immunity** [i'mju:niti] *n.* ①免除; 豁免: enjoy diplomatic *immunities* 享有外交豁免权 ②免疫(力), 免疫性: acquired *immunity* 后天免疫性 / active *immunity* 自动免疫性

immunize ['imju(:)naiz] *vt.* 使免除; 使免疫: ~d from disease 有免疫力 / Vaccination ~s people *against* smallpox. 种牛痘能使人免患天花。‖**immunization** [,imju(:)nai'zeiʃən] *n.*

imp[1] [imp] *n.* ①顽童, 小淘气 ②魔鬼的后代; 小魔鬼 ③[古]孩子, 后代

imp[2] [imp] *vt.* ①移植羽毛以修补(鹰的翅膀或尾巴) ②于…上装翅膀 ③加强, 增大, 补充

impact I ['impækt] *n.* ①冲击, 碰撞; 冲击力: the ~ of the swift current *against* the shore 激流对海岸的冲击 ~ test 【机】冲击试验 ②影响: make a notable ~ *on* literature and art 对文学艺术产生显著的影响 ③【军】弹着; 【宇】(火箭的)着陆(或降落): the point of ~ 弹着点 II [im'pækt] *vt.* ①装紧, 压紧; 楔牢 (into, in) ②塞满 ③冲击, 碰撞 ‖~ion [im'pækʃən] *n.* ①装紧

压紧 ②撞击 ③【医】阻生; 嵌塞: food ~**ion** 食物嵌塞

impair [im'pɛə] *vt.* ①削弱; 减少 ②损害, 伤害: ~ one's health 损害健康 ‖~**ment** *n.*

impale [im'peil] *vt.* ①刺穿; 钉住 ②把…钉在尖桩上; 对…施以刺刑 ③使绝望; 使尴尬: ~ sb. *on* a dilemma 使某人陷于进退两难的境地 ④ [罕]用桩围住; 围住 ‖~**ment** *n.*

impart [im'pɑːt] *vt.* ①把…分给; 给予; 传递: ~ knowledge *to* sb. 把知识传授给某人 / ~ a lyric quality *to* that passage 在那一节上抒情的成分 ②告诉; 透露: I have nothing important to ~ *to* you. 我没有什么重要的事可告知你。‖~**a-tion** [impɑːˈteiʃən], ~**ment** *n.*

impartial [im'pɑːʃəl] *a.* 公正的, 不偏袒的; 无偏见的: be ~ *to* 对…公正无私 ‖~**ity** ['im,pɑːʃiˈæliti] *n.* / ~**ly** *ad.*

impassable [im'pɑːsəbl] *a.* ①不能通行的; 不可逾越的: an ~ swamp 不能通行的沼泽地 ②不可流通的 ‖**impassability** ['im,pɑːsəˈbiliti] *n.* / ~**ness** *n.* / **impassably** *ad.*

impasse [æm'pɑːs; 美 im'pæs] *n.* [法] ①死路, 死胡同 ②绝境; 僵局

impassible [im'pæsəbl] *a.* ①不感疼痛的; 不感苦痛的 ②不能伤害的; 不受伤害的 ③无动于衷的; 无情的 ‖**impassibility** [im,pæsi'biliti] *n.* / ~**ness** *n.* / **impassibly** *ad.*

impassion [im'pæʃən] *vt.* 激起…的热情, 使充满热情, 激动 ‖~**ed** *a.* 充满热情的, 热烈的, 激动的: ~ed language 激动的语言

impassive [im'pæsiv] *a.* ①缺乏热情的, 冷淡的; 无动于衷的; 无表情的: an ~ man 缺乏热情的人 / an ~ face 无表情的面孔 ②无感觉的 ③不易受伤害的 ④不动的 ‖~**ly** *ad.* / ~**ness** *n.* / **impassivity** [,impæ'siviti] *n.*

impatience [im'peiʃəns] *n.* ①不耐烦, 急躁: restrain one's ~ 抑制急躁情绪 ②渴望, 切望

impatient [im'peiʃənt] *a.* ①不耐烦的, 急躁的; 忍受不了的: Don't be ~ *with* your children. 对孩子们不要急躁。/ He was ~ *of* all this waiting. 他等得不耐烦了。②急欲的, 急切的: The children are ~ *for* the arrival of Children's Day. 孩子们切望儿童节的到来。/ He is ~ *to* know what happened. 他急于想知道发生了什么事。‖~**ly** *ad.*

impeach [im'piːtʃ] *vt.* ①控告; 检举, 弹劾: ~ sb. *with* (或 *of*) a crime 控告某人犯罪 / be ~ed *for* treason 被告发犯有叛国罪 ②对…表示怀疑, 不信任; 指责, 非难, 责问: ~ the testimony of a witness 对见证人证词的可靠性提出异议 ‖~**able** *a.* 可控告(或弹劾)的; 可怀疑的 / ~**ment** *n.*

impeccable [im'pekəbl] **I** *a.* ①不会做坏事的; 不易做坏事的 ②没有缺点的; 无瑕疵的: a report written with ~ discretion 一篇以无懈可击的审慎态度所写的报告 **II** *n.* 不会做坏事的人; 无瑕

疵的人 ‖**impeccability** [im,pekə'biliti] *n.* / **impeccably** *ad.*

impecunious [,im-pi'kjuːnjəs] *a.* 没钱的, 贫穷的 ‖**impecuniosity** [,im-pi,kjuːni'ɔsiti] *n.* / ~**ly** *ad.* / ~**ness** *n.*

impede [im'piːd] *vt.* 妨碍, 阻碍; 阻止: ~ sb.'s progress 妨碍某人的进步 / His departure was ~d by the heavy rain. 大雨使他不能离去。

impediment [im'pedimənt] *n.* ①妨碍, 阻碍; 障碍物: an ~ *to* progress 进步的阻碍 / strive *to* get ahead despite all ~s in one's path 不顾道路上的一切障碍奋力前进 ②口吃: He has an ~ in speech. 他讲话口吃。③法定婚姻的障碍(如年龄不足)④[复]行李; 辎重 ‖~**al** [im,pedi'mentl] *a.* 妨碍的, 阻碍的: causes ~al *to* success 阻碍成功的原因

impel [im'pel] (impelled; impelling) *vt.* ①推动, 推进; 激励: ~ sb. to do sth. 推动某人做某事 / ~ sb. *to* greater efforts 促使某人作出更大努力 ②驱使; 迫使; 促成: be *impelled* by necessity 迫不得已 / feel *impelled* to speak 觉得非说不可

impend [im'pend] *vi.* [常用现在分词] ①悬挂 (over): an ~*ing* cliff 悬崖 ②逼近 (over); 即将发生: the danger ~*ing* over sb. 迫在某人眼前的危险 / Rain is ~*ing*. 雨就要来了。/ an ~*ing* storm 即将来临的风暴 ‖~**ent** *a.*

impenetrable [im'penitrəbl] *a.* ①刺不进的; 穿不过的; 透不进的: an ~ shield 刺不穿的盾牌 / an ~ forest 难以通过的森林 / ~ darkness 漆黑 ②费解的, 不可测知的: an ~ mystery 难解的秘密 ③顽固的, 不接受的: a mind ~ *to* (或 *by*) new ideas 不接受新思想的顽固头脑 ④【物】不可入性的 ‖**impenetrability** [im,penitrə'biliti] *n.* / ~**ness** *n.* / **impenetrably** *ad.*

imperative [im'perətiv] **I** *a.* ①绝对必要的; 紧急的; 迫切的: It is ~ that every one of us (或 It is ~ for every one of us to) remould his world outlook. 我们每个人都必须改造自己的世界观。/ an ~ duty 紧急任务 / ~ necessity 迫切需要 ②命令的; 强制的; 专横的: an ~ tone of voice 命令口气 / an ~ manner 专横的态度 ③【语】祈使的: the ~ mood 祈使语气 / an ~ sentence 祈使句 **II** *n.* ①命令; 规则; 必须履行的责任 ②【语】祈使语气; 祈使语气动词 ‖~**ly** *ad.* / ~**ness** *n.*

imperial [im'piəriəl] **I** *a.* ①帝国的; [英][常作 I-] 英帝国的; 有属地的: the ~ preference 英帝国对于从殖民地输入商品的关税优待 / *Imperial Aluminium Company* 帝国铝公司(英国)②皇帝(或皇后)的; 最高权力的: an ~ household 皇室 / an ~ envoy 钦差大臣 ③帝王一般的; 威严的; 堂皇的; 傲慢的 ④特大的; 特等的: on an ~ scale 以特大规模 ⑤(英国度量衡)法定标准的 **II** *n.* ①某种尺寸的写字纸 ②特大品; 特等品 ③留在下唇下面的小绺胡须(因拿破仑三世曾留此须, 又称帝须)④帝俄时代的金币(=15银卢布) ⑤公共马车的车顶; 放在公共马车顶上的行李箱

⑥[I-]【史】神圣罗马皇帝的拥护者(或其士兵) ‖~ly *ad.* / ~ness *n.*

imperialism [im'piəriəlizəm] *n.* 帝国主义

imperialist [im'piəriəlist] I *n.* ①帝国主义者 ②皇帝的支持者；帝制的拥护者 ③[I-]【史】神圣罗马皇帝的拥护者(或其士兵) II *a.* 帝国主义的

imperil [im'peril] (imperil(l)ed; imperil(l)ing) *vt.* 使处于危险，危害

imperious [im'piəriəs] *a.* ①专横的；老爷式的；傲慢的：an ~ gesture 专横的样子 ②紧要的；迫切的：an ~ demand 迫切要求 ‖~ly *ad.* / ~ness *n.*

impersonal [im'pə:sənl] I *a.* ①非个人的；非特指某一个人的；不受个人情感影响的：an ~ criticism 不针对某一个人的批评 ②不具人格的，与人力无关的：~ forces 非人力(指自然力等) ③【语】非人称的：an ~ verb 非人称动词(通常用 it 作主语；真正的非人称动词没有主语，如 methinks, 但现在极少用) II *n.* 非人称动词(=~ verb) ‖~ity [im,pə:sə'næliti] *n.* ①与个人无关；非人格性 ②非人格性的东西(指时间、空间等) / ~ly *ad.*

impersonate [im'pə:səneit] *vt.* ①使人格化；体现 ②扮演；模仿；假冒 ‖**impersonation** [im,pə:sə'neiʃən] *n.* / **impersonative** *a.* / **impersonator** *n.* 模仿者；扮演者

impertinence [im'pə:tinəns], **impertinency** [im'pə:tinənsi] *n.* ①不恰当，不适合 ②不得要领；离题 ③不礼貌，傲慢；鲁莽：have the ~ to say that 竟无礼到说出那样的话来 ④无礼的举动(或言论)

impertinent [im'pə:tinənt] *a.* ①不恰当的，不适合的 ②不得要领的；离题的：a point ~ *to* the argument 离题太远的论点 ③不礼貌的，傲慢的；鲁莽的：ask an ~ question 提一个不礼貌的问题 ‖~ly *ad.*

imperturbable [,im-pə(:)'tə:bəbl] *a.* 沉着的,冷静的 ‖**imperturbability** ['im-pə(:),tə:bə'biliti] *n.* / ~ness *n.* / **imperturbably** *ad.*

impervious [im'pə:vjəs] *a.* ①不可渗透的，透不过的；穿不过的：a fabric ~ *to* moisture 防潮的织品 ②不受影响的，不受干扰的 ③无动于衷的，不接受的：be ~ *to* all reason 不通情理 ‖~ly *ad.* / ~ness *n.*

impetuous [im'petjuəs] *a.* ①激烈的，猛烈的；迅疾的：an ~ wind 狂风 ②鲁莽的，冲动的；性急的，急躁的 ‖~ly *ad.* / ~ness *n.*

impetus ['impitəs] *n.* ①动力；原动力 ②促进；推动；激励：give an ~ to trade 促进贸易 ③动量

impinge [im'pindʒ] ❶ *vi.* ①撞击，冲击(on, upon, against): A strong light ~d on his eyes. 强烈的光刺着他的眼睛。/ the rain impinging upon the earth 冲击着土地的大雨 ②紧密接触(on) ③侵犯；侵害(on, upon): The sovereignty of our country should by no means be ~d upon. 我们

国家的主权绝不容许侵犯。❷ *vt.* (气体等)撞击 ‖~ment *n.*

impious ['impiəs] *a.* ①不虔诚的，不敬神的；邪恶的 ②不敬的；不孝的 ‖~ly *ad.*

implacable [im'plækəbl] *a.* ①不饶恕的，不宽容的；难平息的，不能缓和的: an ~ resentment 极大的怨懑 ②不能改变的 ‖**implacability** [im,plækə'biliti] *n.* / ~ness *n.* / **implacably** *ad.*

implant I [im'plɑ:nt] *vt.* ①插入；嵌入；种植 ②牢固树立，灌输,注入 ③【医】移植 II ['im-plɑ:nt] *n.* 【医】①移植物，移植片 ②(治疗癌症用的镭等放射性物质)植入管: a radium ~ 镭植入管 ‖~ation [,im-plɑ:n'teiʃən] *n.*

implement I ['implimənt] *n.* ①[常用复]工具；器具: new types of farm ~s 新式农具 / household ~s 日用器具 ②家具；服装 ③[苏格兰]【律】履行 II ['impliment] *vt.* ①贯彻；完成；履行(契约、诺言等) ②给…提供方法；为…供应器具 ③把…填满，补充 ‖~ation [,implimen'teiʃən] *n.*

implemental [,impli'mentl] *a.* ①器具的；作器具用的 ②起作用的；有助的

implicate I ['implikeit] *vt.* ①含有…的意思 ②使(某人)牵连(于罪行等之中): be ~d in a plot 卷入阴谋 ③[用被动语态]影响 ④[古]绕住,使缠在一起 II ['implikit] *n.* 包含的东西,暗指的东西 ‖**implication** [,impli'keiʃən] *n.* / **implicative** [im'plikətiv] *a.* ①含蓄的,言外之意的 ②牵连的: be *implicative of* each other 互相牵连

implicit [im'plisit] *a.* ①含蓄的,不言明的: an ~ answer 含蓄的答复 / ~ consent 默许 ②内含的,固有的 ③无疑的；无保留的；绝对的 ‖~ly *ad.*

implied [im'plaid] *a.* 暗指的；含蓄的；不言而喻的：~ consent 默许 ‖~ly [im'plaiidli] *ad.*

imply [im'plai] *vt.* ①含有…的意思: Do you realize what his words ~? 你领会他说话的含意吗? ②暗指,暗示；意指: I do not ~ that you are wrong. 我的意思不是说你错了。

impolicy [im'polisi] *n.* 失策,不智

impolite [,im-pə'lait] *a.* 不礼貌的，失礼的；粗鲁的: It is ~ of you to do so. 你这样做是不礼貌的。‖~ly *ad.* / ~ness *n.*

imponderable [im'pondərəbl] I *a.* ①没有重量的；极轻的 ②不可称量的；无法正确估计的: of ~ weight 重量称不出 / The effect is ~. 这作用是无法正确估计的。II *n.* ①无重量之物；不可量物 ②[复]无法估量的事物(或影响、作用) ‖**imponderability** [im,pondərə'biliti]

import [im'pɔ:t] I ❶ *vt.* ①进口,输入；引入: ~ sth. *from* a country 从某国输入某物 / ~ bicycles *into* a country 把自行车输入某国 / ~ed goods 进口货 ②意味,表明: What does this ~? 这意味着什么? ③[古]对…重要；对…有关 ❷ *vi.* 有关系 II ['impɔ:t] *n.* ①进口,输入,输入商品: an ~ duty 进口税 / an ~ surplus 入超 / an ~ quota 进口限额 / the ~ of cotton 棉花的

口 / ~*s* of cotton 进口棉花 ②意义,含意: grasp the ~ of sb.'s remarks 领会某人说话的含意 ③ 重要(性): a matter of great ~ 重大事情 ‖~**able** *a.* 可进口的 / ~**ation** [,impɔ:'teiʃən] *n.* ①进口,输入 ②进口货,输入品 / ~**er** *n.* 进口商;进口者

importance [im'pɔ:təns] *n.* ①重要(性),重大;价值: a natural resource that is *of* great ~ to industry 工业上极为重要的一种自然资源 / The matter is *of* no ~. 这件事无关紧要。 / a city *of* strategic ~ 战略重镇 ②傲慢,自大: speak with an air of ~ 带着傲慢的态度讲话 ‖**attach ~ to** 重视

important [im'pɔ:tənt] *a.* ①重要的,重大的: details ~ *to* a correct conclusion 对得出正确结论起重大作用的细节 / ~ events in history 历史上的重大事件 ②大量的,许多的;大的: ~ money 大笔的钱 / spend an ~ part of one's time on ... 把自己很大的一部分时间用于… ③有权力的,有地位的;显要的: an ~ figure (或 person) 要人 ④自高自大的: look ~ 看起来了不起 ‖~**ly** *ad.*

importunate [im'pɔ:tjunit] *a.* ①强求的; 缠扰不休的; 讨厌的: an ~ petitioner 一个缠扰不休的请求者 ②迫切的; 坚持的: an ~ request for assistance 对援助的急切要求 ‖~**ly** *ad.*

impose [im'pɔuz] ❶ *vt.* ①征(税等): ~ duties *on* tobaccos and wines 征收烟酒税 ②把…强加: ~ one's company (或 oneself) *on* sb. 硬叫着某人 / ~ oneself as 硬充作,自称为 ③把(坏货、赝品等)硬塞;以…欺骗 ④【印】把…拼版 ❷ *vi.* ①利用 (*on, upon*): ~ *on* sb.'s kindness 利用某人的善意 ②欺骗 (*on, upon*): I am not to be ~*d upon*. 我是不会上当的。 ③施影响 (*on, upon*)

imposition [,impə'ziʃən] *n.* ①征税; 税,税款; 负担 ②强加,强迫接受; 过分的要求: It is indeed an ~ to ask him to do that. 叫他去做那件事真是太过分了。③欺诈;哄骗 ④[英]罚学生做的作业(口语中略作 impo 或 impot) ⑤【宗】按手礼

impossible [im'pɔsəbl] *a.* ①不可能的,办不到的: ~ *of* conquest 不可能征服的 / Nothing is ~ to a willing mind. 天下无难事,只怕有心人。②不可能存在的;不会发生的: an ~ case 不能成立的案例 / It's all ~ to me. 这对我来说完全是不可思议的。③[口]使人受不了的;非常讨厌的;很难对付的: an ~ situation 无法忍受的局面 / an ~ person 十分讨厌的人 / an ~ hat 简直不像样的帽子 ‖**impossibility** [im,pɔsə-'biliti] *n.* 不可能;不可能的事 / **impossibly** *ad.*

impostor [im'pɔstə] *n.* 冒名顶替者; 骗子

imposture [im'pɔstʃə] *n.* 冒名顶替; 欺骗,欺诈: by lying and ~ 靠说谎和冒充 / a thorough ~ 彻头彻尾的欺骗行为

impotent ['impətənt] *a.* ①无力的; 软弱无能的; 虚弱的; 不起作用的: look on in ~ fury 站在一旁白白地冒火(而无能为力) / rid oneself of all

~ thinking 肃清一切软弱无能的思想 ②【医】阳萎的

impound [im'paund] *vt.* ①将(牛等)关在栏中 ② 没收(物件);扣押(人) ③贮(水)备灌溉用

impoverish [im'pɔvəriʃ] *vt.* ① 使穷困 ②使(力量、资源等)枯竭: ~*ed* rubber 失去弹性的橡皮 / ~*ed* soil 贫瘠的土壤 ‖~**ment** *n.*

impracticable [im'præktikəbl] *a.* ①不能实行的, 行不通的: an ~ plan 不能实行的计划 ② 不能用的; 不能通行的: an ~ road 无法通行的路 ③ 难对付的, 顽强的 ‖**impracticability** [im,præktikə'biliti] *n.* / ~**ness** *n.* / **impracticably** *ad.*

imprecate ['imprikeit] *vt.* ① 祈求降(祸): ~ evil *upon* sb. 祈求降祸于某人 ② 诅咒 ‖**imprecation** [,impri'keiʃən] *n.* / **imprecatory** *a.*

imprecise [,impri'sais] *a.* 不精确的; 含糊不清的

impregnable [im'pregnəbl] *a.* ①攻不破的; 坚不可摧的: an ~ bulwark 坚不可摧的堡垒 ②坚定不移的,毫不动摇的: an ~ belief 坚定不移的信念 ‖**impregnability** [im,pregnə'biliti] *n.* / **impregnably** *ad.*

impregnate I ['impregneit] *vt.* ①使怀孕,使妊娠;使受精 ②使充满;使饱和;浸渍;灌注,灌输: be ~*d with* enthusiasm 充满了热情 ③使(土地)肥沃;施肥于 II [im'pregnit] *a.* ①怀孕的,妊娠的 ②充满的;浸透的 (*with*) ‖**impregnation** [,impreg'neiʃən] *n.* ①受孕;饱和;注入 ②【矿】围岩中的浸染矿床 ③【化】浸渗,浸透,浸渍

impress¹ I [im'pres] ❶ *vt.* ①印,压印 ②铭刻;给…极深的印象: ~ sb. *with* the high speed of development 给某人留下高速度发展的深刻印象/ What ~*ed* me most is ... 给我印象最深的是 … / He ~*ed* me favourably. 他给我的印象不错。 ③传递,发送 ④【电】从外电源加(电压或电动势)到线路上 ❷ *vi.* 给人印象,引人注目: Never write or speak merely to ~. 不论写文章还是说话,都不要哗众取宠。 II ['impres] *n.* ①印记,压痕: the ~ of a tractor's tread on the mud 拖拉机履带在泥土上留下的印痕 ②印象;效应

impress² I [im'pres] *vt.* ① 强迫…服役 ② 强征(费用、财产等) ③(在辩论中)利用,引用

impression [im'preʃən] *n.* ①压印; 印记; 压痕 ②【印】印刷; 印数; 印次, 版(指原版的第几次印刷); 印制品; (雕版等的)印痕: The third ~ of the second edition 再版的第三次印刷 / an ~ of 100,000 copies 十万册的印数 ③ (油画的)底色; (作装饰等用的)漆层 ④印象;感想;模糊的观念: eye (或 visual) ~*s* 视觉印象 / sense ~*s* 感性知觉 / make a lasting ~ *on* sb. 给某人留下不可磨灭的印象 / have a false ~ *of* sb. 对某人有不正确的看法 ⑤效果;影响: What I said made practically no ~ *on* him. 我的话对他简直不起作用。⑥【医】(牙齿的)印模 ⑦(绘画、戏剧等中

所用的)漫画式的摹仿表现(或描绘) ‖~**al** *a.* 印象(上)的 / ~**ism** *n.* (绘画、文艺等方面的)印象主义;印象派 / ~**ist** *a.* 印象主义的 *n.* 印象派艺术家

impressionable [im'preʃənəbl] *a.* ①易刻的,易印的;可塑的: ~ paper 适合印刷的纸张 / an ~ plastic material 可塑的塑料 ②易受影响的;敏感的: at the ~ age 在易受影响的年龄(指青少年期) ‖**impressionability** [im,preʃənə'biliti] *n.* 可印性;易感性;敏感性

impressive [im'presiv] *a.* 给人深刻印象的,感人的: an ~ scene 难忘的场面 ‖~**ly** *ad.* / ~**ness** *n.*

imprint I [im'print] *vt.* ①印; 盖(印); 压(印): ~ a paper with a seal 在文件上盖章 / ~ a postmark on a letter 在信上盖邮戳 ②在…上压出记号;使带上…的特征 (on, in): ~ one's personality on one's writing 在作品里表现出个性 ③铭刻;使被牢记 II ['im-print] *n.* ①印: leave an ~ with every footstep 一步(留下)一个脚印 ②痕迹, 特征; 深刻的印象: bear the ~ of the time 具有时代的特征 ③(出版者在标题页或版权页上关于出版时间、地点等的)版本说明(= publisher's ~ 或 printer's ~)

imprison [im'prizn] *vt.* ①关押;监禁 ②限制,束缚 ‖~**ment** *n.* 关押;监禁: be sentenced to five years' ~ment 被判处五年徒刑

impromptu [im'promptju:] I *a. & ad.* 无准备的(地),临时的(地),即兴的(地),即席的(地) II *n.* 即兴演奏;临时讲话;即席之作

improper [im'prɔpə] *a.* ①不适当的,不合适的: a remark ~ to the occasion 不合场合的话 ②不合理的;不正确的,错误的 ③不合礼仪的;不成体统的,不正派的: ~ language 无礼的话 ‖~**ly** *ad.* ‖~ **fraction** 【数】假分数,可约分数

improve [im'pru:v] ❶ *vt.* ①使更好,增进: ~ the living conditions of the people 改善人民生活 / ~ farming methods 改进耕作方法 / ~ oneself in English 提高自己的英语水平 ②利用(机会等): ~ one's leisure by studying 利用空闲时间进行学习 ③抓住(机会)进行开导 ④提高(田地、地产)的价值: ~ a lot by building on it 在一块地上建造房屋以提高地价 ❷ *vi.* ①变得更好: His health is *improving*. (或 He is *improving* in health.) 他的健康状况正在好起来。 / How much you have ~d! 你进步真大! ②增加;升值: The demand for bicycles is *improving*. 对自行车的需求正在增加。 ‖~ **away** 通过改良祛除: ~ away a good point 意图改良反而搞坏 / ~ **upon** (或 on) 作出比…更好的东西;对…作出改进: I am unable to ~ on his suggestion. 我提不出比他更好的建议了。 ‖~**r** *n.* ①改进者; 改进物(尤指促进发酵作用的"助发剂"等) ②[英]学徒,练习生

improvement [im'pru:vmənt] *n.* ①改进; 改良; 增进: Much ~ has been made in the safety devices of the factory. 工厂的安全设备有了很大的改进。 / ~ of soil 【农】土壤改良 ②经改进的东西; 改进措施: city ~s 城市各方面的进步 / The new work procedure is a great ~ on (或 over) the old one. 新工序比起老工序来是一个巨大的改进。 ③(为使田地、地产增值所进行的)改建,经营 ④更优秀(或更进步)的人

improvident [im'prɔvidənt] *a.* 无远见的; 不顾将来的;不注意节约的 ‖~**ly** *ad.*

improvise ['imprəvaiz] *vt.* ①即席创作(诗歌等); 即席演奏(或演唱) ②临时准备,临时凑成: ~ a bed out of leaves 用树叶临时铺成一张床 / an ~d operating room 临时改成的简易手术室 / an ~d makeshift 临时凑合的办法 ‖~**r**, **improvisor** *n.* 即兴诗人;即席演奏(或演唱)者

impudent ['impjudənt] *a.* 厚颜无耻的; 冒失的;无礼的: be ~ enough to pervert the truth 竟无耻到歪曲事实 ‖~**ly** *ad.*

impugn [im'pju:n] *vt.* 指责,非难;对(话、行动、品质等)表示怀疑 ‖~**able** *a.* 可指责的,可非难的;易遭怀疑的 / ~**ment** *n.*

impulse ['impʌls] I *n.* ①推动;冲力: give an ~ to the development of the friendly relations between the two countries 促进两国友好关系的发展 ②冲动;刺激: a man of ~ 易冲动的人; act on ~ (on the ~ of the moment) 凭冲动(一时的冲动) 行事 / be driven by ~ to do sth. 情不自禁地去做某事 ③【物】冲量;脉冲;【医】激动 II *vt.* 推动

impulsion [im'pʌlʃən] *n.* ①推动; 推动力 ②冲动;刺激

impulsive [im'pʌlsiv] *a.* ①冲动的; 由冲动所造成的: an ~ person 容易感情冲动的人 / an ~ action 妄动 ②冲击的: an ~ force 冲力 ‖~**ly** *ad.* / ~**ness** *n.*

impunity [im'pju:niti] *n.* 不受惩罚; 免罪;不受损失;不受损害 ‖with ~ 不受惩罚地;泰然地

impute [im'pju:t] *vt.* 把…归因于,把…归咎于;把(罪名、责任等)推于;把…转嫁于 (to): ~ the guilt to sb. 把罪过推到某人身上

In 【化】元素铟 (indium) 的符号

in [in] I *prep.* ①[表示地点、场所、部位]在…里,在…上;在: in the workshop 在车间里 / work in a factory 在一个厂里工作 / at several cities ~ the province 在那个省的几个城市里 / ~ the world 在世界上 / ~ the universe 在宇宙中 / ~ the distance 在远处 / march ~ the rain 冒雨行军 / be injured ~ the eye 眼部受伤 ②[表示时间]在…期间;在…以后: at two o'clock ~ the afternoon 在下午两点钟 / ~ the twentieth century 在二十世纪 / a man ~ his thirties 一个三十几岁的男子 / The work was done ~ a week. 这工作在一星期内就完成了。 / have not slept ~ several days [美]几天没有睡觉 / I'll come and see you again ~ five days. 过五天我再来看你。 / I'll be with you ~ a minute.

马上就来。

③[表示过程]在…当儿；在…过程中：be killed ～ action 阵亡 / ～ crossing the river 在渡河的当儿

④[表示范围、领域、方面]在…之内；在…方面：～ the realm of the superstructure 在上层建筑领域内 / Victory is ～ sight. 胜利在望了。/ ～ every respect 在每一方面 / The new generator is large ～ capacity, small ～ size and low ～ coal consumption. 这台新发电机发电量大、体积小、耗煤量低。/ the latest thing ～ cars [口]最新式的汽车

⑤[表示状态、情况]处在…中：～ good condition 情况良好 / He is still ～ two minds. 他还没拿定主意。/ be ～ liquor 喝醉了 / a cow ～ milk 正在产奶的牛

⑥[表示职业、活动]从事于；参加着：～ the army 在军队中（服役）/ be ～ rice [美]经营米业 / He is ～ an amateur play. 他参加那个业余剧目的演出。

⑦[表示地位、形式、方式等]以，按照；符合于：～ an advisory capacity 以顾问的身分 / ～ the order of the number of strokes of the surnames 按姓氏笔划为序 / arrange ～ alphabetic order 按字母顺序排列 / buy ～ instalments 以分期付款方式购买 / In my opinion, he is wrong. 在我看来他是错了。/ Do everything ～ the interests of the people. 一切行动都要符合人民的利益。

⑧[表示述意的途径或表示所用的原料、材料]以，用：talk ～ English 用英语交谈 / a telegram ～ cipher 一封密码电报 / a statue ～ marble 一座大理石像 / a book bound ～ leather 一本皮面精装书

⑨[表示服饰]穿着，戴着；带着：a girl ～ red 穿红衣的女孩 / a wolf ～ sheep's skin 披着羊皮的狼 / be ～ irons 戴着镣铐

⑩[表示数量、程度、比例]按，以；在…中：We are agreed ～ the main. 我们在基本上取得了一致意见。/ not ～ the least 一点也不 / Such an occurrence is one ～ a thousand. 这样的事是非常难得碰上的。

⑪[表示方向]朝，向

⑫[表示能力、含有]包含在…之中：Do you think he has ～ him? 你认为他干得了这个吗？

⑬[表示同一性]在…身上，在…上

⑭[表示原因]由于，为了；作为…的表示：rejoice ～ others' achievements 为别人的成就欢欣鼓舞

⑮[表示动作的对象]对于；在于：The cause lies ～ the fact that .... 原因就在于…

⑯[表示动作的方向和结果]进入到…中；成，为 (=into)：come ～ the house 进屋来 / set the machine ～ motion 把机器开动起来 / break sth. ～ two 把某物断成两半

II ad. ①进，入：Bring him ～! 把他带进来！/ welcome ～ the new year 迎来新年 / hand ～

one's exercises 交进作业 / fit a piece ～ 嵌一块进去

②朝里；逼近；在里头：a coat with the woolly side ～ 一件羊毛里子的上衣 / You may count me ～. 把我也算在里面。/ a built-～ cooler 造在机器里边的冷却器

③在屋里；在家：Is there anybody ～? 屋里有人吗？/ have sb. ～ for dinner 请某人到家里来吃饭

④在狱中：What offence is Tom ～ for? 汤姆是因为什么罪名坐牢的？

⑤(季节、车、船等)已到达，已来临：Spring is ～ 春天来了。

⑥(庄稼等)已收进；已成熟；(土地)已耕好：The wheat crop is safely ～ 小麦完好无损地收进来了。

⑦完全成功，取胜：By the end of the performance, the actor was ～. 演出快结束时，那演员的成功是肯定无疑的了。

⑧(服装等)时髦；(食品等)正上市

⑨当政，在朝；(候选人)当选

⑩(火等)燃烧着；(灯)亮着：keep the torch ～ 使火炬一直燃烧着 / The streetlights were ～. 街灯亮着。

⑪(板球)正在攻球

⑫(油井)正出油：The well has come ～. 这口油井开始出油了。

⑬(法令等)在执行中；(证据等)在手头

⑭一致：fall ～ with sb.'s plan 与某人的计划相一致

⑮处于某种关系：be ～ bad with sb. 同某人关系不好

III a. ①在里面的；朝里面的：an ～ door 往里边开的门

②执政的，在朝的：the ～ party 执政党

③(车、船等)到站的，抵港的

④[美口]赚进的：be ～ a million U. S. dollars 赚进一百万美元

⑤时髦的，流行的：the ～ thing to do 流行的事情，时髦的做法

IV n. ①[常用复]在朝派，执政者；知情者

②[常用复](板球)攻球方

③[美口]入口；门路

④[美俚](与大人物的)特殊关系，提携：enjoy some sort of ～ with the manager 在一定程度上得到经理的赏识

‖ *be ～ for* ①必定会遭到，免不了遭受：It looks as if we *are* ～ *for* a big storm. 看来我们这一会碰上一场暴风雨的。②参加(竞争)：*Are* you ～ *for* the basketball match? 你参加篮球比赛吗？/ *be ～ for it* ①骑虎难下，已不能中途退出：Now that you *are* ～ *for it*, you must carry on. 你既然已经干了就得干下去。②势必受罚，势必倒霉 / *be ～ on* [口]参预：*be* ～ *on* a scheme 参预阴谋 / *be ～ on it* [口]熟悉内情 / *be* (或 *keep*) ～ *with sb.* ①与某人友好相处 ②与某人结伙；深得某人 (尤指大人物) 欢心 / *have it* ～

for sb. [口] 对某人怀有仇恨; 伺机想害某人 / **~ and out** ① 进进出出: be ~ *and out* of hospital 常在医院进出; 常生病住院 ② 曲曲弯弯地: The coastline winds ~ *and out* from northeast to southwest. 海岸线蜿蜒曲折地由东北往西南延伸。/ **~ between** 见 **between** / **~ so far as** 见 **far** / **~ that** 见 **that** / **In with it!** (把它) 丢进去! 装进去! / **the ~s and the outs** ① 执政党和在野党 ② (地方、事件、机械等的) 种种复杂详情: know *the ~s and the outs* of an incident 了解事件的全部详情细节
‖**~-and-'~** *a. & ad.* 同种交配的(地); 近亲交配的(地) / **,~-be'tween** *n.* 中间物(或人). No ~-*betweens*, no compromises. 不允许有任何折衷办法, 也不允许有任何妥协。 *a.* 中间性的; 中间派的: an ~-*between* stand 中间立场

in [in] *prep.* [拉] =in (*prep.*) (只接用拉丁语的名词, 构成状语词组, 这些词组多用于法律文件、科技文献等中) ‖**~ absentia** [æb'senʃiə] 缺席 / **~ articulo mortis** [ɑ:'tikjulou 'mɔ:tis] 临终时 / **~ contumaciam** [ˌkɔntju'meiʃiæm] 蔑视法庭 / **~ esse** ['esi] 确实存在着 / **~ extenso** [iks-'tensou] 全部地, 详尽地 / **~ extremis** [iks-'tri:mis] 临终时 / **~ flagrante delicto** [flə-'grænti di'liktou] 在犯罪当场, 在现行中 / **~ forma pauperis** ['fɔ:mə 'pɔ:pəris] 因贫穷准其免付诉讼费用; 作为一个穷人 / **~ loco parentis** ['loukou pə'rentis] 在养父(或养母)地位 / **~ medias res** ['mi:diæs 'ri:z] 在(或进入)事物的中心 / **~ memoriam** [mi'mɔ:riæm] 作为纪念 / **~ perpetuum** [pə'petjuəm] 永久地 / **~ posse** ['posi] 可能存在着 / **~ propria persona** ['proupriə pə'sounə] 亲自(指无律师帮助) / **~ situ** ['saitju:] 在原来位置, 在自然位置 / **~ statu quo** ['steitju: 'kwou] 按原样, 维持现状 / **~ terrorem** [te'rɔ:rem] 作为警告 / **~ toto** ['tou-tou] 全部地, 全然 / **~ vitro** ['vaitrou] 在试管内; 在(生物的)体外

inaccurate [in'ækjurit] *a.* 不精密的; 不准确的; 错误的 ‖**~ly** *ad.*

inadvertent [ˌinəd'və:tənt] *a.* ① 不经心的; 疏忽的 ② 出于无心的, 非故意的

inalienable [in'eiljənəbl] *a.* 不可分割的; 不能让与的 ‖**inalienability** [inˌeiljənə'biliti] *n.* / **inalienably** *ad.*

inane [i'nein] **I** *a.* ① 空的; 空虚的 ② 空洞的; 无意义的; 愚蠢的: make an ~ remark 言之无物 **II** *n.* [the ~] 空洞无物; 无限空间 ‖**~ly** *ad.*

inanimate [in'ænimit] *a.* ① 无生命的: an ~ object 无生物 ② 无生气的, 没精打采的: an ~ conversation 沉闷的谈话 ‖**~ly** *ad.* / **inanimation** [ˌæni'meiʃən] *n.*

inanition [ˌinə'niʃən] *n.* ① 空虚, 空洞 ②【医】虚弱; 食物不足, 营养不足

inapt [in'æpt] *a.* ① 不适当的, 不合适的 (for): an ~ analogy 不适当的比喻 ② 不熟练的, 笨拙

的; 拙劣的 (at) ‖**~ly** *ad.* / **~ness** *n.*

inasmuch [ˌinəz'mʌtʃ] *ad.* [与 as 连用, 起连接词的作用] 因为, 由于

inaugurate [i'nɔ:gjureit] *vt.* ① 开始; 开创 为…举行就职典礼: ~ a president 举行总统就职典礼 ③ 为…举行开幕式; 为…举行落成仪式: The Export Commodities Fair was ~*d* yesterday. 出口商品交易会昨天开幕了。 ‖**inauguration** [iˌnɔ:gju'reiʃən] *n. Inauguration* Day (美国)总统就职日 / **inaugurator** *n.* 主持就职(或开幕等)仪式者; 开创者, 创始人

inborn ['in'bɔ:n] *a.* ① 生来的, 天生的 ② 先天的, 遗传的

inbred ['in'bred] *a.* ① 生来的, 先天的 ② 选种产生的 ③【生】近亲繁殖的, 近交的: ~ line 近交系

inbreed ['in'bri:d] (inbred ['in'bred]) *vt.* ① 使近亲繁殖, 使近交 ② 使在内部发生 (或产生) ‖**~ing** *n.* ①【生】近亲繁殖, 近交 ②(知识等的)限于狭隘范围

incandescent [ˌinkæn'desnt] *a.* ① 白热的; 白炽的: an ~ lamp 白炽灯 / ~ sand flow【地】热沙流 ②极亮的, 灿烂的; 闪闪发光的; 炽热的; 热情的

incandescent lamp

incantation [ˌinkæn'teiʃən] *n.* 咒语; 符咒; 妖术

incapacitate [ˌinkə'pæsiteit] *vt.* ① 使无能力; 使残废: ~ sb. from working (或 for work) 使人不能工作 ②【律】使无资格: be ~*d* from voting 被剥夺选举权 ‖**incapacitation** ['inkəˌpæsi-'teiʃən] *n.*

incapacity [ˌinkə'pæsiti] *n.* ① 无能力: ~ to work (或 for working) 不能工作 / renal ~【医】肾机能不全 ②【律】无资格

incarcerate [in'kɑ:səreit] *vt.* ① 监禁; 禁闭 ②【医】钳闭 ‖**incarceration** [inˌkɑ:sə'reiʃən] *n.*

incarnate I ['inkɑ:neit] *vt.* ① 赋予…以形体; 使成化身; 使实体化 ②使具体化, 体现 **II** [in'kɑ:nit] *a.* ①化身的; 人体化的; 实体化的 ②肉色的; 红的; 玫瑰红的 ‖**incarnation** [ˌinkɑ:'neiʃən] *n.* 化身; 体现;【医】肉化

incendiary [in'sendjəri] **I** *a.* ①放火的, 纵火的; 燃烧的: an ~ bomb 燃烧弹 ②煽动性的 **II** *n.* ①纵火者; 燃烧弹; 可引起燃烧的东西 ②煽动者 ‖**incendiarism** [in'sendjərizəm] *n.* 放火, 纵火; 煽动

incense¹ ['insens] **I** *n.* ①香; 焚香时的烟: mosquito coil ~ 蚊香 ②香气 ③奉承, 恭维 **II ❶** *vt.* 用香熏; 对…焚香 **❷** *vi.* 焚香 ‖**incensation** [,insen'seiʃən] *n.* 熏香 ‖~ **burner** 香炉

incense² [in'sens] *vt.* 使发怒, 激怒: be ~d by sb.'s conduct 被某人的行为所激怒 / be ~d at sb.'s remarks 对某人的话感到愤怒

incentive [in'sentiv] **I** *n.* 刺激; 鼓励: give sb. an ~ to (或 to make) greater efforts 激发某人作出更大的努力 / material ~s 物质刺激 **II** *a.* 刺激的; 鼓励的

incept [in'sept] **❶** *vt.* ①[古]开始 ②接收(入会); [生]摄取 **❷** *vi.* (在英国剑桥大学)取得硕士(或博士)学位 ‖~**ion** [in'sepʃən] *n.* 开始, 发端; (英国剑桥大学)硕士(或博士)学位的取得 / ~**ive** *a.* 开始的; [语]表示动作的开始的 *n.* 表示开始的动词(或短语) / ~**or** *n.* 开始人, 发端者; (英国剑桥大学)取得硕士(或博士)学位者

incessant [in'sesnt] *a.* 不停的, 连续的, 持续不断的; 频繁的: ~ rains 连绵不断的雨 ‖~**ly** *ad.* / ~**ness** *n.*

incest ['insest] *n.* 乱伦

inch¹ [intʃ] **I** *n.* ①英寸, 吋(略作 in.) ②[复]身高; 身材: He is about your ~es. 他的身材和你相仿。③(距离、数量、程度等的)少许, 一点儿: I couldn't see an ~ before me in the dense fog. 在浓雾中我面前一点儿也看不见。/ escape death by an ~ 差点儿送命 **II ❶** *vt.* 使缓慢地移动; 使渐进: The mountaineers ~ed their way up the snow-clad peak. 登山队员一步一步地攀登积雪的山峰。**❷** *vi.* 缓慢地移动; 渐进: Prices are ~ing down. 物价正逐步下降。‖**an ~ of cold iron** 匕首的一刺 / **by ~es** 缓慢地, 一点一点地: kill sb. **by ~es** 把某人慢慢地折磨死 / **by ~ of candle** 通过拍卖(因过去拍卖时点着蜡烛)/ **every ~** 完全, 彻底 / **Give him an ~ and he'll take an ell.** [谚]他得寸进尺。/ **~ by ~** 一点一点地; 渐渐地 / **not yield an ~** 寸步不让 / **to an ~** 精确地, 丝毫不差地: fulfil the requirements **to an ~** 完完全全达到要求 / **within an ~ of** 差点儿: The athlete was *within an ~ of* breaking the record. 那个运动员差点儿打破纪录。/ **within an ~ of one's life** 差点儿丧命 ‖~**ed** *a.* [常用以构成复合词]长…英寸的; 刻有时的

inch² [intʃ] *n.* [苏格兰]小岛

incidence ['insidəns] *n.* ①发生; 影响; 影响的方式: What is the ~ of the tax? 这税会落在谁的身上? ②影响范围; 影响程度; 发生率 ③[物]入射; 入射角: plane of ~ 入射(平)面 / angle of ~ 入射角 ④[空](机翼)倾角; 安装角: ~ wire 倾角线 ⑤[数]关联, 接合: ~ numbers 关联数

incident ['insidənt] **I** *n.* ①附带事件, 小事件; 事情 ②(小说、剧本中的)插曲; 枝节 ③[律]附带事物; 附属于财产的权利(或义务) **II** *a.* ①易发生的; 伴随而来的 (*to*): the difficulties ~ to the

mountaineering 登山过程中要遇到的种种困难 / new duties ~ to increased tasks 随着新增加的任务而来的新的职责 ②[律]附属的 (*to*) ③[物]入射的: light ~ *upon* the surface 投射在表面的光 / ~ rays 入射线

incidental [,insi'dentl] **I** *a.* ①附带的; 伴随的, 非主要的: ~ music *to* the performance 演出的配乐 / ~ expenses 杂费 ②偶然碰到的: an ~ acquaintance 偶然相识的人 ③易发生的: diseases ~ *to* childhood 幼年易得的疾病 **II** *n.* ①附带事件 ②[复]杂项; 杂费 ‖~**ly** *ad.* ①附带地; 偶然地 ②顺便说及地: *Incidentally,* your letter came only this morning. 顺便提一句, 你的信直到今天早上才收到。

incinerate [in'sinəreit] **❶** *vt.* 把…烧成灰; 烧尽; 焚化; 火葬 **❷** *vi.* 烧成灰; 烧尽 ‖**incineration** [in,sinə'reiʃən] *n.* 焚化; 火葬 / **incinerator** *n.* 焚化者; 焚化炉; 火葬炉

incipient [in'sipiənt] *a.* 开始的; 刚出现的; 早期的: ~ light of day 曙光 / (an) ~ cancer 早期癌症 ‖~**ly** *ad.*

incise [in'saiz] *vt.* ①切入, 切开 ②雕刻 ‖~**d** *a.* ①切入的, 切开的: ~d wound [医]刀伤, 割伤 ②[植](叶)有缺刻的 ③雕刻的

incision [in'siʒən] *n.* ①切入, 切开: abdominal ~ [医]剖腹术 ②[植](叶的)缺刻 ③雕刻

incisive [in'saisiv] *a.* ①切入的; 锋利的 ②尖锐的; 深刻的; 透彻的: an ~ criticism 尖锐的批评 / an ~ analysis 透彻的分析 ③[解]切牙的; 门牙的 ‖~**ly** *ad.* / ~**ness** *n.*

incite [in'sait] *vt.* 激励; 刺激; 煽动; 促成: ~ sb. *to* (go into) further investigation 促使某人作进一步的调查 / ~ sb.'s curiosity 引起某人的好奇心 / ~ war 煽动战争 ‖~**ment** *n.*

inclement [in'klemənt] *a.* ①(天气、气候)险恶的, 酷烈的; 寒冷的; 狂风暴雨的 ②(人)严酷的, 无情的

inclination [,inkli'neiʃən] *n.* ①倾斜; 点头; 弯腰: He expressed his consent with an ~ (of the head). 他点头表示同意。②斜坡; 倾度; [数]倾角, 斜角: ~ of an orbit [天]轨道交角 ③倾向; 爱好: follow one's own ~s 随心所欲 / show little ~ to go (或 to going) there 不大想去那儿 / have an ~ for sports 爱好体育运动 ④爱好的事物

incline [in'klain] **I ❶** *vi.* ①倾斜 ②屈身; 低头: ~ *towards* the speaker to hear more clearly 把身体俯向发言的人以便听得更清楚些 ③倾向(于); 赞同, 喜爱: yellow *inclining to* green 黄中带绿 / I strongly ~ *to* the view that.... 我很倾向于…这样的意见。/ ~ *to* corpulence(身体)有发胖的趋势 ④[军]侧转前进: Left ~! 半面向左转走! **❷** *vt.* ①使倾斜; 屈(身); 低(头): an ~d plane 斜面 / ~ one's ear *to* sb. 倾听并赞同某人的话 ②[常用被动语态]使倾向于, 使想要: What he said ~s me *to* think that he will agree to our plan. 他的话使我觉得他会同意我们的计划的. / Do you feel ~*d for* a cup of tea? 你想喝杯茶吗? **II** *n.* 斜面; 斜坡

include [in'klu:d] *vt.* ①包住, 关住: The nutshell ~*s* the kernel. 果壳裹住果仁. ② 包括; 包含; 算入: The freight is ~*d* in the account. 运费包括在帐内. (== ~ terms) ‖**includable, includible** *a.* 可包括在内的

inclusion [in'klu:ʒən] *n.* ①包括; 包含 ②内含物; 【医】包涵物; 【矿】包体; 【冶】夹杂物

inclusive [in'klu:siv] *a.* ① 包围住的; 范围广的 ②包括的: from Monday to Friday ~ 从星期一到星期五, 首尾两天也包括在内 ③ 一切开支(或项目)包括在内的: an ~ fee 一切开支包括在内的费用 (== ~ terms) ‖~*ly ad.* / ~*ness n.*

incognito [in'kɔgnitou] **I** *a. & ad.* 隐匿姓名身分的(地), 微行的(地) **II** *n.* 隐匿姓名身分(者), 微行(者)

income ['inkəm] *n.* 收入; 收益; 进款, 所得: net ~ 纯收入 ‖~ **account** ①收益帐 ②损益计算书 / ~ **statement** 损益计算书 / ~ **tax** 所得税

incoming ['in,kʌmiŋ] **I** *a.* ① 进来的: the ~ tide 涨潮 / an ~ vessel 进(港)口船舶 / the ~ year 即将到来的一年 ②正从外国移入的 ③新来的; 继任的 ④(收益等)正在产生的, 即将取得的: ~ profits 即将取得的利润 **II** *n.* ① 进来, 到来 ② [常用复]收入: ~*s and* outgoings 收支

incommode [,inkə'moud] *vt.* 使感不便; 妨碍, 打扰; 惹恼: Will it ~ you if I keep the book for another week? 那本书我再借用一星期会使你不方便吗?

incomparable [in'kɔmpərəbl] *a.* ①无比的, 无双的: ~ skill 无与伦比的高超技能 ②不能比较的; 无共同衡量基础的 *(with, to)* ‖**incomparably** *ad.*

incomplete [,inkəm'pli:t] *a.* 不完全的; 未完成的; 不完善的: ~ reaction 【化】不完全反应, 可逆反应 ‖~*ly ad.* / ~*ness n.*

incongruity [,inkɔŋ'gru(:)iti] *n.* ① 不调和; 不一致; 不适合, 不相称 ②不协调的事物

incongruous [in'kɔŋgruəs] *a.* ①不调和的; 自相矛盾的, 不一致的 *(with)*: ~ colours 不调和的色彩 / conduct ~ *with* avowed principles 与自己宣称的原则不一致的行为 ②不适合的; 不恰当的; 不合理的 ‖~*ly ad.*

inconsequent [in'kɔnsikwənt] *a.* ①不连贯的, 前后不符的; 不合逻辑的; 不对题的: ~ reasoning 自相矛盾的推论 ② 无关紧要的, 无价值的 ‖~*ly ad.*

inconsequential [in,kɔnsi'kwenʃəl] **I** *a.* ①无意义的; 无关紧要的, 微不足道的 ②不连贯的; 不合逻辑的 **II** *n.* 无关紧要的事物 ‖~*ly ad.*

inconvenience [,inkən'vi:njəns] **I** *n.* ①不方便; 打扰: put sb. to ~ 使某人感到不便 ② 不便之处, 烦扰的事 **II** *vt.* 使感不便: I hope I haven't ~*d* you. 我希望没有打扰你.

inconvenient [,inkən'vi:njənt] *a.* 不方便的, 引起不方便的; 烦扰的: Please come, if it is not ~ to you. 如果你方便的话, 就请来一次.

incorporate [in'kɔ:pəreit] **I ❶** *vt.* ①结合; 合并; 收编: We will ~ your suggestion in the new plan. 我们将把你的建议编到新计划中去. ②使混合 ③ 使具体化; 使实体化; 体现 ④ 使结成社团; 使组成公司; 使加入社团组织: an ~*d* company [美] 【商】股份有限公司 / be ~*d* a member of a learned society 被吸收为学会成员 **❷** *vi.* ①合并; 混合 *(with)* ② 成为社团; 组成公司 **II** [in'kɔ:pərit] *a.* ①一体化的, 合并的 ②紧密结合的 ②掺合的, 混合的 ③ (结成)社团的; (组成)公司的 ‖**incorporation** [in,kɔ:pə'reiʃən] *n.* ①结合; 合并; 社团; 公司 ②掺合, 混合 / **incorporator** *n.* 合并者; 社团成员; 公司创办人

incorrigible [in'kɔridʒəbl] **I** *a.* 难以纠正的; 不可改造的, 不可救药的; 固执的, 难弄的 **II** *n.* 不改悔的人, 不可救药的人 ‖**incorrigibility** [in,kɔridʒə'biliti] *n.* / **incorrigibly** *ad.*

increase **I** [in'kri:s] **❶** *vt.* 增加; 增长; 增殖; 增进: ~ production and practise economy 增产节约 / ~ wages 增加工资 **❷** *vi.* 增加; 繁殖: The per unit area yield of ginned cotton has ~*d* by 15% over the last year. 皮棉单位面积产量比去年增加了百分之十五. / greatly ~ *in* power and prestige 力量和威望大大增加 / ~ *with* years 与年俱增 **II** ['inkri:s] *n.* 增加; 增长; 增殖; 增进: an ~ *in* industrial and agricultural output 工农业产量的增加 ‖**on the** ~ 不断增长; 正在增加: The technical cooperation and cultural exchanges between the two countries are daily *on the* ~. 两国之间的技术合作和文化交流正在与日俱增.

increasingly [in'kri:siŋli] *ad.* 继续增加地; 日益: be ~ prosperous and strong 日益繁荣强盛

increment ['inkrimənt] *n.* ①增长; 增额; 增值: yearly ~*s* 年度增加额 / unearned ~ 【经】自然增值 ②【数】增量

incriminate [in'krimineit] *vt.* ①控告; 显示…有罪 ②连累(某人); 归罪于: ~ oneself 使自己牵连进刑事案件 ‖**incriminatory** [in'kriminətəri] *a.*

incubate ['inkjubeit] **❶** *vt.* ① 孵(卵), 孵育 ②使发展, 把…酝酿成熟 **❷** *vi.* 孵卵; 酝酿成熟 ‖**incubation** [,inkju'beiʃən] *n.* ① 孵卵, 孵化: artificial *incubation* 人工孵卵 ②【医】潜伏: *incubation* period 潜伏期 ③ 酝酿 / **incubative** *a.* 孵卵的; 潜伏期的 / **incubator** *n.* ①孵卵器; 孵卵员 ②早产婴儿保育箱 ③细菌培养器 / **incubatory** *a.* 孵卵的; 孵育用的

inculcate ['inkʌlkeit, in'kʌlkeit] *vt.* ①反复灌输; ②谆谆教诲 ‖**inculcation** [,inkʌl'keiʃən] *n.* / **inculcator** *n.* 反复灌输者; 谆谆教诲者

incumbent [in'kʌmbənt] **I** *a.* ① 成为责任的; 义不容辞的 (*on, upon*): It is ~ *upon* us to do so. 这样做是我们义不容辞的责任。②压(或覆盖)在上面的 (*on*) ③弯垂下来的 ④在职的 ⑤(地层)重迭的, 迭覆的; 上覆的 **II** *n.* ①教会中的任职者; 教区牧师 ②[美]政府(或团体、学术机构等)的任职者

incur [in'kə:] (incurred; incurring [in'kə:riŋ]) *vt.* 招致, 惹起; 遭受: ~ a heavy loss 招致重大损失 / ~ danger 遭受危险 / ~ great expense 带来很大的花费

incursion [in'kə:ʃən] *n.* ① 进入; 流入: the ~ of water through a crack 水从裂缝中的流入 ② 侵入, 袭击; 侵犯: make an ~ into 对…进行入侵

indebted [in'detid] *a.* ① 负债的; 法律上有义务偿还的 ②受惠的; 蒙恩的; 感激的: I am greatly ~ *to* you *for* your criticisms and help. 我非常感激你的批评和帮助。 ‖**~ness** *n.*

indeed [in'di:d] *ad.* ①真正地, 实际上: To investigate a problem is, ~, to solve it. 调查就是解决问题。②[加强语气]确实, 实在 ③[表示让步]当然, 固然: These problems are ~ difficult ones, but I am sure they can be solved. 这些问题固然是些难题, 但我相信它们是能够解决的。④[表示进一层的意思]甚至 ⑤[表示惊讶、轻蔑等]真的; 真是: *Indeed*? You are already going? 什么? 你这么早就要走啦! / A: You must thank him for his kindness. B: Kindness ~! 甲: 你应该谢谢他的好意。乙: 什么好意! / A: What is his name? B: What is it, ~! 甲: 他叫什么名字? 乙: 他叫什么名字! 这你还要问吗? (或: 是啊, 他到底叫什么名字?)

indefatigable [,indi'fætigəbl] *a.* 不倦的; 不屈不挠的: ~ bridge builders 努力不懈的造桥工人们 / work with ~ zeal 以坚持不懈的热情工作 ‖**indefatigability** ['indi,fætigə'biliti] *n.* / **indefatigably** *ad.*

indefinite [in'definit] *a.* ① 无定限的; 无限期的: a strike of ~ duration 无限期罢工 ②不明确的; 模糊的: give an ~ answer 作含糊其词的答复 ③【语】不定的: the ~ article 不定冠词 ④【植】(雄蕊)无定数的 ‖**~ly** *ad.* / **~ness** *n.*

indelible [in'delibl] *a.* ① 去不掉的; 洗不掉的; 擦不掉的; 持久的: ~ ink stains 去不掉的墨渍 / ~ shame 洗刷不掉的耻辱 ②留下不易除去的痕迹的: an ~ pencil 笔迹难擦掉的铅笔 ‖**indelibility** [in,deli'biliti] *n.* / **indelibly** *ad.*

indelicate [in'delikit] *a.* ① 不文雅的, 粗俗的: an ~ remark 粗鄙的话 ②粗鲁的, 粗率的: make an ~ allusion to sb.'s shortcomings 粗鲁地提及某人的缺点 ‖**~ly** *ad.*

indemnify [in'demnifai] *vt.* ① 保障, 保护: ~ sb. *from* (或 *against*) damage 保障某人不受损害 ②使免于受罚 ③赔偿, 补偿: ~ sb. *for* his loss 赔偿某人损失 ‖**indemnification** [in,demnifi'keiʃən] *n.*

indemnity [in'demniti] *n.* ①保障, 保护: a measure that offers ~ *against* further loss 使免受更多损失的措施 ②免罚; 赦免 ③ 赔偿, 补偿 ④赔偿物, 赔款(尤指战败国的): a war ~ 战争赔款

indent[1] **I** [in'dent] ❶ *vt.* ①把…刻成锯齿形, 使成犬牙状; 打缺刻于: an ~ed coastline 锯齿形的海岸线 ②把(一张抄有一式两份或两份以上文件的纸张)按犬牙状割开(以备将来拼拢验证文件真伪之用) ③一式两份(或两份以上)地起草(文件、合同等) ④(印刷或书写中)缩进排(或书写): the first line of each paragraph 把每段第一行缩进几格排印(或书写) ⑤[英](用双联单)订(货) ❻用榫眼接牢 ❷ *vi.* ①刻成锯齿形; 打缺刻 ②订合同 ③[英](用双联单)订货(向…)正式申请 (*on*); 动用 (*on*): ~ *upon* sb. *for* goods 向某人订货 **II** ['indent] *n.* ①锯齿形; 缺刻 ②合同, 契约 ③(印刷或书写中的)缩进, 空格; 缩进排的一行(或段落等) ④ [英]国外订货单 ⑤ [英]征用令

indent[2] **I** [in'dent] *vt.* ①在…上压凹痕 ②压印(图案等) **II** ['indent] *n.* 凹痕

indenture [in'dentʃə] **I** *n.* ①契约; 双联合同 ②[常用复]师徒契约; 定期服务合同: take up one's ~s 学徒期满; 服务期满 ③凭单(如商业上的传票、清单等) ④缺刻, 凹痕 **II** *vt.* 以契约束缚(学徒等)

independence [,indi'pendəns] *n.* ①独立; 自主; 自立 ②足够维持闲居生活的收入(或资产)

independent [,indi'pendənt] **I** *a.* ①独立的; 自治的; 有主见的: a ~ country 独立国家 / ~ thinking 独立思考 / ~ research work 独立的研究工作 ② 不愿受约束的: an ~ manner 不愿受约束的样子 ③(收入等)足够维持闲居生活的; 富裕得无须为生计而操劳的 ④单独的; 不接受外援的; 不承担义务的: an ~ attack 【军】单独进攻 / an ~ grocer 独立经营的杂货商 ⑤无党派的: an ~ voter 无党派的选民 ⑥[I-]【宗】独立派的 ⑦【语】主要的, 主体的: an ~ clause (主从复合句中的)主句 ⑧【数】无关的, 独立的: ~ functions 独立函数 / ~ variable 自变数, 自变量 **II** *n.* ①独立自主的人 ② 无党派者 ③[I-]【宗】独立派教徒, 公理会教徒 ‖**~ of** 独立于…之外的, 不受…支配的: be ~ *of* outside control 不受外界控制 / an objective law ~ *of* man's will 不以人们意志为转移的客观规律 ②与…无关的; 不依赖…的: be ~ *of* each other 相互无关 / be ~ *of* one's parents 不依赖父母而自立 ‖**~ly** *ad.* act ~ly 独立自行动 / *Independently of* what you may think, I have my own opinion. 不管你怎么想, 我有我自己的意见。

indeterminate [,indi'tə:minit] *a.* ①不确定的; 无定限的; 不明确的; 模糊的: an ~ result 不明确的结果 ②不会有结果的; 仍有疑问的; 未决定的, 未解决的: an ~ debate 不会有结果的辩论 / an ~ sentence 【律】规定刑期限度而具体刑期由行政当局视犯人表现而定的判决 ③ 无法预先知道的 ④【语】无确定音值的, 中性的: an ~ vowel

中性元音 (如 ago 中的 a 或 moment 中的 e 的发音) ⑤【数】不确定的; 未定元的: ~ analysis 不定解析(或分析) ⑥【植】总状的; 花被与花萼分隔而未覆盖着的 ‖~ly ad. / ~ness n.

index ['indeks] **I**([复] indexes 或 indices ['indisi:z]) **n.** ①索引; card ~es in a library 图书馆的卡片索引 ②指标; 标准; 标志 ③指数: the cost of living ~ 生活费指数 / price indices 物价指数 ④(刻度盘上的)指针; 【机】(铣床)分度(头); 【印】指标, 示指; 参见号(即 ☞): an ~ pin (plate) 指度针(盘) ⑤食指 (=~ finger) ⑥ [the I-] (天主教的)禁书目录 **II** ❶ **vt.** ①为(书籍等)做索引: The book is well ~ed. 这本书编有很好的索引。②把(资料等)编入索引: All persons and places mentioned in this book are ~ed. 凡本书提及的人名、地名均编入索引。③指向; 指明 ❷ **vi.** 做索引 ‖~er n. 编索引的人 / ~ical [in'deksikəl] a. / ~less a. 无索引的 ‖~ fossil 【地】标准化石 / ~ number 指数

India ['indjə] **n.** 印度[亚洲] ‖~ ink 墨; 墨汁 / ~man ['indjəmən] n. 过去用于与印度做生意的商船 / ~ paper 薄型不透明而坚韧的印刷纸, 字典纸, 圣经纸 (=Oxford ~ paper) / ~ rubber 橡皮; 橡胶; 橡胶套鞋

India ['indjə] 通讯中用以代表字母 i 的词

Indian ['indjən] **I** a. ① 印度的; 印度人的; 印度文化的 ② 印第安人的; 印第安文化的; 西印度群岛的; 西印度群岛文化的 ③玉米制的 **II** n. ①印度人 ②印第安人 ③印第安语 ④过去长期居住印度的欧洲人(尤指英国人) ‖~ agent (美国及加拿大的)印第安事务官 / ~ club (体操用的)瓶状棒 / ~ corn [英]玉蜀黍, 玉米, 苞米 / ~ file 一路纵队: in ~ file 成一路纵队 / ~ giver [口] 送东西给人而日后索回的人; 送东西给人而希望还礼的人 / ~ ink 墨; 墨汁 / ~ meal 玉米粉 / ~ Ocean 印度洋 / ~ red 印度红; 【化】三氧化铁; 氧化正铁 / ~ summer ①(美国北部或其他国家)晚秋的晴暖宜人的气候, 小阳春 ②兴旺的晚期; 愉快宁静的晚年 / ~ weed 烟草

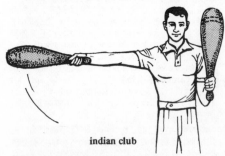

indian club

indicate ['indikeit] **vt.** ①指示; 指出: an arrow indicating the direction of advance 指示前进方向的箭头 / ~ a place on a map 指出地图上的某一地方 ②表明(症状、原因等); 象征; 预示; 暗示:

a high fever that ~s severe illness 表明病重的高烧 ③ 需要; 使成为必要: In this weather, a fire is ~d. 在这样的天气, 需要生火。④ 简要地说明 ‖~d horsepower 【机】指示马力(略作 i. h. p.) / ~d power 【机】指示功率 / ~d work 【机】指示功

indication [,indi'keiʃən] **n.** ① 指示; 指出; 表示 ②象征; 暗示; 迹象: give ~ of a change in the weather 表明天气要变 / There are ~s that .... 有迹象表明… ③【医】指示法; 适效; 指征: 适应症: The immediate ~ is artificial respiration. 立即有效的疗法是人工呼吸。④指示器表示的量(或度数)

indicative [in'dikətiv] **I** a. ① 指示的; 表示的; 象征的; 预示的 ②【语】陈述的, 直陈的: the ~ mood 陈述语气 **II** n. 【语】陈述语气; 动词的陈述语气形式 ‖~ly ad.

indicator ['indikeitə] **n.** ①指示者; 指示物 ②【机】指示器; 示功器: ~ card (或 diagram) 示功图 ③【化】指示剂

indices ['indisi:z] index 的复数

indict [in'dait] **vt.** 控告, 告发, 对…起诉: ~ sb. as a scab 指控某人为工贼 / ~ sb. for sabotage 告发某人的破坏行为 / be ~ed on a charge of 因犯…罪被起诉 ‖~able a. (人或罪行)可被控告的 / ~ion [in'dikʃən] n.

indifference [in'difrəns], **indifferency** [in'difrənsi] **n.** ① 不关心, 冷淡; 不计较: show ~ to (或 towards) personal affairs 不计较个人的事 ②无关紧要, 不在乎: face death with ~ 置生死于度外 / a matter of ~ 无关紧要的事 ③ 中立; 中性

indifferent [in'difrənt] **I** a. ① 不关心的, 冷淡的, 不感兴趣的 ② 无关紧要的, 不在乎的: ~ to hardships and dangers 置艰险危险于度外 ③ 一般的, 质量不高的; 能力平常的; 差得很的: an ~ book 质量不高的书 / an ~ performance 水平不高的演出 / a very ~ footballer 很差的足球运动员 ④无偏袒的; 中立的: remain ~ in a dispute 对争论保持中立 ⑤【物】中性的, 惰性的 ⑥【生】未分化的 **II** n. (在政治或宗教等方面)冷淡的人 ‖~ly ad.

indigenous [in'didʒinəs] a. ①本土的, 土生土长的: use ~ raw materials 就地取材 / make up-to-date products with ~ equipments and methods 用土设备、土办法制造现代化产品 / Giant pandas are ~ to China. 熊猫产于中国。②生来的, 固有的 (to) ‖~ly ad.

indigent ['indidʒənt] a. 贫困的, 贫穷的

indigestible [,indi'dʒestəbl, ,indai'dʒestəbl] a. ① 难消化的, 无法消化的 ② 难理解的, 难领会的 ‖indigestibility ['indi,dʒestə'biliti, 'indai,dʒestə'biliti] n.

indigestion [,indi'dʒestʃən, ,indai'dʒestʃən] **n.** 消化不良, 胃弱; [喻]难理解, 难领会 ‖indigestive [,indi'dʒestiv, ,indai'dʒestiv] a.

indignant [in'dignənt] *a.* 愤慨的, 义愤的: be ~ at (或 over, about) sth. 对某事感到愤慨 / be ~ with sb. 对某人表示愤慨 ‖~ly *ad.*

indignation [,indig'neiʃən] *n.* 愤慨, 义愤: an ~ meeting 声讨大会

indignity [in'digniti] *n.* 无礼, 侮辱; 侮辱的言行: treat sb. with ~ 侮辱某人

indigo ['indigou] *n.* ①靛蓝, 靛青; 靛蓝类染料: ~-blue 靛蓝色 / Chinese ~ 草本靛青 / Indian ~ 木本靛青 ②一种深蓝色 ③【植】能产生靛蓝的植物(尤指槐蓝)

indiscreet [,indis'kri:t] *a.* 不慎重的, 轻率的; 不得体的, 不明智的 ‖~ly *ad.*

indiscriminate [,indis'kriminit] *a.* ①不加区别的, 无选择的, 不分青红皂白的: give ~ praise 一味恭维 / an ~ reading habit 不加选择地阅读的习惯 ②杂乱的; 任性的 ‖~ly *ad.* / ~ness *n.*

indispensable [,indis'pensəbl] **I** *a.* ①必不可少的, 必需的 (to, for): Air is ~ to life. 空气是生命所必需的东西。②不能撇开的, 责无旁贷的: an ~ obligation 不可推卸的责任 **II** *n.* 不可少的人(或物) ‖**indispensability** ['indis,pensə'biliti] *n.* / ~ness *n.* / **indispensably** *ad.*

indisposed [,indis'pouzd] *a.* ①不愿的; 不倾向的; 厌恶的: He is ~ to go. 他不想去。/ be ~ towards sb. 对某人没有好感 ②不舒服的, 有病的: I am ~ with a cold today. 今天我感冒了, 感到不舒服。

indisposition [,indispə'ziʃən] *n.* ①不舒服, 小病: recover from one's ~ 小病痊愈 ②无意; 厌恶: have an ~ to (或 to play) the game 不高兴玩那游戏 / have an ~ towards (或 to) fast life 厌恶放荡生活

individual [,indi'vidjuəl] **I** *a.* ①个人的, 个体的; 个别的, 单独的: give ~ attention (instruction) 给予个别注意(指导) / ~ private ownership 个体所有制 / ~ economy 个体经济 ②独特的; 个性的: an ~ style 独特风格 **II** *n.* ①个人, 个体; 独立单位 ②[俚]人. ‖~**ism** *n.* ①个人主义; 利己主义 ②个性; 独特性 ③不干涉主义, 自由放任主义 / ~**ist** *n.* 个人主义者; 利己主义者 *a.* 个人主义(者)的: an ~**ist** careerist 个人主义野心家 / ~**ly** *ad.* ①以个人资格; 分别地, 各个地; 各自地 ②独特地

individuality [,indi,vidju'æliti] *n.* ①个性; 个人的特征 ②个体; 个人; 独立存在 ③[常用复]个人的趣味(或爱好等)

indoctrinate [in'dɔktrineit] *vt.* ①灌输: ~ sb. with an idea (a belief) 把一种想法(信仰)灌输给某人 ②教, 教训 ‖**indoctrination** [in,dɔktri'neiʃən] *n.*

indoor ['indɔ:] *a.* ① (在)室内的, (在)屋里的: ~ antenna 【无】室内天线 ②室内进行的; 住在室内的: ~ gymnastics 室内运动

indoors ['in'dɔ:z] *ad.* 在屋里; 进入室内: keep (或 stay) ~ 呆在家里, 不外出 / go ~ 进屋里

indubitable [in'dju:bitəbl] *a.* 不容置疑的; 明确的 ‖**indubitability** [in,dju:bitə'biliti] *n.* / **indubitably** *ad.*

induce [in'dju:s] *vt.* ①引诱; 劝使: ~ sb. to do sth. 劝诱某人做某事 / Nothing shall ~ me to go. 我怎么都不去。②引起; 导致: indigestion ~d by overeating 因饮食过多而引起的消化不良 / ~d abortion 人工流产 ③【逻】归纳 ④诱导; 【电】感应: ~d current 感应电流

inducement [in'dju:smənt] *n.* ①引诱; 劝诱 ②诱因, 动机: have much ~ (或 many ~s) to do sth. 很想去做某事 ③【律】提出主张事项前的陈述说明

induct [in'dʌkt] *vt.* ① (通过正式仪式)使就职 (to, into) ②使正式入会; 征调·· 入伍 (to, into) ③介绍(知识等); 使初步入门 ④引入, 引导: ~ sb. into a seat 引导某人就座 ⑤【电】感应, 感生

induction [in'dʌkʃən] *n.* ①就职; 入会; 入伍; 入伍仪式 ②首次经验, 入门 ③[古]前言; 序幕 ④【逻】【数】归纳法, 归纳: ~ principle 归纳法原则 ⑤吸入; 【电】感应, 感应现象 ‖~ **coil**【电】感应线圈, 电感线圈 / ~ **field**【电】感应(磁)场, 感应(电)场 / ~ **furnace**【冶】感应电炉 / ~ **heating**【电】感应加热 / ~ **motor**【电】感应电动机, 异步电动机 / ~ **stroke**【机】吸入冲程 / ~ **valve**【机】吸入阀, 进气门

inductive [in'dʌktiv] *a.* ①引入的; 诱进的 ②【逻】【数】归纳的, 归纳法的: ~ method 归纳法 ③【电】感应的, 电感的: ~ coupling 电感耦合 / ~ reactance 感抗 ④导论的, 绪论的 ‖~ly *ad.* / ~ness *n.*

indulge [in'dʌldʒ] ❶ *vt.* ①使(自己)沉迷; 放纵(感情、欲望); 纵情享受: He no longer ~d himself in smoking. 他不再过度抽烟了。/ ~ a taste for the exotic 纵情赏奇猎异 ②使满足; 纵容; 迁就: ~ a child 纵容孩子 ③【商】容许(某人)延期付款 ❷ *vi.* ①纵情, 沉迷; 沉溺: ~ in the wildest fantasy 一味异想天开 / ~ in self-glorification 大肆自吹自擂 ②[口]酗酒, 嗜酒

indulgence [in'dʌldʒəns], **indulgency** [in'dʌldʒənsi] *n.* ①任性, 放肆; 沉溺, 着迷 ②纵容; 娇养 ③嗜好, 着迷的事物 ④【商】付款延期 ⑤恩惠, 特惠; (天主教的)免罪

indulgent [in'dʌldʒənt] *a.* 纵容的; 宽容的; 溺爱的: be ~ to sb. 宽容(或溺爱)某人 ‖~ly *ad.*

industrial [in'dʌstriəl] **I** *a.* ①工业的, 产业的, 实业的: an independent and integrated ~ system 独立完整的工业体系 / learn ~ production 学工 / ~ arts 工艺劳作(美国中小学的一门课程) / an ~ school 工艺劳作学校(尤指教养青少年犯的机构) ②从事工业的 ③工业高度发达的: an ~ country 工业国 ④供工业用的: ~ alcohol 工业用的酒精 / ~ diamond 工业用的钻石 ⑤因勤奋努力而得到的: an ~ crop 靠劳力而得的收获 **II** *n.* ①工业工人, 产业工人 ②工业公司 ③[商]工业股票 ‖~**ism** *n.* 工业(或产业)主义 / ~**ist**

n. 工业主义者;实业家 / ~**ly** *ad.* ‖~ **archae-ology** 工业考古学(指对过去技术发达时代,尤指工业革命后各阶段的研究) / ~ **park** 工业区(一般在郊区) / ~ **relations** 劳资关系 / **Industrial Revolution** (十八世纪六十年代在英国开始的)产业革命,工业革命 / ~ **union** 同一工业内跨行业的职工工会

industrialize [in'dʌstriəlaiz] ❶ *vt.* 使工业化: highly ~*d* areas (cities) 高度工业化的地区(城市) ❷ *vi.* 工业化 ‖**industrialization** [in,dʌstriəlai'zeiʃən] *n.* 工业化: bring about socialist *industrialization* 实现社会主义工业化

industrious [in'dʌstriəs] *a.* 勤劳的,勤奋的 ‖~**ly** *ad.* / ~**ness** *n.*

industry ['indəstri] *n.* ① 勤劳, 勤奋: build the country with ~ and frugality 勤俭建国 ② 有组织的劳动; 经常的工作 ③工业, 产业; 行业: heavy and light *industries* 重工业和轻工业 / national and local *industries* 中央和地方工业 / state-operated ~ 国营工业 / the ~ of national defence 国防工业 / the automobile ~ 汽车制造业 / the air transport ~ 航空运输业 / the hotel ~ 旅馆业 ④[总称]工业(或产业等)的资方人员

inebriate [i'ni:briit] **I** *a.* 酒醉的 **II** *n.* 酒鬼,酒徒 **III** [i'ni:brieit] *vt.* ①使醉;灌醉 ②使如痴如醉;使兴奋;使发呆

ineffable [in'efəbl] *a.* ①无法表达的,不可言喻的: ~ joy (disgust) 说不出的欢乐(厌恶) ②因神圣而不容称呼的,须避讳的 ‖**ineffably** *ad.*

inept [i'nept] *a.* ①不适当的,不符要求的,不合场面的: ~ remarks 不恰当的言语 ②笨拙的,愚蠢的 ③无能的,不称职的 ‖~**ly** *ad.* / ~**ness** *n.*

inert [i'nə:t] *a.* ① 无自动力的;无活动力的 ② 呆滞的,迟缓的;无生气的 ③【生】【化】惰性的;不活泼的,钝的: ~ gases 【化】惰性气体 / ~ type 【生】安定型,不活泼型 ④【医】不起作用的,无效的;中性的 ‖~**ly** *ad.* / ~**ness** *n.*

inertia [i'nə:ʃjə] *n.* ①[物]惯性;惯量: moment of ~ 转动惯量;惯性矩 / ~ governor 【机】惯性调速器 ②【医】无力 ③不活动;惰性;迟钝

inestimable [in'estiməbl] *a.* ①无法估计的 ②极珍贵的,无价的 ‖**inestimably** *ad.*

inevitable [in'evitəbl] *a.* ①不可避免的,无法规避的;必然(发生)的: the ~ course of history 历史必由之路 ② [口]照例必有的;老一套的 ‖*the* ~ 注定必然的事;不可避免的命运 ‖**inevitability** [in,evitə'biliti] *n.* / ~**ness** *n.* / **inevitably** *ad.*

inexorable [in'eksərəbl] *a.* ①不屈不挠的,坚决不屈的 ② 无情的,毫不宽容的: History is ~. 历史是无情的。‖**inexorability** [in,eksərə'biliti] *n.* / **inexorably** *ad.*

inexperience [,iniks'piəriəns] *n.* 缺乏经验;不熟练 ‖~**d** *a.* 无经验的;不熟练的

inexpressible [,iniks'presəbl] *a.* 表现(或表达)不出的,说不出的,无法形容的 ‖**inexpressibly** *ad.*

inextricable [in'ekstrikəbl] *a.* ①(困境等)无法摆脱的 ②(问题等)不能解决的 ③(疙瘩、结)解不开的 ‖**inextricability** [in,ekstrikə'biliti] *n.* / **inextricably** *ad.*

infamous ['infəməs] *a.* ①声名狼藉的,臭名昭著的 ②丢脸的,无耻的,不名誉的: ~ conduct 丑行 / tell an ~ lie 撒下无耻谎言 ③ 犯有丧失廉耻罪行的 ④【律】(因犯重罪)被褫夺(部分)公权的,[美]被剥夺法律上作证权的 ④ [口]很差的,低劣的: an ~ dinner (house) 质量很差的一顿饭(一所房子)

infancy ['infənsi] *n.* ①婴儿期,幼年期 ②初期;摇篮时代: The factory was then in its ~. 当时该厂处于初建阶段。③【律】未成年

infant ['infənt] **I** *n.* ①婴儿,幼儿 ② 未成年人 **II** *a.* ①婴儿的,幼儿的;幼稚的;初期的: an ~ industry 新建的工业 / ~ fruit 未熟的水果 ②未成年的 ③ 为婴儿(或幼儿)设置的: an ~ school [英]幼儿园

infanticide [in'fæntisaid] *n.* 杀害婴孩;杀婴犯

infantile ['infəntail], **infantine** ['infəntain] *a.* ①婴儿(期)的,幼儿(期)的: ~ diseases 小儿病 / ~ paralysis 【医】脊髓灰质炎,婴儿麻痹 ② 适合于婴儿的;幼稚的,孩子气的 ③早期的,初期的

infantry ['infəntri] *n.* ①[总称] 步兵(部队): five divisions of ~ 五师步兵 / The ~ *is* (或 *are*) equipped with new weapons. 步兵部队是用新武器装备起来的。②步兵团 ‖~**man** *n.* 步兵

infatuate [in'fætjueit] **I** *vt.* ① 使冲昏头脑; 使糊涂: be ~*d* with pride 被骄傲冲昏了头脑 ② 使迷恋,使错爱: be ~*d* with sb. 迷恋某人 **II** *a.* 被冲昏头脑的;迷恋着的 **III** *n.* 变得昏头昏脑的人;迷恋者 ‖**infatuation** [in,fætju'eiʃən] *n.*

infect [in'fekt] *vt.* ①传染;侵染;传播病菌于: be ~*ed* with cholera 传染上霍乱 / a wound ~ with disease germs 使伤口受病菌侵染 ②使受影响;感染: ~ sb. with a theory 用一种理论影响某人

infection [in'fekʃən] *n.* ①传染;侵染: contagious ~ 接触性传染 / general ~ 全身感染 ②传染病 ③影响;感染

infectious [in'fekʃəs] *a.* ①传染的;传染性的: an ~ disease 传染病 / an ~ hospital 传染病医院 / ~ hepatitis 传染性肝炎 ②感染性的;易传播的: an ~ laugh 有感染力的笑声 ③ 有坏影响的,有损害的 ‖~**ly** *ad.* / ~**ness** *n.*

infer [in'fə:] (inferred; inferring [in'fə:riŋ]) ❶ *vt.* ①推论,推断: ~ a motive from an effect 从效果推知动机 ②猜想,臆测 ③意味着;暗示;指出,指明 ❷ *vi.* 作出推论

inferior [in'fiəriə] **I** *a.* ①下等的;下级的: ~ in social position 社会地位低的 / an ~ officer 下级军官 ②(质量等)劣等的,差的,次的: ~ goods 低档货 / be ~ to others in many respects 在许多方面不如人家 ③(位置)下方的,下部的:

the ~ rock strata 下方岩层 / ~ limit【机】下限,最小限度 ④【天】(行星)在地球轨道内侧的;在太阳和地球之间的: ~ conjunction 下合 / ~ planet 内行星 ⑤【植】下位的,下生的 ⑥【解】在下的;下后的;在其他器官之下的: ~ meatus of the nose 鼻下道 ⑦【印】附印(或抄)在字母下的: ~ figures 下附数字(如 H_2SO_4 中的下附的 2, 4) **II** *n.* ①(地位、能力等)低下的人 ②次品 ③【印】下附数字;下附文字 ‖**~ity** [in,fiəri'oriti] *n.* 下等;劣等;下级;下位: a sense of ~ity 自卑感 / ~ity complex【心】自卑情结;自卑感 / **~ly** *ad.*

infernal [in'fə:nl] *a.* ①阴间的,地狱的 ②地狱般的,恶魔似的;穷凶极恶的: ~ cruelty 极度的残酷 ③【口】可恨的;坏透的;该死的 ‖**~ity** [,infə-'næliti] *n.* / **~ly** *ad.* ‖**~ machine**【军】饵雷,诡雷

inferno [in'fə:nou] *n.* ①地狱 ②象地狱的地方;恐怖的景象 ③[I-]《地狱篇》(但丁所作《神曲》的第一部)

infest [in'fest] *vt.* ①(害虫、盗贼等)大批出没于;侵扰: be ~ed with rats 鼠害成灾 ②寄生于: fleas ~ing cats 寄生于猫身上的跳蚤 ‖**infestation** [,infes'teiʃən] *n.* ①大批出没;侵扰 ②【动】(昆虫)传染

infidel ['infidəl] **I** *n.* ①不信仰宗教者 ②【宗】异教徒;不信奉正统宗教者 **II** *a.* ①不信宗教的 ②异教徒的;不信仰的;怀疑的 ‖**~ity** [,infi-'deliti] *n.* ①无宗教信仰 ②不信基督教 ③背信;不信任;不忠诚 ④(夫妇间的)不忠实;不忠实的行为: conjugal ~ity 私通,不贞 / **~ize** *vt.* & *vi.* (使)不信奉宗教

infiltrate ['infiltreit, in'filtreit] **I** ❶ *vt.* ①使(液体等)渗入,透过 (through, into);使浸润: ~ water *into* the sponge 使水渗入海绵中 / ~ the tissue with a local anaesthetic 用局部麻醉剂浸入组织 ②【军】渗透,通过;侵袭 ❷ *vi.* 渗入;混进 **II** *n.* 渗入物 ‖**infiltration** [,infil'treiʃən] *n.* ①渗入;【医】浸润: infiltration tuberculosa 结核浸润 ②【军】渗透,通过;渗透活动 / **infiltrator** *n.* 渗入者

infinite ['infinit] **I** *a.* ①无限的,无穷的;广大无边的: be of ~ power 具有无穷的力量 ②[用在复数名词前]无数的,极多的 ③【语】非限定的(不受人称、数、时态的限制,如动词不定式、动名词等) ④【数】无穷(大)的;无尽的: ~ decimal 无尽小数 / ~ series 无穷极数,无尽极数 **II** *n.* ①无限物(指空间、时间) ②【数】无穷(大);无尽 ③[the I-]【宗】上帝 ‖**~ly** *ad.* / **~ness** *n.*

infinitesimal [,infini'tesiməl] **I** *a.* ①无穷小的,无限小的: (the) ~ calculus 微积分(学) ②细微末节的 **II** *n.*【数】无穷小,无限小,微元 ‖**~ly** *ad.*

infinitive [in'finitiv] **I** *n.*【语】(动词)不定式(不受人称、数、时态的限制,通常前面带 to,如 "He wants to go." 中的 to go 是不定式。但在助动词和某些动词后不带 to,如在 "Can you read it?" 和 "Let me see." 中的 read 和 see 也是不定式)

II *a.*【语】不定式形式的: an ~ form of the verb 动词的不定式形式

infinity [in'finiti] *n.* ① =infinitude ②(数目、数额的)大量,大宗: an ~ of stars 无数的星星 ③【数】无穷大,无穷(符号为∞) ‖**to** ~ 直到无限

infirm [in'fə:m] *a.* ①体弱的,虚弱的: be ~ with age 年老体弱 ② 意志薄弱的;不坚定的,动摇的 ③不牢靠的;不生效的 ‖**~ly** *ad.*

infirmary [in'fə:məri] *n.* 医院;医务室 (尤指学校、教养所等附设的病房或配药处)

infirmity [in'fə:miti] *n.* ①体弱,虚弱 ②疾病,病症: infirmities of age 老年的疾病 ③懦弱;薄弱;弱点

inflame [in'fleim] ❶ *vt.* ① 使燃烧;使炽热 ②使极度激动;引起…的热情;使脸红耳赤;使愤怒: a speech that ~d popular feeling 激动群情的讲话 ③加剧;使火上加油 ④【医】使发炎: ~d boil 发炎的疖子 ❷ *vi.* ①着火 ②激动;发怒 ③发炎

inflammable [in'flæməbl] **I** *a.* ①易燃的: an ~ gas 易燃的气体 ②易激动的;易激怒的;性情暴躁的 **II** *n.* 易燃物 ‖**inflammability** [in,flæmə-'biliti] *n.* / **~ness** *n.* / **inflammably** *ad.*

inflammation [,inflə'meiʃən] *n.* ① 点火;燃烧 ②激动: a state of extreme ~ 极其激动的状态 ③【医】炎: the ~ of the lungs 肺部发炎

inflammatory [in'flæmətəri] *a.* ①使激怒的,煽动性的: ~ speeches (writings) 煽动性的讲话(文章) ②【医】炎性的,炎的: ~ disease 炎症

inflate [in'fleit] ❶ *vt.* ①使充气;使膨胀,使胀大 ②使得意,使骄傲: ~ the arrogance of sb. 使某人妄自尊大 / be ~d with pride 得意扬扬 ③使(通货)膨胀;抬高(物价): ~ the paper currency 滥发纸币 ❷ *vi.* 进行充气;膨胀 ‖**~r** *n.* =inflator

inflated [in'fleitid] *a.* ①充了气的: an ~ tyre 充气轮胎 ② (语言等)夸张的,言过其实的: an ~ style 夸张的文体 ③(通货)恶性膨胀的;(价格)飞涨的 ④【植】空心和张大的;肿胀的;扩大了的: ~ stem (capsule) 空心而张大的茎(英)

inflation [in'fleiʃən] *n.* ①充气;膨胀: ~ inlet【机】充气进口 / ~ pressure【机】充气压力,气胀压力 ② 夸张;自满 ③ 通货膨胀;信用膨胀;物价飞涨 ‖**~ary** *a.* 膨胀的,通货膨胀的;由膨胀引起的;由通货膨胀引起的: the ~ary spiral (通货、物价、工资等的)螺旋性膨胀 / **~ism** *n.* 通货膨胀政策 / **~ist** *n.* 通货膨胀政策的支持者 *a.* 支持通货膨胀政策的

inflect [in'flekt] ❶ *vt.* ①弯曲;使向内弯曲;使屈折 ②【音】变(音);转(调) ③【语】使(词)发生屈折变化 ❷ *vi.* 发生屈折变化 ‖**~ion** [in'flekʃən] *n.* =inflexion / **~ive** *a.*

inflexion [in'flekʃən] *n.* ①弯曲;向内弯曲 ②【音】变音;转调 ③【语】屈折变化(形式) ④【数】拐折,回折;拐点,回折点 ‖**~al** *a.* / **~less** *a.* 无屈折变化的

inflict [in'flikt] *vt.* ① 予以(打击),使遭受(损伤、苦痛等),使承受 ②处(罚),加(刑): ~ the death penalty *upon* the murderer 处杀人犯以死刑 ‖ ~ *oneself* (或 *one's company*) *upon sb.* 打扰某人 ‖ ~**ion** [in'flikʃən] *n.*

inflow ['in-flou] *n.* ①流入: an ~ of air 空气的流入 / an ~ of bank deposits 银行存款的增加 ②流入物 ③【机】流入,吸入,吸风

influence ['influəns] **I** *n.* ① 影响,感化 (*upon, on*): under the ~ of 在…的影响之下 ②势力,权势: within sb.'s sphere of ~ 在某人的势力范围内 / a man of great ~ 很有权势的人 / have ~ *over* 有左右…的力量; 对…有影响 / Will you please use your ~ *with* him not to do it? 请你运用你的影响叫他不要做那事好吗? / use one's ~ in sb.'s favour (或 behalf) 为某人尽力 ③ 有影响的人 (或事物); 有权势的人: an ~ in politics 在政界有影响的人 (或势力) ④【电】感应 **II** *vt.* 影响,感化; 对…有作用,左右: be ~*d* by the weather 受到气候的影响 / The labour enthusiasm of the workers strongly ~*d* us. 工人们的劳动热情强烈地感染了我们。

influent ['influent] **I** *a.* 流入的 **II** *n.* ① 流入 ② 支流 ③(生态学中)一种动物(或植物)对其他生物的影响

influential [,influ'enʃəl] *a.* ①有影响的,施以影响的: be ~ *in* (reaching) a decision 对(作出)某一决定有影响 ②有权势的 ‖ ~**ly** *ad.*

influenza [,influ'enzə] *n.* 【医】流行性感冒 ②(马、猪等的)流行性热病

influx ['inflʌks] *n.* ①流入,注入; 涌进,汇集(指人或物): a strong ~ of light 光的强烈射入 / a great ~ of holiday visitors into a city 假日游客大批涌到某一城市 ②河口; 河流的汇合处

inform [in'fɔːm] ❶ *vt.* ①告诉,通知; 向…报告: Did you ~ them *of* the progress of the work? 你把工作进程告诉他们了吗? / I beg to ~ you that .... 谨通知… / We'll keep you ~*ed*. 我们将随时向你报告情况。 / be well ~*ed about* sth. 精通某事; 对某事消息灵通 / be rightly (wrongly) ~*ed* 得到正确 (错误) 的知识 (或情报) ②使充满; 使活跃 (*with*) ❷ *vi.* 告发,告密 (*against*) ‖ ~**er** *n.* ①通知者; 通报者 ②告密者: a common (或 professional) ~*er* 以告密为业的人 / turn ~*er* on sb. 告发某人

informal [in'fɔːməl] *a.* ①非正式的,非正规的: an ~ visit 非正式的访问 ②不拘礼节的; 日常使用的: an ~ gathering 不拘礼节的集会 / ~ dress 日常服装 (非礼服) / ~ English 日常 (使用的) 英语 / an ~ style 口语体 ‖ ~**ity** [,infɔː'mæliti] *n.* ① 非正式; 不拘礼节 ② 不拘礼节的行动 / ~**ly** *ad.*

informant [in'fɔːmənt] *n.* ① 提供消息(或情报)的人 ②(为语言学调查)提供资料的本地人

information [,infə'meiʃən] *n.* ①通知,报告 ②消息,报道; 情报: a piece of ~ 一则消息; 一份情

报 / ask for ~ *on* (或 *about, concerning*) sth. 打听关于某事的消息 / For fuller ~ please contact our local agent. 欲知详情, 请与我们驻当地的代理人联系。 / official ~ 官方消息 / ~ desk 问讯处 / an ~ bureau 情报局 ③知识,见闻; 资料: a man of wide ~ 博学多闻的人 / accumulate (或 amass) a great amount of ~ 积累大量资料 / firsthand ~ 第一手资料 / For Your *Information* Only 仅供参考 ④(检察官的)起诉,告发: lay (或 lodge) an ~ *against* sb. 告发某人 ⑤【自】信息: theory of ~ (或 ~ theory) 信息论 ‖ ~**al** *a.* 消息(或情报)的; 提供消息(或情报)的,介绍情况的 ‖ ~ **science** ①资料学(研究资料的搜集、分类、储存等的学科) ②【自】信息学

informative [in'fɔːmətiv] *a.* 报告消息的; 提供资料的; 增进知识的: an ~ book 资料丰富的书 ‖ ~**ly** *ad.* / ~**ness** *n.*

informed [in'fɔːmd] *a.* 有知识的,见闻广的; 有情报根据的: ~ public opinion 明达的舆论 / ~ sources 消息灵通人士

infraction [in'frækʃən] *n.* (法规等的)违犯,违背

infringe [in'frindʒ] ❶ *vt.* 违犯; 侵犯; 违反: ~ a rule 犯规 ❷ *vi.* 侵犯,侵害 (*on, upon*): ~ upon sb.'s rights 侵犯某人的权利 ‖ ~**ment** *n.*

infuriate [in'fjuərieit] **I** *vt.* 使发怒,激怒 **II** *a.* 狂怒的 ‖ ~**ly** *ad.* 狂怒地 / **infuriatingly** *ad.* 万分激怒地; 令人发怒地 / **infuriation** [in,fjuəri'eiʃən] *n.*

infuse [in'fjuːz] ❶ *vt.* ①(向…)注入; (向…)灌输: ~ new life *into* sb. (sth.) 赋予某人(某物)以新的生命 ②泡(茶); 浸渍; 泡制(药): ~ tea 泡茶 ③使充满,鼓舞: ~ sb. *with* courage 鼓起某人的勇气 ❷ *vi.* 注; 泡,浸 ‖ ~**r** *n.* 注入器; 浸渍器; 茶壶

infusion [in'fjuːʒən] *n.* ①注入; 灌输 ②【医】注注: saline ~ 盐水输注 ③泡制,浸渍 ④浸液: fresh ~*s* 【医】新鲜浸剂

ingenious [in'dʒiːnjəs] *a.* ①机灵的,足智多谋的; 有独创性的: an ~ mind 机灵的头脑 ②精巧制成的; 巧妙的: an ~ machine 精巧的机器 / flexible and ~ tactics 机动灵活的战术 ‖ ~**ly** *ad.* / ~**ness** *n.*

ingenuity [,indʒi'nju(ː)iti] *n.* ① 机灵,足智多谋; 独创性 ② 精巧; 设计新颖,独出心裁

ingenuous [in'dʒenjuəs] *a.* 坦率的; 天真的,单纯的 ‖ ~**ly** *ad.* / ~**ness** *n.*

inglorious [in'glɔːriəs] *a.* ①不光彩的; 不名誉的; 可耻的 ② 不出名的,湮没无闻的 ‖ ~**ly** *ad.*

ingot ['iŋgət] *n.* 【冶】铸模; 铸块, 锭: ~ iron 锭铁,低碳钢 / ~ dogs (或 tongs) 锭钳

ingrain [in'grein] **I** *vt.* ①【纺】使原纱(或原料)染色 ②使遍体渗透; 使根深蒂固: be deeply ~*ed* in the mind 在头脑中根深蒂固 **II** *a.* ①由染色原纱(或原料)制成的: an ~ carpet (两面花纹颜色相反的)双面提花地毯 ②遍体渗透的; 根深固的; 积习成性的; 固有的: ~ stubbornness 根深

蒂固的顽固性 / an ~ criminal 惯犯 **III** *n.* ①原纱染色,原料染色;用染色原纱纺制的织物 ②固有的品质,本质 ‖**~ed** *a.* 根深蒂固的: an ~*ed* prejudice 根深蒂固的偏见

ingratiate [in'greiʃieit] *vt.* 使讨好,使巴结,使迎合: ~ oneself *with* sb. (或 ~ oneself *into* sb.'s favour) 讨好某人

ingredient [in'gri:djənt] *n.* ①(混合物的)组成部份;配料,成分: the ~*s* of ice cream 冰淇淋的各种配料 ②【化】拼份;拼料

inhabit [in'hæbit] *vt.* 居住于; (动物) 栖居于: a district thickly (thinly) ~*ed* 人口稠密(稀少)的地区 / a small·island ~*ed* by a rich fauna and flora 产有丰富动植物的小岛 ‖**~able** *a.* 可居住(或栖居)的

inhabitant [in'hæbitənt] *n.* ①居民,住户;常住居民: a city of 100,000 ~*s* 有十万居民的城市 ②栖居的动物

inhale [in'heil] ❶ *vt.* ①吸入: ~ fresh air 吸入新鲜空气 ②[美俚]吃(小餐);喝(啤酒或不含酒精的饮料) ❷ *vi.* 吸气: Inhale! Exhale! 吸气!呼气! ‖**~r** *n.* ①吸入器;吸气器: ether ~*r*【医】醚吸入器 ②【化】滤气器,滤气器

inherent [in'hiərənt] *a.* 内在的;固有的,生来的: the ~ laws of things 事物的内部规律 / ~ stability【空】固有稳定性 / Polarity is ~ *in* a magnet. 极性是磁铁的固有性质。 ‖**~ly** *ad.*

inherit [in'herit] ❶ *vt.* ①继承(传统、遗产、权利等) ②经遗传而得(性格、特征等) ❷ *vi.* 接受遗产;成为继承人 ‖**~or** *n.* 继承人,后继者

inheritance [in'heritəns] *n.* ①继承;承受: receive sth. by ~ 继承得到某物 ②继承物;遗产;遗赠 ③继承权;世袭权 ④遗传;遗传的特征: criss-cross ~【生】交叉遗传 ‖**~ tax** [美]遗产税,继承税(英国称 succession duty)

inhibit [in'hibit] ❶ *vt.* ①禁止,阻止: ~ sb. *from* doing sth. 禁止某人做某事 ②抑制,约束: ~ wrong desires 抑制邪念 ❷ *vi.* 有禁止力; 起抑制作用 ‖**~ion** [ˌinhi'biʃən] *n.* 禁止,阻止;抑制;抑制物: central ~*ion*【医】中枢抑制

inhuman [in'hju:mən] *a.* ①无人性的; 非人的 ②野蛮的;残酷的 ‖**~ly** *ad.*

inhumanity [ˌinhju(:)'mæniti] *n.* ①无人性;野蛮,残酷 ②残酷无情的行为

inimical [i'nimikəl] *a.* ①敌意的,不友好的: mutually ~ blocs 敌对的集团 ②有害的,不利的: a habit ~ *to* health 有碍健康的习惯 ‖**~ly** *ad.*

inimitable [i'nimitəbl] *a.* ①不能模仿的 ②无双的,无与伦比的 ‖**~ness** *n.* / **inimitably** *ad.*

iniquitous [i'nikwitəs] *a.* 不公正的,不正直的;邪恶的,罪恶的 ‖**~ly** *ad.* / **~ness** *n.*

iniquity [i'nikwiti] *n.* ①不公正,不正直;邪恶,罪恶 ②不义行为;邪恶的事物

initial [i'niʃəl] **I** *a.* ①最初的, 开始的: the ~ issue of a magazine 杂志的创刊号 / ~ prosperity 初步繁荣 / ~ line【数】极轴 / ~ velocity【物】初速(度) / ~ (boiling) point【化】初馏点(第一滴馏物滴下时的温度) ②词首的: the ~ letter of a word 一个词的首字母 / an ~ signature 仅用姓名首字母的签名 / an ~ word 首字母缩略词(如 NATO) **II** *n.* ①首字母;(书刊文章中的)段落、章节的)特大的大写首字母 ②[复]姓名 (或组织名称) 的开头字母(如 John Smith 的 J. S.; United Nations Organization 的 UNO) **III** (initial(l)ed; initial(l)ing) *vt.* ①标注(或印、签)姓名的首字母于: ~ a note 用缩写签署便条 / an *initial(l)ed* pen 刻上缩写姓名的笔 ②草签(指条约等正式签订前由缔约国代表在审定的草案上的临时签署) ‖**~ism** *n.* 首字母缩略词 / **~ly** *ad.* 最初,开始

initiate **I** [i'niʃieit] *vt.* ①开始;创始;发动: ~ a new plan 开始实行一个新计划 ②使入门 ③正式介绍,引进: ~ sb. into a club 介绍某人加入俱乐部 **II** [i'niʃiit, i'niʃieit] *a. & n.* ①被传授了初步知识的人 ②新入会的人(物)

initiation [iˌniʃi'eiʃən] *n.* ①开始;创始 ②指引,传授 ③(会、社等的)加入;入会式

initiative [i'niʃiətiv] **I** *n.* ①发端;创始;首创精神;主动;积极性: win ~ 赢得主动 / ~ in labour 劳动积极性 ②(公民的)创制权;(立法机关对新法案的)动议权 **II** *a.* 起始的;创始的;初步的 ‖**have the ~** 掌握主动权 / *on one's own* ~ 主动地 / *take the* ~ 带头,采取主动

inject [in'dʒekt] *vt.* ①注射,注入: ~ glucose *into* the veins 把葡萄糖注入静脉 ②注满 ③插进(话);引入 ④【机】喷射;引射 ‖**~or** *n.* ①注射者;注射器,注入器 ②喷射器;喷射泵;注水器: an exhaust steam ~*or* 排气喷射器 / a spray ~*or* 射流式喷嘴

injection [in'dʒekʃən] *n.* ①注射: give sb. an ~ of penicillin 给某人打一针青霉素 / hypodermic (或 subcutaneous) ~ 皮下注射 ②注射剂,针剂 ③充满;注满 ④【机】喷射: fuel ~ 燃料喷射,注油 / ~ pump 喷射泵,喷油泵 ⑤(卫星、宇宙飞船等的)射入轨道;射入轨道的时间(或地点)

injunction [in'dʒʌŋkʃən] *n.* 命令;责戒;【律】指令,禁令: lay ~*s* on (或 *upon*) sb. to do sth. 命令某人做某事

injure ['indʒə] *vt.* 损害,伤害;毁坏: ~ an arm in a car accident 在一场车祸中伤了一只手臂 / ~ sb.'s pride (reputation) 伤害某人的自尊心 (名誉) ‖**~d** *a.* 受伤的;受损害的;被触怒的: the dead and the ~*d* (事故中的) 死亡者和受伤者 / the ~*d* party 受害者 / an ~*d* look 生气的样子

injury ['indʒəri] *n.* ①损害,伤害;毁坏 ②伤害的行为: do sb. an ~ (或 do an ~ to sb.) 伤害某人 ③受伤处 ‖**add insult to** ~ 伤害之外又加侮辱

injustice [in'dʒʌstis] *n.* ①非正义;不公正,不公平;侵犯(别人的)权利 ②非正义(或不公正)的行为: do sb. an ~ 使某人受屈

ink [iŋk] **I** *n.* ①墨水;油墨: Chinese ~ (中国)墨,墨汁 / invisible (或 sympathetic, secret) ~ 隐显墨水(起初无色,经热、光或药品等作用而显字) / printing ~ 印刷油墨 ②(乌贼体内分泌的)墨汁 ③[美俚]咖啡;廉价酒 ④[美俚][贬]黑人 **II** *vt.* ①涂墨水(或油墨)于;用墨水(划)写: a neatly ~ed entry 一笔清楚地用墨水记写的项目 ②用墨水(或油墨)沾污 ③[美俚]签署(契约) ||~ *in* (或 over) 再用墨水描 / ~ *in* a drawing 在铅笔底线上用墨水笔加描 / ~ *out* 用墨水涂去 / *sling* ~ [俚]当作家(或记者),写作;卖文为生 ||~*less a.* 无墨水(或墨汁)的 ||~ *bag* (乌贼的)墨囊 / '~,berry *n.* 【植】光滑冬青 / '~-blot test* [心]墨迹测验 / '~,bottle *n.* 墨水瓶 / '~fish *n.* 乌贼(又称墨鱼)(=cuttlefish) / '~horn *n.* (旧时用角等制的)墨水瓶: smell of the ~horn 有学究气 *a.* 学究气的;卖弄学问的: an ~horn term 从拉丁文(或希腊文)中生造出来的言词;行文用语 / '~pad *n.* 印台 / '~pot *n.* 墨水瓶 / ~ *sac* =~ bag / '~,slinger *n.* [美]作者,作家;办事员;记录员 / ~*stand* *n.* ①墨水台 =~well / '~stone *n.* ①【矿】水绿矾 ②砚;调墨台 / '~well *n.* (镶在桌上或墨水台上的)墨水池 / '~,writer *n.* (电报)印字机

inkling ['iŋkliŋ] *n.* ①暗示;细微的迹象: give sb. an ~ of the matter 给某人一些关于此事的暗示 / have some ~ of a cold 有点伤风的征候 ②略知;模糊的想法: have no ~ as to the real cause 对真正的原因一无所知

inland ['inlənd] **I** *a.* ①内地的,内陆的: an ~ town 内地城市 / an ~ river 内河 / ~ navigation 内河航行 ②国内的: ~ revenue [英]国内税收(不包括关税) / ~ trade 国内贸易 / ~ telegraph 国内电报 **II** *n.* 内地 **III** [in'lænd] *ad.* 在内地;到内地: go ~ 到内地去 ||~er *n.* (生长在)内地的人

in-law ['inlɔ:] *n.* [口][常用复]姻亲

inlay ['in'lei] **I** (inlaid ['in'leid]) *vt.* ①镶嵌,嵌入: ivory *inlaid with* gold 镶金象牙 ②用镶嵌物装饰 **II** ['inlei] *n.* ①镶嵌物;镶嵌所用的材料;镶嵌工艺 ②【医】嵌体 ||~er *n.* 镶嵌者

inlet ['inlet] **I** *n.* ①进口;入口: ~ chamber 【机】进气室 / an ~ passage 【军】进路 / ~ and outlet channels (水库的)进出渠道 ②水湾;小港 ③插入物,镶嵌物 ④【电】引入,输入 **II** (inlet; inletting) *vt.* ①引进 ②嵌入,插入

inmate ['inmeit] *n.* ①同住者(尤指同院病人、同狱犯人、住在同一收容所的人) ②居民

inmost ['inmoust] *a.* 最内的;最深入的;内心深处的: one's ~ thoughts (feelings) 内心深处的思想(感情)

inn [in] **I** *n.* ①小旅馆,客栈(尤指乡村或公路旁的) ②小酒店,小饭店 **II** *vi.* 住旅馆 ||*Inns of Court* 英国伦敦具有授律师资格权的四个法律协会 ||~,keeper, '~,holder *n.* 小旅馆老板

innate ['i'neit] *a.* ①天生的,生来的;固有的

②【生】先天的,遗传的 ||~ly *ad.* / ~ness *n.*

inner ['inə] **I** *a.* ①内部的;里面的;接近中心的(尤指权势): ~ flue 【机】内烟道 / an ~ tube (车轮的)里胎 / ~ complex salt 【化】内络盐 / ~ circle 全体内圈人物;核心集团 ②思想的,精神的;内心的;秘密的: the ~ life of man 人的内心活动;人的精神生活 **II** *n.* ①内部;里面 ②接近靶心部分;射中接近靶心部分的一发 ||*the ~ man* 见 man / *the ~ most a.* 最里面的;最深处的: one's ~most being 灵魂深处 *n.* 最深处 ||'~-di'rected *a.* [美]有自己的看法的,不随俗的 / Inner Light 【宗】灵光

inning ['iniŋ] *n.* ①(荒地,尤指海滩的)围垦;[复]围垦过的土地 ②[~s][用作单或复]【体】局,盘,回合(尤指棒球、板球中的) ③[~s][用作单或复]轮到显身手的机会;掌职期间;(政党的)当权期间 ||*get one's ~s* 得好机会,走运 / *have a good ~s* ①击球得胜 ②享有一段得意时期,寿长 / *have an ~s* ①轮到击球(尤指棒球、板球)②参加某项活动

innocence ['inəsns] *n.* ①清白;无罪 ②天真,单纯 ③无知,头脑简单 ④无害 ⑤无罪的人,清白无辜者 ⑥【医】良性

innocent ['inəsnt] **I** *a.* ①清白的;无罪的: be ~ of a crime 无罪 ②天真的,单纯的: an ~ child 天真的孩子 / do the ~ 装傻 ③无知的,头脑简单的 ④无害的 ⑤【医】良性的:an ~ tumour 良性瘤 ⑥[口]没有…的: a book ~ of illustrations 没有插图的书 **II** *n.* ①天真无邪的人(尤指小孩) ②头脑简单的人,笨蛋 ||*massacre* (或 *slaughter*) *of the ~s* [英俚](议会中趁会期快满而作出的)撤销某些议案的决定 ||~ly *ad.* / ~ passage (船舶在航行中遇险时)未经主权国同意在其港口停泊的权利,无害通过(权)

innocuous [i'nɔkjuəs] *a.* ①无害的;无毒的: an ~ drug 无毒的药品 ②不关痛痒的,不会招怨的;无味的: ~ generalities 不关痛痒的泛泛之谈 ||~ly *ad.* / ~ness *n.*

innovate ['inouveit] *vi.* 革新,创新;变革(in, upon): ~ in techniques 在工艺上革新 ||innovator *n.* 革新者,创新者: technical *innovators* 技术革新者

innovation [,inou'veiʃən] *n.* 革新,创新,改革;新方法,新事物: a vitally important ~ in. industry 一项有重大意义的工业上的革新 ||~al *a.* 革新的,富有革新精神的

innuendo [,inju(:)'endou] **I** ([复] innuendoes) *n.* ①暗讽;影射;暗指: attack by ~ 旁敲侧击,含沙射影 ②[律]文件中的附注句(尤指对被指称为诽谤性词句的注解) **II** ❶ *vi.* 使用暗讽 ❷ *vt.* 用暗讽表现(或表达)

innumerable [i'nju:mərəbl] *a.* 无数的,数不清的 ||innumerably *ad.*

inoculate [i'nɔkjuleit] *vt.* ①【医】给…接种;给…作(预防)注射;移植(细菌等): ~ sb. against cholera 给某人注射霍乱预防针 ②【植】嫁接(枝

芽）；接枝（或芽）于 ③向…灌输：~ sb. *with an idea* 把某一思想灌输给某人 ‖**inoculative** *a.* / **inoculator** *n.* 接种者；注射者；接枝者

inoculation [i,nɔkju'leiʃən] *n.* ①【医】接种；预防注射；(细菌等的)移植：~ *against* typhoid fever 伤寒预防注射 ②【植】接枝，接芽；嫁接：artificial ~ 人工接种 ③(思想等的)灌输 ④【冶】加孕育处理法

inoperable [in'ɔpərəbl] *a.* ①【医】不能行手术的，不宜动手术的：an ~ cancer 不宜动手术的癌 ② 不能实行的；行不通的

inpatient ['in,peiʃənt] *n.* 住院病人

inquest ['inkwest] *n.* ①审讯，审问(尤指有陪审团参加的)；验尸 ②陪审团；验尸团 ③审问后的判决；调查判决报告 ④调查，调查：a three-year ~ into the case 对该案进行的历时三年的调查 ‖*the great* (或 *last*) ~【宗】世界末日的大审判

inquire [in'kwaiə] ❶ *vi.* ①询问：He ~d *of* me *about* (或 *concerning*) our work. 他向我了解我们工作的情况。②调查；查问：~ *into* a matter 对一件事进行调查 ❷ *vt.* ①问，打听：~ sb.'s name (telephone number) 问某人姓名 (电话号码) / We ~d the way *of* a boy. 我们向一个男孩问路。/ He ~d (*of* me) how to proceed with the work. 他问(我)怎样进行这一工作。②调查 ‖~ *after* 问起(某人)的健康情况 / *for* ①询问(商品、地点等)：~ *for* a new picture book 问问有没有一本新的画册出售 ② 要见：~ *for* the comrade in charge 要见负责同志 ③ =~ after ‖~r [in'kwaiərə] *n.* 询问者；调查人

inquiring [in'kwaiəriŋ] *a.* ①爱打听的，好询问的 ②显得好奇的：The boy rolled ~ eyes towards his father. 那个男孩转动着好奇的眼睛盯着他的父亲。‖~**ly** *ad.*

inquiry [in'kwaiəri] *n.* ①询问，打听；质询：Upon (或 On) ~, I learnt that .... 经询问，我得知… / make *inquiries of* sb. *about* sth. 向某人询问某事 / an ~ office 问讯处 / answer sb.'s *inquiries* 回答某人的质询 ②调查：hold an ~ *into* a case 对一桩案子进行调查 ③(真理、知识等的)探究：the scientific method of ~ 科学的探究方法

inquisition [,inkwi'ziʃən] *n.* ①探究；调查 ②【律】讯问，审理 (通常有陪审团参加)；陪审团的判决 ③ [the I-] (中世纪天主教审讯异端的)宗教法庭 ④(对被认为是危险分子的人们的)恣意镇压，严厉刑罚 ‖~**al** *a.*

inquisitive [in'kwizitiv] **I** *a.* ①好询问的；好奇的：an ~ person 爱打破砂锅问到底的人 ②爱打听别人的事情的 **II** *n.* ①好询问的人 ②爱打听别人事情的人 ‖~**ly** *ad.* / ~**ness** *n.*

inroad ['inroud] *n.* ①(突然)袭击，(突然)侵犯 ② [常用复] 损害，侵蚀：make ~s on sb.'s health 使某人的健康受到损害

inrush ['inrʌʃ] *n.* 流入；涌入；闯入：an ~ of fresh air 新鲜空气的流入

insatiable [in'seiʃəbl] *a.* 不能满足的；贪得无厌的：be ~ in learning 学而不厌 ‖**insatiability** [in,seiʃə'biliti] *n.* / **insatiably** *ad.*

inscribe [in'skraib] *vt.* ①刻(写)；雕 ②题写；写；印 ③ 把 (某人) 的名字写到名单中，将…注册；[英] 登记 (证券)：an ~d stock [总称]记名股票 ④题献 (书籍，歌曲等)；题赠：~ one's book *to* a friend 把自己写的一本书赠给一个朋友 ⑤牢记；铭记

inscription [in'skripʃən] *n.* ①铭刻；铭文；碑文；铸币 (或勋章、图章等) 上的刻印文字 ②标题；题词；题献词：an ~ *on* a photograph 照片上的题词 ③编入名单，注册；[英]证券持有者名字登记 ④[英][复]记名证券 ‖~**al** *a.*

inscrutable [in'skru:təbl] *a.* 不可理解的，不可思议的；不可测知的；象谜一样的：an ~ expression 一个令人费解的表情 (或表达方式) / as ~ a mystery as 象…一样不可测知的奥秘 ‖**inscrutability** [in,skru:tə'biliti] *n.* / ~**ness** *n.* / **inscrutably** *ad.*

insect ['insekt] *n.* ①昆虫，虫：a destructive ~ 害虫 / an ~ pest 虫害 / ~ powder 除虫粉 ② 可鄙的人，渺小的人

insects

insecticide [in'sektisaid] *n.* 杀虫药剂：farm ~ 农业杀虫剂，农药 / spray ~ 喷射杀虫剂 ‖**insecticidal** [in,sekti'saidl] *a.* *insecticidal* oil 杀虫油

insensate [in'senseit] *a.* ①没有感觉的，无知觉的；无生气的 ②愚钝的；没有理智的 ③残忍的，无情的 ‖~**ly** *ad.* / ~**ness** *n.*

insensible [in'sensəbl] *a.* ①失去知觉的；麻木的；无感觉的：fall ~ 昏过去 / hands ~ *from* cold 冻麻木了的手 / be ~ *to* pain 不感觉痛 ②不知道的；没察觉到的 (*of*)：be ~ *of* one's danger 不知道自己所临到的危险 ③不被觉察的；极微的：by ~ degrees 极缓慢地，徐徐地 ④ 无感情的，冷淡的 ⑤ 莫明其妙的，无意义的 ⑥不敏感的

‖**insensibility** [in,sensə'biliti] *n.* / **~ness** *n.* / **insensibly** *ad.*

insert I [in'sə:t] ❶ *vt.* ①插入;嵌入;登载(广告等): ~ a key *in* (或 *into*) a lock 把钥匙插入锁里 / ~ a few words 插入几句话 ②(缝纫中)镶;补 ❷ *vi.* 【医】(肌肉)附着 **II** ['insə:t] *n.* 插入物;插页

insertion [in'sə:ʃən] *n.* ①插入;嵌入;登载 ②插入物;插入广告 ③(服装上的)嵌饰,绣饰 ④【医】(肌肉)附着: the ~ of a muscle 肌附着,肌止端 ‖**~al** *a.*

inset I ['in-set] *n.* ①水道;(潮水)流入 ②插入物;插页;(大地图上的)插图;插画 ③镶嵌 **II** ['in'set] (inset 或 insetted; insetting) *vt.* 插入,嵌入

inside [in'said] **I** *n.* ①里面,内部: proceed from the outside to the ~ 由表及里 / the ~ of a box 匣子的内部 ②(人行道、道路的)内侧;(跑道的)内圈,内道 ③内心,内在思想 ④期中: the ~ of a week 一周的当中一段时间 ⑤[口]肚子,肠胃: feel a pain in one's ~ 觉觉肚子痛 ⑥[俚]内幕情报,内情;能通内情的境地 **II** *a.* ①里面的,内部的;在屋里的: the ~ front (back) (杂志等)的封面(底)的背面 / ~ clothing 内衣 / the ~ diameter 内径 / For *Inside* Circulation Only 内部传阅,不得外传 ②内幕的,秘密的: ~ information (或 stuff) 内部消息 / an ~ story 内情,内幕 ③干室内工作的 **III** *ad.* 在里面,在内部: There is nobody ~. 里面没人。 **IV** *prep.* 在…之内: return ~ a week 一周以内回来 ‖**~ of** [口] 在…之内;(时间上)少于: ~ *of* a week (mile) 不到一周(哩) / ~ *out* 里面翻到外面;彻底地: wear a sweater ~ *out* 反穿球衫 / turn everything ~ *out* 翻箱倒柜 / know sth. ~ *out* 透彻了解某事 / *on the* ~ 在(或从)里面: The door is locked *on the* ~. 门反锁着。②[美]知内情的;参与内部机密(或受特别照顾)的 ③[美]在内心深处 ‖**~r** *n.* ①(组织、团体等)内部的人 ②知内情者,了解内幕的人 ‖**~ job** [美口]内部的自己人所作的案;通过内应而作的案 / **~ track** ①内圈跑道 ②(竞争的)有利地位,好机会

insidious [in'sidiəs] *a.* ①阴险的;狡诈的;暗中为害的 ②(疾病)不知不觉之间加剧的 ③伺机陷害的;毒而诱人的 ‖**~ly** *ad.* / **~ness** *n.*

insight ['insait] *n.* ①洞察(力);洞悉;见识: a man of deep ~ 有深远见识的人 / gain an ~ into sb.'s mind 看透某人心思 ②[心]顿悟

insignia [in'signiə] ([复] insignia(s)) *n.* ①勋章;国徽 ②【军】认识符号;徽章

insinuate [in'sinjueit] *vt.* ①使逐渐而巧妙地进入,使潜入: ~ doubts *into* sb.'s mind 使某人慢慢产生疑虑 / ~ *oneself into* sb.'s favour 向某人献媚求宠 / ~ *oneself into* the crowd 暗暗地挤进人群 ②暗示,暗讽: He ~d his doubt of the answer. 他暗示他对这回答有怀疑。‖**insinuation** [in,sinju'eiʃən] *n.* make *insinuations* 含沙射影 / **insinuative** *a.* / **insinuator** *n.* ①献媚者 ②暗

示者,暗讽者

insipid [in'sipid] *a.* ①无味的,淡而无味的: ~ food 淡而无味的食物 ②枯燥乏味的;无吸引力的;无生气的: ~ conversation 枯燥无味的谈话 ‖**~ity** [,insi'piditi] *n.* / **~ly** *ad.* / **~ness** *n.*

insist [in'sist] ❶ *vi.* ①坚持;坚决主张;坚决认为 (on, upon): We ~ *on* (或 *upon*) self-reliance. 我们坚持自力更生。/ He ~s *on* his innocence. 他坚持自己无罪。 ②坚决要求,定要 (on, upon): He ~s *on* going with me (*on* my going with him). 他定要和我同去(我和我同去)。 ❷ *vt.* ①坚持;坚决主张;坚决认为: He ~ed *that* he had done right. 他坚认自己做对了。②坚决要求,定要: He ~s *that* I *shall be* (或 I *should be* 或 I *be*) present. 他定要我出席。/ We all ~ *that* we shall (或 *should*) not rest until we finish the work. 大家都坚决要求不完工就不休息。

insistence [in'sistəns], **insistency** [in'sistənsi] *n.* 坚持;坚决主张;坚决要求: his ~ *on* doing the work himself (或 his ~ *that* he do the work himself) 他坚持自己动手做这工作的主张 / at sb.'s ~ 经某人的坚决要求

insistent [in'sistənt] *a.* ①坚持的: at sb.'s ~ request 在某人一再要求之下 ②逼人注意的;显眼的,显著的: work in the ~ heat 在酷热下工作 ‖**~ly** *ad.*

insolence ['insələns] *n.* ①傲慢,目空一切;无礼蛮横 ②傲慢的态度;侮辱性的行动(或言论)

insolent ['insələnt] *a.* 傲慢的,目空一切的;无礼的;蛮横的,侮慢的 ‖**~ly** *ad.*

insomnia [in'sɔmniə] *n.* 失眠;失眠症

insomuch [,insou'mʌtʃ] *ad.* ①到这样的程度,如此地: He worked very fast, ~ *that* he was through in an hour. 他工作得很快,以致一小时内就干完了。②因为,由于(与 as 连用 =inasmuch as)

inspect [in'spekt] ❶ *vt.* ①检查;审查: ~ outgoing baggage 检查外出的行李 ②检阅;视察;参观: ~ troops 检阅军队 / ~ a factory 视察工厂 ❷ *vi.* 检查

inspection [in'spekʃən] *n.* ①检查,检验;审查: ~ arms 【军】验枪姿势;(口令用语)验枪 / ~ tools 【冶】检验工具,控制工具 / ~ hole 【冶】观察孔,检验孔 / a house-to-house ~ 挨户检查 ②检阅;视察;参观: make an ~ of a school 视察学校 / *Inspection* declined! 谢绝参观!

inspector [in'spektə] *n.* ①检查员;监察员;视察者;检阅者;检查官 ②【军】军械检验员 / an ~ of weights and measures 度量衡检查员 / an *Inspector* of Taxes [英]税务稽查员 ②巡官 ‖**~al** [in'spektərəl], **~ial** [,inspek'tɔ:riəl] *a.* / **~ate** [in'spektərit] *n.* ①检查员(或监察员等)的职责(或身分) ②检查员(或监察员等)的管辖区域 ③[总称]视察人员,视察团 / **~ship** *n.* 检查员(或监察员等)的地位(或职权) ‖**~ general** 监察主任;【军】监察长: the *Inspector General* of the Army (Navy) (美国的)陆(海)军监察长 / the *Inspector General's* Department 监察署·

inspiration [,inspə'reiʃən] *n.* ①吸入, 吸气 ②鼓舞, 激励; 鼓舞人心的人(或事物) ③灵感; 【宗】神灵的启示 ④[口]灵机, 妙想: have a sudden ~ 灵机一动 ⑤授意; 鼓动 ||**~al** *a.* / **~ism** *n.* 灵感论 / **~ist** *n.* 灵感论者

inspire [in'spaiə] ❶ *vt.* ①吸入, 吸(气) ②鼓舞, 激励; 激起, 唤起: ~ sb. *to* greater efforts 激励某人作出更大的努力 / ~ sb. *with* courage 鼓起某人的勇气 / ~ confidence *in* sb. 使某人产生信心 ③引起, 产生: researches that ~d several inventions 产生了多项发明的研究工作 ④注入 ⑤[常用被动语态]使生灵感, 使感悟: a so-called ~d poet 一个所谓的富有灵感的诗人 ⑥授意; 唆使: an ~d article 一篇由别人授意而写的文章 / a rumour ~d by bad elements 由一些坏家伙授意散布的谣言 ❷ *vi.* ①吸入 ②赋予灵感 ||**inspiring** [in'spaiəriŋ] *a.* 鼓舞人心的: an *inspiring* speech 鼓舞人心的讲话

instability [,instə'biliti] *n.* ①不稳定性 ②不坚决, 动摇; 三心两意

instal(l) [in'stɔ:l] (installed; installing) *vt.* ①任命, 使就职: be *installed in* one's office 就任 ②安装: ~ a heating apparatus 安装暖气设备 ③安顿, 安置: He *installed* himself *in* a front-row seat. 他在前排的一个座位上坐定下来. ||**install-er** *n.* 安装者

installation [,instə'leiʃən] *n.* ①就任, 就职; 就职礼 ②安装; 设置; 安置: an ~ diagram 安装图, 装配图 ③装置, 设备: a heating ~ 暖气设备 ④(军事)设施: an ammunition supply ~ 弹药补给机关, 弹药库 / military ~s 军事设施

instal(l)ment [in'stɔ:lmənt] *n.* ①分期付款中的每一期所付的款项: monthly ~s 按月摊付的款项 / pay *by* (或 *in*) ~s 分期付款 ②(分期连载的)一部分: The novel will appear *in* ~s. 这部小说将分期发表. ||**~ plan** 分期付款购货法: buy *on the* ~ *plan* 用分期付款办法购买

instance ['instəns] **I** *n.* ①例子, 事例, 实例: furnish abundant ~s 提供丰富的例证 / There are many ~s of good people and good deeds. 好人好事的例子很多. ②要求, 建议 ③场合, 情况: in your ~ 在你这种情况下 ④诉讼(手续): a court of first ~ 初审法庭 **II** *vt.* ①举…为例, 引证 ②[常用被动语态]用例子说明: His meaning is well ~d in the passage quoted. 他的意思已在那节引文中有充分的说明. ||*at the ~ of* 应…之请, 经…的提议 / *for ~* 例如 / *in the first ~* 首先, 起初

instant ['instənt] **I** *a.* ①紧迫的; 刻不容缓的: a patient in ~ need of first aid 急需抢救的病人 ②立即的; 直接的: The medicine gave ~ relief. 服药后立即感到舒展. ③本月的(用于商业或正式函件中, 常略作 inst.): your letter of the 8th *inst.* 您本月八日的来函 ④(食品)已配制好的;

速溶的: ~ coffee 速溶咖啡 **II** *n.* ①(某一)时刻: Please come this ~. 请此刻就来. / He may arrive any ~. 他随时都可能到达. ②瞬息, 霎时: I couldn't answer *for an* ~. 我一时答不上来. / I'll be with you *in an* ~. 我马上就来. ||*on the* ~ 立即, 马上: We were ordered to march off *on the* ~. 命令我们立即出发. / *the* ~ ——(就) ||*~ly ad.* 立即, 即刻 ——*conj.* ——(就): I recognized her *~ly* I saw her. 我一看见她就把她认出来了. ||*~ replay* 可即时放送的录象

instantaneous [,instən'teinjəs] *a.* 瞬间的; 即刻的: an ~ bomb 瞬发炸弹 / ~ exposure 自动快速曝光 / ~ velocity 【物】瞬时速度 / an ~ response 即刻的反应 ||*~ly ad.* / *~ness n.*

instead [in'sted] *ad.* 代替, 顶替: He is tired, let me go ~. 他累了, 让我去吧. ||*~ of* 代替, 而不是…: He will go ~ *of* you. 他将代你去. / They went there on foot ~ *of* by bus. 他们没乘公共汽车而是步行到那里去的. / That increased ~ *of* decreased our courage. 那不但没有减弱反倒增强了我们的勇气.

instep ['in-step] *n.* ①脚背 ②鞋面; 袜子的脚面部分 ③【动】跖

instigate ['instigeit] *vt.* ①教唆; 怂恿: ~ sb. *to* do sth. (或 *to* an action) 唆使某人去做某事 ②煽动: ~ a rebellion 煽动叛乱 ||**instigation** [,insti'geiʃən] *n.* at the *instigation* of sb. 在某人的煽动下 / **instigator** *n.* 唆使者; 煽动者

instil(l) [in'stil] (instilled; instilling) *vt.* ①滴注 ②逐渐灌输: ~ an idea *into* sb.'s mind 把一种思想逐渐灌输到某人的脑中去

instinct[1] ['instiŋkt] *n.* ①本能; 直觉; *by* ~ 出于本能 / act *on* ~ 凭直觉行动 ②生性, 天性 ||*have an* ~ *for* 生性爱好; 生来就…

instinct[2] [in'stiŋkt] *a.* 充满的: be ~ *with* confidence 充满信心

instinctive [in'stiŋktiv] *a.* 本能的, 天性的: ~ behaviour 本能行为 ||*~ly ad.*

institute ['institju:t] **I** *n.* ①学会, 协会; 学院, (大专)学校;(研究)所,院 ②讲习会, 讲座 ③会址, 院址, 校址, 所址 ④(公认的)基本原理, 基本原则; [复]法理概要 **II** *vt.* ①建立, 设立; 制定: ~ a sound system of meetings 建立健全的会议制度 / ~ rules 制定规则 ②开始; 创立; 实行: ~ an investigation 着手调查 / ~ a suit *against* sb. 对某人起诉 ③任命;【宗】授予…圣职(*into, to*)

institution [,insti'tju:ʃən] *n.* ①建立, 设立; 制定: the ~ of regulations 条例的制定 ②制度; 惯例; 风俗 ③(慈善、宗教等性质的)公共机构; 协会; 学校: public ~s 公共机构(指孤儿院、医院、学校等) / a scientific ~ 科学协会 / ~s of higher learning 高等学校 ④会址, 校址, 院址, 所址 ⑤[口]恪守惯例一成不变的人

instruct [in'strʌkt] *vt.* ①教, 教育; 指导: The old workers ~ the young workers not only in words, but by deeds. 老工人对青年工人不仅言教而且身传。/ ~ a class in history 给一班学生上历史课 ②通知;向…提供事实情况: be ~ed when to start 得到出发时间的通知 ③指示,命令: ~ sb. to do sth. 指示(或命令)某人做某事 ‖~ed a. ① 受教育的 ② 得到指示的; 被委派的: ~ed delegates 委派的代表

instruction [in'strʌkʃən] *n.* ① 教育; 指导; 训练: give ~ in English 讲授英语 ② (长辈等的) 教训,教诲 ③[复]指示,命令: give (receive) ~s to do sth. 下达(得到)命令(或指示)做某事 ‖~al *a.* an ~al film 教学影片

instructive [in'strʌktiv] *a.* ① 教育的; 指导性的; 用于传播知识的 ② 有教益的; 有启发的: ~ experiences (lessons) 有益的经验(教训) / books 有教育意义的书籍 ‖~ly *ad.* / ~ness *n.*

instructor [in'strʌktə] *n.* ① 指导者; 教员 ② [美]讲师 ‖~ship *n.* 讲师的职位

instrument ['instrumənt] I *n.* ① 仪器, 器械, 器具: optical ~s 光学仪器 / an ~ panel (或 board) 仪器板, 仪表板 / ~ flight (或 flying) [军]仪表飞行 / surgical ~s 外科器械 ② 手段; 工具 ③ 乐器 ④【律】证券; 契约; 文件: a negotiable ~ 流通票据, 可转让证券 II *vt.* ①用仪器装备 ②给乐器编(乐曲); 为管弦乐队编(曲) ③ 提交法律文件给

instrumental [,instru'mentl] *a.* ① 仪器的, 器械的, 器具的: ~ errors 仪器误差; 仪表误差 ②作为手段(或工具)的; 有帮助的, 起作用的: be ~ to a purpose 有助于达到某一目的 / This technical innovation is ~ in improving the qualities of our products. 这项技术革新有助于提高我们产品的质量。③乐器(上)的; 为乐器谱的; 用乐器演奏的: ~ music 器乐 / an ~ ensemble 器乐重奏曲 ④【语】工具格的: the ~ case 工具格 ‖~ism *n.* 工具主义(唯心实用主义的一种, 主张"有用即真理"、"为达到目的可以不择手段"等反动观点) / ~ist *n.* ①乐器演奏者 ②工具主义者 *a.* 主张工具主义的; 根据工具主义的 / ~ly *ad.*

insubordinate [,insə'bɔːdənit] I *a.* ① 不顺从的, 不服从的; 反抗的 ② 地位不低(劣)的 II *n.* 不顺从的人; 反抗者 ‖~ly *ad.* / **insubordination** ['insə,bɔːdi'neiʃən] *n.*

insufferable [in'sʌfərəbl] *a.* 难以忍受的; 不可容忍的; 难堪的: ~ insolence 蛮横不堪 ‖**insufferably** *ad.*

insular ['insjulə] *a.* ① 海岛的, 岛屿的; 岛形的: an ~ climate 岛屿性气候 ②岛民的; 象岛民的; 具有岛民特性的 ③在岛上居住的; 位于岛上的 ④象岛似的; 隔绝的, 孤立的: an ~ fortress 孤立无援的城堡 ⑤思想狭窄的; 保守的; 有偏见的 ⑥【医】岛屿状的, 散开的;【解】胰岛的; 脑岛的 ‖~ism ['insjulərizəm], ~ity [,insju'læriti] *n.* 岛国性质; (思想、观点等的)偏狭性 / ~ly *ad.*

insulate ['insjuleit] *vt.* ① 隔离; 使孤立 ②【物】使绝缘; 使绝热: ~d body 被绝缘体 ‖**insulation**

[,insju'leiʃən] *n.* ① 隔离; 孤立 ②【物】绝缘; 绝热: sound *insulation* 声绝缘,隔声 / *insulation* resistance【电】绝缘电阻 / *insulation* material 绝缘材料 / **insulator** *n.*【物】绝缘体, 绝缘子, 隔电子: heat *insulator* 热绝缘体

insult I ['insʌlt] *n.* ① 侮辱, 凌辱: pocket (或 swallow) an ~ 忍受侮辱 ②[古]攻击,袭击 ③ (对身体或其一部分的)损害: environmental ~s 环境对人体的各种危害 II [in'sʌlt] *vt.* 侮辱; 辱骂; 冒犯; 蔑视; 损害 ‖*add ~ to injury* 伤害之外又加侮辱

insulting [in'sʌltiŋ] *a.* 侮辱的, 无礼的: use ~ language 使用侮辱性的语言 ‖~ly *ad.*

insuperable [in'sjuːpərəbl] *a.* ①不能克服的; 难以越过的: an ~ barrier 无法越过的障碍 ②不可战胜的; 无敌的 ‖**insuperability** [in,sjuːpərə'biliti] *n.* / **insuperably** *ad.*

insupportable [,in-sə'pɔːtəbl] *a.* ① 不能容忍的, 难以忍受的 ②无根据的, 理由站不住的: ~ charges 无理的指责 ‖**insupportably** *ad.*

insurance [in'ʃuərəns] *n.* ① 安全保障: provide ~ against floods 为防洪提供安全措施 ②保险; 保险业: labour ~ 劳动保险 / fire ~ 火险 / marine ~ 水险 / life (accident) ~ 人寿(意外)险 / an ~ company 保险公司 ③保险单(通常称 ~ policy) ④保险费(通常称 premium) ⑤保险额

insure [in'ʃuə] ❶ *vt.* ①给…保险: ~ one's house *against* fire 给自己的房屋保火险 / ~ one's life ~d 给自己保人寿险 / an ~d letter 保价信 / the ~d 受保人 ②保证使…得到; 为…提供保证: Carefulness ~s you against errors. 工作过细可使你避免发生差错。❷ *vi.* 投保; 承保 ‖~r [in'ʃuərə] 承保人

insurgence [in'səːdʒəns] *n.* 起义; 暴动; 造反(指行动)

insurgent [in'səːdʒənt] I *a.* ①起义的; 暴动的; 造反的; 反抗的 ②(波涛等)汹涌而来的 II *n.* 起义者; 暴动者; 造反者; 反抗者

insurmountable [,insə(ː)'mauntəbl] *a.* 难以超越的; 不可克服的; 难以制胜的 ‖**insurmountably** *ad.*

insurrection [,insə'rekʃən] *n.* 起义; 暴动; 造反(指行动): armed ~ 武装起义 ‖~al *a.* 起义的; 暴动的; 造反的 / ~ist *n.* 起义者; 暴动者; 支持暴动者; 造反者

intact [in'tækt] *a.* 未经触动的; 未受损的; 完整的: keep (或 leave) sth. ~ 使某物保持原样 (指完整无缺)

intake ['in-teik] *n.* ①吸入; 纳入, 收纳: an ~ tower 进水塔 / an ~ of hundreds of servicemen 几百名军人的征召 ② 纳入(数)量;【物】输入能量;【矿】进风量 ③ (水、气体流入沟、管的)入口;【矿】进风巷道 ④ 被收纳的东西; 被吸收(到团体或组织里)的人 ⑤[英方](从沼泽等圈入的)垦地 ⑥【医】摄取: ~ of food 食物摄取

intangible [in'tændʒəbl] I *a.* ①触摸不到的; 无形

的: ~ value 无形价值 ②不可捉摸的; 难以确定的; 模糊的 **II** *n.* 无形的东西; 不可捉摸的事物 ||**intangibility** [in,tændʒə'biliti] *n.*

integral ['intigrəl] **I** *a.* ①构成整体所必要的; 组成的: an ~ part of the whole 整体的组成部分 ②完整的; 整体的 ③【数】整的; 积分的: ~ equation 积分方程 **II** *n.* ①整体 ②【数】积分: definite (indefinite) ~ 定(不定)积分 / double ~ (二)重积分 ||**~ity** [,inti'græliti] *n.* 完整性 / **~ly** *ad.* || **~ calculus** 【数】积分(学)

integrate **I** ['intigreit] ❶*vt.* ①使结合(*with*); 使并入(*into*); 使一体化: ~ theory *with* practice 使理论联系实际 / an ~d iron and steel works 钢铁联合企业 / ~d circuit 【无】集成电路 ②[美]取消(学校等)的种族隔离; 使 (黑人等)~: an ~d school 兼收黑人与白人学生的学校 ③【数】求…的积分 ④表示(面积、温度等)的总数 ❷ *vi.* (与…)结合起来(*with*); 成一体 **II** ['intigrit] *a.* 完整的; 完全的; 综合的

integration [,inti'greiʃən] *n.* ①结合; 综合; 一体化: the ~ of manual and mental labour 体力劳动与脑力劳动相结合 ②[美]取消种族隔离; 给予(种族上的)平等待遇 ③【数】积分(法) ④【心】整合(作用) ||**~ism** *n.* 取消种族隔离主义 / **~ist** *a.* & *n.* 主张取消种族隔离的(人)

integrity [in'tegriti] *n.* ①完整; 完全; 完善: mutual respect for territorial ~ 互相尊重领土完整 / The ancient pagoda is still there, but not in its ~. 那座古塔还在, 但是不完整了。②正直; 诚实: a man of moral ~ 一个有道德的人

intellect ['intilekt] *n.* ①理智; 智力; 才智: a man of ~ 有才智的人 ②有才智的人: the ~(s) of the age 当代有才智的人士; 当代的知识界 ||**intellection** [,inti'lekʃən] *n.* 理解;智力活动 / **intellective** [,inti'lektiv] *a.* 智力的; 有智力的

intellectual [,inti'lektjuəl] **I** *n.* 知识分子 **II** *a.* ①智力的, 理智的: ~ education 智育 / the ~ faculties 智能 ②用脑筋的, 需智力的: ~ work 脑力工作 ③一味凭理智行事的;旨在打动人的智力的, 理性的 ||**~ism** *n.* ①智力活动 ②唯智论 / **~ist** *n.* ①过度强调智力活动的人 ②唯理智论者 / **~ly** *ad.*

intelligence [in'telidʒəns] *n.* ①智力; 理解力; 聪明: an ~ test 智力测验 / ~ quotient (略作 I. Q.) 智商, 智力商数(资产阶级心理学家进行智力测验的术语) ②情报; 谍报; 情报机构: communications ~ 【军】电信侦察 / current ~ 【军】动态情报 / an ~ agent 情报员,谍报员 / an ~ bureau (department) 情报局(处) ③【宗】神;天使: the Supreme *Intelligence* 神明, 上帝 ||**~r** *n.* ①情报员; 间谍 ②报信者,报道者

intelligent [in'telidʒənt] *a.* 理解力强的, 聪明的; 理智的, 明智的: an ~ child 聪明的孩子 / an ~ decision 明智的决定 / an ~ reader 理解力高的读者 ||**~ly** *ad.*

intelligentsia, intelligentzia [in,teli'dʒentsiə] *n.*

[the ~] [总称]知识分子;知识界

intelligible [in'telidʒəbl] *a.* ①可理解的; 明白的, 易懂的: an ~ explanation 明白易懂的解释 / Do not coin terms that are ~ *to* nobody. 不要生造谁也不懂的词语。/ make oneself ~ 讲得使人懂 ②【哲】仅能用智力了解的, 概念的 ||**intelligibility** [in,telidʒə'biliti] *n.* ①可理解性; 明了 ②可理解的事物 / **intelligibly** *ad.*

intend [in'tend] *vt.* ①想要, 打算: What do you ~ to do (或 ~ doing) next? 你下一步打算做什么? / We ~ him to set out(或 ~ that he (shall) set out) at once. 我们打算要他立刻出发。/ He ~s no harm. 他没有恶意。②打算使…(成)为: They ~ the building *to* be a guest house. 他们打算把这幢房子用作宾馆。/ We ~ this news report *as* teaching material for freshmen. 我们打算把这篇新闻报道作为新生教材。③意指, 意思是: What do you ~ by that remark? 你说这话算是什么意思?

intense [in'tens] *a.* ①强烈的, 剧烈的; 紧张的: ~ feelings 强烈的感情 / ~ heat 酷热 / ~ pain 剧痛 / ~ but orderly work 紧张而有秩序的工作 ②热切的, 热情的; 认真的: an ~ person 热烈认真的人 / an ~ longing 热望, 渴望 / an ~ study 认真的研究 ③【摄】(底片)银影密度高的 ||**~ly** *ad.* / **~ness** *n.*

intensify [in'tensifai] ❶ *vt.* ①加强; 加剧 ②【摄】增高(底片)的银影密度 ❷ *vi.* 强化; 剧化 ||**intensifier** *n.* 【机】增强器; 【摄】增厚剂; 【物】增强剂: spark *intensifier* 【机】火花增强器

intension [in'tenʃən] *n.* ①紧张; 强度; 加强 ②专心致志 ③【逻】内包 ④【数】内涵 ⑤【农】集约经营

intensity [in'tensiti] *n.* ①(思想、感情等的)强烈, 剧烈 ②强度: labour ~ 劳动强度 / current ~ 【电】电流强度 / radiant ~ 【物】辐射强度 ③【摄】(底片)的明暗度

intensive [in'tensiv] **I** *a.* ①加强的; 集中的; 深入细致的: make an ~ study of sth. 对某事作深入细致的研究 / ~ readings 精读材料 / an ~ bombardment 密集炮击 ②【逻】内包的 ③【农】精耕细作的, 集约的: ~ farming 细耕农业, 集约农业 / deep ploughing and ~ cultivation 深耕细作 ④【语】加强语意的 **II** *n.* ①加强器; 加强剂 ②【语】加强语意的词(或前缀等)

intent [in'tent] **I** *a.* ①(目光等)不转移的, 集中的; 热切的: an ~ look 目不转睛的注视; 热切的样子 ②专心致志的; 坚决的: be ~ *on* one's studies 专心学习 / be ~ *on* going 坚决要去 **II** *n.* ①意图; 目的: with murderous ~ behind one's smiles 笑里藏刀 / use one's leisure time *to good* ~ 有益地利用空余时间 ②意义, 含义 ||*to all* ~*s and purposes* 实际上, 实质上 || **~ly** *ad.* / **~ness** *n.*

intention [in'tenʃən] *n.* ①意图, 意向; 打算; 目的: What is your ~? 你的意图究竟是什么? / He did it *by* ~. 他故意地做了这事。/ with good ~s 好心好意地 / have no ~ of staying 无意留

下,不打算留下 ②意义;意旨: the ~ of a clause 条款的意旨 ③[复]婚娶背后隐藏的意图 ④【逻】概念 ⑤【医】愈合

intentional [in'tenʃənl] *a.* 有意(识)的, 故意的 ‖**~ly** *ad.*

inter [in'tə:] (interred; interring [in'tə:riŋ]) *vt.* 埋葬

intercede [,intə(:)'si:d] *vi.* ①代为请求, 说情: ~ with sb. for another person (for sth.) 为另一个人(为某事)向某人说情 ②调解, 调停

intercept [,intə(:)'sept] **I** *vt.* ①拦截;截击(敌军等);截取(情报等);截断(光、热、水等) ②窃听, 侦听 ③【数】(在两点或两线间)截取 **II** ['intə(:)-sept] *n.* ①拦截;截击: an ~ mission【军】截击任务 / an ~ officer【军】截击军官 / ~ heading 【军】截击航向 ②窃听,侦听: an ~ station【军】侦听台 ③【数】截距, 截段: ~ of a line (plane) 线(面)的截距 ‖**~ive** *a.* / **~or, ~er** *n.* ① 【军】截击机 ②【空】遮断器;阻止器;扰流板: ~or plate 翼缝扰流板 ③窃听器

interception [,intə(:)'sepʃən] *n.* ①拦截;截击;截取;截住;截断: ground-controlled ~【空】地面控制截击(设备) / blind ~【空】(用仪表)盲目拦截 ②窃听, 侦听;【空】雷达侦察: long-range ~ 【空】远距离雷达侦察

interchange I [,intə(:)'tʃeindʒ] ❶ *vt.* ①交换,互换: ~ views (或 opinions) 交换意见 / ~ letters 互通信件 / ~ gifts 相互赠送礼物 ②交替(位置等) ③使更迭发生;轮流进行 ❷ *vi.* 交替发生;交换位置 **II** ['intə(:)'tʃeindʒ] *n.* ①交换;交替 ②【建】互通式立体交叉;道路立体枢纽

interchangeable [,intə(:)'tʃeindʒəbl] *a.* ①可交换的;可交替的 ②可互换的 ‖**interchangeability** ['intə(:),tʃeindʒə'biliti] *n.* 可交换性;可交替性;互换性 / **~ness** *n.* / **interchangeably** *ad.*

intercom ['intə(:)kɔm] *n.* 【讯】内部通信联络系统

intercourse ['intə(:)kɔ:s] *n.* ① 交际;往来;交流: diplomatic ~ 外交往来 / commercial ~ 商业往来 / social ~ 社交 ②【生】交合: sexual ~ 性交

interest ['intrist] **I** *n.* ①兴趣;关心,注意;趣味: His report aroused the ~ of all. 他的报告引起了大家的兴趣。/ have ~ (或 take, feel) no ~ in sth. 对某事不感兴趣 / a question of common ~ 共同关心的问题 / This subject has no ~ for(或 to) me. 这题目对我来说没有什么趣味。/ It is of ~ to note that ... 值得注意的是…(或:饶有趣味的是…) ②感兴趣的事,爱好: Table tennis and swimming are his two ~s. 乒乓球和游泳是他的两项爱好。③利益;利害关系;权利;股权: The ~s of the individual must be subordinated to the ~s of the collective. 个人利益必须服从集体利益。/ It is to your ~ to give up smoking. 戒烟对你(的身体)有好处。/ vested ~s 既得利益 / have an ~ in a business 在某一企业中享有股权 ④重要性;影响;势力: a matter of considerable (little) ~ 相当(不大)重要的事 /

have ~ with sb. 能对某人产生影响 ⑤利息: pay 5 per cent ~ on a loan 借款付息五厘 / annual ~ 年利 / simple (compound) ~ 单(复)利 ⑥行业: the shipping ~ 航运界 / the business ~s 商业界 **II** *vt.* ①使发生兴趣;引起…的注意(或关心): This new method will certainly ~ you. 这新方法肯定会引起你的兴趣。②使参与,使发生关系: ~ sb. in sth. 劝使(或说服)某人参与某事 ‖**in the ~(s) of** 为了…的利益;为了 / **lose ~** ①不再感兴趣: He lost ~ in the book. 他对这本书失掉兴趣。②不再引起兴趣: **take (an) ~ in** 对…感兴趣 / **with ~** ①有兴趣地: listen to a story with ~ 津津有味地听故事 ②付利息: [喻]更加重地(回击、报答等): with ~ at five per cent 以百分之五利息 / return a blow with ~ 加重回击 ③通过某种关系: obtain a position with ~ 通过某种关系取得职位 ‖**~-free** *a.* 无息的: an ~-free loan 无息贷款 / **~ group** 利益集团 (指有共同利益的一批人)

interested ['intristid] *a.* ①感兴趣的;注意的,关心的: We shall be ~ to hear about it. 我们很想听到这个消息。/ He is ~ in sports. 他爱好运动。/ with an ~ look 带着感兴趣的样子 ②有(利害)关系的,有份儿的: the ~ parties 有关的当事人 ③有私心的,有偏见的: ~ motives 不纯正的(或自私自利的)动机 ‖**~ly** *ad.*

interesting ['intristiŋ] *a.* 有趣味的;引起兴趣的: an ~ storybook for children 一本有趣的儿童故事书 ‖**in an ~ condition** [英]怀孕 ‖**~ly** *ad.*

interfere [,intə'fiə] *vi.* ①干涉,干预 ②妨碍,打扰 ③(事物)抵触,冲突 (with) ④(马等在行走、奔驰时)一脚碰在另一脚(踝)上 ⑤【物】干扰 ⑥(橄榄球赛中)阻挡;犯规撞人 ⑦【律】对发明专利权提起诉讼

interference [,intə'fiərəns] *n.* ①干涉,干预 ②妨碍,扰乱;阻碍物: linguistic ~ 本族语对于外语学习的干扰 ③抵触,冲突 ④【物】(光波、声波等的)干涉;干扰: constructive ~ 相长干涉 / destructive ~ 相消干涉 / colours 干涉色 / ~ wave 干涉波 ‖**run ~ for** (橄榄球赛中)保护 (带球者)以防对方抢球

interim ['intərim] **I** *n.* 间歇: in the ~ 在间歇的当儿,在过渡期间 **II** *a.* ①间歇的;期间的 ②暂时的;临时的: an ~ report 中期报告,临时性的报告 / an ~ government 过渡(性质)的政府 / ~ dividends 期中股利

interior [in'tiəriə] **I** *a.* ① 内的,内部的: operate on ~ lines【军】内线作战 / ~ guards【军】内卫兵 / ~ decoration【建】内部装饰 / ~ angle【数】内角 ②内地的: an ~ city 内地城市 ③国内的: ~ trade 国内贸易 ④ 内心的,本质的;深藏的: the ~ meaning of a poem 一首诗的深意 **II** *n.* ① 内部;内景: the ~ of a house 房子的内部 ②内地: travel in the ~ 内地旅行 ③内心;内在性质 ④内务,内政: Department of the *Interior* 内政部(美国) / Secretary of the *Interior* (美国)内政部长 ‖**~ity** [in,tiəri'ɔriti] *n.* / **~ly** *ad.*

interject [,intə(:)'dʒekt] *vt.* (突然)插入: ~ a remark 突然插话 ‖**~or** *n.* 插话者;插入物

interjection [,intə(:)'dʒekʃən] *n.* ①【语】感叹词,惊叹词 ②叫喊;感叹声 ③插入;插入物

interlock [,intə(:)'lɔk] **I** *vt. & vi.* (使)联锁,(使)连结 **II** ['intə(:)lɔk] *n.* 联锁;连结;联锁装置 ‖**~ing device** 联锁装置 / **~ing directorate** (美国)联锁董事会(各企业董事中有几个是由某些人共同兼任的,使经营协调,以便控制) / **~ing signals**【讯】联锁信号

interlope [,intə(:)'loup] *vi.* ①侵占他人权利(如营业等) ②闯人;干涉 ③无执照营业 ‖**~r** ['intə(:)-loupə] *n.* (为营利目的而)干涉他人事务者;无执照营业者

interlude ['intə(:)lu:d] *n.* ① 幕间;幕间插入的表演 ② 插曲 ③ 穿插;间歇;穿插事件: a forest with ~s of open meadow 夹有空旷草地的森林

intermediary [,intə(:)'mi:djəri] **I** *a.* ①中间的;居间的 ② 中间人的;媒介的;调解人的 **II** *n.* ①中间人;调解人 ② 中介(物),媒介(物);手段,工具 ③ 中间形态;中间阶段

intermediate [,intə(:)'mi:djət] **I** *a.* 中间的;居间的: ~ elements (forces) 中间分子(力量) / ~ ports 中途口岸 / an ~-range (或 a medium-range) missile 中程导弹 / an ~ zone【军】中间阵地地带,中间地带 **II** *n.* ① 中间体; 媒介物 ② 中间人;调解人 **III** *vi.* 起媒介作用;起调解作用(*between*) ‖**~ly** *ad.* 在中间 / **intermediation** [,intə(:),mi:di'eiʃən] *n.* 调解

interminable [in'tə:minəbl] *a.* 漫无止境的;没完没了的;冗长不堪的 ‖**~ness** *n.* / **interminably** *ad.*

intermittent [,intə(:)'mitənt] *a.* 间歇的; 断断续续的; 周期性的: ~ noise 断断续续的闹声 / ~ insanity【医】间歇性精神病 / ~ load【电】间歇负载 / ~ reaction【化】间歇反应 ‖**~ly** *ad.*

intern[1] [in'tə:n] **I** *vt.* 拘留(俘虏等);扣留(船只等) **II** *n.* =internee

intern[2] ['intə:n] [美] **I** *vi.* 做实习医生 **II** *n.* 实习医生 (=interne)

internal [in'tə:nl] **I** *a.* ① 内的,内部的: the ~ relations of things 事物的内部联系 / ~ resistance【物】内阻力;内电阻 ②内在的,固有的: ~ evidence 内证(指事物本身所提供的证据) ③内心的: ~ monologue 内心独白 ④ 国内的;内政的: an ~ war 内战 / ~ trade (revenue) 国内贸易(税收) / ~ debts 内债 ⑤体内的;内服的: ~ bleeding 内出血 / ~ secretion 内分泌 / an ~ remedy 内服药 / ~ medicine 内科学 **II** *n.* [复]①内脏,内部器官 ② 本质,本性 ‖**~ly** *ad.*

international [,intə(:)'næʃənl] *a.* 国际的,世界的: ~ conventions 国际惯例 / ~ law 国际公法 / ~ private law 国际私法 / an ~ call 国际通话 / the *International* Phonetic Alphabet 国际音标 / the ~ date line 国际日期变更线,日界线 / an ~ bomber 洲际轰炸机 / the *Interna-*tional Court of Justice 国际法院(联合国) ‖**~ity** [,intə(:),næʃi'næliti] *n.* / **~ly** *ad.*

interplay ['intə(:)'plei] **I** *n.* 相互影响;相互作用 **II** *vi.* 相互影响;相互作用

interpolate [in'tə:pouleit] ❶ *vt.* ①窜改 ② 插入(字句等); 插(话) ③【数】插(值);内插,内推 ❷ *vi.* ① 进行窜改 ② 插入 ‖**interpolation** [in,tə:pou'leiʃən] *n.* ① 窜改 ② 插入; 插入物 ③【数】插值法,内插法,内推法 / **interpolator** *n.* 窜改者,插入者

interpose [,intə(:)'pouz] ❶ *vt.* 插入;插(话);干预;提出(异议等): ~ a barrier between 在…中间设置障碍物 / ~ a veto 使用否决权 ❷ *vi.* 插进来;插嘴;干预

interpret [in'tə:prit] ❶ *vt.* ① 解释;说明 ② 把…理解(为),把…看(作): He ~ed the silence as contempt. 他把这沉默看作轻蔑的表示。③(根据本人的理解)表演;表现(剧中人物);演奏(乐曲) ❷ *vi.* 翻译,口译;当译员;解释: ~ for foreign visitors 替外宾当翻译 ‖**~able** *a.* 可以解释的

interpreter [in'tə:pritə] *n.* ①译员,口译者;解释者【军】情报判读员 ③【自】翻译器: electronic ~ 电子翻译器 ‖**~ship** *n.* 译员职务(或身分) / **interpretress** [in'tə:pritris] *n.* 女译员

interrogate [in'terəgeit] ❶ *vt.* 讯问;审问;质问: ~ a prisoner of war 讯问战俘 ❷ *vi.* 提出问题

interrogation [in,terə'geiʃən] *n.* ① 讯问;审问;质问 ②疑问句 ③【语】问号: an ~ mark (或 point, note) 问号

interrogative [,intə'rɔgətiv] **I** *a.* 疑问的,讯问的;质问的: an ~ pronoun (adverb)【语】疑问代词(副词) / an ~ tone 用疑问的口气 **II** *n.* 疑问词 (如 who, which, what 等) ‖**~ly** *ad.*

interrupt [,intə'rʌpt] ❶ *vt.* ① 中断;遮断;阻碍: Traffic was ~ed by a snowstorm. 交通被暴风雪所阻断。/ ~ a view 遮住视线 ② 打断(讲话或讲话的人);扰: His speech was constantly ~ed by applause. 他的讲话频为掌声所打断。/ Don't ~ me. 别打扰我。❷ *vi.* 打断;打扰

interrupted [,intə'rʌptid] *a.* 中断的;被遮断的;被打断的 ‖**~ly** *ad.*

interruption [,intə'rʌpʃən] *n.* ①中断;遮断;打断: ~ of communication 交通中断 / service ~ 业务中断;服务中断(指停电或停自来水等) / alternating current【电】交流(电流)断路 ②障碍物,遮断物 ③中断期;休止期

intersect [,intə(:)'sekt] ❶ *vt.* 横切,横断;和…交叉: The line AB ~s the line CD at E. 直线 AB 与直线 CD 相交于 E 点上。❷ *vi.* (线)相交,交叉: The two roads ~ at the railway. 两条路在铁路处交叉。‖**~ion** [,intə(:)'sekʃən] *n.* ①横断,交叉 ②交叉点;十字街口

intersperse [,intə(:)'spə:s] *vt.* ① 散布,散置 (*between*, *among*) ②点缀: The lawn is ~d with flower-beds in the shape of five-point stars. 草地上点缀着五角星形的花坛。

interval ['intəvəl] *n.* ①(时间的)间隔; 间歇; 幕间(或工间)休息: after a year's ~ 隔一年后 / There is a two hours' ~ to the next train. 下一班火车还要过两小时。/ *Interval*—10 Min. 休息十分钟(常用于演出节目单中) ②(空间的)间隔; 空隙: an ~ of five metres between columns 柱间相隔五米的距离 ③(在品质、地位等方面的)悬殊, 差别 ④【音】音程 ⑤【数】区间 ‖*at ~s* 不时 ②相隔一定的距离: Trees are standing *at ~s* along the street. 沿街相隔不远都有树木。/ *at long ~s* 间或 / *at regular ~s* 每隔一定时间; 每隔一定距离 / *at short ~s* 常常 ‖~ **land**

intervene [,intə(:)'vi:n] *vi.* ①干涉; 干预 ②插进; 介入; 介于 (指时间和空间): The meeting will be held on Monday if nothing ~s. 如果没有什么特殊事情, 会议将于星期一举行。③调停: ~ between the two people quarrelling 在两个争吵者之间进行调停 ④【律】(第三者为保护个人利益)参加诉讼 ‖**intervenor, ~r** *n.* 干涉者; 介入者; 调停者

intervention [,intə(:)'venʃən] *n.* ①干涉; 干预; 妨碍: armed ~ 武装干涉 ②调停 ③插进; 介入 ‖~**ist** *n.* 进行干涉的人; 主张进行干涉的人(尤指对国际事务) *a.* ①干涉的; 干涉者的 ②进行干涉的; 主张进行干涉的

interview ['intəvju:] **I** *n.* ①接见; 会见; 会谈: I thank you very much indeed for this ~. 非常感谢您这次接见。/ give (或 grant) an ~ to sb. 接见某人 / have an ~ with sb. 会见某人 ②(记者的)访问; 访问记 ③对申请工作者(或投考学校者)的口头审查: job ~s 对申请工作者的口头审查 **II** *vt.* 接见; 会见; (记者等)访问 ‖~**ee** [,intəvju'i:] *n.* 被接见者; 被采访者 / ~**er** *n.* 接见者; 会见者; 面谈者; 记者

intestate [in'testit] **I** *a.* 没有留下遗嘱的; 不能根据遗嘱处理的: die ~ 未留遗嘱而死 **II** *n.* 未留遗嘱的死亡者

intestine [in'testin] **I** *a.* 内部的; 国内的 **II** *n.* [常用复]肠: large ~ 大肠 / small ~ 小肠

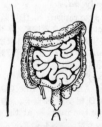

intestine

intimacy ['intiməsi] *n.* ①亲密; 密切; 熟悉 ②[委婉语]不正当的性关系 ③[复]亲昵行为

intimate[1] ['intimit] **I** *a.* ①亲密的; 密切的: an ~ friend 亲密的朋友 / be on ~ terms with sb. 与某人关系密切 ②熟悉的; 经过认真调查研究的: an ~ knowledge of life 熟悉生活 ③内部的; 内心深处的; 本质的: the ~ structure of the atom 原子的内部结构 / one's ~ feelings 内心的感情 ④私人的; 个人的: an ~ diary 私人日记 ⑤[委婉语]发生不正当性关系的 **II** *n.* 熟友, 知己 ‖~**ly** *ad.*

intimate[2] ['intimeit] *vt.* ①宣布, 通知, 通告; 明白表示: ~ one's approval of a plan 表明同意某项计划 ②暗示; 提示

intimidate [in'timideit] *vt.* 恫吓, 恐吓, 威胁: ~ sb. *into doing* sth. 胁迫某人做事 ‖**intimidation** [in,timi'deiʃən] *n.* / **intimidator** *n.* 威吓者

into ['intu, 'intə] *prep.* ①[表示动作的方向]到…里: put the hammer ~ the toolbox 把锤子放进工具箱里 / launch an earth satellite ~ orbit 把人造地球卫星发射进轨道 / change ~ working clothes 换上工作服 / inquire ~ a problem 深入研究一个问题 ②[表示时间]进入到 ③[表示变化]成, 为; 转入: transform wasteland ~ fertile fields 变荒地为良田 / divide one ~ two 一分为二 / bring one's ideas ~ correspondence with the objective laws 使自己的思想合乎客观规律 / talk sb. ~ reason 说服某人使他讲理 ④[数]除: 5 *into* 20 is 4. 五除二十等于四。⑤[罕][数]乘: 4 *into* 5 is 20. 四乘五等于二十。

intonation [,intou'neiʃən] *n.* ①语调; 声调: a rising (falling) ~ 升 (降) 调 ②抑扬 ③【宗】(圣歌等的)起始短句; (圣歌等的)吟咏, 吟诵 ④【音】发声, 转调

intone [in'toun] ❶ *vt.* ①(以单调音等)吟咏, 吟诵(赞美诗、祷文等) ②给…一种特殊音调 ③唱(圣歌等)的起始短句 ❷ *vi.* ①吟咏, 吟诵 ②拖长的声音: The dogs ~d to the strangers. 狗对着生人不停地吠叫。

intoxicant [in'tɔksikənt] **I** *a.* ①致醉的 ②令人陶醉的 ③使中毒的 **II** *n.* ①酒类饮料 ②【医】麻醉剂; 毒药

intoxicate [in'tɔksikeit] *vt.* ①使喝醉: become ~d *from* wine 喝醉了酒 ②使陶醉; 使高兴欲狂: be ~d *by* (或 *with*) one's success 陶醉于自己的成就 / be ~d *with* joy 欣喜若狂 ③使中毒 ‖**intoxication** [in,tɔksi'keiʃən] *n.*

intoxicating [in'tɔksikeitiŋ] *a.* ①醉人的: an ~ beverage 酒类 ②令人陶醉的 ‖~**ly** *ad.*

intrepid [in'trepid] *a.* 无畏的; 勇猛的; 坚韧不拔的 ‖~**ity** [,intri'piditi] *n.* / ~**ly** *ad.*

intricacy ['intrikəsi] *n.* ①错综; 复杂; 缠结 ②[复]错综复杂的事物

intricate ['intrikit] *a.* 复杂的; 错综的; 缠结的; 难懂的: an ~ instrument 复杂的仪器 / a novel with an ~ plot 情节复杂的小说 ‖~**ly** *ad.*

intrigue [in'tri:g] **I** ❶ *vi.* ①阴谋, 诡计 ②私通 ❷ *vi.* 策划阴谋, 捣鬼(*against*); 私通(*with*) ❷ *vt.* ①用诡计取得; [古]哄骗 ②(新闻用语)引起…的兴趣(或好奇心): The news ~d all of us. 这新闻引起了大家的兴趣。‖~r *n.* 阴谋者; 私通者 / **intriguing** *a.* 引起兴趣(或好奇心)的; 有迷惑力的

intrinsic(al) [in'trinsik(ə)l] *a.* ①内在的; 固有的; 本质的: *intrinsic* energy 【物】内能 / *intrinsic* value 内在的价值 ②【解】内部的, 体内的 ‖**intrinsically** *ad.*

introduce [,intrə'dju:s] *vt.* ①带领; 引进: ~ a new course *into* the curriculum 设一门新课程 ②输入, 传入; 采用: ~ new techniques 采用新技术 ③介绍: ~ oneself 作自我介绍 / ~ sb. *to* a new method of work 向某人介绍一种新的工作方法 ④作为(文章、讲话等)的开头 ⑤提出(议案、话题等): ~ a motion *to* the meeting 向会议提出一项动议 ⑥把…插入(*into*): ~ a tube *into* a wound 把管子插入伤口 ⑦推销(商品等) ⑧【化】导入 ‖~r *n.* 介绍人; 传入者; 创始人; 提出人

introduction [,intrə'dʌkʃən] *n.* ①引进; 传入 ②采用; 被采用的东西: ~ of better strains of seeds 良种的采用 / These words are recent ~s. 这些词是新近采用的。③介绍: a letter of ~ 介绍信 ④导言, 引言; 【音】序曲 ⑤入门(书): *An Introduction to Radio* «无线电入门»

introductory [,intrə'dʌktəri] *a.* 介绍的; 导言的: ~ remarks 绪言; 开场白 ‖**introductorily** *ad.*

introspect [,introu'spekt] ❶ *vt.* 对(思想等)进行反省 ❷ *vi.* 进行反省

introspection [,introu'spekʃən] *n.* 内省, 反省 ‖~ist *a.* 内省的, 反省的 *n.* 内省者, 反省者

intrude [in'tru:d] ❶ *vi.* 侵入; 闯入; 打扰: ~ *upon* sb.'s time 占用某人的时间 / I hope I am not *intruding*. 我希望不致打扰。❷ *vt.* ①硬挤; 强加: ~ oneself *into* a meeting 闯进会场 / ~ one's views *upon* others 把自己的意见强加于人 ②【地】使侵入其它地层: ~d rock 侵入岩 ‖~r *n.* 入侵者; 闯入者

intrusion [in'tru:ʒən] *n.* ①侵入; 闯入; 打扰: armed ~s 武装入侵 ②【地】侵入; 侵入岩(浆)

intuition [,intju(:)'iʃən] *n.* ①直觉; 直观 ②直觉到的事物; 直觉知识 ‖~ism *n.* 直觉主义; 直观论 / ~ist *n.* 直觉主义者; 直观论者 *a.* 直观主义的; 直观论的

inundate ['inʌndeit] *vt.* ①淹没 ②使充满: The office was inundated with telegrams of congratulations. 贺电潮水般涌到办公处。‖**inundation** [,inʌn'deiʃən] *n.* 泛滥; 洪水

inure [i'njuə] ❶ *vt.* [常用被动语态] 使习惯(不利条件): be ~d *to* cold 习惯于寒冷 / ~ oneself *to* hardships 使自己习惯于艰苦 ❷ *vi.* 【律】生效; 适用 ‖~ment *n.*

invade [in'veid] *vt.* ①侵入, 侵略(别国); 侵犯(权利等): ~ sb.'s rights 侵犯某人的权利 ②拥入 ③(疾病、感情、声音等)侵袭 ‖~r *n.* 侵略者, 侵入者; 侵犯者; 侵入物

invalid¹ ['invəli:d] I *a.* ①有病的; 病弱的; 伤残的 ②病人用的: an ~ chair (有轮子的) 病人用椅 II *n.* 病人; 病弱者; 伤病员, 伤病军人 III [,invə'li:d] ❶ *vt.* ①使病弱; 使伤残 ②把…作为病员处理: be ~ed out of the army 因伤病而奉命退伍 / be ~ed home 被作为伤病员送回家乡 ❷ *vi.* ①失去健康 ②因病而退伍

invalid² [in'vælid] *a.* (法律上)无效的; 无效力的: declare a decision ~ 宣布决定无效 / an ~ contract (cheque) 无效的契约 (支票) / an ~ argument 站不住脚的论点

invaluable [in'væljuəbl] *a.* 无法估价的, 无价的; 非常宝贵的: an ~ treasure 无价之宝 ‖**invaluably** *ad.*

invasion [in'veiʒən] *n.* ①入侵; 侵略; 闯入: an ~ of locusts 蝗虫的侵袭 ②侵害, 侵犯: an ~ of sb.'s rights 对某人权利的侵害 ③【医】发病; 发作

invective [in'vektiv] I *n.* ①痛骂; 抨击; 恶骂: a speech filled with ~ 充满抨击的演说 ②[复] 骂人的话: utter ~s against sb. 恶骂某人 II *a.* 抨击的; 恶骂的

inveigh [in'vei] *vi.* 猛烈抨击; 痛骂; 申斥 (*against*)

inveigle [in'vi:gl] *vt.* (用甜言蜜语)诱骗; 骗取: ~ sb. *into* sth. (或 *into* doing sth.) 诱骗某人做某事 ‖~ment *n.*

invent [in'vent] *vt.* ①发明, 创造 ②捏造, 虚构: ~ a story (an excuse) 捏造事实(借口)

invention [in'venʃən] *n.* ①发明, 创造; 发明物 ②创造力, 发明才能 ③捏造, 虚构 ④【音】创意曲

inventive [in'ventiv] *a.* 发明创造的; 有发明才能的, 有创造力的: ~ powers 发明创造的能力 ‖~ness *n.* 发明创造能力, 创造性

inventory ['invəntri] I *n.* ①财产目录; 存货清单; 存货盘存 (报表): ~ liquidating 【商】减少存货 / physical ~ 【商】实地盘存 ②存货: an aircraft ~ 【军】编制内飞机总数 II *vt.* 为…编制财产目录; 为…开列存货清单; 把…编入目录

inverness [,invə'nes] *n.* 长披风, 无袖长外套

inverse ['in'və:s] I *a.* 相反的; 倒转的: ~ ratio 【数】反比 / ~ function 【数】反函数 II *n.* 反面: Evil is the ~ of good. 恶是善的反面。III [in'və:s] *vt.* 使倒转; 使成反面 ‖~ly *ad.* 相反地

inversion [in'və:ʃən] *n.* ①反向; 倒转; 倒置; 转换: ~ of relief 【地】地形倒置 ②倒置物; 颠倒现象 ③【机】(四杆机构的) 机架变换 ④【化】转化: ~ point 转化点 ⑤【数】反演 ⑥【医】内翻 ⑦【心】同性恋 ⑧【生】(染色体的)倒位: ~ hybrid 倒位杂种 ⑨【语】(词序) 倒装法; (语音的)卷舌 ⑩【音】倒影进行 ⑪【电】(直流电转变成交流电的)换流; 【自】反相 ⑫【气】逆温, 逆增

invert I [in'və:t] *vt.* ①使颠倒; 使内翻; 使倒转, 使反向; 转换: ~ flight 【军】倒飞 / ~ed engine 【机】倒缸发动机 / ~ed arch 【建】仰拱 / ~ed commas 引号 ②【化】使转化 ③【音】使倒影进行 II ['invə:t] *n.* ①颠倒了的事物 ②同性恋

者 ③【建】仰拱 **III** ['invə:t] *a.* 【化】转化的: ~ sugar 转化糖

invest [in'vest] ❶ *vt.* ①给…着衣;披盖: Fog ~s the city. 大雾笼罩着这座城市。 ② 使带有: be ~ed with mystery 带有神秘色彩 ③授予 (with): be ~ed with full authority 被授予全权 ④【军】包围 ⑤ 投(资);投入(时间,精力等): ~ money in mines 投资于矿山 ❷ *vi.* ① 投资 (in): ~ heavily in an enterprise 对某一企业进行大量投资 ②[口]买进 (in): ~ in a new shirt 买一件新衬衫 ‖~**able** *a.* 可供投资的

investigate [in'vestigeit] ❶ *vt.* 调查,调查研究; 审查: ~ conditions at the grass roots 对基层情况作调查研究 ❷ *vi.* 调查,调查研究: ~ into an affair 调查一件事情 ‖**investigative, investigatory** *a.* 调查的;审查的;爱调查研究的 / **investigator** *n.* 调查者,调查研究者;审查者;侦查员

investigation [in,vesti'geiʃən] *n.* 调查,调查研究: No ~, no right to speak. 没有调查就没有发言权 / make an ~ on (或 of, into) sth. 对某事进行调查研究 / The matter is under ~. 这事正在调查中。

investiture [in'vestitʃə] *n.* ①授职(仪式);授权 ②覆盖物;装饰 ③(封建时代的)封地仪式

investment [in'vestmənt] *n.* ①投资(额);(时间,精力等的)投入;(可)投入资金的东西: an ~ trust 投资信托公司 ②【军】包围;封锁 ③覆盖 ④ 授职(仪式);授权

inveterate [in'vetərit] *a.* 长期形成的;根深蒂固的;积习很深的: ~ conservatives 顽固不化的保守派 / an ~ disease 宿疾,老毛病 / an ~ smoker 烟瘾很深的人 ‖~**ly** *ad.*

invidious [in'vidiəs] *a.* ①(言行等)引起反感的,使人厌恶的;招嫉妒的 ②怀恨的;诽谤的,中伤的 ‖~**ly** *ad.* / ~**ness** *n.*

invigorate [in'vigəreit] *vt.* 使精力充沛;使健壮;使活跃; 鼓舞 ‖**invigorating, invigorative** *a.* 增益精力的;强身的;令人鼓舞的: an *invigorating* climate 高爽的气候 / *invigorating* news 鼓舞人心的消息 / **invigoration** [in,vigə'reiʃən] *n.* 增益精力;滋补;鼓舞 / **invigorator** *n.* 鼓舞者;补药

invincible [in'vinsəbl] *a.* 无敌的,战无不胜的 ‖**invincibility** [in,vinsi'biliti] *n.* / **invincibly** *ad.*

inviolable [in'vaiələbl] *a.* 不可侵犯的;不能违反的;不可亵渎的,神圣的: an ~ promise 不容违背的诺言 ‖**inviolably** *ad.*

inviolate [in'vaiəlit], **inviolated** [in'vaiəleitid] *a.* 不受侵犯的,无损的;不受亵渎的,不被玷污的,纯洁的: keep one's promise ~ 坚守诺言

invitation [,invi'teiʃən] *n.* ①邀请,招待;请帖: at the ~ of sb. 应某人邀请 / accept (decline) an ~ 接受(谢绝)邀请 / receive an ~ to deliver a lecture 接到作演讲的邀请 / send sb. an ~ to

dinner 向某人发出宴会请帖 / admission by ~ only 凭柬入场 / an ~ tournament 邀请赛 ②吸引 ‖~**al** *a.*

invite [in'vait] **I** *vt.* ① 邀请,招待: ~ sb. to a dinner party (a meeting) 邀请某人参加宴会(会议) ② 请求;征求: ~ sb. to consider 请求某人考虑 / Questions are ~d. 欢迎提问。 / ~ tenders 招标 ③引起,招致;吸引: ~ danger 引起危险 **II** [in'vait; 美 'invait] *n.* [俚]邀请 ‖~ *n.* 邀请者

inviting [in'vaitiŋ] *a.* 吸引人的,诱人的 ‖~**ly** *ad.* / ~**ness** *n.*

invocation [,invou'keiʃən] *n.* ①祈祷,乞灵 ②召唤魔鬼;符咒 ③ (法权的)行使;(法规的)援引;发动

invoice ['invois] **I** *n.* ① 发票;装货清单: specification 发票明细单 ②货物的托运: receive a large ~ of goods 接受大宗商品的托运 **II** *vt.* & *vi.* (把…)开发票;(把…)开清单

invoke [in'vouk] *vt.* ①祈求(神灵)保佑,乞灵于;用符咒召唤(魔鬼) ②恳求,乞求: ~ sb.'s help 恳求某人帮助 ③ 行使(法权等);实行: ~ the veto in the dispute 在辩论中行使否决权 / ~ economic sanctions 实行经济制裁 ④援引(法规,条文等) ⑤引起,产生: ~ new problems 引起一些新的问题

involuntary [in'vɔləntəri] *a.* ①非故意的;偶然的: ~ manslaughter 【律】过失杀人 ②非自愿的;不随意的: ~ muscle 【解】不随意肌 ③无意识的;不自觉的·‖**involuntarily** [in'vɔləntərili; 美 in,vɔlən'terili] *ad.* / **involuntariness** *n.*

involve [in'vɔlv] *vt.* ①包缠;卷缠 ②使卷入,使陷入;拖累: be ~d in trouble 卷入纠纷 ③使专注: He was ~d in working out a plan. 他专心一意地订计划。④必须包括;包含,含有: Building this road will ~ the construction of ten bridges. 造这条路须包括建造十座桥梁。/ a task which ~s much difficulty 带有许多困难的任务 ⑤包围,围住;笼罩: The real meaning of his remark is ~d in ambiguity. 他这句话的真正意思是很难捉摸的。⑥【数】把(某数字)乘方 ‖~**d** *a.* 难懂的;复杂的: an ~d sentence 复杂的难句

inward ['inwəd] **I** *a.* ①里面的,内部的;内在的,固有的;精神上的: the ~ organs of the body 身体内部的器官 / ~ happiness 内心的喜悦 ②向内的,进来的;输入的,进口的: an ~ curve 内弯 / ~ correspondence 来信 / ~ charges 入港费 ③内地的;[古]国内的: ~ Asia 亚洲的腹地 ④(声音)低沉的,暗自说着的: Her words were ~ and indistinct. 她说话声音低沉,模糊不清。⑤亲密的;熟悉的 **II** *n.* ①里面,内部;内心;实质 ②[复]内脏,肠胃 ③[英][复]进口商品;进口税 **III** *ad.* ①向内,向中心: slope ~ 向内倾斜 / ~ bound 【海】向内行驶 ② 向着内心,进入心灵 ‖~**ly** *ad.* ①在内部,内里;向内,向中心: bleed ~ly 内出血 ②在心灵深处;思想上,精神上 ③暗

自地: speak ~ly 自言自语 / ~ness n. ①本质; 深意: grasp the ~ness of the text 抓住原文的实质 ②灵性; 精神性 ③思想(或感情)的深度; 诚挚

iodine ['aiədi:n, 'aiədain] n. ①【化】碘: tincture of ~【药】碘酊 ②[口]碘酊

iota [ai'outə] n. ①希腊语的第九个字母(I, ι) ②微小, 小点儿: not change by one ~ 丝毫也不变/ have not an ~ of 没有一点儿…

irascible [i'ræsibl] a. 易怒的; 性情暴躁的 ||**irascibility** [i,ræsi'biliti] n. / **irascibly** ad.

irate [ai'reit] a. 发怒的, 愤怒的, 激怒的

ire ['aiə] n. [诗] 怒火

iris ['aiəris] ([复] irises 或 irides ['aiəridi:z]) n. ①虹; 虹彩; 虹状物; [I-]【希神】(为诸神报信的)彩虹女神 ②【解】虹膜 ③【植】鸢尾属植物, 鸢尾, 蝴蝶花 ④【物】膜片; 可变光阑 ⑤【矿】彩虹色石英 ‖~ **diaphragm**【物】可变光阑

irk [ə:k] vt. 使厌烦, 使厌倦; 使恼怒: It ~s me to stay at home. 呆在家里使我感到厌烦。

iron ['aiən] **I** n. ①铁; [喻]铁一般的刚强, 坚强; 严酷: pig ~ 生铁 / cast ~ 铸铁 / wrought ~ 熟铁, 锻铁 / scrap ~ 废铁 / ~-melting furnace 【冶】化铁炉, 熔铁炉 / muscles of ~ 非常结实的肌肉 / an ~ will (determination) 钢铁般的意志 (决心) ②铁制品; 烙铁, 熨斗: fire ~s 炉子的生火用具(指炉钩, 火钳等) / an electric soldering ~ 电烙铁 / an electric ~ 电熨斗 / Materials are all washable and non or minimum ~. 料子可以洗, 但勿用熨斗烫, 或尽量少烫。③[复]镣铐; 马镫 ④[俚]手枪; 小枪 ⑤[俚](牛羊身上打的)烙印 ⑥【药】铁剂, 含铁补药 ⑦(高尔夫球)铁头球棒 **II** ❶ vt. ①用铁装裹, 用铁包 ②给(犯人等)戴上镣铐; 烫平, 烫平(衣服) ❷ vi. ①烫衣服 ②(衣服等)被烫平: Damp clothes ~ easily. 湿衣服容易烫平。‖a barking (或 shooting) ~ [美俚]手枪 / a man of ~ ①意志坚强的人 ②严酷无情的人 / have too many ~s in the fire 同时要办的事(或要参加的活动)太多 / in ~s ①戴着镣铐; 被监禁着 ②[海](帆船)船头向风难以调向 / ~ out ①烫平(衣服或衣服的皱痕等) ②消除(困难等): ~ out misunderstandings 消除误解 ③[美俚]杀掉 / put (或 lay) all ~s (或 every ~) in the fire 试用种种手段; 用尽一切方法 / Strike while the ~ is hot. [谚]趁热打铁。/ the ~ age (古代神话中描写的)堕落时代, 没落时代 / the Iron Age 铁器时代 / the Iron Curtain 铁幕 / The ~ enters (into) his soul. 他心如刀割。/ with an ~ hand 见 hand ‖~bark n. 【植】(澳大利亚等地生长的)桉树属植物 / '~bound a. ①包铁的 ②坚硬; 不容变通的 ③(海岸)岩石围绕的 / '~clad a. ①穿甲的 ②打不破的: an ~clad proof 铁证 n. 装甲舰 / '~fisted a. 吝啬的; 残忍的 / foundry 铸铁厂, 铸铁车间 / ~ glance 【矿】镜铁矿 / ~ grey 铁灰色 / '~handed a. 铁腕的, 用高压手段的, 严厉的 / ~ hat [美俚]礼帽 / '~'hearted a. 铁石心肠的 / ~ horse [口]火车头; 自行车; 三轮(童)车 / ~ house [美俚]监狱 / ~ lung 人工呼吸器, 铁肺 / ~ man ①钢铁工人; [美俚]体力坚强的运动选手, 铁汉 ②[美俚]银元 / '~,master n. 铁器制造商 / '~,monger n. [英]金属器具商, 小五金商 / '~,mongery n. [英][总称]五金器具, 五金店; 五金业 / '~mo(u)ld n. 铁锈迹, 墨水迹 vt. & vi. (使)弄上锈迹(或墨水迹); (使)生锈(或有墨水迹) / ~ ore【矿】铁矿 / ~ pony [美俚]摩托车 / ~ pyrites【矿】黄铁矿 / ~ sand【矿】铁砂 / '~side ①勇敢的人 ②[Ironsides]【英史】克伦威尔铁甲军 / ~smith n. 锻工; 铁匠 / '~stone n. 【矿】铁石; 含铁矿石; 菱镁矿 / '~ware n. [总称]铁器; 五金器 / '~wood n. 硬质的树木; 坚硬的木料 / '~work n. ①铁工; 铁制的部分 ②[总称]铁制品 / '~,worker n. ①钢铁工人; 铁器工人 ②造铁桥架的工人 / '~works [复] n. [用作单或复]钢铁厂

iron lung

ironic(al) [ai'rɔnik(ə)l] a. ①冷嘲的, 讽刺的; 反话的; 挖苦的: an ~ smile 冷笑 / ~ remarks 讽刺的话, 冷言冷语 ②令人啼笑皆非的: It was ~ that he should . . . . 他竟然…, 真令人啼笑皆非。‖~ly ad.

ironing ['aiəniŋ] n. ①熨烫 ②[总称]烫过的衣服; 要烫的衣服 ‖~ **board** 烫衣板

irony ['aiərəni] n. 冷嘲; 反话; 【语】反语法 ‖an ~ of fate (circumstances) (指事情结果与预期相反的)命运(境遇)的嘲弄 / Socratic ~ 苏格拉底式的装作无知法(辩论中佯装无知, 接受对方的结论, 然后用发问方法逐步引到相反的结论而驳倒对方)

irreproachable [,iri'prəutʃəbl] a. 无可指责的, 无瑕疵的, 无缺点的: an ~ manner 无可指责的举止 ‖**irreproachability** ['iri,prəutʃə'biliti] n. / **irreproachably** ad.

irresistible [,iri'zistəbl] a. 不可抵抗的; 不能压制的: an ~ historical trend 不可阻挡的历史潮流 ‖**irresistibility** ['iri,ziste'biliti] n. / **irresistibly** ad.

irrespective [,iris'pektiv] a. 不考虑的; 不问的, 不顾的: ~ of sex, age or education 不论性别、年龄或教育程度 / ~ of the consequences 不顾后

果 / *Irrespective of* Percentage 【海】无免赔率
||~**ly** *ad.*

irresponsible [,iris'ponsəbl] **I** *a.* ①不承担责任的;
不需负责任的 ②无责任感的,不负责任的 (*for*);
不可靠的: be ~ *for* what one has said 对自己说
过的话不负责任 **II** *n.* 不承担责任的人; 无责任
感的人,不负责任的人 ||**irresponsibility** ['iris-
,ponse'biliti] *n.* / **irresponsibly** *ad.*

irrigate ['irigeit] ❶ *vt.* ①灌溉;~*d* fields 水浇地;
水田 ②【医】冲洗(伤口) ③滋润;使清新 ❷ *vi.*
① 进行灌溉 ②【美俚】饮酒过度 ||**irrigator** *n.*
①灌溉者;灌溉设备,灌溉用具 ②【医】冲洗器

irrigation [,iri'geiʃən] *n.* ①灌溉; 水利: bring the
farmland under ~ 使农田水利化 / an ~ canal
(或 channel) 灌溉渠 / an ~ system (network)
灌溉系统(网) ②【医】冲洗法;[复]冲洗剂 ||~**al**
a. / ~**ist** *n.* 灌溉者;水利专家

irrigation canal

irritable ['iritəbl] *a.* ①易激怒的, 烦躁的 ②【医】
易激动的; 过敏性的: ~ weakness 过敏性虚弱
||**irritability** [,iritə'biliti] *n.* ①易怒, 烦躁;过敏
②【医】应激性,激动性: nervous *irritability* 神经
应激性,神经质的烦躁 / **irritably** *ad.*

irritant ['iritənt] **I** *a.* 刺激的,有刺激(性)的;引起
发炎的: ~ gas 【军】刺激性毒气 **II** *n.* 【医】刺激
物,刺激剂

irritate ['iriteit] ❶ *vt.* ①激怒, 使恼怒; 使烦躁:
be ~*d by* sb.'s insolence 被某人的蛮横态度弄得
恼火 / be ~*d against* sb. 对某人生气 / be ~*d
at* sb.'s inhospitality 因受到某人的冷待而恼怒
②使不舒服;使发炎;使疼痛: The smoke ~*d* my
eyes. 烟熏得我的眼睛怪难受的。③ 刺激,使兴
奋 ❷ *vi.* 引起不愉快;引起恼怒 ||~**d** *a.* ①被
激怒的,生了气的 ②(皮肤等)变粗的;发红的;因
刺激而发炎的

irritating ['iriteitiŋ] *a.* 气人的, 使人不愉快的
||~**ly** *ad.*

irritation [,iri'teiʃən] *n.* ①激怒,恼怒,生气 ②刺激
物 ③【医】刺激;兴奋过度;疼痛;发炎: mechanical
~ 机械性刺激

is [强 iz; 弱 z, s] 见 **be** ||*as* ~ 照现在的样子(指
不再作修理或改进)

island ['ailənd] **I** *n.* ① 岛,岛屿: ~ territories 属
岛 ②岛状物;孤立的地区;孤立的组织 ③【船】航空

母舰(或船)的上层建筑(如舰桥等) ④安全地区
安全岛, 路岛: a pedestrian ~ (交叉口处)行人
安全岛 / a safety ~ (路中)安全岛 / an ~
platform (火车站上的)岛式站台 ⑤【解】岛;
岛; 胰岛: a blood ~ 血岛 ⑥(喷气式飞机等
中的)导管固定部 **II** *vt.* ①使成岛(状):孤立 ②象
岛屿般分布在: a prairie ~*ed with* groves 星星
点点地分布着一些树丛的大草原 ||*the Islands
of the Blessed* 【希神】极乐岛; 西方极乐世界
||~**er** *n.* 岛民,岛上居民 / ~**less** *a.* 无岛屿的
||~**-,hopping** *n.* 【军】越岛作战

isle [ail] **I** *n.* 岛, 小岛: the British *Isles* 不列颠
(诸)岛 **II** ❶ *vt.* 使成岛 ❷ *vi.* 住在岛上

islet ['ailit] *n.* ①小岛;岛状地带,孤立地点 ②【解】
胰岛

isn't ['iznt] [口] =is not

isobar ['aisouba:] *n.* ①【气】等压线 ②【物】【化】同
量异位素

isolate I ['aisəleit] *vt.* ① 隔离; 孤立; 使脱离: an
~*d* patient 被隔离的病人 ②【微】使(细菌)分离;
使与种群隔离 ③【化】使离析 ④【电】使绝缘 **II**
['aisəʊleit] *n.* 【微】分离菌,隔离种群

isolation [,aisə'leiʃən] *n.* ①隔离; 孤立; 脱离; 分
离: an ~ hospital (ward) 隔离病院(病房) ②【物】
隔绝; 绝缘: ~ of noise 噪声隔绝 / an ~ booth
隔音室 ③【化】离析(作用)

isosceles [ai'sosili:z] *a.* 【数】等腰的, 等边的: ~
triangle 等腰三角形

issue ['isju:, 'iʃju:] **I** *n.* ①(血、水等)流出,放出;
流出物 ②出口 ③结果,结局: bring a matter to
a successful ~ 使某事有圆满的结果 ④发行;
行物;一次发行量;(报刊)期号: monetary ~ 货
币发行 / items of ~ (军队的)补给品 / an ~ of
100,000 copies 十万册的发行量 ⑤问题;争端,
争论点: the burning ~ of the day 燃眉之急
的问题 / major ~*s* of principle 大是大非 / a
minor ~ 枝节问题 / raise a new ~ 提出新的争
论点 ⑥【律】子女,后嗣: die without ~ 死后无
子女 ⑦(土地、地产等的)收益 **II** ❶ *vt.* ①使流
出,放出 ②发行;发布: ~ a statement 发表声明
③发给,配给: ~ winter clothing *to* troops 给部
队发冬装 ❷ *vi.* ①出(来),流出 (*from*): They
~*d out* into the street. 他们涌到街上。/ Blood
~*d from* the cut. 血从伤口流出。②由…得出,
由…产生 (*from*); 导致, 造成 (*in*): a mistake
issuing from carelessness 由于不过细而引起的错
误 / That oversight ~*d in* heavy losses. 那一
疏忽造成重大的损失。③(报刊等)发行; 发布 ④
(根据法律或事实)提出抗辩, 进行辩护 ⑤传代,
传下 (*from*) ||*at* ~ 在争论中;不和的; 待裁决
的: the point *at* ~ 争论点 / be *at* ~ with sb. 与
某人争辩 / *in* ~ 在争论中 / *in the* ~ 结果,到
头来 / join ~【律】共同提出争论点供裁决;(按
照双方提出的争论点或一方接受另一方提出的争
论点) 进行辩论 / *join* (或 *take*) ~ *with sb. on
sth.* 就某事与某人争论

isthmus ['isməs] *n.* ①地峡，地颈，土腰 ②【解】峡 ‖**the Isthmus** ①巴拿马地峡 ②苏伊士地峡

it [it] *pron.* ①[指心目中或上下文中的人或事物] 这,那,它:That's ~! 就是这么回事!(或:就要这个! 对啊!)/ He is fifty-two, but doesn't look ~. 他看上去不象一个五十二岁的人。/ Whatever you do and say, ask yourself whether ~ is in the interests of the people. 想想自己的一言一行是否符合人民的利益。

②[指无生命的东西,在性别不详或性别无关紧要时,亦可指动物、幼孩等]它: I threw the ball to him and he caught ~. 我将球抛给他,他接住了。

③[作无人称动词的主语,表示时间、气候、距离等]: It is ten o'clock. 十点钟了。/ It's a fortnight to May Day. 离五一节还有两星期。/ It is raining. 下雨了。/ It's only five minutes' walk now. 现在只剩下五分钟路程了。/ He would have gone, if ~ had not been for my advice. 要不是我劝他,他肯定已经去了。

④[作先行代词,引导后面的短语或从句]这,这一点: It is a great joy *to battle against nature*. 与大自然奋斗,其乐无穷。/ It's no use *trying to keep him in bed*. 他是不肯卧床休息的,你怎么劝也没用。/ It is a nuisance, *this delay*. 这样拖拉,真是讨厌。

⑤[作先行代词,用于表示强调的句型中]: It is that neighbourhood factory *that* we have been wanting to visit. 我们一直想访问的正是那家街道工厂。[注意:本句中斜写的 that 一般不用 which 代。]/ It was here *that* I first met him. 我初次与他见面就在这儿。[注意:本句中的 that 不能用 where 代。]

⑥[接在某些由名词变来的动词之后,无实义,构成习惯性动词短语]: We'll foot (taxi) ~. 我们将步行(坐出租汽车)去。/ lord ~ over others 对别人称王称霸

⑦[用于某些动词或前置词的后面,词义含糊,构成习语]: fight ~ out 决一雌雄; 争辩个明白 / Keep at ~! 别松劲! 干下去! / You'll catch ~! 你可小心点儿! (警告用语) / go ~ alone 单干 / You are in for ~. 这一下你可得干到底了。(或:这下你肯定要倒霉了。)

⑧[口]绝妙的人; 最好的东西: Stop acting as though you were ~. 不要夜郎自大。

⑨[口]性感

⑩[美俚]傻瓜,笨蛋

‖**as ~ is** (或 **was**) 事实上,既然如此: As ~ is, we can hardly get to the station by 6 o'clock. 事实上,我们六点钟前是很难赶到车站的。/ **as ~ were** 似乎,可以说是 / **not in ~** [俚]不足以成其为对手的; 差的,不足道的 / **with ~** [美俚]机灵的; 知内情的; 市面灵通的; 时髦的

italic [i'tælik] **I** *a.* ①【印】斜体的: ~ type 斜体活字 ②[I-]古意大利(人)的; 印欧语系意大利语族的 **II** *n.* ①[常用复]斜体字: in ~(s) 用斜体

②[I-] 印欧语系意大利语族

italicize, italicise [i'tælisaiz] *vt.* 用斜体字印刷; 在(词语)下划单横线(表示印刷时该用斜体字)

itch [itʃ] **I** *n.* ①[前接定冠词或不定冠词]痒; [the ~]【医】疥疮: have (或 suffer from) the ~ 发痒; 长疥疮 ②[前常接不定冠词或物主代词]渴望: have an ~ *for* writing 很想写 / sb.'s ~ *to* climb up the mountain 某人想爬上山去的渴望 **II** *vi.* ①发痒: Are your mosquito bites still ~*ing*? 你给蚊子咬的地方还痒吗? / I ~ all over. 我浑身发痒。②渴望: ~ *for* sth. 渴望得到某物 / ~ *to* have a try 跃跃欲试 ‖**mite** 【动】疥癣虫,痒螨

item ['aitem, 'aitəm] **I** *n.* ①条,项,款数,项目: ~ by ~ 逐条 / an important ~ on the agenda 一项重要议程 / an export ~ 出口项目 / an ~ of business 营业项目 / an ~ of equipment 【军】装备品 ②(新闻等的)一条,一则: local ~*s* 当地新闻 [前用于介绍目录或细目中逐个项目之前]又,同上 ‖**~ize** *vt.* 逐条列记,详细列明: an ~ized account 细帐

itinerant [i'tinərənt] **I** *a.* 巡回的,巡游的: an ~ peddler 行商 / an ~ theatrical troupe 巡回剧团 / an ~ preacher 巡回传教士 **II** *n.* 巡回者(如行商、巡回传教士)

itinerary [ai'tinərəri] **I** *n.* ①旅程; 路线 ②预定的行程,旅行计划 ③旅行记录,行程记 ④旅行指南 **II** *a.* 旅行的; 旅程的; 路线的; 道路的: an ~ pillar (或 column) 路标 / an ~ map 路线图

its [its] *pron.* [it 的所有格]它的: the plan and ~ realization 计划及其实施

it's [its] ①=it is ②=it has

itself [it'self] *pron.* ①[反身代词]它自己,它本身: 正常,健康: His attitude speaks for ~. 他的态度本身就足以说明问题。/ The baby was soon ~ again. 婴孩很快就痊愈了。②[用以加强语气]自身,本身: Doing is ~ learning. 干本身就是学习。‖*by* ~ ①单独地,孤寂地: Put it *by* ~. 把这件东西单独放开。②独力地 / *in* ~ 本身,实质上 / *of* ~ 自行

I've [aiv] =I have

ivory ['aivəri] **I** *n.* ①象牙; (海象等的)长牙: artificial ~ 人造象牙 ②牙质: dental ~ 牙质

ivory

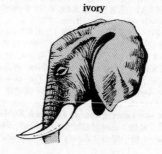

③象牙色，乳白色 ④[复]象牙制品，仿象牙制品 ⑤厚光纸 ⑥[复][俚]钢琴的键；牙齿；骰子；台球，弹子 **II** *a.* ①象牙制成的；似象牙的 ②象牙色的，乳白色的 ‖*show one's ivories* [口] 露出牙齿，咧着嘴笑 / *solid* ~ [美俚]头脑迟钝的人‖~ **black**【化】象牙墨 / '~-**dome** *n.* [美俚]笨蛋 / ~ **nut**, ~ **palm**【植】橡扣树，象牙椰子 / ~ **tower** [喻]象牙塔 / ~ **white**, ~ **yellow** 乳

白色 / '~-'**white** *a.* 乳白色的
ivy ['aivi] **I** *n.*【植】常春藤；~ **buttercup** 常春藤毛茛 **II** *a.* ①学院的；学究式的 ②纯理论的，抽象的；无实用意义的 ‖**Ivy League** (美国东北部哈佛、哥伦比亚等大学的)常青藤联合会；[作定语用]名牌大学的；名牌大学学生派头的(常指富有、保守等) / '~-**leaved** *a.* 常春藤(叶)的；~-*leaved* crowfoot 常春藤毛茛

J

jab [dʒæb] **I** (jabbed; jabbing) ❶ *vt.* ①刺，戳：He got *jabbed* in the lower part of his chest. 他的下胸部被戳。/ ~ a vein [美俚]进行麻醉品注射 ②用(拨火棒等)捅：~ the poker among the grey ashes 用拨火棒捅灰烬 ③用拳猛击 ❷ *vi.* 刺，戳；猛击 (*at*) **II** *n.* 猛刺，猛戳；猛击：receive a ~ in the arm [口]在臂上打一针(或接种) ‖'~-**off** *n.* [美俚]麻醉药的皮下注射；麻醉药注射发生的作用
jabber ['dʒæbə] **I** *vi.* & *vt.* ①急促而不清楚地说 ②闲聊 ③(猴等)吱吱喳喳地叫 **II** *n.* 急促不清的话，莫名其妙的话
jack[1] [dʒæk] **I** *n.* ①[J-]杰克(男子名；也可用作 John 约翰的俗称或昵称) ②[J-]普通人；男人；男孩；家伙；仆人 ③[常作 J-]水手，水兵，海员 ④伐木工人；打杂工；工人 ⑤(烤肉等用的)铁叉旋转器；脱靴器 ⑥【机】起重器，千斤顶；支撑物(如舞台布景后的支柱) ⑦公驴；幼雄鲑鱼；寒鸦；长耳大野兔 ⑧[美俚]钱: make one's ~ 赚大钱 ⑨[J-](纸牌中的)杰克；(赢得的)大量赌注 ⑩(滚球戏中作靶子的)小白球；(抛石游戏中所用的)小石块(或小金属片) ⑪[美](夜间打猎或捕鱼用的)篝灯 ⑫【海】(标志国籍的)船首旗；公司旗 ⑬【电】插座；插口，塞孔；弹簧开关: bridging ~[电]并联塞孔，桥接塞孔 ⑭苹果酒；白兰地酒 ⑮(跳水中前弯身的)一种跳水法 **II** ❶ *vi.* 用篝灯打猎(或捕鱼) ❷ *vt.* ①用起重器举(或顶): ~ (up) a car 把汽车顶起 ②(用篝灯)猎(兽)；(用篝灯)捕(鱼) ③增加；提高(水平、质量、物价、工资等) (up): ~ up expenditure 增加开支 ④责备 (up); 规劝…尽职 (up); 放弃(企图等) (up) ⑤[美俚]拔(枪等) (out) **III** *a.* (动物)雄的 ‖*Jack at a pinch* [口]紧急时有用的人(或物)，临时召来代替的人 / *a Jack in office* 自命不凡的小官吏 / *a Jack in the water* [俚]码头打杂工 / *a Jack of* (或 *on*) *both sides* 骑墙派 / *Jack of straw* ①稻草人 ②无资产者，寄生者 / *before you can* (或 *could*) *say Jack Robinson* 转瞬间，突然，说时迟那时快 / *climb like a steeple* ~ 善于爬山 / *Every Jack has his Jill*

(或 *Gill*). [谚]人各有偶。/ *every man Jack* 人人，每个人 / *Jack and Jill* (或 *Gill*) 少年和姑娘 / *Jack of all trades and master of none* 杂而不精的人，三脚猫 / *Jack Sprat* 矮子，侏儒 / *the Union Jack* 英国国旗 ‖**Jack-a-'dandy** ([复] Jack-a-dandies) *n.* 花花公子 / '**Jack-a-Lent** ([复] Jack-a-Lents) *n.* ①(四旬斋期间游戏中被击的)小玩偶 ②[喻]小人物 / ~**anapes** ['dʒækəneips] *n.* ①猴子 ②自负的人，傲慢的人 ③大胆的顽童 / '~**ass** *n.* ①公驴 ②笨蛋，傻瓜 / ~**assery** ['dʒæk,æsəri] *n.* 愚蠢的行为 / '~**boot** *n.* (过膝的)长统靴 / '~**daw** *n.*【动】寒鸦；严寒 / '~-**fruit**【植】①木波罗(或其果实) ②榴莲 / '~,**hammer** *n.* ①手持式凿岩机 ②气锤 / '**Jack-in-,office** ([复] Jacks-in-office) 自命不凡的小官吏 / '~-**in-the-box** ([复] ~-in-the-boxes 或 ~s-in-the-box) *n.* ①玩偶匣(揭起盖子即有玩偶跳起) ②一种焰火 / '**Jack-in-the-Green** ([复] Jack-in-the-Greens 或 Jacks-in-the-Green) *n.* 花屋中的人(西俗五月一日用冬青花扎成小屋，人居其中上街游行) / **Jack Ketch** [英]绞刑吏 / '~**knife** *n.* ①(可放袋中的)大折刀 ②(跳入水中前弯身的)一种跳水法 *vt.* 用大折刀切(或戳) *vi.* (跳水时)弯身 / '~-**leg** *a.* ①技术不高明的(人)；外行的(人) ②不诚实的(人)，不择手段的(人) ③权宜之计的(行动) / '~**light** *n.* (夜间打猎或捕鱼用的)篝灯 / '**Jack-of-'all-trades** ([复] Jacks-of-all-trades) *n.* ①能做各种事情的人，万能博士 ②杂而不精的人 / '~-o'-,**lantern** *n.* ①磷火 ②行踪不定的人 ③使人迷惑的事物 ④(以南瓜刻成人面形的)灯笼 / ~ **plane**【机】粗刨 / ~ **post** 轴柱 / '~**pot** *n.* ①(赌者须有一对杰克或更好的牌才能赢的)积累的赌注 ②(彩票等的)头奖；(屡次得奖而积累的)大笔钱；(在冒险的事情中获得的)最大成功；意外的成功(或好运): hit the ~*pot* 赢得大笔钱；获得最大成功，运气非常好 ③[美]困境: be in (get into) a ~*pot* 处于(陷入)困境 / '~-'**pudding** *n.* 丑角

'~,rabbit n. (北美西部产)长耳大野兔 / ~ rafter【建】小椽 / '~screw n.【机】螺旋起重器 / '~shaft n. 副轴;变速机传动轴 / '~snipe n.【动】小鹬 / ~ staff 舰首旗杆 / '~stay n. ①【船】天幕边索;支索;舰首旗杆;(汽艇用)分隔索 ②【机】撑杆 / '~straw n. ①稻草人 ②(抽杆游戏用的)麦杆(或细木条) ③[~straws][用作单]抽杆游戏 / '~-'tar n. [常作 J-]水手

jackknife

jack² ['dʒæk] n. ①(中世纪的)无袖皮军衣 ②(外涂柏油的)革制酒杯

jack³ ['dʒæk] n. 一种似面包果的树(或其果实、木材)

jackal ['dʒækɔ:l] n. ①【动】豺,黑背豺 ②走狗,爪牙,狗腿子: ~s of the same lair 一丘之貉 / play the ~ to the tiger 为虎作伥

jacket ['dʒækit] I n. ①短上衣,茄克衫 ②(动物的)皮毛;马铃薯皮: potatoes boiled in their ~s 连皮煮的马铃薯 ③(书籍的)护封;公文套;唱片套;弹壳 ④(软木)救生衣 ⑤【机】套: cooling water ~ 冷水套 / cylinder ~ 气缸套 II vt. ①给…穿短上衣 ②给…包上护封(或装套) ||dust (或 lace, smoke, trim, thrash) sb.'s ~ 殴打某人 / Pull down your ~! 请镇定! 不要激动! / send in one's ~ 辞职 / warm sb.'s ~ 打某人;辱骂某人

jade¹ [dʒeid] I n. ①【矿】玉 ②绿玉色 II a. ①玉制的 ②绿玉色的 ||~ green 绿玉色

jade² [dʒeid] I n. ①老马,驽马 ②(贬)荡妇,轻佻的女子 ③[谑][贬]女人 II vt. & vi. (使)疲倦 ||~d a. 精疲力竭的;过饱的;发腻的

jag¹ [dʒæg] I n. ①织品上的 V 字形凹口(或尖的裂缝) ②锯齿状的突出部 II (jagged; jagging) ❶ vt. ①在…上刻 V 形凹口 ②把…撕成锯齿状,把…切成参差不齐 ③在(衣服)上开叉(或穿饰孔) ❷ vi. ①刺;戳 ②颠簸地移动

jag² [dʒæg] n. ①[口]小驮子 ②[美俚]醉态: on a ~ 酩酊大醉 ③[俚]闹饮,酒席,宴会 ④一阵

jail [dʒeil] [美] I n. & vt. =gaol ||~er, ~or =gaoler ||~bird n. 囚犯,惯犯 / ~break n. 越狱 / ~ delivery 监狱的大出空 (指把囚犯送去法庭受审或指在暴力威逼前释放囚犯) / '~-house n. 监狱

jam¹ [dʒæm] I (jammed; jamming) ❶ vt. ①把…挤进,把…楔进;挤进,塞进: He jammed his clothes into a small suitcase. 他把衣服塞进一只小箱子里。②轧伤,压碎 ③使塞满,使挤满: The bus was jammed full. 公共汽车挤得满满的。④使刹住不动: He jammed the brakes on. 他刹住了车。⑤使(通道等)堵塞 ⑥[无]干扰 ❷ vi. ①堵塞;楔紧;轧住: The overheated machine jammed. 过热的机器轧住了。②拥挤,挤进 ③[美俚]参加爵士音乐即席演奏会 ④[无]干扰 II n. ①拥挤;塞满;阻塞;(机器等的)轧住: a traffic ~ 交通拥挤 ②拥挤的人群;阻塞物 ③[俚]困境: be in (get into) a ~ 处于(陷人)困境 ④[美俚]不费吹灰之力的容易事情 ||~ nut【机】防松螺母 / '~-'packed a. 塞得紧紧的,挤得水泄不通的 / ~ session [美俚]爵士乐即席演奏会

jam² [dʒæm] n. 果酱 ||real ~ [俚]使人愉快的事物;乐事

jamb [dʒæm] n. ①【建】门窗侧壁;侧柱;[复]壁炉侧墙 ②【矿】矿脉中的土石层;矿柱

jamboree [,dʒæmbə'ri:] n. ①大喝大闹;欢乐的聚会 ②大集会;比赛;童子军大会 ③包括多样娱乐的长节目

jangle ['dʒæŋgl] I ❶ vi. ①(铃等)发出不和谐的刺耳声 ②吵架 ❷ vt. ①使发出刺耳声 ②刺耳地发出 ③刺激得…紧张烦乱 II n. ①吵嚷;口角 ②刺耳的刺耳声 ③空谈

janitor ['dʒænitə] n. ①看门人,管门人 ②照管房屋的工友 ||~ial [,dʒæni'tɔ:riəl] a.

January ['dʒænjuəri] n. 一月(略作 Ja., Jan.)

jar¹ [dʒɑ:] I (jarred; jarring ['dʒɑ:riŋ]) ❶ vi. ①发出刺耳声;轧轧地作响 ②使人产生不愉快的感觉,刺激 (upon, on): ~ on sb. 给某人不快之感 ③剧烈震动 ④不一致;不和谐,冲突;吵嘴 (with): His opinions ~ with mine. 他的意见和我的(意见)不一致。❷ vt. ①震动;摇动 ②给…不快之感,刺激(神经): be jarred by the sad news 因噩耗而受刺激 ③使发出刺耳声 II n. ①刺耳声;轧轧声 ②突然的震动 ③刺激;震惊 ④不调和,不一致;口角,争执 ⑤(节奏等的)突然中止;失调

jar² [dʒɑ:] n. ①罐子;坛子;广口瓶 ②一罐所装的量(或物): a ~ of strawberry jam 一罐草莓酱 ③【电】瓶: battery ~ 蓄电池容器,电池槽 ④【电】加耳(= 1/900 微法)

jar³ [dʒɑ:] n. [古]旋转 ||on the ~ (门)微开,半开

jargon ['dʒɑ:gən] I n. [总称] ①多专门术语的话;行话;隐语 ②难懂的话,莫名其妙的话 ③奇特粗俗的语言(或方言),土语 ④混合语 ⑤(鸟等的)喳喳叫声 II vi. ①喊喊喳喳地叫 ②讲难懂的话,写难懂的文章 ||~ize vi. 讲难懂的话,写难懂的文章 vt. ①用难懂的话(或隐语、行话)表达 ②使成为难懂的话

jasmin(e) ['dʒæsmin] n. ①【植】素馨,茉莉;类似素馨的植物(如栀子等) ②淡黄色

jaundice ['dʒɔːndis] I n. ①【医】黄疸 ②妒忌;厌恶;偏见 II vt. ①使患黄疸病 ②使有偏见;使妒忌 ‖~d a. ①害黄疸病的 ②有偏见的;有猜忌心的

jaunt [dʒɔːnt] I vi. 作短途游览 II n. 短途游览

jaunty ['dʒɔːnti] I a. ①[古]斯文的;时髦的 ②活泼的;洋洋得意的;逍遥自在的 II n. [英俚]舰船纠察队长;运输船纠察长 ‖**jauntily** ad. / **jauntiness** n.

javelin ['dʒævəlin] n. 标枪: ~ throw 掷标枪 / a ~ formation【军】(轰炸机的)标枪队形

javelin

jaw [dʒɔː] I n. ①颌,颚: the lower (upper) ~ 下(上)颌 ②[复]上下颚,口部 ③【机】爪;虎钳牙;夹片,夹头 ④[复](山谷、水道等的)狭窄的入口 ⑤[复]危险的境遇: the ~s of death 鬼门关,死地 / get out of the ~s of danger 脱离危险 ⑥[口]饶舌,喋喋不休;讲道,训人: Hold your ~! 别唠叨了!住嘴! ⑦[美俚]闲聊 II ❶ vt. [俚]训斥;对…唠叨 ❷ vi. [俚]唠叨;谩骂 ‖be all ~ 全是空谈而已 / lantern ~s 尖瘦脸 / wag one's ~ 喋喋不休 ‖~bone n. ①颚骨,牙床骨 ②[美俚](财务上的)信用;赊买,借贷;借到的款子 vi. ①[美俚]进行诚挚和讲道理的谈话来达到可以赊买(或借贷)的目的 ②[美俚]赊买给人;借贷给人 vt. ①[美俚]赊买;借到 ②[美俚]利用职权对…施加压力,利用职权企图使…就范 ad. [美俚]凭信用地: buy ~bone 赊买;分期付款购买 / '~,breaker n. ①[口]难发音的字 ②[美俚]一种圆形的硬糖 ③【矿】颚形碎石机

jay [dʒei] n. ①【动】樫鸟 ②[俚]爱唠叨的无礼者 ③[美俚]花花公子;乡下佬,呆汉,易受骗的人 ④中蓝色 ‖scalp sb. for a ~ 欺骗愚弄某人 ‖~,hawker n. ①[美俚](南北战争期间密苏里、堪萨斯州的)废除农奴派游击队员 ②强盗 ③[J-][口]堪萨斯州人

jazz [dʒæz] I n. ①爵士音乐;爵士舞(曲) ②[美俚]带有爵士音乐的特征;活泼,活泼放纵 ③[总称]浮华而陈腐的话(或观点等) II a. 爵士音乐的;不和谐的;颜色过鲜的,花哨的 III ❶ vt. ①把…奏成爵士音乐 ②使有刺激性,使活泼(up) ③加快…的速度 ❷ vi. ①游荡(around) ②奏爵士乐;跳爵士舞 ‖~ist n. 爵士音乐爱好者 / ~y

a. ①有爵士音乐特征的 ②[美俚]活泼放纵的 ‖~man n. 爵士音乐演奏者

jealous ['dʒeləs] a. ①妒忌的;善嫉妒的: be ~ of nobody (nobody's achievement) 不妒忌任何人(任何人的成就) ②猜疑的,留意提防的 ③注意的,戒备的,唯恐失掉的: be ~ of one's rights 小心翼翼注意保护自己的权利 ④(基督教《圣经》中指上帝)要求绝对忠实和崇敬的 ‖~ly ad. / ~ness n.

jealousy ['dʒeləsi] n. ①妒忌;猜忌;嫉妒 ②留意的提防,谨慎戒备

jean [dʒein] n. ①【纺】三页细斜纹布 ②[复](三页细斜纹布做的)工装裤;裤子

jeep [dʒiːp] I n. ①吉普车,小型越野汽车 ②【军】小型航空母舰(指护航航空母舰) II ❶ vi. 乘吉普车旅行 ❷ vt. 用吉普车运送

jeer[1] [dʒiə] vi., vt. & n. 嘲笑;嘲弄

jeer[2] [dʒiə] n. [常用复]【船】(升降下层帆桁的)桁索

jelly ['dʒeli] I n. ①果子冻;肉冻 ②胶状物;糊状物,浆 ③畏惧,犹豫不决 ④[美俚]轻而易举的事;免费得来的东西 II ❶ vt. ①使结冻,使成胶状 ②在…上加胶冻物 ❷ vi. ①结冻;凝结;成胶状 ②[美俚]闲逛着聊天 ‖~graph n. [英]胶版 ‖~ bean ①一种豆形胶质软糖 ②[喻]优柔寡断的人 / '~fish n. ①【动】水母,海蜇 ②[美俚]无骨气的人;优柔寡断的人 / ~ roll ①一种涂果子冻的薄卷饼 ②[美俚]一味追求女人的男子;情人

jeopardize, jeopardise ['dʒepədaiz] vt. 使受险;危害

jeopardy ['dʒepədi] n. ①危险,危难: be in ~ (of one's life) 处于(生命)危险中 ②【律】刑事案件中被告的(危险)处境

jerk[1] [dʒəːk] I ❶ vt. ①猛地一拉(或一推、一翻、一抛等) ②突然,急促、断续地说出 ③配制(苏打) ❷ vi. ①急拉;猛推;扔;猛地一动 ②颠簸地行进 ③痉挛 II n. ①急拉;急推;急扭;扔;急动 ②颠簸,震摇 ③【医】反射;[复](因激动引起的)肌肉的痉挛;急冲病 ④【体】挺举 ⑤[美俚]愚笨(或古怪)的人 ‖in a ~ 立刻,马上 / ~ chin music 谈话 / put a ~ in (或 into) it [俚]使劲干,卖力干

jerk[2] [dʒəːk] I vt. 把(牛肉等)切成长片晒干 II n. 牛肉干;肉干

jerkin ['dʒəːkin] n. ①(旧时)一种短的紧身皮上衣 ②女用背心

jerry ['dʒeri] I a. 草率的,偷工减料的;权宜之计的 II n. [英俚]夜壶 ‖~-build vt. 偷工减料地建造 / '~-,builder n. 偷工减料的营造商 / '~,building n. 偷工减料的建筑工程 / '~-built a. ①偷工减料盖成的 ②草率匆促拼凑的

jersey ['dʒəːzi] n. ①【纺】平针织物 ②卫生衫,运动衫 ③针织紧身上衣 ④[J-]泽西种乳牛

jest [dʒest] I n. ①玩笑;滑稽事 ②笑话;俏皮话 ③戏谑,诙谐;快活 ④笑柄;笑料: a standing ~

经常被嘲弄的对象 **II ❶** *vi.* ①说笑话; 嘲弄 (*at*) ②开玩笑; 打趣; 戏谑; 做滑稽动作 **❷** *vt.* 对…开玩笑, 嘲笑 ‖*break a* ~ 说笑话 / *in* ~ 开玩笑地, 诙谐地 / ~*ing apart* [口] [作插入语用] 言归正传, 说正经话 ‖**~er** *n.* 爱开玩笑的人; 小丑; (中世纪的) 弄臣

jesting ['dʒestiŋ] *a.* 爱开玩笑的; 说着玩的, 打趣的; *a* ~ *fellow* 爱开玩笑的人 ‖**~ly** *ad.*

jet¹ [dʒet] **I** (jetted; jetting) **❶** *vt.* ①喷射出 (烟、水流等) ②用喷气式飞机运送 **❷** *vi.* ①喷出, 射出 ②乘喷气式飞机旅行 **II** *n.* ①【物】喷射; 射流; 喷注; 气流 ②喷嘴, 喷口; 喷射器 ③【空】喷气发动机; 喷气式飞机: travel by ~ 乘喷气式飞机旅行 ④[喻]喷射似涌出的东西: Talk poured from him in a ~. 他滔滔不绝地谈着。**III** *a.* 喷气式 (发动机) 推进的 ‖~ **airplane** 喷气式飞机 / ~ **blower** 【机】喷气鼓风机 / ~ **engine** 喷气式发动机 / ~ **lag** 高速飞行时引起的生理节奏的破坏 / '~,**liner** *n.* 喷气式客机(尤指班机) / ~ **plane** 喷气式飞机 / '~**port** *n.* 喷气式飞机机场 / '~-**pro'pelled** *a.* 喷气式(发动机)推进的; 疾驶的, 强有力的 ~ **propeller** 喷气式推进器, 喷气式螺旋桨 / ~ **propulsion** 【空】喷气推进 / ~ **pump** 【机】喷射泵 / ~ **set** (乘喷气式客机的) 富翁环球游览团, 有条件乘喷气式飞机作环球游览的富人阶层 / ~ **stream** ①【气】急流 ②【空】喷射气流, 喷流

jet² [dʒet] **I** *n.* ①【矿】煤玉; 黑色大理石 ②乌黑发亮的颜色 **II** *a.* ①黑色大理石制的 ②乌黑发亮的 ‖**~-'black** *a.* 乌黑发亮的

jetsam ['dʒetsəm] *n.* ①(船舶遇险时) 投弃的货物 (或船的装备等); (投弃后) 沉入水底的 (或冲到岸上的) 货物 (或船的装备等) ②被抛弃的东西 ‖*flotsam and* ~ 见 **flotsam**

jettison ['dʒetisn] **I** *n.* 【海】【空】(在紧急情况下) 投弃货物(的行为) ②抛弃, 放弃 **II** *vt.* ①抛弃(船上货物) ②抛弃, 丢弃(累赘或无用之物) ③(飞机) 在飞行时投弃(辅助装备、弹药、燃料等)

jetty¹ ['dʒeti] **I** *n.* ①防波堤; 栈桥 ②(突)码头 ③建筑物的突出部 **II** *vi.* 伸出, 突出

jetty² ['dʒeti] *a.* 乌黑发亮的

jewel ['dʒuːəl] **I** *n.* ①宝石 ②宝石饰物; 贵重饰物 ③[喻]受珍视的人(或物) ④(手表内的)(似)宝石轴承 **II** (jewel(l)ed; jewel(l)ing) *vt.* ①用宝石装饰 ②把宝石轴承装进(手表) ‖**jewel(l)er** *n.* 宝石商, 珠宝商; 宝石匠

jewellery, jewelry ['dʒuːəlri] *n.* [总称]珠宝; 珠宝饰物

jib¹ [dʒib] *n.* 【机】臂, 挺杆; 人字起重机的桁: elevator ~ 升降机臂

jib² [dʒib] **I** *n.* 船首三角帆 **II** (jibbed; jibbing) **❶** *vt.* 使(帆、桁等) 从一边转至另一边 **❷** *vi.* (船帆等) 从一边转至另一边 ‖*the cut of sb.'s* ~ 某人的相貌(或仪表)

jib³ [dʒib] (jibbed; jibbing) *vi.* ①(马等)停止不肯前进; 横跑; 后退 ②[喻]踌躇不前 ‖~ *at* [喻]对

…不愿意, 厌恶: He never *jibbed at* hard work. 他总是乐于做艰苦的工作。

jibe¹ [dʒaib] *vi.*, *vt.* & *n.* 嘲笑, 嘲弄

jibe² [dʒaib] *vi.* [美口]一致, 符合(*with*): Our views ~. 我们的看法一致。

jig [dʒig] **I** *n.* ①快步舞; 快步舞曲 ②特种钓鱼钩 ③【矿】跳汰机; 跳汰选(矿法) ④【机】夹具; 钻模; 样板; 装配架: assembly ~ 装配架 / plate ~ 板式钻模 **II** (jigged; jigging) *vt.* & *vi.* ①用快步跳(舞) ②(使)作上下(或前后)的急动 ③用特种钓鱼钩钓(鱼) ④【矿】筛(矿); 用夹具加工 ‖*in* ~ *time* [口]极快地 / *The* ~ *is up.* [美俚]一切都完了。

jilt [dʒilt] **I** *n.* 任意抛弃情人的女子 **II** *vt.* (女子)任意抛弃(情人) ‖**~ee** [dʒil'tiː] *n.* [美]被抛弃者

jingle ['dʒiŋgl] **I** *vi.* & *vt.* ①(使)丁当响 ②(使)(诗或音乐)合于简单的引人注意的韵律 **II** *n.* ①(硬币、小铃、钥匙等的)丁当声; [美俚]电话(指打电话的动作); 发丁当声的东西 ②诗的简单韵律; 具有简单韵律的诗句 ③(爱尔兰或澳洲的)有顶两轮马车 ‖**jingly** *a.* 丁当响的; 合简单韵律的 ‖~ **bell** ①门铃铛; 装在雪橇上的铃铛 ②【海】(通知船速的)信号铃 / '~,**jangle** *n.* ①丁丁当当声 ②[美俚]钱 *vi.* 发出丁丁当当声

jingo¹ ['dʒiŋgou] *n.* 侵略主义者; 沙文主义者; 武力外交政策论者 ‖**~ism** *n.* 侵略主义; 沙文主义 / **~ist** *n.* 侵略主义者; 沙文主义者

jingo² ['dʒiŋgou] *int.* ‖*By* ~! 啊呀! [表示惊异、快乐或加强语气]

jink [dʒiŋk] **I** *vi.* 闪开, 急转 **II** *n.* ①[苏格兰]闪避 ②[复]喧闹的嬉戏: high ~*s* 大吵大闹的嬉戏

job¹ [dʒɔb] **I** *n.* ①工作: make a good (thorough) ~ of it 把这件事做好(做彻底) ②零活: odd ~*s* 零活, 杂务 ③职责, 任务; 作用: The white blood cells have the ~ of fighting infection. 白血球有抵抗感染的作用。 ④[口]职位, 职业: John is *out of a* ~. 约翰失业了。 / He has a ~ *as a* cook. 他担任炊事员的职务。 ⑤[口]费力的事情: It is (quite) a ~ to talk through the noise. 声音这么闹, 谈话可真费劲。 ⑥假公济私的事情 ⑦[俚]犯罪行为(尤指偷窃) ⑧成果, 成品: Your bike is a lovely ~. 你这辆自行车真不错。 / This novel is a superb ~. 这部小说是一部出色的作品。 **II** (jobbed; jobbing) **❶** *vi.* ①做零工, 做临时工, 打杂 ②做股票经纪 ③假公济私, 营私舞弊 **❷** *vt.* ①代客买卖(股票、货物等) ②(商品等)承包; 分包(工程) ③以假公济私的手段办理(或实现、作成)…: ~ sb. *into* a post 用假公济私的手段使某人就职 ④临时租进和出租(车、马等) ⑤[美俚]欺骗, 欺诈 ‖*a bad* ~ 白费力的事, 倒霉事: give sth. up as *a bad* ~ 认为某事无成功希望而放弃 / *a good* ~ 幸运事 / *a* ~ *lot* (廉价)整批买(或卖)的杂货 ②杂乱的一伙(或一堆) / *a put-up* ~ [俚]预谋的事; 骗局,

圈套 / a straight ～ [美俚](无拖车的)载重汽车 / by the ～ 包做,论件: a man paid by the ～ 计件工 / do a ～ on sb.(或 do sb.'s ～) 毁了某人 / lie down on the ～ [口]不卖力,磨洋工 / make the best of a bad ～ 见 best / nose a ～ in everything 处处看到有利可图 / on the ～ [俚](专心)工作着,忙碌着 ‖～less a. 失业的,无职业的; 失业职工的 ‖～ action (警察等的)临时性罢工示威 / Job Corps 职业团(美国政府办的青年就业训练项目) / '～,holder n. ①有职业者 ②[美]公务员 / '～,hopping n. (为图直接经济利益等的)换职业 / ～ hunter [美]求职者, 找工作的人 / ～ printer 承印零星印件的印刷商 / '～,splitting n. 一工分做制(现代资本主义企业采用的一种把全日工改为两半日工的做法) / ～ work ①包工,散工 ②杂项的印刷工作

job² [dʒɔb] **n.**, (jobbed; jobbing) **vt. & vi.** [方] =jab

jockey ['dʒɔki] **I** **n.** ①赛马的职业骑师 ②驾驶员; (机器等)的操作者 ③[英]小伙子; 下属, 帮手 ④[古]马商 **II** **❶** **vt.** ①驾驶; 操作 ②欺骗,诈骗,诱使: ～ sb. into a trap 诱骗某人落入圈套 ③移动 **❷** **vi.** ①当赛马骑师 ②运用手段图谋利益 ‖～ for position 见 position ‖**Jockey Club** ①(英国的)赛马总会 ②[j- c-]赛马俱乐部 / ～ pulley 【机】导轮

jocose [dʒə'kous] **a.** 开玩笑的; 滑稽的; 幽默的 ‖～ly ad. / ～ness n.

jocular ['dʒɔkjulə] **a.** ①诙谐的,滑稽的;喜开玩笑的 ②打趣的,寻乐的

jocund ['dʒɔkənd] **a.** 欢乐的; 快活的 ‖～ly ad.

jog¹ [dʒɔg] **I** (jogged; jogging) **❶** **vt.** ①轻推;轻撞;轻轻摇动: ～ sb. with one's elbow 用肘轻撞某人 ②唤起(记忆); 提醒: ～ sb.'s memory 唤起某人的记忆 ③使(马等)缓步行进 **❷** **vi.** ①颠簸地移动: The old bus jogged up and down. 那辆旧公共汽车上下颠簸着行驶。②慢吞吞地走, 缓步前进 (on, along) ③[喻]缓慢平稳地进行 (on, along): Matters ～ along. 事情在慢慢地进行。④熬过时间 **II** **n.** ①轻推;轻摇;轻撞 ②慢步,缓行 ‖～ trot ①慢步,缓行 ②单调的进程; 常规

jog² [dʒɔg] [美] **I** **n.** ①(面或线上的)凹进;凸出 ②突然的转向 **II** (jogged; jogging) **vi.** ①凹进;凸出 ②突然转向

join [dʒɔin] **I** **❶** **vt.** ①连接; 接合; 使结合: a bridge ～ing the opposite banks of a river 把两岸连接起来的一座桥 / ～ two boards with glue 把两块木板胶合起来 / be ～ed in marriage 结成夫妇 ②参加; 加入, 作…的成员; 和…作伴 ③回到(岗位等) ④[口]邻接,毗连: Their house ～s ours. 他们的家就在我们隔壁。 **❷** **vi.** ①联合;相遇 ②参加,加入;同…一起 (in): ～ in a game (conversation) 参加游戏(谈话) / ～ in with sb. to take a risk 与某人同冒风险 ③邻接,毗连 **II** **n.** ①连接;结合 ②接连处;接合点,

接合线: a ～ in a coat 外衣的接缝 ‖～ forces (with) 见 force¹ / ～ hands (with) 见 hand / ～ issue with sb. on sth. 见 issue / ～ the colo(u)rs 见 colo(u)r / ～ the (great) majority 死 / ～ up [口] ①参军,入伍 ②联合起来

joiner ['dʒɔinə] **n.** ①接合者;接合物 ②细木工人 ③[口]爱参加各种组织的人

joint [dʒɔint] **I** **n.** ①接合;接头,榫;接缝;接合处: air-tight (water-tight) ～ 【机】气密 (水密) 接合 / butt ～ 【机】对接 / rivet ～ 【机】铆(钉接)合 / universal ～ 【机】万向节 ②关节;节[口]: finger ～s 手指关节 ③两条钢轨的连接(物) ④(牛、羊等的)带骨的腿肉(或肩肉、大块肉) ⑤[植]节 ⑥【地】节理 ⑦(硬皮书面的)折合线 ⑧[美俚]下流场所(指赌窟、烟馆、小酒店等);(任何)场所 ⑨[美俚]大麻叶制成的烟卷 **II** **a.** ①连接的,接合的: a ～ pin 连接销 / a ～ pipe 接合管 ②联合的,共同的; 同时的: a ～ communiqué (declaration) 联合公报(声明) / ～ action 联合行动(或战斗、起诉) / ～ efforts 共同努力 / ～ authors 合著者 / ～ exercises (或 manoeuvre) 联合演习 / the Joint Chiefs of Staff 参谋长联席会议(美国) / during their ～ lives (法律用语) 当他们都活着的时候 ③合办的;共有的: a ～ state-private enterprise 公私合营企业 / a ～ property 共有的财产 / ～ owners 有共同所有权的物主 ④连带的: ～ responsibility (或 liability) 连带责任 **III** **❶** **vt.** ①连接,结合: ～ boards 把木板拼起来 ②使有接头、关节处)切断;把(肉)切成带骨的大块 **❷** **vi.** ①贴合 ②【植】生节;长骨节 ‖a juice ～ [美俚] ①果汁摊 ②酒吧间;夜总会 ③(禁酒法废止前的)秘密酒馆 / out of ～ ①脱榫的;脱节的;脱臼的: put one's arm (knee) out of ～ 使自己的臂(膝)脱臼 ②混乱的 ③不协调的 ④不满的 / put sb.'s nose out of ～ 见 nose ‖～ed a. 有接缝的;有节的;有关节的 / ～er n. ①接合人;接合物;接合器 ②(泥工用的)涂缝刨 ③(木工用的)接缝刨,长刨 / ～less a. 无接合的;无关节的 / ～ly ad. 联合地,共同地;连带地 ‖～ account (数人)共有的(银行存款等)帐户 / ～ chair 【建】接座 / ～ committee ①(议会的两院)联合委员会 ②(几个组织的)联合委员会 / ～ing rule 接榫规 / ～ resolution (议会

joints

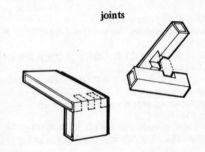

的两院）共同决议 / **~ return**（夫妇）同缴的一笔所得税 / **~ session**（议会的两院）联席会议 / **~ stock** 合股 / **'~-stock company** 股份公司

jointure ['dʒɔintʃə] **I** *n.* ①【律】(丈夫生前指定的)由妻子继承的遗产；寡妇所得产 ②[罕]连接，接合；接合处 **II** *vt.* 使(妻子)继承遗产

joist [dʒɔist] **I** *n.*【建】搁栅；小梁；(地板等的)托梁 **II** *vt.* 为…架搁栅；为…装托梁 ‖**~ ceiling** 搁栅平顶 / **~ steel** 梁钢

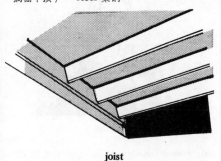

joist

joke [dʒouk] **I** *n.* ①笑话；玩笑：have a ~ with sb. 和某人在一起讲笑话 / He said this in ~. 他说这话是开玩笑的。/ He can't take a ~. 他经不起开玩笑。/ It is no ~. 这可不是开玩笑的事。②笑柄；笑料：be (become) the ~ of the town 是(成为)全镇的笑柄 ③易如反掌的事情；无实在内容的东西，空话：That test was a ~. 那个测验太容易了。**II** ❶ *vi.* 开玩笑：He is only *joking*. 他只是开玩笑罢了。❷ *vt.* 开…的玩笑，戏弄 ‖*a practical ~* 恶作剧 / *a standing ~* 老是被人嘲笑的笑柄 / *be but a ~* 只不过是开开玩笑罢了；完全是一句空话 / *crack* (或 *cut*, *make*) *a ~* 讲笑话；开玩笑 / *joking apart* [口] [用作插入语]言归正传，说正经话 / *make a ~ about sb.* (*sth.*) 以某人(某事)为笑柄 / *play a ~ on sb.* 开某人的玩笑

joker ['dʒoukə] *n.* ①爱开玩笑的人，诙谐者 ②[美](为使法案等失效或含糊而在条文中埋下的)伏笔，曲笔；计策 ③隐蔽的障碍(或挫折) ④(纸牌)百搭(可作任何点数的牌或王牌) ⑤[俚]家伙

joking ['dʒoukiŋ] *a.* 开玩笑的：This is no ~ matter. 这不是开玩笑的事。‖**~ly** *ad.*

jolly ['dʒɔli] **I** *a.* ①快活的，兴高采烈的；有趣的：a ~ young man 快活的年轻人 / a ~ companion 有趣的伙伴 ②[口]令人高兴的；很愉快的，很舒服的；好极的：~ weather 很好的天气 ③[英口]大大的：a ~ fool 一个大傻瓜 ④[英]微醉的：the ~ god 酒神 **II** *ad.* [英口]很，非常：take ~ good care 特别当心 / I'll be ~ glad to help you. 我很高兴帮助你。/ He will be ~ angry. 他会大发脾气的。/ He is so ~ green. 他太天真了。**III** ❶ *vt.* ①[口](用捧、哄或开玩笑等)使高兴，使快活(*along*)：The children *jollied* their mother *along* until she agreed. 孩子们讲得母亲高兴地同意了。②开…的玩笑，戏弄 ❷ *vi.* 开玩笑：~ *with sb.* 同某人开玩笑 **IV** *n.* [英俚]水兵，海军陆战队员 ‖*a ~ dog* [俚]快活人；有趣的伙伴 / *a tame ~* [俚]义勇兵，义勇团丁 / *get one's jollies* [俚]作乐 ‖**jollily** *ad.* 高兴地，快活地 / **jolliness** *n.* 高兴；欢乐 ‖**~ boat** (附于大船的)单座艇 / **~ fellow** ①快活人；有趣的伙伴 ②酒徒 ③[俚]贼 / **Jolly Roger** 海盗旗(饰有白色骷髅等的黑旗) / **'~-up** *n.* ①[俚](非正式的)舞会；跳舞 ②[俚]酒宴；豪饮

jolt [dʒoult] **I** ❶ *vt.* ①使颠簸，震摇 ②(拳击中)给(对手)猛然一击 ③使慌乱 ④(粗暴地)突然干涉 ❷ *vi.* (车辆等)震摇；颠簸 **II** *n.* ①震摇；颠簸 ②突然的猛击(尤指拳击)：pass a ~ 猛然一击 ③[喻]震惊；引起震惊的事情：The unexpected news gave them a ~. 这个意外的消息使他们大吃一惊。④严重的挫折 ⑤少量：pour a ~ of wine 倒一些酒 ‖**'~-,wag(g)on** *n.* [美方]农家牛车

jostle ['dʒɔsl] **I** ❶ *vi.* ①推撞；拥挤：~ *against sb.* 推撞某人 / The crowd ~d into the theatre. 人群挤进了戏院。②贴近②竞争，争夺 ❷ *vt.* ①挤；推，撞：~ *one's way through a crowd* 从人群中挤过去 ②贴近：Many fishing vessels lay *jostling* each other at the riverside. 许多渔船互相紧靠着停泊在河边。③激惹，煽动，使激动 ④与…竞争，与…争夺 **II** *n.* 推撞；拥挤

jot [dʒɔt] **I** *n.* 一点儿；(最)小额；(最)少量：not care a ~ 毫不在乎 / not one ~ or tittle 丝毫也没有，一点也没有 **II** (jotted; jotting) *vt.* 草草记下(*down*)：~ *down sb.'s address* 草草记下某人的地址

journal ['dʒə:nl] *n.* ①日志；日记；航海日记 ②(立法机关、委员会等的)议事录 ③日报；定期刊物，杂志 ④【会计】日记帐 ⑤【机】轴颈：thrust ~ 止推轴颈 ‖**~ box** 【机】①轴颈箱 ②轴颈轴承

journalism ['dʒə:nəlizəm] *n.* ①新闻业；新闻工作；新闻写作；新闻编辑；新闻出版 ②[总称]报刊；报刊文章 ③新闻学

journey ['dʒə:ni] **I** *n.* ①旅行，旅程，路程(常指陆上的)：break one's ~ (at) (在…)中途下车 / I wish you a pleasant ~! (或 A pleasant ~ to you!) 祝你一路顺风！②历程：life's ~ 人生的历程 **II** *vi.* 旅行：~ *on foot* (*by rail*) 徒步(乘火车)旅行 *vt.* 游历 ‖*cheat the ~* 消磨旅途的寂聊 / *Sabbath-day's ~* 见 **Sabbath** ‖**~man** ['dʒə:nimən] *n.* ①雇工，计日工，短工 ②熟练工人 ③[古](学徒期满的)工匠 ④被雇用的人 / **'~work** *n.* ①短工的工作 ②雇佣性的工作

joust [dʒaust] **I** *n.* ①(骑士等用长枪进行的)比武，厮打 ②[复]比赛 ③斗争 **II** *vi.* ①骑着马用长枪比武(或厮打) ②参加比赛

jovial ['dʒouvjəl] *a.* ①[J-]【罗神】(主神)朱庇特的 ②[J-]【天】木星的 ③快活的,愉快的 ‖~ly *ad.* 快活地

joviality [,dʒouvi'æliti] *n.* ①快活,愉快 ②[复]快活的行为(或言语)

jowl [dʒaul] *n.* ①颚骨;颚,下颚;垂肉: a man with a heavy ~ 下颚宽厚(有垂肉)的人 ②颊;猪的颊肉 ③(牛、禽类的)垂肉,喉袋; (鸟的)嗉囊 ④鱼头及头边部分 ‖*cheek by ~ (with)* 见 **cheek**

joy [dʒɔi] I *n.* ①欢乐;高兴 ②乐事;乐趣 II ❶ *vi.* 欢欣,高兴 ❷ *vt.* [古]使高兴;享受 ‖'~-**bells** [复] *n.* (教堂中为喜庆等事而敲的)报喜钟,庆祝钟 / '~**house** *n.* [美俚]妓院 / '~-**juice** *n.* [美俚]酒 / '~**pop** *vi.* [美俚]逢场作戏地吸毒 / '~-,**powder** *n.* [美俚]吗啡 / '~**ride** *n.* [俚] ①乘汽车的兜风(尤指偷车乱开) ②(不顾一切的)追求享乐的行动 / '~,**rider** *n.* [俚]乘汽车兜风的人 / ~ **stick** [俚](飞机的)操纵杆;(汽车的)驾驶盘

joyful ['dʒɔiful] *a.* ①十分喜悦的,高兴的,快乐的: a ~ heart 欣喜的心情 / a ~ face 喜气洋洋的脸容 ②使人喜悦的: ~ news 喜讯 / a ~ occasion 欢乐的节庆 ‖~**ly** *ad.* / ~**ness** *n.*

joyous ['dʒɔiəs] *a.* 快乐的,高兴的: ~ children 快乐的孩子们 ‖~**ly** *ad.* / ~**ness** *n.*

jubilant ['dʒu:bilənt] *a.* 欢呼的;兴高采烈的,喜气洋洋的: The whole nation is ~. 举国一片欢腾。‖~**ly** *ad.*

jubilee ['dʒu:bili:] *n.* ①[常作 J-](犹太史)五十年节 ②【天主教】大赦年 ③(结婚等)五十周年纪念(或庆祝);二十五周年纪念(或庆祝): a silver (diamond) ~ 二十五(六十或七十五)周年纪念 / the Diamond *Jubilee* 英国维多利亚女王统治六十周年纪念(一八九七年) ④欢乐的佳节;欢乐 ⑤[美](歌唱未来幸福时代的)黑人民歌

judge [dʒʌdʒ] I *n.* ①审判员,法官: as grave (或 sober) as a ~ 象法官一样庄重,非常严肃 ②(比赛等的)裁判员;(纠纷等的)评判员: the ~s at a sports meet 运动会的裁判员 ③鉴定人;鉴赏家: a good ~ of cattle 鉴别牲畜的行家 / I am no ~ in such matters. 我对这些事是外行(不会鉴别)。④[J-] 最高审判者(指上帝) ⑤【史】(犹太诸王以前的统治者)士师; [Judges]用作单](基督教《圣经·旧约全书》中的)《士师记》 II ❶ *vt.* ①审判;审理;判决 ②裁判(比赛);评定;裁决(争端等) ③判断;断定: ~ him (to be) a skilled worker. 我断定他是个熟练工人。You can ~ for yourself whether it is good or not. 好不好,你可以自己判断。④鉴定;识别;评价 ⑤认为: We ~d it better not to make a hasty decision. 我们认为最好不要匆忙作出决定。⑥[古]批评;指责 ❷ *vi.* ①下判断;作出裁判: between right and wrong 判断是非 / so far as I can ~ 据我判断,我认为 / *Judging by* (或 *from*) his accent, he must be from the South. 从他的口音判断,他一定是南方人。②作评价(*of*): ~ *of* historical characters 评价历史人物 ‖~**ship** *n.* 审判员的地位(或职权、任期) / ‖~ **advocate** 军法官;军法检查官 / **Judge Advocate General** 军法署署长: *Judge Advocate General's* Department 军法署 / '~-**made** *a.* 由法官(或判决)创造的

judge

judg(e)ment ['dʒʌdʒmənt] *n.* ①审判;裁判;判决: sit *in* ~ *on* a case 审判一个案件 / a ~ *for* (*against*) the plaintiff 裁定原告胜(败)诉的判决 / a ~ *by* default 缺席判决 ②由判决所确定的债务;确定债务的判决书: a ~ debt 判决确定的债务 / a ~ creditor 判决确定的债权人 ③判断;鉴定;评价: form a ~ upon facts 根据事实作出判断 / an error of ~ 判断错误 / pass a ~ *on* a book (man) 对一本书(一个人)作出评价 ④判断力;识(别)力: a man of (good) ~ 判断力强的人 / use (或 exercise) one's ~ 运用判断力 ⑤意见,看法: in sb.'s ~ 照某人看来 ⑥批评;指责 ⑦天罚;报应 ⑧[J-]【宗】上帝的最后审判(日) (=the Last Judg(e)ment) ⑨(基督教《圣经》用语)公正;正义 ‖**Judg(e)ment Day**【宗】上帝的最后审判日;世界的末日 (=the Day of Judg(e)ment) / ~ **seat** 审判员席;法院

judicature ['dʒu:dikətʃə] *n.* ①司法 ②审判员的地位(或职务、职权) ③(审判员或法院的)司法权(或范围) ④法庭;审判制度 ⑤[总称]审判员(或法院): the Supreme Court of *Judicature* 高等法院(英国)

judicial [dʒu(:)'diʃəl] *a.* ①司法的;审判(上)的: the ~ departments 司法部门 / ~ affairs 司法 / ~ powers 司法权 / a ~ assembly 审判大会 / take ~ proceedings against sb. 对某人起诉 ②审判员(或法官)的;法院的;法院判决(或规定)的: the ~ bench [总称]法官 / a ~ sale (separation) 法院判决的拍卖(夫妇分居) ③法官似的;合乎法官身分的 ④公正的;考虑周密的;慎重决定的 ⑤明断的;评判的;批评的: a biography ~ in purpose 一本批判性的传记 ⑥上帝审判的,天罚的 ‖*a ~ murder* 见 **murder**

judicious [dʒu(:)'diʃəs] *a.* 明断的;明智的,审慎的;有见识的 ‖~**ly** *ad.* / ~**ness** *n.*

judo

judo ['dʒu:dou] *n.* [日]现代柔道，现代柔术(日本的一种拳术、摔角术，特别利用运动、平衡和杠杆原理)

jug¹ [dʒʌg] I *n.* ①(有柄、小口、盛水等)大壶，罐，盂: drink a ~ of milk 饮一大壶牛奶 ②壶中物，罐中物 ③[俚]监牢 ④[美俚]银行；保险箱 II (jugged; jugging) *vt.* ①把…放入壶(或罐)中，烧，炖(兔等) ③[俚]监禁，关押 ‖~**ful** *n.* ①满壶，满罐 ②许多(用于下面的短语): not by a ~*ful* [俚]一点也不 ‖'~-,**handled** *a.* ①不匀称的 ②单方面的；片面的 / '~**head** *n.* [美俚]笨蛋，傻瓜

jug² [dʒʌg] I *n.* 模仿夜莺的叫声 II (jugged; jugging) *vi.* 模仿夜莺啼鸣

juggle ['dʒʌgl] I ❶ *vi.* ①(用球、小刀等)玩杂耍；变戏法: ~ with four plates 耍四个盘子 ②玩把戏，耍花招；欺骗: ~ with words (concepts) 作文字(概念)游戏 / ~ with sb. 要弄(或欺骗)某人 ③歪曲，窜改: ~ with history 歪曲历史 ❷ *vt.* ①耍(球、盘等)；要弄: ~ nine balls at the same time 同时耍九个球 ②把…抓住不牢(或摆弄不稳) ③歪曲，窜改，颠倒(事实等): ~ the figures 窜改数字 / ~ black and white 混淆黑白 ④欺骗，诈取: ~ money *out of* sb. (或 ~ sb. *out of* his money) 骗取某人的钱 / ~ sb. *into* doing sth. 骗某人做某事 / ~ sth. *away* 骗掉某物 II *n.* ①玩杂耍；变戏法，魔术 ②耍花招；欺骗，欺诈

juggle

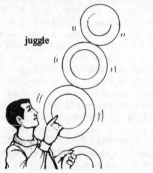

‖~**r** *n.* ①玩杂耍的人；魔术师 ②骗子 / ~**ry** ['dʒʌgləri] *n.* ①杂耍；戏法，魔术 ②把戏，花招 ③欺骗，欺诈

jugular ['dʒʌgjulə] I *a.* ①【解】颈的；喉的；颈静脉的: ~ vein 颈静脉 ②(鱼)喉部有腹鳍(在胸鳍之前)的; (鳍)在喉部的 II *n.* 颈静脉

juice [dʒu:s] I *n.* ①(水果、蔬菜等的)汁，液: orange ~ 柑橘汁 / meat ~ 肉汁 ②[常用复]体液: the ~s 体液 / gastric ~(s) 胃液 ③精，精髓；精力 ④[俚]电，电流；汽油，液体燃料；硝化甘油 ⑤[美俚]酒(尤指威士忌酒) ⑥[J-][美俚](舞台等的)照明员，灯光员 ⑦[俚](赌博、敲诈等所得的)钱，油水; (债主索取的)高利; (从官职等所得的)薪水，收入 II *vt.* ①[口]从…榨出汁(或液); [美俚]从…挤牛奶: ~ a cow 挤牛奶 ②在…中加汁(或液) ‖a ~ joint 见 **joint** / ~ up 使有精力，使有精神；使活跃 / *step on the* ~ 加快；促进 / *stew in one's own* ~ 自作自受 ‖~**less** *a.* 无汁的 / ~**r** *n.* ①榨汁器 ②[美俚]一贯酗酒的人 ③[美俚](剧场、摄影棚的)照明员，灯光员 ‖~**d rehearsal** 电视节目预演 / '~**head** *n.* [美俚]酒鬼

juicy ['dʒu:si] *a.* ①多液汁的: ~ peaches 多汁的桃子 / ~ pork 多汁的猪肉 ②多雨的，潮湿的 ③[口]津津有味的；有趣的；刺激性的(指不健康的故事、见闻、笑话等) ④活力充沛的；有力的: a ~ kick 猛踢 ⑤富于色彩的；绚烂的 ⑥报酬丰厚的，油水多的 ‖**juicily** *ad.* / **juiciness** *n.*

July [dʒu(ː)'lai] *n.* 七月(略作 Jul.)

jumble¹ ['dʒʌmbl] I ❶ *vt.* 搞乱; 使混乱 (*up, together*): ~ up one question and another 混淆两个问题 ❷ *vi.* 混杂; 搞乱; 乱堆 II *n.* ①混乱，杂乱; 混乱的一堆 ②[英]旧杂货义卖; [总称]旧杂货义卖品 ‖~ **sale** [英]旧杂货拍卖(尤指义卖) / ~ **shop** [英](廉价)杂货店

jumble² ['dʒʌmbl] *n.* 环形甜薄饼

jump [dʒʌmp] I ❶ *vi.* ①跳，跳跃: ~ to one's feet 一跃而起 / ~ in the car 跳入汽车 ②(因喜悦、吃惊、紧张等)跃起；跳动；剧跳: ~ at sb.'s unexpected entry 在某人突然进来时吓了一跳 / ~ for joy 欢跃 / He remained calm before danger, his face not turning pale, his heart not ~ing. 在危险面前，他保持镇静，脸不变色，心不跳。③跳越过去(over); 越级升职: ~ over a page or two 跳过一两页 ④暴涨；猛增: Gold prices on Western markets ~ed. 西方市场上的黄金价格暴涨。/ The oil output is ~ing. 石油产量正在猛增。⑤(对结论等)匆匆作出; (对话题、主张等)突然变动: ~ to (或 at) a conclusion 匆匆作出结论 / ~ from one topic to the other 从一个题目跳到另一个题目 ⑥无定见地转移；弃约他就: ~ from job to job 无定见地调换工作，见异思迁 / ~ to another employment 突然另就他业 ⑦猛扑(on, upon); (口头上)攻击，叱责: ~ on the boy for his mischief 由于孩子的恶作剧而加以叱责 ⑧踊跃行动; 奔忙，活跃: On receiving instructions they ~ed at once. 一接到指示，他们立即踊跃行动起来。/ As the Spring Festival is coming, the whole town is ~ing. 春节快到了，全镇在活动中。⑨欣然接受，抢着接受 (at); 急切地投入 (in, into): ~ at the job 抢着接受任务 ⑩符合，一致: His ideas ~ with mine. 他的意见和我一致。/ Our ideas ~ together. 我们意见一致。⑪ (电影中的映象) 歪跳; 颠倒 ⑫(桥牌中) 跳级叫牌 ❷ vt. ①跳过; 越过: ~ a hurdle 跳过栏架 / a chapter 跳过一章 (如讲完第一章就讲第三章) ②使跳跃; 使跳动: ~ a horse across a ditch 纵马跃过沟渠 / a child on one's knees 在膝上颠动小孩 ③使惊起: The news ~ed him out of bed. 这消息使他从床上惊起。④跳上，搭上 (车辆); 跳下 (开动中的火车等): ~ a bus 跳上公共汽车 ⑤使 (物价等) 猛升 ⑥使 (人) 连升几级; 跳过 (几级职位等) ⑦突然离开 (轨道、职位等); [俚] (因欠债等) 逃离: The train ~ed the rail (或 track). 火车出轨了。/ ~ ship 弃职离船 / town 逃离城市 ⑧猛地扑向; (口头上) 猛攻，叱责 ⑨ (赛跑等) 抢在…之前出发: ~ the green light 抢在转绿灯前把车子开过交通线 ⑩非法侵占 (采矿权等) ⑪(把杂志等文章的一部分) 转入 (他页) ⑫(桥牌中) 跳级叫高 ⑬【电】跨接，跳 (线) ⑭把 (石) 冲击打磨 ⑮(在煎锅中) 摇动着煎煮 (土豆等) II n. ①跳跃; 跳跃运动; 一跳的距离; (需跳越的) 障碍物: the high ~ 跳高 / the broad (或 long) ~ 跳远 / ball (篮球) 跳球 / a shot (篮球) 跳投 ②惊跳; [the ~s] 震颤，心神不安: give sb. a ~ 使某人吓了一跳 / give sb. the ~s 使某人心惊肉跳 ③暴涨; 猛增 ④ (空航途中的) 一段短程 ⑤(在起步、出发时的) 占先 ⑥(杂志等文章的) 部分转入他页; (注明下见某页的) 一行附注 ⑦(系列的) 中断; 突然转变: the ~ from liquid to gaseous state 从液态到气态的突变 ⑧【自】跳变; 转移: ~ instructions 跳变指令 ⑨【军】跳伞: a forced ~ 被迫跳伞 ⑩【建】大放脚的梯级 ⑪[俚] (爵士乐等的) 急奏 ‖at a full ~ [美]全速地(的) / be all of a ~ 在紧张状态中，心惊胆战 / from the ~ 从开始 / get (或 have) the ~ on 抢在…之前行动 / ~ off 开始; 开始进攻 / ~ sb. out 叱责某人 / Jump to it! [俚]赶快! 立即动手工作! / on the ~ 在忙碌中; 在移动中: keep the enemy on the ~ 使敌人疲于奔命 / on the keen ~ [美]急忙地; 立即 ‖'~-ed-'up a. 新近获得财势的，暴发的; 自大的; 无耻的 / '~-off n. (赛跑或进攻的) 开始 / ~ seat (在轿车前后座中间的) 折迭式座子; (马车中的) 活动座子 / ~ suit ①伞兵跳伞服; (汽车机械士等穿的) 连衣裤工作服 ②(妇女穿的一种) 紧身衣裤便服

jumper[1] ['dʒʌmpə] n. ①跳跃者; (送货车上) 递送包件的人: a high ~ 跳高运动员 ②跳虫 (如蚤等); 训练成能跳障碍物的马 ③[美] 橇的一种 ④【机】长凿; (钟表的) 棘爪，制轮爪，掣子 ⑤【电】

跳线，跨接线 (=~ wire) ⑥【地】冲击钻杆; 跳动器械 ⑦(稳住桅杆等的) 牵索 ‖~ stay 【船】(前桅与烟囱间的) 横牵索

jumper[2] ['dʒʌmpə] n. ①工作服; (水手穿的) 短上衣 ②(妇女穿的) 无袖套领罩衫; 连兜头帽的皮外衣 ③[复]一种连衫裤的童装

jumping ['dʒʌmpiŋ] a. 跳跃的; 用于跳跃的: a ~ animal 跳跃的动物 / a ~ pole 跳竿 ‖~ **disease** 【医】痉跳病 / ~ **jack** 跳娃娃 (玩具) / ~ **net** [英] =life net / '~-'off **place** ①僻远的地方 ②出发点 ③智穷力竭的地步 / ~ **sheet** [英]失火时用以接住从楼上跳下来的人的布

junction ['dʒʌŋkʃən] n. ①连接; 接合: effect a ~ of two armies 使两军会师 ②接合点; 交叉点; (铁道的) 联轨点 (或站); (河流的) 汇合处: at the ~ of two highways 在两条公路的交叉点 / The power station stands at the ~ of two rivers. 发电站建在两条河流汇合处。/ a ~ station 联轨站, 枢纽站 ③【电】中继线; 【物】接头: 结

juncture ['dʒʌŋktʃə] n. ①接合点; 交界处: at the ~ of four fields 在四块田地的交界处 ②时机; 关头: at this ~ 在这个时候 / at an important historical ~ 在重大的历史关头 ③【语】连音

June [dʒuːn] n. 六月 (略作 Jun.)

jungle ['dʒʌŋɡl] n. ①[常用定冠词]丛林，密林，丛丛: cut a path through the ~ 在丛林中开辟一条路 / ~ warfare 丛林战 / ~ fever 丛林热 (热带恶性疟疾) ②[美俚] (无业游民的) 露营地，集合处; 城市中人口稠密而热闹的居住区 (或工厂区) ③混乱的一堆东西; 错综复杂难以解决的事 ④ (资本主义社会中) 为生存而残酷斗争的地方 ‖**jungly** a. 丛林的; 丛林地带的; 象丛林的 ‖~ **law** 弱肉强食的原则

junior ['dʒuːnjə] I a. ① 年少的，较年幼的(略作 Jr. 或 Jun., 加在姓名后): He is three years ~ to me. 他比我小三岁。/ Tom Brown, *Junior* 小汤姆·布朗(父子同名时对儿子的称呼) / Brown, *Junior* 小布朗(一个集体中有两人同姓时对较年幼者的称呼) ②资历较浅的; 等级较低的: ~ members of the staff 工作人员中年资 (或等级) 较低者 / ~ partners 小伙伴 (即地位较低的伙伴) / a ~ college [美]初级大学(指一二年制大学) / a ~ high school [美]初级中学 ③由青少年组成的; 专为青少年设计的: a *Junior* League [美]的青年女子协会(由上层社会的有闲年轻女子组成，从事于"慈善"事业) / a ~ novel 为青少年写的小说 ④ [美]美国中学或四年制大学中) 三年级 (生)的; 低年级的: the ~ class 三年级 II n. ①年少者: She is my ~ by three years. (或 She is three years my ~.) 她比我小三岁。②等级较低者; 晚辈 ③[美]美国中学或四年制大学中)的三年级生 ④少女衣服尺寸 ‖~ **miss** 少女; 少女衣服尺寸 / ~ **varsity** [美]大学运动队的第二队

juniper ['dʒuːnipə] n. 【植】①桧属植物 ②某些桧属植物的松柏科树(如落叶松等) ‖*Chinese* ~

【植】桧 / common ~【植】欧洲刺柏

junk¹ [dʒʌŋk] **I** *n.* ①(作麻絮、垫料等用的)旧缆绳 ②(金属、玻璃等可重新利用的)废弃的旧物,破烂货;旧货: a yard full of ~ 堆满废弃物的场地 / a ~ market 废旧货市场 ③冒充物,假货;废话,哄骗: ~ jewelry 假珠宝 ④[英](木杆、肉类等的)大块,厚片: a ~ of mutton 一大块羊肉 ⑤(供船上用的)腌牛肉 ⑥[俚]麻醉品,毒品(尤指海洛因) ⑦抹香鲸头部含脑的部分 **II** *vt.* ①[口]把…(当作废物)丢弃 ②把…分成块 ‖**~er** *n.* [美俚] ①吸毒的人 ②破旧得可丢弃的汽车 ‖**~ bottle** 深色厚玻璃瓶 / **~ dealer** 废旧品商人;废旧船具商人 / **~ heap** [美俚]破旧汽车 / **~ mail** (不写收件人姓名、地址的)邮寄宣传品;大量胡乱邮寄的广告 / **'~man** *n.* 废旧品商人 / **~ shop** ①旧船具商店 ②[贬]古董商店

junk² [dʒʌŋk] *n.* 平底中国帆船,舢板 ‖**~man** ['dʒʌŋkmən] *n.* 船工

junk

junket ['dʒʌŋkit] **I** *n.* ①凝乳食品;乳冻甜食 ②野餐;宴会 ③郊游;公费旅游 **II** ❶ *vi.* ①设宴;参加宴会;举行野餐 ②郊游;作公费旅游 ❷ *vt.* 宴请,设宴招待

juridic(al) [dʒuə'ridik(ə)l] *a.* ①审判(上)的;司法(上)的: ~ days 法院开庭日 ②法律(上)的: a ~ person 法人 ‖**juridically** *ad.*

jurisdiction [,dʒuəris'dikʃən] *n.* ①司法;司法权;裁判权,审判权 ②管辖权,权限;管辖范围: have ~ over sb. 对某人有裁判权 ②管辖权,权限;管辖范围: be under the ~ of 在…管辖(权限)之下 ‖**~al** *a.*

jurisprudence ['dʒuəris,pru:dəns] *n.* ①法学,法理学 ②法学的一个分支;一种法律制度: medical ~ 法医学 ③(法院的)裁判规程;判决录

jury¹ ['dʒuəri] *n.* ①[律]陪审团: The ~ finds the prisoner guilty. 陪审团裁定犯人有罪。/ The ~ were divided in opinion. 陪审团意见分歧。/ a hung ~ 由于意见分歧一时未能作出决定的陪审团 / a coroner's ~ (或 a ~ of inquest) (审查死因的)验尸陪审团 / a grand ~ (由十二至二十三人组成的)大陪审团 ②(竞赛时的)评奖团 ‖**hang the ~** [美]使陪审团由于意见分歧而不能作出决定 ‖**~ box** 陪审席 / **~man** ['dʒuərimən] *n.* 陪审员 / '**~,woman** *n.* 女陪审员

jury² ['dʒuəri] *a.* (船上)临时用的;应急的: a ~ anchor 应急锚 / ~ repairs 临时应急的修理 ‖**~ mast** [海]应急桅杆 / '**~-'rigged** *a.*【海】临时配备的 / **~ strut** 应急支柱

just¹ [dʒʌst] **I** *a.* ①正义的;公正的,正直的;公平的: a ~ decision 公正的决定 / be ~ to sb. 对某人公正 / a ~ man 正直的人 ②应得的: a ~ punishment (reward) 应得的惩罚 (报酬) ③合理的;恰当的,正当的;有充分根据的: a ~ opinion 合理的意见 / a ~ claim 正当的要求 / ~ suspicions 有充分理由的怀疑 ④正确的;精确的: in ~ proportions 按正确的比例 ⑤合法的: a ~ title 合法的权利 **II** *ad.* ①正好,恰好: It is ~ two o'clock. 现在正好两点钟。/ It is ~ on two o'clock. 马上就要两点钟了。/ This is ~ how things are in objective reality. 客观事物本来就是如此。/ This is ~ the point. 问题正在这里。/ I was ~ going when he came in. 他进来时我正要走。/ ~ then (there) 正在那时 (那里) ②仅仅,只是: He is ~ a child. 他只是一个孩子。③刚才,方才: He has ~ left here. 他刚刚离开这儿。/ He was ~ here. 他刚才还在这儿。④[常与 only 连用]勉勉强强地,差一点就不能,好不容易才: We could ~ see the roof. 我们勉强看得到屋顶。/ I only ~ caught the last bus. 我刚好赶上末班公共汽车。/ I ~ managed to finish the work. 我好不容易才把这项工作做完。⑤ 直接,就: ~ west of that place 就在那地方的西面 / ~ across from the campus 就在校园对面 ⑥ [口][用于加强语气]真正,非常: The play was ~ splendid. 这出戏真是太好了。/ A: Could he play the violin? B: Couldn't he, ~! 甲: 他会拉小提琴吗? 乙: 他不会? 会得很呢! ⑦[用于祈使语气中]试请,且请: *Just* think of the result! 试想一下后果吧! / *Just* feel it. 你摸摸看。/ *Just* a moment, please. 请稍等一下。‖**~ about** 差不多,几乎: ~ about enough 差不多够了 / I'm ~ about through. 我差不多就要做(或吃)完了。/ **~ as** 正象;正当…的时候 / ~ as you say 正象你说的那样 / **~ as it is** 恰好如此;完全照原样 / **~ as ..., so ...** 正象…一样,…也 / **~ now** 见 now / **~ so** 正是如此,一点不错 / **~ the same** 见 same / **not ~ ... but** 不仅…而且… ‖**~ly** *ad.* 公正地;正当地;应得地 / **~ness** *n.* ①正义(性),正直(性) ②合理,公正 ③正当,正确

just² [dʒʌst] *n. & vi.* =joust

justice ['dʒʌstis] *n.* ①正义;正当;公正,公平;公正原则,公正的赏罚: social ~ 社会正义 / a sense of ~ 正义感 / examine the ~ of a claim 审核要求是否正当 / treat sth. with ~ 公正对待某事 ②正确,确实;正当的理由,合法: There isn't much ~ in these observations. 这些看法不大正确。③司法,审判: a court of ~ 法院 / administer ~ 执法;行使审判权 ④[英]高等法院法官;[美]最高法院法官 ‖**bring sb. to ~** 把某人送交法院

审判，把某人缉拿归案 / do ~ (to) ①公平对待；适当地处理；公平评判: want to see ~ done him 希望看到他得到应有的待遇 / I cannot do ~ to his kindness. 我真无法酬答他对我的好意。/ To do him ~, he is not a bad footballer. 说句公道话，他的足球踢得不坏。②和…酷似（或逼真）: The photograph has done you ~. 这张照片很像你本人。③欣赏；大吃，饱食: do ~ to a dinner 大吃一顿 / do oneself ~ 充分发挥自己的能力；公正待己: He has done himself ~ in performing the work. 他在这项工作中充分发挥了自己的能力。/ in ~ to 为对…公正起见 / Justice of the Peace 兼理一般司法事务的地方官，治安官 / Justice's ~ 执法不当的裁判（用以讽刺治安官不当的判决）/ poetic(al) ~ 理想的赏罚，劝善惩恶 / temper ~ with mercy 宽严并济；恩威兼施 ‖~ship n. 法官的职位；法官任期

justification [,dʒʌstifi'keiʃən] n. ①证明为正当，辩护；正当的理由: He said this in ~ of his action 他说这话是为自己的行为辩护 ②无过失，无咎: It can be said for his ~ that.... 为证明他无咎，我们可以说… ③【印】（活字行间的）整理，整版

justify ['dʒʌstifai] ❶ vt. ①证明…是正当的（或有理的）；为…辩护: The course of events fully justifies our views. 事情的发展完全证明我们的意见是正确的。/ He is fully justified in doing so. 他这样做是完全有道理的。/ ~ oneself for one's conduct 为自己的行为辩护 ②为…提供法律根据；宣誓证明(自己)有财力作保 ③【宗】把…释罪 ❹【印】调整(铅字)的间隔使全行排满 ❷ vi. ①提出充分法律根据；证明合法 ②证明有资格作保证人（或保释人）③【印】调整铅字间隔使全行排满

jut [dʒʌt] Ⅰ (jutted; jutting) ❶ vi. 突出；伸出(out, up): cliffs jutting straight up 矗立着的峭壁 ❷ vt. 使突出；伸出: ~ out one's jaw 使颏突出 Ⅱ n. ①突出；伸出 ②突出部；伸出部

jute [dʒuːt] n. ①【植】黄麻属植物；黄麻；长蒴黄麻 ②黄麻的纤维

juvenile ['dʒuːvinail] Ⅰ a. ①青少年的: ten ~ years of sb.'s life 某人的十年少年时代 / a ~ shock team 少年突击队 ②适合于青少年的；青少年特有的: ~ books 少年读物 / a ~ court 少年法庭 ③幼稚的: ~ behaviour 幼稚的行为 Ⅱ n. ①青少年 ②演少年角色的演员 ③儿童书籍，少年读物 ④羽毛未丰的鸟，雏鸟；两岁的(供竞赛用的)马 ‖~ delinquency 少年犯罪 / ~ delinquent 少年罪犯

juxtapose ['dʒʌkstəpouz] vt. 把…并列，使并置

K

kaleidoscope [kə'laidəskoup] n. ①万花筒 ②千变万化的情景

kaleidoscopic(al) [kə,laidə'skɔpik(əl)] a. 万花筒(似)的；千变万化的 ‖**kaleidoscopically** ad.

kangaroo [,kæŋgə'ruː] n. 【动】大袋鼠 ‖~ closure [英]限制议事法（由议会或委员会中主席决定几个修正案中何者应进行辩论何者应终结辩论不予置议的一种议事规则）/ ~ court [美口]袋鼠法庭(指非法的或不按法律程序的非正规法庭；也指囚犯在狱内举行的模拟法庭) / ~ rat ①鼹(产于澳洲，=rat ~) ②产于美洲的有袋啮齿类动物

karate [kə'rɑːti] n. 日本的一种徒手自卫武术

keel¹ [kiːl] Ⅰ n. ①(船、飞艇等的)龙骨: lay down a ~ 安置龙骨(开工造船) ②【动】龙骨突，脊棱；【植】龙骨瓣 ③[诗]船 Ⅱ ❶ vt. ①给(船等)装龙骨 ②(为了修理等)把(船等)翻转；使倾覆 ❷ vi. (船等)翻身，倾覆 ‖~ over ①倾覆，翻身 ②[口]昏倒 / on an even ~ ①(船)平稳的(地) ②[喻]稳定的(地)，平静的(地) ‖~less a. 无龙骨的 / '~block n. [船]龙骨墩 / '~boat n. 一种有龙骨的内河运货船 / '~haul vt. ①把(某人)用绳子缚在船底拖(作为一种刑罚) ②严斥 / ~ line [船]首尾线；龙骨线

keel² [kiːl] n. ①(运煤的)平底船 ②一平底船的煤 ③[英]煤的重量单位 (=21.2 长吨)

keen¹ [kiːn] a. ①锋利的；刺人的: a ~ knife 锋利的刀 / a ~ scent 刺鼻的气味 / ~ criticism 尖锐的批评 ②激烈的；强烈的: a ~ competition 激烈的竞争 / a ~ sense of responsibility 强烈的责任感 ③敏锐的；敏捷的: a ~ observer 敏锐的观察者 / a ~ intelligence 敏捷的智力，急智 ④热心的；渴望的 ⑤[美俚]极好的，漂亮的 ‖be ~ about 喜爱，对…着迷 / be ~ on [口]喜爱；渴望: be ~ on (playing) table tennis 爱好(打)乒乓 ‖~ly ad. / ~ness n.

keen² [kiːn] Ⅰ n. 哀哭地唱出的挽歌；号哭，痛哭 Ⅱ ❶ vi. 以哀哭唱出挽歌；号哭，痛哭 ❷ vt. 以哀哭唱出挽歌追悼(某人)；哀哭着发出 ‖~er n. 以哀哭唱出挽歌者；痛哭者

keep [kiːp] Ⅰ (kept [kept]) ❶ vt. ①保持；保存；保留；保守(秘密): Will you ~ the seat for me? 替我保留这个座位好吗？ / Does your watch ~ good time? 你的表走得准吗？②使(人或物)保持在(某一状态): ~ the motherland in mind and the whole world (globe) in view 胸怀祖国，放眼世界(全球) / We'll ~ you informed. 我们将随时让你知道情况。 / Sorry to have *kept* you waiting. 对不起,让你等了。 / *Keep* top side up! 请勿倒放!

③履行(诺言等);遵守(惯例等): ~ regular hours 生活作息很有规律

④庆祝,(按民间习俗)过(节或生日等);守(宗教节日等): ~ Spring Festival (或 Chinese New Year) 过春节 / ~ the Sabbath【宗】守安息日

⑤保护;看守: ~ goal 守球门

⑥整理,料理: ~ house 管理家务 / ~ open house 好客

⑦备有(商品等),经售: Sorry, we don't ~ notepaper here. 对不起,我们这儿不卖信纸。

⑧记(日记、帐等): He ~s a diary. 他每天记日记。 / ~ books 记帐

⑨赡养;雇用: John has a wife and six children to ~. 约翰要养活妻子和六个孩子。

⑩饲养: ~ pigs (hens) 养猪(鸡)

⑪经营,开设(商店等)

⑫拘留;留住: ~ sb. in custody 拘留某人 / be *kept* at office until midnight by extra work 因额外工作留在办公室干到半夜

⑬留在(房屋等)内;保持在(座位等)上: ~ one's bed 卧床不起 / ~ the house 足不出户 / ~ the saddle despite the bucking of the horse 不管马怎样跳跃稳坐在马鞍上

⑭继续沿…走: ~ the middle of the road 一直沿着路中间前进

❷ *vi.* ①保持着某一状态: ~ firm in one's proletarian stand 站稳自己的无产阶级立场 / *Keep* silent! 别作声! / *Keep* dry! 切勿受潮!

②[常接 ...ing]继续不断: News of successes ~s pouring in. 捷报频传。

③(食物等)保持不坏: In such weather meat won't ~ long. 在这样的天气,肉放时间长了要坏的。

④搁,拖: The matter will ~ until morning. 这事搁到明晨再说。 / There was much I wanted to ask him, but now it would have to ~. 我有许多事要问他,但现在不得不拖一下。

⑤(学校)上课: Does your school ~ all day? 你们学校全天上课吗?

⑥[口]住,呆

⑦保持某种路线(或方向、活动等)

II *n.* ①保持,保养

②生计,衣食;饲料

③【史】要塞;(城堡的)高楼,最强固部分

④牢监,监狱

‖earn one's ~ ①挣饭吃 ②值得雇用;值得豢养 / for ~s [口]永远地: You may have it *for* ~s. 这个东西你拿去好了。(指不必归还) / play *for* ~s 玩作输赢的游戏 / ~ *at* ①坚持(做);使不停地做: *Keep* at it! 别松劲! 干下去! ②~ = on at / ~ *away* 站开;使离开 / ~ *back* ①留在后面,不前进 ②阻止 ③隐瞒 ④留下 / ~ *down* ①卧下;蹲下 ②镇压,压服;控制 ③缩减:

~ *down* non-productive expenses 缩减非生产性开支 ④保留(食物等) ⑤【印】用小活字排印 / ~ *from* ①阻止;使免于 ②隐瞒: ~ sth. (back) *from* sb. 对某人隐瞒某事 ③抑制 / ~ *in* ①抑制 ②隐瞒,隐藏 ③把…关在里边;把(学生)关学;不出去 ④(火)继续燃烧;使(火)不熄 ⑤【印】(活字)排紧 / ~ *in with* [口]继续和…相好;不断讨好 / ~ *off* ①让开;不接近: *Keep off* the grass! 勿踏草地! ②不让…接近,把…驱开: *Keep* your hands *off* (the exhibits)! 勿用手摸(展品)! / ~ *on* ①[常接 ...ing]继续(进行);继续下去: We *kept on* working in the fields in spite of the rain. 尽管下雨,我们还是坚持在地里劳动。 ②穿(或戴)着…不脱 / ~ *on at* 纠缠,困扰(某人);使烦恼 / ~ *oneself to oneself* [口]不交际,不与人来往 / ~ *out* ①(使)在外: Danger! *Keep out*! 危险! 切勿入内! ②【印】疏排(以增篇幅) / ~ *out of* (使)置身于…之外 / ~ *sb. going in sth.* 供给某人以某物 / ~ *to* 坚持,保持;固守(习惯等): ~ *to* the style of hard struggle and plain living 保持艰苦奋斗的作风 / ~ *to oneself* ①保守秘密 ②不交际,不与人来往 / ~ *under* 压制,控制: The fire has been *kept under*. 火势已被控制住了。 / ~ *up* ①(斗志、价格等)不低落;使不低落: ~ *up* one's courage 鼓足勇气 ②保持,坚持;继续: *Keep* it *up*! 坚持下去! ③使(某人)熬夜 ④【印】用大写正体排印 / ~ *up with* 跟上: ~ *up with* the rapidly developing situation 跟上飞速发展的形势

keeper ['ki:pə] *n.* ①看守人;看护人;(动物园中的)饲养员 ②保管员;管理人 ③(商店、客栈等的)经营人 ④【机】夹头,锁紧螺帽;衔铁 ⑤耐藏的水果(或蔬菜)

keeping ['ki:piŋ] *n.* ①保管,保存;看守: in safe ~ 由可靠的人保管着;保存得很好 ②(诺言等的)遵守 ③供养;饲养 ④一致;协调 ‖in ~ *with* 与…一致;与…协调 / out of ~ *with* 与…不一致;与…不协调 ‖~ *room* [美]家庭起居室

keepsake ['ki:pseik] *n.* 纪念品

keg [keg] *n.* ①小桶(容量通常在三十加仑以下) ②一小桶的东西

ken¹ [ken] I (kenned 或 kent [kent]; kenning) ❶ *vt.* ①[苏格兰]知道 ②[古]看见 ③[方]认识 ❷ *vi.* [苏格兰]知道 (*of*, *about*) II *n.* ①[罕]视野;景象 ②认识范围,知识范围

ken² [ken] *n.* (盗贼、乞丐等的)窝

kennel¹ ['kenl] I *n.* ①狗窝 ②[复]养狗场 ②(狗、野兽等的)群 ③(狐、水獭等的)窝 ④鄙陋的住所 II (kennel(l)ed; kennel(l)ing) ❶ *vt.* ①使进狗窝;使呆在狗窝内 ②使住进鄙陋的住所 ❷ *vi.* ①进狗窝;呆在狗窝内 ②(人)住在鄙陋的住所

kennel² ['kenl] *n.* (路旁的)下水道,阴沟,沟菜

kepi ['kepi] *n.* (有平圆顶及水平帽沿的)法国军帽

kept [kept] I keep 的过去式和过去分词 II *a.* 受人资助和控制的

kerb [kə:b] *n.* [英](街道的)路边镶边石; 井栏 ‖~ **market** 场外证券市场

kerchief ['kə:tʃif] ([复] kerchiefs 或 kerchieves ['kə:tʃivz]) *n.* ①(妇女用)方头巾, 方围巾 ②[诗] 手帕 ‖~ed, ~t *a.* 包着头巾的, 围着围巾的

kernel ['kə:nl] *n.* ①[方](果实的)核; 仁 ② 谷粒 ③[原]原子实; 原子核; [数](积分方程的)影响函数核 ④[喻]核心, 中心: the ~ of dialectics 辩证法的核心

kerosene, kerosine ['kerəsi:n] *n.* 煤油, 火油 (= ~ oil)

ketch [ketʃ] *n.* 一种双桅船

ketchup ['ketʃəp] *n.* 番茄沙司, 番茄酱

kettle ['ketl] *n.* ①(烧水用的)水壶, 水锅 ②[地] 锅穴 (= ~ hole) ‖*a pretty ~ of fish* 混乱, 乱七八槽; 尴尬, 困境 ‖'~drum *n.* ①铜鼓, 定音鼓 ②午后茶会

key¹ [ki:] **I** *n.* ① 钥匙: turn the ~ 转动钥匙(开锁) ②[常用复](钢琴、打字机等的)键 ③(地图等的)图例; 题解; 表解; 图解(如动植物分类特征表等); 符号(或缩写)的解释: the ~ to the code 电码索引 ④(解决事件或问题的)线索; 秘诀; 答案: discover the ~ to the secret 发现揭开秘密的线索(或秘诀) ⑤关键; 要害; 要冲: The ~ to the settlement of the question lies in .... 解决这个问题的关键在于… / a pass known as the ~ to the Northeast 通往东北的要隘 ⑥[音]调; [喻](文章、演说等)的调子, 基调: speak in a high (low) ~ 以高昂(低沉)的声调讲话 / all in the same ~ 单调地, 千篇一律 ⑦[电]电键, 电钥 ⑧ (上钟表发条的)钥匙; [机]销子, 楔, 栓 ⑨[建]拱顶石 ⑩[植]翅果 **II** ❶ *vt.* ①(用钥匙)锁上; 插上(栓、销子等); [建]用拱顶石装饰 ② 向…提供解决的线索(或答案) ③[音]调节…的音调; [喻] (在调子等方面)使和谐 ④用动植物分类特征表鉴定(生物标本) ❷ *vi.* 使用钥匙 **III** *a.* 主要的, 关键的; 基本的: a ~ post 主要岗位(或职位) / a ~ point 要点 ‖*get (或 have) the ~ of the street* [口]被关在屋外; 无家可归 / *hold the ~s of* 控制, 支配 / *in a minor ~* 用低调; 带有阴郁的情绪 / ~ *up* ①使升调 ②使紧张; 使激动; 激励 ~ *up tension* 使紧张状态激化 / The children were all ~ed up over the show of wire-walking. 孩子们在看走钢丝表演时都紧张极了。/ *lay (或 put) the ~ under the door* 闭户而去 ‖~ed *a.* ①锁着的; 用拱顶石连住的 ② (乐器等)有键的; 已调节的, 已被定于某调的 ③[常用以构成复合词]调子…的: a low-~ed address 调子低的演说 / ~er *n.* [无]键控器 / ~less *a.* 无钥匙的; (钟表发条等)不需钥匙开的 ‖'~board *n.* ①(钢琴、打字机等的)键盘 ②挂钥匙的板 *vi.* 操作键盘式排字机 *vt.* 用键盘式排字机排(字) / ~ **club** [美](每一成员各自持有钥匙的)非正式俱乐部 / ~ **fruit** [植]翅果 / ~hole *n.* 锁眼, 钥匙孔 *a.* 显示内情的: a ~*hole* reporter 报道内幕的记者 / '~man *n.* [美](企

业等的)中心人物, 要人 / ~ **money** (房地产经纪人索取的)额外的小费 / '~note *n.* ①[音]调; 主音 ②[喻]主旨, 要旨; 基调: set the ~*note* 定下基调 *vt.* 给…定下基调, 在(会议等)场合发表主要讲话 / '~,noter *n.* 定基调的人, 作主要讲话的人: a conference ~*noter* (通过讲话)给会议定下基调的人 / ~ **ring** 钥匙圈 / '~stone *n.* ①[建]冠石, 塞缝石, 拱顶石; [无]梯形失真(光栅) ②[喻]基本原理, 要旨 / '~way *n.* 锁槽; [机]键槽, 销座

keystone

key² [ki:] *n.* 礁; 暗礁

khaki ['kɑ:ki] **I** *a.* ①土色的, 黄褐色的 ②卡其布的 **II** *n.* ①土黄色 ②卡其布 ③[常用复]卡其布服装(尤指军装)

kick¹ [kik] **I** ❶ *vi.* ①踢: That horse ~s. 那匹马老是要踢。②(枪炮等)反冲 ③[口]发牢骚; 反对, 抗议 (against, at): ~ *against* (或 *at*) harsh treatment 对虐待表示抗议 ❷ *vt.* ①踢: ~ a football 踢足球 / ~ one's way through the thorns 从荆棘丛中踢出一条路 ②(枪炮等)反冲 ③(足球)踢得(分): ~ a goal 踢进一球, 得一分 ④(用强硬手段等)赶出, 驱逐 (out) ⑤戒除(毒瘾) **II** *n.* ①踢; [英]踢足球者: give a ~ at 对…踢一下 / a good (bad) ~ 足球踢得好(槽)的人 / a dying ~ 垂死挣扎 ②反冲; 后座力(指枪炮等); (赛跑等的)冲刺(力) ③[口]牢骚; 反对, 抗议 ④[口]弹力, 反应力; 冲击力: have no ~ left 已无反击力了 ⑤[口](酒等的)刺激力; 极度的快感: get a big ~ out of 从…中得到极大乐趣 / There is much ~ in the wine. 这种酒劲儿很足。⑥[俚]撤职, 解雇: get the ~ 被解雇 ⑦[英俚]六便士的硬币 ⑧(事态或情节等突然或惊人的)转折; 显示 ⑨[美俚]升, 增加(指新金等) ‖*a ~ in one's gallop* 异想天开 / *a ~ in the teeth* 突然(或很大)的挫折(或失败) / *alive and ~ing* 见 alive / (*get*) *more ~s than halfpence* (或 *ha'pence*) 未受优待反遭虐待; 很费力气而获少利; 得不偿失 / ~ *against the pricks* 见 prick / ~ *around* [口] ①粗暴而轻率地对待; 仗势欺(人) ②(人)到处跑来跑去; 常换行业 ③从各个角度考虑(或调查、讨论) / ~ *back* 踢回; 反冲; [口]突然退缩 ②

[美俚]退赔(赃物) ③[美俚]付(佣金、酬金等) / **~ *down the ladder*** 见 **ladder** / **~ *in*** [美俚] ①捐(款);缴付(自己应付的一份) ②死 / **~ *off*** ①踢脱(鞋子等) ②(足球)中线开球;[喻]开始 ③[美俚]死 / **~ *oneself*** [美] 严厉自责 / **~ *one's heels*** 见 **heel**[1] / **~ *out*** ①(足球)把球踢出界[2] ②[口]踢开;解雇 / **~ *over the traces***[2] / **~ *sb. downstairs*** 赶出(或驱逐)某人 / **~ *sb. upstairs*** 以升官爵等为名排斥某人,使某人名升实降 / **~ *the bucket*** [俚]死掉 / **~ *the wind*** (或 **clouds**) 被绞死 / **~ *up*** 踢起;[俚]激起,引起(骚乱等);**~ *up* a dust** (汽车开动时等)扬起灰尘;[喻]引起骚动 / **~ *up a row*** 见 **row**[3] / **~ *up its heels*** 见 **heel**[1] / **~ *up one's heels*** 见 **heel**[1] / **on (off)** *a* **~** [美俚]正(不再)迷恋于某项活动 ‖**~er** *n.* ①踢的人 ②爱踢的马 ③[口]反对者,老是唱反调的人 ④【宇】喷射器;抛掷器 ⑤[俚]出乎意料的结局;隐蔽的难点 ⑥[俚]艇外推进机 / **'~back** *n.* ①剧烈的反应 ②反冲;返程 ③[美俚]退赔的赃款 ④[美俚]佣金,酬金 / **'~off** *n.* (足球等)的开球;[喻]开始 / **'~out** *n.* ①(足球中的)踢球出界 ②[口]撵走;撤职,解雇 / **'~stand** *n.* (自行车等的)撑脚架 / **~ starter** (摩托车等的)反冲式起动器 / **'~'up** *n.* [口]骚乱;大吵大闹

kick[2] [kik] *n.* (玻璃瓶等的)凹底

kickshaw ['kikʃɔː] *n.* ①精美的菜肴 ②华而不实的玩物

kid[1] [kid] **I** *n.* ①小山羊;小羚羊 ②(食用)小山羊肉;小山羊皮;[复]小山羊皮制的手套(或皮鞋等) ③[俚]小孩,少年,儿童 **II** 小山羊皮制的: **~ gloves** 用小山羊皮制的柔软光滑的手套 **III** (kidded; kidding) *vt. & vi.* (山羊或羚羊)生(仔) ‖**handle** (或 **treat**) **with ~ gloves** 见 **glove** / **the ~ lay** (盗贼语)抢夺(或偷窃)外出购物的小孩的钱 / **'~-'glove(d)** *a.* 温和的;过分讲究的;考虑周到的: **~-glove(d) methods** 软的一套手段 / **'~skin** *n.* (用于制手套、皮鞋等的)小山羊皮

kid[2] [kid] [俚] **I** *n.* 欺骗 **II** (kidded; kidding) *vt. & vi.* ①欺瞒,哄骗 ②嘲笑,戏弄

kid[3] [kid] *n.* (水手用以盛食物的)小木桶

kidnap ['kidnæp] (kidnap(p)ed; kidnap(p)ing) *vt.* 诱拐(小孩等);绑架 ‖**kidnap(p)er** *n.* 拐子;绑架者

kidney ['kidni] *n.* ①肾,腰子 ②性格,脾气: a man of the right **~** 脾气好的人 ‖**~ bean** 菜豆;肾形豆

kill[1] [kil] **I** ❶ *vt.* ①杀死,弄死;宰(猪等): prevent the frost from **~ing** the plants 不让严霜冻死植物 ②扼杀,毁掉(希望等): **~ sb.'s appetite** 使某人毫无食欲 ③中和;抵消: throw some alkali in the solution to **~** the acid 在溶液中放些碱使酸中和 ④使终止;使(发动机等)停止;【电】截断(电流): **~** a live circuit 截断通电

电路 / **~** an engine 使(汽车等的)发动机熄火 / **~** the pain with drugs 用药物止痛 / take a snack to **~** one's hunger 吃一顿快餐充饥 ⑤消磨(时间) ⑥[口]使着迷;使感到非常有趣(或可笑): His jokes **~ed** me. 他说的笑话简直把我笑死了。 ⑦否决(议案等): **~** a petition (断然)拒绝请求 ⑧删除 ⑨(网球等中)杀(球) ⑩喝光(酒) ⑪使非常痛苦;使精疲力竭 ❷ *vi.* ①杀死 ②(植物等)被弄死;(家畜等)适于屠宰: Mosquitoes **~** easily when incubating. 蚊子在产卵时易于消灭。 **II** *n.* ①杀,杀伤: mass-**~** weapons 大规模杀伤武器 ②(被打死的)猎获物 ③被击毁的敌机(或敌潜艇,敌舰) ④(网球等中)杀球 ‖**be in at the ~** ①猎物被杀时在场 ②结尾时在场 / **~ off** 消灭,杀光: This new insecticide **~s off** green flies in thousands. 这种新杀虫剂可大量地消灭蚜虫。 / **~ two birds with one stone** 见 **bird** / **~ with kindness** 见 **kindness** / **to ~** [俚]极其,非常;过度地,过分地: do sth. **to ~** 尽力做某事 / be dressed **to ~** 穿着过分考究的 ‖**~ed** *a.* ①被杀死的;被屠宰的 ②【冶】镇静的: **~ed steel** 镇静钢 / **~er** *n.* ①杀人者;嗜杀成性的人(或动物);[英](粗俗的新闻用语)凶手: a **~er** whale 逆戟鲸 ②灭…的东西;宰杀的器具: a weed **~er** 除草药 / a submarine **~er** 防潜舰艇 / a humane **~er** (使动物无痛苦的)屠宰机 ③[口]迷人的人(或物) ④【无】限制器,抑制器;断路器;瞄准器 ‖**~-,devil** *n.* ①假饵 ②[方]西印度群岛的一种甜酒 ③便宜的劣质饮料 / **'~joy** *n.* 扫兴的人 / **'~-time** *n.* 用来消磨时间(或消遣)的事情

kill[2] [kil] [美][常作 K-] (主要用于特拉华州和纽约州的地名中)水道,小河

killing ['kiliŋ] **I** *a.* ①致死的 ②使人疲乏的 ③[口]吸引人的;很滑稽的 **II** *n.* ①杀害,屠杀 ②突然赚得的一笔大钱;突然获得的大成功 ‖**~ly** *ad.* [口]吸引人地

kiln [kiln, kil] **I** *n.* 窑 **II** *vt.* 在窑内烧(或烘干) ‖**~-dry** *vt.* 在窑内烘干 / **'~man** *n.* 烧窑工人

kiln

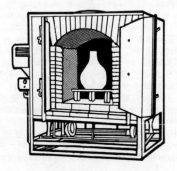

kilo ['ki:lou] *n.* ①公斤,千克: a ~ bomb【军】轻燃烧弹,重一公斤的燃烧弹 ②公里,千米

kilt [kilt] **I** *n.* ①(苏格兰高地男子和苏格兰兵团士兵穿的)褶迭短裙(通常用格子呢做的) ②儿童穿的苏格兰式短裙 **II** ❶ *vt.* [苏格兰] ①卷起(裙等) (*up*) ②使有直褶 ❷ *vi.* 敏捷地移动

kimono [ki'mounou] *n.* [日] ①和服 ②和服式女晨衣

kimono

kin [kin] **I** *n.* ①家族,门第 ②[总称]家属;亲属: We are near ~. 我们是近亲。 ③亲属关系 **II** *a.* 有亲属关系的 (*to*): He is ~ *to* me. 他是我的亲属。 / We are ~. 我们是亲属。‖count ~ *with* [苏格兰] ①和…算亲属关系,和…是近亲 ②和…比血统,和…比门第 / (*near*) *of* ~ 近亲的 / *next of* ~ 最近的亲属(们) ‖~less *a.* 无家属(或亲属)的 / ~ship *n.* 家属(或亲属)关系;类似家属(或亲属)的密切关系

kind[1] [kaind] *n.* ①种;类;[贬]帮,伙: different ~s of animal(s) 各种不同种类的动物 / three ~s of book(s) 三种书 / all ~s of tree(s) 各种树 / What ~ of man is he? 他是怎样的人? / He is not the ~ (of person) to idle away his time. 他不是那种游手好闲的人。 / the best ~ of typewriter 最好的一种打字机 / watches of this ~ (或 [口] these ~ of watches) 这种表 / Hitler and his ~ 希特勒之流 ②性质,本质: These materials differ in strength but not in ~. 这些材料强度不同但性质是一样的。 ③[古]家族 ‖*a* ~ *of* 几分,稍稍: have *a* ~ *of* suspicion that … 有点怀疑… / *in* ~ 以货代款,以实物;[喻]以同样的方法(或手段): provide aid *in* ~ 以实物提供援助 / *~ of* [口] [用作状语] 有点儿,有几分: I ~ *of* thought he would come. 我似乎感到他会来的。 / *of a* ~ ①同一种类的: Things *of a* ~ come together. 物以类聚。 ②徒有其名的;蹩脚的 / *nothing of the* ~ 毫不相似(的事物),决非如此(的事物) / *something of the* ~ 类似的事物

kind[2] [kaind] *a.* ①仁慈的;和蔼的;好意的;友爱的: Will you be ~ enough to (或 so ~ as to) help me? 请你帮帮我的忙,好吗? / It's very ~ of you to repair the lathe for us. 谢谢你为我们修理车床。 ② 亲切的: with ~ regards 祝好(信尾用语) ‖~'hearted *a.* 仁慈的,好心的

kindergarten ['kində,gɑ:tn] *n.* 幼儿园 ‖kindergartner, ~er *n.* ①幼儿园教师 ②幼儿园里的小孩

kindle ['kindl] ❶ *vt.* ①点燃 ②使(人、感情等)激动起来 ③照亮,使明亮 ❷ *vi.* ①着火,燃起 ②(人、感情等)激动起来 ③发亮: Her eyes ~d with joy. 她的眼睛因喜悦而发亮。 ‖kindling *n.* ①点火: the *kindling* point 燃点,着火点 ②[总称]引火物

kindly ['kaindli] **I** *a.* ①仁慈的;和蔼的;友好的;体贴的 ②(气候等)宜人的,温和的 ③[古]合法的 **II** *ad.* ①仁慈地;和蔼地;友好地;有礼貌地: treat sb. ~ 和蔼地对待某人 / be ~ invited to join the evening party 被盛情邀请参加晚会 ②诚恳地,衷心地: Thank you ~. 衷心地感谢你。 ③ 请(用于客套语): *Kindly* tell me your address. 请告诉我你的地址。 ④ 自然地,容易地: take ~ to 自然而然地爱上了… ‖kindlily *ad.* / kindliness *n.*

kindness ['kaindnis] *n.* ①仁慈;和气;好意: out of ~ 出于好意 ②友好的行为;好事: Will you do me a ~? 你能帮我一下忙吗? / *Kindness* of … (信封上用语)烦…转交 ‖kill with ~ ①以溺爱害(人或动物等) ②用过分的好意使(人)不知所措

kindred ['kindrid] **I** *n.* ①宗族 ②血缘关系;亲属关系 ③[总称]亲属,(遗传学用语)血缘族 ④同质;相似 **II** *a.* ①宗族的;亲属的 ②同种的;同源的;同性质的;类似的: ~ languages 同源的几种语言

kinetic [kai'netik] *a.* ①【物】动力(学)的;(运)动的: ~ energy 动能 / the ~ molecular theory 分子运动论 ②活动的;活跃的;能动的;有力的 ‖~s [复] [用作单]动力学 / ~ art 活动艺术(指可用机械力驱动活动部分的雕塑等)

king [kiŋ] **I** *n.* ①王,国王;(部落的)首领,头子: the *King* of Denmark 丹麦国王 / a ~ of the Indians 印第安人的首领 ②(某范围内)最有势力者,大王: the ~ of beasts 百兽之王(指狮子)/the ~ of birds 鸟王(指鹰) ③(纸牌)K;(国际象棋)王;(西洋跳棋)王棋 ④[K-]【宗】上帝,耶稣: *King* of Bliss (或 Glory, Heaven) 上帝,基督 ⑤(水果、植物等中)最佳者 ‖*King's Bench* 英国高等法院 / *King's colour* 英军的团旗(或军旗)/ *King's evil* 瘰疬(昔时迷信,经国王一触即可痊愈) / *King's highway* 水陆交通干线;[喻]大道,正道(指行为等) / *King's picture* (或 *portrait*) [英俚]钱 / *King's pipe* 伦敦船坞内的焚毁炉(旧时焚违禁烟草,现焚烟屑等) / *King's silver* 纯银 / *King's weather* 庆典时的晴朗天气 **II** ❶ *vi.* ①做国王 ②统治 ❷ *vt.* 立…为王 ‖*a King Log* 有名无实的君王,极端放任而无权

kingfisher

威的君主(源出《伊索寓言》) / a ～ of shreds and patches 专事抄袭进行编辑的小文人 / a King Stork 暴君(源出《伊索寓言》) / go up King Street [澳]破产, 倒账 / King Charles's spaniel 一种黑褐色小狗 / ～ it 做帝王, 统治; 称王称霸(over) / King of Arms 英国主管纹章的长官 / King of day 太阳 / King of Kings ①[宗]上帝, 神 ②(过去东方某些国家国王的称号)大皇帝 / King of the Castle (儿童游戏)山寨大王 / Kings have long arms (或 hands). [谚]王权及四海, 勿与帝王争。(或: 百姓强不过官家。) / take the King's shilling 见 shilling / The King can do no wrong. [谚]国王不可能犯错误。/ the ～ of metals 金 / the King of Terrors 死神 / turn King's evidence 见 evidence ‖～less a. 无国王的 / ～ship n. ①君王的身分; 王位; 王权 ②帝王统治 ③(对君王的称呼)陛下(=his ～ship) ‖'～bolt n. 【机】中心立轴; (汽车转向关节)主销; 大螺丝 / '～craft n. 君王的统治权术 / '～cup n. 【植】鳞茎毛茛; 驴蹄草 / '～fish n. (产于大西洋或太平洋沿岸的)食用大海鱼 ②[美口]首领, 头子 / ',fisher n. 翠鸟, 鱼狗(一种食鱼鸟) / '～,maker n. 拥立国王的人; 左右候选人选择的要人, 竞选的后台老板 / '～pin n. ①【机】中心立轴 ②[口]中心人物; 主要成分 / ～ post 【建】中柱, 桁架中柱;【船】吊杆柱 / '～post truss 【建】单柱桁架 / '～-size(d) a. ①特大的, 特长的 ②非寻常的

kingdom ['kiŋdəm] n. ①王国: the United Kingdom 联合王国(大不列颠与北爱尔兰) ②领域;界(生物的最大分界): the ～ of thought 思想领域 / the animal (plant, mineral) ～ 动(植, 矿)物界 ③[K-]【宗】天国; 神政 ‖come into one's ～ [俚]飞黄腾达, 成为富翁(指继承财产) / come [俚]天国; 西天: go to ～ come 上西天, 死

kingly ['kiŋli] I a. ①国王的; 君主地位的 ②国王似的; 适合国王身分的 ③ 君主政体的: the ～ form of government 君主政体的(统治) II ad. 国王似地, 象君主那样地 ‖**kingliness** n.

kink [kiŋk] I n. ①(绳索、头发等的)纽结, 绞缠 ②奇想, 怪念头; 乖僻 ③(奇特的)妙法 ④(颈、背

等处的)肌肉痉挛, 抽筋 ⑤[美](结构或设计等的)缺陷 II ❶ vt. 使绞结, 使绞缠 ❷ vi. 纽结, 打结, 绞缠 ‖'～cough n.【医】百日咳

kinsfolk ['kinzfouk] n. [总称]家属, 亲属

kinsman ['kinzmən] ([复] kinsmen) n. 男亲属

kiosk [ki'ɔsk] n. ①(土耳其、伊朗等国的)凉亭, 亭子 ②报摊; 公用电话间; 音乐台

kipper ['kipə] I n. ①(在雌鲑、雌鳟产卵期中或后的)雄鲑, 雄鳟 ②腌(或熏)的鲑鱼, 鲱鱼 ③[俚]人(尤指小伙子, 孩子) II vt. 腌(或熏、晒干)(鲑鱼、鲱鱼等)

kirk [kə:k] n. [苏格兰]教会: the Kirk (of Scotland) 苏格兰教会(即苏格兰长老会) ‖～man ['kə:kmən] n. ①苏格兰教会的教徒(或支持者) ②[苏格兰]教徒; 教士

kiss [kis] I ❶ vt. ①吻: ～ the baby on the cheek (或 ～ the baby's cheek)吻婴孩的颊 ②(风、波浪等)轻拂, 轻触 ❷ vi. ①接吻 ②轻抚, 轻触 II n. ①吻 ②轻拂, 轻触 ③小糖果; (常含椰子的)蛋白小甜饼 ‖a Judas ～ 奸诈, 口蜜腹剑; 阴险的背叛 / a ～ of death 看上去对人有好处实则具毁灭性的行为 / ～ away ①吻掉(眼泪等) ②由于荒淫而挥霍掉(财产等) / ～ hands (或 the hand) 见 hand / ～ off [俚]①(突然或粗暴地)把…解雇 ②躲避, 逃避 ③杀死 / ～ sb. goodby(e) 吻别某人 / ～ sth. goodby(e) ①无可奈何地失掉某物(如钱等) ②去掉某物 / ～ the book 见 book / ～ the dust 见 dust / ～ the ground 见 ground¹ / ～ the hare's foot 见 foot / ～ the resin (或 canvas) 见 resin / ～ the rod 见 rod ‖～er n. ①接吻者 ②[俚]嘴; 颌; 面孔 ‖～ing bug (咬嘴唇、面孔等的)害虫(如锥鼻虫) / ～ing crust (烘时相粘而成的)面包上的软皮 / ～ing gate [英方](只容一人通过的)小门 / ～ing kind 亲密(200狎昵)的 / '～-me-quick n. ①(垂于额上的)鬈发 ②(十九世纪)一种小的女帽 / '～-off n. [美俚]①粗暴无礼的开除(或遣走) ②死亡

kit¹ [kit] n. ①[英方]木桶 ②成套工具(或用具、物件、器材);配套元件;【军】士兵的个人装具: a carpenter's ～ 一套木工用具 / a travel ～ 一套旅行用物件 / a model-airplane ～ 模型飞机的全套元件 ③装具袋;用具包;工具箱: a first-aid ～ 急救药箱 / a tool ～ 工具箱 ④[口]一套东西; 一群人(常用于下面的短语) ‖～ bag ①长形帆布用具袋 ②【军】(士兵个人的)长形帆布装具袋

kit², **kitt** [kit] n. ①小猫(=kitten) ②软毛小动物; 软毛小动物的毛皮

kitchen ['kitʃin] n. ①厨房, 灶间 ②[集合名词]炊事人员 ③(便于携带的)全套炊具 ‖～er n. ①(尤指修道院的)厨师, 厨房总管 ②厨房用的炉灶 / ～ cabinet ①[厨房用的]食橱, 碗柜 ②[政府首脑的]非正式顾问团 / ～ garden 菜园 / '～maid n. 帮助厨师的女工 / ～ midden (考

古学用语)贝冢,贝丘 / ～ **physic** 滋补身体的食物 / ～ **police** [总称]【军】炊事值勤(员) / '～-**sink** n.①厨房中的洗涤盆(或水池)②[喻]搬不动的东西;乱七八糟的东西 a.[喻](剧本等)表现西方现代生活中肮脏情景的 / ～ **stuff** ①[总称]供烹调的菜蔬 ②厨房下脚(尤指从锅上弄下的油垢) / '～**ware** n.[总称]厨房用具

kite [kait] I n.①【动】鸢 ②贪得无厌的人;骗子,流氓 ③风筝 ④[复](微风时用的)最高的轻帆 ⑤[商]空头支票;抵用票据 ⑥[英]【军】轻型飞机;风筝式飞机;[美俚]飞机 II ❶ vt.①使(物价等)上升 ②[商]用(空头支票)骗钱 ❷ vi.①[口](象风筝般)上升;飘动;翱翔;飞奔 ②用空头支票骗钱 ‖**fly a ～** ①放风筝 ②试探舆论 ③发空头支票 [美俚]写信(尤指狱中私递信件);寄航空信(常指为了要钱或要求帮助而寄) / **higher than a ～** [美俚]极高;大醉 ‖～ **balloon** 系留气球 / '～-**flying** n.(用便于在以后进行否认的方式)发表政治新闻

kith [kiθ] n.[总称]①[古](熟悉的)朋友;邻居 ②亲属 ‖～ **and kin** [总称]亲属;朋友

kitten ['kitn] I n.①小猫;小动物(如小兔等) II vt. & vi. 产(小猫) ‖**have (a litter of) ～s** [美俚]发怒,生气;担忧;兴奋 ‖～**ish** a. 小猫似的;嬉耍的 ‖'～**ball** n.[美]垒球

kiwi ['ki:wi(:)] n.①【动】鹬鸵,几维(新西兰产的一种不能飞行的鸟) ②[K-][口]新西兰人 ③[俚]【军】不飞行的空军军官;未单独飞行过的学员

kiwi

knack [næk] n.①诀窍,窍门;妙法;技巧 ②需要熟练技巧的工作 ③花巧,花样 ④(行为、言语等的)习惯,癖 ⑤玩具,小玩意儿

knacker ['nækə] [英] n.①无用的家畜(或其尸体)的收买者;废马的收买者和屠宰者 ②旧船、旧屋的收买和拆卖者 ③[方]废马 ‖**go to the ～s** (马)被屠宰

knapsack ['næpsæk] n.(军用或旅行用,帆布或皮制的)背包

knave [neiv] n.①流氓,无赖,恶棍 ②(纸牌中的)杰克 (Jack)

knavery ['neivəri] n. 流氓行为,无赖行为;欺诈;恶作剧

knavish ['neiviʃ] a. 无赖的;欺诈的;不正直的 ‖～**ly** ad. / ～**ness** n.

knead [ni:d] vt.①揉,捏(面粉、陶土等);捏制(面包、陶器等) ②按摩(肌肉等) ‖～**ing trough** 揉面槽,揉面钵

knee [ni:] I n.①膝;膝盖;膝关节 ②(裤子、长袜等的)膝部 ③膝状物;【机】弯头(管);膝(形)杆;合角铁;(铣床的)升降台;【建】扶手弯头;曲材;(木船用的)肋材 ④(用膝的)碰击 II vt.①用膝盖碰 ②用弯头管(或合角铁)接合 ③[口]使(裤子)的膝部凸出 ‖**bend one's ～ to**(或 **bow the ～ before**) 向…跪下,屈服于 / **bow the ～ to Baal** 崇拜流行的偶象,信奉流行的信仰 / **bring sb. to his ～s** 迫使某人屈服 / **drop (on) to one's ～s** 跪下 / **fall**(或 **go down) on one's ～s** 跪下(请求等) / **on bended ～s** 屈膝跪着 / **on one's ～s** 在严重的(失败)状态中 / **on the ～s of the gods** 尚未可知的,尚未可定的(指未来的事) ‖～ **action**【机】膝(形)杆动作;膝(形)杆作用: ～ **action** suspension【机】独立悬挂 / **brace**【机】隅撑,角撑 / ～ **breeches** 短裤 / '～**cap** n.【解】膝盖骨 ②护膝 / '～-**deep** a.①(积雪等)齐膝深的,(涉水的人等)没膝的 ②深陷在…中的(in) / '～-**high** a.(袜等)高及膝盖的: ～-**high** to a mosquito(或 duck) 很小的,微不足道的 / '～**hole** n.(写字台等)容纳膝部的地方 / '～ **joint** n.①【解】膝关节 ②【机】弯头接合,肘接 / '～**pad** n. 护膝 / '～**pan** n.【解】膝盖骨 / ～ **swell** [美](风琴的)膝板,增音器

kneel [ni:l] (knelt [nelt] 或 kneeled) vi. 跪下;跪着 (to, before, down) ‖～**er** n.①跪垫 ②跪着的人(如做礼拜时)

knell [nel] I n. 钟声,丧钟声;[喻]死亡(或灭亡、失败等)的凶兆: the ～ of sb.'s hopes 某人的希望破灭的征兆 II ❶ vi.①(丧钟、钟)发出丧钟声 ②发出悲哀(或不祥)之声 ❷ vt.①敲(钟)报丧(或报灾) ②敲丧钟召集(或宣布);发出丧钟声般的声音召集(或宣布)

knelt [nelt] kneel 的过去式和过去分词

knew [nju:] know 的过去式

knickerbocker ['nikəbəkə] n.① [K-] (最初到纽约的)荷兰移民的后代;(泛指)纽约人 ②[复](膝下扎起的)灯笼裤

knickers ['nikəz] [复] n.①[口](膝下扎起的)灯笼裤 ②女用扎口短衬裤

knickknack ['niknæk] n. 零星的装饰物(或珠宝、衣服、家具等);小摆设;小玩意儿

knife [naif] I ([复] knives [naivz]) n.①(有柄的)小刀: a pocket ～(可折合的)小刀 / a table ～ 餐刀 / a ～ and fork (吃西餐用的)一副刀叉 ②匕首 ③(机器上的)刀片(或刀具) II ❶ vt.①(用刀)切,戳,刺 ②[美口](用阴险手段)伤害(或背叛、击败) ③(刀切似地)穿过: birds knifing the sky 一群掠过天空的鸟 ❷ vi.(刀似地)穿开,穿过 ‖**before you can say ～** 说时迟那时快;突然 / **get one's**(或 **a) ～ into sb.**

(恶毒地或报复性地)伤害某人 / *play* (*a good*) ~ *and fork* (胃口很好地) 饱餐一顿, 痛痛快快地吃 / *sharpen one's* ~ *for sb.* 准备惩罚(或攻击)某人 / *the* ~ 外科手术 / *under the* ~ [口] 经受外科手术 / *war to the* ~ 见 war ‖'~board *n.* ①磨刀板 ②[英]公共马车顶上的座位 / '~edge *n.* ①刀口; (门框、舱门等的)刃形边缘 ②(任何)锋利的边缘 ③【机】(天平等的)刃形支承 / '~-edged *a.* (象刀口般)锋利的, 锐利的 / ~ grinder ①磨刀工人 ②磨刀装置; 磨刀石, 砂轮 / ~ machine 磨刀机 / ~ rest (餐)刀架 / ~ switch [电]闸刀开关

knight [nait] I *n.* ①(欧洲中世纪)骑士, 武士 ②爵士(其名前称号用 Sir) ③【英史】郡选议员 (=~ of the shire) ④(古希腊)雅典的第二等级的公民; (古罗马)骑士(奴隶主集团中一个阶层的成员) ⑤贵妇人的护卫者(或侍从) ⑥(对某种事业等的)忠实的拥护者: *Knights* of Labor【美史】(一八六九年成立的秘密的工会)劳动骑士团(成员) ⑦(国际象棋中的)马: queen's ~ 和"王后"同列配置的"马" II *vt.* 封…为骑士(或爵士) ‖a ~ *of the brush* 美术家, 画家 / *a* ~ *of the hammer* 打铁工人, 铁匠 / *a* ~ *of the pen* (或 *pencil*) 文人; 记者; 抄写员 / *a* ~ *of the post*【英史】以作假见证为职业的人 / *a* ~ *of the road* ①流动的推销员 ②流浪汉 ③[古]拦路贼 ‖~age ['naitidʒ] *n.* [总称]骑士; 爵士; 骑士(或爵士)名录; 骑士(或爵士)的地位 / ~hood *n.* ①骑士(或爵士)的地位(或身分) ②骑士精神; 侠义 ③[总称]骑士; 爵士 / ~ly *a.* ①骑士(般)的; 侠义的; 英勇而文雅的 ②由骑士(或爵士)组成的 ③骑士般地; 侠义地 / ~ bachelor 英国最古最低级爵士 / '~-'errant ([复] ~s-errant) *n.* (欧洲中世纪)游侠骑士; 侠客; 堂吉诃德式的人 / '~-'errantry *n.* 骑士风尚; 侠义行为; 堂吉诃德式的行为 / '~head *n.* (船首斜桅的)支撑杆 / Knight(s) of Columbus (美国天主教徒于一八八二年成立的)一种国际性互助与慈善团体的成员 / ~('s) service [史]以服军役为条件的对土地的占有权 / Knight Templar ①(十二世纪初欧洲的)十字军救护团骑士(保护朝圣者) ②共济会一个宗派的成员

knight

knit [nit] (knitted 或 knit; knitting) ❶ *vt.* ①把…编结(或针织): ~ wool *into* a sweater 把毛线结成毛线衫 / ~ a sweater *out of* wool 用毛线结成毛线衫 ③皱起, 皱紧: ~ the brows 皱眉头 ④接合(折骨等); 使紧密结合, 联合(指通过共同利益、婚姻等) ⑤[常用过去分词]使严密, 使紧凑: a closely ~ demonstration 严密的论证 ❷ *vi.* ①编结; 编织, 针织 ②(眉头)皱起, 皱紧 ③(折骨等)接合; 紧密结合 ④[英方](植物)生长, 结果实; (蜂)蜂拥, 成群 ‖~ *up* ①织补 ②[喻]结束(议论等) ‖knitter *n.* ①编结者; 编织工人 ②编织机, 针织机 ‖~ goods 针织品: a ~ goods mill 针织厂

knitting ['nitiŋ] *n.* ①编结(法); 针织(法) ②[总称]编织物; 针织品 ‖stick to (或 tend to, mind) one's ~ 只管自己的事 ‖~ machine 针织机 / ~ needle 手工编结用的针; 针织机上用的针

knives [naivz] knife 的复数

knob [nɔb] I *n.* ①球形突出物; (树干等的)节; (棒等的)圆头 ②疖, 瘤, 疙瘩 ③[俚]头 ③(门、抽屉等的)球形捏手; (旗杆等上的)顶状; 【建】雕球饰, 顶华 ④(收音机等的)旋钮, 调节器 ⑤[美]圆丘; [复]丘陵地带 ⑥[主英]方糖; 煤块 II (knobbed; knobbing) ❶ *vt.* 使有球形突出物; 给(门等)装球形捏手 ❷ *vi.* 鼓起, 突出 ‖*with*~s *on* [俚] 尤其突出地, 更加 ‖knobbed *a.* (树干等)有节的, 多节的; (棒等)有圆头的 ‖~kerrie ['nɔbkeri] *n.* 圆头棒(旧时南非人用作武器)

knock [nɔk] I ❶ *vi.* ①敲; 击, 打: Someone is ~ing. 有人敲门。 / ~ *at* (或 *on*) a door 敲门 ②相撞, 碰撞: ~ *into* sb. 撞在某人身上 ③(发动机等由于故障)发出爆(击)声 ④[美俚]找岔子, 说坏话 ⑤奔忙, 忙乱: ~ *round* in a kitchen 在厨房里忙来忙去 ❷ *vt.* ①敲; 击, 打; 去掉: ~ *in* a nail 把一枚钉敲进去 / ~ sb. *flat* 把某人击倒在地 / An effective remedy for ~ing colds 治感冒的良药 ②使碰撞 ③[英俚]给…强烈印象; 使震惊 ④[美俚]找…的岔子, 说…的坏话 II *n.* ①敲; (狠狠的)一击; 打击: There is a ~ *at* (或 *on*) the door. 有人敲门。 ②[喻]不幸; 挫折; 艰苦, 困苦 ③(发动机等由于故障发出的)爆(击)声; 爆击: a ~-test engine 测爆机 ④[无]敲击信号 ⑤[美俚]指摘, 挑剔: take (或 stand) the ~s 忍受指摘 ⑥[英俚](板球赛的)盘, 回合 ‖get the ~ ①喝酒过量, 喝醉 ②被解雇 / ~ *about* ①[口](指物)碰撞 ②[口]到处流浪, 厮混; 漫游 ③接连打击; (浪等)冲击(船等); 粗暴对待 / ~ *against* =~ up against / ~ *around* [美] =~ about / ~ *back* [俚](一口)喝掉 / ~ *down* ①击倒; 撞倒; 击落; [喻]使屈服 ②拆除; 拆卸: ~ *down* a machine 拆卸机器 ③[口]降低(价格等); 迫使(某人)降价, 迫使(某人的索价)降低 ④(拍卖时)击锤卖出(货物) ⑤获得(收入、薪金等) ⑥[口]要求(*for*): ~ sb. *down for* a song 要求某人唱一支歌 / ~ *for a loop* 见 loop / ~ *head* 叩头 / ~ *into a cocked hat* 见 hat /

~ *it off* [美俚]住嘴! 别笑了! 别说笑话了! /
~ *off* ① 把…敲掉; 把…从…敲落; 击倒: ~ sb.
off his feet 把某人打倒在地 ②[口]停工; 中断
(工作等): When do you usually ~ *off* (work)
for lunch? 中午你们一般什么时候歇手吃饭? ③
[口](从价目中等)减去, 除去 ④[口]很快写出
(文章等): ~ *off* a few lines 匆匆写几句 ⑤[美
俚]杀死; 压倒 / ~ *on the head* 见 **head** /
~ *out* ①敲空: ~ *out* a pipe 敲出烟斗里的灰
②(拳击中)击倒; 打昏; 压倒; 打破; 使震惊
③使失去效能, 使无用; 破坏 ④[~ oneself
out] 使筋疲力尽 ⑤[口]做成(作品); 匆匆制订
出(计划等): ~ *out* an idea 匆匆想出个主意
⑥[无]脱模 ⑦弄倒, 打翻 ②[美俚]
(警察等)袭击, 搜查; 逮捕 ③[美俚]吃掉; 喝下
(酒等) / ~ *sb. into the middle of next week*
见 **middle** / ~ *sb.'s head off* 见 **head** /
the bottom out of 见 **bottom** / ~ *together*
①(使)相撞; (膝等颤抖地)相碰 ②匆匆拼凑成,
草草做成 / ~ *under* (*to*) (向…)屈服 / ~ *up*
①把…往上敲去 ②敲门喊醒; 召唤: Please
~ me *up* at six o'clock. 请在六点钟敲门叫醒我.
③匆匆赶成(或安排): ~ *up* a meal 匆匆做好一
顿饭 ④[英口](使)筋疲力尽 ⑤[英](在板球赛
中)很快得(分) ⑥[美俚]使受孕 / ~ *up against*
碰撞; 同…冲突; 偶然碰见 / *take the* ~ [俚] ①
经济上受到沉重打击 ②喝醉 ‖**~about** *n.* ①单
桅小帆船; 小游艇 ②喧闹的喜剧表演(或演员)
③粗(或牢)的东西 ④厮打, 狠斗 ⑤流浪汉 *a.*
①(喜剧表演等)喧闹的 ②(衣服等)粗的, 牢的
③闲荡的; 漫游的 / '~-**down** *a.* ①击倒的; 压
倒的 ②可拆卸的, 易于拆卸的 ③(拍卖的价格)
最低的 *n.* ①打倒的一击; 击倒 ②易于拆开的
东西 ③厮打, 混战 ④[美俚]介绍 ⑤降低 /
'~-**down**(-**and**)-'**drag-out** *a.* 激烈而无情的 /
'~-**knee** *n.* 膝内翻症; [复]内翻膝 / '~-**kneed**
a. 膝内翻的 / '~**out** *n.* ①(拳击)把对手打倒
在地的一击; 击倒; 被击倒 ②[俚]引人注目的人
物; 轰动的事物 ③联合拍货(互相勾结的一伙人
在拍卖时由一人以低价买进后在同伙内转售); 联
合拍货者 *a.* ①击倒的 ②引人注目的, 轰动的
③使昏迷的: ~*out* drops (放于酒中使人昏迷以
便盗窃的)迷药, 蒙汗药

knoll[1] [noul] *n.* 小山, 圆丘; 土墩

knoll[2] [noul] [古] ❶ *vt.* 敲(钟); 敲钟报(时); 敲
钟召唤 ❷ *vi.* (钟)敲响

knot [not] **I** *n.* ①(绳等的)结; (装饰用的)花结:
tie a ~ in a cord 在绳上打个结 / tie a cord in
a ~ 把绳子打个结 / untie (或 undo) a ~ 解开
一个结 / a reef ~ 平结, 方结 / a granny('s) ~
打错的平结 ②结合(指婚姻等) ③一小群, 一小
队: People are standing about *in* ~s. 人们三
五成群地站着. ④(树木或木板上的)节; 节疤,
节瘤 ⑤难题, 麻烦事; 疙瘩; ~s in the mind 思
想上的疙瘩 ⑥[海]节(=浬/小时); 海里, 浬: a
vessel of 25 ~s 每小时航行二十五浬的船 ⑦[英]

搬运工用的垫肩 (=porter's ~) **II** (knotted;
knotting) ❶ *vt.* ①把…打结; 把…连结; 捆扎:
~ two ropes together 把两根绳子结在一起 ②使
密切结合(指血缘等) ③使纠结, 使纠缠(指藤草
等) ④皱(眉) ❷ *vi.* ①打结; 成结; 作花结(指木
边等) ②纠结, 纠缠 ‖a Gordian ~ ①难解的
结; 难办的事, 棘手问题 ②(问题或故事情节等
的)关键, 焦点 / *cut the* (*Gordian*) ~ 以斩钉
截铁手段解决困难问题, 快刀斩乱麻 / *get into*
~s 困惑不解 / *tie oneself* (*up*) *in* (或 *into*)
~s 陷入困境 ‖'~**grass** *n.* 【植】两耳草; 软花
属植物 / '~**hole** *n.* (木板或树上的)节孔

knot

knout [naut] **I** *n.* (沙皇时代的刑具)皮鞭 **II** *vt.*
(狠毒地)鞭打

know [nou] **I** (knew [nju:], known [noun]) ❶ *vt.*
①知道; 了解, 懂得: ~ oneself 有自知之明 / ~
for certain that ... 确实知道 / Do you ~
how to swim? 你会游泳吗? / We ~ him to be
brave. 我们知道他是勇敢的. / (as) you ~ (或
don't you ~) [用作插入语]你也知道(或: 你是
知道的, 不是吗) / ~ no bounds (或 ends) 无限
度, 无穷; 不知足 ②认识; 熟悉(地方等); 记牢:
I should like to ~ him. 我希望(通过介绍)认识
他. / ~ truth through practice 通过实践认识真
理 / ~ sb. by name 只知某人的名字 / ~ sb.
by sight 同某人只是面熟 / I ~ him only to say
hullo to. 我同他不过是打招呼的朋友. / ~
one's lines (by heart) 背熟自己的台词 ③精通
(语言等) ④认出, 识别; 分辨: I would ~ him
even in a crowd. 即使在人群中, 我也能认出他
来. / I knew her *for* a German. 我看出她是德
国人. / ~ right *from* wrong 分辨是非 ⑤体验,
经历: He never knew fear. 他从不知道害怕. /
History ~s only two kinds of war, just and
unjust. 历史上只有两类战争, 正义战争和非正
义战争. ⑥(基督教《圣经》或法律用语)同(某人)
发生性关系 ❷ *vi.* 知道; 了解, 懂得: How can
I ~? 我怎么知道呢? / I don't ~ *about* that
matter. 我不知道那件事. / Not that I ~ *of*.
据我知道并不是那样. / I don't ~ the
writer, but I ~ *of* him. 我不认识这个作家, 但
我听说过(或知道)他. **II** *n.* [口]知情(用于下

面的短语): in the ~ 知内情的 ‖*all one ~s* 力
所能及的一切; 尽全力地 / *for all I* ~ 见 **all** /
I wouldn't ~. [美]我不知道。 / ~ *a hawk
from a handsaw* 见 **hawk**[1] / ~ *a thing or
two* 见 **thing**[1] / ~ *better* (*than*) 很懂得, 很明
白(而不至于): You ought to have *known better*.
你本来就应该更懂事些嘛。 / She certainly ~s
better than to tackle such problems by herself.
她很明白不能独自去解决这类问题。 / ~ *one's
business* 见 **business** / ~ *one's own mind* 见
mind / ~ *one's stuff* (或 *goods*) 见 **stuff** / ~
the ropes 见 **rope** / ~ *the time of day* 见
time / ~ *all the answers* 见 **answer**
‖'~-**all** *n*. [口]自称无所不知的人, 知识里手 /
'~-**how** *n*. [口]实际知识; 技能; 诀窍: pass
one's technical ~-*how* to others 把技术传授给别
人 / '~-**it-all** *a*. & *n*. 自称无所不知的(人) /
'~-,**nothing** *n*. ①无知的人 ②不可知论者 ③
[K-]【美史】(十九世纪反对外来移民、天主教徒等
的)一种秘密党派的成员 / '~-,**nothingism** *n*.
①不可知论 ②[K-]【美史】(十九世纪反对外来
移民等的)秘密党派的排外主义

knowing ['nouiŋ] **I** *a*. ①知道的; 有知识的; 有见
识的 ②老练的; 世故的; 狡猾的 ③机警的, 灵敏
的 ④会意的: a ~ look 会意的眼色 ⑤故意的
⑥[口](帽子等)时髦的 **II** *n*. 知道; 认识: There
is no ~ when he will come again. 不知道他什
么时候会再来。 ‖~**ly** *ad*. ①故意地: Don't
violate it ~*ly*. 不要明知故犯。②老练地 ③会
意地

knowledge ['nɔlidʒ] *n*. ①知识; 学识; 学问: There
can be no ~ apart from practice. 离开实践的
认识是不可能的。 / genuine ~ 真知 / a working ~ of English (学到)能应用的地步的英语
知识 / a branch of ~ 一门学科 ②认识: *Knowledge* originates in practice. 认识来源于实践。
③知道, 了解; 消息 ④[古]学科 ⑤[古]性关系
(=carnal ~) ‖*come to sb.'s* ~ 为某人得悉, 被
某人知道 / *to sb.'s* (*certain*) ~ 据某人所(确)
知: *To my* ~, they will break ground for the
new project next week. 据我所知, 新工程在下
周破土动工。 / *to* (*the best of*) *sb.'s* ~ 据某人
所知 ‖'~-**box** *n*. ①[俚]头 ②[美俚]校舍 / ~
factory [美]学校(尤指高等院校); 教育机构

knowledgeable ['nɔlidʒəbl] *a*. [口]有知识的, 渊
博的; 有见识的: a ~ critic 有见识的批评家 /
He made some ~ remarks at the meeting. 他
在会上的发言相当有见地。

known [noun] **I** know 的过去分词 **II** *a*. 大家知
道的; 知名的; 已知的: a nationally ~ advanced
unit 全国闻名的先进单位 / ~ number (quantity)【数】已知数(量) ‖*be* ~ *as* 以…知名; 被认
为是 / *be* ~ *for* 因…而众所周知: He is ~
for his readiness to help others. 大家都知道
他乐于助人。/ *be* ~ *to* 为…所知 / *make oneself* ~(*to sb.*)(向某人)作自我介绍 / *make sth.*

~ (*to sb.*) 把某事(向某人)公布

knuckle ['nʌkl] **I** *n*. ①指(关)节 ②(猪等动物的)
膝关节, 脚圈 ③【机】关节; 钩爪; 铰链接合 (=~
joint); (屋顶等的)脊;【船】船尾棱缘: coupler ~
车钩关节 / universal joint ~ 万向接头关节
④[复]指套铜套(套在四指关节上的铜套, 握拳时
铜套向外, 用以打人; =~-duster) **II** ❶ *vt*. 用
指关节敲打(或压、摩、触) ❷ *vi*. (儿童打弹子
时)以指关节贴地 (*down*) ‖*give sb. a rap on*
(或 *over*) *the* ~*s* 见 **rap**[1] / ~ *down* ①开始认
真(或有干劲地)工作 ② =~ under / ~ *under*
(*to sb.*) [口](向某人)承认失败, 屈服 / *near the*
~ [口]近于猥亵(或淫)的 ‖'~-**bone** *n*. ①指
关节骨; (牛羊等的)蹠骨 ②[复]玩蹠骨的游戏 /
~ **joint**【机】铰链接合

knuckle

koala [kou'ɑ:lə] *n*. 【动】考拉(澳大利亚产的一种
貌似小熊的栖于树上的无尾动物)

koala

kosher ['kouʃə] **1** *a*. ①(食物等)按犹太教规的; 清
洁的, 可食的 ②(饮食店)供应按照犹太教规的清
洁食物的 ③[美俚]真正的; 合法的; 诚实的; 合乎
伦理的 **II** *n*. 按犹太教规清洁的食物(或供应清
洁食物的饮食店) **III** *vt*. 使清洁可食(或可用)

kraal [krɑ:l] **I** *n*. ①(南非有栅栏防护的)村庄;
[总称]村中居民 ②(南非)家畜栏 **II** *vt*. 把(家
畜)关入栏

kudos ['kju:dɔs] *n*. [口]荣誉, 光荣; 名声; 威信

L

label ['leibl] **I** *n.* ①标签,签条: attach a ~ to 在
…上加标签 / put ~s on one's luggage 在行李
上贴上标签 ②标记,符号 ③称号,绰号: acquire
the ~ of 得了…的绰号 ④说明性略语(如词典用语
中的[古]、[美]等) ⑤【建】披水石 ⑥带胶的邮票
⑦[古]布条; 带子; 附在文件上带有封印的丝带
II (label(l)ed; label(l)ing) *vt.* ①贴标签于; 用签
条标明: The bottle is label(l)ed poison. 瓶上标
明有毒。②把…称为;把…列为 ③(用放射性同
位素)使(元素或原子)示踪; (用示踪原子)使(化
合物等)示踪

labial ['leibjəl] **I** *a.* ①唇状的;嘴唇的 ②【语】唇
音的 **II** *n.* ①风琴管 ②【语】唇音(如: [b], [p],
[m] 等)

laboratory [lə'borətəri, 'læbərətəri] *n.* ① 实验室,
研究室 ②化学厂,药厂 ③实验课 ‖**laboratorial**
[,læbərə'tɔːriəl] *a.* ‖~ **school** 为学生实习而设
的大学实验学校

laborious [lə'bɔːriəs] *a.* ①勤劳的 ②吃力的: a
~ task 费力的工作 ③(文体等)矫揉造作的,不
流畅的 ‖~**ly** *ad.* / ~**ness** *n.*

labo(u)r ['leibə] **I** *n.* ①劳动: Labo(u)r creates the
world. 劳动创造世界。/ physical (或 manual)
~ 体力劳动 / mental ~ 脑力劳动 / wage ~ 雇
佣劳动 / hard ~ 劳役,苦役 ②努力: With great
~ the workers streamlined the process. 经
过巨大的努力工人们把工序流水作业化了。③工
作; 活计: a ~ that calls for exertion and
precision 一件既要花气力又要求精确的工作 /
inspect sb.'s completed ~s 检查某人所完成的工
作 ④[有时作 L][集合名词]工人,劳方;劳动力:
skilled (unskilled) ~ 熟练(不熟练)工人 / the
struggle between ~ and capital 劳资之间的斗
争 / ~ aristocrats 工人贵族 / cheap ~ 廉价劳
动力 ⑤分娩,阵痛: a woman in ~ 在分娩中的妇
女 / difficult (natural) ~ 难(顺)产 ⑥[L-](英
国或英联邦国家的)工党 (=the Labo(u)r Party):
the Labo(u)r vote 支持工党的选票 **II** ❶ *vi.*
① 劳动: ~ in the fields 在田里劳动 ②苦苦地
干 ③努力争取 (for); 努力: ~ at a difficult
problem 绞尽脑汁地做一道难题 ④费力地前进:
(船只)前后颠簸,纵摇: The car ~ed up the hill.
汽车艰难地爬上山去。/ ~ through a book 费劲
地读完一本书 ⑤分娩 ❷ *vt.* ①在…上过分花费
精力;过于详尽地阐述: I'll not ~ the point. 这
点我就不详细谈了。②麻烦;打扰: I won't ~ you with
the details. 我不拿细节来烦你。③使辛勤地工
作: ~ one's wits over sth. 为某事动脑筋 ‖*a*

of love 爱做的事,出自喜爱而做的事 / ~ one's
way 吃力地前进 / ~ under 为…苦恼: ~
under a mistake (delusion) 因弄错(幻想)而吃苦
头 / *lost* ~ (或 ~ *lost*) 徒劳 / *the* ~s *of
Hercules* (或 *the Herculean* ~s) 需要花巨大
精力去完成的工作 ‖~ed *a.* ①吃力的; 缓慢的:
~ed breathing 困难的呼吸 ② (文体等)不自然
的;矫揉造作的 / ~er ['leibərə] *n.* 劳动者;工
人: a farm ~er 雇农 / a long-term ~er 长工 /
a seasonal ~er 短工 / ~ing ['leibəriŋ] *a.* 劳
动的: the ~ing people 劳动人民 / ~some
['leibəsəm] *a.* 费力的,吃力的 ‖~ **camp** ①劳
动营(对犯人实行强制劳动的场所) ② 流动工人
的营地 / ~ **cost** 人工成本 / ~ **court** 劳资争议
法庭 / Labo(u)r **Day** ①五一国际劳动节 ②(美
国、加拿大的)劳动节(九月的第一个星期一) / ~
dispute 劳资争议 / ~ **exchange** ①物物交易,
交换,产品交换 ②职业介绍所;[主英](劳工部
的)劳工介绍所 / ~ **force** 劳动力: a ~ force of
two hundred 两百个劳动力 / ~ **insurance**
劳动保险 / ~ **market** 劳动力市场 / ~
movement 工人运动 / ~ **organization** 工人
组织 / '~,**saving** *a.* 节省劳力的,减轻劳动的 /
~ **union** 工会

labyrinth ['læbərinθ] *n.* ①迷宫;曲径 ②【喻】(事
情等的)错综复杂,曲折;难以摆脱的处境 ③【解】
(内耳的)迷路: bony ~ 骨迷路 / membranous
~ 膜迷路

lac [læk] *n.* ①【动】紫胶: ~ insect 紫胶虫 ②【化】
虫胶;虫漆;虫脂

lace [leis] **I** *n.* ①鞋带; 系带 ②花边,饰带,编带
③(带有装饰图案的)精细网织品,透孔织品
④(加在咖啡或茶等中的)少量烈性酒 **II** ❶ *vt.*
①缚…的带子,用带子束紧 (up) ②用带子穿过;
交叉: a landscape ~d with countless creeks 溪
流纵横的一幅自然景色 ③用花边装饰;使成彩色
条纹 ④打,鞭打 ⑤加少量烈性酒于;[喻]使有活
气,使更有风味 ❷ *vi.* 缚带子; 用带子束紧 ‖
into [口]打,鞭打; 斥骂 / ~ *sb.'s coat* [俚]鞭
打某人 ‖~d *a.* ①用带子束紧了的 ②饰有花
边的 ③(花)有彩色条纹的; (羽毛)有花边的 /
~**like** *a.* 带子般的;花边状的 / ~**ing** *n.* ①绳;
系带,鞋带 ②(加在饮料中的)少量烈性酒;增添
风味的东西 ③[口]鞭打 ‖'~-'**curtain** *a.* 模仿
中产阶级的; 渴望成为中产阶级的 / ~ **glass** 有
花边状图案的玻璃器皿 / ~ **paper** 花边纸 /
pillow 编织花边时置于膝上的垫子 / '~-**ups**
[复] *n.* [口]绳带的鞋子(或靴子) / '~**work** *n.*
【纺】网眼针织物,花边

acerate ['læsəreit] **I** *vt.* ①撕碎,割碎(软组织等) ②伤害(感情等);使烦恼 **II** ['læsərit] *a.* ①撕碎了的,割碎了的 ②【植】(叶子等)撕裂状的 ③受折磨的,受困扰的 ‖**laceration** [,læsə'reiʃən] *n.* ①撕裂,划破 ②伤口,破口 / **lacerative** *a.*

achrymose ['lækrimous] *a.* ①爱哭的;满是泪水的 ②使流泪的;悲哀的 ‖**~ly** *ad.*

ack [læk] **I** *n.* ①缺乏,不足: show a complete ~ of method 显得毫无条理 / overcome the ~ of technical data 克服技术资料的不足 ②缺少的东西;需要的东西: Logic is a conspicuous ~ in his writings. 他写的文章显然缺乏逻辑性。 **II** ❶ *vi.* 缺乏; 短少; 没有: He is ~ing in responsibility. 他不够负责。 / Nothing is ~ing for our plan. 咱们的计划不短少什么了。 / Space ~s for a detailed description of it. 篇幅有限,不能在此详细描述了。 ❷ *vt.* ①缺乏; 短少; 没有: Your statement ~s detail. 你的叙述不够详尽具体。 / It ~s 5 minutes of eight. 现在是八点缺五分。 ❷需要: What do you ~? (旧时小贩的叫喊声)你要买点什么? / **for** (或 **by, from, through**) ~ **of** 因缺乏…;因没有… / **have no ~ of** 不缺乏… / **supply the ~** 补缺

ackadaisical [,lækə'deizikəl] *a.* 懒洋洋的;没精打采的 ‖**~ly** *ad.* / **~ness** *n.*

ackey ['læki] **I** *n.* ①穿号衣的男仆 ②走狗

aconic [lə'kɔnik] *a.* ①(说话、文章等)简洁的,精练的 ②说话简短的,文章写得简洁的 ‖**~ally** *ad.*

acquer ['lækə] **I** *n.* ①(涂在黄铜等金属上的)漆 ②真漆;中国漆;日本漆 ③硝基漆,清喷漆 ④漆器 **II** *vt.* 用漆涂;使表面光洁 ‖**~er** ['lækərə] *n.* (油)漆工 / **~ing** ['lækəriŋ] *n.* ①上漆 ②漆涂层

actic ['læktik] *a.* 乳的;乳汁的;从酸乳(或乳清)中取得的: ~ acid 【化】乳酸 / ~ fermentation 【微】乳酸发酵

acy ['leisi] *a.* ①(有)花边的,(有)带子的 ②花边状的,带子状的

adder ['lædə] **I** *n.* ①梯子: a scaling ~ 云梯 / a Jack [船]木踏板绳梯 ②梯状物;阶梯;成功发迹的手段: the bottom rung of the social ~ 社会的最底层 ③[英](长统袜等上的)抽丝 **II** *vi.* (长统袜等)发生抽丝现象 ‖*kick down the ~* 过河拆桥(成功后抛弃帮忙的人) / *see through a ~* 看见显而易见的东西 ‖**~like** *a.* 梯状的 / ‖**~-back** *a.* (椅子等)背部有梯格式横档的 / **~-proof** *a.* (袜等)防抽丝的,不抽丝的 / **stitch** 梯形花样的刺绣 / ~ **truck** 装备长梯的救火车

addie ['lædi] *n.* 男孩

ade [leid] (过去式 laded, 过去分词 laded 或 laden ['leidn]) ❶ *vt.* ①装(船);装载(货物) ②舀(水等),汲取 ③塞满;把…压倒 ❷ *vi.* ①装货 ②汲取液体

aden¹ ['leidn] **I** lade 的过去分词 **II** *a.* ①装满了的;充满了的 (with): a ship ~ with chemical fertilizers 装满化肥的船 / a tree ~ with fruit 结满果子的树 / a crime-~ landlord 罪恶累累的地主 ②负了重担的;苦恼的: a ~ heart 沉重的心情

lading ['leidiŋ] *n.* ①装载;汲取 ②船货,客货 ③重量;压力 ‖*a bill of* ~ 提(货)单

ladle ['leidl] **I** *n.* 长柄勺子;【机】铸勺,铁水包: a soup ~ 汤勺 / a bulk (或 giant) ~ 大铸勺 **II** *vt.* (用勺)舀,盛 ‖~ **in** 舀进;插入 / ~ **out** 舀出;端出;提供 ‖**~ful** *n.* 一满勺

lady ['leidi] *n.* ①女士;夫人;小姐: Ladies and gentlemen! 女士们,先生们! (演说和祝酒时用语) / young ~ (称呼)小姐 ②贵妇人 ③[L-] (英国拥有某些爵位的贵族妻女的尊称)…夫人;…小姐 ④女主人(现只用于 ~ of the house 一语中) ⑤妻子;情人;情妇 ⑥[Ladies][用作单] 公共女厕所,女盥洗室 ⑦[用作定语]女性的;[谑]雌的: a ~ doctor 女医生(一般用 a woman doctor) / a ~ dog [谑]母狗 ‖*a ~ of easy virtue* 放荡的女人 / *a ~ of letters* [谑]女文学家 / *a ~ of the bedchamber* [英]宫廷女待 / *Our Lady* 【宗】圣母 / *the first ~ (of the land)* [美]第一夫人,总统夫人(或元首夫人) / *the Old Lady of Threadneedle Street* [英]英格兰银行(Bank of England)的别称 ‖**~hood** *n.* 贵妇人身分;[总称]贵妇人,女士们 / **~kin** *n.* 小贵人(常用有亲热的称呼) / **~like** *a.* ①象贵妇人的;适合于贵妇人身分的 ②(男子)带女人腔的 / **~ship** *n.* 贵妇人身分; 夫人,小姐: your (her) *Ladyship* (对家族有爵位的妇女的称呼)夫人;小姐(用 your 时是直接称呼;用 her 时是间接提及) ‖**ladies' man** = **~'s man** / **ladies' room** 公共女厕所,女盥洗室 / ~ **beetle**,~ **bird**,~ **bug** 瓢虫 / ~ **chair** 两人用手交叉搭成的座架(供抬运伤员等) / ~ **chapel** 大教堂内的圣母堂 / **Lady Day** 【宗】报喜节(三月二十五日);[英]春季结账日(三月二十五日) / **'~-'help** *n.* [英]女助(一种取酬少、在社会地位方面被认为同主妇平等的高级帮佣) / **'~-in-'waiting** *n.* [英]宫廷女侍 / ~ **killer** *n.* 专门勾引女子的人 / **~'love** *n.* 情妇 / **~'s maid** 专管梳妆的贴身女侍 / **~'s man** 喜欢在女人中间厮混的男人 / **~'s slipper** 【植】杓兰属植物,杓兰 / **'~-('s)-smock** *n.* 【植】布谷鸟剪秋罗

lag¹ [læg] **I** (lagged; lagging) ❶ *vi.* ①走得慢;落后;延迟 ②【电】滞后 ③变弱,松懈 ❷ *vt.* 落后;滞后于 **II** *n.* ①落后;迟延,延缓: This work must go forward without ~. 这项工作必须毫不迟延地进行。 / the ~ of the tide 迟潮时间 ②(一个现象和另一个相关现象中间的)相隔时间: a time ~ 时间滞差,时滞(指因和果或一个现象和另一相关现象中间的相隔时间) / the ~ between composition and publication 排字和出版之间的相隔时间 ③(指牛羊等的)落后者,掉队者 **III** *a.* 最后的 ‖**lagger** *n.* =laggard (*n.*)

lag² [læg] **I** *n.* ①桶板 ②(锅炉等的)外套,防护

套: the ~ of a boiler (cylinder) 锅炉(汽缸)的外套 **II** (lagged; lagging) *vt.* 给…加上外套

lag³ [læg] **I** (lagged; lagging) *vt.* ①[俚]把(犯人)押往监狱; 把(犯人)押送去做苦役 ②[英俚]逮捕 **II** *n.* [俚]①囚犯; 犯人; 旧犯: an old ~ 曾经多次坐牢的人, 积犯 ②徒刑期限, 苦役期限 ‖**lagger** *n.* [俚]囚犯; 旧犯

laggard ['lægəd] **I** *n.* 迟钝者; 落后者; 懒散的人 **II** *a.* 落后的; 迟缓的

lagoon, lagune [lə'guːn] *n.* 环礁湖; 咸水湖; 潟湖

laid [leid] lay¹ 的过去式和过去分词 ‖~ **out** [美俚]喝醉了的 ‖~ **paper** 直纹纸; 夫士纸

lain [lein] lie¹ 的过去分词

lair¹ [lɛə] **I** *n.* ①兽穴; 兽窝; 躲藏处 ②[英方]床 ③[英](赶牲口去市场途中用的)围栏 **II** ① *vi.* 进穴; 休息 ② *vt.* ①把…置于穴中, 给…设洞穴 ②作为…的洞穴

lair² [lɛə] [苏格兰] **I** *n.* 泥潭, 泥沼 **II** ① *vt.* 使陷入泥潭 ② *vi.* (在泥水中)打滚

laird [lɛəd] *n.* [苏格兰]地主

laissez-faire, laisser-faire ['leisei'fɛə] [法] **I** *n.* 放任主义, 不干涉主义; 自由放任 **II** *a.* 放任主义的: ~ capitalism 自由资本主义

laity ['leiiti] *n.* [the ~] [集合名词] ①俗人(以别于教士或僧侣) ②外行

lake¹ [leik] *n.* ①湖 ②(贮油或其他液体的)池 ‖*the Great Lake* 大西洋 / *the Great Lakes* 北美洲五大湖 / *the Lakes* 英国北部的湖泊区 ‖~**let** ['leiklit] *n.* 小湖 / ~ **r** *n.* ①湖鱼 ②湖轮(北美大湖上的散装货船) ‖**Lake Country, Lake District** 英国北部的湖泊区 / ~ **dweller** 湖上居民 / ~ **dwelling** (建造在木桩上的)湖上房屋 / '~**land** *n.* 湖水地区 / **Lake Poets, Lake School** 湖畔派(十八世纪末十九世纪初英国的一种消极浪漫主义诗歌流派) / **Lake Success** 成功湖(美国纽约近郊一村庄, 一九五二年以前联合国秘书处所在地, 过去人们常以成功湖作为联合国总部的代称)

lake² [leik] *n.* ①[化]色淀; 沉淀染料: ~ colours 色淀染料 / ~ oil 琥珀油 ②胭脂红

lake³ [leik] ① *vi.* 血球溶解 ② *vt.* 使(血液)发生血球溶解

lamb [læm] **I** *n.* ①羔羊, 小羊; 小羚羊 ②羔羊肉; 羔羊皮 ③羔羊般柔弱的人; (对孩子等的爱称)宝贝儿, 乖乖 ④易受骗上当者(尤指在证券交易方面) ⑤[the L-] [宗]耶稣 **II** ① *vi.* 生小羊 ② *vt.* ①生 (小羊) ②照管(产期中的母羊) ‖*as well be hanged for a sheep as (for) a* ~ 见 sheep / *like a* ~ ①驯顺地, 怯弱地 ②天真烂漫地; 容易受骗的 ‖~**kin** *n.* ①羔羊 ②(对孩子等的爱称)乖乖 / ~**like** *a.* 羔羊般的; 柔弱的; 天真烂漫的 / '~**skin** *n.* 羔羊皮 (尤指带羊毛的); 羔皮革; 羊皮纸

lame¹ [leim] **I** *a.* ①跛的, 瘸的; 残废的: go ~ 变成瘸子 / walk ~ 一瘸一拐地走 / be ~ in (或 of) one leg 一腿跛的 ②僵直而疼痛的 ③站不

住脚的; 有缺陷的: a ~ excuse 站不住脚的借口 / a ~ imitation 低劣的仿制品 ④不合诗韵的 **II** ① *vt.* ①使跛; 使残废 ②使不中用: ~ sb. power of bargaining in the negotiations 使某人在谈判中失去讨价还价的力量 ② *vi.* 跛行 ‖~ *ad.* / ~**ness** *n.* ‖'~-brain *n.* [美俚]笨蛋 ~ **duck** [俚]①[美](任期快满但没有重新当选上的)落选官员(或议员) ②残废的人; 无能的人 ③(交易所投机失败后)无力偿债的人

lame² [leim] *n.* ①(金属)薄板, 薄片 ②[复](古代护身甲上的)重迭金属片

lame³ [leim] *n.* [俚]不知内情的人; 古板守旧的人

lamé [laː'mei] *n.* [法]金银线织物

lament [lə'ment] **I** ① *vi.* 悲痛, 哀悼 ② *vt.* ①为…而悲痛, 哀悼; 痛惜: ~ this great loss 痛惜这一巨大损失 / the late ~ed 死者 ②悲叹 **II** *n.* ①悲哀的表现; 哀诉; 恸哭 ②挽歌; 悼词

lamentable ['læməntəbl] *a.* ①可悲的; 令人痛惜的 ②表现悲哀的 ③质量低的; 糟糕的: a ~ piece of acting 拙劣的表演 ‖**lamentably** *ad.*

lamentation [,læmen'teiʃən] *n.* 悲伤; 哀悼; 恸哭

lamp [læmp] *n.* ①灯: an arc ~ 弧光灯 / blackout ~ 防空灯 / a safety ~ 安全灯 / ultraviolet ~ 紫外线灯 ②[诗]日; 月; 星 ③智慧的源泉; 精神力量的来源 ④[俚]眼睛 **II** *vt.* ①照亮 ②[俚]看; 看到 ‖rub the ~ 很容易地实现自己的愿望 / smell of the ~ (苦心写成但不太自然的作品等)有熬夜用功的迹象 / the Lamp of Phoebus [诗]太阳 / the ~s of heaven 明亮的天体(包括太阳、月亮、星星) ‖~**less** *a.* 无灯的; 未点灯的 ‖'~**black** *n.* 灯黑, 灯烟 / '~ ,chimney *n.* (煤油灯用)玻璃灯罩 / '~ holde (插电灯泡的)灯座 / '~**house** *n.* (仪器上的)光源 / '~**light** *n.* 灯光 / '~**post** *n.* 灯杆, 路灯柱 / '~**shade** *n.* 灯罩 / '~**stand** *n.* 灯台

lampoon [læm'puːn] **I** *n.* ①(针对个人的)强烈的讽刺文 ②略带挖苦性的作品 **II** *vt.* 用讽刺抨击; 嘲讽 ‖~**er**, ~**ist** *n.* 讽刺作家

lance [laːns] **I** *n.* ①旗杆矛, 长矛 ②长矛骑兵 ③矛状的器具; 捕鲸枪 ④[医]柳叶刀, 双刃小刀 **II** ① *vt.* ①用矛刺穿 ②[医]用柳叶刀割开 ③投, 掷 ② *vi.* 急速前进 ‖break a ~ with sb. 和某人交锋; 和某人争论 ‖~**r** *n.* 使用矛的骑兵 ‖~ **corporal** (英国陆军中的)一等兵 / ~ **fis** 【动】=launce / ~ **sergeant** (英国陆军中的)代理中士

lancet ['laːnsit] *n.* ①[医]刺血针; 柳叶刀; 口针 ②[建]矢状饰, 锐尖窗

land [lænd] **I** *n.* ①陆地, 地面: go by ~ 从陆路去 / a ~ campaign 陆战 / a ~ force 地面部队 ②土地; 田地: public (collective) ownership ~ 土地公有(集体所有)制 / open up barre ~ 开荒 / work on the ~ 务农 ③国土, 国家: come home from foreign ~s 从外国归来 ④地带; 境界: no man's ~ 无主地 / [军]真空地带, 无人地带 / the ~ of dreams 梦境 ⑤地

皮;[复]地产,田产 ⑥(枪炮的)阳堂线 ⑦[美][L-](用于惊叹句)老天爷 (=Lord) **II ❶** *vt.* ① 使上岸,使登陆;使(飞机等)降落: ～ the troops at a beachhead 把部队送上滩头阵地 / ～ an aeroplane 使飞机降落 (于地面或水面) ② 使到达,把…送到: The truck ～ed me at the construction site. 卡车把我送到工地。③ 使陷入,处于: ～ oneself in a passive position 使自己处于被动地位 ④把(鱼)捕上岸(或船) ⑤[口]弄到,捞到 ⑥[口]打: ～ sb. one (或 a blow) in the eye 一拳打在某人眼睛上 **❷** *vi.* ①上岸;登陆;降落 ②到达;歇脚;(船)靠岸: ～ (up) at a hotel 在旅馆歇脚 / ~ **flowing with milk and honey** [古]富饶的地方;鱼米之乡 / clear ～ 清除土地上的树木等(以备耕种) / clear the ～ (船只)离岸出海 / Good ～! [美口]天哪! / how the ～ lies 情况如何: find out how the ～ lies 弄清情况 / Land ho! 看到陆地啦! (海员在航行中见到陆地时发出的欣喜叫喊) / ~ on [口]猛烈抨击 / lay (或 shut in) the ～ (船离陆地渐远时,似觉陆地下沉)看不见陆地 / lie along the ～ 沿岸航行 / make ～ 看见陆地,到岸 / see ～ ①看到陆地 ②行将达到目的 / The ～ knows! [美口]天知道! / the ～ o' (或 of) cakes 苏格兰(因居民多吃燕麦饼而得名) / the Land (或 ～) of Promise [喻]希望之乡(基督教《圣经》中上帝赐给亚伯拉罕的 Canaan 迦南地方) / the ～ of the leal 天国 / the ～ of the living 人世,现世 / the never-never ～ 幻想中的地方 ‖～less *a.* 无地的 ‖～ agent 地产经理人,地产商;[英]田产管理(人) / '～-air *a.*【军】①地对空的 ②陆空联合的 / '～ bank (经营土地抵押业务的) 土地银行 / '～-based *a.* 以地面为基地的;岸基的 / ～ breeze 陆风 (指从陆地吹向海洋的风) / crab 陆栖蟹 / '～fall *n.* ①【军】着陆 ②(航程中)第一次见陆地(或靠岸);初见的陆地: a good (bad) ～fall 按(未按)预计时间的靠岸 / '～form *n.* 地形 / ～ girl [英]战时代替男子从事农业劳动的妇女 / '～-,grabber *n.* 抢土地者 / ～ grant 政府的赠与地 / '～,holder *n.* ①土地所有者 ②土地租用人 / '～-,jobber *n.* [英]地产投机商;地皮掮客 / '～,lady *n.* ①女房东;(旅馆等的)女店主 ②女地主 / ～ law [常用复]土地法 / '～line *n.* 陆上通讯(或运输)线 / '～locked *a.* (海湾、港口等)为陆地围住的;(鱼等)为栅栏围住的 / '～lord *n.* ①地主 ②房东;(旅馆等的)店主 / '～lordism ['lændlɔ:dizəm] *n.* 地主所有制 / '～,lubber *n.* ①没有出过海的人;不懂航海的人 ②(水手用语)外行水手 / '～mark *n.* ①界标 ②【海】陆上明显标志 ③(历史上的)里程碑 / '～mass *n.* 大片陆地 / ～ mine ①地雷 ②第二次世界大战中用降落伞投下的薄壳炸弹 / '～,owner *n.* 地主;土地所有者 / ～ plaster (用作肥料的)石膏粉 / '～-'poor *a.* 持有大量无利可图的土地因而周转不灵、经济困难的

power ①陆军力量,地面力量 ②陆军强国 / ～ **reform** 土地改革 / ～'s **end** ①(一国或一地方的)末端地区 ②[L- E-]英国最西端的小村 / ～ **service** 陆军兵役 / ～ **shark** ①向上岸水手行骗的人 ②抢土地者 / '～**slide** *n.* ①山崩;崩塌;塌方 ②压倒的优胜(尤指竞选中选票的一面倒) / '～**slip** *n.* [英]山崩;崩塌;塌方 / ～ **swell** 近岸巨浪 / ～ **tie**【建】着地拉杆 / '～,**waiter** *n.* (英国的)海关税务检查人员 / '～**wash** *n.* ①波浪对海岸的冲击 ② 高潮线 / ～ **wind** =～ breeze / '～,**worker** *n.* 农夫

landed ['lændid] *a.* ①有地的: the ～ class 地主阶级 ②地皮的;不动产的: ～ property 地产

landing ['lændiŋ] *n.* ①上岸,登陆;着陆;降落: effect a soft ～【字】作软着陆 / an emergency ～ 紧急着陆 / Happy ～! 祝你平安! (向上飞机的人告别时说的话) ②码头上装卸货物(或旅客上下)的地方 ③楼梯平台 ④【无】(电子的)沉陷;沉淀 ‖～ craft 登陆艇 / ～ field (飞机等的)着陆场 / ～ force 登陆部队 / ～ gear【空】起落装置,起落架 / ～ net 抄网(用以抄取上钩的鱼等) / ～ party 登陆(分遣)队 / ～ ship 登陆舰 / ～ skid【空】起落橇 / ～ speed 最低着陆速度;着陆速度 / ～ stage 趸船;浮码头 / ～ strip【空】起落跑道;可着陆地区 / ～ tee,～ T【空】(指示飞机着陆的) T 形着陆标识,T 字布

landscape ['lændskeip] **I** *n.* ①(一张)风景画;风景绘画;风景摄影 ②风景,景色 ③地形 ④前景展望 **II ❶** *vt.* 使自然美化(如加铺草地、加栽树木等) **❷** *vi.* 从事自然美化工作 ‖**landscapist** *n.* 风景画家 ‖～ **architect** 以美化环境景色为业的人 / ～ **gardener** 园艺美化专家

lane [lein] *n.* ①狭路;小巷(有时可指我国的里弄) ②(人群间的)通路 ③规定的单向行车道;航道: the inside (outside) ～ 内(外)车道 ④【体】跑道 ‖*It is a long ～ that has no turning.* [谚]路必有弯。(指事情必有转机,常用于安慰灰心丧气的人等场合) / *the Lane* 伦敦的特鲁利 (Drury) 街戏院区 / *the red* ~ 喉咙

language ['læŋgwidʒ] *n.* ①语言;语言课程: learn (master) a foreign ～ 学习(掌握)一门外语 / the English ～ 英语 / the ～ of diplomacy 外交词令 / The idea, in simple ～, is that …. 这个主意,说得简单一点,无非是… ② 使用语言的能力(或风格): a person with an easy flow of ～ 健谈的人,口若悬河的人 ③骂人的话 (=bad) ④【自】(机器)代码 ‖*a dead* ～ 死语言(如古希腊语) / *finger* ～ (聋哑人用的)手势语 / *the ～ of flowers* 花的语言(如以 lily (百合)象征纯洁等) / *legal* ～ 法律用语 / *a living* ～ (正在使用中的)活语言 / *sign* (或 *gesture*) ～ 手势语 / *spoken* (或 *oral*) ～ 口语 / *strong* ～ 强烈的言词,骂人话 / *written* ～ 书面语 / *speak the same* ～ 说同样的语言;有共同的信仰和观点 ‖～ **master** 语言教师(尤指外国语教师)

languish ['læŋgwiʃ] ***vi.*** ①变得衰弱无力；失去活力；(植物等)雕萎：Then the conversation ~*ed*. 接着，谈话就冷下来了。②焦思，因渴望而苦恼(*for*) ③作出惹人爱怜的倦态(或感伤的样子) ‖**~ment** ***n.***

languor ['læŋgə] ***n.*** ①衰弱无力；(精神上的)消沉 ②[常用复]柔情 ③(气候、气氛等引起的)倦怠，沉闷：the ~ of a summer day 夏日令人昏昏欲睡的感觉 ‖**~ous** ['læŋgərəs] ***a.***

lank [læŋk] ***a.*** ①细长的；瘦的；(草)稀少的 ②(头发)平直的，不鬈的

lanky ['læŋki] ***a.*** 过分瘦长的，瘦长得难看的 ‖**lankily** ***ad.*** / **lankiness** ***n.***

lantern ['læntən] **I** ***n.*** ①提灯；灯笼：a signal ~ 信号灯，号志灯 ②灯塔上的灯室 ③【建】(灯笼式的)天窗 ④幻灯 **II** ***vt.*** ①给…装上提灯 ②把…吊在街灯柱上处死 ‖***the parish*** ~ [英方]月亮 ‖~ **fly**【动】白蜡虫 / ~ **jaw** 突出的下巴；瘦长的下巴 / '**~-jawed** ***a.*** 下巴突出的；下巴瘦长的，双颊深陷的 / ~ **pinion** 灯笼式小齿轮 / ~ **slide** 幻灯片

lanyard ['lænjəd] ***n.*** ①船上系物的短绳 ②水手套在颈上的系刀(或系哨子)小绳；勋带 ③【军】(发射火炮等用的)拉火绳

lap[1] [læp] **I** ***n.*** ①(衣服的)下摆；裙兜，衣兜 ②(人坐着时)腰以下及大腿的前面部分：hold a child in (或 on) one's ~ 把孩子抱在膝上 ③山坳：a reservoir built in the ~ of a mountain 建造在山坳中的水库 ④互搭；搭接 ⑤重迭部分；重迭量；【机】余面 ⑥(滚筒上绳索的)一圈；【纺】棉卷，毛卷 ⑦(跑道的)一圈；一段行程；工作阶段：He overtook all the other runners on the last ~. 他在跑最后一圈时超过了所有别的运动员。/ the first hundred-kilometre ~ of the march 行军的第一段一百公里路程 ⑧(磨玻璃、金属等用的)磨盘 ⑨掌管，掌握：drop (或 dump) the whole thing in (或 into) sb.'s ~ 把事情一古脑儿推在某人身上 / Everything falls into his ~. 他事事如意。**II** (lapped; lapping) ❶ ***vt.*** ①用…包住；包住；(环境等)包围：~ a bandage round a wrist (或 ~ a wrist with a bandage) 用纱布包扎手腕 / be *lapped* in luxury 生活奢侈 ②把…抱在膝上；[喻]爱护地怀抱着… ③【纺】使(梳棉后的棉花)成卷 ④使形成部分重迭；部分重迭于…之上：~ roof-slates 迭盖石板瓦 / The second board ~*s* the first. 第二块木板部分迭盖在第一块上。⑤(赛跑中)比(某人)领先一圈(或几圈)；跑完…的一圈 ⑥用磨盘磨(玻璃、金属等) ❷ ***vi.*** ①被包住；围起来：The rough edges must ~ under. 毛边必须包没。②部分重迭；搭接；并排 ‖***in Fortune's*** ~ 走运，运气好 / ***in the ~ of luxury*** 在奢侈环境中 / ***in the ~ of the gods*** 在神的掌管之中，(结果)难以预料 / ***throw oneself into the ~ of*** 投入…的怀抱；投靠 ‖**~ful** ***n.*** 一满兜 ‖'**~dog** ***n.*** 叭儿狗 / ~ **joint** 互搭接头；搭接缝 / ~ **robe** 乘车时盖在膝上保暖用的毯子 / '**~stone** ***n.*** 皮匠放在膝盖上的垫石(或垫铁) / '**~-strap** ***n.*** (飞机座位上用来缚住大腿部的)安全带

lap[2] [læp] **I** (lapped; lapping) ❶ ***vt.*** ①舐；舐食(液质食物)(*up*) ②[口]贪婪地喝(或吃)；爱听(恭维等)(*up, down*) ③(波浪)拍打，泼溅：The sea ~*s* the shore. 波浪拍打海岸。❷ ***vi.*** ①舐 ②(波浪)拍打，泼溅：Waves *lapped against* the sides of the ship. 波浪拍打着船舷。/ ~ *at* the edge of sth. 拍打某物的边缘；稍稍打击着某物 **II** ***n.*** ①舐；一次舐食的分量：take a ~ *at* 舐…一下，稍为吃掉一点… ②波浪拍打声 ③[俚]淡饮料

lapel [lə'pel] ***n.*** (西服上衣延及胸前的)翻领

lapse [læps] **I** ***n.*** ①失误，小错：a ~ of the tongue (pen) 口(笔)误 / a ~ of memory 记错 / a ~ of attention 一时疏忽 ②跌落，下降(尤指气温、气压等) ③失检；偏离：a ~ from respectability 有失体面 ④(时间的)流逝，间隔：with the ~ of time 随着时间的过去 / after a ~ of ten years 事隔十年之后 ⑤(因未履行义务等而引起的)权利终止；权利失效 **II** ❶ ***vi.*** ①失检；背离(*from*) ②堕入，陷入：~ into unconsciousness 晕过去 / ~ backward 落后 ③(时间)流逝 ④(权利、任期等)终止；失效；【律】(因失效而)转归(*to*)：My sub is due to ~ at the end of October. 我的订阅期到十月底为止。⑤消失，终止：Then the conversation ~*d*. 接着谈话就停止了。❷ ***vt.*** 使失效 ‖~ **rate**【气】递减率

larceny ['lɑːsni] ***n.*** ①偷窃 ②非法侵占财产

larch [lɑːtʃ] ***n.*** ①【植】落叶松 ②落叶松木

lard [lɑːd] **I** ***n.*** 猪油 **II** ***vt.*** ①涂油于，搽油于 ②(烹调前)嵌肥猪肉(或腌肉片)于…中 ③加饰物于；润色(文章、谈话等)：a speech ~*ed with* compliments 一篇充满赞词的讲演 ‖'**~-,bucket** ***n.*** [美俚]胖子 / ~ **fruit**【植】猪油果(也称油渣果，油瓜；产于我国华南地区及越南、印度等地) / '**~-head** ***n.*** [美俚]蠢人

larder ['lɑːdə] ***n.*** ①家中藏肉(或其他食物)的地方 ②家中贮藏的食品

large [lɑːdʒ] **I** ***a.*** ①大的，巨大的：a ~ building 巨大的建筑物 / a ~ family 子女多的家庭 / a ~ population 人口众多 / ~ and small sizes 大小尺寸 ②(见解等)广博的，开阔的；(权限等)广泛的：take a ~ view 持有开阔的见解 / have a ~ discretion in settling sth. 在处理某事时有广泛的决定权 ③[古](心胸等)宽广的，宽宏大量的，慷慨的 ④夸大的：~ talk 大话 ⑤(艺术风格)奔放的，粗犷有力的 ⑥【海】(风)顺的 **II** ***ad.*** ①大，大大地 ②夸大地：talk ~ 说大话 ③【海】顺风地 **III** ***n.*** 大(一般只用于 at ~ 和 in (the) ~ 等习语中) ‖***as ~ as life*** ①与原物一般大小 ②[口]亲自；千真万确：He is here *as ~ as life*. 喏，他不明明就在这儿吗？/ ***at*** ~ ①未被捕；逍遥自在地：cattle grazing *at* ~ 放在外面吃草的牛 ②详尽地：talk *at* ~ 详谈 ③普遍的，一般

的;[美]代表整个州的: society (the world) at ~ 整个社会(世界) / a congressman-at-~ [美]全州选出的议员 ④ 笼统地;无的放矢地: preliminary arrangements made at ~ 笼统地作出的初步安排 ⑤ 无目的地: an ambassador-at-~ 无任所大使 / **by and ~** 见 **by** / **in (the) ~** ①大规模地 ②一般地 / **sail ~** 顺风航行 ‖**~ness** *n*. ‖**'~-'handed** *a*. 慷慨的,大方的 / **'~'hearted** *a*. 慷慨的;富于同情心的 / **'~-'minded** *a*. 度量大的;心胸开阔的;思想开通的 / **'~-'scale** *a*. ①大规模的;大型的 ②(地图等)大比例的

argely ['lɑːdʒli] *ad*. ① 大量地: build ~ 大兴土木 ② 主要地: This mistake is ~ due to my carelessness. 这个错误主要是由于我的粗心大意。

ark[1] [lɑːk] *n*.【动】百灵科鸣禽(如云雀) ‖*If the sky falls we shall catch ~s*. 见 **sky** / **rise (或 be up) with the ~** 早起

ark[2] [lɑːk] **I ❶** *vi*. ① 嬉耍,闹着玩: Stop ~*ing* about! 别闹着玩了! ② 骑马越野 **❷** *vt*. ① 愚弄,取笑 ② 骑(马)越野;(骑着马)跳栏 **II** *n*. 嬉耍,玩乐: What a ~! 真有趣! / He said it only for a ~. 他只是说着玩的。 / **have a ~** 玩乐一阵 / **be on a ~** 在闹着玩儿

arva ['lɑːvə] ([复] larvae ['lɑːviː] 或 larvas) *n*.【动】幼虫;幼体: The tadpole is the ~ of the frog. 蝌蚪是蛙的幼体。‖**~l** *a*. ①幼虫的;幼体的 ②幼虫形的;幼体形的

arynx ['læriŋks] ([复] larynges [lə'rindʒiːz] 或 larynxes) *n*.【解】喉

ascivious [lə'siviəs] *a*. ① 好色的;淫荡的 ② 挑动情欲的 ‖**~ly** *ad*. / **~ness** *n*.

ash[1] [læʃ] **I** *n*. ① 鞭打;抽打;突然、猛烈的一击;[the ~] 鞭笞刑罚 ② 鞭子(尤指抽打部分) ③ 责骂,讽刺;尖锐的话,严厉的批评 ④ 眼睫毛 **II ❶** *vt*. ① 鞭打;打 ② 急伸(手、脚)、(动物)猛烈甩动(尾巴等) ③(波浪等)冲击;使(雨水等)急打: The waves ~ed the white cliffs. 波浪冲击着白色的峭壁。 ④ 痛斥;讽刺;嘲笑,挖苦 ⑤ 激使,煽动: ~ sb. into a fury 激得某人大怒 **❷** *vi*. ①猛烈地甩;(雨水、波浪等)冲击: The lion's tail ~ed back and forth. 狮子的尾巴甩来甩去。 ②用鞭打;猛打 ③痛骂 ‖**~ out** ①痛打 ②痛斥: ~ out into strong language 破口大骂起来 ‖**~er** *n*. ①鞭打者;痛斥者 ②[英方]冲过堰的水;堰,堰下水塘 / **~ing** *n*. ① 鞭打 ② 痛斥;非难 / **~ings** [复] *n*. [英]大量,许多(of)

ash[2] [læʃ] *vt*. 用缆(或链等)捆绑 ‖**~ing** *n*. ① 捆绑 ②捆绑用的绳子 ‖**~-up** *n*. ①临时凑成的东西 ② 装置;计划,安排

ass [læs] *n*. ①少女,小姑娘 ②情侣 ③[苏格兰]女佣

assitude ['læsitjuːd] *n*. ① 疲乏;无力 ② 厌倦,无精打采

asso ['læsəu] **I** ([复] lasso(e)s) *n*. (捕捉野马等用的)套索 **II** *vt*. 用套索捕捉

last[1] [lɑːst] **I** *a*. ① 最后的; 唯一剩下的 ②临终的 ③ 最近过去的,紧接前面的: ~ night 昨晚 / ~ week (month) 上星期(月) / ~ year 去年 / ~ Tuesday (或 on Tuesday ~) 刚过去的星期二 / ~ September (或 in September ~) 刚过去的九月 / this day ~ year 去年今日 / in the ~ few months 在最近几个月里 / the night before ~ 前晚 / the ~ time I saw him 我上次看到他的时候 / He did each new job better than the ~. 他每做一件新的工作都比上一件做得更好。④ 极少可能的;最不适合的: He would be the ~ man to say such things. 他决不会说这种话。/ the ~ thing sb. will do 某人最不愿意干的事情 ⑤结论性的;权威性的: the ~ explanation of 关于…的结论性的解释 ⑥极端的: a question of the ~ importance 极端重要的问题 ⑦最新式的;最时髦的: the ~ thing in electric fans 最新式的电扇 ⑧最槽糕的,最坏的: the ~ crime 最恶劣的罪行 ⑨[加强语气用]每一的: every ~ square inch of fertile soil 每一平方时的沃土 **II** *ad*. ①最后: speak ~ at a meeting 在会上最后发言 / Last came the procession of the athletes. 最后走过来的是运动员队伍。②上一次,最近一次: When did you see him ~? 你最近一次见到他是什么时候? ③最后(一点): Last, a few words about our plan for the next week. 最后,谈谈我们下星期的计划。**III** *n*. ①最后;末尾;临终: hold on to (或 till) the ~ 坚持到最后 / He came back the ~ of March. 他于三月底回来。/ I didn't hear the ~ of his report. 我没有听到他报告的结尾部分。② 最后的人(或东西): The ~ out will please shut the door. 最后出去的人请关门。/ the ~ of the southward wild geese 最后一批南飞的雁群 / I received your ~ in May. 我是在五月份收到你最后一封信的。 ③ (指动作的)最后一次: look one's ~ at 朝…看最后一眼 ‖**at (long) ~** 终于 / **breathe one's ~** 断气,死 / **hear the ~ of** 最后一次听到…: You'll never *hear the ~ of* this. 这件事你可得听啦! (指一件不会有个完的) / **but not least** 最后但并不是最不重要的(一点) / **but one (two)** 倒数第二(第三) / **on one's ~ legs** 见 **leg** / **see the ~ of** 最后一次看到…,再也不见到… ‖**~ly** *ad*. 最后 ‖**~ day**【宗】最后审判日,世界末日 / **~ ditch** 最后的防御壕 / **'~=-ditch** *a*. 已无后退余地的,拼死的 / **~ hurrah** 最后的努力 / **Last Judg(e)ment**【宗】上帝的最后审判(日) / **'~=-'minute** *a*. 最后一分钟的,紧急关头的 / **~ sleep** 长眠,死 / **~ straw** (一系列重压、打击中)终于使人不能忍受的最后一击;终于使人不支而垮下的因素 / **Last Supper**【宗】耶稣及其十二门徒的最后晚餐 / **~ word** ①最后一句话;最后决定权;决定性的说明,定论: Who has (或 says) the ~ *word* in this matter? 这件事情谁说了算? ②(同类事物中)最新型式,最先进品种

last[2] [lɑːst] **❶** *vi*. 持续;支持;耐久: The performance ~*ed* two hours. 演出持续了两小时。 / Can you ~ *out*? It's ten *li* yet. 你能坚持吗？还有十里路要走呢。 / This cloth ~*s* well. 这种布很耐穿。 ❷ *vt.* 够…之用，使得以维持下去；经受住: enough provisions to ~ sb. a whole month 足够维持某人整整一个月的食物 / The patient ~*ed* (*out*) the attack. 病人经受住了这场(疾病的)发作。

last³ [lɑ:st] **I** *n.* 鞋楦头 **II** *vt.* 楦(鞋) ‖*stick to one's* ~ 不去管自己不懂的事；做自己分内的事

last⁴ [lɑ:st] *n.* ① 重量单位(因商品不同而异，一般在四千磅上下) ② (英国)谷物容量单位 (=80 蒲式耳) ③ 鲱鱼的计量单位

lasting ['lɑ:stiŋ] **I** *a.* 持久的；耐久的: a ~ friendship 持久的友谊 **II** *n.* 厚实斜纹织物 ‖~*ly ad.* / ~*ness n.*

latch¹ [lætʃ] **I** *n.* ①闩；门闩；窗闩: The door is on the ~. 门上着闩。②碰锁，弹簧锁 **II** ❶ *vt.* 用闩把…闩上；用碰锁把…锁上 ❷ *vi.* 闩上；用碰锁锁上: Will the door ~? 门锁得上吗？ ‖~*key n.* 弹簧锁钥匙；前门钥匙

latch² [lætʃ] *vi.* 抓住；占有；理解 (*on, onto*)

late [leit] **I** *a.* ①迟的: He is never ~ for work (school). 他上班(上学)从不迟到。/ I was ten minutes ~. 我迟到了十分钟。②晚的；晚期的: at a ~ hour 在很晚的时刻 / a week ~*r* 一星期后 / in the ~ afternoon 在下午较晚的时候，傍晚 / in the ~ sixties 六十年代后期 / ~ dinner 晚正餐(别于中午吃的正餐) / a ~ worker 通常工作到很晚的人 / a ~ food store 打烊很晚的食品店 / cater to (the needs of) ~ customers 满足晚来顾客的需要 / We favour ~ marriage. 我们提倡晚婚。/ the ~ rice 晚稻 ③新近的: the ~ developments of science 科学的新发展 ④已故的；去世不久的⑤前任的；不久前才卸任的 **II** *ad.* ①迟: come to work early and leave off ~ 早上工，迟下班 ②晚；在晚期: work ~ into the night 工作至深夜 / ~ in autumn 在深秋 ③最近；不久前: I saw him as ~ as yesterday. 直到昨天我还看见过他。‖*at the ~st* 最迟 / *Better ~ than never.* [谚]迟做总比不做好。/ *early and ~* 从早到晚 / *early or ~* (= *sooner or ~r*) / *It is never too ~ to mend.* [谚]改过不嫌晚。/ *keep ~ hours* 晚睡晚起 / ~*r on* [作状语用]以后，下回 / *no ~r than* 不迟于… / *of ~* 近来，最近: He has made great progress *of* ~. 近来他进步很大。/ *of ~ years* 近年来 / *See you ~.* 再见! / *sit up* ~ 深夜不睡 ‖~*ness n.* ‖~ *fee* [英]过时附加费(指在邮局规定时间之后投递邮件时所付的) / **Late Greek** 从二世纪末至六世纪所用的希腊语(尤指书面语) / '~-,**model** *a.* 新型的

lately ['leitli] *ad.* 最近，不久前: Have you seen them ~? 你最近见到过他们吗？/ It is only (或 just) ~ that I got a copy of it. 最近我才弄到一份。/ He stayed there ~ as October

of last year. 他在那儿呆到去年十月。

latent ['leitənt] **I** *a.* 潜伏的，潜在的，隐而不见的: ~ bud 【植】潜伏芽，休眠芽 / ~ force 潜力 / ~ heat 【物】潜热 / ~ period 【医】潜伏期 **II** *n.* 隐约的指印，潜指印 ‖~*ly ad.*

lateral ['lætərəl] **I** *a.* ①侧面的；旁边的；横(向)的: ~ action 【军】侧翼推进 / a ~ branch (of a family) (一个家族的)旁系 ②【语】(舌)边音的 **II** *n.* ①位于侧面的东西；侧向生长的东西 ②【电】支线 ③【矿】走向平巷 ④【建】横向排水沟 ⑤【语】(舌)边音 ‖~*ly ad.*

laterite ['lætərait] *n.* 红土；砖红壤

latex ['leiteks] ([复] latices ['lætisi:z] 或 latexes) *n.* 【植】乳液；胶乳；橡浆

lath [lɑ:θ] **I** ([复] lath(s)) *n.* 【建】板条 **II** *vt.* 用板条覆盖；给…用板条衬里 ‖*as thin as a* ~ 骨瘦如柴

lathe [leið] **I** *n.* 车床；镟床 (=turning-~): an automatic turret ~ 自动六角车床 / a boring ~ 镗床 / a programme-controlled vertical ~ 程序控制立式车床 / a tool-maker ~ 工具车床 / a universal ~ 万能车床 **II** *vt.* 用车床加工

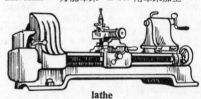

lathe

lather ['lɑ:ðə] **I** *n.* ①(肥皂水等的)泡沫 ②(马等的)汗沫 ③ [喻] 激动；焦躁 **II** ❶ *vt.* ①在…上涂以皂沫；以泡沫布满 ②[俚]狠狠地打 ❷ *vi.* 形成皂沫；起泡沫

Latin ['lætin] **I** *a.* ①拉丁的；拉丁语的；拉丁语系的: the ~ peoples 拉丁系民族(指法兰西、西班牙、意大利等国的民族) ②天主教的(尤用以与东正教相区别) **II** *n.* ①拉丁语；拉丁字母表: old ~ 约公元前七十五年以前的拉丁语 / classical ~ (约从公元前七十五年至公元一七五年的)古典拉丁语 / late ~ 约从公元一七五年至六○○年的拉丁语 / medieval ~ (约从公元六○○年至一五○○年的)中古拉丁语 / modern ~ (从公元一五○○年以来的)现代拉丁语 ②拉丁人(尤指拉丁美洲人)；古罗马人 ③天主教徒 ‖*dog* ~ 不正规的拉丁语 / *silver* ~ "白银时代"的拉丁语(指约从公元十四世纪至一三八年间所用的) / *thieves'* ~ 盗贼的黑话 ‖~ **America** 拉丁美洲 / '~-A'merican *a.* 拉丁美洲的 / ~ **American** 拉丁美洲人 / ~ **Church** 以拉丁语作礼拜仪式的天主教；罗马天主教 / ~ **Quarter** 拉丁区(位于巴黎塞纳河南面，是大学生与艺术家群集之处) / ~ **school**, ~ **grammar school** (十三世纪在欧洲开始出现的)拉丁学校(以拉丁语及希腊语为主科的文科中学，作为大学的预科)

atitude ['lætitju:d] *n.* ①纬度: forty degrees north (south) ~ 北纬(南纬)四十度 ②【天】黄纬 ③[复] 地方，地区 (尤指从温度上而言): high (low) ~s 高(低)纬度地方，离赤道远(近)的地方 ④[罕] 宽度;[古] 范围;幅度 ⑤(言论、行动等的)自由: allow sb. more ~ in the matter 让某人在处理该事时有更多的自由 ⑥ 胶片曝光的时限 ‖**latitudinal** [,læti'tju:dinl] *a.*

atrine [lə'tri:n] *n.* (沟形或坑形的)厕所; 公共厕所

atter ['lætə] *a.* ①后面的;后半的;末了的: the ~ half of the month 后半月，下半月 / the ~ part of the year 一年中的后一段时期 ②(两者中)后者的: Of the two the ~ is far better than the former. 两者中后者比前者好得多。③最近的;现今的: in these ~ days 在最近的这些日子里，现今 ‖**ly** *ad.* [罕]后来;近来 ‖**~-day** *a.* 近代的;现代的

attice ['lætis] **I** *n.* ①格子 ②【物】点阵;网络: crystal ~ 晶体点阵，晶格 ③【建】格构: ~ girder 格构(大)梁，花格(大)梁 / ~ window 格构窗，花格窗 **II** *vt.* ①把…制成格子状 ②用格子(或格子花样)覆盖(或装饰) ‖**~d** *a.* 制成格子状的;装有格子的 ‖**~work** *n.* ①格子 ②[集合名词] 格子;格子细工

aud [lɔ:d] **I** *n.* ① 赞美，称赞; 赞美歌，颂歌 ②[Lauds] [用作单或复](天主教)早祷的赞美歌 **II** *vt.* 赞美，称赞: ~ sb. to the skies 把某人捧上天

augh [lɑ:f] **I** ❶ *vi.* ①(大)笑;发笑: The children are jumping and ~ing. 孩子们边跳边笑。/ His eyes are ~ing. 他的眼里露出笑意。②(山川、草木等)呈现欢欣景象: Green pines ~ in the breeze. 青松迎风欢笑。❷ *vt.* ① 以笑表示: He ~ed his consent. 他笑着表示同意。② 笑得使…: ~ oneself to death 笑得要死 / The child ~ed his mother into a better humour. 孩子笑得使妈妈的心情好起来了。**II** *n.* ① 笑;笑声: break into a ~ 突然笑起来 / raise a ~ 引起一阵笑声 / laugh a hearty ~ 放声大笑 ② 引人发笑的事情: What a ~ to say that! 真可笑，竟说出这种话来! ③ 嘲笑;[复]玩笑: give sb. the ~ for his foolishness 因为某人的愚蠢行为而嘲笑他 / beat sb. for ~s 为了取乐而打某人一顿 ‖**have the last ~** 笑在最后，获得最后胜利 / **have (或 get) the ~ of sb.** 反驳某人 (指使嘲笑别人的某人反受嘲笑) / **have the ~ on one's side** (先被人笑)这回轮到自己来笑别人 / **He ~s best who ~s last.** [谚]谁笑在最后，谁笑得最好。(意为不要高兴得太早或不要在稍受挫折时即认为事已无望) / **~ and grow fat** 心宽体胖 / **~ at** ①因…而发笑: ~ at a joke 听了笑话而发笑 ②嘲笑;取笑: Don't ~ at him. 别嘲笑他。③ 漠视，把…付诸一笑 / **~ away** 用笑来驱除(烦闷、恐惧等);笑着消磨(时间)等 / **~ down** 用笑声来打断(演讲者等);用笑

声来拒绝(建议等) / **~ in (或 up) one's sleeve** 暗暗发笑，窃笑 / **~ in sb.'s face** 当面嘲笑某人，公然蔑视某人 / **~ off** 用笑摆脱(困境等);对…一笑置之 / **~ on (或 out of) the wrong (或 other) side of one's mouth (或 face)** 转喜为忧;哭 / **~ out of court** 对…一笑置之 / **~ over** 笑着谈论: ~ over a letter 笑着谈论一封信 / **the holy ~** 狂笑;歇斯底里的笑

laughable ['lɑ:fəbl] *a.* 可笑的;有趣的 ‖**laughably** *ad.*

laughing ['lɑ:fiŋ] **I** *a.* 笑的，带着笑的; 可笑的: a ~ face 笑脸 / It's no ~ matter. 这可不是闹着玩的事。**II** *n.* 笑: hold one's ~ 忍住笑 ‖**~ly** *ad.* ‖**~ gas** 【化】笑气 / **~ hyena** 【动】斑狼，笑狼 / **~ jackass** 【动】笑鸠 / '**~stock** *n.* 笑柄

laughter ['lɑ:ftə] *n.* ①笑;笑声: roar with ~ 哄笑 / burst into ~ 哈哈大笑起来 ②[古]好笑的事情 ‖**Homeric ~** 放声大笑(原指如荷马史诗中诸神的大笑)

launch[1] [lɔ:ntʃ] **I** ❶ *vt.* ①发射;投掷: ~ a man-made satellite 发射人造卫星 ②使(船)下水 ③发动(战争等);开展(运动、斗争等) ④发出(命令等);提出(抗议等);施以(打击、谩骂等): ~ threats against sb. 对某人发出威胁 ⑤ 开办，发起;使踏上社会自立;使开始从事: ~ a new enterprise 开办新企业 / ~ sb. in (或 into) business 使人进入商界 ❷ *vi.* ① 起飞;(船)下水 ② 投入 (into): ~ into a strong rebuke 作激烈的斥责 ③ 着手进行，开始 (on, upon) **II** *n.* 发射;(船)下水 ‖**~ out** ①(船)下水 ② 开始新的事情 ③大肆挥霍 ④大肆谴责;大讲，详述 / **~ out into** 开始从事，着手进行: ~ out into a series of new experiments 着手进行一系列新的实验 / **~ out into expense (或 extravagance)** 开始大肆挥霍 ‖**~er** *n.* 发射器，弹射器，发射装置，起动装置: a guided missile ~er 导弹发射器 / a grenade ~er 掷弹筒 ‖**~ pad** (火箭等的)发射台 / **~ vehicle** 活动发射装置;运载火箭 / **~ window** (为完成特定任务而发射火箭或宇宙飞船时的)发射时限

launch[2] [lɔ:ntʃ] *n.* 汽艇，游艇: a motor ~ 摩托艇

launching ['lɔ:ntʃiŋ] *n.* ①发射 ② 船下水;下水典礼 ③开办 ‖**~ pad** (火箭等的)发射台 / **~ site** 发射场;发射场中的各种设备 / **~ tube** (鱼雷、导弹等的)发射管 / **~ ways** 【船】下水滑道

launder ['lɔ:ndə] **I** *n.* [矿]流槽;槽洗机 **II** ❶ *vt.* ①洗(衣等) ②(洗后)烫(衣等) ❷ *vi.* ①洗烫衣物 ②经洗;耐烫: This fabric ~s well. 这种织品经洗耐烫。‖**~er** ['lɔ:ndərə] *n.* 洗衣工

laundress ['lɔ:ndris] *n.* 洗烫衣物的女工

laundry ['lɔ:ndri] *n.* ①洗衣 ②洗衣房;洗衣店 ③送洗衣店去洗的东西;洗衣店已洗好的东西 ‖**hang out the ~** [美][军俚]空投伞兵 ‖**~man** *n.* 洗衣男工 (尤指为洗衣店取送顾客衣物的人) / '**~,woman** *n.* 洗烫衣物的女工

laureate ['lɔ:riit] **I** *a.* ①(桂冠)用月桂树枝编成的 ②戴桂冠的 ③配戴桂冠的, 卓越的(尤指诗人) **II** *n.* ①戴桂冠的人; (由于艺术或科学上的成就)获得荣誉者 ②[the L-]桂冠诗人(英国王室御用诗人的称号; =the Poet Laureate) **III** ['lɔ:rieit] *vt.* ①使戴桂冠, 授…以荣誉 ②授…以桂冠诗人的称号 ‖**~ship** *n.* 桂冠诗人的地位 / **laureation** [,lɔ:ri'eiʃən] *n.* 授桂冠; 授荣誉

laurel ['lɔrəl] **I** *n.* ①【植】月桂属植物; 月桂树 ②月桂树叶(古代希腊人用以编成冠冕、授予竞赛的优胜者) ③桂冠; [~s]用作单或复]荣誉, 名声; 胜利; 优(或 gain)~ 得到荣誉 **II** (laurel(l)ed; laurel(l)ing) *vt.* ①使戴桂冠 ②给予…荣誉 ‖**look to one's ~s** 小心翼翼地保持已得的荣誉 / **rest on one's ~s** 满足于已有成就, 吃老本 ‖**laurel(l)ed** *a.* 戴桂冠的; 获得荣誉的

lava ['lɑ:və] *n.* 【地】熔岩

lavatory ['lævətəri] *n.* ①洗脸盆; 【宗】洗礼盆 ②盥洗室; 厕所

lavender ['lævində] **I** *n.* ①【植】薰衣草 ②干薰衣草的花(或叶、茎); ~ water 薰衣草香水 ③淡紫色 **II** *a.* 淡紫色的 **III** *vt.* 用薰衣草薰香 ‖**lay sb. out in ~** [美俚] ①把某人打得不省人事; 打死某人 ②斥骂某人 / **lay up in ~** ①小心保存(衣物等) ②[俚]把…典当(或抵押)出去

lavish ['læviʃ] **I** *a.* ①过分大方的, 浪费的; 慷慨的, 不吝惜的: be ~ of endearments 过分表示亲热 / a man too ~ with his money 花钱过于大手大脚的人 ②过分丰富的, 过度的; 丰富的, 大量的: ~ hospitality 过于好客 **II** *vt.* 过多地赠送; 滥花; 慷慨地给予: ~ praises on sb. 大肆吹捧某人 / ~ money on sth. 在某事上乱花钱 ‖**~ly** *ad.* / **~ment** *n.* 浪费, 滥花 / **~ness** *n.*

law¹ [lɔ:] **I** *n.* ①法律, 法令, 法: the ~ of the land 国法 / abide by the ~ 守法 / break the ~ 犯法 / deal with sb. according to ~ 依法处理某人 ②法治: ~ and order 治安 ③法学; 法律知识: be learned in the ~ 精通法学 / read (或 study) ~ 学法律, 读法科 / His ~ is sound. 他很懂法律。④司法界, 律师行业: practise (或 follow) the ~ 做律师 ⑤诉讼, 法律解决: go to ~ against sb. 跟某人打官司 ⑥[英]成文法和习惯法 ⑦法则, 规律, 定律: the inner ~s of a thing 事物的内部规律 / a ~ of nature (或 a natural ~) 自然法则 / the Law of Nature (或 Reason) 天理 ⑧(艺术、运动、某一生活部门中的)规则, 守则 ⑨【基督教】(摩西)律法(=~ of Moses) ⑩[英]在赛跑中给与弱手的抢先跑的时间(或距离); 宽限期 ‖*civil (criminal)* ~ 民(刑)法 / *common* ~ (英国的)习惯法, 不成文法(区别于 *statute* ~ 成文法) / *international* ~ (或 *the* ~ *of nations*) 国际法 / *the jungle* ~ 弱肉强食的原则 / ~ *of conservation of energy* 【物】能量守恒定律 / ~ *of parity* 【物】字称定律 / ~ *of universal gravitation* 【物】万有引力定

律 / *martial* ~ 军法; 戒严令 **II** ❶ *vi.* 起诉, 控告 ❷ *vt.* [主方]对…起诉 ‖*a* ~ *(或 the ~s) of the Medes* [mi:dz] *and Persians* 不可更改的法律 / *be a ~ unto oneself* 独断独行 / *be at ~* 在诉讼中 / *be good (bad)* ~ (意见、决定等)合(违背)法律 / *be within (outside) the ~* 合(不合)法 / *give the ~ to sb.* 把自己的意志强加于某人 / *have (或 take) the ~ of sb.* 控告某人 / *lay down the ~* 发号施令; 呵斥 (to) / *take the ~ into one's own hands* 擅自处理 / *the ~* [美俚][总称]司法人员; 警察; 警察机关; 监狱的看守人 ‖**~-a.biding** *a.* 守法的 / **~.breaker** *n.* 犯法的人 / **~court** *n.* 法院, 法庭 / **~.giver** *n.* 制定法典者 / **~-hand** *n.* (英国旧时)写法律文件的一种书法 / **Law Lord** (英国)上议院执掌司法的议员(正式职称为 Lord of Appeal in Ordinary) / **~.maker** *n.* 立法者 / **~.making** *n.* 立法 *a.* 立法的 / **~man** ['lɔ:mən] *n.* [美]执法吏(如警察等) / **~ merchant** 商法, 商业习惯法 / ~ **office** [美]律师事务所 / ~ **officer** 司法官(尤指英国的检察长等) / **~suit** *n.* 诉讼(案件): enter(或 bring in) a ~suit against sb. 对某人起诉 / ~ **term** ①法律用语 ②(法庭)开庭期

law² [lɔ:] *int.* [英俚]天哪! 啊呀! [表示惊讶]

lawful ['lɔ:ful] *a.* 合法的; 法定的; 守法的: a ~ act 合法行为 / ~ age 法定年龄 ‖**~ly** *ad.* / **~ness** *n.*

lawless ['lɔ:lis] *a.* ①(国家等)没有法律的; 失去法律控制的 ②不法的, 非法的, 无法无天的: a ~ man 不法之徒 / ~ practices 违法行为

lawn¹ [lɔ:n] *n.* 上等细布; 上等细麻布 ‖**~y** *a.*

lawn² [lɔ:n] *n.* ①草地, 草坪, 草场 ②[古]林间的空地 ‖**~y** *a.* ‖~ **mower** 割草机 / ~ **tennis** 草地网球

lawyer ['lɔ:jə] *n.* ①律师 ②法学家 ‖*a forecastle* ~ [美俚](水手用语)经常要争论(或抱怨、议论)的人 / *a good (bad)* ~ 懂(不懂)法律的人

lax [læks] **I** *a.* ①(肠)宽松的, 易通便的; 腹泻的 ②松弛的; 质地松的 ③不严格的; 不精密的; 马虎的; 不严肃的: ~ discipline 松懈的纪律 / be ~ in morals 行为放荡 ④【植】(花簇)疏松的 ⑤【语】(元音)松(弛)的: ~ (tense) vowels 松(紧)元音 **II** *n.* 【语】松元音 ‖**~ly** *ad.* / **~ness** *n.*

laxative ['læksətiv] **I** *a.* ①缓泻的, 通大便的 ②有轻度腹泻的 ③放松的; 放肆的 **II** *n.* 【药】轻泻剂 ‖**~ly** *ad.* / **~ness** *n.*

lay¹ [lei] **I** (laid [leid]) ❶ *vt.* ①放, 搁: ~ a book on the table 把书放在桌上 / ~ a watch to one's ear 把表放在耳边听 / ~ stress (emphasis) on investigation and study 注重调查研究 ②把…压平; 使倒下: The typhoon *laid* the crops. 台风把庄稼吹倒了。/ ~ sb. low 把某人打翻在地; 打败某人 ③使处于某种状态(或地位): ~ bare a scheme 揭露阴谋 / ~ sb. under (an) obligation (to) 使

某人(对…)承担义务

④铺设;敷设;砌(砖): ~ a railroad track 铺铁路轨道 / ~ a submarine cable 敷设海底电缆 / ~ the foundation of heavy industry 打下重工业的基础

⑤铺;涂: The road is *laid* with asphalt. 这条路是用柏油铺的。/ ~ plaster on the wall 在墙上涂灰泥

⑥布置; 安排; [常用被动语态]设(故事等的场景): ~ an ambush (a snare) 设下埋伏(陷阱) / ~ mines 布雷,埋雷 / ~ the table (准备开饭时)摆好餐具 / ~ a fire 放好木柴等准备生火

⑦拟订(计划等);策划: ~ a plan carefully 精心拟订计划

⑧提出(问题、主张、要求等): ~ the question before a committee 把问题提交委员会 / ~ claim to sth. 对某物提出所有权要求

⑨平息(风浪等); 消除(疑虑等);平服,驱除(鬼怪): The shower *laid* the dust. 阵雨涤荡了空中飞扬的灰尘。/ ~ sb.'s doubts 打消某人的疑虑

⑩下(蛋);(飞机)投(弹);放(烟幕)

⑪归(罪)于;把…归于: The engine trouble was *laid* to faulty inspection. 发动机故障被认为是检查不严的结果。/ ~ a fault *to* sb.'s charge (或 *at* sb.'s door) 归咎于某人 / ~ the blame *on* sb. 责怪某人

⑫把(惩罚、赋税、负担等)加于: ~ a heavy tax *on* land 对土地课以重税 / ~ a burden *on* sb. 把重负加在某人身上

⑬用(棍等)打;用(斧等)砍;施…于: ~ one's axe *to* the tree 用斧头砍树 / think carefully before ~*ing* pen *to* paper 落笔前仔细斟酌

⑭与(某人)以…打赌: I'll ~ you ten to one that he'll come. 我和你打赌他十之八九会来的。

⑮把(炮等)瞄准

⑯搓,编(绳等): ~ *up* a rope 搓绳

❷ *vi.* ①下蛋

②打赌

③[俚]躺下 (=lie)

④【海】就位: ~ aft 到船尾就位

⑤用力干: The sailors *laid* to their oars. 水手们用力划桨。

II *n.* ①位置;(地理)形势: the ~ of the land 地形

②层;隐蔽处

③行动计划

④行业,职业

⑤(销售)条件;价格;(雇佣)条件;(捕鲸船上代替工资的)分红: be sold at a good ~ 以好价售出

⑥(绳索等的)搓合方式;(粗纱的)圈距

⑦下蛋: The hen is in full ~. 这只母鸡下蛋正勤。

‖~ *about* ①向四面八方乱打 ②努力干 ③作准备 / ~ *a* (或 *one's*) *course* 【海】(朝某方向)直驶;[喻]制订计划 / ~ *aside* ①把…放在一边;把…搁置起来: ~ *aside* old prejudices 撇开旧的偏见 / The plan has been *laid aside*. 这项计划被搁置起来了。②把…留待后用;积蓄: ~ *aside* 50 cents a week 每周积蓄五角钱 / ~ *at* 对准…打过去,攻击 / ~ *away* ①把…留待后用;积蓄 ②[美][常用被动语态]埋葬 / ~ *by* ① =~ aside ②收割后贮藏(谷物等) ③停(船);(船)顶风停驶 / ~ *down* ①放下;使躺下;交出;献出(生命) ②*down* one's office 辞职 ②规定,制定(计划、规划、原则等) ③兴建,建造;铺好: ~ *down* a railway 兴建一条铁路 / ~ *down* a solid foundation for 为…打下坚实基础 ④主张,断言;下(赌注);打赌 ⑤将(酒等)贮存在地窖里 ⑥利(田)种(作物);把(土地)变为牧场: They have *laid* their melons *down*. 他们已经种好了瓜。/ ~ *for* 等待(时机);埋伏着等待… / ~ *hands on* 见 **hand** / ~ *hold of* 见 **hold** / ~ *in* 贮存: ~ *in* hay for the winter 贮存干草以备过冬 / ~ *into* [俚]痛打;痛斥 / ~ *it on thick* [俚]拼命恭维;过分责备 / ~ *it on with a trowel* 竭力恭维;过分夸奖 / ~ *off* ①(暂时)解雇 ②停止工作(或活动);休息: The doctor told him to ~ *off* (for) a couple of days. 医生叫他休息几天。③把…搁在一边;[俚]停止;放弃: ~ *off* smoking 戒烟 / *Lay off*! 别烦了! 别再老说别人不好了! ④给…标界,划出;【船】放样;绘图 ⑤把(船)驶离 / ~ *on* ①加(惩罚、赋税、命令等)于人 ②猛攻;接连地打 ③涂(颜料、油漆等) ④[英]安装(水、电、煤气、电话等): a house with gas and water *laid on* 装有煤气和自来水的房子 ⑤[口]组织,安排(演出、服务等): Concerts were *laid on* for the foreign guests. 为外宾们准备了音乐会。⑥长(肉),增(重): These pigs *laid on* flesh quick. 这些猪长肉很快。/ ~ *oneself open to* 使自己遭到(攻击、责难等) / ~ *open* ①=~ *out* ①摆开;布置,安排;设计(花园、版面等);【机】为…定线,为…划样: The work for tomorrow is all *laid out*. 明天的工作都安排好了。③花(钱);投资: ~ *out* a large sum of money *in* purchasing safety devices 拨一大笔钱购买安全设备 ④为(尸体)作殡葬准备 ⑤[俚]打昏;打倒 ⑥[~ oneself out] 竭尽全力: They *laid themselves out* to make the reception a success. 他们竭尽全力使招待会成功。/ ~ *over* ①涂,覆盖 ②压倒,胜过 ③稍作停留 ④使延期 / ~ *to* ①把(功、过)归于 ②努力干: She took a shovel and *laid to* with the others. 她拿起铲子就和大家一起干了起来。③打: ~ *to* in all directions with a stick 用棒四处乱打 ④(船)顶着风停止;使(船)停下 / ~ *up* ①贮存,储蓄: He has *laid up* some money. 他积下了一些钱。/ ~ *up* trouble for oneself 给自己增加麻烦 ②暂停使用;搁置: ~ a ship *up* for repairs 使船入坞修理 ③[常用被动语态](因病等)卧床: be *laid up* with a bad cold 因患重伤风而不能起床 / ~ *wait for* 埋伏着等待… / ~ *waste* 见 **waste** /

the kid (或 *kinchin*) ~ (盗贼语) 抢夺(或偷窃)外出购物的小孩的钱 ‖~ **about** [俚]流浪汉 / '~**a,way plan** 逐月付款的累积购买法 / '~**-by** *n.* ①[英]路旁停车处 ②【矿】矿井中空车皮岔道 / ~ **day**【海】(租船契约所允许的)装卸货物日期中的每一日;港口耽搁日 / ~ **figure** ①人体活动模型(用于服装式样展览) ②傀儡般的人物 / '~**-off** *n.* ①解雇 ②(临时)解雇期 ③关闭;停歇 ④停止活动(或比赛)的时期 / '~**-out** *n.* ①布局;陈设;安排;设计: the ~*out of a factory* 工厂的布局 ②(报纸等的)版面编排 ③一套器具(或工具、衣服等): a miner's ~*out* 矿工的全套装备 ④[美口]事态,情况 ⑤[美]地方(指建筑物及四周环境) / '~**,over** *n.* 中途短暂的停留 / '~**-shaft** *n.*【机】副轴 / '~**-stall** *n.* [英]垃圾堆

lay² [lei] *n.* ①(唱的)短叙事诗,短抒情诗 ②[古]歌曲

lay³ [lei] *a.* ①凡俗的,世俗的(与教会中神职人员相对而言) ②外行的,非专业性的: to the ~ mind 对外行人说来 ‖~ **analyst** 非专业的(心理)分析家 / ~ **brother** 修道院里做杂役的僧侣 / ~ **man** ['leimən] *n.* ①俗人(别于僧侣、牧师) ②门外汉,外行 / ~ **reader** ① 在教堂里主持礼拜的俗人 ② 外行的读者,一般读者 / ~ **sister** 修道院里做杂役的修女

lay⁴ [lei] lie¹ 的过去式

layer ['leiə] **I** *n.* ①层;阶层;地层: a ~ of rock 一层岩石 ②铺设者;敷设工: a brick ~ 砌砖者 / a mine ~ 布雷艇艇【军】瞄准手 ③下蛋的鸡: a good (bad) ~ 生蛋多(少)的鸡 ④【植】压条; [复] (由于生长不结实而)倒伏的庄稼 **II** [lsə, 'leiə] ❶ *vt.* 用压条法培植 ❷ *vi.* ①(庄稼)由于生长不结实而倒伏 ②(植物)借助压条法生根繁殖;分层 ‖~**s and backers** (赛马等的)赌客

layette [lei'et] *n.* 新生婴儿的全套用品(如衣服、被褥、洗涤用具等)

lazy ['leizi] **I** *a.* ①懒惰的; 懒散的 ②慢吞吞的: a ~ stream 水流缓慢的溪流 ③令人懒散的 ④松垮低垂的 **II** *vi.* 懒惰; 懒散 ‖**lazily** *ad.* / **laziness** *n.* / ~**ish** *a.* 有点儿愛惰的; 懒洋洋的 / ~**-back** *n.* 马车坐椅的靠背 / ~**-bed** *n.* [主英]马铃薯培植床 / '~**-bones** [复] *n.* [用作单或复]懒汉,懒骨头 / ~ **guy**【船】吊杆稳索 / ~ **Susan** (餐桌上便于人们取食的)转动大餐盘 / ~ **tongs**【机】惰钳(原来用于钳取远处的东西)

lea¹ [li:] *n.* 草地,牧地

lea² [li:] *n.*【纺】缕, 小绞

lead¹ [li:d] **I** (led [led]) ❶ *vt.* ①领导;率领;指挥: a government delegation *led* by the foreign minister 由外交部长率领的政府代表团 / ~ a campaign 指挥一场战役 ②带领,引导;走在(队伍等)的最前头: ~ the way 带路 / The pipes ~ the water into the fields. 这些管道把水引到田里。③撺;牵(马等) ④致使;诱发;用诱供法讯问(证人等): Investigations *led* us to the foregoing conclusion. 调查研究使我们得出上述

结论。/ What *led* you to think so? 是什么使得你这样想的呢? / You might have been *led* to believe that I was joking. 你或许会(被弄得)以为我在开玩笑。/ ~ sb. astray 把某人引入歧途 ⑤ 过(活),使…过(某种生活): ~ a happy (miserable) life 过着幸福(惨苦)的生活 / ~ sb. a dog's life 使某人过着受折磨的日子 ⑥前置瞄准,超前瞄准(飞鸟、飞机等) ⑦ (打牌时)先出(牌) ⑧(拳击中)向对手打出(一拳) ⑨(尤指在竞选等场合)压倒(对手) ❷ *vi.* ①领导;领路;带头,领先 ②通向, 导致 (to): a road ~*ing* to the foot of a mountain 一条通到山脚下的路 ③首先出牌(或开球等) **II** *n.* ①领导;榜样 ②引导;带头;领先;首位: With him in the ~, all the others followed suit. 在他带动下,其他人也都跟上来了 / gain (或 have) the ~ in a race 在赛跑中领先 / 领先的程度(或距离): have a ~ of ten metres over the other runners 比别的赛跑运动员领先十米 / hold a safe ~ 遥遥领先 ④ 提示,暗示: provide ~s for further research 为进一步的研究提供了线索 ⑤ (戏中) 主角;扮演主角的演员: play the ~ in a film 在一部电影中担任主角 / the juvenile ~ 青年男主角 ⑥(新闻报道开端的)内容提要,导语;(报上)刊登在显著地位的报道,重要报道 ⑦人工水道(尤指引向磨坊的) ⑧【电】导线;引线;超前: phase ~ 相位超前 ⑨【矿】脉 ⑩(牵狗等的)绳索,皮带 ⑪(纸牌游戏中的)出牌权;先出牌;出的头 [复]张牌 ⑫(拳击中)第一拳 **III** *a.* ①领头的,领先的: a bomber 领队轰炸机 / a ~ horse (马群中)领头的马 ②最重要的,以显著地位刊载的: the ~ article in this month's issue 本月这一期中主要的文章 / a ~ headline 重要标题 ‖*follow the ~ of sb.* 效法某人,以某人为榜样 / *give sb. a ~* ①给某人做出榜样,为某人起带头作用 ②提示某人 / ~ *away* 使盲从;把…引入歧途 / ~ *back* ①把…带领回 ②按搭档出牌的花色出(牌) / *off* 开始;开头: ~ *off* a dance 领头起舞 / He led *off* by reading a paragraph from the document. 他读了一段文件作为讲话的开头。/ ~ *on* ①率领(或带领)·前进 ②诱使;继续下去;引诱 / ~ *sb. on to do sth.* 诱使某人干某事 / ~ *out* ①开始 ② 带(舞伴)起舞 / ~ *sb. by the nose* 见 *nose* / ~ *up to* ①把……一直带领到 ②导致 ③渐渐引到(某个话题): That's just what I was ~*ing up to.* 这正是我所要说到的一点。/ *return sb.'s* ~ 跟着某人(指纸牌游戏中的搭档)出同一花色的牌 / *take the* ~ 为首;领先;做榜样 ‖~**able** *a.* 能被领导的;能被指挥的 ‖~**-'in** *n.*【无】引入线 ②介绍,开场白 / '~**-'off** *n.* 开始,开端;打出的第一拳;先发球者 / ~ **time** ① 产品设计至实际投产间的时间 ② 订货至交货间的时间 / '~**-'up** *n.* 导致物

lead² [led] **I** *n.* ①铅;铅制品;笔铅: black ~ 黑铅(石墨的别名) / a ~ pipe 铅管 ② [英] [复] 铅皮;铅皮屋顶 ③【印】插铅,铅条 ④【海】测深锤

水砣 ⑤[总称]子弹: an ounce of ~ 一颗子弹 II ❶ *vt.* ①用铅包; 在…的里面衬上一层铅; 用铅来增加…的重量 ②[印]在…间插铅条 ③加铅(或铅的化合物)于: ~ed gasoline 加铅汽油, 乙基化汽油 ④用铅条固住: ~ed glass 铅条玻璃 ❷ *vi.* ①用水砣测深 ②被铅覆盖住(枪膛等)被铅塞住 ||*arm the* ~ 注兽脂入测深锤底部凹处(以便粘起泥沙而探知海底情况) / *cast*(或 *heave*)*the* ~ 【海】用水砣测深 / *get the* ~ [口]中弹, 饮弹 / *swing the* ~ [英俚]装病(或以其他欺骗手段)逃避分内的工作 ||~*less a.* 无铅的 / ~*y a.* 含铅的; 似铅的 ||~ **acetate** 醋酸铅 / ~ **arsenate** 砷酸铅 / ~ **line**[海]测深绳 / ~ **pencil** 铅笔 / '~-**pipe (cinch)** [美俚]轻而易举的事; 肯定的事情 / ~ **poisoning** 铅中毒 / ~ **wool**【建】(接铅管用的)铅毛(也称 ~ **yarn**) / '~**work** *n.* 铅制品 / ~**works**[复] *n.*[用作单或复]制铅工厂, 铅矿熔炼厂 / '~**wort** *n.* 【植】欧洲蓝茉莉; 白花丹属植物

leaden ['ledn] I *a.* ①铅制的: a ~ box 铅盒 ②铅灰色的: ~ clouds 铅灰色的云块 ③质量差的, 低劣的 ④无表情的; 呆滞的: with heavy ~ eyes 带着沉重呆滞的目光 ⑤沉闷的; 乏味的; 拖拉的: a ~ silence 使人觉得窒息的静默 II *vt.* 使象铅似地沉重

leader ['li:də] *n.* ①领袖, 领导; 首领; 指挥者 ②乐队指挥; 领唱者; 领奏者, 首席演奏者: the ~ of the violin section 首席小提琴手 ③[英](诉讼的)首席律师, 主要辩护人 ④[英]社论; 重要文章 ⑤居首位的事物(如最易传染的疾病、最热门的股票等)⑥先导马; 领舰; 领机 ⑦【建】水落管; 【机】导杆 ⑧[复][印]指引线(指图表上引导视线用的连续的点或短划)⑨【植】顶枝 ⑩[矿]导脉 ⑪[解]腱 ⑫为兜揽生意而以特别廉价出售的商品 ||~*less a.* 无领袖的; 无领导的

leadership ['li:dəʃip] *n.* ①领导: unified ~ 一元化领导 / give correct ~ to the struggle 对这一场斗争实行正确的领导 ②[总称]领导人员 ③领导能力

leading[1] ['li:diŋ] I *a.* ①领导的 ②第一位的, 最主要的: the ~ topics of the hour 当前最主要的话题 ③(戏中)扮演主角的: a ~ lady (man) 演主角的女(男)演员 II *n.* ①领导; 指挥; 指导: men of light and ~ 有才实学的有影响的人们 ②引导: propose a ~ of water to arid lands 建议把水引到旱地去 ||~ **article** [报上的]主要文章; [英]社论 ②为招揽生意的特别廉价商品 / ~ **business** 主要演员常演的角色 / ~ **case**【律】例案 / ~ **current**【电】超前电流 / ~ **edge**[空](机翼或叶片的)前缘 / ~ **fossil**[矿]主导化石, 标准化石 / ~ **light** ①[海]迷标灯 ②突出而有影响的一员 / ~ **motive** 主要动机 ②【音】主导主题, 主导旋律 / ~ **note** =~ **tone** / ~ **question**【律】诱导性的提问 / ~ **rein** 驾驭马的缰绳 / ~ **seaman** (英)海军一等水兵 / ~ **staff** 附在牛鼻环上的棒头 / ~ **strings** 用来教幼孩

学走路的牵引绳带; [喻]管教: be in ~ *strings* 处于幼稚阶段; 象幼孩一样受着管教 / ~ **tone**【音】长音阶第七音; 导音

leading[2] ['lediŋ] *n.* ①铅制的覆盖物(或框架)②[总称]铅皮; 铅条

leaf [li:f] I ([复] leaves [li:vz]) *n.* ①叶; [总称]叶子: This tree has green *leaves* throughout the year. 这树终年常青。/ put forth new *leaves* 长新叶 / a consignment of choice tobacco ~ 一批上等烟叶 ②花瓣: a rose ~ 玫瑰花瓣 ③(书刊等的)一张(即正反两页)④薄的金属片; [总称]箔: a frame covered with gold ~ 包上金箔的框架 ⑤(撑起来或插入即可增大桌面的)活动桌板 ⑥(窗、门等的)页扇 ⑦(汽车等片弹簧的)簧片: a spring ~ 片弹簧 ⑧[英方]帽边 ⑨(步枪的)瞄准尺; 小轮齿 II ❶ *vi.* ①生叶, 长叶(out) ②翻书页: ~ through a book 把书翻阅一遍 ❷ *vt.* 翻…的书页 ||*come into* ~ 长叶 / *in* ~ 生有叶子的; 叶茂的: All the trees are *in* ~ now. 树木现在都长满着叶子。/ *take a* ~ *out of sb.'s book* 学某人的样子 / *the fall of the* ~ 秋天 / *the sere and yellow* ~ 晚年 / *turn over a new* ~ 翻开新的一页; 重新开始; 改过自新 ||~**ed** *a.* 有叶的 / ~**less** *a.* 无叶的 ||~ **bud** 叶芽 / ~ **fat** (猪的)板油 / ~ **mo(u)ld** 腐殖质土(主要成分是腐叶的土壤) / ~ **rust** (谷类等的)叶锈病 / '~**stalk** *n.* 【植】叶柄

leaflet ['li:flit] I *n.* ①小叶, 嫩叶 ②复叶的一片 ③叶状器官(或部分) ④传单; 活页 II (leafletted; leafletting) *vt.* 散发传单给: ~ a rally 在群众大会上散发传单

league[1] [li:g] I *n.* ①(政治性的)同盟, 联盟; 盟约: the *League* (of Nations)【史】国际联盟(1920—1946) ②[运动、文艺等方面的]联合会, 社团; [英](足、篮球等的)竞赛联合会: ~ football matches 足球联赛(参加竞赛联合会各队之间的相互比赛)③种类; 范畴: He is not in your ~. 他和你不是一类人。II *vt.* & *vi.* (使)结盟; 联合 ||*in* ~ *with* 和…联合着; 和…勾结着

league[2] [li:g] *n.* 里格(长度名; 在英美约为为三哩或三浬)

leak [li:k] I *vi.* ①漏; 渗: The ship ~s. 船漏了。/ The water has ~ed out. 水漏出来了。/ The fumes have ~ed in. 气味钻进来了。②泄漏出去: The news has ~ed out. 这消息已泄漏出去了。❷ *vt.* 使(空气、液体等)渗漏; 使(消息等)泄漏 II *n.* ①漏洞; 漏隙: a ~ in the roof 屋顶的漏洞 ②漏, 漏出; 泄漏: officially inspired ~s 官方授意透露的消息 ③[电]漏泄电阻; 漏损 ④漏出物 ⑤[俚]撒尿 ||*spring a* ~ 生漏缝 / *take a* ~ [俚]撒尿 ||~'**proof** *a.* 防漏的; 不漏的

leakage ['li:kidʒ] *n.* ①漏; 漏出; 泄漏: a ~ of information 消息的走漏 / cause a ~ 引起渗漏 / ~ current【电】漏泄电流 ②漏出量; 漏出量 ③【商】许可的漏损率; 漏损量

lean¹ [li:n] **I** (leaned [lent, li:nd] 或 leant [lent]) ❶ *vi.* ①倾斜; 屈身; 倾向, 偏向: The post ~s a little bit. 这根柱子有点倾斜. / ~ *over* the desk 俯身在书桌上 / ~ *out of* the window 身子探出窗外 / ~ *to* (或 *towards*) a view 倾向一种观点 ②靠, 倚; 依赖: ~ *on* the table 靠着桌子 / *against* the wall 倚墙 / Don't always ~ *on* (或 *upon*) others for help. 不要老是依赖别人的帮助. ❷ *vt.* ①使倾斜 ②靠在某种东西上: ~ a ladder against a wall 把一架梯子靠在墙上 **II** *n.* 倾斜; 倾向: a wall with a slight ~ 一堵稍稍有些倾斜的墙 ‖~ *over backward(s)* (为了避免一种倾向而) 走另一极端 ‖**~ing** *n.* 倾斜; 倾向 (*towards*): a reformer with radical ~*ings* 带有激进主义倾向的改革家 ‖**~-to** *n.* 单坡屋顶的小房子; 披屋 *a.* 【建】单坡的

lean² [li:n] **I** *a.* ①(人、家畜等)瘦的; (肉)无脂肪的, 精瘦的 ②贫乏的; 贫瘠的; 缺乏营养的; 收益差的: a ~ year 歉收年 ③(文体等)简朴的 **II** *n.* 瘦肉 **III** *vt.* 使变瘦 ‖**~ness** *n.*

leap [li:p] **I** (leapt [lept] 或 leaped [lept, li:pt]) ❶ *vi.* ①跃, 跳: ~ on a horse 跃上马 / The fish *leapt* out of the water. 鱼跳出水面. / Our hearts ~ed *with* joy at the good news. 听到这个好消息我们的心情万分激动. ②猛然行动; 迅速行动: ~ from one topic to another 从一个话题跳到另一个话题 / ~ *to* conclusions 匆匆武断地下结论 / ~ *at* a chance (或 an opportunity) 抓住机会 ❷ *vt.* ①跃过: ~ a ditch 跃过一条沟 ②使跃过: ~ a horse *over* a hurdle 纵马跃过栅栏 / ~ a horse *across* a ditch 纵马跃过一条沟 **II** *n.* ①跳跃: take a ~ *over* an obstacle 跃过障碍物 ②飞跃; 跃进: a ~ in the process of cognition 认识过程的一次飞跃 ③(必须)跃过的地方; 跃过的距离: a ~ of seven metres 七米的跃距 ‖a ~ *in the dark* 冒险的行动, 轻举妄动 / *by ~s and bounds* 飞跃地, 极迅速地 / *in one* ~ 以一跃 / *Look before you* ~. [谚] 深思熟虑而后行. ‖**~er** *n.* 跳跃者 ‖**~ day** 闰日(指二月二十九日) / **~frog** *n.* ①跳背游戏 ②蛙跳(尤指两栖部队登陆后的前进行动) *vi.* 作蛙跳, 蛙跳般地前进: ~*frogging* tactics 蛙跳战术 *vt.* ①(蛙跳般地)跃过, 越过 ②【军】使(两支部队)交互跃进 / ~ **year** 闰年

learn [lə:n] (learnt [lə:nt] 或 learned [lə:nt, lə:nd]) ❶ *vi.* ①学习; 学: The boy ~s fast and well. 这孩子学得又快又好. ~ *from* past mistakes to avoid future ones 惩前毖后 ②听到, 获悉: I ~ed *of* his departure only yesterday. 昨天我才听说他走了. ❷ *vt.* ①学习; 学; 学会: ~ a foreign language (a new skill) 学一门外语 (一门新技术) / ~ to swim (或~ how to swim) 学游泳 / Have you ~t your lessons? 你的功课学会了吗? / ~ hygiene 学会注意卫生 ②听到; 认识到: I've ~ed that he'll join our science expedition. 我听说他将参加我们的科学考察

队. / We ~ed by actual experience that .... 我们从实际经验中认识到… ③记住: ~ the lines of a play 背台词 / ~ sth. by heart 记住(或背下)某事 ④[俗] 教; 教训: This will ~ you to keep out of mischief. 这将使你得到教训不要去捣蛋了. ‖I am (或 have) yet to ~. 我还得了解了解啊. (常含有不信对方说法之意) ‖**~able** *a.* 可学得的 / **~er** *n.* 学习者; 初学者: an advanced ~er 进修者

learned ['lə:nid] *a.* ①有学问的; 博学的; 精通某门学问的; [英]精通法律的: a ~ man 学者 / my ~ friend (或 brother) (英国律师在下议院等场合对同行的敬称)我那位渊博的同行 ② 学术上的: a ~ periodical 一份学术期刊 / a ~ society 学会 ③[lə:nd 或 lə:nt] 经过训练学到的: ~ skills 学到的技巧 ④ 由学者研究(或应用、从事)的: a ~ language 学者语言(一般指希腊语、拉丁语) / a ~ word 学者造出的词 ‖**~ly** *ad.* ‖**~ profession** 需要学问的职业(尤指牧师、律师、医生等职业)

learning ['lə:niŋ] *n.* ①学习: be good at ~ 善于学习 ②知识; 学问: book ~ 书本知识 / a man of ~ 学问高深的人 ‖*the New Learning* 新学问(指十五—十六世纪时对原文《圣经》及希腊古典作品的研究)

lease [li:s] **I** *vt.* ①出租(土地等) ②租得, 租有(土地等) **II** *n.* ①租约; 租契 ②租借期限 ③租借权 ④租借物 (*a new* ~ *of* (或 *on*) *life* 在大病痊愈等以后的)重生; 富于希望的新生 / *by* (或 *on*) ~ 以租借方式 / *put out to* ~ 出租 ‖**leasable** *a.* 可租借的 ‖**~-back** *n.* 将产权出售同时长期租用该产业的做法 / '**~hold** *a.* 租来的 *n.* ①租得物(尤指土地)②租赁期 / '**~holder** *n.* 租借人 / '**~lend** *n.*, *a.* & *vt.* =lend-

leash [li:ʃ] **I** *n.* ①(系狗等的)皮带, 皮条 ②(打猎用语)(狗、狐等的)三只; 成三的一组 ③【纺】综束, 综框(指提花机上连于同一根综线下的若干线)④[喻]束缚, 抑制 **II** *vt.* ① 用皮带系住 ②[喻]束缚, 抑制 ‖*hold* (或 *have*) *in* ~ 用皮带缚住(猎犬等); [喻]束缚, 抑制 / *slip the* ~ (猎犬等)挣脱皮带; [喻]摆脱束缚 / *strain at the* ~ (猎犬等)牵扯皮带; [喻]急欲摆脱束缚自由行动

least [li:st] **I** *a.* [little 的最高级] ①最小的: the ~ distance 最小的距离 / He hadn't the ~ thought of his own interests. 他丝毫不考虑个人利益. / ~ common multiple【数】最小公倍数 ②最不重要的; 地位最低的: the last but not the ~ 最后的但并非不重要的 ③[美方]年纪最小的; (动、植物)最小种类的 **II** *ad.* [little 的最高级]最小; 最少; 最不: Young people are the ~ conservative. 青年人最不保守. **III** *n.* 最小; 最少: That's the ~ of our worries. 那是我们最不担心的. ‖*at (the)* ~ 至少, 起码; 无论如何: It requires *at* ~ two days. 这事至少需要两天. / *at the very* ~ [用于加强语气] = at (the) ~ / *in the* ~ 一点: A: Are you afraid? B: Not *in the* ~. 甲: 你怕吗? 乙: 一点不怕. / ~ *of all* 最不: something I like ~ *of all* 我最不喜欢的东西 / *Least said, soonest mended.* (或 *The* ~ *said, the soonest mended.*) [谚] 多说反坏事. / *to say the* ~ (*of it*) 至少可以这样说; 退一步说: Such a view is incorrect, *to say the* ~. 至少可以这样说, 这种见解是错误的. ‖~**ways** *ad.* [主方] =~**wise** / ~**wise** *ad.* [口]至少; 无论如何

leather ['leðə] **I** *n.* ①皮革: patent ~ 漆皮 ②皮革制品; [俚] (板球、足球等运动的)球; 皮夹子; [美俚]拳击手套; [复] (骑马用的)皮短裤; 皮绷腿 ③皮肤 ④狗耳的下垂部分 ⑤ [the ~] [美俚]拳击中的一击 **II** *a.* 皮革的; 皮革制的 **III** *vt.* ①用皮革包盖 ② [口] 用皮鞭抽打 ‖*American* ~ [英]油布 / ~ *and prunella* ① 仅在衣着外表上的差别 ② 无关紧要的(东西) / *nothing like* ~ 自己的东西最好 ‖'~**back** *n.* 棱龟, 草龟(一种大海龟) / '~**head** *n.* ① 笨蛋 ② [古] [方]美国宾夕法尼亚州(Pennsylvania)人 ③ [古] [美俚]守夜人, 巡警 / '~**-,hunting** *n.* [俚] (板球的)防守 / '~**,jacket** *n.* 【动】无腹鳍刺鲀 ④ [英]长脚蝇的蛆 / '~**neck** *n.* [美俚]海军陆战队士兵 / '~**wood** *n.* 革木属植物

leave[1] [li:v] (left [left]) ❶ *vt.* ① 离开; 脱离: ~ school 离开学校(指毕业或退学)/~ medicine for art 放弃医学改学艺术 ② 把…留在; 留下; 剩下; 把… 遗赠给: Please ~ your umbrellas in the corridor. 请把伞放在走廊里. / The bullet wound *left* a scar on his chest. 枪伤在他胸口上留下了疤. / I *left* him quite well an hour ago. 一小时前我离开他时, 他还是好好的. / Did he ~ any message for me? 他有话留给我吗? / To be *left* till called for. (邮件等)留局待领. / His heroic action has *left* a deep impression on our minds. 他的英雄行为在我们心里留下了深刻的印象. / ~ no room (或 scope) for doubt 不容置疑 / Four from five ~s one. 五减四剩一. ③ 遗忘; 丢下: I *left* my notebook in the dormitory. 我把笔记本忘在宿舍里了. ④ 使…处于(某种状态): *Leave* the door open. 让门开着吧. / Nothing was *left* undone. 要做的都做了. ⑤ 把… 交给; 委托: ~ sb. sth. (或 ~ sth. *with* sb.) 把某物交给某人 / *Leave* this (*up*) to me. 把这事交给我吧. / ~ sb. in charge of the matter 委托某人负责办理此事 / [美俚]让(=let): *Leave* him to do it himself. 让他自己儿去做这件事吧. / Nothing was *left* to chance. 不是靠运气, 一切都是经过考虑的. / *Leave* him go. 让他去吧. ⑦遗弃(妻、女等); 舍弃: Take it or ~ it—it's up to you. 或取或舍, 由你自己决定. ⑧(从某个方位)经过: *Leave* the monument on the right and cross the bridge. 从右手经过纪念碑, 再往前过桥. ❷ *vi.* 离去; 动身, 出发: We ~ tomorrow. 我们明天动身. / It's time

for us to ~. (或 It's time we *left*.) 我们该走了. ‖*be* (*nicely*) *left* 受骗; 被遗弃 / *be well left* 得大量遗产 / *get left* ① 被遗弃 ② 被击败 / ~ *about* 乱放, 乱丢 / ~ *alone* 不管, 不理会; 不惹动: *Leave* him *alone*. 别管他. (或: 让他去好了.) / *Leave* the tap *alone*. 别耍弄水龙头. / ~ *behind* ① 留下, 忘带: Take care not to ~ anything *behind*. 当心别丢下东西. ② 遗留 ③ 把…丢在后面, 超过 / *in the air* 见 air / *it at that* 够了, 就这样好了, 就到此为止 / ~ *much to be desired* 还有许多有待改进之处 / ~ *nothing to be desired* 完美无缺 / ~ *off* ①(使)停止: ~ *off* talking 停止讲话 / The rain *left off* at daybreak. 破晓时, 雨停了. / Let's ~ *off* here for lunch. 吃饭了, 就到此为止吧! ②不再使用; 不再穿: I've *left off* medicines. 我现在不吃药了. / feel warm enough to ~ *off* the heavy coat 热得穿不住大衣 / ~ *out* ①省去, 略去: decide what to ~ *out* and what to leave in 决定何去何取 ②遗漏: No comma was *left out*. 一个逗号也没漏掉. ③没有考虑, 不考虑: ~ *out* the possibility of sb.'s coming 排除(或不考虑)某人来的可能性 ④[美]离开 ⑤[方](学校等) 结束一天工作 / ~ *over* ① 留下; 剩下: questions *left over* by history 历史上遗留下来的问题 ②[英]把…留待后用; 使…延期: *Leave* this matter over until tomorrow. 这件事明天再说吧. / ~ *sb. in the lurch* 见 lurch[3] / ~ *sb. to himself* (或 *to his own devices*) 听任某人自行其是, 对某人不加干涉 / ~ *sth. as it is* 听任某事自然发展 / *Leave well* (或 *enough*) *alone*. 不要画蛇添足. / ~ *word* 见 word ‖~**r** *n.* 离开的人(常指学校毕业生)

leave[2] [li:v] *n.* ① 许可, 同意: ask ~ to do sth. 请求同意做某事 / You may have our ~ to visit the workshop. 我们同意你去参观那个车间. ② 准假; 休假; 假期: ask for ~ 请假 / grant sb. ~ of absence 准某人假 / a sick ~ of three days 三天病假 / have two ~s in three years 三年中两次休假 / break (或 overstay) one's ~ 超(过)假(期) ③ 离去; 告别: He took his ~ at eight. 他八点钟告辞离去. / take ~ of one's friends 向朋友们告别 ‖*beg* ~ 请允许: I beg ~ to inform you that ... . 请允许我通知您... / *by* (或 *with*) *your* ~ [口]请原谅; 借光, 劳驾 / on ~ 休假: go home on ~ 休假回家 / a sailor on shore ~ 获准离船上岸的水手 / *take French* ~ 不告而别; 擅自离开; 擅自行动 / *take* ~ *of one's senses* 发疯 / *without a "with your* ~" (或 *without a "by your* ~") [口]径自, 未经许可地 ‖~**-,breaker** *n.* 超过假期的人 / '~**-,taking** *n.* 告别

leave[3] [li:v] *vi.* 生叶, 长叶

leaven ['levn] **I** *n.* ①发酵剂; 曲 ②[喻]引起渐变(或致使活跃)的因素, 潜移默化的影响: tell a few funny stories by way of ~ 讲了几个滑稽故事以使气氛活跃起来 ③气味, 色彩 **II** *vt.* ①(加发

酵剂)使发酵 ②[喻]掺杂些东西以影响; 使渐变; 使活跃: a serious style ~ed with wit 一种带点诙谐的严肃文体 ‖*the old* ~ 表明旧习尚未革除的痕迹 ‖~**ing** *n.* ①发酵 ②发酵剂 ③引起渐变(或致使活跃)的因素; 影响; 气味, 色彩

leaves [li:vz] leaf 的复数

leavings ['li:viŋz] [复] *n.* 剩余; 残渣: the ~ of meals 残羹剩饭

lectern ['lektə(:)n] *n.* ①(教堂中的)读经台 ②(演讲人)放讲稿的小台架

lectern

lecture ['lektʃə] **I** *n.* ① 演讲; 讲课; (演讲或讲课的)讲稿: a ~ tour 演讲 (或讲课) 旅行 / attend a ~ 听演讲(或讲课) / a series of ~s on philosophy 一系列有关哲学的演讲 / deliver (或 give) a ~ 讲演; 讲课 ② 严责, 长篇大论的教训: give sb. a moral ~ 一本正经地向某人说教一通 **II** *vi.* 演讲; 讲课: ~ on public hygiene 作关于公共卫生方面的报告 **III** *vt.* ①向···讲演; 给···讲课 ②教训, 训斥: be ~d for being too mischievous 因太淘气而被教训了一顿 ‖*a curtain* ~ 妻子私下对丈夫的训斥 / *read sb. a* ~ 训斥某人一顿 ‖~**r** ['lektʃərə] *n.* ① 讲演者 ② (大学、学院中)的讲师: a group of worker ~rs 工人讲师团 / ~**ship** *n.* 讲师的职位(或资格、身分)

led [led] lead¹ 的过去式和过去分词 ‖~ **captain** 拍马者, 追随者 / ~ **farm** [苏格兰] 主人远居他地的农庄 / ~ **horse** 由马伕牵着的备用的马

ledge [ledʒ] *n.* ①(自墙壁突出的)壁架; 架状突出物 ②[矿]矿脉 ③岩石的突出部 ④(近海岸的)水面下突出物, 暗礁 ‖~**d** *a.* 有壁架的; 有突出物的; 有暗礁的

ledger ['ledʒə] *n.* ① 分类帐: the general ~ 总分类帐, 总帐 ②[建](搭脚手架用的)横木, 卧材 ③(坟墓的)台石 ④ =~ line ‖~ **bait** 底饵(挂在钓鱼丝底部的鱼饵) / ~ **blade** [纺]剪毛机上的固定刀片 / ~ **board** (栅栏的)横顶板; 栏杆的扶手 / ~ **line** 【音】加线(加于五线谱上方或下方的短线) / ~ **tackle** [总称]能使钓饵沉于水底的鱼具

lee [li:] **I** *n.* ①庇护, 保护 ②庇护所; 避风处 ③【海】下风, 背风面 ④[地]背冰川面 **II** *a.* ①避风处的 ②下风的, 背风面的 ③背冰川面的 ‖*under* (或 *in*) *the* ~ *of* 在···庇护之下 ‖~**board** *n.* 【船】(平底船下风边)横漂抵板 / ~ **shore** ①【海】下风岸 ② 危险, 招致毁灭的根源

leech¹ [li:tʃ] **I** *n.* ①[古](内科或外科)医生 ②【动】水蛭 ③吸血鬼, 榨取他人脂膏者 **II** ❶ *vt.* ①用水蛭给···抽血 ②吸尽···的血汗: ~ sb. white 吸干某人的血 ❷ *vi.* (水蛭般)依附于别人 (*on to*) ‖*stick like a* ~ 死死抓牢, 钉住不放 ‖~**craft** *n.* [古]医术

leech² [li:tʃ] *n.* 【船】帆的垂直缘

leek [li:k] *n.* 【植】韭葱 ‖*eat* (或 *swallow*) *the* ~ 被迫收回自己说过的话; 被迫忍受屈辱 / *not worth a* ~ 毫无价值

leer¹ [liə] **I** *n.* 斜眼一瞥(表示敌意、嘲弄、会意等); 秋波 **II** *vi.* 斜眼看; 送秋波 (*at*) ‖~**ingly** ['liərinli] *ad.* 斜着眼地

leer² [liə] *n.* 【化】(玻璃的)退火炉

lees [li:z] [复] *n.* 酒糟; 沉积物; 渣滓 ‖*drink* (或 *drain*) *to the* ~ ①把···喝得杯底朝天 ②尝尽···的辛酸

left¹ [left] leave¹ 的过去式和过去分词 ‖~-,**luggage office** [英]行李寄存处 / ~-'**off** *a.* (衣服等)不用的, 不穿的 / '~-,**over** *a.* 剩余的 *n.* 剩余物; 吃剩的食物

left² [left] **I** *a.* ①左, 左边的, 左侧的 ②左翼的; [常作 L-]左派的: the ~ flank of an army 军队的左翼 **II** *ad.* 在左边; 向左: Left face (或 Left turn)! 向左转! **III** *n.* ①左, 左边, 左方: turn to the ~ 向左转 / Come and sit on (或 at) my ~. 来坐在我左边。 ② (拳击中的)左手 ③[常作 L-]左派; 急进分子们; 议长席左侧的议员们, 左派议员们 ④【军】左翼 ‖*have two* ~ *feet* 极其笨拙 / *over the* ~ [俚]完全不是这样, 恰恰相反: He is punctual—*over the* ~. 他可准时啦—准时个屁! ‖~**ism** *n.* [有时作 L-]左派观点(或主张、运动) / ~**ist** *a.* & *n.* [常作 L-]左派的(人) / ~**most** *a.* 最左的 / ~**ward(s)** *ad.* & *a.* 在左边(的); 向左边(的) / '~-**hand** *a.* ①左边的; 左手的: on the ~-*hand* side of 在···的左边 / the ~-*hand* man (站在某人)左边的人 ② =~-*handed* (*a.*) / '~-'**handed** *a.* ①惯用左手的 ②左手的; 用左手做的 ③笨拙的 ④不诚恳的; 含恶意的: a ~-*handed* compliment 言不由衷的恭维话 ⑤ 反时针的, 向左旋转的: a ~-*handed* screw 左转螺丝 ⑥(婚姻)门第不相当的 *ad.* 用左手: write ~-*handed* 用左手写 / '~-'**hander** *n.* ①用左手的人, 左撇子 ②(拳击中)用左手的一拳 / '~-'**leaning** *a.* 左倾的 / '~-'**wing** (政党等的)左翼; [总称]左翼人士 / '~-'**wing** *a.* 左翼的 / ~-**winger** ['left,wiŋə] *n.* 左翼人士

leg [leg] **I** *n.* ①腿; (猪、羊等)供食用的腿: a ~ of mutton (pork) 一只羊(猪)腿 ②假腿 ③(桌、椅等的)腿脚; 支撑柱条 ④裤脚管; 袜统; 靴统: the ~s of a pair of trousers 裤脚管 ⑤(直角三角形的)勾, 股; 三角形底边外的边 ⑥(船朝某一方向抢

风直驶的)一段航程;一段旅程;(接力赛中每个运动员所承担的)一段赛程: complete the first ~ of a five-nation tour 完成访问五国旅途中的第一段行程 ⑦[电]引线,支线;多相变压器的每一相的铁芯;(多相系统的)一个相 ⑧[英俚]骗子 ⑨(板球)击球员的右后方场地 ⑩ (牌戏等上下两局中的)一局,一盘 II (legged; legging) ❶ vi. ①[口]疾走;急跑(一般用于 ~ it 短语中): He legged it out to the wharf. 他朝码头飞跑而去。②用腿抵住运河隧洞壁推船通过 ②(为…)奔走,卖力(for) ❷ vt. 用腿抵壁把(船)推过运河隧洞 ||as fast as one's ~s could carry (one) 拼命跑 / be all ~s (人)又瘦又长 / be on (或 upon) one's hind ~s [谑] =be on (或 upon) one's ~s 在(或 upon) one's ~s ①站着(尤指演说时) ②(病后)能起来走动 ③发达的,富裕的;已有成就的 / be run off one's ~s 破产 / change the ~ (马)改换步伐 / fall on (或 upon) one's ~s 跌而不伤;运气好;侥幸摆脱困境 / feel (或 find) one's ~s ①(婴孩)开始能站起(或行走) ②开始意识到自己的力量(或能力);有了自信心 / get a ~ in [口]得到…的信任 / get (或 set) sb. on his ~s ① 使某人恢复健康 ②帮助某人在经济上自立 / get up on one's hind ~s [口] 盛气凌人,气势汹汹 / give sb. a ~ up [口] ① 帮某人上马;帮某人越过障碍 ② 助某人一臂之力;扶助某人 / hang a ~ 犹豫不定 / have a bone in one's ~ 难于行走 / have ~s 走得快;有耐力 / have not a ~ to stand on [口](论点等)站不住脚;(人)理屈词穷: He hasn't a ~ to stand on for his behaviour. 他的这种行为是完全没有理由的。/ have sb. by the ~ [美俚]使某人处于不利地位 / have the ~s of 比…跑得快: He had the ~s of me. 他比我跑得快。/ keep one's ~s 站稳,不跌倒 / ~ and ~ 双方得分相等;平分秋色 / ~ before wicket (板球)击球员违犯规则用腿截球(常略作l.b.w.)/ make a ~ 弯一腿行礼(另一腿向后伸)/ on one's last ~s 垂死;临近结束 / pull sb.'s ~ [口]哄骗取笑某人,愚弄某人 / put one's best ~ forward (或 foremost) [口]飞速走(或跑);[喻]全力以赴 / run sb. off his ~s 使某人疲于奔命 / scrape a ~ 见 scrape / shake a ~ ①[口]跳舞 ②[美俚]赶紧 / shake a loose (或 free) ~ 过放荡的生活 / show a ~ [口]起床 / show ~ [美俚]逃跑 / stand on one's own ~s 自立;自主 / stretch one's ~s (坐久后)走一走,散散步 / take to one's ~s 逃跑 / talk the hind ~ off a donkey (或 dog, horse) 唠叨不休 / try it on the other ~ [口]试用所剩的最后方法去做 / walk (或 trot) sb. off his ~s 使某人走得精疲力竭 ||legged a. [常用以构成复合词]有…腿的: a long-legged man 腿长的人 / a three-legged race (两人一组,将每人一腿捆在一起的)三脚竞走游戏 / legging n. [常用复](帆布或革制的)护胫(或护腿);(小孩的)护腿套裤 / leggy a. ①腿过长的;腿长而不灵便的 ②腿长

而美的 ③【植】茎细长的 / ~less a. 无腿的 ||~ bail 逃;give (或 take) ~ bail 逃跑 / ~ guard (运动员的)护腿 / '~-,iron n. 脚镣 vt. 用脚镣锁住 / ~man ['legmən] n. ①(现场)采访记者;记者(尤指自己外出来采访新闻的访员) ②(报馆内)采访新闻及做零星活的助手 ③(因工作需要)到处奔波的人 / '~-of-'mutton a. 羊腿形的 / '~-pull n. 愚弄 / '~-rest n. (病人等用的)搁脚凳 / '~room n. (车辆、飞机上)供乘坐者伸腿的面积 / ~ show (一种由女子表演的低级黄色的)大腿戏 / '~work n. 跑腿活儿;新闻采访工作

legacy ['legəsi] n. ① 遗赠物(一般指动产),遗产 ②传代物

legal ['li:gəl] I a. ① 法律(上)的: a ~ question 法律问题 ②合法的,正当的: one's ~ status 某人的合法地位 / ~ separation (未正式离婚夫妇的)合法分居 ③ 法定的: a ~ tender 法币,法偿 / a ~ holiday 法定假日 / the ~ limit (汽车等行驶的)法定速度 II n. ①法定权利 ②依法必须登报的声明 ③[复]储蓄银行(或信托公司等)依法可以用来投资的证券 ||~ly ad.

legality [li(:)'gæliti] n. ①合法性;法律性 ②[复](法律上的)义务

legalize ['li:gəlaiz] vt. 使合法化;法律上认可,使成为法定 ||legalization [,li:gəlai'zeiʃən] n.

legate[1] ['legit] n. 使者,使节(尤指罗马教皇的使节) ||~ship n. 使节的职权(或任期)

legate[2] [li'geit] vt. 把…遗留给,把…遗赠给

legation [li'geiʃən] n. ①使节的派遣;使节负有的使命 ② 公使馆;公使馆全体人员(指公使及其随员) ③使节的职权

legend ['ledʒənd] n. ①传说;传奇;传奇文学 ②传奇的起源人物(或事件) ③(奖章、硬币等上的)题铭,铭文 ④地图的图例;插图的说明

legendary ['ledʒəndəri] a. 传说(中)的;传奇(中)的;传说(或传奇)似的

legible ['ledʒəbl] a. 易读的,字迹清楚的 ||legibility [,ledʒi'biliti] n. / legibly ad.

legion ['li:dʒən] n. ①古罗马军团(约有三千至六千名步兵,辅以骑兵) ② 军团,大批部队 ③[L-]全国退伍军人协会: the American Legion 美国军团(美国的退伍军人组织之一) ④ 众多,大批: a ~ of followers 大批追随者 / Books on this subject are ~. 关于这个题目的书籍多得不计其数。||~ary a. 军团的,部队的;退伍军人协会的 n. 军团(或部队)的一员;退伍军人协会会员

legislate ['ledʒisleit] ❶ vi. 立法· ❷ vt. 通过立法以使…产生(或成立)

legislative ['ledʒisleitiv] I a. ① 立法的: the ~ power 立法权 ②有立法权的;起立法作用的 ③立法机关的;由立法机关成员组成的 ④根据法规执行的 ⑤立法机关创立的(区别于行政机关或司法机关创立的) II n. 立法机关 ||~ly ad. ||~ assembly [常作 L- A-] ① 美国州(或领地)的两院制议会 ②两院制议会的下院 ③一院制的立法院

(尤指加拿大的省议会) / ~ council [常作 L-C-]
① 英国议会的上院 ② (英国殖民地或美国领地
的)一院制议会 ③美国州议会的常设委员会

legislator ['ledʒisleitə] *n.* 立法机关的成员，议员；
立法者 ‖~ial [,ledʒislə'tɔ:riəl] *a.* / ~ship *n.*
立法机关成员(或立法者)的身分(或地位、资格等)

legislature ['ledʒisleitʃə] *n.* 立法机关

legitimacy [li'dʒitiməsi] *n.* 合法性；正统性

legitimate [li'dʒitimit] **I** *a.* ①合法的；合理的：a
~ claim 合法的要求 / a ~ inference 合理的推
断 ②正统的：the ~ drama 正统戏剧 ③由合
法婚姻所生的，嫡出的 ④(感情等)真实的 **II**
[li'dʒitimeit] *vt.* ①使合法，给…以合法地位(或
权力)；宣布…为合法 ②证明…有理 ‖~ly *ad.* /
legitimation [li,dʒiti'meiʃən] *n.*

leisure ['leʒə; 美 'li:ʒə] **I** *n.* ①空闲，闲暇：I
scarcely have ~ *for* (或 to play) football this
afternoon. 今天下午我没有空踢足球。②悠闲，
安逸：He doesn't like a life of ~. 他不喜欢
过悠闲的生活。**II** *a.* ①空闲的；in one's ~ time
(或 hours, moments) 在空闲时间里 ②有闲的
‖at ~ ①闲着的；有空的：I am quite *at* ~ if
you want me to help you. 你如果要我帮忙，我
完全有空。② 从容不迫地：You may proceed *at*
~. 你尽可从容地进行。/ *at one's* ~ 当有空
的时候；Drop in to see us *at your* ~. 有空时
我们这儿来。/ *wait sb.'s* ~ 等某人有空的时
候：Don't hurry, I can *wait your* ~. 别急，我
可以等到你有空的时候。‖~d *a.* ①有闲的；the
~d class 有闲阶级 ②从容的 / ~less *a.* 无空
闲的

leisurely ['leʒəli; 美 'li:ʒəli] **I** *a.* 从容的，慢慢的：
at a ~ pace 以从容不迫的速度 / He made a ~
inspection of the doors and the windows before
leaving. 离开前，他从容地检查了门窗。**II** *ad.*
从容地，慢慢地：The boat steamed ~ upstream.
这只船缓缓驶向上游。‖**leisureliness** *n.*

lemon ['lemən] **I** *n.* ①柠檬；柠檬树 ②= ~ yellow
③[美俚]不中用的东西，次品；讨厌的家伙；无用
的人 **II** *a.* 柠檬色的；柠檬香的；柠檬味的；柠檬
制的 ‖*hand sb. a* ~ [美俚]把蹩脚东西给某人；
使某人不快 ‖'**~-drop** *n.* 柠檬糖 / ~ kali 用
酒石酸和碳酸氢钠制的起泡饮料 / ~ squash
[英]柠檬苏打水 / '~-,squeezer *n.* 榨柠檬器 /
~ yellow ①柠檬色 ②柠檬黄(铬酸钡或铬酸铅
颜料)

lemonade [,lemə'neid] *n.* 柠檬水

lend [lend] (lent [lent]) **❶** *vt.* ①把…借给：They
lent us their pumps. 他们把水泵借给我们。
②贷(款)；出租(书籍等)；给予；给：~ sb. a box
on the ear 打某人一记耳光 **❷** *vi.*
贷款 ‖~ *itself to* 有助于，适宜于：The rural
environment *lent itself* to the restoration of
his health. 农村环境有助于他恢复健康。/
oneself to 帮助；屈从：~ *oneself* to dishonest
schemes 参与诡诈勾当 ‖~able *a.* 可供借(贷)

的 / ~er *n.* 出借者；贷方

lending ['lendiŋ] *n.* ①出借；出租 ②借出物；租
借物 ‖~ library ①收费图书馆 ②[英](图书馆
的)借书处；公共图书馆

length [leŋθ] *n.* ① 长，长度：a pigsty 15 metres
in ~ and 5 in breadth 长十五米宽五米的猪圈 /
Have you got any fluorescent lamps this ~?
你们有这样长度的日光灯管吗？②(时间的)长
短，期间 ③【语】音长 ④(一)段，(一)节：a
dress ~ (足以缝制一件衣服的)一段衣料 / a ~
of tubing (或 pipe) 一节管子 ⑤(作为长度单位
的)物体的长度，动物的体长：The racing boat
led by three ~s after a quarter of a mile. 这
赛艇在行驶了四分之一哩后三艇身领先。‖*at
arm's* ~ 在手臂伸得到的地方；疏远 / *at full* ~
①极为详细地 ②全身平伸地：lie *at full* ~ on
the grass 伸直身体躺在草地上 / *at* ~ ①最后，
终于 ②详细地：speak at (great) ~ 详细地讲了
好久 / debate a subject *at* ~ 对一个题目进行充
分辩论 / *cannot see beyond the* ~ *of one's
nose* 鼠目寸光 / *go (to) all* ~s (或 *any* ~)
竭尽全力 / *go to great* ~s 竭尽全力 /
go (to) the ~ *of* 走到…这样的极端，甚至
会…：*go (to) the* ~ *of* saying … 甚至说… /
keep at arm's ~ 避免同…亲近 / *know* (或
find, get, have) the ~ *of sb.'s foot* 了解某人
的弱点以便加以控制 / *measure one's* (*own*) ~
全身跌倒在地 / *not the* ~ *of a street* 见
street / *one's* ~ *of days* 一个人的寿命 ‖~ways
ad. 纵长地 / ~wise *ad.* & *a.* 纵长地(的)

lengthen ['leŋθən] **❶** *vt.* 使延长：~ a runway 加
长跑道 / ~ a vowel 【语】延长元音音长 **❷** *vi.*
变长，长起来；延伸：The days are ~*ing*. 白天
长起来了 / Summer ~s (*out*) into autumn.
夏天渐渐转入秋天。/ The shadows ~. 天色渐
黑。(或：年纪渐老。或：死期已近。)

lengthy ['leŋθi] *a.* ①过长的，漫长的 ②(演说、文
章等)冗长的；(讲话人、作者等)罗罗唆唆的
③[口]个子高的 ‖**lengthily** *ad.* / **lengthiness** *n.*

lenient ['li:njənt] *a.* ①宽大的，宽厚的；怜悯的：
give ~ treatment to the prisoners of war 宽大
对待战俘 ②[古]减轻痛苦的 ‖~ly *ad.*

lens [lenz] **I** *n.* ①透镜；(凹、凸)镜片；一组透镜：
a concave (convex) ~ 凹(凸)透镜 ②(眼球的)晶
(状)体 ③(照相机的)镜头 ④双凸透镜状物品
【矿】透镜状油矿，扁豆状矿体 **II** *vt.* 给…摄影
(尤指摄制影片) ‖~ed *a.* 有透镜的 / ~less *a.*
无透镜的 ‖~ louse [美俚]抢电影(或电视)镜头
的人 / ~man ['lenzmən] *n.* [美口]摄影师

Lent [lent] *n.* [基督教]四旬斋；大斋期(指复活节
前的四十天) ‖~en *a* ①四旬斋的；大斋期的
②适合于斋节的，简朴的；严肃的：a ~en face
阴沉的脸 ③无肉的：a ~en pie 无肉斋饼
‖~ lily 水仙 / ~ term 大学的春季学期

lent [lent] lend 的过去式和过去分词

lentil ['lentil] *n.* 小扁豆(指植物或其种子)

leopard ['lepəd] *n.* 豹 ‖*Can the ~ change his spots?* [谚]花豹能改变它身上的斑点吗? (意指本性难移) ‖*-ess n.* 母豹 ‖*~ spot* 豹斑(常指一方在另一方地盘内建立的分散的据点, 在地图上因标色不同, 呈豹斑状)

leopard

leper ['lepə] *n.* ①麻风病患者 ②(由于道德和社会原因)别人避之唯恐不及的人

leprosy ['leprəsi] *n.* ①【医】麻风(病) ②有害的影响; [喻](道德的)堕落, 败坏

less [les] **I** *a.* [little 的比较级]更少(或更小)的, 较少(或较小)的: ~ but better 少而精 / The indigenous method costs ~ money. 土办法少花钱。 / More haste, ~ speed. [谚]欲速则不达。 / a matter of ~ importance 次要的事情 / try to make ~ mistakes 尽量少犯错误 **II** *ad.* [little 的比较级]更少(或更小)地, 较少(或较小)地: The child was ~ hurt than frightened. 这小孩倒伤没有什么, 却受了惊吓。 / Malaria cases are quite common in the tropical areas but ~ so in cold places. 疟疾病例在热带是常见的, 在寒冷地方却不然。 / the ~ known of the two 两者中不大知名的一个 / The better you get to know him, the ~ aloof you'll find him to be. 你越是了解他, 你就越会发觉他并不是那么不可亲近的。 / I was the ~ surprised as I had been informed beforehand. 因为我事前已得到消息, 所以并不感到怎么惊奇。 **III** *n.* 更少(或更小), 较少(或较小): John will not take ~. 约翰一点不肯多拿。 / *Less* of your lip! [口]别饶舌了! / The project was completed in ~ than two years. 工程在两年不到的时间里就完成了。 / expect to see ~ of sb. 不想多见某人 **IV** *prep.* 减去; 少掉: a month ~ two days 一个月差两天 ‖*any the ~* 更少(或更小)一些: He did not work *any the* ~ for his illness. 他没有因为生病而少工作一些。 / *in ~ than no time* 马上, 一眨眼工夫: I'll come *in* ~ *than no time*. 我马上就来。 / *no ~ a person than* 身分(或级别等)不低于 / *no ~ (than)* (和…)一样, 不少(于…), 不亚(于…): She is *no* ~ active than she used to be. 她和从前一样活跃。 / *a no* ~ important question 同样重要的问题 / *none the* ~ 见 **none** /

nothing ~ *than* 见 **nothing** / *still* (或 *much*, *even*) ~ 更不必说, 何况 ‖*'~-than-'carload a.* (铁路运输中的)零担的(略作 L. C. L.) / *'~-than-'truckload a.* 卡车零担的(略作 L. T. L.)

lessee [le'si:] *n.* 承租人, 租户

lessen ['lesn] ❶ *vt.* ①减少, 减轻: ~ production costs 减少生产成本 / ~ tensions 缓和紧张局势 ②缩小; 贬低: ~ the differences between the city and the countryside 缩小城乡差别 ❷ *vi.* 变小, 变小: As the medicine took effect, the symptoms ~ed. 药力奏效, 症状减轻了。

lesser ['lesə] [little 的比较级] **I** *a.* [只作定语]较小的; 更少的; 次要的: a ~ river 小河 / a ~ nation 小国 **II** *ad.* =less (*ad.*)

lesson ['lesn] **I** *n.* ①功课; 课业: prepare and review ~s with the students 跟学员们一起预习和复习功课 / You know your ~ well. 你的功课记得很熟。 ②[常用复]课程: give ~s *in* agricultural knowledge 教农业知识课 / take violin ~s from sb. 跟某人学小提琴 ③一节课; (教科书中的)一课: This textbook has twenty ~s. 这课本有二十课。 / *Lesson* Six 第六课 ④教训; 训诫, 训斥: draw useful ~s from 从…吸取有益的教训 ⑤[宗]日课(指早、晚祷时的《圣经》选读) **II** *vt.* ①给…上课 ②训斥, 教训 ‖*read sb. a* ~ 训斥某人一顿

lessor [le'sɔ:] *n.* 出租人

lest [lest] *conj.* ① [在被连接的状语从句里常用 should 或原形动词]唯恐; 免得: The driver looked over the engine carefully ~ it (should) go wrong on the way. 唯恐车子在路上出毛病, 司机仔细检查了发动机。 ②[用于 fear, worry 一类动词后面, 起连接从句的作用, 并无实际意思]: I was afraid ~ the kid (should) fall down the staircase. 我怕这孩子会从楼梯上跌下来。

let[1] [let] **I** (let; letting) ❶ *vt.* ①[用于第一或第三人称的祈使句中, 表示建议、请求、命令、警告等]让: *Let* them set off at once. 叫他们立刻就出发吧。 / Don't ~ this happen again. 不要再让这种事情发生了! / *Let* them do their worst! (用作挑战语)让他们把最凶恶的绝招都使出来吧! / *Let* there be no mistake about it. 在这一点上不要有什么误解。 ②[用于祈使句]假设: *Let* AB be equal to CD. 设 AB 等于 CD。 ③允许, 让: Please ~ me know. 请告诉我。 / The child was ~ (to) do it. 这孩子被允许去做那件事。 / He ~ it be known that .... 他对人说…… / The patient wanted to go back to work but the doctor wouldn't ~ him. 病员要求回去工作, 但医生不同意。 / ~ sb. through 让某人通过 / ~ drop a hint 露口风 ④使流出, 放出: ~ the water from the pond 把水从池里放掉 / ~ (*out*) a sigh 叹一口气 ⑤让…进入 (或通过): This pair of rubber shoes ~ (*in*) water. 这双套鞋漏水。 ⑥出租, 租给: ~ (sb.) a room 出租(给某人)一间房间 / House to *Let* (广告用语) 房屋

召租 ⑦交付(承包工作等);【经】发包订(约) ❷ *vi.* ①出租 ②(工程等)被承包 II *n.* [英]出租;租出的房屋 ‖~ *alone* ①不干涉,不管;不碰;不弄: *Let* him *alone* to do it. 让他们个儿去干吧。 ②更不用说 / ~ *be* 听任,不打扰: *Let* him *be.* 不要打扰他。(或:由他去。) / ~ *down* ①放下;放低: ~ *down* a curtain 放下幕布 ②使失望,辜负;不支持,不做…的台: Don't ~ me *down.* 别使我失望啊。(或:别抬我台。) ③松动 ④(飞机)减速下降 / ~ *drive (at)* (向…)投掷;(向…)打出: ~ *drive at* sb. with a stone 拿一块石子扔某人 / ~ *drive* with one's right fist 用右拳击出 / ~ *fall* ①让…倒下(或落下) ②无意中说出;有意无意似地说出,露(口风等) ③【数】划(垂线) (*upon, on*) / ~ *fly* 发射,投射; ~ *fly* an arrow 射箭 / ~ *fly at* ①向…发射,向…射出;向…投击 ②骂 / *Let George do it.* [美俚]让别人去干吧。 / ~ *go* ①放开;释放: Don't ~ *go.* 别放手。 / Don't ~ *go (of)* the rope. 抓牢绳子,别松手。 / *Let* me go! 让我走! / *Let go of* me! 放开我! ② 发射: ~ *go* an arrow 射箭 / ~ *in* ①让…进来,放进;招致(祸害等): Please open the window and ~ *in* some fresh air. 请打开窗透透新鲜空气吧。 ②插入,嵌入 ③使陷于,损害,累及 (*for*): ~ sb. *in for* trouble 使某人遭到麻烦 / ~ *into* ①让…进入 ②把…嵌进: ~ a window *into* the wall 在墙上开一扇窗 ③让…知道: ~ sb. *into* the secret 让某人知道秘密 ④拳打;责骂 / ~ *it go at that* 谈论到此为止,停止讨论;不再去想 / ~ *loose* 释放,放出;发出,吐出 / *Let me see.* 让我想想看。(有时在上下文中作插入语,可译作"呃,呃") / ~ *off* ①放掉(蒸气等),放(炮、烟火等);说出(笑话等) ②不惩罚,饶恕;对…从轻处置: ~ sb. *off* easy 轻轻放过某人 ③准许…暂时停止工作 / ~ *on* [口] ①泄露;泄露秘密: Don't ~ *on* (to him) that .... 别(向他)泄露… / Don't ~ *on* (to him). 别(向他)泄露秘密。②假装: He ~s *on* that he doesn't know. 他装着不知道。 / ~ *oneself go* 尽情,情不自禁;忘乎所以: How did you get to ~ *yourself go* like that? 你怎会那样忘乎所以? / ~ *out* ①放掉(水、气等);泄露 ②放大(衣服等);放出(贴边等) ③[美口]放学;散场 ④[美俚]解雇 ⑤出租(车、马等) ⑥打;踢;骂 (*at*) / ~ *pass* 放过,不追究 / ~ *ride* 不管;放任…自流 / ~ sb. *down gently* (或 *easily*) 给某人留面子 / ~ sb. *have it* [美俚]让某人吃顿苦头 / ~ *slide* 不关心,对…漫不经心 / ~ *slip* 放走,松开…的绳索;错过(机会等);无意中说出 / ~ *up* 减小,松弛;减缓;停止,中止: The rain is letting *up* a little. 雨小些了。 / ~ *up on* expenditures 减少开支 / ~ *well alone* 见 well² ‖~'*down n.* ①失望;令人失望的事物 ②松劲 ③下降,减退 ④(飞机准备着陆前的)下降,减低 / '~'*up n.* 放松;停顿: They have been working twelve hours without a ~*up.* 他们已不停地工作了十二个小

时。 / There was a six-day ~*up* in ground fighting. 地面战斗暂停了六天。

let² [let] I (letted 或 let; letting) *vt.* [古]妨碍,阻碍 II *n.* ①障碍 ②(网球等的)球触网(需重发球) ‖*without ~ or hindrance* 无阻碍地

lethal ['li:θəl] I *a.* 致死的,致命的: ~ gas 致死性毒气 II *n.* 【生】致死因子 (=~ gene) ‖-*ity* [li'θæliti] *n.* 致死性 / ~*ly ad.*

lethargy ['leθədʒi] *n.* ①【医】嗜眠症 ②冷淡,冷漠;懒散;无生气

letter¹ ['letə] *n.* [主英]出租人

letter² ['letə] I *n.* ①文字,字;字母: teach a child his ~s 教孩子识字 / a capital (small) ~ 大(小)写字母 / How many ~s are there in the word "struggle"? "struggle" 这个词有几个字母? ②【印】活字,铅字 ③信,函件;[常用复]证书,许可证: pay serious attention to ~s from the people 重视人民来信 / a ~ of introduction 介绍信 / an official ~ 公函 / a ~ of credit【商】信用状 / ~s of administration【律】管理遗产委任状 ④ [~s] [用作单或复]文学;学问: a man of ~s 文人 / the profession of ~s 著作界 / the republic (或 commonwealth) of ~s 文坛 ⑤字面意义: in ~ and in spirit 在字面和精神实质上,在形式和内容上 ⑥[美](运动衣上用校名缩写字母缀合的)学校标志: win one's ~ 当运动选手 II ❶ *vt.* ①用印刷体字母在…上写(或刻印);用字母分类标明: The poster was artistically ~ed. 这张标语是用美术字写(或印)的。②用印刷体字母写(或刻印): He ~ed his name on the flyleaf. 他在书的衬页上用印刷体写上自己的姓名。❷ *vi.* 写(或刻印)印刷体字 ‖*by* ~ 以书信形式: I shall inform him *by* ~. 我将写信通知他。 / *to the* ~ 严格按照字句: carry out an order to ~s 不折不扣地执行一项命令 ‖-*ed a.* ①识字的;有文化的 ②有学问的 ③印有字母的;有文字的 / ~*er* ['letərə] *n.* 字母(或文字)刻写人 / ~*ing* ['letəriŋ] *n.* ①写字;印字;刻字 ②[总称](写或刻印的)字 / ~*less a.* ①没有信件的 ②没有刻印文字的 ‖~ *balance* 信秤 / ~ *board* [印]铅字盘 / ~ *bomb* 书信炸弹(指装在信封内的爆炸物) / ~ *book* (保存或誊录信件的)书信备查簿 / ~ *box* 信箱 / '~*card n.* 封缄信片 / ~ *carrier* 邮递员 / ~ *case* 携带用信件夹 / '~-*drop n.* 邮局(或信箱)的投信口 / ~ *founder* 铸铅字工人 / '~*head n.* 信笺上端所印文字(包括姓名、商店、地址、电话号码等) / ~ *lock* 字锁,暗码锁 / '~*man n.* [美](得奖的)运动员 / ~ *missive* 传达上级命令、任命、许可、邀请的函件 / ~ *paper* 信笺 / '~-'*perfect a.* ①字字正确的,完全正确的;逐字的 ②熟记台词的;对自己扮演的角色完全了解的 / '~*press n.* ①[主英]有插图的书中的正文 ②活版印刷 ③书信复写器 / ~ *sheet* 邮简 / ~s patent 特许证书 / '~*weight* *n.* ①信秤 ②镇纸,纸压 (＝paperweight) / **~ writer** ①写信者;代人写信者 ②尺牍

lettuce ['letis] *n.* ① 莴苣 ②[美俚]纸币

level ['levl] **I** *n.* ①水平面;水平线;水平状态: 4,000 metres above sea ~ 海拔四千米 / the rise and fall of water ~ 水位的升降 / Water seeks its own ~. 水往低处流。②水平;标准: a normal blood-sugar ~ 正常血糖量标准 ③级别; 地位: top-~ talks 最高级会谈 ④水准仪;水平测量: take a ~ 作水准测量 ⑤高度: at eye ~ 齐眼睛那末高 / high ~ bombing 高空轰炸 ⑥平地; 梯形座位各排之间的通道 ⑦【矿】主平巷 / 【电】电平; 能级 **II** *a.* ①水平的;平的: ~ land 平地 ②同高度的;同水平的;同程度的;并进的; 【电】等位的: The tree top is ~ with the roof. 树梢和屋顶一样高。/ be ~ in technique 具有同样的技术水平 / a ~ spoonful of sugar 一平匙的食糖 / a ~ race 势均力敌的赛跑 ③笔直的,直盯着的: give sb. a ~ look 盯某人一眼 ④平稳的;冷静的: keep a ~ head in face of danger 危急时保持冷静头脑 ⑤ 均匀不变的; 平均分布的;平板的: keep a workshop at a ~ temperature 保持车间恒温 / speak (sing) in ~ tones 用平板的声音说(唱) ⑥公平的 **III** (level(l)ed, level(l)ing) **❶** *vt.* ①使成水平;把…弄平;平整: ~ the fields 平整土地 / ~ up (down) the ground 填(铲)平地面 ②夷平,毁坏;击倒 ③使同等;把… (向上或向下)拉平;消除(差别): ~ the output of a factory up to that of the advanced 把一工厂的产量提高到先进厂的水平 ④ 把…对准 ⑤ 使(颜色等)均匀;使(声音)平板 ⑥对(土地)作水平测量 **❷** *vi.* ①变平 ②拉平(with) ③用枪瞄准(at) ④坦率诚实地对待: I'll ~ with you. 我对你开诚布公。‖**do one's ~ best** 全力以赴 / **draw ~ (with)** (和…)拉平,(同…)相齐 / **find one's own ~** 找到相称的位置 / **~ off** ①把…弄平,整平: The bulldozers quickly level(l)ed off the site. 推土机很快就把工地整平了。②变平; 达到平衡,稳定 ③(飞机降落前)平飞 / **on a ~ with** 和…同一水准;和…相等 / **on the ~** [口]公平,坦率,不耍花招 ‖**level(l)er** *n.* ①使平等(或平均)的人(或事物) ② 水准测量员; 校平器 ③ 平等主义者; [L-] (英国十七世纪资产阶级革命时期)平均派的成员 ‖**-ly** *ad.* / **~ness** *n.* ‖**~ crossing** [英](道路等的)平面交叉 / **'~ headed** *a.* 头脑冷静的

level(l)ing ['levəliŋ] *n.* 水准测量;测平;(路型的)整平: a ~ machine (道路)整平机;【冶】钢板矫平机 ‖**~ rod** 水准(标)尺

lever ['li:və; 美 'levə] **I** *n.* ①杆,杠杆: control ~ 【机】控制杆 / timing ~ 【机】定时杆 ②途径;工具;手段 **II** *vt.* ①用杠杆撬动,用杠杆移动 ②用杆操纵 **❷** *vi.* 用杠杆

leverage ['li:vəridʒ; 美 'levəridʒ] *n.* ① 杠杆作用 ②杠杆率 ③力量;影响: have little bargaining ~ 几乎没有什么讨价还价的力量

leviathan [li'vaiəθən] *n.* ①[常作 L-] (基督教《圣经·旧约全书》中象征邪恶的)海中怪兽 ②巨物; 海中巨兽(如鲸等);巨型远洋轮 ③ [常作 L-] 极权主义国家 ④有财有势的人

levity ['leviti] *n.* ①(举止、谈吐等的)轻率,轻浮 ②变化无常 ③[罕]轻

levy ['levi] **I** *n.* ①征收;征税;征收额: make a ~ of 8% on a commodity 对一种商品征收百分之八的税款 ②征集;征兵;被征的兵员: green levies and veteran soldiers 新兵和老兵 **II ❶** *vt.* ①征收(捐税、罚款、贡品等);强索: ~ a tax on sb. 向某人征税 ②征集(兵员) ③(动员人力、物力)发动(战争): ~ war upon (或 against) 对…发动战争 **❷** *vi.* ①征税;抽款 ②【律】扣押财产: ~ on sb.'s property 扣押某人的财产 ‖**~ en masse** (或 **~ in mass**) 国家战时总动员

lewd [lu:d] *a.* ①淫荡的; 淫猥的 ②[古]下流的, 邪恶的,卑劣的 ‖**-ly** *ad.* / **~ness** *n.*

lexicography [,leksi'kɔgrəfi] *n.* 词典编纂法; 词典学 ‖**lexicographical** [,leksikou'græfikəl] *a.*

lexicon ['leksikən] *n.* ①词典,字典(尤指拉丁语等古代语言的词书) ②(某一作家或学科的)特殊词汇,专门词汇

liability [,laiə'biliti] *n.* ①责任;义务: hold no ~ for damages 不负赔偿责任 / limited (unlimited) ~ 有限(无限)责任 ②倾向: ~ to nosebleed 易出鼻血 ③[复]债务,负债: assets and liabilities 资产与负债 ④不利条件

liable ['laiəbl] *a.* ①有(法律)责任的; 有义务的; (财产等)可受(法律)处理的: be ~ for damages 有赔偿损失的责任 / All his property is ~ to pay his debts. 他的所有财产都可依法处理以偿债务。②应受(罚)的; 应付(税)的; 应服从的: be ~ to the penalty 该受罚 / be ~ to the tax 该付税 / be ~ to the driving laws 应遵守行车规则 ③易于…的,有…倾向的(to): He's ~ to seasickness. 他容易晕船。/ Without careful investigation, you're ~ to come to wrong conclusions. 不仔细调查研究,你就会得出错误结论。④[口]可能的,大概的: He's ~ to be there. 他很可能在那儿。

liaison [li(:)'eizɔ:n, li(:)'eizən] *n.* ①【语】连音(尤指法语中第一词词尾与第二词词首的连读) ②(尤指军队中的)联络: a ~ officer 联络官 ③私通 ④(烹调中的)勾芡,起浆作料

liar ['laiə] *n.* 说谎的人

libation [lai'beiʃən] *n.* ①【宗】奠酒(指倒酒在地上祭神);祭奠用的酒 ②[谑]饮酒;酒

libel ['laibəl] **I** *n.* ①【律】诽谤;诽谤罪: write a ~ against sb. 写文章诽谤某人 / sue sb. for ~ 以诽谤罪控告某人 ②侮辱;对人不公平(或有损名誉)的东西: This portrait is a ~ on him. 这幅画像得太难看了。③ (在海事或宗教裁判所中)原告的控诉状 **II** (libel(l)ed; libel(l)ing) **❶** *vt.* ①(发表文章等)诽谤 ②对…不公平 **❷** *vi.* 诽谤 (against, on)

liberal ['libərəl] I *a.* ①自由主义的; [L-] (英国等的)自由党的 ②慷慨的; 大方的: a ~ donation 慷慨的捐赠 / be ~ of (或 with) one's advice 乐于向别人提出劝告 ③丰富的, 丰盛的: a ~ supply 大量的供应 / a ~ table 一桌丰盛的菜 ④心胸宽大的; 不受清规戒律拘束的: a man of ~ views (a man ~ in his views) 见解开明的人 ⑤自由随便的; 不拘泥字面的: a ~ interpretation of sth. 对某事作出的任意的解释 / have a ~ tongue 说话随便 / a ~ translation 意译 II *n.* ①开明的人 ②自由主义者 ③[L-]自由党党员; 支持自由党的人 ‖**~ly** *ad.* ‖**~ arts** 大学文科 / **~ education** 文科教育

liberality [,libə'ræliti] *n.* ①慷慨; 慷慨的施舍物 ②心胸宽大; 公正 ③丰富; 丰满; 宽阔

liberate ['libəreit] *vt.* ①解放, 使获自由, 使脱离奴化生活(或异族统治) ②【化】释出, 放出 ③[俚]用不正当手段取得, 偷 ‖**~d** *a.* 被解放了的

liberation [,libə'reiʃən] *n.* ①解放 ②【化】释出, 放出 ‖**~ism** *n.* 政教分离主义 / **~ist** *n.* 政教分离主义者

libertine ['libə(ː)tain, 'libə(ː)tiːn] I *n.* ①浪子, 放荡的人 ②[罕]持有自由思想的人(尤指在宗教方面); 怀疑论者 ③【史】古罗马获得自由的奴隶 II *a.* 放荡的

liberty ['libəti] *n.* ①自由; 自由权 ②冒昧, 失礼, (对规章等的)违反行为: Excuse my *liberties*. 请原谅我的冒昧。/ detect a kind of ~ in sb.'s translation 发现某人的翻译对原文不太忠实 ③[常用复]特许权, 特权 ④特许; (一定范围内的)自由活动(或使用)权: You may have the ~ of the lab. 你可以随时使用这个实验室。⑤特许区域(尤指英国一些城市中享有某种司法、行政特权的区域) ⑥上岸许可; 上岸许可时间 ⑦[哲]意志自由 ‖*civil* ~ 法律规定的(公民)自由权 / ~ *of conscience* 宗教信仰自由 ‖*at* ~ ①自由; 有权: Each member is *at* ~ to air his views. 每个成员均可自由发表意见。/ set sb. *at* ~ 释放某人; 恢复某人的自由 ②(人)有空, 闲着; (东西)不在使用中: I shall be *at* ~ this evening. 今晚我有空。/ *take liberties* (或 *take* ~) *with* 对…放肆随便; 随意对待: take great *liberties with* grammar 全然不顾语法规则 / *take liberties with* one's health 糟蹋身体 / *take the* ~ *to do* (或 *of doing*) sth. 冒昧做某事: I *took the* ~ *of* using your typewriter while you were away. 你不在时, 我擅自用过你的打字机。‖**~ cap** 自由帽 / **~ hall** 便厅 (指客人可以在此自由自在、不拘礼节的房间) / **'~man** *n.* [英]获准上岸的水手 / **~ pass** 【军】外出许可证; 外出许可; 外出许可时间 / **Liberty Ship** 自由轮(美国在第二次世界大战时大量建造的一种万吨左右的商船)

librarian [lai'brɛəriən] *n.* ①图书馆管理员 ②图书馆管理学专家 ‖**~ship** *n.* 图书馆管理员(或图书馆管理学专家)的职位(或资格)

library ['laibrəri] *n.* ①图书馆: a circulating ~ 流通出租图书馆 / a public ~ (不取费的)公共图书馆 / a reference ~ (只供在内查阅、不供外借的)参考图书馆 ②藏书楼; 藏书室 ③藏书; 收藏的作品(指唱片、手稿等) ④丛书; 文库(指装帧相同的一套书) ‖*a walking* ~ 活学问渊博的人) ‖~ **edition** ①图书馆版(指大本、装帧特牢的书) ②(某一作家所著的)装帧相同的一套作品 / ~ **science** 图书馆学 / ~ **steps** 图书馆用(可折叠的)小梯

libretto [li'bretou] ([复] librettos 或 libretti [li'breti(ː)]) *n.* (歌剧等的)歌词; 歌剧剧本

lice [lais] louse 的复数

license, licence ['laisəns] I *n.* ①许可; 特许: goods exported under special ~ 特许出口商品 / be given full ~ to do sth. 受权放手做某事 ②许可证; 特许证; 执照: apply for (take out) a driving ~ 申请(领取)驾驶执照 / grant a marriage ~ 颁发结婚证书 ③放纵, 放肆 ④(文艺、美术、音乐等的)破格 II *vt.* 发许可证给…; 准许; 批准(书籍、戏剧等)的出版(或上演等): ~ sb. to do sth. (正式)允准某人做某事 ‖~ **plate**, ~ **tag** (汽车等的)牌照

licensed, licenced ['laisənst] *a.* ①得到许可(或批准)的; 领有执照的 ②被允许享有破格自由的 ‖~ **premises** [英]特许的卖烟酒处

licentious [lai'senʃəs] *a.* ①放肆的, 无法无天的; 放荡的 ②[罕](诗体等)破格的, 不顾规则的 ‖**~ly** *ad.* / **~ness** *n.*

lichen ['laiken] I *n.* ①【植】地衣 ②【医】苔癣(病) II *vt.* 使生满地衣 ‖**~ology** [,laike'nɔlədʒi] *n.* 地衣学 / **~ous** ['laikinəs] *a.* ①生满地衣的 ②苔癣病的

lick [lik] I ❶ *vt.* ①舔; 舔吃: The cat ~ed its paws. 猫舔舔脚爪。/ ~ a saucer clean 把碟子舔干净 ②(火舌)卷过, 吞没(up); (波浪)轻轻拍打 ③[俚]揍; 鞭打: be well ~ed 被痛揍一顿 ④[俚]战胜; 超越: That ~s me! 这简直使我不能理解! ❷ *vi.* ①(火焰)象舌头一样伸吐; (波浪)轻轻拍打: They dashed into the house to save the children despite the ~ing flames. 他们不顾四下乱窜的火舌, 冲进屋里抢救孩子们。②[俚]高速行进: go off as hard as one can ~ 飞快地离开 II *n.* ①舔: take a ~ of 舔一下… ②少量: There was not a ~ of rain for forty days. 四十天里一点雨也未下过。③[俚]狠狠的一击: He drove in a peg with a few hard ~s. 他用力敲了几下把木钉敲进去了。④[俚]速度, 步速: at a great ~ 高速地 / (at) full ~ 以全速 ⑤[常用复][俚]轮到的机会: I'll get my ~s later. 下次我就挨得着了。⑥野兽常去舔盐的盐渍地(=salt ~) ⑦[美俚]即兴插入的爵士音乐装饰乐句 ‖*give a* ~ *and a promise* (洗刷、打扫等时)草率地搞一下(待今后再彻底地搞) / *give sb. a* ~ *with the rough side of one's tongue* 对某人出言粗鲁; 出恶言伤害某

人 / ~ *off* 舔掉… / ~ *one's chops* 见 **chop**[1] / *That ~s creation!* 见 **creation** ||~*ing* n. ① 舔 ②[口] 狠狠的一顿揍; 惨败: give sb. a good ~*ing* 狠揍某人一顿 / take the ~*ing* 遭到惨败 ||'**spit(tle)** n. 马屁精, 奉承者

lid [lid] **I** n. ① 盖子; 【生】盖; 囊盖; 孔盖; 萌盖: the ~ of a kettle 水壶盖子 / a trunk (piano) ~ 箱子(钢琴)盖 ② 眼睑 (=eyelid) ③ 制止, 取缔: clap (或 clamp) a ~ on speculation 取缔投机买卖 ④[俚]帽子 **II** (lidded; lidding) vt. 给…装盖子; 给…盖盖子 ||*blow one's* ~ 发脾气, 勃然大怒 / *blow the* ~ *off* [美俚] 揭露丑事 (或罪恶) / *flip one's* ~ [美俚] ①大发脾气 ②失去理智 ③失声狂笑 / *put the* ~ *on* ①禁止, 取缔: The ~ has been put on further leaks of information. 已禁止进一步走漏消息。 ②[英俚] 使到达无以复加的地步; 使到顶: You *put the* ~ *on* it when you said such things in his presence. 你竟当着他的面说这样的话, 真是大错特错了。/ *sit on the* ~ 压制; 镇压叛乱 (或抗议等) / *take the* ~ *off* 揭开…的盖子, 揭露 (丑事) / *with the* ~ *off* 开着盖子; 使丑恶暴露于众也 ||**lidded** a. ①有盖子的; 盖着的 ②[常用以构成复合词] 长着…眼睑的; 眼睑呈…状的: with heavy-*lidded* eyes 眼皮重垂着 ||~**less** a. ①无盖子的 ②眼睛睁得大大的, 留神注视着的

lie[1] [lai] **I** (lay [lei], lain [lein]; lying) vi. ① 躺, 平躺: ~ on a bed 躺在床上 / ~ in bed 卧床 / ~ on one's back (side) 仰(侧)卧 / ~ face downwards 俯卧 ②(东西)被平放: the blueprints *lying* on the table 摊在桌上的蓝图 / Snow ~*s* thick on the fields. 田野里铺着厚厚一层雪。③展现; 伸展 ④处于某种状态: His motives *lay* hidden. 他的动机还不明。/ Don't leave your tools *lying* about. 别把工具四处乱丢。/ How do they ~ to each other? 他们之间的关系怎样? ⑤位于 ⑥(抽象事物)存在, 所在: Where does the crux ~? 关键在哪里? / know where one's interest ~*s* 知道自己的利益所在 ⑦(东西)被存放(尤指安搁在一旁不用或不管): the fund *lying* at the bank 存在银行的基金 ⑧(船)停泊; (猎鸟)不起飞: ~ at anchor (抛锚)停泊着 ⑨(部队)驻扎 ⑩被埋葬: ~ in the cemetery 葬在公墓 ⑪【律】成立; 可受理: This action (appeal, objection) will not ~. 这起诉讼 (上诉,异议)不能成立。**II** n. ①[只用单]位置; 状态: the ~ of the land 地势; [喻]情况 ②(鸟、兽等的)栖息处 ③[英口]小睡; 休息: go and have a ~ 去躺一下 ||*as far as in me* ~*s* 尽我的力量 / ~ *along the land* 沿岸航行 / ~ *at sb.'s door* (过失,罪责)归于某人 / ~ *by* ①躺在…边②近在手边 ③被搁置不用; 使有效无法 use engines that have so far been *lying* by 把那些一直被搁置的发动机有效地利用起来 ④休息, 停歇: We *lay by* for two hours during the heat of the day. 在一天中最热的时候我们歇了两小

时。/ ~ (或 keep) *close* 躲起来 / ~ *doggo* [俚]隐伏不动 / ~ *down* ①躺下 ②(故意)躺下不干: ~ *down* on the job [口] 不卖力, 磨洋工 / ~ *down under* 甘受(侮辱等) / ~ *idle* 被搁置不用 / ~ *in* ①在于: The fundamental cause of the development of a thing ~*s in* its internal contradictoriness. 事物发展的根本原因在于事物内部的矛盾性。②分娩 ③睡懒觉 / ~ *in wait for* 埋伏着等待… / ~ *low* 见 **low**[1] / ~ *off* ①【海】与陆地(或其它船只)保持一定距离 ②[俚](赛跑中)初跑时控制速度 ③暂停工作 / ~ *on* (或 *upon*) ①依赖: ~ *on* the result 取决于结果如何 ②压迫; 折磨(人、良心等) / ~ heavy *on* one's stomach (食物)搁在胃里不舒服 ③是…的责任: It ~*s on* us to accomplish the task. 完成这项任务是我们的责任。/ ~ *on sb.'s hand(s)* 见 **hand** / ~ *over* ①等待以后处理: Let the matter ~ *over* till next week. 把这件事留到下星期再处理吧。②(款项等)逾期未付 / ~ *to* 【海】(船)顶风停住 / ~ *under* 受到, 蒙受: ~ *under* suspicion 受到怀疑 / ~ *up* ①卧床(或不出门): You'd better ~ *up* for a few more days. 你最好再躺几天。②(船)入坞, 停止使用 / ~ *with* ①是…的权利(或义务): It ~*s with* you to decide. 由你决定。②与…性交 / *take* ... *lying down* 甘受(挫败等); 对(挑战等)俯首屈服 ||~-*abed* n. 睡懒觉的人 / '~-*down* n. 小睡, 小憩: go and have a ~-*down* 去躺一会儿 / ~-'*in* n. ①[口]懒觉 ②(在大街等处)卧地示威

lie[2] [lai] **I** (lying) ❶ vi. ①说谎: You are *lying*! 你撒谎! / ~ about sth. to sb. 就某事对某人撒谎 ②造成错觉, 欺骗: Facts never ~. 事实总不会骗人的。/ That thermometer must be *lying*. 那温度计一定不准。❷ vt. ①用谎骗使得…, 诳骗: Be on guard against those who try to ~ themselves *into* our confidence. 警惕那些用谎言来骗取我们信任的人。/ ~ sb. *out of* sth. 从某人处骗取某物 / ~ *away* sb.'s *reputation* 用谎言损坏某人的名誉 **II** n. ①谎话, 谎言: tell a ~ 说谎 / *Lies* cannot cover up facts. 谎言掩盖不了事实。②造成错觉的事物; 假象 ||*act a* ~ 用行动骗人 / *a white* ~ 不怀恶意的谎话 / *give sb. the* ~ 指责某人说谎 / *give the* ~ *to sth.* 拆穿某事的虚伪性 / ~ *in one's throat* 撒大谎 / *like a gas meter* 一味撒谎 / *Lies have short legs.* 谎言总是站不住脚的。/ *live a* ~ 过欺骗人的生活, 做人虚伪 / *nail a* ~ *to the counter* 证明所说不真实, 拆穿西洋镜 / *swap* ~*s* [美口]扯淡, 讲空话 / *the big* ~ ①被不断重复和加油添酱以致似乎确有其事的弥天大谎 ②不断重复谎言以骗取人们相信的宣传伎俩 / *throw a* ~ *in sb.'s face* 当面斥责某人说谎 / *worship a* ~ 盲目崇拜错误的事物 ||~ *detector* 测谎器

lien [lien] n. 【律】(债权人在债务未清偿前对担保品的)扣押权, 留置权

lieu [lju:] *n.* 场所(一般仅用于 in ～ (of) 中) ‖*in ～ (of)* 作为(…的)替代

lieutenant [lef'tenənt, 英海军 le'tenənt; 美 lu:-'tenənt] *n.* ① (英)陆军(或海军陆战队)中尉 ② (英、美)海军上尉 ③副职官员;代理官员 ‖*a first ～* (美)陆军(或空军、海军陆战队)中尉 / *a flight ～* (英)空军上尉 / *a ～ colonel* (英)陆军(或海军陆战队)中校 / *a ～ commander* (英、美)海军少校 / *a ～ general* (英)陆军(或海军陆战队)中将 / (美)陆军(或空军、海军陆战队)中将 / *a ～ governor* (省或地区的)代理总督,副总督; (美)副州长 / *a Lieutenant Junior Grade* (美)海军中尉 / *a second ～* (英)陆军(或海军陆战队)少尉; (美)陆军(或空军、海军陆战队)少尉

life [laif] ([复] lives [laivz]) *n.* ①生命;性命: the origin of ～ 生命的起源 ②[总称]生物 ③寿命;【原】(亚原子粒子的)生命期 ④一生;生涯: Hers is a ～ of struggle. 她的一生是战斗的一生。 / devote one's whole ～ to serving the people 为人民服务一辈子 / tell one's story 讲自己的身世 ⑤传记 ⑥生活: live (或 lead) a happy ～ 过幸福生活 ⑦世事,人生;处世: see much (nothing) of ～ 见过很多(没见过什么)世面 / begin ～ 踏进社会 ⑧生命力,生气: new things full of ～ 充满活力的新事物 / add (或 give) ～ to an article 增加文章的生气 ⑨[喻]支柱,灵魂: This principle is the ～ of the association. 这条原则是这协会的支柱。 ⑩活体模型;实物: a drawing from the ～ 摹拟实物的图画 / a still ～ 静物画 / a ～ class 人体写生课 ⑪无期徒刑: If found guilty, he will get ～. 如证明为有罪,他将被判处无期徒刑。 ⑫无生命物所具有的类似活力的特性,弹性: the ～ of a bow 弓的弹力 ⑬(大难之后的)生命的新开端;新机会: The batsman was given a ～. 击球员获得新机会。 ‖*a bad ～* ①不道德的生活 ②估计活不到(人寿保险所统计出的)平均寿命的人 / *a future ～*【宗】来生 / *a good ～* ①好的生活 ② 有道德的生活 ③ 可能超过(人寿保险所统计出的)平均寿命的人 / *all one's ～* 一生 / *a matter of ～ and death* 生死攸关的事情 / *as large as ～* 见 **large** / *bring to ～* 使苏醒 / *carry one's ～ in one's hands* 手里提着脑袋生活,冒险 / *come to ～* 苏醒过来 / *escape with bare* ～ 仅以身免,死里逃生 / *escape with ～ and limb* 无大损伤而逃脱 / *eternal ～*【宗】永生 / *expectation of ～* (或 [美] *expectancy*) (根据概率统计求得的)估计寿命 / *for dear ～* (或 *for one's ～*) ① (为)逃命 ②拼命地 / *for ～* ①终身: settle down in the countryside *for ～* 在农村安家落户一辈子 ② (为)逃命 / *for the ～ of me* [用于否定句]即使要你的命,无论如何: I cannot *for the ～ of me* recollect where I put it. 我无论如何想不起把它放到哪里去了。 / *gasp one's ～ away* (或

out) 断气,死去 / *get on in ～* 发迹 / *in ～* ①一生中 ②世间 / *lead (sb.) a dog's ～* (使某人)过着受折磨的日子 / *lead sb. a ～* 经常使某人不得安宁 / *live (或 lead) a double ～* 过着双重人格的生活,搞两面派 / *nothing in ～* 毫无,一点也没有 / *on your ～* [口]在任何情况下;无论如何: A: Do you appreciate it? B: Not *on your ～*. 甲:你喜欢这个吗? 乙:一点也不喜欢。 / *'pon my ～* (或 *upon my ～*) [作插入语]我敢打赌说;确实 / *seek sb.'s ～* 想谋害某人 / *see ～* ① 交游广阔 ② 见世面长阅历(尤指通过玩乐挥霍) / *sell one's ～ dearly* 被杀死前杀伤了对方很多人;死得够本 / *take one's ～ in one's hand* 冒生命危险,冒大险 / *take one's own ～* 自杀 / *take sb.'s ～* 干掉某人 / *the ～ of Riley* ['raili] [美俚]放纵的生活 / *the other ～*【宗】来世,来生 / *the time of one's ～* 见 **time** / *this ～*【宗】尘世,今生 / *to the ～* 逼真地: The picture shows him *to the ～*. 这张画(或照片)把他逼真地表现出来。 / *true to ～* 逼真的: The portrait is *true to ～*. 这张画像栩栩如生。 ‖*～like a.* 逼真的,栩栩如生的 ‖*'～-and-'death, '～-or-'death a.* 生死攸关的: the ～-and-death struggle between the two lines 两条路线的生死搏斗 / *～ annuity* 终身年金 / *～ assurance* 人寿保险 / *～ belt* 救生带;安全带 / *'～blood n.* ①生命必需的血液;[喻]生命线,根子 ②嘴唇(或眼睑)的抽搐 / *'～boat n.* 救生艇 / *～ buoy* 救生圈 / *～ cycle* 生命周期 / *～ estate* 非世袭的终身财产 / *'～-force n.* 生命力 / *'～-,giving a.* ① 给予生命的 ②提神的

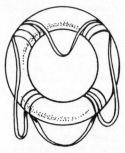

life buoy

'～guard n. 救生员 / *～ history* ① 【生】生活史 ② (个人的)生活经历 / *～ insurance* [美]人寿保险 / *～ interest* 非世袭的终身财产拥有者的财产权 / *～ jacket* 救生衣 / *'～-kiss n.* 口对口人工呼吸 / *'～line n.* ①救生索;潜水员的升降索 ②生命线: the economic *～lines* of the country 国家的经济命脉 / *～long a.* 毕生的,终身的 / *～manship* ['laifmənʃip] *n.* 通过困惑别人(或动摇士气)而使自己占上风的一种手法(如在谈话中或商业上) / *～ net* 救生网(用于在火灾

life preserver

时接救从楼上跳下的人) / **~ preserver** ①救生
衣(或带、圈等) ② 护身棒 / **~ raft** 救生筏 /
'**~,saver** *n.* 救生员;救命物 / '**~,saving** *n.* 救
生(法) *a.* 救生用的;救生的 / **~ sentence** 无
期徒刑 / '**~'size(d)** *a.* 与原物一般大小的 /
'**~'span** *n.* ①寿命 ②平均生命期 / '**~-strings**
[复] *n.* 维系生命之物 / '**~-style** *n.* 生活方式 /
'**~-sup'port system** (宇航员等的) 生命维持系
统 / '**~time** *n.* ① 一生,终身: a ~*time* job 毕
生的工作 / the chance of a ~*time* 唯一难得的
机会 ②[原]寿命: neutron ~*time* 中子寿命 / **~
vest** 救生背心 / **~'work** *n.* 毕生的事业;一生
中最重要的工作 / **~ zone**【生】生命带

lifeless ['laif-lis] *a.* ①无生命的;死的 ②没有生气
的;沉闷的,单调的: a ~ voice 单调沉闷的声音
③没有生物的: That planet is probably ~. 那
行星上或许没有生物。‖**~ly** *ad.* / **~ness** *n.*

lift [lift] **I** ❶ *vt.* ①提起;举起;抬;吊: ~ a pail
of water from the ground 把一桶水从地上提
起来 / ~ weights 举重 / The crane ~ed the
bales into the hold. 起重机将大包吊进货舱。/
~ up one's eyes 向上看 ② 提高;提升;鼓舞:
Water is now ~ed to terraced fields by electric
power. 现在用电力抽水灌溉梯田。/~ prices 提高
价格 / ~ up the hearts of the troops 激励军心
③ 运送;空运: ~ the fire squad to the scene of
the accident 将救火队空运至出事地点 ④ 挖出
(山芋等);拔起(秧苗)以备移植;拔(帐、营) ⑤解
除(封锁、包围等);撤销(命令): ~ the ban on 解
除对…的禁令 / ~ the curfew 解除宵禁 ⑥[俚]
偷;[口]剽窃;断章取义地抽出(词、句等): ~ a
sentence out of context 断章取义地抽出一句来
⑦ 清偿,偿付: ~ a mortgage 偿付抵押债款
⑧ 把(板球)向高空击去 ❷ *vi.* ① 被提(或举)
起;升起: The engine hood will not ~. 发动机
盖揭不开。/ The plane ~ed from the airport. 飞机从机场飞起。②(云、雾等)消散: The fog
~ed and the sun came out. 雾散日出。③ 耸立
④(船)随浪升高 ⑤(地面)隆起 **II** *n.* ①提,吊,
升,举: the ~ of the waves 波浪的升起 / a
sudden ~ in one's voice 嗓门的突然提高 / a ~

of one's eyebrows 眉毛的一扬 / a ~ in costs 费
用的增加 ② 一次提(或吊等)的量: a ~ of sheet
steel 一次吊起的钢板 ③ 情绪激昂; 鼓舞: His
report gave us a tremendous ~. 他的报告给我
们极大的鼓舞。④ 高昂的姿态: walk with a
proud ~ of one's head 昂首走去 ⑤ 地面的隆
起,小丘 ⑥[英]电梯;登山电梯(或吊车): take
the ~ to the twelfth floor 搭电梯到第十三层楼
⑦(修理汽车等用的)千斤顶;起重机 ⑧【空】升
力;空运;空中供应线 ⑨【机】升程;(运河水闸中
水位的)上升程度 ⑩ 鞋后跟皮的一层 ⑪ 帮忙
(如帮助提高地位等);(半路上)搭便车 ‖**a dead
~** ①不用机械的硬搬 ②需要全力以赴的难事 /
give sb. a ~ ① 让某人搭车 ② 帮某人忙 /
sb.'s face 用手术消除某人面部的皱纹,为某人
整容 / **on the ~** [美方]虚弱的(地),弱不禁风
的(地) / **thumb a ~** (竖起拇指向司机做手势)
要求搭车;搭乘便车 ‖'**~boy**, '**~man** *n.* [英]
开电梯的工人 / **~ bridge** 升降吊桥 / '**~-'drag
ratio**【空】阻升比 / '**~ing force** (具有重返大气
层、自行着陆等性能的)宇宙飞行及高空飞行两用
机 / **~ irrigation** 抽水灌溉 / '**~-off** *n.* (飞机
或导弹的)起飞,起离,初动;起飞(或起离)时刻 /
~ pump【机】提升泵,升水泵 / **~ truck** 起重
机车(或车辆)

ligament ['ligəmənt] *n.* ①系带 ②【解】韧带 ‖**~al**
[,ligə'mentl], **~ary** [,ligə'mentəri], **~ous**
[,ligə'mentəs] *a.* 带状的;韧带(似)的

ligature ['ligət∫uə] **I** *n.* ① 绑扎;结扎 ② 带子;
绷带;【医】结扎线,缚线;[喻]连系物 ③【音】连
线;连音 ④[印]连字(如 æ 等);连字弧线 **II** *vt.*
绑扎;结扎

light¹ [lait] **I** *n.* ①光;光线;光亮: The sun gives
~ and heat. 太阳发出光和热。/ The ~ is good.
光线很好。/ The room has poor ~. 这房间
光线不足。
② 日光;白昼;黎明: The ~ began to fail. 天
暗下来了。/ *Light* is breaking. 天破晓了。
③ 发光体,光源;灯;信号灯;灯塔;天体: turn on
(off) the ~ 开(关)灯/ a blackout ~ 防空
灯 / traffic ~s 交通信号灯 / As night fell, ~s
in the sky multiplied. 夜幕降临,满天繁星。
④ 明星;名人,显赫人物: the leading ~s of
diplomacy 外界头面人物
⑤窗;天窗;【律】光线不受(邻居)阻碍权: a studio
with a north ~ 窗子朝北开的画室
⑥ 火花;点火物: Could you give me a ~? 借个
火。/ strike a ~ 擦火柴
⑦ 光觉;[诗]视力;[复][俚]眼睛
⑧ 眼神: A ~ of recognition came into his eyes.
从他的眼神中可以看到他已认出来了。
⑨(绘画中的)明亮部分,投光部分: ~ and shade
明暗 / the high ~s of a picture 画的强光部分
⑩ 显豁,众所周知
⑪[复]帮助理解(或说明)的事实,启发: new ~s
on a question 帮助说明一个问题的新线索

⑫(事物呈现出来的)模样;见解;眼光: see sb. in a new ～ 用新眼光看待某人

⑬[复]智能;处世标准,人生哲学: do one's best according to one's ～s 尽力而为

⑭【宗】灵光

II *a.* ①明亮的: a ～ room 明亮的房间 / It's beginning to get ～. 天在亮了。

②淡色的: a ～ blue 淡蓝色 / a ～ complexion 白皮肤

III (lit [lit] 或 lighted) ❶ *vt.* ①点(火);点燃: ～ (up) a lamp (cigarette) 点灯(香烟)

②照亮;使发亮: A smile of triumph *lit up* her face. 她的脸上闪耀出胜利的微笑。

③用灯光指引: The beacon *lit* the plane to a safe landing. 信标引导飞机安全着陆。

❷ *vi.* ①点着: The match ～s easily. 这火柴容易划着。 / He fished out a cigarette and *lit up.* 他摸出一支烟来点着了。 / It is time to ～ up. 是点灯的时候了。

②变亮: His face *lit up* with happiness. 他脸上喜气洋洋。

‖*before the ～s* 在舞台上;登台(演出) / *be out like ～* [美俚] ①醉得不省人事 ②被击昏;昏睡 / *between the ～s* 在傍晚 (指在日光与灯光之间) / *between two ～s* 在黑夜 / *bring sth. to ～* 使某事显露出来 / *by the ～ of nature* 自然而然地 / *come to ～* 显露出来,暴露 / *expose sth. to the ～ of day* 把某事暴露于光天化日之下 / *go out like ～* [美俚] ①开始醉得不省人事 ②被击昏;开始昏睡 / *hide one's ～ under a bushel* 见 bushel¹ / *in a good ～* 在光线好的地方: hang a map *in a good ～* 把地图挂在光线好的地方 / show sth. *in a good ～* 把某物的长处尽量表现出来 / *in ～* 被光线照着 / *in ～ of* 按照,根据 (=in the ～ of) / *in the ～ of* ①以…的模样: appear *in the ～ of* a greenhorn 看上去是个生手 ②按照,根据 ③当作: We view extravagance and waste *in the ～ of* a grave crime. 我们把奢侈浪费看作极大的犯罪。 / *see ～* 领会: Now I begin to *see ～* on the matter. 现在我对这事开始有所领会了。 / *see the ～* (*of day*) ①出世;(书籍)问世 ②领悟 / *see the red ～* 觉察危险(或灾祸)迫近 / *shed* (或 *throw*) *～ on* (或 *upon*) *sth.* 使某事清楚明白地显示出来 / *stand in one's own ～* ①背光 ②损害自己的利益 / *stand* (或 *be*) *in sb.'s ～* ①挡住某人的光线 ②妨碍某人发迹(或成功等) / *the ～ of one's eyes* 心爱的人 / *the ～ of sb.'s countenance* 某人的嘉许(常作讽刺语)

‖*～ buoy* 【海】灯浮标 / *～ due, ～ duty* 灯塔税 / *'～'fast a.* 耐曝晒的,不褪色的 / *'～house n.* 灯塔: *～house* tube 【无】灯塔管 / *～ meter* 照度计,曝光表 / *～ pen* 【自】光笔,光写入头 / *'～'proof a.* 防光的,不透光的 / *'～ship n.* 灯船 / *～ show* (伴随摇摆舞音乐的)光影闪烁表演 / *'～-s-'out n.* 熄灯号;规定的熄灯时间 / '～

lightship

'struck a. (底片、印相纸等)漏过光的 / *'～'tight a.* 防光的,不透光的 / *～ tracer* 曳光弹 / *～ trap* ①暗室进出口的避光装置(如两重门、幕等) ②灯光捕虫器 / *～ wave* 【物】光波 / *'～wood n.* 易燃的木头;轻材,多脂材 / *'～-'year n.* 【天】光年

light² [lait] **I** *a.* ①轻的: Aluminium is a ～ metal. 铝是一种轻金属。 / ～ industry 轻工业 ②容易承担(或忍受)的: ～ work 轻活儿 / ～ punishment 不重的惩罚 / a ～ loss 轻微的损失 / ～ rule 温和的统治 / patients of ～ illnesses 易燃病病 ③少量的;分量不足的: I had a ～ meal. 我这一顿吃得很少。 / a ～ rain 小雨 / The earlier voting was ～. 早些时候的那次表决票数不足。 / a ～ coin 分量不足的钱币 / give ～ weight 克扣分量 ④轻微的,微弱的: give sb. a ～ pat on the shoulder 在某人肩上轻轻一拍 / ～ applause 微弱的掌声 ⑤(嗓音)柔和的 ⑥轻快的;灵巧的: She's ～ on her feet (或 foot). 她脚步轻快。 / have a ～ hand for knitting (at pastry) 巧于编织(做面点) ⑦轻便的;轻型的;轻装的: a ～ car 轻便汽车 / a ～ bomber 轻轰炸机 / 300 ～ cavalry (or horse) 三百轻骑兵 ⑧(船等)不装货的,轻载的: ～ waterline (船)不装货时的吃水线 / ～ traffic 轻量交通 ⑨不重要的,琐碎的: ～ conversation 随便的闲谈 ⑩轻率易变的;轻浮的,水性杨花的: ～ opinions 轻率的意见 / ～ conduct 轻浮的行为 ⑪轻松愉快的: a ～ heart 轻松愉快的心情 / ～ reading 消遣读物 / ～ music 轻音乐 ⑫易醒的: a ～ sleeper 睡不沉的人 ⑬清淡的;易消化的: a ～ beer 一种淡啤酒 / a ～ soup 清汤 / The doctor advised a ～ diet. 医生建议吃清淡的食物。 ⑭晕眩的: He was a bit ～ after the illness. 病后他有些头晕。 ⑮(食物)酥松的;松的;砂质的: a ～ cake 松软的蛋糕 / ～ soil 轻质土,砂土 / ～ sand 松砂 ⑯精巧的,优美的: ～ architecture 精巧的建筑 ⑰(音节)不重读的 ⑱缺少人员的,人手不足的 **II** *ad.* 轻地;轻装地: sleep ～ 睡得不熟 / travel ～ 轻装旅行 ‖*Light come, ～ go.* [谚]来得容易,去得快。(或: 不义之财,理无久享。) / ～ *in hand* (马等)易于驾驭 / ～ *in the head* ①头晕 ②头

脑简单,愚蠢 / **make ~ of** 轻视,藐视;视…不足道: *make ~ of* sb.'s advice 无视某人的忠告 / **set ~ by** 轻视 / **sit ~ on** (工作等) 对…说来负担不重: Her years *sit ~ on* her. 她上了年纪,但不见老。 ‖**~ air** 软风,一级风 / **'~-'armed** *a.* 轻武器装备的 / **~ artillery** [总称]轻型火炮 / **~ bob** [英]轻步兵 / **~ bread** [美方]用酵母发酵的白面包 / **~ breeze** 轻风,二级风 / **'~-'duty** *a.* (机器等)轻型的;可用轻型机械做成的 / **~ engine** 没有挂列车的机车 / **'~-er-than-'air** *a.* (飞船等)轻于空气的 / **'~-face** *n.* & *a.* 【印】细体活字(的) / **'~-,fingered** *a.* ①手指灵巧的 ②善于摸窃的: a *~-fingered* gentleman [谑]扒手 / **~-foot, '~-'footed** *a.* 脚步轻快的,轻盈的 / **'~-,handed** ① 手巧的;手法高明的 ②缺人手的 / **'~-'headed** *a.* ①头晕目眩的 ②轻率的;轻浮的 / **'~-'hearted** *a.* 轻松愉快的,无忧无虑的 / **~ heavyweight** 轻重量级运动员(体重不超过一百七十五磅) / **'~-'heeled** *a.* ①步子轻快的 ②放纵的;淫荡的 / **~ housekeeping** [总称] ①轻的家务活儿 ②厨房设备简陋的住家中的家务 / **'~-'minded** *a.* 轻率的 / **'~-o'-'love** ([复] ~-o'-loves) *n.* 水性杨花的女人;婊子 / **~ opera** 轻歌剧 / **'~plane** *n.* 轻型飞机(尤指私人小飞机) / **'~-weight** *n.* ①体重在平均以下的人(或动物);轻量级运动员 ②无足轻重的人 ③性格(或智力)不够强的人;不能胜任职务的人 *a.* ①轻量的 ②平均重量以下的 ③无足轻重的

light³ [lait] (lighted 或 lit [lit]) ❶ *vi.* ①[罕]下马;下车 ②停落: The bird *lit on* a branch. 鸟飞落在树枝上。 / ~ *on* one's feet 双脚落地 ③(灾难、好运、打击等)突然降临 (*on, upon*) ④偶然碰到;偶然得到: ~ *upon* (或 *on*) some useful reference material 偶然找到一些有用的参考材料 ❷ *vt.* 【海】拉(绳索);移动(风帆等) ‖**~ into** [美俚]攻击…;骂 / **~ out** [美俚]匆匆离去

lighten¹ ['laitn] ❶ *vt.* ①照亮,使明亮: A full moon ~ed our path to the camp. 一轮明月照亮了我们去营地去的道路。 ②闪出;闪电般地显现出 (*out, forth*) ③调浓(色彩等) ④[古]使明白,启发 ❷ *vi.* ①发亮;变亮: The eastern sky ~ed. 东方亮起来了。 / His face ~ed when he heard the news. 他听到这个消息面露喜色。 ②打闪: It thundered and ~ed. 雷电交作。

lighten² ['laitn] ❶ *vt.* ①减轻…的负荷;减轻: ~ a ship (*of* her cargo) (或 a ship's cargo) 减轻船只的负荷 / ~ sb.'s sorrow 减轻某人的悲伤 / ~ a punishment 减轻处分 / ~ taxes 减轻赋税 ②使轻松;使愉快: The news of the success of the operation ~ed our hearts. 手术成功的消息使我们宽慰。 ❷ *vi.* ①变轻松 ②(船、载货等)分量减轻下来 ②(心情等)变得轻松: His mood ~ed after the solution of the knotty problem. 难题解决了,他的心情愉快起来。

lighter¹ ['laitə] *n.* ①点火者 ②引燃器;打火机

lighter² ['laitə] I *n.* 驳船 II *vt.* 驳运

lighting ['laitiŋ] *n.* ①照明;照明设备;[总称]舞台灯光 ②点火;发火 ③(画面的)明暗分布 ‖**~-'up time** 行驶车辆的规定开灯时间

lightly ['laitli] *ad.* ① 轻轻地;轻微地: The ~ wounded refused to leave the front line. 轻伤员们不肯下火线。 / He wears his seventy years ~. 他简直看不出有七十岁。 ②轻柔地;轻巧地: leap ~ over a ditch 轻轻纵身跳过小沟 ③ 轻率地;轻浮地,轻佻地: The fruits we have won must never be given up ~. 我们的胜利果实决不能轻易放弃。 / Don't take it ~. 可不能等闲视之。 ④ 轻而易举地: get off ~ 轻易逃脱 ‖*Lightly come, ~ go.* [谚]来得容易,去得快。 (或:不义之财,理无久享。)

lightning ['laitniŋ] I *n.* ①闪电;闪电放电: forked (或 chain) ~ 叉状闪电 / heat (或 summer) ~ 无声闪电,热闪 / sheet ~ 片状闪电 ②意外的幸运(尤指在政治上得到提拔) ③ [美俚]劣等威士忌酒 II *a.* 闪电的;闪电似的: a ~ attack 突然袭击 / at (或 with) ~ speed 闪电似地,极快地 III *vi.* (lightninged; lightning) 闪电 ‖*chained* ~ ①叉状闪电 ②[美俚]劣等酒 / *like (greased)* ~ 闪电似地,风驰电掣地 ‖**~ arrester** 避雷器 / **~ bug** [美]萤火虫 / **~ conductor** 避雷装置 / **~ rod** ①避雷针 ②[美俚]喷气式战斗机 / **~ strike** 闪电式罢工 / **~ war** 闪电战

lights [laits] [复] *n.* (供食用的)牲畜肺脏

lightsome¹ ['laitsəm] *a.* ①轻快的,敏捷的;轻盈的 ②轻松愉快的,无忧无虑的 ③轻率的;轻浮的 ‖**~ly** *ad.* / **~ness** *n.*

like¹ [laik] I ❶ *vt.* ①喜欢: I don't ~ smoking. 我不喜欢抽烟。 / He ~s to swim in big rivers. 他喜欢在大河里游泳。 / How do you ~ it? 你觉得它怎么样? (或: 你满意吗?) / A: How do you ~ your tea? B: I ~ it rather strong. 甲: 你喜欢喝怎样的茶? 乙: 我喜欢喝浓一点儿的。 / I ~ his impudence! (反语)哼,我可喜欢他的厚脸皮呢! ② [常与 should, would 连用]希望,想: I *should* (或 *would*) ~ time to read the book. 我希望有时间读一读这本书。 / He *would* ~ to join our discussion. 他希望参加我们的讨论。 / I *should* (或 *would*) much ~ to come. 我很想来。 / I *should* (或 *would*) ~ to know (see).... 我倒想知道知道(看看)… / I *should* (或 *would*) ~ the problem to be discussed at the next meeting. 我希望这问题在下次会上讨论。 ③[用于否定句中]愿意: I don't ~ troubling (或 to trouble) you. 我不愿意打扰你。 ④适合于: I like pepper but it doesn't ~ me. (戏言)我喜欢吃胡椒,但胡椒对我不适合。 ❷ *vi.* ①喜欢;愿意;希望: Do as you ~. 你喜欢怎么做就怎么做。 / You may come whenever you ~. 你愿意什么时候来就什么时候来。 ②[方]赞同 (*of, with*) II *n.* [常用复]爱好: one's ~s and dislikes 好恶；爱憎 ‖if you ~ ①如果你愿意：You may come if you ~. 你愿意就来吧。②如果你愿意这样理解：I am rude if you ~. 就算我没有礼貌吧。[注意：若重读句中的 rude, 句子的含义为"我只不过是粗鲁无礼而已，并无恶意"；若重读句中的 I, 则意为"仅我一人粗鲁，可不能讲别人也是这样"] / I ~ that! (反语)说得真好听！(或：干得好事!) / ~ it or not [用作插入语]不管你喜欢不喜欢

like² [laik] I (more like, most like; [诗][罕] liker, likest) a. ①相象的；相同的；同类的：The two buildings are very ~. 这两座楼很象。/ The picture is not at all ~. 这张画画得一点不象。/ hospitals and ~ institutions 医院以及同类性质的机构 / fabrics of ~ quality 相同质量的织物 ②[方](象要)就要；可能：He is ~ to come any minute. 他随时可能到。II prep. ①象，如；跟…一样：He looks ~ an athlete. 他看上去象个运动员。/ What is he ~? 他是怎么样一个人么？(可指外貌或品行等) / Don't treat me ~ a guest. 别把我当客人。/ That's just ~ him! 他就是干那种事情(或说那种话)的人。②象要；想要：It looks ~ rain. 好象要下雨了。/ It looks ~ another good harvest. 看来又是个好收成。/ Do you feel ~ (taking) a walk? 想去散散步吗？III (more like, most like; [诗][罕] liker, likest) ad. ①[古]一样地 ②[常用于插入语中]可能，多半：Like enough (或 Very ~), the ship will arrive in port tomorrow. 这条船很可能明天进港。③[口]有点儿，可以说得上：I'm thirsty ~. 我有点口渴。IV conj. [口]如同，好象：I hope I can drive the tractor ~ you do. 我希望我开拖拉机开得象你一样好。/ It's hot ~ in midsummer. 天热得象在大伏天一样。V n. ①同样(或同类)的人(或事物)：Hitler and his ~ 希特勒之流 / Have you ever heard the ~ (of it)? 你听见过这样的事情吗？②(高尔夫球中)使与对方击球次数相等的一次击球 (the odd 之对) ‖and the ~ 等等，以及诸如此类：music, painting, and the ~ 音乐、绘画等等 / anything ~ 见 anything / as ~ as chalk and (或 to) cheese 外貌相似而实质不同的 / (as) ~ as not 很可能：As ~ as not, he's already there. 他很可能已经在那儿了。/ as ~ as two peas 一模一样 / had ~ to have done 差点儿就要做了 / ~ anything 象什么似地；非常猛地；拼命地：~ as [主方]如同 (=as) / Like attracts (或 draws to) ~. [谚]物以类聚。/ Like begets ~. [谚]龙生龙，凤生凤。/ Like cures ~. [谚]以毒攻毒。/ ~ for ~ 以牙还牙 / Like knows ~. [谚]英雄识英雄。/ ~ that 就象上述那样的 / nothing ~ 见 nothing / something ~ 见 something / the ~s of me [口]象我这样(不行)的人 / the ~s of you [口]象你这样(了不起)的人 ‖'~-minded a. 有同样想法的，有同样的思想习惯的；志趣相投的

likelihood ['laiklihud] n. ①可能(性)：In all ~, it will rain. 十之八九要下雨。② 可能发生的事物；可能成功的迹象

likely ['laikli] (more likely, most likely; 或 likelier, likeliest) I a. ①很可能的：What is the likeliest (或 the most ~) time to find him in his office? 什么时候最可能在他办公室里找到他？/ be ~ of success 可能成功 / He's not ~ to come. 他不见得会来。/ Take a coat along; it's ~ to be cold down there. 带件上装去，那边可能很冷。/ It's ~ they'll win. 很可能他们赢。②(象是)可靠的，可信的：That's a ~ story! 倒说得象真呐！③有希望的；恰当的：~ regions for the discovery of oil 有希望发现石油的地区 / ~ young men 有希望的青年们 ④漂亮的，吸引人的 II ad. 很可能：He will most (或 very) ~ come right away. 他大概马上就会来的。‖as ~ as not 很可能

liken ['laikən] vt. 把…比喻，把…比拟 (to)：~ one's work to a battle 把工作当作战斗

likeness ['laiknis] n. ①类似，相象：He bears a striking ~ to his brother. 他活象他的兄弟。②肖像，画像，写真；照片；(字画的)真迹：take sb.'s ~ 给某人画像(或照相) ③外象，表象

likewise ['laik-waiz] ad. ①同样地，照样地：They went on foot and I did ~. 他们步行去，我也步行去了。②也；又：A: Pleased to meet you. B: Likewise. 甲：见到你我高兴。乙：我也是。

liking ['laikiŋ] n. 喜欢；爱好 ‖have a ~ for 喜欢… / take a ~ for (或 to) 对…产生好感，喜欢上… / to sb.'s ~ 配某人胃口，合某人的意思

lilac ['lailək] I n. ①丁香花属植物；丁香花，紫丁香 ②淡紫色 II a. 淡紫色的

lilt [lilt] I ❶ vt. 轻快有节奏地唱(或演奏) ❷ vi. ①轻快有节奏地唱，用抑扬的声调说 ②轻快地跳动 II n. ①轻快活泼的歌曲 ②轻快有节奏的摆动；明显的旋律 ③轻快的动作

lily ['lili] I n. ①百合属植物；百合花，百合 ②纯洁的人；洁白的东西 ③[美俚]女人腔的男子 ④[常用复]象征法国王室的百合花徽 II a. 象百合花般纯洁的；洁白的；脆弱的 ‖gild (或 paint) the ~ 作不恰当而过分的修饰，画蛇添足 / lilies and roses 美貌 / ~ of the valley 铃兰 ‖'~-'livered a. 胆小的 / ~ pad 浮在水面上的睡莲叶子 / '~-'white a. ①纯白的；洁白的 n. ①[美]排斥黑人的纯白种运动派的 n. ①[美]排斥黑人的纯白种运动派成员 ②[复][美俚]双手

limb¹ [lim] I n. ①肢，翼，翅膀 ②大树枝 ③分支；突出物：a ~ of a river 河的支流 ④骨干；爪牙 ⑤顽童 ⑥(句子中的)从句 II vt. ①给…截肢；肢解(躯体) ②从(倒下的树)上砍去树枝 ‖a ~ of the devil (或 of Satan) 顽童 / a ~ of the law 律师；警察 / escape with life and ~ 见 life / out on a ~ [口]处于危险的境地 / rest one's tired ~s 使疲倦的四肢休息 ‖~less a. 无肢的；无翼的；无枝叉的

limb^2 [lim] *n.* ①(四分仪等的)分度弧 ②(日、月等天体的)边缘 ③【植】瓣片;冠檐;萼檐

limber^1 ['limbə] I *a.* ① 可塑的; 柔软的, 易弯曲的: ~ terms 可变通的条件 ② 富于弹性的; 思想活跃的; 风格明快的 II ❶ *vt.* 使柔软: ~ (up) one's fingers 使手指变得柔软起来 ❷ *vi.* 变得柔软: ~ up by running 跑一跑使身体柔软灵活起来

limber^2 ['limbə] I *n.* 前车(指拖带火炮和弹药的两轮车辆) II ❶ *vt.* 把(火炮)系在前车上 ❷ *vi.* 连接炮和前车(up)

limbo ['limbou] *n.* ① [常作 L-]【宗】地狱的边境(据说是基督降生前好人和未受洗儿童灵魂所去之地) ②监狱;拘禁 ③丢弃废物的地方;忘却,遗弃: sink into the ~ of oblivion (或 of forgotten things) 湮没无闻, 被忘却 ④ 中间过渡状态(或地带)

lime^1 [laim] I *n.* ① 石灰: quick (或 caustic) ~ 生石灰 / ~ and water 石灰水 / slaked ~ 熟石灰 ②粘鸟胶 II *vt.* ① 用石灰处理; 撒石灰于; 浸…于石灰水中 ② 涂粘鸟胶于; 用粘鸟胶捕捉 ‖'~,burner *n.* 烧石灰工人 / ~ glass 石灰玻璃 / '~kiln *n.* 石灰窑 / '~light *n.* ①(舞台照明用的)灰光灯;石灰光;灰光灯所照射的全部;②众人注目的中心: be fond of the ~light 喜欢引人注目, 爱出风头 / in the ~light 引人注目 *vt.* 把光集中在…上; 使成注目中心, 使显著 / ~ pit 石灰石坑; 石灰窑 / '~stone *n.* 石灰石 / '~twig *n.* (用以捕鸟的)涂有粘鸟胶的小树枝 ④ 陷阱 / '~,water *n.* 石灰水

lime^2 [laim] *n.*【植】酸橙 ‖'~,juicer *n.* [俚] ① 英国船 ② 英国水手;英国佬

lime^3 [laim] *n.*【植】欧椴

limerick ['limərik] *n.* 五行打油诗

limit ['limit] I *n.* ①界线,界限: The diver went into the deep water beyond the danger ~. 潜水员潜到超过危险线的深水中去了。 / at the northern ~ of the valley 在山谷北面的边沿上 ② 限度;限制;[复]范围,境界: set a ~ to the number of passengers 限定乘客人数 / the age ~ for enlistment 入伍的年龄限制 / the city ~s 市区范围 ③ 极限,极点: reach the ~ of one's patience 到了忍无可忍的地步 / ~ value 【数】极限值 ④(规定可以猎取的)猎物的最大限额;(规定的)最大赌额 II *vt.* ①限制,限定: The author will ~ himself to a discussion of these two topics. 作者只准备讨论这两个题目。②减少: ~ the expenses as much as possible 尽量节省开支 ‖*go beyond* (或 *over*) *the* ~ 超过限度 / *go the* ~ (参加球类比赛等时)赛完全局(或全场) / *off* ~s [美]禁止进入的(指禁止军人、受训人员等进入的某些娱乐场所或地区) / *the* ~ [口] 使人无法容忍的事物(或人), 到了绝顶的事物: I've seen bad weather, but this is *the* ~. 坏天气我见过, 可没见过比这更坏的了。/ *the* ~ *man* (赛跑等比赛中)受到最大让步的人 / *the*

superior (**inferior**) ~ ① 最早(最迟)的限期 ② 最大(最小)的限额 / *to the* (**utmost**) ~ 到顶点: strain oneself *to the* ~ 竭尽全力 / *within* ~s 在一定范围之内, 适当地 / *within the* ~s *of* 在…的范围内: *within the* ~s *of* objective conditions 在客观条件许可的范围内 / *without* ~ 无限(制)地 ‖~able *a.* 可限制的 / ~er *n.* ① 限制物 ②【无】限幅器, 限制器 / ~less *a.* 无限制的; 无限的

limitation [,limi'teiʃən] *n.* ① 限制 ② 限度; 局限; 限制因素: This problem will not be dealt with here owing to the ~ of space. 限于篇幅, 这儿就不谈这个问题了。/ know one's ~s 知道自己能力有限, 有自知之明 ③【律】(诉讼)时效

limited ['limitid] I *a.* ① 有限的: ~ monarchy 有限君主制, 君主立宪政体(指君主权力受宪法所限制) ②(指智力方面)狭窄的, 缺乏创见的 ③(火车等)乘客定额的; 停靠少的, 速度快的; 高级的 II *n.* 高级快车 ‖~ly *ad.* / ~ness *n.* ‖~ company, '~-,lia'bility company 股份有限公司 (用在公司名字后时, 作 Limited, 或略作 Ltd.) / ~ service【军】(指装备、器材)不适用于战区;(指人员)不适合担任战斗任务 / ~ war 有限战争

limp^1 [limp] I *vi.* ① 一瘸一拐地走, 跛行; 蹒跚 ② 缓慢费力地进行 II *n.* 跛行: walk with a ~ 一颠一跛地走 ‖~ingly *ad.* 一瘸一拐地

limp^2 [limp] *a.* ① 柔软的;易曲的 ② 软弱的;无生气的,无精神的 ‖~ly *ad.* / ~ness *n.*

limpet ['limpit] *n.* ①【动】蛾, 帽贝 ② 恋栈者(尤指眷恋官职者); 缠住某人(或某事)的人 ③ 水下爆破弹 (=~ mine) ‖*stick like a* ~ 缠住不放, 纠缠不休

limpid ['limpid] *a.* ① 清澈的 ② (文体等)清晰的 ③ 平静的, 无忧无虑的 ‖~ity [lim'piditi] *n.* / ~ly *ad.* / ~ness *n.*

linchpin ['lintʃpin] *n.* ① 车辖;制轮楔 ② 关键: the ~ upon which success or failure depends 成败的关键

linden ['lindən] *n.*【植】椴;欧椴;美洲椴

line^1 [lain] I *n.* ① 线,索,绳;钓线;测量(深度等用的)测平用的绳(或卷尺);[常用复]缰绳(尤指较长的): a strong hemp ~ 一根结实的麻绳 / hang the clothes on the ~ 把衣服挂在绳上 / fishing ~s 钓(鱼)线 ②金属线,电线;线路;管;管路: a three-party ~ 三户合用的电话线 / *Line* engaged! (或 [美] *Line* busy!) (电话)有人在打! / a telegraph ~ 电报线路 / an oil ~ 油管 / a sewage ~ 下水管道, 污水管道 ③【数】线;【无】扫描线; (绘画等中的)线条;【音】乐谱线: a straight (curved, undulating) ~ 直(曲, 波状)线 / translate life into ~ and colour 用线条和色彩描绘实物 ④ 路线, 交通线; 航线; 铁路线; 铁轨; (固定路线的)运输公司: a ~ of supply【军】补给线 / a blockade ~ 封锁线 / open up a new air ~ 开辟一条新的航空线 / the main ~ of a railway 铁路干线 / a shipping ~ 航线; 航运公司 / a belt ~ 环行线电车路; 环行铁路 / This steamship (air) ~ now belongs to the people. 这家轮船(航空)公司现在归人民所有了。

⑤作业线: a production (an assembly) ~ 生产(装配)线

⑥界线, 界限: The ball crossed the ~. 球出界了。 / a dividing ~ 分界线 / go (或 step) over the ~ 超越限度; 越界

⑦[the ~] 赤道: The ship crossed the ~. 船通过赤道。

⑧战线; 前线: the first ~ of defence 第一道防线

⑨(政治)路线; 方法, 方式: lay down a general ~ 制订一条总路线 / a ~ in education 教育路线 / proceed on correct ~s 按照正确方法进行 / What ~ do you expect to take? 你打算采用什么样的方法?

⑩外形, 轮廓; [复]设计, 草图; 船体型线图: the designing of the hull ~ 船体型线图的设计

⑪(一类)货色: the best-selling ~ in scarf 最畅销的一种围巾 / There is a full ~ of electrical supplies. 各种电器一应俱全。

⑫行业, 行当; 擅长: His ~ is chemistry. 他是搞化学的。 / He is in the plumbing ~. 他是干装修水管这一行的。

⑬排, 行列; [军]两列横队; 整列的战舰: a ~ of chairs 一排椅子 / form into (或 draw up in) ~ 排成二列横队 / a ~ abreast (astern 或 ahead) 舰队横(纵)列

⑭[复](英军的)一排营帐(或营房): inspect the ~s 巡视营房

⑮[the ~] (英陆军的)正规军(不包括近卫军等辅助兵种); (美军的)战斗部队(不包括参谋部、后勤部人员); 前线部队

⑯(诗、文的)一行; 短信; [复]一首诗; 台词: page 3, ~ 5 第三页第五行 / Drop me a ~ (或 a few ~s) when you get there. 到达那里之后, 请写封短信给我。 / memorize one's ~s 记台词

⑰[复]结婚证书 (=marriage ~)

⑱一系列相关联的事物(或人); 系统, 家系, 血统: relations in the direct (female) ~ 直(母)系亲属

⑲[复]命运, 运气: Hard ~s! 倒霉!

⑳迹象, 消息: try to get (或 have) a ~ on sb.'s plan 想打听到某人的计划 / give sb. a ~ on sth. 透露给某人一点有关某事的情况

㉑(皮肤上的)条纹, 皱纹; 掌纹: a face seamed with ~s 满是皱纹的脸

㉒(长度单位)十二分之一吋

II ❶ *vt.* ①用线表示; 用线描画; 划线于: ~ off several columns 划出几栏

②使有线条, 使起皱纹: a ~d face 起了皱纹的脸

③使排成一列

④沿…排列: Thousands of people ~d the streets to welcome the visiting delegation. 成千上万的人夹道欢迎来访的代表团。 / a road ~d with trees 两旁种着树的路

❷ *vi.* 排队, 排齐 (*up*)

‖*a* ~ *of least resistance* 见 **resistance** / *all along the* ~ 在全线, 到处; 在每一点上: win victories *all along the* ~ 全线获胜 / *bring* (或 *get*) *into* ~ ①使排齐 ②使协调起来, 使一致: alter the passage to *bring* it *into* ~ *with* the facts 修改这段文章使与事实相符 / *by rule and* ~ 见 **rule** / *come* (或 *fall*) *into* ~ ①排齐 ②同意; 采取协调一致的步骤: I think he will *come into* ~ *with* us if you explain things clearly. 如果你把情况讲清楚, 我想他会同意我们的。 / *down the* ~ [美]①往市中心(去) ②完全地: back sb. *down the* ~ 完全支持某人 / *down the* ~ *for* 全力支持… / *draw the* (或 *a*) ~ ①划一界线 ②划定最后界限: *draw the* ~ *at* going any further 到此截断(或为止)不再往下 / *give sb.* ~ *enough* 暂时放任以便最后收拾某人, 对某人欲擒故纵 / *go up the* ~ 离开后方(或基地)去前线 / *hew to the* ~ 服从纪律, 循规蹈矩 / *hit the* ~ [美] ①(橄榄球赛中)试图带球冲过对方防线 ②勇敢果断地行事 / *hold the* ~ ①(打电话时)等着不挂断 ②坚定不移, 不肯退让 / *hook,* ~, *and sinker* [美口]完全地, 全部地 / *in* ~ ①成一直线, 整齐: stand in ~ 站队; 排齐 ②一致, 协调: 与现行价格(或标准)一致 ③有秩序; 受约束: keep sb. *in* ~ 控制住某人使他规规矩矩 / *in* ~ *for* [美]即将获得; 可以得到 / *in* ~ *with* 跟……一致 / *in sb.'s* ~ ①与某人有关的; 在某人行业范围内的 ②是某人擅长的: Knitting is more *in her* ~ than mine. 编结东西她可比我内行得多。 / *lay* (或 *put*) *it on the* ~ [美俚] ①付钱 ②坦率地说; 提供证据 / ~ *out* ①划线标明, 标出: ~ *out* the route on the map 在地图上把这路线标示出来 ②用条表明; 需删去 ③把…排成行 【植】列植 ④(向某一方向)迅速移动: The plane ~d *out* east. 飞机向东直飞而去。 ⑤ 放声高唱(歌曲) / ~ *through* 划掉, 勾销 / ~ *up* ①(使)整队, 排列起来: people *lining up* at the bus stop 排在公共汽车站上(候车)的人们 / Plenty of canned foodstuffs were ~d *up* on the shelves. 许多罐头食品并排陈列在货架上。 ②(使)集合于一个营垒 / ~ *upon* ~ 一排排地; 稳步向前地 / *on the* ~ ①(油画等挂得)与观赏者的眼睛相平, 在不高不低的地方 ②模棱两可, 在两个不同性质的范畴的交界线上 ③处于危险状态: put one's life *on the* ~ 冒着生命危险 ④立即, 马上: pay cash *on the* ~ 立即付出现金 ⑤(沦)为妓女 / *out of* ~ ①不成一直线 ②不一致, 不协调; 与现行价格(或标准)不符 / *out of sb.'s* ~ ①与某人无关的; 不属某人行业范围的: We don't keep foreign language books. They are *out of our* ~. 我们

这里不卖外文书籍,那不是我们的经营范围。② 非某人所擅长的 / *read between the ~s* 体会字里行间的言外之意 / *ride the ~* [美] 骑马巡行大群牧畜的四周边沿以防疏散 / *shoot a ~* [俚] 吹牛,说大话 / *sign on the dotted ~* 在虚线上署名; [喻] 全部接受,毫不迟疑地同意 / *take a strong ~* 干得起劲 / *take* (或 *keep to*) *one's own ~* 干自己的事,满足于自己的本行 / *take the air ~* 走直线,走最短的路 / *the ~ of beauty* S 形的线条,美的线条 / *the ~ of duty* 值勤,公务: be wounded in *the ~ of duty* 因公负伤 / *the ~ of sight* 视线; 瞄准线 / *toe the ~* ① 准备起跑 ② 听从命令(尤指服从团体或党派的纪律) / *under the ~* 在赤道,正在赤道上的 ‖ **chief** 机场外场保养组组长 / **~ drawing** 线条画(如钢笔画、铅笔画等) / **~ engraving** 线雕; 线雕画 / **'~-haul** *n.* 长途运输 / **~man** ['lainmən] *n.* ①【电】线务员,线路工人,【军】架线兵 ②(铁路)护路工,养路工 ③[美](橄榄球赛的)前锋 ④[测]执线人 / **~ officer** 陆空军战斗兵种的军官; 军舰上的指挥军官 / **'~-,shooter** *n.* 吹牛的人 / **'~-,shooting** *n.* 吹牛 / **'~sman** ['lainzmən] *n.* ①【电】线务员,线路工人,【军】架线兵 ②(铁路)护路工,养路工 ③(某些球类比赛中的)巡边员 ④[英]正规军陆军士兵 / **'~up** *n.* ①(同一兴趣或同一宗旨的)一组人; (同一用途的)一批东西 ②一排人(尤指排队受检查的嫌疑犯) ③比赛时球员的阵容

line² [lain] *vt.* ①给(衣服、箱子等)装里子,加衬里于: ~ a coat with silk 用绸做外衣的衬里 ②用作(衣服、箱子等)的衬里: Strong cloth ~d the trunk. 这箱子用结实的布做衬里。③填(腰包),塞(肚皮): ~ one's pockets 肥私囊

lineage ['liniidʒ] *n.* 血统,世系; 门第

lineal ['liniəl] *a.* ① 直系的: a ~ descendant 直系后裔 ② 世袭的 ③ 世系的; 属同一世系的: ~ relatives 属同一世系的亲属 ④ =linear ⑤ 线的; 线状的 ⑥战斗部队的 ‖**~ly** *ad.*

lineament ['liniəmənt] *n.* [常用复] ①面貌; 面部轮廓 ②特征

linear ['liniə] *a.* ①线的; 直线的 ②长度的 ③【数】一次的,线性的: ~ equation 一次方程(式) / distortion【无】线性失真 ④强调线条的: ~ art 线条艺术 ⑤长条形的: a ~ leaf 长叶片 ‖**~ accelerator**【物】直线性加速器 / **~ measure** 长度; 长度单位制 / **~ perspective** 直线透视(作图)法 / **~ programming** 线性规划

linen ['linin] **I** *n.* ①亚麻布(或纱、线) ②亚麻织物(如台布、床单等) ③似亚麻布的制品(如衬衫、内衣等): change one's ~ 换内衣 ④ 亚麻纤维制成的纸(=~ paper) **II** *a.* ①用亚麻纺成的: ~ thread 亚麻线 ②亚麻布制的;似亚麻布的 ‖*shoot one's ~* 故意抖出内衣的袖子(表示自己是大人物,或表示不安) / *wash one's dirty ~* 谈论隐私(或家丑) ‖**'~,draper** *n.* [主英]亚麻布制品商

liner¹ ['lainə] *n.* ① 画线的人 ② 画线的工具 ③ 班船; 班机 ④(棒球中的)直球,平球

liner² ['lainə] *n.* ①衬里; 【机】衬垫,衬套,套筒 ②制衬里(或衬垫等)的人; 装衬里(或衬垫等)的人

linger ['liŋgə] ❶ *vi.* ① 逗留,徘徊; 闲荡 ②拖延; 苟延: Winter ~ed. 冬天迟迟不去。❷ *vt.* ①拖延; 慢慢地挨过(时间等): The patient ~ed out several more years. 病人又挨过了好几年。②[古]把…推迟 ‖**~ing** ['liŋgəriŋ] *a.* 拖延的; 逗留不去的: a ~ing disease 缠绵的病

lingerie ['lɛ̃:nʒəri:] *n.* [法]女内衣

lingo ['liŋgou] ([复] lingoes) *n.* [贬][谑] 外国话; 行话; 难懂的方言; 隐语

lingua franca ['liŋgwə 'fræŋkə] ([复] lingua francas 或 linguae francae ['liŋgwi: 'fræŋki:]) ① 意大利、西班牙、法兰西、希腊、阿拉伯、土耳其等国语言的混合语(通用于地中海的某些港口) ②(不同民族之间交往或进行交易时用的)混合语 ③混合方言

linguist ['liŋgwist] *n.* ①通晓数国语言的人 ②语言学家

linguistic [liŋ'gwistik] *a.* 语言的; 语言学的 ‖**~ally** *ad.*

liniment ['linimənt] *n.*【药】搽剂,涂抹油; 涂抹剂

lining ['lainiŋ] *n.* ①(衣服、箱子等的)衬里; 衬料; 【机】衬,衬套,套筒; 衬垫 ②装衬里(或衬套等) ③[古]内容

link¹ [liŋk] **I** *n.* ①链环;【机】连杆,链节;(编织物的)链圈: draw ~ 牵引连杆 ②(链状物中的)一节;(多节香肠的)一节香肠;单节小香肠 ③环节; 连接,联系: the ~s in a chain of development 发展过程中的各个环节 / a rail ~ from the port to the interior 一条把港口与内地连接起来的铁路 / cultural (spiritual) ~s 文化(精神)联系 / keep (或 maintain) close ~s with the masses 密切联系群众 ④【常用复】(衬衫袖口的)链扣(=cuff ~s) ⑤【无】通讯线路; 网络节; 固定接线;【电】熔丝;【化】键,键合 ⑥ 令(测量用的长度单位) ⑦[复][方]河道弯曲处 **II** ❶ *vt.* ①用环连接; 连接,联系: friendly neighbouring countries ~ed together as flesh and blood 血肉相连的友好邻邦 / ~ theory with practice 把理论和实践结合起来 ②挽(手臂); 挽(手): ~ one's arm in (或 through) another's 用手臂挽着别人的手臂 ❷ *vi.* 连接起来,联系着: There the irrigation canal ~s up with the reservoir. 这条灌溉渠道在那儿与水库连接起来。 ‖*the missing ~* ① 一系列完整的事物中缺少的一环 ② 设想中存在于类人猿与人类之间的过渡生物 ‖**'~-ing-up ship** 联络舰 / **'~ing-up station** 中继电台 / **~ing verb** = ~ verb / **~ motion** 【机】连杆运动 / **'~-s-and-~s** *a.* (针织品等)双反面组织的: a ~s-and-~s machine 双反面针织机,回复机 / **'~up** *n.* ①连接,联系,会合: plan a ground ~up 计划进行一次空降部队与地面部队的会合 ②连接物 / **~ verb**【语】联系动词

link²[liŋk] *n.* (旧时用的一种)火炬 ‖'**~boy, ~man** ['liŋkmən] *n.* 夜晚手执火炬的引路人

linkage ['liŋkidʒ] *n.* ①联系;连锁;联动 ②[机]链系,联动装置: brake ~ 制动联动装置 ③[化]键合 ④[电]耦合;磁链

links [liŋks] [复] *n.* ①[苏格兰]海边生草的沙地 ②[用作单或复]高尔夫球场 ‖**~man** ['liŋksmən] *n.* 打高尔夫球的人

linoleum [li'nouljəm] *n.* 亚麻油(地)毡;漆布

linseed ['linsi:d] *n.* 亚麻子,亚麻仁 ‖**~ cake** 亚麻子饼 / **~ meal** 亚麻子饼粉 / **~ oil** 亚麻子油,亚麻仁油

lint [lint] *n.* ①皮棉(=~ cotton) ②棉绒 ③(亚麻布或棉布经刮码后的)软麻布(作绷带等用)

lintel ['lintl] *n.* [建]楣,过梁

lion ['laiən] *n.* ①([复] lion(s) 狮子 ②(象征英国的)狮子纹章 ③勇猛的人 ④名人,社交场合的明星 ⑤[英][复]城市中的名胜地(源出游狮教者必去参观的伦敦塔狮子) ⑥[the L-] [天]狮子宫;狮子座 ‖a ~ in the way 拦路虎(尤指臆想的危险)/ a ~'s provider ①豺狼 ②[喻]走狗,爪牙 / beard the ~ in his den 太岁头上动土 / ~ and unicorn ①雄狮和独角兽(指捧着英国王室纹章的动物) ②英国王室军队的支持者 / see the ~s [英]游览名胜 / show sb. the ~s [英]带领某人游览名胜 / the British Lion 英国的别称 / the ~'s mouth 见 mouth / the ~'s share 见 share¹ / the ~'s skin 见 skin / twist the ~'s tail 见 tail¹ ‖**~hood, ~ship** *n.* 社会名流的地位 / **~like** *a.* 像狮子的 ‖**~heart** *n.* ①勇士 ②[L-] 英王理查一世 / '**~,hearted** *a.* 非常勇敢的 / '**~,hunter** *n.* ①猎狮者 ②巴结社会名流的人

lip [lip] **l** *n.* ①嘴唇: the upper (lower 或 under) ~ 上(下)唇 / be as close as the ~s are to the teeth (或 be closely related as ~s and teeth) 唇齿相依 / I heard it from his ~s. 这是我听他亲口说的。②(嘴)唇状物;(器皿或凹洞的)边;(伤口的)边缘;(茶壶等的)嘴;(螺丝钻的)唇;[植]唇瓣: the ~ of a bowl 碗边 ③(管乐器的)嘴;(吹奏时的)嘴形,唇形 ④[俚]无礼(的话);顶嘴: None of your ~! 不许你顶嘴! ⑤[美俚]律师 **II** *a.* ①口头上的,不真诚的: ~ comfort 口头敷衍的安慰 / ~ praise 表面的称赞 ②用嘴唇发(音)的: a ~ consonant 唇辅音 **III** (lipped; lipping) **❶** *vt.* ①用嘴唇触及,吻 ②轻轻地讲;[俚]唱;[美俚]吹奏 ③(波浪等)轻轻拍打 ④把高尔夫球打到(洞口)而未进入 **❷** *vi.* ①用嘴唇对上管乐器的嘴 ②(水)发出激溅声 ‖be steeped to the ~s in 深陷于…之中 / bite one's ~(s) 咬嘴唇(以压抑喜怒等感情) / button up one's ~ [美俚]住嘴;保守秘密 / curl one's ~ 撇嘴(表示鄙夷等) / escape sb.'s ~s (话)溜出某人之口 / hang one's ~ (由于屈辱)耷拉着嘴唇 / hang on sb.'s ~s 专心倾听某人说话,洗耳恭听某人说话 / keep a stiff upper ~ 坚定不移;顽

强不屈 / lick one's ~s 咂咂嘴唇(表示垂涎或满意)/ on sb.'s ~s 就在某人的嘴边: The words were just on my ~s. 话就在我嘴边。/ on the ~s of ① 在…中流传 ② 出诸…之口,挂在…嘴上 / pass sb.'s ~s ①被某人吃(或喝)掉 ②被某人说出口 / shoot out one's ~s 蔑视地噘嘴 / Zip your ~s! [美俚]别开口! ‖**~less** *a.* 没有嘴唇的;(器皿等)没有嘴的 ‖'**~-'deep** *a.* 表面上的,无诚意的 / **~ language** (聋哑人用嘴唇动作交谈的)唇语,视话 / **~ microphone** [讯](戴在讲话人嘴唇上的)唇式传声器 / '**~-read** *vt.* 唇读理解(某人的话)*vi.* 用唇读方法 / '**~,reading** *n.* (教聋哑人从嘴唇的动作了解话意的)唇读法 / '**~salve** *n.* ①防唇裂油膏 ②[喻]奉承,献媚 / **~ service** 口头上说得好听的话,口惠 / '**~stick** *n.* 唇膏;口红 / **~-sync** ['lipsiŋk] *vt.*, *vi. & n.* 对口型(指配音时使口的动作与录好的音相合)

lipping ['lipiŋ] *n.* ①[解](骨的)唇形变 ②(吹管乐器时的)嘴形,唇形

liqueur [li'kjuə] *n.* 味浓性烈的一种(甜)酒

liquid ['likwid] **I** *a.* ①液体的;液态的,流动的:(眼睛)泪汪汪的: ~ phase 液相 / ~ state 液态 / ~ food 流质食品 ②清澈的,透明的;明亮的: a ~ sky 明朗的天空 ③(声音)柔和的,清脆的;(诗等)流利的,流畅的 ④不稳定的,易变的;易变换为现金的: a ~ opinion 易变的意见 / ~ assets 流动资产 / ~ capital 活动资本,流动资本 ⑤[语]流音的 **II** *n.* ①液体 ②[语]流音(如 [l], [r] 等) ‖**~ly** *ad.* / **~ness** *n.* ‖**~ air** 液态空气 / **~ crystal** 液晶(体) / **~ fire** 液体燃烧剂 / **~ measure** ① 液量单位 ② 液体测量器 / **~ oxygen** 液态氧

liquidate ['likwideit] **❶** *vt.* ①清理,清算(破产的企业等) ②清偿,了结(债务等) ③将(资产等)变换现金 ④肃清,消灭,杀掉;取消: ~ the pernicious influence of 肃清…的流毒 **❷** *vi.* 清理,清算 ‖**liquidator** *n.* 清算人

liquidation [,likwi'deiʃən] *n.* ①(债务的)了结;(企业的)清理,清算;(资产的)变现 ②肃清,消灭;取消 ‖a ~ sale 停业清理大拍卖 / go into ~ (公司等)停业清理,破产

liquor ['likə] **I** *n.* ①液,液体;汁: meat ~ 肉汁 ②[药]溶液;液剂 ③(尤指蒸馏制成的)酒: malt ~ 啤酒 / different kinds of spirituous ~s 各种烈酒 / traffic ~ 酒的(非法)买卖 / be under the influence of ~ 有点醉,微醺 **II** **❶** *vt.* ①用液态物质处理,把…浸于水中 ②给(鞋子、皮革等)上油 ③[俚]使喝烈酒(up) **❷** *vi.* [俚]喝大量的烈酒(up) ‖be in ~ (或 be the worse for ~) 喝醉 / carry one's ~ like a gentleman 没有丝毫醉意 / take a ~ (或 ~-up) [俚]喝酒提神 ‖**~ head** 醉汉

lisp [lisp] **I** **❶** *vi.* ①咬舌儿(指将 [s] [z] 音发作 [θ] [ð]) ②(孩子似地)口齿不清地说话 **❷** *vt.* ①咬着舌儿说;口齿不清地说(out) **II** *n.* ①咬舌儿②

口齿不清: speak with a ~ 说话口齿不清 ②咬舌儿发出的声音; (树叶等的)沙沙声 ‖~ingly ad.

lissom(e) ['lisəm] a. ①柔软的 ②敏捷的, 轻快的 ‖lissomely ad. / lissomeness n.

list¹ [list] I n. ①表, 一览表; 目录; 名单: make (或 draw up) a ~ 造表, 列表 / put the newcomers' names on the ~ 把新来人员的名字列入名册 / take that item off the ~ 从表上去掉那一项目 ②[总称](交易所中)各种上市证券 ③ =~ price ‖an active ~ 现役官兵名册 / a casualty ~ 伤亡名单 / an export ~ 出口商品目录 / a free ~ 免税商品表; 免费入场观众名单 / a packing ~ 【商】装箱单 / a price ~ 价目表 / a reading ~ 阅读书目 / a shopping ~ 购物单 / a sick ~ (尤指军队中和船上的)病员名单 II ❶ vt. ①把…编列成表, 把…列入目录 (或名单); 列举: a few reasons 列举几条理由 / as ~ed above (below) 如上(下)所列 ②[~ oneself] 把…算作 (as) ③[古]征召…入伍 ❷ vi. ①列入价目表 ②[古]入伍 ‖head (或 lead) the ~ 居首位, 领衔 / stand first on the ~ 居首位, 列前茅 ‖~ price 目录价格, 价目单定价

list

list² [list] I n. ①布条, 布边, 织边 ②狭条; (木板上截下的)木条 ③田埂 ④【建】边饰; 扁带饰 ⑤[~s][用作单或复]竞技场, 斗技场; 争辩的场所; (竞技场内的)栅栏 ⑥条纹(尤指马背中央的深色条纹) II (list(ed)) vt. ①从(木板)上截下边条 ②犁(地) ③把…排成条 ④给…装布边: ~ a door (为防风)在门的边沿上装上布条 ‖enter the ~s against (尤指辩论时)向…挑战; 接受…的挑战

list³ [list] (list(ed)) ❶ vt. [古]听 ❷ vi. [古]听; 听见

list⁴ [list] I (list(ed)) ❶ vt. [古]称…的心, 中…的意: He did as him ~. 他随心所欲。 ❷ vi. 愿意, 想要 II n. [古]倾向; 个人意愿

list⁵ [list] I (list(ed)) ❶ vi. (船只、房屋、篱笆等)倾侧 ❷ vt. 使倾侧 II n. 倾侧; 倾侧性: That ship has a ~ to port (或 a port ~). 那条船左舷倾侧(即倾向左边)。

listen ['lisn] I vi. ①听; 留神听: He ~ed but could not hear. 他留神地听, 但没有听见。 / ~ for the clock to announce the new year 等着听时钟报新年 ②倾听; 听信 ③[俚]听上去, 听起来: It doesn't ~ right. 这听上去不对。 II n. 听; 倾听: Please have a ~ to this. 请听听这个吧。 ‖~ in ①收听; 监听 ②偷听; 窃听: a ~ing-in device 【军】潜听装置 / on the ~ 在注意地听着

listener ['lisnə] n. 听者; 收听者, 听众之一 ‖~ship n. 听众(人数) ‖~-in ['lisnər'in] n. ①收听者, 听众之一 ②监听者; 偷听者

listening ['lisnin] I n. 听; 监听 II a. ①收听的; 收听无线电广播的; 留神倾听的 ②助听用的: wear a ~ button in one's ear. 戴着耳塞助听器 ‖~ gear 听音器 / ~ post ①情报收集中心; 听音哨; 潜听哨 ②【军】能监听无线电通讯的短波电台 / ~ station 【军】侦察敌人电子器材位置的无线电(或雷达)接收站

listless ['listlis] a. 不想活动的, 倦怠的; 无精打采的 ‖~ly ad. / ~ness n.

lit¹ [lit] I light¹, light³ 的过去式和过去分词 II a. ①照亮的; 点着的 ②[美俚]喝醉了的; 被毒品麻醉了的 ‖be ~ up [俚]喝醉着; 被毒品麻醉着

lit² [lit] n. [美俚]文学课程 (literature 的缩略)

litany ['litəni] n. 【宗】连祷; 应答祈祷: the Litany 祷告书中的连祷文

literacy ['litərəsi] n. 识字, 有文化; 阅读和写作的能力; 精通文学; 善于写作

literal ['litərəl] I a. ①文字(上)的: a ~ error 文字上的错误 ②照词句本义的, 字面的, 逐字的; 原义的: a ~ interpretation of a passage 对一段文章的字面解释 / a ~ translation 直译 / I heard nothing in the ~ sense of the word. 我听是实在没有听到过。(常有"但可能看到过"的含义) ③字母的; 用字母代表的: Codes may be either numerical or ~. 电码可用数字代表, 也可用字母代表。 ④确确实实的, 不加夸张的; 朴实的: have a love of ~ truth 爱实事求是 ⑤只讲实际的, 刻板的; 缺乏想象力的 II n. 文字上的错误; 印刷错误 ‖~ity [litə'ræliti] n. / ~ly ①照字义, 逐字地 ②[口]确实地, 不加夸张地: He ~ly flew into the room. 他简直是飞也似地跑进了房间。 / ~ness n. ‖~ contract 【律】成文契约

literary ['litərəri] a. ①文学(上)的: ~ works 文学作品 ②从事写作的; 精通文学的; 文人的: ~ and art workers 文艺工作者 ③书本的; (词语等)书面语中的; 书卷气的 ‖literarily ['litərərili; 美 ,litə'rerili] ad. / literariness n. ‖~ property (作者的)著作权, 版权

literate ['litərit] I a. ①有阅读和写作能力的, 有文化的 ②精通文学的; 善于写作的 II n. 识字的人, 有文化的人 ‖~ly ad.

literature ['litəritfə] n. ①文学; 文学作品: ~ and art 文学艺术 / read a great amount of ~ 读大量文学作品 ②(关于某学科或专题的)文献, [总称]

作品: The subject boasts of an extensive ~. 这门学科的文献极为丰富。 / disarmament ~ 有关裁军问题的各种论文书籍 ③写作(业): be engaged in ~ 从事写作 ④[口][总称]印刷品(如广告、传单等) ⑤(为某一乐器或一组乐器演奏用的)一组乐曲 ⑥[古]学识,学问

lithe [laið] *a.* ①柔软的; 易弯曲的: make sb.'s muscles ~ 使某人的肌肉柔软灵活 ②轻巧自如的 ‖**~ly** *ad.* / **~ness** *n.*

lithography [li'θɔgrəfi] *n.* 平版(指石版或金属版)印刷术; [总称]平版印刷品

litigant ['litigənt] **I** *a.* (人)在诉讼中的 **II** *n.* 诉讼当事人

litigate ['litigeit] ❶ *vi.* 提出诉讼 ❷ *vt.* ①就…争讼 ②[古]争论,争辩 ‖**litigation** [ˌliti'geiʃən] *n.* 诉讼,打官司,讼争

litigious [li'tidʒəs] *a.* ①好诉讼的, 好打官司的 ②关于诉讼的; (事件等)可引起诉讼的 ‖**~ly** *ad.* / **~ness** *n.*

litmus ['litməs] *n.* [化]石蕊: ~ blue 石蕊蓝 ‖**~ paper** 石蕊试纸

litre ['liːtə] *n.* 升(容量单位)(略作 l.)

litter ['litə] **I** *n.* ①轿,舆 ②担架,异床 ③(供动物睡眠或防植物受冻等用的)稻草,树叶,干草 ④落叶层; 枯枝层 ⑤(猪、狗等多产动物)一胎生下的小动物: a ~ of little pigs 一窝小猪 ⑥[总称]四下乱丢的东西; 杂乱 **II** ❶ *vt.* ①为(动物)铺草荐; 在…上铺草荐: ~ *down* a horse 给马铺草荐 / ~ *down* a stable with fresh straw 在马棚里铺上新稻草 ②(多产动物)产(仔) ③使在…上布满杂乱的东西: Don't ~ (*up*) the floor *with* scraps of paper. 不要在地板上乱丢纸屑。 ④乱丢: Don't ~ scraps of paper over the floor. 不要在地板上乱丢纸屑。 ❷ *vi.* ①产仔 ②四下丢东西 ‖*have a ~ of kittens* 见 **kitten** / *in a ~* 一片杂乱 / *in* ～ (多产动物)正在产仔 ‖**~-bin** *n.* (街上等处的)废物箱 / **'~bug** *n.* 在公共场所乱抛废物的人

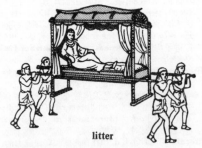

litter

little ['litl] **I** (比较级 less [les] 或 lesser, 最高级 least [liːst]) *a.* ①小的: a ~ group of people 一小群人 / the ~ finger (toe) 小手指(脚趾) / So that's your ~ trick! 原来是你要的小花招! ②(人或动物)幼小的; 小得可爱的: How are the ~

ones? 小孩子们好吗? / the ~ Blakes 布莱克家的小孩子们 / Her child is a nice ~ thing. 她的孩子是个可爱的小家伙。③矮小的: a ~ man 身材矮小的人 ④短暂的: You have only a ~ month to wait. 你只须等待短短的一个月。⑤琐碎的; 微不足道的: He never overlooks any ~ points. 他从不忽视细节。 / a ~ fellow 小人物 ⑥狭小的; 可鄙的: a ~ mind 小心眼儿 ⑦(表示否定语气)少, 不多的; [a ~] (表示肯定语气)一些,一点点: There is (very 或 but) ~ time left. 没剩下多少时间了。[比较: Don't worry, you still have *a* ~ time. 别担心,你还有一点时间呢。] / know (*a*) ~ German 不懂什么(懂一点儿)德语 / go *a* ~ way with sb. 陪某人走一小段路 **II** (比较级 less [les] 或 lesser, 最高级 least [liːst]) *ad.* ❶ 少; [a ~] 稍许, 一点儿: sleep ~ 睡得少[比较: sleep *a* ~ 睡一会儿] / I have seen him very ~ recently. 最近我不大看到他。 / He is ~ better than a bookworm. 他简直跟书呆子差不多。 / That is ~ short of a farce. 那简直是一出滑稽戏。 / feel *a* ~ cold 觉得有点冷 / *a* ~ before ten (o'clock) 十点钟不到一点 ❷[用在 know, suspect, believe, care 等动词之前]毫不: He ~ knows (或 *Little* does he know) what may happen. 他一点不知道可能要发生什么事。 **III** *n.* ① 没有多少; [a ~] 一点,少量: *Little* remains to be done about it. 在这件事上几乎没有什么可做的了。[比较: *A* ~ remains to be done. 还有一点事做一做。] / Every ~ counts. 点点滴滴都是重要的。 / Every ~ helps. 点点滴滴都起作用。/ He did what ~ he could. 他把仅有的一点力量都使出来了。 / Please give me *a* ~. 请给我一点儿。 / know *a* ~ of everything 样样都懂一点 ②短时间; 短距离: I'll be back in *a* ~. 我马上就回来。 / We have only covered *a* ~ today. 今天我们才走了一点点路(或只做了一点点)。 ‖*after a* ~ 过了一会儿: *After a* ~ he felt better. 过了一会儿他觉得舒服点了。 / *by and* ~ ~ 一点点 / *a* ~ 一会儿: May I have your pincers *for a* ~? 我借你的钳子用一会儿好吗? / *in* ～ ①小规模地 ②缩小地: a painting done *in* ～ 一幅小型画 / ~ *by* ~ 一点一点地,逐渐地 / ~ *or nothing* 简直没有 / *make* ~ *of* ①不重视; 不以…为意: He *makes* ~ *of* walking fifty kilometres in a day. 他一天走五十公里路是毫不在乎的。②难了解,不领会: I could *make* ~ *of* what he was saying. 我弄不懂他的话。/ *Many a* ~ *makes a mickle.* 见 **many** / *no* ~ 许多: take *no* ~ pains over sth. 在某事上花费许多精力 / *not a* ～ 许多; 很: give sb. *not a* ～ trouble 给某人带来许多麻烦 / be *not a* ～ bewildered 大惑不解 / *set* ～ *by* 轻视 / *the* ～ ①小人物们,无足轻重的人们 ②仅有的一点: He did *the* ～ that he could. 他已尽到他仅有的一点力量了。/ *think* ～ *of* ①不重

视 ②对…没有多加思索, 对…不踌躇: He thought ～ of swimming for three hours on end. 他连续游泳三小时毫不在乎. ‖**-ness** n. ‖**Little Bear**【天】小熊座 / '～-ease n. 【史】使人立卧不得的牢笼 / ～ **Joe** [美俚](掷骰子戏中的)四点 / ～ **magazine**(刊登试验性文艺作品的非商业性)小杂志 / ～ **Mary** [口]肚子 / ～ **people** 小妖精们 / **Little Rhody** 美国罗德岛州的别名(因该州是美国最小的州) / **Little Rock** 小石城 [美国城市] / ～ **slam**(桥牌中只让对方赢去一副的)小满贯 / ～ **theatre** 小剧场, 实验剧场 / ～ **woman** [美俚]妻子

littoral ['litərəl] **I** a. 海岸的; 沿(海)岸的; 生长在海岸的 **II** n. 沿(海)岸地区 ‖～**ly** ad.

liturgy ['litə(ɔ)dʒi] n.【宗】①礼拜仪式 ②[常作 L-] 圣餐仪式

live[1] [liv] ❶ vi. ① 活着; 活, 生存:～ to a great age 活到高龄 ②生活, 过活 / ～ plainly and frugally 过俭朴的生活 ③ 居住: He ～s near the factory. 他住在工厂附近. / ～ under the same roof 住在同一幢房子里 ④留存在人们记忆中 ⑤享受人生, 生活过得满意 ⑥(船、飞机)渡过危险: The ship ～d in the storm. 这船没有在风浪中沉掉. ⑦[宗]获得永生 ❷ vt. ①过(生活); 度过: ～ a happy life 过幸福生活 ② 实践; 经历: ～ one's belief 实践自己的信仰 / He had ～d what he narrated. 他曾经历过他所讲的那些事. ‖**as I ～**(或 **as sure as one ～s**)[用作插入语]的确是 / **Live and learn!** 真是活到老, 学不了! / ～ **and let** ～ [谚]自己活也让别人活 / ～ **by** 靠…过活: ～ by one's hands 靠双手劳动过活 / ～ **down** 改正行为而使(以往的过错、丑行等)被人遗忘 / ～ **fast** 过放纵的生活 / ～ **high** 过奢华的生活 / ～ **in** 住在工作(或学习)的地方: The room does not seem to be ～d in. 这房间似乎没有人住在里面. ②(佣工)住在雇主家内;(店员)住在店内 / ～ **it up** [俚]① 狂欢一场 ②(一反常规地)纵欲欢乐 / ～ **off** ① 住在…之外 ②靠…生活; 靠…供养 / ～ **on** ①继续活着 ②以…为主食 ③靠…生活; 靠…维持地位(或名誉): ～ on one's wages 靠工资生活 / ～ **out** ① 活过(某一段时间): The patient ～d out another fortnight. 病人又活了两个星期. ② 住在外面, (佣工)不住在雇主家内; (店员)住在店外 / ～ **through** 过; 经受住 / ～ **to oneself** 过孤独的生活 / ～ **up to** 实践(原则、誓言等); 做到 / ～ **well** ① 过有道德的生活 ②过奢华的生活, 吃喝得好 / ～ **with sb.** ①与某人住在一道;与某人同居 ②寄宿在某人处 / **where sb. ～s** [美俚]在某人的要害处: The word goes right *where* I ～. 这句话击中了我的要害. ‖'～**-for,ever** n. 【植】紫花景天

live[2] [laiv] **I** a. [常作定语]①活的, 有生命的:～ fish 活鱼 ②[谑][常接在 real 后]真的, 活生生的: a *real* ～ steam engine 真的蒸汽机(指不是玩具) ③ 精力充沛的, 充满活力的;

a ～ young man 生气勃勃的年轻人 / ～ eyes 炯炯有神的眼睛 ④燃着的: ～ coals 燃烧着的煤块 ⑤目前大家关心的; 尚在争论中的: a ～ issue 尚在争论中的问题 ⑥正在使用着的;(球等)正在玩的: a ～ runway 现用跑道 ⑦(机器等)运转着的; 传动的; 动力发动的: a ～ axle 转轴 ⑧ 装着炸药(或可裂变物质)的;实弹的; 通上电的; 有作用的: ～ shell shooting 实弹射击 / a ～ bomb 真炸弹, 未经爆炸的炸弹 ⑨(稿子等)排好版准备印刷的; 尚未排版的 ⑩(岩石等)未使用过的; 未采掘的, 原状的: a ～ match 没擦过的火柴 ⑪(空气)清新的;(颜色)鲜艳的 ⑫实况播送的;参加实况播送的: a ～ radio programme 无线电实况广播 **II** ad. 活在(或从)表演现场, 以实况: be televised ～ to 向…作电视实况转播 ‖'～-**bait** n. 活的钓饵 / '～-**box** n. 放在河中使鱼虾保持鲜活的箩筐(或栅栏) / ～ **load** 活负载, 动荷载 / ～ **parking** 司机等候在车内的车辆停放 / ～ **steam** 新汽(直接从锅炉出来的高压蒸汽) / ～-**stock** n. [总称]家畜, 牲畜: ～*stock* farm 牧场 / ～ **wire** ①通电的电线 ②生龙活虎般的人

livelihood ['laivlihud] n. 生活; 生计: means of ～ 生活资料 / earn(或 gain, make)a ～ 谋生

livelong ['livlɔŋ, 'laivlɔŋ] a. 漫长的; 整个的: the ～ summer 漫漫长夏 / the ～ day 整整的一天

lively ['laivli] **I** a. ①活泼的, 充满生气的; 活跃的; 快活的: The dock is ～ *with* cranes and vehicles of all descriptions. 码头上到处是各式各样的吊车和运输车辆, 一片蓬勃景象. / a ～ imagination 丰富的想象力 ②(情绪等)热烈的; 强烈的: a ～ discussion 热烈的讨论 ③[谑]紧张的, 惊险的: make things(或 it)～ for sb. 使某人紧张一阵 ④鼓舞的, 提神的 ⑤(色彩等)明快的; 鲜明的 ⑥栩栩如生的, 真实的: a ～ description 生动的描述 ⑦(舞蹈等)轻快的;(球等)弹力足的 ⑧(船)行驶轻快的, 驾驶灵便的 **II** ad. 活泼地; 轻快地 ‖**as** ～ **as a grig** 非常快活 ‖**livelily** ad. / **liveliness** n. a certain *liveliness* [俚]一阵猛烈的炮火

liven ['laivn] vt. & vi. (使)活跃起来, (使)愉快起来(up)

liver[1] ['livə] n. ①肝脏 ②(供食用的鸡、牛等的)肝 ③无脊椎动物类似肝的器官 ‖'～-**com,plaint** n. 肝病 / '～-**wort** n. 【植】欧龙牙草 / '～-**wurst** n. 碎肝制成的红肠

liver[2] ['livə] n. ①[一般与定语连用]过着某种生活的人: a fast(或 loose)～ 生活放荡的人 / a good ～ 有道德的人;考究吃喝的人 ②居住者

livery[1] ['livəri] a. ①像肝的 ②有肝病征象的

livery[2] ['livəri] n. ①(封建贵族侍从、仆人等所穿的)特殊制服, 号衣 ②伦敦各种行会会员的制服; [总称]伦敦同业公会会员 ③[古]侍从, 仆从 ④代客养马; 出租马(车)⑤(出租马、马车的)马车行, 马房(= ～ stable)⑥ 各种车辆出租行 ⑦【律】财产所有权的让渡(批准书)⑧[诗][喻]衣服, 覆盖物: birds in their winter ～ 长着冬季

羽毛的鸟 ⑨[古] (尤指给仆人的)津贴,食粮 ‖*at ~* (马)付费由人代养 / *in (out of)* ~ 穿(不穿)制服 / *sue (for) one's* ~ (继承人)向法院控诉要求让与财产 / *take up one's* ~ 成为同业公会会员 / *the ~ of grief* (或 *woe*) 丧服 / *the ~ of other men's opinions* 别人意见的借用 ‖~ **company** (有特权制服的)伦教同业公会 / ~**man** ['livərimən] *n.* ① (穿特殊制服的)伦敦各种行会的会员 ②马车出租人 ③[古] (穿特殊制服的)侍从,仆从

livid ['livid] *a.* ①青黑色的(指皮肉被打伤而呈现的颜色) ②青灰色的;铅色的: a face ~ with cold (rage) 冷(气)得发青的脸

living ['livin] **I** *a.* ①活的;活着的;现存的: ~ beings 生物 / the greatest event within ~ memory 人们记忆中最伟大的事件 ② 在活动中的;在使用着的;起作用的: ~ water 活水 / ~ coals 燃烧着的煤块 / a ~ language 活的语言 ③充满生气的;活跃的;生动的 ④逼真的: He is the ~ image of his father. 他活象他的父亲。(尤指外貌) ⑤生活的,维持生活的: improve the ~ conditions of the people 改善人民生活条件 / lower the ~ cost 降低生活费用 / raise the ~ standards 提高生活水平 ⑥适于居住的: the ~ area 适于居住的地方 ⑦(岩石等)未经采掘的;未经琢磨过的 ⑧[加强语气用,=very]: scare the ~ daylights out of sb. 把某人吓得半死 **II** *n.* ①生活;生计: the cost of ~ 生活费用 ②活着 ③[英]教士的俸禄 ④[古]财产 ‖*good* ~ 讲究吃喝的生活 / *the* ~ 活着的人们[后接复数动词] / *the* ~ *theatre* 舞台剧(与电影及电视相对而言) ‖~ **death** 活地狱般的生活 / ~ **room** ①起居室 ②= ~ space / ~ **space** ①生存空间(指为满足民族生存和经济自给所需的领土,系第二次世界大战前纳粹德国为向外侵略和扩张所提出的一种反动的地缘政治学理论) ②(房屋的)可居住面积 / ~ **wage** 能维持普通家庭生活的工资;最低生活工资

lizard ['lizəd] *n.* ①蜥蜴: a house ~ 壁虎 ②一种家养的杂色金丝雀 ③[常作 L-]美国亚拉巴马州人 (Alabamian) 的别称

llama ['lɑ:mə] *n.* 【动】美洲驼,无峰驼

llama

load [loud] **I** *n.* ①担子;重载;[喻]负担,重任: be ever ready to bear a heavy ~ on one's shoulders 勇于挑重担 / take a ~ off sb.'s mind 消除某人的思想负担 / a ~ of taxation 赋税的重压 ②(车、船等的)装载量;一车(或一船、一驮、一飞机)货物;(弹药的)一次装入(量): cart full ~s of vegetables to the market 把一车车满载的蔬菜送上市场 / We have to make three ~s of the cargo. 我们得把货物分装三车(或三趟)。③(电机、机器等的)负载,负荷;(发电站的)发电量: the safe (permissible) ~ 安全(容许)载 / the dead ~ 恒载,静(荷)载,自重(指本身及固定附件的重量) / the live ~ 活负载,动荷载(如车上的货物及乘客的重量) / the capacity (full) ~ 满载 / the peak ~ 最大负载,峰负荷 ④工作量: the normal teaching ~ 正常教学工作量 ⑤[复][口]大量,许多,一大堆: ~s of time 充裕的时间 / ~s of friends 大批朋友 ⑥[俚]使人醉醺的量: carry a ~ 喝醉 **II** ❶ *vt.* ①装;装载: ~ a ship (truck) with coal 把煤装上船(卡车) / ~ cargo into the hold 把货装入船舱 ②把弹药装入(枪、炮);把胶卷装入(照相机): Are you ~ed? (或 Have you had your gun ~ed?) 你的枪上了子弹吗? / ~ a camera (with film) 把胶卷装入照相机 ③装满;使负担: ~ one's stomach with food 吃得太多 / ~ sb. with praise (abuse) 对某人大加颂扬(咒骂) / with a heart ~ed with care 心事重重地 ④使(某物)增加重量;用铅加重;用劣物质掺入(以增加重量或增加酒力等) ❷ *vi.* ①装货;上客;装弹药;装料: Load! 【军】装子弹! ②上船(或车等): They ~ed into the boat. 他们上了船。‖*get a* ~ *of* [美俚]仔细地看(或听);打量,估量 / *have a* ~ *on* [美俚]喝醉 / ~ *the dice (against sb.)* (对某人)使用灌铅骰子;[喻]用不正当手段占(某人)便宜 / *take a* ~ *off one's feet* [美俚]坐下休息 ‖~**er** *n.* 装货工人;装货设备;装弹机;装填手 / ~ **displacement** [船]满载排水量 / ~ **draught** [船]满载吃水 / ~ **factor** 【电】负载因数 / '~-,**shedding** *n.* (为防电站超载)对部分地区暂停供电 / ~ **(water) line** 满载吃水线

loaded ['loudid] *a.* ①有负载的,装着货的;有含意的: a ~ question 另有用意的问题 ②装有弹药的 ③加重的,灌过铅的 ④[美俚]喝醉了的 ⑤[美俚]钱很多的,富有的 ‖*for bear* 见 **bear** ‖~ **dice** (赌博中作弊用的)灌铅骰子

loading ['loudin] *n.* ①装货;装卸;装料: ~ and unloading 装卸 ②(车、船等装载的)货;(加在货物上面的)重量;载荷 ③填充物;填料

loaf[1] [louf] ([复] loaves [louvz]) *n.* ①一条面包;一只面包(通常有一定的重量,如一磅、二磅或四磅): two loaves of bread 两只面包 ②圆锥形糖块;[英](卷心菜等的)圆锥形菜心 ③(用肉、鱼等烘制成的)面包形菜肴;面包形食品: a ~ of cheese 长方形大块干酪 ④[英俚]脑袋: Use your

用你的脑袋想一想。‖*Half a ~ is better than no bread.* [谚]有比没有好。/ *loaves and fishes* 物质利益;私利 ‖*~ sugar* 圆锥形糖块

loaf² [louf] **I** ❶ *vi.* ①游荡,闲逛 ②懒散地工作: ~ on the job 磨洋工 ❷ *vt.* 混(日子),消磨(时间) (*away*) **II** *n.* [只用单]游荡: have a ~ 游荡 / on the ~ 在游荡着 ‖*~er n.* ①游手好闲者,二流子;无业游民 ②一种平底便鞋

loam [loum] **I** *n.* ①肥土,沃土;壤土 ②(做铸模等用的)粘泥和砂等的混合物 **II** *vt.* 用肥土填(或覆盖) ‖*~y a.* 肥土(似)的,含肥土的

loan¹ [loun] **I** *n.* ①贷款: a long-term interest-free ~ 长期无息贷款 / domestic (foreign) ~s 内(外)债 / public (or government) ~s 公债 ②借出;借出的东西: a ~ counter (图书馆等的)出借处 ③外来语 (=~word);外来的风俗(或习惯等) **II** *vt. & vi.* [主美]借出 ‖*~able a.* 可借出的 / *~ee* [lou'ni:] *n.* 借入者,债务人 / *~er n.* ①借出者,债权人 ②借用物(如承修某物时暂借顾客使用的代替品) ‖*~ collection* (向收藏者)借来的(文物)展品 / *~ holder* 债券持有人;(押款的)受押人 / *~ office* ①(向私人放贷的)贷款处 ②当铺 ③公债经募处 / *~ shark* [口]高利贷者 / *'~shift n.* 已经部分同化的外来词 / *~ society* 互助储金会 / *~ translation* (照外语字面的)直译语(例如: "处女地"译自"virgin land") / *'~word n.* 外来语

loan² [loun], **loaning** ['lounin] *n.* [苏格兰] ①小路 ②挤牛奶的场地

loath [louθ] *a.* [用作表语]不愿意的;厌恶的: be ~ to do sth. for sb. 不愿与某人干某事 / be ~ that it should be so 不愿意事情成为这个样子 ‖*nothing ~* 很愿意,很乐意: I was *nothing ~*. 我很愿意。

loathe [louð] *vt.* ①厌恶,憎恨 ②[口]不喜欢: I ~ going. 我不想去。‖*loathing n.* 厌恶,憎恨

loaves [louvz] loaf¹的复数

lobby ['lobi] **I** *n.* ①(剧院、旅馆等的)门廊;门厅 ②议会走廊;议会休息室;议会接待室;(英议会)下院会客厅; 赞成及反对的两派议员分别投票时的两个投票厅之一 (=division) ③院外活动集团(也称"第三院",指美国垄断组织为收买或胁迫议员使立法为其服务所派的专人和设的专门机构。因活动在议会走廊、休息室而得名。) **II** ❶ *vi.* ①经常出入议会走廊及休息室 ②对议员(或政府官员)进行疏通活动 ③游说,疏通 ❷ *vt.* ①对(议员等)进行疏通活动: Agents of big U.S. firms often wine, dine, and ~ the legislature. 美国许多大公司的代理人经常用请客吃喝的方法来影响、左右立法机关。②用疏通的方法使(议案、计划等)得以通过 (*through*) ‖*~ism n.* 院外活动;(对政府官员等的)游说,疏通 / *~ist n.* 院外活动集团的成员,专门受雇对议员(或政府官员)进行疏通的人;说客 ‖*~man* ['lobimən] *n.* (戏院、剧场等的)收票员

lobe [loub] *n.* ①耳垂 ②【解】(脑、肺、肝等的)叶

③【植】裂片;圆裂片;浅裂片 ④【机】凸角 ⑤【无】瓣,波瓣 ⑥【空】(气球)舵囊 ‖*~d a.* 有叶的;有裂片的

lobster ['lobstə] *n.* ① 大螯虾;大螯虾肉 ② 龙虾 (=spiny ~);龙虾肉 ③笨拙的人;[美口]易受骗的人 ‖*~-eyed* ['lobstəraid] *a.* 眼睛凸出的 / *~ pot* 捕大螯虾(或龙虾)用的篓 / *~ shift, ~ trick* [美口] ①报馆人员的夜班采访;夜班 ②[总称]报纸发行间隙中的报馆值班人员

local ['loukəl] **I** *a.* ①地方的;当地的;本地的: a ~ adverb 表示地点的副词(如 here, there 等) / ~ industry 地方工业 / ~ nationalism 地方民族主义 / ~ time 当地时间 / ~ news 本地新闻 / ~ colour (文艺作品等的)地方色彩 ②[英](邮件用语)本市的,本县的 ③乡土的,狭隘的: a ~ point of view 狭隘的看法 ④局部的: a ~ war 局部战争 / ~ anaesthesia 局部麻醉 ⑤[美](公共交通)沿途逢站必停的: a ~ train 慢车,普通列车 ⑥【数】轨迹的 **II** *n.* ①当地居民;当地医生(律师、教士) ②(报纸上的)本地新闻 ③[美]地方分会(尤指工会);[常用复]本地球队 ④在一定地区使用的邮票 ⑤慢车(指沿途逢站必停的火车或公共汽车) ⑥[英口]本地酒店,附近的酒店 ⑦[英][复] =~ examination(s) ‖*~ly ad.* ‖*~ examination* [英]地方考试(某些大学在各地举行的考试,对考试及格者发给证书) / *~ government* 地方自治;地方政府 / *~ option, ~ veto* 地方人民抉择权(例如关于禁酒问题) / *~ preacher* 【宗】监理会中被准许在当地讲道的教友

locality [lou'kæliti] *n.* 位置;地点;地方;发生地;所在地: a ~ rich in mineral springs 矿泉丰富的地方 / She has a good sense of ~. 她对于方位有很强的辨识力。

localize, localise ['loukəlaiz] ❶ *vt.* ①使地方化;使限制于局部: Hot applications ~ the infection. 热敷使感染不会扩散。②使(新闻等)带有地方色彩,使有地方性 ③确定(传统等)的起源,确定(传统等起源)的地方 ④集中: ~ attention upon sth. 把注意力集中在某事上 ❷ *vi.* 局限;集中: Their interest ~d on this new discovery. 他们的兴趣集中在这一新发现上。

locate [lou'keit] ❶ *vt.* ①…的地点(或范围) ②把…设置在[常用被动语态]使…坐落于: The hospital is to be ~d in your town. 这家医院将设在你们镇上。/ The factory is ~d near the river. 工厂坐落在河的附近。③探出,找出: ~ a point in a plane 求出一平面上某一点的位置 ❷ *vi.* [美口]居住下来,定居 ‖*~r n.* =locator

location [lou'keiʃən] *n.* ①定位;测位;探测;勘定地界 ②位置;场所;标明特殊用途的场地(如供起居或采矿) ③定线(指铁路在建造前所确定的路线) ④(电影)外景;外景拍摄地: be on ~ 在拍外景 ⑤非洲土著居住的城郊 ⑥(房屋、车辆等的)出租(契约)

loch [lok, lox] *n.* [苏格兰] ①湖 ②(被陆地包围的)狭长的海湾

lock¹ [lɔk] **I** *n.* ①锁;用来锁闭(或固定)的器具: open (fasten) a ～ 把锁打开(锁上) ②制轮楔; 【机】汽塞,锁气室;【军】枪机 ③(运河等的)船闸 ④锁住,固定 ⑤(交通的)阻塞 ⑥(格斗时的)揪扭 ⑦[英]性病医院 (=～ hospital) ⑧【自】同步: phase ～ 相位同步 **II ❶** *vt.* ①锁,锁上: ～ a door (trunk) 锁门(箱子) / ～ up a house 把房屋锁起来 ②把…锁藏起来;秘藏: be ～ed (up) in the drawer 被锁在抽屉里 / ～ a secret in one's heart 严守秘密 ③使固定;使紧密衔接: The ship was ～ed fast in ice. 这条船被冰封住了。④紧抱住,挽住;(格斗时)揪扭: ～ a child in one's arms 紧紧抱住孩子 / a ～ed arms picket line 由纠察队员手挽手组成的纠察线 / be ～ed in a fight 打得难分难解 / be ～ed in contemplation 陷入沉思 ⑤卡住,塞住: The gears are ～ed. 齿轮卡住了。⑥为(运河等)设置船闸;使(船)通过船闸;用水闸隔开(河道) (off): ～ a ship up (down) 使船通过船闸向上(下)游开去 ⑦搁死(资金) (up) ⑧将(曲面印版)装在轮转印刷机滚筒上 (up) **❷** *vi.* ①锁;锁得上: The door ～s easily. 这门容易锁上。/ The safe doesn't ～. 这保险柜锁不上了。②紧闭 ③交接;连接: The parts ～ into each other. 各部件相互紧密衔接。④(齿轮等)卡住,塞住 ⑤(船)过闸,建造船闸 ‖～ on 用雷达波束自动跟踪(目标) / ～ oneself in 把自己关在里面,闭门谢客 / ～ out 把…关在外面: Be back before ten, or you'll be ～ed out. 你必须在十点钟以前回来,否则就要被关在外面。②不准(工人)进厂(资本家用以胁迫工人接受其条件的一种手法) / ～ sb. in 把某人关在屋里 / ～, stock and barrel 一古脑儿,统统;完全地: He will soon take over the duties of his predecessor ～, stock and barrel. 他即将把他前任的所有职责接过来。/ Lock the stable door after the horse has been stolen. 贼去关门。/ under ～ and key 妥善地锁藏着;严密地监禁着 ‖～less *a.* 无锁的;无船闸的 / '～-chain *n.* 锁车轮链条 / '～-fast *a.* [苏格兰]锁牢的 / ～ [美] ～过进 ②占领并封锁建筑物的一种示威行动 / '～-jaw *n.* 【医】牙关紧闭症;破伤风 / '～-keeper *n.* =～sman / '～-nut *n.* 防松螺母,对开螺母 / '～-out *n.* 封闭工厂(资本家压制罢工工人的一种手段) / ～sman ['lɔksmən] *n.* 船闸管理人 / '～-smith *n.* 锁匠 / '～-step *n.* 前后紧接,步伐一致的前进 ②陈旧古板的做法,因循守旧 / '～-stitch *n.* 双线连锁缝纫法 / '～-up *n.* ①锁,闭;锁住: a ～up garage 能上锁的汽车库 ②(学校等)夜晚的关闭(时间) ③拘留所 ④(资金等)的搁死

lock² [lɔk] *n.* ①一绺头发;[复]头发 ②(羊毛、亚麻纤维等的)一簇;【纺】毛绺

locker ['lɔkə] *n.* ①(公共场所供单人存放衣帽等用的)柜,抽屉,小室 ②(船上的)贮藏箱,小舱: a chain ～ 锚链舱 ③冷藏间 ④上锁人;(英国海关的)仓库管理人 ⑤(车轮上的)锁具;锁扣装置 ‖a shot in the ～ 见 **shot²** / go to (或 be in) Davy Jone's ～ 葬身鱼腹 ‖～ paper 冷藏包装纸 / ～ room 衣帽间;(运动员用的)更衣室

locket ['lɔkit] *n.* (挂在项链下的)保藏纪念品的贵重金属小盒

locomotion [,loukə'mouʃən] *n.* ①运动(力),移动(力) ②行进(力) ③旅行

locomotive ['loukə,moutiv] **I** *a.* ①运动的;在动中起作用的: the ～ faculty of animal life 动物的运动能力 ②机动的 ③(动物)非寄生的,能自己移动的 ④[谑]旅行的;爱旅行的: in these ～ days 在当今旅行非常方便的时代中 / a ～ person 爱旅行的人 **II** *n.* ①火车头,机车 ②节奏由慢到快的集体欢呼(常指美国学生一种习惯的欢呼方式) ③能自己移动的动物

locum ['loukəm] *n.* (医生、牧师等的)临时代理 ‖～ tenens ['ti:nenz] ([复] ～ tenentes [tə'nenti:z]) =locum

locust ['loukəst] *n.* ①蝗虫 ②[美]蝉 ③【植】洋槐,刺槐;洋槐(或刺槐)的木材 ④破坏成性的人,贪吃的人 ⑤[美俚]警棍

locution [lou'kju:ʃən] *n.* ①特别的说话风格 ②特别的表达方式,惯用语

lode [loud] *n.* ①矿脉;[喻]丰富的蕴藏 ②[英方]水路;(沼泽的)排水沟

lodge [lɔdʒ] **I** *n.* ①(工厂、学校等的)门房,传达室;(花园宅第大门口的)仆人住宅 ②(临时居住用的)山林小屋;印第安人居住的棚屋;北美印第安住户 ③(游览区的)小旅馆 ④(剧场中的)包厢;前座 ⑤分会 (主要指秘密社团或联谊会的);分会全体会员;分会集会处;分会会议: the grand ～ (秘密组织或联谊会等的)管理机构 ⑥兽穴(尤指聚居动物如水獭的巢穴) ⑦剑桥大学院长的住宅 **II ❶** *vt.* ①供给(某人)住宿,接纳(寄宿者),租房间给(某人)住: We'll be very glad to board and ～ you. 我们将很高兴供给你们膳宿。/ I am well ～d in the reception centre. 我住在招待所里很舒适。②容纳 ③把…射入(或投入,插入): A bullet was ～d in his thigh. 一颗子弹打进了他的大腿。/ a ～d bullet in one's brain 一颗留在头部的子弹 / a blow on sb.'s jaw 一拳打在某人下巴上 ④把…交于;(为安全起见)存放: ～ power in (或 with, in the hands of) sb. 把权力交给某人 / ～ money in the bank 把钱存放在银行里 ⑤提出(申诉、抗议等): ～ a complaint against sb. with the authorities concerned 向有关当局对某人提出控诉 ⑥使(庄稼)倒伏 **❷** *vi.* ①(暂)住;寄宿,投宿 ②(子弹等)射入而停留: This incident has ～d in my memory. 这件事留在我的记忆中了。③(庄稼等)倒伏 ‖～r *n.* 寄宿者;房客: take in ～rs 收房客

lodg(e)ment ['lɔdʒmənt] *n.* ①住所;住宿 ②提出: the ～ of a protest 抗议的提出 ③沉积,沉积物;沉积处;存放,存放物,存放处: a ～ of dirt inside

the radio 收音机里面的积尘 ④立足点;(对敌区
的)进占;(对争议地区的)进驻: make (或
effect) a ~ 取得立足点 / a ~ area 滩点占领区;
空降作战初期占领区

lodging ['lɔdʒiŋ] *n.* ①寄宿: provide board and
~ 供膳宿 ②住所 ③[常用复]租住的一间(或几
间)房间(别于旅馆的房间而言) ④存放处 ⑤(庄
稼等的)倒伏 ‖**~ house** 分间出租的供人住宿用
的房屋: a common ~ house [英]供宿夜铺位的
房屋(一般为极贫穷的人所租用)

loft [lɔft] **I** *n.* ①阁楼;草料棚 ②[美](仓库、工厂
的)统楼层 ③(教堂、讲堂的)楼厢 ④鸽房;鸽群,
通信鸽队 ⑤(高尔夫球的)打高球;(高尔夫球棒端
的)高击斜面 **II** ❶ *vt.* ①把…放在阁楼中 ②把
(鸽子)关在鸽房内 ③(高尔夫球戏中)把(球)高
打出去 ④把…向高处发射 ⑤给…放样(指画出
与船壳或机翼等实物同样大小的图样) ❷ *vi.*
(高尔夫球戏中)打高球

lofty ['lɔfti] *a.* ①高耸的; 极高的: a ~ tower
(peak) 高塔(峰) / a ~ flight 高飞 ②崇高的,
高尚的 ③高傲的, 傲慢的: with an attitude
of ~ scorn 以高傲的蔑视态度 ④地位高的,高
级的 ⑤玄虚的: a ~ abstraction 玄虚的抽象概
念 ‖**loftily** *ad.* / **loftiness** *n.*

log¹ [lɔg] **I** *n.* 原木;圆木;(大)木料;干柴 **II**
(logged; logging) ❶ *vt.* ①伐(林木);把(某地
区)的林木砍掉运走: They logged a large part
of the trees. 他们砍伐了一大片树木。/ They
logged off part of the area. 他们把这一带部分
地区的林木伐运掉了。②把(树木)锯成段木:
the timber into 2-metre lengths 把木材锯成两
米长的段木 ❷ *vi.* 采伐木材 ‖a King Log 见
king / as easy as rolling(或 falling) off a ~
[美] 极其容易 / in the ~ 未经劈削过的 / like
a ~ 象木头一样不能动弹: sleep like a ~ 熟
睡 / Roll my ~ and I'll roll yours. [谚]你帮
我的忙,我也帮你的忙。‖**logger** *n.* ①伐木工,锯木
工 ②将圆木装车的机器 / **logging** *n.* 伐木(业)
‖**~ cabin** 圆木搭建的小木屋 / **~jam** *n.*
①(河道中输送木材时出现的)木材梗塞 ②阻塞;
僵局: break a ~jam in negotiations 打破谈判僵
局 / '**~wood** *n.* 洋苏木树; 洋苏木(作染料用)

log² [lɔg] **I** *n.* ①测程仪,计程仪: sail by the ~
靠测程仪测船位航行 / heave (或 throw) the ~
用测程仪测船速 ②航海日志 ③飞行日志 ④(机器
运转、检修等的)记录;(工程、试验等的)工作记录
簿: a performance ~ (机器等的)运转情况记
录(簿) ④[英](缝纫店日工的)工作时间表 **II**
(logged; logging) *vt.* ①把…记入航海(或飞行)
日志 ②航行;飞行(一定距离、时数): The ship
logged 200 knots that day. 这条船那天的航程
达二百浬。/ How many hours have you logged?
你的飞行时数是多少? ③以…速度航(或飞)行
‖'**~book** *n.* 航海日志;飞行日志 / **~ line** 【海】
测程索

log³ [lɔg] *n.* =logarithm

logarithm ['lɔgəriθəm] *n.* 【数】对数: common ~
常用对数 / natural ~ 自然对数 / table of ~s
对数表

loggerhead ['lɔgəhed] *n.* ①[方言]傻瓜,笨蛋 ②
【动】蠵龟(=~ turtle) ③铁球棒(顶端有一铁
球, 烧烫后用以融解柏油或加热液体) ‖**at ~s
(with)** (与…)不和,(与…)相争 / **fall** (或 **get,
go) to ~s** 互相吵起来

logic ['lɔdʒik] *n.* ①逻辑(学): dialectical ~ 辩证
逻辑 / formal ~ 形式逻辑 / mathematical ~
数理逻辑 ②关于逻辑的著作 ③逻辑性,条理性: I
cannot understand the ~ of her deed. 我不能
理解她的行为的逻辑性。④ 推理(法): At this
point your ~ is at fault. 在这一点上你的推理
是错误的。⑤必然的联系(或结果) / ~ chop ~ 强
词夺理地争辩 ‖**~ core** 【自】【数】逻辑磁心

logical ['lɔdʒikəl] *a.* ①逻辑(上)的: ~ argumen-
tation 逻辑推理 ②符合逻辑的;有逻辑的,有逻
辑头脑的: a ~ conclusion 符合逻辑的结论 / a
~ thinker 思维有逻辑性的人 ③逻辑上必然的:
a ~ result 逻辑上必然的结果 ‖**~ly** *ad.* ‖**~-
ness** *n.* ‖**~ empiricism** 逻辑经验论(即逻辑实
证论) / **~ empiricist** 逻辑经验论者(即逻辑实
证论者) / **~ positivism** 逻辑实证论(现代资产
阶级主观唯心主义的一种哲学流派) / **~ posi-
tivist** 逻辑实证论者

loin [lɔin] *n.* ①[常用复]腰 ②(牛、羊等的)腰肉
③[复]耻骨区;生殖器官 ‖**a fruit** (或 **child) of
sb.'s ~s** 某人生的孩子 / **be sprung from
sb.'s ~s** 某人所生 / **gird up one's ~s** 准备
旅行;准备行动 ‖'**~cloth** *n.* (尤指热带地区原
始民族作为衣服的)缠腰布

loiter ['lɔitə] ❶ *vi.* ①闲逛,游荡,踯躅: He ~ed
on his way. 他一路闲逛(边走边停)。②消磨时
光 (about) ❷ *vt.* 消磨(时间),混(日子): ~
one's time away 虚度光阴 / ~ out the whole
afternoon 消磨掉整个下午 ‖**~er** ['lɔitərə] *n.*
闲逛的人;混日子的人 / **~ingly** ['lɔitəriŋli] *ad.*
懒散地,吊儿郎当地

loll [lɔl] ❶ *vi.* ①懒洋洋地倚靠(或躺);懒散地闲
荡: ~ in a chair 懒洋洋地躺在椅子里 / ~
against the wall 懒洋洋地靠在墙上 / ~ about
the beach 在海滩上懒散地闲荡 ②(头等)垂下:
His head ~ed forward in his sleep. 他垂着头打
瞌睡。③(舌头等)伸出 (out) ❷ *vt.* ①垂,伸(舌
头等) (out) ②把(头、四肢等)懒洋洋地倚靠着
‖**~ingly** *ad.*

lolly ['lɔli] *n.* ①[英]硬糖 ②[英俚]钱

lone [loun] *a.* ①孤独的,无伴的: a ~ flight 单独
飞行 ②寂寞的 ③[谑]独身的;已寡的 ④离群索
居的;人迹稀少的,远僻的 ‖**~some** ['lounsəm] *a.*
①寂寞的;孤单的 ②人迹稀少的;荒凉的 *n.* 自己
‖**Lone Star** (美国)得克萨斯州: the Lone Star
State 孤星州(得克萨斯州的别称)

lonely ['lounli] *a.* ①孤独的 ②寂寞的 ③人迹稀
少的;荒凉的 ‖**loneliness** *n.*

long[1] [lɔŋ] **I** (longer ['lɔŋɡə], longest ['lɔŋɡist]) *a.*
①长的;远的: a ~ coastline 长长的海岸线 / a
railway four hundred kilometres ~ 一条四百
公里长的铁路
②长久的;长期的: I shan't be ~. 我马上就来。/
This period will be two years ~. 这个时期将要
有两年之久。/ a ~ friendship 长期的友谊 / a
~ memory 好记性 / a ~ date (票据等的)远期 /
a ~ note 远期票据
③超过一般长度(或数量)的;过长的,冗长的;缓慢
的: wait three ~ hours 足足等了三个多小时 /
Don't be ~ about it. 别慢吞吞的! / He was ~
(in) deciding. 他迟迟才作出决定。
④达到远处的,长远的: make a ~ arm 伸长手
臂去拿东西 / have a ~ arm 能使自己的权力及
到远处 / take a ~ view of the matter 从长远
考虑来看待这事
⑤高的: a ~ man 高个子的人 / a ~ drink 高
杯酒(或其他饮料)
⑥众多的;充足的;大的: read a ~ list of books
读许多书 / have a ~ family 有很多子女 /
Corn is in ~ supply. 谷物供应充足。/ fetch ~
prices 售得高价
⑦【语】长音的;(诗中的音节)长的,重读的
⑧(股票等投机市场用语)做多头的, 对市价看涨
的: be on the ~ side of the market 做多头
⑨长于⋯的 (on): be ~ on understanding 理解
力强
II (longer ['lɔŋɡə] longest ['lɔŋɡist]) *ad.* ①长
久;长期地: Discussion went ~ into the night. 讨
论直到深夜。/ ~ after midnight 半夜以后很久
②始终: serve the people all one's life ~ 一辈
子为人民服务 / all day (night) ~ 整天(夜)
③遥远地: a ~-travelled person 曾到远处旅行
的人
III *n.* ①长时间;长时期: It will not take ~. 这
不需要很多时间。
②【语】长音节;长元音;长辅音
③(投机市场上)做多头的人
④(服装的)长尺寸;[复]长裤
⑤[英]*~er* [用于否定句](不)再: I can't wait
any *~er*. 我不能再等了。/ as *~* as ①达⋯之
久,长达⋯: as *~* as ten years 十年之久 ②
= so *~* as / at (the) *~est* (指日期)至多,最
晚: five days at (the) *~est* 至多五天 / before
~ 不久以后: The book will be published before
~. 这书不久就要出版。/ for *~* 长久: Will
you be away for *~*? 你要离开好久吗? / *~*
after 在⋯后很久: *~* after World War II 在
第二次世界大战后很久 / *~* before 在⋯以前很
久 / *~* (*,~*) ago 很久 (很久) 以前: That happened *~*, *~* ago. 那件事发生在很久很久以
前。/ *~s and shorts* ①诗(尤指古希腊和古拉
丁)的 ②【建】长短砌合 / *~ since* ①很久以前:
I first met him *~ since*. 我在很久以前第一次遇

到他。②很久以来: This kind of lathe has *~*
since been out of use. 这种车床早已不用了。/
no *~er* 不再 / So *~*! [口]再见! / so *~ as*
只要: We can surely overcome these difficulties so *~* as we are closely united. 只要我们
紧密地团结一致,一定能克服这些困难。/ the *~*
and the short of it 概括的意思,总的意思
‖*~ways ad.* ①纵长地 ②(跳舞)成两直行地 /
~wise ad. 纵长地
‖**'~-a'go** *a.* 从前的,往昔的 / **'~-a,waited** *a.*
被期待已久的 / **Long Beach** 长滩[美国城市] /
'~bow *n.* (手拉的)大弓: draw (或 pull) the
~bow 吹牛 / **'~-,cherished** *a.* 被长期渴望的 /
'~-,dated *a.* 远期的 / **'~-'distance** *a.* ①位于
远处的;长途的: a *~-distance* bomber 远程轰炸
机 ②长途电话的: a *~-distance* call 长途通话
ad. 通过长途电话 / **distance** ①长途电话通
讯 ②长途电话局(或交换机);长途话务员 / **~
division** 【数】长除法 / **~ dozen** 十三个 / **'~-
drawn(-'out)** *a.* 长期的,拖长的: a *~-drawn-out*
war 长期战争 / **'~-'eared** *a.* ①长耳朵的 ②
驴般的,愚钝的 / **~ face** 闷闷不乐(的脸色) /
~ green [美俚]钞票 / **'~hair** *n.* ①留长发者 ②
嬉皮士 ②艺术家;古典音乐爱好者(或演奏者)
[美俚]古典音乐 ③脱离现实搞空头理论的学究 /
'~hand *n.* 普通写法(与 shorthand 速记相对而
言) / **'~-'headed** *a.* ①头颅长的 ②有远见的,
精明的 / **~ hundred** 一百二十;一百多 / **'~-
hundredweight** 长担 (=112磅) / **Long Island**
长岛[美国] / **~ johns** [美口]长内衣裤 / **~
jump** 跳远 / **'~-legged** *a.* 长腿的 / **'~-'lived**
a. 长寿的 / **~ measure** 量长度的单位 / **Long
Parliament** 【史】(英国的) 长期国会 (1640—
1660) / **~ pig** 食人生番嘴里的牺牲品 / **~ play**
'~-'playing record 慢转密纹唱片 / **'~-'range**
a. ①远程的: a *~-range* gun 远射程大炮 ②长
期的,长远的: a *~-range* plan 长期规划 / a *~-
range* weather forecast 长期天气预报 / **~ robe**
律师服装: gentlemen of the *~ robe* 律师界 /
'~-'run *a.* 长远的 / **'~-'short story** 较长的短
篇小说 / **~ shot** ①远投;远射: not by a *~ shot*
[口]一点也没有,全不 ②获胜可能性非常微小的
参加者(指赛马等) ③冒大险图大利的赌注: a *~
shot* gamble 孤注一掷 ④(电影中)远距离拍摄的
镜头 / **'~-'sighted** *a.* ①远视的 ②有远见的 /
'~-,standing *a.* 长期间的,长期存在的: solve
a difficult and *~-standing* problem 解决一个长
期存在的难题 / **'~-'suffering** *n.* & *a.* 长期忍
受苦难(的) / **~ suit** ①长牌(指同花多的一手
牌) ②胜过别人的东西,长处 / **'~-term** *a.* 长
期的: a *~-term* loan 长期贷款 / from a *~-term*
point of view 从长远的观点出发 / **'~-'tested**
a. 久经考验的 / **'~,timer** *n.* ①(在某地)住了
很久的人;长期从事(某项)工作的人 ②惯犯,积
犯 / **Long Tom** 远程大炮 / **~ ton** 长吨 (2,240
磅) / **'~-'tongued** *a.* 长舌的,饶舌的;话多的

~ vacation [英] ①大学暑假 ②法院夏季休庭 / **'~-'winded** *a.* ①气长的,能跑长距离而不喘的 ②冗长的: a *~-winded* speech 冗长的演说

ong² [lɔŋ] *vi.* 渴望,极想念: **~** to visit Yenan 渴望去访问延安 / **~** for the festival 渴望节日来临

ongevity [lɔn'dʒeviti] *n.* ①长寿,长命 ②长期供职,资历

onging ['lɔŋiŋ] **I** *n.* 渴望: have a **~** for sth. 渴望某物 / ungovernable *~s* 难以抑制的渴望 / pine away with **~** 由于渴望而憔悴 **II** *a.* 显示渴望的: a **~** look 渴望的目光 ‖**~ly** *ad.*

ongitude ['lɔndʒitjuːd] *n.* ①经度: the east (west) **~** 东(西)经 ②【天】黄经: the meridian of **~** 黄经圈 ③[谑]长;长度

ook [luk] **I** ❶ *vi.* ①看: He *~ed* in that direction and saw an airplane. 他朝那个方向一看,看见一架飞机。/ *Look*, here he comes. 瞧,他来了。②注意,留神: When you **~** deeper, you'll find some difference between them. 你要是更仔细地研究一下,就会发现它们之间有一些差别了。③朝着;倾向: a cottage *~ing* seaward (或 to the sea) 面朝大海的小屋 / These circumstances **~** to alliance. 这些情况可能导致联盟。④显得;好像: **~** black 面带怒容;面色阴沉 / **~** blue 神色沮丧 / **~** big 做出一副了不起的样子 / **~** small 显得卑劣 / He is now sixty but *~s* about fifty. 他现在已六十岁了,但看上去只有五十岁左右。/ He *~s* to be very strong. 他看上去很强壮。/ It *~s* like rain. 看来要下雨。/ It *~s* as if the coming autumn harvest will be even better than the last one. 看来即将到来的秋收将比去年更好。/ She does not **~** her age. 她看上去不象是有这点年纪的人。/ He *~s* every inch a good athlete. 他看上去十十足足是一个优秀运动员。❷ *vt.* ①瞧;打量: **~** sb. in the face 直视某人的脸(表示不惧怕,挑战等意思) / **~** sb. out of countenance 瞧得某人侷促不安 / **~** sb. up and down 上下打量某人 ②留心,注意: Please **~** what time the train starts. 请留心一下火车什么时候开。/ You must **~** *that* no one lags behind. 你必须注意不使一个人掉队。③用眼色(或脸色)表示出: **~** one's gratitude 用眼色表示感激 / **~** daggers at sb. 用敌视的目光看着某人 ④期待: I **~** to be with you soon. 我希望不久就能和你在一起。**II** *n.* ① 看: May I have a **~** at it? 让我看一看好不好? / give sb. a **~** 对某人看了一眼 / steal a **~** 偷看一眼 ②脸色,神态;外貌,外表: A serious **~** passed over his face. 他脸上显出一副严肃的神色。/ an amused **~** in sb.'s eyes 某人眼中的顽皮神色 / This old factory has taken on a new **~**. 这座老厂换上了新貌。

③[复]面容;美貌: Don't judge a man by his *~s*. 不要凭容貌来判断一个人。/ good *~s* 好相貌 / lose one's *~s* 失去美貌(指女子容颜衰老) ‖**give sb. a dirty ~** 对某人瞪一眼 / **~ about** ① 四下环顾;四处寻找: **~** *about* for one's pen 到处找自己的笔 ②察看,考虑: **~** *about* carefully before making the final decision 在作最后结论前先仔细考虑一下 / **~ about one** ① 察看自己周围的情况 ②花时间考虑自己的行动 / **~ after** ① 目送;眼睛盯着;寻求 ② 照顾,照料,关心: **~** *after* the children 照料孩子们 / **Look alive!** 快些! / **~ around** [美] =**~** round / **~ at** ① 看;查看: This little girl is pretty to **~** at. 这个小女孩很好看。/ The building is not much to **~** at. 这座楼房的式样不怎么好看。/ He came to **~** at the drainage. 他是来检查排水设备的。② 考虑;着眼于: **~** at problems all-sidedly 全面地看问题 / will not **~** at a proposal 不愿考虑某一建议,对某一建议不屑一顾 / What I **~** at is its economy. 我所以想买(或想要)这件东西是因为它经济。/ **~ back** ①回顾 ②[常用于否定句中]停止不前;倒退: Since that time our team has never *~ed* back. 从那时起我们小组就一直不断地进步。/ **Look before you leap.** [谚]深思熟虑而后行。/ **~ down** ①向下看,俯视: The sanatorium *~s* down on the West Lake. 这座疗养院俯瞰西湖。② 看不起,轻视 (*on, upon*): never **~** down on physical labour 从不轻视体力劳动 ③【商】跌价 ④用目光慑服(某人) / **~ for** ①寻找;寻求: be **~** *ing for* trouble 自找麻烦 ②期待: **~** *for* sb.'s arrival 期待某人的到来 / **~ forward to** 盼望: **~** *forward to* hearing from sb. 盼望某人来信 / **Look here!** 喂,注意! : *Look here*, now, I can't agree to that. 注意,对那一点我不能赞同。他完全恢复了。/ **~ in** ①(顺便)看望: promise to **~** *in* (on sb.) 答应去看望一下(某人) / **~ into** ①向…的里面看去,窥视;浏览(书刊等) ② 观察,调查: **~** *into* a problem 调查研究问题 / **~ on** ① 观看 ②面向,面朝;合读,合看 (*with*): a house *~ing on* (to) the street 临街的房子 / May I **~** *on with* you? 我可以跟你合看(这本书)吗? ③旁观: In no case will they **~** on passively. 他们决不会消极旁观。④看待: **~** *on* (或 *upon*) sb. *as* one's good guide 把某人看成自己的好向导 / **~** *on* sb. *with* distrust 不信任某人 / **~ oneself** 看上去和平常一样;不改常态: He is very quite *himself* again. 他完全恢复了。(可指健康或情绪) / **~ out** ①(房间)向外看,把头伸到窗外(看): The room *~s* out on (或 *over*) a square. 这房间朝着一个广场。②留神,提防: *Look out!* There is danger ahead. 当心! 前面有危险。/ *Look out for* the snags! 当心触礁! ③照料,照看: Now the patient is able to **~** *out for* himself. 这病人现在能自己照料自己了。④[主英]搜寻;找出: I have to **~** *out* those letters. 我得把那些信找出来。/ **~ over** ① 从…上面看过去 ② 察看;检查: **~** *over* the examination papers 审阅试卷 ③原谅(过错等) / ~ *round* ①掉头看,环顾;到处寻找(*for*);观光: We found time to ~ *round* (the city). 我们还抽出时间(在城里)观光了一番。②察看;慎重考虑: Look *round* well before taking any step. 在采取任何措施前最好好好考虑一下。/ ~ *sharp* 见 **sharp** / ~ *through* ①透过…看去;看穿: *through* a window 透过窗户看去 ②审核;仔细查看: The auditor ~*ed through* all the vouchers. 查帐员审核了全部凭单。/ He ~*ed through* a number of journals. 他查阅了许多期刊。③浏览;温习 ④从…中显露出来: The cruelty and greed of the hungry wolf ~ *through* its eyes. 饿狼的眼中露出凶残、贪婪的目光。/ ~ *to* ①照管;看管;留心,注意: Look *to* your manners. 你得检点一些。/ Look *to* it that you make no more similar mistakes. 注意今后你不要再犯类似的错误了。②指望: ~ *to* sb. *for* help 期待某人帮助 / ~ *to* sb. *to do* sth. 指望某人去做某事 ③(房屋等)面朝;(人)往…看去 / ~ *toward*(s) ①(房屋等)面朝;(人)往…看去 ②为…作好准备;期待: a policy ~*ing towards* the development of local industries 一项意在促使建立地方工业发展的政策 ③[口]举杯祝贺(某人)健康 / ~ *up* ①向上看 ②尊敬,仰望: ~ *up* to sb. *as* one's teacher 把某人尊为自己的老师 ③好转(尤用于商业上表示价格上升、市场活跃): Things are ~*ing up*. 情况正在好转。④(在词典、参考书等中)查寻: ~ *up* a word in a dictionary 在词典中查一个词 ⑤拜访: On my way home, I ~*ed* him *up*. 在回家的路上,我去看望了他一下。/ ~ *upon* = ~ *on* / ~ *well* (*ill*) ①看上去健康(有病);看上去漂亮(不漂亮) ②(事物)显得不错(很糟) / Look you! 注意! / *to* ~ *at* sb. (sth.) [常用作插入语]从某人(某物)的外表来看 / *upon the* ~ 在找寻着 ‖'~-a'like *n*. [美俚]面貌酷似的人 / '~-'in *n*. ①观察(通常指比较短促的) ②(顺便)拜访: give sb. a ~-*in* 去拜访某人 ③(在体育比赛等中)获胜的希望: have a ~-*in* 有可能取胜 / ~**ing glass** 镜子 / '~-,over *n*. 粗略的一看 / '~-'see *n*. [俚]察看,调查;视察旅行 / '~-'up *n*. 查找 / [自]检查

lookout ['luk'aut] *n*. ①警戒;注意: keep (或 take) a sharp (或 keen) ~ *for* 密切注视(或防备)着… / I'll be *on the* ~ *for* the data you want. 我将注意收集你所需要的资料。②了望台,监视哨;了望员,监视者: a ~ tower 了望塔 / an antiaircraft ~ 对空监视哨 ③景色;远景,前途: a bad ~ *for* sb. 一个对某人说来不妙的前景 ④与个人有关的事: That's his own ~. 那是他自己的事。

loom[1] [lu:m] *n*. ①织机;织造术: a power ~ 动力织机 ②桨柄 ③【空】翼肋腹部

loom[2] [lu:m] I *vi*. ①隐现呈现: A ship ~*ed* (up) through the fog. 一艘船在大雾中隐隐出现。

②赫然耸现;逼近: A hard struggle ~*s* ahead. 一场苦斗迫在眉睫。II *n*. 隐约呈现的形象,巨大的幽影 ‖~ **large** 赫然耸现;显得突出(或严重)

loop [lu:p] I *n*. ①(线、带等打成的)圈,环,环形 ②环状物;搭环;拎环 ③【空】筋斗 ④[无]回路;回线,波腹 ⑤(铁路上的)让车道,环道 ⑥[美]闹市区;[the L-]芝加哥闹市区 II ❶ *vt*. ①打环扣住: ~ the curtains *up* 用绳环把帘系起 ②把(绳等)打成环,使成圈;【电】把(导线)连成回路 ③使作环状运动;【空】翻(筋斗): The airman ~*ed* the loop three times. 飞行员(驾驶飞机)连翻了三个筋斗。❷ *vi*. ①打环,成圈 ②【空】翻筋斗 ③(象尺蠖似地)伸屈前进 ‖*for a* ~ 陷入惊奇(或混乱、激动)的状态;陷入突然的灾难(或不幸、悲伤): They were thrown *for a* ~ when they saw this. 他们看到这个都大惊失色了。/ *knock for a* ~ [美俚]①猛击;打昏;(酒等)把…醉倒 ②给…极好的印象 ③极为出色地通过(或做成) ‖~ **aerial**, ~ **antenna** [无]环形天线 / ~ **line** 环线,圈线 / ,~-the-'~ *n*. ①环路火车(一种娱乐装置,乘客在一段路上借离心力向头部朝下) ②【空】筋斗

loose [lu:s] I *a*. ①松的,宽的;松散的: ~ soil 松土 / ~ clothing 宽大的衣服 / a ~ knot 松的结 / a cloth of ~ texture 稀薄织物 ②没加束缚的;松开的;自由的: the ~ end of a string 绳子松着的一端 / a horse ~ of its tether 没系住的马 / This dog must not be left ~. 这条狗切不可不加约束。③松掉了的: a ~ tooth 松动的牙齿 / I had ~ bowels yesterday. 我昨天拉肚子。④散放的;散装的: ~ cash 散放的钱 / ~ honey 散装蜂蜜 ⑤散漫的;放荡的,荒淫的: have a ~ tongue 惯于随口乱讲,饶舌 / lead a ~ life 荒淫生活 / a ~ woman 放荡的女人 ⑥不严格的,不确切的,不明确的: a ~ thinker 思想不严密的人 / a ~ style 不精练的文体 / a ~ translation 不严格按照原文的译文 ⑦(色、染料等)易退的 ⑧咳得出痰的: a ~ cough 有痰的咳嗽 ⑨(身材等)难看的 II *ad*. 松松地;松散地;不紧凑地;不严格地 III ❶ *vt*. ①释放;把…放开: Wine ~*d* his tongue. 酒后他说话随便起来了。②解开(结等)放(枪);射(箭)(*off*) ❷ *vi*. ①变松;松开;松弛;开火(*at*) ②[主英]放学 / 起锚 IV *n*. ①(箭的)放射 ②放纵 ‖*on the* ~ [口]①无拘束;散漫;逍遥法外: a dog *on the* ~ 没有系住(或关好)的狗 ②放荡;寻欢作乐 / *break* ~ 挣脱出来;迸发出来: The mountain torrents broke ~. 山洪暴发。/ *cast* ~ 【海】解开(缆绳等);解缆放(船);使脱离 / *come* (或 *get*) ~ (结等)松掉 / *cut* ~ ①使脱离约束(或拘禁等) ②摆脱,逃脱: cut ~ *from* that old custom 摆脱那个旧风俗 ③[口]狂欢;尽情作乐 / *give* (*a*) ~ *to* 放纵(感情、想象等) / *hold* ~ 漠然置之 / *in* ~ *order* 【军】以散开队形 / *let* ~ 释放;放出;发出 / *play fas* and ~ 见 play / set ~ 释放; 放出; 发出 / sit ~ 见 sit / turn ~ 见 turn / work ~ (螺丝等)松掉 ‖~ly ad. / ~ness n. ‖'~-'bodied a. (衣服)宽松的 / '~-box n. [英]不把马系住的饲马房 / '~-'fitting a. 配上去稍大的 / '~-'flowing a. 缓缓流着的, 轻轻飘着的 / '~-'jointed a. (铰链)可拆卸的; (关节)活络的 / '~-leaf a. 活页的 / ~ pulley, ~ wheel【机】游滑轮 / smut 散黑穗病 / '~-'tongued a. 饶舌的, 随口乱说的

loosen ['luːsn] ❶ vt. ①解开, 放松: ~ a screw 松开螺丝 / ~ one's tongue 信口开河 ②使(纪律等)松弛 ③使(肠)通畅; 使(咳嗽)咳得出痰来 ❷ vi. 变松; 松开; 松弛 ‖~ up [美口] ① 无顾忌地乱说, 信口开河 ②慷慨解囊 ③松弛下来 ‖~er n. 放松者

loot[1] [luːt] I n. ①[总称]掠夺物, [贬][总称]战利品 ②(官吏的)非法收入, [总称]赃物 ③抢劫, 掠夺 ④[美俚]金钱(尤指大量的) II ❶ vt. ①洗劫(都市等) ②强夺, 掠夺, 抢劫(物品等) ❷ vi. 进行掠夺 ‖~er n. 掠夺者, 抢劫者

loot[2] [luːt] n. [美俚] =lieutenant

lop[1] [lɔp] I (lopped; lopping) vt. ①修剪(树木或藤) ②砍掉(头、肢等): ~ off branches from a tree 砍掉树枝 ③[喻]割裂; 删除(off) II n. ①修剪; 砍, 砍 ②修剪下来的小树枝 ‖lopper n. 修剪树木的工人; 修剪树木的长柄剪刀 / lopping n. [常用复]修剪下来的树枝

lop[2] [lɔp] I (lopped; lopping) ❶ vi. ①软绵绵地下垂 ②吊儿郎当; 闲荡(about) ③大步慢跑 ❷ vt. 垂(耳) II n. [常作 L-] 垂耳兔 III a. 垂下的: ~ ears 垂下的耳朵 ‖loppy a. 下垂的, 低垂的 / '~-ear n. 垂耳兔 / '~-eared a. 垂耳的

lop[3] [lɔp] I (lopped; lopping) vi. 以短而急的浪起伏 II n. 短而急的波浪

lope [loup] I vt. & vi. (使)大步慢跑 II n. (能维持较久的)大步慢跑

loquacious [lou'kweiʃəs] a. ①过于健谈的, 多话的 ②(鸟)啁啾不休的; (水)潺潺不息的 ‖~ly ad. / ~ness n.

lord [lɔːd] I n. ①贵族; 封建领主; 地主 ②君主: our sovereign ~ the King (英国等国对封建君主的称呼)国王陛下 ③勋爵(对侯、伯、子、男爵等贵族或高级官员的尊称); [the Lords] 英国上议院全体议员: the First Lord of the Admiralty (英国)海军大臣 / the Lord Mayor of London 伦敦市长 ④[L-]【宗】上帝; 基督 ⑤大老板, 巨头 ⑥老爷; [谑]丈夫(常作 and master) II ❶ vi. 称王称霸: Gone are the days when a big nation could ~ it over (或 among) small ones. 大国可以对小国称王称霸的日子已经一去不复返了。/ We will not be ~ed over. 决不容许别人在我们头上作威作福。❷ vt. 加封(某人)为贵族, 赐(某人)贵族的爵衔 ‖a Lord in waiting (女王的)宫廷侍从 / a Lord of the Bedchamber (国王的)宫廷侍从 / as drunk as a ~ 酩酊大醉 / live

like a ~ 豪华地生活 / Lord! (或 Lord God! 或 Good Lord!) 老天爷! (表示惊奇等) / Lord bless me (或 bless my soul 或 have mercy)! 老天保祐! 啊呀! (表示惊奇等) / my ~ [mi'lɔːd] (对某些贵族或主教、法官等的尊称)老爷 / the Lord of Hosts (基督教《圣经》中的)万军之主(指耶和华) / the Lord of Misrule ① (英国)主持圣诞节狂欢会的人 (尤指十五、十六世纪时) ② 民间节日庆祝会的主持人 / the Lord's Day【宗】主日(即星期日) / the ~s of creation 万物之灵, 人类; [谑]男人们 / the Lord's Prayer【宗】主祷文 / the Lord's Supper【宗】①圣餐(仪式) ②耶稣及其十二门徒的最后晚餐 / the year of our Lord ... 耶稣纪元…年, 公元…年 / treat sb. like a ~ 阔绰地款待某人 ‖~less a. 无君主的; 无贵族的 / ~ling n. 小贵族, 小老爷 / ~ chancellor (英国)大法官 (兼任上议院议长) / '~-s-and-'ladies [复] n.【植】斑叶阿若母(也称 cuckoopint)

lordly ['lɔːdli] I a. ①贵族的; 贵族似的, 气派十足的 ②高傲的, 傲慢无礼的 II ad. 贵族似地, 气派十足地; 高傲地 ‖lordliness n.

lordship ['lɔːdʃip] n. ①贵族的身分: Your Lordship (直接称呼时用语)爵爷 (有时也用作对一般人或动物的滑稽称呼) ②贵族的权力 ③贵族的领地

lore[1] [lɔː] n. ①学问; 经验知识 ②口头传说 ③[古]渊博

lore[2] [lɔː] n.【动】眼先(鸟的眼与啄之间, 爬虫及鱼的眼与鼻之间的部分)

lorgnette [lɔː'njet] n. [法]长柄眼镜(右镜框边装有握柄); 观剧用的长柄眼镜式望远镜

longnette

lorry ['lɔri] n. ①平台四轮车 ②(在轨道上行驶的)各种运货车辆(如推料车) ③[英]运货汽车, 卡车 (美国通常用 truck)

lose [luːz] (lost [lɔst]) ❶ vt. ①失; 丢失; 丧失: ~ a key 丢失一把钥匙 / ~ one's balance 失去平衡, 跌倒 / ~ one's head 被斩首; 被搞糊涂 / ~ patience (reason) 失去耐心 (理智) / The doctor lost his patient. 医生没把病人治好。(或: 病人另投医生了。) / They lost few cases of gastric ulcer. 他们治胃溃疡, 很少没治好的。②使失去: Such behaviour lost him our trust.

他这种行为使得我们不再信任他了。③抓不住;
听(或看)不见: ~ the thread of an argument
抓不住论据的线索 / I tried hard not to ~ a
word of what he said. 我努力想听清他讲的一
字一句。/ I lost him in the crowd. 我看着他消
失在人丛中了。/ The two ships lost each other
in the fog. 两条船在迷雾中彼此失去联系。④
错过: ~ one's train (a bus) 没赶上火车(公共汽
车) / ~ an opportunity 错过机会 ⑤白费,浪费:
Our labour will not be lost. 我们的努力不会白
费。/ ~ no time in carrying out the plan 立即
着手执行计划 / There is not a moment to ~.
一分钟也不能浪费。⑥迷失;使迷路;使迷糊不
清: ~ one's way 迷路 / ~ oneself (或 be lost)
in the woods 在森林中迷路 ⑦输去;未赢得(奖
品等): ~ a game 输一局 / ~ a battle 打败仗 /
The motion was lost. 这个动议被否决了。⑧使
沉湎于: be lost (或 ~ oneself) in thought 想得
出神 ⑨[用被动语态]使毁灭;使死去;使丧失:
That ship and all hands on board were lost on
the reef. 那条船只连同船员都触礁遇难了。/
be lost to all sense of shame 全不知耻 / be lost
to history 无历史记载可查 ⑩摆脱: I've lost my
cold. 我感冒好了。⑪(赛跑中)超过,领先于 ❷
vi. ① 受损失; 赔钱: The shipping line lost
considerably by it. 这家航运公司为此受到相当
大的损失。②失败,输掉 ③(钟、表等)走慢: Does
your watch gain or ~? 你的表走得快,还是走
得慢? / My watch ~s thirty seconds a day.
我的表一天要慢三十秒。||be lost on (或 upon)
对…不起作用: Our advice was not lost on him.
我们的劝告对他起了作用。/ ~ out [美口](比
赛或竞争中)输掉,失败 / ~ out on [美口]输去
…,未能占…的上风 ||losable a. 能被失去(或输
掉)的

loser ['lu:zə] n. ①损失者;损失物: be a ~ by sth.
因某事而受损失 ②失败者,输者: a good (bad)
~ 输得起(输不起)的人 ③[美]刑事犯 ④[英]
(台球游戏中)击中他球而自己却反落入袋中输掉
的一球

losing ['lu:ziŋ] I a. 看来要失败的;要输掉的:
fight a ~ battle 打一场不可能取胜的仗 II n.
失败;[复](尤指赌博中的)损失

loss [los, lo:s] n. ①丧失;遗失: ~ of sight 视力的
丧失, 失明 ②损失; 亏损; 损耗: suffer heavy
~es 遭受重大损失 / profit and ~ 盈亏 /
reduce friction ~ 减少摩擦损耗 ③失败,输: the
~ of a battle 战败 ④损毁;【军】伤亡;[复]伤亡
及被俘人员 ⑤错过;浪费: ~ of opportunity 错
过机会 ⑥降低: a temperature ~ of 50°C 温度
下降摄氏五十度 ||at a ~ ① 困惑,不知所措: I
found myself at a ~ for words of consolation.
我简直想不出安慰的话来。/ be at a ~ to
recollect sb.'s name 一下子记不起某人的名字 /
be at a (complete) ~ what to do 不知(完然不知)
所措 ②亏本地: sell sth. at a ~ 蚀本出售某物 /
cut a (或 the) ~ 赶紧脱手以免多受损失 / for

a ~ 处于苦恼中: throw sb. for a ~ 使某人苦
恼 / without (any) ~ of time 立即, 马上 ||~
leader 为招揽顾客而亏本出售的商品 / ~ list
【军】伤亡表

lost [lost] I lose 的过去式和过去分词 II a. ①失
去的; 丢失的; 丧失的: a ~ pen 遗失的钢笔
②错过的;浪费掉的: a ~ opportunity 错过的机
会 / ~ time 浪费掉的时间 / ~ labour 徒劳
③迷途的; 不知所措的: a ~ child 迷路的孩子 /
feel ~ 感到空虚而不知所措 ④输掉的, 失败了
的; 无望的: a ~ battle 败仗 / a ~ cause 已注
(或必将)失败的事业(或主张、主义) / cry out ~
and terrible words 喊出绝望可怕的话 ⑤遭难
的,死了的: a ~ ship 沉没了的船 ⑥不再为人所
知的: a ~ city 湮没无闻的城市 / a ~ art 失传
的艺术 ||Get ~! [美俚]走开! 别来磨我! /
give up for ~ 认为…已死;认为…已经没有希
望 ||~ generation 迷惘的一代(指第一次世界大
战前后的美国青年一代) / ~ motion 【机】空动 /
~ river 【地】干河,隐入河

lot [lot] I n. ①签,阄;抽签,拈阄: draw (或 cast)
~s for turns 抽签决定顺序 / The ~ fell upon
(或 came to) him. 他中签了。/ be chosen by
~ 通过抽签被选中 ②份额,份儿 ③命运,运气 ④一
块地; (作特定用处的)地方: a vacant ~ 空地 /
a parking ~ 停车处 ⑤[美]电影制片场 ⑥(商
品、拍卖品或人的)一批,一摞; 某一类的人: The
shop has got a new ~ of underwear for sale.
店里新到了一批内衣出售。/ sell by ~s 分成一
摞摞地出售 / all the parliamentary ~ 所有这些
批议员 / They are indeed a sorry ~. 他们真
是一批糟糕的家伙。⑦[口]许多(一般用于肯定
句中,在否定句及疑问句中则用 many 和 much):
A ~ of (或 Lots of) people went swimming
yesterday. 昨天很多人参加了游泳。/ A ~ of
(或 Lots of) work is to be done this week. 本
周将有许多工作要做。/ I saw quite a ~ of him
last year. 去年我常常看到他。/ I feel a ~ (或
feel ~s) better now. 我现在感觉好多了。/
Thanks a ~. 多谢。/ A ~ you care! (讽刺语)
你真太关心了! ⑧[the ~] 全部,一切: That's
the ~. 整个儿就是这些了。/ take (或全啦!) / get
away, the whole ~ of you! 你们统统走开! ❷
(lotted; lotting) ❶ vt. ①划分,把(商品等)分组:
~ land 划分土地 / ~ out goods in parcels 把货
物分成一包一包 ②[罕]分配 ❷ vi. 抽签,拈阄
||a bad ~ [俚](一个或一帮)坏家伙 / a fat ~
见 fat / a great (或 good) ~ 大量: It will
cost a great ~. 这要花费大量的钱。/ a job ~
见 job¹ / an odd ~ 不成整数的一批货色;不满
一百股的零星股票 / a round ~ (热门股票的)
一百股 (或其倍数); (冷门股票的) 十股 (或其倍
数) / cast (或 throw) in one's ~ with 与…共
命运 / have neither part nor ~ in 见 part /
It falls to sb.'s ~ to do sth. 注定要某人去
做某事。(强调不可避免) / ~ on (或 upon) [美
方] 指望, 期待 / ~s and ~s (of) 许许多多(的

oth [louθ] *a.* =loath

otion ['louʃən] *n.* ①【药】洗液,洗剂 ②洗净 ③[英俚]饮料

ottery ['lotəri] *n.* ①抽彩给奖法: a ~ ticket 彩票,奖券 ②[喻]不能预测的事

otus ['loutəs] *n.* ①【植】莲,荷: ~ roots 莲藕 ②【建】莲饰 ‖'~-,eater *n.* 贪图安逸的人 / ~ land ①安乐乡 ②安逸

oud [laud] **I** *a.* ①(声音)响亮的: a ~ voice 高声 ②发出强声的 ③吵闹的,喧嚷的 ④强调的;坚持的: a ~ denial 断然的否认 / be ~ in one's praises 竭力称赞 ⑤(衣服颜色等)俗艳的,过分花哨的;(举止)招摇的 ⑥(气味)难闻的 **II** *ad.* 大声地;响亮地: laugh ~ and long 大声笑个不住 / Speak ~er. 说得大声点。‖~ly *ad.* / ~ness *n.* ①高声,大声 ②喧闹 ③俗艳 ④【物】响度,音量 ‖'~-'hailer *n.* 扩音器 / '~'mouth *n.* 咭咭呱呱说个不停的人;多嘴的人 / '~-'speaker *n.* 扬声器,喇叭 / '~'spoken *a.* 大声说的

ounge [laundʒ] **I** ❶ *vi.* ①(懒洋洋地)倚,靠,躺 ②闲荡;闲逛 ❷ *vt.* 吊儿郎当地混(时间)(*away*) **II** *n.* ①懒洋洋的姿势;懒洋洋的步子 ②闲逛,漫步;混过的时间 ③起居室;(旅馆等处的)休息室,休息处 ④躺椅 ‖~r *n.* 闲荡的人;吊儿郎当的人 / **loungingly** *ad.* ‖~ **car** (火车的)供休息的车厢 / ~ **chair** 躺椅 / ~ **lizard** [俚]①旅馆休息室中陪伴妇女跳舞的职业性舞伴 ②爱与女人厮混的男人;讲究服装的男子 ③社会寄生虫 / ~ **suit** [主英]普通西装(区别于比较正式的服装)

ouse [laus] **I** ([复] lice [lais]) *n.* ①虱 ②(附于动、植物上的)小虫;寄生虫 ③([复] louses) [美俚]卑鄙的人,不受欢迎的人 **II** *vt.* 在…上捉虱子 ‖~ **around** [美俚]游荡;闲混 / ~ **up** [美俚]①把…弄糟,把…弄坏 ②变糟 ‖~ **cage** [美俚]①帽子 ②(火车的)守车 ③(伐木工的)山中小屋

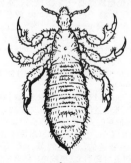

louse

ousy ['lauzi] *a.* ①多虱的,全是虱子的 ②糟糕的;劣等的 ③[美俚]很多的,丰富的(*with*) ④[美俚]卑鄙下流的,讨厌的 ⑤【纺】(丝)茸毛的 ‖**lousily** *ad.* / **lousiness** *n.*

lout[1] [laut] **I** *n.* 蠢人;丑角般人物 **II** *vt.* 把…当作蠢人;愚弄,嘲弄 ‖~**ish** *a.* 蠢笨的;小丑般的

lout[2] [laut] *vi.* ① 鞠躬 ② 屈服

lovable ['lʌvəbl] *a.* 可爱的,讨人喜欢的: a ~ child 可爱的孩子 ‖~**ness** *n.* / **lovably** *ad.*

love [lʌv] **I** *n.* ①爱,热爱;爱戴: ~ of (one's) country 爱国热情 / Give my ~ to your parents. 向你的父母问好。②爱好: ~ of (或 for) sports 对体育运动的爱好 ③恋爱,爱情 ④性爱,男女关系 ⑤亲爱的(夫妇、情侣间,或对孩子的爱称) ⑥[L-]爱的化身,爱神 ⑦(指女性)情人;情妇 ⑧[口]讨人欢喜的人,可爱的东西: It's a ~, isn't it? 真可爱啊,是不是?/ What a ~ of a clay doll! 多么可爱的泥娃娃! ⑨【体】零分: The score is ~ all (one-~). 比分是零对零(一比零)。 **II** ❶ *vt.* ①爱,热爱;爱戴 ②抚爱 ③爱好,喜欢: I'd ~ to, but I'm afraid I can't come tomorrow. 我倒是希望明天能来,但恐怕来不了。 ❷ *vi.* 爱 ‖a *labo(u)r of* ~ 爱做的事,出自喜爱而做的事 / *be in* ~ (*with*) (跟…)恋爱 / *fall in* ~ (*with*) 爱上(…) / *for* ~ *or money* 无论如何 / *for the* ~ *of* 为了…起见,看在…的面上 / *in a cottage* 穷苦而和谐的夫妇生活 / *Love is blind.* [谚]爱情使人对缺点视而不见。/ *Love me,* ~ *my dog.* [谚]爱屋及乌。/ *make* ~ (*to*) (向…)表示爱情;(与…)发生性行为 / *one-sided* ~ 单相思 / *play for* ~ (打牌等)打着玩玩(指不赌钱) / *There's no* ~ *lost between them.* 他们彼此之间毫无感情。(指相互嫌憎) ‖~ **affair** ①恋爱事件;风流韵事 ②强烈爱好 / ~ **beads** [美](颓废派男女挂的)彩色念珠 / '~**bird** *n.* 情鸟(指小鹦鹉类鸟) / ~ **child** 私生子 / ~ **feast** ①(卫理公会等教派的)友好聚餐 ②联谊宴会 / ~ **game** (网球等)输方未获分的比赛 / '~-in-a-'mist *n.*【植】黑种草 / '~-in-'idleness *n.*【植】三色堇 / ~ **knot** 同心结 / ~ **letter** 情书 / '~-lies-'bleeding *n.*【植】(苋科)千穗谷 / ~ **life** 爱情生活 / '~**lorn** *a.* 失恋的;因失恋而憔悴的 / '~,**making** *n.* 调情;性行为 / ~ **match** 出自真正爱情的婚姻 / ~ **seat** 双人坐椅(或沙发) / '~-**sick** *a.* 害相思病的 / ~ **song** 情歌,恋歌 / ~ **story** 恋爱小说;爱情故事 / ~ **token** 爱情纪念品

lovely ['lʌvli] **I** *a.* ①秀丽的,好看的;优美的: a ~ landscape 明媚的景色 ②[口]令人愉快的;美好的: have a ~ afternoon 过一个愉快的下午 ③可爱的 ④[美]高尚的,谦和的 **II** *n.* ①美女 ②漂亮的东西 ‖**loveliness** *n.*

lover ['lʌvə] *n.* ①爱好者: a ~ of table tennis 乒乓球爱好者 ②[复]情侣 ③(指男性)情人,情夫 ‖~**less** *a.* 没情人的 / ~**like** *a.* 情人般的 / ~**ly** *a.* & *ad.*

loving ['lʌviŋ] *a.* 爱的;表示爱的: Your ~ friend (信末用语)你的亲爱的朋友 ‖~**ly** *ad.* Yours ~ly (或 *Lovingly* yours) 您的亲爱的(孩子给父母写信时信末常用的习惯语) / ~**ness** *n.* ‖~

cup ① 宴席上客人们轮饮用的有两个（或数个）柄的大酒杯 ② 纪念杯，奖杯 / '~-'kindness n. 慈爱

low[lou] I a. ①低的；浅的: a ~ house 低矮的房屋 / a ~ forehead 低低的前额 / a ·flight 低飞 / The river is very ~. 这条河很浅。②低声的，低音的；(发音时)舌位放低的: speak in a ~ voice 低声地讲话 / a ~ vowel 低元音 ③(在量、度、价值等方面)少的，低下的: ~ cost 低成本 / a ~ latitude 低纬度 / a ~ price 低廉的价格 ④贬的 ⑤不足的，快枯竭的；缺钱的 ⑥地位低的，卑微的；低等的 a man of ~ origin (或birth) 出身低微的人 ⑦粗俗的，下贱的；卑劣的: a ~ style of writing 粗俗的文体 / a ~ trick 卑鄙手段 ⑧营养差的；体质弱的: a ~ diet 简陋的食物 / be in a ~ state of health 健康状况不好 ⑨没精神的，情绪低落的: feel ~ 情绪不高 / be in ~ spirits 没精打采 ⑩(衣服)袒胸露颈的，低领的；低口的: a ~ dress 低领衣，袒胸衣 / a ~ shoe 低口鞋 ⑪[L-](英国)低教会(派)的 II ad. ① 低，向下地: The village is located ~ on the slope of a hill. 这村庄处在山坡低处。/ bow ~ 深深地鞠躬 / hit ~ 朝下部打 ②低声地；以低音调: talk ~ 轻声交谈 / I cannot get so ~. 我(调门)唱不到这样低。③ 低价地；程度低地: sell (sth.) ~ 廉价出售(某物) / Don't value yourself too ~. 不要把你自己估计得过低。/ play ~ 小赌 ④地位低地，卑微地；下贱地: fall ~ 堕落下去 ⑤营养差地，穷困地 ⑥在较近的年代: as ~ as the 19th century 近至十九世纪 III n. ①[常用复]低地 ②低水平，低点;低数字 ③低速;低排档;低速齿轮: put a car in ~ 把车子放到最低速 ④[气]低气压区 ⑤(体育比赛、纸牌游戏等中)最低的得分；得最低分的人(或队)；最小的王牌 ‖at ~est 至少，最低 / bring ~ 使跌落；使恶化 / burn ~ 快要烧完 / lay ~ 使倒下，击倒；弄死: I was laid ~ by influenza. 流行性感冒把我弄得躺倒了。/ lie ~ ① 平躺;大败;受辱 ②隐匿,潜伏 / play it ~ (down) upon 卑鄙地对待，歧视 / run ~ 减少 ‖~ness n. ‖~-alloy a. [冶]低合金的 / '~-,angle a. 【军】俯冲角的 / ~ beam (低于迎面车辆司机视线的)车头的短焦距光 / ~ blow ①打在腰部以下的一击(拳击中的犯规动作) ②不正大光明的行为，卑劣勾当 / '~'born a. 出身微贱的 / '~'boy n. 带有抽屉的矮衣柜 / '~'bred a. ①出身低微的 ②粗鲁的 / ~'brow a. & n. 缺少文化素养的(人) / '~-'browed a. ①前额低的；(建筑物)入口处低矮的 ②阴暗的 / '~-'carbon a. 【冶】低碳的 / Low Church (英国)低教会派 / ~ comedy 滑稽戏 / Low Countries 低地国家(荷兰、比利时、卢森堡的总称) / '~-down a. 非常低的 / '~-,down n. [俚]内幕，真相: This is the ~down on the whole event. 这就是整个事件的内幕。/ frequency【物】低频 / ~ gear 低排档；低速齿轮 / Low German 低地德语(在德意志北部和

西部使用的德语) / '~-'grade a. ①低质量的，低级的 ②(热度等)低的 / '~-'key(ed) a. ①低调的；有节制的: a ~-key speech 调子低的演说 / Low Latin 中古拉丁语 / '~-'level a. ①低水平的;低级别的 / ~ life n. ①下等社会的人 ②[美俚]卑劣的家伙，下流坯 / '~-'lying a. 地势低洼的: ~-lying land 低洼地 ②低地的: ~-lying hills 低低的群山 / '~-'minded a. 下流的 / '~-'neck(ed) a. (衣服)领口开得低的 / '~-'pitched a. 低调的，低音的；(屋顶)缓斜的 / '~-'pressure a. ①低压的 ②轻松的 / '~-proof a. 酒精成分低的 / ~ relief 浅浮雕 / '~-'rise a. (建筑物)不高的 / '~-'spirited a. 沮丧的，精神不振的 / Low Sunday 复活节后的第一个星期日 / '~-'tension a. 低电压的 / ~ tide 低潮 / ~ water 低水位;低潮: at ~ water 处于低潮 / in ~ water 缺钱

low²[lou] I n. 牛叫声，哞 II ❶ vi. (牛等)哞哞叫 ❷ vt. 牛叫似地说

lower¹['loua] a. ①较低的 ②地位较低的，较低的;下等的: ~ officeholders 低级公职人员 ③低年级的: a ~ school 低年级学校(英国一般指公学中的一至四年级) ④下游的 ⑤南部的 ⑥(日期)较近的 ⑦[L-]【地】早期的: Lower Permain 二迭纪早期 ‖~most a. 最低的 ‖~case【印】小写字母盘 / '~'case a. 小写的 n. 小写字母 vt. 用小写字母排印 / ~ classes, ~ orders 下等社会，下层社会 / ~ classman ['loua-,klɑ:smən] n. [美](大学或中学的)一年级(或二年级)学生 / ~ criticism (对基督教《圣经》的)校勘 / ~ deck ①甲板 ②[英][the l- d-][总称]海军士兵；舰上的低级军官和水手 / Lower Empire【史】东罗马帝国 / ~ house, ~ chamber 下(议)院，众议院 / '~-,middle peasant 下中农 / ~ world 尘世;地狱

lower²['loua] ❶ vt. ①放下，降下;放低: ~ a bucket 放下吊桶 / ~ a sail 落帆 / ~ the aim of a gun 把枪瞄得低一些 ②减低；减弱: ~ the price 减低价格 / ~ one's voice 放低声音 / A cold had ~ed his resistance. 伤风已削弱了他的抵抗力。/ ~ one's sights 降低抱负 ③贬低: ~ oneself 贬低自己的身分 / Such acts ~ed him in our eyes. 这种行为降低了他在我们心目中的地位。❷ vi. ①降落;降低;减弱 ②放下小艇;下帆篷 (away)

lowland ['loulend] I n. [常用复]低地: the Lowlands 苏格兰低地区 II a. 低地的 ‖~er n. ①居住在低地的人 ②[L-]苏格兰低地居民

lowly ['louli] I a. ①谦逊的 ②卑贱的,地位低的;低级的 ③普通的，平凡的 II ad. ①谦逊地;bow ~ 谦逊地鞠躬 ②卑贱地;低贱地;低下地: be ~ priced 价格定得低 ③声音低低地，不响亮地 ‖lowliness n.

loyal ['loiəl] I a. 忠诚的；忠心的: be ~ to the Party 忠于党 II n. [常用复]忠实信徒 ‖~ly ad. / ~ness n.

loyalty ['lɔiəlti] *n.* 忠诚; 忠心: ～ *to* the people 忠于人民

lozenge ['lɔzindʒ] *n.* ①菱形 ②菱形物 ③【药】锭剂, 糖锭: cough ～*s* 咳嗽糖

lubricant ['lju:brikənt] I *a.* ①润滑的 II *n.* ①润滑剂, 润滑油 ②[喻]能减少摩擦的东西: a social ～ 在社交场合用来拉拢关系的东西(如酒) ③[美俚]奶油, 黄油

lubricate ['lju:brikeit] ❶ *vt.* ①使润滑 ②给…涂油, 给…上油 ③[美俚]使饮酒 ④[美俚]收买 ❷ *vi.* ①起润滑作用 ②[美俚]饮酒 ‖～*d a.* [美俚]喝醉了的 / **lubrication** [,lju:bri'keiʃən] *n.* 润滑(作用); 注油: ring *lubrication* 【机】油环润滑(法) / **lubricator** *n.* ①润滑剂; 润滑器 ②加润滑剂的人

lucid ['lju:sid] *a.* ①清楚的, 易懂的: a ～ style 明晰的文体 ②神志清醒的; 头脑清楚的: ～ intervals (精神病患者)神志清醒的时刻 / a ～ thinker 头脑清楚的人 ③透明的, 清澈的: a ～ stream 清澈的小溪 ④[诗]光辉的, 明亮的 ‖～*ly ad.* / ～*ness n.*

luck [lʌk] I *n.* ①运气: Any idea of winning easy victories through good ～ is wrong. 任何靠好运气轻易取胜的想法都是错误的。 / have bad (或 ill, hard, tough) ～ 倒霉 / Good ～ (to you)! 祝你顺利! (或:一路平安!) / try one's (或 trust to) ～ 碰运气 ②好运, 侥幸: a piece of ～ 一件幸运的事 / have no ～ 不走运 / I had the ～ to get a ticket. 我侥幸弄到了一张票。 ③带来运气的东西, 吉祥的东西 II *vi.* 侥幸成功; 靠运气行事 (into, out, through): Don't expect to ～ through without an effort. 别指望不经过努力就能侥幸成功。 ‖*as ～ would have it* 碰巧; 碰得不巧(表示有幸或不幸, 视上下文而定): As ～ would have it, a doctor happened to be there when she fainted. 她晕倒时幸好旁边正有一个医生。 / As ～ would have it, I was out when he called. 不巧得很, 他来访时我正好外出了。 / *be down on one's ～* [口]倒霉 / *be ～ed out* [美俚]倒霉, 遭殃; 被杀死 / *by (good) ～* 幸亏, 侥幸地 / *crowd* (或 *push*) *one's ～* [美俚]在已经很有利的形势下作多余的冒险 / *for ～* 为了表示吉利 / *in (out of) ～* 运气好(不好) / *Just my ～!* 唉, 又是倒霉! / *～ up* [美俚]走运, 交好运 / *play big* [美]走运, 得意 / *play to* (或 *in*) *hard* [美]不走运, 倒霉, 失意 / *rough ～* 倒霉 / *worse ～* [用作插入语]更不幸地, 不幸地: We were caught in a downpour and, worse ～, drenched to the skin. 我们正好碰上一场大雨, 更倒霉的是还被淋得浑身湿透。 ‖～*less a.* 不幸的 / ～'*s-penny*, *money n.* [英]吉利钱(常指旧时出售牲口的人在成交后为求吉利还给买主的一小笔钱)

lucky¹ ['lʌki] *a.* ①幸运的, 侥幸的: a ～ dog (或 beggar) 幸运儿 / I was ～ enough to catch the last bus. 我真幸运, 赶上了最后一班公共汽车。 / a ～ guess (hit, escape) 侥幸的猜中(打中, 逃脱) / touch ～ 交好运 ②吉祥的, 吉利的: a ～ day 运气好的日子, 吉日 ‖**luckily** *ad.* / **luckiness** *n.* ‖～ **bag** ①摸彩袋 ②(军舰上的)失物箱 / ～ **dip** [英]摸彩袋

lucky² ['lʌki] *n.* [英俚]逃跑 ‖*cut one's ～* 逃走

lucrative ['lju:krətiv] *a.* ①有利的; 生利的, 赚钱的: a ～ investment 有利的投资 ②【军】值得作为目标的: a ～ target 有利目标 ‖～*ly ad.* / ～*ness n.*

lucre ['lju:kə] *n.* [贬]金钱上的收益; 钱财: filthy ～ 肮脏钱

ludicrous ['lju:dikrəs] *a.* 荒唐得滑稽的, 荒谬可笑的 ‖～*ly ad.* / ～*ness n.*

lug¹ [lʌg] I (lugged; lugging) ❶ *vt.* ①(用力地)拖, 拉: ～ sb. along 硬拉着某人走 / ～ one's suitcase 吃力地提着衣箱 ②硬扯; ～ irrelevancies into (或 in) a conversation 把题外的东西硬扯到谈话中来 ❷ *vi.* ①(用力地)拖, 拉 (at) ②(印刷墨辊等)沉重地移动, 一跳一跳地转动 II *n.* ①[古](用力的)一拖, 一拉; 被拖(或被拉)的东西 ②[复]装腔作势, 架子 ③[美俚]勒索(尤指政客、警察等敲竹杠); 被勒索的钱财 ‖*put* (或 *pile*) *on ～s* 摆架子 / *put the ～ on* 向…敲竹杠

lug² [lʌg] *n.* ①[苏格兰]耳朵 ②(用作把手或柄等的)耳状物;【机】突缘, 凸出部 ③(马具上的)皮环 ④【电】接线片, 焊片 ⑤[俚]笨家伙

luggage ['lʌgidʒ] *n.* ①[总称]行李(美国一般用 baggage): three pieces (或 articles) of ～ 三件行李 / stowing space for hand ～ (火车等处)堆放手提行李的空间 / check one's ～ 寄存行李; 打行李票 / excess ～ 超重行李 / registered ～ 托运的行李 ②[美](店家出售的)皮箱, 皮包 ③红褐色 ‖～*-carrier n.* (自行车等的)衣架(俗称书包架) / ～*-rack n.* (火车等的)行李架 / ～ **van** [英]行李车 (=[美] baggage car)

lugger ['lʌgə] *n.* (装有一张或多张斜桁用四角帆的)小帆船

lugubrious [lju:'gju:briəs] *a.* 非常悲哀的(尤指故意装出); 阴郁的 ‖～*ly ad.* / ～*ness n.*

lukewarm ['lju:k-wɔ:m] *a.* ①(指液体)微温的: ～ water 温水 ②不热情的; 半心半意的: a ～ attitude 冷淡的态度 ‖～*ly ad.* / ～*ness n.*

lull [lʌl] I ❶ *vt.* ①使安静; 哄(小孩)睡觉: ～ a baby to sleep 哄婴孩入睡 ②哄骗; ～ sb. into a false sense of security 哄得某人产生一种虚假的安全感 ③使平静, 使缓和; 麻痹(斗志等): The raging sea was ～ed. 翻腾的海浪平息了。 / ～ sb.'s suspicions (fears) 消除某人的猜疑(恐惧) ❷ *vi.* 变平静: The wind ～ed. 风停了。 II *n.* ①间歇, 暂停: a ～ in the storm 风暴的暂息 / a bombing ～ 暂时停炸 ②[古]催眠的东西(尤指催眠曲) ‖～*ingly ad.* 催人入眠地

lullaby ['lʌləbai] I *n.* ①催眠曲; 摇篮曲 ②轻柔的声音(如飒飒的风声、潺潺的流水声) II *vt.* 唱催眠曲使…入睡(或安静下来)

lumber[1] ['lʌmbə] **I** *n.* ① 无用杂物;破烂的东西 (如废旧家具等) ② 木材,木料;制材(如木条、木板等) **II ❶** *vt.* ① 以破旧东西堆满;零乱地堆积在…中: a room ~ed up with useless articles 堆满无用物品的房间 ② 伐(树);采伐…的林木 **❷** *vi.* 伐木;制材 ‖~**er** ['lʌmbərə] *n.* 伐木者;集材者/~**ing** ['lʌmbəriŋ] *n.* 伐木(业) ‖'~**jack** *n.* ① 伐木者;集材者 ② 短茄克衫/~ **jacket** 伐木者穿的茄克衫/'~**man** ['lʌmbəmən] *n.* 伐木者;集材者(尤指监工、经理人等)/'~**mill** *n.* 制材厂/'~**room** 破旧东西堆藏室/'~**yard** *n.* 贮木场

lumber[2] ['lʌmbə] **I** *vi.* 笨重地移动;隆隆地行进: He ~ed a little in his walk. 他走路有些蹒跚。/ The tanks ~ed up the steep incline. 坦克隆隆地开上陡坡。 **II** *n.* 隆隆声 ‖~**ing** ['lʌmbəriŋ] *a.* ① 外形笨重的 ② 动作迟缓的,步子沉重的 ③ 笨拙的;表达不流畅的

luminary ['lju:minəri] *n.* ① 发光体(尤指日、月等天体) ② 灯光;照明 ③ (学识等方面的)杰出人物;名人

luminous ['lju:minəs] *a.* ① 发光的,发亮的: a ~ watch 夜光表/~ paint 发光漆 ② 光明的,灿烂的 ③ 照亮着的,照耀着的: a square ~ with sunlight 阳光普照的广场 ④ 明白易懂的: His prose is simple and ~. 他的散文简明易懂。 ⑤ 聪明的;有启发的: full of ~ ideas 富于启发性意见的 ‖~**ly** *ad.* /~**ness** *n.* ‖~**flux** 【物】光通量/~ **intensity** 【物】发光强度

lump[1] [lʌmp] **I** *n.* ① 团,块;土坯;面团: a ~ of clay 一块粘土/a ~ of sugar 一块方糖/break a piece of coal into small ~s 把煤敲成碎块 ② 大量,一大堆;多数;总共: a ~ of money 一笔巨款 ③ 隆起,肿块: have a bad ~ on the forehead 额上肿起一大块 ④ [口]粗笨的人;迟钝的人 ⑤ [复][美俚]责打;指责;应得的责罚 **II ❶** *vt.* ① 把…弄成一团(或一块);把…归并在一起;把…混为一谈: ~ all these items together under the heading "sundry expenses" 把这些费用一并列入"杂费"项下/~ed capacity 【无】集总电容/~ed parameter 【物】集总参数 ② 笨拙地移动;使重重地坐下: The bear ~ed its huge bulk about. 那只熊摆动着笨重的身体来回走着。③ 把…弄成七高八低: The lad's pocket was ~ed with various articles. 那小孩的口袋给各式各样的东西塞得凹凸不平。④ 把全部(赌注)压在 (on) **❷** *vi.* ① 结块;成堆: The milk powder has ~ed. 奶粉结块了。② 笨重地行走 (along),重重地坐下 (down, on) ‖**all of a** ~ 一齐成了一团,全部发肿: His hand is all of a ~. 他的手全肿起来了。/a ~ in the (或 one's) throat (因感情激动而)喉咙哽住/a ~ of selfishness (avarice) 一个彻头彻尾的自私鬼(贪婪鬼)/get (或 take) one's ~s (咎由自取地)挨打(或骂);吃苦头/in a (或 one) ~ 一次全部地/in (或 by) the ~ 总共,全数地;总的说来: Taken in

the ~, the team played well. 总的说来,这个球队打(或踢)得不错。 ‖~ **sugar** 块糖/'~-'**sum** *a.* (金额)一次总付的/~ **work** 总包的工作,包干工作

lump[2] [lʌmp] *vt.* [口]勉强容忍(现一般用于下面的句子中): If you don't like it, you may (或 can) ~ it. 你不喜欢,也得容忍一下。

lump[3] [lʌmp] *n.* 【动】(北大西洋产的)一种海鱼 (=~fish)

lunacy ['lju:nəsi] *n.* ① 疯狂,精神错乱 ② 极端愚蠢的行为;疯狂的行为

lunar ['lju:nə] *a.* ① 月的,太阴的;按月球的运转而测定的: ~ probe 月球探测/the Lunar New Year 阴历新年/a ~ rainbow 月夜的虹;月虹 ② 似月的;新月形的,半月形的: ~ bone 【解】半月状骨 ③ (光等)青冷的,微弱的 ④ 银的;含银的 ‖~**ian** [lju:'nεəriən] *n.* ① (假想中的)月球上的居住者 ② 研究月球的人 ‖~ **calendar** 阴历/~ **caustic** 【化】硝酸银,银丹/~ **distance** 月距(月和太阳或星之间的角距)/~ **eclipse** 月食/~ **mansions** 【天】二十八宿/~ **module** 【宇】登月舱/~ **month** 太阴月(约 29¼ 日)/~ **observation** 太阴观测(为测定经度作计算月距的观测)/~ **politics** 不切实际的问题,空论/~ **year** 太阴年(约 354¼ 日)

lunatic ['lu:nətik] **I** *a.* ① 精神错乱的,疯的 ② 为收容精神病人所用的 ③ 疯狂的;极端愚蠢的 **II** *n.* ① 精神病患者,疯子 ② 狂人,怪人;大傻瓜/~ **asylum** 疯人院,精神病院(现在常称 mental home 或 mental institution)/~ **fringe** 极端分子,极端主义者

lunch [lʌntʃ] **I** *n.* ① 午餐;[美]便餐: Won't you stay and take (或 have) ~ with us? (或 Won't you stay for ~?) 留在这儿吃午饭好吗? ② 午餐(或便餐)的食品: The children take their ~es to school every day. 孩子们天天带午饭到学校去吃。 **II ❶** *vi.* 吃午餐(或便餐): What time do you ~? 你们几点钟吃午饭? **❷** *vt.* 为…供应午餐(或便餐): He ~ed me at his home. 他请我在他家里吃了午饭。 ‖'~-**hooks** [复] *n.* [美俚]【手;手指 ② 牙齿 ③ 非难,恶评/'~**room** *n.* 供应快餐的小饭馆/~ **time** *n.* 午餐时间

lung [lʌŋ] *n.* ① 肺脏,肺(指两肺之一): a disease of the ~s 肺部疾病 ② (无脊椎动物的)呼吸器官 ③ 人离开潜艇升到水面所使用的一种装置 ④ 辅助肺部呼吸的装置: an iron ~ 人工呼吸器,铁肺 ⑤ [英]可供呼吸新鲜空气的空旷地方: the ~s of London 伦敦市内(或附近)的空旷地(如大公园) ‖**at the top of one's** ~s 用尽最大的声音/**have good** ~s 声音洪亮/**try one's** ~s 把嗓门提得极高 ‖~**ed** *a.* ① 有肺的 ② [常用以构成复合词]有(某一种或某一数目的)肺的: deep-~ed 声音洪亮的/one-~ed 单肺的/~**er** *n.* [美俚]患肺结核病者 ‖'~-,**duster**, '~-,**fogger** *n.* [美俚]香烟/~ **irritant** 窒息性毒剂/~ **power** 发声力/~ **sac** 肺囊

lunge¹ [lʌndʒ] **I** *n.* ①(刀、剑等的)刺；戳 ②猛冲：make a ~ at the door 向门口冲去 **II ❶** *vi.* 冲刺；猛向前冲 (at, out) **❷** *vt.* 刺；推

lunge² [lʌndʒ] **I** *n.* ①练马索 ②圆形练马场 **II** *vt.* 用练马索练(马)；在圆形练马场练(马)

lurch¹ [lə:tʃ] **I** *vi.* ①(船)突然倾斜 ②蹒跚，东倒西歪地向前：The drunken man ~ed along. 那个醉汉蹒跚而行。 **II** *n.* ①(船的)突然倾斜；倾侧：The ship gave a ~ to starboard. 船的右舷突然倾侧。②蹒跚，东倒西歪 ③[美]倾向

lurch² [lə:tʃ] **❶** *vi.* [英方](偷偷摸摸地)徘徊，逡巡 **❷** *vt.* [古]欺骗 ‖ *~ing* n. [古]潜行，徘徊，逡巡

lurch³ [lə:tʃ] **I** *n.* ①败北，挫折 ②(牌戏中的)大败 **II** *vt.* ①(牌戏等中)击败 ②[古](在危难中)丢弃(朋友等) ‖ *leave sb. in the* ~ 在某人危难时舍弃不顾

lure [ljuə] **I** *n.* ①用以诱回猎鹰的一束彩色羽毛 ②(捕鱼用的)诱饵 ③诱惑(物)；吸引力，魅力 **II** *vt.* ①用诱物诱回(鹰) ②引诱，诱惑；吸引：The scent ~d the hound *on* (或 *onward*). 臭迹吸引猎犬前进。

lurid [ˈljuərid] *a.* ①(脸色等)苍白的；灰黄的 ②(火焰、云霞等)火红的，血红的 ③可怕的，惊人的，耸人听闻的：a ~ tale 可怖的故事 / the ~ details of a shipwreck 船只失事的惊险细节 ④过分渲染的；(装潢、色彩等)俗艳的：a ~ melodrama 过分渲染情节的闹剧 ‖ *~ly ad.* / *~ness n.*

lurk [lə:k] **I** *vi.* ①潜伏；埋伏：The mantis takes the cicada, but behind him ~s the oriole. 螳螂捕蝉，黄雀在后。②潜藏；潜在：Some anxiety still ~ed in his mind. 他心里还暗暗地有点不放心。③偷偷地行动，鬼鬼祟祟地活动 **II** *n.* ①潜伏；潜在；潜行 ②[英俚]欺诈 ‖ *on the* ~ 暗中潜伏，偷偷侦察 ‖ *~er n.* 潜伏者 ‖ *~ing-place n.* 隐匿处

luscious [ˈlʌʃəs] *a.* ①甘美的；芬芳的：~ grapes 甘美的葡萄 ②[古]过分香甜的，腻味的 ③肉感的；诱惑的 ④(文体等)华丽的，绚烂的 ‖ *~ly ad.* / *~ness n.*

lush¹ [lʌʃ] *a.* ①(草木)茂盛的；葱翠的：the ~ growing crops 茂盛的庄稼 / a ~ pasture 青草繁茂的牧场 ②多汁的；味美的；芬芳的：a ~ pie 美味的馅饼 / a ~ perfume that smells ~ 气味浓郁的香料 ③丰富的；豪华的：~ appropriations 宽裕的拨款 ④繁荣的；有利的：~ industries 繁荣的工业 ⑤肉感的 ⑥[口]花哨的

lush² [lʌʃ] [美俚] **I** *n.* ①(烈性的)酒 ②醉汉，酒鬼 **II ❶** *vt.* 喝(酒) **❷** *vi.* 喝酒 ‖ *~ed a.* [美俚]喝醉的 / *~er n.* [美俚]醉汉，酒鬼 ‖ *~-roller, ~-worker n.* [美俚]摸醉汉口袋的扒手

lust [lʌst] **I** *n.* ①(不纯洁的)欲望；贪欲 ②色欲，淫欲 ③渴望，热烈追求 **II** *vi.* 贪求；渴望 (after, for) ‖ *~er n.* 好色的人 / *~ful a.* ①贪欲的 ②好色的

lustily [ˈlʌstili] *ad.* 精力充沛地，起劲地；健壮地：The boys cheered ~. 男孩们起劲地欢呼。

lustre¹, luster¹ [ˈlʌstə] **I** *n.* ①光泽；光辉；光彩：the ~ of metals (pearls) 金属(珍珠)的光泽 / the ~ of the stars 星星的灿烂光辉 / the ~ of one's eyes 目光的炯炯有神 ②[喻]荣光；显赫：add ~ to (或 shed ~ on) 给…增光 ③有枝玻璃烛台；枝形玻璃灯架；枝形挂灯 ④釉；光瓷 (=~ware) ⑤[主英]一种有光泽的毛织物 **II ❶** *vt.* ①使有光泽；使有光彩 ②给…上釉 **❷** *vi.* 有光泽，发光 ③ ‖ *~less a.* 无光泽的；无光彩的 ‖ *~ware n.* [总称]光瓷

lustre², luster² [ˈlʌstə] *n.* 五年时间

lustrous [ˈlʌstrəs] *a.* ①有光泽的；有光彩的：Chinese silk in ~ colours 色彩鲜艳的中国丝绸 ②(品德、声誉等)光辉的；显赫的：set a ~ example for all 为大家树立光辉的榜样 ‖ *~ly ad.* / *~ness n.*

lusty [ˈlʌsti] *a.* ①强壮的，精力充沛的；朝气蓬勃的：a ~ boy 强健的男孩 ②有力的，强烈的：a ~ shock 强烈的震动 ③贪欲的 ④[古]快乐的

lute¹ [lju:t] **I** *n.* (十四至十七世纪的一种拨弦乐器)诗琴；琵琶 **II ❶** *vi.* 弹琵琶 **❷** *vt.* 用琵琶弹奏

lute

lute² [lju:t] **I** *n.* ①封泥 ②起密封作用的橡皮圈 **II** *vt.* 用封泥封

luxuriant [lʌgˈzjuəriənt] *a.* ①繁茂的；丰饶的：~ soil 肥沃的土壤 ②丰富的：a ~ imagination 丰富的想象力 ③(文体等)绚烂的，华丽的：a piece of ~ prose 一篇词藻华丽的散文 ④奢华的；精美的：a ~ restaurant 豪华的饭馆 ‖ *~ly ad.*

luxuriate [lʌgˈzjuərieit] *vi.* ①茂盛；繁盛：Vegetation ~s in the tropical forests. 热带森林中草木茂盛。②沉溺；尽情享受：They are *luxuriating in* sunshine. 他们在尽情享受日光。

luxurious [lʌgˈzjuəriəs] *a.* ①爱好奢侈的；放纵的；纵欲的：~ habits 奢侈的习惯 ②供有奢侈享受的；非常舒适的：a ~ liner 豪华的班轮 ③精美而昂贵的：~ food 盛馔 ④词藻华丽的：a ~ piece of writing 一篇词藻华丽的作品 ‖ *~ly ad.* / *~ness n.*

luxury ['lʌkʃəri] **I** *n.* ①奢侈; 奢华; 华贵: live in ~ 过奢侈的生活 ②奢侈品; 昂贵难得的东西: impose taxation upon *luxuries* 对奢侈品课税 ③给人以享乐的事物; 舒适的环境 **II** *a.* 奢华的, 豪华的: a ~ hotel 豪华的大旅馆 ‖~ **consumption**【农】过度吸收(指作物对土壤中的氮或钾碱的过度吸收)

lying[1] ['laiiŋ] **I** lie[1] 的现在分词 **II** *n.* 躺的地方 ‖'~-**in** (【复】~s-in 或 ~-ins) *n.* 产期: a ~-*in* woman 产妇

lying[2] ['laiiŋ] **I** lie[2] 的现在分词 **II** *a.* 欺骗的, 不诚实的; 假的 ‖~**ly** *ad.*

lynch [lintʃ] **I** *vt.* 私刑处死; [古] 私刑拷打 **II** *n.* 私刑 (美国反动势力对黑人和进步人士所实行的不经司法途径的残酷杀害) ‖~**er** 施私刑者 /

~**ing** *n.* 私刑 ‖~ **law** 私刑

lynx [liŋks] (【复】lynx(es)) *n.* ①山猫, 猞猁狲 ②猞猁狲皮 ③[the L-]【天】天猫座 ‖'~-**eyed** *a.* 目光锐利的

lyre ['laiə] *n.* ①里拉(古希腊的一种七弦竖琴) ②[the L-]【天】=Lyra ‖~**bird** *n.* (澳洲产的)琴鸟

lyric ['lirik] **I** *n.* ①抒情诗; 抒情作品 ②[复]民歌(或音乐喜剧中)的词句 **II** *a.* ①竖琴的 ②适合于演奏(或歌唱)的; 适合用竖琴伴奏的 ③抒情的: (the) ~ drama 歌剧 / a ~ poet 抒情诗人 / ~ poetry 抒情诗 ④(感情、风格等)奔放的, 不拘束的: explode with ~ wrath 勃然大怒

lyrical ['lirikəl] *a.* =lyric (*a.*) ‖~**ly** *ad.* / ~**ness** *n.*

M

ma [mɑ:] *n.* [口]妈

ma'am *n.* [口] (madam 的缩略) ① [mæm, mɑ:m] (对女王及其他王室贵妇的称呼)夫人, 女士 ② [məm, m] (仆佣对女主人的称呼)太太, 小姐

macabre, macaber [mə'kɑ:br, mə'kɑ:bə] *a.* 以死亡为主题的; 可怕的, 令人毛骨悚然的

macadam [mə'kædəm] *n.* ①[总称](铺路用的)碎石 ②碎石路 (=~ road); 碎石路面

macaroni [,mækə'rouni] *n.* ① 通心面, 空心面; 通心粉 ②[复] macaroni(e)s 十八世纪醉心于仿效欧洲大陆派头的英国少年; 浮华少年, 纨袴子弟

mace[1] [meis] *n.* ①权标, 权杖 ②持权杖者 ③狼牙棒, 钉头锤(一种中古时代武器) ④(旧式击台球用的)平头杆 ‖'~-,**bearer** *n.* 持权杖者

mace[2] [meis] *n.* 肉豆蔻干皮(用作香料或调味品)

machete [mə'tʃeiti] *n.* ①(中美、南美人割甘蔗或当武器用的)大砍刀 ②葡萄牙四弦小吉他

machete

machinate ['mækineit] *vt.* & *vi.* 图谋, 策划 ‖**machination** [,mæki'neiʃən] *n.* ①[罕]图谋, 策划 ②诡计, 奸计; 阴谋 / **machinator** *n.* 策划者; 阴谋家

machine [mə'ʃi:n] **I** *n.* ①机器; 机械: a sewing (printing, cutting) ~ 缝纫(印刷, 切割)机 / simple ~s 简单机械(如滑轮、杠杆等) / farm ~s 农业机械 ②汽车; 自行车; 机动车辆 ③身体器官 ④机械地工作的人(或机构) ⑤机构; (控制政党的)核心小集团: the state ~ 国家机器 / the propaganda ~ 宣传机器 / ~ Democrats 民主党核心人物 ⑥用来产生舞台效果的装置; (文学作品中为取得戏剧效果的)布局, 设计(尤指安排在小说、诗中的超自然力量) ‖a boring ~ 镗床 / a drilling ~ 钻床 / a grinding ~ 磨床 / a milling ~ 铣床 / a planing ~ 刨床 / a punching ~ 冲床 / a shaping ~ 牛头刨床 **II** *vt.* 机制; 用机床加工(如切、削、磨、铣等) ‖~ **building** 机器制造; 机器制造工业 / ~ **carbine** 卡宾枪 / ~ **gun** 机枪 / ma'**chine-gun** *vt.* 用机枪扫射; 用机枪击中 / ~ **gunner** 机枪手 / ma'**chine-'hour** *n.* 一台机器在一小时内的工作量(计算成本、工时的基本单位) / ~ **language** 【自】计算机语言 / ma'**chine-made** *a.* ①机制的 ②刻板的, 机械的 / ~**man** [mə'ʃi:nmən] *n.* ①[英]印刷工 ②钻石工人 / ~ **pistol** 自动手枪 / ma'**chine-'readable** *a.* 可直接为计算机所使用的 / ~ **rifle** 自动步枪 / ~ **screw** 机(器)小螺钉 / ~ **shop** 金工车间 / ma'**chine-'smashing** *n.* 捣毁机器 / ~ **tool** 工作母机, 机床

machinery [mə'ʃi:nəri] *n.* [总称] ①机器, 机械: precision ~ 精密机器 ②(机器的)运转部分 ③(政府等的)机构: the ~ of government 政府机

构 ④方法 ⑤用来产生舞台效果的装置; (文学作品中为取得戏剧效果的)布局, 设计(尤指安排在小说、诗中的超自然力量)

machinist [mə'ʃi:nist] *n.* ① 机工; 机械师: an erecting ～ 装配机工 ② 机器操作工人(尤指缝纫车工) ③海军机械军士长

mackerel ['mækrəl] ([复] mackerel(s)) *n.*【动】鲐鱼(又叫鲭鱼); 欧洲鲐: Spanish ～ 马鲛鱼 ‖～ breeze, ～ gale 【气】鲭风(使水面起微波的风, 常认为适于钓鲭) / ～ sky 【气】鱼鳞天

mackintosh ['mækintɔʃ] *n.* ①轻而薄的防水织物, 防水胶布 ②[主英]雨衣

mad [mæd] **I** *a.* ①发疯的, 发狂的; (狗等)患狂犬病的 ②疯狂的; 狂烈的: go ～ with joy 欣喜若狂 / a ～ wind 狂风 ③狂热的, 着迷的: be ～ about (或 on, for) sth. (sb.) 狂热地迷恋某事(某人) ④愚蠢的; 狂妄的: a ～ idea 狂妄的想法 ⑤[口]恼火的, 狂怒的: be (或 get) ～ at sb. (sth.) 对某人(某事)恼火 ⑥狂欢的, 欢闹的: have a ～ time 欢闹一场 **II** *vt. & vi.* [罕]=madden **III** *n.* 狂怒 ‖(as) ～ as a hatter 发狂的, 发疯的 / (as) ～ as a March hare 像三月(交尾期)时的野兔一样疯野 / (as) ～ as a wet hen [美俚] 非常生气 / be hopping ～ [美口]怒不可遏, 气得跳起来 / have a ～ on 勃然大怒 / like ～ 疯狂地, 猛烈地: run like ～ 疯跑 ‖～ly ad. / ～ness n. ‖'～-'brained a. 狂热的; 鲁莽的 / '～cap a. 鲁莽的; 不顾前后的 n. 鲁莽的人; 狂妄的人 / '～-,doctor n. 精神病医师 / '～house n. ①疯人院 ②吵闹混乱的场所 / '～man ['mædmən] n. 疯子, 狂人 / ～money [俚]女子随身带着的应急用的钱; 私房 / '～,woman n. 女疯子

madam ['mædəm] ([复] madams 或 mesdames ['meidæm]) *n.* ①(对妇女的尊称)夫人, 女士, 太太, 小姐: This way, please, ～. (接待女宾时用)女士, 请这儿走。(复数借用 ladies) / Dear Madam (或 My dear Madam) (书信中对不熟识妇女的称呼)亲爱的女士 (复数用 mesdames 或借用 ladies) ②(用于姓名或职称前)…夫人, …女士, …太太, …小姐: Madam Chairman 主席女士 ③(家庭)主妇 ④[口]喜欢差使别人的女子: What a little ～! 好一副小姐架子! ⑤鸨母

madame ['mædəm; 法 madam] ([复] mesdames ['meidæm] 或 madames) *n.* [法] ① ([复] mesdames) (用于姓名前称呼非英语民族的已婚妇女及有职业的妇女, 相当于 Mrs.; 略作 Mme.) 夫人, 女士, 太太 ②鸨母 ‖*Madame Tussaud's* [tə'sɔ:dz] (伦敦)塔梭滋夫人名人蜡像陈列馆

made [meid] **I** make 的过去式和过去分词 **II** *a.* ①人工制造的: a ～ ground 人工开辟的场地 ②虚构的, 捏造的: a ～ story 编造的故事 ③拼成的: a ～ dish 拼盘 ④保证会成功(或发达)的 ‖'～-to-'order a. 定制的 / '～-'up a. ①制成的; 编排好的: a ～-up garment 制成的服装 / a ～-up page of type 一页排好的(铅)字 ②虚构的, 捏造的: a ～-up excuse 虚构的借口 ③做

作的: a ～-up style 做作的文体 ④坚定的, 决定了的: a ～-up mind 下定的决心; 固定了的思想 ⑤化了妆的; 化了装的

Madonna [mə'dɔnə] *n.* ①[m-] (旧时意大利对妇女的称呼; 相当于 madam) 夫人, 女士, 太太, 小姐 ②[宗]圣母(马利亚); 圣母像 ‖～ lily 【植】白百合(花)

maelstrom ['meilstroum] *n.* ① 大漩涡, 大漩流; [M-] 挪威西海岸的大漩涡 ② 猛烈(或破坏性)的力量; 大动乱

magazine [,mægə'zi:n] *n.* ①杂志, 期刊; (报纸的)星期专刊 ②仓库; (城堡、船舰等的)弹药库, 弹药仓; 库存物; 库存弹药 ③ (枪上的)弹仓, 弹盒, 弹盘 ④(照相机内的)胶卷盒, 底片盒 ‖**magazinist** *n.* 杂志撰稿人; 期刊编辑 ‖～ gun 连发枪, 弹仓式枪

magenta [mə'dʒentə] *n.* (碱性)品红; 洋红

maggot ['mægət] *n.* ① 蛆 ② 狂想, 空想; 怪念头 ‖have a ～ in one's head (或 brain) 异想天开; 想入非非 ‖～y a. ① 多蛆的 ② 抱狂想的; 满脑子怪念头的

magic ['mædʒik] **I** *n.* ①(迷信中的)魔法, 巫术 ② 魔术, 戏法 ③ 魔力, 魅力 **II** *a.* [只作定语] ①巫术的; 魔术的 ②有魔力的, 不可思议的: a ～ weapon 法宝 ‖as if by (或 like) ～ 象使用魔术般地; 不可思议地 ‖～ carpet 魔毯(源自《一千零一夜》, 人站其上可到处飞行) / ～ hand (核反应堆等操作时用的)机械手, 人造手 / ～ lantern 幻灯 / ～ nucleus 【原】幻核 / ～ number 【数】幻数

magisterial [,mædʒis'tiəriəl] *a.* ①地方行政官的; 官吏的 ②教师的; 师长作风的, 威严傲慢的 ③(意见等)权威的, 专横的 ④硕士的: a ～ thesis 硕士论文 ‖～ly ad.

magistracy ['mædʒistrəsi] *n.* ①地方行政官的职位(或职权、任期) ② 地方行政官的管辖区 ③ [the ～] [总称]地方行政官

magistrate ['mædʒistrit] *n.* ①地方行政官: the county ～ 县长 ②文职官员: the first (或 chief) ～ (美国的)总统 ③ 地方法官 ‖～ship *n.* 地方行政官(或法官)的职位(或任期)

magnanimous [mæg'næniməs] *a.* 宽宏大量的; 高尚的 ‖～ly ad. / ～ness n.

magnate ['mægneit] *n.* ① 大官; 权贵; 阔人 ② (资本主义工商业的)巨头, 大王: a steel ～ 钢铁大王

magnesia [mæg'ni:ʃə] *n.* 【化】氧化镁; 【矿】镁氧: ～ brick 镁砖 / ～ cement 镁氧水泥

magnesium [mæg'ni:zjəm] *n.* 镁: a ～ bomb 镁燃烧弹, 镁弹 / a ～ flare 镁光照明弹 / a ～ lamp 镁光灯

magnet ['mægnit] *n.* ① 磁体, 磁铁, 磁石: a bar ～ 条形磁铁, 条形磁体 / a horseshoe ～ 马蹄形磁铁 ②有吸引力的人(或物)

magnetic [mæg'netik] *a.* ①磁的; 有磁性的; (可)磁化的; 由磁性引起的 ② 有吸引力的, 有魅力的

③催眠术的 ‖**~ally** *ad.* / **~s**［复］*n.*［用作单］磁学 ‖**~ compass** 磁罗盘 / **~ equator** 地磁赤道 / **~ field** 磁场 / **~ flux** 磁通量 / **~ mine** 磁性水雷 / **~ moment** 磁矩 / **~ needle** 磁针, 指南针 / **~ north** 磁北 / **~ pole** 磁极 / **~ recorder** 磁录音机;磁记录器 / **~ storm** 磁暴 / **~ tape** (录音等用)磁带

magnetism ['mægnitizəm] *n.* ①磁,磁力;磁学: terrestrial ~ 地磁;地磁学 / animal ~ 动物磁性说 ②魅力,吸引力 ③催眠术 ‖**magnetist** *n.* ①磁学家 ②催眠术家

magnetize ['mægnitaiz] ❶ *vt.* ①使磁化,使生磁性,使有磁力 ②使醉迷,吸引 ③[罕]催眠 ❷ *vi.* 受磁 ‖**magnetization** [,mægnitai'zeiʃən] *n.* 磁化,起磁;磁化强度 / **~r** *n.* 磁化器

magneto [mæg'ni:tou] *n.* 磁电机,永磁发电机,磁石发电机

magnificence [mæg'nifisns] *n.* ①壮丽;宏伟,宏大 ②华丽,豪华

magnificent [mæg'nifisnt] *a.* ①壮丽的;宏伟的,宏大的 ②华丽的,豪华的 ③漂亮得惊人的,极其动人的;(人、动物体型等)优美的,健壮的: a ~ view of the country 乡村极其动人的景色 / a ~ physique 健美的体格 / a ~ grey horse 一匹灰色骏马 ④(思想等)高尚的,高贵的 ⑤[口]极好的: ~ weather 极好的天气 ‖**~ly** *ad.*

magnify ['mægnifai] ❶ *vt.* ①放大,扩大: The microscope *magnifies* the object 100 diameters. 这架显微镜把物像放大一百倍。 ② 赞美,推崇 ③夸张,夸大: You have *magnified* the peril. 你把危险夸大了。 ❷ *vi.* 有放大能力 ‖**~ oneself against sb.** 用抬高自己贬低对方的方法反对某人 ‖**~ing glass** 放大镜 / **~ing power** 放大率

magnifying glass

magniloquent [mæg'niləkwənt] *a.* (文风、语言等)华而不实的,夸张的;(人)使用夸张语言的,唱高调的 ‖**~ly** *ad.*

magnitude ['mægnitju:d] *n.* ①巨大;广大;[古]伟大 ②重大;重要性: an affair of the first ~ 头等重要的事情 ③大小;积;量,数量;音量: the ~ of current 电流量 / the ~ of traffic flow 交通流量 ④【天】星等;星的光度: ~ difference (或 equation) 星等差 ⑤【数】量值

magpie ['mægpai] *n.* ①【动】鹊 ②[喻]爱说话的人,叽叽喳喳的人 ③ 靶子上自外数第二圈;击中靶子自外数第二圈的一枪

magpie

mahogany [mə'hogəni] *n.* ①桃花心木;菲律宾红柳桉木;红木 ② 产桃花心木的树;菲律宾红柳桉树 ③ 赤褐色 ④ 餐桌: have one's knees under sb.'s ~ 在某人家吃饭 ⑤[英] 杜松子酒掺蜜糖;白兰地掺水的烈性饮料

maid [meid] *n.* ①少女;(未婚的)青年女子 ②未婚女子;(老)处女 ③ 侍女;女仆: a lady's ~ 专管女主人化妆的女侍 ‖**a ~ of all work** ①什么活儿都干的女仆 ② 可派多种用场的人 (或用具) / **a ~ of hono(u)r** ①侍候英国女王 (或王后、公主) 的未婚女子 (通常出身贵族) ②(婚礼中) 主要的女傧相 ③ 柠檬杏仁馅酪饼 / **an old ~** ①老处女 ②老处女式的人物 (可指男人) ③ 一种抽对子的简单牌戏 ‖**~ish** *a.* ①少女似的 ②老处女的 / **~y n.** 小女孩 ‖**~-in-'waiting** ([复] ~s-in-waiting) *n.* 女王 (或王后、公主) 的贴身侍女 / **'~,servant** *n.* 女仆

maiden ['meidn] Ⅰ *n.* ① 少女;未婚女子,处女 ②【英史】苏格兰的一种断头机 ③(赛马中)未得过奖的马 ④(板球中)未得分的投球 Ⅱ *a.* ①少女的;未婚女子的,处女的,适合未婚女子的: a ~ aunt 未婚的姑妈(或姨妈) / one's ~ name (女子)未婚前娘家的姓 ②(雌性动物)未交配的;未生育过的 ③(马)未得过奖的;(赛马)为未得过奖的马举行的 ④(植物)从种子长成的 ⑤(士兵等)无经验的;未经考验的;新的,原封未动的 ⑥初次的: a ~ flight 初次飞行 / a ~ work 处女作 ‖**~hood** *n.* 处女性;处女时期 / **~ish** *a.* ①女似的 ②象老处女的 / **~like** *a.* 处女般的;柔和的 / **~ly** *ad.* [古]处女般地 *a.* ①少女(或处女)的,少女(或处女)似的;适合于少女(或未婚女子)的 ②谦逊的;柔和的 / **~hair** *n.*【植】①掌叶铁线蕨;铁线蕨 ②金发薜属的一种 / **~hair tree**【植】银杏树,白果树 / **'~head** *n.*【解】①处女膜 ②处女性;处女时期 / **~ over** (板球中)未得分的投球

mail¹ [meil] Ⅰ *n.* ①邮件: Is there any ~ for me today? 今天有我的信吗? / He has a large amount of ~ to answer every day. 他每天有

大量的信件要回复。②[主美] [the ~] 邮件的一次发送(英国一般用 post): Has the morning ~ come yet? 早班邮件已来了吗? / catch (miss) the 7 o'clock ~ 赶上(误了)七点钟一班的收信时间 ③[美] 邮递; 邮政制度(英国用 post): air ~s 航空邮递 / surface ~s 陆上(或海上)邮递 / send a letter by ~ (或 through the ~) 邮寄信件 / Please reply by return ~. 请即回信(交下次回程邮班寄来)。/ a letter delayed in the ~ 一封被耽误了邮递的信件 ④ 邮递员; 邮政工具(指邮船、邮车等): a Canadian ~ 一艘加拿大邮船 ⑤ (邮局间装运邮件的)邮袋 ⑥ [苏格兰]袋; 旅行包 II vt. [美] 邮寄(英国用 post): a letter (parcel) 寄一封信(一个包裹) ‖~able a. 适用邮寄的; 按规定可作邮件接受的 / ~er n. ① 邮寄者; 经办邮件寄发工作者 ② = ~ing machine ③邮船 ④ 包装邮件用的箱(或匣); 附在信中的广告性印刷品 ‖~bag n. 邮袋 / ~box n. [美]邮筒, 邮箱; (收信人的)信箱 / ~carrier 邮递员 / '~cart n. ①邮车 ②一种童车 / catcher [美] 邮包装卸机(火车行进中将邮包挂上或卸下邮车的装置) / ~ clerk [美] 邮局办事员; (机关、企业中)管理邮件人员 / '~coach n. =~cart / ~ day 邮件截出日 / ~ drop ①邮筒, 信箱; (邮箱、信箱上的)槽口 ②谍报人员用以传递秘密通讯的地址 / ~ing list 通讯(或发送)名单(如出版社新书目录分送对象的名单) / ~ing machine 邮件收发机(指打邮戳、称重等的机器) / '~man n. [美] 邮递员(英国用 postman) / ~ order 函购, 邮购 / '~-order house 以函购为经营方式的商行 / '~plane 邮政飞机

mail² [meil] I n. ①锁子甲, 铠甲 ②(动物护身的)锁子状甲壳 II vt. 使披上铠甲; 给…装甲: be ~ed in armour 穿着铠甲的; 装甲的 ‖~ed a. 披甲的; 装甲的: the ~ed fist 暴力; 武力威胁

maim [meim] vt. 残害, 使残废, 使负重伤 ‖~ed a. 残废的; 负重伤的 / ~er n. 残害者, (给人)重创者

main [mein] I n. ①体力, 力气; 力量 ②主要部分; 要点 ③(自来水、煤气等的)总管道, (电、铁路等的)干线: a gas (water) ~ 煤气(自来水)总管道 / electric ~s 电力网 / a ~s set 用交流电的收音机 ④[诗]海洋, 沧海 ⑤[船]主桅; (主桅上的)主帆 ⑥大陆(对小岛和半岛而言) II a. ①主要的, 最重要的; 总的: ~ forces [军]主力 / a ~ clause [语]主句 / the ~ current 主流 / the ~ lines of communication 交通干线 / the ~ point under discussion 讨论中的要点 ②尽力的, 全力的: with ~ strength 用全力 ③(与主桅或主帆)相近的, 相接的 ④[英][方]相当大的 ‖by ~ force (或 strength) 见 force¹ / have an eye to the ~ chance 见 eye / in (或 for) the ~ 基本上, 大体上: The work has been completed in the ~. 这项工作已经基本完成。/ the Spanish Main 拉丁美洲大陆(尤指南美的北海岸一带; 有时指加勒比海的南部) / with (或 by) might

and ~ 见 might ‖ '~ly ad. 大体上; 主要地: The visitors were ~ly students. 来访者多半是学生。‖ ~ body [军]本队, 主力 / ~ brace [海]系于主桅横杆上的绳索 / ~ course ①(船)(主桅上的)主帆 ②主要课程 ③主菜 / ~ deck [船]主甲板 / ~ drag [美俚]主街, 大街 / '~frame [美俚]主机, 大街 / '~frame 主计算机 / '~ hatch [船]主舱口 / '~land [meinlənd, 'meinlænd] n. 大陆(对小岛和半岛而言) / '~line vt. & vi. [美俚]把(毒品)直接注射入静脉 / ~ line ①主线; (铁路的)干线, 正线 ②[美俚]主血管; 对主血管的海洛因注射 / ~ mast n. [船]主桅 / ~ plane [英][军]机翼 ②主翼 / '~sail n. [船](主桅上的)主帆 / '~sheet n. [船](主桅上的)主帆索 / '~spring n. ①(钟表的)主发条 ②主要动机, 主要动力, 主要原因 / ~ squeeze [美俚]①(一个地区的)重要人物 ②老板; 工头 / '~stay n. ①[船]主牵条 ② 主要的依靠: the ~stay of leadership 领导骨干 / ~ stem ①(铁路的)干线; (河流等的)主道 ②[美俚]主街, 大街 / '~stream n. 主流; 主要倾向 / Main Street ①(小城镇的)大街, 主街 ②[总称]小城镇(或乡村社会)的典型居民 ③ 小城镇周围的地区 ④ 以庸俗狭隘的实利主义为特征的地方(或环境) / '~top n. [船]主桅楼 / '~top gallant mast [船]主二接桅 / ~ topsail [船]主一接帆 / '~topmast n. [船]主一接桅 / ~ topsail [船]主二接帆 / ~ yard [船]主帆的桅横杆

maintain [men'tein] vt. ① 维持; 保持; 继续: ~ public order 维持社会秩序 / ~ high vigilance 保持高度警惕 / ~ close ties with the masses 保持与群众的密切联系 / ~ an open mind on a question 愿意听取对一个问题的不同意见 ② 维持, 保养: ~ machinery (a highway) 维修机器(公路) ③ 坚持; 维护 ④ 供养, 扶养: ~ one's family 养家 / ~ oneself 自立 ⑤(坚决)主张, 强调: He ~ed that it was wrong. 他坚持认为这是错的。/ ~ an opinion 主张一种意见 ‖~able a. ①可维持的; 可保持的 ②可维修的; 可供养的 ③可主张的; 可坚持的

maintenance ['meintinəns] n. ①维持; 保持: ~ of unity 保持团结 ② 维修, 保养: routine ammunition ~ 弹药日常保养 / ~ of way 道路的养护 ③扶养; 生活(费); 生计 ④坚持; 主张; 支持: the ~ of justice 维护正义 ⑤[律]依法应负的对他人赡养义务; 对诉讼一方的非法资助; a ~ order 法院规定一方赡养另一方 (如丈夫给分居的妻子赡养费)的判令 ‖a cap of ~ 见 cap / ~ of membership [美](劳资契约中)工会会员资格保留条款 ‖ ~ man 维修工

maize [meiz] n. ①[主英]玉蜀黍, 玉米: a ~ borer 玉米螟虫 / ~ gruel 玉米粥 ②玉米的颜色, 黄色

majestic [mə'dʒestik] a. 雄伟的, 壮丽的; 庄严的; 威严的; 崇高的 ‖~ally ad.

majesty ['mædʒisti] n. ①雄伟, 壮丽; 庄严; 崇高 ②(帝王的)威仪; 尊严; 威严 ③ 君权; 最高权力;

君主 ④[M-](尊称)陛下: Your *Majesty* 陛下 (直接称呼时用) / His (或 Her) *Majesty* 陛下 (间接提及时用) ⑤【宗】环以光轮的圣象 ‖*His Satanic* (或 *Sable*) *Majesty* [谑]魔鬼

major ['meidʒə] **I** *a.* ①较大的;较多的;较年长的;较重要的;较大范围的: a ~ premise【逻】大前提 / Brown ~【英】大布朗(指姓布朗的兄弟中年长的一个,在学校则指同姓布朗者中年长的或先入学的一个) / a ~ suit 桥牌中实力较强的一手牌(指"黑桃"及"红桃") / the ~ axis (of an ellipse) (椭圆的)长轴 / the ~ part 较多的部分 / the ~ operations 大规模作战 ②主要的;主力的: the ~ industries 主要工业 / a ~ combat 主力战 / a ~ party (有竞选力量的)主要政党 ③(专业课程中)主修的: the ~ subjects 主修(专业)课程 ④成年的 ⑤严重的: a ~ illness 严重的疾病 ⑥【音】大调的,大音阶的: a ~ scale 大音阶 **II** *n.* ①成年人;长者 ②(英)陆军(或海军陆战队)少校;(美)陆军(或空军、海军陆战队)少校;【军team】军士长 ③【逻】大前提 ④【音】大调,大音阶 ⑤[美](大学中的)主课,专业;专业学生: take organic chemistry as one's ~ 以有机化学为主修专业 / He is a history ~. 他是历史专业(科)学生。 **III** *vi.* [美]主修,专攻 (*in*): He ~s *in* physics. 他主修物理。 ‖**~ship** *n.* 少校的职位 ‖**~ general** (英)陆军(或海军陆战队)少将;(美)陆军(或空军、海军陆战队)少将

majority [mə'dʒɔriti] *n.* ①多数;大多数;半数以上: The ~ *were* (或 *was*) for (against) the plan. 多数人赞成(不赞成)这个计划。②得票多的党(或集团),多数党;(选举等中)多得的票数: the ~ leader (议会中)多数党领袖 / be elected by an absolute (an overwhelming, a thin) ~ 得到绝对多数(压倒多数,微弱多数)票而当选 / The proposal was passed *by* a ~ of ten. 这个提议以超过对方十票的多数通过。③成年;法定年龄: reach (或 attain) one's ~ 达到法定年龄 ④【军】少校级 ‖*be in the* ~ 占多数 / *join the* (*great*) ~ 死 ‖~ *rule* 多数裁定原则(指过半数的人裁定的全体必须服从)

make [meik] **I** (made [meid]) ❶ *vt.* ①做,制造;建造;创造: ~ paper 造纸 / ~ cloth 织布 / This factory ~s shoes to last. 这家工厂制造的鞋子耐穿。/ *Make* a thorough job of it! 做得彻底些! / ~ a road 筑路 ②作出(某种举动)[和某些名词连用时,意义上等于相应的动词]: ~ great efforts 作很大努力 / ~ new contributions 作出新贡献,立新功 / ~ a self-criticism 作自我批评 / ~ a summing-up 做总结 / ~ an answer 回答 / ~ a decision 作出决定 / ~ progress 取得进步 / ~ a promise 允诺 ③写作;制定;订立: ~ a poem 作诗 / ~ a sentence 造句 / ~ laws (rules) 制定法律(规章) / ~ a plan (contract) 订计划(契约) / ~ a

price 定价目 ④造成;构成;组成;成为…的组成分子: That event has *made* the headlines. 这事件成了重大新闻。/ One tree does not ~ a wood. 独木不成林。/ Two more will ~ a quorum. 再有两人就足法定人数了。/ *Make* twos (fours)! 成两列(四列)集合! / He *made* the college basketball team. 他成了大学篮球队队员。⑤成为,变成: He will ~ a very good athlete. 他将成为一个很好的运动员。/ That ~s the third time he has succeeded in his experiment. 这次已是他实验成功的第三次了。/ "Come" ~s in the past tense "came". "come" 的过去式是"came"。⑥使成为;使作为;使…看上去成为: They *made* him their team leader. 他们推选他当了队长。⑦使,使得;迫使: We *made* the arid land green. 我们把荒地变成了绿野。/ ~ one's position known 表明立场 / *Make* yourself at home. (招待客人时用语)请不要客气。/ *Make* form serve content. (或 Form must be *made* to serve content.) 形式必须为内容服务。/ ~ the mountains bow and the rivers give way 使高山低头叫河水让路 / Every one must be *made* to understand that…. 必须使每一个人懂得… ⑧使适合;注定: No one is ever *made* to be a hero. 从来没有天生的英雄豪杰。⑨使成功,保证…飞黄腾达 ⑩整理;布置;准备: ~ the beds 铺床 / ~ camp 扎营 / ~ a fire 生火 / ~ tea 泡茶,沏茶 ⑪给…做;为…作成,为…提供(或准备): He is going to ~ us a report. 他将给我们做一次报告。/ This length of cloth will ~ you a suit. 这块布给你做一套衣服够长了。/ We will ~ you a discount of 10 per cent. 我们将给你打个九折。/ He will ~ you a good assistant. 他可以成为你的好助手。⑫引起;产生: ~ trouble 引起麻烦,捣乱 / ~ no sense (difference) 毫无意义(差别) ⑬认为,估计;抱有(怀疑、犹豫等): What time do you ~ it? (或 What do you ~ the time?) 你看现在几点钟了? / I ~ the distance (to be) about 70 kilometres. 我估计这距离约有七十公里。/ ~ no doubt of it 并不怀疑 ⑭获得,挣得;赢得;(比赛中)得(分): ~ profits 获利 / ~ money 赚钱 / ~ a (或 one's) living 维持生活 / ~ friends with sb. 和某人交朋友 ⑮走;保持(航行等速度);到达;把…包括在行程内;赶上: a postman *making* his rounds 正在值勤投递的邮递员 / We have *made* 20 kilometres today. 今天我们已走了二十公里。/ The ship ~s 11 knots an hour. 这船一小时行十一浬。/ We *made* the airport in half an hour. 不到半小时我们就到了机场。/ I don't think he will ~ the morning train. 我看他赶不上早班火车。

⑯实行,进行: ~ social investigations 进行社会调查 / ~ war 开战 / ~ peace 讲和

⑰总计;等于: Three plus six ~s nine. 三加六等于九。/ Twice two ~s four. 二乘二得四。

⑱吃: ~ a hasty lunch 匆匆吃一顿午餐

⑲【海】(开始)看见,发现: We made a cruiser in the distance. 我们看见远处有一艘巡洋舰。

⑳【电】使闭合;使接通

㉑(纸牌中)洗(牌);打满(叫牌数);出(牌)胜一圈;胜(一圈)

❷ vi. ① 开始;似乎要: He made to go. 他要走了。

② 前进,朝某方向走去,行进;指向,趋向: They were making towards the river. 他们正向河边走去。/ The forest ~s nearly to the border. 这森林几乎伸展到边界。/ All the evidence ~s in our favour. 一切证据都有利于我们。

③(潮汐等)增高;增大: The tide is making now. 现在正在涨潮。/ Water was making in the hold. 船舱里的水越来越多了。

④被制造;被处理: Hay ~s better in small heaps. 谷草分成小堆容易晒干。/ Bolts are making (=being made) in this shop. 这车间正在制造螺钉。

⑤[后接形容词,表示某种状态、方式]: ~ bold 敢于,冒昧 / ~ sure 查明,弄确实 / ~ ready 准备好 / ~ merry 寻欢作乐

⑥(纸牌中)洗牌;(一张牌)吃掉旁人的牌

II n. ① 制造(法);构造;样式;(产品)来源: Is this your own ~? 这是你们自己制造的吗? / woolen sweaters of first-class ~ 头等技术制造的羊毛衫 / boilers of various ~s 各种式样的锅炉 / an automobile of a well-known ~ 名厂出品的汽车

②(矿井等某一期间的)产量

③性情;品质;体格: a man of this ~ 这种类型的人 / He has the ~ of an athlete. 他有运动员的体格。

④【电】闭合;接通: the ~ and break of a circuit 电路的接通与切断 / at ~ 在接通位置上

⑤(纸牌中)(轮值)洗牌

‖have (或 have got) it made [美俚]有成功的把握 / ~ after 追逐;跟随 / ~ against 和…相违反;不利于,有害于 / ~ and mend [英]【海】(没有固定任务的)空闲时间(原指给船员缝补衣服的时间) / ~ as if (或 as though) 假装,装作: He ~s as though he didn't hear. (或 He ~s as though not to hear.) 他假装没有听见。/ ~ at 扑向;攻击 / ~ away (赶快)离去;逃走 / ~ away with ①携…而逃 ②摧毁;除去;杀死: ~ away with oneself 自杀 ③浪费;吃掉 / ~ believe 假装 / ~ certain 见 certain / ~ do and mend 修修补补就过去 / ~ do (with) (用…)设法应付,凑合着用(…): ~ do with what little equipment one has 就现有的一点儿设备对付过去 / ~ down 改小(衣服) / ~ for ①走

向;向…前进: ~ for the door 走向门口 ②有利于,有助于;倾向于· Cultural exchanges ~ for mutual understanding. 文化交流有助于相互了解。③向…猛攻,袭击 / ~ free with 见 free / ~ free from 由…制造…,用…为原料制取…(参见 ~ of) / ~ fun of sb. 见 fun / ~ good 见 good / ~ in 向…进大;干涉别人;加入纷争 / ~ into 把…制成…;使转变为: ~ glass into bottles 用玻璃制成瓶子 / ~ it ①规定时间: A: Shall we meet next week? B: Yes, let's ~ it next Sunday. 甲: 下星期我们碰头一次头好吗? 乙: 好的,让我们约定下星期日碰头吧。②办成功,做到;赶到: A: You have just 15 minutes to get your train. B: All right, I guess I can ~ it. 甲: 你只有一刻钟时间去赶乘这班火车了。乙: 没关系,我想我赶得上。/ You can't ~ it to the other shore in this weather. 天气这么恶劣,你可到不了对岸。/ ~ light of 见 light² / ~ like [俚]模仿;扮演 / ~ little of 见 little / ~ love (to) 见 love / ~ much of 见 much / ~ of ①用…制造…: The bridge is made of steel. 这座桥是用钢材造的。[试比较: Steel is made from iron. 钢是由铁炼成的。] ②了解,明白: What do you ~ of his statement? 你怎么理解他的话? ③对待,处理;重视: I know not what to ~ of him. 我不知道怎么对待他才好。/ ~ off (赶快)离开;逃走 / ~ off with 携…而逃 / ~ one ①成为一分子,参加 ②使成为一体;使成婚 / ~ or break (或 ~ or mar) 或成之或毁之 / ~ out ①书写,填写: ~ out a document in duplicate 把文件缮写一式两份 / ~ out a list of books 开书单 ②拼凑;完成: ~ out a sum to settle the account 拼凑一笔款子了结帐目 ③(企图)证明,说明;把…说成: I don't see what you are trying to ~ out. 我不明白你要证明什么。/ This is not such a wasteland as some people ~ out (或 ~ it out to be). 这块地方决不是象有些人所说那样的荒地。/ He made out that he had forgotten about it. 他假装忘记了这事。④理解,了解: I can't ~ out the meaning of this passage. 我不能理解这段文章的意思。⑤ 辨认出: I can't ~ out his handwriting. 我认不出他的字迹。/ I ~ out a bamboo thicket over there. 我隐约看见那边有一片竹林。⑥详细勾划出 ⑦设法应付;[美]进展;过活: He made out with a defective tool and still got the job done. 他将就使用一件不完善的工具而仍然完成了任务。/ He is making out very well in his new job. 他干他那新的一行干得很不错呢。/ How are things making out? 事情进展得怎样? / ~ out of ①用…制造出…: ~ organic fertilizer out of maize and sorghum stalks 用玉米秆和高粱秆制造有机肥料 ②理解;了解 / ~ over ①把(财产)转让,移交 ②改造;把(衣服等)改制(或翻新): ~ nature over 改造自然,改天换地 / ~ the best of 见

best / ~ **the most of** 见 **most** / ~ **through with** 完成 / ~ **up** ①弥补,补偿;赔偿;补足;补(考): ~ **up** deficiency by the surplus 截长补短 / We must ~ it *up* to him somehow. 我们得想个办法赔偿他。 / ~ *up* missed lessons 补课 / ~*up* for lost time 弥补时间上的损失 ②拼凑成;配制;包装: ~ *up* a prescription 配方 / ~ *up* a bottle of medicine 配一瓶药水 / ~ *up* books into bundles 把书扎成几包 ③编排(版面等);编辑,编制(书、表等) ④虚构,捏造(谎言、故事等) ⑤缝制;(材料等)可缝制成衣: Can you ~ *up* this suit length for me? 你能用这个尺寸的料子给我做一套衣服吗? ⑥组成: a mobile medical team *made up* of ten doctors 由十名医生组成的流动医疗队 ⑦调停(纠纷等);和解 ⑧结算(帐目);整理(房间等);准备(床铺等);包装: ~ *up* a bed on the floor for an unexpected guest 给意外的来客搭地铺 (~ up a bed 指临时搭起床铺,与 ~ the beds 铺床有别) ⑨(演员等)化装;打扮 ⑩加燃料使(炉火)不熄 ⑪缔结(协定等);安排(婚姻等) ⑫洗(牌) / ~ **up to** ①接近: A fishing boat *made up to* us. 一艘渔船驶近我们。 ② 巴结,奉承;向(女子)求爱 / ~ **use of** 见 **use** / ~ **with** [美俚]用(眼、口、手、脚等)做动作,作出,产生: He *made with* the shoulders. 他耸耸肩。 / ~ **with** the tears 落泪 / **on the** ~ ①在构成中,在增长中,在改进中 ②热中于追求名利,野心勃勃 ‖'~-be,lieve n. 假装,假托;假装者 a. 假装的;虚假的: ~-*believe* disarmament 假裁军 / '~-**do** n. & a. =~shift / '~-**fast** n. 拴船柱 / '~-**peace** n. 和事佬,调停人 / '~-**shift** n. 权宜之计;临时凑合的代用品: use sth. as a ~*shift* for it 用某物作它的代用品 a. 权宜的;临时凑合的: a ~*shift* bridge 临时便桥 / a ~*shift* policy 权宜的政策 / make a ~*shift* arrangement 作临时的安排 / '~-**up** n. ①组成;构造: the ~*up* of Chinese characters 汉字的构造 ②性格;特质;体格: the national ~*up* 民族性 / He has a stout ~*up*. 他有强壮的体格。 ③虚构,捏造 ④补给,补充: a fuel ~*up* 燃料补给 ⑤(演员的)化装(术);化装用具;(妇女用)化妆品 ⑥(学校的)补考 ⑦【印】排版,拼版;(印刷品的)编排 / '~-**weight** n. (磅秤上)补足重量的东西;[喻]平衡力 ②(补缺的)无关重要的人(或物);(补充说明的)非重要的论点 / '~-**work** n. [美]为提供就业机会而安排的工作

maker ['meikə] n. ①创造者;[the M-]【宗】上帝: ②制造者;制作者;制造商: a pattern ~ 制模工人 / the policy ~s 决定政策的人,决策者 ③期票出票人 ④【电】接合器,接通器 ⑤(桥牌中)定王牌的人 ‖~-**up** ['meikərʌp]([复]~s-up) n. 【印】排版工;[英]制品装配工;服装工人

making ['meikiŋ] n. ①制造,制作;形成;发展: These laboratory instruments are of our own ~. 这些实验室仪器都是我们自己制造的。 / an

economic crisis in the ~ 正在酝酿中的一场经济危机 ②成功的原因(或手段) ③[复]素质,内在因素: have ~s of 具有成为…所需要的素质 ④[复]赚头 ⑤制造物;一次制造量: a ~ of bread 一批出炉的面包 ⑥[复]材料 ⑦[复]【纸俗】卷纸烟用的纸和烟叶 ⑧[复]【矿】截槽煤粉

malady ['mælədi] n. ①病,疾病 ②[喻]弊病;歪风: a social ~ 社会上的歪风

malaria [mə'lɛəriə] n. ①【医】疟疾 ②[古]污浊的空气,瘴气 ‖~l, ~n, **malarious** a.

malcontent ['mælkən,tent] I a. 不满的;对政治现状不满的,反叛的 II n. 不满者;不满于政治现状者;反叛者

male [meil] I a. ①男(性)的;公的,雄的: a deep voice 浑厚的男声 ②由男子组成的: a ~ choir 男声合唱队 ③雄纠纠的;有力的: ~ vigour 刚强 ④【植】雄的,只有雄蕊的: ~ gamete 雄配子 / ~ holly 雄冬青 ⑤【机】阳的: ~ screw 阳螺旋 II n. ①男子;雄性动物;雄性植物 ②【自】插入式配件 ‖~-'**sterile** a.【生】雄性不育的 / ~ **supremacist** 男子霸权论者,大男子主义者 / ~ **supremacy** 男子霸权,大男子主义

malediction [,mæli'dikʃən] n. 诅咒,咒骂;诽谤

malefactor ['mælifæktə] n. 犯罪分子;罪大恶极者;作恶者;坏分子

malevolence [mə'levələns] n. ①恶意,恶毒 ②[总称]用心狠毒的行为

malevolent [mə'levələnt] a. 含有恶意的,恶毒的 ‖~ly ad.

malformation ['mælfɔ:'meiʃən] n. ①畸形(性): congenital ~ 先天畸形 ②畸形物;畸形体

malice ['mælis] n. ①恶意;怨恨: do it out of ~ 出于恶意而做这事 / eyes shining with ~ 闪露凶光的眼睛 ②蓄意犯罪(或害人),【律】预谋 ‖**bear ~ to** (或 **towards**) **sb.** 对某人怀有恶意 / ~ **aforethought** (或 **prepense**)【律】预谋 / **stand mute of** ~【律】对被控罪名拒不答辩

malicious [mə'liʃəs] a. ①恶意的,恶毒的: ~ remarks 恶言毒语 ②蓄意的,预谋的 ‖~ly ad. / ~ness n. ‖~ **mischief**【律】对他人财产的蓄意破坏

malign [mə'lain] I a. ①有害的;邪恶的: a ~ environment 有害的环境 ②恶意的,恶毒的: give sb. a ~ look 用恶狠狠的目光看某人一眼 ③(疾病)恶性的: a ~ lesion 恶性损害 II vt. 诽谤,中伤,诬蔑 ‖~er n. 诽谤者,中伤者 / ~ly ad.

malignant [mə'lignənt] a. ①恶意的,恶毒的 ②有害的,邪恶的 ③【医】恶性的: A cancer is a ~ tumour. 癌是一种恶性瘤。 ‖~ly ad.

malignity [mə'ligniti] n. ①极度的恶意,狠毒 ②(病的)恶性 ③恶意(或恶毒)的言行

malinger [mə'lingə] vi. 装病,托病逃差;开小差: a ~*ing* GI 托病开小差的美国兵 ‖~er [mə'lingərə] n. 装病逃差者(尤指士兵)

malleable ['mæliəbl] *a.* ①(金属)有延展性的,可锻的,韧性的: ～ cast-iron 可锻铸铁,韧性铸铁 ②(性格)柔顺的,顺从的,易适应的,可训练的 ‖**malleability** [,mæliə'biliti] *n.* / ～**ness** *n.*

mallet ['mælit] *n.* ①槌,木槌: a hand ～ 手木槌 / a rawhide ～ 皮槌 ②打槌球(croquet)用的长柄木槌;打马球(polo)用的球棍

malnutrition ['mælnju(ː)'triʃən] *n.* 营养不良

malodorous [mæ'loudərəs] *a.* 恶臭的 ‖～**ly** *ad.* / ～**ness** *n.*

malpractice ['mæl'præktis] *n.* ①不法行为;利用职权营私舞弊;玩忽职守,渎职 ②治疗失当,治疗错误

malt [mɔːlt] **I** *n.* ①麦芽 ②麦芽酒,啤酒 ③麦乳精 **II** ❶ *vt.* 使成麦芽;用麦芽(或麦精)处理(或调制) ❷ *vi.* (麦粒)发芽;制麦芽 ‖～**ing** *n.* ①麦粒发芽;制成麦芽糖 ②麦芽作坊 / ～**y** *a.* 麦芽的 ‖～ **dust** 麦芽糖 麦曲槽 / ～**ed milk** 麦乳精 / ～ **extract** 麦芽膏,麦精 / '～**house** *n.* 麦芽作坊 / ～ **liquor** 麦芽酒(例如啤酒)

maltreat [mæl'triːt] *vt.* ①粗暴地对待;虐待 ②乱用,滥用(机器等) ‖～**ment** *n.*

mamma[1] [mə'mɑː] *n.* [儿语]妈妈

mamma[2] ['mæmə] ([复] mammae ['mæmiː]) *n.* 乳房;哺乳动物雄体的乳房残迹

mammal ['mæməl] *n.* 哺乳动物

mammon ['mæmən] *n.* ①(视作偶像或罪恶源的)钱财;财富 ②[M-](基督教《圣经》中所说的)财神;贪欲之神: worship at the shrine of *Mammon* 崇拜财神,一心想发财 / *Mammon* art 拜金艺术 ‖*the* ～ *of unrighteousness* 不义之财;用于坏事上的钱财 ‖～**ish** *a.* 为金钱驱使的;拜金的,贪婪的

mammoth ['mæməθ] **I** *n.* ①猛犸(已绝种的古代长毛象) ②巨物,庞然大物 **II** *a.* 巨大的,庞大的: a ～ parade 盛大的游行

man [mæn] **I** ([复] men [men]) *n.* ①人(指男人或女人);个人;(任何)人 ②[单][不用冠词]人类;【生】人科: *Man* will conquer nature. 人类将征服自然。(或:人定胜天。) / *Man's* knowledge of things constantly develops. 人类的认识总是不断发展的。③成年男子;男子汉;男子气概: make a ～ of sb. 使某人成人;使某人成器 / Be a ～! 拿出点勇气来! / be only half a ～ 不象个男子汉(指缺乏勇气等) ④丈夫;[方](男)情人: ～ and wife 夫妇 / her young ～ 她的情人 ⑤【史】封臣;佃户;侍从;部下;男仆 ⑥[复]雇工,雇员 ⑦[复]士兵;水手: officers and *men* 官兵 ⑧[用在物主代词后]合适的对象: mistake one's ～ 找(或看)错对象 / If you want a good turner, he's your ～. 如果你要一个好车工的话,他最合适。⑨(亲热、戏谑的称呼)老兄,伙计: Hullo, little ～! 喂,小家伙! ⑩[表示不耐烦、轻蔑等的感叹语]: Hurry up, ～ (alive)! 嗨,赶快! / Nonsense, ～! 胡扯! ⑪[the M- 或 the ～][美]白人社会;白人现存统治体制;法律;执法吏,警察;私人侦探;老板;乐队领队 ⑫球队队员 ⑬(棋)子 **II** (manned; manning) *vt.* ① 给…配备人员: ～ a ship 为一艘船配备船员 ②在…就位;操纵: ～ the side (或 yards)【海】举行登舷礼(指水手在船舷边列队欢迎) / *Man* the guns! (对炮手的口令)就位! / Ho, train coming. *Man* the switches. 喂,火车来了。快去扳道岔。 / ～ a lookout post 守住了望哨 / Ten workers were assigned to ～ the production line. 十名工人被派到生产线上进行操作。③使增强勇气;使振作精神 ‖*a best* ～ 男傧相 / *a dollar-a-year* ～ [美]支取象征性薪俸的人(尤指在政府挂名的大资本家) / *a green goods* ～ [美俚]造(或用)假钞票的人 / *a* ～ *about town* 活跃于交际场中的男子,花花公子 / *a* ～ *born of woman* 凡人 / *A* ～ *is as old as he feels.* 凡人 / *a* ～ *of business* (商业上或法律上的)代理人 / *a* ～ *of God*【宗】①圣徒 ②牧师,教士 / *a* ～ *of his hands* 有手艺的人;武艺家 / *a* ～ *of iron* ①意志坚强的人 ②严酷无情的人 / *a* ～ *of letters* 学者;作家,文人 / *a* ～ *of mark* 名人,显要人物 / *a* ～ *of men* [口]杰出人物 / *a* ～ *of mo(u)ld* (终要入土的)凡人 / *a* ～ *of one's word* 守信的人,说话算数的人 / *a* ～ *of parts* 有才干的人 / *a* ～ *of sin* [古]【宗】反基督教的人;堕落的人,罪人,被神遗弃的人 / *a* ～ *of straw* ①稻草人 ②假想的对手 ③(在非法交易等中)被人用作挡箭牌的人 / *a* ～ *of the world* 深通世故的人 / *a* ～ *on horseback* 权势大到危及现存政府统治的人;军事独裁者 / *a medical* ～ 医生;外科医生 / *a merry* ～ [古]小丑 / *angry young men* 见 **angry** / *an iron* ～ ①铁人;[美俚]体力很强的运动选手 ②[美俚]一块银元 / *(an) odd* ～ *out* ①(其余人成对后)剩下的一人 ②[口]在团体中难以和他人相处的人 ③三人中通过抽签挑出一人的方法 / *as a* ～ ①一致地 ②就他个人的品德而言 / *as one* ～ 一致地 / *a straight* ～ [美俚]喜剧中丑角的助手 / *a tall-water* ～ [美俚]远洋海员 / *a young* ～ *in a hurry* 急躁的改革者 / *be one's own* ～ 不受他人支配;能完全控制住自己 / *between* ～ *and* ～ 在两人中私下讲的 / *dead men* [俚]空酒瓶 / *Dead men tell no tales.* [谚]死人不会告密。 / *every* ～ *jack* 每一个人 / *Man alive!* [口]哎呀! 我的天呀! (或:这是怎么一回事!) / ～ *and boy* 从少年时代起,从小到大: He has worked in this factory, ～ *and boy*, for thirty years.

他在这厂里工作,从小到大,已经三十年了。/ *for* ~ 以一个人对一个人 / ~ *Friday* 忠实的仆人(源出《鲁滨逊漂流记》);得力助手 / *Man proposes, God disposes.* [谚]谋事在人,成事在天。/ *Many men, many minds.* [谚]十个人,十条心。(或: 各有各的主意。) / *men of light and leading* 有真才实学的有影响的人们 / *men of the moment* 当代要人 / *merry men of May* 落潮时的潮流 / *Once a ~ and twice a child.* [谚]一次做成人,两次当小孩。(因人到年老言谈举止都有点象小孩,故称人生一生中要当两次小孩) / *one ~, one vote* (选举)一人一票制 / *one's* (或 *the*) *old* ~ [美俚]①丈夫 ②父亲 ③(招呼用语)老朋友,老兄 ④船长 ⑤(美国兵用的称呼)长官(尤指连长) ⑥老板,主管人;工头 ⑦老资格者;老前辈 ⑧姘夫 / *play the ~* 显示男子的气概 / *put on the new ~* 以改邪归正的行为表示皈依基督教 / *So's your old ~.* [美俚]去你的吧!(对于难以置信的话的轻蔑表示) / *the dead* ~ 冗员 / *the forgotten* ~ [美]被遗忘的人;普通老百姓 / *the inner* ~ ①人的灵魂(或精神) ②[谑]胃. *refresh* (或 *satisfy*) *one's inner* ~ 吃饱肚子 / *the limit* ~ (赛跑等比赛中)受到最大让步的人 / *the ~ at the wheel* ①舵手;驾驶员 ②负责人 / *the ~ higher up* [美]政界巨头 / *the ~ in the moon* 想象中的月中人,虚构的人物 / *the ~ in the oak* 妖怪,恶魔 / *the ~ in* (或 *on*) *the street* 一般人,普通人 / *the Man of Sorrows* 【基督教】耶稣,基督 / *the ~ on the spot* 熟悉当地情况的人 / *the odd* ~ (两选票数相等时)投决定性一票的人 / *the old ~ of the sea* 摆脱不掉的人(或物) / *the outer* ~ 人的外表(指面貌、服装等) / *the right ~ in the right place* 人地相宜;人得其位,位得其人 / *the Sick Man of Europe* 【史】土耳其帝国的别称 / *the wild men* 激进分子 / *to a* (*the last*) ~ 全体无例外地: The committee, *to a* ~, adopted the proposal. 委员会全体一致采纳了这个建议。 || **~less** *a.* 无人的 / **~like** *a.* ①象男人的,男子似的 ②有男子气概的 *ad.* 有男子气概地 || '**~-at-'arms** *n.* 士兵(尤指重骑兵) / '**~-child** *n.* 男孩 / '**~-,eater** *n.* ①食人者 ②食人兽 ③咬人的马 / '**~-,eating** *a.* 食人的,吃人的 / '**~-,engine** *n.* 载人升降机 / '**~-,hater** *n.* 厌恶人类的人;厌世者 / '**~-hole** *n.* (进)人孔(指锅炉等的修理入口等) / '**~-'hour** *n.* 一个人在一小时内完成的工作量 / '**~-hunt** *n.* 对逃亡者的追捕 / '**~-,killer** *n.* 杀人的人(或物) / '**~-,made** *a.* 人造的,人工的: a ~-*made* earth satellite 人造地球卫星 / '**~-'milliner** ([复] ~-milliners 或 men-milliners) *n.* ①女帽(或女子头饰)制造人,女帽(或女子头饰)商 ②忙于琐碎事务的男子 / '**~-of-'all-,work** *n.* 杂差 / '**~-of-'war** *n.* 军舰 / '**~pack** *a.* 单人可携带的 / ~ **power** ①人力 ②【机】人力(相当于 1/10 马力的功率单位) / '**~rope** *n.* (上船用的)把索,绳梯 / '**~-**

,**servant** ([复] menservants) *n.* 男仆 / '**~-shift** *n.* 一人在一班中所作的工作量 / '**~-,size(d)** *a.* [美口] ①大尺寸的;[美俚]数目(或分量)极大的 ②适合于男子的;需由男子担当的 / '**~-,slaughter** *n.* ①杀人罪 ②【律】杀人罪(指非预谋的杀人);误杀 / **~,slayer** *n.* 杀人者 / '**~-'time** ([复] men-times) *n.* 人次 / '**~-to-'** *a.* ①坦率的,诚实的 ②(球赛中)人钉人的 / '**~-trap** *n.* ①捕人(尤指侵入者)的陷阱 ②容易引起事故的场所(或东西) ③潜在危险的根源 / '**~-way** *n.* 【矿】人行巷道 / '**~-'year** ([复] ~-years) *n.* (按每周一般工作日标准计算的)一人一年的工作量

manacle ['mænəkl] **I** *n.* [常用复] ①手铐 ②束缚 **II** *vt.* 给…上手铐;束缚

manage ['mænidʒ] ❶ *vt.* ①管理;处理;经营;安排: ~ a school (corporation, household) 管理学校(企业,家务) / Properly ~*d,* the money can last them three months. 如果安排得好,这些钱够他们用三个月。②运用;操纵,控制;驾驭: ~ a tool dexterously 熟练地使用工具 / ~ the cattle 看管牲畜 / ~ a horse 驭马 ③设法;[谑]弄得 / [口][常与 can, could, be able to 连用]对付;吃: Can you ~ another slice of cake? 你能再吃一片蛋糕吗? ❷ *vi.* 处理,办理;设法对付: I shall be able to ~ without help. 我一个人能行。/ I shall ~ with what tools I have. 我将用仅有的这些工具设法对付。|| **~d currency** 管理通货

manageable ['mænidʒəbl] *a.* ①易管理的;易处理的 ②易驾驭的,驯服的;易操纵的 ③可以设法的 || **manageability** [,mænidʒə'biliti] *n.* / **~ness** *n.* / **manageably** *ad.*

management ['mænidʒmənt] *n.* ①管理;处理;经营;安排: field ~ 田间管理 / personnel ~ 人事管理 / household ~ 家务处理 ②运用;操纵;驾驭: the ~ of a tool (weapon, machine) 工具(武器,机器)的使用 ③手段,经营手腕;经营才能 ④(工商企业的)管理部门;资方: the ~ of the factory 工厂的管理部门 / labour and ~ 劳资双方

manager ['mænidʒə] *n.* ①经理;管理人;干事;当家人: a general ~ 总经理 / a stage ~ 舞台监督 / a good (bad) ~ 善于(不善于)理财(或当家)的人 ②[英](议会中)处理两院共同事务的委员 ③[英]【律】(高等法院指定的)财务管理人 || **~ess** ['mænidʒəres] *n.* 女经理;女管理人 / **~ship** *n.* 经理的职位(或权力)

managerial [,mænə'dʒiəriəl] *a.* ①经理的;管理人的 ②管理上的,经营上的 || **~ly** *ad.*

managing ['mænidʒiŋ] *a.* ①管理的;主管的;善于经营的: a ~ director 总经理;常务董事 / a ~ editor 总编辑 ②喜欢管别人的: a ~ granny 爱多管事的老奶奶 ③节约的,节俭的;吝啬的

mandarin[1] ['mændərin] **I** *n.* ①【史】(中国清朝九品及九品以上的)官员 ②官话(旧时欧美人指的北京方言) ③达官贵人 **II** *a.* ①(服装)中国式身马褂的 ②(作品风格)过分文雅的 || ~ **coat** 清

朝式对襟绣花马褂(现为西方妇女晚礼服外套) /
~ **duck** 鸳鸯 / ~ **fish** 鳜,桂鱼

mandarin² ['mændərin], **mandarine** [,mændəri:n]
n. ①中国柑橘 (= ~ orange); 柑橘树 (= ~ tree)
②一种橙色染料 ③[通常拼写作 ·mandarine] 橘
子香酒 ‖~ **oil** 橘皮油

mandate ['mændeit] **I** *n.* ① 命令, 训令 ② 委任;
(前国际联盟的)委任统治权; 托管地 ③ (选民对
选出的代表、议会等的)授权 ④【律】上级法院给
下级法院的命令;(英国法律中的)财产委托;(罗
马法律中的)委任契约(委任受托人无偿代理的契
约);委任代理契约 **II** *vt.* 把(某地区)置于委任
管理下; 托管: a ~d territory 托管地 ‖**man-
dator** *n.* 命令者; 委任者

mandolin ['mændəlin], **mandoline** [,mændə'li:n]
n. 曼陀林(琴)(一种琵琶类乐器)

mane [mein] *n.* ① (马、狮等的)鬃毛 ② (人的)长
而密的头发 ‖~**d** *a.* 有鬃毛的 / ~**less** *a.* 无
鬃毛的

manganese [,mæŋgə'ni:z, 'mæŋgəni:z] *n.* 【化】
锰: ~ dioxide 二氧化锰 / ~ spar 蔷薇辉石; 菱
锰矿 / ~ steel 锰钢 ‖**manganesian** [,mæŋgə-
'ni:ʒən, ,mæŋgə'ni:ziən] *a.*

mange [meindʒ] *n.* ① 兽疥癣; 癞疥 ② 皮肤的肮脏

manger ['meindʒə] *n.* 马(或牛等的)槽 ‖*a dog in
the* ~ 见 **dog** ‖~ **board** 【船】挡水板

mangle¹ ['mæŋgl] *vt.* ① 乱切, 乱砍;(用拳等)乱打,
弄伤: The body was ~d beyond recognition. 尸
体被弄得血肉模糊使人认不出是谁。② (因大错
而)损坏, 弄糟;(因乱发音)使无法被听懂: The
text was ~d. 原文(因删削、窜改、曲解等)受到
损害。‖~**r** *n.* 乱切者, 乱砍者

mangle² ['mæŋgl] **I** *n.* (轧干洗过的衣服等用的)
轧液机; 砑光机; 轧布机; 轧板机; 钢板矫正辊 **II**
vt. 把(布等)送入轧机中轧压 ‖~**r** *n.* ①轧机操
作人员 ②砑光机;压延机;绞肉机;榨甘蔗汁机

mango ['mæŋgou] ([复] mango(e)s) *n.* ① 杧果树;
杧果(或芒果) ②灯笼椒, 狮头辣椒 ③醋泡甜瓜
(或黄瓜) ‖~ **fish** [动]四指马鲅

mangrove ['mæŋgrouv] *n.* 【植】红树属植物; 美洲
红树

mangrove

manhood ['mænhud] *n.* ① 人的状态 ② (男子的)
成年身分(或资格); 成年期: ~ suffrage 男公民
选举权 / reach ~ (男子)成年 ③男子气概; 勇气;
刚毅 ④[总称]男子

mania ['meinjə] *n.* 【医】躁狂症; 疯狂 ② 狂热,
癖好: a ~ for collecting stamps 集邮癖

maniac¹ ['meiniæk] **I** *a.* ①【医】躁狂的; 疯狂的
③狂热的; 狂乱的 **II** *n.* ①【医】躁狂者 ②疯子:
war ~s 战争狂人 ‖~**ally** *ad.*

maniac² ['meiniæk] *n.* 一种高速电子数字计算机

manicure ['mænikjuə] **I** *n.* ① 修指甲(包括修剪、
洗净、涂水指甲) ② =manicurist **II** *vt.* ① 修…
的指甲; 为…修指甲 ②修剪, 修平: ~ the lawn
修剪草坪 ‖**manicurist** ['mænikjuərist] *n.* 指甲
修剪师

manifest ['mænifest] **I** *a.* 明白的, 明显的, 明了
的 **II** ❶ *vt.* ①表明; 证明 ②显示, 表现
(人的品质、感情等) ③ 把…记在船货单上; 出示
(所运货物)的货单 ④[~ oneself] (事物、现象
等)出现, 显露: No such disease ~ed *itself* in
these years. 这些年来未发生过这种疾病。❷ *vi.*
(鬼等)出现, 显露 **III** *n.* ①显示 ②宣言, 声明
③(飞机或船的)货物清单, 舱单 ④快运货车; 用
快运货车载运的易变质的物品(或牲畜) ‖~**ative**
[,mæni'festiv] *a.* 显然的, 明白的 / ~**ly** *ad.*
‖~ **destiny** 命定说(尤指一种认为某一民族扩张
其领土系天命所定的反动史观)

manifestation [,mænifes'teiʃən] *n.* ① 表现形式;
现象: A disease can often be determined by its
~s. 疾病往往可通过它的现象而诊断出来。②神
秘现象的具体化 ③(政府或政党的)公开声明

manifesto [,mæni'festou] **I** ([复] manifesto(e)s) *n.*
宣言, 声明: issue a ~ 发表声明 **II** *vi.* 发表宣言
(或声明)

manifold ['mænifould] **I** *a.* ① 多样的; 种种的; 多
方面的: ~ industries 多种多样的工业 / ~ wis-
dom 多方面的智慧 ②多种特征(或用途)的; 同时
具有多种功能的; 作成多份的, 由同类的几部分组
成的: a ~ bellpull 能同时操纵几只铃的拉索
③许许多多的 **II** *n.* ①复写本 ②【机】歧管, 多支
管, 集合管; 复式接头 ③【数】簇, 流形 **III** *vt.*
复写: ~ the document with carbon paper 将该
文件用复写纸复写 ‖~**ing** *n.* 歧管装置 / ~**ly**
ad. / ~ **paper** 复写用的薄纸 /
~ **writer** 复写器

Manil(l)a [mə'nilə] *n.* ① 马尼拉 [菲律宾首都]
②吕宋烟(马尼拉产的雪茄烟) ③吕宋绳, 白棕绳
(= ~ rope) ④ 马尼拉麻 (= ~ hemp) ⑤ 马尼拉
纸(以马尼拉麻为原料的包装纸) (= ~ paper)

manipulate [mə'nipjuleit] *vt.* ①熟练地使用, 操作;
处理, 操纵: ~ a dislocated arm joint 给脱臼的手
臂关节上胼 / ~ an electric device 操纵电气装置
② (用权势或不正当的手段)操纵; 摆布: ~ the
stock market 操纵股票市场 ③ 应付, (巧妙地)
处置 ④ 窜改, 伪造 (账目等) ‖**manipulator** *n.*
①操作者; 操纵者; 窜改者 ②操作器, 控制器

manipulation [mə,nipjuˈleiʃən] *n.* ① (熟练的) 操作; 操纵, 控制: Accidents often occurred through carelessness in ~ by the drivers. 事故往往是由于驾驶人员操作上的疏忽而引起的。 / remote ~ 远距离操作, 遥控 ② (使用手段的) 操纵 ③应付, 处理 ④ (对数字、账目等的) 窜改 ⑤【医】手技, 手法, 操作法

mankind *n.* [用作单或复] ① [mænˈkaind] 人类 ② [ˈmænkaind] 男子, 男性

manly [ˈmænli] **I** *a.* ①男子气概的; 雄赳赳的; 果断的 ② 适合男子的: ~ sports 适合于男子的运动 ③ (女子) 有男子气的 **II** *ad.* 男子般地; 雄赳赳地; 果断地 ‖**manliness** *n.*

manna [ˈmænə] *n.* ①吗哪 (基督教《圣经》中所说古以色列人经过旷野时获得的神赐食物) ②不期而获的东西; 振奋精神的东西 ③【医】甘露, 木蜜: ~ in tears (in sorts) 上等 (下等) 甘露 ‖**~ ash** 欧洲白蜡树; 花白蜡树 / ‖**~-croup** *n.* 粗小麦粉

manned [mænd] *a.* 载人的; 人操纵的: ~ space flight 载人的宇宙飞行

mannequin [ˈmænikin] *n.* ① 人体模型 ② (以穿时装供展览为职业的) 女模特儿, 时装模特儿

manner [ˈmænə] *n.* ① 方式, 样式; 方法 ② [复] 礼貌; 规矩 ③态度; 举止; 风度: His ~ showed his frankness. 他的态度说明了他的坦率。 / have ~ as well as good manners 不但很有礼貌而且态度大方 ④ 习惯: It is his ~ to be humorous. 他老是幽默得很。⑤[复]风俗; 生活方式: a novel of ~s 社会风俗小说 ⑥ (文艺上的) 风格; 手法: a ~ of one's own 自成一家的风格 ⑦种类: pay attention to *all ~ of* things 留心各种各样的事情 ‖*by .all ~ of means* 无论如何 / *by no ~ of means* 见 **means** / *have no ~ of right* 毫无权利 / *in a ~* 在某种意义上; 在一定程度上; 有点 / *in a ~ of speaking* [古]不妨这样; 说起来 / *in like ~* 同样地 / *shark's ~* [俚] 贪心, 贪婪 / *to the ~ born* 从小就习惯; 生来就适合 ‖**~ed** *a.* ①[用以构成复合词]礼貌…的: well-~ed 很有礼貌的 ②具有特殊风格的(尤指艺术上矫揉造作等风格的) / **~less** *a.* 没有礼貌的

mannerism [ˈmænərizəm] *n.* ① (常指文艺上矫揉造作的) 个人惯用的格调 (或表现手法), 过分强调独特风格 ② (说话、举止等的) 癖性, 习气

mannerly [ˈmænəli] *a. & ad.* 有礼貌的 (地) ‖**mannerliness** *n.*

manoeuvre [məˈnuːvə] **I** *n.* ①【军】(部队、舰艇的) 机动, 调动; (船只、飞机、车辆的) 机动动作: a mass of ~ 实施机动集团 / Inverted flight is an acrobatic ~ of the plane. 倒飞是飞机的一种特技动作。② [复]【军】对抗演习: carry out grand ~s 举行大规模演习 / anti-air-raid ~s 防空演习 ③策略; 花招 **II** ❶ *vi.* ① (部队、舰艇等) 实施机动, 调动; 演习: The fleet is *manoeuvring.* 舰队正在进行演习。② 用策略; 要花招: He ~d successfully to get them go with him. 他成功地使他们都同意和他一起去。❷ *vt.* ① 调动; 使演习

② 设法使… ③ (敏捷地) 操纵; 使 (飞机) 作特技飞行: ~ a tractor through a muddy paddy field 设法把拖拉机开过泥泞的稻田

manor [ˈmænə] *n.* ①庄园; 庄园中的宅第 ②【英史】采地, 采邑 ‖**~ial** [məˈnɔːriəl] *a.* ‖**~ house** 庄园主的住宅

manse [mæns] *n.* 牧师住宅

mansion [ˈmænʃən] *n.* ① 大厦, 大楼 ②宅第; 官邸 ③[主英][常用复] 公寓大厦 ④ (大楼中的) 一套房间 ⑤【天】宿: lunar ~s 二十八宿

mantel [ˈmæntl] *n.* 壁炉架; 壁炉台 ‖**~-board** *n.* 壁炉架 / ‖**~piece**, ‖**~shelf** *n.* 壁炉台 / ‖**~tree** *n.* 壁炉棚

mantis [ˈmæntis] ([复] mantises 或 mantes [ˈmænti:z]) *n.* 螳螂

mantle [ˈmæntl] **I** *n.* ① 披风, 斗篷 ② 覆盖物; 罩, 幕: a ~ of snow 一层雪 / the ~ of night 夜幕 ③ (煤气灯的) 白炽罩 ④ (高炉的) 环架壳 ⑤ 壁炉架 ⑥【地】地幔 ⑦【解】外表: brain ~ 脑外表 ⑧ (软体动物的) 套膜; (鸟的) 翕 **II** ❶ *vt.* (用披风等) 盖, 罩, 覆盖: The mountains are ~d in silver. 丛山披上了银装。❷ *vi.* ① (液体) 表面上结皮, 被盖上泡沫: The milk ~d in the cup. 杯子里的牛奶面上结了一层膜。② 笼罩; 覆盖: Dawn ~d in the sky. 满天曙光。③(血液)涌上面颊; (脸) 发红, 涨红: The child's face ~d with blushes. 孩子脸上泛起了红晕。④(鹰)展开翅膀 ‖*One's ~ falls on sb.* 衣钵传给某人。/ *take over* (或 *inherit*) *the ~ of sb.* 继承某人的衣钵 ‖**~d** *a.* 披着斗篷的; 覆盖着的

manual [ˈmænjuəl] **I** *a.* ① 手的; 用手 (操作) 的: 手工做的: ~ training (学校等的) 手工课, 手工训练 / a ~ fire engine 手压灭火机 / ~ exercises 【军】步枪操作练习 / a ~ alphabet (聋哑者用的) 手语字母 / a sign ~ 亲笔签名 ② 体力的: a ~ worker 体力劳动者 ③【律】实际占有的 **II** *n.* ①手册, 指南: a shorthand ~ 速记手册 ② (风琴等的) 键盘 ③ (兵器) 教范: the ~ of arms 兵器教范 ‖**~ism** *n.* (对聋哑者的) 手势教法 / **~ly** *ad.* 用手, 用手工操作, 人工地

manufacture [,mænjuˈfæktʃə] **I** ❶ *vt.* ① (大量) 制造, 加工: ~ paper *from* rags (或 ~ rags *into* paper) 用破布造纸 ②粗制滥造 (文艺作品等) ③ 捏造, 虚构 (证据、借口等): a ~d tale 虚构的故事 ❷ *vi.* 制造 **II** *n.* ① (大量) 制造: the ~ of high-precision machine tools 高精密度机床的制造 ② 制造业: the cloth ~ 织布业 / the glass ~ 玻璃制造业 ③制造品, 产品: silk ~s 丝织品 ④ (文艺作品等的) 粗制滥造

manufacturer [,mænjuˈfæktʃərə] *n.* ①制造人; 制造商, 工厂主 ②制造厂

manufacturing [,mænjuˈfæktʃəriŋ] *a.* 制造的, 生产的: a ~ plant 制造厂 / the ~ industry 制造业 / turn a consuming city into a ~ city 把消费城市变为生产城市 / a series of ~ projects 一系列的生产计划

manure [mə'njuə] **I** ***n.*** (人、畜的)粪;粪肥;肥料: barnyard ～ 厩肥 / green ～ 绿肥 / chemical ～ 化肥 / accumulate (或 collect) ～ 积肥 / apply ～ 施肥 / a ～ pit 粪坑 **II** ***vt.*** 给(土地)施肥,施肥于… ‖**manurial** [mə'njuəriəl] ***a.***

manuscript ['mænjuskript] ***n.*** 手稿;打字稿;底稿,原稿;手写本 ‖***in*** ～ 以原稿形式,未付印的: a novel *in* ～ 未付印的小说(稿)

many ['meni] **I** (more [mɔː], most [moust]) ***a.*** [后接复数名词]许多的,多的: How ～ people were there at the meeting? 有多少人到会? / There aren't ～ typhoons this year. 今年台风不多。 **II** ***pron.*** [用作复]许多人;许多: *Many* of them have left for the countryside. 他们中许多人已去农村了。 **III** ***n.*** [用作复] 多数; [the ～] 多数人,群众 ‖***a good*** ～ 很多,相当多 / ***a great*** ～ 许许多多,极多: We have *a great* ～ (things) to do at present. 我们当前有许许多多事要做。/ ***as*** ～ 一样多的,同样数目的: I have called on him three times in *as* ～ days. 我已在三天里访过他三次。 / ***as*** ～ ***again*** 再同样多的,再同样数目的: We have six trucks, but we shall need *as* ～ *again*. 我们有了六辆卡车,可是还需要六辆。/ ***as*** ～ ***as*** 和…一样多: Take *as* ～ *as* you want. 你要多少就拿多少。/ ***as*** (或 ***like***) ***so*** ～ 象同数的…一样: Viewed from the hilltop, the three streams extend *as so* ～ ribbons. 从山顶上看,三条河流伸展出去象三条彩带。/ ***half as*** ～ ***again*** 加半倍,一倍半 / ～ ***a*** (或 ***an, another***) [后接单数名词] 许多的,多的,一个又一个的: ～ *a* time 许多次 / ***Many a little makes a mickle.*** [谚] 积少成多。(或: 集腋成裘。) / ～ ***a long day*** 见 **day** / ～***'s the*** 有许多 / *Many's the* time I have seen him work late into the night. 有好多次我看到他工作到深夜。/ ***one too*** ～ 见 **one** / ***one too*** ～ ***for*** 见 **one** / ***so*** ～ 那么多的;同数目的: Do you need *so* ～? 你需要那么多吗? / pack *so* ～ machines in *so* ～ cases 有几台机器就装几箱 ‖～**fold** ***ad.*** 许多倍地 ‖'～-'**angled** ***a.*** 多角的 / '～-'**headed** ***a.*** 多头的 / '～**plies** [复] ***n.*** [用作单]重瓣胃(反刍类动物的第三胃) / '～-'**sided** ***a.*** ①多边的: a ～*-sided* figure 多边形 ②(才能等)多方面的: ～*-sided* efforts 各方面的努力 / men of ～*-sided* abilities 多面手 / '～'**sidedness** ***n.*** ①多边 ②(才能等的)多面性

map [mæp] **I** ***n.*** ① 地图: a ～ scale 地图比例尺 ②天体图 ③(类似地图的)图: a ～ board 图板 / an outline ～ 略图 / a weather ～ 气象图 ④[美俚] 面孔 ⑤[美俚] (存款不足的) 空头支票 **II** (mapped; mapping) ***vt.*** ①绘制…的地图,在地图上表示出 ②(为制地图而)勘测 ③(详细地)制订,筹划 (*out*): ～ *out* an overall plan 制订全面规划 ‖***off the*** ～ [口] ①不重要的 ②废了的 / ***on the*** ～ [口] ① 重要的 ② 出名的 / ***wipe off the*** ～ [美] 把…消灭掉 ‖～**less** ***a.*** 没有地图的 ‖～**measurer** 量图仪,曲线仪(在地图上滚动以测出两地实际距离的一种仪器)

maple ['meipl] ***n.*** ①【植】槭树,枫树; [M-] 槭属 ②槭木 ③槭树汁味;槭糖味 ④淡棕色;灰黄色 ‖～ **sugar** 槭糖 / ～ **syrup** 槭糖浆,槭树汁

mar [mɑː] (marred; marring ['mɑːriŋ]) ***vt.*** 损坏,毁坏,弄糟: A shower *marred* an otherwise perfect day. 美中不足,那天下了一场阵雨。 ‖***make or*** ～ 见 **make** ‖'～**-plot** ***n.*** 因干预而坏事的人

marabou ['mærəbuː] ***n.*** ①【动】秃鹳(尤指产于非洲和东印度的) ②秃鹳毛 ③【纺】马拉布生丝;单丝经缎

marathon ['mærəθən] **I** ***n.*** [有时作 M-] ①【体】马拉松长跑(全长 42.195 公里) ②(游泳、滑冰等的)长距离比赛;耐力比赛 **II** ***a.*** [有时作 M-] 马拉松式的;耐力的 **III** ***vi.*** 参加马拉松长跑(或比赛) ‖～**er** ***n.*** 马拉松运动员 / ～**ian** [ˌmærə'θouniən], ～**ic** [ˌmærə'θɔnik] ***a.*** ‖～ **race** 马拉松赛跑

maraud [mə'rɔːd] ***vi., vt.*** & ***n.*** 掳掠,抢劫,攫夺 ‖～**er** ***n.*** ①掳掠者,抢劫者: air ～*ers* 空中强盗 ②攫食的动物

marble ['mɑːbl] **I** ***n.*** ①大理石,大理岩,云石;大理石制品 ②大理石状的东西 ③大理石花纹 ④(游戏用的玻璃、石头等做的)弹子; [～s] [用作单] 打弹子游戏 **II** ***a.*** 大理石的;大理石般的: a ～ statue 大理石雕像 / ～ paper 云石纸(作簿面等用) / a ～ breast 铁石心肠 **III** ***vt.*** [常用被动语态]把(书边、纸等)弄上大理石花纹: a book with ～*d* edge 云纹状边的书 ‖***Elgin*** ['elgin] ～***s*** 不列颠博物馆所藏的古希腊大理石雕刻 ‖～**ize** ***vt.*** 把…弄上大理石花纹 / **marbly** ***a.*** 大理石的;大理石般的: a *marbly* building 大理石建筑物 / the *marbly* calm of the lake 平静如镜的湖面 ‖'～**-dome** ***n.*** [美俚]笨蛋 / '～'**hearted** ***a.*** 铁石心肠的,冷酷的

March [mɑːtʃ] ***n.*** 三月(略作 Mar.) ‖～ **brown** 蜉蝣;(钓鱼用的)蜉蝣似的假蚊钩 / ～ **hare** 交尾期的野兔

march[1] [mɑːtʃ] **I** ❶ ***vi.*** ①(齐步)前进,行进;行军: ②走过,通过 ③(事件等)进行,进展 ❷ ***vt.*** 使行进;使行军;迫使前进: The prisoners of war were ～*ed off* to the company headquarters. 战俘被押往连部。**II** ***n.*** ① 行进,行军; (部队一日的)行程: a forced ～ 强行军,兼程行军 / a rapid ～ 急行军 / a ～ column (formation) 行军纵队(队形) / Forward ～! (口令)开步走! ②步伐,步调: a quick (slow) ～ 快步(慢步)走 ③[the ～] 进行,进展: the ～ of events 事情的进展 / the ～ of science 科学的发展 ④长途跋涉 ⑤进行曲: military ～*es* 进行曲 / a dead (或 funeral) ～ 送葬曲 ‖***a death*** ～ 向着死亡的进军(指战俘往集中营的行军) / ***a rogue's*** ～ 旧时将士兵逐出兵营时奏的乐曲;将某人逐出某团体时的起哄声/ ***on the*** ～ 行军中;进行中: The equipment improvement was *on the* ～. 设备改进工作正

在进行中。/ *steal a ~ on sb.* (偷偷地)抢在某人之前 ‖*~er n.* 行进者，行军者；游行者 ‖*~* **past** *n.* 【军】分列式 / '*~-'rally* *n.* 游行集会

march² [mɑːtʃ] **I** *n.* ①【史】边界，边境；[常用复] 英格兰和苏格兰(或威尔士)的接界地区 ②(有争端的)边境地区 **II** *vi.* 交界，交接 (*upon, with*) ‖*~er n.* 边界地区居民

marchioness ['mɑːʃənis] *n.* 侯爵夫人；女侯爵

mare¹ [mɛə] *n.* 牝马，母马；牝驴 ‖*a grey ~* 胜过丈夫的妻子 / *Money makes the ~ (to) go.* 见 **money** / *ride* (或 *go on*) *shanks' ~* [美俚] 走着去，骑着两脚马去 / *The grey ~ is the better horse.* [谚]牝鸡司晨。(指妻子当家) / *win the ~ or lose the halter* 孤注一掷 ‖*~'s nest* ①海市蜃楼般的东西；骗人的东西 ②乱糟糟的地方；混乱，杂乱 / *~'s tail* ①【气】马尾云 ②【植】杉叶藻

mare² ['mɛəri] ([复] **maria** ['mɛəriə]) *n.* ①【天】(月亮、火星表面的)海(指阴暗区) ②海 ‖**clausum** ['klɔːsəm] 领海 / *~ liberum* ['laibərəm] 公海 / *~ nostrum* ['nɔstrəm] 属于一国(或两国、数国共有)的海

margarine [ˌmɑːdʒə'riːn], **margarin** [ˌmɑːdʒə'rin] *n.* 人造黄油，代黄油

margin ['mɑːdʒin] **I** *n.* ①页边的空白；栏外: leave a wide ~ *in* (或 *on*) the page 在纸上留一道宽边 / make notes *on* the ~ 在页边作注释 ②边缘；【军】图廓: the ~ of a lake (forest) 湖(森林)的边缘 ③界限: a joke that is *on* the ~ of good taste 有点不登大雅之堂的笑话 / *~ line*【船】(舱破后水面的安全)限界线 ④ (时间、花费上保留的)余地，余裕 ⑤差数；幅度: increase *by* a wide (或 big) ~ 大幅度地增长 ⑥【商】(成本与售价的)差额，赚头；保证金，垫头: a narrow ~ of profit 微利，薄利 **II** *vt.* ①加边于；成为…的边: trees *~ing* the shore 沿岸的一行树 ②加旁注于: ~ every page with comments 在每页的页边加上注解 ③【商】为…付保证金

marginal ['mɑːdʒinəl] *a.* ①记在页边的；有旁注的: ~ notes 旁注 / a ~ manuscript 有旁注的手稿 ②边缘的，边际的；边沿地区的: ~ people 边远地区的人们 ③介乎两者之间的；(文化等)结合而彼此未同化的: a ~ seat (竞选中双方票数接近)可能为任何一方争得的席位 ④限界的，勉强够格的 ⑤【经】(土地)只有限界价值的，收益仅敷支出的: ~ profits 限界利润，边际利润 / ~ ability 勉强合格的能力 ‖*~ity* [ˌmɑːdʒi'næliti] *n.* / *~ly ad.* 在边上，边沿地: be *~ly* qualified 勉强合格 ‖*utility*【经】边际效用

marguerite [ˌmɑːgə'riːt] *n.*【植】①木茼蒿 ②雏菊 ③青黄菊属植物

marine [mə'riːn] **I** *a.* ①海的；海生的，海产的: ~ geology 海洋地质(学) / the ~ belt 领海 / ~ products 海产物 ②船舶的；船用的；航海的: a ~ engine 轮机 / ~ engineering 船舶工程(学) / a ~ surveyor 验船师 / ~ soap 海水皂(用椰

子油制，可溶解于海水) / a ~ chart 航海图 / a ~ store 船用物品商店 / ~ stores 船舶用具，旧船具 / a ~ railway (曳船上岸的)滑道，船排 ③海上的；海事的；海运的: ~ law 航海法 / ~ insurance 海上保险，水险 ④海军陆战队的: a ~ corps 海军陆战队 / the (U.S.) *Marine Corps* 美国海军陆战队 / ~ barracks 海军陆战队兵营 **II** *n.* ①[只用单][总称](一个国家的)船舶；海运业: the merchant (或 mercantile) ~ [总称](一个国家的)商船 ②海军陆战队士兵(或军官)；[英]两栖突击作战专家: a *Marine* First (Second) Class (英)海军陆战队一(二)等兵 / blue (red) *~s*【史】海军陆战队炮(步)兵 ③(法国等国家的)海军部 ④海景画 ⑤[美俚]空酒瓶 (=dead ~) ‖*Tell that to the ~s.* 谁信你那一套!

mariner ['mærinə] *n.* 水手，海员: a master ~ 商船船长 ‖*~'s compass* 航海罗盘

marionette [ˌmæriə'net] *n.* 活动木偶；提线木偶

marital ['mæritl] *a.* ① 婚姻的 ② [古] 丈夫的 ‖*~ly ad.*

maritime ['mæritaim] *a.* ① 海(上)的，海事的；海运的: a ~ climate 海洋性气候 / ~ law 海商法 / a ~ court 海事法庭 / ~ insurance 海上保险 / the *Maritime* Customs 海关 ②沿海的；近海的: ~ provinces 沿海各省 / ~ people 沿海地区人民 ③海员的: He has a ~ appearance. 他的外貌象个海员。

mark¹ [mɑːk] **I** *n.* ①痕迹；斑点，瘢疤: an ink ~ 墨水渍 / the ~ of an old wound 旧伤痕 ②记号；符号；标记，唛头；商标；邮戳: the *~s* on a box of merchandise 一箱商品上的标记 / send sb. a gift as a ~ of esteem 送给某人礼物以表敬意 ③标识；刻度；【海】(测深线上的)测标: The tower is a ~ for fliers. 飞行员把这座塔楼作为标识。/ a tide ~ 潮标 / Plimsoll ~【海】(船舶)载重线标志 (=load line ~) ④ (文件上代替签名的)花押 ⑤(考试等的)分数；(品行等的)等第: full *~s* 满分 / give sb. a good (bad) ~ 给某人以好的(不好的)评分 ⑥标志，特征 ⑦靶子；目标；指标: hit (miss) the ~ 打中(没打中)目标；达到(没达到)目的 / a ~ of gossips 被人讲闲话的对象 / The production figures for this month have topped the 5,000 ~. 本月份生产数字已超过了五千大关。⑧ 标准；常态: up to (below) the ~ 达到(未达到)标准 ⑨显要；名声: a man of ~ 要人物 ⑩ (深刻的)印象；影响: The new machines on exhibition left their ~ on the visitors. 展出的新机器给观众留下了深刻的印象。⑪ 注意: These technical improvements are worthy of ~. 这些技术上的改进值得注意。⑫起跑线 ⑬ (拳击用语)心窝 ⑭【史】中世纪日耳曼村社的公地 ⑮ [M-] (与数字连用表示武器等的)…型，…式: a *Mark* III tank 三号坦克 **II** ❶ *vt.* ①留痕迹于；作记号于，标明: a dirt road *~ed* with footprints 留有脚印的泥路 / ~ the parcel

"Fragile" and "Handle with care" 在包裹上标明"易碎物品"和"小心轻放" ②[常用被动语态] (人、动物等身上)具有(斑纹等): wings ~*ed* with white lines 有白色条纹的翅膀 ③明显表示,表明: ~ one's approval by nodding 以点头表明赞许 ④ 标志; 表示…的特征: activities ~*ing* the 20th anniversary of 纪念(或庆祝)…二十周年的活动 ⑤记下;记录: ~ in one's notebook the main points of a speech 在本子中记下讲话的要点 ⑥注意,留心: *Mark* my words! 你(留心)听着! / *Mark* carefully how it is done. 注意这话是怎么干的。⑦给(试卷等)打分数 ⑧在…上贴项目(或尺寸等)标签 ⑨给(比赛等)记得分 ⑩使…注定要;预定: The pig is ~*ed* for slaughter next week. 这头猪下星期要杀了。⑪标出…的界限 ⑫[英](球赛中)钉(人) ❷ *vi.* ①作记号(或符号)②注意 ③(比赛中)记得分 ‖*an easy* (或 *soft*) ~ 易受欺骗的人, 傻瓜 / *beside the* ~ 没有打中目标;不切题,不相关 / *beyond the* ~ 越出界限;过度,过分 / *Bless the* ~! =God bless the ~! / *cut the* ~ (箭)未达靶子而先落下 / *get off the* ~ 起跑;开始 / *God bless the* ~! ①不要见怪!(提及令人厌恶的事情时表示道歉)②天哪!(表示惊愕、嘲笑、讽刺等)/ *have a* ~ *on* 喜欢,爱好 / *make one's* ~ 使自己出名 / ~ *down* ①记下: ~ *that down* in one's notebook 把这一点记在本子上 ②标低(商品)的价目 / ~ *off* 划分出: The boundaries are clearly ~*ed off* on the map. 边界的划分在地图上标得很清楚。/ ~ *out* ① ~ *off* ②规划 / ~ *out for* 使…注定要;事先选定 / ~ *sth. with a white stone* 标记某事以示喜庆(或吉利)/ ~ *time* 见 *time* / ~ *up* ①把…标出 ②标高(商品)的价目; 赊欠(帐项)/ *not feel up to the* ~ [口]身体有点不舒服 / *off the* ~ 没有打中目标;不相关 / *On your* ~*s*! (赛跑出发前的口令)各就各位! / *overshoot the* ~ ①过其词 ②做得过分 / *over the* ~ 超过限度 / *pass the* ~ 把身受的事转施于别人 / *Save the* ~! =God bless the ~! / *the* ~ *of mouth* 表示马龄的齿凹 / *toe the* ~ ①(赛跑时)用脚尖踏在起步线上; 严守规则 ②承担责任(或后果)/ *wide of the* ~ ①未击中目标;毫不相关 ‖~*down n.* 降低标价;(价格中)标低的金额 / '~*up n.* ①提高标价;(价格中)标高的金额 ②(加在商品成本上的)毛利

mark² [mɑːk] *n.* ①马克(德意志民主共和国、德意志联邦共和国及旧时德国等的货币单位)②金银的重量单位(约等于八盎斯,旧时用于欧洲大陆)

marked [mɑːkt] *a.* ①打上记号的;有标记的,有唛头的 ②显著的;清楚的: make ~ progress 取得显著的进步 / a man with ~ features 面部特征显著的人 ③被监视的; 受人注目的: a ~ man 被监视的人,可疑人物,受到敌视的人;众所瞩目的人 ‖~*ly* ['mɑːkidli] *ad.* 显著地 / ~*ness* ['mɑːkidnis] *n.* 显著

marker ['mɑːkə] *n.* ①打记号(或分数)的人 ②(比赛中的)记分员; 记分器; [美俚](比赛中的)得分 ③书签 ④[美]纪念碑; 墓碑; 里程碑; 标示物: a boundary ~ 界标 / a street ~ 路牌 ⑤ 标识器; 指示器;【无】指点标: ~ beacon 指点标,标志信标 / ~ light 标识灯光,信标灯光 ⑥【军】标靶兵;标兵, 标杆, 旗标; [英]【军】照明弹

market ['mɑːkit] **I** *n.* ①(交易)市场: the money ~ 金融市场 / the (European) Common *Market* (欧洲)共同市场 ②(集)市; 菜市(场);商业中心; 集市日; 市场中买卖的人群: The next ~ is on 15th. 下次集市是在十五日。/ the free ~ 自由市场 / the black ~ 黑市 / go to (the) ~ to buy food 上菜场去买菜 ③[美]食品店: a meat ~ 肉类食品店 ④市面,市况;行情,市价: ~ supply and demand 市面供求 / ~ value 市面价值(区别于成本和帐面价值)/ a brisk (dull) ~ 兴旺(呆滞)市面 / The ~ rose (fell). 行情上涨(下跌)了。⑤推销地区; 销路; 需要: There is a good ~ for these goods. 这些商品销路很好。**II** ❶ *vt.* (在市场上)销售: ~ one million head of livestock a year 每年销售一百万头牲口 ❷ *vi.* (在市场上)购买(或卖出): go ~*ing* 到市场去买(或卖)东西, 赶集 ‖*at the* ~ 照市价 / *away from the* ~ 照(顾客的)限价(不照市价)/ *be in the* ~ *for sth.* 在市场上觅购某物,想买进某物 / *be on the* ~ 被拍卖出售 / *bull the* ~ 【商】做多头(抬高市场价格)/ *buyer's* ~ 买方有利的市面 / *come into the* ~ 在市场上出售,上市 / *corner the* ~ 囤积居奇 / *engross the* ~ 购进某物的全部存货以便垄断市场 / *hold the* ~ 垄断市面 / *lose the* ~ 失去买卖的机会 / *make a* ~ (为引起对某企业的注意,故意在交易所买进卖出该企业股票)制造兴旺气象 / *make a* (或 *one's*) ~ *of* 把…作为赚钱的机会(或目的)/ *make one's* ~ 出售存货 / *mar one's own* (*sb.'s*) ~ 糟蹋自己(某人)的生意;使自己(某人)遭受损失 / *milk the* ~ [美]操纵市场从中牟利 / *overstand one's* ~ 坚持过高条件太久致失去买卖机会 / *play the* ~ 投机倒把 / *put sth. on the* ~ 把某物拿到市场上出售 / *raid the* ~ (制造恐慌气氛)扰乱市面 / *raise the* ~ *upon* [口]向…要高价 / *seller's* ~ 卖方有利的市面 / *the kerb* ~ 场外证券市场 ‖~*eer* [ˌmɑːkiˈtiə] *n.* 市场上的卖主;市场商人 ②(二十世纪六十年代)主张英国加入欧洲共同市场的人 / ~*er n.* 在市场中买卖的人 ‖~ *cross* 市场中的十字形房屋(常作市场办公用)/ ~ *day* 集市日 / ~ *garden* 以供应市场为目的的菜园 / ~ *overt* 公开市场 / '~*place n.* 市场 / ~ *research* 市场调查(指调查消费者对某种商品或服务的意见等)/ '~*re,search vt.* 调查(消费者)对某种商品(或服务)的意见 / ~ *town* 集镇

marketable ['mɑːkitəbl] *a.* 可销售的;适合市场销售的;有销路的;市场买卖的: a ~ product 可销售的产品 / ~ grain 商品粮 / ~ value 市场价

值 ‖**marketability** [ˌmɑːkitə'biliti] *n.* / **marketably** *ad.*

marketing ['mɑːkitiŋ] *n.* 在市场上购买(或卖出);销售(学): do one's ~ 到市场上去买(或卖)东西 / a supply and ~ co-op 供销合作社 ‖~ **research** 销售调查(指调查市场范围及产品成本等)

marking ['mɑːkiŋ] *n.* ①打记号;作标志;记分: a ~ device 标示器材 ②记号;识别标志: a ground ~ 地面标志 ③(兽皮、鸟羽等的)斑纹 ‖~ **ga(u)ge** 划线规 / ~ **ink** (衬衫、被单等上印记姓名等用的)不褪色墨水 / ~ **iron** 烙印铁

marksman ['mɑːksmən] ([复] marksmen) *n.* ①射手;神枪手 ②[美][军]二等射手;轻兵器射手的最低等级 ‖~**ship** *n.* 射击术,枪法

marmalade ['mɑːməleid] *n.* 果酱;橘子酱

maroon[1] [mə'ruːn] **I** *n.* ①栗色,紫酱色 ②爆竹,鞭炮 **II** *a.* 栗色的,紫酱色的

maroon[2] [mə'ruːn] **I** *n.* ①十七、十八世纪时受压迫而逃亡到西印度群岛等地的黑奴(或其后代) ②被放逐到孤岛的人 **II** *vt.* ①放逐到孤岛(或无人烟的海滩) ②使处于孤立无援(或无法脱逃)的境地 **②** *vi.* ①从奴役下逃亡 ②闲荡 ③[美]去野营,去郊游野餐 ‖~**er** *n.* 海盗;肆无忌惮的冒险家

marquee [mɑː'kiː] *n.* ①大帐篷 ②【建】大门罩

marquis ['mɑːkwis] *n.* 侯爵 ‖~**ate** ['mɑːkwizit] *n.* 侯爵地位(或身分);侯爵领地

marriage ['mæridʒ] *n.* ①结婚;婚姻;结婚生活: freedom of ~ 婚姻自由 / a relation by ~ 姻亲 ②结婚仪式,婚礼: a civil ~ (西方国家中)不采用宗教仪式的结婚 ③密切结合 ‖a ~ of convenience 基于利害关系的结婚(指封建和资本主义社会中为追求社会地位或政治、经济利益的结婚) / a shotgun ~ ①由于怀孕而被迫的结婚 ②强迫的结合(或协调) / give sb. in ~ 把某人嫁出 / take sb. in ~ 娶某人 ‖~**able** *a.* 达到结婚年龄的;(年龄)适宜结婚的 ‖~ **articles**, ~ **contract** (婚前预定财产权、继承权等的)婚姻契约 / ~ **licence** 结婚登记证 / ~ **lines** [英]结婚证书 / ~ **portion** 妆奁,嫁妆 / ~ **settlement** 结婚时分授财产给妻子等的处理

married ['mærid] **I** *a.* ①结了婚(而未丧偶或离婚)的,有配偶的;夫妇的;婚姻的: ~ life 婚后生活 / a newly ~ couple 一对新婚夫妇 ②密切结合的 **II** *n.* [常用复]已婚的人: the young ~s 已婚的青年人

marrow[1] ['mærou] *n.* ①髓,骨髓: the spinal ~ 脊髓 / be chilled to the ~ 寒冷彻骨 ②精髓,精华;实质:the very ~ and substance of the matter 事情的要旨 ③活力,生气 ④[英](南瓜等)葫芦科蔬菜 ‖~**less** *a.* 无髓的 ‖'~**bone** *n.* 髓骨;[复][谑]膝: get (或 go) down on one's ~bones [谑]跪下 / ride in the ~bone coach (或 stage) [俚]坐两脚车去,步行 / '~**fat** *n.* 一种大豌豆

(=~fat pea) / ~ **spoon** (刮骨髓用的)细长匙子

marrow[2] ['mærou] *n.* [苏格兰]配偶;配对物;很相象的人(或物): a pair of gloves that is not ~s 不成对的两只手套

marry[1] ['mæri] **❶** *vt.* ①娶,嫁,和…结婚 ②[常用被动语态]使成婚: They are going to be (或 get) married on New Year's Day. 他们将于元旦结婚。 ③把(女儿等)嫁出 ④(牧师等)为…证婚 ⑤使密切结合;【海】(不增加围长)接合(绳端) **❷** *vi.* 结婚;结合: He married late in life. 他结婚很晚。 / a ~ing man 一个想要结婚的男子 ‖Marry in haste and repent at leisure. [谚]草率结婚后悔多。 / ~ into 结婚后成为…家中的一员 / ~ with the left hand 与门第比自己低的人结婚

marry[2] ['mæri] *int.* [古][方]哎呀,真是 [= "Marry come up!", 表示惊愕、讥讽、愤怒等]

marsh [mɑːʃ] *n.* 沼泽,湿地: reed ~es 芦苇荡 / salt ~es 盐(碱)滩 ‖~ **gas** 沼气,甲烷 / '~**land** *n.* 沼泽地区,沼泽地 / '~**mallow** *n.* ①【植】药用蜀葵 ②果汁软糖 / ~ **marigold** 【植】驴蹄草 / ~ **ore** 【矿】沼铁矿

marshal ['mɑːʃəl] **I** *n.* ①【军】元帅;陆军元帅;相当于陆军元帅的其他军种将领;最高级指挥官;(英)空军元帅 (=Marshal of the RAF): an air chief ~ (英)空军上将 / an air ~ (英)空军中将 / an air vice-~ (英)空军少将 ②(集会的)司仪;(宫廷的)典礼官 ③【史】(中古时期王室的)司令官;宫内司法官 ④【军】宪兵上任 [=provost ~] ⑤美国的联邦法院的执行官;市执法官;市警察局长;消防队长 **II** (marshal(l)ed; marshal(l)ing) **❶** *vt.* ①排列,安排;整理: ~ the guests at a banquet 为参加宴会的客人安排(席位) / carefully ~ the arguments 仔细地整理论据 / ~ troops 集结部队 ②(讲究礼节地)引领; ~ ... into the presence of the minister 引领某人去见部长 ③调度(列车的各部分): ~ railway cars into a train 调配车厢组成列车 **❷** *vi.* 排列,集合 ‖~**cy**, ~**ship** *n.* 元帅的职位(或级别,权力)

marshal(l)ing ['mɑːʃəliŋ] *a.* ①把货车等编组的 ②【军】(营地等)用来集结军队准备出发的 ‖~ **yard** (铁道)编组车场

marsupial [mɑː'sjuːpjəl] **I** *a.* ①【动】有袋(目)的 ②袋状的 **II** *a.* 有袋(目)动物

martial ['mɑːʃəl] *a.* ①军事的,战争的: ~ music 军乐 ②军人的,英勇的,尚武的: the ~ spirit 尚武精神 ③[M-]【罗神】战神的;【天】火星的 ‖~**ism** *n.* 英勇,尚武 / ~**ize** *vt.* 使尚武 / ~**ly** *ad.* 英勇地,尚武地 ‖~ **law** 【军】军事管制法,戒严令: be under ~ law 在戒严期中;在戒严地区内

martin ['mɑːtin] *n.* 一种燕子: a house ~ 欧洲家燕 / a sand (或 bank) ~ 灰沙燕

martinet [ˌmɑːti'net] *n.* ①严峻的军纪官 ②厉行严格纪律的人

martyr ['mɑːtə] **I** *n.* ① 烈士,殉难者 ②殉教者,殉道者 ③ (因疾病等)长期受痛苦的人: be a ～ to rheumatism 长期受风湿病的折磨 **II** *vt.* ①杀害(坚持某种信仰者) ② 折磨 ‖**make a ～ of oneself** (假装)牺牲自己利益(或愿望等)以博得信誉 / **make a ～ of sb.** 使某人殉难;折磨某人 ‖**～dom** *n.* ① 殉难;牺牲 ② 折磨;受苦 / **～ize** ['mɑːtəraiz] *vt.* 使殉难;折磨 *vi.* 成为烈士,殉难

marvel ['mɑːvəl] **I** *n.* ① 令人惊奇的事物; (某一事物的)奇特的例子 (of): the ～s of modern science 近代科学的奇迹 / She is a ～ of patience. 她耐心得出奇。②[古]惊异,惊奇 **II** (marvel(l)ed, marvel(l)ing) ❶ *vi.* 惊异,惊奇 (at) ❷ *vt.* 对…感到惊异

marvel(l)ous ['mɑːviləs] *a.* ① 奇异的,奇迹般的;惊人的,不可思议的: a ～ creation by the workers 工人们奇迹般的创造 / the ～ 不可思议的各种东西 ②[口]了不起的,妙极的: The performance is simply ～! 演出简直好极了! ‖**～ly** *ad.* / **～ness** *n.*

mascot ['mæskət] *n.* (迷信的人认为能带来好运气的)吉祥的人(或动物、东西)

masculine ['mɑːskjulin] **I** *a.* ①男性的;男子气概的: a ～ style 男式 ②(女子)有男子气的 ③(组织、行业等)由男子组成(或控制)的 ④【语】阳性的 **II** *n.* ① 男性的东西 ②男子;男孩 ③【语】阳性;阳性词(如 man, cock 等) ‖**～ly** *ad.* / **～ness** *n.* / **masculinity** [,mæskju'liniti] *n.* / **masculinize** *vt.* 使男子化

mash¹ [mæʃ] **I** *n.* ① 麦芽浆(啤酒原料) ② 谷糠(或麦麸等)煮成的饲料 ③ 捣成糊状的东西;[俚]马铃薯泥: sausage and ～ 香肠和马铃薯泥 ④ 乱糟糟的一团 **II** *vt.* ① 把(麦芽)制成麦芽浆 ② 捣碎,捣烂;压碎: ～ed potatoes 马铃薯泥 ‖**～er** *n.* 捣碎者;捣碎器;制麦芽浆的工人 ‖**～ tub** 捣麦芽的大桶

mash² [mæʃ] *vt.* 向…调情求爱 ‖**～er** *n.* 调情求爱者

mask [mɑːsk] **I** *n.* ① 面具,面罩;防护面具; 口罩: a gas ～ 防毒面具 / an oxygen ～ 氧气面具 / a flu ～ 卫生口罩 ②假面具;伪装;遮盖物,遮蔽物: throw off one's (或 the) ～ 摘下假面具 / a ～ of snow on the ground 掩盖地面的一层雪 ③ (作建筑装饰等用的)假面;面部模型: a death ～ 在死者面部印制的模型 ④假面舞会;假面剧;假面剧剧本 ⑤[印]蒙片;[摄]蔽光框 ⑥(狗、狐等的)面,头;[动](蜻蜓的)脸盖 **II** ❶ *vt.* ① 在(脸)上戴面具 ② 掩饰(感情等);伪装,遮蔽: ～ one's real purpose 掩饰真实目的 / ～ a gun battery 把炮台伪装起来 ③阻碍(敌人)行动;妨碍(友军)射击 ④ 使模糊,使不被觉察: ～ undesirable flavours 使难闻的味道闻不出 / ～ a drug 使药吃起来不苦 ⑤[摄]用蔽光框修改(照相的大小、形状等);[印](制版时)用蒙片修正(底片色调) ❷ *vi.* ① 戴面具,化装;参加化装舞会 ② 掩饰;伪装起来 ‖**～er** *n.*

戴面具的人;参加假面舞会的人

masked [mɑːskt] *a.* ① 戴面具的,化装的: a ～ ball 假面舞会 ②(感情等)被掩饰的;有伪装的,遮蔽了的: ～ guns 伪装了的大炮 / a ～ gun battery 掩蔽的炮台 / ～ pupa 【动】隐蛹 ③潜伏的,潜在的: ～ fever 【医】潜热

mason ['meisn] **I** *n.* ① 石工;砖石工;泥瓦工,圬工 ② [M-] 共济会成员 **II** *vt.* 用石料建造;用石加固 ‖**～ic, Masonic** [mə'sɔnik] *a.* 共济会成员的;共济会的 / **～ry** *n.* ①石工(业);圬工(业) ②砖石建筑 ③ [M-] 共济会纲领;共济会仪式; [集合名词]共济会成员

masque [mɑːsk] *n.* ① 假面舞会 ②(英国十六、十七世纪流行的)假面剧;假面剧剧本 ‖**～r** *n.* 参加假面舞会的人

masquerade [,mæskə'reid, ,mɑːskə'reid] **I** *n.* ① 化装舞会,化装聚会 ② 化装舞会上穿的服装 ③伪装;掩饰 **II** *vi.* ① 化装;参加化装舞会(或聚会) ②假装,冒充 ‖**～r** *n.* 参加化装舞会(或聚会)者;伪装者

Mass, mass¹ [mæs, mɑːs] *n.* 【宗】弥撒(尤指天主教的领圣餐); 弥撒的音乐: high ～ (有烧香、奏乐等的)大弥撒 / low ～ (无奏乐等的)小弥撒 / say ～ for 为…作弥撒,为…念经

mass² [mæs] **I** *n.* ①(聚成一体的)团,块,堆,片,群: a ～ of hot air 一团热空气 / floating ～es of ice 大块大块的浮冰 / a ～ of sand 一堆沙 / a ～ of green 一大片绿色 ②众多;大量,大宗 ③ [the ～es] 群众,民众: from the ～es, to the ～es 从群众中来,到群众中去 ④ 大部分,主体;总体 ⑤【军】集团纵队;密集横队: a ～ of manoeuvre 实施机动集团 ⑥【物】质量: the law of conservation of ～ 质量守恒定律 ⑦【矿】体: tabular ～ 板状体,层状体 / molten ～ 熔融体 / ore ～ 矿体 **II** *a.* ① 群众的,群众性的: a ～ meeting 群众大会 / ～ criticism and repudiation 大批判 / a ～ magazine 通俗杂志 / ～ education 民众教育 ② 大量的;大规模的;大批的: a ～-circulation magazine 大量发行的杂志 / weapons of ～ destruction 大规模毁灭性武器 / ～ production 成批生产 ③整个儿的,总的:the ～ effect of the treatment 总的疗效 ④【军】集中的,密集(队形)的: ～ bombing 集中轰炸,密集轰炸 / ～ flights 大机群飞行 / ～ tactics 密集战术 **III** ❶ *vt.* 集中,聚集: ～ forces for action 集结兵力准备作战 / a ～ed formation 【军】密集队形 ❷ *vi.* 集聚起来: Dark clouds are ～ing in the west. 西方乌云密布。‖**be a ～ of** 遍布着…,遍体是…: He is a ～ of bruises. 他遍体鳞伤。/ **in the ～** 总体上,整个儿地: view a problem in the ～ 总的来看一个问题 / **the (great) ～ of** 大多数,大部分 / **the (great) ～ of** the people 人民的大多数 ‖**～-based** *a.* 有广大群众基础的 / **～ communication** 有广泛影响的宣传工具(指报纸、广播、电视等) / **～ defect** 【物】质量亏损 / **'～-'energy equation** 【物】质能相当性 / **～**

medium =~ communication / ~ **number** (原子)质量数 / **Mass Observation** (英国的)民意调查 / '~-**pro,duce** *vt.* 成批生产: This type of tip-truck is now being ~-*produced*. 这种自动卸货卡车现正在成批生产。 / '~-**pro,duced** *a.* 成批生产的 / ~ **selection**【生】混合选择 / ~ **spectrograph** 质谱仪 / ~ **spectrometer** 质谱测定计

massacre ['mæsəkə] **I** *n.* ①大屠杀;残杀 ②(牲畜的)成批屠宰 **II** *vt.* (大规模地)屠杀;残杀 ‖~ *of the innocents* 见 **innocent**

massage ['mæsɑːʒ] **I** *n.* 按摩;推拿 **II** *vt.* 给(某人或身体某部位)按摩(或推拿) ‖~**r, massagist** *n.* 按摩师 ‖~ **parlo(u)r** 按摩院

masseur [mæ'sɔː] *n.* 男按摩师 ‖**masseuse** [mæ-'sɔːz] *n.* 女按摩师

massive ['mæsiv] *a.* ①大而重的,厚实的;(面貌五官等)粗大的: a ~ pillar 粗大的柱子 / a ~ volume of 800 pages 八百页的一册厚书 / a ~ jaw 大下巴 ②魁伟的,结实的;给人深刻印象的 ③大规模的,巨大的;大量的: ~ retaliation 大规模的报复 / a ~ dose of penicillin 大剂量的青霉素 ④(金银器等)实心的 ⑤【地】块状的;【矿】均匀构造的,非晶质的: ~ mountain 块状山 / ~ structure 整体结构;块状结构 ‖~**ly** *ad.* / ~**ness** *n.*

massy ['mæsi] *a.* ①大而重的,厚实的;【物】有质量的: a ~ volume 厚重的书本 ②实心的: a ~ gold frame 实心的金框 ③大而浓密的: a tree's ~ foliage 树上茂密的叶子 / ~ clouds 浓云,密云 ‖**massiness** *n.*

mast[1] [mɑːst] **I** *n.* ①桅杆,樯: a ~ crane 桅杆(式)起重机 ②杆,柱;天线杆,天线塔: an aerial (或 antenna) ~ 天线杆,天线塔 / a television ~ 电视天线杆(或塔) **II** *vt.* 在…上装桅杆 ‖(*sail*) **before** (或 **afore**) **the** ~ 作为普通水手: He *sails before the* ~. 他是一名普通水手。 ‖~**less** *a.* 无桅杆的

mast[2] [mɑːst] *n.*【植】山毛榉 (或栎树等)的果实(作猪等饲料用)

master[1] ['mɑːstə] **I** *n.* ①(男)主人,主子;户主;雇主;(商船的)船长: ~ and man 老板和工人;主仆 / the ~ of the house 家长 ②师傅;能手;优秀者,获胜者: a ~ in pig-breeding 养猪能手 / make oneself ~ of… 使自己精通… ③男教师;(学院的)院长: a mathematics ~ 数学教师 ④大师,名家;名家作品: a ~ *in* literature 文学大师 / This painting is an old ~. 这幅画是古代名画家的作品。 ⑤[M-] 硕士: a *Master of Arts* (*Science*) 文科(理科)硕士 ⑥[M-](用在人名前作称呼)…少爷;[苏格兰]子爵(或男爵)的长子: *Master Smith* 史密斯少爷 ⑦(用于职位名)长,官: a harbour ~ 港务长 / a ~ of (the) ceremonies 典礼官;司仪 ⑧[the M-]【宗】耶稣,主;[常作 M-] 宗教界的首脑,长老 ⑨[方] 丈夫 ⑩【机】主导装置 ⑪主盘,原版录音片(即唱片的

负片) **II** *a.* ①主人的;支配的,统治的 ②精通的,熟练的;优秀的: a ~ carpenter 手艺高明的木匠师傅 ③主要的;总的: ~ station【电】主控台 / a ~ switch 总开关 / a ~ plan 总计划;蓝图 **III** *vt.* ①做…的主人 ②控制;统治;制服: ~ one's temper 抑制着不发脾气 / Man can ~ nature. 人能征服自然。 ③精通,掌握: ~ the English language 掌握英语 ‖*a passed* (或 *past*) ~ ①能手,老手 ②(行会、帮会、俱乐部等的)前任主持人;以前的头子 / *be* ~ *in one's own house* 不受外人干涉地处理自己的事 / *be* ~ *o* 控制,掌握: *be* ~ *of* the situation 控制局面 / *one's own* ~ 独立,自主 / *Like* ~, *like man* (或 *Such* ~, *such servant.*) [谚]有其主必有其仆。 / *serve two* ~s ①侍奉二主;不忠 ②在两相反的原则间徘徊 ‖~**dom** *n.* =mastery / ~**hood** *n.* ①主人(或师傅等)的身分 / ~**less** *a.* ①无主人的;无主的 ②[古]含义流浪的 / ~**ship** *n.* ①统治;控制 ②校长(或师傅)的身分;硕士学位 ③精通,熟练 ‖~ **clock** (电钟的)母钟 / '~-**hand** *n.* ①能手 ②高超的技艺 / ~ **key** ①万能钥匙 ②(在解决难题中)起作用的事物,关键 ③【电】总电键 / '~-**piece, '~-work** *n.* 杰作;名作;杰出的事 / ~ **sergeant**【美】陆军(或空军、海军陆战队)军士长 / '~-**stroke** *n.* 巧妙的动作,妙举;(政策等的)成功 / '~-**touch** *n.* 显示才华的细节

master[2] ['mɑːstə] *n.* [常用以构成复合词]…桅船: a two-~ 二桅船

masterful ['mɑːstəful] *a.* ①好支配人的,专横的: speak in a ~ manner 用专横的态度讲话 ②熟练的;巧妙的;名家的: write in ~ English 用熟练的英语写 ‖~**ly** *ad.* / ~**ness** *n.*

masterly ['mɑːstəli] **I** *a.* 熟练的;巧妙的;高明的: He did a ~ job. 他干得很出色。 / ~ generalization and summation 高度的概括和总结 **II** *ad.* 熟练地;巧妙地;高明地 ‖**masterliness** *n.*

mastermind ['mɑːstəmaind] **I** *n.* ①具有极大才智的人 ②出谋划策的人 **II** *vt.* 策划: ~ a *coup d'état* 策划一场政变

mastery ['mɑːstəri] *n.* ①控制;统治: ~ of the air (seas) 制空(海)权 / get ~ of a wild horse 驯服野马 ②优势,优胜 ③精通,掌握

masticate ['mæstikeit] **❶** *vt.* ①咀嚼 ②撕碎(橡胶等) **❷** *vi.* 咀嚼 ‖**mastication** [,mæsti-'keiʃən] *n.* ①咀嚼(作用) ②撕捏(作用),捏和(作用) ③【化】(橡胶)素炼

mat[1] [mæt] **I** *n.* ①地席;席子;草席,蒲席 ②(体操或角斗用的)垫子;(放在门口处的)蹭鞋垫;(花瓶、茶杯等的)衬垫 ③丛,簇: a ~ of hair (weed) 一簇头发(野草) ④[俚](航空母舰的)甲板 **II** (matted; matting) **❶** *vt.* ①铺上(或盖上)席子;给…铺上垫子: The room is *matted*. 这房间用草垫铺地。 / ~ *up* the seedlings 把树苗用草席包起来 ②使缠结 **❷** *vi.* 缠结: The weeds ~ together. 野草杂生在一起。 ‖*go to the* ~

参加一场(口头或思想意识上的)激战 / *hit the* ~ 被打倒 / *leave sb. on the* ~ 拒绝接待某人 / *on the* ~ [俚]被上级训斥;受责备,受到严厉批评

mat² [mæt] **I** *a.* ①无光泽的,闷光的: ~ metals 未抛光的金属 ②表面粗糙的,不光滑的: ~ glass 毛玻璃,磨砂玻璃 **II** *n.* ①(画片的)闷光金边 ②(油漆、镀金等的)无光粗糙的一层;褪光 ③[印]字模;铸铅版用的纸型 **III** (matted; matting) *vt.* ①使(金属、玻璃等)褪光 ②给(画)配闷光金边

matador ['mætədɔ:] *n.* ①斗牛士 ②(纸牌戏中的)主要王牌

match¹ [mætʃ] *n.* ①(一根)火柴: a box of ~es 一盒火柴 / strike a ~ 擦火柴 ②导火线,火绳 ‖~**box** *n.* 火柴盒 / '~**lock** *n.* ①火绳枪 ②引发枪机的火绳 / '~**wood** *n.* ①制火柴材的木料 ②碎片: make ~wood of sth. (或 smash sth. to ~wood) 把某物弄得粉碎

match² [mætʃ] **I** *n.* ①比赛,竞赛: play a football ~ 举行足球比赛 ②对手;敌手: find (meet) one's ~ 找到(遇着)对手 / be more than a ~ for sb. 比某人强,胜过某人 / with no ~ in the world 举世无双 / However sly a fox may be, it is no ~ for a good hunter. 狐狸再狡猾也敌不过好猎手。③相配者;配对物;【电】匹配;【机】假型: The cap is a ~ for the coat. 这帽子和上衣很相称。/ a conjugate ~ 共轭匹配 / a sand ~ 砂假型 ④相配的两个(或两个以上)人(或物): The chairs and the desk are a good ~. 这些椅子和这张书桌很相配。⑤婚姻;(婚姻的)对象 **II** ❶ *vt.* ①使较量,使比赛 (*against, with*): ~ one's strength *with* that of another 与另一人较量 ②敌得过;比得上: No one can ~ him in singing. 论唱歌谁也比不过他。③和…相配,和…相称: The picture ~es the story. 这幅图和故事很相称。④使成对,使相配,使相称: ~ words *with* deeds 言行一致 / a design well ~ed in colour 颜色很相称的图案 / Can you ~ (me) this silk? 你能(为我)找一块和这块相配的绸子吗? ⑤使比较: Any story ~ed *with* this seems uninteresting. 任何故事和这个故事相比,任何故事都显得无趣了。⑥使结婚 ⑦抛掷(硬币)后按正反面作决定;同(某人)抛掷硬币以作决定 ❷ *vi.* ①相配,相适合: The colours ~ well. 颜色配合得很好。②结婚 ‖*Let beggars* ~ *with beggars.* [谚]龙配龙,凤配凤。/ *make a* ~ *of it* 结婚 / *play off a* ~ (平局后)再赛以决胜负 ‖~**able** *a.* 敌得过的;相配的;对等的 / ~**less** *a.* 无敌的,无比的 ‖'~**board** *n.* 假型板 / '~,**maker** *n.* ①媒人;好做媒的人 ②安排各种体育比赛(尤指摔角比赛或职业拳击赛)的人 / ~ **point** 比赛中为得胜所需的最后一分

mate¹ [meit] **I** *n.* ①(工人之间的)伙伴,同事;(常用在称呼中)老兄,老弟: Where you going, ~? 老兄,你上哪儿去? ②配偶;配对物;鸟兽的偶 ③【海】(商船的)大副;助手: the chief (或 first) ~ 大副 / the second ~ 二副 / a surgeon's ~ 军医助手 ④(海军的)军士 **II** ❶ *vt.* ①使成配偶;使配对;使(鸟等)交配: ~ (*up*) pigeons 使鸽子交配繁殖 ②使紧密配合: ~ words *with* deeds 言行一致 ❷ *vi.* ①成配偶;成伙伴 (*with*) ②紧密配合: The gears ~ well. 齿轮啮合紧密。③(鸟类等)交尾: the *mating* season (动物的)交配季节 ‖*go* ~*s with* 成为…的伙伴;与…合伙

mate² [meit] **I** *vt.* (象棋中)将死(对方的"王") **II** *n.* (象棋中"王"的)将死 ‖*fool's* ~ 走第二步棋后就出现的败局

material [mə'tiəriəl] **I** *n.* ①材料,原料;物资: raw ~ 原料 / feed ~ into a machine 给机器加料 / strategic ~s 战略物资 ②素材,题材;资料: gather ~ for a novel 搜集小说素材 / teaching ~ 教材 / The book provides much ~ for thought. 这本书中有许多东西是发人深思的。③织物,料子: dress ~s 衣料 ④[复]用具,设备: writing ~s 文具 **II** *a.* ①物质的,实体的,有形的 ②物质性的,肉体的: a ~ force 物质力量 / a ~ noun 【语】物质名词 / a ~ being 有形体 ②身体上的,肉体的: ~ needs 身体上的需要(如衣、食等) ③物欲的,追求实利的;卑俗的 ④重要的;实质性的: neglect no data that is ~ *to* the work 不忽视对工作有重要意义的资料 / a ~ piece of evidence 实质性的证据 / a ~ difference 本质上的区别 ‖~*ly ad.* ①物质上;实质上 ②大大地,相当地 ‖'~**man** [mə'tiəriəlmən] *n.* (尤指建筑工程的)材料供给人

materialistic [mə,tiəriə'listik] *a.* ①唯物主义的;唯物主义者的: the ~ interpretation (或 conception) of history 唯物史观 ②物质第一主义的,实利主义的;实利主义者的 ‖~**ally** *ad.*

materialize [mə'tiəriəlaiz] ❶ *vt.* ①使物质化;使具体化: ~ an idea in words 把一个思想形诸文字 / ~ a lofty aspiration 实现崇高志向 ②使追求物质利益 ③使(鬼魂等)显形 ❷ *vi.* ①物质化;具体化 ②成为事实,(希望、计划等)实现 ③(鬼魂等)显形;突然出现 ‖**materialization** [mə,tiəriəlai'zeiʃən] *n.*

maternal [mə'tə:nl] *a.* ①母亲的;母性的,母亲似的: the death rate during childbirth 分娩过程中的产妇死亡率 / one's ~ language 本国语 ②母方的,母系的: one's ~ grandparents 外祖父母 / ~ plant 【农】母本植物 ‖~**ly** *ad.*

maternity [mə'tə:niti] **I** *n.* ①母性;母道 ②产院,产科医院 (=~ hospital) ③怀孕 **II** *a.* 产妇的;孕妇的: a ~ nurse 产科护士;助产士 / ~ leave 产假 / a ~ dress 孕妇服装

mathematical [,mæθi'mætikəl] *a.* ①数学的,数学上的 ②精确的;确定无疑的: a ~ proof 毋庸置疑的证据 ③可能性极小的: a ~ chance 极小的可能 ‖~**ly** *ad.* ‖~ **logic** 数理逻辑

mathematician [ˌmæθimə'tiʃən] *n.* 数学家

mathematics [ˌmæθi'mætiks] [复] *n.* 【用作单或复】数学: applied ~ 应用数学 / Your ~ are (或 is) not so good. 你的数学(指成绩或实用能力)可不大好啊。

matin ['mætin] **I** *n.* ①[复](天主教的)早课; (英国国教的)晨祷 ②[诗](鸟的)晨歌 **II** *a.* ①【宗】早课的; 晨祷的 ② 黎明的, 早晨的

matinée ['mætinei] *n.* [法] ① 日间的招待会 ② 午后的演出, 日戏

matriarch ['meitriɑːk] *n.* 女家长; 女族长 ‖**~al** [ˌmeitri'ɑːkəl] *a.* 女家长的; 女族长的; 母权制的 / **~y** *n.* 母权制, 母系氏族制

matricide ['meitrisaid] *n.* ① 杀母(罪) ② 杀母者 ‖**matricidal** [ˌmeitri'saidl] *a.*

matriculate [mə'trikjuleit] **I** ❶ *vt.* 录取(大学生等), 准许…注册入学 ❷ *vi.* 被录取; 注册入学 **II** *n.* 被录取者 ‖**matriculation** [məˌtrikju-'leiʃən] *n.* ① 录取入学; 注册入学; 入学典礼 ②(大学的)入学考试

matrimony ['mætriməni] *n.* ① 结婚; 婚礼; 婚姻; 婚姻生活 ② 一种抽对子牌戏

matrix ['meitriks] ([复] matrices ['meitrisiːz] 或 matrixes) *n.* ①【解】子宫 ②【生】基质; 母质: chromosome ~ 染色体基质 / bone ~ 骨基质; nail ~ 甲床 ③发源地,策源地 ④【地】脉石,填质;(岩石中化石等的)痕印 ⑤[冶](合金的)基体 ⑥【数】阵,矩阵,真值表,母式;【无】矩阵变换电路 ⑦ 模型, 型片;【印】字模, (铸铅版用的)纸型: copper ~ 铜质型片

matron ['meitrən] *n.* ①(年长有威望的)已婚妇女, 主妇 ②(学校等的)女总管, 女舍监; (监狱等的)女看守; (妇女团体的)总干事; 护士长 ③母种畜 ‖*a ~ of hono(u)r* (婚礼中)陪伴新娘的已婚妇女 ‖**~age** ['meitrənidʒ] *n.* ①[集合名词]主妇(或女总管等) ②主妇(或女总管等)的身分(或职责) ③主妇(或女总管等)的照料(或监护) / **~hood**, **~ship** *n.* 主妇(或女总管等)的身分(或职责) / **~ize** *vt.* ①使显出主妇(或女总管等)的派头; 使庄重 ②(以女长者身分)监护, 陪伴(青年女子) / **~like** *a.* =**~ly** (*a.*) / **~ly** *a.* ①主妇(或女总管等)的; 主妇(或女总管等)似的; 适合主妇(或女总管等)身分的 ② 尊严的, 庄重的; 沉着的 *ad.* 主妇(或女总管等)似地

matt [mæt] *a., n. & vt.* =mat²

matter ['mætə] **I** *n.* ① 物质; 物料: the motion of ~ 物质运动 / a colouring ~ 着色剂, 色料 / solid (liquid) ~ 固(液)体 / waste ~ 废料 ②物品;文件;邮件: printed ~ 印刷品 / second-class ~ 二等邮件 ③ 事情; 问题; [复]事态, 情况: It's no laughing ~. 这可不是开玩笑的事。/ a ~ in dispute 争执中的问题 / in ~s of principle 在原则问题上 / How did ~s stand? 情况怎样? ④(文章,讲话等的)内容, 素材: The article is devoid of ~. 这篇文章缺乏内容。⑤要紧事, 要紧: It is of no ~. 这无关紧要。/ No ~!

不要紧! 不碍事! ⑥[the ~] 麻烦事, 毛病: What's the ~ (*with you*)? (你)怎么啦? (你)出了什么事? / There's nothing the ~ with the machine. 这机器没有毛病。⑦ 理由, 根据: no ~ for wonder 没有惊奇的理由 ⑧(表示数量)…左右,…上下: a ~ of ten kilometres (ten years) 大约十公里(十年)左右 ⑨【医】脓 ⑩【印】排版; (稿子中的)文字部分 **II** *vi.* ①[主要用于否定句和疑问句]有关系, 要紧: What does it ~? 这有什么关系? / It doesn't ~ much whether we go together or separately. 我们一起去还是分头去都可以。②【医】化脓, 出脓: a ~*ing* wound 化脓的伤口 ‖*a hanging ~* 要处绞刑的案子 / *~ of course* 理所当然的事 / *a ~ of life and death* 生死攸关的事情 / *a ~ of opinion* 看法不同的问题 / *a ~ of record* 有案可查的事 / *as a ~ of fact* 事实上, 其实 / *as ~s stand* (或 *as the ~ stands*) 照目前的情况 / *for that ~* (或 *for the ~ of that*) 就此而言; 至于那个 / *in the ~ of* 在…上, 就…而论 / *no ~ how (what, when, where, who, whether)*... 不管怎样(什么, 何时, 哪里, 谁, 是否)… / *not to mince ~s* 见 mince/ *what ~ if* 即使…又何妨: *What ~ if* we meet with some difficulties? 即使我们会遇到一些困难, 那又有什么可怕呢? ‖**~-of-course** ['mætərəv'kɔːs] *a.* 当然的, 不言而喻的 / **~-of-fact** ['mætərəv'fækt] *a.* ①注重事实的, 讲究实际的 ②平淡无味的, 干巴巴的

matting¹ ['mætiŋ] *n.* ①[总称]地席; 席; 草席, 蒲席 ② 编席的材料; 编席

matting² ['mætiŋ] *n.* ①(金属, 玻璃等的)褪光; 无光泽的表面 ②(画片的)闪光金边

mattress ['mætris] *n.* ① 褥垫, 床垫: a spring ~ 弹簧垫子 ②(土木工程用的)柴排, 沉排, 沉床

mature [mə'tjuə] **I** *a.* ①成熟的: ~ grain 成熟的谷物 / be politically ~ 政治上成熟 / a ~ plan (考虑)成熟的计划 / write ~ English 用老练的英语写作 / ~ soil 【地】成熟土壤 / ~ wine 酿熟的酒 ②成年人的;【地】壮年的 ③(考虑等)慎重的, 周到的: after ~ deliberation 经过周密的考虑 ④【商】(票据等)到期的 **II** ❶ *vt.* 使成熟; 使长成 ❷ *vi.* ①成熟; 长成 ②【商】(票据等)到期

maturity [mə'tjuəriti] *n.* ①成熟 ②【商】(票据等的)到期; 到期日: payable at ~ 到期付款 ③【地】壮年; 壮年期

maudlin ['mɔːdlin] **I** *a.* ①易伤感的; 感情脆弱的 ②酒后伤感的 **II** *n.* 脆弱的感情

maul [mɔːl] **I** *n.* (木制的)大槌 **II** *vt.* ①殴打, 打伤; (用言语)挫伤 ②粗手粗脚地弄(或做) ③用楔和大槌劈开

mausoleum [ˌmɔːsə'liəm] ([复] mausoleums 或 mausolea [ˌmɔːsə'li(ə)]) *n.* ① 陵墓 ② 大而阴森的房屋(或房间)

mauve [mouv] **I** *n.* ① 苯胺紫染料, 碱性木槿染料 ② 紫红色 **II** *a.* 紫红色的

maw [mɔ:] *n.* ①动物的胃(尤指反刍动物的第四胃) ②(鸟的)嗉囊 ③鱼鳔,鱼泡 ④贪吃肉类的动物的咽喉(或食道等) ⑤[谑]人胃 ‖'~-'bound *a.* (牲畜)便秘的 / '~worm *n.* ①肠胃寄生虫(尤指寄生线虫) ②伪君子

mawkish ['mɔ:kiʃ] *a.* ①使人作呕的,令人厌恶的,乏味的 ②假装多情的;感情脆弱的 ‖~ly *ad.* / ~ness *n.*

Maxim ['mæksim] *n.* 马克沁机枪(一种老式机枪)(=~ gun)

maxim ['mæksim] *n.* ①格言,箴言,准则 ②谚语

maximum ['mæksiməm] **I** ([复] maxima ['mæksimə] 或 maximums) *n.* ①最大量,最大数;最大限度: achieve the ~ of efficiency with the minimum of labour 以最少的劳动取得最高的效率 / ~ of eclipse【天】食甚 ②顶点,极限: The excitement was at its ~. 兴奋到极点。③【数】极大(值) **II** *a.* 最大的;最多的;最高的;顶点的: the ~ range 最大射程 / the ~ load 最大载重量 / the ~ draft (或 draught) 最大吃水深度 / a ~ thermometer 最高温度计

May [mei] *n.* ①五月 ②[常作 m-]青春,壮年 ③(英国风俗)五朔节的欢庆活动: Queen of (the) ~ 五朔节游戏中被选为五月女王的女人 ④[m-]山楂属植物;英国山楂;春天开花的绣线菊属植物 ⑤(英国剑桥大学俚语)五月考试;五月赛艇会 ‖'~,apple *n.*【植】(鬼臼属中)盾叶鬼臼;盾叶鬼臼的卵状淡黄色果实 / ~ beetle, ~ bug【动】鳃角金龟科吃植物叶片的甲虫(如跳甲) / ~ Day ①五一国际劳动节: attend ~ Day celebrations 参加五一节庆祝活动 ②(英国风俗)五朔节 / '~day *n.* 无线电话中呼救信号 / '~fair *n.* [英]伦敦西区贵族住宅区 / '~,flower *n.* ①五月花(英国指山楂; 美国指某些银莲花) ②[the ~flower] 五月花号(1620 年英国清教徒初次去美洲时所乘的船) / '~fly *n.*【动】蜉蝣 / '~pole *n.* 五朔节花柱(庆祝时常绕此柱舞蹈游戏) / ~ queen (为游乐活动选出的)五朔节女王 / '~thorn *n.*【植】山楂 / '~tide, '~time *n.* 五月期间 / ~ tree【植】山楂

may¹ [mei] (might [mait]) *v. aux.* [无人称变化,后接不带 to 的动词不定式] ①[表示可能性]能,也许: He ~ be right. 他可能是对的。(表示否定用 He cannot be right. 他不可能是对的。) / He ~ not be right. 他也许不对。/ He was afraid it *might* rain. 他担心会下雨。/ You ~ have been there before. 你以前也许去过那里。②[表示许可或用于请求许可,相当于 can] A: *May* I go now? B: Yes, you ~. 甲: 现在我可以走了吗? 乙: 是的,你可以走了。(表示否定用 No, you must not. 或 No, you cannot. 不,你不能走。) / *May* I make a suggestion? 我可以提个建议吗? / if I ~ say so... 要是我可以这么说的话… ③[用于问句中,表示不确定]会,究竟: Who ~ the man be? 这个人会是谁呢? ④[表示希望、祝愿、祈求等]祝,愿: *May* you succeed! 祝你成功! ⑤[常与 well 连用,表示有充分的理由](完全)能,(满)可以: You ~ *well* say so. 你完全可以这么说。⑥[用于从句中表示目的](以便)能,(使…)可以: Hold the flag higher (so) that all ~ see. 把旗子举得高一些,让大家都能看到。⑦[用于从句中表示让步]不管,不论; 尽管: be that as it ~ 无论如何 / Come what ~, I will try it. 无论发生什么,我总要试一试。⑧[用于从句中表示期望]能够,会: I hope we ~ succeed. 我希望我们会成功。⑨[用于法令条款中,相当于 shall, must] 须,得 ‖as best one ~ 尽最大努力 / as the case ~ be 看情况,根据具体情况 / ~ as well 还是…的好: We ~ *as well* go and have a look. 我们还是去看一下吧。/ ~ *as well* ... *as* ...(做)…与(做)…一样: We ~ *as well* go *as* not. 我们去不去都行。

may² [mei] *n.* [诗]少女

maybe ['meibi:] **I** *ad.* 大概,或许: *Maybe* it is right. 这可能是对的。/ as soon as ~ 尽可能快地 **II** *n.* 疑虑

mayn't [meint] =may not

mayonnaise [,meiə'neiz] *n.* ①(用蛋黄、橄榄油、柠檬汁等制成的)蛋黄酱 ②用蛋黄酱调味的食物

mayor [mɛə] *n.* 市长: the Lord *Mayor* 伦敦(或英国其他某些大城市)的市长 ‖~al ['mɛərəl] *a.* / ~ess ['mɛəris] *n.* 女市长;市长夫人 / ~ship *n.* 市长的职位;市长的任期

maze [meiz] **I** *n.* ①迷宫,迷津;曲径 ②混乱;迷惑: His mind was all in a ~. 他的头脑里一片糊涂。**II** *vt.* ①使如入迷宫 ②使困惑;使为难 ‖~d *a.* 迷惘的,困惑的

me [mi:; 弱 mi] *pron.* [I 的宾格] ①[用作宾语]我: Do you remember ~? 你还记得我吗? / Please give ~ a book. 请给我一本书。/ She stood behind ~. 她站在我后面。②[口][用作表语]我 (=I): A: Who is it? B: It's ~. (=It's I.) 甲: 谁啊? 乙: 是我。③[口][用于 than 后面]我 (=I): He's older than ~. 他比我年纪大。④[用于感叹句]: Ah (或 Dear) ~! 哎哟! ⑤[古]我自己 (=myself): I laid ~ down. 我躺下了。

mead¹ [mi:d] *n.* 蜂蜜酒

mead² [mi:d] *n.* [诗]草地

meadow ['medou] *n.* ①草地,牧草地 ②河(或湖)边肥沃的低草地 ‖~y *a.* ①草地般的 ②有草地的 ‖'~sweet *n.* ①绣线菊属植物(尤指白花绣线菊或绒毛绣线菊) ②合叶子属植物(尤指欧洲合叶子)

meagre, meager ['mi:gə] *a.* ①(人等)瘦的;(土地)不毛的 ②贫乏的,不足的;贫弱的;思想贫乏的 ‖~ly *ad.* / ~ness *n.*

meal¹ [mi:l] **I** *n.* ①膳食;一餐,一顿(饭);进餐(时间): a light ~ 便餐 / a square ~ 丰盛的一餐 / three ~s a day 一日三餐 / make a ~ of noodles 吃一顿面条 / at ~s 在吃饭 / between

~s 在两餐之间 ②[英方]挤奶(时间)，一次挤奶所得量 **Ⅱ** *vi.* 进餐 ‖~ **ticket** ①饭票，餐券 ②[美俚]供给生活(或吃饭)的人 ③[美俚]赖以为生的东西(指手艺、才能、双手等) / '~**time** *n.* 进餐时间

meal² [mi:l] *n.* ①(谷、豆类)未经筛过的粗粉: whole ~ (没去麸的)粗面粉 ②象粗粉的东西: 麦片; 玉米片

mean¹ [mi:n] (meant [ment]) ❶ *vt.* ①(词语等)表示…的意思，作…解释: What does that word ~? (或 What is *meant* by that word?) 那个词作什么解释? ②意指，意谓: I ~ business. 我是当真的.(指非口头说说而已) ③意味着，就是 ④意欲，打算; 怀着: Do you ~ him to read the letter too? 你是否有意让他也读读这封信? / You don't ~ to say so! 你要说的该不会是这个意思吧! / I ~ to accomplish the task, one way or another. 不管怎么样我决意要完成这个任务. / I don't ~ there to be any unpleasantness. 我的意思不是要引起任何不愉快。/ They ~ you no harm. 他们对你不怀恶意。/ Sorry, I didn't ~ it. (向人认错道歉时用语)对不起，我是无意的。 ⑤预定; 指定: This gift is *meant* for you. 这件礼物是准备给你的。/ He was *meant* for (或 to be) an electrician. 本来是准备把他培养成电工的。/ It is *meant* for a joke. 这是说着玩的。❷ *vi.* ①用意: He ~s well (ill) *by* (或 *towards*) us. 他对我们怀着好(恶)意。②具有意义: Your cooperation ~s much (或 a great deal) to us. 你们的协作对我们帮助极大。‖ ***What do you ~ by ...?*** ①你说…的话(或做…的事)是什么意思? ②你怎么胆敢…? 你怎么竟然…?: *What do you ~ by sign-ing the letter for him?* 你为什么竟然代他在信上签名?

mean² [mi:n] *a.* ①卑鄙的; 自私的: a ~ motive 卑鄙的动机 ②低劣的; 平庸的: a man of no ~ ability 一个能力很强的人 / have a ~ opinion of oneself 有自卑感 ③简陋的，难看的: a ~ cottage 简陋的村舍 ④吝啬的，小气的; 刻薄的: be ~ about (或 over) money matters 在金钱问题上很小气 ⑤卑贱的，下贱的 ⑥麻烦的，讨厌的 ⑦不好意思的，惭愧的: feel ~ for not having done one's best 因没有尽力而感到不好意思 ⑧不适的，不舒服的: feel ~ with a cold 因伤风而感不适 ⑨(马等)脾气坏的，难驯服的 ⑩[美俚]出色的; 巧妙的; 有效的 ‖~**ie**, ~**y** ['mi:ni] *n.* [口]小气鬼; 卑鄙家伙 / ~**ly** *ad.* / ~**ness** *n.* ‖~'**spirited** *a.* 卑鄙的

mean³ [mi:n] **Ⅰ** *a.* ①(在位置、时间、顺序等方面)中间的; 中庸的: in the ~ time (或 while) 在此期间 (=in the meantime 或 in the meanwhile) / take a ~ course 采取折衷方针 ②中等的，普通的: of a ~ stature 有一副中等身材 ③平均的: the ~ error 平均误差 / the ~ velocity (temperature) 平均速度(温度) ④【数】中项的:

~ proportional 比例中项 **Ⅱ** *n.* ①中间; 中庸 ②【数】平均(数)，平均(值); 中数: arithmatic (geometric) ~ 等差(等比)中项 ③【逻】(三段论的)中项 ④【音】中音部 ‖~ **sea level** 平均海平面(略作 m. s. l) / ~ (**solar**) **time**【天】平太阳时 / ~ **sun**【天】平太阳

meander [mi'ændə] **Ⅰ** *n.* ①[常用复]曲流，河曲; 弯弯曲曲的路 ②漫步，散步 ③(回纹) 波形饰 **Ⅱ** *vi.* ①蜿蜒而流; 迂回曲折地前进 ②漫步，闲荡; 无目的地讲话，闲谈 ❷ *vt.* ①使蜿蜒曲折: stroll along the ~ed bank 沿着蜿蜒的河岸散步 ②循着(迂回的路)前进: ~ the lower reaches of the river 循着下游迂回的河道前进 ‖~**er** [mi'ændərə] *n.* 漫游者，闲逛者 ‖~ **line**【测】折线

meaning ['mi:niŋ] **Ⅰ** *n.* ①意义，意思; 含意: What's the ~ of this word? 这个词作什么解释? / Beg pardon, I didn't quite catch your ~. 对不起，我没听清楚你的意思。/ exchange glances *with* ~ 含有深意地互使眼色 ②意图: What was his ~? 他的用意何在? ③【逻】内涵 (=~ in intension); 外延 (=~ in extension) **Ⅱ** *a.* ①意味深长的: a ~ smile 意味深长的一笑 ②怀有(某种)意图的: a well-~ (an ill-~) man 善意(恶意)的人 ‖~**less** *a.* 无意义的

meaningful ['mi:niŋful] *a.* 意味深长的，富有意义的: ~ advice 语重心长的忠告 / a ~ experience 有意义的经验 ‖~**ly** *ad.* / ~**ness** *n.*

means [mi:nz] [复] *n.* ①[常用作单]方法，手段; 工具: leave no ~ untried 用尽一切办法 / a ~ to an end 达到目的的方法 / the ~ of production 生产资料 / the ~ of subsistence (或 livelihood) 生活资料 / the ~ of transport 运输工具 / launch ~ 发射(导弹等)的工具 ②财产; 资力; 收入: a man of straitened ~ 经济困难的人 / live within (beyond) one's ~ 量入(不量入)为出 / This foreign firm has not much (或 has little) ~. 这家外国商行没有多大资力。‖ *by all* (*manner of*) ~ ①尽一切办法; 一定，务必: This plan must be realized *by all* ~. 这计划一定要实现。②(表示答应)好的，当然可以: A: May I have one? B: Yes, *by all* ~. 甲: 可以给我一个吗? 乙: 当然可以。/ *by any* ~ 无论如何 / *by fair* ~ *or foul* 用正当或不正当的手段，不择手段地 / *by* ~ *of* 用，依靠: He succeeded *by* ~ *of* perseverance. 他依靠坚持而获得成功。/ *by no* (*manner of*) ~ 决不，并没有: A: Am I wrong? B: No, *by no* ~. 甲: 我错了吗? 乙: 不，一点不错。/ *by some* ~ *or other* 用某种方法: We must get it finished *by some* ~ *or other*. 我们总得想个办法把它完成。/ *The end justifies* (或 *sanctifies*) *the* ~. 见 **end** / *ways and* ~ 见 **way** ‖~ **test** [英](在发放救济津贴前对申请人的)家庭经济况调查

meant [ment] mean¹ 的过去式和过去分词

neasles ['mi:zlz] [复] *n.* [用作单或复] ①【医】麻疹: German ~ 风疹 ②家畜囊虫病

neasly ['mi:zli] *a.* ①患麻疹的 ②(肉类中)含绦虫幼体的, 含囊虫的 ③[口]微不足道的, 小(或少)得可怜的

measurable ['meʒərəbl] *a.* 可测量的: be within the ~ distance of success 接近成功 / within the ~ future 在不久的将来 ‖**measurability** [,meʒərə'biliti] *n.* 可测量性 / **measurably** *ad.* 适度地; 显著地; 觉察得出地: The patient has improved *measurably*. 病人已显著好转.

measure ['meʒə] **I** *n.* ①量度, 测量 ②分量; 尺寸: give full (short) ~ 给足(短少)分量 / clothes made to ~ 依照尺寸定制的衣服 ③计量制度, 度量法: the metric ~ 公制, 米制 / the circular ~ 弧度法 / official weights and ~s 法定度量衡 ④计量单位; (特种商品习惯用的)容积单位(如 bushel 等): A metre is a ~ of length. 米是长度单位. ⑤量具, 量器: a tape ~ 卷尺 / a ~ for liquids 液体量器 ⑥(衡量)标准, 尺度 ⑦程度; 限度, 范围; 适度, 分寸: There is a certain ~ of truth in what you say. 你说的有几分道理. / achieve the highest ~ of success 获得最大限度的成功 ⑧本分, 份儿 ⑨措施, 办法: adopt (或 take) effective ~s to improve one's work 采取有效措施来改进工作 ⑩议案 ⑪(诗歌的)韵律; 【音】拍子; 小节; (慢步而庄重的)舞蹈 ⑫【数】测度; 常 measure ~ 公(剖)度 ⑬【复】【地】层组 ⑭[印]行宽, 页宽 **II** *vt.* ❶ *vt.* ①量, 测量; 计量: ~ the distance 测量距离 / ~ the speed of a car 测定汽车速度 / ~ sb. for a new suit 给某人量尺寸做一套新衣服 ②(按尺寸)划分 (off); (按量)配给, 分派 (out): ~ off 2 metres of cloth 量两米布(指从整块布料上划出) / ~ out a dose of medicine 配一剂药 ③打量; 估量, 衡量: ~ sb. with one's eye (用眼)打量某人 / ~ oneself by a high standard 以高标准要求自己 ④ 拿…作较量: ~ one's strength *with* (或 *against*) another's 同别人比力气 ⑤酌量, 权衡; 调节, 使均衡: ~ one's words 斟酌词句 / ~ the output by the demand 按需要调节产量 ❷ *vi.* ①量: Can you ~ accurately? 你能量得准确吗? / It ~s more easily if spread on a table. 要是把它铺在桌上, 量起来可更容易些. ②有长(或阔,高等): This room ~s 10 metres across. 这房间宽十米. ‖*beyond* (或 *above, out of*) ~ 无可估量, 极度, 过分 / *fill* (*up*) *the* ~ *of* 使(不幸事)达到极点 / *for good* ~ 作为额外添加, 加重分量: add another example *for good* ~ 增添一个实例以利说明 / *in* (*a*) *great* (或 *large*) ~ 大部分 / *in a* (或 *some*) ~ 一部分, 有几分 / *keep* ~*s with* 宽大对待 / *know no* ~ 无止境, 极度: When his wish was realized, his joy *knew no* ~. 当他的志愿实现时, 他高兴极了. / *for* ~ 针锋相对地 / ~ *oneself against* (或 *with*) 同…较量 / ~ *others' corn by one's*

own bushel 拿自己作标准来衡量别人, 以己度人 / ~ *up* 合格, 符合标准: This product does not ~ *up*. 这项产品不合格. / ~ *up to* (或 *with*) 符合, 达到, 够得上: The new techniques ~ *up to* advanced world standard. 这些新技术达到了世界先进水平. / *set* ~*s to* 限制; 约束 / *take sb.'s* ~ 给某人量尺寸; 估量某人(的品格、能力等), 掂着某人的分量: *take sb.'s* waist ~ 给某人量腰围尺寸 / *take sb.'s* ~ *at a glance* 一看出某人是怎样的人 / *take the* ~ *of sb.'s foot* 估量(或了解)某人的品格(或能力)等 / *within* ~ 适当地, 不过分 / *without* ~ 过度, 过分 ‖~*less a.* 无边无际的, 巨大的: a ~*less* expanse of sea 茫茫大海

measured ['meʒəd] *a.* ① 量过的; 按标准的; 精确的 ②(言语)有分寸的, 慎重的, 经过斟酌的 ③整齐的, 有节奏的: march in ~ steps 用整齐的步伐行进 ④韵律的: the ~ forms of verse 诗歌的韵律

measurement ['meʒəmənt] *n.* ① 衡量, 测量: remote ~ 遥测 / the optical ~ of distance 光学测距 ②[复](量得的)尺寸, 大小, 长(或宽,深)度: take ~s with a rule 用尺量尺寸 / the ~s of a room 房间的大小(指长, 阔, 高) ③度量制, 测量法: inside (outside) ~ 内(外)部测量法

measuring ['meʒəriŋ] **I** *n.* 测量 **II** *a.* 测量用的: a ~ glass (或 cup) 量杯 ‖~ **worm**【动】尺蠖

meat [mi:t] *n.* ①食用肉类: butcher's ~ (猪、牛、羊等的)鲜肉; [俚]赊帐的肉食 / chilled (或 frozen) ~ 冻肉 / a slice of ~ 一片肉 / crab ~ 蟹肉 / dark ~ 黑肉(指禽类的腿等部分烧不白的肉) / light (或 white) ~ 白肉(指禽类的胸部和翅膀等处的肉) ②(蛋、贝、果子等的)食用部分, 肉: the ~ of a nut 胡桃肉 / the ~ of an apple 苹果的果肉部分 ③内容, 实质, 要点: There is not much ~ in this argument. 这番议论没有什么内容. ④[古][方]食物: green ~ 青菜 ⑤[古](一)餐: at ~ 在吃饭 / before (after) ~ 餐前(后) ⑥[美俚]爱好; 特长: Table tennis is my ~. 我最喜欢打乒乓. ‖*as full of ... as an egg is of* ~ (头脑等)充满于…, 尽是… / *be and drink to sb.* 对某人来说是无上乐趣 / *be* ~ *for sb.'s master* 对某人说来未免太好 / *cry roast* ~ 自吹自擂 / *make* ~ *of sb.* [俚]杀死某人 / *One man's* ~ *is another man's poison.* [谚]对甲有利的未必对乙也有利. ‖~*less a.* 无肉的; 无内容的 ‖~*-ax(e) n.* ①切肉大菜刀 ②(对问题采取的)毫不容情的措施; (对预算等)大刀阔斧的削减 / ~*ball n.* ①炸肉圆 ②[美俚]讨厌的人, 无趣味的人 ③[美俚]信号旗; 小三角旗(如旗标指旗) ④[美俚](面部上)被击起的肿块 / ~ **by-product** 屠宰牲畜时所得的副产品(如毛、骨头等) / ~ **chopper**, ~ **grinder** 轧肉机, 绞肉机 / [喻]残酷的厮杀 / '~-**,eating** *a.* 食肉的 / ~ **fly** 肉蝇 / '~**head** *n.* [美俚]笨蛋 / '~-**hooks** [复] *n.* [美俚](尤指强壮的人的)手,

拳 / ～ **maggot** 肉蝇的幼虫 / '～**man** *n.* 肉商,屠夫 / ～ **offering** (面粉和油做的)祭品 / '～-,**packing** *n.* 大规模的肉类工业(包括屠宰、装罐及批发) / ～ **pie** 肉馅饼 / ～ **safe** [英](用金属纱罩制的)肉柜,菜橱 / ～ **show** [美俚]卖弄色相的下流表演 / ～ **tea** [英](下午五至六时之间、有肉食冷盆的)正式茶点 / ～ **wag(g)on** [美俚] ①救护车 ②枢车,灵车

mechanic [mi'kænik] **I** *n.* ①技工;机械工;机修工: an air ～ 空勤机械士 / an automobile ～ 汽车修理工 ②[美俚]玩牌时善于作假的人 **II** *a.* ①手工的 ②机械(似)的;老一套的

mechanical [mi'kænikəl] *a.* ①机械(制)的,用机械的: ～ energy 机械能 / ～ drawing 机械制图 / ～ power 机械功率 / ～ advantage 【机】机械利益 / ～ strain 【物】机工肌变,机工应变 / the ～ transport (英陆军)汽车运输队 ②机械学的;力学的;物理的: ～ engineering 机械工程(学) / ～ equivalent of heat 【物】热功当量 ③【哲】机械论的: ～ materialism 机械唯物论 ④机械似的,呆板的: His acting is ～. 他的表演很呆板。 ⑤手工操作的;技工的 ‖～**ly** *ad.* / ～**ness** *n.*

mechanician [,mekə'niʃən] *n.* =mechanic (*n.*)

mechanics [mi'kæniks] [复] *n.* [用作单或复] ①力学,机械学 ②结构;构成法;技巧: the ～ of play-writing 剧本写作技巧

mechanism ['mekənizəm] *n.* ①机械装置;机构;结构;【生】机制: the ～ of a clock 时钟的结构 / a counting ～ 计数装置 / the ～ of government 政府机构 ②(自然现象等的)作用过程;【化】历程: the ～ of seeing (hearing) 视觉(听觉)的作用过程 / the ～ responsible for typhoons 产生台风的自然作用过程 ③手法,途径 ④【哲】机械论

mechanize ['mekənaiz] *vt.* 使机械化;用机械装备: ～ farming 使耕种机械化 / a ～d unit (或 force) 机械化部队 / ～d equipment 机械化设备 ‖**mechanization** [,mekənai'zeiʃən] *n.* 机械化: *mechanization* in agriculture 农业机械化

medal ['medl] **I** *n.* 奖章,勋章;纪念章: a prize ～ 奖章,奖牌 / award sb. with a ～ (或 confer a ～ on sb.) 授予某人奖章 ‖*Medal for Merit* (美国)功绩奖章(对有特殊功绩的非军事人员所发的奖章) / *Medal of Freedom* (美国)自由勋章(授予在战争期间对国家有功绩的国民的勋章) / *Medal of Honor* (美国)荣誉勋章(由国会授予军人;为美国最高勋章) / *Soldier's Medal* (美国)军人奖章(因作战以外的英勇事迹而授予的奖章) **II** (medal(l)ed; medal(l)ing) *vt.* 授予…奖章 ‖*a putty* ～ (对小功劳或小贡献的)小奖赏(常含有讽刺意味) / *the reverse side of the* ～ 问题的另一面,事情的反面 ‖**medal(l)ed** *a.* 受奖章的;佩带勋章的 ‖～ **play** (高尔夫球)以全盘击数计分的比赛

medallion [mi'dæljən] *n.* ①大奖章;大纪念章 ②圆雕饰;【纺】团花;花边装饰纹

meddle ['medl] *vi.* ①干涉,干预: Don't ～ *in* the internal affairs of other countries. 不要干涉别国内政。 / He is always *meddling*. 他老是管闲事。 ②乱弄,瞎弄: Don't ～ *with* the clock. 别乱弄那只钟。 ‖*neither ～ nor make* [古][方]不干涉 ‖～**r** *n.* 干涉者;爱管闲事的人 / ～**some** ['medlsəm] *a.* 好干涉的;爱管闲事的

media[1] ['mediə; 美 'mi:diə] ([复] mediae ['medii:; 美 'mi:dii:]) *n.* ①【语】(尤指希腊语)带声破裂音;(带声)不送气破裂音 ②【解】血管中层;【动】(昆虫的)中脉

media[2] ['mi:djə] medium 的复数

mediate I ['mi:dieit] ❶ *vi.* ①处于中间地位 ②调停,调解: ～ between the two parties 斡旋于双方之间 ❷ *vt.* ①调停,调解 ②作为引起…的媒介;传递,转达(消息等) **II** ['mi:diit] *a.* ①居间的,介于中间的 ②间接的: ～ contacts 间接的接触 ‖～**ly** ['mi:diitli] *ad.*

mediation [,mi:di'eiʃən] *n.* 调停,调解: through the ～ of a third party 经第三者的调解

mediator ['mi:dieitə] *n.* ①调停者;调解国 ②【化】【生】介体 ③[M-]【宗】耶稣基督

medical ['medikəl] **I** *a.* ①医学的;医术的;医疗的: ～ and health work 医疗卫生工作 / ～ college 医学院 / a ～ certificate 健康证明书;诊断书 / ～ examination 体格检查 / ～ inspection 检疫 / free ～ service (或 treatment) 公费医疗 / a ～ team 医疗队 / a ～ orderly 看护兵 / a ～ officer 军医;军医主任 / ～ instruments 医疗器械 ②内科的;医药的: a ～ ward 内科病房 **II** *n.* [口]医科学生 ‖a ～ *man* 医生;外科医生 ‖～**ly** *ad.* ‖～ **examiner** ①验尸员 ②检查体格的医生 ③医生资格考核者 / ～ **jurisprudence** 法医学 / ～ **record** 病历卡

medicament [me'dikəmənt] *n.* (内服或外用)药物,药剂 ‖～**ous** [,medikə'mentəs] *a.*

medicate ['medikeit] *vt.* ①用药治疗 ②用药(剂)浸;加药物于 ‖～**d** *a.* 加入药品的,含药的,药制的: ～d soap 药皂 / ～d wine 药酒 / ～d gauze 药用纱布

medicinal [me'disinl] **I** *a.* ①药的;药用的;治疗的: ～ preparations 药剂,药膏 / ～ crops 药草,药材 / Chinese ～ herbs 中草药 / a ～ leech (医用)水蛭 ②有益健康的;有益的 **II** *n.* 药物,药品 ‖～**ly** *ad.*

medicine ['medsin, 'medisin] **I** *n.* ①医学;医术;内科学: practise ～ 行医 / study ～ as well as surgery 既学外科又学内科 ②内服药(剂): a ～ for colds 感冒药 / take traditional Chinese ～ 服中药 / He took too much ～. 他药吃得太多了。 ③带来幸福的事物 ④(原始民族迷信的)符咒,巫术,魔力 ⑤[美俚][方]情报 **II** *vt.* 给…药,用药给…治病 ‖*take one's* ～ ①忍受不愉快的事情;受到惩罚 ②饮酒 ‖～ **ball** (锻炼身体用的)实心皮球 / '～-**chest** *n.* 药箱,药柜 / ～ **man** 巫医 / ～ **show** 旨在兜售药品的广告性巡

回演出；走江湖卖膏药

medieval [,medi'i:vəl] *a.* ① 中世纪的，中古(时代)的: ~ history 中世纪史 / *Medieval* Greek 中世纪希腊语 ② 类似中世纪的 ③ 古老的；过时的 ||**~ism** *n.* ① 中世纪精神(或特征、状态、风俗、信仰等) ② 对中世纪风味的爱好 ③ 中世纪残存的思想(或风俗等) / **~ist** *n.* ① 中世纪史专家(或研究者)；中世纪文化研究者 ② 中世纪艺术(或文化)的鉴赏者(或爱好者) / **~ly** *ad.* 以中世纪的方式

mediocre ['mi:dioukə] *a.* ① 普普通通的；平庸的；中等的 ② 低劣的

meditate ['mediteit] ❶ *vt.* 考虑；策划，企图: ~ a new experiment 考虑作一次新的实验 ❷ *vi.* 深思，沉思；反省；冥想: sit there *meditating* 坐在那里冥想 / ~ *on* the plot of a play 构思剧本的情节 ||**meditation** [,medi'teiʃən] *n.* ① 深思，沉思；反省；冥想 ② 沉思录 / **meditator** *n.* 深思者；策划者

medium ['mi:djəm] Ⅰ ([复] mediums 或 media ['mi:djə]) *n.* ① 中间；中庸；适中 ② 媒质，媒介物；传导体；(颜料的)溶剂: Air is the ~ of sound. 空气是传播声音的介体。③ 手段；工具；[复]宣传工具: an English ~ school 用英语进行教学的学校 / mass *media* 有广泛影响的宣传工具 (指报纸、广播、电视等) / The *media* have (或 has) flocked to the place where the event took place. 报纸、电视和广播记者已纷纷拥向发生这一事件的现场。④ [喻] 环境，生活条件；[生]培养基: agar ~ 琼脂培养基 ⑤ 中号纸(通常为 18×23 时的印刷纸) ⑥ (舞台上用的)灯光滤光片 ⑦ 调解人，中间人；(搞迷信活动的)关亡人，巫师 Ⅱ *a.* 中等的；中间的；适中的: a ~ range 中距离 / a man of ~ height 中等身材的人 ||*the ~ of exchange* 【商】交换媒介(指货币、支票等) ||**~ frequency** 【无】中频 / **'~-term** *a.* 中期的(指介乎长期和短期之间的) / **~ wave** 【无】中波

medley ['medli] Ⅰ *n.* ① 杂乱的一团；混杂的人群；混合物 ② (诗、文等的)杂集 ③【音】集成曲(几首歌曲的片断凑成的乐曲) ④[古]混战 Ⅱ *a.* 混杂的，混合的 Ⅲ *vt.* 使成杂乱一堆(或一团)；使混杂 ||**~ race** ① 各段距离不等的接力赛跑 ② 各段不同游泳式的游泳接力赛

meed [mi:d] *n.* ① [诗](指荣誉等)应得的一份；[古]挣得的报酬；工资 ② 适当的报答

meek [mi:k] *a.* ① 逆来顺受的，温顺的 ② 缺乏勇气和胆量的 ③ 适中的，柔和的，不猛烈的 ||as ~ as a lamb (或 moses) 非常温顺 ||**~ly** *ad.* / **~ness** *n.*

meet[1] [mi:t] Ⅰ (met [met]) ❶ *vt.* ① 遇见，与…相遇；碰上: I *met* him in the street. 我在街上遇见他。/ The two trains ~ at the bridge. 这两列火车在桥上面对面地驶过。/ ~ ... end on 【海】对遇… ② 认识；会见，会谈: *Meet* Mr. Smith. [美](介绍时用语) 这是史密斯先生。/ Pleased to ~ you. 遇见你很高兴。/ I know of him but I have never *met* him. 我知道他，但不认识他。/ arrange to ~ a friend at 3 o'clock 约好朋友在三点钟碰头 ③ 迎接: Will you ~ her at the station? 你到车站去接她吗? / ~ sb.'s train 到火车站去迎接某人 ④ 满足；符合: ~ the requirements of the consumers 满足消费者的需要 / ~ advanced world standards 达到世界先进水平 ⑤ 对付，应付；如期偿付，践(约): ~ a sudden danger cool-headedly 冷静地应付突然发生的危险 / ~ a bill 准备支付到期的票据 ⑥ 和…接触，与…相遇: ~ the eye (ear) 被看(听)到 ⑦ 与…对抗，与…会战 ⑧ (路等)与…交叉，与…相合: There the brook ~s the river. 在那里小溪汇入河流。❷ *vi.* ① 相遇；相会；相识: Good-bye till we ~ again. 下次再见! ② 接触；接合；会合；交战: His coat won't ~. 他的上衣(因太小)扣不上了。/ The two ends of the line ~ here. 线的两端在此接合。/ The village is located where the two rivers ~. 村庄坐落在那两条河流的汇合处。③ 集合；聚会，开会: The group leaders ~ once a week. 小组长每周碰头一次(开会)。④ (指品质方面)兼备，共存 (in) Ⅱ *n.* ① [美]集会，会: a sports ~ 运动会 / a singing ~ 歌咏会 [注意: 英国一般用 meeting] ②[英](狩猎前)猎人和猎犬的聚集 ③【数】交(集) ||*make (both) ends ~* 见 end / ~ *one's end* (或 fate) 死，送命 / ~ sb. halfway 在半路迎接(或迎战)某人; 迎合某人，迁就某人 / ~ *trouble halfway* 自寻烦恼，杞人忧天 / ~ *up with* 偶尔碰见 / ~ *with* ① (偶尔)遇见；碰到: Such fish are rarely *met with* in the north country. 这种鱼在北方难得看到。② 得到(赞成等)；遭受: The design has *met with* approval. 设计已被批准。/ ~ *(with) one's death* 死去

meet[2] [mi:t] *a.* 适当的，适合的 ||**~ly** *ad.* / **~ness** *n.*

meeting ['mi:tiŋ] Ⅰ *n.* ① 会议；会；集会: call (break up) a ~ 召集(解散)一次会议 / hold a ~ 开会 / address a ~ 向大会致辞；在会上发言 / a sports ~ [英]运动会 ② 聚会；会见 ③ 汇合点，交叉点: the ~ of two great rivers 两条大河的汇合处 ④ 会战；[古]决斗: a ~ engagement 遭遇战 ⑤【宗】(基督教教友会的)聚会；聚会所 ||~ *of minds* 意见一致 ||'~-house *n.* 【宗】(基督教教友会的)聚会所 / '~-place *n.* 会场

megaphone ['megəfoun] Ⅰ *n.* 喇叭筒，喊话筒；传声筒 Ⅱ ❶ *vt.* ① 用喇叭筒说出；用喊话筒喊话 ② 广泛宣传 ❷ *vi.* 用喊话筒喊话

melancholic [,melən'kɔlik] Ⅰ *a.* ① 忧郁的，使人抑郁的，令人忧伤的 ②【医】忧郁症的，患忧郁症的 Ⅱ *n.* 患忧郁症的人 ||**~ally** *ad.*

melancholy ['melənkəli] Ⅰ *n.* ① 忧郁；意气消沉 ②【医】忧郁症 Ⅱ *a.* ① 忧郁的；意气消沉的 ② 令人伤感的，使人抑郁的

mêlée ['melei] *n.* [法] ① 混战，格斗 ② 混乱的一

堆; 混乱的人群: push one's way through a ~ of taxis, bicycles and people 从汽车、自行车、人群中挤过去 ③ 激烈的论战

mellifluous [me'lifluəs] *a.* ① 加了蜜糖的; 流蜜糖的; 甜蜜的 ②(声音、言词等)甜美的, 流畅的 ‖~ly *ad.* / ~ness *n.*

mellow ['melou] *I a.* ①(水果)甘美多汁的; (酒)芳醇的 ②(声音)圆润的; (光、色等)柔和的 ③(土地)肥沃的, 松软的 ④(人)老成的, 成熟的 ⑤[口]温和的; 高兴的; 微醉的 ⑥[美俚]好的, 极好的 *II* ❶ *vt.* ① 使丰美; 使醇香 ② 使圆润; 使柔和 ③ 使老成, 使成熟 ❷ *vi.* ① 变得丰美; 变得醇香; 变得柔和 ② 变得老成, 成熟起来 ‖~ly *ad.* / ~ness *n.* /~y *a.*

melodrama ['melə,drɑ:mə] *n.* ①【戏】情节剧(一种不着重刻划人物, 一味追求情节奇异, 通常都有惩恶扬善结局的戏剧) ② 轰动的事件; 感情夸张的言行

melody ['melədi] *n.* ① 悦耳的音调, 美妙的音乐 ② 歌曲; 可咏唱的诗 ③【音】旋律, 曲调; 主调

melon ['melən] *n.* ① 瓜; 甜瓜: a *Hami* ~ 哈密瓜 ② 圆鼓鼓象瓜似的东西; 突出的肚子 ③[俚]红利; 赃物; 横财 ‖*cut a* ~ [俚]分红; 分赃 ‖~ *cutting* [俚]分红; 分赃, 瓜分 / ~ *tree* 【植】蕃木瓜树

melt [melt] *I* (过去式 melted, 过去分词 melted 或 molten ['moultən] ❶ *vi.* ① 融化; 熔化; (食物)酥融: The snow has ~ed. 雪融化了。 / Glass ~s at a high temperature. 玻璃在高温下熔化。 / This cake ~s in the mouth. 这蛋糕一进嘴就化掉了。 ②溶化; 液解: Salt ~s in water. 盐在水中溶解。 ③[口]感到热极: I am simply ~ing (with heat). 我简直热死了。 ④消散; 消失; (云)化雨: The fog soon ~ed in the morning sun. 在早晨的太阳下雾很快消散了。 ⑤(人、人的心肠或态度等)变软, 软化; (声音)变得柔润 ⑥ 融合: The sea seems to ~ into the sky at the horizon. 在地平线上仿佛海连着天。 ❷ *vt.* ① 使融化; 使熔化; 使溶解: Lead can be ~ed easily. 铅是容易熔化的。 ② 使消散; 使消失 ③ 使软化; 使柔软 ④[俚]把(支票等)兑现 *II n.* ① 熔(或溶)解; 熔化了的金属; 熔(或溶)解量 ② 熔炉的一次装料 ‖~ *away* ① 融掉; 消失; (钱)渐渐花光: The crowd ~ed away. 人群散去了。 ②(使)着迷, (使)神魂颠倒 / ~ *down* ① 熔化; 熔毁: ~ *down* metal scrap 熔化废金属 ②[谑]变卖(财产) / ~ *into* ① 化为, 消散于⋯: ~ *into* air 化为乌有, 烟消云散 / ~ *into distance* 消失在远方 ③因心软而⋯: ~ *into tears* 感动得流泪 ‖~**ability** [,meltə'biliti] *n.* 可熔性 / ~**able** *a.* 可熔的 ‖'~,water *n.* 融化的冰(或雪)水

melting ['meltiŋ] *a.* ① 融化的, 熔化的 ② 温柔的; 感伤的: speak in a ~ voice 充满柔情地说 / a ~ mood 感伤的心情 ‖~**ly** *ad.* ‖~ **point** 熔点 / ~ **pot** 熔化锅: go into the ~ *pot* 被彻

底改革; (感情、心情)变温和, 软化 ②各种族融合的国家(或地方)

member ['membə] *n.* ①(团体、组织等的)成员, 一分子; 会员: ~s of a family 家庭成员 / a ~ nation 会员国 ② [M-] 议员: a *Member* of Congress (美国)国会议员(略作 M. C.) / a *Member* of Parliament (英国)下院议员(略作 M. P.) ③ 部分;【语】子句;【逻】推论的命题 ④【数】元;【机】构件, 部件: driving (driven) ~ 主动(从动)构件 ⑤(政治团体的)部门, 支部 ⑥ 身体的一部分; (人和动物的)器官; 植物体的一部分 ‖*a* ~ *of Christ* 基督教徒 / ~s *above* (*below*) *the gangway* [英]观点与所属政党的政策较密切(较不密切)的下议员 / *the honourable and gallant* ~ (英国议会)军人身分的议员 / *the unruly* ~ 难于控制的器官(指舌头) ‖~**ed** *a.* [常用以构成复合词]有⋯会员的; 有⋯肢体的 / ~**less** *a.* 无会员的 / ~**ship** *n.* ①成员资格; 会员资格: a ~*ship* committee 会员资格审查委员会 ② 全体成员;全体会员 ③ 成员人数; 会员人数: The trade union has a large ~*ship.* 工会有很多会员。/ a ~*ship* of 150 一百五十名成员

membrane ['membrein] *n.* ①【解】【生】膜: mucous ~ 粘膜 / tympanic ~ (耳)鼓膜 ②膜状物, 薄膜 ③ 羊皮纸; 羊皮纸文件中的一页

memento [mi'mentou] ([复] memento(e)s) *n.* ①纪念品 ② 引起人回忆的东西; 引起人警惕的东西 ③ 回忆 ‖*memento mori* ['mɔ:rai] [拉]死的警告; 死的象征(骷髅等)

memo ['mi:mou, 'memou] *n.* [口] =memorandum

memoir ['memwɑ:] *n.* ①[复]回忆录; 自传 ② 传记, 传略; 报道 ③学术论文; 研究报告, 专题报告; [复]学会纪要 ④[罕](外交上的)备忘录

memorable ['memərəbl] *a.* 值得纪念的; 值得注意的; 难忘的 ‖**memorability** [,memərə'biliti] *n.* / ~**ness** *n.* /**memorably** *ad.*

memorandum [,memə'rændəm] ([复] memorandums 或 memoranda [,memə'rændə]) *n.* ①备忘录; (契约等条文的)节略: a ~ book 备忘录 / a protest ~ 抗议书 ②【商】便笺, 便函

memorial [mi'mɔ:riəl] *I a.* ① 记忆的 ② 纪念的, 追悼的: a ~ meeting 追悼会 / a ~ park 陵园, 公墓 / a ~ service【宗】追思礼拜 *II n.* ①纪念物; 纪念日; 纪念碑; 纪念馆: a war ~ 战争纪念碑(乡村中刻有在两次世界大战中阵亡村民名字的纪念碑, 尤指英国乡村中的) ②[复]年代记; 编年史 ③请愿书, 抗议书 ④(外交上的)备忘录; 略 ‖~**ist** *n.* ①请愿者; 请愿书起草(或署名)人 ②回忆录作者, 传记作者 ‖**Memorial Day** ①(美国)阵亡将士纪念日(大多数州定为五月三十日) ②(美国)南方联邦阵亡将士纪念日(纪念南北战争中阵亡将士)

memorize, memorise ['meməraiz] *vt.* ① 记住, 熟记 ②记录 ③【自】存储

memory ['meməri] *n.* ① 记忆; 记忆力: if my ~

serves me 如果我记得不错的话 / speak from
~ 单凭记忆讲 / have a good (bad) ~ 记忆力好
(差) ②留在记忆中的人(或事物); 回忆: His ~
will always live. 他永远不会被人遗忘。/ It
seems already a distant ~. 这对象是很久以前的
事了。/ a ~ of one's boyhood 童年的回忆 ③记
忆期间, 追想得起的年限: be still within living
~ 至今还被人牢记着 ④纪念 ⑤死后的名声: a
man of hon oured ~ 已故的受人尊敬的人 ⑥【自】
存储; 存储器 ‖a convenient (或 an accommodating) ~ 只记住对己有利的事 / beyond the
~ of men 有史以前 / commit sth. to ~ 把某
事记住 / have a ~ like a sieve 记忆力极差,
什么也记不住 / of blessed ~ 先, 故(加于已故
君王等称呼后面, 表示敬意) / slip sb.'s ~ 使某
人一时想不起来: His name slipped my ~. 他
的名字我一时想不起来了。/ to the best of
one's ~ 就记忆所及

men [men] man 的复数 ‖~'s room 男厕所
menace ['menəs] I n. ①威胁, 恐吓: constitute
a ~ to world peace 成为对世界和平的威胁 / spit
angry ~s at sb. 怒气冲冲地用言词恐吓某人
②威胁者; 危险物; 引起烦扰者: That boy is a
~. 那个孩子是个捣蛋鬼。 II ❶ vt. 威胁, 恐吓;
危及 ❷ vi. 进行威胁, 进行恐吓 ‖~r n. 威胁者,
恐吓者 / menacingly ad. 威胁地, 恐吓地
menagerie [mi'nædʒəri] n. ①动物园 ②动物展
览; (马戏团中)囚在笼中的兽群
mend [mend] I ❶ vt. ①修理, 修补; 织补, 缝补:
~ a road 修路 / ~ a hole 补洞 ②改正, 纠正;
改善, 改进: ~ one's ways 改过自新 / ~ the
state of affairs 使事态好转 ③加快; 加(火): ~
one's pace 加快步伐 / ~ the fire 添火 ④治愈,
使恢复健康 ❷ vi. ①渐愈, 好转: The patient
will ~ soon. 病人会很快好起来的。/ wait for
one's injury to ~ 等待创伤好起来 ②改过, 改善
II n. ①修补; 缝补; 修补好的地方: The ~s on
your shirt were almost invisible. 你衬衣上的
补钉简直看不出来。②好转, 痊愈 ‖It's never
too late to ~. [谚]改过不嫌晚。/ Least said,
soonest ~ed. (或 The least said, the soonest
~ed.) 见 least / ~ one's fences 见 fence /
~ or end 不改则废 / ~ or mar 或成之或
毁之 / on the ~ (或 on the ~ing hand)
(病情或事态)在好转中 ‖~able a. ①可修补
的 ②可改正的, 可改善的 / ~er n. [常用以构
成复合词]修补者: a road-~er 修路工
mendacious [men'deiʃəs] a. ①虚假的, 捏造的:
a ~ report 虚假的报道 ②好说谎的, 爱捏造的
‖~ly ad. / ~ness n.
mendicant ['mendikənt] I a. 行乞的; 乞丐的
II n. ①乞丐; 行乞者 ②[常作 M-] (到处化缘
的)托钵僧
menial ['mi:njəl] I a. ①仆人的, 奴仆的 ②奴性
的; 卑下的 II n. ①仆人 ②奴性的人; 卑
下的人 ‖~ly ad.

mensurable ['menʃurəbl] a. ①可量的 ②【音】定
量的, 有固定节奏的 ‖**mensurability** [,menʃurə-
'biliti] n.
mensuration [,mensjuə'reiʃən] n. ①测定, 测量
②【数】求积法, 量法
mental[1] ['mentl] I a. ①精神的, 思想的; 内心的:
~ outlook 精神面貌 / ~ arithmetic 心算 ②脑
力的, 智力的: reduce the difference between
manual and ~ labour 缩小体力劳动和脑力劳动
的差别 / ~ faculties 智力 / ~ age 智力年龄 /
~ deficiency 智力缺陷 ③精神病的: a ~ patient
精神病人 / a ~ specialist 精神病医生 / a ~
hospital (或 home, asylum) 精神病院, 疯人院
II n. [口]精神病; 精神病患者 ‖~ly ad. 精神
上; 在内心; 智力上: be ~ly prepared 有精神
准备
mental[2] ['mentl] a. 【解】颏的
mentality [men'tæliti] n. ①脑力, 智力: persons
of average ~ 一般智力的人 ②精神, 思想; 心理
mention ['menʃən] I n. ①提及, 说起: at the ~
of 在提到…时 ②(战报等中对杰出事迹的)提述;
提名表扬: receive an honourable ~ 得到表扬 II
vt. ①提到, 说起: He ~ed to me that he would
leave soon. 他对我讲起他马上就要走了。/ as
~ed above 如上所述 ②提述; 提名表扬: be ~ed
in the dispatches 在战报中得到表扬 ‖Don't ~
it. (答复别人道谢时用语)不用客气。(或: 不用
谢。) / make ~ of 提及… / not to ~ (或
without ~ing) 更不必说: The boy has not
learnt arithmatics, not to ~ algebra. 这孩子
算术还没学会, 更谈不上代数了。
mentor ['mentɔ:] n. ①[M-] (古希腊史诗《奥德
赛》中)奥德修斯的忠诚朋友; 奥德修斯之子的良
师 ②良师益友 ③私人教师, 辅导教师
menu ['menju:] n. ①菜单 ②饭菜, 菜肴: an
excellent ~ 佳肴; 一顿美餐
mercantile ['mə:kəntail] a. ①商业的, 贸易的; 商
人的 ②重商主义的: ~ system 重商主义
‖~ marine [总称] ①(一个国家的)商船 ②(一
个国家的)商船船员 / ~ paper 商业票据
mercenary ['mə:sinəri] I a. ①为钱的, 唯利是图
的, 贪财的: a ~ marriage 完全着眼于实利的婚
姻 ②被雇佣在外国军队中的; 雇佣的: the ~
system 募兵制 / ~ troops 雇佣军 II n. 外国雇佣
兵 ‖**mercenarily** ['mə:sinərili; 美 ,mə:si'nerili]
ad. / mercenariness n.
merchandise ['mə:tʃəndaiz] I n. [总称]商品, 货
物: general ~ 杂货 II ❶ vi. [美]经商 ❷ vt.
[美]买卖; 推销 ‖~r n. 商人
merchant ['mə:tʃənt] I n. ①(批发)商人(尤指进
出口贸易商人): a wholesale ~ 批发商人 / a ~
of death 死亡商人(指军火商) ②零售商 ③[接
在所经营的商品名后构成复合词]…商: a coal-~
煤炭商 ④[俚]好…的人, 迷于…的人: a speed
~ 喜欢把车子开得飞快的人 II vt. 经营, 买卖
III a. 商人的; 商业的; 商船的: a ~ ship 一艘商

船 / laws ~ [主英]商事法规 ‖**~able** *a.* 可销售的, 有销路的 / **~like** *a.* 商人似的 ‖**~man** ['mə:tʃəntmən] *n.* 商船 / **~ marine, ~ service** [总称] ①(一个国家的)商船 ②(一个国家的)商船船员 / **~ prince** 豪商, 富商 / **~ tailor** (供应衣料或成衣的)定制服装裁缝

merciful ['mə:siful] *a.* 仁慈的, 宽大的 ‖**~ly** *ad.* / **~ness** *n.*

merciless ['mə:silis] *a.* 冷酷无情的, 残忍的 ‖**~ly** *ad.* / **~ness** *n.*

mercurial [mə:'kjuəriəl] **I** *a.* ①水银的, 汞的; 含水银的; 由水银引起的: a ~ barometer 水银气压计 / ~ ointment 含汞药膏 / ~ poisoning 水银中毒, 汞中毒 ②活泼的, 易变的: a ~ temperament 反复无常的性情 ③ [M-] 水星的 ④雄辩的; 狡诈的; 贼性的 **II** *n.* 汞制剂 ‖**~ism** *n.* 水银中毒, 汞中毒 / **~ity** [,mə:kjueri'æliti] *n.* 活泼, 易变 / **~ly** *ad.*

mercury ['mə:kjuri] *n.* ①水银, 汞: a ~-arc lamp 汞弧灯 / a ~-vapour lamp 汞汽灯, 水银灯 / ~ (或 mercuric) chloride 氯化汞, 升汞 ②(温度计等中的)水银柱: The ~ stood at nearly 40°C. 水银柱几乎升到了摄氏四十度。/ The ~ is rising. [喻]天气(或情绪)好起来了。③活泼: He has no ~ in him. 他不活泼。④ [the M-] 【天】水星 ⑤ [M-]【罗神】墨丘利(为众神传信并掌管商业、道路等的神) ⑥[常作 M-](用于报刊名)信使; [古]向导: *Mercury and News* 《信使和新闻》(美国报刊名) ⑦[植]山靛(一种有毒植物)

mercy ['mə:si] **I** *n.* ①怜悯, 宽恕; 仁慈; 恩惠: throw oneself on sb.'s ~ 请求某人的宽容 ②幸运, 侥幸: That's a ~! 那真幸运! **II** *int.* 嗳呀[表示惊奇或假装惊恐等]: *Mercy!* 嗳呀! / *Mercy on me!* 我的天哪! ‖*at the ~ of* 在…支配中, 任凭…摆布: *at the ~ of circumstances* 受环境所支配 / *be left to the tender ~* (或 *mercies*) *of* 任凭…虐待 / *have ~ on* (或 *upon*) 对…表示怜悯 / *sin one's mercies* 幸运而不感恩 / *without ~* 毫不容情地; 残忍地 ‖**~ killing** (使受刑者)减少痛苦的处决 / **~ seat** 【宗】约柜上的金板; 上帝的御座

mere¹ [miə] *a.* ①仅仅的, 只不过的: a paper tiger that can be punctured with a ~ stroke 一戳就穿的纸老虎 ②纯粹的: a ~ nobody 十足的小人物 ‖**~ly** *ad.* 仅仅, 只不过: It is ~ly a matter of time. 这仅仅是时间问题。

mere² [miə] *n.* 池塘

meretricious [,meri'triʃəs] *a.* ①娼妓的 ②浮华的, 耀眼的; 俗气的 ③(论据等)虚夸的, 似是而非的 ‖**~ly** *ad.* / **~ness** *n.*

merge [mə:dʒ] ❶ *vt.* ①使(企业等)合并; 使并入: ~ a company into another 把一家公司并入另一家公司 ②使结合 ③使渐渐消失; 吞没 ❷ *vi.* 合并; 结合; 渐渐消失: ~ into a single whole 合为一体 / Twilight was *merging* into darkness. 暮色渐浓。‖**~r** *n.* (企业等的)合并, 并吞; 合并者

meridian [mə'ridiən] **I** *n.* ①【天】子午圈, 子午线: the prime (或 first) ~ 本初子午圈, 本初子午线 / the ~ of longitude 黄经圈 ②顶点, 极点; 全盛时期: the ~ of life 壮年, 盛年 **II** *a.* ①【天】子午圈的, 子午线的: a ~ circle 子午仪 / a ~ plane 子午面 / ~ transit (或 passage) 中天 ②顶点的, 极点的; 全盛时期的

meringue [mə'ræŋ] *n.* [法] ①(将蛋白、白糖等打和并烘烤成棕色后覆盖在糕、饼上的)蛋白酥皮 ②(用来包裹冰淇淋、水果等的)蛋白酥皮筒 (或卷); 蛋白甜饼

merino [mə'ri:nou] **I** *n.* ①美利奴绵羊(产细密的丝状羊毛) ②美利奴羊毛; 美利奴精纺毛纱; 美利奴毛织物; 棉毛混纺针织物 **II** *a.* 美利奴绵羊的; 美利奴羊毛(织)的

merit ['merit] **I** *n.* ①长处, 优点; 价值: ~s and demerits 优缺点 / appoint people on their ~ 任人唯贤 ②功绩, 功劳; 荣誉 ③[有时用复]功过, 功罪 ④法律意义, 法律依据; [复]是非曲直: decide the case *on* its ~s 根据是非曲直断案 **II** ❶ *vt.* 值得, 应受: It ~s our attention. 这事值得我们注意。❷ *vi.* 应受赏(或罚) ‖*have the ~s* 【律】在诉讼中证明自己有理(但由于法律上的原因不能取得对自己有利的判决) / *make a ~ of sth.* 以某事居功自夸 ‖**~ system** 根据才能任命(或提升)文职人员的制度

meritorious [,meri'tɔ:riəs] *a.* 有功的; 值得称赞的, 可奖励的: ~ deeds 功绩 ‖**~ly** *ad.* / **~ness** *n.*

mermaid ['mə:meid] *n.* ①(传说中的)美人鱼 ②[美]女子游泳健将

merry ['meri] *a.* ①欢乐的, 愉快的, 兴高采烈的: Signs of ~ life could be seen everywhere after the bumper harvest. 丰收以后到处可以看到一片欢乐景象。/ A *Merry* Christmas! 祝圣诞节快乐! ②微醉的 ③轻快的; 激烈的; [用以加强语气]狠狠的: at a ~ pace 用轻快的步伐 / give sb. a ~ hell 狠狠地揍某人一顿 ④[古]令人愉快的; 可爱的: ~ England 可爱的英格兰(英国人从前的说法) ‖a ~ man 见 man / as ~ as a cricket (或 grig, lark) 非常快活 / make ~ 尽情欢乐; 宴乐; 作乐 / make ~ at another's expense 以取笑别人为乐 / make ~ over 嘲弄, 嘲笑 / men of May 见 man / the ~ monarch 见 monarch / merrily 见 merrily ‖**~ment** *n.* ‖**~-andrew** ['meri'ændru:] *n.* 小丑; 江湖医生的助手 / **~ dancers** [英]北极光 / **'~-go-,round** *n.* ①(儿童玩乐用的)旋转木马 ②[美俚](指工作、活动等)高度的繁忙; 走马灯似的打转 / **'~,making** *n.* 作乐; 欢乐; 欢宴 / **'~thought** *n.* [主英](鸟胸的)叉骨

mesh [meʃ] **I** *n.* ①网眼, 网孔; 筛眼, 筛孔; 每平方吋的网孔(或筛孔)数 ②[常用复]网(丝); 网络, 网状结构: steel ~es used for reinforcing concrete 加固混凝土用的钢筋网 ③网织品; 网状物: a ~ handbag 网线袋 / the ~ of irrigation canals 灌溉网 ④[常用复]罗网,圈套; 纠缠,错综复杂: be caught in the ~es of the law 陷入法网 / a ~ of circumstance 错综复杂的情况 ⑤【机】(齿轮的)啮合: The gears are in ~. 齿轮相互啮合。II ❶ vt. ①用网捕捉; 使缠住: Lots of fishes are ~ed today. 今天捕了很多鱼。②使成网状: The city was ~ed in the morning haze. 晨雾笼罩这座城市。③使紧密配合; 【机】使啮合 ❷ vi. ①被网缠住; 落网 ②紧密配合; 【机】相啮合: The two plans ~ed with each other smoothly. 这两个计划互相配合得很好。‖'~work n. 网(丝); 网络; 网织品

mesmerism ['mezmərizəm] n. ①催眠; 催眠状态; 催眠术 ②催眠力; 巨大的魅力

mess [mes] I n. ①伙食团(尤指海陆军的); 食堂; 集体用膳人员; 伙食: be at ~ 在食堂吃饭 / go to ~ 去食堂吃饭 ②一份食品(常指半流质的); (给猎狗等吃的)杂食; [古]一道菜 ③足够一顿吃的量; 一次(抓、捕)所得量: pick a ~ of strawberries 摘了足够吃一顿的草莓 / a ~ of carp 一网鲤鱼 ④混乱; 混杂,大杂烩; 肮脏: a hopeless ~ 不可收拾的局面, 一团糟 / The room is a ~. 这房间又脏又乱。⑤困境: get in (或 into) a ~ 陷入困境 ⑥[美俚]笨人, 傻瓜 II ❶ vt. ①使就餐, 给…供膳; [英方]配给(食物), 分(菜): The guests will be ~ed in the east building. 客人们安排在东大楼就餐。②弄糟; 搞乱; 弄脏: The boy's clothes are all ~ed. 这男孩的衣服都弄脏了。③妨碍; 干扰 ④粗暴地处理 ❷ vi. ①准备伙食; 供膳 ②集体用膳: ~ three times a day aboard ship 在船上食堂里一天吃三餐 / The four friends ~ed together. 四个朋友在一块儿吃饭。③搞乱; 陷入混乱 ④瞎弄, 摆弄; 干涉: ~ing with the spoon and finish your breakfast. 不要把匙子弄来弄去, 快把早饭吃了。‖a ~ of pottage 付出较崇高的精神方面的代价而得到的物质享受 / Benjamin's ~ 最大的份儿 / lose the number of one's ~ (英海军用语)死 / make a ~ of 把…弄糟, 把…搞得一塌糊涂: make a ~ of it (the job) 把事情搞得一团糟 / ~ about [主英] = ~ around / ~ around ①[美俚]浪费时间, 混日子: He is always ~ing around doing nothing. 他老是荡来荡去不做事。②[美俚]粗暴地对待(某人) / ~ up ①搞乱; 弄糟; 弄脏 ②[美俚]陷入困境; 引起麻烦 ③粗暴地处理 ‖'~boy n. (船上的)食堂服务员 / ~ call 就餐号 / '~cook n. =~man / '~deck n. 住舱甲板, 寝居甲板 / ~ gear, ~ kit 餐具; 士兵野战膳食用具 / hall, ~ room 食堂, 餐室 / ~ing allowance 伙食津贴 / ~ jacket 晚餐(礼)服 / ~man ['mesmən] n.(海军)炊事兵 / '~mate n. 同吃的伙伴 / '~tin n. 饭盒子 / '~-up n. [口]混乱

message ['mesidʒ] I n. ①文电, 通讯; 消息, 音信; 祝词: a ~ of greeting (或 a congratulatory

~) 贺电, 贺信 / a ~ centre【军】文件收发所 / Would you mind giving him a ~? 请你带个口信给他好吗? / a New Year ~ 新年祝贺 ②差使: go on a ~ 出外替别人办事 / run ~s for sb. 为某人送信跑腿 ③[美]咨文: the U. S. President's State of the Union ~ to the Congress 美国总统向国会提出的国情咨文 ④启示; 教训; (先知的)预言; 要旨; 寓言 ⑤广告词句: a ~ copywriter 专门撰写广告词的人 ⑥【讯】(无线)电报; 话传电报: a half-rate ~ 半价电报 / an international ~ 国际电报 II ❶ vt. 通知; 发信号传达; 同…通讯联系 ❷ vi. 带信息; 通信联系

messenger ['mesindʒə] n. ①送信者; 使者;【军】通信员, 传令兵 ②顺着风筝线送上天空的纸片 ③【海】引绳 ‖a corbie ~ 一去不返(或回来很晚)的使者(源出基督教《圣经》的《创世纪》) ‖~ cable, ~ wire【电】吊线, 悬线 / ~ call 传呼(电话) / ~ service【军】传令勤务

Messiah [mi'saiə] n. ①弥赛亚(犹太人期望中的复国救主) ②[基督教]救世主, 耶稣; [m-] (民族的)救星 ‖**Messianic** [,mesi'ænik] a. ①救世主的 ②以救世主自居的

Messrs. ['mesəz] [缩] ①[法] Messieurs ② Mr. 的复数

met [met] meet¹的过去式和过去分词

metal ['metl] I n. ①金属; 金属制品; 金属性: a base ~ 贱金属;基底金属(合金中的主要金属); 碱金属 / a precious(或 noble) ~ 贵金属 / a light ~ 轻金属 / a ferrous ~ 黑色金属 / a rare ~ 稀有金属 / an exotic ~ 新金属 ②金属合金; 淦(一种金属合金) ③[英][复]轨道: The train left (或 jumped) the ~s. 火车出轨了。④铸铁熔液;制造玻璃用的熔融态原料 ⑤[印]活字金; 排好活字的(铅)版 ⑥气质; 本质; 勇气 ⑦(一次发出的)炮火力; [英][总称]【军】坦克(或装甲车等) ⑧[主英][铺路用的]碎石料(=road-~) II (metal(l)ed; metal(l)ing) vt. ①用金属包 ②用碎石铺(路): a ~ed road 碎石路 ‖heavy ~ ①重金属 ②[总称]重型坦克(或装甲车) ③难对付的敌手 ‖'~ware n. 金属器皿(尤指家庭用的) / '~work n. 金属制品; 金属制造 / '~,worker n. 金属制造工 / '~,working n. 金属制造; 金属加工 a. (从事)金属制造的

metallic [mi'tælik] I a. ①金属(性)的,金属质的; 金属制的; 含金属的: lustre 金属光泽 / (a) ~ currency 硬币 / a ~ standard 金(或银)本位 ②产金属的 ③(颜色等)象金属的; (态度、声音等)生硬的,刺耳的 II n. [复]金属粒子 ‖~ally ad.

metallurgy [me'tælədʒi] n. 冶金学,冶金术 ‖**metallurgist** n. 冶金学家

metamorphosis [,metə'mɔ:fəsis] ([复] metamorphoses [,metə'mɔ:fəsi:z]) n. ①变形; 变质; 变状 ②魔术引起的变形 ③【生】变态

metaphor ['metəfə] *n.* 【语】隐喻(一种修辞手段) (如说 a glaring mistake); (泛指)比喻的说法 ‖(a) *mixed* ~ 前后不一致的隐喻

metaphysic [,metə'fizik] *n.* 形而上学, 玄学; 玄学体系

mete[1] [mi:t] *n.* 边界, 分界; 分界标志, 界石: ~*s and bounds* 【律】边界, 分界

mete[2] [mi:t] *vt.* ①给予, 派给: ~ *out* rewards 给予报酬 / ~ *out* severe punishment to sb. 严惩某人 ②[古]计量 ‖'~-**wand**, '~-**yard** *n.* [英][喻]评价的标准

meteor ['mi:tjə] *n.* ① 大气现象(如闪电、虹等) ②流星 ③(流星的)曳光

meteoric [,mi:ti'ɔrik] *a.* ① 大气的; 气象(学)的: ~ *water* 天落水,大气水 ②流星的: a ~ *stream* (或 swarm, train) 流星群 / ~ iron 陨铁 ③流星似的; [喻]转瞬即逝的; 闪烁的 ‖~**ally** *ad.*

meteorite ['mi:tjərait] *n.* 陨星: an iron ~ 铁陨星, 陨铁 / a stony ~ 石陨星, 陨石 ‖**meteoritic(al)** [,mi:tjə'ritik(ə)l] *a.*

meteorology [,mi:tjə'rɔlədʒi] *n.* ①气象学: aeronautical ~ 航空气象学 ② (一地区的)气象 ‖**meteorologist** *n.* 气象学家

meter[1] ['mi:tə] I *n.* ①计量器; 计, 表, 仪表: a gas ~ 气量计; 煤气表 / a kilowatt-hour ~ 千瓦小时计, 电度表 / a water ~ 水表 ② 计量人; 计量官 II *vt.* ①用表测量(或计量) ② 计量(或按规定量)供给: Fuel is ~*ed* to the engine. 燃料被置入发动机。③用邮资总付计数器在(邮件)上打戳 ‖~ **maid** 处理违章停车的女警察

meter[2] ['mi:tə] *n.* [美] =metre[1], metre[2]

method ['meθəd] *n.* ①方法, 办法, 法; [美]教学法: use different ~*s* to solve different contradictions 用不同的方法解决不同的矛盾 / native (或 indigenous) ~*s* 土办法 / the dialectical ~ 辩证法 / the deductive (inductive) ~ 演绎(归纳)法 / a ~ of teaching foreign languages 外语教学法 / a course in ~*s* 一门关于教学法的课程 ② 条理; 秩序: If you had used more ~, you wouldn't have wasted so much time. 要是你安排得更有条理些, 就不会浪费那么多时间了。

methodism ['meθədizəm] *n.* ①墨守成规 ②[M-]【基督教】卫理公会; 卫理公会派教义(或仪式、组织) ‖**methodist** *n.* ①墨守成规者 ② [贬]宗教观点死板者; [M-]卫理公会教徒 *a.* [M-]卫理公会的; 卫理公会教徒的

methylate ['meθileit] I *vt.* 【化】向…导入甲基; 在…中加入甲醇 II *n.* =methoxide ‖~**d** *a.* 甲基化了的; 加入甲醇的: ~*d* spirit 用甲醇变性的酒精

meticulous [mi'tikjuləs] *a.* ① 过分注意细节的, 谨小慎微的 ② 过细的, 细致的: in a ~ way 过细地, 细致地 / careful and ~ calculation 精打细算 ‖~**ly** *ad.* 过细地, 细致地: work ~*ly* 过细地做工作 / ~**ness** *n.*

metre[1] ['mi:tə] *n.* ①(诗的)韵律, 格律 ②【音】拍子

metre[2] ['mi:tə] *n.* (公制长度单位)米, 公尺 ‖'~-'**kilogram(me)-'second** *a.* 【物】米·公斤·秒制的: ~-*kilogram(me)-second* system 米·公斤·秒制

metric ['metrik] *a.* 公制的, 米制的: the ~ system 公制, 米制 / the ~ ton 公吨 (=1,000 公斤) ‖~**ally** *ad.*

metrical ['metrikəl] *a.* ①(诗的)韵律的, 格律的: a ~ romance 韵文小说 ② 测量的, 度量的: ~ geometry 度量几何 ‖~**ly** *ad.*

metropolis [mi'trɔpəlis] *n.* ① 主要都市, 大城市, 大都会 (常指首都、首府或文化等的中心): the ~ [英]伦敦 ② (某种商业活动等的)中心城市: a lumber ~ 木材业中心 ③(殖民地的)宗主国(或宗主城市) ④【宗】大主教教区

metropolitan [,metrə'pɔlitən] I *a.* ① 主要都市的, 大城市的, 大都会的 ②【宗】大主教教区的; 大主教的 ③宗主(国)的: a ~ country (或 state) 宗主国 II *n.* ①大城市人; 大城市派头的人 ②大主教 ‖~**ate** *n.* 大主教的教座(或教区) / ~**ize** *vt.* 使大都会化

mettle ['metl] *n.* 气质, 勇气; 精神: a man of ~ 有勇气的人 ‖*be on one's* ~ 鼓起勇气, 奋发 / *put sb. on his* ~ 激励某人, 使某人奋发 ‖~**d**, ~**some** ['metlsəm] *a.* 精神饱满的; 勇敢的; 有生气的

mew[1] [mju:] I *n.* 咪, 喵(猫叫声) II *vi.* 咪咪叫, 喵喵叫

mew[2] [mju:] I *n.* ① 隐蔽处, 密室 ② [英][~s] [用作单或复]马厩 (常指庭院四周的一圈马房), (马厩改建的)汽车房(或平房) ③ [英][~s] [用作单或复]小街, 小巷 ④[古]鹰笼(尤指在鹰换羽毛期用的) II ❶ *vt.* ① 把(鹰)关进笼子; 把(某人)关起来 (*up*) ②[古](鹰)换(羽毛) ❷ *vi.* [古]换羽毛

mew[3] [mju:] *n.* 鸥, 海鸥 (= ~ gull)

mezzotint ['medzoutint] I *n.* ① 金属版印刷法 ②金属版印刷品 II *vt.* 把…制成金属版

Mg 【化】元素镁 (magnesium) 的符号

mica ['maikə] *n.* 【矿】云母: sheet ~ 云母片 ‖'~-**schist** *n.* 【地】云母片岩 / '~-**slate** *n.* 【地】云母板岩

mice [mais] mouse 的复数

microbe ['maikroub] *n.* 微生物; 细菌

microcosm ['maikroukɔzəm] *n.* ①【物】微观世界, 微观宇宙 ② (人类、社会等的)缩影 ‖~**ic** [,maikrou'kɔzmik] *a.* ~*ic salt* 【化】小天地盐 (四水合磷酸氢铵钠的别名)

microfilm ['maikroufilm] I *n.* ① (印刷物等的)缩微胶卷 ② 缩微照片; 缩微放大照片 II ❶ *vt.* 用缩微法拍摄 ❷ *vi.* 摄制缩微胶卷 ‖~**er** *n.* 缩微机; 缩微摄影者 / ~ **reader** 显微阅读器

micrometer [mai'krɔmitə] *n.* 测微计, 微距计; 千分尺: an annular ~ 圆径千分尺 / an eyepiece

~ 目镜千分尺 / an inside (outside) ~ 内径(外径)千分尺 / ~ caliper(s) 千分卡尺

microphone ['maikrəfoun] *n.* (电话、录音、扩音等设备的)传声筒(俗称话筒或麦克风): a lapel ~ 佩带式传声器, 小型话筒 / a lip (hand) ~ 唇式(手持式)传声器 ‖**microphonic** [,maikrə'fɔnik] *a.*

microscope ['maikrəskoup] *n.* 显微镜: a binocular (simple) ~ 双筒(单筒)显微镜 / an electron ~ 电子显微镜 / a metallurgical ~ 冶金显微镜 / a reading ~ 读数显微镜

microscope

mid [mid] **I** *a.* ①中部的; 中间的, 居中的; 当中的: from ~ June to ~ August 从六月中到八月中 ②[常用以构成复合词]中, 中间: the Mid-Autumn Festival 中秋节 / the ~term exams 期中考试 / in the ~-fifties 在五十年代中期 / in ~air 在半空 ③【语】央元音的, 半开元音的(如 "cake" 中的 "a") **II** *prep.* [诗] =amid ‖**most** *a., ad. & n.* 正中, 中间; 最内部 ‖~**day** *n.* 正午, 日中: at ~day 在正午 / the ~day meal 午餐 / '**Mideast** *a.* 中东的: the Mideast situation 中东局势 / '~**,heaven** *n.* 天空中部, 中天; [古]子午圈 / ~**land** ['midlənd] *n.* 中部地方, 内地; [M-]英国中部方言, 美国中部及东部一些州的方言; [the Midlands] 英国中部 / [M-]英国中部的 / '~**,morning** *n.* 上午的中段时间 / '~**night** *n.* 晚上十二点钟, 午夜, 漆黑: ~night sun【天】半夜太阳 / at ~night 在午夜 / burn the ~night oil 工作到深更半夜, 开夜车 / '~**rib** *n.* 【植】(叶的)中脉 / ~**ship** *n.* 船身中部, 船中央 / '~**shipman** ['midʃipmən] *n.* [美]海军军官学校学员; [英]海军候补生 / '~**ships** *ad.* 在船身中部 / '~**stream** *n.* 中流: change horses in ~stream 中流换马 / [喻]在危急时期调换主持人 / '~**,summer** *n.* 仲夏; 夏至(六月二十二日左右): Midsummer Day 施洗约翰节(六月二十四日)(英国四结帐日之一) / ~**summer** madness 极度的疯狂 / '~**town** *n.* (城市的)商业区与住宅区之间的地区 / '~**way** *n.* ①中途 ②[美](博览会等中的)娱乐场, 游艺场 *a. & ad.* 中途(的) / '**Midway Islands** 中途岛[北太平洋] /

'~**'week** *n.* 周中; [M-] (公谊会教友的)星期三 / '~**'winter** *n.* 仲冬; 冬至(十二月二十二日左右) / '~**'year** *n.* 年中; 学年中期; [复]年中考试

midden ['midn] *n.* ①[英]粪堆; 垃圾堆 ②(考古学用语)贝冢, 贝丘 (=kitchen ~)

middle ['midl] **I** *n.* ① 中部, 中间, 当中: the ~ of a month 月中 / the ~ of a room 房间中央 ②身体的中部, 腰部 ③中间物, 中等物 ④中间派 ⑤(希腊语法中的)动词中间态 ⑥[英](报刊上常排在政论文与书评之间的)文学性短文 (=~ article) ⑦[逻]中名词; 【数】中项 (=~ term) **II** *a.* ①中部的, 中间的, 当中的: a ~ road 中间道路 / the ~ finger 中指 ②中等的, 中级的: a ~ school 中学 ③[M-]【语】中古的: Middle English 中古英语 / Middle French 中古法语 ④(希腊语法中的)中间态的 ⑤ 中产阶级的 **III** *vt. & vi.* (把…)放在中间; (把…)对折 ‖in the ~ of 在…当中; 在…的中途: in the ~ of the night 夜半时 / in the ~ of dinner 饭吃了一半时 / in the ~ of nowhere 在偏僻的地方 / knock sb. into the ~ of next week 把某人打得不省人事, 严惩某人 ‖~**most** *a.* [英]正中的, 最当中的 ‖~ **age** 中年 / '~**-aged** *a.* 中年的 / **Middle Ages** 中世纪 / '~**-'aisle** *vt.* [美俚](常后接 it) 结婚 / **Middle America** ①美国中产阶级 ②中部美洲(包括墨西哥及西印度群岛等地) ③美国的中西部 / '~**brow** *a. & n.* [美口]只有中等文化素养的(人); 中产阶级趣味的(人); 自以为渊博其实则浅薄的(人) / ~ **class** 中产阶级 / ~ **distance** ①(图景上的)中景 ②(四百米至一千五百米的)中距离赛跑 / ~ **ear**【解】中耳 / **Middle East** 中东 / '~**man** *n.* 经纪人, 中间人, 中人 / '~**-of-the-'road** *n.* 中间道路 / '~**-of-the= 'roader** *n.* 中间派, 走中间道路的人 / '~**-sized** *a.* 中等尺寸的 / ~ **watch**【海】(船上的)午夜值勤(从午夜到黎明四时) / '~**weight** *n.* 中量级拳手(或摔角)选手 / **Middle West** (美国的)中西部

middling ['midliŋ] **I** *a.* ① 中号的, 中级的, 中等的: a town of ~ size 中等城镇 / I feel only ~. [口]我身体觉得还好。②第二流的 **II** *ad.* [口]一般地; 相当地: ~ good 相当好 **III** *n.* ①中级品, 中等货 ② [~s][用作单或复](作饲料用的)麦麸, 粗粉 ③[美]标准棉花 ‖fair to ~ [口]过得去, 还算好 ‖~**ly** *ad.*

middy ['midi] *n.* ① [美口]海军军官学校学员; [英]海军候补生 ②水手领上衣, 水手领罩衫 ‖~ **blouse** 水手领女套衫

midge [midʒ] *n.* ①【动】蠓, 小蚊 ② 矮人, 侏儒 ③极小的鱼

midget ['midʒit] **I** *n.* ①矮人, 侏儒 ②(同类事物中的)极小者 **II** *a.* 小型的: a ~ submarine 小型潜艇, 袖珍潜艇

midst [midst] **I** *n.* 中部, 中间, 当中 **II** *prep.* [诗] =amidst ‖first, ~, and last 彻头彻尾,

始终 / *from* (或 *out of*) *the ~ of* 自…之中 / *in our* (*your, their*) ~ 在我们(你们,他们)当中 / *in the ~ of* 在…之中: the trees *in the ~ of* the forest 森林深处的树木 / *in the ~ of* cheers 在欢呼声中 / *into the ~ of* 入…之中

midwife ['midwaif] ([复] midwives ['midwaivz]) *n.* 助产士,接生婆 ‖**~ry** ['midwifəri] *n.* 产科学,助产学;接生

mien [mi:n] *n.* ①风度,神采;态度: a serious ~ 严肃态度 / with an easy self-possessed ~ 神色自若地,从容不迫地 ②外表,外貌

might[1] [mait] *n.* ①力量,威力;能力: work with all one's ~ 全力以赴地工作 / a man of ~ 大力士 / beyond one's ~ 超出自己的能力 ②强权;势力 ③[方]大量,很多 ‖**with** (或 **by**) *~ and main* 尽全力

might[2] [mait] (may[1] 的过去式) *v. aux.* [无人称变化;后接不带 to 的动词不定式;只用于表示现在或将来的概念]①[表示可能、不确定、期望、许可等,相当于 may,但更带迟疑、婉转、谦逊的色彩]可能,也许;可以: I'm afraid it ~ rain tonight. 我看今晚恐怕要下雨。/ Who ~ the man be? 这个人会是谁呢? / I wish I ~ find time to go into the question. 但愿我能找到时间去深入研究一下这个问题。/ *Might* I ask a question? 我是否无礼可以提个问题吗? / Well ~ you be surprised! 你满有理由感到惊奇嘛。②[用于表示与事实相反情况的虚拟语气中]会,能: If he were older, he ~ understand. 要是他年龄大些的话,他就可能懂了。/ I ~ have fulfilled the work earlier. 我本可以早一些完成这件工作的。③[表示请求或婉转的责备]请;应该: You ~ post this letter for me. 是否请您代我把这封信寄一下。/ You ~ well try again. 你不妨再试一下。/ You ~ write more frequently. 你该经常写信才是。(或: 请你经常写信。)

mightiness ['maitinis] *n.* ①强大,有力 ②高官,高位; [M-]阁下(对高位者的尊称) ‖**his** (或 **your**) **high ~** [谑]尊贵的阁下(间接提及时用his,直接称呼时用your)

mightn't ['maitnt] =might not

mighty ['maiti] **I** *a.* ①强大的,强有力的 ②巨大的,浩大的:a ~ tempest 大暴风雨 / the ~ ocean 汪洋大海 ③[口]伟大的,非凡的,了不得的: a ~ poet 一个伟大的诗人 / high and ~ 趾高气扬,神气活现 **II** *ad.* [口]非常,很: It is ~ easy. 这容易极了。‖~ **works** 见 work

migrate [mai'greit] ❶ *vi.* ①迁移;移居(尤指移居外国) ②(候鸟等)定期移栖;(鱼群)回游 ③[化][物]移动,游动 ❷ *vt.* 使移居;使徙动

mike[1] [maik] *n.* [口]话筒 (=microphone) ‖**~-fright** 广播时在话筒前的紧张(或胆怯)

nike[2] [maik] [俚] **I** *vi.* 偷懒;鬼混 **II** *n.* 偷懒的行为(或作风): be on the ~ (或 do a ~) 偷懒,吊儿郎当

milch [milt∫] *a.* (家畜)有奶的,生乳的;为取乳而饲养的;适于产奶的 ‖~ **cow** ①乳牛 ②财源,摇钱树

mild [maild] *a.* ①温和的,温柔的: ~ in disposition 性情温和 ②温暖的,暖和的: a ~ climate 温暖的气候 ③(酒、烟等)淡淡的 ④(在动作或作用方面)和缓的;适度的: a ~ medicine 作用和缓的药 ⑤(处罚等)轻微的;宽大的 ⑥【冶】低碳的,软的: ~ steel 低碳钢,软钢 ‖*as ~ as a dove* (或 *May, milk* 等)非常温和 / *draw it ~* 说(或做)得适度,不夸张 ‖~**ly** *ad.* ①温和地 ②适度地: to put it ~*ly* [常作插入语]说得婉转些 / ~**ness** *n.*

mildew ['mildju:] **I** *n.* ①霉 ②【植】霉病: ~ of millet 谷子白发病 **II** ❶ *vi.* 发霉,长霉,生霉 ❷ *vt.* 使发霉 ‖~**ed** *a.* ①发了霉的,长了霉花的 ②陈腐的: a ~*ed* notion 陈腐的想法 / ~**y** *a.* 发霉的;发了霉似的

mile [mail] *n.* ①英里,哩(常略作 mi., M., 或 m.): 80 ~*s* per hour 时速八十哩 / walk for ~*s* 走了好几哩路程 ②距离为一哩的赛跑(或赛马) ③海里,浬 (=nautical ~) ④较大的距离,较大的间隔: feel ~*s* better 觉得好得多 / miss the target a ~ 远远没有击中目标 ‖*an Admiralty ~* [英]=a nautical ~ / *an air* (或 *aeronautical*) ~ 空哩(距离等于海里) / *a geographical ~* 地理哩(距离等于海里) / *a nautical* (或 *sea*) ~ 海里,浬 / *a plane ~* 飞机哩(以一架飞机飞行一哩计算) / *a statute ~* 法定哩(距离等于英里) ‖*not a hundred ~s from* 离…不远;离…不久 / *not a hundred ~s off* (离…)不远;(离…)不久 / *stick out a ~* [俚]显而易见 ‖~ **r** *n.* 参加一哩赛跑的运动员(或马) ‖'~**post** *n.* 哩程标 / '~**stone** *n.* ①哩程碑 ②[喻]里程碑,(个人或人类)历史上的重大事件

mileage ['mailidʒ] *n.* ①哩数;哩程: traffic ~ [交]周转量 ②按哩计数的运费 ③按哩计数的旅费津贴 ④汽车消耗一加仑汽油所行的平均哩程 ⑤好处;利润

militant ['militənt] **I** *a.* ①战斗(性)的,富于战斗性的 ②好战的 ③交战中的,战斗中的 **II** *n.* 富有战斗精神的人;斗士(现尤指美国国内参加各种激进化运动的人) ‖~**ly** *ad.* / ~**ness** *n.*

militarism ['militərizəm] *n.* ①军国主义 ②好战精神;尚武精神 ‖**militarist** *n.* ①军国主义者 ②军事家

military ['militəri] **I** *a.* ①军事的;军用的: ~ training 军事训练 / ~ affairs 军事,军务 / ~ supplies 军需品 ②军人的;军队的: ~ ranks 军阶,军衔 / a man of ~ age 适龄(服兵役的)男子 / ~ discipline and ~ orders 军纪军令 / a ~ chest 军队金库;军队资金 ③陆军的; a ~ attaché 陆军武官 **II** ([复] military 或 militaries) *n.* ①[the ~][总称]武装部队,军方;陆军 ②[the ~][集合名词]军人(尤指军官) ‖**military ['militərili]; 美 ,mili'terili] *ad.* 在军事上,从军**

事角度 ‖ **~ academy** 陆军军官学校; 军事学院 / **~ band** 军乐队 / **~ commission** 特别军事法庭 (专门审讯违犯军法或戒严法公民的军事法庭) / **~ crest** 【军】防界线, 军事倾斜变换线 / **~ engineering** 军事工程学 / '**~-'feudal** *a.* 军事封建的 / **~ fever** 伤寒 / **~ government** (对占领区的)军事管制政府; 军人政府 / **~ intelligence** 军事情报; 军事情报工作; 军事情报部门 / **~ law** 军法 / **~ march** (军乐)进行曲 / **~ offence** 触犯军法 / **~ police** 宪兵队(略作 M.P. 或 MP) / **~ science** 军事科学; (普通学校中的)军事课 / **~ service** 兵役, 现役 / **~ testament, ~ will** 军人口头遗嘱

militate ['militeit] *vi.* 发生影响, 起作用: **~ against the success of the plan** 妨碍计划的成功

militia [mi'liʃə] *n.* ①民军组织; [总称]民兵: a contingent of the people's **~** 一支民兵队伍 ②[英](一九三九年开始征集的)国民军 ③[美](十八至四十五岁未入伍的)全体青、壮年男子; (各军种)编成的后备队; 全体国民警卫队队员 ‖**~man** [mi'liʃəmən] *n.* (男)民兵 / **militia, woman** *n.* 女民兵

milk [milk] **I** *n.* ①乳; 牛奶: breast **~** 人乳 / condensed **~** 炼乳 / skimmed **~** 脱脂乳 ②(植物、果实的)乳液, 乳状物; 【药】乳剂: coco(a)nut **~** 椰(子)汁 / **~** of lime 石灰乳 / **~** of magnesia 镁乳(一种泻药) **II** ❶ *vt.* 挤…的奶; 挤(奶): **~** a cow 挤牛奶 / **~** wholesome milk from healthy cows 从健康的牛挤出好奶 ②抽取(树等)的液汁; 抽取(乳液等); 取出(蛇等)的毒液 ③压, 榨; 榨取: **~** sb. dry 对某人进行敲骨吸髓的压榨 / **~** an enterprise 尽量从企业中榨取好处 ④套出(消息等) / [俚]窃取(电话、电报线)上的消息: **~** news from a source of information 从消息提供人士处套出新闻 ⑤加牛乳于 ❷ *vi.* ①挤乳 ②出奶: The cow **~s** well. 这头母牛出奶率高。‖**cry over spilt ~** 作无益的后悔 / **in ~** 在授乳期中的 / **in the ~** (谷物)因未成熟而呈浆状 / **~ and honey** 多种多样的享受; 丰饶 / **~ for babes** 简易的读物; 粗浅的东西 / **~ the bull** (或 **ram**) 作徒劳无益的事 / **pigeon's ~** 不存在的东西(愚人节时骗人去找的东西) / **That accounts for the ~ in the coco(a)nut.** [谑]啊, 原来如此。/ **the ~ of human kindness** 天生的善心; 人情味 ‖**~er** *n.* ①挤奶的人; 挤奶器 ②乳牛: a good (bad) **~er** 产乳多(少)的牛 ‖**~ abscess** 【医】乳房脓疮, 奶疮 / '**~-and-'water** *a.* 无味的, 缺乏生气的; 软弱无力的 / **~ bar** 卖牛奶、冷饮等的柜台 / '**~-churn** *n.* [主英]有盖的大牛奶桶 / **~ crust** 【医】奶癣 / **~ fever** 【医】产乳热 / **~ float** *n.* [主英]送牛奶的车子 / **~ leg** (产妇)股白肿病 / '**~-,livered** *a.* 胆小的, 懦怯的 / '**~maid** *n.* 挤奶女工 / **~man** ['milkmən] *n.* 卖(或送)牛奶的人 / **~ powder** 奶粉 / **~ run** [美俚]定期的循环轰炸(或搜索)飞行; 容易执行的飞行任务,

无危险的常规任务 / **~ shake** 牛奶和冰淇淋等的混合饮料 / **~ sickness** (曾在美国西部流行的因食病牛的肉、乳引起的)饮乳病, 毒乳病 / '**~sop** *n.* 懦弱的人, 没有骨气的人 / **~ sugar** 乳糖 / **~ tooth** 乳齿 / **~ vetch** [植]黄芪属植物; 紫云英: **~ vetch** honey 紫云英蜜 / **~ walk** 送牛奶人的值勤范围 / '**~weed** *n.* 【植】马利筋属植物 / **~ white** 乳白色 / '**~wort** *n.* 远志科植物

milky ['milki] *a.* ①牛奶的; 掺奶的; 多乳的; 出乳汁的: a **~** food 加了奶的食物 ②像牛奶的; 乳白色的; (液体)混浊不清的, 浊白的 ③柔弱的, 温顺的 ‖**Milky Way** 【天】银河: the *Milky Way galaxy* 银河系

mill¹ [mil] **I** *n.* ①磨坊, 碾磨厂; 面粉厂 ②磨臼; 磨(粉)机, 碾磨机: a coffee **~** 咖啡研磨机 ③制造厂, 工厂; 制造机构: a cotton **~** 棉纺厂 / a paper **~** 造纸厂 ④钱币压印机, 榨汁机; 【冶】轧钢机: a cane **~** 甘蔗榨汁机 / a plate **~** 轧板机 ⑤[机]铣床; 铣刀 ⑥(刻纹滚模的)钢芯 ⑦[美俚]拳击 ⑧[美俚]监狱 ⑨[美俚]机车; (飞机等的)马达 ⑩[美俚]打字机 **II** ❶ *vt.* ①碾磨; 磨碎; 磨出(面粉): **~** grain 碾谷物 / **~** ore 捣碎矿石 ②【机】铣 ③搅拌; 将…打成泡沫 ④[常以过去分词形式出现]在(钱币)上压印花边 ⑤使(畜群)绕圈子转 ⑥[纺]使(织物)缩绒(或缩呢) ⑦[美俚]用拳打 ❷ *vi.* ①(人、家畜)成群地乱转: **~** around within narrow confines 在狭小的圈子里打转 / crowds **~ing** in the theatre lobby 在剧场休息室里转来转去的人群 ②[美俚]殴斗 ③被研磨 ‖**go (put) through the ~** 经受(使经受)磨炼 / **in the ~** 在制造中 / **No ~, no meal.** [谚]不磨面, 没饭吃。/ **The ~s of God grind slowly.** [谚]天网恢恢, 疏而不漏。‖**~er** *n.* ①磨坊主; 面粉厂主: Every **~er** draws water to his own mill. [谚]人人为己。/ Too much water drowned the **~er**. [谚]太多反有害。②磨坊工人 ③铣床; 铣床用工具 ④铣工 ⑤碾磨机(或轧钢机等)的操作工人 ⑥粉翅蛾 ‖'**~board** *n.* 书皮纸板; 麻丝板 / '**~dam** *n.* ①为磨坊提供水力而造的拦河水坝 ②(为发动水车用的)贮水池 / **~ girl** 工厂女工, 纱厂女工 / **~ hand** 工厂工人 / '**~pond** *n.* ①(为发动水车用的)贮水池: like a **~pond** (指海洋)象贮水池一样风平浪静 ②[谑]北大西洋 / '**~race** *n.* ①(推动水车的)水流 ②(水车用)水沟 / **~race** ②(用碾磨测定矿质的)一定量矿砂 ③锯木厂可售出的木材产量 ④普通产品; [喻]平庸普通的人; 平凡的东西 / '**~-'run** *a.* ①刚从机器中生产出来的; 未经检验的; 未分级的 ②一般的, 普通的 / '**~stone** *n.* ①磨石: as hard as the nether **~stone** 铁石心肠 / be caught between the upper and nether **~stone** 被上下夹攻而陷于困境 / drop (或 weep) **~stones** 有铁石心肠, 在巨大悲哀事情前不落泪 / see far into a **~stone** 有特别敏锐的目光, 有神奇的智力(通常用作讽刺

语) ②重担 / '~stone grit【地】磨石粗砂岩 / '~stream n. (水车用)水流;(水车用)水沟 / ~wheel 水(车的)轮(子) / '~wright n. ①水车(或磨坊)设计人 ②磨轮机工,安装工

mill² [mil] n. [美]密尔(等于千分之一美元;只用于统计中)

millennium [mi'leniəm] ([复] millenniums 或 millennia [mi'leniə]) n. ①一千年,千年期 ②千年周年纪念日(或庆典)【基督教】至福一千年(据《圣经·启示录》,耶稣将再来统治人间一千年)④[喻]太平盛世;想象中的黄金时代

millet ['milit] n. ①黍,稷,小米: foxtail ~ 小米,谷子,粟 ②【植】狗尾草属植物

milliner ['milinə] n. 女帽及妇女头饰的设计(或制造,整修,销售)者 ‖~y ['milinəri] n. [总称]女帽,妇女头饰;女帽及妇女头饰商(或制造业)

milling ['miliŋ] n. ①磨粉;碾谷;谷类加工业;碾磨,碾碎【机】铣(法),铣削法;铣出的齿边③[纺]缩绒,缩呢,毡合 ④【矿】选矿 ⑤(钱币等)花边的轧压;轧出的花边 ⑥(家畜的)成群兜圈⑦[俚]殴打 / ~ **cutter**【机】铣刀 / ~ **machine** ①【机】铣床 ②【纺】缩绒机,缩呢机

million ['miljən] I num. 百万;百万个(人或物): one and a half ~s(或 a ~ and a half)一百五十万/ several ~s of(或 several ~)inhabitants 数百万居民 II n. ①百万元(或镑、法郎等): The state invested two ~s. 国家投资两百万元。②[复]无数: ~s of reasons 许许多多的理由 ③[the ~] 大众: Mathematics for the Million 《大众数学》‖~**fold** ad. & a. 百万倍 / ~**th** num. ①第一百万(个) ②一百万分之一(的)

millionaire [,miljə'nεə] n. 百万富翁;巨富 ‖~**ss** [,miljə'nεəris] n. 女百万富翁

mime [maim] I n. ①(古希腊、罗马)(摹拟真人真事的)笑剧;摹拟表演;摹拟笑剧的对白 ②摹拟笑剧的演员;哑剧演员;效颦者;小丑 ③(现代的)摹拟笑剧,滑稽戏 II ❶ vt. 在笑剧中扮演;摹拟,模仿 ❷ vi. 作摹拟表演,演滑稽角色(通常为哑剧)

mimic ['mimik] I a. ①模仿的;好模仿的;摹拟的;假装的: a ~ battle 摹拟战 / ~ crying 假哭 ②[生]拟态的: ~ colouration 拟色 II n. ①好学样者,效颦者;摹拟笑剧的演员,小丑 ②仿制品 III (mimicked ['mimikt]; mimicking ['mimikiŋ]) vt. ①模仿;摹拟: ~ sb.'s voice, gestures and manners 模仿某人的声音、姿势和举止 ②细致地临摹: ~ marble on paper 在纸上临摹大理石的花纹 ③酷似;以…的形象呈现: In a mirage the desert will ~ a lake. 在海市蜃楼中,沙漠有时会现出湖泊的形象。‖~**al** a.

mince [mins] I ❶ vt. ①切碎,剁碎,斩细(用绞碎机)绞碎 ②吞吞吐吐地说;婉转地说 ❷ vi. ①碎步走;扭扭捏捏地走 ②矫揉造作,装腔作势 II n. ~meat ‖not to ~ matters(或 one's words)[用作插入语]直言不讳地说,坦率地说 ‖~r n. ①切碎机;绞肉机 ②说话吞吞吐吐的人: a great ~r of words 说话老爱吞吞吐吐的

人 ③走路扭捏的人;矫揉造作的人 ‖~**meat** n. 剁碎的肉;百果馅,肉馅: make ~meat of 把…剁烂(或切碎);[喻]彻底击溃;把…驳得体无完肤 / ~-'**pie** n. ①碎肉馅饼 ②[复][美俚]眼睛

mincing ['minsiŋ] a. ①(说话、举动等)装腔作势的,矫揉造作的,装得斯文的: a ~ gait 慢条斯理的步伐 / ~ speech 装得斯文的谈吐 / take ~ steps 扭扭捏捏地走 ②剁碎(或切碎)用的: a ~ machine 切碎机;绞肉机 ‖~**ly** ad.

mind [maind] I n. ①头脑;精神;心(神): An idea flashed across his ~. 他脑子里闪过一个念头。/ with the whole situation in ~ 胸中有全局 ②意向,愿望;意见,见解: the public ~ 公众意见 / I'm of your ~. 我同意你的意见。/ Speak your ~ out. 把你的想法说出来吧! / tell sb. one's ~ 把自己的心思告诉某人 ③记忆: come to sb.'s ~ 被某人想起,被某人记起 ④心理,心情,情绪: patriotic ~ 爱国心 / a frame (或 state) of ~ (一种)心情,心境 / ease of ~ 心情的舒畅 ⑤理智;智力,智能;有才智的人: He has lost his ~. 他失去理智了。(或:他发疯了。) ⑥[宗]追思弥撒;[M-]【基督教】上帝;神道: a month's (year's) ~ 人死后一月(一年)举行的追思弥撒 / Divine Mind【基督教】上帝 II ❶ vt. ①注意;听从;留心,当心: Mind that you don't forget to mail the letters. 注意可别忘了寄信。/ The child doesn't ~ his sister. 这孩子不听他姐姐的话。/ Mind what I say. 留心听着我的话。/ Mind the wet paint! 当心,油漆未干! / Mind your head! 小心别碰了头!(或:当心你的脑袋!) ②专心于,从事: ~ one's work 专心于工作 / Mind your own business! 别管闲事! ③[常用于疑问、否定、条件句中]介意;反对: I don't ~ the cold. 我不在乎这样的冷天。/ Would you ~ my smoking? 我抽烟你不反对吗? / A: Would you ~ opening the window? B: Certainly not. 甲:请你把窗子开好吗? 乙:当然好。/ I should not ~ a glass of beer. 我倒想喝一杯啤酒。④(细心地)照看,照料;关心: ~ the baby 照看孩子 / ~ a machine 看管机器 ⑤[方]意欲,想要 ⑥[方]使想起;记得 ❷ vi. ①注意;听话;留心,当心: The boy ~s well. 这孩子很听话。/ Mind (out), there's a bus coming! 当心,公共汽车! ②介意: A: Do you ~ if I smoke? B: I'm sorry, but I do. 甲:我抽烟你不反对吗? 乙:抱歉,请勿吸烟。③关心;照料 ‖**absence of** ~ 心不在焉 / a ~ **reader** 能猜出别人心思的人 / an open ~ 虚心: learn with an open ~ 虚心学习 / apply one's ~ **to** 专心于 / a sound ~ **in a sound body** [谚]有健全的身体才有健全的精神 / be a ~ **to do sth.** [方]希望做某事 / bear in ~ 记住 / be in one's right ~ 精神正常,精神健全 / be in (或 of) two ~s (about) (对…)犹豫不决 / be of one (或 a) ~ 同心协力,相一致 / be of the same ~ ①意见相同 ②保

持原来的意见: *Is he still of the same ~*? 他的意见没变吗? / *be out of one's* 精神不正常,发狂 / *bring* (或 *call*) *to* ~ 使被想起,想起 / *change one's* ~ 改变主意 / *give one's* ~ *to* 专心于 / *give sb. a piece of one's* ~ 对某人直言不讳;责备某人 / *have a* (*good* 或 *great*) ~ *to do sth.* 想做某事 / *have half a* ~ *to do sth.* 有点想做某事 / *have little* (*no*) ~ *to do sth.* 不很(不)想做某事 / *have sth. in* ~ ① 记得某事;想到某事 ② 想要做某事 / *have sth. on one's* ~ 挂虑某事,为某事担忧 / *in sb.'s* ~*'s eye* 见 **eye** / *keep in* ~ =bear in ~ / *keep one's* ~ *on* 专心于 / *know one's own* ~ 有自己的想法,有决断 / *make up one's* ~ ① 下决心,决意 ② 接受,承认(*to*): The arrangement has been made; we must *make up our* ~*s to it*. 安排已定,我们非照办不可。/ *Many men, many* ~*s.* 见 **man** / *meeting of* ~*s* 意见一致 / ~ *one's p's and q's* 谨言慎行, 小心行事 / *Mind* (*you*)**!** [口]听着! (或: 请注意!) / *never* ~ ① 不要紧,没关系: A: Sorry for interrupting you. B: *Never* ~. 甲: 对不起我打扰你了。乙: 没关系。② 不用担心 / *off sb.'s* ~ 不再搁在某人心上 / *on sb.'s* ~ 压在某人心上: There are too many problems *on his* ~. 他心事重重。/ *open one's* ~ *to* 把心里话透露给 / *Out of sight, out of* ~. 见 **sight** / *pass* (或 *go*) *out of* ~ 被忘却 / *poison sb.'s* ~ *against* 使某人对…发生恶感 / *presence of* ~ 镇定,沉着 / *put sb. in* ~ *of sth.* 使某人想起某事,以某事提醒某人 / *set one's* ~ *on* 决心要,很想要 / *sink into the* ~ 留在心头,被铭记在心 / *take sb.'s* ~ *off* (*sth.*) 使某人不想(某事),移开某人(对某事)的注意 / *time out of* ~ 太古时代,很久以前 / *to one's* ~ ① 根据某人的意见,如某人所想 ② 合某人的心意 / *weigh on sb.'s* ~ 使某人担忧,挂在某人心头 ‖**~er** *n.* [英][常用以构成复合词]照料人员,看管人员: a machine-~*er* 看管机器的人 ‖**~,blower** *n.* 动人心弦(或引起幻觉)的东西 / **'~,blowing** *a.* 动人心弦的;(麻醉品等)引起幻觉的 / **'~-set** *n.* 思想的形式 / ~ **stuff** 【哲】精神素材(唯心论脱离客观世界所假定的"心理存在"的初步形式)

minded ['maindid] *a.* ① [常用以构成复合词]有…心的,有…思想的;关心…的;重视…的: absent-~ 心不在焉的 / a noble-~ man 思想高尚的人 / negotiation-~ 倾向于举行谈判的 / air-~ 关心航空事业的 ② [只作表语]有意于…的,心想…的: He could do it well if he were so ~. 要是他真有心的话,他是可以把这件事做好的。

mindful ['maindful] *a.* 留心的,注意的;记住的,不忘的(*of*): be ~ *of* one's duty 认真对待自己的职责 / You ought to be ~. 你要注意些。‖**~ly** *ad.* / **~ness** *n.*

mindless ['maindlis] *a.* ① 没头脑的;愚笨的;无知

觉的: a ~ act 愚笨莽撞的行为 ② 不注意的;不留心的;忘却的(*of*): be ~ *of* danger 对危险满不在乎 ‖**~ness** *n.*

mine¹ [main] *pron.* ① [物主代词]我的(东西);我的家属(或有关的人): Is this pen yours or ~? 这支笔是你的还是我的? / His speciality is physics; ~ is chemistry. 他的专业是物理,我的专业是化学。/ He is a friend of ~. 他是我的一个朋友。/ The game is ~. (比赛结果)是我赢了。/ He was kind to me and ~. 他待我和我的家属很亲切。② [古]我的(=my): ~ eyes 我的眼睛 / daughter ~ 我的女儿

mine² [main] **I** *n.* ① 矿(藏),矿山,矿井;[英]铁矿砂: an opencut coal ~ 露天煤矿 / work a ~ 经营矿山,办矿 ② 宝库,源泉: a ~ of the raw materials for literature and art 文学艺术原料的源泉 ③ 地雷;水雷: lay ~*s* 布雷 / strike (或 hit) a ~ 触雷 / a personnel (an antitank) ~ 防步兵(防坦克)地雷 / an aerial ~ 空投水雷 / a drifting ~ 漂雷 / a moored ~ 锚雷 ④ 坑道,地雷坑 ⑤ (在空中爆发成多种火花的)烟火 ⑥ [动](昆虫的)潜道 **II** ● *vt.* ① 开采(矿物);在…中开采矿物;挖入(泥土);从(水、空气等)中提取;(昆虫)在…下钻洞: ~ oil shale 开采油页岩 / ~ sea water for magnesium 从海水中提取镁 ② 在…下挖坑道;在地下挖(洞) ③ 在…中(或在…下)敷雷;(用雷)炸毁: ~ the entrance to a harbour 在港口敷设水雷 ④ 暗害,破坏 ❷ *vi.* ① 开矿;挖坑道 ② 布雷 ‖*salt a* ~ [俚]把矿石撒于矿山使矿藏看来丰富以进行欺诈 ‖**~r** *n.* ① 矿工; ~*r's* phthisis 【医】矿工痨病,炭末入肺病 ② 地雷工兵 ③ 联合采矿机 ‖**~ barrage** 雷幕 / **~ belt** 雷带 / **~ clearance** 扫雷,排雷 / **~ detector** 探雷器 / **~ dredger** 扫雷艇 / **'~field** *n.* 布雷区,布雷场 / **'~,layer** *n.* 布雷舰艇 / **~ planter** 布雷船;布雷兵 / **'~,sweeper** *n.* 扫雷舰;扫雷器 / **~ thrower** 掷雷筒;扫雷活门 / **~ vessel** 水雷舰 / **~ warfare** 地雷战;水雷战

mineral ['minərəl] **I** *n.* ① 矿物,矿石 ② 【化】无机物 ③ [英][复]矿泉水;苏打水;姜汁啤酒 **II** *a.* ① 矿物的,矿质的 ② 无机的 ‖~ **acid** 无机酸 / ~ **black** 石墨 / ~ **kingdom** 矿物界 / **spring** ~ 矿泉 / ~ **water** 矿泉水,矿质水;苏打水;姜汁啤酒 / ~ **wax** 地蜡 / ~ **wool** 矿渣绒(作防火、防热、隔音等用)

mingle ['miŋgl] ● *vt.* 使混合,使相混: ~ water and alcohol 使水和酒精混合 / with ~*d* feelings 百感交集地,悲喜交加地 / a thunderous ovation ~*d with* the beating of drums and gongs 和锣鼓声交织在一起的欢呼声 ❷ *vi.* 混合起来,相混合: Water and alcohol may ~ *with* each other in any proportions. 水和酒精可按任何比率互相混合。/ ~ *in* (或 *with*) the crowd 混入人群

miniature ['minjətʃə] **I** *n.* ① 小画像,袖珍画(尤指刻在象牙或画在牛皮纸上的); 微小绘画术 ② 雏型;缩样;小型物 **II** *a.* 雏型的;小型的: ~

bearings 微型轴承 / a ～ war 小规模战争 / a ～ camera 小型照相机 / a ～ car 微型汽车 **III** *vt.* 使成小型 ‖*in* ～ 小型的;在小规模上

minimize ['minimaiz] *vt.* ①使减到最少,使缩到最小 ②把…估计得最低;极度轻视 ‖**minimization** [,minimai'zeiʃən] *n.* / ～**r** *n.* 对事情作最低估计的人

minimum ['miniməm] **I** ([复] minima ['minimə] 或 minimums) *n.* ①最小量,最小数;最低限度: reduce sth. to a ～ 把某物减少到最小限度 / achieve the maximum of efficiency with the ～ of labour 以最少的劳动取得最高的效率 ②【数】极小(值) **II** *a.* 最小的;最少的;最低的: a ～ dose 最小剂量 / a ～ thermometer 最低温度计 / a ～ wage 法定最低限度工资

mining ['mainiŋ] *n.* 采矿;矿业: deep ～ 深井开采 / opencut (或 opencast, open-pit) ～ 露天开采 / ～ engineering 采矿工程(学) / the ～ industry 采矿工业

minion ['minjən] *n.* ①奴才,顺从讨好的仆佣 ②宠儿;宠臣;宠物 ③受人崇拜者,偶象 ④僚属 ⑤【印】七点(旧称七磅)的铅字体: be set in ～ 用七点铅字排印 ‖*a ～ of the law* [蔑]警察;监狱看守

minister ['ministə] **I** *n.* ①部长;大臣: a prime ～ 总理;首相 / a ～ of (或 for) foreign affairs (或 a foreign ～) 外交部长;外交大臣;外相 ②公使;(泛指)外交使节: a ～ plenipotentiary 全权公使 / a ～ resident 常驻公使(低于全权公使) ③(基督教新教)牧师;圣餐礼的执行者;(某些教派的)教长(=～-general) ④代理者;执行者 **II** ❶ *vi.* ①伺候;照顾;给予帮助 (to): ～ to a sick man's wants 照顾病人需要 ②执行牧师职务 ❷ *vt.* ①[古]供给 ②举行(祭祀等)

ministerial [,minis'tiəriəl] *a.* ①部长的;部的;公使的; [常作 M-] 内阁的;支持内阁方面的: be given a ～ appointment 被任命为部长 / a conference on a ～ level 部长级的会谈 / *Ministerial* crisis 内阁危机 / ～ benches in the House of Commons (英国)下议院中执政党的席位 ②奉命令做的;代理的;行政(性)的(与 judicial 司法的相对): act in a ～ capacity 以行政的身分执行(即与司法官不同,要执行上级命令,不负独立裁判之责) ③起作用的,作为成因的 (to) ④牧师的 ‖～**ist** *n.* 内阁的支持者 / ～**ly** *ad.*

ministrant ['ministrənt] **I** *a.* 行宗教职务的;服侍的;提供服务的 **II** *n.* 主持仪式的牧师;服侍者;提供帮助者

ministration [,minis'treiʃən] *n.* ①行宗教仪式 ②服务;服侍;帮助: under the tender ～s of the nurses 在护士们的亲切护理下

ministry ['ministri] *n.* ①(政府的)部;部的办公楼: the *Ministry* of National Defence 国防部 ②[常作 M-] (全体)部长;内阁: form a ～ 组阁,组织内阁 ③[the ～] (全体)牧师 ④部长(或公使、牧师)的职位(或任期) ⑤服务

mink [miŋk] ([复] mink(s)) *n.* ①【动】水貂 ②貂皮

minnow ['minou] ([复] minnow(s)) *n.* ①鲤科小鱼 ②用作钓饵的活小鱼(或假小鱼) ‖*a Triton of* (或 *among*) *the* ～*s* 矮中之长,鹤立鸡群者

minor ['mainə] **I** *a.* ①较小的;较少的;较年幼的;较次要的: a ～ premise 小前提 / Smith [英]小史密斯(指姓史密斯的兄弟中年幼的一个;在学校则指同姓史密斯者中年幼或后入学的一个) / a ～ suit 桥牌中实力较弱的一手牌(指"方块"或"草花") / a ～ issue 枝节问题 / a ～ party 少数党 / a ～ part in a play 剧中的配角 ②未成年的 ③(疾病等)不严重的,无生命危险的: a ～ illness 小病 / a ～ operation 小手术 ④【美】(大学中)次要学科的 ⑤【音】小调的,小音阶的: a ～ scale 小音阶 / a ～ third 小三(音)度 ⑥[古]少数的 **II** *n.* ①未成年人 ②【逻】小前提;小名词 ③【音】小调,小音阶 ④【美】(大学中的)次要学科,选修科;选修(或兼修)某种学科的人: English majors and ～s 专修和兼修英语的人 ⑤(天主教)圣芳济派修道士 **III** *vi.* [美]兼修,选作次要学科 (in): ～ in physics 兼修物理 ‖*in a ～ key* 见 key[1] ‖～ **surgery** 小外科 / ～ **term** 【逻】小名词

minority [mai'nɔriti] *n.* ①少数;少数派;少数票: a ～ report (调查委员会等中)持不同意见的少数委员单独提出的报告 ②少数民族: the ～ areas 少数民族地区 ③未成年;未达法定年龄 ‖*be in a ～ of one* 得不到任何人的支持 / *be in the* ～ 占少数

minster ['minstə] *n.* ①附属于修道院的礼拜堂 ②大教堂

minstrel ['minstrəl] *n.* ①中世纪的吟游诗人 ②音乐家;诗人 ③(十九世纪起源于美国常由白人扮演黑人演唱黑人歌曲等的)黑人剧团团员;黑人剧团的演出 (=～ show) ‖～**sy** *n.* ①吟游,游唱 ②[总称]吟游诗人 ③歌谣集

mint[1] [mint] *n.* ①【植】薄荷;薄荷属植物: ～ sauce (吃烤小羊肉用的)薄荷酱 ②薄荷糖;薄荷点心 ③[英]金钱

mint[2] [mint] **I** *n.* ①造币厂;[喻]制造所: a ～ of rumours 谣言制造所 ②巨额,巨大;富源: a ～ of money 巨款 / have a ～ of ideas 主意极多 **II** *a.* 崭新的,完美的;新造的: a stamp in ～ state (或 condition) 一张崭新的邮票 / ～ coins 刚出厂的硬币 **III** *vt.* ①铸造(硬币): ～ five-cent pieces 铸造每枚五分钱的辅币 ②造(字、句等),臆造: a newly ～ed phrase 一个新创造出来的短语 ‖～**er** *n.* 铸币工 ‖'～**mark** *n.* (硬币上表示铸造厂的)印记 / '～**master** *n.* 造币厂厂长

minuet [,minju'et] *n.* ①小步舞 ②小步舞曲

minus ['mainəs] **I** *prep.* ①减(去): Four ～ two is two. 四减二等于二。 ②[口]没有,失去: a man ～ a leg 失去了一条腿的男子 **II** *a.* ①负的;减去的: a ～ sign 负号,减号(即"－") / a ～ quantity 负数,负量 / ～ electricity 阴电,负电 / The temperature is ～ 10 degrees. 温度是零下

十度。/ the plus and ~ factors 有利和不利因素 ②[通常放在被修饰的词之后] 略差一些的: get a grade of A ~ in English 英语得到 A⁻ 的成绩 **Ⅲ** *n.* ①【数】负号，减号；负数，负量 ②不足，缺陷

minute¹ ['minit] **Ⅰ** *n.* ①分(一小时或一度的六十分之一)；分的路程: five ~s to (past) three 三点缺(零)五分 / 37 degrees and 30 ~s 三十七度三十分(可写作 37°30′) / It's only several ~s from here to the cinema. 从这儿到电影院只有几分钟的路程。②一会儿，片刻，瞬间: Just a ~, please. 请等一下。/ I'll do it this ~. 我此刻就做。③备忘录；笔记；底稿；[复]会议记录: make a ~ of sth. 把某事记录下来 / read the ~s of the last meeting 宣读上次会议记录 ④(角度的)弧分 (= ~ of arc) **Ⅱ** *vt.* ①记录，摘录；将…制成备忘录 (*down*); 将…列入会议记录 ②测定…的精确时间: ~ a race 为赛跑测时 ‖*half a* ~ 片刻: I won't keep you waiting more than *half a* ~. 我不会使你久等的。/ *in a* ~ 马上，立刻 / *the* ~ ……(就): I'll tell him *the* ~ (*that*) he comes. 他一来我就告诉他。/ *to the* ~ 一分不差，恰好: The train arrived at three o'clock *to the* ~. 火车准三点到达。/ *up to the* ~ 最新的；最新式的 ‖~**ly** *ad.* **&** *a.* 每分钟地(的)；连续不断地(的) / ~ **book** 会议记录本 / ~ **gun** 分炮(为高级军官举行葬礼或船舶遇险时等每分钟一次的号炮) / ~ **hand** (钟表的)分针，长针 / '~**man** *n.* ①美国独立战争时(命令一下立即应召)的民兵: a *Minuteman* missile (美国的)民兵式导弹 ②[M-] (美国极右组织)民兵 / ~ **mark** 分的符号(即′) / ~ **steak** 快熟薄牛排

minute² [mai'nju:t] *a.* ①微小的，微细的；不足道的 ②详细的；细致的；精密的: a ~ description 细致的描写 ‖~**ly** *ad.* / ~**ness** *n.*

minx [minks] *n.* 顽皮姑娘；[古]轻佻女子

miracle ['mirəkl] *n.* ①奇迹；非凡的事例；令人惊奇的人(或事物): work (或 create, perform) ~s 创造奇迹 / He is a ~ of fortitude. 他那非凡的毅力令人惊奇。②(中世纪表演基督教《圣经》故事的)奇迹剧 (= ~ play) ‖*to a* ~ 奇迹般地；(好得)不可思议地

miraculous [mi'rækjuləs] *a.* ①超自然的，非凡的 ②象奇迹一样的；令人惊叹的，不可思议的 ③能创造奇迹的 ‖~**ly** *ad.* / ~**ness** *n.*

mirage ['mira:ʒ, mi'ra:ʒ] *n.* ①海市蜃楼，蜃景，幻景 ②[喻]幻想

mire ['maiə] **Ⅰ** *n.* 淤泥；泥潭，泥坑；[喻]困境 **Ⅱ** ❶ *vt.* 使溅满污泥，使陷入泥坑；[喻]使陷入困境 ❷ *vi.* 掉进泥坑；[喻]陷入困境 ‖*drag sb.* (或 *sb.'s name*) *through the* ~ 把某人搞臭 / *find oneself in the* ~ 发现自己陷入了困境

mirror ['mirə] **Ⅰ** *n.* ①镜: look at oneself in the ~ 照镜子 / a concave (convex) ~ 凹(凸)镜 / a driving ~ (汽车上供驾驶者察看车后情况的)

反光镜 ②[喻]反映，能反映真相的东西；借鉴: a ~ of the times 时代的反映 **Ⅱ** *vt.* 反映；反射: The glory of the morning is ~ed in the lake. 朝霞映在湖面上。‖~ **image** 【物】镜象 / ~ **machine** 【原】带有磁镜(或塞子)的热核装置 / ~ **writing** 倒写

mirth [mə:θ] *n.* 欢笑，高兴: with suppressed ~ 强忍着笑

misadventure ['misəd'ventʃə] *n.* ①不幸的事，不幸的遭遇；灾难 ②【律】意外事故: death by ~ 意外事故造成的死亡 / homicide by ~ 误杀

miscarriage [mis'kærid3] *n.* ①(计划等的)失败 ②(信件等的)误投，误送: ~ of goods 货物的误送 ③(孕妇的)小产，流产；堕胎: have a ~ 小产 ‖~ *of justice* ①审判不公，误判 ②审判不公的案件，误判案

miscarry [mis'kæri] *vi.* ①(计划等)失败 ②(信件等)被误投，被误送 ③(孕妇)小产，流产

miscellaneous [,misi'leinjəs] *a.* ①混杂的，各种各样杂在一起的: a ~ collection of goods 一批杂货 ②有各种特点的；多方面的；兴趣杂的 ‖~**ly** *ad.* / ~**ness** *n.*

miscellany [mi'seləni, 'misiləni] *n.* ①混合物，杂物: a ~ of fish, dairy products, etc. 鱼、乳制品等一堆杂七杂八的东西 ②[常用复]杂集；杂录

mischance [mis'tʃa:ns] *n.* 不幸，横祸，灾难: by ~ 不幸地 / end without ~ 圆满告终

mischief ['mis-tʃif] *n.* ①(尤指人为的)损害，伤害；危害，毒害: do sb. a ~ 伤害某人，加害某人 ②造成损害的行为；祸根 ③调皮，淘气；捣蛋，恶作剧: eyes full of ~ 充满调皮神色的眼睛 / get into ~ 胡闹起来 / keep out of ~ 不胡闹 / What ~ are you up to? 你在搞什么鬼? ④调皮的人，淘气鬼；捣蛋鬼: You little ~! 你这个小淘气(或小捣蛋)! / a regular ~ 老是调皮捣蛋的人 ⑤[the ~][用于特殊疑问句，作状语]究竟: Where the ~ have you been? 你到底上哪儿去了? ‖*make* ~ (*between*) (在…之间)挑拨离间 / *play the* ~ *with* 把…弄得乱七八糟 ‖~-,**maker** 挑拨离间的人 / '~-,**making** *a.* 挑拨离间的 *n.* 挑拨行为

mischievous ['mis-tʃivəs] *a.* ①有害的，为害的 ②调皮的，淘气的；恶作剧的: a ~ look 调皮的神色 / a ~ child 淘气的孩子 / a ~ trick 恶作剧 ‖~**ly** *ad.* / ~**ness** *n.*

misconceive ['miskən'si:v] ❶ *vt.* 误解，对…有错误看法: ~ the nature of a problem 误解问题的性质 ❷ *vi.* 误解，有错误看法 (*of*): ~ *of* one's duty 对自己的责任有错误的看法

misconception ['miskən'sepʃən] *n.* 误解，看法错误，错觉

misconduct **Ⅰ** ['miskən'dʌkt] *vt.* ①办错，对…处置不当 ②[~ oneself] 使行为不端: ~ *oneself* in office 渎职 / ~ *oneself with* 与…通奸 **Ⅱ** [mis-'kɔndəkt] *n.* ①办错，处置不当 ②(尤指官吏的)胡作非为，渎职 ③不端的行为；通奸

misconstrue ['miskən'stru:] *vt.* 曲解,误解: You have ~d my words. 你误解了我的话。

miscount ['mis'kaunt] I *vt.* & *vi.* 误算;数错 II *n.* 误算; (尤指选票的)数错

miscreant ['miskriənt] I *a.* ①堕落的;恶的,无赖的 ②[古]异端的,异教的,不信教的 II *n.* ①恶棍,歹徒,无赖 ②[古]异端者,异教徒

misdeal ['mis'di:l] I (misdealt ['mis'delt]) *vt.* & *vi.* 发错(牌) II *n.* 发错牌

misdeed ['mis'di:d] *n.* 不端行为;罪行

misdemeano(u)r [,misdi'mi:nə] *n.* ①【律】轻罪 (felony 之对) ②不端行为

miser[1] ['maizə] *n.* 守财奴,财迷;吝啬鬼,小气鬼

miser[2] ['maizə] *n.* ①凿井机;钻探机 ②【矿】管形提泥钻头

miserable ['mizərəbl] *a.* ①痛苦的,悲惨的;可怜的 ②糟糕的;使人难受的: a ~ performance 糟糕的演出 / ~ weather 恼人的天气 ③蹩脚的,粗劣的: a ~ house 蹩脚的房屋 ④可耻的,卑鄙的 ‖**~ness** *n.* / **miserably** *ad.* ①悲惨地 ②糟糕地 ③[口]极其

misery ['mizəri] *n.* ①痛苦,悲惨;[复]痛苦的事,苦难 ②[方]疼痛: have a ~ in the back 背疼 ③[口]老是忧愁的人 ‖*Misery loves company.* [谚]同病相怜。

misfire ['mis'faiə] I *vi.* ①(枪等)不发火,射不出;(内燃机等)发动不起来 ②不奏效,打不中要害: As criticism, this essay ~s. 这篇文章作为批评来讲没有打中要害。 II *n.* ①不发火,射不出;发动不起 ②不奏效,打不中要害

misfit ['misfit, 'mis'fit] I *n.* ①不合身的衣着 ②[喻]不适应环境的人;不称职的人 ③ 不合适,不相称 II (misfitted; misfitting) ❶ *vt.* ①(衣着等) 对…不合身 ②对…不合适,对…不相称 ❷ *vi.* 不合适,不相称

misfortune [mis'fɔ:tʃən] *n.* ①不幸;灾祸;不幸的事: suffer ~ 遭到不幸 / He had the ~ to break his leg. 他不幸折断了腿。 ②[方]生私生子;私生子: have (meet with) a ~ 有 (生) 私生子 ‖*Misfortunes never come singly.* [谚]祸不单行。

misgive [mis'giv] (misgave [mis'geiv], misgiven [mis'givn]) ❶ *vt.* [主语常用 heart, mind, conscience 等] 使疑虑(或担忧、害怕): My heart (或 mind) ~s me. 我感到心中不安。 / His mind *misgave* him about the result. 他担心结果不好。 / My mind *misgave* me that my neglect had been inexcusable. 我怕我的疏忽是不可原谅的。 ❷ *vi.* 疑虑,担忧,害怕 ‖**misgiving** *n.* [常用复]疑虑,担忧,害怕

misguide ['mis'gaid] *vt.* [常用被动语态]错误地引导;使误入歧途: be ~d by erroneous ideas 被错误思想引入歧途 ‖**misguidance** ['mis'gaidəns] *n.* / **~r** *n.* 错误引导者;使误入歧途者

misguided ['mis'gaidid] *a.* 被引导错误的,被指导错的;误入歧途的: ~ conduct 错误的行为 /

a ~ man 误入歧途的人 ‖**~ly** *ad.*

mishap ['mishæp, mis'hæp] *n.* 不幸的事;灾祸: meet with a slight ~ 遇到小小的不幸 / a great ~, such as a landslide 象山崩那样的大灾难 / Trains run on schedule without ~. 列车安全正点运行。

mislay [mis'lei] (mislaid [mis'leid]) *vt.* ①把…布置错;放错;丢失: ~ the table for four instead of six 桌上应该放六副餐具而只放了四副 / I have *mislaid* the dictionary. 我不知道把词典放到哪儿去了。 ②丢弃: never ~ one's principles 从不放弃原则

mislead [mis'li:d] (misled [mis'led]) *vt.* ①把…带错路;引导错: The travellers were *misled* by the guide. 旅游者们被向导领错了路。 ②把…带坏,使误入歧途 ③ 给…错误印象;使误解: be *misled* into thinking that … 被引得误以为… ‖**~er** *n.* 错误引导者,错误领导人 / **~ing** *a.* 引入歧途的;骗人的,使人误解的

misnomer [mis'noumə] *n.* 名词使用不当,用词不当;使用不当的名称: "Fruit", as used to describe potatoes, is a ~. 用"水果"一词来形容土豆是用词不当。 ②(文件中的)人名(或地名)错误

misplace ['mis'pleis] *vt.* ① 把…放错地方,误放 ②把(感情等)寄托于不该寄托的对象: His trust was not ~d. 他没有信错人。 ‖**~ment** *n.*

misprint I [mis'print] *vt.* 印错,误印 II ['mis'print, 'misprint] *n.* 印刷错误: be free from ~s 无印刷错误

misquote ['mis'kwout] *vt.* & *vi.* 错误地引用,误引 ‖**misquotation** ['miskwou'teiʃən] *n.* 引用错误;误引的文字(或语句等)

misrule ['mis'ru:l] I *vt.* 对…施暴政 II *n.* ①暴政,苛政 ②无政府状态;混乱

miss[1] [mis] *n.* ①[M-](用于姓名或姓之前对未婚女子的称呼)小姐: *Miss* (Helen) Smith (海伦·)史密斯小姐 / the *Miss* Greens (或较正式的用法: the *Misses* Green) 格林家的小姐们 ②(不用于姓名前的称呼语)小姐: Good morning, ~! 小姐,早上好! ③ [谑] 姑娘,小女孩;小女学生: a saucy ~ 毛头姑娘 / shoes for Junior *Misses* (商业用语)女式中人鞋 ④[M-](用于地名或行业等名称前指具有代表性的青年女子)…小姐,…之王后(参见 **mister**)

miss[2] [mis] I ❶ *vt.* ①未击中;未得到;未达到: ~ a ball 没接(或击)到球 / ~ one's aim (或 mark) 未达到目的 / ~ one's way 迷路 / ~ one's footing (或 step) 失足,踏空 ②未看到;未听到;未觉察,未领会: You must have ~ed the notice on the blackboard. 你大概没看见黑板上的通知。 / I ~ed the first part of the speech. 我没听到报告的第一部分。 / ~ the point of an argument 没领会一个论据的要点 ③未履行;未出席;未赶上,错过: ~ school 缺课 / ~ a train 没赶上火车 / ~ an opportunity 错过机会 /

the farming season 误农时 ④逃脱,免于: He just ~ed being struck. 他险些儿被打着。 / ~ an accident 免于事故 ⑤发觉没有,觉得遗失;感到…不在,惦念: When did you ~ your pen? 你什么时候发现钢笔丢了的? / I ~ you terribly! 我多么惦记你呀! ⑥遗漏;省去: You've ~ed out one word. 你漏掉了一个词。 / He was in such a hurry that he ~ed his breakfast. 他急急忙忙连早饭也不吃了。 / You may ~ out the third paragraph of the article while reading it. 你读这篇文章时可略去第三段(不读)。 ❷ vi. ①未击中,打偏: He took a cut at the ball but ~ed. 他削球削了个空。②失败: He ~ed (out) at the third round. 在第三回合中他打输了。③(内燃机等)发动不起来 II n. ①击不中;得不到;达不到: hit the target five times without a ~ 五发五中 ②省略;避免: a lucky ~ 侥幸避免 ③(内燃机等的)发动不起 ④[口]流产,小产 ‖A ~ is as good as a mile. [谚]毫末之错仍为错;死里逃生总是生。(指程度虽有不同,性质却是一样) / give sth. a ~ 避开某物;略去某物(或跳过不做某事): The last two lines are not clear, let's just give it a ~. 最后两行不清楚,跳过不看吧! / I'll give the sweet course a ~ 这道甜食我不吃了。 / hit or ~ 见 hit / ~ fire 见 fire / ~ out on sth. [美]未得到某物;在某事上不成功 / ~ the boat 见 boat / ~ the bus 见 bus

misshape ['mis'ʃeip] I (过去式 misshaped, 过去分词 misshaped 或 misshapen ['mis'ʃeipən]) vt. 使成奇形怪状;使成畸形;畸形 ‖~n ['mis'ʃeipən] a. 奇形怪状的;畸形的

missile ['misail; 美 'misəl] I n. ①发射物;投掷物(尤指武器) ②导弹;飞弹: an air-to-air ~ 空对空导弹 / an air-to-surface (或 air-to-ground) ~ 空对地导弹 / an air-to-underwater ~ 空对水下导弹 / an anti~ ~ 反导弹导弹(= a contra-~) / an antiballistic-~ ~ 反弹道导弹的导弹 / an intercontinental ballistic ~ 洲际弹道导弹 / a guided wing ~ 有翼导弹 / a long-range ~ 远程导弹 / a medium-range ~ 中程导弹 / a target-seeking ~ 寻的导弹 / a three-stage ~ 三级导弹 / a cruise ~ 巡航导弹 / ~ sites 导弹发射场 / ~ bases 导弹基地 II a. 可发射的;可投掷的: A hand-grenade is a ~ weapon. 手榴弹是一种投掷武器。 ‖~er [,misi'liə] n. =~man ‖~man ['misəlmæn] n. (协助设计、制造和操纵导弹的)导弹手

missing ['misiŋ] a. 缺掉的,失去的;失踪的,下落不明的: a book with some pages ~ 一本缺了几页的书 / He is said to be ~. 据说他失踪了。 / the ~ [总称](战争中的)失踪者,下落不明的人 ‖~ link ①一系列完整的事物中缺少的一个环节 ②设想中存在于类人猿与人类之间的过渡生物

mission ['miʃən] I n. ①(外交)使团,代表团;使馆: a goodwill ~ 友好访问团 / a trade ~ to Japan 赴日贸易代表团 ②传教团,传教机构;传

教地区;传教活动;[复]传教,布道: a Foreign (Home) Mission (西方国家的)国外(国内)布道团 ③慈善机构,救济机构 ④使命,任务;天职;【军】战斗任务,飞行任务: a historic ~ 历史使命 / complete (或 accomplish) one's ~ 完成使命,完成任务 / a combat ~ 战斗任务 / fly a bombing ~ 执行轰炸任务 ⑤(使团等的)派遣 II vt. ①派遣 ②向…传教 ‖~er n. 传教士 / ~ church 由较大宗教机构资助经费的教会 / ~ school (利用教会进行奴化教育的)教会学校

missionary ['miʃənəri] I a. 教会的,传教的;传教士的 II n. ①传教士 ②(受雇佣来)软化罢工者斗志的人 (= ~ worker)

misspell ['mis'spel] (misspelled ['mis'spelt, 'mis'speld] 或 misspelt ['mis'spelt]) vt. 拼错 ‖~ing n. 拼写错误

misspend ['mis'spend] (misspent ['mis'spent]) vt. 滥用,浪费;虚度: a misspent sum 乱花掉的一笔款子

mist [mist] I n. ①薄雾,霭: trees hidden in a ~ 薄雾笼罩的树木 ②(眼睛的)迷糊不清;眼翳: smile in a ~ of tears 噙着眼泪微笑 ③[喻]起模糊作用的东西;造成理解上困难的事物: hear through the ~ of sleep 睡得迷迷糊糊时听见 / be lost in the ~s of time 随着时间消逝被渐渐遗忘 II ❶ vi. ①下薄雾;被蒙上薄雾: It's ~ing. 起雾了。 / The distant trees ~ed over. 远处的树木被蒙上了雾霭。②变得模糊,迷糊 ❷ vt. 使蒙上薄雾,使模糊 ‖cast (或 throw) a ~ before sb.'s eyes 使某人模糊,使某人眼花缭乱

mistake [mis'teik] I (mistook [mis'tuk], mistaken [mis'teikən]) ❶ vt. ①误解,弄错: ~ sb.'s meaning 误解某人的意思 / ~ the hour 弄错时间 / There is no mistaking what ought to be done. 应该做什么是清楚不过的。 ②把…错认 (for): He mistook me for my brother. 他把我错当作我的兄弟了。 ③挑选错;估计错: ~ a road 走错路 / They ~ their man if they think they can frighten him. 如果他们认为可以把他吓倒,那是认错人了。 ❷ vi. 弄错,搞错: If I ~ not, … 如果我没弄错的话,… II n. 错误,误会: make a ~ 犯错误 / learn from past ~s to avoid future ones 惩前毖后 / I took his umbrella by ~. 我错拿了他的伞。 ‖and no ~ 无疑地,的确: It's raining outside and no ~. 外面确实在下雨,没错。 / make no ~ 别弄错 / Now no ~! 别搞错我的意思!

mistaken [mis'teikən] I mistake 的过去分词 II a. 错误的,弄错的: a ~ idea 错误的想法 / ~ kindness 对不该施仁政的人所表示的仁慈;不该有的仁慈 / If I am not ~, …. 如果我没弄错的话,… / You are ~ about him. 你错看了他了。(或: 你误会他了。) ‖~ly ad. / ~ness n.

mister ['mistə] I n. ①[M-](常略作 Mr. 或 Mr, 复数略作 Messrs.;用于姓名或职称前)先生: Mr.

James 詹姆斯先生 / Mr. President 总统先生
②[口](不用于姓名前的称呼语)先生: Listen to
me, ~! 听我说, 先生! ③ 没有特殊尊称(或头
衔)的人: a plain ~ 普通人 ④丈夫 ⑤[M-](用
于地名或行业等名称前指具有代表性的男子)…
先生,…之王: Mr. Baseball 棒球之王 Ⅱ vt. 称
…先生: Don't ~ me. 别称我作先生。

mistletoe ['misltou] n.【植】槲寄生(西俗用作基督
教圣诞节的装饰物): the ~ family 桑寄生科

mistook [mis'tuk] mistake 的过去式

mistress ['mistris] n. ①女主人, 主妇; 女雇主; 有
支配能力的女子: Is your ~ at home? (客人对
佣人的问语)女主人在家吗? / be one's own ~
(女子)对自己的事情作得了主 / be ~ of the
situation (女子)控制得了局面 ②有专长的妇女;
女能手: a ~ of the science of medicine 医
学家 / a ~ of needlework 做针线的能手 ③
[英]女教师; 女校长; 女主管: the French ~ 法
语女教师 ④[M-][古]…小姐(用于女子姓名前
作称呼);…夫人(现只用缩写 Mrs. ['misiz], 放在
已婚者的夫姓或姓名前) ⑤[苏格兰][M-]子
爵(或男爵)的长女 ⑥情妇;[古]情人, 爱人(指女
子) ⑦称霸的国家; 霸主: be ~ of the world
称霸世界 / the ~ of the seas 海上霸主 ‖*Mistress of the Robes* [英]女王的女侍长 / *the Mistress of the Adriatic* 亚得里亚海的门户
(威尼斯的别称) ‖~-ship n. ①女主人的身分;
女教师的职位 ②(女王的)女侍长职位 ③霸主
权, 霸主地位

mistrust [mis'trʌst] vt., vi. & n. 不信任; 不相信;
怀疑

misunderstand ['misʌndə'stænd] (misunderstood
['misʌndə'stud]) vt. 误解, 误会; 曲解: ~ sb.
(sb.'s intentions) 误解某人(某人的意图) ‖~ing
n. I don't want any ~ing. 我不希望有任何误
会。

misuse ['mis'ju:z] Ⅰ vt. ①误用, 滥用 ②苛待, 虐
待 Ⅱ ['mis'ju:s] n. 误用, 滥用 ‖~r n. 误用者,
滥用者; 虐待者

mite [mait] n. ① 螨; 壁虱; 蛆(尤指乳酪中的)
② 古弗兰米的小铜币; (基督教《圣经》中的)八分
之一旧便士的硬币 ③少量的捐款; 尽力而行的贡
献: contribute one's ~ 贡献一分力量 ④ 少许,
一点儿: not a ~ 毫不, 一点也不 ⑤ 小东西(尤
指小孩, 用时常带同情色彩): Poor little ~! 怪
可怜的小孩! / a ~ of a child 小得可怜的孩子
‖*a millionaire's* ~ 大富翁的小施舍 / *a ~ on an elephant* 大象身上一小虱(指大小悬殊) / *a*
(或 *one's*) *widow's* ~ 少而可贵的捐献

mitigate ['mitigeit] vt. ①使缓和, 使镇静: ~ the
flood 分洪 ② 安慰(忧伤、悲苦等), 平息(怒气
等) ③ 减轻(病痛、惩罚等) ④ 调节(冷、热等)
‖**mitigation** [,miti'geiʃən] n. / **mitigatory**
['mitigətəri] a.

mitre ['maitə] Ⅰ n. ①【宗】主教冠(象征主教、
教皇等的职权); 僧帽 ②斜角缝; 斜接; 斜榫 Ⅱ

mitre

❶ vt. ①给(主教)加冠; 升任(某人)为主教 ②使
斜接 ❷ vi. 斜接 ‖~ box (斜锯时用以定锯路
的)辅锯箱 / ~ gear【机】等径伞齿轮 / ~ joint
斜削接头, 斜面接合, 斜角联接

mitten ['mitn] n. ①连指手套(拇指分开, 其他四
指连在一起) ②(女用)露指长手套 (=mit(t)) ③
[常用复]拳击手套 ‖ get the ~ [俚]①求婚遭
到拒绝 ② 被解职 / give (或 send) sb. the ~
[俚]①拒绝某人的求婚 ②解某人的职 / handle
without ~s 严厉对待; 大刀阔斧地处理 / the
~ sport [美俚]拳击

mix [miks] Ⅰ vt. ①使混合, 搀和: ~ concrete,
sand and stones 把水泥、沙和石子搅和在一起 /
~ cotton into wool 在羊毛中搀棉花 ②使结合;
使结交: ~ work with adequate rest 劳逸结合
③(给…)配制; 调制: The doctor ~ed (me) some
medicine. 医生(给我)配了一些药。 / ~ a cake
拌做糕饼 ④混淆, 搞混: ~ black with white 混
淆黑白 / The price tags on these commodities
are ~ed. 这些商品上的价目标签搞混了。⑤使
杂交 ❷ vi. ① 相混合, 相溶合: Oil and water
will not ~. 油和水不相溶合。② 交往, 交游:
Never ~ with such people. 不要同这种人交
混。/ He doesn't ~ well. 他不善于与人相处。
③ 发生牵连; 参与 (in): ~ in a quarrel 参与争吵
④交配成杂种 ⑤[美俚]殴打 Ⅱ n. ①混合, 搀和
②混合物, 拌和物 ③(由几种成分配合的)调制
品, 速煮(或速溶)食品: an instant coffee ~ 速
溶咖啡 ④糊涂, 迷惑: I am in a ~. 我被弄得
稀里糊涂。‖*be* (*get*) ~ed *up in sth.* (*with sb.*)
与某事(某人)有(发生)牵连 / ~ *it* (*up*) [俚]拚
拳, 猛打 / ~ *up* ①搅匀; 拌和: ~ up flour and
water 把面粉和水搅匀 ②混淆, 搞混: I am all
~ed up. 我完全搞糊涂了。‖~able a. 可以混和
的 / ~er n. ①混合者; 搅拌器: a concrete ~er
混凝土搅拌机 ②【无】混频器 ③[冶]混铁炉
④[口]交际家: a good (bad) ~er 善于(不善于)
交际的人 ⑤[美俚]交谊会 ‖'~-'up n. ①混乱;
迷惑: a ~-up in terminology 术语上的混乱
②混合物 ③[口]厮打, 拳击

mixed [mikst] a. ①混合的; 混杂的; 混淆的; 杂种
的: a ~ marriage 不同民族(或不同宗教信仰)
间的通婚 / a ~ force 混合部队 / a ~ brigade
混成旅 / ~ farming 农业的混合经营(指在同一

农场既种植粮食作物，又种植经济作物、饲料作物，并饲养牲畜等）/ have ~ feelings of surprise and joy 惊喜交集 / ~ number【数】带分数（如 5⅔）②男女混合的: ~ doubles（乒乓球等的）男女混合双打 / a ~ chorus 混声合唱 / a ~ school 男女同校的学校 ③[口]头脑混乱的，(酒醉)糊涂的，无条理的 ④【语】(元音)中央的: a ~ vowel (中)央元音 ‖**~ly** ['miksidli] *ad.* / **~ness** ['miksidnis] *n.* ‖**~ media** ① 艺术的混合效应法（如在演出时同时采用彩色灯光与录音效果）② 混合画法（如在一幅作品上同时采用水彩及蜡笔）/ '**~-'up** *a.* 混乱的；迷惑的

mixing ['miksiŋ] *n.* 混合；【无】混频

mixture ['mikstʃə] *n.* ①混合；混合状态；混合比 ②混合物；混合料；混合气；混合剂: Air is a ~ of gases. 空气是各种气体的混合物。/ heather ~ 混色毛纱 / brown ~ 棕色合剂，复方甘草合剂（常用的咳嗽药水）‖**the ~ as before** 照原来药方配药;[口]照原办法办理

mizzle¹ ['mizl] [方] I *n.* 细雨,蒙蒙雨，毛毛雨 II *vi.* 下蒙蒙雨 ‖**mizzly** *a.* 下着蒙蒙雨的

mizzle² ['mizl] *vi.* [英俚]突然离开，撤走

moan [moun] I *n.* ①呻吟声；呜咽声；悲叹声: utter ~s 呻吟 ②(风、树等的)萧萧声: the ~ of the west wind 西风萧瑟 II ❶ *vi.* 呻吟，呜咽，悲叹: ~ for the dead 哀悼死者 ❷ *vt.* 以呻吟(或呜咽声)声说出 ‖**~ful** *a.* 呻吟的；悲伤的

moat [mout] I *n.* (城堡等的)护城河；壕；深沟 II *vt.* 以护城河(或壕等)围绕

mob [mɔb] I *n.* ①[蔑]暴民；[the ~]下层民众，群氓 ②一群暴徒；乌合之众 ③[美俚](盗贼等的)一伙；一群罪犯 ④一群人；[集俚]被雇用的一伙人 II (mobbed; mobbing) ❶ *vt.* ①成群结队袭击(或骚扰)；成群结队地涌进(或围着) ②成群结队地围着…欢呼 ❷ *vi.* 聚众生事 ‖**swell ~** 衣着时髦的扒手们 / **~ law** 暴民的法律；私刑 / **~ scene** (电影或日常生活中的)群众场面 / **~sman** ['mɔbzmən] *n.* ①暴民中的一成员 ②[英]打扮时髦的扒手

mobile ['moubail, 'moubi(:)l] I *a.* ①运动的，活动的；可动的: ~ warfare 运动战 / a ~ chair 折椅 ②流动的；机动的；装在车上的，用车辆运输的: ~ labour 流动劳动力 / a ~ medical team 巡回医疗队 / ~ troops (或 units) 快速部队 / a ~ loudspeaker 流动广播宣传车 ③易变的，多变的；(在社会地位方面)升降很大的: a ~ face 表情多变的脸 / a ~ mind 多变的心思 ④具有灵活性的 ⑤运动物体的，活动装置的 II *n.* ①运动物体；(由空气流动而转动的)活动装置 ②[美]汽车(automobile 之略) ‖**~ home** [美]住房拖车(指一种改装的由汽车拖拉的活动房屋)

mobility [mou'biliti] *n.* ①运动性；流动性；机动性: ~ of capital 资本的流动性 ②变动性；灵活性 ③[物]动性，迁移率;【化】迁度: ionic ~ 离子迁移率；离子迁度

mobilize ['moubilaiz] ❶ *vt.* ①动员: ~ all

positive factors 调动一切积极因素 ②使可动,使流通 ❷ *vi.* 动员起来 ‖**mobilizable** *a.* 可动员的 / **mobilization** [,moubilai'zeiʃən] *n.* 动员: *mobilization* orders 动员令

moccasin ['mɔkəsin] *n.* ① (北美印第安人穿的)鹿皮(或其他软皮)鞋 ②软鞋；软拖鞋 ③【动】(美国南部产的)一种毒蛇，嚙鱼蛇 ‖**~ flower** 杓兰属植物(尤指美国产的美丽杓兰)

mock [mɔk] I ❶ *vt.* ① (尤指通过模仿进行的)嘲弄，嘲笑；模拟: ~ sb.'s gait 学着某人走路的样子来嘲弄他 ②使失望；欺骗: ~ sb. (或 sb.'s hope) with empty promises 用空洞的诺言欺骗某人 ③使无效，挫败 ❷ *vi.* 嘲弄 (*at*) II *n.* ①嘲弄；嘲弄的对象: make a ~ of sb. 嘲弄某人 ②模仿；仿造；仿造品 III *a.* 假的；虚幻的；模拟的: ~ modesty 假谦虚 / the ~ daylight given by snow 雪(光)所造成的假白昼 / a ~ battle 模拟战 IV *ad.* [常用以构成复合词]虚伪地: ~-serious 假装严肃的 ‖**~er** *n.* ①嘲笑者,愚弄者 ②模仿鸟 ‖**~ duck** 充鸭,假鸭(做成鸭形的猪肉或羊肉肉) / '**~-he'roic** *a.* 嘲弄(或滑稽)地模仿英雄风格的(尤指诗歌等) *n.* 嘲弄(或滑稽)地模仿英雄风格的作品 / **~ moon**【气】幻月(月晕的光轮) / **~ orange**【植】①山梅花 ②桑橙 ③葡萄牙桂樱 ④象橙子的葫芦 / **~ sun**【气】幻日(日晕的光轮) / **~ turtle soup** (用小牛头等煮成的)充甲鱼汤 / '**~-up** *n.* ① (供试验、教练用的机器等的)大模型: a ~*-up* of an aeroplane 飞机模型 ②【军】伪装工事

mockery ['mɔkəri] *n.* ①嘲笑,愚弄: hold sb. (sth.) up to ~ 对某人(某事)加以嘲笑 ②嘲弄的对象,笑柄: make a ~ of 把…作为笑料,愚弄… ③拙劣的模仿,冒牌 ④恶劣(或可鄙)的事例: the ~ of a trial 可鄙的审判；不公正的审判 ⑤ 徒劳

mode [moud] *n.* ①方式，样式: the ~ of operation 操作方式;【军】作战方式 / the ~ of thinking 思想方法 / the ~ of life 生活方式 / the ~ of production 生产方式 ②风气，风尚，时尚: be all the ~ 在风行中 / out of ~ 不流行，过时 ③[语]语气(=mood) ④【逻】程式，样式，论式 ⑤【音】调式: the major (minor) ~ 大(小)调式 ⑥ (统计学中的)众数

model ['mɔdl] I *n.* ①模型，雏型；原型: a ~ of an aeroplane (或 a ~ aeroplane) 飞机模型 / a wax ~ for a statue 塑像的蜡制原型 ②模范，典型: a labour ~ 劳动模范 / This article is a ~ of conciseness and clearness. 这篇文章的简洁明了是典型的。/ a ~ worker 模范工作者 / a ~ test 模型试验 ③[英方]极相似的人(或东西): She is a perfect ~ of her mother. 她酷象她母亲。④样式: the latest ~ of the lorry 卡车的最新式样 / a sports ~ (能高速行驶的)跑车型汽车 ⑤(供画家等作绘示对象的)模特儿;(供顾客挑选服装等用的)时装模特儿(指活人或用木、蜡等制的): stand ~ 做模特儿 II (model(l)ed; model(l)ing) ❶ vt. ①做…的模型 ②按模型制作; 使模仿 (on, upon, after): delicately model(l)ed features 清秀的面貌 ③做模特儿展示(服装等): a model(l)ed hat 模特儿戴着示样的帽子 ④使(图画等)有立体感 ❷ vi. ①做模型: She ~s in clay. 她用粘土做模型。②做模特儿 ||**model(l)er** n. 塑造者; 做模型的人

model(l)ing ['mɔdliŋ] n. ①造型(术); 制作模型的方法 ②模特儿职业 ③(图画等)的立体感

moderate ['mɔdərit] I a. ①中等的, 适度的: a room of ~ size 不大不小的房间 / a ~ distance 中等距离 / ~ health 中等的健康状况 ②温和的; 稳健的; 有节制的: a ~ climate 温和的天气 / be ~ in views 持稳健见解 ③(价钱)公道的; 花费不多的 II n. 温和主义者, 稳健派 III ['mɔdəreit] ❶ vt. ①使和缓; 使减轻; 节制: ~ one's voice 压低讲话的声音 / a moderating influence 起缓和(或节制)作用的影响 ②主持(会议等) ❷ vi. ①变和缓: The wind has ~d. 风小了。②主持会议 ||~**ly** ad. / ~**ness** n. ||~ **breeze** 【气】和风 / ~ **gale** 【气】疾风

moderation [,mɔdə'reiʃən] n. ①中等, 适度 ②温和; 缓和; 节制: in ~ 适中地, 有节制地 ③【原】减速, 慢化, 延时作用 ④[英][复]牛津大学文学士学位第一次考试

modern ['mɔdən] I a. 现代的; 近代的; 新式的: ~ history 近代史 / ~ languages 近代语言(包括德、法、西、英语等, 区别于古希腊、拉丁语) / Modern English 近代英语(指一五〇〇年以后的英语) / Modern Hebrew 现以色列用的犹太语 / ~ electric wiring 现代化电线装置 II n. 现代人; 近代人; 现代派的人: the Modern Athens 现代雅典(英国爱丁堡或美国波士顿的别称) / the Modern Babylon 现代巴比伦(伦敦的别称) / the ~ school (或 side) [英]学校中着重现代学科的部分 ||~**ly** ad. / ~**ness** n.

modernize ['mɔdə(:)naiz] ❶ vt. 使现代化; 使适应现代需要 ❷ vi. 现代化; 用现代方法 ||**modernization** [,mɔdə(:)nai'zeiʃən] n. ①现代化, 维新 ②现代化的事物

modest ['mɔdist] a. ①谦虚的, 谦让的, 谦恭的 ②(尤指妇女)端庄的, 庄重的; 贞节的 ③羞怯的 ④(希望、要求等)有节制的, 不过分的 ⑤朴素的, 朴实的 ||~**ly** ad.

modesty ['mɔdisti] n. ①谦逊, 虚心: Modesty helps one to go forward, whereas conceit makes one lag behind. 虚心使人进步, 骄傲使人落后。②(尤指妇女的)端庄, 稳重 ③羞怯 ④节制, 中肯 ⑤朴素, 朴实

modicum ['mɔdikəm] n. [只用单]一小份, 少量: a ~ of wine 少量的酒 / a falsehood without a ~ of truth in it 弥天大谎

modification [,mɔdifi'keiʃən] n. ①缓和; 减轻; 限制 ②更改; 修改; 改变 ③【语】修饰 ④【语】(用变音符号的)元音改变 (如 Bülow 中的 ü)

modify ['mɔdifai] vt. ①缓和; 减轻: ~ one's tone 缓和语气 / ~ one's demands 减少要求 ②更改; 修改: The equipment was modified to produce locomotives. 这设备被改用来生产火车头了。/ ~ the terms of a contract 修改合同条款 ③【语】修饰: Adjectives ~ nouns. 形容词修饰名词。④【语】用变音符号"‥"改变(元音) ||**modifier** n. ①更改者; 修改者 ②【语】修饰语

modulate ['mɔdjuleit] ❶ vt. ①调整; 调节(声等) ②声调抑扬地唱(歌) ③【音】使转调, 使变调 ④【无】调制: a ~d electric wave 已调波 ❷ vi. ①声调抑扬地歌唱(或演奏) ②【音】转调, 变调: ~ from one key to another 从一个调转到另一个调 ③【无】调制 ||**modulator** n. 调整者; 调节者; 【无】调制者; 调制器

modulation [,mɔdju'leiʃən] n. ①调整; 调节 ②(声调的)抑扬 ③【音】转调, 变调 ④【无】调制: amplitude ~ 调幅, 振幅调制 / audio (或 voice) ~ 音频调制 / frequency ~ 调频, 频率调制

module ['mɔdju:l] n. ①(建筑或一般工业上应用的)模数 ②【数】模; 系数 ③【无】微型组件; 组件 ④(宇宙飞船上各个独立的)舱: a command ~ 指挥舱, 指令舱 / a lunar ~ 登月舱

mohair ['mouhɛə] I n. ①马海毛, 安哥拉山羊毛 ②马海毛织物; 仿马海毛织物 II a. 用马海毛制造的: ~ cloth 马海呢

Mohammedan [mou'hæmidən] I a. (伊斯兰教创立人)穆罕默德(Mohammed)的; 伊斯兰教的 II n. 伊斯兰教徒, 穆斯林 (=Moslem) ||~**ism** n. 伊斯兰教

moiety ['mɔieti] n. ①一半(尤用于法律方面); 均一半 ②组成部分; 一份(尤指政府给告密者的一份报酬) ③(部落的两个基本分支中)一个分支

moil [mɔil] I ❶ vi. 做苦工: toil and ~ 辛辛苦苦地工作 ❷ vt. [方]弄脏; 弄湿 II n. ①苦工; 混乱; 喧闹 ②[英方]泥; 泥潭

moist [mɔist] a. ①潮湿的, 微湿的; 多雨的: the ~ season 雨季 / a ~ wind from the sea 从海面上吹来的潮湿的风 ②含泪的, 泪汪汪的: eyes ~ with tears 泪汪汪的眼睛 ③【医】湿性的, 有分泌物的: ~ gangrene 湿性坏疽 ||~**ly** ad. / ~**ness** n.

moisture ['mɔistʃə] n. ①潮湿, 潮气, 湿气 ②湿度; 水分, 含水量: ~ capacity (或 content) 湿度, 含水量 / ~ determination 含水量测定 ||~**less** a. [古]无水分的; 干的 ||'~proof a. 防潮湿的 vt. 使防潮湿

molar¹ ['moulə] I n. 【解】磨牙, 臼齿 (=~ tooth) II a. ①磨的; 适宜于用来磨的 ②臼齿的

molar² ['moulə] a. 【化】①(体积)克分子的 ②克模的; (体积)克分子(浓度)的 ||~ heat 克分子热 / ~ refraction 克分子折射(度) / ~ solution 容模溶液 / ~ volume 克分子体积; 衡分子体积 / ~ weight 克分子量 ||~**ity** [mou'læriti] n. (体积)克分子浓度; 容模

mole¹ [moul] I n. ①鼹鼠; 鼹鼠皮 ②在黑暗中工作的人 II vi. 掘地道, 打地洞 ||**blind as a ~**

瞎的 ‖**~ cricket** 蝼蛄 / '**~hill** *n.* 鼹鼠窝,鼹鼠丘: make a mountain (out) of a ~*hill* 小题大作 / **~ plough** 挖沟犁,鼹鼠犁 / **~ shrew** 美洲短尾鼩鼱 / **~skin** *n.* ①鼹鼠皮；充鼹鼠皮②厚毛头斜纹棉布 ③[复]厚毛头布裤

mole² [moul] *n.* 【医】① 痣: a pigmented ~ 色(素)痣 / a warty ~ 疣状痣 ②胎块

mole³ [moul] *n.* ①防波堤,堤道 ②有防波堤的海港

mole⁴ [moul] *n.* 【化】①克分子(量),克模 ②衡分子

molecular [mou'lekjulə] *a.* 【化】① 分子的: ~ formula 分子式 / ~ weight 分子量 ②克分子的: ~ conductivity 克分子电导率；克分子传导率 ‖**~ity** [mou,lekju'læriti] *n.* 分子性；分子状态；分子作用 / **~ly** *ad.*

molecule ['mɔlikju:l] *n.* 【化】分子；克分子: gram ~ 克分子 / polar ~ 有极分子 ②微小颗粒

molest [mou'lest] *vt.* 骚扰,干扰；使烦恼 ‖**~ation** [,moules'teiʃən] *n.*

moll [mɔl] *n.* [俚] ① 盗贼的女友(或姘妇)；娼妓 ②女人

mollify ['mɔlifai] *vt.* ①使平静,平息: ~ sb. 使某人平静下来 / ~ sb.'s anger 使某人息怒 / **~ing** remarks 安慰的话 ②使软 ③ 缓和,减轻 ‖**mollification** [,mɔlifi'keiʃən] *n.*

mollusc ['mɔləsk] *n.* 【动】软体动物

mollycoddle ['mɔlikɔdl] I *n.* 女子气的男子；懦夫 II *vt.* 娇养,溺爱: ~ oneself 养尊处优,纵容自己 ‖**~r** *n.* 溺爱者

molten ['moultən] I melt 的过去分词 II *a.* 熔融的,熔化的: ~ steel 钢水

moment ['moumənt] *n.* ①片刻,瞬间,刹那；时刻: Please wait (for) a ~. 请等一下。/ Come here this ~! 此刻就来! / He arrived at the last ~. 他在最后一刻赶到。②重要,重大；【哲】要素,契机: be of great (little, no) ~ 很(不很,不)重要 / decisions of ~ 重要的决定 ③【物】【力】矩: ~ of force 力矩 / ~ of inertia 惯性矩；转动惯量 ④(历史发展的)阶段 ⑤(统计学)动差 ‖**at any ~** 在任何时候,随时 / **at the ~** [用于现在时态中]此刻；[用于过去时态中]那时: I am (was) busy *at the ~*. 我此刻(当时)很忙。/ **for the ~** 暂时；目前: Stop discussing *for the ~*, please. 请暂停讨论。/ **Half a ~!** 稍等片刻! (=Wait a ~!) / **have one's ~s** 走红；得意 / **in a ~** 立即,立刻: I'll come *in a ~*. 我马上就来。/ **in one's extreme ~s** 在临终时刻 / **men of the ~** 当代要人 / **never (或 not) for a ~** 决不；从来没有 / **of the ~** 此刻,现在 / **on (或 upon) the ~** 立刻,马上 / **the ~** [相当于连接词 as soon as]一……(就……)；正当……的一刹那间 / **the ~ of truth** ①斗牛中的最后一剑 ②生死一决,关键时刻 / **the psychological ~** 心理上的适当瞬间；最适当的时机 / **to the ~** 恰好,不差片刻 ‖**~ly** *ad.* 时刻地,随时；一会儿

momentary ['mouməntəri] *a.* ① 瞬息间的,顷刻的,短暂的: not rely on ~ enthusiasm 不凭一时的热情 ②时时刻刻的: in ~ expectation of the arrival of sb. 时刻盼望某人的到来 ‖**momentarily** ['moumentərili; 美 ,moumən'terili] *ad.* / **momentariness** *n.*

momentous [mou'mentəs] *a.* 重大的,重要的；严重的: a ~ decision 重要的决定 ‖**~ly** *ad.* / **~ness** *n.*

momentum [mou'mentəm] ([复] momentums 或 momenta [mou'mentə]) *n.* ①【物】动量；(火箭发动机的)总冲量 ②势头,力量: with the ~ of an avalanche (或 a landslide) 以排山倒海之势 / The movement is gaining ~. 这场运动愈来愈猛烈了。③要素,契机

monarch ['mɔnək] *n.* ① 君主,最高统治者 ②[喻]王,大王: the ~ of the forest 森林之王(指枳树、橡树或狮、虎等) ③(美洲产)一种橙褐色大蝴蝶 ‖**the Grand Monarch** 法王路易十四的别称 / **the merry ~** 英王查理二世的别称

monarchy ['mɔnəki] *n.* ①君主政体,君主制度: an absolute (或 autocratic) ~ 君主专制制度 / a constitutional ~ 君主立宪制度 ②君主国

monastery ['mɔnəstəri] *n.* 修道院；庙宇,寺院: a Buddhist ~ 佛寺,庙 ‖**monasterial** [,mɔnəs'tiəriəl] *a.*

monastic [mə'næstik] I *a.* ①修道院的；庙宇的,寺院的: ~ architecture 寺院建筑 ②修道士的；僧尼的；禁欲生活的 II *n.* 修道士；和尚 ‖**~ally** *ad.* / **~ism** [mə'næstisizəm] *n.* 修道生活,禁欲生活；寺院制度

Monday ['mʌndi, 'mʌndei] *n.* 星期一 ‖**a ~ morning quarterback** [美俚]放马后炮的人(指事后提出劝告或发表议论的人) / **Black ~** [学俚](放假后的)开学第一天 / **blue ~** ①[口]烦闷的星期一(指任何星期一,与欢乐的周末相对而言)；沮丧的时候 ②四旬斋(Lent) 前的星期一 / **Mad ~** (交易所用语)忙乱的星期一(因为这一天交易所特别忙乱) / **St. (或 Saint) ~** 很少工作的星期一,过得懒散的星期一 ‖**~ish** *a.* (由于星期天过于劳累而)在星期一不想做事的,疲倦的 / **~s** *ad.* [美]每星期一；在任何星期一

money ['mʌni] ([复] moneys 或 monies) *n.* ①货币(硬币和纸币)；[复]特种钱币: hard (soft 或 paper) ~ 硬(纸)币 / standard (subsidiary) ~ 本位(辅)币 ②金钱；财富,财产: save ~ 省钱,储蓄金钱；节省资金 / in ~ matters 在金钱问题上 / make ~ 赚钱 / lose ~ 亏本 / raise ~ 筹款 ③[复]金额,款项: public *monies* 公款 / the collection of tax *monies* 税款的征收 ④[总称]富翁；金融界 ⑤(赛马、赛狗中)前三名优胜者；优胜奖金 ‖**be good ~** 是有利可图的投资 / **be made of ~** (人)钱多得用不完 / **coin ~** 暴发,获大利 / **come into one's ~** 继承遗产 / **covered ~** [美](归国会调拨的)国库存款 / **earn good ~** 赚大钱 / **easy ~** 来得容易的钱；[美]低利贷款 / **even ~** 同额赌注 / **fairy ~** 神仙赏赐的钱(相传很快变成枯叶或废物)；[喻]

拾得的钱 / *for love or* ~ 见 *love* / *for* ~ (伦敦证券交易所用语) 现款交易的 / *for one's* ~ [口] 依照本人的意见 / *get one's* ~'s *worth* 花钱划得来 / *have* ~ *to burn* 有花不完的钱 / *in the* ~ [俚] ① 在富裕境遇中, 资金充裕 ② (在赛马、赛狗中) 赌胜 / *lie out of one's* ~ 未得报酬 / *lucky* ~ (佩作护符的) 吉利钱币 / *Money burns a hole in his pocket.* 钱烧口袋漏, 一有就不留。/ ~ *for jam* (或 *for old rope*) [英俚] 不用费力得来的利益, 容易赚的钱 / *Money makes the mare* (*to*) *go.* [谚] 有钱能使鬼推磨。/ ~ *of account* 记帐货币 / ~ *on* (或 *at*) *call* 随时可以收回的借款 (=call ~) / *Money talks.* [美俚] 金钱万能。/ *not every man's* ~ 不是对每个人都有价值 / *out of the* ~ (在赛马、赛狗中) 赌输 (*pay*) ~ *down* (付) 现款 / *put* ~ *into* 投资于… / *put* ~ *on* 在…上打赌 / *sink* ~ 浪费金钱, 投资于无利可图的事业 / *spend* ~ *like water* 挥金如土 / *spill* ~ [俚] 赌输 / *splash one's* ~ *about* 大肆挥霍 / *throw good* ~ *after bad* 想补偿损失反而损失得更多 / *Time is* ~. [谚] 一寸光阴一寸金。/ *wallow in* ~ 腰缠万贯, 钱很多 / ~*er* n. 铸币者 / ~*less* a. 没钱的 / ~*wise* ad. 在金钱方面; 财政上 ‖~**bag** n. ① 钱袋 ② [复] 财富 ③ [~bags] [用作单] 富翁, 守财奴 / ~ **broker** 代办短期借款的经纪人 / ~ **changer** 货币兑换商; 钱币兑换器 / ~ **crop** 专供销售 (或立可销售) 的农作物 / '~**grubber** n. 守财奴 / '~**lender** n. 放债者 / '~**maker** n. 会赚钱的人; 赚钱的东西 (或计划) / '~**man** n. 投资者; 金融家 / ~ **market** 金融市场 / ~ **order** ① 汇票 ② 邮政汇票 (=postal ~ order) / ~ **spinner** [英] 很赚钱的书籍 (或戏剧、电影等); 会赚钱的人 / '~'s-**worth** n. 值钱的东西, 可卖钱的东西 / '~**wort** n. 【植】铜钱状珍珠菜

mongoose ['mɔŋgu:s] n. 【动】① 猫鼬, 獴 ② =~ lemur ‖~ **lemur** (马达加斯加岛产的) 狐猴

mongrel ['mʌŋgrəl] I n. ① 杂种狗 ② 杂种植物 (或动物) ③ [蔑] 杂种, 混血儿 II a. [只作定语] 杂种的, 混血的 ‖~**ism** n. 混血 / ~**ize** vt. 使成混合种 ② (种族主义者污蔑性用语) 使血统混合, 使成杂种

monitor ['mɔnitə] I n. ① (学校的) 班长, 级长; 导生 (指英国学校中协助教师维持秩序、辅导低年级同学的高年级成绩较好的学生) ② (对外国广播等的) 监听员; 监听器; (电视、飞机等的) 监视器, 控制器; (放射性等的) 检验器; (火箭的) 追踪器: a television wave form —— 波形监视器 / an air ~ (空气中) 放射性检验器 ③ 告诫物, 提醒物; [罕] 告诫者, 提醒者 ④ (旧式的) 低舷铁甲舰; 浅水重炮舰 ⑤ (采矿、救火用) 水枪, 水枪喷嘴 (也称 ~ nozzle) ⑥ 【动】巨蜥 (也称 ~ lizard) II ❶ vt. ① 监听 (外国广播等); 监视, 监控 (电视、飞机等); 追踪 (火箭) ② 检验 (放射性污染物); 检查

(机器等); 控制 (操作等等); 调节 (声音): ~ engines 检查引擎 / ~ upper air to collect evidence of atomic explosions 检验高空空气以收集原子爆炸的证据 / ~ the liquid level 控制液面 ❷ vi. 监视, 监听; 检验放射性污染物; 追踪火箭飞行 ‖~ **roof**, ~ **top** 【建】通风顶, 采光顶 / ~ **screen** 电视台检查 (或选择) 播送内容的电视屏

monk [mʌŋk] n. 修道士; 僧侣: a Buddhist ~ 和尚; 喇嘛 ‖~**hood** n. ① 修道士 (或僧侣) 的身分 ② 修道生活; 僧侣生活 ③ [总称] 僧侣 / ~**ish** a. [蔑] 修道士 (似) 的; 僧侣 (似) 的

monkey ['mʌŋki] I n. ① 猴子; 猿; 长毛猴的毛皮: When the tree falls, the ~s scatter. 树倒猢狲散。/ as mischievous as a ~ 像猴子一样调皮 ② [谑] 猴子似的人; 淘气鬼, 顽童; 易受欺的人: What have you done, you young ~! 你干了什么啦, 你这个小捣蛋! / make a ~ of sb. 愚弄某人 ③ 打桩锤: the ~ of a pile driver 打桩机桩锤 ④ (制玻璃用的) 小坩埚 ⑤ [俚] 五百英镑; 五百美元 II ❶ vi. 胡闹, 捣蛋; 瞎弄: Stop ~ing about with the machine! 不要瞎弄机器! ❷ vt. 学…的样; 嘲弄 ‖a ~ with a long tail 抵押 / get (或 have) one's ~ up [英俚] 生气: Don't get your ~ up for nothing. 别无缘无故生气。/ get the ~ off [英俚] 戒除吸毒恶习 / have a ~ on a house (或 up the chimney) 抵押房屋 / have a ~ on one's back [美俚] 毒瘾很深 (以致思想上、经济上负担沉重) / ~ around [美俚] 闲荡, 捣蛋; 瞎弄 / put sb.'s ~ up [英俚] 使某人生气, 激怒某人: Your last word word has really put his ~ up. 你最后一句话实在使他大为生气。/ suck the ~ [英俚] ① 自瓶中饮酒; 用椰子壳饮糖浆 ② 用麦杆 (或吸管) 插入酒桶吸 ‖~ **bread** 【植】猴面包树; 猴面包树果实 / ~ **business** 胡闹; 欺骗; 恶作剧 / ~ **cap** (有带襻住下巴的) 圆顶无边小帽 / ~ **clothes** [美俚] 礼服; 军服 / ~ **drill** [美俚] 柔软体操 / ~ **engine** 打桩机 / ~ **jacket** [口] (水手穿的) 紧身短上衣 / ~ **meat** [美俚] 劣等牛肉 / '~-**nut** n. 落花生 / ~ **puzzle** 【植】智利南美杉, 智利松 / '~-**shine** n. [常用复] [美俚] 恶作剧, 胡闹 / ~ **suit** [美俚] 制服; 军服; 礼服 / ~ **wrench** ① 【机】活动扳手 ② 引起破坏的东西: throw a ~ wrench into negotiations 破坏谈判

monocle ['mɔnəkl] n. 单片眼镜

monocotyledon ['mɔnou,kɔti'li:dən] n. 【植】单子叶植物 ‖~**ous** a.

monogamy [mɔ'nɔgəmi] n. ① 一夫一妻制 ② 一生一婚制 ③ 【动】单配偶, 单配性

monogram ['mɔnəgræm] I n. 交织字母, 花押字 (姓名或公司名等起首字母相互交织成图案状, 用作信笺或商标等的标记) II (monogrammed, monogramming) vt. 把交织字母标在: ~ one's handkerchief 在手帕上缀上 (自己姓名起首字母组成的) 交织字母 ‖**monogrammatic** [,mɔnəgrə'mætik] a.

monograph ['mɔnəɡrɑːf] I n. 专题文章,专题著作 II vt. 写关于…的专题文章 ‖**~er** [mɔ-'nɔɡrəfə] n. 专题文章作者 / **~ic(al)** [,mɔnə-'ɡræfik(əl)] a. 专题(性)的 / **~ist** [mə'nɔɡrəfist] n. =~er

monolith ['mɔnəuliθ] n. ①(柱状或碑状的)独块巨石,整块石料 ②独块石料制品;独石柱(或碑) ③坚如磐石的东西

monologue ['mɔnəlɔɡ] n. ①(戏)独白;独白场面 ②独演剧本;独脚戏;独白式文学作品 ③(使别人无法插嘴的)滔滔不绝的话

monoplane ['mɔnəplein] n. 单翼(飞)机

monopolist [mə'nɔpəlist] I n. ①垄断者,独占者;专利者 ②垄断论者 II a. =~ic ‖**~ic** [mə,nɔpə-'listik] a. ①垄断(者)的,独占(者)的;专利(者)的 ②垄断商品的

monopolize [mə'nɔpəlaiz] vt. 垄断,独占;专营,专利: ~ the market 垄断市场 / ~ the conversation 滔滔不绝使别人插不上嘴地谈话 ‖**monopolization** [mə,nɔpəlai'zeiʃən] n. / **~r** n. 垄断者,独占者;专利者

monopoly [mə'nɔpəli] n. ①垄断,独占;专利: capital 垄断资本,独占资本 / the ~ the capitalist class 垄断资产阶级 / the ~ of a conversation 使别人插不上嘴的滔滔不绝的谈话 ②垄断商品,专利品;专利事业: a government ~ 政府专利品 / make a ~ of some commodity 独家经售某种商品 ③垄断权,专利权: secure a ~ of one's invention 取得发明的专利权 ④垄断者,专利者;垄断集团,垄断企业: the steel monopolies 钢铁垄断资本家(或集团)

monosyllable ['mɔnə,siləbl] n. 单音节词

monotheism ['mɔnəuθi:,izəm] n. 一神教;一神论 ‖**monotheist** n. 信一神教者;一神论者

monotone ['mɔnətəun] I n. ①(语调、文体、风格、色彩等的)单调 ②不变的乐调;单调的歌曲 ③只会用单音调歌唱的人 II a. 单调的 III vt. & vi. 单调地说(或读、唱) ‖**monotonic** [,mɔnə'tɔnik] a. 单调的

monotonous [mə'nɔtənəs] a. ①单音调的,无抑扬顿挫的 ②单调的,一成不变的;使人厌倦的 ‖**~ly** ad. / **~ness** n.

monotony [mə'nɔtəni] n. 单音,单调;无变化,千篇一律

monsieur [强 mə'sjə:; 弱 məsjə] ([复] messieurs ['mesəz]) n. [法] ①先生;[M-]…先生(略作 M.,用于姓名前作称呼,相当于 Mr. 或 Sir) ②法国人 ③[史]法国国王的次子(或大弟)的称号

monsoon [mɔn'su:n] n. ①季风,季节风(在印度洋和亚洲南部,夏为西南风,冬为东北风): the dry ~ 冬季季风,干季风 / the wet ~ 夏季季风,湿季风 ②(印度等地的)夏季季风期,雨季 ‖**~ forest** 季雨林 / **~ rain** 季风雨

monster ['mɔnstə] n. ①怪物,妖怪: ghosts and ~s 牛鬼蛇神 ②畸形的动植物;【医】畸胎 ③巨兽;异常大的东西;可怕的东西: The pumpkin is a real ~. 这南瓜可真大。/ a technological ~ 技术上的庞然大物(如大机器等) ④极丑陋的人;恶人,残忍的人 II a. [只作定语]异乎寻常地大的: a ~ ship 巨舰 / What a ~ potato! 好大的一个马铃薯!

monstrous ['mɔnstrəs] I a. ①畸形的,怪异的: a ~ fetus 怪胎 ②异乎寻常地大的: a ~ tiger 巨虎 / a ~ sum 巨款 ③可怕的;极恶的;极可笑的,荒谬的: ~ crimes 滔天罪行 / ~ slanders 恶毒诽谤 / magnify a blemish to ~ proportions 把一个小缺点夸大到荒谬的程度 ④[用以加强语气]极大的: be awakened by a ~ hammering on the door 被一阵猛烈的敲门声所惊醒 II ad. [方]极,非常 ‖**~ly** ad. / **~ness** n.

month [mʌnθ] n. 月;一个月的时间: this (last, next) ~ 本(上,下)月 / the ~ after next 再下一个月 / the ~ before last 再上一个月 / during the ~ of October 在十月份 / a calendar ~ 历月 / a lunar ~ 太阴月 / a solar ~ 太阳月 / a few ~s 几个月 / a woman in her sixth ~ 怀孕六个月的女人 ‖**a ~ of Sundays** 很长的时间,很久 / **for ~s** 好几个月以来 / **~ after ~** 一月又一月,每月 / **~ by ~** 逐月 / **~ in, ~ out** 月月,每月 / **this day ~** 上(或下)月的今天 ‖**~'s mind** ①【宗】(人死后的)周月弥撒 ②[英]渴望,心意

monthly ['mʌnθli] I a. 每月的,每月一次的;按月计算的;以一个月为期的: a ~ magazine 月刊 / a ~ rose 月季花 / ~ pay 月薪 / a ~ season ticket 月(季)票 / a ~ nurse (照料产妇的)产褥护士 II ad. 每月一次,每月: check ~ 每月检查一次 III n. ①月刊 ②[复]月经 ‖**Monthly Meeting** 【宗】月会(基督教公谊会的地区组织)

monument ['mɔnjumənt] n. ①纪念碑;纪念馆;纪念像;纪念物;纪念性作品;纪念文 ②遗迹,遗址: ancient (或 historic) ~s 古迹,古址 ③有永久价值的作品,不朽的功业: a ~ of learning 不朽的学术著作 ④标石,界石 ⑤墓碑 ⑥[古]纪录;标记 ⑦[the M-](一六六六年)伦敦大火纪念塔

monumental [,mɔnju'mentl] a. ①纪念碑(或物)的;纪念的: a ~ inscription 碑铭 ②巨大的,雄伟的;不朽的: a painting on a ~ scale 巨幅画 / ~ works 不朽的著作 ③[用以加强语气]非常的,极大的: ~ ignorance 极端的无知 ‖**~ly** ad.

mood¹ [muːd] n. ①心境,心情,情绪;(精神)状态: a militant ~ 战斗情绪 / be in the (be in no) ~ to joke (或 for jokes) 有(没有)开玩笑的心境 / The city is in a festive (或 holiday) ~. 全城处在一片节日气氛中。②基调: the emotional ~ of a play 一出戏剧的感情基调 ③[复]喜怒无常: a man of ~s 喜怒无常的人,心情易变的人 ④[古]大怒

mood² [muːd] n. ①【语】语气: the indicative (imperative, subjunctive) ~ 陈述(祈使,虚拟)语气 ②【逻】论式 ③【音】调式

moody ['mu:di] *a.* ①喜怒无常的，易怒的；心情易变的 ②忧郁的，不快的 ‖**moodily** *ad.* / **moodiness** *n.*

moon [mu:n] **I** *n.* ①月球，月亮: a half (full) ~ 半(满)月 / a new (或 crescent) ~ 新月 / an old (或 a waning) ~ 亏月 / the harvest ~ 收获季节的满月(指九月廿二、廿三日后两周内的第一次满月) / the hunter's ~ 狩猎季节的满月(指紧接收获季节满月后的第一次满月) ②朔望月，太阴月；[诗]月(=month) ③月光: There is little ~ tonight. 今晚没什么月光。 ④月状物，新月状物 ⑤卫星 ⑥【天】月相 ⑦[美俚]酒，非法酿造的威士忌酒 **II ❶** *vi.* 闲荡；出神，呆看 (about, around, over) **❷** *vt.* 虚度(时间)(away): ~ the afternoon away 稀里糊涂地过了一个下午 ‖(a) blue ~ 不可能的事；难得遇见的事 / bay the ~ (或 bark at the ~) (狂犬)吠月；空嚷，徒劳 / below the ~ 月下的；尘世的 / cry for the ~ 想做做不到的事，想要得不到的东西 / once in a blue ~ 千载难逢(地) / promise sb. the ~ 对某人作无法兑现的许诺 / shoot the ~ [英俚](为逃避欠租)乘黑夜搬家，夜逃 / the old ~ in the new ~'s arms 新月以后月球的黑暗部分仍然呈现的微光 ‖~ed *a.* 月亮般的；新月状的；有月形纹的 / ~less *a.* 月亮的；无月光的；无卫星的 / ~let ['mu:nlit] *n.* ①【天】小月 ②小卫星；小人造卫星 / ~ward(s) *ad.* 往月球 ‖~beam *n.* (一道)月光 / ~blindness 夜盲，月光盲(马的一种眼病) / ~cake (我国的)月饼 / '~calf *n.* ①傻瓜，笨蛋 ②畸形的动物(或植物)，怪物 / '~craft *n.* 月球探测机 / '~down *n.* =~set / '~eye *n.* 患月光盲的马眼；月光盲 / '~-eyed *a.* ①患月光盲的 ②(因惊奇等)圆睁着双眼的 / '~faced *a.* 圆脸的 / '~fish *n.* 月鱼 / '~flower *n.* 月光花；[英]春白菊，法兰西菊 / ~ gate 月洞门 / '~head *n.* [美俚]傻瓜，笨蛋；神经错乱的人 / '~lit *a.* 月照的，月明的: a ~lit scene 月夜的景色，月景 / ~ month 太阴月 / '~port *n.* 月球火箭发射站 / '~quake *n.* 月震: a ~quake monitor 月震计 / '~raker *n.* ①[主英]笨蛋 ②[英俚]走私贩子 / '~raking *n.* [古]空想 / '~rise *n.* 月出(时) / '~scape *n.* 月亮的表面，月面景色 / '~scooper *n.* (在月球上挖土的)宇宙车 / '~set *n.* 月落(时) / '~shine *n.* ①月光 ②空谈，空想 ③[美俚]非法酿造(或贩卖)的威士忌酒 / '~shiner *n.* [口]非法酿酒的人；夜间进行非法买卖的人 / '~shiny *a.* ①月照的；月光似的 ②空想的 / '~shot *n.* 月球探测器；向月球发射 / '~stone *n.* 月长石 / '~struck *a.* 狂乱的，神经错乱的 / '~walk *n.* 月面行走

moonlight ['mu:nlait] **I** *n.* ①月光: travel by ~ (或 in the ~) 借着月光行路 ②[英俚]杜松子酒 **II** *a.* 月光的；月照的；月光下的: a ~ night 月明之夜 / ~ flit (或 flitting) [英俚](为逃避欠租)乘黑夜搬家，夜逃 / a ~ school (美国南部的)乡村为文盲开办的夜校 **III** *vi.* ①在月光下从事活动；参加夜袭 ②非法酿酒(或贩酒) ③同时兼两个职业‖~er *n.* ①参与夜袭的人 ②非法酿酒(或贩酒)的人 ③同时兼两个职业的人 / ~ing *n.* ①月光下的活动；夜袭 ②同时兼两个职业

moor¹ [muə] *n.* ①[英]荒野，(尤指松鸡的)禁猎地 ②沼，高沼，酸沼 ‖ ~ coal 沼煤 / '~cock *n.* 公红松鸡 / '~fowl, ~ game *n.* 红松鸡 / '~hen *n.* 母红松鸡 / '~land *n.* 高沼地 / '~stone *n.* (英国康威尔地区沼泽所产的)松碎花岗岩

moor² [muə] **❶** *vt.* ①使停泊，系泊(船只)，系留(飞艇等): a motorboat ~ed to a buoy 系缆于浮筒的汽艇 ②使固定，系住: a ~ed mine 【军】锚雷 **❷** *vi.* ①系泊，系留 ②固定，系住

moose [mu:s] [单复同] *n.* 【动】麋，驼鹿

moot [mu:t] **I** *n.* ①【英史】(解决司法、行政等问题的)自由民集会 ②(法科学生的)假设案件讨论会 **II** *a.* ①可讨论的，争论未决的 ②不切实际的；学究式的 **III** *vt.* ①讨论，争论 ②提出…供讨论 ③(在假设法庭上)为(案件)辩护 ‖~ court (法科学生实习的)假设法庭

mop¹ [mɔp] **I** *n.* ①拖把；洗碗刷 ②拖把似的东西；蓬乱的头发 **II** (mopped; mopping) *vt.* 用拖把拖洗；擦，抹: ~ the floor 拖地板 / ~ one's brow 擦去额上的汗水 ‖be (all) ~s and brooms [英俚]半醉的 / ~ up ①用拖把拖洗，擦，抹: ~ up a plate 擦干盘子 ②[口]结束；完成: ~ up arrears of work 做完拖下来的工作 ③痛击；【军】扫荡；肃清 ④吃光，饮尽 ⑤[俚]获取(利润等) ‖'~board *n.*【建】踢脚板 / '~head *n.* ①拖把头 ②头发乱蓬蓬的头；头发乱蓬蓬的人 / '~stick *n.* 拖把柄 / '~-up, 'mopping-up *n.* 扫尾工作；【军】扫荡，肃清残敌: a mopping-up operation 扫荡

mop² [mɔp] **I** *n.* [古]愁脸；鬼脸: ~s and mows 愁脸；鬼脸 **II** (mopped; mopping) *vi.* 作愁脸；扮鬼脸: ~ and mow 作愁脸；扮鬼脸

mop³ [mɔp] *n.* [英]雇工集市(在秋季进行，雇主在此雇用农场工人或仆役)

mope [moup] **I ❶** *vi.* ①忧郁，闷闷不乐 ②闲逛 **❷** *vt.* ①使忧郁，使闷闷不乐: ~ oneself 闹情绪，烦闷 ②闷闷不乐地度过(一段时间)(away) **II** *n.* ①忧郁的人 ②[复]忧郁，烦闷

moped ['mou-ped] *n.* 机动脚踏两用车

moral ['mɔrəl] **I** *a.* ①道德(上)的: ~ standards 道德标准 / the ~ sense 道德感，是非感 / a ~ monster 道德败坏的人 / ~ culture 德育 / ~ philosophy 道德哲学，伦理学 ②合乎道德的，有道德的；道德意义的: a ~ person 有道德的人 / ~ books 道德教育书籍 ③能辨别是非的 ④精神上的，心理上的；道义上的: a ~ victory 精神上的胜利 / a ~ obligation 道义上的责任 ⑤内心确信的: We have a ~ certainty that the experiment will prove a success. 我们完全有把握实验将获得成功。 **II** *n.* ①(由事件、故事

引出的)道德上的教训; 寓意: draw a ~ from
从…引出教训 / The ~ of the story is that
"Solidarity is strength." 这个故事的教益在于
"团结就是力量"。 ②[复]道德, 伦理; (男女的)
品行: a high standard of ~s 高的道德标准
③ [mɔˈrɑːl] 士气 ‖point a ~ 说明(或应用)一
个道德标准 ‖~ly ad. ①道德上;道义上 ②有
道德地,正直地 ③简直

morale [mɔˈrɑːl] *n.* ①士气; 风纪; 精神: heighten
(或 boost)the ~ of 提高…的士气 ②信心, 信念:
Failure did not affect his ~. 失败没有使他泄
气。③道德; 道义

morality [məˈræliti] *n.* ①道德, 美德; 德行; 品行:
new ~ and practices 新道德风尚 ②教训,寓意;
说教 ③道德教育的作品; 道德剧 (=~ play)
④伦理学; [复]道德规范 ‖~ **play** 道德剧(西方
中世纪末一种灌输善恶观念的宗教戏剧, 又称寓
意剧)

moralize [ˈmɔrəlaiz] ❶ *vt.* ①从道德上解释; 从…
引出道德上的教训, 指出…的寓意 ②提高…的德
性, 教化 ❷ *vi.* 论道德问题; 说教 ‖**moralization**
[ˌmɔrəlaiˈzeiʃən] *n.* / ~**r** *n.* 说教者

morass [məˈræs] *n.* ①沼泽, 泥淖 ②陷阱; 困境:
fall into the ~ of 陷入…的泥坑 ‖~**y** *a.* 沼泽
一样的 ‖~ **ore** 褐铁矿

moratorium [ˌmɔrəˈtɔːriəm]([复] moratoriums 或
moratoria [ˌmɔrəˈtɔːriə]) *n.* ① (依法给欠债人
的)延缓偿付权; (欠款的)延缓偿付期 ②(法律义
务的)延期履行权;合法的延缓 ③(行动、活动的)
暂停, 暂禁

morbid [ˈmɔːbid] *a.* ①疾病的;生病的、致病的;患
部的; 病理学的: a ~ condition (或 state) 病
态 / a ~ substance 致病物质 ②~ anatomy
病理解剖学 ②(精神、思想等)不健康的,病态的
③可怕的, 令人毛骨悚然的: ~ details 令人毛骨
悚然的细节 ‖~**ly** *ad.* / ~**ness** *n.*

mordant [ˈmɔːdənt] **I** *a.* ①讥刺的, 尖锐的, 辛辣
的: ~ criticism 尖锐辛辣的批评 ②【化】媒染的:
~ colour (或 dye) 媒染料 ③剧烈的, 热辣辣的:
a ~ pain 剧痛 ④蚀的 **II** *n.* ①媒染剂 ②(金
属)腐蚀剂 ③ =mordent **III** *vt.* 用媒染剂(或腐
蚀剂)处理 ‖~**ly** *ad.*

more [mɔː, məə] **I** *a.* ①[many, much 的比较级]
更多的, 较多的; 更高程度的: do ~ harm than
good 害多益少 / More than one person has made
the suggestion. 不止一人提过这个建议。
②另外的; 附加的: One ~ word. (或 One word
~.) 还有一句话。 / We have a lot ~ work to
do. 我们还有很多工作要做。 / What ~ do
you want? 你还要什么呢? (意指: 难道还不够
吗?) / Would you like to have some ~ tea?
您要不要再喝点茶?
II *n.* ①更多的数量; 较多的数量: forty years
and (或 or) ~ 四十多年 / More of the land is
planted to cabbages than to tomatoes. 种白菜
的地比种西红柿的多。 / There is ~ in it than

you imagine. 其中还有你想象不到的含义。
②额外的数量,另外的一些: Give me a little ~.
再给我一些。 / Take some ~. 再吃点罢。(或:
再拿一些好了。) / I should like as many ~.
我还要同样的数量。 / Say no ~ (about it). 别
再提(它)了。 / There is hardly any ~. 差不
多再也没有了。 / I hope to see ~ of the city.
我希望能多看看这座城市。(意指不仅看其中的一
部分)
III *ad.* ① [much 的比较级,常和两音节以上的
形容词或副词连用]更多; 更: He works ~ and
better than he used to. 他的工作做得比过去更
多更好。 / The work is progressing ~ rapidly
than was expected. 工作进展得比预料的更快。
②倒, 倒不如说: ~ brave than wise 有勇无谋 /
~ in name than in reality 名不副实 / The
child was ~ frightened than hurt. 这孩子
的伤倒不算什么, 只是受惊不小。 / The book
seems to be ~ a dictionary than a grammar.
这本书看来与其说是一本语法书, 倒不如说是一
本词典。
③另外, 再: Read it once ~, please. 请再念
一遍。
④而且: It is a good plan; ~, it is easy to carry
out. 这是一个好计划, 而且容易实行。
‖(and) what is ~ [常用作插入语]更重要的是,
更有甚者, 而且 / all the ~ 更加, 越发 / ~
and ~ 越来越(多): The play gets ~ *and*
~ exciting in the last few scenes. 这
出戏在最后几场中越来越激动人心。 / *More is*
meant than meets the ear. 意在言外。 / ~
or less 或多或少; 左右: We hope our explanation will prove ~ *or less* helpful. 希望我们的
说明多少有些帮助。 / 60 kilometres, ~ *or less*
六十公里左右 / *much* ~ 更加, 何况: It is
difficult to understand his books, *much* ~ his
lectures. 他写的书很难理解, 他的演讲就更难懂
了。 / *neither* ~ *nor less than* 不多不少, 恰
好; 简直: *neither* ~ *nor less than* 100 恰好一百
个 / *neither* ~ *nor less than* absurd 简直荒谬 /
never ~ 决不再 / *no* ~ ①不再: Time lost
will return no ~. 失去了的时间不会再来。
②不再存在, 死了: The old man is no ~. 那
个老年人死了。 ③也不, 也没有: You didn't
come, no ~ did he. 你没有来, 他也没有来。 /
no (或 *not any*) ~ *than* ①不过,仅仅: *no* ~
than five 只有五个 ②同…一样大: I could *no* ~
do that *than* you. (或 I could *not* do that
any ~ *than* you.) 你不能做这件事, 我也不能
做。 / *not* ~ *than* ①至多, 不超过: *not* ~ *than*
five 至多五个 ②不比…更: The new edition is
not ~ expensive *than* the old edition. 新版本
不比旧版更贵。 / *the* ~ 越发, 更: The ~
fool you to believe him. 你如果相信他, 你就越
发显得蠢了。 / *the* ~ *...*, *the* ~ *...* 愈…, 愈
.... The ~, *the* merrier. [谚]人越多越高兴。 /

There is ~ (to it) than meets the eye. 现象背后有文章。

moribund ['mɔ(ː)ribʌnd] I *a.* 垂死的, 即将消灭的 II *n.* 垂死的人 ‖**-ity** [,mɔ(ː)ri'bʌnditi] *n.*

morning ['mɔːniŋ] *n.* ①早晨, 上午: Good ~! (或 *Morning!*) 早上好! 你好! (上午分别时也可用, 表示"再见") / this (yesterday, tomorrow) ~ 今天(昨天, 明天)早上 / in (或 during) the ~ 在早上; 在上午 / on Sunday ~ 星期日上午 / When he woke up, it was already ~. 他一觉醒来已是早上了。/ do ~ exercises 做早操 ②[诗]破晓, 黎明 ③[M-] 黎明女神 ③初期, 早期: the ~ of the world 原始时代 ‖*from ~ till night* 从早到晚地 / of a ~ 往往在早上(指动作的习惯性) ‖**-s** *ad.* [美]每天上午; 在任何上午 ‖**~ call** [英]午后的正式访问 / **~ coat** 晨礼服 / **~ dress** 常礼服 / **~ glory** 牵牛花 / **~ gun** 【军】晨炮(早晨升旗时鸣放的礼炮) / **~ hour** [美]参议院和众议院每天例会时间 / **~ paper** 晨报 / **~ performance** [主英]日戏 / **Morning Prayer** (英国国教的)晨祷 / **~ report** 【军】晨报, 阵中日记 / **~ room** (上午使用的)起居室 / **~ sickness** 孕妇晨吐 / **~ star** 晨星(尤指金星) / **~ watch** 【海】早班值班(上午四时至八时)

morose [me'rous] *a.* ①郁闷的, 愁眉不展的 ②脾气不好的, 乖僻的, 难相处的 ‖**~ly** *ad.* **~ness** *n.*

morrow ['mɔrou] *n.* ①[the ~] 次日, 翌日 ②[喻] 紧接在后的时间 ③[诗]早晨

Morse [mɔːs] *n.* [讯]摩尔斯电码(用点和划表示字母, 可用灯光或无线电发送): ~ flashing light (或 ~ lamp) 闪光信号灯(旧称摩尔斯灯) ‖**~ code**, **~ alphabet** 摩尔斯电码

morsel ['mɔːsəl] *n.* ①(食物的)一口, 一小份, 一小片: a ~ of food 一口食物 / He ate his ~ quickly in the morning. 早上他匆匆忙忙地吃了一点。②少量, 一点点; 片断: ~*s* of information 零星的消息; 片断的知识 ③佳肴; 乐事; 使人愉快的人: exotic ~*s* 异国风味的佳肴 ④微不足道的人 II (morsel(l)ed; morsel(l)ing) *vt.* 使分成小块; 少量地分配

mortal ['mɔːtl] I *a.* ①终有一死的; 死的; 临死的: the ~ remains of (或 all that is ~ of) …的遗体 / ~ agony 临死时的痛苦 ②致死的, 致命的: a ~ wound (blow) 致命的创伤(打击) ③你死我活的; 不共戴天的: a ~ combat 你死我活的战斗 ④世间的, 凡人的; 人的, 人类的: ~ morals 人的道德 ⑤[口]极大的, 极度的; 冗长沉闷的: in a ~ hurry 极其匆忙 / three ~ hours 长得要命的三个钟头 ⑥[与 any, every, no 等连用]想象得出的, 可能的: every ~ thing 世间一切 / It's of no ~ use. 这没有任何用处。⑦【宗】要人地狱的, 不可饶恕的: ~ sins 不可饶恕的大罪 II *n.* ①终有一死的人, 凡人 ②[谑]人 III *ad.* [口][方]极, 非常: be ~ ill 病得很厉害 ‖**~ly** *ad.*

①致命地: be ~*ly* wounded 受致命伤 ②[口]极, 非常: be ~*ly* offended 非常生气

mortality [mɔː'tæliti] *n.* ①致命性, 必死性 ②大量死亡 ③死亡数, 死亡率; (事业等的)失败数, 失败率: a high (low) ~ 死亡率高(低) / greatly reduce the ~ from tuberculosis 使结核病的死亡率大大降低 ④人类 ⑤[古]死 ‖**~ table** 死亡率表

mortar ['mɔːtə] I *n.* ①臼, 研钵: pound sth. in a ~ with a pestle 用杵在臼里捣碎某物 ②灰浆, 砂浆, 灰泥, 胶泥 ③迫击炮;【矿】(试验炸药用的)臼炮 II *vt.* ①用灰浆等涂抹; 用胶泥接合 ②用迫击炮轰击 ‖**~board** *n.* ①灰泥板, 镘板 ②[口]学士帽, 学位帽

mortgage ['mɔːgidʒ] I *n.* ①抵押: raise a ~ (on a house) from a bank (用房子)向银行抵押借款 / pay off the ~ 归还抵押借款 ②抵押契据 ③受押人对抵押品的权利 II *vt.* ①抵押: ~ a house to sb. for £2,000 用房屋向某人押借两千英镑 ②把…当作抵押; 把…许给: ~ oneself to a cause 保证为某一事业努力奋斗 ‖**~e** [,mɔːgə'dʒiː] *n.* 受抵押者, 受押人 / **~r** ['mɔːgədʒə], **mortgagor** [,mɔːgə'dʒɔː] *n.* 抵押人, 出押人

mortify ['mɔːtifai] ❶ *vt.* ①(通过苦行)抑制, 克制: ~ the flesh 禁欲 ②使受辱; 伤害(别人的)感情): be *mortified* at (或 by) sb.'s rudeness 因遭到某人的无礼对待而感到屈辱 ❷ *vi.* ①禁欲, 苦行 ②【医】生坏疽(或脱疽), 腐坏 ③【植】生枯萎, 坏死

mortise ['mɔːtis] I *n.* 榫眼: a ~ chisel 榫凿 / ~ and tenon joint 镶榫接合 II *vt.* ①在…上开榫眼 ②用榫接合, 使上榫; 牢固结合

mortuary ['mɔːtjuəri] I *n.* (丧葬前的)停尸室, (医院的)太平间; 殡仪馆 II *a.* ①丧葬的: ~ rites 丧葬仪式 / the ~ urn 骨灰罐 ②死亡的

mosaic [me'zeiik] I *n.* ①镶嵌工, 镶嵌工艺(品) ②镶嵌图案;【建】镶嵌砖(音译马赛克) ③镶嵌成的东西;【军】镶嵌图(将许多航空照片衔接所构成某一地区的连续空中照相图) ③【无】感光镶嵌幕, 嵌镶光电阴极 ④【植】花叶病 II *a.* ①镶嵌工的, 嵌花式的: a ~ floor 拼花地面 / ~ woolwork 镶嵌式绒线刺绣 ②拼成的: a compilation of various materials 汇编 III (mosaicked; mosaicking) *vt.* ①用镶嵌细工装饰 ②把…组成镶嵌图 ‖**~ist** [mou'zeiisist] *n.* 镶嵌细工师(或艺人) ‖**~ gold** ①彩色金(一种主要含二硫化锡的颜料) ②(用于家具装饰等)仿金的铜合金

mosque [mɔsk] *n.* 伊斯兰教寺院, 清真寺

mosquito [məs'kiːtou] ([复] mosquito(e)s) *n.* ①蚊子 ②[M-] 【军】蚊式飞机; (瑞士)蚊式地对地导弹 ‖*knee-high to a ~* 很小的, 微不足道的 ‖**~cide** *n.* 杀蚊药 / **~ey** [məs'kiːtoui] *a.* 蚊子多的 ‖**~ boat** 【军】快艇; 鱼雷快艇 / **~ craft** [总称]快艇 / **~ curtain** 蚊帐 / **~ fleet** 【军】快艇队, 鱼雷艇队 / **~ hawk** 蜻蜓 / **~ net** 蚊帐 / **~ netting** [纺]蚊帐纱, 网眼纱

moss [mɔs] **I** *n.* ①苔藓；地衣 ②泥炭沼；沼泽 **II** *vt.* 以苔覆盖，使长满苔藓 ‖*A rolling stone gathers no ~*. 见 **stone** ‖*~like a.* 象苔藓的 ‖*~ agate* 【矿】苔纹玛瑙 ‖*back n.* ①背生青苔的老乌龟，绿毛龟；动作呆滞的老鱼；难接近的老牛 ②极端守旧的人，老顽固 / *~,bunker*, *~,banker n.* 一种鲱鱼 / *~-grown a.* 长满苔藓的；古老的 / *~,trooper n.* ①十七世纪英格兰、苏格兰边境沼泽地的劫掠者 ②土匪，强盗

most [moust] **I** [many, much 的最高级] *a.* ① 最多的，最高程度的: get the ~ votes 得到最多的票数 / Who has the ~ need of help? 谁最需要帮助? ② 多数的，大部分的，多半的: Most people think so. 多数人都这样想。**II** *n.* ①最大量，最多数，最高额: Do the ~ you can. 尽你最大的力量去做。② 大多数，大部分; 大多数人: ~ who are present 在场的大部分人 / Most of them are working on the irrigation project. 他们中的多数人都在参加灌溉工程的工作。/ We spent ~ of March ploughing. 三月份的大部分时间内我们在春耕。/ The ~ are on our side. 大多数人在我们这一边。**III** *ad.* ①[much 的最高级,常和两音节以上的形容词或副词连用] 最: Which do you like the ~, apple, orange or peach? 苹果、橘子和桃子三者当中你最喜欢哪一样? ②极，很;十分: The meeting proceeded in a ~ friendly atmosphere. 会见在极友好的气氛中进行。/ We shall ~ certainly come. 我们一定来。③ [英方][美口] 差不多，几乎 (= almost)。*Most* everybody talks about it. 几乎每个人都在谈论这件事。/ ~ anywhere in the world 几乎在世界各地 ‖*at (the) ~* 至多，不超过: The railway will be completed in six months *at (the) ~*. 这条铁路至多过六个月即将完成。/ *at the very ~* =at (the) ~ (但语气较重) / *for the ~ part* 见 **part** / *make the ~ of* ① 尽量利用: In both work and study we ought to *make the ~ of* our time. 不论工作或学习，我们都应该尽量利用时间。② 极为重视: The old worker was *made the ~ of* when he was ill. 这个老工人在生病时受到无微不至的关怀。③ 把…形容尽致: The poem *makes the ~ of* the cruelties of serfdom. 这首诗把农奴制的种种残酷展露无遗。/ *~ and least* [诗]统统；毫无例外 / *~ an end* [英方]经常,通常: I was with him *~ an end*. 我经常和他在一起。‖*~ly ad.* 主要地；大部分；多半；通常: Air is *~ly* nitrogen. 空气中大部分是氮。/ She is *~ly* out on Sundays. 星期天她多半不在家。‖*~= *favo(u)red-*nation clause* 最惠国条款

note [mout] *n.* ①尘埃；微粒，屑 ②瑕疵，小缺点 ‖*a ~ in sb.'s eye* (看不见自己大错误的人所看到的)某人的小缺点

notel [mou'tel] *n.* (附有停车场设施的)汽车游客旅馆

noth [mɔθ] *n.* 蛾；蠹，蛀虫: a grain ~ 谷蛾 / a

clothes ~ 蛀衣服的蠹虫 ‖*~-,eaten a.* 蛀坏了的；破烂的；过时的 / *'~proof a.* 防蛀的，不蛀的 *vt.* 对…作防蛀处理

mother ['mʌðə] **I** *n.* ①母亲，妈妈: a ~ of two 有两个孩子的母亲 ②母爱 ③[M-] (常用于姓氏前)大妈，大娘: *Mother* Li 李大妈 ④女主管人；妇女宗教团体的女主持人 ⑤[喻]根由: Failure is the ~ of success. 失败是成功之母。⑥(动、植物的) 母: a ~ bird 母鸟 / a ~ tree 母树 ⑦ (小鸡等的)人工养育器 (又作 artificial ~) ⑧ 【微】醋母(又作 ~ of vinegar) **II** *vt.* ①生;产生 ②(母亲般地)照管，保护 ③【军】掩护 ④收养 …为子女，承认自己为…的母亲；承认自己是…的作者 ‖*every ~'s son* 人人，所有的人 / *the Mother of God* (或 *God's Mother*)【宗】上帝之母(指圣母玛利亚) / *the Mother of Presidents* 总统之乡(美国弗吉尼亚州的别名,因该州有多人任过总统之故) / *the Mother of States* 各州之母(美国弗吉尼亚州的别名) / *the ~ of (the) months* [诗]月亮 ‖*~hood n.* 母性；母亲身分;[总称]母亲: pass into *~hood* 开始做妈妈 / *~less a.* 没有母亲的 / *~like a.* 母亲般的 / *~ly a.* 母亲般的；慈母般的 *ad.* 慈母般地 / *~y* ['mʌðəri] *a.* 含醋母的;象醋母的 ‖*~ aircraft* 【空】母机 / *Mother Carey's chicken* 一种小海燕 / *~ cell* 【生】母细胞 / *~ church* ①地方上的主要教会 ② 母教会(其下派生出附属教会,或指将某人养育成人的教会) / *~ country* ①祖国 ②发源地 ③(殖民地等的)母国(殖民主义者用以称其本国) / *~ earth* 地上万物之母，大地;土地，地面 / *Mother Goose* 一七六〇年左右出版的一本儿歌集的传说中的作者 / *Mother Hubbard* ①(尤指妇女的) 宽大长罩衣(或套衣) ②一种驾驶室设在锅炉正中顶上的机车 / *~ing* ['mʌðəriŋ] *Sunday* 省亲星期日 (指四旬斋的第四个星期日,按英国旧习俗,在该日带着礼物探望父母) / *~-in-law* ['mʌðərinlɔ:] ([复] *~s-in-law*) *n.* 岳母；婆婆 / *'~land n.* 祖国 / *~ liquor* 【化】母液 / *'~-'naked a.* 象初出娘胎时那样一丝不挂的 / *~-of-pearl* ['mʌðərəv'pə:l] *n.* 珍珠母，螺钿 / *~ right* 母权 / *Mother's Day* (美国、加拿大等的) 母亲节 (五月份的第二个星期日) / *~ ship* [英]【海】母舰 / *~ superior* 女修道院院长 / *~ tongue* 本国语言，本民族的语言 / *~ wit* 天生的智力

motif [mou'ti:f] *n.* [法] ①(文艺作品的)主题 ②(图案的)基本花纹，基本色彩；(衣服的)花边; the colour ~ 色彩基调 ③动机;主旨 ④【物】型主

motion ['mouʃən] **I** *n.* ①(物体的)运动，动: *Motion* itself is a contradiction. 运动本身就是矛盾。/ ~ and rest 运动和静止 / a pendulum in ~ 摆动着的钟摆 / rotational ~ 转动 / the ~ of the planets 行星的运行 / proper ~ 【天】自行 ②手势,眼色;动作，姿势 ③动机,意向: of one's own ~ 自动地，自愿地 ④(会议上的)提议,动议: The ~ was adopted (或 carried). 提议通过了。/ on the ~ of sb. 经某人的提议

⑤【律】(诉讼人向法院提出的)请求,申请 ⑥(钟、表等的)机构,运动机构 ⑦【音】(旋律、曲调的)变移 ⑧大便;[复]粪便 **II ❶** *vi.* ①打手势;摇(或点)头示意: I ~ed to him to come quietly. 我示意叫他轻轻地过来。②(钟表等)摆动,走: The mainspring makes the watch ~. 发条带动表走。**❷** *vt.* 向…打手势;向…摇(或点)头示意: He ~ed me in (或 to enter). 他示意叫我进去。‖*go through the* ~*s (of)* [口]装(…的)样子,做出(…的)姿态 / *put* (或 *set*) *sth. in* ~ 开动某物,使某物运转;调动某物 ‖**~less** *a.* 不动的,静止的 / ~ **picture** 电影 / ~ **sickness**【医】运动病(指晕车、晕船等) / ~ **study** (资本主义国家中为了加强剥削对工人工作所作的) 动作研究(也作 time and ~ study)

motional ['mou∫ənl] *a.* 运动的,动的

motivate ['moutiveit] *vt.* 作为…的动机,促动,激发 ‖**~d** *a.* 有动机的,目的明确的

motivation [,mouti'vei∫ən] *n.* 动机的形成;促动因素,动力 **~al** *a.* ~al psychology 动机心理学

motive ['moutiv] **I** *n.* ①动机;主旨;目的: the unity of ~ and effect 动机和效果的统一 / with ulterior ~s 别有用心地 ②(文艺作品的)主题 (=motif) **II** *a.* [只作定语]发动的;运动的: the ~ power (或 force) 动力 **III** *vt.* =motivate ‖**~less** *a.* 没有动机的;无主旨的;无目的的

motley ['mɔtli] **I** *a.* ①杂色的,五颜六色的 ②穿杂色衣的: a ~ clown 穿彩衣的小丑 ③混杂的,成分杂乱的: a ~ crowd 混杂的人群 / a ~ scene 混乱的场面 **II** *n.* ①杂色呢,杂色布 ②(小丑穿的)彩衣;小丑: wear ~ 扮演小丑 ③混杂物

motor ['moutə] **I** *n.* ①原动力 ②发动机,内燃机,摩托;电动机,马达 ③机动车,汽车 ④[美][复]汽车公司股票 ⑤[解]运动肌,运动神经 **II** *a.* ①原动的;机动的: ~ power 原动力 ②汽车的: a ~ trip 乘汽车的旅行 / the ~ industry 汽车工业 / ~ fuels 汽车燃料 ③【解】运动的;运动神经的: ~ nerve 运动神经 **III** **❶** *vi.* 驾驶汽车;乘汽车: ~ down to the suburbs 开汽车到郊区去 **❷** *vt.* 用汽车运送: The foreign guests were ~ed from the airfield to the hotel. 汽车把外宾从机场送到旅馆。‖**~able** ['moutərəbl] *a.* [英]可行驶机动车辆的 / **~less** *a.* 无动力的,无发动机的,无马达的 ‖**~-assisted** ['moutərə'sistid] *a.* 马达助动的 / **~bike** =~bike / **'~bike** *n.* [口]①机动脚踏两用车 ②摩托车 / **'~boat** *n.* 汽船 *vi.* 乘汽船 / **,boating** *n.*【无】汽船声(低频寄生振荡) / ~ **bus** 公共汽车 / **~cade** ['moutəkeid] *n.* 汽车的长列 / **'~car** *n.* ①汽车 ②[常作 ~car](铁道上的)机动车厢 / ~ **coach** = ~ bus → ~ **court** =motel / **'~cycle** *n.* 摩托车 *vi.* 骑摩托车,坐摩托车 / **'~cyclist** *n.* 骑(或坐)摩托车的人 / 【军】摩托兵 / ~ **drive** 电机驱动装置 / **'~drome** *n.* 汽车比赛场;汽车试车场 / ~ **generator** 电动发电机组 / ~ **home** [美]住房汽车 / ~ **inn** 多层

的汽车游客旅馆 / ~ **launch** 摩托艇,汽艇 / **'~,lorry** *n.* [英]卡车,载重汽车 / **~man** ['moutəmən] *n.* 电车(或电气机车)司机;电动机操作工人 / ~ **meter** 电动机型仪表,电磁作用式仪表 / ~ **mower** 自动割草机 / ~ **pool** 军用汽车集中调度场;(军政机关等的)车场 / ~ **scooter** 低座小摩托车 / ~ **ship** 内燃机船 / ~ **spirit** [英]汽油 / ~ **squadron**【军】汽车队 / ~ **starter** (发动机)起动器 / ~ **torpedo boat** 鱼雷快艇 / **'~truck** *n.* [美] =~-lorry / ~ **vehicle** 机动车;汽车 / **'~way** *n.* [英]汽车道;快车路

motoring ['moutəriŋ] **I** *n.* 驾驶汽车,乘汽车 **II** *a.* [英]汽车的;汽车驾驶(人)的: ~ offences 汽车驾驶违章

motorist ['moutərist] *n.* 驾驶汽车的人;乘汽车旅行的人

mottle ['mɔtl] **I** *vt.* 使呈杂色,使成斑驳 **II** *n.* ①杂色,斑点,斑纹 ②杂色毛纱 ‖**~d** *a.* 杂色的,斑驳的

motto ['mɔtou] ([复] motto(e)s) *n.* ①箴言,座右铭;格言 ②题词;(书籍扉页上或章节前所引用的)警句

mo(u)ld¹ [mould] **I** *n.* ①模子,模型,铸模,铸型 ②【印】(铸铅字的)字模: a casting ~ 铸型 / ~ line [船](表示船壳形状的)型线 ③模制品;铸造物 ③类型. 性状, 气质 ④【建】(装饰)线条,(凹凸)线脚 **II** *vt.* ①用模子做,把…放在模子里做;浇铸: ~ a figure in (或 out of) clay 用模子做泥塑人像 / ~ clay into the shape of a figure 用模子把泥土做成人像 / ~ a stereotype 浇铅版 ②对…产生影响;形成: environmental factors which ~ a child's character 形成小孩性格的环境因素 ③与…的轮廓相符合: a silhouette that ~s the body 显出人体轮廓的剪影 ④【建】用线条(或雕刻)装饰 ⑤[古]把(陶土等)捏成…‖**'~board** *n.* 模板,型板 / ~ **loft** (船厂、飞机厂的)放样间

mo(u)ld² [mould] **I** *n.* ①耕作土壤;松软沃土 ②[方]地面;坟场的泥土 ③材料,物质 **II** *vt.* 用泥土覆盖 ‖*a man of* ~ 见 man ‖**'~board** *n.* 犁壁,翻土犁板

mo(u)ld³ [mould] **I** *n.* 霉;霉菌: ~ rains【气】梅雨 **II** *vi.* [美]发霉

mo(u)lder¹ ['mouldə] *n.* ①制模工;铸工;造型者 ②【印】(复制用的)电铸版

mo(u)lder² ['mouldə] **❶** *vi.* ①崩解;腐朽: the ~ing ruins of an old castle 古堡的废墟 ②衰;退化: Long periods of sickness caused his memory to ~. 长期疾病使他记忆力衰退了。**❷** *vt.* ①使崩碎;使腐朽 ②使消衰,使退化

mo(u)lding ['mouldiŋ] *n.* ①模制;浇铸;造型(法) compression ~ (加)压(模)制 / shell ~ 壳形铸造(法) ②模制件,铸造物 ③【建】(装饰)线条,(凹凸)线脚 ‖**~ board** ①模板, 型板 ②擀面板

mo(u)lt [moult] **I** **❶** *vi.* 换羽;脱毛;脱角;蜕(皮) **❷** *vt.* ①换(羽);脱(毛、角),蜕(皮) ②[喻]

除(旧习惯、旧思想等): ~ one's old notions 去掉旧观念 **II** **n.** ①换羽; 脱毛; 脱角; 蜕皮; 换羽(或脱毛等)期 ②换下的羽; 脱下的毛(或角等); 蜕下的皮

ound¹ [maund] **I** **n.** ①土墩, 土石堆; 土冈, 土丘 ②坟墩 ③(城堡的)护堤 ④(东西的)堆, 垛: a thick ~ of ice 厚厚的一堆冰 / a target ~ 靶垛 **II** **①** **vt.** ①[古]筑堤围住, 筑墙防卫 ②堆起: snow ~ed in cones 积成圆锥形的雪堆 **②** **vi.** 积成堆 ‖**Mound Builder** ①筑堤人(指史前在密西西比河盆地及邻近地区筑护堤的北美印第安人) ②[m- b-]【动】营冢鸟

ound² [maund] **n.** 宝球(用作王权的象征, 球顶常饰有十字架)

ount¹ [maunt] **n.** ①[诗]山, 丘 ②[M-](用于山名前, 略作 Mt.)…山, …峰: *Mount* Tai 泰山 / *Mt.* Jolmo Lungma 珠穆朗玛峰 ③土墩, 土石堆; 土冈

ount² [maunt] **I** **①** **vi.** ①登, 爬上; 骑上马: He ~ed and rode off. 他跨上马走了。 ②增长, 上升: The flush ~ed to her face. 她脸上浮起一阵红晕。 **②** **vt.** ①登上, 爬上(山、梯、王位等); 骑上(马等); 骑在…上: ~ the rostrum 登上主席台 / The town ~s the hills. 这座小镇座落在山顶上。 ②给(某人)备马; 使上马(或车), 扶(某人)上马: ~ the cavalry 给骑兵备好马匹 ③架置; 装有(枪炮等): ~ a gun on a gun carriage 把炮架在炮架上 / The ship ~s six cannon. 这艘军舰装有六门大炮。④安放; 镶嵌(宝石等); 裱贴(画、邮票、照片等): ~ a statue on a pedestal 把塑像安放在像座上 / ~ gems in a gold ring 在金戒指上镶宝石 / a map ~ed on stout paper 用厚纸裱好的地图 / stamps ~ed in an album 插在邮票簿上的邮票 ⑤制作(动植物)的标本, 把(动植物)固定在标本架上; 把(标本等)固定在显微镜的载片上: ~ insects 把昆虫制成标本 / classify and ~ specimens 分类装制标本 ⑥发动(攻势), 进行(袭击) ⑦设置(岗哨); 担任(警卫): ~ a guard at the entrance gate 在大门口设岗 / ~ guard over a camp 警卫营地 ⑧把(剧本)搬上舞台, 上演; 展出 ⑨(雄性动物)与…交配 **II** **n.** ①登, 爬上; 骑上; (赛马时的)骑马机会: leap to the horse's back in a flying ~ 飞身上马 ②可乘骑的东西(如马、车等), 坐骑: army ~s 军马 ③底座, 座架; 炮架 ④(镶宝石的)底板, 托板; (书画等的)装帧, 衬托纸, 裱画纸; (显微镜的)载片 ⑤扇托, 扇骨 ‖*be well (poorly)* ~ed 骑着好马(劣马) / *the high horse* 趾高气扬, 耀武扬威 ‖**~able** **a.** 可登上的 / **~er** **n.** (宝石等)安装工; 装配工; 安装工

mountain ['mauntin] **n.** ①山, 山岳; [复]山脉 ②巨大如山的物; 大堆, 大量: a ~ of a man 巨人 / a ~ of work 一大堆工作 / overcome ~s of difficulties 克服重重困难 ③[the M-] 山岳派(1793 年法国资产阶级革命时期占据国民公会大厅最高处座位的革命民主派) ‖*a ~ of flesh* 高大结实的人 / *If the* ~ *will not come to*

Mohammed [mou'hæmed], *Mohammed must go to the* ~. 大山不肯向穆罕默德移来, 穆罕默德只得往大山走去。(源出穆罕默德向阿拉伯人传教的传说; 意为"若对方不肯按你意旨行事, 你就只得迁就他。") / *make a* ~ *(out) of a molehill* 小题大作 / *remove* ~s 移山倒海, 创造奇迹 / *run* ~s *high* (波浪等)汹涌澎湃 / *the* ~ *in labo(u)r* 费力大收效小(源出大山生出小鼠的希腊谚语) / *The* ~s *have brought forth a mouse.* [谚]大山生出小鼠。(意指费力大收效小) ‖~ **artillery** [总称]山炮; 山地炮兵 / ~ **ash**【植】花楸 / ~ **battery** =~ artillery / ~ **canary** [美俚]小驴子 / ~ **cat** 美洲狮; 赤猞猁 / ~ **chain** 山脉, 山链 / ~ **cork** 石棉 / ~ **crystal** 水晶 / ~ **dew** [俚]苏格兰威士忌酒; 非法酿造的酒 / ~ **division**【军】山地师 / ~ **green** 孔雀石 / ~ **group** 山群 / ~ **gun** 山炮 / ~**-high** **a.** 高如山的 / ~ **howitzer** 山地榴弹炮 / ~ **lion** 美洲狮 / ~ **man** [美]①山地人 ②首批开拓边境者之一 / ~ **railway** 山区铁道 / ~ **range** 山脉 / ~ **rice** 野麦 / ~ **sickness** (缺氧引起的)山岳病, 高山病 / '~**side** **n.** 山腰 / ~ **spur** 山脊 / **Mountain Standard Time** =Mountain time / '~'**stronghold mentality** 山头主义 / **Mountain time** 山区标准时间(指国际时区西七区的区时) / '~**top** **n.** 山顶 / ~ **warfare** 山地战 / ~ **wine** 西班牙南部马拉加出产的白葡萄酒 / ~ **wood** 石棉, 不灰木

mountaineer [,maunti'niə] **I** **n.** ①山地人, 山区人 ②爬山家, 登山运动员 **II** **vi.** 爬山, 登山 ‖**~ing** [,maunti'niəriŋ] **n.** 登山运动

mountebank ['mauntibæŋk] **I** **n.** ①走江湖卖假药的人; 江湖医生 ②江湖骗子 **II** **vi.** 走江湖卖假药(或行医) ‖**~ery** **n.**

mounted ['mauntid] **a.** ①安置在马(或车)上的, 骑在马上的; 由车(或马)输送的: ~ police 骑警队 / ~ troops (或 units) 骑兵部队; 乘车部队 / a ~ point 骑兵尖兵 ②安置于支架(或衬板)上的; (枪炮等)架好的; (书画等)裱好的; 镶嵌上的

mounting ['mauntiŋ] **n.** ①登上; 上马; 上车; 乘骑 ②安置, 安放; 上架; 固定 ③底座, 座架; 炮架; (镶宝石的)底板, 托板; (书画等的)装帧, 衬托纸, 裱画纸

mourn [mɔ:n] **①** **vi.** ①哀痛, 哀悼: ~ for (或 over) the dead 哀悼死者 ②(鸽子似地)咕咕鸣叫 **②** **vt.** ①为(某事)哀痛; 向(某人)致哀: ~ the loss of sb. 为失去某人而哀痛 ②悲哀地说 ‖**~er** **n.** ①哀痛者; 哀悼者; 送葬者 ②【宗】奋兴会上的公开忏悔者

mournful ['mɔ:nful] **a.** 悲哀的, 哀痛的; 令人沮丧的 ‖**~ly** **ad.** / **~ness** **n.**

mourning ['mɔ:niŋ] **n.** ①哀痛; 哀悼: express one's ~ for the dead 对死者表示哀悼 ②举哀; 居丧: go into ~ for three days 举哀三天 / leave off (或 go out of) ~ 服阕, 除服 ③丧服; 戴孝; 表示哀悼的服饰: in deep (或 first) ~ 着

全丧服, 着正式丧服 / in half (或 second) ~ 着半丧服, 着简单丧服 ‖in ~ ① 戴孝 ② [俚](指甲等)肮脏的, 污黑的 ‖'~-band n. (服丧时戴的)黑纱 / '~-coach n. 出殡车 / ~ dove 【动】(美国产的)一种鸣声凄凉的野鸽 / '~-,paper n. 黑边信纸(报丧用) / '~-ring n. 纪念死者的戒指

mouse [maus] **I** ([复] mice [mais]) *n.* ① 鼠, 耗子 ② [俚]胆小怕羞的人 ③ [俚]姑娘, 女人 ④ [俚](眼部等被击伤后起的)青肿, 乌青块 ⑤ 鼠色, 灰褐色 ⑥ [海]缠口结 ⑦ [美俚]小火箭 **II** [mauz] **❶** *vi.* ① 捕鼠: Does your cat ~ well? 你家的猫很会抓老鼠吗? ② 窥探; 偷偷地搜寻; 蹑手蹑脚地走动 **❷** *vt.* 仔细搜寻; 探出 (out) ‖(as) poor as a church ~ 一贫如洗 / like a drowned ~ 像落水老鼠似地狼狈, 处于窘境 / ~ and man 一切生物, 众生 / When the cat's away, the mice will play. [谚]猫儿一跑耗子闹。‖'~,colo(u)red a. 鼠色的, 灰褐色的 / '~-ear n. 【植】有卷耳状叶的植物(如山柳菊、勿忘草) / '~hole n. ①鼠洞, 鼠穴 ② 狭窄的出入口; 小房间; 壁橱 / '~proof a. 防鼠的 / '~trap n. ① 捕鼠器 / ~trap cheese [谑](只好用来喂老鼠的)很差的干酪 ② 诱使对方失败的策略 ③ [美俚]小戏院; 下等夜总会 *vt.* 诱捕; 引诱…入毂

moustache [məs'tɑ:ʃ] *n.* ① 髭, 小胡子 ②(哺乳动物的)触须

mouth I [mauθ] ([复] mouths [mauðz]) *n.* ① 口, 嘴; 口腔 ② 人; 动物: a useless ~ 只吃不做的人 / hungry ~s 饥饿的人们 ③ 口状物, 进出口; 河口; 容器口; 喷口; 枪口; (乐器等的)吹口: the ~ of a pocket (bottle) 袋(瓶)口 / the ~ of a volcano 火山口 ④(表示厌恶或引人发笑的)怪脸, 苦相 ⑤ 话声, 话; 代言人: None of your ~! 住嘴! **II** [mauð] **❶** *vt.* ① 说出; 清楚地读出: learn to ~ the word "box" 学会发准 "box" 这字的音 ② 做作地说, 夸大地说: ~ big phrases 装腔作势地说大话 ③ 假装有; 有口无心地说 ④ 不清楚地说出, 含糊地说 ⑤ 把…放入嘴内, 吃: ~ down a piece of cake 吃下一块糕 ⑥ 用嘴接触, 吻 ⑦ 训练(马)咬马嚼子 **❷** *vi.* ① 做作地说话, 夸大地说话, 夸口 ② 做怪脸 ‖a good (bad 或 hard) ~ 顺从(不顺从)使唤的马 / button up one's ~ 保持缄默 / down in (at) the ~ [口]垂头丧气 / foam at the ~ ① 口吐泡沫 ② 非常愤怒 / from ~ to ~ 口口相传, 广泛流传: The news spread rapidly from ~ to ~. 消息很快就传开了。/ from the horse's ~ (消息等)直接得来的 / give it ~ 滔滔不绝地讲, 慷慨陈词 / give ~ 吠叫 / give ~ to 说出, 讲出 / have a big ~ [俚]大声说话; 过多地说话; 冒失地说话 / in everyone's ~ 大家都如此说 / in the ~ of 出于…之口 / make a ~ ① 做怪脸, 做苦相 ② 训练小马咬马嚼子 / make sb.'s ~ water (或 bring the water to sb.'s ~) 使某人垂涎 / My ~ is closed. 这个我不能说出来。/ One's ~ is full of pap. [俚]

乳臭未干。/ open one's ~ wide 狮子大开口(指索高价) / run at the ~ 流口水 / shoot off one's ~ at the ~ (或 shoot off one's ~) [俚]夸夸其谈, 信口开河 / stop sb.'s ~ 使某人不讲, 用贿赂塞住某人的口 / the lion's ~ 狮口, 虎穴(指极危险处) / with open ~ 张着口; 张口结舌 ‖~er ['mauðə] *n.* 说大话的人 ‖'~-,filling (句子等)很长的; 气势十足的 / ~ organ 口琴 (=harmonica) / '~part n. 【动】口器 / '~-piece n. ① 口状物; 烟嘴口; (乐器的)吹口; 【讯】口器【机】口罩: the ~piece of a transmitter 送话器口承 ② 喉舌, 代言人; [俚](刑事案件的)辩护师 / '~-to-'~ method 口对口人工呼吸法 / '~wash n. 漱口剂, 洗口药

mouthful ['mauθful] *n.* ① 满口, 一口; 少量: swallow sth. at a ~ 一口吞下某物 / take a ~ of sweet country air 吸一口新鲜的乡村空气 ② 很长的词句 ③ [俚]妙语: You said a ~. 你说得真妙。

movable ['mu:vəbl] **I** *a.* ① 可移动的, 活动的; 【律】动产的: a ~ dam 活动坝 / ~ and immovable properties 动产与不动产 ②(指日期)每次变动的, 不固定的: a ~ feast 每年不固定的节日; [谑]不固定时间的进餐 **II** *n.* 可移动的东西; 可搬动的家具; [复]动产(尤指家具) ‖movability [,mu:və'biliti], ~ness *n.* / movably *ad.*

move [mu:v] **I** *vt.* ① 移动, 搬动, 使改变位置(或姿势): ~ a piece (下棋)走一子 / ~ a rock aside from the road 把一块石头从路上搬掉 / ~ troops 调动军队 ② 开动, 使运行; 使前进; 发动: This button ~s the whole mechanism. 一按这个电钮使所有的机械部分都运转起来。/ Move the handle to the right and the door will open. 向右转动把手, 门就会开了。③ 感动; 激起: ~d to tears 感动得流出眼泪 / We were ~ with admiration at the magnificent bridge. 我们望着这座雄伟的大桥, 我们感动得赞赏不已。/ ~ sb. to laughter (anger) 惹某人发笑(生气) ④ 鼓动; 推动, 促使: The inspiring speech ~d them into action. 那鼓舞人心的讲话使他们行动起来。⑤ (在会议上)提议, 动议: I ~ (that) the meeting be adjourned. 我提议休会。⑥ 使(肚子)通便 ⑦ 脱售, 租掉 **❷** *vi.* ① 移动; 离开, 动身; 前进; (事情等)进展; (下棋)走一子: "Move along, please!" said the conductor. "请往里走!" 公共汽车售票员说。/ It is late and I think it is time to be moving. 不早了, 我想该走了。② 运行, 转动; 摇动: The piston ~s by steam pressure. 活塞在蒸汽压力下运动。/ Not a leaf ~d. 树叶一动也不动。③ 迁移; 搬家: ~ to the countryside 迁居农村 / ~ in (或 into) a newly built workers' residential quarter 搬进新建的工人住宅区 ④ 提议; 请求, 申请; 呼吁: ~ for reconsideration of the plan 提议重新考虑这个计划 ⑤ 采取行动; 行动: ~ in the matter 对事情采取行动 / make up one's mind and ~ 下

决心行动起来 ⑥频繁活动, 忙碌; 活跃: Things begin to ~. 情况开始有所发展。⑦在外处境: 生存; 生活, 过活; 生活于(某种环境), 周旋于(in): ~ in publishing circles 常和出版界人士交往 ⑧(肠子)通便 ⑨(商品等)脱手, 转手 **II** *n.* ❶动, 移动; 迁移; 搬家: protection on ~【军】行军警戒 ②步骤, 行动: What's our next ~? 我们下一步怎么做? ③(下棋用语)走棋, 一着: Whose ~ is it? 该轮到谁走了? / One careless ~ loses the whole game. 一着不慎, 满盘皆输。/ a clever ~ 妙棋, [喻]机智的一着 / lose a ~ to sb. 输给人一着 ‖*get a ~ on* [俚]行动起来; 赶快 / *know a ~ or two* 机灵, 精明 / *make a ~* ①走一着(棋) ②搬家; 迁移 ③走(尤指起立离开餐桌); 开始行动 / *~ in* 走来走去; 老是搬家 / *~ heaven and earth* 竭尽全力: ~ *heaven and earth to* raise the grain output 千方百计提高粮食产量 / ~ *in on* [美俚]①(为捕获而)潜近… ②企图夺取(某物); 企图从(某人)处夺取东西 / ~ *off* ①离去, 走掉 ②[口]死 ③(货物)畅销 / ~ *on* ①继续前进; (交通警察用语)朝前走, 朝前走 ②[口]出发: Let's be *moving on.* 让我们走吧! / ~ *out* ①搬出, 搬走 ②【军】开始行动 / ~ (*sb.*) *back* ①(使某人)后缩 ②[美俚](使某人)花费(多少钱) / ~ *sb. on* 指挥某人朝前走 / ~ *up* 提前; 上升; (被)提升 / ~ *upon* 进逼 / *on the* ~ [口]在活动中; 在进展中: The train was just *on the* ~. 火车刚起动。/ *up to a ~ or two* (或 *up to every ~ on the board*) 机灵, 精明 ‖*~-in* *n.* 移入

movement ['mu:vmənt] *n.* ❶运动, 活动; 动作, 姿势: the ~ of the planets 行星的运动 / He stood there without ~. 他一动也不动地站在那里。/ make a violent ~ of the hand 猛烈地挥动手 / graceful ~s 优美的姿势 ②移动; 迁移, 迁居 ③(部队及装备等的)调动, 调遣; 输送; 行进 ④(政治、社会或思想)运动 ⑤倾向; 动向; 动态; 思想动机: Do let me know all your ~s while you're away. 你走了以后, 务必要让我知道你的动向。⑥(诗、故事等情节的)变化, 曲折; (雕刻、绘画等的)动势: The play lacks ~. 这出戏情节平淡。⑦【机】程序; 机构; 装置: the ~ of a clock (watch) 钟(表)的机件 ⑧(市面的)活动, (价格的)变动: downward ~ in stock and shares 股票市面下跌 ⑨【音】乐章; 速度; 【语】节奏; 韵律: quick (slow) ~ 快速(缓徐)调 ⑩通便; 粪便: bowel ~s 大便 ‖*in the* ~ 随时势潮流, 与时代并进

mover ['mu:və] *n.* ①(使…)移动者; (使…)运行者; 搬场工人(替搬家者搬运家具等物): A deer is a fast ~. 鹿跑起来很快。②提议人 ③煽动者 ④发动机; 原动力: a prime ~ 原动机; 会出主意的人

movie ['mu:vi] *n.* ①[口]电影 ②[the ~s] [口] [总称]电影; 电影制片业; [美俚]电影院: Let's go to the ~s. 让我们去看电影去。‖*a ~ fan*

(电)影迷 / *a ~ house* 电影院 / *a ~ star* 电影明星 ‖*~dom* *n.* 电影界 ‖*'~,goer* *n.* 看电影者; 常看电影的人 / *'~-land* *n.* =~dom

moving ['mu:viŋ] *a.* ①(使)活动的, 移动的: a ~ target 【军】活动目标 ②动人的, 令人感动的; 鼓动的: the ~ spirit behind a plan 计划的幕后策动者 ③原动的: the ~ force of a machine 机器的动力 ④运输业的 ‖*~ly* *ad.* ‖*~ picture* 电影 / *~ sidewalk*, *~ walk* 自动人行道 / *~ staircase* 自动楼梯

mow[1] [mou; 美 mau] *n.* ①禾堆, 谷堆; 干草堆 ②(谷仓内)禾、草堆积处 **II** [mou] (过去式 mowed, 过去分词 mowed 或 mown [moun]) ❶ *vt.* ①刈; 割: ~ the grass regularly 定期刈草 ②(像刈草一样)刈倒; 扫除; [喻]扫杀; 摧毁 (*down, off*) ❷ *vi.* 刈草; 收割庄稼 ‖*~er* ['mouə] *n.* 刈割者; 刈草机 ‖*~burnt* ['moubə:nt; 美 'maubə:nt] *a.* (谷、草等)因堆积发热而霉烂的 / *~ing* ['mouiŋ] *machine* 割草机

mow[2] [mau] *n. & vi.* (做)怪脸

Mr., Mr ['mistə] [缩] Mister 先生

Mrs., Mrs ['misiz] [缩] Mistress 夫人

MsTh 【化】新钍 (mesothorium) 的符号

much [mʌtʃ] **I** (more [mɔ:], most [moust]) *a.* 许多, 多; 大量的; 很大程度的: *Much* thanks. 多谢。(今多用 Many thanks.) / There isn't ~ water left. 没剩下多少水了。/ Did you have ~ difficulty in your work? 你工作中困难多不多? / I am afraid I've put you to too ~ trouble. 我怕太麻烦你了。/ *Much* coal has thus been saved. 这样就节约了大量的煤。**II** *n.* ①许多, 大量: learn ~ from the experience 从这一经验中得到许多教益 / There is ~ to be done. 还有大量工作要做。/ *Much* of what you say is true. 你的话有许多是对的。/ I do not see ~ of him. 我不大见到他。②重要(或有意义)的事物: There was not ~ to look at. 没有什么值得一看的。/ He spoke for half an hour, but what he said did not amount to ~. 他讲了半小时, 可是他说的没有多大意义。**III** *ad.* ① (more [mɔ:], most [moust]) 非常, 很: Thank you very ~. 多谢。/ I should ~ like to have your opinion. 我很想得到你的意见。/ I was very ~ pleased to hear of your success. 听到你的成功, 我感到非常高兴。/ I am very ~ afraid that you have given ~ too little care to your work. 我很担心你工作得太不细心了。/ ~ to sb.'s surprise 使某人大为惊奇的是 ② [加强比较级或最高级]…多; 更…: I feel ~ better now. 我现在感觉好多了。/ We must work ~ more carefully. 我们应该更加仔细地工作。/ This is ~ the best. 这是最最好的。③常常; 好久: be ~ with sb. 常和某人在一起 / He went ~ to the park on holidays. 假日他常去公园。/ They are not likely to arrive there ~ before midnight. 他们总要将近半夜才会到达那里。④差不多, 几乎: The two children are ~ of an age. 这两个孩

子年龄差不多。/ We found the place ~ what we had expected it. 我们发现那个地方和我们预想的差不多。/ The patient's condition is ~ the same. 病人的情况差不多没有什么变化。‖as ~ ①同样多少的: Give me as ~ again. 再给我那么多。②同样的事物: I thought as ~. 我也这样想。/ I found him rather careless and said as ~ to him. 我发现他有些粗枝大叶,并直率地向他说了。/ as ~ again 两倍 / as as ①尽…那样多: Take as ~ as you need. 你需要多少就拿多少。/ as ~ as possible 尽可能 / It was as ~ as he could do to help us. 他尽了最大的力量帮助我们。②差不多,几乎等于: He as ~ as admitted the whole story. 他几乎全部承认了。/ That is as ~ as to say . . . 这等于是说。/ as ~ as . . . as . . . 跟…到同一程度: It is as ~ our responsibility as! yours. 这是你们的责任,同样也是我们的责任。/ be too ~ for 非…力所能及,非…所应付得了: It is too ~ for me. 这个我干不了(或受不了)。/ half as ~ again 加半倍,一倍半 / how ~ 这等于是 ~ sugar do you want? 你要多少糖?②什么价钱: How ~ is it? 这要多少钱?③到什么程度: How ~ do you really want to go there? 你究竟有几分想要到那里去的意思?/ leave ~ to be desired 还有许多有待改进之处 / make ~ of ①重视;充分利用: make ~ of an event 重视一事件;大肆宣传一事件 ②悉心照顾;奉承 ③理解/ ~ as . . . 虽然很…. Much as I should like to go, I can't go right now. 我虽然很想去,但现在还不能去。/ ~ at one 几乎相同,几乎等价 / ~ less 更不: I didn't even see him, ~ less speak to him. 我见也没有见到他,更谈不上和他说话了。/ ~ more 更加,何况: It is difficult to understand his books, ~ more his lectures. 理解他的书很难,理解他的讲演更难了。/ ~ of a . . . [常用于否定句或疑问句]了不起的…, 称得上…的: He was not ~ of an oculist. 他并不是一个高明的眼科医生。/ She is not ~ of a cinema-goer. 她不大去看电影。/ not so ~ . . . as 与其…不如: He is not so ~ a writer as a reporter. 他与其说是个作家,不如说是个记者。/ not think ~ of 对…估价不高: I don't think ~ of him as a basketball player. 我认为他篮球打得不怎么好。/ one too ~ for 见 one / so ~ 那么多,全是: So ~ for today. 今天就讲(或做)那么多。/ His talk was so ~ nonsense. 他讲的全是废话。/ that (this) ~ 那(这)样多,那(这)些: We have done that ~ up to now. 到现在为止我们就做了那么多。/ I want this ~ only. 我只要这样多。/ This ~ is certain, that we shall have another fine crop of rice. 这点可以肯定:我们这回稻子又是丰收。/ too ~ ①太多: You have given me too ~. 你给我太多了。②(估价)太高: Don't think too ~ of yourself. 不要自以为了不起。/ too ~ of a good thing 好事过头反成坏事 / up to ~ 有很大价值的:

This report does not seem to be up to ~. 这篇报道似乎没有多大价值。/ without so ~ as 甚至于不…: She left without so ~ as a nod. 她连头也不点一下就离开了。‖~ly ad. [谚]大量地,~ness n. 大量,很多 (只用于下面的短语) much of a ~ness [口]很相象,半斤八两

muck [mʌk] **I** n. ①湿粪;粪肥;腐殖土 ②[口]污秽;污物;讨厌的东西;腐化堕落的事物: oily ~ on the floor of the garage 车库地上的油污 ③[口]乱七八糟的状态 ④[总称]中伤的言论(或作品);废话,胡言乱语 ⑤[开挖或采矿中清出的]废料,垃圾 **II** ❶ vt.①给…施粪肥;弄脏;搞糟: ~ up a plan 把计划搞乱 ③清除…的污物;清除(污物) ❷ vi. [俚]闲逛;鬼混(about) ‖all of a ~ of sweat 浑身大汗 / in (或 all of) a ~ 浑身是泥 / make a ~ of sth. [口]①弄脏某物 ②把某事弄得一团糟 / throw ~ at sb. 中伤某人 ‖~heap, ~hill n. 粪堆 / ~rake n. ①粪耙 ②爱打听丑闻的人 vi. 搜集并揭发社会的丑事 / ~,raker n. 专门报道丑事的人(尤指新闻记者)/ ~worm n. ①粪蛆 ②守财奴 ③街头流浪儿童

mucous ['mju:kəs] a. ①有粘液的;蒙上粘液的;粘液质的 ②像(或像蒙上)粘液的 ③分泌(或含)粘液的

mud [mʌd] **I** n. ①(软)泥,泥浆;泥淖;[喻]毫无价值的脏东西: scrape the ~ off one's shoes 刮掉鞋上的泥 / His name is ~. 他声名狼藉。②[总称]诽谤的话,恶意的攻击 ③[美俚]黑糊糊的食品(如咖啡、巧克力布丁等)④[美俚]黑糊糊的液体(如铁水、石油等)⑤[美俚][总称]不清晰的无线电(或电报)信号 **II** (mudded; mudding) vt. 使沾上污泥,弄脏 ‖consider (或 treat) sb. as ~ (或 as the ~ beneath one's feet) 把某人当作脚下的泥土看待,轻视某人 / fling (或 sling, throw) ~ at 毁谤,中伤 / Here is ~ in your eye! [俚](祝酒时用语)干杯! / stick in the ~ (使)陷入泥淖;(使)停滞不前: The car got stuck in the ~. 汽车陷入了泥淖。‖~ bath 泥浴(如作为风湿病的一种治疗)/ ~ flat 河滨泥地,泥滩 / ~guard n. ①(车子的)挡泥板,叶子板 ②(鞋上的)挡泥皮罩 / ~ hooks [美俚]双脚 / ~ lark ①拾荒者;街头流浪儿童 ②云雀的一种 / ~ puppy [动]泥狗(美洲蝾螈)/ ~sill n. ①底梁,下槛 ②低贱的人 / ~,skipper n. 【动】弹涂鱼;大弹涂鱼 / ~,slinger n. 毁谤者,中伤者 / ~,slinging n. 毁谤,中伤 / ~stone n. 【地】泥岩 / ~ volcano 泥火山 / ~-wall n. 土墙

muddle ['mʌdl] **I** ❶ vt. ①使浑浊,使多淤泥: ~ the water 把水搅浑 ②使糊涂;使泥醉: ~d views 糊涂观点 / be slightly ~d with liquor 有点儿喝醉了 ③使混乱;弄糟: ~ things up (或 together) 把事情搞乱 / ~ a piece of work 把一件工作弄糟 ④糊里糊涂地打发(away): ~ away one's time 浪费时间 ❷ vi. 胡乱对付,鬼混: ~ through (经过纷乱、挫折)终于对付过去 / ~ on

(或 *along*) 混日子,得过且过 / ~ *with* one's work 敷衍了事 **II** *n.* 混乱,杂乱;(头脑)糊涂: be all in a ~ 在一片混乱之中 / make a ~ of sth. 把某事搞得一团糟 ||~ **headed** *a.* 头脑糊涂的;笨拙的

muddy ['mʌdi] **I** *a.* ①多泥的,泥泞的,泥状的: ~ shoes 沾满污泥的鞋 / a ~ path 泥泞小路 ②泥土般的,(在光、色、声音等方面)浑浊与模糊的: a ~ stream 浑浊的小河 / a ~ colour 土色 / a ~ voice 重浊的声音 / a ~ skin 黑皮肤 ③糊涂的,混乱的: ~ ideas 糊涂思想 / a ~ thinker 头脑糊涂的人 ④(道德上)不纯的,下流的: ~ humour 下流的诙谐 **II** *vt.* ①使泥上污泥,把…弄脏;使浑浊,搅浑 ②使糊涂,使混乱

muff¹ [mʌf] *n.* ①(妇女防寒用的)皮手笼,皮手筒 ②【机】套筒

muff² [mʌf] **I** *n.* ①笨拙的人;笨拙的运动员;[美俚]笨蛋: make a ~ of oneself 出丑 ②笨拙的行动;弄糟的行为;接球的失误: make a ~ of sth. 把某事弄糟 **II** ❶ *vt.* ①弄糟 ②漏接(球);[美俚]错过(机会): ~ an easy catch 误失一个容易接的球 ❷ *vi.* ①行为笨拙;做出笨事;[口]失败 ②漏接球

muffin ['mʌfin] *n.* [主英]松饼,小松糕 ||~-**bell** *n.* [英]卖松饼者摇的铃 / '~-**man** *n.* [英]卖松饼者

muffle ['mʌfl] **I** *vt.* ①包裹,裹住;蒙住(某人)的头部(或眼睛): ~ one's throat with a scarf 用围巾围住脖子 / ~ oneself up well 把自己裹得紧紧的 / He ~d his face and went to sleep. 他蒙起脸,睡着了。②抑住,压抑(声音),捂住,用布等将(铃、鼓等)包住使其声音低沉;使…的噪声消失: ~ the noise / ~ one's feelings 抑制自己的感情 **II** *n.* ①围巾,头巾 ②【机】消声器,减音器 ③【化】蒙烘,隔焰甑,闭(式)烤炉 ④(精神病患者带的)无指皮手套 ⑤(反刍动物等的)上唇露肉部分及鼻子 ||~ **furnace** 蒙烘炉,隔焰炉,膛式炉 / ~ **kiln** 隔焰窑,隔焰窑

muffler ['mʌflə] *n.* ①围巾 ②厚手套;拳击用手套 ③消声器,减音器;(钢琴内)裹在琴槌上的绒毡: exhaust ~ 【机】排气消声器 / put the ~ on sb 使某人住嘴

mufti ['mʌfti] *n.* ①(尤指平日着军服或制服者所穿的)便服,便衣: in ~ 穿着便衣 ②[宗]伊斯兰教法典说明官

mug¹ [mʌg] *n.* ①大杯(通常为有柄的);一大杯的量: a beer ~ 啤酒杯 / a ~ of water 一大杯水 ②一种清凉饮料

mug², **mugg** [mʌg] [俚] **I** *n.* ①脸;嘴;下颌: an ugly ~ 一副丑恶的嘴脸 ②装怪相的脸 ③[主英]蠢才,笨蛋 ④粗鲁无礼的人;流氓阿飞,暴徒,罪犯 ⑤面部照片;(警察局存查的)嫌疑犯的照片 **II** (mugged; mugging) ①向(观众)装怪脸 ②对…行凶抢劫 ③给…拍照;为存档给(罪犯)拍照 ||**mugger** *n.* ①装怪脸者,装怪脸以引观众发笑的演员 ②行凶抢劫者 ③人像摄影专家 ④【动】泽鳄 ||~ **shot** 面部照片,(警察局存查的)嫌疑犯照片

mug³ [mʌg] [英俚] **I** *n.* ①拼命用功的人 ②考试 **II** (mugged; mugging) ❶ *vi.* 拼命用功 (*at*) ❷ *vt.* 拼命用功研究: ~ (*up*) a subject 拼命攻读某一门课程

muggy ['mʌgi] *a.* 闷热的,湿热的: ~ weather 闷热的天气 ||**muggily** *ad.* / **mugginess** *n.*

mulberry ['mʌlbəri] *n.* ①桑属植物;桑树 ②桑葚,桑子 ③深紫红色

mulch [mʌltʃ] **I** *n.* ①林地覆盖物(霉烂的麦秆等;常与泥土、粪肥混合);护根物(保护植物根部) ②地面覆盖料(保护地面用的木屑、堆肥、碎石、纸等) **II** *vt.* 用烂麦秆等覆盖(树根等);用覆盖料覆盖(地面)

mulct [mʌlkt] **I** *n.* 罚款;惩罚 **II** *vt.* ①处…以罚款: ~ sb. (*in*) $200 处某人罚款二百美元 ②诈骗;盗取,骗得: be ~ed of one's money 钱被骗走 / ~ £1,000 from sb. 从某人那里骗得一千英镑

mule¹ [mju:l] *n.* ①骡,马骡(公驴和母马所生的种间杂种) ②(动物或植物的)杂种 ③[喻]顽固的人 ④[纺]走锭精纺机 ⑤(拖曳船只、煤车等的)小型电动机车;(在码头等处拖运货车等的)轻便牵引机 ||~ **deer** (北美西部产的)黑尾鹿 / '~=,**driver** *n.* 赶骡人 / ~ **skinner** [美]赶骡人

mule² [mju:l] *n.* 室内用的无后跟女式拖鞋

mullet ['mʌlit] *n.* ①鲻鱼科鱼;鲻鱼 ②鲱鲤科鱼

mullion ['mʌliən] **I** *n.* [建](窗门的)直棂,竖框;石质中棂 **II** *vt.* 装直棂于;用直棂分开 ||~ed *a.* 有直棂的,有竖框的;有石质中棂的

multilingual [,mʌlti'liŋgwəl] **I** *a.* 多种语言(或文字)的;懂(或用)多种语言(或文字)的: a ~ sign-board 写有多种文字的招牌 **II** *n.* 懂多种语言(或文字)的人

multiple ['mʌltipl] **I** *a.* ①复合的,多样的;多重的,多倍的: a ~ jobholder 有多样职业的人 / ~ achievements 多种成就 / be of ~ ownership 为多人共同所有 ②复杂的 ③【电】并联的,多路的,复接的: ~ circuit 多路电路,复接电路 / ~ access 多路通信(即多个地面站共用一个卫星进行通信) ④[植]聚花的 **II** *n.* ①【数】倍数: lowest (或 least) common ~ 最小公倍数(略作 L. C. M.) ②【电】并联;多路系统 ③相联成组: lay mines in ~ 成组地布雷 / several coaches running in ~ 几节联列行驶的客车 ④ [英]联号商店(~ shop 或 ~ store) ||'~-'choice *a.* 从几个答案中选择正确答案的: a ~-*choice* test 选择法测验 / ~ **cropping** 【农】复种 / '~-,**nozzle** *a.* 多喷嘴的: a ~-*nozzle* missile 多喷嘴发动机导弹 / '~-,**party** *a.* 多党的: the ~-*party* system 多党制 / ~ **sclerosis** [医]多发性硬化 / ~ **star** [天]聚星 / ~ **voting** 重复投票

multiplex ['mʌltipleks] *a.* ①复合的,多样的;多重的 ②【讯】多路传输的,多路复用的: ~ telegraphy 多路通报,多路电报 / ~ telephony

多路电话 **II** ❶ *vt.* 多路传输 (几种信号等) ❷ *vi.* 多路传输,多路复用

multiplication [,mʌltipli'keiʃən] *n.* ①增加,增多;倍增 ②增殖,繁殖 ③【数】乘法;乘法运算

multiply[1] ['mʌltiplai] ❶ *vi.* ①增加,增多 ②增殖,繁殖 ③做乘法 ❷ *vt.* ①增加;成倍地增加 ②【数】乘;使相乘: ~ five by three 以三乘五 / ~ five and three 把五和三相乘 ‖ *the earth* 见 **earth** / *~ words* 见 **word**

multiply[2] ['mʌltipli] *ad.* ①复合地;多样地,多重地,多倍地 ②复杂地 ③【电】并联地,多路地

multitude ['mʌltitjuːd] *n.* ①大批,大群; [the ~] 群众,大众: a ~ of heroic figures 大批英雄人物 / a great ~ of people 一大群人 / a noun of ~【语】群体名词 ②众多,大量: like the stars in ~ 多似繁星

mum[1] [mʌm] **I** *a.* 沉默的,缄默的: keep ~ about sth. 不说某事 **II** *n.* 沉默,缄默 **III** *int.* 别说话,别作声 ‖ *Mum's the word!* 别多话! 别声张!

mum[2] [mʌm] *vi.* ①(戴假面化装) 演哑剧 ②(节日中) 化装游玩

mum[3] [mʌm] *n.* ①[英]妈妈 (=[美] mom) ②女士,太太;小姐

mum[4] [mʌm] *n.* 烈性啤酒

mum[5] [mʌm] *n.* [口]菊花

mumble ['mʌmbl] **I** ❶ *vi.* 含糊地说话,咕哝 ❷ *vt.* ①含糊说话,咕哝: He ~d a few words and went off. 他咕哝了几句就走了。②抿着嘴嚼,瘪着嘴嚼 **II** *n.* 含糊的话,咕噜

mummer ['mʌmə] *n.* ①哑剧演员;演员 ②(节日中) 化装游玩的人 ‖ ~**y** ['mʌməri] *n.* ①哑剧演员的表演;哑剧 ②做作可笑的仪式(或表演)

mummify ['mʌmifai] ❶ *vt.* ①使(尸体)成木乃伊,用香料殓藏(尸体) ②使成木乃伊似;使干瘪,使皱缩 ❷ *vi.* 成木乃伊状;干瘪,皱缩 ‖ **mummification** [,mʌmifi'keiʃən] *n.*

mummy[1] ['mʌmi] **I** *n.* ①木乃伊,干尸 ②木乃伊似的人,干瘪的人 ③稀烂的一团 ④【化】普鲁士红,褐色氧化铁粉 **II** *vt.* =mummify ‖ *beat to a* ~ 把…打得稀烂 ‖ **bag** 一种睡袋 / ~ **cloth** ①木乃伊裹布 ②【纺】马米绉;马米布

mummy[2] ['mʌmi] *n.* [英]儿语)妈妈

mump[1] [mʌmp] ❶ *vi.* ①绷着脸不说话,愠怒;故作正经 ②[英方]咧着嘴笑 ③[方]含糊地说话,咕哝 ❷ *vt.* [方]含糊地说,咕哝: ~ one's anger 叽哩咕噜地发脾气

mump[2] [mʌmp] ❶ *vi.* [主英]强行乞讨,行乞;欺骗 ❷ *vt.* [方]欺骗

mumpish ['mʌmpiʃ] *a.* 绷着脸不说话的,愠怒的

mumps [mʌmps] [复] *n.* [用作单或复] ①【医】流行性腮腺炎 ②愠怒

munch [mʌntʃ] ❶ *vt.* ①用力嚼,大声嚼: The cattle were ~ing their fodder. 牛群正在大声嚼饲料。②使(颚)嚼动 ❷ *vi.* 用力咀嚼,大声

咀嚼: ~ away at an apple 一口口地使劲咬苹果

mundane ['mʌndein] *a.* ①世间的,世俗的;庸俗的: ~ affairs 世事 ②宇宙的 ‖ ~**ly** *ad.* / ~**ness** *n.*

municipal [mju(ː)'nisipəl] *a.* ①市的,市政的;市立的,市内办的: ~ administration 市政管理 / a ~ university 市立大学 ②自治城市的,地方自治的;地方(性)的 ③内政的: a ~ law 国内法 ‖ ~**ly** *ad.*

munificent [mju(ː)'nifisnt] *a.* ①慷慨解囊的,毫不吝啬的 ②(所给的东西)大量的 ‖ ~**ly** *ad.*

munition [mju(ː)'niʃən] **I** *n.* [常用复] ①军需品 (尤指枪、炮、弹药),军火: production of ~s 军需品生产 / gas ~s 化学弹药,毒气弹药 / a depot 军械库 ②必需的物质准备 **II** *vt.* 供给军需品: ~ a fort 为要塞配备军火 ‖ ~**eer** [mju(ː),niʃə'niə] *n.* ①军火投机商 ②=~**er** / ~**er** *n.* 军火制造人

mural ['mjuərəl] **I** *a.* ①墙壁的;墙壁上的: a ~ tablet 壁碑 ②似墙壁的: ~ circle【天】墙仪 **II** *n.* 壁画;壁饰 ‖ ~**ist** *n.* 壁画家;壁饰家 ‖ **crown** 城冠(古罗马用以奖给首先登上敌方城墙的士兵)

murder ['məːdə] **I** *n.* ①谋杀,凶杀;谋杀案,谋杀罪;(战争中的)屠杀: wilful ~ 蓄意谋杀(罪) / *Murder!* (惊呼声) 杀人啦! ②极艰险的事 ❶ *vt.* ①谋杀,凶杀;屠杀 ②扼杀(真理、艺术等);糟塌(语言、乐曲等) ③折磨(人心等) ❷ *vi.* 犯杀人罪 ‖ *a judicial* ~ 合法但不公正的死刑判决 / *cry* (或 *shout*) *blue* ~ [口]大声惊呼,大惊小怪地叫喊 / *get away with* ~ [俚]做了坏事而未被发觉;逍遥法外 / *Murder will out.* [谚] ①杀了人终究要败露。②纸包不住火。/ *The* ~ *is out.* 真相大白。(或: 水落石出了。) ‖ ~**er** ['məːdərə] *n.* 杀人犯,凶手 / ~**ess** ['məːdəris] *n.* 女杀人犯,女凶手

murderous ['məːdərəs] *a.* ①杀人的,行凶的: a ~ weapon 凶器 ②凶恶的,杀气腾腾的: a ~ ruffian 杀气腾腾的恶棍 ③厉害的,势不可挡的;要命的: ~ heat 酷热 ‖ ~**ly** *ad.* / ~**ness** *n.*

murky ['məːki] *a.* ①黑暗的,阴沉的;(黑暗)浓密的: a ~ night 黑夜 / Rain poured down from the ~ skies. 雨从阴沉的天空倾盆而下。/ ~ darkness 漆黑 ②朦胧的;有浓雾的,雾状的: The air was ~ with smoke. 空气中烟雾迷漫。③难懂的,隐晦的 ‖ **murkily** *ad.* / **murkiness** *n.*

murmur ['məːmə] **I** *n.* ①低沉连续的声音(如微风的沙沙声、流水的淙淙声等): the ~ of bees 蜜蜂的嗡嗡声 ②咕哝;怨言: go without a ~ 毫无怨言地去 ③低语声,喊喳声: a ~ of conversation 一阵轻轻的谈话声 / a ~ of delight in the audience 观众中欢乐的喊喳喳喳声 ④【医】(心脏)杂音: respiratory ~ 呼吸性杂音 **II** ❶ *vi.* ①发低沉连续的声音: A breeze ~ed in the trees. 树林中微风沙沙作响。②咕哝,低声抱怨

(*against, at*) ❷ *vt.* 低声说: ~ a secret to sb. 低声告诉某人一个秘密

muscle ['mʌsl] **I** *n.* ①肌肉;【解】肌: exercise one's ~s 锻炼肌肉, 活动自己的肌肉 / voluntary (involuntary) ~s 随意(不随意)肌 ②体力,膂力: a man of ~ 大力士 ③[喻]力量;(酒等的)劲道 ④[美俚]大力士;打手 **II** ❶ *vt.* ①强推 ② up a diplomatic approach 以实力作为外交途径的后盾 ③[方]用体力搬运 ❷ *vi.* 用劲走, 用力挤着走: ~ up a cliff 用劲攀上峭壁 ‖*be on the* ~ [美俚]准备动武; 准备蛮干 / ~ *in* [俚]强行进入; 强行分得一份利益, 强夺 / ~ *out* [俚]强行逐出: be ~d out of an organization 被逐出一组织 / *not move a* ~ 一点不动弹; 毫不动容 ②~ 无肌肉的;无气力的 ‖'~-**bound** *a.* ①(因过度运动)肌肉紧张的 ②僵硬的, 死板的 / '~-**man** *n.* ①肌肉发达的男子 ②(被雇用的)打手, 暴徒 / ~ **sense** 【医】肌肉觉

muscle

muscular ['mʌskjulə] *a.* ①肌肉的;【解】肌的: ~ tissues 肌组织 / ~ activity 肌活动 ②肌肉发达的, 强健的; 强有力的: a ~ young man 强壮的年青人 / ~ music 刚健有力的音乐 / a ~ river 水势汹涌的河流 ‖~**ity** [,mʌskju'læriti] *n.* / ~**ly** *ad.* ‖~ **dystrophy** (遗传性)肌肉萎缩症

muse¹ [mju:z] *n.* ①[the Muses]【希神】缪斯(掌管文艺、音乐、天文等的九位女神) ②[the ~] 诗人的灵感,诗才,诗兴 ③[诗]诗人

muse² [mju:z] **I** ❶ *vi.* ①沉思, 冥想: ~ *over* past memories 缅怀往事 / ~ *on* what one has heard 对听到的事左思右想 / The veteran worker's words set his mind *musing*. 老工人的话使他沉思起来。②若有所思地望着: ~ *upon* the rushing torrents of the river 凝视着急流奔腾的河水 ③[古]惊讶, 惊异 ❷ *vt.* 沉思, 冥想 **II** *n.* 沉思, 冥想

museum [mju(:)'ziəm] *n.* ①博物馆, 博物院 ②[美]展览馆, 陈列馆: an art ~ 美术馆 ‖~-**piece** ①博物馆的珍藏物;可供陈列的艺术品(或工业品) ②[贬]老古董(指人或物)

mush¹ [mʌʃ] **I** *n.* ①软糊糊的东西, 软块: ~ of snow 融化中的雪块 ②[美]玉米粥 ③[口]多愁善感, 痴情; 废话, 无聊文字 ④[美俚]嘴巴; 脸

II ❶ *vt.* [方]使成软糊状 ❷ *vi.* (飞机因控制器失灵)半失速飞行; 升不高 ‖*make a* ~ *of* [口] 把…弄得一团糟 ‖'~-**head** *n.* [美俚]笨蛋, 傻瓜 / '~-**mouth** *n.* [美俚]口齿不清的人

mush² [mʌʃ] [美] **I** *vi.* 坐狗拉的雪橇旅行 **II** *n.* 坐狗拉雪橇的行路 **III** *int.* 走! (赶拉雪橇的狗前进的吆喝声) ‖~**er** *n.* 赶狗拉雪橇的人

mush³ [mʌʃ] *n.* [俚]伞

mushroom ['mʌʃrum] **I** *n.* ①蘑菇;食用伞菌,菌类植物: dried ~s 干蘑菇;香菇 ②蘑菇形物;蘑菇形女式扁帽;蘑菇状烟云;[俚]伞: the ~ from an atom-bomb explosion 原子弹爆炸形成的蘑菇云 ③蘑菇似迅速增长的事物;[古]暴发户 **II** *a.* 蘑菇形的; 蘑菇似迅速增长的; 生命象蘑菇一样短暂的: ~ clouds 蘑菇状云, 菌状云 **III** *vi.* ①采蘑菇: go ~ing 采蘑菇去 ②蘑菇似地迅速增长, 雨后春笋般地发展 ③(子弹等)打扁成蘑菇形; (烟云等)喷散成蘑菇状 ④爆炸 ‖*spring up like* ~s 雨后春笋般地涌现

music ['mju:zik] *n.* ①音乐;乐曲;乐谱: folk ~ 民间音乐 / vocal (instrumental) ~ 声(器)乐 / absolute ~ 纯音乐, 无标题音乐(指不用文字标明其题目而通过曲调、结构等反映某种情绪的器乐曲) / programme ~ 标题音乐(根据一定主题构思并用标题提示中心内容的器乐曲) / compose ~ 作曲 / set a poem to ~ 把诗谱成曲 / piano ~ 钢琴曲 / play without ~ 不用乐谱演奏 / Can you read ~? 你识乐谱吗? ②乐队: a field ~ 野战军乐队 ③音乐欣赏力 ④和谐悦耳的声音(如鸟鸣声、泉水声等): the ~ of the nightingale 夜莺的啾鸣 ⑤(猎犬见猎物时的)吠叫声;喧闹 ⑥法律制裁, 惩处 ‖*face the* ~ 勇于承担后果(或批评);临危不惧 / *jerk chin* ~ 谈话 / *rough* ~ (故意使人讨厌的)吵闹, 喧器 ‖~ **book** 乐谱 / ~ **box** [美]自动奏乐器, 百音盒 / ~ **case** 乐谱夹 / ~ **drama** 乐剧(歌剧的一种) / ~ **hall** [英]杂耍剧场; [美]音乐厅 / ~ **paper** 空白五线谱纸 / ~ **stand** 乐谱架 / ~ **stool** 琴凳

musical ['mju:zikəl] **I** *a.* ①音乐的;配乐的: a ~ instrument 乐器 / a ~ performance 演奏 / a ~ clock 音乐闹钟 / the ~ images of positive characters 正面人物的音乐形象 ②音乐般好听的;和谐的, 悦耳的: a ~ voice 好听的嗓音 / a ~ name 悦耳的名称 ③爱好音乐的;精通音乐的;有音乐才能的: a ~ family 爱好音乐的家庭 / be of a ~ turn 有音乐之才, 对音乐有兴趣 ④音乐家的, 音乐爱好者的 **II** *n.* 音乐喜剧 (= ~ comedy); (电影的)音乐片; [古]音乐(晚)会: a film ~ in technicolor 五彩音乐片 ‖~**ity** [,mju:zi'kæliti] *n.* 和谐, 悦耳;音乐才能(或知识) / ~**ly** *ad.* / ~**ness** *n.* ‖~ **box** [英]自动奏乐器, 百音盒 / ~ **chairs** 抢座位游戏(参加游戏的人随乐声绕着一圈椅子走动, 乐声停止时未抢到座位者受罚) / ~ **saw** (演奏用的)钢锯

musician [mju(:)'ziʃən] *n.* 音乐家, 乐师;作曲家 ‖~**ly** *a.* 有音乐家的鉴赏力(或才能)的, 音乐家似的

musk [mʌsk] *n.* ①麝香;【动】麝 ②麝香植物(尤指香沟酸浆) ‖~ **cat** 灵猫, 香猫 / ~ **cow** 母麝牛 / ~ **deer**【动】麝 / ~ **mallow**【植】黄葵, 麝香锦葵 / '~,**melon** *n.* 甜瓜, 香瓜 / ~ **onion** 麝香葱 / '~-**ox** *n.* 麝牛 / ~ **plant**【植】香沟酸浆 / '~**rat** *n.* 麝鼠; 麝鼠皮 / ~ **rose** 麝香蔷薇

musket ['mʌskit] *n.* 滑膛枪, 旧式步枪 ‖'~-**shot** *n.* ①步枪子弹 ②步枪射程

muslin ['mʌzlin] *n.* 平纹细布, 薄纱织物 ‖*a bit of* ~ [俚]女子 ‖~ **delaine** 细薄平纹毛织物 / ~ **weave**【纺】平纹组织

must[1] **I** [强 mʌst; 弱 məst] *v. aux.* (无时态和人称变化, 后接不带 to 的动词不定式) ①[表示义务、命令或必要]必须, 应当: We ~ obey orders. 我们必须服从命令。/ You ~ be there on time. 你务必要按时到达那里。/ I told him what he ~ do. 我告诉过他应该做些什么。/ You ~n't touch the machine, child. 孩子, 不准碰那台机器。/ Cars ~ not be parked here. 此地不准停车。/ A: *Must* you go so soon? B: No, I need not go yet. (Yes, I ~.) 甲: 你那么早就得走吗? 乙: 不, 我没有必要现在就走。(是的, 我得走了。) / I ~ say you're looking much better. 我得说你看上去好多了。 ②[表示不可避免性或肯定性]必然要, 必定会: If he had really been there, I ~ have seen him. 如果他当时真的在那里, 我必定会看到他。③[表示主张]一定要, 坚持要: He ~ always have his own way. 他总是自行其是。/ If you ~ go, at least wait till the storm is over. 如果你坚持要走, 至少也要等这场暴风雨过去了再走。④[表示推定或指具有较大的可能性]很可能, 谅必: This ~ be the book you want. 这谅必就是你要的那本书。/ I think my letter ~ have miscarried. 我想我的信一定是误投了。/ Something ~ have happened or he would have been here. 很可能发生了什么事, 否则他应该已经来了。/ It ~ be time. 该到点了吧。/ You ~ have overcome the difficulties if you had tried harder. 要是你当时多使一把劲的话, 你肯定已克服那些困难了。/ They ~ have been enjoying themselves. 他们谅必玩得很痛快。⑤[表示与说话人愿望相反及不耐烦]偏要: Why ~ you be so stubborn? 为什么你偏要这样固执呢? / As I was sitting down to supper, the telephone ~ ring. 正当我坐下来吃晚餐的时候, 偏偏电话铃响了。⑥[方][表示请求]可以: *Must* I go now? 我现在可以去了吗? **II** [mʌst] *n.* 必须做的事, 不可少的事物 **III** [mʌst] *a.* 绝对必要的 ‖~ *needs* 必须, 不得不

must[2] [mʌst] *n.* ①(未发酵或发酵中的)葡萄汁, 果汁 ②新酿葡萄酒

must[3] [mʌst] *n.* ①麝香 ②霉臭, 霉

mustang ['mʌstæŋ] *n.* ①(墨西哥和美国加利福尼亚州产的)野马 ②[美俚]行伍出身的军官 ③[美][M-]【军】野马式战斗机 ‖~ **grape**【植】白亮葡萄

mustard ['mʌstəd] *n.* ①【植】芥; 芥子, 芥末: black (white) ~ 幽(白)芥 / I don't like ~; it's too hot. 我不爱吃芥末, 这东西太辣了。②芥末色, 深黄色 ③[俚](酒等)的辣劲; 热情; 热烈有劲的事; 热情有劲的人; 优秀飞行员 ‖*a grain of* ~ *seed* 有极大发展前途的小东西 / *cut the* ~ (或 *be up to the* ~)[美俚]符合要求 ‖~ **gas**【军】芥子气(一种糜烂性毒气) / ~ **oil**【化】芥子油 / ~ **plaster**【医】芥末硬膏 / ~ **pot** 芥末瓶

muster ['mʌstə] **I** *n.* ①集合, 聚集; [总称]被集合在一起的人员(或物); 一群, 一堆: call an emergency ~ 下令紧急集合 / a ~ of amateurs 一群业余爱好者 / a ~ of biographical facts 一批传记资料 ②检验; 检阅: troops standing ~ 正在接受检阅的部队 ③清单; 花名册 ④样品: ~s of goods for sale 货物的样品 ⑤孔雀群 **II** ❶ *vt.* ①集合, 召集; 召集…点名: The mate ~ed the ship's company. 大副召集船上全体人员点名。②搜集, 收集: ~ all possible strength 集中一切力量 ③征召; 把…列入名册 ④振起, 鼓起: ~ up one's courage 鼓起勇气 / with all the speed one can ~ 以最快的速度 ⑤合计; 构成, 组成: The movie-going public ~s 70 percent of the population. 人口总数中有百分之七十的人常看电影。❷ *vi.* 集合; 集中; 聚集 ‖~ *in* 征召…入伍 / ~ *out* 使退伍 / *pass* ~ (或 *cut the* ~) 及格, 符合要求: Slipshod work will never *pass* ~. 草率的工作绝对经不起检查。‖'~,**master** *n.* 点名官 / ~ **roll** 花名册

musty ['mʌsti] *a.* ①霉的, 发霉的, 霉臭的 ②陈腐的, 老朽的 ‖**mustily** *ad.* / **mustiness** *n.*

mutable ['mju:təbl] *a.* 可变的; 易变的; 无常的, 不定的 ‖**mutability** [,mju:tə'biliti] *n.* / ~**ness** *n.* / **mutably** *ad.*

mutation [mju(:)'teiʃən] *n.* ①(根本的)变化, 变异, 更换, 转变 ②【生】突变; 变种 ③【语】元音变化; 变音 ④人生的浮沉(或盛衰) ‖~ **plural** 由元音变化而构成的复数(例如由 foot 变出的 feet) / ~ **stop**【音】(使管风琴)和声用的变奏音栓

mute[1] [mju:t] **I** *a.* ①缄默的, 不出声的; 一时说不出话的; 不以言语表达的: stare at sb. in ~ amazement 目瞪口呆地凝视某人 / a ~ appeal 无言的恳求 ②哑的; (猎犬)追猎时不吠叫的; (矿物)敲上去不响的 ③【律】故意不答辩的: stand ~ of malice 对被控罪名拒不答辩 ④【语】不发音的(如 dumb 中的 b, mute 中的 e) **II** *n.* ①哑子; 沉默的人: Acupuncture treatment has enabled many deaf~s to hear and speak. 针刺疗法使许多聋哑人获得了听和讲的能力。②雇用的送丧人; [古](没有台词讲的)无言演员 ③【音】弱音器(装在乐器上使声音变柔和或减弱的装置, 在弦乐器上的是骨片或金属小片, 在管乐器上的是管口的塞头) ④【语】不发音的字母 **III** *vt.* 减弱…的声音; 柔和…的色调: play the violin with ~d strings 用调低了的弦拉小提琴 ‖~ly *ad.* / ~ness *n.*

mute² [mju:t] *vi.* (鸟) 排泄

mutilate ['mju:tileit] *vt.* ①使断肢; 使残废; 切去 (手、足或身体的重要部分) ②使残缺不全; 把… 删改得支离破碎 ‖**mutilation** [,mju:ti'leiʃən] *n.* 肢体残缺

mutter ['mʌtə] I ❶ *vi.* ①轻声低语, 咕哝: ~ and mumble 吞吞吐吐 / ~ to oneself 喃喃自语 ②抱怨 (at, against): ~ against sb. 抱怨某人 ③发出低沉的轰隆声; 发出轻微持续的声音: Thunder was ~ing in the distance. 远处响着低沉的雷声。 ❷ *vt.* ①轻声含糊地说: ~ an answer 轻声含糊地作了回答 ②暗地里说; 抱怨地说, 嘀咕 ③ (号角) 嘟嘟地发出(信号) II *n.* ①轻声低语; 抱怨 ②咕哝的话; 怨言 ‖~er ['mʌtərə] *n.* 喃喃低语者

mutton ['mʌtn] *n.* 羊肉: a ~ chop 羊排 / roast ~ 烤羊肉 ‖*be (as) dead as* ~ 确已僵死了的; 被彻底废弃(或遗忘)的 / *eat* ~ *cold* 受人白眼, 被冷待 / *eat one's* ~ *(with)* (与…一起)进餐 / ~ *dressed like lamb* [口]少妇打扮的老媪 / *to return to one's* ~s [用作插入语]回到本题, 言归正传 ‖'~'chops *n.* 圆形络腮胡子 / ~ *fist* [俚][贬]身体庞大(或两手粗大)的人 / '~head *n.* [口]笨蛋, 呆子

muttony ['mʌtəni] *a.* 羊肉味的; 羊膻气的

mutual ['mju:tjuəl, 'mju:tʃuəl] *a.* ①相互的; 彼此的: give ~ support and inspiration 相互支持并鼓舞 / a ~-aid team 互助组 / a ~ admiration society 一批互相标榜的人 / by ~ consent 经双方同意 / ~ conductance 【电】互导 / ~ inductance 【电】互感 ②共同的; 共有的: ~ efforts 共同的努力 ‖~ly *ad.* ‖~ *fund, ~ investment company* 发行随时可换成现款的股票的投资公司

mutuality [,mju:tju'æliti, ,mju:tʃu'æliti] *n.* ①相互关系; 相关 ②感情的共鸣; 亲密

muzzle ['mʌzl] I *n.* ①(狗、狐等)凸出的口和鼻 ②(动物的)口套, 口络 ③喷口, 喷嘴 ④炮口, 枪口 ⑤禁止, 抑制 II *vt.* ①给(动物)上口络 ②封住…的嘴, 使缄默 ③收(帆) ‖'~,loader *n.* 前装炮; 前装枪 / ~ *velocity* 初速(射弹离开炮口瞬间的速度)

muzzy ['mʌzi] *a.* 迟钝的; 迷惑的; 醉得发呆的 ‖**muzzily** *ad.* / **muzziness** *n.*

my [mai; 弱 mi] *pron.* ①[I 的所有格]我的: ~ schoolmates 我的同学们 / ~ article 我(写)的文章 / This book is ~ own. 这本书是我自己的。 / ~ and her mother 我和她两人的母亲 / ~ and her mother(s) 我的母亲和她的母亲 / What do you think of ~ English? 你以为我的英语水平如何? ②[用于称呼]我的: ~ dear Mr. Snow 亲爱的斯诺先生 / Tell me, ~ little boy. 告诉我, (我的)好孩子。 / My Lord (或 ~ lord) [mi 'lɔ:d] (对某些贵族或主教、法官等的尊称)老爷

③[用于感叹句, 表示惊奇; 有时与 eye, foot 等连用, 表示怀疑或不赞成]: Oh, ~! 哎呀! (或: 喔唷!) / My goodness! 天哪!

mycology [mai'kɔlədʒi] *n.* [微]真菌学

myriad ['miriəd] I *n.* ①无数, 极大数量: ~s of changes 千变万化 ②[诗]万, 一万 II *a.* ①无数的 ②含有无数方面(或因素)的 ‖~-'minded *a.* 极有才能的

myrrh [mə:] *n.* ①[药]没药 ②没药树; 没药树脂 ‖~ic ['mə:rik] *a.* 没药的; 没药树(脂)的

myrtle ['mə:tl] *n.* [植]①桃金娘科植物(尤指爱神木) ②长春花属植物 ③加州桂 ④铜钱状珍珠菜 ‖'~,berry *n.* 爱神木的果实

myself [mai'self] *pron.* ①[反身代词]我自己:I'm going to get ~ a new suit. 我将替自己买一套新衣服。 ②[用以加强语气]我亲自, 我本人: as for ~ 至于我自己 / I saw it ~. 这是我亲眼目睹的。 ③[用于 be, become, come to 等之后]我的正常情况(指健康、情绪等): I'm not quite ~ today. 今天我有点不舒服(或不正常)。 ‖*(all) by* ~ ①我独自地 ②我独力地

mysterious [mis'tiəriəs] *a.* ①神秘的, 不可思议的; 难以理解的 ②故弄玄虚的 ‖~ly *ad.* / ~ness *n.*

mystery¹ ['mistəri] *n.* ①神秘的事物, 不可思议的事物; 难以理解的事物: It's a ~ to me 对我来说是个谜。 / make a ~ of 把…搞得神秘化 / the *mysteries* of nature 自然的奥秘 ②神秘, 秘密: an air of ~ 神秘的气氛 / be wrapped in ~ 包在秘密中 ③故弄玄虚 ④神秘小说(或故事, 戏剧), 侦探小说 ⑤[复](古希腊、罗马的)秘密的宗教仪式 【宗】[Misteries] (基督教的)圣餐礼 ⑦神秘剧(欧洲中世纪一种宣传宗教的戏剧) (= ~ play) ⑧[美俚]菜肴 ‖~ *ship, ~ boat* 伪装猎潜舰

mystery² ['mistəri] *n.* [英][古]手艺; 行业; 行会: art and ~ 技术和手艺

mystic ['mistik] I *a.* ①神秘的, 不可思议的; 难以理解的; 引起惊奇(或畏惧)的 ②神秘主义的, 神秘主义者的 ③秘密仪式的 II *n.* 神秘主义者

mystical ['mistikəl] *a.* ①[宗](心灵上)具有象征意义的: the ~ rose 【宗】象征圣母玛利亚的玫瑰 ②根据直觉的 ③ 神秘的, 不可理解的, 隐秘的 ④秘密仪式的 ‖~ly *ad.*

mysticism ['mistisizəm] *n.* ①神秘主义; 神秘教 ②玄想; 基于玄想的谬说

mystification [,mistifi'keiʃən] *n.* ①神秘化; 故弄玄虚; 迷惑 ②神秘的事物; 使人迷惑的事物

mystify ['mistifai] *vt.* 使神秘化; 蒙蔽, 迷惑

myth [miθ] *n.* ①神话: a Hercules ~ 一则关于大力神赫拉克勒斯的神话 / distinguish modern fiction from ~ 区别现代小说作品与神话故事 ②神话式人物(或事物) ③虚构的故事; 荒诞的说法

mythology [mi'θɔlədʒi] *n.* ①[总称]神话 ②神话学 ③神话集, 关于神话的书

N

nab [næb] (nabbed; nabbing) *vt.* [口] ①猛然抓取 ②逮捕, 捉住(现行犯等)

nacreous ['neikriəs], **nacrous** ['neikrəs] *a.* ①真珠质的; 象真珠质的 ②产生真珠质的 ③虹彩般的; 有光彩的

nadir ['neidiə] *n.* ①【天】天底 ②最低点; 极度消沉的时刻: at the ~ of 在…的最低点

nag[1] [næg] **I** (nagged; nagging) ❶ *vt.* ①唠唠叨叨地责骂; 不断地找…的岔子 ②(问题等)困扰 ❷ *vi.* ①唠叨; 责骂不休; 老是催促(at) ②恼人(at): The aching tooth kept *nagging* at me. 牙痛得我不得安宁。 **II** *n.* ①唠叨; 不停的责骂; 不断的催促 ②[口]爱唠叨的人(尤指妇女)

nag[2] [næg] *n.* ①小马 ②[口]马(尤指老马或驽马)

nail [neil] **I** *n.* ①(手、脚的)指甲; 爪: pare one's ~s 修指甲 ②钉: drive (或 knock) in a ~ 把钉敲进去 / fasten sth. with ~s 用钉子把某物钉牢 ③(软嘴鸟及鸭子等)喙上的硬瘤 ④纳尔(英旧制量布长度单位, 相当于 2¼ 吋) ⑤[俚]香烟 **II** *vt.* ①钉, 将…钉牢; 使固定: ~ a lid on a box 给箱子钉上盖子 / ~ a notice on (或 to) the bulletin board 把通知钉在布告栏上 ②使(目光、注意力等)集中于: ~ one's eyes on sth. 盯住某物看 ③揭露, 揭穿 ④拦住, 留下: ~ sb. before he leaves 在某人离开前把他拦下 ⑤[口]抓住, 捕获 ⑥成交(一笔生意) ⑦[美俚]击, 打③(棒球用语)使(跑垒者)被开出场 ‖*as hard as* ~*s* ①身体结实 ②冷酷无情 / *drive a* ~ *into sb.'s coffin* (忧愁、烟酒等)促某人早死 / *hit the (right)* ~ *on the head* 说得中肯; 猜中; 打中要害; 做得恰到好处 / ~ *a lie to the counter* 见 **lie**[2] / ~ *down* ①用钉钉住 ②*down* a carpet 将地毯钉住 ②束缚(to): ~ sb. *down* to his promise 使某人遵守诺言 / ~ sb. *down* to a definite statement 使某人明确表态 ③明确, 确定(做法、契约等) / ~ *one's colo(u)rs to the mast* 见 **colo(u)r** / ~ *up* ①把…钉牢; 把(门、窗等)钉死 ②将…钉在墙上 (或较高处) / *on the* ~ [口]①立即; 当场: pay *on the* ~ 立即付钱 ②在讨论中: a topic *on the* ~ 人们正在谈论的话题 / *right as* ~*s* 见 **right** / *tooth and* ~ 见 **tooth** / *to the* ~ 极其; 完全: His analysis was correct *to the* ~. 他的分析极其正确。 ‖**~er** *n.* ①制钉者; 敲钉者 ②自动敲钉机; 操纵自动敲钉机的人 ③[俚]能手, 好手 ④[俚]远胜于同类各种事物的东西 / **~less** *a.* ①没指甲的 ②不用钉的 ‖**~-biting** *n.* ①咬指甲 ②束手无策 / ~ **brush** 指甲刷 / ~ **clippers** 指甲钳, 指甲刀 / ~ **file** 指甲锉 /

'**~head** *n.* 【建】钉头饰 / '**~-,headed** *a.* 钉头状的 / '**~hole** *n.* ①钉眼 ②(折刀上为便于开启而设的)指甲孔 / ~ **puller** 起钉钳 / '**~sick** *a.* ①因多次钉过钉而变得不结实的: Don't patch the roof with ~*sick* boards. 不要用多次钉过钉而不结实的木板修补屋顶。 ②钉病的(指钉眼引漏水的): a ~*sick* boat 有钉病的船

naïve [nɑːˈiːv], **naive** [neiv; 美 nɑːˈiːv] *a.* ①天真的; 幼稚的 ②朴素的, 朴实的: ~ materialism 朴素唯物论 ③(鼠、兔等)首次用来作(某种)实验的 ‖**~ly** *ad.* / **~ness** *n.*

naked ['neikid] *a.* ①裸体的, 光身的: be stark ~ 一丝不挂 ②无遮蔽的; 无保护的, 无防备的; (灯火)无罩的; (房屋等)未加陈设的; (土地等)无树木的, 暴露的: a ~ sword 出鞘的剑 / a ~ light 没有灯罩的灯 / the ~ eye 肉眼 / with ~ fists 赤手空拳地 ③无掩饰的; 坦白的, 直率的; 赤裸裸的: ~ facts 赤裸裸的事实 / the ~ truth 真相 / The fallacy has been exposed in its ~ absurdity. 这谬论的荒诞性已被充分揭露。 ④无证据的; 无保证的: a ~ assertion 无论据的主张 / a ~ contract 无担保的契约 ⑤裸的; 无毛的; 无鳞的; 无贝壳的: ~ barley 裸麦 / a ~ tree 秃树 ‖*as when one was born* 赤条条, 裸体 ‖**~ly** *ad.* / **~ness** *n.* ①裸; 裸体 ②无掩饰 ③光秃; 无防备状态: the ~*ness* of the land 国家(或个人、团体)的无资力(或无防备)状态 ‖~ **dance** [美俚]裸体舞

name [neim] **I** *n.* ①名字; 姓; 姓名; 名称: What's his ~? 他叫什么名字? / What's the ~ of this farm tool? 这件农具叫什么? ②名义; 名目: exist in ~ only 有名无实 / worthy of the ~ 名副其实的 ③[只用单]名誉; 名声: a good (an ill) ~ 好(坏)名声 / have a ~ for bravery 以勇敢著称 ④名人: Don't be intimidated by big ~*s* and authorities. 不要被名人、权威所吓倒。 ⑤族姓, 家族 ⑥【逻】概念的名称; 名词 ‖*an assumed* ~ 化名 / *a common* ~ 【语】普通名词(=a common noun) / *a double-barrelled* ~ (欧美人以两个姓合成的)双姓 / *a false* ~ 假名 / *a family* ~ 姓 / *the first* (或 *given*, *Christian*) ~ (欧美人的)名字, 教名 / *the middle* ~ 当中的名字(有些欧美人姓与名中间的名字) / *a pen* ~ 笔名 / *a proper* ~ 【语】专有名词(=a proper noun) / *a real* ~ 真名 **II** *vt.* ①给…取名: ~ the boy after (或[美] for) his grandfather 以祖父的名字为男孩取名 (如祖父名 George, 孙子也取名叫 George) ②正确叫出…的名字; 列举: Can you ~ these plants?

你叫得出这些植物的名称吗? / He ~d some of the measures that had been taken. 他列举了一些已经采取的措施。③ 任命,提名: ~ sb. (as) manager 任命某人为经理 ④ 说出,提到;指定: ~ no names 不点名,不指出名字 / ~ the price 说出价格 / ~ a date 指定一个日子 ⑤ [英] (下院议长因议员不服从裁决等而)点名警告 ‖ **III** *a.* ①姓名的: a ~ tag 写姓名用的标签 ②(作品等)据以取名的;取某人名字的: the ~ article of an anthology 选集所据以取名的文章(指选集中的某篇文章) / sb.'s ~ child 照某人的名字取名的孩子 ③[美口]著名的;有声誉的: a ~ brand 名牌 / a ~ band 著名的乐队 ‖*a ~ to conjure with* 威力巨大的名字 / *answer to the ~ of* 名叫,叫做 / *by ~* ①名叫···: He met a man, John *by ~*. 他遇到一个名叫约翰的人。②用名字;凭名字: call sb. *by ~* 叫某人名字 / I knew him only *by ~*. 我只知道他的名字。(指没见过其人) / *by* (或 *of, under*) *the ~ of* 名叫: a U.S. newsman *by* (或 *of*) *the ~ of* Newton 一个名叫牛顿的美国记者 / go *by* (或 *under*) *the ~ of* 以···的名字出现;名叫 / *call sb. ~s* 谩骂某人 / *drag sb.'s ~ through the mire* 把某人搞臭 / *get* (或 *make*) *a ~ (for oneself)* 成名;得到名声 / *Give a dog a bad* (或 *an ill*) *name and hang him.* 见 **dog** / *Give it a ~.* [口]你要什么,请讲。/ *have one's ~ up* 成名,扬名 / *in one's own ~* 以自己的名义(指未经授权) / *in the ~ of* ①以···的名义;代表···②凭···: in the ~ *of common sense* 凭常识而言(用于疑问句中,有时作"到底","究竟"解) / *keep one's ~ on the books* 保留学籍(或会籍等) / ~ *it* (把自己所希望的东西等) 讲出来 / *not to be ~d on* (或 *in*) *the same day with* 与···不可同日而语,比···差得多 / *of ~* 有名的 / *put one's ~ down for* ①申请成为···的候选人 ②答允为···捐钱 / *take a ~ in vain* 滥用名字(尤指用神名发誓等) / *take one's ~ off the books* 退学(或退会等) / *to one's ~* 属于自己所有: *without a ~* 无名的;名字说不出的‖**~d** *a.* 被指名的;指定的: arrive on the ~d date 在指定的日子到达 ‖**'~board** *n.* 招牌;站名牌(或船名牌等) / '~-,calling *n.* 骂人 / ~ *day* 命名日(欧美人常以圣徒名取名,该圣徒的生日即为此人的命名日) / ~ *part* 成为剧名的角色(如《奥赛罗》中的奥赛罗) / '~plate *n.* ①门上刻姓名的牌子②(印在报头上或封面上的)报刊名 ③商标 / '~sake *n.*同姓名的人(尤指根据另一人取名的人);同名的物: He is my *~sake*. 他与我同姓(或同名)。

nanny ['næni] *n.* [主英] ①保姆 ②雌山羊 (=~ goat)

nap[1] [næp] **I** (napped; napping) *vi.* ①(白天)小睡,打盹 ②疏忽,不留神 **II** *n.* (白天的)小睡,打盹,瞌睡: have (或 take) a ~ 睡午觉,打盹 ‖*catch sb. napping* 发现某人在打瞌睡;乘某人不备时抓住他的疏忽之处(或错误等)

nap[2] [næp] **I** *n.* ①(织物上面的一层)绒毛 ②(某些植物表面的) 短茸毛 **II** (napped; napping) *vt.* ①使起绒,使拉毛 ②修整,使平滑 ‖**~less** *a.* 无绒毛的

nap[3] [næp] **I** *n.* ①一种牌戏 ②孤注一掷 **II** (napped; napping) *vt.* 预测···为可能获胜的马 ‖*a ~ hand* 一手可获全胜的牌; 冒险一下可获全胜的地位 / *go ~ on* 对···孤注一掷,把一切押在···上

napalm ['neipɑ:m] **I** *n.*【化】凝汽油剂;凝固汽油: a ~ bomb 凝固汽油弹 **II** *vt.* 用凝固汽油轰炸;用喷火器攻击

nape [neip] *n.* 项,颈背,后颈

naphtha ['næfθə] *n.*【化】①石脑油 ②石油 ③可作溶剂的易挥发可燃的碳氢化合物液体(如煤焦油石脑油、页岩石脑油、乙醚等)

napkin ['næpkin] *n.* ①(吃西餐用的)揩嘴布,餐巾 ②[英方]手帕;头巾 ③[主英]尿布 ‖*lay up* (或 *hide*) *in a ~* 把···藏着不用 ‖~ *ring* 束餐巾的环

narcissus [nɑ:'sisəs] *n.* ① [N-]【希神】那喀索斯(因爱恋自己在水中的影子而憔悴致死的美少年;死后化为水仙花) ②([复] narcissuses 或 narcissi [nɑ:'sisai]) 水仙花; [N-]【植】水仙属

narcissus

narcotic [nɑ:'kɔtik] **I** *a.* ① 麻醉(性)的,麻醉剂的 ②在精神上起麻痹作用的 ③吸毒成瘾者的;护理(或照料)吸毒成瘾者的 **II** *n.* ①麻醉剂 ②起麻痹作用的东西 ③吸毒成瘾的人 ‖**~ally** *ad.*

narrate [næ'reit] ❶ *vt.* 讲(故事);叙述: ~ the process of an experiment 叙述一个实验的过程 ❷ *vi.* 讲述,叙述 ‖**narrator** *n.* 讲述者,叙述者

narrative ['nærətiv] **I** *a.* 叙述的;叙事体的: ~ literature 叙事文学 / a ~ poet 叙事诗作家 **II** *n.* ①记事,叙述(可指文章或讲话),记叙文: give a clear ~ of the incident 对事件作清晰的叙述 ②记叙体 ‖**~ly** *ad.*

narrow ['nærou] **I** *a.* ①狭的,狭窄的; (布匹等)狭幅的(通常指十八吋以下) ②范围狭小的: ~ nationalism 狭隘民族主义 / in a ~ sense 在狭义上 / move in a ~ circle of friends 生活在狭小的朋友圈子中 ③眼光短浅的; 有偏见的;自我中心的 ④气量狭小的; [方]吝啬的 ⑤勉强的: ~ majority 勉强的多数 ⑥(收入等)勉强维持生

活的: live. in ～ circumstances 生活在贫困中 ⑦精细的,严密的: a ～ inspection 精密的检查 ⑧[语]窄(音)的: a ～ vowel 窄元音 **II ❶** *vi.* 变狭;收缩;(眼睛)眯成一条缝 **❷** *vt.* 弄窄; 使缩小;使(观点等)变得狭隘: ～ the gap between 缩小…与…两者间的差距 **III** *n.* ①(山谷、道路等)狭窄部分 ②[常作 ～s]用作单或复]海峡: the *Narrows* (美国纽约)斯塔腾岛(Staten Island)和长岛间的海峡;达达尼尔海峡的最狭窄部分 ‖*a ～ escape* 九死一生 / *a ～ squeak* 见 **squeak** / *the ～ bed* (或 *cell, house*) 墓 ‖*~ness a.* ‖'*~-gauge a.* ①[也作 *~-gage*] (铁道)狭轨的 ②[口]胸襟狭窄的 / *～ seas* 英吉利海峡和爱尔兰海 / *～ way* 正直(源出基督教«圣经»)

nasal ['neizəl] **I** *a.* 鼻的;鼻音的: the ～ organ [谑]鼻子 / a ～ sound 鼻音(如 [m], [n]) **II** *n.* ①鼻音;鼻音字母 ②[解]鼻骨 ③(头盔上的)护鼻 ‖**-ity** [nei'zæliti] *n.* 鼻音性 / *~ly ad.* 以鼻音

nasty ['nɑːsti] *a.* ①龌龊的,极脏的; (气味等)令人作呕的: a ～ smell 臭味,难闻的气味 ②淫秽的,下流的: ～ stories 猥亵的故事 ③(天气等)非常恶劣的;使人感到极不愉快的: a ～ storm 狂风暴雨 ④平庸的;俗丽的 ⑤脾气不好的; (手段等)卑鄙的;恶意的: turn ～ 发怒 / Don't be ～. 别发火。/ a ～ remark 恶毒的话 ⑥险恶的;非常有害的;严重的: a ～ look 一付凶相 / a ～ illness 严重的疾病 ⑦难处理的,问题多的;别扭的: be ～ to sb. 跟某人闹别扭 ‖*a ～ one* ①责骂 ②使人一蹶不振的打击 / *a ～ piece of work* ①[口]讨厌的家伙,下流坯 ②恶意行为,阴谋 / *leave a ～ taste in the mouth* 见 **taste** ‖**nastily** *ad.* / **nastiness** *n.*

natal ['neitl] *a.* ①出生的; 诞生时的: one's ～ day 生日 ② =native (a.)

nation ['neiʃən] *n.* ①民族: the Chinese ～ 中华民族 / the Scottish ～ 苏格兰民族 ②国家: a member ～ of the UNO 联合国会员国 ③[总称]国民 ④(北美印第安人等的)部落;部落联盟;部落(或部落联盟)的领地 ⑤(中世纪或一些苏格兰大学中)同乡(或同国)的学生们 ‖*the law of ～s* 国际公法 / *the League of Nations* 【史】国际联盟 / *a most favoured ～* 最惠国 / *the ～s* (基督教«圣经»用语)非犹太的各民族; [诗] 世界各民族 / *the United Nations (Organization)* 联合国(组织) ‖**-hood** *n.* 作为一个国家的地位: emerge into ～*hood* 成为国家 / *'~-'state n.* 民族国家,单一民族国家 / *'~'wide a.* 全国性的: make a ～*wide* call 向全国发出号召 *ad.* 在全国范围内: Gains ～*wide* amount to . . . annually. 全国每年收益达…

national ['næʃənl] **I** *a.* ①民族的: the ～ independence and liberation movement 民族独立解放运动 / be ～ in style 具有民族风格 ②国家的;国民的: ～ salvation 救国 ③全国性的: a ～ newspaper 全国性的报纸 ④国有的;国立的: a ～ railway 国有铁路 / a ～ university 国立大

学 ⑤国家主义的 ⑥爱国的 ⑦各党联合的 **II** *n.* ①国民(尤指侨居于外国的): German ～*s* in France 在法国的德国侨民 / the consul's relations with his own ～*s* 领事与其侨胞的联系 ②[常用复]全国性体育竞赛: *the Grand National* (每年三月举行的)英国大赛马 / a ～ *anthem* (或 *air, hymn*) 国歌 / *～ boundaries* 国界 / *～ costume* 民族服装 / *National Day* 国庆日 / *the National Debt* 国债 / *～ defence* 国防 / *the ～ economy* 国民经济 / a ～ *flag* 国旗 / *the National Guard* (美国)国民警卫队 / a ～ *holiday* 国庆日; 国定假日 / *～ income* 国民收入 / *～ mobilization* 全国总动员 / *～ self-determination* 民族自决 / *～ socialism* 国家社会主义,纳粹主义 / *a ～ state* 民族国家 ‖*~ly ad.* 在全国范围内;全国性地

nationalism ['næʃənəlizəm] *n.* ①民族主义 ②国家主义 ③民族性;民族特征(或习惯、惯用语) ④工业国有化主义

nationalist ['næʃənəlist] **I** *a.* ①民族主义的: a ～ state (或 country) 民族主义国家 ②国家主义的 ③ [N-] 民族主义(或国家主义)政党的 **II** *n.* ①民族主义者 ②国家主义者 ③ [N-] 民族主义(或国家主义)政党成员

nationality [,næʃə'næliti] *n.* ①国籍: What's your ～? 你是什么国籍? / dual ～ 双重国籍 ②民族;族: the Han ～ 汉族 / the Chinese people of all *nationalities* 中国各族人民 / the minority *nationalities* 各少数民族 ③民族性 ④民族主义 ⑤国民身分 ⑥独立国地位

nationalize ['næʃənəlaiz] *vt.* ①把…收归国有,使国有化: ～ the railways and mines 将铁路和矿山收归国有 ②使具有某国国籍: ～*d* Germans in the U. S. A. 美国的美籍德国人 ③使组成国家 ④使民族化 ‖**nationalization** [,næʃənəlai-'zeiʃən] *n.*

native ['neitiv] **I** *a.* ①出生的;出生地的: one's ～ place 出生地 / one's ～ country (或 land) 祖国 ②本土的;本国的;土生的: one's ～ language 本族语;本国语 / a ～ son 本地人 / a ～ industry 本地工业,地方工业 / the ～ plants of Asia 亚洲的土生植物 / The yak is ～ to Tibet. 牦牛为西藏所产。③天生的: The ability to swim is ～ to fish. 鱼天生会游泳。④朴素的, 不做作的 ⑤(金属等)天然的,自然的: ～ rubber 天然橡胶 / ～ gold [矿]自然金 ⑥[主澳](动植物)英国种的 ⑦土人的,土著的;非欧美(人)的 **II** *n.* ①本地人;本国人 ②当地人与暂居者相对) ③[贬]土人,土著 ④当地产的动(或植)物: The panda is a ～ of west China. 熊猫是中国西部产的动物。⑤英国本地人工培育的牡蛎 ‖*go ～* (在殖民地的欧洲人)过土人的生活方式 ‖*~ly ad.* / *~ness n.* ‖'*~-'born a.* 本地生的;本国出生的

nativity [nə'tiviti] *n.* ①出生,诞生;出生的情况 ②出生地 ③ [N-] 【宗】耶稣诞生;耶稣诞生图;圣母玛利亚诞生 ④ [N-] 【宗】耶稣诞生节

(=Christmas); 圣母玛利亚诞生节 ⑤(占星术的)算命天宫图

natural ['nætʃərəl] **I** *a.* ①自然界的; 关于自然界的: ~ phenomena 自然现象 / (a) ~ science (一门)自然科学 / be prepared against ~ disasters 备荒(直译: 预防自然灾害) ②天然的: ~ gas 天然气 ③自然的, 不加做作的: a ~ style 自然的风格 / a ~ voice 自然的嗓音 ④物质的, 物质世界的, 非精神的: the ~ world 物质世界 ⑤合乎自然规律的, 正常的; 惯常的: ·a ~ outcome 自然的结果 / die a ~ death 因年老而死 ⑥天生的 ⑦自然状态的, 蒙昧的; 野生的; 未开垦的: animals living a ~ life 野生的动物 / land in its ~ state 未开垦的土地 ⑧逼真的 ⑨私生的, 私生关系的: a ~ son (daughter) 私生子(女) ⑩[主方](父母)生身的, (子女)有血统关系的(别于领养的) ⑪【数】自然数的; 真数的: ~ sine 正弦真数 ⑫【音】本位的; 标明本位号的: a ~ note 本位音 / the ~ scale of C major C 大调 ‖ ~ classification【生】自然分类 / the ~ day 白天; 自然日(一昼夜) / ~ frequency【物】固有频率 / ~ graft【植】自然嫁接 / ~ group【生】自然类群 / a ~ historian 博物学家 / ~ history 博物学; 博物学论著 / ~ law 自然法则;【律】自然法 / one's ~ life 寿命 / the ~ man 蒙昧的人, (迷信说法)未经神明启示的人 / a ~ person【律】自然人(别于"法人") / ~ philosophy 自然哲学(旧时用以指自然科学, 特别是物理学) / ~ religion 自然宗教(宣称以人的本性为依据的宗教) / ~ resources 自然资源 / ~ selection【生】自然选择 / the ~ sign【音】本位号 **II** *n.* ①没有正常智力的人; 傻子; 白痴 ②[口](似乎)在某方面有天生才能的人 ③[口]可望获得显著成功的事物 ④【音】本位音; 本位号(♮); (钢琴等的)白键 ‖ come ~ to sb. 对某人来说是轻而易举的 ‖ ~ness *n.* ①自然(指性质或状态) ②【无】逼真度 ‖ ~-'born *a.* 生来的, 生来的: a ~-born citizen 本国出生的公民(区别于经政变国籍而成的公民)

naturalist ['nætʃərəlist] **I** *n.* ①自然主义者; 自然主义作家 ②博物学家(尤指直接观察动植物者) ③[英](行业用语)买卖玩赏动物的商人 ④[英](行业用语)动物标本剥制者 **II** *a.* =naturalistic

naturalize, naturalise ['nætʃərəlaiz] ❶ *vt.* ①授与…以国籍, 使入国籍 ②使(动, 植物)顺化; 移植; 移养: A number of tropical plants have been ~d in central China. 好些热带植物已移植到华中来了。 ③采纳(外国语词, 风俗等): These French words have been ~d in English. 这些法国词已为英语所采用了。 ④使自然化; 使摆脱习俗 ⑤用自然法则解释(发生的事); 使摆脱神秘性 ❷ *vi.* ①入国籍 ②(动, 植物)顺化, 归化 ③(语词等)被采纳 ④研究博物学 ‖ **naturalization** [,nætʃərəlai'zeiʃən] *n.* ①入国籍 ②(动, 植物)顺化, 归化 ③(外国语词等的)采纳

nature ['neitʃə] *n.* ①[拟人化时作 N-] 大自然, 自然界; 自然力: conquer ~ 征服自然 / a law of ~ 自然法则 ②本性 ③ 性格, 性情; 具有某种性格的人: good ~ 善良的性情 / buoyant ~s 快活的人们 ④性质; 种类: Iron and wood have different ~s (或 are different in ~). 铁和木头性质不同。 / questions of an ideological ~ 思想意识性质的问题 / things of this ~ 这类事情 ⑤生命力, 生命机能; 人体的本能(或需要) ⑥(人的)原始状态; 裸体; (动、植物的)野生状态: be in a state of ~ 处于原始状态; 裸体; 野生 ⑦风景 ⑧(艺术上的)自然, 逼真 ⑨【宗】(人的)未赎罪的状态 ⑩树脂; 树液 ‖ *a call of* ~ 要大便(或小便)的感觉 / *against* ~ 违反自然的(地); 奇迹般的(地) / (be) true to ~ 逼真 / by ~ 生性, 本性上 / contrary to ~ = against ~ / ease (或 relieve) ~ 大便; 小便 / in ~ ①性质上 ②实际上 ③[用于疑问句、否定句及包含 最高级的句子中, 以加强语气]在世界上, 在任何地方; 究竟: What in ~ do you mean? 你究竟是什么意思? / in the course of ~ 见 course / in (或 of) the ~ of 具有…的性质的: a counter-offensive in the ~ of a decisive engagement 带决战性的反攻 / in (或 by, from) the ~ of things (或 of the case) 理所当然地, 必然地 / Nature's engineering 天工 / pay the debt of ~ (或 pay one's debt to ~) 死 / second ~ 第二天性 ‖ ~ printing【印】(把树叶等原物直接压成印版的)自然印刷法 / ~ study 粗浅的自然研究, 初级博物

naught [nɔ:t] **I** *n.* ①无: bring sth. to ~ 使某事成泡影 / come to ~ (计划等)落空 ②【数】零: ~ point five 零点五 (=0.5) **II** *a.* 无价值的, 无用的 ‖ *all for* ~ 徒然, 无用 / *a thing of* ~ 无价值的东西, 无用之物 / care ~ for 对…不感兴趣; 对… 毫不关心; 认为…无价值 / set at ~ 蔑视, 轻视

naughty ['nɔ:ti] *a.* ①顽皮的, 淘气的, 不听话的: a ~ child 顽皮的孩子 / That's very ~ of you. 你太淘气了。 ②猥亵的, 下流的: a ~ novel 黄色小说 ‖ **naughtily** *ad.* / **naughtiness** *n.* ‖ ~ pack [古]坏蛋; 荡妇

nausea ['nɔ:sjə] *n.* ①恶心; 晕船: feel ~ 欲呕 ②极端的憎恶(或厌恶): be filled with ~ at the sight of 看到…就感到十分厌恶

nauseate ['nɔ:sieit] ❶ *vt.* ①使恶心; 使作呕 ②使厌恶 ❷ *vi.* 作呕; 厌恶 (at)

nauseous ['nɔ:sjəs] *a.* ①令人恶心的, 令人作呕的 ②使人厌恶的 ‖ ~ly *ad.* / ~ness *n.*

nautical ['nɔ:tikəl] *a.* 航海的; 海员的; 船舶的; 海上的: a ~ almanac 航海天文历 / a ~ term 航海用语 ‖ ~ly *ad.* 在航海方面 ‖ ~ mile 浬, 海里(合 1.852 公里或 1852 米)

naval ['neivəl] *a.* 海军的; 军舰的; 船的: a ~ architect 造船工程师 / a ~ port 军港 / a ~ battle 海战 / a ~ officer 海军军官; 美国财政部驻海关官员 / a ~ force 海军部队 ‖ ~ly *ad.* 在海军方面 ‖ ~ stores ①海军补给品 ②松脂; 松脂制品

nave[1] [neiv] *n.* (轮)毂

nave[2] [neiv] *n.* ①早期教堂中殿(座位所在部分) ②(铁路车站等建筑的)中间广场

nave

nave

navel ['neivəl] *n.* ①脐,肚脐 ②中心(点) ‖~ **orange**【植】脐橙(一端有脐状凹陷的无核大橙) / ~ **string**【解】脐带

navigable ['nævigəbl] *a.* ①(河、海等)可航行的, 可通航的: a ~ river 可通航的河流 / ~ waters 通航水域 ②(船舶等)具备航行条件的;可操纵航向的: a ~ ship 可航行的船只 / a ~ balloon 可操纵航向的汽球 ‖**navigability** [,nævigə'biliti] *n.* (河、海或船舶等的)适航性

navigate ['nævigeit] ❶ *vi.* ①航行;航空: ~ up a river 向上游航行 ②驾驶船舶(或飞机等) ③(醉汉等)行走 ❷ *vt.* ①航行于: cargo ships that can ~ inland waters 可在内陆水道航行的 货船 ②驾驶,操纵(船舶、飞机等) ③使通过: ~ a bill through Parliament 使议案在议会通过 ‖**navigator** *n.* ①(船舶、飞机的)驾驶员;领航员 ②航海者,航行者;早期的航海冒险者 ‖**navigating officer** 航海长;航海人员

navigation [,nævi'geiʃən] *n.* ①航行;航海;航空: aerial ~ 空中航行 / inland ~ 内河航行 / a certificate 适航证书 ②航海术;航行学 ③导航; 领航: radar ~ 雷达导航 ④海上交通 ‖**coal** ~ 锅炉煤,蒸汽煤

navvy ['nævi] *n.* ①[英](运河、铁路、道路等工程中)挖土工;不熟练工人: a ~ pick (挖)土镐 ② 【机】挖泥机

navy ['neivi] *n.* ①海军: an officer in the ~ 海军军官 / the Department of the *Navy*(美国)海军部 / the Secretary of the *Navy* (美国)海军部长 ②[古][诗]船队,舰队 ③藏青色 (=~ blue) ‖~ **blue** 藏青色 / **Navy Cross** (美国的)海军十字勋章 / ~ **cut** [英]切成细片的块形烟草 / ~ **yard** 海军造船厂

nay [nei] **I** *ad.* ①[古]否,不 ②不仅如此,而且; 甚至: I suspect, ~, I am quite sure, that you are mistaken. 我怀疑,不,我可以确定,你搞错了。 / It is peculiar, ~, unique. 这不但是特殊的,而且是独一无二的。 **II** *n.* ①否定,否认;拒绝;否定的答复: will not take ~ 不许不答应 ②反对票;投反对票的人: the yeas and ~s 赞成和反对的数目(或票数) / vote among the ~s 投反对票 / *Let your yea be yea and your* ~ *be* ~. 见 **yea** / *say* ~ *to sth.* 拒绝某事,不批准

某事 / *say sb.* ~ 拒绝某人的要求 / *yea and* ~ 见 **yea**

Nd 【化】元素钕 (neodymium) 的符号

neap [ni:p] **I** *n.* 小潮;最低潮 **II** *a.* 小潮的;最低潮的: (a) ~ tide 小潮 **III** ❶ *vi.* (潮水)趋向小潮;达小潮最高点 ❷ *vt.* (由于小潮)使(船)受阻: The ship was ~ed. 这船因小潮而搁浅。

near [niə] **I** *ad.* ①(空间、时间)接近,近: A bosom friend afar brings a distant land ~. 海内存知己,天涯若比邻。 / International Labour Day is drawing ~. 国际劳动节即将来到。 ②差不多,几乎: dark brown coming ~ to black 与黑色差不多的深棕色 / be ~ dead with fright 几乎吓死 [注意:现通常用 ~ly] ③亲近地,亲密地 ④节俭地;吝啬地 **II** *a.* ①(空间、时间)近的: The tractor station is quite ~. 拖拉机站就在附近。 / in the ~ future 在不久的将来 / on a ~ day 在近日内 ②接近的,近似的;勉强的: a ~ translation 接近原文的翻译 / ~ silk 象真丝的人造丝 / Though the game was won, it was a very ~ thing. 虽然比赛赢了,但比分非常接近。 ③关系接近的,亲密的: a ~ relation 近亲 ④(车轮等)在左侧的: the ~ front wheel of a car 汽车的左前轮 / the ~ side of the road 路的左侧 ⑤(路等)直达的,近的 ⑥[古]吝啬的 **III** *prep.* 接近,靠近: He is ~ fifty. 他近五十岁了。 / This new freighter is ~ completion. 这艘新货轮即将完工。 / The experimental farm is ~ the waterpower station. 实验农场在水电站附近。 / come (或 go) ~ being drowned 几乎淹死 / The picture does not come ~ the original. 这幅复制的画走了样。 **IV** ❶ *vt.* 接近;走近,驶近: The ship was ~ing the wharf. 船正驶近码头。 ❷ *vi.* 接近;走近,驶近: The harvest season ~s. 收获季节快到了。 ‖*a* ~ *escape* 九死一生 / *far and* ~ 见 **far** / ~ *and dear* 极亲密的 / *upon* (时间)将近: It was ~ *upon* nine o'clock when we came back. 我们回来时已将近九点钟。 ‖~**ness** *n.* ‖~ **beer** 淡啤酒 / **Near East** 近东 / '~-'**miss** 靠近弹,近失弹(炸弹等虽未命中目标,但弹着点距目标很近,仍可造成一定损失) / ~ **point** 【医】近点 / '~'**sighted** *a.* ①近视眼的 ②眼光短浅的 / '~'**sightedness** *n.* ①近视 ②眼光短浅 / '~-'**sonic** *a.* 【空】近音速的 / ~ **work** 需要眼睛靠近看的工作

nearly ['niəli] *ad.* ①差不多,几乎: It's ~ five o'clock. 差不多五点钟了。 / *Nearly* everyone knows it. 几乎每个人都知道这个。 / be ~ completed 即将完成 ②密切地;亲密地: examine sth. ~ 仔细检查某物 / The matter concerns him ~ 这事与他有密切关系。 / be ~ related 是至亲 ③吝啬地 ‖**not** ~ 远非,相差很远: It's *not* ~ so easy as you think. 这远不是你所想的那么容易。

neat[1] [ni:t] *a.* ①整洁的;简洁的;整齐的: a ~ room 整洁的房间 / a ~ speech 简练的演说 / ~ handwriting 工整的笔迹 ②匀称的;样子好的: a ~

figure 匀称的身材 / a ～ dress 简朴雅致的女服
③熟练的; 灵巧的: a ～ worker 做事干净利落的
人 / a ～ piece of work 一件灵巧的成品 / make
a ～ job of it 干得利落 / a ～ answer 巧妙的回
答 ④平滑的, 光滑的: ～ silk 光滑的丝绸 ⑤纯净
的; 不掺水的: a ～ profit [罕]净利 / ～ brandy
纯白兰地酒 ⑥[俚]好的, 美妙的 ‖～ *as a* (*new*)
pin 十分整洁, 干干净净 ‖～ly *ad.* / ～ness *n.*
‖'～-'handed *a.* 手巧的

neat² [ni:t] [单复同] *n.* ①牛类动物; 牛 ②[总称]
家牛 ‖'～herd *n.* 牧牛人 / ～ house 牛棚 /
'～'s-tongue *n.* (食用)牛舌

nebula ['nebjulə]([复] nebulae ['nebjuli:] 或 neb-
ulas) *n.* ①【天】星云 ②【医】角膜翳; (小便的)
溷浊; 喷雾剂

nebulous ['nebjuləs] *a.* ①星云的; 星云状的 ②模
糊不清的; 曚昽的 ③[古]多云的

necessary ['nesisəri] I *a.* ①必要的, 必需的: It is
～ that he (should) do so. 他必须这样做。/
These reference books are ～ to scientific workers. 这些参考书是科学工作者所必需的。②必
然的, 不可避免的: a ～ conclusion 必然会作出
的结论 / the ～ outcome of the affair 事情的必
然结局 ③强制的, 非做不可的; 被迫的, 非自愿的
II *n.* ①[常用复]必需品: the *necessaries* of life
生活必需品 ②[the ～] 必需的钱; 必须做的事:
provide the ～ 提供必需的钱 / do the ～ 做必
须做的事 ③[美方]厕所 ‖*if* ～ 如果必要的话
‖necessarily ['nesisərili, ,nesi'serili] *ad.* 必定,
必然: It must *necessarily* be so. 必然如此。/
It is not *necessarily* so. 未必如此。‖～ condition 【逻】必要条件

necessitate [ni'sesiteit] *vt.* ① 使被需要; 使成为必
需: The increase of production ～*s* a greater
supply of raw materials. 随着生产的增加, 原料
的供应必须增多。② [常用被动语态]迫使: be
～*d* to make a choice 被迫作出抉择 ‖necessita-
tion [ni,sesi'teiʃən] *n.* 迫使; 被迫

necessitous [ni'sesitəs] *a.* ① 贫困的 ② 紧迫的 ③
必需的; 不可避免的 ‖～ly *ad.* / ～ness *n.*

necessity [ni'sesiti] *n.* ① 需要; 必要性 ② 必然
(性): historical (logical) ～ 历史的 (逻辑的) 必
然 / physical ～ 必然; 命运 / ～ and contingency 必然性和偶然性 / ～ and freedom 必然
和自由 ③ 必需品: the *necessities* of life 生活必
需品 / daily *necessities* 日常必需品 ④ 贫穷; 困
难; 危急: in dire ～ 在贫困中 / in case of ～ 在
危急时 ‖*be under the* ～ *of doing sth.* 必须做
某事, 不得不做某事 / *bow to* ～ 屈服于需要, 做
不得不做的事 / *make a virtue of* ～ 见
virtue / *Necessity is the mother of invention.*
[谚]需要是发明之母。/ *Necessity knows no
law.* [谚]需要面前无法律。(做事不择手段的
辩解语) / *of* ～ 必然地, 不可避免地: It must
of ～ be so. 必然是这样的。

neck¹ [nek] I *n.* ①(头)颈, 脖子 ②(动物)颈肉:

a ～ of mutton 一整段羊颈肉 ③ (衣服的)领圈:
a V ～ V 字形领圈, 尖领圈 ④(物的)颈状部分:
the ～ of a bottle 瓶颈 / the ～ of a gourd 葫芦
的颈 ⑤ 狭窄地带, 隘口: 地峡; 海峡 ⑥[地]岩
⑦[建]颈弯饰 ⑧[俚]厚脸: have the ～ to do
sth. 厚着脸皮做某事 II ❶ *vt.* ① 割颈杀死(家
禽) ② 缩小…的口径使成颈状 (*down, in*): ～
down a cylinder 给圆筒轧上颈状凹槽 ③[俚]
与…接吻, 爱抚 ❷ *vi.* ①[俚]接吻, 爱抚 ②收缩,
缩小 ‖*a stiff* ～ 硬领子 ②固执, 顽固 ③固执
的人 / *break one's* ～ 折断颈骨; 折颈致死 /
break the ～ *of* 做完(工作等)的最难部分 / *by
a* ～ ① (在赛马中) 以一颈之差 (得胜 或 输去)
② (在其他竞赛中) 以些微之差 (得胜或输去) /
get it in the ～ [俚]遭殃; 受严厉的申斥; 受重
罚 / *harden the* ～ 变得顽固 / ～ *and crop*
干脆, 彻底: throw sb. out ～ *and crop* 干脆把某
人赶走 / ～ *and* ～ (在赛马及其他竞赛中)并驾
齐驱, 不分上下 / ～ *of the woods* ①林区的居
住地 ②一带, 区域: We haven't been in that ～
of the woods for a long time. 我们好久没有
到那一带地方去了。/ ～ *or nothing* 铤而走
险地, 孤注一掷地 / *on* (或 *over*) *the* ～ *of*
紧跟在… 后面 / *risk one's* ～ 冒生命危险 /
save one's ～ ①免受绞刑 ②免于遭殃 / *shot
in the* ～ [美俚]醉; 半醉 / *stick* (或 *shoot*)
one's ～ *out* [俚]招麻烦; 惹祸殃 / *talk
through* (*the back of*) *one's* ～ 吹牛, 讲蠢话 /
tread on the ～ *of* 骑在…头上, 压迫 / *up to
one's* ～ *in* 齐颈陷在…中; 深陷于…中 ‖'～-
band *n.* ① (作衣饰用的)领圈, 领巾 ② 领口
③衬衫领子 / '～cloth *n.* ①(旧时男装的)领饰
②颈巾, 开领 / ～lace ['neklis] *n.* 项圈 / '～line *n.* 领
口, 开领 / '～piece *n.* ①领饰, 皮围巾 ②(衣服
的)领圈 ③盔甲的护颈部分 / '～-rein *vi.* (马)
随缰绳的控制转向 *vt.* 用缰绳控制(马)的方向 /
'～tie *n.* ①领带 ②[美俚]绞索: a ～*tie* party
绞死; 私刑 / '～wear *n.* [总称]颈部服饰(领子、
围巾、领带等)

neck² [nek] *n.* [英]最后收割下的一束谷物

nectar ['nektə] *n.* ①[希神]众神饮的酒 ②甘美的
饮料 ③【植】花蜜 ‖～ed *a.* [古]充满美酒的; 芳
香甜蜜的

née, nee [nei] *a.* [法]母家姓…的(表示已婚妇女的
母家姓): Mrs. Smith, ～ Jones 母家姓琼斯的
史密斯夫人

need [ni:d] I *n.* ① 需要, 必要: There is a great
～ for (或 of) a new dictionary. 急需一本新词
典。/ There is no ～ for him to come. 不需要
他来。②[复]需用的东西; 需求: from each ac-
cording to his ability, to each according to his
～*s* 各尽所能, 按需分配 ③ 贫穷; 困窘; 危急: help
sb. in his (hour of)～ 在某人困难时帮助他 II ❶
vt. 需要, 必需: This farm tool ～*s* repairing (或
～*s* to be repaired). 这件农具需要修理。/ Does

anybody ~ to see the doctor? 有谁需要看医生吗? ❷ *vi.* ①生活贫困 ②是需要的,是必要的: be more (less) than ~s 比所需要的为多(少) ❸ *v. aux.* [无时态、人称变化。多用于疑问句和否定句]需要, 必须: A: *Need* we buy any new equipment? B: No, we ~n't. 甲:我们需要购置新的设备吗?乙:不,不需要。[注意:相反情况说 Yes, we *must.* 是的,需要的。] / Your elder brother ~ not have come last night. 你哥哥昨天晚上本来无需来的。[注意: ~ not have come 指"来了,但实际不必来"; did not ~ to come 则表示"不必来,实际上没有来"] ‖*at* ~ 紧急时: Tincture of iodine is good *at* ~. 碘酒紧急时有用。/ *be* (或 *stand*) *in* ~ *of* 需要… / *do one's* ~s 解大(小)便 / *had* ~ 应该, 必须[后接不定式, to 可略] / *have* ~ *of* (或 *for*) 需要… / *have* ~ *to do sth.* 必须做某事: I've ~ *to go* to town. 我必须到城里去。/ *if* ~ *be* 如果需要的话: *If* ~ *be,* we'll go and have a look. 如果需要, 我们就去看一看。/ *Need makes the old wife trot.* [谚]事急老妪跑。/ *What* ~(*s*)? 为什么要这样? ‖~*s test* 经济情况调查(如对申请救济金的失业人员和年老者的调查)

needful ['ni:dful] I *a.* 需要的,必要的 II *n.* ①需要的事物: do the ~ 做需要做的事 / summer ~s 夏令必备品 ②[俚]钱 ‖~*ly ad.* / ~*ness n.*

needle ['ni:dl] I *n.* ①针;缝针;编织针;唱针;注射针: a ~'s eye 针眼 ②指针;磁针: a compass ~ 罗(盘)针 / a magnetic ~ 磁针 ③【植】针叶;【矿】针状结晶体;针状物(如尖岩、方尖塔等): pine ~s 松叶 ④【建】横撑木 ⑤放射性材料容器 II *vt.* ①用针缝;用针刺;用针对…进行手术;穿针似地穿过: ~ a blister until it bursts 挑开水泡 / ~ one's way through a crowd 在人群中穿过 ②用横撑木支撑 ③[口]刺激,煽动;戏弄 ④加强(讲话等)效果, 使更尖锐辛辣; 掺酒精使(饮料)浓烈: ~ a speech with criticism 用批评增加讲话锋芒 / ~ the beer 在啤酒里掺酒精 ❷ *vi.* ①缝纫;刺绣 ②成针状结晶 ‖*Adam's* ~ 【植】丝兰属植物 / *a devil's darning* ~ 蜻蜓 / (*as*) *sharp as a* ~ 非常机敏,非常敏锐 / *get* (或 *have*) *the* ~ 恼怒;抑郁 / *hit the* ~ 击中要害;射箭中靶 / *look for a* ~ *in a bottle* (或 *bundle*) *of hay* 大海捞针 / *on the* ~ 注射毒品成瘾 / *pins and* ~s 见 pin ‖~*ful n.* 穿在针上的一次所用的线 ‖'~*bar n.* 【纺】针床;针座;(缝纫机的)针天心 / ~ *bath* 一种淋浴 / ~ *beam* 【建】簪梁 / '~*craft n.* =~work / '~*fish n.* 【动】颌针鱼; 海龙属鱼 / ~ *lace* [纺]针绣花边 / '~*point n.* 针尖;针绣花边 / ~ *valve* 【机】针阀 / '~*woman n.* 缝纫女工 / '~*work n.* 刺绣活;缝纫业

needless ['ni:dlis] *a.* 不需要的: *Needless* to say, I agree. 不用说,我是同意的。‖~*ly ad.* / ~*ness n.*

needy ['ni:di] *a.* 贫困的: the poor and ~ 穷苦的人们 ‖**needily** *ad.* / **neediness** *n.*

negation [ni'geiʃən] *n.* ①否定;否认;否定性的话(或学说) ②虚无,不存在 ③【逻】命题的否定 ‖~ *of* ~ 否定之否定 ‖~*ist n.* 否定论者

negative ['negətiv] I *a.* ①否定的; 否认的: a ~ answer 否定的回答 / a ~ proposition 【逻】否定命题 ②反面的;消极的: a teacher by ~ example 反面教员 / positive and ~ historical lessons 正反两方面的历史经验 / turn ~ factors into positive ones 把消极因素转化为积极因素 ~ evidence 【律】反证 ③【数】负的;【电】阴性的,负的;【医】阴性的;【摄】底片的: ~ angle 负角 / ~ sign 负号 / ~ pole 阴极,负极 II *n.* ①否定词;否定语;否定的观点: Two ~s make an affirmative. 负负得正。/ His request received a ~. 他的请求被拒绝。②否决权 ③消极的属性 ④【数】负数;【电】阴电,阴极板;【摄】底片 III *vt.* ①否定; 否认; 驳斥: Practical experience ~d this theory. 实践的经验驳斥了这一学说。②否决;拒绝 ③抵销, 使中和 ‖*in the* ~ 否定地: answer *in the* ~ 回答说"不" / be decided *in the* ~ 遭到否决 / His request received a ~. ‖~*ly ad.* 否定地;消极地 / ~*ness n.* 否定性;消极性 ‖~ *income tax* [美] 对收入低于法定标准的家庭的联邦补助 / ~ *proton* 【物】阴质子,负质子

neglect [ni'glekt] I *vt.* ①忽视, 忽略: ~ one's meals and sleep 废寝忘食 ②疏忽, 玩忽; 漏做(某事): ~ one's duties 玩忽职责 / ~ed to wind the clock. 我忘了开钟。II *n.* 忽略;疏忽,玩忽: He showed no ~ of duty. 他不曾玩忽职守。/ in a state of ~ 处于无人管理的状态 / treat sb. with ~ 怠慢某人 ‖~*ed a.* 被忽视的;未被好好照管的

neglectful [ni'glektful] *a.* 疏忽的,不注意的 (*of*): be ~ of one's appearance 不注意自己的仪表 ‖~*ly ad.* / ~*ness n.*

negligence ['neglidʒəns] *n.* ①疏忽,粗心大意,玩忽;疏忽行为: ~ of dress 不修边幅 ②【律】过失 ③(文学作品等)风格的奔放

negligent ['neglidʒənt] *a.* 玩忽的,疏忽的,粗心大意的: be ~ in one's work 工作马虎 / be ~ of one's duties 玩忽职守 ‖~*ly ad.*

negligible ['neglidʒəbl] *a.* 可以忽略的, 微不足道的: a ~ quantity 可忽略的量(或因素);无足轻重的人 ‖**negligibly** *ad.*

negotiable [ni'gouʃjəbl] *a.* ① 可谈判的,可协商的 ②(票据、证券等)可转让的,可流通的: ~ instruments 流通票据, 可转让票据 ③(道路、河流等)可通行的: a road normally ~ by trucks 在正常情况下可行驶卡车的道路 ‖**negotiability** [ni,gouʃə'biliti] *n.*

negotiate [ni'gouʃieit] ❶ *vi.* 谈判,协商: ~ with sb. *about* (或 *over*) sth. 与某人谈判(或协商)某事 ❷ *vt.* ①议定,议妥;通过谈判使…: ~ peace 议和 / ~ a peace treaty 议订和约 / ~ sb. into making concessions 通过谈判使某人作出让步 ②转让; 兑现(票证等) ③处置,处理;解决(难

题等) ④通过,越过(障碍等): ~ rugged mountains and turbulent rivers 越险岭过激流 / ~ a turn 顺利地拐过弯去 ⑤完成(旅程等)

negotiation [ni,gouʃi'eiʃən] n. 谈判, 协商: enter into ~s (或 open ~s) with sb. 开始与某人进行谈判 / the resumption (suspension) of all-round ~s 全面谈判的恢复(中止) / a point of (或 under) ~ 正在谈判中的问题 / be in ~ with sb. over sth. 与某人协商某事

Negro ['ni:grou] I ([复] Negroes) n. ①黑人 ②具有黑人血统的人 II a. ①黑人的: ~ minstrels 黑人(或由其他肤色的人扮作黑人的)歌舞剧 ②黑色的 ||**negro ant** 黑蚁 / **negrohead** n. ①黑色压缩烟砖 ②低劣的橡胶

neigh [nei] I vi. (马)嘶; 发马嘶般的声音 II n. 马嘶声

neighbo(u)r ['neibə] I n. ①邻居; 邻人, 邻座; 邻国; 邻接的东西: next-door ~s 隔壁邻居 / our ~s across the Channel 海峡对面的邻居(英国人用语; 指法国人) / one's immediate ~ in the classroom 上课时紧靠自己坐的人 / a good-~ policy 睦邻政策 / The falling tree brought down its ~. 树在倒下时把旁边那一棵也带倒了。②世人 ③(对不知姓名者的称呼)朋友: Say, ~, give me a hand. 喂, 朋友, 帮我一帮。II a. 邻接的; 邻近的 III ❶ vt. 邻接; 邻接于 ❷ vi. ~ 结邻 ❷ vi.: 住在邻近处; 位于附近 ②友好往来; 有睦邻关系 (with) ||~ed a. 有某种邻居(或环境)的: a beautifully ~ed town 环境优美的市镇 / ~ing ['neibəriŋ] a. 邻近的, 附近的; 接壤的: ~ing villages 邻近的村庄 / ~less a. 无邻居的 / ~ship n. [古]附近; 邻居关系

neighbo(u)rhood ['neibəhud] n. ① 邻接; 邻近; 附近 ②邻居关系 ③四邻, 街坊; 街道, 地区 / The whole ~ is stirred. 整个街坊都动起来了。 / a ~ workshop 街道工厂 ④【数】邻域 ||**in the ~ of** [口] ①在…附近 ②大约

neither ['naiðə, 'ni:ðə] I a. (与单数名词或代词连用)既非此又非彼的, (两者)都不: Neither sentence is correct. 两句句子都不对。/ In ~ case will he come. 不论在哪种情况下他都不会来。 (指两种情况) II pron. 两者中无一: Neither of them was in good health, but both worked very hard.他们两人身体都不好, 但都努力地工作。III conj. 也不: The enemy couldn't make any advance, ~ could they retreat. 敌人进不得, 也退不得。IV ad. ①也不: The first one was not bad, and ~ was the second. 第一个不坏, 第二个也不坏。②[口]也(=either): I don't know that ~. 那个我也不知道。||~ here nor there 见 here / ~ . . . nor . . . 既不…也不…: Neither he nor I know. (或 Neither I nor he knows.) 他和我都不知道。

nem. con. ['nem 'kɔn] [缩][拉] nemine contradicente ['ni:mini: ˌkɔntrədai'senti] 无异议地; 全体一致地 (=no one contradicting): The resolu-

tion was passed nem. con. 决议案无异议地通过。

nemesis ['nemisis] ([复] nemeses ['nemisi:z]) n. ①[N-]【希神】复仇女神, 报应女神 ② 给以报应者; 复仇者; 难以对付的敌手 ③公正的惩罚; 报应

neolithic [ˌni:ou'liθik] a. ①[常作 N-] 新石器时代的 ②过时的

neon ['ni:ən, 'ni:ɔn] n. ①【化】氖 ②氖光灯, 霓虹灯 (=~ lamp 或 ~ light) ③霓虹灯广告牌 (=~ sign) ||~ ribbons [美俚]军功勋章

nephew ['nevju(:), 'nefju(:)] n. ①侄子; 外甥 ②教士的私生子

nepotism ['nepətizəm] n. 重用亲戚, 裙带关系 ||**nepotist** n. 重用亲戚的人

nerve [nə:v] I n. ① 神经 ② [诗]筋, 腱 ③勇敢; 沉着, 果断: a man of ~ 一个有胆量的人 / a task that requires ~ 需要沉着对待的任务 ④ (力量、行动等的)中枢, 核心 ⑤ 力量, 精力; 活力 ⑥[口]厚颜; 鲁莽: Did he have the ~ to say that? 他竟有脸说这话吗? ⑦[复] 神经质, 神经紧张: never know what ~s are 神经从不紧张 / suffer from ~s 有神经质毛病 / have a fit of ~s 发一阵歇斯底里 / a war of ~s 神经战 ⑧痛处; 难弄的问题 ⑨【动】翅脉;【植】脉 II vt. 给…以力量; 给…以勇气 ||**be all ~s** 高度不安, 神经紧张 / **get on sb.'s ~s** [口]使某人心烦, 使某人不安 / **have iron ~s** (或 **have ~s of steel**) 神经坚强, 有胆量 / **lose one's ~** 变得慌张, 不知所措 / **~ oneself** 鼓起勇气, 振作起来: ~ oneself for a difficult task (to face difficulties) 鼓起勇气去做一件困难的工作 (去对付困难) / **regain one's ~** 恢复镇静 / **strain every ~** 竭力 ||~ **cell** 【解】神经细胞 / ~ **centre** ①【解】神经中枢 ② 中枢, 核心 / ~ **fibre** 【解】神经纤维 / ~ **gas** 【军】神经毒气, 中毒性毒气 / ~ **impulse** 【医】神经冲动 / '~-,racking, ',wracking a. 使人心烦的, 伤脑筋的

nerveless ['nə:vlis] a. ①没有劲的; 无生气的 ②(文体) 松散的 ③沉着的, 镇静的 ④【动】无翅脉的; 【植】无叶脉的 ⑤【解】无神经的 ||~ly ad. / ~ness n.

nervous ['nə:vəs] a. ①神经的, 神经方面的: the ~ system of the human body 人体的神经系统 / a ~ breakdown 精神崩溃 ②神经元的, 神经元构成的 ③ 易激动的; 神经质的, 紧张不安的: The patient is in a ~ state. 病人处于神经不安状态。/ feel ~ about (或 at) sth. 为某事而心中忐忑不安 ④胆怯的, 害怕的 (of) ⑤ [古] 强有力的 ⑥(文体等)简练的, 刚劲的 ⑦摇摆不定的: a ~ canoe 摇晃的独木船 ||~ly ad. / ~ness n. ||~ **Nellie** ['neli] 胆子很小的人, 无用的人

nervy ['nə:vi] a. ①易激动的; 紧张不安的 ②镇静的, 有胆量的 ③[俚]厚脸的, 粗鲁的 ④[俚]使人心烦的

nest [nest] I n. ①巢, 窝; 穴 ②安逸的处所; 住所, 家; 荫蔽处: a machine-gun ~ 【军】机枪掩体 ③(盗、贼的)窟; (罪恶等的)渊薮, 温床: a ~ of crime and vice 罪恶的渊薮 ④(盗、贼等的)(一)伙 ⑤(同栖一巢的鸟、昆虫等的)群 ⑥一组同类物件;(相互套得起来的)一套物件: a ~ of tables 套几,一套茶几 ⑦【矿】矿藏 ⑧【建】蜂窝(混凝土缺陷) **II** ❶ *vi.* ①筑巢;巢居 ②找鸟巢,摸鸟蛋: go ~*ing* 摸鸟巢去 ❷ *vt.* ①为…筑巢;把…放入巢中 ②使套入 ‖*a mare's* ~ 幻想的东西,不存在的东西 / *a stolen* ~ 母鸡不在本窝而在别处生的一窝蛋 / *bring* (或 *raise, arouse) a hornets'* ~ *about one's ears* 捅马蜂窝;树敌招怨;惹麻烦 / *feather one's* ~ 营私,自肥 / *foul* (或 *befoul) one's own* ~ 说自己人坏话,家丑外扬 / *stir up* (或 *arouse) a* ~ *of hornets* 捅马蜂窝;树敌招怨;惹麻烦 / *take a* ~ 摸鸟巢,摸取巢中的蛋(或雏) ‖~**er** *n.* ①筑巢的鸟 ②[美方]占据无主牧草地定居下来的自耕农 / ~**ful** *n.* (一)满巢 / ~**like** *a.* 巢状的 ‖~ **egg** ①留窝鸡蛋(引诱母鸡继续把蛋生在窝中之用) ②储备金(或物);继续积累的基础

nestle ['nesl] ❶ *vi.* ①舒适地安顿下来;安卧: ~ down in bed 上床休息 ②偎依: ~ up to sb. 偎依到某人身旁 ③半隐半现地处于: a village *nestling* in the valley 山谷中半隐半现的村庄 ❷ *vt.* ①抱;使紧贴: She ~*d* the child's head close against her. 她把孩子的头紧紧抱在怀里。②使舒适地安顿下来: ~ oneself in bed 安卧在床上

nestling ['neslin] *n.* ①(未离巢的)雏鸟 ②婴儿

net[1] [net] **I** *n.* ①网;网状物: a table-tennis ~ 乒乓球网 / a fishing ~ 渔网 / a mosquito ~ 蚊帐 / be caught in a ~ 落入网中 ②【纺】网眼织物;(花边的)地网 ③罗网: encircle the enemy forces completely and let none escape from the ~ 四面包围敌人不使一个漏网 ④网状系统;通信网: a radar ~ 雷达网 / a radio (communication) ~ 无线电(通信)网 ⑤(乒乓、网球等的)落网球,不过网的球 **II** (netted; netting) *vt.* ①把…编结成网状物;用网制作: ~ a bag 编网袋 ②用网覆盖;用网拦住: ~ fruit trees 用网覆盖果树 / ~ a river 在河里张网捕鱼 ③用网捕: ~ fish 用网捕鱼 ④抓住 ⑤打(球)落网 ❷ *vi.* 编网;结编网状物 ‖~**ful** *n.* (一)满网 / ~**like** *a.* 网状的 ‖~ **ball** 落网球,不过网的球 / '~**ball** *n.* 一种与篮球相近似的球戏

net

net[2] [net] **I** *a.* ①纯净的: a ~ weight 净重 / ~ profit 净利,纯利 / a ~ income 净收益 ②基本的;最后的: the ~ result 最后结果 **II** (netted; netting) *vt.* ①净得,净赚: The sale *netted* £1,000. 这笔买卖净赚一千镑。②得到;使得: ~ sb. a sense of security 使某人获得一种安全感 **III** *n.* ①净数;净重;净价;净值 ②要点,要旨

nether ['neðe] *a.* ①下面的: one's ~ lip 下唇 / ~ garments [谑]裤子 ②地下的: the ~ regions 地狱,阴间 ‖*as hard as a ~ millstone* 铁石心肠 ‖'~**world** *n.* ①阴间 ②下层社会

netting ['netiŋ] *n.* ①网,网状(织)物: wire ~ 金属网 / mosquito ~ 蚊帐纱 ②结网 ③网鱼;捕鱼权

nettle ['netl] **I** *n.* 荨麻; [N-]【植】荨麻属 **II** *vt.* ①以荨麻鞭打;以荨麻刺 ②惹怒,使烦恼: be ~*d* by sth. 因某事着恼 / look ~*d* 表现出恼怒神情 ‖*grasp the* ~ 迎着艰险全上;大胆抓起棘手问题 ‖~**some** ['netlsəm] *a.* 恼人的 ‖~ **rash** 荨麻疹,风疹

network ['netwə:k] **I** *n.* ①【纺】网眼织物 ②网状物,网状系统(如道路网、运河网等): a ~ of railways 铁路网 ③广播网;电视网;广播(或电视)联播公司 ④【无】网络,电路 **II** *a.* 【无】电视网(或电视网)中各台同时播放的 **III** *vt.* ①使组成网状 ②(广播网、电视网)联播;使加入联播公司

neurotic [njuə'rɔtik] **I** *a.* ①神经(机能)病的 ②神经过敏的 **II** *n.* 神经过敏者;神经病患者 ‖~**ally** *ad.*

neuter ['nju:te] **I** *a.* ①【语】(名词等)中性的;(动词)不及物的: the ~ gender 中性 ②【植】【动】无性的;无生殖器的;生殖器发育不完全的 ③中立的: stand ~ 保持中立 **II** *n.* ①【语】中性;中性词;中性形式 ②无性植物(或动物);生殖器发育不完全的动物(如工蜂、工蚁等) ③已阉割的动物 ④守中立的人(或团体) **III** *vi.* 阉割

neutral ['nju:trəl] **I** *a.* ①中立的;中立国的: remain ~ 保持中立 / a ~ nation 中立国 / ~ ships 中立国船只 ②非彩色的(指黑、灰或中色的,尤指灰色的): ~ tints (各种)灰色 ③【植】【动】无性的;被阉割过的;生殖器发育不完全的 ④【化】中性的;【电】不带电的: ~ reaction 【化】中性反应 ⑤【语】(元音)松弛的,中性的 **II** *n.* ①中立者;中立国 ②中立国的国民 ③非彩色(指黑、灰或白色,尤指灰色) ③【机】空档(指传动装置空转状态): slip the gear into ~ 拉到空档 ‖~**ly** *ad.* / ~**ness** *n.*

neutrality [nju(:)'træliti] *n.* ①中立;中立地位: declare ~ 宣布中立 / maintain strict ~ 严守中立 / armed ~ 武装中立 ②中性

neutralize ['nju:trəlaiz] ❶ *vt.* ①使中立化 ②使成为无效;抵销;【军】压制(火力) ③【化】【电】使中和 ❷ *vi.* ①中立化 ②成为无效 ③中和

never ['neve] *ad.* ①永不,决不;从来没有 ②不,没有 (=not,但语气较强);不要 (=do not,

但语气较强）: He ~ said (或 said ~) a word the whole two hours. 整整两个小时他一句话也没有说。/ *Never fear.* 别怕。/ *Never mind.* 没关系。③[口][表示惊异或不信]不会…吧; 不可能…吧: You ~ left the key in the lock! 你总不会把钥匙留在锁上吧。/ A: He beat me 21-2. B: *Never!* 甲: 他以二十一比二把我打败了。乙: 不可能吧。‖*Better late than* ~. 见 late / ~ *a one* 没有一个(人) (=none) / *Never is a long word* (或 *day*). 不要轻易讲"决不"。(指不要轻易放弃、绝望或作否定的预测) / *Never say die.* 不要失望。/ He ~ *so much as* winked. 他连眼也没眨一下。/ ~ *the* [后接比较级]毫不(更…): For all your advice I am ~ *the* wiser. 虽然有你的指点, 我还是(和以前一样)莫名其妙。/ *Now or* ~! 见 now / *Well, I* ~ (*did*)! (表示惊讶)我真没想到过(或听到过、见过等)! ‖'~-ending *a.* 永远不会完结的 / '~-'failing *a.* (友谊、恩惠等)永远不变的, 永不辜负期望的 / '~-get-'overs [复] *n.* [美俚]不治之症 / '~-'setting *a.* 永远不落的 / '~-to-be-for'gotten *a.* 永远不会被遗忘的 / '~-was ([复] ~-weres) *n.* [美俚]从未取得成功的人

nevermore ['nevə'mɔ:] *ad.* 永不再, 决不再

nevertheless [,nevəðə'les] **I** *conj.* 然而, 不过: The news may be unexpected; ~, it is true. 这消息可能是出乎意料的, 然而是真实的。**II** *ad.* 仍然, 不过: He succeeded ~. 不过他还是成功了。

nevus ['ni:vəs] ([复] nevi ['ni:vai]) *n.* =naevus [医]痣

new [nju:] **I** *a.* ①新的: ~ people and ~ things 新人新事 / take on a completely ~ look 呈现出全新的面貌 ②新近出现的; 新制成的; 新就任的: ~ peas 新摘的豌豆 / the ~ poor [总称]新近沦为贫民的人 / a young worker ~ from school 新从学校出来的青年工人 / a ~ 10,000-tonner 新造成的万吨轮 ③ 精神恢复了的, 健康恢复了的; 改变了的: Rest has made him a ~ man. 休息后他恢复过来了。④新发现的: a ~ chemical element 新发现的化学元素 / This is ~ to me. 这一点我现在才知道。⑤ (土地)新开发的 ⑥重新开始的, 周而复始的: Let's make a ~ start. 我们重新开始吧。/ the ~ moon 新月 / Another ~ day dawned. 又是新的一天开始了。⑦ 不熟悉的, 不习惯的; 没经验的: Though he is ~ to the work (或 Though the work is ~ to him), he is doing it very well. 他虽然对这项工作没经验, 却干得很出色。⑧另加的, 附加的 ⑨[N-] (语言)中世纪以来所用的, 现代的: New Greek 现代希腊语 **II** *ad.* [常用以构成复合词]新; 最近: ~-built 新建的 / the threshing ground ~ washed by rain 新近为雨水冲洗过的打谷场 **III** *a.* 新的东西; 新: wear the ~ off the shoes 把鞋穿旧 ‖**~ness** *n.* ‖'~-blown *a.* (花)新开的 / '~born *a.* ①新生的: a ~born child

新生婴儿 / the ~born period 初生阶段 / vigorous ~born things 生气勃勃的新生事物 ②再生的 *n.* ([复] ~born(s)) 新生者 / '~-build *vt.* 重建 / ~ chum ①[主澳]新的移民(尤指来自英伦三岛者) ②[美俚]新手 / '~-coined *a.* (尤指词)新造出来的 / '~comer *n.* 新来的人; 移民; 新手 / ~ deal 新政 / ~ dealer 主张实行新政者 / '~,fangled *a.* ①新花样的, 新奇的: ~fangled gadgets 新奇的小玩意儿 ②爱好新奇的 / '~'fashioned *a.* 新式的; 新流行的; 入时的 / '~'found *a.* 新发现的 / '~-front *vt.* 给…装上新门面 / '~,furnish *vt.* 为(房间等)重新配上家具 / '~-,laid *a.* (蛋)才生下来的 / New Left "新左派"(二十世纪六十年代起源于美国, 以学生为主体) / New Look [美俚](头发、衣服等的)时髦式样 / '~'made *a.* 新做的 / '~-'model *vt.* 改组; 改建 / '~'mown *a.* ①新割下来的: ~mown hay 新割下来的干草 ②(草地等)新近才割过草的 / '~-rich *n.* 新发迹的人 *a.* 新发迹的; 暴发户的 / New Testament (基督教《圣经》的)《新约全书》 / '~-type *a.* 新型的 / ~ wave [常作 N- W-] 新浪潮 / ~ woman 新女性(尤指十九世纪末反抗传统势力的女子) / New World 西半球; 美洲 / New Year 新年: New Year's Day 元旦 / New Year's Eve 除夕 / I wish you a happy New Year! 祝你新年好!

newly ['nju:li] *ad.* ①新近, 最近: a ~ built plant 一座新建的工厂 ② 重新; 以新的方式: a ~ arranged reception room 重新布置过的接待室 ‖'~wed *n.* 新结婚的人

news [nju:z] [复] *n.* [用作单] ①新闻, 消息; 新闻报道: the latest ~ 最新消息 / Any ~? 有什么新闻吗?(英美人同事间见面时的常用语) / a piece (some pieces) of good ~ 一(几)个好消息 / Here is the ~. (广播用语)现在报告新闻。/ That's (no) ~ to me. 那对我(不)是新闻。/ grapevine ~ 小道新闻 ②[N-] (作报刊名用)…报: ... Daily News 《…日报》‖be in the ~ 在新闻报道中出现, 被报道 / break the ~ to sb. 把坏消息告诉某人 / Good ~ goes on crutches. [谚]好事不出门。/ Ill ~ flies apace. [谚]坏事传千里。/ No ~ is good ~. [谚]没有消息就是好消息。(因坏消息传得快,所以没有消息就表示没有坏事发生) ‖~less *a.* 没有新闻的 ‖~ agency 通讯社 / '~,agent *n.* [英]报刊经售人 / '~ analyst *n.* 新闻分析员, 评论员 / '~ beat *n.* 新闻记者的采访区域 / '~ boy *n.* 报童 / '~cast *n.* 新闻广播 / '~,caster *n.* 新闻广播员, 评论员 / '~,casting *n.* & *a.* 新闻广播(的) / ~ cinema (放映新闻片、动画片等的)新闻电影院 / ~ conference 记者招待会 / ~ dealer [美]报刊经售人 / ~ film 新闻短片 / '~flash *n.* 简短的新闻报道 / '~hawk, '~hound *n.* [美俚]新闻记者 / '~hen *n.* [美俚]女新闻记者 / '~letter *n.* ①定期出版的时事

通讯，新闻信札 ②(公司等刊印的)业务通讯 / '~‚magazine n. (一般为每周出版的)新闻杂志，时事刊物 / '~man n. ①卖报人;送报人 ②新闻记者 / '~‚monger n. 传播新闻的人;饶舌的人 / '~print n. 新闻纸,白报纸 / '~reel n. 新闻短片 / '~room n. ①(报馆、广播电台或电视台的)新闻编辑室 ②(图书馆等的)报刊阅览室 ③报刊出售室 / ~'sheet n. ①单张报纸 ②=~letter / ~ stall [英] =~stand / '~stand n. 报摊;报刊柜 / ~ theatre =~ cinema / ~ vendor 卖报人 / ~ window 新闻图片栏 / '~‚worthy a. 有新闻价值的,值得报道的

newspaper ['nju:s‚peipe] **I** n. ①报纸,报: run a ~ well 办好报 ②新闻纸,白报纸 ③[美俚]监禁三十天的判决 || a daily ~ 日报 / a ~ office 报社 / a ~ report 新闻报道 / the ~ world 新闻界 **II** vi. 从事报纸工作(可指办报、编辑、采访等) ||'~man n. 新闻记者 / '~‚woman n. 女新闻记者

next [nekst] **I** a. ①紧接(在后面)的,其次的: Let's take the ~ train. 咱们搭下一班火车吧。/ the ~ two chapters 以下的两章 / the ~ page before 前一页 ②贴近的;隔壁的: the house ~ to ours 我们隔壁的那所房子 ③紧接着来到的;下(年、月、日等): We'll celebrate National Day ~ Friday (或 on Friday ~). 下个星期五我们将庆祝国庆。/ (the) ~ week (year) 下星期(明年) / the week (year) after ~ 下下星期(年) / The harvest will have been got in (the) ~ time you come. 你下次来的时候,庄稼将已收好了。④ [the ~] 任何别的: He can swim as well as the ~ boy. 他游泳游得象其他男孩一样好。**II** ad. ①其次;然后: What comes ~? 接下去是什么? (或: 接下去干什么?) / the ~ tallest boy 第二个最高的男孩 ②贴近: the house standing ~ to the hospital 医院隔壁的那幢房子 ③下次: When shall we meet ~? 下一次我们什么时候见面? **III** prep. 靠近,贴近: sit ~ sb. 坐在某人旁边 / wear a shirt ~ one's skin 贴身穿衬衫 **IV** n. 下一个人(或物): Next, please! 下一位! (或: 请提出下一个问题!) / I'll tell you in my ~. 我将在下一封信里告诉你。/ to be continued in our ~ (杂志等用语)下期续登 ||get ~ to sb. [俚]讨好某人;与某人接近 / in the ~ place 其次,第二点 / ~ door 见 door / ~ door to 见 door / ~ of kin 见 kin / ~ to 几乎: He has eaten ~ to nothing. 他几乎什么也没吃。/ the ~ best 仅次于最好的 / the ~ but one 下下个 / What ~? ①(店员用语)还要什么? ②还有比这更荒唐(或更料想不到)的吗? ||~ friend 【律】未成年人或其他无行为能力者的诉讼代理人

nib [nib] **I** n. ①鹅毛管笔笔尖;钢笔尖 ②(鸟的)嘴 ③(工具等的)尖头,尖端 ④(大镰刀的)短柄 ⑤[复]咖啡(或可可豆)的碎粒 **II** (nibbed; nibbing) vt. 削尖(鹅管笔);修(笔)尖;在(笔杆)上装笔尖

nibble ['nibl] **I** ❶ vt. 啃,一点一点地咬(或吃);一点一点地去掉 ❷ vi. ①啃,一点一点地咬(或吃);小心谨慎地对付(或进攻) (at): nibbling operations 【军】蚕食活动 ②吹毛求疵,找错儿 (at) ③[喻](对交易、建议、诱惑等)显出有意接受的样子 (at) **II** n. ①啃;轻咬 ②咬一口的量;很少量

nice [nais] a. ①美好的,合宜的,令人愉快的;和蔼的,友好的: ~ weather 好天气 / be ~ to sb. 对某人友好 ②有教养的;贞洁的;正派的: a ~ girl 好姑娘 / a ~ guy 好人(尤指正派可靠) / It's not ~ of little boys to do such things. 小孩子做这种事可不好。/ be not over ~ in one's dealings 行事不太老实 ③须慎重对待的;微妙的;细微的: a ~ experiment 需要谨慎进行的试验 / a ~ question 微妙的问题 / There is a ~ distinction between these two words. 这两个字有着细微的区别。④细心的; 精密的; 慎重的: a ~ observer 细心的观察者 / a ~ ear for sound 敏锐的听觉 / the ~ handling of a difficult matter 对困难问题所作的慎重处理 ⑤挑剔的,难以满足的: be very ~ in one's food 对吃的东西挑三拣四 ⑥拘泥的;多考虑的: be too ~ about form 太拘泥于形式 ⑦[反语]困难的; 糟透的: get oneself in a ~ fix 使自己处于困境 ||more ~ than wise 因要面子而损害自己的实际利益 / ~ and 很,挺: It feels ~ and soft. 这东西摸上去挺软。/ The bus is running ~ and fast. 这辆公共汽车跑得挺快。/ weigh sth. in the ~st scales 见 scale[2] ||'~ness n. ||'~-looking a. 好看的,漂亮的 / ~ Nelly ['neli] ①装得规规矩矩的人 ②委婉语 / '~-‚Nelly a. ①装得规矩的②委婉的

nicely ['naisli] **I** ad. ①恰好地: fit ~ 恰恰合适 ②谨慎地;拘泥地 ③令人满意地;令人愉快地;很好地: The patient is doing ~. 病人情况进展良好。**II** [主方] a. 健康的

nicety ['naisiti] n. ①美好,优美;优美的东西 ②准确,精确: ~ of one's powers of observation 精确的观察力 ③微妙: a question of great ~ 极为微妙的问题 ④ [常用复]细微的区别; 细节: observe niceties of syntax 注意句法上细微之处 ⑤拘泥;挑剔 ||to a ~ 精细入微地;恰到好处地: The character of the hero is depicted to a ~. 英雄的性格刻划得很细腻。

niche [nitʃ] **I** n. ①壁龛(放置雕像、花瓶等的墙壁凹入处) ②合适的职务(或地位等) ③[生]小生境 **II** vt. ①[常用被动语态] 把(雕像等)放在壁龛中 ② [~ oneself 或用被动语态] 把…安顿(在适当位置) ||have a ~ in the temple of fame 留芳百世

nick [nik] **I** n. ①槽口;刻痕;裂口;缺口 ②[印]铅字边的凹槽 ③(骰子赌博中)赢的一掷 ④[俚]监狱 **II** ❶ vt. ①刻痕于;弄缺(刀口等)用刻痕记(数);摘记: ~ a tree as signal 在树上刻痕作为记号 ②割短(马尾等);浅刻 ③(恰好)赶上,赶

中, 猜中: ~ it 猜中, 说中 / ~ an opportunity 抓住机会 / ~ a train 赶上火车 ④(掷骰子)掷出(赢的点子) ⑤[英俚]逮捕 ⑥[俚]诈骗 ❷ **vi.** ①狙击 ②杂交(产生良种) ③(赛跑、打猎中)抄近路追过 ‖**in the ~ (of time)** 正是时候, 正在关键时刻

nickel ['nikl] **I** *n.* ①[化]镍: ~ silver 德银(镍铜锌合金) / ~ steel 镍钢 ②(美国和加拿大的)五分镍币 (=nickle) **II** *vt.* 把…镀镍 ‖***Don't take any wooden ~s.*** [美俚](告别时叮咛用)当心别找麻烦。‖~ **note** [美俚]五元的钞票 / ~ **nurser**[美俚]守财奴 / '**~-plate** *vt.* 把…镀镍

nickname ['nikneim] **I** *n.* ①绰号, 浑名 ②教名的略称(或爱称) **II** *vt.* ①给…起绰号 ②以绰号(或爱称)称呼 ②[罕]误称: ~ patience cowardice 把忍耐说成是怯懦

nicotine['nikəti:n]*n.*【化】烟碱, 尼古丁: ~-stained fingers 被尼古丁熏黄的手指

niece [ni:s] *n.* 侄女; 甥女

niggardly ['nigədli] **I** *a.* ①小气的, 吝啬的 ②很少量的: a ~ sum 少得可怜的数目 **II** *ad.* 吝啬地 ‖**niggardliness** *n.*

nigh [nai] **I** *ad.* ①(地点、时间、关系等)(接)近地, 靠近地 (on, onto): for ~ on forty years 将近四十年之久 ②几乎 **II** *a.* ①(接)近的; 亲密的 ②[主方]直接的, 短的: take a ~ cut 抄近路 ③在左侧的: the ~ horse 在左边的那匹马 ④[主方]吝啬的 **III** *prep.* (接)近 **IV** *vi.* & *vt.* [古]接近, 靠近

night [nait] *n.* ①夜, 夜间: in the stillness of the ~ 夜阑人静时 / We saw the play on the first ~. 这戏上演的第一夜我们就看了。/ ~ operations 【军】夜战 ②黑夜, 黑暗: go out into the ~ 走向夜晚的黑暗里去 / under cover of ~ 在黑夜掩护下; 趁黑夜 ③夜晚的活动(如晚会、游戏等) ④黑夜般的状况; 黑暗时期; 悲伤的时刻; 死亡: be wrapped in the ~ of ignorance 处于蒙昧无知状态 ⑤黄昏 (=~fall) ‖*a dirty ~* 雨夜, 暴风雨之夜 / *all ~ (long)* 整夜: The nurse sat by the patient *all ~ (long).* 护士整夜守在病人身旁。/ *as black (或 dark) as ~* 昏黑, 漆黑 / *at ~* ①天黑时; 在夜里 ②(用于下午六时至午夜的时间词组后)晚上…: 6 o'clock *at ~* 晚上六点钟 / *at ~s* 在夜里经常…: have dreams *at ~s* 夜里常做梦 / *a white ~* 失眠之夜; 【天】白夜 / *by ~* 在夜间; 趁黑夜 / *Good ~!* 晚安! 再会! (晚上分别时用语) / *have a good (bad) ~* 一夜睡得好(不好) / *have a ~ out* (或 *off*) 在外玩一晚上; 一个晚上不上班 / *make a ~ of it* 痛快地玩一晚上, 通宵宴庆 / *~ after ~* 一夜又一夜地, 日以继夜地, 日夜不停地 / *o'* (=on) *~s* [口]在夜晚; 晚上经常: can't sleep *o' ~s* 晚上经常不能入睡 / *sb.'s ~ to howl* 任某人尽情欢乐的时候 / *turn ~ into day* 以黑夜当白昼 (指把一般是在白天做的事放在晚上做) / *under ~* 乘黑夜; 秘密 / *What is done

by ~ appears by day.* [谚]若要人不知, 除非己莫为。‖'**~-bell** *n.* 夜间用的门铃 / ~ **bird** ①夜间活动的鸟(尤指猫头鹰、夜莺) ②晚睡者 ③夜出活动 (常指做坏事) 的人 / ~ **blindness** 【医】夜盲(症), 昼视症 / ~ **bomber** 【军】夜间轰炸机 / '**~cap** *n.* ①睡帽 ②临睡前喝的酒 ③一天中的最后一场比赛 / ~ **cart** 粪车 / ~ **cellar** 低级的地下室酒店 / '**~clothes** [复] *n.* 睡衣 / '**~club** *n.* 夜总会 / ~ **court** (办理即决刑事案件的)夜间法庭 / ~ **crawler** 晚上爬出来的大蚯蚓 / ~ **crow** 夜啼鸟(尤指夜鹭) / '**~dress** *n.* 妇女(或孩子)穿的睡衣 / '**~fall** *n.* 黄昏 / '**~flower** *n.* 夜里开的花 / '**~ glass(es)**, ~ **binoculars** 夜用望远镜 / '**~gown** *n.* = ~ **dress** / ~ **hag** ① 夜间飞行空中的女魔 ② 梦魇 / '**~hawk** *n.* ①(北美产的)夜鹰 ②=~jar ③晚睡的人 ④夜间服务的出租汽车 ⑤牧场的夜工(尤指看马人) ⑥夜间行窃(或干其他坏事)的人 / ~ **heron** 【动】夜鹭 / '**~jar** *n.* 【动】欧夜鹰 / ~ **key** 弹子门锁的钥匙 / ~ **landing** 【军】夜间着陆; 夜间登陆 / '**~latch**, ~ **lock** 弹子门锁 / ~ **letter**, ~ **lettergram** (减价收费的)夜间电报, 夜信电(电报局用语, 常用缩写 NLT) / ~ **life** 夜生活(指在夜总会等处的活动) / '**~-light** *n.* 夜灯 (通常指为病人等通宵点着的小支光灯或蜡烛) / ~ **line** (连饵留在水中过夜的)夜钓绳 / '**~long** *a.* & *ad.* 通宵的(地) / ~ **man** *n.* ①掏粪工(一般在夜里工作) ②[也作 ~ man]夜间工作的人(特指夜看守) / ~ **mare** ['naitmɛə] *n.* ① 梦魇; 恶梦 ② 经常的恐惧; 可怕的事物 / '**~marish** ['naitmɛəriʃ] *a.* ①梦魇似的 ②经常使人恐惧的; 可怕的 / ~ **owl** ①猫头鹰 ②晚睡的人 / ~ **piece** 夜景(画); 以夜景为题材的诗文 / ~ **porter** (旅馆门口搬行李的)夜班侍者 / ~ **raid** 【军】夜间空袭; 夜间袭击 / ~ **rider** (美国南部)夜间蒙面骑马从事恐怖活动的秘密组织成员 / ~ **school** 夜校 / '**~shade** *n.* 茄属植物 (如龙葵、颠茄、天仙子等) / ~ **shift** ①夜班 ②[总称]夜班工人 / '**~shirt** *n.* 男用长睡衣 / ~ **soil** 大粪(通常夜间取走) / ~ **stick** *n.* [美]警棍(尤指夜间用的) / '**~stool** *n.* 便桶 / '**~stop** *vi.* (长途飞行飞机在机场等)停飞过夜 / ~ **stop** (长途飞行飞机的)夜停 / ~ **suit** (一套)睡衣 / ~ **sweat** 盗汗 / '**~tide** *n.* ①[诗] =~time ②夜潮 / '**~time** *n.* 夜间: in the ~*time* 在夜间 / '**~walker** *n.* ①晚上爬出来的大蚯蚓 ②梦游病患者 ③晚上行窃者 ④妓女 / ~ **watch** ①守夜, 值夜 ②值夜的人们 ③值夜时间 ④[常用复]值夜的班次(古代希伯来人和罗马人把一夜分成三至四班): in the ~ *watches* 在夜晚焦虑之际不能成寐之际 / ~ **watcher** 守夜的人, 值夜的人 / ~ **watchman** (专职的)守夜人 / '**~wear** *n.* [总称]睡衣 / ~ **work** *n.* (必须在)晚上干的活, 夜间工作, 夜工

nightingale ['naitiŋgeil] *n.* ①夜莺, 哥鸲 ②(泛指)夜间鸣叫的鸟

nightly ['naitli] **I** *a.* ①晚上的, 夜间的 ②每夜的: *Nightly* visits are made by the house physicians. 住院医师每夜查病房。③[诗]夜的, 适于夜晚的 **II** *ad.* 在夜间; 每夜

nil [nil] *n.* 无, 零: three goals to ～ (球赛中)三比零 / The result of the game was 3—0 (读作 three-nil 或 three-nothing). 比赛结果是三比零.

nimble ['nimbl] *a.* ① 灵活的, 敏捷的: ～ fingers 灵巧的手指 / a ～ leap 轻捷的一跃 ② 聪明的, 机智的, 多才的: have a ～ tongue 能说会道 / a ～ reply 巧妙的回答 ‖*(as)* ～ *as a squirrel* 身手灵活, 举动轻捷 ‖**～ness** *n.* / **nimbly** *ad.* ‖'～-'witted *a.* 聪敏的, 机智的

nincompoop ['ninkəmpu:p] *n.* 傻子; 无用的人

nine [nain] **I** *num.* 九; 九个(人或物); 第九(卷、章、页等)(用例参看 **eight**) **II** *n.* ①九个(人或物)一组(尤指棒球队) ②[the N-]【希神】九个文艺女神 ③九岁 ④九点钟 ‖*A cat has ～ lives.* [谚]猫有九命. (指生命力强) / *a ～ days' wonder* 轰动一时(便被遗忘)的事物 / *～ tenths* 十之八九, 几乎全部 / *～ times out of ten* 几乎每次, 十之八九, 常常 / *Possession is ～ points of the law.* [谚]占有者在诉讼中总占上风. / *to the ～* 完美(特别用于下面的短语中): dressed up *to the ～s* 打扮得极为华丽 ‖**'～fold** *a. & ad.* 九倍; 九重 ‖'**～holes** [复] *n.* [用作单] ①九孔戏 ②困境: in the ～*holes* 处于困境 / '**～pin** *n.* 九柱戏的木柱; [～pins] [用作单] 九柱戏: fall (或 be knocked) over like ～*pins* 东倒西歪

nineteen ['nain'ti:n] **I** *num.* 十九; 十九个(人或物); 第十九(卷、章、页等)(用例参看 **eight**) **II** *n.* ①十九岁 ②十九点钟(即下午七点) ‖*talk* (或 *speak*) *～ to the dozen* 喋喋不休

ninetieth ['naintiiθ] *num.* ①第九十(个) ②九十分之一(的)

ninety ['nainti] **I** *num.* 九十; 九十个(人或物); 第九十(页等)(用例参看 **eight**) **II** *n.* 九十岁 ‖**～-nine out of a hundred** 百分之九十九, 几乎全部

nip[1] [nip] **I** (nipped; nipping) ❶ *vt.* ①夹, 钳, 掐, 捏, 咬: ～ a child between one's knees 把孩子夹在双膝当中 / get one of the fingers *nipped* in the door 一个手指被门轧住 ②剪断, 夹断; 摘取 ③阻止, 制止; 使受挫折 ④(风、霜等)摧残; 冻伤 ⑤[俚]攫夺; 偷 ❷ *vi.* ①夹, 钳, 掐, 捏, 咬 ②(寒冷等)刺骨: The wind ～s pretty hard today. 今天寒风刺骨。③[英口]敏捷地走, 飞快地跑 (*off, away, about*); 跳, 跃: ～ *off* 急忙离开 / ～ *along* 快速前进 / ～ *on* (*out of*) a bus 跳上(下)公共汽车 **II** *n.* ①夹, 钳, 掐, 捏, 咬; 被掐(或咬)下的东西 ②寒冷: There is a ～ in the air. 天气冷飕飕。③讥刺 ④(乳酪的)刺鼻的气味 ⑤少量: a ～ of cheese 少量乳酪 ‖*～ and tuck* 势均力敌, 不相上下: a ～ and tuck contest 一场势均力敌的比赛 / *～ in* [英口]①飞快地跑进来 ②插嘴 / *～ in the bud* (或 *blossom*)

见 **bud**[1] ‖'*～-up* *n.* (从仰卧姿势)一跃而起

nip[2] [nip] **I** *n.* 一小口(酒), 一呷: take a ～ of whisky 呷一口威士忌酒 **II** (nipped; nipping) *vi.* 喝一小口酒

nipple ['nipl] *n.* ①乳头; 橡皮奶头; 奶头罩 ②(皮肤、金属、玻璃面等的)乳头状隆起 ③【机】螺纹接套; 喷灯嘴: close ～ 螺纹接口(管) ④【军】(枪炮的)火门

nitric ['naitrik] *a.* (含)氮的: ～ acid 硝酸 / ～ oxide 氧化一氮

nitrogen ['naitridʒen] *n.* 【化】氮: ～ fixation process 固氮法 / ～ monoxide 一氧化二氮 / ～ oxide 氧化氮 / ～ mustard gas [军]氮化芥子气

nitroglycerine ['naitrou-glisə'ri:n] *n.* 【化】硝化甘油

No 【化】元素锘(nobelium)的符号

no [nou] **I** *a.* ①没有: There are ～ clouds in the sky. 天上没有云。②很少, 很小: They finished the task in ～ time. 他们很快就完成了任务。/ It's ～ distance to the post office. 到邮局没有多少路。③并非, 决非: This is ～ trifle. 这可不是一件小事。/ He is ～ poet. 他根本不是诗人。④[用于下列省略结构或固定结构中]不许; 没有; 不要: *No* admittance except on business. 非公莫入。/ *No* thoroughfare. 此路不通。/ a ～ confidence vote 不信任投票 / ～ gains. [谚]不劳则无获。/ in a state of "～ war, ～ peace" 处于"不战不和"的状态 / There is ～ smoke without fire. [谚]无风不起浪。/ It's raining hard and ～ mistake. 雨的确下得很大嘛。⑤[用于 there is ～ ... ing 结构中]不可能: *There is ～* denying (the fact) that . . . . ……(这个事实)是不能否认的。/ *There was ～* knowing when he would be back. 无法知道他什么时候回来。**II** *ad.* ①[用在形容词、副词的比较级前]并不, 毫不: We went ～ farther than the bridge. 我们走到桥边就不再往前了。②[用以表示否定的回答]不, 不是 (yes 之对): A: Do you smoke? B: *No*, I don't. 甲: 你抽烟吗? 乙: 不, 我不抽。[注意: 回答反问句时, yes 和 no 的用法和汉语习惯不同。如: A: You don't smoke, I suppose? B: *No*, I don't. 甲: 你不抽烟吧? 乙: 是的, 我不抽。/ A: Isn't this book yours? B: *No*, it isn't. 甲: 这本书不是你的吗? 乙: 是的, 这本书不是我的。] ③[用以加强否定语气]不: I don't believe it, ～, not I. 我不相信这事, 不, 我才不信哩! ④[用以表示惊奇、怀疑或不信]不: `A: He left yesterday. B: *No*! A: Yes, he did. 甲: 他昨天走了。乙: 不会吧! 甲: 他是走了。⑤[用于 or 之后]…与否: Pleasant *or* ～, the news is true. 不管是好是坏, 反正消息是真的。⑥[用于委婉的说法中]不, 并非: in ～ smal measure 在不小的程度上 / in ～ uncertain terms 用十分明确的言词 **III** ([复] no(e)s) **n.** ①不, 拒绝; 否定, 否认: will not take ～ for an answer 不许别人回答个"不"字 / Two ～es make a yes. 否定的否定就是肯定。②反对票; 反对的决定 ③[复]投反对票者: The ～es had it. 投反对票者得胜。‖～ less (than) 见 less / ～ longer 见 long[1] / ～ more 见 more / say ～ (to) 拒绝(…), 不批准(…); 否认(…) ‖～-ac'count, '～-'count **a.** & **n.** 无价值的(人), 不足道的(人) / '～-,being **n.** 不存在 / '～-'good **a.** 无价值的, 无用的; 无希望的: It's ～-good waiting. 等待是没用的。**n.** 无用的人(或物) / '～-man **n.** 惯常反对别人意见(或拒绝别人要求)的人(yes-man 之对) / '～-'man's-land **n.** ①荒地 ②无主土地; 所有权争执未定的土地 ③【军】真空地带, 人无地带 / '～-'nonsense **a.** 不胡闹的; 讲究实际的; 严肃的 / '～-'show **n.** 在火车(或轮船、飞机)上预订了座位而未到的人 / '～-'trump **n.** (桥牌)"无将","无主";一手打"无将"的牌 / ～-'trumper **n.** (桥牌)一手(可)打"无将"的牌 / ～ whit [作状语用,常用在比较级前]并不,一点也不

noble ['noubl] **I a.** ①贵族的; 显贵的(指贵族出身、称号、头衔等) ②(品质、思想等)高尚的, 崇高的: a ～ mind 崇高的思想 / a ～ deed 高尚的行为 ③壮丽的, 宏伟的: a ～ view 壮观的景色(或场面) / a ～ edifice 宏伟的大厦 / The whole project is planned on a ～ scale. 整个工程计划十分宏伟。④极好的, 杰出的: a ～ horse 骏马 ⑤(金属)贵重的; (气体)惰性的: ～ metals 贵金属(指金、银、铂等) **II n.** ①贵族 ②古时一种英国金币(相当于英国旧币六先令八便士) ③[美俚]雇来破坏罢工的工贼头子 ‖～ness **n.** ‖～-art, ～man 拳击 / ～man ['noublmən] **n.** 贵族 / '～-'minded **a.** 思想高尚的 / '～,woman **n.** 女贵族

nobly ['noubli] **ad.** ①高贵地; 高尚地; 豪侠地, 豁达地 ②壮丽地, 宏伟地 ③出身于贵族: ～ born 出身贵族的

nobody ['noubədi] **I pron.** 谁也不; 没有人, 无人: There is ～ there. 那儿一个人也没有。/ Nobody else but I went. 除我以外, 谁也没去。**II n.** 无足轻重的人, 小人物: a mere ～ 一个微不足道的无名小卒 / "somebodies" and "nobodies" "大人物"和"小人物" ‖～ home [美俚](作感叹语用)愚蠢, 低能

nocturnal [nɔk'tə:nl] **a.** ①夜的; 夜间发生的; 夜间开放的; 夜间活动的, 夜出的: a ～ journey 夜间旅行 ②【音】夜曲的 ‖～ity [,nɔktə:'næliti] **n.** 夜间活动性 / ～ly **ad.**

nod [nɔd] **I** (nodded; nodding) **❶ vi.** ①点头(表示同意或打招呼等): ～ in approval 点头表示赞

同 / ～ to sb. in greeting 向某人点头打招呼 ②打盹, 瞌睡: The child sat nodding by his side. 孩子坐在他旁边打瞌睡。③不当心而弄错 ④(树梢、花等)上下(或前后)摆动; (建筑物等)倾斜 **❷ vt.** ①点(头) ②点头表示; 向…点头示意: He nodded approval (agreement). 他点头表示赞同(同意)。/ ～ sb. a welcome 向某人点头表示欢迎 / ～ sb. back 点头示意某人回来 **II n.** ①点头: give sb. a ～ 向某人点头 ②打盹, 瞌睡 ③(树梢等的)上下(或前后)摆动 ④(点头表示)同意: give a plan the ～ 同意一个计划 ‖a nodding acquaintance 点头之交 / A ～ is as good as a wink to a blind horse. 对瞎马点头和眨眼是一样的。(指反正都看不见) / be at (或 be dependent on) sb.'s ～ 看某人点头而定, 受某人支配 / have a nodding acquaintance with ①和…有点头之交 ②对…略知一二 / Homer sometimes ～s. [谚] 智者千虑, 必有一失。/ ～ to its fall 摇摇欲坠 / on the ～ [俚] 赊购 / the Land of Nod (或 the land of Nod) 睡乡

noel [nou'el] **n.**【基督教】① [N-] 圣诞节 ②庆祝耶稣诞辰的欢呼声; 圣诞颂歌

noise [nɔiz] **I n.** ①喧闹声, 嘈杂声: Don't make so much ～. 不要这样吵闹。/ There was a great ～ over there. 那边嘈杂极了。②响声; 不寻常的声音: the ～ of the rain 雨声 / Do you hear those (queer) ～s? 你听到那些不寻常的声音吗? ③噪声, 杂音: a ～ suppressor 噪声遏抑器 / the urban ～ problem 城市噪音问题 / the ～ rules (主管当局对飞机、车辆等所作的)噪音规定 **II ❶ vt.** 哄传, 谣传: It was ～d about that …. 外界谣传说… **❷ vi.** ①大声讲话 ②喧闹 ‖a big ～ [俚] ①耸人听闻的声明(或事实) ②有影响的人物; 有势力的人物 ③重磅炸弹 / make a ～ (about sth.) (为某事而)吵吵嚷嚷 / make a ～ in the world 名噪一时 ‖～ful **a.** 喧闹的 / ‖～,maker **n.** 发出嘈杂声的人; 发噪音器(尤指狂欢等时用来凑热闹的汽车喇叭、铃铛等) / ～ pollution 噪音污染 (指汽车、喷气机等的噪音危害) / '～'proof **a.** 防杂音的, 隔音的

noiseless ['nɔizlis] **a.** 无声的; 声音很轻的: a ～ typewriter 无声打字机 ‖～ly **ad.** / ～ness **n.**

noisome ['nɔisəm] **a.** ①有害的, 有毒的 ②恶臭的 ③可厌的, 令人不快的 ‖～ly **ad.** / ～ness **n.**

noisy ['nɔizi] **a.** ①嘈杂的, 喧闹的; 熙熙攘攘的 ②(颜色、服装等)过分鲜艳的; (文体)过分渲染的 ‖noisily **ad.** / noisiness **n.**

nomad ['nɔmæd] **I n.** ①游牧民中的一员 ②流浪者 **II a.** ①游牧的 ②流浪的 ‖～ism **n.** ①游牧生活 ②流浪生活

nomadic [nou'mædik] **a.** ①游牧的; 游牧生活的: a ～ tribe 游牧部落 ②流浪的; 流浪生活的

nomenclature [nou'menklətʃə] **n.** ①名称, 术语: the ～ of biology 生物学的专门名词 ②命名(过程), 命名法 ③(某一学科的)术语表, 术语集

nominal ['nominl] **I** *a.* ①名义上的,有名无实的: a ~ director 挂名的主任 / the ~ value of the shares 股票的票面价值 ②名字的,列名的: a ~ list of the personnel 人员名单 ③【语】名词性的: a ~ compound predicate 名词性合成谓语 ④(金额)微不足道的: a ~ sum 微小的数目 ⑤按计划进行的,令人满意的: Everything was ~ during the rocket launch. 火箭发射时一切进行顺利。 **II** *n.* 名词性的词(指名词、形容词、代词) ‖~ism *n.*【哲】唯名论 / ~ist *n.* 唯名论者 / ~ly *ad.*

nominate ['nomineit] *vt.* ①提名: The candidates were ~d today. 今天提了候选人名单。 / ~ sb. for the Presidency 提名某人为总统候选人 ②任命,指定: a board of six ~d and six elected members 由六名指定委员和六名选举产生的委员组成的委员会 ③命名 ④(赛马中)登记(马名)

nomination [,nomi'neiʃən] *n.* ①提名;任命 ②提名权;任命权 ③(赛马中)马名的登记

nominative ['nominətiv] **I** *a.* ①主格的: the ~ case 主格 / a ~ ending 主格词尾 ②被提名的;被任命的: the ~ and elective members 任命的成员及选举产生的成员 ③具有姓名的: ~ shares 记名的股份 **II** *n.*【语】主格 ‖~ absolute, ~ independent【语】独立主格

nominee [,nomi'ni:] *n.* 被提名者(尤指被提名为候选人者);被任命者

non [non] *ad.* [拉] 不 (=not)

nonce [nons] **I** *n.* 眼下,当前(只用于以下短语): for the ~ 目前,暂且 **II** *a.* 一度发生(或使用)的 ‖~ word (为了特殊需要而)临时造的字

nonchalant ['nonʃələnt] *a.* 漠不关心的;冷淡的,若无其事的,不激动的 ‖~ly *ad.*

nondescript ['nondiskript] **I** *a.* (因无特征而)难以归类的;难以形容的: a ~ mixture of feelings 难以名状的感情交织 **II** *n.* 难以形容(或归类)的人(或物)

none [nʌn] **I** *pron.* [用作单或复] ①没有人;没有任何东西: None have (或 has) arrived yet. 还没人来。 / I need some carbon paper badly but there is ~ at hand. 我急需复写纸,可是手边一张也没有。 ②…中任何一个人(或任何事物、任何部分)都不(of): None of us are (或 is) afraid of difficulties. 我们当中没有一个人害怕困难。 / There is ~ of it left. 那东西一点儿也没有剩下。 / It's ~ of your business. 这事根本与你不相干。 / None of your impudence! 你别厚颜无耻! **II** *a.* [用于文学体裁中,被修饰的名词通常提前或省略]没有: Money Tom has ~. 汤姆没有钱。 **III** *ad.* [与the 加比较级连用,或与 so, too 连用]一点也不: The machine is working ~ the worse for its long service. 这部机器并不因长久使用而运转不良。 / be ~ the wiser for 并不因…而有所开窍 / We arrived at the station ~ too soon. 我们到达车站,时间很不早了。 / be ~ so fond of sth. 并不那么喜欢某物 ‖~ but 只有: None but the aged and the sick stayed at home. 只有年老和生病的人留在家里。 / ~ other than 见 other / ~ the less 仍然,依然: For all his years, he is ~ the less vigorous and active. 他虽年老,但仍然生气勃勃,精力旺盛。

nonentity [no'nentiti] *n.* ①不存在;不存在(或虚构)的东西 ②【哲】不存在的实质 ③无足轻重的人(或物): a political ~ 政治上无足轻重的人

nonplus ['non'plʌs] **I** ([复] nonplus(s)es) *n.* 困惑;为难;窘境: put (或 reduce) sb. to a ~ 使某人为难 / stand at a ~ 进退维谷,左右为难 **II** (nonplus(s)ed; nonplus(s)ing) *vt.* 使迷惑;使为难;使狼狈: be nonplus(s)ed for a moment 一时不知所措 / be nonplus(s)ed over sth. 对某事一筹莫展

nonsense ['nonsəns] **I** *n.* ①胡说,废话;胡闹,愚蠢的举动: talk ~ 胡说八道;说废话 / I want no more of your ~. 我不许你再胡闹(或胡说)了。 There is no ~ about him. 他决不容许胡闹。 / This is nothing short of a ~, silly ~. 这全是一派胡言,愚蠢之极的胡言。 ②无价值的东西,无用的装饰品 **II** *int.* 胡说! 废话!

nonsensical [non'sensikəl] *a.* 无意义的;愚蠢的,荒谬的 ‖~ly *ad.*

noodle[1] ['nu:dl] *n.* ①笨蛋,傻子 ②[俚]脑袋瓜: have a foggy ~ 头脑糊里糊涂

noodle[2] ['nu:dl] *n.* [常用复]面条,鸡蛋面

nook [nuk] *n.* 凹角;偏僻隐蔽的角落;隐蔽处,匿处: every ~ and corner 每一个角落

noon [nu:n] **I** *n.* ①中午,正午 [一般不加 the]: a little before ~ 中午前一会儿 / at high ~ 正午时 / a ~ meal 午餐 ②最高点;全盛期: the ~ of one's life 在壮年时 **II** *vi.* [主方] 午休;歇手进午餐 ②达最高点 ‖(as) clear as ~ 一清二楚 / the ~ of night [诗]午夜 ‖'~-mar n.【天】(正)午标,(正)午线 / '~tide *n.* ①午,正午 ②最高点 / '~time *n.* =~tide *a.* 午的,正午的

noonday ['nu:ndei] *n.* 中午: at ~ 在中午 summer ~ heat 夏天中午的酷热 ‖(as) clear (或 plain) as ~ (或 (as) clear as the sun at ~)一清二楚

noose [nu:s] **I** *n.* ①绞索;套索 ②羁绊,束缚 ③套;陷阱: put one's head in the ~ 自投罗网 *vt.* ①用套索捕捉;使落入圈套 ②把(绳索)套成活套 ③把…处绞刑 ‖The ~ is hanging. [俚]万事俱备,只等开场。

noose

nor [nɔ:] *conj.* ① [常与 neither 或 not 连用,有时也与 no, never 等表示否定的词连用] 也不: We fear *neither* hardship ~ death. 我们一不怕苦,二不怕死。/ *Neither* he ~ I was there. 当时我和他都不在那里。/ *Not a* fly ~ a mosquito was to be found. 无论苍蝇还是蚊子一只也找不到。/ I *never* saw him again, ~ did I hear from him. 我再也没有见到他,也没有收到过他的信。② [用在肯定句后] 也不; 不: The article is too long; ~ is the style easy. 文章太长,文笔也不流畅。/ All that is true, ~ must we forget about it. 那全是真实的,我们可不能忘记。③ [方]比 (=than): He does better ~ you. 他比你做得好。‖(~) … ~ … [古] [诗] 既不…又不…; 既非…又非… (=neither … nor …)

normal ['nɔ:məl] I *a.* ① 正常的,正规的; 标准的: a ~ phenomenon (state) 正常现象(状态) / the frontier guards on ~ patrol duty 在执行正常巡逻任务的边防战士 ② 智力正常的; 精神健全的 ③【化】中性的; 规度的; 当量的;【物】简正的: ~ concentration【化】规(定浓)度,标准浓度; (克)当量浓度 ④【数】垂直的,正交的,法线的: ~ line 法线 / ~plane 法面 / ~ angle 法角 ⑤【生】不受感染的 ⑥【经】按产品最高成本定价的 II *n.* ①[只用单]正常的状态(或数量、程度等); 标准: above (below) ~ 标准以上(以下) / return to ~ 恢复正常 ②【数】垂直线,法线 ‖~ly *ad.* ‖~ distribution (统计学用语)正态分布,正规分布 / ~ **school** 师范学校

north [nɔ:θ] I *n.* ① 北, 北方: ~ by east 北偏东 (即正北偏东 11°15′, 写作 N 11°15′E) / ~ by west 北偏西(即正北偏西 11°15′, 写作 N 11°15′ W) / a cold wind from the ~ 北方吹来的寒风 ② [N-] (一国或一地区的)北部 ③ [常作 N-] 地球的北部(尤指北极地区) ④北风 II *a.* ①北的,北方的: the ~ latitude 北纬 ② [N-] (一国、一洲或一地区)北方的 ③朝北的: a ~ window 北窗 ④ 从北面来的: a ~ wind 北风 / ~ *polar regions* 北极地区 III *ad.* 向北方; 在北方; 自北方: lie ~ of 位于…的北面 / sail ~ 向北航行 ‖*too far* ~ 精明的,不会受骗的 / ~ **light** (适宜于绘画的)北面来的光线 / (画室等)北窗 ③ 北极光 / **North Pole** 北极 / **North Star** 北极星

northerly ['nɔ:θəli] I *ad.* & *a.* ①在北方(的);向北方(的) ②来自北方的(的) II *n.* 北风

northern ['nɔ:ðən] I *a.* ① [常作 N-] (一国或一地区的)北方的 ② 来自北方的 ③ 朝北的; ④有北方地区特征的: ~ habits and customs 北方的风俗习惯 II *n.* ① =~er [常作 N-] 美国北部方言 ‖~er *n.* [常作 N-] ①北方人; 居住在北方的人 ②美国的北方人 ‖**Northern Hemisphere** 北半球 / ~ **lights** 北极光

northward ['nɔ:θwəd] I *ad.* 向北方: sail ~ 向北航行 II *a.* 向北的 III *n.* 向北的方向; 北方的地区 ‖~ly *ad.* & *a.* 向北方(的); 向北的(的)

northwards ['nɔ:θwədz] *ad.* 向北方

nose [nouz] I *n.* ① 鼻子; (动物的)鼻口部; 吻: the bridge of the ~ 鼻梁 ②嗅觉: have a good ~ 嗅觉灵敏 / develop a good ~ for 提高对…的嗅觉 ③气味; 凭气味追踪的能力 ④鼻状物(如喷嘴、管口、鼻锥、机件的凸头、弹头): the ~ of a missile 导弹头部 / a projectile ~ (子弹的)弹头 ⑤突出部分(如船头、飞机机首、突出的岩角): ~ wheel【空】前轮, 鼻轮 ⑥ [俚]暗探, 告密者 II ❶ *vt.* ①闻出; 探出, 侦察出: ~ *out* something fishy 嗅出什么可疑 ② 用鼻子触,用鼻子擦; 把鼻子塞入: The dog ~d the door open. 狗用鼻子顶开了门。③(船、飞机等)用头部探(路)前进: The steamer ~d its way along the winding creek. 汽船沿着弯曲的河道探路前进。④(在赛马或比赛中)以微小差距胜过(out) ❷ *vi.* ①嗅,闻 (at, about) ②探听; 干涉: ~ *around* everywhere 嗅探着到处活动 / ~ *into* other people's affairs 探听(或干涉)别人的事情 / ~ *for* information 探听消息 ③(船等)缓慢小心地前进: The ship ~d in towards the shore. 船徐徐驶向岸边。④(地层)下倾(in); 露出(out) ⑤[俚]做暗探,告密: ~ *on* sb. 告发某人 ‖*a dog's* ~ 一种杜松子酒搀啤酒的混合饮料 / ~ *of wax* ① 没有主意的人, 耳朵软的人 ② 容易塑捏的东西 / a ~ *to light candles at* [俚]酒鬼的红鼻子, 酒槽鼻子 / (as) *plain as the* ~ *in your face* 一清二楚 / *bite sb.'s* ~ *off* 气势汹汹地回答某人 / *blow one's* ~ 擤鼻子 / *by a* ~ (指赛马或比赛中的输赢)以些微之差: win *by a* ~ (赛马)仅以一鼻之差而获胜, 险胜; 侥幸取胜 / *cannot see beyond (the length of) one's* ~ 鼠目寸光 / *count* (或 *tell*) ~s 数人数(尤指支持者的人数); 凭人数决定问题 / *cut off one's* ~ *to spite one's face* 发脾气时做了害自己的事 / *follow one's* ~ ①笔直走 ②凭本能行事 / *fuddle one's* ~ 酩酊, 泥醉 / *have sb.'s* ~ *out of joint* =put sb.'s ~ out of joint / *(in) spite of sb.'s* ~ 不顾某人的反对 / *keep one's* ~ *clean* [美]不喝酒 / *keep one's (sb.'s)* ~ *to the grindstone* 使某人(某人)埋头从事辛苦的劳动 / *lead sb. by the* ~ 牵着某人的鼻子走, 完全支配某人 / *look down one's* ~ *at* 瞧不起 / *make a long* ~ 作蔑视的手势(把拇指搁在鼻端,其余四指张开) / ~ *down* (飞机机首朝下)俯冲; 使俯冲 / ~ *over* (飞机着陆失事时)机首着地而翻转 / ~ *to* ~ 面对面地 / ~ *up*(飞机机首朝上)升起; 使升起 / *on the* ~ [美俚] ①(赛马或比赛时某一赛者)将第一个到达终点 ②正是,正好 / *pay through the* ~ 被敲竹杠, 付出过高的代价 / *poke* (或 *push, thrust*) *one's* ~ *into* 探究; 干涉(别人的事情) / *pull sb.'s* ~ (或 *pull sb. by the* ~) 拉某人的鼻子(一种侮辱性的动作) / *put sb.'s* ~ *out of joint* ① 打乱某人的计划 ②挤掉某人 (使自己得宠) / *run at the* ~ 流鼻涕 / *snap sb.'s* ~ *off* =bite sb.'s

~ off / *speak through one's* ~ 带鼻音说话 / *the parson's* (或 *pope's*) ~ (煮熟供食用的)鸡(或其它家禽的)屁股 / *thumb one's* ~ (*at*) (对…)作蔑视的手势(把拇指搁在鼻端,其余四指张开) / *turn up one's* ~ *at* 对…嗤之以鼻,瞧不起 / *under sb.'s* (*very*) ~ ①就在某人眼前 ②当着某人的面,公然 ‖**～less** *a.* 无鼻子的;无喷嘴(或其他鼻状物)的 ‖**～ bag** 挂在马等脖子上的草料袋 / '**～band** *n.* (牲口的) 鼻羁 / '**～bleed** *n.* 鼻出血 / ~ **candy** [美俚]嗅用麻醉品 / ~ **cone** 火箭式导弹的头部,前锥体 / ~ **dive** ①头朝下的俯冲: The plane made a ~ dive. 飞机垂直俯冲。②(价格等)猛跌,暴落 / '**～-dive** *vi.* ①俯冲 ②(价格等)猛跌,暴落 / ~ **drops** [复]滴鼻药水 / ~ **gas** 喷嚏性毒气 / '**～gay** *n.* 花束 / ~ **paint** [美俚]酒(尤指威士忌) / '**～piece** *n.* ①(头盔上的)护鼻 ②(牲口的)鼻羁 ③形状(或位置)象鼻子的东西;喷嘴,管口;显微镜的物镜旋座 ④眼镜的鼻梁架 / ~ **rag** [俚]手帕 / ~ **ring** 鼻环

nosey ['nouzi] *a.* & *n.* =nosy

nostalgia [nɔs'tældʒiə] *n.* ①怀乡病 ②留恋过去,怀旧

nostril ['nɔstril] *n.* ①鼻孔 ②鼻孔内壁 ‖*a breath of one's* ~s 见 **breath** / *stink in sb.'s* ~s 使某人厌恶

nosy ['nouzi] **I** *a.* ①大鼻子的 ②[俚]好打听别人事情的,爱管闲事的 ③(发霉的干草等)发臭味的;对臭味敏感的 ④(茶)香的 **II** *n.* 大鼻子的人 ‖**Nosy Parker** [英]爱管闲事的人

not [nɔt] *ad.* ①不: He is ~ a mechanic, but a welder. 他不是机匠,而是焊工。/ He told us ~ to spray too much insecticide. 他告诉我们不要让农药喷洒得太多。/ I know ~. [古]我不知道。(=I don't know.) [注意:与助动词连用时, not 常简缩为 n't, 如 don't, can't, wouldn't] ②[用在动词 think, suppose, believe, expect, fear, fancy, trust, hope, seem, appear 等、副词 perhaps, probably, absolutely 等和词组 be afraid 等的后面,代表否定的从句]不会: A: Will they come tomorrow? B: I suppose ~. (=I suppose they will ~ come tomorrow.) 甲: 他们明天会来吗? 乙: 我想不会吧。/ A: Will it rain this afternoon? B: Probably ~. 甲: 今天下午会下雨吗? 乙: 大概不会。[注意: 作肯定回答时用 I suppose so. 或 Probably so. 等] ③[用在其他省略结构中, 代替词、短语或句子]: If it clears up, we will go out; if ~, ~. 如果天放晴, 我们就出去, 要不, 我们就不去。/ Correct or ~, the expression is unpopular. 不管正确与否, 这个表达法是不通俗的。/ They will not be discouraged, ~ they. 他们不会灰心——他们才不会呢! ④[与 all, both, every 等词连用, 表示部分否定]: All is ~ gold that glitters. [谚]发亮的东西不一定都是金子。/ Not every horse can run fast. 不是每匹马都能快跑的。⑤[用

于委婉的说法中]: ~ a few 不少 / ~ too well (身体或情况)不太好 / ~ (so) bad 很好 / ~ reluctant 相当乐意 / ~ without reason 不无理由, 颇有理由 ‖*as likely as* ~ 很可能 / *as soon as* ~ 再也乐意不过地: I'd go there as soon as ~. 我非常愿意去那儿。/ ~ *a* 一个也不: ~ *a* drop of rain 一点雨水也没有 / ~ *all that* 不那么…(地): It is ~ *all that* urgent. 这事不那么危急。(=It is ~ as urgent as all that.) / A: D'you like fish, by the way? B: Not all that much, I prefer meat. 甲: 顺便问一下, 你喜欢鱼吗? 乙: 不太喜欢, 我宁可吃肉。/ ~ *at all* 见 **all** / ~ *but that* (或 ~ *but what*) 虽然: He is very strong —— ~ *but that* he will catch cold sometimes. 他身体很强壮, 虽然他有时要患感冒。/ ~ *dry behind the ears* [美俚]乳臭未干的,无经验的 / ~ *half* 见 **half** / ~ *it* 见 **it** / ~ *only* ... *but* (*also*) ... 见 **only** / ~ *so much as* 见 **much** / ~ *that* 并不是说: If he ever said so —— ~ *that* I ever heard him say so —— he was mistaken. 如果他曾经这样说过——并不是说我曾听见他这样说过——那末他是错了。/ ~ *that* ... *but that* ... 不是(因为)…而是(因为)…: Not *that* she forgot to do her homework, *but that* she was busy nursing a sick classmate. 不是她忘记了做作业, 而是她忙着照顾一个生病的同学。/ *Not that I know of*. 据我所知并不是那样。‖'**～-self** *n.* =nonego

notability [,noutə'biliti] *n.* ①名人,显要人物 ②值得注意(指性质或状况)

notable ['noutəbl] **I** *a.* ①值得注意的;显著的 ②著名的,显要的 ③[化]可觉知的 ④(有时读作 ['nɔtəbl]) [方](主妇)会当家的,能干的,勤勉的 **II** *n.* ①名人,显要人物 ②[N-]【史】法王召开紧急会议时所召集的知名人士 ‖**notably** *ad.* 显著地;著名地

notary ['noutəri] *n.* 公证人,公证员(常称 ~ public 或 public ~)

notation [nou'teiʃən] *n.* ①标志;标志法 ②【数】符号,用号;记法: decimal ~ 十进制记数法 ③【音】乐谱;记谱法 ④注释 ‖**～al** *a.*

notch [nɔtʃ] **I** *n.* ①(V 字形)槽口,凹口 ②[美]山峡,峡谷 ③(记数等用的)刻痕 ④[口]等,级: a ~ above (或 higher than) the others 比其他的高一等 **II** *vt.* ①在…上开槽口 ②刻痕记(数等) ③赢得 ④把(箭)搭在弦上 ‖**～ed** *a.* ①开凹口的 ②【生】具缺刻的 ‖'**～board** *n.* 【建】楼级搁板 / '**～wing** *n.* 卷叶蛾科昆虫

note [nout] **I** *n.* ①笔记,记录: speak from ~ (without a ~) 根据草稿(不用草稿)发言 / the ~s of a journey 旅行笔记 ②按语,评注: the editor's ~ 编者按(语) / ~s to (或 on) an article 文章的注解 ③短笺,便条: I left a ~ to tell him to attend the meeting this evening. 我留下条子通知他今晚来开会。/ a ~ of invitation 请帖 / a ~ of thanks 感谢信 ④(学术或科技

的)短文 ⑤(外交上的)照会: a ~ of protest 抗议照会 / Notes were exchanged between the two governments. 两国政府互换了照会。⑥票据; 借据; 纸币: a promissory ~ (或 a ~ of hand) 期票 / a demand ~ 即期票据 / ~s payable (receivable) 应付(应收)票据 / a bank ~ 钞票 / a five-yuan ~ 票面为五元的纸币 ⑦口气, 调子; 特征: change one's ~ 改变口气 / There was a ~ of pessimism in what he said. 他的讲话带着悲观的调子。⑧显要, 名望: a person of ~ 名人 ⑨符号; 标记: a ~ of exclamation (interrogation) 惊叹(问)号 ⑩【音】音调; 音符; 琴键: a whole (half, quarter) ~ 全分(二分, 四分)音符 ⑪[诗]曲调, 歌子 ⑫叫声, 声音; 鸟鸣声 ⑬注意: things worthy of ~ 值得注意的事物 ⑭暗示, 提示: a ~ of admonition 表示警告的一种暗示 II vt. ①记下, 摘下: ~ down one's impressions of a city 记下对一座城市的观感 ②注意; 注意到: Please ~ how the machine is operated. 请注意机器的操作方法。/ I failed to ~ that he had left. 我没有注意到他已经走了。③特别观察 ④指明, 表明 ⑤对…加注释 ⑥【音】用音符记出 ‖compare ~s 对笔记; 交换意见 / make (或 take) a ~ (或 ~s) of 把…记下来 / strike (或 sound) a false ~ 说(或做)得不恰当 / strike the right ~ 说(或做)得恰当 / take ~ of 注意(到) / take (或 make) ~s 记笔记 ‖~less a. 不被注意的; 不著名的 ②音调不和谐的 ‖~r n. 摘记者, 做笔记者 ‖~book n. 笔记簿; 期票簿 / '~case n. [英]皮夹子 / '~,paper n. 信纸, 便条纸

noted ['noutid] a. 著名的, 知名的: a ~ scientist 著名的科学家 / a ~ personage 知名人士 / a town ~ for its pottery 以陶器著名的市镇 / ‖~ly ad. / ~ness n.

noteworthy ['nout,wə:ði] a. 值得注意的; 显著的 ‖noteworthily ad. / noteworthiness n.

nothing ['nʌθiŋ] I n. ① 没有东西, 没有什么: Nothing in the world is difficult for one who sets his mind to it. 天下无难事, 只怕有心人。/ There is ~ wrong with this tractor. 这辆拖拉机没有什么毛病。②不存在; 不存在的东西 ③微不足道的事物(或人): A: Sorry to have interrupted you. B: Oh, it's ~. 甲: 打扰了你真是对不起。乙: 没有什么。/ the little ~s of life 人生琐事 【数】零: Multiply 6 by ~, and the result is ~. 六乘以零等于零。/ He is five foot ~. 他身高刚好五呎。⑤ [作表语, 前不加冠词] 不属于任何教派的人; 无神论者; 不可知论者 II ad. 一点也不, 并不: It is ~ surprising. 这毫不奇怪。/ Nothing daunted, they dived into the icy water. 他们毫无惧色地跳入冰冷的水中。‖all to ~ 百分之百的: It is all to ~ that they will succeed. 他们定会成功。/ be ~ to ①对…来说无足轻重 ②不能与…相比 / come to ~ 失败, 没有结果; 到头来一场空 / dance upon (或 on) ~ 被绞死 / for ~ ①免费, 不要钱 ②徒然,

没有结果: These investigations are not done for ~. 这些调查工作自然不是白做的。③没有理由: They quarrelled for ~. 他们无端大吵一场。/ have ~ in one ①不足道, 无可取 ②没有个性 / have ~ on sb. [美]对某人毫不占优势, 不拥有表明某人确有罪的证据 / have ~ to do with 和…无关; 和…不往来 / have ~ to show for 在…方面没有成绩可言 / leave ~ to be desired 完美无缺 / like ~ on earth 世间稀有的, 珍奇的 / make ~ of ①对…等闲视之 / make ~ of working ten hours at a stretch 对一下子连续工作十小时毫不在意 ②不能理解 ③不能解决(或应用、对付) / neck or ~ 见 neck[1] / no ~ 什么也没有: ~ but 除了…以外什么也不; 只有; 只不过: Don't worry for my illness; what I need is ~ but a few days' rest. 不要为我的病担心, 我只要稍微休息几天就会好的。/ Nothing doing! [俚] ①(拒绝别人要求时说)不行! 不干! ②(失败时说)糟了! 完了! / ~ else but (或 than) = ~ but / ~ if not 极其: The situation is ~ if not fine. 形势好极了。/ ~ in life 见 life / ~ less than 和…一模一样, 完全是: That's ~ less than a miracle. 那完全是一个奇迹。/ ~ like 没有什么能比得…: In summer there is ~ like swimming as a means of keeping fit. 在夏天再没有比游泳更好的锻炼方式了。/ ~ like (或 near) as (或 so) ... as ... 远远不象…那样…: The book is ~ like as difficult as I expected. 它远远没有我想象的那么难懂。/ ~ like leather 见 leather / ~ loath 见 loath / ~ much 很少: A: Anything interesting? B: Nothing much. 甲: 有什么有趣的东西吗? 乙: 没什么有趣的东西。/ ~ of the kind 见 kind[1] / ~ short of 见 short / Nothing succeeds like success. [谚]一事成功, 事事顺利。/ ~ to write home about 不值得大书特书的事情 / Nothing venture, ~ have. [谚]不入虎穴, 焉得虎子。/ there is ~ for it but to 除了…以外别无他法: There is ~ for it but to rush the injured man to hospital. 只有赶快把伤员送到医院去罗。/ There is ~ in it. ①里面没有什么内容 ②这是不真实的。③这是不重要的。④这里面无利可图。/ think ~ of 把…看成平常; 把…看成不重要 / to say ~ of 更不必说 ‖~ness n. ①无, 虚无; 不存在: fade into ~ness 渐渐隐没 ②无价值(的事物), 微不足道(的事物) ③死

notice ['noutis] I n. ①通告, 布告; 通知: put up a (public) ~ 贴出布告 / Notice is hereby given that ……, 特此布告。②预先通知(尤用于雇主、雇员或房东、房客之间): a ~ to quit 解雇(或迁出)通知 / give one's employee a month's ~ 通知雇员一个月后离职 / give one's employer a month's ~ 通知雇主一个月后辞职 / The tenant (landlord) received two months' ~. 房客得到(房东得到房客)两个月后迁出的通知。/

Will you allow us ten minutes' ~? 请你在十分钟前通知我们好吗? / The aeroplane will take off at a moment's ~. 一接到通知这架飞机立即就可起飞。③注意: bring sth. into public ~ 使某事为公众所注意 ④警告; 被警告的状态: We put them on ~ that they should keep out of bounds. 我们警告他们不得越界。⑤招呼; 客气对待 ⑥(报刊上对图书、戏剧等的)短评; 介绍: a book ~ 书评 / the play under ~ 正在评论中的戏剧 **II ❶** *vt.* ①注意; 注意到: Please ~ the regulations overleaf. 请注意本页反面的规章(或使用须知)。/ I ~d that he came early. 我注意到他来得早。/ I ~d him enter(ing) the office. 我看到他走进(正在走进)办公室。②通知: The aeroplane was ~d to take off at six o'clock. 这架飞机被通知在六点钟起飞。③评论, 介绍: The book will be ~d in our periodical before long. 这本书不久将在本刊评介。④提到, 谈到: ~ sb.'s merits in a speech 在讲演中提到某人的功绩 ⑤招呼; 客气对待 ❷ *vi.* 注意 ‖*at short* ~ 一俟通知(马上就…): We are ready to start *at short* ~. 我们已准备好, 一接到通知马上就出发。[注意: 在美国有时说 on short ~] / *be beneath sb.'s* ~ 被某人认为不值得一顾 / *bring sth. to sb.'s* ~ 使某人注意某事 / *come into* ~ 引起注意 / *come to sb.'s* ~ 引起某人的注意 / *give* ~ ①通知: He *gave* me ~ to hand in the application by the end of the week. 他通知我至迟在本周末交上申请书。②通知…离职(或迁出等): The boss has *given* John ~ to quit. 老板已通知约翰离职。/ *have* ~ 接到通知: I *have* ~ to report for duty on Monday. 我已接到通知, 要我星期一去报到。/ *serve* ~ ①正式通知; 宣布(*on*) / *sit up and take* ~ 蓦地注意起来 ②(病人)健康渐渐恢复 / *take* ~ ①注意: *take* no ~ of others' comments 不理会别人的议论 ②(婴孩)开始懂事 / *take sb.'s* ~ 得到某人的通知(关于离职或迁屋) / *till* (或 *until*) *further* ~ 在另行通知以前: The library will be open only in the afternoon *till further* ~. 在另行通知以前, 图书馆只在下午开放。/ *without* ~ 不预先通知地; 不另行通知: leave *without* ~ 擅自离去, 不告而别 / The schedule is subject to change *without* ~. 时间表随时可能改变, 不另行通知。‖~ **board** 布告栏

notifiable ['noutifaiəbl] *a.* (疾病)须报告卫生当局的, 应具报的

notification [,noutifi'keiʃən] *n.* ①通知 ②通知单, 通知书

notify ['noutifai] *vt.* ①通知: ~ sb. *of* the change of one's address 将自己地址的更改通知某人 / I *notified* him that the meeting had been postponed. 我通知他会议已延期。②报告; 宣告: ~ a birth 报出生

notion ['nouʃən] *n.* ①概念: have a vague ~ *about* sth. 对某事物有模糊的概念 / I have no ~ (*of*) what he means. 我不懂他是什么意思。②想法; 看法, 见解: have a ~ that . . . 认为… ③打算, 意图: have no ~ of doing sth. 不打算做某事 ④精巧的小玩意儿; [美][复]个人衣物(指针线等小件日用品) ‖'~-,counter *n.* [美]出售针线等小件用品的杂货柜 / '~-,store *n.* [美]出售针线等小件用品的杂货店

notorious [nou'tɔːriəs] *a.* ①臭名昭著的, 声名狼藉的: a ~ scoundrel 劣迹昭彰的人 ‖~ly *ad.* / ~ness *n.*

notwithstanding [,nɔtwiθ'stændiŋ] **I** *prep.* 尽管: They travelled on, ~ the storm. 尽管有暴风雨, 他们仍然继续赶路。/ this ~ 尽管如此 **II** *ad.* 尽管; 还是: Whatever you may say, they will do it, ~. 无论你怎样说, 他们还是要做。**III** *conj.* [古]虽然, 尽管: I would go ~ (that) he advised me not to. 尽管他劝我不要去, 我还是要去。

nought [nɔːt] *n. & a.* =naught

noun [naun] *n.* [语]名词: an abstract (a material) ~ 抽象(物质)名词 / an attributive ~ 作定语用的名词 / a collective (an individual) ~ 集合(个体)名词 / a common (proper) ~ 普通(专有)名词 / a countable (an uncountable) ~ 可数(不可数)名词 / a ~ of multitude 群体名词

nourish ['nʌriʃ] *vt.* ①养育; 施肥于: ~ the soil 给土地施肥 ②怀抱(希望、仇恨等) ‖~ing *a.* 养的, 富于营养的 / ~ment *n.* ①食物; 滋养品 ②营养情况

novel ['nɔvəl] **I** *a.* 新的, 新颖的; 新奇的: be on the lookout for whatever is ~ 追求新奇 **II** *n.* ①(长篇)小说 ②[常用复](罗马法律)新法, 附律 ‖~ist *n.* 小说家

November [nou'vembə] *n.* 十一月(略作 Nov.)

novice ['nɔvis] *n.* ①[宗]见习修道士(或修女)新皈依的教徒(尤指新基督教徒) ②新手; 初学者: a ~ *at* motorboating 摩托赛艇活动中的新手 / a ~ pilot 新飞行员

novitiate, noviciate [nou'viʃiit] *n.* ①[宗]修道士(或修女)的见习期(或见习处) ②(新手的)见习期 ③ =novice

now [nau] **I** *ad.* ①现在, 此刻, 目前; 直到现在: Everything is ready ~. 现在一切都准备好了。/ for several centuries ~ 几个世纪以来 / a good many years ago ~ 许多年以前 ②立刻, 马上: You must write ~, or it will be too late. 你必须马上写信, 否则就太晚了。③(在叙述中表示所涉及的时间)于是, 然后; 当时: The child was ~ five years old. 这时孩子已五岁了。④(不表示时间, 而表示说话者的语气, 包含说明、命令、请求、警告、安慰等意): *Now* listen to me 且听我讲。(命令口气) / No more talking ~ 别再讲话啦! (命令口气) / *Now* what do you mean? 你到底是什么意思? (不耐烦的口气) / *Now*, ~, don't cry. 好了, 好了, 别哭了。(安慰的口气) **II** *n.* [常用在前置词后]现在, 此刻

read the future in the ~ 从现在推测未来 **III conj.** 既然，由于: *Now (that) I am well again, I can go on with my work.* 我既然恢复了健康，那就可以继续工作了。/ *Now (that) you mention it, I do remember.* 你这样一提，我就记起来了。**IV a.** 现在的，现任的: the ~ chairman of the association 现任的协会主席 ‖*(every) ~ and again* =(every) ~ and then / *(every) ~ and then* 时而，不时: *We go to the films (every) ~ and then.* 我们常常去看电影。/ *from ~ on* 从现在开始，今后 / *just ~* ①刚才，一会儿以前: *The foreign guests arrived just ~.* 外宾刚到。②现在，眼下；立即，马上: *I am busy just ~.* 我此刻正忙。/ *~ . . ., ~ . . .* 时而…，时而…: *The weather is ~ hot, ~ cold.* 天气一会儿热，一会儿冷。/ *Now or never!* 机不可失! / *~ then* (用于句首，表示 警告、抗议或引起注意) 喂: *Now then, a little less noise, please.* 喂，请安静一点。/ *~ . . ., then . . .* = *~ . . ., ~ . . .* / *up to ~* 到目前为止

nowadays ['nauedeiz] **I ad.** 现今，现在(常用于将现在的风俗习惯等与过去相比时) **II n.** 现今，当今

nowhere ['nouʰwɛə] **I ad.** ①任何地方都不: *He went ~ last Sunday.* 上星期天他什么地方都没去。/ *The book is ~ to be found.* 到处找不到这本书 ②远远地在后面: *leave one's rivals ~* 把自己的敌手远远地抛在后面 **II n.** ①无处: *There is ~ to sit in the crowded room.* 房间里人很挤，无处可坐。②不知道的地方: *A tiger appeared from ~.* 蓦地出现了一只老虎。‖*be ~* ①一无所得；一事无成；失败 ②(在比赛等中)远远地落在后面；未得名次 / *get ~* 见 **get** / *~ near* 离…很远: *The jar is ~ near full.* 这缸还远远没有装满。

noxious ['nɔkʃəs] **a.** ①有害的，不卫生的，有毒的: a ~ gas 毒气 ②使道德败坏的 ③讨厌的 ‖*~ly ad.* / *~ness n.*

nozzle ['nɔzl] **n.** ①(茶壶等的)嘴；管嘴；喷嘴: oil ~【机】喷油嘴 / an exit ~ (排气)喷管 ②[俚]鼻子

Np【化】元素镎 (neptunium) 的符号

nuclear ['nju:kliə] **a.** ①核心的，中心的: the ~ part of a city 城市的中心部分 ②原子核的；原子能的；原子弹的；核动力的: ~ weapons 核武器 / a ~ bomb 核(炸)弹 / a ~ war 核战争 / ~ tests, atmospheric and underground 大气层及地下核试验 / a ~ power 核国家 / a ~ umbrella 核保护伞 / go ~ (指国家)走上利用核动力(尤指制造核武器)的道路 ‖*~-'armed a.* 用核武器装备的 / *'~-'capable a.* 可携带核武器的 / *~ chemistry* (原子)核化学 / *~ deterrent* 核威慑力量 / *~ energy* 核能 / *~ fission*【物】核分裂，核裂变 / *'~-'free zone* 无核区 / *~ fusion* 核聚变，核合成 / *physics* 原子核物理学 / *'~-'powered a.* 核动

力的 / *~ reactor* (原子)核反应堆 / *'~-'tipped a.* 有核弹头的

nucleus ['nju:kliəs] ([复] nuclei ['nju:kliai] 或 nucleuses) **n.** ①核；核心，中心: a ~ of leadership 领导核心 / play the role of a ~ 起核心作用 ②【生】细胞核；核 ③【天】彗核 ④【原】(原子)核: atomic ~ 原子核 ⑤【化】环; (晶)核

nude [nju:d] **I a.** ①裸体的 ②(房间等)无点缀品的；光秃的: a ~ hillside 光秃秃的山坡 ③肉色的(尤指袜子) ④【律】(契约等)无偿的 **II n.** ①[the ~] 裸体 ②裸体画(或雕像等) ③裸体者 ‖*in the ~* ①赤身裸体 ②公开的；赤裸裸的 ‖*~ly ad.* / *~ness n.*

nudge [nʌdʒ] **I vt.** ①用肘轻推(以引起注意或暗示) ②[喻]引起…注意 ③接近: *The circulation of the book is nudging the two million mark.* 这本书的发行量已近二百万册。**II n.** 用肘轻推

nugget ['nʌgit] **n.**【矿】(天然)块金；矿块

nuisance ['nju:sns] **n.** ①损害，妨害: relieve the ~ of fumes from factories 减轻工厂烟雾的污害 ②讨厌(或有害)的东西(或事情、行为等)；讨厌(或麻烦)的人: *The mosquitoes are a ~.* 蚊子是讨厌的东西。/ *What a ~!* 真讨厌! / *That fellow is a perfect ~.* 那家伙讨厌极了! ‖*~ raid*【军】扰乱性袭击 / *~ tax* (直接对消费者征收的)小额消费品税

null [nʌl] **I a.** ①无束缚力的，无效的 ②不存在的，等于零的 ③无价值的，无用的: as ~ as nothing 毫无价值 ④无(个性)特征的，没有表情的 ⑤指针为零的，零(位)的 ‖ ~ indicator【数】零位指示器 **II n.** ①【数】零；空 ②【无】零讯号，微弱讯号 ‖*~ and void* 无效: *declare a treaty ~ and void* 宣布条约无效

nullify ['nʌlifai] **vt.** ①使无效，废弃，取消 ②使无价值，使无用

numb [nʌm] **I a.** ①麻木的；失去感觉的: ~ with cold 冻僵了的 ②愚蠢的；注意力不集中的 **II vt.** 使麻木；使麻痹 ‖*~ly ad.* / *~ness n.*

number ['nʌmbə] **I n.** ①数；数字: an even (odd) ~ 偶(奇)数 / a cardinal (an ordinal) ~ 基(序)数 / a known (an unknown) ~ 已知(未知)数 ②(略作 No., 复数略作 Nos.) 号码；…号; (报刊等的)期，册: a telephone ~ 电话号码 ③数目；[复]大批，数量上的优势: ~s (a large ~) of people 很多人 / *Visitors came in (great) ~s.* 参观访问者蜂拥而来。④一群人，一帮人: *He is not of our ~.* 他可不是我们中的一分子。/ *be among the ~ of the dead* 已死 ⑤[复]算术: *the science of ~s* 算术 / *be skilled in ~s* 精于算术 ⑥[美俚]人(尤指活泼而动人的姑娘)；商品的某一型号(或式样): a new nylon ~ 新的尼龙品种 ⑦[语]数: the singular (plural) ~ 单(复)数 / *The noun "oxen" is plural in ~.* 名词 "oxen" 是复数形式。⑧(一个)节目; (歌剧的)部分: the first ~ on the programme 第一个节目 / the solo ~s of an opera 歌剧的独唱部分 ⑨【音】

节奏; [复]拍子，调子 ⑩ 韵律; [复]韵文，诗 ⑪ [Numbers]《民数纪》(《旧约全书》第四篇) ⑫ [the ~s]用作单或复]一种把赌注押在数字上的彩票赌博 (=~s pool 或 game racket) II ❶ vt. ①给…编号: ~ the pages of a manuscript 给手稿编页码 ②达…之数,总计: The students in our class ~ thirty. 我班总共有三十多个学生。③把…算作,认为 (among, in, with): ~ sb. among one's friends 认为某人是朋友 ④ [常用被动语态] 使在数目方面受到限制 ⑤ 计算,数: ~ one's friends by the dozen(s) 有好几十个朋友 ⑥ [古] 列举 (up) ⑦ [古] 活了…岁 ❷ vi. ①计: visitors ~ing in the thousands 数以千计的参观者 ②报数: ~ from the right in fours 从右首开始一至四报数 ‖a back ~ ①过期的一期刊物 ②过时的人(或物) / a hot ~ [美俚] ①感情热烈的女子 ②热门货,销路广的商品 / a ~ of 若干; 许多: A ~ of new products have (或 has) been successfully trial-produced. 许多新产品已试制成功。/ any ~ of 许多 / beyond ~ 多得数不清 / by the ~s ①合拍地; 【军】以规定的动作并按"一, 二, 一"的口令 ②系统地; 按常规地; 机械地 / get sb.'s ~ [俚] 发现某人的本质(或动机) / have sb.'s ~ 了解某人的能力(或性格) 心中有数 / in ~ 在数字上; 总共: They exceed us in ~. 他们在数目上超过我们。/ We are fifteen in ~. 我们总共十五人。/ in round ~s ① (舍弃零数)以整数表示; 以约数表示 ② [喻] 大概; 总而言之 / lose the ~ of one's mess (英海军用语) 死 / ~ one (略作 No. 1) ① [英俚] (负责船的保养和整洁的) 舰务官 ②自己; 自己的利益: look after (或 take care of) ~ one 顾着自己的利益 ③头号的(的); 头等(的) / One's ~ is (或 goes) up. [俚] 某人的死期 (或遭难的日子) 已到。/ one's (或 the) opposite ~ 对等的人(或物) (指在不同机构中职位相当的人或不同国家中互相对应的机构或官员等) / to the ~ of 达到…的数目,合计数为… / without ~ 多得数不清: times without ~ 无数次 ‖~less a. ①无号码的 ②数不清的 ‖~ing ['nʌmbərin] machine 号码机 / ~ plate 号码牌 (如汽车的号码牌,房子的门牌)

numeral ['nju:mərəl] I a. 数的; 示数的 II n. ①数字: the Arabic ~s 阿拉伯数字 (如 1,2,3 等) / the Roman ~s 罗马数字 (如 I,II,III 等) ② [语] 数词: the cardinal (ordinal) ~s 基(序) 数词 / fractional ~s 分数词 ③ [美] [复] (奖给在课外活动某一方面有显着成绩的班级的) 荣誉年号: win ~s in basketball, baseball and track 在篮球、棒球和径赛方面赢得荣誉年号

numerator ['nju:məreitə] n. ① 【数】分子 ②计算者; 计数器, 计数管

numerical [nju:(')merikəl] a. 数字的, 用数字表示的; 数值的: ~ aperture 【物】数值孔(或口) 径 / a ~ order 号数 / the ~ strength 人数, 兵数 / ~ value 数值 ‖~ly ad. 在数字上

numerous ['nju:mərəs] a. ① [修饰单数名词]为数众多的: a ~ acquaintance 很多熟人 / a ~ army 大军 / a ~ class 大班 / a ~ family 子女众多的家庭 / a ~ library 书多的图书馆 / a ~ [修饰复数名词]许多: ~ libraries 许多图书馆 / too ~ to enumerate 不胜枚举的 ③ (散文、诗歌等)有节奏的,和谐的 ‖~ly ad. / ~ness n.

nun [nʌn] n. 修女; 尼姑: ~'s cloth 【纺】修女黑色薄呢 / ~'s thread 【纺】细白线 / ~'s veiling 【纺】修女薄纱

nunnery ['nʌnəri] n. 女修道院; 尼姑庵

nuptial ['nʌpʃəl] I a. ①婚姻的, 结婚的; 婚礼的 ②交配季节所特有的 II [复] n. 婚礼

nurse [nə:s] I n. ①保姆 (通常称 dry ~); 奶妈 (常称 wet ~); 保育员 ②护士, 看护: a hospital ~ 医院的护士 / a trained (或 graduate) ~ 经过护士学校训练的护士 ③ 养育者; 保护者; 养成所, 发祥地 (of) ④ (森林中起屏障作用的) 保护树; 【动】保育虫 (一种群居性昆虫, 如保护幼蚁的工蚁等); 为非己生的幼兽哺乳的母兽 ⑤养育; 护理 II ❶ vt. ①给 (婴孩、幼畜) 喂奶; 带养; 看顾 ②吸…的奶 ③看护, 护理 (病人、疾病等): ~ sb. back to health 护理某人使恢复健康 ④ 培养; 培育; 精心节俭地管理 (事业): ~ new authors 培养新作家 / ~ young plants 培育幼苗 ⑤小心操纵; 节约地使用 (或消耗): ~ a horse 开始时不使马过于劳累 / ~ a crippled plane 小心驾驶失灵的飞机 / ~ resources 节约资源 / ~ a cup of coffee 慢饮慢呷一杯咖啡 ⑥紧抱; 爱抚 ⑦怀有 (希望、仇恨等) ❷ vi. ①喂奶; 吃奶 ②看护病人; 照料孩童 ‖at ~ 由保姆 (或奶妈) 领养中 / ~ a constituency (候选人或当选人) 笼络选区的选民 / put ... (out) to ~ 将…寄养于人; 把 (地产) 交人管理 ‖~r n. ① 培育者; 促使…发展者 (of) ②奶瓶 ‖~ frog 【动】产婆蛙 / '~maid n. 保姆 / ~ship [英] (保护鱼雷艇、潜水艇等的) 母舰

nursery ['nə:sri] n. ①托儿所; 保育室; 儿童室 (私人家里专供儿童游戏、吃饭等用的房间): a day (night) ~ 日 (夜) 间托儿所 ②养成所 ③苗圃; 养鱼池; 动物繁殖场 ‖~ governess 保育员 / '~maid n. 保姆 / ~ rhyme 童谣 / ~ school 幼儿园 (一般接纳五岁以下幼儿)

nurture ['nə:tʃə] I n. ①营养物, 食物 ②养育, 教养 ③ [总称]环境因素 II vt. ①给…营养物 ②养育, 培育, 教养

nut [nʌt] I n. ①坚果 (如胡桃、栗子等); 坚果仁 ②难事; 难题; 难对付的人 ③ [俚]脑袋: be off one's ~ 发疯 ④ 【机】螺母, 螺帽: check (或 lock) ~ 防松螺母 / grip ~ 夹紧螺母 ⑤ [复]小煤块

nut

⑥[美俚]疯子; 傻瓜; (行为或信仰方面的)怪人; 狂热者; [罕]花花公子: a ~ house (或 college, factory, farm, foundry, hatch) 精神病疗养院; 疯人监狱; 疯人医院 / a football ~ 足球迷 ⑦[复][美俚]睾丸 ⑧[音](弦乐器的)琴马 ⑨[印] 对开 Ⅱ (nutted; nutting) vi. 采坚果, 拾坚果: go nutting 采拾坚果去 ‖a hard (或 tough) ~ to crack 棘手的问题; 难对付的人 / a tough ~ ①大胆果断的人 ②暴躁的人; 无赖汉 / (can't do sth.) for ~s [俚]一点也(不会做某事) / not care a (rotten) ~ 毫不在乎 / the ~s [美俚]极出色的人(或物) ‖~let ['nʌtlit] n. ①小坚果 ②果核 ‖'~-brown a. 深棕色的, 栗色的 / ~ butter 坚果制成的奶油(代用奶油) / '~,cracker n. ①[常用复]轧碎坚果的钳子(一端有铰) ②[动]星鸟(一种鸟类) ③瘪嘴; a ~-cracker face 瘪嘴脸 / '~gall n. [药]没食子 / '~hatch n. [动]鹌 / ~ oil 坚果制成的油(如胡桃油等) / '~pick n. ①挑取坚果果仁的工具 ②[美俚]精神病医生 / '~-tree n. 坚果树(尤指榛树)

nutmeg ['nʌtmeg] n. 【植】肉豆蔻(树) ‖~ **apple** 肉豆蔻的果实 / ~ **liver** 【医】豆蔻肝(一种肝病) / ~ **tree** 【植】肉豆蔻树

nutrition [nju(ː)'triʃən] n. ①营养, 滋养 ②营养物, 滋养物; 食物

nutritious [nju(ː)'triʃəs] a. 有营养的, 滋养的 ‖~**ly** ad. / ~**ness** n.

nutshell ['nʌt-ʃel] n. ①坚果(如胡桃、栗子等)的外壳 ②小的东西, 小数量(或范围)的东西; 小容器; 小住所 ‖in a ~ 简括地说, 一句话: He explained the situation in a ~. 他概括地说明了情况。

nuzzle ['nʌzl] ❶ vi. ①(用鼻子或用鼻子般地)掘, 擦, 触, 伸入 ②舒服地躺着; 紧挨地躺着 ❷ vt. ①用(鼻子等)挨擦 (against); 把(鼻子等)伸入 (into) ②[~ oneself] 使舒服地躺着; 使紧挨地躺着

nylon ['nailən] n. ①【纺】耐纶, 尼龙(聚酰胺纤维的统称) ②耐纶制品; [复]耐纶长袜

nymph [nimf] n. ①[希神]居于山林水泽的仙女 ②[诗]美女 ③(昆虫的)若虫, 蛹 ‖~**al** a.

O

O [ou] int. ①[用在称呼前]…啊; 哦: O Time, how fast you fly! 时间啊, 你流逝得真快! ②哎呀; 唉 [表示惊讶、痛苦等]: O dear me! 哎呀! / O for a cup of water! 唉!有杯水喝多好!

oak [ouk] Ⅰ n. ①【植】栎属植物; 栎, 橡 ②栎木 ③栎树叶(常作装饰用) ④栎木家具, 栎木器具 ⑤[英俚]栎木大门 ⑥[诗]木船 Ⅱ a. 栎木的; 栎木制的 ‖a heart of ~ 坚强勇敢的人(或物) / sport one's (或 the) ~ [英俚]闭门谢客 ‖~ apple, ~ gall

oak

栎五倍子 / ~ **bark** 栎树皮 / ~ **leather** 栎树皮鞣革

oakum ['oukəm] n. 麻絮, 填絮(用于填塞船缝等)

oar [ɔː] Ⅰ n. ①桨; 橹: a pair-~ 双桨船 / a four-~ 四桨船 ②划手; 桨手: a practised ~ 老练的划手 ③桨状器官(如鳍、臂等) Ⅱ ❶ vt. 划, 划动: ~ a boat forward 把船划向前 ❷ vi. 划行; 划行似地前进: ~ slowly across a river 慢慢地划过河去 ‖be chained to the ~ 长时间地被迫做苦工 / bend to the ~s 用力划桨 / boat the ~s 停划并把桨收到船内 / have an ~ in everyman's boat 多管闲事 / ~ one's way 划桨前进 / pull a good ~ 划得一手好桨 / pull a lone ~ 独自干 / put (或 shove, stick) one's ~ in 干涉, 干预 / rest (或 lie) on one's ~s ①搁桨停划 ②停下来息一会儿 / take (或 have, pull) the labo(u)ring ~ 担任最繁重的工作 / toss ~s 举桨致敬 ‖'~lock n. U 形桨架 / ~sman ['ɔːzmən] n. 划手;划桨能手 / ~smanship ['ɔːzmənʃip] n. 划艇法;划艇技能 / '~s,woman n. 女划手

oasis [ou'eisis] ([复] oases [ou'eisiːz]) n. ①(沙漠中的)绿洲 ②(不毛之地中的)沃洲 ③(存在于枯燥或不愉快的环境中的)慰藉物, 宜人的地方

oat [out] n. ①[常用复]燕麦; 燕麦属植物: naked ~s 油麦 / wild ~s 野燕麦 ②[常作 ~s]用作单或复]种燕麦的田地; 燕麦种子 ③[常作 ~s] [用作单]燕麦粥, 麦片粥 ④[诗]麦笛; 田园诗, 牧

歌 ‖*feel one's* ~s [美俚] ①兴高采烈; 活跃 ②自命不凡 / *sow one's wild* ~s (年轻时)放荡 ‖~'**cake** n. 燕麦饼 / ~ **grass**【植】燕麦草属植物 / ~**meal** n. 燕麦片; 燕麦粥 / ~ **opera** 以美国西部作背景的影片(或广播剧、电视剧)

oath [ouθ] ([复] oaths [ouðz]) n. ①誓言, 誓约; 宣誓: an ~ of allegiance (office) 效忠(就职)宣誓 / bind sb. by ~ 用誓约约束某人 ② (咒骂或强调所陈述之事时)妄用神名; 诅咒; 渎神的言词; 咒骂语 ‖*grind out an* ~ 切齿诅咒 / *on* (或 *upon, under*) ~ 发誓 / *put sb. on* (*sb.'s*) ~ 使某人立誓 / *take* (或 *make, swear*) *an* ~ 宣誓, 发誓

obduracy ['ɔbdjurəsi] n. ①冷酷无情 ②顽固不化 ③执拗, 倔强

obdurate ['ɔbdjurit] a. ①冷酷无情的 ②顽固不化的 ③执拗的, 倔强的 ‖~**ly** ad.

obedience [ə'bi:djəns] n. ①服从, 顺从: in ~ to orders 遵照命令 / hold sb. in ~ 使某人顺从 / blind ~ 盲从 / filial ~ 孝顺 ②【宗】管辖; 管辖区; [总称]管区的教徒

obedient [ə'bi:djənt] a. 服从的, 顺从的, 恭顺的: be ~ to 对…服从 / Your ~ servant [英]您的恭顺的仆人(公文末尾署名前的套语; 过去也在说话时用作自谦的称呼, 今作诙谐语) ‖~**ly** ad. Yours ~*ly* (或 *Obediently* yours) 您的恭顺的(公文末尾署名前的套语)

obeisance [ou'beisəns] n. ①敬礼(指鞠躬、屈膝礼等): make an ~ to sb. [古]向某人致敬礼 ②敬意: do (或 make, pay) ~ to sb. 向某人致敬

obelisk ['ɔbilisk] n.【建】方尖塔; 方尖碑; 方尖碑形物

obese [ou'bi:s] a. (人)过度肥胖的, 肥大的

obesity [ou'bi:siti] n. ① 过度肥胖, 肥大 ②【医】肥胖症; 多脂

obey [ə'bei] ❶ vt. ①服从, 顺从; 听从; 执行: The part should ~ the whole. 局部必须服从全局。/ make oneself ~ed 使别人听从自己 / ~ orders 服从命令 ②按照…行动; 按照理智行动 / The ship ~s the helm. 船随舵转动行驶。❷ vi. 服从; 听话

obituary [ə'bitjuəri] I n. (常附死者传略的)讣告, 讣闻 II a. 报告死亡的; 有关死者的: an ~ notice 讣告 ‖**obituarist** n. 讣告作者

object ['ɔbdʒikt] I n. ①物, 物体: cultural ~s 文物 / a luminous ~ 发光体 ②对象: an ~ of study 研究对象 ③[口]外表可笑的(或可鄙的、可怜的)人(或物): What an ~ you have made (of) yourself! 瞧你把自己搞成了什么怪样子! ④目的: attain one's ~ 达到目的 / Money no ~. (待聘人员在报上登广告时用语)报酬不论。⑤[语]宾语: a direct (an indirect) ~ 直接(间接)宾语 ⑥【哲】客体, 客观: ~s in themselves 自在的感性客体 II [əb'dʒekt] ❶ vi. ①反对; 抗议: I ~ to the proposal. 我反对这个提议。/ We ~ to leaving him alone. 我们反对丢下他不管。②抱反感, 不赞成: I don't ~ to a glass of

hot water. 我很想喝杯开水。❷ vt. 提出…作为反对的理由(或根据): He ~ed that I was not careful enough. 他提出了反对, 说我不够谨慎。/ I ~. [英](下议院用语)我反对(这个提案)。‖~**less** a. 无目的的 / ~**or** [əb'dʒektə] n. 反对者: a conscientious ~*or* (为了道德或宗教上的原因而)拒服兵役者 ‖ **glass,** ~ **lens** (显微镜、望远镜等的)物镜 / ~ **lesson** ①实物教学课, 直观教学课 ②足资教训的实例 / ~ **plate** 检镜片(显微镜的载物玻璃片) / ~ **staff** (测量用的)准尺 / ~ **teaching** 实物教学, 直观教学

objection [əb'dʒekʃən] n. ① 反对, 异议; 不喜欢: have no (have an) ~ to the plan 不反对(反对)这计划 / take (或 make an) ~ to 对…表示反对 / lodge (或 utter) an ~ against 对…提出异议 / feel an ~ to getting up late 不喜欢晚起 ②缺点, 缺陷: The chief ~ to the story is its tediousness. 这本小说的主要缺点是沉闷乏味。③妨碍: There can be no ~ to your doing so. 你这样做不会有什么不可以的。④反对的理由: present one's ~s 提出反对的理由

objectionable [əb'dʒekʃənəbl] a. ①引起反对的; 要不得的 ②令人不愉快的, 讨厌的 ‖~**ness** n.

objective [əb'dʒektiv] I a. ①【哲】客观的; 真实的: an ~ law 客观规律 / ~ reality 客观现实 / transform the ~ and the subjective world 改造客观和主观世界 ② (作品)如实的; (人)无偏私的: an ~ description 客观如实的描绘 ③目标的: an ~ point 【军】出击目标; 弹着点 ④【语】宾位的: the ~ case 宾格 ⑤【医】(病状除本人感觉也为)他人感觉的: an ~ symptom 他觉症状 II n. ①目标, 目的;【军】出击目标 ②(显微镜等的)物镜 ③【语】宾格 ‖~**ly** ad. 客观地 / ~**ness** n. 客观(性) ‖~ **test** 由是非题、选择题等组成的测验

oblation [ou'bleiʃən] n.【宗】① 供奉 ② 供物, 祭品

obligation [,ɔbli'geiʃən] n. ① (道义上或法律上的)义务; 职责, 责任: the ~s of a citizen 公民的义务 / a matter of ~ 义不容辞的事情 ②合约, 契约; 证券 ③恩惠; 感恩 ④ 偿付债务的款项 ‖*be* (或 *lie*) *under an* ~ *to sb.* 受某人的恩惠 / *lay an* ~ *on sb.* 使某人负有义务 / *put* (或 *place*) *sb. under an* ~ 施恩于某人, 使某人负有义务 / *repay an* ~ 报恩

obligatory [ɔ'bligətəri] a. ① (道义上或法律上)须履行的, 应尽的, 强制性的: Physical education is ~ 体育课是必修的。②【生】专性的

oblige [ə'blaidʒ] ❶ vt. ① 迫使; 责成 ②以誓言(或契约等)束缚(某人): ~ oneself to settle one's father's bills 根据契约代父亲清账 ③施恩惠于; 答应…的请求; 使满足: Will you ~ me by closing the windows? 劳您驾替我关上窗好吗? / A: Can you ~ me with one or two dollars? B: Sorry I can't ~ you. 甲: 你能借给我一两元吗? 乙: 抱歉, 我不能答应你的请求。/ Please ~ me with your presence. 务请光临。④[用被动语态]使感

激: We are much ~d to you for your help. 非常感激你给我们的帮助。/ Much ~d! [口] 谢谢! ⑤[口]为…表演: He ~d us with a song. 他为我们唱了一个歌。❷ vi. 做某事表示好意: Will you ~ with a song? 请唱一个歌, 好吗?‖~r n. 施惠于人者

oblique [ə'bli:k] I a. ①斜的, 倾斜的; 偏斜的: an ~ compartment【军】倾斜地形 / We set a course ~ to the other ships. 我们采用了一条和其他的船偏斜的航线。/ ~ leaf【植】歪叶(两侧不对称的)/ ~ muscles【解】斜肌 ②【数】非直角的; 非垂直的: ~ angle 斜角 / ~ cone 斜圆锥 ③转弯抹角的, 不坦率的, 不直截了当的: make ~ accusations 指桑骂槐 / make ~ thrusts 旁敲侧击 ④躲躲闪闪的; 无诚意的; 不光明正大的 ⑤间接的: the ~ case【语】间接格(指主格或呼格外的格)/ ~ oration (或 narration, speech)【语】间接叙述 / an ~ reference to sth. 对某事的间接提及 ⑥【军】(照片)从空中倾斜摄制的: an ~ aerial photograph 倾斜航空照片 II vi. ①倾斜; 歪: The road ~s from the river. 这条路与河岔开了。②【军】斜行进, 与原方向成四十五度角前进 III n. ①倾斜物 ②【解】斜肌(尤指腹部的肌肉)③【军】倾斜航空照片 IV ad. 成四十五度角地: To the right ~, march!【军】向右成四十五度角, 前进!‖~ly ad. / ~ness n.

obliterate [ə'blitəreit] vt. ①涂抹, 擦去; 去掉…的痕迹: ~ one's signature 擦掉签名 ②使被忘却, 使湮没: ~ sth. from one's memory 忘却某事 ③使消失; 除去‖**obliteration** [ə,blitə'reiʃən] n. ①涂抹, 灭迹, 消灭; 湮没; 消失 ②【医】管腔闭合

oblivion [ə'bliviən] n. ①忘却, 被忘却; 健忘 ②被忘却的状态(或事实): be rescued from ~ 幸免遗忘(或湮没)③湮没; 漠视 ④大赦, 赦免‖an Act (或 a Bill) of Oblivion 大赦令 / be buried in ~ 被人们忘掉 / fall (或 sink) into ~ 渐被忘却; 废而不用

oblivious [ə'bliviəs] a. ①忘却的; 健忘的: be ~ of what has taken place 忘记了已发生的事情 ②不在意的, 不以为意的: They are working hard, ~ of all fatigue. 他们不顾疲劳地努力工作。/ be ~ to all the risk 不顾一切危险 ③[诗]使忘却的‖~ly ad. / ~ness n.

oblong ['ɔblɔŋ] I n. 长方形; 椭圆形 II a. 长方形的; 椭圆形的; 拉长的

obloquy ['ɔbləkwi] n. ①大骂; 强烈的指责 ②(由于被人强烈指责而引起的)坏名声, 丑名; 耻辱

obnoxious [əb'nɔkʃəs] a. ①令人非常不快的, 引起反感的, 讨厌的: an ~ person 讨厌的人 ②易受…的: ~ to harm 易受伤害的 ③【律】有责任的 ④应受谴责的‖~ly ad. / ~ness n.

obscene [əb'si:n] a. ①猥亵的; 淫泆的 ②可憎的; 污秽的; 令人厌恶的‖~ly ad.

obscenity [əb'si:niti] n. ①猥亵; 淫泆 ②[常用复]猥亵的话(或行为)

obscure [əb'skjuə] I a. ①暗的, 昏暗的, 黑暗的;

朦胧的: an ~ view 朦胧的景色 / ~ glass 毛玻璃 ②模糊的; 含糊的, 不清楚的, 不分明的; 晦涩的, 难解的: an ~ sound 模糊的声音 / Is the meaning still ~ to you? 你对这意义还不清楚吗? / an ~ malady 起因不明的疾病 / an ~ passage 难解的一段文章 ③不引人注目的; 偏僻的; 隐蔽的: the ~ regions 偏僻的地区 ④无名的; 微贱的: an ~ poet 无名诗人 / be of ~ origin (或 birth) 出身微贱 II vt. ①使暗, 使黑暗; 遮掩: The moon was ~d by dark clouds. 月亮被乌云遮蔽了。/ ~ the evil 掩盖罪恶 ②使难理解; 搞混: ~ the issue 把问题搞混 ③使不分明; 使失色: Don't let the negative roles ~ the brilliant heroic figures. 不要让反面角色遮去英雄的光辉形象。/ His success ~d his failures. 他的成功使他的失败显得微不足道。III n. =obscurity‖~ly ad. / ~ness n.

obscurity [əb'skjuəriti] n. ①暗, 暗淡; 朦胧 ②模糊; 含糊, 不清楚, 不分明; 晦涩, 难解: an article full of obscurities 一篇充满难解之处的文章 ③不引人注目; 偏僻; 隐匿: retire into ~ 退隐 ④无名(的人); 微贱(的人): sink into ~ 湮没无闻

obsequies ['ɔbsikwiz] [复] n. 葬礼, 丧礼

obsequious [əb'si:kwiəs] a. ①谄媚的, 奉承的, 巴结的 (to) ②[罕] 顺从的, 忠实的, 孝顺的‖~ly ad. / ~ness n.

observable [əb'zə:vəbl] I a. ①可遵守的, 应遵守的 ②可庆祝的, 应庆祝的: an ~ holiday 应予庆祝的节日 ③看得见的, 观察(或观测)得到的; 可辨别的: This is an ~ phenomenon. 这是一个观察得到的现象。④值得注意的, 显著的 II n. ①(可直接或间接)感觉到的(或看得见)的事物; 现象 ②[古] 值得注意的东西‖**observably** ad.

observance [əb'zə:vəns] n. ①(法律、习俗、规章等的)遵守, 奉行: the strict ~ of the doctor's directions 严遵医嘱 ②(节日、生日等的)纪念, 庆祝 ③惯例, 习惯 ④礼仪, 仪式: social ~s 社交礼仪 / religious ~s 宗教仪式 ⑤注意, 观察 ⑥教规; [O-] 天主教教规 ⑦[古]敬意, 恭顺

observant [əb'zə:vənt] I a. ①严格遵守…的: be ~ of laws (customs) 严格遵守法律(习俗) ②留心的, 当心的: be ~ to avoid mistakes 谨防犯错误 ③观察力敏锐的: an ~ boy 观察力敏锐的男孩子 II n. [O-](天主教方济各会的)严格遵守教规的教徒‖~ly ad.

observation [,ɔbzə(:)'veiʃən] n. ①注意, 监视; 观察, 观测: come (或 fall) under sb.'s ~ 被某人注意到 / keep sb. under ~ 监视某人; 观察某人(如病人等)/ ~ of natural phenomena 对自然现象的观察 / take an ~【海】测天(船舶、飞机驾驶员在航行中观测天体以求出所在处地理坐标的方法)②观察力: a man of keen (narrow) ~ 观察力敏锐(有限)的人 ③[常用复]观察(或观测)资料(或报告): firsthand ~s 第一手观察资料 / ~s on the growth of peanuts 对花生生长情况的观察报告 ④(观察后发表的)言论, 意见: He made some valuable ~s on the work. 他对工作

提出了一些宝贵的意见。‖an ~ balloon【军】观测气球 / an ~ battalion【军】观测营 / an ~ car 火车的游览车厢 / an ~ plane 侦察机 / an ~ post (或 point, station)【军】观察所, 观测所 / an ~ tower 了望台

observatory [əb'zə:vətəri] *n.* ①天文台（=astronomical ~）②气象台（=meteorological ~）③了望台

observe [əb'zə:v] ❶ *vt.* ①遵守, 奉行(法律、习俗、规章等) ②(按传统习惯)纪念, 庆祝(节日、生日等) ③看到, 注意到; 监视; 观察, 观测(天体、气象等): I have never ~d him do otherwise. 我从未看到他不是这样做的。/ ~ sb. stealing out of that room 看到某人正从那房间里偷偷地走出来 /We ~d that it had turned cloudy. 我们注意到天转阴了。/ ~ a suspected person 监视可疑的人 ④说; 评述, 评论: He ~d (to me) that our work was very well done. 他(对我)说我们的工作做得很好。❷ *vi.* ①注意; 观察 ②说; 评述, 评论(on, upon) ‖the ~d of all observers 众人所瞩目者

observer [əb'zə:və] *n.* ①遵守者, 奉行者: an ~ of one's promises 遵守诺言者 ②注视者; 监视人 ③观察者, 观测者, 测候员: an astronomical ~ 天文观察者 ④【军】观察员, 观测员: an ~'s cockpit (飞机的)观察员舱 ⑤评述者 ⑥(出席会议的)观察员 ⑦旁观者

obsess [əb'ses] *vt.* ①(魔鬼、妄想等)迷住, 使着迷; 缠住 ②使窘困, 使烦扰 ‖**~ion** [əb'seʃən] *n.* 着迷, 缠住; 摆脱不了的思想(或情感等): be under an ~ion of 在思想(或情感)上被…缠住

obsolescent [ˌɔbsə'lesnt] *a.* 逐渐被废弃的, 正在废退的, 在逐渐过时中的

obsolete ['ɔbsəli:t] **I** *a.* ①已废弃的, 已不用的: an ~ word 已废的词 ②过时的, 陈腐的, 老式的: ~ guns 老式的枪炮 ③【生】(器官)不明显的; 不发育的 **II** *n.* 被废弃的事物 ‖**~ly** *ad.* / **~ness** *n.*

obstacle ['ɔbstəkl] *n.* 障碍(物), 妨碍: an ~ to progress 进步的障碍 / throw ~s in sb.'s way 妨碍某人 / There are ~s to overcome. 有需要排除的障碍。‖**~ race** 障碍赛跑

obstinacy ['ɔbstinəsi] *n.* ①固执, 顽固 ②顽强; 不易克服性 ③(病痛等)难治, 难解除, 难抑制

obstinate ['ɔbstinit] *a.* ①固执的, 顽固的: be ~ in argument 在辩论中固执己见 ②顽强的, 不易克服的: ~ resistance 顽强不屈的抵抗 ③(病痛等)难治的, 难解除的, 难抑制的: ~ fever 经久不退的热度 ‖**~ly** *ad.*

obstruct [əb'strʌkt] ❶ *vt.* ①阻塞, 堵塞: ~ the traffic 阻塞交通 ②阻挡, 阻止, 阻碍: ~ sb. in (或 from) doing sth. 阻挠某人做某事 ③挡住(视线); 遮住 ❷ *vi.* 设置障碍(尤指在议事进程中) ‖**~or** *n.* 阻塞者, 阻碍者

obstruction [əb'strʌkʃən] *n.* ①阻塞, 堵塞: intestinal ~【医】肠梗阻 ②阻挡, 阻止, 阻碍: advance

without ~ 毫无阻碍地前进 ③障碍物 ④妨碍议事进程(辩论中故意拖延时间) ‖**~ism** *n.* 故意妨碍议案通过 / **~ist** *n.* 故意妨碍议案通过者 *a.* 故意妨碍议案通过(者)的 ‖**~ guard** (铁路机车的)护栏

obstructive [əb'strʌktiv] **I** *a.* ①引起阻塞的 ②障碍的, 阻挡的 ③妨碍议事的 **II** *n.* ①障碍物 ②妨碍议事者(尤指英下议院议员) ‖**~ly** *ad.* / **~ness** *n.*

obtain [əb'tein] ❶ *vt.* 获得, 得到; 买到: ~ knowledge through practice 通过实践获得知识 / Where can I ~ the book? 我从哪里可以买到这本书? ❷ *vi.* ①(习惯等)流行, 通行; 得到公认: These views no longer ~. 这些看法已经过时了。/ This ~s with most people. 这是大多数人公认的。②[古]成功 ‖**~ment** *n.*

obtainable [əb'teinəbl] *a.* 可获得的; 可取得的; 可买到的: be ~ for one dollar each 一元可以买到一个

obtrude [əb'tru:d] ❶ *vt.* ①挤出, 冲出 ②强加, 强行: ~ one's views *upon* others 把自己的观点强加于人 / ~ oneself *upon* (或 *into*) 硬要插手干扰 ❷ *vi.* 强加于人; 闯入, 打扰: ~ *upon* sb.'s privacy 打扰某人的安静 ‖**~r** *n.* 强加者; 闯入者

obtrusive [əb'tru:siv] *a.* ①伸出的, 突出的 ②炫耀的, 夸耀的 ③强迫人的; 闯入的; 冒失的 ‖**~ly** *ad.* / **~ness** *n.*

obtuse [əb'tju:s] *a.* ①钝的, 不尖的; 不锐利的: ~ knife 钝刀子 ②【数】(角)钝的: ~ triangle 钝角三角形 ③(感觉)迟钝的; 愚钝的 ④(印象等)不鲜明的, (疼痛)不剧烈的: an ~ pain 隐隐疼痛 ⑤【植】(叶子尖)钝(形)的; 圆头的 ‖**~ly** *ad.* / **~ness** *n.*

obviate ['ɔbvieit] *vt.* ①排除, 消除: ~ difficulties 排除种种困难 ②预防; 避免: ~ the possibility of a mistake 事先排除出错的可能性

obvious ['ɔbviəs] *a.* ①明显的, 显而易见的; 显著的: It is ~ that he is wrong. 显然他错了。/ an ~ effect 显著的效果 / ~ to everybody 对任何人都很清楚的 ②[古]挡在面前的; 挡路的; 阻碍的 ‖**~ly** *ad.* / **~ness** *n.*

occasion [ə'keiʒən] **I** *n.* ①场合; (重大的)时刻; 时节: a formal (great) ~ 正式(盛大)的场面 / on numerous ~s 无数次 / on the ~ of ... 值此…之际 / National Day is an ~ for general rejoicings. 国庆节是举国欢腾的日子。②时机, 机会: choose one's ~ 选择时机 ③偶然原因; 诱因, 近因: the ~ of the strike 引起这次罢工的近因 ④理由; 必要, 需要: There is no ~ to doubt the truth of the statement. 没有理由怀疑这话的真实性。/ We have had no ~ to go there recently. 近来我们没有必要到那里去。/ We shall never have any ~ for theory which is divorced from practice. 我们永远不需要脱离实际的理论。⑤[复][古]事务: go about one's lawful ~s 从事本分工作 **II** *vt.* 引起: ~ (sb.)

inconvenience 带来(给某人带来)不便 / ～ sb. to do sth. 使某人做某事 ‖*as* (或 *when*) *requires* 在必要时 / *as* 或 *serves* 一有适当的机会,当时机有利时 / *give* ～ *to* 引起: That remark gave ～ *to* a burst of laughter. 那句话引起了一阵笑声。/ *improve the* ～ 乘机说教;因势利导 / *on* ～ 间或,有时: He visits the city on ～. 他有时进城去。/ *rise to the* ～ 起来对付紧急局面;应付裕如 / *take* (或 *seize*) ～ *by the forelock* 抓住时机 / *take* ～ *to* 利用机会…,乘机…: take ～ to say a few words 趁机会讲几句

occasional [ə'keiʒənl] *a.* ①偶然的,非经常的: an ～ cause 偶然原因;诱因,近因 / There will be showers during the day. 白天有时有阵雨。②特殊场合的: an ～ driver 临时驾驶员 / an ～ licence [英] (限制时间、地点的)酒类临时贩卖执照 / an ～ poem 应景诗 ‖**～ism** *n.* [哲]偶因论 / **～ist** *n.* 偶因论者 / **～ity** [ə,keiʒə'næliti] *n.* 偶然性,非经常性 / **～ly** *ad.* 偶然,非经常地

Occident ['ɔksidənt] *n.* (也作 o-) [诗]西方 ② [the ～] 亚洲以西的全部国家;欧洲;西欧;欧美;美洲;西半球;西方文明

occult [ɔ'kʌlt] **I** *a.* ① 隐藏的;看不见的 ② 秘密的;秘传的;不公开的 ③神秘的;玄妙的;超自然的;难以理解的: the ～ arts (应用炼金术、占星术等的)秘术 **II** *vt.* & *vi.* ① (使)隐藏 ② 【天】掩(星) **III** *n.* [the ～] [总称] 神鬼(或神秘)之事 ‖**～ly** *ad.* / **～ness** *n.*

occupant ['ɔkjupənt] *n.* ①占有人,占用者; 居住者: the ～ of the seat 占这位子的人 ②任职者

occupation [,ɔkju'peiʃən] ①占领,占据;占领状态;占领军(当局): an army of ～ (或 an ～ army) 占领军 ②占有,占用;居住: The new house is ready for ～. 新屋可以居住了(指已落成)。③占有(或占用、居住)期间 ④职业;工作;消遣: a sideline (或 side) ～ 副业 ‖**～ist** *n.* 军事占领者‖ ～ **bridge** (土地占有者的)专用桥梁 / ～ **franchise** [英]租地人投票权

occupy ['ɔkjupai] *vt.* ①占领,占据 ②占(时间、空间),占有,占用;住(房子等): His speech *occupied* only three minutes. 他的讲话只占了三分钟。/ Is this seat *occupied*? 这座位有人吗? / "*Occupied*" (厕所、浴室等)"有人(在使用)" / The house is *occupied*. 这房子已有人住。③处于(某种地位);担任(职务): contradictions ～*ing* a secondary position 处于次要地位的矛盾 ④ 使忙碌,使从事: I am *occupied*. 我没空。/ He is *occupied* (*in*) repairing (或 *with* the repair of) farm tools. 他正忙着修理农具。/ ～ oneself *with* (*in* doing) some work 从事(正从事)某项工作 ‖**occupier** *n.* ① (土地、房屋等的暂时)占用者 ②军事占领者

occur [ə'kə:] (occurred; occurring [ə'kə:riŋ]) *vi.* ①发生: Don't let the mistake ～ again. 不要让这样的错误再次发生。/ if anything should

～, ... 如果发生什么事的话,… ②出现;存在: These plants ～ in Africa only. 这些植物只在非洲才有。③被想到: A fresh idea *occurred to* him. 他想到了一个新主意。/ Did it ever ～ to you that ...? 你是否想到过…? / It never *occurred to* me to phone you. 我根本没有想到要打电话给你。

occurrence [ə'kʌrəns] *n.* ① 发生;出现: be of frequent (rare) ～ 经常(很少)发生 ②(偶发)事件;事变;发生的事物: daily ～s 日常发生的事 ③【矿】存象,(矿床等的)埋藏: ore ～ 矿藏,矿石存象

ocean ['ouʃən] *n.* ① [总称]海洋 [诗]海: an ～ voyage 海洋航行 ②[O-] [地]洋: the Pacific (*Ocean*) 太平洋 ③[喻]无限;无际;[常用复][口]大量;许多: an ～ of sand 一望无际的沙漠 / ～s of time 大量的时间 ‖**～'going** *a.* 远洋航行的: an ～going destroyer 远洋驱逐舰 / an ～going submarine 远洋潜水艇 / an ～going freighter in the 10,000-ton class 万吨级远洋货轮 / **'～'grey, '～'gray** *n.* & *a.* 淡银灰色(的) (尤指第二次世界大战中美国军舰的颜色) / ～ **greyhound** 远洋快轮 / ～ **lane,** ～ **route** 外洋航线 / ～ **liner** 远洋定期客轮 / ～ **tramp** 不定航线的远洋货轮

ochre ['oukə] **I** *n.* 【矿】赭石: red ～ 代赭石,红赭石(一种赤铁矿) / uranium ～ 铀华 / yellow ～ 黄赭石(一种颜料) ②赭色,黄褐色 ③[俚]金钱 **II** *vt.* 涂赭色于 ‖**ous** ['oukriəs] *a.* 赭石质的;赭石色的

o'clock [ə'klɔk] …点钟 (of the clock的略写;只用于正点): What ～ is it? 现在几点钟? / It is just eight ～. 正好八点。‖*know what* ～ *it is* 什么都知道,熟悉情况;为人机敏: He is wide-awake and *knows what* ～ *it is*. 他是机灵的,什么都知道。/ *like one* ～ ①非常迅速地,马上 ②非常带劲地;津津有味地

octagon ['ɔktəgən] *n.* ①【数】八边形 ②八角形物体 ‖**al** [ɔk'tægənl] *a.* 八边形的

octave ['ɔktiv, 'ɔkteiv] **I** *n.* ①八个一组的事物 ②【音】八音度,一音阶;高(或低)八度音;低频程;风琴上的高八度音栓 ③八行(体)诗;十四行诗的前八行 ④(击剑中)八种防守姿势的第八式 ⑤【宗】节日起第八天;节日算起的八天 ⑥[英]容量为十三加仑半的酒桶 **II** *a.* 八个一组的;八行的 ②【音】高八度音的 ‖**～,coupler** *n.* 【音】(风琴)高低八度同奏的音栓 / ～ **flute** 【音】(风琴)高八度的音栓

October [ɔk'toubə] *n.* 十月(略作 Oct.)

octogenarian [,ɔktoudʒi'nɛəriən] *a.* & *n.* 八十至八十九岁的(人)

octopus ['ɔktəpəs] *n.* ①[O-][动]章鱼属 ②章鱼属动物;章鱼,蛸 ③[喻]章鱼状物(尤指多方面伸手进行控制的势力或团体)

ocular ['ɔkjulə] **I** *a.* ①眼睛的;视觉(上)的: an ～ disease 眼病 / ～ illusions 眼睛的错觉 ②用眼的;凭视觉的: ～ measurement 目测 / an ～ demonstration 直观演示 ③目击的: an ～ witness 目击者 / ~ testimony 目睹的证据 ④象眼睛的; 起眼睛作用的 **II** *n.* 目镜; the ~ of a microscope 显微镜的(接)目镜 ‖**~ly** *ad.*

oculist ['ɔkjulist] *n.* 眼科医生, 眼科专家 ‖**~ic** [,ɔkju'listik] *a.*

odd [ɔd] **I** *a.* ①奇数的, 单数的: ~ numbers 奇数, 单数 / the ~ houses 单号门牌的房子 / the ~ months 大月(指有三十一天的月份) ②单只的, 不成对的; 零散的: an ~ shoe (glove) 单只的鞋(手套) / some ~ numbers of a periodical 一种期刊的零星几期 ③有零数的; 带零头的: sixty thousand ~ 六万挂零 / sixty ~ thousand 六万几千 / thirty-~ years 三十多年(过去也作 thirty and ~ years) ④临时的, 不固定的; 额外的: an ~ hand (或 man) 打杂的短工 / do ~ jobs 打杂; 做额外的零星活儿 / an ~ player (在人数固定的游戏中)多出的一人 / at ~ times (或 moments) 有空的时候; 偶尔 ⑤奇特的, 古怪的: How ~! 好奇怪! ⑥偏僻的: in some ~ corner 在偏僻的角落里 **II** *n.* [the ~] (高尔夫球中)多于对方的一次击球 ‖**(an) ~ man out** 见 **man** / **~ and even** 猜单双的游戏 / **the ~ man** 见 **man** ‖**~ly** *ad.* 奇特地, 古怪地: ~*ly* enough [用作插入语]说来也奇怪 / **~ness** *n.* 奇特, 古怪 ‖**'~ball** *a.* & *n.* 古怪的(人) / **'~-job** *vi.* 做零活 / **~ trick** (打牌时双方各赢六墩后的)第十三墩牌

oddity ['ɔditi] *n.* ①奇特, 古怪 ②怪人; 古怪的事(物); 怪癖

oddment ['ɔdmənt] *n.* ①[常用复]残余的东西; 零散物 ②古怪的事(物) ③[复]【印】书的本文以外的部分(如内封等)

odds [ɔdz] [复] *n.* [用作单或复] ①不平等: make ~ even 拉平, 使平等 ②差异: It makes no ~ whether he comes or not. 他来不来都没有什么关系。/ What's the ~? 那有什么要紧? ③力量(或形势等)对比下的差距, 差额: The ~ are in our favour. 形势对我们有利。④(事物发生的)可能性, 机会: be within (over) the ~ 可(不可)能 / It is (long) ~ (或 The ~ are) that he will come. 大约他会来。/ It is long ~ against his coming. 大约他不会来。⑤(比赛或打赌时给对方的)让步: give (receive) ~ 提出(接受)让步 / lay (或 give) ~ of three to one 提出以三比一的赌注打赌(指若输就给对方三份, 赢则只拿对方一份) / take ~ of three to one 接受以三比一的赌注打赌(指若赢就拿对方三份, 输则只给对方一份) ‖**ask** (或 **beg**) **no** ~ [美]不要求照顾 / **at** ~ 争执; 不一致: set the two at ~ 使二者不和(或不一致) / be at ~ with 与…有争执; 与…不一致 / **by** (**long** 或 **all**) ~ (相比之下)远远地, 大大超过地: This is *by all* ~ the easier way. 这是容易得多的办法。/ **even** ~ 成败(或正反)机会均等 / **~ and ends** 残缺(或零星)的东西; 零碎的事情 / **shout the** ~ [口](尤指在比赛中)说大话, 夸海口 ‖**'~-'on** *a.* 大半有希望赢的: an

~-*on* candidate 大有把握当选的候选人

ode [əud] *n.* 颂诗; 颂歌

odious ['əudjəs] *a.* 可憎的; 丑恶的; 令人作呕的: an ~ smell 臭味 ‖**~ly** *ad.* / **~ness** *n.*

odo(u)r ['əudə] *n.* ①气味; 香气; 臭气 ②味道; 迹象: The word has an ~ of antiquity about it. 这个词有古意。③名誉, 声誉: an ~ of sanctity 圣洁的声誉, 德高望重 ④[古][常用复]香料 ‖**be in bad** (或 **ill**) ~ 名誉不好 ‖**~less** *a.* 没有气味的

of¹ [强 ɔv; 弱 əv, v, f] *prep.* ①(属于)…的: a topic ~ conversation 话题 / a friend ~ sb.'s 某人的一个朋友 / That's no fault ~ his. 这不是他的过错。

②(关于)…的: tell sb. ~ sth. 把某事告诉别人 / I have heard ~ him. 我听到过他。

③[表示同位]: the month ~ May 五月 / the fact ~ my having seen him 我见过他这个事实 / a mountain ~ a wave 象山般的巨浪 / a fool ~ a man 傻里傻气的人

④[表示具有某种性质、内容、状况等]: a man ~ ability 能干的人 / a congress ~ unity 团结的大会 / a matter ~ great importance 很重要的事情 / a cup ~ tea 一杯茶 / a friend ~ ten years 有十年交情的朋友 / vegetables ~ sb.'s own growing 某人自己种的菜

⑤[表示…的数量或种类]: a sheet ~ paper 一张纸 / two tons ~ coal 两吨煤 / a kind ~ oil 一种油

⑥[表示…的部分或全部]: three ~ us 我们中的三人(指部分) / the three ~ us 我们三人(指全部)

⑦[表示…中最突出的]: He is (They are) the best ~ teachers. 他(他们)是最好的教师。/ the hero ~ heroes 最杰出的英雄 / in sb.'s heart ~ hearts 在某人心坎的最深处

⑧[表示在…方面]: be slow ~ speech 讲话慢 / be quick ~ eye 眼快 / be difficult ~ access 难以进去(或接近)

⑨[表示在…一方]: It's very kind ~ you to help us. 谢谢你给了我们帮助。

⑩来自…的; 从…: I often ask advice ~ him. 我时常向他请教。

⑪由于; 因为: He came ~ his own accord. 他自动地来了。/ do sth. ~ necessity 不得不做某事 / die ~ cancer 患癌症而死

⑫由…组成(或做成)的: a committee ~ seven 七人委员会 / a distance ~ 50 *li* 五十里的距离 / a table (made) ~ wood 木头(做的)桌子

⑬表示动作的对象]: love ~ one's country 爱国

⑭[表示动作的主体]: the arrival ~ the delegation 代表团的到来

⑮[表示除去、剥夺等]: cure sb. ~ a disease 医好某人的病 / rid a warehouse ~ rats 消灭仓库里的老鼠 / deprive sb. ~ sth. 剥夺某人的某物

⑯[表示方位、时间等的范围]: within an hour ~ sb.'s departure 在某人出发后一小时之内 / fulfil a plan ahead ~ schedule 提前完成计划 / three minutes ~ ten [美]十点缺三分

⑰[表示在…时候或时期]: He comes ~ a morning (an afternoon, an evening, a Sunday). 他经常上午(下午,晚上,星期天)来。/ The baby was born ~ a Monday. 娃娃是星期一生的。/ ~ recent years 近年来

‖*all ~ a* ... 在(暂时的)…状态中: *all ~ a* sweat 一身大汗;惊恐万分 / *all ~ a* tremble 浑身发抖地 / *all ~ a* sudden 突然间 / *~ all* ... 在所有的,中偏偏(或竟然): Why ask him to go, ~ *all* people? 为什么不叫别人而偏叫他去? / They all came that day ~ *all* days. 他们偏偏都在那天来了。/ ~ *course* 当然,自然 / ~ *it* [用在名词后,加强语气]: make a good job ~ *it* 把事情做好 / have a nice time ~ *it* 过得快乐,好好乐一阵 / ~ *late* 见 late / ~ *old* 见 old / ~ *oneself* 自然而然地;自动地

off [ɔ(:)f] **I** ad. ①离,距: The town is two miles ~. 城在两哩路外。/ May Day is only a week ~. 离"五一"节只一星期了。/ The completion of the bridge is not far ~. 离桥的完工已不远了。②(离)开,(走)开: We're ~! (或 *Off* we go!) 我们出发了! / I must be ~. 我该走了。/ Be ~! 去! 滚! / Where are you ~ to? 你到哪里去? ③(脱离)掉: The paint has come ~. 油漆脱落了。/ take one's coat ~ 脱掉上装 ④(断)掉;(休)止: turn ~ the radio (gas, light) 关掉无线电(煤气,电灯) / The negotiation is (broken) ~. 谈判中断了。/ That dish is ~. (菜单上的)那样菜已卖完。/ take (ask for) a day ~ 休(请)假一天 / take time ~ for lunch 歇工吃午饭 ⑤ 完,光: drink it ~ 把它喝完 / kill ~ vermin 把害虫消灭光 / pay ~ a loan 还清贷款 ⑥[表示情况]: be well (badly) ~ 生活过得好(不好) / How are you ~ for fuel? 你们的燃料情况怎样? ⑦(剧本的舞台说明)台后,台旁: Shouts ~. 内喊声。**II** prep. ①从;从…离开(或脱离、去掉): buy (borrow) sth. ~ sb. 向某人买(借)某物 / step ~ the train 下火车 / A button is ~ my coat. 我的上装的一颗钮扣掉了。/ He's ~ smoking (liquor). [口]他戒烟(酒)了。②与…相隔;离: a village a little way ~ the main road 离大路不远的一个村子 / islands ~ the coast of Fukien 福建沿海的岛屿 / She is 3 years ~ 30. 再过三年她满三十岁了。③(路等)从…分岔 ④靠(养活、赚钱等) ⑤低于…;从…扣除: a dollar ~ the list price 比价目表价格便宜一元 / take 5 per cent ~ the price 减价百分之五 **III** a. ①(离人)较远的(一边);反(面)的: go round to the ~ side of the wall 绕到墙后面去 / the ~ side of a coin 硬币的反面 ②(车轮等)在右侧的;(船的)向海一边的: the ~ front wheel 右前轮 / the horse's ~ hind leg 马的右后腿 / The ship kept the buoy on her ~

side. 这船使浮标保持在船身向海的一边。③(路等)分支的;非主要的: an ~ branch of a river 河的支流 / an ~ street 小街 / an ~ issue 枝节问题 ④停止了的;休歇的;空闲的: The motor is ~. 马达停了。/ an ~ day 休假日 / ~ hours 空闲时间 ⑤低于通常水平的;较差的;(可能性)极小的: an ~ season 淡季 / an ~ year for apples 苹果的小年 / an ~ grade of oil 质量差的(石)油 / There is an ~ chance of finding him at home. 在他家里找到他的可能性很小。⑥[口]有点怪的;不对头的: He seems to be a bit ~. 他(头脑)似乎有点失常。/ be ~ in one's calculations 计算(或估计)错误 / The meat is slightly ~. 这肉有点变味了。**IV** ❶ vt. ①[口]宣布中止(谈判、合同等);取消与…的约定 ②[美俚]杀掉 ❷ vi. 走开;离开 ‖*be ~ one's game* 见 game[1] / ~ *and* [口]忽然,意外地: He ~ *and* left the room. 他忽然离开了房间。/ ~ *and on* (或 *on and* ~) 断断续续地: It rained ~ *and on* all day. 整天断断续续地下着雨。②(船)时而靠岸时而离岸地 / ~ *of* [美口]从(=~): Take the bag ~ *of* the peg. 把袋从挂钉上拿下来。/ ~ *with* [用于祈使句]去;去掉: *Off with* you! 去! 滚! / *Off with* him! 把他撵走! / *Off with* your hats! 脱帽! / *right* (或 *straight*) ~ 立刻 ‖**~ward** ad. 【海】(离岸)向海面 ‖**'~-balance** a. & ad. 不平衡的(地) / **'~beat** n. 【音】弱拍 a. [口]非常规的,不落俗套的 / **~ Broadway** 非百老汇戏剧(界)(指纽约百老汇大街以外的专业戏剧或戏剧界) n. 正在摄像而未送出电波信号的电视摄像机 / **'~-camera** ad. & a. 在电影(或电视)镜头之外(的) / **'~cast** a. & n. 被抛弃的(人或物) / **'~-colo(u)r** a. ①颜色不对头的 ②脸色不好的,身体不舒服的: She felt rather ~-*colo(u)r*. 她感到身体不大舒服。③[俚](笑话、歌曲等)下流的 / **'~-course** n.【无】偏离航向 / **'~-key** a. ①走音的,走调的 ②不合适的;不正常的;不协调的: sense something ~-*key* about it 感到这事有点不对头 / **'~-licence** n. [英]只许外卖酒类(不许堂饮)的执照 / **'~-line** a. ①不在铁路沿线的 ②[美]离线的: ~-*line* operation 脱机操作 / **'~-load** vt. 卸(货);下(客) / **'~-~-'Broadway** [美] a. 纽约的非商业性戏剧的(指在教室、咖啡馆内的小规模的实验性演出) ad. 非商业性地,实验性地(指戏剧演出) n. [总称]纽约的非商业性戏剧;纽约先锋派戏剧(界) / **'~-'peak** a. (交通、用电等)非高峰(时间)的: ~-*peak* hours 非高峰时间 / **'~print** n. (书刊中选文的)单行本 vt. 将…印成单行本 / **'~'screen** a. 在观众视线以外发生(或产生)的: ~*screen* voice 插话声音,画外音 / **'~'shore** a. ①离岸的;向海的: ~*shore* fisheries 近海渔业 / ~*shore* patrol【军】外海巡逻(队) / an ~*shore* wind (从陆地)吹向海面的风 / ②[美]国外的: ~*shore* purchases 国外采购 ad. 离岸;近海岸;向海面 / **'~'side** n. ①后面;反面;较劣的一面 ②[主英](车、马等的)

右边 ③(足球运动等中的)越位 / '~·**stage** *ad.*
& *a.* 台后(的),幕内(的) / '~·'**street** *a.* 不靠
街面的: an ~·*street* parking lot 不靠街面的停
车场 / '~·**the·'record** *a.* (谈话等)秘密的,不许
发表(或引用)的 / '~·**white** *n.* & *a.* 米色的(的),
灰白色(的) / ~ **year** ①(水果等的)小年 ②[美]
非大选年: an ~ *year* election 中期选举

offal ['ɔfəl] *n.* ①废物;垃圾;碎屑;渣滓 ②(家畜、
家禽等被宰杀后的)内脏,下水 ③腐肉; 廉价鱼
④[常用复]糖;麸皮;谷类的副产品 ⑤次品:
wood 次木料

offence [ə'fens] *n.* ①冒犯;触怒: No ~! 没有冒
犯你的意思!(或: 请勿见怪!) / give (或 cause)~
to sb. 得罪某人 It. 因某事而生气
②犯法(行为);罪过:过错: commit an ~ against
a rule 犯规 / a military ~ 触犯军法的行为
③讨厌的东西,引起反感的事物: an ~ to the ear
刺耳的声音 ④[罕]罪源; 绊脚石 ⑤进攻, 攻
击: weapons of ~ 进攻性武器 ⑥进攻的一方
‖~**less** *a.* ①不冒犯人的 ②无力进攻的

offend [ə'fend] ❶ *vt.* ①冒犯;触怒;伤害…的感
情: I'm sorry if I've ~ed you. 如有冒犯之
处,请原谅。/ be ~ed with (或 by) sb. for his
conduct 因某人的行为而对他生气 / be ~ed at
(或 by) sb.'s words 对某人的话感到生气 ②使
不舒服: ~ the ear (eye) 刺耳(眼) / ~ sb.'s
sense of justice 触犯某人的正义感 ❷ *vi.* ①犯
过错;违犯;犯罪(*against*): In what have I ~ed?
我犯了什么过错? / ~ *against* custom 违反习
惯 / ~ *against* the law 犯法 ②引起不舒服;引
起愤怒 ‖~**edly** *ad.* 生气地 / ~**ing** *a.*

offender [ə'fendə] *n.* 冒犯者;罪犯: a first (an old)
~ 初(惯)犯 / a juvenile ~ 少年犯

offensive [ə'fensiv] Ⅰ *a.* ①冒犯的; 唐突的: ~
language 无礼的话 ②讨厌的; 令人作呕的: an
~ sight 令人生厌的景象 / an ~ odour 臭气
③进攻的,进攻性的,攻势的: an ~ and defensive alliance 攻守同盟 / ~ formation 攻击队
形 / ~ weapons 进攻性武器 / a good ~ player
善于进攻的选手 Ⅱ *n.* 进攻,攻势: an all-out ~
大举进攻 / a political ~ 政治攻势 / a peace ~
和平攻势 ‖*assume* (或 *take, act on*) *the* ~ 进
攻,采取攻势 ‖~**ly** *ad.* / ~**ness** *n.*

offer ['ɔfə] Ⅰ ❶ *vt.* ①提出;提供: ~ advice (an
opinion) 提出劝告(意见) / ~ warm congratulations 热烈祝贺 / ~ sb. a cup of tea 给某人端
上一杯茶 / ~ lessons in French 设有法语课程
②奉献;贡献: ~ (*up*) prayers 做祷告 ③ 试
图;表示要: ~ to help sb. 表示愿意帮助某
人 ④ 出(价);开(价);提供出售: This shop
~s various daily necessaries. 这家商店供应各
种日常必需品。⑤呈现出; 使出现: Each stage
of the work ~s its own characteristic problems.
工作的每一阶段有它自己特有的问题。/ till a
better chance ~s itself 等到更好的机会来到时
⑥演出: ~ a new comedy 上演一出新的喜剧

❷ *vi.* ①出现: We shall visit the place as occasion (或 opportunity) ~s. 有机会时我们要访问
那个地方。②献祭 ③提议;求婚 ④[古]试图
(*at*): ~ *at* sth. 尝试某事 Ⅱ *n.* ①提供;提议:
make an ~ of help (support, food) 表示愿给以
帮助(支持,食物) / accept (refuse) an ~ 接受
(拒绝)建议 ②意图;想做: make an ~ to catch
the ball 想要接住那球 ③【商】报价;发价: He 出
open to an ~. 他愿考虑(买主的)出价。/ a firm
firm ~ (一定期限内有效的)固定发价 ④求购
‖ *battle* 挑战 / ~ *one's hand* 见 hand ‖~
出售中(的);供出售(的)

offering ['ɔfəriŋ] *n.* ①提供;提出 ②礼物;捐献
物;(给教会的)捐款;祭品: a peace ~ (为修复友
谊的)友好赠品 ③出售物: ~s on the vegetable
market 菜场上出售的东西 ④课程: new ~s in
the history department 历史系的新设课程

offertory ['ɔfətəri] *n.* 【宗】① 圣餐礼拜中的奉献
仪式(或祷词、歌唱的圣诗、捐款) ② 做礼拜时的
捐款

offhand ['ɔ:f'hænd] Ⅰ *ad.* 立即,当下;事先无准备
地: I couldn't give the figures ~. 我一下子说
不出数字来。Ⅱ *a.* ①即席的;临时的;随便的:
an ~ speech 即席发言 / act in an ~ way 不加
思考地行动 ②简慢的: be ~ with sb. 对某人简
慢无礼 ③无依托的站立姿势的: ~ shooting 无
依托立射

office ['ɔfis] *n.* ①办公室,办事处;事务所,营业所;
[美]诊所: work in an ~ 当职员 / go to the
~ 去办公 ②处,局,社,行,公司: a booking
(box) ~ 车站(剧场)售票处 / an inquiry ~ 问
讯处 / a post (telegraph) ~ 邮政(电报)局 / a
newspaper ~ 报社 / a head (branch) ~ 总(分)公
司(或社、行等) ③[O-]政府机关:[英]部;[美]司
局:the Foreign (War) Office (英国的)外交(陆军)
部 / the Office of Education (美国的)教育局
④公职;官职: hold public ~ 担任公职 / take
(或 come into, enter upon) ~ 就职,上任 /
leave (resign) ~ 离(辞)职 / the party in (out
of) ~ 执政(在野)党 ⑤职责;功能: do the ~
of host 尽主人之责 / The ~ of the mind is to
think. 头脑的功能是思考。⑥[复]照料,帮助:
by (或 through) the good (ill) ~s of sb. 由于
某人的斡旋(破坏) / do sb. kind ~s 帮某人忙
⑦[英][复]下房(指厨房、贮藏室等) ⑧礼仪;【宗】
祭礼,圣餐,祷告: perform the last ~s to (或
for) sb. 为某人举行葬礼 / the Divine Office (天
主教的)每日祷告 ⑨[俚]暗号,暗示: give sb. the
~ 暗示某人 ⑩[俚]飞机驾驶员座舱 ‖ *a Jack in*
~ 见 jack¹ / *the Holy Office* (天主教的)宗教
法庭 ‖~·**bearer** *n.* [英]官吏 / '~·**block** *n.*
[英]办事处集中的街区 / ~ **boy** (办公室的)勤
杂员 / ~ **building** 办公楼 / ~ **clerk** 职员,办
事员 / ~ **copy** 公文正本; 正式抄本 / '~·**holder**
n. 官员 / ~ **hours** 办公(或营业)、门诊时间
/ ~ **hunter**, ~ **seeker** [美]谋求官职的人 / ~
work 办公室工作

officer ['ɔfisə] **I** *n.* ①官员;办事员: a press ~ 新闻发布官 / the ~s of state 政府各部部长 / a customs ~ 海关关务员 / a quarantine ~ 船舶检疫员 ②(团体、组织等的)干事,高级职员(如主任、秘书、司库等) ③军官: the unity between ~s and men 官兵一致 / a Naval (an Army, an Air Force) ~ 海(陆,空)军军官 / a commanding ~ 指挥官,司令官 / an ~ of the day 值日军官 / an ~ of the watch 【军】舰上值班军官 ④警官;法警,执达员: an ~ of the court 法院执达官 ⑤高级船员: a chief (second, third) ~ (船上的)大(二,三)副 / ~s and crew 全船工作人员 **II** *vt.* (常用被动语态)①给…配备军官(或高级船员) ②指挥,统率 ‖*a parade* ~ 只懂得上操和检阅的军官

official [ə'fiʃəl] **I** *a.* ①官员的;公务(职务)上的: an ~ title (residence) 官衔(邸) / ~ duties 公务 / an ~ letter 公函 / an ~ gazette 官方通报 / routine 例行公事 ②官方的,法定的;正式的: news coming from an ~ source 官方消息 / the ~ exchange rate 官方外汇牌价 / an ~ statement (visit) 正式声明(访问) ③官气十足的;讲究形式的: discard ~ airs 放下官架子 ④【医】依据药典(配制)的 **II** *n.* ①官员; 行政人员, 高级职员: government ~s 政府官员 / bank ~s 银行高级职员 ②【宗】宗教法庭推事 ‖*(the President's) ~ family* [美](新闻用语)(总统的)内阁 ‖~**dom** *n.* [总称]官员;官场 ②官僚作风 / ~**ly** *ad.*

officiate [ə'fiʃieit] **❶** *vi.* ①行使职务: ~ (as chairman) at a meeting 主持会议 ②【宗】司祭,司仪 **❷** *vt.* ①执行(公务) ②司(仪) ③充当(比赛的)的裁判

officious [ə'fiʃəs] *a.* ①过分殷勤的; 好管闲事的 ②(外交上)非官方的,非正式的 (official 之对): an ~ statement 非正式声明 ‖~**ly** *ad.* / ~**ness** *n.*

offset ['ɔ(ː)fset] **I** *n.* ①分支,旁支;(山的)支脉;支族,后裔 ②抵销;补偿: an ~ to the loss 对损失的补偿 ③陪衬物 ④【军】开端,出发 ⑤【建】壁阶 ⑥【植】短匍茎 ⑦【机】偏置,偏距;支管;迂回管 ⑧【印】胶印 (经过橡皮滚筒转印的间接印刷法)/(油墨未干造成的)污损 ⑨【地】水平断错 ⑩【船】型值(船体型线对基线的坐标);船体尺码表 ⑪【测】支距: perpendicular ~ 交距,垂直支距 **II** (offset; offsetting) **❶** *vt.* ①抵销;补偿 ②建壁阶 ③【机】偏置 ③用胶印法印刷 **❷** *vi.* ①形成分支 ②(印刷中由于油墨未干)造成污染

offshoot ['ɔ(ː)fʃuːt] *n.* ①分枝;分株 ②支脉,支流,支线 ③支族(的后裔);旁系(的一员)

offspring ['ɔ(ː)fspriŋ] ([复] offspring(s)) *n.* ①儿女;子孙,后代: a mother of numerous ~ 子女众多的母亲 / John is her only ~ 约翰是她唯一的后代。②结果,产物: the ~ of modern times 近代的产物 ③幼苗;仔,崽

often ['ɔ(ː)fn] (比较级 oftener 或 more often, 最高级 oftenest 或 most often) *ad.* 经常,常常:

We ~ go to the countryside. 我们经常下乡。/ How ~ do the buses run? 这公共汽车多少时间一班? ‖*as ~ as* 每当 / *as ~ as not* 往往: As ~ as not the buses are late on foggy days. 每遇多雾天气, 公共汽车往往脱班。/ *every so ~* [口]时常,不时: We meet *every so* ~ and compare notes. 我们不时碰头, 交换意见。/ *more ~ than not* 多半 / *and* ~ 经常 / *once too ~* 见 once ‖~**time(s)** *ad.* =often

ogle ['ougl] **I** *n.* 媚眼, 秋波; [俚]眼 **II ❶** *vt.* 对…做媚眼; 贪婪地看 **❷** *vi.* 做媚眼, 送秋波 (at) ‖~*r n.* 做媚眼的人

ogre ['ougə] *n.* ①吃人的妖魔; ~s of all kinds 形形色色的牛鬼蛇神 ②残暴的人; 可怕的东西 ‖~**ss** ['ougris] *n.* 女妖魔

oh [ou] *int.* 嗬,哦;唉呀!哎哟[表示惊讶、恐惧、痛苦等]: Oh, what a wonder! 嗬,真是奇迹! / Oh, mama! Will you come here, please? 哦, 妈妈!你过来好吗? / Oh, yeah? [美口]哦,是吗?(意为不见得吧)

oil [ɔil] **I** *n.* ①油;[复]油类: animal (vegetable, mineral) ~(s) 动物(植物,矿物)油(类) / edible ~ 食油 / cod-liver ~ 鱼肝油 / hair ~ 生发油 / tar ~ 煤焦油 / (non-)drying ~s 【化】(非)干性油类 ②石油: crude ~ 原油 / ~ seepage 【矿】油苗 / ~ mat 【建】沥青面层 ③[常用复]油画颜料; 油画作品: a portrait in ~s 一幅油画 / ~s by a worker-painter 一位工人画家的油画作品 ④[常用复]油布; 油布雨衣; 油布衣裤 ⑤[口]奉承话; [美俚]鬼话,废话; (贪污的)钱财 **II ❶** *vt.* ①加油于; 给…加润滑油: ~ the bearings of a machine 给机器的轴承加润滑油 / ~ a lock 给锁加油 ②使涂满(或浸透)油 (使(脂肪等)融化 ③贿赂: ~ sb. (或 sb.'s hand, sb.'s palm) 贿赂某人 **❷** *vi.* ①(轮船等)加燃料油 ②(脂肪等)融化 ‖*burn the midnight* ~ 工作到深更半夜;开夜车 / ~ *and vinegar* 截然不同(或水火不相容)的东西 / ~ *one's tongue* 见 tongue / ~ *the wheels* 见 wheel / *pour* ~ *on the flame(s)* (或 on fire) 火上加油 / *pour* ~ *on the (troubled) waters* 平息风波; 调停争端 / *smell of* ~ (作品等)有熬夜赶制的痕迹 / *strike* ~ ①发现油矿 ②一下子发了财;飞黄腾达 ‖~**ed** *a.* ①上了油的,浸透油的;用油润滑了的 ②[俚]醉了的 / ~**er** *n.* ①加油工,润滑工 ②加油器,油壶 ③正产着油的油井 ④油轮船;用油作燃料的轮船 ⑤[复]油布衣裤 / ~**less** *a.* ①缺油的 ②未经油润的 ③不需加油的 ‖~ **box** 油箱, 润滑油盒 / ~ **bunker** 油库;燃油舱 / ~ **burner** 燃油的发动机(或轮船、加热器) ②[美俚]耗油极多的破旧车辆(或船只) / ~ **bush** 【机】充油套管 / ~ **cake** (作饲料或肥料用的)油渣饼(如豆饼、棉子饼等) / '~**can** *n.* 加油器, 油壶 / '~**cloth** *n.* 油布, 漆布 / ~ **colo(u)r** ①[常用复]油画颜料;油漆 ②油溶性染料 / ~ **field** 油田 / '~-'**fired** *a.* 燃油的 / '~-'**ga(u)ge** *n.* 油类比重

测定计 / **~hole** *n.*(机器上灌入润滑油的)油孔 / **'~man** *n.* ①制油工 ②油商，油画颜料商 ③石油大王(指企业家) / **~ meal** (作饲料或肥料用的)油渣粉 / **~ paint** ①油画颜料 ②油漆 / **~ painting** ①画油画；油画艺术 ②油画作品 / **'~ paper** *n.* 油纸 / **~ plant** 油料作物 / **~ press** 榨油机 / **'~-rich** *a.* 石油藏量丰富的 / **'~-silk** *n.* (做雨衣等用的)油绸 / **'~skin** *n.* 油布；油布雨衣；[复]油布衣裤 / **~ slick** (水面上的一层)浮油 / **'~-spring** *n.* 石油泉 / **~stone** *n.*(磨刀用的)油石 / **~stove** *n.* 煤油炉，石油炉 / **~ tanker** ①油轮；油罐车 ②加油飞机 / **~ well** 油井

oily ['ɔili] *a.* ①(含)油的；油状的 ②涂满油的，浸透油的；油腻的 ③(言行等)圆滑的，讨好人的

ointment ['ɔintmənt] *n.* 软膏；油膏；药膏

old [ould] **I** *a.* ①年老的；年代久的；古老的；古时的：an ~ man 老人 / ~ age 老年，晚年 / get (或 grow) ~ 老起来，上年纪 / look ~ 显出老态 / an ~ tree 老树 / ~ wine 陈酒 / a customer of ~ standing 老顾客 / an ~ civilization 古老文明
②(指年龄)…岁的；(指时间)…久的：How ~ are you? 你多大岁数? / at twenty years ~ 在二十岁时 / The house is two hundred years ~. 这房子已历时二百年的历史。 / a six-month-~ strike 已历时六个月的罢工
③旧时的；过去的：(the) ~ society 旧社会 / ~ customs and habits 旧风俗旧习惯 / the ~ year 刚刚过去(或即将过去)的一年 / the ~ country 故国(移居外国的人对本国的称呼：常特指欧洲) / sb.'s ~ students 某人从前的学生
④陈旧的；破旧的；废弃的：~ clothes 旧衣服 / ~ rags 破烂
⑤熟悉的：an ~ story 惯见的事物；老一套 / an ~ friend 老朋友 / ~ familiar faces 老相识的人们
⑥老练的，老资格的：be ~ in diplomacy 外交上很老练 / an ~ hand at sth. 进行某事的老手
⑦暗褐色的
⑧[口](招呼用语，表示亲密)：Old Zhang! 老张!
⑨[口][用在名词前，加强语气]：have a fine (或 good, high) ~ time 过得极愉快 / Any ~ thing (time) will do. 随便什么东西(时候)都行。
II *n.* ①古时；旧时(只用于 of ~ 一习语中)
②…年岁(或月、周)的人(或动物)：a four-year-~ 四岁的孩子(或马等) / a group of ten-year-~s 一群十岁的孩子
③[the ~]旧事物
‖**A man is as ~ as he feels.** [谚]老不老，自己晓。(意为你觉得多老就多老) / **an ~ head on young shoulders** 少年老成 / **as of ~** 一如从前，照旧 / **as ~ as the hills** 极老，极旧 / **be ~ enough to know better** 岁数不小应更懂事些了 / **for ~ sake's sake** 为了老交情 / **from of ~** 自古以来；很久以来 / **of ~** ①

古时的；从前的：the men *of* ~ 古时的人们 / in days *of* ~ 在古时；在从前 ②从前；很久前：have heard it *of* ~. 我很久前就听见过这事了。 / **~ and young** (或 **young and ~**) 老老少少 / **the Old One** 见 **one**
‖**~ boy** ①老同学 ②孩子气的老头 ③(招呼用语)老朋友! 老兄! ④[the O- B-]魔鬼 / **'~-'clothesman** *n.* 旧衣商 / **Old English** 古代英语(450—1150 年间通用的英语) / **'~-'fangled** *a.* 老式的；守旧的 / **'~-'fashioned** *a.* ①老式的；过时的 ②守旧的 ③[英方](目光等)责备的，含义深刻的 / **Old Fashioned** [美]用威士忌酒做成的鸡尾酒 / **~ fog(e)y** 见老守旧派，落后于时代的人 ②老家伙 ③领养老金的老兵 / **'fog(e)yish** *a.* 守旧的，落后于时代的 / **Old Glory** [美]美国国旗的别称 / **~ goat** [美俚]讨厌的老家伙 / **~ guard** [总称]某一事业(或主张)的老一辈的维护者(尤指政党内当权的保守派) / **~ hat** [俚]老式的；反动的 / **~ lady** ①妻子 ②母亲 ③老处女式的人物(可指男人) / **'~line** *a.* ①老资格的；老牌的：an ~-*line* inhabitant 老居民 / the ~-*line* imperialists 老牌帝国主义者 ②守旧的 / **~ liner** ①政治上保守的人；[英][O- L-]保守党党员(或支持者) ②守旧者 / **~ maid** ①老处女 ②老处女式的人物(可指男人) ③一种抽对子的简单牌戏 / **'~maidish** *a.* 带点老处女脾气的；象老处女的 / **~ man** [美俚]①丈夫 ②父亲 ③老板，主管人；工头 ④船长；(美国兵用的称呼)长官(尤指连长) ⑤老资格者；老前辈 ⑥(招呼用语)老朋友，老兄 ⑦妹夫 / **~ master** ①(十八世纪前的)大画家 ②古代大画家的作品 / **~ saw** [美俚]老话，民间流传的格言 / **~ school** [总称]守旧派 / **Old Sol** [谑]太阳 / **~ style** ①老式的东西 ②一种老式铅字 ③[O- S-]西洋旧历 / **Old Testament** (基督教《圣经》的)《旧约全书》 / **'~-time** *a.* ①古时的；旧时的 ②老资格的 / **'~-,timer** *n.* ①老资格的人，老前辈；老手 ②上了年纪的人 ③守旧的人 ④老式的东西 / **'~-,tim(e)y** *a.* (东西、方法等)旧时的，早期的 / **~ woman** ①妻子 ②母亲 / **'~-'womanish** *a.* 婆婆妈妈的 / **Old World** 东半球(与美洲大陆相对而言；尤指欧洲)/**'~-world** *a.* ①旧时代的 ②东半球的(尤指与美洲新大陆相对) ③旧式的，古老风味的

olden ['ouldən] **I** *a.* [古][诗]古昔的：in ~ times (或 in ~ days) 古昔；昔时 **II** *vt.* & *vi.* (使)变老，(使)衰弱

oligarchy ['ɔligɑːki] *n.* ①寡头政治，寡头统治 ②实行寡头独裁的政府(或国家) ③寡头政治集团 ④少数人垄断的组织

olive ['ɔliv] **I** *n.* ①齐墩果属植物；齐墩果；橄榄(旧译，现仍沿用)橄榄树 ②橄榄色，茶青色 ③(作为和平象征的)橄榄叶，橄榄枝，橄榄枝叶圈 **II** *a.* 橄榄的；橄榄色的 ‖**~ branch** ①橄榄枝(和平的象征)：hold out the ~ branch 伸出橄榄枝，建议讲和 / **~ drab** ①草绿色，草黄色 ②草绿色布

呢绒) ③草绿色制服 / ~ green 橄榄绿,茶青色 / ~ oil ①橄榄油 ②[美俚]再会

omelet(te) ['ɔmlit] *n.* 煎蛋卷,炒蛋,煎蛋饼 ‖*You can't make an ~ without breaking eggs.* [谚]有失才有得。

omen ['oumen] **I** *n.* 预兆,兆头: a good ~ 吉兆 / an evil ~ 凶兆 **II** *vt.* 预示,预告: The clouds ~ rain. 这乌云预示要下雨。

ominous ['ɔminəs] *a.* ①不祥的,不吉的 ②预示的,预兆的 (*of*) ‖~**ly** *ad.* / ~**ness** *n.*

omit [ou'mit] (omitted; omitting) *vt.* ①省略;删去: You may ~ the second paragraph from the article. 这篇文章的第二段你可以略去。/ Not a single one can be *omitted.* 缺一不可。②遗漏;忽略;忘记: Don't ~ locking (或 to lock) the door. 别忘了锁门。

omnibus ['ɔmnibəs] **I** *n.* ①公共汽车,公共马车: a hotel ~ 载运旅客往返于车站和旅馆之间的客车 / a private (或 family) ~ (铁路公司提供的)载运旅客和行李往返车站的专用车 ②选集;文集的廉价普及本 (=~ book) **II** *a.* 总括的;多项的;多种用途的 ‖~ **bill** 混合议案

omnipotence [ɔm'nipətəns] *n.* ①全能;无限权力;无限威力 ②[O-]【宗】上帝

omnipotent [ɔm'nipətənt] **I** *a.* 全能的,有无限权力的;有无上权威的 **II** *n.* 万能者; [the O-]【宗】上帝 ‖~**ly** *ad.*

omniscience [ɔm'nisiəns] *n.* ①无所不知;无限知识 ②[O-]【宗】上帝

omniscient [ɔm'nisiənt] **I** *a.* 无所不知的;有无限知识的 **II** *n.* 无所不知者; [the O-]【宗】上帝 ‖~**ly** *ad.*

omnivorous [ɔm'nivərəs] *a.* ①什么食物都吃的,【动】杂食性的 ②[喻]什么书都读的,博览群书的: an ~ reader 什么书都读的人 ‖~**ly** *ad.* / ~**ness** *n.*

on [ɔn] **I** *prep.* ①在…上: a book ~ the table 桌上的书 / an oil painting ~ the wall 壁上的一幅油画 / a blister ~ the sole of one's foot 脚底上的水泡 / float ~ the water 浮在水面上 / ~ the construction site 在工地上 / Have you any matches (any money) ~ you? 你身上有火柴(钱)吗?
②在…旁,靠近…: He sat ~ my right. 他坐在我右边。/ a town (situated) ~ the river 临河的城镇 / a house ~ the main road 临大街的房子
③向着…,对着…: smile ~ sb. 对着某人笑 / draw one's knife ~ sb. 拔刀向某人砍去 / frown ~ sth. 不赞成某事
④在…的时候;在…后立即: ~ Sunday 在星期天 / ~ Sunday afternoon 在星期天下午 / (the morning of) May the 1st 在五月一日(上午) / He comes ~ Saturdays. 他常在星期六来。/ ~ the instant 立刻,当下 / *On arriving*

there, we all set to enthusiastically. 我们一到那里马上就甩开膀子干起来。/ ~ examination (analysis) 经审查(分析)后
⑤根据…,凭…,靠…: act ~ sb.'s advice (instructions) 按照某人的劝告(指示)做 / know sth. ~ good authority 从可靠方面得知某事 / a theory based ~ practice 基于实践的理论 / *On* what ground? 凭什么理由? / buy sth. ~ credit 赊购某物 / live ~ rice 主食大米 / live ~ one's salary 靠薪金过活
⑥关于…: a report ~ the international situation 关于国际形势的报告 / exchange views ~ questions of common concern 就共同关心的问题交换意见 / *On Practice* 《实践论》/ be keen ~ (doing) sth. 热衷于(做)某事,爱好(做)某事
⑦(是)…的成员: be ~ the committee (staff) 担任委员(职员)
⑧在从事…中;处于…情况中: workers ~ strike 在罢工的工人 / go ~ an errand 办差事 / be ~ leave 在休假
⑨通过…;以…的方式: I heard the happy news ~ the radio. 我从收音机里听到这喜讯。/ cut one's finger ~ a knife 手指被刀划破 / talk ~ the telephone 在电话里交谈 / leave ~ an early train 乘早班火车离开 / do sth. ~ the sly (quiet) 秘密(暗暗)地做某事
⑩由…支付(指费用等): This lunch is ~ me. 这顿午饭我来付钱。
⑪(一个)接(一个);…又…: The enemy suffered defeat ~ defeat (loss ~ loss). 敌人接二连三地吃败仗(损人折马)。
II *ad.* ①(安置)上去; (连接)上去: put the kettle ~ 把水壶放在火上 / He has new shoes ~. 他穿上新鞋了。/ turn ~ the radio (water, light, gas) 开收音机(自来水,电灯,煤气)
②向前去; (进行)下去; (继续)下去: Go ~! 往前走! (或: 说下去!) / further ~ 再向前 / later ~ 后来 / from now (that day) ~ 从现在(那天)起 / He is getting (well) ~ in years. 他年纪(很)大了。/ struggle (work, speak, sing) ~ 斗争(工作,说,唱)下去
III *a.* ①在发生 (或活动着) 的;起着作用的: What's ~ at that theatre? 那剧场上演着什么戏? / The battle against drought was ~. 抗旱的战斗在继续中。/ Is there anything ~ tomorrow? 明天有什么事吗? / Is the water ~ yet? 自来水通了吗?
②[口]同意的;乐意参加的: Are you ~? 你同意(或乐意去)吗?
③[俚]醉了的: He is a bit ~. 他有点醉了。
‖*and so* ~ 等等 / *be* ~ *it* [美口] ①准备就绪(常用以指准备从事战斗) ②决定动手做某事 / *be* (或 *get*) ~ *to* …: ①知道,意识到(情况);识透(某人)的意图 ②对(某人)找岔子 / *have something* ~ *sb.* [口]掌握某人的一些事实(指证据等) / *just* ~ 差不多(=almost): *just* ~ a

year ago 差不多一年前 / just ~ 10 dollars 差不多十块钱 / **~ and off** (或 **off and ~**) 见 **off** / **~ and ~** 继续不停地 / **~ with** ①穿上、戴上: On (I'll help you ~) with your coat. 把(我来帮你把)衣服穿上。②开始;继续: On with the training. 开始(或继续)训练吧。

‖**'~-a͵gain, 'off-a͵gain** 时有时无的,断断续续的: **~-again, off-again** headaches (negotiations) 断断续续的头痛(谈判) / **'~-͵coming** a. ①迎面而来的;即将到来的: ~coming traffic【交】对向交通,迎面车流 ②正在兴起的,新兴的 n. 接近 / **'~fall** n. 攻击,袭击 / **'~-flow** n. 滚滚向前 / **'~-͵going** a. 不断前进中的,不断发展中的 n. ①[复](常指古怪或偶然的)事件;行动,行为 ②前进,发展 / **'~-͵licence** n. 不许外卖酒类(只许堂饮)的执照 / **'~-͵line** a. 【自】在线的 / **'~load** vt. 装载: ~load cargo 装货 / **'~͵looker** n. 旁观者;袖手旁观者: The ~looker sees most of the game. [谚]旁观者清。/ **'~͵looking** a. (袖手)旁观的 / **'~rush** n. ①猛冲,直冲;冲击 ②奔流: the ~rush of molten iron 铁水的奔流 / **'~͵rushing** a. 冲势迅急的,汹涌奔流的 / **'~set** n. ①攻击,袭击 ②开始;突然开始: the ~set of labour (分娩前的)阵痛发作 ③【印】利用静电作用通过印版和滚筒间的空隙使油墨涂在纸上的一种印刷法 / **'~shore** a. & ad. ①朝着岸(的) ②在岸上(的);在近岸处(的) ③在国内(的) / **'~'side** n. (足球运动等的)不越位 / **'~'slaught** n. 冲击,猛击;猛攻 / **'~'stage** a. & ad. 在前台(的) / **'~-'stream** ad. 在生产中: A new plant will go ~-stream. 一座新工厂将投入生产。/ **'~-the-'job** a. ①在职时的: ~-the-job training 在职训练 ②工作现场的 / **'~-the-'spot** a. 现场的;当场的: an ~-the-spot investigation (meeting) 现场调查(会议)

once [wʌns] I ad. ①一次: I have been there ~. 我曾到过那儿一次。/ ~ a week 每星期一次 / ~ or twice 一两次 / not ~ 一次也没有 ②曾经,一度;从前 ③[用于否定句]一次也(不…),完全(不…): Don't ~ leave a mistake uncorrected. 决不要放过一个错误。/ I couldn't ~ understand what they meant. 我完全不能理解他们的意思。④[用于条件句等]一旦…: If one ~ (或 When ~ one) loses confidence, he can never expect to do his work well. 一旦失去信心,就甭想做好工作。⑤乘以一: Once one is one. 一一得一。⑥(指亲属间行辈上)小一辈(指程度上)相差无几: a cousin ~ removed 堂(或表)兄弟的孩子,堂(或表)姊妹的孩子 II conj. 一旦…(就…): Once (that) the principal contradiction is grasped, all problems will be readily solved. 一旦抓住了主要矛盾,一切问题就迎刃而解。III n. 一次: Will ~ be enough? 一次就够了吗? IV a. 从前的: a ~ province of the Northeast 从前东北的一个省 ‖**all at ~** ①突然: He left all at ~. 他突然离开。②同时: Don't talk all at ~. Speak one by one. 不要大家同时发言,一个一个轮流讲。/ **at ~** ①立刻,马上: Do it at ~, please. 请马上做吧。②同时 / **~ ... and ...** 既…又…: at ~ simple and forceful 既简明又有力 / **every ~ in a while** 见 **every** / **(for) this ~** (或 **for ~** 或 **just for ~**) 就这一次: Let him go this ~. 这次就(作为例外)让他去吧。/ He beat me for ~. 他只有这一次赢了我。/ **more than ~** 不止一次: I have read the book more than ~. 我不止一次读过这本书。/ **~ again** 再一次: try ~ again 再试一次 / **~ and again** 一而再,再三 / **~ and away** =~ (and) for all / **~ (and) for all** 一次了结地;一劳永逸地;彻底地,永远地 / **Once bit twice shy.** [谚]一次被咬,下次胆小。(或:从经验取得教训。) / **in a way** 只有一次,只有一度 ②偶尔,间或 / **~ in a while** 偶尔,间或: He went to see them ~ in a while. 他偶尔去探望他们。/ **~ more** =~ again / **~ over** =~ again / **~ over lightly** 从头到尾马马虎虎地 / **~ too often** 又(多了)一次: He exceeded the speed limit ~ too often and was criticized. 他再次(开车)超速,受到了批评。/ **~ upon a time** 见 **time** ‖**'~-,over** n. [口]草率的检查;大略一看;草草了事

one [wʌn] I num. 一;一个(人或物);第一(卷、章、页等)(用例参看 **eight**): the viewpoint of ~ dividing into two 一分为二的观点 / ~ half 一半 II pron. ①一个(任何)人;本人: He is ~ who never troubles about his personal interests. 他是一个从不计较个人利益的人。/ little (dear) ~s 孩子(亲人)们 / One is rather busy just now. 人家(指本人)现在正忙着呢。②一个: The task is ~ of great importance (或 a very important ~). 这是个很重要的任务。/ compare the new edition with the old ~s 把新版本同几种老版本作比较 / Which ~s do you want? 你要哪一个? ③[表示与别的对照]这一个: proceed from the ~ to the other 由此及彼 / One has come, the others have not. 一个人来了,其他人还没来。III a. ①一致的,同一的: I'm ~ with you on this subject. 在这个问题上我同你(看法)一致。/ We are all going in ~ direction. 我们都在向同一个方向前进。②完整的,一体的: be ~ and undivided 是不可分的一个整体 ③唯一的,单独一个的: the ~ way to do it 做这事的唯一方法 / No ~ man could lift it. 一个人举,谁也举它不动。④某一: ~ day (night, morning) 在某一天(晚上,上午) / I heard the news from ~ Wu. 我从一个姓吴的人那儿听到这消息。⑤[表示与别的对照]这一: from ~ side to the other 从这一边到另一边 / with a pick in ~ hand and a rifle in the other 一手拿镐,一手拿枪 IV n. ①一元(或镑等)的钞票 ②怪人: He's a ~. 他真是个怪人。③一岁 ④一点钟 ⑤一击 ⑥(食物的)一客 ‖**a fast ~** ①(棒球中的)急球 ②[俚]诡计,骗局: pull a fast ~ on sb. 设计欺骗某人 / a *hot* ~ [美俚]异常滑稽的笑话 / *a nasty* ~ ①责骂 ②使人一蹶不振的打击 / *a quick* ~ [美俚]匆匆一口喝下的威士忌酒 / *be all* ~ 都一样: It's all ~ to me whether you go or not. 你去不去对我都一样。/ *be at* ~ 一致: I'm at ~ with you (We are at ~) on that point. 在那点上我和你(我们)是一致的。/ *become* ~ ①成为一体, 结合 ②结婚 / *by* ~*s and twos* 三三两两地, 零零落落地 / *for* ~ 举个例说(表示作为其中一人): I, for ~, will not go. 拿我来说, 我就不会去。/ *for* ~ *thing* 见 **thing**[1] / *go* (*sb.*) ~ *better* 见 **better**[1] / *have* ~ *over the eight* [英俚]醉得七颠八倒: It is a book of English phonetics, grammar and usage (all) *in* ~. 这是一本英语语音、语法和习惯用法的综合性著作。/ *in the year* ~ 很久以前, 早年 / *lay* ~ *on sb.* [美俚]给某人一拳/ *make* ~ 见 **make** / *never a* ~ 没有一个(人) / *number* ~ 见 **number** / *One above* 【宗】上帝 / ~ *after another* 一个接一个地, 接连地: ~ *after the other* = ~ *after another* / ~ *and all* 个个都, 全都: We are ~ *and all* in favour of the decision. 我们全体拥护这个决定。/ ~ *and only* ①唯一的, 独一无二的 ②[美俚]情人 / ~ *and the same* 同一个(的), 完全一样, 完全一回事 / ~ *another* 互相: help *another* 互相帮助 / ~ *by* ~ 一个一个地, 依次地: *One down!* [美俚] ①来一客吐司! ②第一个障碍排除了! / ~ *man*, ~ *vote* (选举)一人一票 / ~ *of these days* 日内; 总有一天, ~ *of these fine days* 总有一天 / ~ *of those things* 见 **thing**[1] / ~ *or other* (几个中间中)或者这个, 或者别个: One or other of us will go there. 我们中间总要去一个人。/ ~ *or two* 一、两个; 很少的: He has been away only ~ *or two* days. 他才去了没几天。/ ~ *too many* ①多余的一个(尤指在旁碍事的人或东西) ②[美俚]过量的酒, 使人醉倒的酒 / ~ *too many* (或 *much*) *for* 胜过…, 非…所能敌: He was ~ *too many for us.* 他胜我们一筹。/ *taken* (或 *taking*) ~ *with another* 总的看来 / *ten to* ~ 十有八九, 很可能 / *the all and the* ~ 全部, 整体 / *the Evil One* 【宗】魔鬼 / *the Holy One* =One above / *the Old One* 魔鬼; 原始宗教中的主神, 造物主 / *tie* ~ *on* [美俚]闹饮 / *young* ~ ①[常用于称呼]年轻人, 孩子 ②幼兽 ‖'~-'armed **bandit** [俚]吃角子老虎(一种赌具) / '~-'arm **joint** [俚]吃角子老虎(一种赌具) / '~-'arm **joint** [俚]吃角子老虎(一种赌具) / '~-'arm **joint** [俚]下等饭馆 / '~-'eyed *a.* ①独眼的 ②[俚]简陋的; 次要的, 小的 / '~-'handed *a.* 只有一只手的; 用独手干的 / '~-'horse *a.* ①用一匹马的 ②[俚]简陋的; 次要的, 小的: a ~-*horse* town 乡村小镇 / ,~-,**hundred-per'center** *n.* =hundred-percenter / '~-i'dea'd, '~-i'deaed *a.* 想法单一的, 思想狭隘的 / '~-'legged *a.* ①一条腿的 ②[喻]片面的, 不公道的 / '~-'man *a.* ①只需要一个人的 ②由一个人组成的

③由一个人做(或经营)的 / '~-pair *a.* & *n.* [英]二楼的(房间或一套房间) / '~-'seater *n.* 单只座位的汽车(或飞机) / '~-shot *a.* ①一次完成的: ~-*shot cure* 【医】一次疗法 ②只有一次的 *n.* [美俚] ①(在报刊上)一次登完的作品 ②只此一次、下不为例的事 / '~-'sided *a.* ①只有一边的; 一面发达的: a ~-*sided* street 一边有房子的街 / a ~-*sided* plant 一面枝叶茂盛的植物 ②片面的, 单方面的: a ~-*sided* view 片面的看法 / a ~-*sided* decision 单方面的决定 / '~-step *n.* 一种狐步舞(曲) *vi.* 跳一种狐步舞 / '~-time *a.* & *ad.* 从前(的), 一度(的) / '~-to-'~ *a.* 一对一的 / '~-'track *a.* ①单轨的 ②狭隘而刻板的: a ~-*track* mind 狭隘而刻板的思路 ③专一不变的 / '~-'two *n.* [美俚](拳击中)迅速连击两次 / '~-up [美口] *a.* 胜人一筹的: be ~-*up on sb.* 胜某人一筹 *vt.* 胜…一筹, 占…的上风 / ~-**upmanship** [wʌn'ʌpmənʃip] *n.* 胜人一筹的本事 / '~-'way *a.* ①单程的, 单行的: a ~-*way* street 单行道 / ~-*way* traffic 单向交通 / a ~-*way* guy [美俚]直肠肠的人 ②片面的, 单方面的

onerous ['ɔnərəs] *a.* ①繁重的; 艰巨的; 麻烦的: an ~ task 繁重的任务 ②【律】负有法律义务的 ‖~**ly** *ad.* / ~**ness** *n.*

oneself [wʌn'self] *pron.* ①[反身代词]自己, 自身 ②[用于加强语气]亲自 ‖*by* ~ ①(人)处于正常状态(指身体、精神等方面) ②显得自然(或真诚) / *by* ~ 单独地, 独自地 / *come to* ~ 见 **come** / *for* ~ ①为自己 ②独自地; 亲自地: One can't do such a thing *for* ~. 这样的事情, 独自一个人是做不起来的。/ *of* ~ 见 **of**[1]

onion ['ʌnjən] **I** *n.* ①洋葱, 洋葱头; 【植】葱属植物: ~ bulbs 洋葱头 / green Chinese ~ 大葱 ②[俚]头, 脑袋; 脸 ③[美俚]讨厌的家伙; 笨蛋 ④[美俚]搞糟的事 ⑤[美俚]一元钱 **II** *vt.* 用洋葱擦(眼睛)使掉泪 ‖*flaming* ~*s* [俚]【军】在空中爆炸时的高射炮弹(或球形曳光弹)火光 / *know one's* ~*s* [俚]精明干练 / *off one's* ~(*s*) [俚]神智失常 ‖~ **couch** 【植】燕麦草 / '~**grass** *n.* 【植】鳞茎臭草 / '~-**shell** *n.* 圆形船 / '~**skin** *n.* ①洋葱皮 ②葱皮纸(一种薄而半透明的纸)

only ['ounli] **I** *a.* ①唯一的: the ~ way out 唯一出路 / an ~ son 独子 ②最好的, 独一无二的: He is the ~ man for the task. 他是完成这项任务的最合适的人。/ It is said that this kind of plastic is the ~ thing these days. 据说这种塑料是现在最理想的。**II** *ad.* ①只; 仅仅; 才: *Only* he knows. 只有他知道。/ We can ~ try. 我们只能试试看。/ He is ~ a child. 他还不过是个小孩。/ He came ~ yesterday. 他昨天才来。②反而; 结果却; 不料: The failure ~ strengthened our determination. 失败反而使我们的决心更坚定了。**III** *conj.* 可是, 不过: You may use any of these tools, ~ you must replace it after use. 这些工具你都可以使用, 但是用后必须归还原处。‖*not*

~ ... *but* (*also*) ... 不但…而且…: He *not* ~ had read the book *but* (*also*) remembered what he had read. 他不但读过此书，而且还记得所读的内容。 / ~ *just* 刚刚才；恰好: They've (或 They) ~ *just* got up. 他们刚刚起身。 / We were ~ *just* in time. 我们恰好赶上。 / ~ *not* 简直是，几乎跟…一样: He is ~ *not* a boy. 他简直象个孩子。 / ~ *that* 要不是: I would go with you, ~ *that* I am too busy. 要是我不太忙的话，我是愿意同你们一起去的。 / ~ *too* 非常，实在: We shall be ~ *too* pleased to hear from you further. 我们非常欢迎你再来信。 / That's ~ *too* true. 那是千真万确的。

onus ['ounəs] *n.* ①[只用单]义务；责任；负担 ②过失 ③耻辱 ④ =*onus probandi* ‖*onus probandi* [prou'bændai] [拉] 提出证据的责任

onward ['ɔnwəd] **I** *a.* 向前的: an ~ march 前进 **II** *ad.* =onwards

ooze [u:z] **I** *n.* ①河床(或海底等)的沉淀物，淤泥，软泥；沼地 ②鞣皮用的浸液(用栎树皮和黄栌、单宁等煎制) ③渗出；分泌 ④渗出物；分泌物 **II ❶** *vi.* ①渗出；冒出；分泌出: The spring ~s out of a rock. 泉水从岩石中渗出。②[喻](秘密等)泄露 (*out*)；(勇气等)逐渐消失 (*away*): The secret ~d out. 秘密泄露了。③[美俚]偷偷溜走 **❷** *vt.* ①渗出；冒出；分泌出: The wound ~s blood. 伤口出血。 / He was *oozing* sweat. 他在出汗。②似乎散发出: confidence 显出一副充满信心的样子 ‖~ **calf** 染制成的小牛皮

opal ['oupəl] *n.* ①[地]蛋白石: fire ~ 火蛋白石(红色或黄色，带有火样的反射) ②乳色玻璃 (=~ glass)

opaque [ou'peik] **I** *a.* ①不透光的，不透明的: an ~ body 不透明体 ②不反光的，不发亮的；暗的: an ~ colour 暗色 ③不传导的 ④难理解的，晦涩的 ⑤愚钝的，迟钝的 **II** *n.* ①不透明体 ②[the ~] 黑暗 ③[摄]遮光涂料 ‖~**ly** *ad.* / ~**ness** *n.*

open ['oupən] **I** *a.* ①开(着)的: an ~ window 开着的窗 / The flowers are all ~. 花都开了。 / leave a book ~ 让书打开着 ②开阔的，空旷的；敞开的: an ~ field 旷野 / an ~ car 敞篷车 / an ~ drain 明沟 ③开始工作的，营业着的；活动着的: The meeting is now declared ~. 现在宣布会议开始。 / The shops are not ~ yet. 商店还没有开始营业。 / The exhibition is ~ on Sundays. 展览会星期天开放。 ④开放的；可被自由参加的；(赌博等)不受禁止的: the ~ season (渔、猎等)开放期 / an ~ market 公开市场 / an ~ competition 公开比赛 ⑤公开的；坦率的: an ~ letter 公开信 / an ~ secret 公开的秘密 / an ~ heart 坦率的胸怀 / an ~ manner 直率的态度 ⑥悬而未决的；空缺未用的: an ~ question 未解决的问题；容许争论的问题 / leave a matter ~

把事情搁起来暂不解决 / The match seems to be an ~ one. 这场比赛看来胜负未定。 / The position is still ~. 这职位仍空缺着。 / keep one day each week ~ for meetings 每星期留一天用来开会 ⑦散开的，稀疏的: ~ ranks [军]前后列离开一步的队形 / ~ order [军]散开队形 / ~ population 稀疏的人口 / ~ soil 疏松的泥土 ⑧(河流、港口等)不冰封的；(气候)温和的，无冰冻的: The river is ~ in May. 这条河五月里能航行。 / an ~ winter 无冰冻的冬天 ⑨不设防的: an ~ city 不设防城市 ⑩[音]不用指按的 ⑪[医]畅通的: ~ bowels 大便畅通 ‖an ~ account 还在往来的帐户 / an ~ cheque 普通支票(划线支票之对) / ~ circuit [电]开路，断路 / an ~ policy 预定保险单 / an ~ port 不冻港；通商口岸 / the ~ sea 公海 / an ~ syllable 开音节 / an ~ vowel 开元音

II ❶ *vt.* ①(打)开；张开；展开: *Open* the window! 开窗! / *Open* your book at page ten. 把书翻到第十页。 / ~ one's eyes 张大眼睛(表示惊讶) / The flower ~s its petals. 花开。②开放；开始；开立；开设: ~ a library 开放图书馆 / The new railway will soon be ~ed to traffic. 这条新铁路不久就可通车。/ ~ a debate (session) 开始辩论(会议) / ~ an account 开立帐户 / an embassy 开设大使馆 / ~ a new store 开一爿新店 ③开出；开发，开垦；开辟: ~ a well 打井 / ~ ground 开垦土地 / ~ a new road 开辟新路 ④揭开，表明: ~ one's designs 讲明自己的打算 ⑤[医]切开；使畅通: an abscess 开脓肿 ⑥弄松；疏开(队列) ⑦[海](改变船位)避开挡住视线的障碍物而看见: We sailed on until we ~ed a bay. 我们继续航行直至看到一个海湾。⑧撤回(判决等) ⑨(牌戏中)开始(叫牌)；开始(出牌) **❷** *vi.* ①开(放)；张开，展开；发展: The door ~s to the south. 这道门是朝南开的。/ The exhibition does not ~ on Sundays. 展览会星期天不开放。/ The wound ~ed under the strain. 伤口崩开了。/ His understanding ~ed with the years. 随着年龄的增长他的理解力也发展了。②开始；(开始)谈: School ~s next Monday. 星期一开学。/ The programme ~ed with the chorus .... 节目以合唱…开始。/ He ~ed upon the fiscal question. 他开始谈财政问题。/ He did not ~ on the subject. 他没有谈那个问题。③展现；被看见: A magnificent view ~ed before our eyes. 一幅宏伟的图景展现在我们眼前。/ The wonders of astronomy were ~ing to him. 他渐渐了解了天文学的奥秘。/ The harbour lights ~ed. 港口的灯光看得见了。④(猎狗)开始吠起来；[贬](人)开口讲起来 ⑤(牌戏中)开始叫牌；开始出牌

‖an ～ book 见 book / be ～ to ①对…开放的 ②愿接受(或考虑)…的: be ～ to advice 愿接受劝告 / be ～ to an offer 愿考虑(买主的)出价 ③易受…的;可…的: be ～ to infection 易受感染 / be ～ to discussion 可供讨论 / break ～ ∼ 研 / in the ～ 在户外,在野外 / into the ～ ①公开化: The struggles soon came into the ～. 斗争不久就公开化了。②出现 / keep one's eyes ～ 留心看着;注意;保持警惕 / lay ～ ①摊开(书等) ②揭露: lay ～ a plot 揭露阴谋 ③擦伤;弄破: lay one's face ～ 擦伤脸 / ～ fire 见 fire / ～ into (或 on, onto) 通往: The room ～s into a corridor. 这房间通走廊。/ The door ～s on the street. 这扇门通大街。/ ～ out ①(打)开,张开,展开 ②开发;开辟 ③展现;揭示,表明 ④畅谈,直言: ～ out to each other 相互畅谈 ⑤[物]加速 / ～ sb.'s eyes to 使某人看清… / ～ sesame 见 sesame / ～ up ①(打)开,张开,展开 ②开发;开辟 ③揭露;展现 ④开始;开火;发动攻击 ⑤[口]滔滔不绝地谈 / throw ～ ①突然打开,大开 ②开放,取消对…的限制 ‖～ly ad. 公开地,公然地;直率地,坦率地 / ～ness n.

‖'～-'air a. 户外的,野外的 / '～-and-'shut a. 一目了然的 / '～-'armed a. 热诚的 / '～-'book a. 开卷的: an ～-book examination 开卷考试 / ～ chain 【化】开链 / '～-cut, '～-cast a. & ad. 露天开采的(地) n. 露天开采的矿山 / '～-'door a. ①公开的 ②(对外关系上)开门的 / ～ door 门户开放(政策) / '～-'eared a. 倾耳静听的 / '～-'end a. ①开放的: an ～-end mortgage 开放抵押(指凭原抵押品可续行借贷的一种抵押) / an ～-end investment company 发行随时可换成现款的股票的投资公司 / an ～-end contract 开口合同(指一定时间内随时要满足买方提出的各种产品需要的合同) ② =～-ended / '～-,ended a. 无尽头的,无限制的;不固定的,随便的: an ～-ended crisis 无尽头的危机 / an ～-ended discussion 漫谈 / '～-'eyed a. ①睁着眼的;留神的 ②惊讶的 / '～-'faced a. ①露面的 ②坦率的 / '～-'handed a. 慷慨的 / '～-,hearted a. ①坦率的,直率的 ②和善的,慈善的 / ～ hearth 【冶】平炉 / '～-'heart surgery 体外循环心脏手术 / '～-'jaw n. 不完全的飞机来回飞(指不飞回起飞地点的长途来回飞) / '～-'minded a. 虚心的;坦率的 / '～-'mouthed a. ①张嘴的 ②发呆的;吃惊的 / '～-pit a., ad. & n. =～cut / ～ shop 自由雇佣企业(指不论是否工会会员一律招雇的商店或工厂) / ～ skies 开放领空(指我军时双方相互让对方从空中视察军事设施) / '～work n. 透孔细工;透孔织物

opening ['oupniŋ] I n. ①开 ②穴,孔,空隙;通道: an ～ in a hedge 篱笆上的一个洞 ③(林中)空地 ④开始;开端: ～ time (营业等)开放时间 / the ～ night (戏等)上演的第一夜 / the ～ of a book 书的开始部分 ⑤(职位的)空缺;机会 ⑥(象棋等

的)开局 II a. 开首的: one's ～ remarks 开场白

opera ['ɔpərə] n. ①歌剧 ②歌剧的总乐谱;歌剧脚本;歌剧艺术 ③一场歌剧的演出 ④歌剧院 ‖～ glass(es) 观剧用的小望远镜 / ～ house 歌剧院,剧场

operate ['ɔpəreit] ❶ vi. ①操作,工作;运转: ～ in deep water 在深水操作 / The tractor ～s on diesel oil. 拖拉机用柴油开动。②起作用;(药物等)奏效: These reasons ～d on the mind of the hearer. 这些道理在听者思想上产生了作用。/ These factors ～ to (against) our advantage. 这些因素对我们有利(不利)。/ The medicine began to ～ at once. 药立刻开始见效。③施行手术,开刀: ～ on (或 upon) sb. for a tumour 为某人施行切除肿瘤手术 / ～ on the eyes of the patient 给病人眼部做手术 ④[军]作战: ～ against the invaders 对入侵敌人作战 ⑤从事投机(指证券、商品等) ❷ vt. ①操作;开动(机器等): ～ a car 开车 / ～ a machine 开机器 ②[主美]经营,管理(=manage): ～ factories and mines 经营工矿 ③对…施行手术,对…开刀: ～ a malignant growth 切除恶性肿瘤 / ～ a patient on the head 为病人头部做手术 ④完成;引起(变化等): Energy ～s changes. 能量引起变化。

operation [,ɔpə'reiʃən] n. ①操作,工作;运转(方式): the ～ of a machine 机器操作;机器运转 / tunnel ～s 坑道作业 / cycle ～ 循环操作(法) / under-capacity ～ 开工不足(低于运转能量) ②作用;效力: the ～s of nature 大自然的作用(指大自然引起的变化) / the ～ of a drug 药物的效力 / extend the ～ 扩大有效范围;延长有效期限 ③(外科)手术: undergo an ～ on the abdomen 经受腹部手术 / perform an ～ on a patient for appendicitis 为病人施行割除阑尾炎手术 ④[常用复]作战;军事演习;行动计划;[复]【空】地面指挥所: round-the-clock ～s 二十四小时连续作战 / Operation X (用代号进行的)X 行动计划;(工、商业等的)X 运动 ⑤[美]经营;业务: the ～ of a steel mill 经营炼钢厂 / the cost of ～ 业务费;经营费 ⑥交易;投机买卖: black market ～s 黑市交易 ⑦【数】运算: the four ～s 加减乘除,四则 / ～s research [美]运筹学(=[英] operational research) ‖come (或 go) into ～ 施行;生效;开始工作(或运转) / in ～ ①操作中,运转着: The plant has been in ～ for several weeks. 这工厂已开工几个星期了。②生效;实施中: the law in ～ 施行中的法律 / put into ～ 使实施,使生效;使开始工作(或运转): A number of mechanized pits have been put into ～. 已有许多机械化的矿井投入生产。

operator ['ɔpəreitə] n. ①操作人员: a milling (punching) machine ～ 铣(冲)床操作工人 / a telephone ～ 接线员;【军】电话兵 / a telegraph ～ 报务员 / ～s of motor vehicles 司机,驾驶员 ②(外科)手术员 ③[美](厂、矿、铁路、农场等的)经营者;(股票、商品等的)经纪人;投机商人: a mine (farm) ～ 矿(农场)主 / an ～ in real estate 房地产投机商 ④骗子；精明圆滑的人 ⑤【数】(运)算子，算符

opiate ['oupiit] **I** *n.* 鸦片剂；麻醉剂 **II** *a.* 含鸦片的；安眠的；安神的；麻醉的 **III** ['oupieit] *vt.* ①使与鸦片混合 ②使缓和；使减轻(痛感)；使麻醉

opinion [ə'pinjən] *n.* ①意见；看法；主张，见解: be of (the) ～ that … 认为… / give (或 express) one's ～ on (或 upon) … 对…发表意见 / in sb.'s ～ 依照某人的看法 / public ～ 舆论 ②[用单数，并常加不定冠词和形容词]评价: have a good ～ of sb. (sth.) 对某人(某事)评价好 / have no ～ of sb. (sth.) 认为某人(某事)不行 ③(医生、专家等的)鉴定；判定: get (或 have) another ～ 另外请人鉴定 / obtain a medical ～ of the case 取得医生对此病(或此案)的意见 ‖*act up to one's ～s* 照自己主张行事 / *a matter of* ～ 看法不同的问题 / *have the best* ～ 请教高明的专家(如医师、律师) / *have the courage of one's ～s* 见 **courage** ‖～ **poll** 民意测验

opinionated [ə'pinjəneitid] *a.* 固执己见的 ‖～**ly** *ad.* / ～**ness** *n.*

opium ['oupjəm] **I** *n.* ①鸦片 ②起鸦片作用的事物；麻醉剂 ③【动】寄生群落 **II** *vt.* 用鸦片处理 ‖～ **den** 鸦片窟，鸦片烟馆 / ～ **poppy** 【植】罂粟 / **Opium War** 【史】鸦片战争

opponent [ə'pounənt] *a.* 对立的，对抗的；反对的，敌对的: ～ muscle 【解】对抗肌 **II** *n.* ①对手,敌手;反对者: ～s to a bill 议案的反对者 ②【解】对抗肌

opportune ['ɔpətjuːn] *a.* ①(指时间)恰好的,适宜的: You've arrived at a most ～ moment. 你来得正是时候。/ Time (或 The present) is ～ for doing that. 现在正是做那件事的时候。②(行动、事情等)及时的;适时的: ～ criticism 及时的批评 / an ～ rain 及时雨 ‖～**ly** *ad.* / ～**ness** *n.*

opportunist ['ɔpətjuːnist] **I** *n.* 机会主义者: an old-line ～ 老机会主义者 **II** *a.* 机会主义的;机会主义者的

opportunity [,ɔpə'tjuːniti] *n.* 机会; 良机: make an (或 the) ～ of doing (或 to do) sth. 创造做事的机会 / at (或 on) the first ～ 一有机会(就…) / have an ～ for doing (或 to do) sth. 有机会做某事 / have no (little, not much) ～ for doing sth. 没有(很少有,有不多的)机会做某事 / in search of new *opportunities* 寻求新的机会 / I take this ～ of thanking you. 我趁此机会感谢你们。‖*Opportunity makes the thief.* [谚] 疏忽招盗贼。

oppose [ə'pouz] **❶** *vt.* ①反对;反抗 ②使相对;使对抗: ～ black *to* white 使黑白相对 / ～ oneself *to* sth. 反对某事 **❷** *vi.* 反对 ‖**－less** *a.* 不可抵抗的,不可反驳的 / **－r** *n.* 反对者;反对注册某一商标者

opposite ['ɔpəzit] **I** *a.* ①对面的;相对的: on the ～ side of the street 在马路对面 / take a seat ～ to sb. 在某人对面坐下 / the ～ sides of a square 正方形相对的边 ②相反的;对立的: go in the ～ direction 向相反的方向去 / Idealism is ～ *to* (或 *from*) materialism. 唯心论和唯物论是对立的。③【植】对生的;(花部)重迭的: ～ leaves 对生叶 **II** *n.* 对立面;对立物: I thought quite the ～ 我想的刚相反。**III** *prep.* 在…的对面: live ～ the post office 住在邮局对面 **IV** *ad.* 在对面;对过: He stood ～. 他站在对面。‖*one's* (或 *the*) ～ *number* 见 **number** ‖～**ly** *ad.* / ～**ness** *n.*

opposition [,ɔpə'ziʃən] *n.* ①反对,反抗 ②面对,相对: the houses *in* ～ *to* each other 面对面的房子 ③相反;对立: find oneself *in* ～ to sb. on a question 发现自己在某问题上与某人意见相反 ④[常作 O-]反对党: the leader of the *Opposition* 反对党领袖 / the *Opposition* benches (议会中的)反对党席位 / whether in ～ or in office 不论在野在朝 ⑤反对物(如反对派的政策等);反对派 ⑥【天】冲 ⑦【逻】对当,对当法 ‖～**al** *a.* 反对的;对抗的 / ～**ist** *n.* 反对党人;主张(或实行)反对政策者

oppress [ə'pres] *vt.* ①压迫；压制 ②压抑；使感沉重;使烦恼: feel ～ed with the heat 热得难受

oppression [ə'preʃən] *n.* ①压迫；压制 ②压制物 ③沉闷,压抑；苦恼

oppressive [ə'presiv] *a.* ①压迫的；压制的；暴虐的 ②沉重的；烦闷的；难以忍受的: ～ heat 闷热 ‖～**ly** *ad.* / ～**ness** *n.*

oppressor [ə'presə] *n.* 压迫者

opprobrious [ə'proubriəs] *a.* ①辱骂的；无礼的: ～ language 骂人的话 ②该骂的；可耻的 ‖～**ly** *ad.* / ～**ness** *n.*

opprobrium [ə'proubriəm] *n.* 责骂；轻蔑；不名誉,耻辱

optical ['ɔptikəl] *a.* ①眼的;视力的;视觉的 ②光学的: an ～ gas mask 【军】光学防毒面具 / ～ instruments 光学仪器 / an ～ pyrometer 光学高温计 / an ～ spectrum 光谱 ③有助于视力的 ‖～**ly** *ad.* ‖～ **activity** 【物】旋光性 / ～ **art** ＝op

optician [ɔp'tiʃən] *n.* ①眼镜商;光学仪器商 ②镜(或光学仪器)制造者

optimism ['ɔptimizəm] *n.* 乐观；乐观主义 ‖**optimist** *n.* 乐观者;乐观主义者

optimistic(al) [,ɔpti'mistik(əb)] *a.* 乐观的；乐观主义的 ‖**optimistically** *ad.*

option ['ɔpʃən] *n.* ①选择；选择权；选择自由: at one's ～ 随意 / have no ～ but to do sth. 不得不做某事 / make one's ～ 进行选择 / I haven't much ～ in the matter. 我对这个问题没有什么选择的余地。②(供)选择的事物: There are three ～s open to us. 我们有三个选择对象。③【经】买卖的特权(指在契约期内按照规定价格买卖指定的股票、货物等的权利) ④在规定时间内要求

履行合同的特权 ⑤被保险人对赔款方式的选择权

optional ['ɔpʃ(ə)nəl] a. 可任意选择的；非强制的：～ subjects at school 学校选修课 / sign ～【自】任意符号(正或负) ‖～**ly** ad.

opulent ['ɔpjuələnt] a. 富裕的；富饶的；繁盛的；丰富的 ‖～**ly** ad.

or [ɔ:, 弱 ə] conj. ①[表示选择]或，或者；还是：Which do you prefer, white, grey ～ black 你喜欢哪种颜色，白的、灰的、还是黑的？/ *Were* you ～ he there? 那时是你还是他在那儿？/ *Either* you ～ I am to go. 不是你去就是我去。/ I don't know *whether* he will come ～ not. 我不知道他是否来。②[表示不明确]大约，或许：two ～ three miles 两三哩 / sooner ～ later 迟早 / a month～so 一个月左右 ③[引导同义词或同义短语]或者说：It is a pillar, ～ more correctly, a column. 这是一根柱子，或说得更正确些，一根圆柱。/ botany, ～ the science of plants 植物学，即关于植物的科学 ④[常和 else 连用]否则，要不然：Hurry up, ～ (else) you'll be late. 赶快，否则你要迟到了。/ Lay down your arms ～ die! 缴枪不杀！⑤[诗][在 either ... or 中代 either] 不是…(就是)

oracle ['ɔrəkl] n. ①【宗】(古希腊、罗马)神谕宣示所；(古犹太)神殿的至圣处；神龛 ②【宗】神使，传神言者；神谕，神的显示(或启示) ③预言；圣言；至理名言 ④预言者；大智者；明断者 ⑤绝对可靠的检验物(或指示器) ⑥[复]基督教《圣经》‖*Sir Oracle* 说话象神谕般的人 / *work the* ～ ①贿赂僧人获得神谕 ②诱人赞助使计划成功 ‖～ **bone** 卜骨

oracular [ɔ'rækjulə] a. ①神谕的；象神谕的 ②明哲的；预言的；圣言的 ③玄妙深奥的；隐晦的：～ utterances 玄妙难解的话 ‖～**ity** [ɔ,rækju'læriti] n. / ～**ly** ad.

oral ['ɔ:rəl] I a. ①口头的，口述的：an ～ examination 口试 / ～ instruction 口授 ②【解】口的，口部的：～ cavity 口腔 ③【动】口的；前的，前面的 ④【语】(语音)口腔发声的 II n. [口]口试 ‖～**ly** ad.

orange ['ɔrindʒ] I n. ①橙(树)；柑(树)；橘(树)：a mandarin(e) ～ 中国柑橘 ②【植】柑橘属植物 ③橙色，橘色，赤黄色 II a. ①橙(或柑、橘)的：peel 橙(或柑、橘)皮 ②橙色的，橘色的，赤黄色的 ‖*a squeezed* (或 *sucked*) ～ 被榨干了的人(或物) / *squeeze* (或 *suck*) *the* ～ ①榨橙汁 ②吸取脂膏 ‖～ **blossom** 香橙花 / '～,colo(u)red a. 橙色的，橘色的，赤黄色的 / ～ **tip** 粉蝶科蝴蝶 / '～**wood** n. & a. 橙木(的)

orang-outang [ɔ:'ræŋ'u:tæŋ], **orang-utan** ['ɔ:rəŋ'u:tæn] n. 【动】猩猩

oration [ɔ:'reiʃən] n. ①演说，演讲：deliver an ～ 发表演说 ②【语】引语：direct (indirect 或 oblique) ～ 直接(间接)引语

orator ['ɔrətə] n. ①演说者；以技巧、雄辩著称的演讲者；雄辩家 ②(大、中学校毕业典礼等场合)被选出发表演说的学生代表 ③【律】请愿人；原告 ‖*a Public Orator* 英国大学中在重大场合发表演说的校方代表 ‖**oratress** ['ɔrətris] n. 女演说家；女雄辩家

oratorical [ɔrə'tɔrikəl] a. ①演说的；演说家的：an ～ contest 演讲比赛 / in an ～ way 以演说家的方式 ②演说术的；雄辩术的；修辞的 ‖～**ly** ad.

oratorio [,ɔrə'tɔ:riəu] n. 【音】(通常以基督教《圣经》故事为主题的)清唱剧；圣乐

oratory ['ɔrətəri] n. ①演讲(术)；雄辩(术)；修辞 ②小礼拜堂；祈祷室 ③[O-] (天主教)一五六四年由 Saint Philip Neri 创办的一种崇尚通俗说教的神父团体

orb [ɔ:b] I n. ①【军】环；圆；圆面 ②球；球体；天体 ③【军】(行星等的)轨道 ④(星球、行星等的)影响范围 ⑤[诗]眼；眼珠 ⑥(象征王位的)顶上有十字架的圆球 ⑦集合体；(有组织的)整体 II ❶ vt. ①使形成球体(或圆面) ②[诗]包围 ❷ vi. ①[古]沿着轨道移动 ②[诗]形成球体 ‖～**ed** a. 球形的；圆的

orb

orbit ['ɔ:bit] I n. ①眼窝，眼眶 ②(鸟或昆虫)复眼缘的狭部 ③(天体等的)运行轨道：put a man-made earth satellite into ～ 把人造地球卫星送入轨道 / the ～ of the earth 地球轨道 ④势力范围；活动范围；生活常规：bring sth. within the ～ of 把某事纳入…的轨道 / the trading ～ of a country 一个国家的贸易圈 II ❶ vt. ①环绕(天体)作轨道运行：a satellite ～*ing* the earth 环绕地球运行的(人造)卫星 ②使进入轨道运行：a satellite ～ 把(人造)卫星送入轨道 ❷ vi. ①(卫星等)沿轨道运行；环行：a plane ～*ing* over a landing field 在着陆场上盘旋的飞机 ②把人造装置射入轨道 ‖～**al** a. 轨道的；眼窝的：～*al* elements 【天】轨道要素 / ～*al* motion 【天】轨道运动 / ～**er** n. 沿轨道运行的东西(尤指绕天体作轨道运行的宇宙飞船) ‖～**ing laboratory** 【宇】(绕)轨道实验室：a manned ～*ing laboratory* 载人(绕)轨道实验室 / ～**ing station** (人造卫星)轨道站 / ～ **trajectory** 【军】轨道弹道

orchard ['ɔ:tʃəd] n. ①果园：an apple ～ 苹果园 ②果园里的全部果树 ‖～**ist** n. 果园主；果园管理人；果树培养人 ‖～**man** ['ɔ:tʃədmən] n. =～ist

orchestra ['ɔ:kistrə] n. ①管弦乐队；管弦乐队的全部乐器：a symphony ～ 交响乐队 ②古希腊剧场舞台前供合唱队用的半圆形场地 ③(剧场中的)乐队席 ④古罗马剧场舞台前的半圆形贵宾

席; 剧场正厅的全部前排座位; 剧场的正厅 ‖~ l
[ɔ:'kestrəl] a. ①管弦乐队的; 供管弦乐队演奏的:
~l instruments 管弦乐器 ②管弦乐队所演奏的;
有管弦乐队风格的: an ~l performance 管弦乐
队的演出

orchid ['ɔ:kid] I n. ①【植】兰, 兰花 ②淡紫色
③[常用复]【喻】称赞, 祝贺; 恭维话 II a. 淡紫
色的

ordain [ɔ:'dein] ❶ vt. ①委任(某人)为牧师,任命
(某人)任圣职 ②(法律等)制定,规定; 命令: what
the law ~s 法律所规定的内容 ③(神、命运等)注
定 ❷ vi. 颁布命令

ordeal [ɔ:'di:l] n. ①(对品格或忍耐力的)严峻考
验; 苦难的经验; 折磨 ②神裁法(古条顿族施行的
判罪法); 例如将嫌疑犯的手浸于沸水中,受神主宰,
手无损, 则定为无罪: ~ by water(fire) 探水(探
火)神裁法

order ['ɔ:də] I n. ①次序, 顺序: be arranged in
alphabetical ~ 按字母次序排列 / in ~ of age
(importance) 按年龄(重要性)的次序 ②有条理;
整齐; 正常状况: in good ~ 很整齐 / 状况正常 /
love of ~ 爱整齐 / put one's ideas into ~ 理
理自己的思想 / The machine is in good working
~. 这部机器运转良好。③秩序; 制度; (会议等
的)规程; 程序: the new (old) ~ 新(旧)秩序 /
public ~ 社会秩序 / keep ~ 维持秩序 / a
point of ~ 有关议事规程问题 ④【军】队形; 序
列: advance in open(close) ~ 以疏散(密集)队形
前进 / an ~ of battle 战斗序列 ⑤等级; 种类; 概
数, 大约:【生】目(介于纲和科之间): considerations
of quite another ~ 从完全不同角度出发的考
虑 / a population of the ~ of 100,000 十万左
右的人口 ⑥阶层; 界; 团体: all ~s and degrees
of men 各阶层的人 / the higher (lower) ~s 上
(下)层社会 / the military ~ 军界 / a monastic
~ 修士会 ⑦勋章; 勋位; 获得勋章(或勋位)
的一批人: ~ of merit, first class 一等功
⑧[复]牧师职; 牧师授职仪式: take (holy) ~
成为牧师 ⑨[常用复]命令: resolutely carry out
~s 坚决执行命令 / give ~s for sth. to be done
命令把某事做完 / take (obey) ~s 接受(服从)命
令 / await ~s【军】待命 / a cease-fire ~ 停战令
⑩【律】(法院等的)决议(指非最后的判决) ⑪定
购; 定货单; (待)交付的定货; (点)一份菜; (叫)一
客饭: give a factory an ~ for ... 向工厂定购
... / fill (或 execute) an ~ 交付定货 / an ~ for
three lathes 三台车床的定单 / I'll have an ~
of fish. 我要一客鱼。⑫汇票, 汇单: a postal (或
post-office, money) ~ 邮政汇票 ⑬(转让产业
的)许可证, 授权证明书; (剧院等的)优待券, 免费
入场券: an ~ to view (a house) (房屋)察看许可
证 ⑭【数】阶, 级 ⑮【建】柱式(尤指古典建筑的柱
型); 式样 II ❶ vt. ①整理; 安排: ~ one's affairs
料理事务 / ~ one's life well 把生活安排好 ②命
令; 指令: ~ an advance 命令前进 / ~ mobilization 下动员令 / He ~ed that the work (should)

order

be started at once. 他命令立即开始工作。/ The
regiment was ~ed to the front. 这个团被调往
前线。/ ~ sb. arrested [美]下令逮捕某人 ③定
购: ~ fertilizer from a shop 向商店定购肥料 /
~ a suit 定制一套衣服 / ~ a meal 叫一客饭
④任命(某人)为牧师, 授圣职给 ❷ vi. ①发命
令, 指挥 ②定货 ‖a large (或 tall) ~ [口]难办
到的事; 难供应的东西 / a marching ~【军】个
人携带的装备 / an Order in Council (英国)
咨询枢密院后不经议会同意而颁布的敕令 / a
review ~ ①检阅队形 ②全副装备 / a short ~
(点)快餐 / by (或 at the) ~ of 奉...之命 /
call to ~ ①叫(人)遵守议事规程 ②宣布开
(会) / draw up in ~ 使排整齐 / in apple-pie
~ 整整齐齐【军】以散开队形 / in ~ ①整齐; 秩序井然: put a room in ~ 把房间
整理好 ②状况良好: Everything is in ~. 情况
良好。③符合(会议等的)规程 ④适宜; 妥当: The
following suggestions may be in ~. 下列建议
可能是合适的。/ Is your pass in ~? 你的出入
证办妥了没有? / in ~ that ... 为了..., 以...为
目的: They flew there in ~ that they might be
in time to attend the opening ceremony. 他们
飞往那里以便能及时参加开幕典礼。/ in ~ to
为了..., 以...为目的: We started early in ~ to
arrive before dark. 为了在天黑前到达, 我们
早早地动了身。/ in short ~ 在短期内; 迅速
地 / made to ~ 定制(的) / march(ing) ~
【军】行军命令 / on ~ 已定(购)而尚未交货的
on the ~ of 属于...同类的, 跟...相似的 / Order
of the Patrons of Husbandry 见 patron /
Order! Order! ①安静! 安静!: Order! Order!
The meeting is going to begin. 安静! 安静! 马
上就要开会了。②违章! 违章! / out of ~ ①要
把某人差来差去 / out of ~ ①次序颠倒 ②不整
齐 ③状况不佳; 发生故障: My stomach (watch)
is out of ~. 我的胃(表)出毛病了。④不符(会
议)规程 ⑤不适宜; 不妥当 / place an ~ for
sth. with 向...定购某物 / rise to (a point of)
~ (议员)起立质询有关违背议事规则的事 /
standing ~s ①议事规则 ②【军】现行命令; 标

准作战规定 ③【会计】制造费用单 / *take ~ to* (do) 采取适当手段去(做…) / *take ~ with* 安排,处理 / *the ~ of nature* 自然的规律 / *the ~ of the day* ①议事日程: put sth. on *the ~ of the day* 把某事提到议事日程上 ②风气: Co-ordination and mutual help have become *the ~ of the day*. 协作和互相帮助已蔚然成风。 / *under the ~s of* 受…指挥;奉…之命: *under the ~s of* a doctor 遵医嘱 ‖~**ing** ['ɔ:dəriŋ] *n.* 【物】有序化 ‖~ **book** ①定货簿 ②[常作 O-B-] (英国下议院的)动议议事登记簿(也作 Order Paper) ③【军】命令簿 / ~ **cheque** 记名支票,抬头支票 / ~ **form** 定货单

orderly ['ɔ:dəli] **I** *a.* ①整洁的;整齐的;有条理的: an ~ desk 整洁的书桌 / The room is in ~ condition. 房间整齐清洁。 / an ~ bin [英] (路旁的)废物箱 / an ~ person 有条理的人 ②有秩序的;守纪律的: intense but ~ work 紧张而有秩序的工作 / an ~ crowd 守纪律的人群 ③【军】关于命令的传达(或执行)的: an ~ book 命令簿 / an ~ man 传令兵 / an ~ officer 值班军官 / an ~ room (军营内的)文书室 **II** *n.* ①【军】传令兵;勤务兵;通讯员 ②护理员(尤指军医院的);勤杂工: a medical ~ 卫生员 ③街道清洁工 **III** *ad.* ①依次地,顺序地 ②有规则地;适当地 ③有条理地

ordinal ['ɔ:dinl] **I** *a.* ①依次的,顺序的: ~ numbers 序数(如 first, second, twentieth 等) ②【生】"目"的 **II** *n.* ①序数 ②[O-]【宗】仪式书;圣职授任礼书;弥撒规则书

ordinance ['ɔ:dinəns] *n.* ①法令;条令;条例: a government ~ 政府法令 ②【宗】仪式(尤指圣餐) ③传统的风俗习惯 ④(神或命运)注定的事

ordinary ['ɔ:dinəri] **I** *a.* ①普通的,平常的;平凡的: ~ workers 普通劳动者 / ~ forces【军】常规部队 / in ~ dress 穿着平常的衣服 ②差劲的,低等的;不精致的: very ~ wine 劣等酒 ③【律】有直接管辖权的;直隶的 **II** *n.* ①【律】推事 ②[英]【宗】罪犯的忏悔牧师;[the O-]大主教,教区主教 ③记载宗教仪式规程的书典 ④[英]客饭;小酒店;定时供膳的小餐馆 ⑤[美]查验遗嘱的法官 ⑥(纹章中的)普通图记 ‖*in ~* ①(职务等)常任的 ②(待修的舰船等)闲搁着的 / *out of the ~* 不平常的,非凡的 ‖**ordinarily** ['ɔ:dinərili] *ad.* / **ordinariness** *n.* ‖~ **seaman** (英国海军)新水兵

ordination [.ɔ:di'neiʃən] *n.* ①排成等级;分类 ②委任;受委任 ③【宗】圣职授任;授予圣命 ④颁布法令

ordnance ['ɔ:dnəns] *n.* ①[总称]大炮 ②军械,军用器材: an ~ depot 军械库 / an ~ factory 兵工厂 ③军械署,军械部门 ‖~ **officer** 军械军官;军械主任 / ~ **stores** 军械器材

ore [ɔ:] *n.* 矿;矿砂,矿石: iron ~ 铁矿 / a piece of ~ 一块矿石 / an ~ deposit 矿床 ‖~ **body** 矿体 / ~ **dressing** 选矿

organ ['ɔ:gən] *n.* ①器官;【机】元件: the ~s of speech (或 the vocal ~s) 发音器官 / the ~s of vegetation (植物的)营养器官 ②嗓音: a singer with a magnificent ~ 嗓音洪亮的歌手 ③机构,机关: state ~s 国家机关 / the ~s of political power 政权机关 ④喉舌;报刊: ~s of public opinion 舆论的喉舌 ⑤管风琴,风琴;类似风琴的乐器: a pipe ~ 管风琴 / a reed ~ 簧风琴 / a mouth ~ 口琴 ‖~ **blower** 操作风琴风箱的人;风琴风箱的操作装置 / ~ **builder** 风琴制造人 / '~-,**grinder** *n.* 在街头演奏手摇风琴营生的人 / ~ **loft** (教堂等)放置管风琴的楼厢 / '~-**stop** *n.* 音栓(即管风琴上定音各异而音色相同的一排管子) ②音栓发声装置中的轴柄

organism ['ɔ:gənizəm] *n.* 生物体;有机体

organist ['ɔ:gənist] *n.* 风琴演奏者,风琴手

organization [.ɔ:gənai'zeiʃən] *n.* ①组织(指动作或状态);体制,编制: be engaged in the ~ of a strike 从事于组织罢工的工作 / Only with ~ can the wisdom of the collective be given full play. 只有组织起来,才能充分地发挥集体智慧。 / war (peace) ~ 战时(平时)编制 ②(政党、社会、企业等)的组织,团体: a social ~ 社会团体 ③【生】有机体,机构: The human body has a very complex ~. 人体具有很复杂的机构。 ‖~ **man** (组织机构内)驯顺的成员;(大公司内)听话的职员

organize ['ɔ:gənaiz] ❶ *vt.* ①[常用被动语态]使有器官;使有机化,使成有机体 ②组织;编组: ~ (the peasants into) mutual aid teams 组织(农民加入)互助组 / ~ an attack 组织进攻 / ~ a fire-net 组织火力网 / ~ an army 编组军队 ③[美]使(工人)组成工会;在(工厂、行业)组织工会 ④使有条理 ⑤给…化妆,给…打扮 ❷ *vi.* ①成有机体 ②组织起来;建立组织 ③[美]组织工会 ‖~**r** *n.* ①组织者,建立者 ②工会组织人 ③【生】形成体

orgy, orgie ['ɔ:dʒi] *n.* ①[常用复](古希腊、罗马)祭酒神的秘密宗教仪式 ②[复]纵酒宴乐;狂欢;狂舞 ③无节制;放荡: an ~ of bloodshed 大规模的血洗

orient ['ɔ:riənt] **I** *n.* ①[诗]东方 ②[the O-]东方;亚洲;远东;东亚;地中海以东的国家 ③优质的珍珠;珍珠的光泽 **II** *a.* ①[诗]东方的 ②光辉夺目的;珍贵的 ③[诗](太阳等)升起的;新生的 **III** ['ɔ:rient] ❶ *vt.* ①使(建筑物等)朝东;建筑(教堂等)使其圣坛在东端 ②调整;定…的位;[喻]使适应;使认清形势: We must ~ our work *to* the needs of the people. 我们必须使我们的工作适应人民的需要。 / ~ oneself *to* new surroundings 使自己适应新环境 / a therapy-~ed, not a research-~ed medical establishment 一所着重治疗不着重研究的医学机构 ③【化】使定向 ❷ *vi.* ①面向东;面对一定的方向 ②适应形势

oriental [.ɔ:ri'entl] **I** *a.* ①[O-]东方的;东方国家的;东方人特有的;远东的 ②(珍贵等)最优质的;珍贵的;有特殊光泽的 **II** *n.* [O-]东方人(尤指中国人和日本人) ‖~**ly** *ad.*

orientation [ˌɔːrienˈteiʃən] *n.* ①向东 ②定位; 定向; 方针(或态度等)的确定 ③方向; 方位; 倾向性: the general ~ 大方向 ④(对周围环境等的)倾向性 ⑤某些动物(如鸽等)的回家本能 ‖~al *a.*

orifice [ˈɔrifis] *n.* 孔, 口, 洞口; 通气口

origin [ˈɔridʒin] *n.* ①起源; 由来; 起因: the ~(s) of civilization 文明的发源 / a word of Latin ~ 源自拉丁语的词 / a certificate of ~【商】(出口商向进口商品国家提出的)商品产地证明书 / the ~ of a dispute 争执的起因 ②出身; 血统: be of noble (humble) ~ 出身高贵(微贱) ③【数】原点: ~ of coordinates 坐标的原点 ④【解】起端: ~ of muscle 肌起端

original [əˈridʒən*ə*l] **I** *a.* ①最初的, 最早的; 原始的, 原先的: an ~ edition 原版(指未经修改的最初版本) / the ~ inhabitants of the country 这国家最早的居民 / the ~ plan 原计划 ②新颖的; 非抄袭的 ③有独创性的; 有独到见解的: ~ views 独到的(或创造性的)见解 / an ~ thinker 有创见的思想家 ④原创作者的; 原作品的: the ~ picture 画的原作 **II** *n.* ①[the ~]原物, 原作品; 原文: This is a reproduction, not the ~. 这是复制品, 不是原作。 ②原型(指文艺作品中描绘形象所依据的真人或真事) ③有独创性的人 ④脾气古怪的人 ⑤[古]来源, 起因 ‖~ly *ad.*

originality [əˌridʒiˈnæliti] *n.* ①创造力; 独创性; 创见; 创举: display much ~ 显示出很大的创造力 / a man of great ~ 很有创见的人 ②新颖

orinasal [ˌɔːriˈneiz*ə*l] *n.* & *a.*【语】鼻化元音(的)

ornament I [ˈɔːnəmənt] *n.* ①装饰物, 装饰品: a shelf crowded with ~s 摆满装饰品的架子 ②装饰, 修饰: add sth. by way of ~ 加添某物作装饰 ③添光彩的人(或物) (to) ④[常用复]【宗】礼拜用品(如圣坛、圣杯等) ⑤[常用复]【音】装饰音 **II** [ˈɔːnəment] *vt.* 装饰; 美化: ~ a hall with paintings 用画装饰大厅

ornamental [ˌɔːnəˈment*ə*l] **I** *a.* 装饰的; 作装饰用的 **II** *n.* ①装饰品 ②观赏植物 ‖~ism *n.* 讲究装饰的倾向 / ~ist *n.* 装饰家 / ~ly *ad.*

ornate [ɔːˈneit] *a.* ①装饰华丽的; 过分装饰的 ②(文体)华美的, 绚丽的; 矫揉造作的 ‖~ly *ad.* / ~ness *n.*

ornithology [ˌɔːniˈθɔlədʒi] *n.* ①鸟学, 禽学 ②鸟学论文 ‖ornithologist *n.* 鸟学家, 禽学家

orphan [ˈɔːfən] **l** *n.* ①孤儿 ②失去生母的幼小动物 **II** *a.* ①无父母的; 无父(或母)的; 孤儿的: an ~ asylum 孤儿院 ②(幼小动物)失去生母的: ~ pigs 失去母猪的猪崽 **III** *vt.* 使成孤儿: be ~ed in babyhood 婴儿时就成为孤儿 ‖~hood *n.* 孤儿身分, 孤儿状态

orphanage [ˈɔːfənidʒ] *n.* ①孤儿身分, 孤儿状态 ②孤儿院 ③[总称]孤儿

orthodox [ˈɔːθədɔks] *a.* ①正统的(尤指宗教方面); 传统的, 习俗的; 保守的: ~ ideas 正统观念 / be very ~ in one's behaviour 在行为方面拘于习俗, 从不越轨 ②[O-]【宗】东正教(会)的: the *Orthodox* Eastern Church 东正教(会) ‖~y *n.* ①正统性; 正统观念; 正统做法 ②【宗】正教

orthography [ɔːˈθɔgrəfi] *n.* ①正字法, 缀字法 ②表音法(指用文字或印刷符号标出某一语言的音) ③【建】面图投影 ④【数】正交射影 ‖**orthographic(al)** [ˌɔːθəˈgræfik(ə)l] *a.*

oscillate [ˈɔsileit] ❶ *vi.* ①摆动; 振动;【物】振荡: an *oscillating* axle 摆动轴 ②动摇; 犹豫: ~ in one's opinions 打不定主意 ③【无】发杂音 ④(银行利率等)在中间值上下波动 ❷ *vt.* 使摆动; 使动摇 ‖**oscillation** [ˌɔsiˈleiʃən] *n.*

osier [ˈouʒə] **I** *n.* ①柳树; 杞柳, 紫皮柳; 青刚柳 ②柳条 **II** *a.* 柳条做的: an ~ basket 柳条篮子 ‖~-bed *n.* 柳园; 柳林

ostensible [ɔsˈtensəbl] *a.* ①可公开的; 显然的: have different ~ properties 具有显然不同的特性 ②外表的, 表面的; 诡称的: one's ~ motive (purpose) 表面的动机(目的) ‖**ostensibly** *ad.*

ostentation [ˌɔstenˈteiʃən] *n.* 夸示; 卖弄; 铺张; 风头主义: detest ~ in any form 憎恶任何形式的虚饰 / be free from individual heroism and ~ 没有个人英雄主义和风头主义

ostentatious [ˌɔstenˈteiʃəs] *a.* 夸示的; 卖弄的; 铺张的; 炫耀的 ‖~ly *ad.* / ~ness *n.*

ostler [ˈɔslə] *n.* 旅店中料理马(或骡)的人

ostracism [ˈɔstrəsizm] *n.* ①(古希腊)贝壳放逐法, 陶片放逐法(由公民将他认为对国家有危害的人的名字记于贝壳或陶片上进行投票, 逾半数者, 则被放逐国外十年或五年) ②流放; 放逐 ③排斥: suffer political (social) ~ 受到政治上的(社会的)排斥

ostracize [ˈɔstrəsaiz] *vt.* ①(古希腊)用贝壳放逐法放逐 ②流放; 放逐 ③把…排除在团体之外; 排斥

ostrich [ˈɔstritʃ] *n.* ①鸵鸟; 鸵鹋: bury one's head in the sand like an ~ 鸵鸟似地把头埋进沙里(据说鸵鸟遇危险时常这样做, 自以为把头藏起人们便看不见它) / an ~ policy 鸵鸟政策 ②鸵鸟似的人; 自以为不正视危险便可避开危险的人: try to play ~ 想实行鸵鸟政策 ‖*have the digestion of an* ~ 消化力强 ‖~ism *n.* 故意无视现实; 自我陶醉 / ~like *a.* 鸵鸟般的 ‖~ farm 鸵鸟养殖场

other [ˈʌðə] **I** *a.* ①另外的, 其他的: ask some ~ people 问其他的人 / Any ~ suggestions? 还有什么别的建议吗? / I'll come again some ~ day. 我改日再来吧。 ②[常加定冠词](两个中)另一的; 其余的: Now open your ~ eye. 好啦, 睁开你另一只眼睛吧。 ③不久前的; 以前的: the ~ day 几天前 / in ~ times 从前 ④第二的, 隔一个的: every ~ day 每隔一天 / Write on every ~ line. 隔一行写。 ⑤更多的, 额外的 ⑥不同的 **II** *pron.* ①[复]另外的人(或事物), 其他的人(或事物): I don't like these. Can you show me any ~s? 我不喜欢这几个, 你能不能另外拿

几个给我看看？ / Some are ploughing, ~s seeding. 一些人在耕地,其他人在播种。 / do good to ~s 为别人做好事 ②[常加定冠词](两个中)另一个人(或事物);[复]其余的人(或事物): Each of us helped the ~. 我俩互相帮助。 / Of the two contradictory aspects, one must be principal and the ~ secondary. 矛盾着的两方面中,必有一方面是主要的,他方面是次要的。 / This article is better than the ~s. 这篇文章比其余的好。 / (the) two ~s (或 the ~ two)另外两个 ③不同者;对立物 **III** *ad.* 另外地,不同地‖*each / none ~ than* 不是别人(或他物)而正是: *of all* ~s在所有的当中(表示唯一、突出等): He is the man *of all* ~s for the role. 在所有人中只有他适合演这个角色。 / The one thing *of all* ~s we detest is treason. 我们最恨的是叛徒行为。/ *one after the* ~ 见 one / *one or* ~ 见 one / ~ *from* 不同于: ~ *than* ① 不同于,非: The truth is quite ~ *than* what you think. 事实真相同你想的完全不同。 ② 除了: All parts of the house ~ *than* the windows were in good condition. 除了窗子外,屋子的其他部分都很好。 / I cannot read the long letter ~ *than* cursorily. 这封长信我只能草草地读一下。/ ~ *things being equal* 见 thing¹ / *quite* ~ 完全不同的: It must be decided by *quite* ~ considerations. 必须另行考虑来决定。/ *some ... or* ~ 见 some

otherwise [ˈʌðəwaiz] **I** *ad.* ①另外,别样: He thinks ~. 他不这样认为。/ I could do no ~ *than* laugh. 我不能不笑起来。②在其他方面: The article is long, but not ~ blameworthy. 这篇文章就是长,其他倒没什么不好。/ an ~ perfect picture 除某一缺点点得以改正则是完美无缺的一幅画 ③要不然;否则: He reminded me of what I should ~ have forgotten. 他提醒了我,要不然我就会把这事给忘了。 **II** *a.* ①另外的,不那样的: if conditions were ~ 假使情况不是这样的话 ②其他方面的: sb.'s ~ equals 在其他方面同某人不相上下者‖*and* ~ 等等;及其他: He helped me with advice *and* ~. 他通过向我提出劝告等方式给我帮助。/ *or* ~ 或其反面: the merits *or* ~ of the method 这方法的优点或缺点 ‖~-ˈminded *a.* ①想法不同的 ②思想逆潮流的

otter [ˈɔtə] ([复] otter(s)) *n.* ①【动】獭,水獭: a sea ~ 海獭 ②水獭(毛)皮

otter

Ottoman [ˈɔtəmən] **I** ([复] Ottomans) *n.* ①土耳其(族)人 ②[o-] 有垫矮凳;无靠背的睡榻;垫脚凳 ③[o-]【纺】粗横棱纹织物 **II** *a.* 土耳其(人)的; 土耳其民族的; 土耳其帝国的 ‖~ **Empire** 【史】奥斯曼(或鄂斯曼)帝国,奥托曼帝国

ouch¹ [autʃ] *int.* ①(突然受痛时的叫声)哎哟 ②[表示不满]哎

ouch² [autʃ] **I** *n.* ①[古](皮带等的)扣环 ②胸针,饰针(妇女用饰物,尤指镶有宝石的) ③镶嵌宝石的底框 **II** *vt.* [古]用饰针装饰

ought¹ [ɔ:t] **I** *v. aux.* [无时态和人称变化,后接动词不定式] ①[表示责任、合适性、可能性等]应当,应该;总应该: There ~ not to be much noise in a hospital. 医院里不该喧闹。/ If he started at seven, he ~ to be here now. 要是他七点钟出发,这会儿总应该到了。②[后接动词不定式的完成式]早应该,本应,本当: You ~ to have done the work yesterday. 你昨天就该把这工作做好了。/ The child ~ not to have been allowed to go alone. 本不应该让这孩子一个人去。 **II** *n.* 应尽的义务,责任

ounce [auns] *n.* ①盎司,英两,啢(常衡=¹/₁₆磅; 金衡及药衡=¹/₁₂磅;略作 oz.) ②少量;一分(力量): If you had had an ~ of resolution, that would not have happened. 你要是稍有一点决断的话,那事本来是不会发生的。/ exert every ~ of energy 用尽一切气力 ③流量啢,液啢

our [ˈauə] *pron.* [we 的所有格] ①我们的: ~ country 我们的国家 / in ~ midst 在我们中间 ②(报刊编者等用语)我(们)的: in ~ opinion 据我(们)看来 ③(帝王在正式场合用以代替 my)朕的,寡人的 ④(用以指对谈话双方都有关系或感兴趣的人)我们那个…: *Our* newcomer works marvellously. (我们)那个新来的同志工作很出色。‖*Our Father*【宗】天父,上帝;主祷文 / *Our Lady*【宗】圣母玛利亚 / *Our Saviour*【宗】耶稣

ours [ˈauəz] *pron.* ①[物主代词]我们的(东西);我们的家属(或有关的人): Victory is ~! 胜利属于我们! / a friend of ~ 我们的一个朋友 ②(报刊编者等用语)我们自己的: Subheads are ~ 小标题是我们加的。③[英]我们的部队

ourselves [ˌauəˈselvz] *pron.* ①[反身代词]我们自己: contradictions between ~ and the enemy 敌我矛盾 / We shall give ~ the pleasure of calling (on you). 我们将高兴地去拜访(你)。②[用以加强语气]我们亲自,我们自己: We ~ made it. 这是我们自己造的。③(报刊编者等用语)我(们)自己(有时用 ourself): We cannot persuade ~ (或 ourself) that .... 我(们)没法相信… ④ [用于 be, become, come to 等之后]我们的正常情况(指健康、情绪等): Wounds healed, we *are* quite ~ again. 伤治好后,我们都又健壮如前了。‖*(all) by* ~ ①我们独自地 ②我们独力地,全靠自己地 / *between* ~ 只限于咱俩之间(不得外传)

oust [aust] *vt.* ①驱逐,撵走: ~ sb. *from* office 把

某人撤职 ②剥夺 (*of*) ③取代: Take care that quantity does not ~ quality. 注意不要一味追求数量而忽视了质量。

out [aut] **I** *ad.* ①出; 在外: go ~ 出去 / Come ~! 出来! / dine ~ 在外吃饭 / live ~ 住在外面 / wear a coat inside ~ 反穿着上衣 / pick (point) ~ 挑(指)出 / sing ~ the old year 用歌声送走旧岁 / find a way ~ 找到出路 / be ~ at sea (船或人) 出航在海上 / have an evening ~ 在外度过一个夜晚(指外出看戏等) / The librarian told me that No. 71929 was ~. 图书馆管理员告诉我 71929 号图书借出去了。
②出声地: call (或 cry) ~ 叫出声来
③现出来, 显露出来; 已问世: The moon will soon be ~. 月亮快出来了。/ The roses are ~. 玫瑰花开。/ The chickens are ~. 小鸡出壳。/ let a secret ~ 泄漏秘密 / be ~ at elbows (衣服) 破损得露出肘部 / [喻] (人) 穷困潦倒 / His article will come ~ in tomorrow's papers. 他的文章将在明天的报上登出。/ Mrs. Green's daughter is ~. 格林太太的女儿已出来参加社交活动了。
④到竭尽点; 处于正常(或到期、荒疏)状态: Summer is ~. 夏天过去了。/ Supplies were running ~. 给养将尽。/ The wind is dying ~. 风正在停息。/ The tide is ~. 潮退了。/ put the fire (light, cigarette) ~ 把火(灯, 香烟)熄掉 / This dress is ~. 这种女服已过时了。/ This lease is ~. 这项租约到期了。/ My hand is ~. 我的技能荒疏了。
⑤明显地, 突出地: bring ~ the hidden meaning 把含义明显地表达出来 / tell sb. sth. straight ~ 将某事直截了当地告诉某人
⑥从头至尾地, 彻底地: hear sb. ~ 听某人把话说完 / fight it ~ 决一雌雄 / have one's sleep (cry) ~ 睡(哭)个够 / feel tired ~ 精疲力竭 / wait till it dries ~ 等它干透
⑦有差错地; 不一致地: Your guess was a long way ~ (或 was far ~). 你的猜测差得远呢。/ They fell ~ over some trifles. 他们因为一些小事闹翻了。
⑧脱漏地: leave ~ a word 漏掉一个词
⑨一份一份地; 以分类形式: portion sth. ~ 把某物一份一份地分配出去 / sort sth. ~ 把某物区分、挑选出来
⑩处于在野状态; 处于缺席状态; 在罢工中: vote sb. ~ 投票使某人下台 / be ~ because of sickness 因病缺席
⑪处于无知觉状态: He passed ~. 他昏过去了。/ knock sb. ~ 把某人打昏
⑫(板球、棒球等运动中) 以使对方球员出局退场的击法; 处于出局(或退场)状态
⑬(无线电通话用语) "报文完, 不必回话"
II *a.* ①外面的; 往外去的; 外围的: an ~ match 外出访问比赛 / the ~ train 开出去的列车 / the ~ islands 外围岛屿
②在野的, 下台的

③特大的: a coat of an ~ size 特大尺寸的上衣
④(板球、棒球等运动中)出局的
⑤[美俚]最新式的
III *n.* ①外面, 外部
②外出; 旅游
③在野党人; [复]在野党: the ins and the ~s 执政党与在野党 / The ~s are against the signing of the treaty. 在野党反对签该条约。
④外观, 体面: make a poor ~ of it 失体面, 出洋相
⑤推脱的借口; 脱身之计; 出路: a possible ~ 可能的推托(或解决办法)
⑥(货品等的)缺点; (境遇的)不利处
⑦[英][复]付出的钱, 税款
⑧[印](字句的)漏排
⑨脱销货
⑩(板球等的)出局人; (网球等的)出界球
IV ❶ *vt.* ①赶出, 驱逐
②[英俚]击倒, 击昏
③(在板球等运动中)使出局; 使退场
❷ *vi.* ①外出; 旅游
②暴露; 成为人所共知: Truth will ~. 真相终将大白。
③拿出; 说出(*with*): He ~s *with* the whole story 他把全部事情都说出来了。
V *prep.* ①通过…而出: run ~ the door 跑出门去
②沿着…而去: drive ~ the wooded road 沿着树木茂密的道路驶去
‖**all** ~ 见 **all** / **at** (或 **on the**) ~**s** (**with sb.**) (同某人)不和 / **be down and** ~ 见 **down**[1] / **be** ~ **for** 力图要; 一心为 / **from** ~ (**of**) 从…中出来: From ~ the cellar came a strange odour. 从地窖里传出一股怪味道。/ **from** ~ **to** ~ 从一端到另一端: the width of the building *from* ~ *to* ~ 大楼两侧间的宽度 / **have it** ~ (**with sb.**) 见 **have** / ~ **and about** (尤指病人在病愈后)能够外出走动 / ~ **and away** 远远地, 大大地: This is ~ *and away* the best method I know. 据我所知, 这是最好的方法了。/ ~ **and home** 往返, 来回 / ~ **and** ~ 十足地, 彻头彻尾地 / ~ **from under** [口]脱离危难 / ~ **of** ①在…外; 离开…; 从…里面: Fish cannot live ~ *of* water. 鱼离了水就不能活。/ This animal is not found ~ *of* certain areas in Africa. 这种动物只在非洲的某些地区有。/ copy a paragraph ~ *of* a book 从一本书上抄下一段 / drink ~ *of* a bottle 从瓶子里喝 / one ~ *of* every ten 每十个中的一个 ②出于, 由于 ③缺乏; 没有: We are ~ *of* tea. 我们的茶叶用完了。/ This book is ~ *of* stock (print). 这本书脱销(绝版)了。/ ~ *of* practice 缺乏练习; 荒疏 / ~ *of* work 失业的 ④放弃; 丧失: talk sb. ~ *of* doing sth. 说服某人不做某事 / reason sb. ~ *of* his fears 说明道理使某人不怕 / be done ~ *of* sth. 被骗去某物 ⑤越出…

之外: ~ *of* the ordinary 不平常的,非凡的 / ~ *of* control 控制不了 / times ~ *of* number 无数次 / sing ~ *of* tune 唱得走调 ⑥用…(制成): make a box ~ *of* old planks 用旧木板做一只箱子 ⑦来自;(指动物)由…所生殖 / ~ *of it* ①不加入;不在内,没有份 ②(因没有份而)闷闷不乐;感到向隅: He couldn't understand what they were saying and felt simply ~ *of it*. 他听不懂他们讲些什么,非常纳闷。③跟不上,脱节;搞错: You're absolutely ~ *of it*. 你完全搞错了。/ ~ *to*(do)力图要,一心要 / *Out upon you!* [古] (表示厌恶,斥责等)呸! 咄! / ~ *with* ①拿出;说出: Out with it! 拿出来! 说出来! ②赶出;逐出: *Out with* him! 赶他出去! ③与…不和: be ~ *with* sb. 同某人闹翻

‖'~-and-'~ *a.* ①十足的,彻头彻尾的: This is ~-and-~ big-power chauvinism. 这是彻头彻尾的大国沙文主义。②公开的,明目张胆的 / '~-and-'~er *n.* 过激分子,极端派 / '~-of-'date *a.* 过时的 / '~-of-'dateness *n.* 过时 / '~-of-'door *a.* 室外的,露天的 / '~-of-'doors *a.* =~-of-door *ad.* 在室外,在露天 *n.* [用作单]室外,露天 / '~-of-the-'way *a.* ①偏僻的 ②罕见的,少有的;破例的

outbid [aut'bid] (过去式 outbid 或 outbade [aut-'beid], 过去分词 outbid 或 outbidden [aut'bidn]; 现在分词 outbidding) *vt.* 出价高于(别人): ~ each other 互相抬高价钱

outbound ['autbaund] *a.* 开往外地的;开往外国的: an ~ ship 开往外地(或外国)的船 / ~ freight 出口货

outbreak ['autbreik] *n.* ①(战争、叛乱、愤怒等的)爆发;(瘟疫、虫害等的)突然蔓延: the ~ of war 战争的爆发 ②暴动,反抗: a slave ~ 奴隶暴动

outbuilding ['aut,bildiŋ] *n.* 【建】外屋(指车库、谷仓等)

outburst ['autbə:st] *n.* ①(感情等的)爆发: an ~ of anger 勃然大怒 / an ~ of cheers 一阵爆发性的欢呼 ②迸发;激增 ③(火山等的)喷发;喷出: an ~ of tears 眼泪的夺眶而出

outcast ['autkɑ:st] I *a.* 被遗弃的;被放逐的;无家可归的 II *n.* ①被遗弃者;被逐出者;流浪者: a social ~ 被社会所排斥的人 ②[英方]争吵

outclass [aut'klɑ:s] *vt.* 大幅度地super过;比…高一档

outcome ['autkʌm] *n.* ①结果;后果;成果: a direct (final) ~ 直接(最后)结果 / the ~ of scientific experiments 科学研究成果 ② =outlet

outcrop I ['autkrɔp] *n.* 【地】①(矿脉等的)露头;露出地面的岩层: ~ of the fault 断层露头 ②爆发,迸发 II [aut'krɔp] (outcropped; outcropping) *vi.* 露头;显现出

outcry I ['autkrai] *n.* ①喊叫,吆喝,呐喊: make an ~ 发出呐喊 ②强烈抗议(或反对)(*against*);强烈要求(*for*) ③拍卖;喊价 II [aut'krai] ❶ *vi.* 喊叫 ❷ *vt.* 叫喊得比…响

outdistance [aut'distəns] *vt.* (指赛跑或竞赛中)把

…远远抛在后面;大大超越

outdo [aut'du:] (outdid [aut'did], outdone [aut-'dʌn]) *vt.* ①胜过,超越: The newcomers have *outdone* the old hands. 后来者居上。/ ~ sb. in kindness 比某人更仁慈(或客气) ②战胜,制服 ‖~ *oneself* ①超过自己原有水平 ②尽了自己最大的努力

outdoor ['autdɔ:] *a.* ①户外的,室外的;露天的,野外的: ~ labour 室外劳动 / ~ sports 室外运动 / an ~ theatre 露天剧场 / an ~ life 野外生活 ② 对不住在贫民院的贫民进行施舍的: ~ relief 对不住在贫民院的贫民的施舍

outdoors ['aut'dɔ:z] I *ad.* 在户外;在野外: go ~ for military training 到野外进行军事训练 II *a.* =outdoor III [复]*n.* [用作单] ①露天 ②野外 ‖~y *a.* 有野外特点的;爱好野外活动的

outer ['autə] I *a.* ①外部的,外面的;外侧的: the ~ covering 外面的覆盖物 ②远离开中心的: an ~ region 边远地区 ③【哲】客观外界的;物质的 II *n.* (射击)靶子环外,环外命中 ‖the ~ man 人的外表(指面貌、服装等) / the ~ world [总称]外界;外部世界 ‖~most *a.* 最外面的;远离中心的 ‖~-di'rected *a.* 符合客观外界标准的 / ~ space 外(部)空间,星际空间 / '~wear *n.* [总称]外衣,外套;户外穿的服装

outface [aut'feis] *vt.* ①盯得…偏促不安,逼视…使其将眼目光移开 ②面对…而无惧色;蔑视

outfit ['autfit] I *n.* ①装备(指动作): The ~ of the exploring party took only half a month. 探险队整装只化了半个月的时间。②全套工具,全部用品;全套装备: a dentist's ~ 牙医用的全套器械 ③[喻]精神方面的素质 ④(在一定场合穿着的)全套衣装: an ~ for camp 露营衣装 ⑤(指班、组、队等)有组织的团体、单位(尤指部队);(某人手下的)全班人马 ⑥牧场;庄园 II (outfitted; outfitting) ❶ *vt.* 装备,配备 ❷ *vi.* 得到装备 ‖**outfitter** *n.* ①服饰用品商店 ②出售旅行及野营用具的商店 ③【船】安装机器的机工

outflank [aut'flæŋk] *vt.* ①【军】对…进行翼侧包围 ②迂回绕过(或避开) ③阻挠,挫败

outgrow [aut'grou] (outgrew [aut'gru:], outgrown [aut'groun]) *vt.* ①生长速度超过,长得比…快 ②长(或发展)得超过(某事物)的作用范围;长(或发展)得不再要(某事物): He has *outgrown* these toys. 他已长大,不再要这些玩具了。/ a habit 随着年龄长大戒掉了某一习惯 / The boy has *outgrown* this suit. 这男孩已长大,穿不下这套衣服了。

outgrowth ['autgrouθ] *n.* ①长出,派生 ②旁枝;支派 ③副产品;结果

outhouse ['authaus] *n.* ①外屋,附属的小屋 ②(户外)厕所

outing ['autiŋ] I *n.* ①出游;户外活动(尤指远足野餐): an ~ at the beach 海滨小游 / go for an ~ 外出游玩 ②体育比赛;划船练习;跑马练习;

score a victory in the second ～ 在第二次比赛中获胜 II *a.* 供户外活动用的 ‖～ **flannel** 软绒布

outlandish [aut'lændiʃ] *a.* ①外国气派的 ②希奇古怪的; 粗鲁笨拙的 ③偏僻的; 边远的 ‖～**ly** *ad.* / ～**ness** *n.*

outlast [aut'lɑːst] *vt.* 比…经久; 比…活得长

outlaw ['aut-lɔː] I *n.* ①被剥夺公民权者; 被放逐者 ②被查禁的组织 ③歹徒; 逃犯; 亡命之徒 ④难驯服的动物(如马) II *vt.* ①剥夺(某人)的公民权; 将(某人)放逐 ②宣布…在法律上失效; 宣告…为不合法 ‖～**ry** *n.* ①公民权的(被)剥夺; 放逐 ②宣布非法, 非法化 ③逍遥法外 ‖～ **strike** [美俚]未经工会批准同意的罢工

outlay I [aut'lei] (outlaid [aut'leid]) *vt.* 支付; 花费 II ['aut-lei] *n.* 支出; 费用

outlet ['aut-let] *n.* ①(河流等的)出口; 出路; 通风口(或孔): an ～ for export produce 出口商品的口岸 ②发泄(感情或精力等)的方法(或机会); 排遣: an ～ for the emotions 发泄情感的途径(或机会) ③销路; 批发商店 ④[电]输出口; 引出线; 电源插座

outline ['aut-lain] I *n.* ①轮廓, 外廓: a broad ～ 大概的轮廓 ②略图; 素描 ③大纲, 提纲; 草案; 概要; [复]要点, 主要原则: a detailed ～ for the investigation 调查细目 / an ～ of English grammar 英语语法概要 / give an ～ of the story 概要说明故事内容 ④隐夜没下的钓鱼线 II *vt.* ①画出…的轮廓; 打…的草图: The railway bridge is ～d by brilliant electric lights. 灿烂的灯光勾划出铁路桥的轮廓。②概括; 提出…的纲要; 略述

outlive [aut'liv] *vt.* ①在(某人)死时尚未死; 比(某物)经久; 度过(风暴、危机等)而健在: ～ one's contemporaries 比同时代的人活得长 / The ship has ～d the storm. 这只船从暴风雨中脱险出来了。②老到超过…的程度: This car has not yet ～d its usefulness. 这辆车还没有老到无用的地步。

outlook ['aut-luk] *n.* ①眺望处; 望楼 ②(眺望中的)景色, 风光: a room with an ～ on the sea 面临海景的房间 ③观点, 看法; 眼界, 视野: a correct ～ on life 正确的人生观 / a man of broad ～ 眼界广阔的人 ④展望; 前景: the political (economic) ～ 政治(经济)前景 / further ～, dry and sunny (天气预报用语)前景: 干燥, 晴朗 ‖**on the** ～ 眼望着, 留心着: He has been *on the* ～ for an opportunity. 他一直等待着机会。

outlying ['aut,laiiŋ] *a.* ①远离中心(或主体)的: an ～ district 边沿区 / an ～ island 外围岛屿 ②无关的; 题外的

outnumber [aut'nʌmbə] *vt.* 在数量上超过: be ～ed 2 to 1 以二比一被超过

outpatient ['aut,peiʃənt] *n.* 门诊病人: an ～ department 门诊部

outpost ['autpoust] *n.* ①[军]前哨; 前哨基地; 警

戒部队: an ～ area 警戒地区 / an ～ line of resistance 警戒部队抵抗线 ②边区村落

output ['autput] *n.* ①产量(尤指某一特定时期的); [总称]产品: the annual ～ of steel 钢的年产量 / the total value of industrial and agricultural ～ 工农业总产值 / the literary ～ of the 1970's 二十世纪七十年代的文学作品 ②(力、能等的)输出量 ③[讯]输出功率; 输出信号; 输出 ④[医]排泄量; 排泄物

outrage ['aut-reidʒ] I *n.* ①蛮横逞凶; 暴行 ②伤害; 凌辱; 蹂躏: an ～ *against* (或 on, upon) society (justice) 对社会(正义)的严重损害 ②严重的违法(或败坏道德的)行为 ③(因暴行而引起的)义愤, 痛恨 II *vt.* ①对…施暴行/伤害; 凌辱; 违(法): an act that ～*s* public opinion 违反民意的行为 / ～ sb.'s sense of justice 粗暴地伤害某人的正义感 ②引起…的义愤 ③强奸

outrageous [aut'reidʒəs] *a.* ①蛮横的; 残暴的 ②无耻的; 使人憎厌的; 令人不能容忍的 ‖～**ly** *ad.* / ～**ness** *n.*

outright ['aut-rait] I *a.* ①直率的; 无保留的: an ～ manner 坦率的态度 ②彻底的; 全部的: an ～ rogue 彻头彻尾的恶棍 / the ～ cost of an undertaking 企业的全部费用 II [aut'rait] *ad.*

outset ['aut-set] *n.* 开端, 开始: at (或 in) the ～ 在开头时 / from the ～ 从一开始

outside ['aut'said] I *n.* ①外部, 外面, 外侧 ②外表, 外表: Don't judge a thing from the ～. 别从外表看事物。/ The building has a magnificent ～. 这座大楼外观宏伟。③外界: impressions from the ～ 来自外界的印象 / those on the ～ 外界人士; 局外的人们 ④(英国旧时四马大车等的)车顶坐位(或乘客) ⑤[复]一令纸最外层的上下两张 II *a.* ①外部的, 外侧的; 表面的, 外面的: ～ measurements (物体)外围的尺寸 / ～ repairs (房屋)外部的修理 ②外界的: Ask the switchboard operator for an ～ line. 叫(电话)接线员接外线。/ ～ help 外援 ③(英国旧时四马大车等)顶上的: an ～ seat 车顶(或近末端的)坐位 ④最大限度的: an ～ price (estimate) 最高的价格(估计) ⑤[美俚]私生的: an ～ child 私生子 ‖*an* ～ broadcast 不在播音室内进行的播音(指实况转播等) / *an* ～ broker 一般经纪人(指不入证券交易所的经纪人) / *an* ～ cadre 外来干部 (与 local cadre 本地干部相对而言) / *an* ～ chance 不大可能的机会 / *the* ～ edge (花样滑冰的一种)以单只冰刀的外刃滑冰 / *an* ～ opinion 外界(尤指英国议会外人士)的意见 / *an* ～ porter 向车站外送行李的搬运工 / ～ work 不在工作场所(而拿回家中)做的工作 / *the* ～ world 外界 III *ad.* ①向外面, 在外面; 向室外, 在室外 ②向海上, 在海上; 在露天 ③外表上, 外观上 ④[体]出线, 出界 ⑤在车顶坐位: ride ～ 乘坐车顶坐位 IV *prep.* ①向…外; 在…外: walk (wait) ～ the house 走向(等候在)屋子外 ②超出…(的范围): ～ the law 超出法律范围 ③[口]除了: No one objected ～ one or two. 除了一两个人外没有人反对。‖*at the* (*very*) ～ 至多,充其量: There were only fifty people *at the* (*very*) ～. 充其量不过五十个人。/ **get** ～ **of** [俚][谑]吃;喝 / ～ **and in** 里里外外 / ～ **in** 里面翻到外面;彻底地 / ～ **of** =outside (*prep*.)

outsider ['aut'saidə] *n*. ①外人,局外人;非会员②外行,门外汉 ③[口](资产阶级社交上所谓)不受欢迎的粗俗人 ④(比赛中)不大可能获胜的选手(或赛马) ‖*The* ～ *sees the best* (或 *the most*) *of the game*. [谚]旁观者清。

outskirt ['aut-skə:t] *n*. [常用复]外边;郊区

outspoken [aut'spoukən] **I** outspeak 的过去分词 **II** *a*. 直言的,坦率的,毫无保留的: ～ **in** the expression of one's opinions 率直地发表意见 / ～ criticism 坦率的批评 / ～**ly** *ad*. / ～**ness** *n*.

outstanding [aut'stændiŋ] **I** *a*. ①凸出的 ②杰出的;显著的 / ～ contributions 卓越的贡献 ③未完成的,未解决的;未付款的: an ～ issue 悬而未决的问题 / an ～ cheque 未兑现支票 ④(股票、公债等)已公开发行并售出的 **II** *n*. [复]未偿清的贷款;未清算的账目 ‖～**ly** *ad*.

outstay [aut'stei] *vt*. ①比…住得久;住得超过(限度): He ～*ed* the other visitors. 他比其他来宾逗留更久。/ ～ one's welcome 因耽搁太久而不再受欢迎 ②在持久力上超过

outstrip [aut'strip] (outstripped; outstripping) *vt*. ①越过 ②胜过,超过: ～ a country *in* 在…方面超过某一国家

outward ['aut-wəd] **I** *a*. ①外面的;外表的: the ～ appearance of things 事物的表面 / For ～ application only. (药品标签用语)只供外用 ②明显的;可见的;公开的 ③向外的;外出的: an ～ voyage 海外航行 ④肉体的;外界的: the ～ man 【宗】肉体;[谑]衣服,丰采 / the ～ eye 肉眼(别于 the mind's eye) / ～ things 周围世界,物质世界 ⑤[英方]嗜酒的;放荡的 **II** *ad*. 向外,(船等)往海外 **III** *n*. ①外表;外形 ②[复]外在事物;周围世界 ‖*to* ～ *and* 从表面上看来 ‖～**ly** *ad*. / ～ **to** ①向外 ②外表上;在外 / ～**ness** *n*. ①客观存在;客观存在性 ②对周围世界的关心,对外在事物的敏感 ‖～-'**bound** *a*. 开往外国(或外地)的

outwit [aut'wit] (outwitted; outwitting) *vt*. ①智胜: ～ one's enemy 斗智克敌 ②哄骗,使上当

outwork[1] ['aut-wə:k] *n*. ①[常用复]【军】简易外围工事 ②户外工作;在(商店、机关等)外部进行的工作,外勤工作

outwork[2] [aut'wə:k] *vt*. ①工作比…做得更好(或更快、更勤);[古]手艺上超过 ②圆满地完成

oval ['ouvəl] **I** *a*. 卵形的;椭圆形的 **II** *n*. ①卵形(物) ②【物】卵形度;【数】卵形线 ‖～**ly** *ad*.

ovation [ou'veiʃən] *n*. ①(古罗马)次于英雄凯旋的一种欢迎仪式,小凯旋式 ②热烈鼓掌,热烈欢迎: a thunderous ～ 雷鸣般的鼓掌欢呼 ‖～**al** *a*.

oven ['ʌvn] *n*. ①炉,灶: hot from the ～ 刚出炉的;刚出笼的 / coke ～ 【冶】炼焦炉 ②烘箱 ‖*in the same* ～ 处于相同的困境

over ['ouvə] **I** *prep*. ① 在…上方;在…上面: A lamp hung ～ us. 在我们(头顶)的上方悬挂着一盏灯。/ a bridge ～ a river 河上的一座桥 / spread a cloth ～ a table 把台布铺在桌上 / hit sb. ～ the head 打中某人的头 ②[表示地位、职权、势力等]高于…,在…之上: He is ～ me in the office. 他职务比我高。/ lose control ～ oneself 失去自制力 ③[表示数目、程度]在…以上,超过: He is ～ fifty. 他五十开外了。/ He spoke (for) ～ an hour. 他讲了一个多小时。/ cost ～ five dollars 价在五元以上 / hold a big lead ～ the others 大大超过别人 ④越过…;从…边缘上往下: jump ～ a trench 跳过壕沟 / climb ～ a mountain 爬过山 / look ～ a hedge 从篱笆上面看过去 / He spoke to me ～ his shoulder. 他转过头来跟我说话。/ The child fell ～ the balcony. 小孩从阳台上掉了下来。⑤在…对面: a city ～ the border 边界对过的一城市 / friends ～ the sea 海外朋友 ⑥[表示时间]在…期间;直到…过完: ～ several decades 在几十年中 / work ～ night 通宵工作 / Can't you stay ～ Sunday? 你不能呆到星期天再走吗? ⑦遍及;(指在温习、检验等时)从头至尾经过…: show a guest ～ the house 领客人走遍全屋参观 / go ～ one's notes 把笔记从头至尾看一遍 ⑧在(做)…时: He sang ～ his work. 他边工作边唱歌。/ We'll discuss it ～ our dinner. 我们吃饭时再谈谈这个问题。/ The bargain was made on June 21st ～ (cups of) cherry. 这笔交易是于六月二十一日在喝樱桃酒时作成的。⑨在…方面,关于;由于: take pains ～ study 在学习上下功夫 / Debates arose ～ some technical questions. 在一些技术问题上产生了争论。/ mourn ～ sb.'s death 哀悼某人的去世 ⑩通过…的通讯途径: listen to a newscast ～ the radio 听无线电新闻广播 **II** *ad*. ①翻倒;翻转过来: knock a bottle ～ 把瓶打翻 / He fell ～ on the ice. 他摔倒在冰上。/ Please turn ～. 请阅背面。(略作 P. T. O., 或只写 Over) ②从一边到对过一边: swim ～ to the other side of the river 游到河对岸去 / I'll come ～ and see you after work. 下班后我来看你。/ Hand that spade ～ to me. 把那把铁锹递给我。/ win sb. ～ 把某人争取过来 ③(越)出: climb (jump) ～ 爬(跳)过 / The milk boiled ～. 牛奶煮得溢了出来。④在另一处,在那边: The post office is ～ there. 邮局在那一边。⑤从头至尾地;全部地;通盘地: Let's talk (think) it ～. 让我们详谈(细想)一下。/ read a book several times ～ 把一本书通读好几遍 / paint a door ～ 把门全部漆遍 / The wound healed ～. 伤口全部愈合了。⑥剩下来;多一些: questions left ～ from history 历史上遗留下来的问题 / citizens of eighteen and ～ 十八岁和十八岁以上的公民 /

one metre and a bit ~ 一米多一点 ⑦过分地; 太: He is ~ polite. 他太客气了。/ He hasn't done it ~ well. 这事他干得不太好。 ⑧结束; 完了: The storm is ~. 暴风雨过了。⑨再:do it ~ 再做一次 ⑩(无线电通话用语)"报文完, 请回复。" **III** *a.* ①上面的; 上级的 ②外面的 ③过分的 **IV** *vt.* 跳过; 越过 **V** *n.* ①额外(或多余)的东西 ②【军】远弹(超过目标落下或爆炸的射弹) ‖ all ~ 见 all / ~ again 再一遍, 重新 / ~ against 在…对面; 与…相反 / ~ all 遍; 从一头到另一头 / ~ and above ①在…之上, 高于…; 重于… ②在…之外(还): We gave them two tons ~ and above the amount agreed to. 除洽定的数字外我们还给了他们两吨。/ ~ and ~ (again) 反复, 再三

overact ['ouvər'ækt] ❶ *vt.* 过火地表演(某一角色); 过分地做(某事) ❷ *vi.* 演得过火; 做得过分

overall ['ouvərɔ:l] **I** *n.* ①[复]工装裤 ②[英][复](军礼服中的)紧身军裤 ③[英](一般在家里穿的)宽大的罩衫 **II** *a.* ①包括一切的; 全面的; 综合的: ~ consideration 全盘考虑 / an ~ settlement 全面解决 / a person in ~ charge 总负责人 ②从头至尾的: ~ length 全长 **III** [,ouvər'ɔ:l] *ad.* ①总体上; 总的说来: *Overall, it is a good book.* 总的说来, 这是一本好书。②从船头到船尾

overall

overawe [,ouvər'ɔ:] *vt.* 威慑; 吓住: Don't be ~d by authorities and big names. 不要被权威、名人所吓倒。

overbalance [,ouvə'bæləns] **I** ❶ *vt.* ①使失去平衡: ~ oneself 身子一歪 ②重于; 压倒; 超过 ❷ *vi.* 失去平衡; 歪倒下来 **II** *n.* ①超过; 超值; 超重: an ~ of exports 出超 ②失去平衡

overbear [,ouvə'bɛə] (overbore [,ouvə'bɔ:], overborne [,ouvə'bɔ:n]) ❶ *vt.* 压倒; 制服; 超过 ❷ *vi.* 结果实过多; 繁殖过度

overboard ['ouvəbɔ:d] *ad.* 向船外; 从船上落(或抛)入水中: A man ~! 有人落水! ‖ go ~ for 过分爱好; 狂热追求 / throw ~ 把…扔到船外; [喻]废除; 抛弃: throw sb. ~ 把某人从船上推落水中; 抛弃某人, 不再支持某人

overcast ['ouvə-ka:st] **I** *n.* ①覆盖; 多云的天, 阴暗的天空 ②【矿】风桥 ③(鱼网等的)过远的一撒 **II** *a.* ①遮盖的 ②多云的, 阴暗的: an ~ night

密云满布的夜晚 ③郁闷的, 忧愁的 ④包边缝纫的 **III** ['ouvə-ka:st] (overcast) ❶ *vt.* ①覆盖, 遮盖 ②使阴暗 ③过远地撒(网等) ④包(边)缝纫, 拷(边), 锁(边) ❷ *vi.* 阴暗起来: It's ~ing for rain. 天阴暗起来要下雨了。

overcoat ['ouvəkout] *n.* 大衣

overcome [,ouvə'kʌm] (overcame [,ouvə'keim], overcome) ❶ *vt.* ①战胜; 克服: ~ difficulties 战胜困难 / ~ one's shortcomings 克服缺点 ②[常用被动语态]压倒: We were ~ with joy. 我们喜出望外。 ❷ *vi.* 得胜

overdo [,ouvə'du:] (overdid [,ouvə'did], overdone [,ouvə'dʌn]) ❶ *vt.* ① 把…做得过头; 对…使用过度; 对…作过火表演: ~ the fertilizing 施肥过多 / Show some politeness to him, but don't ~ it. 对他应该有些礼貌, 但不要过分。/ Don't ~ literary allusions. 不要过多地使用文学典故。/ ~ a part in a play 在剧中表演过头 ②[常用被动语态]把…煮得太久(或太熟): The meat is a bit *overdone*. 肉煮得太烂了一点。③使劳累; 耗尽: ~ a horse 使马劳累过度 / ~ one's strength 使尽力量, 疲劳不堪 ❷ *vi.* 做过头; 演得过火

overdraft, overdraught ['ouvədra:ft] *n.* ①透支; 透支额 (常略作 O. D.) ②(在炉火上面掠过的)气流; 【冶】过度通风

overdraw ['ouvə'drɔ:] (overdrew ['ouvə'dru:], overdrawn ['ouvə'drɔ:n]) ❶ *vt.* ①把…描绘过分, 把…说得过分 ②透支(存款帐户) ③把(弓等)拉得过度 ❷ *vi.* 透支

overdress **I** ['ouvə'dres] *vt.* & *vi.* (使)穿得太讲究, (使)装束过分 **II** ['ouvədres] *n.* 外衣

overdue ['ouvə'dju:] *a.* ①过期(未付)的: an ~ bill 过期未付的帐单 ②迟到的, 延误的: The train is ~. 火车误点了。③过度的: give sth. an ~ share of attention 对某事过分注意 ④期待已久的; 早就成熟的: a reform that was long ~ 早该实行的改革

overgrown ['ouvə'groun] **I** overgrow 的过去分词 **II** *a.* ①簇叶丛生的 ②长得太大的; 过度发展的: an ~ lad 长得太大(或太高)的小伙子

overhang **I** ['ouvə'hæŋ] (overhung ['ouvə'hʌŋ]) ❶ *vt.* ①悬于…之上; 突出于…之上 ②用悬挂物(如吊帘等)装饰 ③(危险、灾难等)逼近; 威胁 ❷ *vi.* ①悬垂 ②伸出; 突出 **II** ['ouvəhæŋ] *n.* ①悬垂物; 伸出物; 延伸量: the ~ of a cliff 悬崖 ②【船】(水线以上)船尾(或船首)突出部 ③【建】挑出屋顶; 挑出楼房(指突出于底层墙外的) ④【空】多翼机的上翼伸出下翼的长度

overhaul [,ouvə'hɔ:l] **I** *vt.* ①彻底检修; 详细检查: have the metallurgical furnace ~ed 对冶金炉进行大检修 / go to the doctor to be ~ed 找医生检查身体 ②赶上, 追上: ~ the other two countries in steel output 在钢产量方面赶上另两个国家 ③解松(船的缆绳) **II** [,ouvə'hɔ:l] *n.* 大检修; 详细检查: undergo a thorough ~ 受彻

底检查 ‖**～er** *n.* 彻底检修(或检查)者 / **～ing** *n.* 彻底检修(或检查)

overhead ['ouvəhed] **I** *a.* ①在头顶上的;在上头的;架空的: an ～ cableway 高架索道 / an ～ crane 高架起重机, 桥式吊车(俗称行车) / ～ welding 仰焊 / ～ fire 超越射击(超越己方军队上方所进行的射击) ②(企业)通常开支的: ～ charges (或 expenses) 企业一般管理费用 **II** *n.* ①企业一般管理费 ②天花板;船舱的顶板 ③(网球等的)扣杀 ④【化】塔顶馏出物 **III** ['ouvə'hed] *ad.* 在头顶上;在上头;高高地: people in the room ～ 在上面一间房间里的人

overhear [,ouvə'hiə] (overheard [,ouvə'hə:d]) *vt.* ①无意中听到;偶然听到 ②偷听

overjoy [,ouvə'dʒɔi] *vt.* 使狂喜;使非常高兴 ‖**～ed** *a.* 极度高兴的: be ～ed at (或 with) the good news 听到喜讯非常高兴

overlap **I** [,ouvə'læp] (overlapped; overlapping) ● *vt.* ①与…交搭, 选盖住 ②与…部分一致; 与…部分巧合 ● *vi.* ①交搭, 选盖: The tiles ～. 瓦片相互交搭。②部分一致; 部分巧合: His visit and mine *overlapped.* 他的访问期与我的访问期有几天重选。**II** ['ouvəlæp] *n.* ①交搭, 重选 ②重选部分, 交搭处 ③【数】交选, 相交; 复合;【地】超复 ④航空照片的重选部分 ‖**～ area** 【军】①防空警报区外围 ②防空警报标示板阴暗区

overlay **I** [,ouvə'lei] (overlaid [,ouvə'leid]) *vt.* ① 在…上铺(或盖、涂)(with): be *overlaid with* sand 铺着沙 ②遮掩, 遮暗 ③盖得使窒息 ④[古] 使负担过度, 压倒 ⑤【印】加上衬于 **II** ['ouvəlei] *n.* ①覆盖物, 涂盖层 ②【印】轮廓纸, 上衬;【军】透明图 ③[苏格兰]领带; 被单; 小台布

overlook **I** [,ouvə'luk] **I** *vt.* ①眺望; 俯瞰: a valley from a hill 从山上俯视山谷 / a tower ～ing the city 俯瞰全市的塔楼 ②耸出 ③检查; 监督: carefully ～ the accounts 仔细检查帐目 ④看漏; 忽略: ～ a printer's error 放过一处印刷错误 ⑤放任, 宽容: ～ a fault 宽容错误 ⑥看得一心慌意乱; 用眼光迷住 **II** ['ouvəluk] *n.* ①了望四周的高地 ②俯瞰中的景色 ③眺望; 视察 ‖**～er** *n.* 监工, 工头

overnight ['ouvə'nait] **I** *ad.* ①在前一天晚上: make preparations ～ for an early start 头天晚上做准备以便一早动身 ②一夜(间); [喻]突然, 一下子: stay ～ at a friend's house 在朋友家里过夜 / Our success is not won ～. 我们的成功不是一下子得来的。**II** *a.* ①前一天晚上的 ②一夜(间)的; 突然出现的: make an ～ stop 停留一晚 / an ～ guest 过(一)夜的客人 / an ～ millionaire 暴发户 ③短途旅行(用)的; 短期访问(用)的: an ～ bag 短途旅行包 **III** *n.* 前一天的晚上

overpower [,ouvə'pauə] *vt.* ①制服; 压倒: No heat could ～ him. 天再热他也顶得住。②供给一过强的力量: The motorcycle was ～ed. 这摩托车马力过足了。‖**～ing** [,ouvə'pauəriŋ] *a.* 不可抗拒的; 压倒(优势)的; 极强大的

overrate ['ouvə'reit] *vt.* 对…估计(或估价)过高: ～ sb.'s abilities 过高估计某人的能力 / an ～d book 一本受到过分赞扬的书

overreach [,ouvə'ri:tʃ] ● *vt.* ①因伸展过长而超越: ～ the mark 因打(或射、投、伸)得过远而未中的 ②赶上; 追上 ③铺盖 ④(以奸诈)取胜于; 哄骗 ● *vi.* ①延伸过远 ②过火; 夸张; 狭行 ③(马等)后蹄踢到前蹄 ‖**～ oneself** 由于好高骛远而失败; 手伸得太长; 弄巧成拙

override [,ouvə'raid] **I** (overrode [,ouvə'roud], overridden [,ouvə'ridn]) *vt.* ①奔越过 ②践踏过 ③制服, 压倒; 把…搁在一边; 使无效: an *overriding* task 压倒一切的任务 / ～ a veto 使否决无效 ④把(马等)骑得过累; 对…驱使过度 ⑤(折骨端)与…重选 ⑥根据代销额给(经理人)以佣金 **II** *n.* 代理佣金

overrule [,ouvə'ru:l] *vt.* ① (上级权力机构)否决; 驳回; 宣布…无效: ～ sb.'s claim 对某人的要求不予受理 ②统治; 制服; 压倒; 对…施加影响

overrun **I** [,ouvə'rʌn] (overran [,ouvə'ræn], overrun; overrunning) ● *vt.* ①溢出; 泛滥; (杂草等)蔓延于 (虫害等)侵扰: be ～ with weeds 杂草丛生 ②(侵略军等)横行于; 窜犯; 蹂躏 ③(思想、风尚等)流行于 ④超越(期限、范围等): His speech *overran* the time allowed. 他的发言超过了规定时间。⑤[古]比…跑得快 ⑥使跑得过度; ～ oneself 跑过度而伤了自己的身体 ⑦[印]因移行重排(行、版面) ● *vi.* ①溢出; 泛滥 ②超过限度;【机】超限运动 **II** *n.* ①泛滥成灾; 横行为害 ②风行一时 ③超越限度; 超出量 ④(空)清除区(机场跑道两端的备用地区)

oversea(s) ['ouvə'si:(z)] **I** *ad.* (向)海外; (向)国外: go ～ 到国外, 出国 **II** *a.* ①外国的; 与外国有关的 ②向海外的; 舶来的: ～ trade 对外贸易 / an ～ broadcast programme 对外广播节目 ②在海外的; 在国外的: an ～ Chinese 华侨

oversee ['ouvə'si:] (oversaw ['ouvə'sɔ:], overseen ['ouvə'si:n]) *vt.* ①俯瞰; 了望 ②监督; 监视 ③检查; 视察 ‖**～r** ['ouvəsi(:)ə] *n.* ①监工; 监督 ②[英]教区中专管救济的人员(=～r of the poor)

oversight ['ouvəsait] *n.* ①失察; 疏忽出错; 忽略: whether by ～ or intention 不管出于疏忽或有意 ②监督; 看管; 细心照料: under the ～ of a nurse 在护士细心照料之下

overstate ['ouvə'steit] *vt.* 把…讲得过分; 夸大: Don't ～ your case. 不要把你的情况夸大了。‖**～ment** *n.*

overstep ['ouvə'step] (overstepped; overstepping) *vt.* 逾越; 违犯: ～ the scope of 超过…的范围 / ～ one's authority 越权

overstrung *a.* ①['ouvə'strʌŋ] 绷得太紧的; 紧张过度的; 神经过敏的 ②['ouvə-strʌŋ] (钢琴)把琴弦斜向交叉着装的

overt ['ouvə:t] *a.* 公开的; 明显的: ～ hostility 公然的敌意 ‖**～ly** *ad.*

overtake [,ouvə'teik] (overtook [,ouvə'tuk], overtaken [,ouvə'teikən]) **vt.** ①追上；赶上；超过： a car 超车 / learn from the advanced and ~ them 学先进，赶先进 ②突然侵袭；压倒： be ~n by a storm 遭受暴风雨袭击 / be ~n by (或 with) surprise 惊奇得目瞪口呆 / be ~n in drink 喝醉

overthrow I [,ouvə'θrou] (overthrew [,ouvə'θru:], overthrown [,ouvə'θroun]) **vt.** ①推翻；打倒；废除 ②(棒球等运动中)把球扔出(垒)外；把球扔得比…远 **II** ['ouvə-θrou] **n.** ①推翻；打倒 ②(棒球等中)扔得过远的球

overtime ['ouvətaim] **I n.** ①超过规定的时间，超时；加班加点的时间： be on ~ 加班加点 ②(体育比赛中赛成和局后的)延长时间 ③加班费 **II a.** 超过规定的，超时的；加班的： ~ pay 加班费 **III ad.** 在规定(工作)时间之外：~ 加班加点 **IV** ['ouvə'taim] **vt.** 【摄】使(曝光等)超过时间

overture ['ouvətjuə] **I n.** ①(常用复)主动的表示，提议： make peace ~s to 对…作出愿意和平的表示 ②开端，序幕；(歌剧等的)前奏曲；序诗 ③(长老教会中)最高教会法庭向长老提出的建议(或问题等) **II vt.** 把…作为提议提出；向…作主动表示，向…提议

overwhelm [,ouvə'hwelm] **vt.** ①打翻；倾覆 ②覆盖；淹没 ③制服，压倒；使不知所措： be ~ed with excitement 极为兴奋 ‖ **~ing a.** 势不可挡的；压倒之势的： an ~ing majority 压倒的多数

owe [ou] **❶ vt.** ① 欠(债等)；应该向(某人)付出： I ~ you for your help. 由于你的帮助我还得谢谢你呢。 / I ~ you an apology. 我得向你道歉。 ②应该把…归功于(to)： I ~ it to you that I finished my work in time. 亏得你帮忙，我才及时完成了工作。 ③怀有： ~ sb. ill will 对某人怀有恶意 **❷ vi.** 欠钱： Henry still ~s for his clothes. 亨利还欠着买衣服的钱。

owl [aul] **I n.** ①【动】鸱鸺，枭，猫头鹰 ②惯于晚上活动的人；夜生活者 ③表情严肃的人；聪明面孔笨肚肠的人 ④[美]深夜行驶的电车(或火车等) **II vi.** [方]像猫头鹰一样地叫(或凝视) **III a.** 深夜(或通宵)活动的： an ~ train 夜间行驶的火车 / an ~ show 深夜演出的电影(或戏剧等) ‖ **as blind (stupid) as an ~** 瞎(笨)透了 / **as drunk as a boiled ~** [美俚]烂醉如泥 / **bring (或 carry, send) ~s to Athens** 多此一举(因雅典盛产猫头鹰，而且希腊神话中雅典城守护神的标志是猫头鹰) / **fly with the ~** 晚间活动；夜游 ‖ **'~-light n.** 傍晚；黄昏

own¹ [oun] **a.** [用在所有格后面，加强语气] ①自己的： I saw it with my ~ eyes. 我亲眼看见的。 / My ~ people told me so. 我家里的人告诉我是这样。 / The workers took him as one of their ~. 工人们把他当作自己人。 / have (或 keep) sth. for one's ~ 把某物据为己有 / She makes all her ~ clothes. 她所有的衣服都是自己做的。 ②特有的： This fruit has a flavour all its ~. 这水果有独特的味道。 ③[不用所有

格] 嫡亲的： ~ brother (sister) to sb. 某人的亲兄弟(姊妹) ‖ **call sth. one's ~** 声称某物为自己所有 / **come into one's ~** ①得到自己名分应得的东西(如信用、名誉等) ②进入繁盛期，盛行起来 / **hold one's ~** 坚守住，不被打败；坚持住，支撑住： The patient is holding his ~. 病人还能够支持。(指没垮) / **of one's ~** 属于某人自己的： She has a mind of her ~. 她颇有主见。 / **on one's ~** ①[口]独自地： I'm (all) on my ~ today. 今天只是我一个人。②独立地；凭自己力量： tackle problems on one's ~ 独立解决问题 ③主动地： They helped fetch water on their ~. 他们主动帮忙提水。

own² [oun] **❶ vt.** ① 有，拥有 ②承认： ~ one's mistakes 承认错误 / ~ oneself (to be) defeated 承认自己失败 / I must ~ myself no supporter of your scheme. 我该说明白我可并不赞成你的计划。③承认是…的作者(或主人、父、母)： a cap that nobody will ~ 无人认领的帽子 ④顺受，服从 **❷ vi.** 承认(to)： ~ to having done wrong 承认做错 / ~ up [口]坦白；爽快承认： You had better ~ up. 你还是坦白的好。

owner ['ounə] **n.** 所有人，物主： the ~ of the building 楼房的主人 ‖ **at ~'s risk** (损失等)由物主负责 / **the ~** [俚]【海】船长 ‖ **~less a.** 无主的；不知道属于谁的： ~less land 无主地 / **~-ship n.** 有(权)；所有制： land of uncertain ~ship 所有权不明的土地 / state (collective, individual) ~ship 国家(集体,个人)所有制 ‖ **~ driver** 自己驾驶自备汽车的人： an ~ driver cabby 自己驾驶自备出租汽车的人 / **'~-'occupied a.** (房子等)自己住的,不出租的 / **'~-'occupier n.** 自己房子自己住的人 / **'~-'peasant n.** 自耕农

ox [ɔks] ([复] oxen ['ɔksən]) **n.** ① 牛(不分性别的通称) ②公牛；阉牛 ‖ **The black ~ has trod on sb.'s foot.** 灾祸已降临到某人头上。(或：某人已人老珠黄。) ‖ **'~-eyed a.** 有如牛眼一般的大眼睛的 / **'~-fence n.** 牛栏

oxide ['ɔksaid] **n.** 【化】氧化物 ‖ **oxidic** [ɔk'sidik] **a.** oxidic film 氧化膜

oxidize ['ɔksidaiz] 【化】 **❶ vt.** ① 使氧化；使生锈 ②使脱氢(尤指由于氧的作用) ③使增加原子价；使(原子、离子)除去电子 **❷ vi.** 氧化 ‖ **~r n.** 氧化剂

oxygen ['ɔksidʒən] **n.** 【化】氧，氧气： blast ~ 氧炼钢 ‖ **~ acid** 含氧酸 / **~ mask** 氧(气)面具 / **~ tent** (急救输氧用的)氧气帐篷

oyster ['ɔistə] **n.** ①【动】牡蛎，蚝 ②鸡背肉 ③沉默寡言的人： an ~ of a man 很少讲话的人 / as close as an ~ 嘴很紧,不会漏嘴 / as dumb as an ~ 很少讲话 ④可以从中得到个人好处的东西 ‖ **~ bed, ~ farm** 牡蛎养殖场 / **'~bird n.** 【动】蛎鹬(也称 ~ catcher) / **'~shell n.** 牡蛎壳

ozone ['ouzoun] **n.** ①【化】臭氧；[口]新鲜空气 ②能使人兴奋的力量

P

Pa【化】元素镤 (protactinium) 的符号

pace [peis] **I** *n.* ① (一) 步; 步度 (指一步跨出去的长度。如美军规定行走时每步为三十吋, 跑步时每步为三十六吋): He stands five ～s behind me. 他站在我后面五步远的地方。②步速; 速度; 进度: follow at a snail's ～ 跟在后面爬行 / at the ～ of three miles an hour 以每小时三英里的步速 / quicken the ～ of technical innovation 加速技术革新的进度 ③步态; 步调: walk with faltering ～ 蹒跚地走 / the ～ of wartime living 战时生活的步调 ④流畅: write with ～ 流畅地写 ⑤溜蹄 (马的同侧两蹄同时并举的步法) ⑥【建】楼梯平台 **II** ❶ *vi.* ①踱步, 慢慢地走: ～ up and down the corridor 在走廊里踱来踱去 ②(马) 溜蹄 ❷ *vt.* ①用步子测: ～ out (或 off) a distance of thirty metres 用步子量出三十米的距离 ②踱步于: ～ a room 在房间里踱步 ③为…定步速 (或速度) ④跑在…前面; 为…的标兵 ⑤ (以) 溜蹄步法跑完; 训练 (马) 的步法 ⑥和…并速前进: The speed of the machine may be regulated to ～ the packing operation. 机器的速度可调节得同包装速度一致。‖*at a good* ～ 相当快地 / *go the* ～ ① 飞快地走 ② [喻] 挥霍, 放荡 / *keep* ～ (*with*) (跟…) 齐步前进; (和…) 并驾齐驱: He walked so fast that the child could hardly keep ～. 他走得那么快, 孩子跟不上了。/ *mend one's* ～ 放快步子 / *off the* ～ 跑在第一名之后 / *put sb. through his* ～s 检验某人的本领 (或能力), 掂掂某人的斤两 / *set* (或 *make*) *the* ～ (在赛跑等中) 领头, 定步速; [喻] 起带头作用, 树榜样 / *show one's* ～s (马) 显出步法 (或速度); [喻] 显出自己的本领 / *try sb.'s* ～s = put sb. through his ～s ‖**～r** *n.* ① = ～maker ② 溜蹄的马 ‖**～maker** *n.* ① 定步速者, 带步人; 标兵 ②【医】起搏器; 起搏点 / '**～making** *n.* 定步速; 当标兵 / '**～setter** *n.* 定步速者; 带步人; 标兵

pace ['peisi] *prep.* [拉] 对不起… (在表示不同意见时用的客气话): ～ tua ['tju:ei] 对不起 (可是…); 冒昧得很 (可是…) / ～ Mr. Smith 对不起史密斯先生 (可是…)

pacific [pə'sifik] **I** *a.* ①和平的; 爱好和平的; 和解性的 ②温和的; 平静的: ～ disposition 温和的性情 ③ [P-] 太平洋的: the *Pacific* Ocean 太平洋 / the *Pacific* countries 太平洋沿岸各国 **II** *n.* [the P-] 太平洋 ‖**～ally** *ad.*

pacification [,pæsifi'keiʃən] *n.* ①镇定; 平定; 绥靖; 媾和 ②和约

pacifism ['pæsifizəm] *n.* ①和平主义 ②不抵抗主义; 消极态度 ‖**pacifist** *n.* 和平主义者; 不抵抗主义者; 持消极态度者 *a.* = pacifistic / **pacifistic** [,pæsi'fistik] *a.* 和平主义的; 不抵抗主义的; 持消极态度的

pacify ['pæsifai] *vt.* ①使镇静; 抚慰 (占领区人民等) ②平定; 绥靖 ‖**pacifier** *n.* ①抚慰者; 平定者 ②(哄婴孩用的) 橡皮奶头

pack¹ [pæk] **I** *n.* ①包; 捆; 包裹: a ～ of cloth 一捆布 / a pedlar's ～ 小贩背上的包裹 ②[美] 小包, 小盒: a ～ of cigarettes 一包香烟 / a ～ of canned goods 一小箱罐头物品 ③ (猎犬、野兽、飞禽等的) 一群: a ～ of wolves 一群狼 / grouse in ～s 成群的松鸡 ④ [常贬] (追求同一目的的) 一伙 (人), 一帮 (人): a ～ of liars (thieves) 一伙骗子 (窃贼) ⑤大量, 一大堆: a ～ of lies 连篇的谎话 / a man with ～s of courage 很有胆量的人 ⑥包装货物的标准重量 (或数量等) 单位 (如羊毛包为二百四十磅, 亚麻纱包为六万码) ⑦ (纸牌的) 一副 ⑧【军】背包; 驮包; 驮载; 降落伞包: a field ～ 背包 ⑨ (作战飞机或舰艇的) 一队 ⑩ (海里成堆的) 大块浮冰 (= ～ ice) ⑪【医】(包) 裹 (疗) 法, 湿 (或干) 裹法, 冷 (或热) 裹法; (裹法所用的) 裹布; 冰袋; 包扎 ⑫ (一季或一年中食物的) 装罐量, 包装量: this year's ～ of fruit (fish, meat) 今年的水果 (鱼, 肉) 装罐量 ⑬包装; 包装法; 包装材料 ⑭容器: plastic ～s for jelly 装果子冻的塑料容器 ⑮[摄] 一叠装到照相机内的散页软片, 软片包; 一组同时曝光的彩色软片 (或硬片) ⑯ (依次排列的) 一堆舞台背景屏 ⑰润肤膏; 头油; 发浆 ⑱ (橄榄球) 一队的全体前锋 ⑲ [无]【自】单元; 部件, 组 (合) 件 **II** ❶ *vt.* ①捆扎; 包装; 把…打包 (或装箱等); 打 (行李), 整 (装): ～ clothes into a trunk 把衣服装进箱子 / a ～ed lunch 装盒的午餐 / ～ one's bags 打行李 / ～ (up) one's things 整理行装 ②把 (食品等) 装罐: ～ meat (fruit) 把肉 (水果) 装罐 ③挤满; 塞满; 装满: The audience ～ed the hall. 听众挤满了大厅。/ The bus was ～ed with people. 公共汽车里挤满了人。/ ～ all the speeches into an hour 把所有的发言排在一小时内讲完 / a day ～ed with events 多事的一天

④填塞(空隙、漏缝等);把…包(或垫)起来: ~ a leaking joint in a pipe 填塞管子的裂漏接头 / glass ~ed in straw 包在稻草里的玻璃
⑤压紧;捣固;夯实: ~ed earth 压得坚实的泥土
⑥使(牲口等)驮载: ~ a mule 使骡子驮货物
⑦背运;驮送(货物等): ~ ammunition to the front 把弹药驮运到前线
⑧经常备带(装备等);配有,备有: ~ a gun 携带枪支 / weapons ~ing nuclear warheads 配备有核弹头的武器
⑨把…裹起来;【医】(用裹布)包裹
⑩把…打发走;撵走,解雇: ~ the boy off to school 打发男孩上学去 / ~ sb. off 叫某人卷铺盖,把某人解雇;赶走某人
⑪使(猎犬)集成队形
⑫把(全副纸牌)叠在一起
⑬[俚](拳击时)猛击…一拳
❷ vi. ①包装(或捆扎)货物;收拾装备;整理行装
②用牲口载运着行李去旅行
③(牲口等)驮载货物: camels used for ~ing 驮运货物的骆驼
④挤: The passengers ~ed into the train. 乘客挤入火车。
⑤被包装;能被捆紧: These books ~ easily. 这些书易于包装捆扎。/ This suit ~s well. 这套衣服能摺紧包装起来。
⑥增加密度,变结实
⑦匆忙离去(off)
⑧群集,聚集
Ⅲ a. ①用于(或适宜)捆扎的,用于(或适宜)包装的
②成包的,成捆的
③(人)背负的,(牲口)驮的;背负(或驮载)用的: ~ equipment 驮载装备 / a ~ flamethrower 背囊式喷火器 / a ~ train 驮畜行列,驮子队
‖~ in 停止: Why don't you ~ in, when you feel dizzy? 你在头晕为什么不停止工作? / ~ it in [俚] ①结束,停止 ②[美俚]充分利用有利条件(以赢得名利地位等) ③[美俚]承认失败 / ~ it up 停止; 不往下讲 / ~ (on) all sail 见 sail / ~ up ①把…打成捆;打包;收拾行李;解雇: He was told by the boss to ~ up. 老板要他解雇了。②[口]收拾工具;停止工作: It's time to ~ up. 到收工的时候了。/ The company will probably ~ up and move south. 这公司可能要停业南迁了。③[俚]出故障,不运转,渐渐停止: The motor ~ed up. 马达坏了。/ ~ [俚]死 / send sb. ~ing 叫某人立即卷铺盖;撵走某人 / spend (或 eat) the ~ [俚]耗尽所有
‖~ed a. ① [常用以构成复合词]充满…的,塞满了…的: an action-~ed story 充满紧张情节的故事 ②压坚实的: ~ed sand 坚硬的沙土 / hard-~ed snow 结实的雪块 ③挤得满满的,满座的
‖~animal n. 驮畜,驮子 / ~ drill 【军】①驮载教练 ②带着全副行军武装往返行走(旧军队中一种处罚) / '~horse n. 驮马 / '~house n.

仓库;(肉类、果品等的)加工包装厂 / ~ ice (海里成堆的)大块浮冰 / ~man ['pækmən] n. 小贩 / ~ rat ①一种北美鼠 ②[美俚]小偷;不可靠的人;旅馆侍应生 / '~sack n. (徒步旅行用的)背包 / '~,saddle n. 驮鞍 / '~thread n. (粗而牢的)包装用线;两股线,缝线
package ['pækidʒ] Ⅰ n. ①(中、小型的)包裹;包;捆;(商品、产品等的)(一)件,件头: a ~ of towels 一包毛巾 / ~s of explosives 炸药包 ②包装用物(如纸、盒、箱、封套等): design a ~ 设计包装 ③整套的广播(或电视)节目: a two-hour TV ~ 两小时的一套电视节目 ④【无】(晶体管的)管壳,外壳;【自】插件;(标准)部件,组件 ⑤(通过工会出面集体交涉取得的)合同上的利益(如福利条件、养老金等) ⑥一揽子交易 ⑦[古]打包,包装(指动作或过程) Ⅱ vt. ①把…打包;包装 ②用花哨的包装使(商品)吸引顾客 ③把…作整体推销(或提出) Ⅲ a. 一整套的: a ~ tour 由旅行社全部代办的旅游 ‖packaging n. (效率高的、美观的)包装法;打包 ‖~ deal 一揽子交易 / ~ store 不供顾客堂饮的小酒店
pact [pækt] n. ①合同,契约 ②条约;公约;盟约: the Warsaw Pact 华沙条约
pad¹ [pæd] Ⅰ n. ①垫;衬垫;(球类运动等中用的)护垫;(骑者用的)鞍褥: a shoulder ~ 垫肩 ②打印台,印色盒 ③(狗、狐狸等动物的)爪垫,肉趾 ④水生植物的浮叶 ⑤(可一张张扯用的)本子,便笺簿: a writing ~ 拍纸簿 / a blotting ~ 吸墨水纸簿 ⑥(简易机场的)起落地带 ⑦(导弹、火箭等的)发射台(=launch(ing) ~) ⑧(外科敷伤口用的)纱布块;垫料;【海】【机】缓冲器,垫手柄 ⑩(一)捆,(一)束(尤指送入卷烟机的烟叶束) ⑪[美俚]睡椅;床: ~ duty [谑]睡觉 ②[美俚]吸毒窝;娼妓窝;安乐窝 Ⅱ (padded; padding) vt.①(用软物)填塞,衬填: a cotton-padded jacket (或coat)棉袄 / ~ a box with soft cloth 用软布把箱子 ②(用废话等)拉长,铺张(文章等) ③[美]虚报(帐目等): a padded bill 虚报的帐单 / ~ one's age 虚报年龄 ④减弱…的声音,使(声音)沉闷 ⑤把(散张纸头)装订成拍纸簿 ‖hit (或 knock) the ~ [美俚]上床睡觉 ‖padding n. 填塞;垫料;(句子、文章等中的)铺张词藻 ‖padded cell (精神病院等处禁锢重病人的)墙上装有衬垫的病房
pad² [pæd] Ⅰ n. ①[英俚]路: a gentleman (或 knight, squire) of the ~ 拦路抢劫的盗匪 ②[古][英俚]拦路贼 ③缓步而行的马 Ⅱ (padded; padding) ❶ vt. 走(路) ❷ vi. 步行;放轻脚步走(或跑) ‖~ it (或 ~ the hoof) [俚]走,拖着步走
pad³ [pæd] n. 低沉的拍打声(或脚步声)
pad⁴ [pæd] n. 量水果等用的大篓子(或篮子)
paddle¹ ['pædl] Ⅰ n. ①(短而阔的)桨 ②桨状物;(桨状)搅拌器;捣衣棒;扁形刑杖 ③(船的)明轮

翼 ④鳍；鳍状肢 ⑤小闸门 **II ❶** *vi.* (依靠桨或明轮)在水中行进；划小船，荡桨 **❷** *vt.* ①用桨划(独木舟等) ②(用划桨的船)运送 ③(用桨状物)搅，打；(用扁形刑杖)鞭挞 ‖～ **one's own canoe** 见 **canoe** ‖'～**board** *n.* (水上救生者用的)狭长浮板 / '～**fish** *n.* 白鲟(尤指北美产的匙吻白鲟) / ～ **steamer** 明轮船 / ～ **wheel** 蹼轮；(船的)明轮(推进器)

paddle[2] ['pædl] *vi.* ①在浅水中行走，涉水；(用脚)玩水

paddock[1] ['pædək] **I** *n.* ①(用来放牧、驯马等的)围场 ②(赛马前)马的集中场 ③[澳]围起来的土地 ④【矿】(井口附近的)矿石临时堆放场地 **II** *vt.* ①把…关入围场 ②临时堆集(矿石)

paddock[2] ['pædək] *n.* [方]蟾蜍；蛙

paddy ['pædi] *n.* ①稻，谷: the two-crop ～ 双季稻 ②水稻田 (=～ field)

padlock ['pædlɔk] **I** *n.* 挂锁，扣锁 **II** *vt.* ①(用挂锁)锁上；把…上锁 ②(官方)正式关闭(公共场所或建筑物)

padre ['pɑ:dri] *n.* (意大利、西班牙、葡萄牙和拉丁美洲的)教士；[俚]随军牧师

pagan ['peigən] **I** *n.* ①异教徒；非基督教徒 ②没有宗教信仰的人 **II** *a.* 异教的；非基督教的；不信教的 ‖～**dom** *n.* ①[总称]异教徒 ②异教徒居住区 / ～**ish** *a.* 有点异教徒味道的；异教(徒)的 / ～**ism** *n.* 信奉异教；异教；异教徒的信仰(或仪式等)

page[1] [peidʒ] **I** *n.* ①页 (略作 p.): the fourth paragraph *on* ～ three 第三页第四段 / the photographs *at* ～s 15, 16 and 17 在第十五、十六和十七页上的照片 / turn *to* ～ ten 翻到第十页 / turn the ～ over 翻过一页 / See ～s five to seven. 参见第五页至第七页。/ read ～ after ～ 一页一页读下去 ②[常用复]记录: the ～s of history 历史的纪录 ③(值得记载的)事件，插曲 ④(报刊的)专页，专栏: the editorial ～ 社论专页 / the sports ～s 体育专栏 ⑤【印】一页版面: a fat ～ 空白多的版面 / a full ～ 全满的版面 **II ❶** *vt.* 标记…的页数，给…标页码 **❷**

page[2] [peidʒ] **I** *n.* ①(中世纪骑士的)小听差，小侍从；受训练做骑士的青年 (有身分者的)青年侍从 ②王室侍从官员的职称 (旅馆、办事处等处穿制服的)小听差，僮仆，侍者 ⑤[美]议会中的侍者 **II ❶** *vt.* ①给…当听差，侍候 ②[美](旅馆等的侍者)当众呼唤名字以找寻(某人): Mr. Brown is being ～d. 有人在叫布朗先生的名字要找他。 **❷** *vi.* 当听差，当侍从，当僮仆 ‖～**hood**, ～**ship** *n.* 听差(或僮仆等)的身分(或地位) ‖～ **boy** ①做小听差的男孩 ②[常作～boy](女子)向下弯的齐肩发型

pageant ['pædʒənt] *n.* ①露天表演(尤指当地历史事件等的古装演出，并伴以音乐) ②庆典；华丽的展览；壮丽的行列(或游行，常伴有彩车) ③虚饰，炫耀 ‖～**ry** *n.* ①[总称]壮丽的行列(或表演) ②壮观 ③夸耀，虚饰

pagoda [pə'goudə] *n.* ①(东方国家的)塔，宝塔；塔式建筑物 ②(印度十九世纪二十年代之前通用的)一种金币 ‖～ **tree** *n.*【植】槐；印度榕树；(白)鸡蛋花 ②[喻]传说能产金币的树: shake the ～ *tree* (在印度)暴发致富

pagoda

paid [peid] **I** pay 的过去式和过去分词 **II** *a.* ①支薪金的，受雇的: a ～ advisor 支薪金的顾问 ②已付的；付清的: a ～ cheque 付讫支票 / a debt 还清的债款 ‖*put "～" to* 了结… ‖～**-in** *a.* (会员等)已缴纳会费的 / ～**-up** *a.* 已付的；付清的: ～*-up* capital 已缴入资本，实收资本 / a ～*-up* loan 还清的贷款

pail [peil] *n.* 桶，提桶；一桶的量: a ～ of water 一桶水 ‖～**ful** *n.* 满桶，一桶

pain [pein] **I** *n.* ①(肉体上的)痛，疼痛: stomach ～s 肚子痛，胃痛 / He has ～s (或～, a ～) in the arm. 他手臂痛。②(精神、感情上的)痛苦，悲痛: It gave us much ～ to learn of the sad news. 我们听到这不幸的消息十分悲痛。③[复]辛苦，刻苦；努力；苦心；操心: You may save your ～s. 你不必费心。(或: 你不要白辛苦。) ④[复]分娩阵痛 ⑤惩罚(现仅用于下列短语): ～s and penalties 刑罚 / on (或 upon, under) ～ of (death) 违者处(死) ⑥[美]讨厌的人(或事物)；厌恶 **II ❶** *vt.* 使(疼)痛；使痛苦: We're ～ed to see such wastefulness. 我们看到这种浪费现象很痛心。**❷** *vi.* 作痛；觉得痛: My tooth is ～ing. 我牙痛。‖a ～ in the neck [美俚]①讨厌(或可恶)的家伙 ②使人厌烦的责任(或义务) / at ～s (或 at the ～s) 尽力；用心；下苦功: She is at ～s to find (或 at the ～s of finding) facts. 她正在努力了解事实真相。/ be in ～ 疼痛；在苦恼中 / feel no ～ ①不觉得痛 ②[俚]醉倒 / for (all) one's ～s 尽管费尽心气(或心思) / go to great ～s 费很大劲儿 / No ～s, no gains. (或 No gains without ～s.) [谚]不劳则无获。/ spare no ～s 不遗余力，全力以赴 / take ～s 尽力；费苦心；耐心: take ～s with one's work 努力工作 ‖～**ed** *a.* 痛苦的；(感情上)受了伤害的 ‖'～**-killer** *n.* 止痛药

painful ['peinful] *a.* ①使疼的；使痛苦的: a ～ leg 疼痛的腿 / ～ lessons 惨痛的教训 / a long and even ～ process of tempering 长期的甚至痛苦的磨练过程 ②(需要)费力的；费心的，伤脑筋的，

棘手的: with ~ care 煞费苦心地 / a ~ problem
棘手的问题 ③ 讨厌的, 麻烦的: with ~
slowness 慢得使人厌烦地 ‖~ly ad. / ~ness n.

painless ['peinlis] a. 无痛(苦)的, 不痛的:
surgery 无痛外科手术 / a ~ extraction 无痛拔
牙 ‖~ly ad. / ~ness n.

painstaking ['peinz,teikiŋ] I a. ①苦干的, 辛勤
的; 费力的, 艰苦的: be ~ with one's work 辛勤
地工作 / require ~ effort 需要下苦功 ②(煞费)
苦心的; 刻苦的: make ~ investigations 进行过
细的调查 / draw up a project with ~ accuracy
十分周密地制订计划 II n. 苦干, 辛勤; 煞费苦
心 ‖~ly ad.

paint [peint] I ❶ vt. ①(用颜料等)画, 绘: ~ a
picture in oils (watercolours, Chinese ink) 画
一幅油画 (水彩画, 水墨画) / ~ a landscape
from nature 画一幅风景写生 ②描写; (用语言、
文字等)描绘: ~ a scene 描写一个场面 ③油漆;
着色于; 刷(标语等): ~ the windows 油漆窗户/
~ the gate red 把大门漆成红色 / slogans on
walls 在墙上刷标语 ④(用油漆、涂料等)修整,
装饰, 点缀: The city has been ~ed up for
festival celebrations. 为庆祝节日, 市容已修整一
新。⑤(用油漆、涂料等)涂掉, 刷掉; 覆盖; [喻]
掩盖: ~ defects 掩饰缺点, 文过饰非 ⑥涂, 搽
(伤口、药、化妆品等): ~ a wound with ointment
(iodine) 用软膏(碘酒)搽伤口 ❷ vi. ①(用颜料
等)绘画 ②搽脂抹粉(或化妆品) II n. ①涂绘; 绘
画作品: a ~ job 油漆工作 / a great piece of ~
一幅绘画杰作 ②颜料; [复](一套)颜料(包括若干
管或若干块颜料): a tube of ~ 一管颜料 / a
box of ~s 一盒颜料 ③油漆; 一层漆(皮); 涂料:
Wet (或 Fresh) ~! 油漆未干! / give the door
two coats of ~ 将门涂两层漆 / The ~ on the
wall is chipping off. 墙壁上的漆在剥落。④胭
脂, 香粉; (演员化装用)油彩 ‖~ sb. black 给某
人抹黑, 把某人描写成坏人 / ~ sth. in 把某物
画于图中: ~ in the foreground 画出前景 / ~
sth. out (用油漆、涂料等)涂样某物 / ~ the lily
见 lily / ~ the town red 见 town ‖~ box 颜
料盒 / ~brush n. 画笔; 漆刷, 漆帚

painted ['peintid] a. ①(图画、照相等)着色的
②上了漆的 ③色彩鲜明的, 颜色瑰丽的: ~
china 彩釉瓷器 / ~ glass 彩色玻璃 ④假装的,
虚伪的: a ~ sepulchre 伪君子 ‖~ lady ①【动】
苎胥(蝶的一种)②【植】红花除虫菊; 波状延龄草/
~ woman ①娼妓 ②荡妇

painter[1] ['peintə] n. ①(油)漆工; 画家, 绘画者: a ~
in oils (watercolours) 油画 (水彩画)家 / a ~ and
decorator 油漆装饰工 ‖~'s colic 【医】铅中毒绞
痛 (=lead colic)

painter[2] ['peintə] n. (小船的)船头系缆绳, 系船索,
拖缆 ‖cut the ~ ①使船漂流 ②[喻]使分离;
(殖民地等)与宗主国脱离关系; 独立

painting ['peintiŋ] n. ①上油漆; 油漆业务; 着色
②绘画; 绘画艺术, 画法 ③(一张)油画, 水彩画

画: a gallery of ~s 画廊 / traditional Chinese
~ 中国画

pair [pɛə] I ([复] pair(s)) n. ①一对, 一双: a ~
of shoes (socks) 一双鞋(短袜) / a ~ of spectacles
一副眼镜 / a ~ of scissors (tongs) 一把剪刀(钳
子) / two ~(s) of trousers 两条裤子 / a ~ of
eyes (hands) 一双眼睛(手) ②一对(已婚或未婚)
夫妇 ③(有共同特征的或相互关联的)一对(人或
物) ④(桥牌等中的)搭档, 对子 ⑤(相约对某议
案不投票的)对立政党的两个议员; 对立政党两个
议员之间的不投票协议; (比赛、竞争中)两人的对
伴关系 ⑥(动物的)一对; (同挽并排的)两匹马;
双套马: a carriage and ~ 双马马车 ⑦(成对用
的)另一只: Where is the ~ to this sock? 这双
袜子的另一只在哪里? ⑧(纸牌等)同点子的一对
⑨[方](指楼梯等的)一段: a ~ of stairs (steps)
一段楼梯(台阶) ⑩[方]一串(或一套)小东西(如
念珠、项链等) II ❶ vi. ①成对, 配对 ②合作,
配合 ③组成对; 分成对 ④结婚; (动物)交配,
交尾 (with) ❷ vt. ①使成对; 把(人或物)组成对;
使成为配偶: ~ the pupils in question and
answer drills 把小学生们组成一对对来作问答练
习 ②使(对立政党议员)成为同意对某议案不投
票的一对 ‖a ~ of colo(u)rs 【军】(一团军队的)
国旗和军旗 / a pigeon ~ 一男一女的双胞胎;
(只有)一个儿子和一个女儿 / in ~s 成对地, 成
双地: The students practise English conversation
in ~s. 学生们成对地练习英语会话。 / ~ off
①把…分成一对一对 ②成对而去 / ~ off with
[口] 同…结婚 / show (或 take) a clean (或
fair, light) ~ of heels 逃走, 滑脚溜走, 逃之夭
夭 / That's (quite) another ~ of shoes. 那
(完全)是另外一回事。‖~ed-as'sociate learning (外语生词等的)成对联想学习法 / '~-horse
a. 双马的 / ~-oar ['pɛərɔ:] n. & a. 双桨艇
(的) / ~ production 【原】偶产生, 对产生

pal [pæl] I n. [口] ①伙伴; 好友 ②同谋, 同党
II (palled; palling) vi. 结成好友 (with)

palace ['pælis] n. ①宫, 宫殿; [英](大主教或主教
的)邸宅 ②宏伟的建筑物; 华丽的公共娱乐场所: a ~
hotel 豪华的旅馆 / a ~ car [英]豪华的(火车)车厢 / a ~ of culture
文化宫 ‖the ~ 宫廷显贵 ‖~ revolution 宫廷
政变

palanquin, palankeen [,pælən'ki:n] n. (东方国
家)四人(或六人)抬的轿子

palatable ['pælətəbl] a. ①好吃的, 可口的, 美味
的 ②[喻]惬意的, 合趣味的

palate ['pælit] n. ①腭: the hard (soft) ~ 硬(软)
腭 / cleft ~ 缺唇, 豁嘴 ②味觉; 嗜好; 鉴赏力:
suit sb.'s ~ 合某人的口味 / have a good ~ for
wines 精于品评酒类 ‖~ bone 【解】腭骨

palatial [pə'leiʃəl] a. 宫殿(似)的; 宏伟的, 壮丽的

pale[1] [peil] I a. ①苍白的, 灰白的: look ~ 面色
苍白 / be ~ with fright 吓得面无人色 ②淡的,
暗淡的; 软弱的, 无力的: ~ blue 淡蓝色 / a ~

moon 暗淡的月光 / be ~ before (或 beside, in comparison to) 在…前相形见绌 / make ... ~ by comparison 使…相形见绌 **II ❶** *vi.* 变苍白; 变暗淡; 失色: ~ by comparison 相形见绌 **❷** *vt.* 使变苍白; 使暗淡; 使失色 ||**~ly** *ad.* / **~ness** *n.*

pale² [peil] **I** *n.* ①(做栅栏用的)尖板条, 桩 ②栅栏, 围篱 ③篱 (某一范围内或管辖权下的)地区 ④界限, 范围: beyond (within) the ~ of law 在法律范围以外(内) **II** *vt.* 用栅栏(或篱笆)把…围起来

palette ['pælit] *n.* ①调色板 ②调色板上的或某画家用的)一套颜料 ||**~ knife** 调色刀

palisade [,pæli'seid] **I** *n.* ①栅, 木栅, 栅栏 ②[复] (河边的)岩壁, 绝壁 **II** *vt.* 用栅围护, 用栅防卫

pall¹ [po:l] **I** *n.* ①棺罩; 柩衣; 墓布; (内有尸体的)棺材 ②[宗]圣杯(或祭台等)的罩布; (教皇、主教的)披肩 ③[喻](阴暗色的)遮盖物, 幕: a ~ of darkness 夜幕 / a ~ of smoke 烟幕 **II** *vt.* 给…盖上棺罩; 覆盖 ||**~, bearer** *n.* 丧礼中抬棺材的人

pall² [po:l] **❶** *vi.* ①[古](酒等)走味, 失味 ②不发生作用; 丧失吸引力 (on, upon): Sight-seeing never ~ed on him. 外出观光从不使他生厌。 ③感到腻烦, 厌倦: ~ of too much oily food 讨厌吃过多的油腻食物 **❷** *vt.* 使变得平淡无味; 使生厌

pallet ['pælit] *n.* ①草荐 ②地铺; 简陋的小床

palliate ['pælieit] *vt.* ①减轻, 缓和(痛苦、疾病等) ②掩饰(罪过等) ||**palliation** [,pæli'eiʃən] *n.* ①减轻, 缓和, 掩饰 ②使减轻(或缓和)之物; 辩解; 掩饰的言词

palliative ['pæliətiv] **I** *a.* ①减轻的; 缓和的; [医]姑息的; 治标的: ~ treatment 姑息疗法 ②掩饰的 **II** *n.* ①[医]姑息剂, 治标剂 ②辩解; 用以掩饰之物 ||**~ly** *ad.*

pallid ['pælid] *a.* ①无血色的, 苍白的; 病状的: a ~ countenance 苍白的面色 ②无生气的 ||**~ly** *ad.* / **~ness** *n.*

pallor ['pælə] *n.* (脸色等的)苍白, 灰白

palm¹ [pɑ:m] **I** *n.* ①手掌, 手心 ②掌尺(以手掌的宽度或长度为尺, 约三寸至四寸不等) ③(手套等的)掌部 ④掌状物 ⑤桨的扁平部 ⑥(缝帆时顶针用的)掌盘 ⑦[海]锚爪 **II** *vt.* ①用手(掌)抚摩; 与…握手 ②(变戏法、打牌时)把…藏在手掌内(以哄骗他人) ③(用欺骗手段)把…硬塞给(或卖给): They can't ~ off that tale on us. 他们那套话骗不了我们。||**cross sb.'s** ~ (用钱币)在某人手心中划一个十字(指把钱币付给算命者); [喻]贿赂某人 / **grease the** ~ of 买通…, 向…行贿 / **have an itching** ~ [口]贪财, 贪钱 / **know sth. like the** ~ **of one's hand** 对某事了如指掌 ||**~ful** *n.* 一手心(的量) ||**~ grease, ~ oil** [美俚]贿赂的钱; 小费

palm² [pɑ:m] *n.* ①棕榈(树) ②棕榈叶(或枝)(常作为胜利的象征) ③胜利 ④[军]荣誉勋章 ||**bear** (或 **carry off**) **the** ~ 得胜; 获奖; 得到

莫大的荣誉 / **yield the** ~ **to sb.** 承认被某人打败, 输给某人 ||**~ house** 温室(栽培棕榈等用) / **~ oil** 棕榈油 / **Palm Sunday** [宗]复活节前的星期日

palpable ['pælpəbl] *a.* ①摸得出的; 容易感觉到的; 明显可知的: a ~ lie 露骨的谎话 / a ~ mistake 明显的错误 / ~ results 具体可见的成果 ②[医]可触知的, 可按得的(指触诊) ||**palpably** *ad.*

palpitate ['pælpiteit] *vi.* ①(心脏)悸动, 突突跳; 急速地跳动 ②颤抖: ~ with fear 吓得直发抖 ||**palpitation** [,pælpi'teiʃən] *n.* ①跳动, 颤动 ②[医]心悸

palter ['po:ltə] *vi.* ①说模棱两可的话, 闪烁其词, 搪塞: ~ with sb. 对某人支支吾吾 ②争论不休; 讨价还价: ~ with sb. about sth. 就某事与某人争论不休 ③瞎谈一番; 敷衍了事: ~ with sth. 马马虎虎对付某事

paltry ['po:ltri] *a.* ①没价值的; 微不足道的: a ~ sum 微不足道的款项 / a ~ trifle 无足轻重的琐事 ②可鄙的 ||**paltriness** *n.*

pamper ['pæmpə] *vt.* ①纵容, 姑息; 娇养: ~ a child 溺爱一个孩子 ②使满足 ③[古]使吃得过饱

pamphlet ['pæmflit] *n.* 小册子: be published in ~ form 用小册子形式出版 / a single-article ~ 单行本

Pan [pæn] *n.* ①[希神]潘, 潘神(人身羊足、头上有角的畜牧神) ②顺乎自然的精神; 信奉异教; 基督教前的世界 ||**~'s pipes** 潘神箫(芦杆制的乐器); 排箫

pan¹ [pæn] **I** *n.* ①平锅; 盘子; 一满锅; 一满盘(指容量) ②盘状器皿; (天平的)秤盘; [矿]淘盘: a gold ~ 淘金盘 ③(旧式枪的)火药池 ④盘状凹地, 盆地: a salt ~ 盐田, 晒盐池 ⑤小块浮冰 ⑥(不透水的)硬土层 ⑦头盖 ⑧[俚]脸 **II** (panned; panning) **❶** *vt.* ①(用平锅)烧(菜) ②(用淘盘)选淘(金子或含金的矿石等) (off, out) ③[口]严厉批评 **❷** *vi.* ①(用淘盘法)淘金; 出金, 产金 ②[口](结果)成为; 成功 (out): How did it ~ out? 结果怎么样? / The plan is sure to ~ out. 这计划一定会成功。||**pots and ~s** 见 pot / **savo(u)r of the** ~ 见 **savo(u)r** / **shut one's** ~ [俚]沉默, 不动声色 ||**~ful** *n.* 一满锅; 一满盘 / **~fish** *n.* 煎食的小鱼

pan² [pæn] *n.* 蒌叶(一种胡椒)的叶子; (用蒌叶的叶子等制成的)开胃生津的咀嚼物

pan³ [pæn] **I** (panned; panning) **❶** *vi.* ①摇镜头, 拍摄全景 ②(镜头)被摄动 **❷** *vt.* 摇动(镜头), 使拍摄全景 **II** *n.* 摇镜头, 摄全景

panacea [,pænə'siə] *n.* 治百病的灵药, 万应药 ||**~n** *a.*

panada [pə'nɑ:də] *n.* (由面包屑或面粉加糖等煮成的)浆, 面糊(煮汤等用)

panchromatic ['pænkrou'mætik] *a.* [摄]全色的, 泛色的: ~ film 全色胶片(或软片) / ~ plate 全色干片

pancreas ['pæŋkriəs] *n.* 【解】胰(腺)

panda ['pændə] *n.* ① 小猫熊,小熊猫 (=lesser ~)
② (大)猫熊,(大)熊猫 (=giant ~)

panda

Pandemonium [,pændi'mounjəm] *n.* ① 魔窟,阎
王殿;地狱 ② [p-] 无法无天,乌烟瘴气,大吵大
闹;大混乱

pander ['pændə] **I** *n.* (淫乱之事的)勾引者,拉皮
条者;为妓女拉客的人;(坏事或情欲等的)怂恿
者;迎合者 **II** ❶ *vi.* 勾引,拉皮条;怂恿;迎合
(*to*) ❷ *vt.* 【古】为…拉皮条

pane [pein] **I** *n.* ①窗格玻璃;(棋盘图案式的)长
方格,长方块: a ~ of glass 一片玻璃 ②(门或
墙上的)嵌板 ③(螺帽、钻石等的)边,面 **II** *vt.*
嵌玻璃于: ~ a window 在窗上嵌玻璃 ‖~d *a.*
① 用布片拼做的 ②[常用以构成复合词]嵌有…
玻璃的;具有…边(或面)的: a small-~d window
嵌有小块玻璃的窗 / a 6-~d nut 六角螺帽 / ~-
less *a.* 无窗格玻璃的

panegyric [,pæni'dʒirik] *n.* ① 颂词(指演讲或文
章): a ~ *on* (或 *upon*) sb. (sth.) 对某人(某事
物)的颂扬 ② 推崇备至

panel ['pænl] **I** *n.* ①陪审员名单;全体陪审员 ②
[英]为参加国民健康保险者治病的医师的名单
③(选定的)专门小组;(广播或电视中)就重大问
题进行公开讨论的小组;猜谜节目的表演小组:
a foreign aid ~ 援外问题专门研究(或顾问)小
组 / a ~ discussion 小组讨论;三五人在电台(或
电视台)就某一问题进行的公开讨论会 ④(有代
表性的)一组调查对象;对一组典型对象进行的调
查: interview a consumer ~ 访问一组有代表性
的用户(征求意见) ⑤面,板: the ~ of a medal
勋章的牌面 / the trademark printed on the front
~ 印在正面的商标 ⑥【建】嵌板,镶板;节间;板
条 ⑦【机】控制板,操纵盘(或台);仪表盘,面板
⑧成组作品中的一部 ⑨【空】(飞机的)翼段 ⑩
【军】信号布板(地面对空中飞机作目视信号联络
用的布片)⑪【电】配电盘;控电板⑫油画板;油画
板上的画 ⑬长方形大型相片 (=~ photograph)
⑭(苏格兰法律中的)被告 ⑮(缝缀在衣服上

的)不同质料(或颜色)的布块 ⑯鞍褥;软鞍 **II**
(panel(l)ed; panel(l)ing) *vt.* ①(用嵌板等)嵌镶
(门、墙等);(以杂色或不同质的布块)缝(服装):
a *panel*(l)ed ceiling 格子平顶 ②在…背上设鞍褥
③选定(陪审团) ④(苏格兰法律中)对…起诉,控
告 ‖**be in the ~** (苏格兰法律中)在受审中 / **be
on the ~** 已登记为替参加国民健康保险者治
病的医师;是小组成员 ② =be in the ~ ‖**~ist**
n. 专门小组成员;参加广播(或电视)公开讨论会
的成员,演出小组成员 / **panel(l)ing** *n.* ①嵌板
细工 ②[总称]镶板,门心板 ‖**~ heating** (将热
水管或电导体嵌置在内的)壁板供暖 / **~ house**
设有暗门密室的下流场所 / **~ truck** (四面都有
挡板的)小型运货汽车

pang [pæŋ] **I** *n.* (肉体上的)一阵剧痛;(精神上的)
一阵极度悲痛 **II** *vt.* 使剧痛;使极度痛苦,折磨

pangolin [pæŋ'goulin] *n.* 【动】鲮鲤(俗名穿山甲)

panic[1] ['pænik] **I** *n.* ①恐慌,惊慌: be seized (或
struck) with (a) ~ 惊慌失措 / get up a ~ 起恐
慌 ②(金融方面的)大恐慌 ③[俚]非常滑稽的人
(或事、物) **II** *a.* 恐慌的;起于恐慌的,莫名其妙
的: a ~ price 【商】恐慌价格 / a ~ fear 莫名其
妙的恐惧 **III** (panicked; panicking) ❶ *vt.* ①使
恐慌 ②使狂热,使喝采: ~ an audience 引起观
众的狂热叫好 ❷ *vi.* 十分惊慌: ~ *over* sth. 对
某事感到惊慌失措 ‖**'~-,monger** *n.* 制造恐慌
的人 / '**~-,stricken,** '**~-struck** *a.* 惊慌失措的

panic[2] ['pænik] *n.* 【植】黍,稷,糜子 (=~ grass)

panicky ['pæniki] *a.* ①恐慌的;由恐慌引起的 ②
易恐慌的

pannier ['pæniə] *n.* ① (挂在驮兽两侧的)驮篮;背
篓(尤指用于山地搬运的) ②(装外科器械和药
品的)军用盖篮 ③(旧时女人用来撑开裙子的)鲸
骨框,裙撑

pannikin ['pænikin] *n.* [英] ①小盘;小锅 ②金属
小杯;杯中饮料

panoply ['pænəpli] *n.* ① 全副甲胄(常用作比喻)
② 礼服 ③ 壮丽的陈列(或装饰) ④防护物 ‖**pan-
oplied** *a.* ①披戴全副甲胄的 ②盛装的

panorama [,pænə'rɑ:mə] *n.* ①回转画;活动画景
②风景的全貌;全景照片 ③全景,概观;概记:
look at the vast ~ of problems 全面地观察各种
问题 / a ~ of English history 英国通史 ④变
化不停的景象(或事件);对于一系列事件的印象
‖**panoramic** [,pænə'ræmik] *a.* 全景的,全貌的:
a *panoramic* camera 全景照相机 / a *panoramic*
sight 【军】全景瞄准镜 / a *panoramic* novel 包罗
万象的长篇小说

pansy ['pænzi] *n.* ①【植】三色堇,三色紫罗兰 ②
[俚][蔑]无丈夫气的男子;搞同性关系的男子

pant [pænt] **I** *n.* ①气喘 ②心跳 ③(机车等的)喷
气 **II** ❶ *vi.* ①气喘 ②(心等)悸动,剧跳 ③(机
车等)喷气 ④渴望 (*for, after*) ❷ *vt.* 气喘吁吁
地讲 (*out, forth*): He ~ed out his message. 他
气喘吁吁地讲出口信。

panther ['pænθə] *n.* ①豹;黑豹 ②美洲狮 ③ a

Black Panther 黑豹党人 / *the Black Panther Party* 黑豹党(美国一黑人组织) ‖**ess** ['pæn-θəris] *n.* ①母(黑)豹 ②母美洲狮

pantomime ['pæntəmaim] **I** *n.* ①(古罗马或现代的)哑剧;舞剧;哑剧演员 ②[英](圣诞节演出的)童话剧 ③手势,表演动作 **II ❶** *vt.* 用手势表达 **❷** *vi.* 演哑剧

pantry ['pæntri] *n.* ①餐具室;食品室;冷菜厨房 ②[美俚]胃 ‖**~man** ['pæntrimen] *n.* 餐厅管理员;管理饭厅的助手

pants [pænts] [复] *n.* ①[美口]裤子 ②[英]男用短衬裤;(商业用语)紧身长衬裤 ③[美](儿童或妇女穿的)紧身短衬裤 ④【空】(减少飞机起落架阻力的)罩: wheel ~ 机轮减阻罩 ‖*catch sb. with his ~ down* 出其不意地对某人下手;使某人来不及对付 / *have ants in one's ~* 见 **ant** / *Keep your ~ on.* [美俚]镇定! (或:别着急!) / *wear the ~* (妇女)掌权当家 / *with one's ~ down* 处于尴尬境地 ‖**~ suit** =pantsuit

pap[1] [pæp] *n.* ①[主方]奶头 ②奶头状物;[复]奶头状双峰

pap[2] [pæp] *n.* ①(婴儿或病弱者吃的)软食,半流质食物 ②政治上的恩惠(或津贴等) ③缺乏实质的东西 ②幼稚的话; 只供消遣而无文学价值的作品 ‖*give ~ with a hatchet* ①以粗暴的方式做好事 ②假装让人尝甜头 (实为惩罚) / *One's mouth is full of ~.* [俚]乳臭未干。

papa [pə'pɑ:] *n.* [主англ][儿语]爸爸

papacy ['peipəsi] *n.* ①罗马教皇的职位(或权力、任期) ②教皇的继承;教皇世系 ③[the P-] 罗马天主教教会制度;教皇统治

papal ['peipəl] *a.* 罗马教皇的;罗马教皇职位(或权力)的;罗马天主教教会的 ‖**~ism** *n.* 教皇统治;罗马天主教教会制度 / **~ist** *n.* 天主教徒

papaya [pə'paiə] *n.* 【植】番木瓜树;番木瓜

paper ['peipə] **I** *n.* ①纸;一张纸: a sheet (或 piece) of ~ 一张纸 / a blank sheet of ~ 一张白纸 ②官方文件;[复]个人(或家庭)书信文件集: a white ~ 白皮书 ③文章,论文;书面作业;考卷: a term ~ 学年论文 / have many ~s coming in weekly 每周有许多作业缴来 / Your history ~ is due. 你的历史课作业该缴了。④(装有东西的)一纸包;一纸板: a ~ of hairpins 一板发夹 ⑤报纸;类似报纸的出版物;[俚][总称]广告单: a morning (an evening) ~ 晨(晚)报 / a school ~ 校刊 ⑥[总称]证券;票据;纸币: pass bad ~ 用假支票(或假钞票) ⑦[总称](戏院等的)免费入场券;持免费入场券的观众: Most of the first-night audience was ~. 观看第一夜演出的观众大部分都是凭赠券入场的。⑧[复]证件,身分证: a ship's ~s 船证,船照 ⑨糊墙纸 ⑩象纸的东西(如纸草等) ⑪[美俚]纸牌 ‖*asphalt* ~ 柏油纸 / *blotting* ~ 吸墨纸 / *carbon* ~ 复写纸 / *commercial* ~ 商业票据 / *graph* ~ (或[英] *section* ~) 方格纸 / *kraft* ~ 牛皮纸 / *manifold* ~ (打字、复写用的)薄纸 / *sensitive* ~ 感光纸 /

tracing ~ (半透明)描图纸 **II** *a.* ①纸做的;硬板纸做的;制型纸做的: a ~ bag 纸袋 ②象纸的;薄薄的 ③文书工作的 ④纸上的;名义上的,仅在理论上存在的: ~ warfare 纸上论战,笔墨官司 / a project still in the ~ stage 尚处在纸上规划阶段的工程 / ~ profits 假设可以得到的利润 ⑤持免费入场券的 ⑥作为纸币发行的 **III ❶** *vt.* ①用纸包装(或覆盖);用纸裱糊;用纸折叠: ~ a wall (room) 用纸裱糊墙壁 (房间) ②(发免费入场券等)使 (剧院等)满座 ③[古]在纸上写下;用文字描绘 ④弥补,掩饰: ~ over the cracks 弥补裂痕,掩盖分歧 **❷** *vi.* 贴糊墙纸 ‖*commit sth. to* ~ 把某事写下来 / *lay* ~ [美俚]开空头支票;用假钞票 / *on* ~ ①以书面形式;凭统计数字判断 ②在纸上;在名义上;只在理论上: a scheme on ~ 停留在纸上的计划 / democracy on ~ 假民主 / *peddle one's* ~s [美俚]不管闲事;走开 / *put pen to* ~ 着手写,下笔 / *send in one's* ~s 辞职 / *set a* ~ 出考题 / *walking* ~s [美俚]解雇通知;(朋友等的)拒绝;要人走开的表示 ‖**~back** *n.* 纸面本,平装本 *a.* =**~-backed** / **~-backed** *a.* (书)纸面的,平装的 / **~board** *n.* 卡纸,卡纸板 / **~ boy** 报童,送(或卖)报人 / ~ **chase** (一些人假扮兔子在前撒纸屑,另一些人假扮猎犬的)追逐游戏 / ~ **clip** 纸夹 (指纸夹、回形针等) / ~ **currency** 纸币 / **~-cut** *n.* 剪纸 / ~ **cutter** ①裁纸刀 ②切纸机 / ~ **gold** 【经】"纸黄金"(即"特别提款权") / **~‚hanger** *n.* 裱糊工人 / ②[美俚]开空头支票的人;用假钞票的人 / **~‚hanging** *n.* ①裱糊 ②[美俚]伪造支票 / ~ **knife** ①裁纸刀 ②切纸机的切刀 / ~ **machine** 造纸机 / **~‚maker** *n.* 造纸工,造纸者 / **~‚makers' alum** 【化】造纸明矾 / **~‚making** *n.* 纸的生产,造纸 / ~ **match** 纸梗火柴 / ~ **mill** 造纸厂 / ~ **money** 纸币 / ~ **mulberry** 【植】构树 (其树皮可作桑皮纸原料) / ~ **pulp** 纸浆 / **~-thin** *a.* 薄如纸张的;极薄弱的 / ~ **tiger** 纸老虎 / **~- weight** *n.* 镇纸,压纸器 / ~ **work** 日常文书工作

papier-mâché ['pæpjei'mɑ:ʃei] [法] **I** *n.* ①[印]纸型 (= ~ mould) ②(纸浆中混入树胶等制成具有高度韧性的)制型纸 **II** *a.* ①制型纸做的: a ~ box (mask) 制型纸做的盒子(面具) ②人造的;假的: a ~ facade 虚饰的门面

papist ['peipist] [贬] **I** *n.* 罗马天主教徒;教皇至上的信仰者 **II** *a.* 罗马天主教(徒)的

papyrus [pə'paiərəs] ([复] papyri [pə'paiərai] 或 papyruses) *n.* ①[植]纸莎草,大伞莎草 ②纸莎草心髓(古埃及人等用以造纸) ③纸莎草纸;(古代写在纸莎草纸上的)文稿;抄本

par[1] [pɑ:] **I** *n.* ①(两种货币间对比的)制定等价,平价: a ~ of exchange 汇兑牌价,外汇平价 / a mint ~ of exchange 法定平价(指两国货币兑换的法定价) ②(股票等的)票面价值 (= ~ value): a nominal (或 face) ~ 票面价值 ③同等 ④常态,一般标准(或水平) ⑤(高尔夫球的)标准打数

II *a.* ①与票面价值相等的,平价的 ②常态的,平均的,一般标准(或水平)的 ‖*above* (*below*) ~ ①在票面价值以上(下) ②在标准以上(下),一般水平以上(下): He feels *below* ~ today. 他今天感觉不舒服。/ *at* ~ 与票面价值相等 / *on a* ~ (*with*) (和…)同等(或同价) / *up to* ~ 达到水平(或标准)

par² [pɑ:] *n.* 【动】幼蛙

parable ['pærəbl] *n.* (道德说教性的)寓言;比喻

parachute ['pærəʃu:t] **I** *n.* ①降落伞: a ~ drop zone 跳伞区,空投区 / a ~ flare 伞投照明弹 / ~ troops 伞兵部队 ②(在形状或作用方面)像降落伞的东西 ③【植】风散种子(如蒲公英) 【动】翅膜;(鳞翅目的)领片 **II** ❶ *vi.* 用降落伞降落 ❷ *vt.* 用降落伞投送,伞投 ‖~r, parachutist *n.* 跳伞者;伞兵 / **parachutic** [ˌpærə'ʃu:tik] *a.*

parade [pə'reid] **I** *n.* ①游行: take part in a ~ 参加游行 / hold a ~ 举行游行 / be on ~ 在游行 ②(军队等的)检阅: a dress ~ 阅兵典礼 ③阅兵场 ④供散步的广场;在广场上散步的人群 ⑤陈列,展览;炫示,夸耀: make a ~ of one's abilities 炫示自己的才能 **II** ❶ *vt.* ①在…游行;在…散步: ~ the streets 在街上游行 ②使(军队等)集队行进(以受检阅或操练): ~ the troops 使军队列队行进 ③使游街 ④夸耀;标榜: ~ oneself (sb., sth.) as . . 把自己(某人,某物)标榜为… / ~ one's knowledge 夸示自己的知识 ❷ *vi.* ①游行;列队行进: a *parading* procession 游行队伍 ②夸耀,自吹: ~ as . . 自吹为… ③散步 ‖*a program(me)* ~ (广播或电视)节目预报 ‖~**r** *n.* 游行者 ‖**pa'rade-ground** *n.* 练兵场,阅兵场

paradise ['pærədais] *n.* ①[P-]【宗】伊甸乐园;天国 ②乐园,福地,天堂;极乐;至福 ③(养禽兽供狩猎的)苑 ‖*a fool's* ~ 虚幻的乐境,黄粱美梦 ‖**paradisiac** [ˌpærə'disiæk], **paradisiacal** [ˌpærə-di'saiəkəl], **paradisial** [ˌpærə'diziəl] *a.* 天堂的;极乐的 ‖~ **bird** 【动】风鸟(又称极乐鸟、雾鸟)

paradox ['pærədɔks] *n.* ①(与通常见解对立的)反论 ②似非而可能是的论点 ③自相矛盾的话(或事、物、人等);谬论,怪事,妄人 ④【物】佯谬 ‖~**er**, ~**ist** *n.* 反论家

paradoxical [ˌpærə'dɔksikəl] *a.* ①反论的 ②似非而可能的 ③自相矛盾的;荒谬的 ‖~**ity** [ˌpærə,dɔksi'kæliti] *n.* / ~**ly** *ad.*

paraffin ['pærəfin], **paraffine** ['pærəfi:n] **I** *n.* ①石蜡;硬石蜡: ~ scale (wax) 粗石蜡 / ~ oil 石蜡油 ②【化】链烷属烃 ③[主英]煤油,火油 **II** *vt.* 用石蜡涂(或浸透)

paragon ['pærəgən] **I** *n.* ①(尽善尽美的)模范(或典型) ②十分优秀的人(或物),完人,珠品 ③(一百克拉以上的)纯粹钻石;圆形大珍珠 ④【印】二十点(一种欧美活字大小的旧称, 约为我国的二、三号间的铅字) **II** *vt.* ①[诗]比较 ②[诗]与…匹敌 ③[古]胜过

paragraph ['pærəgrɑ:f] **I** *n.* ①(文章的)段,节

②段落号 (即 ‖,也用作参看符号) ③(报刊的)短评,短讯(往往没有标题): an editorial ~ 短评 / miscellaneous ~s 杂评 **II** ❶ *vt.* ①写短文报道 ②将…分段 ❷ *vi.* (为报刊)写短评(或杂评) ‖~**er**, ~**ist** *n.* 短评(或杂评)作者

parakeet ['pærəki:t] *n.* 【动】长尾小鹦鹉

parallel ['pærəlel] **I** *a.* ①平行的,并行的: ~ lines 平行线 / The highway runs ~ to the river. 这条公路和河流平行。②相同的;类似的: a ~ case (development) 相同的事例(发展) ③【电】并联的: ~ circuit 并联电路 / ~ connection 并联 / ~ feed 并联馈电 ‖~ *flow turbine* 【机】平射涡轮,平射卧轮 / *the* ~ *middle body* (船体)中部平行部分,平行中体 / ~ *resonance* 【无】并联谐振 / a ~ *ruler* 平行规(或尺) / ~ *sailing* 【海】纬线航法,正东西航法 / ~ *veins* 【植】平行脉 / ~ *vice* 【机】平行虎钳 **II** *n.* ①平行线(或面) ②类似的(可相比拟的)事(或物、人、情况等): a historical ~ 历史上类似的事(或人) / a great event without ~ in history 史无前例的伟大事件 ③比较: draw a ~ between . . . 在…之间做个比较 ④纬线;纬圈 ⑤平行号(即 ‖) ⑥【电】并联 ⑦【军】平行堑壕 **III** (parallel(l)ed; parallel(l)ing) *vt.* ①使成平行;与…平行 ②比较…(with): one thing *with* another 把一件事与另一件事作比 ③比得过,配得上,与…相应 ‖~**ism** *n.* ①平行 ②类似;对应 ③【哲】心身平行论 ④【语】对句法 ⑤【生】【数】平行性,平行现象 ‖~ *bars* 【体】双杠

paralyse, paralyze ['pærəlaiz] *vt.* ①使麻痹,使瘫痪: His left arm is ~d. 他的左臂麻痹了。②使无力,使无能为力;使气馁;使惊呆 / be ~d with terror 吓得目瞪口呆 ‖**paralysation** [ˌpærərəlai'zeiʃən] *n.* / ~**d** *a.* 麻痹的;瘫痪的;呆的

paralysis [pə'rælisis] ([复] **paralyses** [pə'ræli:si:z]) *n.* ①【医】麻痹;瘫痪: cerebral ~ 大脑性麻痹 / infantile ~ 小儿麻痹症 ②完全无力,停顿: a ~ of trade 贸易停顿 ‖~ *agitans* ['ædʒitænz] 【医】震颤(性)麻痹

paralytic [ˌpærə'litik] **I** *a.* 麻痹的;瘫痪的;患瘫痪的 **II** *n.* 麻痹病人 ‖~**ally** *ad.*

paramount ['pærəmaunt] **I** *a.* 最高的,至上的;卓越的,首要的: a matter of ~ importance 首要的事 / This duty is ~ to all the others. 没有比这更重要的义务了。**II** *n.* 最高掌权者;元首 ‖~**cy** *n.* ①最高权位 ②至上,首要

parapet ['pærəpit] *n.* ①【军】胸墙(为防止敌人观察和射击而在堑壕和掩体前方构筑的土埂) ②(阳台、桥等旁边的)栏杆;护墙;女儿墙 ‖~**ed** *a.* 筑有胸墙(或栏杆、护墙)的

paraphernalia [ˌpærəfə'neiljə] [复] *n.* ①随身用具 ②设备,装置;工具: the ~ of a circus 马戏团的道具 / lighting ~ 照明设备 ③【律】已婚妻子可自由处理的动产(如衣服、首饰等)

paraphrase ['pærəfreiz] **I** *n.* 释义,意译: a prose ~ of a poem 一首诗的散文释义(或意译) **II ❶** *vt.* 将…释义(或意译): ~ a passage in modern English 用现代英语意译一段文章 **❷** *vi.* ~ 释义,意译 ‖**paraphrastic(al)** [,pærə'fræstik(əl)] *a.*

parasite ['pærəsait] *n.* ①寄生虫;寄生菌;寄生(植)物: a ~ on cattle 牛身上的寄生虫 ②食客,清客 ‖**parasitism** *n.* ①寄生(现象);寄生状态;寄生习惯 ②【医】寄生物传染; 寄生虫引起的疾病 ‖~ **aeroplane** 子机(由飞行中的母机携带或发射的飞机) / ~ **drag** 【空】废阻力,寄生阻力

parasol [,pærə'sɒl] *n.* ①(女用)阳伞 ②【空】伞式单翼机 ‖a Chinese ~ (tree) 梧桐

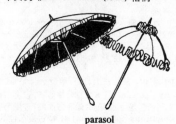

parasol

parcel ['pɑ:sl] **I** *n.* ①小包,包裹: a postal ~ 邮政包裹 ②(货物的)一宗 ③(土地的)一块 ④(常带贬义)一批,一群,一组(人、兽、物) **II** (parcel(l)ed; parcel(l)ing) *vt.* ① 把…划成部分后分配 (out): The experimental plot was ~ed out to the students. 实验田已分给学生们耕种了。 ②打包,捆扎 (up) ③【海】用帆布条包(绳索等);用帆布条和沥青填缝(缝) **III** *a.* 部分的;部分时间的 **IV** *ad.* [古]部分地,局部地 (=partly) (用于下列词语): ~ blind 半盲的 / ~-gilt 部分镀金的 ‖**part and** ~ 见 **part** ‖~ **post** 包裹邮递;包裹邮务处;[总称]邮包,包裹邮件

parch [pɑ:tʃ] **❶** *vt.* ①烘,烤 ②使焦干,使干透: ~ed fields 焦干的田地 / be ~ed with thirst 口渴得要命 ③ 使冷干软缩 **❷** *vi.* 焦干,干透,烤干 ‖~**ing** *a.* 烘烤似的,燃烧般的

parchment ['pɑ:tʃmənt] *n.* ① 羊皮纸;(羊皮纸似的)上等纸 ②羊皮纸文稿;大学毕业文凭

pardon ['pɑ:dn] **I** *n.* ① 原谅,饶恕,宽恕 ②【律】赦免: general ~ 大赦 ③【宗】赦罪;免罪符 **II** *vt.* ①原谅,饶恕: Pardon me for interrupting (you). 对不起打扰(你)了。②【律】赦免 ‖**I beg your** ~. (或 **Beg your** ~.) 对不起, 请原谅。 (常用于下列情况: ①做了错事道歉时 ②谈话中提出异议前 ③没听清楚对方的话,希望他重复一遍时,这里也可升调 (此时用"Beg ~." 或 "Pardon." 说时用升调) ‖~**er** *n.* ①宽恕者 ②【宗】(中世纪)获准售卖天主教免罪符的人

pardonable ['pɑ:dnəbl] *a.* 可以原谅的,可以宽恕的 ‖~**ness** *n.* / **pardonably** *ad.*

pare [pɛə] *vt.* ① 削(果子等)的皮;剪,修(指甲等): ~ an apple 削苹果 / ~ one's nails to the

quick 把指甲剪到肉根 ②修掉(角、边等) (off, away) ③(逐渐)削减,减少 (down, away): ~ down expenses 削减费用

parent ['pɛərənt] **I** *n.* ①父亲;母亲;[复]双亲;祖先: His ~s are still alive. 他的父母都还活着。/ our first ~s 【基督教】人类的始祖(指亚当和夏娃) ②(动、植物的)亲本,母体 ③起源,根源;原因 **II** *a.* 母(体)的;作为渊源(或来源)的: a ~ firm (或 company) 母公司 ‖~**hood** *n.* 父母的身分: planned ~hood 计划生育

parentage ['pɛərəntidʒ] *n.* ① 出身,家系,门第 ②来源 ③父母的身分

parental [pə'rentl] *a.* ①父母的;父的;母的;【生】亲本的: ~ care 父母(般)的照料 ②作为渊源(或来源)的 ‖~**ly** *ad.* ‖~ **home** 问题儿童教养院

parenthesis [pə'renθisis] ([复] parentheses [pə'renθisi:z]) *n.* ①[常用复]圆括号: Put these two words in parentheses. 把这两个词括在圆括号里。②【语】插句,插入语 ③【喻】插曲 ‖**by way of** ~ 附带地: I should like to mention this by way of ~. 我想附带地提起这点。

parenthetic(al) [,pærən'θetik(əl)] *a.* ①作为插入语的 ②作为附带说明的,作为附加注解的 ③放在括号里的 ④【喻】插曲的 ‖**parenthetically** *ad.*

pariah ['pæriə] *n.* ① 贱民(印度等的受压迫的低等级或不列级的成员) ② 为社会所遗弃者,流浪者 ‖~ **dog** (印度等地的)无主的杂种狗

parish ['pæriʃ] *n.* ① 教区(郡下的分区,有教堂和牧师) ② 教区的全体居民 ‖**go on the** ~ 接受教区救济 ‖~ **clerk** 教区执事 / ~ **council** (英国的)农村教区行政团体 / ~ **lantern** [英方]月亮 / '~-**pump** *a.* [英]地方范围的;目光偏狭的;利益狭隘的 / ~ **register** 教区记事录(记录教区居民的洗礼、命名、婚、丧等事)

parity ['pæriti] *n.* ①同等,平等: be on a ~ with 和…平等 / ~ of treatment 同等待遇 ②【逻】类似,相同: by ~ of reasoning 由此类推 ③平价(指官定货币汇兑比值);价值对等 ④(两方兵力的)对峙,相持;均势: atomic ~ 原子均势 / military ~ 军事均势 ⑤【物】宇称(性),奇偶性: law of ~ conservation 宇称守恒定律 / ~ nonconservation 宇称不守恒 ‖~ **check** 【自】奇偶校验

park [pɑ:k] **I** *n.* ①公园;公共游憩场 ②【律】(英国国王特许的)猎园 ③(乡村别墅四围的)园林 ④(汽车等的)停车场 ⑤【军】(枪炮、军需品等的)放置场;(放置场上所放置的)全部东西: an artillery ~ 停炮场 **II ❶** *vt.* ① 停放(车辆、飞机等): Can we ~ the car here? 我们可以在这儿停车吗? / an aircraft ~ing area 停机坪 ②把(某地)圈为公园(或游憩场) ③把(炮车等)安排在放置场 ④[美俚]寄放,留放,搁置: He ~ed his baby at his aunt's. 他把婴儿寄放在姑母处。 **❷** *vi.* ①停放车辆: No Parking Here! 此处禁止停车! ②坐下一时不走 ‖~**er** *n.* 停放车辆的人 ‖~**ing lot** (露天)停车场 / ~**ing**

meter （计算汽车停放时间的）停车计时器 / ~ing orbit 【宇】驻留轨道 / ~ing ticket 警察给违反停车规则者的传票

parlance ['pɑ:ləns] *n.* ①[总称] 说法, 用语: in common ~ 照一般的说法 / in legal ~ 用法律上的话来说 / in rural ~ 用乡里话说 ②(尤指正式辩论或谈判中的) 发言, 讲话

parley ['pɑ:li] I *n.* 会谈; (与敌方的)谈判: beat (sound) a ~ 击鼓(吹号)要求休战谈判 II ❶ *vi.* 会谈; 谈判 (*with*) ❷ *vt.* 讲(外国语等)

parliament ['pɑ:ləmənt] *n.* ①议会, 国会: convene (或 summon) a ~ 召开议会 / dissolve a ~ 解散议会 ② [P-] (英国或加拿大等的)议会: *Parliament* sits (rises). 议会开会(休会)。 / a Member of *Parliament* (英国)下院议员(略作 MP) / enter *Parliament* 成为下院议员 / open *Parliament* (君王) 宣布议会开会 ③ (法国革命前的)高等法院 ④薄姜饼 (=~ cake)

parliamentarian [,pɑ:ləmen'tɛəriən] *n.* ①议会法规专家 ②议会中的雄辩家 ③国会议员 ④[常作 P-]【英史】内战时期反对查理一世的议会党人

parliamentary [,pɑ:lə'mentəri] *a.* ①议会的, 国会的; 议会政治的: ~ buffoonery 议会丑剧 / ~ cretinism 议会迷 ②议员的 ③(合于)议会法规的 ④[英义]内战时期反对查理一世的议会党人的, 追随议会的 ||~ language 慎重有礼的言语 / ~ train [英](原指)每英里客运价格不超过一便士的列车; 廉价列车

parlo(u)r ['pɑ:lə] I *n.* ① 客厅, 会客室; 起居室 ②(旅馆中的)休息室, 私人谈话室 ③ [美](装璜得很好的)营业室: an ice-cream ~ 冷饮室 / a hairdresser's ~ (尤指女子)理发室 II *a.* ①客厅的; 适于客厅用的 ②只有高谈阔论无实际行动的: a ~ pink 只会空谈的温和激进派 ||~ boarder 住在校长家里的寄宿小学生 / ~ car (有单人坐椅供日间旅行的)豪华的铁路客车 / '~maid *n.* (负责餐桌侍候、开门等的)客厅女仆

parlous ['pɑ:ləs] I *a.* ① 危险的 ② 不易对付的 **parochial** [pə'roukjəl] *a.* ① 教区的 ② 地方范围的; 狭隘的 ||~ism, ~ity [pə,rouki'æliti] *n.* ①教区制度 ②地方观念; 眼界狭小 / ~ize *vt.* ①使成教区 ②使地方化; 使眼界狭小

parody ['pærədi] I *n.* ① (为嘲弄某作者或某作品而作成的)模仿滑稽作品 ② 拙劣的模仿 II *vt.* ①模仿(某作者或某作品)而作成滑稽作品 ② 拙劣地模仿 ||**parodist** *n.* 模仿某作者(或某作品)而作滑稽作品的人

parole [pə'roul] I *n.* ① (俘虏)宣誓(如保证永不逃脱等) ②(卫队军官进一步查问用的)特别口令, 特用暗号 ③ [美]有条件的释放; 假释 II *vt.* ① 凭誓释放(俘虏) ②[美]假释 ||**be on** ~ ①(俘虏)凭誓获释 ②[美]被假释 / **break one's** ~ (企图)违誓脱逃 ||**parolee** [pə,rou'li:] *n.* [美]假释犯

paroxysm ['pærəksizəm] *n.* (疾病、感情等的)突然发作, 阵发: a ~ of laughter 一阵大笑 ||**al**

[,pærək'sizməl] *a.* 发作性的; 爆发性的

parquet ['pɑ:kei] I *n.* ① 镶木地板, 席纹地面 ②[美](剧场的)正厅前排 II *vt.* 铺镶木地板于; 用镶木制 ||~ry ['pɑ:kitri] *n.* 镶木细工; 木条镶花 / ~ circle [美](剧场的)正厅后排

parricide ['pærisaid] *n.* ① 杀父母者; 杀近亲者; 杀长上者 ② 杀父母; 杀近亲; 杀长上 ③ 叛国者 ④ 忤逆罪; 叛逆罪 ||**parricidal** [,pæri'saidl] *a.*

parrot ['pærət] I *n.* ① 鹦鹉 ②应声虫, 人云亦云者, 学舌者 II *vt.* ①鹦鹉学舌般地复述 ②训练(某人)使机械地复述 ||~ry *n.* 学舌 / '~-cry *n.* 模仿别人或机械的机械的叫喊 / ~ disease, ~ fever 【医】鹦鹉病 (=psittacosis) / ~ fish 【动】隆头鱼; 鹦嘴鱼

parry ['pæri] I ❶ *vt.* ①挡开, 避开: ~ a weapon 挡开武器 / ~ a blow 避开打击 ② 回避: ~ a question 回避问题, 避而不答 ❷ *vi.* ① 挡开武器(或打击) ②回避 II *n.* ①挡开; 避开 ②回避; 遁词

parse [pɑ:z] *vt.* 从语法上分析, 解析(词、句等)

parsimony ['pɑ:siməni] *n.* ①异常俭省, 过度节俭 ②吝啬, 小气 ③[喻](在用词等方面的)过度节省 ||**parsimonious** [,pɑ:si'mounjəs] *a.* 过度节俭的; 吝啬小气的

parsley ['pɑ:sli] *n.*【植】欧芹(可供食用)

parsnip ['pɑ:snip] *n.*【植】欧洲防风; 欧洲防风块根

parson ['pɑ:sn] *n.* ①教区牧师 ②[口]牧师 ||~'s nose 见 nose ||~age ['pɑ:snidʒ] *n.* (教区)牧师住所 / ~ic(al) [pɑ:'sonik(əb)] *a.* 牧师(似)的

part [pɑ:t] I *n.* ① 一部分, 部分; 局部: *Part* (或 A ~) of it was spoilt. 这东西中的一部分已坏了。 / *Part* (或 A ~) of the books have arrived. 一部分书已经到达了。 / the upper ~ of the face 脸的上半部 / the greater ~ of a highway (an hour) 一条公路(一小时)的大部分 / The annoying ~ of the matter is that .... 这事麻烦就麻烦在… / subordinate the interests of the ~ to those of the whole 使局部利益服从整体利益 ② …分之一, 等分: A second is the sixtieth ~ of a minute. 一秒钟是一分钟的六十分之一。 / a solution of one ~ of sulphuric acid and three ~s of water 一份硫酸和三份水的溶液 ③ 基本构成成分, 要素: Libraries are a ~ of modern education. 图书馆是现代教育中不可缺少的组成部分。 ④ 本份, 职责; 份儿; 作用: It was no ~ of his to interfere. 他不应该插手干涉。 / have a small ~ in 在…中只有很小的一份; 在…中只起很小的作用 ⑤ (剧中的)角色; (角色的)台词: know one's ~ 背熟台词 ⑥ 地区, 区域: a perfect stranger in these ~s 对这一带完全陌生的人 / That ~ of the country is colder than the rest. 国家的那一地区比其他部分都冷。 ⑦(争论、交易等中的)一方; …方面 ⑧[常用复]才华: a man of ~s 有才华的人 ⑨(文艺作品等的)分部: a novel in three ~s 一本分

为三部分的小说 / *Part III* 第三部分 ⑩(头发)分开的缝 ⑪【语】词类: ~*s of speech* 各种词类 ⑫零件: spare ~*s of a machine* 机器的备件 ⑬【数】整除部分; 部分分数; 部分分式: aliquot ~ 整除部分 ⑭【音】声部; 乐曲的一部: the soprano (bass) ~ 女高音(男低音)部 ⑮(身体的)部位; [复]阴部, 私处: the affected ~ 患部 / the injured ~ 受伤部位 / the private (或 secret) ~*s* 阴部, 私处 **II ❶ *vt.*** ①分, 使分开: A huge rock ~*s* the stream. 巨岩使溪水分流。 / ~ one's hair in the middle 从中间把头发分开 / The two were ~*ed from* each other years ago. 许多年前他们两人就分开了。 ②断绝(关系、联系) ③区别, 辨别(学说、理论等) ④(用提炼等化学方法)分解出; 分解出【海】斩断(缆索、锚链等); 使(缆索、锚链等)断裂 ⑤把···分成若干份; 分配 ⑦[英方]放弃, 丢掉(财产等) **❷ *vi.*** ①分开, (河流等)分叉, 分道: The crowd ~*ed* to let him pass. 人群让开一条路让他通过。 ②断裂: The cord ~*ed.* 绳子断了。 / The piece of three-ply wood has ~*ed from* the glue. 三夹板胶胶裂开了。 ③分手, 分别; 中止联系, 断绝关系: They two ~*ed* at the door. 他们两人在门口分别。 / ~ *from* (或 *with*) sb. 同某人分手(告别) ④放弃: hate to ~ *with* sth. 不肯放弃某物 ⑤离开; 死(去) ⑥[口]出钱, 付款 **III *a.*** 部分的; 局部的 **IV *ad.*** 部分地 ‖*bear a ~ in* 在···中参与, 参与··· / *for one's ~* 尽自己职责, 尽自己一份力量 / *for one's ~* 至于某人; 对某人来说: I, *for my ~*, have no objection. 至于我, 可没什么反对意见。 / The girls undertook the kitchen work and the boys, *for their ~*, gathered firewood. 女孩们负责伙房工作, 而男孩子们则去拾柴火。 / *for the most ~* 就绝大部分而言; 在极大程度上; 多半: Their designs, *for the most ~*, correspond to actual needs. 他们的设计绝大部分符合实际需要。 / *have neither ~ nor lot in* 未参与···; 与···不相干 / *in ~* 在某种程度上; 部分地: The article runs *in ~* as follows: . . . . 文章的一部分内容如下: ··· / *on the ~ of* 就···而言; 在······一边: The agreement has been kept *on our ~*. 我们这方面遵守了协议。 ②由···表现出来的; 由···所经历的; 由···所作出的: an indiscretion *on sb.'s ~* 某人的一个不慎的举动 / *~ and parcel* 重要的部分 / *~ brass rags with* sth. 见 rag¹ / *~ company* (*with*) 见 company / *~ friends* 见 friend / *play* (或 *act*) *a ~* ①扮演一个角色 ②装腔作势 ③在···中起一份作用, 参与··· (*in*) / *take . . . in good ~* 很乐意地接受(···), 不因···见怪 / *take ~* (*in*) 参与(···), 参加(···): For all our advice to the contrary he refused to *take ~*. 尽管我们劝说过他, 他还是拒绝参加。 / *take* an active ~ *in* collective productive labour 积极参加集体生产劳动 / *take ~ with* (或 *take the ~ of*) 与···站在一边, 袒护, 支持 / *the best ~* 最大(或最多)的部分: for *the best ~* of the week 在一周中的绝大部分时间

内 / *the better ~* ①较好的办法(或计策): He thought discretion *the better* ~. 他认为还是谨慎为好。 ② 较大(或较多)的部分: the better ~ of the way. 一路上我大部分时间是骑马的。 / *the ninth ~ of a man* [贬]裁缝 ‖**~ly *ad.*** 部分地, 不完全地; 在一定程度上 ‖**~ music** 合唱(或合奏)乐曲 / **~ owner** 共有者(尤指同船主之一) / **'~-song** *n.* (尤指无伴奏的四声部)合唱歌曲 / **'~-'time** *a.* 部分时间的, 非全日的: (教师等)兼职的, 兼任的: a ~*-time* job 非全日性工作, 零活 / a ~*-time* teacher 兼任教师 *ad.* 花部分时间; 兼任地, 兼职地: This worker teaches ~*-time* in our school. 这位工人在我们学校兼任教学工作。 / **'~-'timer** *n.* [口]零工, 非全日工

partake [pɑ:'teik] (partook [pɑ:'tuk], partaken [pɑ:'teikən]) **❶ *vi.*** ①参与, 参加: ~ *of* most of the activities 参加大部分活动 ②分享; 分担; 同吃(或喝等): ~ *in* each other's joys and sorrows 同甘共苦 / ~ *of* a meal with sb. 和某人一起吃一顿饭 ③[口]吃光, 喝光: ~ *of* three bowls of rice 吃完三碗饭 ④带有某种性质(或特征等): feelings *partaking of* joy and surprise 惊喜交集的感情 **❷ *vt.*** ①分享; 分担 ②同吃 (或喝等); 单独吃 (或喝等): ~ a meal with sb. 同某人一起吃一顿饭 / ~ one's meals in the school dining hall 在学校食堂吃饭 ‖**~r** *n.* 参与者; 分担者; 共享者: a ~*r in* guilt 同谋犯

partial ['pɑ:ʃəl] **I *a.*** ① 偏袒的, 不公平的: a ~ opinion 偏见 / be ~ *to* one while neglecting the other 厚此薄彼 ②癖好的; 过分错爱的 (*to*) ③部分的, 不完全的: ~ success 部分成功 / ~ paralysis 部分瘫痪 / the ~ transfer of power 权力的部分转移 / a ~ eclipse of the moon 月偏食 **II *n.*** 【音】陪音, 泛音 ‖**~ly *ad.*** ‖**~ fraction** 【数】部分分数; 部分分式 / **~ tone** 【音】陪音, 泛音; 【物】谐音

partiality [,pɑ:ʃi'æliti] *n.* ①偏心, 不公平 ②特殊爱好, 偏爱; 癖好: a ~ *for* chess 下棋的癖好

participant [pɑ:'tisipənt] **I *n.*** 参加者, 参与者: a ~ *in* the table-tennis tournament 参加乒乓球比赛的人 / treaty ~*s* 条约参加国 **II *a.*** 有份的, 参与的 (*of*) / ~ observation (人类学家、社会学家等)通过亲自参加研究对象的活动进行的现场观察研究

participate [pɑ:'tisipeit] **❶ *vi.*** ① 参与, 参加 ② 分享; 分担: ~ *with* sb. *in* his sufferings 与某人同患难 ③含有, 带有: ~ *of* the nature of satire 带有讽刺的性质 **❷ *vt.*** 分享; 分担 ‖**participating** *a.* ① 由多人一起参加的: *participating* sponsorship 由多人 (或多方) 一齐参加的集体发起 ②(股票等)使持有人有权参与分享的 / **participation** [pɑ:,tisi'peiʃən] *n.* 参与, 参加; 分享: **participator** *n.* =participant (*n.*)

participial [,pɑ:ti'sipiəl] *a.* 【语】分词的: a ~ phrase 分词短语 / a ~ adjective 分词形容词 ‖**~ly *ad.*** 作为分词

participle ['pɑ:tisipl] *n.* 【语】分词: a present (past) ~ 现在(过去)分词

particle ['pɑ:tikl] *n.* ①粒子,微粒: ~s of dust 尘埃 ②极小量: There is not a ~ of truth in it. 其中没有一点真实性。③【物】【数】粒子,质点 ④【语】小品词(例如 yes, no); 虚词,不变词(如冠词、前置词、连接词等); 词缀(例如 un-, -ness)

parti-colo(u)red ['pɑ:ti,kʌləd] *a.* ①杂色的,斑驳的 ②多样的

particular [pə'tikjulə] Ⅰ *a.* ① 特殊的;特别的; 【逻】特称的: from the ~ to the universal 从特殊到普遍 / for no ~ reason 并非因为任何特别的理由 / take ~ trouble to be precise 力求精确 / a ~ (universal) proposition 【逻】特称(全称)命题 ②特定的; 各个的; (人)个别的; 特指的: a ~ period 特定阶段 / It happened on that ~ day. 事情就发生在那一天。/ choose a ~ person for the job 选某一个人去做这件事 / examine every ~ item 逐一审查每个项目 / criticize without naming any ~ person 不点名地进行批评 ③特有的,独特的 ④分项的,列举的; 细致的,详细的 ⑤(过于)讲究的;苛求的,挑剔的: be ~ about (as to) what one eats (wears) 过于讲究吃(穿) / a ~ customer 挑剔的顾客 Ⅱ *n.* ①(可分类或列举的) 项目;(消息、情报等的) 一条,一项,一点: a bill of ~s 【律】分列细节的原告起诉书(或被告答辩书) / be different in every ~ 每一点都不同 ②细节;[复]详细情况: generalize from ~s 从个别概括一般 / For ~s please contact our local office. 欲知详情请询问我驻当地机构。③特点;特色: the London ~ 伦敦的特点(指浓雾) ‖go (或 enter) into ~s 详细叙述 / in ~ 特别,尤其: He stressed that point in ~. 他特别强调那一点。‖~ly *ad.* ① 特别,尤其,格外: It's a ~ly fine day. 天气特别好。② 详细地,细致地: describe a scene ~ly 详细地描写一种景象

particularism [pə'tikjulərizəm] *n.* ①【宗】特殊神宠论 ②完全忠于一党(或一个宗派、一种制度等) ③允许各州(或各邦)政治上独立的政策(或原则); 主张各政治团体有权独立发展自身利益的一种理论 ④以单一因素阐明社会复杂现象的倾向

particularity [pə,tikju'læriti] *n.* ① 特殊性; [常用复]特征: the ~ of contradiction 矛盾的特殊性 / the particularities of the current situation 当前形势的特征 ②个性;癖性 ③细致,详细;精确性 ④过分讲究;苛求,挑剔

particularize [pə'tikjuləraiz] *vt. & vi.* ① 列举;分列 ②特别举出(或讲述);详述 ‖**particularization** [pə,tikjulərai'zeiʃən] *n.*

particulate [pə'tikjulit] Ⅰ *n.* 微粒, 颗粒, 粒子 Ⅱ *a.* 微粒的,颗粒的: ~ inheritance 【生】颗粒遗传(说)

parting ['pɑ:tiŋ] Ⅰ *a.* ①分开的,分离的,分隔的: ~ sand 【机】(翻砂用的)隔砂 / ~ strip 【建】(结构的)分隔条(或带) ②离别的,临别的: a ~ gift

临别纪念品 / ~ words (或 a piece of ~ advice) 临别赠言 ③临死的,临终的 Ⅱ *n.* ①分裂,分离 ②分界处;分界线(或点); (头发的)分缝,头路 ③分开物,分离物; 【冶】分金(指有色金属如金银的分离); 【机】【铸工】分离砂,分离材料 ④分手;告别;离别: on ~ 在离别时 ⑤死亡 ‖at the ~ of the ways 在十字路口

partisan[1], **partizan**[1] [,pɑ:ti'zæn, 'pɑ:ti'zæn] Ⅰ *n.* ①党人,党徒;坚决支持者 ②骚扰部队成员; 敌后游击队员 Ⅱ *a.* ①党徒的;党派性的;有偏袒的: in a ~ spirit 党派观念十足地 ②由一个党派组成(或控制)的 ③ 游击队的 ‖~ship *n.* 对党派的效忠;党派偏见

partisan[2], **partizan**[2] ['pɑ:tizn] *n.* 戟(十六、十七世纪时的一种兵器)

partition [pɑ:'tiʃən] Ⅰ *n.* ① 分开;被分开;分割;划分 ②隔开物;隔墙;隔板: a plywood ~ between two rooms 两个房间中间的夹板墙 / a hall subdivided by movable ~s 用活动隔板隔开的大厅 ③部分;隔开部分;隔开的房间: ~s in a ward 病房里的隔开部分 ④【律】分财产 ⑤【逻】(把一个类别)分成部分 Ⅱ *vt.* ①把…分成部分 ②(用隔板等)隔: ~ a house into rooms 把房屋隔成若干房间 / These two lots of cargo should be ~ed off from each other. 这两批货物应当隔开。

partner ['pɑ:tnə] Ⅰ *n.* ① 伙伴,合作者; 合股人,合伙人: ~s in trade 合股做生意的人们 / a sleeping ~ 隐名合伙人(指不参加经营管理、不为外界所知的出资人) ② (乒乓等运动中的) 合作者,配手; (桥牌等游戏中的)搭档; (双人舞中的)舞伴: pairs of ~s in practising conversational English 练习英语会话的一对对的搭档 / a dancing ~ 舞伴 ③配偶(指夫或妻): one's life ~ 终身伴侣 ④[常用复]【船】桅孔加固板 Ⅱ ❶ *vt.* ①同…合作(或合伙),做…的伙伴 ② 使有配偶(或搭档) ❷ *vi.* 做伙伴;当配手 (with) ‖~less *a.* 无伙伴的; 无配手的 / ~ship *n.* 合伙(或合作)关系,伙伴关系; 合股关系; 全体合伙(或合股)人; 合伙(或合股)契约: enter into ~ship with sb. 同某人结成伙伴关系; 与某人合股 / a limited ~ship 两合公司 / an unlimited ~ship 无限公司

partook [pɑ:'tuk] partake 的过去式

partridge ['pɑ:tridʒ] *n.* 鹧鸪, 斑翅山鹑(又称斑鸡); 石鸡(又称嘎嘎鸟、红腿鸡) ‖~-wood *n.* 一种红色硬木(可做手杖、家具等)

party ['pɑ:ti] Ⅰ *n.* ①党,党派,政党: the democratic parties 民主党派 ②结党,党派活动: ~ politics (不顾公众利益的) 党派政治 ③ (条约、会议、诉讼等有关的) 一方; 当事人,参与者: both parties 双方 / the other ~ 另一方 / the contracting parties 缔约国; 缔约当事人 / the parties to a dispute 争论的各方 ④ (参加共同活动的)一批,一组,一伙人; 随行人员: a survey (hunting) ~ 测量(狩猎)队 / a ~ on line work (道路工程等的)路线勘测队 / the Foreign Minister and his ~ 外交部长及其随行人员 ⑤【军】(担任某种特殊任务的)临时编组,特遣队(或组): a landing ~ 登陆特遣部队 / a firing ~ 行刑队 ⑥(社交性或娱乐性的)聚会: a dinner ~ 宴会 / a cocktail ~ 鸡尾酒会 / a garden ~ 游园会 / a quilting ~ 妇女在一起边缝被子边闲谈的聚会 / give (或 hold) a ~ 举行宴会(或茶会等) ⑦[俚][谑](一个)人: an old ~ with spectacles 戴眼镜的老头儿 II ❶ vi. 举行(或参加)社交聚会 ❷ vt. 为…举行社交聚会 ‖~-,colo(u)red a. = parti-colo(u)red / ~ girl ① 社交聚会的女招待 ② 一心想参加社交聚会的女子 / ~ line ① 政党的路线 ②【讯】合用线 ③ 分界线 / ~ man 政党的忠实支持者

pass [pɑːs] **I** (过去式 passed, 过去分词 passed 或 past [pɑːst]) ❶ vt. ① 经过,穿过;越过,超过: The ship ~ed the channel. 船通过海峡。/ This information will never ~ my lips. 我决不泄漏这个消息。/ ~ the summit of a mountain 越过山顶 / Soon their car ~ed ours. 他们的车很快超过了我们的车。② 通过(考试、检查等);使通过;批准(议案等);被…批准(或通过): ~ an examination 考试及格 / a pupil on a test 评定小学生测验及格 / The report has ~ed the committee. (或 The committee has ~ed the report.) 报告已由该委员会批准通过。/ ~ the Customs 得到海关批准 ③ 度过: How will you ~ your holiday? 你打算怎样度过假日? ④ 超出,超越(能力、范围、限度等): It ~es my comprehension. 这非我所能理解。⑤ 传递(用具等);传达(命令、消息等);传(球): Please ~ me the spade. 请把铲子递给我。/ ~ sign the attendance sheet and ~ it on to others 在签到单上签名后把单子传给其他人 / Please ~ the word to him. 请把这个命令(或这句话)传给他。/~the ball to the centre forward 把球传给中锋 ⑥ 使(货币等)流通,传播(谣言等): ~ bad cheques 使用假支票 ⑦ 使移过;使行进: ~ one's eyes over a list of names 使眼光扫过一张名单 / ~ one's hand through the hair 用手顺着头发抹过去 / ~ the rope round a tree 用绳把树圈拴起来 / ~ the troops in review 使部队列队行进接受检阅 ⑧ 把…略过不提,忽略: ~ trivial details 略过细微末节 ⑨ 宣布(判决等);提出(批评、意见等);宣(誓),发(誓): ~ sentence on sb. 对某人判刑 / ~ a critical remark on sth. 对某事提出批评 / ~ one's word 发誓 ⑩ 排泄,通(大、小便);分泌: ~ water 小便 ❷ vi. ① 经过,穿过;越过(思想、眼光等)掠过: A bus ~ed by just a moment ago. 一辆公共汽车刚开过去。/ Please let me ~. 请让我过去。/ ~ through a village 穿过村庄 / No ~ing permitted. 不准超车。/ An idea ~ed through his mind. 他心中闪过一个念头。② 变化,转化;(在所有权等方面)转换;(时间)推移,流逝: Water ~es into steam at boiling

point. 水在沸点时变成蒸汽。/ ~ from youth to age 从青年到老年 / A week ~ed quickly. 一个星期很快地过去了。③ (货币等)流通,通用;(文件等)被传阅 ④(问候等)交流,来往: Greetings ~ed between them. 他们互相问候。⑤ (在考试、试验中)及格,合格;被通过,被批准;宣判,判决: We cannot let inferior products ~. 我们不能放过次品。/ The judgement ~ed against him. 判决宣告他败诉。/ ~ upon a case 宣判案件 ⑥ 发生: What ~ed in my absence? 我不在的时候发生了什么事? ⑦ 终止,消失;离开;死亡: The child's fever has ~ed. 孩子热度退了。⑧ 被忽略过去: let sb.'s remarks ~ 对某人的话不予追究(或驳斥等) / His remarks ~ed unnoticed. 他的话未引起人注意。⑨ 以某种身分(或名义)出现;(黑人后裔)自称白人 ⑩(纸牌戏中)不叫牌,放弃叫牌 ⑪(球类运动中)传递 **II** n. ① 穿过,经过 ② 关口,要隘;海峡: a strategic ~ 战略要隘 ③ 情况,状况,境遇(常指不利处境) ④ 及格;及格分数;及格证书: a ~ mark 及格分数 ⑤ 入场证;通行证;护照: No admittance without a ~. 无证(或票)不得入内。⑥ 一次操作(如轧钢机中的一次轧压等) ⑦ 传球动作;(击剑中的一次)戳刺 ⑧ (飞机、人造卫星等的)一次掠过(或飞过) ⑨(纸牌戏中)(一次)放弃叫牌(或补牌) ⑩(魔术、牌戏等中的)手法 ⑪[俚]勾引手段,过分举动 ‖ a pretty (或 fine, nice) ~ [口] 困境;不幸(或危急)的局面 / hold the ~ 把关;[喻]捍卫一种主义(或事业) / make a ~ at sb. [俚] 对某人作非礼举动 / ~ away ① 终止,停止 ② 死亡 ③ 消磨(时间等) / ~ current 见 current / ~ for 被认为…,被当做…: He ~es for a learned man. 他被认为是个有学问的人。/ ~ in one's checks 见 check / ~ muster 见 muster / ~ off ① (感觉等)终止,停止: Has the pain ~ed off yet? (问病人)不痛了吧? ②(事件等)发生,进行到最后: The transaction ~ed off without a hitch. 这笔生意顺利地做成了。③ 故意不去注意… / ~ out [俚] 失去知觉,昏倒;死 / ~ over 不注意,忽略;省略 / ~ (round) the hat 见 hat / ~ sth. (sb.) by 不注意(或忽视)某事物(某人),放过某人(某人): We cannot ~ the matter by in silence. 对这件事我们不能保持沉默。/ ~ sth. (sb.) off as (或 for) 把某物(某人)充作…;以某物(某人)冒充… / ~ the buck to 见 buck[2] / ~ the time of day (with sb.) 见 time / ~ up [美俚] 放过,拒绝(机会等) / sell the ~ [喻]放弃一种主义(或事业),背叛 ‖~less a. 无路可走;走不通的 / ~'book n. ① 银行存折 ② 顾客赊欠帐簿 / ~ degree (英国大学中的)学士学位(最普通的学位) / '~key n. 万能钥匙;(大门等的)私人钥匙 / '~man n. 取得及格成绩的大学生 / 'Pass,over n.【宗】(犹太人的)逾越节 / '~port n. ① 护照 ② 获得允许的手段;保障: a ~port to success 获得成功的保证 / '~word n. 【军】(通过警戒线等时使用的)口令

passable ['pɑːsəbl] *a.* ① 可通行的, 能通过的: a ~ path 可通行的小路 / a ~ forest 能穿过的森林 ②合格的;过得去的,还好的,尚可的: She has a ~ knowledge of Japanese. 她的日语(知识)还可以。③(钱币等)可流通的;真的 ④(建议的法律条文等)可制订的 ‖**passably** *ad.* 可通行地;还好

passage[1] ['pæsidʒ] **I** *n.* ① 通过, 经过; 过渡: the ~ of time 时间的推移 / block the ~ of information 封锁消息 ②迁移, 移居: a bird of ~ 候鸟;[喻]漂泊不定的人 ③(法案等的)通过 ④(海上、空中)航行;船上的旅客供应设备;船费(包括膳宿): have a smooth (rough) ~ 航行顺利(困难) ⑤自由通过权 ⑥通路, 通道, 管; 航道; 小径: force a ~ through a crowd 从人群中挤过去 / a ~ of current 电流通路 / air ~【机】气道, 【医】呼吸道 / exhaust ~【机】排气通路 ⑦走廊, 过道 ⑧[复]交流, 交换(指两人间彼此信任、共立誓约、发生争执等): have angry ~s with sb. 与某人争得面红耳赤 ⑨(文章、讲话、乐曲等的)一段, 一节;(绘画等艺术作品的)细节, 细部;【音】经过句 ⑩【医】(大小便的)排出;排便 ⑪【生】病原体(如病毒)的培育 ②已发生(或完成)的事情或事件) **II** *vi.* ①通过, 经过; 横过, 穿过 ②航行, 旅行 ③参加争执(或殴斗) ‖*a ~ of* (或 *at*) *arms* 交战; 争论 / *work one's ~* 在船上做工充作船费;(非正式受雇人员) 做事取得报酬 ‖'~·**way** *n.* 走廊, 过道

passage[2] ['pæsidʒ] ❶ *vi.* (马或骑手)以斜横步前进 ❷ *vt.* 使(马)以斜横步前进

passenger ['pæsindʒə] *n.* ① 乘客, 旅客; 过路人: a ~ cabin 客舱 / a ~ plane 客机 / ~ traffic 客运 / a ~ tunnel 旅客地道 / a ~ footbridge 人行天桥 / The streets are full of ~s. 街上行人熙攘。②[口](球队、船员等队伍中)不中用的成员 ‖*wake up the wrong* ~ [美口]错怪了人, 骂错了人 ‖~ **car** ①[指火车]客车 ②[指汽车]小客车, 轿车 / ~ **liner** ①班轮, 邮船 ②班机 / ~ **list** (船长交给海关人员的)旅客名单 / '~·**train car** (火车)载行李、邮件等的车厢

passion ['pæʃən] *n.* ①激情, 热情; [复]感情(与理智相对而言) ②爱好, 热爱; 热望占有的东西: have a ~ for 对…有强烈的爱好 ③ 恋爱; 情欲 ④大怒, 激怒: fly (或 work oneself up) into a ~ 大怒, 大发雷霆 / be subject to fits of ~ 动不动就发怒 ⑤[古]病痛 ⑥[the P-]【宗】(十字架上)耶稣的受难 ‖~**al** *a.* 热情的;感情的;情欲的 *n.* (基督教的)圣徒(或殉教者)的受难记 / *Passionist n.* (天主教的)受难会修道士 ‖~**less** *a.* 没热情的, 不动情的, 冷淡的 ‖'~·**flower** *n.* 【植】西番莲 / **Passion music**【宗】耶稣受难曲 / **Passion play**【宗】耶稣受难剧 / **Passion Sunday**【宗】耶稣受难日

passionate ['pæʃənit] *a.* ① 热情的; 热烈的, 激昂的: make a ~ speech 作热情洋溢的讲话 ② 易动情的 ③ 易怒的, 性情暴躁的 ④ 被情欲所支

配的 ‖~**ly** *ad.* / ~**ness** *n.*

passive ['pæsiv] **I** *a.* ① 被动的, 受动的; 守势的; 【语】被动的: ~ operations 守势作战 / the ~ voice 被动语态 ② 消极的; 驯服的; 缺乏精力的: ~ resistance 消极抵抗; 不顺从 ③【物】【化】钝性的; 钝态的; 无源的 ④无利息的: ~ bonds 无利息债券 **II** *n.* ① [常用复]被动消极的东西; 被动性 ②【语】被动语态; 被动式 ‖~**ly** *ad.* / ~**ness** *n.*

passivity [pæ'siviti] *n.* ① 被动; 被动性; 消极状态 ② 忍受; 服从 ③【物】【化】钝性; 钝态, 无源性 ④【语】被动语态的结构

past [pɑːst] **I** pass 的过去分词 **II** *a.* ① 过去的; 刚过去的 / for the ~ few days 过去几天以来 / for some time ~ 前些时候 / It happened ten years ~. 这发生在十年以前。②【语】过去(时)的: the ~ tense 过去时 ③前任的, 曾任的: a ~ president 前任会长(或主席) **III** *n.* ①过去, 昔日: in the ~ 在过去 ②往事; 经历(尤指秘密的、不可告人的丑史): a man *with* a ~ 有不可告人的经历的人 ③【语】过去时;(动词的)过去式 **IV** *prep.* ① (指时间、地点、数量、程度等)过: at half ~ seven 在七点半 / She is ~ sixty. 她六十多岁了。②(指范围、限度、能力等)超过: It's ~ repair. 这个东西没法修补了。/ It's ~ all belief. 简直不可思议。③(指行动的性质、方式等)超过 **V** *ad.* 过: run ~ 跑过去 / The train is ~ due. 火车误点了。‖*a ~ master* 见 **master**[1] / *be ~ praying for* 见 **pray** / *not put it ~ sb.* 相信某人可能会(做某事)

paste [peist] **I** *n.* ① (做点心等用的)加油脂的面团 ②一种软糖 ③糊, 酱;糊状物: fish ~ 鱼糊 / bean ~ 豆瓣酱 / tooth ~ 牙膏 ④浆糊: a bottle of ~ 一瓶浆糊 ⑤(制陶、瓷器用的)湿粘土 ⑥(做人造宝石等用的)玻璃质混合物;制成的人造宝石 **II** *vt.* ① 用浆糊贴粘: ~ up a big-character poster 贴大字报 ② ~ things together 把东西贴在一起 ③ 裱糊; 用粘贴物(或糊状物)覆盖: ~ the window with paper 用纸糊窗子 / bread thickly ~d with butter 涂有厚厚一层黄油的面包

pasteboard ['peistbɔːd] **I** *n.* ① 纸板 ② 名片 ③ 纸牌 ④ 门票; 火车票 **II** *a.* ①纸板做的 ②薄弱的, 不坚实的; 假冒的

pastel I [pæs'tel] *n.* ① 菘蓝染料; 【植】菘蓝 ②色粉笔; 彩色蜡笔 ③彩色粉笔画(或画法); 彩色蜡笔画(或画法); 粉画(或画法) ④轻松的小品文 ⑤淡而柔和的色彩 **II** ['pæstl] *a.* ①彩色粉(或蜡)笔的; 彩色粉(或蜡)笔画的; 粉画的 ②(色彩)柔和的, 淡的: ~ shades 轻淡优美的色彩 ③虚弱的

pasteurize ['pæstəraiz] *vt.*【医】用巴氏法对…消毒(或灭菌); 对…进行消毒(或灭菌): ~d milk 消毒牛奶 ‖**pasteurization** [ˌpæstərai'zeiʃən] *n.* 巴氏灭菌法, 低热灭菌

pastime ['pɑːs-taim] *n.* 消遣; 娱乐

pastor ['pɑ:stə] *n.* ① (基督教的)牧师; 精神生活方面的指路人 ②牧人, 牧羊人 ③【动】粉红椋鸟 ‖**~ship** *n.* 牧师的职权(或任期)

pastoral ['pɑ:stərəl] **I** *a.* ①牧(羊)人的; (关于)牧人的生活方式的 ②畜牧的; 以畜牧为基础的 ③乡村的; 描写牧人(或乡村)生活的; 田园诗的: ~ poetry 田园诗 ④牧师的; 主教的 **II** *n.* ①牧师(或主教)写给教区教友的公开信 ②田园诗(或剧、画), 牧歌; 【音】田园曲 ③乡村景色 ④主教的权杖 (= ~ staff) ⑤论述牧师职能的书 ‖**~ism** *n.* ①田园作品的风格(或性质) ②畜牧; 以畜牧为基本经济活动的社会组织 / **~ist** *n.* ① 田园诗(或剧等)的作者 ②放牧者, 畜牧者 ③【澳】畜牧场主 / **~ly** *ad.*

pastry ['peistri] *n.* 面粉制的糕点 (如馅饼、蛋糕等); 一块糕点: a good hand at ~ 做糕饼的能手 ‖**'~cook** *n.* 糕饼师傅

pasture ['pɑ:stʃə] **I** *n.* ①牧场 ②牧草 ③牲畜饲养, 放牧 **II** ❶ *vt.* (牛、羊)吃(草); 放(牛、羊)吃草; 把(土地)作为牧场 ❷ *vi.* (牛、羊)吃草 ‖**'~=ground**, **'~land** *n.* 牧场

pasty[1] ['peisti] *a.* 面糊似的; 苍白的; 不健康的 ‖**'~-'faced** *a.* 面色苍白的

pasty[2] ['pæsti] *n.* 馅饼, 肉馅饼

pat[1] [pæt] **I** *n.* ①(用掌或扁平物)轻拍, 轻打 ②有节奏的轻拍声 (黄油等的) 小块; 似小块黄油的东西 **II** (patted; patting) ❶ *vt.* ① 轻拍; 轻拍…使平滑(或成形) ② 轻拍…表示抚慰(或赞同) ❷ *vi.* ①轻拍, 轻敲 ②发出轻的拍打声(如跑时) ‖**~ *sb.* on the back** 见 **back** ‖**'~-a-cake** *n.* 儿童的一种拍手游戏

pat[2] [pæt] **I** *a.* ①恰合适的, 完全适时的: a ~ hand (in poker) (玩纸牌时) 一手好牌(打牌时常用此语表示不要重新补牌等) / A ~ tale aroused a big laugh. 一个贴切适时的故事引起一场大笑。②过于巧合的; 人为的 ③学(或记)得一点不差 ④准备好的 ⑤坚定的, 不屈服的; [美俚]固定不变的 **II** *ad.* 适当地, 及时地; 立即 ‖**come ~** 来得正好: The sentence came ~ to his purpose. 这句句子正合他的意思。/ **have sth.** ~ ①对事物了解(或记忆)得一点不差 ②准备好某事物随时可用: have one's excuse ~ 想好了托词随时可用 / **know sth.** ~ 对某事物了解(或记忆)得一点不差 / **stand** ~ ① (玩纸牌时) 不再补新牌 ②坚持, 不改变主张

patch[1] [pætʃ] **I** *n.* ① 补钉, 补片, 补块 ②(贴于伤口的)膏药; 裹伤(胶)布; (保护病眼或伤眼的)眼罩 ③(缀于肩部下面袖子上的)臂章 ④ 小块土地: a potato ~ 一小块种土豆的地 ⑤ 碎片, 碎屑; 与周围不同的斑片; 【医】斑: a ~ of white on the dog's head 狗头上的一块白斑 ⑥饰颜片(十七、十八世纪欧洲贵族妇女脸上的黑色圆形贴片) ⑦[主英]时期, 季节 **II** *vt.* ①补缀, 修补; [喻]弥补, (暂时)掩盖: 平息: ~ *up* worn-out clothes 缝补破衣 / ~ *up* a quarrel 平息一场争吵 ②(匆忙)拼凑(*up*) ‖**be not a ~ on** 比不上…: What

he accomplished *was not a* ~ *on* what he had planned. 他所取得的成绩比不上他原先的计划。/ **make a ~ against** 可与…相比 / **strike a bad** ~ 倒霉, 遭受不幸(或困难) ‖**~ pocket** 贴袋 / **'~ test** [医](检验过敏性病症的)皮肤接触测验 / **'~work** *n.* ①缝缀起来的各色布片 ②拼凑的东西, 混杂物: the ~*work* assemblage of puppet troops 伪军的拼凑集结

pate [peit] *n.* 头; 头顶; [蔑] 头脑: a bald ~ 秃头 / an empty ~ 没头脑的家伙

patent ['peitənt, 'pætənt] **I** *a.* ①专利的, 获得专利权(或专利证)保护的; 特许的: a ~ right 专利权 / the ~ medicines 专卖药 / letters ~ ['pætənt] 专利证 ②[口]首创的, 独出心裁的: a ~ notion 独特的见解 ③(门)开着的; 公开的; 显然的: It is ~ to all that .... 大家都明白… ④【生】张开的, 伸展的 **II** *n.* ①专利; 专利权; 专利证; 专利品: get (或 take out) a ~ for 得到…的专利权(或证) ②独享的权利, 特权 **III** *vt.* ①给予…专利权(或证) ②取得…的专利权(或证) ‖**~able** *a.* 可给予(或可取得)专利权(或证)的 / **~ee** [,peitən'ti:, ,pætən'ti:] *n.* 专利权的获得者 / **~ly** *ad.* 显然地, 一清二楚地 / **~or** *n.* 专利权的授予者 ‖**~ anchor** 【海】无档锚 / **~ flour** 上等面粉 / **~ leather** 漆皮 / **~ log** 【海】拖曳式计程仪 / **Patent** ['pætənt] **Office** 专利局 / **~ pool** 专利权共享互用的一组企业 / **~ rolls** [英]专利登记簿

paternal [pə'tə:nl] *a.* ①父亲的; 象父亲的: ~ care 父亲(般)的关怀(或操心) ②父方的; 父系的; 得自(或传自)父亲的: one's ~ grandfather 祖父 ‖**~ly** *ad.* 父亲似地

paternity [pə'tə:niti] *n.* ①父亲的身分; 父权; 父系 ②[喻]渊源; 来源, 出处

path [pɑ:θ] *n.* ① (走出来的)路, 小道, 小径 ② (公路旁的)人行道 ③(竞走或自行车比赛用的)跑道: a cinder ~ 煤屑跑道 ④(思想、生活、行为等的)道路, 途径 ⑤路线; 路程; 轨道: approach ~ 【空】进场航线 / optical ~ 【物】光程 / the ~ of a projectile 【军】弹道 ⑥【天】道, 带: ~ of a total eclipse 全食带 / moon's ~ 白道 ‖**a beaten ~** 踏出来的路; [喻]常规, 惯例, 陈套 / **a ~ strewn with roses** 安乐的一生 / **break (或 blaze) a (new)** ~ 开辟一条(新)路 / **cross sb.'s** ~ 碰见某人 ②挡住某人去路, 阻碍某人 / **set sb. on the right** ~ 使某人走上正路 ‖**~less** *a.* 没路的, 未被踩踏过的: ~*less* jungles 人迹未到的丛林 ‖**'~,breaker** *n.* 开路人; 开拓者; 闯将 / **'~-,finder** *n.* ①探路者, 探索者; 开拓者 ②导航人员; 导航飞机; 导航雷达 / **'~,finding** *n.* 领航, 导航; 寻找目标 / **'~way** *n.* 小路, 小径

pathetic [pə'θetik] *a.* ①哀婉动人的, 可怜的 ②悲哀的, 忧郁的 ③感情(上)的, 情绪(上)的 ‖**~ally** *ad.* ‖**~ fallacy** 感情的误置(指对自然界现象或无生命事物的拟人化; 如把汹涌的大海称为 an angry sea)

pathology [pə'θɔlədʒi] *n.* ①病理学 ②病理, 病状 ③[喻]反常, 变态 ‖**pathologist** *n.* 病理学家

pathos ['peiθɔs] *n.* ① (事件、作品、言词等中)引起怜悯(或同情)的因素; 怜悯, 同情 ② 悲怆, 哀婉 ③【心】精神病苦 ④偶然因素; 暂时性

patience ['peiʃəns] *n.* ①忍耐; 容忍; 耐心, 忍耐力; 坚韧: with ~ 耐心地 / Have ~! 忍耐一下! (或: 耐心一点!) ②[主英]单人纸牌戏 ‖*be out of ~ with* 对…耐不住 / *have no ~ with* 不能容忍… / *It would try the ~ of a saint.* 这样的话(或行为等)使圣人也要发脾气。 / *My ~!* [口]啊呀! 啊! / *Patience is a plaster for all sores.* [谚]忍耐可减轻一切痛苦。 / *the ~ of Job* 极度的忍耐

patient ['peiʃənt] **I** *a.* 忍耐的, 容忍的; 有忍耐力的, 有耐心的; 坚韧的: Be ~! 耐心点儿! / be ~ *with* sb. 对某人有耐心 **II** *n.* ①(接受治疗的)病人 ②(美容院等的)顾客 ‖*~ of* ①能忍受…的: be ~ *of* pains 忍受疼痛 ②容许(或具有)…意义的: This sentence is ~ *of* two interpretations. 这句子可作两种解释。 ‖**~ly** *ad.*

patriarch ['peitriɑ:k] *n.* ①家长; 族长 ②(宗教、学派等的)创始者, 鼻祖 ③可尊敬的老人; (一群人中的)最年长者 ④(基督教的)早期的主教; (罗马天主教和东正教的)最高一级的主教 ‖~**ate** ['peitriɑ:kit] *n.* ①主教的职权(或任期、管辖区、住所) ②=~y / ~**y** *n.* ①父权制 ②父权制社会

patrician [pə'triʃən] **I** *n.* ①(古罗马的)贵族; (罗马帝国在意大利及非洲各地的)行政长官; (中世纪意大利各城市共和国的)显贵 ②(一般的)贵族; 地位高的人 ③有教养的人 **II** *a.* 贵族的; 贵族似的

patrimony ['pætriməni] *n.* ①祖传的财物; 遗产 ②教会的基金(或财产) ③[喻]继承物

patriot ['peitriət, 'pætriət] *n.* 爱国者, 爱国主义者

patriotism ['pætriətizəm, 'peitriətizəm] *n.* 爱国主义; 爱国精神, 爱国心

patrol [pə'troul] **I** *n.* ①巡逻, 巡查: frontier guards *on* ~ 巡逻中的边防战士 / *on* duty 在执行巡逻任务中 / a ~ boat 巡逻艇 / a ~ route 巡逻线 / a ~ dog 警犬 / maintain a constant sea and air ~ 保持经常的海空巡逻 ②巡逻兵; 斥候; 巡逻队; 巡逻艇队; 巡逻机队 ③[美]童子军小队 **II** (patrolled; patrolling) *vt. & vi.* 巡逻; 巡查 ‖**pa'trolman** *n.* [美]巡警, 警察 / **wag(g)on** 囚车

patron ['peitrən] *n.* ①庇护人, 保护人; 恩主 ②赞助人, 资助人 ③老顾客, 主顾 ④(旅店等的)老板 ⑤(英国教会中)有圣职授与权的人 ⑥[宗]保护圣徒, (教堂、城镇等的)守护神 ‖~**ess** *n.* 女庇护人(或保护人、赞助人等) ‖~ **saint** ①保护圣徒, 守护神 ②(团体等的)最初的领导人; 最高的典范

patronage ['pætrənidʒ] *n.* ①庇护人(或保护人、赞助人等)的身分(或影响、作用等) ②庇护, 保护; 赞助, 资助 ③恩赐的态度; (以恩赐的态度施予的)恩惠 ④ 光顾, 惠顾 ⑤任意授与官职(或特权)的权力; 官职的恩赐; 被恩赐的官职 ⑥[宗]圣职授与权

patronize ['pætrənaiz] *vt.* ①庇护, 保护; 赞助, 资助 ②光顾, 惠顾 ③对…以恩人自居; 对…摆出屈尊俯就的样子

patter[1] ['pætə] **I** *n.* (急促的)嗒嗒声: the ~ of footsteps 嗒嗒的脚步声 / the ~ of rain 嗒嗒的雨声 **II** ❶ *vi.* ①发出嗒嗒声: Raindrops came ~*ing* on the windowpanes. 雨点嗒嗒地打在玻璃窗上。 ②嗒嗒地跑: The children ~*ed* down the stairs. 孩子们嗒嗒地跑下楼梯。 ❷ *vt.* 使发出嗒嗒声

patter[2] ['pætə] **I** *n.* ①行话; 黑话, 切口 ②(小贩等的)连珠炮似的话, 顺口溜 ③(滑稽演员的)急口词, 快板; (滑稽歌曲的)快板插词, 歌词 ④喋喋不休的废话, 饶舌 **II** ❶ *vt.* 喋喋不休地说; 念经似地说 ❷ *vi.* ①喋喋不休 ②祷告, 念经 ③念职口溜; 唱节奏快的滑稽歌曲 ‖~ **song** 节奏快的滑稽歌曲

pattern ['pætən] **I** *n.* ①模范, 榜样; 典范 ②型, 式样; 纸样; (浇铸用的)模, 模型: a sentence ~ 句型 / behaviour ~ 【心】行为型式 / after the ~ of 照…的式样 / a dressmaker's ~ 女式服装样 ③样品 ④(糊墙纸等的)图案, 图样; (电视的)帧面图象: a geometrical ~ 几何图案 / frost ~s 霜冻的花纹 ⑤方式; 形式; 格局; (文艺作品的)格调: the vivid ~s of life and struggle 生动的生活形式和斗争形式 ⑥一段衣料 ⑦(炮弹等的)散布面; (靶上的)子弹洞图 ⑧(飞机的)着陆航线 **II** ❶ *vt.* ①摹制, 仿造: ~ a coat on a Chinese model 一件仿照中国式样做的上装 ②以图案装饰, 给…加上花纹 ③[英方]与…相等, 与…相比 (to, with); 学…的样, 模仿 ❷ *vi.* 形成图案 ‖~**ed** *a.* 被组成图案的的 / ~**ing** *n.* ①图案结构, 图形: the ~*ing* of a carpet 地毯的图案结构 ②(行为、社会习惯等的)特有型式 / ~**less** *a.* 无图案的 ‖~ **bargaining** 工会要求资方按某一理想方案签订合同所进行的谈判 / ~ **bombing** 【军】定形轰炸 / '~,**maker** *n.* 制模工; 制作图案者 / '~-**room**, '~-**shop** *n.* (翻砂厂的)制模车间

pattie, **patty** ['pæti] *n.* ①小馅饼 ②小片糖 ‖~**pan** *n.* 烘馅饼的锅 / ~ **shell** 小馅饼皮子

paucity ['pɔ:siti] *n.* ①少量, 少许 ②缺乏, 贫乏

paunch [pɔ:ntʃ] **I** *n.* ①肚子, 腹; 大肚皮 ②【动】瘤胃(即反刍动物的第一胃) ③[海](防帆桁磨损的)防磨席 (= rubbing ~) **II** *vt.* 把…剖腹; 剖腹取出…的内脏

pauper ['pɔ:pə] *n.* ①靠救济过活的人; 乞丐 ②穷人, 贫民 ③[律](可免交诉讼费用的)贫民起诉人 ‖~**dom** *n.* =~ism / ~**ism** ['pɔ:pərizəm] *n.* ①[总称]穷人, 贫民 ②贫穷

pause [pɔ:z] **I** *n.* ①中止, 暂停; 停顿; 停留: during a ~ in the conversation 谈话暂停时 / a bombing ~ 停炸 / He came to a ~ and then went on reading. 他顿了一下后又继续念下去。 / without

~ 不停地 ②蹒跚 ③(书写或印刷中的)停顿符号(如句号、逗号等);(诗中)节奏的停顿 ④【音】延长号(⌢ 或 ⌣) II vi. ①中止;暂停;停顿;停留:He ~d upon the threshold to survey the room. 他在门槛上停了停把室内打量一下。/ ~ on a point 在一点上停留 ②蹒跚 ‖give ~ to 使踌躇 / ~ and ponder 停一停仔细考虑;踌躇

pave [peiv] vt. ①铺,筑(路等);作铺路…之用: ~ a path with bricks 用砖铺小路 / These bricks are to ~ the courtyard. 这些砖要用来铺院子。②铺设;密布: a garden well ~d with flowers 长满了花的花园 ‖~ the way for (或 to) 见 way ‖~r n. ①铺路工;铺设人 ②铺筑材料;铺设材料 ③铺路机

pavement ['peivmənt] n. ①铺筑过的地面(或路面);铺过的道路: a crazy ~ (花园里的)碎纹石小道 ②[英]人行道(= [美] sidewalk) ③铺筑材料: Concrete makes good ~. 混凝土是很好的铺筑材料。‖pound the ~(s) [美俚] ①徘徊街头找职业(或行乞);找职业 ②(警察)巡行街道 ‖~ artist [英] (用彩色粉笔在人行道上画图讨钱的)马路画家 / ~ light【建】(地客等的)顶窗

pavilion [pə'viljən] I n. ①(尖顶)大帐篷;帐篷形物,穹形物 ②(公园等中)小巧玲珑的建筑;亭子,楼阁;(博览会的)馆 ③(大楼等的)装饰华美的突出部分;(医院等建筑物的)分隔部分 ④【解】耳郭 II vt. ①给…搭帐篷;用帐篷覆盖 ②笼罩

paw [pɔ:] I n. ①脚爪,爪子 ②[口]手(尤指笨拙的大手);笔迹 II ❶ vt. ①(用脚爪等)抓;扒: be ~ed by a lion 被狮子抓了一下 / The horses ~ed the dust of the street. 马群刨起了街上的尘土。②笨拙地搔;粗鲁地摸弄;乱抓 ❷ vi. ①(用脚爪等)抓;扒: The cat ~ed at a mouse. 猫向老鼠抓去。②笨拙地搔;粗鲁地摸弄;乱抓 ‖a velvet ~ ①(猫的)肉爪 ②笑面虎;笑里藏刀 ‖~ foot 家具上的兽爪撑脚

pawky ['pɔ:ki] a. [主英]狡诈的;机警的 ‖pawkily ad. / pawkiness n.

pawn[1] [pɔ:n] I n. ①典,当,押: be at (或 in) ~ (物品等)当掉,押出 / give (或 put) sth. in ~ 当掉某物 ②当出物;抵押品;人质 II vt. ①当;抵押 ②[喻]用…作担保(或抵押): ~ one's word 口头担保 ‖~ sth. off as 把某物冒充为…押(或拿)出去 ‖~ee [pɔ:'ni:] n. 承典人,接受抵押品的人 / ~or, ~er 典出人,当出人 ‖~, broker n. 当铺老板 / ~, broking n. 典当业 / ~shop n. 当铺 / ~ ticket 当票;抵押凭据

pawn[2] [pɔ:n] n. ①(西洋象棋)兵,卒 ②[喻]马前卒;爪牙,工具

pay[1] [pei] I (paid [peid]) ❶ vt. ①支付,付清;缴纳: How much did you ~ for that book? 你买那本书花了多少钱? / ~ a bill 付帐 / ~ one's membership dues 缴会费 / ~ the penalty 缴纳罚金 ②付给(某人),给…以报酬;出钱雇: ~ the barber 付钱给理发员,付理发费 / be paid by the piece (hour) 计件(计时)取酬 ③偿还,补偿

His efforts were well paid in the end. 他的努力终于得到了很好的结果。④对…有利,对…合算: It doesn't ~ one to be dishonest. 不老实的人总要吃亏。⑤有…收益;(职位等)有(若干)报酬: an investment ~ing 5 percent 能获利百分之五的投资 / jobs ~ing lower wages 低薪职位 ⑥给予(注意等);致以(问候等);进行(访问等): ~ attention to investigation and study 注重调查研究 / ~ one's respects to sb. 向某人表示敬意 / ~ visits to 访问 ⑦[过去式和过去分词用 payed] 松出(绳索等)(out) ❷ vi. ①付款,付清: ~ in advance 预付 / ~ by instalments 分期付款 / ~ on delivery【商】货到付款 ②偿还;付出代价;[喻]受到惩罚,得到报应(for): ~ for the damage 赔偿损坏 / ~ in kind 以实物支付;[喻]以同样的东西(或手段)偿还 ③有利,合算: It will ~ to read that book. 读读那本书是值得的。④有收益,(职位等)有报酬: a ~ing enterprise 有收益的企业 II n. ①支付;受雇用 ②偿还;报答;报应 ③雇用;工资,薪金(尤指军饷);津贴: equal ~ for equal work 同工同酬 / full (half) ~ 全(半)薪 / draw one's ~ 领薪水 / travel ~ 出差津贴 ④有支付能力的人;按期付款的人;有信用的人 ⑤有大量矿藏的土(或岩,砂);可采矿石;产(石)油地带,产油层 III a. ①含贵重矿物的;矿物丰富的: ~ gravel 含矿砾 / ~ ore 富矿石 / a ~ bed (或 horizon) 产油层,生产层 ②[美]需付费的,收费的;自动收费的: a ~ audience (听演讲等)付费的听众 / a ~ library 收费图书馆 ③有关支付的: a ~ clerk 出纳员 ‖be good (bad) [口]能(不能)偿清债务 / in the ~ of [贬]受…的雇用 / ~ as you go ①帐单到期即付 ②量入为出 ③领到薪金即付所得税 / ~ back 偿付(借款等);报答;向…报复: ~ back a social obligation 尽社会义务 / How can I ~ you back for all your kindness? 你的这番好意我该怎么报答呢? / ~ sb. back blow for blow 对某人以牙还牙地报复 / ~ down ①用现金支付 ②(分期付款购货时)先支付(部分货款) / ~ home 充分报复;全力反击 / ~ in (或 into) 解款,把(款项等)解入: ~ a cheque into the bank 将支票解入银行 / ~ off ①付清(某人)的工资,付清工资解雇(某人);偿清(欠款等) ②对(某人或某事)进行报复 ③使人得益;有报偿 ④【海】使(船)掉转向下风;(船)转向下风 ⑤松出(绳索等) ⑥贿赂 / ~ one's way 见 way / ~ out ①付出(款项等) ②对(某人)进行报复 ③松出(绳索等) / ~ sb. back in his own coin 见 coin / ~ the debt of nature (或 ~ one's debt to nature) 死去 / ~ through the nose 见 nose / ~ up 全部(或按时)付清 / Something is to ~. [美口]情况不妙。(或:有点不对头。)/ What is to ~? 出了什么事? ‖~ee [pei'i:] n. 受款人,收款人 / ~er, ~or ['peiə] n. 付款人 ‖'~-as-you-'earn n. [英] (从薪金中扣除所得税的)所得税预扣法(略作 PAYE) / '~-cheque n. 付薪金用的支票;

薪金, 工资 / '~day *n.* ①发薪日 ②【商】交割日, 过户结帐日 / ~ dirt ①(含矿丰富)可开采而获利的土(或砂等): strike ~ *dirt* 发现矿藏; [喻]发横财 ②有利可图的发现(或东西) / ~ envelope [美]工资袋; 工资 / '~load *n.* ①(工厂、企业等的)工资负担 ②(运输工具的)净载重量, 有用载重量; (导弹的)有效载荷, 有效负荷 / '~,master *n.* (发放薪饷的)出纳员; 军需官: a ~*master* general 军需部长;(英国财政部的)主计长 / '~off *n.* ①发工资; 分配盈利; 分赃 ②盈利; 报酬; 报偿; 报应 ③(事件、叙述等的)高潮 ④出乎意料(或不可思议)的事 ⑤决定性的事; 决定因素 *a.*得出结果的; 决定的 / '~out *n.* 花费, 支出 / ~ packet [英]工资袋; 工资 / '~roll *n.* ①工资名单; 饷金名单: names on (off) the ~*roll* 受雇(解雇)人员名单; 在职(解职)人员名单 ②发放的工资额 / '~-,roller *n.* [美]领薪金者; 受津贴者(尤指政府的雇员) / ~ sheet [英] =~- roll / ~ station 公用自动收费电话亭

pay² [pei] (payed 或 paid [peid]) *vt.* 在 … 上涂柏油(或其它防水剂)

payable ['peiəbl] *a.* ①可支付的; (到期)应支付的: bills ~ 应付票据 / a cheque ~ at sight 见票即付的支票 ②(矿山投资等)可获利的 ‖**payably** *ad.* 可获利地

payment ['peimənt] *n.* ①支付; 支付的款项; 作为支付的东西: a cheque in ~ for rent 付房租的支票 / accept sth. as ~ for a debt 接受某物作为对债务的抵偿 ②报偿; 报应 ‖*suspend ~* 【商】无力支付, 宣布破产

pea [pi:] ([复] peas(e) [pi:z]) *n.* ①豌豆; 豌豆属植物: new ~*s* 新鲜豌豆 / green ~*s* 青豆 / split ~*s* 去皮干豌豆 ②豌豆般的东西 ‖*as like as two ~s* 一模一样 ‖**~like** *a.* ①豌豆般的 ②(花)艳丽的, 蝶形的 ‖~ coat (水手等穿的)粗呢上装 / ~ flour 豌豆粉 / ~ green 青豆色, 嫩绿色 / ~ jacket =~ coat / '~,shooter *n.* 射豆枪, 玩具枪 / ~ soup ①豌豆汤 ②[俚]无用的人, 饭桶 ③=~-souper / '~-souper *n.* 黄色浓雾 / '~-'soupy *a.* 黄色浓雾似的

peace [pi:s] I *n.* ①和平; 和平时期: world ~ 世界和平 / preach (an) "honourable ~" 鼓吹"体面(或光荣)的和平" / wreck (restore, maintain) ~ 破坏(恢复, 维护)和平 ②和约: a negotiated ~ 经谈判后达成的和约 ③[常作复]治安, 社会秩序: a breach of the ~ 扰乱治安的行为, 闹事 / the queen's(或 king's) ~ (指王国的)治安, 社会安宁 ④ 和睦, 和好: live together in ~ 和睦相处 ⑤平静, 安宁; 寂静: disturb sb.'s inward ~ 扰乱某人的内心平静 / ~ of mind 心情的平静 / the ~ of the deep forest 密林中的沉寂 ‖a ~ conference 和会 / Peace Corps (美国)和平队 / a ~ fraud 和平骗局 / ~ negotiations (或 talks) 和平谈判 / a ~ offensive 和平攻势 / a ~ rally 和平集会, 反战集会 / a ~ settlement 和平解决 / a ~ zone 和平区 II *vi.* [一般用于祈使句]安静下来 ‖*at ~* ①处于和平(或和睦)状态 ②处于平静状态 / *be sworn of the ~* 被委为治安官 / *hold (或 keep) one's ~* 闭口不说 / *keep the ~* 守法; 防止扰乱治安 / *make one's (sb.'s) ~ with* 同 (使某人同)…言归于好 / *make ~ (with)* (与…)讲和, (与…)休战; (与…)言归于好 / *Peace to his ashes (或 memory, soul)!* (愿死者)安息吧! / *swear the ~ against sb.* 控告某人图谋行凶(以勒令其保证不违法) ‖**~nik** ['pi:snik] *n.* [美]反战运动分子 ‖**~,breaker** *n.* 破坏和平的人; 扰乱治安者, 肇事者 / '~-'loving *a.* 爱好和平的 / '~,maker *n.* 调解人, 和事佬/ '~,making *n.* 调解, 调停 *a.* 调解的, 调停的 / '~,monger *n.* [美]一味乞求和平的人 / ~ offering ①和平礼物; 和平仪式(或建议) ②(感谢上帝的)祭品 / ~ officer 治安官(如警官、司法官等) / ~ pipe 长杆烟斗(北美印第安人用以表示和睦的象征) / '~time *n.* 和平时期, 平时(wartime 之对)

peaceable ['pi:səbl] *a.* ①平和的, 息事宁人的; 安静的 ②和平的, 太平的 ‖**~ness** *n.* / **peaceably** *ad.*

peaceful ['pi:sful] *a.* ①和平的; 爱好和平的: ~ evolution 和平演变 / a ~ nation 爱好和平的国家 ②安静的, 平静的; 安宁的, 太平的: a ~ bay 风平浪静的海湾 ③和平时期的, 平时的: an air-raid shelter used as a ~ warehouse 平时用作仓库的防空洞 ④ 平和的 ‖**~ly** *ad.* / **~ness** *n.*

peach¹ [pi:tʃ] *n.* ①桃子; 桃树: honey ~ 水蜜桃 ②桃色, 桃红色 ③[俚]受人喜欢的人(或物); 杰出的人, 极好的东西; 漂亮女子: a ~ of a cook 出色的厨师 / What a ~ of a room! 多好的一间房间! ‖~ blossom 桃花 ‖~ blossom *n.* 桃红色 / '~-blow *n.* (中国瓷器上的)桃色釉 / ~ brandy 桃子酒 / '~-,colo(u)red *a.* 桃色的

peach² [pi:tʃ] ❶ *vt.* 告发; 出卖(某人) ❷ *vi.* 告密: ~ against (或 upon) an accomplice 告发同谋者

peacock ['pi:kok] I *n.* ①雄孔雀; 孔雀 ②爱炫耀自己的人, 虚荣的人 II *vi.* 炫耀, 招摇; 装模作样地走 ‖*a ~ in his pride* 开屏的孔雀 / *(as) proud as a ~* 非常高傲 / *play the ~* 炫耀自己 ‖~ery *n.* 炫耀, 招摇; 虚荣 / ~ish, ~like *a.* 孔雀似的; 炫耀的, 虚荣的 / ~y *a.* 孔雀似的; 炫耀的, 虚荣的; 色彩艳丽的 ‖~ blue 孔雀蓝(染料) / ~ ore 黄铜矿, 斑铜矿 / ~ stone 孔雀石

peak¹ [pi:k] I *n.* ①山顶, 巅, 山峰 ②最高点, 高峰, 顶端: the ~ of flow (水位)的洪峰 / at the ~ of struggle 在斗争的高峰 / reach a new ~ 达到新的高度 ③(物体的)尖端, 尖儿: the ~*s* of a roof 屋顶尖 ④ (衣着上的)尖形突出部分; 帽檐 ⑤[船](船首或船尾的)尖舱 II *a.* 最高的, 高峰的: the ~ year (in production) (生产的)最高年份/ the ~ output 最高产量 / ~ hours 交通、用电等的)高峰时间 / ~ gust 【气】最大阵风 III *vi.* 达到最高点, 达到高峰: Production ~*ed* from July to September. 七月到九月生产达到了高

峰。 **❷** *vt.* ① 使尖起，使成峰状: ~ one's eyebrows 竖起眉尖 ② 使达到最高点，使达到高峰 ‖~ed [pi:kt] *a.* 有峰的；尖的 / ~y *a.* 有峰的，多峰的 ‖ **load** (交通、用电等的)高峰负荷，最大负载

peak² [pi:k] *vi.* ① 消瘦，憔悴 ② 减少；缩小 (out) ‖~ **and pine** 消瘦；憔悴 ‖~ed [pi:kt; 美 'pi:kid], ~y *a.* 消瘦的；憔悴的

peal [pi:l] **I** *n.* ① 钟声；(一组钟奏出的)钟乐；(奏钟乐的)编钟 ② 连续的洪亮的响声，隆隆声: ~s of artillery 隆隆的炮声 / ~s of spring thunder 隆隆的春雷 / a ~ of applause (laughter) 一阵响亮的鼓掌声(笑声) **II ❶** *vt.* 使鸣响；大声发出，大声说: ~ one's ideas 大声说出自己的想法 **❷** *vi.* 大声响，轰响: The bells began ~ing. 钟声噹噹地响了。

pear [pɛə] *n.* 梨子；梨树 ‖'~-shaped *a.* ① 梨子形的 ② (声音)圆润的；无鼻音的

pearl [pə:l] **I** *n.* ① 珍珠；珍珠母: cultured ~s (人工)养殖的珍珠 / pass off fish eyes for ~s 鱼目混珠 / ~ buttons 珠母纽扣 ② 珠状物(如露珠、洁白的牙齿等) ③ 珍品；杰出的人；优秀的典型 ④ 珍珠色，蓝灰色 ⑤ (煤、金属等的)碎片；(大麦等揉搓成的)小圆粒 ⑥ [方] [医] 白内障 ⑦ [印] 珠型活字(即五点小型活字) **II ❶** *vt.* ① 用珍珠镶嵌(或装饰) ② 使成珠状；使成小圆粒 ③ 珠子似地散布在…上: The grass was ~ed with dew. 草上点缀着露珠。 / Sweat ~ed his forehead. 他额上满是汗珠。 ④ 使呈珍珠色(或光泽) **❷** *vi.* ① 成珠子状 ② 采珍珠: go ~ing 去采珍珠 **III** *a.* ① 珍珠(制)的；珍珠似的；镶珍珠的 ② 小粒的 ‖*cast* ~s *before swine* [谚]明珠暗投；把珍贵的东西送给不识货者 ‖~er *n.* ① (潜水)采珠人；采珠船 ② 碾麦机 / ~y *a.* ① 珍珠似的，珠母似的 ② 产珍珠的，产珠母的 ③ 用珍珠(或珠母)装饰的 ④ 珍贵的 ‖~ **ash** 珍珠灰(一种不纯的碳酸钾) / ~ **barley** (揉搓成的)大麦粉粒 / ~ **diver**, **fisher** (潜水)采珠人 / ~ **eye** ① 鸟的眼睛 ② [医]白内障 / '~-**,fishery** *n.* 采珠业；采珠场 / ~ **grain** 珍珠克拉(珍珠的重量单位；=¼ carat) / **Pearl Harbor** ① 珍珠港[美国军港] ② (珍珠港事件式的)偷袭: pull a *Pearl Harbor* on sb. 对某人进行突然袭击 / ~ **oyster** 【动】珍珠贝 / ~ **plant** 【植】紫草；麦家公 / ~ **powder** (作化妆品用的)珍珠粉；珠光粉 / '~-'**sago** *n.* 珠粒西米 / ~ **shell** 珍珠贝，珠母贝 / ~ **white** ① 锌钡白(一种白色颜料) ② 鱼鳞粉(人造珍珠的原料)

peasant ['pezənt] *n.* ① 农民(常指非英语国家的自耕农或雇农): the alliance of the workers and ~s 工农联盟 / the poor and lower-middle ~ 贫下中农 / a ~ movement 农民运动 / a ~ association 农会 / ~ labour 农活，庄稼活 ② 庄稼人；乡下人 ‖a *hired-hand* ~ 雇农(又称a farm labourer) / a *middle* ~ 中农 / an *owner* ~ 自耕农 / an *upper-middle* ~ 上中农 / a *rich* ~ 富

农 / a *semi-owner* ~ 半自耕农 / a *tenant* ~ 佃农 / a *well-to-do* ~ 富裕中农 ‖~ **proprietor** 自耕农，占有土地的农民

peasantry ['pezəntri] *n.* ① [总称]农民 ② 农民的地位(或特点)

peat¹ [pi:t] *n.* 泥炭，泥煤 ‖~ery *n.* 泥炭产地，泥炭沼 / ~y *a.* 产泥炭的；泥炭似的；泥炭气味的 ‖~ **bog**, ~ **moor**, ~ **moss** 泥炭沼 / '~-**reek** *n.* 泥炭烟

peat² [pi:t] *n.* ① 放浪的女子 ② [古]姑娘；美女

pebble ['pebl] **I** *n.* ① 卵石，细砾 ② 水晶；水晶透镜 ③ (印在皮革、纸张等上的)卵石花纹 **II** *vt.* ① (用石子等)连续扔 ② (用卵石等)铺，盖 ③ 在(皮革、纸张等)上印卵石花纹 ‖*not the only* ~ *on the beach* 并非独一无二的(指人) ‖**pebbly** *a.* 多卵石的；有卵石花纹的 ‖~ **powder** 粒状火药 / ~**stone** *n.* 小卵石 / '~**ware** *n.* [总称]一种斑纹陶器

peccadillo [,pekə'dilou] ([复] peccadillo(e)s) *n.* 轻罪；小过失

peck¹ [pek] *n.* ① 配克(英美干量名，=8 夸脱，略作 pk.); 一配克的容器 ② 许多，大量: a ~ of troubles 一大堆麻烦事

peck² [pek] **I ❶** *vt.* ① 啄；啄起，啄穿，啄成: The bird was ~ing the bark. 鸟啄着树皮。 / hens ~ing grain 啄食谷子的母鸡 / The chicken ~ed a hole in the sack. 小鸡在布袋上啄了一个洞。 ② (用尖头的工具)凿，琢: ~ figures into the rock 在岩石上琢出图形 ③ [口]匆忙地吻 **❷** *vi.* ① 啄；啄起，啄穿 ② 凿，琢 ③ 连续敲击: ~ at the keys of a piano 连击钢琴键 ④ 斯文地吃，一点一点地吃；吃: ~ at one's food 吃一点点东西；[喻]胃口不好 / Are you going to ~ with them? 你是否准备合同他们一起吃饭? ⑤ 找岔子，吹毛求疵 (at) **II** *n.* ① 啄；凿，琢 ② 啄痕，琢痕；啄(或琢)出的洞 ③ [口]匆忙的一吻 ④ [俚]食物；[美俚](卡车驾驶员等用语)短暂的进餐时间 ‖*off one's* ~ [俚]失去胃口 / ~ *and perch* [俚]吃和住 ‖~ **(ing) order** ① 禽鸟的等级 (指最凶的可啄次凶的，次凶的可啄一般的，依此类推) ② 社会等级

peck³ [pek] [俚] **❶** *vt.* 扔(石头) **❷** *vi.* 扔石头 (at)

peculiar [pi'kju:ljə] **I** *a.* ① (个人或一个团体)特有的，独具的: customs ~ to these tribes 这些部落所特有的风俗习惯 / Language is ~ to mankind. 语言是人类特有的。 ② 特别的，特殊的: a matter of ~ interest 具有特殊意义的事情 / ~ star 【天】特殊星 ③ 罕见的；奇怪的；乖僻的: ~ dress 奇装异服 / He has always been a little ~. 他总是有点古怪。 **II** *n.* ① 特有财产；特权 ② (不受当地司法机关管辖的)特殊教会(或教区) ③ [P-] 【基督教】上帝的特选子民(指基督徒)；犹太人 ‖~**ly** *ad.* [总称] 【基督教】上帝的特选子民(指基督徒)；犹太人 ② [P- P-] (十九世纪)反对医药并迷信神能治病的基督教教派

peculiarity [pi,kju:li'æriti] *n.* ① 独特性，特色，特

质 ②特殊的东西; 奇怪的东西 ③怪癖

pecuniary [pi'kju:njəri] *a.* ①金钱的: ~ aid 资助 / a ~ unit 货币单位 ②应罚款的: a ~ offence 应罚款的违法行为 ‖**pecuniarily** [pi'kju:njərili; 美 pi,kju:ni'erili] *ad.*

pedagogue ['pedəgɔg] *n.* ① 教师, 教员 ② [贬]卖弄学问的教师, 学究式的教师, 教书匠

pedagogy ['pedəgɔgi] *n.* 教育学; 教学法; 教师职业

pedal ['pedl] **I** *a.* ①【动】足的 ②踏板的; 脚踏的: a ~ brake 脚踏闸, 脚刹车 ②【数】垂足的: ~ curve 垂足曲线 **II** *n.* ①(自行车、缝纫机等机械的)踏脚, 踏板, 脚蹬 ②管风琴的脚踏键; (钢琴的)踏板: loud ~ 强音踏板 **III** (pedal(l)ed; pedal-(l)ing) **❶** *vi.* ①踩踏板 ②骑自行车 **❷** *vt.* 踩…的踏板 ‖~ point 【音】持续音部 / ~ pushers 长及小腿的女式裤(原为骑自行车用)

pedant ['pedənt] *n.* ①卖弄学问的人; 空谈家 ②迂腐的教师; 书呆子, 学究 ‖~ic [pi'dæntik] *a.* 卖弄学问的; 迂腐的, 学究式的 / ~ry *n.* 卖弄学问; 自称有学问; 迂腐

peddle ['pedl] **❶** *vi.* ①沿街叫卖, 挨户兜售 ②忙于琐事 **❷** *vt.* ① 叫卖; 零卖: ~ one's old wares 贩卖陈货 ②兜售(理论等), 散播(传闻等): ~ gossip 说闲话, 传播小道新闻 / ~ fish stories 吹嘘自己的业绩, 吹牛 ‖~ one's papers 见 **paper**

pedestal ['pedistl] **I** *n.* ①【建】柱脚, (雕像等的)垫座; (书桌的)基座; 【机】轴架, 支座 ②基础, 支撑 ③受人尊敬的地位 **II** (pedestal(l)ed; pedes-tal(l)ing) *vt.* ① 把…搁在垫座上; 给…装上座子 ② 提高…的地位; 颂扬 ‖put (或 set) sb. upon (或 on) a ~ 把某人当偶像崇拜

pedestrian [pi'destriən] **I** *a.* ①徒步的, 步行的: a ~ race 竞走 ②(作品风格等)缺乏想象力的; 平淡的, 沉闷的 **II** *n.* 步行者, 行人: a ~ crossing 人行横道 ‖~ism *n.* ①步行; 对步行锻炼的爱好 ②平凡, 单调 / ~ize *vi.* 徒步旅行; 步行

pedicab ['pedikæb] *n.* 三轮车, 三轮人力车

pedigree ['pedigri:] *n.* ①家谱; 【生】谱系: ~ chart 谱系图 ②家系, 血统; 门第, 出身; 名门出身 ③(事物的)起源和历史; 【语】词源: the ~ of a docu-ment 文件的来由和发展 ④(家畜的)种, 纯种: ~ cattle 纯种牛 ‖~d *a.* 有血统来历的

pedlar, pedler ['pedlə] *n.* ① (挨户兜售的)小贩, (沿街叫卖的)商贩, 货郎 ②[喻](谣言、闲话等的)兜售者, 传播者 ‖**pedlary** ['pedləri] *n.* ①小贩的货物 ②小贩的营生

peek [pi:k] **I** *vi.* ①从缝隙(或隐蔽处)看 ②偷看, 窥视 **II** *n.* 偷偷的一看; 一瞥

peel[1] [pi:l] **I** *n.* 果皮; 蔬菜皮; 幼苗皮; 嫩芽: can-died ~ 蜜饯果皮 / seasoned orange ~ 陈皮 **II** **❶** *vt.* 剥(皮), 削(皮); 剥(或削)…的皮 : ~ an orange 剥橘子 **❷** *vi.* ①(树木等)脱皮; 被剥(或削)去皮; (蛇等)蜕皮: These potatoes ~ easily. 这些土豆的皮很容易剥。②(树皮、油漆、壁纸等)剥落: The wallpaper is ~ing off. 壁纸在剥落下来了。③脱衣服 ‖keep one's eyes ~ed 见

eye / ~ it [美俚] 使劲跑 / ~ off (飞机)离队俯冲目标(或降落) / ~ out [美俚]离开, 不告而别 / scattered and ~ed [古] 被劫掠 ‖~ing *n.* ①剥皮 ②[复](马铃薯等)剥下内皮

peel[2] [pi:l] *n.* (烤面包时用的)长柄铲形器具

peep[1] [pi:p] **I** *n.* ①偷看, 窥探; 一瞥; 不完全的景象: have a ~ at sb. 偷看某人 / take a quick ~ at the past 迅速地回顾一下过去 / get a ~ of a distant cottage through the trees 从树丛中瞥见处的农舍 ②初现, 隐约的显现: at the ~ of day (或 dawn) 在黎明时分 ③ 窥视孔 **II** **❶** *vi.* ①(从缝隙等中)偷看, 窥探: ~ through a keyhole 从锁眼中偷看 / ~ behind the scenes 在幕后窥探 ②从隐蔽处出现 (out); [喻] (品质等)露出真相: The moon ~ed out from behind the clouds. 月亮从云层中隐约出现。 **❷** *vt.* 微微伸出(头部等) ‖~er *n.* ①窥视者 ②[常用复][俚]眼睛 ③[俚]私家侦探 ‖~'-bo *n.* =peekaboo[1] / ~'hole *n.* 窥视孔, 窥探孔: a ~'hole view 一孔之见 ②【军】瞄准孔, (坦克的)展望孔 / peeping Tom (尤指下流的)偷看者 / ~ show 西洋景; 透过小孔看的(下流)表演 / ~ sight 【军】觇视孔, 准门, 照门

peep[2] [pi:p] **I** *n.* ①(小鸟、鼠等的)唧唧声, 啾啾声 ②(表示埋怨、抗议等的)嘀咕 **II** *vi.* ① (小鸟、鼠等)唧唧叫 ②嘀咕 ‖~er *n.* ①唧唧叫的鸟(或鼠) ②雨蛙 ③嘀咕的人

peer[1] [piə] *vi.* ① 凝视, 盯着看 (at, into): ~ at the traffic lights 注视着交通灯 / ~ into the distance 凝视着远方 ② 隐约出现; 出现: The sun ~ed through a vast cloud. 太阳从大块云朵中隐约出现。

peer[2] [piə] **I** *n.* ① 同等的人; 同等地位的公民: a jury of sb.'s ~s 由某人同等地位的公民组成的陪审团 / without a ~ 无比 ② (英国)贵族(可指公、侯、伯、子、男中的任何一种爵位); 可成为上议院议员的贵族 (= ~ of the realm) **II** *vt.* ①与…相比; 与…同等 ②封…为贵族 ‖~age ['piəridʒ] *n.* [总称]贵族; 贵族爵位; 贵族名册 / ~ess ['piəris] *n.* ①女贵族; 贵妇 ②上议院贵族夫人 / ~less *a.* 无比的, 无可匹敌的

peevish ['pi:viʃ] *a.* ①易怒的, 暴躁的, 乖戾的 ②闹别扭的; 倔强的 ③带怒气的: a ~ accent 带怒的语气 ‖~ly *ad.* / ~ness *n.*

peg [peg] **I** *n.* ①木(或金属)钉; 栓; 短桩; 【建】测标; (桶)塞; (弦乐器的)弦轴 : a coat (hat) ~ 衣(帽)钉 / a tent ~ 系帐篷的桩 ②(用以抓、撕、钩的)尖状物, 爪; (晒衣用的)衣夹 ③栓与栓的间隔; [喻]等, 级; (物价等的)限定标准 ④主题; 借口, 遁词: He has not a ~ to hang on. 他一点借口也找不出来。⑤[复][口]腿; 裤子: be knocked off one's ~s 被击倒 ⑥[口]木腿; [美俚]装假腿的人 (= ~ leg) ⑦[主英]含酒的饮料 ⑧(一)扔 **II** (pegged; pegging) **❶** *vt.* ①用木钉钉; 用短桩固定 (down, in, out): ~ a tent down 用木桩把帐篷固定 ②[主英]用木夹把(洗的)衣服夹在晒衣绳上 ③固定, 限制;

限定(价格、工资等); 鉴定: ～ sb. **down** 约束某人的行动 / ～ sb. as a bad guy 把某人说成是坏蛋 ④用木桩在地上标出; 用木钉记(分数): The surveyor *pegged out* the plot of land. 测量员用木桩标出那块地。⑤扔: ～ a ball 扔球 ❷ *vi.* ①坚持不懈地工作(*away*); ～ *away at* (或 *on*) sth. 孜孜不倦地做某事 ②用木钉记分数 ③急忙前行(*along*) **III** *a.* =～-top ‖*a round* ～ *in a square hole* (或 *a square* ～ *in a round hole*) 不适宜担任某一职务的人 / *off the* ～ 〖口〗现成的(指服装) / ～ *out* 〖美俚〗死 / *put sb. on the* ～ 〖军俚〗把某人弄到法庭上去受审 / *take* (或 *bring, let*) *sb. down a* ～ *or two* 下某人的面子; 杀某人的威风; 挫某人的锐气 ‖～ **top** ①木制梨形陀螺 ②〖复〗(臀部宽大、踝部狭小的)陀螺形裤子 / '～-top *a.* (裤子)陀螺形的

pelican ['pelikən] *n.* 【动】鹈鹕 (又名塘鹅、淘河)

pellet ['pelit] *n.* ①小团, 小球; 药丸 ②(中世纪作战用的)石弹; 炮弹, 子弹, 弹丸 ③(鼠、兔等的)屎粒 ④硬币上的圆形浮雕 **II** *vt.* ①使形成小球(或丸子等) ②用子弹射击; 用小球扔 ‖～ **bomb** 珠型炸弹 / ～ **mo(u)lding** 【建】丸子饰

pell-mell ['pel'mel] **I** *ad.* ①混乱地, 乱七八糟地 ②匆促地 **II** *a.* 混乱的, 乱七八糟的; 匆促的 **III** *n.* 纷乱, 混乱; 杂乱

pelt¹ [pelt] **I** *n.* ①毛皮; (去毛待鞣的)生皮 ②(做衣服用的)皮货 ③〖谑〗(人的)皮肤 **II** *vt.* 剥去…的皮

pelt² [pelt] **I** ❶ *vt.* ①(连续地)向…投击; 连续打击 ②投、扔(飞弹等) ③〖喻〗对…猛烈攻击, 连续抨击: ～ sb. with questions 连珠炮似地质问某人 ❷ *vi.* ①(连续地)投击; 打击; 开火(*at*) ②(雨等持续地)大降; 猛落: The rain was ～*ing* down. 大雨倾盆。③迅猛前进 **II** *n.* ①投掷; 打击 ②抨击; 质问 ③(雨等的)大降, 猛落 ④速度 ⑤〖英方〗一阵大怒 ‖*go* (*at*) *full* ～ 拼命; 开足马力

pelvis ['pelvis] (〖复〗pelvises 或 pelves ['pelviːz]) *n.* 【解】骨盆: ～ major 大骨盆, 假骨盆 / ～ minor 小骨盆, 真骨盆

pem(m)ican ['pemikən] *n.* ①干肉饼; 牛肉干 ②(报告等的)摘要, 提要

pen¹ [pen] **I** *n.* ①笔; 笔杆; 笔尖: a ball-point ～ 圆珠笔 / a ruling ～ 鸭嘴笔 / a slip of the ～ 笔误 ②(旧时的)鹅毛(管)笔; 钢笔; 自来水笔 ③(作家等的)笔调, 笔法; 写作: live by one's ～ 以写作为生 ④作家: a scene no ～ can fully describe 没有哪一个作家能够描写得淋漓尽致的景象 ⑤【动】(枪乌贼的)羽状壳 **II** (penned; penning) *vt.* 写: ～ a letter 写信 / ～ a declaration of one's determination 写决心书 ‖～ *and ink* 书写工具, 笔墨; 写作 / *put* ～ *to paper* 着手写, 下笔 ‖～**ful** *n.* (自来水笔)一满管(指墨水) / **penner** *n.* (文件用的)执笔人; 写作人 / '～**-and**-'**ink** *a.* 用钢笔写(或画)的: a ～*-and-ink* sketch 钢笔素描 / '～**craft** *n.* ①书法; 笔法 ②写作; 写作的技巧; 作家的业务 / '～-**driver** *n.* =～-

pusher / '～-**friend** *n.* (从未见过面的)通信朋友, 笔友 / '～-**holder** *n.* ①笔杆 ②笔架 / '～-**knife** *n.* ①削(或修)鹅毛(管)笔的小刀; 削铅笔刀 ②(随身带的)单开小刀 / '～**light**, '～**lite** *n.* 钢笔形小手电筒 / ～ **name** 笔名 / ～ **pal** =～-friend / ～ **point** 〖美〗(钢)笔尖 / '～**pusher** *n.* 〖口〗用笔工作的人(指办公室职员、抄写员、簿记员、作家等) / '～**wiper** *n.* 擦笔(尖)布

pen² [pen] **I** *n.* ①(家畜的)栏, 圈, 棚; 一栏(或圈等)家畜: a sheep (cattle) ～ 羊(牛)栏 ②小围栏; (堆积货物等用的)栅栏; (小河中的)拦水坝 ③(供修理潜水艇用的)掩体, 坞 ④(西印度群岛的)畜牧场, 种植园 **II** (penned 或 pent; penning) *vt.* 把(家畜)关入栏圈; 把…关起来

pen³ [pen] *n.* 雌天鹅

penal ['piːnl] *a.* ①刑事的, 刑法上的: a ～ code 刑事法典 / a ～ law 刑法 ②受刑罚的, 当受刑罚的: ～ servitude 监禁时的劳役 / a ～ offence 刑事罪 ③刑罚场所的: a ～ colony (罪犯的)充军地; 监禁场 / a ～ farm 劳役农场 ‖～**ly** *ad.*

penalize ['piːnəlaiz] *vt.* ①对…处以刑事惩罚, 处罚: ～ unlicensed drivers 处罚无照驾车者 ②使处于严重不利地位 ‖**penalization** [,piːnəlai-'zeiʃən] *n.*

penalty ['penlti] *n.* ①处罚, 惩罚; 刑罚 ②罚款 ③【体】犯规的处罚; (桥牌中的)罚分 ④(行为等造成的)痛苦; 不利后果: the ～ *of* poor quality 质量差造成的不良后果 ‖*under* (或 *on*) ～ *of* 否则受…之罚 ‖～ **area** (足球等的)罚球区 / ～ **box** (冰球运动中)被罚暂时下场的球员的座席 / ～ **clause** 〖美〗私人冒用者必罚(印在政府免费邮件上的字样) / ～ **envelope** 〖美〗印有"私人冒用者必罚"字样的信封 / ～ **kick** (足球等的)罚球

penance ['penəns] **I** *n.* ①(赎罪的)苦行, 苦修: do ～ for one's crime 以苦行赎罪 ②【天主教】补赎 **II** *vt.* 使(某人)以苦行赎罪

pence [pens] penny 的复数

pencil ['pensl] **I** *n.* ①铅笔: a lead ～ 石墨铅笔 / a red ～ 红铅笔 / a coloured ～ 颜色铅笔 ②小画笔; (古)画笔 ③(画家等的)笔调, 笔法 ④笔状物 (如药管、眉笔等): a diamond ～ (划玻璃用的)金钢钻刀 / a styptic ～ 止血药管 ⑤〖美俚〗左轮手枪 ⑥【物】光线锥; 【数】束: a ～ of rays 一锥光线 / a ～ of lines (circles, planes) 线(圆, 面)束 **II** (pencil(l)ed; pencil(l)ing) *vt.* ①用铅笔写(或画、标); 用画笔画(或描) ②用药笔治; 用眉笔涂 ‖**pencil(l)ed** *a.* ①用铅笔写的; 用画笔画的 ②(禽类羽毛等)有彩色细纹的 ③【物】成锥状的; 【数】成束的 / **pencil-(l)er** *n.* ①用铅笔写(或画)的人 ②〖英俚〗(赛马赌博的)记帐员 / **pencil(l)ing** *n.* ①铅笔画; 毛笔画 ②(墙上沿着砖缝画成的)白色(或其它色)线条 ③(禽类羽毛等的)彩色细纹 ‖～ **case** 铅笔盒 / ～ **ore** 〖矿〗笔铁矿 / ～ **pusher** 〖美〗①用笔工作的人(指办公室职员、抄写员、簿记员、

记者等) ②[俚]轰炸机的领航员 / ~ **sharpener**
卷笔刀 / ~ **sketch** 铅笔画(或素描);草图 / ~
stone 石笔石,滑石 / ~ **vase** 笔筒

pendant ['pendənt] **I** n. ①下垂物,垂饰;挂表壳
上系表链的环: ear~s 耳环 ②【建】悬饰;吊灯
架 ③(成对物中的)一个; (书的)姐妹篇,附录
④[海]短索:三角旗,尖旗 **II** a. =pendent (a.)

pending ['pendiŋ] **I** a. ①悬而未决的: a ~ case
未决案件,悬案 ②迫近的: a ~ danger 迫在眉
睫的危险 **II** prep. ①在…期间: ~ the negotiations 在谈判期间 ②在…以前: ~ sb.'s arrival
在某人到达之前

pendulum ['pendjuləm] n. ①(钟等的)摆: a
simple ~ 单摆 / a compound ~ 复摆 ②[喻]摇
摆的人(或物): the ~ of public opinion 舆论的
动荡 │the swing of the ~ 见 **swing**

penetrate ['penitreit] ❶ vt. ①穿过,穿透;刺入;
透过: The rays of the sun ~d the mists. 阳光
透过迷雾。②看穿,看透;识破: ~ the phe-
nomena of things to study their essence 透过
事物的现象研究其本质 / ~ sb.'s disguise 识
破某人的伪装 ③渗透入;弥漫于;扩散于 ④(思
想、感情等)深入于,打动 ❷ vi. ①穿入;刺入;
透过: The arrow ~d through the target. 箭射
穿靶子。②看穿,看透;识破 ③渗透;弥漫;扩散
④(思想、感情等)深入人心,打动人心 │**pene-
trator** n. ①穿入者;渗透者;侵入者 ②【军】侵
入式飞机

penetrating ['penitreitiŋ] a. ①穿透的,贯穿的;渗
透的: ~ rays 穿透的光线 / ~ radiation 【物】
贯穿辐射 / a ~ gas 渗透性毒气 ②(目光等)尖
锐的,深刻的,透彻的: ~ insight 敏锐的洞察
力/sum up in a ~ way 深入地总结 ③(声音等)响
亮的,尖利的: a ~ cry 尖声大叫 / a ~ smell 刺
鼻的气味 ④(伤口等)深的 │**~ly** ad.

penetration [,peni'treiʃən] n. ①穿入,穿透;穿透
能力;穿透深度: ~ frequency 【物】穿透频率
②渗透;侵入: ~ and level dying 【纺】渗透匀
染 ③【军】突破;(空战中)深入敌方飞行: a force
of ~ 突破部队 / a ~ fighter 远程战斗机 ④
(目光等的)尖锐;洞察力: He writes with ~. 他
写的文章尖锐深刻。

penguin ['peŋgwin] n. ①企鹅(南半球产的一种不
会飞的海鸟) ②[美俚]非飞行航空人员 ③[美俚]
跑龙套

peninsula [pi'ninsjulə] n. ①半岛 ②[the P-]【史】
(一八〇八至一八一四年"半岛战争"中指)伊比利
亚半岛;(第一次世界大战中指)加利波利半岛

peninsular [pi'ninsjulə] **I** a. ①半岛的;半岛状的
②[常作 P-]伊利亚半岛的;伊比利亚半岛战争
的 **II** n. ①半岛居民 ②[P-]参加伊比利亚半岛
战争的士兵

penitence ['penitəns] n. 悔罪,悔过;后悔,忏悔:
~ for a fault 悔过

penitent ['penitənt] **I** a. 悔罪的,悔过的;后悔的,

忏悔的 **II** n. 悔罪者,悔过者;忏悔者 │~ly ad.

penitential [,peni'tenʃəl] **I** a. 后悔的,忏悔的;苦
行赎罪的 **II** n. ①悔罪者,悔过者;忏悔者
②【宗】苦行赎罪的规则(书) │~ly ad.

penitentiary [,peni'tenʃəri] **I** n. ①(罪犯)教养
所;[英]妓女收容所;[美]州(或联邦)监狱 ②
(天主教主教所任命的)对教徒悔改事项的处理者
II a. ①教养的;监禁的;引起监禁处分的 ②
=penitential (a.)

pennant ['penənt] n. ①【海】短索;尖旗,三角旗
②(运动比赛中的)三角锦旗

penny ['peni] ([复] pennies 或 pence [pens]) n.
①便士 (英国辅币单位): Please give me six
pennies for this six*pence*. 请给我把这个六便
士的硬币换成六个一便士的硬币。[注意: 复数
pence 用于数词后构成复合词, 如 sixpence, ten-
pence, eighteen pence] ②(美国或加拿大辅币)
分 (=cent); (古罗马的)一枚钱;一银币;一笔
钱 ③[英][用于数词后构成复合词, 作定语, 表
示价格]…便士: a ten~ supper 一顿十便士的
晚餐 / four~ nails (每百枚价格)四便士的钉
子(现常表示钉子的规格) │*A ~ for your
thoughts!* 你呆呆地在想什么啦! / a ~ plain
and twopence colo(u)red (对庸俗的华丽的嘲笑
语)不值钱的花花绿绿 / a pretty (或 fine) ~
[口]一大笔钱 / in for a ~, in for a pound 一
旦开始就干到底;一不做,二不休 / pennies from
heaven 不费力(或不花钱)而得到的东西; 意外
得到的好处 / ~ wise and pound foolish 小
处精明,大处浪费;小事聪明,大事糊涂 / pinch
pennies 精打细算 / spend a ~ [口]上(公共)
厕所 / Take care of the pence, and the
pounds will take care of themselves. [谚]
(金钱)积少自然成多。(或: 小事谨慎,大事自
成。) / The ~ dropped. 目的已达到。(或: 话
已听明白。) / turn (或 earn) an honest ~ 用
正当手段(如干零活)挣一点钱 │'~-a-'line a.
每行一便士稿酬的;稿酬低的 ②(文章等)整版
的 / '~-a-'liner n. 取低稿酬的文人,穷文人,雇
佣文人 / ~ ante (打扑克等)赌注小的赌博;琐
碎小事 / ~ dreadful, ~ blood 廉价的恐怖(或
惊险)小说;刊登恐怖故事的廉价书刊 / ~ gaff
[英]票价低廉的剧场(或娱乐场) / '~-in-the-
'slot n. 自动售货机 / '~-pinch vt. 对…吝啬 /
~ pincher 吝啬鬼 / '~'royal n. 【植】(产于北
美的)除蚤薄荷(油) / '~weight n. 英钱(音译
本尼威特,英国衡单位: =1.555 克) / '~-
'wise a. 小处精明的;谨小慎微的 / '~-wort,
'~wort n. 【植】破铜钱属植物 / '~worth
['penθ, 'peniwə(ː)θ] n. 一便士的价值;一便
士价值的东西;少量: not a ~*worth* 一钱不值;丝
毫不 ②交易: a good ~*worth* 便宜货 / sell
Robin Hood's ~*worth* 廉价(或半价)出售

pension¹ ['penʃən] **I** n. ①抚恤金;年金;养老金,
退休金: retire on a ~ 领取养老金退休 ②(艺
术家等所领的)津贴,补助金 **II** vt. 给予…抚恤
金(或养老金等) │~ sb. off 发给某人养老金

其退休; 发给某人年金令其退职 ‖ **~able** *a.* 可领取抚恤金(或养老金等)的 / **~ary** *a.* ① 抚恤金(或养老金等)的 ② 领取抚恤金(或养老金等)的; 依靠抚恤金(或养老金等)生活的 *n.* ① = **~er** ② 为金钱所收买的人; 帮佣 / **~er** *n.* ① 领取抚恤金(或养老金等)者 ②(英国剑桥大学的)自费生 / **~less** *a.* 没有抚恤金(或养老金等)的

pension² ['pɑ̃:ŋsiɔ̃:ŋ] *n.* ①(欧洲大陆国家的)膳宿学校; 膳宿公寓 ②膳宿费 ‖ *live en* **~** 在公寓膳宿

pensive ['pensiv] *a.* 沉思的; 忧郁的 ‖ **~ly** *ad.* / **~ness** *n.*

pent¹ [pent] **I** pen² 的过去式和过去分词 **II** *a.* 被关禁的, 被关起来的 ‖ **'~-'up** *a.* 被抑制的; 被关住的: **~-up** emotion 被抑制的情感

pent² [pent] *n.* 单斜顶棚; 庇檐 ‖ **~ roof** 【建】单坡屋顶

pentagon ['pentəgən] *n.* ①五边形, 五角形 ②[the P-] 五角大楼(美国国防部的办公大楼) ‖ **~al** [pen'tægənl] *a.* 五边形的, 五角形的

penthouse ['penthaus] *n.* ①(靠在大楼等边上搭的)披屋;(建于大楼平顶上的)楼顶房屋; 小棚屋 ②(靠墙的)单斜顶棚; 庇檐 ③遮篷, 雨篷

penult [pi'nʌlt], **penultimate** [pi'nʌltimit] **I** *a.* 倒数第二的; 倒数第二音节的: on the **~** day of the week-long meeting 在历时一周的会议结束的前一天 **II** *n.* 倒数第二位; 倒数第二音节

penury ['penjuri] *n.* 赤贫; 缺乏

peony ['pi:əni] *n.* 芍药属植物; 芍药, 牡丹

people ['pi:pl] **I** *n.* ①人民 ②民族; 种族;(某国的)国民: the English-speaking **~s** 使用英语的(各)民族 / a great **~** 伟大的民族 / the American **~** 美国人民 ③人, 人类(以别于其他动物而言) ④(泛指)人, 人们: Most **~** think so. 大多数人这样想。/ Fifty **~** were present. 五十个人出席。/ **~** of (或 from) all walks of life 各界人士 / *People* say that . . . . 人们说…(或: 据说…) ⑤[口]家族; 家人, 亲属(尤指父母); 祖先: Would you come and meet my **~**? 你来见见我家的人好吗? ⑥(某一个阶级、地区、团体、行业的)人: the customhouse **~** 海关人员 ⑦公民, 选民 ⑧平民, 老百姓 ⑨仆从; 随员;(武装)随从 ⑩【基督教】教区内的教徒 ⑪(某种或某一特定场合的)小动物: the little **~s** of field and forest 田野与森林中的(各种)小动物 **II** *vt.* ①使住着(或住满)人: a thickly (sparsely) **~d** area 人口稠密(稀少)地区 / **~** the new lands 向新开发地区移民 ②栖息在; 布满 ‖ *of all* **~** 在所有(或许多)人中(偏偏…): They chose him *of all* **~**. 他们恰恰就挑选了他。/ *the best* **~** [口]上流社会人士 / *the Chosen People* 【基督教】上帝的特选子民(指基督徒); 犹太人 ‖ **~-to-'** *a.* 人与人之间的: **~**-*to*-**~** contacts and exchanges 人民之间的联系和交流

pep [pep] [美俚] **I** *n.* 锐气, 劲头, 活力: be full of **~** 劲头十足 **II** (pepped; pepping) *vt.* 激励,

给…打气, 叫…加油: **~** sb. *up* 激励某人 ‖ **~ pill** [美俚]兴奋药片 / **~ rally** 鼓舞士气的(集)会 / **~ talk** (对球员等)鼓励士气的讲话

pepper ['pepə] **I** *n.* ①[P-]【植】胡椒属 ②胡椒; 胡椒粉 ③辛辣(或富于刺激性、尖刻)的事物(如评论等) ④[美俚]活力, 精力; 劲头; 勇气 ‖ *black* **~** 黑胡椒(用未成熟的胡椒子晒干后做的胡椒粉) / *cayenne* **~** 【植】辣椒 / *water* **~** 【植】蓼; 美洲线叶苹 / *white* **~** 白胡椒(用成熟去皮的胡椒子做的胡椒粉) **II** *vt.* ①加胡椒粉于 ②雨点

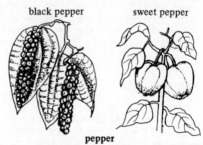

black pepper   sweet pepper

pepper

般地撒(或掷、射): **~** sb. with stones (shots, questions) 雨点似地向某人扔石头(射击, 提问题) ③使(文章等)尖刻(或富于刺激性) ④殴打, 鞭打;[美俚]连续打击(某人) ‖ *take* **~** *in the nose* 发脾气, 勃然大怒 ‖ **'~-and-'salt** *a.* (布料)黑白点子混合而呈灰色的 *n.* 椒盐色; 椒盐色料子 / **'~box** *n.* ①胡椒盒(或瓶) ②急性子的人 / **~ caster**, **~ castor** 胡椒盒(或瓶) / **'~corn** *n.* ①胡椒子 ②空有其名的租金 ③微不足道(或空有其名)的答礼 / **'~grass** *n.* 【植】独行菜 / **'~-mill** *n.* 磨胡椒子的小罐 / **'~mint** *n.* ①【植】胡椒薄荷; 薄荷 ②薄荷油 ③薄荷糖 / **~ pot** ①胡椒盒(或瓶) ②(西印度群岛的)红胡椒炖肉(或鱼) ③辣味什锦砂锅; 辣味浓汤

peppery ['pepəri] *a.* ①胡椒的; 胡椒似的; 加了很多胡椒的 ②胡椒味的; 辣的 ③(讲话、文章等)辛辣的, 尖刻的 ④易怒的, 暴躁的

per [强 pə:; 弱 pə] *prep.* [拉] ①经, 由, 靠: **~** post 经(由)邮局 / **~** rail 经(由)铁路 / **~** bearer 由来人 ②每: **~** day (month, year) 每日(月, 年) ③按照, 根据: **~** list price 按照表上价格 / as **~** enclosed document 按照附上的文件 / as **~** usual [谑]照常 ‖ *per annum* 每年 / *per capita* ['kæpitə] *per capita* output of grain 按人口计算的粮食(平均)产量 / *per centum* 每百中, 百分之… / *per contra* 相反的, 反之 / **~** *diem* ['daiem] 每日 / *per mensem* ['mensem] 每月 / *per mill, per mille, per mil* [mil] 每千 / *per procurationem* [.prɔkjureiʃi'ounem] 由…所代表 / *per saltum* ['sæltəm] 一跃 / *per se* [sei, si:] 本身; 本来, 本质上

peradventure [.pərəd'ventʃə] **I** *ad.* [古] 或者, 可

能: if ~ 如果, 万一 **II** *n.* 疑惑, 不确定: beyond (或 without) ~ 无疑地, 必定

perambulator ['præmbjuleitə, pə'ræmbjuleitə] *n.* ①漫步者, 闲荡者; 巡行者, 巡视者; 察勘者 ②[主英]童车 ③【测】路程计, 测程器

perceive [pə'si:v] *vt.* ① 察觉, 发觉; 看见, 看出: ~ the danger 看出危险 ② 领悟; 理解 ||**perceivable** *a.* 可察觉的, 可看到的; 可理解的 / **perceivably** *ad.*

percentage [pə'sentidʒ] *n.* ① 百分数, 百分率: ~ of hits 【军】命中率 / the lowest ~ 最低的百分比 ②比例; 部分: A large (small) ~ of the people came. 大(小)部分人来了。③【商】手续费, 佣金 ④ 利润, 赚头; 好处; 用处: There is no ~ in worrying. 担忧是于事无补的。⑤(根据统计得出的)可能性

perceptible [pə'septəbl] *a.* ① 感觉得到的, 察觉得到的; 看得出的: a ~ smell of paint 感觉得到的(轻微)油漆气味 ② 可领悟的; 可理解的, 可认识的 ||**perceptibility** [pə,septə'biliti] *n.* 感觉力, 觉察力; 领悟能力, 认识能力 / **perceptibly** *ad.*

perception [pə'sepʃən] *n.* ①感觉; 知觉: a man of keen ~ 感觉敏锐的人 / sense ~ (通过感官的)知觉, 感觉 ②知觉过程, 知觉作用; 感性认识; 观念, 概念 ③直觉; 洞察力; 理解力 ④【律】(地租等的)征收, (农作物的)收获 ||**~al** *a.*

perceptive [pə'septiv] *a.* 知觉的; 感觉灵敏的; 有察觉力的; 有理解力的: a good ~ article 一篇富有洞察力的好文章 ||**~ly** *ad.* / **~ness** *n.*

perch[1] [pə:tʃ] **I** *n.* ① (禽鸟的)栖木; 悬挂东西的横条: The bird took its ~. 鸟停歇在栖木上。② (尤指在高处的)休息处, 有利的地位, 高位 ③【机】(联系前后车轴的)连杆, 主轴; 架: front spring ~ 前弹簧架 ④ 杆(英国长度单位, =5¼ 码); 石料容量单位 (=24¾ 立方呎) ⑤【纺】验布架 ⑥ 皮革的致柔; 皮革破绽的弥补 ⑦【海】浮筒顶标 **II ❶** *vi.* 栖息, 停歇; 坐 (或落) 在高处 **❷** *vt.* ① 使(鸟)栖息; 放置(人或物)于高处(或危险处): a pagoda ~ed on a cliff 耸峙在悬崖上的宝塔 ②验(布) ||**come off one's** ~ 不再骄傲自大 / **hop the** ~ 死 / **knock sb. off his** ~ 把某人毁掉, 打败某人 ||**~er** *n.* ①栖木类鸟; 居于高处的人(或物) ② 验布工

perch[2] [pə:tʃ] *n.*【动】河鲈

percolate ['pə:kəleit] **I ❶** *vt.* ①滤, 使渗滤; 使渗透: ~ water through sand 用沙滤水 ②(用渗滤壶)煮(咖啡) **❷** *vi.* 渗开; 滤过 **II** *n.* 滤过液; 渗(或滤)出液 ||**percolator** *n.* 滤器; 咖啡渗滤壶

percussion [pə:'kʌʃən] *n.* ①敲打, 叩击; 碰撞 ②(由敲、击产生的)震动, 声响 ③【医】叩诊(法) ④【军】击发, 着发 ⑤【音】打击; (乐队的)打击乐器组 ||**~ist** *n.* 敲奏打击乐器的人 / **bullet** 【军】爆破枪弹 / **~ cap** 【军】雷管, 火帽 / **~ cap composition** 引火药 / **~ fuse** 【军】着发引信 /

~ **instrument** 【音】打击乐器 / ~ **lock** 【军】击发装置 / ~ **powder** 【军】起爆药 / ~ **primer** 【军】起爆管

perdition [pə:'diʃən] *n.* ① 毁灭, 沉沦 ②【宗】永灭; 地狱

peremptory [pə'remptəri] *a.* ① 断然的; 命令式的: a ~ tone 命令式的语气 ② 高傲的, 专横的, 独断的 ③【律】绝对的, 最后决定的: a ~ mandamus 强制执行命令书 / a ~ writ 强制被告出庭的传票 ||**peremptorily** *ad.* / **peremptoriness** *n.*

perennial [pə'renjəl] **I** *a.* ①四季皆有的, 终年的: ~ ice and snow 终年不化的冰雪 ② 长期的; 持久不断的; 循环呈现的: ~ efforts 持续的努力 ③ 多年生的: a ~ plant 多年生的植物 / a ~ colony 多年群体 **II** *n.* 多年生植物 ||**~ly** *ad.*

perfect ['pə:fikt] **I** *a.* ①完美的; 无瑕的; 极好的; 理想的: He speaks ~ English. 他说一口极好的英语。 / a ~ method of production 完善的生产方法 / ~ weather 极好的天气 / ~ gas 【物】理想气体 ②完全的, 完备的; 全然的, 纯然的; 绝对的, 毋容置疑的: in ~ silence 鸦雀无声地 / a ~ stranger 完全陌生的人 / a ~ scoundrel 十足的无赖 ③ 熟练的; 精通的: a ~ table-tennis player 熟练的乒乓球运动员 ④ 正确的, 精确的; 忠于原文的: a ~ copy 与原本完全一致的文本 ⑤法律上有效的 ⑥【语】完成的: the ~ tense 完成时 ⑦【植】雌雄(蕊)同花的; 具备的: ~ flower 具备花 ⑧【印】两面印的: make ~ 两面印刷 **II** *n.* 【语】完成时, 完成式: the present (past, future) ~ 现在(过去, 将来)完成时 **III** [pə(:)'fekt, 'pə:fikt] *vt.* ① 使完美, 使完善; 改善 ② 使熟练, 使精通: ~ oneself in French 使自己精通法语 ||**~ly** *ad.* / **~ness** *n.* / **~or** [pə(:)'fektə] *n.* 【印】双面印刷机 ||~ **binding** 【印】无线胶粘装订 / ~ **square** 【数】整方, 完全平方

perfection [pə'fekʃən] *n.* ① 尽善尽美, 完整无缺; 登峰造极: reach (或 attain) ~ 臻于完善, 达到极致 / He aims at ~ in everything he does. 他做任何事情都指望尽善尽美。②无比精确, 圆满成熟: strive for ~ in the ballet 力求芭蕾舞艺的高度熟练 ③完成; 改善 ④理想的人(或物); 完美的典型 ⑤[复]才艺, 造诣; 优点 ||**to** ~ 完全地; 好极: She sings to ~. 她唱得好极了。 ||**~ism** *n.* ① 至善论, 圆满论(认为人在现世可达到道德、宗教、社会等方面圆满的境地) ②过度追求尽善尽美 / ~**ist** *n.* 至善论者; 圆满论者 ② 追求尽善尽美者(有时带戏谑, 指过分挑剔者)

perfidy ['pə:fidi] *n.* 背信弃义; 叛变, 出卖

perforate ['pə:fəreit] **I ❶** *vt.* ① 穿孔于, 打眼于 ② 打一排孔于(邮票等)以便于撕开 **❷** *vi.* ①穿孔: The ulcer has ~d. 溃疡已穿孔。②穿过; 刺穿; 刺穿(into, through) **II** ['pə:forit] *a.* (邮票等)有孔的, 穿孔的(尤指有一排孔的) ||**perforation** [,pə:fə'reiʃən] *n.* ①穿孔, 打眼; 贯穿 ② 孔状缝 / **perforator** *n.* ①穿孔器, 钻孔器, 打眼器

剪票铁 ②穿孔(或打眼)的人

perforce [pə'fɔːs] *ad.* 必然地,必要地;不得已地

perform [pə'fɔːm] ❶ *vt.* ①履行; 执行,完成(事业等): ~ what one has promised 履行诺言 / ~ a task 执行任务 / ~ a surgical operation on sb. 给某人施行外科手术 / ~ deeds of merit 立功 / ~ calculations with surprising speed 以惊人的速度完成演算 ②演出,表演,演奏: ~ a part in a play 在剧中扮演一个角色 ❷ *vi.* ①行动;进行: not only promise but ~ 不但许诺而且做到/The new machine is ~*ing* very well. 新机器运行良好。②演出;表演,演奏: ~ perfectly on the piano 熟练地演奏钢琴 ③(驯兽)表演把戏 ‖ **~able** *a.* 可履行的;可完成的;可演出的 / **~er** *n.* ①履行者,执行者 ②表演者,演奏者 / **~ing** *a.* 表演的,会表演的: the ~*ing* arts 表演艺术 / a ~*ing* bear 会表演把戏的熊

performance [pə'fɔːməns] *n.* ①履行,执行;完成: faithful ~ of a task 忠实执行任务 ②行为,行动;工作;成绩;功绩: This novel is really a remarkable ~ 这部小说确实是一部出色的作品。③演出;演奏; 表演; 把戏: on a tour of ~*s* 在巡回演出中 / two ~*s* a day 一天上演两场 / give (或 put on) a ~ 演出 / put a dog through its ~*s* 使狗玩种种把戏 ④(机械的)性能,特性: a ~ test 性能试验

perfume I ['pəːfjuːm] *n.* ①香味,芳香 ②香料;香水 II [pə(ː)'fjuːm] *vt.* 使发香;洒香水于 ‖ *~d talk* [美][讽]坏话, 骂人话 ‖ **~r** [pə(ː)'fjuːmə] *n.* ①香料商;香料制造者 ②洒香水的人(或器具) / **~ry** [pə(ː)'fjuːməri] *n.* ①香料;香料制造法 ②香料厂;香料店 ③[总称]香料,香水类

perfunctory [pə(ː)'fʌŋktəri] *a.* 敷衍塞责的,草率的,马马虎虎的: a ~ inspection 草率的检查 / in a ~ manner 马马虎虎地 ‖ **perfunctorily** *ad.*

pergola ['pəːgələ] *n.* ①凉亭 ②藤架,蔓藤花棚;(藤架等底下的)散步小径

perhaps [pə'hæps, præps] I *ad.* 也许,可能;多半,大概: Perhaps they are in need of our help. 也许他们需要我们的帮助。/ Perhaps he will be there—but ~ he won't. 他可能会在那里,但也可能不在。/ Perhaps so. 大概如此。 II *n.* [常复]假定,设想; 尚属疑问的事(或物): hamper oneself with ~*es* 用种种设想来妨碍自己

peril ['peril] I *n.* ①(严重的)危险: be in ~ of one's life 有生命危险 / in the hour (或 time) of ~ 在危险时刻 ②危险的事物: the ~*s* of the ocean 海洋上的风险(指风暴、船只失事等) ③冒险: You do it at your ~! 要干的话,你自己承担风险! / Keep off at your ~! 站开,否则发生危险自己负责! II (peril(l)ed, peril(l)ing) *vt.* 置…于危险中: ~ one's life 冒生命危险

perilous ['periləs] *a.* 危险的; 冒险的: a ~ peak 险峰 ‖ **~ly** *ad.* / **~ness** *n.*

perimeter [pə'rimitə] *n.* ①周,周边,周界线;周

长: the ~ of a circle 圆的周长 ②(兵营或工事外的)环形防线(或防御带): a barbed-wire ~ 有刺铁丝网的环形防线 / ~ defence 环形防御 ③[医]视野计

period ['piəriəd] I *n.* ①时期;时代;期间: in the Fourth Five-Year Plan ~ 在第四个五年计划期间 / the prehistoric ~ 史前时代 ②[the ~] 现代,当代: the youth of the ~ 现代青年 / the costume of the ~ 当代的服饰 ③周期,期;[地]纪;[常用复]月经期: ~ of incubation 【医】潜伏期 / the ~ of gestation 妊娠期 / ~ of rotation (revolution) 【天】自转(公转)周期 / natural ~ 【物】固有周期 / ~ of a circulating decimal 【数】小数的循环节 / Devonian ~ 【地】泥盆纪 ④学时,课时;(比赛的)一节时间: a lesson (或 teaching) ~ 一节课 ⑤句号,句点;结束,终止 ⑥整句(常指复合句);[复]矫饰的(或华丽的)词藻 ⑦[语]掉尾句,圆周句 (=periodic sentence) ⑧【音】乐段 II *a.* (关于)过去某一特定历史时期的;像过去某一特定历史时期的: ~ furniture [仿]古式家具 / a ~ novel 一本描写特定历史时期的小说 III *int.* 没有了(强调话已讲完): He hates dogs, ~! 他就是讨厌狗,其他没什么好讲的了! ‖ **come to a ~** 结束,告终 / **put a ~ to sth.** 结束某事 ‖ **~= lumi'nosity curve** 【天】周光曲线

periodic[1] [ˌpiəri'ɔdik] *a.* ①周期的;定期的;间歇的,间发性的;循环的: the ~ motion of a planet 行星的周期运动 / ~ disease 【医】间发性病,定期性病 / ~ attacks of malaria 疟疾的间歇发作/ ~ decimals 【数】循环小数 ②一定时期的 ③【语】用掉尾句的,用圆周句的 ‖ **function** 【数】周期函数 / ~ **law** 【化】周期律 / ~ **sentence** 【语】掉尾句,圆周句(通常指主句在最后出现的一种复合句,例如: Yesterday while I was walking down the street I met him.) / ~ **table** 【化】周期表

periodic[2] [ˌpəːrai'ɔdik] *a.* 【化】高碘的: ~ acid 高碘酸

periodical [ˌpiəri'ɔdikəl] I *a.* ①定期的,周期的;间歇的 ②定期刊行的: newspapers and ~ publications 报纸和期刊 ③期刊的: book reviews 期刊中的书评 / a ~ room in a library 图书馆的期刊阅览室 II *n.* 期刊,杂志: a weekly (monthly) ~ 周(月)刊 / an illustrated ~ 画刊 ‖ **~ly** *ad.*

peripatetic [ˌperipə'tetik] I *a.* ①徒步游历的;走来走去的 ②[P-] 亚里士多德学派的,逍遥学派的(古希腊哲学家亚里士多德在学园内逍遥步讲学,故有此称) II *n.* ①徒步游历者;[谑]行商 ②[P-] 亚里士多德学派的人,逍遥学派的人 ③[复]到处走动;游历 ‖ **~ally** *ad.*

periscope ['periskoup] *n.* 潜望镜: ~ binoculars 潜望镜式双筒望远镜 / a furnace scanning ~ 熔炉观测镜

perish ['periʃ] ❶ *vi.* ①灭亡,消灭;死去;暴卒,

天折 ②枯萎; 腐烂, 腐朽: Flowers ~ in frost.
花遇霜枯萎。/ The rubber belt on this machine
has ~ed. 这机器上的橡皮带已经失去弹性。
❷ vt. ① 毁坏; 使死去: Oil will ~ your rubber
boots. 油会毁坏你的橡胶鞋。② 使困顿; 使麻
木: be ~ed with cold 冻僵了 ‖**Perish the
thought!** 见 thought² ‖**~er** n. [俚]讨厌鬼

perishable ['periʃəbl] **I** *a.* 容易腐烂的; 易死的;
不经久的: Fruits are ~ in transit. 水果在运
送中容易腐烂。**II** *n.* [复]容易腐坏的东西(尤指
食物) ‖**perishability** [,periʃə'biliti] *n.* / **~ness**
n. / **perishably** *ad.*

periwig ['periwig] *n.* 假发

periwinkle ['peri,winkl] *n.* ①【动】荔枝螺, 滨螺,
海螺 ②【植】长春花

perjure ['pə:dʒə] *vt.* [~ oneself] 使发假誓, 使作伪
证 ‖**~d** *a.* 发假誓的, 作伪证的 / **~r** ['pə:dʒərə]
n. 发假誓者, 作伪证者

perjury ['pə:dʒəri] *n.* 假誓, 伪证; 伪证罪

perk¹ [pə:k] ❶ *vi.* ① 昂首; 蓦气洋洋 ② 振作(病
活跃起来(尤指消沉或疾病之后) ❷ *vt.* ① 竖起
(耳朵等); 昂(首); 翘(尾) ② 打扮, 修饰

perk² [pə:k] *vt.* & *vi.* [口]过滤, 渗透

perk³ [pə:k] *n.* [常用复][俚]额外津贴, 赏钱, 小账

permanent ['pə:mənənt] **I** *a.* 永久的; 持久的: a
~ force【军】常备军 / a ~ committee 常设委员
会 / a ~ magnet 永久磁铁 **II** *n.* 电烫的头发
(= ~ wave) ‖**~ly** *ad.* / **~ness** *n.*

permeable ['pə:mjəbl] *a.* 可渗透的; 具渗透性的:
~ plastics 可透塑料 / ~ soil 渗透性土 ‖**~ness**
n. / **permeably** *ad.*

permeate ['pə:mieit] ❶ *vt.* 渗入, 透过; 弥漫, 充
满: Water will ~ blotting paper. 水能渗透吸
水纸。/ The banquet was ~d with an atmosphere
of friendship. 宴会洋溢着友谊的气氛。❷ *vi.*
渗透, 透入 (through, among) ‖**permeation**
[,pə:mi'eiʃən] *n.*

permissible [pə(:)'misəbl] *a.* 可允许的; 容许的,
许可的, 准许的: a ~ error 容许误差 / a ~
explosive 安全炸药, 合格炸药 / a ~ load 容许
荷载 ‖**permissibility** [pə(:),misə'biliti] *n.* /
~ness *n.* / **permissibly** *ad.*

permission [pə(:)'miʃən] *n.* 允许, 许可, 同意: You
have my ~ to leave. 我允许你离开。(或: 你可
以走了。) / ask for ~ 请求许可 / with sb.'s ~
在某人许可的情况下 / without ~ 未经许可

permit I [pə(:)'mit] (permitted; permitting) ❶ *vt.*
允许, 许可: Permit me to say a few words. 请
允许我说几句话。/ Smoking is not *permitted*
here. 此地不准吸烟。❷ *vi.* 容许: Such
hydropower stations have been set up in all
places where conditions ~ 在条件许可的地方
都建立了这样的水电站。/ We'll go, weather
permitting. 天气许可的话, 我们就去。/ This
task ~s of no delay. 这项任务不允许有任何耽
搁。**II** ['pə:mit] *n.* ① 许可 ② 执照, 许可证

pernicious [pə(:)'niʃəs] *a.* 有害的, 有毒的; 致命
的: a climate ~ to health 对健康有害的气候 /
~ habits 恶习 / ~ anemia【医】恶性贫血
‖**~ly** *ad.* / **~ness** *n.*

pernickety [pə'nikiti] *a.* [口] ① 爱挑剔的, 吹毛
求疵的 ② 难应付的, 需要十分小心对待的; 要求
极度精确的

peroxide [pə'rɔksaid] *n.*【化】过氧化物: hydrogen
~ 过氧化氢

perpendicular [,pə:pən'dikjulə] **I** *a.* ① 垂直的,
成直角的, 正交的 (to): The plumb line is always
~ to the horizontal plane. 铅垂线总是垂直于
水平面的。② 陡峭的, 垂直的: a ~ cliff 绝壁
③ [P-]【建】垂直式的(指十四到十六世纪英国哥
特式建筑的一种特点) ④[俚]站着的 **II** *n.* ① 垂
直: The wall is a little out of (the) ~. 墙壁有
些倾斜。② 垂直线; 垂直面 ③ 垂规, 铅垂线
④ [英俚]客人站着的进餐 ‖**~ity** [,pə:pən,dikju-
'læriti] *n.* ① 垂直; 直立 ②【机】垂直度 /
~ly *ad.*

perpetrate ['pə:pitreit] *vt.* 犯(罪); 作(恶), 做
(坏事) 胡说: ~ a crime 犯罪 / ~ a hoax on
(或 upon) sb. 叫某人上当 / ~ a joke 乱开玩笑
‖**perpetration** [,pə:pi'treiʃən] *n.* / **perpetrator**
n. 作恶者; 行凶者; 犯罪者

perpetual [pə'petjuəl, pə'petʃuəl] **I** *a.* ①永远的,
永恒的; (职位等)终身的 ② 四季开花的: a ~
rose 四季开花的蔷薇 ③ 不断的, 重复不停的:
She is tired of their ~ chatter. 她对他们没完
没了的唠叨感到厌烦。**II** *n.* 多年生植物; 四季
开花的蔷薇 ‖**~ly** *ad.* / **~ calendar** 万年历

perpetuate [pə(:)'petjueit, pə(:)'petʃueit] *vt.* 使
永久存在; 使不朽 ‖**perpetuation** [pə(:),petʃu-
'eiʃən, pə(:),petju'eiʃən], **perpetuance** [pə(:)'pe-
tjuəns, pə(:)'petʃuəns] *n.* / **perpetuator** *n.* 使
永存者, 使不朽者

perpetuity [,pə(:)pi'tju(:)iti] *n.* ① 永久, 永恒; 不
朽: in (或 to, for) ~ 永远地 ②终身年金 ③【律】
永久所有权; (产业的)永远(或长期)不得转让;
永远(或长期)不得转让的产业

perplex [pə'pleks] *vt.* ① 困惑; 难住: be ~ed for
an answer 不知怎么回答才好 ② 使复杂化, 使纠
缠不清: Don't ~ the problem. 不要使问题复
杂化。

perplexed [pə'plekst] *a.* ① 困惑的, 茫然不知所
措的: a ~ look 茫然不知所措的神色 ② 复杂的,
纠缠不清的: a ~ question 错综复杂的问题 ‖**~ly**
[pə'pleksidli] *ad.* / **~ness** [pə'pleksidnis] *n.*

perplexity [pə'pleksiti] *n.* ① 困惑; 窘困: stare in
~ 茫然不解地瞪着眼 ② 令人困惑的事物 ③ 纠
缠, 扭结

perquisite ['pə:kwizit] *n.* ① (工资以外的)额外所
得, 津贴 ② 赏钱, 小账, 酒钱 ③ 特权享有的东西

persecute ['pə:sikju:t] *vt.* ① (尤指因政治、宗教信
仰不同)迫害, 残害 ② 困扰, 为难 ‖**persecutor**
n. 迫害者, 虐待者

persecution [ˌpə:si'kju:ʃən] *n.* 迫害, 残害; 困扰: suffer (或 be subjected to) ~ 遭受迫害

perseverance [ˌpə:si'viərəns] *n.* 坚持, 坚忍不拔, 不屈不挠

persevere [ˌpə:si'viə] *vi.* 坚持, 不屈不挠 (*in, at, with*): ~ *with* an arduous task 坚持进行艰巨的工作 / ~ *to* an end 坚持到底

persist [pə(:)'sist] *vi.* ① 坚持; 固执 (*in*): ~ *in* taking the road of self-reliance and hard work 坚持自力更生、艰苦奋斗的道路 ②持续, 存留

persistence [pə(:)'sistəns], **persistency** [pə(:)'sistənsi] *n.* ① 坚持; 固执: with ~ 坚持地 / be annoyed by sb.'s ~ 被某人的固执所激怒 ②持续, 存留 【无】持久性; (荧光屏上余辉的)保留时间: the ~ of a fever 寒热不退 / the ~ of vision 视觉暂留

persistent [pə(:)'sistənt] *a.* ① 坚持的; 固执的: a ~ effort 坚持不懈的努力 ②持续的, 持久的, 不断的: ~ gas 【军】持久性毒气 / ~ attacks of malaria 疟疾的不断发作 ③【植】宿存的 ④【动】持续生存的 ‖~ly *ad.*

person ['pə:sn] *n.* ① 人: a courageous ~ 勇敢的人 / a young ~ 年轻人(常指女子) / a ~ of importance 重要人物 / a committee of nine ~s 由九人组成的委员会 / an artificial ~ 【律】法人 / a natural ~ 【律】自然人 ②[贬]家伙: Who is this ~? 这家伙是谁? / that stupid ~ 那个笨蛋 ③ 人, 身体: freedom of the ~ 人身自由 / an unlawful search of the ~ 非法的人身搜查 / have sth. on one's ~ 身上藏有某物 ④本人, 自身 ⑤容貌, 外表; 风度: He has a fine ~. 他风度很好。⑥【语】人称: the first (second, third) ~ 第一(二,三)人称 ⑦[古](戏剧、小说中的)人物, 角色 ⑧[宗](三位一体的)位 ‖*accept the ~ of* 偏爱…, 偏袒… / in ~ ① 亲自: He will come *in* ~ (或 *in* his own ~ 或 *in* his proper ~). 他将亲自来。/ You may ask him *in* ~. 你可以亲自问他。②身体上; 外貌上: He was tall and strong *in* ~. 他长得又高又健壮。/ *in the* ~ *of* ①以…的资格, 代表…: speak *in the* ~ *of Daily News* 代表《每日新闻》讲话 ②体现于…; 叫做…的人 / *no less a* ~ *than* 身分(或级别等)不低于 ‖'~*-to-*'~ *a.* ①(长途电话)在指名受话人受话后才索费的 ② 通过个人接触进行的 *ad.* ①个人对个人地 ②面对面地

persona [pə:'souə] ([复] personae [pə:'souni:]) *n.* [拉] ① *n.* ~ (non) grata ['greitə]受(不受)欢迎的人(一般指外交官) / *in propria* ~ 亲自 ②(小说、戏剧中的)人物, 角色: *dramatis personae* 【戏】剧中人 ③([复] personas)(在社交场合装出的)一种伪装外表

personable ['pə:sənəbl] *a.* 漂亮的, 美貌的; 风度好的 ‖~ness *n.*

personage ['pə:sənidʒ] *n.* ① 要人, 名流, 显贵 ②人, 个人: democratic ~s 民主人士 ③(历史、小说中的)人物, 角色

personal ['pə:sənl] **I** *a.* ① 个人的, 私人的/~ affairs 私事 / ~ history 履历 / a ~ letter 私人信件/a~opinion个人的意见 one's~acquaintance 个人的相识 ②本人的, 亲自的: a ~ interview 亲自会见 ③身体的; 容貌的: ~ appearance 容貌; 风度 / ~ hygiene 个人卫生 ④人身的, 涉及个人的; 攻击个人的: make ~ abuse 进行人身攻击 / become ~ 变成对个人的攻击(或议论) ⑤[语]人称的: a ~ pronoun 人称代词 ⑥【律】属于个人的; 可动的: ~ property 动产 **II** *n.* [美][常用复]报纸上有关个人的简讯 ‖~ly *ad.* ①亲自地: He conducted me ~ly through the mansion. 他亲自带我在大楼各处参观。②作为一个人 ③就自己而言: *Personally* I see no objection to your leaving at once. 就我个人而言, 我不反对你马上就走。‖~ **effects** 动产, 私有物 / ~ **equation** ①【天】人差 ②个人在观察上的误差 / ~ **foul** 【体】撞人犯规 / ~ **shopper** (百货商店等处)代客挑选货物的人

personality [ˌpə:sə'næliti] *n.* ①人的存在; 人 ②个性; 人格: a man with a strong ~ 个性强的人 / multiple ~ 【心】多重性格 ③人物(尤指有名的): *personalities* of the screen 电影界名人 ④[常用复]人身攻击; 人物评议: refrain from *personalities* 避免对别人进行人身攻击 ⑤ [罕] =personalty ‖~ **cult** 个人崇拜

personification [pə(:),sonifi'keiʃən] *n.* ① 拟人, 人格化;【语】拟人法 ②化身, 体现; 典型

personnel [ˌpə:sə'nel] *n.* ①[集合名词]全体人员, 全体职员: naval ~ 海军人员 / engineering and technical ~ 工程技术人员 / an anti-~ bomb 【军】杀伤炸弹 / a ~ mine 【军】防步兵地雷 ②人事(部门): the ~ department 人事处 / ~ administration 人事管理

perspective[1] [pə(:)'spektiv] **I** *n.* ①透视; 透视画法; 透视图: linear ~ 直线透视 ②正确观察事物相互关系的能力, 眼力: lack ~ 缺乏眼力 ③远景, 前景; 展望, 前途; 景象 ④ 观点, 看法 ⑤ 事物相互关系的外观, 整体各个部分的比例(或关系) **II** *a.* 透视的, 透视画的 ‖*in* ~ ①显现在脑海中的(地)展望中的(地) ②合乎透视画法的(地) ③(观察)真实的(地): see things *in* ~ 正确地观察事物 ‖~ly *ad.*

perspective[2] [pə(:)'spektiv] *n.* 透镜; 望远镜

perspicacious [ˌpə:spi'keiʃəs] *a.* ① 颖悟的, 敏锐的 ②[古]眼光锐利的 ‖~ly *ad.* / ~ness *n.*

perspicacity [ˌpə:spi'kæsiti] *n.* (判断、理解力的)颖悟, 敏锐

perspicuous [pə(:)'spikjuəs] *a.* (文章)意思明白的; (人)表达清楚的 ‖~ly *ad.* / ~ness *n.*

perspiration [ˌpə:spə'reiʃən] *n.* ①排汗 ②汗

perspire [pəs'paiə] ❶ *vi.* 排汗 ❷ *vt.* 排出(汗) ‖**perspirable** [pəs'paiərəbl] *a.* 汗液可通过的; 可随汗液排出的 / **perspiratory** [pəs'paiərətəri] *a.* 排汗的; 引起排汗的

persuade [pə(:)'sweid] ❶ *vt.* ①说服, 劝服: ~ sb.

to do (或 *into* do*ing*) sth. 说服某人做某事 / He ~*d* me *out of* the idea of dropping the experiment. 他劝得我打消了中断试验的想法。 / We ~*d* him to our way of thinking. 我们使他接受了我们的想法。②使(某人)相信: I ~*d* him *of* its truth (或 *that* it was true). 我使他相信这是真的。❷ *vi.* 被说服: He ~s easily. 他容易被说服。‖**persuadable** *a.* 可说服的；可使相信的 / ~**r** *n.* ①劝说者 ②[美]威慑物(如鞭、枪等)

persuasion [pə(ː)'sweiʒən] *n.* ①说服，劝服；劝说: the method of ~ and education 说服教育的方法 ②说服力 ③劝说的论点，劝说的话 ④ 主张，见解；信念；(宗教的)信仰: writers of different ~s 持不同见解的作家 ⑤(持某一见解的)派别，集团；教派 ⑥[口][谑]种，类；性别: the male ~ 男性

persuasive [pə(ː)'sweisiv] **I** *a.* 有说服力的；劝导性的；劝诱的: a ~ speaker 有说服力的演说家 / a ~ manner 劝诱的态度 **II** *n.* [罕]引诱物 ‖~**ly** *ad.* / ~**ness** *n.*

pert [pəːt] *a.* ①没有礼貌的，冒失的 ②活跃的；精神抖擞的 ③(服装等)整齐而时髦的，别致的 ④ (言语等)辛辣的，痛快的 ‖~**ly** *ad.* / ~**ness** *n.*

pertain [pə(ː)'tein] *vi.* ①从属，附属 (to) ②关于，有关 (to): His remark did not ~ to the question. 他的话同这问题不相干。③适合，相称 (to)

pertinacious [,pəːti'neiʃəs] *a.* ①坚持的；固执的，执拗的 ②难消除的；顽固的: a ~ illness 痼疾 ‖~**ly** *ad.* / **pertinacity** [,pəːti'næsiti] *n.* 执拗；顽固

pertinent ['pəːtinənt] *a.* ①恰当的，贴切的；中肯的: The students made some ~ comments on the teaching material. 学生对教材提了一些中肯的意见。②有关的，相干的 (to): data ~ to the design of a new machine 有关新机器设计的资料 ‖~**ly** *ad.*

perturb [pə(ː)'təːb] *vt.* ①使不安，烦扰 ②使紊乱，扰乱 ③【天】使摄动 ‖~**ance** *n.* / ~**ative** [pə(ː)'təːbətiv] *a.* 烦扰性的；扰乱性的

peruke [pə'ruːk] *n.* 长假发

peruse [pə'ruːz] *vt.* ①细阅，细读；阅读: ~ a newspaper 仔细读报 ②仔细察看 ‖**perusal** *n.* 细阅，细读；阅读: The article deserves careful *perusal*. 这篇文章值得细读。/ ~**r** *n.* 细读者；阅读者

pervade [pə(ː)'veid] *vt.* 弥漫，渗透；遍及，充满 ‖**pervasion** [pə(ː)'veiʒən] *n.*

pervasive [pə(ː)'veisiv] *a.* 弥漫的，渗透的；遍布的，充满的: ~ influences 普遍性的影响，深入的影响 ‖~**ly** *ad.* / ~**ness** *n.*

perverse [pə(ː)'vəːs] *a.* ①不正当的，堕落的；邪恶的 ②违反常情的，反常的: ~ behaviour 反常行为 ③坚持错误的，刚愎的；任性的 ④(情况等)违背意愿的 ⑤[律](判决等)不合法的 ‖~**ly** *ad.* / ~**ness** *n.*

pervert [pə(ː)'vəːt] **I** *vt.* ①使走入邪路，使堕落；

使变坏: ~ (the mind of) sb. 腐蚀某人(的思想) ②使违反常情，使反常 ③误用，滥用 ④歪曲，曲解: ~ the text 曲解原文 / ~ the truth 颠倒是非 **II** ['pəːvəːt] *n.* ①走入邪路者，堕落者 ②反常者；【心】性反常者 ‖~**ible** *a.* ① 可引入邪路的；易反常的 ②易被滥用的 ③易被歪曲的；易被曲解的

peseta [pə'setə] *n.* 比塞塔(西班牙货币单位)

pessimism ['pesimizəm] *n.* 悲观；悲观主义，厌世主义 ‖**pessimist** *n.* 悲观者，悲观主义者；厌世者

pessimistic [,pesi'mistik] *a.* 悲观的；悲观主义的，厌世的 ‖~**ally** *ad.*

pest [pest] *n.* ①有害动物，害虫；有害植物: eliminate the four ~s 消灭四害 / garden ~s 园中害虫 / ~ control 虫害控制 ②讨厌的人，害人虫；有害的东西 ③[罕]瘟疫，鼠疫 ‖*Pest on* (或 *upon*) *him!* (诅咒语)让他遭殃! ‖'~**hole** *n.* 瘟疫区 / '~**house** *n.* 隔离医院，传染病医院

pester ['pestə] *vt.* 烦扰，纠缠: be ~ed with flies 为苍蝇所扰 / ~ sb.. for sth. 缠住某人讨取某物

pestle ['pesl, 'pestl] **I** *n.* (捣研用的)杵，碾槌: a ~ and mortar 杵和臼 **II** *vt.* & *vi.* (用杵)捣，研碎

pet[1] [pet] **I** *n.* ①供玩赏的动物；爱畜 ②宠儿；宝贝儿 ③受 ~ of sb. 宠爱某人 **II** *a.* ①作为玩赏动物豢养的；宠爱的: a ~ bird (dog) 供玩赏的鸟(狗) ②表示亲昵的: a ~ name 昵称，小名 ③最得意的: one's ~ and darling work 得意之作 ④[谑]第一号的；特别的: a ~ aversion 第一号的讨厌东西；痛恶的事物 / a ~ peeve 特别令人气恼的事情 **III** (petted; petting) ❶ *vt.* ①把…当作宠儿 ②抚弄，爱抚 ③钟爱，宠爱 ❷ *vi.* 拥抱；接吻；爱抚 ‖~ **cock** 【机】小型旋塞，龙头

pet[2] [pet] **I** *n.* 生气，愠怒，不开心: be in a ~ 不开心 / take the ~ 生气 **II** (petted; petting) *vi.* 生气，不开心

petal ['petl] *n.* 花瓣

peter ['piːtə] *vi.* 逐渐枯竭；渐趋消失 (out): The storm ~ed out. 暴风雨渐息。

petition [pi'tiʃən] **I** *n.* ①请愿，申请，请求，祈求: the right of ~ 请愿权 ②请愿书；【律】(向法院递交的)请求书: present a ~ to sb. 向某人递交请愿书 / a ~ in bankruptcy 申请宣布破产的请求书 **II** ❶ *vt.* 向…请愿，请求，祈求: ~ sb. for sth. 为某事向某人请愿 / ~ sb. to do sth. 祈求某人做某事 ❷ *vi.* 请愿，祈求: ~ for sth. 请求得到某物 / ~ to be allowed to do sth. 请求准许做某事 ‖~**ary** *a.* 请愿的，请求的 / ~**er** *n.* 请愿人，请求者；离婚诉讼的原告

petrel ['petrəl] *n.* ①鹱科海鸟；海燕科海鸟 ②海燕

petrify ['petrifai] ❶ *vt.* ①【地】使石化: *petrified* wood 石化木，木化石，硅化木 ②使僵化，使麻

失活力 ③使(因恐惧、惊慌等而)发呆: stand *petrified* with terror 吓得呆呆地站着 ❷ *vi.* ①【地】石化 ②变僵硬

petrol ['petrəl] *n.* ①[英]汽油(美国称 gasoline): a ~ station 汽油加油站 ②[古]石油

petroleum [pi'trouljəm] *n.* 石油: crude (或 raw) ~ 原油 / the ~ industry 石油工业 ‖~ **ether** 石油醚(石油的低沸部分) ②~ **jelly** 凡士林

petticoat ['petikout] **I** *n.* ①衬裙; (旧时妇女或幼儿穿的)裙子 ②[口]女人, 少女; [复]女性 ③裙状物 **II** *a.* 女性的; 女人主持的: ~ government (家庭里或政治上的)女人当权 ‖*in* ~*s* ①穿着裙子的; 女性的: She is her father again *in* ~*s*. 她象是她父亲的化身, 只是性别不同。②幼年时: I have known him since he was *in* ~*s*. 我从他小时候起就认识他了。‖~**ed** *a.* 穿裙子的; 有裙状物的 / ~**less** *a.* 未穿(衬)裙的; 无裙状物的

pettifogging ['petifɔgiŋ] *a.* ①讼棍般的; 诡计多端的 ②为小事而烦恼的; 过分注重细节的

petty ['peti] *a.* ①小的, 微小的; 小规模的; 次要的: ~ commodities 小商品 / a ~ proprietor (shopkeeper) 小业(店)主 / a ~ quarrel (offence) 小争吵(过失) ②琐小的, 不足道的; 器量小的; 偏狭的; 派头小的; 卑劣的: a ~ and mean action 卑鄙的小动作 ③地位低微的, 下级的: a ~ official 小官吏 / ~ **cash** 小额现金收入(或支出) ②零用现金 / ~ **jury** 小陪审团(由十二人组成, 判决前审理、评定事实) / ~ **larceny** 【律】轻窃盗罪 / ~ **officer** 海军军士: a chief ~ *officer* (英)海军上士; (美)海军军士长 / a *Petty Officer* First Class (英)海军中士; (美)海军上士 / a *Petty Officer* Second Class (英)海军下士; (美)海军中士 / a *Petty Officer* Third Class (美)海军下士

petulant ['petjulənt] *a.* ①易怒的; 使性子的; 脾气坏的 ②[古]无礼的 ‖~**ly** *ad.*

pew [pju:] **I** *n.* ①教堂内的靠背长凳 ②坐在教堂座位上的人们, 会众 ③[口]座位 **II** *vt.* ①为(教堂)装备座位 ②使在教堂座位中就座 ‖~ **chair** 教堂靠背长凳旁的添座

pew

pewter ['pju:tə] **I** *n.* ①【冶】白镴(锡基合金) ②锡镴器皿 ③[英俚]奖杯; 奖金 **II** *a.* 白镴制的

phalanx ['fælæŋks] ([复] phalanxes 或 phalanges [fæ'lændʒi:z]) *n.* ①(古希腊的)方阵 ②密集队

为共同目标而集结的一批人 ③([复] phalanges)【解】指骨; 趾骨 ④【植】雄蕊束 ⑤(傅立叶空想社会主义中的)法郎吉(即法伦斯泰尔)

phantasm ['fæntæzəm] *n.* ①幻觉, 幻影; 幻想; 幽灵 ②幻象, 假象: a ~ of hope 虚假的希望 ③事物呈现在脑中的形象

phantom ['fæntəm] **I** *n.* ①幽灵, 鬼怪; 阴影, 令人恐惧的东西 ②[P-]鬼怪式飞机 ③幻象 ④影子, 有名无实的人(或物); [美俚]在工资单上挂虚名的人: a ~ of a king 有名无实的君王 ⑤(脑海中的)印象: the ~s of things past 往事的影子 ⑥(抽象品性等的)化身: a ~ of delight 快乐的化身 ⑦人体模型; (机器等内部部分结构的)剖视图 **II** *a.* ①幽灵(似)的, 鬼怪(似)的 ②幻象的; 幻觉的: a ~ target 幻象目标, 假目标 / a ~ circuit 幻象电路 / a ~ tumour (常在歇斯底里病人腹部等处长出的)虚瘤, 假瘤 / a ~ limb 被截肢者感到被截肢体依然存在的幻觉, 幻肢(感) ③无形的 ④虚拟的, 傀儡性的: a ~ regime 傀儡政权 ⑤部分剖视的 ‖~**like** *ad.* & *a.* 象鬼影一样地(的)

Pharaoh ['fɛərou] *n.* ①法老(古埃及君王称号) ②暴君 ‖**Pharaonic** [,fɛərei'ɔnik] *a.* 法老(似)的 ‖~**'s chicken**, ~**'s hen** 【动】王鸡(产于埃及等地的一种兀鹰) / ~**'s mouse**, ~**'s rat** 【动】埃及鼷 / ~**'s serpent** 法老蛇(一点火就现成蛇形的化学玩物)

pharmacy ['fɑ:məsi] *n.* ①药学 ②制药; 配药 ③药房, 药店 ④(一批)备着的药品: a family ~ 家庭备用药品

phase [feiz] **I** *n.* ①阶段; 状态: a combat ~ 【军】战斗阶段 / the launch ~ (火箭等的)起飞阶段, 加速时间 ②方面, 侧面: This is but one ~ of the problem. 这只不过是问题的一个方面。③【天】【物】相, 周相; 相位: ~s of the moon 月相(指"新月"、"上弦"、"满月"、"下弦"等) / gaseous (liquid, solid) ~ 气(液, 固)相 ④【动】型; 期: theory 变型学说 **II** *vt.* ①使调整相位, 使定相: ~ the recorder to the incoming signal 调整记录器使与输入讯号相同 ②使分阶段进行; 使按计划进行: a ~d withdrawal 分阶段的逐步撤出 ③逐步采用 ‖*in* ~ 【物】①同相的 ②同时协调的(地) / *out of* ~ 【物】①异相的(地) ②非同时协调的(地): The windshield wipers were *out of* ~. 挡风玻璃上的刮水器动作不协调。 / ~ *in* 分阶段引入, 逐步采用: ~ *in* new machinery for increased automation 逐步采用新机器以提高自动化程度 / ~ *out* ①使逐步结束; 使逐步淘汰; 逐步撤出: ~ *out* a war 逐步结束一场战争 / ~ *out* troops 分阶段逐步撤军 ②逐步停止生产(或活动等): That company has ~*d out* of the truck manufacturing business. 那家公司已逐步停止了卡车生产。③逐步转入(*into*) ‖**phasic** *a.* 相的, 阶段的 / ~**-'contrast** *a.* 相衬显微镜的 / ~ **microscope** 【物】相衬显微镜 / ~ **modulation** 【无】调相, 相位调制 / '~**out** *n.*

(生产、军事行动等的)逐步停止;逐步撤出

pheasant ['feznt] ([复] pheasant(s)) *n.* 雉, 野鸡 ‖**~ry** *n.* 养雉场 ‖**'~'s-eye** *n.* 【植】红口水仙

phenomenal [fi'nɔminl] *a.* ①现象的;关于现象的;从感官认识到的 ②非凡的,出众的 ‖**~ly** *ad.*

phenomenon [fi'nɔminən] ([复] phenomena [fi'nɔminə]) *n.* ①现象: the *phenomena* of nature 自然界的各种现象 / a transient ~ 暂时现象 ②稀有现象,奇迹: a publishing ~ 出版方面的一个奇迹 ③非凡的人,杰出人材: quite a ~ at tennis 网球运动中的健将

phial ['faiəl] *n.* 管形瓶;小药瓶

philander [fi'lændə] *vi.* ① 追求女性;调戏妇女 ②玩弄 (*with*) ‖**~er** [fi'lændərə] *n.* 追求女性者;(在爱情方面)不专一的男子

philanthropist [fi'lænθrəpist] *n.* 慈善家

philanthropy [fi'lænθrəpi] *n.* ①慈善,善心;博爱主义 ②善行;慈善性赠与物;慈善事业

philately [fi'lætəli] *n.* 集邮 ‖**philatelist** *n.* 集邮家

philology [fi'lɔlədʒi] *n.* ①语文学 ②语文文献学 ③历史比较语言学;语言学 ‖**philologist** *n.* 语文学家;语言学家

philosopher [fi'lɔsəfə] *n.* ①哲学家 ②思想家,学者 ③能泰然自若地对待危难的人;达观者,逆来顺受者 ④阐明(…方面的)哲理的人 (*of*) ⑤爱卖弄大道理的人 ⑥[古]炼金术士 ‖**~'s stone** 点金石 (炼金术士所寻求的能使其他金属变成金银的一种实际上不存在的东西)

philosophic(al) [ˌfilə'sɔfik(əb)] *a.* ①哲学家的;哲学(上)的: ~ works 哲学著作 / ~ thinking 哲学思想 ②有哲人态度的;镇静的;达观的,逆来顺受的 ③富于哲理性的 ‖**philosophically** *ad.*

philosophy [fi'lɔsəfi] *n.* ① 哲学;哲学体系: the Marxist ~ of dialectical materialism 马克思主义的辩证唯物论哲学 / establish a new ~ 建立一个新的哲学体系 ②哲理: There is much ~ in it. 这其中大有哲理。③人生观;宗旨: relentlessly criticize the "~ of survival" 狠批"活命哲学" / a sound ~ of life 健康的人生观 / the ~ of an institution 一个机构的宗旨 ④(某一门学科的)基本原理: the ~ of history 历史哲学 ⑤(除医学、法律、神学外的)所有学科;[古]自然科学: a doctor of ~ in architecture 建筑学方面的哲学博士 ⑥伦理学 ⑦哲人态度;达观;镇静: use ~ 采取哲人态度(可指临危不惧或逆来顺受等) ⑧对知识的热爱(或探究)

philtre, philter ['filtə] I *n.* ①春药 ②有魔力的药 II *vt.* 用春药迷惑;使兴奋,刺激

phlegm [flem] *n.* ①痰 ②粘液(古生理学所称四种体液之一,能使人迟钝) ③迟钝;冷淡;不动感情 ‖**~y** *a.* 痰的;似痰的;含痰的

phobia ['foubjə] *n.* (病态的)恐惧;憎恶

phoenix ['fi:niks] *n.* ① (埃及神话中阿拉伯沙漠的)不死鸟,长生鸟(相传此鸟每五百年自行焚死,

然后由灰中再生): rise ~-like (或 like a ~) from the ashes 象长生鸟一般从灰烬中再生;不可抑制 ②(中国古代传说中的)凤凰 ③毁灭后会再生的事物 ④尽善尽美的模范(或典型);十分优秀的人(或物),完人,殊品 ⑤ [the P-]【天】凤凰座 ⑥【植】海枣;[P-] 海枣属 ‖**~ tree** 梧桐

phone¹ [foun] I *n.* ①[口]电话;电话机(=telephone): A ~ for you. 你有电话。/ You are wanted on the ~. 有人叫你听电话。(或: 你有电话。) / make a ~ call 打个电话 / a ~ booth 电话间,电话亭 ②受话器,耳机: hang up the ~ 挂断电话 II [口] ❶ *vt.* ①给…打电话: *Phone* the doctor at once. 马上打电话给医生。②打电话通知(一件事): ~ a message to sb. 打电话告诉某人一件事 ❷ *vi.* 打电话 (to) ‖**~ meter** 【讯】通话计数器

phone² [foun] *n.* 【语】单音

phonetic [fou'netik] *a.* ①语音的;语音学的: ~ exercises (或 drills) 语音练习 ②表示语音的;形音一致的: the international ~ alphabet (或 symbols) 国际音标 / ~ transcription 标音(法) / Russian spelling is ~. 俄语的拼法是表音的。 ‖**~ally** *ad.* 根据语音;在语音上: words spelt ~*ally* 根据语音拼写的词 / ~*ally* similar 语音上相似的

phonetician [ˌfouni'tiʃən] *n.* 语音学家

phonograph ['founəgrɑ:f] *n.* [美]留声机,唱机 (=[英] gramophone): an electric ~ 电唱机 / a ~ pickup 唱机拾音器 / a ~ record 唱片

phosphate ['fɔsfeit] *n.* 【化】磷酸盐;磷酸酯: ~ fertilizer 磷肥 / ~ rock 磷酸盐岩

phosphorescence [ˌfɔsfə'resns] *n.* 磷光(现象)

phosphorescent [ˌfɔsfə'resnt] *a.* 发磷光的: a ~ substance 磷光体

phosphorus ['fɔsfərəs] *n.* ①【化】磷 ②磷光体

photograph ['foutəgrɑ:f] I *n.* ①照片: have one's ~ taken (或 pose for one's ~) 请人给自己拍照 / have a ~ taken with … 和…合影 ②逼真的描绘(或印象) II ❶ *vt.* ①为…拍照: have (或 get) oneself ~ed 请人给自己拍照 ②逼真地描绘;把…记入脑中 ❷ *vi.* ①拍照 ②被照相: I always ~ badly. 我照相老是照不好。(指不上照) ‖**~er** [fə'tɔgrəfə] *n.* 摄影师;摄影者

photography [fə'tɔgrəfi] *n.* 摄影术: colour ~ 彩色摄影术 / frame ~ 分幅摄影术 / smear ~ 扫描(快速)摄影术

phrase [freiz] I *n.* ①【语】短语,片语,词组: an adjective ~ 形容词短语 / an adverb(ial) ~ 副词短语 / a noun ~ 名词短语 / a prepositional ~ 前置词短语 / a set ~ 固定词组 ②习惯用语 ③措词,用语: be expressed in simple ~ 用简单的话表达 / felicity of ~ 措词之巧妙 ④警句 ⑤【音】短句 ⑥[复]空话,废话: mere ~ 空洞词句 II *vt.* ①用话表示;措辞描述(或限定): a neatly ~d report 措词简洁的报告 / Thus he ~d it. 他是这样措词的。②(苏格兰)谄媚,奉承

③【音】把…分成短句 ‖**phrasal** *a.* 短语的,片语的: a *phrasal* verb 短语动词,动词词组 ‖**~ book** 短语集,熟语集 / '**~,monger** *n.* 爱用漂亮句子的人 / '**~-,mongering** *n.* 空谈, 讲漂亮话

phraseology [,freizi'olədʒi] *n.* ①措词,用语;表达方式 ②术语 ③熟语集

phyllade ['fileid] *n.*【植】鳞状叶

physic ['fizik] **I** *n.* ①[口]药品;泻药: a dose of ~ 一服药 ②[罕]物理学 ③[古]医术; 医学; 医业 **II** (physicked; physicking) *vt.* ①给…服药; 给…服泻药 ②治愈

physical ['fizikəl] **I** *a.* ①物质的,有形的;确确实实的: the ~ world 物质世界 / the ~ depreciation of machinery 机器的有形损耗 / This ~ evidence completely shattered that story. 这一确凿的证据完全粉碎了那一说法。②自然(界)的;自然科学的;按自然法则的: ~ geography 地文学,自然地理学 / man's ~ environment 人类的自然环境 / a ~ impossibility 违反自然法则的不可能的事 ③物理的: (a) ~ change 物理变化 / ~ chemistry 物理化学 / ~ therapy 物理疗法,理疗 ④身体的,肉体的: ~ constitution 体格 / ~ education (或 culture) 体育 / ~ training 体育锻炼 / ~ exercise 体育活动 / ~ jerks [英俚]体操;体育活动 / ~ punishment 肉刑(包括监禁、鞭打、处死等);体罚 ⑤一味追求肉欲的 (=~ examination): the Navy induction ~ 海军入伍体格检查 ‖**~ity** [,fizi'kæliti] *n.* 肉体性 / **~ly** *ad.* ‖**~ science** 自然科学(指物理、化学、天文、地理等)

physician [fi'ziʃən] *n.* ①医生;内科医生: a chief ~ 主任医生 / a house (或 resident) ~ 内科住院医生 ②(解除精神痛苦等的)医治者,抚慰者

physicist ['fizisist] *n.* ①物理学家 ②[古]自然科学家

physics ['fiziks] [复] *n.* [用作单或复] ①物理学: applied ~ 应用物理学 / nuclear ~ 核物理学 ②物理过程; 物理现象; 物理成分: the ~ of the living cell 活细胞的物理现象 / the ~ of different soils 不同土壤的物理成分

physiognomy [,fizi'onəmi] *n.* ①相法,观相术 ②相貌,容貌 ③[俗]脸,面孔 ③(土地等)的外形,外观;特征: the ~ of a mountain 山的形势 / the social and economic ~ of a country 一个国家的社会经济面貌 ‖**physiognomist** *n.* 观相家,相士

physiology [,fizi'olədʒi] *n.* 生理学: plant ~ 植物生理学 / animal ~ 动物生理学 ‖**physiologist** *n.* 生理学家

physique [fi'zi:k] *n.* 体格: a man of strong (slender) ~ 体格健壮(瘦小)的人 / build up a powerful ~ 锻炼出强健的体格

pianist ['pjænist] *n.* 钢琴家; 钢琴演奏者

piano ['pjænou, pi'ænou] *n.* 钢琴: a cottage ~ 小型竖式钢琴 / a grand ~ 大钢琴 / an upright ~ 竖式钢琴 / At the ~ will be . . . . 将由…担任钢琴伴奏。 / play (on) the ~ 弹钢琴 ‖**~ accordion** 键盘式手风琴 / **~ organ** 回转式自鸣钢琴 / **~ player** ①钢琴演奏者 ②钢琴自动弹奏机

piano ['pja:nou] [意]【音】**I** *a.* & *ad.* 微弱的(地); 轻轻的(地) **II** *n.* 轻奏乐段

piccolo ['pikəlou] [意] **I** *n.* 短笛 **II** *a.* (乐器)小型的

pick¹ [pik] *n.* ①鹤嘴锄, 镐 ②用来挖掘的尖状物; 牙签 ③(弹弦乐器用的金属或角质)拨子 ④撬锁工具; 撬锁贼 (=~lock) ‖**~ax(e)** *n.* 鹤嘴锄, 镐 *vt.* & *vi.* 用鹤嘴锄掘

pick² [pik] **I** ❶ *vt.* ①(用鹤嘴锄等)凿, 掘, 挖; 凿成(洞 等): ~ the hard clay 掘硬土 ②(用手指等)挖(鼻子、耳朵等); 剔(骨头、牙齿等); 剔去: ~ meat from bones 剔去骨头上的肉 ③摘, 采(花朵、果实等); 拔(禽类)的羽毛: ~ cotton (apples) 摘棉花(苹果) / ~ spring tea 采春茶 / ~ a fowl 拔禽毛 ④(鸟类)啄(食); (人)少量地(或挑精拣肥地)吃 ⑤撕开, 扯开(纤维等): ~ oakum (rags) 撕开麻絮(破布) ⑥挑选, 选择: ~ the best seeds 挑选最好的种子 / ~ one's words 精选用词 ⑦找(碴儿); 寻找机会吵(架): ~ flaws 找碴儿 / ~ a quarrel with sb. 寻机会和某人吵架 ⑧拨(琴弦), 弹(弦乐器等): ~ a guitar 弹六弦琴 ⑨撬(锁); 扒窃(别人衣袋)中的东西: ~ a lock with a wire 用铁丝撬锁 ❷ *vi.* ①(用鹤嘴锄等)凿, 掘, 挖 ②(被)采摘: Ripe apples ~ easily. 熟了的苹果容易摘下来。 / the ~ing season (果实等的)采摘收获季节 ③啄食; 少量地(或挑精拣肥地)吃: The chickens ~ed about the yard. 小鸡在院子里到处啄食。④挑选 ⑤偷窃, 扒窃 **II** *n.* ①凿, 掘 ②选择; 选出物; 一次采摘的作物 ③ [the ~] (人或物的)精华; 最好的部分 ‖**have a bone to ~ with sb.** 见 **bone** / **~ a hole** (或 **holes**) **in** 见 **hole** / **~ and choose** 挑挑拣拣;挑剔 / **~ and steal** 扒窃,小偷小摸 / **~ apart** (或 **to pieces**) ①把…撕成碎片 ②把…攻击得一钱不值 / **~ at** ①用指尖拉 ②少量(或挑精拣肥)地吃: ~ at one's dinner 挑精拣肥地进食 ③老是挑剔(某人) / **~ off** ①摘下,摘掉 ②逐个地(或有选择地)瞄准射中 / **~ on** ①老是挑剔(某人);(偏偏)挑中(某人)(进行责骂、批评或叫他干不愉快的事等);作弄(某人);惹恼(某人) ②挑中,选中(也作 ~ upon) / **~ one's way** 见 **way** / **~ out** ①选出;拣出: ~ out the best table-tennis players 选出最好的乒乓球运动员 ②区别出,辨别出;看出;嗅出: ~ out an old friend in a crowd 在人群中认出一位老朋友 / ~ out a scent 闻出味道 ③领会: ~ out the meaning of a poem (passage) 领会一首诗(一段文章)的含义 ④(用另一种颜色)衬托(底色) ⑤(弹钢琴等时)凭听觉(或一个音一个音地)弹奏(曲调) / **~ over** 在…里挑;分档挑选: ~ over a basket of oranges 在一篓橘子中进行挑选(如把坏的拣掉) / **~ sb.'s**

brains 见 **brain** / ～ *up* ① (用鹤嘴锄等) 掘 (地) ② (跌倒后) 使 (自己) 爬起: He slipped and fell, but quickly ～ed himself *up*. 他失足滑倒, 但马上就站了起来。③ 拾起, 捡起: ～ *up* sb.'s hat 拾起某人的帽子 ④ (偶然地、无意地) 获得 (收益、生计、知识、消息等); 学会 (语言): ～ *up* a foreign language (未经听课等) 学会一种外语 / ～ *up* some knowledge of physics 偶然获得一些物理知识 ⑤ (未经正式介绍) 随便地结识 (常指异性): ～ *up* an acquaintance *with* sb. 结识某人 ⑥ (依靠探照灯、雷达等) 测知, 看到; (在无线电里) 收听到 ⑦ (车辆等) 中途搭 (人), 中途带 (货): The train stopped to ～ *up* passengers. 火车停下来搭乘客。⑧ 重新找到 (路); 重提 (话题) ⑨ 使恢复精神; 振作起 (精神), 恢复 (健康等): A bite of something might ～ you *up*. 吃一点东西也许能使你振起精神。 / ～ *up* flesh 恢复体重 / ～ *up* one's courage 鼓起勇气 ⑩恢复健康, 恢复活力, 振起精神: He is beginning to ～ *up*. 他的健康正在渐渐恢复。⑪ 加快 (速度): The train ～*ed up* speed. 火车加快速度。⑫ 加速: Let's see how fast you can ～ *up* from a standing start. 看看你站着起跑后能加速多快。⑬ 收拾; 整理: ～ *up* tools 收拾工具 / ～ *up* a room 整理房间 ⑭逮住, 捉牢 (罪犯等) / ～ *up on* [美俚] 与…熟悉起来 / *the ～ of the basket* (或 *bunch*) 一批中最好的, 精华

pick[2] [pik] 【纺】I *vt.* 投 (梭) II *n.* 纬纱; 投梭

picket ['pikit] I *n.* ①桩, 尖桩; 站桩刑 (古时使罪犯以一只脚站在桩上的刑罚); 站桩刑用的桩 ② [军] 前哨; 警戒哨 (或队、船、飞机): an aerial ～ 空中巡逻飞机 / a ～ ship 雷达哨舰, 雷达警戒飞机 ③ [复] (罢工时工会派出的) 一队纠察员 II *vt.* ①用尖桩围住; 用围篱 (或栅栏) 护围 ②把 (马等) 拴在桩上 ③派…担任警戒哨; 用警戒哨保卫 ④在 (工厂等) 设置 (或担任) 纠察; 用纠察包围 ❷ *vi.* 担任纠察 (或警戒哨) ‖～**er** *n.* 纠察员 ‖～**boat** *n.* 雷达哨艇 / ～ **line** ① 哨兵线, 前哨线; 纠察线: a locked arms ～ *line* 由纠察队员手挽手组成的纠察线 ② 拴马 (或骡) 索 / ～ **pin** 拴马桩

pickle ['pikl] I *n.* ① (腌鱼、蔬菜等的) 盐水, 泡菜水; 醋 ②腌制食品; 腌菜, 泡菜 ③ (清洁金属表面的) 稀酸浴, 酸洗液 ④ (皮革的) 泡腌 ⑤逆境, 困境: be in a sad (或 sorry, nice) ～ 处境困难 ⑥ [军] 空投鱼雷 ⑦ [口] 顽皮孩子 II *vt.* ① (以盐水或醋) 腌制, 腌渍 ②酸洗 ‖*have a rod in ～ for* sb. 见 **rod** / ～ *barrel bombing* 【军】极精确的轰炸, 对极小目标的轰炸 ‖～**d** *a.* ①盐渍的, 醋泡的 ② [俚] 醉的, 酩酊的

pick-me-up ['pikmi(:)ʌp] *n.* [口] 浓烈的兴奋饮料; [喻] 兴奋剂

pickpocket ['pik,pɔkit] *n.* 扒手

pickup ['pikʌp] I *n.* ①拾起 ②加速; (汽车等的) 突然加速能力 ③小吨位运货汽车 ④偶然结识; 偶然结识的人 ⑤ (商业等的) 好转 ⑥ [口] 兴奋剂,

刺激品; 刺激 ⑦ 拾波, 拾音; 唱头, 拾音器, 拾波器; 电视摄象; 电视摄象管 ⑧实况转播地点; 连接实况转播的电路系统 II *a.* [口] 临时拼凑的: a ～ jazz band 临时拼凑成的爵士乐队

picnic ['piknik] I *n.* ① (自带食物的) 郊游, 野餐; 各人自备食品的聚餐: go out on a ～ 去野餐 ② [口] 愉快的经历, 轻松的工作: It is no ～. 这可不是轻松的事情。II (picnicked; picnicking) *vi.* (去) 野餐, 参加野餐

pictorial [pik'tɔ:riəl] I *a.* ①绘画的 ②图片的; 由图片组成的; 用图片表示的: a ～ record 用图片的记实 / a ～ biweekly 双周画刊 ③图画似的; 形象化的 II *n.* 画报 ‖～**ly** *ad.*

picture ['piktʃə] I *n.* ①画; 画像; 图片; 照片: have one's ～ taken (请人给自己) 照相 ②美景, 美的事物 (或人): The park is a ～ itself. 这公园美景如画。③ (用语言文字的) 生动的描写, 写照: The article gives an excellent ～ of the student activities. 这篇文章对学生活动作了出色的描写。/ put sb. in the ～ [口] 把情况告诉某人 (使有身历其境之感, 或使能掌握形势) ④相似的形象, 化身; 体现: She is the ～ of her mother. 她跟她母亲长得一模一样。/ The child looks the ～ of health. 这孩子非常健康。⑤心象; 情景; 局面, 状况: in one's mind ～s 在某人的想象之中 / paint a black (rosy) ～ …说得漆黑一团 (光明乐观) ⑥影片; [the ～s] 电影 / [口] 图象: adjust the TV set for a brighter ～ 调节电视机使图象更清晰 II *vt.* ① 画; 用图表示 (抽象的东西) ② (生动地) 描写, 描述 ③ 想象: Picture to yourself the brilliant future ahead of us. 想象一下我们光明灿烂的前途。④ 把…摄成电影 ‖*be high up in the ～s* (或 *be in the ～*) [美俚] 取得成功, 成为要人 / *come into the ～* 引起人们注意; 被牵涉到, 牵连进去: I don't think you *come into the ～* at all. 我认为这根本没你的份儿。(或: 我认为这根本与你无关。) / *out of the ～* 不相干的; 在本题以外的: In discussing the question, we shouldn't keep this point *out of the ～*. 讨论这个问题时, 我们不该把这一点看作不相干的事。‖～ **book** 图画书 / ～ **card** ① (纸牌中的) 花牌 ②美术明信片 / '～**drome** *n.* [英] 电影院 / ～ **element** 【无】象素, 象点 / ～ **frame** ①画框 ② [美俚] 绞索 / ～ **gallery** ①绘画展览室; 画廊 (或收藏的) 一批画 / ～**,goer** *n.* [英] 常看电影的人 / ～ **hat** 妇女的阔边花式帽 / ～ **house** [英] 电影院 / ～ **palace** [英] 电影院 / ～ **phone** 电视电话 / ～ **postcard** 美术明信片 / ～ **puzzle** 画谜, 拼图游戏 / ～ **show** ①画展 ②电影; 电影院 / ～ **theatre** [英] 电影院 / ～ **tube** 【无】显象管 / ～ **writing** 用图画记载 (或通讯) 的方法; 象形文字

picturesque [,piktʃə'resk] *a.* ① (景色等) 似画的: a ～ village 景色如画的村庄 ②别致的: a ～ style of architecture 别致的建筑风格 ③ (语言等) 生动的, 形象化的: a ～ account 十分生动、形象的叙述 ‖～**ly** *ad.* / ～**ness** *n.*

pidgin ['pidʒin] *n.* ① (不同语种的人们在商业交往中发展起来的)混杂语言, 混杂行话 ②洋泾浜英语, 不纯粹的英语(尤指在旧中国港口等地所用的混杂英语)(巴布亚、新几内亚等地的)皮钦语 (=~ English) ③事务, 工作: That's not my ~. 那不是我的事。

pie¹ [pai] *n.* ①(西点)馅饼, 攀; 馅饼状物: an apple ~ 苹果攀 / a mud ~ (小孩玩耍做成的)泥饼 ②[俚]轻而易举的事情; 容易击败的软弱对手: That's ~ for him. 那件事对他来说真是易如反掌。 ‖**a resurrection ~** [俚]用剩肉做的馅饼 / **as easy as ~** [俚] 极容易 / **eat humble ~** 忍辱含垢 / **have a finger in the ~** 见 **finger** / **~ in the sky** 天堂, 死后的乐园; 渺茫的幸福; 空头支票 / **put one's finger in another's ~** 见 **finger** ‖**'~ card** [美俚]工会会员证 / '**~counter** *n.* [美俚] 政治上的恩赐(或分脏) / '**~crust** *n.* ①做馅饼的糊 ②馅饼皮 / **~man** ['paimən] *n.* 做(或卖)馅饼的人 / '**~plant** *n.* [主方]食用大黄(常用作点心馅) / **~wag(g)on** *n.* 流动小吃车 ②押送囚犯的警车

pie² [pai] I *n.* ①[印]混杂活字 ②杂乱 II *vt.* 使混杂; 弄乱(铅字或排版)

pie³ [pai] *n.* ①[动]喜鹊 ②[古]爱说话的人

pie⁴ [pai] *n.* 派(印度和巴基斯坦旧辅币名)

piebald ['paibɔːld] I *a.* ①(马)黑白斑的, 花斑的 ②斑驳的 II *n.* 有花斑的动物; 花马

piece [piːs] I *n.* ①碎片, 断片, 切片; 部分, 部件: fall to ~s 跌碎 / cut sth. into ~s 把某物切成碎片 / There's a ~ missing. 少了一个部件。 / He took the clock to ~s. 他把钟全拆开了。 ②块, 片, 段: a ~ of bread 一块面包 / a ~ of paper 一张纸 / a ~ of wood 一块木材 / a ~ of furniture 一件家具 / a ~ of water 一片池塘 / a ~ of land 一块地 ③项, 番: a ~ of news 一则新闻 / a ~ of advice 一个忠告 / a ~ of kindness 一番好意 ④(按固定规格生产或发售的)件; 匹; 桶: a ~ of wallpaper 一卷糊墙纸 (通常为十二码) / a ~ of muslin 一匹平纹细布 ⑤(文艺作品的)篇, 出, 首, 幅; 文艺作品: a ~ of poetry 一首诗 / a dramatic ~ 一出戏 / a snow ~ 一幅雪景画 / a fine ~ of sculpture 一件完美的雕塑品 / They played three Korean ~s in a row. 他们一连演奏了三支朝鲜乐曲。 ⑥(按件计算的)工作量 ⑦(成套中的)件, 个: a tea service of twenty-four ~s 一套二十四件的茶具 ⑧[常用以构成复合词]轻武器; 枪炮: a field~ 野战炮 / a ~ of artillery 一门炮 ⑨钱币; 标志物; 筹码: a five-fen ~ 一枚五分的硬币 / a ~ of silver 一块银元 ⑩棋子; (国际象棋)卒以上的棋子 ⑪[用以构成复合词] (乐器的)演奏者: an eighty-~ symphony orchestra 八十人的交响乐队 II ❶ *vt.* ①修理; 修补 (up); 添补 ②拼合 (together); 拼凑; 串成 (out): a quilt (用布头)拼缝被子 / together odds and ends of cloth 把零头碎布拼拢 / ~ one thing to another 把一件东西拼凑到另一件东西上 / ~ out a chain of evidence 把一连串的证据连贯起来 ❷ *vi.* ①[纺]接头 ②[口]不在正餐时吃, 零吃: ~ on sth. 不在正餐时吃某物 ‖**all to ~s** ①[美]完全地, 彻底地 ②(破得)粉碎地 ③失去控制地 / **a nasty ~ of work** ①[口]讨厌的家伙, 下流坯 ②恶意行为, 阴谋 / **a ~ of cake** [口]轻松(或愉快)的事情 / **a ~ of eight** 一种西班牙古银币 / **a ~ of goods** [贬]女人; 人 / **a ~ of work** ①一件工作; 一件作品 ②难事 ③骚动 / **break into (或 to) ~s** (使)成为碎片 / **by the ~** 按件计算: be sold by the ~ 只论件出售 / **pay by the ~** 计件付酬 / **give sb. a ~ of one's mind** 对某人直言不讳; 责备某人 / **go to ~s** ①崩溃, 瓦解 ②身体(或精神上)垮下来 / **of a (或 one) ~ (with)** (与…)一致的; (与…)同一性质的 / **~ by ~** 一点一点地; (与…)同一性质的 / **pull (或 pick) to ~s** ①把…撕成碎片 ②把…攻击得一钱不值 / **speak one's ~** ①[美口]诉苦; 申诉 ②[美口]求婚 ‖**~r** *n.* ①拼补者 ②[纺]接头工; 接经器 ‖**~-dye** *vt.* 【纺】成匹染(布): ~-dyed cloth 匹染色布 / **~goods** [总称]【纺】匹头, 布匹 / **~-meal** *ad.* 一件一件地; 零碎地; 零星地: work done by ~meal 零碎做出的工作 *a.* 一件一件的; 逐渐的; 零碎的 *n.* 块, 片: by ~meal 一件一件地; 逐渐地; 零碎地 / **~ rate** 计件工价 / '**~work** *n.* 计件工作, 件工 / '**~,worker** *n.* 计件工

pièce de résistance ['pjes də ˌreizis'tɑːns] [法] ①一餐中的主菜 ②主要项目; 主要事件

pier [piə] *n.* ①(桥)墩 ②(凸式)码头, 直码头; 防波堤: a floating ~ 浮码头 ③【建】窗间壁, 户间壁, 扶壁; 支柱, 方柱 ‖**~ glass** 穿衣镜; 窗间镜

pierce [piəs] ❶ *vt.* ①刺穿; 刺破; 突入, 突破(防线等): The cold ~d him to the bone. 他感到寒冷刺骨。 / A ray of light ~d the darkness. 一道亮光刺破黑暗。 ②穿(洞、孔) ③看穿, 洞察: ~ the mysteries of the universe 揭开宇宙的秘密 ④打动, 感动: ~ sb. to the core 深深打动某人 ❷ *vi.* 穿入, 刺入; 突破 (into, through)

pierrot ['pierou] *n.* ①(法国哑剧中的)丑角 ②搽白脸穿宽大白衣的走江湖小丑

piety ['paiəti] *n.* ①虔敬, 虔诚 ②孝顺, 孝敬 ③虔敬行为

piffle ['pifl] I *n.* [总称]废话, 蠢话; 笨事, 无聊事 II *vi.* 说无聊话; 做傻事

pig [pig] I *n.* ①猪; 小猪; 野猪 ②猪肉; 宰好的小肉猪; 猪皮: roast ~ 烤猪肉 ③[口]猪一般的人(指肮脏、贪吃等的人) ④[美俚]警察, 密探; 荡妇; 赛马用的马 (尤指劣马); (调车场用的)火车头; 牵 [美俚]警察局 / the ~ forces [美俚] 警察 ⑤[常用以构成复合词]猪一般的动物 ⑥生铁块(或锭); 生铁 ⑦橘子的瓣 II (pigged; pigging) ❶ *vi.* ①生小猪 ②像猪一样过活: ~ together 像猪一般肮脏地挤在一起(过活) ❷ *vt.* 生(小猪) ‖**bring one's ~s to a fine (或 a pretty, the wrong) market** 卖得吃亏; 失算; 失败 / **buy a ~ in a poke** (未见实物而)

瞎买东西 / *drive one's ~s to market* 打鼾 / *in a* (或 *the*) *~'s eye* 见 **eye** / *in a ~'s whisper* [俚] 低声地; 顷刻间 / *in ~* 怀小猪的 / *live like ~s in clover* 见 **clover** / *between two sheets* [美俚] 火腿三明治 / *~ it* ① 像猪一样生活; 过困苦的生活 ②[美俚] 停止奔跑; 放慢速度;(因慑怯) 退却 / *Pigs might fly (if they had wings).* [谑] 奇事也许会发生。/ *please the ~s* [谑] 如果老天保佑的话; 如果运气好的话 / *teach a ~ to play on a flute* 教猪吹笛; 做荒谬(或不可能做到)的事 / *when ~s fly* 永不; 决不; 决不可能 ‖*~ bed* ① 猪圈 ②【冶】(高炉的) 铸床, 出铁场 / *'~boat n.* [美俚] 潜水艇 / *~ iron* ①【冶】生铁 ②[美俚] 非法酿造的劣酒 / *'~-jump n.* (马) 举四腿跃起 / *~ Latin* 任意颠倒(或打乱) 英语词的字母顺序而成的黑话 / *~ lead* [总称]【冶】铅锭 / *'~nut n.* 【植】①[英] 块茎; 铁荸荠; 花生 ②山核桃树; 山核桃 / *'~pen n.* ① 猪圈 ② 肮脏的地方 / *'~skin n.* ① 猪皮 ②[口] 马鞍 ③[美俚] 橄榄球 / *'~stick vi.* ①(骑在马上用长矛) 猎野猪 / *'~,sticker n.* ①(骑在马上用长矛) 猎野猪者; 屠夫 ②长刀折刀; [美俚] 刺刀; 刀, 剑 / *'~,sticking n.* ① 用长矛猎野猪 ② 宰猪 / *'~sty n.* ① 猪圈 ②[喻] 肮脏的住所 / *'~'s-wash n.* =*~wash* / *~ sweat* [美俚] 啤酒; 劣酒 / *'~tail n.* ① 辫子 ② 卷成细条的烟草 / *'~tailed a.* 梳辫子的 / *'~wash n.* 泔脚 / *'~weed n.* 苋属植物; 蔾

pigeon ['pidʒin] **I** *n.* ① 鸽子(包括野鸽和家鸽): a carrier (或 homing) ~ 通信鸽 ②[俚] 傻瓜; 易受骗的人, 受骗上当者 ③(抛入空中作为射击目标的) 粘土制圆盘, 土鸽 ④ 特别关心的事物(或人): Football is not his ~. 他不怎么喜欢踢足球。 ⑤[美] 少女, 少妇 **II** *vt.* 诈骗(尤指赌博时) ‖*a ~ pair* 见 **pair** / *pluck a ~* 诈骗傻瓜的钱财 ‖*~ breast* 【医】鸡胸 / *'~-,breasted a.* 【医】鸡胸的 / *~ carrier* ① 通信鸽输送兵 ② 鸽笼 / *~ company* 【军】通信鸽连 / *'~gram n.* 鸽子带的信 / *'~hearted a.* 懦怯的 / *~ house* 鸽舍, 鸽棚 / *'~-'livered a.* 温柔的 / *'~-toed a.* 【医】足内翻的 / *'~wing n.* ① 一种顿脚的花色舞步 ② 鸽翼式花色溜冰动作

pigeonhole ['pidʒinhoul] **I** *n.* ①(鸽棚中隔开的) 鸽巢; (门、墙上的) 鸽子出入孔 ②(书橱中、书桌上鸽笼式的) 分类架, 文件架, 信件架 ③ 极小的房间 **II** *vt.* ①把(文件等) 插入分类架中; 把(文件等) 分类(或归档) ②把(计划等) 搁置, 把…束之高阁: The plan was ~d. 这个计划被搁置了。/ *~ an article* 扣压一篇文章 ③把(事物等)记在脑子里

pigment ['pigmənt] *n.* ① 颜料; 色料 ②【生】色素: ~ granule 色素粒 ‖*~al* [pig'mentl], *~ary a.* (含有) 颜料的; (含有) 色素的 / *~ation* [,pigmən'teiʃən] *n.* ① 色素淀积, 着色(作用) ②【医】色素沉着

pigmy ['pigmi] *n. & a.* =**pygmy**

pike[1] [paik] **I** *n.* ① 长矛, 长枪; 矛头, 枪刺; (行人防滑用的) 尖头杖 ②【动】狗鱼 ③[英方](英国湖畔地方) 有尖峰的(高) 山; 尖峰(常用作地名) ④[英] 鹤嘴锄, 镐 **II** *vt.* 用矛刺穿(或刺伤、刺死) ‖*trail a ~* 当兵, 服役 / *'~d a.* 尖的, 有尖头的 ‖*'~man* ['paikmən] *n.* ① 长矛兵 ②[英] 用镐的矿工

pike[2] [paik] **I** *n.* ① 收税栅, 收费门, 关卡 ② 通行税 ③ 税道, 收税路 **II** *vi.* [美俚] 走; 离开(*along*) ‖*'~man* ['paikmən] *n.* 税道关栅看守人

pilchard ['piltʃəd] *n.* 沙丁鱼, 沙脑鱼

pile[1] [pail] **I** *n.* ① 堆: a ~ of books (logs) 一堆书(木头) ② 火化堆(火化尸体等的燃料堆) ③ 高大的建筑物; 一群建筑物: a stately ~ 巍峨的大厦 ④[口] 大量; 大数目; 大笔钱财 ⑤【电】电池: a dry ~ 干电池 ⑥【原】核反应堆 **II** ❶ *vt.* ① 堆叠; 累积; 积聚(*up, on*): ~ arms [军] 叉枪, 架枪 / ~ *more coal on* 堆上更多的煤 / ~ (*up*) *stones* 叠起石头 ② 在…上堆东西: ~ a cart with straw 给大车装满稻草 ❷ *vi.* ① 堆积, 堆起; 积累: Work has ~d up during his absence. 在他离开期间工作堆积起来了。/ New production records ~d up rapidly. 新的生产纪录迅速出现。②拥, 挤; 进(入)(*in, into*), 走(出)(*out, off*): They ~d out of the theatre. 他们挤出了剧场。 He ~d into a car. 他跨进了汽车。 ‖*a ~ of shit* [美俚] 胡说八道; 废话; 破烂的废物 ③ 可鄙的人 / *make a* (或 *one's*) ~ 发财 / *~ it on* 夸张 / *~ up* ① 堆积; 积聚;(汽车等) 挤在一起 ②(船) 搁浅; 使(船) 搁浅 ③(汽车、飞机等) 撞毁; 撞毁(汽车、飞机等) / *~ up* (或 *on*) *the agony* 渲染悲痛的事情 ‖*'~-up n.* ①[口] 数辆汽车(或数名球员等) 同时碰撞事件 ②(繁重任务等的) 堆积

pile[2] [pail] **I** *n.* 桩; 桥桩: a foundation ~ 基桩 / a sheet ~ 板桩 / drive (raise 或 draw) ~s 打(拔) 桩 **II** *vt.* ① 把桩打入 ② 用桩支撑, 用桩加强 ‖*~ driver* 打桩机; 打桩者 / *~ dweller* 湖边桩屋居民 / *~ dwelling* 湖边桩屋

pile[3] [pail] *n.* ① 绒面, 软绒 ② 绒毛, 绒头, 毛茸

pile[4] [pail] *n.* [常用复] 痔疮

pilfer ['pilfə] *vt. & vi.* 小偷小摸; 偷窃 ‖*~er* ['pilfərə] *n.* 小偷

pilgrim ['pilgrim] **I** *n.* ① (在国外) 旅行者; 流浪者 ② 香客, 朝山进香的人, 朝拜圣地者 ③ 最初的移民; [P-] 一六二〇年移到美洲的英国清教徒 ④ 新来的移民 **II** *vi.* 朝圣般地行进; 朝圣 ‖*Pilgrim Fathers* 一六二〇年移到美洲建立普利茅斯殖民地的一批英国清教徒 / *Pilgrim's Progress* 《天路历程》(十七世纪英国作家班扬(Bunyan) 讽刺贵族阶级的寓言式作品)

pilgrimage ['pilgrimidʒ] **I** *n.* ① 朝圣, 朝觐: go on (a) ~ 去朝圣 ② 远游 ③ 人生历程 **II** *vi.* 朝圣

pill[1] [pil] **I** *n.* ① 药丸, 丸剂; [the ~] (女用) 口服避孕药 ② 讨厌而必须忍受的事; 屈辱: a bitter

~ to swallow 不得不忍受的苦事 ③[俚]讨厌的家伙；医生 ④[俚]炸弹,炮弹,子弹；棒球,网球 ⑤[英][复]弹子戏,台球戏 ⑥[美俚](鸦片)烟泡；镇静剂；香烟 II vt. ①把…做成药丸 ②使服药丸 ③(用秘密投票)拒绝,挫败 ‖a ~ to cure an earthquake 软弱的措施,不彻底的办法 / Bitter ~s may have wholesome effects. [谚] 良药苦口。 / gild (或 sugar) the ~ 把苦药包上糖衣；使苦事容易被接受 ‖~ pad [美俚]鸦片窝；吸毒窝 / ~ roller n. [俚]医生；医科学生

pill² [pil] vt. ①[古]掠夺(某地)的财物,抢劫(某人)的财物 ②[方]去掉(树木、橘子等)的皮

pillage ['pilidʒ] I n. ①掠夺,抢劫(尤指战争中的) ②[古]掠夺物 II ❶ vt. ①在(某地)进行掠夺；抢劫(某人)的财物 ②偷窃 ❷ vi. 掠夺,抢劫 ‖~r n. 掠夺者,抢劫者

pillar ['pilə] I n. ①柱,柱子 ②[喻]栋梁,支柱: a ~ of the state 国家的栋梁 ③柱形物(如水柱、火柱等) ④[建]墩；[矿]矿柱,煤柱 II vt. 用柱支持,用柱加固 ‖be driven from ~ to post 被逼得四处奔走；被逼得走投无路；到处碰壁 ‖'~box [英]邮筒,信筒

pillion ['piljən] I n. ①后鞍,添鞍(设于骑手背后以供妇女等乘用者) ②摩托车后座 II ad. 坐在后鞍上: ride ~ 骑在后鞍(或摩托车的后座)上

pillory ['piləri] I n. ①颈手枷(用以将罪犯示众的古代刑具) ②使受公众嘲笑的办法 II vt. ①给…上颈手枷,处…以枷刑 ②使受公众嘲笑

pillow ['pilou] I n. ①枕头 ②[机]轴枕,垫座 ③[美俚]拳击用手套；(棒球中的)垒 II ❶ vt. ①把…搁在枕上；使靠在(on): ~ one's head on one's arm 把头枕在手臂上 ②给…当枕头；垫: Her arm ~ed the sleeping child. 她的手臂枕着熟睡的孩子。 ❷ vi. 靠在枕上 ‖take counsel of one's ~ (或 consult one's ~) 通夜思考 ‖~ block [机]轴台 / '~case n. 枕套 / '~ fight ①儿童在临睡前用枕头打闹着玩 ②打闹,小争吵 / '~-,puncher n. [美俚](收拾卧室的)女佣 / '~slip n. =~case

pilot ['pailət] I n. ①领港员；领航员；引水员；舵手；航海指南 ②飞行员,飞机驾驶员；(美空军的)二级驾驶员: a jet ~ 喷气飞机驾驶员 / a first ~ 正驾驶员 / a senior (command) ~ (美空军的)特级)驾驶员 / a ~-navigator 领航驾驶员 / a robot ~ 自动驾驶仪 ③[喻]向导,带路人；领导人 ④(机车前的)排障器；[交][建]导洞: ~ drive 导洞开挖(或掘进) ⑤[机][电]领示,导向器；指示灯 II vt. ①给(船等)领航(或领港)(on, in, over) ②驾驶(飞机等)③带领；指引,引导: III a. ①引导的；向导的,领示的: a ~ car 先驱车 / a ~ bearing 导航承 / a ~ tunnel 导挖隧道 / a ~ cell 领示电池 ②[机][电]辅助的；控制的 ③(小规模)试验性的,试点的: a ~ scheme (或 project) (小规模)试验计划 / a ~ plant (小规模)试验厂 / investigation 试点调查 ‖a hangar ~ [美俚]好

胡吹而实不会驾驶飞机的人 / drop the ~ 不听忠告；抛弃良师益友 ‖~ing n. 领港 / ~less a. 无人驾驶的: a ~less aircraft 无人驾驶飞机；(非正式用法)导弹 / a ~less high-altitude reconnaissance plane 无人驾驶高空侦察机 / a ~less missile [军俚]导弹,弹道导弹 ‖~ balloon 测风气球 / ~ boat 领港艇；领航艇 / ~ bread (船上等用的)硬面包,硬饼干(也作 ~ biscuit 或 hardtack) / ~ chart 航空气象简图 / ~ chute [空]引导伞 / ~ cloth [纺]海昆厚绒呢 / ~ engine 清路机车,先驱机车,压道(机)车 / ~ fish [动](常与鲨鱼同游的)舟鰤 / ~ flag, ~ jack 领港旗；领航旗；引水旗 / '~house n. 操舵室 / ~ lamp 指示灯,信号灯；领航灯 / ~ light ①指示灯,信号灯；领航灯 ②(煤气炉中常燃的)小火(用于引燃大火) / ~ officer (英)空军少尉 / '~-tube 【空】空速指示器 / ~ whale 【动】巨头鲸 / ~ wire 【电】控制线,领示线,操作线

pilotage ['pailətidʒ] n. ①领港；领航；引水；[喻]响导: radar ~ 雷达领航 / a ~ chart 领航图 / ~ water 引水区 ②领航术；驾驶术；目视飞行术 ③领港费；领航费

pimple ['pimpl] n. [医]丘疹；脓疱 ‖~d, pimply a. 有丘疹的；多脓疱的

pin [pin] I n. ①针,别针,大头针: groove ~ 【机】槽针 / a safety ~ 安全别针；饰针(反面有别针的)徽章,像章；针状物 ③钉；轴钉；销；栓；枢；(弦乐器上调弦用)弦轴,轸子,扣手；发夹: a drawing ~ 图画钉 / a split ~ 开尾书钉；开尾销 / a cotter ~ 开尾销,扁销 ④插头；(电子管的)管脚；引线 ⑤[海]桨架脚,桡座(舷缘桨架的两期之一) ⑥(容量为四加仑半的)小桶 ⑦(钥匙)插入锁孔的部分 ⑧琐碎物,小东西 ⑨[常用复][口]腿: be quick on one's ~s 跑得快 II (pinned; pinning) vt. ①(用别针等)别住；(用钉等)钉住；(用针等)刺穿: ~ a badge on one's jacket 在外套上别一枚徽章 / ~ up an announcement on a notice board 在布告板上钉一张通告 / ~ papers together 用针把文件别起来 ②(用栅栏等)圈住；使不能行动,牵制: ~ sb. against the wall 使某人无处可逃 / a pinning attack 【军】牵制性攻击 ③ 把…归罪于(on): ~ the theft on sb. 说东西是某人偷的 III a. ①针的；销的 ②(皮革商)粒状(如针头)的 ‖neat as a (new) ~ 十分整洁,干干净净 / not care a ~ 毫不在乎 / not worth a ~ 一钱不值 / on one's ~s 活着；身体健康 / on ~s and needles 如坐针毡,坐立不安,急得要命 / ~ down ①使受约束 ②阻止,牵制；压住 / ~ one's faith on 或 faith / ~ one's hope(s) on 见 hope / ~s and needles (手、脚的)发麻 / ~ up ①钉住,钉起来；(用针)扣住,别住 ②【建】托换…的基础,加固；(以基础)支撑 / pull the ~ [美俚] ①(原铁道用语)拆开 ②离开某地 ③离职 ④遗弃妻子,抛弃家属(或朋友等) / put (或 keep) in the ~ [俚]停止(尤指戒酒) ‖'~ball *n.* 弹球戏(把小球打入插钉的板上的凹洞中) / '~cushion *n.* 针插 / '~head *n.* ①针头;钉头 ②(口)小东西,微不足道的东西 ③傻瓜;笨蛋;(畸形小头的)白痴 / ~,headed *a.* 愚蠢的 / '~hole *n.* ①针刺的孔; 小孔: a ~hole camera (无透镜的)针孔摄影机 ②插针(或钉、栓)的孔 / ~ money 零用钱(尤指男人给女人买衣服等用的钱) / '~prick *n.* ①针刺的孔 ②[喻]使人烦恼的事物;刺耳的话 / '~stripe *n.* (织物上的)细条子;细条子衣服 / '~tail *n.* ①针尾鸭 ②针尾松鸡 / '~up *a.* ①可钉在墙上的: a ~up lamp 壁灯 ②(女子)其照片可供倾慕者钉在墙上的 *n.* 钉在墙上的东西(如壁灯、妖艳女子的照片等) / '~wale *a.* (织物)细棱条的 / '~wheel *n.* ①玩具风车 ②彩色焰火 ③[俚]直升飞机 / '~work *n.* [纺]撤纱工艺;(针绣花边的)细小突出饰纹

pinafore ['pinəfɔ:] *n.* (小孩的)围涎; 防脏的围裙

pincers ['pinsəz] [复] *n.* [用作单或复] ①铁钳,钳子: a (pair of) ~ 一把钳子 ②[动]螯;尾铗 ‖pincer(s) movement [军]钳形运动

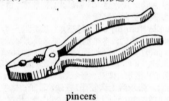

pincers

pinch [pintʃ] I ❶ *vt.* ①捏, 拧; 夹痛, 轧痛: ~ the boy's arm 在男孩臂上拧一下 / The shoe ~es me. 我的鞋子太紧(轧痛脚)。/ ~ one's fingers in the doorway 手指被门轧住 ②掐掉(嫩枝等), 修剪(out, off, back): ~ off (back) the young shoots 把嫩枝掐掉(掐短) ③使不舒服, 使苦恼 ④使消瘦; 使萎缩: be ~ed with cold 冷得缩手缩脚 ⑤使贫拮据,使感缺乏: be ~ed for money 手头拮据 ⑥勒索,诈取(钱财等) (from, out of) ⑦[俚]盗窃;不告而取;对(人)进行抢劫 ⑧[俚]逮捕;拘留 ⑨[海]使(船)紧抢风行驶 ⑩[英](赛马时)催(马)快跑 ❷ *vi.* ①(向里)挤压,收缩(in);(鞋等)紧得使人感到痛 ②节省;吝啬 ③(矿脉等)狭缩,变瘦 II *n.* [物]箍缩,收缩: give the child a ~ on the cheek 在孩子脸颊上拧一下 ②(一)撮,微量: a ~ of salt 一撮盐 ③(匮乏等的)压力,重压;匮乏: the ~ of poverty 贫困的重压 ④紧急情况,紧要关头 ⑤[俚]盗窃 ⑥[俚]逮捕;拘留 ‖at a ~ 在紧要关头,急需时: We can put up five people for the night at a ~. 必要时我们可以留宿五个人。/ drop a ~ of salt on the tail of 见 salt / ~ and scrape (或 screw) 省吃俭用 / ~ pennies 见 penny / when it comes to the ~ =at a ~ / where the shoe ~es 见 shoe / with a ~ of salt 有保留地,不全信地 ‖~beck *n.* 金色

铜(铜与锌的合金, 用来假冒金质饰物等); 冒牌货; 廉价货 *a.* 金色铜制的; 假冒的; 廉价的 / '~cock *n.* (夹在软管上调节液流的)弹簧夹; 节流夹 / '~fist *n.* 吝啬鬼,守财奴 / '~hit *vi.* ①(棒球赛中)在紧要关头代打球 ②紧急时代替(for) / ~ hitter ①(棒球赛中)紧急时上场的代打者 ②代替者,代理人 / '~,penny *a.* 吝啬的

pine¹ [pain] *n.* ①松树; 松木 ②[口]凤梨, 波罗 ‖~ barren (美国南部)长有稀疏松树的沙地(或泥炭地) / ~cone *n.* 松球, 松果 / ~ needle 松叶 / ~ nut ①松果 ②松子 / ~ overcoat [美俚]棺材(尤指蹩脚棺材) / ~ tar 松焦油 / '~wood *n.* ①[常用复]松林 ②松木

pine² [pain] *vi.* ①衰弱,憔悴,消瘦 (away) ②渴望 (for, after): ~ to do sth. 渴望做某事

pineapple ['pain,æpl] *n.* [植]凤梨, 波罗 ②[俚]炸弹; 手榴弹 ‖~ cloth [纺]波罗纤维织物; 巴拿马麻布; 上浆全丝薄纱

pinion¹ ['pinjən] I *n.* ①(鸟的)翅膀; 羽毛, 翮 ②昆虫翅的前部 II *vt.* ①缚住(鸟)的翼; 剪断(鸟)的翅膀 ②缚住(双翅或双臂) ③绑住…的双臂; 把…绑住,把…缚住 ‖~ed *a.* ①有翅膀的 ②被捆住的

pinion² ['pinjən] *n.* [机]小齿轮: lazy ~ 惰轮

pink¹ [piŋk] I *n.* ①[植]石竹; 石竹花 ②桃红色, 粉红色: be dressed in ~ 穿着粉红色衣服 ③极致;化身,典型: the ~ of perfection 十全十美 / He is the ~ of politeness. 他真是客气极了。④穿着入时的人; [the ~] [总称]名流 ⑤[有时作 P-]政治观点有点左倾的人; a parlour ~ 会空谈的温和激进派 ⑥[英]猎狐者穿的红色上衣; 猎狐者 ⑦[美俚]汽车驾驶执照 II *a.* ①粉红色的 ②有点左倾的, 有点激进的 ③面红耳赤的, 激怒的 III *vt. & vi.* (使)变粉红色 ‖in the ~ (of condition) 非常健康 / tickle sb. ~ 见 tickle / ~ly *ad.* / ~ness *n.* / ~ elephants (狂饮或吸毒后呈现的)幻觉 / '~eye *n.* ①火眼(触染性急性结膜炎) ②马的传染性热病 / ~ lady 由白兰地、柠檬汁等调制而成的鸡尾酒 / ~ slip 解雇通知书 / ~ tea ①(非常讲究仪式的)午后茶会 ②正式的社交活动

pink² [piŋk] *vt.* ①刺, 扎, 戳 ②(用讽刺、嘲笑等)刺伤,刺痛 ③在(布、皮、纸等)上打饰孔 ④把(布等)的边剪成锯齿形 ⑤装饰

pink³ [piŋk] *vi.* (内燃机)发爆声

pink⁴ [piŋk] *n.* 尖尾船

pinnace ['pinis] *n.* ①(大)舢板(常用作军舰等的供应船) ②(任何种类的)舰载艇

pinnacle ['pinəkl] I *n.* ①(主要指哥特式建筑上的)小尖塔; 尖顶 ②山顶,山峰 ③顶峰,极点,顶点: the ~ of prosperity 极度繁荣 II *vt.* ①把…置于小尖塔之上;把…放在极高处 ②在…之上造小尖塔

pint [paint] *n.* ①品脱(英美干量或液量名,= 1/2 夸脱,略作 pt.) ②一品脱壶(或其他容器) ‖~-'size(d) *a.* 小的,小型的

pioneer [ˌpaiə'niə] **I** n. ①拓荒者,开辟者 ②先驱者,先锋;倡导者 ③【军】轻工兵: ～ work 轻工兵作业 / ～ tools 轻工兵工具 ④【生】先驱生物 **II** ❶ vt. 开辟;倡导: ～ wilderness 开拓荒野 / ～ an enterprise 创办企业 ❷ vi. 当先驱,当先锋 **III** a. ①最早的;原先的: ～ form【生】发端类型 ②开拓的;先驱的;首创的

pious ['paiəs] a. ①虔诚的, 敬神的; 虔奉宗教的 ②[古]孝顺的;尽本分的 ③虚伪的;道貌岸然的 ④可嘉的;有善良意向的: a ～ effort 值得嘉许的努力 ‖～ly ad. / ～ness n.

pip¹ [pip] n. ①(苹果、橘子、梨等的)果仁,种子 ②[美俚]出众的人(或物) ‖～less a. 无果仁的,无种子的

pip² [pip] (pipped; pipping) [英口] ❶ vt. ① 投票反对,排斥;挫败(计划等) ② 射击;击伤;击死 ❷ vi. 死(out)

pip³ [pip] n. [the ～] ①家禽的一种传染病(喉头生粘液或舌上生痂) ②形容不出的小毛病,无以名状的疾病;[俚]梅毒 ③烦躁;抑郁,闷闷不乐: That gave me the ～. 那使我感到不舒服。

pip⁴ [pip] n. ①(纸牌、骰子、骨牌上的)点 ②【无】(雷达的)反射点, 尖头信号; (荧光屏上的)脉冲 ③(英国军官肩章上表示等级的)星

pip⁵ [pip] n. (广播中的)报时信号: broadcast the six ～s of the time signal 广播六声报时信号

pip⁶ [pip] (pipped; pipping) ❶ vt. (小鸡等)啄破(壳) ❷ vi. ①(小鸡等)叽叽地叫 ②(小鸡等)破壳而出

pipe [paip] **I** n. ①管子,导管,输送管: a water (gas) ～ 水(煤气)管 / a drain (street) ～ 放出(进给)管 / a seamless steel ～ 无缝钢管 ②(人或动物的)管状器官; [常用复]嗓子; 声带; 呼吸器官 ③ 乐器; (管风琴的)管; [复](苏格兰)风笛 (=bagpipes);【海】水手长的哨子,哨子声 ④ 歌声;鸟叫声 ⑤烟斗,旱烟筒;一斗烟丝;[美俚]雪茄 ⑥最大桶(英美液量单位,=105英加仑或126美加仑);(同等容量盛酒、油等的)大桶 ⑦[俚]容易干的活儿; 容易成功的工作 ⑧【矿】筒状(矿)脉;【地】筒状火成砾岩;火山筒 ⑨[美俚]短信;交谈 **II** ❶ vt. ①为…装管子; 用管道输送(液体、气体等) ②用乐器吹奏(曲调);【海】吹水手长的哨子召集(或吹笛);吹笛子引诱 ③用尖嗓子讲(话) ④为(衣服等)拷边,为…滚边; 为(糕饼)浇饰花边 ⑤[美俚]传递(消息等);谈论,透露;【电】(用导线或同轴电缆) 传送 (广播或电视节目等) ⑥[美俚]看,看见;注视;注意到 ❷ vi. ①吹奏管乐 ②尖声叫嚷; 发出尖音 ③吹水手长的哨子传递命令 ‖dance to sb.'s ～ 跟着某人亦步亦趋 / hit the ～ [美俚]①吸鸦片 ②吸毒 / ～ away 发出开船信号 / ～ down【海】吹哨子通知(水手等)下班 ②[俚]安静下来;不过于自信 / ～ in 用电讯设备传送 / ～ off ①把…列入黑名单;宣布…不受欢迎 ②向警察告发 / ～ one's eye 见 eye / ～ up 开始吹奏(或唱歌); 尖声地说 / put sb.'s ～ out 使某人无法获得成功;使某人的计谋

不能实现 / Put that in your ～ and smoke it. (斥责或劝告用语)你自己好好考虑吧。 / smoke the ～ of peace 表示和睦; 言和 (北美印第安人有以旱烟筒敬外来人从而表示亲善的风俗) ‖～ful n. 满满一烟斗 / ～less a. 无管的 ‖clay ～ 管土(制烟斗或涂白皮带等用的一种白粘土); [喻]军队中对服装的过分讲究 / '～-clay vt. 用管土涂白(皮带等) / ～ cleaner 烟斗通条 / ～ course [美俚]容易对付的课程 / ～ dream [美] (鸦片鬼的)幻想; 白日梦; 想入非非的计划 / '～fish n. 【动】海龙 / ～ fitter 管道安装工(或修理工) / ～ fitting ①管道安装工作 ②接管零件(如弯头、阀门等) / '～,layer n. ①铺管工人,管道安装工 ②[俚]政治阴谋家 / '～line n. ①管道,管线: an oil ～line 输油管 ②传送途径: a ～line of information 情报渠道 ③ (从制造商到零售商或消费者的)商品供应线 vt. ①用管道输送 ②为…装管道 / ～ major 风笛乐队的主要吹奏手 / ～ organ 管风琴 / ～ rack 烟斗架 / '～stone n. 印第安人用以制烟斗的淡红色泥质岩石 / ～ stop 管风琴的音栓 / ～ wrench【机】管扳手

piped [paipt] a. ①(服装)拷边的,滚边的 ②[俚]酒醉的

piper ['paipə] n. ① 吹奏人(尤指流浪艺人);吹风笛的人 ②管道工 ③拷边工;(缝纫机上的)拷边装置 ④【动】鲂鮄,绿鳍鱼 ⑤气喘的马 ⑥幼鸽 ⑦[英](用以诱捕猎物的)囮鸟,诱犬 ‖pay the ～ (and call the tune) 出资(而作主); 承担费用(而有决定权)

piping ['paipiŋ] **I** n. ①吹笛;笛乐;尖声 ②管(道)系(统);管道: gas ～ 煤气管道 ③(衣服等的)拷边, 滚边 ④(蛋糕上的)糖制花色条纹, 花饰边 **II** a. ①吹笛的 ②(管乐)乐声平和的,和平的 ③尖音的,高音的 **III** ad. 炽热地,沸腾地: ～ hot soup (food) 滚烫的汤(食物)

piquant ['pi:kənt] a. ①辛辣的,开胃的: a ～ sauce 辣酱油 ②泼辣的,使人兴奋的,痛快的; 活泼有趣的: ～ comments 泼辣的评论 / a ～ anecdote 妙趣横生的轶事 ③调皮的,淘气的: a ～ face 淘气的脸 ④[古]尖刻伤人的 ‖～ly ad. / ～ness n.

pique [pi:k] **I** n. 生气,呕气;愠怒;不满: do sth. in a fit of ～ 赌气做某事 / take a ～ against sb. 生某人的气 **II** vt. ①使生气;激怒: be ～d at sb.'s indifference 因某人无动于衷而生气 ②刺激,激发,激起(好奇心、兴趣等) ③[～ oneself]夸耀 (on, upon): ～ oneself on having a good memory 自夸记忆力好

piqué ['pi:kei] n. [法]【纺】凹凸织物,凸纹布

pirate ['paiərit] **I** n. ①海盗;掠夺者 ②海盗船 ③侵犯版权者,非法翻印者 ④非法广播者 ⑤[英]私自招徕乘客的私营公共汽车(或马车) **II** ❶ vt. ①(以海盗方式)掠夺 ②非法翻印 ③挖(别人所雇用的人) ❷ vi. 做海盗;从事劫掠 ‖swear like a ～ 破口大骂

pirouette [ˌpiru'et] **I** n. ①(芭蕾)舞蹈中以脚尖

立地旋转 ②(马在飞跑时)突然起立以后脚为轴心旋转(骑马术中的一种高级动作) **II** *vi.* 用脚尖旋转;(马)急转

pistol ['pistl] **I** *n.* ①手枪 ②信号手枪: best the ~ (赛跑时)在枪响前冲出,偷跑 **II** (pistol(l)ed; pistol(l)ing) *vt.* 用手枪射击 ‖ **carbine** 驳壳枪 / ~ **grip** (枪枝或工具上的)手枪式握把 / ~ **shot** ①手枪射程: within (beyond) ~ *shot* 在手枪射程之内(之外) ②善于用手枪射击的人 / '~-**whip** *vt.* 用手枪柄打(尤指打头部)

piston ['pistən] *n.* ①【机】活塞: steam ~ 蒸汽活塞 ②【音】(铜管乐器的)直升式活塞 ‖ ~ **ring** 活塞环 / ~ **rod** 活塞杆

pit¹ [pit] **I** *n.* ①坑,地坑;深洼;【军】散兵坑;靶壕;炮兵掩体: A fall in the ~, a gain in your wit. 吃一堑,长一智。/ a rifle ~ 散兵壕 / a machine-gun ~ 机枪掩体 ②(藏农作物等的)地窖 ③深渊; [the] ~ 地狱; [方]坟墓 ④陷阱; [喻]圈套: dig a ~ for sb. 给某人设圈套 ⑤煤矿,矿井,坑洞,窑(如石灰窑、炭窑): an open ~ 露天矿 / a salt (stone, sand) ~ 采盐(石,砂)坑 ⑥[英](剧场)楼下正厅(尤指正厅后座); 正厅后座观众;(剧场舞台前的)乐队池 ⑦兽栏;斗兽场;斗鸡场 ⑧躯体凹部: the ~ of the stomach 胸口,心窝(指腹上部) ⑨(平面上的)小凹陷;天花疤痕,麻子 ⑩[美](交易所中)某种商品的交易场: the wheat ~ 小麦交易场 ⑪(赛车中途的)加油站,修理站 **II** (pitted; pitting) **❶** *vt.* ①把…放进坑内,窖藏: ~ vegetables (grapes) 窖藏蔬菜(葡萄) ②使成凹,使凹下; 挖坑于: The ground was *pitted* by the heavy rain. 大雨使坑地成洼。③使留下疤痕: be *pitted* by smallpox 留有天花疤痕,有麻子 ④把(鸡等)放进斗场内使互斗;使相斗; 使对立; 使竞争(against) **❷** *vi.* ①起凹点; 变成坑坑洼洼: Does that metal ~ after contact with acid? 那种金属同酸接触后是否会起凹点? ②[医](浮肿者的皮肤被揿后的)凹陷 ‖ ~ **boss** [美俚]矿井工头; 工头; 赌场老板 / '~**fall** *n.* ①陷阱;圈套 ②隐藏着的危险;易犯的错误 / '~**head** *n.* 矿井口 / ~**man** ['pitmən] *n.* ([复] ~men) 矿工,煤矿工人; 下锯木工(通常站在坑内) ②([复] ~mans)[美]【机】连杆,联接杆 / '~**pan** *n.* (中美洲的)平底独木舟 / '~**prop** *n.* 【矿】(支持矿井巷道顶用的)临时木支柱 / ~ **saw** 双人竖拉大锯(一人站在木材上端,另一人站在坑内) / ~ **sawyer** 下锯木工

pit² [pit] [美] **I** *n.* 果核(如桃、杏、梅子等的核) **II** (pitted; pitting) *vt.* 除去…的核

pitch¹ [pitʃ] **I** *n.* ①沥青 ②(针叶树的)树脂 ③人造沥青;人造树脂 **II** *vt.* 用沥青涂,用沥青覆盖 ‖ *touch* ~ 参与不可告人的交易;与坏人有来往 ‖ '~-'**black**, '~-'**dark** *a.* 漆黑的 / '~**blende** *n.* 沥青铀矿 / ~ **coal** ①沥青煤 ②倾斜煤层 / ~ **pine** 【植】北美油松 / '~**stone** *n.* 【地】松脂石

pitch² [pitʃ] **I** **❶** *vt.* ①搭(帐)、扎(营): ~ tents

pitch

for shelter 搭帐篷居住 / ~ a camp 扎营 ②投,掷,扔: ~ hay onto a stack (用叉子)把干草叉上草堆 / ~ a spear 掷标枪 / ~ sb. out 把某人撵出去 ③把…定得,把…定在: ~ the roof steep 使屋顶陡斜 ④【音】为…定音高; 为…定调; [喻]用特定文体表达: ~ a tune high (low) 把曲调定高(低) ⑤(竭力地)推销,叫卖; [主英]陈列(商品) ⑥(用石子等)铺(路) ⑦[英俚]讲(故事) ⑧装腔作势地讲(或念) ⑨(棒球等中)以…为投手; 作为投手打(一局球等) **❷** *vi.* ①安营;搭起帐篷;站定位置: The surveying team ~ed on the mountain. 测量队在山上搭起帐篷。②投掷(头向下)坠落,摔倒;跳入: ~ on one's head 头朝地跌倒 / ~ on one's head into the swimming pool 头朝下跳入游泳池 ④(地面、道路等)倾斜 ⑤(船只)前后颠簸,纵摇(区别于 roll 横摇): The ship ~ed and rolled in the rough sea. 船在波涛汹涌的海上纵横摇动。⑥吹牛,说大话 ⑦(棒球等中)当投手 **II** *n.* ①投掷;投掷物;投掷量;投球 ②前倾;(船只的)纵摇 ③坡度;【建】(屋顶)斜度,高跨比;(地层或矿脉的)倾斜,斜角 ④【机】螺距;(齿轮的)齿节,节距 ⑤【空】螺距(飞机螺旋桨一次旋转的前进距离); 螺旋线间隔 ⑤【语】【音】音高;【音】(调整乐器所依据的)音高标准: the ~ of a sound 一个音的音高 / a high (low) ~ sound 高(低)音 ⑥程度;强度: The excitement of the audience was at a high ~. 观众异常激动。⑦商贩摆摊处; [英](街头艺人等的)表演场所: a high ~ 摆在车上的小摊 / a low ~ 地摊 ⑧上市的商品量 ⑨(摊贩等的)行话;竭力推销商品的话; 广告 ⑩[美俚]情况,现状: Do you get the ~? 情况你清楚了吗? ‖ *at concert* ~ 处于高效能(或充分准备)状态 / *in there* ~*ing* [美口]拼命地干,劲头十足地干 / *make a* ~ *for* [美俚]为…说好话,替…作宣传 / *make one's* ~ [美口]定居;落户 / ~ *in* [口]开始使劲干活,努力投入工作: ~ *in* where hardships abound 到很艰苦的地方去大干 / ~ *into* [口]①投入,投身于: The medical team ~ed *into* action to save the wounded worker. 医疗队积极投入抢救受伤工人的战斗。/ ~ *into* work (struggle) 投入工作(斗争) ②猛烈攻击: ~ *into* sb. 猛烈攻击某人 ③大吃大嚼 / ~ *on* (或 *upon*) (偶然)选中,选定 / *queer sb.'s* ~ (或 *queer the* ~ *for sb.*) 破坏某

人成功的机会;打乱某人计划 ‖'~-and-'toss *n.*
一种向目的物投掷铜币的游戏 / ~ed battle ①
对阵战 ②激战 / ~man ['pitʃmən] *n.* ①[俚](出
售珠宝或珍奇杂物的)摊贩 / ~ pipe【音】定调
管,律管 / '~-wheel *n.* 相互啮合的齿轮

pitcher[1] ['pitʃə] *n.* ①(有嘴和柄的)大水罐 ②【植】
瓶状叶 ‖*Little ~s have long* (或 *large*) *ears.*
[谚] 小孩子耳朵长。(指当心别让小孩子听到) /
Pitchers have ears. [谚]隔墙有耳。‖~ful *n.*
(一)满水罐 ‖~ plant【植】猪笼草,瓶子草

pitcher[2] ['pitʃə] *n.* ①投掷者;(棒球)投手 ②[英]
摊贩 ③[英]铺路石

piteous ['pitiəs] *a.* ①引人哀怜的;乞怜的;可怜
的 ②[古]慈悲的,怜悯的 ‖~ly *ad.* / ~ness
n.

pith [piθ] I *n.* ①木髓 ②【解】髓,骨髓 ③核心;精
髓,要旨: the ~ and marrow of a speech 演说的
要旨 ④ 重要性,意义: a matter of ~ and
moment 意义重大的事件 ⑤[古]精力;力气
II *vt.* ①除去(茎)中的木髓 ②(用切断动物脊髓
的方法)杀死;使瘫痪 ‖~less *a.* 没有髓的 ‖~
cavity【植】髓孔

pity ['piti] I *n.* ①怜悯;同情: in ~ of 因为可
怜… / out of ~ 出于怜悯 / feel ~ for sb. 同情
某人 / For ~'s sake! 发发慈悲吧! / have (或
take) ~ on (或 upon) 怜悯…;同情… ②可惜的
事,憾事: It is a ~ (a thousand *pities*) that you
cannot come. 你不能来真是遗憾(遗憾之极)。/
The ~ is that …. 可惜的(或:遗憾的是)/
…, (the) more's the ~. …尤属憾事。/ What
a ~! 真可惜! 真是遗憾! / The ~ of it! 真
遗憾! II ❶ *vt.* 可怜;对…觉得可怜又可鄙 ❷
vi. 觉得可怜 ‖~ingly *ad.* 怜惜地

pivot ['pivət] I *n.* ①枢,枢轴,支枢,支点: conical
~【机】锥形枢 / turn on the ~ 在枢轴上转动
②【军】基准,轴兵 ③中枢,枢纽;要点,中心点
④回转运动 II *a.* 在枢轴上转动的; 枢轴的;
枢要的 III ❶ *vi.* ①在枢轴上转动;转过身 ②
随…转移;依…而定(*on, upon*) ❷ *vt.* 装枢轴于;
把…放在枢轴上;使绕枢轴转动: a ~ed mechanism 有枢轴的机构 / ~ bearing【机】立式
止推轴承 / ~ bridge【建】旋开桥,开合桥 / ~
man【军】基准兵(指行进队伍变换方向时作为基
准的士兵) / ~ tooth【医】柱(牙)冠

placard ['plækɑ:d] I *n.* ① 招贴,布告;标语牌
②(钉在门上的)小牌子 II *vt.* ① 张贴布告于,
悬挂布告于 ②(用布告或招贴)公布;替…做广
告;用招贴,悬挂

placate [plə'keit] *vt.* 安抚,抚慰;使和解 ‖**placa-
tion** [plə'keiʃən] *n.*

place [pleis] I *n.* ①地方,地点;地区;位置: time
and ~ 时间和地点 / He has been to many ~s.
他到过许多地方。/ There is no ~ for doubt.
没有怀疑的余地。②住所,寓所: Come round to
my ~ sometime next week. 下星期什么时候
请到我家来。③(有特定用途的)场所: a ~ of

amusement 娱乐场所 / a ~ of worship 礼拜场
所(如教堂等) ④(身体或表面的)特定位置: a
sore ~ on the leg 腿上伤痛处 ⑤(固定或指定
的)席位,座位: take one's ~ 就座 / the host's
~ (宴会等)主人的席位 ⑥名次;(第…)名,
(第…)位;(赛马)前几名中的任何一名(英国指前
三名;美国指前二名,尤指第二名): give first ~
to sth. 把某事物放在首位 / get the first ~ in
a contest 比赛中得第一名 ⑦地位;处境: the
important ~ of agriculture in economic construction 农业在经济建设中的重要地位 /
If I were in your ~, …. 假使我处于你
的地位,… ⑧职位,公职;职责,职权: take (be
offered) a ~ as … 应聘(被聘请)担任… / It is
not his ~ to make final decisions. 他无权作最
后决定。⑨【数】位: calculate to three decimal
~s 算到小数点后第三位 ⑩(书刊的)段落,页:
use a bookmark to keep one's ~ 用书签标示
读到哪里 / I've lost my ~. 我读到哪里,
找不到了。⑪[常用于专有名词]广场,街道;
别墅 II ❶ *vt.* ①放置,安置: ~ books in the
proper order 把书整理好 / ~ a problem on
the agenda 把问题提到议事日程上 ②寄托
(希望等);给予(信任等) ③安插,任命;安置(难民
等): ~ sb. as … 任命某人为… ④ 完全认定,
认清(人): The man seemed familiar, but I
could not ~ him. 这人很面熟,但是我记不得
在哪里见过他。/ That man was difficult to ~.
那人的身分很难断定。⑤投(资),存(款)
(订单) / ~ an order *for* chemical fertilizer
with a factory 向某厂订购化肥 ⑥销售(存货等)
⑦(唱歌、讲话时)调整(嗓音) ⑧(赛跑、赛马等)
定出(选手)的名次 ❷ *vi.* 名列前茅,得名次(赛
马时)得第二名: ~ third in a contest 竞赛中得
第三名 ‖~ [英](在下院指)上院;[谑]
(剑桥指)牛津,(牛津指)剑桥 / a ~ *in the sun*
好的境遇;显要的地位 / *a wide ~ in the road*
[美俚] 小城镇 / *give ~ to* 让位于…; 被…所代
替 / go ~s [美](即将)获得成功 / in ~ ①在
适当的地位: Every tool is *in* ~. 每一件工具
都放在应放的位置。② 适当的,恰当的,相称的:
I don't think your proposal quite *in* ~. 我
认为你的建议不很恰当。/ *in* ~ *of* 代替: use
plastics *in* ~ *of* wood or metal 用塑料来代替木
材或金属 / *in the first* ~ 首先,第一点;原先,
本来 / *in the next* ~ 其次,第二点 / *know
one's* ~ 知道自己的地位(或身分);知趣,识
相 / *make* ~ *for* ① 为…腾出地方 ②让位
于… ③ 退居…之后 / *out of* ~ ① 不在适当
的地位 ②不适当的,不恰当的,不相称的:
Your remarks were a bit *out of* ~. 你的话有
点不恰当。/ *put sb. in his* ~ 使某人不敢越轨,
使某人安分 / *supply the* ~ *of* 代替 / *take* ~
发生,产生;进行,举行: The May 4th Movement
took ~ in 1919. 五四运动发生于一九一九年。/
When will the football match *take* ~? 足球比

赛什么时候举行? / *take the ~ of* 代替: Nylon has *taken the ~ of* cotton in making some textiles. 在某些纺织品中耐纶已经代替了棉花。 ||**~able** *a.* 可被确定位置的 / ||**~less** *a.* 没有固定位置的 ||~ **brick** 半烧砖,未烧透的砖 / ~ **card** (正式宴会等中的)座位姓名卡 / '**~-kick** *n.* (足球等的)定位踢 / **~man** ['pleismən] *n.* [主英][常贬]官吏 / '**~-name** *n.* 地名

placid ['plæsid] *a.* 平静的,安静的,温和的: a ~ lake 平静的湖 / in a ~ mood 心平气和 ||**placidity** [plæ'siditi] *n.* / ~**ly** *ad.*

plagiarize ['pleidʒjəraiz] ❶ *vt.* 剽窃,抄袭(别人的学说、著作等) ❷ *vi.* 剽窃,抄袭 ||**~r** *n.* 剽窃者

plague [pleig] Ⅰ *n.* ①瘟疫; [the ~]鼠疫,黑死病 ②天灾,灾害,祸患: a ~ of locusts 蝗灾 / a ~ of hail 雹灾 ③[口]讨厌的人(或东西): What a ~ that fellow is! 那家伙真是讨厌极了! Ⅱ *vt.* ①使染瘟疫;使得灾祸 ②折磨;烦扰;使苦恼: be ~d to death 烦得要死 ||*Plague on it (him)*! 该死的(人)! / *Plague take it (him)*! 该死的(人)! ||**~some** *a.* ①讨厌的,麻烦的 ②瘟疫的 ||~ **spot** ①【医】鼠疫斑 ②瘟疫区 ③道德败坏的征象;罪恶的渊薮

plaice [pleis] *n.* 【动】鲽;太平洋拟庸鲽

plaid [plæd] *n.* ①方格花呢披衣(苏格兰高地人穿的民族服装) ②(苏格兰)方格呢,方格布 ③方格花纹 ||**~ed** *a.* ①穿格子花呢披衣的 ②方格呢制的 ③方格花纹的

plain [plein] Ⅰ *a.* ①清楚的,明白的;平易的: This is ~ to everybody. 这是大家都明白的。 / speak ~ English 讲平易的英语 ②简单的;朴素的;单纯的,不搀杂的: living and hard struggle 艰苦奋斗 ③(景色等)清晰的,无障碍的: be in ~ view (或 sight) 能被清晰看到,一览无遗 ④无装饰的,无花纹的;(图画等)不着色的; 【纺】平(纹)的,素(色)的: ~ cloth 平布,平纹织物 / ~ gauze 纱罗 / ~ bar 【建】素钢筋 / ~ tile 【建】无楞瓦 ⑤坦白的,直率的,爽快的: to be ~ with you [用作插入语]坦白对你讲 / ~ speaking 讲话直率(的) ⑥普通的,平凡的: the ~ people 普通人,一般的人们 / ~ common sense 普通的常识 / ~ language 普通语言;(指电报等中不用电码或密码的)普通文字 ⑦家常的;(相貌等)平常的,不好看的: in ~ clothes 穿着便衣 / a ~ meal 一顿便饭 ⑧十足的,彻底的: ~ cheating 彻头彻尾的欺骗 / The invaders suffered a ~ defeat. 入侵者遭到惨败。 ⑨[古]平的,平坦的 Ⅱ *n.* ①平原,旷野: the Great *Plains* (美国密西西比河流域以西的)大平原 ②[常用复]平(纹)布;素色布 Ⅲ *ad.* 清楚地;平易地: learn to speak ~ 学习简单明了地讲话 Ⅳ *vi.* [古]抱怨(=complain); 哀悼 ||(*as*) ~ *as daylight* (或 *noonday, a pikestaff, the nose in your face*)一清二楚 / ~ *sailing* 见 *sailing* ||**~ly** *ad.* / **~ness** *n.* ||'**~chant** *n.* =~song /

'**~clothes** *a.* 穿便衣的: a ~*clothes* policeman 便衣警察 / '**~'clothesman** *n.* 便衣警察;侦探 / ~ **dealing** 坦白直率(的),光明磊落(的) / ~ **sail** (船上用的)普通帆布 / '**~song** *n.* (基督教仪式中用的)无伴奏齐唱乐 / '**~spoken** *a.* 直言不讳的,坦率的 / ~ **weave** 【纺】平纹组织 / ~ **work** ①平缝 ②(凿平的)石面

plaintiff ['pleintif] *n.* 【律】原告

plaintive ['pleintiv] *a.* 表示哀愁的,表示悲痛的: a ~ melody 哀调 / a ~ cry 哀鸣 ||**~ly** *ad.*

plait [plæt; 美 pleit] Ⅰ *n.* ①褶,裥 ②辫子 ③辫状物 Ⅱ *vt.* ①在(布)上打褶 ②把…编成辫 ③打辫编成

plan [plæn] Ⅰ *n.* ①计划;规划;方案;打算: a five-year ~ 五年计划 / draw up a ~ for increasing production 制订增产计划 / develop socialist economy according to ~ 按计划发展社会主义经济 ②方法,办法: the best ~ to prevent diseases 预防疾病的最好办法 ③进程表,程序表,时间表 ④平面图(=~ view, ~ sheet);设计图,轮廓图,图样;设计: a general ~ 总图 / a working ~ 施工图;工作程序图 ⑤(城、镇、区或公园等的)详图 ||*the American* ~ 美国旅馆收费方式(房金与伙食合计) / a battle ~ 战斗计划 / a campaign ~ 战役计划;竞选活动计划 / *the European* ~ 欧洲旅馆收费方式(房金与伙食分计) / *an instalment* ~ 分期付款的销售方式;分期付款计划 / a perspective ~ 透视图 / a *position indicator* 平面位置雷达指示器(略作 PPI) / a rough ~ 设计草图 / a strategic ~ 战略计划 Ⅱ (planned; planning) ❶ *vt.* ①计划;打算;部署: We're *planning* to start next week. 我们打算下星期出发(或开始)。 / in a *planned* way 有计划地 / ~ (out) a battle 部署战役 ②设计;绘制…的平面图: ~ a theatre (park) 设计剧场(公园) ❷ *vi.* 订计划;想办法 ||~ **on** [口]打算,想要

plane¹ [plein] Ⅰ *n.* ①平面: a horizontal ~ 水平面 / an inclined ~ 斜面 / a ~ of reflection 反射平面 ②程度;水平;阶段,级: The talks between the two countries will be held on a higher ~. 两国之间的谈判将在更高一级举行。 ③飞机(aeroplane 的缩略): a reconnaissance ~ 侦察机 / a jet ~ 喷气机 ④【空】机翼: elevating ~ 升降翼 / tail ~ 尾翼 / ~ cell 翼组 Ⅱ *a.* 平的,平坦的;平面的: a ~ angle 平面角 / a ~ curve 平面曲线 / a ~ figure 平面图 Ⅲ *vi.* ①翱翔 ②(水上飞机等高速运动时)在水面滑行,在水面掠过 ③乘飞机飞行 ||~ **geometry** 平面几何 / ~ **table** (测量用)平板仪,平板绘图器

plane² [plein] Ⅰ *n.* ①刨 ②(泥水工的)镘 Ⅱ ❶ *vt.* ①刨平 ~ sth. smooth 把某物刨平 ②刨掉(*down, away*) ③[古]弄平,使平滑: ~ the way 把路弄平 ❷ *vi.* 刨: a *planing* machine 刨床;刨机 ||**~r** *n.* ①刨;刨床;刨工 ②刨路机;路刮;(地面)整平机

plane³ [plein] **n.** 悬铃木属树木（包括法国梧桐、美国梧桐等）(=~ tree)

planet ['plænit] **n.** 行星: superior ~s 外行星 / inferior ~s 内行星 / major ~s 大行星 / minor ~s 小行星 ‖**~-struck**, **'~-,stricken a.** ①受行星所变的, 倒霉的(迷信传说中认为行星能带来厄运) ②惊慌失措的, 狼狈的

plank [plæŋk] **I n.** ①板(条); 厚板: a ~ bed 木板床 / a ~ bridge 木板桥 ②木板制成物(如桌、凳、板桥等) ③支持物, 基础: the ~s of a system 制度的基础 ④政纲条目; 政党要点: the main ~ in a country's foreign policy 一个国家对外政策的主要点 **II ❶ vt.** ①在…上铺板 ②[口]放下, 摆下 ③[美口]立即支付 (down, out, up) ④把(鱼、鸡等)摆在板子上再于板上供食 ❷ vi. 睡在木板(或其他硬的表面)上 ‖**burn the ~s** 长走, 久坐 / ~ **it** 睡在木板(或其他硬的表面)上 / **prick for a (soft) ~** (海员用语)找最舒适的卧处 / **walk the ~** ① 蒙着眼在突出舷外的板上行走而掉落海中(十七世纪海盗用以残杀俘虏的一种方法) ② 被迫辞职

plant [plɑːnt] **I n.** ①植物; 作物 ②幼苗; 插枝 ③生长, 发育: in ~ 在生长发育中 / lose ~ 枯死 / miss ~ (种籽)不发芽 ④ 工厂; 车间: a power ~ 发电厂 ⑤(医院、学校等)的全部设备 ⑥[俚]欺诈; 搞欺诈的人; 用以欺诈的东西 ⑦[俚]歹徒的巢穴; 赃物的贮藏所; 隐藏着的赃物 ⑧[俚]间谍; 警探 **II vt.** ①栽种; 播种; 栽培: ~ the slopes to tea (或 ~ tea on the slopes) 在斜坡上种茶树 / ~ seeds 播种 / ~ crops 种庄稼 ②养殖(鱼秧等) ③插(旗子等); 安插(尤指安插间谍、奸细等) ④灌输, 使(思想等)生根 ⑤移植(植物) 殖民(动物) 建立; 设立(城镇、教会等) ⑨殖(民); 移居于(某一地点) ⑧[俚]编造; 谋划(诡计等): a ~ed story 谎言 ⑨[俚](对准目标)给予(打击) ⑩[俚]窝藏(赃物等); 栽(赃): ~ stolen goods on sb. 栽赃于某人 ⑪[俚]布置(人或物)行骗; 埋(沙金等)于矿里诱骗购买者 ⑫抛弃(人) ❷ vi. 种植 ‖**~oneself** ①站立不动 ②找到职位安顿下来 / ~ **out** ①把…移植到户外 ②以一定行距种植(幼苗等) / ~ **food** ①植物养料 ②肥料 / ~ **louse** 蚜虫

plantain ['plæntin] **n.** 【植】 ①车前草 ②大蕉

plantation [plæn'teiʃən] **n.** ①种植园, 大农场: a rubber ~ (或 a ~ of rubber) 橡胶园 / a ~ owner 种植园主 / work on a ~ 在种植园干活 ②栽植; 植树造林; 人造林 ③移民; 殖民; 殖民地; 新开地 ‖**~ song** 旧时北美棉花农场上黑奴所唱的歌

plaque [plɑːk] **n.** ①(用金属、象牙、陶瓷等制的)匾, 饰板 ②襟上饰物; 名誉奖章, 徽章 ③【医】斑; 血小板; 【微】噬菌斑

plasmoquine ['plæzməkwain] **n.** 【药】扑疟喹啉

plaster ['plɑːstə] **I n.** ①(涂墙等用的)灰泥 ②硬膏; 膏药: put a ~ on a sore 贴膏药于患处 / adhesive ~ 橡皮膏 ③熟石膏: a ~ figure 石膏

像 / ~ of Paris 烧石膏, 熟石膏 **II vt.** ①在…上涂灰泥; 厚厚地涂抹: The child rose from the ground ~ed over with yellow clay. 孩子满身沾着黄泥从地上爬起来。 ②在…上敷贴膏药 ③安慰; 减轻 ④粘贴; 使紧贴: The downpour ~ed his shirt to his body. 倾盆大雨把他的衬衫湿淋淋地贴在身上。 ⑤用熟石膏处理 ⑥在…上加一层掩饰(或装饰); 在…上过多地放上(或贴上) ⑦重创(敌手等) ‖**~ed a.** [美俚]喝醉的 / ~**er** ['plɑːstərə] **n.** 涂灰泥工人; 泥水匠 / ~**ing** ['plɑːstəriŋ] **n.** ①涂灰泥; 敷石膏 ②灰泥面; 石膏层 ③重创 / ~**y** ['plɑːstəri] **a.** 灰泥状的 ‖**'~-board n.** 糊墙纸板, 灰胶纸柏板 / ~ **cast** 石膏模型; 石膏绷带 / ~ **stone** (生)石膏

plastic ['plæstik, 'plɑːstik] **I a.** ①可塑的, 塑性的; 粘的: a ~ substance 可塑物质 / ~ deformation 塑性变形 / a ~ explosive 可塑炸药(在正常温度下可塑成任何形状) / a ~ state 粘态 ②塑料的; 塑料制的, 合成树脂做的: a ~ tablecloth 塑料台布 ③造型的, 塑造的; 产生立体感的: the ~ arts 造型艺术, 塑造术(指雕塑、陶瓷器制造等) / a ~ figure in painting 画中产生立体感的图像 ④柔顺的, 易受影响的: the ~ affections of children 孩子们易受影响的感情 ⑤有形成力的, 有创造力的: the ~ forces in nature 自然界的创造力 ⑥【医】整形的, 成形的, 修补的: a ~ operation 整形(或成形)手术 / ~ surgery 整形(或成形)外科(学) ⑦【生】有适应力的; 能进行新陈代谢的, 形成活组织的 **II n.** ①[常用复]塑料, 塑料制品: the ~s industry 塑料工业 ②[~s][用作单或复]【医】整形外科, 成形外科 ‖**~ally ad.**

plate [pleit] **I n.** ①(金属)板, 片, 盘; 钢板(常指厚度在六毫米以上的) ②金属牌子(尤指刻有居住人姓名等的黄铜门牌) ③制铠甲的金属片, 装甲板; 铠甲 ④【印】印版; 图版; (书中用另一种纸张印刷的)插图 ⑤[总称]金银餐具; 镀金(或镀银)餐具: silver ~ 银餐具 / a piece of ~ 一件餐具 ⑥盘子, 盆子: a dinner ~ 餐盘 / a soup ~ 汤盆 ⑦(一)满盘; (一)盘菜; 一道正菜; 一顿饭菜: a ~ of strawberries 一盘草莓 / a fruit ~ 一道水果 / a dinner at fifty cents a ~ 五角钱一客的饭菜 ⑧(教堂中的)捐款盘, 奉献盘 ⑨(幼虫的)盾片; (鱼的)棱鳞 ⑩【建】(墙顶承梁用的以及窗框套顶或底部的)横木板: wall (或 roof) ~ 承梁板 ⑪假牙托; 一副假牙 ⑫【电】(电子管的)屏极, 阳极; (蓄电池的)极板; 电容器板 ⑬【摄】底片, 感光板 ⑭=~ rail ⑮【微】平皿, 培养皿 ⑯(棒球中的)本垒; 体育比赛(尤指赛马); 金(或银)奖杯 **II vt.** ①镀; 电镀: a silver ~d spoon 镀银匙 ②给(船体等)装镀板; 给…装甲 ③[印]给…制铅版(或电铸版) ④用板固定 ‖**foul a ~ with** 和…共餐 / **read one's ~** [美俚] ①做饭前祷告 ②埋着头不声不响地吃饭 ‖**~ful n.** (一)满盘 / ~ **basket** (放叉、匙等的)餐具篮 / ~ **glass** (制镜子或商店橱窗等用

的)厚玻璃板 / '~͵holder n.【摄】干片夹,硬片夹 / ~ iron 熨板,铁板,铁皮 / '~͵layer n. (铁路的)铺路工,养路工 / ~ mark ①证明金银等纯度的印记 ②印刷时印版边部的凹凸记号在湿纸上压出的印记 / ~ powder 擦银粉 / ~ printing 铜版(或锌版)印刷 / ~ rack 餐具架 / ~ rail ①[主英]钣轨(一种早期的铁轨) ②壁上供竖着安放盘、盆或装饰物的狭长架子 / ~ wheel [机]盘轮

plateau ['plætou, plæ'tou] **I** ([复] plateaus 或 plateaux ['plætouz, plæ'touz]) *n.* ①高原 ②【心】学习高原(指学习上无进步也无退步的一段);平稳时期,停滞时期: reach a ~ 开始停滞不前 ③(作摆设用的)碟,托盘;[墙等上的]饰匾 ④平顶女帽 **II** *vi.* 达到稳定的时期(或状态)

platform ['plætfɔːm] **I** *n.* ①平台;台: ~ deck 【船】平台甲板 / launching ~【宇】发射台 ②(铁路等的)站台,月台;[美](火车、电车上的)乘客上下平台: a ~ ticket 月台票 / a ~ bridge 天桥 ③讲台;戏台 ④【军】炮手站台;炮床;【地】地台,台地;【油】(海洋钻井的)栈桥 ⑤(政党等的)党纲,政纲;宣言 **II** [the ~] (讲坛) **II** *vt.* ① 把…放在台上 ② 为…设月台 ❷ *vi.* (在台上)演讲 ‖*be at home on the* ~ 善于(或惯于)说议 ‖ **car** (铁路的)平板货车 / ~ **scale**, ~ **balance** 台秤 / ~ **truck** 平板大卡车

platinum ['plætinəm] *n.*【化】铂,白金 ‖ **black** 铂黑,铂墨 / ~ **blonde** 有淡黄色头发的(女)人 / ~ **sponge** 铂绵

platitude ['plætitjuːd] *n.* ① 老生常谈,平凡的话,陈词滥调 ②平凡,陈腐

platter ['plætə] *n.* ① 大浅盘(通常为椭圆形) ②[俚](留声机)唱片 ③[俚](棒球中的)本垒 ‖*on a* ~ ①用盘子奉上 ②现成地;不费力地

plaudit ['plɔːdit] *n.* [常用复] 拍手;喝采;称赞,赞扬

plausible ['plɔːzəbl] *a.* ① 似乎有理的,似乎可能的 ②嘴巧的,善于花言巧语的 ‖ **plausibility** [͵plɔːzə-'biliti] *n.* / **plausibly** *ad.*

play [plei] **I** ❶ *vi.* ① 玩,游戏;装扮;假装: The kids are ~ing in the nursery garden. 孩子们在托儿所的花园内玩耍。/ The children are ~ing at catching a spy. 孩子们在做抓特务的游戏。/ ~ dead 装死(躺下) ② 开玩笑;嘲弄;(对人或物)玩弄: ~ at sb. in print 用文字嘲弄某人 / ~ with sb. 开某人的玩笑(或玩弄某人) / Whoever ~s with fire gets burnt. 玩火者必自焚。③ 进行体育(或文娱)比赛: Our team ~ed in several major games last month. 我队上月参加了好几次大的比赛。/ ~ at chess 下棋 / ~ at basketball 打篮球 ④演奏,弹(或吹)奏;(乐器)奏鸣: ~ on the violin 拉小提琴(现在通常用 ~ the violin) / We heard an organ ~ing. 我们听见有人在弹风琴。⑤表演,(戏剧等)演出: What's ~ing at the

theatre? 剧场里在演什么戏? ⑥(乐器)适于吹奏(或弹奏);(戏剧等)适于演出: The new piano ~s well. 这架新钢琴弹起来很好。/ That drama will ~. 那出戏适宜上演。⑦赌博: ~ for money 赌钱 ⑧ 跳来蹦去;闪动;飘动,飞舞;浮现: Flashes of lightning ~ed across the sky. 空中电光闪闪。/ Sea gulls ~ed about the ship. 海鸥围着船只翱翔。/ A smile ~ed on (或 about) his lips. 他嘴上露出一丝微笑。/ His imagination ~ed that queer idea. 他老是想着那个怪念头。⑨ (机器部件等)运转自如: The piston can be heard ~ing within the cylinder at a moderate speed. 可以听到活塞在汽缸内以不快的速度往返运动着。⑩(唱片、录音机等)放音: a record ~ing at a rate of 转速为…的唱片 / a long-~ing record 慢转唱片;密纹唱片 ⑪(接连)发射;(泉水等)喷射;(光)照射 (*on, over, along*): Scores of hoses ~ed on the flames. 几十根水龙带向火喷水。⑫发生影响: See that direct heat does not ~ on it. 当心别让它直接受热。⑬[方]怠工,罢工 ❷ *vt.* ① 做(游戏),玩;装扮: ~ cards 玩牌 / ~ the hero 逞英雄 / ~ the despot 称王称霸 ②开(玩笑);嘲弄,愚弄;耍(花样等),玩弄: ~ a joke on sb. 对某人开玩笑 / ~ sb. a dirty trick 对某人玩弄卑劣的手段 / ~ tricks with sb.'s tools 胡乱使用某人的工具 ③玩(球戏等),打(球),踢(球);同…比赛;使上场: ~ football 踢足球 / ~ a friendly match 举行友谊比赛 / Will you ~ me at chess? 你同我下一盘棋好吗? / We are ~ing the cadre school team next Sunday. 下星期日我们将同干校代表队比赛。/ The coach ~ed him at centre. 教练叫他担任中锋。④ 演奏,弹(或吹)奏;奏乐迎(或送): ~ *The Internationale* on the piano 用钢琴演奏《国际歌》/ Does she ~ the flute? 她会吹笛子吗? / Won't you ~ us some folk songs? 你给我们奏些民歌好吗? / ~ sb. home 一路奏乐把某人送回家 ⑤扮演;演出,上演于(某地、某剧场等) ⑥赌,与(某人)打赌,对(赛马等)打赌;打出(牌)走(一着棋子): ~ a trump 打出王牌 / ~ a pawn 走小卒 ⑦使跳动,使闪动,使飘动: ~ a flashlight *upon* 用手电在…上闪照 ⑧(接连)发射;使(泉水等)喷射: ~ guns *on* the enemy lines 向敌人阵地接连开炮 ⑨ (灵敏地或用劲地)使用,挥舞(刀、剑等): ~ a good fork and knife 大吃 / ~ a good stick 舞得一手好剑 ⑩利用;操纵,摆布: ~ sb. for selfish ends 为了私利而利用某人

⑪(耍手腕)对待, 对付: ~ the conversation in a gay manner (故作)谈笑风生 / He ~ed me just the way I had expected. 他以我所预料到的那种手段来对付我。

⑫(恶作剧地)造成, 引起: ~ havoc 造成破坏

⑬让上钩的(鱼)不停地拉动钓线而致疲乏

II *n.* ①游戏, 玩耍; 消遣: The children are *at* ~. 孩子们在玩耍。/ It is mere child's ~ to him. 这事对他说来极为容易。

②玩笑; 玩弄; 调戏; 花样, 把戏: He said it *in* ~. 他这样说只是开玩笑罢了。/ a ~ *of* words 文字游戏, 玩弄词藻 / a ~ *on* (或 *upon*) words 双关语; 俏皮话

③(体育)运动; 比赛作风(或进程): rough ~ (比赛时)粗野的作风 / It's your ~. 该你走棋了。(或: 轮到你打球(或发球)了。)

④剧本, 戏剧; 表演: a ~ *in* five acts 五幕剧 / go to the ~ 看戏去

⑤赌博, [美俚]一次赌局的赌注总数

⑥跳动; 闪动; 飘动; 波动: the ~ *of* colours 彩色缤纷/[矿]变彩, 变色 / the ~ *of* waves 浪的起伏 / the ~ *of* wind 风的吹拂

⑦(对刀剑或工具等灵巧的)使用, 挥舞

⑧活动的范围(或余地); 作用, (才智等的)运用; [机]间隙, 游动, 游隙: Give the rope more ~. 把绳子放松些。/ The new rising forces are in full ~. 新生力量在充分发挥作用。/ free ~ 空转; 齿隙 / end ~ 端隙

⑨交易; (投机性)企业: a land ~ 地产交易 / an oil ~ 石油企业

⑩停止工作(指罢工等)

‖*allow* full ~ *to* 使充分活动(或发挥) / *as good as a* ~ (象戏剧那样)有趣味的 / *bring* (或 *call*) *into* ~ 发挥, 发扬; 发动, 调动: bring all positive factors *into* ~ 调动一切积极因素 / *come into* ~ 开始活动(或起作用) / *fair* ~ ①公平的(或按照规则的)比赛 ②[喻]公平对待, 条件均等; 光明磊落 / *foul* ~ ①不公平的(或犯规的)比赛 ②[喻]不公平; 奸诈; 暴行(如谋杀等) / *give free* ~ *to* 使任意活动(或发挥): give free ~ to one's emotions 发泄感情 / *high* ~ 大赌, 下大笔赌注的赌博 / *hold* (或 *keep*) *in* ~ 牵制(敌人等) / *in* ~ ①开玩笑地 ②在赌博中 ③(纸牌)尚在手中未打出 ④(球赛中用语)不是死球(即按规则可继续比赛) / *make a* ~ *for* [口]挖空心思吸引(某人); 想尽办法获得(某物) / *make* ~ 行动有效; 激得落后者(或追逐者)用劲赶(尤指赛马、打猎等时) / *out of* ~ (球赛中用语)死球(即按规则须暂停比赛) / ~ *a lone hand* 见 **hand** / ~ *along with* 参与; 与…合作: ~ along with sb.'s plot 参与某人的阴谋 / ~ *a part* 见 **part** / ~ *at* ①做(游戏), 打(球、牌等), 下(棋); 参加(比赛); 以…消遣 ②假装 / ~ *away* ①(球队)在外地比赛 ②赌输掉(钱等); 浪费(时间、精力等) / ~ *back* 播放(录音带、唱片) /

ball 见 **ball**[1] / ~ *booty* 见 **booty** / ~ *both ends against the middle* 见 **end** / ~ *by ear* 见 **ear**[1] / ~ *down* 降低; 贬低; 减弱; 缩小: ~ down the tune 降低调子 / ~ *down* one's massive image 藏头纳尾避免招摇 / ~ *ducks and drakes* 见 **duck**[1] / ~ *fast and loose* 玩弄, 反复无常 / ~ *first* (*second*) *fiddle* 见 **fiddle** / ~ *for time* 为争取时间而拖延 / ~ *hard* 行为卑鄙, 不择手段/ ~ *high* 进行输赢很大的赌博 / ~ *hookey* [美俚]逃学 / ~ . . . *in* (*out*) 奏乐迎…进场(送…出场) / ~ *into the hands of sb.* 见 **hand** / ~ *it* (*low*) *on* (或 (*low*) *down on*) [俚]用卑鄙手段欺骗… / ~ *off* ①使暴露弱点, 使出丑; 嘲弄 ②把…冒充; 把…假装 / ~ . . . *off against one another* (或 *each other*) 在…之间挑拨离间(从中渔利) / ~ *off a match* (或 *a draw, a tie*) (平局后)再赛以决胜负 / ~ *one's cards well* 见 **card**[1] / ~ *opposite* 演与(主角)相对的异性角色: He ~ed opposite her. 他与她分演男女主角。/ ~ *out* ①把(戏)演完; 把(比赛)进行到底 ②放出, 放松(绳索等) ③[喻]使筋疲力尽; 用完; 使输光, 使破产; 使成为无用(或过时): The pie was ~ed out. 馅饼吃完了。/ ~ *safe* 求稳, 不冒险 / ~ *sb.'s game* 见 **game**[1] / ~ *smash with* [美俚]摧毁…, 打碎 … / ~ *the deuce with* 弄糟…, 有害于…; 使失败 / ~ *the game* 见 **game**[1] / ~ *the man* 见 **man** / ~ *the market* 见 **market** / ~ *truant* 见 **truant** / ~ *up* ①[尤用于祈使句](在比赛等中)加油, 用劲 ②开始奏乐 ③使恼火 ④[口]大肆宣扬, 鼓吹; 渲染 / ~ *upon* (或 *on*) (狡猾地或不择手段地)利用: ~ upon sb.'s fears (credulity) 利用某人的恐惧(轻信) / ~ *up to* ①(在演戏中)同…配合得好; 支持 ②[口]向…讨好, 巴结, 奉承 / *see fair* ~ 公平裁判; 公平对待, 公平处理

‖**~act** *vi.* ①表演 ②装扮; 假装, 装腔作势 *vt.* 演出, 表演 / **'~,acting** *n.* ①演戏 ②装扮; 假装 / **'~,actor** *n.* 演员 / **'~back** *n.* (录音等的)播放, 放音; 放像; 放音(或放像)设备 / **'~bill** *n.* 演出海报; 剧场节目单 / **'~book** *n.* 剧本, 剧本集 / **'~box** *n.* 玩具箱; 私人用品箱(尤指寄宿学校中的) / **'~boy** *n.* 花花公子, 追求享乐者 / **'~-by-'~** *a.* ①(比赛时)现场报道评述的 ②详细叙述的, 详尽的 / **'~day** *n.* ①(学校)假日 ②[英](矿工等非例假日的)休息日 ③(几所学校运动员混合组成的各队之间的)非正式比赛/ ~ *debt* [古]赌债 / **'~,fellow** *n.* 游戏的伙伴 / **'~game** *n.* 儿戏, 不足道的事 / **'~,goer** *n.* 经常看戏的人, 戏迷 / **'~ground** *n.* (学校的)操场, 运动场; (儿童)游戏场: The students were all in the ~ground. 学生们都在操场上。/ the ~ground *of* Europe 欧洲游乐场(指瑞士) / **'~-house** *n.* ①剧场 ②儿童游戏室 / **'~land** *n.* =~ground / **'~,mate** *n.* =~fellow / **'~off** *n.* (因不分胜负而进行的)延长赛; (实力最强的运动队之间的)锦标赛 / **'~pen** *n.* 供婴孩在内

爬着玩的携带式围栏 / '~**room** *n.* ①儿童游戏室 ②文娱活动室 / '~**suit** *n.* (妇女、儿童穿的)运动衫,运动裤 / ~**therapy**【心】演剧疗法; 游戏疗法 / '~**thing** *n.* 玩具; 被玩弄的人,玩物 / '~**time** *n.* 游玩(或娱乐)时间 / '~**wright** *n.* 剧作家 / '~,**writing** *n.* 剧本创作

playful ['pleiful] *a.* ① 爱玩耍的, 嬉笑的; 顽皮的: a ~ kitten 顽皮的小猫 ②开玩笑的, 幽默的, 滑稽的: in a ~ manner 开玩笑地 ‖~**ly** *ad.* / ~**ness** *n.*

plea [pli:] *n.* ①【律】抗辩;[古]诉讼: a special ~ 特殊抗辩(被告接受原告的指控,但提出特殊的或新的情况使诉讼不能成立) / the Court of Common *Pleas* (英国的)高等民事法庭;(美国某些州的)中级民事及刑事法庭 ②托词, 口实: under (或 on) the ~ of a headache 借口头痛 ③请愿, 恳求, 请求: make a ~ for aid 恳求援助 ‖**cop a** ~ [美俚]为避免查出后遭重罚而自己招认有罪; 避重就轻地认罪

plead [pli:d] (pleaded 或 pled [pled]) ❶ *vt.* ① 为(案件)辩护: ~ a client's case 为某一当事人的案子辩护 ② 以…作为答辩, 以…为理由, 以…为借口: ~ ignorance 以不知道情况为借口 / He ~ed illness as the reason for his absence. 他以生病作为缺席的理由。❷ *vi.* ①辩护, 抗辩; 申明: ~ for sb. 为某人辩护 / ~ against sb. 反驳某人 / ~ guilty (to a crime) 服罪 / ~ not guilty (或 ~ unguilty) 不服罪 ②恳求: ~ (with sb.) for mercy 恳求(某人)宽恕 ‖~**able** *a.* 可辩护的, 可作为抗辩的理由的 / ~**er** *n.* 抗辩人; 辩护律师; 代为求情者

pleasant ['pleznt] *a.* ① 令人愉快的, 舒适的, 合意的: ~ weather 令人愉快的天气 / enjoy sb.'s company 跟某人在一起很愉快 / be ~ to the eye 悦目 / be ~ to the taste 可口 ②举止文雅的; 外貌悦人的 ③[古]滑稽的 ‖~**ly** *ad.* / ~**ness** *n.*

please [pli:z] ❶ *vt.* ①使高兴; 使喜欢; 使中意: The children's performance ~d the audience. 孩子们的演出使观众很满意。 / a picture that ~s the eye 悦目的图画 / It ~d him to do so. 他喜欢这样做。 / a person hard to ~ 难以讨好的人 ②[用于祈使语气]请: Please come in. (或 Come in, ~.) 请进来。 / Please don't laugh. 请不要笑。 / Will you ~ pass me the pencil? 请把铅笔递给我好吗? / Those in favour of the suggestion ~ sign your names. 赞成这个建议的人请签名。 ❷ *vi.* ①满意, 中意; 讨人喜欢, 讨好: be anxious to ~ 急于讨好 ②欢喜, 愿意: *if you* ~ ①请; 对不起: I will have another cup of tea, *if you* ~. 对不起,请再来一杯茶。 ②你看(怪不怪), 竟然: The missing letter was in his pocket, *if you* ~! 你看怪不怪,那封遗失的信竟在他口袋里哩! / ~ *God* 见 **God** / ~ *oneself* 愿意怎样就怎样; 感到满意: *Please yourself.* 请便。 / ~ *the pigs* 见 **pig**

pleased [pli:zd] *a.* ① 高兴的, 喜欢的: I'm ~

meet you. 我很高兴见到你。 / be much ~ *at* the good news 听到好消息很高兴 ② 满意的: We are very ~ *with* his work. 我们对他的工作很满意。 / a ~ look 满意的表情 ‖(*as*) ~ *as Punch* 非常高傲

pleasurable ['pleʒərəbl] *a.* 令人愉快的, 舒适的 ‖~**ness** *n.* / **pleasurably** *ad.*

pleasure ['pleʒə] **I** *n.* ① 愉快, 快乐, 高兴; 满足: It gives me much ~ to hear of your progress. 听到你的进步我很高兴。 ②乐事;乐趣: The work is a ~ to me. 这工作对我是件乐事。 / May I have the ~ of going with you? 我可以跟您一起去吗? / Will you do me the ~ of dining with me? 请您跟我一起吃饭好吗? ③ 肉体享乐;放荡(行为): a man of ~ 浪荡子 ④ 愿望, 意向: consult sb.'s ~ 询问(或顾及)某人的意向 / during sb.'s ~ 乘某人高兴时 / Is it your ~ to go at once? 你愿意立刻就去吗? / You may go or stay at your ~. 愿去愿留,随你的便。 **II** ❶ *vt.* 使高兴, 使喜欢, 使满意 ❷ *vi.* ①高兴, 喜欢, 喜爱(*in*) ②追求享乐; 游荡: ~ round (或 around) all day long 整天闲荡 /~ *for* ~ 为了取乐, 作为消遣: It was not *for* ~ that I did it. 我做那件事不是为了消遣。 / take (a) ~ *in* 以…为乐, 喜欢: take ~ *in* the calamity of others 幸灾乐祸 / take ~ *in* playing tennis 喜爱打网球 / *with* ~ ①愉快地, 高兴地: He did the work *with* ~. 那工作他干得很愉快。 ②十分服从: A: Will you play my accompaniment? B: *With* ~. 甲: 请你给我伴奏好吗? 乙: 好的。 ‖~-**boat** *n.* 游船 / ~ **ground** 游乐场, 娱乐场 / ~ **principle**【心】(精神分析中的)快乐原则 / '~-,**seeker** *n.* 追求享乐的人 / '~-,**seeking** *n.* 享乐主义 / ~ **trip** 游览

pleat [pli:t] **I** *n.* 褶; 褶状皱起物 **II** *vt.* ①使成褶: a ~ed skirt 百褶裙 ②把…编成辫;编织

plebeian [pli'bi(:)ən] **I** *n.* ① (古罗马的)平民 ②[蔑]老百姓; 卑贱粗俗的人 **II** *a.* ①平民的, 庶民的 ②卑贱的, 粗俗的 ‖~**ism** *n.* ① 平民特点; 带有平民特点的行为(或言词) ② 粗俗; 卑贱 / ~**ize** *vt.* 使平民化

plebiscite ['plebisit] *n.* ①公民投票 ② (古罗马的)平民表决

pledge [pledʒ] **I** *n.* ① 誓言; 誓约; 保证: make a solemn ~ 庄严宣誓 / redeem one's ~ 履行誓言,践约 / be under ~ of secrecy 誓不泄密 ②保证物,信物;象征(物): a ~ of friendship 友谊的信物(或保证) / a ~ of love 爱的象征) ③抵押(品); 典当(物); 保人,保证人: be in ~ 在抵押中,典当着 / put (或 lay) sth. in ~ 以某物作抵押,典当某物 / take sth. out of ~ 赎回某物 ④ 祝酒,干杯 ⑤立誓加入秘密社团的人 **II** *vt.* ①使发誓; 保证; 决心(做): be (或 stand) ~d to a cause 立誓忠于一项事业 / ~ oneself to fulfilling the task ahead of time 保证提前完成任务 / ~ one's honour (或 word) 发誓, 保证

one's resolute support for 对…保证予以坚决支持 / I have ~d to do my best. 我已保证尽最大努力。②抵押；典当: the ~d assets 出质资产 ③向…祝酒；为…干杯 ‖*take* (或 *sign, keep*) *the* ~ 发誓戒酒 ‖**pledgee** [ple'dʒi:] *n.* 接受抵押(或典当)的人 / **pledg(e)or** *n.* 抵押者，典当者 / **~r** *n.* (戒酒等的)发誓人；举杯祝酒的人

plenary ['pli:nəri] *a.* ①完全的，充分的；绝对的: ~ powers 全权 ②全体出席的: a ~ session (或 meeting) 全体会议 ‖ **indulgence**【天主教】大赦 / ~ **inspiration**【宗】完全灵感

plenipotentiary [,plenipə'tenʃəri] **I** *n.* 全权委任的人；全权大使；全权大臣 **II** *a.* 有全权的: an ambassador extraordinary and ~ 特命全权大使 / an envoy extraordinary and minister ~ 特命全权公使

plenteous ['plentjəs] *a.* [诗]丰富的，丰硕的: ~ crops 丰收 / a ~ year 丰年

plentiful ['plentiful] *a.* 富裕的，丰裕的；多的: a ~ supply of food 充裕的食品供应 ‖**~ly** *ad.* / **~ness** *n.*

plenty ['plenti] **I** *n.* 丰富，充足；大量: live in ~ 生活富裕 / There are good books in ~. 好书多得很。 / There is ~ of time. 时间很充裕。 / There are ~ of eggs in the basket. 篮里鸡蛋多得很。 / That will give you ~ to do. 那样一来你可有许多事情干了。 **II** *a.* 很多的；足够的: Six will be ~. 六个足够了。 **III** *ad.* [口]充分地，十分: It is ~ big enough. 这足够大了。

pleurisy ['pluərisi] *n.*【医】胸膜炎，肋膜炎

pliable ['plai-əbl] *a.* ①易弯的，柔韧的: the ~ twigs of willows 杨柳的柔条 ②柔顺的，顺从的；圆通的 ③能适应的 ‖**pliability** [,plai-ə'biliti] *n.* 柔韧(性)；柔顺(性)；能适应(性) / **pliably** *ad.*

pliers ['plaiəz] [复] *n.* [用作单或复]钳子，老虎钳，手钳: a pair of ~ 一把钳子 / cutting ~ 剪钳

plight[1] [plait] *n.* 境况；困境，苦境: be in a sorry (或 pitiable, wretched) ~ 处境困窘

plight[2] [plait] **I** *vt.* 保证；给…订婚: one's ~d word 某人的誓言 / ~ oneself to sb. 和某人订婚 **II** *n.* 誓约；婚约

plinth [plinθ] *n.*【建】底座，勒脚；柱础

plod [plɔd] **I** (plodded; plodding) **❶** *vi.* ①沉重缓慢地走 (on, along) ②努力从事；沉闷地苦干: ~ away at one's work 苦苦地干活 **❷** *vt.* 沉重缓慢地走(路): one's weary way back 拖着疲乏的步子走回去 **II** *n.* ①沉重缓慢的脚步(或脚步声) ②沉闷的苦干 ‖**plodder** *n.* ①拖着沉重步子走的人 ②沉闷苦干的人: a routine *plodder* 忙忙碌碌的事务主义者

plot [plɔt] **I** *n.* ①小块土地，小块地皮: an experimental ~ of cotton 一块棉花试验田 ②基址 ③标绘图；地区图 ④情节: The ~ thickens. 情节渐渐复杂起来了。 / a novel almost without ~ 几乎没有什么情节的长篇小说 ⑤秘密计划；阴谋 **II** (plotted; plotting) **❶** *vt.* ①把…划成小块地；划分: ~ out one's time 分配自己的时间 ②标绘，绘制…的图: ~ a ship's course on a chart 把一艘船的航线标绘在航海图上 ③测定(点、线)的位置；作图表示(方程式) ④为(文学作品)设计情节 ⑤密谋，策划: ~ a conspiracy 搞阴谋 / ~ treason 谋反 **❷** *vi.* ①密谋，策划: ~ for sb.'s assassination (或 ~ against sb.'s life) 阴谋暗杀某人 ②设计作品情节

plough [plau] **I** *n.* ①犁: a two-wheeled double-share ~ 双轮双铧犁 ②犁过的地；耕地: 200 *mu* of ~ 两百亩耕地 ③犁形器具；雪犁，扫雪机；【矿】煤犁，刨煤机；【建】路犁; (木工的)沟刨；【印】手动切书机: an ice ~ 切冰机 / an activated ~ 动力刨煤机 ④[the P-]【天】北斗七星 ⑤[英俚](主考人评定)不及格 **II** **❶** *vt.* ①犁，耕: ~ (up) the field 犁田 / ~ out the weeds 犁除杂草 / ~ up the roots 用犁翻根 ②用犁掘(畦)，挖(沟、槽)；刨(煤),用刨煤机采(煤) ③[喻]使起皱纹: a face ~ed with wrinkles 有皱纹的脸 ③开(路)，破(浪): The prospecting team ~ed their way through the snows. 勘探队排雪前进。 / Our gunboats ~ed the waves. 我军炮艇破浪前进。 ④投(资): ~ a hefty sum into a project 对一项工程进行巨额投资 ⑤[英俚]使考试不及格 **❷** *vi.* ①犁，耕；用犁: the season for spring ~ing 春耕时节 / deep ~ing and intensive cultivation 深耕细作 ②可耕: The field ~s well after the rain. 雨后土地易耕。 ③开路；跋涉；[喻]钻研: ~ through the mud 在泥泞中跋涉 / ~ through one's studies 刻苦学习 ‖*follow the ~* 种田，务农 / *~ a lonely furrow* 见 **furrow** / *~ around* [美俚]试探 / *~ back* 把(草等)犁入土中(作肥料) / [喻]把(利润)再投资 / *~ into* 干劲十足地投入(工作等) / *~ the sand*(s) 见 **sand** / *~ under* 使消失；埋葬掉；压倒 / *put* (或 *set*) *one's hand to the* ~ 见 **hand** ‖**~boy** *n.* ①牵引耕畜的孩子 ②农家孩子 / '**~land** *n.* ①(一块)耕地；可耕地 ②【英史】可耕地面积单位 (约合八头牛一年中可耕的面积) / **~man** ['plaumən] *n.* ①把犁人 ②庄稼汉 / '**~share** *n.* 犁铧，犁头 / '**~staff** *n.* (清除犁铧上泥土等用的)小铲 / '**~tail** *n.* 犁柄；[喻]农活，耕作: at the ~tail 种田，务农 / '**~wright** *n.* 制犁(或修犁)的人

pluck [plʌk] **I** **❶** *vt.* ①采，摘，拔: ~ tea 采茶 / ~ apples 摘苹果 / feathers from a hen 拔下母鸡的毛 ②拔…的毛: ~ a chicken 拔去鸡的毛 ③扯，拉: ~ the notice down from the wall 从墙上撕下布告 / ~ aside the curtain 拉开帷幕(或窗帘) / ~ the paper to pieces 把纸扯碎 / ~ sb. by the sleeve to catch his attention 拉拉某人的衣袖引起注意 ④拨；弹: ~ the strings of a guitar 拨吉他的弦 / a *pi-pa* 弹琵琶 ⑤拆毁 (down): ~ down a cabin 把小木屋拆去 ⑥杀…的威风 (down) ⑦[俚]诈骗 ⑧[英]不录取: He was (或 got) ~ed in the examination. 他没考上。⑨使(军官)退伍; 调动…的职务(尤指提升) ⑩【地】(冰川)冲走(岩石), 拔成 ❷ vi. 拉, 拽; 想抓住 (at): ~ at the chance 抢机会 Ⅱ n. ①(一)拉, (一)拖, (一)扯 ②(家畜等供食用的)内脏 ③采(或摘、拔、扯)下的东西; 拨弹的工具: a ~ of wool 拔下的一把羊毛 / the ~ for the guitar (套在手指上的)吉他拨弹器 ④精神, 勇气: be full of ~ 很有勇气 ⑤[英](考试的)不及格 ⑥(图画等的)鲜明, 清晰 ‖*have a crow to ~ with sb.* 见 **crow**[1] / ~ *a pigeon* 见 **pigeon**[1] / ~ *up* ① 鼓起, 振作; 振作精神 = ~ *up one's courage* 鼓起勇气 ② 拔起: ~ *up a tree* 把一棵树连根拔起 ‖~*less a.* 没有勇气的, 没胆量的

plug [plʌg] Ⅰ n. ① 塞子, 栓; 堵塞物(如龋齿的填齿料) ②【电】插头; 针形接点: insert the ~ in the socket 把插头插入插座 ③(内燃机的)火花塞 ④ 消防龙头, 消防栓 ⑤(压制的)扁形烟草块, 口嚼烟草块 ⑥拳击; [俚]拳术 ⑦[俚]拳术: take a ~ at a tiger 向虎射击 ⑦(切下作为样品的)心子, 楔形块 ⑧【地】岩颈 ⑨[俚]广告(尤指插入电台节目中的); 捧场; 推荐: put in a ~ for 为…做广告, 为…作宣传 ⑩ 不中用的东西 (尤指年老无力的马); 安稳沉着的马 (通常指轻的或中等重量的) ⑪(配有一组或数组钩钓的)人造鱼饵 ⑫[美俚](男子用)高顶礼帽 (= ~ hat) ⑬[英](抽水马桶的)抽水装置 Ⅱ (plugged; plugging) ❶ vt. ① 塞, 堵 (up): He used his body to ~ up a hole in the dyke. 他用身体堵住水堤的裂口。②[俚]枪击; 拳打 ③ [俚]大肆宣传(某一歌曲、理论、政策等) ④从(西瓜等)上切下一楔形小块以鉴定质量 ❷ vi. ①被塞住, 被堵住 (up) ②[口]苦干: ~ away at one's work 埋头干活 ③[俚]枪击; 拳打 (at) ‖~ *in* (使)插上插头以接通电源: ~ *in the wireless set* 使收音机接通电源 ‖~ **cock**【机】旋塞 / ~ **cord**【电】① 插头(软)线 ② 塞绳 / **fuse**【电】插塞式熔丝, 插入式保险丝 / '~*-in a.* 【电】插入式的, 组合式的, 带插头接点的

plum [plʌm] n. ①李属植物; 洋李; 梅: ~ *rains* 【气】梅雨 / (用于布丁及糕中的)葡萄干: ~ *pudding* 葡萄干布丁 ③ 糖果 ④ 最好的东西, 佳品(如书中的一段精彩文章); 期望得到的东西(尤指待遇好的职位), 美缺 ⑤梅红色 ⑥[古]十万英镑 ⑦意外的财产增值; 意外的金钱收益 ⑧ 混凝土用毛石块

plumage ['plu:midʒ] n. ①羽衣, (鸟的)全身羽毛 ②漂亮精致的衣服

plumb [plʌm] Ⅰ n. 铅锤, 测锤, 垂球: out of ~ (或 off ~) 不垂直的 Ⅱ a. ①垂直的: The wall is ~. 这墙是垂直的。②[口]完全的, 绝对的: It's ~ nonsense. 这全是胡说八道。Ⅲ ad. ①垂直地: fall ~ down 垂直地落下 ②恰恰; 正: southwards 正南, 向正西 ③[主方]完全 Ⅳ ❶ vt. ① 用铅锤测量 ②用铅锤校正…的垂直度; 使垂直: ~ a wall 使墙垂直 ③ 探测, 查明; 了解: sb.'s motives 探测某人的动机 ④ 灌铅以增加…

的重量; 用铅封: The trunk was ~ed by the inspector. 箱子被检查员加上铅封。⑤给…装设铅管: ~ the new building 给新建的大楼装设铅管 ❷ vi. ①垂直: The mast ~s perfectly. 这桅杆是完全垂直的。②做(铅)管工 ‖~*less a.* 深不可测的 / ~ **bob** 铅锤, 测锤, 垂球 / ~ **line** 铅垂线; 准绳 / '~*-line vt.* ①用铅垂线检查…的垂直度; 用铅垂线测量 ②探测, 检查 / ~ **rule** 【建】垂规

plumber ['plʌmə] n. ①管子工; 铅管工 ②[美](调查政府人员泄密情况的)堵漏防漏人员 ‖~ **block** 【机】轴台

plumbing ['plʌmiŋ] n. ①铅锤测量 ②铅管业; 管子工作 ③[总称]管件 ④[the ~]抽水马桶

plume [plu:m] Ⅰ n. ①羽毛; 大羽, 正羽; 羽衣 ②羽饰 ③多毛的尾; 羽状物; 【植】羽状部: a ~ of smoke 一缕烟 ④[喻]荣誉的标志; 奖品 Ⅱ vt. ① (鸟)整理(羽毛); [~ itself] (鸟)整理羽毛; [~ oneself] 打扮 ②用羽毛装饰, 翎饰 ③[~ oneself] 自夸, 自矜; 自庆: He does not ~ himself on these achievements. 他并不因这些成就而自夸。④ 使成羽毛状; 在…内形成羽毛状物: The locomotive ~d steam. 火车头喷出一缕缕蒸汽。/ The chimney ~d the sky. 烟囱把出一大股烟喷入空中。‖*borrowed ~s* 向别人借来的漂亮衣服; 靠别人得来的期望 / *shear off sb.'s ~s* 砍掉某人盔上的羽毛; 打下某人的威风 ‖~*like a.* 羽毛状的

plump[1] [plʌmp] Ⅰ a. ① 丰满的: a ~ figure 丰满的身段 ②(钱包等)饱满的, 鼓起的 Ⅱ ❶ vt. 使丰满; 使鼓起 (up) ❷ vi. 变丰满; 鼓起 (out, up) ‖~*ly ad.* / ~*ness n.*

plump[2] [plʌmp] Ⅰ ❶ vi. ①扑地地坠下; 猛地触地 ②突然进入 (in); 蓦地冲出 (out) ③投票赞成; 坚决拥护 (for) ④[主英](在规定选举二人或二人以上时)只投票选一人 ❷ vt. ① 扑通地放落: ~ stones into the water 扑通地把石块投入水中 ② 冲口说出 (out) ③为…说好话; 宣扬 Ⅱ n. ①(沉重的)坠落, 坠下; 碰撞 ②突然跳进; 猛冲 ③扑通声; 冲撞声: fall into the stream with a ~ 扑通一声落入河中 Ⅲ a. ① 爽直的; 老实的; 直率的, 直截了当的: a ~ refusal 干脆的拒绝 / answer with a ~ "No" 给予一个直截了当的否定答复 ② 一次付清的 Ⅳ ad. ①扑通一声地, 沉重地: sit down ~ 扑通一声坐下 ②突然, 蓦地 ③直截了当地, 坦白地: Say it out ~! 老实讲出来! ‖~*ly ad.* / ~*ness n.*

plump[3] [plʌmp] n. ① [主方]群; 束; 丛 ②一群水鸟: a ~ of ducks 一群鸭子

plunder ['plʌndə] Ⅰ ❶ vt. ① 掠夺, 劫掠, 抢劫: ~ a country of its resources 掠夺一国的资源 ②掠夺, 劫掠, 抢劫 Ⅱ ❷ vi. 掠夺, 抢劫 Ⅱ n. ① 掠夺, 抢劫; 盗窃 ②掠夺物; 赃物 ③[主方]利润, 收益 ④[主方] 行李; 货物; 配备用品: camping ~ 野营用品 / house ~ 家庭用品 ‖~*able* ['plʌndərəbl] a. 易受掠夺的 / ~*er* ['plʌndərə]

n. 掠夺者; 盗窃者 ‖'**~bund** n. (商业、政治集团或财团联合组成的) 剥削公众利益的集团

plunge [plʌndʒ] **I ❶** vt. ①使投入; 使插入; 使刺进: ~ one's hand into water (a bag) 把手伸进水(袋)中 ②使陷入, 使遭受: ~ sb. into debt 使某人负债 / ~ a country into war 使一个国家陷入战争 / be ~d into poverty 陷入贫困 ③把(栽有植物的盆)埋入地中 ❷vi. ①投(入); 跳(入); 冲: ~ into a swimming pool 跳入游泳池 / ~ up (down) stairs 冲上(下)楼梯 ②陷(入): ~ into a difficulty 陷入困境 ③ 下降, 急降; (道路、坡度等)陡峭地下倾 ④ (船只)颠簸; (马等)猛烈前冲 ⑤[口]盲目投资(或投机); 滥赌; 负债 **II** n. ①投身入水的地方; 游泳池 ②跳水; 游水 ③跳水落下; 下跌: the downward ~ of the stock market 证券市场行情的猛跌 ④投入; (突然、猛烈的)冲击 ⑤[口]盲目投资(或投机) ⑥阵雨 ⑦[主方]为难, 窘迫 ‖**take the ~** 冒险尝试; (经过踌躇后)采取断然行动 / ‖~ **bath** (可以纵身而入的)浴池; 池浴 / **plunging fire** (火炮等的)俯射

plural [ˈpluərəl] **I** a. ①【语】复数的: a ~ noun (verb) 复数名词(动词) / the ~ number 复数 ②由复数组成的, 包含复数的: a ~ society (由多人种组成的)复性社会 **II** n. 【语】复数; (词的)复数形式; 复数形式的单词: The form "sheep" is used also in the ~. "sheep" 这一形式也可作为复数用。‖~**ly** ad. 以复数形式 / ~ **executive** 复数主管人 (指决策并主持日常事务的董事会等) / ~ **vote** 一人多选区投票(权)

plus [plʌs] **I** prep. 加, 加上: Four ~ one equals five. 四加一等于五。 **II** a. ①正的; 【商】贷方的: the ~ sign 正号, 加号(即 "+") / a ~ ion 正离子 / on the ~ side of the account 在帐户的贷方 ②有增益的; 附加的: Jack is ~ a dollar. 杰克赚得一元。/ the ~ and minus factors 有利和不利因素 ③[通常放在被修饰的词之后][口]略大(或略高)的; 标准以上的: get a grade of B ~ in English 英语得到 B+ 的成绩 / a $5 million-~ appropriation 五百余万美元的拨款 / have personality ~ 极有个性 ④【植】(菌丝体)阳性的, 雄性的 ~ (高尔夫球戏中)先加上分数的, 有让分的 **III** n. 【数】正号, 加号 ②附加物; 附加额; 【数】正数, 正量 ③增益 ‖~ **fours** [复]宽大的运动裤, 灯笼裤

plush [plʌʃ] **I** n. ①长毛绒 ②[复](差役等穿的)毛绒裤 **II** a. ①长毛绒(做)的 ②[俚]奢侈豪华的; 漂亮的; 舒服的 ‖~**ly** ad. 奢侈豪华地; 漂亮地; 舒服地 / ~**y** a. 长毛绒(似)的; 奢侈豪华的; 漂亮的; 舒服的

plutocracy [pluːˈtɔkrəsi] n. ①富豪统治, 财阀统治 ②富豪(或财阀)统治集团

plutocrat [ˈpluːtəkræt] n. ①富豪, 财阀 ②[口]有钱的人

plutocratic [ˌpluːtəˈkrætik] a. 富豪统治的; 富豪(般)的, 财阀(般)的

ply[1] [plai] **I** n. ①厚度; 折迭; 层片; 股: be composed of 3 plies of cloth 由三层布迭成 / three-~ wood 三夹板 / a two-~ rope 一根双股的绳子 / ~ yarn 合股纱 ②倾向, 性癖: take a ~ 有某种倾向(或习癖) **II** vt. 折; 弯; 使绞合: ~ two single yarns 绞并两股纱 ‖'~**wood** n. 胶合板, 层压木板

ply[2] [plai] **❶** vt. ①使劲挥舞; 勤奋地使用: ~ one's oars 使劲划桨 / ~ a hoe in a cornfield 在玉米地里不断挥动锄头 / ~ one's needle 忙于缝纫 ②(努力)从事, 经营: ~ a trade 努力从事某一项商业(或手艺) ③不断供…以饮食; 缠扰: ~ sb. with liquor 强劝某人喝酒 / ~ a donkey with a whip 不断用鞭子抽打驴子 / ~ a speaker with questions 向讲演人问个不休 ④(船等)来回于, 往返于 **❷** vi. ①努力从事: ~ in a just cause 为一正义事业孜孜不倦地工作 ②(车、船等)定期地来回, 定期地往返 (between); [诗]驾驶; 把舵 ③【海】(帆船)逆风换舱, 沿锯齿形折线逆风行驶 ④(出租汽车司机、船夫等)候客, 待雇

pneumatic [njuːˈmætik] **I** a. ①空气的, 气体的; (可)充空气(或气体)的 ②装有气胎的 ③由压缩空气推动(或操作)的, 气动的; 风动的 ④【动】有气腔的 ⑤精神的, 灵魂的 ‖a ~ boat 橡皮船 / a ~ brake 气闸, 风闸 / a ~ cushion 气枕, 气垫 / a ~ drill 风钻 / a ~ gun 气枪 / a ~ hammer 气(力)锤, 气压锤 / a ~ jack 气力起重机, 气压千斤顶 / a ~ tyre 气胎 **II** n. ①气胎 ②有气胎的车辆 ‖~**ally** ad.

pneumatics [njuːˈmætiks] [复] n. [用作单]【物】气体力学

poach[1] [pəutʃ] vt. 水煮(荷包蛋) ‖~**er** n. (内有数个浅碟的)水煮荷包蛋器

poach[2] [pəutʃ] **❶** vi. ①侵入他人地界)偷猎(或偷捕鱼): ~ on a neighbour's land 侵入邻人地界偷猎 / ~ for pheasants 偷猎野鸡 ②边走边陷入泥中; (泥土等)被踏即成泥浆(或陷落成洞): The swamp country is inclined to ~ in winter. 这片沼泽地带在冬季一踏就陷下去。③(网球赛中)抢打 **❷** vt. ①侵入(他人地界)偷猎(或偷捕鱼); 偷猎, 偷捕(鱼) ②(赛跑时)以不正当手段取得(先跑权、优势等); 窃得: ~ a start in a race 比赛中偷跑 ③把…踏成泥浆; 在…上踏出泥洞 ④抢打(网球) ⑤把(棒、手指等)戳入 (into) ⑥漂洗(纸浆) ‖~**er** n. 侵入他人地界偷猎(或偷渔)者

pock [pɔk] **I** n. 痘疱; 痘凹 **II** vt. 使留有痘痕, 使有麻点

pocket [ˈpɔkit] **I** n. ①小袋; 钱袋; 衣袋; [英]一袋(一种大小不一的重量单位, 尤指称蛇麻布用的 168 磅): a coat (trouser) ~ 衣(裤)袋 ②钱; 财力: He has suffered in his ~. 他在经济上受到了损失。③贮器, 容器, 囊; (弹子球台四角的)球囊; (袋鼠等动物的)球囊 ‖【机】套: a spring ~ 弹簧套 ④(孤立的)小块地区, (被敌军包围或占领的)孤立地区; (赛跑中)被挤轧的不利情况 ⑤【空】(大气中的)气阱 (=air ~) ⑥死胡同 ⑦

【矿】矿穴; 小矿藏; 矿囊 **II** *a.* ① 可放在衣袋内的, 袖珍的, 小型的: a ~ dictionary (atlas) 袖珍词典(地图册) ②压缩的, 紧凑的: a ~ lecture 紧凑的讲课 ③金钱上的: one's ~ interest 某人的金钱上的利益 ④ 放在袋中作零用的 **III** *vt.* ①把…装入袋内; 包藏, 封入 ② 侵吞, 盗用(款项) ③忍受; 深藏; 压制, 压抑: ~ an insult 忍受侮辱 / ~ one's pride 抑制自尊心, 忍辱 ④阻挠, 搁置(议案等)使之不通过 ⑤ (在弹子戏中)击(球)落袋 ‖*an empty* ~ 没钱的人 / *be in* (*out of*) ~ 赚(赔)钱: John *is* 5 pounds *in* (*out of*) ~ *by* this transaction. 约翰在这笔交易中赚(赔)了五英镑. / *be prepared to put one's hand in one's* ~ 准备花钱; 准备解囊捐献 / *have sb. in one's* ~ 可以任意支配某人 / *line one's* ~*s* 赚大钱, 肥私囊 / *out-of-*~ *expenses* (或 *out of* ~ *expenses*) 现金支付, 实际的花费, 实际支出 / *pick a* ~ 扒窃 / *put one's pride in one's* ~ 抑制自尊心, 忍辱 ‖'~*ful n.* (指容量)一袋 ‖'~*book n.* ①袖珍本; 笔记本 ②(放钞票等的)皮夹子 ③[美](妇女用的)钱袋, 手袋 ④财力; 进账; 经济利益 / ~ **borough** (英国)议会改革前由个人(或一个家族)操纵的选区 / ~ **edition** ①袖珍本, 袖珍版 ②小型的东西 / ,~-'**handkerchief** *n.* ①(放在袋中的)手帕 ②小型物: a ~-*handkerchief of land* 小块土地 / a ~-*handkerchief lawn* 小块草地 / '~**knife** *n.* 随身携带的小折刀 / ~ **money** 零用钱 / ~ **veto** [美](总统或州长对议案的)搁置否决权(美国会通过的议案送交总统签字时, 如被搁置至国会休会后十日不签, 该议案即被否决)

pod[1] [pod] **I** *n.* ①[豆荚, 英果 ②蚕茧; (蝗虫等的)卵囊 ③(海豹等的)一群 ④[矿]近圆柱形矿体, 扁豆形矿体, 透镜形矿体 ⑤[空]容器; 塔门吊舱; (发动机)吊舱; (翼梢等上的)发射架; (宇宙飞船的)可分离的舱 **II** (podded; podding) ❶ *vt.* ①把 (豆等) 剥出荚 ②驱(海豹等)成群 ❷ *vi.* 生荚, 结荚 ‖~**pepper**【植】朝天椒

pod[2] [pod] *n.*【机】①(某些钻头及螺旋钻的)纵槽; 有纵槽的螺旋钻 ②手摇钻的钻头承窝

podgy ['pɔdʒi] *a.* 矮胖的

poem ['pouim] *n.* ①诗, 韵文; 诗体文: a lyric ~ 抒情诗 / a prose ~ 散文诗 / write (或 compose) a ~ 写诗, 作诗 ②诗似的事物, 富有诗意的东西

poet ['pouit] *n.* ①诗人: a romantic ~ 浪漫主义诗人 / a realistic ~ 现实主义诗人 ② 富有想象、善于抒情的艺术家 ‖~**ess** *n.* 女诗人 ‖~ **laureate** 桂冠诗人 / **Poets' Corner** ① 英国伦敦威斯敏斯特教堂埋有英国大诗人并设纪念碑的一隅 ② [谑]报纸上的诗栏

poetic [pou'etik] *a.* ①诗的; 韵文的; 用诗写成的: ~ works 诗作品 / ~ diction 诗的用语 / in ~ form 以诗的形式 ②诗人的; 爱好(或善于)写诗的; 富有诗意的; 具有想象力的 ‖~ **justice** 理想的赏罚, 劝善惩恶 / ~ **license** 诗的破格

poetical [pou'etikəl] *a.* ① =poetic ②理想化了的 ‖~**ly** *ad.* / ~**ness** *n.*

poetry ['pouitri] *n.* ①[总称]诗, 诗歌; 诗作; 诗集: prose ~ 散文诗 / Chinese ~ 中国诗歌 / write ~ 写诗 ②作诗; 作诗法 ③诗意; 富有诗意的东西: the ~ of motion (芭蕾舞蹈等的)动作的诗意 / add ~ to an article 使一篇文章带上诗意 / Her dancing is pure ~. 她的舞蹈非常富于诗意.

poignant ['pɔinənt] *a.* ①辛辣的 ②尖锐得伤人感情的; 深深打动人的: ~ remarks 尖锐的指责 / ~ satire 尖刻的讽刺 / a ~ spectacle 令人心碎的景象 ③强烈的; 生动透彻的: a feeling too ~ to endure 过于强烈、难以忍受的感情 ④恰当的; 针对的 ‖~**ly** *ad.*

poinsettia [pɔin'setiə] *n.*【植】一品红, 猩猩木; 戟属植物

point [pɔint] **I** *n.* ①(几何、物理等概念中的)点; 小数点; (文字中的)标点(尤指句号); 【音】点符; (温度计等的)度: a ~ of sight 视点; 瞄准点 / a ~ of contact 接触点;【数】切点 / the decimal ~ 小数点 / five ~ three 五点三(写作 5.3) / a full ~ 句号 / the boiling (freezing, melting) ~ 沸(冰, 熔)点 / The temperature has gone up four ~s. 温度升高了四度. / a ~ target 【军】点状目标(指飞机、坦克、火炮掩体等) ②(空间的)一点, 地点; [英](警察值勤的)固定岗位; (球类运动员的)位置, (在某一位置上的)球员: a strategic (fortified) ~ 战略(据)点 / a ~ of impact【军】弹着点 ③(时间上的)一点; (特定)时刻, 瞬间: a ~ of departure 出发点, 起点 / a crucial ~ 严重关头, 关键时刻 ④要点; 要害; 论点; (言论、论证等的)有力, 中肯: This is the first ~ I want to make. 这是我要说的第一点. / That's just the ~. 对啦, 这才是要害! / You have a ~ there! 你的话极有道理! / His deeds give ~ to his words. 他的行动给他的言语添加了分量. ⑤ 细目, 条款: explain a problem ~ by ~ 逐点逐条地解释一个问题 ⑥特点, 特征: one's strong and weak ~s 某人的长处和短处 / judge the ~s of a horse (根据体格特征)判断马的品种优劣 ⑦意义; 目的; 用途: What's the ~ of acting like this? 这样做有什么意思呢? / There is no ~ in doing so. 这样做毫无意义. ⑧尖(端); 尖状物; (常用在专有名词中)岬; 峰顶: the ~ of a needle (knife, pen) 针(刀, 钢笔)尖 / the towering ~ of a mountain 高耸的山峰 ⑨针绣花边 (= ~ lace) ⑩【军】尖兵: a ~ of advance (rear) guard 前卫(后卫)尖兵 / a ~ company 尖兵连 ⑪(身体上突出部分的)尖端, 顶端(如鹿角叉等) / [复]动物的四肢(尤指马蹄等): the ~ of the jaw 颚端(拳击中常指此处以击倒对方) ⑫(针灸、推拿等的)穴位: the key acupuncture

~s 主要针刺穴位

⑬分(数); (比赛等的)得分; [美] (修毕某一课程所得的)学分; 点数,点(配给等的计算单位): work ~s 工分 / put a commodity on ~s 对一种商品实行配给 / ~s food 配给的食物

⑭【商】(证券、商品等市场价格计算单位)点,磅音

⑮【海】罗盘主方位,罗经点; 两罗经点间的差度(=11¼度): the 32 ~s of the compass 罗盘上的三十二个罗经点

⑯【印】(活字大小单位)点(相当于 ¹/₇₂ 吋或 0.3478 毫米)

⑰[英] [常用复] (铁路的)辙尖,岔尖

⑱(插头等的)接触点; [主英] (电)插座

⑲【音】短促曲调; 军号短调讯号; (弦乐器)弓的顶端,弓尖

⑳(猎犬发现猎物时)站住以头指向猎物的动作

‖a critical ~ 临界点; 关键时刻 / a firing ~ 发射点 / a fusion (或 fusing) ~ 熔点 / a relay ~ 中继站,转播站 / a release ~【军】投弹点

Ⅱ ❶ vt. ①弄尖,削尖: ~ a pencil with a knife 用刀削尖铅笔

②使尖锐; 加强,强调: ~ (up) an argument with facts 用事实来加强论据

③指出; 指向; 把…对准,使对准: ~ out a mistake 指出错误 / ~ the boat northward 使船又驶向北方

④给…加标点; 给…加小数点 (off); 【语】给…加元音符号· ~ off the last figure of 215 在215的末位数字前加上小数点

⑤(泥水工用灰泥等)嵌填,勾抹 (墙缝等) (up); (用锹尖)把(肥料)插入土中 (in),翻 (土) (over): ~ up the brickwork 勾抹砖缝

⑥(猎犬)站住以头指向(猎物)

❷ vi. ①指,指向; 面向 (to, at, towards): ~ to sb. 指着某人 / ~ at the map (用手等)指着地图 / a signpost ~ing to the north 指向北方的路牌 / The building ~s to the east. 这所大楼朝东。

②表明,暗示 (to, at, towards): All the facts ~ to the same conclusion. 所有事实都说明同样的结论。

③(船)几乎迎风行驶

④(猎犬)站住以头指向猎物

⑤(为参加比赛)进行有的放矢的训练 (for)

⑥[英] (脓肿等)起脓头

‖a point of hono(u)r 为维持面子必须做的事(尤指为了面子必须决斗) / a ~ of no return 见 return / a ~ of safe return 见 return / a ~ of view 观点; 着眼点 / at all ~s 在各方面,充分地: be armed at all ~s 全副武装 / at swords' ~s 剑拔弩张准备打架 / at the ~ of 靠近,接近; 将近…的时候 / at the ~ of the sword 在暴力威胁之下 / beside the ~ 离题,不中肯: What you said is beside the ~. 你讲的与本题无关。 / carry (或 gain) one's ~ 说服别人同意自己的观点; 达到目的 / come to a ~ ①变

尖; 变尖锐 ②到紧要关头 ③(猎犬)停住以头指向猎物 / give ~s to (在比赛中)让分给(对方) / in ~ 恰当的,中肯的,切题的: a case in ~ 恰当的例子 / in ~ of ... 就…而言,关于: in ~ of fact 实际上,就事实而论 / keep to the ~ 扣住主题 / make (或 score) a ~ ①立论,证明论点,赢得他人对争论之点的同意 ②(比赛等)得一分 / make a ~ of doing ... 决心(或坚持)做…/ not to put too fine a ~ on (或 upon) it 坦率地说,说实话 / off (或 away from) the ~ 不切题,离题 / on (或 upon) the ~ of 即将…之时,正要…的时候 / on the ~ 拘泥于细节 / stretch (或 strain) a ~ ①破例作出让步 ②(在论证等时)作过度的延伸,作牵强附会的说明 / to a ~ 在每一点上 / to the ~ 中肯; 扼要: Be concise and to the ~. 请简明扼要一点。 / to the ~ of 到达…的程度

‖~-'blank a. ①【军】(火力)近距离平射的: fire at ~-blank range 近距离射击 ②直截了当的,干脆的: a ~-blank answer (refusal) 直截了当的回答(拒绝) ad. ①近距离平射地; 在一条直线上: fire ~-blank 近距离射击 ②直截了当地; 断然: I tell you ~-blank it won't do. 我干脆告诉你,断然不行。 / refuse ~-blank 断然拒绝 / ~ count 数点子(桥牌中计算一手牌实力的一种方法) / ~-de'vice a. & ad. [古]过分精致的(地); 完全正确的(地) / ~ duty [英] (交通警察在固定岗位上的)值勤,站岗 / ~ lace 针绣花边 / ~sman ['pointsmen] n. [英] ①(铁路的)扳道工,扳闸手,转辙手 ②(有固定岗位的)交通警察 / ~-to-' n. 越野赛马: a ~-to-~ race (打猎时骑马者的)越野赛跑

pointed ['pointid] a. ①尖的,尖角的 ②(言语等)尖锐的,犀利的; 直截了当的,率直的; 有所指的; 中肯的 ③显然的,突出的 ‖~ly ad. / ~ness n.

pointer ['pointə] n. ①指示者,指示物; (钟表、仪表、天平秤等的)指针 ②教鞭 ③一种短毛大猎犬 ④[口]暗示,线索,点子: Give us some ~s on how to do the job. 这工作怎么搞法,你给我们出一些点子。 ⑤[the Pointers]【天】(大熊星座中的)两颗指极星 ⑥【军】瞄准手

pointless ['point-lis] a. ①无尖头的,钝的 ②无意义的; 不得要领的; 空洞的,乏味的: a ~ life 无意义的生活 / a ~ retort 不得要领的反驳 ③(比赛等)未得分的: a ~ draw 零比零 ‖~ly ad. / ~ness n.

poise [poiz] Ⅰ ❶ vt. ①使平衡,使保持均衡: walk along with a water jar ~d on one's head 头上平稳地顶着水坛子向前走去 / The gymnast ~d herself on the balance beam. 体操运动员在平衡木上保持平衡。 ②使(头部等)保持一种特殊的姿态; 使悬着: ~ one's head forward 使头向前倾 / The earth is ~d in space. 地球悬于太空之中。 ③使作好准备 ❷ vi. ①平衡; 悬着 ②作好准备 ③犹豫不决,踌躇 Ⅱ n. ①平衡,均衡

②沉着,泰然自若;自信 ③静谧,安静,沉静 ④(身体或头部的)姿态 ⑤悬而不决,犹豫 ⑥砝码,秤锤 ⑦【化】泊(粘度单位)

poison ['pɔizn] I *n.* ①毒;毒药;毒物: use ~ as an antidote to~ 以毒攻毒 / drink ~ to quench one's thirst 饮鸩止渴 ②毒害;败坏社会的学说(或主义等): the ~ of bad example 坏样的毒害 ③[俚]劣酒 ④抑制剂: a catalyst ~ 催化剂毒(抑制催化剂作用的物质) II ❶ *vt.* ①使中毒;毒杀;放毒于;使感染而中毒(或发炎): ~ mice 毒杀老鼠 / a ~ed finger 因感染而发炎的手指 / blood ~ed by infection 因感染而中毒的血液 ②毒害,败坏,伤害;玷污: ~ sb.'s mind 毒害某人的思想 / ~ the friendship of 破坏…的友谊 ③阻碍,抑制(催化剂等) ❷ *vi.* 放毒,下毒 III *a.* ①有毒的: a ~ plant 有毒的植物 / a ~ tongue 刻毒的嘴 ②加了毒的: a ~ arrow 毒箭 ‖*hate each other like* ~ 互相恨透 / *What's your* ~? [口]你要喝点什么? (特指酒类) ‖*~er n.* 毒害者,毒杀者;放毒者 / *~ing n.* ①中毒 ②毒害 ③布毒 ‖~ **gas** 毒气 / ~ **gland**【动】毒腺 / ~ **hemlock**【植】芹叶钩吻 / ~ **ivy**【植】毒漆树属植物 / ~ **oak**【植】①美国西部一种灌木状毒漆树 ②=~ sumac / '~-**pen** *a.* 恶意中伤的;匿名写的: a ~-pen letter 匿名信 / ~ **sumac**【植】美国毒漆

poisonous ['pɔiznəs] *a.* ①有毒的;有害的: ~ weeds 毒草 / the remaining ~ influence 余毒 / a ~ play 一出毒草戏 / be ~ to sb.'s mind 对某人的思想有害 ②恶毒的,有恶意的: ~ words 恶毒的话 / give sb. a ~ look 恶狠狠地看某人一眼 ③[口]讨厌的,不愉快的: The heat is simply ~. 热得讨厌极了。/ an absolutely ~ horse 一匹极难对付的马 ‖*~ly ad.*

poke[1] [pouk] I ❶ *vt.* ①(用棍棒等)戳,刺,捅;拨弄: ~ a hole in the wallpaper 在糊壁纸上戳一个洞 / ~ a stake into the earth 把桩子插进泥土 / ~ (up) the fire 拨旺炉火 ②(用手指、肘等)触,碰;[美俚](用拳)揍,击;打(一拳): ~ sb. in the ribs with one's elbow 用肘轻触某人(以引起注意或表示亲密) / ~ sb. a blow 打某人一拳 ③伸(头等);放置;把…指向(或指向): ~ one's head 弯着背把头向前伸着 / ~ one's head out of the window 把头伸出窗外 / ~ one's finger at 把手指指向… ④[口]使蛰居于狭隘简陋的地方(up): ~ oneself up in a small room 呆在小房间里不出去 ⑤[美俚]赶,牧(牛、羊等) ⑥[美俚]激励 ❷ *vi.* ①戳,刺,捅;拨弄,翻弄: ~ among the waste materials with a stick 用棒在废料堆中东翻西戳 / ~ at that policy 攻击那项政策 ②(头等)伸出;[喻]探听,刺探;瞎管,干涉: I saw his head *poking* through the window. 我看见他的头伸出窗外。/ ~ *into* sb.'s private affairs 探听(或干涉)某人的私事 ③摸索地走,逛,闲荡(*along, about, around*): ~ *about* in a secondhand bookstore 逛旧书店(找想买的书) /

~ *around* at home 在家过无聊日子,蛰居家中 II *n.* ①戳,捅;拨;触;[美俚]一拳;(棒球赛等中的)一击: give the fire a ~ 拨一下炉火 ②懒汉,游手好闲的人;慢性子的人(=slow ~);蠢得讨厌的人 ③触处颈轭(前面有一长棒,斜搭及地,用来防止牛、马等闯出栅栏) ④朝前撑起的阔边(女帽)朝前撑起的阔边 ⑤[美俚](美国西部的)骑马牧者,牛仔 ‖~ *and pry* 管闲事,打听消息 ‖~ **bonnet** 朝前撑起的阔边女帽 / '~-**out** [美俚] ①给乞丐吃的东西 ②用柴(或炭)烧的野餐

poke[2] [pouk] *n.* ①[方]小袋,囊 ②放金块(或金砂)的袋 ③[俚]钞票夹,皮夹子;积起的一笔钱,一叠钞票 ④颈部肿大(尤指羊颈部的袋状肿大) ‖*buy a pig in a* ~ 见 **pig**

poke[3] [pouk] *n.*【植】美洲商陆(=~weed)

poker[1] ['poukə] I *n.* ①戳(或拨弄)的人 ②拨棒,火钳 ③(在白木上)烙画的用具 II *vt.* 烙制(图案等)用烙画装饰 ‖*as stiff as a* ~ (指姿态、态度)生硬,刻板 / *by the holy* ~ [谑](发誓用语)一定 ‖~ **work** 烙画,焦笔画

poker[2] ['poukə] *n.* 扑克牌戏,纸牌戏 ‖~ **face** [口]没有表情的脸,一本正经的面容;面无表情的人 / '~-**faced** *a.* 面无表情的;一本正经的;表示与己无关的

pole[1] [poul] I *n.* ①杆,柱;帐篷的支柱;电线杆;旗杆;撑竿跳的竿;圆篙;(车的)辕杆: a carrying (或 shoulder) ~ 扁担,杠棒 ②杆(长度名,=5½码) ③在齐胸高的地位直径为四时至十二时的树 II ❶ *vt.* ①用杆支撑,用篙跳 ②用篙撑(船等) ❷ *vi.* ①用篙撑船 ②用雪橇杆撑行以加快速度 ‖*under bare ~s*【海】不张帆 / *up the* ~ [俚] ①处于困境,进退两难 ②微狂的 ‖~ **ax(e)** *n.* ①长柄战斧,钺;短柄斧 ②屠牛斧 *vt.* 用斧砍倒 / ~ **jump(ing)**, ~ **vault** 撑竿跳

pole[2] [poul] *n.* 极(点);磁极;【电】电极: the North (South) *Pole* 北(南)极 / the positive (negative) ~ 阳(阴)极 / ~ strength (磁)极强(度) / the ~ of a circle (line) 圆(线)的极点 ‖~*s apart* (或 *asunder*) 南辕北辙,截然相反: Their opinions are ~*s asunder.* 他们的意见截然相反。‖~**ward(s)** *ad.* 向极 ‖~ **piece** 极靴,磁极片 / '~**star** *n.* ①[the ~star]【天】北极星 ②指导原则;目标;有吸引力的中心

polemic [pɔ'lemik] I *a.* 争论的;爱争论的 II *n.* ①攻击,驳斥 ②[~s]用作单或复]争论,辩论;论战;辩论法,辩论术: be engaged in open ~s on 就……进行公开论战 ③辩论者,爱争论者 ④[~s][用作单或复](基督教神学中)对错误的驳斥

police [pə'li:s] I [单复同] *n.* ①[常作 the ~]警察当局;警务人员: the marine ~ 水上警察队 / the mounted ~ 骑警队 / the military ~ [美]宪兵队 / the riot ~ 防暴警察队 / The ~ are on the track of the criminal. 警察部门正在追踪该犯。②警察(=policemen): two (many) ~ 名(许多)警察 ③警察性组织;警察性组织的人

员: railway ～ 铁路警察 ④ 治安,公安 ⑤［美］【军】(兵营内的)打扫,整顿;内务值勤;内务值勤人员 **II** *vt.* ①维持…的治安,警备; 在…实施警察制度; 在…设置警察: ～ the street 维持街上的治安 ②管辖;控制 ③［美］整理…的内务;打扫,整顿(兵营等)(up) ④［古］统治 ‖～ **action** 警察行动 / ～ **constable** ［英］普通警员 / ～ **court** 违警罪法庭 / ～ **dog** 警犬 / ～ **force** 警察力量;［总称］警察 / ～ **magistrate** 违警罪法庭推事 / ～**man** [pə'li:smən] *n.* ① 警察: a people's ～*man* 人民警察 / a ～*man* in plain clothes 便衣警察 ②【化】淀帚 / ～ **office** ［英］=～ station / ～ **officer** 警官,警察;内务军官 / ～ **post** 派出所 / ～ **reporter** 专门负责采访治安消息的记者 / ～ **state** 警察国家 / ～ **station** (地方的)警察局,警察分局 / po'lice,woman *n.* 女警察

policy[1] ['pɔlisi] *n.* ① 政策,方针: domestic (foreign) ～ 国内(对外)政策 / establish (或 shape) an editorial ～ 制订编辑方针 / follow (或 pursue) the ～ of unity 奉行团结的方针 ②策略(性);贤明(性);精明的行为;权谋: for reasons of ～ 由于策略上的原因 ‖*the ～ of the big revolver* 见 **revolver** ‖'～,maker *n.* 制订政策的人

policy[2] ['pɔlisi] *n.* ①保险单: a fire insurance ～ 火灾保险单 / a floating ～ 总保 (险)单 / a voyage ～ 航行保险单 / take out a ～ *on* one's life 保人寿险 ②［美］一种每日以数字打赌的彩票 ‖'～,holder *n.* 投保人,保险客户

polish ['pɔliʃ] **I ❶** *vt.* ①磨光;擦亮;琢磨: ～ arms 擦枪 / ～ furniture 擦家具 ②使优美,使精练;润饰 **❷** *vi.* 发光;变光滑;变优美: Steel ～*es* well. 钢能擦得很亮。**II** *n.* ①磨光;擦亮;琢磨: give a good ～ to sth. 把某物好好擦一擦 (或琢磨一下) ②光泽,光滑;优美,完善: a desk with a high ～ 表面光泽极好的书桌 / The ～ has worn off. 表面的光泽已脱落了。③擦光剂;擦光油: shoe ～ 鞋油 ‖～ *off* ［口］赶快做完,草草做完: ～ *off* a meal 匆匆吃完一餐饭 ②打败;干掉(竞争者,敌人等) / ～ *up* ①［口］改善,修饰 ②［美俚］［只用被动语态]使喝醉 ‖～ed *a.* ①擦亮的,磨光的: ～*ed* rice 白米 ②精练的,无瑕的 / ～er *n.* ①擦亮者;磨光工人 ②磨光机

polite [pə'lait] *a.* ①有礼貌的;殷勤的;温和的: a ～ answer 有礼貌的答复 / You're too ～. 你太客气了。②有教养的,斯文的,文雅的: ～ language 文雅的话 / the so-called ～ society 所谓的上流社会 ③(文学作品等)优雅的: ～ letters 纯文学(指希腊、罗马古典文学等) ‖～ly *ad.* / ～ness *n.*

politic ['pɔlitik] *a.* ①(人)精明的,有策略的;狡猾的 ②(计划、言行等)考虑周到的,得策的 ③［罕］政治的: a body ～ 国家

political [pə'litikəl] *a.* ①政治的;政治上的: ～ power 政权 / ～ affairs 政治 / a ～ party 政党 / a ～ instructor 政治指导员 / ～ economy 政

治经济学 / ～ science 政治学 / ～ consciousness 政治觉悟 / a ～ line 政治路线 / a ～ writer 政论撰稿人 ②党派政治的 ‖～ly *ad.* become ～ly conscious 有了政治觉悟

politician [,pɔli'tiʃən] *n.* ①从事政治者;通晓政事者;政治家 ②［贬］政客,专搞党派政治的人

politics ['pɔlitiks] ［复］*n.* ［用作单或复］①政治;政治学: Politics is the commander, the soul in everything. 政治是统帅,是灵魂。②政治活动;政治生活: talk ～ 谈论政治 / enter ～ 入政界 ③政纲;政见;策略;党派关系: What are your ～? 你的政见如何? / It is not good ～ to do so. 这样做不策略。‖*lunar ～* 不切实际的问题,空论 / *play ～* 玩弄权术;要阴谋诡计以达到个人目的

poll[1] [poul] **I** *n.* ①人头(尤指顶部、后部或头发);颈背: scratch one's ～ 搔头 ②(一群人中的)一名;人头税 ③选举投票: on the eve of the ～ 在选举投票的前夕 ④记票及数票;投票记录,投票数: declare the ～ 宣布投票结果 / have a ～ 得票最多 / a heavy (light) ～ 高(低)得票率 ⑤［常用复］投票处: go to the ～*s* 去投票处投票 / be defeated (successful) at the ～*s* 落(当)选 ⑥民意测验;民意测验记录 ⑦ (锤等的)宽平端 **II** *vt.* ①收受及登记…的选票 ②个别征求…中成员对候选人的取舍意见 ③得到(若干票数);得到(某一类投票者)的选票 ④对…进行民意测验 ⑤剪掉(或剪短)…的头发(或羊毛);剪(羊毛等) ⑥剪去(树木)的顶部枝桠;截去(牛等)的角 **❷** *vi.* 投票 ③ *a.* (牛等)被截去角的 / ～ee [pou'li:] *n.* 民意测验的被测对象 / ～er *n.* 剪羊桠的人 ②民意测验者 ‖'～book *n.* 选举人名册 / clerk 选举投票工作人员(尤指记票人) / ～ing booth (临时设立的)投票站 / ～ing place 投票所 / ～ing station ［主英］=～ing place / ～ tax 人头税

poll[2] [pɔl] *n.* ［也作 P-] 养驯的鹦鹉;［喻］老是说些陈词烂调的人 (=～ parrot)

poll[3] [pɔl] *n.* ［英］(剑桥大学俚语)以普通学位毕业的学生们;［用作定语］普通学位: go out in the Poll 取得普通学位 / a ～ degree 普通学位 / a ～ man 普通毕业生

pollard ['pɔləd] **I** *n.* ①截去了梢的树;去了角的牛(或羊等) ②含有少量面粉的细糠 **II** *vt.* 截去(树)梢

pollen ['pɔlin] **I** *n.* ①【植】花粉 ②【动】粉面(常指双翅目昆虫的易落粉) **II** *vt.* 传花粉给,用花粉覆被

pollinate ['pɔlineit] *vt.* 【植】传花粉给 ‖pollination [,pɔli'neiʃən] *n.*

pollute [pə'lju:t] *vt.* ①弄脏,沾污,污染: air ～d by radioactive fallout 被放射性尘埃污染的空气 ②玷污,亵渎,败坏(道德等)

pollution [pə'lju:ʃən] *n.* ①污染: environmental (airborne) ～ 环境(空气)污染 / the ～ of the atmosphere 大气层的污染 ② 玷污, 亵渎, 败坏 ③【医】遗精

polo ['poulou] *n.* 【体】①马球 ②水球 (＝water ～) ‖～**ist** *n.* 打马球(或水球)的人 ‖～ **shirt** (开领短袖式)马球衬衫 / ～ **stick** 马球棍

polygamy [pə'ligəmi] *n.* ① 多配偶, 一夫多妻, 一妻多夫 ②【动】多配性, 一雄多雌;【植】杂性式

polyglot ['poliglot] **I** *n.* ① 通晓数种语言的人 ②[P-] 有数种文字对照的书(尤指数种文字对照的基督教《圣经》) ③数种语言的混合 **II** *a.* ①多种语言的; 通晓(或使用)多种语言的: a ～ population 多语种的居民 ②有数种文字对照的: a ～ dictionary 有数种文字对照的词典 ③ 数种语言混合组成的

polygon ['poligən] *n.* 【数】多边形, 多角形 ‖～**al** [pɔ'ligənl] *a.*

polysyllable ['poli,siləbl] *n.* 多音节词,三音节以上的词

polytechnic [,poli'teknik] **I** *a.* (传授)多种工艺的,多种学艺的,多种科技的: a ～ school 工艺(或科技)学校 / a ～ college 专科大学 / a ～ exhibition 工艺展览会 **II** *n.* 综合性工艺学校; 工业学校(或大学)

pomade [pə'mɑːd] **I** *n.* 润发脂;润发油 **II** *vt.* 用润发脂(或油)搽

pomegranate ['pom,grænit] *n.* 石榴; 石榴树

pommel ['pʌml] **I** *n.* ①(刀剑柄上的)圆头 ②(马鞍的)前桥 **II** (pommel(l)ed; pommel(l)ing) *vt.* (用刀剑柄上圆头)击,打;用拳头连续搂

pomp [pomp] *n.* ① 华丽;壮丽;(典礼等的)盛况,壮观;(节日或庆祝的)游行行列 ②浮华,虚饰;好夸耀的姿态(或举动),浮夸

pompous ['pompəs] *a.* ①壮丽的; 豪华的 ②浮华的,浮夸的;夸大的;自负的: ～ language 夸大的言词 / in a ～ manner 以自负(或浮夸)的态度 ‖～**ly** *ad.* / ～**ness** *n.*

pond [pond] **I** *n.* ①池塘 ②[谑]海: the big (或 herring) ～ [谑]北大西洋 **II** *vt.* 堵(流水)成池 (back, up) **②** *vi.* 筑成池塘 ‖～ **life** 在池中生活的动物(尤指无脊椎动物) / ～ **lily** 【植】睡莲 / ～ **snail** 【动】生殖于池中的螺(尤指膀胱螺属) / '～**weed** *n.* 【植】眼子莱属植物;角果藻

ponder ['pondə] **①** *vt.* ① 默想,深思;考虑: ～ a question 考虑问题 ② 衡量,估量: ～ sb. and what he has done 衡量某人及其所做的事情 **②** *vi.* 默想,沉思,深思 (on, over): ～ deeply over the matter 反复思考这件事 ‖～**ation** [,pondə'reiʃən] *n.*

ponderable ['pondərəbl] **I** *a.* ① 可衡量的; 可估量的,可估计的 ②(重量)可称的 **II** *n.* [复]有重量的东西;可估量的事物;可考虑的情况

ponderous ['pondərəs] *a.* ①极重的,沉重的,笨重的: a ～ burden 沉重的负担 / ～ furniture 笨重的家具 ②(文章、谈话等)冗长的,沉闷的,平凡的: a ～ explanation 冗长的解说 / ～ words 沉

闷的话 ‖～**ly** *ad.* / ～**ness** *n.*

poniard ['ponjəd] **I** *n.* 短剑,匕首 **II** *vt.* 用短剑戳

pontiff ['pontif] *n.* ①(古罗马)最高祭司团成员,大祭司; 主教 ② 教皇 (＝ sovereign ～)

pontoon[1] [pon'tuːn] **I** *n.* ①浮桥;(架设浮桥用的)平底船,浮舟; (装在飞机上使从水面浮起的)浮筒,浮囊: wing tip ～【空】翼梢浮筒 ② 趸船; 起重机船;浮码头; a ～ crane 水上起重机 ③潜水钟;潜水箱;沉箱 **II** *vt.* 架浮桥于;用浮桥渡(河等) ‖～ **bridge** 浮桥

pontoon[2] [pon'tuːn] *n.* [英]二十一点牌戏

pony ['pouni] **I** *n.* ①矮种马;小马 ②赛马用的马 ③ [美口]小酒杯;一小杯酒 ④[美俚](滑稽歌剧等中的)小个子舞女 ⑤[英俚](赛马用语)二十五镑 ⑥[美俚](外国文学书、外语教科书的供学生抄袭用的)直译本,考试作弊用的夹带 **II** *vt.* & *vi.* [美俚]①付清 (up) ② 借助注解书翻译,借助夹带翻译 **III** *a.* ①小(型)的: a ～ glass of beer 一小杯啤酒 ② 每日摘要(性)的: a ～ report 每日摘要的新闻报道 ‖an iron ～ [美俚]摩托车 ‖～ **engine** 小火车头 / ～ **express** 用小马快递的邮政制度 / '～**tail** *n.* 女孩的马尾发型

poodle ['puːdl] **I** *n.* 长卷毛狗 **II** *vt.* 把(狗)的毛剪修成卷曲状

pooh [phuː, puː] **I** *int.* 呸, 啐[表示轻蔑、不耐烦、不赞成等] **II** *vt.* & *vi.* =pooh-pooh

pooh-pooh [puː'puː] **①** *vt.* 藐视,漠视; 嘲笑: ～ the idea 表示瞧不起那个意见 **②** *vi.* 发"呸"声(表示轻蔑、不耐烦等) ‖～ **theory** 【语】感叹说(指语言起源于感叹词)

pool[1] [puːl] **I** *n.* ① 水塘;水池;游泳池 (＝swimming ～) ② 小水坑,潭,渊: in a ～ of blood 在血泊中 ③ 油田地带; 石油层; 瓦斯层 **II ①** *vi.* ①汇合成塘(或小潭) ②(血)郁积 **②** *vt.* ①(采矿或采石时)开(楔眼) ② 采掘(煤等) ③ 在…中形成塘(或小潭) ④使(血)郁积

pool[2] [puːl] **I** *n.* ①(赌博者所下的)全部赌注;(某一项目上的)赌注总额;贮放赌金的容器 ②(赢得独得全部赌注的)一种弹子戏; 落袋弹子戏(有六只袋,通常用十五只球) ③ 合伙经营; 联营; 集合基金(尤指用来操纵证券或商品行情者); 合伙经营者 ④集中备用的物资; 备用物资贮存处(如血库等): a metabolic ～ 代谢库,代谢池 ⑤集合剑术比赛(两组人员全体轮流比赛) **II ①** *vt.* ①合伙经营;拿(资金等)入伙 ②集中(智慧等);共享,分享: ～ (together) our efforts 共同协力 ③合伙经营; 联营; 组织(操纵市场的)共同基金 ‖'～**room** *n.* ①(赛马等赌博的)收赌注处 ②弹子房

poop[1] [puːp] **I** *n.* 【海】船尾楼;船尾楼甲板 (＝ deck); 船尾 **II** *vt.* (浪)冲打(船)尾;船尾受(浪)冲打

poop[2] [puːp] *n.* [俚](官方或非官方的)消息,材料;(有关的)事实 ‖～ **sheet** ①(官方的)书面声明(或材料汇编等) ②(书面的)详细指示

poop³ [pu:p] [俚] **❶** *vt.* [常用被动语态] 使筋疲力尽;使喘不过气来 **❷** *vi.* 疲乏;筋疲力尽 (out)

poop⁴ [pu:p] **I ❶** *vi.* ① 发出啪啪声 ② 放枪 ③[俗]放屁 **❷** *vt.* 啪啪地放射 **II** *n.* ①啪啪声 ②[俗]通便: take ～ 大便 ③[俗]屁

poop⁵ [pu:p] *n.* [俚]傻子;无用的人

poor [puə, poə] *a.* ① 贫穷的,贫困的 ② 贫乏的,缺少的;贫瘠的 ③ 粗劣的;蹩脚的,不好的: make high-quality products with ～ equipment 用差的设备造出优质产品 / a ～ composition 不通的作文 / a ～ memory 不好的记忆力 / a ～ hand at chess 不高明的棋手 / a ～ excuse (apology) 不能自圆其说的借口 (辩解) / in ～ health 健康不佳 ④ 可怜的,不幸的: a ～ fellow 可怜的家伙 ⑤卑劣的,可鄙的: a ～ creature 卑劣的人 ⑥乏味的,无聊的,没意思的: have a ～ time 过一段乏味的时间 ⑦浅薄的;不重要的: in my ～ opinion 依愚见看来;照我的肤浅看法 ⑧已故的 (= late, deceased) ‖(as) ～ as a church mouse 一贫如洗 / the ～ [总称]穷人,贫民: the urban ～ 城市贫民 ‖~ness *n.* ‖~ box (教堂里的)济贫捐款箱,施舍箱 / '~house *n.* (资本主义社会中的)贫民院,养育院 / ～ law (英国等的)济贫法;[复]恤贫法令 / '~-mouth *vi.* 以贫穷作为借口 *vt.* 把…说得一钱不值 / ～ rate 济贫税,贫民救济税 / '~-'spirited *a.* 胆怯的,懦弱的;可鄙的 / ～ white [美][常蔑](美国南部的)贫困白人(常指佃农) / ～ white trash [美][总称][蔑](美国南部的)贫困白人(常指佃农)

poorly ['puəli] **I** *a.* [只用作表语][口]身体不舒服的,健康不佳的: He is (looking) very ～. 他(看上去)身体很不舒服。 / feel rather ～ with the low grade fever 由于有低热而感到不舒服 **II** *ad.* ①贫穷地;贫乏地 ②拙劣地,蹩脚地: a ～ lighted room 光线很暗的房间 ‖~ off 贫困的,没钱的 / *think* ～ of 对…评价低;低估

pop¹ [pop] **I** *n.* ①砰的一声;爆破声: The cork flew off with a ～. 砰地一声瓶塞飞出去了。 ②枪声;枪: take a ～ at the wolf 对准狼砰地一枪打去 ③[美俚]有气的瓶装饮料 (汽水、啤酒等) ④(迅速打上的)记号,点痕(尤指打在羊身上的印记) ⑤[英俚]典当: in ～ (东西)在当铺里 ⑥[美俚]尝试 **II ❶** *vi.* ①(突然)爆开;(开枪)射击: ～ *at* a target 向目标射击 ②(意外地,突然地)出现,发生;(突然地,迅速地)行动,来,去: An idea *popped into* his mind like a flash. 他脑里突然闪过一个念头。 / ～ in and out 跳进跳出 / ～ over to the market 到商场去 ③(眼睛)瞪出,张大;突出: His eyes *popped (out)* with surprise. 他吃惊得眼睛都瞪出来了。 **❷** *vt.* ①[美]爆(玉米等);开枪打: ～ rice (corn) 爆炒米(玉米)花 / ～ a rabbit (开枪)打兔子 ②(突然)伸出;抛出;提出(问题等): ～ a series of questions *at* sb. 向某人(迅速地)提出一连串问题 / ～ *out* one's head (突然)伸出头去 ③[英俚]典当(东西) **III** *ad.* 砰地(一声);突然地:

Pop went the gun. 砰地一声枪响了。 ‖～ off ①突然离去,匆匆离去 ②[俚]突然死掉;杀死 ③怒气冲冲(或漫不经心)地乱讲(或乱写) / ～ *the question* [俚]求婚 / ～ *to* 喀嚓一声立正 ‖'~-corn *n.* 爆玉米(花) / '~-eyed *a.* (因惊讶等)瞪出眼睛的;眼球突出的 / '~ fly (棒球)打得短促而高的飞球 / '~-gun *n.* (儿童玩具)气枪;蹩脚的枪 / '~-off *n.* ①大声(或东拉西扯)讲话的人;盛怒之下乱说乱讲的人 ②(供烧过程中)爆脱的搪瓷块 / '~over *n.* 薄脆空心松饼 / '~,shop *n.* [英]当铺 [美俚]突然袭击式的测验 / ～ valve【机】突开阀

pop² [pop] **I** *a.* (音乐、绘画、电影等)流行的;(尤指通过报纸、电台等)普及的: ～ music 流行音乐 / a ～ singer 流行歌曲演唱家 / a ～ painter 流行画家,流行艺术画家 / a ～ society 普及文化协会 **II** *n.* ①[美口]流行音乐,流行歌曲;流行(歌曲等)唱片 ②[复][口]流行音乐会 ③流行艺术(= ～ art) ④普及文化 / ～ art 流行艺术(以罐头、招牌等杂物为题材,并常把实物嵌入画面或雕塑品) / ～ artist (颓废派)流行艺术家

pop³ [pop] *n.* [美俚] ①爸爸 ②(常用作对老年人的昵称)大爷,老爹

pope¹ [poup] *n.* ① [P-] (罗马天主教的)教皇 ②[喻]自以为(或被认为)一贯绝对正确的人 (希腊东正教的)教区牧师 ‖~dom *n.* 教皇的权力;教皇的在职时期;教皇的辖区 ‖~'s nose (煮熟供食用的)鸡(或其它家禽的)屁股

pope² [poup] **I** *n.* 大腿上被打时极痛(或发麻)的部位: take sb.'s ～ 打某人腿上要害处 **II** *vt.* 打(某人)大腿上极易感痛(或发麻)的部位

poplar ['poplə] *n.* 杨属植物,白杨;杨木

poplin ['poplin] *n.* [纺]府绸;毛葛: ～ broche 织花府绸;织花毛葛 / cotton ～ 棉府绸

poppy ['popi] *n.* ①罂粟属植物;罂粟属植物的花;药用罂粟汁: the opium ～ 可提制鸦片的罂粟 ②有罂粟般麻醉性的东西;鸦片 ③芙蓉红 (= ～ red) ‖~cock *n.* 胡扯,废话 / '~head *n.* 【建】顶花饰

populace ['popjuləs] *n.* ① 平民;大众 ② 人口 ③[蔑]群氓

popular ['popjulə] *a.* ① 民众的,大众的,人民的: ～ election 普选 / a ～ opinion poll 民意测验 / win (lose) ～ support 得(失)人心 ② 普及的;通俗的,大众化的;(价格)低廉的: a ～ edition 普及本 / ～ science readings 科普读物 / in ～ language 用通俗的话 / sell at ～ prices 以廉价出售 ③ 流行的;大众(或某种人)喜爱的;(民间)流传的;为一般人接受(或认为)的: a ～ song 流行歌曲 / These artistic handicrafts are very ～ *with* foreign friends. 外国朋友很喜爱这些工艺美术品。 / ～ medicinal herbs 民间流传的草药 / a ～ misconception 一般人的误解 ④ 受欢迎的;被爱戴的: a ～ writer 受人欢迎的作家 ‖~ly *ad.* ①通过民众: a ～ly elected government 民

选政府 ②通俗地;一般地: be ~*ly* known as ... 一般称作…(或俗称…) ‖ ~ **sovereignty** 【美史】人民主权论 (南北战争前一种政治上的主义,主张各州人民有权处理其内政,并决定是否容许奴隶制)

populate ['pɔpjuleit] *vt.* ①居住于…中;在…中占一席地位 ②使人口聚居在…中;移民于;殖民于: a densely (sparsely) ~*d* area 人口稠密(稀少)地区

population [,pɔpju'leiʃən] *n.* ① 人口(数字);全体居民: have a ~ of 有…人口 / the peasant ~ 农业人口 / a ~ centre 居民点 / the density of a region 一个地区的人口密度 / zero ~ growth 零点人口增长率(即主张人口增长率应与死亡率相平的社会改革方案) / the entire adult male ~ of the city 那个城市里的全体成年男子 ②(人或物的)全体,总数: the student ~ of a university (或 the campus ~) 一个大学的全体学生 / The tractor ~ increased. 拖拉机的总数增加了。 ③(人口的)聚居: encourage ~ of remote border regions 鼓励向偏僻的边境地区移民 ④【数】(对象)总体,全域 ⑤【物】布居;密度;组,族,个数 ⑥【生】种群(量);群体;虫口 ‖ ~**ist** *n.* 主张控制人口增长论者 ‖ ~ **explosion,** ~ **boom** 人口骤增

populous ['pɔpjuləs] *a.* ① 人口稠密的 ② 众多的 ③挤满的 ‖ ~**ly** *ad.* / ~**ness** *n.*

porcelain ['pɔ:slin] **I** *n.* 瓷; [总称]瓷器: a piece of ~ 一件瓷器 **II** *a.* ① 瓷制的;瓷的: ~ glaze 瓷釉 / ~ insulator 【电】陶瓷绝缘子 ② 精美的 ③ 脆的,易碎的 ‖ ~**ize** *vt.* 使成为瓷一般的东西;涂瓷于(金属器皿) / ~ **clay** 瓷土,高岭土 / ~ **enamel** 搪瓷 / ~ **shell** 【动】宝贝属的贝类

porch [pɔ:tʃ] *n.* ① (上有顶棚的)门廊;入口处 ② [美] 走廊,游廊 ③ [the P-] (公元前四世纪)斯多葛 (即斯多亚) 派哲学家芝诺 (Zeno) 在雅典讲学的柱廊;斯多葛学派 ‖ ~**ed** *a.* 有门廊的

porch

porcupine ['pɔ:kjupain] *n.* 豪猪,箭猪

pore[1] [pɔ:] ❶ *vi.* ①注视,凝视: ~ *over* the microscope 通过显微镜仔细观察 ② 钻研,熟读: ~ *over* a book 全神贯注地读书 ③默想,沉思: ~ *on* (或 *upon, over*) a problem 深入思考一个问题 ❷

vt. 因凝视过度而使…疲劳: ~ one's eyes out 因凝视过度而使眼睛疲劳不堪

pore[2] [pɔ:] *n.* 毛孔;气孔;细孔,微孔 ‖*at every* ~ 全身,浑身 / *sweat from every* ~ ①极热 ②受惊吓;极兴奋 ‖ ~**d** *a.* 有孔的

pork [pɔ:k] *n.* ①猪肉: a ~ chop 猪排 ② [美俚]政客假公济私给手下人的好处(如金钱、职位等) ‖ ~ **barrel** [美俚] (为讨好、报答支持者的)政治分肥(如从州的赋税中拨出用于地方福利的款项) / ~ **butcher** 杀猪的屠夫 / '~,**chopper** *n.* '~**pie** *n.* 猪肉饼 / '~**pie hat** 卷边低平顶帽

porous ['pɔ:rəs] *a.* ①多孔的;有气孔的; [喻]多漏洞的 ②能渗透的: Sandy soil is ~. 沙土是渗水的。 ③素烧(瓷)的 ‖ ~**ly** *ad.* / ~**ness** *n.*

porpoise ['pɔ:pəs] *n.* 【动】海豚

porridge ['pɔridʒ] *n.* 麦片粥;粥 ‖*keep* (或 *save*) *one's breath to cool one's* ~ 省点力气别开口(指说了也没用)

port[1] [pɔ:t] *n.* ① 港; [喻]避风港: clear a ~ 出港 / make(或 enter, reach)~ 入港 / close a ~ 封港 / touch at a ~ 靠港 ②港市;口岸 ③机场;航空港 ④(驻有海关关员的)对外开放港口 输入港(== ~ of entry) ‖*an admiralty* ~ 海军要塞 / *a close* ~ 河流上游港口 / *a commercial* ~ 商港 / *a free* ~ 自由港 / *an ice-free* (或 *a non-freezing, warmwater*) ~ 不冻港 / *an intermediate* ~ 中途转运港 / *a naval* ~ 军港 / *an open* ~ 对外贸易港;全年不冻港 / *an admiral* 海军要塞司令 / *a* ~ *of call* (沿途)停靠港 / *a* ~ *of delivery* 交货港 / *a* ~ *of discharge* (或 *unloading*) 卸货港 / *a* ~ *of distress* (或 *refuge*) 避难港 / *a* ~ *of recruit* 补充港,接应港 / *a* ~ *of registry* 船籍港 / *a river* ~ 内河港 / *a treaty* ~ 按条约规定(向缔约国)开放的港口 ‖*any* ~ *in a storm* 危难时不择好坏的出路 / *in* ~ 在港内,碇泊: There are many vessels *in* ~. 许多船停泊在港内。 ‖ ~ **charge** 入港税

port[2] [pɔ:t] *n.* ①[苏格兰]门(尤指城门口) ②【海】(船只的)舷窗;(装卸货物的)舱口 ③(装甲车、工事等的)炮眼,枪眼,射击孔;展望孔 ④【机】口;汽门;水门 ‖ ~**hole** *n.* ① 舷窗,舱口 ② 炮眼;射击孔

port[3] [pɔ:t] **I** *n.* (船、飞机的)左舷: a ~ anchor 左舷锚 / the ~ guns (军舰的)左舷炮 / the ~ engine of a bomber 轰炸机的左侧发动机 / put the helm to ~ (或 put the helm a-~) 转左舷 / on the ~ bow (quarter) 在左舷船首(尾) **II** ❶ *vt.* [主要用作命令语] 转(舵) 向左 (使船头右转): Port the helm! 左舵! ❷ *vi.* 转舵向左 ‖ ~'**side** *a.* ① 左边的;左派的 ② [美俚] 惯用左手的 / '~,**sider** *n.* [美俚] ①(垒球中的)左手投手 ② 左撇子

port[4] [pɔ:t] **I** *n.* ①举止,样子 ②含意;意义 ③(枪筒向上,自左肩至右胯)斜持枪支的持枪姿势 **II** *vt.* 持(枪): Port arms! (口令)持枪!

port[5] [pɔ:t] *n.* 葡萄酒 (原指葡萄牙产的一种深红

色或白色葡萄酒;=~ wine)

portable ['pɔ:təbl] **I** *a.* 轻便的;手提(式)的;便于携带的;可移动的: a ~ railway 轻便小铁道 / a ~ typewriter 手提打字机 / a ~ test instrument 便携式测试仪器 **II** *n.* ①手提打字机;手提式收音机(或电视机) ②可移动的房屋;可移动的校舍 ‖**portability** [ˌpɔ:təˈbiliti] *n.* 可携带性;轻便

portage ['pɔ:tidʒ] **I** *n.* ①搬运;运输 ②水陆联运;(两条水路间的)陆上运送路线 ③[古]搬运费,运费 **II** *vt.* & *vi.* 水陆联运(货物等);(由于激流等不能行驶而)把(船)搬经陆地运过去后再放入河中 (*the mariner's* ~ 准许水手存放所带私货的地方(旧时船上常以划出这种地方以代替付给水手的工资)

portal ['pɔ:tl] **I** *n.* ①门,入口(尤指大建筑物的正门) ②桥门;隧道门 ③[诗][喻]门,入门: the ~ of knowledge 知识之门 **II** *a.* 【医】门的;肝门的;门静脉的 ‖**'~-to-'~** *a.* 工人从(厂、矿等的)进口处到工作场所上下班所花回所花的时间的 / ~ vein 【医】门静脉

portcullis [pɔ:tˈkʌlis] **I** *n.* 城堡的吊闸; 吊门 **II** *vt.* 给…装吊门;用吊门关闭

portend [pɔ:ˈtend] *vt.* 预示;为…的兆头;给…以警告

portent ['pɔ:tent] *n.* ①不祥之兆;预兆;警告 ②预兆不祥之事;奇事,奇物,怪物

portentous [pɔ:ˈtentəs] *a.* ①预兆的,凶兆的,不祥的 ②怪异的;奇特的;可惊的 ③自命不凡的,自大的 ‖**~ly** *ad.*

porter[1] ['pɔ:tə] *n.* [主英]守门人,门房

porter[2] ['pɔ:tə] *n.* ①搬运工人;(火车站、旅馆等的)搬行李工人 ②(卧车或特等列车的)服务员 ③(银行、商店等的)杂务工,清洁工 ④黑啤酒 (=~'s beer) ‖**'~house** *n.* ①[美][古]小酒馆,小饭馆 ②上等牛排 (=~house steak) / ~'s **knot** [英] 搬运工用的垫肩

portfolio [pɔ:tˈfouljou] *n.* ①(皮制)公事包;文件夹: a lecture ~ (教师用的)讲义夹 ②大臣职;部长职: resign one's ~ 辞去大臣(或部长)职 / a minister without ~ 不管部大臣 (或部长) ③(保险)业务量;业务责任;【商】有价证券 ④(艺术家等的)代表作选

portico ['pɔ:tikou] ([复] portico(e)s) *n.* 【建】(有圆柱的)门廊

portion ['pɔ:ʃən] **I** *n.* ①一部分,一份: a large ~ of the products 大部分产品 / for the great ~ of one's life 一生中的大部分时间 / distribute in equal ~s 按份儿平均分配 / the through ~ for London (火车)直达伦敦的一部分车厢 ②(食物的)一份,一客: order a ~ of fried eggs 要一客煎蛋 ③遗产 (或赠与的财产) ;嫁妆 ⑤[只用单]命运 **II** *vt.* ①把…分成份额;分配 (out): ~ out food (land, property) 分配食物(土地,财产) ②给…嫁妆: ~ a daughter 给女儿嫁妆 ‖**~less** *a.* 没有份儿的(尤指得不到遗产或嫁

妆的)

portly ['pɔ:tli] *a.* ①肥胖的;粗壮的,魁梧的(常指年长者) ②[主方]举止庄重的 ‖**portliness** *n.*

portmanteau [pɔ:tˈmæntou] **I** ([复] portmanteaus 或 portmanteaux [pɔ:tˈmæntouz]) *n.* ①旅行皮包;旅行皮箱 ②[喻](两词音义合并的)混成词 (= ~ word; 如 motel 由 motorist 与 hotel 组成) **II** *a.* 多用途的;多性质的

portrait ['pɔ:trit] *n.* ①肖像,画像;相片: a ~ painter 肖像画家 ②半身像;雕像 ③生动的描写;人物描写 ④[喻]型式;相似 ‖**~ist** *n.* 肖像画家,画像者;照相者

portraiture ['pɔ:tritʃə] *n.* ①肖像画法 ②肖像,画像;照相 ③生动的描写(或描绘)

portray [pɔ:ˈtrei] *vt.* ①画(人物、风景等);描绘,描述,描写 ②扮演 ‖**~al** *n.* ①描绘;描写: the ~al of heroic characters 英雄人物的刻划 ②画像,肖像

pose[1] [pouz] **I** ❶ *vt.* ①使摆好姿势;把…摆正位置: The photographer ~d him carefully. 摄影师细心地使他摆好姿势。/ ~ one's spectacles 扶正眼镜 ②提出;造成,形成: ~ a problem (condition) 提出问题(条件) / ~ an obstacle (a threat) to 成为…的障碍(威胁) ❷ *vi.* ①摆好姿势: ~ for a group photo with a friend 摆好姿势和朋友合影 ②摆样子(或架子);装腔作势;假装: ~ as a scholar 摆出学者的样子 ③(西洋骨牌戏中)打出第一张牌 **II** *n.* ①(摄影、画像、表演时的)姿势,姿态: a dramatic (或 stage) ~ 舞台亮相 ②装腔作势;作态: overawe people by striking a ~ 靠装腔作势吓唬人 / put on a ~ of 装出…面貌(或样子)

pose[2] [pouz] *vt.* (用难题等)难住,使困惑

poser[1] ['pouzə] *n.* 装腔作势的人;伪装者

poser[2] ['pouzə] *n.* 难题,怪题

posh [pɔʃ] **I** *a.* [俚] ①豪华时髦的 ②优雅的,漂亮的;第一流的,极好的 **II** *int.* 呸[表示蔑视] ‖**~ism** *n.* 奢侈主义 / **~ly** *ad.* / **~ness** *n.* / **'~-looking** *a.* 漂亮的

position [pəˈziʃən] **I** *n.* ①位置;方位: the ~ of a city on a map 城市在地图上的位置 / fix a ship's ~ in the sea 测定船在海上的方位 / a football player's ~ 一个足球队员的位置 ②地位;身分: a man of ~ 有地位的人 ③职位;职务: She holds the ~ as (或 of) accountant for the production team. 她担任生产队会计的职务。④形势,状况,境况: in a favourable (difficult) ~ 处于有利(困难)地位 ⑤姿势;姿态: a ready ~ 【军】射击准备姿势 ⑥主张,见解;立场,态度: one's ~ on this problem 某人对这问题的看法 / a ~ paper 阐明自己对各种(或某一)问题的立场的论文 / make one's ~ known 表明立场态度 ⑦【军】发射阵地;阵地: warfare 阵地战 / get (或 go) into ~ 进入阵地 / an advance (或 a forward) ~ 前沿阵地 / occupy the ~s on the cultural front 占领文化战线上的阵地 ⑧【音】(左手在提琴指板上的)把位 ⑨【语】(音节中)元音的位置 II **vt.** ①把…放在适当的位置; 给…定位 ②【军】屯(兵), 驻扎(部队) ‖in a ~ to (do sth.) 能够(做某事): I'm sorry I'm not *in a ~* to help you right now. 很抱歉, 我不能马上帮你的忙。/ *in* (out of) ~ 在(不在)适当的位置 / *jockey for* ~ ①(赛马时)挤其他骑师以占有利位置 ②【喻】运用(欺诈)手段谋图利益 / (*put sb.*) *in a false* ~ (使某人)处于违反原则行事的地位; (使某人)处于被误解的地位 ‖~ **buoy** 雾标, 指示浮标 / ~ **light** (飞机的)航行灯; 锚位灯

positive ['pɔzətiv] I **a.** ①确定的, 明确的; 确实的: a ~ fact 无可怀疑的事实 / a ~ proof 确证 ②确信的; 有自信的: I am ~ that he is correct. 我确信他是正确的。/ Can you be ~ about what you saw? 你能肯定你看得真切吗? ③过于自信的; 独断的 ④绝对的 ⑤积极的; 建设性的, 确有助益的; 肯定的: ~ criticism 积极的批评 / make ~ contributions (to victory) (为胜利)作出积极的贡献 / bring all ~ factors into play 调动一切积极因素 / ~ help 确有助益的帮助 / a ~ reply 肯定的答复 / state in a ~ way 正面阐明 / ~ and negative historical lessons 正反两个方面的历史教训 ⑥实证的; 实际的, 实在的: ~ philosophy 实证哲学, 实证论 / a ~ mind 实事求是的人 ⑦(协定、习惯等)规定的: ~ laws 成文法 ⑧【口】完全的, 纯粹的: a ~ fool 大傻瓜 ⑨【语】原级的: a ~ adjective (adverb) 原级形容词(副词) / the ~ degree 原级 ⑩【数】正的: a ~ angle 正角 / a ~ number 正数 / a ~ sign 正号 ⑪【物】正的; 阳性的: ~ charge 阳电荷, 正电荷 / ~ electricity 阳电, 正电 / ~ ray 阳极射线 / ~ pole 正极, 阳极 / ~ reaction 阳性反应, 正反应; 正反力 ⑫【摄】正片的, 正像的 ⑬【生】(刺激源)向性的, 趋性的 II **n.** ①明确, 实在; 确实 ②正面; 【摄】正片, 正像 ③[the ~]【语】原级 ④(电池的)阳极板 ⑤【数】正数 ‖~**ly ad.** / ~**ness n.**

possess [pə'zes] **vt.** ①占有, 拥有(财产等); 使占有, 使拥有 (of, with): ~ landed property 拥有地产 / ~ sb. of sth. 使某人占有(或拥有)某物 ②具有(品质、才能等) ③掌握(思想、语言、知识、技能等) ④(常指心情方面)保持; 克制, 抑制: ~ oneself 自制, 保持镇定 / ~ one's soul (或 mind) in patience 耐心等待 ⑤支配, 控制: be ~ed with (或 by) an idea 一心想着一个念头 / What ~ed him to do such a thing? 什么东西使他干出这种事来? ⑥(妖魔、情欲等)迷住, 缠住: like one ~ed 着了魔似的 / be ~ed with (或 by) a lust for gain 利欲熏心 ‖be ~ed ①疯了; 鬼迷心窍 ②一心想做某事; 渴望占有某物 ③镇静 / be ~ed of 拥有, 占有; 具有: be ~ed of a strong fighting spirit 具有旺盛的战斗精神 / be ~ed of good health 身体健康 / like

all ~ed [美]极其猛烈地; 拼命地 / ~ oneself of 取得, 获得; 把…占为己有: ~ oneself of the necessary material 取得必要的材料

possession [pə'zeʃən] **n.** ①有, 所有, 拥有: the information in sb.'s ~ 某人拥有的消息(或情报) ②所有权; 占有 ③[常用复]占有物, 所有物; 财产: personal ~s 个人财产(或财物) ④[常用复]领地, 属地, 殖民地 ⑤自制, 镇定自若: in full ~ of one's senses 神智十分清醒 ⑥(指人)着魔 ‖come into ~ of sth. 占有(或获得)某物 / come into sb.'s ~ (某物)被某人占有 / demand (give) ~ 要求(给予)引渡 / in ~ of sth. 占有某物: put sb. in ~ of the information 让某人知道这消息 / in the ~ of sb. 为某人所有 / *Possession is nine points of the law.* [谚]占有者在诉讼中总占上风。/ take ~ of 占有; 占领

possessive [pə'zesiv] I **a.** ①占有的, 所有的; 占有欲的 ②【语】(词、词组、形态变化等)所属关系的, 所有格的: the ~ case 所有格 II **n.** 【语】[the ~] 所有格; 所有格的词, 物主代词, (表示)所属关系的词(或词组等) ‖~**ly ad.** / ~**ness n.** ‖~ **adjective**【语】所有格形容词 / ~ **pronoun**【语】物主代词

possessor [pə'zesə] **n.** 占有人, 所有人; 持有人

possibility [ˌpɔse'biliti] **n.** ①可能, 可能性: is there any ~ of our getting there in time? 我们还能准时赶到那里吗? / There is no ~ of his coming back this week. 他本星期不可能回来。/ be within the bounds (或 range) of ~ 在可能范围内 ②[常用复]可能的事, 可能发生的事: What are the *possibilities*? 有哪些可能发生的情况? (或: 前景如何?) / I see great *possibilities* in the experiment. 我看实验成功的可能性很大。‖a bare ~ 万一的事情 / by any ~ 有可能, 万一, 也许: If I could by any ~ manage to do it, I would. 假使有可能设法做的话, 我一定做。/ He cannot by any ~ do such a thing. 他决不会做这种事。

possible ['pɔsəbl] I **a.** ①可能的; 可能存在(或发生, 做到)的; 潜在的: the best ~ means (或 the best means ~) 尽可能好的办法 / ~, if not probable 即使不见得会发生, 至少是可能的 [注意: probable 和 possible 二词都有 '可能的' 意思, 但 probable 所指的可能性更大些] / a ~ site for an industrial base 可能作为工业基地的地点 / It is entirely ~ for us to fulfil the task ahead of schedule. 我们完全有可能提前完成任务。/ It is ~ (that) he will be here in time. 他也许会及时来这儿的。②合理的; 可允许的: two ~ solutions to the problem 两种可以用来解决问题的办法 ③[口]过得去的; 可以接受的; 还算可以的: a ~ football player 还算不错的足球运动员 II **n.** ①可能(性); 潜在性 ②[常用复]可能的人(或物); 可能出现的事物: a trial game between ~s and probables （为选拔为正式队员而进行的）预备队员间的一次预赛 / the ~ in scientific research 科学研究中可能出现的事物 ③最高分,最优等成绩(尤指射击): He scored a ~ at 200 metres. 他在二百米射击中得到最优等的成绩。④[复]必ზ物品(尤指金钱、给养等) ‖as … as ~ 尽可能…,愈…愈好: Come as early as ~. 尽可能早点来。/ do one's ~ 尽力,竭力/ if ~ 如果可能的话/ ~ of 可能…的: be ~ of attainment (realization, solution) 可能达到(实现,解决)

possibly ['posəbli] ad. ①可能地;合理地②也许,或者: It may ~ be so. 也许是这样的。③[用于否定句、疑问句]无论如何,不管怎样: Could he ~ agree? 难道他会同意吗?/ He cannot ~ forget it. 他无论如何也不会忘记。

post[1] [poust] I n. ①柱;桩;杆;标柱,标杆: a boundary ~ 界桩,界柱/ bed ~s 床杆/ door ~s 门柱/ a distance ~ 路程标/ a lamp ~ (路)灯杆/ a sign ~ 标杆/ the starting (winning) ~ (赛跑、赛马等的)起跑点(终点)的标志/ a screw ~ 千斤顶柱;螺旋柱 ②[矿]煤柱,矿柱;厚砂岩层;厚石灰岩层 ③(枪膛前方的)准星 II vt. ①贴出(布告、通告等);(把布告等)贴在…上(up): Post no bills! 禁止招贴! / ~ up a notice on the bulletin board 在布告板上贴出通知 ②(用布告)宣布,公告: the ~ed price 牌价/ names ~ed for holiday duty 公布的假日值班名单 ③把…登入榜;[英](大学)宣布(不及格学生)的名单 ④(出布告、用布告牌等)警告;禁止进入(某地);(出布告)公开揭发,公开谴责: ~ one's land [美](出公告宣布)地内禁猎 ⑤公布(失事或失踪船只): a ship ~ed as missing 已宣布为失踪的船只 ⑥得(分) ‖beat sb. on the ~ (赛跑中)以一胸之差胜过某人

post[2] [poust] I n. ①邮政(制度);邮寄: ~ and telecommunication 邮电/ send books by ~ 邮寄书籍 ②[英](一批)邮件(=[美] mail);邮件的一次发送(或收进) There is a heavy ~ today. 今天邮件很多。/ When does the first ~ go out (come in)? 头班邮件什么时候发出(收进)?/ I missed the morning ~. 我没赶上早班邮件(寄邮时间)/ catch the last ~ 赶上末班邮件(寄邮时间) ③[英]邮局;邮筒;[方]邮递员 ④驿马;邮车;邮船 ⑤[古]驿站;(两驿站之间的)行程,路程 ⑥[作名称用]邮报,报纸 ⑦一种信笺或抄写纸的尺寸 II ❶ vi. ①乘驿马旅行 ②快速旅行;赶紧走 ❷ vt. ①[主英]投寄,邮寄(=[美] mail);[古]急派(某人) ②过(帐),誊(帐)(尤指把日记帐记入分类帐),登入(总帐): ~ (up) export sales 把出口销售金额记入总帐/ ~ up a ledger 过入总帐 ③[常用被动语态]使熟悉,使了解: keep sb. ~ed (up) in the developments of the experiment 让某人了解实验的进展情况 III ad. ①乘驿马 ②快速地,加急地 ‖by return of ~ (原指)由原送信人带回;(现指)由下一班回程邮递带回/ ~ off 匆匆出发 ‖'~bag n. [主英] ①邮袋 ②一

次发送(或收进)的邮件/ ~ boat [英]邮船;(往返于某地间的)客船/ '~box n. 信箱;邮筒/ '~boy n. ①用驿车送信的人 ② =postil(l)ion / '~card n. 明信片;非邮局发行的明信片(常指附有图画、需贴邮票的)/ ~ chaise (旧时)驿递(或驿站)马车/ '~'free a. [主英]免付邮资的;邮费付讫的/ '~'haste ad. 尽可能快速地,急速地 n. [古]火速,火急,赶紧/ ~ horn (十八、十九世纪)驿车上用的一种喇叭/ '~-horse n. (旧时)驿马/ '~house n. ①(旧时)驿馆,驿栈 ②[古]邮局/ ~man ['poustmən] n. 邮递员;邮差/ the ~man's route 邮递员的投递路线/ '~mark n. 邮戳 vt. 盖邮戳于/ ~master n. ①邮政局长 ②驿站站长/ '~,master general 邮政部长/ ~ mistress 女邮政局长/ ~ office 邮局/ '~-,office box 邮政信箱/ '~,office order [英]邮政汇票/ '~'paid a. 邮费付讫的/ ~ road 驿路/ ~ town (某一地区内)设有邮局的市镇

post[3] [poust] I n. ①岗位(尤指哨兵站岗位置);哨所;站/ a command ~ 指挥所/ an observation ~ 观察所,观测哨/ a radar ~ 雷达哨 ②(部队的)驻地;兵营,营区;守备部队 ③职位;职守/ fill successively the ~s of 历任…等职/ stick to one's ~ 坚守岗位 ④[英][军](熄灯号(声): the first (last) ~ 头次(末次)熄灯号 ⑤[美](退役军人的)地方分会 ⑥商埠,贸易站;租界;(证券交易所中的)地面交易站 II vt. ①布置(岗哨等): ~ sentries around the camp 在营地周围布置岗哨 ②[军]任命,派任(尤指军职) ③(隆重地)把(国旗)带到指定地点/ ~ (国旗)带到指定地点/ ~ with 把(证券等)交有关当局 ‖ captain [英史]小军官的舰长/ ~ exchange 陆军消费合作社(美国)(略作 PX)

post [poust] ad. [拉] 在后 ‖ meridiem [mə'ridiem] 午后,下午(略作 p.m. 或 P.M.)

postal ['poustəl] I a. 邮政的;邮局的: ~ matter 邮件/ ~ rates 各种邮件的邮资/ a ~ delivery department 邮递部门 II n. [美口]明信片 ‖ ~ card [美]明信片/ ~ course [英]函授课程/ ~ order [英]邮政汇票

poster[1] ['poustə] n. ①(贴在公共场所的大型)招贴;标语;广告(画): ~ paper 广告纸,招贴纸 ②贴标语(或广告、招贴等)的人

poster[2] ['poustə] n. ①驿马 ②[古]快速旅行者

poste restante ['poust 'restɑ̃:nt] [法] ①(信封上的附注)留局待领邮件 ②[主英](邮局的)待领邮件科;待领邮件业务

posterior [pos'tiəriə] I a. ①(时间上)以后的;(次序上)其次的;(位置上)后面的: ~ to the year 1949 一九四九年以后的/ a ~ limb 后肢/ a ~ branch (树木)后部的叉枝 II n. [常用复]臀部;后部 ‖ ~ly ad.

posterity [pos'teriti] n. 后裔,子孙;后代,后世: go down to ~ 传至后代

postil(l)ion [pəs'tiljən] n. (两匹或多匹马拉马车或驿车的)骑在左马上的驭者

postpone [poust'poun] ❶ *vt.* ①延迟,使延期,延缓: The meeting is ~d until (或 to) next week. 会议延期至下星期举行。/ be ~d for six months 延期六个月 / ~ sending an answer 暂缓答复 ②把(人或事物)放在次要地位;【语】把(某种词等)放在后面(或句尾): ~ an adjective 把形容词放在后面 ❷ *vi.* (疾疫等)延缓发作(或复发) ‖**postponable** *a.* 可以延缓的 / **~ment** *n.* 延迟,延期: demand a ten-day ~ment 要求延期十天 / after numerous ~ments 在无数次的延搁以后

postulate ['postjuleit] Ⅰ ❶ *vt.* ①要求: the claims ~d 要求事项 ②假定;以…为基点 ③【数】公设,假设: ~d point 假设点 ❷ *vi.* 要求: ~ for certain conditions 要求某些条件 Ⅱ ['postjulit, 'postjuleit] *n.* ①假定 ②先决条件;必要条件 ③【数】公设,假设 ④基本原理 ‖**postulation** [ˌpostju'leiʃən] *n.* ①假定: postulation formula 【数】假定公式 ②要求 / **postulator** *n.* 假定者;要求者

posture ['postʃə] Ⅰ *n.* ①姿势,姿态;态度: in an erect (a reclining) ~ 直立(斜靠)着 / draw sb. in three ~s 画出某人在三种不同姿态时的样子 / assume a ~ of superiority 摆出高人一等的样子 ②情形,形势: in the present ~ of 在目前…的情况下 ③心情;心境: good ~ 愉快的心境 Ⅱ ❶ *vt.* 使作出某种姿势(或态度) ❷ *vi.* 取某种姿势(或态度);故作姿态 ‖**~r** ['postʃərə] *n.* ①作出某种姿势的人;装腔作势的人 ②擅长作出怪样的卖艺人 / **posturise, posturize** ['postʃəraiz] *vi.* 摆姿势 ‖**~-ˌmaker** *n.* 演杂技的人;擅长作出怪样的卖艺人 / **~-ˌmaster** *n.* 柔软体操教师

posy ['pouzi] *n.* ①[古](刻在戒指上的)诗句(或格言、纪念性词句) ②花束

pot [pot] Ⅰ *n.* ①[常用以构成复合词]罐;锅;壶: a glass ~ 玻璃罐 / a sauce~ 煮物锅(如家用钢精锅) / a watering ~ 浇水壶,洒水壶 / an ink-~ 墨水瓶 / a flower~ 花盆 / a tea~ 茶壶 ②一罐(或锅、壶)的容量: a ~ of soup 一锅汤 / a ~ of tea 一壶茶 ③[冶]锅,罐,坩埚: melting ~ 熔化锅 ④罐状物(尤指捕鱼虾等用的篓笼) ⑤(运动会等的)奖杯;奖品 ⑥大笔(款子): a ~ (或 ~s) of money 大笔钱 ⑦(纸牌戏的)一局;赌注的总额;奖金的总额;(一个团体的)基金总额 ⑧一壶酒;酒;饮酒;酗酒: crush a ~ 喝酒 ⑨[美俚]大麻叶 ⑩ =~shot (n.) ⑪一种书写(或印刷)用纸(也作 pott) ⑫[俚]大肚皮 ⑬(台球戏中)把球打入袋中的一击 ⑭[俚]电位计 Ⅱ (potted; potting) ❶ *vt.* ①把…放在罐(或锅)里;把…装罐(或装坛): potted ham 罐装火腿 ②把…栽在花盆里 ③删节;摘录 ④[俚]从…取得食物则向…射击;用乱枪射死(动物);获得(猎物)抓住,捕获 ⑤把(台球)打入袋中 ❷ *vi.* 射击;乱射 (at) ‖**a big ~** 大人物,要人 / **A little ~ is soon hot.** [谚]壶小易热。(或:量小易怒。) /

A watched ~ never boils. [谚]心急水不沸。/ **betray the ~ to the roses** 泄漏秘密 / **go into the melting ~** 经受锻炼 / **go to ~** 遭毁坏,垮掉;破产,潦倒;(营业等)衰落,萧条 / **in the ~** 醉了 / **keep the ~ boiling** 谋生,维持生活;(游戏等)使生动活泼地进行下去 / **make the ~ boil** 糊口,谋生,维持生活 / **~s and pans** 炊事用具;坛坛罐罐 / **The ~ calls the kettle black.** [谚]指责别人,而不怪自己有同样的过失。(或:责人严而律己宽。) ‖**~ful** *n.* 一罐,一锅,一壶(指容量) ‖**~ ale** 酒糟 / **~ˌbarley** 去壳大麦 / **~ˌbellied** *a.* 大肚皮的,大腹便便的 / **~ˌbelly** *n.* 大肚皮;大肚皮的人 ②(一种家用取暖的)大腹火炉 / **~boil** *vi.* 为混饭吃而粗制滥造(指文艺作品) / **~ˌboiler** *n.* ①为混饭吃而粗制滥造的文艺作品 ②为混饭吃而粗制滥造作品的人 / **~-bound** *a.* (植物等)根生满花盆没有伸展余地的 / **~ boy** *n.* (酒馆中的)侍者 / **~ˌhanger** *n.* (炉火上的)挂锅钩(或搁锅子的装置) / **~ hat** 硬质礼帽 / **~ˌhead** *n.* [美俚]吸大麻成瘾的人 / **~herb** *n.* ①野菜 ②调味用的香草(如薄荷) / **~hole** *n.* ①[地]锅穴,壶穴 ②(路面上的)坑洼 / **~hook** *n.* ①(把锅、罐等吊在火上煮或从火上钩起的)S形锅钩 ②(初学者写的)歪歪斜斜的笔划 / **~house** *n.* [英]小酒馆,小旅馆 / **~ˌhunter** *n.* ①(为了获得食物而乱猎的)猎人 ②[英]为获奖而参加比赛的人 / **~ lead** 石墨(尤指涂赛船底部用的) / **~ˈluck** *n.* 家常便饭: Come along and take ~luck. (请)来吃便饭。/ **~ˌman** *n.* =~boy / **~ metal** ①一种铜和铅的合金(供制造大型容器用) ②一种铸铁(供制锅等用) ③(熔解时着色的)有色玻璃 / **~pie** *n.* 菜肉馅饼 / **~ roast** 炖熟的肉 / **~-roast** *vt.* 炖 / **~sherd** *n.* 陶瓷碎片 / **~ˈshot** *n.* ①(为取得食物而猎的猎人的)射击 ②近距离射击;乱射;任意的射击 ③肆意的抨击,突然的抨击 *vt. & vi.* (…)乱射 ②肆意抨击 / **~ still** 壶形(式蒸)馏器 / **~stone** *n.* [矿]不纯皂石 / **~-ˌvaliant** *a.* 酒(醉)后胆壮的 / **~ˈwalloper** *n.* ①【英史】自己成家从而有选举权的人(也作 ~waller) ②[英俚]行动笨拙的人,重手重脚的人 ③[美俚]洗碗工;(伐木营地的)厨师 ④[海]厨师的助手

potash ['potæʃ] *n.* 【化】钾碱(泛指碳酸钾,也称苛性钾): caustic ~ 苛性钾碱(氢氧化钾的俗称)

potato [pə'teitou] ([复] potatoes) *n.* ①马铃薯,土豆: sweet (或 Spanish) ~ 甘薯,白薯,山芋 / white (或 Irish) ~ 马铃薯,土豆(即普通的白马铃薯) / mashed ~(es) 马铃薯泥(捣烂的熟马铃薯) ②[美]甘薯 ③[美俚]头;脸(尤指难看的脸) ④[美俚]一元钱 ⑤[美俚]球(尤指垒球) ‖**a hot ~** 棘手的问题 / **~es and point** (肉少得可怜的)一锅马铃薯烧肉 / **small ~es** (或 **a small ~**) [美俚]微不足道的人(或物) / **the clean ~** [俚]最好(或最正确、最适当)的事物 ‖**chip ~** 马铃薯薄片 / **po'tato-head** *n.* [美俚]笨蛋

~ **masher** ①熟马铃薯捣烂器 ②一种木柄手榴弹 / ~ **ring** (爱尔兰旧时用以)垫碗(或钵等)的银围圈 / **po'tato-trap** *n.* [美俚]嘴

potent ['pəutənt] *a.* ①有力的,强有力的;有势力的 ②(药、酒等)有效力的,有效验的;烈性的;(议论等)有说服力的: ~ reasons 使人信服的理由 ③(茶等)浓的 ④(男性)有性交能力的 ‖~**ly** *ad.*

potentate ['pəutənteit] *n.* 有权势的人;当权者,统治者;君主

potential [pə'tenʃəl] **I** *a.* ①潜在的;【物】势的,位的: ~ resources 潜在的资源 ②有可能性的;【语】可能(语气)的: the ~ demand of the market 市场上可能达到的需求量 / the ~ mood 可能语气(原形动词加助动词 may 等) ③[罕]有力量的 **II** *n.* ①潜势;潜能;潜力: industrial (military) ~ 工业(军事)潜力 / tap the ~ of production 挖掘生产潜力 ②【物】势,位: electric ~ 电势,电位 ③【语】可能语气 ‖~**ly** *ad.* 潜在地 ‖~ **difference** 【物】势差,位差; 电位差 / ~ **energy** 【物】势能,位能 / ~ **transformer** 【电】变压器

potion ['pəuʃən] *n.* ①一服药水(或药剂): sleeping ~ 安眠药 ②一服麻醉药(或毒药)

potter[1] ['pɔtə] *n.* 陶工 ‖~**'s asthma** 【医】陶工喘症 /~**'s bronchitis** 【医】陶工支气管炎 /~**'s clay**, ~**'s earth** 陶土 / ~**'s field** 义冢地(源出基督教《圣经》) / ~**'s wheel** 陶人旋盘

potter[2] ['pɔtə] [英方] ❶ *vi.* ①松松垮垮地做事: ~ at (或 in) one's occupation 吊儿郎当地混饭吃 ②闲逛,闲荡 (about, around) ❷ *vt.* 混(日子),浪费(时间等) (away)

pottery ['pɔtəri] *n.* ①[总称]陶器 ②陶器制造(术) ③陶器制造厂(或作坊)

potty[1] ['pɔti] *a.* [英俚] ①琐碎的,微不足道的: ~ little details 琐碎的细节 / ~ questions (试卷中)容易回答的问题 ②傻的;有些疯狂的;迷恋的,着迷的 (about) ③傲慢的;势利的

potty[2] ['pɔti] *n.* (小孩用的)便罐,尿壶 ‖'~-**chair** *n.* (小孩用的)拉屎坐椅(座上开圆孔,下置容器)

pouch [pautʃ] **I** *n.* ①(随身携带的)小袋,烟草袋; [古]钱袋 ②皮制弹药袋: an ammunition ~ 子弹盒 ③邮袋 ④[苏格兰](衣服的)口袋 ⑤【动】(袋类动物体腹面的)育儿袋,肚囊;(某些猴的)颊袋 ⑥【植】短角 ⑦【解】陷凹,憩室 **II** ❶ *vt.* ①把…放入袋中;把…占为己有 ②把(衣服的一部分)做成袋子;使成袋状,使鼓起 ③[古](鱼、鸟等)吞下 ④[英俚]付小帐给 ❷ *vi.* ①成袋状;悬垂如袋 ②用邮袋递送 ‖~**ed** *a.* 有袋的;悬垂如袋的: ~ed mammals 有袋哺乳动物(如袋鼠等) /~**y** *a.* 有袋的;袋形的

poulterer ['pəultərə] *n.* 家禽贩

poultice ['pəultis] **I** *n.* 【医】泥罨(敷)剂 **II** *vt.* 敷泥罨(敷)剂于

poultry ['pəultri] *n.* [总称]家禽: a ~ farm 家禽饲养场 ‖~**man** ['pəultrimən] *n.* (尤指为了营利的)家禽饲养者;家禽商

pounce[1] [pauns] **I** *n.* ①(猛禽等的)猛扑,飞扑: make a ~ upon 向…猛扑 / be on the ~ 正在扑过去 ②(猛禽的)利爪 **II** ❶ *vi.* ①猛扑;突然袭击 (on, upon); 猛抓 (at) ②[喻]攻击 (on, upon): ~ upon sb.'s slip of tongue 抓住某人的一时失言而大做文章 ❷ *vt.* 扑过去攫住

pounce[2] [pauns] **I** *n.* ①(旧时用来防止墨水渗开的)吸墨粉 ②(撒在镂花模板上以印出图案的)印花粉 **II** *vt.* ①用擦粉把…擦得光滑 ②撒吸墨粉于(纸)上 ③用印花粉印出

pound[1] [paund] *n.* ①磅(重量单位,一般指常衡磅): an avoirdupois ~ 常衡磅(略作 lb., 或 lb. av.; 合 0.454 公斤); 金银、药品以外的重量单位) / a troy ~ 金衡磅(略作 lb. t.; 合 0.373 公斤; 金银重量单位) / an apothecaries' ~ 药衡磅(略作 lb. ap.; 合 0.373 公斤; 药品重量单位) / three hundred ~s 三百磅 (常写作 300 lbs.) ② 英镑 (= ~ sterling) (符号为 £): five ~s 五英镑 (常写作 £5) / a (five-~) note 一英镑 (五英镑) 票面的钞票 / pay 25 pence in the ~ 欠款每英镑归还二十五便士 ③镑 (爱尔兰、马耳他、苏丹等的货币单位) ‖a ~ of flesh (源出莎士比亚剧本《威尼斯商人》) 合法但极不合理的要求: The moneylender intends to have his ~ of flesh. 这放债人企图尽量榨取。/ in for a penny, in for a ~ 见 penny / penny wise and ~ foolish 见 penny / ~ cake 重油蛋糕 / '~-'foolish *a.* 大数目上马虎的;大事情上糊涂的 / ~ sterling 英镑

pound[2] [paund] **I** ❶ *vt.* ①捣碎;舂烂: ~ rice in a mortar 在臼中舂米 / ~ sth. into a jelly 把某物舂成冻状物 ②(连续)猛击;(猛烈)敲打: ~ nails into a board 把钉子敲进木板 / ~ the typewriter 劈劈啪啪地打字 / be ~ed on all sides 四面挨打 ③(不断重复地)灌输: This truth is being ~ed home to them. 正在不断地使他们理解这个道理(或事实)。④(沉重地或持续地)沿着…移动: The heavy bomber ~ed her way down the runway. 这架重轰炸机在跑道上沉重地滑行。❷ *vi.* ①(连续)撞击;(猛烈)敲打: The two fleets ~ed away at each other. 两支舰队彼此猛轰。/ hear sb. ~ing at the door 听到有人在砰砰敲门 / feel one's heart ~ing 觉得心在剧跳 ②脚步沉重地走 (或跑);隆隆行驶(或飞行): ~ up the stairs 脚步沉重地上楼梯 / A tractor was ~ing down the road. 一辆拖拉机沿着道路隆隆地驶过去。③(持续地)苦干: keep ~ing away at one's work 持续地努力工作 **II** *n.* 重击;重击声 ‖~ **out** 连续猛击而产生: ~ out a list on the typewriter 在打字机上劈劈啪啪打出一张单子 / ~ a song on the piano 在钢琴上砰砰地(乱)弹出一支歌曲 / ~ the pavement(s) 见 pavement

pound[3] [paund] **I** *n.* ①(走失的牲畜)待领场 ②(关禁无执照或未驯养的牲畜的)牲畜栏; 诱捕

兽类的栏 ③(捕鱼或养鱼的)鱼塘; 养龙虾池; 鲜活龙虾出售处 ④[喻]拘留所; 拘留; 围住; 圈紧 ⑤(扣压的财物等)待赎所, 待赎所 II vt. ①[古]把(走失的牲畜)关进待领场 (up); [喻]监禁, 拘留 ②[古]筑坝拦(水)

pour [pɔ:, poə] I ❶ vt. ①倒;灌;注: ~ sugar out of a bag into a pot 把糖从袋中倒入罐内 / ~ sb. a cup of tea 为某人倒一杯茶 / ~ concrete (steel) 浇注混凝土(钢水) ②倾注, 源源输送: After every match the stadium ~s thousands of people into the surrounding streets. 每场比赛后, 成千上万的人从体育场散入周围街道。 / a large sum of money into a project 把大笔资金投入一项工程 ③倾吐, 诉说 out, forth): ~ oneself out 倾诉自己的想法(或感情等) ❷ vi. ①倾泻, 不断流出: Sweat ~ed down from his face. 汗珠不断从他脸上流下。 ②涌出, 涌来; 源源而来: People ~ed out to the rally. 人们踊跃参加群众大会。 / Reports of new successes keep ~ing in. 捷报频传。③下倾盆大雨 (雨)倾盆而下: It is ~ing. 在下倾盆大雨。 / The rain ~ed down. 大雨如注。 / a ~ing day 下大雨的日子 ④ 在茶桌上当主妇(西方风俗,招待客人饮茶时由主妇斟茶) II n. ①倒、倾泻; 浇注;一次浇注(入模)的量 ②倾盆大雨 ‖It never rains but it ~s. 见 rain / cold water on 对…泼冷水 / it on [美俚]①大肆吹捧 ②加油干, 努力干 ③飞速行进 / ~ oil on the flame(s) (或 on fire) 见 oil / ~ oil on the (troubled) waters 见 oil ‖~er ['pɔ:rə] n. ①倒(茶水等)的人 ②浇注工

pout[1] [paut] I ❶ vi. ①撅嘴, 板脸;不高兴 ②撅起; 凸出, 板起: The paper ~ed up in flames. 纸被烧得卷了起来。 ❷ vt. ①撅起(嘴唇等);使凸出; 使(羽毛等)张开 ②撅嘴板脸地说 II n. ①撅嘴 ②[常用复]生气, 不高兴: have (或 be in) the ~s 撅着嘴不高兴 ‖~er n. ①撅嘴生气的人 ②【动】凸顶鸽 / ~y a. 生气的

pout[2] [paut] ([复] pout(s)) n. 【动】大头鱼类(如鳕、棉鳕、鲶等)

poverty ['pɔvəti] n. ①贫穷, 贫困: abject ~ 赤贫 / live in ~ 过着穷苦的生活 ②贫乏, 缺少: ~ in vitamins 维生素的缺乏 ③(土地等)的贫瘠 ④虚弱 ‖live in genteel ~ 家境贫寒却虚摆场面 ‖~-stricken a. 贫穷的, 贫困的; 贫乏的

powder ['paudə] I n. ①粉末: reduce (grind) sth. to ~ 把某物弄成(磨成)粉末 ②香粉;粉: tooth ~ 牙粉 / talcum ~ 滑石粉; 爽身粉 / curry ~ 咖喱粉 ③(一服)药粉;粉剂: take a ~ after each meal 每顿饭后吃一服药粉 ④火药;炸药; [喻]推动力;爆炸力 ⑤雪糁;泥土的屑粒, 尘土 ⑥[美俚]一杯酒 ⑦[美俚]逃跑, 逃遁: take a ~ 逃跑;离开 II ❶ vt. ①洒粉于; (用粉状物)覆盖 (with): The leaves were ~ed with dust. 树叶上积着尘土。②在…上搽粉 ③(用圆点或微小的图案)装饰 (with): a piece of red cloth ~ed

with white spots 一块有白点的红布 ④使成粉末 ❷ vi. ①变成粉末 ②搽粉 ③[美俚]离开; 逃跑 ‖foolish ~ [美俚]海洛因 / keep one's ~ dry 时刻准备着, 作好准备 / ~ and shot 子弹, 军用品: not worth ~ and shot 不值得射击的; 不能得争取的 ‖~ed a. 弄成粉末(状)的: ~ed milk 奶粉 / ~ed fuel 粉末燃料 ‖~ blue 氧化钴(一种深蓝色颜料);深蓝色 / ~ cart 弹药车 / ~ chamber (炮膛中的)药室 / ~ factory 火药制造厂 / ~ flask, ~ horn (牛角制的)火药筒 / ~ keg ①(金属制的)小型火药(或炸药)箱 ②易爆炸的东西 / ~ magazine 火药库 / ~ metallurgy【冶】粉末冶金 / ~ monkey ①(旧时舰上)为火炮搬运火药的人 ②[美](矿山中)搬运药的人;负责装炸药的人 / ~ puff ①粉扑 ②机灵的拳斗手 ③轻击 / ~ rocket 固体燃料火箭 / ~ room ①(舰上)药包舱 ②女用盥洗室,化妆室;休息室 ③浴室 / ~ snow 雪糁

powdery ['paudəri] a. ①粉的;粉状的 ②易碎成粉末的 ③布满粉状物(或尘埃)的 ‖powderiness n.

power ['pauə] I n. ①能力: do everything in one's ~ to help 尽力帮助 ②(生理)机能;体力;精力;才能: the ~ of vision 视力 / tax sb.'s ~s to the utmost 需要某人尽力 / a man of varied ~s 多才多艺的人 ③力, 力量;动力, 电力;功率, 率: electric (water) ~ 电(水)力 / military ~ 军事力量 / ~ in kilowatts 以瓩计算的功率 ④权,政权;权力;势力: organs of state ~ 国家权力机关 / a political party in ~ 执政党 / have ~ over 对…有控制权 ⑤权力范围, 权限: exceed one's ~s 超越自己的权限 ⑥(授权的)证书: ~ (或 letter) of attorney 授权书, 委托书(授权给代理人的法定证件) ⑦强国, 大国: an industrial ~ 工业强国 ⑧有权力的人;有影响的机构 ⑨【数】幂, 乘方: the fourth ~ of x x 的四次幂(即 x^4) ⑩(光学上的)放大率;透镜的焦强 ⑪[俗]许多,大量: a ~ of people 许多人 / do a ~ of work 做大量工作 ⑫神, 神仙 II vt. 用动力发动;赋与…动力 ‖come into ~ (开始)执政, 当权; 上台 / have sb. in one's ~ 控制住某人, 能摆布某人 / More ~ to your elbow! (表示鼓励或赞同的用语)加把劲! 使劲干吧! / the ~ of the keys 【基督教】司钥权, 教皇享有的最高教权 / the ~s that be 当局 ‖~boat n. 动力艇, 汽艇 / ~ brake 机力制动(器), 机动闸 / ~ dive 动力俯冲 / ~-dive vt. & vi. (使)进行动力俯冲 / ~-driven a. 动力传动的 / ~ gas 动力气体 / ~house n. ①发电站 ②(影响等的)源泉 ③权力大的人 ④[美俚]有实力的运动队(尤指橄榄球队); 强健的运动员 (尤指橄榄球员); 强壮的男子 / ~ lathe 机力车床 / ~ loom 动力织机 / ~man ['pauəmən] n. 发电机专业人员 / ~ mower 电动割草机 / ~ pack 电源组 / ~ plant ①发电站, 发电厂 ②(机动车辆等的)动力设备 / ~ politics 强权政治 / ~ series 【数】幂

级数 / ~ **shovel** (单斗) 挖土机; 机铲 / ~ **station** 发电站 / ~ **structure** (社会、组织等的)权力结构 / ~ **take-off** (卡车、拖拉机上输出动力以推动绞盘、泵等机械的)动力输出装置 / ~ **transmission** 输电, 电力传输

powerful ['pauəful] **I** a. ① 强有力的, 强大的: a ~ motive force 强大的(或)动力 / 强大的, 作用大的: a ~ remedy 强效药 ③有权威的, 有影响的; 权力大的 ④[美方]很多的, 相当的: a ~ crop 很可观的收获 **II** ad. [美方] 很, 非常: be ~ glad 非常高兴 ‖**~ly** ad.

powerless ['pauəlis] a. ① 无力量的, 软弱的; 无资源的 ② [常接不定式]无权力的; 无能力的, 无能为力的: be ~ to do so 没有能力这样做 ‖**~ly** ad. / **~ness** n.

practicable ['præktikəbl] a. ① 能实行的; 行得通的: a ~ method (plan) 切实可行的办法(计划) ②适用的; (舞台布景等)能实际使用的: a ~ tool (weapon) 适用的工具(武器) ③ 可行的: This road is ~ for automobiles. 这条路可通行汽车。‖**practicability** [ˌpræktikə'biliti] n. ① 可行性; 实用性 ②实用物 / **~ness** n. / **practicably** ad.

practical ['præktikəl] a. ① 实践的; 实际的: activities 实践活动 / ~ work 实际工作 / a ~ question 现实问题, 实际问题 ②事实上的; 实际上的; 实事求是的: the ~ value 实际价值 / set an example in being ~ 树立实事求是的榜样 ③注重实践(或实际)的; 有实际经验的; [贬] 只讲实用的: a ~ mind 注重实际的头脑 / a vulgar "~ man" 庸俗的事务主义者 ④可行的; 有实效的; 实用的: a ~ proposal 切实可行的建议 / ~ chemistry 实用化学 ‖**for (all) ~ purposes** 实际上: worthless for ~ purposes 实际上毫无价值 / **~ism** n. 求实主义, 实际主义 / **~ness** n. 实际精神; 实践性 ‖**~ art(s)** 实用工艺 / ~ **joke** 恶作剧, 耍弄别人的玩笑 / ~ **joker** 爱恶作剧 (或耍弄别人)的人 / ~ **nurse** 未经正式训练但有实践经验的护士 / ~ **politics** 可实施的政治 / ~ **unit** 实用单位

practically ['præktikəli] ad. ①实际上; 事实上; 实用上: Practically speaking, such a view is wrong. 实际上, 这种观点是错误的。/ This coat is a ~ perfect fit. 这件上衣确实穿十分合身。②从实际出发; 通过实践: look at a question ~ 从实际出发观察问题 ③[口]几乎; 简直: It rained ~ all night. 几乎整夜下着雨。/ ~ impossible 简直不可能

practice ['præktis] **I** n. ①实践; 实际; 实行: The standpoint of life, of ~, should be first and fundamental in the theory of knowledge. 生活、实践的观点, 应该是认识论的首先的和基本的观点。/ from ~ to knowledge 由实践到认识 / unite (或 integrate) theory with ~ 使理论和实践相结合 ②练习, 实习; 熟练: do ~ in speaking English 练习讲英语 / target ~

射击练习 / firing ~ 实弹射击 ③惯例, 习惯做法; 习俗: according to the international ~ 按照国际惯例 / a regular ~ 习惯(或常规的)做法 / the good ~ of summing up one's experience from time to time 不时总结经验的好作风 ④(医生、律师等)业务; 开业; (一批)主顾: commence the ~ of law 挂牌做律师 / a physician with a large ~ 有许多病人求诊的(开业)医生 ⑤【律】诉讼手续 **II** vt. & vi. [美] =practise ‖**in ~** ① 在实践中; 实际上: This plan works well in ~. 这个计划很行得通。② 在不断练习中; 熟练的: keep (oneself) in ~ 经常练习, 不荒疏 ③(医生、律师等) 在开业中 / **in ~ if not in profession** 虽不明讲而实际如此 / **make a ~ of** 经常进行… / **out of ~** 久不练习, 荒疏: I am out of ~ on the piano. 我好久不练习弹钢琴了。/ **Practice makes perfect.** [谚]熟能生巧。/ **put in (或 into) ~** 实行, 实施: put theory into ~ 把理论付诸实践 / put the law into ~ 实施这项法令 / **sharp ~** 狡诈的手段, 不正当的手段 ‖**~ teacher** 教学实习生 / ~ **teaching** (学生的)教学实习

practise ['præktis] **❶** vt. ①实践; 实行: ~ strict economy 厉行节约 / ~ what one preaches 以身作则 ②练习, 实习; 使练习; 训练: ~ shooting (running) 练习射击(跑步) / ~ the flute 练习吹笛子 / ~ pupils in penmanship 教小学生练习书法 / ~ children in discipline 培养孩子们遵守纪律 ③ 惯常地进行: He ~s early rising. 他经常早起。④开业从事: ~ medicine (the law) 开业行医(做律师) **❷** vi. ①实践; 实行 ②练习, 实习: ~ with the rifle 练习打步枪 / ~ in instrumental music 练习器乐 ③ (医生、律师等)开业: ~ at the bar (或 as a barrister) 开业做律师 ④[古]策划阴谋; 诈骗 ‖**~ upon (或 on)** 利用(别人的弱点等); 欺骗(某人): ~ upon sb.'s credulity 利用某人的轻信 ‖**~d** a. 有经验的; 精通的, 熟练的: a ~d marksman 射击能手 / a ~d skill 一种熟练的技能 / **practising** a. 在从事职业 (或活动等)的: a practising physician 开业医生

practitioner [præk'tiʃənə] n. ① 开业者(尤指医生、律师等): a general ~ 普通医生(通看各科的开业医生) ② 从事者, 实践者

pragmatical [præg'mætikəl] a. ① 爱管闲事的 ②独断的, 固执己见的; 自负的 ③实际的; 重实效的 ④【哲】实用主义的 ‖**~ly** ad. / **~ness** n.

prairie ['preəri] n. 大草原: A single spark can start a ~ fire. 星星之火, 可以燎原。‖~ **chicken**, ~ **hen** (北美产)一种松鸡 / ~ **dog**, ~ **marmot**, ~ **squirrel** (北美产)草原犬鼠 / ~ **fire** 草原上的野火; 燎原烈火 / ~ **oyster** 吞吃的生鸡蛋 / ~ **schooner**, ~ **wag(g)on** [美](早期移民过大草原时用的)有篷大车 / **Prairie State** 美国伊利诺斯州的别称

praise [preiz] **I** n. ①赞扬, 表扬; [复]赞词, 赞美

的话: win high ~ 受到高度赞扬 / be loud in sb.'s ~(s) 对某人大大表扬 / give ~ to (或 bestow ~ on) 表扬… ②[古] 受赞扬的人(或物);值得赞扬之处;值得赞扬的理由 ③【宗】(基督教用语)赞美;崇拜;荣耀: a service of ~ 赞美礼拜 II ❶ vt. ① 赞扬,表扬;歌颂: He is warmly ~d for his spirit of absolute selflessness. 他毫无自私自利之心的精神受到人们的热烈赞扬。② 吹捧: ~ sb. (up) to the skies 把某人捧上天 ❷【宗】赞美(上帝) ❷ vi. 赞扬,表扬 ||beyond (all) ~ 赞美不尽 / in ~ of 为颂扬…,为歌颂… / more ~ than pudding 恭维多而实惠少 / pudding rather than ~ 宁要实惠而不要恭维 / sing one's own ~s 自吹自擂;夸奖自己 / sing sb.'s ~s (或 sing the ~s of sb.) 颂扬某人;夸奖某人

praiseworthy ['preiz,wə:ði] a. 值得赞扬的,可嘉的: a ~ act 值得称赞的行动 / What is ~ of him is that .... 他值得表扬的地方在于… ||**praiseworthily** ad. / **praiseworthiness** n.

pram[1] [prɑ:m] n. ①(波罗的海等上的)平底小船;平底货船;平底炮艇 ②(斯堪的纳维亚一带)大船上附带的小艇

pram[2] [præm] n. [英口] ① 婴儿车,童车(perambulator 的缩略) ②(送牛奶用的)手推车

prance [prɑ:ns] I ❶ vi. ①(马)腾跃 ②(人)跃马前进 ③ 昂首阔步,神气活现地走(或骑马) ④欢跃 (about);快活地走(或骑马) ❷ vt. 使(马)腾跃 II n. ①(马的)腾跃 ②昂首阔步 ③欢跃(尤指舞蹈中双膝轮流举起的一种动作) ||~r n. ①腾跃的马;烈性的马 ② 骑烈马者 ③ 欢跃者;舞蹈者

prank[1] [præŋk] n. 胡闹,恶作剧;开玩笑: play ~s on (或 upon) sb. 作弄某人 ②(机器等)反常的运转 ||~ish a. 爱开玩笑的;恶作剧的 ②开玩笑(或恶作剧)性质的 / ~ster ['præŋkstə] n. 开玩笑者;恶作剧者

prank[2] [præŋk] ❶ vt. 装饰;打扮: villages ~ed with newly-built white houses 点缀着新建的白色房屋的村庄 / ~ oneself up (或 out) with 用…把自己打扮起来 ❷ vi. 打扮得漂亮

prate [preit] I ❶ vi. 唠叨;空谈,瞎聊 (about): ~ about a theory 空谈一种理论 ❷ vt. 瞎说: ~ nonsense 胡说八道 II n. 唠叨;空谈,瞎谈 ||~r n. 唠叨者;空谈者

prattle ['prætl] I ❶ vi. ①空谈;胡说;唠叨 ②发出小孩喃喃般的声音,发出连续而无意义的声音: The water ~d over the rocks. 水在石上淙淙地流过。❷ vt. 天真地说;轻率地说: He ~d the secret to the stranger. 他竟轻率地把秘密向陌生人吐露了。II n. ①空谈;胡说,废话 ②孩子气的话;连续而无意义的声音(如流水声) ||~r n. 空谈者;喃喃学语的小孩

prawn [prɔ:n] I n. 对虾,明虾;斑节虾 II vi. 捉对虾

pray [prei] ❶ vt. ①请求,恳求;【宗】祈祷,祈求:

~ sb. to do sth. 请求某人做某事 / ~ sb. for sth. 向某人恳求某事 / ~ permission 请求允许 ②请(= I pray you 或 please): Pray tell me the time. 请问现在是什么时间。/ What is the use of that, ~? 请问那有什么用处呢? ❷ vi. 请求,恳求;【宗】祈祷: ~ for sb. 为某人祈祷 / ~ for sb.'s pardon 请(求)某人原谅 ||be past ~ing for 无可挽救,不可救药 / ~ down (或 out) 求神伏(某人) / ~ in aid of [古] 求助于…(尤指讼时呈请由人帮助辩护)

prayer [prɛə] n. ①祈祷,祈求: a morning (an evening) ~ 早(晚)祷 / a house of ~ 教堂 / a person at ~ 在做祷告的人 / kneel down in ~ 跪下祈祷 ②[常用复]祈祷式;祈祷文: say (give) one's ~s 做祷告 / a book of ~s 祈祷书,经书 ③恳求;恳求(或祈求)的事物 ④[复]祝福,祝愿: Whatever you decide, you have my ~s. 不论你怎样决定,我都祝你成功。⑤ ['preiə] 祈祷者;恳求者 ||the Lord's Prayer 【宗】主祷文 / wrestle in ~ 热忱祈祷 ||~less a. 不做祷告的 ||~ bones [美俚]膝盖 / ~ book 祈祷书 / meeting 祷告会 / ~ rug, ~ mat (穆斯林祈祷时用的)跪毯 / ~ wheel (喇嘛教使用的、刻有祈祷文的)祈祷轮,地藏车

preach [pri:tʃ] I ❶ vt. ①【宗】布讲,宣讲;讲(道): ~ the Gospel 布讲福音 / a sermon 讲道 [喻]劝诫;说教 ② 说教;由于说教而…: ~ oneself hoarse 说教说得嗓子都哑了 ❷ vi. ①讲道;说教 ②宣扬,鼓吹 ③(唠叨地)劝诫: ~ to (或 at) 向某人唠叨地劝诫 II n. [口]讲道;说教;训诫 ||~ down 贬损;(用说教或讲话)当众折服(或否决) / ~ up 吹捧;赞扬 ||~er n. 传道士,说教者;鼓吹者 / ~ment n. [贬]讲道,说教(尤指冗长而令人生厌的)

preamble [pri(:)'æmbl] I n. ①(法规、条约等的)序言,绪论; ②开场白 ②开端;预兆性事件 II vi. 作序言(或绪论) ||without ~ 直截了当地;开门见山地

precarious [pri'kɛəriəs] a. ①不稳定的,不确定的;不安全的,危险的: make a ~ living 过着朝不保夕的生活 / a ~ foothold 不稳的立足点 ②前提有问题的,根据不充足的,靠不住的: a ~ assumption (assertion) 靠不住的假定(论断) ③[古]由他人摆布的 ||~ly ad. / ~ness n.

precaution [pri'kɔ:ʃən] I n. ①预防;警惕;谨慎: by way of ~ 为了小心(或预防) ②[常用复]预防措施: take ~s against fire 采取预防火灾的措施 / air-raid ~ (空袭)预备警报 II vt. 预先警告,使提防 ||~ary a. 预防的: ~ary measures 预防措施

precede [pri(:)'si:d] ❶ vt. ①先于…,位于…之前;比…优先;(地位等)高于…: The motorcade was ~d by motorcycles. 摩托车队为车队作先导。②在…前加上;为…加上引言 (by, with): ~ one's speech with a welcome to the guests 讲话前先向来宾表示欢迎 ❷ vi. 在前面,居前,领先: in the chapters that ~ 在前面各章中

precedence [pri(:)'si:dəns] **n.** ①(次序、时间、重要性等的)领先,在前;优先 ②(正式场合、举行仪式等时的)优先地位,上座;(按地位的)先后次序 ||*take* (或 *have*) ~ *of* (或 *over*)优先于…,地位在…之上: a question that *takes* ~ *over* the others 比其他问题更重要(或优先考虑)的一个问题

precedent[1] ['presidənt] **n.** ①先例,前例;【律】判例: set (或 create) a ~ for 为…创先例 / have no ~ to go by 无先例可援 / without ~ in history 史无前例的 ②惯例

precedent[2] [pri'si:dənt] **a.** 在前的,在先的;优先的: a condition ~ (财产转让、合同生效等前的)先决条件 ||**~ly** *ad.*

precept [pri'sept] **n.** ①教训;戒律;格言,箴言 ②(技术上的)规则,方案 ③令状,命令书 ||*Example is better than* ~. [谚]以身作则胜于口头训海。 ||**~ive** [pri'septiv] **a.** 教训的,告诫的

precinct ['pri:siŋkt] **n.** ①(教堂等的)围地,境域 ②[美]管辖区;(选举)区: an election ~ 选举区 / a police ~ 警察管区 ③[复](城镇)的周围地区 ④分界;分区: within the city ~s 在市区内 / a shopping ~ 商店区 ⑤(思想)境界

precious ['preʃəs] **I a.** ①宝贵的,珍贵的: ~ metals 贵金属(指金、银、白金) / ~ stones 宝石,钻石 / ~ words 珍贵的话 / my ~ 我的亲爱的(=my dear) ②[口]十足的,大大的: make a ~ mess of sth. 把某事搞得一团糟 / It costs a ~ sight more than you think. 这东西的价格比你想的要贵得多。 / a ~ rascal 十足的无赖 ③(语言、工艺等)过分讲究的,矫揉造作的 **II ad.** [口]很,非常: know ~ little about sth. 对某事知道得极少 / take ~ good care of sth. 非常细心地照管某物 ||**~ly** *ad.* / **~ness n.**

precipice ['presipis] **n.** ①悬崖,峭壁,巉岩 ②危急的处境(或形势),灾难的边缘

precipitate [pri'sipiteit] **I ❶ vt.** ①猛抛,猛投;猛然抛下;把(某人)猛然摔下: The cataract ~s itself between the mountains. 瀑布在山间急泻而下。 ②使突然陷入 (*into*): ~ a country *into* a crisis 使一个国家突然陷入危机 ③使突然发生;加速;促使: ~ sb.'s ruin 加速某人的破产(或毁灭) / ~ the extinction of sth. 使某事物消灭 ④【化】使沉淀;【气】使(水蒸气)凝结 **❷ vi.** ①猛然落下(或摔下来);陡斜地落下 ②突然陷入(指状态等) ③仓卒行事,鲁莽地行动 ④【化】沉淀;【气】水蒸气凝结成雨(或露等) **II** [pri'sipitit] **a.** ①猛然落下(或摔下)的;陡斜地落下的;猛冲的 ②急躁的,鲁莽的;仓卒的 ③突然的 **III** [pri'sipitit] **n.** 【化】沉淀物;【气】凝结的水蒸气(指雨、露等) ||**~ly** [pri'sipititli] *ad.* / **precipitating a.** 【化】起沉淀作用的,导致沉淀的 / **precipitator n.** ①促使者;促使物 ②【化】沉淀器;除尘器 ③沉淀器操作者

precipitation [pri,sipi'teiʃən] **n.** ①猛然落下(或摔

下);猛冲 ②急躁,鲁莽;仓卒: act *with* ~ 仓卒地行动 ③促使;催促 ④【化】沉淀(作用) ⑤(雨、雪、冰雹等的)降下;降(雨)量,雨量: the annual ~ in the district 该地区的每年雨量 ||**~ hardening** 【冶】沉淀硬化,弥散硬化

precipitous [pri'sipitəs] **a.** ①(似)悬崖峭壁的,险峻的,陡峭的 ②急躁的,鲁莽的;仓卒的 ||**~ly** *ad.*

précis ['preisi:] [法] **I** ([复] précis ['preisi:z]) **n.** 摘要,概要,大意,梗概 **II vt.** 摘…的要点,写…的大意

precise [pri'sais] **a.** ①精确的,准确的;讲究精确的: the ~ meaning of a word 一个词的确切意义 / a ~ order 严格的命令 / a ~ researcher 一丝不苟的研究者 ②明确的;说话清晰的: speak with a ~ northern accent 用十足的北方口音讲话 / to be ~ [用作插入语]确切地讲 ③[加强语气]恰好的: at that ~ moment 恰恰在那个时刻 ④刻板的,拘泥(陈规)的 ||**~ly** *ad.* ①精确地;明确地: speak ~ly 说话精确 ②刻板地,拘泥(陈规)地 ③正好,恰恰: ~ly because ... 恰恰因为… ④[用于肯定性答复;相当于 "yes",但语气更强调或正式]对;确实如此: *Precisely* so. 正是这样。 ||**~ness n.** ①精确,确切 ②拘泥

precision [pri'siʒən] **I n.** ①精确,精确度;精密度: point out with scientific ~ 以科学的精确性指出 **II a.** 精确的,精密的: ~ bombing 精确轰炸,瞄准轰炸 / a ~ instrument 精密仪器 ||**~ist n.** (在语言等方面)讲究精确的人

preclude [pri'klu:d] **vt.** ①预防;排除,消除: ~ all doubts 排除一切疑虑 ②阻止,妨碍: A prior engagement will ~ me *from* coming. 我因有约在先,不能来了。

precocious [pri'kouʃəs] **a.** ①(人)发育过早的;早熟的,早慧的,(行为、知识等)过早发展的 ②(植物)早成的,早开花的 ||**~ly** *ad.* / **~ness n.**

preconceive ['pri:kən'si:v] **vt.** 预想,事先想好(意见等): ~d ideas 先入之见

preconception ['pri:kən'sepʃən] **n.** ①预想 ②先入之见;偏见

precursor [pri(:)'kə:sə] **n.** ①先驱者;先锋 ②前辈;前任 ③预兆,先兆

predatory ['predətəri] **a.** ①【动】捕食其他动物的,食肉的 ②掠夺(性)的,掠夺成性的: a ~ war 掠夺性战争 ||**predatorily** ['predətərili; 美,predə-'tɔ:rili] *ad.* / **predatoriness n.**

predecessor ['pri:disesə] **n.** ①前辈;前任者: one's immediate ~ 某人的直接前任者 ②(被取代的)原有事物: The new proposal is better than its ~. 新的建议比原有的建议好。 ③[古]祖先

predestinate I [pri(:)'destineit] **vt.** ①【宗】(命中)注定 ②[古]预先确定 **II** [pri(:)'destinit, pri(:)'destineit] **a.** 命定的,宿命的;[古]预定的 ||**predestination** [pri(:),desti'neiʃən] **n.** 【宗】宿命论,命定论;预定;命运

predestine [pri(ː)ˈdestin] *vt.* ①预先指定, 预先决定 ②【宗】(命中)注定

predicable [ˈpredikəbl] **I** *a.* 可被论断为…的属性的 (*of*): Length is ~ *of* a line. 长度是线的属性。**II** *n.* 可被作为属性而断定的事物; 同类对象的共同属性; [复](亚里士多德逻辑学中的)五种宾词 (指"类"、"种"、"特异性"、"固有性"、"偶然性")

predicament [priˈdikəmənt] *n.* ①困境, 尴尬的处境; 危境: be in an awkward ~ 处在困境中 ②【逻】(可)被论断的事物; 范畴; [复](亚里士多德的)十大范畴

predicate [ˈpredikit] **I** *n.* ①【语】谓语 ②【逻】谓项, 谓词, 宾词 ③ 本质; 属性 **II** *a.* 谓语的; 谓项的 **III** [ˈpredikeit] ❶ *vt.* ①论断, 断言, 断言…为某物的属性: ~ the earth to be round (或 ~ *of* the earth that it is round 或 ~ roundness *of* the earth) 断言地球是圆的 ②使依据, 使基于: be ~*d* on the principles of 以…的原则为基础 ③意味着, 具有…的含义 ④宣布, 声明 ❷ *vi.* 作出论断; 断言 ‖**predication** [ˌprediˈkeiʃən] *n.*

predicative [priˈdikətiv] **I** *a.* ①(在某一对象的属性方面)起论断作用的, 论断性的 ②【语】表语的; 用作表语的: a ~ adjective 表语形容词 **II** *n.* 表语 ‖~**ly** *ad.*

predict [priˈdikt] *vt. & vi.* 预言; 预告, 预示 ‖~**or** *n.* ①预言者; 预告者 ②【军】活动目标预测器; 水雷发射预测器 ③【气】预报因子

predictable [priˈdiktəbl] *a.* 可预言的; 可预报的

prediction [priˈdikʃən] *n.* ①预言; 预告 ②被预言的事物; (气象等的)预报

predispose [ˈpriːdisˈpouz] *vt.* ①预先安排(或处理) ②使先倾向于; 使易感染(或接受): His manner of speaking ~*s* people in his favour. 他说话的态度就使人先有好感。/ Fatigue ~*s* one to colds (或 to catch cold). 疲劳使人易患感冒。‖~**d** *a.* ①先倾向于…的 (to) ②事先安排好的 / **predisposition** [ˈpriːˌdispəˈziʃən] *n.*

predominance [priˈdɔminəns] *n.* ①优势, 优越 ②显著, 突出

predominant [priˈdɔminənt] *a.* ①占优势的; 支配其他的 (over) ②主要的; 突出的, 最显著的: the ~ feature of sb.'s character 某人性格的主要特征 ③流行的 ‖~**ly** *ad.*

predominate **I** [priˈdɔmineit] ❶ *vi.* 居支配地位, 统治; 占优势(尤指在数量上): ~ over sb. 支配(或统治)某人 / Red and scarlet ~ in these flowers. 这些花中大都是红色和鲜红色的。❷ *vt.* 支配, 统治: Pines ~ the forest there. 那里的森林中松树最多。**II** [priˈdɔminit] *a.* =predominant ‖~**ly** *ad.* / **predomination** [priˌdɔmiˈneiʃən] *n.*

preeminent [priˈeminənt] *a.* 卓越的, 杰出的 ‖~**ly** *ad.*

preemphasis [ˈpriːˈemfəsis] *n.* 【无】预加重, 预修正, (频应)预矫

preen [priːn] ❶ *vt.* ①(鸟)用嘴整理(羽毛) ②[~ oneself] (人)打扮(自己) ③[~ oneself] 赞扬(自己), 夸耀(自己) ❷ *vi.* ①把自己打扮得漂亮 ②自满, 自负

prefabricate [ˈpriːˈfæbrikeit] *vt.* ①预制: a ~*d* house 预制房屋, 活动房屋(指构件已定规格先制成, 到施工现场装配即成的房屋) / ~*d* parts 预制构件 ② 预先构想 ‖**prefabrication** [ˈpriːˌfæbriˈkeiʃən] *n.*

preface [ˈprefis] **I** *n.* ①序言, 前言, 绪言; 引语: in the ~ to his book 在本书的序言中 ② [P-]【宗】(弥撒的)序诵, 序祷 **II** *vt.* 给…作序; 作为…的开端(或开言); 开始; 导致: ~ a book with an introduction 给一本书作序 / He ~*d* his remarks by an apology. 他以道歉的话作为开场白。❷ *vi.* 作序

prefect [ˈpriːfekt] *n.* ①(古罗马的)长官, 高级文武官员 ②(法国的)县长; (巴黎的)警察局长 ③(英国指某些公立学校中, 美国指某些私立学校中的)级长, 负责维持纪律的学生 ‖~**oral** [priˈfektərəl], ~**orial** [ˌpriːfekˈtɔːriəl] *a.*

prefer [priˈfəː] (**preferred**; **preferring** [priˈfəːriŋ]) *vt.* ①宁可, 宁愿(选择); 更喜欢: I should ~ you not to stay (或 that you did not stay) there too long. 我倒希望你不要在那儿呆得太久。/ We ~ that the plan should be fully discussed before being put into execution. 我们宁愿在计划实施前加以充分讨论。②提出(声明、请求、控诉等): ~ a charge against sb. 对某人提出控告 ③[古]提升, 提拔 (to); 推荐, 介绍 ④优先偿付(对债权人) ⑤建议; 申请 ‖**preferred stock** [美]优先股(持有者有权优先领取股息, 并在有权在公司清理时优先取回股金)

preferable [ˈprefərəbl] *a.* 更可取的, 更好的 (to): The first choice is ~ to the second. (两种选择中)第一种比第二种更可取。‖**preferably** *ad.* 更可取地, 宁可: You may come, *preferably*, in the morning. 你还是早晨来更好。

preference [ˈprefərəns] *n.* ①偏爱; 优先: have a ~ for 偏爱…, 特别喜爱… / have a ~ of sth. to (或 over) another 喜爱某物甚于喜爱另一物 / in ~ to 优先于… ②偏爱物: This is his ~. 这是他偏爱的东西。③选择权, 选择机会: The guests will have their ~ of seats. 客人可以优先选择座位。④优先权; (关税等方面的)特惠: ~ stock (或 share, bond) [英]优先股 (=[美] preferred stock) ⑤【律】受优先偿还的权利

preferential [ˌprefəˈrenʃəl] *a.* ①优先的; 优待的: ~ treatment 优先处理; 优待 ②特惠的: a ~ tariff 特惠关税(率) ‖~ **shop** (根据契约)优先雇用(或提升)工会会员的商业机构 / ~ **voting**, ~ **system** 选择选举制(选举人可在选票中注明对几个被选举人的优先选择次序)

preferment [priˈfəːmənt] *n.* ①提升, 升级 ②显赫的职位; 肥缺, 有利可图的职位 ③(购置财产的)优先权 ④(控告等的)提出

prefix I ['pri:fiks] *n.* ①【语】前缀，词头 ②人名前用的尊称 (如 Mr., Dr., Sir 等) **II** [pri'fiks, 'pri:fiks] *vt.* ① 给…加前缀(或标题等) ②把…放在前: ~ a title *to* one's name 在姓名前加头衔 ③[古]预先指定

pregnancy ['pregnənsi] *n.* ①怀孕，怀胎; 怀孕期 ②[喻]充满; 富有意义

pregnant ['pregnənt] *a.* ①怀孕的，怀胎的; [喻]孕育着的,充满的,富有的 ②意义深长的,含蓄的: ~ construction【语】简洁体(如将 Let him go out. 说成 Let him out.) ③富于想象力的, 有创造力的: ~ artists 有创造力的艺术家 ④富于成果的; 多产的: ~ years 丰产年 / a ~ cause 富于成果的事业 ||~**ly** *ad.*

prehistoric ['pri:his'tɔrik] *a.* ①(有记载的)历史以前的, 史前的 ②[口]古老不堪的, 陈腐的 ||~**ally** *ad.*

prejudge ['pri:'dʒʌdʒ] *vt.* 预先判断; 过早判断; 【律】不审而判 ||**prejudg(e)ment** *n.*

prejudice ['predʒudis] **I** *n.* ①偏见, 成见: have a ~ *against* (*in favour of*) sb. 对某人有偏见(偏爱) ②【律】损害, 侵害; 不利: to the ~ of sb.'s rights 有损于某人的权利 ③歧视 **II** *vt.* ① 使抱偏见, 使怀成见 ②损害, 侵害; 不利于: His mistake ~*d* the outcome. 他的错误使结局受到了不利的影响。 ||*without* ~ *to*【律】不使(合法权利等)受损害 ||~**d** *a.* 有偏见的, 有成见的: a ~*d* opinion 偏见

prejudicial [,predʒu'diʃəl] *a.* ①引起偏见的; 有成见的 ②有损害的; 不利的: be ~ to sb.'s interest 有损于某人的利益 ||~**ly** *ad.*

prelate ['prelit] *n.* 高级教士(如主教等)

preliminary [pri'liminəri] **I** *a.* ①预备的; 初步的; 序言(性)的; 开端的: a ~ examination 初试, 预考 / a ~ hearing 预审 / ~ measures 初步措施 / ~ remarks 前言; 开场白 / ~ groundwork 创建工作 **II** *n.* ①(对学生等的)预考, 初试 ②【体】预赛; 淘汰赛; (主赛前的)次要比赛(如拳击) ③[常用复]初步, 开端; 预备(指步骤、措施等) ④[复]正文前的书页, 正文前的内容(如序言等) ||**preliminarily** [pri'liminərili; 美 pri,limi'nerili] *ad.*

prelude ['prelju:d] **I** *n.* ①序言; 序幕, 开场戏; 序曲; 前奏曲 ②预兆 **II** ❶ *vi.* 作序言; 演开场戏; 作序曲; 奏序曲 ❷ *vt.* 为…作序; 成为…的序曲(或序幕); 成为…的预兆

premature [,premə'tjuə, ,pri:mə'tjuə] **I** *a.* ①早熟的; 不成熟的 ②过早的; 不到期的: a ~ decision 过早的决定 / a ~ birth 早产 / a ~ fall of snow 早雪 **II** *n.* ①早产的婴儿 ②过早爆发的炮弹 ③过早发生的事物 ||~**ly** *ad.*

premeditate [pri(:)'mediteit] *vt.* & *vi.* 预先思考; 预先计划; 预谋 ||**premeditation** [pri(:)-,medi'teiʃən] *n.*

premier ['premjə] **I** *n.* 总理; 首相: *Premier of the State Council* 国务院总理 **II** *a.* ①首位的,

首要的; 最前的: take (或 hold) the ~ place 占首位; 占首席 ②最早的 ||~**ship** *n.* 总理职位(或职权); 首相职位(或职权)

premise I ['premis] *n.* ① 前提: major (minor) ~【逻】大(小)前提 / on the ~ of (或 that) ... 在…前提下 ②[复]房屋(及其附属建筑、基地等): business ~*s* 办公室; 事务所 / to be drunk (或 consumed) on the ~*s* 只供堂饮(指酒等) ③[复]【律】(契据等用语)上述各点, 上述房屋(或让渡物件、当事人等, 尤指编号起部分) **II** [pri'maiz] ❶ *vt.* ①预述(条件等); 引导(论述等) ②提出…为前提 ③假定 ❷ *vi.* 作出前提

premium ['pri:mjəm] *n.* ①奖赏, 奖励; 奖金: *Premium* Bonds [英]政府有奖债券 / a ~ for 为…而发的奖(金) ②佣金; (利息、工资等以外的)酬金; 额外费用 ③保险费: ~ tariff 保险率表 ④【商】贴水, 升水 ⑤【商】溢价: bond ~ 债券溢价 ⑥习艺费, 学费 ||*at a* ~ 在票面(或一般)价值以上; [喻]非常珍贵, 很受重视 / *put a* ~ *on* 奖励; 鼓励; 重视; 助长: *put a* ~ *on* punctuality 很重视准时 / *put a* ~ *on* fraud 助长欺诈的歪风

premonition [,pri:mə'niʃən] *n.* ①预先的警告(或告诫) ②预感; 预兆

preoccupation [pri(:),ɔkju'peiʃən] *n.* ①先占, 先取 ②偏见, 成见 ③全神贯注; 出神: ~ *with* the public interest 专心于公益 ④使人全神贯注的事物; 急务

preoccupy [pri(:)'ɔkjupai] *vt.* ①先占, 先取 ②[常用被动语态]使对…全神贯注, 使专心于; 使出神, 迷住,吸引住 be *preoccupied by* some troubles 心事重重 ||**preoccupied** *a.* ①被先占的 ②出神的; 全神贯注的; 一心想…的; 心事重重的 ③【生】(种或属的名称)不能再以新义使用的

preordain ['pri:ɔ:'dein] *vt.* 先期注定; 预先规定

prep [prep] *n.* ①[英](学生用语)准备功课; 家庭作业 ②预备学校, 预科(=preparatory school); 预备学校的学生 **II** *a.* [美口]预备的,准备的: a ~ school 预备学校 **III** (prepped; prepping) ❶ *vi.* ①进预备学校 ②进行预备训练(或学习); 自我训练, 自修 ❷ *vt.* 预备, 准备; 给(病人)作手术前的准备

preparation [,prepə'reiʃən] *n.* ①准备, 预备; [常复]准备工作, 准备措施: mental ~ 精神(或思想)准备 / begin ~ of the land for sowing 平整土地准备播种 / finish all necessary ~*s* 完成所有必要的准备工作 ②预习; 备课; 预习(或备课)时间 ③制备; 制剂: the ~ of samples 样品的制备 ④一种解剖(或病理)标本 ⑤配制好的食物 ||*be in* ~ 在准备中: The book *is in* rapid ~. 这本书正在迅速编写 / *in* ~ *for* 作为…的准备: collect new material *in* ~ *for* the experiment 收集新资料为实验作准备 / *make* ~*s against* 为对付(或防止)…作准备: *make* ~*s against* natural disasters 为防止自然灾害作好准备 / *make* ~*s for* 为…作准备: *make* ~*s for* the conference 为会议作准备

preparatory [pri'pærətəri] **I** *a.* 准备的，预备的；筹备的: a ～ command (口令的)预令 / ～ training 预备训练 / a ～ committee for a congress 大会的筹备委员会 **II** *n.* 预备学校，预科(在美国指为升入大学作准备的学校，在英国一般指为升入高级中学作准备的学校; =～ school) **III** *ad.* 作为准备；在先前 ‖～ **to** 作为…的准备；在…之前: get things together ～ *to* a journey 收拾东西准备旅行 / pack sth. up ～ *to* sending it by post 邮寄前把某物包好 ‖**preparatorily** [pri'pærətərili; 美 pri,pærə'tɔːrili] *ad.*

prepare [pri'pɛə] ❶ *vt.* ① 准备，预备；筹备: ～ one's lessons 准备功课 / ～ the table 准备开饭 / ～ land *for* summer crops 整理土地准备种夏季作物 / ～ public opinion for ... 为…造舆论 ② 使有准备；为…作准备: Be ～*d against* war, be ～*d against* natural disasters, and do everything for the people. 备战、备荒，为人民。/ be well ～*d* (或 *to* do) sth. 对做某事有充分准备 / ～ sb. *for* (或 *to* hear) the news 使某人对这消息有思想准备 ③ 训练；配备，装备: ～ oneself as a basketball player 为使自己成为篮球运动员而进行锻炼 / ～ an expedition 为探险(或考察)队作各方面的配备 ④ 作出，制订 ⑤ 配制，调制: ～ a prescription 配药 / ～ a meal 做饭菜 / bread ～*d* from the best flour 用最好的面粉做的面包 ❷ *vi.* 预备，作好准备: ～ *for* struggle 准备斗争 / ～ to receive foreign visitors 准备接待外宾

prepared [pri'pɛəd] *a.* ①有准备的，准备好的: ～ installations【军】既设工事 ②特别处理过的，精制的: ～ lard (tar) 精制猪油(焦油) ‖～**ly** [pri'pɛədli, pri'pɛəridli] *ad.*

prepay ['priː'pei] (prepaid ['priː'peid]) *vt.* 预付，先付(邮资等): ～ a reply to a telegram 预付复电(报)费 ‖～**able** *a.* 可预付的 / ～**ment** *n.*

preponderance [pri'pɔndərəns] *n.* (数量、重量、力量、影响或重要性上的)优势，优越: have the ～ *over* 比…占优势

preponderant [pri'pɔndərənt] *a.* 优势的；压倒的: concentrate ～ forces 集中优势兵力

preponderate [pri'pɔndəreit] ❶ *vi.* ① 超过，占优势: ～ *in* number 数量上占优势 / reasons that ～ *over* other considerations 优先考虑的理由 ② 重量上胜过；偏重；(天平盘)一端下沉 ❷ *vt.* [古]重于；压倒

preposition [,prepə'ziʃən] *n.* ①【语】前置词，介词 ②前面的位置；放在前面

prepossessing [,priːpə'zesiŋ] *a.* 给人好感的；令人喜爱的，有吸引力的: of ～ manners 举止大方的 ‖～**ly** *ad.*

prepossession [,priːpə'zeʃən] *n.* ①预先形成的印象(或信念等)；偏爱，偏见 ②全神贯注；着迷 ③[古]先占

preposterous [pri'pɔstərəs] *a.* ①反常的，乖戾的；十分荒谬的；愚蠢的: What a ～ idea! 多么荒谬的想法! ②[古](次序等)颠倒的 ‖～**ly** *ad.*

prerequisite ['priː'rekwizit] **I** *a.* 必须先具备的，先决条件的，必要的 (to) **II** *n.* 先决条件，前提；必要条件 (for)

prerogative [pri'rɔgətiv] **I** *n.* ① 特权；[英]君权: a political ～ 政治特权 / the ～ of mercy 赦免权 / It is within his ～ to do so. 他是有权这样做的。②[英](学究式的用语)优先投票权 ③ 天赋的特权(或能力等) ④ 特性，特点；显著的优点 **II** *a.* ①(有)特权的 ②【史】(古罗马)有优先投票权的 ‖～ **court** ①【英史】(审查遗嘱等的)大主教法庭 ②【美史】(英国殖民统治时期)总督委任组成的法庭

presage ['presidʒ] **I** *n.* ①预示，预兆: the ～ of a storm 风暴的预兆 ②预知；预感 ③[古]预言 **II** ❶ *vt.* ①预示，预兆 ②预言；预先警告 ③预知；预感 ❷ *vi.* 预言

prescient ['presiənt] *a.* 预知的，有先见之明的 ‖～**ly** *ad.*

prescribe [pris'kraib] ❶ *vt.* ①命令，指示；规定: a ～*d* form (textbook) 规定的表格(课本) ②处(方)；开(药)；嘱咐，建议: The doctor ～*d* his patient a receipt. 医生给病人开了一张药方。/ ～ medicinal herbs 开草药 / The doctor ～*d* total abstinence (long rest). 医生嘱咐(病人)戒酒 (作长期的休息)。③【律】使(过期限而)失效(或不合法) ❷ *vi.* ①命令；指示；规定 ②处方: ～ *for* (或 *to*) a patient 给病人处方 / ～ *for* a complaint 对症处方 ③【律】(通过长占有等而)要求(权利等) (to, for) ④【律】(因过期限而)失效，不合法

prescription [pris'kripʃən] *n.* ①命令，指示；规定；法规 ②药方，处方；处方的药: a medical ～ 药方 / write out a ～ 开药方 / make up a ～ 配方 ③旧习，惯例；传统 ④【律】(根据传统或长期使用而)要求权利；(由于长期使用等而)获得权利；(由于长期使用而获得的)权利 ‖**negative** ～【律】可提出诉讼(或要求)的法定期限 / **positive** ～【律】(在法定期限内等的)长期使用，长期占有；(由于长期使用等而获得的)权利

presence ['prezns] *n.* ①出席，到场: Your ～ is requested. 请你出席。/ We shall be very glad to have your ～. 你如能出席，我们将感到很高兴。②在，存在；存在的人(或物): the ～ of argon in the air 空气中氩的存在 / a ～ behind the scenes 一个在幕后操纵的人 ③面前，眼前；[英][the ～]御前: speak *in the* ～ of a large audience 在许多听众面前讲话 / be admitted to sb.'s ～ 被允许谒见(或会见)某人 ④风采；风度;(能引起观众亲切感的)表演风度: a man of (a) noble ～ 仪态高贵的人 ⑤(感到在面前的)精灵，鬼怪 ‖～ *of* **mind** 镇定，沉着: lose one's ～ *of mind* 心慌意乱 / with (great) ～ *of mind* 镇定自若地 / **saving your** ～ 恕我冒昧 ‖～ **chamber** (君主或显要人物的)接见厅

present¹ ['preznt] **I** *a.* ①现在的,目前的;现存的: at the ~ time(或day)在目前 / the ~ government 政府,本届政府 / the ~ social system 现存的社会制度 ②出席的,在座的;到场的: be ~ in the process of development 存在于发展过程中 / the ~ company 在座的人(指全体) / Present! (点名时的回答)到! ③正在处理(或考虑)中的;本,此: in the ~ case 在这件事中;照目前这个情况 / the ~ volume 本书 / the ~ writer 作者,笔者 ④[古]即刻有用的;应急的;随时的 **II** *n.* 现在,目前;【语】现在时(态): make the past serve the ~ 古为今用 / work out a plan for the immediate ~ 制订一个从当前着眼的计划 / a verb in the ~ 现在时(态)的动词 ‖*at* ~ 现在,目前 ‖ *by these* ~*s* [讼][律]根据本文件 / *for the* ~ 暂时,暂且: stop doing sth. *for the* ~ 暂时停止做某事 / I can't remember it *for the* ~. 我一时记不起来了。/ That will do *for the* ~. 暂且就这样好了。/ ~ *to* 出现在…: A vivid picture is ~ *to* his eye. 一幅生动的画面出现在眼前。/ *up to the* ~ 直到现在,至今 ‖'~-'**day** *a.* 当前的;当代的: ~-*day* English 当代英语 / ~ **participle**【语】现在分词 / ~ **perfect**【语】①现在完成时(的) ②现在完成时的动词 / ~ **tense**【语】现在时(态)

present² [pri'zent] **I** ❶ *vt.* ①介绍;引见: Allow me to ~ Mr. Brown to you. 请允许我把布朗先生介绍给你。/ The ambassador was ~ed to the president. 大使被引见总统。②赠送,给予;呈献: ~ a book *to* sb. (或 ~ sb. *with* a book) 送某人一本书 / ~ compliments to sb. 向某人问候 / Samples are ~ed free. 样品免费赠送。③提出;呈递: ~ an application to the committee 向委员会提出申请(书) / ~ a cheque at the bank 向银行兑付支票 ④呈现;描述;出示: The characters in the novel are vividly ~ed. 小说中人物描写得很生动。/ ~ an invitation card at the entrance 在入口处出示请帖 ⑤上演;使扮演 ⑥以(武器)瞄准;举(枪等)敬礼: ~ a pistol *at* 用手枪对准… / ~ arms 举枪致敬 ⑦【律】控告 ⑧【宗】推荐(牧师)任圣职 ❷ *vi.* ①举枪瞄准;举枪致敬 ②【宗】推荐牧师任圣职 ③【医】(分娩时婴儿)露出,先露 **II** *n.* ①(举枪)瞄准;瞄准时枪的位置: bring the rifle down to the ~ 使步枪横下处于瞄准状态 ②举枪致敬 ‖~ *itself* 出现,呈现: The question ~ed *itself* for our attention. 这个问题引起我们注意。/ ~ *oneself* 出席,到场: He ~ed *himself* for a checkup at the hospital. 他到医院受体格检查。

present³ ['preznt] *n.* 礼物,赠送物: a birthday ~ 生日礼物 / exchange ~s 互赠礼物 / make (或give) a ~ to sb. 给某人送礼 / I'm buying it for a ~, so please wrap it up nicely. 我买这东西是送人的,因此请扎得漂亮一点。‖*make a ~ of sth. to sb.* (或 *make sb. a ~ of sth.*) 把某物赠送给某人: Will you *make* me a ~ *of* your photograph?

把你的相片送给我一张好吗?

presentable [pri'zentəbl] *a.* ①拿得出的,像样的;经得起挑剔的 ②中看的,见得了人的 ③可介绍的,可推荐的 ④适宜赠送的 ‖**presentability** [pri,zentə'biliti] *n.* / **presentably** *ad.*

presentation [,prezen'teiʃən] *n.* ①介绍;引见 ②赠送;礼物;授予仪式: a ~ copy 赠送本 / ~ of colours (medals) 授军旗(勋章)仪式 ③提出;呈递: the ~ of a plan 计划的提出 / the ~ of credentials 国书的呈递 / payable on ~ 交银行即可兑现(指支票等) ④呈现;展示;描述: the ~ of history as it actually occurred 展示(或描述)历史的本来面目 / give a systematic ~ of 对…作系统的陈述 ⑤上演,演出: the successful ~ of a new play 新剧本的成功的演出 ⑥【无】图象;显示,扫描: a ~ on a radar screen 雷达屏上出现的图象 / aural ~ 方向显示 ⑦【宗】(圣职的)推荐 ⑧【哲】【心】表象 ⑨【医】先露,产式: head ~ (分娩时的)头先露 ‖~**al** *a.* ①表象(论)的 ②上演的,演出的 ③(词、语等)本身有意义的;描述性的

presentiment [pri'zentiment] *n.* 预感 (尤指不祥的)

preservation [,preze(:)'veiʃən] *n.* ①保存;保管;储藏;保护: in a good state of ~ 保存得很好 / the ~ of food 食品保藏 / ~ from decay 防腐 ②保持;维护: the ~ of world peace 维护世界和平

preservative [pri'zə:vətiv] **I** *a.* 有保存力的;防腐的 **II** *n.* ①防腐剂;防腐料;保护料;预防药;预防法: Salt is a common food ~. 盐是一种常用的食物防腐剂。②起维护作用的原则(或因素等)

preserve [pri'zə:v] **I** ❶ *vt.* ①保护;防护;维护;维持: ~ forests 保护森林 / ~ one's eyesight 保护视力 / ~ order 维持秩序 ②保存,保藏;防腐: Salt ~s food from decay. 盐能防止食物腐烂。③腌(肉等);把…做成蜜饯(或果酱);把…制成罐头(食品): ~ peaches 制桃子酱(或糖水桃子) / ~ eggs in salt 腌蛋 ④使(某人的名声)流传;把(某人)铭记在心;使(诗歌等)留存 ⑤禁猎;把…圈为禁地: ~ game 禁猎鸟兽 / Fishing in this river is strictly ~d. 此河严禁捕鱼。❷ *vi.* ①制蜜饯;制果酱;制罐头(食品) ②禁猎;圈为禁地 **II** *n.* ①[常用复]蜜饯;果酱;罐头水果 ②禁猎地;(畜养鸟兽的)苑,林;鱼塘 ③独占的事物(或范围);禁区: poach on another's ~ 侵犯他人的活动(或利益等)范围 ④防护物;[复]护目镜,防风镜;太阳眼镜 ‖~**d** *a.* [美俚]喝醉的 / ~**r** *n.* ①保护者;保存者;防腐物;防护物 ②鸟兽保护者

preside [pri'zaid] *vi.* ①作会议的主席;主持 (*at, over*): ~ *at* (或 *over*) a meeting 主持会议 / ~ *at* tea (主持)招待客人吃茶(点) ②统辖;指挥;负责 (*at, over*): ~ *over* a radio programme 负责安排广播节目 ③主奏 (*at*): ~ *at* the piano (在音乐会上)主奏钢琴 ‖~**r** *n.* (会议的)主席;主持者

presidency ['prezidənsi] *n.* ①总统(或校长、会长、行长等)的职位(或职权、任期) ②管辖；主宰，支配 ③(美国)总统直辖的政府机构(包括决策机构等) ④[P-]【史】管辖区(指前英属印度的马德拉斯等三大管辖区之一) ⑤(摩门教的)三人评议会：the First *Presidency* 最高(三人)评议会

president ['prezidənt] *n.* ①总统 ②长官；大臣；(院长的)议长；【律】院长；庭长：the Lord *President* of the Council (英国)枢密大臣 ③(美国大学)校长；(英国大学)院长 ④会长，社长；(会议)主席：(the) *President* of the China-Japan Friendship Association 中日友好协会会长 / (the) *President* of the U. N. General Assembly 联合国大会主席 ⑤(银行等)行长；总裁；董事长；总经理 ⑥【史】州长；(殖民地)总督 ‖**~ess** *n.* ①女总统(或女校长等) ②总统夫人(或校长夫人等) / **~ship** *n.* 总统(或校长等)的职位(或任期) ‖**~-e'lect** *n.* 新当选(尚未就职)的总统

presidential [,prezi'denʃəl] *a.* ①总统(或校长等)的；总统(或校长等)职务的：the ~ election 总统选举 / the ~ year 总统选举年 / the ~ inauguration 总统就职典礼 ②统辖的，主宰的，支配的 ‖**~ly** *ad.* ‖**~ government** 总统制政体

press¹ [pres] I ❶ *vt.* ①压；揿，按；扳：~ sth. (down) with a stone 用石头压(下)某物 / ~ the button 按电钮；[喻]开始采取决定性行动 / ~ the trigger (of a rifle) 扣(枪的)扳机 ②压榨，榨取(汁等)；压缩，压制；熨平；压印(花纹等)：~ grapes 榨葡萄(取汁) / ~ oil from soya beans 榨取豆油 / ~ a shirt 熨衬衫 / ~ed fuel 压制的燃料(如煤饼) ③使贴紧；紧抱；紧握：~ one's ear to an instrument 把耳朵贴在仪器上(倾听) / ~ sb.'s hand 紧握某人的手 ④逼迫；进逼：~ sb. *for* an answer 迫使某人回答 ⑤使苦恼；使窘迫：be ~ed *with* want 迫于贫困 ⑥敦促，(极力)劝说：~ the guests to taste the new-strain apples 硬要客人尝尝新品种的苹果 ⑦ 迫使接受；把…强加于(*upon, on*)：~ food *upon* sb. 硬要某人吃东西 / ~ one's opinion *upon* sb. 把自己的意见强加于某人 ⑧ 坚持；坚决进行；贯彻：~ one's way *against* the cold wind 冒着寒风坚持前进 / ~ a policy (强行)贯彻一项政策 / ~ a demand 坚持要求 ⑨ 用模子压制(唱片) ❷ *vi.* ①压；重压 ②紧迫：Time ~es. 时间紧迫。③催；逼；迫切要求(*for*)：This problem ~es for solution. 这个问题急待解决。④奋力前进；挤向前：~ *on* in the face of difficulties 迎着困难奋勇向前 / ~ *forward* (或 *ahead*) through a crowd 在人群中向前挤 ⑤ 拥挤，密集：~ *about* (或 *round*) sb. 拥挤在某人周围 ⑥承压，受压：This fabric ~es well. 这种织物容易熨平。II *n.* ①压；揿，按；榨；熨；挤；紧握：give sth. a light ~ 把某物轻轻压(或按、扳) / give sb. a ~ of the hand 把某人的手紧紧握一下 ②人丛；拥挤；蜂拥向前；繁忙；繁忙：make one's way through a ~ of people 挤过密集的人群 / be carried forward in the ~ of the masses 被蜂拥的人群推向前 / the ~ of work (business) 工作(事务)繁忙 ③ 压榨机；压机：an oil ~ 榨油机 / a drill ~ 钻床 / a hydraulic forging ~ 水力锻压机 / a punch(ing) ~ 冲床 ④印刷机；印刷所；印刷(术)；印刷业：The book is *in* to ~. 这本书正在印刷。/ go (或 come, be sent) to (the) ~ 付印 / be off the ~ 已印好；发行 / at ~ time (报刊用语)在发稿时 / 到发稿时为止 / correct the ~ 改正校样，校对 ⑤ 新闻报道；[the ~] [总称]报刊(包括广播及电视新闻报道)；新闻界；出版界；出版社；通讯社：a ~ communique 新闻公报 / a ~ campaign (或 stunt) (为竞选目的而进行的)报纸上的宣传 / He is *on* the ~. 他在报界工作。/ according to ~ reports 据新闻报道 / freedom of the ~ 出版自由 / Foreign Languages *Press* 外文出版社 / the Associated *Press* (美国)联合通讯社(简称美联社) ⑥报刊上的评论：have a good ~ 受到报刊好评 ⑦衣橱；柜橱 ⑧夹具；(网球拍等的)夹子 ⑨(举重中的)推举 ‖a ~ *of sail* (或 *canvas*)【海】满帆 / be hard ~ed 被紧紧赶上(或催逼) / be ~ed for 缺少，缺乏：be ~ed for time 时间紧迫 / ~ on (或 *forward*) with 加紧 / ~ on with one's work 加紧工作 / 决心继续；~ *on* with one's work 加紧工作 ‖**~er** *n.* ①压者；压具 ②熨衣工 / **~or** *a.* 加压的，使机能亢进的，增高血压的 ‖**~ agent** (公司、剧团等或个人雇用的)新闻广告员；报刊宣传员，~ **box** (运动会等的)新闻记者席 / '~.**button** *n.* 按钮，电钮：a ~-button war 按钮战争(指按动电钮以发射导弹等武器的战争) / **clipping**，~ **cutting** [英]剪报 / '~ **conference** 记者招待会 / **~ gallery** (议会等中的)新闻记者席 / **~man** ['presmən] *n.* ①印刷工人 ②[英]新闻工作者 / '**~mark** *n.* (图书馆藏书上印的)书架号 / '~-**pho'tographer** *n.* 摄影记者 / **~ proof**【印】(正式付印前的)清样；机样(印版装上印刷机后打出的校样) / **~ reader** 清样的校对人 / **~ release** ①(通讯社发布的)通讯稿 ②(向记者发布的)新闻稿 / '**~room** *n.* ①印刷间 ②(政府机关中的)记者室 / '~**work** *n.* 印刷(术)；印刷业务；[总称]印刷物，印刷品

press² [pres] I ❶ *vt.* ①强征…入伍(或服劳役等) ②征用 ❷ *vi.* 强迫征募；抓壮丁 II *n.* 强迫征募；抓壮丁 ‖**~ *into service*** (因急需而)暂用；要求…帮一下忙：~ a passing car *into service* to help send the patient to hospital 要一辆过路的汽车帮忙把病人送医院 ‖'**~-gang** *vt.* 强征…入伍(或服劳役等)

pressing ['presiŋ] I *a.* ①紧迫的，迫切的：Time is ~. 时间很紧。/ a ~ task 一项紧急任务 / ~ need 迫切的需要 ②恳切的；再三要求的：a ~ invitation 恳切的邀请 II *n.* ①压；按；榨；冲压；压制 ②冲压件；模压制品 ③唱片；[总称]同一次压制的唱片：the first ~ of that song 那首歌的第一批制出的唱片 ‖**~ly** *ad.* / **~ness** *n.*

pressure ['preʃə] **I** *n.* ① 压; 按; 榨; 挤: the ~ of a crowd 人群的拥挤 ② 压力; 强制; 紧迫; 艰难: exert ~ upon 对…施加压力 / the ~ of affairs 事务繁忙 ③【物】压力,压强; 电压 ④ 大气压力 (=atmospheric ~) **II** *vt.* ① 对…施加压力,迫使: ~ sb. *into* doing sth. 迫使某人做某事 ② 使 (高空飞行的飞机的机舱等) 增压; 密封 (用加压蒸煮器) 蒸煮 ‖*bring ~ to bear on* (或 *upon*) 对…施加压力 / *under (the) ~ of* 在…的压力下: *under (the) ~ of* circumstances 在环境(或形势)的逼迫下; 逼不得已 / *work at high ~* 紧张地工作; 使劲干 ‖~ **cabin**【空】增压舱,气密座舱 / ~'**cook** *vt.* & *vi.* 用加压蒸煮器蒸煮 / ~ **cooker** 加压蒸(汽速)煮器 / ~ **ga(u)ge** ①压力计,压强计; 气压计 ②(置于火炮药室内测量的) 膛压表 / ~ **suit** (高空飞行用的)增压(衣)服 / ~ **vessel** 压力容器(如锅炉等)

pressurize ['preʃəraiz] *vt.* ① 使(高空飞行的飞机的机舱等)增压; 密封: a ~d cabin 增压舱,气密座舱 ② 对…加压(力); 使压入(油井等): a ~d compartment 加压室 / a ~d accelerator 高压壳内的加速器 ③ 使(飞机的机身等)耐压 ‖**pressurization** [,preʃərai'zeiʃən] *n.* ① 压力输送; 挤压 ② 气密,密封 ③增压; 加压

prestige [pres'tiːʒ] *n.* 威信,威望; 声望;(由于财富等而产生的)显赫: a man of high ~ 威信高的人 / sweep every bit of sb.'s ~ into the dust 使某人威信扫地 / international ~ 国际声誉

presume [pri'zjuːm] **❶** *vt.* ①擅自,敢于(用于第一人称时为客套语): ~ to order people about 擅自对人发号施令 / I won't ~ to disturb you. 我不敢打扰你。② 假定,假设;(没有证据地)相信: Let's ~ that he has told the truth. 我们姑且认为他说的是真话。/ We ~ the story (to be) true. 我们认为这传闻大概是可靠的。/ You had better ~ no such thing. 你最好不要这样设想。③ 足以推定,意味着: A signed invoice ~s receipt of the shipment. 经过签收的发货单表示运去的货物已收到。**❷** *vi.* ①擅自行动,放肆 ②设想: Mr. Wilson, I ~? 你是威尔逊先生吧? ‖~ **upon** (或 **on**) ①把期望寄托在…,指望: We must not ~ too much *on* the reliability of such sources. 我们不应过分指望这类消息来源的可靠性。②(不正当地)利用; 滥用: ~ *upon* sb.'s good nature 利用某人的好脾气 / ~ *on* one's position 滥用职权 ‖~**r** *n.* ①冒昧的人; 放肆的人 ②假定者,(无根据地)设想的人

presumed [pri'zjuːmd] *a.* 假定的; 推测的 ‖~**ly** [pri'zjuːmidli] *ad.* 据推测,大概

presumption [pri'zʌmpʃən] *n.* ① 专横,自以为是; 傲慢;冒昧;放肆 ② 假定,设想,推测,推断: *Presumption* is not reality. 设想不等于现实。/ The ~ is that he had lost his way. 看起来,他当时是迷了路。③作出推论的根据(或理由,证据): There is a strong ~ in favour of the truthfulness of their statement. 有一个有力的根据

足以推定他们所讲是真实的。④【律】事实的推断(从其他的已知事实推断某事)(=~ of fact) ‖~ *of law* ① 法律上的假定 ② (在一定情况下普遍适用的)法定推论

presumptive [pri'zʌmptiv] *a.* ① 可据以推定的: ~ evidence 推定证据 ②假定的,设想的: an heir ~ 假定继承人(指有血统更近的继承人出生时即失去继承权者) ‖~**ly** *ad.*

presumptuous [pri'zʌmptjuəs] *a.* 专横的,自以为是的; 傲慢的; 冒昧的; 放肆的: It is too ~ of him to do so. 他这样做太放肆了。‖~**ly** *ad.* / ~**ness** *n.*

presuppose [,priːsə'pəuz] *vt.* ① 预先假定; 预料,推测 ②以…为先决条件; 含有: Effects ~ causes. 有其果必有其因。‖**presupposition** [,priːsʌpə'ziʃən] *n.* 预想(的事); 预先假定(的事); 先决条件

pretence [pri'tens] *n.* ① 假装; 矫饰; 虚伪; 做作: make a ~ of ignorance 假装无知(或不知道) / be devoid of all ~ 毫不虚伪(或做作) / a man without ~ 不装腔作势的人 ②借口,托词,口实: *on* the ~ of (或 that ...) 以…为借口 / You shouldn't scold him *on* the slightest ~. 你不应该以一点点借口就责骂他。/ *under* the ~ of helping (friendship) 以帮助(友谊)为借口 ③ 自命,自称; 自吹: have (或 make) no ~ to being learned 不以有学问自居 ④ (无事实根据的)要求; 虚假的理由 ⑤ [罕] 目的; 企图 ‖*false ~s* 【律】欺诈(手段)

pretend [pri'tend] **❶** *vt.* ①假托,借口; 假装;(演戏等中)装扮: ~ innocence (sickness) 假装无辜(有病) / ~ to know 装懂 / ~ to be asleep 装睡 / boys ~*ing* that they are old men 装扮为老人的男孩们 ② 自命,自称: He does not ~ to be a scientist. 他并不自命为科学家。**❷** *vi.* ① 假装,装作: He ~s as though he were not guilty. 他假装无罪。② 自封,自称; 妄求,觊觎 (*to*): ~ *to* talent 自称有才能 / ~ *to* the throne 觊觎王位 ③【古】向身分高的女方求婚(to) ‖~**edly** *ad.*

pretender [pri'tendə] *n.* ① 妄求者,妄想者; 觊觎王位者: the Old and the Young *Pretender*【英史】(十八世纪)觊觎王位者(指詹姆士二世的儿子和孙子)②伪装者,冒充者: a ~ in medicine 冒牌医生

pretension[1] [pri'tenʃən] *n.* ① 要求; 主张; 权利: have no ~ to the title 配不上这个称号 ②抱负; 意图 ③借口,托词 ④自称,自命: make no ~s to intelligence 并不自称聪明 ⑤ 矫饰,做作,虚荣

pretension[2] ['priː'tenʃən] *vt.*【建】预张,预拉: ~ed concrete 先张法(或预应力)混凝土

pretentious [pri'tenʃəs] *a.* ①自负的,自命不凡的,狂妄的: a ~ writer 一个自命不凡的作家 / a ~ speech 一篇夸夸其谈的演说 ② 矫饰的,做作的 ③ 用力的,使劲的; 需要技巧(或才能)的 ‖~**ly** *ad.* / ~**ness** *n.* shed the ugly mantle of ~*ness* 放下臭架子

preterhuman [,pri:tə(:)'hju:mən] *a.* 超人的，异乎常人的

preterit(e) ['pretərit] **I** *a.* ①【语】过去的: the ~ tense 过去时态 ②[罕][谑]过去的，已往的 **II** *n.* 【语】过去时态；过去时的动词

pretext **I** ['pri:tekst] *n.* 借口，托词: find a ~ *for* 为…找借口 / make a ~ *for* 以借口来辩解… / on some ~ or other 用某种借口 / on (或 *under*, *upon*) the ~ of 以…为借口 **II** [pri'tekst] *vt.* 借口，假托

pretty ['priti] **I** *a.* ①漂亮的，标致的，俏的；美丽的，秀丽的: a ~ garden (valley) 美丽的花园(山谷) ②优美的，悦耳的；(游戏等)有趣的，愉快的: a ~ piece of music 优美的乐曲 ③(常作讽刺语)好的，妙的；浮华的: A ~ mess you have made of it! 你可搞得真"好"呀! (或: 你搞得太糟了!) / in a ~ state of affairs 情况(或处境)不妙 ④机灵的；(手腕等)巧妙的；狡猾的: a ~ hypocrite 狡猾的伪君子 ⑤十分恰当的，贴切的: a ~ example 很恰当的例子 ⑥[口]好多的，相当大的: a ~ sum of money 相当大的一笔钱 / It will cost a ~ penny. 这要花相当多钱。⑦[古][苏格兰]健壮的；勇敢的 **II** *ad.* 相当，颇: well 相当好 / ~ soon 不久 / ~ certain 相当可靠(或有把握) / I feel ~ tired. 我感到相当疲倦了。**III** *n.* ①漂亮的人(常指孩子) ②漂亮的东西；[复]漂亮的衣服 ③[英](酒杯等)的凹纹: fill it up to the ~ 把酒斟到齐杯子的凹纹 ④(高尔夫球)球的正规通路 **IV** *vt.* 使漂亮，使可爱，美化 (up) ‖*a kettle of fish* 见 kettle / ~ *much* [口]几乎(全部): ~ *much* the same thing 差不多一样 / *sit* ~ 见 sit ‖**prettily** *ad.* / **prettiness** *n.* / ~**ish** *a.* 有些漂亮的 / ~**ism** *n.* (文体或态度等的)矫揉造作；过分讲究修饰 ‖'~-,~ *a.* 专门讲究修饰(或打扮)的，只想漂亮的；装饰(或打扮)得俗气的 *n.* [复]小玩意儿，小装饰品；无用的装饰(品)

prevail [pri'veil] *vi.* ①胜(过)，优胜 (over, against); 成功；奏效: Truth will ~. 真理必胜。/ ~ *against* the enemy 胜过敌人 ②流行，盛行；普遍: This custom does not ~ now. 这种风俗现在已经不流行了。‖~ *on* (或 *upon*, *with*) 说服，劝说；诱使: ~ *upon* sb. to accept an invitation 劝得某人接受邀请 / He is liable to ~ *upon* (或 *with*). 他是容易说服的。

prevalence ['prevələns] *n.* ①流行，盛行；普遍 ②[罕]优势

prevalent ['prevələnt] *a.* ①流行的，盛行的；普遍的 ②[罕]优势的 ‖~**ly** *ad.*

prevaricate [pri'værikeit] *vi.* ①支吾，搪塞，推诿 ②撒谎 ‖**prevarication** [pri,væri'keiʃən] *n.* / **prevaricator** *n.* 推诿的人；撒谎的人

prevent [pri'vent] ❶ *vt.* ①防止，预防(或制止)战争 / ~ diseases (accidents) 预防疾病(事故) ②阻止，阻挡；制止；妨碍 (from): What (Who) ~ed him *from* going (或 ~ed him

going 或 ~ed his going)? 什么事(谁)阻止了他去? ③[古]先做；预先迎合(愿望等)；预先应付(问题等)；【宗】引领 ❷ *vi.* 妨碍；阻止: We shall come tomorrow if nothing ~s. 如果没有什么阻碍的话，我们明天来。

preventable [pri'ventəbl] *a.* 可防止的，可预防的；可阻止的 ‖**preventability** [pri,ventə'biliti] *n.*

prevention [pri'venʃən] *n.* 预防，防止；阻止；妨碍: 预防法。Prevention is better than cure. 预防胜于治疗。

preventive [pri'ventiv] **I** *a.* 预防的，防止的: ~ measure against rats 防鼠措施 / a ~ war 先发制人的战争 / Preventive (Coastguard) Service [英]海关缉私部 **II** *n.* 预防法，预防措施；预防药；预防物 ‖~ **medicine** ① 预防医学 ② 预防药，预防剂

previous ['pri:vjəs] **I** *a.* ①先的，前的，以前的: a ~ engagement 先约 / as sb. mentioned on a ~ occasion 如某人上次所提到的 / a criminal with ~ convictions 以前判过刑的罪犯，惯犯 ②[口]过早的，过急的: He was a little too ~ in making the decision. 他作出这个决定太匆忙了些。**II** *ad.* 在前，在先，在…以前 (to): make full investigations ~ *to* reaching a conclusion 先充分调查再下结论 ‖~**ly** *ad.* / ~**ness** *n.* ‖**Previous Examination** [英](剑桥大学文学士学位的)初考 / ~ **question** (议会中)先决问题(或动议)

prey [prei] **I** *n.* ①被捕食的动物: The deer fell a ~ *to* the lion. 鹿被狮子捕食了。②[喻]牺牲品，牺牲品: be (或 fall) a ~ *to* 成为…的牺牲品；被…折磨(或蹂躏) ③捕食: a beast (bird) of ~ 食肉兽(鸟)，猛兽(禽) ④[古]掠夺品；战利品 **II** *vi.* ①(猛兽等)捕食，攫食 (on, upon) ②掠夺，劫掠；诈取 (on, upon) ③(疾病等)折磨，损害 (on, upon): Remorse ~ed upon his mind. 悔恨使他内心痛苦。

price [prais] **I** *n.* ①价格，价钱: In our country, ~s are stable. 我国物价稳定。/ set a ~ *on* (或 *upon*) sth. 定某物的价格 / sell at a fair ~ 以公平价格出售 / reduce (raise) a ~ 减低(提高)价格 / be worth the ~ 是值这个价钱的 ②(对杀死或捉拿某人者的)赏金；(贿赂的)金额 ③代价: the lesson gained *at* the ~ *of* blood 以血的代价取得的教训 / pay a high ~ *for* 为…付出很高代价 ④价值: above (或 beyond, without) ~ 极其珍贵的，无价之宝的 / of great ~ 十分宝贵的，价值很高的 ⑤(赌博中)赌注与赢款的差额 ‖*an administrated* ~ [美](由大垄断资本控制的不受市场供求规律支配的)垄断价格 / *the asking* ~ 卖主的开叫价 / *a cost* ~ 成本价格 / *current* ~*s* 时价，现行价格 / *famine* ~*s* 缺货市 / *fixed* (或 *set*) ~ 固定价格 / *a long* (或 *heavy*) ~ 昂价，高价 / *a net* ~ 实价 / *the* ~ *of money* 贷款利率 / *a reduced* ~ 折扣价格 / *a selling* (*retail*, *wholesale*) ~ 售(另售，批发)价 / *a unit* ~ 单价 **II** *vt.* ①给…定价；给…标价: be ~d 5 yuan 定

价五元 / All our goods are clearly ~d. 我们所有的货物都标明了价目。 ② 由于抬价过高而使…: ~ one's goods (或 oneself) out of the market 漫天讨价以致减少(或没有)销路 ③[口]问…的价格 ‖at any ~ 无论花多少代价;无论如何 / at a ~ 以很高代价;以比市价高的价钱 / fetch a good ~ 可售得好价钱 / set (或 put) a ~ on sb.'s head 悬赏缉拿某人(不论生死) / What ~ ...? [英俚] ①(比赛的马等)胜算如何? ②有可能…吗?: What ~ fine weather for Sunday? 星期日天气会不会好? ③(嘲笑失败的某事物)…算个什么东西? …有什么用处呢? ‖~d a. 有定价的;定价的。a ~d catalogue 列有定价的目录单 / high-~d 高价的 / low-~d 廉价的 ‖~ control 价格管制,物价控制 / ~ current 市价表 / '~-,cutter n. (为了挫败竞争者等的)削价者 / ~ index 物价指数 / ~ level 物价水平 / ~ list 定价表;价目单 / ~ support [美] ①对预定价格标准的维持(通常由政府采取措施) ②为维持一定价格的贷金,价格补偿金 / ~ tag ①价格标签 ②价格 / ~ war 一再削价的商业竞争,价格战

priceless ['praislis] a. ①无价的;贵重的;无法估价的。a ~ treasure 无价之宝 ②[俚]极有趣的;极荒唐的

prick [prik] I ❶ vt. ① 刺(穿),扎(穿),戳(穿): ~ holes in paper 在纸上刺孔 / ~ blisters on one's sole with a needle 用针挑破脚底上的水泡 ② 刺伤;刺痛: get one's finger ~ed by a thorn 手指给刺扎痛了 / Remorse ~ed him. 悔恨使他不安。 ③(刺小孔或用小点点)标出;(在名单等上做小记号)挑选出: ~ an embroidery pattern 刺出绣花样 / ~ a candidate 挑选候选人 ④ 竖起(耳朵): ~ (up) one's ears 侧耳倾听;警觉起来 / ~ up its ears (犬、马等警觉地)竖起耳朵 ⑤(用靴刺或刺棒)刺(踢); [喻]驱使 (on, off): His sense of duty ~ed him on to do so. 他的责任感使他这么去做。 ⑥ 追踪(野兔等) ⑦ 缝合(篷、帆等) ⑧移植(幼苗) (in, out, off) ⑨使(酒等)发酸 ❷ vi. ①刺;(感到)刺痛: Thorns ~. 荆棘刺人。/ The wound ~s badly. 伤口痛得厉害。②[古]用靴刺驱马;策马前进: ~ across a plain 策马驰过平原 ③(耳朵)竖起;耸耸: The dog's ear ~ed up at the sound. 狗听到声音而竖起耳朵。/ steeples ~ing toward the sky 耸入云霄的尖塔 ④(酒等)发酸 II n. ①一刺,一扎: A slight ~, and the injection was over. 轻轻的一扎,针就打好了。②刺痛;刺伤: I can still feel the ~. 我仍有刺痛的感觉。/ ~s of conscience 良心的责备 ③刺痕;刺点;刺孔;野兔的足迹: the ~ made by a needle 针的刺痕 ④(植物的)刺;(动物的)突出的器官(或部位) ⑤尖形器具(或武器);[古](赶牲畜用的)刺棒 ⑥(箭靶的)靶心 ⑦[音]符点 III a. 竖起的(指耳朵) ‖kick against the ~s 以卵击石;螳臂挡车 / ~ a bubble 见 bubble / ~ for a (soft) plank (海员用语)找最舒适的卧处 / ~ near 与…不相上下 / ~ off (或 out)

①挑选出 ②移植(幼苗) ③【海】(实地观察后)将(船)的位置和进程记于海图上 / ~ up ①(用灰泥等)粗涂,打底子 ②(风)加剧 / ~ up oneself 打扮自己;炫耀自己 ‖~er n. ①刺(或扎、戳)的人 ②供刺(或扎、钻孔)用的工具(如刺孔针、锥子等) ③鞭棘,刺 ④轻骑兵 / ~ing n. 刺;刺痛感 ‖'~-eared a. ①(狗等)竖起耳朵的 ②(人)耳朵显露的

prickle[1] ['prikl] I n. ① (动植物的)皮刺,刺;棘 ② 针刺般的感觉,刺痛 II ❶ vt. ① 针一般地刺 ② 使感到刺痛 ❷ vi. 引起刺痛;感到刺痛

prickle[2] ['prikl] n. [英] 柳条篮子

prickly ['prikli] a. ① 多刺的,满是针刺的: a ~ shrub 多刺灌木 ② 针刺般的: a ~ sensation 针刺般痛的感觉 ③ 易动怒的;敏感的 ‖~ heat 痱子 / ~ pear【植】霸王树(仙人掌科);霸王树的梨状果实

pride [praid] I n. ① 骄傲,傲慢,自大: be puffed up with ~ 妄自尊大 ②自满;得意 ③自豪;自尊(心): a sense of national ~ 民族自尊心 ④引以自豪的人(或事物) ⑤最优秀部分,精华(指一部分人等);全盛(期);顶点: in the ~ of one's life 在年富力强的时期 ⑥[古]华丽,壮观;美观 ⑦(马的)精力,勇气 ⑧(鸟、兽等的)群 II vt. [~ oneself] 使得意 (on, upon): ~ oneself upon one's ability 自夸能力大 ‖a peacock in his ~ 见 peacock / false ~ 妄自尊大 / in ~ (或 prime) of grease (猎物)正肥,适宜于狩猎 / Pride goes before a fall. (或 Pride will have a fall.) [谚]骄者必败。/ ~ of place 头等重要的地位;高位;傲慢: give ~ of place to the positive characters in a play 使剧中的正面人物处于显著地位 / proper (或 honest) ~ 自尊心 / put one's ~ in one's pocket 抑制自尊心,忍辱 / take (a) ~ in 以…自豪;对…感到得意 / the ~ of China (或 India) 檀香 / the ~ of the desert 骆驼 / the ~ of the morning 早晨的雾(或阵雨)(天晴的预兆) ‖~ful a. 十分骄傲的,傲慢的;得意的;自豪的

priest [pri:st] I n. ①【基督教】教士;牧师;神父;(英国国教或天主教位于执事及主教之间的)僧侣 ②(基督教以外的宗教的)祭司;和尚;术士 ③[爱尔兰](用来打死已上钩的鱼的)木槌 II vt. 使成为教士;任命…为祭司(或牧师等);使做和尚 ‖a ~ of Bacchus 酒鬼 ‖~ess n. (基督教以外的)尼姑;女祭司;女术士 / ~hood n. ①教士(或祭司等)的职位(或身分) ②(教会的)全体教士(或牧师、僧侣) / ~like a. 似教士的;适于教士的 / ~ling n. 小教士;小和尚 ‖'~-craft n. 教士(或僧侣)的权术(或谋略) / '~-,ridden a. 受教士控制(或压制)的

priestly ['pri:stli] a. 教士的;象教士的;适于教士的 ‖**priestliness** n.

prig[1] [prig] n. ①一本正经的人;自命不凡者;道学先生,学究气的人 ②讨厌的人

prig[2] [prig] I (prigged; prigging) ❶ vt. [英俚]偷

❷ *vi.* [苏格兰] 争论;讨价还价 **II** *n.* [英俚] 贼,扒手

priggish ['prigiʃ] *a.* 自负的,自命不凡的,沾沾自喜的;一本正经的,古板的 ‖**~ly** *ad.* / **~ness** *n.*

prim [prim] **I** (primmer, primmest) *a.* ①整洁的,端正的: a ~ garden 整洁的园子 ②一本正经的,拘谨的,古板的 **II** (primmed; primming) **❶** *vt.* ① 使(脸、嘴)显出一本正经的表情 ② 整洁地打扮(或装饰) **❷** *vi.* 做出一本正经的样子 ‖**~ly** *ad.* / **~ness** *n.*

primacy ['praiməsi] *n.* ①第一位,首位;卓越 ②大主教的职责(或身分、权力) ③【天主教】教皇的最高权力

primary ['praiməri] **I** *a.* ① 最初的; 原始的: the ~ stage of civilization 文明(或文化)的初期 / a ~ forest 原始(森)林 ②原有的,本来的;原著的,第一手的; (颜色)原色的: the ~ meaning of a word 一个词的原义 / ~ colours 基色,原色(指红、黄、蓝三色) ③基本的;基层的;初级的,初等的: a ~ party organization 基层党组织 / a ~ unit 基层单位 / a ~ school 小学 / ~ education 小学教育,初等教育 ④首要的,主要的: a matter of ~ importance 头等重要的事情 ⑤【电】一次的;第一级的: ~ cell 一次电池,原电池(指不能再充电使用的) / ~ coil 初级线圈,原线圈 ⑥【地】原生的: ~ minerals 原生矿物,未氧化的矿物 ⑦【植】初生的: ~ wall 初生壁 ⑧【化】伯的;连上一个碳原子的; (无机盐)一代的: ~ alcohol 伯醇 / ~ carbon atom 伯碳原子 / ~ arsenate 一代砷酸盐 / a ~ accent【语】主重音(符号) / a ~ assembly (或 meeting) 候选人选拔会 / a ~ election (选民直接选出候选人的)初选 / a ~ road 公路网中的干线 / ~ star【天】主星 / ~ tenses【语】主要时态(指拉丁文和希腊文等语法中的现在、将来、完成和将来完成时) / a ~ trainer 初级教练机 / ~ vowel sounds【语】基本元音 **II** *n.* ①(次序、质量等)居首位的事物 ②原色,原色感 ③候选人选拔会;初选 ④【天】主星 (=~ star) ⑤[常用复][动]初级飞羽; (昆虫的)前翅 ⑥【电】初级线圈,原线圈 ‖**primarily** ['praiməri] 美 prai-'merili] *ad.* ①首先;起初,原来 ②首要地,主要 ③根本上

primate ['praimit, 'praimeit] *n.* ① 大主教: the Primate of all England (英国的)坎特伯雷 (Canterbury) 大主教 ②[罕]首领 ③['praimeit] 灵长目动物

prime¹ [praim] **I** *a.* ①最初的; 基本的; 原有的: the ~ reason 基本的理由 ②首要的,主要的;首位的: a political task of ~ importance 头等重要的政治任务 / life's ~ want (或 need) 生活的第一(或基本)需要 ③最好的,第一流的: ~ beef 上等牛肉 / tobacco of ~ quality 优质烟草 ④【数】质数的,素数的 ‖**~ cost** 主要成本 / ~ meridian【天】本初子午线,本初子午圈 / a ~ minister 总理;首相 / a ~ mover 原动力,主导力;原动机(如汽轮机等),牵引车 / a ~ number【数】质数,素数 / a ~ pump【机】起动注油泵 /

~ rate 最优惠利率,头等贷款利率 / ~ time [美] (无线电、电视的)听众(或观众)最多的时候(尤指晚间) / ~ vertical【天】卯酉圈 **II** *n.* ①最初,初期: the ~ of the moon 新月 ②春;青春;全盛时期: the ~ of the year 春天 / in the ~ of life 在壮年时期 / be past one's ~ 已过壮年 ③精华,最好部分 ④【数】质数,素数 ⑤黎明;【宗】晨祷 ⑥【音】同度 ⑦符号"′": A and A′ A 和 A一撇(读作 A and A prime) ⑧(击剑中八个防御姿势的)第一姿势 **III** *ad.* 极好地 ‖in ~ of grease (猎物)正肥,适宜于狩猎 ‖**~ly** *ad.* / **~ness** *n.*

prime² [praim] **❶** *vt.* ①灌注,装填; 为…装雷管(或火药): a lamp with oil 把油注入灯内 / ~ a mine 为地雷装雷管 ②(注入水或油等)使起动: ~ a pump (注入水等)使泵起动 ③在…上涂底漆(或底色): ~ the wall with white paint 在墙上涂白漆打底 ④使准备好,使完成准备工作 ⑤事先给…指导;事先为…提供消息(或情报等): be ~d with the latest news 掌握最新消息 ⑥[口]使吃饱,使喝足 **❷** *vi.* ① (为枪等)装火药,装雷管 ②注水入泵引动; (蒸汽机)让水雾与压入汽缸的蒸汽混合 ③涂底漆(或底色) ④事先提供消息(或情报等) ⑤质量变好 ‖~ the pump 见 pump

primer¹ ['praimə, 'primə] *n.* ①识字课本, 初级读本 ② 入门书; 入门 ③['primə] 一种铅字的名称: a great ~ 十八点铅字(旧称十八磅铅字) / a long ~ 十点铅字(旧称十磅铅字)

primer² ['praimə] *n.* ① 雷管,火帽,底火,发火药;导火线 ②装火药者 ③底漆;首涂油 ④【机】初注器: engine ~ 发动机起动注油器 ⑤【生化】引物 ‖asphalt ~ 路面头道沥青; 沥青底漆 / a delay ~ 迟发起爆药包 / a percussion ~ 碰炸起爆药包;击发式底火 / a cartridge ~ 起爆药筒 / a charge ~ 点火药 / a ~ pump 起动注油泵(=prime pump)

primeval [prai'mi:vəl] *a.* 原始的,早期的,远古的: a ~ forest 原始森林,原生林 ‖**~ly** *ad.*

primitive ['primitiv] **I** *a.* ①原始的,远古的;早期的: a ~ forest 原生林 / ~ organisms 原始生物 / ~ society (communes) 原始社会(公社) / ~ accumulation 原始积累 / ~ soil 生荒地,未开垦的土地 ②粗糙的,简单的;未开化的 ③纯朴的,自然的 ④ 原来的; 基本的; 非派生的: a ~ function 原函数 ⑤自学而成的;自学的艺术家所创作的 **II** *n.* ①原(始)人;原始事物 ②(一种文化运动或艺术流派的)早期艺术家;原始派艺术家;模仿早期风格的艺术家;原始派艺术家 ③文艺复兴以前时期的艺术家(或其作品) ④ 自学而成的艺术家;风格朴素的艺术家 ⑤ 纯朴的人 ⑥【语】原词,根词 ⑦【数】本原,原始 ‖**~ly** *ad.* / **~ness** *n.* / **primitivism** *n.* (生活方式或艺术上的)原始主义;原始(或质朴)的风格;尚古主义

primrose ['primrouz] **I** *n.* ①【植】报春(花)属植物;樱草;樱草花: the Chinese (或 Tibetan) ~ 藏报春 / the Japanese ~ 七重草 ②樱草色,淡黄色 **II** *a.* 樱草色的;樱草色的,淡黄色的 ‖**~ path** (of dalliance) ①享乐之路，追求享乐使人堕落的放荡生活 ②最易走也最易出乱子的路

prince [prins] *n.* ①王子；王孙；亲王：a ~ of the blood 男王族 / the Crown *Prince* 太子，王储 / the ~ royal 太子(王或女王的长子) / *Prince* of *Wales* 威尔士亲王(英国太子的称号) ②(封建、公国或小国的)君主；诸侯 ③(英国以外国家的)公爵,侯爵,伯爵；…公,…侯：a great (或 grand) ~ (帝俄时代等的)大公 ④[诗]帝王,君主 ⑤[喻]巨头；大王；名家：a merchant ~ 豪商 / the ~ of poets 诗坛宗匠，最杰出的诗人 / the ~ of liars 说谎专家 ⑥[美俚]好人 ‖*Hamlet without the Prince of Denmark* 去掉了本质的东西 / *Prince of Denmark* 丹麦王子(指莎士比亚剧中主角 Hamlet 汉姆雷特) / *Prince of Wales's feathers* 英国太子的纹章 / *the ~ of darkness* (或 *the air, the world*) 撒旦,魔鬼 / *the Prince of Peace* 耶稣 / *the ~ of the* (*Holy Roman*) *Church* 罗马天主教红衣主教的称号 ‖~**dom** *n.* ①小国君主(如亲王、侯等)的权位 (或领地) ②公国，侯国 / ~**kin** *n.* 幼君；小君主 / ~**let** ['prinslit], ~**ling** *n.* (领地、势力等较小的)小诸侯，小公子 / ~**like** *a.* ①君主般的；王子般的；诸侯般的 ②高贵的；威严的；慷慨大方的 / ~**ship** *n.* ①君主(或王子、诸侯等)的身分(或权威) ②君主(或王子、诸侯等)在位的时期 ‖*Prince Albert* [美口](男子)礼服大衣 / '~-'**bishop** *n.* 兼任主教的公国君主 / ~ **charming** 女子理想中的求婚者;对女子假装殷勤的男子 / ~ **consort** 女王的丈夫 / ~ **regent** 摄政王 / '~'s-'**feather** *n.*【植】硬穗苋；荭草 / '~'s-'**metal** *n.* 一种铜锌合金,黄铜(作廉价饰物用)

princely ['prinsli] *a.* ①王侯的;王子的 ②王侯般的;王子似的;象殿公子的 ③高贵的,堂皇的,庄严的 ④与王侯(或王子)相称的;豪华的;奢侈的,挥霍的 ‖**princeliness** *n.*

princess [prin'ses; 作定语时 'prinses] *n.* ①公主;王妃;亲王夫人：a ~ of the blood 女王族 / a ~ royal 大公主(王的长女) / a Crown *Princess* 皇太子之妃 / *Princess* of *Wales* 英国太子之妃 / *Princess* Anne 安妮公主 ②(英国以外君主国的)公爵夫人,侯爵夫人 ③[古]女王 ④女巨头,女名家：a ~ of seamstresses 女缝纫名手 ‖~ **regent** 女摄政王;摄政王的夫人

principal ['prinsəpəl] **I** *a.* ①主要的,首要的,最重要的：~ food 主食 / the ~ points 要点 / the ~ aspect of a contradiction 矛盾的主要方面 / the ~ persons concerned 有关的主要人员 ②负责人的,首长的 ③资本的,本金的 ‖the ~ boy (girl) [英]哑剧中扮演男(女)主角的女演员 / a ~ clause (或 *sentence*)【语】(复合句中的)主句 / the ~ force 主力部队 / a ~ offender【律】主犯 / a ~ office 总社;总店;总部 / the ~ parts【语】动词的主要变化形式 / the ~ section 主截面 **II** *n.* ①长,首长;负责人;校长：a lady ~ 女校长 ②主要演员,主角 ③【律】主犯：a ~ in the first (second)

degree 主(从)犯 ④(经纪人或代理人所代表的)委托人,本人：I must consult my ~. 我必须与委托人商量。⑤资本;本金;基本财产：pay off the ~ and interest 付清本息 ⑥【建】(主要)屋架 ⑦【音】主音栓;(音乐会的)主奏者;独奏者,独唱者 ⑧(艺术作品的)主题 ‖~**ly** *ad.*

principality [,prinsi'pæliti] *n.* ①公国,侯国;封邑 ②公国君主的职位(或权力、领地) ③首长(或校长)的职位(或权力) ④[复](神学中)天使的九个等级之一 ‖*the Principality* (英国地方)威尔士(Wales) 的别称

principle ['prinsəpl] *n.* ①原则;原理：a cardinal ~ 根本(或主要)原理 / a matter (或 question) of ~ 原则性的问题 / These two instruments work *on* the same ~. 这两种仪器的工作原理是一样的。②主义;节操：moral ~ 道义 / the conservative ~ 保守主义 / a man of high ~ 有高度道德原则的人 ③本原,源泉：the first ~ of all things 万物的本原 ④天然的性能(或倾向),本性;天赋的才能 ⑤【化】素,要素：bitter ~ 苦味素 / odorous ~ 香臭要素 (=essential oil) ‖*in* ~ 原则上,大体上：We are agreed *in* ~ but not in detail. 我们在原则上是一致的,但在细节上不一致。/ *on* ~ 根据原则,按照原则：refuse *on* ~ 根据原则加以拒绝 / *on the* ~ *of* 根据…的原则,按照…的原则：distribute *on the* ~ *of* equal pay for equal work 按照同工同酬的原则进行分配

principled ['prinsəpld] *a.* 原则的,原则性的,有原则的：~ argument 原则上的争论 / persist in a ~ stand 坚持原则立场 / be high-~ 有高度道德原则的

print [print] **I** ❶ *vt.* ①印;铭刻;打上(印记等)：The child's feet ~ed the sand. 孩子的脚在沙土上留下了脚印。/ ~ a seal *in* wax 在火漆上打印记 / ~ sth. *on* sb.'s memory (或 mind) 使某事铭记在某人心上,使某人牢记某事 ②印刷;把…付印,把…用书面发表：~ a book (poster) 印一本书(一张宣传画) / Has he consented to have his talk ~ed? 他已同意印发他的谈话了吗? ③用印刷体写：Please ~ your names. 请用印刷体写姓名。④在(织物)上印花;印(花)：~ed cloth 印花布 ⑤【摄】印,晒印;复制(电影拷贝等) (*off*, *out*)：How many copies shall we ~ (*off*) from the negative? 用那张底片,我们要印几张像片? ⑥[美俚]取…的指纹 ❷ *vi.* ①印刷,刊印;从事印刷;印：The new press ~s rapidly. 新的印刷机印得很快。/ This paper (negative) ~s well. 这种纸(底片)印起来很好。②用印刷体写字 **II** *n.* ①印痕,痕迹；[复][美俚]指纹：a finger~ 指印,指纹 / a foot~ 脚印,足迹 / His experiences left deep ~s on him. 他的经历在他身上留下了深刻的烙印。②印刷;印刷术;印刷业：put an article into ~ 把一篇文章付印 / appear (或 come out) in ~ (被)印成,(被)印出来 / rush into ~ 草率地发表文章(或出版书等);急于把作

品付印 ③印出的字体; 印刷字体: in large (small) ~ 用大(小)号铅字印的 / clear ~ 清晰的印刷字体 / uneven ~ 排列不齐的印刷字体 ④[主美]印刷品, 出版物(尤指报纸) ⑤图片; 晒图; 版画; 【摄】正片, 照片: a colour ~ 彩色图片 / old Chinese ~s 中国的古代版画 ⑥印花布; 印花布服装; 印花布制品: a ~ dress 印花布女服 ⑦打印器; 印章, 戳子 ⑧【冶】型心座(=core ~) ⑨打着印痕的东西; 印模制物: a ~ of butter (印模压成的)一块黄油 ⑩版本; 印次 ‖in ~ ①已出版的, (书等)在销售的 ②(书等)还能买到的, 书店有售的 / out of ~ (书等)已售完的; 已绝版的 ‖~able a. ①可印刷的; 印得出的 ②可刊印的, 适于出版的 / ~less a. 无印痕的; 不留印痕的 ‖~ed circuit 印刷电路 / ~ed matter 印刷品 / ~ effect (录音)复制效应, 转印效应 / ~ hand 用印刷体写的字 / '~out n. 【自】印出(指以打印方式表示的计算机计算结果) / '~-,seller n. 图片(或版画)商 / '~shop n. ①图片(或版画)店 ②印刷所 / '~works [复] n. [用作单或复](棉布等的)印花厂

printer ['printə] n. ①印刷工(包括排字工人): a ~'s error 排字错误, 误植 ②印花工 ③【摄】晒片机, 印象机; 【讯】印字机 ④印刷商 ‖~gram n. 印字电报 ‖~'s devil 印刷所学徒 / ~'s ink ①(印刷)油墨 ②印刷品 / ~'s mark (版权页等上)出版商的商标 / ~'s pie ①铅字的乱堆 ②[喻]混乱

printing ['printiŋ] n. ①印刷; 印刷术; 印刷业: coloured ~ 彩印 / three-coloured ~ 三色版印刷(术) ②【纺】印花: ~ and dyeing 印染 ③【摄】印像; (电影拷贝等的)复制 ④(书等的一次)印数 ⑤[复]供印刷用的纸 ‖印刷字体 / ~ house 印刷厂 / ~ ink (印刷)油墨 / ~ machine [主英](电动)印刷机 / ~ office 印刷所 / ~ press 印刷机(一般指电动的)

prior[1] ['praiə] I a. ①在先的, 在前的; 居先的: have a ~ engagement 已另有约会 ②优先的, 更重要的: ~ claims 优先要求权 / This task is ~ to all others. 这项任务比所有其他任务都重要。 II ad. 在前; 居先 (to): It happened ~ to my arrival. 这发生在我到达以前。

prior[2] ['praiə] n. ①(大修道院)副院长 ②(小修道院)院长 ‖~ate ['praiərit] n. ① 修道院院长职位(或职权、任期) ② =priory / ~ess ['praiəris] n. (大的女修道院)副院长; (小的)女修道院院长 / ~ship n. 修道院院长职位(或职权、任期)

priory ['praiəri] n. 小修道院; 小的女修道院: a ~ alien (或 an alien ~) 从属于外国大修道院的小修道院

prism ['prizəm] n. ①【数】棱柱(体), 角柱(体): oblique (regular, right, triangular) ~ 斜(正, 直, 三)棱柱 ②棱镜; 棱晶: ~ glasses 棱镜望远镜 / a reversing ~ 反像棱镜 ③【物】光谱; [复]光谱的七色 ④折光物体 ‖**prunes and** ~ 见 **prune**[1]

prison ['prizn] I n. ①监狱; 监禁: go to ~ 入狱, 被监禁 / be in ~ 在狱中, 被监禁着 / cast (或 put) sb. into ~ 把某人关进监狱 / be taken to ~ 被关入监狱 / break (out of) ~ 越狱 ②看守所, 拘留所; 羁押室, 禁闭室 II vt. [诗][方]监禁, 关押 ‖~ bird 囚犯, 惯犯 / ~ breaker 越狱者 / ~ breaking, ~ breach 越狱 / ~ camp ①战俘集中营 ②(监禁一般犯人使服劳役的)拘禁营地 / ~ fever 【医】斑疹伤寒 / ~ house 牢房

prisoner ['priznə] n. ①囚犯 ②刑事被告; 拘留犯, 羁押犯: a ~ at the bar 刑事被告 / a ~ of State (或 a State ~) 政治犯 ③俘虏: take (或 make) sb. ~ 俘虏某人 / a ~ of war 战俘(略作 POW, P. O. W. 或 PW) ④失去自由的人(或动物等): A bad cold kept me a ~ to my room. 重伤风使我不得不呆在房间里。 / He made the boy's hand a ~. 他抓住那男孩的手不放。 ‖~ at large (只准在舰上或营房内自由走动的)受约束处分的海军人员 / yield oneself ~ 投降做俘虏 ‖~'s base 抓俘房游戏(参加游戏者分作两队, 划定地界, 相互捕捉对方队中的越界人员

privacy ['praivəsi, 'privəsi] n. ①隐退, 隐居; (不受干扰的)独处: live in ~ 隐居 / I must have disturbed your ~. 我一定打扰了你, 使你不能清静了。②[古]退隐处, 隐居处 ③秘密, 私下: strict ~ 完全私下地(的)

private ['praivit] I a. ①私人的, 个人的; 私有的: ~ affairs 私事, 个人的事 / a ~ opinion 个人的见解 / ~ property 私有财产 / ~ ownership 私有制 / ~ study 自学 / at one's ~ house 在自己的屋内 ②私营的; 私立的; 民间的: a ~ enterprise 私营企业 / a ~ school 私立学校 ③不让人知道的, 私下的; 保密的, 秘密的; (信件等)亲启的: The matter was kept ~. 这事没有让人知道。 / for ~ reasons 仅仅私下地, 不足为外人知道 / a ~ conversation 密谈 / This is for your ~ ear. 这是我私下对你说的。 / a letter marked "~" 一封标明"亲启"(或"保密")的信 ④非公开的: a ~ door 便门 / a ~ view (绘画等公开出前的)预展 / The news came through ~ channels. 消息是私下传出来的。⑤非官职的; 士兵的: a ~ citizen 平民 / a ~ soldier 列兵, 士兵 ⑥(地方等)隔绝的, 隐蔽的, 幽僻的: a ~ dining room (与大厅隔开的)小间餐室, 雅座 / a ~ valley 幽谷 ⑦不宜公开谈论(或显露)的: one's ~ parts 阴部, 生殖器 ‖~ clothes 便衣 / ~ means 工资以外的收入 / a ~ teacher (或 coach, tutor) 私人教师, 家庭教师 / ~ theatricals (仅供亲友观看的)业余演出 II n. ①[复]阴部, 生殖器 ②职位低的人 ③列兵; (英)陆军二等兵; (美)陆军(或海军陆战队)二等兵; 士兵: a Private First Class (美)陆军(或海军陆战队)一等兵 / a basic ~ (美)陆军三等兵 ④[古]退隐者, 隐士 ‖in ~ 私下的(地); 秘密的(地): irresponsible criticism in ~ 不负责任的背后批评 / comply in public but oppose in ~ 阳奉阴违 ‖~ly ad.

‖ **~ bill, ~ act** 关于个人(或社团、公司)利益的议案 / **~ detective** (个人或单位雇用的) 私人侦探 / **~ eye** [俚] =**~ detective** / **~ law** (处理私人关系、财产等的) 私法 / **~ member (of Parliament)** (非内阁成员的)下院议员 / **~ practice** 私人开业 / **~ secretary** 私人秘书 / **~ treaty** (买卖双方直接议定条件的) 财产出让(契约)

privateer [ˌpraivəˈtiə] **I** *n.* ① (战时特准攻击敌方商船等的)武装民船, 私掠船 ②私掠船船长(或船员) **II** *vi.* 私掠巡航 ‖**~ing** [ˌpraivəˈtiəriŋ] *n.* 私掠巡航, 掠捕对方商船 ‖**~sman** [ˌpraivəˈtiəzmən] *n.* 私掠船船长(或船员)

privation [praiˈveiʃən] *n.* ①丧失; 缺乏: Cold is the ~ of heat. 所谓冷就是缺乏热量。 ② (生活必需品的)匮乏, 贫困: suffer many ~s 备尝苦困 ③ [罕] 剥夺

privilege [ˈprivilidʒ] **I** *n.* 特权; 优惠; 特免; 特殊的荣幸: enjoy ~s 享受特权(或优惠) / an exclusive ~ 专有特权 / grant sb. the ~ of doing sth. 赋予某人做某事的特权 / To converse with him is a ~. 同他交谈是件很荣幸的事。 **II** *vt.* ① 给予…特权(或优惠) ② 特免: ~ sb. *from* a tax 特免某人纳税 ‖ *a bill of* **~** 见 **bill**¹ / *the* **~** *of clergy* 教士的特权(犯罪时可不受普通法院审判); 受过教育者的特权(初次犯罪可免予判刑) / *the* **~** *of Parliament* (英国)议会(或议员)的特权 ‖ **~ cab** [英]特许在车站候客的马车

privileged [ˈprivilidʒd] *a.* ① 有特权的; 特许的: the ~ classes 特权阶级 ② (由于特殊情况)不受一般法规节制的: a ~ statement 不受一般法规节制的声明 ③ 【天主教】(祭坛等)庆祝大赦的弥撒中特设的 ‖**~ communication** 见 **communication**

privy [ˈprivi] **I** *a.* ① 个人的, 私人的 ② (地方、物等)秘密的; 隐蔽的; (行为)暗中参与的: ~ parts 阴部, 生殖器 / be ~ to a conspiracy 参与阴谋 **II** *n.* ①【律】有利害关系的人 ② 厕所 ‖**Privy Council** (英国)枢密院 / **~ counsellor, ~ councillor** [英]枢密院官员; 枢密顾问官 / **~ purse** [英](王室)内库: Keeper of the *Privy Purse* (英国)王室司库 / **~ seal** [英]御玺: Lord *Privy Seal* (英国)掌玺大臣

prix [pri:] [单复同] *n.* [法] ①奖金, 奖品 ②价格 ‖**~ *fixe*** [fi:ks] (一客)定好价钱的客饭, 公司餐 (=*table d'hôte*); 定价客饭的价格

prize¹ [praiz] **I** *n.* ① 奖赏, 奖金, 奖品; 赠品: be awarded a ~ for 为了…而获奖 / carry off (或 win) a ~ 得奖 / consolation ~s (体育比赛的)安慰奖 / the Nobel *Prize* 诺贝尔奖金 ② [喻]众人争夺的东西, (值得)竞争的目标; 极好的东西 **II** *a.* ① 得奖的; 作为奖品的; 为得奖而参加的: a ~ essay (novel) 得奖的论文 (小说) / a ~ cup 奖杯 ② [口] (有时含讽刺意)第一流的, 第一的: a ~ idiot 大傻瓜 **III** *vt.* ① 珍视, 珍藏: a ~d collection of books (自己)珍视的藏书 ② 估价;

评价 ‖ *play one's* **~** 图私利 / *run* **~***s* (为得奖而)参加比赛 ‖**~less** *a.* 未获奖的; 非杰出的 ‖**~ fellow** 得奖学金的人 / **~ fellowship** 成绩优良奖学金 / '**~fight** *n.* 职业拳击赛 / '**~ˌfighter** *n.* 职业拳击家 / '**~ˌfighting** *n.* 职业拳击 / **~man** [ˈpraizmən] *n.* 得奖人 / **~ ring** 拳击场; 拳击练习 / **~ scholarship** =**~ fellowship** / '**~ˌwinner** *n.* 获奖人

prize² [praiz] **I** *n.* ①捕获(尤指战时在海上捕获敌方的船、货等)②俘获品, 战利品; (战时)捕获的船只(或货物): make ~ of (战时)捕获(敌船等) ③ [喻]意外的收获; 横财 **II** *vt.* 捕获 ‖**~ court** 处理战利品的(海军)军事法庭 / **~ crew** 押送捕获船的船员 / **~ master** 捕获船押送官 / **~ money** 捕获赏金(旧时出售捕获船的货物等后分给立功官兵的赏金)

prize³ [praiz] **I** *vt.* (用杠杆)撬, 撬动 (*up, off, out*): ~ a box open 撬开箱子 / ~ *up* the lid of a box 撬开箱盖 **II** *n.* [方]杠杆; 撬杠, 撬棒; 杠杆作用

pro [prou] **I** *ad.* 在赞成方面, 正面地: argue the matter ~ and con 从正反两方面辩论问题 **II** *n.* 赞成者; 赞成的意见; 赞成的(投票): the ~s and cons 赞成者和反对者; 赞成和反对的票数; 正面和反面的理由 ‖**'~-and-'con** *vt.* & *vi.* 辩论

probability [ˌprobəˈbiliti] *n.* ①有或; 可能性, 或然性; 【逻】盖然性(介于 certainty 和 possibility 之间的性质): The ~ is that .... 很可能是… / There is every ~ of his coming. (或 There is every ~ that he will come.) 他多半会来的。 ② 有或的事; 可能的结果: The *probabilities* are in our favour (against us). 趋势对我们有利 (不利)。 ③ 【数】概率, 几率, 或然率: ~ curve 概率曲线 / the ~ of hitting 【军】预期命中率, 命中公算 ‖*in all* **~** 很可能, 多半, 十之八九

probable [ˈprobəbl] **I** *a.* ①或有的, 或然的, 大概的, 很可能的: a ~ error (大)概(误)差, 或然误差 / It is ~ that he forgot. 很可能他是忘了。 / the ~ zone 【军】预期命中地带 / the ~ cost 大概费用 ② 象真实的, 似确有的; 很有希望的: Rain is possible but not ~ before evening. 傍晚前可能下雨, 但不一定。 / ~ evidence 大概确实的证据 / a ~ candidate 大有希望的候选人[注意: probable 所指的可能性比 possible 或 likely 所指的为大] **II** *n.* ① 很可能的事(或情况) ② 很可能被选中(或获胜)的人, 大有希望的候补(或候选)者 ‖**probably** *ad.* 很可能, 大概, 或许

probate [ˈproubit] **I** *n.* 【律】①遗嘱检验 ②验讫的遗嘱 **II** *a.* 【律】遗嘱检验的 **III** [ˈproubeit] *vt.* ① 检验(遗嘱) ② 处(犯人)以缓刑 ‖**~ court** 遗嘱检验法庭 / **~ duty** 立遗嘱人死后的动产税

probation [prəˈbeiʃən] *n.* ①检验, 验证; 鉴定: a ~ report 鉴定报告 ② 试用; 见习; 试读 ③ 试用期; 见习期; 试读期; 预备期 ④察看(以观后效); 【律】缓刑 ‖**on** ~①作为试用; 作为见习 ②察看; 【律】缓刑: place(或 put) an offender *on* ~ 处犯人以缓刑 ‖**~al, ~ary** *a.* ① 试用的; 见习的; 预备

期的 ②缓刑中的 / ~**er** *n.* ①试用人员;见习生;见习护士 ②缓刑犯 ‖~ **officer** [美] 监督缓刑犯的官员

probative ['proubətiv], **probatory** ['proubətəri] *a.* ①检验的,鉴定的 ②证明的,提供证明的

probe [proub] **I** *n.* ①【医】探针,探子;【物】试探电极 ②(对伪处等的)针探,探查 ③刺探;探索;查究,彻底调查 (*into*): mount a massive ~ of sb.'s death 大举调查某人之死 ④【宇】探测器,探测飞船 ⑤【空】(飞机)空中加油管 **II** ❶ *vt.* ①用探针(或探测器)探查 ②刺探;探索;查究,彻底调查: ~ a matter to the bottom 对一件事进行彻底调查 ❷ *vi.* 探查,探索;深查,深挖 (*into*): ~ into the essence of things 探索事物的本质

probit ['probit] *n.* 概率单位(根据常态频率分配平均数的偏差计算的统计单位)

probity ['proubiti] *n.* 正直;诚实,笃实

problem ['problem] **I** *n.* ①问题;疑难问题;令人困惑的事(或人、情况等): the ~ of "for whom" 为什么人的问题 / tackle a ~ 对付一个问题 / a key 一个关键问题 / Her conduct is a ~ to me. 她的行为使我莫名其妙。 ②(下棋时,须按规定的)布局问题 ③【数】【物】习题,问题;几何作图题 **II** *a.* ①成为问题的,难对付的: a ~ child 【心】问题儿童,难管教的儿童;【喻】难处理的事情 ②关于社会问题的: a ~ play (社会)问题剧 ‖*sleep on* (或 *upon, over*) a ~ 把问题留到第二天解决

problematic(al) [,probli'mætik(əl)] *a.* ①成问题的,有疑问的;疑难的;未定的 ②【逻】盖然性的,或然性的 ‖**problematically** *ad.*

procedure [prə'si:dʒə] *n.* ①过程;步骤: ~ in production 生产过程 / break the normal ~ 打破常规 / His first ~ was to make a thorough investigation. 他首先采取的步骤是进行彻底调查。②程序: legal (scientific) ~ 法律(科学)程序 / set-up ~ 【自】准备程序 ③传统的做法;(外交、军队等的)礼仪,礼节

proceed [prə'si:d] *vi.* ①进行: The talks ~ed in a friendly atmosphere. 会谈是在友好的气氛中进行的。/ His thinking did not ~ this way. 他不是这样进行思考的。②继续进行;继续做下去;继续讲下去: ~ from the outside to the inside 由表及里 / ~ with one's work 继续工作下去(尤指停顿后) / Let us ~ to the next item on the agenda. 让我们进入下一项议程。/ "On this point," he ~ed, "our attitude is clear." 他接着说:"在这点上我们的态度是明确的。" ③开始;着手,出发: ~ to take off one's coat 开始脱掉上衣 / ~ from objective realities 从客观实际出发 / ~ from the interests of the people 从人民利益出发 ④发出;出(自): diseases that ~ from negligence of hygiene 不讲究卫生而引起的疾病 / Sobs were heard to ~ from that room. 从那房间里传出呜咽声。⑤起诉: ~ against sb. for sth. 为某事对某人起诉 ⑥[英]升到(高一级的学位) (*to*);获得(硕士以上)学位: ~ to

the degree of M. A. (或 ~ M. A.) 得硕士学位

proceeding [prə'si:diŋ] *n.* ①程序;进程;进行 ②行动;举动;做法: the best way of ~ 最好的行动方式 / a high-handed ~ 专横的举动 / suspicious ~s 可疑的(或鬼鬼祟祟的)行径 ③[复]事项;活动: the ~s at the meeting 会议事项 / business ~s 商业活动 ④[复]诉讼: take (或 institute) legal ~s against sb. 对某人起诉 ⑤[复](学会或其它团体的)会议录;活动记录;记录汇编

proceeds ['prousi:dz] [复] *n.* (从事某种活动或变卖财物等的)收入,收益

process[1] ['prouses; 美 'prɔses] **I** *n.* ①过程,进程;变化的过程;作用: a ~ in cognition 一个认识的过程 / the ~ of digestion 消化过程 / go through the same ~ again 重复同一过程 / the ~ of history 历史的进程 / in (the) ~ of time 随着时间的推移;逐渐地 / a psychological ~ 心理作用 ②工序;制作法: develop a new ~ of dyeing 创造一种新的染色法 【印】照相制版术;照相版图片;三原色印刷: offset ~ 胶印法 ④诉讼;(法律)手续: change one's name by legal ~ 通过法律手续更改名字 ⑤传票: serve a ~ on 对…发出传票 ⑥(动、植物)机体的突起,隆起;突: vermiform ~ 【解】蚓突(即阑尾) **II** *vt.* ①加工: ~ medicinal herbs 给草药加工 / ~ed leather 经过加工的皮革 / a ~ing workshop 加工车间 ②处理;初步分类,分理;办理: ~ polluted water 处理污水 / ~ data 分理数据(对数据作迅速的检查和分析) / ~ a loan 办理贷款手续 / ~ the recruits 对新兵进行初步分类 / a prisoner-of-war ~ing station 战俘处理站 ③对…起诉;(要求)对…发出传票 ④用照相版影印 **III** *a.* ①经过特殊加工的;(用人工合成法等)处理过的: ~ cheese 混合乳酪,精制干酪 ②【印】照相版的;三色版的: ~ ink 三色版油墨 ③(电影镜头等)有幻觉效应的 ‖ *in* ~ 在进行中: Changes are *in* ~. 正在发生变化。/ *in* (*the*) ~ *of* 在…的过程中: The machine is *in* (*the*) ~ *of* repair. 那部机器在修理中。‖ ~ **engraving** 【印】三色版(一般指三色网目铜或锌凸版) / ~ **plate** 【印】套色版(一般指三色原版) / ~ **printing** 彩色套印 / ~ **server** 递送传票的司法人员 / ~ **shot** 伪装镜头(为使场面中增添假象而用特种技巧拍摄的电影镜头)

process[2] [prə'ses] *vi.* [主英] 列队行进

procession [prə'seʃən] **I** *n.* ①(列队的)行进: It happened during the ~. 事情发生在行进途中。②(人或车辆等的)行列,队伍: form a ~ 排成行列 / parading ~s 游行队伍 / go (或 walk) in ~ 列队行进 ③一(长)列,一(长)排: a ~ of trees 一长排树 ④竞争不激烈的赛跑 **II** ❶ *vi.* 列队行进;在队伍中行进 ❷ *vt.* 沿着(街道)行进 ‖~**al** *a.* 列队行进的;列队行进时用的(或唱的) *n.* 列队行进时唱的歌;【宗】行列仪式书(书中规定列队行进的仪式) / ~**ary** *a.* 列队前进的 / ~**ist** *n.* 在行列中走的人

proclaim [prə'kleim] *vt.* ①宣告;宣布,公布;声

明: ~ a law 公布一项法令 / ~ (the country) a republic 宣布共和国成立 / ~ war 宣战 / ~ sb. (to be) a traitor 宣布某人为叛徒 ②公开赞扬 ③表明, 显示: His accent ~ed him a southerner. 他的口音表明他是南方人。④宣布禁止(集会等); 宣布对(某地区等)加以法律管制

proclamation [ˌprɔkləˈmeiʃən] *n.* ①宣布, 公布; 声明: ~ of martial law 宣布戒严 / ~ of neutrality 宣布中立 ②公告, 布告; 宣言; 声明书: issue (或 make) a ~ 发布公告; 发表声明 / the Potsdam *Proclamation* 波茨坦公告

proclivity [prəˈkliviti] *n.* 癖性; 倾向(尤指坏的倾向) *(to, towards, for)*: snobbish *proclivities* 势利成性 / a ~ *towards* being vicious (或 a ~ *to* vice) 作恶的倾向 / have no ~ *for* riding 不喜爱骑马

procrastinate [prouˈkræstineit] *vi. & vt.* 拖延, 耽搁, 因循 ||**procrastinator** *n.* 拖延者, 因循者

procrastination [prouˌkræstiˈneiʃən] *n.* 拖延, 耽搁, 因循 ||*Procrastination is the thief of time.* [谚]拖延即浪费时间。(或: 拖延错过时机。)

proctor [ˈprɔktə] **I** *n.* ①代理人; 【律】代诉人 ②监督者; (大学的)学监, 监考人 **II** *vt.* 监(考) ||*King's* (或 *Queen's*) *Proctor* (英国)王室的讼监(有权监察离婚、遗嘱等件的官员) ||~ial [prɔkˈtɔːriəl] *a.*

procure [prəˈkjuə] **❶** *vt.* ①(努力)取得, (设法)获得, 为…获得; 采办: Please ~ me some specimens. 请设法给我搞一些标本。②实现, 达成; 完成: ~ an agreement 达成协议 / a systematic theory 建立系统性的理论 ③[古]促使, 引起: His pride ~d his downfall. 他的骄傲使他垮台了。④介绍(娼妓); 为…作淫媒 **❷** *vi.* 介绍娼妓; 作淫媒, 拉皮条 ||~ment *n.* 获得, 获得的条件: the ~ment of materials 物资的采办 / ~r [prəˈkjuərə] *n.* 拉条者, 作淫媒者 / ~ss [prəˈkjuəris] *n.* 老鸨; 作淫媒的女人

prod [prɔd] **I** *n.* ①刺, 戳: give sb. a ~ with sth. 用其物戳某人一下 ②刺(或戳)的东西; 刺针, 刺棒; 锥: an electric ~ (赶牛等用的)通电刺棒 ③刺激(物); 促使, 推动: under the ~ of 在…的推动下 **II** (prodded; prodding) **❶** *vt.* ①刺, 戳: ~ an ox with a stick 用棒戳牛 ②刺激, 惹起; 促使, 激励: ~ one's memory 促使自己回忆 / ~ a lazy boy 激励一个懒惰的孩子 **❷** *vi.* 刺, 戳 *(at)* ||*on the* ~ [美方]大发脾气

prodigal [ˈprɔdiɡəl] **I** *a.* ①非常浪费的, 挥霍的, 奢侈的 ②不吝惜的, 十分慷慨的 *(of)*: be ~ *of* praise 赞不绝口 ③(物产等)丰富的, 大量的 **II** *n.* ①浪费者 ②浪子: the return of the ~ 浪子回头 ||~ly *ad.* ||~ son ①回头的浪子; 忏悔的罪人(源出基督教《圣经》) ②【动】军曹鱼(一种可食用的海鱼)

prodigalize [ˈprɔdiɡəlaiz] *vt.* 浪费, 挥霍

prodigious [prəˈdidʒəs] *a.* ①巨大的; 庞大的: a ~ amount of work 大量工作 ②异常的; 惊人的, 奇

妙的: a ~ view 奇异的景象 ③[古]预兆的; 不吉利的 ||~ly *ad.*

prodigy [ˈprɔdidʒi] *n.* ①奇迹, 奇事; 奇物, 奇观: *prodigies* of nature 自然界的壮观 ②奇才, 天才(尤指神童) ③[古]预兆

produce **I** [prəˈdjuːs] **❶** *vt.* ①生产, 出产, 制造; 生: grain (petroleum) 生产粮食(石油) / lathes (medicines) 制造车床(药品) / an egg (a calf)生蛋(小牛) ②产生; 引起 ③提出; 展现; 出示: ~ evidence (reasons) 提出证据(理由) / ~ one's driver's licence 出示驾驶执照 ④上演, 演出; (电影)制(片), 放映; 出版; 创作 ⑤ 使(线)延长; 使(面)扩展: ~ a side of a triangle 使三角形的一边 **❷** *vi.* 生产, 制造; 创作: an oil well that no longer ~s 不再出油的油井 / a *producing* lot [美俚]电影制片厂 **II** [ˈprɔdjuːs] *n.* ①产量, 出产 ②[总称]产品; 农产品(尤指水果、蔬菜等): the agricultural (或 farm) ~ 农产品 / the native ~ 土特产品 ③结果, 成果 ④(通常指雌性动物的)后代 ||~d [prəˈdjuːst] *a.* (叶子等)畸形地伸长的, 引长的

producer [prəˈdjuːsə] *n.* ①生产者, 制造者: an agricultural ~s' co-operative 农业生产合作社 ②(为演出提供资金的)演出者; 舞台监督; (电影)制片人, 监制人; (广播节目等)负责安排者 ③【机】发生器; 煤气发生炉 ④【讯】振荡器 ⑤(油)生产井 ||~-,city *n.* 生产城市 / ~ gas (发生)炉煤气 / ~ goods 生产物资(用于生产其他产品的物资, 如工具、原料等)

product [ˈprɔdəkt] *n.* ①产品, 产物; 产量; 出产: industrial and agricultural ~s 工农业产品 / a finished (semifinished) ~ 成(半成)品 / a substandard (spoiled) ~ 等外(废)品 / the packing of ~s 产品包装 ②结果, 成果: the ~ of one's labour 劳动成果 ③作品, 创作 ④【数】(乘)积: The ~ of 4 and 7 is 28. 四和七的乘积是二十八。

production [prəˈdʌkʃən] *n.* ①生产: the struggle for ~ 生产斗争 / the movement for increasing ~ and practising economy 增产节约运动 / the relations of ~ 生产关系 / a means (mode) of ~ 生产资料(方式) / go (或 be put) into ~ 开始生产, 投产 ②制作; (电影、戏剧等的)摄制, 演出; (演戏般)夸张的行动, 小题大做 ③产品; 总产量; množ(文艺)作品 ④拿出, 提供 ||*mass* ~ 大量生产 / *mass serial* ~ 成批生产 / a ~ *line* (或 *chain*) 流水(作业)线 / a ~ *quota* 生产指标 / a ~ *team* 生产队 / *war* ~ 军工生产 ||*make a* ~ *(out) of* [美口]对…作不必要的发挥; 令人讨厌地对…小题大作 ||~al *a.*

productive [prəˈdʌktiv] *a.* ①生产的, 生产性的: the ~ forces 生产力 / ~ capacity 生产能力 / ~ labour 生产劳动 ②丰饶的, 多产的: ~ soil 沃土 / ~ fishing waters 大量产鱼的水域 / a ~ writer 多产的作家 ③出产…的, 产生…的 *(of)*: a method ~ *of* results 富于成效的方法 ④不断

构成新词的: Un- is a ~ prefix. un- 是一个构词力活跃的前缀。⑤分泌粘液的, 生痰的: a ~ cough 痰咳 ‖~ly *ad.* / ~ness *n.*

productivity [ˌprɔdʌk'tiviti] *n.* ①生产率; 生产能力: labour ~ 劳动生产率 / increase (或 raise) ~ 提高生产率 ②丰饶, 多产

profane [prə'fein] **I** *a.* ①渎神的, 亵渎的, 不敬(神)的; 不圣洁的; 好咒骂的 ②世俗的, 非宗教的: ~ art 世俗的艺术(宗教艺术之对) ③异教的 ④未受秘传的(尤指关于教规); 无专门知识的, 外行的 **II** *vt.* 亵渎(圣物); 玷污 ‖~ly *ad.*

profanity [prə'fæniti] *n.* ①渎神; 使用亵渎的言语 ②[复]亵渎的言语

profess [prə'fes] **❶** *vt.* ①表示, 声称; 承认: ~ one's readiness (或 ~ oneself ready) to do sth. 表示愿意做某事 / I ~ that I was surprised at the news. 我承认这个消息使我感到惊奇。②自称; 冒充, 假装: ~ ignorance 自称(或假装)不知情 / He does not ~ to have exhausted the subject. 他并不自称对这题目已作了详尽无遗的研究。 / ~ to uphold justice 假装维护正义 ③宣布信奉(宗教等); 立(誓)信教; 正式接受…入教 ④以…为业: ~ medicine 行医 / ~ the violin 以奏小提琴为职业 ⑤当…学科的教授; (以教授身分)教, 讲授: ~ history (以教授身分)讲授历史 **❷** *vi.* ①表白; 承认 ②正式入教 ③当教授

professed [prə'fest] *a.* ①公开表示的, 公开声称的: a ~ opponent of 公开声称反对…的人 ②自称的; 假装的: ~ neutrality 假装的中立 ③专业的, 专门的 ④已立誓信教的, 已受戒的 ‖~ly [prə'fesidli] *ad.* 公开声称地; 自称地; 自认地; 假装地

profession [prə'feʃən] *n.* ①职业(尤指从事脑力劳动或受过专门训练的): the ~ of (a) doctor 医生的职业 / the teaching ~ 教书的职业 / be a carpenter by ~ 以木工为业 / exercise the ~ of journalism 从事新闻业 / make it a ~ to do sth. 以做某事为业 / without ~ 无职业 ②[the ~] [总称]同业, 同行; [英俚]演员们 ③明言, 声明; 表白; 诈称: ~s of loyalty 效忠的表白 / Accept my sincere ~s of regard. 请接受我真诚的致意。④ 立誓信教; 入教的誓言; 信奉的宗教 ‖*in practice if not in* ~ 虽不明讲而实际如此 / *the learned* ~s (西方所谓)学者的职业(指牧师、律师、医生等的职业) / *the oldest* ~ [谑]卖淫 ‖~less *a.* 没有职业的

professional [prə'feʃənl] **I** *a.* ①职业的, 专业的, 业务的: ~ knowledge (skill) 专业知识(技术) / ~ proficiency 业务能力 / ~ men 专门家(尤指医生、律师等) ②职业性的, 非业余的: a ~ tennis player 职业网球运动员 ③职业上的, 同行中的: ~ etiquette 同行中遵守的规矩 **II** *n.* ①以某种职业为生的人(如自由职业者、职业运动员等) ②专业人员; 内行 ‖~ism [prə'feʃənəlizəm] *n.* ①职业特性, 职业作风 ②职业化(尤指雇用或当职业选手等) / ~ly *ad.*

professor [prə'fesə] *n.* ①(大学)教授; [美](泛指)教师, 教员: *Professor* Strong 斯特朗教授(略作 Prof. Strong) / a ~ of chemistry (或 a chemistry ~) 化学教授 / an associate ~ 副教授 / an assistant ~ [美]助理教授(地位在副教授与讲师之间) / an emeritus ~ 或 a ~ emeritus (退休或光荣退职后的)名誉教授 / a ~'s chair 讲座; 教授的职位 / a ~ of military science and tactics 军事学及战术教官 ②公开表示信仰(宗教等)的人, 声称…的人 (of) ③[俗][谑](跳舞、拳术、魔术等的)专家, 教授; 带眼镜的书呆子 ④[美俚](酒吧间)奏乐的人; 弹钢琴者 [prə'fesərit] *n.* ①教授职务, 教授地位 ②教授任期 ‖~ial [ˌprɔfe'sɔːriəl] *a.* 教授的; 教授似的 / ~iate [ˌprɔfe'sɔːriit] *n.* ①(一个大学的)全体教授, 教授会 ②教授职位(或身分) / ~ship *n.* 教授职位(或身分)

proffer ['prɔfə] **I** *vt.* 提供, 贡献; 提出: ~ a gift 献礼物, 送礼 / ~ services 表示愿意效劳 / ~ to help sb. 表示要帮助某人 **II** *n.* 提供, 贡献; 提议, 建议

proficiency [prə'fiʃənsi] *n.* 熟练, 精通 (*in*): acquire ~ in a foreign language through practice 通过实践熟练地掌握一门外语

proficient [prə'fiʃənt] **I** *a.* 熟练的, 精通的 (*at, in*): be ~ in doing sth. 做某事很熟练 / be ~ at (或 *in*) an art 精通一种技艺 **II** *n.* 能手, 专家 ‖~ly *ad.*

profile ['proufail] **I** *n.* ①侧面(像): a portrait drawn *in* ~ 侧面画像 ②外形, 轮廓; 外观, 形象: the ~ of a distant hill 远山的轮廓 / lower the international ~ of a country 有损一个国家在国际上的形象; 使一个国家在国际上以不太令人注目的形象出现 ③传略, 人物简介 ④纵断面(图), 纵剖面(图) ⑤[美]个人能力(或特征)测验图 **II** *vt.* ①描(或显出)…的轮廓: a line of ~d against the night sky 夜空衬托出的隐约的群山 ②给…画侧面图; 给…作纵断面图 ③给…铣出轮廓: a *profiling* machine 靠模铣床, 模制机, 仿形铣床 ④写(某人)的传略 ‖**profilist** *n.* 侧面图制作人; 侧面像画家

profit ['prɔfit] **I** *n.* ①益处, 得益: gain ~ from 从…得到益处 / do sth. *to* one's ~ (或 *with* ~) 做某事而得益 ②[常用复]利润; (财产等的)收益: gross ~s 总利润, 毛利 / net ~s 纯利润, 净利 / a ~ and loss account (statement) 损益帐(表) / sell sth. *at* a ~ 出售某物而获利 ③利润率 ④红利 **II** ❶ *vt.* 有益于: We hope our criticisms will ~ you. 我们希望我们的批评会对你有益。❷ *vi.* ①有益; 有利: something that ~s 有利的事情 ②得益; 利用 (*by, from*): I hope to ~ *by* (或 *from*) your comments. 我希望从你的评语中得益。/ The ~ed *by* the interval to tell us about the excavation. 他利用间歇时间对我们谈了些发掘(文物)的情况。 ‖*in* ~ [英方][澳](乳牛)在产乳期的 ‖'~-ˌhungry *a.* 求利润的 / ~ **margin** 利润率 / ~ **system**

利润制(指资本主义的自由竞争) / ~ **taking** 获利了结,靠买空卖空的差额而获利润

profitable ['prɔfitəbl] *a.* ①有益的;有用的: ~ information 有用的情报(或消息) ②有利(可图)的 ||**profitability** [,prɔfitə'biliti] *n.* / ~**ness** *n.* / **profitably** *ad.*

profiteer [,prɔfi'tiə] I *n.* (趁物资缺乏等时)牟取暴利的人;投机商,奸商 II *vi.* 牟取暴利: a ~ing merchant 奸商 ||~ing [,prɔfi'tiəriŋ] *n.* 牟取暴利,投机活动

profligacy ['prɔfligəsi] *n.* ①放荡,荒淫 ②恣意的挥霍,极度的浪费

profligate ['prɔfligit] I *a.* ①放荡的,荒淫的②恣意挥霍的,极其浪费的 II *n.* ①放荡的人,浪子 ②恣意挥霍的人

profound [prə'faund] I *a.* ①意味深长的,意义深远的;深奥的: a ~ theory 一种深奥的理论②渊博的,造诣深的: ~ knowledge 渊博的学识③深厚的;深刻的;深切的;深深的;极度的: ~ lessons (understanding) 深刻的教训(理解) / a ~ bow 深深的鞠躬 / a ~ sleep 酣睡 / a ~ sigh 长叹 / a ~ gangrene 恶疸 / take a ~ interest 感到很大的兴趣;十分关切 II *n.* [诗] 深渊;深海;(灵魂)深处 ||~**ly** *ad.* 深深地,深切地: be ~ly moved 深受感动 / apologize ~ly 十分恳切地道歉 / ~**ness** *n.*

profundity [prə'fʌnditi] *n.* ①深度;深渊;深处②深奥;深刻;深厚: the ~ of feeling 感情的深厚 ③[常用复]深奥的事物;深刻的思想;意义深刻的话

profuse [prə'fju:s] *a.* ①毫不吝惜的,十分慷慨的;挥霍的,浪费的 (*in, of*): He is ~ *in* his hospitality. 他招待得十分周到。/ be ~ *of* one's money 挥金如土 ②极其丰富的,充沛的;过多的: a ~ variety of minerals 多种多样的矿藏 ||~**ly** *ad.* talk ~ly about peace 侈谈和平 / sweat ~ly 大汗淋漓 / ~**ness** *n.*

profusion [prə'fju:ʒən] *n.* ①慷慨;挥霍,浪费,奢侈 ②充沛,丰富,大量: a ~ of fruits on the market 市场上大量的各种水果 / flowers blooming in ~ 盛开的花朵

progeny ['prɔdʒini] *n.* ①子孙,后裔;(动植物的)后代 ②[喻] 结果,成果

prognosticate [prɔg'nɔstikeit] *vt.* 预言,预示;预兆 ||**prognostication** [prɔg,nɔsti'keiʃən] *n.* / **prognosticator** *n.* 预言者,预测者

program(me) ['prougræm] I *n.* ①节目单,说明书;节目,表演: the ~ of the concert 音乐会节目单 / What's *on* the ~? 演出些什么节目? / the first item *on* the ~ 第一个节目 / a theatre (broadcasting, television) ~ 一个演出(广播,电视)节目 / The ~ was a great success. 演出很成功。②纲领,纲要;(教学)计划,提纲: the maximum (minimum) ~ 最高(最低)纲领 / announce the ~ of political action 宣布施政纲领 / a teaching ~ 教学大纲 ③计划,方案;程

序表,计划表: the reservoir to be built under this year's ~ 按本年度计划行将兴建的水库 / draw up a ~ of prevention 制订预防计划 / What is the ~ for today? 今天有些什么活动? ④【自】程序: ~- controlled computer 程序控制计算机 ⑤ 布告 II (program(m)ed; program(m)ing) ❶ *vt.* ①为…安排节目;把…列入节目 ②为…制订计划(或规划) ③【自】为…编制程序; 使按程序工作 ④为(自学教科书)配习题及题解 ❷ *vi.* 安排节目;编制程序 ||**programmatic** [,prougrə'mætik] *a.* ①纲领性的,有纲领的: a *programmatic* document 纲领性文件 ②标题音乐的 ③计划性的,有计划的 / **programmer** *n.* ①排节目者;订计划者 ②【自】程序编制员;程序设计器 ||**program(m)ed instruction** 循序渐进的教学(法) / ~ **director** (广播电台或电视台的)负责安排节目的人 / **program-(m)ed learning** 利用有习题解答的教科书进行的自学 / ~ **music** 【音】标题音乐(根据一定主题构思并用标题提示中心内容的器乐曲)

progress I ['prougres; 美 'prɔgres] *n.* ①前进;进展: The building of the bridge is in ~. 桥梁正在建造中。/ the ~ of a battle 战斗的进展 / a ~ chart 进度表 ②进步,上进;发展: Study well and make ~ every day. 好好学习 天天向上 ③ (帝王等的)巡行,游历 II [prə'gres] *vi.* 前进;进行,进展;进步: The construction of the new railway is ~ing successfully. 那条新铁路的建设在顺利进行。/ ~ from place to place 从一处到又一处 / Medical science is ~ing rapidly in our country. 我国的医学进展很快。||**report** ~ 报告到当时为止的进展情况: move to *report* ~ (在英国下院)提议暂停辩论

progression [prə'greʃən] *n.* ①前进,行进: modes of ~ 行进的方式(指走,骑,爬等) ②(行为,动作,事件等的)接续,连续,一系列 ③进步;上升④【数】级数: arithmetical ~ 算术级数, 等差级数 / geometrical ~ 几何级数,等比级数 / harmonic ~ 调和级数 ⑤【音】(乐音或和弦)的相继进行;(各声部的)和谐进行 ||~**al** *a.* 向前进的;连续的;级数的

progressive [prə'gresiv] I *a.* ①进步的,先进的: ~ views 进步的观点 / ~ elements 进步人士②向前进的: ~ motion 向前的行动 ③渐次的,逐渐的;渐进的;累进的: ~ concentration 【军】逐次集中射击 / ~ taxation 累进税(制) / ~ education 循序渐进的教育 ④主张进步的;[常作P-]进步党的 ⑤【医】进行性的 ⑥【语】进行(时)的: the ~ tense 进行时 ⑦(几组桥牌中)搭档的人(或几张桌子间)进行轮换的 II *n.* ①进步分子,进步人士;革新主义者 ②改良主义者 ③[P-](美国)进步党党员 ||~**ly** *ad.* / ~**ness** *n.* ||**Progressive Conservative** (加拿大)进步保守党;进步保守党的 / ~ **jazz** (本世纪五十年代的)一种爵士音乐

prohibit [prə'hibit] *vt.* 禁止;阻止: Smoking

strictly ~ed. 严禁吸烟。/ ~ed articles (或 goods) 违禁品 / ~ sb. *from* going 不许某人前往 / be ~ed *from* riding bicycles on the sidewalk 被禁止在人行道上骑自行车 ‖~er, ~or n. 禁止者;阻止者

prohibition [,proui'bi∫ən, ,prouhi'bi∫ən] n. ① 禁止 ②禁令;禁律 ③【律】(上级法院禁止下级法院对无权审理的案件起诉的)诉讼止令 ④禁酒;[P-]【美史】禁酒时期: the ~ law 禁酒法

prohibitive [prə'hibitiv] a. ① 禁止(性)的 ②(对使用、滥用或购买等)起阻止作用的,抑制的: a ~ tax 寓禁税 / a ~ price 抑制购买的价格;高得使人不敢买的价格 ‖~ly ad. / ~ness n.

project I ['prɔdʒekt] n. ① 方案,计划,规划: a ~ to develop (或 for developing) local industries 发展地方工业的规划 ② 工程: an irrigation ~ 灌溉工程 ③科研项目;(辅助课堂教学的)课外自修项目 II [prə'dʒekt] ❶ vt. ①设计,规划: ~ a new canal 规划新的运河 ②投掷,发射;喷射: a guided missile 发射导弹 ③ 投射(光线、阴影等);映: ~ a film *on* a screen 把影片放映在银幕上 ④ 使凸出;突出: The wall is ~ed in the middle. 墙壁中部凸出。⑤表明…的特点,使…的特点呈现;生动地表演: The author tries to ~ how primitive men lived. 作者企图说明原始人是怎样生活的。/ ~ one's country overseas 向海外介绍自己的国家 ⑥作…的投影图 ⑦【心】投射;使(思想、感情等)形象化,使(观念等)具体化;设想 ❷ vi. 凸出,伸出: a balcony that ~s over the entrance 在入口处上面突出的阳台 ‖~ oneself ① 突出自己,表现自己;使自己显得象…(as) ② 设想自己处身于(into): ~ oneself *into* the future world 设想自己处身于未来的世界

projectile I ['prɔdʒiktail; 美 prə'dʒektil] n.【物】抛射体 ② 射弹(如子弹、炮弹等): a gas ~ 毒气弹 ③ 自动推进的武器(如火箭) II [prə'dʒektail; 美 prə'dʒektil] a. ①抛射的;射弹的: ~ motion【物】抛体运动;【军】射弹运动 ②供抛掷用的 ③【动】(触角等)能伸出的

projection [prə'dʒek∫ən] n. ①设计,规划 ②投掷;发射;喷射 ③凸出;凸出物 ④投射;投影;投影图;投影图法: conical ~ 圆锥形投影 ⑤放映: a film ~ team 电影放映队 / a ~ room (或 booth) 放映室 / a ~ lantern 幻灯,映画器 ⑥【心】投射;(观念等的)具体化: ~ of sensation 感觉的投射 ⑦(根据趋势所作的)预测,推算,估计 ⑧(古代炼金术中所说的)金属的嬗变 ‖~al a.

projector [prə'dʒektə] n. ①计划人,规划人;(投机性公司等的)发起人 ②(电影)放映机;幻灯,映画器 ③探照灯 ④发射装置;发射器: a rocket ~ 火箭发射装置 / a flame ~【军】喷火器 ⑤(制图)投影线

proletarian [,proule'tɛəriən] I n. 无产者

prolific [prə'lifik] a. ①多产的,多育的;富于创造力的: a ~ writer 多产作家 / as ~ as rabbits 像兔子般多育的 ②丰富的,富饶的;富于…的

(*of, in*): ~ *in* the production of fruit 盛产水果的 ‖~ally ad. / ~ness n.

prolix ['prouliks] a. 冗长的,罗唆的: a ~ article (speech) 冗长的文章(演说) ‖~ity [prou'liksiti] n.

prolog(ue) ['proulɔg] I n. ①序言;序诗;(戏剧的)开场白;(正戏开始前通常由主要角色朗诵的)诗白;序幕 ②[喻](一系列事件等的)开端,序幕(*to*): the ~ *to* the French Revolution 法国大革命的序幕 ③作开场白的演员 II vt. ①为…作序言(或序诗) ②作(戏剧等)的开场白 ‖prologize ['proulɔdʒaiz, 'proulɔgaiz], prologuize ['proulɔgaiz] vi. 作序言,作序诗;作开场白

prolong [prə'lɔŋ] vt. ① 延长;拉长;拖延: The treaty has been ~ed for another ten years. 条约延长十年。/ the runway of an airfield 加长机场跑道 / the experience of ~ed struggle 长期斗争的经验 ② 拖长(音节等)的发音 ‖~able a. 可延长的;可拉长的;可拖延的;可拖长的

promenade [,promi'na:d, ,promi'neid] I n. ①(为散心或炫耀等所作的)散步;骑马;开车(兜风) ②散步场所(如大街、海滨大道、剧场走廊等) ③[美](大学生等的)舞会;(舞会开始时全体参加者的)列队行进 II ❶ vi. ①散步;骑马;开车(兜风) ②(舞会中)列队行进 ❷ vt. 在(某处)散步;炫耀地带着(某人)散步(或兜风): ~ one's child along the seashore 带着孩子在海滨散步 III ['promina:d] a. 散步(用)的;走动的 ‖~ concert [英]场内无座位、听众站立或走动着听的音乐会 / ~ deck (客轮的)上层甲板,散步甲板

prominence ['prominəns], **prominency** ['prominənsi] n. ① 突起;凸出;凸出物: a ~ in the middle of a plain 平原中间的一块高地 ②突出;显著;杰出,卓越;声望: give ~ to the key points 突出重点 ③【天】日珥

prominent ['prominənt] a. ① 突起的;凸出的: a ~ chin 凸出的下颏 ② 突出的;显著的;杰出的,卓越的;重要的;著名的: occupy a ~ position 占有显要的位置 / a ~ figure 知名人物 ‖~ly ad. This article is ~ly featured. 这篇文章是以显著地位刊登的。

promiscuous [prə'miskjuəs] a. ① 混杂的;杂乱的,乱七八糟的: a ~ heap of clothes 乱堆在一起的衣服 ② 不加区别的;不分男女的;男女乱交的: ~ hospitality 不加区别的款待 / a ~ massacre 不分男女老少的大屠杀 ③ [口]偶然的,随意的: take a ~ stroll 漫步 ‖~ly ad.

promise ['promis] I n. ① 允诺,诺言;字据: make a ~ of help 答应帮助 / give a ~ to write to sb. 答应给某人写信 / keep (carry out) a ~ 遵守(履行)诺言 / break a ~ 不守诺言 ②允诺的东西,约定的事项: I claim your ~. 我要求得到你所允诺的东西。③(有)指望,(有)出息,(有)前途: The crops are full of ~. 庄稼大有希望。/ writers and artists of ~ 有出息的文学家和艺术家们 / hold some ~ of success 有希望获得成功 II ❶ vt. ① 允诺,答应: He ~d (me) a quick answer. 他答应(我)从速答复。 / I ~*d* (him) to attend to the matter promptly. 我答应(他)立即处理这件事。 ② 给人以…的指望,有…的可能: This year ~*s* to be another good one for harvests. 今年看来又是个丰收年。 / The dark clouds ~ rain. 乌云密布,看来会下雨。③[口]向…保证,向…断言: It is not so simple, I ~ you. 我敢向你保证,事情并不那么简单。 ④ 把(某人)许配(给) (to) ❷ *vi.* ① 允诺;作出保证 ②有指望,有前途: a research item that ~*s* well 大有前途的科研项目 ‖*Promise is debt.* [谚]许愿要还。(或:欠债要清。) / ~ *oneself* 指望,指望获得: I ~ *myself* a fruitful discussion with you. 我指望跟你进行一次有成效的讨论。/ *the Land of Promise* 见 land ‖~*r n.* 作出诺言的人

promising ['prɔmisiŋ] *a.* 有指望的,有希望的,有出息的,有前途的: ~ crops 长势很好的庄稼 / a ~ iron deposit 有开采价值的铁矿床 / The weather is ~. 天气可望好转。‖~*ly ad.*

promissory ['prɔmisəri] *a.* 表示允诺的;约定的: a ~ note 【商】本票,期票 / a ~ oath 允诺(或保证)的誓言

promontory ['prɔməntəri] *n.* ① 岬(角);海角 ②【解】岬,隆突: ~ of the tympanum 鼓岬

promote [prə'mout] *vt.* ①促进;发扬;助长,引起: ~ growth (prosperity, understanding) 促进生长(繁荣,谅解) / ~ physical culture 发展体育运动 / ~ what is right 提倡(或发扬)正确的东西 / ~ disorder (jealousy) 引起混乱(猜忌) ②提升;使(学生)升级: be ~*d* (to be 或 to the rank of) first mate 被提升为大副 ③发起,创立(企业等) ④[美]宣传,推销(商品等) ⑤设法通过(法律、议案等) ⑥[美俚](用不正当的手段)获得 ⑦(国际象棋中)使(卒)升格(为女王等) ‖~*r n.* ①促进者;助长者 ②(企业等)的发起人,创办人;推销商 ③[美](营业性体育比赛的)包办人,出资人 ④【化】促进剂;助催化剂

promotion [prə'mouʃən] *n.* ①促进,增进;发扬;助长: ~ of friendship 友谊的增进 ②提升: ~ by merit 以功绩为标准的提升 ③(企业等)的发起,创立 ④[美](商品等的)宣传,推销: a ~ worker 推销员 ‖~*al a.* 提升的;发起的;推销的

prompt [prɔmpt] **Ⅰ** *a.* ①立刻行动的,敏捷的,迅速的;干脆的,果断的: a ~ assistant 敏捷的助手 / be ~ in responding (to respond) 立刻响应 / a ~ decision (reply) 迅速的决定(答复) / ~ assistance (medical treatment) 及时的帮助(医疗) ②【商】当场交付的: for ~ cash 须当场付款(的) / ~ goods 当场交货的商品;现货 ③(演剧中的)提白员的,提词员的 **Ⅱ** *ad.* 准时地;正(指时间): at seven o'clock ~ 在七时正 **Ⅲ** *vt.* ①敦促,使促;激励,鼓舞;怂恿: be ~*ed* by sb.'s example 受某人榜样的带动 ②引起,激起: Our discussion ~*ed* some questions worthy of consideration. 我们的讨论引起了一些值得考虑

的问题。③为(演员)提白,给…提词 **Ⅳ** *n.* ①催促;提醒;催款单 ②付款期限;付款期限协定: What is the ~? 付款期限是哪一天? ③(对演员的)提白,提词 ‖~*er n.* ①敦促者;鼓舞者,激励者 ②提白员,提词员: opposite ~*er* 在提词员的对面(英国指舞台上演员的左方;美国指舞台上演员的右方) / ~*ly ad.* / ~*ness n.* ‖~*book*, ~ *copy n.* 供提白员用的剧本 / ~ *box* 提白员藏身处 / ~ *day* 【商】交割日 / ~ *note* 【商】期货金额及交割日期通知单 / ~ *side* [英]舞台上演员的左方;[美]舞台上演员的右方(略作 P. S.)

promulgate ['prɔmʌlgeit] *vt.* ① 颁布,公布: a constitution 颁布宪法 / a decree 公布法令 ② 散播,传播(信仰、知识等) ‖**promulgation** [ˌprɔmʌl'geiʃən] *n.* / **promulgator** *n.* 颁布者,公布者;传播者

prone [proun] *a.* ① 俯伏的,面向下的: fall ~ on the ground 面朝下地跌倒在地上 / ~ fire 【军】卧射 ② 有…倾向的,易于…的 (to): be ~ to anger 动辄发怒 / be ~ to accidents (或 be accident ~) 易出事故 / be ~ to compromise 倾向妥协,易于妥协 / be ~ to jump to hasty conclusions 易于作出轻率的结论 ③倾斜的;陡的: a ~ stretch of ground 一片向下倾斜的地 / ~ bombing 俯冲轰炸 ④卑躬屈节的 ‖~*ly ad.* / ~*ness n.* ‖~ **pressure method** 俯仰人工呼吸法

prong [prɔŋ] **Ⅰ** *n.* ①叉子;干草耙 ②尖头,(叉、耙的)尖;齿尖;鹿角尖 **Ⅱ** *vt.* (用叉等)刺,戳;耙开(泥土等)

pronoun ['prounaun] *n.* 【语】代(名)词: a personal ~ 人称代词 / a possessive ~ 物主代词 / a relative ~ 关系代词

pronounce [prə'nauns] ❶ *vt.* ①宣布;宣(判): ~ a sentence of three years *on* sb. 宣判某人服徒刑三年 ②宣称,宣告;断言;表示: The patient has been ~*d* out of danger. 病人已宣告脱险。/ ~ oneself against (in favour of) a decision 表示反对(赞成)一个决议 ③发…的音;注…的音: How do you ~ c-l-e-r-k? 你怎么念 c-l-e-r-k 这词? / We do not ~ the "b" in "doubt". "doubt" 一词中的"b"不发音。/ The two dictionaries ~ the word differently. 两本词典把这个词的音注得不一样。❷ *vi.* ① 发表意见;作出判断;表态: ~ *on* a proposal (subject) 对一个建议(论题)发表意见 / ~ for (against) 对…表示赞成(反对) ② 发音: ~ distinctly 发音清楚 ‖~*able a.* 可发音的,读得出的

pronounced [prə'naunst] *a.* ① 发出音的;讲出来的 ② 显著的,明显的;明确的;决然的: a ~ tendency 显著的倾向 / the ~ symptoms of influenza 明显的流行性感冒症状 / ~ opinions 明确的意见 ‖~*ly* [prə'naunstli, prə'naunsidli] *ad.*

pronunciation [prəˌnʌnsi'eiʃən] *n.* 发音;发音法: He has a good ~. 他的发音很好。/ This word has two ~s. 这个词有两种读法。 / Received *Pronunciation* (英国的)标准发音 ‖~al *a.*

proof [pru:f] **I** *n.* ①证据;物证;【律】(口头或书面)证词: require ~(s) of a statement 要求对陈述提供证据 / be full ~ *that* ... 是…的充分证据,充分证明… ②证明;论证: Is that capable of ~? 那个能被证明吗? / give eloquent ~ of ... 雄辩地证明… / produce evidence *in* ~ of one's innocence 拿出证明自己是无辜的证据 ③检验,考验: put (或 bring) sth. to the ~ 检验某物 / The new product has stood a severe ~. 新产品经受了严格的考验。 ④(火器或爆炸物的)试验(或试验场所) ⑤试管 ⑥【印】校样;(版画或照相的)样张: pass the ~*s* for press 同意把校样付印 / read ~*s* 读校样;校对 ⑦(酒精、酒类的)强度标准: be 20% below ~ 比标准酒精度低百分之二十 ⑧【数】证,证明,证法 ⑨[古](盔甲等的)不穿透性,坚固性 **II** *a.* ①不能穿透的;能抵挡的(*against*): The room is ~ *against* sound. 这房间是隔音的。②验证用的,检验用的:a ~ sample 试样 / a ~ test 验收试验,复核试验 ③规定的;(酒等)合乎标准的 **III** *vt.* ①检验,试验;试印;把…印成校样 ②校对 ③使(某物)不被穿透,使有耐力;使(布等)不透水,使防水 ④发(面) ‖*The ~ of the pudding is in the eating.* [谚]要检验布丁,就要吃一吃。(或:空谈不如实验。) ‖~**er** *n.* ①印校样的工人 ②发面机 ‖~**less** *a.* 无证据的 ‖'~**mark** *n.* (枪炮等的)验讫印记 / ~ **plane** 验电板 / '~**read** *vt.* 校对 / '~,**reader** *n.* 校对员 / '~**room** *n.* 校对室 / ~ **sheet** 校样 / ~ **spirit** ①规定酒精,定强酒精 ②标准强度的酒(含酒精量约为50%) / '~**test** *vt.* 试验,检验(枪等)

prop[1] [prɔp] **I** *n.* ①支柱;撑材;支持物 ②(机关、企业等的)支持者,拥护者;后盾;靠山 **II** (propped; propping) ❶ *vt.* 支撑;支持;维持: sit with one's chin *propped* in one's hands 双手托住下巴坐着 / ~ (*up*) a roof 撑住屋顶 / ~ a ladder *against* a wall 把梯子靠着墙 ❷ *vi.* (马等)前腿挺直地停住

prop[2] [prɔp] *n.* 【戏】道具 ‖'~**man** *n.* 道具管理人

prop[3] [prɔp] *n.* [口]【空】螺旋桨 ‖~'**jet** *n.* 涡轮螺旋桨喷气发动机

propaganda [,prɔpə'gændə] *n.* ①宣传机构,宣传组织 ②宣传;宣传方法;宣传运动: carry on active ~ 大力宣传 / a ~ organ (department) 宣传机器(部门) / dismiss ... as mere ~ 把…看作仅仅是宣传伎俩而不予理睬 ③[P-](罗马天主教的)传道总会(由红衣主教组成,负责海外传教)

propagate ['prɔpəgeit] ❶ *vt.* ①繁殖,增殖: ~ a new breed of cattle 繁殖新品种的牛 ②遗传(特征等) ③传播,宣传;普及 ④使(疾病等)蔓延 ⑤[物]传播 ❷ *vi.* ①(动物、植物)繁殖,增殖: Rabbits ~ rapidly. 兔子能迅速繁殖。 ②蔓延 ‖**propagator** *n.* 繁殖者;传播者;宣传物

propagation [,prɔpə'geiʃən] *n.* ①繁殖,增殖 ②传播,宣传;普及 ③蔓延 ④【物】传播: wave ~ 波的传播 / rectilinear ~ 直线传播 ‖~**al** *a.*

propel [prə'pel] (propelled; propelling) *vt.* 推进,推动: a ship *propelled* by steam 用蒸汽推动的船 / ~ history forward 推动历史前进 / a *propelling* pencil 活动铅笔 / a self-*propelled* gun 自行火炮

propensity [prə'pensiti] *n.* (性格上的)倾向;嗜好,癖好: a ~ *to* exaggerate (或 *for* exaggerating 或 *to* exaggeration) 动辄爱夸大的倾向

proper ['prɔpə] **I** *a.* ①适合的,适当的,恰当的: a ~ arrangement 适当的安排 / do sth. the ~ way 以恰当的方式做某事 / He said something ~ for the occasion. 他说了一些适合时宜的话。 / Do as you think ~. 你认为怎么合适就怎么办吧。 ②合乎体统的;正当的;规矩的,正经的;高尚的: ~ behaviour 正当的行为 / ~ children 循规蹈矩的孩子们 ③特有的;专门的(*to*): the weather ~ *to* the North 北方特有的天气 / the literature ~ *to* this subject 专门有关这个题目的参考书刊 / a ~ noun (adjective) 【语】专有名词(形容词) / a ~ name 专(有)名(称) ④固有的,本来的;正确的: in tLe ~ sense of the word 按照这个词的本来意义 ⑤自己的: see with one's (own) ~ eyes 亲眼看到 ⑥[用在名词后面]严格意义上的,本身的: the dictionary ~/architecture ~ 狭义建筑学(不包括铺管道、雕刻装饰等) ⑦(纹章)本色的: peacock ~ 天然色彩的孔雀(纹章) ⑧[主英][口]完完全全的,彻底的;大大的: The fellow is a ~ terror! 这家伙简直讨厌透了! / a ~ mess 一团糟 ⑨出色的,极好的;[主方]漂亮的,好看的 ‖~ **energy** 【物】原能 / ~ **fraction** 【数】真分数 / ~ *integral* 【数】正常积分,常义积分 / ~ *mass* 【物】静质量 / ~ *motion* 【物】固有运动;【天】自行 **II** *ad.* [主方]完完全全地,彻底地 **III** *n.* 【宗】特定节日专用的仪式(或祷词等)

properly ['prɔpəli] *ad.* ①适当地;正当地 ②严格地(说来): That is not, ~ speaking, a dictionary, but a grammar. 严格地说来那不是一本词典,而是一本语法书。 ③[主英]完完全全地,彻底地;大大地: be ~ puzzled 感到极其困惑

property ['prɔpəti] *n.* ①财产,资产,(房)地产: protect state ~ 保护国家财产 / personal ~ 动产 / real ~ 不动产 / a piece of ~ 一项财产 / a ~ man 一宗房地产 / a man of ~ 有产者 / The news (joke) is common ~. 这个消息(笑话)大家都知道。 ②财产权,所有权: ~ in land 土地所有权 ③性质,性能;特性,特征: the *properties* of nature 自然的性质 / the healing *properties* of medicinal herbs 草药的医疗效能 ④[逻]非本质特性 ⑤(戏剧或电影的)道具 ‖~ **line** 【建】地界线,建筑红线 / ~ **man**, ~ **master** ①道具管理员 ②煤矿装备管理员 / ~ **room** 道具室

prophecy ['prɒfisi] *n.* 预言；预言能力；【宗】预言书

prophesy ['prɒfisai] ❶ *vt.* 预言，预示: ~ a storm 预言将有风暴 ❷ *vi.* 预言，预示: ~ of change 预示将有改变

prophet ['prɒfit] *n.* ① 预言者，预言家；先知 ②(主义等的)宣扬者；提倡者 ③[俚]赛马输赢的预言者 ‖the Prophet (伊斯兰教祖)穆罕默德；(摩门教创始人)史密斯 / the Prophets (基督教《圣经》中的)各种预言书(或其作者) ‖~ess *n.* 女预言家

prophetic(al) [prə'fetik(əl)] *a.* 预言的；预示的 (of)；预言家的: a sign ~ of 预示…的征象 ‖prophetically *ad.*

prophylactic [ˌprɒfi'læktik] I *a.* 【医】预防(性)的 II *n.* ①预防剂；预防器；预防法 ②避孕用品(或药物)

propinquity [prə'piŋkwiti] *n.* ①(时间、地点上的)接近，邻近 ②[血统上的]近亲关系 ③(性质、观念等的)类似，近似

propitiate [prə'piʃieit] *vt.* ① 劝解；抚慰；使息怒 ② 谋求…的好感 ‖propitiation [prəˌpiʃi'eiʃən] *n.* ① 劝解；抚慰 ② 赎罪；(为赎罪而献给神的)牺牲 / propitiator *n.* 劝解者；抚慰者 / propitiatory *a.* 劝解的；抚慰的；谋求好感的 *n.* 【宗】上帝的御座

propitious [prə'piʃəs] *a.* ①(神等)慈悲的 ②吉祥的，吉利的: a ~ omen 吉兆 ③ 顺利的；有利的，适合的(for, to): ~ winds 顺风 / conditions ~ to the development of sth. 有利于某事物发展的条件 ‖~ly *ad.* / ~ness *n.*

proportion [prə'pɔːʃən] I *n.* ①比，比率；比例: the ~ of three to one 三与一之比 / the ~ of births to the population 人口出生率 / direct (inverse) ~ 正(反)比例 ②均衡，相称，调和: in perfect ~ 非常匀称 ③部分，份儿: a large ~ of the earth surface 地球表面的大部分 ④[复]面积；容积；大小: a building of grand ~s 宏大的建筑物 II *vt.* ①使成比例；使相称；使均衡: ~ the expenses to the receipts 量入为出 / one's pace to the march 调整步子使与行军的步伐一致 ②分摊，摊派 ‖in ~ as 按…的比例；依…的程度而变 / in ~ to 与…成比例；与…相称 / out of ~ 不成比例；不相称 ‖~ed *a.* 相称的，成比例的: well ~ed 很匀称的

proportional [prə'pɔːʃənl] I *a.* ①比例的，有比例性的: be directly ~ to 与…成正比例 / ~ representation 比例代表制 ②相称的，均衡的，调和的 II *n.* 【数】比例项: mean ~ 比例中项 ‖~ly *ad.*

proportionate [prə'pɔːʃənit] I *a.* 成比例的；相称的；均衡的 II *vt.* 使成比例；使相称，使均衡

proposal [prə'pəuzəl] *n.* ①(建议等的)提议，建议；计划: offer ~s for peace 提出和平建议 / a ~ concerning … 关于…的建议 ②求婚: have a ~ 被求婚

propose [prə'pəuz] ❶ *vt.* ①提议，建议，提出: ~ a motion 提出一项动议 / ~ an early start 建议及早开始(或出发) / We ~ that the house (should) be repaired. 我们建议对房屋进行修理。/ ~ a toast to 提议为…干杯 ②提(名)，推荐: be ~d as a candidate for 被推荐为…的候选人 ③打算，计划: ~ to act (或 ~ acting) immediately 打算立即行动 ④求(婚): ~ marriage to 向…求婚 ❷ *vi.* ①作出计划，打算 ②求婚(to) ‖Man ~s, God disposes. 见 man ‖~r *n.* 提议者，提出者

proposition [ˌprɒpə'ziʃən] I *n.* ① 提议，建议；计划 ②陈述，主张 ③【逻】【数】命题 ④【语】主题: an absolute (或 a predicative) ~ 定言命题，直言判断 / a major (minor) ~ 大 (小) 前提 / Euclid, Book I, ~ 5 《欧几里得几何学》第一卷，命题五 ④[口]事业，企业: a paying (losing) ~ 赚钱(蚀本)生意 ⑤[口]事情；目的；问题；家伙: an awkward ~ 一件尴尬事情 / a queer ~ 怪人 / a tough ~ 一个难对付的家伙 ⑥[美口]下流的建议，猥亵的要求 II *vt.* [美口]向…提出要求(尤指猥亵下流的要求) ‖~al *a.*

propound [prə'paund] *vt.* ① 提出(问题、计划等)供考虑(或讨论)，建议，提议: ~ a question 提出一个问题供考虑 ②【律】(为求确定合法性向有关方面)提出(遗嘱等) ‖~er *n.* 提议者，建议者

proprietary [prə'praiətəri] I *a.* ① 所有(人)的，业主的: ~ rights 所有权 ② 有财产的: the ~ classes 有产阶级 ③ 专有的，专卖的: ~ articles 专利品，专卖品 / a ~ medicine 特许专卖药 / a ~ name 专利商标名 II *n.* ① [指个人或总称]所有人，业主: the landed ~ [总称]土地拥有者 ② 所有(权) ③【美史】(独立前，英王特许独占某块殖民地的)领主 ④ 专卖药 ‖colony 【美史】(独立前，英王特许领主)独占的殖民地 ‖ ~ company ① (占有其他公司股票的全部或几乎全部的)控股公司 ②[英]土地兴业公司 ③[英]独占公司(股票由经营人支配，不向外界发售)

proprietor [prə'praiətə] *n.* ① 所有人，业主: a landed ~ 土地拥有者 / the ~ of a hotel 旅馆老板 ②【美史】(独立前，英王特许独占某块殖民地的)领主 ‖~ial [prəˌpraiə'tɔːriəl] *a.* 所有(权)的: ~ial rights 所有权 / ~ship *n.* 所有(权)

proprietress [prə'praiətris] *n.* 女所有人，女业主

propriety [prə'praiəti] *n.* ① 适当，妥当；正当；得体，合宜: the ~ of a term 一个用语的贴切性 / ~ of language 言语得体 / a breach of ~ 失礼行为 ③[复]礼仪，礼节: observe the proprieties 遵守礼节 / diplomatic proprieties 外交礼节

propulsion [prə'pʌlʃən] *n.* 推进；推进力；推进器: jet ~ 喷气推进 / rocket ~ 火箭推进

prorogue [prə'rəug] ❶ *vt.* ①使闭会；使休会(指议会等) ②[罕]使延期 ❷ *vi.* 闭会；休会

prosaic [prou'zeiik] *a.* ①散文的；散文体的 ②无诗意的；平凡的；无聊的: ~ views 平凡的见解 / a ~ speech (speaker) 乏味的演说(演说者) ③如

实的: a ~ statement of weather conditions 对天气情况的如实的叙述

proscribe [prouˈkraib] *vt.* ①(古罗马)公布(死囚等)的姓名 ②剥夺…的公权,使失去法律保护 ③把…充军,把…放逐 ④排斥;禁止

prose [prouz] **I** *n.* ①散文;平铺直叙的文体 ②平凡;单调 ③无聊 ④乏味的议论 ⑤【天主教】续唱 **II** ❶ *vi.* ①写散文 ②平铺直叙地写;乏味地讲 (*about*) ❷ *vt.* 把(诗等)改写成散文 **III** *a.* ①散文的;用散文写的: ~ style 散文体 / a ~ poem 散文诗 ②平凡的;乏味的;无想象力的 ③如实的 ‖~r *n.* ①散文家 ②乏味的人(指在讲话、写作方面)

prosecute [ˈprɔsikjuːt] ❶ *vt.* ①彻底进行;执行: ~ an investigation 彻底进行调查 ②从事,经营: ~ a trade 从事一门行业 ③ 对…起诉,告发;检举;依法进行: ~ a claim 依法提出要求权 / sb. for theft 告发某人犯盗窃罪 / Trespassers will be ~d. 闲人莫入,违者法办。(用于告示) ❷ *vi.* ①起诉,告发 ②作检察官 ‖**prosecuting attorney** [美]检察官

prosecution [ˌprɔsiˈkjuːʃən] *n.* ①彻底进行;实行,执行: ~ of one's duties 履行职责 ②从事,经营 ③起诉,告发;检举;被告发: a criminal ~ 刑事诉讼 / start a ~ against sb. 检举某人 ④[总称]原告及其律师 ⑤检察当局: the Director of Public *Prosecutions* [英]检察官

prosecutor [ˈprɔsikjuːtə] *n.* 原告,起诉人;检举人: a public ~ 检察官;检察员

proselyte [ˈprɔsilait] **I** *n.* ①改变宗教信仰(或政治信仰、意见等)的人;改宗者;改入他党者 ②[古](从异教)皈依犹太教者 **II** ❶ *vt.* ①使改变宗教信仰(或政治信仰、意见等) ②[美]劝诱,搜罗(运动员等) ❷ *vi.* ①改变宗教信仰(或政治信仰、意见等) ②[美]劝诱运动员;搜罗人员

prosody [ˈprɔsədi] *n.* ①诗体学,韵律学,作诗法 ②(某诗人特用的)韵律 ‖**prosodist** *n.* 诗体学者,韵律学者

prospect I [ˈprɔspekt] *n.* ①展望;视野;景色;景象;境界: The hill commands a fine ~. 从这座山上可以眺望美景。/ This experience opened a new ~ to his mind. 这一经验为他的思想开拓了新的境界。/ a house with a southern ~ 朝南的房屋 ②指望;预期;盼望的事物: A rich harvest is *in* ~. 丰收在望。③[常用复]前景;前程,前途: young people with brilliant ~s 前程无量的青年 / open up broad ~s for 为…开辟广阔的前景 ④[美]可能成为主顾(或委托人)的人;有希望的候选人 ⑤有希望开出矿产的地区;正在勘探的矿地;矿石样品中取得的矿物量 **II** [ˈprɔspekt] ❶ *vt.* 勘探(矿藏);勘察(地区): ~ a mine 勘探矿藏 ❷ *vi.* ①找矿,勘探 (*for*): ~ *for* oil 勘探石油矿 ②(指矿产量)有希望,有前途: The mine ~s ill (well). 这个矿没有(大有)开采前途。‖**~or** [ˈprɔspektə] *n.* (矿藏等的)勘探者

prospective [prəsˈpektiv] *a.* 预期的,盼望的;未来的: ~ achievements 预期中的成就 / a ~ teacher 可能成为教师的人 / a ~ statute 将会生效的法令 / sb.'s ~ neighbour 某人未来的邻居 ‖**~ly** *ad.* / **~ness** *n.* ‖**~ glass** 小型轻便望远镜

prospectus [prəsˈpektəs] *n.* ①(创办学校、企业等的)计划书,发起书;说明书 ②(即将出版的书等的)内容介绍,简介

prosper [ˈprɔspə] ❶ *vi.* 繁荣,昌盛;成功: Our great motherland is ~ing with each passing day. 我们伟大的祖国蒸蒸日上。❷ *vt.* 使繁荣,使昌盛;使成功

prosperity [prɔsˈperiti] *n.* 繁荣,昌盛;幸运;成功: the ~ of a cause (country) 事业(国家)的兴旺

prosperous [ˈprɔspərəs] *a.* ①繁荣的,昌盛的;成功的;富裕的: make a country ~ 使国家昌盛 / a ~ voyage 一次成功的航行 / bring a plan to a ~ issue 使计划获得成功 ②有利的;顺利的,幸运的: wait for a more ~ moment 等待更有利的时刻 / a ~ wind 顺风 ‖**~ly** *ad.*

prostitute [ˈprɔstitjuːt] **I** *n.* ①妓女,娼妓 ②[喻]出卖节操者(如贪钱而粗制滥造的文人等) **II** *vt.* ①使沦为娼妓: ~ oneself 卖淫 ②[喻]出卖(名誉等);滥用(才能等): ~ one's honour (为图利而)出卖荣誉 **III** *a.* ①卖淫的 ②堕落的‖**prostitution** [ˌprɔstiˈtjuːʃən] *n.* 卖淫;滥用,糟蹋

prostrate I [ˈprɔstreit] *a.* ①俯卧的;平卧的;倒在地上的 ②(表示尊敬或顺从等)匍伏的,拜倒的: lie ~ at the feet of sb. 拜倒在某人脚下 ③被征服的;降伏的;屈服的 ④衰竭的,疲惫的;沮丧的 [prɔsˈtreit] *vt.* ①使倒伏,使平卧;弄倒: The typhoon ~d hundreds of trees. 台风吹倒了数百棵树。②[~ oneself]使(自己)俯卧;使拜倒,使匍伏;使屈从: ~ *oneself* at a shrine 拜倒在神像前 / ~ *oneself before* sb. 拜倒在某人面前 ③使屈服;使衰竭,使疲惫: be ~d *by* the heat 热得昏倒 / be ~d *with* fear 胆颤心惊‖**prostration** [prɔsˈtreiʃən] *n.* ①俯卧;平卧 ②拜倒;屈服 ③衰竭,疲惫;【医】虚脱

prosy [ˈprouzi] *a.* ①散文(体)的 ②单调的;平淡乏味的;嚕苏的: a ~ talk 冗长乏味的谈话

protagonist [prouˈtægənist] *n.* ①(戏剧、小说等)主角,主人公 ②领导者;提倡者;拥护者;积极的参加者 ③通过收缩引起某种运动的肌肉

protect [prəˈtekt] *vt.* ①保护;警戒: ~ plants *from* the cold 保护植物使不受冻 / be ~ed *against* surprise attacks 对于突然袭击作好戒备 / a ~ed state 保护国 ②【经】对进口物资征收保护性关税以保护(国内工业): ~ed trade 保护贸易 ③备款以应(期票等)的支付 ④在…上装防护(或保险)装置以避免伤害: ~ed rifles 保险枪

protection [prəˈtekʃən] *n.* ①保护;警戒: under the ~ of 在…的保护下 / on move 【军】行军警戒 ②保护者;防护物: various ~s *against* fire 各种防火装置 / a ~ *from* the wind 防风设施 ③护照;通行证 ④保护贸易制度 ⑤[美口](罪犯

等通过贿赂而取得的)免于起诉;(歹徒所勒索的)
保护费

protective [prə'tektiv] *a.* ①保护的;防护的: ~
colouration (动物的)保护色 / ~ custody 保护
性拘留 / ~ foods (含必要的维生素的)各种保健
食物 / ~ mimicry【动】保护性拟态 / clothing
【军】防毒衣 / a ~ screen【军】掩护幕 ②保护贸
易的: a ~ tariff (对进口物资征收的)保护(性)
关税 / the ~ system 保护关税制 ‖~ly *ad.* /
~ness *n.*

protector [prə'tektə] *n.* ①保护者;防御者 ②保护
装置,保护器: a point ~ 铅笔套 ③摄政者; [the
P-]【英史】护国公 (=Lord Protector, 指十七
世纪英国共和国时代的摄政者克伦威尔) ‖~al
[prə'tektərəl] *a.* 保护者的(或摄政的)

protectorate [prə'tektərit] *n.* ① (尤指 1653—
1659 英国克伦威尔父子摄政时期的) 摄政政体;
摄政者的职位(或任期) ② (较强国对较弱国的)
保护关系;保护国,保护领地 ③ 对保护国行使的
权力

protégé ['prouteʒei] *n.* 被保护人,门徒

protein ['prouti:n]【生化】I *n.* 朊,蛋白质 II *a.*
(含)蛋白质的 ‖~aceous [,proutii'neiʃəs], ~ic
[prou'ti:inik], ~ous ['prouti:inəs] *a.* 朊的,蛋白
质的

protest I [prə'test] ❶ *vt.* ①明言,断言;主张;(坚
决)表示: ~ one's friendship 保证友谊 / ~ one's
innocence 申明自己无罪 ② 抗议;反对: ~ a
decision 反对一项决定 ③【商】拒付 (票据等)
❷ *vi.* ①明言,断言;主张 ②抗议;反对 (against)
II ['proutest] *n.* ①明言;主张 ②抗议;异议;反
对;抗议书: make (或 lodge, enter) a ~ against…
对…提出抗议 / a ~ strike (集会) 表示抗议的
罢工(集会) ③【律】(公证人对汇票等的)拒付证
书;船长证明书(证明船的损坏由灾难造成);(缴
付人对苛捐等的)抗议书 ‖under ~ 抗议着;持
异议地;极不乐意地: do sth. under ~ 虽做某事
但有异议;不得已地干某事 ‖~ation [,proutes-
'teiʃən] *n.* ①明言,断言;主张 ②抗议;异议;反
对 / ~or, ~er [prə'testə] *n.* ①[古]声明者 ②
抗议者;持异议者 ③(汇票等的)拒付者

Protestant ['protistənt] I *n.* ①新教徒,耶稣教徒
②[复]抗罗宗,抗议宗(指一五二九年德国国会中
对天主教诸侯提出抗议的新教诸侯) ③ [p-] 抗
议者,异议者 II *a.* ① 新教(教徒)的,耶稣教(徒)
的 ② [p-] 抗议的,异议的 ‖~ism *n.* ① 新教,
耶稣教;新教徒的制度(或信仰、教义等) ②[总称]
新教教会(或新教教徒)

protocol ['proutekol] I *n.* ①(条约等的)草案,草
约;(外交)议定书;会谈记录(或备忘录) ②礼仪;
外交礼节: according to ~ 根据礼仪 / the
Protocol (法国等的)外交部礼宾司 II (proto-
col(l)ed; protocol(l)ing) ❶ *vi.* 拟定(或颁布)议
定书 ❷ *vt.* 把…写入议定书

proton ['prouten] *n.* 【物】质子,气核: a ~
synchrotron 质子同步加速器,同步稳相加速器

prototype ['proutetaip] *n.* ①原型: a production
~ 生产原型 (指用特定方法生产出的第一件物
品) ②典型,范例,样板 ‖**prototypal**,
prototypic(al) [,proute'tipik(əl)] *a.*

protract [prə'trækt] *vt.* ①延长,拖延: ~ one's
stay for some days 多呆几天 / a debate 延长
辩论 ②(用量角尺或比例尺)绘制 ③【动】伸展,
突出 ‖~ion [prə'trækʃən] *n.*

protractor [prə'træktə] *n.* ①延长者,拖延者 ②量
角器,分度规 ③【解】牵引肌 ④【医】异物取除器,
钳取器

protrude [prə'tru:d] ❶ *vt.* 使伸出,使突出: ~
one's tongue 伸舌 ❷ *vi.* (高大房屋等) 耸出

protuberance [prə'tju:bərəns] *n.* ①隆起,突出
②隆起部,突出物: a cancerous ~ 癌肿

protuberant [prə'tju:bərənt] *a.* ①隆起的,突出的
②[喻]显著的;突兀的;引人注意的

proud [praud] *a.* ①骄傲的,妄自尊大的,自高自
大的: (as) ~ as Punch (或 a peacock) 非常高傲 /
He is too ~ to ask questions. 他太骄傲了,总不
问人。②自尊的,有自尊心的 ③自豪的;得意的;
高兴的: be ~ of sb.'s acquaintance (或 be ~
of knowing sb.) 以和某人结识为荣 / I am ~ to
be a member of this organization. 我以属于这
个组织而感到光荣。④辉煌的,壮丽的;值得夸耀
的: ~ achievements 辉煌的成就 / a ~ sight 壮
丽的景象 / a ~ period in the country's history
国家历史上的全盛期 ⑤ (马等) 元气充沛的 ⑥
(河流等)涨了水的,泛滥的 ‖do oneself ~ [口]
自奉优厚,养尊处优 / do … ~ 使…感到荣幸
‖~ly *ad.* ‖~ flesh (伤口愈合后凸现出来的)
疤;【医】浮肉 / '~'hearted *a.* 骄傲的;傲慢的

prove [pru:v] (过去式 proved, 过去分词 proved 或
proven ['pru:vən]) ❶ *vt.* ①证明,证实: Facts
have ~d that the creative power of the
masses knows no limits. 事实证明群众的创造力
是无穷的。/ ~ the truthfulness of sb.'s statement 证明某人的话是真实的 / ~ oneself (to be)
an outstanding fighter 证明自己是一个出色的战
士 ②检验;试验;考验: ~ gold 验金 / ~ a new
weapon 试验新武器 / a proving ground 器材试
验场;检验场 ③勘探;钻探;探明 (up): ~ sb.'s
honesty 考验某人是否诚实 ③勘探;钻探;探明 (up): ~d
oil land 探明的含油地区 ④【数】
证,证明 ⑤检定 (遗嘱等) ⑥发(面团) ⑦试印,
把…印成校样 ❷ *vi.* 证明是,表明是: The method
~d (to be) highly effective. 这方法证明是非常
有效的。‖~ out 证明是适合的;证明是令人满意
的 ‖~n *a.* 被证实的;证据确凿
的叛徒 / not ~n [苏格兰]【律】罪证不足

provender ['provində] *n.* ①(家畜的)干饲料,粮秣
②[谑](人的)食物

proverb ['provə(:)b] I *n.* ①谚语,格言,箴言: as
the ~ runs (或 says) 俗语说;常言道 / the (Book
of) Proverbs (基督教《旧约全书》的)《箴言》②尽
人皆知的话柄,笑柄: pass into a ~ 传为话柄 /

He is a ~ for carelessness. 他的粗心是人所共知的。 ③[复](猜)谚语游戏 **II** *vt.* ①使成为谚语;使成为话柄 ②用谚语表达 ‖*to a* ~ 到尽人皆知的地步: He is fickle *to a* ~. 他的任性是人所共知的。

proverbial [prə'vɜːbjəl] *a.* ①谚语的,格言式的: ~ wisdom 谚语中表达的智慧 / ~ style 谚语风格 ②众所周知的;臭名昭著的 ‖~**ly** *ad.*

provide [prə'vaid] ❶ *vt.* ①提供: ~ guidance (a powerful backing) *for* 为…提供指导(有力的支持) / ~ food and clothes *for* one's family 供给家里人衣食,养家活口 / Many hands ~ great strength. 人多力量大。 ②装备;供给 (*with*): a ship *with* radar equipment 为船只装上雷达设备 / You must ~ yourselves. 你们必须自备必需品。 ③规定,订定(*that*): The agreement ~*s that* the two sides shall meet once a month. 协议规定双方每月会晤一次。 ④[古]准备,预备 ❷ *vi.* ①作准备(*for*);预防 (*against*): ~ *for* the entertainment of one's guests 为招待客人作准备 / ~ *against* emergencies 为应付紧急情况作准备 ② 赡养;提供生计 (*for*): ~ *for* one's children 赡养孩子女 ③ 规定,订定(*for, against*): measures ~*d for* (*against*) by law 法律规定(禁止)的措施 ‖~**d school** [英]地方公立小学

provided [prə'vaidid] *conj.* 以…为条件,假如: ~ (that) circumstances permit 假如情况允许的话

providence ['prɔvidəns] *n.* ①远见,远虑 ②[古]节俭 ③[常作 P-] 天意,天道,天命: a special ~ 天祐 / visitation of *Providence* 天灾 ④[P-] 天公,上帝

provident ['prɔvidənt] *a.* ①有远见的,远虑的: a ~ statesman 一个有远见的政治家 ②节俭的

providential [,prɔvi'denʃəl] *a.* ①上帝的,天意的 ②天祐的,神助(似)的 ③幸运的,凑巧的: a ~ escape 幸运的逃脱 ‖~**ly** *ad.*

province ['prɔvins] *n.* ①省 ②[复]地方(指首都或大都市以外的地方);乡间: the ~*s* 外省;地方;[英](伦敦以外的)各地 ③本分,职权,(学术)领域;部门;(活动)范围: be outside (within) sb.'s ~ 在某人职权范围外(内);不是(是)某人的本分 / in the ~ of literary criticism 在文艺批评的领域中 ④【史】古罗马在意大利以外的行省 ⑤(旧时)英国在北美的殖民地 ⑥[宗]大主教辖区

provincial [prə'vinʃəl] **I** *a.* ①省的: a ~ governor 省长 ②外省的;地方的;乡间的: a ~ paper 地方报纸 ③乡气的;粗野的;地方性的;偏狭的: a ~ accent 地方口音;乡土音 / a ~ outlook 偏狭的观念(或眼界) ④(家具的装饰风格等)朴素的,家常的 **II** *n.* ①地方居民;外省人;乡下人 ②兴趣(或眼界)狭窄的人;粗野的人 ③【宗】(管辖教区的)大主教 ④[复]地方部队 ‖~**ly** *ad.*

provision [prə'viʒən] **I** *n.* ①供应;(一批)供应品: a ~ of meat 一批肉类供应品 ②预备;防备: make ~ *for* the future 为将来作好准备 / make ~ *against* attack by air 预防空袭 ③[复]存粮;粮食;食物;口粮;给养: *Provisions* are plentiful. 粮食充足。 / lay in a store of ~s 贮存粮食 ④规定;条款: general ~s 总则 / Both sides have to act according to the ~s of the agreement. 双方都应按照协议条款办事。 an express ~ 明文(规定) ⑤【宗】圣职的委任(尤指教皇对尚未出缺的圣职的预先委任) **II** *vt.* 向…供应粮食(或必需品等): ~ a ship *for* a long voyage 为长途航行的船准备好粮食等必需品 ‖~**ment** *n.* 粮食供应

provisional [prə'viʒənl] **I** *a.* 临时的,暂时性的,暂定的: a ~ government (contract) 临时政府(契约) / a ~ order 紧急命令 **II** *n.* (正式邮票发行前的)临时邮票 ‖~**ly** *ad.*

proviso [prə'vaizou] ([复] proviso(e)s) *n.* 附文,但书,限制性条款;(附带)条件: make it a ~ that ... 以…为附带条件 / with the ~ that ... 以…为条件

provocation [,prɔvə'keiʃən] *n.* ①挑衅;挑拨;惹起;激怒;刺激: ~ of disorder 煽动骚乱 / ~ and estrangement 挑拨离间 / fly into a rage at (或 on) the slightest ~ 为了点小事就大发脾气 / do sth. under ~ 被激做某事 ②激怒的原因;惹人恼火的事: give ~ 激怒

provocative [prə'vɔkətiv] **I** *a.* ①挑衅的;挑逗的;激起…的(*of*);激怒的;刺激的: a ~ tone 用挑衅的口吻(or) / ~ remarks 惹人恼火的话 / be ~ of mirth 引人发笑 ②引起争论(或议论,兴趣等)的: a ~ novel 一本引起争论的小说 **II** *n.* 刺激物,吊胃口的东西

provoke [prə'vouk] *vt.* ①对…挑衅;挑拨;煽动;激怒;刺激: ~ a riot 煽动骚乱 / ~ sb. to anger 激怒某人 ②激起,引起;挑起;诱发: ~ sb.'s interest (indignation) 引起某人的兴趣(义愤) / ~ sb. to do sth. (或 into doing sth.) 惹得某人做某事

provoking [prə'voukin] *a.* 惹人恼火的;使人烦恼的: ~ behaviour 使人恼火的行为 ‖~**ly** *ad.*

provost[1] ['prɔvəst] *n.* ①(牛津、剑桥等大学的某些学院的)院长;(美国某些大学的)教务长 ②【基督教】大教堂的教长 【史】宗教团体的首脑 ③[苏格兰]市长 ④监督者,负责官员 ⑤监狱看守

provost[2] [prə'vou] *n.* 宪兵司令 ‖~ **court** (处理军民犯轻罪的)宪兵法庭 / ~ **guard** (在无宪兵时,与地方当局合作维持秩序并受宪兵司令管辖的)纠察队 / ~ **marshal** 宪兵主任 / ~ **sergeant** 宪兵军士

prow[1] [prau] *n.* ①船头;(飞机)机首;突出的前端 ②[诗]船

prow[2] [prau] *a.* [古]英勇的,勇猛的

prowess ['prauis] *n.* ①英勇,勇猛: show (或 display) one's ~ 发挥威力 ②杰出的才能(或技巧等);技术;本领: one's ~ in debate 杰出的辩才 / technical ~ 专门技术

prowl [praul] **I ❶** *vi.* ①(野兽等)四处觅食;[喻]暗中来回寻觅: beasts ~ing after their prey 四处觅食的野兽 ②徘徊,潜行(想偷窃等): ~ about the city 在城中徘徊 **❷** *vt.* 徘徊(某地);潜行于: ~ the forest for hours 徘徊林中数小时 **II** *n.* ①四处觅食;暗中来回寻觅 ②徘徊, 潜行 ‖*on the* ~ 徘徊;潜行(想偷窃等): be still on the ~ around the streets at dead of night 夜深人静时仍在街上徘徊 ‖~**er** 四处觅食的野兽;徘徊者;小偷 ‖~ **car** [美]警备车

proximity [prɔk'simiti] *n.* 最近;接近;亲近;近似: in the ~ of 在…附近 / in close ~ to 与…靠得很近 / ~ of blood 近亲 ‖~ **fuze** (炸弹、导弹等的)无线电引信,变时引信,近发引信

proxy ['prɔksi] *n.* ①代理(权);代表(权) ②代理人;代表人: be (or stand) ~ for sb. 担任某人的代理人 / vote by ~ 由代表投票 ③(对代理人的)委托书

prude [pru:d] *n.* 过分拘谨的人;装作正经的人(尤指女人)

prudence ['pru:dəns] *n.* ①谨慎;慎重;深谋远虑 ②精明 ③节俭

prudent ['pru:dənt] *a.* ①谨慎的;慎重的;深谋远虑的: be modest and ~ 谦虚谨慎 ②精明的 ③节俭的 ‖~**ly** *ad.*

prudery ['pru:dəri] *n.* 过分拘谨;装作正经

prudish ['pru:diʃ] *a.* 过分拘谨的;装作正经的 ‖~**ly** *ad.*

prune¹ [pru:n] *n.* ①洋李脯,梅脯,梅干 ②深紫红色 ③[美俚]乏味的人,讨厌的人;傻瓜 ‖*full of* ~*s* [美俚] ①愚蠢透顶的;完全错误的;浮夸的 ②活跃的;兴高采烈的 / ~*s and prism* 吞吞吐吐;转弯抹角;装腔作势

prune² [pru:n] **❶** *vt.* ①修剪(树枝等): ~ *away* (或 *off, down*) branches 修剪树枝 / ~ the bushes 修剪灌木 ②[喻]删除;删节;削减(预算等): ~ an article *of* its superfluities 删去文章中的冗语 / ~ *away* the unnecessary adjectives 删去不必要的形容词 **❷** *vi.* 删除,删节 ‖**pruning hook** 修枝钩刀

prurient ['pruəriənt] *a.* ①好色的,荒淫的;淫欲的 ②(焦躁地)渴望的

prussic ['prʌsik] *a.* ~ **acid** 【化】氢氰酸

pry¹ [prai] **I** *vi.* 窥探,盯着看(*into, about*);打听,探问(*into*): ~ *about* 到处窥探 / ~ *into* other people's affairs 打听别人的事情 **II** *n.* ①窥探;打听 ②过于好奇(或爱打听)的人

pry² [prai] **I** *vt.* ①(用杠杆等)撬,撬起,撬动: ~ the lid open 把盖撬开 / ~ up a floorboard 撬起一块地板 ②[喻]挖;用尽方法使脱离: ~ a secret out of sb. 从某人口中探出秘密 / ~ sb. *away* from an organization 用尽方法使某人脱离一个组织 **II** *n.* ①杠杆;撬具 ②杠杆作用

psalm [sɑ:m] **I** [宗] *n.* ①赞美诗;圣诗;圣歌: the (Book of) *Psalms* (或 the *Psalms* of David) (基督教《圣经》中的)〈诗篇〉 **II** *vt.* 唱(赞美诗);詠(诗篇) ‖~**ist** *n.* 赞美诗作者;诗篇作者: the *Psalmist* 《诗篇》作者,大卫(David) 王

pseudo ['psju:dou] *a.* 假的,伪的,冒充的

pseudonym ['psju:dənim] *n.* 假名,笔名: write under the ~ of 用…的笔名写作

pseudonymous [psju:'dɔniməs] *a.* ①用假名(或笔名)写的;签有假名(或笔名)的 ②用假名(或笔名)的

pshaw [pʃɔ:] **I** [pɑ:] *int.* 啐,哼[表示轻蔑、不耐烦或讨厌] **II** *n.* 啐声,哼声 **III** **❶** *vi.* 啐一声,哼一声(*at*) **❷** *vt.* 对…啐一声

psychiatry [sai'kaiətri] *n.* 精神病学 ‖**psychiatric(al)** [,saiki'ætrik(əl)] *a.* 精神病学的,医精神病的 / **psychiatrist** *n.* 精神病医生;精神病学者

psychic ['saikik] **I** *a.* ①精神的,灵魂的,心理的: ~ blindness 精神(性)盲 / ~ mechanics 心理机械学 / ~ research 心灵研究 ②对超自然力量敏感的,通灵的 **II** *n.* ①对超自然力量敏感的人,通灵的人;巫师,女巫 ②灵媒 ③精神上的现象,超自然的现象(如精神感应等) ‖~ **energizer** 抗抑郁麻醉毒品

psychoanalysis [,saikouə'næləsis] *n.* 精神分析(学)

psychological [,saikə'lɔdʒikəl] *a.* 心理(上)的;心理学的: a ~ factor 心理上的因素 / ~ warfare 心理战 / the ~ moment 心理上的适当瞬间;最适当的时机 ‖~**ly** *ad.* 心理上;从心理(学)角度

psychologist [sai'kɔlədʒist] *n.* 心理学者;心理学家

psychology [sai'kɔlədʒi] *n.* ①心理学: abnormal ~ 变态心理学 ②心理: the ~ of the adolescent 青春期心理 / understand sb.'s ~ very well 很理解某人的心理 ③心理学论文 ④心理学体系

ptomain(e) ['toumein] *n.* 尸毒,【化】尸碱 ‖**Ptomain(e) Domain** [美][军俚]食堂 / ~ **poisoning** 【医】尸碱中毒;食物中毒

pub [pʌb] *n.* [英口] ①小酒店 ②小旅馆,客栈 ‖~**-crawl** *vi.* & *vt.* [英俚](在…)进行逐店闹饮 / '~-,**crawler** *n.* 进行逐店闹饮者

puberty ['pju:bə(:)ti] *n.* 发身;青春期: reach the age of ~ 到达发身期

public ['pʌblik] **I** *a.* ①公(有)的,公众的: socialist ~ ownership 社会主义公有制 / ~ affairs 公众事务 / the ~ good 公益 / ~ health 公共卫生 / a ~ holiday 公定假日 ②政府的;公家的,公立的: a ~ document 政府文件,公文 / a ~ subsidy 公家补助,政府补助 / a ~ elementary (secondary) school 公立小(中)学 / a ~ officer 公职人员,公务员 ③公众事务的,社会的;为公的: ~ life 公共生活,社会生活 / volunteer for ~ work 志愿参加社会工作 / a ~ man 从事社会活动的人;关心公益的人 / ~ spirit 热心公益的精神 ④公用的,公共的: a ~ telephone 公用电话 / a ~ library 公共图书馆 / ~ baths 公共

浴室 / a ～ comfort room (或 station) [美] 公共厕所(或盥洗室) / ～ welfare 公共福利 ⑤公开的; 当众的: make a ～ protest 提出公开抗议 / make a secret ～ 揭露秘密 / a ～ address 当众的演说 ⑥知名的,突出的: a ～ figure 知名人士 ⑦全国的; 国际的; 普遍的: ～ ownership of the railways 铁路国有 ⑧[英]大学的; 代表大学的: ～ lectures (examinations) 大学讲座(考试) ⑨可感知的,物质性的 **II** ***n.*** ①[the ～] [用作单或复]公众,民众; 众人 ②(某一方面的)大众,群众: the reading ～ 读者大众 / the theatre-going ～ 经常看戏的观众 / The book attracted a large ～. 这本书的读者很多。③ [英] ＝～ house ‖***in*** ～ 公开地,当众: make a speech *in* ～ 当众发表演说 ‖**～ly** ***ad.*** ①当众; 公开地; 明显地 ②由公众; 由政府 (出资或持有等) ‖～ **act**＝～ law / '**～-ad'dress system** 扩音装备; 扩音系统, 有线广播 / ～ **bill** (议会的)公共关系法案 / ～ **bond** 公债券 / ～ **debt** 公债 / ～ **defender** 公设辩护人(指律师) / ～ **domain** ①(美国政府的)公有土地 ②不受版权(或专利权)限制的状态: The book is in the ～ *domain.* 这本书并无版权。/ ～ **enemy** ①全国(或各国)的公敌 ②社会公敌; (公众协助查缉的)要犯 / ～ **house** ①小旅馆, 客栈 ②[主英]小酒店 / ～ **law** 公法 / '**～-'minded** ***a.*** ＝～-spirited / ～ **nuisance**【律】公妨犯; 社会的害物 / ～ **opinion** 舆论; 民意: a ～ *opinion* poll 民意测验 / ～ **prosecutor** 检察官 / ～ **relations** (通过宣传手段建立的)与公众的联系: a ～ *relations* officer 新闻发布员; 对外联络员 / ～ **sale** 拍卖 / ～ **school** ①(英国的)公学 ②(美国的)公立中学(或小学) / ～ **servant** ①公仆,官员,公务员 ②从事公用事业的个人(或团体) / ～ **service** ①公用事业 ②公益服务 ③公职 / ～ **speaking** 演说; 演说术 / '**～-'spirited** ***a.*** 热心公益的, 为公的 / ～ **television** (播送有关文化知识和情况介绍等内容、一般不插播广告的)大众电视 / ～ **utility** ①公用事业 ②[常用复]公用事业公司股份 / ～ **works** 公共建筑; 公共工程; 市政工程

publican ['pʌblikən] ***n.*** ①[英]酒店(或客栈)老板 ②(赋税或贡物的)征收员; (古罗马的)收税人

publication [ˌpʌbli'keiʃən] ***n.*** ①发表, 公布: the ～ of a *communiqué* 公报的发表 ②出版; 发行 ③出版物: a list of new ～*s* 新书 (或新刊等) 目录

publicist ['pʌblisist] ***n.*** ①国际法专家, 国际法研究者 ②(报纸等的)时事评论员 ③广告员, 宣传员 ‖**～ic** [ˌpʌbli'sistik] ***a.***

publicity [pʌb'lisiti] ***n.*** ①公开(性): in the ～ of the street 在街道上大家都看得见的情况下 ②(公众的)注意; 名声: avoid (或 shun) ～ 避免惹人注意; 不要出名 / court (或 seek) ～ 求名 / in the full blaze of ～ 在众目睽睽之下 ③宣传; 宣扬; (向报界等散发的) 宣传材料; 广告: There has not been much ～ about this conference. 对这次会议没有作什么宣传。/ a ～ stunt 宣传伎俩 / a ～ drive 宣传运动; 广告运动 / be engaged in producing ～ for the student movement 为学生运动准备宣传材料 ‖***give*** ～ ***to*** 公布; 宣传: ‖～ **agent** 广告员; 宣传员

publicize ['pʌblisaiz] ***vt.*** ①宣传; 公布 ②为…做广告

publish ['pʌbliʃ] ❶ ***vt.*** ①公布, 发布: ～ a plan (statement) 公布计划(声明) ②发表; 宣传: ～ one's views in a big-character poster 用大字报发表自己的看法 / ～ an article in the press 在报刊上发表文章 ③出版; 发行; 刊印: When will the book be ～*ed*? 这书什么时候出版? / ～*ed* symphonies 已出版的交响曲(总谱) ④出版…的著作: a ～*ed* author 出版过著作的作者 ⑤使用(假钞票等) ❷ ***vi.*** ①出版; 发行: Be conscientious and make a good job of ～*ing*. 认真作好出版工作 / keep a paper ～*ing* 使报纸不间断地出版 / ～ for a university 为大学出版书刊 ②(著作人)发表著作 ‖**～able** ***a.*** 可发表的; 适于出版的 / **～er** ***n.*** ①书籍出版者 ②[英]报刊发行者 ③[美]报刊出版者 ④发表者; 公布者 ‖**～ing house** 出版社

pucker ['pʌkə] **I** ❶ ***vt.*** 折迭; 使起皱; 使缩拢: a ～*ed* fabric 皱纹织物 / ～ *up* one's brows (face) 皱起眉头(脸) ❷ ***vi.*** 折迭; 皱起; 缩拢: ～ *up* at the shoulders (衣服)肩部皱起 **II** ***n.*** 皱纹; 皱褶,襞 ‖***in a*** ～ 激动; 慌张; 烦恼 / ～ ***up*** 发脾气

pud [pʌd] ***n.*** [儿语] ①(小孩的)手 ②(动物的)前脚

pudding ['pudiŋ] ***n.*** ①布丁(西餐中一种松软的甜点心); 布丁状物: milk (lemon) ～*s* 牛奶(柠檬)布丁 ②[方]香肠,腊肠 ③【海】(由帆布等制成的护船用)船尾碰垫 ④[俚](贼给看屋狗吃的)毒肝 ‖***more praise than*** ～ 恭维多而实惠少 / ～ ***rather than praise*** 宁要实惠而不要恭维 / **～*s and pies*** 眼睛 / ***The proof of the*** ～ ***is in the eating.*** 见 **proof** / ***the*** ～ ***house*** [俚]胃, 肚子 ‖～ **face** 肥大的脸 / ～ **head** 傻瓜 / ～ **heart** 懦夫 / ～ **pie** [英]肉馅布丁 / ～ **stone**【矿】圆砾岩

puddle ['pʌdl] **I** ***n.*** ①水坑, 泥潭, 洼 ②胶土(粘土和水混成的塑性土, 不透水): a ～ wall 胶土墙 **II** ❶ ***vt.*** ①把(湿土和沙)捣成糊状; 搅浑; 用胶土填塞 ②【冶】搅炼 ③【农】湿土培育(稻秧等) ❷ ***vi.*** 搅泥浆; 在污水中泼溅 (或打滚) (*about*) ‖**～r** ***n.*** ①捣泥浆者; 搅炼者 ②【冶】搅炼棒, 拨火棒; 搅炼炉 / **puddling** ***n.*** 捣成泥浆;【冶】搅炼 / **puddly** ***a.*** ①多水坑的 ②象泥潭的; 混浊的 ‖～ **jumper** [美俚] ①小火车; 小型公共汽车 ②小型低空侦察机 ③小汽艇

puerile ['pjuərail] ***a.*** 幼稚的, 孩子气的; 不成熟的; 傻的 ‖**～ly** ***ad.***

puff [pʌf] **I** ***n.*** ①(一)喷, (一)吹; 一阵, 一股(气味、烟雾等); 噗的一声: a ～ of breeze 一阵微风 / ～*s* of smoke 喷出的一团团烟雾 / the ～*s* of a distant locomotive 远处机车的喷气声 / have a ~ at a pipe 从烟斗中抽一口烟 ③隆起的小块, 小肿胀 ③蓬松的一团; 衣服的蓬松部分; 蓬松的发卷: a ~ of feathers 一团羽毛 ④ 粉扑 ⑤(奶油)松饼 ⑥被子; 鸭绒被 ⑦吹捧性的短文(或书评、广告等) **II ❶** *vi.* ①一阵阵地吹(或喷);吹气;喷烟(而驶去) *(away, out)*: A fresh breeze ~ed across the river. 凉爽的微风一阵阵吹过河面。/ The kettle is ~*ing.* 水壶在冒气了。/ a steamboat ~*ing* along the river 喷着烟沿河航行的汽艇 ②喘气;喷着气走: ~ upstairs 喘着气走上楼梯 ③趾高气扬, 盛气凌人, 表示轻蔑: ~ at sb.'s remarks 对某人的话嗤之以鼻 ④ 肿胀, 肿起 *(up)* ⑤膨胀; 爆开, 爆裂: The parachute ~ed. 降落伞噗地张开了。/ Fireworks ~ed all around. 到处在放烟火。⑥[英](拍卖时)为抬价而喊价 **❷** *vt.* ①(一阵阵地)吹: The wind ~ed the clouds away. 风把云吹散了。/ ~ out a candle 吹熄蜡烛 ②喷(烟等)①使气急: He ran and ran till he was ~ed. 他直跑得喘不过气来。④喘着气说: ~ out a few words 喘着气说了些话 ⑤ 使充气, 使膨胀 *(out)*: ~ out one's chest (cheeks) 鼓起胸脯(双颊) ⑥使骄傲自大,使趾高气扬 *(up)*: Never let anything ~ you up. 决不要因任何事而骄傲自大。⑦吹捧(书等); 为(商品)作广告 ⑧ 使成蓬松的一团团(或一卷卷) ‖*be out of* ~ [口] 气喘吁吁 / ~ *and blow* 喘气, 气急 ‖~ *adder* (非洲)鼓腹毒蛇, 鼓腹蟒 / ~*ball n.* 【微】马勃 / ~ *paste* 做千层饼的生面 / ~-~ *n.* (火车的)喷气声; [儿语]火车; 火车头

puffin ['pʌfin] *n.* 【动】善知鸟; 海鹦

puffy ['pʌfi] *a.* ① 一阵阵地吹(或喷)的: a ~ southeast wind 一阵一阵吹着的东南风 ② 气喘吁吁的; 容易气急的 ③肿大的, 鼓起的; 肥胖的: a ~ face 虚胖的脸 ④虚荣的, 爱炫耀的 ⑤蓬松的, 松的 / '*pillow ~* 松软的枕头 ‖*puffiness n.*

pugilism ['pju:dʒilizəm] *n.* 拳击(术) ‖*pugilist n.* 拳击家, 拳师; [喻] 有力的争辩者 / **pugilistic** [,pju:dʒi'listik] *a.* 拳击家的; 拳击(术)的

pugnacious [pʌg'neiʃəs] *a.* 好斗的; 好战的; 爱吵架的

pugnacity [pʌg'næsiti] *n.* 好斗; 好战; 爱吵架

pull [pul] **I ❶** *vt.* ① 拉, 拖, 牵: *Pull* the door open. 把门拉开。Don't push it. 把门拉开。别推。/ He ~ed my sleeve (或 ~ed me by the sleeve). 他拉了拉我的衣袖 (引我注意)。/ The locomotive ~ed a long line of freight cars. 这台机车拖了一长列货车。② 拔; 抽出; 采, 摘(玉蜀黍、花等): ~ a tooth 拔一只牙齿 / ~ a knife (pistol) on sb. 拔出刀子(手枪)对准某人 / ~ The seam of his coat is ~ed. 他外套上的线缝被撕开了。④ 搬走: ~ a crankshaft 移出曲轴 ⑤划(桨、船), (船)被…划动; 划运: ~ a boat to the shore 把船划到岸边 / This boat ~s four oars.

这船是用四枝桨划的。⑥过分用力而弄伤, 拉伤: He ~ed the muscles in the leg. 他把腿部的肌肉弄伤了。⑦吸引, 招揽; 获得 ⑧ 放慢(赛马)速度故意跑输 ⑨ 手印: ~ a proof 用手打印校样 ⑩(棒球、高尔夫球等中)从右手把(球)向左侧击去 ⑪放肆地打, 干(勾当); 犯(罪), 犯…的过错: ~ a holdup 进行拦路抢劫 / ~ a boner 闹大笑话 ⑫[美俚]逮捕; (派警察)突然袭击(赌窟等) ⑬号召进行(罢工); 号召…罢工: ~ a strike 号召进行罢工 / ~ the plant 号召全厂罢工 **❷** *vi.* ①拉, 拖; 拔: The tractor ~s well. 这台拖拉机拉力大。② 能被拉(或拖、拔): These roots ~ easily. 这些根很好拔。③ 拔枪(或刀) ④行驶; (船)划动; 划船: The train ~ed into the station. 火车进站了。/ The boat ~ed for the shore. 船向岸划动。⑤有吸引力; 吸引顾客 ⑥深表同情; 鼓劲 *(for)* ⑦ (在赛马中) 故意放慢速度而输掉 ⑧ 大口喝 *(at)*; 猛抽, 深吸 *(at)*: ~ at one's pipe 猛吸烟斗 ⑨ 费力地前进: ~ up the hill 吃力地爬山 **II** *n.* ①拉, 拖; 拔: give a ~ at the rope 拉一下绳子 ②拉力, 拖力, 牵引力 ③供拉的东西; 拉手, 把手: a wooden ~ for a drawer 抽屉上的木拉手 ④划船: go for a ~ on the lake 到湖上去划船 ⑤费力的前进; 爬高 ⑥提携, 门路; (进行竞争等的)有利条件 ⑦吸引(力) ⑧【印】草样, 校样 ⑨ 勒马减速(尤指赛马时) ⑩一口(酒等); 一口(烟): take a long ~ at the bottle 从瓶里喝一大口酒 / take a ~ at a cigarette 抽一口香烟 ‖*have the ~ of* (或 *over*) sb. 胜过某人; 控制某人 / ~ *about* ①把…拖来拖去 ②粗暴对待 / ~ *apart* ① 扯断, 撕开 ②找出…错处; 批评 / ~ *at* ①用力拉: ~ at a handle 使劲地拉着把手 ②大口喝; 深吸 / ~ *away* 脱身, 脱出; 离开 / *Pull devil,* ~ *baker!* (拔河等时鼓励双方的用语)大家加油, 加油! / ~ *down* ①拉倒; 摧毁: ~ *down* an old house 拆毁一所旧房子 ②使降低; 使(价格等)下跌 ③ 使体质减弱; 使精神不振: Since his illness, he is very much ~ed down. 病后他身体差多了。④领取(工资等) / ~ *in* ①(列车)进站, 停站; (船)靠岸, 靠岸: The special train ~ed in at 9 a.m. 专车于上午九时进站。②勒(马) ③紧缩; 缩减开支 ④[俚]逮捕 / ~ *it* [俚]逃走 / ~ *off* ①脱(帽、衣等) ②努力实现; 赢得: ~ *off* a plan 努力实现计划 / ~ *on* ①穿, 戴(袜子、手套等) ②继续划(或划) / ~ *oneself together* 振作起来, 恢复镇定 / ~ *out* ①拔出, 挖出: have a bad tooth ~ed out 拔掉一只蛀牙 ② 离开; 撤走 ③(车、船)驶出 ④渡过难关; 恢复健康 / ~ *out of the fire* 使转败为胜 / ~ *over* ①把…拉过来: ~ the blanket over the child 拉毯子盖在孩子身上 ② (把…)划到岸边; (把…)开到路边, ~ *oneself* signalled him to ~ over. 我们招呼他(把车)开过来。/ ~ *round* (使)恢复健康; (使)复原: He quickly ~ed round. 他很快就恢复了健康。/ ~ *through* (使)渡过危机; 使渡过(危险等); (使)恢复健康: ~ sb.

through 使某人脱离险境 / ～ sb. *through* difficulties (a crisis) 使某人渡过困难(危机) / At length he ～ed *through*. 他终于渡过了难关。(或:他终于恢复了健康。) / ～ *together* 齐心协力: ～ *together* for the good of the people 为着人民的利益同心干 / ～ *to pieces* (或 *bits*) ①把…撕成碎片 ②把…攻击得一钱不值 / ～ *up* ①拔起(树、草等) ②(使)停下: The driver ～ed up (his car) at the gate. 司机在门口停车。/ The car ～ed up at the gate. 车在门口停下。③阻止;斥责 ④(在赛马等中)追上 (to, with) ‖'**～-back** *n.* ①阻力; 逆境 ②反动家伙 / a ～*back* of troops 撤军 / '**～-in** *n.* [英]沿路休息处;路边咖啡馆 / '**～-on** *n.* 套穿上去的衣物(如手套、汗衫等) *a.* 套穿的 / '**～-out** *n.* ①拔,拉 ②撤离;撤军 ③书刊中折着的供参阅用的大张插页;书刊中可取出的附录(或附件) ④【军】(飞机的) 改出动作(俯冲后恢复水平飞行的动作) / '**～-over** *n.* 套衫(如羊毛套衫等) *a.* 套领的,套的 / '**～-through** *n.* 枪筒清扫竿 / '**～-up** *n.* [英]沿路休息处;路边咖啡馆 ②【军】(飞机的)拉起动作,急升动作(特指从平飞位置转入急升的动作) ③[体](单杠)引体向上

pullet ['pulit] *n.* ①(未满一岁的)小母鸡 ②[美俚]小姑娘

pulley ['puli] *n.* [机]滑轮,滑车;辘轳;皮带轮: a fixed (或 fast) ～ 定(滑)轮 / a movable ～ 动(滑)轮 ‖**～ block** 滑轮组,滑车组

pulp [pʌlp] I *n.* ① 动植物体(或器官)中的肉质(或髓质)部分 ②果肉;(植物的)髓;牙髓 ③浆状物;纸浆;矿浆: reduce to (a) ～ 把…捣成浆状;把…打个稀烂 / meat ～ 肉浆 ④[常用复][美俚]低级杂志,黄色杂志 II ❶ *vt.* ① 使捣成浆状; 使化为纸浆: ～ old books 把旧书做成纸浆 ②除去(咖啡豆等)的果肉 ❷ *vi.* 成浆状 ‖**～wood** *n.* 纸浆原材

pulpit ['pulpit] *n.* ①【宗】布道坛,讲坛 ②[the ～] 教士职务;教士们: be denounced alike by ～ and platform 受宗教界和政界双方面的谴责 ③(用于书名)布道讲集 ④(机器)操纵台

pulpit

pulsate [pʌl'seit, 'pʌlseit] *vi.* ①(脉等)搏动,(心脏)跳动;有节奏地鼓动 ②震动;抖动;【物】脉动

pulse[1] [pʌls] I *n.* ①脉搏; 脉的一次跳动; 有节奏的跳动(或拍打): feel sb.'s ～ 给某人诊脉;[喻]试探某人意图 / His ～ was at a hundred. 他的脉搏是(每分钟)一百次。②【物】脉冲,(光波、声波等的)脉动;[喻](感情等的)激动 ③意向,动向;情绪: the ～ of the nation 全国的动向 / stir sb.'s ～s 鼓动某人的情绪 ④【音】拍子,律动 II ❶ *vi.* 搏动;跳动 ❷ *vt.* ①使跳动;使产生脉动 ②用脉冲输送(血液等) (in, out) ③脉动地产生(或调节) ‖**～less** *a.* 没有脉搏的; 没有生气的 ‖**～ code** [无]脉冲(编)码 / '**～ frequency** [无]脉冲频率 / '**～-jet** *n.* 脉动式空气喷气发动机 / ～ **radar** 脉冲雷达

pulse[2] [pʌls] *n.* 豆类植物;[复]豆子

pulverize ['pʌlvəraiz] ❶ *vt.* ① 使成粉末;研磨;把(液体)喷成雾 ② 粉碎,彻底摧毁 ❷ *vi.* 变成粉状;变成尘埃 ‖**～r** *n.* 粉碎器;粉磨机;粉碎者

puma ['pju:mə] *n.* ①美洲狮 ②美洲狮皮

pumice ['pʌmis] I *n.* 轻石(块),浮石(块)(其粉末常用于去污和磨光) (=～**stone**) II *vt.* 用浮石磨擦

pump[1] [pʌmp] I *n.* ①泵,抽(水)机,唧筒: a centrifugal ～ 离心泵 / a reciprocating ～ 往复泵 / a bicycle ～ 打气筒 / a breast ～ 吸奶器 ②抽吸;一抽,一吸 ③[喻]盘问,追问,探问;很会探问出消息的人 ④[美俚]心 ⑤[喻](昆虫的)吸盘 II ❶ *vt.* ①用抽机抽(液体);用抽机抽吸…的液体: ～ water from a well 从井里抽水 / a ～

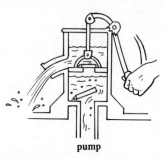

pump

well dry 把井抽干 ② 用打气筒打(气); 为…打气: ～ air *into* a tyre 把气打入轮胎 / ～ *up* a tyre 把轮胎打足气 ③ [喻]盘问,追问; 以追问(或巧妙方式)探出(秘密等) (out): ～ sb. *for* information (或 ～ information *out of* sb.) 从某人那里探出消息 ④[喻] 把(功课等)灌注(入脑) (into); 倾注 (upon): ～ abuses *upon* sb. 破口大骂某人 ⑤使疲惫; 使剧烈喘息: be ～ed out 累极; 喘得上气不接下气 ⑥使劲地握(手) ❷ *vi.* ①用抽机抽水(或油等);操作抽机 ②盘问 ③(象唧筒把手或活塞)上下往复行动;(气压计中水银柱)猛升猛降 ‖*fetch a* ～ 注水于泵使产生吸力而开

pump 始抽水 / *prime the* ~ 采取措施促使某事物发展(尤指以政府资金促使经济发展等) ‖~**er** *n.* ①司水者 ②装有水泵的消防车;抽水机 ③[美]要用泵才能抽出油来的油井 / ~**ing** *n.* 抽水;泵送: a ~*ing* station 抽水站 / an oil ~*ing* station 石油泵送站 ‖~ **brake** 唧筒的把手(尤指较长者);液压制动器 / ~ **handle** ①泵的把手 ②[口]使劲的握手 / '~-,handle *vt.* [口]使劲握(手) / ~ **priming** 意在诱导自力发展经济的政府投资 / ~ **room** ①(温泉疗养地的)药用矿水配制处 ②水泵房 / '~ship *vi. & n.* [海俚]小便,撒尿

pump² [pʌmp] *n.* (与晚礼服一起穿的跳舞用的)一种浅口无带皮鞋

pumpkin ['pʌmpkin] *n.* ①南瓜;南瓜藤 ②[美俚]重要人物,大亨 ③[美俚]头,脑袋瓜 ④[美俚]乡村小镇 ‖~ **head** [美俚]傻瓜

pun¹ [pʌn] **I** *n.* (修辞中的)双关 **II** (punned; punning) ❶ *vi.* 用双关语: ~ *on* (或 *upon*) a word 使一个词有双关意思 ❷ *vt.* 用双关语说服(或促使)

pun² [pʌn] (punned; punning) *vt.* [英]把(土、碎石等)捣结实;用夯把…打紧密 (*up*)

punch¹ [pʌntʃ] **I** *n.* ①冲压机,冲床;冲头 ②(纸、纸板等的)打孔器,穿孔机 ③(木工用的)钉锥 ④ 打印器;突模冲头 ⑤(冲出或打出的)孔,切口 **II** *vt.* ①(用冲床)冲(某物),(用打孔器)在…上打孔: ~ a bus ticket 用剪票夹在公共汽车票上打孔 ②(用冲床)冲(孔),(用打孔器)打出(孔) ③(用钉锥)打进(或起出)(钉子等) ④(用打印器)打印,(用突模冲头)冲印 ‖~**er** *n.* ①电报凿孔机 ②冲床工,钻床工;[俚]报务员 ‖~(**ed**) **card** 打孔的资料卡 / ~ **pliers** 打孔钻 / ~ **press** 冲床

punch² [pʌntʃ] **I** ❶ *vt.* ①用拳猛击: ~ sb. on the nose 对着某人的鼻子打一拳 ②用力击,用力按: ~ (the keys of) a typewriter 按打字机(的字键) ③(用棒)戳,刺 ④ 赶(牲口),放牧(牲口) ⑤猛力推挤: The rocket ~*ed* its way out of the atmosphere. 火箭猛力冲出了大气层。❷ *vi.* ①用拳猛击 ②用力击,用力按 **II** *n.* ①拳打: give sb. a ~ 给某人一拳 ②力量,活力;效力: a boxer with a strong ~ 击拳有力的拳击家 / The speech has a ~. 这讲话很有力。‖*pull one's ~es* ①(拳击中)故意不用力打 ②(攻击、批评等时)故意不猛烈 / ~ *in* (*out*) (在装有上下班时间记录钟的工厂等中)打上班(下班)钟片: ~ *out* and go home 打下班钟片而回家 ‖~**er** *n.* 牧人 / ~**y** *a.* ① 有力的,生气勃勃的 ② =~-drunk ‖'~-**drunk** *a.* ① (拳击中)被打得晕头转向的 ②摇摇晃晃的;惶惑的 / ~**ing bag** (练习拳击用的)吊袋/[喻]攻击目标 / ~**ing ball** (练习拳击用的)吊球 / ~ **line** 妙句,妙语 / '~-**up** *n.* [英俚]大吵大闹的殴斗;打群架

punch³ [pʌntʃ] *n.* ①(果汁、香料、茶、酒等搀和的)混合甜饮料 ② 饮混合甜饮料的聚会 ‖~ **bowl** ①放混合甜饮料的大钵 ②山坳

punch⁴ [pʌntʃ] *n.* ① [P-] 英国木偶剧 *Punch and Judy* 中驼背的滑稽角色 ② [P-] 《笨拙》周刊(英国幽默插画杂志) ③(英国索夫克郡产的)矮脚驮马;[方]矮胖子;粗而短的东西 ‖(*as*) *pleased* (或 *proud*) *as Punch* 非常高傲

punctilious [pʌŋk'tiliəs] *a.* 拘泥细节的;谨小慎微的 ‖*as* ~ *as a Spaniard* 极其拘泥于细节的 ‖~**ly** *ad.* / ~**ness** *n.*

punctual ['pʌŋktjuəl, 'pʌŋktʃuəl] *a.* ①严守时刻的;准时的;不误期的: be ~ for class 准时去上课 / be ~ in the payment of one's rent 按期付租金 ②(表达方式等)正确的,精确的 ③点状的; 【数】点的 =punctilious ‖~**ity** [,pʌŋktju-'æliti, ,pʌŋktʃu'æliti] *n.* 严守时刻;准时; 按期 / ~**ly** *ad.* ①守时地;准时地;按期地 ②正确地,精确地

punctuate ['pʌŋktjueit, 'pʌŋktʃueit] ❶ *vt.* ①加标点符号于,标点(文章等) ②强调,加强: He nodded to ~ his approval. 他点点头表示他完全同意。 ③不时打断: a speech ~*d* with cheers 不时被欢呼声打断的讲话 ❷ *vi.* 点标点 ‖**punctuation** [,pʌŋktju'eiʃən, ,pʌŋktʃu'eiʃən] *n.* ① 点标点;标点法 ② 全部标点符号 / **punctuative** *a.* 标点的;作为标点的 / **punctuator** *n.* 点标点者

punctulate ['pʌŋktjuleit] *a.* 【生】具小刻点的;有细孔的 ‖**punctulation** [,pʌŋktju'leiʃən] *n.*

puncture ['pʌŋktʃə] **I** *n.* ①刺,穿刺 ②刺痕,(车胎等的)刺孔 ③【生】刻点 **II** ❶ *vt.* ①(用针)刺,刺穿;戳破: ~ the skin with a needle 用针刺破皮肤 ②揭穿;使无用 ❷ *vi.* ①被刺穿;被戳破 ②(自行车或骑自行车者)车胎遭到刺破 ‖**puncturable** ['pʌŋktʃərəbl] *a.* 可刺穿的;可戳穿的 / ~**d** *a.* 【生】具刻点的

pundit ['pʌndit] *n.* ① =pandit ② [谑]博学的老师 ③权威性的评论者;(某一学科的)权威

pungent ['pʌndʒənt] *a.* ①(气味等)刺激性的,刺鼻的,辣的: ~ gas 刺鼻的气体 / ~ sauce 辣酱油 ②(语言等)辛辣的,尖刻的,尖锐的: ~ sarcasm 辛辣的讽刺 / a ~ remark 尖刻的话 / ~ criticism 尖锐的批评 ③【生】尖形的 ‖~**ly** *ad.*

punish ['pʌniʃ] ❶ *vt.* ① 罚;惩罚,处罚: ~ sb. *for* an offence 因某人犯罪而惩罚他 / ~ an offence *with* (或 *by*) imprisonment 以徒刑惩处犯罪行为 ②粗暴地对待,痛击;折磨;损害: ~ one's opponent 痛击对手 ③[口]大量消耗,耗尽: ~ the food 大吃 ❷ *vi.* 惩罚,处罚 ‖~**er** *n.* 惩罚者,处罚者

punishment ['pʌniʃmənt] *n.* ①罚;处罚,惩罚;刑罚: inflict a ~ on a criminal 处罚罪犯 / capital ~ 极刑,死刑 ②猛烈的对待,痛击;折磨;损害

punitive ['pju:nitiv] *a.* 给予惩罚的,惩罚性的;刑罚的 ‖~ *expedition* 为惩罚叛乱者的征伐,讨伐 / ~ *damages* (要肇事者付给的)惩罚性补偿费 / ~ *police* (印度)派往闹事地区而由该区居民承担费用的警察队 ‖~**ly** *ad.* / ~**ness** *n.*

punka(h) ['pʌŋkə] *n.* [印地] ①大葵扇 ②(吊在天花板上拉动产生风的)布风扇,拉风

punt¹ [pʌnt] I *n.* (用篙撑的)方头平底船 II ❶ *vt.* ① 用篙撑(方头平底船) ② 用方头平底船运载 ❷ *vi.* 乘方头平底船 ‖~er *n.* 撑方头平底船的人

punt² [pʌnt] I ❶ *vt.* 踢(从手中扔下而未着地的足球) ❷ *vi.* 踢悬空球 II *n.* 踢悬空球

punt³ [pʌnt] I *vi.* ① (打纸牌时)向庄家下赌注 ②赌博 II *n.* =~er ‖~er *n.* 向庄家下赌注者;赌博者

puny ['pju:ni] *a.* ① 小的, 弱小的; 软弱无力的 ②不足道的,次要的

pup¹ [pʌp] I *n.* ①小狗,幼犬 ② 幼畜,幼兽(尤指小海豹) II (pupped; pupping) *vi. & vt.* 生(小狗) ‖*a conceited* ~ 傲慢的小伙子 / *in* ~ (母狗等)怀胎的 / *sell sb. a* ~ 欺骗某人(尤指卖给某人某种使他相信将来能增加价值的东西)‖~tent (楔形)小帐篷

pupa ['pju:pə] ([复] pupae ['pju:pi:] 或 pupas) *n.* 蛹 ‖~l *a.*

pupil¹ ['pju:pl, 'pju:pil] *n.* ① 小学生; 学生; 门生, 弟子: To be a good teacher, one must first be a good ~. 要作好先生,首先要作好学生。②【律】(有监护人的)未成年人 ‖**pupil(l)ary** ['pju:piləri] *a.* ‖~ **load** 一名教师所负责的学生总数 / ~ **teacher** 小先生(边读书边教其他小学生的学生)

pupil² ['pju:pil] *n.* 【解】瞳孔 ‖**pupilar** ['pju:pilə] *a.*

puppet ['pʌpit] *n.* ①(演木偶戏用的)木偶; 玩偶: a glove (或 hand) ~ (套在手上表演的)布袋木偶 ②受他人操纵的人(或集团); 傀儡: a ~ state 傀儡国家 / a ~ government 傀儡政府, 伪政府 / ~ troops 伪军 / a ~ regime 伪政权 ‖~**eer** [ˌpʌpi'tiːə] *n.* 操纵木偶的人; 演木偶戏的人 / ~**ry** *n.* ①[总称]木偶,傀儡 ② 木偶(戏)艺术 ‖~ **play**, ~ **show** 木偶戏 / ~ **valve** 【机】提升阀

puppet

puppy ['pʌpi] *n.* ①(不满一岁的)小狗,幼犬 ②幼小的动物(尤指幼鲨鱼) ③ 自负的青年 ‖~**dom** *n.* ①[总称]小狗,幼犬 ② =~hood / ~**hood** *n.* (狗等的)幼年时期 / ~**ish** *a.* ① 小狗似的 ②自负的 / ~**ism** *n.* 自负 ‖~ **fat** 少年在青春期前显现的肥胖 / ~ **love** 初恋

purchase ['pə:tʃəs] I *n.* ①买,购买,购置;所购物: make a ~ 买件东西 / fill the truck with ~s 把卡车装满买来的东西 / a good ~ 便宜货 ②获得物; 赃物 ③(地产等以年计的)收益, 价值: be sold at ten years' ~ (房屋等)以相当于十年租金的价格出售 / The man's life is not worth a day's ~. 那人生命危在旦夕。④【史】买取军官职位(的做法) ⑤【律】(房屋、地产等)置得(非继承所得的) ⑥紧握, 紧抓(以拉或举某物, 或防止其落下): get (或 secure) a ~ on sth. 抓住某物 ⑦【机】起重装置; 杠杆作用;【海】绳索; 绞辘; 滑轮 II *vt.* ①买,购买,购置: ~ a car 购买一辆汽车 ②赢得,(用牺牲等)换得 ③【律】置得(房屋、地产等) ④用起重装置(或杠杆作用等)举起(或移动): ~ an anchor 【海】起锚 ‖**purchasable** *a.* ①可买的,买得到的 ②(用贿赂)可收买的 / ~**r** *n.* 买主,购买人;采购人 ‖~ **money** 买价;定价 / **purchasing power** (人或货币的)购买力

purdah ['pə:da:] *n.* [印地] ①(印度等地使妇女不被陌生人看见的)帘子, 帏幔 ②(印度等地的)深闺制度 ‖**live in** ~ 生活于深闺中

pure [pjuə] *a.* ① 纯粹的, 不搀杂的; (颜色)纯的: ~ gold 纯金 / ~ alcohol 纯酒精 / ~ white 纯白色 ②纯净的, 洁净的; 无垢的: ~ water (food) 洁净的水(食物) ③无瑕的, 无错的; 完美的; 纯正的: speak a very ~ English 讲非常纯正的英语 / the ~ and original text (未经窜改的)真本 ④(品德等)纯洁的, 清白的; 贞洁的: ~ in mind and body 身心纯洁 ⑤(马等)纯种的; 纯血统的 ⑥ 完全的, 十足的: ~ nonsense 十足的废话 / a ~ waste of time 十足的浪费时间 / It was a ~ accident. 这全然是意外事故。⑦纯理论的; 抽象的: ~ science 纯科学(区别于 applied science 应用科学) / ~ chemistry 理论化学 / ~ literature (为文学而文学的)纯文学 ⑧(康德哲学中的)非经验论的 ⑨(声音)清亮的, 圆润的 ⑩【语】(元音)在另一元音后面的; (词根)以元音结尾的; (辅音)不与其它辅音相连的 ‖~ **and simple** 完完全全的, 十足的 / *the* ~ *in* (或 *of*) *heart* 心地纯洁的人们 ‖~**ly** *ad.* / ~**ness** *n.* ‖'~**blood** *a. & n.* 纯血统的(动物) / '~**bred** *a. & n.* 纯种的 (动物或植物) / **Pure Land** 【佛教】西方净土,西方极乐世界 / ~ **line** 【生】纯系

purgative ['pə:gətiv] I *a.* ①净化的;清洗的 ②通便的 II *n.* 泻药

purgatory ['pə:gətəri] I *n.* ①【宗】炼狱;(在炼狱中的)涤罪 ②暂时受苦的地方;暂时的苦难 II *a.* =purgative (*a.*) ‖**purgatorial** [ˌpə:gə'tɔ:riəl] *a.* 炼狱的;(在炼狱中)涤罪的

purge [pə:dʒ] I ❶ *vt.* ① 使洁净;使净化;清除;清洗: ~ water by distillation (用蒸馏法净水 / ~ metal of dross 或 ~ away dross from metal) 清除金属中的浮渣 / ~ sb. oneself) of a charge 洗涤某人(自己)的罪名 / be ~d of (或 from) sin 被涤除罪过 ②【律】以认错作为…

的补偿；~ one's contempt 在藐视法官(或法庭)后认错 ③ 用药物使(肠)通便；使(人)通便 ❷ vi. ①净化；清除；清洗 ②通便 II n. ①净化；清除；清洗 ②泻药 ‖**purgee** [pə:'dʒi:] n. 被清除者 / ~**r** n. 清除(别人)者

Puritan ['pjuəritən] I n. ①清教徒(基督教新教的一派) ② [p-] 清教徒似的人；宗教(或道德)上极端拘谨的人 II a. ①清教徒的 ② [p-] 清教徒似的；宗教(或道德)上极端拘谨的 ‖~**ism** n. ①清教徒的习俗和教义，清教主义 ② [p-] 宗教(或道德)上的极端拘谨

purloin [pə:'lɔin] vt. & vi. 偷窃

purple ['pə:pl] I n. ①紫色，紫红色 ②紫色染料(或颜料)；[古]泰尔红紫(从海螺中浸出的紫色染料) ③紫色布；紫衣；紫袍 ④ [the ~] [喻]帝位，王位；显位；红衣主教的职位: be raised to the ~ 升为红衣主教 II a. ①紫的，紫红的；[古]泰尔红紫的: become ~ with rage 气得脸色发紫 ②帝王的 ③词藻华美的；华而不实的 ④亵渎的 III vi. & vt. (使)成紫色 ‖**born to** (或 **in**) **the ~** 出身王室(或显贵)的 ‖~ **emperor** [动]闪紫蝶 / '~-**flowered garlic** 【植】紫花蒜 / **Purple Heart** (美国的)紫心勋章(授予作战中负伤的军人) / ~ **medic** 【植】苜蓿 / ~ **passage**, ~ **patch** 词藻绚丽的段落；华而不实的章句

purport ['pə:pət, 'pə:pɔ:t, pə(:)'pɔ:t] I n. ①(文件、演说等的)意义，涵义，主旨: the main ~ of one's speech 演说的要点 II vt. ①意味着；似乎有…的意义；大意是: His letter may ~ his forthcoming arrival. 他的来信可能意味着他快要到达了。②声称，号称: a letter ~ing to be written by sb. 一封声称是某人写的信 ③意图；意欲

purpose ['pə:pəs] I n. ①意图；目的: What is his ~ in coming? 他来的意图是什么? / answer (或 serve) the ~ 管用，能解决问题 / for military (scientific) ~s 为了军事上(科学上)的目的 ②意志，决心: be firm (wanting) in ~ 意志坚定(薄弱) ③效用，效果；意义: time spent to good (no) ~ 花得有成效(无意义)的时间 / live to some ~ 活得有些意义 ④(讨论中的)论题；(进行中的)行动: a novel with a ~ 为宣传一种主张而写的小说 II vt. 决意(做)，打算(做): We ~ (making 或 to make) another trial. 我们打算再试一下。/ We ~ that the experiment shall be carried out before long. 我们决意不久就做这项实验。‖**for** (**all**) **practical ~s** 实际上 / **in** ~ [古]故意地 / **of** (**set**) ~ 有意地；故意地 / **on** ~ ①为了: He came here on ~ to discuss it with you. 他到这儿来是要与你讨论这事的。②故意地: do sth. on ~ 故意做某事 / **to the** ~ 得要领的，中肯的；合适的: He said something that was (not) to the ~. 他说了一些中肯(不中肯)的话。‖~**ly** ad. ①特意地 ②故意地

purposeful ['pə:pəsful] a. ①有意义的；有目的的；

有意义的: ~ activities 有目的的活动 ②意志坚强的，有决心的: a ~ man 有决心的人 ‖~**ly** ad. / ~**ness** n.

purr [pə:] I n. ①(猫等的)满足时鸣鸣的叫声 ②低沉的颤动声(如汽车引擎声等) II ❶ vi. ①(猫等)满足地鸣鸣叫 ②(汽车引擎)发出震颤的声音 ③用愉快的声调表示满意 ❷ vt. 以愉快的声调表示；愉快满意地说: She ~ed her approval of the suggestion. 她高兴地表示赞同这个建议。

purse [pə:s] I n. ①钱包，小钱袋；(女用)手提包 ②(钱包形的)小袋，小包 ③金钱，资金；财力: a common ~ 公共资金 / be beyond sb.'s ~ 非某人财力所及，为某人所买不起 ④募集(或捐赠)的作为奖金(或奖赏等)的款项: make up a ~ 捐募一笔款子 / put up (或 give) a ~ 捐赠奖金(如给比赛优胜者等) ⑤【解】蘘，蘘状部 II ❶ vt. ①[古]把…放进钱袋(up) ②缩拢；皱起: ~ (up) one's lips 噘起拉嘴 ❷ vi. 缩拢；皱起 ‖**a heavy** (或 **long**) ~ 充实的钱包；富裕 / **a light** (或 **lean**) ~ 空空的钱包；贫穷 / **A light** ~ **makes a heavy heart.** [谚]为人无钱心事重。/ **dip into one's** ~ 乱花钱 / **One cannot make a silk out of a sow's ear.** [谚]巧妇难为无米之炊。/ **open one's** ~ 解蘘，出钱 / **the privy** ~ 岁收中拨给王室的费用 / **the public** ~ 国库 / **Who holds the ~ rules the house.** [谚]有钱就有势。‖~**ful** n. 一钱袋 / ~ **bearer** [英]保管金钱的人；会计员 / ~ **net** (捕兔等用的)袋网 / ~ **pride** 富有引起的傲慢 / '~-**proud** a. 因富有而傲慢的 / ~ **seine** (用两只船拖曳的)大型渔网 / ~ **strings** ①钱袋口上的绳子 ②金钱；财力: hold the ~ **strings** 掌管金钱 / loosen the (或 one's) ~ **strings** 乱花钱，浪费 / tighten the (或 one's) ~ **strings** 节省用钱

purser ['pə:sə] n. (轮船、班机等的)事务长

pursuance [pə'sju(:)əns] n. ①追赶(或追踪等)；追求 ②进行，实行；从事；继续进行: in ~ of a plan (resolution) 在执行计划(决议)时

pursue [pə'sju:] ❶ vt. ①追赶；追踪；追捕；追击: ②追随,跟踪;(疾病、灾祸等)纠缠: The ship ~d a northern course. 船向北航行。/ Illness ~d him till his death. 疾病一直纠缠着他，直到他去世。③追求,寻求;向…求爱: ~ a lofty goal 追求崇高的目标 ④进行，实行；从事；继续: ~ correct policies 执行正确的政策 / ~ a subject of discussion 继续讨论一个题目 ❷ vi. ①追，追赶 (after) ②继续进行 ③[苏格兰]起诉 (for) ‖~**r** n. ①追赶(或追踪等)者；追求者 ②从事者，研究者 ③[苏格兰]起诉者；原告

pursuit [pə'sju:t] n. ①追赶；追踪；追捕；追击: come in ~ 追踪而来 ②追求，寻求 ③追赶(或追求等)的对象 ④事务；职业；消遣: daily ~s 日常事务 / mercantile (或 commercial) ~s 商业 / engage in scientific ~s 从事科学研究 ⑤[美]驱逐机 (=~ plane)

purulent ['pjuərulənt] *a.* 化脓的; 脓性的; 含脓的

purvey [pə'vei] ❶ *vt.* 承办, 供应(伙食等) ❷ *vi.* (为…)办伙食 (*for*)

purveyor [pə'veiə] *n.* ①办伙食者; 伙食供应商 ②【英史】食物征发官

purview ['pə:vju:] *n.* ①权限; 范围: outside (within) the ~ of studies 在研究范围之外(之内) ②视界, 眼界 ③某一法律的条款部分

pus [pʌs] *n.* 脓; 脓液

push [puʃ] Ⅰ ❶ *vt.* ①推; 推动; 推进: ~ a door open 把门推开 / ~ a cart 推车 / ~ up (down, aside) 把…向上(向下, 向旁边)推 / ~ the frontline forward 把战线向前推进 ②使突出, 使伸出, 使延伸: Some plants ~ their roots deep into the soil. 有些植物的根深深长入土中。 / ~ one's nose into other people's affairs 干涉别人的事情 / ~ a new road across the grassland 筑一条新路穿过大草地 ③大力推进, 推行: ~ a campaign 大力推进一场运动 / ~ a bill in the legislature 在立法机关竭力要求通过某一法案 / ~ a claim 坚持要求 / ~ a political line 推行某一政治路线 ④逼迫, 催逼, 促使: be ~ed for time 感到时间紧迫 / ~ sb. to continue doing sth. 促使某人继续做某事 / ~ a truck to a high speed 把卡车开得飞快 ⑤使引人注意; 提携(人); 推销(商品); [俚]贩卖(毒品): ~ oneself forward 使人家注意自己, 出风头 / ~ one's wares 推销货物 ⑥扩展, 扩大, 增加: ~ the production of daily necessities 增加日用品的生产 ❷ *vi.* ①推: Don't ~ against me! 别推我! ②推进, 努力前进 ③伸展; 扩展; 增加: a dock that ~es far out into the river 远远伸入江中的码头 ④奋力争取, 力求取得 (*for*): ~ *for* the passage of a bill 力图取得法案的通过 Ⅱ *n.* ①推; 推动; 推进; 促进: give the door a ~ (或 give a ~ at the door) 把门推一下 / The good tidings gave us a vigorous ~. 这喜讯给了我们有力的推动。 / a tremendous ~ to industry 对工业的巨大促进 ②奋斗, 奋力; 奋进: Let's make a ~ to get it done tonight. 让我们加把劲今夜把它干完。③攻击, 攻势; 推销运动: an economic ~ on a product 一种产品的推销运动 ④急迫, 紧迫; 紧要关头: when it comes to the ~... 临到紧要关头… ⑤劲头; 进取心; 事业心: a man of ~ and go 劲头十足的人 ⑥[英俚]解雇: give sb. the ~ 把某人解雇 / get the ~ 被解雇 ⑦一批人; [英]一帮贼(或罪犯等) ⑧(刀锋或兽角等的)刺, 中, 触 ‖*at a* ~ 没有(别的)办法时, 急迫时 / *be in the* ~ [俚]熟悉情况, 知情 / ~ *ahead with* 推动, 推进; 推行: ~ *ahead with* one's work 推进工作 / ~ *ahead with* a policy (line) 推行一项政策(一条路线) / ~ *around* ①把…推来推去 ②摆布; 烦扰; 欺侮 / ~ *back* ①把…向后推; 向后拥 ②[俚]吞下 / ~ *off* ①(用桨等撑开)使船离岸 ②离开, 走: It's time to ~ *off*. 该走啦。/ ~ *on* ①推动,

推进: ~ sb. *on* 促使某人干下去 ②努力向前 / ~ *on* to one's destination 努力向目的地(或目标)前进 / ~ *on* with one's work 加紧干工作 / ~ *over* 推倒: ~ sb. *over* 把某人推倒 / ~ *through* ①促成, 完成: ~ a matter *through* 促成一件事 ②挤着穿过: ~ (one's way) *through* the crowd 从人群中挤过去 / ~ (*up*) *daisies* 见 **daisy** ‖~**er** *n.* ①推者, 推动者; 推动器 ②推销者; (毒品等的)贩卖者 ③推进式飞机 (= ~airplane) / ~**ful** *a.* 有进取心的; 有冲劲的 ‖~ **bicycle**, '~**-bike** *n.* [英]自行车(区别于机动脚踏两用车或摩托车) / ~ **button** *n.* 电钮, 按钮 / '~**-button** *a.* 按钮的, 按钮式的; 按电钮操纵的: a ~**-button** switch 按钮开关; 按钮式机键 / a ~**-button** war 按钮战争(指按动电钮以发射导弹等武器的战争) / ~ **car** ①(铁道工程用的)运料车 ②(机车把列车车厢推上渡轮时用的)居间车 / '~**cart** *n.* 手推车; 婴孩推车 / ~ **cycle** = ~ **bicycle** / ~**-down** *n.* ①【空】推下 ②【自】迭式存储器, 后进出存储器 / ~ **money** 给推销员的佣金 / '~**,over** *n.* ①容易击败的对手, 弱敌 ②容易被吸引的人; 容易受骗的人 ③轻易做成的事 ④(导弹、火箭)沿弹道水平方向的位移 ⑤= ~**-down** / '~**pin** *n.* ①(一种儿童玩的)针戏 ②微不足道的东西 ③[美]高顶图画钉 / '~**-'pull** *a.*【无】推挽式的 / '~**-up** *n.*【体】俯卧撑

puss [pus] *n.* ①(爱称)小猫; 少女, 小姑娘 ②[英]兔子; 老虎 ③[美俚]脸; 嘴 ‖~ *in the corner* [美]抢壁角游戏 ‖~ **moth** 天蛾的一种

pussy[1] ['pusi] *n.* ①[儿语]猫儿 ②有柔毛的东西 ②少女, 小姑娘 ③褪色柳的柔荑花序 ‖~ *wants a corner* [美]抢壁角游戏 ‖~ **willow** 褪色柳

pussy[2] ['pʌsi] *a.* 多脓的; 似脓的

put[1] [put] Ⅰ (put; putting) ❶ *vt.* ①放, 摆; 装: *Put* the hammer into the tool box, please. 请把锤子放入工具箱。/ ~ a horse to the cart 把马套上车 / ~ a handle to a hoe 为锄头装柄 / ~ a play on the stage 上演一出戏 / ~ the children to bed 料理孩子们上床睡觉 / ~ faith in 相信…; 信任… ②移动, 拨动; 【矿】推(煤车): ~ the hands of the clock back 把时钟的针向后拨 ③使穿进, 使穿过: ~ one's arm through a sleeve 把手伸进袖子 / ~ one's pen through a word 划掉一个词 / ~ a nail into a board 把钉子敲入木板 ④投掷; 发射: ~ the shot 推铅球 / ~ a satellite into orbit 把人造卫星射入轨道 ⑤使渡(过), 使航行: ~ a person (boat) across a river 使人(船)渡过一条河 ⑥使处于(某种状态): ~ politics in command 政治挂帅 / be ~ into action 被实行; 被付诸实践 / be ~ out of action (机器等)受损坏而不能应用; (敌军等)被歼灭 / be ~ into production 被投入生产 / ~ sb. to death 把某人处死 / ~ sth. to (good) use (充分)利用某物 / ~ sb. to school 送某人去上学

⑦写上，标上：~ a tick against a name 在名字上打上记号 / ~ one's signature to a contract 在合同上签名

⑧提出：Who ~ the question? 这问题是谁提的？/ I ~ a question to him (或 ~ him a question). 我向他提出一个问题。/ ~ a matter before a committee 把一件事提交委员会(讨论)

⑨表达，表述；翻译：~ one's feelings in words 用言语表达感情 / to ~ it bluntly (more concretely) [用作插入语]直率地(更具体地)说来 / You have ~ the case clearly. 你把情况讲清楚了。/ What a way you have of putting things! 瞧你这人的那种表达方式！/ ~ an article into English 把一篇文章译成英语

⑩使从事；把…用于；使受到 (to)：~ oneself to the study of medicine 开始学医 / ~ sb. to processing the data 指派某人分析数据 / ~ sb.'s mind to a problem 开始思考问题 / ~ sb. to trial (shame) 使某人受到考验(耻辱)

⑪驱使，迫使，促使：~ one's horse over (或 at) a fence 纵马跳过篱笆 / be ~ to flight (one's trumps) 被迫逃跑(打出王牌)

⑫估计：I ~ the capacity of the generator at 100,000 kilowatts. 我估计这部发电机的发电量为十万瓩。/ He ~ the time of the accident as about a quarter to two. 他估计出事的时间大约是一点三刻。

⑬课(税)；投(资)；下(赌注)：~ a tax on sth. 对某物课税

⑭赋予，给与，推诿 (on)：~ the proper interpretation on a clause in the agreement 对协定条款作出正确的解释 / ~ the blame on others 把罪责推给别人

⑮为…配(曲)：~ a poem to music 为一首诗谱曲

❷ vi. ①出发，走；匆忙离开

②(向…)航行：The ship ~ (off 或 out) to sea. 船出海航行。

③发芽

④流入(或流出)：The river ~s into a lake. 这条河流入一个湖。

Ⅱ n. ①(铅球等的)掷，推

②在一定期限以一定价格交售一定数量股票(或商品)的选择权；卖方的选择

Ⅲ a. 固定不动的：Stay ~ until I come back. 我回来前不要走开。

‖ be hard ~ to it 陷入困境：be hard ~ to it to find a way out 陷入困境而找不到出路 / ~ about ①(使…)转向；(使…)向后转 ②散布，宣称：He ~ it about that he would do no such thing. 他宣称不愿做这样的事。③麻烦，打扰；使烦恼：Don't ~ yourself about! 别烦恼啦！(或：你别忙啦！) / feel ~ about 感到烦恼 / ~ across ①做成，搞成(尤指用不正当手段)：~ a deal across 做成一笔交易 ②使被理解，使被接受；欺骗：~ an idea across to the public 使公

众接受一种想法 / You can't ~ that across me. 你甭想骗我相信那事。③有效地(或有力地)传达，表达：He knows how to ~ a song across. 他知道如何唱好一支歌。/ ~ apart 留开，拨出 / ~ aside ①把…放在一边；撇开：~ aside one's book 放下书 ②储存；备用：~ aside grain as collective reserves 留集体储备粮 / ~ away ①把…收起来，放好：~ away one's tools after work 工作完毕把工具收拾好 ②储存；备用 ③处理掉；抛弃；放弃(想法等) ④[俚]吃掉；喝掉 ⑤[口]把…送进监狱；把…送进疯人院 ⑥[俚]把…处死，杀掉；葬掉 ⑦[俚]当掉 ⑧[古]离弃(妻子) / ~ back ①把…放回原处 ②向后移，拨回：~ back the clock 把时钟向后拨；[喻]倒退 ③推迟；阻碍；使后退：~ back acting 推迟行动 ④(船或船员们)返航 / ~ behind one 拒绝考虑(某事) / ~ by ①把…放在…旁边：~ the dictionary by the textbook 把词典放在教科书旁边 ②储存…备用 ③把…搁在一边；回避，忽视：~ an idea (a person) by 把一个想法(一个人)搁在一边 / ~ down ①放下；拒绝：~ down airs 放下架子；~ one's foot down 把脚踏下；[喻]坚决反对；表示很坚决 ②平定；镇压；取缔：~ down a rebellion 镇压叛乱 ③使安静下来：~ down the gossip 制止流言蜚语 ④记下；写下…的姓名：~ down sb.'s address 记下某人的地址 ⑤贬低，轻蔑；羞辱；使降职 ⑥削减(开支等) ⑦贮藏(食物等) ⑧估计 (at, as)；认为 (as, for) ⑨把…归因于 (to)：~ the dispute down to some misunderstanding 把争论归因于某种误会 / ~ forth ①放出；长出(树叶等) ②发表，颁布 ③提出(理论、意见等) ④使出，用出：~ forth all one's strength 使出自己全部力量 ⑤起航 / ~ forward ①放出，拿出；提出(理论、意见等)：~ forward a suggestion (slogan, task) 提出一个建议(口号,任务) ②推举出；使突出：~ sb. forward as a candidate 推举某人为候选人 ③把(时针等)向前拨 / ~ in ①把…放进；伸进 ②提交，提出：~ in a claim for £50 damages 提出一项五十英镑赔偿费的要求 / ~ in orders for building materials 订购建筑材料 ③使就职；把…选入议会：~ in a janitor 请一个看门人 ④插入：~ in a (good) word for sb. 为某人说句好话 / ~ in a blow 打中一拳 ⑤干(一段时间的工作)；[口]度过(时间)：~ in half an hour's practice before breakfast 在早饭前练习半小时 / ~ in a hard day 大干一天 / There's an hour to ~ in before we set off. 我们还得待一小时才出发。⑥种植：~ in crops 种庄稼 ⑦进港；进入 ⑧申请 (for) / ~ inside 把…送进监狱 / ~ into ①把…放进；使进入…(状态)：~ into operation 使运转；使开动 / ~ into practice 实行…；落实…/ ~ into effect 使生效；执行 / ~ 把…翻译成…③把…(在土地上)种植 / ~ it across (或 over) sb. 责罚某人；向某人报复；责怪某人 / ~ it on [口] ①夸张地表示感情；装出重要的样子 ②(说话或行动)装腔作势

② 夸大，夸张 ③ 要高价 / ~ *it over* [美俚] ① 获得成功；获得推广 ② 欺骗，作弄 (on) / *Put it* (*right*) *there!* (讲和时或表示同意时用语)来握手吧! / ~ *it to sb.* 提出这点请某人考虑: I ~ *it to you.* 关于这一点，我吁请你判断。/ I ~ *it to you that . . . .* 我希望你会同意… / ~ *off* ① 推迟；拖延 / ~ *off* a meeting till Saturday 把会议推迟到星期六 / Don't ~ *off* until tomorrow what can be done today. 今天可以做的事情不要拖到明天去做。/ ~ *off* going to a place 延期去某处 ② 设法使…等待；推迟与…的约会；搪塞: ~ the contractor *off* for a month 设法使承包人等待一个月 / refuse to be ~ *off* with vague promises (excuses) 拒绝被空洞的诺言(借口)所搪塞 ③ 阻止, 劝阻 (from); 使打消原有意图 ④ 脱掉；去掉；扔掉: ~ *off* one's coat 脱外衣 / ~ *off* one's doubts (fears) 摆脱疑虑(惊恐) ⑤ 使分心；使从…分心；使厌恶: He's thinking things over; you must do nothing to ~ him *off*. 他正在细细考虑，你别弄得他分心。/ ~ sb. *off* his guard 使某人失去警惕 / ~ sb. *off* his meal 使某人感到吃不进饭 ⑥ 用欺骗手段卖掉；混用(假钞票等): ~ *off* a fake (on 或 upon sb.) 卖赝品(给某人) ⑦ 出航；~ *on* ① 把…放在…上 ② 穿上；戴上: They ~ *on* their safety helmets before starting to work. 他们在开始工作以前戴上安全帽。③ 装出；假装；伪称为: ~ *on* an air of innocence 装出无辜的样子 / ~ *on* airs 摆架子 ④ 增加, 添上: ~ *on* speed (pressure) 增加速度(压力) / ~ *on* weight 增加体重 / ~ *on* extra buses during the rush hours 高峰时刻加开公共汽车 ⑤ 上演(戏剧等) ⑥ 使(球员等)上场 ⑦ 拨快: ~ the clock *on* an hour 把时钟拨快一小时 ⑧ 使靠(某种饮食)维持生命: The doctor ~ him *on* a diet (bread and water). 医生要他只吃规定的饮食(只吃面包和水)。⑨ 把…施加于；把…推诿给 ⑩ 哄骗；欺骗 / ~ *out* ① 放出, 摆出；伸出；挖出(眼睛): The doctor told him to ~ *out* his tongue. 医生要他伸出舌头。/ ~ one's hand *out* 伸出手 ② 生产, 出产；出版；发布: ~ *out* 20,000 tons of steel (rice) 生产二万吨钢(大米) ③ 使出, 用上；作出努力: ~ *out* great effort 作出巨大努力 ④ 熄灭；关熄；消灭, 消除: ~ *out* a fire 熄掉炉火；扑灭火灾 / ~ *out* the light (gas) 关掉电灯(煤气) ⑤ 困扰, 使不安；使不便；激怒: He is never ~ *out* by unexpected questions. 他从不被意外的问题所窘住。be easily ~ *out* by trifles 常因小事情感到不安(或发怒) ⑥ 麻烦, 打扰: Don't ~ yourself *out* for us! 不要为我们忙吧! ⑦ 发放出: ~ *out* money at interest 放利, 放债 / ~ *out* the washing 把衣服送出去洗 ⑧ 使脱臼: He fell and ~ his shoulder *out*. 他跌得肩胛脱臼。⑨ 使(球员等)退场；把…逐出 ⑩ 出航 / ~ *over* ① 使…放在…之上 ② 使转向: ~ the wheel *over* and steer N. E. 转动舵轮使船朝东北驶行 ③ 推迟；拖延 ④[口] (尤指用不正当手段)搞成, 做成 ⑤ 使被理

解；使被接受；使受欢迎 ⑥ 航行到对面, 驶过: ~ *over* to the other side of the harbour (船)驶到港的另一面 / ~ *"paid" to* 见 *paid* / ~ sb. *next* (或 *wise*) [美俚] 使某人事先心中有数, 使某人知情: I think he'll ~ us *next* about the whole business. 我想他会把整个事情的内情告诉我们的。/ ~ *sb. on to* 引某人对…注意起来 / ~ *through* ① 使穿过 ② 使从事；使经受: ~ sb. *through* drills (a trial) 使某人受训练(考验) ③ 做成(工作等) ④(电话用语)把…接通: *Put* me *through* to the repair shop, please. 请接修理车间。/ Your call has been ~ *through*. 要的电话接通了。/ ~ *to* (船只因避风等而)靠岸 / ~ *together* ① 把…放在一起；把…加起来: You two had better ~ your heads *together*. 你们两人最好商量一下。② 使构成整体；装配: ~ *together* a dictionary 编成一部词典 / ~ one's thoughts (或 ideas) *together* 整理思路 / ~ a machine *together* 把机器装配起来 / ~ *to it* [常用被动语态]逼使, 使感困难: when one is ~ *to it* 紧要时；没有别的办法时 / ~ *under* ① 使处于…之下 ② 在(土地)上种植 / ~ *up* ① 举起, 抬起；打开(伞) / ~ *up* a flag 挂起一面旗 / *Put* your hands (或 *Put* 'em) *up*! 举起手来! / ~ *up* the signboard of 打起…的招牌(或幌子) ② 进行, 作 ③ 推举, 提名；参加竞选: ~ sb. *up* for M. P. (for a club) 提名某人竞选议员(参加俱乐部) / Are you going to ~ *up* for the borough again? 你还要做那个区的国会议员的候选人吗? ④ 提供(资金等)；悬(赏)；下(赌注) ⑤ 建造(房屋)；搭起, 张起(篷帐等) ⑥ 为…提供食宿；招待 ⑦ 住宿；得到食宿: You can ~ *up* here for the night. 你可以在这里过夜。⑧ 提高；抬价(租金等): ~ *up* productivity (prices) 提高生产率(价格) ⑨ 包装；把(食物等)装罐；贮藏: ~ the buns *up* in a bag 把圆面包装在袋里 ⑩ 配制(药品等)；配(方) ⑪ 把…搁起不用 ⑫ 把…拿出(供拍卖或竞争): ~ sth. *up* for (或 to) auction 把某物拿出拍卖 ⑬ 张贴(布告、相片等)；公布: ~ *up* a portrait 挂起一张相片 / ~ *up* an idea for criticism 谈出想法供批评 ⑭ 表现出, 显示出: ~ *up* a bluff 虚张声势 ⑮ 上演(剧本) ⑯[口]密谋…，预谋… ⑰ 把(长发)向上梳卷 ⑱ 惊起(飞禽等)；使(禽、兽等)离巢穴 ⑲[古]把(剑)插入鞘 ⑳ 提出(请愿)；作(祷告) / ~ *upon* 欺骗；使成为牺牲品: be ~ *upon* by sb. 上某人的当 / ~ *up or shut up* ①要就拿出钱来赌东道要就闭嘴 ②要就拿出行动来要就闭嘴 / ~ *up to* [口] ①唆使…做…: ~ sb. *up to* (do 或 doing) mischief 唆使某人捣乱 ②通知…(某事), 告诉…做…, 指导…做…: ~ sb. *up to* his duties 告诉某人他的职责是什么 / ~ *up with* 忍受；容忍(讨厌的人或事物等)

‖'~-*down* n. ①平定 ②贬低；贬低的话, 轻蔑的话 ③(飞机的)降落 / '~-*off* n. ①推迟 ②搪塞 / '~-*on* n. ①假装；欺骗 ②(滑稽或讽刺性的)模仿剧, 模仿作品: a ~-*on* of pretentious

films 模仿浮夸影片的戏剧 *a.* 假装的 / '~out
n. (垒球)出局 / '~-'up *a.* 用不正当手段安排
好的,预先商定的: a ~*up* job (或 thing) [俚]预
先布置的勾当;骗局,圈套 / '~upon *a.* 受虐待
的;受愚弄的;被占去便宜的

put² [pʌt] I (putted; putting) ❶ *vt.* 在平地上把
(高尔夫球)轻轻打进洞 ❷ *vi.* 击高尔夫球 II *n.*
(使高尔夫球进洞的)轻轻一击

put³ [pʌt] *n.* 笨蛋; 怪人

putrefy ['pju:trifai] *vt. & vi.* ①(使)化脓 ②(使)
腐烂,(使)腐败 ③(使)堕落

putrescent [pju:'tresnt] *a.* ① 正在腐烂(或腐败)
的 ② 正在堕落的 ③ 关于腐烂(或腐败)的

putrid ['pju:trid] *a.* ①腐烂的,腐败的: turn ~
烂掉 / ~ fish 腐烂的鱼 / ~ fever 斑疹伤寒 /
~ sore throat 坏疽性咽炎 ② 堕落的,道德败坏
的 ③[口]坏透的,极讨厌的: ~ weather 讨厌
的天气 ‖~ity [pju:'triditi] *n.* ①腐烂, 腐败
②腐烂(或腐败)的东西 ③堕落

puttee ['pʌti] *n.* (布或皮的)绑腿, 裹腿

putty ['pʌti] I *n.* ①【建】油灰, 腻子;油灰状粘性
材料: glaziers' ~ 粘玻璃(或填塞孔缝)用的油
灰 / plasterers' ~ 粉刷用的外层细料 ②(织品)
淡褐灰色至淡灰褐色之间的颜色 ③ 易于被人摆
弄的人 II *vt.* 用油灰接合(或填塞): ~ up a
hole 用油灰塞洞 ‖a ~ medal(对小功劳或小
贡献的)小奖赏(常含有讽刺意味) ‖'~-head *n.*
[美俚]蠢货 / ~ powder 氧
化锡擦粉,油灰粉(擦玻璃及金属等用)

puzzle ['pʌzl] I *n.* ①难题 ②测验智力的问题
(或玩具),谜: a Chinese ~ (七巧板、九连环等)
中国玩具; [喻]复杂难懂的事物 ③[只用单]迷

puzzle

惑,困惑: be in a ~ about the matter 对这件事
大惑不解 II ❶ *vt.* ① 使迷惑; 使为难, 使窘困:
The question ~*d* me. (或 I was ~*d* by the
question.) 这个问题把我难住了。/ I am ~*ed*
what to do. 我不知道怎样做才好。~ one's
brains *about* (或 *over*) sth. 为某事大伤脑筋 ②
思索而得 (*out*): ~ *out* the meaning of a sentence

推敲出句中的涵义 ③冥思苦想地进行: ~ one's
way *through* geometry 费一番苦工夫搞通几何学
❷ *vi.* ①迷惑 ②苦思: ~ *over* a question 为解
决问题而苦思 ‖~dom *n.* 为难,困境 / ~ment
n. 困惑,苦思 / ~r *n.* 使人为难的人(或物),难
题 ‖'~,headed, '~,pated *a.* 思想混乱的 /
'~-peg *n.* [英]装在狗的下巴上的木片(使其鼻
不能着地)

pygmy ['pigmi] I *n.* ① [P-] (分布在中非、东南亚
和大洋洲一带的身体矮小的)俾格米人 ②矮人;
侏儒 ③[喻]智力低的人;微不足道的东西(或人)
④小仙人,小精灵 II *a.* ① [P-] 俾格米人的
②矮人的;矮小的 ③ 微少的,微薄的;无足轻重
的: one's ~ effort 微力,绵薄

pyjama [pə'dʒɑ:mə] *n.* ①[常用复](宽大的)睡衣
裤: a suit of ~*s* 一套睡衣裤 / a ~ coat 睡衣 /
~ trousers 睡裤 ②[复](印度和巴基斯坦的伊斯
兰教徒穿的)宽松裤 ‖*the cat's* ~*s* [俚]正对头;
妙极了

pylon ['pailən] *n.* ① 塔门,两旁有塔形建筑的门道
②(飞机场等的)路标塔,标杆;架高压电缆的铁塔
③(机身下悬挂副油箱或炸弹等的)吊架

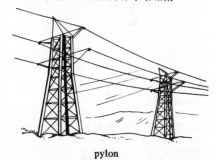

pylon

pyramid ['pirəmid] I *n.* ① (古代埃及的)金字塔
②【数】棱锥(体),角锥(体) ③角锥状物;角锥形的
一堆东西; 长成(或剪成)角锥形的树 ④宝塔诗;
倒宝塔诗 ⑤金字塔现象(指基础广阔,越到上面
越狭窄) ❶ *vi.* ①成尖塔(或角锥)形;聚成一
堆 ②(为了积累利润而)连续投机 ③(步步)升级,
(节节)增加 ❷ *vt.* ①使成尖塔形,使成角锥形;
使成堆 ②(为了积累利润而)使用(或经营) ③使
步步升级, 使节节增加: ~ arguments upon
a hypothesis 给假设添上许多论据 ‖~al
[pi'ræmidl] *a.* =~ic(al) / ~ bone【解】锥骨(即腕的楔
骨) =~al bone) / ~ic(al) [,pirə'midik(əb] *a.*
金字塔的; 角锥体的; 金字塔形的, 角锥状的 /
~ist, ~alist [pi'ræmidəlist] *n.* 对埃及金字塔抱
神秘观点者; 埃及金字塔的结构和历史的研究者

pyre ['paiə] *n.* 供燃烧的大堆木料;火葬用的柴堆

python ['paiθən] *n.* ①【希神】阿波罗神所杀死的巨
蛇 ②大蟒(尤指蚺蛇属的) ③ 巫;预言者 ‖~ess
['paiθenes] *n.* (阿波罗神的)女预言者; 女巫 /
~ic [pai'θɔnik] *a.* ① 预言的 ②大蟒似的

Q

quack¹ [kwæk] **I** *vi.* ①(鸭子)嘎嘎地叫 ②大声闲聊;发吵闹声 **II** *n.* ①鸭子的叫声 ②嘈杂声 ‖~-'~ *n.* [儿语] 鸭子

quack² [kwæk] **I** *n.* ①庸医,江湖医生 ②冒充内行的人,骗子 **II** *a.* ①庸医的;冒充内行医病的: a ~ doctor 庸医,江湖郎中 ②冒充内行者所用(或卖)的;骗人的,骗子用的;胡吹的: ~ remedies 骗人的药 / a ~ politician 胡吹的政客 **III** ❶ *vi.* ①用骗术行医 ②胡吹 ❷ *vt.* ①卖(假药) ②胡吹,(用广告等)吹嘘

quadrangle ['kwɔ,dræŋgl] *n.* ①四角形,四边形(尤指正方形和长方形): ~ roof 【建】方形屋顶 ②(有建筑物围着的)四方院子;围着四方院子的建筑物 ③(美国国家地质测量机构颁布的)标准地形图上的一方格(通常为南北十七英里,东西十一至十五英里)

quadrangular [kwɔ'dræŋgjulə] *a.* 四角形的,四边形的 ‖~ly *ad.*

quadrant ['kwɔdrənt] *n.* ①四分之一圆周,九十度弧;四分之一圆 ②扇形体 ③【天】【海】象限仪 ④【数】象限 ‖~ *elevation* 【军】仰角;水平射角 / *radio navigation* ~ 【空】无线电导航区 ‖~al [kwɔ'dræntl] *a.*

quadrilateral [ˌkwɔdri'lætərəl] **I** *a.* ①四边的,四边形的 ②四方面的 **II** *n.* ①四边形 ②四边形物;周围有四座堡垒防御的地区

quadruped ['kwɔdruped] **I** *n.* 四足动物(尤指哺乳动物) **II** *a.* 有四足的;四足动物的

quadruple ['kwɔdrupl] **I** *a.* ①四倍的: a height ~ (或 ~ of, ~ to) that of the tree 四倍于这棵树的高度 ②四重的;由四部分组成的: a ~ alliance 四国联盟 ③【音】四节拍的: ~ time (或 measure) 四拍子 **II** *ad.* 四倍地 **III** *n.* 四倍,四倍量 **IV** *vt. & vi.* (使)成四倍;以四乘

quadruplet ['kwɔdruplit] *n.* ①[复]一胎生的四个孩子,四胞胎 ②四胞胎中的一个孩子 ③成套的四件东西 ④四人同乘的自行车

quaff [kwɑːf] **I** *vt. & vi.* 大口地喝(或吞);痛饮,畅饮 **II** *n.* 大口的喝(或吞);畅饮;一饮而尽的酒

quagmire ['kwægmaiə] *n.* ①沼泽地;泥潭,泥坑 ②(难以解脱的)困境: be bogged down in a ~ 陷入困境

quail¹ [kweil] ([复] quail(s)) *n.* ①【动】鹑,鹌鹑: a ~ pipe (引诱鹑的)鹑笛 / a ~ call 鹑鸣;鹑笛声 ②[美俚]漂亮姑娘,青年女子 ‖'~-'roost *n.* [美俚] (大学)女宿舍

quail² [kweil] ❶ *vi.* 胆怯,畏缩 (*at, before, to*):

He (或 His courage) never ~s *before* difficulties. 在困难面前,他从不丧失勇气。 ❷ *vt.* [古]使胆怯;威吓

quaint [kweint] *a.* ①离奇的,古怪的;富有奇趣的;古雅的: a ~ notion 一个怪念头 / a ~ old-fashioned dress 希奇古怪的老式衣服 ②(工艺、设计等)灵巧的,精致的 ③(仪态等)英俊的,漂亮的;(语言等)优雅的 ‖~ly *ad.* / ~ness *n.*

quake [kweik] **I** *vi.* ①震动;颤动 ②颤抖,发抖 (*with, for*): ~ *with* cold (fear) 冷(怕)得发抖 **II** *n.* 震动;颤抖;[口]地震: a ~ looter 乘地震抢劫者 ‖quakingly *ad.* ‖quaking aspen 【植】颤杨

Quaker ['kweikə] *n.* ①(基督教的一个教派)贵格会教徒,公谊会教徒,教友派教徒 ②[q-]发抖的人;震动的东西 ‖~ism ['kweikərizəm] *n.* 贵格会(或公谊会、教友派)教义 ‖~ gun (木制)炮 / ~ meeting ①贵格会教徒的祈祷会(会上常保持长时间的静默) ②[喻]有许多沉默时刻的会议(或集会)

qualification [ˌkwɔlifi'keiʃən] *n.* ①资格,合格性;合格证明: a teacher's ~s (通过训练与考试而获得的)教师的资格 / political and physical ~s for a pilot 一个飞行员应具有的政治上和体质上的条件 / a ~ test 合格考试 ②限制条件;限定: be hedged with ~s 受着种种条件限制 / accept sb.'s statement without ~ (with certain ~s) 毫无保留地(有些保留地)接受某人的声明 ③称作,认作: The ~ of such a course of action as conservative is too mild. 把这种行动方针称作保守是太轻了。

qualify ['kwɔlifai] ❶ *vt.* ①使具有资格,使合格: His selfless spirit *qualifies* him *for* the task. 他的无私的精神使他适合担当这个任务。 / be *qualified as* a doctor 有资格当医生 / be *qualified* to do (或 *for* doing) the work 能胜任这件工作 ②限制,限定;【语】修饰,限定 ③把…称作;形容,描述: ~ a proposal *as* practical 认为建议是切实可行的 ④证明…合格: This certificate *qualifies* the product. 这份证书证明产品是合格的。 ⑤授法权予,准予: ~ a jury 授陪审团以法权 ⑥缓和,减轻: ~ sb.'s anger 减轻某人的怒气 ⑦改变(液体)的浓度(或风味): ~ spirits with water 在酒中掺水 ❷ *vi.* 取得资格;具备合格条件: ~ *as* a typist 够格做打字员 / ~ *for* the vote (依法)取得选举权

qualitative ['kwɔlitətiv] *a.* ①质的,质量的;性质上的: a ~ change 质变 / ~ sound changes 音质

的变化　②定性的: ～ analysis【化】定性分析 ||～ly *ad.*

quality ['kwɔliti] **I** *n.* ①质,质量: a change in ～ 质变 / good (high, poor) ～ 好(高, 差)质量 / control 质量控制 / Without quantity there can be no ～. 没有数量也就没有质量。/ enhance the military ～ of our armed forces 加强我军军事素质 ②优质: products of ～ 优质产品 / have ～ 质量好 ③品质,特性: keep the fine *qualities* of the working people 保持劳动人民的优良品质 / One ～ of this material is that it can endure much stress. 这材料的一个特性就是能承受很大的应力。 ||to produce quality in five *qualities* 生产五样品种的货物 ⑤身分,地位: advise sb. in the ～ of a friend 以朋友的身分劝告某人 ⑥才能,本领: give a taste of one's ～ 显本领 ⑦音质,音色 ⑧(色泽的)鲜明(性) ⑨【逻】(命题的)性质(指肯定的或否定的) ⑩[古][俗]社会地位; 高的地位; 贵族: a man of ～ 地位高的人 ||*flying* ～ 飞行性能; 飞行数据 / ～ *of reproduction*【物】保真度 **II** *a.* ①优质的, 高级的: ～ leather 优质皮革 ②上流社会的, 贵族化的 ||*have the defects of one's qualities* 见 **defect**

qualm [kwɔ:m] *n.* ①一阵眩晕;一阵恶心: ～s of seasickness 一阵阵的晕船 ②疑惑,不安(尤指对所做的事是否正当的疑虑): feel no ～s about one's actions 对自己的行为问心无愧 ||*～ish a.* 有点发晕的;有点疑虑不安的

quandary ['kwɔndəri] *n.* 窘境;犹豫不定: be in a ～ (*about* 或 *as to*) (对…)左右为难

quantitative ['kwɔntitətiv] *a.* ①量的,数量的: ～ change 量变 / ～ inheritance【生】数量遗传 ②定量的: ～ analysis【化】定量分析 ③【语】音量的(尤指诗歌的音节等) ||*～ly ad.*

quantity ['kwɔntiti] *n.* ①量,数量;分量: a great ～ 大量 / a small ～ of water 少量的水 / a large ～ of flowers 许多花 / Without ～ there can be no quality. 没有数量也就没有质量。/ a rapid increase in ～ 数量上的迅速增长 / What ～ do you want? 你要多少? / ～ of heat【物】热量 ②[常用复]大量,大宗: have *quantities* (或 a ～) of water pipes 有大批的水管 / buy cotton *in* ～ (或 *in large quantities*) 大量购买棉花 ③【语】(元音,音节等的)音量 ④【逻】(命题的)量 ⑤【数】量 ||*a negligible* ～ ①【数】可忽略的量 ②无足轻重的人;可忽略的因素 / *an unknown* ～ ①未知量 ②难以预测的人(或事) ||～ **mark**【语】(标于元音之上的)音量符号 / ～ **surveyor** [英]【建】估算师

quarantine ['kwɔrənti:n] **I** *n.* ①(对港口船舶等的)检疫,留验;检疫处;检疫期: be put *under* ～ (或 be *in* ～) 被隔离检疫 / be *out of* ～ 被撤销留验 / a ～ flag (被检疫的船上挂的)黄色检疫旗 ②(因传染流行而对人、畜等的)隔离; 隔离区 ③四十天 **II** *vt.* ①对…进行检疫 ②(在政治等方面)隔离,使孤立

quarrel[1] ['kwɔrəl] *n.* ①(古代用的)方镞箭 ②(窗格上小块的)方形(或菱形)玻璃板 ③方头的东西(如石工用的方头凿)

quarrel[2] ['kwɔrəl] **I** *n.* ①争吵,吵架;吵闹;不和: have a ～ *with* sb. *about* sth. 就某事跟某人争吵 / make up a ～ (争吵后)言归于好 ②争吵的原因;怨言,责备: That is part of my ～ *with* (或 *against*) them. 那是我与他们争吵的部分原因。 **II** (quarrel(l)ed; quarrel(l)ing) *vi.* ①争吵,吵架; 不和: ～ *with* sb. 与某人吵架 / They *quarrel(l)ed among* themselves. 他们相互吵架。 ②责备;埋怨;挑剔 (*with*): ～ *with* Providence 埋怨上帝; 怨天怨地 ||*Bad workmen ～ with their tools.* (或 *An ill workman ～s with his tools.*) 见 **workman** / *fight one's ～s for sb.* 帮某人争吵 (为了主持公道或帮某人取得赔偿等) / *find ～ in a straw* 吹毛求疵,找碴儿 / *in a good* ～ 争吵得有理 / *pick* (或 *seek*) *a* ～ 寻衅 / ～ *with one's bread and butter* 见 **bread** / *take up* (或 *espouse*) *another's* ～ 帮别人争吵 ||**quarrel(l)er** *n.* 争吵者;吵架者

quarrelsome ['kwɔrəlsəm] *a.* 好争吵的;好争论的 ||～ly *ad.* / ～ness *n.*

quarry[1] ['kwɔri] **I** *n.* ①(采)石场,石坑,石矿 ②菱形(或方形)的玻璃片(或石、瓦等) ③消息(或资料等)的来源 **II** ❶ *vt.* ①(采石),挖掘: ～ (out) a block of marble 挖掘出一块大理石 ②(在古书等中)极力搜索(证据等),发掘 ❷ *vi.* 费力地搜寻 ||～**man** *n.* 采石工人

quarry[2] ['kwɔri] *n.* ①猎物(指鸟、兽等) ②追求物,追逐的目标

quart[1] [kwɔ:t] *n.* ①夸脱(英美干量或液量单位, =2品脱;略作 qt.) ②一夸脱的容器 ||*put a ～ into a pint pot* 用小者去容纳大者; 做不可能做到的事

quart[2] [kɑ:t] *n.* ①(击剑中的)一种防御姿势 ②(纸牌戏中的)四张同花顺子

quarter ['kwɔ:tə] **I** *n.* ①四分之一;四等分: a ～ (of a) *li* 四分之一里 / three ～s of a *li* 四分之三里 / the first ～ of this century 本世纪的最初二十五年 / divide sth. into ～s 把某物四等分 / buy sth. for a ～ (of) the price 以四分之一的价格购买某物 ②一刻钟: a ～ to (past) three 三点差(过)一刻 / Some clocks strike the ～s. 有些钟每一刻钟报时一次。/ It has gone the ～. 一刻钟已敲过。 ③季度;付款的季度;按季度付的款项: pay one's rent at the end of each ～ 每一季度末付房租 ④(每学年分为四学期制度中的)一学期 ⑤(美国、加拿大的)两角五分钱;两角五分的辅币 ⑥四分之一英担(英国为 28 磅, 美国为 25 磅) ⑦四分之一码;四分之一哩 ⑧四分之一呎: a ～ five $5\frac{1}{4}$ 呎 / a ～ less five $4\frac{3}{4}$ 呎 ⑨(计量谷物等的容量单位)八蒲式耳 (=$\frac{1}{4}$ 吨) ⑩包括整条腿的大块肉: a ～ of beef 包括整条腿的大块牛肉

⑪[常用复](活的四肢动物的)一肢;臀腰部: fore (hind) ~s 前(后)半身
⑫(受刑者被肢解后的)四分之一尸体
⑬(罗盘针)方位,方角
⑭(罗盘上)四个主要点中的一点;(罗盘上三十二点中任何两点之间距离的)四分之一;象限
⑮方向;地区;方面: What ~ is the wind in? 风向如何?/(或:事情的动向怎样?)/ flock in from all ~s 从四面八方汇集 / the ~s concerned 有关方面 / have the news from a good ~ 消息得自可靠来源
⑯(城市中的)地区;一区中的居民: an industrial (a residential) ~ 工业(住宅)区 / the Jewish ~ 犹太居民区
⑰[复]住处;【军】营房: find ~s at a hotel 在旅馆里找到住处 / Take up your ~s with us. 跟我们住在一起吧。/ winter ~s 冬季营房(或住房)
⑱[常用复](船员或水兵的)岗位;[复](船员的)集合: battle ~s (水兵等的)战斗岗位
⑲船(舷)的后部: on the port (starboard) ~ 在船的左舷(右舷)后部 / the ~ ladder 船尾楼梯
⑳(鞋帮等的)后侧部
㉑月球公转的四分之一;弦: the moon at the first (in its last) ~ 上(下)弦月
㉒(橄榄球赛等的)四分之一场
㉓(机器零件的)相互垂直
㉔(纹章中的)盾形的四分之一
㉕(对投降者的)生命保障,(对敌人的)宽恕: give ~ 饶命,饶命 / receive ~ 得到饶恕
㉖四分之一哩的赛跑: win the ~ [口]在四分之一哩赛跑中获胜
Ⅱ ❶ vt. ①把…分为四部分;把…四等分
②供…住宿;使(部队)驻扎: ~ troops on the villagers 安置军队于村民家中
③(猎犬等)到处来回搜索(某地区)
④[古]把(受刑者)肢解为四部分
⑤(机器中)使(曲柄等)与机器连结部分成直角
⑥将(纹章)置于四分之一的盾面上;将(别家的纹章)置于自家的分成四份的盾面上;纵横划分(盾面)为四部分
❷ vi. ①住宿;驻扎 (at, with)
②(猎犬)到处来回搜索
③【海】(风)向船后侧吹来
‖a bad ~ of an hour 不愉快的短暂时刻 / at close ~s 逼近地,接近地 / beat up the ~s of 拜访… / close ~s 狭隘的住所 / cry (或 ask for) ~ 请求饶命 / not a ~ 远不是,远不象: not a ~ as good as it should be 远不及本来应该那样的好 / on the ~ 【海】在船尾部 / take up one's ~s ①住下来 ②(水兵)进入岗位
‖~age ['kwɔːtəridʒ] n. ①按季收付的款项;季度工资;季度税;季度津贴 ②供给军队的住处 ③供给住宿 ④住宿费用
‖~back n. ①(橄榄球赛中指挥反攻的)四分卫 ②四分卫所站的位置 vt. ①指挥(橄榄球队)进攻 ②对…发号施令;操纵 vi. 担任四分卫 /

'~-bell n. 每一刻钟报时的钟铃 / ~ bill (海军)战斗部署表 / ~ binding (书的)皮脊装订 / ~ boards 舰尾的防波板 / ~ boat 舰尾小艇 / '~-'bound a. (书)皮脊装订的 / '~-breed n. 有四分之一异族血统的人(尤指血统四分之三为白人、四分之一为印第安人者) / crack (马的)裂蹄 / ~ day 季度的第一天;季度清帐日 / '~-deck n. ①(军官用的)后甲板 ②[英](the ~deck) [总称]海军军官舰上的军官 / '~'final a. & n. 四分之一决赛(的) / '~'finalist n. 参加四分之一决赛的运动员(或运动队) / ~ hour 一刻钟 / ~ ill 【动】气肿疽 / '~-jack n. 钟内每一刻钟报时的装置 / ~ left 【军】靠左四分之一直角 / ~ light [英](车的)边窗 / ~ line 舰船的雁行队形 / '~,master n. ①军需军官,军需主任 ②【海】(兼管信号等的)舵手,航信士官 / 'Quarter,master Corps 陆军军需兵(种) / '~,master depot 军需补给仓库 / 'Quarter,master General 陆军军需兵司令兼军需局局长 / '~,master sergeant 军需军士 / '~,master unit 军需部队 / ~ miler 参加四分之一哩赛跑者 / ~ note 【音】四分音符 / ~ plate 3¼ 时×4¼ 时的照相感光板 (或用这种感光板照的相片) / ~ right 【军】靠右四分之一直角 / '~saw vt. 把(原木)纵向锯成四块(再锯成木板) / section 约四分之一平方哩的地 (=160 英亩) / ~ sessions (英国)每季开审的地方法庭;(美国某些州的)地方法庭 / '~staff n. (英国农民古用作武器的)铁头木棍;用铁头木棍进行的战斗(或游戏) / ~ tone, ~ step 【音】四分音 / wind 【海】船尾风

quartz [kwɔːts] n. 【矿】石英: arenaceous ~ 石英砂 / milk (violet) ~ 乳(紫)石英 / smoky ~ 烟晶 / ~ clock 石英晶体钟

quasi ['kwɑːzi(ː)] conj. 即;宛如(用于说明语源,略作 qu.)

quatrain ['kwɔtrein] n. 四行诗(每节四行,韵律一般为 a b a b 或 a b b a)

quaver ['kweivə] Ⅰ ❶ vi. ①震动;颤抖 ②发颤音 ❷ vt. 用颤声唱;用颤音演奏;用颤声说 (out) Ⅱ n. ①颤音 ②【音】八分音符

quay [kiː] n. 码头,埠头 ‖age ['kiːidʒ] n. ①码头(使用)费 ②码头面积 ③[总称](一组)码头 ‖'~side n. [常作定语]码头区

quay

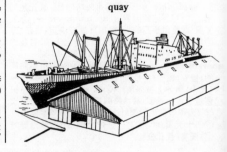

queasy, queazy ['kwi:zi] *a.* ①不稳的,动荡不定的: a ~ stock market 不稳定的股票市场 ②催人呕吐的,使人眩晕的; (人)要呕吐的;易呕吐的: the ~ motion of the waves 使人眩晕欲呕的波浪的起伏 ③使人不自在的;局促不安的,不舒服的: become ~ at the sight of sb. 一见某人就感到不自在 ④脆弱的,动辄要烦恼的;谨小慎微的;挑剔的 ‖**queasily** *ad.* / **queasiness** *n.*

queen [kwi:n] **I** *n.* ①王后(也称 ~ consort);酋长夫人: a ~ dowager 太后(已故君主之妻) / a ~ mother 太后(在位君主之母) / a ~ regent 摄政(或执政)的王后 / a ~ regnant 执政的王后 ②女王;女酋长;女首脑: Queen Victoria (英国)维多利亚女王 ③(权力、地位、相貌等)出众的女人;(资本主义社会中)"美女比赛"的第一名 ④女神 ⑤心爱的女子(指妻子、女儿等) ⑥〔喻〕出类拔萃的事物;胜地: the ~ of roses 玫瑰之王 / the ~ of summer resorts 避暑胜地 ⑦(蜜蜂、蚂蚁等)的女王 ⑧(纸牌中的)王后, Q; (国际象棋中)的王后: sacrifice the knights in order to save the ~ 〔喻〕丢车保帅 / ~'s bishop (knight) (国际象棋中)与王后同列配置的象(马) ⑨雌猫 ⑩〔俚〕乱搞同性性关系的男子 ‖Queen's Bench 英国高等法院 / Queen's colour 英军的国旗(或军旗) / Queen's Counsel 英国王室法律顾问 / Queen's English (英国"上流社会"所谓的)标准英语 / ~'s weather 庆典时的晴朗天气〔注意:以上五例用于英国 queen 当政时,如为 king 当政则相应用 King's 或 king's〕 **II** *vt.* ①立…为女王(或王后) ②使成为电影界(或交际界等)的王后 ③(国际象棋中)使(卒子)成为王后(指将卒子攻至敌方底线以取得纵、横、斜自由行走的资格) ❷ *vi.* ①做女王;象女王般行事: ~ it over (或 among) the girls 在女孩子中称大王 ②(国际象棋中)成为王后 ‖a ~ of hearts 美人 / Queen Anne is dead. 早知道了。(指消息已过时) / the Queen of grace 【基督教】圣母玛利亚 / the Queen of heaven 朱诺 (神话中的天后) / the Queen of love 维纳斯 (神话中的爱神) / the Queen of night 狄安娜 (神话中司狩猎的女神;月神) / the ~ of the Adriatic 亚德里亚海之王(指意大利港市威尼斯) / the Queen of May 五月女王(指五月一日花魁日的游戏中被选中做女王的女子) / the ~ of the meadows 【植】绣线菊 / the ~ of the seas 海上霸王(旧时英帝国的别称) / to the ~'s taste 见 taste ‖~dom *n.* ①女王统治的王国 ②女王(或王后)的地位(或身分) / ~hood, ~ship 女王(或王后)的地位(或身分) / ~less *a.* 无女王(或王后)的 / ~like *a.* =queenly (*a.*) ‖~ bee ①蜂王 ②社交界女王 / '~cake *n.* 心形的葡萄干小软饼 / ~ post 【建】双柱架 / '~-size *a.* 大号的,仅次于特大号的 / '~sware, '~'s-ware *n.* 〔总称〕(英国的)奶油色陶器

queer [kwiə] **I** *a.* ①奇怪的,古怪的;神经不很正常的: speak in a ~ way 怪腔怪调地说 / That's ~ indeed! 真奇怪! / What a ~ fellow (或

fish 或 card)! 真是个怪人! ②〔口〕可疑的: a ~ character 可疑人物 / There's something ~ about him. 他有些可疑之处。③眩晕的;不舒服的;想呕吐的: feel ~ 感到头晕;觉得不舒服 ④ 对…着了迷的 (for, on, about) ⑤〔俚〕假的,伪的;无价值的: ~ money 伪币 ⑥〔俚〕搞同性性关系的 ⑦〔英俚〕喝醉的 **II** *ad.* =~ly **III** *vt.* ①把…弄糟,破坏: ~ sb.'s plans 破坏某人的计划 ②使陷于不利地位(或窘境) **IV** *n.* 〔俚〕①〔the ~〕伪造的货币: pass the ~ 使用伪币 ②搞同性性关系的男子 ‖~ sb.'s pitch (或 ~ the pitch for sb.) 见 pitch[2] ‖~ish ['kwiəriʃ] *a.* 有点古怪的;有些可疑的;有些不舒服的 / ~ly *ad.* 奇怪地,古怪地;可疑地;眩晕地 / ~ness *n.* ‖Queer Street 窘境,困境(尤指经济方面)

quell [kwel] **I** *vt.* ①镇压;平息 ②消除;减轻: ~ fears 消除恐惧 **II** *n.* 〔古〕屠杀 ‖~er *n.* 镇压者;平息者

quench [kwentʃ] ❶ *vt.* ①熄灭,扑灭: ~ a fire 灭火 / ~ a lamp 熄灯 / ~ sb.'s hope 断绝某人的希望 ②压制,抑制;解(渴): ~ one's desire 遏制欲望 / ~ one's thirst 止渴 ③〔俚〕迫使(反对者)住嘴 ④【冶】把…淬火,使骤冷;使淬硬;【物】猝熄: ~ steel 淬钢 ❷ *vi.* ①熄灭;冷却 ②平静下来;平息: The talking ~ed. 谈话停止了。‖~able *a.* 可熄灭的;可冷却的;可压制的 / ~er *n.* ①扑(或熄)灭者;扑灭物,熄灭器;【物】猝灭剂 ②压制者 ③〔俚〕饮料 / ~less *a.* 不(可)熄灭的;不(可)冷却的;不(可)被压制的

querulous ['kweruləs] *a.* 爱发牢骚的;抱怨的;易怒的 ‖~ly *ad.* / ~ness *n.*

query ['kwiəri] **I** *n.* ①质问;询问;疑问,怀疑: suppress *queries* 压制质问 / raise a ~ 提出质问(或疑问) ②〔引导问句,或用作插入语〕略作qu.: 请问: *Query*, when did I ever say so? 请问我几时这么说过? ③疑问号(画于校样、文件等的边上,表示怀疑) **II** ❶ *vt.* ①询问;质问: ~ a witness 讯问证人 ②作为问题提出: ~ the matter to one's superiors 把这件事作为问题向上级提出 ③对…表示怀疑: I ~ whether his word can be relied on. 我怀疑他的诺言是否靠得住。④画疑问号于 ❷ *vi.* 询问;表示怀疑

quest [kwest] **I** *n.* ①寻找,追求;探索: the ~ for scientific laws 科学规律的探索 ②调查 ③验尸陪审团;〔英〕〔古〕验尸官: a coroner's (或〔俗〕crowner's) ~ 验尸官的验尸 ④(中世纪骑士的)探求(物) **II** ❶ *vi.* ①(狗等)跟踪搜寻;吠叫: ~ about for game 到处寻找猎物 ②追求;探索: ~ eagerly for improvements 力求改进 ❷ *vt.* ①寻找;探索 ②要求

question ['kwestʃən] **I** *n.* ①发问,询问: ask sb. a ~ (或 ask a ~ of sb.) 向某人提一个问题 / ~s and answers 问与答 ②问题;议题: a boundary (racial) ~ 边界(种族)问题 / a ~ of principle 原则问题 / a cardinal ~ of right and wrong 大是大非的问题 / It's only a ~ of time. 这只是时

间问题。③疑问,不确定: There is no ~ about his honesty. 他的诚实是毫无疑问的。④【语】疑问句: a direct (an indirect) ~ 直接(间接)疑问句 / a special (an alternative) ~ 特殊(选择)疑问句 ⑤(法庭上的)争端;(大会上的)争论点(或议题) ⑥(对问题的)投票表决;付表决的问题 ⑦审问;[古]拷问: put sb. *to the* ~ 拷问某人 ⑧可能性,机会: no ~ of escape 没有逃走的可能 II **❶ vt.** ①询问;讯问;审问: ~ sb. *on* his views 询问某人的看法 / ~ a witness 讯问证人 ②怀疑,对…表示疑问: ~ the accuracy (importance) of ... 对…的精确性(重要性)表示怀疑 / It cannot be ~*ed but* (或 *that, but that*) the new method is superior to the old one. 新方法比旧方法好,这是毫无疑义的。③争论 ④分析;探究 **❷ vi.** 询问;探究: a ~*ing* mind 好问的精神 ‖*an open* ~ 未解决的问题;容许争论的问题 / *a rhetorical* ~ 反诘句(Who doesn't know? 谁不知道呢? =Everybody knows.) / *a sixty-four dollar* ~ 最后的也是最难解答的问题;最重要的问题 / *beg the* ~ 用未经证明的假定来辩论 / *beside the* ~ 和本题无关;离题 / *beyond (all)* ~ 毫无疑问;无可争辩 / *call in* ~ ①对…表示怀疑: *call* sb.'s honesty *in* ~ 对某人是否诚实表示怀疑 ②对…表示异议 ③要求…的证据 / *come into* ~ 被讨论;成为有实际重要性 / *in* ~ ①正被谈论的: the book *in* ~ 该书 ②可怀疑;被争论;成问题 / *make no* ~ *of* 对…不加怀疑;承认 / *out of* ~ [罕]毫无疑问 / *out of the* ~ 不可能的,办不到的;不必谈的 / *past* ~ 无疑地 / *pop the* ~ [俚]求婚 / *put a* ~ *to sb.* 向某人提问题 / *put the* ~ 要求投票决定;提付表决 / **Question!** ①(在集会上对发言人发出的喊声)别扯到题外去! ②(对发言的真实性有怀疑时)有疑问! / *sleep on* (或 *upon, over*) *a* ~ 把问题留到第二天解决 / *That is not the* ~. 那不是我们讨论的问题。(或:那是题外的话。) / *there is no* ~ (*but*) *that* … 是毫无疑问的 / *there is no* ~ *of* ① …是毫无疑问的: There is no ~ *of* his veracity. 他说话诚实,那是毫无疑问的。②…是不可能的;…是未经提出讨论过的: There is no ~ *of* our leaving on such a rainy day. 这样的雨天我们才不会动身呢。/ There was no ~ *of* his being asked to become a member. 请他作成员这事没有提出来讨论过。/ *to the* ~ 针对所讨论的题目;对题 / *without* ~ 毫无疑问 ‖~*er n.* 询问者;讯问者;审问者 / ~*less a.* ①不发问的;不发疑问的 ②无疑的 *ad.* 无疑地 ‖~*mark* 问号(often) / '~-,**master** *n.* (广播或电视争中)答问节目的主持人 / ~ *time* (英国议会中)议员可对大臣提问题的一段时间

questionable ['kwestʃənəbl] *a.* 可疑的;(品德等)有问题的;不可靠的: a ~ person 可疑的人 / a ~ conduct 可疑的行为 / a ~ statement 不可靠的陈述 ‖**questionably** *ad.*

question(n)aire [,kwestiə'nɛə, ,kwestʃə'nɛə] *n.* [法]①调查情况用的一组问题,问题单 ②调查

表,征求意见表 ③用调查表进行的调查

quetzal [ket'sɑ:l] ([复] quetzals 或 quetzales [ket'sɑ:leis]) *n.* ①中美产的一种毛色鲜艳的鸟 ②格查尔(危地马拉货币单位)

queue [kju:] I *n.* ①辫子 ②(人或车辆等的)行列,长队: a movie ~ 排队买电影票的行列 / form a ~ 排队 / join a ~ 参加长列队伍 / stand in a ~ 排队等候 / a ~ of cars held up by the traffic lights 被交通指挥灯拦住的一长列汽车 II (queue(e)ing) **❶** *vt.* 把(发)梳成辫子 **❷** *vi.* (成长)队;排队等候 (*up*): ~ *up* for a bus 排队等候公共汽车 ‖*jump the* ~ ①不按次序排队;插队 ②企图抢先获得某物;获得优惠待遇

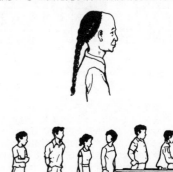

queue

quibble ['kwibl] I *n.* ①遁辞,诡辩;支吾: use ~*s* in a dispute 在争论中用遁词(或诡辩) ②吹毛求疵的意见 ③[古]双关语 II **❶** *vi.* ①使用遁辞;诡辩;争辩琐屑的事(或小的分歧) (*over*) ②吹毛求疵,找碴子 ③[古]说双关语,用双关语 **❷** *vt.* 对…进行诡辩 ‖~*r n.* 诡辩者 / **quibbling** *n.* ①诡辩 ②吹毛求疵,找碴子 *a.* 吹毛求疵的,挑剔的

quick [kwik] I *a.* ①快的,迅速的,急速的: Be ~! 快点! / come in ~ succession 迅速地接连而来 / do a ~ mile 急速地行过一哩路 / a ~ one (或 drink) 匆匆一口喝下的酒 / a ~ profit 暴利 ②敏捷的,灵巧的;灵敏的,伶俐的: be ~ *of* sight 眼睛尖 / be ~ *of* apprehension 理解力强 / be ~ *at* figures 能很快地计算数字 / be ~ *to* learn new things 新事物学得快 / He has a ~ ear *for* any sound of a defective mechanism. 他的耳朵很灵敏,机械装置有了毛病就能听出来。/ a ~ hand *at* …方面的快手 / a ~ child 伶俐的孩子 / a ~ mind 敏慧 / ~ wits 机智,急智 ③性急的;易怒的: have a ~ temper 性子暴躁 ④活泼的;活跃的;[古](溪水等)流动的 ⑤急

剧的: a ~ turn in the road 路上的急转弯 ⑥[古]怀孕达到胎动期的: be ~ with child (或 with ~ child) (孕妇)感觉到胎动 ⑦[古]活的: the ~ and the dead 生者和死者 ⑧[古]灼热的,(烧得)发光的: the ~ flames 红通通的火焰 ⑨ =~set (a.) II ad. [用在口语中或复合词中]快: Run as ~ as you can. 你要尽快地跑。/ ~-hardening cement【建】快硬水泥 III n. ①(皮肤下,尤指指甲下的)活肉;伤口的嫩皮;感觉敏锐的部位;感情的中枢 ②要点,本质;核心: the ~ of the matter 事情的实质 ③ = ~set (n.) ④ =quickie (n.) ⑤[古]生物;真实(或现实)的事物 IV vt. & vi. [古] =quicken ‖(as) ~ as thought 极快地,一闪而过地 / be ~ in (或 on) the uptake 理解很快 / be ~ on the draw ①动不动就会很快拔出武器 ②[美俚]思想敏捷;理解很快 / to the ~ ①触到活肉: cut the fingernail to the ~ (剪指甲)剪着了指甲下的肉 ②触及痛处,触及要害: The criticism touched him to the ~. 这批评触到了他的痛处。/ sting sb. to the ~ 刺痛某人的心 ③彻头彻尾: He is a conservative to the ~. 他是个十足的保守派。‖~ly ad. / ~ness n. ‖~ assets 现钱和即可兑现的资产,速动资产 / ~ bread 快速发酵面团制成的糕饼 / '~-change a. (演员等)迅速换装而演另一角色的;(工具零件等)可迅速调换的 / '~-'eared a. 听觉灵敏的 / '~-'eyed a. 眼睛尖的 / '~-fire,'~-,firing a.【军】急射的,速射的: a ~-fire rifle 急射步枪 / '~-,firer n. 速射枪(或炮) / '~-freeze vt. 使(食物)速冻,速冻 / '~lime n. 生石灰 / '~-'lunch n. 快餐: a ~-lunch bar (或 counter) 快餐柜台 / ~ march【军】齐步行进 / ~ match【军】速燃导火索 / ~ push [美俚]容易受骗上当的人;易被击败的运动员(或运动队) / ~sand n. ①流沙(区) ②动荡的捉摸不定的事物,易使人上当(或毁灭)的事物 / '~set n. [主英]插条(尤指作树篱用的山楂);种作树篱用的树木;树篱(尤指山楂篱) a. 插树做成的: a ~set hedge [主英](尤指山楂)树篱 / '~-'sighted a. 眼睛尖的 / '~,silver n. ①水银,汞 ②(气质或心情的)易变 vt. 涂水银于 a. 水银似的;易变的 / '~-,step n. ①【军】齐步 ②轻快疾步 ②快速进行曲 / ~ study 学新东西学得很快的人 / '~-'tempered a. 性情急躁的,易怒的 / ~ time【军】齐步行进的步速(通常每分钟走一百二十步) / '~-'witted a. 机智的,机灵的,有急智的

quicken ['kwikən] ❶ vt. ①加快: ~ one's steps (或 pace) 加快步伐 ②刺激;鼓舞;使活跃: one's imagination 使想象力活跃 ③使活,使复活 ④使(曲线)更würe;使(斜坡)更陡 ❷ vi. ①加快,变快: The patient's pulse ~ed. 病人的脉搏加快了。 ② 变活跃,变生动 ③活过来,生长: The seeds ~ed in the soil. 种子在土壤中生长起来。 ④(胎)动;(孕妇)进入胎动期: watch the dawn ~ing in the east 看着东方渐渐发白 ‖~ing n.【医】胎动初觉;胎动期 a.

加快的;(使)活跃的

quid[1] [kwid] n. 含在口中咀嚼的烟草块;咀嚼物

quid[2] [kwid] ([复] quid(s)) n. [英俚]一镑

quiescent [kwai'esnt] a. ①静止的;沉寂的: a ~ area 沉寂的地区 ②(昆虫等)静止期的,休眠的 ③(尤指疾病)被遏制的;没有症状的 ‖~ly ad.

quiet ['kwaiət] I a. ①寂静的;静止的: a ~ sea 风平浪静的海洋 / The winds are ~ now. 现在风已止了。②安静的,轻声的,不出声的: Be ~! 安静些! / Ask them to keep ~. 叫他们保持安静。/ ~ footsteps 轻轻的脚步声 / Why is he so ~ all the while? 为什么他老是不说话? ③温和的;不易激动的;文静的: a ~ disposition 温和的性情 / a ~ mind 宁静的心境 / a ~ manner 文静的举止 ④朴素的;不显眼的: ~ clothes 朴素的衣服 / a ~ colour 素净的颜色 ⑤闲适的,从容的: do some ~ reading 从容地读些书 ⑥ (环境、生活方式等)单调的,无变化的 ⑦僻静的: a ~ street 僻静的街道 ⑧暗中的: keep sth. ~ 将某事保密 / harbour ~ resentment 心怀不满 / have a ~ dig at sb. 暗中刺某人一下 / a ~ dinner party 非正式的宴会 ⑩(商业)清淡的,不活跃的 II n. ①寂静;平静: in the ~ of the night 在夜阑人静时 / a period of ~ 一段平静的时期 ②安静,清静: live in ~ 过安静的生活 ③(社会、政治状况的)安定,和平: years of ~ 安定的岁月 ④ 沉着的举止 III vt. ①使静;使平静;使(争论等)平息: ~ sb.'s fears 消除某人的恐惧 ②抚慰,安慰 ❷ vi. 平静下来(down): The children soon ~ed down. 孩子们不久就静下来了。/ The storm ~ed down. 暴风雨停止了。 IV ad. 平静地 ‖at ~ 平静: grow more at ~ with oneself 变得较为安静 / on the ~ 秘密地,私下地 / ~ title 见 title ‖~ly ad. / ~ness n.

quietude ['kwaiitju:d] n. 平静,寂静;宁静

quill [kwil] I n. ①羽毛管,羽(毛)根,翮 ②羽毛管制成的东西;羽毛管状物,鹅毛笔;(弦乐器上用的)拨子;(钓鱼用的)浮标,浮子;羽毛制牙签;(芦茎制的)芦笛 ③[纺]纡管;纬管 ④(刺猬或豪猪的)刺 ⑤[药](桂皮或金鸡纳皮等的)一小卷 ⑥[机]套管轴 ⑦(炸药的)导火线 II vt. ①(用羽毛管等)刺穿;拔掉…的羽毛管 ②把(线或纱)绕在筒管上 ③在(布)上打褶裥 ④[俚]拍…马屁 ‖drive the ~ 写字,挥笔 ‖~-,coverts [复] n.【动】翮羽(翮部细毛) / '~-,driver n. 作家;抄写员;新闻记者

quilt [kwilt] I n. 被(子);被状物 II ❶ vt. ①缝(被);用垫料填塞 ②绗缝(衣服等);把(钱等)缝入两层布中 ③在多层布上缝出(花样) ④摘抄剪贴地编辑;东拼西凑地做 ⑤[主方]痛打 ❷ vi. 制被;缝被子 ‖~er n. ①缝被子的人;绗缝的人 ②(缝纫机的)绗缝附件 / '~ing n. ①被子绗缝: a ~ing bee (或 party) 女子在一起绗缝被子的联谊会 ②绗缝料子 ③(衣服)的管状褶裥

quince [kwins] n.【植】榅桲;榅桲树

quinine [kwi'ni:n, 'kwini:n; 美 'kwainain] *n.* 【药】奎宁;【化】金鸡纳碱 ‖**quinism** ['kwainizəm] *n.* 奎宁中毒,金鸡纳中毒

quintet(te) [kwin'tet] *n.* ①【音】五重唱(曲);五重奏(曲);五重唱(或五重奏)演出小组 ②五人一组;五件一套 ③男子篮球队

quip [kwip] **I** *n.* ①讽刺话,嘲弄;妙语 ②遁辞 ③奇怪行为,怪事 **II** (quipped; quipping) ❶ *vi.*

quire[1] ['kwaiə] *n.* ①一帖(四张纸对折叠成的八张);对折的一叠纸(用来钉成书等) ②(纸的)一刀(共二十四张或二十五张): buy (sell) paper *by the ~* 按刀购买(卖)纸 ‖*in ~s* ①(书本)未装订成册的 ②按(纸张的)刀数

quit [kwit] **I** (quitted 或 quit; quitting) ❶ *vt.* ①离开;退出;放弃(思想、行动、职业等): ~ office 离职 / ~ school 退学 / sb. in anger 怒然离开某人 / ~ hold of 撒手放开… ②解除,免除: ~ oneself of fear 消除恐惧 ③偿清(债务等);报答: ~ love with hate 思将仇报 ④ [~ oneself] 使行动,表现: They quitted themselves like heroes. 他们表现得很英勇。/ Quit you like men. [古] 行动要象男子汉。⑤[美]停止: ~ work 停止工作 / Quit muttering! 别嘀咕! / Quit your nonsense! 别胡说! / Quit it out! 住嘴! (或: 住手!) ❷ *vi.* ①离开;搬出,迁出: give sb. notice to ~ 通知某人离职(或迁出)②停止,停下来;放弃斗争,认输 ③[口]辞职 **II** *a.* [只作表语]摆脱了…的,自由的: be ~ of sb. (the trouble) 摆脱了某人(麻烦) / get ~ of one's debts 了清债务 **III** *n.* ①离开;退出: a fighter with little ~ in him 不会退却的战士 ②退职;辞职

quite [kwait] *ad.* ①完全,十分,彻底: Quite right. 完全对。/ It's (或 That's) ~ all right. 没关系! (对别人道歉的回答) / You are ~ mistaken. 你完全弄错了。/ The baby has ~ recovered. 婴儿已完全恢复健康。/ not ~ proper 不十分妥当(或正当) / That's ~ another story. 那完全是一回事。②相当,颇;或多或少: He is ~ a good player. 他是一个相当不错的球员。/ We spent ~ a long time rehearsing the play. 我们花了相当长的时间排练这出戏。/ be ~ ill 病得相当重 ③的确,真正: Quite a man! 真是个男子汉! ‖*He isn't ~.* [英口]他不大象个绅士(或正人君子)。(=He isn't ~ a gentleman.) / ~ *a few* 见 few / *Quite* (*so*)! 正是这样! 不错! / ~ *the thing* 见 thing[1]

quits [kwits] *a.* [只作表语](因报复或偿清而)抵销的;对等的;不分胜负的: We are now ~. 现在我们两相抵销了。(或: 现在我们谁也没有对不起谁。) ‖*be ~ with* 向…报复 / *call it ~* (暂时)停做某事;停止争吵(或搏斗等) / *cry ~* 承认彼此不相上下;同意不再争(或吵)下去

quiver[1] ['kwivə] **I** ❶ *vi.* (轻微地)颤动,抖动: ~ing leaves 颤动的树叶 / ~ with cold 冷得发抖 ❷ *vt.* 使颤动;(鸟等,尤指云雀)抖动(翅膀) **II** *n.* ①颤动,抖动;颤声 ②一闪: a ~ of light-

ning 电光的一闪 ‖~ing ['kwivəriŋ] *a.* 颤动的,抖动的

quiver[2] ['kwivə] **I** *n.* ①箭袋,箭筒 ②箭袋内的箭

quiver

③(能装一套东西的)容器 ④大群;大队 **II** *vi.* (箭)落入箭袋中;稳稳地射中: The arrow ~ed in its mark. 箭稳稳地射中目标。‖*a ~ full of children* 子女众多的大家庭 / *have an arrow* (或 *a shaft*) *left in one's ~* 还有本钱;还有办法 ‖~*ful* *n.* ①箭筒容纳量: a ~ful of arrows 满筒的箭 ②大量,许多: a ~ful of children 许多孩子

quiver[3] ['kwivə] *a.* [古]迅速的;敏捷的;活泼的

quiz [kwiz] **I** ([复] quizzes) *n.* ①恶作剧;挖苦,嘲笑,戏弄 ②小型考试,测验;提问;(广播节目中的)一般知识测验,答问比赛,猜谜 ③挖苦者,嘲笑者,戏弄者;[罕]怪人,举止奇特的人;容貌古怪的人 **II** (quizzed; quizzing) *vt.* ①挖苦,嘲弄 ②(嘲弄地或无礼地)盯着…看,(好奇地)张望 ③对(学生或班级)进行测验 ④盘问 ‖*a drop* (或 *shotgun*) ~ [美俚]突击测验 ‖~ *game* (广播或电视节目中的)答问比赛 / ~ *kid* 极聪明的孩子 / '~,*master* *n.* (答问比赛节目中的)提问者 / ~ *program*(me) 答问比赛节目 / *quizzing glass* 有柄单眼镜

quizzical ['kwizikəl] *a.* ①古怪的;可笑的 ②爱挖苦的;嘲弄的: a ~ smile 嘲弄的微笑 ③探询的,好奇的;疑惑的: a ~ look 好奇的(或疑惑的)眼光 ‖~*ly* *ad.*

quod [kwɔd] [英俚] **I** *n.* 监狱: in ~ 在监狱中 **II** (quodded; quodding) *vt.* 关押,监禁

quoit [kɔit] **I** *n.* ①(掷环游戏中用的)铁圈(或绳圈)②[~s]用作单或复]掷(铁)圈游戏 **II** *vt.* 掷,抛

quorum ['kwɔ:rəm] *n.* ①[古](英国法庭开庭时必须达到的)治安法官人数 ②[英][总称]治安法官 ③挑选出的一群人: a ~ of athletes 一批优秀运动员 ④法定人数: form (procure, lack) a ~ 形成(达到,不足)法定人数

quota ['kwoutə] *n.* 定额;分配额;限额(尤指政府对进口货物或移民人数的控制的): output ~s 产品定额 / hiring ~s [美]雇员分配额 (指政府为企业单位等规定的雇员中各人种的比例限额)

overfulfil the ～ 超额完成 / the ～ system 定额分配制
quotation [kwou'teiʃən] *n.* ①引用,引证 ②引文,引语;语录 ③【商】行情(报告);报价单,估价单: the ～s for wheat 小麦行情 / a ～ of prices 报价(单) / a ～ for building a workshop 建造一所车间的报价(单) ④【印】(填空白用的)嵌块,空铅 ‖～ **mark(s)** 引号(即"")
quote [kwout] **I** ❶ *vt.* ①引用,引证;引述,复述: a passage ～d from the editorial 引自社论的一段文章 ② 把…放在引号内,用引号把…括起来 ③【商】报…的价,开…的价;报(价),开(价): ～

a commodity at ten dollars 将一件商品开价十元 ❷ *vi.* ①引用,引证 **II** *n.* ①[口]引语,引文 ②引号 ‖～r *n.* ①引用者 ②报价者 ③记录保险单红利并计算其应付利息的职员 ‖'～,**worthy** *a.* 值得引用的,值得引证的
quoth [kwouθ] *vt.* [古][过去式;用于第一人称和第三人称]说 (=said): "Very true," he. 他说: "很对。"
quotient ['kwouʃənt] *n.* ①【数】商: differential ～ 微商 / respiratory ～ (或 ratio)【生】呼吸商(呼出的二氧化碳与吸入的氧气的容积之比) ②份额,应分得的部分

R

rabbi ['ræbai], **rabbin** ['ræbin] *n.* ①犹太的法学博士 ②(犹太人的尊称)先生,老师 ③犹太教教士 ‖*the rabbins* (二世纪至十三世纪间的)犹太法学权威们
rabbit[1] ['ræbit] **I** *n.* ①兔;野兔 ②兔子的毛皮 ③[英口]蹩脚的运动员(尤指板球、网球等的) ④一种融开后涂在烤面包上并加调味品的干酪 (=Welsh ～) **II** *vi.* 打兔子,猎兔: go ～ing 去打兔子 ‖*like* (或 *as thick as*) ～*s in a warren* 挤得水泄不通 / ～ **burrow** 野兔穴 / ～ **ears** ①[美口](电视机的)兔耳形室内天线 ②[美俚](运动员)对场外观众嘲讽的敏感 / ～ **fever** 【医】兔热病 / '～**fish** *n.* 河豚 / ～ **hole** =～ burrow / ～ **hutch** 兔棚 / ～ **punch** 打在头背近颈部处的一击 / ～ **warren** 养兔场
rabbit[2] ['ræbit] *vt.* [俗](诅咒语)让…见鬼去吧,该死: Odd ～ it! 他妈的!
rabble[1] ['ræbl] **I** *n.* ①乌合之众;乱民,暴民 ②[the ～][蔑]下层民众,下等人 ③(动物或昆虫的)一群;(东西)混乱的一堆 **II** *vt.* 聚众袭击(或侮辱) ‖～**ment** *n.* 暴民;(暴民等的)吵闹;暴动 ‖'～**rouser** *n.* (暴动等的)煽动者
rabble[2] ['ræbl] **I** *n.* ①【冶】拨火棒 ②【矿】长柄耙;焙烧炉的机械搅拌器 **II** *vt.* 用拨火棒搅动
rabid ['ræbid] *a.* ①狂暴的;狂怒的: be ～ in one's hatred of 痛恨… ②偏激的;固执的;狂热的;无理性的: be ～ on the subject of 在…问题上走极端 / a ～ football fan 狂热的足球迷 ③(患)狂犬病的;疯狂的 ‖～**ly** *ad.* / ～**ness** *n.*
rabies ['reibi:z] [单复同] *n.* 【医】狂犬病
race[1] [reis] **I** *n.* ①(速度上的)比赛,竞赛,竞争: a horse (boat) ～ 赛马(船) / run a 1,500-metre ～ with sb. 和某人进行一千五百米赛跑 / a ～ against time 和时间赛跑 / the ～ for president 总统竞选 / strongly condemn the two super-powers' armament ～ 强烈谴责两个超级大国的

军备竞赛 ②[复]赛跑会(尤指赛马会): go to the ～s 去看赛马 ③(江、海的)急流;水道 ④日(或月)的运行;人生的历程 ⑤【空】滑流 ⑥【机】(滚珠轴承的)座圈,滚道;(织布机的)梭道,走梭板: inner (outer) ～ 内(外)座圈;内(外)环滚道 **II** ❶ *vi.* ①比速度;参加竞赛;参加赛马,以赛马为业: ～ with sb. 与某人赛跑(或竞赛) / The builders of the power station decided to ～ against the floods. 建设电力站的工人下决心抢在洪水前完成任务。 ② 疾走,全速行进;(机件因阻力过大或负荷减少而)猛转: Ships ～d along on the river. 船只在河上疾驶而过。 / a campaign *racing* across the country 席卷全国的运动 ❷ *vt.* ①和…比速度(或竞赛) ②使(马等)参加比赛 ③使疾走,使全速行进;使(发动机)空转: ～ the bill through the House 使议案在议院迅速通过 / Don't ～ the engine. 不要让发动机空转。 ④(在速度上)试图超过 ‖*a rat* ～ 激烈的竞争 / *a straight* ～ 全力以赴的竞赛 ‖'～**course** *n.* 赛马场;跑道(尤指赛马所用的);水道 / '～**horse** *n.* 比赛用的马 / ～ **meeting** [主英]赛马会 / ～ **runner** 【动】(北美产的)一种蜥蜴 / '～**track** *n.* (体育比赛用的)跑道 / '～**way** *n.* 水道;电线管
race[2] [reis] *n.* ①人种;种族,民族: the black ～s 黑色人种 / the Mongolian (Caucasian) ～ 蒙古(高加索)人种 / ～ prejudices 种族偏见 ②家族;世系 ③(动、植物的)属,种;(人、生物的)宗,类: the human ～ 人类 / the feathered (finny) ～ [谑]鸟(鱼)类 / a rust-resistant ～ of wheat 抗锈病的小麦品种 ④(有同样活动、习惯、思想等的)一批人: the ～ of painters 画家们 ⑤(食物、酒等)独特(或强烈)的风味;(语言的)尖锐泼辣 ‖～ **suicide** 种族自杀(指某一种族把出生率控制过低而引起的逐渐消亡)
race[3] [reis] *n.* 姜根
rack[1] [ræk] **I** *n.* ①饲草架(盛饲草喂牲畜用的架

子) ②搁物架, 挂物架; 格状文件分类架;【军】(飞机的)炸弹架: a tool ~ 工具架 / a rifle ~ 枪架 ③(火车、客机等座位上面的)行李架 ④【机】齿条; 齿轨 **II ❶** *vt.* ①[主英]在饲草架中装满草料喂(马等); 把(牲畜)系在饲草架前 ②把…放在架子上 ③在架上制作(或处理)(皮革、矿石等) ❷ *vi.* 把饲草架装满干草; 把牲畜系在饲草架前 ‖*in a high* ~ [英方]居高位 / *off the* ~ (衣服)现成做好的 ‖~ **rail** 齿轨 / ~ **railway**, ~ **railroad** 齿轨铁道 / ~ **wheel** 齿(车)轮

rack² [ræk] **I** *n.* ①拉肢刑架(拷问犯人时拉其四肢使关节脱离的一种刑具) ②极大的苦痛; 绞动; 痛苦的根源 **II ❶** *vt.* ①把…放在拉肢刑架上施刑 ②使苦痛, 折磨: a ~*ing* headache 折磨人的头痛 / be ~*ed* with anxiety 极为焦虑不安 ③使猛力摇动; 扭伤: The cough seemed to ~ his whole body. 他咳得全身震动。④ 压榨(尤指索取高额租金), 榨取: The landlords ~*ed* the tenants. 地主对佃户进行残酷剥削。/ ~ heavy rents 榨取重租 ⑤过度使用(土地)而把它弄得贫瘠 ❷ *vi.* 变形, 倾斜 ‖*be on the* ~ ①受酷刑; 受极大折磨 ②极度焦虑不安 / ~ *one's brains* 绞脑汁 / ~ *up* [俚]①获(胜); 得(分) ②彻底击败 ③击倒 ‖~ **rent** 与地产年产值相等(或相近)的租金; 高额租金 / ~**-renter** *n.* ①付高额租金的人 ②勒索高额租金的人

rack³ [ræk] **I** *n.* [书面语]行云, 流云 **II** *vi.* (云)随风飘动

rack⁴ [ræk] *n.* 破坏 ‖*go to* ~ *and ruin* (或 *go to* ~ *and manger*) 被破坏掉, 陷于毁灭

rack⁵ [ræk] **I** *n.* (马)小步跑, 轻跑(速步和常步中间的一种步法) **II** *vi.* (马)小步跑, 轻跑

rack⁶ [ræk] *n.* 烧酒 **II** *vt.* 从渣滓中榨出(酒等)

racket¹ ['rækit] *n.* ①(网球、羽毛球等的)球拍; 乒乓球拍 ②[~s][用作单](在四周有围墙的院子里玩的)一种网球戏 ③球拍形雪鞋

racket² ['rækit] **I** *n.* ①[只用单]喧嚷, 吵闹声: What a ~! 多么吵闹! ②繁忙的社交活动; 忙乱, 纷乱 ③放荡生活: go on the ~ 过花天酒地的生活 ④[口]敲诈, 骗钱; 骗局; 非法的买卖(或职业); 容易赚钱的生计: be in on a ~ 参与敲诈 ⑤严格考验, 苦痛的经历 ⑥[俚]生意, 职业 **II** *vi.* ①喧嚷, 大声吵闹 ②忙于社交活动; 过放荡的生活 (*about*) ‖*make* (或 *kick up*) *a* ~ 大声喧闹 / *stand the* ~ ①经受住考验 ②承担后果(或费用); 接受责备

racy¹ ['reisi] *a.* ①保持原味的; 显出特色的; 新鲜的: ~ fruit 保持原味的水果 ②活泼的, 充满活力的 ③(讲话、文章等)生动的; 辛辣的【美】(讲话、文章等)猥亵的, 挑逗性的 / ~ *of the soil* ①具有原来特征的 ②生动活泼的; 刺激的

racy² ['reisi] *a.* ①(体格)适于赛跑的 ②(动物)体高而瘦的

radar ['reidə] (radio detecting and ranging 的首字母缩略词) *n.* 雷达, 无线电探测器, 无线电定位装置; 无线电定位: follow the flight of an aircraft by ~ 用雷达跟踪飞机 ‖*an air surveillance* ~

对空监视雷达 / *a marine* ~ 船用雷达 / *a beacon* 雷达信标 / *a* ~ *bombing* 雷达轰炸 / *a* ~ *control* 雷达控制 / *a* ~ *fence* 雷达警戒网 / ~ *installations* 雷达装置 / ~ *jamming* 雷达干扰 / *a* ~ *operator* 雷达员, 雷达操作人员 / ~ *screen* 雷达荧光屏 ‖**~man** *n.* 雷达员 / **'~scope** *n.* 雷达显示器, 雷达示波器

radiant ['reidjənt] **I** *a.* ①光芒四射的, 光辉灿烂的; 绚丽的: the ~ sun 光芒四射的太阳 ②(人、面容等)喜悦的, 容光焕发的: wear a ~ face 红光满面 / be ~ with joy 喜气洋洋 ③放射的, 辐射的: ~ energy (heat) 辐射能(热) / ~ rays 辐射线 ④发出辐射热的 **II** *n.* ①发光(或发热)的物体, 光点 ②(电炉或煤气炉的)白炽部分 ③【天】(流星)辐射点 (= ~ point) ‖**~ly** *ad.*

radiate ['reidieit] **I ❶** *vi.* ①发射光线; 放射能量; 发射电磁波; 闪闪发光 ②(光、热等)辐射, 散发: heat that ~*s* from a fireplace 从壁炉中散发出的热气 ③(感情等)流露, 显出: joy that ~*s* from sb.'s eyes 某人的眼光中流露出的欢乐 ④ 辐射状发出, 从中心向各方伸展出: streets *radiating* from the central square 从中央广场伸展出去的各条街道 ❷ *vt.* ①发射(光、热等): The sun ~*s* light and heat. 太阳放射出光和热。②照明, 照亮 ③散发; 传播 ④(通过无线电或电视)广播: ~ a programme 播送节目 **II** *a.* 有射线的; 具辐射部的; 辐射状的 ‖**~ly** *ad.*

radiation [,reidi'eiʃən] *n.* ①放射, 发光, 发热; 辐射: cosmic ~ 宇宙辐射 / electromagnetic ~ 电磁辐射 / nuclear ~ (原子)核辐射 / thermal ~ 热辐射 ②放射物;[总称]辐射线; 辐射能 ③辐射状排列, 放射形 ④(暖气设备等的)散热器 ⑤【医】射线疗法 ‖~ **damage** 辐射线损伤 / **radi'ation-'proof** *a.* 防辐射的 / ~ **sickness** 辐射病, 射线中毒

radiator ['reidieitə] *n.* ①辐射体; 辐射器; 辐射源 ②(暖气设备等的)散热器; (汽车的)水箱; 冷却器: nose ~ 【机】机头散热器 ③取暖电炉(或油炉) ④【无】发射天线

radical ['rædikəl] **I** *a.* ①根本的, 基本的: make ~ changes 作根本的(或彻底的)改变 / a ~ cure 根治; 彻底治愈 / a ~ principle 基本原理 ②激进的, 激进派的: a ~ democrat 激进的民主主义者 / take ~ measures 采取激进手段 ③【数】根的;【植】根生的;【化】基的, 原子团的: ~ sign 【数】根号 / ~ expression 【数】根式 / ~ weight 【化】基团量 ④【语】词根的;【音】根音的: a ~ word 【语】根词 **II** *n.* ①根部; 基础; 基本原理 ②[常作 R-]激进分子; 激进党派的成员 ③【数】根数, 根式; 根号【化】基, 原子团: ~ centre 【数】根心, 等幂心 / acid ~ 【化】酸根 ④【语】词根, 词干 ⑤(汉语中的)部首 ‖**~ism** *n.* 激进主义 / **~ly** *ad.*

radio ['reidiou] **I** *n.* ①无线电, 射电; 无线电话; 无线电报: send a message by ~ 拍发无线电报 / receive a ~ 收到一份无线电报 ②无线电传收机

无线电广播: We heard the news *over* (或 *on, upon*) the ～. 我们从无线电广播中听到了这新闻。/ listen *in* to the ～ 收听无线电广播 / speak *over* the ～ 作广播讲话 ③无线电设备;收音机: a portable ～ 便携式收音机 / turn (或 switch) on (off) the ～ 开(关)收音机 / tune a ～ to a certain wavelength 把收音机调拨至某波长 ④无线电广播台: a ～ announcer 电台广播员 **II ❶ vt.** ①向…发无线电报(或无线电话) ②用无线电发送(或广播) ❷ *vi.* 用无线电通讯,用无线电传送 ‖～ **astronomy**【天】射电天文学 / ～ **beacon** 无线电航空信标 / ～ **beam** 无线电射束 / ～ **bomb**【军】无线电引信炸弹 / ～ **car** 无线电通讯(船) / ～ **communication** 无线电通讯 / ～ **compass** 无线电罗盘 / ～ **control** 无线电操纵 / ～ **direction finder** 无线电测向器,无线电定向仪 / ～ **electrician** (海军)无线电军士长 / ～ **engineering** 无线电工程 / ～ **field intensity** 电磁场场强 / ～ **fix** 无线电定位 / ～ **frequency** 射频,无线电频率 / ～ **knife**【医】高频手术刀 / ～ **navigation** 无线电导航(法) / '～-'**phonograph** *n.* 收音电唱两用机 / ～ **range** 无线电航向信标;无线电测得的距离 / ～ **receiver** 无线电接收机 / ～ **set** 收音机;无线电收发报机;无线电台 / ～ **silence** 停止发报(时期);无线电静寂 / ～ **star** 无线电星,电波星,射电星 / ～ **station** 无线电台 / ～ **telescope** 无线电望远镜 / ～ **transmitter** 无线电发射机 / ～ **tube** 无线电真空管 / ～ **wave** 无线电波

radiograph ['reidiougrɑ:f]【物】**I** *n.* 射线照片(尤指 X 射线照片) **II** *vt.* 拍…的射线照片 ‖**~ic** [,reidiou'græfik] *a.* / **~y** [,reidi'ɔgrəfi] *n.* 射线照相(术)

radish ['rædiʃ] *n.* (红或白的)小萝卜(可放在色拉中生吃)

radium ['reidjəm] *n.*【化】镭 ‖**~ emanation** 镭(放)射气 / ～ **therapy**【医】放射疗法,镭疗法

radius ['reidjəs] ([复] radii ['reidiai] 或 radiuses) *n.* ①辐射光线;【无】径向射线 ②辐射状部分;【植】(菊科的)边花;(车轮上的)半径 ③半径;半径距离;半径范围: a ～ of action【军】活动半径;有效破坏半径 / There was no house within a ～ of three kilometres. 周围三公里内没有房子。④界限,范围: a ～ of visibility【军】有效观察界 / within the ～ of sb.'s capacity 在某人力所能及的范围内 ⑤【解】桡骨;【动】(昆虫的)径脉 ‖**~ vector**【数】矢径,辐

raffia ['ræfiə] *n.* ①【植】酒椰(=～ palm) ②酒椰纤维

raffle[1] ['ræfl] **I** *n.* (常为义卖等实行的)抽彩售货(法) **II ❶** *vi.* 抽彩: ～ *for* a watch 抽彩买表 ❷ *vt.* 以抽彩法出售: ～ (*off*) a watch 以抽彩法售表

raffle[2] ['ræfl] *n.* [总称] ①废物;杂物 ②(船上的)绳索什具

raft[1] [rɑ:ft] **I** *n.* ①(伐下的树木扎成的)木排;木筏,筏子;救生筏 ②妨碍航行的流木(或浮冰等) ③(某些昆虫的)卵筏 **II ❶** *vt.* ①筏运(木材) ②把(木头等)扎成筏子 ③用筏子运(人、货物等) ④用筏子渡过(或通过) ❷ *vi.* 乘筏子;使用筏子 ‖**~ bridge** 筏桥,浮桥 / ～**sman** ['rɑ:ftsmən] *n.* =rafter[2]

raft[2] [rɑ:ft] *n.* [口]一大堆,大量

rafter[1] ['rɑ:ftə] **I** *n.*【建】椽: angle ～ 角椽 / common ～ 普通椽木 **II** *vt.* ①装椽子于 ②[英]犁(地)使泥土向一边堆成畦 ‖*from cellar to* ～ 见 **cellar**

rafter[2] ['rɑ:ftə] *n.* 筏夫,撑筏人;木材筏运人

rag[1] [ræg] **I** *n.* ①破布,碎布;抹布: The shirt was worn to ～s. 这件衬衫已穿得很破了。/ clean a table with a ～ 用抹布擦桌子 ②碎片,残片: There is not a ～ of evidence. 没有丝毫证据。/ flying ～s of cloud 飘动的残云 ③[复]破旧衣服;[谑]衣服 ④[复]制造优质纸的破布 ⑤破布似的无价值的东西;[贬]旗子;手帕;帷幕;报纸;微不足道的事 ⑥【海】小块风帆: spread every ～ of sail 张起所有的小风帆 ⑦ 橘络 ⑧ [the R-] [英俚]陆海军俱乐部 ⑨[俚]钱币,钞票: without a ～ 分文没有 / not a ～ (left) 一点钱也没有(剩下来) ‖*chew the* ～ [俚]①聊天,闲谈 ②争论 ③发牢骚 / *feel like a boiled* ～ 觉得非常不舒服(或虚弱) / *glad* ～s [俚]华丽的服装;晚礼服 / *part brass* ～s *with sb.* [俚]不再同某人保持亲密关系 ‖**~ baby** (碎布做成的)玩具娃娃 / '～**bag** *n.* ①放备用碎布的布袋 ②一袋杂七杂八的东西 / ～ **bolt**【机】棘螺栓 / ～ **cutter** (造纸用的)切布机 / ～ **doll** ① =～ baby ②(试验种子萌发用的)湿布卷条 / ～ **fair** 旧衣市场 / '～**man** *n.* 收买破旧货的人 / ～ **paper** (破布制成的)优质纸 / '～,**picker** *n.* 捡破烂的人 / '～**tag** *n.* 乌合之众: a ～tag army 杂牌军 / '～**tag and bobtail** =～tag / ～**weed** *n.*【植】豚草 / ～ **wheel**【机】抛光轮,布轮

rag[2] [ræg] *n.* ①【建】石板瓦 ②[主英]坚硬石灰岩: Kentish ～ 坚硬砂质石灰岩

rag[3] [ræg] **I** (ragged; ragging) **❶** *vt.* [俚]①和…开玩笑;对…恶作剧 ②责骂 ❷ *vi.* 喧闹 **II** *n.* [英俚]恶作剧;喧闹

rage [reidʒ] **I** *n.* ①(一阵)狂怒,盛怒: be in a ～ with sb. 对某人大发脾气 / fall (或 fly) into a ～ 勃然大怒 / be hot with ～ 气得发火 ②(风、浪等)狂暴,凶猛: the ～ of the waves 波涛的汹涌 ③风行一时的人(或物) ④强烈的感情;热情;士气的激昂;狂热: a ～ for collecting stamps 集邮热 **II** *vi.* ①大怒: ～ *at* (或 *against*) sb. (sth.) 对某人(某事)大发脾气 ②(风)狂吹;(浪等)汹涌: The storm ～d for hours. 风暴猛刮了好几个小时。③盛行,流行;(病等)猖獗 ‖*be* (*all*) *the* ～ 风靡一时,流行一时: This song *was all the* ～ *then.* 这首歌在当时十分流行。/ ～ *itself out* (暴风雨等)肆虐后平息下来

raid [reid] **I** *n.* ①(突然)袭击: an air ～ 空袭

②(警察的)突然搜查,搜捕 ③(对公款等的)非法盗用;抢劫 ④(对竞争对手等的)突然行动;故意造成股票价格猛跌的行为 **II** *vt.* & *vi.* ①袭击;侵入 ②搜查,搜捕 ‖**~er** *n.* ①袭击者;侵入者 ②劫掠商船的武装快船 ③袭击(用)飞机 ④[R-](美国海军陆战队的)近战兵

rail [reil] **I** *n.* ①横条,横杆;扶手,栏杆;围栏: a towel ~ 挂毛巾用的横杆 / the side ~s of a ladder 梯子两边的扶手 ②(门等的)横档 ③铁轨,钢轨;轨道;铁路: a single (double) line of ~s 单(双)线铁轨 / send goods by ~ 由铁路运送货物 ④[复]铁路股票;铁道网 **II** *vt.* ①用栏杆围进(in);用栏杆隔开(off);用栏杆围出(out) ②[英]由铁路运输 ‖*free on* ~ 见 free / *off the* ~*s* (火车等)出轨的;[喻]越轨的,混乱的;*on the* ~*s* ①顺利地进行着 ②在正常的轨道上 / *ride sb. on a* ~ 把某人骑在杆上抬着而起出集体(一种惩罚的方法,常在受罚者身上涂上柏油,插上羽毛) ‖'**~car** *n.* (单节)机动有轨车 / '**~chair** (铁路的)轨座 / **~fence** 栅栏,篱笆 / '**~head** *n.* ①(战场上军用物资转运的)铁路末站 ②铁路线的终点(或起点);建造中的铁路已经到达的最远点 / **~man** ['reilmən] *n.* ①铁路职工 ②(船上装卸货时打信号的)码头工人 / '**~-motor** *a.* 铁路公路联运的

raillery ['reiləri] *n.* ①善意的嘲笑;戏弄 ②戏弄人的行为(或话)

railway ['reilwei] **I** *n.* ①[主英]铁道,铁路: build a new ~ 筑新铁路 / a broad-gauge (narrow-gauge) ~ 阔(狭)轨铁路 ②[主英]铁路系统,铁道部门: work on the ~ 在铁路上工作 ③(轻便车辆等的)轨道: a street ~ 有轨电车道 / a cash ~ in a department store 百货商店中的货款传送线 **II** *vi.* 乘火车旅行 ‖*at* ~ *speed* 见 speed ‖ ~ **carriage** [英]火车车厢 / ~ **corps** 铁道兵(种) / ~ **letter** [英]由铁路部门经营邮递的信件 / **mail car** (运送途中分拣信件的)铁路邮车 / '**~man** *n.* 铁路职工 / ~ **station** 火车站

rain [rein] **I** *n.* ①雨,雨水;一场雨;下雨;[复]季节雨,一阵一阵的雨: walk out in the ~ 冒雨走出去 / a heavy (light, fine) ~ 一阵大(小,细)雨 / It looks like ~. 象要下雨了。/ the ~s (热带的)雨季;[the Rains](大西洋上北纬四度至十度间的)雨区 ②(雨点般的)落下;(下雨般的)一阵: a ~ of bullets 一阵弹雨 / a ~ of congratulations 一连串的祝贺 **II** ❶ *vi.* ①下雨;降雨: It's ~*ing*. 下雨了。/ It ~*s* in. 漏雨了。②雨点般地落下;雨水般地淌下 ❷ *vt.* ①使(雨等)大量降下;使…如雨而下: It has ~*ed* out. 雨停了。/ His eyes were ~*ing* tears. 他泪如雨下。②大量地给;厚施: ~ influence on … 给…很大影响 / ~ praises on sb. 连声称赞某人 ‖*It never ~s but it pours.* [谚]不雨则已,一雨倾盆。(指事情不发生则已,一旦发生便接踵而来) / ~ *cats and dogs* 见 cat / ~ *or shine* 不论晴雨,无论如何: The sports meet will be held ~ *or shine*. 运动会风雨无阻,照常举行。/ ~ *out* 因下雨而取消;因下雨取消(或中断): Today's football match has been ~*ed* out. 今天的足球赛因下雨而取消了。/ ~ *pitchforks* 倾盆大雨 / *right as* ~ 见 right ‖'**~less** *a.* 缺少雨的,无雨的 ‖'**~band** *n.* 【气】雨带(指太阳光谱中黄色部分内的黑带) / ~ **belt** 雨区 / ~ **boot** 雨鞋 / ~ **box** 舞台上发出雨声的音匣 / ~ **cap** 雨帽 / ~ **cape** 雨披 / ~ **check** ①(球赛等因下雨而中断后)留作下次继续使用的票根 ②延期: give a ~ *check* on a dinner 推迟举行宴会 / ~ **cloud** 【气】雨云 / '**~coat** *n.* 雨衣 / '**~drop** *n.* 雨点 / '**~fall** *n.* ①一场雨 ②(降)雨量 / ~ **forest** (热带)雨林 / ~ **ga(u)ge** 【气】雨量器 / ~ **glass** 气压表,晴雨计 / '**~hat** *n.* 雨帽: a bamboo ~-hat 笠帽 / '**~maker** *n.* ①求雨者(尤指印第安人的巫医) ②[口]参加人工降雨工作的气象学家(或飞行员等) / '**~making** *n.* 求雨;人工降雨 / '**~proof** *a.* 防雨的: a ~-proof bag 防雨袋 ‖ *n.* 雨衣;雨披 ‖ *vt.* 使能防雨 / '**~spout** *n.* ①水落管;排水口 ②龙卷风卷起的水柱,海龙卷 / '**~storm** *n.* 暴(风)雨 / '**~tight** *a.* 不漏雨的 / '**~wash** *n.* 雨水的冲刷;被雨水带走的东西 / '**~water** *n.* 雨水;软水 / '**~wear** *n.* [总称]雨衣(或雨披等) / '**~worm** *n.* 蚯蚓

raise [reiz] **I** ❶ *vt.* ①举起;使升高: ~ a dumbbell from the ground 把哑铃从地上举起来 / ~ one's eyes 举目(向上)看 / ~ one's hand to sb. 向某人举起手(做出要打的样子) / ~ one's hat to sb. 向某人举帽致敬 / ~ one's glass to sb. 举杯祝某人健康 / Heavy rains ~*d* the river stage. 暴雨使河水水位升高。②使起来;使立起: ~ sb. from a bed of sickness 使某人从病床上起来 / ~ a building 造起一所房子 ③唤起;引起;惹起(骚乱等);扬起;(从巢穴中)赶起(猎物): The remark ~*d* a laugh. 这话引起了笑声。/ ~ a cloud of dust 扬起一片尘土 ④提高,增加;提升,提拔: ~ the living standard of the working people 提高劳动人民的生活水平 / ~ a captain to the rank of major 将上尉提升为少校 ⑤使出现;使复活;使苏醒: ~ the dead 死人复活 / ~ sb. from the dead 使某人起死回生 ⑥提出;发出: ~ a question for discussion 提出问题供讨论 / ~ a shout 发出叫喊声 ⑦筹(款);招;召集;集结: ~ funds 筹集资金 / ~ a loan 借款 / ~ a regiment 招募一团兵 ⑧解除;使终止: ~ a siege 解围 / ~ an embargo 解除禁运 ⑨使隆起;(皮肤上)起(水泡);【纺】把(布)拉绒,使起绒 ⑩使(面团等)发酵 ⑪种植;饲养;养育: ~ crops 种庄稼 / Where was he ~*d*? [美]他是在哪儿长大的? ⑫[数]使自乘 ⑬[海]看得见(地平线上起的事物): The ship ~*d* land at dawn. 黎明时在船上看见了陆地。⑭(用涂改等欺骗手法)增加(支票)的票面价值 ⑮(赌牌时)下赌注超过(前面的赌注或最高的赌注) ⑯和…建立无线电联系 ❷ *vi.* ①[方]上升 ②[口]咳出痰 ③(赌牌时)加赌注 **II** *n.* ①举起,升起;

加(尤指工资): a pay ~ [美] 工资的增加 ③路的高处 ④【矿】天井,上山 ‖ *make a ~ of* 收集到,弄到,筹集到(钱或贵重物品) / ~ *a dust* 见 dust / ~ *the wind* 见 wind[1]

raisin ['reizn] *n.* 葡萄干(常指无核的)

raja(h) ['rɑːdʒə] *n.* [印地](印度等的)王公;首领

rake[1] [reik] I *n.* ①(长柄的)耙子,钉齿耙,草耙;(马或拖拉机等牵引的)耙机 ②耙状的用具 ③(赌台上用的)钱耙 II ❶ *vt.* ①(用耙子)耙;耙松: ~ the soil level 把土耙平 / ~ *up* (或 *together*) dead leaves 把枯叶耙在一起 / ~ *out* a fire 把炉灰耙出来 / ~ the grass *off* (或 *from*) the lawn after mowing 修剪后把草耙出草坪 ②搜索,探索: ~ one's memory 竭力回忆 / ~ all history for proofs 从全部历史中寻找证据 ③迅速(或大量)取得(钱财等)(*in*) ④痛骂,痛斥 (*over*) ⑤撩过,掠过: The clouds ~*d* the mountain summits. 云朵掠过山峰。⑥扫视;(窗等)俯瞰: He ~*d* the horizon with a telescope. 他用望远镜扫视地平线。⑦【军】扫射,纵射 ❷ *vi.* ①(用耙)耙 ②搜索,探索: ~ *among* (或 *in, into, through*) old documents 在旧文件中翻找 ③撩过,掠过 (*over, across*) ‖~ *sth. up* 重新提起某事(尤指不愉快的事): ~ *up* the past 重提往事;翻旧帐 ‖'~-off *n.* 佣金,回扣(尤指在非法交易中所获得的)

rake[2] [reik] I *n.* ①斜度,倾角 ②【船】(帆樯等的)倾斜;船首(或船尾)向龙骨外面的突出 ③【矿】倾伏;斜脉;【空】倾度 ④戏院(或舞台)的地面倾斜 II ❶ *vi.* ①(船首或船尾)突出于龙骨之外 ②倾斜 ❷ *vt.* 使倾斜

rake[3] [reik] I *n.* 放荡的人;浪子;流氓 II *vi.* 放荡;过浪荡生活

rakish[1] ['reikiʃ] *a.* ①(船等)外形灵巧的,看上去速度快的 ②不拘俗套的;扬扬自得的 ‖~ly *ad.* / ~ness *n.*

rakish[2] ['reikiʃ] *a.* 放荡的;浪荡的;(象)浪子的 ‖~ly *ad.* / ~ness *n.*

rally[1] ['ræli] I ❶ *vt.* ①(重新)集合,重整(溃败的军队等) ②召集;团结 ③振作(精神等);恢复(元气等): ~ one's energy 振作精神 / ~ one's courage 鼓起勇气 ❷ *vi.* ①(重新)集合,重整②团结 ③(在健康、精力等方面)恢复,复元 ④(网球、羽毛球等)连续对打 ⑤(股票市场等)价格止跌,回稳 II *n.* ①(重新)集合;重整旗鼓;恢复;振作 ②(群众性的)大会,集会: hold a mass ~ 举行群众大会 / a celebration ~ 庆祝大会 ③汽车竞赛会 ④(网球、羽毛球等的)连续对打 ⑤(市场的)价格止跌,回稳

rally[2] ['ræli] *vt. & vi.* 嘲笑,挖苦 ‖~ingly *ad.*

ram[1] [ræm] I *n.* ①公羊 ②[R-]【天】白羊(星)座 ③(旧时攻城用的)撞墙锤;(旧时军舰舰首的)金属撞角;装有撞角的军舰 ④(起重机等的)撞杆,撞锤;夯;压头;(压力泵的)柱塞 II (rammed; ramming) ❶ *vi.* ①猛撞 ②迅速移动 ❷ *vt.* ①猛击,撞击,锤击;夯紧(土等) ②塞,压;【军】装(弹药): ~ clothes into a trunk 把衣服塞进箱子 / ~ a charge into a gun 把弹药装入枪内 ③迫使别人

接受;灌输(思想、知识等): ~ an idea home 反复说得别人接受一个想法 ‖*milk the ~* 作徒劳无益的事 / ~ *sth. down sb.'s throat* 见 throat

ram[2] [ræm] *n.* [英]船的总长度

ramble ['ræmbl] I ❶ *vi.* ①闲逛,漫步 (*about, over*) ②漫谈,聊天;漫笔 ③(草木等)蔓生,蔓延 ❷ *vt.* 在…闲逛;漫步于… II *n.* ①闲逛;漫步 ②随笔,漫笔 ‖~**r** *n.* ①漫游者(或漫谈者等) ②蔓生植物;攀缘蔷薇

rambling ['ræmbliŋ] *a.* ①闲逛的;漫步的 ②(说话、文章等)散漫的,不连贯的 ③(草木等)蔓生的,蔓延的 ④(街道、建筑等)凌乱的,杂乱无章的 ‖~ly *ad.*

ramify ['ræmifai] ❶ *vt.* ①使分枝,使分叉 ②使成网状: Railways are *ramified* over the country. 铁路线分布全国。❷ *vi.* ①分枝,分叉 ②成网状

ramp[1] [ræmp] I *n.* ①斜面;斜坡;(弯曲的)坡道 ②【建】弯子(楼梯扶手的弯曲部分) ③【空】客机梯子,梯升 II *vt.* ①使有斜面;使有斜坡 ②【建】使弯

ramp[2] [ræmp] I *vi.* ①(狮等)用后脚立起,跃立 ②作恫吓的姿势;暴跳;乱撞;猖獗 ③(草木等)蔓生,蔓延 II *n.* ①(狮等的)跃立 ②恫吓的姿势;猖獗

ramp[3] [ræmp] [英俚] I *n.* (指租金等)索取高价;敲诈;诓骗 II *vi. & vt.* 索取高价;敲诈

rampage [ræm'peidʒ] *n. & vi.* 暴跳;横冲直撞 ‖*go* (或 *be*) *on the* (或 *a*) ~ 暴跳如雷;横冲直撞

rampant ['ræmpənt] *a.* ①繁茂的;蔓生的: ~ beds of roses on the lawn 草坪上玫瑰盛开的花坛 ②(疾病、恶习等)蔓延的;猖獗的: run ~ 猖狂,横行 ③(行为、态度、说话等)猛烈的;不能控制的 ④(狮等)用后脚立起的;跃立的 ⑤具有一个比一个高的拱座(或桥台)的: a ~ arch 陂拱 ‖~ly *ad.*

rampart ['ræmpɑːt] I *n.* ①(城堡周围堤状的)防御土墙,壁垒;(堤状防御土墙顶部的)通路 ②防御物,保护物 ③(碎石等堆成的)土墙状狭长隆起物 II *vt.* (用壁垒)防护

rampart

ramrod ['ræmrɔd] I *n.* ①【军】推弹杆;(枪的)通条 ②严格执行纪律者 II *a.* 笔直不弯的;死板的;生硬的;严厉的

ramshackle ['ræm,ʃækl] *a.* ①倒塌似的,摇摇欲坠的: a ~ house 东倒西歪的房子 ②草率建成的 ③放荡的;任性的

ranch [rɑ:ntʃ, ræntʃ] **I** *n.* (北美洲的)大牧场,大农场;专业性的牧场(或农场): a fruit ~ 大果园 / a poultry ~ 家禽饲养场 **II** ❶ *vi.* ①经营牧场(或农场) ②在牧场(或农场)工作 ❷ *vt.* ①在…经营牧场(或农场) ②在牧场饲养 ‖~er *n.* ① 大牧场(或农场)主(或管理人) ② 大牧场(或农场)工人 ‖~ **house** ①牧场(或农场)主的住宅 ②(通常附有汽车房的)平房建筑 / ~**man** ['rɑ:ntʃmən, 'ræntʃmən] *n.* =~er / ~ **wag(g)on** 旅行(汽)车;客货两用车

rancid ['rænsid] *a.* 有陈腐脂肪臭味的;败坏的;恶臭的 ‖~**ity** [ræn'siditi] *n.* (食品等的)腐败,败坏;恶臭

rancorous ['ræŋkərəs] *a.* 充满(或表示)仇恨的 ‖~**ly** *ad.*

ranco(u)r ['ræŋkə] *n.* 深仇;积怨

random ['rændəm] **I** *n.* 偶然的(或随便的)行动(或过程)[现只用于 at ~ 中] **II** *a.* ① 胡乱的;随便的,任意的: a ~ guess 瞎猜 / a ~ remark 随便说的话;漫评 / a ~ sample 随意抽取的样品 / a ~ selection 任意选择的东西 ②(石料建筑等)石块形状不规则的;不一律的 ③【数】随机的,机遇的;【物】无规则的: ~ access 随机存取 / ~ process 随机过程 / ~ variable 随机变数 **III** *ad.* 胡乱地;随便地 ‖*at* ~ 胡乱地,随便地,任意地: shoot *at* ~ 胡乱射击;无的放矢 / Soiled dishes were piled *at* ~. 脏碟子乱七八糟地堆着。‖~**ly** *ad.* / ~**ness** *n.*

rang [ræŋ] ring² 的过去式

range [reindʒ] **I** *n.* ①排,行;一系列: a ~ of buildings 一排房屋 / a whole ~ of strategy and tactics 一整套战略战术 ②山脉: a mountain ~ (或 a ~ of mountains) 山脉 ③范围,区域: a wide ~ of choice 广泛的选择范围 / widen the ~ of irrigation 扩大灌溉区域 / His reading is of very wide ~. 他的阅读范围很广。④变动范围;视域(或听觉)范围;理解范围: the annual ~ of temperature 全年的温度较差(或气温变化幅度) / The ~ of prices was great (narrow). 价格涨落变动很大(不大)。/ the ~ of one's voice (vision) 音(视)域 / What you ask is out of my ~. 你问的问题我不懂。/ the ~ of a radio transmitter 无线电发射机的有效范围 / a subject outside sb.'s ~ 不在某人研究范围内的题目 ⑤动植物的生产区,分布区;放牧区;猎区 ⑥【军】射程;距离;(加足燃料后车辆等的)最大行程: a grazing (或 horizontal) ~ 水平射程 / the effective ~ 有效射程 ⑦射击场,靶场: a shooting (或 gunnery) ~ 射击场 ⑧方向,位置: The ~ of the strata is east and west. 地层的走向是从东到西。⑨徘徊;漫游 ⑩炉灶: a kitchen ~ 厨房中固定的(或可移动的)炉灶 / a gas ~ 煤气灶 ⑪一种,一类 ⑫【数】变程,量程;

值域 ⑬(统计学中的)全距 ⑭[美](公地测量中)相距六哩的两子午线间的一排市镇 **II** ❶ *vt.* ①排列,将…排成行: ~ books on a shelf 把书排列在书架上 / ~ the fighters in line 使战士排列成行 ②使并列;使进入行列 ③把…分类;使系统化 ④把(枪、炮、望远镜等)对准 ⑤在…来回走动;在…徘徊;沿(海岸)巡航: ~ the woods in search of game 在树林中来回寻找猎物 ⑥放牧(牛、羊等) ⑦解开(锚索)放在甲板上 ❷ *vi.* ①平行;列成一行: a line of cliffs *ranging with* the river 与河道平行的一排峭壁 / ~ *along* the coast 沿海岸航行 ②绵亘,延伸: The Himalayas ~ from west to east. 喜马拉雅山脉从西向东绵亘。/ a boundary that ~s north and south 一条南北走向的边界 ③漫游;探寻;涉及: ~ *through* woods 在森林里来回走 / researches *ranging over* a wide field 范围很广的研究 / The speaker ~d far and wide. 演说者讲到许多方面。④(在一定范围内)变动,变化: The increase ~d from several to several dozen times. 增长几倍至几十倍不等。⑤[军]测距,试射测距;射程为: ~ for line 方向试射 ⑥(动植物)生长,栖息: The kangaroo ~s in Australia. 袋鼠生长在澳大利亚。‖*at close* ~ 接近地 / *in* (或 *within*) ~ 在射程内 / *in* ~ *with* 和…并列 / *out of* (或 *beyond*) ~ 在射程外 / ~ *oneself* ①安定下来(例如结婚后) ②在社会上获得固定地位 / ~ *short* (炮弹等)中途落下 ‖~ **finder** 测距计,测远仪;【军】(测定由枪炮至目标间距离的)光学测距仪 / ~ **oil** 厨房炉灶用油 / ~ **table** 【军】射程表

rank¹ [ræŋk] **I** *n.* ①排,横列;【军】行列: the rear ~ 后列 / stand in two separate ~s 分两排站着 [注意: rank 指"横列",file 指"纵列"] ②[复]队伍; 军队;士兵: serve in the ~s 服兵役 ③秩序;队形: fall into ~ 排队,列队 ④社会阶层;【军】军阶,军衔: people of all ~s and classes 各阶级各阶层的人 / hold the ~ of colonel 领有上校军衔 ⑤等级;地位,身分;显贵: a painter of the first ~ 第一流的画家 / be appointed with the ~ of ambassador 受到大使级的任命 / a man of ~ 有地位的人 / persons of ~ 贵族们 ⑥棋盘上横的一排方格 ⑦[主英]出租汽车站,出租汽车停放处 ⑧【数】秩: ~ of a determinant 行列式的秩 **II** ❶ *vt.* ①把…列成横列;把…列队: ~ the new books on a shelf 把新书排列在书架上 / The troops were perfectly ~ed. 部队排得整整齐齐。②把…分等;把…评级: The population ~s the city third in the province. 按人口,这城市在省内居第三位。/ All ~ed him as an excellent teacher. 大家都评他为优秀教师。③[美]等级(或级别)高于: A colonel ~s a major. 上校的级别高于少校。❷ *vi.* ①列为: ~ next to 仅次于 / ~ second on the list 在名单上列第二 / ~ *with* (或 *among*) the world's eminent scientists 名列世界著名的科学家之中 ②列队;【军】列队前进(*past, off*) ③

【律】对破产者的财产有求权 ‖*break* ～ 打乱队伍 / *break (the)* ～*s* 走出队伍,【军】列队; 掉队; 解散队伍; 溃散 / *close (the)* ～*s* ①使队伍靠拢 ②[喻]紧密团结 / *in the front* ～ ①在第一排,在前列 ②[喻]著名; 显著 / *keep* ～ 保持队形 / *other* ～*s* 普通士兵们 / *pull one's* ～ *on* [美俚]滥用职权对…强迫命令 / ～ *and fashion* 上流社会 / *reduce sb. to the* ～*s* 把某人降为士兵 / *rise from the* ～ (军官)出身行伍; (靠个人奋斗)由寒微发迹 / *swell the* ～*s of* 扩大…的队伍; 增加…的数目 / *take* ～ *with* (或 *among*) 和…并列 / *the* ～ *and file* 普通士兵们; 老百姓们; 普通成员们 / *the* ～*s* 普通士兵们 ‖*'*～*-and-'filer n.* 普通士兵; 普通成员,一般人员

rank² [ræŋk] *a.* ❶繁茂的; 丛生的; 过于茂盛的: a ～ growth of weeds 丛生的杂草 / These plants are growing ～. 这些植物长得过盛。❷多杂草的; 易生杂草的 ❸过于多产的; 过于肥沃的: ～ soil 过于肥沃的土壤 / a garden ～ with weeds 杂草滋生的庭园 / land too ～ to grow beans 太肥而不宜种豆类的土地 ❹臭气难闻的; 腥臭的; (味道等)令人讨厌的: ～ tobacco 臭气难闻的烟叶 / ～ with filth 污秽难闻的 / purify the ～ air 净化污浊的空气 ❺粗鄙的,下流的: ～ language 下流话 ❻极坏的; 极毒的; [贬]十足的: a ～ lie 弥天大谎 / ～ poison 剧毒 / ～ opportunism 不折不扣的机会主义 ‖～**ly** *ad.* / ～**ness** *n.*

rankle ['ræŋkl] ❶ *vi.* ①引起怨恨,使人痛恨 ②怨恨 ③[古](创伤)化脓,发炎; 使人疼痛不已 ❷ *vt.* 激怒; 使怨恨

ransack ['rænsæk] *vt.* ①彻底搜查; 在…中仔细搜查: ～ a room for a lost key 满屋子寻找丢失的钥匙 / ～ one's memory for suitable words 苦苦思索恰当的词语 ②洗劫,抢劫,掠夺

ransom ['rænsəm] **I** *n.* ①(释放俘虏等的)赎金 ②赎; 赎身,赎救 ③[宗]赎罪法 ④敲诈,勒索 **II** *vt.* ①赎; 赎回,赎出 ②掳(人)勒赎 ③向(某人)勒索赎金 ④得赎金后释放(某人) ⑤[宗]赎(罪) ‖*a king's* ～ 一笔巨款 / *hold sb. to* ～ 劫持某人勒取赎金; 绑架某人的票 ‖～ **bill,** ～ **bond** (被掳船只的)付赎保证书

rant [rænt] **I** ❶ *vi.* ①喧嚣夸张地说话; 激昂地说话 ②咆哮,怒吼; 大声责骂 ③[英方]狂欢 ❷ *vt.* 喧嚣夸张地说; 激昂地说(out); 装腔作势地朗诵: ～ out one's denunciation 激昂地指责 / an actor who ～*s* his part 把角色演得过分的演员 **II** *n.* ①喧嚣夸张的话,激昂的长篇演说; 夸夸其谈 ②[英方]狂欢 ‖～**er** *n.* 喧嚣夸张地说话的人

rap¹ [ræp] **I** *n.* ①叩击(声); 敲击(声); 急拍(声): There's a ～ on the door. 有敲门声。②责备; 责骂; 严厉批评 ③[美俚]刑事责任; (不利的)后果; 罪犯身分的验明; 罪名; 徒刑: be under a murder ～ 被控犯谋杀罪 **II** (rapped; rapping) ❶ *vt.* ①叩击; 敲击; 急拍 ②突然说出; 厉声说出 (out);

(迷信者搞的降神会鬼魂)以敲击表达: ～ out an oath 粗声咒骂 ③敲击致使: ～ the occupants of the room awake 敲门使屋里的人醒来 / ～ the meeting to order 敲桌子使会场安静下来 ④严厉批评 ⑤[美俚]逮捕; 处…以刑罚 ❷ *vi.* ①敲击; 急拍: ～ at the door 敲门 / ～ on the table 敲桌子 ②发出敲门声; 发出急促尖锐的声音 ③说粗野的话 ‖*beat the* ～ 逃避刑事责任(或责罚) / *give sb. a* ～ *on* (或 *over*) *the knuckles* ①敲打某人的手指关节(对小孩的一种体罚) ②谴责某人,责骂某人 / *take the* ～ 承担刑事责任; (常指为别人)受责备

rap² [ræp] (rapped 或 rapt [ræpt]; rapping) *vt.* ①抢走,夺去 ②使着迷,使销魂 ‖～ *and rend* ①夺取,盗窃 ②不择手段地拼凑 (或收罗)

rap³ [ræp] *n.* ①(旧时爱尔兰的)半便士的膺币; 无价值的东西 ②[口]极少的一点儿 ‖*not care* (或 *give*) *a* ～ 毫不在乎 / *not worth a* ～ 毫无价值

rap⁴ [ræp] [美俚] **I** (rapped; rapping) *vi.* ①交谈: ～ *to* sb. 对某人说话以表示认识他 ②理解: He *rapped to* it right away. 他马上领会了。**II** *n.* 交谈(尤指联谊性的) ‖～ **session** 座谈会

rapacious [rə'peiʃəs] *a.* ①掠夺的,强取的 ②贪婪的; 贪得无厌的,贪吃的 ③(猛禽等)捕食生物的 ‖～**ly** *ad.* / ～**ness** *n.*

rapacity [rə'pæsiti] *n.* ①掠夺,强取 ②贪婪; 贪得无厌

rape¹ [reip] **I** *vt.* ①强奸 ②强夺 ③洗劫(城市等) **II** *n.* ①强奸; 强奸罪 ②强夺 ③洗劫 ‖～**r** *n.* =rapist

rape² [reip] *n.* ①(挤去葡萄汁后供制醋用的)葡萄渣 ②(过滤葡萄渣等用的)过滤器

rape³ [reip] *n.* 油菜 ‖～ **cake** [总称]菜子饼 / ～ **oil** 菜油 / ～**seed** *n.* 菜子 / ～**seed** oil 菜油

rapid ['ræpid] **I** *a.* ①快的,迅速的; 动作快的: a ～ current 急流 / a ～ worker 做起事来动作快的人,快手 ②(斜坡)陡的,险峻的: a ～ rise in the highway 公路上陡然上升的坡道 **II** *n.* [常用复]急流; 湍滩 ‖～**ness** *n.* ‖～ **fire** 【军】速射 / '～-'fire, '～-'firing *a.* ①(枪等)速射的 ②(讲话等)快而尖声的 / '～-'firer *n.* 速射枪(或炮) / ～ **transit** 高速交通: a ～ transit line 高速交通线

rapidity [rə'piditi] *n.* ①快,迅速: with great ～ 非常迅速地 ②陡,险峻

rapier ['reipjə] *n.* (决斗或剑术中用的)轻剑: a ～ glance 锐利的一瞥 / a ～ thrust [喻]机智灵敏的对答(或反驳)

rapt [ræpt] **I** rap² 的过去式和过去分词 **II** *a.* ①着迷的,销魂的 ②全神贯注的: listen with ～ attention 凝神静听 / be in one's work 专心地工作着 ③欣喜若狂的 ‖～**ly** *ad.* / ～**ness** *n.*

rapture ['ræptʃə] **I** *n.* ①着迷,销魂 ②全神贯注 ③[复]欢天喜地,狂喜 **II** *vt.* 使欢天喜地,使狂喜 ‖*be in* ～*s over* (或 *about*) 对…欣喜若狂; 对…狂热; 狂热地谈论着… ‖～**d** *a.* 欢天喜地的,狂喜的

rapturous ['ræptʃərəs] *a.* 欢天喜地的,狂喜的;引起狂喜的 ‖**~ly** *ad.* / **~ness** *n.*

rare[1] [reə] I *a.* ① 稀薄的: the ~ air on the mountain top 山顶的稀薄空气 ②稀有的,罕见的;不常发生的: a ~ metal 稀有金属 / on occasions 难得,不常,偶尔 / It is ~ for him to come late. 他很少迟到。③杰出的;珍贵的: a ~ ballerina 杰出的女芭蕾舞演员 / a ~ book 珍本书,善本书 ④[口]非常的,极端的: have ~ fun (或 a ~ time) 玩得高兴极了 / make a ~ fuss over sth. 对某事大惊小怪 II *ad.* [口]很,非常: a ~ fine view 极好的景色 ‖**~ly** *ad.* ①很少,难得 ②极好地 ③不平凡地,非常地 / **~ness** *n.* ‖**~-'earth element**【化】稀土元素 / **~ earths**【化】稀土族

rare[2] [reə] *a.* (肉类)半熟的,煮得嫩的

rarity ['reəriti] *n.* ①稀有;希罕 ②罕见的事物(或人);希罕的东西: Such a hailstorm was a ~ in that region. 这样的冰雹在那个地区是很少见的。③稀薄;稀疏 ④杰出;珍贵

rascal ['rɑːskəl] I *n.* ①流氓,无赖,恶棍 ②[谑]小淘气,(小) 坏蛋: You little ~! 你这个小淘气! II *a.* [罕]下贱的,卑鄙的 ‖**~ism** *n.* 流氓行为,恶事

rash[1] [ræʃ] *n.* ①【医】(皮)疹 ②一下子大量出现的事物

rash[2] [ræʃ] *a.* ①急躁的,性急的,鲁莽的: a ~ young man 莽撞的小伙子 ②草率从事的,轻率的: a ~ statement 不顾后果的话 / He did something ~ and repented forever. 他做了件轻率的事而一直为之后悔。‖**~ly** *ad.* / **~ness** *n.*

rasher ['ræʃə] *n.* 咸肉(或火腿)薄片

rasp [rɑːsp] I *n.* ①粗锉(刀),木锉 ②锉磨的声音,粗厉的刺耳声 II ❶ *vt.* ①用粗锉刀锉;粗锉;锉掉(*away, off*) ②伤(感情);刺激(神经),使焦躁 ③粗声粗气地说,生气地说: ~ out a command 粗声粗气地发号施令 ❷ *vi.* ①粗锉,粗擦 ②发出刺耳的声音 ‖**~er** *n.* ①锉刀;锉机;用锉刀的人 ②(打猎时)难越过的高栏 / **~y** *a.* ①发刺耳声的 ②焦躁的,易怒的

raspberry ['rɑːzbəri] *n.* ①【植】悬钩子,木莓,山莓: ~ canes 悬钩子的新枝 / ~ jam 木莓果酱 ②[俚](表示憎恶、嘲笑、不赞成等的)咂舌声(或姿势): get the ~ 被咂舌嘲笑 / give sb. the ~ 咂舌嘲笑某人 ③[俚]辞退

rat [ræt] I *n.* ①老鼠,耗子: A ~ crossing the street is chased by all. 老鼠过街,人人喊打。/ catch ~s by the trap 用夹子捉老鼠 ②讨厌鬼;可耻的人;叛徒,变节者;告密者,密探 ③破坏罢工的工人,工贼 ④[口]假发卷 ⑤[美俚]新学生 ⑥[美俚]下流女人 II (ratted; ratting) ❶ *vi.* ①捕鼠: go *ratting* 去捕鼠 ②叛变,变节;当密探;当工贼: ~ on sb. 密告(或背弃)某人 ❷ *vt.* [美]把(毛发)弄得蓬蓬松松 ‖a ~ leaving a *sinking ship* 不能共患难的人 / a ~ race 见 **race**[1] / *die like a* ~ 被毒死 / *have a* ~ *in a*

garret ①不安 ②想入非非;近于疯癫 ③[口]抱着难实现的希望 / *like a drowned* ~ (湿得)象落汤鸡 / *like a* ~ *in a hole* 象瓮中之鳖 / ~ *out* [美俚]失面子后离开 / *Rats!* [俚]胡说! / *smell a* ~ 感到有可疑之处;感到事情不妙: I smelt a ~ in the matter. 我感到这件事里面有问题。‖**like** *a.* 老鼠的;像老鼠的 ‖**~-bite fever**【医】鼠咬热 / ~ **cheese** (工厂出品的)一般硬奶酪 / **'~-face** *n.* [美俚]阴险卑鄙的人 / '**~-fish** *n.* 银鲛科鱼 (船上穿在绳缆上的)防鼠隔,鼠挡 / ~ **snake** 吃老鼠的蛇 / '**~-tail** *n.* ①没毛的马尾巴 ②长有细长圆柱状短粗刺的植物 / '**~-trap** *n.* ① 捕鼠夹,老鼠琼 ②东歪西倒的肮脏房屋 ③[喻]绝境;困境 / ~ **unit**【医】鼠单位(一种生物鉴定单位)

ratchet ['rætʃit], **ratch** [rætʃ] I *n.* 【机】棘轮机构;棘轮;棘爪 II *vt.* 安装棘轮机构于 ‖~ **wheel** 棘轮

rate[1] [reit] I *n.* ①比率,率: the ~ of finished (spoiled) products 成品(废品)率 / the ~ between the U. S. dollar and the pound sterling 美元与英镑间的兑换率 ②速度,速率: The train was going at the (或 a) ~ of 80 kilometres an hour. 火车正以每小时八十公里的速度前进。/ increase at a great ~ 迅速地增长 / an aircraft with a good ~ of climb 上升速率高的飞机 ③价格;估价: be sold at a high (low) ~ 以高 (低)价出售 / value sth. at a low ~ 低估某事物 ④等级: of the first ~ 头等的 ⑤房地产税率;[英]地方税: ~s and taxes 地方税和国家税 ⑥钟表快慢的差率: the daily ~ 每天的慢差率 ‖a birth ~ 出生率 / a death ~ 死亡率 / a discount (或 bank) ~【商】贴现率 / postal ~s 邮资 / a ~ of fire (或 firing ~)【军】射速 / a ~ of flow 水流量 / a ~ of (foreign) exchange (外汇)兑换率 / a ~ of interest (或 an interest ~) 利率 / a survival ~ 成活率 II ❶ *vt.* ①对…估价;对…评价; 对…评定: He did not ~ the machine above its real value. 他没有对机器估价过高。/ ~ an achievement high 高度评价一项成就 ②认为;列为: He is ~d (as) a good electrician. 他被看作是好的电工。/ This heavy-duty truck is ~d among the best of its kind. 这种载重汽车在同类型中是最好的。③定(货物)的运费 ④估定…的保险费 ⑤[口]值得,应得: special attention 值得特别注意 ⑥[英][常用被动语态]向…征地方税;为了征收地方税而估计(财产)的价值 ⑦【海】定(船员)的等级;定(船)的等级 ⑧调整(钟表)的快慢差率;找出(钟表)的快慢差率 ❷ *vi.* 被评价,被列入等级;有价值: ~ high in sb.'s estimation 受到某人很高的评价 / The ship ~s as second. 这船列入二级。‖at an easy ~ 廉价地;很容易地,不费力地 / at any ~ ①无论如何: At any ~, the medical supplies will reach you within a week. 无论如何,医疗备将于一星期内送到你处。②至少 / at that ~

那样的话; 照那种情形: If you go on *at that* ~, you will injure your health. 那样下去的话, 你会把身体搞垮的。/ *at this* ~ 这样地; 这样的话 / *be on the* ~s (在英国等)领取公共救济金 / ~ *up* 向(易遇险的人等)征收较高的保险费 / ~ *with sb.* 受某人好评 ‖~d **horsepower** (飞机等的)额定马力 / ~d **load** (机器等的)额定负载 / '~,**payer** *n.* [英]纳税人

rate² [reit] ❶ *vt.* 责骂, 怒斥 ❷ *vi.* 责骂, 怒斥 (*at*)

rather ['rɑːðə] *ad.* ①宁可, 宁愿; (与其⋯)倒不如: ~ die than surrender 宁死不屈 / I *would* (或 *had*) ~ you post*ed* the letter right away. 我倒希望你把这封信立即寄出。/ I, ~ *than* you, should do the work. 该做这工作的是我, 而不是你。②更确切地: He worked till late last night, *or* ~, early this morning. 他一直工作到深夜, 或者更确切地说, 到今天凌晨。③相当, 颇; 有点儿: a ~ hot day (或 ~ a hot day) 相当热的一天 / You've done ~ well. 你做得相当好。/ I ~ think so. 我倒是这样想的。④相反地: The patient was no better but ~ grew worse. 病人情况不但没有见好, 反而进一步恶化了。⑤['rɑː-ðə] [英口]当然, 的确(回答问题时用): A: Do you like the film? B: *Rather*! 甲: 你欢喜这部片子吗? 乙: 当然啦! ‖~ ... *than otherwise* 不是别的而是⋯: It is ~ cold *than otherwise*. 天还是挺冷的。/ ~ *too* 稍微⋯一点: This one is ~ *too* large. 这一个稍微大了一点。/ *the* ~ *that* 何况; 因为⋯所以更加: I'll not go now, *the* ~ *that* it's too late. 因为太迟了, 所以我现在更不想去了。‖~**ish** ['rɑːðəriʃ] *ad.* 颇, 相当; 有点儿, 有几分

ratification [,rætifi'keiʃən] *n.* 批准; 认可: exchange instruments of ~ 互换批准书

ratify ['rætifai] *vt.* 批准; 认可: ~ a convention 批准公约 ‖**ratifier** *n.* 批准者; 认可者

rating¹ ['reitiŋ] *n.* ①级别, 等级; 军阶 ②额定值; 定额; [无]标称值 ③[主英]海军入伍士兵 ④(商人、商店等的)信用程度 ⑤[美](电台、电视台经典型调查后确定的)节目受欢迎程度

rating² ['reitiŋ] *n.* 责骂, 申斥: give sb. a severe ~ 严厉申斥某人

ratio ['reiʃiou] *n.* 比, 比率: be in the ~ of five to seven 成五与七之比 / the direct (inverse) ~ 正(反)比 / turns ~ 【电】匝数比 ②【经】复本位制中金银的法定比价

ration ['ræʃən] **I** *n.* ①(食物等的)定量, 配给量: a ~ card (book) 定量供应卡(簿) / ~ bread 配给面包 / ~ the gasoline ~ for the month 每月的汽油配给量 ②[常用复][军]给养; 口粮; 食物: marching ~s 行军干粮 / draw ~s 领取给养 / a dry ~ bag 干粮袋 ③(配给物的)一份 **II** *vt.* 配给, 定量供应; 分发: be ~ed with sugar 配给到食糖 / The army is well ~ed. 部队给养良好。/ ~ out the bread 分发面包 / ~ the water

限制用水 ‖*an iron* (或 *emergency*) ~ (备急用的)浓缩食物, 军用干粮 / *on short* ~s 处于配给量不足的情况中 / *put on* ~s 对(居民等)实行配给应制

rational ['ræʃənl] **I** *a.* ①理性的; 推理的: perceptual knowledge and ~ knowledge 感性认识和理性认识 ②有理性的; 有推理能力的; 有理解力的 ③出于理性的; 合理的; 适度的; 明事理的: a ~ act 合理的行为 / ~ readjustment 合理调整 / a perfectly ~ explanation 完全合乎情理的解释 ④【数】有理的, 命分的 **II** *n.* 有理数 (= ~ number) ‖~**ism** *n.* ①理性主义 ②【哲】唯理论 / ~**ist** *n.* ①理性主义者 ②【哲】唯理论者 / ~**ly** *ad.*

rattan [rə'tæn] *n.* ①【植】白藤属植物; 藤 ②藤条, 藤杖

rattle ['rætl] **I** ❶ *vi.* ①发出格格声: The windows were *rattling* in the wind. 窗在风中不断格格作响。/ The machine gun ~d away. 机枪嗒嗒地响个不停。/ He ~d at the door. 他把门摇得格格地响。②嘎拉嘎拉地行进(或掉下): The handcart ~d along. 手推车嘎拉嘎拉地前行。③喋喋不休 ❷ *vt.* ①使发出格格声: Who is *rattling* the door handle? 谁在把门弄得格格地响? ②急促地讲(或背诵); 匆忙地做; 使迅速移动(或通过): ~ a bill through the House 使议案在议会中匆匆通过 / ~ up the anchor 把锚迅速收起 ③[口]使慌乱; 扰乱: The basketball players were ~d by their opponents' tactics. 篮球运动员们被对方的战术搞乱了阵脚。/ a speaker by heckling 不断的诘问扰乱发言者 ④使觉醒, 使振作 (*up*) ⑤从(草丛)中赶出猎物 **II** *n.* ①格格声; 吵闹声 ②喋喋不休的话; 喋喋不休的人 ③拨浪鼓(一种幼儿玩具) ④喉部发出的哮吼声(如人临死前所发出的); [the ~s]【医】哮吼; 一种喉炎(旧名格鲁布) ⑤响尾蛇尾部的(全部)响环 ⑥果实成熟时在荚中格格作响的种籽 ‖*the sabre* 见 sabre ‖'~**box** *n.* ①格格响的玩具匣 ②【植】猪屎豆 / '~**brain,** '~**head,** '~**pate** *n.* 头脑空虚的人; 愚蠢而饶舌的人 / '~**brained,** '~,**headed,** '~,**pated** *a.* 头脑空虚的; 愚蠢而饶舌的 / '~**snake** *n.* 响尾蛇 / '~**trap** *n.* ①破旧得格格响的东西; 旧车辆 / [俚]饶舌的人; 嘴 ②古玩; 零碎东西 *a.* 破旧的; 格格响的, 破旧的

raucous ['rɔːkəs] *a.* ①沙哑的; 粗声的: the ~ cries of the crows 乌鸦的粗哑叫声 ②喧闹的 ‖~**ly** *ad.* / ~**ness** *n.*

rave¹ [reiv] **I** ❶ *vi.* ①胡言乱语; 狂骂; 激烈地说话: The patient began to ~. 病人开始说呓语。/ ~ wildly *against* sb. 破口大骂某人 ②醉心地说, 痴心地说 (*about, of*) ③(风等)呼啸, 咆哮; 迅猛前进: The wind ~d through the mountains. 风呼啸着掠过群山。❷ *vt.* ①语无伦次地说, 狂乱地说 ②醉心地说, 痴心地说 ③[~ one-self] 使叫嚷(或呼啸)得⋯: He ~d *himself*

hoarse. 他叫嚷得嗓子也哑了。 / The storm
~d itself out. 暴风雨狂袭了一阵后停了。 II n.
①胡言乱语; 狂骂; 呼啸, 咆哮 ②疯狂, 狂乱 ③
[俚]醉心, 痴心; 醉心的话: a ~ review of a play
对一出戏的热烈的好评

rave² [reiv] n. [常用复](运货车四周的)栏板

ravel ['rævəl] I (ravel(l)ed; ravel(l)ing) ❶ vt.
①使纠缠; 使混乱, 使错综复杂: the ravel(l)ed
skein of life 错综复杂的人生 ②拆散, 解开(out):
~ (out) a rope's end 拆开绳头 ③弄清(复杂的事
件) ❷ vi. ①(编织物等)散开, 松散 ②解除, 得
到解决(out): The difficulty will soon ~ out. 困
难会很快得到解决。 II n. ①纠缠的东西; 纷乱的
一撮; 错综复杂的一团 ②(编织物等的)散开部分
||**ravel(l)er** n. ①使纠缠者; 使变得错综复杂者
②拆散者, 解开者 / **ravel(l)ing** n. [常用复]
被拆散的东西(尤指拆下的线), 被解开的东西 ②
纠缠; 混乱 ③拆散, 解开 / ~**ment** n. 纠缠; 混
乱

raven¹ ['reivən] I n. [动]渡鸦 II a. 乌亮油的, 墨
黑的: ~ locks 乌油油的头发

raven² ['rævən] I ❶ vi. ①贪食, 狼吞虎咽 ②悄
悄地捕食 ③掠夺, 抢劫 ❷ vt. 狼吞虎咽地吃 II
n. =ravin / ~**er** n. ①强夺者, 强盗 ②贪食的
人 ③贪食的野兽

ravenous ['rævinəs] a. ①贪婪的; 狼吞虎咽的 ②
饿极了的, 受饥的 ③渴望的 ||~**ly** ad. / ~**ness**
n.

ravine [rə'vi:n] n. 沟壑; 深谷

ravish ['ræviʃ] vt. ①强夺; 抢去: be ~ed from the
world by death 被死神夺去生命, 死 ②使出神, 使
陶醉: be ~ed by the beauty of the West
Lake 被西湖的秀丽迷住 ③强奸 ||~**er** n. 强夺
者; 强奸者 / ~**ment** n. 强夺; 陶醉, 狂喜; 强奸

raw [ro:] I a. ①未煮过的, 生的: ~ meat 生肉 /
eat shrimps ~ 吃生虾 ②未加工的; 半加工的;
处于自然状态的: ~ cotton 原棉 / ~ ore 原矿
石 / ~ sugar 粗糖 / ~ data 原始材料; 素材 ③
(酒精等)未稀释的, 纯的: ~ spirit 无水酒精
④生疏的, 未经训练的, 无经验的: a ~ hand 生
手 / a ~ wind 阴冷的风 / a ~ winter day 阴湿
的冬日 ⑦(伤口等)露肉的, 擦掉皮的; 刺痛的; 赤
裸的; (织物)毛边的: a ~ edge (of cloth) (布的)
毛边 / a ~ wound 刺痛的伤口 ⑧[口]粗鄙的,
下流的: a ~ remark 下流话 / pull a ~ one 讲
粗俗下流的笑话 ⑨[俚]苛刻的; 不公正的, 粗暴
的 II n. 擦伤处; 红肿发炎处 III vt. 擦破(马背
等) ||**in the** ~ ①处在自然状态; 不完善的 ②
裸露的, 裸体的 / **touch sb. on the** ~ 触到某人
的痛处 ||~**ly** ad. / ~**ness** n. ||~'**boned** a.
骨瘦如柴的 / ~ **deal** 不公平的待遇 / '~**head**
n. (用来吓唬孩子的)妖怪: ~head and bloody

bones 骷髅头和交叉的腿骨(死的象征); (吓唬孩
子的)妖怪, 可怕的东西 / '~**hide** n. 生牛皮; 牛
皮鞭 a. 生牛皮的 / ~ **material** 原料 / ~ **silk**
生丝 / ~ **water** 未经净化的水

ray¹ [rei] I n. ①光线; 射线; (热、能等的)辐射线
②辐射状的直线; (图画中)表示光的线 ③光辉;
一线光芒: a ~ of intelligence 一线智慧的光芒
④微量, 丝毫: a ~ of hope 一线希望 ⑤[数]半
直线; [军]半径 ⑥[植]伞形花序枝; 星状毛分枝;
【动】辐肋; 鳍刺 ||alpha ~s α 射线 / anode
(cathode) ~s 阳(阴)极射线 / beta ~s β 射线 /
cosmic ~s 宇宙射线 / gamma ~s γ 射线 /
infrared ~s 红外线 / Roentgen ~s 伦琴射线
(即 X 射线) / ultraviolet ~s 紫外线 II ❶ vi.
放射光线; (思想、希望等)闪现; 向周围放送 ❷
vt. 放射, 射出(光线等); 显出(智慧、才能等)
||~**less** a. 无光线的; 昏暗的 ||~ **flower** 【植】
(盘)边花

ray² [rei] n. 【动】鳐鱼; 虹鱼

rayon ['reiɔn] n. ①人造丝, 人造纤维, 嫘萦 ②人
(造)丝织物

raze [reiz] vt. ①铲平; 把(城市、房屋等)夷为平
地; 拆毁; 毁灭: a city ~d by an earthquake 被
地震彻底破坏的城市 ②刮去, 削去(out); 抹去,
消除(印象等): ~ sb. from one's remembrance
有意忘却某人 ③[军]使负轻伤; 擦伤 ||~ **to the**
ground 把…夷为平地

razor ['reizə] I n. 剃刀: a safety ~ 保安剃刀 II
vt. ①[罕]剃, 刮 ②[美俚]瓜分(赃物) ||as
sharp as a ~ 厉害的; 机警的 / be on a ~'s
edge (或 ~-edge) 在锋口上; 处于十分危险的境
地, 在危急关头 ||~**back** n. ①【动】剃刀鲸; (美
国南部的)半野猪 ②[美俚]干体力活的人; 看门
人 / '~-**back(ed)** a. (有)尖削背脊的 / '~=
'edge n. ①剃刀的锋口 ②尖削的山脊 ③危急
关头 ④鲜明的分界线 / ~ **fish** 【动】隆头鱼科的
一种鱼 / ~ **shell** 【动】竹蛏 / ~ **strop** 磨剃刀的
皮带

re¹ [ri:; 美 rei] n. 【音】七个唱名之一(在固定唱
名法中相当于音名 D)

re² [ri:] prep. 关于: ~ your letter of yesterday
关于你昨天的来信 ||in ~ 关于 / ~ infecta
[in'fektə] 未完成

reach [ri:tʃ] I ❶ vt. ①抵达, 到达; 达到: Your
letter ~ed me this morning. 你的信我今天早
上收到。 / The news ~ed every part of the
world. 这消息传到了全世界。 / The two sides
have ~ed an identity of views. 双方取得了一
致的看法。 / ~ adolescence (maturity) 达到青少
年期(成熟期) ②伸出(手、树枝等): He ~ed his
hand (out) for the book. 他伸手拿那本书。
③伸手(或脚等)及到: Can you ~ the top shelf?
你(的手)能够到那最高的架子吗? ④ 把…递来:
Please ~ me the newspaper. 请把报纸递给我。
⑤影响, 对…起作用: This rule does not ~ the
case. 这条规则不适用于这种情况。 ⑥与…取得

联系: I couldn't ～ him by phone this morning. 今天早晨我给他打电话打不通. **❷** *vi.* ①达到; 延伸: Our campus ～es down to the river. 我们的校园一直延伸到河边. / a peak ～*ing* into the clouds 高耸入云的山峰 / as far as the eye can ～ 就眼力所能及; 极目 ②伸出手(或脚): ～ (out) *for* the dictionary 伸出手去拿词典 / I can't ～ so high. 我够不到这么高. / Excuse my ～*ing over* you. (伸手越过他人拿东西时的用语)对不起, 我拿一下东西. ③竭力想得到: ～ *after* personal fame and gain 追求个人名利 ④传开, 深入: The sound ～ed to the back of the hall. 声音直传到大厅的后面. ⑤【海】横风行驶 **II** *n.* ①伸, 伸出: make a ～ *for* sth. (sb.) 伸手拿某物(抓某人) / get sth. by a long ～ (费力地)伸长着手拿到某物 ②到达距离: be out of ～ of guns 在大炮射程以外 ③(智力、影响等)能及的范围: We don't believe it's beyond the ～ of human power. 我们不相信这是人力所能办到的. / have a wonderful ～ of imagination 有很丰富的想象力 ④区域;【地】河段; 河流流程: a ～ of woodland 一片林地 ⑤岬 ⑥【海】横风行驶 ⑦一段旅程: arrive at the destination after three ～*es* 全程分三段走完后到达目的地 ⑧车辆前部与后轴的连杆 ‖'**～-me-down** [主英] *a.* ①现成的(常指廉价而劣质的) ②旧的; 别人用过的 ③[美俚]无个性的, 千篇一律的; 不真诚的 *n.* [常用复] ①现成(或穿旧)的衣服 ②旧事物

react [ri(ː)'ækt] *vi.* ①起反应 (to): The eye ～*s* to light. 眼睛对光起反应. / The audience ～*ed* readily to his speech. 听众对他的演说立即起了反应. ②有影响; 起化学反应; 起作用 (on, upon): Applause ～*s on* (或 *upon*) a speaker. (听众的)鼓掌对讲演者有影响. / Sulphuric acid ～*s on* (或 *upon*) zinc. 硫酸对锌起反应. / ～ *on* (或 *upon*) each other 相互起作用 / ～*ing* weight 反应量 ③反抗 ④回复原状 ⑤【军】反攻 ⑧受到化学反应

re-act ['riː'ækt] *vt.* ①重作, 再做 ②重演, 再演

reaction [ri(ː)'ækʃən] *n.* ①反应, 感应: What was his ～ *to* our proposal? 他对我们的提议有什么反应? / evoke powerful ～*s* among the audience 在听众中引起强烈的反应 ②【化】反应;【物】反应作用力: chain ～ 连锁反应 / organic ～ 有机反应 / fusion ～ 【原子核】聚合反应 / bearing ～ 轴承反应力 ③【医】反应; (由神经紧张、过度刺激等所引起的)体力下降 ④反作用: action and ～ 作用和反作用 / the ～ of the superstructure *on* the economic base 上层建筑对于经济基础的反作用 ⑤反动; 极端保守 ⑥回复原状【无】反馈, 回授 ⑧【军】回击 ‖**～ism** *n.* 反动主义; 极端保守主义 / **～ist** *n.* 反动分子 *a.* 反动的 / **～ engine** 喷气发动机 / **～ time** 【心】反应时间

reactor [ri(ː)'æktə] *n.* ①引起(或经受)反应作用的人(或物);【化】反应器 ②【电】电抗器, 扼流圈 ③【原】反应堆: nuclear ～ 核反应堆 ④【医】(对外来物质)呈阳性反应的人(或动物)

read[1] [riːd] **I** (read [red]) **❶** *vt.* ①读, 阅读; 默读; 朗读: We ～ newspapers every day. 我们每天读报. / Will you please ～ me this poem? 请你把这首诗读给我听好吗? / ～ out a statement 宣读声明 / ～ over an article 把文章读一遍 ②看懂, 辨认; 觉察: He ～*s* English, but doesn't speak it. 他看得懂英文, 但不会讲. / The child can ～ the clock now. 孩子现在会看钟了. / ～ shorthand 看懂速记 / ～ sb.'s mind 看出某人的心思 / ～ the sky 观天色 / ～ malice in sb.'s compliment 在某人的恭维话中觉察出恶意 ③解释, 理解; 解答; 预言: How do you ～ this passage? 这一段话你怎么解释? / Do not ～ my silence as consent. 不要把我的沉默看作同意. / ～ a riddle 猜出谜语 / ～ an ill omen 预卜凶兆 / ～ sb.'s hand 看某人的手相 ④读到, 获悉: He ～ the news only yesterday. 他昨天才读到这条新闻. ⑤攻读, 学习: ～ law at a university 在大学读法律 ⑥记明, 标明; (在雷达屏上)定出(我方飞机)的位置: The thermometer ～*s* 15℃. 温度计标明摄氏十五度. ⑦(指不同版本等中词语的特定形式)(印)作: This edition ～*s* "hurry", not "harry". 这个版本印作 "hurry", 不作 "harry". ⑧(在勘误表等中)用…去代替: In the fifth line, ～ "hurry" *for* "harry". 在第五行中, 将 "harry" 改为 "hurry". ⑨演奏(乐曲等) ⑩使…读得: ～ oneself *to* sleep 看书看得睡着了 / ～ oneself hoarse 读得喉咙都哑了 / 校对 **❷** *vi.* ①读, 阅读; 朗读: have enough time to ～ (或 *for* ～*ing*) 有足够的时间看书报 / learn how to ～ and write 学习读书写字 ②读到, 获悉 (*about, of*): ～ *about* the arrival of the foreign guests 读到关于外宾到达的消息 ③攻读, 学习 ④(文章等)内容是; 读起来: The full text ～*s* as follows: .... 全文如下:… / This poem ～*s* well. 这首诗读起来很好. / I wonder how the letter would ～ to her. 我不知道她读到这封信会有怎么样的感觉. / That article ～*s* like a translation. 那篇文章读起来象一篇译文. **II** *n.* [主英]一段阅读时间: have a good ～ in the train 在火车上阅读了好一会 / have a short (long) ～ 读了一会儿(长时间) ‖**～ aloud** 朗读 / **～ back** 【军】重复, 复述 / **～ between the lines** 见 **line**[1] / **～ into** 把…塞进对…的理解中去: Don't ～ your own thoughts *into* the poem. 不要把你自己的想法硬加在这首诗中. / **～ (oneself) in** [英](在当众朗读三十九个信条后)就任牧师职位 / **～ out** ①宣告开除 ②把…读出声来 ③【自】读出(指把计算机存储器中的资料取出等) / **～ sb. a lesson** (或 *lecture*) 训斥某人一顿 / **～ up** 攻读, 熟读: ～ *up* (on) space rockets 攻读宇宙火箭学 ‖**'～-in** *n.* ①【自】写入 ②宣读活动(如议员在国会宣读某种文件以反对某事) / **'～out** *n.* ①宣读 ②宣告开除 ③指示数字的装置;【自】读出: sum ～*out* 和数读出

read² [red] **I** read¹ 的过去式和过去分词 **II** *a.* 书看得多的,有学问的: a well-~ man 博学的人 / be deeply (little) ~ in the classics 精通 (不大熟悉)古典文学

readable ['ri:dəbl] *a.* ①(书等)易读的;使人爱读的,有趣味的 ②(笔迹等)可看懂的,清楚的

reader ['ri:də] *n.* ①读者;朗诵者 ②读物,读本;文选: an English ~ 英语读本 / a G. B. Shaw ~ 萧伯纳选集 ③(出版物的)审稿人;校对人: ~'s marks 校对符号 ④(水、电等的)抄表员 ⑤【宗】读经师 ⑥代教授阅卷的助教;(英国某些大学的)高级讲师: a ~ in European literature 欧洲文学讲师 ⑦【化】读数镜;【自】读出器: a punch card ~ 穿孔卡片阅读器 ⑧[美俚]营业(或演出)执照 ⑨[美俚]缉捕通知 ⑩(注明售价等的)标签 ‖a mind ~ 能清出别人心思的人 ‖**ship** *n.* ①读者(或审稿人、讲师等)的身分 ②(某一书刊等的)读者们,读者总数: increase the ~*ship* of a magazine 增加杂志的读者数量

reading ['ri:diŋ] **I** *n.* ①读,阅读;朗读: intensive ~ 精读 / extensive ~ 泛读 ②朗诵会;朗读的章节 ③读书;学识: a man of wide ~ 博览群书的人 ④读物,阅读材料: ~s in Chinese literature 中国文学读本 ⑤读起来…的东西: The book is good (dull) ~. 这本书读起来有趣(枯燥)。/ This article makes heavy ~. 这篇文章读起来费劲。⑥【物】读数,仪器指示数: the ~s on the thermometer 温度计读数 / staff ~ 水准尺读数 ⑦(不同版本的)异文: There were several ~s for the passage. 这一段有几种异文。/ the right ~ 各种异文中正确的一种 ⑧ 解释,看法: What is your ~ of the facts? 你对这些事实怎么看法? ⑨(对剧本人物等的)表演;(对乐曲等的)演奏: His ~ of the hero of the play is excellent. 他演主角演得很出色。⑩(议会的)读议案: the first ~ 一读 (提出议案供审议) / the second ~ 二读 (辩论议案采纳与否) / the third ~ 三读(对委员会所修正的议案的最后辩论) **II** *a.* 阅读的: the ~ public 广大读者 / a ~ report 书面报告 ‖**book** 读本 / ~ **desk** 斜面书桌;【宗】读经台 / ~ **glass** (看小字用的)放大镜 / ~ **lamp** 台灯 / ~ **room** ①阅览室 ②(印刷厂的)校对室

ready ['redi] **I** *a.* ①[用作表语]准备好的: Are you ~? 你准备好了吗? ②[用作表语]思想有准备的;愿意的,乐意的 ③[用作表语]快要…的;易于…的,动辄…的: be ~ to launch an attack 即将发动进攻 / be ~ to suspect 多疑 ④快的,迅速的: give a ~ reply 脱口而出地回答 / the readiest way to do it 做这事的最简便的方法 ⑤敏捷的,机灵的: He has a ~ pen. 他下笔很快。/ a ~ worker 熟练的工作者,快手 / ~ wit 机敏 ⑥立即可得到的;用起来便利的;预先准备好的,现成的: Reference materials are ~ to (或 at) hand. 参考资料就在手边。**II** *ad.* ①预先准备好: The products are packed ~. 产品已预先包装好。/ buy food ~ cooked 买熟食 ②[常

用比较级或最高级]迅速: He answered *readiest*. 他回答得最快。**III** *n.* ①【军】射击的准备姿势: come to the ~ 托枪(准备射击) ②[常作 the ~] [口]现款: be well supplied with the ~ 现金充足 **IV** *vt.* 使准备好: The two sides are readying themselves for negotiations. 双方正在为谈判作好准备。/ Rolled plates are being *readied* for shipment. 轧制钢板正在准备装运。‖**get** ~ (使)准备好: *get* ~ for an expedition 作好远征的准备 / *get* the players ~ for the game 使运动员们准备好参加比赛 / *make* ~ 准备好: We must *make* the spare bedrooms ~ for the new students. 我们必须把空的寝室准备好,让新学员来住。/ *Ready all!*【军】各就各位! / *Ready, present, fire!*【军】预备,瞄准,放! / ~ *up* [俚]即付;用现金支付 ‖**~-'made** *a.* ①现成的,预先制成的: ~-made clothes 现成衣服 ②(卖)现成物品的: a ~-made shop 卖现成衣服的店 ③平凡的;陈旧的,非创新的: ~-made opinions 陈旧的意见 / '~-'mix *a.* 掺水(或液体)即可用的: ~-mix concrete【建】预拌混凝土 / ~ **money** 现款 / ~ **reckoner** 计算便览,简便计算表 / ~ **reserve**【军】第一类预备役 / ~ **room**【军】(空勤人员的)待命室 / '~-to-'wear *a.* (衣服)现成的 / '~-'witted *a.* 灵敏的,机智的

real¹ [riəl] **I** *a.* ①真的,真正的: Is it rayon or silk? 这是人造丝还是真丝? / ~ knowledge 真知 / effect a ~ cure 根治 / a ~ man 真诚的人;真正的人(指品质高尚的人) ②现实的,实际的;真实的: in ~ life 在现实生活中 / ~ income 实际收入 / the ~ reason 实际的理由(同 the good reason 表面宣称的理由相对) ③【律】(产业等)不动的: ~ estate (或 property) 不动产,房地产 /【哲】实在的 ‖~ **account**【商】实帐 / ~ **image**【物】实像 / ~ **money** 现金;[总称]硬币 / ~ **number**【数】实数 / the ~ **thing** 真货;上等品 **II** *n.* ①实在的东西;【数】实数 ② [the ~] 现实 **III** *ad.* [口]真正: I am ~ pleased to meet you. 遇到你我真高兴。/ ~ gone 极度地,彻底地 ‖**for** ~ [美俚] ①真的,实在的;可能的: Are you *for* ~? (你讲的)是真的吗? ②很,非常 ‖**'~-life** *a.* 真实的,非想象的 / ~ **McCoy** [美俚] ①出色人物(或东西) ②纯威士忌酒 / **Real Presence** (基督教教义)圣体实在 (指举行圣餐时吃的面包与酒确实是耶稣的身体和血)

realism ['riəlizəm] *n.* ① (文艺的)现实主义,写实主义: critical ~ 批判现实主义 / socialist ~ 社会主义现实主义 ②【哲】唯实论,实在论 ③(对人对事的)现实主义态度

realist ['riəlist] **I** *n.* ①现实主义者;现实主义作家 ②【哲】唯实论者,实在论者 ③采取现实主义态度的人 **II** *a.* =realistic

realistic [riə'listik] *a.* ①现实主义的;现实主义派的: a ~ novel 一本现实主义小说 ②逼真的: Their acting was ~. 他们演得逼真。③现实的,实际的: take a ~ attitude 采取现实的态度 ④【哲】唯实论的,实在论的 ‖**~ally** *ad.*

reality [ri(:)'æliti] *n.* ①现实; 实际存在的事物: the *realities* of the day 当前的现实 / an objective ~ 客观现实 / make sth. a ~ 实现某事 ②真实: believe in the ~ of the statement 相信这说法是真的 ③逼真: describe a scene with ~ 逼真地描写情景 ④【哲】实在 ‖**bring sb. back to** ~ 使某人面对现实 / **in** ~ 实际上,事实上

realize ['riəlaiz] ❶ *vt.* ①实现: ~ one's hopes (aspirations) 实现希望(愿望) ②认识到,认清,了解: It must be ~d that .... 必须了解… ③使显得逼真: These details help to ~ the scene. 这些细节使场面显得逼真。④ 把(证券、产业等)变为现钱 ⑤(因出售、投资等而)获得(利润等) ❷ *vi.* 变卖产业 (或产权等)为现钱 ‖**realization** [,riəlai'zeifən] *n.*

really ['riəli] *ad.* ①真正地: a ~ hot day 真正炎热的天 / Do you ~ want to go? 你真的要去吗? ②实在; 真实地: It was ~ not his fault, but mine. 这实在不是他的错,而是我的错。/ reflect things as they ~ are 如实地反映事物 ③[表示关心、惊讶、怀疑、异议等]: A: He is leaving tomorrow. B: Oh, ~? (Not ~!) 甲: 他明天就走了。乙: 啊,真的吗? (不会吧!) ‖*~ and truly* — *a ~ and truly* magnificent sight 真正壮丽之极的景象 / Do you ~ *and truly* say so? 你真这样说吗?

realm [relm] *n.* ①王国;国土,领土: an independent ~ [喻]独立王国 / advance from the ~ of necessity to the ~ of freedom 从必然王国走向自由王国 / the laws of the ~ 王国的法律 ②领域,范围: the ~ of literature and art 文学艺术领域 / in the ~ of the superstructure 在上层建筑领域里 / within the ~ of possibility 属于可能的范围,有可能性的 ③(生物地理学中生物的)类,门

realty ['riəlti] *n.* 【律】不动产,房地产

ream[1] [ri:m] *n.* ① 令 (纸张的计数单位,一般为500 张左右): a printer's ~ 令印刷纸 (516 张) ②[常用复][口](指纸张、写作等)大量: He wrote ~s on the subject. 关于这题目他写了很多。

ream[2] [ri:m] *vt.* ①(用铰刀等)铰大,钻大(孔);铰大(枪等)的口径 (*out*) ②铰除(疵点等) (*out*) ③榨出(水果等)的汁;榨取(果汁等) ④ 折进(子弹壳等)的边

reap [ri:p] ❶ *vt.* ①收割,从…收割庄稼;收获: ~ the rice 收割稻子 / ~ a field of wheat 收割田里的小麦 / ~ a rich cotton crop 获得棉花丰收 ②获得,得到: ~ profits through (或 from) 从…获得利润 ❷ *vi.* ①收割; 收获 ②遭到报应;得到报偿 ‖*As a man sows, so he shall* ~. (或 *You must* ~ *what you have sown.*) 种瓜得瓜,种豆得豆。/ ~ *where one has not sown* 自食其果 / ~ *where one has not sown* 不劳而获 / *sow the wind and* ~ *the whirlwind* 见 **wind**[1] ‖*~ing hook* 镰刀 / *~ing machine* 收割机

rear[1] [riə] **I** *n.* ①后部; 后面: The hall is *in* the ~ of the building. 大厅在建筑物的后部。/ The storehouse is *at* the ~ of the workshop. 仓库在车间后面。/ I saw them far *in* the ~. 我看见他们远远地在后面。②【军】后方,(部队、舰队等)的后尾 ③背面,背后: the ~ of a bookcase 书架的背面 ④[英口] 厕所 ⑤[口]臀部 **II** *a.* ①后部的; 后面的: ~ wheels 后轮 / the ~ lamps of a car 汽车的后灯 / the ~ entrance of a bus 公共汽车后部的门 ②【军】后方的;殿后的: a ~ base 后方 (空军) 基地 / a ~ ship 殿后舰 / a ~ area 【军】后方地域 / a ~ party 后卫尖兵群 / a ~ point 后卫尖兵 / a ~ rank 【军】后列 / ~ service 后方勤务 ‖*bring up the* ~ (或 *close the* ~) 殿后 / *front and* ~ 在前后 / *hang on the* ~ *of* 跟在…后面伺机袭击 ‖*~most a.* 最后面的;最后的 / *~ward n.* 后部; 后面; (军队的)后卫 *a.* *in the ~ward* 在后面 / *to the ~ward of* 在…的后面 *a.* 在后面(或后部)的,向后面(或后部)的 / *~wards ad.* 在后面,向后面 ‖*~ admiral* 海军少将 / ~ *arch* 【建】背拱 (=rere-arch) / ~ *echelon* 【军】后方指挥所 / ~ *end* 后部; 臀部 / ~ *guard* 后卫,殿后: make a ~ *guard* for the procession 为行进队伍殿后 / '*~guard action* 【军】后卫战斗; [喻]维护旧制度的努力 / ~ *sight* 【军】表尺(距枪机最近的瞄准装置) / '*~view mirror* (装在车辆上可以照见车后情况的)反照镜,后视镜

rear[2] [riə] ❶ *vt.* ①抚养,培养: ~ children 抚养孩子 ②栽种,培植; 饲养: ~ crops 培育庄稼 / ~ cattle 饲养家畜 ③竖起,举起; 使(马等)用后腿站起 ④树立,建立 ❷ *vi.* ① 高耸: a steeple ~ing far into the sky 高耸入云的尖塔 ②(马等)用后腿站起 ③[喻]暴跳 (*up*)

reason ['ri:zn] **I** *n.* ①理由;原因: There is no ~ for us to be conceited and arrogant. 我们没有理由骄傲自大。/ Give your ~ for changing the plan. 把你改变计划的理由讲一下。/ The ~ *that* (或 *why*) it should be so is now clear. 应当如此的理由现在清楚了。②理智,理性;清醒的头脑(或神志): One must use ~ to solve this problem. 必须用理智来解决这个问题。/ be restored to ~ 恢复清醒的头脑(或正常的神志) / lose one's ~ 发疯 ③道理,情理;明智: There is ~ in what you say. 你讲的有道理。/ It stands to ~ that .... …是合乎情理的。/ bring sb. to ~ 说服某人变得明智些; 使某人讲道理 ④【逻】前提 (尤指推论的次序颠倒时在结论后面的小前提) ⑤(德国古典哲学中的)理性(与 understanding 知性相对) **II** ❶ *vi.* ①推论,推理,思考: ~ from general laws 从一般规律推论 / man's ability to ~ 人类的思考能力 / I ~ in this way on the matter. 对于这件事我是这样想的。②评理;劝说 (*with*): ~ *with* sb. for (against) 为了赞成(反对)…和某人评理 ❷ *vt.* ①推论,推理: He ~ed that .... 他推想道… / ~ *out* a conclusion 通过推理作出结论 ②与…评理; 劝说 (*out of, into*): ~ sb. *out of* his prejudice 说服某人消除成见 / ~ sb. *into* accepting a proposal 说服某人接受建议 ③ 辩论, 讨论: We need to ~ that point. 我们有必要讨论这一点。/ ~ whether it is right 讨论这是否正确 / set forth facts and ~ things out 摆事实讲道理 ‖*as* = *was* 根据情理 / *by* ~ *of* 由于, 因为: We succeeded *by* ~ *of* good organization. 因为组织得好, 我们成功了。/ *by* ~ *that* 因为…, 由于… / *for no other* ~ *than that* 只是因为… / *in* (*all*) ~ 明智, 合情合理; 在道理上: I would do anything in ~. 只要是合情合理的事我都愿意做。/ They cannot, *in* ~, doubt what he says. 在道理上, 他们不能怀疑他说的话。/ *listen to* (或 *hear*) ~ 听从道理, 服理 / *out of all* ~ 无理的, 不可喻的 / ~ *of State* 执政者的理由 (指替政府的不正当行为的辩护) / *see* ~ 看出…的理由: *see* ~ *to suspect* sb. 认为怀疑某人是有道理的 / I *saw* no ~ for your doing it. 我看不出你做这事的理由。/ *the* (或 *a*) *woman's* ~ 不成其为理由的“理由”, 讲不出道理的“理由” (如“我不喜它, 就是因为我不喜它。”) / *with* (*without*) ~ 有 (没有) 道理; 合乎 (不合乎) 情理: He argued *with* much ~. 他辩论得头头是道。/ *without rhyme or* ~ 见 **rhyme**

reasonable ['ri:znəbl] *a.* ①合情合理的, 有道理的; 适当的: be ~ *in* one's demands 合情合理地要求 / a ~ excuse 合理的辩解 / a ~ size 适当的尺寸 ②(价钱)公道的, 不贵的: be sold at a ~ price (或 rate) 售价公道 / Fresh vegetables are ~ in winter too. 冬季新鲜蔬菜的价钱也不贵。③通情达理的, 讲道理的: a ~ man 讲道理的人 ④有理智的, 有理性的; 明智的: a ~ being 有理智的动物, 人 ‖**~ness** *n.* / **reasonably** *ad.*

reassure [,ri:ə'ʃuə] *vt.* ①使放心, 使消除疑虑 ②再向…保证; 再对…进行保险 ‖**reassurance** [,ri:ə'ʃuərəns] *n.*

rebate ['ri:beit, ri'beit] **I** *n.* (付款总额的)减少; 回扣, 折扣: a 10% ~ for immediate payment 如立即付款可打九折 **II** ❶ *vt.* ①给予(某一数额)的回扣; 给(某人或票据)打折扣 ②减少; 削弱 ③使变钝 ❷ *vi.* 给予回扣; 打折扣

rebel I ['ri'bel] (rebelled; rebelling) *vi.* ①造反; 反叛; 反抗, 对抗(*against*) ②嫌恶, 反感: ~ *at* the very idea of 一想到…就有反感 **II** ['rebəl] *n.* ①造反者; 反抗者; 反叛者 ②[美][常作 R-](南北战争中的)南军士兵 **III** ['rebəl] *a.* ①造反的; 反抗的; 反叛的 ②造反者的; 反抗者的; 反叛者的 ‖**~dom** ['rebəldəm] *n.* 全体造反者; 造反者控制的地区; [美](南北战争中的)南方各州

rebellion [ri'beljən] *n.* ①造反 ②叛乱 ③反抗, 对抗

rebellious [ri'beljəs] *a.* ①反叛的; 反抗的; 反叛的 ②难对付的, 难管束的: ~ circumstances 难对付的情况 / a ~ temper 倔强的脾气 ③(疾病等)难治的 ‖**~ly** *ad.* / **~ness** *n.*

rebound[1] ['ri:'baund] rebind 的过去式和过去分词

rebound[2] [ri'baund] **I** ❶ *vi.* ①弹回, 跳回: The ball ~ed from the opponent's racket. 球从对手的球拍上弹了回来。②返回; 报应: His evil doings ~ed upon himself. 他干坏事而自食其果。③(从挫折中)重新振作; 跃起: ~ from disappointment 从失望中振作起来 ④(再)回响 ❷ *vt.* ①使弹回, 使跳回; 使返回 ②使回响 **II** *n.* ①弹回, 跳回; 返回: hit a ball *on the* ~ 击弹回的球 ②弹回的球; 接弹回的球 (主要指篮球) ③振作; 跃起: a sharp ~ *in* prices 价格激增 ④(遭受挫折等后情绪上的)波动, 反应: take (或 catch) sb. *on* (或 *at*) *the* ~ 利用某人(遭受挫折后)的情绪波动(而劝其改变行径)

rebuff [ri'bʌf] **I** *n.* 断然的拒绝; 冷淡; 挫败: meet with (或 suffer) a ~ (from sb.) 受到(某人的)拒绝 **II** *vt.* ①断然拒绝; 漠视: ~ an invitation from sb. 回绝某人的邀请 ②挫败, 击退: ~ the enemy attack 击退敌人的进攻

rebuke [ri'bju:k] **I** *vt.* ①指责, 非难; 训斥: ~ sb. *for* his neglect of duty 斥责某人失职 ②成为对…的指责: His industry ~s me. 他的勤劳使我感到惭愧。③阻碍, 制止 **II** *n.* 指责, 非难; 训斥: administer ~ to sb. 斥责某人 / be without ~ 无可非议, 无可指摘

rebut [ri'bʌt] (rebutted; rebutting) ❶ *vt.* ①【律】辩驳; 反驳, 驳回 ②揭露, 戳穿 ③抗拒; 击退 ❷ *vi.* 辩驳; 反驳, 驳回 ‖**~ment** *n.* 辩驳, 反驳, 驳回 / **rebuttable** *a.* 可辩驳的; 可反驳的, 可驳回的 / **rebuttal** *n.* ①辩驳; 反驳, 驳回(尤指法律方面) ②反驳的证据, 反证 / **rebutter** *n.* ①辩驳(或揭露等)的人; 反驳的论点 ②(被告的)第三(次)答辩

recall [ri'kɔ:l] **I** *vt.* ①回想, 回忆; 使回忆: I can't ~ having met him before. 我记不起以前曾见到过他。/ The sight ~ed the days of childhood to me. 那情景使我想起了童年。②叫回, 召回: ~ all members on leave 召回所有休假人员 / ~ an ambassador from his post 召回大使 ③收回, 撤销; 取消: ~ one's words 收回前言 / ~ an order 撤销定货单 / ~ a decision 取消决定 ④使复活; 恢复: ~ sb. to life 使某人苏醒 **II** *n.* ①回想, 回忆 ②叫回, 召回: letters of ~ (对大使等的)召回公文; 解任状 ③收回, 撤销; 取消 ④【军】归队信号; 收操号; 【海】召唤小船回大船 (或舰只回舰队) 的信号旗: sound the ~ 吹收操号 ⑤[美](由公民投票对官员的)罢免; 罢免权 ‖*beyond* (或 *past*) ~ ①记不起的 ②不能撤销 (或挽回) 的 ‖**~able** *a.* ①可回忆的, 记得起的 ②可召回的; 可撤销的

recant [ri'kænt] ❶ *vt.* 宣布放弃(信仰、主张等); 宣布撤回(声明等) ❷ *vi.* ①放弃信仰(或主张等); 撤回声明: rather die than ~ 宁死不放弃信仰 ②公开认错 ‖**~ation** [,ri:kæn'teiʃən] *n.*

recapitulate [,ri:kə'pitjuleit] *vt.* & *vi.* 扼要重述, 摘要说明; 概括 ‖**recapitulation** ['ri:-kə,pitju-

'leiʃən] **n.** ①扼要的重述 ②【生】重演 ③【音】再现部

recast ['ri:'kɑ:st] **I** (recast) **vt.** ①重新铸造,再铸造: ~ a bell 重铸一口钟 ②彻底改动;重做: ~ a sentence 重写一个句子 / ~ the notions of (完全)改变对…的观念 ③ 重算,重计 ④ 重新安排(戏剧等)的角色 **II n.** ① 重新铸造(或重做等) ②经重铸(或重做等)的事物

recede¹ [ri(:)'si:d] **vi.** ①退,退去;退远: The tide ~d. 潮水退了。/ The coast ~d slowly as our ship sailed out to sea. 我们的船向海驶去时,海岸就渐渐远去了。/ Memories of childhood are gradually receding. 童年的事渐渐记不清了。②缩进;向后倾斜: a receding chin (forehead) 向后削的下巴(前额) ③ 收回,撤回 (from): ~ from an opinion (a promise) 收回意见(诺言) / ~ from a bargain 撤销买卖合同 ④ 降低;缩减: Prices have ~d. 物价已经降低。/ ~ in importance 重要性减小 ‖ ~ into the background 见 **background**

recede² ['ri:'si:d] **vt.** 归还(领土);交还

receipt [ri'si:t] **I n.** ①收到: I beg to acknowledge (the) ~ of your letter. (商业信件等用语)来函已收到。/ We sent out the goods on ~ of your postal order. 我们收到你的邮汇后立即将货物发出了。/ be in ~ of 已收到… ②收条,收据: write out and sign a ~ 开收据并在上面签名 / a ~ book 收据簿 ③【复】收到的物(或款项);收入: ~s and expenditures 【商】收入和支出 ④ =recipe ⑤[古]税务局 **II vt.** ①开…的收据;承认收到 ②上注明"收讫"(或"付清"): ~ a bill 在帐单上签字或盖章,表明帐款已收讫

receive [ri'si:v] ❶ **vt.** ①收到,接到:~ a letter收到一封信 / Received from...(收据用语)今从…处收到/ ~ instructions from higher authorities 接到上级指示 ② 得到;受到: ~ support from sb. 得到某人的支持 / ~ much acclaim from the audience 博得听众的喝采 / ~ severe punishment 遭到严厉的惩罚 / ~ a mortal wound 受致命伤 ③接受;接纳;承认: a theory universally ~d by the scientists 科学家公认的一种理论 ④ 接待,接见;欢迎: ~ foreign guests 接待(或接见)外宾 / These new books on sciences are favourably ~d. 这些新的科学书很受欢迎。⑤容纳: The new auditorium can ~ 4,000 people. 新的大礼堂能容纳四千人。⑥ 承受;挡住,抵挡: The pillars ~ the weight of the roof. 柱子承受屋顶的重量。/ prepare to ~ cavalry (对步兵的命令)准备阻击骑兵 ⑦听取;受理: ~ sb.'s confession (牧师)听取某人的忏悔 / ~ a petition 受理请愿书(或起诉状) ⑧窝藏(赃物) ❷ **vi.** ①收到;得到;接受 ②会客,接待: We do not ~ on Thursdays. 我们星期四不接待。③【无】接收 ④【宗】受圣餐: attend without receiving 参加圣餐礼而不吃圣餐 ⑤(网球等)接发(过来)的球 ‖ **be on the receiving end** 见 **end** ‖ ~**d** **a.** 被普遍接受的;公认的;标准的: the ~d view 普遍的看法;公认的观点 / the ~d text (version) 标准本(译本) / Received Pronunciation (英语的)标准发音 / Received Standard (English) 标准英语 ‖ **receiving antenna, receiving aerial** 接收天线 / **receiving blanket** [美] 婴儿的包被(浴后等用) / **receiving line** (正式场合的)迎宾队列 / **receiving order** [英]【律】法院委派破产者产业管理人的委任书 / **receiving set** (广播、电视等的)接收机 / **receiving ship** 海军接待船

receiver [ri'si:və] **n.** ①收受者; 收件人; 收款人 ②接待人 ③【无】接收机: a radio ~ 无线电接收机; 收音机 / a colour (monochrome) television ~ 彩色(黑白)电视机 ④电话听筒,受话器: take up (put down) the ~ 拿起(放下)听筒 / hang up the ~ 挂断电话 ⑤【化】接受器,容器 ⑥窝赃者 ⑦【律】破产案产业管理人;涉讼财产管理人 ‖ ~**ship** **n.** 破产案产业管理人的职务(或职位)

recent ['ri:snt] **a.** ①新近的,最近的;近来的,近代的: ~ news 最近的消息 / in ~ times 在近代 / a ~ acquaintance 新近的相识;新朋友 ②[R-]【地】全新世的: the Recent epoch 全新世;冲积世 ‖ **recency n.** / ~**ly ad.** / ~**ness n.**

receptacle [ri'septəkl] **n.** ①容器,贮藏器;贮藏所 ②【植】花托;囊托 ③【电】插座,插孔

reception [ri'sepʃən] **n.** ①接待,接见;欢迎: prepare for the ~ of the foreign guests 准备接待(或接见)外宾 / The book had a favourable ~. 这本书很受欢迎。②招待会;欢迎会;宴会: give (或 hold) a grand National Day ~ 举行盛大的国庆招待会 / a reciprocal ~ 答谢酒会 ③接纳: have a great faculty of ~ 有很大的接受能力 / be honoured by ~ into 获得加入…的荣誉 ④【无】接收,接收力: Reception of the television programmes is excellent here. 这里电视节目接收情况极为良好。‖ ~**ist n.** (旅馆、照相馆、牙医诊所等的)接待员 ‖ ~ **centre** (新成员的)报到站 / ~ **clerk** [美](旅馆等的)接待员 / ~ **desk** (旅馆的)接待处 / ~ **room,** ~ **chamber** 接待室;会客室

receptive [ri'septiv] **a.** ①接受的;接纳的,容纳的 ②有接受能力的;(对新思想等)善于接受的,接受得快的: a mind ~ of new ideas 善于接受新思想的头脑 ③感受的,感官的,感受器的 ‖ ~**ly ad.** / ~**ness, receptivity** [risep'tiviti] **n.**

recess [ri'ses] **I n.** ①休息;(学校等的)短暂的休假;休会: take a ten-minute ~ 休息十分钟 / The court is in ~. 法庭暂停开庭。②(墙壁、山脉等的)凹进处;壁龛: a ~ in a coastline 海岸线的凹进处 / a ~ with a bust in it 放有半身雕像的壁龛 ③[常用复]深处,幽深处: in the ~es of the forest 在森林深处 / in the innermost ~es of the heart 在内心深处 ④【解】隐窝 **II** ❶ **vt.** ①把…放在隐蔽处: ~ a house from the line of a road 把房屋造在远离道路的地方 ②使凹进,

使有凹进处: ~ a wall 做壁龛 ❷ vi. [美]休息；休假；休会

recession[1] [ri'seʃən] n. ①后退，退回；撤回 ②凹处 ③(工商业的)衰退；(价格的)暴跌 ④【基督教】(做完礼拜后牧师和唱诗班)退场时的行列 ‖ **~al** a. ①后退的，退回的；撤回的 ②[英]议会休会期的 n. 【基督教】退场时唱的赞美诗 (=~al hymn)

recession[2] ['ri:'seʃən] n. (领土的)归还；交还

recipe ['resipi] n. ①【医】处方(符号R)；照处方配成的药 ②烹饪法；食谱，(糕饼等的)制法 ③诀窍，方法: a ~ for success 成功的窍门

recipient [ri'sipiənt] I a. 接受的；领受的；容纳的；能接受的，善于接受的: a ~ country 受援国 II n. 接受者，领受者；接受器，容器

reciprocal [ri'siprəkəl] I a. ①相互的；互惠的；有来有往的；交互的: a ~ trade agreement 互惠贸易协定 / ~ cultural missions 互派的文化代表团 / on ~ terms 互惠地 / a ~ banquet 答谢宴会 ②相应的，相互补足的 ③相应而相反的: a ~ mistake 彼此相反的错误 (例如我误认他为学生而他误认我为教师) ④【数】反商的，倒数的: ~ function 反商函数 ‖ ~ action 交互作用 / cross ~【生】正反交 / ~ pronouns【语】相互代词 (如 each other) / ~ transformation 相互转化 / a ~ treaty 互惠条约 II n. ①互相起作用的(或有互相关系的)事物 ②【数】反商，倒数 ‖~ly ad.

reciprocate [ri'siprəkeit] ❶ vt. ①使(机件)往复移动 ②互给，互换: They ~ hospitality (enmity). 他们互相款待(敌对)。③报答，酬答: ~ sb.'s good wishes 报答某人的好意 ❷ vi. ①往复移动；互换位置: a reciprocating engine 往复式发动机 ②互给，互换 ③报答，酬答

recite [ri'sait] ❶ vt. ①背诵，朗诵，当众吟诵 ②叙述，详述；列举: ~ the dates of important historical events 列举重大历史事件的日期 ③【律】书面陈述(事实) ④[美]背(课文)；回答(关于课文的提问) ❷ vi. ①背诵；朗诵 ②[美]回答(关于课文的)提问 ‖~r n. 背诵者；朗诵者；讲述者 ‖ **reciting note**【音】朗吟符

reckless ['reklis] a. ①不注意的；不在乎的；粗心大意的: be ~ of expenditure 乱花钱 ②鲁莽的；妄动的；不顾一切的，不顾后果的: ~ driving 乱开车 / be ~ of the consequences 不顾后果 ‖~ly ad. / ~ness n.

reckon ['rekən] ❶ vt. ①计算: ~ the cost of production 计算生产成本 / ~ up the bill 加起帐单上的各个项目 / I ~ 28 of them. 我算来总数是二十八。②认为，把…看作: ~ the problem (as) important 认为这问题重要 / They ~ed him (as) an experienced welder. 他们认为他是一个有经验的焊工。/ ~ sb. among one's friends 认为某人是自己的朋友 ③估计；推断: We ~ the output will increase by 40%. 我们估计产量将增加百分之四十。④[主美]想，料想: We've been doing the work for years and we ~ we know

something about it. 我们做这工作已多年，想来对它有所了解。❷ vi. ①数，计算；算帐: The child can ~ from 1 to 100. 这孩子能从一数到一百。②估计；推断 ③指望；依赖: ~ on (或 upon) sb.'s help 指望某人的帮助 ④[主美]想，料想: He will come soon, I ~. 我想他很快就会来的。‖ ~ sth. in 把某事物计算在内；把某事物考虑在内: Did you ~ in the time needed for unloading the cargo? 你把卸货所需的时间算进去了吗? / ~ with ①和…算帐；[喻]向…清算 ②将…加以考虑，认真对付: an opponent to be ~ed with 一个需要认真对付的对手 / ~ without one's host 见 host[1] / the day of ~ing 见 day ‖ ~er n. ①计算者 ②计算手册；帮助计算的东西

reckoning ['rekəniŋ] n. ①计算；估计；算帐: be out in one's ~ 计算错误；估计错误 ②帐单: pay the ~ 付帐 ③【海】(用观测天象等法进行的)船位推算: dead ~ (无法观测天象时)仅根据测程器和罗盘进行的船位推算 ‖ a Dutch ~ 荷兰式结帐(客人越嫌贵，帐单上的金额越增加)

reclaim [ri'kleim] I vt. ①开垦，开拓: ~ wasteland 开垦荒地 / ~ fields from the sea 拦海拓地 ②改造，使悔改，感化(犯错误者、犯罪者等): ~ sb. from vice 使某人弃邪归正 ③(从废料或副产品中)回收: ~ valuable raw materials from industrial waste water 从工业废水中回收有价值的原料 / ~ed rubber【化】再生橡胶 II n. 改造，感化: be past (或 beyond) ~ 无法改造，不可救药 ‖~able a. 可开垦的；可改造的，能悔改的；可回收的

re-claim ['ri:'kleim] vt. 要求收回，要求恢复；要求重得；试图取回: ~ lost territory 要求收回失去的领土 / ~ one's job 要求恢复职业

reclamation [,reklə'meiʃən] n. ①开垦，开拓: land ~ 垦荒 / a large-scale ~ project 大规模的开垦计划 ②改造，感化 ③要求归还；收复 ④(废料等的)再生，回收

recline [ri'klain] ❶ vt. 使向后靠，使斜倚: ~ one's head on the pillow 把头靠在枕上 ❷ vi. ①斜倚；躺 ②[喻]依赖；信赖 (on, upon)

recluse [ri'klu:s] I a. 隐居的，遁世的；孤寂的 II n. 隐士；遁世者

recognition [,rekəg'niʃən] n. ①认出；识别；认识: The place has changed beyond ~. 这地方已变得认不出来了。/ My ~ of him was immediate. 我一眼就把他认出来了。/ a ~ officer【军】识别军官(负责识别敌我舰只、飞机等) ②承认: the ~ of a new state 对一个新成立的国家的承认 ③认识；赏识；重视: a medal in ~ of a service 因功授予的奖章 / gain international ~ 得到国际上的公认 / receive (或 meet with) universal ~ 受到普遍重视 ④招呼，致意: give sb. a passing ~ 对某人匆匆招呼而过 ⑤认可；准许发言: by the chair of one rising to speak 主席对起立发言者的认可

recognize ['rekəgnaiz] ❶ *vt.* ①认识;认出;辨认: ~ a word 认得一个词 / ~ one's long lost brother 认出失散已久的兄弟 / ~ sth. in disguise 辨认出伪装的某物 / ~ a tune 听出一首曾听到过的曲子 ②承认: ~ a country's independence 正式承认一个国家的独立 / be ~d as the legitimate representative 被承认为合法代表 / ~ sb.'s claims as justified 承认某人的要求是正当的 ③清楚地认识到;自认: ~ one's duty 认清自己的职责 / He ~d that he was not qualified for the work. 他认识到他对这项工作是不够格的。④公认;赏识: Acupuncture anaesthesia has been ~d to be of great use in surgical operations. 在外科手术中针刺麻醉已被公认为非常有用。⑤招呼(某人)以示相识: refuse to ~ sb. any longer 不再理睬某人 ⑥认可;准许(某人)发言 ❷ *vi.* 【律】具结

recoil [ri'kɔil] I *vi.* ①撤退;退缩,畏缩: ~ in terror 吓得退缩 / ~ from doing sth. 对做某事畏缩不前 ②跳回,弹回;产生反作用;(枪等)产生后坐力,反冲: The vessels ~ed at the collision. 船只相撞而弹回。③[喻]报应: The damage ~s upon his own head. 他害人害己。II *n.* ①撤退,后退;退缩,畏缩 ②跳回,弹回;反作用;(枪等)的后坐(力);后坐距离;反冲: a ~ indicator 后坐指标 / ~ electrons 反冲电子 ‖~less *a.* 无后坐力的: a ~less gun 无后坐力炮

recollect [,rekə'lekt] ❶ *vt.* ①回忆,追忆;想起: ~ one's childhood days 回忆起童年的日子 / I ~ having heard him say so. 我记得听到他这样讲过。/ I can't ~ the exact words. 我回想不起确切的话了。②[~ oneself]使(自己)想起一时忘掉的事: "Now I know!" he exclaimed, ~ing himself. 他想起来了,就嚷道:"我知道啦!" ❷ *vi.* 回忆,记忆: if I ~ correctly 假如我没记错的话 / as far as I ~ 就我记忆所及

re-collect ['ri:-kə'lekt] ❶ *vt.* ①再集合,重新集合 ②[,rekə'lekt, 'ri:-kə'lekt] 恢复,振作(精神等);使(自己)镇定: ~ one's courage 重新鼓起勇气 / ~ oneself (或 one's thoughts) 使自己镇定下来 ❷ *vi.* 再集合,重新集合 ‖~ion ['ri:-kə'lekʃən] *n.* 重新集合

recollection [,rekə'lekʃən] *n.* ①回忆,追忆;记忆力: be beyond (或 past) ~ 已无法被回忆起 / have a vivid (dim) ~ of sth. 清晰地(模糊地)记得某事 / to the best of sb.'s ~ 就某人记忆所及 / It is in my ~ that he was present. 我记得他当时在场。②[常用复]回忆起的事物,往事;回忆录: The letter brought many happy ~s to my mind. 这封信使我想起了许多愉快的往事。/ He is writing his ~s. 他正在写他的回忆录。③心境平静;【宗】冥想

recommend [,rekə'mend] *vt.* ①推荐,介绍: ~ (sb.) a book (向某人)推荐一本书 / ~ sb. as a good electrician 推荐某人说他是一个好电工 ②劝告,建议: The doctor ~ed the patient to do some light manual labour. 医生劝病人做一些轻微劳动。/ They ~ that the machine be overhauled. 他们建议把机器检修一下。③使成为可取,使受欢迎: His proposal has quite a few points to ~ it. 他的建议有好些可取之处。④托,托付: ~ a child to sb. (to sb.'s care) 把小孩托给某人(托某人照管) ‖~able *a.* ①可推荐的;值得推荐的 ②得当的;明智的 / ~atory *a.* ①推荐的;博得欢迎的;引起重视的 ②劝告的

recommendation [,rekəmen'deiʃən] *n.* ①推荐,介绍:speak in ~ of sb. (sth.) 口头推荐某人(某物) / buy sth. on the ~ of a friend 因朋友推荐而买某物 / a letter of ~ 介绍信,推荐的信 ②介绍信;推荐的话 ③可取之处(指品质、才能等) ④劝告: follow sb.'s ~s 听从某人的劝告

recompense ['rekəmpens] I *vt.* ①酬报;回报(赏或罚): ~ good with evil 以怨报德 / ~ sb. for his misdeeds 由于某人的罪行而惩罚他 ②赔偿,补偿: ~ sb. for his loss 补偿某人的损失 / agree to ~ all losses 同意赔偿一切损失 II *n.* ①报酬,报答;酬金: work hard without ~ 没有报酬地努力工作 ②赔偿,补偿

reconcile ['rekənsail] *vt.* ①使和解,使复交,使和好: ~ two quarrelling men 使争吵的两人和解 / ~ sb. to (或 with) another person 使某人与另一人重新和好 / be (或 become) ~d with sb. 同某人言归于好 ②调解,调停;调和: ~ differences (disputes) 调解分歧(争执) ③使和谐,使一致,使符合: fail to ~ one's statement with the fact 不能自圆其说(因与事实不符) / ~ work and rest 使劳逸结合 ④使顺从(于),使听从(于);使甘心(于): be ~d to doing sth. 安于做某事(指无可奈何) ⑤(造船时)使(木条)妥贴地接合 ⑥【宗】使(遭亵渎的神殿等)恢复洁净 ‖~ment *n.*

reconciliation [,rekənsili'eiʃən] *n.* ①和解,复交,(重新)和好 ②调解,调停 ③和谐,一致 ④甘愿,顺从 ‖~ statement 【会计】对帐表

recondite [ri'kɔndait, 'rekəndait] *a.* ①深奥的;难解的,晦涩的: ~ principles (knowledge, studies) 深奥的原理(学识,研究) ②很少人知道的;隐秘的 ‖~ly *ad.* / ~ness *n.*

recondition ['ri:-kən'diʃən] *vt.* ①修理,修复,修整: a ~ed car 经过修整的汽车 ②改革,改善;纠正

reconnaissance [ri'kɔnisəns] *n.* ①【军】侦察: ~ of position 阵地侦察 / a pilotless high-altitude ~ plane 无人驾驶高空侦察机 / make a ~ of the work to be done 对要进行的工作先做一番调查研究 ③侦察队 ④侦察车 (= ~ car)

reconnoitre, reconnoiter [,rekə'nɔitə] *vt. & vi.* ①【军】侦察;搜索 ②勘察,踏勘 ‖**reconnoitrer** [,rekə'nɔitrə], **reconnoiterer** [,rekə'nɔitərə] *n.* 侦察者;踏勘者

record ['rekɔːd] I *n.* ①记录,记载;提供证据(或资料)的东西: original ~s 原始记录 / a ~ of events 大事记　②履历；经历: have a good (an honourable) ~ 有良好(光荣)的履历 / a school ~ 学生成绩报告单 / That air line has a bad ~. 那条航线历来办得不好。(指飞机常出事等) ③案卷，档案；【律】诉状；公判录: ~s disposition 档案处理 / the (Public) *Record* Office 伦敦档案局　④最高纪录；最佳成绩；从未到达的最高(或最低)限度: set a new world ~ *in* men's high jump 刷新男子跳高的世界纪录 / Two ~s fell during the sports meet. 在运动会中两项纪录被打破了。/ Production ~s have been broken. 生产纪录打破了。⑤唱片；录了音的磁带: play a ~ on the radiogram 在电唱机上放唱片　**II** [ri'kɔ:d] ❶ *vt.* ①记录，记载　②标明；(仪器等)在刻度上指示　③将(声音、景象等)录下: ~ a speech 把演讲录下　❷ *vi.* ①进行录音　②被录音: His voice ~s well. 他的声音录下来很好听。**III** *a.* 创纪录的: ~ grain harvests 创纪录的粮食丰收 / surpass the ~ year in steel production 超过钢产量最高的一年 ‖*a matter of* ~ 见 **matter** / *bear* ~ *to* 给…作证: I can *bear* ~ *to* his honesty. 我能证明他是诚实的。/ *break* (或 *beat, cut*) *the* (或 *a*) ~ 打破纪录 / *go on* ~ 公开表明见解；被记录下来 / *hold the* ~ *of* 保持…的纪录 / *keep to the* ~ 不扯到题外 / *off the* ~ 【口】不得引用的(地)，不得发表的(地)；非正式的(地): speak *off the* ~ 非正式地说 / These remarks are *off the* ~. 这些话不得发表(或引用)。/ *on* ~ 记录在案的；公开宣布的: the greatest earthquake *on* ~ 纪录上最大的地震 / *travel out of the* ~ 扯到题外；离开说题 ‖**~ breaker** 打破纪录者 / **~-, breaking** *a.* 打破纪录的: a ~-*breaking* crop of rice 打破纪录的稻谷收成 / **~ changer** (电唱机的)自动换片装置 / **~ holder** 纪录保持者 / **~ player** 电唱机

recording [ri'kɔ:diŋ] **I** *n.* ①记录；录音: tape (disc, wire) ~ 磁带(唱片，钢丝)录音 / The ~ is taking place at the studio. 录音正在播音室进行。②唱片，录了音的磁带　③录音的节目 ‖**~ disc** 录音盘 / **~ film** 录音胶片 / **~ meter** 自记仪表

recount¹ [ri'kaunt] *vt.* ①详细叙述，描述: ~ one's experiences 叙述自己的经历　②列举: ~ sb.'s faults 列举某人的过失

recount² ['ri:'kaunt] **I** *vt.* 重新计算，再数　**II** *n.* 重计

recoup [ri'ku:p] ❶ *vt.* ①【律】扣除　②赔偿，补偿，偿还: ~ sb. for a loss 补偿某人的损失　③重获: ~ one's strength 恢复力气　❷ *vi.* 补偿损失 ‖**~ment** *n.*

recourse [ri'kɔ:s] *n.* ①求助，求援: get over one's difficulties without ~ *to* outside help 不求外援克服困难　②求助的对象；力量的源泉: No ~ was left. 无可依赖了。③【律】追索权: with (without) ~ 有(无)追索权的 ‖*have* ~ *to* 求助

于，求援于: *have* ~ *to* law (force) 诉诸法律(武力)

recover [ri'kʌvə] ❶ *vt.* ①重新获得；重新找到: ~ one's lost pen 找回遗失的钢笔 / a lost scent (猎犬)重新找到失去的臭迹　②恢复，使恢复原状: sit down to ~ one's breath 坐下来喘口气 / ~ one's appetite (consciousness, sight) 恢复胃口(知觉，视力) / ~ oneself 恢复知觉(或镇静)；恢复控制(四肢等)的能力 / ~ one's feet (或 legs) (跌倒后)又站起来/ The patient is perfectly ~*ed from* his illness. 病人已完全好了。③挽回，弥补: ~ losses 弥补损失 / We worked hard to ~ lost time. 我们加紧工作，以弥补失去(或浪费)的时间。④(根据法律程序)取得: ~ damages 取得赔偿 / ~ judgement against the defendant 获得不利于被告的判决；胜诉　⑤使(物)重新有用；使(人)改过自新: ~ land from the sea 围垦(海)滩地　⑥[罕]到达　❷ *vi.* ①痊愈，复原；恢复，恢复原状: ~ *from* fatigue 恢复疲劳 / ~ *from* the effects of the natural disasters 从自然灾害的影响下恢复过来　②回复原来的防御(或预备)姿势 (指击剑、划剑等)　③【律】胜诉

re-cover ['ri:'kʌvə] *vt.* ①再盖，重新盖　②给…换新面子: I'll have my umbrella ~*ed*. 我要给我这把伞换个新面子。/ ~ the lamp with a new lampshade 换新灯罩

recovery [ri'kʌvəri] *n.* ①重获; 复得: the ~ of a lost thing 失物的找回　②复原，痊愈；恢复，恢复原状: make a quick ~ 迅速复原 / ~ *from* influenza 流行性感冒的痊愈 / battlefield ~ 战场的打扫 / ~ facilities 抢救用的器材 / a ~ ship (helicopter) (把从太空回来的宇宙航行员从海面等处捞起来的)载回船舶(直升飞机)　③恢复所需的时间，恢复期　④(击剑、划船等)防御(或预备)姿势的回复　‖**~ room** 手术后特别病房

recreant ['rekriənt] **I** *a.* ①讨饶的；怯懦的　②不忠的；叛逆的，变节的　**II** *n.* ①懦夫，胆小鬼　②背叛者，变节者

recreation [,rekri'eiʃən] *n.* ①消遣，娱乐；娱乐活动: do sth. for ~ 为了消遣而做某事 / To him, walking is a ~. 对他来说，散步是一种消遣。/ an innocent ~ 无害的娱乐活动　②(身心的)休养 ‖**~al** *a.* 消遣的，娱乐的: ~*al* activities 文娱活动 ‖**~ ground** 娱乐场，游乐园 / **~ room** 娱乐室 / **~ vehicle** 周末旅游汽车(车内设有厨房、床铺等，可作活动住房)

re-creation ['ri:-kri'eiʃən] *n.* ①再创造，再创作；重新创造(或创作)　②再创造的事物

recruit [ri'kru:t] **I** ❶ *vt.* ①征募(新兵)；吸收(新成员): ~ soldiers 征兵　②(增加人员)充实(部队等): ~ a regiment 充实团的兵力　③补充: ~ supplies 补充供应品 / ~ technical force 补充技术力量　④使恢复；使复原: ~ one's energies (health) 使自己恢复精力(健康) / ~ oneself after an excess of work 过度工作后使自己恢复一下　❷ *vi.* ①征募新兵；吸收新成员　②得到补

充 ③恢复健康,复原: ～ after an illness 病后恢复健康 **II** *n.* ①新兵;新成员;新手;(英)陆军(或海军陆战队)新兵: a ～ training centre 新兵训练中心 / a raw ～ 新兵;新手 ②补充品 ‖**~er** *n.* 征兵人员 / **~ment** *n.* ①新兵征召;新成员的吸收;征召新兵的数量 ②补充,充实 ③恢复健康,复原 ‖**~ing officer** 新兵征召军官 / **~ing station** 新兵征召站 / **~ing system** 征兵制

recrystallization ['ri:,kristəlai'zeiʃən] *n.*【化】再结晶,重结晶

rectangle ['rek,tæŋgl] *n.*【数】矩形,长方形 ‖**~d** *a.*

rectangular [rek'tæŋgjulə] *a.*【数】矩形的,长方形的;成直角的 ‖**~ity** [rek,tæŋgju'læriti] *n.* / **~ly** *ad.*

rectification [,rektifi'keiʃən] *n.* ①纠正,矫正;整顿: errors needing ～ 需纠正的错误 ②调整;校正 ③【化】精馏 ④【电】整流 ⑤【数】求长(法)

rectify ['rektifai] *vt.* ①纠正,矫正;整顿: errors 纠正错误 / ～ the style of work 整顿工作作风 / ～ one's life 改过自新 ②调整;校正: ～ an instrument 校正仪器 / ～ the calendar 调整历法 ③【化】精馏: *rectified* spirit 精馏酒精 ④【无】整流;把…检波 ⑤【数】求(曲线)的长度 ‖**rectifiable** *a.* ①可纠正的;可调整的 ②【化】可精馏的 ③【数】(曲线)可求长的 / **rectifier** *n.* ①纠正(或调整)的人;矫正器 ②【化】精馏器 ③【电】整流器,整流管 ④【无】检波器,检波管: silicon controlled *rectifier* 硅可控整流器,可控硅 / phase-sensitive *rectifier* 相敏检波器 ‖**~ing device**【电】整流装置【无】检波装置

rectitude ['rektitju:d] *n.* ①正直,严正 ②(判断、程序等的)正确 ③直,笔直

rector ['rektə] *n.* ①(英国国教、天主教等的)教区长 ②(修道院、宗教学校等的)院长,校长 ③(某些学校、学院、大学的)校长 ④主任;负责人 ‖**~ial** [rek'tɔ:riəl] *a.* / **~ship** *n.* 教区长(或宗教学校校长等)的职位

recumbent [ri'kʌmbənt] *a.* ①躺着的;斜靠的: a ～ statue 雕塑的卧像 ②【生】横卧的,斜倚的 ③休息着的;不活动的

recuperate [ri'kju:pəreit] ❶ *vt.* ①使复原;恢复(健康、元气等): ～ the patient 使病人复原 / ～ one's health 恢复健康 ②挽回,弥补(损失等) ❷ *vi.* ①复原,恢复健康: ～ *from* a minor ailment 小病后复原 ②弥补损失 ‖**recuperation** [ri,kju:pə'reiʃən] *n.* ①复原;恢复;挽回,弥补 ②【化】同流换热(法)

recur [ri'kə:] (recurred; recurring [ri'kə:riŋ]) *vi.* ①再发生;(疾病等)复发: correct one's mistakes thoroughly so that they may not ～ 彻底改正错误以免再犯 ②重新提起 (*to*): I shall ～ to the subject later on. 关于这个问题我后面还要提到。③(往事等)重新浮现 (*to*): The scene often ～s *to* his mind (或 memory). 这景象常在他脑海中重现。④依赖,借助于 (*to*): ～ *to* arms 诉诸

武力 ⑤【数】递归,循环: *recurring* decimal (series) 循环小数(级数)

recurrence [ri'kʌrəns] *n.* ①再发生;复发: Let there be no ～ of this error. 不要再犯这种错误。/ Acupunctural treatment cured his headache, which had been of frequent ～. 针刺疗法治好了他经常复发的头痛。②重新提起 ③(往事等)重新浮现 ④【数】递归,循环: ～ theorem 循环定理

recurrent [ri'kʌrənt] **I** *a.* ①再发的;经常发生的;周期性发生的: ～ expenses (房租、水电等)经常性开支 ②【解】(神经、血管等)返的;回归的: ～ nerve 返神经 / ～ fever【医】回归热 **II** *n.* 回归神经;回归动脉 ‖**~ly** *ad.*

red [red] **I** *a.* ①红色的: ～ cloth 红布 ②[也作 R-]红的,红色的 ③胀红的;充血的: be ～ with anger 因发怒而脸胀红 / with ～ eyes 以充血的(或哭红的)眼睛 ④赤热的: ～ slag 烧红的铁渣 ⑤流血的,暴力的;火烧的: a ～ battle 血战 / ～ hands 沾满血的手 / ～ ruin 火灾 ⑥有红内发的 ⑦有微红肤色的: a *Red* Indian (或 a *Red* Man)(北美)印第安人 ⑧[英]英国的(由于英国在地图上常用红色标示): an all-～ route (cable) 只通过英国领土和英帝国控制地区的路线(海底电缆) **II** *n.* ①红色 ②红颜料,红染料 ③[复][常作 R-](北美)印第安人 ④红色物(如红衣、红布、红棋子、红球等);红色毛皮的动物: a little girl *in* ～ 穿红衣的小女孩 ⑤赤字,负债,亏损: be in the ～ 亏损;负债 / get out of the ～ 不再亏空 ⑥[美俚]一分钱 ⑦[英史]红舰队(从前英国红、白、蓝三种舰队之一) ‖*paint the town* ～ 见 town / *see* ～ 发怒,冒火 / *turn* ～ *in the gills* 发怒 ‖～ alert 警报(空袭)紧急警报 / ～ ball [美俚]快运货车;快车 / '～-blind *a.* 红色色盲的 / ～= 'blooded *a.* ①(人)充满活力的,健壮的 ②(小说等)情节丰富的,紧张的 / ～ box [英]大臣用的文件匣 / '~breast *n.*【动】欧鸲,知更鸟 / 'Red'brick *n.* [英](地方设立的)较新的大学 (Oxbridge 较老的大学之对) / '~cap *n.* ①[美]车站的搬运工 ②[英口]宪兵 ③(欧洲产)金翅雀 / ～ carpet 红地毯 ‖[喻]隆重的接待(或欢迎): roll out the ～ carpet for sb. 展开红地毯隆重地欢迎某人 / '~-'carpet *a.* 铺红地毯的,[喻]隆重的: give sb. a ～-*carpet* reception 隆重地接待某人 / ～ cell【解】红血球,红(血)细胞 / ～ cent [美口]一分钱: not worth a ～ cent 一文不值 / not care a ～ cent. 我一点也不在乎。/ '~coat *n.* [常作 R-](美国独立战争时期的)英国兵 / **Red Crescent** (土耳其

等国的相当于红十字会的)红新月会 / **Red Cross** 红十字(会) / ～ **deer**【动】赤鹿 / ～ **earth** 红土 / ～ **ensign** 英国商船旗(角上标有英国国旗的红色旗帜) / **'～-eye** *n.* 廉价威士忌酒 / **'～fish** *n.* 鲑鱼 / ～ **flag** ①(铁路等作为危险信号的)红旗 ②引起愤怒的事物 / ～ **gold**【古】[诗]纯金;金钱 / **'～green blindness** 红绿色盲,部分色盲 / **'～-'handed** *a.* ①有沾满血的手的 ②正在犯罪的,现行犯的: be caught ～-handed (犯罪者)被当场捉住 ③流血的,暴动的 / ～ **hat** ①红衣主教的帽子;红衣主教的职位;红衣主教 ②[英](英国)参谋军官 / **'～head** *n.* ①红头发的人 ②红头啄木鸟 / ～ **heat** 赤热,炽热;赤热状态 / ～ **herring** ①熏青鱼: neither fish, flesh, nor good ～ herring 非驴非马,不伦不类 ②转移注意力的话(或事物) / **'～-'hot** *a.* ①赤热的,炽热的 ②非常恼怒的;十分激动的 ③(新闻等)最新的,最近的 / ～ **ink** 红墨水;赤字,亏本: go into ～ ink 亏空 / ～ **lead**【化】铅丹,红丹(即四氧化三铅) / **'～-'letter** *a.* (日历上)用红字标明的;可纪念的;喜庆的: a ～-letter day 纪念日;大喜日子 / ～ **light** 危险信号;(交通灯)红灯;红色危行灯: see the ～ light 觉察危险(或灾祸)迫近 / **'～-'light district** 妓院很多的地区 / ～ **meat** 牛肉,羊肉 / **'～-neck** *n.* [蔑](美国)南部农民;乡下佬 / **'～out** *n.* 红视(航空中因向心加速度使头部充血而引起的头痛和视野变红) / **'～-pencil** *vt.* ①(以检查官身分)检查;删除;改正,修正 / **phosphorus**【化】赤磷,红磷 / ～ **pole**,**poll**【动】金翅雀;无角的红毛牛 / ～ **prussiate**【化】赤血盐,铁氰化物 / ～ **rag** ①刺激牛发怒的红布;激怒人的事物 ②[英]谷物的锈病 / **ribbon** ①授给(竞赛中)亚军的红绶带 ②[英]斯勋章的红绶带 / **Red Sea** 红海[亚洲、非洲之间] / **'～shank** *n.*【动】红脚鹬 / ～ **shift**【天】红向移动 / **'～-'short** *a.*【冶】热脆的 / **'～skin** *n.* [贬](北美)印第安人 / **Red Square** (莫斯科的)红场 / **'～start** *n.*【动】红尾鸲 / ～ **tab** [俚](英国的)参谋军官 / ～ **tape** 官样文章,烦琐和拖拉的公事程序 / **'～-'tapism** *n.* 文牍主义,烦琐和拖拉的工作作风,官僚作风 / **'～-'tapist** *n.* 文牍主义者,工作作风烦琐和拖拉的人 / **'～-'tasselled spear** 红缨枪 / ～ **triangle** (基督教男青年会的)红三角标记 / ～ **water**【医】(牛、羊的)血尿病 / **'～wing** *n.*【动】红翼鸫 / ～ **wood** *n.*【植】红杉 ②红木树似;红木

redden ['redn] ❶ *vt.* 使红 ❷ *vi.* 变红;脸红

redeem [ri'di:m] *vt.* ①买回;赎回: ～ a mortgage 赎回抵押品 / ～ pawned goods 赎回当掉的物品 ②重获;恢复;挽回: ～ one's position 恢复地位 / ～ one's honour 挽回名誉 ③偿还,还清: ～ all the national bonds 还清全部公债 ④赎救,解救,拯救;【宗】(上帝)使免罪: ～ a prisoner from captivity 赎救被监禁的囚犯 / ～ oneself 赎身 ⑤履行(诺言等): ～ one's obligation 履行

义务 ⑥补偿,补救: ～ an error 弥补过失 ⑦改善;修复 ⑧兑换(纸币)成硬币;变卖(证券)为现款 ‖**～able** *a.* ①可赎回的 ②(证券等)可换成现款的 ③能改善的,能改过自新的

redeemer [ri'di:mə] *n.* ①赎回者;赎买者 ②挽回者;偿还者 ③补救者;(诺言等的)履行者 ④赎救者,拯救者 ⑤[the R-]【宗】救世主(指耶稣基督)

redemption [ri'dempʃən] *n.* ①买回,赎回;赎买: the policy of ～ 赎买政策 ②重获,恢复;挽回 ③偿还,还清: the ～ of debts 债务的偿还 / the ～ of the unused portion of a season ticket 未用完的月季票的退款 ④赎救;拯救;赎身;【宗】赎罪 ⑤履行: the ～ of a promise 诺言的履行 ⑥补偿,补救;补救的事物: the ～ of an error 对过失的弥补 ⑦改善;修复 ⑧(纸币的)兑成硬币;(证券的)变卖成现款 ⑨[主英](对地位、资格的)出钱购买 ‖**beyond** (或 *past, without*) ～ 不可救药;不可挽回 / **the year of our** ～ ... 耶稣纪元...年,公元...年 ‖**～al** *a.*

redo [ri'du:] (redid [ri'did], redone ['ri:dʌn]) *vt.* ①再做,重做;重演 ②重新装饰

redolent ['redoulənt] **I** *a.* ①芬芳的,馥郁的 ②...气味的(of): The air is ～ of rape flowers. 空气中弥漫着菜花香。 ③有...气息的,使人联想(或回想)起...的(of): a letter ～ of sb.'s life at the ‖**redolence** ['redoulens],**redolency** ['redoulensi] *n.* ‖**～ly** *ad.*

redouble [ri(:)'dʌbl] ❶ *vt.* ①使加倍;加强: ～ one's efforts 加倍努力 / The audience ～d their applause. 观众更加热烈地鼓掌。 ②重复;再说;再做 ❷ *vi.* ①加倍,倍增;加强: His courage ～d. 他勇气倍增。 / The noise doubled and ～d. 噪声越来越大。 ②重折,重迭 ③(桥牌中,给对方加倍过的牌)再加倍

redoubtable [ri'dautəbl] *a.* ①可怕的,厉害的,令人惊骇的: a ～ opponent (controversialist) 厉害的敌手(争论者) ②可敬畏的 ③著名的;杰出的

redound [ri'daund] *vi.* ①增加(利益、信誉、耻辱等);促进,有助于(to): ～ to the interests of the collective 增进集体的利益 ②回报;返回到(upon)

redress[1] [ri'dres] **I** *vt.* ①纠正,改正,矫正: ～ abuses 矫正流弊(或陋习) / ～ one's errors 改正错误 / ～ a grievance 伸冤 ②调整;赔偿,补偿;补救: ～ damage 赔偿损失 **II** *n.* ①纠正,改正,矫正 ②调整;赔偿;补偿;补救: get legal ～ 得到法律上的补救 ‖**seek** ～ ①要求赔偿;寻求纠正的办法(如设法伸冤等) ③设法解除烦恼

redress[2] ['ri:'dres] *vt.* ①重新给...穿衣 ②重新修整 ③重新敷裹(伤口)

reduce [ri'dju:s] ❶ *vt.* ①减少,减小;缩减: ～ pain 减少痛苦 / ～ pressure 减小压力 / ～ the production costs 降低生产成本 / ～ the staff (或 personnel) 裁减人员 / ～ the distance 缩短距离 / ～ the flood 分洪 ②使处于(某种状

态) (to); 使艰难 (指处境); [常用被动语态] 迫使 (to): sb. to discipline (silence) 使某人服从纪律(住嘴) / a chaotic room to order 把乱糟糟的屋子整理得井井有条 / live in ~d circumstances过着比原来贫困的生活 / be ~d to despair 陷入绝望 ③使化为，使变为 (to): ~ sth. to ashes 把某物化为灰烬 / ~ wood to pulp 把木头变成纸浆 / a rule to practice 把规则付诸实践 / ~ a profound discourse to plain terms 把深奥的论述变为平易的词句 / ~ one's thoughts to writing 把自己的思想写成文字 ④降服；攻陷 ⑤使降级，使降职: ~ an officer to the ranks 把军官降为士兵 ⑥把…归纳，把…归并: ~ all the questions to one 把所有的问题归纳为一个 / ~ the animals to classes 把动物归类 ⑦把…弄碎；把…分解;把…分析: ~ a compound to its components 把化合物分解为各个组分 / ~ water by electrolysis 将水电解 / ~ argument to an absurdity 揭露一个论点的实质使显得荒谬可笑 ⑧使变胖，使变瘦: be ~d by illness 因病消瘦 / be ~d to skin and bones (或 to a skeleton) 变得骨瘦如柴 / be ~d to nothing 瘦得不成样子 ⑨把(油漆)调稀 ⑩把…折合(成较小单位): ~ the days to hours 把日数折合成时数 ⑪【数】简化，约简: ~ an equation (a fraction) 约简方程式(分数) ⑫【化】使还原 ⑬【医】使(脱臼)复位;使(骨折)恢复原状: ~ a dislocation 把脱臼接合好 ⑭【矿】从(原油)中蒸去轻质油 ⑮【生】使(细胞)减数分裂 ⑯【摄】把(底片等)减薄，减低强度 ⑰【语】把(重读音)变为非重读音 ❷ vi. ①减少，减小; 缩减 ②变瘦，减轻体重 ③归纳为，化为 (to) ④【生】减数分裂 ‖reducing agent 【化】还原剂 / reducing division 【生】减数分裂 / reducing furnace 【化】还原炉 / a reducing machine 磨碎机 / a reducing pipe 渐缩管 / a reducing valve 减压阀 ‖~r n. ①缩减者；变形者 ②【机】减压器;减速器;渐缩管 ③【化】还原剂；还原器；退粘剂 ④【摄】减薄剂，减薄液

reduction [ri'dʌkʃən] n. ①减少，缩减: make a 30% ~ in the prices of medicines 把药品降价百分之三十 / ~ of armament 裁军 / division 【生】减数分裂 ②缩小了的东西(如缩图、降低的价格等);缩减的量 ③变形;变化 ④降服，攻陷 ⑤降级，降职 ⑥归纳，归并 ⑦弄碎;分解 ⑧折合 ⑨【数】简化，约简: ~ of a fraction 约分 / ~ of fractions to a common denominator 通分母 ⑩【化】还原(作用) ⑪【医】复位术 ⑫减速: a ~ gear 减速齿轮 ⑬【摄】减薄 ‖~ to absurdity 【逻】间接证明法，归谬法 ‖~ism n. 简化(法);简化论

redundant [ri'dʌndənt] a. ①过多的，过剩的，多余的(常用来指劳动力、工作人员等);累赘的;冗长的: ~ words 多余的词句，赘言 / a ~ literary style 冗长的文体 / ~ population 过剩的人口 ②丰盛的，丰富的 ‖**redundance** [ri'dʌndəns], **redundancy** [ri'dʌndənsi] n. ①过多，多余;累赘;冗长 ②多余的东西，多余部分 ③【自】多余

度,冗余度;冗余位 ④【无】冗余码;多余信息 / ~ly ad. ‖~ check 冗余检验 / ~ member 多余的支撑架，冗余杆 / ~ verb 【语】有一种以上形式(如过去式)的动词

reed [ri:d] I n. ①芦苇;芦杆;[总称]芦丛: as flexible as a ~ 象芦苇般易弯曲的 / ~ beds 芦苇地 ②[复](盖屋顶用的)干芦苇;[英](盖屋顶用的)麦秸 ③不可依靠的人(或物): lean on a ~ 依赖不可靠的人(或物) ④芦笛;象征田园诗的芦笛 ⑤[音]簧片;簧(或管)乐器 ⑥[诗]箭 ⑦【建】小凸嵌线 (= ~ mould) ⑧【纺】筘,钢筘· ~ density 筘齿密度 II vt. ①用芦苇(或茅草)盖(屋顶) ②【建】用小凸嵌线装饰 ③在(乐器)上装簧片 ‖a broken ~ 不可靠的人(或物) / ~ instrument 簧(或管)乐器 / ~ mace [英]【植】宽叶香蒲 / ~ organ 簧风琴 / ~ pipe 牧笛;簧管 / ~ stop (管风琴的)变音簧管组;簧管组变音钮

grass   clarinet
reed

reef¹ [ri:f] n. ①礁;暗礁;礁脉;[喻]危险的障碍: strike a ~ 触礁 / wreck on a ~ (船)触礁而撞破 ②矿脉

reef² [ri:f] I n. 【海】缩帆 II ❶ vt. 缩(帆) ❷ vi. 缩帆 ‖take in a ~ ①缩帆 ②[喻]小心行进;紧缩费用 ‖~ knot 缩帆结,平结,方结 / ~ point 收帆索

reek [ri:k] I n. ①[方]烟 ②水蒸气;雾 ③臭气;吴烟味: the ~ of tobacco 烟臭 / live amid ~ and squalor 住在又臭又脏的地方 II ❶ vi. ①冒烟;冒水蒸气(或雾气) ②发臭气，充满臭气;具有强烈的气息 (of, with): ~ of garlic 发出大蒜臭 / a novel ~ing with sentimentalism—本充满着感伤主义的小说 ③(烟气等)散发 ❷ vt. ①用烟(或水蒸气)熏 ②散发(烟、水汽等);发出…的气息: ~ prosperity 显出兴旺的样子(或气象) ‖Where there's ~, there's heat. 有果必有因。(或:无风不起浪。)

reel¹ [ri:l] I n. ①(电线、棉纱等的)卷轴,卷筒;卷线车;(钓竿上的)绕线轮;[英](缝纫机线团的)木芯: an aerial ~ 天线卷轴 ②(电影胶片、磁带、水龙带等的)卷盘 ③(电线、棉纱等的)一卷;(电影胶片、磁带等的)一盘 ④(转动的)烘衣架

II ❶ *vt.* ①卷,绕 (*in*);(从卷轴等上)放出 (*out*);抽出 (*off*): ~ thread *in* (*out*) 绕(放)线 / ~ the silk thread *off* cocoons 从茧中抽出丝 ②(卷着)拉起 (*in, up*): ~ *up* a tail of fish (收绕钓丝)钓起一条鱼 ③【纺】缫(丝) ④滔滔地讲(或背诵);流畅地写 (*off*): ~ *off* a story 滔滔不绝地讲故事 / ~ *off* a list 接连不断地读名单 ❷ *vi.* (蚱蜢等如卷线车转动似地) 唧唧叫 ‖(*straight* 或 *right*) off the ~ [口]不停地;滔滔不绝地: Words came *off* the ~. 话说个没完。‖~able *a.* 可卷的,可绕的 / ~er *n.* ①卷(或绕)的人;【纺】摇纱工;缫丝工 ②卷(或绕)的器具;【纺】摇纱机;缫丝机 ③[用以构成复合词]有…盘胶片的影片: a two-~er 有两盘胶片的影片

reel² [ri:l] **I ❶** *vi.* ①旋转;似在旋转: Everything ~ed before his eyes. 他感到一切都在眼前旋转。②眩晕;震颤: The unexpected news made her mind ~. 这意外的消息使她内心感到震动。③摇晃,摇摆;蹒跚: ~ to and fro 前后摇摆 / The ship ~ed in the storm. 船在风暴中颠簸。/ He ~ed down the street. 他在街上蹒跚而去。④倒退,退缩 ⑤猖獗;骚乱: in the ~ing days of 在…的骚乱的时期 ❷ *vt.* 使旋转;使眩晕;使摇晃 **II** *n.* ①旋转;摇晃 ②蹒跚,蹒跚的步伐: without a ~ or a stagger 脚步很稳健

reel³ [ri:l] **I** *n.* ①轻快的苏格兰双人舞(或舞曲) ②美国的一种乡村舞蹈(或舞曲),弗吉尼亚舞 **II** *vi.* 跳苏格兰双人舞(或弗吉尼亚舞)

refectory [ri'fektəri] *n.* (修道院、神学院等的)食堂,餐厅 ‖~ **table** 狭长的餐桌

refer [ri'fə:] (referred; referring [ri'fə:riŋ]) ❶ *vt.* ①把…归诸,认为…起源(于)②把…归类(于),把…归属(于)③把…委托,把…提交: ~ a question *to* a committee 把问题提交委员会(去解决) / ~ a patient *to* a physician 把病人交给医生 ④指点;使求助于,使向…请教: The teacher *referred* him *to* Chapter III. 教师叫他去查第三章。/ I was *referred* to the information desk. 人家叫我到问讯处去问。/ Henry *referred* the manager to his former employer. 亨利告诉经理关于他的(品行、能力等)情况可以向他以前的雇主了解。❷ *vi.* ①谈到,提到;涉及,有关: I'll ~ to this point again. 我还会提到这一点的。/ the question *referred to* 所谈到的问题 / source materials *referring* to cattle breeding 有关家畜饲养的资料 / The numbers ~ to footnotes. 数目字指脚注。/ That remark does not ~ to you. 那句话不是指你说的。②查阅,参考;查询,打听: ~ *to* the map (schedule) 查阅地图(时间表) / The speaker often *referred* to his notes. 演讲者常看他的笔记。/ ~ *to* sb. for information 向某人打听消息 / *Refer* to drawer. [商]请询问出票人。(或:请与出票人接洽。)(略作 R. D.) ‖~ *oneself to* 依赖,求助于 / ~ *to* sb. (sth.) *as* 称某人(某物)为 ‖~able [ri'fə:rəbl] *a.* 可归诸…的;与…有关的:

The disease is ~*able to* excessive smoking. 这病与吸烟过度有关。

referee [,refə'ri:] **I** *n.* ①受委托者,受托处理者;公断人,仲裁人;(足球、拳击等的)裁判员 ②【律】(受法庭委托的)鉴定人,审查人 **II** *vt.* & *vi.* (为…)担任裁判;(为…)担任仲裁;(为…)担任鉴定

reference ['refrəns] **I** *n.* ①参考: This is *for* your ~ only. 仅供你(们)参考。/ ~ material 参考材料 / ~ frequency【无】基准频率,参考频率 / frame of ~【物】参照构架,参照系 ②出处;参照;参考书目: The author does not give ~s. 作者没有注明(所引资料)的出处。/ cross ~ (同一书或文件等中的)相互参照 / the list of ~s appended to the essay 论文所附的参考书目 ③参照符号 ④提及;涉及 ⑤关系,关联: The parts of a machine all have ~ to each other. 机器的各部分都是互相关联的。/ have no ~ to 与…无关系 ⑥提交,委托: the ~ of a bill to a committee 向委员会提交议案 ⑦职权范围: keep to the terms of ~ 不超出职权(或调查、审查)范围 ⑧(关于品行、能力等的)证明,介绍;证明书,介绍书;证明人,介绍人: ~s from sb.'s former colleagues 某人以前的同事对某人的证明(书) ⑨(关于品行、能力等的)查询,了解: make a ~ to sb.'s friends 向某人的朋友了解某人的情况 **II** *vt.* 给(书等)加上参考书目(或注明资料来源) ‖*without* ~ *to* ①不论 ②与…无关 / *with* (或 *in*) ~ *to* 关于: *with* ~ *to* the context 根据上下文(确定意义等) ‖~ **book** 参考用的工具书(如词典、地图册等) ②(图书馆中只供室内阅览的)参考书 / ~ **ga(u)ge**【建】考证规 / ~ **library** (不外借的)参考书阅览室 / ~ **mark** ①参照符号(例如 *, †, §) ②【建】参考标记 / ~ **point**【建】参考点,控制点;[喻]衡量的标准: use sth. as a ~ *point* for judging ... 以某事物为标准来衡量… / ~ **room** 图书参考室

referendum [,refə'rendəm] ([复] referenda [refə'rendə] 或 referendums) *n.* ①(关于政治措施、法律等的)公民投票;公民投票权;公民所投的票;复决投票;复决权 ②(外交官对本国政府的)请示书

refine [ri'fain] ❶ *vt.* ①精炼,提纯;精制: ~ oil (ores) 炼油(矿石) ②提去(杂质等) (*out, away*) ③使精练,使优美;使文雅(语言、文体、仪态等) ❷ *vi.* ①精炼,提纯;精制 ②变得优雅(或精练) ③琢磨,推敲: ~ upon (或 on) the methods of teaching 使教学方法精益求精 / ~ upon (或 on) the wording 字斟句酌 ‖~r *n.* ①精炼者;精制者 ②精制机;精制机 ④匀料机;匀浆机 ‖**refining equipments** 精炼设备 / **refining furnace** 精炼炉 / **refining methods** 精炼法 / **refining mill** 精研机 / **refining solvent** (选择性)精制溶剂

refined [ri'faind] *a.* ①精炼的;精制的: ~ oil 炼油 / ~ salt 精盐 / ~ gold 纯金 ②优美的;

文雅的;讲究的: ~ manners 文雅的举止 ③精练的;精确的,精细的: ~ analysis (calculations) 精细的分析(计算) ④过于讲究的: speak in an unnaturally ~ accent 用过于讲究的不自然的语音说话 ‖~ly [ri'fainidli] ad.

refinement [ri'fainmənt] n. ① 精炼,提纯;精制: the ~ of metals 金属的提纯 ②优美;文雅;讲究: lack of ~ 粗俗 ③ 细致的改进;为了改进的设计(或装置);精心的安排;巧妙的发挥: introduce ~s into a machine 对机器作精心的改进 / ~(s) of torture 挖空心思的折磨(或拷打) ④ 精确,精细;精致,细腻: the ~s of logic (reasoning) 逻辑(推理)的精细

refinery [ri'fainəri] n. 精炼厂,提炼厂: an oil ~ 炼油厂 / a sugar ~ 制糖厂

refit ['ri:'fit] I (refitted; refitting) ❶ vt. 整修;重新装配;改装: ~ a classroom into a laboratory 把一间教室改成实验室 ❷ vi. 整修;重新装配;改装: The ship returned to ~. 船驶回来整修。 II n. 整修;重新装配;改装 ‖~ment n.

reflect [ri'flekt] ❶ vt. ① 反射(光、热、声音等);反照: Mirrors ~ light. 镜子能反射光线。 / This wall ~s heat waves. 这墙壁能反射热。 / trees ~ed in the water 映在水中的树影 / shine with ~ed light 以反射的光照耀;[喻]借别人的光炫耀自己 ②反映,表现 ③带给,招致(on, upon): ~ credit (discredit) upon sb. 给某人带来荣誉(耻辱) ④思考,考虑;想到;反省: ~ how to fulfil the task 考虑怎样完成任务 ⑤ 投回,弹回(声音等) ❷ vi. ①反射;映出: the light ~ing from the water 由水中反射出的光 / clouds ~ing on the lake 映在湖中的云影 ②反射光(或热、声音等);映出形象: The brass plate can ~. 铜片能映出形象。 ③思考,考虑;沉思;反省 (on, upon): ~ upon a problem 思考一个问题 / ~ on what to do next 考虑下一步怎么办 ④丢脸;责备,指摘;怀疑 (on, upon): His arrogance only ~s upon himself. 他的傲慢无礼只能使他自己出丑。 / ~ on sb.'s conduct in one's speech 在讲话中指责某人的行为 / The investigation ~s on her character. 调查(的结果)表明她的品格是有问题的。 ⑤有影响,有关系 ‖~ible [ri'flektəbl] a. 可反射的;可映出的

reflection [ri'flekʃən] n. ①反射;反照: the ~ of heat 热的反射 / angle of ~【物】反射角 ②反射光(或反射热等);映象,倒影: the ~ of a bridge in the water 桥在水中的倒影 ③(指言行、思想等方面)酷似的人(或物): The apprentices are a ~ of their masters. 学徒们很象他们的师傅。 ④反映 ⑤思考;考虑,沉思;反省: On ~, we decided to change our plan. 经考虑后,我们决定改变计划。 / be lost in ~ 陷入沉思中 ⑥ 想法,见解: ~s on the European situation 对欧洲局势的看法 ⑦丢脸;责难;责难(或丢脸)的话;丢脸的行为: cast a ~ on sb.'s intelligence 指责某人的愚蠢 / a grave ~ upon sb.'s reputation 使某人丢

尽脸的事 ⑧【生】反射(作用) ‖~al a. 反射的;反照的;反映的;反省(或反照)引起的

reflective [ri'flektiv] a. ① 反射的;反映的: ~ glare of the beach 海滩反射的强光 ②思考的,沉思的 ③【罕】【语】反身的 ‖~ly ad. / ~ness n.

reflector [ri'flektə] n. ①反射器;反射镜;反射物;【原】反射层 ②反射望远镜 ③反映者;反映物: a true ~ of public opinion 舆论的真实的反映者 ‖~ize [ri'flektəraiz] vt. ①加工(某物)使能反射光线 ②在…上装反射器(或反射镜)

reflex ['ri:-fleks] I n. ① 反射: the ~ of light (sound) 光(声)的反射 ②反射光;反射热 ③映象,倒影;酷似物;复制品: the ~ of the moon in water 水中月影 ④ 反映: A man's behaviour is the ~ of his world outlook. 人的行为是他的世界观的反映。 ⑤(美术中)由明面反射到暗面的光 ⑥【生】反射(作用);[复]反应能力: conditioned (unconditioned) ~ 条件(无条件)反射 / knee jerk ~ 膝跳反射 ⑦习惯性思维(或行为)方式 ⑧【无】来复;来复式收音机,来复式接收机 II a. ①反射的;a ~ action 反射作用 ②折转的;折回的: ~ condenser【化】回流冷凝器 ③内省的,反省的 ④反作用的 ⑤【无】来复的: ~ circuit 来复电路 / ~ receiver 来复式收音机,来复式接收机 ⑥【数】优角的: ~ angle 优角 III [ri'fleks] vt. ①把…折转;折回: a ~ed current in a river 江中的回流 ②使经历反射过程 ‖~ed [ri'flekst] a. 【植】下弯的,反折的: ~ed leaves 反折的叶子 / ~ible [ri'fleksəbl] a. 可反射的;可折转的 / ~ly ad. 反射地;折回地;反省地 ‖~ arc 【生】反射弧 / ~ camera 反射式照相机

reflexive [ri'fleksiv] I a. ①反射的;折转的,折回的 ②内省的;反省的 ③【语】反身的: a ~ pronoun 反身代词(如 oneself) / a ~ verb 反身动词 (如 "He hurt himself." 中的 hurt) II n. 【语】反身代词;反身动词 ‖~ly ad.

reform[1] [ri'fɔ:m] I ❶ vt. ①改革,革新;改良: ~ outdated and irrational rules and regulations 改革旧的不合理的规章制度 ②革除(弊端等) ③改造: ~ a criminal through labour 通过劳动改造犯人 / ~ oneself 改过自新 ④【化】重整(指将石油等裂化): ~ed gasoline 重整汽油 ❷ vi. 革新;改过;改邪归正 II n. ①(政治、社会等方面的)改革;改良: democratic ~ 民主改革 / land ~ 土地改革 / a ~ in teaching methods 教学方法的改革 / the Reform Movement of 1898【史】戊戌政变 / farm tool ~ 农具改良 ②改过,自新 ‖~atory n. (少年罪犯等的)教养院 a. 改革的,革新的 / ~ism n. 改良主义 / ~ist n. 改良主义者 a. 改良主义的 ‖Reform Bill [英史]一八三二年议会选举法修正法案 / Reformed Church (基督教)新教 / ~ school (少年罪犯等的)教养院

reform[2] ['ri:'fɔ:m] ❶ vt. 重新组成;重新形成 ❷ vi. 重新组成;重新形成;【军】(尤指飞机在攻击后)重新编队

reformation[1] [ˌrefə'meiʃən] n. ① 改革,革新: ~ of the old educational system 旧教育制度的改革

②(罪犯等的)改过自新 ③ [the R-] (十六世纪欧洲的)基督教改革运动 ‖~al a.

reformation² ['ri:fɔ:'meiʃən] n. 重新组成; 重新形成

reformer [ri'fɔ:mə] n. ① 改革者,革新者;改良者 ② [R-] (十六世纪欧洲) 基督教改革运动的领袖 ③【英史】(一八三一年至一八三二年的)议会改革运动的鼓吹者与参加者

refract [ri'frækt] vt. 【物】① 使折射: Glass ~s light. 玻璃使光折射。/ a ~ed ray 折射线 ②测定…的折射度,对…验光 ‖~able a. 可折射的,折射性的 / ~or n. ①折射器 ②折射望远镜 (=~ing telescope)

refraction [ri'frækʃən] n. ①【物】折射(作用);折射度: index of ~ 折射率 / angle of ~ 折射角 ②(对眼睛的)折射度测定 ‖~al a.

refractory [ri'fræktəri] I a. ① 倔强的, 难驾驭的, 执拗的 ②耐熔的,耐火的: ~ bricks 耐火砖 ③ 难医的,难治疗的; (肌体组织)不起反应的, 麻木的 ④能抵抗疾病(或病菌)的 II n. ① 倔强的人; 难驾驭的东西 ② 耐火材料; 耐熔物质 ‖**refractorily** ad. / **refractoriness** n.

refrain¹ [ri'frein] ❶ vi. 忍住; 抑制, 制止; 戒除 (from): ~ from laughing (tears) 忍住不笑(不哭) / ~ from retorting 抑制住不反驳 / ~ from smoking 戒烟 ❷ vt. [古] 忍住; 抑制, 制止: can hardly ~ oneself 几乎不能抑制自己 ‖~ment n.

refrain² [ri'frein] n. (诗歌或乐曲的)迭句; 副歌 ‖**take up sb.'s** ~ 为某人帮腔

refresh [ri'freʃ] ❶ vt. ① 使清新, 使清凉 ②(以食物、睡眠等)使精力恢复,使精神振作: ~ oneself with a cold shower 用冷水淋浴来恢复精神 ③使更新; 使得到补充; 使恢复: ~ a fire (添燃料)使火再旺 / ~ a storage battery 将蓄电池充电 / The host ~ed our teacups. 主人又为我们斟了茶。/ ~ sb.'s memory 使某人重新想起 ④使(脱水蔬菜等)吸水返鲜 ❷ vi. 恢复精神,振作精神; 吃点心, 喝饮料 ③补充(或装上)供应品

refreshing [ri'freʃiŋ] a. ① 使精力恢复的,使精神振作的; 使人清爽的: a ~ breeze 凉爽的微风 ② 使人耳目一新的, 使人喜欢的: Your letter is ~ beyond words. 你的来信使我高兴得无法形容。‖~ly ad.

refreshment [ri'freʃmənt] n. ①(精力或精神上的)恢复; 爽快: feel ~ of mind and body 感到身心爽快 ② 使恢复精力(或精神)的事物(如食物、休息等) ③ [常用复] 茶点, 点心, 便餐; 饮料: take some ~s 吃些点心 / provide (或 serve) ~s 供应点心与饮料 ‖~ car (列车上)供应点心与饮料的车厢 / ~ room (车站等处的)茶点室, 小吃部

refrigerate [ri'fridʒəreit] vt. ① 使冷, 使凉 ②冷冻, 冷藏(食物等): a ~d van 冷藏车 ‖**refrigeration** [ri,fridʒə'reiʃən] n. / **refrigerative** a.

refrigerator [ri'fridʒəreitə] n. 冰箱; 冷冻机; 冷藏室, 冷藏库: a ~ car (火车上的)冷藏车(厢)

refuge ['refju:dʒ] I n. ①避难; 庇护: take ~ in a dugout 躲在掩蔽洞里 / seek ~ from the floods (设法)躲避洪水 / give ~ to sb. 庇护某人 / take ~ in silence 用沉默来回避(无礼的问题等) ② 庇护者; 避难所: a house of ~ (难民等的)收容所 ③安全地带; 隐蔽处; 安全岛(街道中心供行人避车等的凸起的地方) ④ 权宜之计 ⑤ 借以凭藉的事物 II vt. 庇护 ② vi. 躲避, 避难

refugee [,refju(:)'dʒi:] I n. 避难者; 流亡者; 难民: a political ~ 政治避难者 / a ~ camp 难民营 / a ~ government 流亡政府 II vi. 避难

refund¹ [ri:'fʌnd] I ❶ vt. ① 归还, 偿还: ~ the excess on a tax 归还多收的税款 ② 归还给, 偿还给(某人) ❷ vi. 归还, 偿还 II ['ri:-fʌnd] n. ①归还,偿还 ② 归还额,偿还款: obtain a ~ of a deposit 获得保证金的退款 ‖~able a. 可归还的,可偿还的

refund² ['ri:'fʌnd] vt. ① (用销售债券的收入)偿还(债务) ② (通常以较低利率发行新债券)代替(旧债券)

refusal [ri'fju:zəl] n. ①拒绝: the ~ of an offer (invitation) 对提议(邀请)的拒绝 / give sb. a flat ~ 断然拒绝某人 / He will take no ~. 他非要别人答应不可。②优先取舍权 (或购买权), 优先取舍的机会: have the ~ of 对…有优先取舍权(或购买权) / give sb. the (first) ~ of the lease of a house 给某人租屋的优先权

refuse¹ [ri'fju:z] ❶ vt. ① 拒绝; 拒受; 拒绝; 不愿: ~ sb. 拒绝某人 / ~ a gift 拒收礼物 / ~ sb. admittance 不让某人进入 / ~ one's consent 不同意 / The motor ~d to start. 马达开不动。②(马)不肯跃过: The horse ~d the brook. 马不肯跳过小溪。③ (纸牌戏中) 打不出(某一花色的牌) ❷ vi. ① 拒绝 ②(马)不肯跃过: The horse ~d at a fence. 马不肯跳过篱笆。③(纸牌戏中)打不出某花色 ‖~r n. ①拒绝者 ②不肯跃过的马

refuse² ['refju:s] I n. 废料, 废物; 渣滓; 垃圾: a ~ dump 垃圾堆 II a. 扔掉的,无用的: ~ wood 废木料 / ~ matter 废物

refute [ri'fju:t] vt. 驳斥,反驳, 驳倒: ~ an argument 驳斥一种论点 / ~ an opponent 驳倒对方 / be ~d down to the last point 被驳得体无完肤 ‖**refutation** [,refju(:)'teiʃən] n.

regain [ri'gein] vt. ①收回,复得;恢复(健康、原职等): ~ consciousness 恢复知觉,苏醒 ② 重到,回到(故乡等): ~ one's native country 返回祖国 ‖~ one's feet 见 foot

regal ['ri:gəl] a. ① 国王的, 王室的: the ~ government 王政 / the ~ office 王位 / the ~ title 王的称号 ②庄严的,豪华的: live in ~ splendour 过着象国王般豪华的生活 ‖~ism n. 王权至上说(尤指国王有权控制教会的论说) / ~ly ad.

regale [ri'geil] I ❶ vt. ①盛情招待; 款待: ~ the honoured guests with a feast 以盛宴款待贵宾 ②[~ oneself]使(尽情地)吃喝, 使享用 (with, on)

③使快乐,使喜悦: a scene that ~s the eye 悦目的景象 / ~ one's friends *with* an amusing tale 讲有趣的故事使朋友们喜悦 ❷ *vi.* (讲究)吃喝,享用 (on) II *n.* 盛宴;佳肴;(饮食方面的)款待;一份食物(或饮料) ‖~ment *n.*

regalia [ri'geiljə] [复] *n.* ① 王室的特权,王权 ② 王位(或王权)的标志(如王冠、王节等) ③(等级、社团等的)标记,徽章 ④华丽的服饰 ‖*in full ~* [喻]威风凛凛地;全副武装地

regard [ri'gɑːd] I ❶ *vt.* ① 把…看作,把…认为 (as): ~ sth. *as* difficult 认为某事是困难的 / They are ~ed *as* the most promising table-tennis players. 他们被认为是最有希望的乒乓球运动员。②[主要用于否定句]注意,注意,考虑: He did not ~ my advice at all. 他根本不把我的劝告放在心上。/ Don't ~ this very seriously. 对此不必过分注意。③ 注视,凝视;看待,对待: ~ sb. sternly 严厉地注视某人 / ~ sb.'s behaviour with suspicion 对某人的行为有怀疑 ④尊敬 ⑤与…有关: Your argument does not ~ the question. 你的论点与这个问题无关。❷ *vi.* ①注视②注重,注意 II *n.* ①注重,注意,考虑;关心: pay ~ to public opinion 重视舆论 / act without ~ to other people's feelings 做事不顾别人的感情 / Regard must be had (或 paid) to general principles. 必须注意总的原则。②注视,凝视: turn one's ~ on sb. 转而注视某人 / look at sb. with a kind ~ 和蔼地看着某人 ③尊敬,尊重; 敬意: have a high (low) ~ for sb.'s opinion 尊重(不尊重)某人的意见 / hold sb. in high ~ 十分尊敬某人 ④ 关系: His remarks have special ~ to the question at issue. 他的话对这个争论中的问题特别有关系。⑤ [复]问候,致意: with kind ~s 谨致问候 ⑥理由;动机 ‖*as ~s* 关于,至于 / *in ~ to*(或 *of*)关于: *In ~ to* his suggestions, we shall discuss them fully. 关于他的建议,我们将充分地讨论。/ *in this ~* 在这点上;关于此事 / *without ~ to* 不考虑,不顾到: *without ~ to* the consequences 不考虑后果 / *with ~ to* 关于

regardful [ri'gɑːdful] *a.* ① 留心的,注意的;关心的 (*of*): be ~ *of* one's duties 注意自己的职责 / be ~ *of* one's promises 遵守诺言;守信 / be ~ *of* the needs of the people 关心人民的需要 ② 恭敬的,表示尊敬的 (*for*) ‖~ly *ad.* / ~ness *n.*

regardless [ri'gɑːdlis] I *a.* 不留心的,不注意的;不关心的: crush sth. with ~ tread 不留心踩坏某物 II *ad.* ①[口]不顾一切地;不管怎样地;无论如何: Everything's been done ~. 不管怎样一切都已做好了。②[俚]不惜花费地;过分地: dress ~ 穿着奢华 ‖*~ of* 不注意;不关心;不顾;不管: ~ *of* wind or rain 不顾风雨;风雨无阻 / ~ *of* the consequences 不顾后果 / ~ *of* party affiliation 不论属何党派 ‖~ly *ad.* / ~ness *n.*

regatta [ri'gætə] *n.* 划船比赛;赛船会

regenerate I [ri'dʒenəreit] ❶ *vt.* ①(精神上)使新生;(道德上)使提高 ② 使获得新力量;使恢复原来的力量(或性质);【化】【生】使再生: ~ a battery 将电池重新充电 / a workshop for *regenerating* waste oil 废油再生车间 / ~d rubber 【化】再生橡胶,翻造橡胶 ③ 改革,更新(社会、组织等) ④ 重新生出;更生: The lizard can ~ its lost tail. 蜥蜴能重新长出失去的尾巴。⑤【无】使回授,使反馈 ⑥【机】使回热 ❷ *vi.* 新生,再生,更新,更生 II [ri'dʒenərit] *a.* 新生的,再生的,更新的,更生的

regeneration [ri,dʒenə'reiʃən] *n.* ① 新生,再生,更新,更生: ~ through one's own efforts 自力更生 / national ~ 国家复兴 ②【无】正回授放大 ③【化】交流换热(法) ④【机】回热

regent ['riːdʒənt] I *n.* ①摄政者 ② [古] 统治者;总督 ③ [美](州立大学的)评议员,(大学等董事会的)董事 II *a.* ① [用在名词后] 摄政的: the Prince *Regent* 摄政王 / the Princess *Regent* 女摄政王;摄政王的夫人 ②[古]统治的 ‖~ship *n.* 摄政者的地位(或任期)

regime, régime [rei'ʒiːm] *n.* ① 政体,政权;统治(方式): a puppet ~ 傀儡政权 ② 社会制度 ③ 摄生法(如用指定的食物或休养等);经系统安排的生活方式(如运动员为了锻炼所采用的)

regiment I ['redʒimənt] *n.* ①【军】团 ② 一大群;大量: ~s of ducks 大群鸭子 ③[罕]统治,管辖 II ['redʒiment] *vt.* ①【军】把…编成团 ②把…编成组 ③严密地组织;管辖 ‖~al [,redʒi'mentl] *a.* 【军】团的: a ~al commander 团长 / ~al headquarters 团部 / ~als [复]团的制服;军装: in full ~als 穿着全套军装 / ~ation [,redʒimen'teiʃən] *n.* ①【军】编成团 ②严密地组织;管辖

region ['riːdʒən] *n.* ① 地区,地带;行政区: a fertile ~ 肥沃地区 / a forest ~ 林区 / build up the border ~s 建设边区 / an autonomous ~ 自治区 / a special administrative ~ 专区 ②【解】部,部位: the abdominal (lumbar) ~ 腹(腰)部 ③(艺术、科学的)领域,范围: the ~ of literature 文学领域 ④(动植物地理学的)区: the Nearctic ~ 新北区 ⑤ (大气、海水等的)层: the upper (middle, lower) ~ of the sea 海水的上 (中,下)层 ‖*in the ~ of* 在…的左右: *in the ~ of* 50 yuan 在五十元左右 / *the lower ~s* 地狱,冥界 / *the ~ beyond the grave* 阴间 / *the upper ~s* 天;天国

regional ['riːdʒənl] *a.* ① 地区的; 局部的: ~ troops 地方部队 ② 整个地区的: a ~ planning 全地区规划 ‖~ism *n.* ①行政区的划分;行政区划分的原则 ② 地方主义;(文艺中的)地方色彩(或倾向) ③地区性,地区特征

register ['redʒistə] I *n.* ①登记;注册;(邮件的)挂号: a ~ office 登记处;注册处 ②登记簿(或表);注册簿;花名册: a household ~ 户口登记簿 / a ~ of births and deaths 生死登记簿 / a parish ~ 教区记录簿(记载受洗、结婚、丧葬等) / the Parliamentary *Register* (或 the *Register* of voters) [英] 选民名册 / Lloyd's *Register* (of British and Foreign Shipping) 劳埃德船舶年鉴(以劳埃德命名的英国商船协会出版,载明吨位、等级等) ③登记员;注册员 ④登记簿中的项目 ⑤(自动)记录器;记数器;【自】寄存器;自动记录的数: a timing ~ 自动计时器 / a programme ~ 程序寄存器 / a cash ~ 现金出纳机 ⑥通风装置;调温装置;节气门 ⑦【音】(人声的)换声区域;(乐器的)音域;一组音管,音栓: the upper (middle) ~ 上(中)音域 / the ~ of a clarinet 单簧管的音域 ⑧【印】(纸张正反面印刷的)对齐,定位;(套色印刷的)套准: be out of (be in) ~ (印刷时纸张正反面)对得不齐(对得齐) ⑨【摄】(焦距屏和感光片位置的)对准;(彩色照相中感光片的)重合,配准 **II ❶** *vt.* ①登记;注册;【喻】记住: ~ the birth of a child 登记小孩的出生 / ~ oneself *with* the proper authorities 向有关部门登记 / ~ the students 给学生注册 / ~ sth. in one's memory 把某事记在心里 ②(仪表等)指示;自动记下: The thermometer ~s 20°C. 温度计上是摄氏二十度。/ Both industrial and agricultural output in our country ~ed a sharp rise last year. 去年我国工农业生产均有大幅度的增长。③(用表情、动作)显示,表达: His face ~ed both surprise and joy. 他脸上流露出惊喜交集的表情。④把(邮件)挂号;【印】托运: I'd like to ~ this letter. 我要把这封信挂号。/ ~ luggage on a railway 把行李交铁路托运 ⑤【印】对齐;套准: ~ a colour print 套准彩色印画 **❷** *vi.* ①登记;注册;挂号: ~ at a hotel 住旅馆时登记姓名 / ~ for the new school year 新学年开始时进行注册 ②登记为选民 ③【口】留下印象: His name simply didn't ~ with me. 我对他的名字简直没有什么印象。④【印】对齐;套准 ‖*~ oneself* 在选民名册上登记姓名

registrar [ˌredʒisˈtrɑː] *n.* ①管登记(或注册)的人(尤指大学中对学生注册的主管者) ②负责登记股票转让的信托公司

registration [ˌredʒisˈtreiʃən] *n.* ①登记;注册;(邮件的)挂号 ②登记簿中的项目 ③登记人数;注册人数 ④登记证;注册证 ⑤(仪表的)记录;读数 ⑥【印】对齐,定位;套准

registry [ˈredʒistri] *n.* ① 登记;注册;(邮件的)挂号 ②登记处;注册处;(邮局的)挂号处 ③登记簿;登记簿中的项目 ④ 船舶的国籍: a certificate of ~ 船舶国籍证 / a ship of Greek ~ 希腊籍船 / the port of ~ 船籍港 ‖*a servants'* ~ 佣工介绍所 / *be married at a* ~ (*office*) 登记结婚(指不举行宗教仪式) ‖~ **office** ①出生、结婚、死亡登记处 ②佣工介绍所

regret [riˈgret] **I** (regretted; regretting) **❶** *vt.* ①懊悔,悔恨: I ~ not to have started (或 not having started) earlier. 我懊悔没有早一点出发(或开始)。/ She *regretted that* she had missed the train. 她没有赶上火车感到很懊恼。/ ~ one's past mistakes 悔恨过去的错误 ②抱歉,遗憾: I ~ (to say) that I cannot come. 很抱歉,我不能来。/ He *regretted* being unable (或 his

inability) to help us. 他因不能帮助我们而感到抱歉。/ It is much to be *regretted* that .... 使人很遗憾的是… ③哀悼,沉痛地怀念: ~ to have to announce the death of sb. 不得不悲痛地宣布某人的逝世 / He died *regretted* by all. 他死了,大家都感到悲痛。**❷** *vi.* 感到懊悔;感到抱歉 **II** *n.* ①懊悔,悔恨: feel ~ *for* one's past misdeeds 对自己过去的过失感到后悔 ②抱歉,遗憾: Much to my ~, I am unable to accept your kind invitation. 不能接受您的盛情邀请,深为抱歉。/ express ~ *for* (或 *at, over*) sb.'s action 对某人的行为表示遗憾 / refuse with much ~ (或 with many ~s) 婉言拒绝 ③[复]歉意;表示谢绝的短束: Please accept my ~s. 请接受我的歉意。(表示婉言谢绝等时用语)

regretful [riˈgretful] *a.* 懊悔的,悔恨的;遗憾的: be ~ *for* what one has done 懊悔自己所做的事 ‖~**ly** *ad.* ~**ness** *n.*

regrettable [riˈgretəbl] *a.* 令人遗憾的;使人悔恨的;可惜的;不幸的: a ~ fact 憾事 / a most ~ loss 非常不幸的损失 ‖**regrettably** *a.* a *regrettably* small amount 少得可怜的数量

regular [ˈregjulə] **I** *a.* ①规则的,有规律的;固定的: a ~ pulse 【医】规则脉 / keep ~ hours 生活有规律,按时作息 / ~ people 生活有规律的人们 / a ~ income 固定收入 / ~ work 固定工作(或职业) ②整齐的,匀称的;有系统的: blocks of the workers' residential quarters 一排排整齐的工人住宅 / a ~ flower 【植】整齐花 / a man of ~ features 五官端正的人 / a ~ nomenclature 有系统的命名法 ③【数】等边(或等角、等面)的,正则的: a ~ polygon 正多边形 / ④定期的: have the machines overhauled at ~ intervals 定期检修机器 ⑤ 经常的,习惯性的: [美]普通的: a ~ meeting 例会 / a ~ size coat 普通尺寸的上衣 ⑥正式的;合乎礼仪的;合格的: without a ~ introduction 未经正式介绍 / ~ warfare 正规战争 / a ~ doctor 合格的医生 / What is the ~ dress for such occasions? 这种场合该穿什么衣服才合适? / ~ procedure 合乎规定的手续 ⑦【军】常备军的;由常备兵组成的: ~ soldiers 常备兵 ⑧【语】按规则变化的: a ~ verb 规则动词 ⑨[口]十足的;彻底的: a rascal 十足的流氓 / a ~ flood 一场大水 / The machine had a ~ overhauling. 这机器经过彻底的检修了。⑩ [口]愉快的,可亲的;可靠的: a ~ guy (或 fellow) 受大家欢迎的人 ⑪属于宗教组织的,受教规约束的 ⑫[美]忠于某一党派的领导的 **II** *n.* ①正规兵 ②(球队的)正式队员 ③老顾客;固定职工,长工 ④[美]忠于领导(或候选人)的某一党派的成员 ⑤适合普通身材的衣服 ⑥修道士,僧侣 **III** *ad.* ①[口]规则地,经常地: come (happen) ~ 经常来(发生) ②[俗]十分,非常: be ~ angry 非常生气 ‖~**ly** *ad.* ‖**Regular Army** (美国)正规陆军 / ~ **army** 常备军,正规军 / ~ **marriage** 【宗】合法婚姻

regularity [,regju'læriti] *n.* ①规则性,规律性;一致性: do one's work with ~ 有条不紊地工作 / ~ of attendance at school 经常按时到校上课 ②整齐;匀称: ~ of form 形状(或形式)的整齐 ③正规 ④经常,定期

regularize ['regjuleraiz] *vt.* ①使有规律;使规则化,使系统化 ②使合法化;使正确;调整: ~ one's position 使自己的地位合法化 / ~ the proceedings 调整程序 ‖**regularization** [,regjulerai'zeiʃən] *n.*

regulate ['regjuleit] *vt.* ①管理,控制;使遵守规章: ~ the traffic 管理交通 / ~ expenditure 控制费用 ②调整,调节;校准: ~ the speed 调整速度 / ~ the heat 调节热量 / ~ a clock 把钟对准 / ~ food supplies 调节食物供应 ③使有条理,使整齐

regulation [,regju'leiʃən] I *n.* ①规则,规章;法规: traffic ~s 交通规则 / the safety ~s of a factory 工厂的安全规则 / reform irrational rules and ~s 改革不合理的规章制度 ②管理;控制: the ~ of affairs 事务管理 ③调整,调节;校准;稳定: ~ of body heat 【医】体温调节 / voltage ~ 【电】电压调节;稳压 ④【生】调整(指胚胎发育中物质的重新分配);(维持早期胚胎正常发育的)调节机制: a ~ egg 调整卵 II *a.* ①规定的: a ~ uniform 制服 / exceed the ~ speed 违章超速 ②普通的,正常的;正式的: of the ~ size 普通大小(或尺寸)的

regulator ['regjuleitə] *n.* ①管理者;调整者;校准者 ②【机】调节器,校准器;【无】稳定器: pressure ~ 压力调节器;电压调节器 / current ~ 电流调节器;稳流器 ③调节剂: growth ~ 【生】生长调节 ④标准时钟,标准计时仪

rehabilitate [,ri:ə'biliteit] *vt.* ①恢复…的地位(或权利、财产、名誉等): ~ oneself 恢复自己的名誉;雪耻 ②修复,整顿;使复兴,更新 ③使(身体)复原,使(残废者等)恢复正常生活 ④(通过给与职业训练等)使(失业者等)恢复就业资格 ‖**rehabilitation** ['ri:ə,bili'teiʃən] *n.* the *rehabilitation* of a national economy 国民经济的恢复

rehearsal [ri'hə:səl] *n.* ①排练,排演: a dress ~ 彩排 ②练习;演习 ③背诵 ④详述;复述

rehearse [ri'hə:s] ❶ *vt.* ①排练,排演;使排练: ~ a play 排戏 / ~ a part in a play 排练戏中的角色 / The orchestra has been ~d many times for the programme. 管弦乐队已经为这个节目排练了好多次。②练习;演习;训练(某人): ~ an action 练习一个动作 ③背诵 ④详述;复述: ~ the events of the day 列举当天发生的各种事情 ❷ *vi.* ①排练,排演 ②练习;演习

reign [rein] I *n.* ①君主统治;统治: under the ~ of 在…的统治下 / at the beginning of Smith's ~ as president of the college 在史密斯任学院院长的初期 ②(君主等)统治时期: in (或 during) the ~ of 在…的统治时期 ③支配;盛行:

the ~ of law in nature 自然界中法则的支配 / Night resumes her ~. 夜幕又降临了。④[罕]王国;领域 II *vi.* ①(君主等)统治;称王 ②支配;盛行;占优势: With a bumper harvest in sight, joy ~ed over us. 丰收在望,我们满怀喜悦。/ Silence ~s everywhere. 万籁俱寂。‖*a ~ of terror* 恐怖统治 / *Better to ~ in hell than serve in heaven.* (或 *It is better to ~ in hell than serve in heaven.*) [谚]宁为鸡口,毋为牛后。/ *the Reign of Terror* 【法史】恐怖时期 (资产阶级历史家用以指法国大革命中一七九三至一七九四年的时期)

reimburse [,ri:im'bə:s] *vt.* ①偿还,付还(款项) ②赔偿,补偿: ~ sb. for a loss 赔偿某人损失 ‖~**ment** *n.*

rein [rein] I *n.* ①[常用复]缰绳: give a horse the ~s (或 a free ~) 放松缰绳任凭马走去 ②[常用复]驾驭,控制,箝制;统治: hold the ~s of government 执政 / hand over the ~s of office 交出职权 II ❶ *vt.* ①给…配缰绳 ②(用缰绳)勒住: ~ in a horse 勒住马 / ~ up a horse 勒马使前蹄跃起 / ~ back a horse 勒马后退 ③驾驭,控制,箝制;统治: ~ in one's temper 揿住火气 ❷ *vi.* ①勒缰绳使马止步(或慢行) (in, up) ②止住,放慢 (in, up): ~ in on the brink of a precipice 悬崖勒马 ‖*assume the ~s of government* 开始执政;上台 / *draw ~* ①勒马;慢下来;停止 ②放缓努力;节省费用 / *drop the ~s of government* 不再执政;下台 / *give the ~s to* (或 *give ~ to*) 对…放任;使…自由发挥 / *keep a tight ~ on* 对…严加约束(或控制) / *ride* (或 *drive*) *with a loose ~* 放松缰绳;放任,纵容 / *take the ~s* 掌握,支配 / *throw the ~s to* 对…不加约束 ‖~**less** *a.* ①没有缰绳的 ②不受限制(或控制)的 ‖~**sman** ['reinzmən] *n.* 驾马车者;骑师

reincarnate I [,ri:'inkɑ:neit] *vt.* 赋予(灵魂)新的肉体,使再生 II ['ri:in'kɑ:nit] *a.* 赋予新的肉体的,再生的 ‖**reincarnation** ['ri:,inkɑ:'neiʃən] *n.*

reindeer ['reindiə] ([复] reindeer(s)) *n.* 【动】驯鹿

reindeer

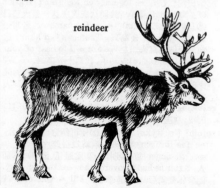

reinforce [ˌriːinˈfɔːs] I ❶ *vt.* ①增援；支援：the army at the front 增援前线部队 ②加强；增加…的数量(或厚度)：a ~d platoon 【军】加强排 / ~ one's argument with fresh points 用新的论点加强论证 / ~ a garment 修补一件衣服使之厚实耐穿 / ~ a wall with mud 用泥把墙加厚 ❷ *vi.* 求援；得到增援 II *n.* ①加固物 ②枪炮后膛的较厚部分 ‖~ment ❶ *n.* ①增援；支援；加强，加固 ②一支增援力量；[常用复]援军：receive a ~ment of 30,000 men 得到三万人的增援 ③[常用复]加固物 ‖~d concrete 钢筋混凝土

reinstate [ˈriːinˈsteit] *vt.* ①使恢复原状(或原位)；恢复(权利等)：~ sb. in his former office 恢复某人原来的职务 ②使(身体)复原；使正常 ‖~ment *n.*

reiterate [riːˈitəreit] *vt.* 反复做；反复讲；重申；重作：~ one's views 重申己见 ‖**reiteration** [riːˌitəˈreiʃən] *n.* ①重复，反复；重申：the *reiteration* of a motif (乐曲等的)主题的反复出现 ②[古](正面已印过的纸上的)反面印刷；反面印刷物 / **reiterative** [riːˈitərətiv] *a.*

reject I [riˈdʒekt] *vt.* ①拒绝；抵制：a request 拒绝请求 / a diplomatic note 拒绝接受一份外交照会 ②丢掉，抛弃：~ weak plants 剔除长得不好的植物 ③驳回；否决：~ an appeal 驳回上诉 / ~ a bill 否决议案 ④呕出；排泄 II [ˈriːdʒekt] *n.* ①遭拒绝的东西；被抛弃的东西；次品；废品 ②遭拒绝者；被抛弃者；落选者 ‖~ee [riˌdʒekˈtiː] *n.* 遭拒绝者；被剔除者(尤指被征兵处剔除的兵役对象) / ~er [riˈdʒektə] *n.* 拒绝者；否决者；抛弃者

rejection [riˈdʒekʃən] *n.* ①拒绝；抵制：a slip (编辑部等的)退稿附条 ②抛弃 ③驳回；否决 ④遭拒绝的东西；被抛弃的东西；呕出物；排泄物

rejoice [riˈdʒɔis] ❶ *vi.* ①欣喜，高兴：~ over a victory 为胜利感到欢欣鼓舞 / We ~ at the good news. 我们为这个好消息而感到欣喜。/ ~ in others' achievements 为别人的成就感到高兴 / I ~ to see you here. 我很高兴能在这儿见到你。②庆祝；欢乐：~ together on the grand occasion of National Day 共同欢庆国庆这一盛大节日 ③[谑]有，享有 (in)：~ in the name of 名叫… ❷ *vt.* 使欣喜，使高兴：The news ~d him. 这消息使他很高兴。/ We are ~d to hear of your success. 听到你们成功了，我们十分高兴。/ We are ~d that you have recovered. 我们为你的健康的恢复而感到高兴 / ~ sb.'s heart 使某人极为高兴

rejoicing [riˈdʒɔisiŋ] *n.* ①欣喜，喜悦，高兴 ②[复]庆祝；欢庆

rejoin[1] [ˈriːˈdʒɔin] ❶ *vt.* ①使再结合；使再聚合：~ the broken pieces 重新拼接碎片 / ~ a severed finger 重接断指 ②重返(队伍等)；再加入：After he had recovered, he ~ed the company. 他身体复原后，重返连队。/ I'll ~ you soon. 我马上就来和你在一起。❷ *vi.* 重新结合；重新结合

rejoin[2] [riˈdʒɔin] ❶ *vi.* ①回答 ②【律】(被告对原告)作第二(次)答辩 ❷ *vt.* (再)回答说

rejoinder [riˈdʒɔində] *n.* ① 回答；反驳：His remarks met with no ~. 他的话没有得到回答。/ draw the sharpest ~s 招致极其尖锐的反驳 ②【律】(被告对原告的)第二(次)答辩

rejuvenate [riˈdʒuːvineit] ❶ *vt.* ①使返老还童；使恢复活力；【生】使复壮 ②使复原 ③【地】回春，使更生：~d river 回春河 / ~d fault scarp 更生断崖层 ❷ *vi.* 返老还童；恢复活力；复原 ‖**rejuvenation** [riˌdʒuːviˈneiʃən] *n.*

relapse [riˈlæps] I *n.* ①旧病复发：The patient has had a ~. 病人旧病复发了。②故态复萌；恶化；沉陷：a ~ of the stock market 股票行情(回升后)再下跌 II *vi.* ①(病等)复发：~ into coma 再陷入昏迷 ②沉陷：~ into obscurity 变得默默无闻 ③堕落；退步；故态复萌：~ into errors 重犯错误 ‖**relapsing fever** 【医】回归热

relate [riˈleit] ❶ *vt.* ①叙述，讲：~ a story vividly 生动地讲故事 ②使联系；显示出…与…的关系：~ the results *with* (或 *to*) the cause 把结果与原因联系起来 / ~ theory and practice 说明了理论与实践的关系 ❷ *vi.* ①有关，涉及 (*to*)：*To* what events did your remarks ~? 你的话指的是什么事? / This paragraph ~s to the international situation. 这一段讲的是国际形势。②符合：What he has said doesn't ~ well *with* the facts. 他所说的和事实不太符合。③相处好好：~ well *to* people 与人们相处得好 ‖*relating to* 与…有关 / ~r *n.* 叙述者，讲述者

related [riˈleitid] *a.* ①叙述的，讲述的 ②有联系的，相关的；有亲戚关系的：two neighbouring countries as closely ~ as the lips and teeth 唇齿相依的两个邻邦 / painting and the ~ arts 绘画及与此有关的艺术 / a church-~ college 与教会有关的大学 / be ~ to sb. 和某人有亲戚关系 ③【音】有密切和声关系的 ‖~ly *ad.* / ~ness *n.*

relation [riˈleiʃən] *n.* ①关系，联系；[复]交往，事务：the ~ between internal and external causes 外因与内因的关系 / The report has ~ to agriculture. 这报告和农业有关。/ correctly handle the ~ of the individual *to* the collective 正确处理个人与集体的关系 / have friendly ~s *with* sb. 与某人有友好关系 / establish diplomatic (trade) ~s between the two countries 建立两国间的外交(贸易)关系 / The ~s between them are rather strained. 他们之间的关系相当紧张。/ break off all ~s *with* sb. 与某人绝交 ②家属，亲属；亲属关系：a near ~ of mine 我的一个近亲 / Is he any ~ to you? 他是你的亲属吗? / He is no ~. 他不是(我的)亲属。/ a ~ by marriage 姻亲 ③叙述；叙述的事，故事 ④[主英]【律】(向检察总长控告使之起诉的)告发 ⑤[复]男女关系，性交 ‖*be out of all ~ to* (与

bear no ~ to) 与…极不相称: The expense *was out of all ~ to* the results. 支出的费用与成果极不相称. / *in* (或 *with*) ~ *to* 关于,涉及,有关: I have a lot to say *in ~ to* that affair. 关于那件事,我有好多话要说. / The project was outlined *with ~ to* available funds. 这方案是根据可以获得的经费而拟订的.

relationship [ri'leiʃənʃip] *n.* ①关系,联系 business ~s 事务上的联系 ②家属关系,亲属关系

relative ['relətiv] **I** *a.* ①有关系的,相关的: the facts ~ *to* the problem 与这问题有关的事实 / a ~ pronoun【语】关系代词 ②相对的;比较的: ~ truth 相对真理 / the period of ~ stability 相对稳定时期 / He made another attempt with ~ coolness. 他比较冷静地又试了一次. ③成比例的;相应的 ④【音】关系的(指有相同调号的) **II** *n.* ①亲属,亲戚: elderly ~s 年长的亲属 ②有关的东西 ③相对物 ④【语】关系词 ‖~**ly** *ad.* 相对地;比较地: ~*ly* speaking 相对地说 / analyse problems in a ~*ly* all-sided way 比较全面地分析问题 ‖~ **humidity**【物】相对湿度 / ~ **motion**【物】相对运动 / ~ **velocity**【物】相对速度

relax [ri'læks] ❶ *vt.* ①使松弛,放松; 使软弱无力: ~ the muscles 放松肌肉 / ~ one's hold 松开手 / a ~*ing* climate 使人懒洋洋的气候 ②缓和;放宽,减轻 ③使松懈: ~ one's pace 放慢步伐 ④使休息;使轻松: ~ one's mind 使脑子得到休息 ❷ *vi.* ①松弛,放松 ②松懈;缓和;放宽: We must not ~ in our efforts. 我们决不能松劲. / His manner ~*ed.* 他的态度缓和下来了. ③变得不拘束;解除顾虑;变得从容: ~ into a smile 从拘谨(或紧张)状态转而微笑起来 ④休养;休息; 娱乐: He lay back and let his mind ~. 他躺下使脑子休息一会儿. / ~ at the seashore 到海边休养 ⑤通便

relaxation [ˌriːlæk'seiʃən] *n.* ①松弛,放松 ②松懈;缓和;放宽;(处罚、课税等的)减轻 ③休养;休息;解闷;娱乐 ④【物】张弛;弛豫

relay[1] ['riːlei] *n.* ①驿马,替换的马(或猎狗);补充物资 ②接替人员;替班: work *in* (或 *by*) ~s 轮班工作 ③【机】继动器;【自】替续器;【电】继电器 ④【无】转播,中继; 转播的无线电节目: ~ station 转播站,中继站 ⑤【体】接力赛跑 (=~ race);接力赛中的一程 ⑥(消息、信号、球等的)分程递送;传达;转运 **II** ['riːlei, ri'lei] ❶ *vt.* ①分程传递;传达;【无】转播 ②使接替;给…换班 ③用继电器(或继动器等)控制 ❷ *vi.* ①得到接替(或补充) ②【无】转播

relay[2] ['riː'lei] (relaid ['riː'leid]) *vt.* ①再放;重新放 ②重新铺设 ③重新涂

release [ri'liːs] **I** *vt.* ①释放,解放: ~ war prisoners 释放战俘 / ~ the productive forces 解放生产力 ②放松;放出: ~ one's hold of sth. 松手放开某物 / ~ a bomb (from an aircraft) (从飞机上)丢炸弹 ③豁免;赦免; 免除: ~ sb. *from* his debt 豁免某人欠款 / ~ sb. *from* anxiety 使某人不忧虑 / ~ sb. *from* his promise 使某人不必履行诺言 ④发表(消息等);发行(书、影片等): ~ a news item 发表一个消息 / a recently ~*d* film 新发行的电影 ⑤【律】放弃,让与(权利、财产等) **II** *n.* ①释放,解放: an order for sb.'s ~ *from* prison 释放某人出狱的命令 ②豁免;赦免;解除: obtain (a) ~ *from* an obligation 得到同意不再承担义务 ③释放(或豁免)的证书 ④放松;放出 ⑤【机】释放装置; 排气装置;【电】断路器: ~ lever 放松杆,离合器压盘分离杆 / ~ valve 排气阀,溢流阀 ⑥(消息、影片等的)发布; 发行 ⑦发布的消息; 发行的书(或影片等): a news ~ 新闻稿 ⑧【律】弃权,让渡; 弃权(或让渡)的证书

re-lease ['riː'liːs] *vt.* 再出租;重订契约出租

relegate ['religeit] *vt.* ①驱逐,放逐; 使湮没无闻 ②使降级: be ~*d* to a secondary position 被降到次要的地位 ③把…归类,使归属某等级(或范围等): ~ a work *to* philosophy 把一本著作归入哲学类 ④把…委托给,把…移交给 (*to*): ~ a question *to* a committee 把问题委托给委员会处理 ‖**relegation** [ˌreli'geiʃən] *n.*

relent [ri'lent] *vi.* ①发慈悲,怜悯;变宽厚,变温和 ②减弱,缓和: The wind blast has ~*ed.* 风力已减弱了. ‖~**ingly** *ad.* 仁慈地;怜悯地;宽厚地

relentless [ri'lentlis] *a.* ①不仁慈的,无情的,严酷的: ~ criticism 不留情面的批评 ②坚韧的,不屈不挠的;不懈的: a ~ pursuer 毫不放松的追赶者 ‖~**ly** *ad.* / ~**ness** *n.*

relevant ['relivənt] *a.* ①有关的,贴切的,中肯的,恰当的: ~ *to* the present question 和目前的问题有关的 / ~ testimony 有关的证据 ②成比例的;相应的 ‖~**ly** *ad.*

reliable [ri'laiəbl] *a.* 可靠的;可信赖的;确实的/ It is reported on ~ authority that .... 据可靠方面消息 ‖**reliability** [ri,laiə'biliti] *n.* *reliability* trials (汽车等的)长距离耐久试验 / ~**ness** *n.* / **reliably** *ad.*

reliance [ri'laiəns] *n.* ①信任,信赖; 信心; 依靠 (*upon, on, in*): put ~ *on* (或 *in*) sb.'s promises 信赖某人的诺言 / Our ~ should be *in* our own efforts. 我们应该依靠自己的努力. ②信赖的人(或物);依靠的人(或物)

reliant [ri'laiənt] *a.* ①信赖的;依靠的 (*on*): He is ~ *on* his brother for news of the family. 他是通过他的兄弟得到家里的信息的. / be ~ *on* sleeping pills (经常)靠安眠药才能睡着 ②信赖自己的;自力更生的 (=self-~)

relic ['relik] *n.* ①遗物,纪念物;遗风,遗俗: a ~ of one's grandfather 祖父的遗物 / ~s of one's youth 青年时代的纪念物 / ~s of superstition 迷信的遗俗 ②残片;遗迹;废墟: unearthed cultural ~s of the Han Dynasty 出土的汉代文物 / ~s of an ancient city 古城的废墟 ③【宗】圣骨;圣物 ④[复]遗体,尸体 ⑤【生】残遗体,残遗种

relief [ri'li:f] *n.* ①(痛苦、捐税、压迫等的)减轻; 解除,免除; 宽慰: Acupuncture anaesthesia brought ~ *to* the patient. 针刺麻醉免除了病人的疼痛。/ give ~ *to* sb.'s sorrow 减轻某人的悲伤 / heave a sigh of ~ 宽慰地舒一口气 / To our great ~, the accident caused little damage. 事故造成很小的损失,这使我们大为欣慰。/ *from* active duty【军】解除现役职务 ②救济; 救济品: ~ food 救济粮 / a ~ fund 救济金 / send ~ *to* the disaster area 把救济品送到灾区 ③援救(解围): ~ troops 援兵 ④换班,代替; 换班的人;【军】换防; 接防部队: a ~ lesson 代(别人上的)课 / a ~ pilot 接班的飞行员 / ~ *in* place【军】原地换班 ⑤(单调事物或紧张场面的)调剂; 娱乐: by way of ~ 作为调剂 / wide stretches of moorland without ~ 一大片景色单调的荒野 / a blank wall without ~ 一堵无门窗的墙 / a comic ~ (戏剧等中作为调剂的)滑稽场面 ⑥浮雕; 浮雕品: wooden carvings in ~ 浮雕木刻 ⑦轮廓鲜明; 形象突出; 生动; 对比(*against*): The peaks stood out in sharp ~ *against* the azure sky. 在蓝天的映衬下,山峰的轮廓极为明显。/ The essential difference between them stands out in high ~. 他们之间的根本区别十分鲜明地显示出来。/ set off sth. in bold ~ (绘画等中)使某物的形象突出 / cast sth. in stark ~ 使某事物大暴露 ⑧地势的起伏 ⑨封建时代封臣的后裔在承继领地时对领主所付的钱 ⑩申诉虐待,伸冤 ⑪【机】保险;放泄;离隙 ‖*indoor* (*outdoor*) ~ [英]给济贫院内(外)的人的救济 / *in high* (*low*) ~ 高(低)浮雕的 / *on* ~ 接受救济的 ‖ ~ **map** 地形图,立体地图(以模型或颜色表示地势高低) / ~ **printing** 凸版印刷 / ~ **road** 间道,分担交通的道路 / ~ **telescope**【军】体视望远镜 / ~ **television** 立体电视 / ~ **tube** 便溺管(飞机上的设备) / ~ **valve** 安全阀;开放阀 / ~ **works** 失业救济工程(如修筑道路等)

relieve [ri'li:v] **I** *vt.* ①减轻;解除(苦痛、忧愁等): The injection can ~ pain. 注射这一针能止痛。②使解除(苦痛、忧愁等);使宽慰: ~ sb.'s arm *of* pain 使某人的手臂不痛 / ~ sb. *from* anxiety 消除某人的忧虑 / We were ~*d* to hear the news. 我们听到这消息后感到宽慰。③救济;援救;供应食品(或物资等)给 ④使解除,使免除; [谑]偷,窃去: Let me ~ you *of* your trunk. 让我替你拿箱子吧。/ He was ~*d of* his post. 他被免职了。/ ~ sb. *from* active duty【军】解除某人现役职务 / The pickpocket ~*d* her *of* her purse. 扒手偷了她的钱袋。⑤换…的班;派人换…的班代替;为…代课: ~ a garrison 换防 / ~ guard 换岗 / The sentry will be ~*d* at half past five. 哨兵将在五点半换班。/ ~ a sick teacher 为生病的教师代课 ⑥调剂,使不单调,使不乏味: The brown hills are ~*d* by patches of green. 褐色的群山因缀有绿色小斑块而显得不单调。⑦衬托,使显著;使成浮雕: The mountain is ~*d against* the blue sky. 在蓝天的衬托下,这座山显得轮廓分明。❷ *vi.* ①救济 ②【军】接防 ③成浮雕 ‖ ~ **oneself** (或 ~ **nature**) 大小便 / ~ **one's feelings** 见 **feeling** ‖ **relieving arch**【建】辅助拱 / **relieving officer** [英]从事救济贫民工作的官员 / **relieving unit** 接防部队

religion [ri'lidʒən] *n.* ①宗教 ②宗教信仰;信仰; 一心追求的目标: Cleanliness is a ~ to her. 她注意清洁简直有点过分了。③宗教生活,修道生活: His name in ~ is Father Peter. 他在宗教生活中的名字是彼得神父。④有关良心的事(自己感到)应做的事: make a ~ of doing sth. 自己认为必须做某事 ‖ *the Buddhist* ~ 佛教 / *the Christian* ~ 基督教 / *established* ~ 国教 / *the Mohammedan* ~ 伊斯兰教 / *natural* ~ 自然教 / *revealed* ~ 天启教(自然教之对) ‖ *enter into* (或 *be in*) ~ 出家,修道 / *get* (或 *experience*) ~ [谑]皈依宗教 / *profess* ~ 公开表明信教;立志修道出家 ‖ ~**ism** *n.* ①笃信宗教; 宗教狂 ②虚伪的宗教信仰 / ~**ist** *n.* 笃信宗教者;宗教狂者

religious [ri'lidʒəs] **I** *a.* ①宗教的,宗教上的: a ~ belief (或 faith) 一种宗教信仰 / a ~ believer 一个宗教信徒 / ~ obscurantism 宗教迷信;宗教蒙昧主义 ②虔诚的,笃信宗教的,虔敬的 ③修道的,出家的: a ~ house 修道院;寺院 ④认真的,严谨的: do sth. with ~ care (或 exactitude) 非常细心地做某事 **II** [单复同] *n.* ①修道士;修女;和尚;尼姑 ②[the ~] [总称]宗教信徒 ‖ ~**ly** *ad.* / ~**ness** *n.*

relinquish [ri'liŋkwiʃ] *vt.* ①放弃;撤回;停止: ~ a project 放弃一项计划 / ~ bad habits 戒除坏习惯 ②松手放开: ~ one's hold of a rope 松手放掉抓着的绳子 ③让与(权利、财产等);把…交给(*to*) ‖ ~**ment** *n.*

relish ['reliʃ] **I** *n.* ①滋味;特殊的味道;风味;美味: a ~ of garlic in the stew 炖菜中的大蒜味 / Hunger gives ~ to any food. 肚子饿时吃什么都香。②意味,寓意,含意: There's a ~ of satire in his words. 他的话中有刺。③食欲;乐趣;爱好: eat (read) *with* ~ 津津有味地吃(阅读) / lose ~ for one's food 食欲不振 / find much ~ in 在…中得到很大乐趣 / have no ~ for tragedy 不喜欢看悲剧 ④饶有趣味的事物,引起乐趣的事物;吸引力: These toys will lose their ~ when the child grows older. 孩子长大后,这些玩具就将失去吸引力了。⑤调味品,作料;(主菜前的)开胃食品 **II** ❶ *vt.* ①加味于,给…调味 ②吃干,爱好: ~ doing sth. 乐于做某事 / She does not ~ the prospect of a long journey. 她不喜欢预期中的长途旅行。③津津有味地吃(或尝);欣赏,玩味: ~ one's food 津津有味地吃东西 / ~ a work of art 赏玩一件艺术品 ❷ *vi.* 具有某种滋味(或风味): find ways in which the food can be made more ~*ing* 想办法把饭菜做得更可口 / a conversation which ~*es* of wit 富有机智的谈话

reluctance [ri'lʌktəns], **reluctancy** [ri'lʌktənsi] *n.* ①不愿; 勉强: show ~ to do sth. 表示不愿做某事 / leave with ~ 勉强地离去 / obey without ~ 甘心服从; 欣然从命 ②[罕]反抗, 反对 ③【电】磁阻

reluctant [ri'lʌktənt] *a.* ①不愿的; 勉强的: be ~ to do sth. 不愿做某事 / a ~ follower 胁从分子 / ~ assistance 勉强的协助 ②难得到的; 难驾驭的; 难处理的: a soil ~ to the plough 一种难耕的土壤 ③[罕]反抗的, 反对的 ‖~ly *ad.*

rely [ri'lai] *vi.* ① 依赖, 依靠; 依仗 (on, upon): ~ on one's own efforts (或 strength) 自力更生 / ~ upon sb. for help 指望某人的帮助 ②信赖, 信任, 对⋯有信心 (on, upon): You may ~ upon it that she won't be late. 你可以放心, 她不会迟到的。/ I ~ upon you to finish the work today. 我相信你今天能完成这工作。/ Rely (或 You may ~) upon it. 放心吧。(含有"错不了"之意)

remain [ri'mein] *vi.* ①剩下, 余留: ~ in one's memory 留在记忆中 / You may have all those that ~. 你可以把剩下的那些全拿去。/ Nothing ~ed of them. 他们(或它们)什么痕迹也没留下。/ Much work ~s to be done. 还有许多工作要做。/ It ~s to them to do it. 这留待他们去做。②继续存在: The old pagoda ~s. 古塔还在。③(人)留下; 逗留: Remain here till I return. 留在这里, 直到我回来。④ 保持, 仍是: ~ modest and prudent 保持谦虚谨慎 / His fine working-class qualities ~ unchanged. 他的优秀的工人阶级品质保持不变。/ I ~ yours truly (或 respectfully 等) . . . . ⋯敬上(信末署名前的客套语) ‖**with** 属于, 归于

remainder [ri'meində] **I** *n.* ①剩余物; 残余部分; 遗迹: the ~ of the porridge 剩下的粥 / the ~ of one's life 余生, 余年 ②剩下的人: Twenty of us went to reap wheat and the ~ worked in the cotton fields. 我们之中二十人去割麦, 其余的人在棉花田里劳动。③【数】(减后、除后的)余数; 余项, 余部: Take 5 from 8 and the ~ is 3. 八减五, 余数是三。④【律】地产的指定继承权(如转让地产给甲, 指定甲死后由乙继承): the ~ man 指定继承人 ⑤(爵位、地位的)继承权 ⑥因滞销而减价出售的书, 剩书: dispose of the ~s 处理剩书 **II** *a.* ①剩余的: the ~ biscuit 吃剩的饼干 ②出售处理书籍的: a ~ counter 卖处理书的柜台 **III** *vt. & vi.* 廉价出售(剩书)

remains [ri'meinz] [复] *n.* [通常用作复, 也可用作单] ① 剩下的东西, 残余; 余额: the ~ of strength 余力 / the ~ of a fortune 剩余的财产 / The ~ of the supper were (或 was) taken away. 晚餐吃剩的东西被收走了。② 废墟, 遗迹; 遗物; 遗风: Here is the ~ of a temple. 这里是一所寺院的废墟。③残存者 ④遗体: pay last respects to sb.'s ~ 向某人的遗体告别 ⑤ 遗稿; (古代作家) 尚存的著作: publish sb.'s literary ~ 出版某人的文学遗著

remake ['ri:'meik] **I** (remade ['ri:'meid]) *vt.* 重制; 翻新; 改造; 修改: ~ nature 改造自然 / ~ a plan 修订计划 **II** *n.* ① 重制; 翻新; 改造; 修改 ②重制物; 重新摄制的影片

remand [ri'mɑ:nd] **I** *vt.* ①送回; 召回 ②【律】还押(被控告人), 押候; 发回(案件)交下级法院处理 **II** *n.* ① 送回; 召回 ②【律】还押, 押候; 被还押者; (案件的)发回: detention on ~ 在押; 还押 ‖~ home [主英]青少年拘留所

remark [ri'mɑ:k] **I** ❶ *vt.* ①注意到; 觉察; 看见: ~ the resemblance between the two things 注意到两者的相似处 / He ~ed the changes of his hometown. 他看到了故乡的变化。② 评论, 谈论, 议论; 说起, 谈到; 说: The editor ~ed that the article was well written. 编者评论说那篇文章写得很好。/ I should like to ~ that . . . 我认为⋯ / "Very impressive," he ~ed. "给人很深刻的印象," 他说。❷ *vi.* 评论, 谈论, 议论: ~ upon (或 on) the prosperous look of the country-tryside 谈论农村的繁荣景象 **II** *n.* ①注意; 觉察; 看: a report worthy of special ~ 值得特别注意的一篇报道 ②评论, 谈论, 议论; 陈述; 话: pass ~ about (或 at) sb. 议论某人 / You should not let it pass without ~. 你不应该随它去而不置可否。/ a theme of general ~ 大家谈论的话题 / make no ~ 不加评论 / make a few ~s (upon) (就⋯)讲几句 ③ =remarque

remarkable [ri'mɑ:kəbl] *a.* 异常的; 非凡的, 卓越的; 值得注意的; 显著的; 奇怪的: make ~ achievements 取得显著成就 / be ~ for one's bravery 以勇敢著称 / make oneself too ~ (使自己)锋芒毕露 / It is ~ that I should not have been told. 人家竟然没有告诉过我, 这是出乎意外的。‖~**ness** *n.* / **remarkably** *ad.*

remedial [ri'mi:djəl] *a.* ① 治疗的; 治疗上(用)的 ②补救的; 纠正的; 修补(用)的: ~ measures 补救办法 ③补习的: ~ instruction (补习性的)辅导 ‖~ly *ad.*

remedy ['remidi] **I** *n.* ①治疗; 治疗法; 药物: a good ~ for colds 治感冒的良药 / a sovereign ~ 特效药 / a toothache ~ 牙痛药 ②补救(法); 纠正(法): There is no ~ but . . . . 除⋯外别无补救办法。/ be past (或 beyond) ~ 不可救药 ③【律】赔偿, 补偿 ④(制造硬币上的)公差 **II** *vt.* ①医治, 治疗 ②补救; 纠正, 改善; 去除(弊病等): Your faults of pronunciation can be remedied. 你的发音缺陷是可以纠正的。③修补, 修缮: ~ a leak in a pipe 修补管子上的漏缝

remember [ri'membə] ❶ *vt.* ①记得; 想起, 回忆起: I ~ seeing him once. 我记得曾经见过他一次。/ try to ~ a telephone number 想把电话号码回忆起来 ②记住; 牢记, 不忘: Remember to post the letter for me. 别忘了替我把信寄掉。③(因感谢或怀恨等而)铭记: ~ sb.'s kindness 把某人的好意铭记在心 / Please don't ~ this unpleasant matter against me. 请别因为这件

不愉快的事而一直对我有意见。④送礼给…; 遗赠财产给…; 付小费给…: ~ sb. in one's will 在遗嘱中把部分财产赠与某人 / ~ the waiter 给待者小费 ⑤代…致意, 代…问好: Please ~ me *to* your brother. 请代我向你兄弟问候。⑥记录; 纪念: History has not ~ed his name. 历史上没有提到他的名字。⑦在祷告中提到 ⑧[古]使记起, 提醒: ~ sb. of the truth of sth. 提醒某人关于某事的真相 ❷ *vi.* 记得; 记起; 记住: If I ~ rightly .... 如果我没有记错的话… ‖ *~ oneself* (犯过失后)反省 ‖ **~able** [ri'membərəb] *a.* 可记得的; 可记起的; 可记住的; 可纪念的 / **~er** [ri'membərə] *n.* 记得者; 记起者; 记住者

remembrance [ri'membrəns] *n.* ① 记忆; 回忆: bear (或 keep) it in ~ 把它记在心头 / have no ~ of 记不起… / It has escaped my ~. 我记不起这个了。②记忆力, 记性 ③能记住的一段时间 ④纪念, 追忆: in ~ of 纪念…; 回忆… ⑤纪念品 ⑥[复]问候, 致意 ‖ *call to ~* 想起, 回忆起 / *have in ~* 记得 / *put in ~* 使想起 ‖ **Remembrance Day** [主英] (纪念第一、二次世界大战阵亡者的)休战纪念日(每年十一月十一日或这天前的星期日)

remind [ri'maind] *vt.* 提醒; 使记起, 使想起: If I forget, please ~ me. 如果我忘了, 请提醒我。/ Please ~ me that I must call him up before noon. 请提醒我在中午前给他打个电话。/ He ~s me *of* his father. 他使我想起他的父亲。

reminder [ri'maində] *n.* ①提醒者; 提醒物(如书信); 令人回忆的东西; 纪念品 ②暗示; 提示 ③【商】催单

reminiscence [,remi'nisns] *n.* ① 回忆, 缅怀往事, 怀旧; 话旧 ②回忆的往事: The scene awakened ~s of my youth. 这景象唤起了我青年时代的往事。③[复]回忆录; 回忆的话 ④引起联想的相似物: There is a ~ of her mother in the way she talks. 她讲话的神态使人联想起她的母亲。⑤【哲】(柏拉图先验论中)不朽灵魂对理念的回忆: the Platonic doctrine of ~ 柏拉图的回忆说

reminiscent [,remi'nisnt] **I** *a.* ①回忆往事的; 缅怀往事的; 怀旧的; 话旧的: a ~ mood 缅怀往事的心情 / tend to be ~ 易于怀旧的 ②提醒的; 暗示的; 使人联想…的 (*of*) **II** *n.* 往事的叙述者 ‖ **~ly** *ad.*

remiss [ri'mis] *a.* ①疏忽的, 粗心的; 不负责任的; 懈怠的: be ~ in one's duties 对自己的职责疏忽 / That was very ~ of you. 你那样做太粗心大意了。/ ~ discipline 松懈的纪律 ②无精打采的, 懒洋洋的 ‖ **~ly** *ad.* / **~ness** *n.*

remission [ri'miʃən] *n.* ①宽恕; 赦免 ②(债务、捐税等的)免除, 豁免 ③缓和; 减轻: the ~ of a fever 热度的减退

remit [ri'mit] **I** (remitted; remitting) ❶ *vt.* ①宽恕; 赦免 ②豁免(捐税、债务等), 免除(处罚): The taxes have been *remitted*. 捐税已豁免了。

③缓和; 减轻, 减退: ~ one's efforts 松劲 / ~ a siege 解围 / ~ one's anger 息怒 ④提交, 移交(问题等); 【律】把(案件)发回下级法院; 还押; 叫(某人)请教(另一人或某书者) (*to*): ~ a question *to* a special committee 把问题移交给专门委员会(解决) ⑤使恢复原位(或原状等), 使复职 ⑥延, 推迟 (*to, till*): ~ consideration of the matter *till* next session 把此事推迟到下届会议考虑 ⑦送, 传送; 汇寄: ~ goods by railway 由铁路运货 / I hope you'll ~ me the money in time. 我希望你能及时把钱汇给我。❷ *vi.* ①缓和; 减轻; 松弛: His pain began to ~. 他的痛开始缓和了。②汇款: Kindly ~ by cheque. 请汇支票付款。**II** *n.* 移交的事件; 呈交当局解决的事项

remittance [ri'mitəns] *n.* 汇款; 汇款额: make a ~ 汇款 ‖ **~ man** (侨居外国的)靠国内汇款生活的人

remnant ['remnənt] **I** *n.* ①残余; 剩余; 残迹: the ~s of a feast 筵席的剩菜 ②(削价出售的)零料, 零头布: a ~ sale 零料出售 ③[常用复]残存者 **II** *a.* 残余的; 剩余的; 残留的

remonstrance [ri'monstrəns] *n.* ①抗议; 抗辩: say in ~ that ... 抗议说… ②规劝, 告诫 ③【英史】谏书: the Grand *Remonstrance* (一六四一年英国下院为反对苛政而呈国王的)大抗议书

remonstrate [ri'monstreit] ❶ *vi.* ①抗议; 抗辩 (*against*) ②规劝, 告诫: ~ with sb. regarding (或 on, upon, about) his bad habits 就其不良习惯进行规劝 ❷ *vt.* 抗议地说; 抗辩地说 ‖ **remonstration** [,ri:mɔns'treiʃən] *n.* / **remonstrative** [ri'mɔnstrətiv] *a.* / **remonstrator** *n.* 抗议者; 规劝者

remorse [ri'mɔ:s] *n.* ①懊悔, 悔恨; 自责: ~ *for* a crime 悔罪 ②同情(心) ‖ *without* ~ 无情的(地)

remote [ri'məut] *a.* ①相隔很远的; 偏僻的: a town ~ from the sea 远离海边的城镇 / go to the ~ mountain areas 到偏僻的山区去 ②很遥远的, 很久的: in the ~ future 在遥远的将来 / cultural relics of ~ ages 古代文物 / from ~ antiquity up to modern times 从上古到现代 ③关系远的; (亲戚)远房的: a question ~ from the subject 同主题关系很少的问题 / a ~ kinsman 远亲 ④冷淡的, 疏远的: be ~ and cold in one's manner 态度冷漠 ⑤很少的, 细微的; 模糊的: a ~ possibility 极小的可能性 / I have only a very ~ idea of what he means. 对他讲的意思我只有一点很模糊的概念。/ The portrait bears not the ~st resemblance to her. 这画像一点也不象她本人。⑥ 间接的; (原因等)远的: ~ effects 间接影响 / the ~ causes 远因 ⑦遥控的 ‖ **~ly** *ad.* / **~ness** *n.* ‖ **~ control** 遥控 / **~ damages** 【律】间接损害

removable [ri'mu:vəbl] *a.* ①可移动的; 可拆除的: a ~ partition 可拆装的隔板 ②可去除的: a ~ evil 可去除的弊害 ③可免职的 ‖ **removability** [ri,mu:və'biliti] *n.*

removal [ri'mu:vəl] *n.* ①移动;调动: the ~ of furniture 搬掉家具 ②迁移;迁居: a ~ to a new house 迁入新居 ③除掉,切除: the surgical ~ of a cancer 恶性肿瘤的手术切除 ④排除: the ~ of obstacles 障碍(物)的排除 ⑤撤换,免职

remove [ri'mu:v] I ❶ *vt.* ①移动,搬开;调动: the spirit of the Foolish Old Man who ~d the mountains 愚公移山的精神 / Kindly ~ the dishes. 请把碗盏端走。②脱掉;去掉,消除: ~ one's hat 脱帽 / ~ the dirt 去掉灰尘 / ~ sb.'s doubts 消除某人的疑虑 / ~ a name from a list 从名单上除名 / ~ the causes of disease 消除疾病的根源 ③使离去;把…免职;撤去: be ~d from office 被撤职 / ~ sb. from school 开除某人出校 / ~ a military base 撤除军事基地 ④[用被动语态](一道菜)被(另一道菜)替换 ⑤除掉,杀掉;暗杀 ⑥【律】移交(案件) ❷ *vi.* ①迁移,搬家: ~ from the city to the countryside 从城里搬到农村 ②[诗]离开 ③移动: a bottle cap that ~s easily 一个容易开的瓶盖子 II *n.* ①移动;迁移,搬家 ②距离,间隔: at a short ~ upon the same platform 在同一月台上的不远处 ③[主英](学校中的)升级;(某些学校的)班级: get one's ~ 升级 ④[主英]替换的一道菜 ⑤程度;阶段;(亲属关系的)远近: The word is but one ~ from slang. 这个词差不离就是俚语。/ a cousin of the fortieth ~ 很远的亲族 ‖ ~ *furniture* 见 **furniture** / ~ *mountains* 见 **mountain** / ~ *oneself* 走开 / *Three ~s are as bad as a fire.* [谚]三次搬家有如一次失火。‖ ~**r** *n.* ①搬运工 ②去除剂: a paint ~r 去涂料剂;去漆剂 ③【律】(案件的)移交

removed [ri'mu:vd] *a.* ①(亲族关系)隔了…代的: a first cousin once ~ 嫡表(或嫡堂)兄弟(或姊妹)的子女 ②远离的,无关的: a language ~ from French 与法语关系疏远的语言 / be ~ from self-interest 没有自私自利之心

remunerate [ri'mju:nəreit] *vt.* 酬报,酬劳;给…补偿(或赔偿) ‖ **remuneration** [ri,mju:nə'rei-ʃən] *n.*

remunerative [ri'mju:nərətiv] *a.* ① 有报酬的 ②有利的 ‖ ~**ly** *ad.* / ~**ness** *n.*

renaissance [rə'neisəns] 法 rənɛsɑ̃:s] I *n.* ①[the R-](欧洲十四至十六世纪的)文艺复兴;文艺复兴时期;文艺复兴时期的风格(指艺术、建筑等方面) ②[R-]文艺(或艺术、学术)的复兴 ③新生;复兴;复活: a postwar ~ 战后的复兴 II *a.* ①[R-]文艺复兴的;文艺复兴时期(或风格)的: *Renaissance* painters (architecture) 文艺复兴时期的画家(建筑) ②[R-]文艺复兴时期的建筑风格的 ‖ **renaissant** *a.* ①[R-]文艺复兴的;文艺复兴时期(或风格)的 ②新生的;复兴的

rend [rend] (rent [rent]) ❶ *vt.* ①撕碎,扯破: be rent to pieces 被撕成碎片 ②因愤怒(或忧虑、失望)而扯(头发或衣服等) ③割裂;分裂: be rent in two 被分裂成两半 ④夺去 ⑤(声音)刺破,响

彻: The stillness was rent by thunderous applause. 雷鸣般的掌声打破了寂静。/ ~ the air (喊声等)震天响 ⑥伤…的感情: ~ sb. with scorn 用蔑视来伤某人的感情 ❷ *vi.* 撕开,裂开;分开

render ['rendə] I ❶ *vt.* ①提出(理由等);呈递;汇报;开出(帐单);作出(判决等): ~ a report to 向…提出报告(或作汇报) / ~ an account of one's actions 说明自己的行动 / ~ a bill 开帐单 / an account ~ed 已开来但未付的帐单 / A verdict of … was ~ed against them. 判处他们… ②放弃;让与(up): ~ (up) a city 放弃城市 ③报答;归还(back): ~ thanks 答谢 / ~ sb. his due reward 给某人应得的报酬 / ~ back sb.'s money 把钱归还某人 ④(使)反映;(使)反响 ⑤表示;给予,提供(帮助等): ~ obedience to sb. 对某人表示顺从 / ~ sb. a service 替某人服务(或效劳) / Thank you for the help you have ~ed us. 感谢你对我们的帮助。⑥使得;使变为 ⑦表达;描绘 ⑧(艺术上)再现形;表演,扮演;朗诵;演奏;处理(绘画等的主题): The piano concerto was well ~ed. 钢琴协奏曲演奏得很好。⑨给…重新措词;翻译;复制: a play into English 把一个剧本译成英语 / The documents were ~ed in their original Chinese. 文件以汉语原文复制。⑩执行,行使,实施;做…的动作: ~ justice 进行审判 / ~ a salute 致敬礼 ⑪煎熬;提取(脂肪): ~ (down) lard 熬猪油 ⑫(用钱、货物或劳役)缴纳 ⑬【建】给…初涂(或打底);粉刷;抹灰 ❷ *vi.* 给予补偿 II *n.* ①(用钱、货物或劳役对佃租等的)缴纳 ②【建】(墙壁的)初涂,打底;粉刷;抹灰 ‖ ~, *float and set* 【建】三层涂抹(指打底,搂平,结砌)

rendezvous ['rondivu:] [法] I ([复] rendezvous ['rondivu:z]) *n.* ①(军队或舰队的)指定集合地;集合 ②聚会的地方;公共场所;人们常去(游憩)的地方: a favourite ~ for anglers (artists) 钓鱼的人(美术家)喜欢常去的地方 ③约定;约会;幽会;约会(或幽会)地点;宇宙飞船(或其他空间飞行器)的会合(点) II *vt. & vi.* (使)在指定地点集合(或聚会、相见)

renew [ri'nju:] ❶ *vt.* ①使更新;使复原;使恢复: ~ one's youth 返老还童 / ~ one's health 恢复健康 / with ~ed efforts 以新的努力 ②使新生;使自新;使苏醒: ~ the heart and mind 使精神面貌焕然一新 ③使复活;使重新记起;复兴;重建: ~ a building 对一幢建筑物进行翻修 ④换新;修补;补充;加强: ~ provisions 补充新鲜食物 / a rubber tire 更换新轮胎 / The trees ~ their foliage every spring. 每年春天树木都苍青。/ ~ the water in the tank 使水箱里再充满水 / ~ the garrison 增援守军 / a coat ~ed in places 补订好几个补钉的上衣 ⑤重新开始;继续: ~ an attack 重新进攻 ⑥重复;重申;重做: ~ a bill 重提议案 ⑦准予(契约)展期;续借(图书等): ~ a contract (lease) 使合同(租约)展期 / ~ a library book for another two weeks 把一本

图书馆的书续借两星期 **❷** *vi.* ①更新; 恢复原状 ②重新开始, 继续 ③(契约等)展期

renounce [ri'nauns] I **❶** *vt.* ①放弃, 抛弃: ~ one's old habits 戒绝旧习惯 / ~ one's religion 放弃宗教信仰 / ~ one's claim *to* an inheritance 放弃遗产继承权 ②与…脱离关系, 拒绝承认(子女等) ③(纸牌戏中出另一花色的牌来)表示缺少(某种花色) **❷** *vi.* ①【律】放弃权利(或财产等) ②(纸牌戏中因打不出应跟的花色而)垫牌 II *n.* 垫牌 ‖ *the world* 退隐 ‖~**ment** *n.*

renovate ['renouveit] *vt.* ①革新, 更新 ②修复, 修理, 整顿 ③恢复(精神、活动等) ④使干净; 刷新 ‖**renovation** [,renou'veiʃən] *n. renovations* of old buildings 对老建筑物的整顿翻新 / **renovator** *n.* 革新者; 修复者; 恢复者; 刷新者

renown [ri'naun] I *n.* 名望, 声誉: of great (或 high) ~ 很有声誉的 II *vt.* 使有名望, 使有声誉 ‖~**ed** *a.* 有名望的, 著名的: be ~*ed* for 因…而著名; 以…著称

rent¹ [rent] *n.* ① (衣服等的)破裂处; 裂缝; 缝隙: mend a ~ in a sleeve 缝补衣袖上的裂缝 / a ~ in the clouds 云间的罅隙 ② [喻] 分裂, (关系等的)破裂

rent² [rent] I *n.* ①租金, 租费; 租: pay a high ~ for a house 付昂贵的房租 ②出租的财产(指房、地产等) II **❶** *vt.* ① 租入, 租用: ~ a house *from* 向…租房子 ②出租: ~ (*out*) a machine *to* 把机器租给… ③ 向…收租: ~ sb. high (low) 向某人收昂贵(低廉)的租金 **❷** *vi.* 出租: The room ~*s at* (或 *for*) £5 a week. 这房间每星期租金五英镑。 ‖*for* ~ 出租的 ‖~**able** *a.* 可租的; 可收租金的 ‖~ **charge** 租费 / '~**-free** *a.* & *ad.* 不收租金的(地) / ~ **party** [美俚]为筹措房租而举行的舞会(参加舞会者须向舞会主人付少量的钱以供他缴房租) / '~**-roll** *n.* 地租(或房租)帐; 租册 ②房地租总收入 ‖~ **service** [主英]代替租金的劳役

rent³ [rent] I rend 的过去式和过去分词 II *a.* ①撕裂的 ②分裂的: be ~ with mutual strife 因互相倾轧(或争夺)而四分五裂

rental ['rentl] I *n.* ①租费; 租金收入 ②租赁; 出租; 出租业 ③租摺, 租册 ④出租的财产(指房屋等) II *a.* ①租用的 ②出租的; 出租业的 ‖~ **library** (商店等内设的)出租书籍处

renunciation [ri,nʌnsi'eiʃən] *n.* ①放弃, 抛弃 ②脱离关系; (对子女等的)拒绝承认 ③克制自己 ④【律】(对权利等的)放弃声明书

repair¹ [ri'pɛə] I *vt.* ① 修理; 修补: ~ a watch (the roads) 修表(路) / ~ a glove (puncture) 补手套(小洞) ②补救, 纠正: ~ a mistake 纠正错误 ③恢复: ~ one's health 使自己恢复健康 ④弥补, 补偿(损失等): ~ a wrong 补偿自己对别人做过的错事 II *n.* ①修理; 修补: a ship under ~ 正在修理的船 / a ~ workshop 修理车间 / [常用复]修理工程; 修理工作: ~*s* on the school building 校舍的修理工程 / The shop is closed

during ~*s.* (商店)内部整修, 暂停营业。/ *Repairs done while you wait.* 修理东西, 立等可取。/ ~ running ~ 小修补 ③ 维修状况: out of ~ (或 in bad ~) 失修 / in (good) ~ 维修良好 / need (putting into) ~ 需要维修 ④ (细胞等的)修复, 再造: ~ of tissue 组织修复 / natural ~ 自愈 ‖~**er** [ri'pɛərə] *n.* 修补者, 修理者: boot and shoe ~*ers* 补鞋工人 ‖~**man** [ri'pɛəmən] *n.* 修理工人

repair² [ri'pɛə] I *vi.* ①去; 经常去; 大伙儿去: We are ~*ing* to the country to help get in the harvest. 我们将去农村帮助收庄稼。/ ~ to the seaside in summer 夏天经常到海滨去 / ~ to sb. for aid 去求助于某人 ②聚集, 集合 II *n.* [古] (人们)常去的地方: a place of great (little) ~ 热闹(冷静)的地方

repairable [ri'pɛərəbl] *a.* ① 可修理的, 可修补的: Is this pair of shoes ~? 这双鞋子还可补一下吗? ② 可补救的, 可纠正的 ③ 可恢复的 ④ 可弥补的, 可补偿的

reparable ['repərəbl] *a.* ①可修理的; 可修补的 ②可补救的; 可纠正的 ③可补偿的; 可赔偿的: a ~ loss 可补偿的损失 ④可治愈的: a ~ injury 可治愈的伤处

reparation [,repə'reiʃən] *n.* ① 补偿; [常用复](战败国须付的)赔款, 赔偿: war ~*s* 战争(损失)赔偿 / ~ in kind 实物赔偿 ② 弥补, 补救; 恢复 ③修理(现常用 repair); 整修工作, 维修工程(现常用 repairs)

repartee [,repɑ:'ti:] I *n.* 巧妙的回答, 妙语; 机智的反驳, 巧辩: have a great power of ~ 具有敏捷答辩的才能 II *vi.* [罕]巧妙地回答(或反驳)

repast [ri'pɑ:st] ‖书面语‖ I *n.* ①餐, 饮食; 宴: a luxurious ~ 美餐; 盛宴 / a slight ~ 便饭 / partake of a ~ 就餐 ②就餐; 就餐时间 II *vi.* 就餐; 设宴

repatriate I [ri:'pætrieit] **❶** *vt.* 把…遣返回国: ~ prisoners of war 遣返战俘 **❷** *vi.* 回国 II [ri:'pætriit] *n.* 被遣返回国者 ‖**repatriation** ['ri:,pætri'eiʃən] *n.*

repay [ri:'pei] (repaid [ri:'peid]) **❶** *vt.* ①偿还, 付还(钱等); 还钱给(某人); 补偿 ②报答; 报复; 报敬: ~ sb. for his hospitality 报答某人的款待 / ~ a visit 回访 **❷** *vi.* 偿还; 报答; 报复 ‖~**ment** *n.* ①偿还; 报答; 报复: bonds due for ~*ment* 到期应偿付的债券 ②偿付的款项(或物)

repeal [ri'pi:l] I *vt.* ① 撤销(决议等); 废除(法令等) ②放弃; 否定 II *n.* ①撤销, 废除 ②【英史】取消联合(十九世纪初, 爱尔兰独立运动领袖奥康诺等反对与英国并成联合王国的主张) ‖~**er** *n.* ①撤销者; 废除者 ②撤销某一法令的法令

repeat [ri'pi:t] I **❶** *vt.* ①重说, 重做; 跟着别人讲(或念): ~ a signal 再发同样的信号 / Please ~ what I said. 请重复一遍我的话。/ Don't ~ the mistake. 不要再犯同样的错误。/ We regret that we cannot ~ this article. 很遗憾, 我们不能再供应这种商品。 ② 把(别人的话等)讲出去: Don't ~ the secret to anybody. 不要把这秘密

讲给任何人听。③背诵: ~ a poem 背诵一首诗
④使再现; 再经历: History will not ~ itself. 历
史决不会重演。⑤复制 ❷ *vi.* ①重复说(或做)。
His words will not bear ~*ing*. 他的话实在不
能再重复。(指说不出口) ②(数字中)重复出现:
The last two figures ~. 最后两个数码相同。(如
1655) ③ (食物)留有味道: Do you find that
onions ~? 你有没有发觉吃洋葱后嘴里还留有味
道? ④[美](违法地)重复投票 **Ⅱ** *n.* ① 重复; 重
演(尤指应观众要求); 重播: a ~ performance 重
演 / There will be a ~ of this programme next
week. 下星期将重播这档节目。②【音】复奏(或
复唱)部分; 反复符号 ③(糊墙纸等上)同样的图
案 ④[商]再订同类货(单) ‖~ **oneself** 不自觉
地重复说 (或做) ‖~**ing decimal** 循环小数 /
~**ing rifle** 转轮枪, 连发枪 / ~**ing watch** 打簧
表 (=repeater)

repeated [ri'pi:tid] *a.* 反复的, 再三的, 屡次的; 重
复的: an often ~ excuse 经常用的一个借口
‖~**ly** *ad.*

repel [ri'pel] (repelled; repelling) ❶ *vt.* ① 击退,
抵制: ~ an attack (the assailants) 击退进攻(进
攻者) / ~ a temptation 不受诱惑 ②拒绝; 排斥:
~ a plea 拒绝请求 / ~ sb.'s advances 拒绝某
人献殷勤 ③使厌恶, 使反感 ④ 抗, 防: A plastic
coating ~s moisture. 塑料涂层能防潮。/ Water
~s oil. 油水不相容。❷ *vi.* 击退; 抵抗; 引起反
感: a *repelling* odour 难闻的气味 / a manner
that ~s 使人讨厌的举止

repellent [ri'pelənt] **Ⅰ** *a.* ① 击退的; 排斥的 ②讨
人厌的, 令人反感的 ③【化】相斥的; 防水的 **Ⅱ** *n.*
①防水布 ②[药]驱虫剂; 消毒药 ③防护剂 ‖~
ly *ad.*

repent[1] [ri'pent] ❶ *vi.* 悔悟; 悔改; 后悔; [宗]忏
悔: ~ and start anew 悔过自新 / ~ of one's
carelessness 对自己的粗心大意表示后悔 / ~ of
having missed a good opportunity to learn 后悔
失去一个学习的好机会 / too late to ~ 悔之莫
及 ❷ *vt.* 悔恨; [古]懊悔后悔: She ~ed her
rashness. 她后悔太急躁。

repent[2] ['ri:pent] *a.* 【植】匍匐生根的; 【动】爬行的

repentance [ri'pentəns] *n.* 悔悟; 悔改; 后悔; 忏悔:
show ~ (for sth.) (对某事)表示后悔

repentant [ri'pentənt] *a.* 悔悟的; 悔改的; 后悔的;
忏悔的: be ~ of one's fault 对自己的过失后悔

repercussion [,ri:pə(:)'kʌʃən] *n.* ①击回, 弹回, 反
冲 ②被击回(或弹回)的东西; 回声; 反射 ③相互作
用; [常用复]反响, 反应; 影响: have ~s all over
the world 在全世界产生反响 ④[医]散解法; 消
疹法; 浮动诊(胎)法 ⑤[音](赋格曲中间插段后
的)主题的再现, 答句(音调或和弦的)重复

repertoire ['repətwɑ:] *n.* ① (准备好能演出的)全
部剧目, 全部节目; 保留剧目: The pianist has a
large ~. 这个钢琴家能演奏许多乐曲。② 全部
技能; 所有组成部分: the ~ of a goalkeeper 守
门员应有的各种技能 / a biochemical ~ 生物化
学的各种组成科目

repertory ['repətəri] *n.* ① 仓库; 库存, 贮藏物 ②
积贮, 搜集(指事实等): He is a ~ of technical
knowledge. 他的技术知识很丰富。③(准备好能
演出的)全部剧目, 全部节目 (=repertoire): a
theatre 由某一剧团定期换演剧目的剧场 / a ~
company 定期换演剧目的剧团

repetition [,repi'tiʃən] *n.* ① 重复; 反复 ② 重说, 重
做; 反复讲(或做): after many ~s 经过多次的
反复 ③ 重复的事物; 复制品; 副本 ④背诵; 背诵
的材料(如诗等); 【音】(乐器)复奏的性能 ‖~**al** *a.* /
~**ary** *a.* / **repetitive** [ri'petitiv] *a.*

repine [ri'pain] *vi.* ①不满, 烦恼, 埋怨, 发牢骚 (at,
against) ②(因不满现状等而)想望, 向往 (for)

replace [ri(:)'pleis] *vt.* ①把…放回(原处); 使恢复
(原职): *Replace* the newspapers after reading.
报纸阅后放回原处。②取代; 以…代替 (by, with):
接替, 替换; 更换: ~ a worn tire 调换旧轮胎/
~ coal by (或 with) gas 用煤气代替煤作燃料 ③
归还; 赔还: ~ borrowed money 还借款 /
embezzled funds 退赔盗用的公款 ‖~**able** *a.*
可放回原处的; 可代替的; 可替换的

replenish [ri'pleniʃ] ❶ *vt.* ①(再)填满, (再)装满:
~ a petrol-tank *with* gasoline 给油箱装满汽油 /
keep one's glass ~ed 使杯中不断斟满酒 ②补充
(兵力等); 添加, 添足: ~ the stock (of goods) 补
充存货 / ~ the fire 给炉火加燃料 / ~ one's
wardrobe 添置服装 ③ 使住满人(或动物); 使充
满精神力量 ❷ *vi.* (再)装满; 充满 ‖~**er** *n.*
①(再)装满者; 补充者; 补充物: a soil ~er 肥料
②[摄]显像剂, 显影剂 / ~**ment** *n.* manpower
~ment 人力补充

replete [ri'pli:t] *a.* ①饱满的; 充分供应的 ②充满
的; 充实的 ③塞满的; 吃饱的; 狼吞虎咽的; 肥
胖的 ‖**repletion** [ri'pli:ʃən] *n.*

replica ['replikə, ri'pli:kə] *n.* ① 艺术复制品(尤指
出于原作者之手的) ② 复制品; 拷贝; 完全一样
的事物: the ~ of an institution (a conversation)
一模一样的机构(谈话) ③【音】(主题的)进入;
(乐谱中的)重复: *senza* ~ 不带重复

replier [ri'plaiə] *n.* 回答者, 答复者

reply [ri'plai] **Ⅰ** ❶ *vi.* ①回答, 答复: ~ to sb. 回
答某人 / ~ to a question 回答问题 / Please
~ at your earliest convenience. 请尽早答复。
②(以行动)答复; 回击: ~ by a blow 回以一击 /
~ to the enemy's fire 回击敌人炮火 ③反响, 回
响 ④(原告对被告)答辩 ❷ *vt.* 回答: I don't
know what to ~. 我不知该回答什么。/ He
replied that he might go. 他回答说他可能去。
Ⅱ *n.* ①回答, 答复: in ~ to 为答复… / make
no ~ 不作答复 / wire a ~ 拍复电 / the letter
under ~ 本函所答复的来信 ②(原告对被告的)
答辩 ‖~ **for sb.** 代表某人作答(或答辩); 代表
某人谢祝酒 / ~ **paid** (拍电人已将)回电费
付讫

report [ri'po:t] **Ⅰ** ❶ *vt.* ①报告; 汇报: ~ the discovery of new coal mines 报告发现新煤矿 /

phone to ~ a fire 打电话报火警 / ~ the state of affairs to higher authorities 向上级汇报情况 ②传说; 转述: It is ~ed that .... 据说… / My actual words and those ~ed to you were quite different. 我实际上说的同别人传给你听的根本不同。 / ~ed speech 【语】间接引语 / ~ing verb 【语】引出间接引语的动词 ③记录(以供发表等); 报道: ~ a speech 记录(或报道)一次讲话 / be ~ed in the press 在报上登载(或报道) / listen to the commentator ~ing a table-tennis game 听广播评述员报道乒乓比赛实况 ④告发, 揭发: ~ sb.'s sabotage 揭发某人的破坏活动 ⑤ [~ oneself] 使报到: ~ oneself at a new post 到新岗位报到 ❷ vi. ①报告; 汇报 ②说出对…的印象 (of): He ~s well of the prospects. 他说他认为前景很好。 / be well (badly) ~ed of 名声好(坏) ③写报道 ④报到: ~ (in) to sb. 向某人报到 / ~ for duty at the construction site 到工地报到(或上班) II n. ①报告; 汇报: make a ~ 作报告 / the State Council's ~ on 国务院关于…的报告 / a school ~ 学校的成绩报告单 / an accounting ~ 财务报表 / a laboratory ~ 化验结果(或报告) ②传说; (公众)议论; 名声: Report has it (或 The ~ goes) that .... 据传说… / Don't listen to idle ~s. 别听信无稽之谈。 / of good (evil) ~ 名声好(坏) ③报道, 通讯; (会议等的)正式记录: newspaper (或 press) ~s 报纸上的报道 ④ [复]【律】笔录; 意见书; 判决书; (给上级法院的)申请书; 案件(或判例)汇编 ⑤爆炸声, 爆裂声: the ~ of a gun 枪炮声 / the ~ of a burst tire 轮胎爆裂声 ‖ ~ out (立法委员会经讨论及修正后)将(提案等)交回议会辩论并表决 / through good and evil ~ 不管名声好坏; 不管舆论如何 ‖ ~able a. ①值得报告(或汇报、报道)的 ②应该报告的 ~er n. ①报告人; 汇报人 ②记者, 通讯员; 新闻广播员: a sports ~er 体育新闻记者 ③【律】判决(或诉讼)发布人; 笔录人 ‖ ~ card (学生的)成绩报告单 / ~ stage (英国)议会在三读前对修正案的讨论与处理阶段

repose[1] [ri'pouz] I ❶ vt. 使休息; 把(头部等)靠着休息: ~ oneself on the bed 在床上躺着休息 / ~ one's head on the pillow 把头靠在枕上休息 ❷ vi. ①(躺着)休息: ~ on a couch 在躺椅上休息 ②长眠, 安息 ③静卧; 蕴藏: The land ~s in the dusk. 大地在暮色中沉寂着。 ④被安放; 座落 (on): The statue ~s on a pedestal. 塑像置于台座上。 / The shale ~s on a bed of limestone. 油页岩在石灰岩岩层上面。 ⑤建立于, 基于(on) ⑥ [古]依靠, 信赖(in) II n. ①休息; 安眠: disturb sb.'s ~ 打扰某人的休息(或安眠) ②宁静; 镇静; 静止; 平静: ~ of mind 心绪宁静; 泰然自若 / His manner lacks ~. 他举止忙乱。 / The volcano was in ~. 火山静止着。 / a face in ~ 平静的脸容 ③(图画等色彩、结构的)和谐, 恬静

repose[2] [ri'pouz] vt. ①[罕]放; 置 ②把…寄托于(in): ~ one's hope in 把希望寄托在… /

confidence in sb. (in sb.'s promises) 信赖某人(某人的诺言) ③授予(管辖、使用等权)

repository [ri'pozitəri] n. ①贮藏所, 仓库; 贮物器(如箱、柜等): repositories for sb.'s manuscripts 藏某人手稿的地方 / This book is a ~ of useful information. 这本书里有许多有用的知识。 / He is a ~ of curious information. 他知道许多稀奇古怪的事情。 ②博物馆; 陈列室; 店铺 ③资源丰富地区 ④墓地 ⑤亲信; 知己

reprehensible [.repri'hensəbl] a. 应受严责的; 应受指摘的; 应受申斥的 ‖ **reprehensibly** ad.

represent[1] [.repri'zent] ❶ vt. ①描绘; 描述: The painting ~s the scene of a bumper harvest. 这幅画描绘丰收的景象。 / I can only ~ it to you by metaphors. 我只能用隐喻来向你描述它。 ②讲述, 阐述; (强烈)指出; 主张: ~ the atomic theory to an audience 向听众阐述原子理论 / We must ~ our determination to the masses. 我们必须向群众表明我们的决心。 ③声称: He ~ed himself as .... 他声称他是… ④代表; 代理; 为…的国会议员: How many countries are ~ed at the meeting? 有多少国家的代表出席了那次会议? / M. P.'s ~ing urban constituencies 代表城市选区的国会议员们 ⑤象征; 体现; 表示; 相当于: troops ~ing a just cause 正义之师 / This glorious achievement ~s the principle of self-reliance. 这个光辉成就体现了自力更生的方针。 / X ~s the unknown. X表示未知数。 ⑥演出; 扮演 ⑦回忆 ❷ vi. 提出异议, 提出抗议 ‖ ~ sth. to oneself 想象出某事物

represent[2] ['ri:pri'zent] vt. 再赠送; 再献; 再提出; 再上演: ~ a cheque at the bank 再向银行兑支票 / ~ a play 再上演某剧

representation [.reprizen'teiʃən] n. ①描写; 表现; 表示: a vivid ~ of rural life 农村生活的生动描写 / the school of the "art of ~" of the 19th century (艺术方面的)十九世纪的表现派 ②(绘画等)艺术作品: a ~ in ivory of peony 牙雕牡丹 ③ [常用复]陈述; 请求; 正式抗议: His ~ influenced them to investigate. 他的陈述促使他们去调查。 / make ~s to the judge about an unjust decision 向法官抗议不公正的判决 ④ [总称]代表; 代表制; 代理: diplomatic ~ 外交代表 / demand ~ on the school committee 要求在校务委员会里有代表 / the right of legal ~ 法定代理权 ⑤演出; 扮演 ⑥【律】继承; (促使另一方订契约的)陈述 ‖ ~al a.

representative [.repri'zentətiv] I a. ①描写的; 表现的; 表示的: a narrative ~ of army life 描写军队生活的故事 / strictly ~ art 纯粹的表现派艺术 ②代表性的, 典型的: samples ~ of the latest industrial development 代表工业上最新发展的样品 ③代表的; 代表制的; 代理的: ~ organs 代表机关 / be ~ of the people 代表人民 / a ~ government 代议制政府 ④【生】相当的, 类似的 II n. ①典型 ②代表; 代理人;【律】继承人: a people's ~ 人民代表 / ~s from various quar-

ters 各方面的代表 / a legal ~ 法定代理人 ③
[美][R-] 众议院议员: the House of *Representatives* 众议院 ‖**~ly** *ad.* / **~ness** *n.*

repress [ri'pres] **❶** *vt.* ① 镇压 ② 抑制(感情等);
忍住; 压制, 约束(行动等): ~ one's tears 忍住
眼泪 / ~ one's child 把孩子管得太严 ③【心】
把(冲动等)压入(潜意识) **❷** *vi.* 采取高压手段
‖**~ed** 被镇压的;被抑制的;受约束的 / **~ion**
[ri'preʃən] *n.* 镇压;抑制;约束 / **~ive** *a.* 镇压
的;抑制的;约束的

reprieve [ri'priːv] **I** *vt.* ①【律】缓期执行(死刑
等) ② 暂缓(痛苦、危险、困难等) **II** *n.* ① 缓刑
(令) ② 暂缓;暂止

reprimand I ['reprimɑːnd] *n.* 惩戒;(尤指当权者
所作的)谴责 **II** ['reprimɑːnd, ˌrepri'mɑːnd] *vt.*
惩戒;谴责: ~ sb. for sth. 为某事申斥某人

reprisal [ri'praizəl] *n.* ①【史】(受害国进行报复的)
没收;拘押 ②(国际法)(除战争外所施行的)报复
性暴力行为 ③ 报复(行为): a ~ raid 报复性空
袭 / make ~(s) 进行报复 ④ [常用复] 赔偿

reproach [ri'prəutʃ] **I** *vt.* ① 责备,申斥;指责,非
难: ~ sb. *with* (或 *for*) carelessness 指责某人粗
心大意 / His eyes ~ed me. 他对我投以责备的
目光。② 使丢脸; 有辱…的名誉: Such doings
will ~ him. 这种行径会使他丢脸。**II** *n.* ① 责
备,斥责;指责: a term (look) of ~ 谴责的话(眼
色) / heap ~es on sb. 痛责某人 / above (或
beyond) ~ 无可指责 ② 耻辱;不名誉: bring (或
draw) ~ on sb. 使某人受辱 ‖**~able** *a.* 可责备
的;应受斥责的 / **~less** *a.* 无可责备的;无可非
难的

reprobate ['reprəubeit] **I** *vt.* ① 谴责, 斥责,指责
② 拒绝; 摈弃 ③【宗】(上帝)摈弃; (天)罚 **II** *a.*
① 堕落的,放荡的, 道德败坏的;邪恶的; 罪恶深重
的 ② 为上帝摈弃的 **III** *n.* ① 堕落者,放荡者;恶
棍 ② 为上帝摈弃的人 ‖**reprobation** [ˌreprəu-
'beiʃən] *n.*

reproduce [ˌriːprə'djuːs] **❶** *vt.* ① 繁殖, 生殖 ②
再生产,再造;再生长(器官) ③ 复制; 翻版;复写,
重演, 再上演; 描绘…的图象: ~ music from a
gramophone record 由留声机唱片重播音乐 / ~
a face on canvas 在画布上描绘脸容 ④在脑海中
再现(过去的情景等) **❷** *vi.* ① 繁殖, 生殖 ② 进
行再生产; 复制: The original ~s clearly in a
photocopy. 原本影印得很清楚。‖**~able, repro-
ducible** *a.* 能繁殖的;能再生产的;能再生长的;
能复制的;能复印的;能再现的 / **~r** *n.* ①扬声
器 ②【无】再现设备

reproduction [ˌriːprə'dʌkʃən] *n.* ① 再生(产); 再
生产过程 ②繁殖, 生殖 ③复制; 复制品(尤指艺
术品);翻版 ④(果生的)幼树

reproductive [ˌriːprə'dʌktiv] **I** *a.* 再生(产)的; 生
殖的;复制(品)的: ~ organs【解】生殖器官, 生
殖器 **II** *n.* (实际或潜在的)母体(尤指有性繁殖
的群居昆虫)

reproof [ri'pruːf] *n.* 谴责,申斥;责备: a glance of
~ 谴责的一瞥 / a word of ~ 责备的话

reprove [ri'pruːv] *vt.* ① 责骂, 谴责: ~ sb. *for*
sth. 为某事责备(或谴责)某人 ② 指摘,非难,不
赞成 ‖**reprovingly** *ad.*

reptile ['reptail] **I** *n.* ①【动】爬行动物;爬虫 ②两
栖动物 ③ 卑躬屈节的人,卑鄙的人 **II** *a.* ①(像)
爬行动物的;(像)爬虫的 ②卑躬屈节的,卑鄙的,
鬼鬼祟祟的

reptilian [rep'tiliən] **I** *a.* ①(像)爬行动物的;(像)
爬虫的 ②卑躬屈节的,卑鄙的, 鬼鬼祟祟的 **II** *n.*
爬行动物;爬虫

republic [ri'pʌblik] *n.* ① 共和国; 共和政体: a
constitutional ~ 立宪共和国 ②(成员具有平等
权利的)团体, 界: the ~ of letters 文坛, 文学界

republican [ri'pʌblikən] **I** *a.* ①共和国的, 共和政
体的 ②共和政体论(者)的;共和主义的 ③ [R-]
(美国)共和党的 ④(鸟类等)群栖的 **II** *n.* ①拥
护共和政体者, 共和主义者 ② [R-] (美国) 共和
党党员; 拥护共和党的人 ‖**~ism** *n.* ①共和论;
共和主义 ②共和国政府; 共和体制 ③对共和体
制的拥护 ④ [Republicanism] (美国)共和党纲
领;共和党;[总称]共和党人 / **~ize** *vt.* ①使成
共和国 (或共和政体) ②按共和原则改组

repudiate [ri'pjuːdieit] *vt.* ① 与(妻)离婚; 遗弃
(妻子); 抛弃(孩子); 与…断绝关系: ~ an old
friend 与老朋友绝交 / ~ any connexion with
sb.(sth.)与某人(某事)完全断绝关系 ②拒绝接受;
否认(权威或效力等);否定: ~ an obligation
拒绝履行义务 / ~ a contract 否认合同有效
③(私人或国家)拒付(债款) ‖**repudiation** [ri-
ˌpjuːdi'eiʃən] *n.* 遗弃,抛弃;否认;否定; 拒付债
务 / **repudiator** *n.* 抛弃者;否认者;拒绝支付者,
赖债者

repugn [ri'pjuːn] *vi.* & *vt.* [古]反对;反抗

repugnance [ri'pʌgnəns], **repugnancy** [ri'pʌgnən-
si] *n.* ①不一致; 不相容; 矛盾, 抵触 (*of, between,
to, with*): ~ of statements 说法的不一致 ②不
一致的地方,矛盾之处 ③厌恶; 深恶痛绝; 极为反
感 (*to, against*): feel a ~ to 对…极为反感

repugnant [ri'pʌgnənt] *a.* ①不一致的;不相容的,
矛盾的 (*to, between*): actions ~ to one's words
言行不一 ② 令人厌恶的, 使人反感的 (*to*): a ~
odour 令人厌恶的气味 / a ~ proposal 使人反感
的建议 ③ 对抗性的, 敌对的, 相斥的 (*with*): ~
forces 相斥的力

repulse [ri'pʌls] **I** *vt.* ① 打退(敌人等), 击退(攻
击等);【喻】(争论中)挫败(对方) ②(以无礼、冷
淡等)排斥;严厉拒绝: ~ an unreasonable request
严厉拒绝不合理的要求 ③厌恶,憎恶 **II** *n.* ①打
退,击退 ②严拒

repulsion [ri'pʌlʃən] *n.* ① 排斥; 严拒 ② 反感;厌
恶: feel ~ for sb. 对某人有反感 ③【物】推斥;
斥力

repulsive [ri'pʌlsiv] *a.* ①排斥的;严拒的 ②使人
反感的;令人厌恶的; 可憎的: a ~ smell 令人厌
恶的气味 ③【物】推斥的,斥力的: ~ force 推斥
力 ‖**~ly** *ad.* / **~ness** *n.*

reputable ['repjutəbl] *a.* ① 声誉好的，可尊敬的: quite a ~ man 声誉非常好的人 / ~ conduct 可敬的行为 ②规范的: ~ use (speech) 规范的用法(语言) ‖**reputably** *ad.*

reputation [,repju(:)'teiʃən] *n.* ① 名誉; 名声: of high ~ 名誉很好的 / of no ~ 默默无闻的 / have a ~ for courage (或 have the ~ of being courageous) 以勇敢闻名 / make an evil ~ for oneself 弄得声名狼藉 ② 好名声，声望: live up to one's ~ 不负盛名 / lose one's ~ 失去声望 ③荣誉，信誉，体面; 著名: a person of ~ 有信誉的人,体面的人 / be held in ~ 享有名望 / win a high ~ 赢得高的信誉

repute [ri'pju:t] **I** *n.* ①名誉; 名声: of good (bad) ~ 名誉好(坏)的 / in high (low) ~声望高(低)的 / know sb. by ~ 因某人的名气而知道某人 ②好名声, 声望, 美名: authors of ~ 著名作家 **II** *vt.* [常用被动语态] 称为,认为: He is ~d (to be 或 as) a good doctor in serving the people. 他被称为是为人民服务的好医生。/ be ~d for 以…著称 ‖**be well (ill) ~d** 有好(坏)名声 / **through good and evil ~** 不管舆论如何; 不管人们怎样认为

reputed [ri'pju:tid] *a.* ① 声誉好的,驰名的 ②挂名的,号称的: a ~ pint [英]号称一品脱装的酒 (事实上不足一品脱) ‖**~ly** *ad.*

request [ri'kwest] **I** *n.* ① 请求，要求; 恳求: Catalogues of our books will be mailed on ~. 书目承索即寄。/ a written ~ 书面要求(或申请) / make a ~ for instructions 请示 / a ~ stop (公共汽车的)招呼站 ② 要求的事物; 请求的话: grant sb.'s ~s 答应某人所要求的东西 / What's your ~? 你要求什么? ③需要 **II** *vt.* 请求,要求; 恳求: ~ sth. from sb. 向某人要求某物 / ~ sb.'s presence 请某人出席 / Visitors are ~ed not to touch the exhibits. 观众请勿抚摸展览品。/ All I ~ of you is that you (should) be punctual. 我只要求你准时。

requiem ['rekwiem] *n.* ① [常作 R-]【宗】(天主教) 安灵弥撒; 追思弥撒; (做弥撒时唱的)安灵歌,安灵曲 ②挽歌,哀悼歌 ③悲歌,哀诗

require [ri'kwaiə] *vt.* ① 需要: These young seedlings will ~ looking after carefully. 这些幼苗需要细心照料。/ ~ a clear-cut stand 要有鲜明的立场 / The emergency ~s that it should be done. 情况紧急,非这样做不可。②要求; 命令: I am ~d immediately to report to the headquarters. 要我立即向司令部报到。/ They ~ that I (should) go at once. 他们要求我立刻去。

requirement [ri'kwaiəmənt] *n.* ①需要; 需要的东西: a tremendous ~ of this material 对这种材料的大量需要 / military ~s 军需 ② 要求; 必要的条件: fulfil quality ~s 达到质量要求; 符合规格

requisite ['rekwizit] **I** *a.* 需要的; 必要的,必不可少的: Decision is a quality ~ to a commander.

果断是指挥员必不可少的品质。/ have the ~ perseverance *for* a heavy task 对承担一项艰巨任务具有不可缺少的毅力 **II** *n.* 必需品: a ~ *for* life 生活的必需品 / the ~s *for* a long march 长途行军所必需的东西

requisition [,rekwi'ziʃən] **I** *n.* ① 正式请求，正式要求; 申请;【律】引渡犯人的要求: a ~ *for* money 拨款要求 ②(要求拨给物、料、人员等的)通知单,调拨单; 申请书; 征用文书: send a ~ to the purchasing department 送一张请购单到采购科 / a material ~ on quota 限额领料单 / a ~ *for* supplies 征用补给的文书 ③ 需要; 使用; 征用: The limousine was *in* (或 *under*) constant ~ for bringing passengers to and from the airdrome. 经常开出交通车来接送飞机乘客。/ Every sort of vehicle was *put in* (或 *brought into, called into*) ~ during the war. 战争期间各种车辆都被征用。/ make a ~ *on* the citizens for supplies (占领军等)向市民征用补给品 **II** *vt.* 要求; 征用: ~ a house *for* a soldiers' billet 征用民房供军队住宿 / ~ sb.'s services 强迫某人服役 / ~ a city for motor vehicles 征用全市机动车辆

requital [ri'kwaitl] *n.* ① 报答; 回报; 报复: *in* ~ *of* (或 *for*) sb.'s service 作为某人服务的报答 ②报答的事; 酬谢之物; 补偿

requite [ri'kwait] *vt.* ① 报答; 回报: ~ like *for* like 以恩报恩; 以怨报怨 / ~ kindness *with* ingratitude 以怨报德 / ~ an obligation 报恩; 还人情 ② 酬答(某人); 向(某人)报复: ~ sb. *for* his kindness 答谢某人的好意

rescind [ri'sind] *vt.* 废除,取消; 撤回,撤消; 解除: ~ the unreasonable rules 废除不合理的规章 / ~ a judgement (contract) 取消判决(合同)

rescue ['reskju:] **I** *vt.* ① 援救; 营救; 挽救: heal the wounded and ~ the dying 救死扶伤 / ~ sb. *from* danger 营救某人脱离危险 ②【律】非法劫回(被扣留的人或物); 对(被围困地)以武力解围 **II** *n.* ①援救; 营救: come (go) to sb.'s ~ (来)援救某人 / a ~ party 抢救队 / a ~ bid (桥牌中使搭档脱离困境的)救援叫牌 / ~ work on the battlefield 战地救护工作 ②【律】(对被扣的人或物的)非法劫回 ‖**~r** ['reskjue] *n.* 援救者; 营救者; 救星 ‖**~ home** (妓女)济良所 / **~ work** (济贫助人或改造妇女、儿童的)救济事业

research [ri'sə:tʃ] **I** *n.* ①调查; 探究: a ~ *for* (或 *after*) facts 为寻找事实而进行的调查 ② 研究工作; [常用复] 学术研究; 创造性研究: make scientific ~es *on* 进行…的科研工作 / a ~ worker 研究人员 / be engaged in ~ work 从事研究工作 / ~ *into* the causes of cancer 癌的病原的研究 / ~es *in* Asian and African literatures 亚非文学的研究 / Their ~es have been fruitful. 他们的研究已有成果。**II** *vi.* ① 调查; 探究: ~ *into* a problem 研究问题 ②进行学术研究 ‖**~er**, **~ist** *n.* 调查者; 探究者; 学术研究者

resemblance [ri'zembləns] *n.* ①相似; 相似性; 相似点; 相似程度: He bears a strong ~ to his

father. 他长得很象他父亲。/ There are striking
~s between the twin sisters. 这对双生姐妹许多
地方长得一模一样。②相似物; 肖像, 像 ③[古]
外貌; 外形特征

resemble [ri'zembl] *vt.* 象, 类似: ~ each other in
appearance or nature 外表或本质上彼此相象

resent [ri'zent] *vt.* 对…忿恨; 对…不满; 怨恨: ~
sb.'s action 对某人的行动不满 ‖~ment *n.* 忿
恨, 不满, 怨恨: bear (no) ~ment against 对…有
(无)怨恨

resentful [ri'zentful] *a.* ①忿恨的; 不满的; 易怨恨
的 ②忿恨引起的; 显然不满的 ‖~ly *ad.*

reservation [,rezə'veiʃən] *n.* ①保留: I accept your
statement without ~. 我完全相信你的话。/
agree to a plan with certain ~s 有某些保留
地赞同计划 ②(旅馆房间、剧院座位等的)预定:
Reservations can be arranged through …. 可
通过…进行预定。/ Have you made your ~s?
你预定好了吗? ③[美]保留地; 居留地; 专用地;
禁猎地: an Indian ~ 印第安人居留地 / a
military ~ 军用地 ④【宗】(供病人等用的)保留
部分圣餐的习惯 ⑤【宗】(教皇)圣职任命权的保
留; (高级圣职者)赦罪权的保留 ⑥【律】(让与或
租赁财产时的)权益保留; 保留权益

reserve [ri'zə:v] **I** *vt.* ①储备, 保存: ~ one's
strength (或 oneself) for the next battle 养精蓄
锐准备下次战斗 ②保留; 留给; 留出: 【宗】保留
(赦罪权); 留出(部分圣餐): All rights (are) ~d.
保留版权。/ The first three rows are ~d for
foreign guests. 前三排留作外宾席。/ seek common ground on major questions while reserving
differences on minor ones 求大同, 存小异 ③推
迟, 延迟: The court will ~ judgement. 法庭将
延期判决。④预定: ~ seats in a theatre 向剧
院定座 / All seats ~d. 所有座位必须预定。
II *n.* ①储备(物), 保存(物); (矿产等)储藏量:
have (或 keep) grain in ~ 贮存粮食 / war ~s
军需储备品 / the gold ~ 黄金储备 / workable
~s【矿】可采储量 / a great ~ of food 大量的食
物储备 / ~s of energy 保存的精力 ②[常用
复]【军】后备军, 后备队(员); 预备役; 预备役军
人;【体】预备队员; (展览品等的)预备奖: call up
the ~s 召集后备军 / be placed on the ~ (军舰)
被编入后备舰队 / ~ duty 预备役 / ~ rations
紧急干粮 ③专用地; 专用林地: a forest ~ 保留林,
预备林 ④保留; 限度: I agreed with (without)
~. 我有(无)保留地同意了。/ a ~ price 最低
价格 ⑤自我克制; 沉默寡言; 含蓄; 冷淡; (艺术手
法)不夸张, 节制: speak with ~ 说话谨慎 / ~
of manner 态度的冷淡 / break through sb.'s
~ 打破某人的缄默 ⑥未透露的消息, 秘密 ⑦储备
金; 准备金; 公积金: the bank's ~s 银行储备金 /
a ~ bank 储备银行 ⑧【生化】(溶液、血液等的酸
或碱的)储量 ⑨代替品

reserved [ri'zə:vd] *a.* ①保留的, 留作专用的; 预定
的; 预备的: ~ seats 预定的座位 / a ~ list [英]

海军预备军官名册 ②沉默寡言的, 缄默的; 含蓄
的; 冷淡的 ‖~ly [ri'zə:vidli] *ad.*

reservoir ['rezəvwɑ:] **I** *n.* ①水库; 蓄水池(或槽);
贮液器;【动】贮液囊; 储蓄器: a storing ~ 贮水
池 / the ~ of a fountain pen 自来水笔的贮墨
水胆 / air ~ 气槽 ②[喻](知识、精力等的)储藏,
蓄积 ③(寄生物或病菌的)贮主, 储主 **II** *vt.* (在
水库、水槽或贮器等中)储藏, 蓄积

reside [ri'zaid] *vi.* ①[正式用语]居住 (in, at);
(官吏)驻扎 ②(权力、权利等)属于, 归于(in): The
power of decision ~s in the higher authorities.
决定权属于上级机关。③(性质等)存在于(in):
The universality of contradiction ~s in the
particularity of contradiction. 矛盾的普遍性存
在于矛盾的特殊性之中。

residence ['rezidəns] *n.* ①居住; 驻扎; 居留: take
up (one's) ~ in a new house 住入新屋 ②住处;
住宅; 公馆: an official ~ 官邸 ③居住期间 ④
(在大学等处)积极从事学术性工作(或研究等)的
一段时期 ‖in ~ (官员)住在任所的; (大学师生)
住校的 / Residence is required. (官员等)须
住在任所。

residency ['rezidənsi] *n.* ①住处 ②[史]英国驻印
度各邦的总督代表的官邸 ③(驻扎官在保护国的)
管辖区 ④(医学专业毕业后的)高级训练阶段, 实
习阶段

resident ['rezidənt] **I** *a.* ①居住的; 居留的; 常驻
的; (鸟等)不迁徙的: the ~ population of a town
城中的居民人口 / ~ aliens 外侨 / a ~ physician
住院医生 / ~ birds 留鸟 ②归属于…的, 存在于
…的 (in): powers of sensation ~ in the nerves
神经的感觉力 **II** *n.* ①居民: local ~s 当地居
民 ②驻外政治代表; 驻扎官(尤指派驻保护国的
官员) ③留鸟, 留兽 ④住院医生

residential [,rezi'denʃəl] *a.* ①居住的; 住宅的; 作
住家用的: the ~ qualifications for voters 选举
人必须具备的居住资格 / ~ construction 住宅
建设 / a ~ quarter 住宅区 / a ~ hotel 作住家
用的旅馆 ②供学生住宿的: a ~ college 供住宿
的专科学院 ‖~ly *ad.*

residue ['rezidju:] *n.* ①残余, 剩余; 渣滓 ②【化】滤
渣; 余渣; 残余物 ③【数】残数, 留数, 余数 ④【律】
(偿债、纳税、遗赠等后的)剩余遗产

resign [ri'zain] ❶ *vt.* ①放弃; 辞去: ~ one's right
(all hope) 放弃权利(一切希望) / ~ one's posi-
tion (as secretary) 辞去(秘书)职务 / ~ office 辞
职 ②把…交托给 (to, into): ~ a task to sb. (或
into sb.'s hands) 把任务交给某人 / ~ a child to
the care of sb. 把孩子交给某人照管 ③[~
oneself] 使听从(于); 使顺从 (to): ~ oneself to
another's guidance 听从别人指导 / ~ oneself to
one's fate 听天由命 / ~ oneself to meditation 陷
入沉思 ❷ *vi.* ①辞职: ~ from the Cabinet 辞
去内阁职务 / He has ~ed. 他辞职了。②屈从
(于); 听任: ~ to sb.'s will 屈从某人的意志

re-sign ['ri:'sain] *vt. & vi.* 再签署, 再签字(于)

resignation [ˌrezigˈneiʃən] *n.* ① 放弃; 辞职; 辞职书, 辞呈: the ~ of a right 弃权 / send in (或 give, tender) one's ~ 提交辞职书, 递辞呈 ②屈从, 听从, 顺从: accept failure with ~ 无可奈何地接受失败

resigned [riˈzaind] *a.* ① 已放弃的; 已辞去(职务)的: a ~ post 已辞去的职务 / a ~ government official 已辞职的政府官员 ② 屈从的, 顺从的: with a ~ mind 逆来顺受 ‖~ly [riˈzainidli] *ad.*

resilience [riˈziliəns] *n.* ①跳回; 回弹(性); 回能; 弹能 ②(活力、精神的)恢复力, 复原力; 迅速恢复的愉快心情

resilient [riˈziliənt] *a.* ① 有回弹力的; 有弹性的; 能回复原来位置(或形状)的 ②恢复活力的; 恢复精神的; 心情愉快的

resin [ˈrezin] **I** *n.* ① (天然或合成的)树脂; 松香, 松脂 ② 树脂制品 **II** *vt.* 涂树脂于; 用树脂处理 ‖*kiss the ~* [美理](在职业性拳击中)被击倒

resist [riˈzist] **I** ❶ *vt.* ① 抵抗, 反抗, 对抗: ~ aggression 抵抗侵略 ② 抗; 耐: ~ infection 抗感染 ③ 抵制; 抗拒; [常用于否定句]忍住: ~ erroneous leadership 抵制错误的领导 / ~ temptation 不受引诱 / She can never ~ a joke. 她听到笑话总忍不住要笑出来。(或: 她想起笑话总忍不住要说出来。) / I cannot ~ peanuts. 我见到花生米就想吃。❷ *vi.* 抵抗, 反抗, 抵制 **II** *n.* (印染花布等用的)防染剂: ~ dye 防染印浆 ‖~er *n.* 抵抗者; 反抗者: a draft ~er 反抗征兵者

resistance [riˈzistəns] *n.* ① 抵抗, 反抗; 抵抗方法; [R-](被占领国家中的)秘密抵抗的组织(或运动) ②(对疾病等的)抵抗力; (物质的)耐力: (good) ~ to wear 耐磨; 耐穿 ③抵制, 反对: arouse ~(s) in the public 引起公众的反对(或反感) ④ 阻力; 【电】电阻; 阻抗; 电阻器 ‖*a line of least ~* 阻力最小的方向; [喻]最容易的方法, 最省力的途径: take (或 follow) the *line of least ~* 采取最容易的方法 / *passive ~* 消极抵抗; 不顺从 ‖ *coil ~* 电阻线圈 / ~ *welding* 电阻焊接

resistless [riˈzistlis] *a.* 不可抵抗的; 不可避免的; 不抵抗的; 无抵抗力的 ‖~**ly** *ad.*

resolute [ˈrezəljuːt] **I** *a.* 坚决的, 坚定的; 果敢的, 果断的; 不屈不挠的: be true in word and ~ in deed 言必信, 行必果 / a ~ man 果敢(或坚定)的人 **II** *n.* 果敢的人; 果敢的人 **III** *vi.* [美]作出(或通过)决议 ‖~**ly** *ad.* / ~**ness** *n.*

resolution [ˌrezəˈljuːʃən] *n.* ①坚决, 坚定; 决心; 决心要做的事; 果断, 不屈不挠: take the firm ~ to fight to the finish 下定决心战斗到底 / show great ~ 表示极大的决心 / good ~s 做好事(或改好)的决心 / a man of great (not much) ~ 极其(不大)果断的人 ②决定, 决议(案): pass (或 adopt) a ~ for (against, on) sth. 通过一项支持(反对, 关于)某事的决议(案) ③消除; (炎症等的)消退; 解答;解决: ~ of doubt 疑团的消除 ④分解,解体; 解析; 【自】分辨能力: the ~ of a compound into

its elements 化合物的分解为元素 / high (或 fine) ~ 高分辨能力 ⑤转变, 变形 (into) ⑥【音】(不协和和音或和弦转为协和和音或和弦的)转变(或解决) ⑦(希腊、拉丁韵律学)代替(指以二短音节代替一长音节) ⑧(剧本等中, 主要戏剧性情节的)解决

resolve [riˈzɔlv] **I** ❶ *vt.* ① 使分解, 使解体; 解析; 分辨: Water may be ~d *into* oxygen and hydrogen. 水可以分解成氧和氢。/ A telescope can ~ a nebula *into* stars. 望远镜能使星云中的群星显得分明。/ ~ the lines of a spectrum 分辨光谱的谱线 ②解决; 解答; 消除; 消退(炎症等): ~ a contradiction 解决矛盾 / ~ all doubts 消除一切疑问 ③决心, 决定; (使)决意; 决议: The circumstances ~d him *to* go (或 *upon* going). 情况使他决定要去。/ The assembly ~d that .... 大会决议···/ *Resolved, that this meeting is opposed to* (is in favour of) .... (会议记录语)决议: 会议反对(赞成)··· ④(通过投票等)使转为; 归结为(into); 【音】使(不协和和音或和弦)转为协和和音 (或和弦): The discussion ~d itself *into* an argument. 讨论到后来变成了争论。❷ *vi.* ①决心, 决意; 决定: ~ *upon* amendment 决心改正 ② 分解, 解体; 溶解; 解析; 分辨: *resolving power* 【物】分辨本领; 分辨率 ③【医】(炎症等)消退 ④【音】转为协和和音(或和弦) **II** *n.* ①决心, 决意: make a ~ to do sth. 决心要做某事 ②[书面语]坚决, 坚定; 刚毅: a man of ~ 刚毅的人 / deeds of high ~ 非常坚决的行为

resolved [riˈzɔlvd] *a.* 决心的, 坚决的, 坚定的: ~ to go 决心去 ‖~**ly** [riˈzɔlvidli] *ad.*

resonant [ˈrezənənt] *a.* ①反响的; 由共鸣而加强的, 洪亮的: a ~ voice 洪亮的声音 / a ~ slap 一记响亮的耳光 ②(木材、墙壁等)引起共鸣的: a violin of fine ~ wood 用共鸣声良好的木料所制的小提琴 ③(厅堂等)回响的; 共鸣的; 共振的, 谐振的 (with): the great hall ~ *with* applause 声回响的大厅 ‖~**ly** *ad.*

resort [riˈzɔːt] **I** *vi.* ① 求助; 凭借; 诉诸; 采取(某种手段等) (to): ~ to force 诉诸武力 / ~ to all kinds of methods 采取一切办法 ② 常去; 成群地去: Visitors ~ to that city in summer. 夏天人们常去那城市游玩。/ a place to which sb. is known to ~ 人们所知道的某人常去的地方 **II** *n.* ①求助; 凭借; 采取: have ~ to sb. 求助于某人 / without ~ to compulsion 不用强制手段地 / 所求助的东西; 所求助的人; 凭借方法(或手段): A repetition of practices is the ~ of gaining genuine knowledge. 反复实践是取得真知的方法。③常去; 成群去; 常去的人群: a place of popular ~ 人们常去的地方 ④ 常去之地; 胜地: a health ~ 疗养地 / a summer ~ 避暑胜地 ‖*in the last ~* (其他一切都失败后)作为最后一着 ‖~**er** *n.* 常去休养地的人; 常去胜地的人

re-sort [ˈriːˈsɔːt] *vt.* 使再分开; 把···再分类

resound [riˈzaund] ❶ *vi.* ①(厅堂等)回响; 充满声

音 (*with*): The hall ~ed *with* songs. 大厅中洋溢着歌声。 ② (声音、乐器等)鸣响;反响,回荡 ③ (名声、事件等)传播,传颂,驰名: This achievement ~ed throughout the land. 这一成就传遍全国。 ❷ *vt.* 使回响;使(声音等)回荡;颂扬,传播(某人的名声等)

re-sound ['riː'saund] *vt.* & *vi.* (使)再发声;(使)重发音

resource [ri'sɔːs] *n.* ① [常用复]资源;物力,财力: exploit natural ~s 开发自然资源 / treasure manpower and material ~s 爱惜人力物力 / the ~s in men and ammunition 兵员和弹药的来源 ②办法,对策;智谋,机智;应变的能力: as a last ~ 作为最后一着 / at the end of one's ~s 智穷才尽 / a man of ~ 足智多谋的人;机智的人 ③ 消遣,娱乐: Is playing chess your only ~? 下棋是你唯一的消遣吗? / a healthy ~ for children 对儿童有益的娱乐 ④有助的事物;有助于避掉麻烦的事物;[常用于否定句]得到援助(或恢复)的可能性: be lost without ~ 无可挽回地失败(或完蛋)了

resourceful [ri'sɔːsful] *a.* ①资源(或物力、财力)丰富的 ②善于随机应变的,机智的,足智多谋的 ‖~ly *ad.* / ~ness *n.*

respect [ris'pekt] I *n.* ①尊敬;尊重: be held *in* great ~ 备受尊敬 / have (或 show) ~ *for* sb. (sb.'s opinions 尊重某人(某人的意见) ② [复]敬意;问候: give (或 send) one's ~s to sb. 向某人问候 ③考虑;重视,关心: *without* ~ *to* the results 不考虑后果地 / He spoke *without* ~ *of* persons. 他并不看人说话。(尤指不趋炎附势) ④关系;方面,着眼点: *with* ~ *to* that question 关于那个问题 / *In* ~ *of* (或 *to*) the content this essay is admirable, but it is unsatisfactory. *in other* ~s. 就内容而言,这篇文章很好,但其他方面还不够令人满意。 / They resemble one another *in no* (*some*) ~s. 他们毫不(有些)相象。 II *vt.* ①尊敬;尊重: ~ed Mr. Minister 尊敬的部长先生 ②考虑;重视: ~ sb.'s wishes 重视某人的愿望 / ~ sb.'s silence 让某人保持沉默 ③遵守;不妨害: ~ an agreement 遵守协议 ‖*in* ~ *that* 因为…;考虑到… / *pay last* ~s *to* 向(死者)告别 / ~ *oneself* 自重(指不做使旁人看不起自己的事)

respectable [ris'pektəbl] I *a.* ① 可敬的;值得尊敬的 ②有相当身分的;正派的,高尚的;体面的,像样的,高雅的: ~ English 讲究的英语,高雅的英语 / a ~ appearance 体面的外表 / a ~ address 像样的演说 / What he did is not quite ~. 他做的事不很正派。 / a ~ coat 雅观的上装 ③(质量等)过得去的,不错的;(数量等)不少的;相当大的;可观的: His work is ~ but not outstanding. 他的工作还不错,但不算突出。 / ~ talents 相当的才能 / a ~ attendance 相当多的出席人数 / a ~ amount 可观的数量 II *n.* [常用复]体面的人;高尚的人 ‖**respectability**

[ris,pektə'biliti] *n.* ① 可敬;体面;高尚;有社会地位 ② [总称]体面的人们 ③ [常用复]习俗: the *respectabilities* of social life 社会生活中的各种习俗 / **respectably** *ad.*

respectful [ris'pektful] *a.* 恭敬的;尊敬人的,尊重人的: a ~ bow 恭敬的一鞠躬 / be ~ *of* tradition 尊重传统 / be ~ *to* sb. 尊敬某人 / stand at a ~ distance from sb. (表示恭敬)站得离某人有一定的距离 ‖~ly *ad.* [常用于致长者书信的结尾,作客套语]: Yours ~ly (或 *Respectfully* yours), James Kent 詹姆斯·肯特敬上 / ~ness *n.*

respecting [ris'pektiŋ] *prep.* ① 关于 (=with regard to): problems ~ air pollution in cities 关于城市空气污染的问题 ②由于,鉴于 (=in view of): *Respecting* these facts, a special committee is to be appointed. 由于这些事实,必须成立一个专门委员会。

respective [ris'pektiv] *a.* 各自的,各个的: We go back to our ~ domitories after work. 下班后我们回到各自的宿舍里去。 / according to the ~ needs of the different departments 根据不同部门的各自需要 / You and I shall get a ~ holiday of two and three weeks. 你和我将分别有两星期和三星期的假期。 ‖~ly *ad.* 各自地;分别地: We shall discuss the two questions ~ly. 我们将分别讨论这两个问题。

respiration [,respə'reiʃən] *n.* ① 呼吸(作用);一次呼吸: artificial ~ 人工呼吸 ②植物的呼吸 ③生物的氧化(作用)

respire [ris'paiə] ❶ *vi.* ①呼吸(尤指连续地) ②松口气 ❷ *vt.* 呼吸;[罕]呼出,发出(气味等)

respite ['respait; 美 'respit] I *n.* ①暂缓;展延(尤指不乐意的事情);(死刑等的)缓期执行 ②暂时的休息(或喘息);(痛苦等的)缓解,暂止: a brief ~ from one's work 工作后的稍事休息 / gain a ~ 获得喘息(时间) II *vt.* ①使暂息;使(痛苦等)缓解 ②缓期执行(死刑等);延期(处分等)

resplendence [ris'plendəns], **resplendency** [ris-'plendənsi] *n.* 灿烂,光辉;辉煌,华丽

resplendent [ris'plendənt] *a.* 灿烂的,光辉的;辉煌的,华丽的 ‖~ly *ad.*

respond [ris'pɔnd] I ❶ *vi.* ①作答;[宗](会众对牧师的)例行应答;回报: ~ *to* a question 答复问题 / ~ *with* a smile 以微笑表示回答 / ~ *with* a blow 报以一击 ②响应;有反应: The illness quickly ~ed *to* proper treatment. 疾病经适当治疗后很快好转。 / The plane ~s well *to* the controls. 这飞机对操纵反应灵敏。 ③[律]承担责任: ~ *in* damages 承担赔偿费用 ❷ *vt.* 回答 II *n.* ① =responsory ② [建]壁联 ‖~er *n.* ①回答者;响应者 ②[无]响应器;应答机

response [ris'pɔns] *n.* ①作答,回复;[宗]礼仪式中会众对牧师)轮流应答(或吟唱)的祈祷文: They made a quick ~ *to* my inquiry. 他们对我的询问很作了答复。 ②响应;反应;[无]灵敏度;特

性曲线: call forth 'no ~ in sb.'s breast 在某人心中不起反应

responsibility [ris,ponsə'biliti] *n.* ①责任; 责任心: bear ~ *for* 对… 负有责任 / take the ~ *for* (*of doing*) sth. 负起对(做)某事的责任 / one's sense of ~ 责任感 / a man lacking *in* ~ 责任心不强的人 ②职责; 任务 ③【无】响应性, 响应度 ④(指财务等方面的)可靠性; 可信赖性; 偿付能力 ‖*do sth. on one's own* ~ 自己负责(或自行而非受命)做某事

responsible [ris'ponsəbl] *a.* ①有责任的, (应)负责的: Our duty is to hold ourselves ~ to the people. 我们的责任, 是向人民负责。/ The pilot of the plane is ~ *for* the passengers' safety. 飞机驾驶员应对旅客的安全负责 / The weather is ~ *for* the delay. 由于天气关系才耽搁了。② 认真负责的, 尽责的; 可靠的, 可信赖的: a ~ teacher 认真负责的教师 ③责任重大的: have a ~ position 担任要职 ④(对议会或全体选民)在政治上应负责的; (议会通过不信任案时)应进行改选的(尤指英国的内阁): ~ government 责任政府制 ‖**responsibly** *ad.*

responsive [ris'ponsiv] *a.* ① 应答的, (表示)回答的; (礼拜仪式)用应答(或吟唱)的祈祷文的: a ~ gesture 表示回答的手势 ②响应的, 易起反应的, 敏感的 ‖~**ly** *ad.* / ~**ness** *n.*

responsory [ris'ponsəri] *n.* (礼拜仪式中会众同牧师)轮流应答(或吟唱)的祈祷文

rest¹ [rest] **I** *n.* ①休息, 歇息; 睡眠; 安息, 长眠; 【军】稍息: Let's stop and take a ~. 我们停下来歇会儿吧。/ They had several ~s on the way up the mountain. 他们在上山途中休息了几次。/ go (或 retire) to ~ 去休息; 去睡 / have a good night's ~ 一晚上睡得很好 / take one's ~ 休息; 睡觉, 就寝 / go to one's (final) ~ 长眠, 死 ②安静, 安宁 ③静止; 停止; (朗读中的)停顿; 【音】休止; 休止符 ④休息处; 住宿处; [用作定语] 疗养(处): a seamen's ~ 海员之家(供海员歇息、住宿、娱乐的场所) / a ~ centre 疗养中心 ⑤撑架, 支座, 托, 垫; (放工作物的)台; 刀架: a rifle ~ 步枪架 **II** ❶ *vi.* ①(躺下)休息; 睡; 安息, 长眠; (农田)休闲 ~ (up) from one's work 停下工作来(好好地)休息一下 ②安心, 安宁 ③静止; 停止: waves that never ~ 永不平静的波浪 / The matter cannot ~ here. 事情不能到此为止。④被支撑(在), 搁(在); (视线等)停留(在): His hand ~ed *on* the table. 他的手放在桌子上。/ His eyes ~ed *on* me. 他的目光落在我身上。/ clouds ~ing *upon* the mountain top 笼罩在山顶上的云 ⑤依据, 依赖; 信赖: Our policy should ~ *on* the basis of self-reliance. 我们的政策要放在自力更生的基点上。/ I ~ *in* (或 *on*) your word. 我相信你说了话是算数的。⑥取决(于), 归(于): It ~s *with* you to decide. (或 The decision ~s *with* you.) 要由你来作决定。⑦【律】自动停止提出证据 ❷ *vt.* ①使休息; 使轻松; 使安息; 使(农田)休闲; 【军】使稍息: He stopped to ~ himself (his horse). 他停下来休息(让马休息)一下。/ Are you quite ~ed? 你睡够了吗? / These dark glasses ~ my eyes. 这副墨镜使我眼睛感到舒适。②使支撑(在), 使搁(在); 使(视线等)停留(在): *Rest* the ladder *against* the wall. 把梯子靠在墙上。/ ~ one's head *on* the pillow 把头枕在枕头上 ③使基(于); 把…寄托(于): ~ one's argument *on* facts 以事实作为论据 / ~ one's hopes *on* sb. 把希望寄托于某人 ④【律】自动止对(案件等)提出证据 ‖*at* ~ ①安眠; 安息, 长眠 ②静止; 安静: a volcano *at* ~ 静止的火山 / The child is never really *at* ~. 这孩子老是手脚不停的。/ set a question *at* ~ 把问题解决 / put sb.'s mind *at* ~ 使某人安心 / *come to* ~ (活动物体)停止移动 / *lay to* ~ ①埋葬 ②[喻]消除: lay sb.'s fear *to* ~ 使某人不害怕 / *on one's oars* 见 **oar** ‖'~**balk** *n.* 【农】不耕种的垄 / ~ **cure** 卧床疗养法 / ~ **day** 休息日; [军]星期日 / ~**,harrow** *n.* 【植】芒柄花属植物 / ~ **home** 疗养院, 疗养所 / ~ **house** 客栈; (无旅馆地区的)招待所 / ~ **mass** 【物】静质量 / ~ **period** 【植】休眠期 / ~ **room** (公共场所或机关内附设盥洗间的)休息室

rest² [rest] **I** *n.* ①[the ~] 剩余部分; 其余的人; 其余: He took ten and gave the ~ to others. 他拿了十个, 把剩下的给了别人。/ Three of us will go; the ~ are to stay here. 我们去三个人, 其余的人将留在这里。/ The ~ needs no telling. 其余就不必细说了。/ for the ~ of one's life 在有生之年 ②[英]【商】盈余; (银行的)储备金; 盘货和结算 ③(网球等的)一阵连续回球 **II** *vi.* ①[后接表语]依然是; 保持: The affair ~s a riddle. 这件事仍是个谜。/ not ~ content (或 satisfied) *with* a smattering of knowledge 不满足于一知半解 / You can ~ assured that they will come. 你放心好了, 他们会来的。②[古]余下, 留下 ‖*among the* ~ 在其中: The whole group started off; I myself was *among the* ~. 全组的人出发了, 我自己也在里面。/ *and (all) the* ~ (*of it*) 以及其它一切; 以及其它等等(指可能提到的) / *for the* ~ 至于其余; 至于其它: This is all I know about it; *for the* ~, you may ask others. 对这件事我就知道这些, 至于其他情况, 你可以问别人。

restaurant ['restərɔ:ŋ, 'restərɔnt] *n.* 餐馆, 饭店, 菜馆 ‖~**eur** [,restərɔ:'ŋtə:, ,restərɔn'tə:] *n.* 餐馆老板

restful ['restful] *a.* 宁静的; 悠闲的; 使(感到)平静的: a ~ scene 宁静的景色 / a colour ~ to the eye 悦目的颜色 ‖~**ly** *ad.* / ~**ness** *n.*

restitution [,resti'tju:ʃən] *n.* ①归还; 赔偿: make ~ of sth. to sb. 向某人归还(或赔偿)某物 ②恢复原状; 【物】(弹性体的)复原 ③【律】要求恢复原状的诉讼: ~ of conjugal rights 要求恢复夫妻同居权的诉讼

restive ['restiv] *a.* ① (人群等)难控制的; 倔强的; 不安静的,不安定的; 烦躁的: a ~ crowd 骚动的人群 ②(马等)难驾驭的,不肯前进的 ‖~**ly** *ad.* / ~**ness** *n.*

restless ['restlis] *a.* ① 得不到休息的: a ~ night 不眠之夜 / ~ sleep 不安宁的睡眠 ② 不静止的,永不宁静的: a ~ sea 不平静的大海 ③ 不安定的; 焦虑的, 烦躁的; 不满足的: a ~ child 坐立不定的孩子 / The audience was getting ~. 听众开始不耐烦(或坐不住)了。 ‖~**ly** *ad.* / ~**ness** *n.* ‖~ **cavy** (拉丁美洲产)野豚鼠

restoration [ˌrestəˈreiʃən] *n.* ① 恢复, 回复; 复位; 复辟: ~ to health and strength 健康与体力的恢复 ②归还: the ~ of the lost watch to its owner 失表归还原主 ③ (受损文物的)修补; 修复(物); 重建(物); (已绝迹动物等的)模型: Closed during ~s. 修建期间, 暂不开放。 / This castle is a mere ~. 这城堡仅仅是(按原样)重建的。 ④[the R-]【英史】(一六六〇年查理二世的)王政复辟; (指查理二世统治的、有时也指包括詹姆斯二世统治期的)王政复辟时期

restorative [risˈtɔrətiv] Ⅰ *a.* 恢复健康(或体力)的; 滋补的 Ⅱ *n.* 营养食品; 恢复剂; 补药 ‖~**ly** *ad.* / ~**ness** *n.*

restore [risˈtɔː] *vt.* ① (使)恢复, (使)回复; 使(帝王等)复位, (使)复辟: His health is entirely ~d. 他的健康完全恢复了。 / ~ sb. to consciousness 使某人恢复知觉 ②归还; 交还: ~ borrowed books 归还所借的书 / ~ a lost child to its parents 把迷失的孩子交还他的父母 ③修补(受损文物等); 修复; 重建: ~ an ancient text 校勘古本 / ~ an old building 修建老房屋 / ~ an extinct kind of animal 制作绝种动物的模型

restrain [risˈtrein] *vt.* ① 抑制, 遏制; 制止: can hardly ~ tears (one's anger) 抑制不住眼泪(怒气) / ~ oneself 克制自己 / ~ a child *from* (doing) mischief 制止小孩胡闹 / ~ one's surprise *from* being visible 尽量不让自己的惊奇表露出来 ②管束; 监禁(疯人、犯人等) ③限制; 约束: ~ trade 限制贸易 ‖~**able** *a.* 可抑制的, 可遏制的; 可制止的; 可管束的 / ~**er** *n.* 抑制的人(或物);【化】抑制剂(尤指摄影中用的溴化钾等)

restraint [risˈtreint] *n.* ① 抑制, 遏制; 制止: His rage was beyond ~. 他怒不可遏。 ②管束; 监禁; 约束; 约束力: the ~s of illness and poverty 贫病交困 / without ~ 无节制地; 不拘束地, 自由自在地 ③(文体等的)谨严; (态度等的)拘谨; 克制, 节制; 谨慎 ‖*be laid* (或 *put*) *under* ~ ① 被监禁 ②(疯人等)被送入精神病院

restrict [risˈtrikt] *vt.* 限制; 限定; 约束: be ~ed *within* narrow limits 限于狭窄的范围内 / be ~ed *to* 30 km. an hour (速率)被限制在每小时三十公里 / be ~ed *in* one's movements 行动受约束 / The woods ~ed our vision. 树林挡住了我们的视野。

restriction [risˈtrikʃən] *n.* 限制; 限定; 约束: ~ of expenditure 限制费用 / impose (或 place) ~s on 对…实行限制 / currency ~s 货币限额 ‖~**ism** *n.* 限制主义(如限制贸易的政策, 垄断政策等) / ~**ist** *n.* 限制主义者 *a.* 限制主义的; 限制主义者的

restrictive [risˈtriktiv] Ⅰ *a.* 限制(性)的; 约束(性)的: ~ sight distance 受到限制的视距 / ~ practices in industry 工业方面的限制性措施 / a ~ clause【语】限制性从句 Ⅱ *n.* 限制性词语 ‖~**ly** *ad.* / ~**ness** *n.*

result [riˈzʌlt] Ⅰ *n.* ①结果; 成果; 效果; [复]【体】比分: In given conditions, a bad thing can lead to good ~s. 在一定的条件下, 坏的东西可以引出好的结果。 / His limp is the ~ of a fall. 他的跛腿是摔跤摔的。 / announce election ~s 宣布选举结果 ②【数】(计算)结果; 答案 ③[美](议院等的)决议; 决定 Ⅱ *vi.* ①(作为结果)发生, 产生 (*from*) ②结果, 终归; 导致 (*in*) ‖*as a* ~ (*of*) 作为(…的)结果 / *in* ~ 结果 / *without* ~ 毫无结果地

resume [riˈzjuːm] ❶ *vt.* ① 恢复; 重新占用: ~ traffic (one's liberty) 恢复交通(自由) / ~ one's spirits 重新振作起来 / ~ one's seat 回到原座 / ~ one's former name 重用原名 ②重新开始; (经打断后)再继续: ~ firing (或 fire) (暂停射击后)继续射击(可用作口令) / ~ one's hat 重新戴上帽子 / ~ reading 重新读下去 / ~ one's work (a conversation) 再继续工作(谈话) / "As I said just now," he ~d, "we are all ready." "正如我刚才所说," 他继续说道, "我们都准备好了。" ③取回; 收回: ~ one's gift 收回礼物 / ~ lost territory 收复失去的领土 ④概述 ❷ *vi.* 再开始; 继续讲: Well, to ~, ... 好吧, 我继续讲下去, …

resumption [riˈzʌmpʃən] *n.* ① 恢复; 再开始; (中断后)再继续: the ~ of one's duties 重新履行职责 ②再取回; 重新占用 ③恢复硬币支付

resurrect [ˌrezəˈrekt] ❶ *vt.* ① 使复活; 复兴; 恢复; 使再现; 使再受注意: ~ an old word 恢复用一个旧词 / ~ "dead letters" 使"死信"复活 ②(从坟墓中)掘出, 盗掘; [口]掘起 ❷ *vi.* 复苏; 复活

resurrection [ˌrezəˈrekʃən] *n.* ①复活; 复兴; 恢复: nature's ~ in the spring 大地的回春 / the ~ of one's hopes 希望的复萌 ②[the R-]【基督教】耶稣复活(节); (上帝最后审判时)全体死者的复活 ③ 掘墓盗尸 ‖~**al** *a.* / ~**ist** *n.* ①盗尸者 ②使复活者; 使复兴者 ③相信复活的人 ‖~ **man** 盗尸者

resuscitate [riˈsʌsiteit] *vt. & vi.* (使)苏醒; (使)复活; (使)复兴; (使)恢复精力 ‖**resuscitation** [riˌsʌsiˈteiʃən] *n.* / **resuscitative** *a.* / **resuscitator** *n.* 使苏醒(或复活)的人;【医】复苏器

retail ['riːteil, riːˈteil] Ⅰ *n.* 零售, 零卖: sell *by* (或 *at*) ~ 零售 Ⅱ *a.* 零售的; 零售商品的: a ~ dealer (price) 零售商(价格) Ⅲ *ad.* 以零售方式: buy

~ 零买 **IV** [ri:'teil, 'ri:teil] ❶ *vt.* ①零售,零卖 ②细谈; 到处传播: ~ gossip 传播流言 ❷ *vi.* 零售,零卖 ‖**~er** [ri:'teilə] ①零售商 ②(流言等的)传播人

retain [ri'tein] *vt.* ① 保持; 保留; 保有: eliminate the false and ~ the true 去伪存真 ②留住; 挡住: a vessel to ~ water 盛水的容器 / a dyke ~*ing* the flood waters 防洪堤 ③ 记住: ~ these distinctions 记住这些区别 ④ 聘, 雇 (律师等) ‖a ~*ing fee* 律师费 / a ~*ing force* 牵制部队 / ~*ing wall* 【建】挡土墙, 拥壁 / ~*ing works* 拦水工程; 蓄水工程; 挡土工程 / a ~ *ring* 扣环 ‖**~able** *a.* 可保持的; 可保留的; 可记住的; 可聘请的,可雇用的

retaliate [ri'tælieit] ❶ *vi.* ①报复,以牙还牙 ②征收报复性关税 ❷ *vt.* 回报,报复(伤害、侮辱等) ‖**retaliation** [ri,tæli'eiʃən] *n.* / **retaliative** *a.* / **retaliatory** [ri'tæliətəri] *a.* 报复(性)的: *retalia-tory* fire 报复性射击 / *retaliatory* tariff 报复性关税

retard [ri'tɑ:d] **I** ❶ *vt.* ①延迟;放慢;使停滞;【物】使减速 ②阻止, 妨碍: ~ the progress of sth. 阻碍某事物的进展 ❷ *vi.* 减速;延迟(尤指潮汐、天体运行等) **II** *n.* 延迟;放慢;妨碍;耽误 ‖**~ant** *a.* 使延迟的 *n.* 【化】抑止剂 / **~ative** [ri'tɑ:də-tiv], **~atory** [ri'tɑ:dətəri] *a.* 使延迟的; 阻止的; 妨碍的;减速的 / **~ed** *a.* 智力上迟钝的 / **~er** *n.* 【化】阻滞剂; 【工】减速器, 延时器

retch [ri:tʃ, retʃ] **I** ❶ *vi.* 干呕, 作呕, 恶心: I did ~ quite a bit. 我真觉得有点恶心。❷ *vt.* 呕吐 **II** *n.* 干呕(声),恶心

retention [ri'tenʃən] *n.* ①保持;保留; 留置 ②保持力;保留物 ③记忆(力) ④【医】停滞;固位: ~ of urine 闭尿症 / post-treatment ~ 疗后固位

retentive [ri'tentiv] *a.* ①保持的; 有保持力的: a ~ soil 能保持水分的土壤 / be ~ *of* moisture 能保持湿度 / ~ material 【电】硬磁材料 ②(记忆力)强的: a ~ mind 记忆力强的头脑 / be ~ *of* details 能记住细节 ③【医】固位的 ④吝啬的 ⑤拘留的 ⑥沉默寡言的 ‖**~ly** *ad.* / **~ness** *n.* / **retentivity** [,ri:ten'tiviti] *n.* 保持力

reticence ['retisəns], **reticency** ['retisənsi] *n.* ①沉默寡言, 缄默; 言不尽意, 保留: speak one's mind without ~ 畅所欲言 / a man of few ~s 坦率的人 ②(艺术风格等的)节制,谨严

reticent ['retisənt] *a.* ①沉默寡言的;爱缄默的;言不尽意的,有保留的: be ~ *about* (或 *on, upon*) what one knows 知而不言 ②(艺术风格等)有节制的,谨严的 ‖**~ly** *ad.*

retinue ['retinju:] *n.* [总称](高级官员等的)随员

retire [ri'taiə] **I** ❶ *vi.* ①退下;离开;(部队等主动地)退却, 撤退: The captain ~*d* to his cabin. 船长回到了自己的舱房。/ The ladies ~*d* (into the drawing-room). 女士们离开了餐室(到客厅去)。(西方餐后风俗) / The football player ~*d* hurt. 那个足球运动员受伤退场了。②引退;退

隐;退休; 退职; 退役: ~ from man 离群索居 / ~ from the world 退隐; 隐居 / ~ from office (service) 退职(役) / ~ from the sea 不再过海上生活 / ~ on a pension 领养老金退休 / ~ backstage 退居幕后 ③[正式用语]就寝: ~ to bed (或 to rest) 就寝 ④(波浪等)后退;(海岸等)似乎后退 ❷ *vt.* ① (主动)撤退, 命令…退却: ~ the troops 撤退军队, 命令部队退却 ② 使引退(或使休息等); 辞退: ~ a clerk 辞退职员 ③ 收回(纸币等);付清(证券等的本息) **II** *n.* 退兵信号: sound the ~ 吹退兵号, 鸣金收兵 ‖**~ into oneself** 退隐,不和人交往;沉默

retired [ri'taiəd] *a.* ①退休的; 退职的; 退役的; 歇业的: a ~ veteran worker 退休的老工人 / a ~ grocer 歇业的杂货商 / ~ pay 退休金;养老金 ②引退的;退隐的: a ~ life 退隐 (或隐居)生活 ③隐僻的,幽静的: a ~ valley 幽谷 ‖**~ list** 退役军官(或士兵)名册 / **Retired Reserve**【军】第三类预备役 ‖**~ly** *ad.* / **~ness** *n.*

retirement [ri'taiəmənt] *n.* ①退休;退职;退役;引退 ②退休的实例: There have been several ~*s* in our factory recently. 最近我们工厂里有几个职工退休了。③(主动的)退却, 撤退 ④退隐; 居处; 幽静处 ‖live in ~ 过退隐(或隐居)生活 ‖**~ pay** 退休金; 退役金

retiring [ri'taiəriŋ] *a.* ①退休的; 退职的; 退役的; 引退的: reach ~ age 到达退休(或退职)年龄 / a ~ pension (或 allowance)退休金; 养老金 ②孤独的, 缄默的; 腼腆的; 谦让的: a man of a ~ disposition (或 a ~ man) 性情孤独的人;谦让的人 ③【军】退却的 ‖**~ly** *ad.* / **~ness** *n.* ‖**board** 【军】退役调查委员会 / **~ room** ①休息室 ②厕所

retort¹ [ri'tɔ:t] **I** *n.* ① 曲颈瓶, 曲颈甑 ② 蒸馏器(用于净化水银, 制煤气等) **II** *vt.* (在蒸馏罐中加热而)提纯(水银等)

retort² [ri'tɔ:t] **I** ❶ *vt.* ①反击,回报: ~ sarcasm for sarcasm 反唇相讥 ②反驳: "It's your fault, not his," I ~*ed.* 我反驳道:"这是你的错, 不是他的错。" / ~ an argument against sb. 反驳某人的论点 ❷ *vi.* 反击; 回嘴; 反驳: ~ *upon* sb. 反驳某人 **II** *n.* 反击; 回嘴; 反驳: say a few words *in* ~ 反驳几句

retouch ['ri:'tʌtʃ] **I** ❶ *vt.* ① 润饰, 润色(画、文章等);改进(化妆等) ② 修正,修描(底片等) ❷ *vi.* 润饰;润色 **II** *n.* ①润饰; 润色 ②润色(或润色)时的增删部分 ③ 修描过的照片(或底片等)

retrace [ri'treis] *vt.* ① 折回, 折返: ~ one's steps (或 way) 顺原路返回; [喻]走回头路, 走老路 ② 再追溯, 再探查 ③回忆; 回顾 ④再修描, 再描画

retract [ri'trækt] ❶ *vt.* ①缩回, 缩进(爪、触角、爪等);缩卷(舌等): A cat *can* ~ its claws. 猫能缩进爪子。 ② 撤回, 收回, 取消(声明、诺言、意见等) ❷ *vi.* ①缩回, 缩进 ②收回; 撤消: ~ from an engagement 取消约会 ‖**~able** *a.* 可收回的;可撤消的; 可缩回的, 可缩进的: a ~*able* missile hook 收缩式导弹挂钩

retreat [ri'tri:t] **I ❶** *vi.* ①(被迫)退却,后退,退去: They watched his ~*ing* figure. 他们看着他走远的身影。 ②〔喻〕放弃,退出(*from*): ~ *from* a controversy 退出论战 ③(眼睛)下陷;(颊、额)后塌 ④(飞机翼梢)后斜 **❷** *vt.* 退(棋) **II** *n.* ①撤退;退却: make good one's ~ 安全撤退 ②退却的信号;(日暮时兵营的)降旗号,降旗式: sound the ~ 吹退兵号,鸣金收兵 ③退避,逃避;隐退;【宗】静修: this ~ *from* reality 这种对现实的逃避 ④隐避所;避难所,收容所;(休养所): a summer ~ 避暑地 ‖*beat a* ~ (匆匆)撤退 ②〔喻〕放弃(指事业等);打退堂鼓

retrench [ri'trentʃ] **❶** *vt.* ① 减少,紧缩,节省(经费等) ② 删除,省略(章节等) ③ 为…筑堑壕(或胸墙) **❷** *vi.* 紧缩,节省 ‖~**ment** *n.* ①紧缩,节省 ②删节 ③内线防御工事(指堑壕等)

retribution [ˌretri'bju:ʃən] *n.* ①惩罚;【宗】(来世)报应;果报 ②报酬,报答 ‖**retributive** [ri'tribju-tiv], **retributory** [ri'tribjutəri] *a.*

retrieve [ri'tri:v] **I ❶** *vt.* ①重新得到;取回,收回,恢复: ~ a lost piece of luggage 找回一件遗失的行李 / He ~*d* his spirits. 他精神恢复了。/ a gas-smoke *retrieving* apparatus 烟气净化回收器 ②挽回,补救;补偿;纠正;挽救;拯救: ~ one's honour 挽回名誉 / ~ an error 纠正错误 / make a fish jump to ~ a ball 鱼跃救球 ③(猎犬)找回,啣回(被击中的猎物) ④追溯,回忆 **❷** *vi.* (猎犬)找回猎物;取回扔出物 **II** *n.* ① =retrieval ②(打球时的)回击险球,救险球 ‖*beyond* (或 *past*) ~ 不可恢复;不可挽回 ‖~**r** *n.* ①重新得到者;挽救者;取回者: a ~*r* boat 驾驶员救援船 ②啣回猎物的猎犬

retroactive [ˌretrou'æktiv] *a.* ① 倒行的;回动的;反作用的 ②【律】追溯既往的,有追溯效力的 ③ 补发增加的工资的: ~ pay 补发的增加工资 ‖~**ly** *ad.* / **retroactivity** [ˌretrouæk'tiviti] *n.*

retrograde ['retrougreid] **I** *a.* ①后退的;向后的;逆行的: a ~ policy (step) 倒退的政策(一步) / ~ motion 【天】逆行 ②次序颠倒的,反常规的(如书写从右往左等) ③退步的,衰退的;恶化的;【生】退化的 **II** *vi.* ① 后退,倒退;【天】逆行;〔喻〕扼要地重述 ②退步;衰退;恶化;【生】退化 **III** *ad.* 后退地;向后地;颠倒地 ‖**retrogradation** [ˌretrougrə'deiʃən] *n.*

retrogression [ˌretrou'greʃən] *n.* 倒退;退步;衰退;【生】退化;【天】逆行

retrogressive [ˌretrou'gresiv] *a.* 倒退的;退步的;衰退的;【生】退化的 ‖~**ly** *ad.*

retrospect ['retrouspekt] **I** *n.* 回顾,回想;追溯;〔罕〕追溯力: review one's work of the past years *in* ~ 回顾个人以往几年的工作 **II** *a.* =retrospective (*a.*) **II ❶** *vi.* 回顾,回想;追溯(*to*): ~ *to* an early period 追溯到早期 **❷** *vt.* 回顾;追溯 ‖~**ion** [ˌretrou'spekʃən] *n.*

retrospective [ˌretrou'spektiv] **I** *a.* ① 回顾的,回想的;追溯的: a ~ exhibition of an artist's work

艺术家过去某个时期的个人作品展览 ②(法律、付款等)追溯既往的;有追溯效力的 ③(风景等)在(房屋等)后面的 **II** *n.* (画家等)某个时期的作品展览

return [ri'tə:n] **I ❶** *vi.* ①回,回来;返回: ~ home 回家;回乡;回国 / ~ from abroad 从国外回来 / ~ to duty 返任;回到岗位 / ~ to the base 返航,返回基地 / He is gone, never to ~. 他一去不复返了。②(话题、言行等)回复,恢复: I shall ~ to this subject later. 我以后还要讲到这个题目。/ His health ~*ed* quickly. 他很快恢复了健康。~ to power 重新掌权 ③送还,归还: In case of non-delivery, ~ to the sender. (邮作用语)无法投递时,退回原处。/ It has ~*ed* to the original owner. 此物已归原主。④回答;反驳 **❷** *vt.* ①还,归还: *Return* everything you borrow. 借东西要还。/ ~ the books to the library 把书还给图书馆 ②回以,回报;报答: ~ sb. a visit 回访某人 / ~ thanks 答谢(尤指对祝酒等) / ~ the compliment 还礼;回报 / ~ the ball 回球 / ~ fire 【军】回击 / ~ sb. an angry look 对某人报以怒视 / ~ blow *for* blow 以牙还牙 / ~ kindness with ingratitude 恩将仇报 ③回答说;反驳道: "I don't know," ~*ed* the boy. 这孩子回答道:"我不知道。" ④获得,产生(利润等): an investment that ~*s* good profits 利润很大的投资 ⑤反射(光);回响(声): ~ an echo 响起一声回音 ⑥报告,汇报;申报;正式宣布: The wrecked ship was ~*ed* unfit for service. 呈报遇难的船已不堪使用。/ The liabilities were ~*ed* at $100,000. 申报负债为十万美元。/ be ~*ed* guilty 被宣告有罪 ⑦(选区)选举,选出: ~ sb. to Parliament 选举某人为国会议员 ⑧(纸牌戏中)跟着打出(搭档曾出过的同花色的牌) ⑨【建】使(墙壁、嵌线等)转延侧面 **II** *n.* ① 回来;返回;回程;回来票;【电】回路: welcome the ~ of the delegation 欢迎代表团归来 / a first-class ~ to Paris 到巴黎的头等车来回票 ② 归还;偿还;【律】(向法院的)送还(指传票等): ask for the ~ of a book 索还所借的书 / the ~ of loans 借款的偿付 ③回复;恢复;再现: the ~ of the blood pressure to normal 血压的回复正常 / a ~ of rheumatism 风湿病的复发 / Many happy ~*s* (of the day). (生日或节日贺词)祝你长寿。(或:敬祝佳节。) / ~ of man to himself 【哲】人性的复归 ④回答 ⑤报答;回报: I can make little ~ for your kindness. 我难以答谢你的好意。/ expect no ~ 不望报答 ⑥退还之物;〔复〕(向出版商)退还的未售出的出版物 ⑦〔常用复〕利润,利润率;成果: yield ~*s* 产生利润 / ~*s* on an investment 投资所得利润 / the law of diminishing ~*s* 报酬递减律(资产阶级政治经济学的一种理论) / show ~*s* for his long years of study 显示出多年研究的成果 ⑧〔常用复〕报告书;统计表;(选举)结果报告;申报;汇报: ~*s* of losses 【军】伤亡报告 / census ~*s* 人口(或户口)统计表 / income tax ~ 所得税申

报书 / the election ~s 选举结果报告 / make a ~ of 申报；汇报 ⑨候选人当选的宣布；[主英]当选国会议员：secure one's ~ for 当选为…选区的议员 ⑩[建](墙壁、嵌线等的)转延侧面 ⑪(纸牌戏)出搭档曾出过的同花色的牌 ⑫(网球等)球；(击剑)迅速回刺 ⑬[英][复]一种和润的板烟 **Ⅲ** *a.* ① 返回的；回程的：a ~ ticket 来回票 / the ~ half (来回票的)回程票 / the ~ voyage 返航 ② 报答的；回报的：a ~ visit 回访 / a ~ courtesy 回礼 / a ~ game (或 match) 再次比赛 (使第一次败者再有机会获胜) ③ 反向的；折回的：a ~ current 反流 / a ~ line (或 pipe) 回水管；回汽管 / a ~ bend 回转弯头 ④重现的；回复的：the ~ period 重现期；回复期 ‖*a point of no* ~ 航线临界点(长途航行等时，因所带燃料不足以返回原地而必须继续前进的地点)；无还点；[喻]只能进不能退的地步 / *a point of safe* ~ 安全返航点 (能安全返回的航线最远点) / *by* ~ *of post* (原指)由原送信人带回；(现指)由下一班回程邮递带回：Please send a reply *by* ~ *of post.* 请即回信，赶上下一班的回邮。/ *in* ~ 作为报答；作为回报：present sth. *in* ~ 赠送某物作为答谢；回赠某物 / *in* ~ *for* 作为…的交换；作为…的报答：hand money *in* ~ *for* a receipt 付款取收据 / *on sale or* ~ 见 sale / *like for like* 以牙还牙 / *to* ~ *(to one's muttons)* [用作插入语]回到本题，言归正传 ‖~*able a.* ① 可退回(再用)的：~*able* bottles 可退回的瓶子 ② 允予退还的：a ~*able* deposit 允予退还的保证金 ③【律】(在指定时间、地点) 依法必须送还 (或答辩) 的 /~**ed** *a.* ① 已回来的；已回国的：a ~*ed* overseas Chinese 归国华侨 ②退回的；回收的：~*ed* empties 退回的空瓶 (或空箱等) ‖~**ing officer** [英]一地区内负责选举的官员

reunion ['ri:'ju:njən] *n.* ①再结合；再联合；再会合 ②重聚；(亲属的)团聚；(同班同学离校后的)联欢会 ‖~**ist** *n.* 重新联合论者(尤指主张使英国国教与天主教重新成为一体的人)

reveal [ri'vi:l] **I** *vt.* ①展现，(显)露出：The rising curtain ~*ed* a countryside scene. 幕启时展现了一幅农村景象。/ The painting ~s the painter. 这幅画显示了这个画家的特色。/ ~ itself (事物)出现，呈现 ② 揭示；揭露，暴露；泄露：one's identity 揭示身分 / a secret to sb. 对某人泄露秘密 ③【宗】(神) 启示，默示：~*ed* religion 天启教(自然教之对) **Ⅱ** *n.*【建】(外墙与门或窗之间的)窗侧，门侧 ‖~**able** *a.* 可展现的；可揭露的 /~**er** *n.* 展示者；揭露者；【宗】启示者，天启者 /~**ment** *n.*

reveille [ri'væli] *n.*【军】①起床号，起床鼓：sound the ~ 吹起床号；击起床鼓 ②(起床号后的)列队，集合

revel ['revl] **I** (revel(l)ed; revel(l)ing) ❶ *vi.* ①狂欢，欢宴；作乐 ②扬扬得意：~ *in* success 因成功而扬扬得意 ③ 十分爱好；着迷 *(in)*：~ *in* sports 非常喜爱运动 / ~ *in* gossip 好讲闲话 ❷ *vt.*

在狂欢中浪费(金钱等)：~ away the time 狂欢作乐虚度光阴 **Ⅱ** *n.* ① 狂欢，欢宴；作乐 ②[常用复](喧闹的)宴会；节庆 ‖**revel(l)er** *n.* 狂欢者；欢宴者 /~**ry** *n.* 狂欢，(喧闹的)宴会

revelation [,revi'leiʃən] *n.* ①展现，显现；揭露 ② 揭露的事物；意想不到的事；新发现：The ease of his driving was a ~ to me. 他居然能驾驶自如，这是我意想不到的。/ some ~ of the laboratory 实验室中的某些新发现 ③【宗】启示，默示；[the Revelation(s)] (基督教《圣经·新约》中的)《启示录》 ‖~**al** *a.* 展现的；揭露的；启示的，天启的

revenge [ri'vendʒ] **I** *vt.* ①替…报仇：~ sb. 为某人报仇 ②报复；洗雪：~ an insult 雪耻 **Ⅱ** *n.* ① 报仇；报复 (指行为或欲望)：have (或 take) one's ~ on sb. for sth. 因某事向某人报仇 / do sth. in ~ (out of ~) 报复性地 (出于报复而) 做某事 ② 雪耻机会；使败方有机会获胜的再次比赛：give sb. his ~ 给某人雪耻机会

revengeful [ri'vendʒful] *a.* 报复的；充满仇恨的；一心想报仇的 ‖~**ly** *ad.* / ~**ness** *n.*

revenue ['revinju:] *n.* ①(国家的)岁入；税收：the main source of a country's ~ 一国岁入的主要来源 / inland ~ 国内岁入；国内税收 / ~ tax 为增加国家岁入而征收的)财政税(区别于为保护本国工商业而征收的税) / the Public Revenue 国库收入，财政收入 ②收入，收益；[复]总收入：~ expenditure (或 charge) 营业支出，收益支出 / one's ~s 个人的总收入 ③税务署(或局)：defraud the ~ 漏税，逃税 ‖*a ~ cutter* (海关)缉私船 / *a ~ officer* 税务(或关)官员 / *a ~ stamp* 印花税票 / ~ *tariff* 财政关税 ‖~**r** *n.* ①[美口]财政部税务官(尤指取缔非法酿酒业者) ②(海关)缉私船

reverberate [ri've:bəreit] **I** ❶ *vt.* ① 使反响，使回响；使回荡 ②反射(光、热等) ③【化】反(焰) ③放…于反射炉处理 ❷ *vi.* ①反响，回响；回荡 ②(光、音等)反射；(反射炉中的热、焰)反回 ③(球等)回跃，回弹 **Ⅱ** *a.* 回响的；反射的；反焰的 ‖**reverberation** [ri,ve:bə'reiʃən] *n.* ①回响，反响；回荡 ②【物】交混回响，混响 ③(光、声波、热的)反射；反焰 ④在反射炉中的处理 ⑤反射物(如反射光等) / **reverberative** [ri've:bərətiv] *a.* 反响(性)的；反射(性)的 / **reverberator** *n.* 反射器；反射灯；反射炉 / **reverberatory** [ri've:bərətəri] *a.* 回响的；反射的；反焰的 *n.* 反射炉

revere[1] [ri'vie] *vt.* 尊敬，崇敬；敬畏

reverence ['revərəns] **I** *n.* ① 尊敬，崇敬；敬畏：hold sb. (sth.) *in* ~ 尊敬某人(某事物) / pay ~ to sb. 向某人致敬 / regard sb. *with* ~ 敬畏(或敬重)某人 / show ~ *for* 对…表示崇敬 ②敬礼；鞠躬：make a ~ 鞠一个躬 ③敬望，威望：stand great ~ 获得崇高威望 ④ [R-] (英国旧时用于对牧师等的尊称，现为粗俗或幽默的用语)尊敬的…阁下：his (或 your) Reverence the Bishop 尊敬的主教阁下 (间接提及时用 his，直接称呼时用

your) **II** *vt.* 尊敬,崇敬;敬畏: ~ the country's laws 尊重国家法律 ‖*saving your* ~ [古][用作插入语]冒昧陈辞,有渎清听

reverend ['revərənd] **I** *a.* ①可尊敬的;可敬畏的;应受尊敬的: ~ sir (用作称呼)可尊敬的先生 ② [the R-] 对牧师(或神父等)的尊称(对教长则用 the Very Reverend, 对主教用 the Right Reverend, 对大主教用 the Most Reverend; 常略作 the Rev.): the *Rev.* John Morris 约翰·莫里斯牧师 (也可称 the *Rev.* J. Morris 或 the *Rev.* Mr. Morris; 不可用 the *Rev.* Morris) / the ~ gentleman 那位牧师先生 ③教士的;圣职的 **II** *n.* [常用复]教士;牧师: ~s and right ~s 教士们和主教们

reverent ['revərənt] *a.* 恭敬的;虔诚的 ‖~ly *ad.*

reverential [,revə'ren∫əl] *a.* ① 恭敬的;出于虔诚的: ~ awe 敬畏 ② 令人肃然起敬的;可敬的 ‖~ly *ad.*

reverie ['revəri] *n.* ①梦想,幻想;白日梦: indulge in ~s 沉溺于幻想中 ② 沉思, 出神: be lost in (a) ~ 出神 ③[音]幻想曲

reversal [ri'və:səl] *n.* ① 颠倒: reverse the ~ of history 把颠倒的历史颠倒过来 ②反向,倒退,倒转;相反: cause a ~ of the state of affairs 把形势扭转过来 / the ~ of the seasons in the two hemispheres 两半球 (指南、北半球)季节的恰好相反 ③(判决等的)推翻;变更;撤销 ④[摄]正负片之间的转换

reverse [ri'və:s] **I** ❶ *vt.* ①颠倒;翻转: ~ a procedure 颠倒程序 / Their positions are ~d. 他们的地位颠倒过来了。/ *Reverse* arms! 倒枪! (行葬礼时使枪口向下的命令) / the verdict 翻案 / ~ the charge 由接电话者付电话费 ②使倒退,使倒转;使反向;[机]使回动 ③使变得相反: ~ a policy (one's attitude) 完全改变政策(态度) / ~ oneself *about* (或 *over*) sth. 完全改变对某事的看法 ④[律]推翻;撤销: ~ the decision of a lower court 否定下级法院的判决 ❷ *vi.* 倒退,倒转;反向;[机]回动: The dancers ~d. 舞蹈者转向相反的方向。**II** *n.* ①相反: do the ~ of what one is expected to do 做与别人对自己期望相反的事 / His opinion is the ~ of favourable. 他不赞成。/ It struck me the ~ of favourably. 那给我的印象不好。②背面,反面:the ~ of a coin (gramophone record)硬币(唱片)的背面 / the ~ of a book lea 一页书的反面 / see the ~ as well as the obverse of things 不但看到事物的正面, 也看到事物的反面 ③挫折;败北;倒霉: financial ~s 经济上的挫折 ④倒退,倒转;反向;[机]回动;回动装置(或齿轮): The car is *in* ~. 汽车在往后倒开。/ There's something wrong *in the* ~. 回动装置出毛病了。**III** *a.* ① 颠倒的: in ~ order 倒序地 ② 相反的;反向的;[机]回动的: in the ~ direction 往相反方向 / a ~ transformation 相反的转化 / the ~ current 反向电流 / a ~ turn

倒转 ③ 背面的,反面的: the ~ side of a medal 徽章的背面 / the ~ side of the coin 硬币的背面;[喻]事物的相反面;事情的另一面 / ~ fire 背面火力 ‖~ly *ad.* ‖ **osmosis** 逆渗透(一种从污水、盐水中提取纯净淡水的方法) / ~ **reaction**【化】逆反应 / ~ **repeater**【机】反围盘

reversible [ri'və:səbl] **I** *a.* ①可逆的: a ~ chemical reaction 可逆化学反应 ② (正反)两面可用的: a ~ fabric 双面织物 / a ~ coat 双面式上衣 ③(判决等)可撤销的 **II** *n.* 双面织物;双面式上衣 ‖**reversibility** [ri,və:sə'biliti] *n.* 可逆(性);两面可用(性);可撤销(性)

revert [ri'və:t] **I** ❶ *vi.* ① 回复 (*to*): ~ *to* the original state 回复原状 / ~ *to* the original topic of conversation 回到原来的话题上来 ②【律】(财产等)归还,归属 (*to*) ③【生】回复变异;返祖遗传 ❷ *vt.* ①使颠倒,使回转 ②把(眼睛等)转向后 **II** *n.* 恢复原来信仰的人

review [ri'vju:] **I** ❶ *vt.* ①再检查,再考察;回顾;复习;【律】复审: ~ the day's work 检查(或回顾)一天的工作 / ~ the past 回顾过去 / ~ last week's lessons 复习上星期的功课 ②考察;检阅: ~ the situation 观察形势 / ~ a guard of honour 检阅仪仗队 ③ (用文字)评论: ~ a new novel 给一本新出版的小说写书评 / be ~ed favourably 得到好评 ❷ *vi.* ①复习功课 ②写评论: ~ for a magazine 为一本杂志写评论 **II** *n.* ①复习;回顾;复习;【律】复审: a general ~ 总复习 ②考察,检查;检阅(式): a ~ board 检查委员会 / under ~ 在检查中 / hold a military ~ 举行阅兵式 ③评论(文章);评论性刊物: a ~ copy of a book (出版者给杂志编辑)供评论用的赠阅本 ④ =revue ‖*a* ~ **order** 见 **order** / *pass in* ~ ① (使)(队伍等)行进接受检阅 ②(被)回顾;(被)检查: pass sth. *in* ~ 回顾某事 ‖~**able** *a.* 可回顾的;可检查的;可评论的 / ~**er** *n.* 评论者;书评作者;报刊评论家

revile [ri'vail] *vt.* & *vi.* 辱骂,谩骂 ‖~**r** *n.* 谩骂者

revise [ri'vaiz] **I** *vt.* ① 修订, 校订: ~ a dictionary 修订词典 / ~ the printers' proofs 看校样 / the *Revised* Version [英] 基督教《圣经》钦定译本的修订本 / the *Revised* Standard Version [美]基督教《圣经》标准译本的修订本 ②修改,修正: ~ a document (contract) 修改文件(合同) / five days ahead of the ~d schedule 比修改后的计划提前五天 / ~ one's opinions of sb. 改变对某人的看法 ③【生】对…重新分类 **II** *n.* ①[印]再校样,二校样 ②[罕]修订;修正 ‖~**r**, **revisor** *n.* 修订者;修改者;修改者;校对员,再校员 ‖~**d edition** 修订版 / **revising barrister** (英国)每年修订各区议员选举人名册的律师

revision [ri'viʒən] *n.* ① 修订, 校订;修改,修正: after four ~s 经过四次修订 ②修订本,修订版 ‖~**ary** *a.* 修订的,校订的;修改的,修正的

revival [ri'vaivəl] *n.* ①苏醒;复活;再生 ②复兴;再流行: the *Revival* of Learning (或 Letters, Literature) 【史】文艺复兴 (=the Renaissance) ③(电影等)重新上演;(书刊等)重新出版 ④(精力、活动、兴趣等的)恢复 ⑤【宗】信仰复兴(期);鼓动性的福音布道会 ⑥【律】(契约等的)再生效 ‖~ism *n.* ①【宗】信仰复兴精神 ②(旧习惯、制度等的)复兴倾向 ‖~ist *n.* ①【宗】信仰复兴者(尤指福音传教士) ②(旧习惯、制度等的)复兴者

revive [ri'vaiv] ❶ *vi.* ①苏醒;复活;再生: Hope ~d in her. 她又有了希望。/ The withered plants ~d in the rain. 枯萎的植物在雨中又活了。②恢复精力(或活动能力);振奋 ③复兴;(风俗等)再流行 ④再生效 ⑤(金属)还原 ❷ *vt.* ①苏醒;使复活;使再生: ~ a fainted person 使昏倒的人苏醒 ②使恢复精力(或活动能力);使振奋 ③使复兴;使再流行 ④使再生效 ⑤回想起: ~ a scene in one's mind 回忆一个景象 ⑥重演(戏剧等) ⑦使(金属)还原 ‖~r *n.* ①使复活者;使复兴者 ②刺激物,兴奋剂 ③[俚]刺激性饮料,酒 ③(衣服、建筑物等的)翻新者 ④[俚]生色剂

revocation [,revə'keiʃən] *n.* 撤销;废除,取消;【律】(对订契约的建议的)撤销: the ~ of all the unequal treaties 一切不平等条约的废除

revocatory ['revəkətəri] *a.* 废除的;撤销的

revoke [ri'vouk] Ⅰ ❶ *vt.* ①撤回,撤销;取消(法律、允诺等): ~ a decision 取消一项决议 / ~ a driving licence 吊销驾驶执照 ②回想;召回 ❷ *vi.* (纸牌戏中)有牌不跟 Ⅱ *n.* ①有牌不跟 ②[罕]撤销;废除: beyond ~ 不能撤销(或废除)的

revolt [ri'voult] Ⅰ ❶ *vi.* ①反抗,造反;起义;叛: ~ *from* one's allegiance to 对…不再忠诚 ②厌恶,憎恶;反感: The stomach ~s *at* such food. 这种食物使人倒胃口。❷ *vt.* 使厌恶;使反感;使恶心 Ⅱ *n.* 反抗,造反;起义;反叛: rise *in* ~ 起来反抗;举行起义 / armed ~s 武装起义(或叛乱) ‖~ed *a.* 起来反抗的;起义的;反叛的

revolution [,revə'lu:ʃən, ,revə'lju:ʃən] *n.* ①革命;剧烈的变革,彻底的改革: a ~ in modern physics 现代物理学的大变革 ②旋转;绕转;【天】公转:~s per minute (略作 r. p. m.)每分钟转数 ③循环;周期: the ~ of the seasons 季节的循环 ‖the *Agrarian Revolution* 土地革命 / the *American Revolution* 美国独立战争(1775—1783) / the *French Revolution* 法国大革命 (1789—1794) / the *in dustrial* ~ 产业革命,工业革命(十八世纪后半期始于英国) / *technical* ~ 技术革命

revolutionary [,revə'lu:ʃənəri, ,revə'lju:ʃənəri] Ⅰ *a.* ①革命的;大变革的: a ~ sweep 革命气概 ②[美][R-]美国独立战争(时期)的 ③[罕]旋转的;绕转的 Ⅱ *n.* 革命者;革命党人 ‖**Revolutionary Calendar** 共和历(法兰西第一共和国时期的革命历法, 1792 年—1806 年)

revolutionize [,revə'lju:ʃənaiz] *vt.* ①使革命化 ②彻底改革 ‖**revolutionization** [,revə,lju:ʃənai-'zeiʃən] *n.* / ~d *a.* 革命化的;被彻底改革的

revolve [ri'vɔlv] ❶ *vt.* ①使旋转;使绕转 ②细想,默想: ~ a scheme 反复思考方案 ❷ *vi.* ①旋转;绕转: The earth ~s both round the sun and on its own axis. 地球既公转又自转。②周期地(或间断地)出现: Seasons ~. 季节周期性转换。③沉思;(念头等)使人再三考虑: Ideas ~d in his mind. 他思虑再三。

revolver [ri'vɔlvə] *n.* ①左轮手枪 ②旋转器;旋转式装置;【冶】转炉 ‖*the policy of the big* ~ 用报复关税权威胁他国的政策

revue [ri'vju:] *n.* [法](有小型歌舞的)时事讽刺剧

revulsion [ri'vʌlʃən] *n.* ①收回;(突然)抽回: the ~ of capital 资本的抽回 ②(感情等的)突变,急剧反应: a ~ of mood 情绪的突变 ③嫌恶,反感 (*against*) ④【医】诱导(法)

reward [ri'wɔ:d] Ⅰ *n.* ①报答;报应;报偿: *in* ~ *for* sb.'s work 作为对某人工作的报答 ②报酬;赏金,奖赏;赏格: offer a ~ of £5 for the finder of a lost watch 给拾得失表者酬谢五镑 / give a ~ to sb. for sth. 为某事给某人报酬(或赏金) Ⅱ *vt.* ①报答;酬劳;奖赏: ~ sb. for his help 答谢某人的帮助 / His efforts were ~ed by success. 他的努力获得了成功。/ feel amply ~ed 觉得已得到充分的报偿 ②报应;惩罚(坏人或坏事) ‖~ing *a.* ①报答的 ②有得益的;值得做的: a ~ing book 值得一读的书 / ~less *a.* 无报酬的,徒劳的

rhapsody ['ræpsədi] *n.* ①(古希腊适于一次吟诵的)叙事诗,叙事诗的一部分 ②狂文,狂诗,狂言 ③[音]狂想曲 ‖**rhapsodist** *n.* ①史诗吟诵者;狂诗作者 ②狂想曲作曲家 ③狂热的写作(或说话)者

rhetoric ['retərik] *n.* ①修辞学;修辞学书 ②运用语言的技能,辩术 ③花言巧语;(措词、文体的)夸与修饰 ④言语,讲话

rhetorical [ri'tɔrikəl] *a.* ①修辞的;修辞学的;用来产生修辞效果的 ②浮夸的 ③口头的 ‖~ly *ad.* ‖~ **question** (不必回答,只为加强印象或获取效果的)反问,反诘

rhetorician [,retə'riʃən] *n.* ①修辞学者,修辞学师;雄辩家;演说家 ②说话雄辩而浮夸的人;词藻华丽而浮夸的作家

rheumatic [ru(:)'mætik] Ⅰ *a.* ①(患)风湿病的;患风湿病似的: a ~ walk 患风湿病人的走路样子 / a ~ elevator 开起来摇摇晃晃的电梯 Ⅱ *n.* ①风湿病患者 ②[复][方]风湿病 ‖~ally *ad.* ‖~ fever 风湿病

rheumatism ['ru:mətizəm] *n.* 【医】风湿病: acute (chronic) ~ 急性(慢性)风湿病 / articular (muscular) ~ 关节(肌肉)风湿病

rhinoceros [rai'nɔsərəs] *n.* ①[复] rhinoceros(es) 或 rhinoceri [rai'nɔsərai] 犀牛 ②[R-] 犀属(包括印度和马来亚的犀牛)

rhubarb ['ru:bɑːb] **n.** ①【植】大黄属植物; 大黄 ②激烈的争论

rhyme [raim] **I n.** ① 韵, 韵脚; 同韵的词(如尾音 相同的 love 和 above, witty 和 pretty): single (或 male, masculine) ~ 一音韵, 阳性韵 / double (或 female, feminine) ~ 二重韵, 阴性韵 / "Is it" and "visit" give ~. "is it" 和 "visit" 为同韵。/ I can't find a ~ to "teacups". 我不能找到和 "teacups" 同韵的词。②押韵; 押韵的词; 韵文: a nursery ~ 摇篮歌, 幼儿曲 / ~ royal 每行十音节的七行诗 / ~ scheme (诗的) 韵律安排 / I prefer ~ to blank verse. 我喜欢押韵诗胜过无韵诗。**II ❶ vi.** ①作押韵诗; 作诗 ②押韵 (with, to): "Profound" ~s with "sound". "profound" 和 "sound" 同韵。③(诗、音乐)和谐 **❷ vt.** ①用韵诗叙述(或歌颂) ②把…写成诗; 写(押韵诗); 使步韵(with): ~ "law" with "four" 使 "law" 步 "four" 的韵 ③使押韵; 用(某字)作韵脚: ~d verse 押韵诗 / a rhyming dictionary 诗韵词典; 韵府 ④以作诗来消磨(时间) (away) ‖ neither ~ nor reason 既无音韵又无情节; 既杂乱又无意义; 一无可取 / without ~ or reason 莫名其妙; 无缘无故; 毫无道理

rhythm ['riðəm] **n.** ①(诗中的)韵律; 格律 ②【音】节奏; 节奏的格调; (乐队中)击节拍的乐器 ③律动; 律动的模式: the ~ of an engine 引擎的律动 / the ~ of speech 语调的抑扬 / the ~ of the seasons 季节的循环 ④(艺术上各部分间的)调和, 匀称: the ~ of a statue 塑像各部分之间的匀称 ⑤【医】节律: ~ of heart 心动节律; 心律 ‖ ~ and blues 节奏极强的一种美国黑人音乐 ‖ ~less a. 无节奏的; 无韵的; 不匀称的 / ~ist n. ①研究韵律(或节奏)的人 ②诗(或韵文)的作者; 作曲者 ③有节奏感的人 ‖ ~ method 一种根据女子经期推算的避孕法 / ~ section 交响乐队中用以烘托乐曲节奏的乐器(指鼓、大提琴等)

rhythmic(al) ['riðmik(əl)] **a.** 有韵律的; 有节奏的 ‖ rhythmically ad.

rib¹ [rib] **I** (ribbed; ribbing) **vt.** [俚]开…的玩笑, 戏弄, 逗 **II n.** ①玩笑, 戏谑 ②(仿他人文体的)滑稽诗文, 讽刺诗文

rib² [rib] **I n.** ①(肉类)肋条, 排骨;【解】肋, 肋骨: a false (或 floating, short) ~ 假肋 / a true (或 sternal) ~ 真肋 / ~(s) of pork (beef) 大块猪(牛)排 ②[谑]妻(源出《圣经·创世纪》, 上帝取亚当肋骨做成其妻夏娃) ③【纺】棱纹, 凸条, 罗纹 ④【植】(叶)主脉;【动】翅脉 ⑤类似肋骨(作用)的东西;【空】翼肋;【建】拱肋, 扇形拱; (拱桥的)弯梁; (船等的)肋材; 伞骨;【矿】(矿区)侧壁; 矿柱: wheel ~ 轮辐 **II** (ribbed; ribbing) **vt.** ①装肋状物于, 用肋状物围(或加固) ②【纺】在…上起棱纹 ‖ dig (或 poke) sb. in the ~s 诡谲地触某人肋骨(促其注意或向他表示欣赏某笑话) / smite under the fifth ~ 刺死 / stick to sb.'s ~s [美俚](丰美的食物)撑满肚子 ‖ ~band ['ribənd] **n.**

【船】木桁 **vt.** 供…以木桁; 用木桁固定 / '~-grass, '~wort **n.** 【植】长叶车前

ribald ['ribəld] **I a.** 开下流玩笑的; (言词或人)下流的: ~ language 下流话, 脏话 **II n.** 开下流玩笑的人, 讲下流话的人

ribbon ['ribən] **I n.** ①缎带, 丝带: the ~s on the wreaths 花圈上的缎带 / the ~-cutting ceremony 剪彩仪式 ②带; 系带; 带状物; 钢卷尺; 带锯; (打字机的)色带 ③【建】条板 ④(勋章等的)缓带;【军】肋表(军服左上袋上方所佩颜色鲜明的条带, 用以代表勋章): win a blue ~ 获得蓝缓带(英国最高荣誉 Garter 嘉德勋章的缓带) ⑤[常用复]破碎条儿: be torn to ~s 撕成碎片 ⑥[复][口]缰绳: handle (或 take) the ~s 赶车 ⑦【船】木桁 **II ❶ vt.** ①用缎带装饰 ②把…撕成条带(或碎片) **❷ vi.** 形成带状 ‖ ~ building, ~ development (由市区到郊区)沿干道发展的一系列建筑

rice [rais] **I** [单复同] **n.** 稻; 米; 饭: a ~ plant 一株稻 / every grain of ~ 每一粒米 / the land of ~ and fish 鱼米之乡 / thresh (hull) ~ 打(舂)谷 / husk ~ 舂米 / broken ~ 碎米 / cargo ~ 糙米 / early (middle-season, late) ~ 早(中、晚)稻 / glutinous ~ 糯米 / ground ~ 米粉 / long-shaped ~ 籼米 / paddy (upland) ~ 水(旱)稻 / polished ~ 精白米 / round-shaped ~ 粳米 / single-crop (double-crop) ~ 单(双)季稻 / unhusked ~ 谷子 **II vt.** ①舂(米) ②把(马铃薯等)捣成米糊状 ‖ bin 米仓; 米箱 / '~bird **n.** ①爪哇麻雀 ②(美国南部产的)食米鸟 / ~ blast 稻瘟病 / ~ borer 水稻螟蛾幼虫 / ~ bran 米糠 / ~ Christian 为物质利益而信奉基督教者 / ~ flour 米粉 / '~-milk **n.** (加米煮成的)牛奶糊 / ~ paper 宣纸 / seeding bed 秧田 / ~ sprouts, ~ shoots 秧 / ~ transplanter 水稻插秧机 / ~ water (供伤病员喝的)稀粥

rich [ritʃ] **a.** ①富的, 富裕的, 有钱的 ②丰富的; 富饶的, 多产的: a ~ harvest 丰收 / ~ soil 沃土 / ~ practical experiences 丰富的实践经验 / a country ~ in natural resources 自然资源丰富的国家 ③贵重的; 珍贵的: a ~ prize 贵重的奖品 / ~ gifts 珍贵的礼物 ④(服装、家具、首饰等)富丽的, 奢华的; (色彩)浓艳的: a ~ landscape (sunset) 瑰丽的景色(日落) ⑤(食物)味浓的, 油腻的; (酒)醇厚的, 芳烈的; (气味)强烈的: a ~ diet 含脂肪蛋白多的食物 ⑥(声音)圆润的; 低沉的: the ~ voice of the baritone 男中音的低沉的声音 ⑦繁茂的: ~ meadows 青葱的草地 ⑧(近乎)纯的: ~ coal 肥煤 / ~ lime 肥石灰 ⑨有意义的, 丰富多采的: ~ allusions 富有含义的典故 / a ~ language 丰富多采的语言 ⑩[口]逗人的, 有趣的; 荒唐的: a ~ joke 有趣的笑话 / That's ~! 真可笑! 真荒唐! ⑪[与过去分词或现在分词连用]…华丽(或丰富、精美等)的: ~-clad 衣着华丽的 / ~-bound 装帧精美

的 / ~-glittering 金碧辉煌的 ⑫(内燃机的混合燃料等)可燃成分高的, 极易起燃的: a ~ fuel mixture 极易起燃的燃料混合物 ‖as ~ as **Croesus** 非常有钱的 / **strike it** ~ 见 **strike** ‖~ly ad. ①富饶地; 丰富地; 浓厚地; 华丽地 ②(与 deserve 连用)完全地, 彻底地, 充分地: ~ly deserve (of) praise 完全应受表扬 / ~ness n.

riches ['ritʃiz] [复] n. 财富; 财宝; 房地产; 富; 丰富 ‖**Riches have wings.** [谚]钱财易散。

rick [rik] I n. 一垛干草(或稻草等); 一堆木料 II vt. 把…堆成垛

rickets ['rikits] [复] n. [用作单或复]【医】佝偻病, 软骨病

rickety ['rikiti] a. ①佝偻病的; 患佝偻病的; 似佝偻病的: a ~ symptom (似)佝偻病的病症 ②连接处不牢固的; 摇晃的, 东倒西歪的: a ~ old man 蹒跚的老人 / ~ stairs 摇摇晃晃的楼梯 / be like an old ox pulling a ~ cart 像老牛拉破车似的

ricochet ['rikəʃet, 'rikəʃei] I n. ①(石片、子弹等接触地面、水面等后的)跳飞, 回跳, 漂掠 ②跳飞的石片; 【军】跳弹: ~ fire (bombing)【军】跳弹射击(轰炸) II (ricochet(t)ed; ricochet(t)ing) ❶ vi. 跳飞, 漂掠: The bullet ~ed. 子弹跳飞。❷ vt. 使跳飞; 用跳弹攻击(或瞄准)

rid [rid] (rid 或 ridded; ridding) vt. ①使摆脱; 使去掉(of) ②[古]救, 救出 ③[方]迅速了结(工作); 除去, 扫除; 打扫, 收拾 ‖be ~ of 摆脱, 去掉: He is ~ of fever. 他不发烧了。/ **get** ~ **of** 摆脱, 去掉, 除去: He can't get ~ of the cold. 他伤风老是不好。/ get ~ of a bad style 去掉不良作风

riddance ['ridəns] n. 摆脱; 清除: ~ from adversity 摆脱困境 ‖**good** ~ (**to bad rubbish**) 可喜的摆脱(指摆脱讨厌的人或事物): He was indeed a good ~. 他真是不在的好。

ridden ['ridn] I ride 的过去分词 II a. [常用以构成复合词]受…支配的; 受…压迫的; …横行的: crisis-~ 充满危机的 / crime-~ 罪大恶极的 / be ~ by fears 十分恐惧的

riddle¹ ['ridl] I n. ①谜, 谜语: propose (ask) a ~ 出谜 / solve (know the answer to) a ~ 解(能解)谜 ②闷葫芦; 难以捉摸的人; 莫名其妙的事物 II ❶ vt. 解(谜等); 给…出谜; 迷惑: Riddle me this. 你猜一猜这个谜。(或: 请你为我解决这疑难。) ❷ vi. 出谜; 说谜似的话

riddle² ['ridl] I n. (筛谷物、砂石等的)粗筛 II vt. ①筛(谷物、砂石等) ②把…打得布满窟窿: Bullets ~d the car. 子弹把汽车打得尽是窟窿。③检查, 鉴定(证据等) ④(用接连质问等)难倒, 驳倒 ⑤批评, 非难 ⑥使完全败坏; 充满于; 弥漫于

ride [raid] I (rode [roud], ridden ['ridn]) ❶ vi. ①骑马(或自行车等), 乘(on, in): ~ astride 跨坐在鞍上骑马 / ~ sidesaddle 侧坐在鞍上骑马(指两腿都放在马鞍的同一边) / The boy was riding on his father's shoulders. 男孩骑在他父亲的肩上。/ ~ in (或 on) a train (boat, plane) 乘火车(船, 飞机) ②(车、马等)适于乘(或骑); (道路等)骑起马(或行起车)来(觉得舒服、不舒服等): The car ~s smoothly. 这汽车乘起来很平稳。/ The ground rode hard after the frost. 降霜后骑起马来觉得地面很硬。③漂浮; 航行, 停泊: The ship rode on the waves (at anchor in the harbour). 船乘浪前进(停泊在港内)。/ eagle riding on the wind 迎风翱翔的鹰 ④支撑在…上而动; 随…而定, 依靠(on): The wheel ~s on the axle. 轮子在轴上转动。/ a man riding on the waves of popularity 孚众望的人 / The plans rode on his nomination. 这些计划要在他被任命后才有可能实施。⑤ [俚]照旧进行: I'll let the matter ~ a few months. 这件事我让它去, 过几个月再说。⑥(骑师等出赛前)称体重 ⑦(折骨等)重叠; (绳子等)绞合 ⑧押作赌注 ❷ vt. ①骑(马等); 乘(车等): children riding the merry-go-round 骑着旋转木马的孩子们 ②骑马(或乘车)通过; 骑马(或乘车)进行(比赛等): ~ the prairies (a ford) 骑马驰草原(浅滩) / ~ a race with sb. 与某人赛马(或赛自行车) ③…骑(或乘); 搭载: ~ a child on one's back 让孩子骑在背上 / He rode a shipment of machines in the truck on his return trip. 他开卡车回来时搭运了一批机器。④乘(风、浪等): Our gunboat rode the waves. 我们的炮舰乘浪前进。⑤经受住, 渡过(难关等)(out): ~ out the gale 经受住大风 / The large ship rode the storm. 大船顶住了风暴。⑥缠住; 控制; 压制, 骑在…头上; [俚]使苦恼, 嘲弄: Don't ~ me. 别缠住(或欺负)我。⑦(系)留, 使停泊 ⑧重叠在…上 ⑨顺势退缩以减轻(对方来击)之势 II n. ①骑; 乘车; 乘坐; 骑马(或乘车)旅行: give a child a ~ on the shoulders 让小孩骑在肩上 ②(尤指供骑马用的)林间道路 ③(儿童公园中)供骑、乘的玩具(如旋转木马等) ④绑架谋杀; 欺骗, 诈骗 ⑤交通工具 ⑥[英]【军】新募的骑兵队 ‖~ and tie 两人轮流乘一匹马旅行 / ~ double 两人合骑一马(或自行车) / ~ down ①骑马赶上 ②骑马撞(倒); 践踏 ③骑得(马等)筋疲力尽 ④克服 / for a fall 见 fall / ~ high 得意扬扬, 神气十足 / ~ off 岔开去: ~ off on a side issue 岔到枝节问题上去 / ~ out ①安然渡过风暴 ②喻]平安渡过困难(或攻击等) / ~ over ①骑马而来: They rode over to see us last week. 上星期他们骑马来探望我们。②(赛马场中)从容胜过 ③骑在…头上, 压制, 欺凌 / ~ roughshod over 横暴地对待, 欺凌: ~ sb. off (马球用语)驱马迫使某人让开 / ~ sb. on a rail 见 rail¹ / ~ to death ①把…骑得累死: He rode his horse to death. 他把马骑得累死了。②讲(或做)得过分而使…失效(或惹人厌): ~ a method to death 把一种方法用得太多而失效 / ~ a jest to death 玩笑开得过分反而乏味 / ~ up (穿着的衣服)向上拱, 缩上去 / take sb. for a ~ [美俚]①

(用汽车等)绑架杀害某人 ② 欺骗(或诈骗)某人 ‖~ meter 测震仪(测量路面行驶质量的仪器)

rider ['raidə] *n.* ①骑马(或自行车等)的人;乘车的人: He is no ~. 他不善于骑马。/ a dispatch ~骑摩托车(或骑马)的通讯员(或传令兵) ②(文件后面的)附文;(议会议案的)附加条款 ③(机件等)架在上面的部分 ④【海】(加固船体的)盖顶木料(或钢板);【物】游码;制动器;【建】(支墙)斜撑 ⑤(数)(复习定理的)应用习题;系 ‖~ship *n.* 全体乘车者;乘客数

ridge [ridʒ] **I** *n.* ①(动)脊 ②(山、屋、堤等的)脊;岭;山脉;分水岭 ③(狭长的)隆起部: the ~ of the nose 鼻梁 / a ~ on an ocean bottom 海洋底的脊 / ~s on a piece of cloth 布上的织纹 ④垄,埂 ⑤(气象图上)狭长的高压带: ~ of high pressure【气】高压脊 **II** ❶ *vt.* ①装(屋)脊;使成脊状;使起皱 ②给…培土;翻(土)作垄: ~ the land for watermelons 翻地作垄种西瓜 ③种(黄瓜等)于垄上 ❷ *vi.* 成脊状地延伸;起皱: ~ northward 成脊状地向北延伸 / The sea ~s under the wind. 风吹海水起皱纹。‖~pole, '~beam, '~piece *n.* 【建】栋梁, 栋木 / ~ tile 脊瓦 / '~tree *n.* [古] =~pole / '~way *n.* 山脊(道)路

ridicule ['ridikju:l] **I** *n.* ① 嘲笑, 嘲弄; 奚落: hold sb. (sth.) up to 嘲笑某人(某事物) / pour ~ on sb. (sth.) 尽情讥笑某人(某事物) ②[古]笑柄; 荒谬: lay oneself open to 使自己成为笑柄 **II** *vt.* 嘲笑,嘲弄; 奚落

ridiculous [ri'dikjuləs] *a.* 可笑的, 荒谬的; 滑稽的: a ~ idea 荒谬的(或可笑的)想法 ‖~ly *ad.* / ~ness *n.*

rife [raif] *a.* [只作表语] ①流行的, 盛行的; 普遍的 ②充满的;众多的 (*with*): a language which is ~ *with* idioms 习语很多的一种语言

riffraff ['rifræf] *n.* ① [the ~] 下等人, 群氓, 贱民 ②地痞流氓, 坏蛋, 社会渣滓 ③废物; 碎屑

rifle¹ ['raifl] **I** *n.* ①步枪, 来复枪; 来复线, 膛线: an automatic ~ 自动步枪 ②[复]步枪队 **II** *vt.* 在(枪、枪管、枪膛)内来复线 ‖~ry *n.* 步枪打靶 / rifling *n.* (在枪膛里)制来复线;来复线;膛线 ‖~ corps 志愿步枪队 / ~ ground, ~ range 步枪射击场 / '~man *n.* 步兵 / ~ pit 散兵壕 / '~scope *n.* 步枪上的望远镜瞄准具 / '~shot *n.* 步枪射程(或射手, 子弹)

rifle² ['raifl] ❶ *vt.* ①搜劫,抢劫,掠夺,抢(或偷)光: ~ sb. 搜劫某人 / ~ a safe *of* its contents 把保险箱盗窃一空 ②偷去;抢走; 带走 ❷ *vi.* 搜劫, 抢劫, 掠夺

rift [rift] **I** *n.* ①裂缝; 空隙: a ~ in the clouds 云间隙隙 ②[地]断裂; 断层线; 长狭谷; 河流浅石滩 ③(意见)分裂, 不和 **II** ❶ *vt.* ①劈开; 分开 ②穿透; 渗入 ❷ *vi.* 裂开; 断裂: Mists ~ed. 雾散了。‖a little ~ *within the lute* 发展后会破坏整体的裂痕, 最初的分歧(或不和); 发狂

的预兆 ‖ ~ valley 【地】地堑; 裂谷

rig¹ [rig] **I** (rigged; rigging) *vt.* ① 装配 (*out, up*); 给(船等)装配帆(或索具等);装(帆、索具等)于船桅(或帆桁等)上面; 给(飞机)装配机翼(或机身等): ~ a ship (the main mast) with new sails 给船(主桅)装上新帆 ②拼凑着做成; 临时赶造; 草草做成 (*up*): ~ *up* a tent for the night 草草搭个帐篷过夜 ③[口]束装(尤指以华美或式样奇特的服装),打扮: be *rigged out* (或 *up*) in one's best 穿着盛装 / ~ *oneself out* as a vagabond 把自己打扮成流浪汉 **II** *n.* ①【海】帆装(一只船特有的帆、桅型式) ②成套器械, 用具;【矿】钻塔, 钻车: oil-drilling ~ 打(油)井机 ③马车(全套) ④[口](尤指华美或奇特的)服装: in full ~ 穿着漂亮

rig² [rig] **I** (rigged; rigging) *vt.* ①(用欺骗等手段)操纵, 控制: ~ the market 操纵市场 / ~ an election 控制选举 ②(为达到预期的目的而)事先决定(比赛的输赢、测验好坏等) **II** *n.* ①[主英]嘲弄, 戏弄; 欺诈, 骗局; 恶作剧, 捣蛋 ②囤积居奇

rig³ [rig] *n.* [英]发育不全(或部分阉割)的动物

rigging ['rigin] *n.* ①【海】帆缆; 索具; 支索: running (standing) ~ 活动(固定)索具 / ~ screw 夹索螺旋夹具; [英] 松紧螺旋扣 ②(舞台用)索具; 传动装置 ③服装 ‖*climb the* ~ [俚]发脾气

right [rait] **I** *a.* ①正确的, 对的: Your opinions are quite ~. 你的看法很正确。/ What's the ~ time now? 现在的正确时间是几点钟? / You were ~ to refuse. 你拒绝是对的。/ You were ~ *in* your decision. 你的决定是对的。/ You were ~ *in* deciding not to go. 你决定不去是对的。
②恰当的; 顺利的; 井井有条的: He is the ~ man for the job. 他做这工作最恰当。/ do the ~ thing at the ~ time 在适当的时候做适当的事情 / make things ~ 把事情搞得井井有条 ③正常的, 好的, 健全的: be ~ in one's head (或 be in one's ~ mind) 神志正常 / All's ~. 一切都好。/ Are you ~ now? 你这会儿(身体感觉)好了吗? ④正直的, 正当的; 正义的: a ~ man 正直的人 / a ~ cause 正义事业 ⑤如实的; 真正的, 名符其实的: give a ~ account of sth. 如实地叙述某事 / a chest of ~ Chinese tea 一箱地道的中国茶 / the ~ heir 合法继承人 ⑥正(面)的: the ~ side of cloth 布的正面 / the ~ side up (out) 正面朝上(向外) ⑦(线)笔直的[仅用于 a ~ line 及 ~-lined 中];(角等)垂直的, 有直角的: at ~ angles with 与…成直角 / a ~ cone 直立圆锥 / a ~ triangle 直角三角形 / ~ sailing 【海】正东(或南、西、北)向航行 / ~ ascension 【天】赤经 ⑧右, 右边的; 右翼的; [常作 R-]右派的: one's ~ hand (arm) 右手(臂); [喻]得力助手 / the ~ side of the road 路的右侧

II *ad.* ①对,不错: guess ~ 猜得对 / if I remember ~ 如果我记(忆)得不错的话 / hold the pen ~ 笔握得对
②顺利,好: All came ~ in the end. 结果一切顺利。/ Nothing goes ~ with .... …干什么都不顺当。(或:…什么都不顺利。)
③正直地,正当地;公正地: act ~ 行为正当;做得对
④如实地: tell sth. ~ 如实谈某事
⑤直接地,径直地: go ~ home 直接回家 / walk ~ on 不拐弯地一直走
⑥ [加强语气] 正好,恰恰;就;立刻;完全: ~ opposite 正对面;正相反 / ~ in the middle of 在正中 / ~ here and now 就在此时此地 / I'll be ~ back. 我马上就回来。/ turn ~ round 转一整圈;完全转过身来 / The pear is rotten ~ through. 这只梨全烂了。
⑦非常,十分: be ~ glad to hear ... 非常高兴听到… / know ~ well 知道得很清楚;很懂得
⑧在右边,向右: Right dress (或 Eyes ~)! 向右看齐! / Right face (或 Right turn)! 向右转!
III *n.* ①正确,对: distinguish between ~ and wrong 分清是非
②正当;公正,正义: defend the ~ 维护正义 / ~ and might 公理和强权
③ [复]实况,真情: hear the ~s of the matter 听取事情真相
④ 权利 【商】(股东以低于市场价格购买增资股票的)优惠权: ~s and duties 权利与义务 / have a (或 the) ~ of veto 有否决权 / have a (或 the) ~ to vote (或 of voting) 有选举权 / mineral ~s (矿藏)开采权 / the film ~s of a novel (作者的)改编小说为电影的权利 / the divine ~ 上帝赋予之权,天赋之权(指君主等) / the ~ of asylum (国际法中的)庇护权;避难权 / the ~ of search (交战国军舰在公海上对中立国船只的)搜查权 / the ~ of flights beyond 【空】以远权
⑤右,右边,右方;右手;【军】右翼: Keep to the ~. 靠右走。/ A house was on our ~. 我们的右边是一幢房子。/ go up the staircase on the ~ 从右边楼梯上去
⑥ [常作 R-] 议长席右侧的议员;右派议员;右派
IV ❶ *vt.* ①扶直,使正;整理;整顿: ~ a fallen pole 把倒下的木杆扶直 / ~ the helm 拨正船舵 / ~ oneself (人或船)恢复平稳 / ~ the room 收拾房间
②纠正,矫正;补偿;为…伸冤,为…报复;拯救: ~ an error 纠正错误 / ~ a wrong 矫枉;雪冤
❷ *vi.* (船等)恢复平稳
‖*all* ~ 见 **all** / a ~ *guy* 见 **guy**² / a ~ of *way* =~-of-way / *be in the* ~ 站在正义的一边 / *by* ~ *of* ... 凭借…,由于… / *by* ~ (*s*) have told you. 按理说;正当地: I should not *by* ~(*s*) have told you. 按理我不该告诉你的。/ *dead to* ~*s* 见 **dead** / *do sb.* ~ 公平对待某人 / *get* ~ 恢复

正常 / *get sth.* ~ ①彻底搞清楚某事: Let's *get* this ~ before we pass on to the next problem. 我们转到下一个问题前先把这件事搞清楚。②使某事物恢复正常 / *in one's own* ~ 凭本身的头衔(或资格、质量等) / *in* ~ *of sb.* 依仗某人的头衔(或权利等) / *of* ~ 按绝对权利; 按照法律(或道义上的要求): Retiring pensions are given as *of* ~. 退休金作为应享的权利而发给。/ *on the* ~ *side of* 见 **side** / *put* (或 *set*) *oneself* ~ (*with sb.*) (向某人)辩白自己 / *put* (或 *set*) ... ~ ①使恢复正常: The doctor soon *put* him ~. 医生很快使他恢复了健康。/ *put* a watch ~ 把表拨正 ②纠正…的错误: It is our duty to *put* him ~. 我们有责任纠正他的错误。/ *put* (或 *set*) *sth. to* ~*s* 使某事物恢复正常(或有秩序): *put* matters *to* ~*s* 整顿事情 / *put* the rooms *to* ~*s* 整理房间 / ~ *along* 继续地,不断地 / ~ *and left* ① 向(或从)左右两边: The crowd divided ~ *and left*. 人群向左右分开。② 到处,四面八方: be surrounded ~ *and left* 四面被围 / look ~ *and left* 左顾右盼 / ~ *as rain* (或 *a trivet* 或 *nails*) 丝毫不错,十分正确 / ~ *away* (或 *off*) 立刻 / *Right oh*! [英俚] [表示同意](你做得或说得)对! 行! 好! / ~ *on* [美俚] ① [用作感叹句]对啊! 你说对啦! 你说得好啦 ② 老于世故的,知情的 / ~ *or wrong* 不管对不对;不管怎样 / *Right* (*you are*)! [口] =Right oh! / *serve sb.* ~ 给某人应得的报应: It *serves* him ~. 他活该。/ *stand on* (或 *assert*) *one's* ~*s* 坚持自己的权利 / *the Bill of Rights* 见 **bill** / *the* ~*s and wrongs* 是非曲直 / *the* ~ *way* 见 **way** / *Too* (*bloody*) ~! 当然!
‖~*ly ad.* ① 正确地;恰当地 ② 正直地,正当地;正义地 / ~*ness n.* ① 正确(性);恰当 ② 正直,正当;公正,正义 / ~*ward*(*s*) *ad.* & *a.* 在右边(的);向右边(的)
‖~-'*angled a.* 成直角的,有直角的: a ~-*angled* street 九十度转弯的街道 / '~-*down a.* 彻底的;真正的: a ~-*down* scab 彻头彻尾的工贼 *ad.* 彻底地;真正地: It's ~-*down* bad. 这简直坏极(或槽透)了。/ ~ **field** (棒球)右翼外场 / ~ **fielder** (棒球)右翼外场球手 / '~-**hand** *a.* ① 右边的;[喻]得力的: one's ~-*hand* man 同一排上右边的人;[喻]得力助手 ② =~-handed (*a.*) / '~-'**handed** *a.* ① 惯用右手的 ② 供右手用的;右手的: a ~-*handed* glove 右手的手套 / a ~-*handed* blow 用右手的一击 ③ 顺时针方向的,向右旋转的: a ~-*handed* propeller 向右转动的螺旋桨 *ad.* 用右手 / '~-'**hander** *n.* ① 惯用右手的人 ② 用右手打的一击 / **Right Hono**(**u**)**rable** 对有爵位者(或高级官员)的尊称 / '~-'**minded** *a.* 正直的,有正义感的 / '~-'**mindedness** *n.* 正直;正义感 / '~-'**to-work** *a.* (法律等)禁止强行要求工人加入工会的 / ~ **whale** 【动】露脊鲸 / ~ **wing** (政治方面或建筑物等的)右翼 / '~-'**winger** *n.* 右翼分子

righteous ['raitʃəs] *a.* ①正直的; 正当的: a ~ man 一个正直的人 / the ~ and the wicked 好人和坏人 ②正义的: a ~ act 正义的行动 / in ~ indignation 义愤地 ‖~ly *ad.* / ~ness *n.*

rightful ['raitful] *a.* ①正义的, 公正的: ~ actions 正义的行动 ②合法的; 依法有正当要求权的: one's ~ owner of a house 房屋的合法所有人 / one's ~ position 合法地位 ③恰当的, 合适的: proceed in the ~ order 按合适的顺序进行 ‖~ly *ad.* / ~ness *n.*

rigid ['ridʒid] *a.* ①刚硬的, 坚硬的; 不易弯的: a ~ metal girder 刚度大的金属大梁 / a ~ bar 坚硬的棍棒 ②僵硬的, 刻板的; 严峻的,严厉的; 严格的: a ~ taskmaster 严厉的监工 / ~ old forms and habits 呆板的旧形式和旧习惯 / ~ economy 严格节约 / ~ adherence to rules 严守规则 ③【物】刚性的: ~ body 刚体 / ~ structure 刚性结构 ④【空】硬式的(如有构架的轻体航空器) ‖~ly *ad.*

rigidity [ri'dʒiditi] *n.* ①刚硬, 坚硬; 不变: the ~ of one's belief 信仰的坚定不移 ②僵化, 刻板; 严峻,严厉;严格: a ~ coming into one's face 脸上出现的严峻表情 ③【物】刚性, 刚度: torsional ~ 抗扭刚度;扭转刚度

rigmarole ['rigməroul] I *n.* ①冗长的废话; 胡言乱语; 前言不搭后语的讲述 ②烦琐的仪式程序 II *a.* 条理不清的, 前言不搭后语的

rigorous ['rigərəs] *a.* ①(性格等)严峻的, 严厉的; 苛刻的; 严酷的: stand up to the ~ tests of any kind 经得住各种严峻的考验 / ~ rules 严格的规则 ②(气候)严酷的 ③严密的, 精确的: ~ scholarship 严谨的治学态度; 精确的学识 ‖~ly *ad.*

rigo(u)r ['rigə] *n.* ①(性格等)严峻, 严厉; 苛刻; 严格: the ~ of martial law 森严的戒严令 / enforce discipline with ~ 严格实施纪律 ②[常用复](生活)艰苦, (气候)严酷: the ~(s) of a northern winter 北方冬天的严寒 ③严密, 精确: logical ~ 逻辑的严密性 ‖~ism ['rigərizəm] *n.* (生活、宗教、艺术风格等)严格(或严峻)的作风 / ~ist ['rigərist] *n.* 作风严肃的(或要求严格的)人

rile [rail] *vt.* ①[口]激怒 ②[美]搅浑

rill[1] [ril] I *n.* 小河, 溪流 II *vi.* 小河般地流, 潺湲

rill[2], **rille** [ril] *n.* 【天】(月面)谷

rim [rim] I *n.* ①边(尤指圆物的);【机】缘; 轮辋, (眼镜)框; (帽)边: the ~ of a cup 杯口 / ~ of gear 【机】齿轮辋 ②边缘: close to the ~ of war 接近战争边缘 ③海面, 水面 II (rimmed; rimming) ❶ *vt.* 装边于; 装轮辋于; 作…的边 ❷ *vi.* 形成边状, 显出边缘 ‖the golden ~ 王冠 / ~less *a.* 无边(缘)的: ~less spectacles 无框眼镜 ‖~ brake 轮圈刹车 / '~land *n.* 心脏地区的周围地带

rime [raim] I *n.* ①[诗]白霜(=hoarfrost) ②结壳; 结晶 II *vt.* [诗]使蒙上霜(或霜状物)

rimy ['raimi] *a.* 被霜蒙着的, 一片白霜的

rind [raind] I *n.* ①树皮; 果(或蔬菜)皮; (黑肉、干酪等的)外皮 ②表面, 外观 II *vt.* 削…皮, 剥…皮 ‖~ gall 树皮上的伤疤, 伤皮愈合

ring[1] [riŋ] I *n.* ①环形物(如圈、环、戒指等): a key ~ 钥匙圈 / a wheel ~ 轮圈 / a piston ~ 活塞环 / a basket ~ 【体】篮圈 / the swinging (或 flying) ~s 【体】吊环 / an ear~ 耳环 / a wedding ~ 结婚戒指 / Ring of Saturn 【天】土星光环 ②圈状, 环状; 网状;【化】【数】环: a ~ of encirclement 包围圈 / close the ~ around 【军】缩紧包围 / a ~ of light 光环 / stand in a ~ 站成一圈 / a spy ~ 间谍网 ③(树的)年轮 (=annual ~) ④圆形场地(如牲畜展览场、马戏场、赛马场等) ⑤拳击场; 摔角场 ⑥[the ~]拳击 ⑦竞赛; 竞选: toss one's hat in the ~ 宣布参加竞选(或竞赛) ⑧[the ~][总称]以赌赛马为业者 ⑨集团: a price ~ 操纵物价的集团 II ❶ *vt.* ①包围 (round, about, in); 围拢 (牛羊等): be ~ed on three sides by mountains 三面环山 / ~ in the isolated enemy 包围孤立的敌人 ②给(牛鼻子等)扣环 ③(投环游戏等)套住; (用铅笔等)圈出 ④环剥(树皮); 旋着削(苹果等)的皮 ❷ *vi.* ①成环形 ②(鹰等)盘旋上升; (被猎的狐狸等)兜圈子奔跑 ‖make (或 run) ~s round *sb.* (跑路或做事)比某人快得多; 轻易地大大超过某人: He was *making* ~s *round* the other boys. 他比其他孩子干得快得多。/ ~ upon ~ 层层; be surrounded ~ *upon* ~ 被层层包围 ‖'~bolt *n.* 环端螺栓 / '~bone *n.* (马的)附骨赘 / '~dove *n.* 斑尾林鸽 / ~ fence 圈地的围栅(或围墙) / ~ finger 无名指(尤指左手的) / '~leader *n.* 头目, 魁首 / ~ lock 环锁, 暗码锁 / '~man ['riŋmən] *n.* [英]以赌赛马为业者 / '~master *n.* 马戏团领班; 马戏团导演 / '~neck *n.* 颈上有环纹的鸟(或野兽等) / '~neck(ed) *a.* 颈上有环纹的 / ~ net (捕鱼用)围网 / ~ road [主英]环形道路; 环城公路 / '~side *n.* 比赛场的外围; 能看清表演的地方 *a.* & *ad.* 紧靠着比赛场 / '~streaked *a.* (身上)有环纹的 / '~worm *n.* 【医】金钱癣

ring[2] [riŋ] I (rang [ræŋ], rung [rʌŋ]) ❶ *vi.* ①(钟、铃等)鸣, 响: The bell has *rung* for the class. 上课铃响过了。/ A shot *rang* out from the opposite bank. 对岸传来一声枪声。/ My ears are ~*ing*. 我耳鸣。②按铃; 摇铃; 敲钟: Someone is ~*ing* at the door. 有人在按门铃。/ The patient *rang* for the nurse. 病人按铃叫护士。③回响; 响彻 ④听起来: His words *rang* true. 他的话听上去是真诚的。/ The drama ~s true. 这个戏剧很逼真。❷ *vt.* ①按(铃), 摇(铃); 敲(钟等); 敲(硬币等)以鉴别真伪: ~ a coin 敲硬币检验真假 ②响钟声报(时、丧等): an alarm 敲起警钟 II *n.* ①铃声, 钟声; 洪亮的声音: the ~ of triumphant laughter 响亮的胜利欢笑声 ②按铃; 打电话: I'll give you a ~ this evening. 今天晚上我打电话给你。③（表示某种性质的）声调；味儿，口气 ④（教堂钟声的）一套钟 ‖ ~ **in** ①宣布来临；用勤钟记录个人上班时间；上班：~ the old year out and the new in 送旧岁，迎新年 ②[美俚]（赛马等）暗中掉换；冒名顶替 / ~ **off** 挂断电话；停止讲话 / ~ **out** 宣布离去；用考勤钟记录个人下班时间；下班 / **the bell** 见 bell / ~ **up** ①[英]打电话：~ sb. up 打电话给某人（=[美] call sb. up）②[美]把（款项）打在现金收入记录机上 / *That* ~*s a bell.* 见 bell ‖'~-a-'ding [美俚] *a.* 疯狂刺激的 *n.* 疯狂的刺激性；具有疯狂刺激性的人（或东西）

ringlet ['riŋlit] *n.* 小环；（长）卷发 ‖**ringletted** *a.* 有（长）卷发的；成（长）卷发的

rink [riŋk] I *n.* ①（室内）溜冰场；滑冰场 ②滚球草场；冰球场 ③滚球队；冰球队 II *vi.* （尤指穿有轮的溜冰鞋）溜冰 ‖**er** *n.* 溜冰者

rinse [rins] I ❶ *vt.* ①冲洗；轻洗（发、手等）；漂清（衣服等）②涮，漱（out）：~ a bottle 涮瓶 / ~ out the mouth 漱口 ③漂掉，冲洗掉（out, away）：~ the soap out of the washed clothes 把肥皂从洗过的衣服上漂掉 ④（用水或液体）吞下（食物）（down）❷ *vi.* 漂净：a soap that ~s easily 一种容易漂净的肥皂 II *n.* ①漂清，冲洗：give sth. a ~ 漂清（或冲洗）某物 ②（冲洗或漂洗用的）清水 ③染发液

riot ['raiət] I *n.* ①暴乱，骚动 ②狂欢（声）；狂闹（声）；闹饮，闹宴；放荡 ③[只用单][与不定冠词连用]（色彩等）的丰富；（感情等的）放纵：a ~ of colour 色彩缤纷 ④[口]轰动的演出；极其有趣的人：The film was a ~ when it was shown in Paris. 这部电影在巴黎放映时轰动一时。 II ❶ *vi.* ①闹事，骚乱 ②放纵，沉溺于(in)：~ in drink 狂饮 / ~ in cruelty 狂暴 ❷ *vt.* 挥霍，浪费 ‖**read the Riot Act** 见 act / run ~ ①（猎狗）跟错踪迹 ②乱跑，胡闯；肆无忌惮，无法无天 ③（植物等）茂盛 ‖**er** *n.* ①暴乱者，暴徒 ②放荡的人，纵情享乐的人 喧闹的作乐的人 ‖~ **gun** 短筒防暴枪 / ~ **police** 防暴警察

riotous ['raiətəs] *a.* ①暴乱的，骚动的；煽动暴乱的 ②狂欢的，狂闹的；放纵的，放荡的 ③（色彩等）丰富的：be ~ with colour 色彩缤纷的 ④（植物等）茂盛的

rip¹ [rip] I (ripped; ripping) ❶ *vt.* ①撕，扯，剥；划破：~ open a letter 撕开一封信 / ~ the cover (lining) off 撕掉面子（里子）/ ~ up rice plants 拔稻 / ~ away (或 off) the mask of a hypocrite 剥掉伪君子的画皮 / The tyre was ripped up. 轮胎划破了。/ The dog has its belly ripped up. 狗的肚子被撕裂了。/ Lightning ripped the cloudy night sky. 闪电划破乌云密布的夜空。②劈，锯（木材等）；凿开（岩石等）③拆（衣、屋顶等）④[古]重新翻出（宿怨、往事等）(up) ❷ *vi.* ①撕裂，裂开 ②（车、船等）猛冲，猛冲：Let her rip. 让它猛冲下去。 II *n.* 裂口，裂缝 ‖**let**

things ~ 让它去；听其自然 / ~ *into* 猛攻；抨击 / ~ *off* 偷窃 / ~ *out* 狠狠地发出(诅咒等) / ~ *up the back* 背后攻击，背后说人坏话 ‖~ **cord** 【空】开伞索，气囊拉索 / '~**-off** *n.* 偷窃、骗钱 / ~ **panel** 【空】裂幅 / '~**-'roaring**, '~**-'roarious** *a.* [美]欢闹的 / '~**saw** 粗齿锯 / '~**snorter** *n.* [俚] ①喧闹狂暴的人（或事物，如暴风雨）②突出的人（或物）/ '~**snorting** *a.* ①喧闹狂暴的 ②突出的

rip² [rip] *n.* ①不中用的(老)马；不中用的东西 ②浪子；荒淫的人

rip³ [rip] *n.* 巨澜 ‖~ **current**, ~ **tide** 岸边巨澜的回流，激流

ripe [raip] I *a.* ①熟的；成熟的；时机成熟的，准备好的：~ apples 成熟的苹果 / a ~ field 一片成熟庄稼的田地 / The rice is ~ for harvest. 稻已熟，可以收割了。/ ~ judgement (experience) 成熟的判断（经验）/ a ~ worker-engineer 一个成长了的工人工程师 / The problem is ~ for settlement. 解决这问题的时机已经成熟。/ a plan ~ for execution 准备就绪即可实行的计划 ②（贮存后）适于食用的：~ wine 醇酒 ③成年的；年高的；老练的：a person of ~(r) years 成年人 / of ~ age 成年的，有经验的 / He lived to the ~ age of ninety. 他活到九十高龄。④【医】(疖等)已化脓的；(白内障等)可开刀的 II *vt.* & *vi.* [主诗] =ripen ‖**Soon ~, soon rotten.** [谚]早熟早烂。(或:[喻]早慧早衰。) ‖~**ly** *ad.* / ~**ness** *n.*

ripen ['raipən] ❶ *vt.* ①使熟；使成熟：~ the fruit by means of ethylene 用乙烯催熟水果 ②(经贮存等)使(乳酪、牛肉等)鲜美 ③【医】(疖等)适于开刀 ❷ *vi.* 成熟

ripple¹ ['ripl] I *n.* 麻梳(用来梳除亚麻茎上籽、叶等的粗钢梳) II *vt.* (用麻梳)梳

ripple² ['ripl] I *n.* ①涟漪，细浪；波纹(头发、丝带等的)卷纹 ②小湍流 ③潺潺声，起伏声：a ~ of conversation (laughter) 轻快的谈话（笑）声 ④【物】脉动，波动 II ❶ *vi.* 起细浪；作潺潺声；波动，飘动 ❷ *vt.* 使起细浪(的)；使作潺潺声；使波动，使飘动 ‖~ **mark** (砂、岩等上的)浪痕；【植】波状纹

ripplet ['riplit] *n.* 小涟漪；小波纹

rise [raiz] I (rose [rouz], risen ['rizn]) ❶ *vi.* ①起立；起床；直立：The house rose at (或 to) the dancers. 全场起立向舞蹈演员鼓掌。/ ~ with the lark 早起 / The horse rose on its hind legs. 马用后腿站起。/ The horse rose to a fence. 马跃起准备过栅栏。/ His hair rose on his head. 他觉得毛骨悚然。②升起，上升：The barometer is rising. 气压计的水银柱在上升。/ His voice rose in excitement. 他激动得声音响起来了。/ His anger rose at the remark. 听到那话他就发怒了。③上涨；增长，增多：The river (price) rose. 河水（价格）上涨。/ The demand (funds) rose sharply. 需要（资金）急剧增长。/ Our confidence

~s. 我们的信心增强。/ The wind is *rising*. 在起风了。/ His colour (spirits) *rose*. 他气色 (情绪)好起来了。④高耸,高出;高起,隆起: above the clouds 耸入云霄 / ~ above the ordinary level 超出一般水平 / ~ out of the sea 拔海而出 / The ground ~s gradually. 地势渐渐高起。/ The bread won't ~. 这面包发不起来。/ Blisters ~ on my heel. 我脚跟起泡了。⑤起义;起来反抗;起反感: ~ (up) in arms 武装起义 / ~ in one's strength 坚强地起来反抗 / My gorge ~s at it. 我一看见这东西就恶心。 ⑥地位升高;兴起: ~ in the world 飞黄腾达 / ~ in sb.'s estimation (或 opinion) 受某人看重 ⑦浮起;浮现,现出: Bubbles *rose*. 水泡浮起来了。/ The fish were *rising*. 鱼浮上水面来了。/ An idea ~s before (或 in) the mind. 一个想法浮现心头。⑧发源;起因: The river ~s in the mountains. 河发源于群山中。/ The quarrel *rose* from a mere trifle. 争吵由小事引起。⑨闭会;休会: The assembly will ~ next Friday. 大会将在星期五闭幕。⑩死而复生,复活 ⑪起而应付 (to): ~ to an emergency (a crisis) 起而应付一个紧急事件(一个危机) ❷ *vt.* ①使(鸟)飞起;诱(鱼)浮上水面 ②【海】驶近时使(另一船)渐现在视野中 ③[主方]抬高(价格) ④[俚]饲养;抚养 **II** *n.* ①升起,上升: at ~ of sun (或 day) [书面语]日出之时 / a vertical ~ 垂直上升 ②上涨;增长: a ~ in temperature 温度的升高 / a ~ (=[美] raise) in wages 工资的增加 / marked ~s in the number of livestock 牲畜头数的显著增长 / on the ~ 在上涨;在增长 ③高地,岗;斜坡;(楼梯的)级高 ④(弓形的)矢高 ⑤(地位、权力、价值、音调等的)升高;兴起: a ~ in social position 社会地位的提高 / a ~ in life(或 the world) 飞黄腾达 / the ~ to power 上台;得势 / the ~ and fall of a country 一国的兴亡 ⑤出现;(鱼吞饵时的)浮起;再生,复活: not a sign of a ~ 毫无浮鱼吞饵的迹象(指鱼吞饵) ⑥起源;发生: have (或 take) its ~ 源自 发源于 / ‖*get* (或 *take*) *a ~ out of sb.* 惹得某人恼怒 / *give ~ to* 引起;使发生: Social practice alone *gives ~ to* human knowledge. 只有社会实践能产生人的认识。/ ~ *again* 死而复生 / ~ *to a bait* (或 *the fly*) (鱼)上钩;(人)入圈套,上当

rising ['raiziŋ] **I** *a.* ①上升的;~ the ~ sun 朝阳 / the ~ tone 升调 ②上涨的;增长的: a ~ market 上涨的行情 ③渐高的;向上斜的: a ~ ground 丘 ④勃兴的,正在发展的: the new and ~ forces 新兴的力量 / the ~ generation 年青的一代 **II** *n.* ①起立;起床 ②上升,升起 ③上涨;增长 ④高地;突出部分 ⑤起义,造反;叛乱: the peasant ~s 农民起义 ⑥脓疱;疮;丘疹 ⑦复活,复苏 **III** *prep.* ①[口]将近···(岁): She is ~ fifteen. 她快十五岁了。②[美口]超过···(数);(数)以上: *Rising (of)* 10,000 tons of steel were shipped away. 一万吨以上的钢铁运走了。

risk [risk] **I** *n.* ①危险,风险: There is the ~ of your catching cold. 你可能会伤风。/ do sth. *at the* ~ *of one's life* 冒着生命危险做某事 ②(保险业用语)···险;危险率;保险金(额);保险对象 (包括人和物): fire (war) ~ 火 (兵) 险 / a poor ~ for insurance 风险大的保险户 **II** *vt.* ①冒···的危险;使遭受危险: ~ one's life 冒生命危险 / ~ everything on a single throw 孤注一掷 ②冒险干: ~ the jump (a battle) 冒险跳一下(打一仗) ‖*at all* ~*s* (或 *at any* ~) 无论冒什么危险;无论如何 / *at one's own* (*the owner's, the buyer's*) ~ (损失等)由自己(物主,买主)负责 / *run* (或 *take*) *a* ~ (或 ~*s*) 冒险 ‖~**er** *n.* 冒险者;投机者 / ~**ful** *a.* 危险的 / ~**less** *a.* 无危险的 ‖'~-,**money** *n.* (出纳员的)差少补偿津贴

risky ['riski] *a.* ①危险的;冒险的;爱冒险的,大胆的: a ~ undertaking 冒险事业 ② =*risqué* ‖**riskily** *ad.* ①冒险地 ②近乎淫猥地 / **riskiness** *n.*

rite [rait] *n.* ①仪式,典礼 ②【宗】礼拜式 ③习俗,惯例: the ~s of hospitality 招待客人的礼节

ritual ['ritjuəl] **I** *n.* ① 仪式,典礼; 宗教仪式 ②(宗教)仪式的程序 ③仪式书;[复]仪式的奉行 **II** *a.* (宗教)仪式的,典礼的 ‖~**ism** *n.* 仪式主义;(宗教)仪式研究 / ~**ist** *n.* 精通(或研究)仪式的人;仪式主义者 / ~**ly** *ad.* 举行仪式般地;按照仪式地 ‖~ **murder** 祭神的杀牲

ritualistic [,ritjuə'listik] *a.* 仪式的;仪式主义的;遵守仪式的 ‖~**ally** *ad.*

rival ['raivəl] **I** *n.* ① 竞争者,对手: defeat one's ~ 击败对手 ② 匹敌者; 可与之相比的东西: Plastics have become ~s of many metals. 塑料已经比得上多种金属。/ without a ~ 无可匹敌 **II** *a.* 竞争的: ~ business firms 竞争的商行 **III** (rival(l)ed, rival(l)ing) ❶ *vt.* ①与···竞争 ②与···相匹敌;比得上: This natural silk ~s the best in the world. 这种天然丝可与世界上最好的相匹敌。/ None of us can ~ him in strength. 我们当中没有人力气比他大。❷ *vi.* 竞争 ‖~**ship** *n.* =rivalry

rive [raiv] **I** (过去式 rived,过去分词 riven ['rivən] 或 rived) ❶ *vt.* ①撕开,扯裂;劈开;断;拧去,扭去 (*off, away, from*): ~ *off* a branch 折去树枝 / trees *riven* by lightning 被闪电劈开的树 ②使(精神等)沮丧;使(心)碎 ❷ *vi.* 裂开;撕开;破裂 **II** *n.* [英方]拉;裂缝 ‖~**r** *n.* 劈木工人

river ['rivə] *n.* ①江,河;水道: temper oneself in big ~s and seas 在大江大海中锻炼自己 / a dry ~ 干水道 ②巨流;[复]大量: a ~ of lava 熔岩的巨流 / drink ~s of tea 喝大量茶 ③生与死的界线: cross the ~ (of death) 死掉 ‖*row sb. up Salt River* [美俚] 使某人在政治上失败,使某人落选 / *sell sb. down the* ~ 欺骗某人;出卖某人 / *up the* ~ [美俚]入狱,在狱中 ‖~ **basin** 江河流域 / '~'**bed** *n.* 河床 / '~**boat** *n.* 江河

中行驶的船 / '~head *n.* 河源 / ~ horse【动】
河马 / ~ novel =*roman-fleuve* / '~side *n.* 河
岸 *a.* 河岸上的,河边的: a ~side park 河滨公园

rivet ['rivit] I *n.* 铆钉 II *vt.* ① 铆,铆接,铆牢
② 敲打(螺钉)使成铆钉头(以铆牢) ③ 固定;钉牢:
a ~ed error 根深蒂固的错误 ④ 集中(目光、注
意力);吸引: He ~ed his eyes on the 32-ton
dumper. 他注视着三十二吨自动卸货车。 / The
32-ton dumper ~ed our attention. 三十二吨自
动卸货车吸引了我们的注意力。‖~er *n.* 铆工;
铆钉枪

rivulet ['rivjulit] *n.* 小河,溪流

road [roud] I *n.* ①路,道路;公路; [美]铁路: ~
safety 安全行车 / ~ accidents 车祸,交通事故 /
~ toll 路上交通事故造成的伤亡 ②行车道 ③途
径 ④【常用复】【海】(开敞)锚地 (=~stead) ⑤
[美][the ~] 巡回演出(或比赛等)的路线(或地
点) II *vt.* (狗)闻着嗅迹追 ‖*All ~s lead to
Rome.* [谚]条条大路通罗马。(或: 殊途同归。) /
by ~ 由公路: Send the goods *by ~*, not by
rail. 由公路而不是由铁路运输这批货物。 / *for
the ~* 以示送行: give sb. one (或 a final glass)
for the ~ 斟上最后一杯送某人上路 / *get out
of the* (sb.'s) ~ (给某人)让路;不妨碍(某人) /
hit the ~ [美俚]离开;离去 / *in the* (sb.'s) ~
挡住(某人)的路;妨碍(某人): You are *in* my
~. 我的路给你挡住了。(或: 你妨碍着我。) /
on the ~ 在旅途中(尤指商人、剧团): How long
were you *on the ~*? 你路上化了多少时间? /
royal ~ 捷径,坦途: There's no *royal ~* to
learning. 学无坦途。 / *take the ~* ①出发,动
身 ②走…道路: *take the* socialist ~ 走社会主
义道路 / *take the ~ of* 占先,居…之上 / *take
to the ~* ①出发,动身 ②[古]做强盗 / *the
rule of the ~* 见 rule / *the Silk Road* [史]丝
绸之路 ‖~less *a.* 无路的 / ~ agent [美]拦路
强盗 / '~bed. ①路基,路床;路基(表)面 ②
行车道 / '~block *n.* 路障 *vt.* 在…设置路障 /
'~book *n.* (尤指标有路线、距离的)旅行指南 /
~ hog 妨碍其他车辆行驶的司机 / '~house *n.*
(郊外的)小旅馆,客栈 / ~ man ['roudmən] *n.*
修路工人 / ~ map 汽车司机的行车图 /
mender =~man / ~ metal 铺路碎石,道碴 /
~ roller 压路机 / ~ sense 行车判断能力,安全
行车本领 / ~ show[美] ①巡回演出 ②新片的
特约放映(通常票价较高) / '~side *n.* 路边 *a.*
路边的: ~side inn 路边客栈 / '~stead *n.*
【海】(开敞)锚地 / ~ test ①(对车辆的)试车
②对(车辆)进行试车 / '~-train *n.* 一支车队 /
'~way *n.* ①道路,路面 ②车行道(区别于人行
道);(铁道的)路线 / '~work *n.* (拳击选手等
的)越野长跑训练 / '~worthy *a.* (适于)在道
路上用的;(人)适于旅行的

roam [roum] I ① *vi.* 漫步;漫游,游历 ~ *about*
the world 漫游世界 ② *vt.* 在…漫步;漫游,游历
II *n.* 漫步;漫游,游历 ‖~er *n.* 徘徊者;漫游

者,游历者

roan[1] [roun] *a.* & *n.* 皮毛红棕色夹杂着白(或灰)
色的(马或其他动物);花毛的(马或其他动物)

roan[2] [roun] *n.* (装订书籍用的) 柔软羊皮

roar [rɔː] I ① *vi.* ①(狮、虎等)吼叫;(海、风等)怒
号,呼啸;(雷、炮、马达等)轰鸣: The lion ~ed.
狮吼。 / The waves are ~ing. 波涛在呼啸。 /
The pumping station ~ed into action. 抽水
站隆隆响着开始工作了。 ② 呼喊,大喊大叫;哄
笑;高声歌唱: ~ with rage 咆哮如雷 / ~ with
pain 痛苦地号叫 / You needn't ~. 你不必大声
嚷嚷嘛。 / The audience ~ed at the farce.
闹剧使观众哄堂大笑。 ③ (会场等)喧闹;回响
(*again*) ④(马)喘鸣 ② *vt.* ①呼喊;大声喊出;
高唱: ~ approval of a resolution 大声表示赞成
决议 / ~ out a song 引吭高歌 ②叫喊着使…: ~
oneself hoarse 喊哑喉咙 / ~ sb. down 大声压倒
某人讲话声 ③ 使轰鸣: ~ an engine 使引擎发
出轰鸣声 II *n.* ①吼,啸;怒号,咆哮;轰鸣声;喧
闹声: the ~s of a tiger 虎啸 / the ~ of guns
大炮的轰鸣声 / the ~ of the traffic 往来车辆的
喧闹声 ② 呼叫;大笑声: ~s of laughter 大笑
声 / ~s of anger 怒骂声 / set the table (room)
in a ~ 引起全桌(哄堂)大笑 ‖~er ['rɔːrə] *n.*
①怒吼者;呼号者 ②患喘鸣症的马

roast [roust] I ① *vt.* ①烤,炙;烘;【冶】焙烧: ~
meat 烤肉 / ~ coffee beans 烘制咖啡豆 / You've
made a fire fit to ~ an ox. 你生的火很旺,足以
烤一头牛了。②(烤得)使灼热(或烫): ~ oneself
(one's hands) at the fire 烤火(烘手)取暖 / The
sun no longer ~ed the valley at dusk. 黄昏时
太阳不再晒得山谷发烫了。③ 捉弄,嘲笑;苛责
② *vi.* ①烤;炙;烘;焙: The meat is ~ing in the
oven. 肉在炉子里烤着。②(烤得)变热(或烫):
I'm simply ~ing. 我简直热死了。 / lie in the
sun and ~ 躺在太阳下取暖 II *n.* ①烤;炙;烘;
焙 ②烤肉,炙肉 ③ 烤食聚餐会 ④捉弄,嘲笑;
苛责 III *a.* 烤过的: ~ ducks 烤鸭 ‖*rule the
~* 当家,作主,处于支配地位 ‖~er *n.* ①烤(或烘)
的人 ②烤(或烘)的器具(如炉子等);【冶】焙烧炉
③适于烤的食物(如小猪、家禽等) ‖~ing jack
(烤肉用的)铁叉转动器

rob [rob] (robbed; robbing) ① *vt.* ①抢劫,劫取;
盗取: ~ a man of his money 抢人钱财 / ~ an
orchard 劫窃果园(指强摘园中的果子) ② 非法
剥夺;使丧失: ~ sb. *of* his rights 非法剥夺某人
的权利 / The shock robbed him *of* speech. 他震
惊得说不出话来。② *vi.* 抢劫,劫掠;盗窃

robber ['robə] *n.* 强盗,盗贼 ‖~ baron (封建
时代)对路过自己领地的旅客进行抢劫的贵族 /
[美]十九世纪末靠残酷剥削致富的美国资本家

robbery ['robəri] *n.* ①抢劫,劫掠;盗取;抢劫案:
two robberies 两起抢劫案 ②【律】强盗罪

robe [roub] I *n.* ① 长袍,罩袍;(婴孩穿的)罩衣;
[美] 晨衣,(化妆时穿的)长衣;浴衣 ②【常用复】
礼服;官服;制服;法衣 ③(毛皮、织物等制的)披
肩,覆盖物;车毯: a lap ~ 盖膝的毯子 II *v.* &

vi. (给…)穿上长袍(或罩袍等);(给…)披上法衣 ∥***gentlemen of the ~*** 律师们 / ***the long ~*** 法官服;教士服

robin ['rɔbin] ***n.*** ① 欧鸲 ② 知更鸟 ∥**Robin Goodfellow** (英国民间故事中)顽皮而善良的小精灵 / ~ **snow** [美]春天的小雪

robot ['rɔubɔt] ***n.*** ①机器人;自动机;自动仪器;遥控机械装置;自动控制导弹,飞弹;自动交通信号:a ~ **bomb** 自动操纵的飞弹 / a ~ **bomber** 遥控轰炸机,无人驾驶轰炸机 ②机器般工作的人

robust [rə'bʌst, rou'bʌst] ***a.*** ① 强健的,茁壮的,健全的:a man of ~ health 身体强健的人 / plants 茁壮的植物 / a ~ intellect 健全的智力 / a ~ appetite 旺盛的食欲 / the ~ vitality of new things 新生事物的强大生命力 ②(运动等)需要很强体力的: ~ work 强体力劳动 ③ 坚强的,坚定的;直爽的,粗犷的,粗野的: ~ stories 粗野的故事 ⑤ 浓的: ~ coffee 浓咖啡 / splendidly ~ soups 美味浓汤 ∥~**ly** ***ad.*** / ~**ness** ***n.***

rock[1] [rɔk] **I** ❶ ***vt.*** ①摇,轻摇;[喻]抚慰: ~ a cradle 摇动摇篮 / ~ a baby to (或 into) sleep 摇婴儿入睡 / be ~ed into a false sense of security 被抚慰得误以为相当安全 ②使动摇,使摇晃;使震动;使震惊: The waves ~ed the boat. 浪涛使船摇晃。 / sb.'s beliefs 动摇某人的信念 / Stormy applause ~ed the hall. 暴风雨般的掌声震动了大厅。 / The news ~ed the household with surprise. 这消息使全家震惊。 ③【矿】用洗矿箱摇洗(矿砂) ④(制铜版时)弄毛(版面) ❷ ***vi.*** 摇,摆动;震动: sit ~ing in one's chair 坐在椅子里摇着 / The speedometer was ~ing between 60 and 65. 速度表在60与65之间摆动着。 / The tower ~ed under the impact of the hurricane. 塔在飓风冲击下摇动。 / with laughter 笑得浑身抖动 **II** ***n.*** ①摇动;摇摆 ②摇摆舞: a ~ band 摇摆舞乐队 / [美俚]美国颓废派男青年(一般穿彩色运动衫、留长发、跳摇摆舞) ∥~ **the boat** 见 **boat** ∥~ **and roll, ~ 'n' roll** [,rɔkn'roul] 摇摆舞(曲) / '~**shaft** ***n.*** 摇(臂)轴

rock[2] [rɔk] ***n.*** ① 岩,岩石;磐石;礁石: as firm as (a) ~ 坚如磐石 / igneous (intrusive) ~ 【地】火成(侵入)岩 ②石头,石块: lift a ~ only to drop it on one's own toes 搬起石头打自己的脚 / throw ~s at sb. 向某人掷石块 ③柱石;基石;靠山 ④[常用复]暗礁;灾难,危险: run (或 strike) against (或 upon) the ~s 触礁 / see ~s ahead 看到有触礁危险;看到前途有危险 ⑤[美俚]一块一块钱,[复]钱;[俚]钻石,宝石 ⑥一种硬糖: almond ~s 杏仁硬糖 ⑦[the R-] 直布罗陀(Gibraltar) 的别名 ⑧ = ~ **dove** = ~**fish** ∥**be built** (或 **founded**) **on the** ~ 建立在磐石上;基础坚固 / **on the** ~s ① 触礁;毁坏,遭难: His plan has landed itself *on the* ~s. 他的计划遭到失败。 ② 手头拮据;破产 ③(酒)倒在小方块冰上的 / **split**

on a ~ 遭遇意外的灾难(或危险);趋于灭亡 / **the Rock of Ages** 【宗】耶稣基督 ∥~ **bottom** 底;(物价等)的最低点: at ~ *bottom* 根本上 / '~-'**bottom** ***a.*** 最低的: ~*bottom* prices 最低价格 / '~-**bound** ***a.*** 被岩石包围的;多岩的 / ~ **cake** 一种表面粗硬的糕点 / ~ **candy** 冰糖 / ~ **cork** 淡石棉 / ~ **crystal** 水晶 / ~ **dove** 野鸽,原鸽(也称 blue ~) / ~ **drill** 钻石机 / **Rock English** 杂有直布罗陀方言的英语 / **Rock fever** 直布罗陀流行的伤寒病 / '~-**firm** ***a.*** 坚如磐石的,坚定不移的,屹立不动的 / '~**fish** ***n.*** 生活在海底岩石间的鱼 / ~ **garden** 种植岩生植物的岩石花园;有假山的花园 / ~ **goat** 原山羊 / '~-**hewn** ***a.*** 岩石凿成的 / ~ **hound** [美口]采集奇石成癖的人 / ~ **leather** 一种石棉 / ~ **oil** 石油 / ~ **pigeon** = dove / ~ **plant** 岩生植物 / '~-**ribbed** ***a.*** ①岩石的;多岩脊的: ~*ribbed* coasts 多岩脊的海岸 ②坚定不移的: a ~*ribbed* policy 坚定不移的政策 / ~ **salmon** 角鲨(商品名) / ~ **salt** 岩盐,石盐 / **Rock scorpion** 直布罗陀出生的人(绰号) / ~ **tar** 石焦油 / ~ **wool** 石棉,石毛 / '~**work** ***n.*** ①假山 ②天然岩石群 ③攀岩技术

rock[3] [rɔk] ***n.*** 手工纺纱杆,老式锭子

rocket[1] ['rɔkit] **I** ***n.*** ①火箭;火箭发动机: a space ~ 宇宙火箭 / launch a manned (carrier) ~ 发射载人(运载)火箭 / a step (three-stage) ~ 多级(三级)火箭 / a solid propellant ~ 固体燃料火箭 / a ~ booster 火箭助推器 ②火箭式投射器;火箭弹; 由火箭推进的飞船(或导弹等): ~ apparatus【海】救生索投射器 ③一种烟火 ④[英俚]斥责 **II** ❶ ***vt.*** ① 用火箭运载 ② 用火箭轰击 ❷ ***vi.*** ①飞速上升;急速高飞;(马等)猛跃 ②飞驰 ③ 乘火箭旅行 ∥~ **base** 火箭(试验)基地 / ~ **bomb** 火箭助推炸弹,火箭弹 / ~ **jet** ① 火箭喷管 ②火箭喷(气)流 / ~ **launcher** 火箭发射装置;火箭筒 / ~ **motor** 火箭发动机 / ~ **plane** 火箭飞机;发射火箭的飞机 / '~-**pro-'pelled** ***a.*** 用火箭推进的: a ~-*propelled* missile 火箭推进的导弹 / a ~-*propelled* vehicle 火箭弹 / ~ **propulsion** 火箭推进 / ~ **range** 火箭靶场;火箭试验区 / ~ **ship** 火箭宇宙飞船 / ~ **sonde** 火箭测候器 / ~ **target** 火箭推进式靶机

rocket[2] ['rɔkit] ***n.*** 【植】芝麻菜;紫花南芥

rod [rɔd] ***n.*** ①(树的)枝条;柳条 ②杆,竿,棒(如钓竿、标尺、牧羊杖、避雷针等);测杆;【微】杆状体,杆菌;【解】视网膜杆: a piston ~ 活塞杆 / a calculating ~ 计算尺 ③(拷打用的)荆条,棍棒; [the ~] 拷打,鞭笞;责,节(标志职权的棍杖);权势;暴政 ⑤[度量单位]杆(=5¼码);平方杆(=30¼平方码) ⑥[美俚](左轮)手枪 ⑦钓鱼者 ⑧(基督教《圣经》用语)家系,世系;种族 ⑨[美俚]把旧汽车拆卸减重而成的汽车(=hot ~) ∥**have a** ~ **in pickle for sb.** 伺机惩罚某人 / **kiss the** ~ 甘心受罚 / **make** (或 **prepare**) **a** ~ **for one's own back** 自讨苦吃;自找麻烦 /

ride (或 *hit*) *the* ~*s* (躲在车厢下面)不买票乘车 / *Spare the* ~ *and spoil the child.* [谚]孩子不打不成器。‖~ **cell** 杆细胞 / ~ **man** ['rɔd-mən] *n.* 钓鱼人;【测】司尺员,立尺员,标杆员

rode [roud] ride 的过去式

rodent ['roudənt] **I** *a.* ①咬的,嚼的 ②【动】啮齿目的 ③【医】侵蚀性的 **II** *n.* 啮齿动物(如兔、鼠等) ‖~**icide** [rou'dentisaid] *n.* 杀鼠剂

rodeo [rou'deiou] *n.* ①(美国西部)驱集牛马;(集中牛马的)圈地 ②(美国西部牧场牧人等的)竞技表演 ③(摩托车驾驶术等的)花式表演

roe [rou] *n.* 【动】①(西亚、欧洲产)牝麅鹿 ②鱼(或甲壳动物等的)卵 ③(木材锯开后显出的)黑斑纹 ‖'~**buck** ([复]~buck(s)) *n.* (雄)麅 / ~ **deer** 麅

rogue [roug] **I** *n.* ①流氓,无赖;[古]流浪汉 ②[谑]淘气鬼,爱捉弄人者 ③(赛马、打猎时)偷懒的马;凶猛而离群的野兽(尤指象,=~ elephant) ④【农】劣种,杂种 **II** *vi.* ①游手好闲;耍无赖 ②【农】除去劣种(或杂种) **②** *vt.* ①欺诈 ②【农】除去(劣种、杂种);除去(地)里的劣种(或杂种) **III** *a.* (野兽)凶猛的 ‖*a* ~'*s march* 见 **march**[1] / *the* ~*s' gallery* 见 gallery

roguery ['rougəri] *n.* ① 流氓行为,无赖行为;诈骗 ② 淘气,[复]恶作剧;捣蛋

roguish ['rougiʃ] *a.* ① 流氓的,无赖的;不老实的 ② 淘气的,调皮的,恶作剧的:as ~ as a kitten 像小猫一样调皮 ‖~**ly** *ad.* / ~**ness** *n.*

roister ['roistə] *vi.* ①大摇大摆,摆架子 ②喧闹;闹饮 ‖~**er** ['roistərə] *n.* 喧闹者;闹饮者

role, rôle [roul] *n.* ① 角色: play the leading ~ in a film 在一部电影中扮演主角 ②作用;任务: play an important ~ in developing agriculture 在发展农业中起重要作用

roll [roul] **I ❶** *vi.* ① 滚动;打滚: Stones ~ed down the hillside. 石块沿山坡滚下。/ The kids ~ed around on the lawn. 孩子们在草坪上打滚。/ send sb. ~ing 使某人在地上翻滚 ②滚动而动: The wheel of history keeps ~ing on. 历史的车轮不断滚滚向前。/ waves ~ing in 滚滚而来的波涛 / Smoke ~ed up. 烟囱袅上升。③行驶,乘车行驶;飘流;流浪 ④ 左右摇晃,摇摆;蹒跚地走: The ship ~ed and heaved (or pitched). 船摇晃颠簸。/ The drunkard ~ed up to Tom. 醉汉向汤姆蹒跚走去。⑤ 流逝: The years ~ed on (or by). 岁月流逝。⑥ (地势)起伏;伸展: The golden wheat fields ~ed to the south. 金黄色的麦田向南伸展。⑦发出隆隆声;咆鸣: The thunder ~ed in the distance. 远处雷声隆隆。/ The drums ~ed. 鼓声震天。⑧(眼睛等)转动;循环运行: Planets ~ on (or in) their courses. 行星在轨道上运行。⑨卷,裹;绕;卷缩: The string ~ed into a ball. 线绕成一团。/ The hedgehog ~s up when attacked. 刺猬遭到袭击就卷缩起来。⑩辗,轧;擀;滚动起来: The steel ~ed out in plates. 钢轧成了钢板。/ This dough

~*s* well. 这面团很好擀。⑪玩滚球 ⑫(车辆等)出发;开始动作(或行动): The fire engines ~ed while the alarm bell was still ringing. 火警钟还在响,救火车就出发了。/ The cameras were ready to ~. (电影等)拍摄即将开始。⑬ 发展,进展: get business ~ing at a high speed 使营业高速发展 / The strike ~ed into its tenth month. 罢工进入了第十个月。**❷** *vt.* ①使滚动;滚成: ~ logs into a river 把大木头滚入河中 / ~ sb. over 把某人打翻在地 ②使滚滚而动 ③(车)行驶(路程);用车载运: ~ a handcart 推手车 / I believe the hardest miles were ~ed. 我想最难走的一段路已驶过了。/ ~ a baby in a pram 用婴儿车推婴孩 ④ 使摇摆(前进): The waves ~ed the ship along. 波浪使船摇曳前进。/ He ~ed himself from side to side. 他左右摇晃。⑤擂(鼓);发(卷舌音或颤音);在(弦)上弹琵音 ⑥使(眼睛等)转动: ~ one's eyes on sb. 眼睛对着某人骨碌碌转 ⑦卷,裹;绕;搓;铺: ~ a cigarette 卷纸烟 / ~ one's own [俚]自己卷纸烟 / ~ up one's sleeves 卷起袖子 / ~ up one's umbrella 收起伞 / [喻]准备大干 / ~ oneself (up) in a blanket 用毯子裹身 / ~ the wool into a ball 把绒线绕成团 / The child was ~ing a marble between his palms. 孩子手中搓着一粒弹子。/ ~ one's bed on the floor 打地铺 / ~ one's stockings on 穿上长统袜 ⑧辗,轧;擀;烫平;烫面 / ~ steel rails 轧钢轨 / ~ (out) dough 擀面团 / ~ a road surface 滚平路面 ⑨掷(骰子)⑩把油墨滚在…上 ⑪开动(摄影机等): ~ a movie camera 开拍电影 / "Quiet—and ~ 'em!" "静——开拍!" ⑫[俚]盗窃(睡着、喝醉的人等)口袋里的东西 **II** *n.* ①(一卷)卷轴;卷状物;面包卷,卷饼;烟卷;(装物用)卷包,卷套;做成卷状的头发: a steamed ~ 花卷 / a sausage (jelly) ~ 香肠(糖酱)卷饼 / a toilet-~ 卫生卷纸 / ~ of film 一卷胶片 / a ~ of cloth 一匹布 / He has ~ of fat on him. 他胖得圆滚滚的。②一卷钞票;[美俚]手头的钱;目录;公文;案卷,档案: the ~ of honour 阵亡将士名册 / an honour ~ 光荣榜 / a muster ~ 花名册 / remove sb.'s name from the ~s 除某人的名 / ~s of parliament 国会档案 / the Master of the *Rolls* (英国上诉法院)保管案卷的法官 ④(服装的)翻边: a ~-collar 大翻领 ③滚筒机,压路机;【印】(封面)压型机;(打字机等的)滚筒【建】(柱头的)旋涡饰: a lowering ~ (造纸用)落刀 ⑥滚动;打滚;(杂技、舞蹈等的)翻滚,翻筋斗;【空】滚: a ~-top desk 有活动顶板的书桌 / The kitten was enjoying a ~ on the floor. 小猫在地板上尽情打滚。/ a snap ~ 【军】快滚 / take-off ~ 起飞滑跑 ⑦(波浪的)翻滚;(话音的)滔滔不绝;(船等的)摇晃: walk with a nautical ~ 象水手般摇晃着行走 ⑧隆隆声,袅响声;(鼓)急敲声: the ~ of cannon 炮声隆隆 ⑩【音】(和弦)琶音;(金丝雀等的)啭鸣 ⑪(地形)起伏;隆起 ‖*be* ~*ing in* 在…中打滚;富于;沉溺于: *be* ~*ing in* wealth

豪富 / *be* ~*ing in* luxury 极其奢华 / *call the* ~ 点名 / ~ *around* ① (时间) 流逝: Five months have ~*ed around* since then. 从那时到现在五个月已经过去了。②(季节等)重临,循环: Another Sunday ~*ed around*. 又是星期日了。/ ~ *back* ① (政府) 把(价格)压低到标准(或原来)水平 ② 使退却,击退: ~ *in* ① 滚滚而来 ② 纷至沓来,蜂拥而来: Good news about production is ~*ing in* from all parts of our country. 生产捷报从全国各地频频传来。③ [美俚] 就寝 (=go to bed) / ~ *into* ① (使)滚进… ② (使)卷成: The kitten ~*ed* itself *into* a ball. 小猫把身体蜷曲成一团。③ 使合为(一体): poet and historian ~*ed into* one 既是诗人又是历史学家 / ~ *one's hoop* 见 **hoop**[1] / ~ *out* ① 辗平;铺开: ~ *out* the red carpet for sb. 展开红地毯隆重地欢迎某人 ② 洪亮地讲出(或唱出): ~ *out* verses 朗诵诗句 ③ [美俚] 起床 ④ 动身,离开 / ~ *the bones* 见 **bone** / ~ *up* ① (烟雾) 袅袅上升 ② 卷起;裹起;卷缩: ~ *up* a map 卷起地图 ③ (乘车)到达: They ~*ed up* to the hotel. 他们乘车到达旅馆。④ [口]到场;出现: A few latecomers ~*ed up*. 几个迟到者来了。⑤ 渐次增加;积累成: ~ *up* a huge fund 积累大笔资金 / ~ *up* a large majority 逐渐取得大多数的支持 ⑥【军】卷击(侧翼) / *strike off the* ~*s* 把(律师等)除名,开除 ‖ ~**back** *n.* ① (政府将价格)压低到标准(或原来)水平 ② 击退 / ~ **booster** *n.* 火箭绕纵轴回转的)助推器,(绕纵轴)回转加速器 / ~ **call** 点名;点名号(或时间) / ~ **film** (摄影用的)胶卷 / ~**man** ['roulmən] *n.* 滚轧机操纵者 / '~**-out** *n.* (飞机)初次公开展出 / '~**past** *n.* (重兵器)分列行进 / '~**way** *n.* 滚木坡;准备运走的原木堆

rolled [rould] *a.* 辗压的;轧制的,辊轧的: ~ steel 辊轧钢,钢材 / ~ gold 金箔

roller ['roulə] *n.* ① 打滚的人;滚动的东西 ② 滚柱;滚筒;辊;辗子;滚轴;【印】油墨辊: a garden-~ 辗草坪机 / a ~ conveyer 滚轴运输机 ③ 滚路机,压路机;滚轧机 ④ 绷带卷;卷轴 ⑤ 巨浪 ⑥ 翻头鸽;(德国种的)金丝雀 ‖ ~ **bandage** 卷绷带卷 / ~ **bearing** 滚柱轴承 / ~ **coaster** (公园等中供游乐用的)滑行铁道 / ~ **skate** 四轮滑冰鞋 / '~**-,skate** *vi.* 穿四轮滑冰鞋滑冰 / ~ **towel** (两头缝结、套在轴上用的)环状毛巾

roller bearing

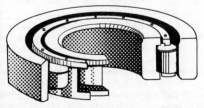

rollick ['rɔlik] *vi. & n.* 嬉戏;欢闹 ‖ ~**ing** *a.*

rolling ['roulin] I *a.* ① 滚的;可滚动的 ② 周而复始的: the ~ seasons 循环的季节 ③ (眼睛等)转动的 ④ (衣领等)翻转的 ⑤ 摇摆的,摇晃的: a ~ walk (或 gait) 摇摆的步态 ⑥ 滚滚的: ~ waves 滚滚的波涛 / ~ smoke 滚滚浓烟 ⑦(雷声等)隆隆的;(金丝雀等)啭鸣的 ⑧ (地形)起伏的,伸展的: a ~ prairie 绵延起伏的草原 II *n.* ①滚动;打滚,翻滚 ②隆隆声;啭鸣声 ‖*A* ~ *stone gathers no moss.* 见 **stone** / ~ **barrage** 【军】徐进弹幕射击 / ~ **bridge** 滚轮活动桥 / ~ **hitch**【海】轮结(一种绳结) / ~ **hospital** 随军医院 / ~ **kitchen** 随军炊事车 / ~ **mill** 轧钢厂;轧钢机;滚轧机 / ~ **pin** 擀面杖 / ~ **press** 压平压力机;滚动印刷机 / ~ **stock** (铁路或汽车公司的)全部车辆 / ~ **stone** 居无定居的人;见异思迁的人 / [the Rolling Stones] 滚石乐队(英国继甲壳虫乐队 (the Beatles) 后风靡一时的摇摆舞乐队) / ~ **strike** 持续的罢工

Roman ['roumən] I *n.* ①古罗马人,罗马人; [蔑] 罗马天主教徒; [复] 古罗马基督教徒: *Epistle to the* ~*s* (基督教《圣经·新约》中的)《罗马书》② [常作 r-] 【印】罗马字,罗马字体,正体字; 罗马体铅字(略作 rom.): set this word in *roman* 把这字排成正体字 ③罗马人讲的意大利语 II *a.* ① (古)罗马的;(古)罗马人的;拉丁的 ② [常作 r-] 罗马字(体)的,正体的; 罗马数字的 ③ 罗马天主教的;罗马教廷的: the ~ rite 天主教仪式 ‖*the* ~ *alphabet* 罗马字母,拉丁字母 / a ~ *arch* 半圆拱 / a ~ *balance* (或 *beam, steelyard*) (普通的)秤,提秤 / *the* ~ *calendar* 罗马历 / a ~ *candle* 罗马焰火筒 / *the* ~ *Catholic Church* 罗马天主教会 / ~ *cement* 罗马水泥,天然水泥 / ~ *Curia* 罗马教廷 / *the* ~ *Empire* 古罗马帝国 / ~ *fever* (旧时)罗马流行的疟疾 / ~ *law* 罗马法 / ~ *letters* 罗马体铅字 / ~ *nose* 鹰鼻;鹰钩鼻,正体字 / ~ *numerals* 罗马数字(如 I, II, V 等) / *the* ~ *order* 罗马柱型,混成柱型 / a ~ *road* 古罗马道路的遗迹 / *the* ~ *school* 拉斐尔 (Raphael) 画派(十七世纪流行于罗马) / a ~ *snail* 罗马蜗牛(欧洲产的一种食用蜗牛) / *the* ~ *type* =~ *letters* / ~ *vitriol* 罗马矾(即硫酸铜)

romance [rə'mæns, rou'mæns] I *n.* ① (中世纪)骑士故事,罗曼司,传奇;(虚构的)冒险(或恋爱)故事 ② 传奇文学;浪漫文学 ③ 传奇气氛;浪漫倾向;夸大的描述;生动的虚构 ④风流韵事,浪漫事迹;离奇的遭遇;虚幻的事物 ⑤【音】浪漫曲(指有伴奏的抒情独唱曲,或旋律性的器乐曲) II ❶ *vi.* ① 写传奇;讲传奇故事 ② 渲染,夸大;虚构,幻想 ③ [口] 谈情说爱,追求 ❷ *vt.* [口] 信口开河的人 / **romancist** *n.* 传奇作家

romantic [rə'mæntik, rou'mæntik] I *a.* ① 浪漫的;风流的,热烈的(尤指爱情) ②传奇(式)的;富于浪漫色彩的: ~ tales (adventures) 传奇式的故事(冒险) / ~ scenes 富于浪漫色彩的情景(或

景色) ③耽于幻想的; 不切实际的; 虚构的; 荒诞的; 夸大的: a ~ scheme 不现实的计划 / a ~ report 夸大的报道 ④[常作 R-](文艺等)浪漫主义的, 浪漫派的: the Romantic Movement 浪漫主义运动 / the ~ poets 浪漫派诗人 II n. ①浪漫的人 ②[常作 R-]浪漫主义作家(或艺术家等) ③[复]浪漫思想(或言行等) ‖~ally ad. / ~ism [rə'mæntisizəm] n. ① [常作 R-]浪漫主义(运动); 浪漫(精神或倾向等) ~ism 革命浪漫主义 ②浪漫精神(或倾向等) / ~ist [rə'mæntisist] n. [常作 R-] 浪漫主义作家(或艺术家等) / ~ize [rə'mæntisaiz] vt. 使浪漫化; 使幻想化 vi. ① 有浪漫主义思想; 幻想化 ②以浪漫主义手法描述人物(或细节等)

romp [rɔmp] I n. ①顽皮孩子(尤指女孩) ②蹦跳嬉戏; 欢闹; 顽皮的游戏 ③(在赛马、竞赛等中)轻松取胜的步法(或速率): win the political race in a ~ 在政治竞争中轻易取胜 II vi. ①(儿童等)蹦来跳去, 嬉闹玩耍; 蹦蹦跳跳地走; 愉快活跃地行进 ②[俚] 轻易地取胜, 迅速地成功: ~ through one's examinations 轻而易举地通过考试 ‖~ home (或 in) 轻易取胜 / ~er n. ①嬉耍的人 ②[常用复]儿童宽松的连裤外衣

roof [ru:f] I n. ① 屋顶; 车顶; [喻]住屋, 家: a flat (gable) ~ 平(人字)屋顶 ② 顶, 顶部: the ~ of heaven 天穹 / the ~ of the world 世界屋脊 / the ~ of the mouth 上颚 ③【矿】顶板 ④(飞机)机身上部的包皮 ⑤担任空中掩护的飞机 ⑥[俗]【空】绝对上升限度 II vt. ①给…盖上屋顶; 做…的屋面 ②遮蔽; 庇护 ‖hit the ~ [美口]勃然大怒 / raise the ~ [俚]①喧闹, (在屋内)吵翻天 ②大声抱怨 / under sb.'s ~ 住在某人家作客 ‖~er n. ① 盖(或修)屋顶的人 ② 盖屋顶的木料; 低级木板 ③ [英口](客人离开后所写感谢款待的)感谢信 / ~less a. 无屋顶的; 无住屋的, 无家可归的 ‖~ garden 屋顶花园 / ~,spotter n. [英](由非军人担任的)屋顶对空了望员 / ~top n. 平顶房的屋顶 / '~tree n. 栋梁; 屋脊梁

rook¹ [ruk] n. (国际象棋的)车

rook² [ruk] I n. ①【动】秃鼻乌鸦, 白嘴鸦 ②(以赌博营生的)赌棍, 骗子 II vt. (用赌博)骗(某人)钱, 诈取; 敲诈(顾客): get ~ed 受骗 ‖~ pie 用小白嘴鸦肉做的馅儿饼 / ~ rifle 打白嘴鸦的小口径枪

room [rum, ru:m] I n. ① 房间, 室; [复]一套房间, 寓所: He lives at Room 124. 他住在 124 室。/ Come and see me in my ~s this evening. 今晚到我家来找我。/ take ~s in the suburbs 住在郊外(的寓所) ② 地位, 空间: This new-type machine takes up little ~. 这台新型机器占地很少。/ There is ~ for more cargo on the truck. 卡车上还有些地位可装货。/ There's only standing ~ in the bus. 公共汽车上只有站的地位了。③ 余地; 机会: There is (much) ~ for improvement in our work. 我们的工作有(大有)改进的

余地。④全室的人: The whole ~ was silent. 房间里鸦雀无声。/ set the ~ in a roar 引起哄堂大笑 II ❶ vi. 住宿, 寄宿, 居住 ❷ vt. 留…住宿 ‖in sb.'s ~ (或 in the ~ of sb.) 处于某人的地位; 作为对某人的接替 / make ~ for sb. (sth.) 让出空地方给某人(某物) / no ~ to turn in (或 no ~ to swing a cat) 没有活动的余地, 地方狭窄 / ~ and board (供)膳宿处 / the parcels ~ [美]衣帽间 / would rather have sb.'s ~ than sb.'s company 希望某人走开 ‖~er n. [美]房客; 寄宿者 / ~ful n. ① 满房间: a ~ful of people 一屋子的人 ② 全室的人(或物) ‖~ clerk 为旅客登记房间的旅馆职员 / ~ing house [美]供寄宿的房屋; 可出租单个房间的公寓 / '~mate n. 住在同室的人 / ~ service 送酒菜到房间的旅馆服务(部)

roomed [ru:md] a. [用以构成复合词]有…房间的: a four-~ apartment 有四个房间的一套公寓房间

roomy ['ru:mi] I a. 宽敞的; 宽大的: a ~ hall 宽敞的大厅 / a ~ raincoat 宽大的雨衣 II n. =roomie ‖**roomily** ad. / **roominess** n.

roost [ru:st] I n. ①栖木; 栖息处; 鸡棚 ②群栖的家禽 ③[口]憩息处; 卧室; 床 II ❶ vi. 栖息, 进窝 ②憩息, 过夜 ❷ vt. 为…设置栖息处; 送去栖息 ‖at ~ 栖于枝上; 憩息着; 睡着 / come home to ~ 得到恶报: Curses (,like chickens,) come home to ~. [谚]咒人反害己。/ go to ~ [口]去卧室休息; 就寝 / rule the ~ 当家, 作主; 称雄

rooster ['ru:stə] n. ①公鸡; 雄鸟 ②[美]狂妄自负的人

root¹ [ru:t] I n. ①根; 根茎, 地下茎; 块根; [复]块根植物: the ~ of a tree 树根 / the ~ of a tooth (a hair, the tongue) 牙(发, 舌)根 / the ~s of a mountain 山麓 / ~ hair【植】根毛 ②根子; 根本, 根基; 本质: the ~ of one's life 命根子 / He has the ~ of industry in him. 他有勤劳的品质。/ be identical at ~ 在根本上是一致的 / the ~ cause 根本原因 ③根源, 来源: get at (或 to) the ~s of things 追究事物的真相; 寻根究底 ④祖先; (基督教《圣经》用语)子孙 ⑤【数】根(数): square (或 second) ~ 平方根 / cube (或 third) ~ 立方根 ⑥【语】词根; 根词 ⑦【音】(和弦的)基础音 II ❶ vt. ①使生根; 使扎根; 使固定: ~ a cutting in the earth 插枝植树 / Fear ~ed him to the ground. 他吓得呆若木鸡。②根除, 肃清 (up, out) ❷ vi. ①生根; 固定 ②根源在于, 来源于 (in) ‖lay the ax(e) to the ~ (或 ax(e).) / pull (或 pluck) up by the ~s 连根拔起; 根除 / ~ and branch 彻底地, 全部地 / strike at the ~ of 打击…的根基; 摧毁 / take (或 strike) ~ 生根; 扎根 ‖~less a. 无根的; 无根基的; 不生根的: ~less nomads 不定居的游牧人 / ~let ['ru:tlit] n. 小根, 枝根 ‖~ borer 钻进植物根部的虫 / ~ cellar 储藏

块根植物(或蔬菜)的窖 / ～ **climber** 根攀(缘)
植物 / ～ **crop** 块根植物, 根可供食用的植物 /
～ **rot** 【植】根腐病 / **'～stock** *n.* ①【植】根茎
②根源, 来源

root² [ru:t] ❶ *vi.* ①(猪等)用鼻拱土: hogs ～*ing*
for food 用鼻拱土觅食的猪 ②翻, 搜, 寻找: ～
about among piles of papers 在文件堆里翻来翻
去寻找 ③[美口](为生计等)努力工作, 苦干 ❷
vt. ①(猪等)用鼻拱, 用鼻拱掘翻出 (*out*) ②搜
出; 发现 (*out*) ‖～**er** *n.* (筑路用)翻土机 ‖**~-**
'hog-or-'die *n.* [美俚] ①苦干则全胜, 不然就
大败 ②不是全力支持, 就是彻底拒绝

root³ [ru:t] *vi.* [美俚] ①(为比赛者等)鼓气, 捧
场; 欢呼, 喝采 ②赞助, 支持(*for*) ‖～**er** *n.* 啦啦
队员; 热情的支持者

rope [roup] **I** *n.* ①绳, 索; [the ～s] (拳击场等四
周的)栏索: tie sth. with (a) ～ 用绳子捆某物
②[the ～] 绞索; 绞刑 ③一串(东西): a ～ of
onions (pearls) 一串洋葱(珠子) ④(啤酒等饮料
中产生的)丝状粘质 ⑤[美俚]雪茄烟 ⑥[美]套
(马)索 ⑦[the ～s] 内情; 规则, 做法 **II** ～ *vt.*
①捆, 扎, 缚, 绑; 用绳系住, 用绳拖: ～ a box 用
绳捆住箱子 / The mountain climbers were ～*d*
together. 爬山的人用绳子相互系在一起。②用
绳围起(或隔开) (*in*, *off*, *out*): ～ *off* the streets
near the fire 把火区附近的街道用绳子拦开 /
Part of the ground was ～*d in.* 部分场地用绳子
圈了起来。③[英](赛马时为了故意输)勒(马)慢
跑 ④[美]用套索套捉(牛马等) ❷ *vi.* ①拧成绳
(状) ②(啤酒等)产生丝状粘质: The candy is
cooked until it ～*s*. 糖煮到成丝状粘质。③(爬
山者)系上绳子串连起来 ④ [英](赛马时为了故
意输)勒马慢跑; (运动员为了故意输掉)不尽全力
‖ a ～ of sand ①用沙结的绳; 不牢固的结合; 不
坚固的事物 ②无结果的事; 无益的事 / a ～'s
end 见 end / at the end of one's ～ 见 end /
be on the ～ (爬山者)用绳子相互系在一起 /
dance on a ～ 被绞死 / give sb. ～ (*enough*)
(或 give sb. plenty of ～) to hang himself 放
任某人使他自取灭亡 / know (learn, show sb.,
put sb. up to) the ～s 知道(学会, 向某人指出,
告诉某人)事情的内情(或窍门, 规则, 做法等) /
on the high ～s [口] ①兴奋, 得意; 趾高气扬
②发怒, 被激怒 / on the ～s ①(拳击时被击)倒
在栏索上 ②[俚]即将完蛋 / ～ sb. in [俚]拉某
人参加; 使某人上当 ‖**~**,**dancer** *n.* (杂技团的)
走(钢)索演员 / **'～,dancing** *n.* 走(钢)索 / ～
ferry [军]绳渡 / ～ **ladder** 绳梯 / **～manship**
['roupmənʃip] *n.* 走索(或爬绳)的技术 / ～ **quoit**
(做投套游戏的)绳圈 / ～ **walk** ①制造绳索的
狭长走道 ②内有制造绳索的狭长走道的低矮小
屋 / **～,walker** *n.* =～dancer / **'～,walking**
n. =～dancing / **'～way** *n.* (运输用的)架空索
道: ～*way* buckets 架空索道的吊桶 / ～ **yard**
=～ walk / ～ **yarn** ①制绳索的股线 ②[喻]
无足轻重的东西, 区区小事 / **'～yarn Sunday**
[俚]一星期内不工作的一个下午

rosary

rose¹ [rouz] rise 的过去式
rose² [rouz] **I** *n.* ①蔷薇科植物; 蔷薇花, 玫瑰花:
a monthly ～ 月季花 / ～ of May 【植】白水仙
②玫瑰色, 玫瑰红; [复]红润的面色: lose one's
～*s* 失去红润的脸色 / bring back the ～*s* to
one's cheeks 使脸上又复红润; 使恢复健康 ③玫
瑰香(料) ④(洒水壶或水管等的)莲蓬式喷嘴 ⑤
玫瑰状宝石(或钻石) ⑥【海】罗经卡 ⑦玫瑰花饰
(如玫瑰花结等); 玫瑰花形纹章(尤指英国国徽)
⑧【建】圆花窗 ⑨ (兽角根部或鸟眼周围的)隆起
部分 ⑩[the ～]【医】丹毒 **II** *a.* ①蔷薇色的, 玫
瑰花的; 作玫瑰花用的; 含有玫瑰花的 ②玫瑰色
的; 玫瑰香的 **III** *vt.* ①使成玫瑰色, 使(脸等)变
红 ②使有玫瑰香味 ‖ *a bed of* ～*s* 见 **bed** / *a*
path strewn with ～*s* 见 **path** / *gather* (*life's*)
～*s* 寻欢作乐 / *No* ～ *without a thorn.* [谚]
没有无刺的玫瑰。(或: 没有十全十美的幸福。) /
not all ～*s* 并非完美, 有某种困苦(或不利) / *the*
Golden ～ 【宗】金玫瑰(教皇在四旬斋的第四个
星期日赠给信奉天主教的君主或都市的被邪物) /
the ～ *of* …地方最漂亮的女子 / *the Wars*
of the Roses 【英史】玫瑰(或蔷薇)战争 (1455—
1485) / *the white* ～ *of innocence* (或 *virginity*)
白玫瑰似的纯洁 / *under the* ～ 秘密地, 私下地:
He told me *under the* ～. 他私下告诉我。‖～*like*
a. 玫瑰花似的 ‖**'～bed** *n.* 玫瑰花坛 / **'～bud**
n. ①玫瑰花苞 ②[美]漂亮的姑娘, 初入社交界
的少女 / **'～bush** *n.* 蔷薇树, 玫瑰树 / **'～-,col-**
o(u)r *n.* 玫瑰红; [喻]美好 / **'～-,colo(u)red**
a. ①玫瑰色的, 玫瑰红的 ②乐观的, 愉快的:
take ～-*colo(u)red* views 抱乐观的看法 / see
things through ～-*colo(u)red* glasses 过分乐观地
看事物 / **'～-drop** *n.* 一种皮肤病(皮肤上生一
块块红斑) / ～ **engine** 用于车曲线花样的车床
附件 / **'～leaf** *n.* 玫瑰花瓣, 蔷薇花瓣 / ～ **oil**
玫瑰油 / ～ **pink** 淡粉红色 / **'～-'red** *a.* 玫瑰
红的 / ～ **water** 玫瑰香水; [喻]奉承话; 温和的

做法: treat with ～ *water* 用温和的办法对待 /
'～,**water** *a.* ①有玫瑰香水香味的; 象玫瑰香水
的 ②(作品等)故作细腻的, 矫揉造作的; 感伤
的 / ～ **window** 圆花窗 / '～**wood** *n.*【植】青
龙木; 黑黄檀

roseate ['rouziit] *a.* ① 玫瑰似的; 玫瑰色的, 玫瑰
红的 ②美好的; 愉快的; 乐观的 ‖～**ly** *ad.*

rosette [rou'zet] *n.* ①玫瑰花形物(如徽章等); 玫
瑰花饰(如玫瑰花结等) ②【建】圆花窗, 圆花饰
③【电】(天花板)接线匣, 插座 ④【植】莲座(叶)丛

roster ['roustə] *n.* ①【军】官兵勤务名册 ②花名
册; 逐项登记表: a membership ～ 成员名册

rostrum ['rɔstrəm] ([复] rostrums 或 rostra
['rɔstrə]) *n.* ① 演讲台; 坛, 讲坛 ②(古罗马战舰
的)嘴形舰首 ③【动】头部的嘴状突起(如额剑、吻
突等)

rosy ['rouzi] *a.* ①玫瑰色的, 玫瑰红的; 红润的;
(因害羞等)涨红脸的: ～ cheeks 红润的脸颊
②美好的, 光明的; 乐观的: ～ prospects 美好的
前景; 光明的前途 / a ～ view 乐观的看法 ‖～
about the gills 气色好; (酒后)两腮红润

rot [rɔt] **I** (rotted; rotting) ❶ *vi.* ①烂, 腐坏; 腐
败, 堕落 ②(在狱中等)消瘦, 憔悴 ③[英俚]用进
行时态①开玩笑; 讲起苦话: He was only *rotting*.
他不过是开玩笑。❷ *vt.* ①使腐烂; 使腐朽; 使腐
败; 使堕落: The continual rain will ～ the
wheat. 连绵不断的雨会使小麦腐烂。/ Oil and
grease will ～ the rubber of the tyres. 油污会
腐蚀轮胎的橡胶。②[俚]弄糟: ～ the whole
plan 打乱整个计划 ③[英俚]嘲弄; 挖苦 ④把
(麻等)浸水软化 **II** *n.* ①腐烂; 腐朽; 腐败; 堕落:
Rot has set in. 开始腐烂了。②腐烂的东西; 腐
朽的事物 ③【农】腐烂病; 【医】肝双盘吸虫病;
[the ～] 羊肝蛭病: ～ on sweet potatoes
【农】甘薯黑斑病 ④[俚]废话; 蠢事; 荒唐: Don't
talk ～! 别胡说! / It is perfect ～ to trust him.
信任他简直是荒唐。⑤(板球、战争等一方的)突
然遭到的一连串失败: A ～ set in. 开始遭到一
连串的失败。(或: 倒霉的事不断来了。) **III** *int.*
[表示厌恶、蔑视、烦恼等]胡说! 混蛋! 糟了! ‖*Rot
it* (或 *um, 'em*)! 胡说! 混蛋! 糟了! / *tommy*
～ [俚]废话; 蠢事; 荒唐

rota ['routə] *n.* ①[主英]花名册; 值勤人员表; 勤
务轮值表 ②[R-] (天主教的)最高法庭

rotary ['routəri] **I** *a.* ①旋转的, 转动的: ～ motion 转动 / a ～ engine 转缸式发动机 / a ～
furnace 回转炉 ②轮转(印刷)的: a ～ press 轮
转印刷机 / a ～ plate 轮转印刷版 ③循环的, 轮
流的: a ～ hiring system 轮流雇佣制 **II** *n.* ①
旋转运行的机器(如轮转印刷机、旋转钻井机、转
缸式发动机等) ②[美]【交】(几条道路环绕圆形
广场、单向通行的)环行交叉(＝～ intersection)
③ [(the) R-] "扶轮国际"(＝Rotary International; 原名扶轮社)
‖**Rotary Club** "扶轮国际"的地方分社 / ～
cultivator 旋转耕耘机 / '～-**wing aircraft** 旋
翼飞机

rotate **I** [rou'teit] ❶ *vi.* ①旋转, 转动: The earth
～s around the sun. 地球绕着太阳转。②循环,
轮流: The seasons ～. 四季循环。❷ *vt.* ①使旋
转, 使转动: ～ the crankshaft 旋转曲轴 ②使轮
流, 使交替; 【农】轮作: ～ crops 轮种庄稼 ③轮
换(人员等) **II** ['routeit] *a.* 【植】辐状的

rotation [rou'teiʃən] *n.* ① 旋转, 转动; (旋转的)
圈; 【天】自转: the daily ～ of the earth 地球每
天的自转 / make ten ～s in a second 每秒钟旋
转十圈 ②循环, 轮流, 交替; 【农】轮作: a ～ of
duties 轮流值勤 / ～ of crops【农】轮作制 / in
(或 by) ～ 轮流地, 交替地 ③【物】旋度; 旋光(本
领) ‖～**al** *a.*

rote [rout] *n.* ①死记硬背: learn *by* ～ 死记硬
背地学习 / repeat a lesson *by* ～ 死背课文 ②
老一套, 机械的方法; 生搬硬套: do (copy) sth. *by*
～ 机械地做(照搬照抄)某事

rotisserie [rou'tisəri] *n.* ①烤肉店, 烤肉铺 ②携带
式电热轮转烤肉器

rotten ['rɔtn] *a.* ①腐烂的, 发臭的; 腐败的, 腐朽
的; 堕落的 ②(石)风化的, 易碎的 ③虚弱的, 不健全
的, 不中用的: feel ～ 感到身体很不行 ④[俚]
蹩脚的; 讨厌的; 槽糕的: a ～ book 一本蹩脚的
书 / ～ weather 讨厌的天气 / What ～ luck!
真倒霉! ⑤(羊)患肝蛭病的 ‖*Rotten Row* 见
row[1] / *Something is* ～ *in the state of Denmark.* 情况很糟糕。(或: 情况令人不满。) ‖～**ly**
ad. / ～**ness** *n.* ‖～ **borough** ①具有同等选
举权但居民比其他选区少得多的选区 ②【英史】
一八三二年前已失去选区实质但仍选举议员的市
镇 / '～**stone** *n.* 磨石

rotund [rou'tʌnd] *a.* ①圆形的 ②圆胖的: a ～
little man 矮胖子 ③(声音)洪亮的, 圆润的 ④
(文体、谈吐)华丽的, 浮夸的 ‖～**ly** *ad.*

rotunda [rou'tʌndə] *n.* (有圆顶的)圆形建筑物;
圆形大厅; (旅馆等的)中央大厅

rotunda

otundity [rou'tʌnditi] *n.* ①圆; 圆形物 ②圆胖 ③(声音的)洪亮, 圆润 ④(文体等的)华丽, 浮夸

ouge [ruːʒ] **I** *n.* ① 胭脂; 口红 ②红铁粉, 铁丹 **II** *vt. & vi.* (在…上)搽胭脂(或口红)

rough [rʌf] **I** *a.* ① 表面不平的; 毛糙的; 粗糙的: a ~ road 崎岖的道路 / ~ hilly country 地势崎岖的山乡 / a book with ~ edges (未切边的)毛边书 / ~ hands 粗糙的手
②毛茸茸的; 蓬乱的: a face ~ with beard 胡子粗硬蓬乱的脸 / ~ hair 乱蓬蓬的头发
③未加工的; 粗加工的, 粗制的; 干粗活的: ~ rice 未春的稻谷 / a ~ stone 未经琢磨的石头 / ~ food 粗食 / a ~ carpenter 粗木工
④粗略的, 大致的, 初步的; 粗率的: a ~ draft 草稿 / ~ justice 大致上的公平合理 / a ~ estimate 约略的估计 / a ~ circle 不精确的圆 / a ~ translation 粗糙的译文
⑤粗陋的, 简陋的; 不讲究的: ~ accommodation at a small inn 小客栈的简陋招待设备 / a ~ makeshift 马马虎虎暂时代用一下的东西 / a ~ but hearty welcome 虽不周到但热情诚心的欢迎 / a ~ style of writing 不讲究的文体
⑥粗暴的, 粗鲁的; 粗野的, 粗俗的: a ~ temper 粗暴的脾气 / a ~ customer 粗暴无礼的家伙 / ~ handling 粗暴的对待(或处置) / have a ~ tongue 说话粗鲁
⑦暴风雨的; 狂暴的; 剧烈的: ~ weather 狂风暴雨的天气 / ~ waters 汹涌的海面 / a ~ voyage 历尽风浪的航程 / ~ exercises 剧烈运动 / That horse has ~ paces. 那匹马跑起来颠得很厉害。
⑧笨重的, 需要体力的: ~ work (或 labour) 粗活, 力气活
⑨(声音等)粗糙刺耳的; (酒等)烈性的; (药物等)强烈的
⑩艰难的; 难受的: a ~ assignment 艰巨的任务 / the ~ life of the explorers 勘探人员的艰苦生活 / have a ~ time 吃苦, 受难
⑪【语】送气的
II *n.* ①高低不平(或杂草丛生)的地面; (高尔夫球场上生杂草的)障碍区域
②粗糙的东西(或部分); (马蹄上的)防滑钉
③未加工状态, 粗加工状态; 粗制品, 毛坯
④梗概, 要略; 草样, 草图: discuss a question in ~ 扼要地讨论一个问题
⑤[主英]粗暴的人; 流氓, 无赖, 暴徒: a gang of ~s 一群暴徒(或无赖)
⑥艰难(的)苦难方面: the ~s and the smooths 艰难与顺利; 苦与乐; 人世的甘苦
III ❶ *vt.* ①使不平, 使毛糙; 给(马等)装防滑钉: Satin is very easily ~ed. 缎子是很容易起毛的。/ ~ the edges of glass 把玻璃的边磨毛
②使(毛发、稻草等)蓬乱
③粗制, 制(玉石雕琢品等)的毛坯: ~ (out) a lens 粗制成镜片的毛坯
④草拟, 画…的轮廓 (in, out): ~ out a plan 草拟计划

⑤粗暴对待; 殴打 (up); (球赛中)向(对方)作粗暴动作
⑥初步驯服(马匹等)
⑦试弹几下(钢琴)以调音
❷ *vi.* ①变粗糙
②粗鲁行事
IV *ad.* ①粗糙地; 粗略地
②粗暴地: play ~ (在比赛等中)耍粗暴作风, 作粗暴动作 / treat sb. ~ 粗暴地对待某人
‖*be* ~ *on sb.* ①对某人粗暴苛刻 ②使某人倒霉 / *cut up* ~ [口]发脾气, 发怒 / *in the* ~ ①未加工; 未完成: a picture *in the* ~ 尚未完成的图画 / The plan is still *in the* ~. 这计划还不成熟。②粗略, 大致上: be worth ten dollars *in the* ~ 约值十元 / be true *in the* ~ 大体上真实 ③[口]处于困境 ~ *it* 生活简单; 过艰苦的生活 / ~ *luck* 见 **luck** / ~ *sb. up the wrong way* 见 **way** / *take the* ~ *with the smooth* 既能享乐也能吃苦; 是好是歹, 一起承受 / *the* ~*er sex* 见 **sex** / *the* ~ *quarter of the town* 城市中粗野人的居住区
‖~**ish** *a.* 有点粗糙的; 有点粗暴的 / ~**ly** *ad.* 粗糙地; 粗略地; 粗鲁地说来; 粗暴地 / ~**ness** *n.*
‖**'~-and-'ready** *a.* ① (方法等)粗糙但尚能用的; (估计等)大致上差不多的 ②(人)鲁莽但尚能顶用的 *n.* [Rough-and-Ready] 美国第十二任总统 Z. 泰勒 (Zachary Taylor) (又作 Old Rough-and-Ready) / **'~-and-'tumble** *a.* 乱糟糟的, 乱作一团的; 杂乱无章的: a ~-*and-tumble* fight 混战 / a ~-*and-tumble* life 无秩序的生活 *n.* 混战, 乱作一团的打闹; 杂乱无章的一片 / '~-**cast** *n.* ①【建】(由石灰、石子等混和而成、涂在建筑物外墙上的)粗灰泥; (墙的)粗灰泥表面 ②毛坯 *a.* ①(墙等)涂粗灰泥的 ②(计划等)草草作成的 *vt.* ①用粗灰泥涂(墙等) ②制…的毛坯; 粗略地作成: ~*cast* a plan 草拟一项计划 / ~ **coat** (石灰、油漆等的)底层 / ~ **coating** =~*cast* (*n.*) / ~ **diamond** ① 未琢磨的钻石 ②举止粗鲁但本质好 (或能力强)的人 / '~-**dry** *vt.* ['rʌf'drai] 晾干而不熨平 (衣服等) *a.* ['rʌf-drai] (衣服等)洗净晾干而未熨的 / '~-'**footed** *a.* (鹰类等)足上有羽毛的 / '~-'**hew** *vt.* ①凿(或砍)出…的毛坯, 粗凿: ~*hew* a statue out of a block of marble 从一块大理石中凿出塑像的毛坯 ②草率地作成; 草拟 / '~-'**hewn** *a.* ①粗凿成的; 毛坯的 ②没有教养的, 粗鲁的 / '~-**house** *n. & a.* ①(尤指室内的)打闹玩笑(的) ②室内大混战(的), 室内暴力行为(的) *vt.* ①同…打闹玩笑 ②粗暴对待, 用暴力对付 ③粗鲁地逗弄(小孩等) *vi.* 参与打闹 / ~ **leaf** [英]【植】(子叶后生出的)第一片真叶, 糙叶。in the ~ *leaf* 出生阶段 / '~-**legged** *a.* (马或鸟)腿上有毛的 / ~ **music** 大声喧闹(尤指以捣蛋为目的的) / '~-**neck** *n.* [美俚] ①粗鲁的人; 无赖 ②油井修建工 ③马戏团工人 / '~-,**rider** *n.* ①驯马人; 善骑烈马的人 ②非正规的骑兵 ③ [R-] (一八九八年美国—西班牙战争中)美国第一义勇骑兵团的骑

兵 / **'～scuff** *n.* =riffraff / **'～shod** *a.* ①(马匹)钉有防滑蹄铁的 ②残暴的: ride ～shod over sb. 横暴地对待某人,欺凌某人 / **'～-'spoken** *a.* 说话粗鲁的 / **～stuff** [美俚] ①暴力行为 ②黄色文学;下流的东西 / **'～-up** *n.* [俚]大打出手 / **'～-'wrought** *a.* 经初步加工的

roughen ['rʌfən] *vt. & vi.* (使)变粗糙,(使)变毛糙

roulette [ru(ː)'let] **I** *n.* ①轮盘赌 ②【机】压花刀具,滚花刀具 ③【数】旋轮线 ④刻压连续点子(如邮票之间的骑缝)的滚轮 ⑤转轮式卷发器 **II** *vt.* 在…上滚压连续点子(或孔)

round[1] [raund] **I** *a.* ①圆的;球形的;圆柱形的;半圆的,弧形的;【语】圆唇的: a ～ plate (post) 圆碟(柱) / The earth is ～. 地球是圆的。/ a ～ arch 半圆拱 / a ～ vowel 圆唇元音
②滚圆的,丰满的;匀称的: ～ arms 滚圆的手臂 / ～ cheeks 丰满的面颊
③圈状的;绕圈的;来回的: a ～ dance 圆舞,华尔兹舞 / a ～ trip 来回的旅行
④整整的,十足的: a ～ ton (dozen) 整整一吨(打) / a ～ lie 十足的谎话
⑤巨大的,可观的: a ～ sum 可观的一笔款子 / buy at a good ～ price 以巨价购进
⑥用十(或百、千等)一类整数表示的;大概的,约略的: 500 is a ～ number for 498, 503, etc. 500 是 498, 503 等的近似百位整数。/ a ～ guess 大致不错的猜测
⑦(声音)圆润的,嘹亮的: a ～ voice 圆润的嗓子
⑧轻捷的,迅速而有力的: a ～ pace 轻快矫健的步子
⑨(文体、风格等)完美流畅的;(人物等)刻划得完美生动的: a ～ style of writing 流畅的写作风格 / The characters and their motives are ～ and deep. 人物和他们的动机刻划得完美而深刻。
⑩率直的,毫不含糊的,直言不讳的;耿直的: a ～ oath 明白无误的誓言 / ～ dealing 光明正大的做法 / a ～ unvarnished tale 真情实话
⑪(笔迹)圆润的
⑫严厉的,粗暴的: give sb. a ～ beating 把某人狠狠地打了一顿
II *n.* ①圆形物;(牛的)圆腿肉;扶梯级棍,横档;[英](面包的)一片: this earthly ～ 地球 / a ～ of beef 一块牛腿肉 / the ～s of a ladder 梯级,梯子的横档 / a ～ of toast [英]从圆形烤面包上切下的一片
②圆舞; [the ～] 圆雕(relief 浮雕之对)
③兜(一)圈,巡回,巡视,巡逻,(时间的)循环,周期: the earth in its daily (yearly) ～ 自(公)转着的地球 / go for a good ～ 出去好好兜一圈 / a postman's ～ 邮递员的一圈投递值勤 / the doctor's ～ of visits to the homes of his patients 医生对病人的巡回探视出诊 / the daily ～ 日常工作,日常事务 / the ～ of the hours 时间的循环 / the life ～ of a fly 苍蝇的生命周期
④(比赛、谈判等的)(一)轮,(一)回合,(一)场;

(牌戏的)(一)局,(一)圈,(酒的)一巡: the semi-final ～ 半决赛轮 / another ～ of diplomat talks 另一轮的外交谈判 / be knocked out in th third ～ 在第三个回合中被击倒 / a ～ of go 一局高尔夫球 / have a ～ of cards 打一圈牌 serve out a ～ of spirit 斟一巡酒
⑤(弹药的)(一)发,(枪炮等的)(一次)齐发;呼等的)一阵;(事情、行动等的)一连串,一系列 two ～s of ball cartridge 两发实弹 / a nine-rifle 九响步枪 / fire a salute of 21 ～s 鸣二十一响礼炮 / His speech drew (或 won) ～ afte ～ of enthusiastic applause. 他的讲话博得一阵又一阵的热烈掌声。/ a ～ of gaiety (parties 一连串的欢乐(社交聚会)
⑥一群人;一簇东西
⑦范围: the whole ～ of knowledge 整个的知识范围
⑧【音】轮唱
⑨【建】圆形饰
⑩圆路,环行路;迂回路,弯弯曲曲的路
III *prep.* ①围(绕)着: He put the scarf ～ hi neck. 他围上围巾。/ sit ～ the table 围桌而坐 / The moon moves ～ the earth. 月亮绕着地球转。/ a tour ～ the world 环球旅行
②在…周围;在…附近: post sentries ～ the bar racks 在营房四周设岗哨 / the farmland ～ th school 学校附近的农田
③绕过: The traffic flowed ～ the obstruction i the road. 来往车辆绕过路上的障碍物行驶。The post office is just ～ the corner. 邮局就在拐弯处。
④在…各处; 向…四周: look ～ the room 朝房间里四下看看 / The news went ～ the papers 报纸都登载了这条消息。
⑤(在时间方面)横贯过: He worked ～ the day 他工作了一整天。
IV *ad.* ①兜着圈子;围绕地: run ～ in the field 在场上兜着圈子跑 / His waist measures forty inches ～. 他腰围四十吋。
②循环地;从头至尾地: Spring came ～. 春天又来了。/ work the (whole) year ～ 一年到头地工作
③在周围;在附近: A crowd soon gathered ～. 一群人马上围了上来。/ The meadows extended ～. 草地向四面延伸。/ He visited all the people ～. 他访问了附近所有的人。/ ～ there 在那里附近
④朝反方向;转过来: the other way ～ 正好相反;用正好相反的方法 / He turned ～. 他转过身来。/ win sb. ～ 把某人争取过来 / bring sb. ～ after a faint 使某人从昏迷中苏醒过来
⑤迂回地: go a long way ～ 绕道走,走远道 / Jump or go ～? 跳过去,还是绕道走?
⑥在各处;往各处: show sb. ～ 陪某人(四处)参观 / go ～ visiting patients 巡回出诊 / The news soon got ～. 消息很快传开了。
⑦逐一,挨次: hand cigarettes ～ 把香烟递给周

围各人 / I haven't got enough candy to go ~. 我没有足够的糖果可让每人都分到。
⑧到某(指定)地点: Order the car ~. 叫汽车开过来。 / Come ~ and see me tomorrow. 明天过来看我吧。
Ⅴ ❶ vt. ①使成圆形;用圆唇发(音): ~ the lips 圆起嘴唇 / ~ the angles 磨光棱角 / ~ the hair 把头发剪短剪齐
②环绕…而行;拐(弯): ~ the world 环绕世界一周 / ~ the cape 绕过海岬 / ~ the corner of the street 在街角拐弯
③完成,使圆满结束;使(文体等)完美: The performance was ~ed off with a one-act play. 演出以一个独幕剧圆满结束。 / ~ (off 或 out) an essay 润色一篇散文
④赶拢;使集拢;围捕,兜捕 (up): ~ up the cattle 把牛赶到一块儿 / She ~ed up the children and took them to the zoo. 她把孩子集合起来,带他们到动物园去。
⑤【数】把…四舍五入: 2.538 ~ed to two decimals becomes 2.54. 2.538 四舍五入到二位小数是 2.54。
⑥[罕]使转到相反方向: ~ a boat off 【海】掉转船头迎着浪
❷ vi. ①变圆;发胖;丰满起来: Her body is beginning to ~ out. 她身体开始丰满起来了。
②兜圈,环行;拐弯: The runners ~ed into the home stretch. 赛跑者拐弯进入了接近终点的一段距离。
③进展,成长 (into): The talk ~ed into a plan. 从这次谈话发展出一个计划。 / The century has ~ed into its eighty decade. 本世纪已进入了八十年代。
④[罕]转到相反方向: ~ on one's heels 向后转身
‖**all** ~ (在…)周围,(在…)各处 / **ask sb.** ~ 请某人来家 / **cut** ~ 卖弄,故意做给人看 / **go** (或 **make**) **one's** ~**s** ①按户投递 ②查病房;出诊: The doctor is making his ~s. 医生正在查病房。
③巡回;巡视;巡逻 / **go the** ~(**s**) ①传遍: The news quickly went the ~(s) of the village. 消息很快传遍了全村。 ② 巡回;巡视;巡逻 / **in** ~ **numbers** (或 **figures**) 见 **number** / **in the** ~ ①圆雕: a statue in the ~ 立体像 ②全面地: A doctor must see his patients in the ~. 医生必须全面地考虑病人的病情。③舞台在剧场中央的: a theatre in the ~ 舞台设在观众座位中央的剧场 / **look** ~ 见 **look** / **out of** ~ 不圆;不很圆 / **right** ~ ①就在(…)周围;就在(…)附近: right ~ here 就在这里附近 ②整整一圈地;完全朝着相反方向: The hour hand of a clock goes right ~ in twelve hours. 钟的时针十二小时恰好转一圈。 / turn right ~ 完全转过身来 / **about** ①(在…)周围,(在…的)四面八方 ②向相反方向 ③迂回地;兜着圈子地,不直接地,不直截了当地: He came ~ about to these conclusions.

他兜了半天圈子才得出这些结论。④大约: Please come ~ about 5 o'clock. 请在五点钟左右来。 / ~ **and** ~ 旋转不息地: turn ~ **and** ~ 团团转 / **talk** ~ **and** ~ **a problem** 在一个问题的表面上谈论来谈论去 / ~ **in** 【海】拉(绳),牵(索) / ~ **on** (或 **upon**) **sb.** ①反驳(或攻击)某人(指自己人);向某人反戈一击 ②告某人的密,出卖某人 / ~ **to** (船)掉头顶风停下 / **taking it all** ~ 全面地来看 / **the clock** ~ (或 ~ **the clock**) 连续一整天(或一昼夜): work the clock ~ 连续工作一昼夜(或一整天)
‖**~let** ['raundlit] n. 小圆,小的圆形物 / **~ness** n.
‖**~-arm** a. & ad. 臂挥到齐肩高度的(地) / '**~-'backed** a. 驼背的 / '**~-'eyed** a. 圆睁着眼的: listen with ~-eyed wonder 圆睁着眼好奇地听 / ~ **hand** 正楷字体,工整的手笔 / '**~-hand** n. 手臂齐肩(投球) / '**~head** n. ①【英史】圆颅党 (1642—1652 英内战期间的议会派分子,头发都剪短,故名) ②短(或阔)头颅的人 / '**~house** n. ①(有旋转式修理圆台的)圆形机车修理房(或车库) ②后甲板舱室 ③【史】拘留所,监狱 ④(拳击中)弯着肘使劲的一击 / [美俚]使劲挥臂的,厉害的 / ~ **robin** ①(分不清签名者先后的)圆形签名请愿书(或抗议书等);联名声明 ②由许多人传递阅读(读后签名,有时并加注意见)的信件 ③【体】循环赛 = ~ table ⑤一系列,一阵 ⑥【军】[军]不着陆往返飞行 / '**~-shot** n. 旧式圆形炮弹(与 shell 相对) / '**~-'shouldered** a. 曲背(以致肩部呈圆形的) / ~ **table** ①[the R-T-] 亚瑟王 (King Arthur) 及其骑士们坐的席位不分主次的大圆桌;亚瑟王的全体骑士们 ②协商会议;协商会议的全体参加者 / '**~-table** a. 圆桌的,协商的: a ~-table conference 圆桌会议 / '**~-the-clock** a. 连续二十四小时的;连续不停的: The shop gives ~-the-clock service. 这家商店日夜服务。 / '**~-'trip** a. 来回旅程的: a ~-trip ticket 来回票 / '**~up** n. ①赶拢;集拢;围捕,兜捕 ②赶拢牲畜的人(或马);(人、物等)被集拢的一群 ③综述;摘要: Following is a ~up of some of the activities. 下面是其中某些活动的综述。 / '**~worm** n. 蛔虫;任何圆体不分节的虫(如蛲虫及钩虫)
round² [raund] [古] ❶ vi. 耳语;低声说话 ❷ vt. 低声讲,悄悄地说;悄悄地对…说: ~ sb. in the ear that ... 悄悄地告诉某人…
roundabout ['raundəbaut] **I** a. ①迂回的;(说话等)兜圈子的,不直接的,不直截了当的: The car has to come a ~ way. 车子只得绕道而来。 / I heard the news in a ~ way. 我是间接听到这消息的。②圆滚滚的,胖的 **Ⅱ** n. ①道路交叉处的环形路;环形路线;兜圈子的话(或文章等) ②[英]旋转木马 ③[美]男用紧身短外套 ‖**What you lose on the swings you get back on the ~s.** 见 **swing**
rounder ['raundə] n. ①巡行者(如巡官、看夜人等) ②车圆的工具(或人) ③[英] [R-] 卫理公会

牧师 ④[美口]浪荡子;酒鬼;惯犯 ⑤[~s][用作单]圆场棒球(一种类似棒球的英国球戏)

roundsman ['raundzmen] ([复] roundsmen) *n.* 巡官;看夜人;[英]商业推销员,跑街

rouse¹ [rauz] I ❶ *vt.* ①唤醒;唤起,使觉醒: ~ sb. (*up*) *from* sleep 唤醒某人 ②激起(情感等);激怒;使振奋: ~ sb.'s bile 激起某人的大怒 / ~ sb. *to* action (或 *from* inaction) 使某人行动起来 / He wants *rousing*. 他需要别人激励一番。③惊起,吓出(猎物等): The boat ~*d* wild ducks *to* flight. 船使野鸭受惊飞起。④搅动(液体) ⑤【海】使劲拉 (*in, out, up*) ❷ *vi.* ①醒来;奋起 (*up*): ~ *up* at 6 in the morning 早晨六时醒来 ②(猎物等)被惊起 II *n.* ①觉醒;奋起 ②【军】起床号 ‖*Rouse and bitt!* 【海】起床! / *Rouse and shine!* 【军】起床! ‖~**r** *n.* ①唤醒者;唤起者 ②(啤酒发酵时的)搅拌器 ③弥天大谎

rouse² [rauz] *n.* [古]狂饮;干杯;闹宴: give a ~ 举杯祝酒 / take one's ~ 闹饮

rout¹ [raut] I *n.* 溃败,溃退 II *vt.* 击溃,打垮;使溃退 ‖*put to* ~ 打垮,击溃

rout² [raut] ❶ *vi.* ①(猪等)用鼻子拱地(觅食) ②翻,搜,寻 ❷ *vt.* ①用鼻子拱(地);挖出,掘出,剔出 (*out*);翻,搜,寻 ②(在金属、木料上)挖,刻(沟,纹) ③(从床上或室内等)唤起;唤出 (*up, out*) ④赶出,驱逐 (*out*)

rout³ [raut] *n.* ①乌合之众,嘈杂的人群;【律】意图聚众闹事 ②混乱,骚动 ③盛大交际会,晚会

rout⁴ [raut] *vi.* [英方](牛等)哞哞叫

route [ruːt] I *n.* ①路;路线;航线: a train (bus) ~ 火车(公共汽车)路线 / a ~ march 【军】旅次行军 / supply ~*s* 供应线 / a ~ formation 【军】疏开飞行队形 / take one's ~ (*to*) (向…)行进,(向…而)去 ②(规定行军路线、司令部地点等的)行军命令: give (get) the ~ 发出(接到)行军命令 II *vt.* ①按规定路线发送 ②给…定路线;安排…的程序 ‖*en* ~ [法]在途中(的) ‖~**man** ['ruːtmen] *n.* 按指定路线售货(或发货)的推销员 / ~-,**proving flight** 新航线的试飞

routine [ruːˈtiːn] I *n.* ①例行公事;日常工作;例行手续,常规;惯例;机械方式;程序: daily ~ 日行公事;日常工作 / the business ~ of import and export trade 进出口贸易的例行业务手续 / follow the (old) ~ 墨守成规 / break the ~ 打破常规 / the input ~ (电子计算机的)输入程序 ②(经常重演的)固定剧目 II *a.* (一般只用作定语)日常的;例行的;常规的: be on the ~ patrol 执行例行巡逻 / a ~ report 例行报告 / a ~ test 定期测验 / a ~ treatment 常规疗法 ‖~**ly** *ad.*

rove¹ [rouv] I *n.* 【纺】粗纱 II *vt.* ①纺(纤维)成粗纱 ‖~**r** *n.* 【纺】三道粗纺机 (=roving frame)

rove² [rouv] I ❶ *vi.* ①流浪;漫游;无一定方向地移动: ~ from one city to another 从一个城市流浪到另一个城市 / His glance ~*d* over the pictures. 他浏览图画。/ Her thoughts ~*d* far into the past. 她遐想往事。②用活饵曳钓 ❷ *vt.*

流浪于;漫游: ~ the woods 漫游森林 II *n.* 流浪;漫游 ‖~**r** *n.* ①流浪者;漫游者 ②海盗;海盗船 ③高年级童子军 ④任意选定的射箭靶子;远距离射箭靶子: shoot at ~*rs* 远距离射箭

row¹ [rou] I *n.* ①(一)排,(一)行;(剧场等)一排(座位): a ~ of soldiers 一列士兵 / a ~ o buildings 一排建筑物 / plant out ~ *upon* ~ o cabbages 种植一行行的卷心菜 / sit in the fron ~ 坐在第一排(座位) ②街,路;(主要为某种专业占用的)街道;地区: Rochester *Row* 罗彻斯特街(伦敦一街名) / an automobile ~ 汽车业集中的街道 / the diplomatic ~ 使馆区 II *vt.* 使成排(或行) (*up*) ‖*a hard* (或 *long*) ~ *to hoe* 难办的事;乏味的工作;*hoe one's own* ~ 干自己的事;自扫门前雪 / *in a* ~ ①成一长行: stand *in a* ~ 站成一排 ②连续,一连串: We have had good harvests for ten years *in a* ~. 我们连续十年获得了丰收。/ *on a* ~ *of stumps* 见 *stump*¹ / *the Row* (或 *Rotten Row*) 伦敦海德公园 (Hyde Park) 中的骑马道 ‖~ **house** 联立(或成排)房屋中的一幢

row² [rou] I ❶ *vt.* ①划(船等);划运,划渡: ~ 40 (strokes) *to* the minute 一分钟划桨四十次 / Shall I ~ you up (down, across) the river? 要不要我把你们划到上游(下游, 对岸)去? ②担任…号手;用…名(划手);(船)用…支(桨): He ~*s* 5 in the crew. 他在划船队中当五号手。/ The team ~*ed* two new men. 这划船队有了两名新划手。/ The boat ~*s* 6 oars. 这小艇有六支桨划。③参加(赛船);与…进行划船比赛: ~ a race 参加划船比赛 / ~ the champion in the annual race 在年度划船比赛中与冠军保持者比赛 ❷ *vi.* ①划船;荡桨 ②(划桨似地)划行;划动: The eagles ~*ed* by on slow wings. 鹰群缓慢地飞过。③参加赛船 II *n.* 划船;划船游览;划程: go for (或 have, take) a ~ 去划船 / a long and tiring ~ 又长又累的一次划船 ‖*look one way and* ~ *another* 见 **way** / ~ *down* (赛船中)追上,赶过 / ~ *dry* 不使水花飞溅地划桨 / *Rowed of all!* (口令)停划! / ~ *out* (赛船中)从容胜过 / ~ *sb. out* 使某人划得筋疲力尽 / ~ *sb. up Salt River* 见 **river** / ~ *wet* 水花飞溅地划桨 ‖~**er** *n.* 划船者,划手 ‖~**boat** *n.* 划艇 / ~**lock** ['rolek] *n.* [主英]桨架,桨叉

row³ [rau] I *n.* ①[口]吵嚷,骚动;吵架,口角: What's the ~? 吵嚷些什么? / make a ~ 吵闹喧嚷;抗议 / a ~ street 街头吵架 ②受斥责: get into a ~ for 为了…挨骂 II *vt.* [口]痛斥,狠骂: ~ sb. *up* 痛斥某人 ❷ *vi.* [口]争吵,吵闹: ~ *with* sb. 同某人争吵 ‖*Hold your* ~! [口]住口!别吵! / *kick up a* ~ [口]大吵大闹,起哄;滋事

rowdy ['raudi] I *n.* 好吵闹的人;粗暴的人;无赖 II *a.* 吵闹的;粗暴的 ‖**rowdily** *ad.* / **rowdiness** *n.* / ~**ish** *a.* 有点吵闹的;有点粗暴的 / ~**ism** *n.* 粗暴(或吵闹)的行为;流氓作风

royal ['rɔiəl] **I** *a.* ①王的,女王的;王室的: the ~ family (或 the blood ~) 王室,皇族 / a ~ edict 敕令,圣旨 / His (或 Her) *Royal* Highness 殿下(间接提及时用) / a ~ princess 公主 / the Princess *Royal* 大公主 ②[R-] (英国)皇家的;英国的: the *Royal* Academy (英国)皇家艺术学会 / the *Royal* Society (英国)皇家学会 / the *Royal* Air Force (英国)皇家空军 / the *Royal* Army (英国)皇家陆军 / the *Royal* Engineers (英国)皇家陆军工兵 / the *Royal* Exchange 伦敦交易所 / the *Royal* Marines (英国)皇家海军陆战队 / the *Royal* Navy (英国)皇家海军 / the *Royal* Observer Corps (英国)皇家民间防空监视队 / the *Royal* Scots (英国)皇家步兵第一团 ③堂皇的,盛大的;庄严的;高贵的: give sb. ~ entertainment 给某人盛大的招待 / a ~ bearing 庄严的仪态 ④ 极大的;第一流的: of ~ dimensions 尺寸(或面积)极大的 / a battle ~ 大规模战斗 / a ~ view 极美的景色 **II** *n.* ①[口]皇族的一员; [the Royals] (英国)皇家步兵第一团 (=the Royal Scots); (英国)皇家海军陆战队 (=the Royal Marines) ② =~ paper ③ =~ sail ④ =~ stag ‖**have a ~ time** 见 time / **in ~ spirits** 见 spirit / **~ road** 见 road ‖**~ly** *ad.* ‖~ **arch** 共济会(Freemasonry)中的一种级别 / ~ **blue** 品蓝,红光蓝 / ~ **burgh** (英王特许的)苏格兰自治市 / ~ **cell** (白蚁巢中的)王房 / ~ **evil** 瘰疬 / ~ **fern** 【植】王紫萁 / ~ **jelly** (昆虫的)王浆 / **Royal Martyr**【英史】被国会处决的查理一世 / ~ **mast** 【船】最上桅 / ~ **purple** 深紫红色 / ~ **sail** 【船】最上桅的帆 / ~ **stag** (六岁以上的)有十二个以上角叉的牡鹿 / ~ **standard** 王旗

royalist ['rɔiəlist] **I** *n.* ①保皇主义者; 保皇党人 ②[R-] (拥护英王查理一世的)保皇党员; (美国独立战争时期)支持英国方面者; (法国资产阶级革命时期)波旁王朝的拥护者 ③[美]保守的实业界巨头 **II** *a.* 保皇主义的; 保皇主义者的,保皇党人的

royalty ['rɔiəlti] *n.* ①王位; 王权; 王威 ②[常用复]王的特权 ③王族,皇亲: a ~ 一个皇亲 / among the ~ 在王族之间 / the economic ~ 经济上的特权阶层 ⑤[古]王的领土,皇畿 ⑥(国王授予私人或公司的采矿等)特许权; 专利权税;版税; (公司等付给土地所有者的)矿区使用费: oil *royalties* 石油产地使用费 ⑦堂皇;庄严;高贵

rub [rʌb] **I** (rubbed; rubbing) ❶ *vt.* ①摩擦,擦; 使札擦: He bent over and *rubbed* his sore ankle. 他弯身去揉擦疼的脚踝。/ ~ a glass with a cloth 用布擦玻璃杯 / ~ one's hands 搓手(得意的表示) / ~ one's coat *against* some wet paint 使上衣沾了些未干的漆 / My shoe is *rubbing* my heel. 我的一只鞋子硌脚跟。②用…擦;擦上: ~ knuckles *in* one's eyes 用手指节揉眼睛 / ~ oil *on* (或 *over*) one's skin 在皮肤上擦油

③把…摩擦得: ~ one's hand sore (dry, clean) 把手擦痛(干,干净) ④触痛,惹怒(某人) ⑤摹拓(墓碑等) ⑥[美俚]杀害 ❷ *vi.* ①摩擦,擦到 (on, against): The journal ~s *against* the bearing surface. 轴颈在轴承面上摩擦。② 被擦掉 (off, out): This ink stain won't ~ out. 这墨水渍擦不掉。③ (皮肤等)擦痛,擦破; (衣服等)磨损 ④(事情等)使人恼火(或烦恼) **II** *n.* ①摩擦,擦: give the table a good ~ 把桌子好好擦一下 ②磨损处,擦痛处 ③阻难;疑难点;要点: There's the ~. 难就难在这里。/ Do you get the ~? 你抓住要点了吗? ④伤人感情的嘲笑(或挖苦、批评等) ⑤[方]磨石,砥石 ‖~ **along** ①(两人以上的人们)勉强地相处; 一起过日子: ~ *along* unhappily (owing to frequent quarrels) (由于经常吵闹)不愉快地勉强相处 / ~ *along* together 不吵不闹地一起过日子 ②(一个人)不太困难地生活,平平过日子 / ~ **away** ①擦掉;磨去 ②消除(羞怯等) / ~ **down** ①用力擦遍;按摩: ~ oneself *down* with a towel 用毛巾用力地擦全身 ②彻底梳刷: ~ *down* a horse 把马梳洗得光滑 ③把…擦亮;使磨平;使磨损(或擦小等) ④[口]对(犯人等)全身搜查 / ~ **in** (或 *into*) ①把…用力擦入: ~ the ointment *into* the skin 把油膏在皮肤上擦透 ②反复讲(令人不愉快的事) / ~ *it in* [俚](故意)反复讲别人不爱听的事; 触人痛处 / ~ **off** ①擦掉,磨去: ~ *off* the finger mark from the painting 擦掉图画上的指印 ②消除(羞怯等) / ~ **on** 勉强度过;尽力度过 / ~ **out** ①擦掉;磨去: ~ *out* the pencil marks 擦掉铅笔记号 ②[俚]杀死: ~ sb. *out* 干掉某人 / ~ *sb.* **the right way** 讨好某人;抚慰某人 / ~ *sb.* **the wrong way** 触犯某人,惹怒某人 / ~ *shoulders* **with sb.** 见 shoulder / ~ **through** 勉强度过,挨过 / ~ **up** ①揉和(颜料等) ②擦亮,把…磨光滑: ~ *up* silver spoons 擦亮银汤匙 ③重温: ~ *up* one's mathematics 复习数学 / ~ *up* one's memory 重温一下 / ~ *the ~s and worries of life* 人生的辛酸 ‖**rubbing** *n.* ①摩擦,擦;擦亮;擦痛 ②摹拓本 ‖'~**down** *n.* 摩擦,擦; (浴后等的)用力擦身 / ~ **rail** (汽车等防止擦坏的)防擦横档 / '~**stone** *n.* 磨石,磨刀石

rubber[1] ['rʌbə] **I** *n.* ①(摩)擦的人;按摩师; (蒸气浴室的)按摩员 ②(摩)擦的工具;砥石;粗锉;橡皮(擦子); (擦火柴的)砂皮; (机器)借助摩擦转动的装置 ③防擦物 ④橡胶; 橡胶状物; 合成橡胶: a ~ plantation 橡胶种植园 / ~ cloth 橡胶布 / a ~-insulated cable 胶包电缆 / a ~-sheathed flexible cord 橡皮软电线 ⑤橡胶制品; 橡皮筋 (= band); 橡胶套鞋; [美俚]汽车轮胎 ⑥障碍,麻烦 ⑦[美俚]职业杀人者 **II** ❶ *vt.* 给…涂上橡胶 ❷ *vi.* [美俚]好奇地盯着看 ‖*peel* [美俚](驾车时)突然加大油门 ‖~ **cement** 橡胶胶水 / ~ **cheque**, ~ **check** (因存款不足)银行拒付的支票,空头支票 / ~ **drink** [美俚]致醉的最后一口(或一杯)酒 / ~ **heel**[美俚]侦探 / ~ **joint** [美俚]低级下流的舞厅 / '~-

neck *n.* ①伸长脖子(或好奇地盯着)看的人;爱问长问短的人 ②(跟着响导)游览的人 / a *~neck bus* 游览车 *vi.* ①伸长脖子(或好奇地盯着)看;好奇地听 ②(跟着响导)游览 / **~ plant** 橡胶植物 / **~ stamp** ①橡皮图章 ②人云亦云的人,无主见的人 ③不经考虑就批准的人(或机构); (不经考虑的)官样文章式的批准,照常规的批准 ④老一套的话;刻板文章 / '**~-'stamp** *vt.* 不经审查就批准;官样文章式地通过;在他人的示意下批准: a parliament which *~-stamped* the war budget 奉令通过战争预算的议会 *a.* 经(或作出)官样文章式批准的

rubber² ['rʌbə] *n.* ①(由连续三盘或五盘等成单的盘数构成的)一局纸牌戏 ②(三盘中赢了两盘从而)赢得的一局 ③不分输赢时的决赛盘 (=~ game)

rubbish ['rʌbiʃ] *n.* ①垃圾;废物: be thrown on to the ~ heap of history 被扔进历史的垃圾堆 ②废话;无聊的思想: He is talking ~. 他在说废话。/ *Rubbish!* 废话! (或: 胡说!)

rubble ['rʌbl] *n.* 碎石,碎砖,破瓦;【建】毛石,块石: ~ concrete 【建】毛石混凝土 ‖**rubbly** *a.* ‖'**~work** 【建】毛石工(程),乱石工(程)

rubicund ['ru:bikənd] *a.* (脸色、肤色)红润的,血色好的 ‖**~ity** [,ru:bi'kʌnditi] *n.*

rubric ['ru:brik] **I** *n.* ①(古代书本等中的)红字,红标题;(章或节的)标题;法律(或法典中某一部分)的标题 ②祈祷书中的仪式指示(通常印成红色) ③成规,成例 ④(编辑的)按语 **II** *a.* ①用红色写(或刻)的印红字的: a ~ day 节日 ③祈祷书中仪式指示所规定的;按照仪式的

rubus ['ru:bəs] *n.* 悬钩子属植物

ruby ['ru:bi] **I** *n.* ①红宝石;红宝石做的东西(如钟表轴承等)②红宝石色,红玉色;颜色象红宝石的东西 ③脸上(或鼻上)的红酒刺 ④[英]五点半的细铅字 ⑤红葡萄酒 ⑥巴西蜂鸟 **II** *a.* 红宝石色的 **III** *vt.* 把…染成红宝石色;使带有红宝石色 ‖**~ glass** 宝石红玻璃,玉红玻璃 / **~ laser** 红宝石光激射器

ruck¹ [rʌk] **I** *n.* 皱,褶 **II** ❶ *vt.* 弄皱;折叠 (up) ❷ *vi.* 变皱,起皱 (up)

ruck² [rʌk] **I** *n.* ①一堆(物);一群(人)②(赛马中的)落后马群;落伍的一批竞赛者;跟在先锋后的人群(或事物);一般的人(或物): the (common) ~ 普通人,一般事物 **II** *vt.* [方]把…耙成一堆

rucksack ['ruksæk, 'rʌksæk] *n.* (登山或旅行者用的)帆布背包

rudder ['rʌdə] *n.* ①(船等的)舵;(飞机等的)方向舵 ②[喻]指导原则;指针 ③(制麦芽浆时的)搅拌棒 ‖**~less** *a.* 无舵的 ‖'**~fish** *n.* 追船鱼

ruddy ['rʌdi] **I** *a.* ①红润的,血色好的;红的;微红的: in ~ health 红光满面;非常健康 ②[英俚]讨厌的,可恶的;(谎言等)极度的,十足的 **II** *vt.* & *vi.* (使)变红 ‖**ruddily** *ad.* / **ruddiness** *n.*

rude [ru:d] *a.* ①原始(阶段)的;未开化的;未加工

的: ~ times 原始时代 / a ~ steam engine 简陋的蒸汽机 / ~ savages 未开化的野蛮人 / ~ ore 原矿 / ~ cotton 原棉 ②加工粗糙的;简陋的;拙劣的: a ~ bench 做工粗糙的板凳 / ~ fare 粗陋的食物 / a ~ style (writer) 拙劣的风格(作家)③粗略的,大略的: a ~ version 粗略的译文 / ~ classification (estimates) 大致的分类(估计)/ a ~ drawing 草图 / a ~ observer 观察(问题等)不细致的人 ④崎岖不平的;荒野的: a ~ path 崎岖的道路 / ~ scenery 荒芜的景色 ⑤不做作的;直率的: ~ truth 直言不讳的真话 / ~ simplicity 质朴 ⑥粗野的;无礼的;粗鲁的: ~ people 粗野的人 / a ~ reply 无礼的回答 / be ~ to 对某人粗暴无礼 / say ~ things 说粗鲁话 ⑦狂暴的;猛烈的;突然的: a ~ blast of wind 一阵狂风 / ~ passions 大怒 / a ~ awakening 猛然的醒悟;强烈的失望 ⑧茁壮的,强健的: the ~ health of the children 孩子们健壮的身体 ⑨(声音)刺耳的,不和谐的 ‖**~ly** *ad.* / **~ness** *n.*

rudiment ['ru:dimənt] *n.* ①[复]基础,基本原理;初步,入门: the ~s of grammar 语法入门 ②[复]雏形;萌芽: the ~s of a plan 计划的雏形 ③发育未全的器官;退化器官

rudimental [,ru:di'mentl], **rudimentary** [,ru:di-'mentəri] *a.* 基本的;初步的,起码的;发展不全的;残留的,退化的: ~ knowledge 起码知识;初步知识 / a ~ organ 退化器官;痕迹器官

rue¹ [ru:] **I** *n.* [古]后悔,悔恨;悲叹 **II** ❶ *vt.* 懊悔,后悔,悔恨;悲叹: You shall ~ it. 你会后悔的。/ You'll live to ~ it. 你总有一天要后悔的。❷ *vi.* 懊悔,后悔,悔恨;悲叹

rue² [ru:] *n.* 【植】芸香

ruff [rʌf] **I** *n.* ①【动】翎颌;流苏鹬;【机】轴环 ②(十六及十七世纪的人所戴的)宽而硬的轮状皱领 ③一种旧式的纸牌戏;出王牌: cross (或 double) ~ 与搭档者对出王牌 **II** ❶ *vt.* 用王牌胜过 ❷ *vi.* 出王牌

ruffian ['rʌfjən] **I** *n.* 流氓,暴徒 **II** *a.* 残暴的,凶恶的 ‖**~ism** *n.* 流氓习气;暴徒行为 / **~ly** *a.* 流氓般的,暴徒似的;残暴的,凶恶的

ruffle¹ ['rʌfl] **I** ❶ *vt.* ①弄皱;弄毛糙: The wind ~s the surface of the water. 风吹皱了水面。②弄乱(头发等);(鸟受惊时等)竖起(羽毛)③把(布等)打褶裥;给…装褶边 ④触怒,使生气: He (或 His temper) is easily ~d. 他动不动就生气。⑤洗(纸牌);很快地翻动(书页等): ~ the pages to find an illustration 很快地翻书找一张插画 ❷ *vi.* ①变皱,变成表面不平: The flag ~s in the breeze. 旗子在微风中飘动。②烦恼,生气 ③傲慢,自高自大 **II** *n.* ①大吵大闹 ②[~边,皱纹 ②(鸟等)颈上的一圈毛 ③(水面等的)波纹 ④烦恼,生气 ⑤骚动,吵闹 ‖**~r** *n.* ①傲慢的家伙 ②(缝纫机上的)打裥装置

ruffle² ['rʌfl] **I** *vt.* & *vi.* 连续地轻轻擂(鼓等) **II** *n.* 轻擂

rug [rʌg] *n.* 小地毯;炉边地毯;[英](旅行等用的)毛毯 ‖**~ joint** [美俚]高级豪华的夜总会

Rugby ['rʌgbi] *n.* 橄榄球;橄榄球戏 (=~ football)

rugged ['rʌgid] *a.* ①不平的,崎岖的;多岩石的;有皱纹的: ~ mountains 崎岖的山脉 / ~ features 粗犷的容貌 / ~ bark 多皱的树皮 ②粗鲁而朴实的: ~ manners 粗鲁而朴实的态度 ③(声音)刺耳的,难听的: a ~ tone 刺耳的音调 ④(生活)艰难的;(气候)严酷的;狂风暴雨的: a ~ life 艰难的生活 / ~ weather 狂风暴雨的天气 ⑤粗壮的,强健的 ‖~ly *ad.* / ~ness *n.*

rugger ['rʌgə] *n.* [英俚] =Rugby

ruin ['ru(:)in] **I** *n.* ①毁灭;崩溃,覆灭;毁坏: the ~ of an illusion 幻想的破灭 / The castle has fallen into ~. 城堡已坍圮了。/ bring ~ upon oneself 自取灭亡 / come to ~ 毁灭;毁灭 / lie (或 be laid) in ~ (房屋等)倾圮 ②倒毁的东西(如建筑物等);[复]废墟,遗迹: The building is now a ~. 这座楼房现在坍圮了。/ lie in ~s 成为废墟 / the ~s of Rome 古罗马的遗迹;罗马帝国制度的残余 ③倾家荡产;丧失地位;(道德上的)堕落: bring sb. to ~ 使某人破产;使某人丧失地位 ④[只用单]祸因: This carelessness will be his ~ (或 the ~ of him). 他这样粗心大意是要倒霉的。**II** ❶ *vt.* ①使毁灭;使覆灭;毁坏 ②使成废墟 ③使破产;诱奸(女子) ❷ *vi.* ①毁灭;覆灭;毁坏 ②变成废墟 ③破产;堕落 ④[诗]坍头向下地跌落;哗啦地坍下 ‖blue ~ ①劣酒 ②灾难;大失败,大丑 / go to rack and ~ 见 rack[4]

ruination [rui'neiʃən] *n.* ①毁灭;毁坏 ②祸因

ruinous ['ru(:)inəs] *a.* ①毁灭性的;破坏性的;灾难性的 ②倾圮的: a ~ heap 一堆,废墟 ‖~ly *ad.* / ~ness *n.*

rule [ru:l] **I** *n.* ①统治(期),管辖(期);控制,支配: under (during) the ~ of 在…统治下(期间) / be entrusted with the ~ of 受托统治(或管辖)… / bear ~ 支配;统治 ②规定,规则,章程,条例;[宗]教规;[律](对某一案例的)裁决,裁定: a ~ for the admission of new members 接纳新成员的规定 / the ~s of basketball 篮球比赛规则 / standing ~s (公司、团体等的)章程 / ~s and regulations 规章制度 / lay down the ~ that … 规定… / a ~ absolute [律]确定性命令,通例;规律,法则: The ~ of the house is to rise early in the morning. 这家人有早起的习惯。/ He makes it a ~ to do (或 makes a ~ of doing) morning exercises everyday. 他每天必做早操。/ Rainy weather is the ~ there during April. 四月里那儿总是多雨。/ the ~ and the exception 普遍规律(或现象)与例外 ④准则,标准;刻度尺,界尺: a 2 ft. ~ 两呎长的尺 / a carpenter's ~ 木工尺 ⑤[印]嵌线;嵌线图案;破折号: a dotted ~ 点线 / a wave ~ 曲线 / an en (em) ~ 短(长)破折号 ⑥[the ~s][英史](设在监狱旁)供特殊犯人(如无力偿债者)居住的区域 ⑦[英史]居于特殊犯人区的权利: He was a prisoner on ~. 他是居于特殊犯人区的犯人。**II** ❶ *vt.* ①统治,管辖;控制,支配: ~ a country 统治国家 / ~ one's

passions 控制感情 / be ~ed by 受…支配;由…控制 ②裁决,裁定: The chairman ~ed me (或 my motion 或 that my motion was) out of order. 会议主席裁定我的动议不合程序。③(用尺)在纸上划(直线),在(纸)上划平行线;把…排成直线 ❷ *vi.* ①统治,管辖;控制,支配: ~ over a country 统治国家 ②作出裁决,作出裁定: The court will ~ on the matter. 法院将对此事作出裁决。/ ~ against a motion 否决动议 ③(价格等)保持某一水平: Prices (Corn, The market) ~ed high (low). 物价(谷物价格,市场价格)普遍偏高(低)。/ Crops ~ good. 庄稼情况普遍都不错。‖as a (general) ~ 通常;一般说来: As a ~, we get up about six o'clock. 我们通常是六点左右起床。/ by ~ 按照规则地;墨守成规地,刻板地 / by ~ and line 准确地;精密地 / ~ off (用尺)划线隔开: ~ off a column of figures 划线把一行数字隔开 / ~ of thumb 单凭经验来做的方法;比较粗糙的方法;约略的衡量(或估计) / ~ out ①(用直线)划去: ~ out a misspelt word 划掉拼错的词 ②排除,取消;拒绝考虑: Gastric carcinoma cannot be ~d out in this case. 在这病例中不能排除胃癌的可能性。/ Bad weather ~d the excursion out for that day. 恶劣的天气使那天不能出游。/ the golden ~ 金科玉律;指导原则;(基督教《圣经·新约》中的)待人规则(指你想人家怎样待你,你也要怎样待人) / the ~ of the road (水上或陆上的)交通规则 / [海]避碰规则 / the ~ of three 比例的运算法则 (指两内项的积等于两外项的积) / work to ~ (故意)死扣规章而减低生产;怠工 ‖~less *a.* 无规则的;无约束的,无法无天的 ‖~joint (木工用曲尺等只能朝单一方向弯折的)活动接头

ruler ['ru:lə] *n.* ①统治者;管理者;支配者 ②(在纸等上)划平行线的人(或机器) ③尺,直尺;划线板 ‖~ship *n.* 统治地位;统治权

ruling ['ru:liŋ] **I** *a.* ①统治的;支配的;主导的: the ~ class 统治阶级 / the ~ ideas of an age 一个时代的主导思想 ②普遍的,流行的: the ~ price 时价 **II** *n.* ①统治;支配 ②裁决,裁定: a ~ on a motion 对动议的裁决 ③(用尺的)划线;(用尺的)量度 ④划出的线 ‖~pen 直线笔,鸭嘴笔

rum[1] [rʌm] *n.* 朗姆酒,(甘蔗汁制的)糖酒;[美]酒 ‖~-runner *n.* [美口]酒类走私贩;酒类走私船 / ~-running *n.* [美口]酒类走私

rum[2] [rʌm] *a.* ①[英俚]古怪的,离奇的: a ~ fellow 古怪的家伙 / a ~ start 惊人的事件 ②[英俚]难对付的,危险的: a ~ customer 怪家伙(尤指不好惹的人或动物) ③蹩脚的: a ~ joke 拙劣的笑话 ‖~ly *ad.*

rumba ['rʌmbə] **I** *n.* ①伦巴舞(古巴黑人的一种舞蹈或类似的交际舞) ②伦巴舞曲 **II** *vi.* 跳伦巴舞

rumble[1] ['rʌmbl] **I** ❶ *vi.* ①(雷、炮等)隆隆响: the thunder *rumbling* in the distance 远方隆隆的雷声 / The long corridor ~d with their footsteps. 长廊中回响着他们沉重的脚步声。② (车辆)辘辘行驶: The freight train ~d past. 载货列车隆隆驶过。③低沉地讲话; (肚子)咕咕作响 ❷ *vt.* ①使隆隆响; 使辘辘行驶 ②低沉地说: ~ *out* (或 *forth*) a few remarks 用低沉的声音说出几点意见 ③在磨箱里磨光(金属零件等); 在滚转筒里混合 **II** *n.* ①隆隆(声); 辘辘(声): the ~ of tanks and armoured cars 坦克和装甲车的隆隆声 ②马车背后的座位(或放行李处) ③磨箱; 滚转筒 ④普遍的怨声; 吵嚷; [美俚](尤指青少年在街头的)打群架 ‖**rumbling** *n.* & *a.* 隆隆声(的); 辘辘声(的) ‖~ **seat** [美](旧式)汽车车厢背后的敞开座位 / '~-,**tumble** *n.* ① 马车背后的座位 ②行驶时发辘辘声的载重车辆 ③剧烈的摇动

rumble² ['rʌmbl] *vt.* [英俚]彻底了解; 洞察; 察觉

ruminate ['ruːmineit] *vi.* & *vt.* ①反刍; 再嚼 ②沉思默想; 反复思考 (*over, about, of, on*) ‖**rumination** [,ruːmi'neiʃən] *n.* / **ruminator** *n.* 沉思默想者; 好思索者

rummage ['rʌmidʒ] **I** *n.* ① (彻底的)查查; (海关人员的)检查 ②搜出的物件; 杂物(堆) ③供义卖的捐献物 **II** ❶ *vt.* ①翻找; 搜查; 仔细检查: ~ a ship 检查船只 ② 搜出, 查出 (*up, out*) ❷ *vi.* 翻找; 搜查; 仔细检查: ~ *in* a drawer 在抽屉里翻寻东西 / ~ *about* among old papers 在旧文件堆里翻找 ‖*a* ~ *sale* 见 **sale** ‖~**r** *n.* 搜查者; 检查者

rumo(u)r ['ruːmə] **I** *n.* ①谣言, 谣传; 传闻, 传说: *Rumo(u)r* has it (或 There is a ~) that .... 据谣传… / start a ~ 造谣 / spike a ~ 辟谣 ②喃喃细语 **II** *vt.* [常用被动语态записы]谣传: It is ~ed that .... 谣传…(或: 听说…) / He is ~ed to have escaped. 据说他已逃走了。‖'~,**monger** *n.* 造谣者 / '~,**mongering** *n.* 造谣: a ~*mongering* campaign 谣言攻势

rump [rʌmp] *n.* ① (鸟的)尾部; (兽的)臀部; [谑](人的)臀部 ② 后臀部的牛排 (=~ steak); (牛的)臀部肉 ③渣滓 ④(大部分成员已离去或已被开除因而无代表性的)残余议会; (自称代表全体的)叛离集团; 余党

rumple ['rʌmpl] **I** *vt.* & *vi.* 弄皱, 压皱; 弄乱 **II** *n.* 褶纹; 皱褶 ‖**rumply** *a.* 弄皱的, 压皱的; 弄乱的

rumpus ['rʌmpəs] *n.* [口]喧嚷, 吵闹; 口角 ‖*raise a* ~ 引起骚乱 ‖~ **room** (常设于地下的)娱乐室

run¹ [rʌn] [rʌn [ræn], run; running] ❶ *vi.* ①跑, 奔: ~ very fast 跑得很快 / ~ upstairs 跑上楼 / ~ to meet sb. 跑去迎接某人 ②逃跑 ③跑步; (参加)赛跑: Are you *running* in the 100 metres? 你参加一百米赛跑吗? / ~ second 跑第二名 ④ 竞赛; 竞选: ~ for Congress [美]参加国会议员竞选 / ~ for office (the presidency) 竞选公职(总统) / ~ for mayor 竞选市长 ⑤赶紧; 赶去: We *ran* to his aid. 我们赶去帮助

他。/ I'll ~ over (或 up, down) and see you after work. 下班后我来看你。
⑥(车、船)行驶: ~ aground 搁浅 / ~ on a reef 触礁
⑦(鱼在产卵期)洄游
⑧(机器等)运转; (工作等)进行, 继续不断: The diesel engine ~s perfectly well. 这台柴油机运转十分良好。/ How your tongue ~s! 瞧, 你讲个没完!
⑨流, 淌; 滴; (墨水等)渗开; (固体)熔化: The river ~s clear (thick). 水流清澈(浑浊)。/ The child's nose is *running*. 孩子在流鼻涕。
⑩变(成), 变得: ~ low 缺乏, 不足 / ~ short 不足; 快用完 / ~ rampant 横行, 猖狂
⑪蔓生; 蔓延; 传播: The vine ~s over the porch. 葡萄藤在门廊上蔓生。The news *ran* like wildfire. 这消息象野火般很快传播开来。
⑫伸展; (演出等)连续; (合同等)继续有效: The street ~s from north to south. 这条街是南北向的。/ The fence ~s round the house. 栅栏围绕着屋子。/ The film has ~ *for* a month. 这影片已连续放映了一个月。/ The novel has ~ *into* ten editions. 这本小说已经出到第十版了。
⑬(思想、曲调等在头脑中)萦绕
⑭(念头等)闪过; (感觉等)通过; (光阴)流逝
⑮写着, 说着: The resolution ~s as follows: .... 决议如下:… / So the story *ran*. 据说(事情)是这样的。
⑯有倾向 (*to*); (特征等)贯穿; (价格、产量等)平均: ~ *to* extremes 趋向极端 / The theme ~s *through* the play like a red thread. 这主题象一根红线贯穿全剧。/ The apples ~ big this year. 今年苹果长得很大。
⑰(针织品)脱针, 抽丝
❷ *vt.* ①使跑, 使奔: ~ sb. (clean) off his legs 使某人疲于奔命
②在…上跑来跑去; 跑过, 穿过: ~ the streets (小孩)在街上玩耍; 流浪街头 / The fever (heat) has ~ its course. 热度(暑气)已开始退了。
③参加(赛跑、竞赛); 同…比赛; 使(马等)比赛: ~ a race 参加赛跑 / ~ sb. hard (或 close) (在比赛中)紧紧钉住某人; 紧追某人
④提出(候选人); 提出(某人)参加竞选: ~ a candidate in the presidential election 提出竞选总统的候选人 / ~ sb. *for* mayor 提名某人参加市长竞选
⑤追捕(猎物等); 追查, 探究: ~ a rumour *back to* its source 追查谣言的来源
⑥放牧(牛、羊等)
⑦驾驶, 开; 放(车辆): ~ a taxi 驾驶出租汽车 / ~ extra trains during holidays 节日期间开加班(火)车
⑧运载; 偷运(走私货物等)
⑨开动(机器等)
⑩办; 管理, 经营; 指挥(运动等); 奔走着做: ~ a factory 办(或管理)工厂 / ~ a study class 办学习班 / ~ all enterprises with diligence and

frugality 勤俭办一切事业 / ~ errands (为别人) 奔走, 跑腿 / ~ messages (为别人) 送信, 传信息 ⑪流; 使流; 倒注; 浇铸, 熔铸; 提炼: The wound *ran* blood. 伤口流血。/ ~ the water off 把水放掉 / ~ molten iron into a mould 将铁水注入模子 / ~ bullets 浇铸子弹 / ~ oil 提炼石油 ⑫使处(于) (*into*); 冒(危险等): ~ sb. *into* difficulties 使某人陷入困境 / ~ the risk of 冒…的危险(或风险) ⑬使通过, 使穿过; 使扫视: ~ a thread *through* an eyelet 把线穿过小孔 / ~ cards *into* a file 把卡片插入卡片夹中 / ~ one's eyes *down* a list 匆匆看一下单子 ⑭把…刺; 刺, 戳: ~ a splinter *into* one's toe 脚趾上戳进一根刺 ⑮使撞(或碰) ⑯使伸展: ~ a simile too far 把一个明喻用得牵强附会 ⑰感染: ~ a fever (或 temperature) 发烧 ⑱(连续)刊登; 刊印: a book to be ~ on lightweight paper 将用轻质纸刊印的一本书 ⑲【体】连续得(分) ⑳匆忙地缝 ㉑划, 描: ~ a contour line on a map 在地图上画等高线 ㉒使(帐目等)累积, 积欠: ~ an account at the grocery 在食品杂货店里积欠欠帐 **II** *n.* ①跑; (长距离)赛跑; (跑的)气力;【空】滑行(距离): break into a ~ 突然奔跑起来 / After the race he still has a lot of ~ in him. 赛跑以后他的体力还很充沛。/ a takeoff ~ (飞机)起飞滑跑 ②短期旅行; 路程, 航程: a two-hour ~ by train 两小时火车的路程 / a day's ~ (船)一昼夜的航程 ③(车、船等的)路线, 航线; 班次: a bomb ~ 【军】轰炸航线 / make an extra ~ (车、船)增开一班次 / The milkman has finished his ~. 送牛奶的人已送完牛奶。④趋势, 动向; (矿脉、木纹等的)走向: the general ~ of things 一般情况(或趋势) / the ~ of events 事态的趋势 / the ~ of the cards 打牌的手气(或牌运) ⑤(普通)类型; 普通产品; 一批产品: be out of the common ~ 不平常, 不普通, 不同凡响 / the ~ of the mill (工厂的)普通产品 ⑥一次生出的(或一起饲养的)动物; (产卵期)洄游的鱼群; 鱼群的洄游 ⑦(野兽出没的)路径; (羊等的)放牧场; (鸡等的)饲养场 ⑧流动; 流量; 水槽, 水管; [美方]小河 ⑨(长度、时间等的)连续: a ~ of office 任期 / a ~ of misfortunes 接二连三的不幸 ⑩连续的演出(或展出、刊登等): a long (limited) ~ 长期(限期)演出 / have a ~ of 20 days 连续演出(或展出)二十天 / a long ~ of power 长期掌权(或执政)

⑪(机器的)运转; 运转期: a trial ~ (机器、汽车等的)试车; (船等的)试航 ⑫[口]使用(或出入)的自由: give sb. the ~ of the reference books 允许某人随意使用参考书 ⑬挤提存款, 挤兑; 抢购; 畅销; 流行: ~s on banks 向银行挤提存款 / The book has a considerable ~. 这本书销路很好。⑭突降: The temperature came down *with a* ~. 温度突然下降。⑮(按音阶顺序的)速奏, 急唱 ⑯脱针, 抽丝 ⑰(板球、棒球等的)得分单位, 一分 ⑱(滑雪等的)滑道 ⑲【船】船尾尖部

‖*a* ~ *for one's money* ① 花了钱(或力气)而得到的一些满足 ② 剧烈的竞争 / *at a* ~ 跑着 / *get the* ~ *upon* (*sb.*) 占(某人的)上风; 能嘲弄(某人) / (*have*) *the* ~ *of one's teeth* 免费吃饭 / *He who* ~*s may read.* 通俗者易懂。/ *hold* (或 ~) *with the hare and* ~ (或 *hunt*) *with the hounds* 两面讨好 / *in the long* ~ 从长远的观点看来; 终究, 毕竟; 最后, 结果 / *in the short* ~ 从短期看来; 在短期内 / *It's all in the day's* ~. 应看作正常(或普通)的事。/ *keep the* ~ *of* [美口]接近…保持接触; 经常了解…/ *on the* ~ ①跑着 ②逃跑 ③奔走, 奔波 ④被警局追缉的; (被警察局追缉而)离开常去地方的 / ~ *across* ① 跑着穿过 ②偶然碰见 / ~ *afoul* (或 *foul*) *of* ① 与…相撞; 与…冲突: *foul of* the law 触犯法律 ② 与…纠缠 / ~ *after* ①追捕; 跟踪 ②追求 / ~ *against* ①撞 ②偶然碰见 ③ 违反 / ~ *along* 走掉; 离开 / ~ *amuck* (或 *amok*) 横行; 乱冲乱杀 / ~ *at* 冲过去袭击 / ~ *away* ①潜逃; 私奔 ②失去控制: Don't let the car ~ *away*. 别让车开得太快而失去控制。/ ~ *away with* ①携(某物)潜逃 ②带(某人)私奔 ③在(比赛等)中轻易取胜; 获得(奖品等) ④消耗(时间、金钱) ⑤轻易得出(结论等); 轻易接受(意见等) ⑥失去控制: His fancy *ran away with* him. 他胡思乱想。/ ~ *back over* 回顾 / ~ *counter to* 违反…, 与…背道而驰 / ~ *down* ①跑下 ②在…上跑下 ③(因发条走完)停掉; 用完: The battery has ~ *down*. 电池里的电用完。④用尽筋疲力尽; (健康情况)逐渐变坏 ⑤(房子、公路等因失修而)坏下去; 减低价值 ⑥与…相撞; 撞倒 ⑦追捕到; 捕杀; 追查到 ⑧探究…的根源, 追溯 ⑨贬低, 说…的坏话 ⑩浏览, 扫视 / ~ *false* (猎狗等)不跟臭迹而直追猎物 / ~ *for it* 为躲避大雨或危险等)快跑 / ~ *in* ①跑进来 ②非正式地访问, 顺便探望: He lives close by and ~*s in* (to us) whenever he likes. 他住在附近, 高兴就来探望(我们)。③把(牲畜)赶入栏内 ④[俚]拘留, 逮捕(罪行较轻的人) ⑤对(汽车等)试车;【机】试转 ⑥插入, 补入; [印]使不间断, 使不分段; 接排 ⑦使当选用于开始短兵相接地作战 / ~ *into* ①跑进②(使)撞: The car *ran into* a wall. 汽车撞在墙上。/ The careless driver *ran* his car *into* a wall.

粗心大意的驾驶人把汽车撞在墙上。③偶然碰见(人)④(使)陷于: ~ into debt 开始负债 / He never let anything ~ him into debt. 不管发生什么事情，他决不借债。⑤(累积而)达到 / ~ **off** ①(使)逃跑: ~ off with money 携款卷逃 ②从…流掉 ③使流掉 ④(火车等)出(轨) ⑤流畅地写出(或背出)⑥印出; 打印出 ⑦把(比赛)进行到底; 以决赛决定(赛跑)的胜负; 进行决赛: When will the race be ~ off? 赛跑什么时候进行决赛? ⑧进行(试验)⑨完成(演奏等)⑩私自赶走, 偷(牛等)/ ~ **on** ①连续; (字母)连写 ②【印】不分段, 不换行; 接排(排印材料); 把(词典中词目等)放于一项的结尾 ③喋喋不休(或滔滔不绝)地讲 ④(时间)流逝 ⑤(病情等)继续进展 ⑥涉及: Our talk ran on world events. 我们谈论了世界大事。/ ~ **oneself out** 跑得筋疲力尽 / ~ **out** ①跑出; 离开 ②完成; 跑完(赛跑)③流出; 流逝 ④期满 ⑤(粮食等)被用完; 将尽: Their carbon paper is running out. 他们的复写纸快用完了。/ My patience is running out. 我快要耐不住了。⑥(绳子)放出去; 把(绳子)放出去去; 【空】放下(起落架襟翼)⑦突出, 伸向: a pier running out into the sea 伸向海中的码头 ⑧逐出 ⑨【印】用空铅(或点线等)填入 ⑩【印】把(一段的第一行)排成向左伸出 / ~ **out of** 用完: They have ~ out of ink. 他们墨水用完了。/ ~ **over** ①(跑)过去(或过来): I shall ~ over to the village this afternoon. 我将在今天下午到那个村庄去。/ He sometimes ~s over to my place to talk about our work. 他有时到我这里来谈工作。②溢出; (杯中水等)满出; 超出限度: The water is running over. 水在溢出。/ The delay is running over. 耽搁得太久了。③扼要复述 ④匆匆排练(或唱) ⑤匆匆看过(或读过), 浏览 ⑤(车辆等)辗过: She was ~ over yesterday when she was crossing the street. 昨天她穿过街道时被车子辗过了。/ ~ **through** ①跑着穿过 ②戳, 刺 ③划掉 ④匆匆看过; 匆匆处理; 不间断地排练 ⑤挥霍; 很快用完 ⑥贯穿 / ~ **to** ①跑到 ②(费用等)达到…; 伸展到; 发展到 ③有钱做(某事); (钱等)足够做(某事): John said, "I can't (或 my money won't) ~ to that." 约翰说:"我没有足够的钱去做那件事。" ④(人、植物等)趋向: ~ to fat 发胖 / ~ to waste 被浪费 / let seed 见 **seed** / ~ **up** ①向上跑; 在…向上跑 ②升(旗等)③很快地缝, 赶做(衣服等); 匆匆搭起(建筑物等)④(债款等)迅速积累; 迅速积累(债款等); (迅速)加起(数字等)⑤抬高(价格); (物价)高涨 ⑥很快生长 ⑦使(飞机发动机)高速转动 / ~ **up against** ①意外地碰到(困难等)/ ~ **up** ②撞着 / ~ **upon** ①(思想等)萦绕着: His thoughts were always running upon the perfection of the machine. 他老是在想怎样使这台机器完善。②偶然碰见(人或物)③(船)撞, 触(礁等)/ ~ **up to** ①跑到 ②(积累而)达到(某一数目); (物价)高涨到…; 把…积累到… / Sunday ~ [美俚]①长距离 ②(流动推销员等用语)星期日的旅行

‖ '**~about** n. ①轻便小汽车; 轻便汽艇; 轻便运货车 ②流浪者 a. 流浪的 / ~**agate** ['rʌnəgeit] n. ①逃亡者; 背叛者 ②流浪汉 / ~**around** n. [美俚]借口; 躲闪, 拖延(尤指对付索款者、谋职者等) / '~**away** n. ①逃跑, 逃亡 ②逃跑者; 脱缰的马 ③脱离控制 ④压倒的优胜 a. ①逃跑的; 私奔的; (工厂、企业等)为逃避某地工会势力(或赋税)而迁移的 ② 脱离控制的; (物价)飞涨的, 易起急剧变化的: ~away inflation 无法控制的通货膨胀 ③(比赛)轻易取胜的; (胜利)决定性的 / '~**down** n. ①(军备等的)裁减 ②简要的总结, 纲要; 分列项目的报告 / '~-**down** a. ①(钟表等)发条走完的, 停了的 ②精疲力竭的; 衰弱的 ③(房屋等)失修的, 颓败的, 坍倒的 / ~'-**in** n. ①口角, 争吵 ②【军】(发动机)试车 ③【军】飞机向目标(或指定地点)的飞行 ④【印】插入部分, 补加部分 / '~'**off** n. ①(雨水、融雪等的)径流(量); 流量 ②决赛 ③决定性竞选 / '~-**of-'paper** a. (由编辑)随意决定登载位置的: ~-of-paper advertisements 在报上随意插排的广告 / '~-**of-(the-)'mill** a. (在质量上)一般性的, 不突出的 / '~-**of-the-'mine** a. ①(煤)不按规格、质量分等级的; 粗制的 ② =~-of-(the-)mill / '~-**on** n. 【印】(不移行而)接排的材料(如词典的词目) a. (诗行之间)词意连贯的 / '~-**on sentence** ①用错逗号的句子(该用连接词而用了逗号) ②乱加从句的冗长句子 / '~-**out** n. 逃开, 避开 / '~-**over** a. (排印材料)超过篇幅的 / '~**over** n. ①超篇幅的排印材料 ②(报刊等文章的)转页部分 / '~-**through** n. ①浏览 ②概要 ③从头至尾的排练 / '~-**up** n. ①飞机发动机试验 ②涨价 ③(跳高时的)跑近起跳线 / '~**way** n. ①(机场的)跑道 ②河床, 河道 ③(运木材等的)斜坡滑道 ④动物踏出的路; (通向动物饮水处的)小径; (动物等用的)过道, 通道; (供鸡等在内自由活动的)家禽围场

run[2] [rʌn] a. ①熔化的; 融化的 ②浇铸的, 模铸的: ~ metal 铸金属 ③(鱼因产卵而)洄游的 ④(蜂蜜等)提取的, 抽出的 ⑤[口]被走私的, 被偷运的: ~ goods 走私货物 ⑥跑得筋疲力尽的; 跑得气喘的

rung[1] [rʌŋ] ring[2] 的过去式和过去分词

rung[2] [rʌŋ] n. ①棍子; (椅子等的)横档; 车辐; 梯级 ②(地位上升的)一级 ‖the lowest (topmost) ~ of Fortune's ladder 倒霉(幸运)之极

runner ['rʌnə] n. ①赛跑的人(或动物等); (棒球赛中的)跑垒者; (足球赛中的)盘球者 ②(商行等的)出差者; 送信者; 外勤员; 跑街, 推销员; 收款员; 接待员 ③(走私者)走私船; 偷越封锁线的人(或船) ④(机器等的)操作者; 火车司机 ⑤(装饰用)狭长桌布; (楼梯等用的)狭长地毯 ⑥十八世纪伦敦巡官(或警探) ⑦【动】普通秧鸡; 鳝属的鱼; 黑蛇 ⑧【植】长匍茎, 纤匍枝; 蔓藤植物: scarlet ~ 红花菜豆 ⑨滑行装置; (雪车等的)滑橇; (溜冰鞋的)冰刀; (抽屉等的)滑槽, 滑道; (移动重物的)承辊; (窗帘等的)滑圈 ⑩[冶]流道 ⑪转

动的磨石 ⑫【海】游动绞辘 ‖**~ bean** [主英]红花菜豆

runt [rʌnt] *n.* ①发育不全的矮小的植物(或动物);(一胎猪中)最小的猪;小种的牛 ②[口][贬]发育不全的矮小的人 ③[苏格兰][英方]植物的硬茎;腐朽的根株;老牛;干瘪老太婆

rupee [ru:'pi:] *n.* 卢比(印度等的货币单位)

rupture ['rʌptʃə] **I** *n.* ①破裂,裂开 ②决裂;不和;(国家之间的)敌对;交战 ③【医】破裂;疝,突出:~ of the heart muscle 心肌破裂 **II** ❶ *vt.* ①使破裂 ②断绝(关系等) ❷ *vi.* ① 裂开,破裂 ②断绝 ‖**~d duck** [美俚](美军)荣誉退役证上的飞鹰标识

rural ['ruərəl] *a.* ①农村的;田园的:a ~ survey 农村调查 / a ~ base area 农村根据地 ②生活于农村的 ③农业的:~ economy 农业经济 ‖**~ly** *ad.* ‖**~ dean** [英](主管若干教区的)乡区牧师 / **~ (free) delivery** [美](对不设邮局的)乡村免费邮递 / **~ route** (乡村免费邮递区的)邮道

ruse [ru:z] *n.* 诡计;计策

rusé ['ru:zei] *a.* [法]诡计多端的,狡猾的

rush¹ [rʌʃ] **I** ❶ *vi.* ①冲;奔;闯;急流:~ at (或 on, upon) the enemy 冲向敌人 / ~ into (out of) the room 奔进(出)房间 / The river ~es past. 河流奔腾而过。/ Avalanches ~ed down. 崩坍的冰雪倾泻而下。②仓促行动 (to, into):~ to conclusions 匆匆下结论 / ~ into print 仓促地出版(或付印、发表)/ ~ into extremes 不加思索地走极端 ③突然出现,涌现:The stars ~ed out. 星星一下子都出来了。/ An idea ~ed into my mind. 我蓦地想起一个主意。④抢先;赶紧:~ for the ball (足球赛中)争球 ❷ *vt.* ①使冲,使急行;急送;猛推:~ troops to the front 急调部队到前线去 / ~ sb. to the hospital 火速送某人进医院 ②匆忙地做:~ one's work 赶做工作 / The bill was ~ed through. 议案匆匆通过了。③催促 ④突然袭击;冲过去占领(建筑物等) ⑤蜂拥地抢占(会议讲台等):~ the boats 抢着上船 ⑥飞速跃过:~ the barricades 冲过路障 ⑦[俚]向…索高价:How much did they ~ you for this? 在这东西上他们敲了你多少钱的竹杠? ⑧[美俚]向(女子等)献殷勤 ⑨[美](用开舞会招待等办法)试图要…加入大学生联谊会 **II** *n.* ①冲;奔;急速行进(或流动):the ~ of the current 激流的奔腾 ②忙碌(一阵):a ~ of work 一阵匆忙的工作 / Why all this ~? 为什么这样忙乱? ③(突然产生的)一大批:a ~ of prohibitions 突然发布的一连串禁令 ④(突然的)迫切需要;抢购;蜂拥前往:the Christmas ~ 圣诞节(前夕)的购买热潮 / a ~ for (或 on) gold 涌往新金矿(或有利可图的地方),淘金热;抢购黄金 / a ~ for the door 拥往门口 ⑤(感情的)一阵激动 ⑥突然袭击,猛攻 ⑦[美](大学各年级学生间争夺奖品等)一种比武 ⑧(社交活动中)献殷勤 ⑨[常用复](电影摄制中未经剪辑的)样片 **III** *a.* ①急需的:a ~ order 紧急定货 ②匆忙的;繁忙的:~ hours (公共车辆

等的)高峰时间,拥挤时刻 / the ~ season 忙季,旺季 ‖**~ sb. off his feet** 见 **foot** / **with a ~** 猛地,哄地一下子 ‖**'~-,harvest** *vt.* 抢收:~-harvest the early rice 抢收早稻 / **'~-plant** *vt.* 抢种

rush² [rʌʃ] **I** *n.* ①【植】灯心草;灯心草属植物:a ~ product (mat) 蒲制品(蒲席) ②无价值的东西 **II** *vt.* 用灯心草做(或铺) ‖not care a ~ 满不在乎 / not worth a ~ 毫无价值 ‖**~ candle, '~-light** ①灯草芯蜡烛 ②微光;微不足道的人;孤陋寡闻

russet ['rʌsit] **I** *n.* ①黄褐色;赤褐色 ②黄褐色(或赤褐色)土布 ③(粗皮有斑的)赤褐色苹果 **II** *a.* ①黄褐色的;赤褐色的 ②黄褐色(或赤褐色)土布制的 ③[罕]乡下的;简朴的

rust [rʌst] **I** *n.* ①铁锈,锈:rub the ~ off a knife 擦去刀子上的锈 ②(脑子等的)发锈,衰退;惰性:keep one's mind from ~ 使头脑不生锈 ③铁锈色,赭色 ④【植】锈病;锈菌 **II** ❶ *vi.* ①生锈;氧化:Iron ~s. 铁会生锈。②(脑子等)发锈,衰退:not allow one's faculties to ~ 使自己的能力不衰退 ③成铁锈色:The leaves slowly ~ed in autumn. 秋天叶子慢慢变成红褐色了。④【植】患锈病 ❷ *vt.* ①使(金属)生锈 ②使(脑子等)发锈(或衰退) ③使成铁锈色 ‖better wear out than ~ out 见 **wear¹** ‖**~less** *a.* 无锈的,不锈的:~less steel 不锈钢 / **'~-proof** *a.* 防锈的,不锈的

rustic ['rʌstik] **I** *a.* ①乡村的,农村的 ②乡村式的;庄稼人样子的,质朴的;[贬]土气的,粗俗的:~ simplicity 淳朴 / ~ manners 土里土气的样子 ③(桌、椅等)用带皮树枝做成的;做工粗糙的;粗面石工的:a ~ bridge (用带皮树干搭成的)粗木桥 / ~ furniture 用带皮树枝做成的家具 **II** *n.* ①农村中的人,庄稼人 ②[贬]乡巴佬,粗汉 ‖**~ally** *ad.*

rustle¹ ['rʌsl] **I** ❶ *vi.* (绸衣、树叶、纸等)沙沙作响 ❷ *vt.* 使沙沙作响 **II** *n.* 沙沙声,瑟瑟声

rustle² ['rʌsl] [美口] ❶ *vi.* ①使劲干;急速动 ②觅食 ③偷牛(或马等) ❷ *vt.* ①弄到(食物等) ②把(牛)赶拢 ③偷牛(或马) ‖**~ up** 弄到(食物等)

rusty¹ ['rʌsti] *a.* ①生锈的;锈的:a ~ needle 生锈的针 / a ~ spot 锈斑 ②(脑子等)发锈的,变迟钝的,衰退的:a ~ mind 变迟钝的头脑 / My English is ~. 我的英语荒疏了。/ I'm a ~ ~ in chess. 我好久不下棋,技术不大行了。③铁锈色的,赭色的;(衣服等)已褪色的:a ~ old coat 颜色泛黄的旧上衣 ④陈旧的,过时的:a ~ joke 听腻了的笑话 / a ~ old fellow 迂腐的老家伙 ⑤(笑声等)嘶哑的,刺耳的 ⑥【植】患锈病的;(水果等)有锈斑的 ‖cut up ~ 发脾气,发怒 ‖**rustily** *ad.* / **rustiness** *n.*

rusty² ['rʌsti] *a.* [方]发脾气的,恼火的:be (turn) ~ 在发(开始发)脾气

rusty³ ['rʌsti] *a.* (肉类等)腐烂发臭的

rut¹ [rʌt] **I** *n.* ①车辙;踏成的路;凹槽;沟 ②常规,

惯例; 老规矩, 老一套 **II** (rutted; rutting) *vt.* 在
…形成车辙; 在…挖槽 ‖*get into a* ~ 开始墨守
成规 / *lift sb. out of the* ~ 使某人摆脱旧习惯
(或常规)
rut² [rʌt] **I** *n.* ① (雄鹿等的)发淫, (周期性的)春
情发动 ② 发淫期 **II** (rutted; rutting) *vi.* (雄鹿

等)发淫, 春情发动
ruthless ['ru:θlis] *a.* 无情的; 冷酷的; 残忍的 ‖~**ly**
ad. / ~**ness** *n.*
rye¹ [rai] *n.* ①【植】黑麦, 裸麦 ② 黑麦威士忌酒
‖~ **bread** 黑面包 / ~ **grass**【植】黑麦草
rye² [rai] *n.* 绅士(尤指吉普赛绅士)

S

Sabbath ['sæbəθ] *n.* ①【宗】安息日, 主日(犹太教
徒为星期六, 基督教徒为星期日)(=~ day) ②
[s-] 休息期 ‖*break the* ~ 不守安息日(指在安息
日工作或娱乐) / *great* (或 *holy*) ~ 大安息
日(复活节的前一天) / *keep the* ~ 守安息日
(在安息日敬神或休息) / ~*-day's journey* 安
息日旅程(约三分之二哩的行程); 轻松的旅行 /
witches' ~ 传说中每年一度妖魔鬼怪在半夜聚
会的日子 ‖~**less** *a.* 不守安息日的 ‖~ **school**
【宗】主日学, 星期日学校
sable¹ ['seibl] **I** *n.* ① 黑貂 ② 黑貂皮 ③[复]黑貂
皮外衣(或衣领) ④ 貂毛制的画笔 **II** *a.* 黑貂皮
制的
sable² ['seibl] **I** *n.* ①[诗]黑色; 深褐色 ②[复]丧
服 ③ =~ antelope **II** *a.* ① 黑的; 深褐色的
②[诗](夜)阴暗的; (命运)可怕的 ‖*His Sable
Majesty* [谑]魔鬼, 魔王 ‖~**d** *a.* 穿丧服的; 黑
色的; 染黑的 / **sably** *ad.* ‖~ **antelope** (产于南
非的)一种大羚羊(公的为黑色)
sabotage ['sæbətɑ:ʒ] **I** *n.* ①(对财产等的)故意毁
坏 ②阴谋破坏, 破坏活动 **II** ❶ *vt.* 破坏: ~
an agreement 破坏协定 ❷ *vi.* 进行破坏, 从事
破坏活动 (*on*)
saboteur ['sæbə'tə:] *n.* 破坏者; 怠工者
sabra ['sɑ:brə] *n.* 土生土长的以色列人
sabre ['seibə] **I** *n.* ① 马刀, 军刀; (击剑或决斗用的)
长剑 ②[the ~] 武力; 黩武政治 ③[复]【史】骑
兵队; 骑兵: 3,000 ~s 三千骑兵 ④(制造玻璃时)
撇去熔化的玻璃表面浮质的铜器 **II** *vt.* 用马刀
砍 (或杀) ‖*rattle the* ~ 以战争恫吓 ‖'~**cut** *n.*
① 马刀的劈砍 ❷ 被马刀砍的伤口 (或伤疤) /
'~**rattler** *n.* 黩武主义者 / ~ **rattling** 战争叫
嚣; 武力威胁; 张牙舞爪 / '~**toothed** *a.* (动物)
长着锐利的长犬牙的
sachet ['sæʃei] *n.* ①(熏衣用的)香囊; 小香袋 ②香
粉 (=~ powder)
sack¹ [sæk] **I** *n.* ①袋;粗布袋; 麻袋; 硬纸袋 ②(一)
袋,(一)包: two ~s of cement 两袋水泥 ③[古]
妇女宽身长服; (妇孺穿的)宽大上衣; (附着于衣
服肩上的)丝绸褶裥长抱纱 ④ [the ~] [口]开
除; 解雇: give sb. the ~ 开除某人 / get the ~
被解雇 ⑤[美俚]床; 睡袋; 睡觉 ⑥(棒球)垒

II ❶ *vt.* ① 装…入袋: ~ flour 表面粉入袋
②[口]开除; 解雇 ③(在竞赛等中)胜过 ❷ *vi.*
[美俚]上床, 睡觉 (*in, up*) ‖*a sad* ~ [美俚]
① 讨厌、难相处的人; 不讨人喜欢的女孩子 ② 好
心办坏事的人(或士兵) / *hit the* ~ [美俚]就
寝 / *hold the* ~ [美俚] ①两手空空; 在分配物
中只得到最差的一份; 受骗 ② 独担(本应与他人
共同承担的)全部罪责 / ~ *out* [美俚]上床睡觉;
睡个够 / ~ *time* [美俚]睡觉时间 ‖~**ful** *n.* 一
满袋: a ~*ful* of grain 一满袋谷子 / ~**ing** *n.*
粗平麻布, 麻袋布 ‖'~**cloth** *n.* ① 粗平麻布, 麻
袋布 ②丧服: in ~*cloth* and ashes【宗】哀悔, 悲
切忏悔 / ~ **coat** 男式便装短上衣 / ~ **race** 套
袋赛跑(指腿上套着袋, 跳跃前进的一种赛跑)
sack² [sæk] **I** *n.* [the ~] 劫掠 **II** *vt.* 劫掠; 洗劫
(被攻陷的城市等) ‖~**er** *n.* 劫掠者 / ~**ing** *n.*
劫掠
sack³ [sæk] *n.* (十六、十七世纪时从欧洲南部输入
英国的)白葡萄酒
sacral ['seikrəl] *a.* ①【解】骶的; 荐骨的 ② 宗教仪
式的; 神圣的 ‖~**ize** *vt.* 使神圣化
sacrament ['sækrəmənt] **I** *n.* ①【基督教】圣礼, 圣
事(如洗礼、坚振等仪式) ②[常作 the S-]【基督
教】圣餐; 用作圣餐的面包和葡萄酒; 圣餐面包 ③
神圣的东西; 神秘的东西 ④庄严的誓言 (或诺言)
II *vt.* 使立誓, 使宣誓
sacramental [,sækrə'mentl] **I** *a.* ①(用于)圣礼的;
(用于)圣餐的 ②受圣礼 (或誓言) 约束的; 神圣的
II *n.* 象圣礼的仪式(如用圣水等)
sacred ['seikrid] *a.* ①【宗】上帝的, 神的, 神圣的;
宗教的: ~ writings 宗教经典 / ~ history
《圣经》中记载的历史 / ~ music 圣乐 / a ~
number 宗教上神圣之数(如七) ② 神圣的; 不可
侵犯的; 庄严的; 郑重的 ③祭祀(某神)的; 献给
…的; 专供…用的 (*to*) ‖~**ly** *ad.* / ~**ness** *n.*
‖**Sacred College**【天主教】罗马教廷枢机主教
团 / ~ **cow** (印度)圣牛; [谑]神圣不可侵犯的
人(或事物)
sacrifice ['sækrifais] **I** *n.* ① 牺牲; 牺牲品: fear
no ~ 不怕牺牲 / make ~s (或 a ~) 作出牺牲;
付出代价 / at some ~ of regularity 以打乱一
些常规为代价 ②亏本出售, 贱卖; 损失; 亏本出售

的商品: sell sth. at a ~ 亏本出售某物 ③【宗】献祭;祭品;基督的献身(指钉十字架);(表示感恩的)圣餐 ④(棒球比赛中为救球而作的)牺牲的一击 (=~ hit) **II ❶** *vt.* ①牺牲;献出: ~ one's life to save others 为救别人而牺牲自己的生命 ②亏本出售 ③ 献祭 **❷** *vi.* ① 献祭 ②(棒球比赛中)作牺牲的一击 ||*the great*(或 *last, supreme*) ~ 为国(或理想)献身

sacrificial [ˌsækri'fiʃəl] *a.* 牺牲的; 献祭的: a ~ object 牺牲品,殉葬品 ||**~ly** *ad.*

sacrilege ['sækrilidʒ] *n.* ① 渎圣; 渎圣罪; 亵渎 ②盗窃圣物罪

sacrilegious [ˌsækri'lidʒəs] *a.* ① 渎圣的; 亵渎的 ②盗窃圣物的 ||**~ly** *ad.* / **~ness** *n.*

sacrosanct ['sækrousæŋkt] *a.* 极神圣的; 不可侵犯的 ||**~ity** [ˌsækrou'sæŋktiti] *n.*

sacrum ['seikrəm] ([复] sacra ['seikrə]) *n.* 【解】骶骨; 荐骨

sad [sæd] (sadder, saddest) *a.* ①悲哀的; 令人悲痛的 ②[口]糟透的, 坏透的: a ~ coward 十足的胆小鬼 ③(颜色)黯淡的 ④(面包、点心等)未烤透而粘糊的; 发得不好的 ||*in* ~ *earnest* 一本正经地, 十分严肃 ||**~ly** *ad.* / **~ness** *n.* ||**'~iron** *n.* (两端尖并有可拆卸的柄的)大熨斗

sadden ['sædn] **❶** *vt.* ①使悲哀, 使悲痛 ②使(颜色)黯淡; 使阴暗 **❷** *vi.* 悲哀, 悲痛

saddle ['sædl] **I** *n.* ①鞍子, 马鞍; (自行车、农业机械等)鞍座; (马背等的)鞍部 ②鞍状物; 鞍状山脊; 书脊; (鞋面的)镶皮脊 ③(带脊骨与肋骨的)脊肉; (雄禽的)背部的羽毛 ④【机】座板, 滑动座架; 滑板, 锅炉座: an axle ~ 轴鞍 / a cylinder ~ 鞍形汽缸座 ⑤浮桥(或电线杆上)的托梁;【船】圆枕木 **II** **❶** *vt.* ①给(马等)装鞍 ②使负担; 强加: ~ a burden *on* (或 *upon*) sb. 使某人负重担 / ~ sb. *with* an obligation 把义务强加在某人身上 / be ~d *with* an ever-deepening economic crisis 陷入日益严重的经济危机 **❷** *vi.* 跨上马鞍 ||*be in the* ~ 骑着马; [喻]执政, 掌权 / *for the* ~ (马)供骑用的 / *get into the* ~ 上马; [喻]就职; 开始掌权 / *put the* ~ *on the right* (*wrong*) *horse* ①责备应该(不该)责备的人 ②[罕]夸奖应该(不该)夸奖的人 ||**'~back** *n.* ①鞍状物; 鞍状山脊;【建】两山头房顶【动】黑背鸥; 北海豹 *a.* 鞍形的 / **'~backed** *a.* ①鞍形的 ②有鞍形花纹的 / **'~bag** *n.* ①鞍囊, 马褡裢 ②(自行车等鞍座后的)挂包, 工具包 / **'~bow** *n.* 鞍的前弓 / **'~cloth** *n.* 鞍褥, 布鞍垫 / **'~fast** *a.* 稳坐马上的 / ~ *horse* 驮马, 可骑的马 / **'~leather** 鞍皮 / **'~-pin** *n.* (自行车等支撑鞍座的)鞍栓 / ~ *roof* 【建】两山头房顶 / ~ *shoe* 鞋帮中段用黄(或褐)色皮的浅口缚带白便鞋 / ~ *soap* 一种洗皮革用的肥皂 / ~ *sore* ①马背上的鞍疮 ②骑者的鞍疮 / **'~tree** *n.* ① 鞍架 ②【植】美国鹅掌楸

saddler ['sædlə] *n.* ① 鞍工, 马具工; 卖鞍子(或马

具)的人 ②(骑兵团中)管马具的人 ③驯马, 可骑的马 ④北海豹 ||**~y** ['sædləri] *n.* ①鞍工术, 马具术 ②[总称]马具; 马具业; 马具店

Sadducee ['sædjusiː] *n.* 撒都该人(古代犹太教一个派别的成员; 该派否定死人的复活、灵魂的存在、来世和天使) ||**~ism** *n.* 撒都该人的信仰(或教义)

sadism ['sædizəm] *n.* ①施虐淫, 性虐待狂, 残暴色情狂 ②虐待狂; 极度残暴

sadist ['sædist] *n.* ① 施虐淫者, 性虐待狂者 ②虐待狂者 ||**~ic** [sæ'distik] *a.* ①施虐淫的, 性虐待狂的 ②虐待狂的

safari [sə'fɑːri] *n.* ①(尤指在东非和中非的)旅行; 狩猎远征 ②狩猎远征队及其装备

safe¹ [seif] *a.* ① 安全的, 保险的; 平安的; 无损的: ~ driving (operation) 安全驾驶(操作) / a ~ stopping distance 安全停车距离 / be ~ *from* attack 不会遭到攻击 / Is the rope ~? 这根绳牢吗? / The secret will be quite ~ *with* her. 她会严守秘密的。/ He arrived there ~. 他平安地到达那里。/ see sb. ~ home 把某人平安送到家 / The glassware came ~. 玻璃器皿已安然运到。②无害的; 不能为害的: Is this dog ~? 这只狗会咬人吗? / The rascal is ~ in jail. 那个坏蛋关在牢里不能害人了。③谨慎的; 可靠的; 稳健的: a ~ driver 谨慎的驾驶者 / a ~ critic 温和的批评家 / from a ~ quarter (指消息来源等)据可靠方面 ④一定的, 有把握的: a ~ winner 必胜者 / a ~ first 有把握的第一名 / be ~ to win 有把握得胜 / It would be ~ to say so. 这样说错不了。⑤【自】稳定的 ⑥(棒球运动员)安抵垒的 ||*get sb.* ~ 使某人不能逃脱(或不能害人) / *on the* ~ *side* 见 **side** / *play* ~ 求稳, 不冒险 / ~ *and sound* 安然无恙: The scouts returned ~ *and sound* from their mission. 侦察兵们执行任务后安然返回。/ *Safe bind,* ~ *find.* [谚]藏得好, 找得到。(或: 捆得牢, 逃不了。) ||**~ly** *ad.* ①安全地, 平安地 ②可靠地; 有把握地: We may ~ly say so. 我们这样说错不了。/ **~ness** *n.* ||**'~-'conduct** *n.* ①通行许可(指通过禁区等可免遭逮捕或伤害): give sb. ~-conduct through the lines 让某人安全通过防线 ②(尤指战时的)安全通行证, 护照 ③护送持有安全通行证者的卫兵 *vt.* ①发安全通行证给 ②护送…通过 / **'~'keeping** *n.* 妥善保护; 妥善保管: The document is *in* ~*keeping with* the secretary. 这个文件由书记妥善保管着。/ **'~-light** *n.*【摄】(暗室冲晒用)安全灯 / ~ *load* 安全载重 / ~ *period*【医】(女子行经前后的)避孕安全期

safe² [seif] *n.* ① 保险箱 ② 冷藏柜; (防止苍蝇等的)菜橱, 纱橱 ||**'~,cracker** *n.* 撬开保险箱的盗贼 / **'~-de,posit** *n.* (放置保险箱等的)保险仓库, 保管库 *a.* 保藏的, 提供保管的: a ~-*deposit* company 保管公司

safeguard ['seifgɑːd] **I** *n.* ①保护措施; 保证条款

②防护设施,安全装置;防护器　③(尤指战时的)安全通行证,护照(=safe-conduct)　④保护者;护送者;警卫员　**II** *vt.* 保护,捍卫,维护: ～ national independence and state sovereignty 维护民族独立和国家主权 / ～*ing* duties (为消除不平等的竞争条件对进口货征收的)保护关税

safety ['seifti] **I** *n.* ①安全,保险: ～ measures 安全措施 / ～ in production 安全生产 / public (road) ～ 公共(交通)安全 / be *in* ～ 安全 / cannot do sth. ～ 做某事不能没有危险 ②安全设备,保险装置;(枪炮等的)保险机;有保险机的武器: ～ devices (或 installations) 安全设备 ③低座自行车 (=～ bicycle) ④(棒球)安打(指保险的一击); (美式足球)把球掷过本队球门线(结果使对方得二分); 最后方的后卫 **II** *vt.* 保护,防护,使保险: ～ a rifle 使步枪保险(不走火等) **‖play for** ～ 稳扎稳打,不冒风险 / *seek* ～ *in flight* 溜之大吉 / *There is* ～ *in numbers.* [谚]人多保险。‖～ **belt** 救生带;(飞机乘客,高空操作者等用的)安全带 / ～ **bicycle** 低座自行车 / ～ **bolt,** ～ **catch** 保险销,保险机 / ～ **curtain** (剧场用)防火幕 / ～ **factor,** **coefficient** 安全系数 / ～ **film** (电影用)安全胶片,不燃性胶片 / ～ **fuse** 熔丝,保险丝;保险信管;安全导火线 / ～ **glass** 保险玻璃,不碎玻璃 / ～ **island** 【交】安全岛,站台(供公共车辆乘客用) / ～ **lamp** (尤指矿工用)安全灯 / ～ **lock** 保险锁;(武器的)保险机 / ～ **match** 安全火柴 / ～ **pin** (安全)别针;安全销 / ～ **razor** 保安剃刀 / ～ **valve** ①安全阀(或活门) ②[喻]使强烈的感情(或旺盛的精力等)得到发泄的事物(或方式): sit on the ～ *valve* 采取压制手段 / ～ **zone** =～ island

saffron ['sæfrən] **I** *n.* ①【植】藏红花,藏花,番红花 ②藏红花的干燥柱头 ③藏红色;橘黄色 **II** *a.* 藏红色的;橘黄色的 ‖～**y** *a.* 藏红色的;橘黄色的 / ～ **oil** 藏花油

sag [sæg] **I** (sagged; sagging) **❶** *vi.* ①(尤指中部)下垂;下陷;下弯: The ceiling is *sagging.* 天花板往下垂了。②倾斜,一边倒 ③(面部等)松垂;(精神)萎靡 ④(电影,小说等)失去吸引力: Though it ～*s* in the middle, the novel is readable on the whole. 这部小说虽然中间部分比较乏味,但总的说来尚可读。⑤【商】萧条;(物价)下跌: a sagging tendency 跌风; 下跌趋势 ⑥【海】漂流: ～ to leeward 随风漂流 **❷** *vt.* 使下垂;把(船或板等)弯压 **II** *n.* ①下垂;下陷;下弯 ②下垂度 ③(道路等的)陷下处 ④经济萧条;物价下跌 ⑤【海】随风漂流

saga ['sɑːgə] *n.* ① 中世纪北欧传说 ② 英雄传奇 ③ (长篇)家世小说 (=～ novel) ④长篇的详细叙述

sagacious [sə'geiʃəs] *a.* ①有洞察力的;有远见的;精明的;明智的 ②(动物)有灵性的;伶俐的 ‖～**ly** *ad.* / ～**ness,** sagacity [sə'gæsiti] *n.*

sage[1] [seidʒ] **I** *a.* ①贤明的,聪明的;明智的;审慎

的 ②[谑]一本正经的;一副聪明相的 **II** *n.* ①哲人,贤人,圣人;年高望重的人 ②[谑]道貌岸然的人 ‖～**ly** *ad.* / ～**ness** *n.*

sage[2] [seidʒ] *n.* 【植】①鼠尾草;蒿属植物;北美艾灌丛 (=～brush) ② 洋苏叶 ‖～ **green** 鼠尾草色,灰绿色 / ～ **oil** 洋苏叶油

sago ['seigou] *n.* 【植】① 西(谷)米 ② 西谷椰子(树)属植物 (=～ palm)

sahib ['sɑːhib] *n.* 先生(印度等地旧时对上层欧洲人或有地位的人的尊称);[口]绅士: Colonel *Sahib* 上校先生 / Jones *Sahib* 琼斯先生 / a pucka ～ (属于统治阶级的)真正的欧洲人;道地的绅士 / the rule of the ～*s* 欧洲人的统治

said [sed] **I** say 的过去式和过去分词 **II** *a.* (法律,商业等文件用语)上述的,该…… (the) ～ contract 上述契约 / (the) ～ witness 该证人

sail [seil] **I** *n.* ① 帆,篷: hoist (lower) ～ (或 ～*s*) 扬(下)帆 ②[单复同]船,船只: not a ～ in sight 看不到一条船 / a fleet of 10 ～ 一支由十条船组成的船队 / Sail ho! 嗨,看见船了! ③帆状物;(风车的)翼板;(旗鱼的)脊鳍;(鹦鹉螺的)触器;(甲板、矿井上用的)漏斗状 帆布通风筒: solar ～【空】太阳帆,太阳反射器(在星际飞行中利用太阳能的一种设备) ④航行;乘船旅行(或游览);航程: go for a ～ 乘船游览 **II** **❶** *vi.* ①航行;(坐船)游览: ～ along the coast 沿海岸航行 / ～ into the har bour 驶进港口 ②启航,开船: ～ with the tide 涨潮时开船 ③(鸟,飞机等)翱翔;(鱼,云等)浮游,飘,平稳地行进: The bird ～*ed* across the sky. 鸟儿平稳地飞过天空。④(尤指女人)仪态万方地走 **❷** *vt.* ① 航行于;飘过,飞过 ②驾驶(船只);(根据指南针、海图等)导航 **‖back the** ～*s* 整帆使船倒退 / **crowd** (on) ～ 张起异常多的帆 / **fill the** ～*s* 使帆满风 / (in) full ～ 全部张帆地;[喻]全力以赴地 / in ～ 张着帆 / **lower one's** ～ 认输,甘拜下风 / **make** ～ ①张帆 ②启航 / **pack (on) all** ～ 扯足风帆 / ～ *about* 逛来逛去 / ～ *against the* **wind** 见 **wind**[1] / ～ *before the wind* 见 **wind**[1] / ～ *in* [口] ①仪态万方地走进来 ②开始殴打起来 ③劲头十足地行动起来: He ～*ed in* and finished the job. 他一鼓作气完成了任务。/ ～ *into* [口] ①痛骂,攻击;殴打(某人) ②干劲十足地开始进行(某事);开始大嚼(食物) ③仪态万方地走进(房间等) / ～ *large* 顺风航行 / ～ *near* (或 *close to*) *the wind* 见 **wind**[1] / ～ *through* ① 轻快地走过 ②[俚]轻易地取得成功 / *set* ～ ① 张帆待航 ②启航 / ～ *shorten* ～ 收帆减速 / *strike* ～ ①(因暴风)突然下帆 ②下帆致敬 / *take in* ～ ①收帆减速 ②减少活动;收敛气焰 / *take the wind out of sb.'s* ～*s* 见 **wind**[1] / *trim the* ～*s* 随风使帆 / *under* ～ ①张着帆 ②在航行中 ‖～**er** *n.* 帆船;船: a good (bad) ～*er* 航力好(差)的船 ‖～ **arm** 风车的翼板 / ～ **axle** 转动风车翼板的轴 / '～**boat** *n.* 帆船 / '～**cloth** *n.* 制帆篷等的布 / '～**fish** *n.*

旗鱼属的鱼；旗鱼；姥鲛 / '～ˌflying n. 翱翔飞行 / '～plane n. 翱翔机

sailor ['seilə] **n.** ① 水手；海员；水兵 ② 乘船旅行者：a bad (good) ～ 常晕船(不晕船)的人 ③扁平的硬边草帽 ‖**～ing** ['seiləriŋ] **n.** 水手的生活(或职责、职业) / **～ly a.** ① 水手的；水手般的 ② 精明的，能干的 ‖**～ hat** ① 扁平的硬边草帽 ②(儿童戴的)水手帽 / **'～man n.** 水手 / **～s' home** 取费低廉的海员宿舍 / **'～'s-knot n.** ①水手结 ②水手式领结 / **～ suit** 男孩的水手服

saint [seint] **I n.** ①(教会正式承认的)圣徒，圣者 ② 进入天国的死者；天使 ③上帝的选民；基督教徒 ④虔诚慈善的人；道德高尚的人；圣人 ⑤ [S-] (加在圣徒、教会、学校、街道等名字前，单数略作 St. 或 S.，复数略作 Sts. 或 SS.) 圣…：*St. Paul's* (伦敦)圣保罗大教堂 **II a.** 神圣的 **III vt.** 承认(死者)为圣徒，使成为圣徒 ‖***All Saints' Day***【宗】万圣节(十一月一日) / ***It would provoke*** (或 ***try the patience of***) ***a ～.*** 这样的话(或行为等)使圣人也要发脾气。/ ***the departed ～*** 死者(葬礼用语) / ***Young ～s, old devils*** (或 ***sinners***). [谚]小时圣洁，大时邪恶。‖**～dom n.** 圣徒身分；圣洁 / **～ed a.** 成为圣徒的；神圣的；死去的 / **～ess n.** 圣女，女圣徒 / **～hood n.** 圣徒身分；[总称]诸圣 / **～like a.** 象圣徒一样的；圣洁的

saintly ['seintli] **a.** 象圣徒一样的；圣洁的 ‖**saintliness n.**

Saint-Simonian [sn*t*sai'mouniən] **I a.** (法国空想社会主义者)圣西门 (Saint-Simon) 的；空想社会主义的 **II n.** 圣西门学派，空想社会主义者 ‖**～ism n.** 圣西门主义；空想社会主义

saith [seθ] 动词 say 的第三人称单数现在式 says 的古体

sake [seik] **n.** 缘故：for all their ～*s* (或 for the ～ of them all) 为了他们所有的人 / for safety('s) ～ 为了安全起见 / for the ～ of convenience (或 for convenience' ～) 为了方便起见 ‖***art for art's ～*** 为艺术而艺术，艺术至上主义 / ***for any ～*** 无论如何 / ***for God's*** (或 ***goodness'*** 或 ***mercy's***) ***～*** (用于加强请求的语气)看在上帝面上；务请 / ***for old ～'s ～*** 为了老交情 / ***without ～*** 无缘无故

salaam [sə'lɑ:m] **I n.** ① 额手礼(印度等民族用右手抚额鞠躬的礼节) ②敬礼，致敬 **II ❶ vt.** 向…行额手礼 **❷ vi.** 行额手礼：～ to sb. 向某人行额手礼

salable ['seiləbl] **a.** 可出售的；卖得出的，有销路的 ‖**salability** [ˌseilə'biliti] **n.**

salad ['sæləd] **n.** ① 色拉(西餐中的一种凉拌菜) ②生菜(尤指莴苣) ‖**～ *days*** ① 青春年少之时(指没有经验或大胆莽撞等) ②(创作家等的)最佳时期，全盛时期 ‖**～ dressing** 拌色拉的调味汁 / **～ oil** 色拉油，冷餐油

salaried ['sælərid] **a.** ① 拿薪水的：the high-～ stratum 高薪阶层 ② 有薪水的

salary ['sæləri] **I n.** 薪水 **II vt.** [常用被动语态]给…薪水

sale [seil] **n.** ①卖，出售：put sth. up *for* ～ 拿出某物来卖 / a ～ for cash 现金交易，现卖 / a ～ on credit 赊销 ②(尤指存货)减价出售；拍卖：the winter ～*s* 冬季大贱卖 / buy goods at the ～*s* 买廉价货 / a clearance ～ 清仓拍卖 ③销路；销售额：command (或 have) a ready ～ 获得畅销 / Will there be any ～ for these goods? 这些货物会有销路吗？/ be dull of ～ 滞销 / *Sales* are up (down) this season. 这一季度销售额上升(下降)。/ the ～*s* volume 销售量 ‖***a distress ～*** 扣押物的拍卖 / ***a liquidation ～*** 停业清理大拍卖 / ***a rummage ～*** ① 清仓拍卖 ②捐赠品义卖 / ***for ～*** 待售；出售的：(a) house *for* ～ 房屋待售(招贴、广告等用语) / Are these machines *for* ～? 这些机器是卖的吗？/ ***not for ～*** 不出售的；非卖品 / ***on ～*** 出售的；上市的 / ***on ～ or return*** 无法销售可以退货(指发给零售商的货物) / ***～ by bulk*** 趸卖，成批出售 / ***～ of work*** (教会主持的)义卖 / ***wash ～s*** 虚伪交易(证券市场用语) ‖**～ price** 廉价 / **～ ring** 拍卖人周围的顾客 / **～s account** 销货帐 / **～sclerk** ['seilzklɑ:k] **n.** [美]售货员 / **～s department** 营业部 / **～sgirl** ['seilzgə:l], **'～sˌlady n.** [口]女售货员 / **～s manager** 营业主任 / **'～sˌperson n.** ＝～sclerk / **～s promotion** 打开(或扩大)销路的活动 / **～s resistance** ①(对兜售的货物的)拒绝购买 ②(对某人鼓吹的思想、建议等的)抵制 / **～sroom** ['seilzru(:)m] **n.** 商品出售处；拍卖场 / **～s talk** 兜揽买卖的话；[喻]游说 / **～s tax** 营业税 / **'～sˌwoman n.** 女售货员；女推销员

salesman ['seilzmən] **n.** ① 售货员，店员；推销员 ②(思想、计划的)兜售者，游说者 ‖**～ship n.** 售货(术)；推销(术)；游说(术)；善于推销(或游说)

salient ['seiljənt] **I a.** ①(角等)突出的；凸起的 ② 显著的：～ features 显著的特征 ③ 跳跃的，跳跳蹦蹦的 ④(水等)喷射的，涌出的 **II n.** ①凸起；突出 ②突角；突出部分；【军】突出部 ‖**～ly *ad.***

saline I ['seilain] **a.** 盐的；含盐的；咸的 **II** [sə'lain] **n.** ①盐湖；盐泉；盐碱滩；盐渍地 ②(有利泻作用的)镁、碱金属盐及其溶液

saliva [sə'laivə] **n.** 涎，唾液

sallow[1] ['sælou] **I a.** (人、肤色)灰黄色的，菜色的 **II vt. & vi.** (使)变灰黄色(或菜色) ‖**～ish a.** 微带灰黄色的，微带菜色的 / **～ness n.**

sallow[2] ['sælou] **n.**【植】① 阔叶柳，黄华柳(山毛柳) ②柳枝，柳条

sally ['sæli] **I n.** ①(被围军队的)突围，出击：make a successful ～ 成功地发动一次突围 ②(感情等的)迸发 ③远足；漫游 ④俏皮话；妙语 ⑤[罕]越轨行为 ⑥【建】凸出部；钝角 **II vi.** ① 突围，出击 (*out*) ②[罕](血等)涌出 ③ 外出；出发 (*forth, out*)：Let's ～ *forth* and look at the town. 我们

出去看看市容吧。‖~ **port** (碉堡等的)出击口

salmon ['sæmən] ([复] salmon(s)) *n.* ①【动】鲑,大麻哈鱼; [复]鲑鳟类 ②鲑肉 ③鲑肉色, 橙红色 ‖~ **colo(u)r**, ~ **pink** 鲑肉色, 橙红色 / '~**,colo(u)red** *a.* 鲑肉色的, 橙红色的

salon ['sælɔ̃ːŋ] *n.* [法] ① 雅致的大会客室; (旅馆等的)大厅; (客轮上的)交谊室 ② 沙龙(西方社会中在社会名流家里定期举行的社交聚会): literary ~s 文艺沙龙 ③ 美术展览馆; 画廊; [the S-] (一年一度在巴黎举行的)当代画家作品展览会 ④营业性的高级服务室(如美容院等)

saloon[1] [sə'luːn] *n.* ① 雅致的大会客室; (旅馆等的)大厅; (客轮上的)交谊室 (=*salon*) ② 沙龙 (=*salon*) ③ 大型客机上的客舱 ④ (作某一用途的)公共大厅, …室: a dining ~ 餐厅 / a hairdressing ~ 理发室 / a billiard ~ 弹子房 ⑤[美]酒馆; 酒吧间 ⑥ = ~ car ‖~**ist** *n.* [美]酒吧间老板 (或管理人) ‖~ **car** [英] ① (火车的)客厅式车厢 ② 可容纳四至七个乘客的大轿车 / ~ **deck** 【船】客舱甲板 / **sa'loon,keeper** *n.* = ~ist

saloon[2] [sə'luːn] *n.* 从气球上发射的人造卫星 (*satellite launched from a balloon* 的缩略)

salt [sɔːlt] **I** *n.* ①盐: common (或 table) ~ 食盐 / sea (或 bay) ~ 海湾盐 / rock ~ 岩盐 / solar ~ 晒制盐 ②【化】盐类; [复]泻盐 (=Epsom ~(s)); 嗅盐 (=smelling ~s): ~ hydrates 水合盐 / ~ of tartar 酒石盐 / inert ~ (安全炸药用)惰性盐 ③风趣; 兴味; 刺激: a talk full of ~ 饶有风趣的谈话 ④ 现实态度, 常识; 慎重态度, 保留 ⑤ [口]老练的水手 (=old ~) ⑥(餐桌上的)盐碟, 盐瓶(=~cellar) ⑦盐沼; 盐碱滩 (=~marsh) ⑧[复]冲入河流的海水 **II** *a.* ①含盐的; 咸味的; 腌的; 加盐调味的: a ~ solution 盐水, 食盐溶液 / ~ beef 咸牛肉 ②(土地)被海水淹没的; (植物)生长于盐沼(或盐碱滩)的; 海生的 ③风趣的; 尖锐的 ④(故事、笑话等)猥亵的 ⑤ 辛酸的; 沉痛的 ⑥[俚](帐单、费用等)浮报的, 过高的: That's rather too ~! 指旅馆帐单上所开列的费用)太贵了! **III** *vt.* ①加(或撒、擦)盐于; 腌, 盐渍; 以盐喂(动物): ~ed meat 腌肉 ②使(谈话等)风趣: ~ one's conversation with wit 使谈话妙趣横生 ③【化】用盐(或盐的混合物)处理(照相纸等); (把…)撒于 (with): ~ clouds *with* dry ice 撒干冰于云层(进行人工降雨) ④[俚]浮开, 虚报(帐目、价格等); 用贵重的矿物虚饰(矿山)以诱骗买主: ~ an account 虚报帐目 / ~ the books in 帐册中虚报收益 ‖**above** (**below**) *the* ~ 在上席(下席)(源于旧时宴礼, 上席是离席上盐瓶最近的席位) / *a* **covenant** *of* ~ 不可背弃的盟约 / (*as*) ~ *as* **fire** 极咸 / **Attic** ~ 文雅的机智 / *be not made of* ~ 不怕雨淋 / *drop a pinch of* ~ *on the tail of* (源于教孩子撒盐在鸟尾巴上捕鸟这一取笑的话)诱捕, 使落圈套; 诱惑 / *eat* ~ *with sb.* 在某人处作客 / *eat sb.'s* ~ 在某人处作客; 做某人的食客 / ~ *away* ① 腌(肉等)

② [口]贮存, 积蓄(钱等) / ~ *down* ① = ~ away ②[美口]训斥 / ~ *out* 【化】盐析 / *spill* ~ 泼翻盐(迷信认为不吉利) / *the* ~ *of the* **earth** 社会中坚; 高尚的人 / *with a grain* (或 *pinch*) *of* ~ 见 grain / *worth one's* ~ 称职, 胜任; 值得雇用 ‖~**ed** *a.* ① 用盐处理的; 腌的, 盐渍的 ②(动物或人)服水土的; 有免疫力的 ③ [口](对职业、工作等)有经验的, 老练的 / ~**er** *n.* ① 制盐人; 卖盐人 ②腌制者 ③[俚]矿山骗子 / ~**ing** *n.* [主英][常用复]经常为潮水淹没的土地 / ~**ness** *n.* ① 咸性; 含盐度 ②(话等)的尖锐性 ‖~ **cake** 芒硝, 盐饼 / '~**,cellar** *n.* (餐桌上的)盐碟, 盐瓶 / ~ **field** 盐场 / ~ **glaze** 【化】盐釉 / ~ **horse** [俚]咸牛肉 / ~ **junk** 咸牛肉干 / **Salt Lake City** 盐湖城[美国城市] / ~ **lick** 野兽常去舐盐的盐渍地 / ~ **marsh** 盐沼; 盐碱滩 / ~ **mine** 盐矿 / ~ **pan** 盐田; 盐盆 / ~ **pit** 盐坑 / ~ **pond** 盐池 / '~-,**rising** *a.* 用陈面团发酵的 / ~ **spoon** 盐匙 / '~,**water** *a.* ① 咸水的: a ~*water* lake 咸水湖 ②生活在咸水中的: ~*water* fish 咸水鱼 / ~ **water** ① 咸水; 海水 ②[俚]泪水 / ~ **well** 盐井 / '~**works** [复] [用作单或复](制)盐场 / ~**wort** *n.* 【植】生于海边(或盐沼)的藜科植物(尤指猪毛菜和海蓬子)

salubrious [sə'ljuːbriəs] *a.* ①(气候、空气等)有益健康的: a ~ climate 宜人的气候 ②健康的, 有利的: a ~ situation 有利的形势 ‖~**ly** *ad.* / ~**ness** *n.*

salutary ['sæljutəri] *a.* ①有益健康的; 有治疗作用的 ②有益的: a ~ lesson 有益的教训

salutation [,sælju(ː)'teiʃən] *n.* ① 招呼, 致意; 行礼; [复]问候: raise one's hat in ~ 举帽致意 ②颂词; (书信或发言开头的)客气称呼 ③[罕]敬礼(现多用 salute) ‖~**al** *a.*

salute [sə'ljuːt] **I** *n.* ①招呼; 行礼; 敬礼; [the ~] 敬礼姿势: give (或 make) a ~ 行礼 / acknowledge (或 answer) a ~ 答礼, 回礼 / stand at (the) ~ 立正敬礼 ②礼炮; 鞭炮: fire a ~ of 21 guns (或 a 21-gun ~) 鸣礼炮二十一响 ③[古][谑]表示致敬的接吻 **II** ❶ *vt.* ①向…打招呼(或致意); 向…行军礼; 向…致敬; 以正式军事仪式纪念: ~ the colours 向军旗敬礼 ②迎接; 呈现在…之前: a friend with a smile 笑迎友人 ③赞扬, 颂扬 ④[古](见面或分别时)吻 ❷ *vi.* ①打招呼, 行礼; 致敬: ~ with eyes (rifle, hand) 行注目(持枪, 举手)礼 ②放礼炮 ‖**national** ~ ①[美]为国家元首(或国旗)鸣放的二十一响礼炮 ②美国国庆礼炮(=Salute to the Union) / *take the* ~ 接受(被检阅者的)敬礼, 行答礼

salvage ['sælvidʒ] **I** *n.* ①海上救助; (疾病的)抢救; (局面等的)挽救 ②救助报酬 ③被救船舶; 救出的货物; 脱险人员; 得救的病员(或肢体等) ④遭难船只及货物的打捞: a ~ company 打捞公司 ⑤ (保险业用语)火灾时财产的抢救; 抢救出的财产; 抢救费; 残(贬价)值; 出售残货的所得款项 ⑥废

物利用; 可利用的废品: a ~ point 废品收集处 II *vt.* ① 救助; 营救; 抢救: The doctors succeeded in *salvaging* the patient. 医生们成功地抢救了病人。②打捞: ~ a sunken boat 打捞沉船 ③ 利用(废物、损坏的货物等) ‖~ corps (火灾保险公司的)救火队,消防队 / ~ money 救难费,救难偿金

salvation [sæl'veiʃən] *n.* ① 救助; 拯救: the road of ~ 生路 / work out one's own ~ 设法自救 ②【宗】灵魂的拯救; 救世: the Salvation Army 【基督教】救世军 ‖*find* ~ ①【宗】信教; 皈依 ②[谑]找到改变宗旨的借口

salve[1] [sɑːv, sælv] I *n.* ① 油膏剂; 药膏; 止痛药, 治疮药 ②涂在羊身上的油膏 ③安慰(物); 缓和物 (*for*) ④ 阿谀, 奉承 II *vt.* ①[古]敷油膏于(伤口等) ②涂油膏于(羊身) ③安慰; 缓和, 减轻(悲痛) ④排除(困难), 解除(疑虑); 保持(荣誉、信用等) ⑤奉承

salve[2] [sælv] *vt.* ①救助(船舶); 抢救 ②打捞

salver ['sælvə] *n.* (金属)托盘; 盘子

salvo[1] ['sælvou] *n.* ①【律】保留条款; 保留 ②遁词; 借口 ③(名誉等的)保全手段; (感情等的)缓和方法

salvo[2] ['sælvou] ([复] salvo(e)s) *n.* ①(炮火)齐射; (炸弹等的)齐投, 连续投; 齐射的炮弹; 齐投的炸弹: ~ bombing 全部炸弹齐投目标的轰炸 ②【军】翼次射(炮兵连的一种发射法) ③(礼炮)齐鸣: a ~ of 21 guns 礼炮二十一响 ④突然爆发; (掌声、欢呼声等的)一阵: ~(e)s of applause (praise) 阵阵掌声(赞扬声)

same [seim] I *a.* ①同一的: stand on the ~ front 站在同一条战线上 / live under the ~ roof and eat at the ~ table 同吃同住 / She is the ~ age as you. 她和你同年。/ He works in the ~ shop as (或 that) I do. 他和我在同一个车间干活。②依然如故的, 同样的: Don't make the ~ mistake again. 不要重犯同样的错误。/ The patient is *about* (或 *much*) the ~. 病人差不多还是那样。/ One should speak clearly and it is *the* ~ *with* writing. 讲话要清楚, 写文章也要如此。③[与 this, that, these, those 连用, 强调语气或含贬义]刚才提到(或想到)的, 上述的: This meter is mounted on *that* ~ panel. 这表就装在上述那块仪表板上。④千篇一律的, 单调的: the ~ old story 老一套 / the fear of being too ~ 怕落俗套 II *pron.* ①同样的人; 同样的事物: The mother scrubbed the floor and her child did the ~. 母亲擦洗地板, 孩子也跟着干。/ A: Good health! B: The ~ to you! (或 I wish you the ~!) 甲: 祝你健康! 乙: (也)祝你健康! ②[法律、商业上的旧用法; 常略定冠词]该人; 上述事物; 上述情况: We have heard from your branch office and have replied to ~. 你处分公司来函收悉, 并已回复。III *ad.* 同样地: think the ~ *of* (或 feel the ~ *to*) sb. 对某人有同样的看法; 对某人的看法和过去一样 ‖*all the* ~

(虽然…)还是, 仍然: It was raining hard, but we got there in time *all the* ~. 那时下着大雨, 但我们还是准时到达那里。/ Thank you *all the* ~. 尽管如此, 还是要谢谢你。/ *at the* ~ *time* 见 time / *be all* (或 *just*) *the* ~ *to* ... 对…说来都一样, 对…无所谓: A: Would you have a cup of tea or coffee? B: It's *all the* ~ *to* me, thanks. 甲: 你喜欢喝茶还是喝咖啡? 乙: 随便, 谢谢。/ *come* (或 *amount*) *to the* ~ *thing* 见 thing[1] / *just the* ~ ① 完全一样 ② =all the ~ / *one and the* ~ 同一个(的), 完全一样, 完全一回事 / ~ *here* [口]我也同样 / *the very* ~ [强调语气]正是这个; 完全相同的: This is *the very* ~ point I want to make. 我要说明的恰恰也是这一点。‖~**ness** *n.* ① 同一, 一致(性); 同样 ②千篇一律, 单调

sampan ['sæmpæn] *n.* [汉]舢板

sample ['sɑːmpl] I *n.* ①样品; 试料; 货样: take a ~ for examination and test 取样检验 / a ~ room 样品间 ②实例; 标本: give a ~ of one's courage 用行动表示自己的勇气 ③(统计学中的)样本; (从总体中选出)供典型调查的部分, 典型部分调查(指人口等) II *vt.* ①从…取样检验; 提供…的样品 ②尝试; 初次体验 ③对…进行典型部分调查 ‖*be up to* ~ (货物)符合样品规格 ‖~**-card** *n.* (衣料等的)样品卡

sanatorium [ˌsænə'tɔːriəm] ([复] sanatoria [ˌsænə'tɔːriə] 或 sanatoriums) *n.* 疗养院; 休养地: a workers' ~ 工人疗养院

sanctify ['sæŋktifai] *vt.* ①使神圣; 把…奉若神明: *sanctified* airs 装出的神圣不可侵犯的气派, 道貌岸然 ②使圣洁, 洗清…的罪孽 ③(道义上)证实…为正当; 尊崇 ‖*The end sanctifies the means.* 见 end ‖**sanctification** [ˌsæŋktifi'keiʃən] *n.*

sanctimonious [ˌsæŋkti'mouniəs] *a.* 假装神圣的, 伪装虔诚的: ~ guarantees 伪善的保证 ‖~**ly** *ad.* / ~**ness** *n.*

sanction ['sæŋkʃən] I *n.* ① (尤指教会的)法令 ②使法律得到遵守的附加条款(如赏、罚等); 使誓约有约束力的事物 ③(为维持法律所作的)制裁; [常用复]国际制裁 ④维护道德的约束力(如习俗、良心等) ⑤认可; 批准: Official ~ has not yet been given. 尚未获得正式批准。⑥(习俗上对行为等的)赞许; 支持; 鼓励 II *vt.* ①认可; 批准 ②同意; 支持; 鼓励: The wrong use of the word is ~ed by usage. 这词的误用已约定俗成了。

sanctity ['sæŋktiti] *n.* ①圣洁; 神圣; 尊严; 神圣不可侵犯性 ②[复]神圣的义务(或权利); 神圣的感情; 神圣的东西

sanctuary ['sæŋktjuəri] *n.* ①圣所; 圣殿; 教堂; 寺院; 内殿; 祭坛; (犹太教堂)至圣所 ②避难所, 庇护所: the right of ~ 庇护权 ③(教堂等的)庇护权 ④鸟兽禁猎区 ‖*break* (或 *violate*) ~ 侵入教堂强行抓人(或打人、杀人等) / *take* (或 *seek*) ~ (在教堂等处)避难

sanctum ['sæŋktəm] *n.* ①圣所 ②(不受干扰的)

私室,书斋 ‖~ **sanctorum** [sæŋk'tɔ:rəm] ①(犹太教堂的)至圣所 ②[谑]密室,私室

sand [sænd] **I** *n.* ①沙,沙子 ②[常用复]沙滩;沙洲;沙地: play on the ~s 在沙滩上玩 ③[常用复]沙粒; 计时沙漏中的沙子 ④顷刻,瞬间; [复]生涯;寿命: the ~s of a man's life 人的寿命,毕生的岁月 ⑤[医][复]沙状结石: urinary ~ 尿沙 ⑥含(石)油沙沙层 ⑦[冶]模沙; 粗矿石; 尾矿 ⑧[美俚]刚毅;胆量: have plenty of ~ 很有胆量 ⑨沙色,带红的黄色 ⑩[美俚]沙糖 **II** *vt.* ① 撒沙于; 撒沙似地布满,铺沙于; 填沙于: a clear night ~ed with stars 满天星斗的夜晚 ②挫沙于(糖等) ③用沙(或沙纸)擦 ④把(船)开上沙滩 ‖*built on (the)* ~ 建立在不牢靠基础上的,不稳固的 / *numberless as the* ~(*s*) 多如恒河沙数的 / *plough the* ~(*s*) 白费力气 / *put* ~ *in the wheels* (或 *machine*) 妨碍,捣乱 / *raise* ~ [美俚]引起骚乱;喧闹 / *The* ~*s are running out.* 剩下的时间不多了。(或: 期限将到。) ‖~**ed** *a.* ①撒上沙的; 铺上沙的; 填满沙的 ②被沙阻塞的 ③有小斑点的 / '~**bag** *n.* 沙袋,沙囊: ~*bag* revetment 【建】沙袋护坡 *vt.* ①堆积沙袋于; 用沙袋阻塞; 用沙袋加重: ~*bag* bomb shelters 用沙袋堆防空洞 ②用沙袋打,用沙袋打昏 ③[口](粗暴地)强迫,强制 / '~**bank** *n.* 沙坝; 沙洲; 沙滩 / '~**bar** *n.* 沙洲,沙坝 / ~ **bath** 沙浴;【化】沙浴器 / 【地】沙盘(用于土质分析) / '~ **bed** *n.* 沙层 / '~**blast** *n.* 【机】喷沙,喷沙清除法; 喷沙器 *vt. & vi.* 沙喷 / 沙吹 / '~-**blind** *a.* 视力极差的,半瞎的 / '~**box** *n.* ①沙箱 ②玩具沙箱 ③吸墨水沙匣 / '~**boy** *n.* ①叫卖沙子的男孩: jolly (或 happy) as a ~*boy* 极快活 ②沙蚤 / '~ **break** *n.* 田野中的沙地; 防沙林 / ~ **casting** 【机】沙型铸造 / ~ **cloud** 因沙漠热风引起的沙云,沙烟 / ~ **crack** ①马裂蹄 ②因走在热沙上引起的脚底裂破 ③(由于调拌不匀而产生的)砖上裂缝 / '~,**culture** *n.* 【农】沙基培养 / ~ **drift** 沙丘 / ~ **fly** [动]白蛉(虫) / '~**glass** *n.* 计时沙漏 / ~ **hill** 沙丘,沙冈 / '~**hog** *n.* [美]水下隧道工人;地下工程工人;挖沙工 / ~ **hopper** 【动】沙蚤 / ~ **jack** 【建】沙箱千斤顶 / ~ **la(u)nce** 【动】玉筋鱼属的鱼(＝~ eel) / '~**man** *n.* (童话中撒沙于孩童眼上使其睡着的)睡魔 / '~,**paper** *n.* 沙纸 *vt.* 用沙纸擦 / '~,**piper** *n.* [动]鹬鸟 / '~**pit** *n.* 沙坑;采沙场 / '~ **pump** 【机】扬沙泵,抽沙泵 / '~**shoe** *n.* 沙地上穿的橡皮底或(大麻底)帆布鞋 / ~ **spout** 沙漠旋风刮起的沙柱 / '~**stone** *n.* 【地】沙岩 / '~**storm** *n.* 【气】沙暴

sandal¹ [sændl] **I** *n.* ①凉鞋;便鞋: straw ~s 草鞋 / plastic ~s 塑料凉鞋 ②浅口橡胶套鞋 ③鞋襻 **II** (sandal(l)ed; sandal(l)ing) *vt.* ①给…穿上凉鞋(或便鞋) ②用鞋襻系(鞋); 给(鞋)上鞋襻 ‖**sandal(l)ed** *a.* 穿凉鞋(或便鞋)的

sandal² [sændl] *n.* 【植】檀香(木);白檀 (＝white ~): red ~ 紫檀 ‖~**wood** *n.* 檀香(木);白檀

sandwich [sænwidʒ, sænwitʃ] **I** *n.* ①夹心面包

片,三明治: ham ~ 火腿三明治 ②三明治形物;夹在一起的东西: a ~ of good and bad 好坏夹在一起的东西 **II** *vt.* ①把…做成三明治 ②夹入,挤进: be ~ed in between two other persons 被挤在二人中间 ‖~ **board** 挂在身前身后的广告牌 / ~ **man** 身前身后挂着广告牌的人

sane [sein] *a.* ①没有疾病的,健全的 ②心智健全的,神志正常的 ③稳健的,明智的,合情合理的: a ~ policy 稳健的政策 / a ~ proposal 合情合理的建议 ‖~**ly** *ad.*

Sanforized [sænfəraizd] *a.* 【纺】桑福赖整理的 (源出商标名,指织物经机械防缩整理,残余缩水率在1% 之内)

sangaree [,sæŋgə'ri:] *n.* 加糖水和香料的冷饮酒

sanguinary [sæŋgwinəri] *a.* ①血淋淋的,血腥的: a ~ conflict 流血冲突 ②好杀戮的,嗜血成性的; 残忍的; (法律)动辄处死刑的 ③[英]充满咒骂的: ~ language 充满咒骂的言语 ‖**sanguinarily** [sæŋgwinərili; 美 ,sæŋgwi'nerili] *ad.* / **sanguinariness** *n.*

sanguine [sæŋgwin] **I** *a.* ①血红的; 红润的; 有血色的: a ~ complexion 红润的脸色 ②血的; 含血的 ③怀着希望的; 乐观的; 自信的; [心]多血质的: a ~ report 乐观的报道 / a ~ person 乐天派 / be ~ of (或 about) success 对成功抱乐观 ④嗜血成性的; 残忍的 **II** *n.* ①血红色 ②用氧化铁制的红粉笔; 红粉笔画 **III** *vt.* [诗]血染;染红 ‖~**ly** *ad.* / ~**ness** *n.*

sanitary [sænitəri] **I** *a.* ①关于环境卫生的: ~ science 环境卫生学 / ~ regulations 卫生规则 / a ~ inspector 卫生检查员 ②(保持)清洁的,卫生的: a ~ cottage 洁净的农舍 / ~ chopsticks 卫生筷 / a ~ belt (或 napkin, towel) 月经带 / a ~ dustbin 有盖垃圾箱 **II** *n.* (有抽水设备的)公共厕所 ‖**sanitarily** [sænitərili; 美 ,sæni'terili] *ad.* / **sanitariness** *n.* ‖~ **engineering** 卫生工程(学) / ~ **sewer** 污水管(道) / ~ **ware** [总称]卫生器具(如浴缸、抽水马桶等)

sanitation [,sæni'teiʃən] *n.* ① (环境)卫生; 环境卫生的提倡(或维持) ②卫生设备(尤指下水道设备)

sanity [sæniti] *n.* ①心智健全; 神志正常 ②明智; 判断正确; 稳健

sap¹ [sæp] **I** *n.* ①树液 ②体液(如血、涎、淋巴、精液);元气,活力: the ~ of life 元气 / the ~ of youth 青春的活力 ③ ＝~wood ④[美]棍棒,警棍 ⑤[美俚]威士忌酒 **II** (sapped; sapping) *vt.* ①使(树)排出液汁; 去掉(木材)的白木质 ②使伤元气; 耗竭; 使衰弱: be *sapped* by disease 因疾病而衰弱不堪 ③用棍棒打倒 ‖~ **up on sb.** [美俚]殴打某人(尤指围攻) ‖~**ful** *a.* 树液多的 / ~**less** *a.* 无树液的; 枯萎的; 无生气的 ‖~ **green** 绿色颜料; 暗绿色 / '~,**sucker** *n.* (吸树液的)美洲啄木鸟 / '~**wood** *n.* (树皮下较软的)白木质,边材(心材外增生的木质部)

sap² [sæp] **I** *n.* ①【军】坑道 ②坑道的挖掘 ③

中的破坏；逐步的削弱 **II** (sapped; sapping) **❶** *vi.* ①挖掘坑道 ②通过坑道接近敌人阵地 **❷** *vt.* ①挖坑道袭击 ②在…下面挖使受损；(潮水等)逐渐侵蚀：～ a wall 挖墙脚 ③渐渐削弱 ‖～**head** *n.* 坑道头

sap³ [sæp] **I** (sapped; sapping) *vi.* [学俚]用功读书 **II** *n.* ①[英]用功读书的人；努力工作的人 ②[美俚]笨蛋；傻瓜，容易上当的人：Don't be a ～. 别那么头脑简单。③[英]令人厌倦的工作，苦差使，麻烦事：It is such a (或 too much) ～. 这事真吃力。‖～**head** *n.* [口]笨蛋，傻瓜

sapper ['sæpə] *n.* ①坑道工兵；地雷工兵 ②挖掘者；挖掘器

sapphire ['sæfaiə] **I** *n.* ①【矿】蓝宝石：false ～ 蓝萤石 ②宝石蓝(色)，天蓝色 **II** *a.* 深蓝色的，天蓝色的

sarcasm ['sɑ:kæzəm] *n.* ①讽刺，挖苦，嘲笑 ②讥讽语，挖苦话 ③讽刺性

sarcastic [sɑ:'kæstik] *a.* ①讽刺的，挖苦的，嘲笑的 ②用讥讽语的；好挖苦人的 ‖～**ally** *ad.*

sarcophagus [sɑ:'kɔfəgəs] *n.* 石棺

sardine¹ [sɑ:'di:n] ([复] sardine(s)) *n.* 鲻鱼，沙丁鱼；供做罐头食品的小鱼：be packed like ～s 装得极满；拥挤不堪 ‖～ **oil** 沙丁(鱼)油(用作润滑剂及肥皂原料)

sardonic [sɑ:'dɔnik] *a.* 讥讽的，挖苦的，嘲笑的：a ～ smile 冷笑 ‖～**ally** *ad.*

sari, saree ['sɑ:ri(:)] *n.* (印度妇女的)莎丽服(用整段的布或绸包头裹身或披肩裹身的服装)

sarong ['sɑ:rɔŋ, sə'rɔŋ] *n.* ①莎笼，围裙(马来民族服装) ②用作莎笼的布料

sartorial [sɑ:'tɔ:riəl] *a.* ①裁缝的；缝纫的；(尤指男式)服装的：a ～ triumph [谑]做工极好的服装 ②【解】裁缝肌的

sash¹ [sæʃ] **I** ([复] sash(es)) *n.* 框格；[罕]窗扉 **II** *vt.* 给(门、窗)装上框格 ‖～**ed** *a.* 装有框格的 / ～**less** *a.* 无框格的 ‖～ **cord**, ～ **line** 吊窗绳，曳窗绳 / ～ **pulley** 吊窗滑轮 / '～**-tool** *n.* 漆工等用的小刷子 / ～ **window** 框格窗；上下推拉窗

sash² [sæʃ] **I** *n.* ①(妇女、儿童用的)腰带；彩带 ②[军]饰带，肩带；值星带 **II** *vt.* 给…系上腰带(或饰带等) ‖～**ed** *a.* 系有腰带(或饰带)的

sat [sæt] sit 的过去式和过去分词

Satan ['seitən] *n.* 【基督教】撒旦，魔鬼，恶魔，魔王 ‖～**ic(al)** [sə'tænik(əl)] *a.* 魔鬼(似)的；邪恶的；穷凶极恶的：His ～ic Majesty [谑]撒旦，魔王 / ～**ism** *n.* ①恶魔崇拜 ②恶魔般的性格；恶魔般的行为

satchel ['sætʃəl] *n.* (皮或帆布的)书包，小背包；小提包；【军】图囊：～ charges [军]炸药包

sate [seit] *vt.* 使充分满足；使饱享；使厌腻：～ oneself with pleasure 享尽欢乐 / be ～d with sleep 睡腻了

satellite ['sætəlait] *n.* ①卫星：launch an artificial ～ 发射人造卫星 ②人造卫星：a manned ～ 载

人卫星 / a reconnaissance ～ 侦察卫星 / a ～ for lunar probes 月球探测卫星 / a ～ station 小型接力电台；中型中继台；卫星电台 / a ～ band 卫星波段，卫星频带 ③卫星国；卫星城镇 ④附属物；仆从：～ troops 仆从军 ‖**satellitic** [,sætə'litik] *a.*

satiate ['seiʃieit] *vt.* 使充分满足；使饱享；使过饱生厌，使厌腻：be ～d with sth. 对某物厌腻 **II** ['seiʃiit] *a.* 餍饱的；厌腻的 ‖**satiation** [,seiʃi'eiʃən] *n.* 充分满足；饱享；(因过多而)厌腻

satiety [sə'taiəti] *n.* 饱足；过饱，厌腻：feast *to* ～ 吃喝得过饱 / have a ～ *of* sth. 饱享某物以致厌腻

satin ['sætin] **I** *n.* ①缎子：figured ～ 花缎 / tapestry ～ 织锦缎 ②【纺】缎纹；经缎组织 ③[俚]杜松子酒 **II** *a.* 缎子做的；缎子般的；光亮柔滑的：～ finish (银器等的)擦亮 / ～ paper 缎面纸 **III** *vt.* 使(纸张等)的表面具有缎子般的光泽 ‖～ **stitch** 缎纹刺绣针迹 / ～ **straw** (编草帽用的)柔软麦秸 / '～**wood** *n.* 缎木(一种适合制造家具的木料)

satire ['sætaiə] *n.* ①讽刺作品 ②讽刺文学 ③讽刺 (*on, upon*)：a scathing ～ *on* sb. 对某人的锐利的讽刺

satirical [sə'tirikəl] *a.* ①好挖苦的 ② =satiric ‖～**ly** *ad.*

satirist ['sætərist] *n.* ①讽刺作家 ②爱说挖苦话的人

satirize, satirise ['sætəraiz] **❶** *vt.* 讽刺；用讽刺文抨击；讽刺地描绘 **❷** *vi.* 写讽刺文；讲讽刺话

satisfaction [,sætis'fækʃən] *n.* ①满意，满足；称心：We watched the performance with great ～. 我们非常满意地观看了演出。/ express one's ～ *at* (或 *with*) 对…表示满意 / find ～ *in* 在…中得到满足 ②[常用单]快事，乐事；愉快：The happy news was a ～ to us all. 喜讯传来，人人高兴。③赔偿；还债；履行义务；赔偿物；【宗】苦行赎罪：in ～ *of* 作为…的赔偿 / make ～ *for* 赔偿…，偿还… ④决斗；报复 ‖**demand** ～ 要求赔偿 / **enter** (**up**) ～ 在法院备案表示债款已还 / **give** ～ 使满意，使满足；答应决斗，接受挑战 / **to the** ～ **of** 使…满意

satisfactory [,sætis'fæktəri] *a.* ①令人满意的；符合要求的，良好的 ②【宗】赎罪的 ‖**satisfactorily** *ad.* / **satisfactoriness** *n.*

satisfy ['sætisfai] **❶** *vt.* ①满足，使满足：～ the people's needs 满足人民需要 / ～ the eye 悦目 ②使满意：The result of the experiment *satisfied* us. 试验结果使我们很满意。/ be *satisfied* with the answers (lectures) 对回答(讲课)感到满意 ③符合，达到(要求、标准、规定等)：～ a definition 符合定义 ④说服；使相信；向…证实：I am *satisfied* of the truthfulness of his statement. (或 I am *satisfied* that his statement is true.) 我相信他的话是真实的。/ He *satisfied* me that it was so. 他使我相信事实如此。⑤消

除(顾虑等): ~ one's fears (doubts) 消除恐惧
(疑虑) ⑥偿还(债务); 履行(义务、契约等); 向…
偿清: ~ a debt (或 a creditor) 还清债务 ⑦赔
偿(受损失者); 赎(罪) ❷ *vi.* ①令人满足; 令人
满意 ②【宗】(基督)替人赎罪 ‖*rest satisfied
(with)* (对…)心满意足 / ~ *oneself* 确实弄明
白, 彻底搞清楚

saturate ['sætʃəreit] I *vt.* ①使饱和; 使中和 ②
浸透; 渗透; 使充满 ③【军】对…进行饱和袭击 II
a. ①[诗]浸透的; 渗透的; 饱和的 ②(颜色)深的,
浓的 ‖~*d a.* ① 饱和的: ~*d* solution 【化】饱和
溶液 / ~*d* rock 【地】饱和岩 ②浸透的; 湿透的
③(颜色)未用白色冲淡的

saturation [,sætʃə'reiʃən] *n.* ① 饱和(状态) ② 浸
透; 浸润 ③【物】磁性饱和 ④(颜色的)浓度; 章度
⑤【商】(市场的)足量供应 ⑥(兵力、火力等)压倒
优势的集中: ~ bombing 饱和轰炸 / ~ cam-
paigning 饱和竞选(指作最大限度的竞选活动)
‖~ **point** 饱和点

Saturday ['sætədi] *n.* 星期六 ‖*a Hospital ~* 见
hospital ‖~**s** ad. [美]每星期六; 在任何星期六
‖'~-**night** special [美俚]一种便于隐藏携带的
小口径廉价枪支(因罪犯在周末作案时多用此枪,
故名) / '~-**to-'Monday** *n.* & *a.* 周末(的)

saturnine ['sætə(:)nain] *a.* ①(表情等)阴沉的; 忧
郁的 ②讥讽的: a ~ smile 冷笑 ③铅的; 铅中毒
的: ~ poisoning 铅中毒

satyr ['sætə] *n.* ①【希】(性好欢娱及耽于淫欲
的)森林之神 ②性欲无度的男人; 色情狂者 ③蛱
眼蝶科的蝴蝶 ④[罕]猩猩 ‖~**ic** [sə'tirik] *a.*
①森林之神的 ②色情狂的

sauce [sɔːs] I *n.* ①调味汁; 酱汁: tomato ~ 番茄
酱 / pungent (或 chilli) ~ 辣酱油 / soy (或
soybean) ~ 酱油 ②[美]炖煮的水果; 罐头水果
③[喻]增加趣味的东西 ④[口]莽撞; 冒失无礼:
None of your ~! 不要无礼! ⑤[方]蔬菜; 肉类的
配菜 ⑥[美俚]烈酒: be on the ~ 大量喝酒, 喝酒
成瘾 II *vt.* ① 给…调味; 浇酱汁于 ② 使增加趣
味; 使增添风味: ~*d* with wit 风趣横生的 ③
[口]对…莽撞; 对…轻率无礼 ‖*a carrier's* (或
poor man's) ~ [俚]饥饿 / *eat* ~ [口]莽撞无
礼 / *have more* ~ *than pig* [口]鲁莽无礼, 极
端无礼 / *Hunger is the best* ~ [谚]饥者口
中尽佳味。/ *serve sb. with the same* ~ 以其
人之道还治其人之身 / *The ~ is better than
the fish.* 喧宾夺主。(或: 本末倒置。) / *What
is ~ for the goose is ~ for the gander.* [谚]
适用于甲者也适用于乙。(或: 对别人怎样对自己
也应怎样。) ‖'~-**boat** *n.* 船形调味汁壶 / '~**box**
n. [口]冒失鬼; 莽撞的孩子 / ~**pan** ['sɔːspən] *n.*
长柄有盖的深平底锅

saucer ['sɔːsə] *n.* ①茶托; 浅碟: a cup and ~ 带茶
托的茶杯 ②(放在花盆下防水流干的)垫盆 ③浅
碟形物; 浅碟形凹地 ④[复][口]眼睛; 睁得又圆
又大的眼睛; 大眼睛 ‖~-**eyed** ['sɔːsəraid] *a.*
眼睛睁得又大又圆的; 眼睛睁得又大又圆的

saucy ['sɔːsi] *a.* ①莽撞的; 无礼的 ②活泼的, 愉
快的 ③漂亮的, 时髦的: a ~ automobile 漂亮
的汽车 ‖**saucily** *ad.* / **sauciness** *n.*

sauna ['saunə] *n.* (芬兰式的) 蒸汽浴(室)

saunter ['sɔːntə] I *vi.* ①闲逛 ②逍遥: ~ through
life 闲混日子; 逍遥一生 II *n.* 闲逛; 漫步 ‖~**er**
['sɔːntərə] *n.* 闲逛者; 漫步者

sausage ['sɔsidʒ] *n.* ① 香肠, 腊肠 ②香肠状物;
【军】圆柱形系留气球 (= ~ balloon) ③[贬]德国
人 ‖~ **meat** 腊肠肉用碎猪肉 / ~ **roll** (包以面
糊的)香肠卷

savage ['sævidʒ] I *a.* ①野性的; 凶猛的; 残酷的;
猛烈的: a ~ beast 野兽, 猛兽 / a ~ blow 猛烈
的打击 ②[罕]荒野的; 未开发的: ~ scenery 荒
凉的景象 / a ~ forest 未开发的森林 ③(部落
等)原始的; 未开化的; 野蛮的: ~ art 原始艺术 /
a ~ tribe 原始部落 ④粗鲁的: ~ bad manners
粗暴无礼的举止 ⑤[口]狂怒的: get ~ with sb.
对某人大发脾气 II *n.* ①原始时代(以渔猎为生)
的人; 未开化的人 ②残酷成性的人 ③粗鲁的人
III *vt.* ①(马)乱撞, 乱咬, 乱踩 ②凶猛地打击; 粗
暴地对待 ‖*cut up* ~ 发脾气, 发怒 ‖~**ly** *ad.* /
~**ness** *n.*

savanna(h) [sə'vænə] *n.* ① (美国东南部的)无树
平原 ②(亚)热带的大草原

savant ['sævənt; 美 sə'vɑːnt] *n.* 博学多闻的人; 专
家; 学者

save[1] [seiv] I ❶ *vt.* ①救, 搭救, 挽救: cure the
sickness to ~ the patient 治病救人 / ~ a child
from drowning 救起溺水儿童 ②节省, 省去; 避
免(损失等): ~ unnecessary expenses 节省不必
要的开支 ③储蓄; 贮存: ~ (*up*)10 percent out of
one's monthly pay 储蓄月薪的十分之一 / ~
surplus grain 贮存余粮 ④顾全, 保全; 保留:
~ (one's) face 顾全面子 / Will you please ~ a
seat for me? 请给我留一个座位好不好? ⑤赶
上…时间; 不失…时机: He wrote hurriedly to
~ the post. 他赶紧写了信, 以便赶上邮递班次。
⑥(球类比赛中)救(球等); 阻碍对方得(分): ~
the game 救出险球; 扭转败局 ⑦【宗】替…赎罪;
拯救 ❷ *vi.* ①救, 挽救 ②节省, 节约: ~ on coal
节约煤炭 ③积蓄金钱; 贮存物品; [口](鱼类、水
果等)耐贮藏, 搁得住: food that ~*s* 耐贮藏的食
物 ④ 救球 II *n.* (球类运动)救球; 阻碍对方得
分; (桥牌)扭转败局的一招 ‖*Save me from my
friends!* 这样的好意我可受不了啦! / ~ *sb.'s
(one's) bacon* 见 **bacon** / ~ *the tide* 见
tide / *~ us!* (表示惊讶)天哪! ‖~**able** *a.*
=savable / ~**r** *n.* ①救助者; 储蓄者; 节省的人
②[常用以构成复合词]节省…的装置 (或器具):
a great labo(u)r-~*r* 大大节省劳动力的装置

save[2] [seiv] I *prep.* 除…以外; 除外: all ~ sb. 除某人以
外所有的人 / The screen was all dark ~ *for*
one bright spot. 除一个光点外屏幕上一片黑
暗。/ ~ and except [加强语气用]除…以外 II
conj. ①若不是; 只是: A similar timetable has

been adopted, ~ *that* the morning break is shorter. 已采用了(大体上)相同的时间表,只是早上休息时间缩短了。②除去: No one knows it ~ she. 这事除了她谁也不知道。③[古]除非(= unless)

saving[1] ['seiviŋ] **I** *a*. ①搭救的;挽救的 ②节约的;节俭的 ③保留的: a ~ clause 保留条款 ④补偿的: He has the ~ grace of modesty. 他有谦逊这一可取之点。**II** *n*. ①搭救;挽救 ②节约;节俭: a ~ *on* fuel 燃料的节约 / a ~ of ten percent 节省百分之十 ③[复]储蓄(金),存款: a steady rise in the people's ~s deposits 稳步上升的人民储蓄存款 / a ~s bank 储蓄银行 / a ~s account book (银行)存(款)折 ‖*Saving is getting.* [谚]节约等于增加收入。‖**~ly** *ad*.

saving[2] ['seiviŋ] **I** *prep*. ① 除…以外 ② 顾到,考虑到: ~ your presence (或 reverence) [古]请恕我冒昧 **II** *conj*. =save[2] (*conj*.)

savio(u)r ['seivjə] *n*. 救助者; 挽救者; 救星 ‖*the* (或 *our*) *Savio(u)r*【宗】救世主; 耶稣基督

savo(u)r ['seivə] **I** *n*. ①滋味;气味;[喻]风味;特点: a poem with a ~ of the epic 一首有史诗风味的诗 ② 引起兴趣(或食欲等)的力量; 吸引力 ③ 食欲;嗜好: one's ~ for sea food 对海味的嗜好 ④[古]名声 **II** ❶ *vi*. 具有…的滋味;带有…的意味(*of*): His argument ~*ed of* sophistry. 他的论点有些诡辩的味道。❷ *vt*. ①给…加调味品: ~ the meat with salt 给肉加上盐 ②使有风味 ③尝到;经历到 ④品尝;欣赏;[古]爱好 ‖~ *of the pan* 露出本来面目,漏底 ‖**~less** *a*. 缺少滋味的;缺少风味的

savo(u)ry ['seivəri] **I** *a*. ①美味可口的;芳香开胃的;饶有趣味的: a ~ dish 一道美味的菜 / a ~ story book 一本饶有趣味的故事书 ②咸的;香辣的: a ~ omelette 咸的煎蛋饼 ③[常用于否定句]宜人的,适意的;体面的: a none too ~ district 不太令人适意的地区 / a not very ~ reputation 不太好的名声 **II** *n*. [英][餐前或餐末吃的]开胃的菜肴 ‖**savo(u)rily** *ad*. / **savo(u)riness** *n*.

saw[1] [sɔː] see[1] 的过去式

saw[2] [sɔː] **I** *n*. ① 锯子; 锯状器; 锯床: a crosscut ~ 横切锯 / a ~ machine 锯床 ②[动]锯齿状部; [复](昆)产卵锯 ③[美俚]票面十元的钞票 **II** (过去式 sawed, 过去分词 sawn [sɔːn] 或 sawed) ❶ *vt*. ①锯;锯开;锯成: ~ a log in two 把木头锯成两半 / ~ a log into planks (或 ~ planks out of a log) 把木头锯成木板 / ~ sth. up 把某物锯成小段 ②拉锯般来回移动; 拉(曲调): ~ one's knife through a beefsteak 用刀割牛排 / ~ a tune out on a fiddle 在提琴上拉出音调 ③在(书刊等)上切口(以便装订) ❷ *vi*. ①用锯,拉锯;锯用: The timber ~s smoothly (badly). 这木材容易(不易)锯开。②(拉锯般)移动: ~ *at* the reins 抖动缰绳 ‖*run a* ~ *on* 嘲笑,讽刺(某人或某事物) / ~ *the air* 见 **air** / ~ *wood* 见 **wood** ‖**~ blade** 锯条 / **~bones** *n*. [俚]外科

医生(也可指其他医生) / '**~buck** *n*. ①[美]锯木架 ②[美俚]票面十元的钞票; 十块钱 / ~ **doctor** 锯齿制作器 / '**~dust** *n*. (锯)木屑; 锯屑: let the ~*dust* out of ... 使原形毕露, 使出丑(原指从玩偶中取出填塞物) / as dry as ~*dust* 枯燥乏味 *a*. ①木屑填塞的 ②(马戏、杂技会等)在天篷下举行的 ③无实质的, 无内容的: a ~*dust* answer 空洞的答辞 / '**~fish** *n*.【动】锯鳐 / '**~fly** *n*.【动】叶蜂 / ~ **gin** 有锯齿装置的轧棉机 / '**~horse** *n*. 锯木架 / '**~log** *n*. 可锯木 / '**~mill** *n*. 锯木厂; 锯床 / ~ **set** 锯齿修整器 / '**~tooth** *n*. 锯齿 *a*. 锯齿形的 / '**~-toothed** *a*. 锯齿形的

saw[3] [sɔː] *n*. 格言; 谚语: an old ~ 古谚 / a wise ~ 名言

saxophone ['sæksəfoun] *n*.【音】萨克斯管 ‖**saxophonist** [sæk'sɔfənist] *n*. 萨克斯管吹奏者

saxophone

say [sei] **I** (said [sed]; 第三人称单数现在式 says [sez]) ❶ *vt*. ①说,讲: ~ all one knows 知无不言 / *Say* it again in English. (请)用英语再说一遍。/ *Say* it out. 直说出来吧。/ He *said*, "Never mind." (或 "Never mind," *said* he.) 他说:"没关系。" / have something to ~ 有话要说 / I can't ~ much for the picture. 我觉得这幅画并不怎么高明。/ We mean what we ~. 我们说了话是算数的。/ I have heard ~ that .... 我听说… / It is *said* (或 They ~) that .... 据说… / Well *said*. 说得好! / What do you ~ (或 What ~ you) *to* a game of chess? 下盘棋好吗? / Who shall I ~? (传达者问来客)我该报什么姓名? (或: 请问贵姓?) / I wish I could ~ when he will return. 我要是能说得出他什么时候回来就好了。②说明; 宣称; 表明: What do these figures ~? 这些数字说明什么? / My watch ~s ten to four. 我的表上是三点五十分。/ a glance that ~s much 含意很深的一瞥 ③念; 背诵: This poem can be both *said* and sung. 这首诗既可以念又可以唱。/ ~ one's lesson (part) 背课文(台词) / ~ grace【宗】饭前(或饭后)祈祷

④ 写道; 报道: What ~s the editorial? 社论中怎么说? / The radio ~s heavy rain in the afternoon. 广播中预报今天下午有大雨。⑤ [常用于虚拟语气、祈使句] 比如说; 即使说; 大约 (=let's ~): Shall we start sometime later this week, ~, Friday? 我们是不是在本周中的晚些时候再出发? 星期五怎么样? / Well, ~ it were true, what then? 好吧, 就算这是真的, 又怎样呢? / Most students, let's ~ five hundred of them, will go camping. 多数学生, 大约五百人, 要去参加野营。

❷ vi. ① 说, 讲; 发表意见: Say on! 说下去! / It is hard to ~. 很难说(定)。 / I cannot ~. 我说不上来。(或: 我不知道。) / You may well ~ so. 你完全可以这么说。(或: 你说得对。) / And so ~ all of them. 他们也都是这个意见。② [美口] 叫, 要: She said (for me) to send you the letter. 她叫我把这封信带给你。

II n. [一般只用单] 要说的话, 意见; 发言机会; 发言权; [常用 the ~] 决定权: You've had your ~, haven't you? 不是已经给你机会让你说话了吗? / I have a (no, not much) ~ in the matter 对这件事有(没有, 不太有)发言权 / have all the ~ 有决定一切的权力 / Who has the (final) ~? 谁说了(最后说了)算?

‖as much as to ~ 等于说 / Easier said than done. [谚] 说来容易做来难。 / go without ~ing 不言而喻, 理所当然: It goes without ~ing that he will be invited as well. 当然, 他肯定也会被邀请的。 / I dare (或 should) ~ [作插入语] 我想, 大概 / I ~ (或 [美] Say) ① (引起话头) 喂: I ~, John, who's that fellow? 喂, 约翰, 那个人是谁? ② (表示惊奇或反感) 啊呀, 唷: Say, what a melon! 唷, 好大的瓜呀! / I ~, you've gone too far! 嗨, 你太过分啦! / Least said, soonest mended. (或 The least said, the soonest mended.) 见 least / No sooner said than done. 说到做到。 / not to ~ 虽不能说…: It is rather cool, not to ~ cold. 天气虽不能说冷, 也算相当凉了。 / a good word for sb. 见 word / Say away! 有话就说吧! / ~ nay to sth. 见 nay / ~ no (to) 见 no / ~ one's ~ 把话说完, 畅所欲言 / ~ over 背诵… / ~ sb. nay 见 nay / Says you! [美俚] (表示不相信等)听你胡扯! / ~ the word 见 word / ~ (或 cry) uncle 见 uncle / ~ yes (to) 见 yes / so to ~ 见 so / So you ~. 你这么说嘛! (意即: 事实并非如此。) / That is ~ing a great deal. 这可了不得。 / that is to ~ [作插入语] 那就是说, 即; 换句话说: two weeks from today, that is to ~, the 1st of March 从今天起两星期后, 即三月一日 / He didn't go, that is to ~, it is not recorded that he did. 他没有去, 换句话说, 他去的这个事实无案可查。 / There is much to be said on both sides. (争论的)双方都有自己的一番大道理。 /

There is no ~ing .... 说不准… (或: 无法断定…): There is no ~ing when it will cease raining. 说不准雨什么时候会停。 / to ~ nothing of 见 nothing / to ~ the least (of it) 见 least / You can ~ that again! [口] 我同意你! / You don't ~ so. 不会这样吧。(或: 不见得吧。或: 不至于吧。) / You said it. [口] 对了, 正是如此。 / when all is said (and done) 结果, 毕竟 ‖~able a. 可说的; 可有力(或流利)地说出来的 / ~er n. 说话的人: a mere ~er of "how-d'you-dos" 只是说说"你好"的人(指无实权、只是出面应付的人物)

saying ['seiiŋ] n. ① 话, 言语; 言论: Saying and doing should agree with each other. 言行应该一致。② 谚语, 俗话; 格言: a common ~ 常言, 谚语 / as the ~ goes (或 is) 正如俗话所说

scab [skæb] I n. ① 痂 ② 动物的皮肤病(尤指羊的); (家畜的)疥癣 ③【植】斑点病 ④ 金属材料表面的疤; 搪瓷上的疵瑕 ⑤ [俚] 卑劣的家伙, 恶棍, 无赖 ⑥ 拒不参加工会者; 拒不参加罢工者; 破坏罢工者, 工贼: a ~ (trade) union 黄色工会 II (scabbed; scabbing) vi. ① (伤口等)结痂 ② 当工贼 ‖~land n.【地】(土壤瘠薄的)崎岖地

scabbard ['skæbəd] I n. 鞘: a bayonet ~ 刺刀鞘 II vt. 把(剑或刺刀等)插入鞘中 ‖fling (或 throw) away the ~ 破釜沉舟; 决心战斗到底 ‖~ fish 安哥拉带鱼

scabbard

scabies ['skeibii:z] [单复同] n.【医】疥疮; 疥螨病

scaffold ['skæfəld] I n. ① 【建】脚手架; 临时搭起的台架; 支架 ② 断头台; 绞刑架: go to (或 mount) the ~ 上断头台; 被处绞刑 / send sb. to the ~ 处某人以绞刑 ③ 骨架 ④ [总称] 搭脚手架的材料 II vt. 搭脚手架于; 搭架于

scaffolding ['skæfəldiŋ] n. ① 【建】脚手架; 脚手组; 搭脚手架的材料 ② 台架, 支架; [喻] (论点等)的支柱 ‖~-pole n.【建】脚手木

scald[1] [sko:ld] I ❶ vt. ① (用沸水等)烫伤 ② 用水(或蒸汽)清洗, 烫洗: ~ (out) a cup 烫洗杯子 ③ 把…烫到接近沸点: ~ milk 烫热牛奶 ④ 把…灼焦 ❷ vi. 烫; 烫痛; 烫伤 II n. ① 烫伤: an ointment for ~s and burns 供烫伤和烧伤用的药膏 ② 烫洗 ‖get a good ~ on [方]在…方面极为成功 ‖~ing a. ① 滚烫的; 灼人的: ~ing water 沸水 / ~ing tears 热泪, 伤心泪 / the ~ing sun 炎炎烈日 ② (文章等)尖锐辛辣的

scald² [skɔ:ld] *n.* (古代北欧的)吟唱诗人

scale¹ [skeil] I *n.* ①鳞,鱼鳞;介壳: scrape the ~s off a fish 刮去鱼鳞 ② 鳞状物; 鳞片;【植】鳞苞; (树木的)鳞皮; (皮肤的)鳞屑 ③ (眼中的)翳障; [复][喻]障眼物 ④铁屑;水锈,水垢,齿垢: boiler (kettle) ~(s) 锅炉(水壶)的水垢 ⑤ 介壳虫;介壳虫害 II ❶ *vt.* ① 刮去…的鳞片; 剥去…的介壳; 除去…的积垢: ~ a fish 刮去鱼鳞 / ~ peas 剥豆 / ~ iron 除铁屑 / ~ one's teeth 剔齿垢 ② 使生鳞(或鳞屑等);使生水垢: Water ~s the boiler. 水使锅炉生垢。 ③ 用(石片等)打水漂 ❷ *vi.* ① (鳞片般地)剥落,脱落(off): paint (plaster) scaling off a wall 从墙上剥落的漆(灰泥) ②生鳞(或鳞屑等);生水垢 ‖remove the ~s off (或 from) sb.'s eyes 擦亮某人的眼睛 ‖~d *a.* ①有鳞(斑)的;有鳞状物的 ②(鸟)有鳞羽的;(珠宝等)有鳞纹的 ③ 瓦片盖叠的; 带比鳞次的 ④ 剥去鳞的 ‖ armo(u)r 鱼鳞铠甲 / '~board *n.* (镜框等)背板,衬板 / '~-,borer *n.* (用于锅炉管等的)除垢器 / ~ insect, ~ louse 介壳虫(一种害虫) / ~ moss【植】叶苔科植物;叶苔 / '~wing *n.* 蛾;蝴蝶 / '~-winged *a.* 鳞翅目的 / '~-work *n.* (细工等)鳞状排列

scale² [skeil] I *n.* ① 天平盘,秤盘 ② [常用复]天平;磅秤,秤: weigh grain *in the* ~s 把粮食过秤 / a livestock ~ 称家畜的磅秤 ③ (尤指牲畜的)重量;大小: The new breed possesses lots of ~. 新畜种分量很重。 ④ [the Scales]【天】天秤座 (= Libra) II ❶ *vt.* ①把…过秤 ②按重量把…分成均等部分: ~ dough into loaves 把面团分成同样重的块块 ❷ *vi.* 重(若干) ‖*be in the* ~(s) 悬而未决; 面临紧急关头 / *hold the* ~s *even* 公平裁判,不偏不倚 / *redress the* ~s 作公平的调整; 主持公道 / *throw one's sword into the* ~ 用武力强求 / *turn* (或 *tip*) *the* ~(s) ① 使平衡起作用; 起决定性作用; 扭转局面 ②[口]称起来重为…(*at*) / *weigh sth. in the nicest* ~s ① 把某物放在最精确的秤上称 ②对某事作极为周密的考虑

scale³ [skeil] I *n.* ①标度,刻度;尺度;刻度尺: the ~ on a ruler (thermometer) 尺(温度计)的标度 / a ~ in centimetres 用厘米标示的刻度 ②(指实物与图表等之间的)比例,比率;比例尺;缩尺: a map on the ~ of one-millionth 百万分之一比例的地图 / be drawn *to* ~ 按比例绘制 ③ 等级; 级别: wage (或 pay) ~s 工资级别 / pay a worker the union ~ (资本主义国家中)按工会会员的工资级别付工资给工人 / the ~ of clothing (英国军队的)服装补给标准 ④ 大小;规模: on a large (或 big, vast) ~ 大规模地(的),广泛地(的) ⑤ 进位制;计数法;换算法: the binary (ternary, decimal) ~ 二(三,十)进位计数法,二(三,十)进位制 ⑥[音]音列,音阶: major (minor) ~ 大(小)调音阶 / He sings ~s every morning. 他每天早晨练声(即吊嗓子)。 / run over ~s (on the piano) (在钢琴上)练指法 ⑦ (对木材中可用部分

的)估量 ⑧[古]梯子;阶梯 II ❶ *vt.* ①攀登(悬崖、墙等);到达…的顶点;(用云梯)进攻: ~ new heights of science and technology 攀登科学技术新高峰 / Firemen ~d the building. 消防员攀登大楼。 ②(按比例)排列;(用比例尺)测量;(按比例或标准)绘制,调节;衡量(木材等)的可用部分: ~ a building (map) 按比例绘制建筑物图(地图) / Prices were ~d down (up) 5 percent. 价格按照比例下降(上升)了百分之五。 ❷ *vi.* ①攀登;(逐步)升高 ②衡量 ‖'~-down *n.* (按比率)缩减,降低;[无]分频: a ~-down of prices 按比率降价 / '~-up *n.* (按比率)增加,扩大,升高: a ~-up of wages 按比率加工资 / scaling ladder 云梯,爬城梯;消防梯

scalp [skælp] I *n.* ① (人的)头皮; (狗、狼等的)头顶皮; 鲸鱼头的上部 ② 带发头皮(从前北美印第安人把它从敌人头上割下来作为战利品); [喻]战利品 ③[方]光秃的圆山顶; 突出的岩石 ④ [口](从事小投机买卖所得的)薄利 II ❶ *vt.* ① 剥下…的头皮; 剥去(土地或物)上面一层 ② 筛(矿石等) ③剥夺…的职位(或权势)/打败(对手) ④ 使饱受嘲弄,使受辱; 猛烈抨击 ⑤[口]转手买卖(股票等)以牟取薄利; 倒卖(戏票等) ❷ *vi.* ① 剥取头皮 ②[口]从事小投机买卖; 倒卖戏票 ‖*have the* ~ *of sb.* 击败某人;征服某人 / *out for* ~s 出猎头皮; [喻]蓄意寻衅; 决心打败对手; 猛烈抨击 / ~ *sb. for a jay* 欺骗愚弄某人 / *take sb.'s* ~ 剥取某人头皮;战胜某人;向某人报仇 ‖~ **lock** 印第安人剃光的头顶上的一绺头发 (作为向敌人挑战的标志)

scalpel [ˈskælpəl] I *n.* 解剖刀,外科用小刀 II (scalpel(l)ed; scalpel(l)ing) *vt.* 用解剖刀割;解剖

scamp¹ [skæmp] *n.* ①流氓,坏蛋; 饭桶 ②[谑]小淘气 ③[古]拦路强盗 ‖*go on* (或 *upon*) *the* ~ 趁火打劫,顺手牵羊

scamp² [skæmp] *vt.* 草率地做(工作等)

scamper [ˈskæmpə] I *vi.* ① (孩子等)跳跳蹦蹦 (*about*) ② (动物等)惊惶奔跑; 奔逃 (*off, away*) ③匆忙游览;浏览 (*through*) II *n.* ① 蹦跳; 奔跑; 短距离的快走(或疾驰): take the dog for a ~ 带着狗出去溜溜腿 ②匆忙的游览; 浏览: take a ~ *through* Europe 匆忙地游览欧洲 / take a ~ *through* Dickens 浏览狄更斯的作品

scan [skæn] I (scanned; scanning) ❶ *vt.* ①细看;审视 ②(用电子装置等)校验(磁带或穿孔卡)③粗略地看;浏览 ④标出(诗)的格律(指划分音步等);有顿挫地吟诵 ⑤(电视、雷达光束等)扫描,扫掠 ❷ *vi.* ①(诗)符合格律,顿挫合拍: The verses ~ smoothly. 这些诗读起来很合格律。 ② 标出诗的格律 ③扫描,扫掠 II *n.* ①细看;审视 ②粗略一看;浏览 ③眼界 ④扫描,扫掠

scandal [ˈskændl] I *n.* ①丑事,丑闻: a public ~ 众所周知的丑事 ②干出丑事的人;耻辱: be a ~ *to* 是…的耻辱 ③反感;愤慨: to sb.'s ~ 使某人反感的是 / cause (或 give rise to) ~ *in the* neighbourhood 在街坊中引起公愤 ④ 流言蜚语;

恶意的诽谤: talk ~ 讲坏话 Ⅱ (scandal(l)ed; scandal(l)ing) vt. [方] 讲…坏话，恶意诽谤 ‖'~,monger n. 恶意中伤的人; 传播丑闻的人 / ~ sheet ① 以较大篇幅登载社会丑闻和杂谈的报刊; 黄色报刊 ②[美俚]商人的费用帐 / ~ soup [美俚]茶

scandalize ['skændəlaiz] vt. ① 使生反感，使感愤慨; 使感震惊: He was ~d at the news. 那消息使他大为愤慨。② 诽谤，中伤 ‖~r n. 恶意中伤者

scar[1] [skɑ:] Ⅰ n. ① 伤疤，伤痕; (精神上的)创伤: a vaccination ~ 牛痘疤 / grief that has left a ~ 难以忘怀的悲痛 ②【植】瘢痕 Ⅱ (scarred; scarring ['skɑ:riŋ]) ❶ vt. 使留下伤痕: a scarred leg 带有伤痕的腿 / a war-scarred town 被战争弄得疮痍满目的城市 ❷ vi. 结疤; (伤口)愈合 (over)

scar[2] [skɑ:] n. 孤岩; 山腰露岩; 断层

scarab ['skærəb] n. ①【动】金龟子科甲虫，圣甲虫 ②(古埃及人作护身符用的)刻有圣甲虫的宝石

scarab

scarce [skɛəs] Ⅰ a. ① [一般作表语]缺乏的，不足的: Water being ~ on the mountains, we built many reservoirs. 由于山间缺水，我们修建了许多水库。②稀有的，珍贵的: ~ metals 稀有金属 / a ~ book 珍本，难得的书 Ⅱ ad. [古][诗] =scarcely ‖*make oneself* ~ [口]溜走，悄悄离开; 不露面 ‖~ness n.

scarcely ['skɛəsli] ad. ① 仅仅; 刚刚 ② 几乎不，简直不,几乎没有: He ~ knew a word of English. 他对英语几乎是一无所知。③决不: This can ~ be true. 事实决不会是这样的。④[相当于 "not" 的减弱语气]不很; 大概不: I ~ think so. 我可不这么想。/ A more suitable man for the work could ~ have been found. (当时)要找一个更恰当的人来担任这工作，怕是不可能的了。

scarcity ['skɛəsiti] n. ① 缺乏，不足; 萧条(时期)，荒(年): capital ~ 资金不足 / ~ of labour (rain) 劳动力(雨量)不足 ②稀少，罕见 ‖~ economics 限制产量以保证利润的经济理论

scare [skɛə] Ⅰ ❶ vt. ①惊吓，使恐慌: ~ sb. stiff 把某人吓呆 / be ~d to death (或 out of one's wits) 吓得要死 / The boy was more ~d than hurt. 这孩子吓倒不算什么，并不是受惊不小。② 把…吓跑 (away, off) ③ 把…吓出来; 把(猎物)吓

出隐蔽处(out, up): ~ the wits out of sb. 把某人吓得要死 / ~ a confession out of sb. 吓唬某人招供 ❷ vi. 受惊 (at) Ⅱ n. 惊恐; 大恐慌: You did give me a ~. 你可真把我吓了一跳。/ a war ~ 战争恐慌 ‖*run* ~*d* [俚](在竞选等中因担心失败而)行动小心翼翼，战战兢兢 / ~ *up* (费力地)张罗; 凑合: ~ *up* a supper for unexpected guests 给一些突然来到的客人张罗一顿晚餐 / *throw* ~ *into sb.* 吓坏某人。/ ~*d a.* 惊慌的; 吓坏了的: a ~*d* child (look) 受惊的孩子(脸色) / ~**y** ['skɛəri] a. =scary ‖~ **buying** (因战争恐慌等引起的)抢购 / '~-**crow** n. ① (竖在田里吓鸟的)稻草人 ②吓唬人的东西 ③衣衫褴褛的人; 骨瘦如柴的人 / '~**head**, ~ **headline** n. 耸人听闻的大标题 / '~,**monger** n. 散播骇人消息的人

scarf[1] [skɑ:f] Ⅰ ([复] scarves [skɑ:vz] 或 scarfs) n. ① 围巾; 肩上的披巾; 头巾 ② 领带; 领巾: a red ~ 红领巾 ③ (装饰用的)狭长枱布 ④[军] (制服肩部或腰部表示军衔的)绶带 Ⅱ vt. ① 围(围巾); 披(披巾) ②用围巾(或披肩等)围(或披、包) ‖~-**pin**, '~-**ring** n. 领带别针 / '~**skin** n. 外皮，表皮(尤指指甲角质层)

scarf[2] [skɑ:f] Ⅰ n. ① 嵌接 ②(嵌接的)斜面，切口，截面; (斜嵌)槽 Ⅱ vt. 嵌接; 凿槽于 ‖~ **joint** 嵌接 / '~**weld** n. 嵌焊，斜面焊接

scarlet ['skɑ:lit] Ⅰ n. ① 猩红色，绯红色，鲜红色 ②鲜红的布; 红色制服，红衣 Ⅱ a. ① 猩红的，绯红的，鲜红的: He turned ~ with rage. 他气得脸色通红。② 淫荡的; 罪恶昭彰的 ‖~ **admiral** 一种红蝴蝶 / ~ **fever** 【医】猩红热 ②[谑] (女子的)军人崇拜 / ~ **hat** 红衣主教的帽子; [喻]红衣主教的职位 / ~ **letter** 红 A 字(美国在殖民地时期用以标志通奸罪) / ~ **runner** (**bean**)【植】红花菜豆 / ~ **woman** [贬]淫妇 ②(新教徒用以指责罗马教皇的用语)异教徒的罗马; 俗世精神

scatter[1] ['skætə] Ⅰ ❶ vt. ① 使消散; 使分散; 使溃散: Clouds were ~ed by the wind. 风把云吹散。/ ~ sb.'s hopes to the four winds 使某人的希望化为乌有 / Don't ~ your strength. 不要分散精力。/ ~ the enemy troops 击溃敌军 ②撒; 散于…上; 散布; 散布在…上: ~ gravel on the road (或 ~ the road with gravel) 把砂砾撒在路面上 / ~ the factories instead of concentrating them in a single area 把工厂分散布局而不是集中在一个地区 ③ 散播，撒播: ~ seed over a plot 把种子撒播在一块地里 ④【物】【军】散射 ⑤ [古] 挥霍掉 ❷ vi. ① 消散; 分散; 溃散: The crowd soon ~ed. 人群很快地散了。②零落地出现 ③(炮火等)散射 Ⅱ n. ① 消散; 分散; 溃散; 散射; (炮火的)散射面 ②散布; 撒播 ③散布的东西; 稀疏的少量: a ~ of applause 稀稀拉拉的掌声 ④[美俚]猎枪; 机关枪 ‖~*ed and peeled* [古]被劫掠 ‖~**ed** a. ①分散的; 散乱的: serve the ~ed population of a mountain region 为山区分散的

居民服务 / concentrate ~ed and unsystematic ideas 把分散的无系统的意见集中起来 ② 散的 ③【植】星散的 / ~er ['skætərə] n. 分散者; 撒播者;【物】散射体 / ~ing ['skætəriŋ] n. ①分散; 散射 ②稀疏的少量: a ~ing of visitors 零零落落的来访者 a. ① 四散开的, 分散的: ~ing votes 不集中(于某一名候选人)的选票 ② 稀疏散乱的 ‖~ bomb 散飞性燃烧弹 / ~brain n. 注意力不集中的人; 轻率浮躁的人 / '~brained a. 不专注的; 轻率的, 浮躁的 / '~good n. 大肆挥霍的人 / '~-gun n. [美俚]猎枪; 机关枪 / ~ rug 小块地毯 / '~shot a. 漫无目标的: a ~shot approach 漫无目标的做法

scatter² ['skætə] n. [美俚] ① 酒馆; 违法售酒处 ②秘密碰头的地方; 藏身处

scavenger ['skævindʒə] n. ① [主英]清道夫; 拾垃圾的人; 清扫工 ② 清除剂; 净化剂 ③ 食腐动物 ④黄色作家

scenario [si'nɑːriou] n. [意] ① 剧情说明; 歌剧剧情说明 ② 电影剧本; 电影拍摄剧本: a ~ writer 电影剧本作者 ②方案

scene [siːn] n. ① [古] 舞台(现只用于比喻): on the world ~ 在国际舞台上 ② (事件或故事的)发生地点 ③(戏剧、电影等的)一场;(戏剧、故事中的)一段情节;(电影的)一个镜头;(实际生活中的)一个场面 (或场面特写): Act I, Scene ii 第一幕第二场 / selected ~s 折子戏 / a stirring ~ 鼓舞人心的场面 ④ [常用复]道具; 布景; 场景: change the ~s 换布景 / a ~ painted by sb. 某人绘制的布景 ⑤ 景色; 景象: ~s in a mountain district 山区风光 / a ~ of prosperity 一派繁荣景象 ⑥当众吵嘴, 发脾气: make a ~ 当众大吵一场 ‖a change of ~ 改换环境(尤指通过旅行) / behind the ~s 在后台; 在幕后: go behind the ~s 到后台去; 探问内幕 / manoeuvre behind the ~s 幕后策划 / come on the ~ 出现, 登场 (常用于比喻) / make the ~ [美俚]①露面, 到场 ②积极参预其中 / quit the ~ ①下台 ②死去 ‖~ dock 舞台旁存放布景处 / ~man ['siːnmæn], '~,shifter n. 换布景者 / ~ painter 布景画师 / ~ painting 布景绘制 / ~ plot (为了卖弄自己)设法把观众注意力吸引到自己身上的配角演员

scenery ['siːnəri] n. ① [总称]舞台布景: a piece of ~ 一幅布景 ②[总称]风景, 景色: natural ~ 自然风景 / a region of attractive ~ 风景动人的地区 ③[罕]风景画

scenic ['siːnik] I a. ① 舞台的; 布景的: ~ effects 舞台效果 ②自然景色的; 景色优美的: a ~ spot 风景区 ③ 描绘情景(或事件)的: a ~ bas-relief 描绘故事的浅浮雕作品 ④戏剧性的; 装腔作势的 II n. 风景影片; 风景照片(或图片); 画有故事的糊墙纸 ‖~ally ad. II ~ railway (大型博览会、游乐场里)沿途可观看人造风景区的小铁路

scent [sent] I n. ① 气味; 香味: the sweet ~ of flowers 花的芳香 / ~s of roses and jasmin 玫瑰

和茉莉的香味 ② 香水: a bottle of ~ 一瓶香水 ③(猎物的)遗臭, 臭迹; 踪迹, 线索: a hot ~ 强烈的(易于追踪的)臭迹 / a cold ~ 微淡的(难于追踪的)臭迹 / give sb. a false ~ 给某人以假线索 ④迹象: a ~ of trouble 要出现麻烦的迹象 ⑤嗅觉; 察觉能力: hunt by ~ 凭嗅觉追猎 / have a keen ~ for 对…有敏锐的嗅觉 ⑥打猎(或钓鱼)用的一种诱饵 / a ~ of sulphur. 这个试管有硫磺的气味。⑦(儿童游戏"狗捉兔子"中)撒在地上的纸屑 II ❶ vt. ① 嗅, 闻; 嗅出, 闻到 (out) ② 察觉; 怀疑: ~ spring in the air 觉察到春天的气息 / ~ danger 发觉有危险 / ~ a plot 觉察其中有阴谋 ③ 使充满气味; 洒香水于: the air ~ed with roses 充满玫瑰花香味的空气 ❷ vi. ① 嗅猎 ② 发出气味 (of); 具有迹象 (of): This tube ~s of sulphur. 这个试管有硫磺的气味。‖be on a wrong (或 false) ~ 追踪的线索不对头; 探究的路子不对头 / be on the ~ (凭臭迹)追踪着猎物; (凭线索)探究着; 获得线索: We are on the ~ of an important discovery. 我们掌握了一条以能导致重要发现的线索。/ follow up the ~ 跟踪 / lose (recover) the ~ 失去(重新找到)线索 / put (或 throw) sb. off the ~ 使某人失去线索, 使某人无法追踪 ‖~ed a. ①有香味的; 洒了香水的: a cake of ~ed soap 一块香皂 ② 有嗅觉的: a keen-~ed hound 嗅觉灵敏的猎狗 / ~less a. ① 无气味的; 无香气的 ②缺乏嗅觉的; 无臭迹的 ‖~ bag ①香袋 ②【动】臭腺 / '~-,bottle n. ② [俚]厕所 / ~ gland【动】臭腺

scepsis ['skepsis] n. 怀疑; 怀疑哲学

scepter ['septə] n. & vt. = sceptre

sceptic ['skeptik] n. ① [S-]【哲】古希腊的怀疑论派成员 ②【哲】怀疑论者; 不可知论者 ③怀疑基督教(或所有宗教教条)的人; [口]无神论者 ④惯抱怀疑态度的人; 对某事物抱怀疑态度的人

sceptical ['skeptikəl] a.【哲】怀疑论的; 不可知论的 ②怀疑宗教教条的 ③怀疑的: be ~ about sth. 对某事怀疑 ‖~ly ad.

scepticism ['skeptisizəm] n. ①【哲】怀疑论 ②怀疑态度; 怀疑主义

sceptre ['septə] I n. 君主的节杖(权位的象征); [喻]君权; 统治权 II vt. 授…以节杖; 授…以王权 ‖lay down the ~ 退位 / seize the ~ 夺王位 / sleep's leaden ~ [诗]睡魔的力量 / wield the ~ 掌握统治权, 掌握大权 ‖~d a. ① 持有君王节杖的; [喻]握有帝王权力的; 掌握统治权的 ②帝王的

schedule ['ʃedjuːl; 美 'skedʒul] I n. ①一览表; 细目单: a ~ of freight rates 运费一览表 ② [美]时间表; 课程表 (=timetable): a train ~ 火车行车时刻表 / a sailing ~ 航运时刻表 / plan (或 map out, lay out) a ~ of games 排出比赛时间表 ③ 计划表, 程序表; 议事日程: a progress ~ (生产等的)进度表 / a visitor with a heavy ~ 日程排得很紧的来访者 / What's your ~ for tomorrow? 你明天的日程安排如何? II vt. ①将

scheme 838 school

…列表; 将…列入计划表(或程序表、时间表等):
~ one's receipts and expenditures 将收支列成
细目单 / ~ a new train (在行车表上规定)增开
一列火车 ②[美]排定; 安排: the ~d speakers
at the rally 排定的大会发言人 / ~ a match for
the next week 在下星期内安排一次比赛 / The
plane is ~d to take off at 4. 飞机定于四时起
飞。/ The ship sailed for Africa as ~d. 船按照
预定计划开往非洲。‖according to ~ 按照预
定计划: accomplish a task according to ~ 按照
预定计划完成任务 / ahead of ~ 提前: The
production plan was fulfilled ahead of ~. 生产
计划提前完成了。/ behind ~ 落后于预定计划
(或时间) / on ~ [美]按照预定时间: The train
arrived on ~. 火车准时到达。/ to ~ [美]按照
预定时间 ‖~r n. (一览表、时间表、程序表等的)
制表人; 程序机(一种生产用计算机)

scheme [ski:m] I n. ①计划, 规划; 方案: an irrigation ~ 灌溉规划 / a ~ of operations 作战计
划 / a ~ for the term's work 学期工作安排 /
lay (或 map, work) out a practical ~ 订出切实
可行的计划 ②组合, 配合; 系统, 体制: a delightful colour ~ 悦目的配色 / the ~ of society
社会结构 ③诡计, 阴谋 ④图解; 大纲; 摘
要 ⑤[古]数学图表; (占星)天象图 II ❶ vt. ①
计划; 设计(out): ~ (out) a new method of bridge
building 设计一种新的造桥法 ②策划(阴谋等):
~ to do sth. 策划搞某事 / try to ~ an escape
企图策划逃跑 ❷ vi. ①计划; 设计 ②搞阴谋:
~ for power 阴谋夺权 / ~ against each other
彼此勾心斗角 ‖~r n. ①计划者 ②阴谋家 /
scheming a. 富于心计的; 诡计多的

schism ['sizəm] n. ①(政治组织等的)分裂, 不和
②【宗】教会分立; 分立教会的罪行 ③(由于分裂
而产生的)教会宗派

schismatic [siz'mætik] I n. 分裂(论)者; 教会分
立(论)者 II a. 分裂(论)的; 教会分立(论)的

schnorkel ['ʃnɔːkəl] n. (潜水艇或潜游者的)通气
管

scholar ['skɔlə] n. ①学者(尤指古典语言和文学方
面的): a ~ in (或 of) English 英语学者; 精通英
语者 / a Greek ~ 希腊语学者 ②有文化者; 能写
会读的人: I'm not much of a ~. 我的文化程度
不高。③奖学金获得者, 津贴生 ④学习者; 门徒;
[古]小学生: Old as he is, he is still a ~. 他活
到老, 学到老。‖~ism ['skɔlərizəm] n. 学术, 学
问(尤指故弄玄虚的) / ~ly a. ①学者派头的,
学者风度的 ②博学的 ③好学的 / ~ship n.
①学业成绩; 学术成就; 学问, 学识 ②奖学金
‖'~,bureaucrat n. 士大夫 / '~,tyrant n.
学阀

scholastic [skə'læstik] I a. ①学校的, 学院的; 学
术的: a ~ year 学年 / a ~ education 学校教
育 / a ~ life 学院生活 / ~ attainments 学
业成绩; 学术成就 ②教师的; 教育的: a ~ post
教师的职位 / the ~ profession 教师的职业 /

a ~ agency 教师职业介绍所 ③学究的, 烦琐的;
故弄玄虚的 ④[S-]经院的: Scholastic philosophy 经院哲学 II n. ①[S-]经院哲学学者 ②
烦琐哲学家; 学究; 拘于形式者 ③(艺术上的)墨
守成规者 ④学生; 学者 ‖~ally ad.

school¹ [sku:l] I n. ①学校; (学校)建筑物, 校舍;
全校师生; 全校学生: In all its work the ~ should
aim at transforming the student's ideology. 学
校一切工作都是为了转变学生的思想。/ a pri-
mary (middle 或 secondary) ~ 小(中)学 ②
(大学里的)学院: the Medical (Law) School 医
(法)学院 ③[不用冠词]上学; 学业, 功课; 学期;
上课: Is the child old enough for ~? 孩子到上
学年龄了吗? / put (或 send) a child to ~ 送孩
子入学 / School begins at 8 o'clock. 学校八点
钟开始上课。④学派, 流派; [复]学术界; (中世
纪)书院, 经院: different ~s of thought 各种
不同学派 / the French Impressionist ~ 法国
印象派 / a man of the old ~ (风俗习惯、生活
方式等方面的)老派人, 守旧派 ⑤[英]大学学位
考试科目; 学位考试试场; [复]学位考试 ⑥锻炼;
军事训练, 军训教程(或章): go through the
hard ~ of adversity 经受逆境的磨炼 / the ~
of the soldier 士兵的训练 II vt. ①把…送进学
校培养; 负担…的学费 ②教育; 训练; 约束; 使(自
己)习惯(或适应)于: be well ~ed in foreign
languages 在外语方面受过很好的训练 / ~ a
horse 训练马 / refuse to be ~ed 拒受约束 / ~
oneself to (或 in) patience 培养自己的耐心 ‖after
~ 下课后, 放学后: have physical exercises
after ~ 下课后进行体育锻炼 / at ~ ①在学校
②在上课 ③在求学: My younger brother is
still at ~. 我弟弟还在读书。/ begin (或
start) ~ 开始求学: She began ~ at seven
years old. 她七岁开始上学。/ finish ~ 完成
学业 / go to ~ ①开始求学 ②到校上课: I go
to ~ at 7:30 every morning. 我每天早上七点
半到校上课。/ go to ~ to sb. 跟某人学; 模仿
某人 / in for one's ~s [英]准备学位考试 /
in ~ 在求学: She is in ~ again. 她复学了。/
in the ~s [英]接受(或主持)牛津大学学位考
试 / leave ~ ①退学 ②(毕业)离校 ③放学回
家 / stay away from ~ (或 cut ~) 旷课 /
teach ~ [美]教书, 当教师 / tell tales out
of ~ 见 tale / the modern ~ [英]学校
中着重现代学科的部分 ‖~ age (儿童入学的)
学龄 / '~,ager n. 学龄儿童 / '~bag n. 书
包 / ~ board 地方上的教育委员会 / '~book
n. 教科书 / '~boy n. & a. (中、小学)男生
(的) / ~ bus 校车 / '~,day n. 上课的日子
(指非假日) / '~-days [复] n. 学生时代 / ~
fee 学费 / '~,fellow n. =~mate / '~girl
n. & a. (中、小学)女生(的) / ~ guard 护送
小学生在学校附近穿过大街的人 / '~house n.
(小学或乡村学校)校舍; [英][the ~house] (小
学)校长住宅 / ~ leaver [主英]未毕业而停学
的(中、小)学生 / '~ma'am, ~marm ['sku:l-

ma:m] *n.* [美口](乡村或小城市小学的)女教师；女学究 / '**~man** *n.* ①[S-](中世纪欧洲书院的)教师；经院哲学家 ②[美]教师；学校行政人员 / '**~,master** *n.* ①男教师 ②(中、小学)校长 ③教练，教导者 / '**~mate** *n.* 同学 / ~ **miss** 怕羞的女学生(或女孩) / '**~,mistress** *n.* (中、小学)女教师 / '**~room** *n.* 教室 / ~ **ship** 教练船(舰) / '**~,teacher** *n.* (中、小学)教师 / '**~,teaching** *n.* 教学；教学职业 / '**~time** *n.* ①(上课或自修)学习时间 ②训练期间 ③[常用复]学生时代，读书时代 / '**~work** *n.* 学校作业，家庭作业 / '**~yard** *n.* 校园，操场 / **~ year** 学年

school² [sku:l] **I** *n.* 鱼群；同类水生物群 **II** *vi.* (鱼、鲸等)成群地游

schooling ['sku:liŋ] *n.* ①正规学校教育；教育：shorten the period of ~ 缩短学制(或教育年限) / have much (little) ~ 受的教育很多(很少) ②学费，学校的膳宿杂费 ③练马；骑术训练

schooner ['sku:nə] *n.* ①纵帆船 ②[美]大啤酒杯；[英]一种量啤酒的杯子 ③[美]有篷四轮大马车

science ['saiəns] *n.* ①科学；科学研究：*Science* means honest, solid knowledge. 科学是老老实实的学问。②(一门)科学，学科：(a) natural (或 physical) ~ (一门)自然科学 / pure ~ (纯)理论科学 / applied ~ 应用科学 / the ~ of tactics 战术学 / moral ~ 伦理学 / 自然科学：a Bachelor of *Science* 理学士 / a Doctor of *Science* 理学博士 ④专门的技巧，技术：the ~ of boxing 拳术 ⑤[古]知识 ‖**~ fiction** 科学幻想小说

scientific [,saiən'tifik] *a.* ①科学(上)的：~ studies (或 researches) 科学研究 / ~ experiments 科学实验 / a ~ method 科学方法 ②符合科学规律的；系统的，精确的：~ socialism 科学社会主义 / a ~ classification 精确的分类 / a conclusion 符合科学的结论 / ~ farming 科学种田 / a ~ thinker 思想谨严的人 ③用于自然科学的：a ~ apparatus 科学仪器 / ~ books 科学书籍 / ~ terminology 科学词汇 ④有技术的；经过严格训练的，需要技术的：a ~ game 一种需要熟练技巧的比赛 ‖**~ally** *ad.*

scientist ['saiəntist] *n.* (自然)科学家 ‖**scientism** *n.* ①科学态度，科学方法 ②唯科学主义

scintillate ['sintileit] **❶** *vi.* ①发出火花 ②(星等)闪烁，闪耀 ③焕发：~ *with* wit 才华焕发 **❷** *vt.* ① 发出(火花、闪光等) ②闪耀出：~ witticisms 妙语横生

scion ['saiən] *n.* ①[植]接穗；(栽种或接枝用的)幼枝，幼芽 ②子孙，后裔(尤指名门或显贵)：a ~ of royalty 皇室子孙

scissor ['sizə] **I** *vt.* ①剪：~ *off* a length of wire 剪掉一段铁丝 / ~ *out* a paragraph from a newspaper 从报上剪下一段新闻 / ~ *up* a piece of paper 把一张纸剪碎 ②删除；削减：items *~ed* from the budget 从预算中削减的项目

II *n.* (一把)剪刀 ‖**~ing** ['sizəriŋ] *n.* ①剪裁 ②[复](从布、报纸等)剪下来的条条 ‖**~bill** *n.* [美方] ①下等人，愚笨的人 ②不关心工人阶级利益的工人；不参加工会的工人 / '**~bird** *n.* =~tail / '**~-cut** *n.* 剪纸 / '**~tail** *n.* [动](产于美国南部和墨西哥的)一种具有铁尾的鸟(属鹟科) / ~ **tooth** (食肉动物的)裂牙，裂齿

scissors ['sizəz] [复] *n.* ①[有时用作单]剪刀，剪子：Give me *a pair of* ~ (或 *a* ~). 给我一把剪刀。/ Where *are* my ~? 我的剪刀在哪里？/ These ~ *are* very sharp. 这些剪刀很锋利。/ ~ movement of prices 【经】价格的剪刀差 ②【体】作剪刀开合状的腿部运动；用双腿钳住对方的摔角姿势 ‖**~ and paste** 剪贴加浆糊；没有创造性的编辑工作 ‖**~bill** *n.* =scissorbill / '**~bird** *n.* =scissortail / ~ **chair** 打开后成 X 形的折椅 / '**~-,grinder** *n.* ①欧夜莺 ②(产于澳洲的)一种小的属鹟科的鸟 / ~ **kick** 侧游的踢脚法 / '**~tail** *n.* =scissortail

sclerotomy [skliə'rɔtəmi] *n.* 【医】巩膜切开术

sclerous ['skliərəs] *a.* 硬化的；骨质的

scobs [skɔbz] [复] *n.* 锯屑；刨花；锉屑；渣滓

scoff¹ [skɔf] **I** *n.* ①嘲弄，嘲笑；嘲弄的话 ②笑柄：be the ~ of the town 成为全城的笑柄 **II** **❶** *vi.* ①嘲弄，嘲笑(*at*)：~ *at* sb. (sth.) 嘲弄某人(某事) ②藐视：~ *at* difficulties 藐视困难 **❷** *vt.* 嘲弄；嘲笑 ‖**~er** *n.* 嘲弄者；嘲笑者 / **~ingly** *ad.* 藐视(或违犯)法令者(尤指违犯交通和禁酒法者)

scoff² [skɔf] [俚] **I** *n.* 食品；饭食 **II** **❶** *vt.* ①贪婪地吃 ②抢劫；偷窃 **❷** *vi.* 狼吞虎咽

scold [skould] **I** *n.* ①老爱责骂的人；好骂街的泼妇 ②责骂：a writing that is a ~ 骂人的文章 **II** **❶** *vi.* 责骂；大声叱责 **❷** *vt.* 申斥；怒骂：Don't ~ the child. It's not his fault. 不要责备这个孩子，这事不是他的过失。‖**~er** *n.* 责骂者 / **~ing** *n.* 责骂；申斥：get a good *~ing* for sth. 为某事挨一顿臭骂 / give sb. a *~ing* 训斥某人一顿

scone [skɔn] *n.* 烤饼

scoop [sku:p] **I** *n.* ①勺子，杓；戽斗；【医】匙，勺：an ear ~ 耳刮匙 ②铲斗，煤斗：a ~ dredge 斗式挖泥机 ③舀，铲；一勺，一铲斗：at one ~ 一勺子；一下子 / a ~ of coal 一铲煤 ④穴，口，凹处：ventilator ~ 【机】通风口 ⑤[口](投机或买卖中)抢先赚得的暴利 ⑥[口]抢先刊载的独家新闻；当前的重要内幕消息 **II** *vt.* ①用勺(或铲)取出，舀：They rowed out in boats to ~ *up* mud. 他们划船出去舀泥。/ ~ *out* half a basket of maize from the bin 从箱里舀出半篮子玉米 ②挖空；挖成；挖出：~ *out* a hole in the sand 在沙中挖个洞 ③[口]收集(*in*) ④[口]抢先赚得(利润) ⑤[口](报纸、电台等)抢在(别家)前面发布某条新闻；抢先获得(某条新闻) ‖**make a ~** ①走运；赚大钱 ②抢先得到新闻 / **on the ~** 饮酒无度；流连忘返 / ~ **out** 【军】接应(轰炸机返航时，由战斗机接应，助其摆脱敌机的攻击) ‖**~er**

n. 舀取者, 挖掘者; 雕刻工具 / **~ful** ***n.*** 一满勺, 一满斗 ‖**~ net** (捕鱼的) 掬网, 浅的抄网 / **~ wheel** 斗式挖泥车轮; 戽水水车

scoot [skuːt] **I** ***vi.*** [口]迅速跑开; 溜走: *Scoot*, or you will be late. 快走, 否则你将太迟了。**II** ***n.*** [口]迅速跑开; 溜走

scooter ['skuːtə] ***n.*** ①(儿童游戏用的) 踏板车 ②低座小摩托车(=motor ~) ③(在水上或冰上行驶的)有滑橇的平底帆船; 滑行艇

scope[1] [skoup] ***n.*** ①(活动、影响等的)范围: an investigation of wide ~ 大规模的调查 / the ~ of a history book 一本历史书所涉及的范围 / be within (beyond) the ~ of sb.'s understanding 是某人所能(不能)理解的 ②(发挥能力等的)余地; 机会: There is ample ~ for our abilities in the countryside. 我们在农村是大有可为的。/ seek ~ for one's energies 找发挥力量的机会 ③视界; 眼界: a mind of wide (limited) ~ 广博(狭隘)的见识 ④导弹的射程; 【海】(抛出的)锚缆长度 ⑤[古]目的, 意图

scope[2] [skoup] ***n.*** ①观察仪器(如显微镜、望远镜、示波器等) ②[美俚](潜艇中所用的)潜望镜 ③(算命用的)星占图, 天宫图

scorch [skɔːtʃ] **I ❶** ***vt.*** ①烧焦, 烤焦, 使枯萎: ~ one's clothes by staying too near the fire 因太靠近炉火而烤焦衣服 / The long drought ~ed the grass. 久旱使青草都枯萎了。②苛责, 用话刺痛 ③(军队撤退前)烧光(某地)的一切: a ~ed earth policy 焦土政策 ④【化】使(橡胶)过早硫化: ~ed rubber 早期硫化橡胶 ⑤[英方]切; 砍 **❷** ***vi.*** ①烧焦, 烤焦; 枯萎 ②苛苦, 刺痛人 ③[口]高速驾驶, 飞驶 **II** ***n.*** ①烧焦; 焦痕 ②(草木等的)枯黄 ③[口]高速驾驶, 高速行驶的时间

score [skɔː] **I** ***n.*** ①刻痕; 抓痕; 伤痕; 划线: ~s on a rock 岩石上的痕迹 ②帐目; 欠帐(源于旧时版店用粉笔划线记录顾客欠帐); [喻] 宿怨, 旧仇: pay one's ~ 付清帐目 ③点, 方面; 理由, 根据: Nobody has any doubt *on that* ~. 对那一点没人怀疑。/ retire *on the* ~ *of* age 因年老退休 ④(比赛中的)得分(记录), 比数; (测验的)成绩, 评分: A: What is the ~? B: The ~ is 2 to 1. 甲: 比分怎样? 乙: (比分是)二比一。/ win by a ~ of 10 to 9 以十比九得胜 / level the ~ 把比分拉平, 打平 / make a good ~ 得分多; 成绩好; 成功 ⑤【音】总谱, 乐谱; (电影、戏剧、歌舞等的)配乐 ⑥(赛跑等的)起跑线, 起步线; 终点线 ⑦[单复同]二十; (指称猪、牛等用的重量单位)二十(或二十一)磅: a (three) ~ of people 二十(六十)人 ⑧[复]许多, 大量: ~s of visitors 一大批来访者 / ~s of years ago 许多年前 / I have been there ~s of times. 我曾多次去那里。⑨赤裸裸的事实, 现实情况; 真相: know the ~ (或 know what the ~ is) 知道真相 ⑩[英俚]占上风的一着(或一句话); 好运气: What a ~! 真走运! ⑪【海】(滑车的)带槽 **II ❶** ***vt.*** ①刻痕于; 划线于, 打记号于: ~ timber 在木材上刻记号 / The

flood has ~d out a deep channel through the valley. 洪水在山谷里冲刷出一条很深的水道。②把…记入帐内; 把…记下(*up*) ③获得(成绩、胜利等); (体育比赛中)得(分), 使(某人)得分: ~ a great victory (success) 取得很大胜利(成功) / ~ a goal 踢进一球 / ~ a point 赢得一分 / ~ a game 胜一盘 ④给…评分; 评价: ~ a test (an examinee) 给测验(应试者)评分 ⑤将…写成总谱; 把…谱成管弦乐曲; 为(影片等)配乐 ⑥[美]严厉批评; 责备 **❷** ***vi.*** ①刻痕; 划线 ②(比赛中)记分: Will you ~? 你来记分好吗? ③得分; 得胜; 成功: Team A ~d *against* (或 *over*) Team B. 甲队胜了乙队。/ That's where he ~s. 那一点就是他占上风(或走运)之处。‖**Death pays all ~s.** [谚]一死百了。/ **go off at (full)** ~ ①(赛跑等时)全速起跑; 精神抖擞地出发 ②兴高采烈地大谈喜爱的话题 ③失去自制 / **have a ~ to settle with sb.** 要跟某人算帐; 要责问某人 / **in** ~ 【音】用总谱, 以总谱方式排列 / **in** ~**s** 很多地, 大批地 / **keep the** ~ (在比赛中)记分 / **make a** ~ **off one's own bat** 独力making / **make a** ~ **off sb.** 驳倒某人, 说得某人没话讲 / **on more** ~**s than one** 为了种种理由 / **on that** ~ 在那点上 ②因此 / **pay (或 pay off, settle, wipe off) old** ~**s** (或 **an old** ~) 报宿怨, 雪旧仇 / **play to the** ~ 随机应变; 见机行事 / **quit** ~**s with sb.** 对某人进行报复; 与某人清帐 / ~ **off sb.** [英俚]驳倒某人; 占某人的便宜 / ~ **out** 划掉, 删去(字句等) / ~ **under** 在(某字句)下划线; 强调 / ~ **up** 把…记入帐内; 把…记下 / **three** ~ **and ten** 人生七十年, 一辈子, 一般人的寿命 ‖**~less** *a.* 没得分的 / ~**r** ['skɔːrə] *n.* ①记分员 ②得分者 ‖'~**board** *n.* (体育比赛中的)记分牌 / '~**book** *n.* (比赛、牌戏等的)记分簿 / '~**card** *n.* (比赛)记分卡; 运动员姓名、体重等登记卡 / '~**keeper** *n.* (比赛的)记分员

scorn [skɔːn] **I** ***n.*** ①轻蔑; 藐视: dismiss a suggestion with ~ 轻蔑地驳回一个建议 / express one's ~ for sb. 对某人表示轻视 ②嘲笑; 嘲弄; 奚落: point the finger of ~ at sb. 奚落某人 ③藐视(或嘲笑)的对象: be a ~ to (或 be the ~ of) 是…的嘲笑对象 **II** ***vt.*** ①轻蔑; 藐视: ~ all difficulties 蔑视一切困难 ②摈斥; 不屑做: ~ to reply (或 ~ replying) to the charge 不屑答复那指控 ‖**hold in** ~ 藐视, 瞧不起 / **laugh sb. to** ~ 嘲弄某人 / **think** (或 **hold**) **it** ~ **to** (do) 不屑(做) / **think** ~ **of** 藐视 ‖~**er** *n.* 藐视者; 嘲笑者

scornful ['skɔːnful] *a.* 轻蔑的; 藐视的: a ~ attitude 藐视的态度 / be ~ *of* the forces of convention 藐视习惯势力 ‖~**ly** *ad.* / ~**ness** *n.*

scorpion ['skɔːpjən] ***n.*** ①蝎子 ②[S-]【天】天蝎座 ③蝎尾鞭(打人凶器); (古代的)弩炮 ④螫针般的刺激 ⑤刻毒的人 ‖~**fish** 【动】锯鲉

scotch [skɔtʃ] **I** ***vt.*** ①[古]切; 抓; 刻痕于; 给…开槽 ②使暂受伤; 使受伤残: ~ a snake 把一条

蛇弄得半死 ③镇压;扑灭;粉碎 ④戳穿(谣言、谬论等) ⑤制止(车轮等)转动;阻止 **II** *n.* ①刻痕;砍痕;划伤 ②(儿童跳格游戏中)划在地上的格线 ③(防止车轮或木材滚动的)木楔,木块;障碍物

scoundrel ['skaundrəl] **I** *n.* 坏蛋,恶棍,流氓 **II** *a.* 恶棍(般)的;卑鄙的 ‖**~ism** *n.* 恶棍性格;恶棍行为 / **~ly** *a.* 有恶棍性格的;恶棍(般)的

scour¹ ['skauə] **I ❶** *vt.* ①擦亮;擦净;洗涤: ~ the tools till they gleam 把工具擦得亮亮的 / ~ out the pot 洗刷锅子内部 / ~ wool 洗涤羊毛 ②冲洗(阴沟、管道等);灌(肠): a pipe ~ 洗管道 ③擦掉;洗掉;冲刷;清除(谷类中的)杂物 (off, away): ~ the rust off 擦去锈迹 / ~ the stains away with soap 用肥皂洗掉污迹 / The flood ~ed away (或 off) mud and sand. 洪水冲走了泥沙。④冲刷成;冲出 (out): The torrents ~ed (out) a channel down the hillside. 急流沿着山腰冲出一条水道。⑤【冶】侵蚀 ❷ *vi.* ①擦;擦亮;洗刷;冲洗: ~ at rusted spots 擦锈斑 ②(牲畜等)腹泻,患痢疾 **II** *n.* ①擦,洗;冲刷;冲刷过的地方(如河床等): give the dirty pot a good ~ 把肮脏的锅子好好洗刷一下 / ~ of the tide 潮水的冲刷 ②[~s]【用作单或复】(畜类等的)腹泻,痢疾 ③除垢剂;洗涤剂 ‖**~er** ['skauərə] *n.* ①擦洗者 ②冲洗阴沟者 ③洗刷器

scour² ['skauə] **❶** *vt.* 急速穿过;走遍(某地)搜索: ~ the forest for sb. 走遍森林搜寻某人 / ~ the library for references 在图书馆寻找参考资料 **❷** *vi.* 急速穿行;追寻: ~ over the hillside for games 在山上追寻猎物

scourge [skə:dʒ] **I** *n.* ①(用作刑具的)鞭 ②惩罚的工具;惩罚 ③苦难的根源;带来灾难的人;灾祸(如瘟疫等): the special ~ of a region 某一地区内的大害(或一霸) **II** *vt.* ①鞭打,鞭笞 ②严斥,痛斥 ③严惩 ④使痛苦;蹂躏 ‖*the white* ~ 一种地方性肺病

scout¹ [skaut] **I** *n.* ①侦察员;侦察机;侦察舰;搜索救援飞机: a ~ platoon 侦察排 / a ~ bomber 侦察轰炸机 ②侦察;搜索: on the ~ 在侦察中 ③守望员 ④(一个)童子军: the Boy (Girl) Scouts 男(女)童子军 ⑤ 四出物色新人材(如演员、运动员等)的人;【体】派去了解对方战术者: a talent ~ 物色人材者 ⑥[英](牛津大学的)校工 ⑦[英](专门协助汽车协会或皇家汽车俱乐部司机的)公路巡逻人员 ⑧【动】海鸟;海鸠;善知鸟 ⑨[俚]人,家伙 **II ❶** *vi.* ①搜集敌方情报,侦察: be out ~ing 外出侦察 ②搜索;寻找: ~ about (或 around) for sth. (或 go about ~ing for sth.) 到处搜寻某物 ③积极参加童子军活动 ❷ *vt.* ①侦察;跟踪;搜索;监视: ~ a village 侦察一个村子的情况 ②观察(运动员、演员等)的表现以对其才能作出估价 ③(经过寻找)发现;觅得 ‖**~ car** ①军用敞篷装甲侦察车 ②警察巡逻车 / '**~-,master** *n.* 童子军领队

scout² [skaut] **❶** *vt.* ①蔑视地拒绝(提议、意见等) ②讥笑;嘲弄 ❷ *vi.* 嘲笑 (at)

scowl [skaul] **I** *n.* ①皱眉,愁眉苦脸 ②怒容 **II ❶** *vi.* 皱眉头,沉着脸,怒视 (at, on) ❷ *vt.* ①瞪眼怒视着使…,瞪眼怒视着把…压下去: ~ sb. into silence 把某人瞪得不敢作声 / ~ down sb.'s gripe 瞪着眼使某人不敢再抱怨 ②以怒容表示(不快等)

scowlingly ['skauliŋli] *ad.* ①皱着眉头,愁眉苦脸地 ②怒视地

scraggy ['skrægi] *a.* ①瘦的,皮包骨的 ②凹凸不平的;参差不齐的 ‖**scraggily** *ad.* / **scragginess** *n.*

scramble ['skræmbl] **I ❶** *vi.* ①爬行,攀爬;(植物)攀缘上架: ~ up a steep hillside 爬上陡峭的山坡 ②不规则地生长,杂乱蔓延 ③(乱槽槽地)争夺,抢夺 (for): ~ for power and wealth 争权夺利 ④勉强拼凑: ~ for a living 勉强凑合着过日子 / manage to ~ along somehow 设法勉强对付过去 ⑤仓促地行动;【空】紧急起飞应战: ~ to one's feet 匆忙站起 / ~ into one's clothes 匆忙穿起衣服 ❷ *vt.* ①攀登 ②使混杂;搅乱: Bad weather ~d the air schedules. 恶劣的天气把飞行班次打乱了。/ ~ the pages of a manuscript 把手稿的页码搞乱 ③杂乱地收集,匆促凑成 (up) ④炒(蛋) ⑤抛出(硬币等)使抢夺 ⑥改变频率使(通话)不被窃听 ⑦【空】命令(截击机组)紧急起飞 **II** *n.* ①爬行,攀登 ②争夺,抢夺 (for) ③混乱;混乱的一团 ④(摩托车的)越野比赛;越野试车 ⑤【空】紧急起飞 ⑥[无]扰频,倒频 ‖**~r** *n.* ①爬行者;攀缘植物 ②[无]扰频器,倒频器,保密器

scrap¹ [skræp] **I** *n.* ①碎片,零屑;[喻]少许,点滴: ~s of bread 面包碎屑 / a few ~s of news 几则新闻 / not a ~ of evidence 没有丝毫证据 / ②(文字等的)片断;(从书报上剪下的)图片,短文: ~s of a letter (conversation) 函件(谈话)的片断 ③废金属;切屑;废料: metal ~ 废旧金属 / rubber ~ 橡胶碎料 / collect ~ 收集废物 ④[复]残羹剩饭 ⑤[复](动物的)油渣: pork ~s 猪油渣 **II** *a.* ①零碎的,片断的;剩余的 ②用过的;废弃的: ~ steel 废钢 **III** (scrapped; scrapping) *vt.* ①敲碎,拆毁,炸碎: ~ a battleship 拆毁(报废的)军舰 ②废弃: ~ outworn methods 废弃陈旧的方法 ‖*a* ~ *of paper* ①碎纸片 ②[讽]等于一张废纸的条约(或诺言) ‖**'~book** *n.* 剪贴簿 / '**~-cake** *n.* (作饲料用的)鱼脂渣饼 / ~ *heap* ①废铜烂铁堆 ②垃圾堆,废物堆: the ~ heap of history 历史的垃圾堆 / a ~ heap policy (对事物)一过时立即抛弃的政策 / throw (或 cast, toss) ... on the ~ heap 把…作为废物丢掉

scrap² [skræp] [俚] **I** *n.* ①打架;吵架: have a ~ with sb. 跟某人打架(或争吵) ②职业拳击赛 **II** (scrapped; scrapping) *vi.* 打架;吵架

scrape [skreip] **I ❶** *vt.* ①刮,擦;刮落,擦去 (off, out, away): ~ one's boots 刮去靴底的泥 / ~ one's chin 剃胡子,刮脸 / ~ one's plate 吃净

盘中食物 / ～ a ship's bottom 刮船底(指刮掉附着的藻类、贝壳等) / ～ scales *off* a fish 刮鱼鳞 / ～ *off* the paint 刮掉油漆 / ～ out a sticky pan 擦净油腻的锅子 / ～ out a word 擦掉一个字 ②擦掉;刮擦(某物)使发出刺耳声: ～ one's knee on the stone 在石头上擦伤膝盖 / The bow ～s the fiddle. 弓在提琴上拉出刺耳的声音。③(尤指用手指或手)挖出;挖成(out): ～ out the ashes from a furnace 扒出炉灰 / ～ (out) a hole 挖成一个洞 ④(艰难地)凑集,积蓄,积攒(up, together); ～ *together* a little sum 好不容易积几个钱 / ～ a living 勉强糊口 **②** *vi.* ①刮,擦;擦过;勉强通过: branches *scraping* against the window 擦着窗子的树枝 / ～ along the wall 擦墙而过 / ～ through a narrow opening 钻过狭洞 / just ～ through an examination 考试勉强及格 ②刮(或擦)出刺耳声 ③(鞠躬时)一脚擦地后退 ④勉强过日子:(艰难地)积攒钱财 **II** *n.* ①刮;擦;挖: rocks worn by the ～ of glaciers 为冰川所擦损的岩石 ②擦伤;擦痕: a ～ on the knee 膝盖擦伤处 ③刮擦声: the ～ of sb.'s pen on paper 某人的笔尖在纸上发出的沙沙声 / the ～ of footsteps on the stairs 上楼时嚓嚓的脚步声 ④(自己招致的)困境,窘境: get into a ～ (或 into ～s) 陷入困境 / get sb. out of (his) ～s 使某人摆脱窘境 ⑤[美俚]剃胡子,刮脸 ‖a ～ *of the pen* ①签字 ②便条 / *bow and* ～ 打躬作揖,过分恭敬 / *pinch and* ～ / *a leg* (深深欠身)鞠躬, 打躬作揖 / ～ *along* 勉强糊口 / ～ *and screw* 省吃俭用 / ～ *down* (用脚擦地板的噪声)阻止(演讲者)说下去 / ～ (*up*) *an acquaintance with sb.* 硬要同某人交朋友 ‖~-,penny n. 吝啬鬼,守财奴

scraper ['skreipə] *n.* ①刮(或擦)的人 ②刮板;削器器,刮除机;刮土机,铲运机 ③吝啬鬼,守财奴

scratch [skrætʃ] **I ❶** *vt.* ①搔;抓;抓破,抓伤: ～ an itch (a mosquito bite) 搔痒(蚊子咬处) / hands much ～ed with thorns 被荆棘划破的手 ②(用爪子等)扒出,挖出: ～ (out) a hole 挖出一个洞 / ～ up a few stray seeds 扒出几颗散落的种子 ③擦;刮: ～ a match 擦火柴 / ～ the paint off the wall 刮掉墙上油漆 ④(潦草地)涂写;乱画: ～ a few lines to a friend 给朋友草草写封短信 ⑤勾划掉(out);把(马等)撤出比赛;勾去(候选人)的名字以示不赞成;在(政党候选人名单)上勾去一些名字以示抵制: ～ out (或 off) a name from a list 从名单上划去一个名字 ⑥(辛苦地)凑集(金钱等)(up, together) **❷** *vi.* ①搔痒;扒;扒寻: ～ where it itches 搔痒 ②作刮擦声: This pen ～es. 这支钢笔写起来沙沙地钩纸。③退出比赛;未能践约 ④勉强糊口,艰难地谋生(along): ～ for oneself at an early age 从很小的时候起就开始自己挣饭吃 ⑤在政党候选人名单上勾掉一些名字 **II** *n.* ①搔;抓;抓痕;擦伤;

【建】刮痕: It's only a ～. 这不过是一点儿擦伤罢了。/ escape without a ～ 安然无恙地逃脱 ②刮擦声 ③乱涂;乱画 ④[只用单,不用冠词]起跑线;(拳击赛中的)角斗起始线 ⑤零 ⑥(台球游戏中)引起罚分的一击;未中的一击;侥幸的击中 ⑦退出比赛的马;[美俚]无名小卒,无足轻重的人 ⑧[美俚]钱,现钞; 借款: raise fresh ～ 再筹款子 / make a ～ 借钱 ⑨[复]马脚葡萄疮 **III** *a.* ①碰巧的,偶然的: a ～ shot 碰巧中的一击 ②凑合的,匆匆组成的: a ～ dinner 临时准备的一顿便饭 / We'll have to play a ～ team today. 今天我们只得临时凑几个人上场比赛了。③打草稿用的 ④(在体育比赛中)无让分优待的,大家从零开始的 ‖a ～ *of the pen* 签名; 简单手令 / *no great* ～ [俚]没有什么了不起;不重要 / *Old Scratch* 魔鬼 / ～ *about for* 到处扒寻;四出搜寻 / *Scratch a Russian, and you('ll) find a Tartar.* [谚]文明不能改变本性。/ *Scratch me and I'll* ～ *you* (或 *yours*). [谚]你捧我,我就捧你。/ ～ *one's head* 搔头皮;(对某事)迷惑不解(over) / ～ *the surface (of)* 见 **surface** / *start from* (或 *at, on*) ①从起跑线开始;从零开始 ②从头做起;白手起家 / *toe the* ～ ①(赛跑时)用脚尖踏在起步线上;严守规则 ②承担责任(或后果) / *up to* ～ ①踏上起跑线,准备起跑(或竞赛) ②[口]准备好迎接困难;准备好动手干干: bring oneself *up to* ～ before an examination 准备好迎接考试 / He'll come *up to* ～ by that time. 到那时候他便可以准备好了。③[口]达到标准,合乎规格 ‖~**back** *n.* 搔背用的扒子(俗称"不求人") / '~**cat** *n.* 凶狠的女人(或小孩) / ～ **coat**【建】打底子的水泥层;(灰涂)打底 / ～ **line** 起跑线;起跳线;(标枪等的)起掷线 / ～ **pad** 便笺簿 / ～ **paper** 便条纸 / ～ **race** 无让分优待的赛跑

scrawl [skrɔ:l] **I ❶** *vt.* 潦草地写(或画): ～ a few lines 潦草地写几行 **❷** *vi.* 乱写,乱涂: ～ all over the wall 在墙上到处乱涂 **II** *n.* 潦草模糊的笔迹;潦草涂成的字句(或书信、图画等): His signature was an illegible ～. 他的签名象鬼画符。

scream [skri:m] **I ❶** *vi.* ①尖叫;放声大笑: ～ for help 尖叫救命 / ～ with laughter 放声大笑 ②(机器、汽笛等)发出尖锐刺耳的声音;(风)呼啸: The wind ～ed through the trees. 风呼啸着穿过林子。/ A jet ～ed past overhead. 一架喷气式飞机发着啸声从头顶掠过。③令人震惊: A bold black headline ～ed out from the front page. 在(报纸的)头版上出现了一条令人触目惊心的粗黑体大字标题。④(歇斯底里地)强烈要求(for);大叫大嚷着抗议(about) **❷** *vt.* ①尖叫着说;尖叫着发出: A newsboy was ～ing an extra. 一个报童正在尖声叫卖号外。/ ～ out one's laughter 放声大笑 ②[～ oneself]尖叫得使…: ～ oneself hoarse 尖叫得把嗓子叫哑了 ③大叫大嚷着要;大叫大嚷着宣传: ～ to do sth. 大叫

大嚷着要做某事 / ~ the news all over the city 大叫大嚷着把消息传遍全城 **II** *n.* ①尖叫；尖锐刺耳的声音 ②[口]引人捧腹大笑的人(或事物)： He is a perfect ~. 他这人真滑稽极了。

screech [skri:tʃ] **I** *n.* ①(表示惊恐、痛苦、愤怒等的)尖叫；尖锐刺耳的声音：the ~ of car brakes 尖锐刺耳的汽车刹车声 ②[俚]经常抱怨找岔子的女人；泼妇 **II** ❶ *vi.* 发出尖锐刺耳叫声 ❷ *vt.* 用尖叫声发出(或表示) ‖~y *a.* 尖叫的 ‖~ owl [动]叫声很尖的枭；仓鸮

screed [skri:d] *n.* ①冗长的文章(或书信、讲话) ②[苏格兰]裂缝 ③[建]样板，(混凝土修正机的)整平板

screen [skri:n] **I** *n.* ①屏；幕；帘；帐；隔板；(教堂的)祭坛屏饰：a folding-~ 折迭屏风 ②(金属、塑料等材料制的)纱窗，纱门 ③掩蔽物；警戒幕；屏护部队：a ~ of trees 一排树篱 / a smoke ~ 烟幕 / a cavalry ~ 骑兵屏护部队 ④掩护；包庇：under ~ of night 在夜幕的掩护下 / put on a ~ of indifference 装作无所谓的样子 ⑤(电影、幻灯的)银幕；(电视的)屏幕；[the ~]电影；电影业：a wide ~ film 宽银幕电影 / a ~ actor (actress) 电影演员(女演员) / a star 电影明星 / make a ~ version of the novel 将那部小说改编成电影剧本 ⑥[电]屏蔽；荧光屏；帘栅极：electric ~ 电屏蔽 / radar ~ 雷达屏 ⑦(有网罩或玻璃盖的)布告板 ⑧(粗眼)筛子，圆眼筛；滤网，过滤器：a coal ~ 煤筛 / a dust ~ 防尘网 / an oil ~ 滤油网 ⑨[印]网屏,网版(照相版将银粒的浓淡色调变变为网目的工具) **II** ❶ *vt.* ①掩蔽；遮护；包庇：~ one's face *from* the fire with a mask 用面具护脸以防火灼 / ~ sb.'s faults 掩盖某人的过失 / ~ sb. *from* blame 包庇某人 ②放映(电影、幻灯片)；(用电影拍摄机)拍摄 ③把(故事、戏剧等)搬上银幕；使在影片中演出：He was ~ed in the male leads of several pictures. 他在几部影片中演男主角。④给…装帘(或纱窗等)：~ a house against mosquitoes and flies 给房子装纱窗纱门以防蚊蝇 ⑤筛(煤等)；筛分(out)；甄别；审查：a ~ing committee 甄别委员会 / ~ visa applications 审查护照签证申请书 ⑥[电]屏蔽 ❷ *vi.* 拍电影；出现在银幕上：That play (actor) ~s well (badly). 那个剧本(演员)适(不适)于拍电影。‖~land *n.* 电影界 / '~play *n.* 电影剧本 / ~ test 试镜头(测验一个人是否适合当电影演员的片断镜头) / '~,writer *n.* 电影剧本作者

screw [skru:] **I** *n.* ①螺旋；螺杆，螺丝；螺(丝)钉；螺旋状物：a ~ bolt (nut) 螺丝钉(母) / drive in a ~ 把螺钉拧进去 ②螺孔 ③螺旋桨 ④(螺旋的)一拧；(螺旋式的)旋转；[英](弹子戏等中的)转球：Give it another ~! 再拧一下子! ⑤[英]一小纸卷(或纸包)：a ~ of tea (tobacco) 一小包茶叶(烟草) ⑥[英俚]工资，薪水 ⑦[主英]吝啬鬼；守财奴；心狠手辣的卖(或买)主 ⑧(监狱)看守人；拇指夹(旧时的刑具) ⑨[英]驽马 **II** ❶ *vt.*

①(用螺旋)操纵，调节；(用螺丝)拧紧；(用螺钉)钉住：~ the two pieces together 用螺钉把两部分拧在一起 ②旋；拧：~ a lid on (off) a jar 把瓶盖拧上(拧开) ③加螺纹于 ④(用拇指夹)夹(人) ⑤扭歪；皱起；眯紧：~ one's head round 扭过头去(看) / ~ one's face *into* wrinkles 皱起面孔 / ~ up one's eyes 眯紧眼睛 ⑥加强；振作；鼓舞(up)：~ oneself *up* to doing sth. 使自己振作起来干某事 ⑦强迫；压榨；榨取；勒索：~ consent *out of* sb. 迫使某人同意⑧[美俚]奸污 ❷ *vi.* ①(螺丝等)转动；作螺旋形转动：~ smoothly 旋转灵活 / ~ to the right 向右旋转 ②旋,拧(*off, on, together*)：The lid ~s on (off). 盖子可拧上(可拧开)。③(球)旋ành运动；(人)摇晃,扭动 ④进行压榨(或勒索) ⑤拼命节省；用钱吝啬 ⑥急忙地离开 ‖*apply the ~ to sb.* (或 *give sb. another turn of the ~*) =put the ~ on (或 to) sb. / *(have) a ~ loose* [俚](发生)故障，(出)毛病；(有点)古怪(或乖僻)；精神不太正常，(有点)疯疯癫癫：There is *a ~ loose* somewhere. 什么地方出毛病了。/ *have one's head ~ed on the right way* 见 head / *pinch and ~* 省吃俭用 / *put the ~ on* (或 *to*) *sb.* 对某人施加压力(向他勒索或威胁) / ~ *down* ①拧紧；钉住 ②使减低价格(或租金) / ~ *up* ①拧紧(琴弦等)；[喻]加强，鼓起(勇气)：~ *up* one's courage 鼓起勇气 / ~ *up* discipline 加强纪律 ②[俚]搞糟，破坏：Somebody has ~ed things *up*. 不知什么人把事情弄糟了。/ *tighten the ~s* 拧紧螺丝；加强控制 / *turn (the) ~s at sb. (sth.)* 对某人(某事)施加压力(或加强控制) ‖~ed *a.* ①有螺纹的 ②扭曲的，弯弯曲曲的 ③[英俚]酒醉的 / ~*ball* *n.* ①(棒球)投手拋出的怪球 ②[俚]怪僻的人，疯疯癫癫的人 *a.* 怪僻的；疯疯癫癫的 / ~ *cap* (瓶、罐等)螺旋盖；螺旋帽 / ~ *coupling* 螺旋联接器 / '~,driver *n.* 旋凿，(螺丝)起子 / ~ *eye* 环首木螺钉；螺丝眼 / ~ *gear* 螺旋轮；螺旋蜗轮装置 / ~ *hook* 有钩螺钉 / ~ *jack* 螺旋起重器，螺旋千斤顶 / ~ *pile* 螺旋桩 / ~ *pine* 露兜树属的一种植物 / '~-pitch ga(u)ge 螺距规 / ~ *plate* 螺丝钢板 / ~ *press* 螺旋压机 / ~ *propeller* 螺旋桨 / ~ *tap* (制螺母用的)螺丝攻；丝锥 / ~ *thread* 螺纹 / '~-'topped *a.* (瓶等)有螺旋盖的；口上有螺纹的 / ~ *wrench* 螺旋扳手

scribble[1] ['skribl] **I** *vt. & vi.* 潦草书写；乱涂；草率写作 **II** *n.* ①潦草的笔迹；乱涂 ②拙劣作品 ‖~r *n.* ①笔迹潦草的人 ②拙劣的作家，粗制滥造的作者 ‖**scribbling-block** *n.* 拍纸簿

scribble[2] ['skribl] *vt.* 【纺】粗梳(羊毛等) ‖~r *n.* 粗梳机，预梳机(=scribbling machine)

scribe [skraib] **I** *n.* ①(古时)犹太法律学家 ②抄写员(尤指印刷术发明前以抄写书籍为职业的人) ③文牍，书记 ④作家；新闻记者 ⑤【建】划线器 **II** ❶ *vi.* 担任抄写员(或书记、文牍等)；缮写 ❷ *vt.* 用划线器在(木、砖等)上划线；用划线器划(线) ②(木工)雕合 ‖~r *n.* 划线器；划片器

scrimmage ['skrimidʒ] **I** ***n.*** ① 小战斗，散兵战 ② 扭打；混战 ③ =scrummage (*n.*) **II** ❶ ***vt.*** 并列争(球)；把(球)放在并列争夺的位置 ❷ ***vi.*** 参加混战 ‖**~r** ***n.*** 参加混战者；(橄榄球赛的)前锋

script [skript] **I** ***n.*** ①手迹；笔迹；手写体 ②手稿；打字原稿；正本 ③(戏剧、电影)剧本(尤指原稿)；广播(原)稿 ④【印】书写体铅字 ⑤[英]考生的笔试卷 **II** ***vt.*** 把…改编为演出本(或广播节目)：~ a novel into a movie 把一部小说改编为电影剧本 ‖**~ed** ***a.*** 照原稿宣读(或广播)的：a ~*ed* discussion 照讲稿宣读的讨论 ‖'**~ˌwriter** ***n.*** 电影剧本作者；广播节目撰稿者

scriptural ['skriptʃərəl] ***a.*** [常作 S-] 基督教《圣经》的；根据基督教《圣经》的 ‖**~ly** ***ad.***

scripture ['skriptʃə] ***n.*** ① 手稿；文件；权威性的著作 ②[常作 S-]基督教《圣经》(也作 Holy Scripture 或 the Scriptures)：a doctrine not found in *Scripture* 不见于基督教《圣经》的教义 / a ~ lesson 基督教《圣经》课 ③[常作 S-]基督教《圣经》中的文句 ④(基督教以外其他宗教的)经文，圣典：the Buddhist ~ 佛经

scroll [skroul] **I** ***n.*** ①羊皮纸卷轴，纸卷；写成卷轴的古书 ②名册；刻有铭辞的纹章饰带；[古]函件 ③(加在签名后面的)花押；涡卷形字体 ④卷形物；【建】(石刻上的)漩涡饰；【机】涡形管；【音】(提琴的)涡卷形头；【数】涡卷 **II** ❶ ***vt.*** ①使成卷形；用漩涡形装饰 ②在卷轴上题(字) ❷ ***vi.*** 成卷形；成漩涡形 ‖***on the ~ of fame*** 名垂史册 ‖**~ed** ***a.*** 漩涡形装饰的 ‖'**~head** ***n.*** 船头涡形装饰 / **~ saw** 钢丝锯；云形截锯 / **~ wheel**【机】涡形齿轮 / '**~work** ***n.*** 涡形装饰；钢丝锯锯成的装饰

scrub[1] [skrʌb] **I** (scrubbed; scrubbing) ❶ ***vt.*** ① 擦洗；擦净：~ the floor 擦洗地板 / ~ oneself with a towel 用毛巾使劲擦身 ②擦掉；摩擦：~ dirt from the wall 把墙上的尘土刷掉 / ~ one's eyes 擦眼睛 ③(施行外科手术前)洗(手、臂)并消毒 ④【化】使(气体)净化；(从气体中)分离出，提出(*out*)：a *scrubbing* tower 涤气塔 ⑤[俚]取消；剔除：~ *out* an order 取消命令 ❷ ***vi.*** ①擦洗干净 ②(施行外科手术前)进行手臂消毒 **II** ***n.*** ①擦洗，擦净：The floor needs a good ~. 这地板需要好好地擦洗一下。②擦洗者；做苦工者 ‖**scrubber** ***n.*** ①擦洗者 ②刷子；【化】涤气器；洗涤器 ‖**~ brush** 硬毛刷子，洗衣刷，板刷 / '**~-up** ***n.*** 彻底擦洗(尤指手术前的) / '**~ˌwoman** ***n.*** 女清洁工；临时女帮工

scrub[2] [skrʌb] **I** ***n.*** ①矮树；灌木；灌丛；丛林地 ②矮小的人；地位低微的人 ③矮小动物；杂种家畜；杂种狗 ④[口]非校一级的球队(或非正规球队)的运动员，二流运动员；[复]二流球队；队员不足的棒球比赛 ⑤用秃了的毛刷；用旧了的扫帚 ⑥短髭 **II** ***a.*** ①低劣的；次等的 ②矮小的；瘦小的 ③非校一级的球队的；非正规球队的 ④即兴的；临时凑合的：a ~ game 临时凑合的比赛 ‖**scrubber** ***n.*** ①住在丛林地的人 ②[澳]杂种牲口 ‖'**~-team** ***n.*** [口]非正规球队，二流球队

scruff [skrʌf] ***n.*** 颈背：take (或 seize) sb. by the ~ of the neck 抓住某人的颈背

scruffy ['skrʌfi] ***a.*** 褴褛的；邋遢的；可鄙的；无价值的

scruple[1] ['skru:pl] **I** ***n.*** (由于道德上的原因而感到的)迟疑不安，踌躇，顾虑，顾忌：a man of no ~*s* 无所顾忌的人，不择手段的人 / have (no) ~*s about* doing sth. 对做某事有(没有)顾忌 / make no ~ to do (或 *about* doing, *of* doing) sth. 做某事没有顾忌 / without ~ 毫无顾忌地 **II** ❶ ***vi.*** 感到迟疑不安，有顾虑：~ at nothing 肆无忌惮 / not ~ to say 毫无顾虑地说 ❷ ***vt.*** [古]对…感到迟疑不安，对…有顾虑

scruple[2] ['skru:pl] ***n.*** ①吩(英美药衡单位；=1.295 克) ②微量

scrupulous ['skru:pjuləs] ***a.*** ①多顾虑的；审慎的 ②严格认真的；拘泥细节的：with ~ precision 以一丝不苟的精确性 ‖**~ly** ***ad.*** / **~ness** ***n.***

scrutinize ['skru:tinaiz] ***vt.*** & ***vi.*** 细看，细阅；仔细检查

scrutiny ['skru:tini] ***n.*** ①细看；细阅：make a ~ of the day's newspaper 仔细地阅读当天的报纸 ②详尽的研究；仔细检查；调查：make a ~ *into* sth. 对某事进行详尽的研究 / His actions do not bear ~. 他的行为经不起检查。③监视 ④选票的复查：demand a ~ 要求复查选票

scuffle ['skʌfl] **I** ***vi.*** ①扭打；混战 ②拖着脚走 ③敷衍了事 **II** ***n.*** ①扭打；混战 ②拖脚行走；拖脚行走的脚步声

scull [skʌl] **I** ***n.*** ①(双桨小艇的)短桨；橹 ②(比赛用)小划艇 **II** ❶ ***vt.*** 用桨划(船)；用橹摇(船) ❷ ***vi.*** 划船 ‖**~er** ***n.*** ①划桨者；摇橹者 ②单人双桨小划艇

scul(l)duggery [skʌl'dʌgəri] ***n.*** = skul(l)duggery

scullery ['skʌləri] ***n.*** 碗碟、蔬菜等的洗涤处；碗碟贮藏室 ‖'**~-maid** ***n.*** 帮助厨子做洗碗碟等事的女仆

sculptor ['skʌlptə] ***n.*** 雕刻家；雕塑家 ‖**sculptress** ['skʌlptris] ***n.*** 女雕刻家；女雕塑家

sculptural ['skʌlptʃərəl] ***a.*** 雕刻的；雕塑的；有雕刻(或雕塑)风味的：the ~ arts 雕塑艺术 ‖**~ly** ***ad.***

sculpture ['skʌlptʃə] **I** ***n.*** ①雕刻(术)；雕塑(术)：be skilled in ~ 精于雕刻(或雕塑) ②雕刻品；雕塑品：clay ~*s* 泥塑 / an ivory ~ 牙雕工艺品 ③【地】刻蚀：~ of earth surface 地形面刻蚀 ④【动】刻纹 **II** ❶ ***vt.*** ①雕刻；雕塑；塑造：~ a statue out of ivory 雕刻象牙雕像 ②以雕刻装饰 ③【地】刻蚀：The river has ~*d* the rock. 河水刻蚀了岩石。❷ ***vi.*** 当雕刻(或雕塑)师；从事雕刻(或雕塑)行业

scum [skʌm] **I** ***n.*** ①(煮沸或发酵时发生的)泡沫；浮渣，浮垢 ②渣滓，糟粕；社会最低层；下贱的人，卑贱者 ③[学俚]服侍高年级学生的低年级学生 **II** (scummed; scumming) ❶ ***vt.*** 去除(浮垢)，撇去 ❷ ***vi.*** 形成泡沫；盖满渣垢

scupper[1] ['skʌpə] *n.* ①【船】排水孔 ②［美俚］妓女

scupper[2] ['skʌpə] *vt.* ［英俚］① 伏击; 出其不意地杀死 ②使(船、全体船员)沉没; 使处于危难中

scurf [skə:f] *n.* ① 皮(肤)屑; 头皮屑 ② 鳞片状的附着物; 附着物的残垢 ③【植】粗皮病; 糠秕 ‖~**y** *a.* ①皮屑似的; 长满皮屑的; 产生皮屑的 ②【植】糠秕状的: 有糠秕的

scurrilous ['skʌriləs] *a.* 庸俗下流的; 满口下流话的; 含有粗鲁辱骂的: make ~ attacks upon sb. 对某人漫骂攻击 ‖~**ly** *ad.* ‖~**ness** *n.*

scurry ['skʌri] I *vi.* ①急匆匆地跑; 急赶: ~ *away* (或 *off*) 匆忙跑开 / ~ *through* one's work 匆促地赶完工作 ②乱转, 急转: ~*ing* snow whirls 回旋飞舞的雪片 II *n.* ① 急促的奔跑; 急促奔跑声 ②奔忙, 急赶; 急转 ③短距离赛跑(或赛马)

scurvy[1] ['skə:vi] *a.* ①卑鄙的, 下流的 ②长满皮屑的 ‖**scurvily** *ad.* / **scurviness** *n.*

scurvy[2] ['skə:vi] *n.*【医】坏血病 ‖**scurvied** *a.* 患坏血病的 ‖~ **grass**【植】辣根草, 坏血病草

scuttle[1] ['skʌtl] *n.* ①煤斗, 煤桶 ②篮, 筐

scuttle[2] ['skʌtl] I *vi.* ①急促奔跑; 急赶 (*away, off*) ② 匆忙撤退(或放弃、摆脱): ~ out of one's responsibilities 逃避责任 II *n.* ①急速的逃走(或离去); 匆忙的撤退(或放弃); 懦怯的逃避: a policy of ~ 逃避政策 ②(短距离的)快跑

scuttle[3] ['skʌtl] I *n.* ①【建】天窗; 气窗 ②【船】小舱口; 船底(或船侧)的孔洞; 舷窗, 舱口盖 II *vt.* ①(在船底等处凿孔)使(船)沉没, 凿沉 ②完全毁坏 ③全部放弃 ‖~**butt** *n.* ①【船】淡水桶; 饮水柜台 ②［美俚］谣言, 闲话

scythe [saið] I *n.* 长柄大镰刀 II *vt.* 用长柄大镰刀割

sea [si:] *n.* ① 海, 海洋: territorial ~ rights 领海权 / swim in the ~ 在海中游泳 / an arm of the ~ 海湾 / the command of the ~ 制海权 / the freedom of the ~s 海上自由贸易权 / the mistress of the ~(s) 海上霸王 / The ~ covers almost three-fourths of the earth's surface. 海洋几乎占地球表面的四分之三。② ［用于专有名词中］海; 内海, 大(淡水)湖: the China *Sea* 中国海 / the Yellow *Sea* 黄海 / the Mediterranean *Sea* 地中海 / the Baltic *Sea* 波罗的海 / the Caribbean *Sea* 加勒比海 / the Caspian *Sea* 里海等 ③［一般与不定冠词连用, 或用复数］海面动态; 海浪, 波涛: a calm (rough 或 heavy) ~ 平静(波涛汹涌)的海面 / a long (short) ~ 长波阔浪(急浪翻腾)的海面 / The ~s were mountains high. 海上巨浪如山。④ 大量; 浩瀚, 茫茫一片 (*of*): a ~ *of* troubles 无穷的麻烦 / a ~ *of* flame 一片火海 / ~s *of* blood 血海, 大流血 ⑤ 航海生活, 海员生活: retire from the ~ (年老退休)不再过航海生活 ‖*at* ~ ① 在茫茫大海上: a voyage *at* ~ 海上航行 / be buried *at* ~ 葬海海中 ② 茫然, 迷惑, 不

知所措: be all *at* ~ as to what to do next 全然不知下一步怎么做才好 / *between the devil and the deep* ~ 见 **devil** / *beyond* (或 *across, over*) *the* ~(s) 在海外; 往海外: For many years he had lived *beyond the* ~(s). 他曾在海外住了多年。/ *by* ~ 由海路, 乘船: travel *by* ~ and land 经海陆两路旅行 / *by the* ~ 在海边, 在海岸上 / *follow the* ~ 做海员, 当水手 / *go* (*down*) *to the* ~ 到海滨去(过假期) / *go to* ~ ① 去当水手: When he was a boy, his greatest wish was to *go to* ~. 他小时候最大的愿望就是去当水手。② 出航 / *half* ~s *over* 酒喝得太多, 酒醉 / *on the* ~ ① 在海上; 在船上 ② 在海边, 在海岸上 / *put* (*out*) *to* ~ 离港出海, 出航 / *ship a* ~ (船等)被海浪打进来: The boat *shipped a* ~. 那条船灌进了海水。/ *sweep the* ~s ①(船等)在海上到处航行 ②横扫海上一切敌人 / *the four* ~s ［英］围绕英国的四海 / *the high* ~s 公海 / *There's as good fish in the* ~ *as ever came out of it.* 见 **fish**[1] / *the seven* ~s 世界七大海洋; 全球: He has travelled *the seven* ~s. 他航行过全球。/ *when the* ~ *gives up its dead*【宗】在耶稣复活的时候 ‖~**most** *a.* ① 向海的, 临海的 ② 从海上来的 *ad.* = ~**wards** *n.* 朝海的方向; 临海地点 / ~**wards** *ad.* 向海, 临海 ‖~ **air** 海边的空气 / '~-**air** *a.* 海空的: a ~-*air* naval operation 海空联合作战 / ~ **anchor** 浮锚, 海锚 / ~ **anemone**【动】海葵 / '~**bag** *n.* 水手放杂物的圆筒形帆布袋 / '~**bathing** 海水浴 / ~ **beach** 海滨, 海滩 / ~**bed** *n.* 海底 / '~**bird** 海鸟 / ~ **biscuit** (船员吃的)硬饼干, 硬面包 / '~**board** *n.* 海岸线; 海滨; 沿海地区 *a.* 海滨的, 沿海的 / '~**boot** *n.* (水手、渔民穿的)高统靴 / '~-**born** *a.* ①生于海中的, 在海中的: a ~-*born* nymph 海中女妖 ②源自海中的, 从海里生长出来的: a ~-*born* isle 从海中长出来的小岛 / '~**borne** *a.* 海运的, 由海轮装运的: ~*borne* trade (与外国的)海运贸易 ② 漂浮在海上的; 来自海上的: a ~*borne* invasion 来自海上的入侵 / ~ **bread** = ~ biscuit / ~ **breeze** (白天吹向内陆的)海风 / ~ **brief** = ~ letter / ~ **cabin** (驾驶台上的)应急舱 / ~ **captain** (商船)船长 / ~ **change** 海上生活而发生的变化 ②显著的改变 / ~ **chest** ① 水手用的贮物箱 ②【船】通海吸水箱 / '~**coast** *n.* 海岸, 海滨 / ~ **cock** ①(船壳上的)海底阀, 通海旋塞 ②【动】黑腹鹩 / ~ **cow**【动】①海牛 ②海象 ③河马 / '~**craft** *n.* ① 海轮 ② 航海术 / ~ **cucumber**【动】海参 ① 海豹 ③ 有经验的水手(尤指英国伊丽莎白一世时代的船长) ④ 海盗 / '~**drome** *n.* 海面机场 / ~ **dust** ① 从干旱陆地吹向海上的红尘(常引起海上血雨) ②［俚］盐 / ~ **duty** ① 出海勤务 ②(美海军的)海外勤务 / ~ **eagle**【动】①鹗 ②一种捕食鱼类的鹰 / '~-**ear** *n.*【动】石决

明(旧误称鲍鱼,现仍沿用) / ~ **fan**【动】石帆,海团扇,柳珊瑚 / '~ˌ**farer** *n.* 海员,水手;航海者/ '~ˌ**faring** *a.* 以航海为业的;在航海中发生的;关于航海的 *n.* 航海业;海员的职业;海上航行 / ~ **feather**【动】海鳃 / ~ **fight** 海战 / ~ **fire** 海洋中的生物性发光 / '~-**foam** *n.* ①海面泡沫 ②【矿】海泡石 / '~**folk** *n.* [总称]海员,水手;航海者 / '~**food** *n.* 海味 / '~**front** *n.* 滨海区;城镇的面海区域(指海滨马路、房屋等) / ~ **frontier** [美]海疆防御指挥部(负责滨海地区及沿海海面的防御任务) / ~ **gate** 通往海洋的门户(常指通海的运河) / '~**girt** *a.* 四面环海的 / '~ˌ**going** *a.* ①适于远洋航行的 ②[美俚]式样奇特的;特大的;神气十足的 / '~ˌ**going bellhop** [美俚] 海军陆战队队员 / ~ **green** 海绿色 / '~-'**green** *a.* 海绿色的 / ~ **gull** ①【动】海鸥 ②[美俚]跟着丈夫出航的女人 ③[美俚]舰载飞机 ④[美俚]贪吃的人 / ~ **horse** ①【动】海象;海马,龙落子;马头鱼 ②(神话中的)半马半鱼的怪兽 ③白色的浪峰 / ~ **jeep** 水陆两用吉普车 / '~ˌ**keeping** *a.* 经得起海上风浪的 / ~ **king** 北欧国家的海盗头子 / ~ **lace** [常用复]【植】绳藻 / '~-**lane** *n.* 航路,海上交通线 / ~ **language** 水手的语言 / ~ **lawyer** ①[口]好争辩的水手;会油嘴滑舌地推卸责任的人 ②鲨鱼 / ~ **legs** 在颠簸的海船甲板上走动的能力;不晕船 / ~ **letter** (战时对中立国船只离港时发给的)海上通行证 / ~ **level** 海平面;(高低潮间的)平均海面: 2,000 metres above ~ *level* 海拔二千米 / '~**lift** *a.* 海上输送的,海上补给的: troops provided with a rapid ~*lift* and airlift capacity 具有快速海运和空运条件的部队 / ~ **line** ① 海岸线;海平线 ② 深海渔业用钓绳 / ~ **lion**【动】海狮;海驴 / **Sea Lord** [英]海军部四个海军首长之一 / '~-**maid(en)** *n.* 美人鱼;海中女神 / '~**mark** *n.* ①航海标志(如灯塔等) ②潮汛线 / ~ **mile** 海里,浬 / ~ **monster** ① 海怪 ② 任何巨大(或奇异可怕)的海中动物 / '~**mount** *n.* 海底山 / ~ **mouse**【动】海毛虫 / ~ **mule** 方形小机动船 / ~ **pass** =~ letter / ~ **pen**【动】海鳃 / '~**piece** *n.* 海景画 / '~**plane** *n.* 水上飞机 / '~**port** *n.* 海港;港市 / ~ **power** ① 海军强国 ② 海上力量 / '~**quake** *n.* 海底地震,海啸 / ~ **return** (雷达)海面反射讯号 / ~ **room** ①(船只)可实施机动(或通航)的宽广海面 ②自由活动的余地 / ~ **route** 航线,海路 / ~ **rover** 海盗;海盗船 / '~-**run** *a.* (海鱼)为产卵而游入江河的 / '~**scape** *n.* 海景(画) / ~ **scout** 受航海训练的童子军 / ~ **service** 海上勤务 / '~'**shore** *n.* 海岸,海滨,海边 / '~**sick** *a.* 晕船的 / '~ˌ**sickness** *n.* 晕船 / '~'**side** *a.* 海边的,海滨的: a ~*side* resort 海滨浴场;海滨避暑地 *n.* 海滨(胜地);滨海城镇: go to the ~*side* for one's holidays 去海滨度假 / '~ˌ**sider** *n.* 住在海滨的人;到海滨去避暑的人 / ~ **slug** 海参 / ~ **snake**【动】蛇婆,海蛇 / ~ **steps** 船侧登舷梯 / ~ **stock,** ~ **stores** [总称]船上食粮,海上供应品 / '~**strand** *n.* =~-shore / ~ **tangle**【植】昆布属海草;墨角藻 / ~ **train** ① 火车车厢运输船 ② 海上运输队 / ~ **urchin**【动】海胆 / '~'**wall** *n.* 海堤,防波堤 / '~**ware** *n.* [总称]作肥料用的海生植物 / '~**way** *n.* ① 海上航路,可航海区 ② 波涛汹涌的海面 ③ 船只在海上的航进 ④(可行驶远洋大船的)内河深水航道 / '~**weed** *n.* 海草,海藻 / '~**wise** *a.* 受过航海锻炼的 / ~ **wolf** ①【动】狼鳚 ②任何贪食的大海鱼 ③海盗 ④潜艇 / '~-**worn** *a.* 被海水冲刷侵蚀的;在海上航行中被磨损的 / '~ˌ**worthiness** *n.* (船的)适航性 / '~ˌ**worthy** *a.* (船)适于航海的,经得起风浪的: a ~*worthy* ship 适于航海的船

seal[1] [si:l] **I** ([复] seal(s)) *n.* ①【动】海豹 ② 海豹(毛)皮;人造海豹皮;海豹皮制品 ③带灰黄的深褐色 ④[美俚][贬]黑人妇女;黑人 **II** *vi.* 捕海豹 ‖~**er** *n.* 捕海豹的人(或船) / ~**ing** *n.* 捕海豹 ‖~ **fishery** ① 捕海豹业 ② 捕海豹场,海豹群集地 / '~**skin** *n.* ①海豹皮 ②海豹皮制的服装

seal[2] [si:l] **I** *n.* ①封蜡;封铅;火漆;封印,封条: a leaden ~ 铅封 / put a ~ *on* a box 在箱上贴封条 / break (或 take off) the ~ 启封,拆封 ②【机】密封垫;焊接;【物】绝缘 ③印记;图章;玺: engrave a ~ 刻图章 / affix one's ~ *to* an official letter 在公函上盖章 / a document *under* sb.'s hand and ~ 由某人亲自签名盖章的文件 / the *Seal* of State 国玺 / the Great *Seal* (英国)国玺 / Lord Privy *Seal* (英国)掌玺大臣 / the Fisher's *Seal* (刻有圣彼得渔猎图的)罗马教皇的玺 ④ 印信;保证;批准;誓约: put the ~ of approval *on* a scheme 批准某一方案 / be *under* (the) ~ of confession (或 confidence, secrecy, silence) 保证严守秘密 ⑤象征;标志: Their handshake was a ~ of friendship. 他们的握手是友谊的象征。**II** *vt.* ① 封,密封;糊住: ~ an envelope (或 a letter) 封信 / ~ *up* a tin 密封罐头 / ~ the doors before fumigating 在熏烟消毒前把门关紧 / Her lips were ~*ed* by a promise. 她的嘴被她的诺言封住了。②盖章于;(盖章)对…提出确证;保证;在(度量衡器等商品)上盖检验印: The agreement has been signed and ~*ed*. 协定已经签字盖章。/ ~ a promise with a handshake 握手保证践约 / Have these scales been ~*ed*? 这些磅秤已经检验盖印了吗? ③决定,确定;解决: ~ a bargain 成交 / ~ sb.'s fate 决定了某人的命运 ④【电】使(插头与插孔等)紧密接触 ⑤用水泥等填塞: ~ the cracks in the wall 填嵌墙上的裂缝 ⑥【宗】(摩门教)使(婚姻等)成为正式和有约束力;为…举行婚礼(或过继仪式等) ‖***have the ~ of death on one's face*** 有死亡将至的征兆,显出快死的样子 / ***~ off*** 把…封锁起来 / ***set one's ~ to*** ①在…上盖章 ② 保证;批准 / ***set the ~ on*** 使确定下来;使生效 / ***the ~s*** 英国上议院议长(或国务大臣)的公章;上议院议长(或国务大臣)的官职 / ***under***

flying ~ (*to . . .*) (外交用语) (在…地方) 启封 / *under* ~ 盖上公章的: a contract *under* ~ 盖上公章的契约 ‖~**er** *n.* ①盖章人 ②(度量衡器等的)检验员 ③(瓶、袋等的)封口人 ④封口机;封口机操作者 ⑤保护层 ‖~**ing wax** 封蜡;火漆 / ~ **ring** 印章戒指 / '~**wort** *n.* 【植】黄精;平铺漆姑草

seam [si:m] I *n.* ①线缝;缝口: ~ slippages 缝口脱开处 ②接缝;接合线(面): a rivet ~ 铆缝 / ~ welding 缝焊, 滚焊 / boundary layer ~ 【空】附面层表面 ③【船】(船板间的)缝隙; 接合处: The ship's ~s want caulking. 船缝需要填塞。④【解】骨缝 ⑤伤痕;皱纹 ⑥(铸件等的)接痕 ⑦【矿】【地】层;矿层;节理;煤层: a workable ~ 可采煤层;可采矿层 II ❶ *vt.*: ①缝合;接合;焊合;铆合;加热使闭合: ~ up a dress 缝制一件衣服 ②使留下伤痕;使生皱纹: be ~ed with wounds 留有伤痕 / a face ~ed with care 因忧虑而布满皱纹的脸 ③(在袜子等上)织桃线 ❷ *vi.* ①裂开, 生裂缝: land drying and ~ing in the heat 在高温下干裂的土地 ②[方] 缝纫 ③织桃线 ‖~**er** *n.* 缝纫工; 缝纫机: a can ~er (食品工业等的)封罐机 / ~**less** *a.* 无缝的: ~less steel tubes 无缝钢管

seamstress ['semstris; 美 'si:mstris] *n.* 女裁缝,女缝工

seamy ['si:mi] *a.* ①露出线缝的;有线缝的;有裂缝的: a ~ rock 有裂缝岩石 ②讨嫌的;丑恶的;(环境等)肮脏的 ‖**the** ~ **side** ①(衣服的)里面 ②(生活等的)阴暗面

sear[1] [sie] I *a.* 干枯的;凋谢的: the ~ and yellow leaf 晚年 II ❶ *vt.* ①使干枯;使凋谢 ②烧焦;烧灼;烙 ③使变为冷酷无情 ❷ *vi.* 干枯;凋谢 III *n.* 烙印;焦痕 ‖~**ing-iron** ['sierinaien] *n.* 烙铁

sear[2] [sie] *n.* 击发阻铁(枪炮中一种保险装置,用以卡住击针)

search [se:tʃ] I ❶ *vt.* ①在…中搜寻;搜查: ~ the woods for a lost child 在树林搜寻一个走失的小孩 / His hand ~ed his pocket for a match. 他的手在衣袋中到处摸着找火柴。/ ~ sb. 搜查某人的身体 ②细看; 细细检查; (用外科仪器)探(伤): ~ the records of a case 仔细查阅某一案件的卷宗 / ~ sb.'s face 察看某人的脸色 / ~ one's heart (或 conscience) 检查自己的内心深处, 自我反省 ③(风等)刺透;穿过: The cold wind ~ed the streets. 寒风吹过街道。④使(火力)向纵深展开 ❷ *vi.* ①搜寻;搜查 (*for*) ②探究;调查 (*into*): ~ *into* a matter 调查一件事 II *n.* ①搜寻;搜查: the right of ~ (交战国军舰在公海上对中立国船只的)搜查权 / make a ~ *for* one's subject books 寻找有关自己学术专业的书籍 ②检查;探索,调查 ‖*in* ~ *of* 寻找;寻求 / ~ *after* 探索;寻找: ~ *after* truth 追求真理 / **Search me!** [美]我可不知道! (或: 我回答不出!) / ~ *out* 寻找;找到: He ~ed out the book and handed it to me. 他找出那本书,交给了我。

‖~**er** *n.* ①搜查者; 检查者 ②搜寻者;追求者 ③【无】搜索器;【军】大炮检查器;【医】膀胱石探杆 ‖~**light** *n.* ①探照灯(光) ②=flashlight / ~ **party** 搜救援组 / ~ **warrant** 搜查证

searching ['se:tʃiŋ] I *a.* ①(搜寻、检查等)彻底的,无孔不入的 ②(目光等)洞察的,锐利的; (风等)彻骨的: a ~ look 锐利的目光 / a ~ cold 刺骨的寒冷 II *n.* 搜寻; 搜索; 检查: ~s of heart 内心的反省 (也作 heart-~s) ‖~**ly** *ad.* ‖~ **fire** 【军】纵深射击

season ['si:zn] I *n.* ①季, 季节; 时节, 时令: the four ~s 四季 / at all ~s 一年四季,一年到头 / the dry (rainy) ~ 旱(雨)季 / the monsoon ~ (印度洋及南亚)季风期, 雨季 / the Spring Festival ~ 春节 / the Christmas ~ 圣诞节前后 / a busy (slack) farming ~ 农忙(闲)季节 / The spring-sowing ~ has set in. 春播季节到来了。②当令期;旺季;(文娱、社交、商业等的)活跃季节: the grape ~ 葡萄当令季 / an off (或 a dull) ~ 淡季 / the theatrical ~ 戏剧季节 / the holiday ~ 休假(旅行)的旺季 / the swimming ~ 游泳季节 / an open ~ 狩猎期 / a close ~ 禁猎期 / the social ~ 社交忙季 / London in the ~ 社交忙季(指初夏)中的伦敦 / the ~ opener 比赛季节的第一次比赛 ③一段时期: a ~ of inaction 暂时的不活动期 ④[口]月季票;定期车票;(剧院等的)长期票: show one's ~ 出示月季票 II ❶ *vt.* ①给…调味;加味于;[喻]使增添趣味: a highly ~ed dish 味道很浓的菜 / fish ~ed *with* vinegar and sugar 糖醋鱼 / a conversation ~ed *with* wit 妙趣横生的谈话 ②使得到锻炼; 使适应; 使服水土: The young people from the South have been ~ed *to* the severe cold of the North. 南方来的青年人已经适应了北方的严寒。/ a ~ed sailor 饱经风霜的海员 ③处理(木材等)以备应用; 使合用: ~ed timber 干燥可用的木料 ④缓和, 使温和 ❷ *vi.* 变合用; (木材)变干: Timber ~s quickly in the wind. 木材在风里干得很快。‖*for a* ~ 一会儿 / *in good* ~ 及早; 及时地 / *in* ~ ①(水果、蔬菜等)应时的,当令的: Tomatoes are *in* ~. 蕃茄正当令。②(猎物)狩猎期内猎得的 ③及时的, 合时宜的: a word *in* ~ 及时的劝告 ④及早的 ⑤(动物)正在发情期中 / *in* ~ *and out of* ~ 任何时候,一年到头; 不管适时不适时 / *out of* ~ 已过时的;不合时令的 / *rush the* ~ [美]预赶季节(如未到夏季先穿夏装) / *the silly* ~ 新闻饥荒期(指八、九月份) ‖~**er** *n.* ①用调味品的人 ②调味品 / ~**ing** *n.* ①调味品, 作料: There's not enough ~ing in the sausage. 这香肠里作料不够。②增加兴趣的东西 ③【物】时效 ‖~ **ticket** 月季票;定期车票;长期票

seasonable ['si:znebl] *a.* ①合时令的: ~ weather 合时令的天气 ②及时的, 合时宜的: a ~ time for discussion 适宜于讨论的时刻 / a ~ rain 及

时雨 / ～ aid 及时的援助 ‖～ness *n.* / **sea-sonably** *ad.*

seasonal ['si:zənl] *a.* 季节的；季节性的；随季节而变化的：～ rates 按季度计算的费用率 / a ～ trade 季节性行业 / the ～ migration of birds 鸟类的季节性迁移 ‖～ly *ad.*

seat [si:t] **I** *n.* ①座，座位：the front (back) ～ of a car 汽车的前(后)座 / The classroom has ～s for fifty. 这教室有五十个座位。/ Does this ～ belong to anybody? 这座位有人么? / book ～ in a theatre 在剧院中订座 ②(椅等的)座部；(机器的)座子；(人体或裤子的)臀部：a chair with a cane ～ 有藤座的椅子 / a ～ cushion 座垫 / a spindle ～ 轴座 ③所在地；活动中心：the ～ of war 战场 / an ancient ～ of learning 古老学府 / The disease has its ～ in the lungs. 病在肺部。④邸宅；别墅 ⑤席位；会员资格：sb.'s lawful ～ 属于某人的合法席位 / have a ～ on the commission 在委员会中有一席位 ⑥坐的姿势；骑马(或自行车)的坐法：a rider with a good ～ 姿势很好的骑者 **II ❶** *vt.* ①使坐下，使就座；帮助…找到座位：～ a baby on one's knees 让孩子坐在膝上 / ～ oneself at a desk (in a chair, on a stool) 在桌子边(椅子里，凳子上)坐下 ②(房间等)供给…座位，坐得下…人；为(房间等)设座位：a great hall that ～s over 10,000 persons 可坐一万多人的大会堂 / This airliner is ～ed for 40. 这架班机设有四十个人的座位。③使得席位，使当选就职；使登位：～ a candidate 使候选人当选 / The queen of that country was ～ed last year. 那个国家的女王是去年登位的。④修补…的座部；为(机器等)装底座：a wornout pair of trousers 给破裤子补后裆 / ～ a chair with cane 给椅子装藤座 / ～ a machine on its support 把机器装在底座上 **❷** *vi.* (机器等)安装在底座上‖be ～ed 坐着；坐定；坐下：Please be ～ed. 请坐。②坐落在，位于…／ *fly by the ～ of one's pants* [俚]凭感官判断(不凭仪器)驾驶飞机 / *keep one's ～* 守住座位；安坐不动 / *lose one's ～* 座位被人占去 / *take a ～* 坐下：Won't you take a ～? (或 Please take a ～.) 请坐。/ *take one's ～* 就座 / *the driver's ～* 见 **driver** / *win (lose) a ～* 在国会选举中当(落)选 ‖～ed *a.* [常用以构成复合词] ①有…的座垫的：a soft-～ed chair 软垫坐椅 / double-～ed trousers 臀部用双层布加固的裤子 ②固定的，扎根的：a deep-～ed disease 痼疾 / well-～ed prejudices 根深蒂固的偏见 ‖～ belt (系于飞机座位上的)安全带 / '～mate *n.* (火车等处的)同座人 / ～ mile 客运哩程(计算客运量的统计单位，指一个旅客一英里的旅程) / '～-pack parachute (可作座垫用的)座包式降落伞

secede [si'si:d] *vi.* (从宗教、政治等组织)退出，脱离 (*from*) ‖～r *n.* ①退出者；退党者；退教者 ②[S-] [常用复] 【史】一七三三年脱离国教的苏格兰长老派

secession [si'seʃən] *n.* ①(从宗教、政治等组织的)退出，脱离 ②[S-] 【美史】脱离联邦 (特指一八六一年南方十一州的脱离联邦)：the War of *Secession* 美国南北战争 (1861—1865) ③退隐 ④【建】直线派，直线式(起源于奥地利) ‖～al *a.* 脱离的；苏格兰长老派的 / ～ism *n.* 脱离主义 / ～ist *n.* 脱离主义者

seclude [si'klu:d] *vt.* ①使隔离；使孤立；使隐退：～ oneself from society 与世隔绝，退隐 ②隔开；把…隐蔽起来

secluded [si'klu:did] *a.* ①隐退的：a ～ life 隐居生活 ②僻静的；隐蔽的：a ～ spot 僻静的地方 ‖～ly *ad.* / ～ness *n.*

seclusion [si'klu:ʒən] *n.* ①隔离；孤立：a policy of ～ 闭关自守政策 ②隐居，隐退：a life of ～ 隐居生活 ③偏僻的地方；隐蔽的地方

second[1] ['sekənd] **I** *num.* 第二(个)：the ～ edition 第二版，再版 / the ～ largest city in China 中国第二大城市 **II** *a.* ①二等的，次等的；次要的：the ～ cabin (客轮的)二等舱 / cloth of ～ quality 次等布 / the teaching of French as a ～ foreign language 作为第二外国语的法语教学 ②【语】第二格的；【音】第二度音程的；低音部的 ③另一的，又一的；类似的；另加的，附加的：every ～ year (month, day) 每隔一年(月，天) / write on every ～ line 每隔一行写 / take a ～ helping of meat 又吃了一份肉 ④副的；辅助的：occupy the ～ leading post 当第二把手 ⑤非独创的，模仿的；非天生的，后天得到的 **III** *ad.* ① 居第二位，列第二等，归第二类：come (in) ～ in the 100-metre dash 在百米赛跑中获得第二名 ②第二，其次 **IV** *n.* ①第二名，第二位，二等奖；(指汇票)第二份；(前述者以外的)另一人(或物)：get a ～ 获得第二名 / the ～ of exchange 【商】(一式三份中的)第二张汇票 / You are the ～ to tell me the news. 你是第二个告诉我这个新闻的人。②【音】第二度音程，二度；低音部 ③支持者；(决斗中的)助手，副手 ④附和，赞成；附议 ⑤副职人员；副司令员，副指挥员 ⑥[the S-] (帝王)二世：William the *Second* 威廉二世 ⑦[复]乙级商品，次货；粗面粉；粗面粉做的面包；[美俚]二煎咖啡：These socks are ～s and have some slight defects. 这些短袜是次品，略有毛病。⑧(汽车)第二档速率；第二排挡 ⑨[～s] [用作单或复] [口]添菜 ⑩(月的)第二日：the ～ of February 二月二日 **V** *vt.* ①(决斗中)当…的助手；作…的后援 ②支持；赞成(提案等)：～ a motion to adjourn 附议休会的动议 ③ [si'kɔnd] [英]【军】调任，调派：～ sb. for special duties 调派某人任特殊职务 ‖～ to none 比谁都好，首屈一指 ‖～ly *ad.* 第二(点)；其次(列举条目等时用) / ～ment [si'kɔndmənt] *n.* [英]【军](被)调任(特殊职务) ‖**Second Advent** 【宗】基督再临 / ～ **ballot** 决选投票制(在选举中，如没有人得票超过半数时，以得票最多和次多的两人为被选举人而进行的第二次投票) / ～ **banana** [美俚] ①在戏里演出

角的人 ②随从式人物 / ~ **base** (棒球)二垒 /
'~-'**best** *a.* 居第二位的,仅次于最好的 / ~
best ① 居于第二位者,仅次于最好的东西 ②居
第二位: come off ~ *best* 居第二; 败于对手 / ~
chamber (两院制的) 上(议)院 / ~ **childhood**
老年人的智力衰退时期 / '~-'**class** *a.* ①第二流
的,二等的: a ~-*class* railway carriage 二等客
车 ②平庸的; 次劣的; 社会地位低下的: a ~-*class*
mind 平庸的头脑 *ad.* 乘坐二等: travel ~-*class*
乘二等车(或舱)旅行 / ~ **class** ① 二等,二类
②车(或舱)的二等 ③[美]二类邮件(尤指报刊杂
志等) / **Second Coming** =Second Advent /
~ **cousin** 父母的堂(或表)兄弟(或姊妹)的子(或
女) / '~-**cut file** [机]中细锉 / **Second Empire**
①[史]法兰西第二帝国 (1852—1870) / ~ **estate**
欧洲封建时代的第二等级(贵族); [英]上院全体
贵族议员 / ~ **fiddle** ①(乐队的)第二小提琴手
(中的一员) ② 次要角色; 次要作用: play ~
fiddle (to) 充当(…的)副手 / ~ **floor** [英]三楼;
[美]二楼 / ~ **front** (第二次世界大战时的)第
二战场 / '~-'**guess** *vt.* ① 事后劝告(或批评)
② 猜出…的意图(或动向); 预言 / '~-'**hand** *a.*
① 间接的,第二手的: ~*hand* information 间接
消息 / a ~*hand* witness 陈述间接听到的话的证
人 ② 用过的; 旧的: ~*hand* goods (clothes,
furniture) 旧货(衣服,家具) ③ 经营旧货的: a
~*hand* bookstore 旧书店 *ad.* ①间接地: know
sth. ~*hand* 间接地得知某事 ②通过旧货店(购
买): buy a bicycle ~*hand* 买一辆旧的自行车 /
~ **hand** ① 中间人; 间接: at ~ *hand* 间接
地,第二手得来地 ② 助手工人 ③旧货 / '~-**in-**
com'mand *n.* 副司令员,副指挥员 / **Second**
International 【史】第二国际 (1889 年在巴黎
成立) / ~ **lieutenant** (英) 陆军(或海军陆战
队)少尉; (美)陆军(或空军、海军陆战队)少尉 /
'~-'**line** *a.* 第二线的: ~-*line* troops 第二线兵
力 / ~ **mate** 【海】二副 / ~ **nature** 第二天性
/ ~ **nerve** 【解】视神经 / '~-**pair back** [英]三楼
后房 / '~-**pair front** [英]三楼前房 / ~ **person**
【语】第二人称 / '~-'**rate** *a.* ①二等的 ②第二
流的,平庸的 / '~-'**rater** *n.* 平庸的人 / ~
reading (议会中对提案的)二读 / **Second**
Republic 【史】法兰西第二共和国 (1848—1852)/
~ **run** (电影)二轮放映 / ~ **self** 心腹朋友; 左
右手 / ~ **sight** 超人的视力,预见力 / '~-'**sight-**
ed *a.* 有超人的视力的,有预见力的 / ~ **sound**
【物】第二声 / ~ **stor(e)y** =~ floor / '~-
'**stor(e)y man** 盗窃,窃贼(尤指从楼上窗口爬进去
的) / '~-'**string** *a.* [口] ①(球员)替补的 ②(在
地位、重要性等方面)从属的,较差的 / ~ **teeth**
成人齿 / ~ **thought(s)** 重新考虑(而得出的意
见): On ~ *thoughts* I am for making a new
plan. 经重新考虑后,我赞成制订新计划。 / '~-
,**timer** *n.* 第二次犯罪的人

second² ['sekənd] *n.* ① 秒 (= 1/60 分): the ~
hand of a clock 时钟的秒针 / Every ~ counts.

一寸光阴一寸金。(或: 分秒必争。) ②片刻,瞬间:
The plane will take off *in a* ~. 那飞机一会儿
就要起飞了。③(角或度的单位)秒 (= 1/60 分)
‖ ~ **mark** (表示时间或角度) 秒的符号 ("): 2° 8'
30" (读作 two degrees eight minutes and thirty
seconds) 二度八分三十秒

secondary ['sekəndəri] **I** *a.* ① 第二的; 第二位的;
第二次的; 中级的: ~ education 中等教育 /
a ~ technical school 中等技术学校 /
flight training 中级飞行训练 ②次要的,副的;从
属的; 辅助的; 非原著的,第二手的: a question of
~ importance 次要问题 / a ~ product 副产
品 / a ~ organ 附属机构 / a ~ accent (副
stress)【语】次重音 / the ~ tenses 【语】从属时
态 / ~ evidence 【律】间接证据 ③【医】继发性
的; 第二期的: ~ infection 继发感染 ④【化】仲
的; 副的; 二代的: ~ carbon atom 仲碳原子 /
~ salt 二代盐; 副盐 ⑤【电】产生感应电流的,
次级的: ~ voltage 次级电压 / ~ coil 次级线圈
⑥【地】次生的 **II** *n.* ① 副手; 次要人物; 代表,代
理人【天】双星中较小较暗的一个; 卫星 ③【动】
(鸟的)次级飞羽(即生在前膀上的羽毛); (昆虫的)
后翅 ④【电】次级绕组; 次级线圈 ‖**secondarily**
['sekəndərili; 美 ,sekən'derili] *ad.* / **secondari-**
ness *n.* ‖~ **cell** 蓄电池 / ~ **colo(u)r** 合成
色 / ~ **(electron) emission** 【电】二次电子放
射 / ~ **planet** 【天】卫星 / ~ **radiation** 【原】次
级辐射 / ~ **sex characteristic** 【生】第二性征,
副性征

seconder ['sekəndə] *n.* 附议者(指会议中赞成某项
动议的人)

secrecy ['si:krisi] *n.* ① 秘密,秘密状态: do sth.
with great ~ 极秘密地做某事 / keep the matter
in ~ 把事情保守秘密 / *in the* ~ *of* one's heart
在内心深处 ② 保密(习惯); 保密能力: promise
~ 答应不泄漏秘密 / rely on sb.'s ~ 相信某人
会保守秘密 / There need be no ~. 不需要保密。

secret ['si:krit] **I** *a.* ①秘密的,机密的: a ~ code
密电码 / a ~ treaty 秘密条约 / ~ diplomacy
(negotiation) 秘密外交(谈判) ②隐蔽的,暗藏的:
a ~ enemy 隐藏的敌人 / a ~ passage 暗道 /
~ joint 【机】暗榫接合 ③ 暗中进行的; 内心感
觉的,秘而不宣的: ~ alarm (rejoicing) 暗自惊
慌(高兴) ④ 神秘的; 奥秘的: There's nothing
~ about it. 其中并无奥妙。⑤ 偏僻的; 人迹罕
到的: a ~ harbour 偏僻的海港 / a ~ valley
幽谷 ⑥嘴紧的; 能保守秘密的: as the grave
守口如瓶 ⑦ (人体)阴部的: the ~ parts 阴部,
私处 **II** *n.* ①秘密,机密; 内情: (a) top ~ 绝密 /
an open ~ 公开的秘密 / let out a ~ 泄漏秘密 /
make no ~ of sth. 对某事毫不掩饰 / We
have no ~s from you. 我们对你毫无隐瞒。②
神秘,奥秘: the ~s of nature 自然界的奥秘
③ 秘诀,诀巧; 秘方: the ~ of health 养身秘诀
④[常用复](人体)阴部,私处 ⑤[S-]【天主教】默
祷(弥撒中,祭司在供献后的低声祷告) ‖*a dead*

~ 还未泄露的秘密 / *be in the* ~ 知道内情;参与秘密: *Is he in the* ~? 他知道这件事的内情吗? / *in* ~ 暗地里;秘密地: meet *in* ~ 秘密会见 / *keep a* (或 *the*) ~ 保守秘密 / *keep sth. a* ~ *from sb.* 不把某事告诉某人 / *keep sth.* ~ 把某事保守秘密 / *let sb. into a* (或 *the*) ~ 使某人知道(或参与)某项秘密 ‖~**ly** *ad.* ‖~ **agent** 特务 / ~ **ballot** 无记名投票 / ~ **ink** 隐显墨水 (起初无色,经热、光或药品等作用而显字) / ~ **police** 秘密警察 / ~ **process** (一种虽非专利但受法律保护的商品等的)秘密制造方法 / ~ **service** ①(政府的)特务机关: a ~ *service man* 谍报人员,特工人员 / ~ *service money* (国家支付的)特工经费 ②[S-S-](美国)联邦经济情报局(隶属美国财政部) / ~ **society** 秘密社团

secretarial [ˌsekrəˈtɛəriəl] *a.* ① 秘书的;有关秘书事务的: the ~ staff 秘书处全体人员 ②书记的;部长的;大臣的

secretary [ˈsekrətri] *n.* ① 秘书: He is (private) ~ to the minister. 他是部长的(私人)秘书。/ a first (second) ~ of the embassy 大使馆一(二)等秘书 ② 书记 ③ (协会等负责书信往来、档案记录等的)干事;文书: an honorary ~ 名誉干事 ④大臣;部长: the *Secretary* of State (英国)国务大臣;(美国)国务卿 / the *Secretary* of State for Foreign (Home) Affairs (英国)外交(内务)大臣 / the *Secretary* of State for War (英国)陆军大臣 / the *Secretary* of Defense (美国)国防部长 ⑤写字桌;上部附有书橱的写字桌 ⑥[印]草书体大铅字 ‖~**ship** *n.* 秘书(或书记,干事等)的职务(或任期) ‖~ **bird** [动]鹭鹰 / '~-'**general** ([复] secretaries-general) *n.* ①秘书长: the *Secretary-General* of the United Nations 联合国秘书长 ②总书记

secrete [siˈkriːt] *vt.* ① 藏匿(人或物): ~ oneself 把自己藏匿起来 ② 私行侵吞 ③【生】分泌 ‖se-**cretion** [siˈkriːʃən] *n.* ①藏匿 ②分泌;分泌液

sect[1] [sekt] *n.* 派别;宗派;【宗】分裂出来的教派(尤指异端)

sect[2] [sekt] *n.* 部分;节,段

sectarian [sekˈtɛəriən] I *a.* ① 宗派的; (分裂性)教派的 ②闹宗派的;思想狭隘的,偏执的: guard against ~ tendencies 防止宗派主义的倾向 II *n.* ① 宗派主义者;分裂教派的一员 ② 思想偏狭者 ‖~**ism** *n.* 宗派主义 / ~**ize** *vt.* 使宗派化 *vi.* 闹宗派

section [ˈsekʃən] I *n.* ①切断;切开 ②切下的部分,切片;断面,剖面: the ~ of a diseased bone 病骨的切片 / a cross ~ (横)截面,横断面,横剖面 / show sth. in ~ 把某物以断面显示出来 ③ (事物的)一段,一部分;(机器的)零件;(文章等的)节;(条文等的)款,项: a ~ of a pipe 管子的一段 / the last ~ of a journey 最后一段旅程 / the sports ~ of a newspaper 报纸中专登体育运动消息的部分 / a large ~ of the inhabitants 居民中的大部分人 / build in ~s 分段制造 / fit

together the ~s of a machine 把机器各段装配拢来 / The chapter falls into three ~s. 这一章共分三节。④处;科;股;组;【军】分排,小队;(乐队的)乐器组: the string ~ (交响乐队中的)全部弦乐器 ⑤(铁路)路段; 同班次的火车车辆之一;车厢中的卧铺段 ⑥地区;区: a rural ~ 乡村地区 / the Negro ~s of New York 纽约的黑人区 / the residential ~s of a city 城市的住宅区 ⑦阶层,界: all ~s of the people 各界人民 ⑧【生】(指分类单位)派;(果子的)瓣: the ~s of an orange 桔子瓣 ⑨分节号(即§) II ❶ *vt.* …分成段(或组)等;将…切片: a class for oral drills 对大班分成小组进行口语练习 ❷ *vi.* 被切割成片(或段) ‖**Section Eight** [美俚] ①(由于性格、习惯不良)开除军籍(美陆军条例第八节);被开除军籍者 ②神经不正常者 / ~ **gang** (铁路)路段道工组 / ~ **hand** (铁路)路段道工组工人 / ~ **house** (铁路)分段工房 / ~ **mark** 分节号(即§) / ~ **paper** [英]制图用的格纸 / ~ **plane** 剖面

sectional [ˈsekʃənl] I *a.* ① 截面的,剖面的: a ~ drawing 截面图 ② 部分的;局部的: ~ interests 局部的利益 ③段落的;章节的 ④地区的;地方性的: a ~ map of Africa 非洲的分区地图 / a ~ dialect 方言 ⑤ 由可拆卸的部件拼制成的: a ~ sofa 可拆成若干单人坐椅的长沙发 II *n.* 可拆卸(或拼拢)使用的家具 ‖~**ism** *n.* 地方主义 / ~**ist** *n.* 地方主义者 / ~**ize** *vt.* ①把…分成段(或部分等): ~ized continuous brick laying method 【建】分段连续砌砖法 ②使地方主义化 / ~**ly** *ad.*

sector [ˈsektə] I *n.* ①【数】扇形;扇形面: the ~ of a circle 圆的扇形 / ~ scanning (电视、雷达等的)扇形扫描 ② 两脚规;函数尺 ③部分;成分;部门: the different ~s of national economy 国民经济的各部门 / the socialist ~ of the economy 社会主义经济成分 / the industrial ~ (经济中的)工业部门 ④【军】防御分区,防区 II *vt.* ①把…分成扇形 ② 使分成部分 ‖~**al** [ˈsektərəl] *a.* ‖~ **gear** [机]扇形齿轮

secular [ˈsekjulə] I *a.* ① 现世的,世俗的;非宗教(或教会)的: ~ concerns 凡夫俗子所关心(或忧虑)的事情 / a ~ court 非宗教法庭 / ~ education 世俗教育 / the ~ power (或 arm) 俗权(指非教会的权力) ② 不受修道誓约约束的,修道院外的: the ~ clergy [总称]寺院外的教士,教区僧侣 ③怀疑宗教教义的;反对教会教育的 ④每世纪(或一个长时期)发生一次的 ⑤ 延续几个世纪的;长期的: the ~ rival between Church and State in European history 欧洲历史上延续好几个世纪的政教之争 / the ~ upheaval of land 地面的长期缓升 / ~ acceleration 【天】长期加速度 / a ~ trend 长期趋势 / ~ fame 不朽的声望 II *n.* ①修道院外的教士,教区僧侣 ②俗人 ‖**the** ~ **bird** 不死鸟,凤凰 ‖~**ism** [ˈsekjulərizəm] *n.* ①现世主义;非宗教主义 ②宗教与教育分离论

~ist ['sekjuⱺrist] *n.* 现世主义者; 非宗教主义者; 宗教与教育分离论者 / ~ity [,sekju'læriti] *n.* ① 现世性, 世俗性 ② 世俗的考虑; 俗事 / ~ly *ad.*

secure [si'kjuⱺ] I *a.* ① 安心的, 无忧虑的; 有把握的: have one's mind ~ 放下心 / feel ~ *about* (或 *as to*) one's future 对未来感到放心 / be ~ *of* victory 有必胜的信念 ② 安全的; 牢固的; 保险的, 可靠的: evacuate the wounded to a ~ place 把伤员转移到安全的地方去 / a ~ foundation 牢固的基础 / Is the ladder ~? 这梯子靠得住吗? / keep a prisoner ~ 把囚犯牢牢地监禁着 / a powerful and ~ backing 坚强可靠的后盾 / be ~ *against* assault 坚不可摧, 固若金汤 / be ~ *from* harm (interruption) 不致受到危害(打扰) ③ [古] 盲目信任的 II ❶ *vt.* ① 使安全; 掩护, 保卫: ~ a supply line *with* heavy gunfire 用密集炮火掩护运输线 / build breakwaters to ~ a harbour *against* waves 修筑防堤使港口免受浪潮冲击 / ~ oneself *from* a repetition of the same mistakes 防止重犯同样的错误 ②保证; 为(借款等)作保; 向(债权人)提供保证: a loan ~d by mortgage (on landed property) 以抵押(以地产)作担保的贷款 ③关紧; 把…弄牢: ~ the hatches of a ship 把舱盖关紧 ④ 把…弄到手, 获得; 替…弄到; 促成, 招致: A million signatures have been ~d. 已征集到一百万人的签名。/ ~ one's ends 达到自己的目的 / ~ sb. a ticket 替某人弄到一张票子 / Perfect teamwork ~s a better performance. 相互配合得好可以表演得更加出色。⑤ 解除(海军人员)的值勤任务 ❷ *vi.* ①(海军人员)停止操作; 值勤完毕 ②(船)停靠码头; 抛锚 ‖*Secure arms!* 【军】挟枪! ‖~ly *ad.* ① 安全地 有把握地 ② 无疑地 ③ 牢牢地 / ~ment *n.* ① 把握, 稳当性 ② 获得, 取得 / ~r [si'kjuⱺrⱺ] *n.* 保卫者; 担保者; 把…弄到手的人 (*of*)

security [si'kjuⱺriti] *n.* ① 安全; 安全感: safeguard the ~ of one's motherland 保卫祖国的安全 / a sense of ~ 安全感 / ~ of person 人身安全 / feel great ~ in the knowledge (belief) that ... 因知道(确信)…而觉得十分安全 ② 使免遭危险的东西, 保护物; 【军】防御物: A good fire is a ~ *against* wild beasts. 生一堆大火可确保不受野兽侵扰。/ give sb. *securities from* further molestation 确保某人不再受干扰 ③治安防卫; 安全防卫措施; [常作 S-] 治安防卫当局: the public ~ organs (personnel) 公安机关(人员) / a ~ cadre 治保干部 / a ~ risk 可能危害国家安全的危险人物, 政治危险人物 / the maximum (medium, minimum) ~ cellblocks 实行最大(中等, 最低)程度防备措施的监房区 / *Security* prevents the reporting of some production figures. 出于安全保卫原因, 某些生产数字不能公开报道。④保证; 保障; 担保: employment ~ 就业保险(如失业津贴等) / guarantee for old age ~ 给老年人提供

各方面的保障 ⑤ 把握; 可靠性: have the ~ of sb.'s devotion 对于某人的忠心很有把握 / The instrumentalist played with great ~. 演奏家满有把握地演奏着。/ the ~ of a knot 一个绳结的牢靠性 ⑥保证人, 担保人; 抵押品; 保证金: lend money *on* ~ 凭抵押品贷款 / give sth. as a ~ *for* 以某物作为…的抵押 ⑦ [常用复]证券, 债券: government *securities* 公债券 ‖*go* (或 *enter into*, *give*) ~ (*for*) (为…)作保 / *in* ~ 安全地 / *in* ~ *for* 作为…的担保(或保证) ‖sə-'curity-'conscious *a.* 常为安全问题提心吊胆的/ **Security Council** (联合国)安全理事会

sedan [si'dæn] *n.* ①轿子 ②轿车 ③单舱汽艇 ‖~ chair 轿子

sedan

sedate[1] [si'deit] *a.* ① 安静的 ② 稳重的, 严肃的 ‖~ly *ad.* / ~ness *n.*

sedate[2] [si'deit] *vt.* 给…服镇静剂

sedative ['sedⱺtiv] I *a.* 镇静的; 止痛的 II *n.* 【药】镇静剂; 止痛药

sedentary ['sedntⱺri] I *a.* ①坐着的; 需要(或惯于)久坐的: a ~ posture 坐着的姿势 / lead a ~ life 过着案牍生活 ② (鸟等)定居的; (昆虫)静止的; (贝壳)固定附着的 II *n.* ① 惯于久坐的人 ② 坐巢蜘蛛 ‖**sedentarily** ['sednt
ⱺrili; 美 ,sedn-'terili] *ad.* / **sedentariness** *n.*

sediment ['sedimⱺnt] *n.* ① 沉积; 沉淀 ②【地】沉积物

sedition [si'diʃⱺn] *n.* ① 煽动叛乱(或闹事); [罕] 叛乱, 暴动 ②煽动性的言论(或行为): a speech abounding in ~ 充满煽动性的发言 ‖~ary *n.* 煽动叛乱者, 煽动分子

seditious [si'diʃⱺs] *a.* 煽动(性)的; 参与煽动的; 犯煽动罪的: ~ writings 煽动性的作品 ‖~ly *ad.* / ~ness *n.*

seduce [si'dju:s] *vt.* ①诱惑; 诱使…堕落(或犯罪); 诱奸, 勾引: ~ sb. from his duty 诱使某人放弃职责 ②以魅力吸引 ‖~ment *n.* / ~r *n.* 引诱者; 诱奸者; 勾引者

seduction [si'dΛkʃⱺn] *n.* ①诱惑; 诱奸, 勾引 ②魅力; 有魅力的东西; 诱饵

seductive [si'dΛktiv] *a.* 诱惑的; 诱人堕落的; 富有魅力的 ‖~ly *ad.* / ~ness *n.*

sedulous ['sedjuləs] *a.* ①勤勉的；孜孜不倦的 ②小心周到的：with ~ care 小心翼翼地 / ~ flattery 百般的奉承 / play the ~ ape（在文学创作方面）依样画葫芦 ‖**~ly** *ad.* / **~ness** *n.*

see[1] [si:] (saw [so:], seen [si:n]) ❶ *vt.* ①看见，看到：He looked round but *saw* nobody. 他转过头去看了一下，但没有看见什么人。/ Can（或 Do）you ~ that light in the distance? 你看见那远处的灯光吗？/ ~ someone move（或 moving）about 看见有人走动 / ~ a guided missile launched 看见发射导弹的情景 / He was *seen to* leave（或 was *seen* leaving）the room. 有人看见他离开房间的。/ ~ the whole 看到全体 / I was surprised to ~ him so much changed. 我很惊讶地看到他大大的变样了。/ I *saw* at a glance that.... 我一眼就看到…[注意：~ 主要指"看见"，look（at）主要指"看着"，watch 主要指"注视"]
②察看，查看：Watch and ~ how others do it. 好好看着人家是怎么干这事的。/ *seen* fire【军】目视射击 / Please ~ who's at the door. 请去看看谁在门口。/ Go and ~ if the tractor needs oil. 去看一下拖拉机是否要加油。/ Let me ~ your pass. 出示你的出入证（或通行证）。
③遇见；会见，约见；访问（尤指看医生、找律师等）；接待：I *saw* her at the exhibition the other day. 前几天我在展览会上碰见她。/ I'm glad to ~ you. 我很高兴同你见面。/ *See* you again（或 later）. 再见！回头见！/ *See* you. [美俚]再见！/ I'm ~*ing* him this evening. 今天晚上我将会见他。/ ~ sb. ill to ~ anyone 病重得不能会见任何人 / When will you come and ~ us? 你什么时候来看望我们？/ You'd better ~ a doctor. 你还是去看看医生吧。/ We ~ no visitors during study hours.（我们在）学习时间不会客。
④观看（戏剧等）；参观；游览：~ a play 看戏 / Go and ~ our new workshop. 去看看咱们的新车间。
⑤看出，发现；领会，理解；认为：~ no reason to worry 看不出有什么好烦恼的 / make sb. ~ sense about sth. 使某人看到（做）某事是有意义的 / We *saw* that the plan would work. 我们看出（或知道）这个计划是行得通的。/ *See*（或 You ~ 或 Do you ~）what I mean? 你懂了我的意思吗？/ I don't（或 can't）~ your point. 我不明白你说的要点是什么。/ as we ~ it 照我们的看法；我们认为 / Do you ~ any advantage (use) of doing so? 你认为这样做有好处（用）吗？/ ~ it fit to do sth. 认为做某事是合适的
⑥（从报刊等）得悉，知道：We ~ that the delegation has already started for home. 我们（从报上）知道代表团已经动身回国了。
⑦参看，参见…；see note below. 参看下面注解。/ *See* page 321. 见第三百二十一页。
⑧看中，喜欢；同意：What does he ~ *in* the offer? 他看中这项提议的哪一点呢？/ Hope you'll be

able to make him ~ it. 希望你能使他喜欢它。/ He will not ~ being made use of. 他不愿受人利用。
⑨目睹；经历：He has *seen* a great deal (of life). 他见多识广（或阅历丰富）。
⑩陪，送：~ sb. home 陪某人回家 / ~ sb. out (to the door) 送某人出去（到门口）
⑪听凭，任凭；宁愿让：We wouldn't ~ you go all alone. 我们不能让你一个人去。/ would ~ oneself shot before yielding 宁死不屈
⑫在幻觉中看见；设想，想象：~ sb. in a dream 梦见某人 / Can you ~ what he looked like ten years ago? 你能想象他十年前是什么样子吗？/ I simply can't ~ him as a crook. 我实在不能想象他可能是个骗子。
⑬照料，使能维持下去：have enough food to ~ one to the end of the year 有足够的食物可维持到年底
⑭注意；当心，留神；务必使…；考虑：*See* (that) you don't catch cold. 当心别伤风。/ We'll ~ that the boy is properly educated. 我们一定设法使这男孩受到很好的教育。/ Well, let's ~ what can be done. 好吧，我们来考虑一下怎么办。
⑮与（对方）押同样赌注，以同样赌注对（赌）
⑯[美俚]贿赂，收买
❷ *vi.* ①看，看见；观看：How far can you ~? 你能看得多远？/ He ~s poorly with his left eye. 他左眼视力不好。/ It's getting dark, I can't ~ to read. 天黑下来了，我看不清书了。/ None is so blind as those who will not ~. 不愿意正视（事实）的人简直不如瞎子。/ A band was passing and the children ran out to ~. 军乐队正在经过，孩子们都跑出去看了。
②[常用于祈使句]瞧；注意，当心：*See*, here they come! 瞧，他们来啦！/ Wait and ~. 等着瞧吧。/ *See*, the train is coming! 注意，火车来啦！
③看出，理解；知道：as everybody can ~ 众所周知 / as far as I can ~ 就我所能理解的说来 / I ~. You are on leave. 我明白了，你是在休假。/ You shall ~. （以后）你一定会明白的。
④想，考虑；查看，调查：Let me ~, what was I saying? 让我想一想，刚才我说什么来着？/ We can't give you an answer yet, but we shall ~. 现在我们还不能答复你，我们再考虑考虑。
‖~ *about* 查看，查询；留意于；负责弄…：We can't decide now, but we'll ~ *about* it. 我们现在还不能决定，但我们会考虑的。/ I'll ~ *about* the fuel. 我负责去弄燃料。/ ~ *after* 照应，照顾 / ~ *double*（酒醉眼花时）把一物看成二形 / ~ *eye to eye* (*with sb.*) 见 **eye** / ~ *for oneself* 自己去看，亲眼看：If you don't believe it, go and ~ *for yourself*. 不信你自己去看！/ *See here*! [美口]（引起对方注意）喂！(=Look here! 或 I say!) / ~*ing* (*that*) 鉴于…，由于…的缘故：*Seeing that* he is ill, we'll do the

work for him. 既然他病了,我们来代他做这件工作吧。/ ~ *into* 调查,了解…的性质(或意义等): Let's ~ *into* the matter first. 让我们先了解这件事的情况吧。/ ~ *one's way* (*clear*) *to do* (或 *to doing*) *sth.* 见 **way** / ~ *over* (为租或买而)察看(房屋等) / ~ *red* 见 **red** / ~ *sb. coming* [俚]使某人上当,欺骗某人 / ~ *sb. damned* (或 *hanged, blowed, dead* 等) *first* (或 *before* ...)(表示坚决拒绝)死也不肯: I'll ~ *you dead before* I accept your terms. 见鬼去吧,我才不接受你的条件呢。/ ~ *sb. off* 为某人送行 / ~ *sb. through* 关心(或帮助)某人使渡过难关;使某人得以维持过…: We will ~ *you through* the difficulty. 我们会帮你们克服困难的。/ This padded coat has *seen* me *through* many severe winters. 我穿着这件棉衣过了好几个寒冬。/ ~ *sth. through* (或 *out*) 办好某事;使某事顺利通过…; 把某事进行到底: I'll ~ everything *through* the Customs for you. 我会帮你办好所有海关手续的。/ ~ a performance *out* 看完表演 / ~ *the back of sb.* 见 **back** / ~ *the elephant* 见 **elephant** / ~ *the last of* 见 **last**[1] / ~ *through* 看穿,识破: ~ *through* a double-dealer 识破两面派 / ~ (*to it*) *that* ...要注意使…;务必使…;保证使…: *See to it that* there is enough leeway. 要留有充分余地。/ ~ *with* 同意: I cannot ~ *with* you (在那点上)我与你不同意你的意见。/ ~ *with half an eye* 见 **eye** / *will never* ~ **40** (**50,** ...) *again* 过四十(五十,…)岁了 / *you* ~ [用作插入语]①你瞧: There, *you* ~, the rain's stopped. 瞧,雨停了。②你是知道的: Acupuncture, *you* ~, is a very effective cure. 你是知道的,针刺是很有效的疗法。③ 你听我说,你懂吧,要知道: It's a serious problem, *you* ~. 要知道,这是个很严肃的问题。
‖'~-through *a.* (衣料、衣服等)透明的

see[2] [si:] *n.* 【宗】主教教座(或教区);主教的地位(或权威、管辖权): the *See* of Rome (或 the *Holy See*)【天主教】罗马教皇职位;罗马教廷

seed [si:d] **I** ([复] seed(s)) *n.* ①种(子);籽;[喻]萌芽,开端;起因: a bag of ~(s) 一袋种子 / a rape ~ 油菜籽 / a sesame ~ 芝麻籽 / potato ~s 马铃薯种 / be kept *for* (或 *as*) ~ 被留作种子 / ~ selecting 选种 / ~ grain 种子粮 / sow the ~ in spring 春播 / introduce better strains of ~ 采用良种②家系;子孙,后代③精液;芽胞;虫卵④ 幼蚝,蚝种 (=~ oyster) ⑤[口]种子选手: the No.1 ~ in a table-tennis championship 乒乓球赛中的第一号种子(选手)⑥结籽(期);产卵(期): in ~ 在结籽(或产卵)中⑦种子状的东西;(玻璃中的)小气泡 **II** ❶ *vt.* ①在…中播种(种): ~ the fields *with* wheat 在田里播种小麦 / ~ land *to* grass 在土地上种草②催…发育(或成长);催(云)化雨(指人工降雨): a breeder reactor ~ed *with* plutonium 用钚加速的增殖反应堆 / ~ clouds 人工降雨③去…的核;脱…的

籽: ~ dates 去掉枣核 ④挑选(某人)作种子选手;安排(种子选手或种子队) ❷ *vi.* ①(植物)结实,生子②脱苞③播种 ‖ *go* (或 *run*) *to* ~ ①花谢结子②变得衰弱无用;退化 ②(人)变得不修边幅,不再注意服饰外表 / *raise up* ~ 繁殖子孙后代 / *the* ~ *of Abraham* 希伯来人,犹太人 ‖~**er** *n.* ①播种者;播种机 ②去核器 ③人工造雨者 / ~**less** *a.* 无核的: ~*less* raisins 无核葡萄干 ‖'~**bed** *n.* 苗床;种子田;[喻]温床,策源地 / '~'**cake** *n.* 含芳香植物种子的饼 / ~ **corn** 谷种;[美]玉蜀黍籽 / ~ **cotton** 籽棉 / ~ **crystal** 【物】籽晶;晶种 / ~ **fish** 产卵期的鱼 / '~**ing=ma,chine** *n.* 播种机 / ~**ing plough** 自动播种耕作机 / '~**leaf** *n.* 一种宽烟叶(用于制雪茄烟) / ~ **leaf, ~ lobe** 【植】子叶 / ~ **money** [美](用来吸引更多资金的)种子基金 / ~ **pearl** 小粒珍珠 / ~ **plant** 种子植物 / ~**-plot** *n.* = ~**bed** / ~**sman** ['si:dzmən] *n.* 播种人;种子商 / ~ **stock** 留出的一批种子;留种的动物 / '~**time** *n.* 播种期;[喻]准备期 / ~ **vessel**【植】果皮,囊果皮 / '~**-wool** *n.* 籽棉

seedling ['si:dliŋ] *n.* ①秧苗,籽苗: grow ~s 育苗 / lift (transplant) ~s 拔(插)秧 ②树苗

seek [si:k] (sought [sɔ:t]) ❶ *vt.* ①寻找;探索;追求: ~ shelter from the rain 找躲雨的地方 / The cause is not far to ~. 不难找到原因。/ ~ truth from facts 实事求是 / ~ a quarrel 寻衅 / ~ fame 追求名誉 / ~ a job as typist 谋求打字员的工作 ②在…中搜索,搜查遍(某地) (*through*) ③[一般后接不定式]试图,企图: ~ to kill sb. (或 ~ sb.'s life) 谋害某人 ④ 征求;请求: ~ sb.'s advice 向某人请教 ⑤往,朝…而去: Water ~s its own level. 水往低处流。/ ~ one's bed 上床,就寝 ❷ *vi.* ①寻找;探索 ②搜索;搜查 ‖*be* (*much*) *to* ~ 还(远)没有找到;(大大)缺乏: A better way *is* yet *to* ~. 还得找一种更好的办法。/ He *is to* ~ in grammar. 他还没有掌握语法。/ ~ *after* (或 *for*) 寻找;探索;追求: ~ *for* a missing pen 找失落的钢笔 / These articles are much *sought after*. 这些商品很受人欢迎。/ *Seek dead!* 去找! (叫猎狗去找打死的猎物) / ~ *out* 搜寻出;(在一群中)挑出;竭力找(某人)作伴 ‖~**er** *n.* ① 探索者;追求者;搜查者: a ~*er after* truth 追求真理的人 ②(导弹的)自导头部,自动导引头部;自导导弹 (=target ~er)

seem [si:m] *vi.* ①好象,在外表上显出;似乎: Be what you ~ (to be). 要表里一致。/ make others ~ pallid by comparison 使其他的相形见绌 / You don't ~ to be quite yourself today. 你今天好象不大对头。(指身体或情绪) / He doesn't ~ to appreciate it. 他对这个好象并不领情。/ There ~s (to be) no point in refusing. 看来没有道理拒绝。②[与引导代词 it 连用]看来好象,似乎: *It* ~s (that) you were lying. 看来你在撒谎吧。/ *It* ~s as if it is going to rain. 看来快下雨了。/ *It would* not ~ proper to do so.

看来这样做不太合适吧。[注意: 此句中的 would 起婉转语气的作用] / You are mistaken, *it* ~s (to me). 看来你搞错了。 / I shall act as ~s best. 我将按照我认为最好的方法去做。③[与人称代词 I 连用]感到好象, 觉得似乎: I ~ to have seen him somewhere before. 我觉得好象以前曾在什么地方见到过他。 / I ~ unable (或: [美口] I can't ~) to solve it right now. 看来我无法立刻解决它。

seeming ['si:miŋ] **I** *a.* ①表面上的; 似乎真实的: a ~ friend 表面上的朋友 / the loyalty of a double-dealer 两面派的表面忠诚 **II** *n.* 外观, 外貌(尤指假象) ‖**to outward** ~ 从表面上看来 ‖~**ly** *ad.*

seemly ['si:mli] **I** *a.* ①好看的, 美貌的 ②吸引人的; 像样的; 匀称的 ③合适的; 适宜的; 得体的; 合乎礼仪的 **II** *ad.* [罕]合适地; 合礼仪地 ‖**seemliness** *n.*

seep [si:p] **I** *vi.* 渗出; 渗漏: water ~ing in through a crack in the ceiling 从天花板裂缝中渗进的水 **II** *n.* ①小泉 ②地下水(或油等)渗出成坑的地方 ‖~**age** ['si:pidʒ] *n.* ①渗出; 渗漏 ②【矿】油苗

seer ['si(:)ə] *n.* ①观看者 ②预言家, 先知 ③(凝视水晶球而占卜未来的)占卜者(=crystal gazer)

seesaw ['si:-sɔ:] **I** *n.* ①跷跷板; 跷跷板游戏: The children are riding on a ~ (are playing a) ~. 孩子们骑在跷跷板上(在玩跷跷板)。 ②(类似跷跷板的)一上一下(或一前一后)的动作; (双方)交替占优势的竞争: a ~ between the attackers and the defenders 攻守双方之间的拉锯战 **II** ① *vi.* ①玩跷跷板 ②上下(或前后)摇动: the ~ing deck of a ship 船的摇晃不定的甲板 ③交替(物价、温度等)起伏, 涨落: The score had been ~ing from the very start. 从一开始比分就成拉锯局面。 ② *vt.* 使作跷跷板式运动: ~ sb. skywards (象在跷跷板上似地)把某人抛得很高 **III** *a. & ad.* 忽上忽下的(地); 忽前忽后的(地); 摇摆不定的(地): Then the lead went ~ between the two runners. 接着两名赛跑运动员就拉锯似地忽而甲领先, 忽而乙领先。 ‖~ **battle** 拉锯战

seethe [si:ð] **I** ① *vi.* ①煮沸 ②沸腾; 激动(with): a street *seething with* people 人群闹哄哄的街道/ ~ *with* joy 喜气洋洋 / The whole industrial front is *seething with* activity. 整个工业战线热气腾腾。 ② *vt.* ①使煮沸 ②使浸湿, 使浸透 **II** *n.* 沸腾

segment ['segmənt] **I** *n.* ①部分; 切片: the affected ~ of the bowel 肠的受感染部分 / every ~ of the economy 各经济部门 / a ~ of a tribe 一个部落中的各氏族 / a few ~s of garlic 几瓣大蒜 ②【数】段, 节; 弓形; 圆缺; 球缺: a ~ of a circle 弓形 ③【机】扇形体 ④【动】(体)节; 环节 **II** *vt. & vi.* 分割; (使)分裂开 ‖~ **gear** 【机】扇形齿轮, 扇形齿条

segregate ['segrigeit] **I** ① *vt.* 使分离, 使分开 使隔离: ~ people with infectious diseases 隔离传染病患者 ② *vi.* ①分离, 分开; 受隔离 ②施行种族隔离政策 ③【化】分凝; 【物】【冶】偏析 ④【生】分异; (成熟分裂时等位基因)分离 **II** ['segrigit] *a.* =~d **III** ['segrigit] *n.* 被隔离的人 ‖~d *a.* ①被分离的; 被隔离的 ②实行种族隔离政策的: a ~d school (state) 实行种族隔离的学校(州) ③【冶】偏析的: ~d band (spot) 偏析带(区)

segregation [,segri'geiʃən] *n.* ①分离, 分开; 隔离: ~ into accelerated classes 分到进度较快的班级 / the notorious policy of racial ~ 臭名昭著的种族隔离政策 ②被隔离的部分 ③【生】分异; (等位基因的)分离: ~ index 分离指数 ④【化】分凝; 【物】【冶】偏析(区); 熔析 ‖~**ist** *n.* (尤指种族)隔离(或分离)主义者

seism ['saizm] *n.* 地震

seismic ['saizmik] *a.* 地震(引起)的; 与地震有关的: the ~ focus (或 origin) 地震源 / a ~ detector 地震检波器 / a ~ ray 地震线 / a ~ region 地震区 ‖~**ally** *ad.*

seismograph ['saizməgrɑ:f] *n.* 【地】地震仪 ‖~**er** [saiz'mɔgrəfə] *n.* 地震学者 / ~**ic(al)** [,saizmə'græfik(əl)] *a.* 地震学的; 地震仪的; 地震记录(法)的 / ~**y** [saiz'mɔgrəfi] *n.* 地震学; 地震记录(法)

seize [si:z] ❶ *vt.* ①抓住; 逮捕; 俘获: ~ a rope 抓住绳子 / ~ sb. *by* the arm (collar) 抓住某人的手臂(衣领) ②夺取; 占领 ③(依法)没收, 把…充公; 扣押; 查封: ~ smuggled goods 没收走私货物 ④【律】占有(尤指终身或世袭领地)(=seise) ⑤抓住(时机等); 掌握, 理解: *Seize* the day, ~ the hour! 只争朝夕! / ~ an opportunity 抓住机会; 趁机 / ~ the essence of the matter 掌握问题的实质 / I can't quite ~ your meaning. 我不十分领会你的意思。⑥[常用被动语态](疾病)侵袭; (情绪)支配: be ~d *by* apoplexy 中风 / be ~d *with* an illness 害病 / be ~d *with* panic 惊惶失措 ⑦【海】(用细索等)捆, 扎 ❷ *vi.* ①抓住; 夺取; 占有 (on, upon) ②利用, 采用 (on, upon): ~ *on* a chance 趁机 / ~ *upon* an idea 采用一个主意 ‖**be** (或 **stand**) ~**d** (或 **seised**) **of** (依法)占有着 / be ~d (或 seised) of some important papers 占有着某些重要文件 ②拥有(情报等); 知道(消息)等) / ~ **hold of** 抓住; 占领 / ~ **up** ①(机器由于过热、摩擦、压力等)失灵, 轧住 ②【海】(指要鞭打时)把(某人)捆绑在索具上 ‖~**r** *n.* ①=seizor ②猎犬 ③捕捉器

seizure ['si:ʒə] *n.* ①抓住, 攫取; 捕捉 ②夺取; 占领: the ~ of power by armed force 武装夺取政权 ③依法占有; 没收, 充公: the ~ of contraband by the Customs 海关对违禁品的没收 ④(疾病的)发作: a heart ~ 心脏病的发作

seldom ['seldəm] **I** *ad.* 很少, 不常, 难得: I have ~ met (或 *Seldom* have I met) him recently. 最近我很少碰到他。 / We have very ~ seen such big melons. 我们极少见过这么大的瓜。/ He ~, if ever, falls ill. 他几乎从不生病。**II** *a.* 罕有的,很少的,少见的 ‖*not* ~ 往往,时常 / ~ *or never* 极难得;简直不: He ~ *or never* drinks. 他简直可以说从不喝酒。‖**~ness** *n.*

select [si'lekt] **I❶** *vt.* 选择; 挑选, 选拔 **❷** *vi.* 选择; 挑选 **II** *a.* ①挑选出来的; 精选的 ②优等的, 杰出的, 卓越的 ③(协会、学校等)选择成员严格的: a ~ club 选择会员严格的俱乐部 ④明辨的; 挑剔的: ~ appreciation 明辨的鉴赏(指对作品等) **III** *n.* [常用复]被挑选者 ‖**~ed** *a.* 挑选出来的; 精选的 / **~ee** [,selek'ti:] *n.* 选征合格的士兵 / **~ness** *n.* ‖**~ committee** [英](在下议院中受命作某项特别调查的)小型特别委员会 / **~man** [si'lektmən] *n.* (美国新英格兰地区的)市镇行政管理委员会成员

selection [si'lekʃən] *n.* ①选择; 挑选, 选拔: a ~ committee (挑选新教员等)选拔委员会 / seed (或 strain) ~ 选种 ②待选择物; 精选物; 选集; 选手: This department store has a good ~ of radios. 这家百货商店有很多收音机可供挑选。【生】选择; 淘汰: natural ~ 自然选择 ‖**~ist** *n.* 自然选择论者

selective [si'lektiv] *a.* ①选择的; 挑选的, 选拔的: ~ subjects 选修科目 ②有选择力的 ③【无】选择性的: ~ calling 选择呼叫 ‖**~ly** *ad.* / **~ness** *n.* ‖**~ service** 选征兵役制

selector [si'lektə] *n.* ①挑选者; 选择器 ②【无】调谐旋钮; 波段开关 ③(澳大利亚)挑选公地来定居的人; 小农

self [self] **I** ([复] selves [selvz]) *n.* ①自我, 自己: the consciousness of ~ 自我意识 ②本性, 本质; 个人的正常情况(指健康等): His true ~ was revealed. 他的本来面目被揭露了。/ He looked just like his old ~. 他看上去和他过去一模一样。③私心, 私利: have no thought of ~ 不考虑个人利益 ④本人: your good ~ (*selves*) (旧式商业用语)台端(贵处) / his own (或 very) ~ 他本人 / Caesar's ~ 恺撒(古罗马皇帝)本人 (=Caesar himself) / pay to ~ 向签票人本人支付 / a ticket admitting ~ and friend 限本人和朋友用的入场券 ⑤[谑]我(或你、他)自己: to our noble selves (干杯时用的诙谐语)为我们这些高贵的人, 为我们自己(干杯) ⑥本身(指一种抽象性质的东西): be beauty's ~ 是美的化身; 美绝了 ⑦【植】单色花, 原色花(指未经人工培育变色的) **II** *a.* 同一性质的; 单色的; (材料、花样等)同一类型的: a ~ flower 单色花, 原色花 / a ~ lining 同一种料子的衣服里子 **III ❶** *vt.* ①使近亲繁殖; 使同种繁殖 ②【植】使自花授精 **❷** *vi.* 【植】自花授精 ‖*one's better* (*worse*) ~ 本性中良好(低劣)的一面 / *Self do,* ~ *have.* [谚]自作自受。/ *support one's* ~ 振作精神 ‖**~dom** *n.* 个人的本质; 个性 / **~ness** *n.* ①自私 ②个性; 人格

self-assertion ['self-ə'sə:ʃən] *n.* ①自作主张; 一意

孤行, 专断 ②坚持自己的权利(或要求) ③突出自己 ‖**self-assertive** ['self-ə'sə:tiv] *a.*

self-centred, self-centered ['self'sentəd] *a.* ①自我中心的; 自私自利的 ②自给自足的; 不受外界影响的 ③(作为其他事物运动的中心而)静止的, 固定的 ‖**~ly** *ad.* / **~ness** *n.*

self-colo(u)red ['self'kʌləd] *a.* ①单色的, 一色的: ~ cloth 单色布,本色布 ②原色的,本色的: a ~ flower 单色花,原色花

self-command ['selfkə'mɑ:nd] *n.* 自制

self-conscious ['self'kɔnʃəs] *a.* ①自觉的; 自我意识的: He is keenly ~ about his responsibility. 他强烈地意识到自己的责任。/ ~ instinct 【心】自觉的本能 ②不自然的; 忸怩的, 害羞的 ‖**~ly** *ad.* / **~ness** *n.*

self-contained ['selfkən'teind] *a.* ①沉默寡言的; 有自制力的; 不易冲动的 ②整套装在一起(并带有动力设备)的: a small ~ iron and steel complex 配套的小型钢铁联合企业 ③设备齐全的; (厨房、浴间等)独用的, 单门出入的 ④(社会团体等)自给自足的; 独立的 ‖**~ly** *ad.* / **~ness**,

self-determination ['selfdi,tə:mi'neiʃən] *n.* ①自决, 自主; 民族自决: the right of national ~ 民族自决权 ②【哲】(强调自由意志的)自我决定

self-evident ['self'evidənt] *a.* 自明的, 不需证明的, 不言而喻的

self-made ['self'meid] *a.* ①自己做的; 独自搞的 ②靠个人奋斗而成功的, 白手起家的

self-possessed ['selfpə'zest] *a.* 有自制力的; 沉着的, 冷静的, 镇定的 ‖**~ly** ['selfpə'zesidli] *ad.*

self-possession ['selfpə'zeʃən] *n.* 自制; 沉着, 冷静, 镇定

self-preservation ['self,prezə(:)'veiʃən] *n.* 自我保存; 自卫本能

self-reliance ['self-ri'laiəns] *n.* 信赖自己; 依靠自己; 自力更生: We stand for ~. 我们是主张自力更生的。‖**self-reliant** *a.*

self-righteous ['self'raitʃəs] *a.* 自以为公正善良的; 自以为有道德的; 伪善的 ‖**~ly** *ad.* / **~ness** *n.*

self-sacrifice ['self'sækrifais] *n.* 自我牺牲 ‖**~r** *n.* 自我牺牲者

selfsame ['selfseim] *a.* 完全一样的, 同一的: They arrived on the ~ day. 他们就在那同一天到达。

self-seeking ['self'si:kiŋ] *n. & a.* 追求私利(的); 追求个人享乐(的)

self-service ['self'sə:vis] *n. & a.* 顾客自理(的); 无人售货(的)(指食品或商品由顾客自行选择,于离店时付款)

self-sufficient ['selfsə'fiʃənt] *a.* ①自给自足的 ②过于自信的; 傲慢的 ‖**self-sufficiency** *n.*

sell [sel] **I** (sold [sould]) **❶** *vt.* ①卖, 销售, 经售: ~ sb. sth. 把某物卖给某人 / ~ sth. at a bargain 廉价出售某物 / ~ goods by retail (wholesale) 零售(批发)货物 / ~ sth. by auction

拍卖某物 / This shop ~s a wide variety of goods. 这店经售各色货物。②出卖，背叛: ~ one's country 卖国 / ~ one's honour 出卖荣誉 ③ 使卖出，有助于销出(某物); 向(某人)推销: The good quality ~s our goods. 我们的货物因质量好而畅销。/ John invited the customer to dinner so that he could ~ him. 约翰请那顾客吃饭以便向他推销货物。④[口]宣传(某事物); 说服(某人), 使接受: ~ sb. on an idea (on a political party) 说服某人接受某一主意(某一政党的观点) ⑤[俚][常用被动语态]欺骗; 使失besides: I've been *sold*! 我被欺骗了! / *Sold* again! 又上了一次当! ❷ *vi.* ①卖, 销售; 有销路; 具有售价(*for, at*): ~ well 销路广 / an item that doesn't ~ 没有销路的货品 ②[口]被广泛接受: Do you think the idea will ~? 你认为这个意见会被广泛接受吗? Ⅱ *n.* ①[俚]欺骗 ②失望: What a ~! 真失望! ③卖; 推销术: hard ~ 硬行推销 ‖ ~ *like hot cakes* (或 *like wildfire*) 见 **cake** / ~ *off* 廉价出清(存货) / ~ *oneself* ①卖身; 出卖自己 ②[口]自我宣传; 自荐 / ~ *one's life dearly* 见 **life** / ~ *out* ①卖完; 出售货物: The new products were *sold out* in a few days. 新产品几天之内都卖完了。/ ~ *out* at a loss 亏本出售 ②[美俚]出卖, 背叛; 受贿 ③为清偿债务出卖(债务人)的货物 ④出卖(股票或商品)以抵偿欠款 ⑤[史]出卖军职而退役 / ~ *sb. a pup* 见 **pup**[1] / ~ *sb. down the river* 欺骗某人, 出卖某人 / ~ *short* ①卖空(指股票投机等) ②低估: make the mistake of ~*ing sb. short* 犯了低估某人的错误 / ~ *the pass* 见 **pass** / ~ *up* ①卖光 ②为偿债而变卖(某人的财产、货物等) ‖~**er** *n.* ①卖者, 销售者: a ~*ers' market* 对卖方有利的市面(指货少价高) ②行销货: a best ~*er* 畅销品 / ~**ing** *a.* 卖的, 出售的; 销路好的: the ~*ing price* 售价 / a ~*ing race* 赛后拍卖胜马的跑马比赛 / the ~*ing point* (某商品)在推销时被大肆宣扬的特色 ‖'~**-off** *n.* 证券的跌价 / '~**out** *n.* [口] ①背叛; 出卖 ②(商品的)售缺 ③票子全部售完的演出(或比赛等), 客满的演出

selvage ['selvidʒ] *n.* ①【纺】织边, 布边 ②(纸等准备切去的)边 ③边缘 ④【地】断层泥 ⑤锁孔板 ‖~**d** *a.*

semaphore ['seməfɔ:] Ⅰ *n.* ① (铁路的)臂板信号(机); 信号灯; 信号装置 ②旗语通信(法): ~ flags 手旗 Ⅱ ❶ *vi.* 打信号; 打旗语 ❷ *vt.* 打信号通知

semblance ['sembləns] *n.* ①外表, 外貌: in ~ 在外表上 / bear the ~ of an angel but have the heart of a devil 具有天使的外表和恶魔的心肠; 人面兽心 ②假装, 伪装: put on a ~ of anger 假装生气的样子 / under the ~ of 在…的幌子下 ③相似; 貌似物: have no ~ of truth 没有一点真实性

semester [si'mestə] *n.* ①半年 ②(美、德等国学校的)学期, 半学年

semicolon ['semi'koulən] *n.* 分号(即 ;)

semidetached ['semidi'tætʃt] *a.* (房屋)一侧与他屋相连的, 半独立的

semifinal ['semi'fainl] *n. & a.* 【体】半决赛(的) ‖~**ist** ['semi'fainəlist] *n.* 参加半决赛的选手

seminar ['seminɑ:] *n.* ①(大学的)研究班 ②研究班课程; 研究班讨论会; 讨论室 ③[美]专家讨论会; 讨论会

seminary ['seminəri] *n.* ①发源地; 温床: a ~ of vice and crime 罪恶的渊薮 ②高等中学; 学院(尤指私立女子学校或学院) ③ 神学院 ④(大学的)研究班 ‖**seminarist** *n.* 神学院学生

senate ['senit] *n.* [S-] (美、法等的)参议院, 上院: the U. S. *Senate* Appropriations Committee 美国参议院拨款委员会 / a U. S. *Senate* subcommittee 美国参议院的一个小组委员会 ②参议院会议厅 ③(剑桥大学等的)评议会 ④(古罗马的)元老院 ⑤ 立法机构; 立法机构全体成员; 立法程序

senator ['senətə] *n.* ①参议员, 上议员 ②(大学)评议员 ③(古罗马的)元老院议员 ‖~**ship** *n.* 参议员(或评议员等)的职位(或任期)

senatorial [,senə'tɔ:riəl] *a.* ①参议院的; 参议员的: the ~ office 参议员的职位 ②由参议员组成的 ③(选区)有权利选举参议员的 ④元老院的; 元老院议员的 ⑤(大学)评议会的 ‖~ **courtesy** [美]参议院的礼貌否决(指当总统对某州官员的任命受到该州执政党参议员反对时, 参议院为对这些参议员表示礼貌起见对总统任命不予认可) / ~ **district** 参议员选举区

send[1] [send] (sent [sent]) ❶ *vt.* ①送; 寄发: a message 送个信, 捎信 / ~ sb. a telegram 给某人发个电报 ②派遣; 打发: ~ a delegation to the UN 派代表团到联合国去 ③发射(子弹、球、箭等); 放出(光、声等): ~ a blow straight to sb.'s chin 对准某人下巴一击 ④使变成; 使陷入, 使处于: ~ sb. mad 使某人发疯 ⑤(旧时指神、上帝)赏赐; 施; 降: God ~ it may not be so! 但愿不是这样! / whatever fate may ~ 不管命运怎样摆布 ⑥[俚]使兴奋; 使心荡神驰 ❷ *vi.* ①寄信, 送信; 派人: If you want me, please ~. 如果你需要我, 请捎个信来。②播送 ‖~ *along* 发送; 派遣: We'll ~ the goods *along* immediately. 我们将立即把货发出去。/ ~ *away* ①派遣; 发送; 把…送往远处 ②驱逐; 解雇 / ~ *back* 退还, 送还 / ~ *down* ①[英](大学)勒令…停学, 开除 ②把…向下发送; 使(温度、价格等)下降 / ~ *flying* 见 **fly**[1] / ~ *for* 派人去叫, 召唤; 遣人去拿: Send *for* the doctor, please. 请叫医生来。/ ~ *forth* 发出, 放出(光、热等); 长出(树叶等): ~ *forth* a loud cry 大叫一声 / ~ *forth* new leaves 长出新叶 / ~ *in* 呈报; 递送; 递(名片等); 送…参加比赛: ~ *in* an application 呈递申请书 / ~ *in* dinner 送上饭菜 / The coach *sent* two players *in*. 教练员送两名球员上场参加比赛。/ ~ *in one's jacket* 见 **jacket** / ~ *in one's papers* 见 **paper** / ~

off ①寄出，发出；派遣: ～ the packages *off* 寄出邮包 ②解雇 ③给…送行 / ～ **on** ①预送: He had his baggage *sent on* ahead. 他已把他的行李先送走了。 ②转送 / ～ **out** ②派遣 ②放出；长出(树叶等) / ～ **over** 发送，运送 / ～ **round** ①使传阅 ②发送;派遣 / ～ **sb.** **about** **his business** 见 **business** / ～ **sb.** **packing** 见 **pack**¹ / ～ **to the right-about** ①使溃退 ②驱逐，撵走 / ～ **up** ①发出;射出: ～ *up* a rocket 发射火箭 ②把(报告、议案等)上送，呈递; 使(价格、温度等)上升 ③[口]把…送进监狱 ④[英俚](通过模仿对方作品的风格等)使显得滑稽可笑 ‖～**er** **n.** ①发送者; 送信人: the ～*er* of a telegraph 发报人 ②【讯】发射机,发信机;发送器；(天线)引向器;记发器;(电报的)电键 ③[美俚]善奏留声机音乐的人 ‖～'**off** **n.** ①[口]送行,欢送: be given a warm ～-*off* 被热烈欢送 ②(在事业开始时的)鼓励；赞扬性的书评 ③[美俚]送葬,葬礼 / '～**out** **n.** 送出量，输出量: the daily ～*out* of gas 煤气每天输出量 / '～**up** **n.** [英俚](假装严肃的)讽刺性模仿

send² [send] **I** **n.** 波浪的推进力；船受浪推动时的向上抬起 **II** **vi.** (船)被波浪抬起

senile ['si:nail] **a.** ①老年的；衰老的；年老所致的: I may be senescent,but I'm not yet ～. 我可能有点显老了,但还没有老得不中用。 / ～ dementia 老年痴呆 / ～ decay 年老体衰 ②【地】老年期的: ～ river 老年河

senility [si'niliti] **n.** 衰老; 老迈; 老态龙钟

senior ['si:njə] **I** **a.** ①年长的,年纪较大的(常略作 Sen. 或 Sr.，加在姓名后);已届退休年龄的: He is three years ～ to me. 他比我大三岁。/ John Smith, *Senior* 老约翰·史密斯(父子同名时对父亲的称呼) / Smith, *Senior* 大史密斯(一个集体中有两人同姓时,对较年长者的称呼) / a ～ citizen 已届退休年龄的公民 ②地位(或级别)较高的;资格较老的;资历较深的: a ～ high school [美]高级中学 / a ～ officer 高级军官 / a ～ member of a committee 资历较深的委员 / the ～ partner in a firm 商行的主要合伙人；大股东 ③[英](大学)高年级的; [美](大学)四年级的; (中学)最高年级的: a ～ man [英](大学一年级以上)高年级生 / the ～ class [美](大学)四年级; (中学)最高年级 ④(债券、股票对企业财产、红利而言)有优先权的: a ～ security 有优先分红权利的证券； 优先股 **II** **n.** ①年长者 ②前辈，资历较深者；上级: He was my ～ by two years at the university. 他在大学时比我高两班。 ③[英](大学一年级以上的)高年级生； 评议员;[美](大学)四年级生;(中学)最高年级生 ‖*the* ～ *service* 见 **service**

seniority [ˌsi:ni'ɔriti] **n.** 年长;资历深；职位高: Should promotion go by ～ alone? 难道提升可以只根据资历吗? ‖～ **rule** [美]资历规定(指国会把在某委员会内任职最久的多数党议员任命为该委员会主席的规定)

sensation [sen'seiʃən] **n.** ①感觉，知觉: have (或 feel) a ～ of coldness (dizziness, happiness) 有寒冷(眩晕,快乐)的感觉 ②轰动，激动；轰动一时的事件(或人物、新闻): The new invention has created a great ～. 这项新发明引起了很大的轰动。/ a three days' ～ 一时的轰动 / a literary ～ 轰动文坛的作品

sensational [sen'seiʃənl] **a.** ①感觉的 ②轰动的,耸人听闻的, 激起情感的: a ～ news report 耸人听闻的新闻报道 ③非常的,巨大的,惊人的: a ～ victory 巨大的胜利 ‖～**ism** **n.** ①(新闻报道中)耸人听闻的手法(或题材);危言耸听 ②[哲]感觉论 / ～**ist** **n.** ①爱采用耸人听闻手法的人 ②感觉论者 / ～**ize** **vt.** 使引起轰动; 耸人听闻地报道(或描绘) / ～**ly** **ad.**

sense [sens] **I** **n.** ①感官; 官能: the ～ of sight (hearing, smell, taste, touch) 视 (听, 嗅, 味, 触)觉 (统称 the five ～*s* 五种官能) / the sixth ～ 第六官能, 运动觉；直觉 / the pleasures of ～*s* 感官上的享受 / have a keen political ～ of smell 具有敏锐的政治嗅觉 ②感觉;辨别力;观念;意识: a ～ of warmth (hunger, pain, pleasure) 温暖(饥饿, 疼痛, 快乐)的感觉 / a ～ of locality 对方位的辨别力 / a ～ of humour (beauty) 幽默(审美)感 / a good language (musical) ～ 良好的语言(音乐)感 / be lost to all ～ of shame 全无羞耻心; 不识人间有羞耻事 ③见识；情理, 道理: common ～ 普通的见识; 常识 / a man of ～ 通情达理的人 / There is some ～ in what he says. 他所说的话有些道理。/ What is the ～ of doing that? 干那件事有什么道理呢? / There's no ～ in going. 去是没有什么意思的。/ Haven't you ～ enough to ask somebody else to help you? 你难道还不知道可以请别人帮一下忙吗? ④[复]神觉; 理智, 理性: lose (recover) one's ～*s* 失去(恢复)知觉; 丧失(恢复)理智 / bring sb. to his ～*s* 使某人觉醒过来 ⑤意义, 意思 ⑥公众意见(或情绪): take the ～ of a meeting 了解与会者的总的意见 ⑦方向, 指向: the ～ of rotation 旋转方向 / a ～ indicator (飞机上的)航向指示器 **II** **vt.** ①感觉, 觉察, 意识到: ～ danger 意识到有危险 ②了解, 领悟: I did not ～ his meaning. 我没有领会他的意思。③【自】自动检测 ‖**come to one's** ～*s* ①(昏迷后)苏醒过来: She soon *came to her* ～*s* after a blood transfusion. 输血后她很快就苏醒过来。②醒悟过来: We hope he'll *come to his* ～*s* and correct his mistakes. 我们希望他能觉悟过来, 改正错误。/ **have more** ～ **than to** (或 **have too much** ～ **to**) 聪明得不至于: You should have *had more* ～ *than to* do such a foolish thing. 你本应当更有头脑而不至于干出这种蠢事的。/ **in all** ～*s* 在任何意义上说 / **in a** ～ 在某种意义上说: What you say is *in a* ～ true. 你所说的话, 在某种意义上说是正确的。/ **in every** ～ (**of the word**) 在各种意义上说: It's a lie *in every* ～ *of the word*. 这是不折不扣的谎

话。/ *in no* ~ 决不 / *in one's* (*right*) ~*s* 有
理性;神志清醒 / *in the proper* (*strict, literal,
figurative*) ~ 在本来(严格,字面,比喻)的意义
上说 / *make* ~ 讲得通;有意义: This sentence
doesn't *make* ~. 这句子毫无意义。/ *make* ~
of 弄懂…的意思: Can you *make* ~ *of* this
telegram? 你弄得懂这电报的意思吗? / *out of
one's* ~*s* 失去理性,精神错乱: frighten sb. *out
of his* ~*s* 把某人吓得魂不附体 / *stand to* ~
[口]通情达理 / *take leave of one's* ~*s* 见
leave[2] / *talk* (或 *speak*) ~ 说话有道理 ‖ ~ **cell**
感觉细胞 / ~ **datum** 【心】感觉资料 / ~ **finder**
【无】单值无线电测向器 / ~ **impression** 感觉印
象 / ~ **organ** 感觉器官 / ~ **perception** 感觉,
感官知觉,感性知觉

senseless ['senslis] *a.* ①无知觉的,无感觉的: fall
~ to the ground 昏倒在地 / knock sb. ~ 把某
人打得昏过去 ②愚蠢的;无意义的: a ~ person
糊涂人 / a ~ action (proposal) 无意义的行动
(建议) ‖ ~**ly** *ad.* / ~**ness** *n.*

sensibility [,sensi'biliti] *n.* ①感觉(力): tactile ~
触觉 ②敏感性;感受性: ~ *to* pain (praise) 对
疼痛(别人的赞扬)的敏感 / the ~ of an artist
艺术家的敏感性 ③[常用复]情感: sense and
理智和情感 / a man of strong *sensibilities* 有强
烈情感的人 / expose mistakes without sparing
anyone's *sensibilities* 不讲情面地揭发错误 ④(诗
歌的)感伤情调

sensible ['sensəbl] I *a.* ①感觉得到的,可觉察的;
明显的: no ~ difference 没有多大区别 / a ~
error 明显的差错 ②知道的,觉察的: I am ~ *of*
your kindness. 我知道你的好意。③明白事理
的,明智的: a ~ man 聪明人 / That was ~ *of*
you. 你做得明智。④(计划等)切合实际的;合理
的; 实用的: a ~ plan 切合实际的计划 / ~
clothing 实用的衣服 ⑤[古]易感的,敏感的 II *n.*
感觉得到的东西 ‖ ~**ness** *n.* / **sensibly** *ad.*

sensitive ['sensitiv] *a.* ①敏感的; 容易感受的: a
~ skin 容易受伤的皮肤;敏感的皮肤 / a ~
market 行情易起波动的市场 / His ears are
highly ~ *to* any unusual sound in the machine.
他的耳朵对机器中任何不正常的声音十分敏感。
②神经过敏的;容易生气的;(由于某种疾病而)过
敏的: be ~ *to* ridicule 对别人的嘲笑容易生气/
be ~ *about* one's appearance 过分注意外表 /
Asthmatic patients are especially ~ *to* odour.
气喘病人对气味特别过敏。③灵敏的、感光的:
~ *to* light 对光的变化灵敏的 / ~ weighing
scales 灵敏度高的天平 / ~ paper (照相用的)感
光纸 ④高度机密的;极为微妙的 ⑤[罕]感觉的,
感官的;传导感觉的 ‖ ~**ly** *ad.* / ~**ness** *n.* ‖ ~
plant 【植】含羞草

sensitivity [,sensi'tiviti] *n.* ①敏感(性);感受性;
灵敏性;过敏 ②灵敏度: a microphone's ~ 传
声器的灵敏度 / light ~ 感光敏度,光敏度

sensitize ['sensitaiz] ❶ *vt.* ①使敏感: ~ sb. *to*
sth. 使某人对事物有所觉察(或感觉起来)

②【物】使敏化(尤指使胶片等具有感光能力)
❷ *vi.* 变敏感;【物】敏化 ‖ **sensitization** [,sensitai-
'zeifən] *n.* 【物】敏化(作用),【医】敏感(作用),感受
(作用) / ~**r** *n.* 【物】敏化剂;【医】激敏物

sensory ['sensəri] *a.* 感觉的;传递感觉的: a ~
nerve 感觉神经

sensual ['sensjuəl] *a.* ①肉体方面的; 耽于声色口
腹之乐的;肉欲的 ②肉感的,色情的,淫荡的 ③世
俗的 ④感觉的 ⑤【哲】感觉论的 ‖ ~**ism** *n.* 耽
于声色;肉欲主义;【哲】感觉论 / ~**ist** *n.* 耽于
声色的人; 肉欲主义者;【哲】感觉论者 / ~**ity**
[,sensju'æliti] *n.* 耽于声色; 好色,淫荡 / ~**ly**
ad.

sensuous ['sensjuəs] *a.* ①感官方面的;感觉上的
②激发美感的,给人以美的享受的: a ~ painting
引起美感的绘画 / a ~ poet 给人以美的享受的
诗人

sentence ['sentəns] I *n.* ①【律】判决,宣判; 课刑:
pass ~ *on* (或 *upon*) sb. 判某人刑 / under ~
of death 被判处死刑 / serve a ~ of five years
服五年徒刑 ②【语】句子: a simple (compound,
complex) ~ 简单(并立,复合)句 / the ~ stress
(或 accent) 句重音 ③[古]结论意见; 警句,格言
④[音]乐句 ⑤【逻】命题 II *vt.* 宣判,判决;使
遭受: be ~*d* to six years' imprisonment 被判
处六年徒刑

sententious [sen'tenfəs] *a.* ①(说话、文体)简洁
的;多格言警句的 ②好用格言警句的;故作庄重
的;说教式的 ‖ ~**ly** *ad.* / ~**ness** *n.*

sentient ['senfənt] *a.* 有知觉能力的;有感觉的,有
知觉的 ‖ ~**ly** *ad.*

sentiment ['sentimənt] *n.* ①思想感情; 情操 ②感
情;(文艺作品等的)情趣: be full of ~ 充满感情/
express friendly ~*s* 表示友好感情 ③情绪: a
rising ~ against sth. 不断增涨的反对某一事物
的情绪 / have hostile ~*s* towards sb. 对某人有
敌意 ④意见;观点: share sb.'s ~*s on* this problem 在这个问题上与某人有同样的看法 / public
~ 舆论;民情 ⑤[贬]柔情,感伤;多愁善感
⑥祝词; 感想: conclude one's speech with a ~
用祝词结束演说 / call upon sb. for a song or a
~ 要求某人唱支歌或发表感想 ‖ *Them's my*
~*s.* [谑]这就是我的看法。

sentimental [,senti'mentl] *a.* ①感伤的: a ~
novel 感伤小说 / strike a ~ note (演说等时)
发出感伤的调子 ②多愁善感的;易动情的;感
情用事的: a ~ person 多愁善感的人 ③情感
(上)的: for ~ reasons 出于情感上的缘故
‖ ~**ism** *n.* 感伤主义 / ~**ist** *n.* 感伤主义者 /
~**ly** *ad.*

sentimentality [,sentimen'tæliti] *n.* 感伤;多愁
善感,感情脆弱

sentinel ['sentinl] I *n.* 哨兵; 步哨; 卫兵; 看守:
post a ~ 设岗哨; 设看守 II (sentinel(l)ed;
sentinel(l)ing) *vt.* ①警戒;守卫 ②设岗哨于 ‖ *stand*
~ 站岗,放哨

sentry ['sentri] **I** *n.* ①卫兵; 步哨: a ～ squad 警卫班 / be on ～ 站岗; 执行步哨勤务 / come off ～ 下岗 / relieve a ～ 换哨 / stand ～ 站岗, 放哨 ②看守, 警卫; keep ～ 警戒 **II** ❶ *vt.* 设岗哨于: be heavily *sentried* 布满岗哨 ❷ *vi.* 站岗, 放哨 ‖～ **box** 岗亭 / ～ **go** ①换哨命令 ②步哨勤务

separable ['sepərəbl] *a.* 可分离的; 可分隔的; 可分开的; 可区分的 ‖～**ness** *n.* / **separably** *ad.*

separate ['sepərit] **I** *a.* ①分离的; 分隔的; 不相连的: Cut it into three ～ parts. 把它切成三份。/ live ～ 分居 / ～ maintenance 丈夫给妻子的分居瞻养费 ②各别的; 单独的; 独立的: the ～ parts of the body 身体的各个部分 / I want a ～ room. 我要一个独用房间。/ a ～ battalion 【军】独立营 / ～ estate 【律】属于妻子的不受丈夫支配的财产 ③[古]孤独的 ④脱离肉体的, 灵魂的 **II** *n.* ①(杂志、文章等的)单行本, 抽印本 ②[复]妇女不配套穿的衣服 **III** ['sepəreit] ❶ *vt.* ①使分离, 使分开; 使分散; 把…分类: Theory should by no means be ～d from practice. 理论绝不应该脱离实际。/ England is ～d from France by the Channel. 英法两国由英吉利海峡隔开。/ ～ sth. into several portions 把某物分成几份 / ～d cottages at the foot of the mountain 分散在山脚下的农舍 / ～ mail 把邮件分类 ②区分; 识别: It is not difficult to ～ a butterfly from a moth. 区别蝴蝶和蛾并不难。③使分居; 使脱离关系; 使解除契约; 使退役: be ～d from the army 从军队中退役 / 使离析; 从…中提取: ～ metal from ore 从矿石中分离出金属 / ～ cream out of milk 从牛奶中提取奶油 ❷ *vi.* ①分离, 开; 脱离; 分手, 分散: We did not ～ until two o'clock. 我们直到两点钟才分手。②分居 ③离析, 析出 ‖～**ly** *ad.* / ～**ness** *n.*

separation [,sepə'reiʃən] *n.* ①分离, 分开; 分类 ②分隔物; 分隔点; 间隔: ～ cloth 【海】(装货的)隔票垫料 ③(夫妇)分居; 脱离: judicial ～ 法院判定的夫妇分居 / ～ allowance (战时士兵按期给予妻子并由政府补贴的)分居津贴 / ～ from military service 脱离军队, 退役 / a ～ centre 【军】复员转业中心 ④离析: ～ coal 精选煤 ⑤【电】(导线的)间距, 间隙: contact ～ 接点间隙 ‖～**ist** *n.* 主张脱离(或分裂)者

sepia ['si:pjə] **I** *n.* ①[S-]【动】乌贼属 ②乌贼的墨汁; 乌贼墨色 ③乌贼墨颜料: a ～ drawing 乌贼墨画 ④深棕色的照片(或印刷品) **II** *a.* ①乌贼墨的 ②深棕色的

September [səp'tembə] *n.* 九月(略作 Sep. 或 Sept.)

septic ['septik] **I** *a.* ①引起腐烂的; 腐败性的 ②【医】脓毒性的; 败血病的: ～ disease 脓毒性病; 败血性病 / ～ infection 败血病; 败血性感染病 / ～ intoxication 腐血症; 腐败质中毒 **II** *n.* 腐烂物; 腐败剂 ‖～ **tank** 化粪池

septuagenarian [,septjuədʒi'nɛəriən], **septuagenary** [,septjuə'dʒi:nəri] *a. & n.* 七十至七十九岁的(人)

sepulchral [si'pʌlkrəl] *a.* ①坟墓的; 埋葬的: a ～ stone 墓石 / ～ customs 丧葬的风俗 ②坟墓似的; 令人想到埋葬的; 阴森森的; 阴沉忧郁的: a ～ look 阴森森的脸色 / a ～ voice 阴沉的声音 ‖～**ly** *ad.*

sepulchre, sepulcher ['sepəlkə] **I** *n.* ①坟墓; 石墓; 墓穴 ②圣物置放处 **II** *vt.* 埋葬 ‖*a whited* ～ 伪君子, 伪善者 / *the Holy Sepulchre* 【宗】耶稣的墓, 圣墓

sequel ['si:kwəl] *n.* ①继续; 继之而来的事 ②(文艺作品的)续集, 续编: the ～ *of* a novel 小说的续集 ③后果; 结局; 余波: the ～ *of* (或 *to*) an event 事件的后果 / The ～ of the film is a happy reunion. 影片的结局是大团圆。④[罕]推论 ‖*in the* ～ 后来; 结果: win *in the* ～ 结果获胜

sequence ['si:kwəns] **I** *n.* ①连续; 继续; 一连串: a ～ of bumper harvests 连续的大丰收 / The enemy are suffering heavy defeats in rapid ～. 敌人接二连三地遭到惨败。②次序; 顺序; 先后; 关联: the ～ of events 事情发生的先后次序 / the ～ of attacks 【军】攻击次序 / in historical (alphabetical) ～ 按历史(字母)顺序 / ～ in the process of cognition 认识过程的先后 / the ～ of tenses 【语】时态的呼应 ③相关联的一组; (同一主题的)组诗; (牌戏中的)同花顺子 ④【音】用不同音调反复演奏一组乐句; 【天主教】宣讲福音前唱的圣歌 ⑤【数】序列; 【无】指令序列, 定序 ⑥后果; 结果 ⑦(电影中表现同一主题的)连续的镜头(或场景); 片断; 插曲 **II** *vt.* 把…按顺序排好 ‖～**r** *n.* 【无】序列发生器, 定序器; 程序装置

sequester [si'kwestə] *vt.* ①使隔绝; 使分离; 使隐退: ～ oneself from society (或 the world) 与世隔绝; 退隐 ②【律】扣押(债务人的地产等); 把(有争议财产)交第三者保管 ③没收; 查封 ‖～**ed** *a.*

seraglio [se'rɑ:liou] *n.* ①闺房(尤指伊斯兰教徒妻妾的) ②【史】(土耳其)宫殿(包括政府机关在内)

seraph ['serəf] ([复] seraphs 或 seraphim ['serəfim]) *n.* ① 六翼天使(相传为最高天使) ② 天使般的人

serenade [,seri'neid] **I** *n.* ①【音】小夜曲 ②月下情歌 **II** ❶ *vt.* 对…唱(或奏)小夜曲 ❷ *vi.* 唱(或奏)小夜曲 ‖～**r** *n.* 唱(或奏)小夜曲的人

serene [si'ri:n] **I** *a.* ①安详的: a ～ look (smile) 安详的神情(微笑) ②晴朗的; 明朗的; 无云的: ～ weather 晴朗的天气 ③平静的; 宁静的: a ～ lake 平静的湖 / a ～ life 宁静的生活 ④ [S-]尊贵的(用于对欧洲某些皇室的称呼): His *Serene* Highness 尊贵的殿下(间接提及时用) **II** *n.* (天空等的)晴朗; (水面等的)平静 **III** *vt.* [诗]使(天空等)明朗; 使平静 ‖*All* ～. [英俚]一切安然无恙。‖～**ly** *ad.*

serenity [si'reniti] *n.* ①安详 ②晴朗；明朗 ③平静；宁静 ④ [S-] 尊贵的殿下(对欧洲某些皇室的尊称)：Your (或 His) *Serenity* 尊贵的殿下(直接称呼时用 your, 间接提及时用 his)

serf [sə:f] *n.* ①农奴：a ~ owner 农奴主 ②受压迫者；做苦工的人 ‖~**age** ['sə:fidʒ] 农奴地位；农奴境遇 / ~**dom** ①农奴制 ②农奴地位，农奴境遇；奴役 / ~**hood** *n.* ①[总称]农奴 ②=~-age

serge [sə:dʒ] *n.* 哔叽 ‖~ **canvas** 小方块纹哔叽 / ~ **cloth** (背面起毛的)哔叽呢

sergeant ['sɑ:dʒənt] *n.* ①【军】军士；(英)陆军(或空军、海军陆战队)中士；(美)陆军(或海军陆战队)中士：a staff ~ (英)陆军上士；(美)空军参谋军士 / a technical ~ (美)空军(或海军陆战队)技术军士 / a *Sergeant* First Class (美)陆军上士 / a master ~ (美)陆军(或空军、海军陆战队)军士长 / a flight ~ (英)空军上士 / a colour ~ (英)海军陆战队上士 / a aviator 军士级航空员 ②警官，巡佐：the ~ of the guard 警卫班长 ③(担任礼仪或维持议会、法庭等处秩序的)警卫官 ④【英史】(在皇家法庭具有特权的)高级律师 (=~-at-law) ‖~**fish**【动】军曹鱼 / ~ **major**【军】军士长

serial ['siəriəl] **I** *a.* ①连续的；一连串的；一系列的：~ numbers 连着顺序的号码 / put sth. into ~ production 把某物投入成批生产 ②分期刊载的；连载的：a ~ story 连载故事 ③分期偿还的：~ bonds 分期偿还的债券 **II** *n.* ①连载小说(或图画等)；连本影片；连本电视节目 ②(分期连载作品的)一个部分 ③期刊 ④【军】行军梯队 ‖~**ly** *ad.* / ~ **number** ①【军】军号，入伍编号 ②(装备、人员、文电等的)编号 / ~ **rights** 连续刊载的版权

series ['siəri:z] [单复同] *n.* ①连续；系列：a ~ of good harvests 连年的丰收 ②(邮票)套；辑；组：the first ~ 第一辑 / a ~ of targets【军】目标组 ③【化】系，系列(根据一定规则系统排列的一连串化合物)：~ of compounds 化合物系 / ~ notation 系列标志 ④【地】统,(岩系的)段 ⑤【数】级数：~ expansion 级数展开 / geometrical ~ 等比级数,几何级数 / arithmetical ~ 等差级数,算术级数 ⑥【电】串联：~ circuit 串联电路 / machine 串行计算机 / ~ winding 串激绕组,串联绕组 ⑦ 交替的一组元音字母(如 *sing, sang, sung* 中的 *i, a, u*) ⑧【动】列,组 ‖*in* ~ ①连续地；按顺序排列 ②【电】串联

serious ['siəriəs] *a.* ①严肃的,庄重的：look ~ 表情严肃 / a ~ young man 一个持重的年轻人 ②认真的；不是开玩笑的,当真的：and now to be ~ [用作插入语]现在谈正经的 ③重要的；须认真对待的：a ~ task 重要的任务 ④严重的；危急的；令人担心的：The state of affairs is very ~. 情况十分严重。/ a ~ warning 严重警告 / a ~ illness 重病 / a ~ accident 严重的事故 / I hope it's nothing ~. 我希望情况不严重。⑤[古]宗教的,伦理学的；[谑]虔诚的 ⑥热中的,极感兴趣的：a ~ chess player 热中下棋的人 ‖~**ly** *ad.* 严肃地；认真地；严重地：deal with sth. ~**ly** 认真对待某事 / be ~**ly** ill 生重病 / ~**ness** *n.* 严肃；认真；严重性：point out *in all* ~*ness* that … 严正指出… ‖~-**'minded** *a.* 心情严肃的；认真的

sermon ['sə:mən] *n.* ①【宗】布道,讲道 ②训诫；喋喋不休的说教 ③(受自然界物启示而作的)道德上的反省：~*s* in stones 木石的启示 ‖~**ic** [sə:'mɔnik] *a.*

serpent ['sə:pənt] *n.* ①蛇(尤指大蛇或毒蛇) ②阴险毒辣的人 ③金蛇飞舞的烟火 ④ [the S-]【天】巨蛇座 ⑤古代木制蛇状吹奏乐器 ‖*the* (*old*) *Serpent* 撒旦,魔鬼 ‖~-**charmer** *n.* 要蛇的人 / '~'s-**tongue** *n.*【植】瓶尔小草属的一种

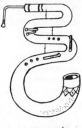

serpent

serpentine ['sə:pəntain] **I** *a.* ①蛇(状)的 ②蜿蜒的；迂回的；盘旋的,螺旋形的：the ~ course of the river 弯曲的河道 / ~ cooler【机】蛇管冷却器 ③阴险毒辣的,狡猾的 **II** *n.* ①蛇形物,蜿蜒的东西 ②【地】蛇纹岩 ③(溜冰的) S 形曲线 **III** *vi.* 蜿蜒 ‖~ **verse** 头尾词相同的诗句

serried ['serid] *a.* (行列、树木等)密集的,排紧的

serrulate(d) ['serjuleit(id)] *a.* 有细锯齿(边)的 ‖**serrulation** [ˌserju'leiʃən] *n.* 细锯齿状；细锯齿；成细锯齿形

serum ['siərəm] ([复] serums 或 sera ['siərə]) *n.*【医】浆液；血清 ‖~ **albumin** 血清白蛋白 / ~ **globulin** 血清球蛋白

servant ['sə:vənt] *n.* ①仆人,佣人,雇工：engage (keep) a ~ 雇(雇着)仆人 / an indoor ~ 室内仆佣(如厨子、女仆等) / an outdoor ~ 室外仆佣(如园丁、马夫等) ②公务员；雇员：a public ~ 公仆；政府官员 / a civil ~ 文职人员；公务员 / always be ~*s* of the people 永远做人民的勤务员 / Your obedient ~ [英]你的恭顺的仆人(公务信件末尾署名前的客套语) ③[美]奴仆 ④忠实的门徒(或信徒) ⑤有用的工具：make atomic energy a ~ of the people 使原子能为人民所用 / Fire and water may be good ~*s*, but bad masters. [谚]水火是忠仆,用之不慎成灾主。‖*the* ~ *of the* ~*s* 上帝的最低下的仆人(罗马教皇的自称) ‖~-**girl**, '~-**maid** *n.* 保姆,女仆

serve [sə:v] **I ❶** *vt.* ①为…服务;为…服役;为…尽责: ~ the people 为人民服务 / ~ one's country 为国尽力 ②做…的帮佣;给…干活 ③经历;度过: ~ time (或 a sentence) 服刑 / ~ one's apprenticeship 当学徒 ④招待(顾客等);端上,摆出(饭菜等): What may I ~ you *with*? (营业员对顾客用语)您要些什么? / Dinner is ~d. 饭已准备好了。/ This restaurant ~s nice food. 这家餐馆供应的饭菜不错。/ fish ~d up nearly cold 端上来时几乎已凉了的鱼 / ~ the soup 上汤 ⑤对…恭顺,尊崇 ⑥供应;分发: Our power station ~s the entire city. 我们这个电站供应全市的用电。/ ~ out ammunition 分发弹药 / ~ round rations 挨次发给食粮 ⑦符合;对…适用;对…有用 ⑧ 对待;对付: ~ sb. a trick 作弄某人 ⑨送交(传票等);向…送交(令状等): ~ a summons *on* sb. (或 ~ sb. *with* a summons)向某人送传票 ⑩ (网球等中)发(球),开(球);操作(火炮) ⑪(马等)与(雌性)交配 ⑫【海】卷缠(绳索等) **❷** *vi.* ①服务;服役 ②帮佣 ③招待,侍应;上菜,斟酒(或其他饮料): ~ at table 做招待员;帮助上菜 / ~ in a department store 在百货商店做营业员 ④适合;适用;有用: when the tide ~s 当适于驶离港口的时候 / as occasion ~s 一有适宜的机会 / as a model 作为榜样 / This nail is too short to ~. 这个钉子太短了,不适用。/ The box will ~ *for* a seat. 这只箱子能当个座儿。/ A simple example will ~ to illustrate the point. 一个简单的例子就足以说明这一点。⑤发球,开球: ~ well (badly) 开球开得好(不好) ⑥(弥撒时)充当助祭者 **II** *n.* 发球,开球;轮到发球: Whose ~ is it? 该谁发球了? / a wrong ~ at tennis 网球发球出界 / win a game with powerful and accurate ~s 以有力而准确的发球赢得比赛 ‖*First come, first ~d.* 见 *first* / (*~ sb. out* (*for sth.*).)(为某事)向某人报复;使某人(因其所做之某事)受罚 / *sb. right* 给某人应得的报应: It ~s *him right.* 他活该! ‖**~r** *n.* ①服务员,侍者 ②送交者 ③发球人 ④ 弥撒时的助祭者 ⑤ 菜盘;托盘 / **~ry** ['sə:vəri] *n.* 餐室与厨房间放菜肴和餐具的小间

service ['sə:vis] **I** *n.* ①服务;帮助: perform new meritorious ~s 立新功 / You have done me a great ~. 你帮了我一个大忙。/ offer one's ~s 主动提供帮助 ②帮佣;服侍;招待;供应: 上菜,斟酒(或其他饮料): be *in* ~ 当佣人 / give good ~ 服务周到 / No ~ charge accepted. 不收服务费。③行政部门;服务机构;[总称]部门人员,机构人员: the civil ~ [总称]文职人员;(军队以外的全部)行政机构 / the consular ~ 领事馆;领事业务 / the secret ~ 特务机关;特务人员 / be in the diplomatic ~ 在外交部门工作 ④军种;勤务部队;服役,勤务: technical ~s 技术勤务兵 ⑤公共设施(尤指交通设施);公用事业: the public ~s 公用事业 / There is a bus ~ between the two cities. 两

城之间有公共汽车相通。⑥(厂商出售物品后给予顾客的)检修,维修,保养: send the car in for ~ every 2,000 kilometres 每行驶二千公里把汽车送厂检修一次 ⑦(全套)食器: a dinner (tea) ~ for twelve 供十二人用的一套餐(茶)具 ⑧发球;发球方式;轮到发球: a smash (twist) ~ 发叫(转)球 / another ~ (裁判员用语)重发(球) / Whose ~ is it? 该谁发球? ⑨(传票、命令等的)送达: personal ~ (传票等的)直接送达当事人 / ~ by substitution (或 substituted ~)代理送达(指传票等由别人代收) / ~ by publication 公示催告,公示送达 ⑩(仪式的)礼拜式;礼拜乐曲: a burial (marriage) ~ 葬(婚)礼 / attend morning ~ 参加早礼拜 ⑪(通过祈祷等)对上帝的尊崇 ⑫(马等的)交配 ⑬【海】(为防绳索擦损而进行的)卷缠;缠素材料(纱线、帆布或金属丝) **II** *vt.* ①检修,维修,保养;为…服务: ~ a typewriter 检修打字机 / have the car ~d regularly 定期把汽车送厂检修 / technicians for *servicing* the airstrips 保养简易机场的技术员 / an accounting department *servicing* the manufacturing and sales programmes 为生产和销售计划服务的会计部 ② 支付(国债等)的利息及提存偿债基金 ③(雄畜)与(母畜)交配 **III** *a.* ①武装部队的;服现役时用的: a ~ uniform 现役军服 ②服务性的;提供保养(或维修等)服务的: the ~ trades 服务性行业 / an all-night ~ store 通宵服务商店 ③仆人的;仆人用的: a ~ door 仆人用的门 ④适用的,耐用的;适于平时使用(或穿着)的 ‖*at sb.'s* ~ 听候某人吩咐;听凭某人使用: The typewriter is *at your* ~. 这台打字机归你使用。/ *be in sb.'s* ~ 在某人家帮佣 / *be of* ~ *to* 对…有用: Can I *be of* ~ *to* you? 我能帮你什么忙吗? / *do yeoman('s)* ~ (一旦有事时)给予有效的援助 / *enter (sb.'s)* ~ 去当(某人的)佣工 / *enter the* ~ 入伍 / *feudal* ~ 徭役 / (*give*) *my* ~ *to* 代我向…致意 / *go into* (或 *out to*) ~ 去当佣工 / *in active* ~ ①在服现役 ② 在职 / *long* ~ [英]长期服役的兵役制(如为期十二年等) / *On His* (或 *Her*) *Majesty's Service* [英]为英王(女王)陛下效劳(英国公函免付邮费的戳记)(常略作 O. H. M. S.) / *on* ~ =in active ~ / *pay lip* ~ *to* 对…口头上说得好听;对…口惠而实不至 / *press into* ~ (因急需而)暂用;要求…帮一下忙 / *see* ~ ①具有经验(尤指参加作战): He has *seen* ~ in the Northeast. 他曾在东北参加过战斗。② 使用很多而变旧: This coat has *seen* ~ 一件穿旧了的上衣 / *take sb. into one's* ~ 雇用某人 / *take* ~ *with* 在…处帮佣 / *take the* ~ 发球,开球 / *the senior* ~ [英]海军(与陆军相对而言) ‖**~ area** ①【无】(广播电台的)有效作用区 ②【军】勤务区域 / **~ book** 【宗】礼拜仪式书;祈祷书 / **~ calls** 集合号;上班号 / **ceiling** 【空】使用升限 / **~ club** ①同行福利俱乐部(常为全国性或国际性组织的一部分) ② 士兵俱乐部 / **~ depot** ①=~ station ②【军】

勤务兵科仓库 / ~ **dress** 军便服 / ~ **flat**
[英]供给伙食并有佣工服务的一套公寓房间 / ~
hatch [英]把菜从厨房送进餐室的小窗口 / ~
line 发球界线 / '~**man** *n.* ①军人·②维修人
员 / ~ **medal** 服役奖章 / ~ **module** (宇宙飞
船的)机械舱 / ~ **pipe** (由总管通入屋内的)给
水(或煤气)管 / ~ **rifle** 军用步枪 / ~ **road**
辅助道路,便道 / ~ **station** ①加油站 ②服务
站,修理站 / ~ **telegram** [讯]公电 / ~ **tree**
【植】花楸果

serviceable ['sə:visəbl] *a.* ①有用的;肯帮忙的: a
~ friend 有用的朋友 ②经用的,耐用的;适于
平时使用(或穿着)的: a pair of ~ shoes 一
双耐穿的鞋 ‖ **serviceability** [,sə:visə'biliti],
~**ness** *n.* / **serviceably** *ad.*

serviette [,sə:vi'et] *n.* [主英]餐巾

servile ['sə:vail; 美 'sə:vil] *a.* ①奴隶的;奴隶般的:
the ~ class 奴隶阶级 ②奴性的,奴态的;十足
依附的, 缺乏独立精神的 ③【语】本身不发音而
只表示其前的元音字母发长音的: The "e" in
"stone" is ~. "stone" 中的 e 不发音,而表明
其前的"o"发长音。④【语】词中表示派生(或词
形变化、语法关系)的部分的(如 reads, pupil's,
books 中的 s) ‖~**ly** *ad.* / ~**ness** *n.* ‖~ **works**
【宗】礼拜天(或主要教会节日)禁作的低下活

servility [sə: viliti] *n.* 奴态;奴性;卑从,屈从

servitude ['sə:vitju:d] *n.* ①奴隶状态;奴役 ②(作
为刑罚的)苦役,劳役: penal ~ 劳役监禁 ③【律】
地役权

sesame ['sesəmi] *n.* 【植】芝麻,脂麻: ~ seeds 芝麻
籽 / ~ oil 麻油, 香油 ‖*open* ~ 开门咒;秘诀;
关键(源出《一千零一夜》中一故事)

session ['se∫ən] *n.* ①会议;一届会议;会期: the
next ~ 下一届会议 / go into secret ~ 开秘
密会议 / have a long ~ 开长时间的会 / the
autumn ~ (英议会)秋季会期 ②开庭;开庭期;
[复]法庭: petty ~s [英]即决法庭 / the Court
of *Session* [英]苏格兰最高民事法庭 ③[美][苏
格兰]学期;[美]上课时间: the summer ~ 夏季
学期 / Some crowded schools have double ~s.
有些学生众多的学校每天分两批上课。④(从事
某项活动的)一段时间(或集会);[口]难捱的一阵
子: a recording ~ 一段录音的时间 / have quite
a ~ with sb. 和某人纠缠了一阵子 ⑤【商】(证
券交易等的)市,盘: the morning (afternoon) ~
上(下)午市, 前(后)市 ⑥基督教长老会的执行
理事会 ‖*in* ~ 在开会; 在开庭; 在上课: The
committee is *in* ~. 委员会正在开会。‖~**al** *a.*
开会的;会议的;开庭的;法庭的: the ~*al* programme 会议议程

set [set] **I** (set; setting) ❶ *vt.* ①放;竖立;使贴着
(to): ~ a pot on the fire 把锅放在火上 / ~ a
ladder against the wall 把梯子靠在墙上 / ~
flowers in a vase 把花插在花瓶里 / ~ a receiver
to the ear 把(电话)听筒放到耳边 / ~ pen *to*
paper 动笔,下笔

②安置,装置;安排: ~ the wheel on the axle 把
轮子装在轴上 / ~ a place for a guest (在餐桌
上)为客人安排位置 / ~ a lathe for screw
cutting 在车床上作车螺丝的准备 / ~ the table
for dinner 在桌上摆设餐具准备开饭

③配置, 布置(岗哨等): ~ sentries round the
camp 在营地周围布置哨兵 / ~ a watch 布置哨
兵(或看守人员等) / ~ the watch 【海】布置哨兵
值勤

④使就座;使就位(如赛跑等): ~ sb. on horseback
使某人骑在马上

⑤使(鸡)孵卵;使(卵)受孵

⑥种植: ~ seeds 下种 / ~ seedlings 植苗

⑦点燃;放(火): ~ a match (或 light) *to* a pile
of dead leaves 擦火柴点燃一堆枯树叶 / Forests
are sometimes ~ ablaze by lightning. 森林有
时因雷击而着火。

⑧签(字);盖(印);印上(痕记);写,记录: ~ one's
hand and seal *to* a document 在文件上签名盖
章 / The years have ~ their mark on his brow.
年岁在他的额上打下了印记。 / ~ *down* all the
items 记下所有的项目

⑨镶,嵌;点缀: ~ a diamond in (或 on) a ring
在戒指上嵌钻石 / ~ the top of a wall with
broken glass 在墙头上嵌碎玻璃 / The sky was
~ with myriads of stars. 无数星星点缀着
夜空。

⑩使朝向;使移动;运送(乘客等): ~ one's face
toward the sun 使脸朝太阳 / The rapid current
~ them northward. 急流把他们推向北去。 /
~ sb. ashore 使某人登岸 / ~ the ferry ~ them
across the river. 渡船把他们送到了对岸。

⑪倾注;使下决心: ~ one's heart *on* the common
good 一心为公 / ~ one's hope *on* becoming a
flyer 渴望成为飞行员 / ~ one's affections *on* sb.
(sth.) 热爱某人(某事) / Nothing in the world
is difficult for one who ~s his mind *to* it. 世上
无难事, 只怕有心人。

⑫使处于某种状态(或位置): This medicine
will ~ you right. 这药会把你的病治好。 / ~
sb.'s heart at rest (或 at ease) 使某人放心 /
~ the table in (或 on) a roar 使同桌的人大笑
起来 / ~ one's house in order 把屋子整理收拾
好;[喻]进行内部整顿 / ~ the machines in
motion 开动机器 / ~ sb. in the way 指点某人
路途 / ~ sb. on his way [古]陪某人走一段路,
送某人一段路 / ~ the bells a-ringing 使铃响起
来 / ~ the door ajar 把门半开着 / These
words ~ me thinking. 这些话引起我的深思。

⑬使(某人)做某事: ~ sb. *to* a task 使某人干某
项工作 / He ~ the boys *to* chop wood (或 *to*
woodchopping). 他叫男孩们去劈柴。 / *Set* a
thief *to* catch a thief. [谚]以贼捉贼。 (或: 以毒
攻毒。)

⑭使凝结, 使凝固; 使牢固; 使固定; 使(骨等)复
位; 使(头发)成波浪形: Cold ~s jellies. 冻胶因

冷而凝结。/ ～ a butterfly 把蝴蝶钉住作标本 / ～ a broken leg 接合断腿 / have one's hair ～ (妇女)把头发做成波浪形

⑮定(日期、限度、价格等);制定(规则等);颁布;估计;评价: 决定会议日期 / ～ the targets of production 定生产指标 / ～ the selling prices (terms of payment) 定售价(支付条件) / ～ a rule 制定规则 / ～ sb.'s promises at naught 把某人的诺言看得一文不值

⑯树立(榜样等);创造(纪录等): He has ～ us a good example in practising economy. 他在节约方面为我们树立了好榜样。/ ～ a new production record 创造新的生产纪录

⑰分配, 提出(任务), 指定(作业); 出(题目等): The new age has ～ new tasks for our literature and art. 新时代给我们的文学艺术提出了新的任务。/ The papers for an examination 出试题 / The teacher ～ the boys a problem. 老师给男孩们出了一个题目。

⑱调整, 校正(仪器等);拨准(钟表);锉(锯齿),调整(锯齿)的倾角;磨快,修平(剃刀等): ～ the camera lens for a long range shot 为拍摄远景调整照相镜头 / ～ the alarm clock 拨好闹钟 / a plough 调整犁头至待用位置 / ～ one's watch by the radio time signal 按无线电报时信号对表 / ～ a razor 修平剃刀刀锋

⑲排(铅字);为(原稿)排版: ～ (up) type 排铅字 / A few pages have been ～ up. 有几页版已排好。

⑳设(陷阱), 张(罗网);扬(帆);用(钩子)钩住鱼颚: ～ a trap for a mouse 放置捕鼠器 / ～ sail 起帆;[喻]开航

㉑为(诗、文等)谱曲;(为诗、文等)谱(曲);设置(布景、背景);为…布景;是…的背景: ～ words to music 为词谱曲 / ～ a piece of music for the violin 为小提琴编曲 / ～ the stage 为舞台布景 / The story is ～ in the early days of World War II. 这故事是以第二次世界大战初期为背景的。

㉒使(身体等)长好;使(性格)定型;使(果实)结成;使(面团)发酵: The peach trees failed to ～ fruit. 这些桃树没有结果子。

㉓(猎狗)蹲住以指示(猎物)的所在

㉔(桥牌中)打败(对方),使打不到(叫牌数)

❷ vi. ①(日、月等)落, 下沉: John thought that his star had ～. 约翰认为他的好运已过去了。

②凝结, 凝固;固定;定型;(颜色等)变牢固: This concrete ～s quickly. 这种混凝土凝结得很快。/ His face ～. 他的脸板起来了。/ His body has ～. 他的身体已发育好了。/ The dumplings ～ heavily on his stomach. 糊团使他腹胀。

③着手, 从事: He has ～ to learning English. 他已开始学习英语。

④(植物、花)结果; (果子)结成: The apples ～ well this year. 今年的苹果结得很好。

⑤(鸡)孵卵

⑥(风)吹;(潮水等)流;显出(或感到)某种倾向: The wind is setting from the east. 风从东方吹来。/ The current ～s to the east. 潮水向东流去。/ The tide has ～ in his favour. 舆论的倾向对他有利。

⑦(衣服等)合身;适合: The new dress ～s well. 新衣服很合身。/ His behaviour does not ～ well with his years. 他的行为和他的年龄不太相称。

⑧(骨)接合;(金属)永久变形

⑨(猎物)蹲住以指示猎物所在

⑩(方形舞中与舞伴)相对而舞

⑪[方]坐

II a. ①决心的, 一心一意的; 急切的: We are ～ on (或 upon) transforming the barren hills into well-cultivated land. 我们决心变荒山为良田。

②规定的, 指定的: ～ hours of study 规定的学习时间 / a ～ policy 既定的方针 / a ～ form 规定的格式

③故意的;预先准备的: do sth. of ～ purpose 故意地做某事 / a ～ speech 事先准备好的演讲

④不变的; 顽固的; (天气等)稳定的, 持久的: be ～ in one's ways 一成不变 / a man of ～ opinions 固执己见的人 / ～ rains 连绵不断的雨

⑤不动的, 固定的; 装好的: a ～ stare 凝视 / a ～ frown 皱紧的眉头 / a ～ scene 装定的布景

⑥习用的; 老一套的: a ～ phrase 固定词组, 成语

⑦准备停当的; (赛跑等中)作好预备姿势的; (棒球、板球中)稳住身体准备出击的: Ready, ～, go! (赛跑口令)各就各位, 预备, 跑!

⑧(两军)对阵的: a ～ battle 对阵战

⑨凝结的, 凝固的

III n. ①[只用单][诗][日]落: at ～ of sun 日落时

②(一)套, (一)副, (一)批, (一)部: a complete ～ of equipment 成套设备 / a bedroom ～ 一套卧室家具 / a ～ of rules 一套规章

③(网球等的)一盘

④(一批)同伙; 一群同伴: a literary ～ 一批爱好文艺的趣味相投者 / be not of one's ～ 不是自己一伙里的人 / a teen-age ～ 一批十几岁的青少年 / the fast ～ 不务正业之流

⑤[只用单]形状;身材; 姿势;(服装穿在身上的)样子: There was a stubborn ～ to his jaw. 他紧闭着嘴。(或: 他紧绷着下巴。)

⑥[只用单](风、水流等的)方向;倾向, 趋势;【心】定向: the ～ of the tide 潮水的方向; 潮流 / The ～ of opinion was toward building a new irrigation canal. 大家的意见倾向于修建一条新的灌溉渠。

⑦(液体等的)凝结, 凝固; (金属因受压等而形成的)永久变形: cold (hot) ～ 冷(热)凝固

⑧籽苗, 秧, 插枝;球茎: a ～ of a willow 供栽种的柳树插枝 / an onion ～ 洋葱球茎

⑨【无】接收机; 电子仪器; 装置, 设备;【数】集(合): a radio (receiving) ～ 收音机 / a TV ～

电视接收机 / a radar ~ 雷达装置 / a mains ~ 用交流电的收音机 ⑩锯齿的倾角;铅字宽度 ⑪成套扳子;成套冲头;(煤矿巷道中的)支架,棚子;(铺路用的)花岗石板;(墙壁上的)最后一道粉饰 ⑫(舞台、电影等的)布景 ⑬(土风舞、方形舞中跳舞者所列的)基本队形 ⑭卷做头发 ⑮一窝蛋: Ten out of the ~ of twelve were hatched. 一窝十二个蛋中孵出了十个。 ⑯[英](獾的)洞穴 ⑰猎狗蹲住以指示猎物所在的姿势 ||*a dead* ~ ①猎狗蹲住以指示猎物所在的姿势 ②(言词的)猛烈攻击;敌对态度: make *a dead* ~ at sb. 猛烈攻击某人 ③(为获得目的物所作的)坚定的努力(尤指女子竭力吸引合意对象的努力) / *be all* ~ 准备就绪: He *is all* ~ for an early morning start. 他已作好清晨出发的一切准备。 / *be dead* ~ (*on*) 坚决,决计: *be dead* ~ *on* having one's own way 一意孤行 / *be hard* ~ ①饿极 ②凝固 ③(蛋)已在孵化中 / ~ *about* ①开始,着手: ~ *about* a task 着手一项工作 / ~ *about* cultivating the wasteland 开始垦荒 ②散布(谣言等) ③[口]攻击 / ~ *against* ①使平衡,使补偿 ②把⋯和⋯对比 ③(使)和⋯对立,(使)反对: Public opinion is *setting against* this practice. 舆论是反对这种做法的。 / ~ *apart* 留出,拨出: ~ *apart* a sum for new equipment 留出一笔款项添置新设备 / ~ *aside* ①留出,拨出: ~ *aside* ample reserve grain 留出充足的储备粮 ②不顾,把⋯置于一旁;略去: ~ *aside* all objections 不顾一切反对 / ~ *aside* all formality 不拘形式 ③取消,驳回;宣布⋯无效: ~ *aside* a claim 驳回一项权利要求 / ~ *at* 袭击 / ~ *back* ①把(钟、表等)往回拨;阻碍;使受挫折: ~ *back* the clock 把时钟往回拨;[喻]倒行逆施 / ~ *back* the hands of the watch one hour 把表拨慢一小时 ②使(房屋等)缩进: The house is well ~ *back* from the street. 这房屋离街面有一段距离。 ③[美俚]使(人)花费: How much did it ~ you *back*? 这使你花多少钱? / ~ *before* 把⋯放在⋯面前; 把⋯放在⋯之先: the spirit of *setting* friendship *before* competition 友谊第一,比赛第二的精神 / ~ *books* 见 **book** / ~ *by* 把⋯搁开; 把⋯留作未来之用: The proposal was ~ *by* for further consideration. 这个提议留待进一步考虑。 / ~ ... *by the ears* 见 **ear**[1] / ~ *by the heels* 见 **heel**[1] / ~ *down* ①放下;使(乘客)下车; 使(飞机)着陆: ~ *down* a load 放下担子 / This bus will ~ you *down* at your destination. 这辆公共汽车会把你送到目的地。 ②记下,记入;登记,记载: It's all ~ *down* in the notebook. 全记在笔记簿上了。 / ~ it *down to* sb.'s account 把它记在某人的帐上 ③把⋯归于 ④把⋯看作;把⋯解释为: ~ sb. *down as* a knave 把某

人看作恶棍 ⑤制定(规则等) ⑥[口]申斥,责骂 ⑦(在游戏或比赛中)击败(对方) / ~ *eyes on* 见 **eye** / ~ *foot* 踏上(*on*),进入(*in*) / ~ *forth* ①阐明;宣布: ~ *forth* one's views 阐述自己的意见 ②陈列 ③出发,动身 / ~ *forward* ①促进 ②提出: The proposal he ~ *forward* is practicable. 他提出的建议是可行的。 ③把(钟、表等)拨快 ④出发 / ~ *going* 见 **going** / ~ *in* ①到来;开始: Spring has ~ *in* very early this year. 今年春季来得很早。 / The weather has ~ *in* rainy. 天气已变得阴雨连绵。 / go to the dentist before decay of the teeth ~s *in* 在牙齿开始腐烂前去看牙医生 ②(潮水)上涨;(水)向岸流;(风)向岸吹来: The tide is *setting in*. 开始涨潮了。 ③插入,嵌入;缝上: ~ *in* a sleeve of a dress 缝上衣服的袖子 ④将(船)驶向岸 / ~ *little* (或 *light*) *by* 轻视 / ~ *loose* 见 **loose** / ~ (*much, great, little, no*) *store by* 见 **store** / ~ *off* ①出发,动身: They ~ *off* for the North yesterday. 他们昨天北上了。 ②使爆炸;使爆发;引起;使(某人)开始(做某事) ③衬托,使更明显;点缀: The green leaves ~ *off* the red flower. 绿叶衬托红花。 ④抵销 ⑤分开,划分: ~ *off* a clause by a comma 用逗点把从句分开 ⑥(未干油墨)粘脏(另一印张) / ~ *on* ①攻击 ②前进;迎击 ③怂恿;唆使: ~ a dog *on* a person 唆使狗咬人(或追人) ④使开始,使着手 / ~ *oneself against* 坚决反对,坚决与⋯相对立 / ~ *oneself up as* 以⋯自居 / ~ *one's face against* 见 **face** / ~ *one's hand to the plough* 见 **hand** / ~ *out* ①出发;开始: Let's ~ *out* before six. 让我们在六点之前动身。 / ~ *out* to undertake technical innovations in a big way 开始大搞技术革新 ②装饰;陈列: The wall was ~ *out* with pictures. 墙上装饰着图画。 / They ~ *out* the pieces and began playing chess. 他们摆出棋子,开始下棋。 ③宣布,陈述,表明: He ~s *out* his ideas clearly in this article. 在这篇文章中他清楚地表明了自己的思想。 ④散栽;种植;移植: ~ *out* rice shoots 插秧 ⑤打算,企图: She could be very eloquent when she ~ *out* to be so. 她要真讲起来是很会讲的。 ⑥设计⋯的布局: ~ *out* a garden (city) 设计一个花园(城市)的布局 ⑦测定,标出(位置) ⑧(潮水)退出,向外流 ⑨把(砖石)砌出一点 ⑩[印]用完(架上铅字);排松(铅字) / ~ *over* ①置⋯于⋯上: a cupboard ~ *over* the fireplace 壁炉上面的一只碗橱 ②指派⋯管理;指定⋯为监督人: He was ~ *over* the workshop. 他被指定为车间的负责人。 ③让渡,移交 / ~ sb. (sth.) *on his* (*its*) *feet* 见 **foot** / ~ *the ax(e) to* 见 **ax(e)** / ~ *the ball rolling* 见 **ball** / ~ *the Thames on fire* [英]做出惊人的事来;成为杰出的人物 / ~ *to* ①开始认真干起来,大搞起来: The workers ~ *to* and repaired the bridge speedily. 工人们大干起来,很快把桥修

好了。②开始大吃: They were hungry and ~ *to* as soon as food was put on the table. 他们很饿，食物一上来就狼吞虎咽地吃起来了。③（人们、动物群等）打起来；争吵起来 / ~ *to work* (使)开始工作: On receiving the assignment, we immediately ~ *to work*. 一接到任务，我们立即开始了工作。/ ~ *up* ①竖立；升高；揭示: ~ *up* a tent 搭起帐篷 / ~ *up* a flag 升旗 / ~ *up* a notice 张贴布告 ②树立（榜样等）: ~ ·*up* an example 树立榜样 ③开办；设立；创立；建立: ~ *up* a shop 开店 / ~ *up* defences 设防 ④资助；使自立,(使)开始从事某种职业: His parents ~ him *up* as a carpenter. 他的父母使他从事木工的职业。/ He ~ *up* for himself as a grocer. 他开始经营杂货。⑤使掌权；使就位 ⑥提出: ~ *up* a new theory 提出新理论 ⑦大声发出: ~ *up* a protest 大声抗议 ⑧[常用被动语态]（充分）供给,准备: The students were well ~ *up* with books for the vacation. 假期内学生们有许多书可读。⑨使恢复健康；（经过锻炼）使体格壮健；【军】教练,锻炼: A few days' rest will ~ you *up*. 几天的休息将使你恢复健康。/ What a well ~ *up* young man! 多么壮健的小伙子! / ~ *up* recruits 训练新兵 ⑩使高兴,使得意；[口]使兴奋；使醉 ⑪引起；惹起(疾病等): The added sugar ~*s up* a fermentation. 加了糖引起发酵。⑫装置,装配: ~ *up* a printing press 装置印刷机 ⑬把…装制成标本 ⑭排(铅字);为(原稿)排版 ⑮策划 ⑯请客喝(酒)；款待; ~ *sb. up to* a meal 请某人吃饭 ⑰使紧固；绞紧(弦)以提高音调；拉紧(索具等) ⑱发挥作用,开始被使用 / ~ *up for* [口]自认为,自称为: He ~*s up for* a scholar. 他以学者自居。/ ~ *upon* 猛烈攻击,袭击
‖'~**back** *n.* ①挫折；失败；倒退；(疾病的)复发: Since that time there has never been any ~*back* in production. 从那时起生产上就一直没有倒退过。②逆流；涡流 ③【建】退进,收进 / '~**down** *n.* 申斥,辱骂 / '~-**fair** *a.* (天气)晴朗无变化的,晴定了的。 *n.* 镘平的灰泥面 / '~-**in** *a.* ①装入的,嵌进在里面的: a ~-*in* bookcase 壁橱式书架 ②缝上的,装进的: ~-*in* sleeves 装袖 / ~-*in* pockets 开叉式衣袋 *n.* ①(冰霜雨雪等的)来临;来临时节 ②嵌入物,插入物·/ '~**line** *n.* 有一排钩子的长钓鱼线 / '~-'**off** *n.* ①装饰品；陪衬物 ②(债务的)抵销;用以抵销债务的权利 ③【印】粘脏(未干油墨从一印张粘到另一印张) ④【建】墙壁的凸出部 / '~**out** *n.* ①开始,开头: at the first ~*out* 最初,一开始 ②布置；设备,装备；装束；马车的全套配备 ③(食物、餐具、物品等的)陈列 ④宴会；招待 / '~**over** *n.* 超过位置;【机】偏置,偏距 / ~ **piece** ①按照固定形式创作的艺术作品 ②燃烧时成一图案的烟火表演 ③一件舞台布景 ④(军事、外交等方面)事先精心布置好的行动(或场面) / **square** 三角板(三只角为 90°、60°、30° 或 90°、45°、45°) / ~ **theory** 【数】集(合)论 / '~-'**to** *n.*

殴斗；吵架 / '~**up** *n.* ①机构；组织体系,体制: the administrative (economic, military) ~*ups* 行政(经济,军事)体制 / the ~*up* for professional work 业务班子 ②[美口](身体的)姿势,姿态；体格 ③装置；(仪器等的)装配;(机器、电子设备等操作用的)调整,准备: an experimental ~*up* 实验装置 ④[美俚](故意布置得)容易做的工作,容易取胜的比赛；容易得到的东西,容易完成的事；参加必败比赛的拳击手 ⑤计划,方案 ⑥(准备取景的)摄影机位置；摄影机在一个取景位置上拍摄的胶卷长度 ⑦ 菜馆铺排好的一席(或一客)台面(常已放有面包、黄油) ⑧(台球的)有利位置 ⑨[美俚]给顾客调制自备烈酒的材料(指茹打水、冰块等)⑩[无]调定

settee[1] [se'ti:] *n.* 长靠椅；中、小型沙发椅

settee[2] [se'ti:] *n.* 地中海的一种船(尖船首,三角帆,二或三桅)

settle[1] ['setl] ❶ *vt.* ①安排；料理；整理: ~ one's affairs 安排自己的事(尤指立遗嘱) / ~ a room 整理房间 ②安放: ~ oneself in an armchair 在扶手椅里坐下 / ~ a child in its crib 把小孩放进小床 ③使定居;使移居(尤指海外拓殖);殖民于: be ~*d* in the countryside 在农村落户 ④使平静,使镇定,使安宁: ~ one's nerves 使神经平静下来 / ~ the agitated mind 使激动的心情平静下来 / ~ the stomach 去除消化不良引起的难过(或恶心) ⑤[口](通过责骂等)使规矩,使就范 ⑥调停；解决；决定: ~ a dispute 调停争执 / The internal affairs of each country should be ~*d* by its own people. 各国的内政应由各国人民自己去解决。/ That ~*s* the matter. 事情就这样决定了。/ ~ which way to go 决定走哪一条路 / ~ the succession 确定继承人 / ~ a waverer 使三心二意的人打定主意 ⑦使固定;使稳定: ~ the system of work 使工作程序固定下来 ⑧支付,结算: ~ a bill 付帐,结帐 ⑨使(液体)澄清;使沉降,压紧;使(路等)平硬: The rain will ~ the dust. 雨将使尘埃平息。/ an apple to ~ one's dinner 帮助消化的饭后苹果 / ~ the contents of a bag by shaking it 摇动袋子压紧里面的东西 / Such fine weather will ~ the roads quickly. 这样的晴天很快就会使道路干硬的。⑩【律】通过法律手续指定把(财产、年金等)授与(on): He ~*d* his property *on* his nephew. 他决定把财产传给侄子(或外甥)。❷【动】使受孕。❷ *vi.* ①停息;停留: The bird ~*d* on the wire. 鸟停在电线上。/ A cold has ~*d* in my chest. 我伤风咳嗽一直发好。②(地基等)下陷,下沉;沉淀;沉落,降下: The ship was *settling* by the stern. 船尾渐渐下沉。/ wait for the coffee grounds to ~ 等咖啡渣渣滓沉淀 / Dust has ~*d* on the furniture. 家具上积起了灰尘。/ Silence ~*d* over the room. 房间里静了下来。③(因澄清沉淀而)澄清;(因摇动下沉而)变坚实: Let the wine ~ for a while before pouring. 让酒澄清一下再倒。④决定: ~ *on* a

plan 决定计划 / ～ to do sth. 决定做某事 ⑤变
稳定;镇定下来,平定下来: The weather has ～d
at last. 天气最后总算稳定下来了。 / ～ into
sleep 慢慢地进入睡乡 ⑥ 了结,清算;偿付: ～
with the bank once a month 每月与银行结算一
次 ⑦安家,定居,定居;殖民 ⑧【动】怀孕 ‖have an
account (或 a score) to ～ with sb. 见 account /
～ down ① 定居;从事固定的职业;过安定的
生活 ②平静下来;安下心来;专心致志于 (to):
let the excitement ～ down 让激动情绪平息下
来 / ～ down to write an article 静下心来写一
篇文章 / ～ down to one's work 安定下来专心
工作 / ～ down to dinner 坐定下来吃饭 / ～
for 对…感到满足,满足于: He demanded a
hundred dollars but had to ～ for half that
amount. 他要求一百元,但只得以得到半数而了
结。/ ～ in 迁入(新居);帮助…迁入新居 / ～
into shape 见 shape / ～ sb.'s hash 见
hash / ～ up 清偿,付清; 了结 / ～ with
①和…取得谅解 ②与…了结,与…清算;偿付:
～ with creditors (经双方妥协后)偿付债权人
③与…商谈生意;与…成交 ④与…算帐(指报仇)
‖settling day [英](交易所每两周一次的) 结
算日

settle² ['setl] n. 木制有扶手的高背长椅(座位下常
为一柜子)

settlement ['setlment] n. ①解决: the ～ of an
issue 问题的解决 / the terms of ～ 和解的条件 /
come to (或 reach) a peace ～ with 与…达成一
项和平解决办法 ② 清算,结帐: international
～s 国际结算 / I enclose a cheque in ～ of my
account with you. 附上支票一张以清帐。②殖
民;殖民地;拓居;新拓居地;租界;村落;新住宅区
④殖民团体; 新拓居地的人群 ⑤沉降; (房屋等
的)沉陷;澄清 ⑥(资本主义国家内)在贫民区进
行福利工作的社会改革团体 ⑦【律】(通过法律手
续的)财产授与; 依法设定的财产: make a ～ on
(或 upon) sb. 授与某人财产 / a marriage ～ 结
婚财产授予授财产给妻子的处理

settler ['setle] n. ①移居者;殖民者;开拓者: the
new ～s 外来移民 ②【化】澄清器 ③[俚]决定性
的一击(或论据、事件等)

seven ['sevn] I num. 七;七个(人或物);第七(卷、
章、页等)(用例参看 eight) II n. ① 七个(人或
物)一组 ②七岁 ③七点钟 ‖at sixes and ～s
见 six / seventy times ～ 很大的数目 ‖～fold
a. & ad. 七倍;七重 ‖Seven Champions (of
Christendom) (基督教的)七守护神 / 'Seven-
'Hill City 罗马的别称 (=the city of (the) Seven
Hills) / '～-league a. 一步跨七里格的: the
～-league boots (童话中)一步跨七里格的靴子 /
make progress at ～-league strides 一日千里地
向前发展 / ～ sages (古希腊)七贤 / ～ seas
世界七大海洋;全球

seventeen ['sevn'ti:n] I num. 十七;十七个(人
或物);第十七(页等)(用例参看 eight) II n. 十

七岁;十七点钟(即下午五点) ‖sweet ～ 妙龄十
七 ‖'～-'year locust 【动】十七年蝉(其幼虫在地
下须经十三至十七年才羽化)

seventeenth ['sevn'ti:nθ] I num. ① 第十七(个)
②十七分之一(的) II n. (月的)第十七日

seventh ['sevnθ] I num. ①第七(个) ②七分之一
(的) II n. ①【音】七度音程; 七度和音; 第七音
②(月的)第七日: the ～ of July 七月七日 ‖the
～ heaven 见 heaven ‖～ly ad. 第七(列举条
目等时用) ‖Seventh Avenue 纽约市第七街;
纽约市女子服装业 / '～-day a. ① 星期六的
②[宗]以星期六为安息日的

seventieth ['sevntiiθ] num. ①第七十(个) ②七十
分之一(的)

seventy ['sevnti] I num. 七十; 七十个(人或
物); 第七十(页等)(用例参看 eight) II n. ①
[复](世纪的)七十年代 ②[复]七十到七十九岁
的时期 ③七十岁 ④[俚]快转唱片 ‖～ times
seven 很大的数目 ‖'～-'eight num. 七十八(个)
n. 78 转/分的唱片,快转唱片 / '～-'five num.
七十五(个) n.【军】法国的 75 毫米口径大炮

sever ['seve] ❶ vt. ①切断, 割断; 把…割下: ～
the cable 把电缆割断 / ～ the head from the
body 把头割下 / rejoin the ～ed hand 再植断手
②把…分隔开; 使分离 ③断绝, 中断: ～ friend
ship 中止友谊 ❷ vi. ①断,裂开: The rope ～ed
under the strain. 绳子拉紧后绷断了。②被
分开 ‖～able ['severebl] a. 可割断的;可分开的

several ['sevrel] I a. ①几个,数个(至少三个): ～
times 几次,数回 / ～ bicycles 几辆自行车 / ～
people 几个人 ② 各自的, 各别的: each ～ part
各部分 / They went their ～ ways. 他们各
走各的路。/ on three ～ occasions 在三个不
同的场合 / the ～ steps in a process 工序中的
各个步骤 / a ～ judgement (对一群被告人的)
分别判决 / a joint and ～ responsibility 连带责
任 ③专有的,独占的: a ～ fishery 个人专有的渔
场 ④不同的,分歧的: the ～ opinions of the
different people 不同人的不同意见 ⑤[主方]大
量的 II pron. 几个, 数个: ～ of us 我们中间
的几个人 / Do you keep postcards? We want
～. 你们有明信片出售吗? 我们要买几张。
‖～fold ad. ① 有几部分地; 有几方面地 ②几
倍地 a. ① 有几部分的; 有几方面的 ②几倍的:
a ～fold increase 几倍的增长 / ～ly ad. All
the points were discussed, first ～ly and then
collectively. 各点均经讨论,先分开来讨论,然后
再总起来讨论。

severe [si'vie] a. ①严肃的,正经的: ～ looks 严肃
的神色 ② 严格的; 严密的: ～ discipline 严格
的纪律 / ～ reasoning 严谨的推理 ③严厉的;
苛刻的;尖锐的;讽刺的: be ～ in criticism 批评
起来很严厉 / be ～ with oneself and lenient
towards others 责己严而待人宽 / be ～ upon
(或 on) sb. 对某人很严厉 / a ～ sentence 重刑
判决 / ～ remarks 讽刺话 ④严重的; 剧烈的;

凛冽的: a ~ wound 重伤 / a ~ attack of toothache 牙痛的剧烈发作 / a ~ winter 严冬 ⑤严峻的;激烈的;艰难的: a ~ test 严峻的考验 / (a) ~ competition 激烈的竞争 / a ~ economic depression 极度的经济萧条 ⑥纯洁的;朴素的: ~ architecture 朴素建筑 / a ~ style 纯朴的文体;【建】纯洁式 ‖~ly *ad.* / ~ness *n.*

severity [si'veriti] *n.* ①严肃;严格;严厉 ②严重;凛冽;激烈: the ~ of the winter 冬天的严寒 ③严密,严谨 ④纯洁;朴素 ⑤[复]严厉的对待,严酷的惩罚;艰苦的经验

sew [sou] (过去式 sewed, 过去分词 sewn [soun] 或 sewed) ❶ *vt.* 缝制;缝合;缝补;缝: ~ a coat 缝制上装 / ~ two pieces of cloth together 把两块布缝合 / ~ the scattered sheets of a book 把书的散页重新装订成册 / ~ *on* a button 钉钮扣 / ~ money into a belt 把钱缝在腰带里 / ~ *in* a patch 打补钉 ❷ *vi.* 缝纫: She has been ~*ing* all morning. 她早上一直在做针线活。‖~ **up** ①缝合,缝拢: ~ up a wound 把伤口缝合 ②把…缝入,把…缝进 ③[美俚]垄断,独占(选票等);独占(某人)的感情 ④[俚]使累极;[常用被动语态]使喝醉 ⑤解决,决定: It has ~*ed* the whole thing up. 这就把整个事情解决了。

sewer[1] [sjuə; 美 'su(:)ə] **I** *n.* 阴沟,污水管,排水管,下水道: a ~ tunnel 污水隧道 / a ~ pipe 污水管 **II** *vt.* ①为…修建下水道 ②用下水道排除…的污水 ‖~ **gas** 【化】沟道气,阴沟气 / ~ **rat** 【动】褐鼠

sewer[2] ['sju:ə] *n.* 【史】(中世纪)负责安排筵席和进菜等的管家

sewer[3] ['souə] *n.* 缝纫者;缝具

sewerage ['sjuəridʒ; 美 'su(:)əridʒ] *n.* ①(阴沟等处的)污水,污物 ②污水排除;污物处理 ③排水系统;沟渠系统 ④肮脏思想;下流话

sewing ['souiŋ] *n.* ①缝纫 ②缝制物 ③(书的)锁线订,串线订 ‖~ **machine** 缝纫机 / ~ **needle** 缝纫针 / ~ **press** (书的)锁线装订机

sewn [soun] sew 的过去分词

sex [seks] **I** *n.* ①性别: without distinction of age or ~ 不分男女老幼 / the male (female) ~ 男(女)性 ②[总称]男;女: both ~es 男人们和女人们 ③性的活动;关于性行为的内容;性欲;性感 ④性交 **II** *vt.* ①区别…的性别: chicks 鉴别小鸡的雌雄 ②增强…的性感;引起…的性欲(*up*) ‖*the fair* (或 *gentle, weaker*) ~ 女性 / *the sterner* (或 *rougher, stronger*) ~ 男性 / ~*ist a.* 性别歧视的 *n.* 主张性别歧视者 ‖~ **appeal** ①性的魅力,性感 ②吸引力 / ~ **hygiene** 性卫生 / '~-**linked** *a.* 【生】性连锁的 / ~ **pot**, ~ **kitten** [美俚]性感的女人

sextant ['sekstənt] *n.* 【天】六分仪: ~ altitude 六分仪高度

sexton ['sekstən] *n.* 教堂司事(担任管理教堂、敲钟、挖掘墓地等工作)

sexual ['seksjuəl] *a.* ①性的;性别的: ~ equality 男女平等 / ~ characteristics 性特征 ②关于两性的;关于性生活的: ~ organs 生殖器官 / ~ intercourse (或 commerce, relations) 性交 / ~ appetite 性欲 ③【生】有性的: ~ generation 有性世代 / ~ selection 性选择 ‖~ly *ad.*

shabby ['ʃæbi] *a.* ①破旧的;失修的: a ~ street 穷街陋巷 ②褴褛的: be ~ in dress 衣衫褴褛 / look ~ 看上去一副寒酸相 ③卑鄙的;不公平的: play a ~ trick 玩弄卑鄙的手法 / a ~ villain 卑劣的坏蛋 ④菲薄的;吝啬的: a ~ gift 菲薄的礼物 / the ~ way in which a guest is received 对客人的简慢接待 ⑤低劣的,蹩脚的: ~ reasoning 拙劣的论证 ‖**shabbily** *ad.* / **shabbiness** *n.* ‖'~-**gen'teel** *a.* 穷了还要面子的,穷了还摆架子的

shack [ʃæk] **I** *n.* ①简陋的小木屋,棚屋 ②(作某种用途的)房间,小室: an ammunition ~ (小型)弹药库 / a guard's ~ 警卫室 **II** *vi.* 居住;暂住 ‖~ **up** (*in*) ①过夜(*in*) ~ 与…同居,与…同住(*with*) ‖~ **fever** [美俚](流浪汉的)疲乏;睡意 / ~ **job** [美俚]情妇,姘头

shackle ['ʃækl] **I** *n.* ①[常用复]镣铐;(马的)脚镣:a pair of ~s 一副镣铐 ②[复][喻]束缚,枷锁: the ~s on the mind 思想包袱 ③束缚装置;【机】钩环: ~ bolt 连钩螺栓 / anchor ~ 锚钩环 ④十五呎长的缆绳(或缆链) ⑤【电】绝缘器 **II** *vt.* ①给…带上镣铐 ②束缚,羁绊 ③给…扣上钩环 ‖'~-**bone** *n.* [苏格兰]腕

shade [ʃeid] **I** *n.* ①荫,阴凉处 [复]阴暗,黑暗: under the ~ of a tree 在树荫下 / Store the bottle of medicine in the ~. 把这瓶药放在阴凉处。/ the ~s of night (evening) 夜(暮)色 ②遮光物;遮光簾;遮罩;灯罩;簾,幕: a window ~ 遮光帘 ③(图画、照相等的)阴暗部分: There is not enough light and ~ in this picture. 这幅画的明暗色调不够明显。④(色彩的)浓淡;[喻]形形色色;细微的差别: various ~s of red 各种深浅不同的红色 / all ~s of opinion 各种各样意见 / These two words have delicate ~s of meaning. 这两个词在意义上有细微的差别。⑤[常用复]隐蔽处 ⑥虚幻的事物;鬼,幽灵 ⑦少量,少许: I am a ~ better today. 我今天好些了。⑧愁容,忧郁的表情 ⑨[复]酒窖 ⑩[复][美俚]太阳眼镜 ⑪[美俚]代贼窝赃者 **II** ❶ *vt.* ①荫敝,遮蔽: Trees ~ the streets. 街道旁绿树成荫。/ ~ the window with curtains 用帘子遮窗 ②使阴暗;使黯然失色: a face ~d with melancholy 带着哀愁的脸容 ③画阴影于;使(色彩)逐渐变化: the ~d parts on a picture 图画的阴影部分 ④使逐渐发生细微变化 ⑤使(风琴管)音调变弱 ⑥降减(价格) ❷ *vi.* (色彩等)渐变;(意义等)出现细微的差别: ~ from blue *into* green 从蓝色渐渐变成绿色 ‖*in the* ~ 在荫凉处;在阴暗处 ②逊色 / *the* ~s ①夜色 ②阴间: go down to the ~s 到阴间去,死 ③鬼魂 /

throw (或 **cast, put**) **into the ~** 使逊色, 使相形见绌: The publication of this new handbook has *thrown* the old one *into the ~*. 这本新手册的出版使旧作相形见绌。|| **~less** *a.* 无荫蔽的, 无遮蔽的

shadow ['ʃædou] **I** *n.* ①阴影; 荫; 影子: in the ~ of a tree 在树荫下 / He is afraid of his own ~. 他胆小得不得了。/ The willow's ~ falls on the lake. 垂柳的影子倒映在湖面上。②[复]日落后渐暗的天色; (房间、画等的)阴暗部分: the ~s of evening 暮色 / ~s under (或 round) the eyes (由于少睡等原因)眼睛周围起黑圈 ③阴郁 ④幻影; 幽灵, 鬼 ⑤预兆, 蛛丝马迹 ⑥微量, 少许 ⑦形影不离的人; [美俚]侦探; 食客 ⑧极相似的人(或物) ⑨隐退, 隐蔽处; 掩蔽, 庇护: live in the ~ 隐居 ⑩[美俚][贬]黑人 **II** ❶ *vt.* ① 投阴影于, 覆阴影于; 遮蔽; 使阴暗, 使朦胧: A glint of displeasure ~ed his eyes. 他的眼里微露不悦之色。② 暗示, 预示 (*forth, out*) ③(如影子一样地)钉…的梢, 尾随: The cruiser was ~ed by a submarine. 这艘巡洋舰被一艘潜艇紧紧尾随着。④[古]掩蔽, 保护 ❷ *vi.* ①渐变: The mountains were ~*ing* into blackness. 群山渐渐消失在黑暗中。②变阴暗, 变朦胧 ||*be the ~ of one's former self* (或 *be worn to a ~*) 瘦得不成样子 / *catch at ~s* (或 *run after a ~*) 捕风捉影, 徒劳 / *Coming events cast their ~s before.* [谚]未来之事先有朕兆。/ *in the ~ of* 与…很接近; 在…的附近 / *May your ~ never grow less!* [古]祝君永昌! / *quarrel with one's own ~* (容易)莫明其妙地无事生气 / *the ~ of a shade* 虚幻 / *under the ~ of* ① 与…很接近; 在…的附近 ② 在…的阴影笼罩之下 ③在…的保护下 ||**~less** *a.* 无投影的; 无阴影的 / **~like** *a.* =shadowy / **~ box** (放展览品等的)玻璃盖匣 / '**~box** *vi.* ①与假想的对手作拳击练习 ②谨慎地对付对手; 避免作出主动(或决定性)的行动 / '**~,boxing** *n.* ①与假想对手作的拳击练习 ②太极拳 / **~ cabinet** 影子内阁 / **~ factory** 战时可改而生产军需品的工厂 / **~land** *n.* 虚幻境界 / **~ play** 皮影戏, 影子戏

shady ['ʃeidi] *a.* ①成荫的; 多荫的; 背阴的, 阴凉的: the ~ side of the street 街道的背阴面 ②阴暗的; 隐蔽的: a ~ night 阴暗之夜 ③[口]可疑的, 靠不住的: a ~-looking man [口]形迹可疑的家伙 / a ~ transaction 不正当的交易 ||*keep ~* [美口](不声不响)避免人家注意 ②匿藏 / *on the ~ side of* 见 **side**

shaft [ʃɑ:ft] **I** *n.* ①箭杆, 矛柄; 箭; 矛; 箭一般的东西: ~s of lightning 一道道闪电 / ~s of satire 一支支讽刺的利箭 ②杆状物; (工具的)长柄; 旗杆; 烛台扦 ③车杠, 辕 ④[建]树干, 茎; 羽干 ⑤[机]轴 ⑥[建]柱身; 塔尖, 井穴; [矿]矿井; 竖井: an inclined ~ 斜井 / ~ excavation 井筒掘进, 凿井 ⑧[冶]炉身: ~ walls 炉墙 ⑨(电梯的)升降机井; 通风管道; (屋顶上的)烟囱

⑩(古生物的)主突起茎 ⑪[复][美俚](人的)大腿 **II** *vt.* ①在…上装杆(或手柄、轴等) ②[俚]欺骗; 利用 ||*get the ~* [俚]受骗 / *give* (*sb.*) *the ~* [俚]欺骗(某人) / *have a ~ left in one's quiver* 还有本钱; 还有办法

shaggy ['ʃægi] *a.* ①长满粗毛的; 有粗毛的 ②(毛发等)粗浓蓬松的: ~ eyebrows 粗眉 ③(人)邋遢的, 不修边幅的 ④草木丛生的; (树)有粗糙树枝的; 表面粗糙的 ⑤粗野的 ||**shaggily** *ad.* / **shagginess** *n.* ||'**~-'dog story** 冗长、杂乱、冒充滑稽的故事; 内有会说话的动物的滑稽故事

shake [ʃeik] **I** [shook [ʃuk], shaken ['ʃeikən] ❶ *vt.* ①摇, (猛力)摇动; 抖动: ~ one's head (*over* 或 *at* sth.) 摇头 (对某事表示不赞成) / To be ~*n* before taking. (药瓶标签用语)服前摇匀 / ~ *sb. by* the shoulder 抓住某人的肩膀猛摇 / ~ hands 握手 / ~ sand *from* (或 *out of*) one's shoes 抖掉鞋里的沙子 ②使震动; 使发抖; 使心绪不宁: be badly ~*n* by the news 对这个消息大为震惊 ③动摇; 减弱: Nothing can ~ our determination. 什么也动摇不了我们的决心。/ ~ the credit of 损害…的信誉 ④挥舞: ~ one's fist *at* sb. (或 *in* sb.'s face) 向某人挥拳(表示威胁等) ⑤[俚]摆脱, 抛弃: ~ (off) a bad habit 改掉坏习惯 / ~ one's pursuers 摆脱追赶者 ⑥[音]使发颤音 ⑦(掷出前)把(骰子)拿在手心里抖动 ❷ *vi.* ①震动, 颤动: The whole house *shook* during the earthquake. 地震时整个房子都震动了。/ sails *shaking* in the wind 在风中抖动的帆 ②发抖: She was *shaking* with cold. 她冷得直打颤。/ His hand ~s. 他有手颤的毛病。③动摇; 动荡, 不稳 ④握手: ~ and be friends 握手结交 (或言归于好) ⑤[音]发颤音 **II** *n.* ①摇动; 震动; 握手; [口]地震: Give it a (good) ~. 把它(用力地)摇一下。②[常用复]颤栗; [the ~s]疟疾 ③[口]一刹那; (原子物理学等计时单位)百分之一微秒 ④(石)的裂缝, (木的)轮裂; (从圆木上锯下的)盖屋板 ⑤[音]颤音 ⑥牛奶(或鸡蛋等)和冰淇淋搅成的饮料 ⑦解雇, 撵走 ⑧[美俚]敲诈, 勒索; 贿金 ||*a fair ~* 公平交易, 公平的处置 / *all of a ~* 发抖, 哆嗦 / *give…the ~* 撵走…, 摆脱… / *in a brace of ~s* (或 *in half a ~* 或 *in two ~s* 或 *in two ~s of a duck's tail* 或 *in two ~s of a lamb's tail*) 马上, 立刻 / *no great ~s* [口]不太出色的(人); 不太重要的(人); 平凡的(人): He is *no great ~s* at his new work. 他做这新工作不太行。/ *on the ~* [美俚]参与犯罪活动(尤指搞贿赂、勒索等) / *put sb. on the ~* (或 *put the ~ on sb.*) [美俚]向某人勒索钱财 / *a leg* 见 **leg** / **~ down** ①摇落(果实等); 摇匀摊平(米谷等) ②(用毯子等)临时搭床铺; 占据临时床铺; 临时寄宿 ③适应新环境; 安顿下来: The new staff members are *shaking down* nicely. 新来的工作人员逐渐很好地适应了他们的工作和环境。④精简, 缩减 ⑤对(船只等)进行试航 ⑥[美俚]勒索, 敲诈; 对…进行搜查 / **~ it up** [美俚]赶快 / **~ off** ①抖落, 掸

去 ②撵走，摆脱：~ off the conservative ideas 抛弃保守思想 / ~ *off* the cold 驱除感冒 / ~ *oneself together* 振作起来，聚精会神起来 / ~ *out* ①把…抖干净；摇(或抖)出(器皿、衣服等)里面的东西；摇(或抖)出 ②抖开，打开(旗、帆等) ③把(实力薄弱的投机商)吓出投机市场 / ~ *up* ①摇匀：~ up a bottle of medicine 摇匀药水 ②摇松…(以使整齐)：~ up a cushion (pillow) 摇松靠垫(枕头)(使恢复原来样子) ③摇醒，使操作 ④把…打散后重新组合；使(想法等)经历剧变 ⑤震动，震惊：He looks a little ~*n* up. 他有点震惊的样子。‖ **~able** *a.* =shakable /

shaking *n.* ①摇动，震动：give sth. a good *shaking* 使劲摇动某物 / deserve a good *shaking* 该好好地揍一顿 ②[复]摇落的东西(船上填缝用的)废绳和帆布碎片等杂物 ③冷颤；疟疾 ‖ **~-'down** *n.* ①地铺；临时床铺 ②喧闹的舞蹈 ③彻底的搜查：give a room a first-class ~*down* 对一个房间进行最严密彻底的搜查 ④调整；调整时期 ⑤[美俚]勒索，敲诈 *a.* (飞机、船只等)试航的：a ~*down* cruise 试航 / a ~*down* flight 试飞 / **'~-hands** [复] *n.* [用作单]握手 / **'~-off** *n.* 摔脱，摆脱 / **'~-out** *n.* ①抖出，摇出；抖开 ②(经济危机中)实力薄弱的投机商的被淘汰 / **'~-'up** *n.* ①摇动，震动；操作，激励 ②草率搭成的房屋；作为权宜之计的东西 ③(政策、人员等)剧变，大改组：a personnel ~*-up* 人事大变动

shaky ['ʃeiki] *a.* ①摇动的，摇晃的；发抖的：a ~ table 摇晃的桌子 / a ~ voice 发抖的声音 ②不稳定的；不坚定的，不可靠的：~ voters 三心两意的投票人 / His English is rather ~. 他的英语不大行。③(木材)轮裂的 ④衰弱的，有病的：look ~ 样子很衰弱 ‖ **shakily** *ad.* / **shakiness** *n.*

shale [ʃeil] *n.* 【地】页岩 ‖ ~ **oil** 页岩油

shall [强 ʃæl；弱 ʃəl，ʃl] (过去式 should [强 ʃud；弱 ʃəd，ʃd]) (shall not 的缩写为 shan't [ʃɑːnt]) *v. aux.* ①[表示单纯的将来，用于第一人称。第二人称只用于问句。美国人常用 will 代替。口语中可缩写为 'll] 将要；会：I'll be twenty next month. 到下月我将满二十岁。/ I'm afraid I *shan't* be able to come. 我恐怕不能来。/ *Shall* we be back in time? 我们会及时回来吗？/ *Shall* you be free tonight? 今天晚上你有空吗？ ②[表示说话者的意图、允诺、警告、命令、决心等，用于陈述句的第二、第三人称中] 必须，应，可：You ~ get the answer right this afternoon. 今天下午你就可以得到答复了。/ You ~ not leave your post. 你不得离开岗位。/ No, he *shan't* go. 不，他不能去。③[在条约、规章、法令等文件中表示义务或规定，一般用于第三人称]应，必须：The new regulation ~ take effect on June 1st. 新章程自六月一日起施行。④[在问句中表示征求对方意见，主要用于第一、第三人称]…好吗？要不要…？：*Shall* I

fetch the hammer? 我去把锤子拿来好吗？ / *Shall* we take umbrellas with us? (或 Let's take umbrellas with us, ~ we?) 我们带雨伞去好吗？ / *Shall* he come to see you? 要不要他来看你？ / *Shall* those goods be sent over to you at once? 那些货物要不要马上给你送来？ ⑤[用在表示意图、要求等的从句中]应该，要：I wish that you ~ stay at home tonight. 我希望今晚你会留在家里。/ He desires that we ~ go there with him tomorrow. 他希望明天我们和他一起到那儿去。/ I am anxious that it ~ be done in time. 我急于要把这件事及时做好。/ My demand is that you ~ get it ready before five. 我要求你在五时前把它准备好。 ⑥[用于将来时态的间接引语中，与直接引语中的 shall 相应]将：He says that he ~ be glad to see you. (=He says: "I ~ be glad to see you.") 他说他将乐意来看你。[注意：这里也可用 will]

shallow ['ʃælou] I *a.* ①浅的：a ~ stream 浅溪 / a ~ dish 浅底盘 ②(知识、议论等)浅薄的，肤浅的：a ~ man 浅薄的人 / ~ talk 肤浅的谈话· II *n.* [常用复]浅水(处)，浅滩 III *v.t. & vi.* (使)变浅 ‖ **~ly** *ad.* / **~ness** *n.* ‖ **~-'brained**, **'~-'headed**, **'~-'pated** *a.* 头脑简单的，知识浅薄的

shalt [强 ʃælt；弱 ʃəlt，ʃlt] *v. aux.* [古] =shall (只用于 thou shalt 中，等于 you shall)

sham [ʃæm] I *n.* ①假冒，哄骗 ②假冒者，骗子 ③假的东西，赝品 ④(摆设用的)绣花枕套(或床罩) II *a.* 假的；虚伪的；劣等的：a ~ battle (练兵用的)摹拟战 / a ~ plea 【律】(为了拖延时间的)虚伪的抗辩 / ~ tea 劣等茶叶 III (shammed; shamming) *vt.* ①假装：~ headache (a faint) 假装头痛(晕倒) ②[古]欺骗 ❷ *vi.* 装假：~ dead 装死 / He is not asleep; he is only *shamming*. 他没睡着，他只是装睡。‖ ~ *Abraham* 装病

shamble ['ʃæmbl] I *vi.* 蹒跚，拖沓地走 II *n.* 蹒跚，拖沓的步子

shambles ['ʃæmblz] [复] *n.* [用作单或复] ①[古]肉店；肉市场 ②屠宰场；[喻]屠杀场所，大流血场所 ③混乱，一团槽；毁坏的景象，废墟：in (a) complete ~ 一片混乱 / clean up the ~ of bombing 打扫轰炸后的废墟

shame [ʃeim] I *n.* ①羞耻(心)，羞愧(感)：feel ~ at having bungled 因工作做得不好而感到羞愧 / flush with ~ 因羞惭而脸红 / hang one's head *for* (或 *from, in*) ~ 羞愧得低下头来 / have no ~ (或 be quite without ~, be lost to ~, be dead to ~, be past ~) 恬不知耻，厚颜无耻 / For ~! 真丢脸! (对做错事而不表示惭愧的人的责备语) ②羞辱，耻辱：put sb. to ~ 羞辱某人；[喻]使某人黯然失色；胜过某人 / bring ~ on oneself 给自己带来耻辱 / *Shame* on you! (你)真丢脸! ③可耻的事(或人)：a ~ to the family 家庭中的一个败类 ④[口]不应该的事，遗憾的事：It is a ~ that they were cheated. 他

们真不应该受骗。/ It is a ~ (或 What a ~) to treat him like that. 这样对待他太不象话了。 **II** *vt.* ① 使难为情，羞(人)： ~ sb. for his ill conduct 使某人为自己的不良行为而感到羞愧 ② 使蒙受羞辱，使丢脸 ③ 使痛感羞愧而： ~ sb. *into* apologizing 使某人出于惭愧而道歉 / ~ sb. *out of* doing sth. 使某人感到难为情而不再做某事 ‖*cry ~ on* (或 *upon*) 说…应自觉惭愧；责备，非难

shamefaced ['ʃeimfeist] *a.* ① 害羞的，羞怯的；谦卑的，不惹人注目的 ② 惭愧的，羞耻的 ‖~**ly** *ad.* / ~**ness** *n.*

shameful ['ʃeimful] *a.* ① 可耻的，丢脸的： ~ conduct 可耻的行为 ② 不道德的,不体面的；猥亵的,淫猥的‖~**ly** *ad.* / ~**ness** *n.*

shameless ['ʃeimlis] *a.* 无耻的，不要脸的；伤风败俗的：a ~ exploiter 无耻的剥削者 / a ~ betrayal 无耻的背叛 ‖~**ly** *ad.* / ~**ness** *n.*

shampoo [ʃæm'pu:] **I** *vt.* ① 用洗发剂洗(头、发) ② 洗…的头(或头发) ③ [古]给…按摩(或推拿) **II** *n.* ① 洗头,洗发: give sb. a ~ 给某人洗头 ② 洗发剂

shamrock ['ʃæmrɔk] *n.* 【植】① 白花酢浆草(爱尔兰的国花) ② 三叶苜蓿 ③ 天蓝

shank [ʃæŋk] **I** *n.* ① 胫，小腿；腿部;胫骨 ②【动】(昆虫的)胫节 ③ 牛(或羊)的腿肉 ④ (工具的)柄,杆;锚杆;匙柄;钉杆;针杆;(植物的)秆,梗,柄 ⑤(钻、凿等插入柄中的)凸出部分;钮扣背面的凸出部分 ⑥【印】铅字身 ⑦鞋底中间狭窄部分；袜统 ⑧[口]末梢, 后部; 较晚的一段时间: the ~ of a journey 旅行的最后一程 **II** *vi.* (花等)从病梗上枯萎脱落 ‖*the ~ of the evening* [口]黄昏将尽时,夜晚的开始 ‖~ **painter**【海】锚杆索

shanty ['ʃænti] *n.* 简陋小屋，棚屋 ‖~**town** *n.* 棚户区；贫民窟; [总称]棚户区居民

shape [ʃeip] **I** *n.* ① 形状,形态；样子,外形: have the ~ of the letter U 呈 U 字形 / rocks of various ~s 各种形态的岩石 / a fiend in human ~ 披着人皮的恶魔 ② 定形；(具体)形式；体现,具体化: get (或 put) one's ideas into ~ 理清思路 / give ~ to a plan 使计划形成(或具体化) / knock (或 whip) sth. into ~ 把某物敲打成形; 大力推动某事物使成形(或合格)；把某事物整理好 ③[口]情况,状态: in good financial ~ 经济情况好 / The patient is in better ~. 病人的情况有所好转。/ the ~ of things to come 未来事物的状态，未来(发展)的情况 ④朦胧的形象, 模糊的人影; 幽灵 ⑤种类: dangers of every ~ 各种危险 ⑥模型；模制胶状物: a hat ~ 帽型 ⑦戏装;戏装衬垫 **II ❶** *vt.* ① 使成形,使具有…形状；塑造,制作;形成: The metal piece is ~d like a new moon. 这个金属部件制成新月状。/ ~ clay into a pot 将粘土塑成罐子 / ~ public opinion 影响(或左右)舆论 ②提出，想象; 使具体化: ~ a conspiracy 策划阴谋 / ~ an answer 作出回答 / ~ a folktale into a narrative

poem 根据民间故事写成叙事诗 ③使符合,使适合 (*to*): ~ one's plans *to* specific conditions 使计划适合具体情况 / a dress ~d *to* sb.'s figure 做得很合某人身材的衣服 ④使朝向: 决定…的进程(或做法): ~ history (the course of events) 决定历史的进程(事件的进展) **❷** *vi.* ①[口]成形;成型;形成 (*up, into*) ②成长,发展: The way events are shaping in the world is encouraging. 国际形势的发展令人鼓舞。③[罕]发生 ‖*in any ~ or form* 以任何形式(或任何种类): He has so far made no suggestions *in any ~ or form*. 他至今没有提出任何建议。/ *in no ~* 决不, 无论如何不, 完全不 / *in ~* ①在形状上，在外形上: *In* ~ the flask resembles a gourd. 这烧瓶的形状象葫芦。②处于良好(或固有)状态: do exercises to keep *in* ~ 做体操保持身体健康 / *in the ~ of* 呈…的形状；以…的形式: They showed us politeness *in the ~ of* a banquet. 他们设宴对我们表示礼待。/ *lick into* ~ 塑造, 使象样；把…训练好, 使有效能 / *settle into* ~ (事情等)有头绪，上正轨 / *~ in with* [美俚]与…厮混在一起 / *~ one's course* 见 **course** / *~ up* [口]成形; 成型; 形成;顺利发展 / *take* ~ 成形;形成,具体化;有显著发展: Completely new relations between teachers and students are *taking* ~ in our schools. 崭新的师生关系正在我国的学校中形成。/ *wear to one's* ~ (衣服)穿过一阵变得合身(或服贴) ‖**~-up** *n.* 码头临时工的挑选(由工会指派的工头在聚集待雇的工人中挑选出当日或当班所需的临时工)

shapeless ['ʃeiplis] *a.* ①无形状的;不定形的 ②破相的,不匀称的,不象样的 ‖~**ly** *ad.* / ~**ness** *n.*

shapely ['ʃeipli] *a.* ① 样子好的，匀称的，美观的 ② 定形的；有条理的: a ~ conception 条理清楚的概念 ‖**shapeliness** *n.*

share[1] [ʃɛə] **I** *n.* ① 一份，份儿: shoulder one's ~ of responsibility 担负起自己的一份责任 / have a ~ in the profits 得一份利润 / He had a large ~ in bringing it about. 他在促成这一事中出过一份很大的力。②份额;分担量: I'll have (或 bear) my ~ of the expenses. 我愿意承担我那一份费用。/ That is your fair ~. 那是你应得的(或应承担的)一份。/ do one's full ~ of work 全部完成分配给自己的工作量 / She did not take much ~ in the conversation. 谈话时她说得很少。③股份; [英][复]股票 (=[美]stock): ordinary (preference) ~s 普通(优先)股 / hold 200 ~s in a company 在某公司中持有二百股 **II ❶** *vt.* ① 均分;分摊；分配: ~ out the work 把工作平均地分派 ②分享,分担;共同具有, 共同使用: ~ a room with sb. 与某人合用一个房间 / I'll ~ the cost with you. 我和你分担费用。**❷** *vi.* 分享, 分担: ~ in the work 分担工作 ‖*fall to sb.'s ~* 由某人承担；归某人享有 / *go ~s* 分享,分担；合伙经营: I'll *go* ~s with you in the travelling expenses. 我和你分

担旅费。/ on ~s 分摊盈亏 / ~ (and ~) alike 平均分享; 平均分担 / the lion's ~ 最大(或最好)的份额 ‖~r ['ʃeərə] n. 分担者; 分享者; 分配者; 参与者 ‖~,broker n. [英]股票经纪人 / '~crop vi. & vt. [主美]交谷租种(田) / '~,cropper n. [主美](尤指美国南方)用谷物交租的佃农 / '~,holder n. 股票持有人, 股东 / ~list [英]股票行情表 / ~-out ['ʃeəraut] n. 均分; 分摊 / '~,pusher n. [英口]硬推销不值钱的股票的掮客

share² [ʃeə] n. 犁头, 犁铧

shark [ɑ:k] I n. ①鲨鱼: ~'s fins (鲨)鱼翅 ②贪婪狡猾的人, 敲诈勒索者, 骗子: a loan ~ 高利贷者 / a land ~ 专门诈诳上岸水手的人 / the big ~s 垄断资本家 ③[俚]内行, 能手, 老手; 专家 ④[美俚]旷课的学生; 旷课; 杰出的学生, 免修课程的优等生 ⑤[英俚]海关官员 II ❶ vt. 敲诈, 骗取, 用不正当手段搜括 (up); 贪婪地吞咽 ❷ vi. 敲诈, 诈骗: ~ for a living 以诈为生

sharp [ɑ:p] I a. ①锋利的, 锐利的; 尖的: a ~ sword 锋利的剑 / a ~ pin 尖利的大头针 / ~ sand 多角砂 ②敏锐的, 机警的: ~ eyes 敏锐的目光 / ~ ears 灵敏的听觉 / a child 机灵的孩子 / be ~ at figures (或 arithmetic) 算得快 / The sentinel kept a ~ lookout. 哨兵警惕地守望着。③ 线条分明的, 轮廓鲜明的; 明显的 ④陡的, 急转的; 急剧的, 激烈的 ⑤尖刻的, 苛刻的; 严厉的, 易怒的: a ~ tongue 利嘴 / criticism 尖锐的批评 / a ~ temper 易怒的脾气 ⑥(感觉、味道等)强烈的, 辛辣的; 刺耳的, 刺骨的: a ~ pain 剧痛 / a ~ smell 刺鼻的气味 / a ~ voice 刺耳的语声; 严厉的语调 / a ~ frost 刺骨的严寒 / a ~ soap 苛性皂 ⑦敏捷的; 生气勃勃的: take a ~ walk 轻快地散步 / ~ work 紧张而热烈的工作 ⑧精明的, 厉害的; 狡猾的, 不择手段的: a ~ trader 精明厉害的商人 / ~ practice 不择手段的行为 ⑨[音]偏高的, 升半音的: The piano is ~. 钢琴的音偏高了。/ C ~ 升 C (调) ⑩[语]不带声的, 清音的 ⑪[美俚]时髦的, 漂亮的 II ad. ①正(指时刻): arrive at 4 (o'clock) ~ 于四时正到达 ②锐利地; 机警地; 急剧地; 突然地: turn ~ to the left 向左急转 ③[音]偏高地, 升半音地: sing ~ 用升半音唱 III n. ①锋利的刀刃; 纤细的长缝衣针 ②[音]升音; 升号 (♯) ③[口]骗子 (=sharper) ④[美俚]内行, 专家 ⑤[英][复]粗面粉 IV ❶ vt. 把(音调)提高半音 ❷ vi. 提高音调演唱(或演奏) ‖as ~ as a razor 厉害的, 机智的 / look ~ 留神, 注意; 赶快, 赶紧 / Sharp's the word. (催人时说)赶快。(或: 快点。) ‖~er n. 骗子(尤指骗人的赌徒) / ~ly ad. / ~ness n. ‖'~-,angled a. 尖角的 / '~='cut a. 切削得锋利的; 分明的, 鲜明的 / '~='eared a. 耳朵尖的; 听觉敏锐的 / '~='edged a. 刀刃锋利的 / '~='eyed a. 眼快的; 目光敏锐的 / '~-'fanged a. 尖齿的; 讥刺的, 挖苦的 / '~-'freeze vt. 使(食物等)速冻 / '~=

'nosed a. 尖鼻子的; 嗅觉灵敏的 / '~-'set a. ①饥饿的 ②渴望的 (upon, after) ③使边缘锋利的 / '~-,shooter n. 狙击手; 一等射手 / '~-'sighted a. 眼快的, 目光敏锐的; 机智的, 灵敏的 / '~-'tongued a. 利嘴的, 说话尖刻的, 挖苦的 / '~-'witted a. 机智的, 灵敏的, 聪明的

sharpen ['ʃɑ:pən] ❶ vt. ①削尖; 磨快: ~ a pencil 削铅笔 / ~ a razor 磨快剃刀 ②使敏锐; 使敏捷: ~ one's vigilance 使边境警惕 / 强; 使剧烈; 使尖锐: ~ the pain 加重痛苦 / the appetite 增进食欲 / ~ one's speech 把话讲得尖刻 ④[英][音]把(音调)提高半音 ❷ vi. ①变尖; 变锋利 ②尖锐化, 急剧化 ‖~ one's knife for sb. 准备惩罚(或攻击)某人 ‖~er n. 磨削器; 磨削者: a knife-~er 磨刀石(或器) / a pencil ~er 卷笔刀 / cutter ~er [机]刀具刃磨器

shatter ['ʃætə] I ❶ vt. ①使散开; 震落; 吹散 ②粉碎, 砸碎: The glass was ~ed to pieces. 玻璃被砸得粉碎。③破坏, 毁坏: ~ed nerves (重大刺激等造成的)极度神经衰弱 ❷ vi. ①破碎; 粉碎 ②损坏, 毁坏 ③嘎嘎地响, 哗啦地响: The heavy rain ~ed on the roof. 大雨哗啦啦地落在屋顶上。④落花, 落叶, 掉果 II n. ①碎片, 裂片: be in ~s 一片破碎 / break into (或 to) ~s 粉碎 ②粉碎; 毁坏 ③[地]震裂 ③(过早的)落花, 落叶, 掉果 ④(一阵)喷散, 迸溅 ‖'~proof a. 防~的: ~proof glass 不碎玻璃; 防震玻璃

shave [ʃeiv] I (过去式 shaved, 过去分词 shaved 或 shaven ['ʃeivn]) ❶ vt. ①剃, 刮(胡须等); 修剪(草坪等): ~ (off) one's beard 剃掉胡须 / ~ oneself (自己)修面, 刮脸 / ~ a patient before operation 开刀前为病人剃光毛发 ②削(或刨)去…的薄薄一层; 把…切削成薄片; [口]削减(价格等) ③擦过, 掠过: The aeroplane ~d the top of a tree. 飞机掠过树梢。④[口]杀价买进(期票等) ⑤[英方]诈取, 强夺 ⑥[美俚]勉强胜过 ❷ vi. ①修面, 刮脸 ②勉强挤过(或挤进); 擦过: ~ through a gap in the fence 从篱笆隙缝里挤过去 ③(做交易时)很会讨价还价, 很精明 II n. ①刮刀, 剃刀; 刨刀; 削片, 薄片 ②修面, 刮脸: have a ~ and a haircut 修面理发 ③[口]擦过, 掠过; 幸免 ④[英]欺诈 ‖a close ~ 剃光头发(或胡须) ②侥幸的脱险 ‖~r n. ①修面的人 ②刨削, 电动剃刀; 刨刀 ②[美俚]小伙子 ⑤ 杀价买进期票的人; 善于讨价还价的人; a note ~r 以超过法定利率贷放票据的人 ⑥[古]骗子

shaven ['ʃeivn] I shave 的过去分词 II a. 修过面的; 修剪过的: a clean-~ face 刮得光洁的脸 / a smooth-~ lawn 修剪得平整的草坪

shaving ['ʃeiviŋ] n. ①刮, 削, 刨 ②修面, 剃须 ③[常用复]刨花; 削片, 薄片 ‖~ brush 修面刷 / ~ horse 刨工台 / ~ lotion 修面等用的香液

shawl [ʃɔ:l] I n. (长)方形的披巾, 围巾(主要指妇女用的) II vt. 用披巾(或披巾状物)包裹

she [ʃi:; 弱 ʃi] I pron. [主格] ①她 ②(作为国

家、地球、月亮、船等的代词)她,它 **II** [ʃiː] (〔复〕 shes [ʃiːz]) *n.* 女;雌: The baby is a ~. 这婴儿是女的。/ a ~-cousin 表(或堂)姐妹 / a ~-goat 雌山羊 ‖'~-'**woman** *n.* 女性十足的女人

sheaf [ʃiːf] **I** (〔复〕 sheaves [ʃiːvz]) *n.* ①捆,束: a ~ of wheat 一捆麦 / a ~ of arrows 一束箭 (一般二十四支) ②扎: a ~ of papers (manuscripts) 一扎文件(手稿) ③【军】火制正面,射面: a ~ of fire 集束弹道 **II** *vt.* 捆,束,扎

shear [ʃiə] **I** (过去式 sheared 或〔古〕 shore [ʃɔː], 过去分词 shorn [ʃɔːn] 或 sheared) **❶** *vt.* ①〔诗〕(用刀、剑)砍;斩 ②剪;剪…的毛(或发);修剪: ~ a sheep 剪羊毛 / ~ a lawn 修剪草坪 / ~ cloth 修剪布(去掉细毛) ③切;切断: A jet plane ~*ed* the blue sky. 一架喷气式飞机划破蓝空。④〔苏格兰〕(用镰刀)收割 ⑤剥夺(*of*): be *shorn of* one's right 被剥夺权利 / His recent illness has *shorn* him *of* strength. 他最近的一场病使他的体力大为减弱。/ come home *shorn* 蚀(或输)得精光回来 **❷** *vi.* ①剪;修剪;剪羊毛: We shall be ~*ing* soon. 我们明天要剪羊毛了。②切断;【物】切变: The torpedo boat ~*ed* through the waves. 鱼雷快艇破浪前进。③〔苏格兰〕(用镰刀)收割 **II** *n.* ①剪;切 ②〔复〕大剪刀;【机】剪切机,剪床: a pair of ~s 一把大剪刀 ③【物】切变;切力,剪力 ④【常用复】起重三角架,人字起重架 ⑤剪下的东西(如羊毛) ⑥(羊的)年岁: a sheep of two ~s 剪过两次毛的羊,两岁的羊 ‖~ **off** *sb.'s* **plume** 砍掉某人盔上的羽毛;打下某人的威风 ‖~**er** ['ʃiərə] *n.* ①剪切者;剪切工人;剪羊毛者 ②可以剪毛的羊 ③剪切机,剪床;【矿】直立横截煤机 / ~**ing** ['ʃiəriŋ] *n.* ①剪切;~*ing* force 剪切力,切力 / ~*ing* stress 【物】切应力 ②剪羊毛;剪下的羊毛: at ~*ing* time 在剪羊毛时节 / sheep ready for the ~*ing* 已能剪毛的羊 / ~*ing* machine 【机】剪切机;剪(羊)毛机;【纺】切布机,刮布机 ‖~ **legs** 起重三角架,人字起重架 / ~ **steel** 【冶】剪钢 / '~-ˌwater *n.* 海鸥,鹱

sheath [ʃiːθ] **I** *n.* ①(刀、剑等的)鞘;(枪)壳;套;护套 ②【生】【解】鞘,兜: dentinal ~ 牙质管鞘 ③(电子管的)屏极;(电缆的)铠装: ~ loss 电缆铅耗,包皮损耗 ④女式紧身服装: a ~ corset 紧身束腹 ⑤河边防泛石堤 **II** *vt.* =sheathe

sheathe [ʃiːð] *vt.* ①插…入鞘 ②包;覆盖: a cable ~*d* with lead 铅包电缆 ③把(剑等)刺入皮肉 ④缩回(爪)

shed[1] [ʃed] **I** (shed;shedding) **❶** *vt.* ①流出;流下: ~ tears 流泪 ②使泻去: Oilskin ~*s* water. 油布能泻去水。③【生】排出(孢子等) ④散发;放射: ~ warmth and light 发出热和光 ⑤脱落;蜕(壳等);脱去: The trees began *shedding* their leaves. 树木开始落叶。/ ~ skin 蜕皮 / ~ one's clothes 脱掉衣服 ⑥摆脱;抛弃: ~ the ugly mantle of pretentiousness 放下臭架子 ⑦〔方〕把…分开 ⑧【电】减少(负荷) **❷** *vi.* ①流出;溢出;泻去 ②散发;散布 ③蜕皮(或壳等);脱

落 **II** *n.* ①分水岭 ②【纺】(织机的)梭口,梭道 ‖~ **blood** 见 **blood** / ~ **light on** (或 **upon**) *sth.* 见 **light**[1]

shed[2] [ʃed] **I** *n.* ①棚,小屋: a livestock ~ 牲畜棚 / a milking ~ 牛奶棚 ②货棚;工棚;车库: an aeroplane ~ 飞机库 **II** (shed; shedding) *vt.* 把…放入棚内

shed

sheen [ʃiːn] **I** *n.* ①光辉,光彩;光泽: the ~ of silk 丝绸的光泽 ②华丽的服装;有光泽的纺织品 **II** *a.* 〔诗〕华丽的;灿烂的 **III** *vi.* 发出光彩;闪光

sheeny[1] ['ʃiːni] *a.* 有光泽的;闪耀的

sheep [ʃiːp] 〔单复同〕 *n.* ①羊,绵羊: a flock of ~ 一群羊 / A ~ is bleating. 羊在咩咩叫。/ keep (或 tend) ~ 养羊 ②羊皮;羊皮革 ③害羞而忸怩的人;胆小鬼;蠢人;驯服的人 ④〔复〕〔谑〕(牧师教化的)教徒,教区居民 ‖a *black* ~ 败家子;败类,害群之马;拒绝参加罢工的工人 / a *lost* ~ 迷途的羊;误入歧途的人 / *as well be hanged for a* ~ *as* (*for*) *a lamb* 一不做,二不休;索性蛮干 / *a wolf in* ~*'s clothing* 披着羊皮的豺狼 / *cast* ~*'s eyes at sb.* 对某人做媚眼 / *follow like* ~ 盲从 / ~ *without a shepherd* 没有牧羊人的羊群;乌合之众 / *the* ~ *and the goats* 好人与坏人 ‖~ **cot(e)** 〔古〕羊栏,羊圈 / '~-**dip** *n.* 洗羊药水 / ~ **dog** 护羊狗 / ~ **farmer** 牧羊业者 / '~ˌfold *n.* 羊栏,羊圈 / '~ˌherder *n.* 〔美〕牧羊人 / '~-**hook** *n.* 牧羊杖 / '~ˌmaster *n.* 牧羊业者 / ~ **pen** 羊栏,羊圈 / ~ **run** 大牧羊场 / '~-**shank** *n.* ①羊的小腿 ②(将绳子暂时缩短的)缩结 ③〔苏格兰〕无价值的东西,不重要的东西 / '~-**shead** ['ʃiːpʃed] *n.* ①(食用的)羊头 ②【动】羊肉鲷(一种食用鱼) ③蠢人 / '~ˌshearer *n.* 剪羊毛的人;剪(羊)毛机(或工具) / '~ˌshearing *n.* 剪羊毛;剪羊毛的时节(或节日) / '~-**skin** *n.* ①绵羊皮革;羊皮袄;(带毛的)羊皮毯;(用作书面等的)羊皮纸;(写在羊皮纸上的)文件;毕业文凭 / **sorrel** 【植】小酸模 / '~-**walk** *n.* 牧羊场

sheepish ['ʃiːpiʃ] *a.* ①(像羊一般)驯顺的,胆怯的 ②忸怩的,害羞的,侷促不安的 ‖~**ly** *ad.* / ~**ness** *n.*

sheer¹[ʃiə] **I** *a.* ①全然的,十足的;彻底的,绝对的: ~ rubbish (或 nonsense)一派胡言 / by ~ chance 纯属偶然地 / by ~ force (determination) 全凭武力(决心) / a ~ fraud 彻头彻尾的骗局 / a ~ impossibility 绝对不可能 ②纯粹的,不掺杂的: ~ brandy 纯白兰地酒 ③(织物)极薄的;透明的: ~ muslin 薄(麦斯林)纱 / stockings of ~ silk 透明丝袜 ④陡峭的;垂直的: a ~ cliff 悬崖,峭壁 **II** *ad.* ①全然,彻底,十足: be torn ~ out by the roots 被连根拔掉 ②垂直地: a rock rising ~ from the water 屹立在水面上的巉岩 **III** *n.* 透明薄纱;透明薄织物;透明薄织物制的衣服 ‖~ly *ad.* / ~ness *n.*

sheer²[ʃiə] **I** *n.* ①[船]舷弧 ②[海]偏航,偏荡;转向 ③以单锚系泊的船位 **II** ❶ *vi.* 偏航,偏荡;转向,避开 (off, away) ❷ *vt.* 使偏航,使偏荡;使转向 ‖~ draft [船]船型线图 / '~legs [复] *n.* 起重三角架,人字起重架 / ~ plan [船]船舶侧视图

sheet [ʃi:t] **I** *n.* ①被单: put clean (或 fresh) ~s on the bed 在床上铺上干净的被单 ②裹尸布 ③[诗]帆 ④纸张;一张(纸);[复]书页;印刷品;(尤指黄色、下流的)报纸(或其他刊物);整版邮票: a ~ of notepaper 一张信纸 / The book is in ~s. 这本书尚未装订。 / mimeographed ~s of teaching materials 油印活页教材 / a supplementary ~ (报刊的)增页 / a hate ~ 煽动仇恨(尤指种族仇恨)的报纸 / a souvenir (或 miniature) ~ 一整版的纪念邮票 ⑤表格,单子;[美俚]罪犯的档案: a work ~ 工作记录单 / a pay ~ [英]工资单 (=[美] payroll) ⑥大片: The rain fell in ~s. 大雨滂沱。 ⑦成幅的薄片,薄板;(一)片,(一)块:a ~ of iron 一块薄铁板 / ~s in coils 金属薄板卷 ⑧[地]岩席 ⑨[海]缭绳,帆脚索 **II** ❶ *vt.* ①给…铺上被单;用裹尸布包;覆盖: ~ a bed 在床上铺被单 / the ~ed dead 包着寿衣的死人 / Mist ~s the valley. 雾笼罩着山谷。②铺开,展开,使成一大片: ~ed rain 大雨 ❷ *vi.* 大片地落下;成片铺开;大片地流动: The fog ~ed in from the sea. 雾从海上弥漫过来。 **III** *a.* ①滚压(或展开)成片的;片状的: steel ~ 薄钢板 ②制金属薄片的: a ~ mill 薄板轧机 ‖a blank ~ 一张空白纸;一张白纸似的心灵 / a clean ~ 清白的历史;品德良好的人 / a ~ in (或 to) the wind [俚]微醉 / get between the ~s 就寝 / put on (或 stand in) a white ~ 公开忏悔;公开认错 / ~ home ①迎风扯紧帆脚把帆(帆)张平 ②把(罪行等)归咎于 (to): ~ it home to sb. 确定某人对该事应负责任 / take a ~ off a hedge 公然盗窃 / three ~s in (或 to) the wind [俚]大醉 / white as a ~ 苍白如纸 / with flowing ~s [海]放松帆脚索 ‖~ anchor ①[船]备用大锚 ②[喻]最后的希望;最后的手段;最后的(或主要的)靠山 / ~ copper (紫)铜片 / ~ iron 黑钢皮,铁皮,铁板 / ~ lightning 片状闪电 / ~ metal 金属片,钢皮 / ~ music 活页乐谱

sheik(h) [ʃeik, ʃi:k] *n.* ①(阿拉伯国家的尊称)酋长;族长;村长 ②(伊斯兰教)教长 ③有威信的丈夫(或情人);[俚]美男子;[俚](妇女)迷人的男子 ‖~dom *n.* 酋长国 ‖Sheik(h) ul [ul] Islam 【史】(土耳其的)伊斯兰教法典权威

shelf [ʃelf] ([复] shelves [ʃelvz]) *n.* ①(壁橱、书橱等内)搁板;架子: replace the books on the shelves 把书放回书架 / a store ~ 商品陈列架 ②搁板上的东西;搁板的容量 ③搁板状物;突出的扁平岩石 ④沙洲,暗礁 ⑤【地】陆架;陆坡:continental ~ 大陆架 ⑥【矿】锡沙矿基岩 ⑦(支撑木船甲板梁的)承梁材 ⑧[俚]告密者(尤指同犯或同伙) ‖off the ~ [俚]复活 / on the ~ ①在搁板上 ②束之高阁,废弃的;不再流通的;不再流行的 ③(商业用语)推迟的,缓行的(指计划等)④(妇女)无结婚希望;[俚](解除婚约的女子)不活跃的,不交际的 ⑤[古]在当铺内 ⑥(盗贼用语)被流放了 ⑦[俚]死了 ‖~ life (罐装食品等的)货架寿命

shell [ʃel] **I** *n.* ①壳,果壳;荚: an egg ~ 蛋壳 / the ~ of a walnut 胡桃壳 / ~ roof 【建】薄壳屋顶 ②贝壳,甲: a tortoise ~ 乌龟(甲)壳 / cast the ~ 脱壳 ③壳状物,外壳,壳体;饼壳;套,罩;小啤酒杯 ④有甲壳的软体动物(尤该钻进壳内似的)缄默;冷淡,矜持 ⑤外表;外貌 ⑦(计划等的)梗概,轮廓 ⑧炮弹;猎枪子弹;爆破筒: an incendiary ~ 燃烧弹 / a tear (gas) ~ 催泪(毒)气弹 / a ~ body (case) 弹身(壳) / fire ~s at the enemy's stronghold 对准敌人据点开炮 ⑨地壳;坚硬岩层 ⑩[复原](原子的)电子壳层 ⑪轻快的赛艇 ⑫内棺 ⑬(剑把或刀柄上的)护手 [诗]竖琴,七弦琴 ⑮[英](学校的)中级班级 ⑯(船的)壳板;(房屋的)框架,骨架;内部未竣工的建筑物 **II** ❶ *vt.* ①剥…的壳,剥;使(小麦等)脱粒: ~ beans 剥豆 ②用贝壳铺;给…装售壳体 ③炮轰;射击: ~ the enemy's headquarters 炮轰敌军司令部 ❷ *vi.* ①(金属等)剥落,落成碎片 (off)②(壳;(颗粒)脱落,脱出 ③采集贝壳 ‖an old ~ 水手 / come out of one's ~ 去掉冷淡(或矜持)的态度,开始愿与别人交谈 / go (或 retire) into one's ~ 摆出冷淡(或矜持)的态度,开始保持缄默 / ~ out [口]交付,付出 ‖~er *n.* 剥壳者,脱粒者 / 剥壳器,脱粒机 / ~-less *a.* 无(贝)壳的 / ~-like *a.* 似壳的 ‖'~back *n.* ①老海员,老水手 ②越过赤道的航海者 / ~ bean 去壳吃的豆(以别于刀豆、豇豆等) / '~fire *n.* 炮轰;炮火 / '~fish *n.* 水生贝壳类动物 / ~ game [美]一种骗人的打赌游戏;骗局 / ~ gun 平射炮 / ~ heap, ~ mound (考古学用语)贝冢 / ~ jacket ①军用短身茄克衣 ②男式紧身茄克衣 / ~ lime 贝壳灰 / '~proof *a.* 防炮弹的 / ~ shock 【医】炮弹休克;弹震症 / '~shocked *a.* 患炮弹休克的 / '~work *n.* (装饰用)贝壳工艺品

shelter ['ʃeltə] **I** *n.* ①隐蔽处,掩蔽部;躲避处;避难所: a bus ~ 公共汽车站旁的候车亭 / a ~

from the wind 避风处 / an air-raid ～ 防空掩蔽部, 防空洞 / a fallout ～ 放射性微粒掩蔽所 ②掩蔽, 遮蔽; 庇护, 保护: get under ～ 隐蔽起来 / ～ trenches【军】掩壕 / find (或 take) ～ from the rain in a hut 在棚屋内避雨 / give ～ to sb. 庇护某人 / under the ～ of 在…的庇护下; 受…的保护 II ❶ vt. (使)掩蔽, 遮蔽; 庇护, 保护: The trenches ～ed us from enemy gunfire. 战壕掩蔽我们使不受敌人炮火袭击。 ～ sb. for the night 收容某人过夜 ❷ vi. 躲避; 避难: behind a hedge 躲在篱笆后 / ～ from trouble 避开麻烦 ‖an Anderson ～[英](上铺铁板的拱形)家庭简易防空洞 / lend the ～ of one's name and position to sb. 用自己的名誉地位庇护某人 / ～ed trades[英]不受外国竞争影响的行业(如建筑、国内运输等) / ～ oneself ①掩护自己 ②替自己找借口, 为自己辩护 ‖～less a. 无遮盖的; 无处藏身的 ‖～ area【军】战地宿营地区 / '～belt n. 防护林带 / ～ half【军】半幅双人帐篷(每人各带半幅, 以备战地应用) / ～ tent【军】双人帐篷

shelve¹ [ʃelv] vt. ①装搁板(或架子)于: ～ a closet 在壁橱内装搁板 ②把…放在搁板(或架子)上: ～ books 把书放上书架 ③搁置, 暂缓考虑: The proposal was ～d. 这建议被暂时搁置了。④把(某人)解雇; 使(军官等)退役

shelve² [ʃelv] vi. (渐次)倾斜, 成斜坡

shepherd [ˈʃepəd] I n. ①牧羊人, 羊倌 ②牧师 ③(保护羊群的)牧羊狗 II vt. ①牧(羊), 护(羊) ②看管; 护送; 带领; 指导: ～ the pupils on an excursion 带领小学生去远足 ③[军俚]使陷入困境 ④[俚](为诈骗等目的)跟踪, 盯…的梢; (在足球赛等中)盯住(对手) ‖the Good Shepherd【宗】耶稣 ‖～less a. 没有牧羊人的; 没有指导的 ‖～ dog 牧羊狗 / Shepherd king 古埃及喜克索王朝(或称"牧人王朝")的国王 / ～('s) check 黑白小格子花纹; 黑白格子布 / ～'s crook 牧羊杖 / ～'s pie 肉馅马铃薯饼 / ～('s) plaid =～('s) check / ～'s trade ①作田园诗 ②【宗】耶稣的业绩

sheriff [ˈʃerif] n. ①[英][常作 High S-] 郡长; (某些城市的)行政司法长官 ②[美]县的行政司法长官

sherry [ˈʃeri] n. (西班牙等地所产浅黄或深褐色的)葡萄酒, 雪利酒

shield [ʃiːld] I n. ①盾: a spear and a ～ 矛和盾 ②保护者; 庇护者 ③防护物; 护罩, 遮护板, 挡板 ④盾状物; 盾形徽章; [美]警察徽章 ⑤(腋下等的)吸汗垫布 ⑥【动】背甲; 头胸甲; 龟甲板 ⑦[地]地盾; [矿]掩护支架 ⑧【电】屏蔽; 铠装 II ❶ vt. ①保护; 保卫: ～ one's eyes from the light 遮住光线保护眼睛 ②庇护; 包庇; 掩盖 ③挡开, 避开(off): These trees will ～ off arid winds and protect the fields. 这些树林能挡住旱风, 保护农田。❷ vi. 起盾的作用; 起保护作用 ‖the other side of the ～ ①盾的反面 ②问题的另一面(或不太明显的方面) ‖Shield of David 大卫王的盾牌(犹太教的六芒星形标志)

shift [ʃift] I ❶ vt. ①替换; 转移, 移动; 转变, 变: ～ the scenes 换布景 ②推卸, 转嫁: Don't try to ～ the responsibility on to others. 不要企图把责任推给别人。③变(速), 调(档) ④【语】使音变(尤指辅音) ⑤[方]换(衣服); 使(某人)换衣服 ❷ vi. ①转换; 转移, 移动; 转变: ～ from the defensive to the offensive 由防御转入进攻 / The wind has ～ed to the north. 风已转入北面吹来。/ The cargo has ～ed. (因船的颠簸)船货移动了位置。②设法应付(或谋生), 想办法: ～ as one can 尽力设法应付 / ～ for oneself 自己尽量想办法(过日子等) ③推托; 欺骗 ④变速, 调档 ⑤【语】辅音音变 ⑥[方]换衣服 II n. ①换换; 转移; 转变: a ～ of crops 庄稼的轮作 / a strategic ～ 一次战略转移 / The plan shows a ～ in emphasis. 这个计划表明侧重点有了改变。②手段, 办法; 权宜之计: resort to desperate ～s 采取不顾一切的手法 / do sth. for a ～ 做某事来凑合一下 ③轮班; 轮班职工; 轮班工作时间: the day (night) ～ 日(夜)班 / go on (off) ～ 上(下)班 / work in three ～s 分三班工作 ④推托; 哄骗: a ～ of responsibility 推卸责任 ⑤【语】辅音的音变 ⑥[方]换衣服; [方]衬衫, 女用衬衫 ⑦[地]变位; (断层)平移 ⑧(演奏时)手在乐器上的移动 ‖make (a) ～ (在困难等条件下)尽力设法应付(或利用): The workers made ～ with what was on hand to improve the machine. 工人们尽力设法利用现有材料来改进机器。/ He had to make ～ without help. 他当时只能独自应付。/ ～ gears 见 gear / ～ off ①推卸(责任); 逃避(义务等); 回避(论点) ②用借口(或狡猾手段)把…打发走 / ～ one's ground =lose ground‖ ‖～er n. ①搬移东西者 ②回避论点者 ③(铁矿等的)领班; (煤矿中的)辅助工 ④【机】移带器; 移动装置; 开关 ‖～ key (打字机的)字型变换按钮

shiftless [ˈʃiftlis] a. ①无能的, 想不出办法的; 无计谋生的 ②偷懒的; 得过且过的 ‖～ly ad. / ～ness n.

shifty [ˈʃifti] a. ①足智多谋的, 随机应变的 ②惯耍花招的, 狡猾的; 躲躲闪闪的 ③变化多端的; 不稳定的 ‖shiftily ad. / shiftiness n. ‖'～-eyed a. [俚]躲躲闪闪的; 卑鄙的; 不能信任的

shilling [ˈʃiliŋ] n. ①先令(原英国货币单位, 二十先令为一镑, 十二便士为一先令; 略作 s., sh.) ②先令(坦桑尼亚、肯尼亚等的货币单位) ③美国早期的货币单位 ‖cut off one's heir with a ～ 见 heir / take the King's (或 Queen's) ～ 入伍当兵 / want twopence in the ～ 脑子不灵; 精神失常

shimmer [ˈʃimə] I ❶ vi. 发微光, 闪烁: the ～ing moonlight on the sea 海面上闪烁的月光 / waves ～ing before one's eyes 眩眼的波浪 ❷ vt. 使闪烁 II n. 微光, 闪光

shin [ʃin] I n. ①【解】胫; (昆虫的)胫节 ②牛的小

腿肉 **II** (shinned; shinning) ❶ *vi.* ①攀, 爬: ~ up a mast (tree) 爬上桅杆(树) / ~ down a drainpipe 沿着排水管爬下来 ②快步走 ❷ *vt.* ①(比赛时)踢(对手)的胫 ②攀, 爬 ‖'~bone *n.* 【解】胫骨 / '~dig *n.* 盛大舞会; 盛大社交聚会 / '~dig dancer (夜总会等处)表演色情舞蹈的女人 / ~ guard (运动员用的)护胫 / '~-plaster *n.* ①贴在胫部的伤膏药 ②私营银行印发的纸币(尤指不可靠和贬值的纸币) ③辅币

shine [ʃain] **I** (shone [ʃon; 美 ʃoun]) ❶ *vi.* ①照耀; 发光, 发亮: The sun ~s bright(ly). 阳光照耀。 / The star shone red on his cap. 他军帽上的红星闪闪发光。 / Her eyes shone with excitement. 她兴奋得两眼闪光。 / Happiness shone from her face. 她面露喜色。②显得出众, 杰出: He does not ~ in conversation. 他不善于谈吐。 / She ~s as a teacher. 她当教师很出色。 / a shining example 杰出的榜样 ❷ *vt.* ①使发光, 使发亮: Please ~ your flashlight over here. 请把手电筒往这儿照。②[过去式和过去分词用 shined] 擦亮: ~ shoes 擦皮鞋 **II** *n.* ① 光(亮), 擦(亮); 光辉, 光泽; 光彩: put a good ~ on the brasses 把铜器擦得金晃晃的 / give one's shoes a ~ 擦皮鞋 / works with a high literary ~ 光辉夺目的文学作品 ②阳光; 晴天: Rain or ~, we'll set out tomorrow. 不管天气好坏, 我们明天出发。③[常用复][俚]鬼把戏, 恶作剧 ④[俚]骚动; 吵闹 ‖ up to sb. [美俚]百般讨好某人 / take a ~ to [美俚]喜欢, 喜爱 / take the ~ off (或 out of) ① 使…的光泽消失 ②使黯然失色, 使相形见绌

shingle¹ [ˈʃiŋgl] **I** *n.* ①【建】木(片)瓦, 盖屋板 ②[美口]小招牌(尤指医生、律师的营业招牌): hang out (或 put up) one's ~ 挂牌开业 ③女子短发式样 **II** *vt.* ①用木瓦盖(屋顶) ②使象瓦片般重迭 ③把(女人头发)理成短式

shingle² [ˈʃiŋgl] *n.* ①(海滩)圆卵石 ②铺满圆卵石的海滩

shingle³ [ˈʃiŋgl] *vt.* 【冶】锻; 压

shingles [ˈʃiŋglz] [复] *n.* [用作单或复]【医】带状疱疹

shiny [ˈʃaini] *a.* ①晴朗的; 发亮的, 闪耀的 ②有光泽的; 擦亮的: ~ boots 擦亮的靴 ③磨光的; 磨损的: a ~ coat 因磨损而发亮的外衣 ‖shinily *ad.* / shininess *n.*

ship [ʃip] **I** *n.* [常用作阴性; 代词用 she, her] ①(大)船; 海船; 舰: a passenger ~ 客轮 / a sister ~ of (或 to) …的姊妹舰, 与…同型号的船只 / a ~ in (out of) commission 现(退)役舰 / a capital ~ 主力舰 / a free ~ 中立国船只 / take ~ 乘船 ②三桅帆船, 全装帆船 ③[俚]赛艇 ④全体船员 ⑤[美口]飞船, 飞机 **II** (shipped; shipping) ❶ *vt.* ①把…装上船 ②用船运; 装运, 运送: ~ goods by train 用火车运送货物 ③在舷侧进(水): The boat shipped a good amount of water. 船里进了大量的水。④安装(舵、桅杆等) ⑤把…放进船内: ~ the gangplank

把跳板收进船内 / ~ oars 把桨从桨架上取下放入船内 ⑥雇用…为船员 ⑦[美俚]解雇, 撵走; 开除(学生) ❷ *vi.* ①上船; 乘船 ②在船上工作, 做水手: ~ as bosun 在船上当水手长 ‖About ~! (对舵手发的命令)换向! / a ~ of the line (旧时备有七十四门炮的)大战舰 / dress ~ (为表示庆祝等)给船舰悬挂旗帜 / free alongside ~ 见 free / heave a ~ to [海]顶风停船 / a sea ~ [海]适于远航的船 / over ~ 重新进海军服役 / spoil (或 lose) the ~ for a ha'p'orth (或 halfpennyworth) of tar [谚]因小失大 / the ~ of the desert 沙漠之舟(即骆驼) / when one's ~ comes home (或 in) 当发财的时候; 当期望实现的时候 / wind a ~ 【海】掉转船头 ‖~less a. 无船的 / shippable a. 可装运的 ‖~ biscuit 硬饼干 / '~board n. 船; 船舷: meet on ~board 在船上碰见 / '~-breaker n. 收购和拆卸废船的承包人 / ~ broker 经营船舶买卖(或租赁、保险)的代理人, 船舶掮客 / '~-builder n. 造船技师; 造船工人 / '~building n. 造船(业) / 造船学 a. 造船(用)的 / ~ canal 能供海船航行的运河 / ~ chandler 船具商 / chandlery 船具业; 船具 / ~ fever 斑疹伤寒 / '~fitter n. 造船装配工, 船钳工 / '~load n. 船货; 船只运载量; [喻]大量: ~loads of merchandise 整船的商品; 大量商品 / ~man [ˈʃipmən] n. ① =~master ② 海员, 水手 / '~master n. (商船等的)船长 / ~mate n. 同船水手 / ~ money 【英史】造舰税 / '~-owner n. 船舶所有人; 船舶公司股东 / ~ railway 移船轨道 / '~-rigged a. 有横帆的 / ~'s articles 雇用船舶条例 / ~'s company 全体船员 / '~shape ad. & a. 整洁地(的), 整齐地(的), 井井有条地(的) / ~'s husband 船舶代理人(在岸上代表船方从事供应、修理等工作) / '~side n. 码头 / ~'s papers 船证, 船照 / ~'s service [美]舰上小卖部 / '~way n. ①造船台, 下水台 ②航道 / '~worm n. 【动】船蛆 / '~wreck n. 船只失事; 失事船的残骸; [喻]毁灭; 失败: suffer ~wreck 遭受船难 / make (或 suffer) ~wreck of one's hopes 希望破灭 vt. 使(船只)失事; 使(旅客等)遭受船难; 使毁灭 vi. 船只失事; 遭受毁灭 / '~wright n. 造船木工; 修船木工 / '~yard n. 船坞; 造船厂; 修船厂

shipment [ˈʃipmənt] *n.* ①装货, 装船; 装运: a ~ request 装运申请书 ②装载的货物(量)

shipper [ˈʃipə] *n.* 发货人; 托运人

shipping [ˈʃipiŋ] *n.* ①装运, 运送; 海运 ②航行: take ~ for the continent 乘船去大陆 ③[总称](一国或一海港的)船舶; 船舶吨数 ‖~ agent 运货代理商 / ~ articles 船员雇用合同 / ~ bill 船货清单, 舱单 / ~ office 运输事务所; 船员雇用管理处 / ~ order 装货单, 装货通知单

shirk [ʃəːk] **I** ❶ *vi.* ①溜掉, 偷偷跑掉; 开小差 ②逃避义务(或责任) ❷ *vt.* 逃避(义务、责任等): ~ one's duty towards 逃避对…的责任 /

~ school 逃学 **II** *n.* =~er ‖~er *n.* 逃避(义务)者;开小差的人

shirt [ʃəːt] *n.* ①(男式)衬衫: a work ~ 工作衫 / a sports ~ 短袖衬衫,运动衫 / have not a ~ to one's back [喻]穷得衣不蔽体 ②内衣;汗衫: a T-~ 短袖圆领紧身男汗衫 / a sweat ~ 圆领长袖运动衫 ③女用(仿男式)衬衫 ‖ *a boiled* ~ [美俚] ①浆过的衬衫,礼服中穿的衬衫 ②拘泥形式的人(或活动) / *a fried* ~ [美俚] 浆过的衬衫,礼服中穿的 / *get sb.'s* ~ *off* [俚]惹怒某人 / *give sb. a wet* ~ 使某人劳累得汗流浃背 / *keep one's* ~ *on* [俚]耐着性子,不发脾气;忍耐;镇静 / *lose one's* ~ 丧失全部财产 / *Near is my* ~, *but nearer is my skin.* [谚]首先考虑自己。 / *put* (或 *bet*) *one's* ~ *on* (或 *upon*) [俚]把全部家当押在…上 / *stripped to the* ~ 剥得只剩衬衫;只剩下最低限度的需要 / *wave the bloody* ~ ①(美国南北战争后)挑拨南北党派间的敌对情绪 ②挑唆冲突斗争 ‖~ed a. 穿着衬衫的 / ~ing *n.* 衬衫料子 ‖~band *n.* (衬衫领子、袖口等的)衬布 / ~ front 衬衫的前胸;衬衫的假前胸 / ~ sleeve 衬衫袖子: be in one's ~ sleeves 只穿衬衫未穿外衣 / ~-sleeve *a.* ①只穿衬衫(未穿外衣)的;[喻]不拘形式的,非正式的,随便的: a ~-sleeve audience (衣着随便的)衬衫观众(或听众) ② 朴素;切合实际的: ~-sleeve diplomacy 因作风坦率、随和而有成果的外交 / ~-tail *n.* ①衬衣下摆(尤指背部) ②[美俚](报刊的)社论栏;报纸文章后的附注 *a.* [美口]幼小的;小的;短的;(亲戚)远房的 / ~-waist *n.* 女用(仿男式)衬衫

shiver[1] [ˈʃivə] **I** ❶ *vi.* ①颤抖,哆嗦: ~ with cold 冷得发抖 / a ~ing fit 一阵寒颤(如发疟疾) ②(帆)迎风飘动 ❷ *vt.* 使(帆)迎风飘动 **II** *n.* 冷颤;战栗: send cold ~s down sb.'s back 使某人背上一阵发麻 / give sb. the ~s 使某人战栗

shiver[2] [ˈʃivə] **I** *n.* [常用复]碎块,裂片 **II** *vt.* & *vi.* (被)打碎,(被)敲碎;粉碎

shoal[1] [ʃoul] **I** *a.* (水)浅的 **II** *n.* ①浅滩;(退潮时露出的)沙洲: strike on a ~ 搁浅 ②[常用复][喻]暗礁,陷阱,潜伏的危机 **III** ❶ *vi.* 变浅 ❷ *vt.* ①使变浅 ②驶入(浅水等) ‖~er *n.* 沿海贸易商船(或水手)

shoal[2] [ʃoul] **I** *n.* 鱼群;大量,大群: receive letters of congratulation in ~s 收到大量的祝贺信 / ~s of people 成群结队的人 **II** *vi.* (鱼等)成群,群集

shock[1] [ʃɔk] **I** *n.* ①冲击,冲撞;震动,震荡: the ~ of tides on the seashore 海滨潮汐的冲击 / earthquake ~s 地震引起的震动 / bang the door with a ~ 砰地把门关上 ②震惊,(对神经的)震扰;引起震惊的事件(或东西);打击: His sudden death was a great ~ to his family. 他的突然逝世使他的家属大为震惊。 / It is meant for ~ effects only. 这只是为了耸人听闻而搞出来的。 ③突击: a ~ worker 突击手 ④(电流通过身体

引起的)电震,电击: get a ~ from a wire 碰着电线而触电 ⑤[医]休克;中风;心脏病引起的昏厥(尤指冠状动脉栓塞形成的): go into ~ three times within 48 hours 四十八小时中休克三次 / a case of shell ~ 炮弹休克症 / insulin ~ 胰岛素休克,惊厥 **II** ❶ *vt.* ①使震动,使震荡;使电震;使休克 ②使震惊(或愤慨,厌恶等): be very much ~ed at the sight (by the news) 看到这情景(知道这消息)感到非常震惊(或愤慨、厌恶等) ③震惊得使…: His senses were ~ed out of him for the moment. 他因震惊一时神志不清。 / ~ sb. *into* a stupor 把某人震惊得目瞪口呆 ❷ *vi.* ①震动;相撞击: His teeth ~ed against each other. 他的牙齿直打战。 ②使人感到震惊,吓唬人 ‖~ absorber [机]减震器 / ~-proof *a.* 防震的 / ~-re,sistant *a.* 抗震的 / ~ stall [空]激波失速,激波分离 / ~ treatment, ~ therapy (对精神病人的)电休克疗法 / ~ wave 冲击波,激波

shock[2] [ʃɔk] **I** *n.* (竖放在田里使干燥的)禾束堆 **II** *vt.* 把…做成禾束堆 ❷ *vi.* 捆堆禾束

shock[3] [ʃɔk] **I** *n.* 乱蓬蓬的一堆: an untidy ~ of hair 一团蓬乱的头发 **II** *a.* 蓬乱的,浓密的 ‖~-,headed, '~-head *a.* 头发蓬乱的

shocking [ˈʃɔkiŋ] **I** *a.* ①令人震惊的,骇人听闻的: ~ news 令人震惊的消息 ②不正当的;十分丑恶的;十分讨厌的: ~ conduct 十分丑恶的行为 ③[口]极坏的,糟糕的: ~ handwriting 很拙劣的书法 **II** [口][用于加强语气]很, 极: a ~ bad cold 很厉害的伤风 ‖~ly *ad.* ①令人震惊地 ②极糟地 ③极度地,极厉害地

shod [ʃɔd] **I** shoe 的过去式和过去分词 **II** *a.* ①穿着鞋的 ②装有轮胎的 ③(马)装有蹄铁的 ④裹了金属包头的

shoddy [ˈʃɔdi] **I** *a.* ①长弹毛的,软再生毛的 ②质量差的,以次货充好的 **II** *n.* ①[纺]长弹毛,软再生毛;软再生毛织物 ②冒充的好货;赝品 ‖shoddily *ad.* / shoddiness *n.*

shoe [ʃuː] **I** *n.* ①鞋: put on (take off) one's ~s 穿(脱)鞋 / a pair of homemade cotton ~s 一双自制布鞋 / have one's leather ~s resoled (reheeled, revamped) 把皮鞋送去换底(换后跟,换鞋面) ②蹄铁 ③鞋状物;[喻]似鞋的)金属包头 ④轮胎,外胎 ⑤[建]桩靴 ⑥制动器;[机]闸瓦 ⑦[电]端;靴;管头 ⑧防磨(或防滑)的装置;[空]尾撑;导向板,发射导轨 ⑨[复][喻]地位,境遇 **II** (shod [ʃɔd] 或 shoed) *vt.* ①给…穿上鞋;给(马)钉蹄铁 ②给…装上鞋状物;用金属片包覆: a pole shod with iron 包了铁头的杆子 ‖another pair of ~s 另外一回事 / die in one's ~s (或 die with one's ~s on) 不死在床上,横死,暴死 / fill one's ~s 就位 / in another's ~s 处于别人的地位(或境遇) / lick sb.'s ~s 巴结某人,向某人摇尾乞怜 / over ~s over boots 将错就错,一不做二不休 / put the ~ on the right foot 责

备该受责备者; 表扬该受表扬者 / **shake in one's ~s** 两腿直哆嗦, 怕得发抖 / **~ the goose** (或 **gosling**) 见 **goose** / **stand in the ~s of sb.** 取得某人的位置; 处在某人的境遇 / **step into the ~s of sb.** 接替某人的职位 (或位置); 步某人后尘 / **The ~ is on the other foot.** 位置完全颠倒了。/ **wait for dead men's ~s** 等待别人死去以求继承遗产 / **where the ~ pinches** 症结所在; 困难 (或烦恼、痛苦) 之处 ‖**~less** *a.* 不穿鞋的; 赤脚的; 没有鞋的 / **~r** *n.* 钉蹄铁工人 ‖**~black** *n.* 擦皮鞋的人 / **~ buckle** 鞋扣 / **'~horn** *n.* 鞋拔 *vt.* 把…硬塞 (或硬挤) 进去 / **'~lace** *n.* 鞋带 / **~ leather** 制鞋用的皮革; 皮鞋 / **~ lift** 鞋拔 / **'~maker** *n.* 制 (或补) 鞋工人; 鞋铺老板 / **'~making** *n.* 制鞋业 / **'~pac(k)** *n.* (冬天穿在厚袜外的) 缚带防水鞋 / **~ polish** 鞋油 / **'~shine** *n.* ①擦皮鞋 ②擦皮鞋者 ③擦亮的皮鞋面 / **'~string** *n.* ①鞋带 ②[美口]少额资本:. **on a ~string** 小本经营地 *a.* ①鞋带一样狭长的 ②小本经营的; 小规模的, 小范围的 ③微小的, 微弱的: **a ~string** majority 微弱多数 ④近踝部的 / **~ tree** 鞋楦

shoo [ʃuː] **I** *int.* ①嘘! (驱赶鸟禽等的声音) ②滚开! **II ❶** *vi.* "嘘嘘" 地赶 **❷** *vt.* "嘘" 的一声赶走, 吓走

shoot [ʃuːt] **I** (shot [ʃɔt]) **❶** *vt.* ①发射, 放射; 射出 (光线等); 开 (枪), 放 (炮): **~ a bullet** 发射子弹 / They are going to **~** live ammunition today. 他们今天要实弹射击了。/ **~ the arrow at the target** 对着靶射箭 / 有的放矢 / **a rifle** 开枪 / ②射中; 射伤; 射死; [喻] 损毁; 使破灭: **be shot in the head** 头部中弹 / **~ sb. (dead)** 击毙某人, 枪毙某人 / This mechanism has been **shot** by prolonged misuse. 这个机械装置由于长期滥用而毁坏了。③投射 (视线等); 挥出, 抛出; 连珠炮似地说出 (问难等): **~ an indignant look at sb.** (或 **~ sb. an indignant look**) 怒气冲冲地瞪某人一眼 / **~ one's fist at sb.** 朝某人挥拳打去 / **~ questions at a speaker** 向演讲者提出一连串问题 / **~ a fishnet across a river** 拦河撒鱼网 ④打 (猎物); 在…中射猎: **~ tigers** 猎虎 / **a covert** 在树丛中打猎 ⑤伸出 (苗头等), 突出; 发 (芽): The trees are **~ing out** new branches. 树在长新枝。⑥(船等) 飞速通过; 急送, 急遣; 使 (船等) 飞速行进: **~ a bridge** 迅速从桥底穿过 / **~ the rapids** 迅速通过急流 / **~ sb. over to headquarters** 火速派某人去司令部 ⑦拍摄: **~ sb. from various angles** 从各种不同的角度给某人拍照 / They have **shot** several scenes this week. 本星期他们已拍摄了 (影片的) 好几个场景。⑧闩 (门闩等); 拔出 (门闩等); 【纺】投 (梭): **~ a bolt** 闩上 (或拔出) 门闩 ⑨把…兜底倒出, 倾卸; 挥霍, 耗尽: **~ rubbish** 倾倒垃圾 / What, you have **shot** your roll already? 什么, 你的钱已经化完了? ⑩把…刨精确, 刨光: **~ the edge of a board** 把板边刨准确 ⑪测量 (星辰等) 的高度: **~ the sun** (用六分仪) 测量太阳高度 ⑫点着; 使爆炸; 炸开; 用爆破法开采 (煤矿等): **~ a charge of dynamite** 爆破一包炸药 / **~ off the firecrackers** 放鞭炮 ⑬(足球运动中) 射 (门); (篮球运动中) 投 (篮); 击 (球); 掷 (骰子); 赌 (钱): **~ a basket** 投篮得分 / **~ the ball into the goal** 把球踢进球门 / **~ a round of golf** 打一盘高尔夫球 ⑭给…注射: have the children **shot for diphtheria** 让孩子们都打了白喉预防针 ⑮[美俚] 把 (食物) 递给 (to): Will you **~** the salt *to* me? 把盐递给我好吗? **❷** *vi.* ①射出; 放出; 抛出; (箭一般地) 飞驰, 飞快地移动: The guns **~** many miles. 这些炮能射好几哩远。/ blood **~ing** from the wound 从伤口喷出来的血 / The yacht **shot** forward. 游艇飞也似地向前驶去。/ The meteor **shot** across the sky. 流星飞快地掠过天空。/ The elevator **shot** upward. 电梯飞快地上升。/ An idea **shot** into his mind. 他突然想到一个主意。②射击; 射猎: Do you (Does your gun) **~** straight? (你的枪) 打得准吗? / He was out **~ing.** 他出去打猎了。③突出, 伸展; (幼芽、枝叶等) 长出: Buds are **~ing** early this year. 今年抽芽早。④拍电影; 拍照 ⑤(门闩) 被闩上; 被拔出; 【纺】投梭: The shuttle **shot** across the loom. 梭子在织机上一穿而过。⑥(疼痛等) 刺激: The tooth **~s.** 牙齿一阵阵剧痛。⑦射门; 投篮; 打高尔夫球; 掷骰子 ⑧[美国] 把话讲出来: All right, **~** and be quick. What's happened? 好, 讲吧, 快讲! 发生了什么事? **II** *n.* ①发芽; 抽枝; 嫩枝, 芽, 苗: bamboo **~s** 笋 / rice **~s** 禾苗, 秧苗 ②射猎 (队); 射猎会; 射猎权; 射猎场; 射击会; (射击比赛的) 一轮 ③发射; 射出; (火箭、导弹等的) 试验发射: **a moon ~** 向月球进行的发射 ④拍摄 ⑤(飞箭一般的) 急速动作; 奔流; 供急流通过的水道; 【矿】滑槽: **a ~ of one's arms** 双臂急速的一伸 ⑥(疼痛、愉快等的) 刺激 ⑦推力; (冰块、土块的) 崩落 ⑧(划桨时) 两划间的间隔时间 ⑨一道光线: **a ~ of sunlight** 一道阳光 ⑩垃圾源? ‖**I'll be shot if....** (否定时的强调语气) 假如…的话, 那我就不得好死。/ **~ ahead** 飞速向前; (比赛中) 迅速超过对手: Towards the end of the run, he **shot** ahead. 赛跑近终点时, 他猛然冲到前面去了。/ **~ at** ①向…射击; 朝…投去: **~ at the target** 打 (或射) 靶 / **~ at the basket** (篮球运动中) 投篮 ②[口] 力争, 为…而努力: **~ at a high output** 力争高产 / **~ away** ①不停地射击 ②打光 (子弹等), 射完: They have **shot away** all their ammunition. 他们把子弹都打完了。/ **~ down** 击落; 击毙; 击伤 / **~ for** [口] 争取, 为…而努力: **~ for a good result** 力争一个好结果 / **~ forth** 射出; (芽等) 抽出, 苞出 / **~ off** ①发射; 击毙; 击落; 打掉: He **shot off** seven cartridges. 他打了七发子弹。/ **~ off a gun** 放炮 / He had his leg **shot off.** 他的腿给打断了。②参加射击会决赛 ③夸夸其谈, 信口开河 / **~ off one's mouth** 见 **mouth** / **~ out** ①抛出; 射出: He was **shot out** in the collision of the cars. 两车相撞时他被摔出车外。/ The boat *shot out* from the reeds. 小船飞也似地从芦苇丛中穿出。②击灭(灯火等) ③(突然)伸出; 抽出(枝、芽等) / ~ *out* one's tongue (突然)伸出舌头 / ~ *out* buds 长出新芽 ④用武力解决 / ~ *straight* (或 *square*) 言行正直 / ~ *up* ①射出, 喷出: The flames ~ *up*. 火舌向上喷出。②(植物)发芽; (儿童等)长大, 长高: The boy is ~*ing up* fast. 这小孩长得很快。③急升(价格等)暴涨 ④[俚]注射麻醉剂 ⑤[美俚]向...乱开枪:The intruders *shot up* the town. 入侵者在镇上乱打了一阵枪。/ *take a* ~ (船不在大河行驶而)在激流中驶过; 走近路 / *the whole* ~ 一切, 全部 ||~*able* *a.* 可射击的; 适于射猎的 / ~*er n.* ①射手, 炮手; (油井等的)爆破手 ②流星 ③[常用以构成复合词]手枪: a six-~*er* 六响枪 ④(板球中的)擦地球 ||'~-'em-,up *n.* 描写枪击凶杀的影片(或电视节目) / '~-off *n.* (射击比赛的)决赛 / '~-out *n.* 交火; 开枪决斗 / '~-the='chutes [复] *n.* [用作单或复]滑雪驾涛游戏(指乘着平底船由陡峭滑入水中的游戏)

shooting ['ʃu:tiŋ] *n.* ①射击; 射杀, 持枪杀人 ②射猎, 游猎; [主英]射猎权; 猎场 ③刺痛, 剧痛 ④(篮球)投篮; (足球)射门 ||~ **box** [主英]狩猎者狩猎季节住的小屋 / ~ **brake** ①(旧时)狩猎用马车 ②[英]旅行汽车 / ~ **gallery** ①打靶场, 射击场 ②[美俚]有毒瘾者注射麻醉剂的场所 / ~ **iron** [俚]火器, 手枪 / ~ **match** ①射击竞赛 ②整个儿, 全部: be tired of the whole ~ *match* 对整个儿事情感到厌烦 / ~ **range** 打靶场, 射击场 / ~ **script** ①(电影)拍摄用的剧本, 分镜头剧本 ②(电视节目)演出用的定稿剧本 / ~ **star** ①流星 ②[美俚]流星花 / ~ **stick** (顶端可打开作坐凳的)手杖 / ~ **war** 热战(指真枪实弹的战争, 与冷战、神经战相对而言)

shop [ʃɔp] **I** *n.* ①[主英]商店, 店铺(=[美] store): a chemist's ~ 药房 / a fruit-~ 水果店 ②[美](大店内的)专业零售部; 专业服务部(也作 shoppe [ʃɔp]): a sport ~ (大商店内的)体育用品部 ③车间, 工场; 工厂: an assembly ~ 装配车间 / a foundry ~ 铸工车间, 翻砂车间 / a car-penter ~ 木工场 / a machine ~ 机械车间;机器厂 / a runaway ~ [美](为逃避赋税或工会压力而迁移的)外逃工厂 ④本行; 与职业有关的事; 行话 ⑤工作室; 工作处 ⑥[美俚]办事处 ⑥(教手艺用的)学校实验室; 工艺(学) **II** (shopped; shopping) ❶ *vi.* ①到商店去买东西; 到处选购商品 (*around*): ~ for clothes 到商店去买衣服 / go *shopping* 去买东西 ②到处寻找 (*around*) ❷ *vt.* ①[方]逮捕;拘禁; 告发(同犯)使人狱 ②选购(商品);在(商店)内选购商品(以期得到有关商品的消息等)浏览(报纸、商品目录等) ③把(车辆等)送去检修 ||*all over the* ~ [俚]零乱, 到处(散置着): His things are *all over the* ~. 他的东西丢得到处都是。/ *look for sth. all over the* ~ 到处寻找某物 / *a slap-bang* ~ (不能赊帐的)小饭店 / *come* (或 *go*) *to the wrong* ~ [口]

(指求助、询问等)找错对象 / *cut the* ~ 不再谈论本行的事 / *keep a* ~ 当店主, 开店兼管店务 / *keep* ~ 照管店务 / *set up* ~ 开店; 开业 / ~ *around* [美] ①逐店进行搜购 ②到处寻找好职位(或主意等) / *shut up* ~ ①关店, 打烊; 歇业 ②[口]停止做某事 / *sink the* ~ 不谈有关本行的事; 隐瞒自己的职业 / *smell of* ~ 本行气息十足 / *talk* ~ 说行话, 三句不离本行 / *the other* ~ 竞争的对手 / *the Shop* [英俚]英国陆军士官学校 ||~ **assistant** [英]店员 / '~-**bell** *n.* (装在店门口顾客进门时作响的)店铃 / '~**boy** *n.* 青年男店员 / ~ **card** (工会发给按劳资契约经营的商店的)营业卡, 营业证 / ~ **chairman**, ~ **deputy** = ~ steward / ~ **committee** (资本主义国家)厂矿中代表劳方跟资方谈判的委员会 / ~ **drawing** 制造图, 工作图 / '~**girl** *n.* 女店员 / '~**hours** [复] *n.* 营业时间 / '~-**in** *n.* [美]黑人针对实行种族歧视的自动商店采取的一种示威行动 / '~**keeper** *n.* 店主: a nation of ~*keepers* 店主之国(对英国的蔑称) / '~,**keeping** *n.* 店务管理 / '~,**lifter** *n.* 冒充顾客进商店行窃的扒手 / '~,**lifting** *n.* 冒充顾客进商店行窃 / ~**man** ['ʃɔpmən] *n.* 店主; 店员 / '~-**soiled** *a.* =~worn / ~ **steward** (资本主义国家)工厂(或车间)的工人代表 / '~**talk** *n.* 行话; 有关本行的谈论 / '~,**walker** *n.* 大商店中的巡视员, 顾客招待员 / '~,**window** *n.* 商店橱窗: dress a ~window 布置橱窗 / put all one's goods in the ~window (或 have everything in the ~window) [喻](指肤浅的人)拼命卖弄才能 / '~**worn** *a.* 在商店里陈列得旧了的; 陈旧的

shore[1] [ʃɔ:] *n.* ①滨;岸: go on ~ 上岸 / troops of the ~ arms [军]岸上部队 / Show me your ~ pass, please. 请出示登陆证。 ②【律】涨潮线与落潮线之间的地带 ||*in* ~ 近岸, 靠岸: steer a ship *in* ~ 驶船靠岸 / *off* ~ ①离岸 ②在离岸不远处 ||~**less** *a.* ①无岸的 ②无边无际的 / ~**ward** *a.* 向海岸的 *ad.* =~wards / ~**wards** *ad.* 向海岸 ||'~-**based** *a.* [军]①以陆上为基地的 ②以海岸为基地的, 岸基的 / ~ **bombardment** 舰炮对岸上的轰击 / ~ **dinner** 以新鲜海货作菜肴的一顿饭 / ~ **leave** 海员上岸假期 / '~**line** *n.* 滨线, (海)岸线 / ~ **party** ①两栖作战中的海岸后勤工作队 / ~ **patrol** (美国海军或海军陆战队的)岸上宪兵, 基地宪兵(常略作 SP) / ~**sman** ['ʃɔ:zmən] *n.* (渔业等海上事业的)陆上勤务人员

shore[2] [ʃɔ:] **I** *n.* (房屋、船等的)斜撑柱 **II** *vt.* 用斜撑撑住; 支持 (*up*)

short [ʃɔ:t] **I** *a.* ①短的; 近的: a ~ story 短篇小说 / a ~ ~ story 超短篇小说(通常只占杂志上一页篇幅, 情节发展快, 结局突兀) / The coat is a bit too ~ *on* him. 这件上衣他穿起来太短了些。/ The bus stop is a ~ way off. 汽车站离这儿不远。②短期的, 短暂的, 短促的: a ~ bill 短期票据 / a ~ time ago 不久以前 / in the space of a few ~ years 在短短的几年中 / The hero's life was ~ but brilliant. 英雄的一生是短暂而光辉的。/ set out at ~ notice 临时接到通知出发 ③矮的;低的: He is ~ in stature. 他身材矮小。/ a ~ smokestack (轮船等的)低烟囱 ④短缺的,不足的;缺钱用的: He emerged from the war, a brother ~. 战争中他失去了一个兄弟。/ These goods are in ~ supply. 这些货物供应不足。/ That has left him temporarily ~. 这使得他暂时手头拮据。⑤(智力等方面)弱的, 浅薄的;(记忆力)差的: a man long on ideas but ~ on knowledge 看问题目光短浅的人 / take ~ views 看问题目光短浅 / a ~ memory 不好的记性 ⑥简慢的, 唐突的;暴躁的: He was very ~ with me today. 他今天对我很简慢无礼。/ a ~ temper 急性子, 暴躁的脾气 ⑦简短的;简略的;缩写的: His answer was ~ and to the point. 他的回答简短扼要。/ make a long story ~ 长话短说, 简而言之 / "Doc" is ~ for "doctor". "doc"是"doctor"的缩写。⑧(金属等)脆的, 松脆的;易裂(成片、块)的: This biscuit eats ~. 这饼干吃起来很松脆。/ ~ clay 粘性很差的粘土 / ~ mortar 砂砾过多的灰浆 / ~ ink【印】颜料含量高的不稠的油墨 ⑨波涛汹涌的: a ~ sea 波涛汹涌的大海 ⑩(酒类)不掺水的, 烈性的;少量的: a ~ drink 烈酒 / 餐前喝的少量鸡尾酒 / have a drop of something ~【口】喝一点烈酒 / a ~ beer 一小杯啤酒 ⑪(股票投机等)卖空的, 空头交易的: a ~ sale 卖空 / a ~ contract 空头交易合同 ⑫【语】(元音)短音的;(音节)非重读的;(诗歌)短音节的 II ad. ①简短地: talk ~ with everyone present 在场的每个人简短地交谈 ②唐突地; 突然地, 出其不意地: bring (或 take) sb. up ~ 唐突地打断某人的话 / pull up ~ 突然停住 / be caught ~ 被当场发觉(或抓住) ③达不到目标地: The shells dropped ~. 炮弹没有达到目标。④以空头方式(指股票投机等) III n. ① [the ~] 扼要, 实质: The ~ of it is .... 这事情的要点是… ②【语】短音;短音节;【音】短音符 ③(电影)短片;(报刊等的)短讯, 短篇特写 ④矮个子的衣服尺码;[复]短裤 ⑤[复]细麸粉(磨面粉的副产品);废料,下脚 ⑥[复]次品;半成品(或半制品);废品,次品(或额) ⑦接近目标但未命中的射弹 ⑧不足规定长度的东西; 长度在法定可捕标准以下的鱼(或龙虾) ⑨不掺水的(烈性)酒 ⑩【电】短路 ⑪【商】空头(户);[复]短期债券 ⑫(棒球)游击手 ⑬[美俚]汽车 IV vt. ①故意少给…找头;欺骗;【电】使短路 ‖be on ~ commons 见 common / be ~ and sweet (说话)简短扼要 / be taken ~【口】突然觉得要大便 / break ~ 见 break¹ / cut ~ 见 cut / fall ~ (of) 见 fall / for ~ 简称,缩写: Robert, called "Bob" for ~ 罗伯特,简称"鲍勃" / go ~ (of) 匮乏(…), 缺乏(…) / in ~ 总之, 简言之: In ~, we must be prepared. 总而言之, 我们要有准备。/ little (或 nothing) ~ of 简直不比…差,简直可以说…: Their achievements are

little (或 nothing) ~ of miraculous. 他们的成就简直是奇迹。/ make ~ work of sth. / on ~ time 见 time / run ~ (of) 缺少(…);用完(…): Gasoline was running ~ on the car. 汽车的汽油不够了。/ sell ~ 见 sell / ~ of ①缺乏,不足: Short of tools, we made our own. 没有工具, 我们自己造。/ be no longer ~ of doctors 不再缺少医生 ②达不到: We will never stop ~ of the goal. 不达目的, 决不罢休。③除了…以外: take all measures ~ of war 采用除战争外的一切手段 ④只要没有…, 只要不…: Short of unexpected delay on his way, he'll arrive by tomorrow. 只要路上没有意外的耽搁,他最迟将在明天到达。/ squeeze the ~s 轧空头,迫使卖空者用高价补进 / the ~ and (the) long 要旨, 概略 ‖~ly ad. ①立刻; 不久: The plane will take off ~ly. 飞机马上要起飞了。/ ~ly before (after) noon 中午前(后)不久 ②简短地;唐突地,简慢地: answer rather ~ly 相当简慢地回答 / ~ness n. ①短; 矮; 低 ②缺乏, 不足: ~ness of breath 气急 ③简短, 简略: for the sake of ~ness 为了简短 ④松脆;(金属等的)脆性: cold ~ness【冶】冷脆性, 常温脆性 ‖~ ballot 限于对少数主要官员(或议员等)的选举 / '~bread, ~cake n. 脆饼, 松饼 / ,~'change vt. 故意少给…找头, 欺骗 / ~ circuit【电】短路 / '~-'circuit vt. ①使短路 ②简化, 缩短(程序) ③阻碍; 葬送(友谊等) / '~clothes, ~coats [复] n. 婴儿脱离褓褓后所穿的童装 / '~coat vt. 给(过了婴儿期的孩子)开始穿童装 / ~'coming n. 缺点, 短处 / '~cut n. 近路, 捷径 / '~'dated a. (票据等)短期的 / '~day a. 【植】短日照的 / ~ division 【数】(不写明演算过程的)简短除法 / ~ end (打赌等)处于劣势的一方,接受让步条件的一方;输掉的一方 / '~fall n. 缺少,不足;亏空 / ~hand n. 速记: take down the conversation in ~hand 用速记把谈话记录下来 / '~'handed a. 缺乏人手的 / ~ head [英](赛马中)不到一个马头的距离: win by a ~ head 小胜 / '~-'head vt. [英](赛马中)以不到一个马头的距离胜过; 略胜 / '~horn n. ①[常作 S-] 短角牛 ②[美俚]刚到边远(或新辟)地区的人;生手 / '~-'landed a. (货物)卸下后发货短少的,短剑的 / ~ line 短程交通路线 / ~ list (供最后挑选用的)人数已缩减的候选人(或谋职业者)名单 / '~-list vt. 把…列入缩减的候选人(或谋职业者)名单 / ~-lived ['∫ɔ:t'livd; 美 '∫ɔ:t'laivd] a. 短命的;短暂的 / ~ order (点)快餐 / '~-'paid a. 欠资的: a ~-paid airmail letter 一封欠资航空信 / ~ range 近射程, 近距离 / '~-'run a. 短期的 / '~-'shipped a. (货物)已报出口但未装船(或重行起岸)的, 退关的 / '~'sighted a. 近视的;目光短浅的 / ~ snort [俚]快饮(指饮酒) / ~ snorter 远航俱乐部的成员(须有横越海洋的飞行经历) / '~-'spoken a. 说话简短的;简慢的,无礼的 / ~ stop ①(棒球)游击手(位置)

②【摄】速显液 / ～ **subject** (与正片同时放映的)电影短片(如动画片等) / **'～-'tempered** *a.* 急性子的, 脾气暴躁的 / **'～-term** *a.* 短期的: ～-term training classes 短期训练班 / a ～-term loan 短期贷款 / **'～-,termer, '～-,timer** *n.* 服短期徒刑的犯人 / ～ **ton** 短吨 (=2,000 磅) / **'～'wave** *n.* 【无】短波; 短波无线电发射机 *vt.* 用短波无线电发射 / **～-winded** ['ʃɔːt'windid] *a.* ①气短的, 气急的; 容易生气的 ②简短的; 不连贯的

shortage ['ʃɔːtidʒ] *n.* 不足, 缺少; 不足额: make up for labour and material ～s 补劳动力和材料的不足 / a ～ of 100 tons of coal 一百吨的短缺额

shorten ['ʃɔːtn] ❶ *vt.* ①弄短, 缩短; 减少: ～ a long article 缩短一篇长文 / ～ the period of schooling 缩短学制 / Please have this coat ～ed. 请把这件上衣改短。/ ～ sail 【海】缩帆 / Their pleasures were ～ed by the bad weather. 他们因天气不好而兴致不高了。②减小…的力量, 减低…的效能 ③使松脆 ④给(孩子)穿童装 ❷ *vi.* 变短, 缩短, 缩小: The days begin to ～ after the summer solstice. 夏至以后白天开始变短。‖ **～ing** *n.* ①缩短 ②使糕饼松脆的油

shot[1] [ʃɔt] **I** *n.* ①发射; 射击, 开枪; 射击声: a ～ of lightning 一道闪电 / fire a rocket ～ at the moon 向月球发射火箭 / a flying ～ 对飞翔物的射击 / exchange ～s 交火 / Shots rang through the forest. 森林中枪声回响。②[单复同]弹丸, 子弹; 炮弹; 霰弹; 铅沙粒;【体】铅球: a case ～ 霰弹, 开花炮弹 / a chilled ～ 穿甲铅弹头 / Shot does (或 do) well for cleaning bottles. 用铅沙粒洗玻璃瓶效果很好。/ put the ～ 推铅球 ③射程; 范围: be out of ～ 在射程之外 ④射击手: a crack (或 dead) ～ 神枪手 ⑤尝试; 猜测, 推测: That's a very good ～. 猜得很准。/ make a lucky ～ 碰巧猜着 ⑥拍摄; (电影等一次曝光的)镜头, (一段)影片; 照相: an exterior ～ 外景拍摄 / a special ～ 特写镜头 / a long (close) ～ 远(近)景 / take a ～ of sb. 给某人拍照 ⑦【矿】爆破; 炮眼;(一次爆破所用的)炸药: tunnel through the mountain with a chain of ～s 用一连串爆破打通山 ⑧注射;[美俚](吗啡等的)一次注射;一服: have (或 get) a penicillin ～ 注射青霉素 / a malaria ～ 治疗疟疾用的注射(剂) / The asthmatic patient was given a ～ of oxygen. 气喘病人接了一次氧气。⑨(烈酒等的)一口, 一杯;(清凉饮料等的)一份, 一客 ⑩中肯的话, 一针见血的评语 ⑪【体】(一次)射门, 投篮; (乒乓等的)一击: fast block ～s 快速挡接 ⑫(一次)撒网;【纺】(一次)投梭: bag a large quantity of fish at one ～ 一网打了许多鱼 ⑬[口](酒吧间等的)应付帐: pay one's ～ 付帐 ⑭[口]机会; 可操胜算的赌注 **II** (shotted; shotting) *vt.* ①给…装弹; 给…加铅粒(使变得沉重) ②(用喷射法)使成颗粒状 ‖ **a bad ～** ①不准的射击; 不行的射击手 ②猜错 ③错误, 失策 / **a big ～** 大人物, 大亨, 有权势的人 / **a gallery** ～ (赛球或演戏时)

卖弄技巧的表演, 为博得喝采的表演 / **a long ～** ①不大会成功的尝试;[口]冒险打赌 ②[口]无获胜(或成功)机会的人(或事) / **as a ～** 作为猜测: As a ～, I should say she's about forty. 我猜她大概四十岁左右。/ **a ～ in the arm** [美俚]麻醉针皮下注射; 兴奋剂; 刺激因素 / **a ～ in the eye** [口]恶意的行为; 敌对的举动 / **a ～ in the locker** ①战舰弹仓内存下的最后一弹 ②备用钱; 最后的办法: not a ～ in the locker 身无分文; 毫无办法 / **call the ～s** 定调子; 发号施令; 操纵 / **have (或 take) a ～ at (或 for)** [口]试着去做(或打、夺、赶等)…: I'll have a ～ for the train. 我想试一试, 看能不能赶上这班火车。/ **like a ～** 飞快地; 立刻, 马上 / **not by a long ～** 绝对没有希望; 远没有; 决不 / **powder and ～** 见 powder ‖ **～ effect** 【无】散粒效应 / **'～gun** *n.* 猎枪; 滑膛枪; [美俚]机关枪 *a.* ①(用)猎枪的; (用)滑膛枪的: a ～gun shell. 霰弹 ②(以武力等)强迫的; 爱用武力的: a ～gun agreement 强迫达成的协议 / a ～gun marriage (或 wedding) 为怀孕所迫的结婚; [喻]强迫的结合(或协调) ③笼统的, 漫无目标的: a selective, not ～gun investigation 有重点的而非笼统的调查 *vt.* ①(用滑膛枪)射击 ②(以武力等)强迫 / ～ **hole** ①爆破井; (地震的)爆破坑; 炮眼 ②(木头上的)蛀洞 / ～ **metal** 霰弹原料 / ～ **put** 推铅球 / **'～-,putter** *n.* 推铅球的人 / ～ **tower** (采用滴铅入水法的)制弹塔

shot[2] [ʃɔt] *a.* ①闪色的; 杂色的: ～ cloth (或 silk) 闪光绸, 闪色绸 / ～ effect 【纺】闪色效应, 闪光效应 / His hair was ～ with grey. 他头发花白。②交织着的; 渗透的: be ～ through with wit 充满着机智 ③丸粒状的: ～ copper 铜粒 ④点焊的 ⑤[美俚]筋疲力尽的; 病弱的; 用坏的, 破旧的; 毁灭的, 破灭的; 失败的: These machines are pretty well ～. 这些机器都坏得一塌糊涂了。/ be ～ down [口] 被完全驳倒 / His chances are ～. 他失去机会了。⑥[俚]喝醉的

should [强 ʃud; 弱 ʃəd, ʃd] (shall 的过去式) *v. aux.* ①[表示过去将来时; 常用于间接引语]将: The group leader announced that we ～ begin to work soon. 小组长宣布, 我们不久就将开始工作了。②[表示语气较强的假设]万一, 竟然: Should it rain tomorrow (或 If it ～ rain tomorrow), the meeting would be postponed. 万一明天下雨, 会议就延期。③[用于第一人称时表示某种条件下会产生的结果; 用于第二、第三人称时表示说话者的意愿]就, 该: If you were here, I ～ be very glad. 要是你能在这儿的话, 我就很高兴了。/ I ～ have seen you if you had been at the meeting. 要是你当时参加会议的话, 我该看到你的。/ If the book were in the library, you ～ have it. 这本书如果在图书馆里, 我就让你借了。/ He ～ not have gone if I could have prevented it. 如果我能够阻止的话, 他就不会去了。④[表示可能性、推测或推论]可能, 该

⑤[表示义务、责任]应当，应该 ⑥[表示委婉、谦逊]可，倒: You are mistaken, I ~ say. 据我看，你可能搞错了。/ Should you like tea? 你可喜欢喝茶吗? ⑦[用于表示必要、适当、惊奇、遗憾等的从句中]应该; 竟然会: It is necessary that we ~ bring in all the crops in a week's time. 必须在一星期内把庄稼都收进来。/ It is most desirable that he ~ attend the conference. 非常希望他能出席会议。/ It is proper that no hasty decision ~ be made. 不应当作出匆促的决定。/ It is simply a miracle that rice ~ grow in such a place. 稻子竟能在这样的地方生长，实在是奇迹。⑧[与 why, who, how 等连用，表示意外、惊异等]竟会: How ~ I know? 我怎么会知道呢? / Why ~ you be so late today? 你今天怎么又来得这么晚? ⑨[用于表示建议、命令、决定等的从句中]应该，必须: The young doctor proposed that he ~ try the experiment on himself. 青年医生建议在他自己身上作试验。⑩[用于表示目的或由 lest 等引导的从句中]可以，会; 万一: We worked hard so that we ~ fulfil our task ahead of schedule. 我们努力工作，争取提前完成任务。/ I'll remind him lest he ~ forget it. 为了怕他忘记，我会提醒他的。/ Write to me in case you ~ need my help. 如果需要我帮助，可以写信告诉我。

shoulder ['∫əuldə] **I** *n.* ①肩，肩膀，肩胛; 肩膀关节: a man with square (或 broad) ~s 肩膀阔的人 / shrug one's ~s 耸耸肩(表示无可奈何等) / with ~s thrown back 挺着胸 / with a rifle *on* one's ~ 肩上扛着枪 / a satchel slung *across* the ~ 挂在肩上的书包 / reduce a dislocated ~ 使脱臼的肩膀复位 ②[复]上背部; [喻]担当的能力: His ~s bowed with age. 因年老的关系，他的上背部佝偻了。/ The task rested squarely on our ~s. 这个任务全部落在我们肩上了。/ His ~s are broad enough to bear the responsibility. 他完全担当得起这个责任。③(衣服的)肩部: The boy's coat is narrow *across* the ~s. 这孩子的上衣肩部窄小。④[复](肉类)带肩肉的前腿肉 ⑤[动](昆虫的)肩角; 肩角; ⑥肩状物; 肩状突出部; 【军】(碉堡堡面与侧面构成的)肩角; 【地】山肩，谷肩; 岾: the northwest ~ of Europe 欧洲的西北角 ⑦【军】挦枪姿势 ⑧【建】路的边缘; 路肩 **II** ❶ *vt.* ①肩起，挑起; 承担: Shoulder arms! 枪上肩! / ~ firearms all at once 立即扛起枪 / be prepared to ~ any heavy burden 随时准备挑重担 / ~ the responsibility 承担责任 ②用肩膀推(挤): one's way through the crowd 用肩膀在人群中挤过去 / be ~ed to one side 被挤在一边 / ~ sb. off (粗暴地)用肩膀挤开某人 ❷ *vi.* 用肩推挤 ‖*an old head on young* ~s 见 **head** / *be up to one's* ~s 深深地陷着; He is up to his ~s in work. 他工作忙得不可开交。/ *cry on sb.'s* ~ 企求某人的同情(或安慰); 向某人倾诉苦楚 / *have broad* ~s 身体扎实; 能挑重担; 能担当重任 / *have on one's* ~s 承担着(责任等): What a heavy task he has on his ~s! 他肩上的任务多重啊! / *head and* ~s above 见 **head** / *lay the blame on the right* (*wrong*) ~s 见 **blame** / *put one's* ~ *out* 使肩膀脱臼 / *put* (或 *set*) *one's* ~ *to the wheel* ①助肩推车; 出一把力 ②努力工作，尽力完成任务 / *rub* ~s *with sb.* 与某人(尤指名人、要人)有来往 / *shift the blame* (*on*) *to other* ~s 见 **blame** / ~ *to* ~ 并肩地; 齐心协力地: fight ~ *to* ~ 并肩作战 / *square one's* ~s ①挺直地站立 ②表示厌恶 / *straight from the* ~ ①(拳击等)狠狠的(地); 很准的(地) ②(批评、驳斥等)直截了当; 一针见血 / *turn* (或 *give*) *a* (或 *the*) *cold* ~ *to sb.* 对某人冷淡; 讨厌某人; 疏远某人 / *with one's* ~ *to collar* 辛勤地，使劲地 ‖~ **blade**【解】肩胛; 肩胛骨; 胛 / ~ **bone** *n.* 【医】(儿童)驼背矫正器 / ~ **emblem** 臂章 / ~-**brace**【医】帮助脊梁伸直的绷带，胸带 / '~-**high** *ad. & a.* 齐肩高的(地) / ~ **knot** ①(仆佣等制服的)肩饰 ②肩章 / ~ **loop** [美](陆军、空军、海军陆战队的)肩章 / ~ **mark** [美](海军)肩章 / '~-**of-'mutton sail** (小艇用的)三角帆 / ~ **patch** 臂章 / '~-**pegged** *a.* (马)肩膀僵直的 / ~ **pole** 扁担，杠棒 / ~ **strap** ①肩章 ②保护衣服肩部的衬垫 / ~ **weapon**【军】手持武器，肩挂枪枝(如步枪、马枪等)

shout [∫aut] **I** *n.* ①呼喊; 喊叫声: ~s of victory 胜利的欢呼声 / utter a ~ of warning 高呼报警 ②[俚]感叹号，惊叹号 **II** ❶ *vi.* ①呼喊，喊叫: ~ out to sb. to do sth. 高声叫喊要某人做某事 / ~ for joy 欢呼 / ~ with laughter 大笑 ②嚷; 大声说: ~ at sb. 对某人大声叫嚷 / She is quite deaf, you'll have to ~ in her ear. 她耳朵很聋，你必须在她耳边大声地说。③引人注目，触目; 大肆张扬 ❷ *vt.* ①高呼; 嚷着说出; 大声叫: ~ (out) orders 大声发布命令 / ~ one's disapproval 大声叫喊表示不同意 / wait for the conductor to ~ the stations 等(公共车辆)售票员大声报站名 ②叫喊得使…: ~ oneself hoarse 叫得声嘶力竭 / ~ sb. *up* from the bed 大声把某人喊醒起床 / ~ *down* rival opinions 以叫喊声压倒对立的意见 ‖*It's my* ~. [俚]该我(买酒)请客。/ *Now you're* ~ing. [俚](你)讲得好。(或: 你抓住了要害。) / ~ *sb. down* 大声叫喊着压倒某人的声音; 比某人叫得响 ‖~**er** *n.* 高呼者; 喊叫者 / ~**ing** *n.* ①呼喊: It's all over but (或 bar) the ~ing. 比赛已经结束，只待观众欢呼散场了。②【军】喊话 / ~**ing distance** 叫得应的地方; 不远的距离: within ~ing *distance* of 在…叫得应的地方; 在…的附近 / ~ **song** 【宗】领唱与会众应答轮唱的歌曲

shove [∫ʌv] **I** ❶ *vt.* ①推，猛推 ②强使: ~ a bill through the legislature 强使立法机关通过一项法案 ③[口]乱塞; 硬推(掉): ~ the letters in the drawer 把信件胡乱地往抽屉里一塞 / ~ a job off onto others 把一件工作硬推给别人去干 / ~ the queer 使用伪币 ❷ *vi.* ①(使劲)推 ②连

推带挤地走; (冰川等)涌流: ～ up to the counter 涌向柜台 II n. 推 ‖give sb. a ～ off 帮助某人开个头(常指从事某种行业等) / on the ～ [俚]在活动中; 在进展中 / ～ off ①(用桨撑岸等)开船; 乘船离去 ②[俚]离开

shovel ['ʃʌvl] I n. ① 铲;铁锨;铁锹: a giant ～ 铲土机 / stoke coal ～ after ～ 一铲又一铲地加煤 ②一铲的量 ③铲状物 ④(教士等戴的)宽边帽 (=～ hat) II (shovel(l)ed; shovel(l)ing) ❶ vt. ① 铲, 铲起; 用铲子掘起(或开出): ～ a path through the snow 用铲子在积雪中开出一条路来 ②把…大量倒入: ～ food into one's mouth 大口地吃 ❷ vi. 铲 ‖put to bed with a ～ 见 bed ‖~ful n. 【动】[俚]指 ‖'~bill n. 【动】琵嘴鸭 / '~man n. 用铲子的人 / '~nose n. 【动】鲸鲛; 犁头鲛 / '~-nosed a. 鼻(或头、喙)阔而扁平的

show [ʃou] I (过去式 showed, 过去分词 shown [ʃoun] 或 showed) ❶ vt. ①给…看, 出示;显示, 显出: Will you kindly ～ us that coat over there? 请把那儿的上衣拿给我们看看好吗? / Show your tickets, please. 请出示票子。/ ～ sb. the door 指着门要某人出去;把某人赶走 / ～ heroism 显示英雄气概 / A dark shirt will not ～ the dirt. 深色衬衫耐脏。/ ～ one's face 露面 ②展出, 陈列, 演出; 放映: The photo you mentioned is ～n at the exhibition. 你提到的那张照片现在展览会展出。/ ～ new spring suits 陈列新式春季服装 / What film are they ～ing this week? 这星期放映什么影片? ③表明, 说明; 证明: Plenty of evidence ～s that he is guilty (或 ～s him to be guilty). 大量证据表明他是有罪的。/ I'll ～ the truth of his point. 我来证明他的论点是正确的。④指示, 指出: Our grain output has ～n another steep rise. 我们的粮食产量又有了激增。/ A lighted tower clock ～ed the time to be 12:00 p. m. 塔楼上的夜光钟指示着时间是午夜十二点。⑤带引,带领: ～ a guest in (out) 领客人进来(出去) / ～ the visitors round a plant 引领访问者参观工厂 ⑥炫耀, 卖弄(off) ⑦给与;赐与 ⑧(通过示范)教, 告知: Can you ～ me how to do it? 你能告诉我怎样做么? ⑨[律]陈述;辩护: ～ cause 陈述案情;为一个案件辩护 ❷ vi. ①显现,显出;露面: Does the stain still ～? 污迹还看得出吗? / The buds are just ～ing. 嫩芽初露。/ The mark of the wound ～ed red. 伤痕呈现红色。/ Dawn is beginning to ～ in the east. 东方露出曙光。②演出 ③[美](在赛马中)得第三(或第三以上)的名次 II n. ①表示, 显示: vote by (a) ～ of hands 举手表决 / make a false ～ of strength 虚张声势 ②展览(会): a tractor ～ 拖拉机展览 / His paintings are on ～ here this month. 他的绘画作品本月在这里展览。③虚饰, 炫耀, 卖弄: be fond of ～ 喜欢炫耀;讲究排场 / do sth. for ～ 为了装门面而

做某事 ④外观,表面: pierce beneath the ～s of things 透过事物的表面 / There is a ～ of reason in his proposal. 他的建议看来似乎有道理。/ offer a ～ of resistance 作出抵抗的样子 ⑤景象;奇观;丑相; 出丑的人: What a fine ～ of blossoms! 好一片鲜花盛开的景象! / The waves rolled on, a mighty ～. 波涛滚滚,真是壮观。/ He is a boast and a ～. 他专门吹牛,十分可笑。⑥演出; 节目; 娱乐: a film ～ 一场电影 / a radio (television) ～ 一个广播(电视)节目 / go to a ～ 去看戏 (或电影等) ⑦[俚]表现: put up a good (poor) ～ 表现得好(不好) / put up a rival ～ against 同…唱对台戏 / Good ～! [主英]干得好! ⑧[口][只用单](表现、表白等的)机会: give sb. a fair ～ 给某人一个好机会 / not to have a ～ of winning (trying) 没有获胜(试一试)的机会 ⑨(正在从事的)事情,事业 ⑩【矿】(指示附近有矿脉露头的)初现浮散矿;迹象: oil (gas) ～ 石油(天然气)迹象 ⑪【医】(分娩时的)现血 ⑫[美](赛马)第三名 ‖a **fleeting** (或 **passing**) ～ 瞬息即逝的景象 / **be the whole** ～ [美]当主要角色;包办代替 / **do a** ～ 去看戏(或电影等) / **give the** ～ **away** 露出马脚; 泄露内幕 / **have nothing to** ～ **for** 在…方面没有成绩可言 / **in dumb** ～ 用哑剧表演;用手势表示 / **make a** ～ **of oneself** 出丑, 出洋相 / **put** (或 **get**) **the** ～ **on the road** [美俚]开始干起来;开办企业 / **run** (或 **boss**) **the** ～ ①主持演出 ②主持; 操纵 / ～ **itself** 呈现, 露头: A tendency has ～n itself. 出现了一种倾向。/ ～ **off** ①炫耀, 卖弄: ～ off one's knowledge 炫耀知识 ②使显眼, 使夺目 / ～ **oneself** 露面, 在公开场合)出现 / ～ **up** ①揭穿, 揭露 ②露出,显出: The mark ～s up only in the strong sunlight. 那斑痕只在强烈的阳光下才显出来。③[口]出席, 到场: Why didn't you ～ up at the meeting yesterday? 昨天开会时你怎么没到场? ④[口]大大胜过 / **stand** (或 **have**) **a** ～ [口]有一个 (较婉委的) 机会 / **steal the** ～ (处于次要地位的人)抢出风头 / **stop the** ～ (因表演精彩)被观众的热烈掌声打断演出 ‖ **bill** (演出等的)海报; 招贴,广告 / ～ **biz** =～ business / '~**boat** n. ①[美]有戏剧表演的轮船,水上舞台 ②[美俚]卖弄的人 vi. [美俚]卖弄 / '~**bread** (犹太教)祭神用的面包 / ～ **business** 娱乐性行业(指戏院、电影院等) / ～ **card** n. = bill / ～**case** n. 陈列柜;显示人(或物)优点的东西 vt. 使显出优点 / '~**down** n. 摊牌; 最后的一决雌雄: call for (force) a ～down 要求(迫使)对方摊牌 / ～ **girl** (夜总会等处的)歌舞女伶, 歌女 / '~**house** n. ①剧院 ②花草陈列馆 / '~-**how** n. 工序等的)示范 / '~**jumping** n. 骑马越障的技术表演 / ～**man** ['ʃoumən] n. ①(戏剧等)主持(或安排)演出者;(马戏团等的)主持人 ②善于安排演出(或吸引观众)的人 / '~**manship** n. 安排演出(或吸引观众)的窍门; (马戏团等的)经营

术;招徕生意的手腕 / '~-me a. 非要人家举出
证据不可的;怀疑的,不轻信的 / '~-off n. ①炫
耀,卖弄 ②爱炫耀的人,爱吹牛的人 / '~piece
n. 展览品;供展览的样品 / '~place n. ①供参
观的场所 ②展出地 / '~room n. 陈列室,展览
室 / '~shop n. ①剧院 ②把商品公开展览的商
店 / '~stopper n. 因特别精彩而被观众掌声
打断的表演(或表演者) / '~up n. ①揭露
被警察排起来供检查与辨认的一队人 (=~up
line) / ~ window 橱窗

shower[1] ['ʃouə] n. 出示者;显示者;展出者;指示器

shower[2] ['ʃau-ə] I n. ①阵雨;冰雹(或风雪等)的
一阵: be caught in a ~ 遇到阵雨 / a
~ of applause 一阵热烈的掌声 / a postcard ~
接踵而来的大批明信片 / Reports of victory came
in ~s. 捷报频传。③[美](为新娘等举行的)送
礼会 ④淋浴: take a cold ~ every morning 每
天早晨洗冷水淋浴 ⑤【物】簇射: cosmic ray ~
宇宙线簇射 II ❶ vi. ①下阵雨;阵雨般落下:
Letters ~ed on him. 大批信件雪片似地向他飞
来。②淋浴 ❷ vt. ①浇,溅,使湿透: The wave
~ed spray over us. 一个浪头迎头扑来,把我们
溅得满身是水。②倾注;大量地给与: ~ affections
on (或 upon) sb. 钟爱某人 / ~ sb. with gifts 给
某人送大量的礼品 / ~ bath ①淋浴;淋浴装置;
淋浴室 ②[喻]淋湿,湿透

showery ['ʃau-əri] a. 阵雨(般)的;多阵雨的
‖**showeriness** n.

showing ['ʃouiŋ] n. ①显示;展览,陈列: a ~ of
evidence 证据的提出 / an advanced ~ 预展
②表演;表现 ③夸耀 ④陈述,叙述: on sb.'s
own ~ 据某人自己说 ⑤外表;迹象: On present
~, the patient has little hope of recovery. 照目
前迹象看,病人不大有希望康复。

showy ['ʃoui] a. ①[常贬]浮华的,(过分)艳丽的;
显眼的,惹眼的: a ~ dress 过分华丽的女服
②炫耀的,卖弄的: a ~ play (赛球等时的)卖
弄技巧 ‖**showily** ad. / **showiness** n.

shram [ʃræm] (shrammed; shramming) vt. [英方]
[常用被动语态] 使冷得麻木 (with)

shrank [ʃræŋk] shrink 的过去式

shrapnel ['ʃræpnəl] n. ① (炮弹、水雷等的)弹片
②榴霰弹,子母弹

shred [ʃred] I n. ①碎片,碎条;破布: meat ~s
肉片 ②少量剩余;最少量 II (shredded 或 [古]
shred; shredding) vt. & vi. 撕碎;切碎

shrew [ʃru:] n. ①【动】鼩鼱(一种似鼠的小动物)
②泼妇,悍妇

shrewd [ʃru:d] a. ①机灵的,敏锐的;精明的;伶俐
的: a ~ answer 机敏的回答 / a ~ eye 敏锐的
目光 / ~ bargaining 精明的讨价还价 / a ~
guess 相当准的猜测 ②厉害的,狠狠的: a ~
blow 狠狠的一击 ③凛冽的;剧烈的: a ~ wind
凛冽的寒风 / a ~ pain 剧痛 ‖**ly** ad. / ~
ness n. ‖'~-'brained, '~-'headed a. 头脑机
灵(或精明)的 / '~-,looking a. 看上去很机灵
(或精明)的

shriek [ʃri:k] I ❶ vi. ①尖声喊叫;发出尖声: ~
with pain 痛得直叫 / ~ with laughter 尖声狂
笑 / The siren ~ed. 警报(器)尖啸着。②(尖
叫似地)促人注意: a ~ing headline 耸人听闻的
大标题 ❷ vt. ①尖声发出: ~ an alarm 尖声报
警 / ~ (out) curses at sb. 尖声咒骂某人 ②耸
人听闻地报道 II n. ①尖叫(声);尖声: the sudden
~ of chalk on a blackboard 粉笔划在黑板时突
然发出的刺耳的吱吱声

shrift [ʃrift] n. ①[古](对牧师所作的)忏悔:(牧
师对忏悔者的)赦免,宽恕 ②承认,招认;泄露
‖a short ~ ①临终前的忏悔 ②将死(或处刑前)
的短暂时间: a man condemned to a short ~
by the physician 被医生判定没几天好活的人 /
get short ~ from sb. 受到某人漠不关心(或简
慢无礼)的对待: This kind of idle talk gets
short ~ from us. 我们不要听这种空谈。/ give
short ~ ① 对…漠不关心; 对…简慢无礼 (to)
②很快解决(或做成)… (to) ③允给的时间太少 /
make short ~ of 很快解决(或做成)…;对(工
作等)敷衍了事

shrill [ʃril] I a. ①尖声的;伴有尖声叫喊的: a ~
whistle 刺耳的汽笛声 ② (批评等)硬要人听的;
哀切的: a ~ complaint 哀诉 ③强烈的: a ~
light 强烈的光 / The outline became ~er. 轮廓
变得分明了。④(怒气等)过度的,无节制的 II ad.
[古]尖声地 ‖❶ vi. 发出尖锐刺耳的声音 ❷ vt.
尖声地叫(或讲) IV n. 尖声 ‖**ness** n.

shrimp [ʃrimp] I (复 shrimp(s)) n. ①(小)虾,
褐虾,河虾: dried ~s 虾干 / shelled ~s 虾仁
②[谑]矮小的人;小东西 II vi. 捕(小)虾 ‖~
pink 深红色,暗红色

shrine [ʃrain] I n. ①神龛;圣祠;神殿 ②圣陵;圣
骨匣;圣物柜 ③圣地;神圣场所 II vt. =en-
shrine ‖worship at the ~ of Mammon 崇拜
财神,一心想发财

shrink [ʃriŋk] I (过去式 shrank [ʃræŋk] 或
shrunk [ʃrʌŋk], 过去分词 shrunk 或 shrunken
['ʃrʌŋkən]) ❶ vi. ①收缩;蜷缩;皱缩: ~ with
cold 冷得缩成一团 / Woollen fabrics ~ in the
wash. 毛织物一洗要缩水。②缩小;减少: a
~ing market 范围在缩小的市场 / The person-
nel of this office has shrunk to skeleton size.
这机关的人员已减少到最低限度。③退缩,畏缩:
We will never ~ back before difficulties. 我们
在困难面前决不退缩。/ The child ~s from
meeting strangers. 这孩子怕见陌生人。❷ vt.
①使收缩;使缩绒;使缩小 ② (织物等的)缩
水,收缩: How much must we allow for the ~?
要留多少缩水长度? ③畏缩,退避 ③[美俚]神经
科医生 ‖~ into oneself 缩做一团; 变得沉默寡
言 / ~ on 【机】红套,乘其热胀时把…套上: ~ a
wheel-tire on 趁轮胎热胀时套上(冷却后缩紧)
‖**able** a. 会收缩的: a ~able fabric 要缩水的
织物 ‖**ing violet** 羞怯的人,怕见场面的人(尤
指不爱当众发表扬的人)

shrinkage ['ʃriŋkidʒ] *n.* ①收缩；皱缩，缩水：There has been much ~ of the clothes in the wash. 这些衣服洗后已缩了很多。②减少；低落：a ~ in the water supply 供水的减少 / a ~ in market values 市价的低落 ③收缩量；收缩程度；【物】缩误：a ~ of two inches in the length 长度上二吋的缩短量 ④(牲畜在运输或咸肉类在加工的过程中)重量的损耗

shrive [ʃraiv] (过去式 shrove [ʃrouv] 或 shrived, 过去分词 shriven ['ʃrivn] 或 shrived) [古] ❶ *vt.* ①(牧师)听忏悔后赦免…的罪 ②[~ oneself] 以忏悔赎(自己)的罪 ❷ *vi.* ①听忏悔 ②忏悔以赎罪

shrivel ['ʃrivl] (shrivel(l)ed; shrivel(l)ing) *vi. & vt.* ①(使)皱缩；(使)枯萎 ②(使)束手无策；(使)变得无用，(使)失效

shroud [ʃraud] I *n.* ①裹尸布，寿衣 ②遮蔽物；幕；罩：a ~ of mystery 笼罩着的神秘气氛 ③【机】护罩；管套；(水车的)侧板：canvas ~ 帆布罩 / exhaust ~ 排气管套 ④[复][船](桅的)左右支索 ⑤(降落伞的)吊伞索 II *vt.* ①给…覆盖裹尸布 ②覆盖；掩蔽：a peak ~ed in mist and cloud 云雾缭绕的山峰

shrub¹ [ʃrʌb] *n.* 灌木

shrub² [ʃrʌb] *n.* ①(掺白兰地等的)果汁甜酒 ②冰果汁水

shrug [ʃrʌg] I (shrugged; shrugging) *vt. & vi.* (为表示冷漠、无奈、蔑视、不满等)耸(肩) II *n.* 耸肩：with a ~ of despair 表示失望地一耸肩 ②一种女式短上衣 ‖~ **off** ①耸肩对…表示不屑理睬；轻视，贬低 ②抖去；摆脱 ③一扭身子而脱掉(衣服)

shudder ['ʃʌdə] I *vi.* 震颤，战栗，发抖：~ with cold 冷得发抖 / ~ at the sight of something terrible 看到某种可怕的东西而战栗 / He ~s to think .... 他一想到…就不寒而栗。II *n.* 震颤，战栗，抖动：give sb. the ~s 使某人怕得发抖

shuffle ['ʃʌfl] I ❶ *vt.* ①拖着(脚)走、(站着或坐时)把(脚)在地上滑来滑去；跳(曳步舞)：Don't ~ your feet *along*. 别拖着脚步走。②搅乱；弄混；洗(牌)；把…移来移去：a pack of cards 洗一副纸牌 / ~ sb. to and fro 把某人差来遣去(或调来调去) ③推开；推诿：~ sth. out of sight 把某物塞在看不见的地方 / ~ off a duty upon others 把一件工作推给别人 ④笨拙地穿上(或脱去)(衣服等)：~ one's clothes on (off) 笨拙地穿上(脱掉)衣服 ❷ *vi.* ①拖着脚走(along)；跳曳步舞 ②狡猾地摆脱(或混入)：manage to ~ out of responsibility 狡猾地设法摆脱责任 ③蒙混；推诿，搪塞：Don't ~, give a definite answer. 别含糊其词，给一个明确的答复。④洗牌 ⑤马虎地做(through)；笨拙地穿(或脱)：~ through one's work 敷衍了事 / ~ into (out of) one's clothes 笨拙地穿上(脱下)衣服 II *n.* ①曳行，曳步；曳步舞 ②杂乱的一堆，一团糟：a ~ of papers 杂乱的一堆文件 ③改组；混合；搅乱：a ~ of the

Cabinet 内阁的改组 / After a hasty ~ through his papers, the speaker began to talk. 演讲者匆匆翻阅讲稿后便开始讲话了。④蒙混；推诿，搪塞 ⑤洗牌；洗牌的轮值：It's your ~. 轮到你洗牌了。‖*lose in the* ~ 在混乱中把…遗漏(或忽略)掉 / ~ *off this mortal coil* 见 **coil²** / *the cards* 进行角色大调动；改变方针政策 / *up* 草草作成 ‖~ **r** *n.* ①曳步而行者 ②洗牌者；轮到洗牌的人 ③做事漫不经心者 ④蒙混者 ⑤[动]潜鸭 ‖~**board** *n.* (在甲板等上)掷木盘于有号码的方格上的游戏；供做掷木盘游戏的平台板

shun¹ [ʃʌn] (shunned; shunning) *vt.* 避免；回避，躲开：~ subjectivity (one-sidedness) 避免主观性(片面性) / ~ publicity 避免抛头露面(或出风头) / ~ society 避开社交活动 ‖~**pike** *n.* (为避免超级公路上的拥挤等而使用的)支路

shun², **'shun** [ʃʌn] *int.* (口令)立正!(是Attention! 的词音的缩略)

shunt [ʃʌnt] I ❶ *vt.* ①使(火车)转轨：Freight Train 422 has been ~ed on to Track 6. 第 422 次货车已调到 6 股道。②[电]装分路器于，使分路，使分流 ③改变(谈话)的路子：~ the conversation on to a new topic 把谈话转向一个新题目 ④把(人)撇在一边；推延，搁置(计划等)：feel ~ed 感到被人冷落 / ~ sb. aside 把某人撇在一边 ❷ *vi.* ①转向一边，靠边；(火车)调轨，调车 ②来回运行，往返 II *n.* ①[主英](铁道的)转辙器 ②调轨，调车 ③【电】分路器，分流(器) ‖~**-wound** ['ʃʌntwaund] *a.* 【电】并联的

shut [ʃʌt] I (shut; shutting) ❶ *vt.* ①关上，闭上，关闭：*Shut* the door after you. 随手关门。/ ~ the door *against* sb. (或 *upon* sb., *in* sb.'s face) 把某人关在门外；飨某人以闭门羹 / ~ the door *upon* negotiations 关上谈判的大门，拒绝谈判 / ~ one's mouth 闭口不语 / ~ one's eyes to the facts 闭眼不看事实 / ~ one's ears *to* all advice 不听劝告 ②合拢；折拢：~ a book 合上书 / an umbrella 收拢雨伞 / ~ a knife 合拢小刀 ③封闭：~ every pass through the mountains 封锁通过山间的各条狭路 ④把…关住；禁闭：~ the chickens in a pen 把小鸡关在栅栏里 ⑤(暂时或永久地)使停止营业；停止开放：All the shops were ~. 商店都打烊了。/ The picture show will be ~ for a week. 画展将暂停开放一星期。⑥轧住；夹进：~ one's finger (dress) in the door (关门时)手指(衣服)被夹在门里 ❷ *vi.* 关上：The door ~ with a bang. 门砰地一声关上了。/ The window won't ~. 这窗关不上。/ The post office will not ~ until 8 p.m. 邮局到下午八时才关门。II *n.* ①关闭；关闭的时间：at ~ of evening 夜幕降临时 ②(金属的)焊缝 ③【机】冷塞 ‖*be* (或 *get*) ~ *of* sb. [俚] 摆脱掉某人 / ~ *down* ①放下来关住(窗等)；(夜等)降临；(雾等)浓起来：~ *down* the lid of a box 关上箱盖 / The night ~ *down* early. 天黑得早。②(使)停工；(使)关闭(常指临时性的)：~ *down* a factory (school) 关闭工厂(学校) / ~ *down* an engine 关闭发动机 / ~ *down on* (或 *upon*) [口]制止; 压制 / ~ *in* ①关进; 禁闭 ②围住; 笼罩: The village is ~ *in* by hills. 这个村子四周环山。/ Evening has ~ *in*. 天色已经暗下来了。/ ~ *off* ①关掉(煤气等) ② 切断: ~ *off* the road from ordinary traffic 禁止一般车辆在这条路上通行 ③使隔绝, 脱离: Don't ~ yourselves *off* from the masses. 不要脱离群众。/ ~ *out* ①关出, 把…关在外面: ~ sb. *out* of the room 把某人关在房门外 ②遮住, 把…挡在外面: A high wall ~ *out* the light. 高墙遮住了光线。③排除(可能性等); (在比赛等中)使(对方)不能得分 / ~ *to* 关上(门等); (门等)关上: He ~ the door *to*. 他把门关上了。/ The door ~ *to*. 门关上了。/ ~ *up* ①关闭; 把(房屋等)的门窗全部关闭上锁: ~ *up* shop 关店; 打烊 / ~ *up* a house (room) 把房屋(房间)关起来 ②保藏; 监禁: ~ *up* the valuables in a safe 把贵重物品藏在保险箱中 / ~ sb. *up* in prison 把某人关进监牢 ③[口](使)住口; 停止写: Tell him to ~ *up*. 叫他住口。‖ '~**down** *n*. (工厂、车间等的)停工, 关闭(常指临时性的); (机器的)停车 / a ~*down* inspection 停工检查 / '~**-eye** *n*. [美俚]①睡眠 ②昏厥 / '~**-in** *n*. 被关在屋里的人; 卧病在床的人 *a*. ① 被关在屋里的; 卧病在床的 ②诡秘的 ③避免与外界交际的 ④被包围在当中的 / '~**off** *n*. ① 停止, 中止 ②关闭器 / '~**out** *n*. ①闭厂, 停业 (资本家要挟工人的一种手段) ②被关在外面的人 ③(比赛中)不让对方得分的比赛 ④(月经)停; (桥牌中)为封住对方而故意抬高的叫牌

shutter ['ʃʌtə] I *n*. ①关闭者 ②百叶窗, 窗板(窗户的活动遮板) ③(照相机的)快门, (光)闸 ④(风琴等的)开闭器, 闸门 ⑤[美俚]安眠药片 II *vt*. ①为…装窗板(或快门等) ②用窗板关闭; 关上…的窗板(或快门) ‖*put up the* ~s (店铺)打烊; 关店, 停业 ‖ '~**bug** *n*. 摄影爱好者, 摄影迷

shuttle ['ʃʌtl] I *n*. ① (织机的)梭; (缝纫机的)滑梭 ②穿梭般的来回; 短程穿梭运输(线); 短程穿梭运输工具: a round-the-clock ~ between the construction site and the warehouses 在建筑工地和各仓库间昼夜不停的来回穿梭运输 / a ~ bus (train) 区间公共汽车(列车) II *vt. & vi.* ①(使)穿梭般来回移动 ②短程穿梭般输送 / ~ **armature** 【电】梭形电枢 / ~ **bombing** 往复轰炸, 穿梭轰炸 / ~ **race** 直线两队接力赛跑

shy[1] [ʃai] I (shier 或 shyer, shiest 或 shyest) *a*. ①易受惊的; 胆怯的: a ~ bird 易受惊的鸟 ②害羞的; 怕羞的, 怕陌生的: a ~ smile 羞怯的微笑 / be ~ in the presence of strangers 在陌生人面前显得腼腆 ③迟疑的, 有戒心的; 畏缩的(of): Don't be ~ of telling us what you want. 你需要什么尽管告诉我们, 不要有顾虑。/ His eye trouble made him ~ of light. 眼病使他怕光。④隐蔽的, 幽僻的; 晦涩的, 费解的 ⑤(树等)果实不丰硕的 ⑥[俚]不足的, 缺乏的 (of, on): be ~ of (或

on) funds 资金不足 ⑦[俚](纸牌戏中)欠赌注的 ⑧(酒吧、赌场等)声名狼藉的 II *vi.* ①(马等)惊退; 惊逸: The horse *shied at* the sight of a passing train. 那马看到驶过的火车惊得往后倒退。② 厌恶 (*from*): ~ *from* publicity 不爱抛头露面 ③ 避开 (*away*, *off*) III *n*. (马等的)惊退; 惊逸 ‖**fight** ~ *of* 躲避, 避开, 不与…接触 / **Once bit** (或 **bitten**) **twice** ~. 见 bite ‖~**ly** *ad.* / ~**ness** *n*.

shy[2] [ʃai] I *n*. ① 投掷; 乱丢 ②[口]嘲弄, 讥刺 ③[口]尝试, 企图 II *vt*. 乱丢; 投掷 ‖*have* (或 *take*) *a* ~ *at* sb. 嘲弄某人 / *make* (或 *have*) *a* ~ *at* sth. ①试图掷中某物 ②试图获得某物

Shylock ['ʃailɔk] *n*. ①夏洛克(莎士比亚剧本《威尼斯商人》中的角色, 放高利贷的犹太人, 狠毒的报复者) ② [喻]敲诈勒索的放债者; 冷酷无情的(放)人

sial ['saiæl] *n*. 【地】硅铝带

sialagogue, sialogogue [sai'æləgɔg] 【医】I *n*. 催涎剂 II *a*. 催涎的

sick[1] [sik] I *a*. ①有病的, 患病的; 病人的: a ~ man 病人 / be ~ with influenza 患流行性感冒 / He has been ~ for three weeks. 他已病了三星期了。/ a ~ ward 病房 / the ~ 病人们, 病员们 ②[英][只作表语]嘔心的, 要吐的: feel (或 turn) ~ 觉得要呕吐 / be ~ in the car 晕车 ③[口]不愉快的, 懊丧的 (at, about): ~ at heart 伤心; 忧心忡忡 / He was ~ with me for being so late. 他对我到得那么晚心里很不高兴。/ She was rather ~ at missing the train. 她没能赶上这班火车感到很懊丧。④[口]厌倦的, 发腻的; 厌恶的 (of): ~ of waiting 等得不耐烦 / It makes me ~ to think of it. 一想起它我就讨厌。⑤渴望的, 想望的 (for): be ~ for (one's) home 想家 ⑥有病容的, 苍白的; (月经)行经的; 没有生气的; (比赛等中)大大落后的: a ~ skin 苍白的肤色 / The girl in green looks ~ in the contest. 穿绿衣服的那个女孩在这场比赛中显得很差。⑦ (精神或道德上)不健全的, 败坏的 ⑧(思想上或感情上)混乱的, 病态的: ~ thoughts 不健康的思想 ⑨(船只等)需要修理的, 有毛病的 ⑩(土壤)长不好某种作物的; 有病菌的: wheat-soil 长不好小麦的土壤 / a ~ field 有病害的田地 ⑪(葡萄酒)走味的; (铸铁等)脆的, 易碎的 II *vt*. [口]呕吐 (up) ‖*fall* ~ 患病 / *go* (或 *report*) ~ 【军】①去医生处治病 ②告病不能工作; 装病告假 / ~ *and tired* (*of*) (对…)十分厌倦 / ~ *as a dog* (或 *horse*) [俚]病得厉害 / *to death of* 对…极厌倦, 对…腻得要命 / ~ *unto death* ①病得厉害, 病入膏肓 ②极度厌倦 / *take* ~ [口]生病 / *the Sick Man of Europe* 【史】土耳其帝国的别称 ‖~ *bay*, ~ *berth* ①船上诊所; 船上救护所 ②病房; (学校等的)医务室 / '~**bed** *n*. 病床; [喻]卧病 / ~ **benefit** 给予因病请假者的津贴 / ~ *call* 【军】门诊伤病员集合

(每日召集未住院的伤病员往军医处进行检查); 门诊伤病员集合号(或时间) / ~ **flag** (检疫站或船的)传染病信号旗,(黄色)疫旗 / ~ **headache** 偏头痛;呕吐性头痛 / ~ **leave** ①病假 ②(雇员等) 可照拿工资的每年病假天数; 病假工资 / ~ **list** 病人名单,病人册: be on the ~ *list* 害着病 / ~ **pay** 病假工资 / '~**room** *n.* 病房

sick[2] [sik] *vt.* 嗾使(狗等)去咬(或攻击、骚扰): ~ a dog upon sb. (sth.) 嗾使狗去咬某人(某物) / *Sick!* 去咬!

sicken ['sikn] ❶ *vt.* 使生病;使作呕;使厌恶;使厌倦: His manner of talking ~*s* us. 我们真讨厌他那种讲话的方式。❷ *vi.* ①生病;[英]初步显出症状: The child is ~*ing for* something. 这孩子怕在生什么毛病了。②嗯心,作呕;厌恶;厌倦: ~ at the sight of (或 ~ to see) 看到…简直要作呕 ‖~ *of* (或 *be ~ed of*) 厌恶…;对…厌倦 ‖~**er** *n.* ① 容易致病之物;过量的药物 ②[口]使人厌恶的东西;厌倦的感觉;[俚](学生用语)讨厌的家伙

sickening ['sikəniŋ] *a.* ①引起疾病的;引起呕吐的 ②使人作呕的,令人厌恶的: a ~ sight 令人厌恶的情景 ‖~**ly** *ad.*

sickle ['sikl] *n.* ①镰刀 ② [the S-]【天】(狮子座中的)镰刀形的六颗星 ‖'~**bill** *n.* 弯嘴鸟 / ~ **cell** 镰形血球 / ~ **feather** 公鸡的镰形尾羽

sickly ['sikli] **I** *a.* ①有病的;多病的: a ~ child 一个多病的孩子 ② 因疾病而产生的;病态的;苍白的: a ~ complexion 病容 ③ 易引起疾病的,有碍健康的;疾病流行的: a ~ climate 易致病的气候 / a ~ season 疾病流行的季节 ④好象有病的;弱的,无力的;阴沉的;黯淡的: a ~ tree 病树 / a ~ smile 苦笑 / ~ moonlight 黯淡的月光 ⑤令人作呕的;使人厌恶的: a ~ smell 令人作呕的气味 **II** *ad.* 病态地 **III** *vt.* 使现病容 (*over*) ‖**sicklily** *ad.* / **sickliness** *n.*

sickness ['siknis] *n.* ①疾病: mountain ~ 高山病 / recover from a ~ 从病中复原 / There hasn't been much ~ here this year. 今年这儿疾病不多。②嗯心,呕吐

side [said] **I** *n.* ①边;旁边;面;侧面: the ~ of a triangle 三角形的一边 / stand by the ~ of the road 站在路旁 / Is the factory (on) this ~ of the river? (或 Is the factory on this ~ the river?) 工厂是在河的这一边吗? / A cube has six ~*s*. 立方体有六个面。/ A box has a top, a bottom and four ~*s*. 一只箱子有顶、底和四个侧面。②(纸、布等的)面,半面;(一个)方面: write on one ~ of the paper 在纸的一面书写 / the right and wrong ~*s* of cloth 布的正反面 / the debit (credit) ~ of an account 帐目的借(贷)方 / look on the bright (dark) ~ of things 看事物的光明面(黑暗面) / There are two ~*s to* every question. 每一问题总有两个方面。③胁;(身体的)侧边: be wounded in the left ~ 左胁受伤 / sit by (或 at) sb.'s ~ 坐在某人身旁 ④(动物从脊骨一分两半的)半边躯体;肋肉: a ~ of beef 牛的肋肉 ⑤(敌对的)一派,一方;[英](比赛的)队: Justice is on our ~. 正义在我们方面。/ both ~*s* in a battle 作战双方 / two ~*s* of eleven players each (比赛中)各方为十一人的两队 ⑥家系,血统: the grandfather on one's mother's ~ 外祖父 / distaff (spear) ~ 女(男)系 ⑦[常用以构成复合词]坡,山坡;岸: on the ~ of a mountain 在山坡上 / on the river~ 在河岸上 ⑧【船】舷侧 ⑨[英俚]架子;傲慢,自大: put on (或 have too much) ~ 摆架子 / have no ~ 很谦虚 ⑩[美俚]一段台词;一张供某一角色练习用的台词纸 ⑪[英](台球中)侧击引起的旋转 **II** *a.* ①旁边的,侧面的;边的: a ~ door 边门 ② 从侧面来的;向一侧的: a ~ blow 侧击 ③枝节的;次要的;附带的: a ~ issue 枝节问题 / a ~ job 附带做的工作 / a ~ occupation 副业 **III** ❶ *vt.* ① 同意,支持;站在…的一边 ② 收拾;搁开,放开: ~ dishes 把菜盆收去 ③ 给…装上侧面;给(木房)钉上披迭板 ④ 刨平(木料等)的侧面 ❷ *vi.* 赞助,支持;袒护;与…站在一边 (*with*) ‖***born on the wrong ~ of the blanket*** 私生的 / ***born on the wrong ~ of the tracks*** 见 **track**[1] / ***by the ~ of*** ①在…旁边,在…附近 ②和…在一起比较: The building looks tall *by the ~ of* the small houses. 和那些矮房子一比较,这幢楼就显得很高了。/ ***clear ~*** 船舶在水上的露出部分 / ***come down on one ~ or the other of the fence*** 支持两方中之一方 / ***come down on the right ~ of the fence*** 附和胜利的一方 / ***from all ~s*** (或 ***from every ~***) 从各方面;到处: We must study the question *from every ~*. 我们必须从各方面研究这个问题。/ People came running *from all ~s* to see what had happened. 人们从四面八方奔来看发生了什么事情。/ ***get up on the wrong ~ of (the) bed*** (或 ***get out of bed on the wrong ~***) 心绪不好,闹脾气 / ***give sb.*** (***a lick with***) ***the rough ~ of one's tongue*** 对某人出言粗鲁;出恶言伤害某人 / ***go over the ~*** [美俚]私自离开船只(或基地) / ***hold*** (或 ***burst, shake, split***) ***one's ~s*** (***with laughter***) 捧腹大笑 / ***laugh on*** (或 ***out of***) ***the wrong*** (或 ***other***) ***~ of one's mouth*** (或 ***face***) 转喜为忧;哭 / ***no ~*** (橄榄球中)比赛完毕 / ***off*** (***on***) ~ (足球等比赛中)在不合(合)规则的位置 / ***on all ~s*** (或 ***on every ~***) 在各方面;到处: There were mountains *on all ~s*. 四面都是山。/ ***one's blind*** (或 ***weak***) ***~*** 弱点,缺点 / ***on the high*** (***low***) ~ (价格)偏高(低) / ***on the hither*** (***thither***) ***~ of*** (或 ***on the right*** (***wrong***) ***~ of***) 不满(已过)…岁: He is *on the right* (*wrong*) *~ of* fifty. 他还不满(已过了)五十岁。/ ***on the plus ~ of the account*** 【商】在贷方 / ***on the safe ~*** 安全的,可靠的: It didn't look like rain, but she took her umbrella to be *on the safe ~*. 天不象会下雨,但她仍带

雨伞以防万一。/ **on the ~** 作为兼职;另外:
take a night job *on the ~* 兼任一项夜间的工作 /
give one dollar *on the ~* 另外再给一元钱 / **on
the ~ of the angels** ①(旧用法)主张从精神上
来解释事物的;道德完善的 ②(现在用法)(指别
人在争论中)站在我们这一边 / *on the small ~*
略小,较小 / *on the sunny (shady) ~ of* [俚]
不满(已过)…岁 / *on the windy ~ of* 在…的
势力所不及的地方 / *on the wrong ~ of the
door* 被关在门外 / *on this ~ the grave* 在人
世,在今生 / *over the ~* [作状语用]上船;下
船 / *put sth. on one ~* 把某物置于一边;不理
会某事 / *~ by* 肩并肩地;一起 / *stand by
sb.'s ~* 站在某人旁边;道义上支持某人 / *take
sb. on one ~* 把某人拉到一边;置某人于一旁 /
take ~s with sb. (或 *take the ~ of sb.*) 同意
某人,支持某人;袒护某人 / *the modern ~* [英]
学校中着重现代学科的部分 / *the other ~ of
the shield* ①盾的反面 ②问题的另一面(或不
太明显的方面) / *the reverse ~ of the medal*
见 **medal** / *the seamy ~* ①(衣服)的里面
②(生活等的)阴暗面 / *the wrong ~ out* 表
里倒置地,反面外露地: wear one's socks *the
wrong ~ out* 反穿袜子 / *this ~ of* 在…以前,
在…以下,不超过: I don't think he will arrive
this ~ of four o'clock. 我想他在四点钟以前
不会到。/ Try to keep your sketch *this ~
of* 500 words. 你的短文请不要超过五百字。
|| **~ling** *ad.* 斜着,斜向一边 *a.* 斜的,斜向一边
的;倾斜的 *n.* [方]斜坡 / **~long** *ad. & a.*
横(的);斜(的);侧面地(的);间接地(的) / **~-
ward(s)** *a. & ad.* 侧面的(地);向旁边的(地),从
旁边的(地) / **~ways** *ad.* 斜着;斜向一边地;自
一边地;一边向前地: look at sb. *~ways* 斜视某
人 *a.* 横斜的;斜向一边的: a *~ways* glance 斜
视 / **~wise** *a. & ad.* =~ways || **~ arms**
①随身武器;佩剑;佩刀 ②[美俚](餐桌上的)调
味品 / **~band** [无]边(频)带,旁频带 / **'~-bar**
a. 兼任的;非主要的: a *~bar* job 兼职;零星工
作 / **~bet** (打牌等)超过一般赌注的打赌 / **~-
board** *n.* ①餐具柜 ②[复][俚]=~-whiskers /
'~bone *n.* ①(家禽翅膀下面的)叉骨 ②[复]
(马蹄的)不正常的软骨骨化 / **'~burns** [复] *n.*
[美](短的)连鬓胡子;鬓脚 / **'~car** *n.* ①(附于
机器脚踏车旁的)单轮侧车,边车 ②一种鸡尾酒
③(爱尔兰流行的)轻便二轮马车 / **~ chapel** (教
堂旁或其走廊内的)附属小礼拜堂 / **~ circuit**
[电]实线电路 / **~ dish** 正菜以外的附加菜 / **~
drum** (军乐队中的)小鼓 / **~ effect** (药物等
的)副作用 / **~ elevation** 侧面图,侧视图 / **~
face** 侧面;侧面地 / **'~-glance** *n.* ①斜视;侧视
②暗示 / **~hill** *n.* 山坡,山边,山侧 *a.* 山坡
的;适宜于山坡上用的: a *~hill* attachment for
farm machinery 山坡上的农机附加装置 / **~
horse** [体] 鞍马 / **'~kick** *n.* [美俚] ①伙伴,
朋友;帮手 ②(裤子两边的)插袋 / **'~light** *n.*

①侧光;边灯,侧灯;[复][海]舷灯 ②边窗 ③(对
问题等的)偶然启示,间接说明;侧面消息;(报刊
上的)杂闻 ④[复][英俚](海员用语)眼睛 / **'~-
line** *n.* ①旁线;横线;侧道 ②附带销售的货类
③副职,兼职;副业: farm and *~line* products 农
副产品 ④[复](球场等的)界线;界线外(观众观
看)的场地: on the *~lines* (因不能参加比赛)在
场外旁观 ⑤局外人的观点,旁观者的看法 *vt.* 使
退出比赛场地: The player was *~lined* with a
sprained ankle. 这运动员因踝部扭伤而退场。/
'~man *n.* (尤指爵士音乐的)乐队队员,伴奏者 /
'~note *n.* 旁注 / **'~piece** *n.* 边件,侧部 / **~
reaction** =~ effect / **~ road** 岔路,小道 /
'~saddle *n.* 女鞍,横鞍,偏座鞍 *ad.* 在女鞍
上,在偏座 / **'~seat** *n.* 背靠车身的座位,边座 /
~ shaft [机]侧轴 / **'~show** *n.* ①(正戏中的)
穿插表演,杂耍 ②附属活动;附带事件;枝节问
题 / **'~slip** *vi.* 横滑,侧滑 *n.* ①横滑,滑向一边
②[空]侧滑,机翼侧滑,沿横轴方向的运动 ③嫩
枝,枝条;[喻]私生子 / **~ ~** 舞台侧边操作布景的地
方 / **~sman** ['saidzmən] *n.* 教区副执事 / **'~-
spin** *n.* 侧旋 / **'~,splitter** *n.* 极滑稽的故事,
令人捧腹的笑话 / **'~,splitting** *a.* 令人捧腹大
笑的,滑稽透顶的 / **'~step** *n.* ①(拳击中为躲
避打击而向旁)横跨的一步 ②(侧面的)台阶;
梯级;马车两边的踏步 *vt.* (拳击等时)横跨一步
躲避(打击);[喻]回避(困难等),逃避(责任等):
It's no good *~stepping* reality. 回避现实是没
有用处的。/ *~step* responsibility 逃避责任 *vi.*
躲避打击;回避问题(或责任等) / **'~stroke** *n.*
& vi. 侧泳 / **'~swipe** *vt.* 沿边擦过,擦边撞击
n. 擦撞 ②顺带的批评,附带的贬损(或暗讽) /
'~tone *n.* (电话机的)侧音 / **'~track** *n.*
①(铁路的)侧线,旁轨 ②(可能降入的)次要地位
vt. ①将(火车)转入侧线 ②转移(某人)的目标;
转变(话题);使降到次要地位;缓议(提案等);使
受牵制 ③[美俚]逮捕 / **~ view** 侧视图,侧面
图;侧面形状 / **'~walk** *n.* [美]人行道: hit the
~walks (挨户)寻找工作 / **'~walk
superintendent** [美俚]逛马路以观看房屋拆建
工程为消遣的人 / **'~wall** *n.* ①边墙,侧壁 ②
轮胎侧壁 / **'~way** *n.* 小路,岔路 *ad. & a.* =
~ways / **'~-wheel** *a.* (汽船)二侧有轮翼的 /
'~-,wheeler *n.* ①[美]明轮船 ②[美俚]惯用左
手的人 ③[美俚]遛蹄的马 / **'~-,whiskers** [复]
n. 连鬓胡子,络腮胡须 / **'~wind** ①侧风 ②间
接的影响;间接手段: I only learnt the news by
a *~ wind*. 我只是间接知道这个消息的。/ **'~-
wind** ['saidwind] *a.* 间接的;不正当的,不法的 /
~winder ['said,wainder] *n.* ①侧击,横击 ②美
国西南部的一种响尾蛇;[S-](美国)响尾蛇导弹
③[美俚]动辄打架的大汉;保镖,花钱雇用的打
手

siding ['saidiŋ] *n.* ①(铁路的)侧线,旁轨(=side-
track) ②[建]披迭板 ③[船](船材的)边宽
④[古]偏袒,党同伐异

sidle ['saidl] **I** *vi.* & *vt.* (使) 侧身而行(尤指羞怯地或鬼鬼祟祟地) **II** *n.* 侧身而行

siege [si:dʒ] **I** *n.* ① 包围,围攻,围困;围城;围攻期间: ~ warfare 围攻战 / press a ~ 猛烈围攻 / stand a ~ 抵住围攻 / undergo a ~ 被围攻 / a ~ of two months 历时两月的围困 ② 再三的努力: after a ~ in doing a great deal of persuasion 在做了大量的说服工作之后 ③ [口](病等的)长期折磨;(灾难等的)不断袭击: a ~ of illness 疾病的长期折磨 **II** *vt.* 包围,围攻 ‖*a state of* ~ 戒严状态 / *lay* ~ *to* ① 包围,围攻: *lay* ~ *to* a fortress 围攻要塞 ② 企图赢得;努力追求 / *raise the* ~ 解…的围 ‖~ **artillery** [总称]攻城炮兵,攻城炮 / '~-,**basket** (盛土、石用的)篾筐(或金属筐) / ~ **coin** =~ piece / ~ **gun** 攻城加农炮 / ~ **piece** 城市被围时所发行的临时钱币 / '~=**works** [复] *n.* 攻城设施

siesta [si'estə] *n.* (在气候炎热国家中的)午睡,午休

sieve [siv] **I** *n.* ①(细)筛;格筛;滤网 ②粗编的篮子(作量器用,容量约一蒲式耳) ③ [喻]嘴快的人,不能守秘密的人 ④ [美俚]防守极不严密的球队 **II** *vt.* 筛;筛分;滤 ‖*draw water with a* ~ (或 *pour water into a* ~) 见 **water** / *have a memory* (或 *head*) *like a* ~ 记忆力极差,什么也记不住 ‖~ **cell** 【植】筛(细)胞 / ~ **plate** 【植】筛板 / ~ **tube** 【植】筛管

sift [sift] **❶** *vt.* ①筛;筛分;过滤: ~ flour 筛面粉 / ~ (out) the wheat from the chaff 把小麦的壳筛掉 / ~ gold from sand 沙里淘金 ②撒(糖等)(*on to*) ③细查;详审: ~ the evidence 审查证据 ④选拔,精选,挑选: ~ out the best 挑出最好的 **❷** *vi.* ①筛 ②被筛下;(象通过筛具般地)落下,通过 (*through, into*): The flour ~ed through. 面粉被筛了下来。/ Snow ~ed through a chink in the window. 雪通过窗缝刷刷地飘了进来。③细查,探究 ④选拔,精选 ‖**~er** *n.* ①家庭用的筛具;(面粉厂的)筛机 ②筛者 ③细查者 / **~ing** *n.* ①筛;过滤 ②[复]筛(或滤)过的东西;筛(或滤)下来的杂质

sigh [sai] **I** *n.* ①叹气,叹息;叹息声: heave a ~ of relief 松一口气 ②(风、树等的)啸声,悲鸣声 **II** **❶** *vi.* ①叹气,叹息,悲叹 ②渴望;思慕 (*for*) ③(风、树等)呼啸,悲鸣 **❷** *vt.* ①叹息地说 (*out, forth*) ②叹息着度过(光阴等) (*away*) ‖**~er** *n.* 叹息者;呼啸的风;发悲鸣声的树

sight [sait] **I** *n.* ①视力;视觉: have good (poor) ~ 视力好(差) / lose (regain) one's ~ 丧失(恢复)视力 / have long (short 或 near) ~ 患远(近)视 ②见,瞥见: Their first ~ of land came after seven days at sea. 他们在海上航行七天之后才第一次见到陆地。③视域,眼界: He lives in ~ of the school. 从他的住处可以看到那所学校。(指住在离学校很近的地方) ④审阅;阅读: This letter is for your ~ only. 这封信只是给你看的。⑤见解;意见,看法: Do what is right in your own ~. 按照你心目中认为正确的去做吧。⑥情景;奇观;[常用复]名胜;风景: The sunrise at the seaside was quite (或 certainly) a ~ to behold. 海滨日出真是个奇观。⑦[口]滑稽可笑的景象: make a ~ of oneself (用穿奇装异服等方式)使自己惹人注目,出洋相 / What a ~ it is! 这样子多怪(或多难看)呀! ⑧瞄准;观测;瞄准器;观测器: take a careful ~ before firing 发射前仔细瞄准一下 / take a ~ at the sun (为测定船的位置等)观测太阳 / a telescopic ~ 望远瞄准器 ⑨[常用复]目标;志向: set one's ~s high 有远大抱负 ⑩[口]很多,大量: a ~ of money (troubles, boys) 许多钱(麻烦,男孩) / think a ~ of sb. 非常想念某人 / This is a *long* ~ better than that. 这个比那个好得多。**II** **❶** *vt.* ①(初次)看见: Several whales were ~ed. 发现了几条鲸鱼。②(用观测器)观测;(用瞄准器)瞄准: ~ a target 瞄准靶子 ③调整(枪、炮等)的瞄准器;装瞄准器于(枪、炮等) **❷** *vi.* ①单凭(或要求)当场认识(或理解)的,事先无准备的,即席的: ~ translation (事先无准备的)即席翻译 ②【商】见票即付的: a ~ draft 即期汇票 ‖*a ~ for sore eyes* [口]乐于看见的人(或物);极受欢迎的人(或物) / *a* ~ (或 *feast*) *for the gods* 不寻常的东西,极为精美的东西;惊人的场面 / *at first* ~ 乍一看(之下): At first ~ these two problems do not seem to be connected with each other. 这两个问题看着起来似乎彼此并无关连。/ *fall in love with ... at first* ~ 对……一见钟情 / *at* (或 *on*) ~ 一见(就): a draft payable *at* (或 *on*) ~ 见票即付的汇票 / *shoot at* ~ 一见就射击 / *play music at* ~ 事先无准备地看谱演奏 / *at* (*the*) ~ *of* 一看见 / *catch* (或 *have, get*) (*a*) ~ *of* 看到,发现 / *Get out of my* ~! 走开! 滚开! / *in* (或 *within*) ~ 被见到: The land came *in* ~. 看见陆地了。/ Another rich harvest is *within* ~. 另一个丰收已经在望。/ *in* (或 *within*) ~ *of* 在见得到…的地方: We are now *in* ~ *of* land. 现在我们见到陆地了。/ *know sb. by* ~ 跟某人只是面熟(并不相识) / *lose* ~ *of* 不再看见;忽略;忘记: We must not *lose* ~ *of* the fact that .... 我们必须看到……这样一个事实。/ *not by a long* ~ 远不;根本不 / *out of* ~ 在视程之外,在看不见的地方;[口](标准等)高得达不到: The train was soon *out of* ~. 那火车很快就看不见了。/ *out of* ~ *of* 在不能看见…的地方;在离…很远处: We are still *out of* ~ *of* land. 我们仍然看不见陆地。/ *Out of* ~, *out of mind.* [谚]眼不见,心不想。/ *put out of* ~ 把…藏起来;对…不予理会 / ~ *unseen* [美](指购货等时)事先未看现货;未经察看(或查验): buy a thing *unseen* 不看实物买东西 / *take a* ~ *of* (或 *at*) *sb.* [俚]以拇指顶着鼻尖张翕其余四指向某人表示嘲笑 ‖~**ed** *a.* [常用以构成复合词]…的: *far*~ed 远视的;有远见的 / *short*~ed 近视的;目光短浅的 / ‖'~-**read** *vt.* 事先无准备地一见便

读(外文等); 事先无准备地演奏(音乐) *vi.* 事先无准备地看着读(或演奏、演唱) / '~-see *vi.* 观光, 游览 / '~-,seeing *n.* & *a.* 观光(的), 游览(的) / '~-,seer *n.* 观光者, 游客 / '~,singing *n.* 视唱(事先无准备地看着谱即唱) / '~,worthy *a.* 值得看的

sightless ['saitlis] *a.* ①盲的, 无视力的 ②[诗]看不见的 ‖~ly *ad.* / ~ness *n.*

sign [sain] **I** *n.* ①符号, 记号: mathematical ~s 数学符号(如 +, -, ×, ÷) ②招牌; 标记; 指示牌: the barber's ~ 理发店招牌 / traffic ~s 交通标志 ③征兆; 迹象; 【医】(病)症: Very often dark clouds are a ~ of rain. 乌云常常是下雨的预兆。/ understand the ~s of the times 认清时代的趋势 / These clothes are showing ~s of wear. 这些衣服看得出已穿旧了。④(手、头等的)示意动作: deaf-and-dumb ~s 聋哑人的手势 / give sb. a ~ to withdraw 示意某人退下 ⑤(动物的)足迹, 踪迹 ⑥【天】宫: ~s of the zodiac 黄道十二宫 ⑦【宗】(表示神的意志的)神迹, 奇迹 **II** ❶ *vt.* ①签(名), 署(名); 签字于(信、文件等): ~ (one's name *to*) a cheque 在支票上签字 / ~ a legislative bill into law 签字批准法案使其成为法律 / By doing so he has ~ed his own doom. 他这样做就是注定了自己必然完蛋的命运。②以手势(或其他动作)表示: He ~ed his approval with a nod. 他点头表示同意。③(通过签订合约)雇用 ④(天主教徒等)对…划十字 ❷ *vi.* ①签名: a ~ing ceremony 签字仪式 ②以动作示意: He ~ed to me to stop. 他做手势叫我停止。‖*in* ~ *of* 作为…的表示: shake hands *in* ~ *of* friendship 握手表示友好 / *make the* ~ *of the cross* (天主教徒等)用手划十字 / ~ *and countersign* 口令; 暗语, 切口 / ~ *away* 签字让与(财产等); 签字放弃(权利等) / ~ *in* ①签到 ②记录(某人)的到达时间 / ~ *off* ①(电台)停止广播 ②[俚]停止讲话; 停止活动 / ~ *on* ①签约雇用(工人等); 签约受雇用 ②(电台)开始广播 / ~ *out* 用签名(或在考勤卡上打印等)方法记录离去的时间 / ~ *over* ~ *away* / ~s *and wonders* 奇迹 / ~ *up* ①签约参加工作(或组织等); 报名从军; 签约承担义务 (*for*) ②签约雇用(工人等); 使签约承担义务 ‖~er *n.* ①签名者 ②使用手势语者 ‖'~board *n.* 招牌; 广告牌 / ~ language (聋哑人等的)手势语 / '~manual (尤指国王的)亲笔签名 ②手势 / '~-off *n.* (电台的)停止广播 / ~ painter 画广告牌的人; 写招牌的人 / '~post *n.* (十字路口等的)路标 / '~,writer *n.* 写招牌的人; 广告牌上写字的人

signal ['signəl] **I** *n.* ①信号; 暗号: go into action at a given ~ 在约定的信号发出时投入战斗 / traffic ~s 交通信号 / a ~ of distress (船之distress ~) (船只等的)遇难信号 ②近因; 导火线 (*for*): His remark was the ~ *for* the argument. 他的这番话引起了这场争论。③传

递信息的工具; 信号机, 信号器 **II** *a.* ①作为信号的 ②显著的, 非凡的: a ~ victory 巨大的胜利 **III** (signal(l)ed; signal(l)ing) ❶ *vt.* ①用信号发出(或报告); 标志: ~ a message 用信号发送消息 / The ship signal(l)ed her position hourly. 该船每小时用信号报告它的位置。②用信号通知; 以动作向…示意: ~ the fleet to turn back 用信号通知舰队返航 / He signal(l)ed me to enter. 他做手势叫我进去。❷ *vi.* 发信号; 打信号: ~ with flags (lights) 用旗子(灯光)发信号 ‖~ly *ad.* 显著地, 非凡地 ‖~ book 旗语通信手册 / ~ box (铁路上的)信号所; 信号塔 / ~ code 通信密码 / ~ fire 烟火信号 / ~ flag 手旗, 信号旗 / ~ generator 信号发生器 / ~ gun 信号枪; 号炮 / ~ lamp 信号灯 / ~man ['signəlmən] *n.* 信号员; 通信兵 / ~ officer 【军】通信主任 / ~ plate (电视摄影机的)信号板 / ~ rocket 烟火信号弹 / ~ station 信号站

signatory ['signətəri] **I** *n.* (协议、条约等的)签署者; 签约国: the *signatories to* a treaty 缔约的各国 **II** *a.* 签署的; 签约的

signature ['signitʃə] *n.* ①署名, 签名: put one's ~ *to* a letter 签名于信件 ②(一项广播节目开始或结束时的)信号调, 信号曲 (=~ tune) ③(药方上的)用法说明 ④【印】书帖(印好后依页码次序可折成一迭的书页); 帖码(印在书帖首页下部指示装订顺序的标记) ⑤【音】调号(=key ~); 拍号 (=time ~) ⑥(旧时认为表明其医疗用途的)植物外形特征(或特性)(如心脏形的叶子被认为可用于治疗心脏疾病)

significance [sig'nifikəns] *n.* ①意义, 意味: far-reaching historical ~ 深远的历史意义 / with a look of deep ~ 用意味深长的表情 ②重要性, 重大: be of no ~ 无关紧要

significant [sig'nifikənt] *a.* ①有意义的; 意义(或意味)深长的 ②表明…的(*of*): actions ~ *of* one's real purposes 说明某人真实目的的行动 ③重要的, 重大的; 值得注意的 ④有效的: ~ figures 【数】有效数(字) ⑤非偶然的: Statistically ~ correlation exists between vitamin deficiency and disease. 从统计数字角度看来, 维生素缺乏和疾病之间存在一定关系。⑥(语言上)表示有别的, 区别的; (词缀等)有实义的 ‖~ly *ad.*

signification [,signifi'keiʃən] *n.* ①正确意义, 含义; 字义 ②[罕]表示, 表明; 正式通知 ③[主方]重要, 重大

signify ['signifai] ❶ *vt.* ①表示, 表明; 意味: What does this word ~? 这个词表示什么意思? / He *signified* his agreement by nodding. 他点头表示同意。②预示 ❷ *vi.* ①要紧, 有重要性: It does not ~. 这没有什么关系。②[美俚]冒充内行 ‖**signifier** *n.* 表示者, 意味者; 记号

silage ['sailidʒ] **I** *n.* 青贮饲料: a ~ cutter 切草机 **II** *vt.* 青贮

silence ['sailəns] **I** *n.* ①沉默, 默不作声: maintain a strict ~ on sth. 对某事保持严格的沉默 / buy

sb.'s ～ 用贿赂堵住某人的口　② 静默，默念:
③ 无声,寂静: the ～ of midnight 子夜的寂静 /
a dead ～ 死沉沉的寂静 / *Silence* reigned in the
hall. 会场内一片肃静。/ international radio
～ 国际无线电寂静时间 ④ 湮没，忘却 ⑤ 未提
到; (作家等的)不创作,无声息: The document's
～ on this point is amazing. 文件没提到这一
点令人惊讶。⑥ 无音信;无联系: Forgive me for
my long ～. 请原谅我好久没给你写信。**II** *vt.*
① 使沉默; 使哑口无言; 使安静: ～ the slanderers
驳得诽谤者哑口无言　② 消灭(噪音)　③压制(意
见 等)　④ 打哑(敌人火力)　**III** *int.* 安静! 别
作声!‖*break* ～ 打破沉默,开口讲话 / *in* ～ 沉
默地,无声地: We cannot pass over the matter
in ～. 我们对这件事不能保持缄默。/ listen to
sb. *in* ～ 默默地听某人讲 / *keep* ～ 保持沉默,
不讲话 / *pass into* ～ 湮没于无声无息之中 /
put sb. to ～ ① 驳得某人哑口无言,驳倒某人:
A series of ironclad facts *put* him *to* ～. 一
系列铁的事实驳得他哑口无言。② 杀死某人 /
Silence gives consent. [谚]沉默即同意。/
Speech is silver, ～ is golden. 见 **speech**
‖～*r n.* ① 使沉默者　② 消音器;灭声器

silent ['sailənt] *a.* ① 沉默的,不作声的;寡言的:
be ～ about what happened 对发生的事情默
不作声　② 寂静无声的: the ～ hills 寂静的群山
③未说出的,明言的: ～ longing 内心的渴望 /
a ～ prayer【宗】默祷　④ 未作记述的; 未被提到
的: History is ～ about (或 upon) it. 历史对这
事没有记载。⑤静止的,不活动的;不参加具体经
营的: a ～ volcano 死的火山 / a ～ partner
不参加具体经营(或无发言权)的合伙人; 隐名合
伙人　⑥无声的;无对话的;【语】不发音的: a ～
film 无声电影 / the ～ drama 哑剧 / a ～ letter
不发音的字母(如 doubt 中的 b)　‖～**ly** *ad.* ‖～
butler "哑仆"(指用来收集餐桌上残渣、倾倒烟灰
等的有盖带柄盛器) / ～ cop "无声警察"(设置
在十字路口指挥交通的机械装置) / ～ service
[美] ①海军 ②潜艇部队 / ～ system 禁止犯
人相互交谈的监禁制度 / ～ treatment 沉默相
待(指蔑视性的不理睬) / ～ vote 秘密投票

silhouette [‚silu(ː)'et] **I** *n.* ① 侧面影像,黑色轮廓
像,剪影: an aiming ～ 人像靶　② 轮廓: the ～
of a new-model automobile 一辆新型汽车的轮廓
II *vt.* 把…画成侧面影像(或黑色轮廓像); 使现
出轮廓 (on, against): trees ～d *against* the evening sky 在晚空的背景上现出轮廓的树木 ‖*in*
～ 成黑色轮廓像,成剪影; 呈轮廓状

silk [silk] **I** *n.* ① 蚕丝,丝;丝织品,绸: tussah (或
tusser) ～ 柞蚕丝 / raw ～ 生丝 / ～ reeling 缫
丝 / spun ～ 绢丝,绢丝纺(绸) / thrown ～
经纬丝线,加拈丝线　②[复]绸服;[美](骑师、拳
击手、杂技演员等的)绸制服: be dressed in ～s
and satins 衣着华丽　③[英]王室法律顾问的绸
制服;[英口]王室法律顾问　④丝状物;[美]玉蜀
黍的须　⑤(宝石等的)光泽　⑥降落伞　**II** *a.* ①丝
的; 丝织的: ～ muslin 全丝薄纱　②象丝的

III *vi.* [美](玉蜀黍)长须;开花　‖*hit the* ～ [美
俚]用降落伞降落 / *take* ～ [英]当上王室法律
顾问 / *the Silk Road*【史】丝绸之路　‖～ **cotton**
丝光木棉 / ～ **floss** 丝绵;绣花丝线 / ～ **gland**
【动】绢丝腺 / ～ **gown** [英]王室法律顾问的绸
制服;王室法律顾问 / ～ **hat** 大礼帽 / ～ **man**
['silkmən] *n.* 丝织品的制造者(或出售者) / ～
mantle (汽灯用)丝质纱罩 / ～ **painting** 绢画,
帛画 / '～-'screen process 绢网印花法 / '～■
'stocking *a.* ① 穿着华丽的;奢侈的　② 贵族的;
有钱的　③【美史】联邦党的 / ～ **stocking** ①长
统丝袜　②穿着华丽的人;贵族;有钱人　③【美史】
联邦党人,辉格党人 / '～**worm** *n.* 蚕: a ～*worm*
cocoon 蚕茧 / ～*worm* breeding 养蚕 / ～ **yarn**
丝线;针织丝线;绣花丝线

silken ['silkən] *a.* ①[古][诗]丝制的　②穿丝衣的
③ 丝一样的;柔软的;光润的: ～ hair 柔软光滑
的头发　④圆滑的,讨好的: ～ flattery 曲意奉承
⑤温柔的;柔和的: a ～ voice 柔和的嗓音　⑥风
雅的

silky ['silki] *a.* ①丝 的　②丝一样的;柔滑的;有光
泽的　③ 奉承讨好的　④ 有细毛(或羽、鳞)的
‖**silkily** *ad.* / **silkiness** *n.*

sill [sil] *n.* ①【建】基石,底木　②(门、船坞、船闸等
的)槛;窗台　③【地】岩床,海底山脊　④【机】(车休
底框的)梁　⑤【矿】底梁;平巷底

silly ['sili] **I** *a.* ①傻的,戆的;愚蠢的; 糊涂的:
Don't be ～! 别傻! / ～ remarks 戆话 / a ～
question 愚蠢的问题　②无聊的: a ～ story 无聊
的故事　③[口]眼花的;失去知觉的: be knocked
～ 被打得昏头转向　④[古]无助的,弱的　⑤朴素
的,乡村风味的　**II** *n.* [口]呆子,傻瓜　‖**sillily**
ad. / **silliness** *n.* ‖～ **Billy** 笨蛋 / ～ **season**
新闻饥荒期(指八、九月份)

silo ['sailou] *n.* ①(贮藏青饲料的密封的)地窖,筒
仓;地下仓库　② 导弹仓库(用钢筋混凝土制造的
地下仓库,并设有发射装置)

silo

farm silo

military silo

silt [silt] **I** *n.* ①淤泥 ②(河边等地的)淤泥沉积处 **II ❶** *vt.* 使淤塞(*up*): The passage is ~ed up. 水道被淤泥堵塞。**❷** *vi.* 淤塞(*up*)

silvan ['silvən] **I** *a.* ①森林的;住在森林中的;在森林中发现的 ②树木多的 ③乡村的,农村的 **II** *n.* ①住在森林中的人 ②森林之神

silver ['silvə] **I** *n.* ①银: fine (或 pure) ~ 纯银 / German (或 nickel) ~ 德银,镍银(锌镍铜合金) / cat ~【矿】银云母 ②(作为商品或交换媒介的)银子;银币;钱;[美俚](五角以下的)零钱 ③银器;银皿,银制用具: table ~ 银餐具 / clean the ~ 擦干净银器 ④银白色;银白色涂料(如镜子的涂料) ⑤(用于摄影等的)银盐 **II** *a.* ①银的;银质的,银制的;含银的;产银的;镀银的: a ~ cup 银杯 / a ~ dollar 银元 / ~ oxide【化】氧化银 ②白银似的;银白色的,有银白光泽的: the ~ moon 明月 / ~ hair 银丝般的白发 ③(货币)银本位的: the ~ bloc 银本位集团 ④(声音)清越的: a ~ tone 银铃般的音调 ⑤雄辩的: a ~ tongue 流利的口才 ⑥次于最好的;第二流的 ⑦二十五周年的 **III ❶** *vt.* ①镀银于 ②使成银白色: trees ~ed with snow (因积雪)披着银装的树木 **❷** *vi.* 变成银白色 ‖ **~age** 白银时代(指次于"黄金时代"的兴盛时期) / **~ bath** 银盐溶液槽 / **~ berry** *n.*【植】银果胡颓子 / **~ birch**【植】白桦 / **~ carp**【动】白鲢 / **~ cedar**【植】落矶山桧 / **~ doctor** 钓鱼用的假饵 / **~ fish** *n.* ①鲻鱼 ②银汉鱼 / **~ foil** 银箔 / **~ fox**【动】银狐;银狐皮 / **~ gilt** 镀金的白银 / **~ grey** 银灰色 / **'~-'haired** *a.* 发白如银的;长着银灰色头发的 / **~ Jeff** [dʒef] [美俚] ①二角五分 ②镍币;五分钱 / **~ leaf** 银箔 / **~ lining** 云朵边缘的白光;困难中看到的光明(或慰藉) / **~ paper** ①包银器的白色薄纸 ②锡纸 / **~ plate** 银器;镀银的器皿 / **'~-'plate** *vt.* 镀银于 / **~ point** 银的熔点 (960.8℃) / **~ print**【摄】银盐感光照片 / **~ screen** 银幕;电影(界) / **'~side** *n.* [英]牛腿肉的最好部分 / **'~smith** *n.* 银匠 / **~ spoon**[喻]财富(尤指遗产): born with a ~ spoon in one's mouth 生在富贵人家 / **~ standard** (货币)银本位 / **~ streak** [英]英吉利海峡的别名 / **'~-'tongued** *a.* 口才流利的,雄辩的 / **'~ware** *n.* [总称]银器,银制品;银餐具 / **~ wedding** (西方风俗)银婚,结婚二十五周年纪念 / **~ wing** [美俚]半元银币,五角钱

silvery ['silvəri] *a.* ①似银的;有银色光泽的 ②(声音)银铃般的,清脆的 ③含银的;银制的 ‖ **silveriness** *n.*

similar ['similə] **I** *a.* 相似的,类似的(*to*): A is ~ to B in many ways. 甲在好多方面同乙相象。/ ~ triangles 相似三角形 **II** *n.* 相似的东西,类似物 ‖ **~ly** *ad.*

similarity [ˌsimi'læriti] *n.* ①类似,相似: the ~ of a cat *to* a tiger 猫和虎的相似 ②[复]类似点,类似物;相似事例: Are there any *similarities* between the two? 两者之间有什么相似之处吗?

simile ['simili] *n.*【语】直喻,明喻(例如: brave as a lion 像狮子一般勇敢; quick like lightning 闪电般迅速)

simmer ['simə] **I ❶** *vi.* ①煨,炖: Let the meat ~ for a few minutes. 让肉再煨几分钟。②(危机等)处于酝酿状态 ③内心充满(*with*): ~ with laughter 忍俊不禁 / ~ with rage 怒火中烧 **❷** *vt.* (以文火)慢慢地煮 **II** *n.* 将沸未沸状态: bring the water to a ~ 把水煮得冒泡 ‖ *at a* ~ (或 *on the* ~) 处于将沸未沸状态;处于将爆发未爆发状态 / ~ *down* ①被煮浓 ②被总括起来: It all ~*s down* to a matter of world outlook. 归根结蒂是世界观问题。③平静下来;缓和

simper ['simpə] **I** *n.* ①痴笑,傻笑 ②假笑 **II ❶** *vi.* 痴笑;假笑 **❷** *vt.* 傻笑着(或假笑着)说 ‖ **~er** ['simpərə] *n.* 痴笑(或假笑)的人

simple ['simpl] **I** *a.* ①简单的;简易的;简明的: a ~ question 简单的问题 / It's just as ~ as that. 就是那么简单的一回事。/ give a ~ explanation 作简明的解释 ②朴素的,简朴的;单纯的;直率的,坦率的: cultivate the habit of ~ and plain living 养成朴素的生活作风 / ~ clothes 朴素的衣服 / a ~ diet 粗茶淡饭 / a ~ style of writing 简朴的文风 / as ~ as a child 象孩子一样单纯 ③头脑简单的;糊涂的,愚蠢的: a ~ soul 头脑简单的人 / They are not so ~ as to believe all that. 他们不至那么糊涂,会相信那一套。④不折不扣的;绝对的,无条件的: The ~ fact is that …… 事情无非就是… / a ~ impossibility 简直不可能 / pure and ~ 地地道道的,不折不扣 ⑤(出身、地位)低微的;微不足道的 ⑥结构单一的,因素单纯的;初级的,原始的: a ~ sentence【语】简单句 / ~ harmony【音】简单和声,初级和声学 / ~ fracture【医】单纯性骨折 / the ~ forms of life 生物的初级形态 **II** *n.* ①出身低微者 ②无知者;傻子 ③[英][复]愚蠢的行为 ④单一成分 ⑤药草;(单味的)草药 ‖ **~r** *n.* 药草采集者 ‖ **~ equation** 【数】一次方程式 / **'~-'hearted** *a.* 心地纯洁的,天真无邪的;真诚的 / **~ hono(u)rs** (桥牌中)一方独占的三张主要王牌 / **~ interest**【商】单利 / **~ machine** 【机】简单机械 / **'~-'minded** *a.* 纯朴的;头脑简单的;笨的

simpleton ['simpltən] *n.* 傻子,笨人;易受骗者

simplicity [sim'plisiti] *n.* ①简单;简易;简明: The method is ~ itself. 这一方法再简单也没有了。②朴素;单纯;直率 ③天真: childlike ~ 孩子般的单纯 ④无知;愚蠢

simplify ['simplifai] *vt.* 简化,精简;使单纯,使易做,使易懂: ~ working process 简化工序 / a *simplified* edition 简写本 ‖ **simplification** [ˌsim-plifi'keiʃən] *n.* / **simplifier** *n.* 简化物

simply ['simpli] *ad.* ①简单地;简明地;简易地 ②朴素地,简朴地 ③坦白地,直率地,单纯地 ④仅仅,只不过: This is ~ a question of procedure. 这只是个手续(或程序)问题。⑤简直,

完全: ~ marvelous (ridiculous) 简直妙极(荒谬)

simulate ['simjuleit] *vt.* ①假装,冒充: ~ enthusiasm (goodness) 装作热心(善良) ②模仿,模拟; 看上去象: The insect ~s a twig. 这种昆虫看上去象一根小树枝。 ‖**simulation** [,simju-'leiʃən] *n.* ‖**simulated rank** 【军】(文职人员获得的)相当于某一军衔的地位

simultaneous [,siməl'teinjəs, ,saiməl'teinjəs] *a.* 同时发生的,同时存在的; 同时的,一齐的: This event was almost ~ *with* that one. 这件事几乎是与那件事同时发生的。/ ~ interpretations 同声翻译 ‖~**ly** *ad.* / ~**ness** *n.* ‖~ **equations** 【数】联立方程式

sin [sin] **I** *n.* ①(宗教或道德上的)罪,罪孽,罪恶: commit a ~ 犯罪 / an unpardonable ~ 不可赦免的罪行 ②(违犯礼节、习俗的)过失; 失礼; 不合常情的事: a ~ *against* good manners 违反礼节的过错 **II** (sinned; sinning) ❶ *vi.* ① 犯罪; 造犯教规 ②犯过失: ~ *against* modesty 不谦虚 ❷ *vt.* ①犯(罪): ~ a sin 犯罪 ②过罪恶生活而糟蹋掉(健康等)(*away*) ‖*a besetting* ~ 容易陷入的罪过;最易犯的恶习 / *a man of* ~ [古]反基督教的人; 堕落的人,罪人,被神遗弃的人 / *deadly* (或 *mortal*) ~*s* 【宗】不可宽恕的罪行 / *for my* ~*s* [谑]自作自受 / *like* ~ [俚]猛烈地: hate the enemy *like* ~ 痛恨敌人 / *live in* ~ 姘居 / *more sinned against than sinning* 别人负己甚于己负别人; 受到过于严厉的惩罚 / *original* ~ 【宗】原罪(《圣经》中亚当犯下的罪,基督教徒认为因此人类具有犯罪的本性) / *one's mercies* 见 *mercy* / *visit the ~s of another person upon sb.* 使某人因他人所犯之罪而受责罚

since [sins] **I** *conj.* ①从…以来; …以后: How have you been ~ I saw you last? (从上次见到你后)这一向你好吗? ②因为; 既然; 鉴于: He didn't come, ~ he was busy. 他因为忙,所以没有来。/ *Since* this method doesn't work, let's try another. 既然这种方法不行,我们就试用另一种吧。 **II** *prep.* 从…以来,自从: He is happy ~ then. 从那时以来他一直很愉快。/ I have not heard from him ~ writing last. 自上次写信以后,我没有接到过他的信。 **III** *ad.* ①[与完成时态连用]从那时以后;后来: This dam has stood the trial of several floods. 从那时起这水坝已经受了几次洪水的考验。 ②以前(=ago): It happened many years ~. 这事是多年以前发生的。 ‖*ever* ~ 从那时起一直到现在; 此后一直: *ever* ~ he graduated (或 his graduation) 从他毕业以来 / *long* ~ 很久以前; 早已

sincere [sin'siə] *a.* ①(人)真诚的; 笃实的; 诚恳的; 直率的: a ~ friend 真诚的朋友 ②(感情、行为)真挚的;表里一致的: have a ~ desire to help 真心实意地想帮助 / It is my ~ belief that .... 我深信… ③不掺假的, 纯净的 ‖~**ness** *n.*

sincerely [sin'siəli] *ad.* 真诚地; 诚恳地; 真挚地: We ~ hope that .... 我们衷心希望… / Yours ~ (或 *Sincerely* yours) 您的忠诚的(致友人等信末署名前的客套语)

sincerity [sin'seriti] *n.* ①真诚; 诚意; 真挚 ②真实

sinecure ['sainikjuə] *n.* ①挂名职务;闲职: hold a ~ 领干薪 / His is hardly a ~. 他的职务决不是挂挂名的。 ②(意指职务繁重)②(教会中)不担任教化工作的领薪职务

sinew ['sinju:] **I** *n.* ①[解]腱 ②[复]肌肉,筋肉 ③体力,气力; 精力 ④[常用复]主要支柱,砥柱;资源: the ~s of war 军费(或军备等) **II** *vt.* ①象腱般连结 ②支持,加强 ‖~**less** *a.* 无腱的; 无精力的; 无气力的

sinful ['sinful] *a.* ①罪孽深重的;有罪的 ②邪恶的,不道德的 ‖~**ly** *ad.* / ~**ness** *n.*

sing [siŋ] **I** (过去式 sang [sæŋ] 或 sung [sʌŋ], 过去分词 sung) ❶ *vi.* ①唱; 演唱: ~ in chorus 合唱 / ~ in (out of) tune 唱得合(不合)调子 / ~ *to* the piano 和着钢琴唱 ②(鸟等)啼, 鸣, 唱: The birds (crickets) are ~*ing*. 鸟儿(蟋蟀)在歌唱。 ③(水壶、风、小河、蜂等)作响, 发出嗡嗡声(或嗖嗖声等);(耳)鸣: The kettle is ~*ing*. (水将沸时)水壶响了。 / My ears are ~*ing*. 我耳鸣。 ④ 欢乐: His heart *sang* for joy. 他欢乐得心儿在歌唱。 ⑤作诗;用诗歌赞美,歌颂(*of*): ⑥[美俚](向警方、法院)自供; 告密 ❷ *vt.* ①唱; 演唱: Will you ~ us a song (或 *sing* a song for us)? 你给我们唱一首歌好吗? ②吟咏; 歌颂 ③唱着使 **II** *n.* ①嗖嗖声; 嗡嗡声: the ~ of arrows overhead 在头顶上嗖嗖飞过的箭声 ②[美口]合唱; 合唱会 ‖~ *out* [口]大声讲,叫喊;[美俚]自供; 告密: *Sing out* if you want anything. 你要什么就大声说吧。 / ~ *small* 在受责备(或受屈辱)后变谦逊,变沉默 / ~ *up* 更用力地唱 ‖~**'a,long** *n.* [口](非正式的)歌唱聚会,(朋友间的)歌咏会

singer[1] ['siŋə] *n.* ①歌唱家,歌手 ②诗人 ③鸣禽

singer[2] ['sindʒə] *n.* ①(屠宰场的)燎毛工; 【纺】烧毛工 ②【纺】烧毛机

singing ['siŋiŋ] *n.* ①唱歌; 唱歌声 ②嗖嗖声;嗡嗡声;耳鸣声 ③[无]啸声,振鸣 ‖~ **bird** 鸣禽;雀类鸟 / '~-,**master** *n.* 音乐教师 / ~ **voice** 歌唱时的嗓音

single ['siŋgl] **I** *a.* ①单一的; 单个的: a ~ track (铁路)单轨 / a ~ ticket 单程票(=[美] a one-way ticket) / walk in ~ file 成列单走 / ~ consonants 单辅音 / ~ standard 单一的标准,统一的标准 ②个别的: not make one ~ concession 不作任何一点让步 / drive out every ~ one of the aggressors 把侵略者一个不剩地赶出去 / examine each ~ piece 逐件一一检查 ③独身的; 孤独的: a ~ man (woman) 独身男子(女子) / remain ~ 尚未结婚 / ~ life (state) 独身生活(状态) / ~ blessedness [谑]未婚,独身 ④单人的: a ~ bed (room) 单人床(房间) ⑤一对一的: ~ combat 一对一的决斗 ⑥专一的;单纯的 ⑦独一无二的,无比的: that unique and ~

gymnast 那位十分杰出的体操运动员 / sb.'s ~ most important contribution 某人极为重大的贡献 ⑧[英](啤酒等)淡的 ⑨【植】单瓣的: a ~ rose 单瓣玫瑰 ⑩【无】单次的, 单工的: ~ sideband communication 单边带通信 **II** *n.* ①一个; [美俚]独自干活的人; 单人演出的节目, 单脚戏 ②(网球等的)单打: play ~s 举行单打比赛 / men's (women's) ~s 男子(女子)单打 ③(棒球的)一垒打 ④单程票 ⑤[常用复]单股头的线 ⑥单瓣花 **III** ❶ *vt.* 选拔; 选拔 (out): ~ out the principal contradiction from among a complexity of contradictions 在错综复杂的矛盾中找出主要矛盾 / ~ sb. *out* for special training 挑选出某人加以特殊训练 ❷ *vi.* ① (棒球中)作一垒打 ②(马)单步行进 ‖~ness *n.* 单一; 单身; 专一 ‖'~-'breasted *a.* 单排钮的 / ~ entry (簿记用语)单式 / '~-'eyed *a.* ① 单纯的, 真诚的 ② 独眼的 / '~-'foot *n.* 单步(马的一种步法) *vi.* (马等)单步行进 / '~-'handed *a.* ① 单独的; 独力的, 单枪匹马的: a ~-handed journey 单独一人的旅行 / a ~-handed cook 没有帮手的炊事员 ② 独手的; 只用一只手的 *ad.* 单独地; 独力地, 单枪匹马地: fight ~-handed 单枪匹马地战斗 / '~-'hearted *a.* 真诚的; 忠心的 / '~-'loader *n.* 单发枪 / '~-'minded *a.* 真诚的;忠心的;一心一意的, 专心致志的 / '~-'seater *n.* 单人车; 单座飞机 / '~-'space *vt. & vi.* 单行打字(或印刷) / '~-'stage *a.* 单级的: a ~-stage rocket 单级火箭 / '~-'stick *n.* 单棍搏斗; 单剑刺杀; 单棍;单剑 / '~,sticker *n.* 单桅船 / '~-'tax 【经】单一税(论) / '~-'track *a.* ① 单轨的 ②狭隘而固执的

singlet ['siŋglit] *n.* ①[英](男式)汗衫, 背心 ②【物】单线

singly ['siŋgli] *ad.* ① 单身地: live ~ 过单身生活 ② 各自地; 独自地; 单枪匹马地: He ~ and successfully defended the position. 他独自一人成功地守住了阵地。③ 个别地; 逐一地: deal with the questions ~ 一个个地处理问题 ④ 直截了当地,真诚地

singsong ['siŋ-sɒŋ] **I** *n.* ①即席演唱会; (朋友们凑在一起的)歌咏会 ② 单调的节奏; 节奏单调的歌(或诗): in a ~ 节奏单调地 **II** *a.* 节奏单调的: in a ~ voice 声音单调地 **III** *vt. & vi.* (节奏单调地)唱, 说, 诵

singular ['siŋgjulə] **I** *a.* ① 单一的; 独个的 ②非凡的; 卓越的; 独一无二的: beauty 非常美 / a man of ~ courage 胆略超群的人 / a ~ specimen 独一无二的标本 ③ 异常的; 奇异的: ~ habits 怪僻的习惯 / ~ to say [用作插入语]说也奇怪 ④ 持异议的: We are not ~ in our judgement. 我们的判断并不是标新立异的。⑤【语】单数的: the ~ number 【语】单数 / "Tooth" is ~. "tooth" 是单数形式。**II** *n.* 【语】单数: "I" is the ~ of "we". "I" 是 "we" 的单数。This noun is in the ~. 这个名词是单数。‖*all and* ~ 见 all ‖~**ly** *ad.*

singularity [,siŋgju'læriti] *n.* ①单一, 独个 ②异常;非凡 ③ 奇特; 怪僻; 奇特的事物

sinister ['sinistə] *a.* ① 不吉祥的; 凶兆的 ② 阴险的; 邪恶的; 凶恶的: a ~ design 阴谋 / a ~ countenance 凶相 ③不幸的; 导致灾难的 ④左首的, 左边的; 在盾章本身的左半边的 ‖~**ly** *ad.* / ~**ness** *n.*

sink [siŋk] **I** (过去式 sank [sæŋk] 或 sunk [sʌŋk], 过去分词 sunk 或 sunken ['sʌŋkən]) ❶ *vi.* ① (船等)下沉; 沉没; (日、月)落, 没: The ship *sank* to the bottom of the river. 船沉入河底。②(面颊、眼睛)下陷: His eyes (cheeks) have *sunk* in. 他的眼睛(面颊)凹下去了。③(水面)低落; (地面)陷落, 斜下去; 倒下: After the spring floods the brooks ~. 春潮以后小溪的水浅了。/ The foundations have *sunk* three inches. 地基下陷了三吋。/ He *sank* to the ground badly wounded. 他受重伤倒在地上。/ ~ into a chair 一屁股坐进椅子 ④(头、目光等)下垂: His eyes *sank*. 他的目光下垂。/ His head *sank* on his chest. 他的头垂在胸前。⑤(声音、火、风、价格等)降低;减弱; (在视野中)消失: His voice *sank* to a whisper. 他的声音降低为耳语。⑥堕落; 衰微; 衰竭; 消沉: ~ into vice 堕入恶习 / ~ into insignificance 陷入渺小的境地 / He is ~ing fast. 他已频于死亡。/ His spirits *sank*. 他的情绪低落。⑦渗透; 深入; 沉入: Water *sank* rapidly through topsoil. 水很快地渗透了表土。/ The lesson had *sunk* in. 教训非常深刻。/ ~ into a deep sleep 沉沉入睡 ❷ *vt.* ① 使下沉; 使陷入; 把…插入: He was *sunk* in deep thought. 他陷入沉思。②使下垂: He *sank* his head in his hands. 他把头埋入双手。③ 挖掘; 刻, 雕: ~ a well 掘井 / ~ words in stone 在石上刻字 ④ 降低(声音、名誉、地位等); 使(河等)变浅 ⑤ 投(资)[因投资而损失掉; 偿还(债务) ⑥ 抑制(激情、骄傲等); 隐匿(证据、身分等);排除(分歧、自身利益等), 把…放在一边 ⑦搞垮, 使完蛋 **II** *n.* ①阴沟; 污水坑 ②(厨房内洗菜、碟等的)洗涤槽 ③[喻]巢窟, 藏垢纳污的场所: a ~ of iniquity 罪恶的渊薮 ④[美]污水洞, 渗沉 ⑤ 舞台布景升降口 ⑥[美俚]海洋 ‖~ *or swim* 沉浮全凭自己: leave sb. to ~ *or swim* 让某人去自找生路 ②不论好歹: *Sink or swim*, I will try. 无论如何我要试一下。/ *tumble down the* ~ (大口地)饮 ‖~*able a.* 会沉的; 可被沉没的 ‖'~**hole** *n.* ①阴沟口; 污水坑 ②【地】落水洞, 灰岩坑 / ~**ing fund** 偿债基金

sinker ['siŋkə] *n.* ①掘矿井工人; 雕刻者: a die ~ (钢型、硬模)开模工 ②(钓丝等的)锤, 坠子 ③[美俚]银元 ④[美口]炸面圈 ‖*hook, line, and* ~ [美口]完全地, 全部地

sinless ['sinlis] *a.* 无罪的, 清白的; 圣洁的 ‖~**ly** *ad.* / ~**ness** *n.*

sinner ['sinə] *n.* ① (宗教、道德上的)罪人 ②无赖

sinuous ['sinjuəs] *a.* ①蜿蜒的，弯曲的；起伏的 ②曲折的，错综复杂的 ③动作柔软的 ④不正的；不老实的 ⑤【植】(叶子)具弯缘的，具深波状边缘的 ‖**-ly** *ad.* / **~ness** *n.*

sip [sip] **I** (sipped; sipping) ❶ *vi.* 啜饮 ❷ *vt.* ①呷，啜；~ tea 喝茶，啜茗 / ~ the glass dry 把玻璃杯内饮料呷干 ②从…中呷吸：~ a flower 吸花蜜 **II** *n.* ①呷，啜 ②一呷之量：take a ~ of brandy 呷一口白兰地酒

siphon ['saifən] **I** *n.* ①虹吸，虹吸管 ②苏打水瓶 (= ~ bottle) ③【动】呼吸管；(昆虫的)管形口器；(蚊幼虫的)管形突；(头足类的)体管；(软体动物的)水管；(软体、棘皮动物的)虹管 ④【建】存水弯 **II** ❶ *vi.* 通过虹吸 ❷ *vt.* ①用虹吸管吸出(或输送)：~ gasoline from a tank 用虹吸管从油桶中吸出汽油 ②吮吸(民脂民膏)(*off*) ‖**~age** ['saifənidʒ] *n.* 虹吸作用 / **~al, ~ic** [sai'fɔnik] *a.* 虹吸的；虹吸管状的 / **~ barometer** 虹吸气压计 / **~ recorder** 虹吸记录器 / 【无】波纹收报机

sir [强 sə:; 弱 sə] **I** *n.* ①先生，阁下(英美人通常对不相识的男子、上级、长辈或对从事某一职务者的尊称)：Yes (No), ~. 是(不)，先生(或长官)。/ *Sir* 先生(正式公函中的称呼) / Dear *Sir* (或 My dear *Sir*) 亲爱的先生(一般信件中的称呼) / Dear *Sirs* (或 *Sirs*) 诸位先生(致公司、团体等信件中的称呼) / ~ judge 法官先生 ② [S-]…爵士(用在姓名或名字前面，但不可用在姓前)：*Sir* John White 约翰·怀特爵士(也可称 *Sir J. White, Sir John*) ③[谑]老兄；"先生"(对被申斥者、孩子等的挖苦)：Will you be quiet, ~! 嗳，老兄，静一点! / ~ grouch 爱发牢骚的先生 **II** *vt.* …为先生：Don't ~ me! 别叫我先生!

sire ['saiə] *n.* ①[古]陛下 ②[诗]父；男性祖先 ③(四脚动物的)父兽；种马 ④创始人；作者 **II** *vt.* ①(指种马等雄性动物而言)生殖 ②创办；创作

siren ['saiərin] **I** *n.* ①[S-]【希神】塞壬(半人半鸟的海妖，常以美妙歌声诱惑经过的海员而使航船触礁毁灭) ②歌声动人的女歌手 ③迷人的美女 ④汽笛；警报器：an air ~ 汽笛 / an ambulance (a fire) ~ 救护(救火)车上的警报器 / an air-raid ~ 空袭警报器 ⑤【动】土鳗属两栖动物 ⑥【动】海牛目动物 **II** *a.* 诱惑的，迷人的 **III** *vi.* (警车、救火车等)响着警报器开道前进

sirloin ['sə:lɔin] *n.* 牛的上腰部肉，牛腰肉

sisal ['saisəl] *n.* 【植】西沙尔麻，波罗麻(= ~ hemp，可制绳索)

sister ['sistə] **I** *n.* ①姐妹；姐；妹：an elder ~ 姐姐 / a younger ~ 妹妹 / a ~ of the whole blood (或 a whole ~, a full ~) 同胞姐妹，同父母的姐妹 ②同父异母(或同母异父)姐妹(= half ~) ③姑子；姨子；嫂子；弟媳 ④[常用S-](天主教)修女；尼姑；(基督教)女会员 ⑤亲如手足的女子；女同事；女好友 ⑥[英]护士长；护士 ⑦相同类型的东西：~ ships (按同一设计图纸建造的)姐妹船 ⑧(由下等动物的同一母体出生的)同胞雌性动物 ⑨[俚](对陌生女子的直接称呼)小妹妹，大姐 **II** *vt.* 姐妹般地对待 ‖*the fatal* ~s【希神】[罗神]命运三女神 ‖**~hood** *n.* ①姐妹身分；姐妹关系 ②妇女会；妇女的宗教团体 / **~less** *a.* 无姐妹的 / **~ly** *a.* 姐妹的；姐妹般的 ‖**~'-german** ([复] ~s-german) *n.* 同胞姐妹，同父母的姐妹 / **~ hook**【机】双抱钩 / **~-in-law** ['sistərinlɔ:] ([复] ~s-in-law) *n.* 姑子；姨子；嫂子；弟媳

sit [sit] **I** (sat [sæt]; sitting) ❶ *vi.* ①坐；就座：on a chair 坐在椅子上 / ~ in an armchair 坐在扶手椅里 / The rider ~s well. 这骑手骑马姿势很好。②坐落；占地位，占位置：The city ~s on a hill. 城市位于山上。/ The clock has sat there for years. 这只钟放在那里已经好几年了。③(鸟等)栖息不动；(鸡等)伏窝，孵卵：This hen doesn't ~ this year. 这只母鸡今年不孵蛋。④(被画像或被照相时)摆好姿势；做模特儿：~ to an artist (或 ~ for one's portrait) 摆好姿势让画家给自己画像 ⑤占议席；当代表：~ for a borough in Parliament 代表某一选区在议会当议员 / ~ on a committee 担任委员会的委员 ⑥(议会等)开会；(法院)开庭 ⑦参加考试(*for*)：~ for a fellowship 参加奖学金考试·⑧(衣服等)合身；适合：That dress ~s well on her. 那件衣服她穿起来很合身。/ His principles ~ loosely on him. 他的那些原则对他自己并没有多少约束力。⑨(风从某方向)吹(*in*)：The wind ~s in the west. 正在刮西风。⑩临时替人照看(*with*)：~ with a baby 临时替人照看婴孩 ⑪搁置不用：The car ~s in the garage unused all week. 汽车在车房里搁了整整一个星期。❷ *vt.* ①使就座；使坐：The mother sat the child at a little table. 母亲把孩子放到小桌旁坐好。/ a story that ~s one up straight 使人端坐聚精会神谛听的精彩故事 ②骑：~ a horse 骑马 ③使就…坐：The car will ~ six people. 这汽车可坐六人。④(鸡等)孵(卵) **II** *n.* ①坐；[口]坐着等候的一段时间 ②(衣服的)合身 ‖**~ back** ①(在紧张活动之后)宽舒地休息 ②不采取行动 / **~ by** 抱无动于衷的态度 / **~ down** ①坐下：Sit down, please. 请坐。②扎营(于…前)；开始围攻(before)：~ down before a fortress 扎营围攻要塞 ③坐下来进行商讨(或谈判) ④(因满足或疲劳而)停手不干 ⑤(飞机等)降落 / **~ down under** 对(侮辱等)逆来顺受 / **~ easy on** = **~ light on** / **~ heavy on** (工作、食物等)对…说来负担过重 / **~ in** ①加入纸牌戏 ②(作为被邀请者)参加，出席(on)：be invited to ~ in on a rehearsal 被邀请观看彩排演 ③[英口]代人临时照看孩子 / **~ light on** (工作等)对…说来负担不重 / **~ loose** 不注意，忽视：~ loose to one's responsibilities 玩忽自己的职责 / **~ on** (或 upon) ①为(陪审团、委员会等)的一成员 ②开会讨论案件：The jury sat on the case. 陪审团开会讨论案件。③扣押(新闻、提案等) ④[俚]责备；压制：He wants sitting on. 得好好责备他一顿才行。/ **~ on one's hands** 见 hand / **~ out** ①坐在一旁不参加(跳舞等)；对

…袖手旁观 ②比…坐得久: ~ *out* other guests 比其他客人坐得久 ③一直坐到(戏等)结束: ~ *out* a long speech (play) 一直坐到冗长的演说(演出)结束 ④ 坐在户外 / ~ *over* ①(打桥牌时)坐在…左手(即有利的位置) ②靠边坐让出地盘 / ~ *pretty* ①处于极为有利的地位 ②[美俚]成功; 过舒服的生活 / ~ *through* 一直挺到…结束; (虽无兴趣而强忍着)听完; 看完 / ~ *tight* ①挺腰坐着; 稳坐着 ②固执己见; 坚持自己的主张 ③稳守不动; 潜伏着; 耐心等待 / ~ *under* 听取(牧师等)的说教; 听(教师)的讲课 / ~ *up* ①(使)坐起; (使)端坐: The patient is now able to ~ up. 病人现在已能坐起来了。②迟睡, 熬夜: The doctor *sat up* all night with the patient. 医生彻夜守着病人。③[口]警觉起来; 突然大感兴趣: ~ *up* and take notice 突然关切(或忧虑)起来 / '~-down n. ①坐下; 坐的地方 ②静坐罢工 (=~-down strike) ③坐着吃的一顿饭 / '~-,downer n. 静坐罢工者 / '~-in n. ①(室内)静坐抗议; (室内)占座抗议: stage a ~-in 举行一次静坐抗议 ②(室内)静坐罢工 / '~-,inner n. 参加(室内)静坐示威(或罢工)的人 / '~-up, '~up n. [体]仰卧起坐 / '~-upon n. ①屁股 ②远足野营者用的方形防水油布

site [sait] **I** n. ①(建造房屋等的)地点; 地基: a construction ~ 工地 / a suitable ~ for a factory 适宜于造工厂的地点 ②场所; (事故等的)现场: the launching ~ for a rocket 火箭发射场 / a nuclear test ~ 核试验场 ③遗址: the ~ of an ancient city 古城遗址 **II** vt. 定…的地点: Where have they decided to ~ the new factory? 他们决定把新工厂造在什么地方? / a well ~d store 地点好的商店

siting ['saitiŋ] n. 建设地点的决定; (道路的)定线

sitting ['sitiŋ] **I** n. ①坐; 就座; 一次连续坐着的时间: finish reading a book at one ~ 坐着一口气读完一本书 / In this dining hall 1,500 people can be served at one ~. 这个大饭厅可同时供一千五百人就餐。②(议会等的)开会; (法院的)开庭; 会期; 庭期 ③坐着供人画像: The artist wants you to give him three ~s. 那画家要你来三次坐着供他画像。④孵卵(期); (一次的)孵卵数 ⑤(教堂、剧院中的)一个座位 **II** a. ①坐着的; 就座的; 坐着做的: a ~ shot 坐式射击 ②在立法(或司法)机构中占席位的; 在任期内的 ③孵卵中的: a ~ hen 伏窝的鸡 ④ 易击中的; (牌戏等)易打的: a ~ target 容易打中的靶子 ⑤[英]租用着房屋(或土地)的: a ~ tenant 租用着房屋(或土地)的人 ‖~ **duck** ①易被击中的目标 ②(敲诈等)容易上钩的对象 / ~ **room** 起居室

situate ['sitjueit] **I** a. [古] =~d **II** vt. ①使位于 ②使处于 ‖~d a. ①位于…的, 坐落在…的: The school is ~d in the suburbs. 这所学校位于郊外。②处于某种境地的: He is awkwardly ~d. 他处境困难。

situation [,sitju'eiʃən] n. ①(建筑物等的)位置; 地点 ②地位; (尤指仆役等的)职位, 工作: be in (out of) a ~ 有(失去)职业 ③处境, 境遇; 在一定时间内作用于生物的内外总刺激; [心]情境: be in an embarrassing ~ 处境尴尬 ④形势; 情况; 局面: the international (domestic) ~ 国际(国内)形势 / the political ~ 政局 ⑤ (戏剧、小说的)紧张场面 ‖*save the* ~ 挽回局势; 解救危局 ‖~al a. / ~ism n. [心]情境决定行为论

six [siks] **I** num. 六; 六个(人或物); 第六(卷、章、页等)(用例参看 **eight**) **II** n. ①六个一组(尤指六人的球队或划船队): be arranged by ~es 按六个一组排列 ②六汽缸发动机(或汽车) ③[复]一磅共六支的蜡烛 ④六岁 ⑤六点钟 ‖*at ~es and sevens* ①乱七八糟 ②不和 / *be ~ of one and half a dozen of the other* 见 **dozen** / *knock . . . for* ~ 彻底打败…; 完全打垮… / ~ *and eight* (*pence*) 六先令八便士(英国以前付给律师的一般费用) / ~ *to one* 六对一; 相差悬殊 / ~ *ways to* (或 *for*) *Sunday* [美俚]在许多方面; 在各方面; 完全; 彻底 ‖~-fold a. & ad. 六倍; 六重 ‖~ **bits** [美俚]七角五分 / '~-by n. [美俚]大卡车 / '~-by-'four n. 有四个驱动轮的六轮卡车 / '~-by-'~ n. 有六个驱动轮的卡车 / '~-'footer n. 六呎长的东西; 身高六呎的人 / '~-'gun n. 六响枪 / '~-o'~ n. 【药】六〇六(即胂凡纳明) / '~-pack n. 装着六个瓶装(或罐头)食品的纸匣 / ~pence ['sikspəns] n. 六便士; (英国旧时的)六便士硬币: not care a ~pence 毫不在乎 / ~penny ['sikspəni] a. ①六便士的 ②廉价的; 不值钱的 ③(钉子)两吋长的 / ~'score n. & a. 一百二十 / '~-'shooter n. 六响枪

sixteen ['siks'ti:n] **I** num. 十六; 十六个(人或物); 第十六(卷、章、页等)(用例参看 **eight**) **II** n. ①十六个一组 ②十六岁 ③十六点钟(即下午四点) ‖*in* ~s [印]以十六开 ‖~th num. ①第十六(个) ②十六分之一(的) n. ①【音】十六分音符 ②(月的)第十六日

sixth [siksθ] **I** num. ①第六(个) ②六分之一(的): five ~s 六分之五 **II** n. ①【音】六度音程; 六度和音; 第六音 ②[英]六年级 ③(月的)第六日: the ~ of March (或 March (the) 6th) 三月六日 ‖-ly ad. 第六(列举条目等时用) ‖~ **sense** 第六官能; 直觉

sixtieth ['sikstiiθ] num. ①第六十(个) ②六十分之一(的)

sixty ['siksti] **I** num. 六十; 六十个(人或物); 第六十(页等) **II** n. ①六十岁 ②[复](世纪的)六十年代 ③[复]六十到六十九岁的时期 ‖a ~-*four dollar question* [口]最后的也是最难解答的问题; 最重要的问题 / *like* ~ [美俚]飞快地; 十分有力地: run like ~ 跑得飞快 / '~-fourmo [,siksti'fo:mou] n. 六十四开(指纸张、书页); 六十四开本 / '~-four note 【音】六十四分音符

sizable ['saizəbl] a. 相当大的; 大的: a ~ man 大

个子 / a ~ battle 一场大仗 ‖~ness *n.* / **sizably** *ad.*

size[1] [saiz] **I** *n.* ①大小, 尺寸, 体积; 规模; 身材: a building of vast ~ 巨大的建筑物 / houses all of a (或 one, the same) ~ 一样大的房屋 / *Size matters less than quality.* 体积不如质量重要。/ the ~ of a delegation (an army) 一个代表团(一支军队)的规模 / bring class ~ *down to* around fifteen students 把班级的大小缩小至 (每班)十五名左右的学生 / keep sth. *down to* ~ 把某物限制在一定规模内 / He is about your ~. 他身材和你差不多。②(服装等的)尺码: 7 gloves 七号手套 / What ~ shoes do you wear? 你穿什么尺码的鞋子? / This is two ~s too big (或 large). 这个尺寸大了两号。/ We haven't anything your ~. 我们这儿没有你要的尺码。③巨大: The ~ of the book makes it awkward to hold. 这书太大,捧在手里不方便。④ 身价; 声望; 才干: The governorship is too big for the ~ of him. 他的声望够不上当州长。⑤真相, 实情; 真面目: That's about the ~ of it. 大体就是这么回事。⑥ 量珠子的工具(尺或筛) ⑦[古](饮食的)定量 **II** ❶ *vt.* ① 依大小排列(或分类); 依一定的尺寸制造: ~ a platoon 按身材高低排列一个排的士兵 ② 估计(物)的大小; [口]估量, [口]估计(情况)(up): ~ *up* a situation 估计形势 ❷ *vi.* (在大小、质量等方面)可比拟, 不相上下 (up to, up with) ‖*cut down to* ~ [口]降低…的威望(或重要性); 还…的本来面目 / *for* ~ ①为了试尺码; 为了试试是否合适 ②按不同尺码 / ~ *down* 由大逐渐到小地排列 ‖**able** *a.* =sizable / ~ **stick** (鞋匠用的)量脚尺 / '~**-up** *n.* 估量, 估计

size[2] [saiz] **I** *n.* (使纸张光润、布匹坚挺的)胶料, 浆糊 **II** *vt.* 把…上胶, 对…施浆

sizzle ['sizl] **I** ❶ *vi.* ①(油炸食物或水滴于热铁时)发咝咝声; 作哧哧声: a *sizzling* hot day 大热天 ②充满忿怒; 充满怨恨 ❷ *vt.* (咝咝地)烧灼 **II** *n.* 咝咝声; 哧哧声 ‖~**r** *n.* [美口]咝咝发烫的东西; 热得要命的一天

skate[1] [skeit] **I** *n.* ① (滑)冰鞋 (=ice ~); 四轮溜冰鞋 (=roller ~): a pair of ~s 一双冰鞋 ②滑冰; 溜冰: go for a ~ 去滑(或溜)一会儿冰 **II** *vi.* ①滑冰; 溜冰: go *skating* 去滑(或溜)冰 ②滑过; 掠过 (over): ~ *over* a delicate subject 一个微妙的问题一笔(或一语)带过 ③[美俚]躲债 **II** *n.* 滑冰者; 溜冰者 ‖**skating rink** 滑冰场; 溜冰场

skate[2] [skeit] ([复] skate(s)) *n.* 【动】鳐

skate[3] [skeit] *n.* ① 驽马; 老马 ② 可鄙的人 ‖*a cheap* ~ [美俚]吝啬鬼(尤指躲避不付自己该付的一份费用者)

skein [skein] **I** *n.* ①(纱、线、丝等的)(一)束, (一)绞 ②(野禽的)(一)群 ③(口槽)纠缠在一起的东西 **II** *vt.* 把(线等)绕成绞

skeleton ['skelitn] **I** *n.* ① 骨胳; 骸骼 ② (建筑物等的)残骸; 【建】骨架 ③骨瘦如柴的人(或动物):

be reduced to a ~ (因贫病等)变得骨瘦如柴 ④ (文艺作品等的)梗概; 轮廓: the ~ of a plan 计划纲要 ⑤ 基干, 骨干 ⑥【植】(叶子的)脉络, 筋 ⑦ 不可外扬的丑事 **II** *a.* ① 骨胳的; 骨胳般的: a ~ hand 青筋暴起的瘦手 ②轮廓的; 概略的 ③ 基干的, 骨干的: a ~ crew (或 staff) 基干人员 ‖*a ~ at the feast* 扫兴的人(或东西) / *a ~ in the cupboard* (或 *closet*) 家丑 / *a walking* ~ 骨瘦如柴的人 / *the family* ~ 家丑 ‖~ **clock** 机件外露的钟 / ~ **key** 万能钥匙

sketch [sketʃ] **I** *n.* ①略图, 草图; 粗样; 草稿 ②述写, 素描 ③概略, 梗概 ④短篇作品, 小品(如见闻录、特写、随笔) ⑤ (滑稽的)短剧; 独幕剧; 短曲 (常指用钢琴演奏的) ⑥ 言行古怪可笑的人 **II** *vt.* & *vi.* ①(给…)绘略图; (给…)写生, 速写 ②草拟; 概略地叙述 (out) ‖~**er** *n.* 画略图者; 作素描者; 舞台布景设计者 ‖~**book** *n.* ①写生簿, 素描簿 ②短文集, 随笔集 ‖~ **map** 略图, 草图, 示意图

sketchy ['sketʃi] *a.* ①粗略的; 大概的; 略图似的 ②肤浅的; 不完全的: He has a rather ~ knowledge of geography. 他的地理知识很肤浅。‖**sketchily** *ad.* / **sketchiness** *n.*

skewer [skjuə] **I** *n.* ①(烤肉用的)串肉扦, 烤肉叉 ②扦状物, 叉状物 ③[谑]剑; 刀 **II** *vt.* (用串肉扦等)串

ski [ski:] **I** ([复] ski(s) 或 skiis) *n.* 滑橇, 滑雪屐: a pair of ~(s) 一双滑雪屐 **II** *vi.* 滑雪: go ~*ing* 去滑雪 ‖~ **boot** 滑雪靴 / ~**joring** ['ski:'jɔ:riŋ] *n.* 由马 (或车辆) 拖曳滑雪者的冬季运动 / ~ **jump** ①滑雪跳跃 ②滑雪跳跃比赛用的斜坡(或跑道) / ~ **lift** 使滑雪者(或游览者)登上长斜坡(或山腰)用的机动运送设备(或吊索设备) / ~**meister** ['ski:ˌmaistə] *n.* 滑雪能手; 职业滑雪运动员; 滑雪教练员 / ~**mobile** ['ski:moubi:l] *n.* 履带式雪上汽车 / '~**-plane** *n.* [空]雪上飞机 (以滑雪屐代替起降轮的飞机, 适于雪地降落) / ~ **pole**, ~ **stick** 滑雪杖 / ~ **run** 滑雪坡, 滑雪道 / ~ **suit** 滑雪服 / ~ **tow** =~ lift / ~ **troops** 滑雪部队

skid [skid] **I** *n.* ①刹车, 制动器 ②(使重物易于滑动的)滑动垫木; 滑行器 ③(支承重物的)垫木; 低平台(有时带有轮子) ④[复](船侧的)护舷木 ⑤【空】起落橇, 滑橇 ⑥ (车辆在结冰的道路上或高速行驶急转弯时所引起的) 车轮的打滑, 溜滑 ⑦ [复][喻]下坡路: He has been on the ~s for some time. 一段时期以来他一直在走下坡路。**II** (skidded; skidding) ❶ *vt.* ①(用刹车)刹住, 使减速 ②(用滑动垫木)滚滑, 溜滑; 堆…于垫木(或平台)上 ③使(车轮等)打滑 ❷ *vi.* ①(汽车等)打滑; 滑向一侧; (飞机在转弯时)外滑 ②(营业额等)急剧下降 ‖*hit the* ~s [美俚]走下坡路, 倒霉, 落魄 / *put the* ~s *under* (或 on) sb. [美俚]使某人走下坡路; 使某人无所施其技 / ~ **fin** (飞机的)翼上垂直面 / ~**-lid** *n.* [俚](骑摩托车者的)头盔 / '~**proof** *a.* (道路、车轮等)防滑的, 抗滑的 / ~ **road** ①伐木场中供木材滑下

的滑道 ②城镇中伐木工人出入的地区 ③ =~
row / ~ row 城镇中的破旧下等地区(内多低级
酒吧间、廉价客店及职业介绍所等)

skill [skil] *n.* ① 技能;技巧;技艺: the ~ of a surgeon 外科医生的技术 ② 熟练: play the
piano with ~ 钢琴弹得熟练; 巧妙: play the
piano with ~ 钢琴弹得熟练; 巧妙: a task that
calls for ~ 要求有熟练技术的工作 ③ [只用单]
[总称]熟练工人: the outgoing flow of ~ 技术
熟练工人的外流 ‖~ed *a.* ①熟练的;有技能的:
a ~ed worker 熟练工人 / be ~ed in (或 at)
carpentry 擅长木工 ② 需要技能的: ~ed work
需要技能的工作,技术性工作

skil(l)ful ['skilful] *a.* ① 灵巧的;熟练的: a ~ de-
bater 善辩论的人 / be ~ at painting 善于绘画 /
be ~ in negotiation 善于谈判 ② 制作精巧的:
~ handicrafts 精巧的手工艺品 ‖~ly *ad.* /
~ness *n.*

skim [skim] I (skimmed; skimming) ❶ *vt.* ① 撇
去(液体)的漂浮物;从液体表面撇去(奶油、浮渣
等);从…中提取精华;从…中取得最易获得的东
西: ~ the milk of its cream 撇去牛奶上的奶油 /
~ the cream from the milk 从牛奶上撇取奶油 /
~ off the grease 撇去油脂 ② 掠过,擦过;使掠
过,使擦过: He *skimmed* a flat stone across the
creek. 他扔出条扁石使之漂掠过小溪。③ 使
盖上一层薄膜(或薄层): a pond *skimmed* with
ice 结上了一层薄冰的池塘 ④ 略读,快读,浮光掠
影地看 ❷ *vi.* ① 掠过,擦过; 滑过 (over, along,
through): The swallows were *skimming* over
the water. 燕子掠过水面。②浏览,略读 (over,
through): ~ over a newspaper 浏览报纸 / This
book is worth *skimming through*. 这本书值得这
读一下。③ 结上薄的覆盖层; 涂上最后一道灰泥
(或漆等): The puddles *skimmed* over during
the cold night. 夜间寒冷,水潭结上了薄冰。II *n.*
① 脱脂乳;表面一层被撇去了的东西 ② 掠过,擦
过 ③ 表面的薄覆盖层 III *a.* 表面一层被撇去
了的 ②脱脂乳制成的 ‖~ milk, skimmed milk
脱脂乳

skimp [skimp] [口] I ❶ *vt.* ①少给,克扣;对…吝
啬 ②马马虎虎地做 ❷ *vi.* 吝啬;省俭 II *a.* 少
的, 不足的 ‖~ingly *ad.* 吝啬地,小气地

skin [skin] I *n.* ① 皮,皮肤: true (或 inner) ~
【解】真皮 / wear one's sweater next to the ~
贴身穿着球衣 ②兽皮;毛皮;(尤指小牛及小动物
的)皮革,生皮: rabbit ~s 兔皮 ③ (植物、果实等
的)外皮;壳: a banana ~ 香蕉皮 ④ (盛液体用
的)皮囊: wine ~s 皮酒囊 ⑤ 奶皮(指煮沸的
牛奶上结成的薄层) ⑥ 外壳(层);船壳(板);(飞
机的)蒙皮;珍珠的外层 ⑦ [口]生命 ⑧ [美俚]
吝啬鬼 ⑨ [美俚]骗子 ⑩ [美俚]一元;一元
纸币 ⑪[美俚]老而无用的马(尤指赛马);老而无
用的耕畜 ⑫[美俚](军队或学校中的)过错;官
方申斥令 ⑬[复][美俚]爵士乐队中的一套鼓 II
(skinned; skinning) ❶ *vt.* ① 剥去…的皮;擦破
(身体某一部位)的皮; [口]使脱去紧身衣: ~ a

rabbit 剥兔子皮 ② 使蒙上皮; 使(伤口)愈合
③[俚]诈骗,骗取…的钱财: ~ sb. of all his
money 骗掉某人的全部钱财 ④[美俚](比赛中)
打败(对方) ⑤申斥,非难;给…记过处分 ⑥驱赶
(牲口等) ❷ *vi.* ①(伤口)愈合 (over); 长出新皮
② 蜕皮 ③攀,爬 (up, down) ④ 勉强穿过 (by,
through): The truck barely *skinned through* the
gate. 卡车勉强地穿过大门。⑤[俚]逃走 ⑥[美
俚](考试、背诵等时)作弊 ‖*be in sb.'s* ~ 处于
某人的地位,换做某人: I wouldn't *be in your*
~. 我才不愿意处于你的地位呢。/ *be no* ~
off sb.'s back [俚]与某人丝毫不相干 / *be only*
~ *and bone(s)* 瘦得皮包骨 / *change one's* ~
改变本性(意指不可能) / *escape* (或 *get off*)
by (或 *with*) *the* ~ *of one's teeth* [口]幸
免于难 / *get under sb.'s* ~ [口] ① 激怒某人
② (在感情等方面)攫住某人 / *give sb. some*
[美俚]与某人握手 / *have a thin* (thick) ~ 脸
皮厚(薄); 敏(不敏)感 / *in a bad* ~ 发着脾气 /
in (或 *with*) *a whole* ~ [口]身未受伤; 安然无
恙 / *in one's* ~ 裸体 / *jump out of one's* ~
惊喜若狂; 大吃一惊 / *keep one's eyes skinned*
见 **eye** / *save one's* ~ [口]免受损伤; 安然
逃脱 / ~ *alive* ① 活活地剥去(人或动物)的皮
② [口]严厉申斥,严厉责骂 ③ [口]决定性地击
败 / *the lion's* ~ 假勇气 / *under the* ~ 在本
质上;在内心 / *wet to the* ~ 全身湿透 ‖~*ful n.*
一皮囊;一肚子(尤指酒) / ~*less a.* ① 无皮的
②易受感动的;敏感的 ‖'~*bound a.* ① 皮绷得
紧紧的 ② 【医】患硬皮症的 / '~-'deep *a.* 表面
的;肤浅的 / ~ *dive* (只带面罩而不穿潜水衣地
在深水)潜游 / '~-,diving *n.* 潜游运动 / ~
effect 【无】集肤效应 / ~ *flick* 裸体黄色影片 /
'~*flint n.* 吝啬的人,小气鬼 / ~ *game* 骗局 /
~ *grafting* 【医】表皮移植 / '~*head n.* [美俚]
① 剃光头的人 ② 秃头(指人) ③ 海军陆战队新
兵 / '~,popping *n.* 皮下注射麻醉毒品 / ~
test 【医】皮试试验 / '~-'tight *a.* 紧身的,包身
的 *n.* 紧身衣服

skinny ['skini] *a.* ①皮的;似皮的;膜状的 ②皮包
骨的,极瘦的 ③(体积)小的;(数量)少的;(质量)
低劣的;缺乏意义的 ④ [美俚]吝啬的 ‖**skinnily**
ad. / **skinniness** *n.* ‖'~-**dip** *vi.* & *n.* [美口]
光着身子游泳

skip[1] [skip] I (skipped; skipping) ❶ *vi.* ① 跳,蹦:
~ over obstacles 跳越障碍物 ② 跳绳: Children
are fond of *skipping*. 孩子们喜欢跳绳。③急速
改变: He always ~s from one subject to another. 他总是一会儿说到这件事,一会儿又扯到
另一件事。④(看书、写字时)略过;遗漏 (over)
⑤作短期旅行; [口]匆匆离开;悄悄离开 ⑥【机】
不发火 ⑦(学校里)跳级 ❷ *vt.* ①跳过;使跳:
a stone across a pond 使石子飞掷过池塘的水面
②跳读;遗漏;略过 ③不参加(会议等) ~ schooI
逃学 ④[口]匆匆离开;悄悄离开(某地) ⑤(学校
里)使跳(级) II *n.* ①轻跳;边走边跳 ②看漏;跳

过；略过；漏看的东西；略过的东西 ③【自】跳跃
(进位)；(计算机)"空白"指令 ‖~ **it** ①[口]逃走
②[美][用于祈使句]不要紧! 没关系! / ~ **bail**
见 **bail**¹ / ~ **bomb** 【军】对…进行跳弹轰炸(一
种超低空轰炸) / ~ **distance** 【无】跳跃距离 /
~ **floor** 【建】(指公寓大楼)每隔一层有公共走
廊的(在这种大楼中，上下两层房间构成一户，每
户有专用楼梯接通) / '~**jack** *n*. ①【动】在水
面跳跃(或嬉戏)前进的鱼(如鲣鱼) ②【动】叩头
虫 ③(用鸟类叉骨制成的)跳跃玩具 / ~ **rope**
=skipping-rope / ~ **tracer** 找寻失踪者(尤指
债务人)的调查员

skip² [skip] **I** *n*. ① (足球、板球等球队的)领队
② =skipper² **II** (skipped; skipping) *vt*. 当…的
领队

skip³ [skip] *n*. 【矿】箕斗；斜井用四轮车

skipper¹ ['skipə] *n*. ① 跳跃者；跳绳者；略读者
②【动】叩头虫；水蝇；酪蛆 ③【动】弄蝶科蝴蝶
④[动]长颌竹刀鱼

skipper² ['skipə] *n*. ① (小商船、渔船或游艇的)船
长 ②(飞机上的)机长；正驾驶员

skirl [skə:l] [苏格兰] **I ❶** *vi*. (风笛)发尖锐声
❷ *vt*. 用风笛演奏 **II** *n*. 风笛吹出的尖锐声

skirmish ['skə:miʃ] **I** *n*. ①【军】小规模战斗 ②小
争论，小冲突 **II** *vi*. ① 进行小规模战斗；进行小
争论 ②侦察；搜索 ‖~**er** *n*. 散兵

skirt [skə:t] **I** *n*. ①女裙：a divided ~ 裙裤 ②(衣
服的)裾，下摆 ③[常用复]边缘；(地区的)边界
④[复]郊区，郊外：on the ~s of a city 在市
郊 ⑤马鞍两边挂下的皮垂 ⑥[俚]女人；姑娘
II ❶ *vt*. ① 位于…的边缘；绕过…的边缘：Fish-
ing villages ~ed the shore. 沿岸有渔村。/ The
workers ~ed the edge of the cliff on a geologic
survey. 工人们沿着悬壁作一次地质勘查。②给
…装边；给…装防护罩 ③避开(危险等)；回避(问
题等) **❷** *vi*. 位于边缘；沿边走 (along, around)：
The path ~s along the edge of the lake. 路沿
着湖边蜿蜒。/ ~ around a reef 绕过暗礁
‖*clear sb.'s ~s* 为某人洗去耻辱；表明某人清
白无辜 / *like a bit of* ~ [口]喜欢与妇女做伴 /
~ *the coast* 见 **coast** ‖~**ing** *n*. ①边缘 ②裙
料 ③[英]【建】踢脚板，壁脚板(=~ing board)

skit¹ [skit] *n*. ① 讽刺话 ② 讽刺短文；幽默故事
③滑稽短剧

skit² [skit] *n*. [口]若干；一群；[复]许多：~s of
things 许多东西

skittish ['skitiʃ] *a*. ①(马等)易惊的 ②(尤指女人)
轻佻的 ③三心二意的；不可靠的 ④羞怯的；胆小
的 ‖~**ly** *ad*. / ~**ness** *n*.

skittle ['skitl] **I** *n*. ①[~s][用作单]九柱戏，撞柱
戏(沿球道以球击倒数个瓶状木柱的游戏) ②九
柱戏的木柱 **II ❶** *vt*. (板球中)接二连三地使(击
球者)出局 (out) **❷** *vi*. 做九柱戏游戏 ‖*knock
over like* ~s 一下子打倒；驳倒 / *not all beer
and* ~s (人生)并不全是吃喝玩乐 / *Skittles!*
[俚]胡说!

skulk [skʌlk] **I** *vi*. ① (尤指出于懦怯或不良企图
而)躲藏 ②偷偷摸摸地走 ③[主英]装病；逃避职
责 **II** *n*. ① =~er ② 一群狐狸 ‖~**er** *n*. ①躲
藏者 ②[主英]装病者；逃避职责者 / ~**ingly** *ad*.
偷偷摸摸地；躲躲闪闪地；懦怯地

skull [skʌl] *n*. ①颅骨，脑壳，头盖骨 ②头脑：have
a thick ~ 笨头笨脑 ③【冶】渣壳 ④[美俚]杰出
的学生(或工人、演奏者等) ‖~ **and cross-
bones** 骷髅画；骷髅旗(为死亡之象征，昔时海盗
用作旗帜) ‖~**ed** *a*. [常用以构成复合词]有…
脑壳的：thick-~ed 笨头笨脑的 ‖'~**cap** *n*. ①室
内便帽 ②【植】黄芩属植物；美黄芩 / ~ **practice**
[美俚](足球队等的)战术研究课 / ~ **session**
① 头头的决策会议 ② 非正式的学术性讨论 =~
practice

skul(l)duggery [skʌl'dʌgəri] *n*. [美俚]欺骗，诈骗，
诡计

skunk [skʌŋk] **I** *n*. ①【动】臭鼬；臭鼬毛皮 ②[口]
卑鄙的人；可恶的人 **II** *vt*. [美俚]①(牌戏等中)
战胜，击败(对方) ②欺骗；赖…的债 ‖~ **cabbage**
【植】臭菘属植物；臭菘

sky [skai] **I** *n*. ①天，天空：a blue ~ 蔚蓝的天空 /
the stars in the ~ 天上群星 / under the open
~ 在户外，露天 ②[the ~][宗]天堂，天国；西天
③[常用复]天气；气候；风土：The papers forecast
clear *skies* tomorrow. 据报纸的天气预报，明日
天气晴朗。/ under a foreign ~ 在异乡；在
异国 **II** (skied 或 skyed) **❶** *vt*. ① 将(板球)击
向空中 ② 将(画)挂在墙上高处；将(某人)的画
挂在墙上高处 **❷** *vi*. (物价等)高涨，猛涨 ‖*be
raised to the skies* 升天，死去 / *If the ~ falls
we shall catch larks.* [谚]天塌下来正好抓云
雀。(指何必杞人忧天) / *out of a clear* ~ 晴天
霹雳似地；出乎意外地；突然 / *The* ~ *is the
limit.* 没有限制。/ *to the* ~ (或 *skies*) 无保
留地；过分地：praise (或 laud, extol) sb. *to
the skies* 极力称赞某人；大肆吹捧某人 ‖~**less**
a. 看不见天的；为云所遮蔽的；多云的 /
~**ward** *ad*. & *a*. ①向着天空(的) ②向上(的)
‖~**blue** 天蓝色，淡蓝色，蔚蓝色 / '~-**blue** *a*.
天蓝色的，淡蓝色的，蔚蓝色的 / '~**borne** *a*. 空
降的，空运的，机载的：~*borne* troops 空降部
队 / '~-**cap** *n*. 机场行李搬运员 / '~-**clad** *a*.
[谑]裸体的 / '~-,**diving** *n*. 尽量延缓张伞的跳
伞运动 / '~-**high** *ad*. ① 天一般高；极高：be
flung ~-*high* 被抛到半空中 / lift sb.'s spirit
~-*high* 使某人情绪高昂 / extol sth. ~-*high*
满口称赞某事物 ②粉碎：blast a fallacy ~-*high*
驳倒谬论 *a*. 极高的；昂贵的 / '~-**jack** *vt*. 空中
劫持(飞机) / '~-**jacker** *n*. 空中劫持飞机的人 /
'~**lab** *n*. 天空实验室 / ~**lark** *n*. 云雀 *vi*. 嬉
戏，开玩笑；爬船索娱乐 / '~**larker** *n*. 嬉戏者 /
'~**light** *n*. ①天上的光 ②(屋顶、舱舱的)天窗 /
'~**line** *n*. ①地平线 ②(建筑物、山等)以天空为
背景映出的轮廓：the ~*line* of a city 城市
高大建筑物的空中轮廓 / ~**man** ['skaimən] *n*.

[美俚]伞兵; 飞机驾驶员 / '~ˌmaster *n.* 巨型客机 / ~ pilot ① [俚]牧师; 随军牧师 ②飞机驾驶员 / '~ˌraider *n.* 【军】"空中袭击者"战斗机 / '~rocket *n.* 焰火; 高空探测火箭 *vi.* [口]突升; (物价)猛涨 *vt.* ①使上升; 使猛涨 ②弹射; 使一举而成: ~rocket sb. to affluence 使某人成暴发户 / '~sail *n.* 【船】第三层帆 / '~scape *n.* 天空景色画 / '~scrape *vi.* 建造摩天楼 / '~ˌscraper *n.* ① 摩天楼; 高烟囱 ②=~sail / ~ screen "空网" (一种用来观测导弹弹道横偏差的光学仪器) / ~ sign (高楼大厦顶上的)广告牌 / '~sweeper *n.* (装有雷达瞄准设备的)一种口径 75 毫米的高射炮 / '~ˌtrooper *n.* 伞兵 / ~ truck (大型)运输机 / ~ wave 【无】天波 / '~way *n.* ①【空】航路 ②高架公路 / '~ˌwriting *n.* 飞机放烟以形成空中文字(或空中广告); 空中文字; 空中广告

slab[1] [slæb] **I** *n.* ① 平板; 厚板; 厚片: a ~ of stone 一块石板 / a ~ of bread 厚厚的一片面包的包 ② 混凝土路面 ③背板(锯木材成板时最外面的有皮的板块) **II** (slabbed; slabbing) *vt.* ① 把…分成厚片, 使成厚片 ②去掉(木材)的背板 ③用石板铺(路等) ④ 厚厚地涂: ~ butter on the bread 给面包涂上一层厚厚的黄油 ‖'~-'sided *a.* [口]①侧面平的 ②瘦的; 高的; 细长的 / '~stone *n.* 板石; 铺路石

slab[2] [slæb] *a.* [英方]粘的

slack [slæk] **I** *a.* ①懒散的; 懈怠的; 疏忽的; 马虎的: be ~ in one's work 干活马马虎虎 ②行动迟缓的; 有气无力的, 没精打采的: a ~ pace 慢吞吞的步子 ③松弛的, 不紧的: a ~ rope 松弛的绳 ④呆滞的; 萧条的 (商业上的)淡季 ⑤温的, 微热的; 未烧干的, 未干透的: a ~ oven 微热的炉灶 / ~ bread 未烘干的面包 ⑥ 不坚定的; 软弱的: ~ control 软弱无力的控制 ⑦不完善的 ⑧漏水的, 透水的 ⑨(石灰)熟化的 ⑩【语】松弛的: a ~ vowel 松弛元音 **II** *ad.* ① 马虎地; 松懈地 ②缓慢地; 没精打采地 ③清淡地, 呆滞地 ④松弛地, 宽松地 ⑤[用以构成复合词]不透地: ~-baked bread 未烘透的面包 **III** *n.* ① 静止不动; 停止流动 ②(绳、带、帆等的)松垂部分: take up the ~ of a rope 拿起绳子松着的一头 ③[复]宽松的裤子, 便裤 ④淡季; 萧条期 ⑤煤屑 ⑥[口]闲散; 休息时间: have a good ~ 舒舒服服地休息一下 ⑦[英方]厚板 ⑧[美口]峡谷; 凹地; 沼泽 **IV** ❶ *vt.* ① 马虎从事, 松垮垮地做(工作等) ②放松(绳索等) ③使缓慢; 使缓和: ~ one's pace 放慢步子 / ~ up one's effort 松劲 ④ 使(石灰)熟化 ❷ *vi.* ① 松懈, 怠惰; 偷懒: Don't ~ off in your studies. 不要放松学习。②减低速度; 减弱, 减退 (up): Slack up before you reach the crossroads. 到达十字路口前减速。/ The wind ~ed. 风力减弱。③(绳索等)松弛 ④[口]休息; 懒散 ⑤(石灰)熟化 ‖pull up one's ~s [口]振作起来 / ~ in stays (帆船)掉头时放慢速度的 ‖~er *n.* 懒惰的人; 敷衍塞责的人; 逃避责任的

人; 战时逃避兵役的人 / ~ly *ad.* / ~ness *n.* ‖~ suit 一套宽松的衣服, 便装 / ~ water, ~ tide 平潮; 平潮期

slacken ['slækən] ❶ *vt.* ① 放松; 松懈: ~ one's muscles 放松肌肉 / ~ one's efforts 松劲 / We must not ~ our vigilance against the enemy. 我们决不可放松对敌人的警惕性。②使缓慢; 放慢: The car has ~ed its speed. 车速放慢了。❷ *vi.* ① (绳索等)变松弛; 松劲 ② (商业)呆滞 ③ (风等)减弱; 变缓慢: The fire ~ed. 火势减弱了。/ The ship's speed ~ed. 船速慢了下来。

slag [slæg] **I** *n.* ①矿渣, 熔渣, 炉渣: a ~ brick 矿渣砖 ② 火山渣 **II** (slagged; slagging) *vt. & vi.* (使)成渣; (使)成渣状 ‖'~-heap *n.* (工厂倒出的)熔渣堆 / ~ wool 渣棉, 渣绒(将熔融的炉渣用蒸汽或压缩空气吹散而成, 用作防火、隔音、隔热材料)

slain [slein] slay 的过去分词

slake [sleik] ❶ *vt.* ① 消除; 平息; 使缓和; 满足: ~ one's thirst 解渴 / ~ one's anger 息怒 ②熄灭; 减弱(火焰) ③ 使(石灰)熟化: ~d lime 熟石灰, 消石灰 ❷ *vi.* ① [古]消除; 平息; 缓和 ② (石灰)熟化 ‖~less *a.* 无法消除的; 不能平息的

slam[1] [slæm] **I** (slammed; slamming) ❶ *vt.* ① 使劲关, 砰地关上(门等); 砰地放下: Don't ~ the door. 不要把门关得太响。② 猛投; 猛击: ~ rockets into the enemy's positions 向敌军阵地猛烈发射火箭 ③[美口]猛烈抨击; 辱骂 ❷ *vi.* ①发出砰声; 砰地关上: The door slammed (to). 门砰的一声关上了。② 猛攻; 使劲干: ~ into one's work 使劲干起活来 ③[美口]猛烈抨击; 辱骂 **II** *n.* ①砰(如关门声); 砰地一关 ② 猛击; 猛击; 撞击 ③[美口]猛烈的抨击 / ~ off [美俚] ① 离开 ②死去 / ~ the door 见 door / ~ the door in sb.'s face 见 door ‖'~-'bang *a. & ad.* ①砰然一声的(地); 猛烈的(地) ② 鲁莽的(地), 轻率的(地)

slam[2] [slæm] **I** *n.* (桥牌等等)满贯: a grand ~ 大满贯(赢十三墩牌) / a little (或 small) ~ 小满贯(赢十二墩牌) **II** (slammed; slamming) *vt.* ①打成满贯战胜(对方) ②打垮

slander ['slɑːndə] **I** *n.* 诽谤, 诋毁, 造谣中伤; 【律】(口头的)诽谤罪: a ~ on sb. 对某人的诽谤 **II** *vt.* 诽谤, 诋毁, 造谣中伤 ‖~er ['slɑːndərə] *n.* 诽谤者, 造谣中伤者

slanderous ['slɑːndərəs] *a.* 诽谤的, 诋毁的, 造谣中伤的 ‖~ly *ad.* / ~ness *n.*

slang [slæŋ] **I** *n.* ①俚语: army ~ 军队俚语 / schoolboy ~ 学生俚语 ②行话; (盗贼等用的)切口, 黑话 **II** ❶ *vt.* ① [主英]用俚语骂 ②[英俚]欺骗; 诈取 ❷ *vi.* 用粗话(或下流话)骂

slangy ['slæŋi] *a.* ①俚语的; 俚语性的 ②好用俚语的 ‖slangily *ad.* / slanginess *n.*

slant [slɑːnt] **I** ❶ *vt.* ①使倾斜, 使斜向; 使歪 ② [美]根据某种观点(或偏见)报道(新闻等); 使

(报道等)带上色彩: ~*ed* reports 带有偏见的报道 ❷ ***vi.*** ①倾斜; 歪向; [喻]倾向(*towards*) ②[美俚]走开 **II *n.*** ①倾斜; 斜面, 斜线, 斜向; 斜线号(即/): on the (或 a) ~ 倾斜着 ②[方]挖苦, 讥刺 ③[美口](考虑某事时的)倾向性; 观点; 态度; 意见; (叙述等中的)偏见, 歪曲: consider sth. from a new ~ 从新的角度考虑某事物 / You have a wrong ~ on the problem. 你对这个问题的看法不正确。④[口]一瞥; 斜视 ⑤[俚]机会 **III *a.*** 斜的, 倾斜的 ‖***a ~ of wind***【海】一阵顺风 ‖'**~-eye** ***n.*** 斜视的人; [美俚][贬](有蒙古人种血统的)东方人

slap [slæp] **I** (slapped; slapping) ❶ ***vt.*** ①(用扁平的东西等)掴; 拍; 掌击; 猛地关(门等): ~ sb.'s face (或 ~ sb. in the face) 打某人的耳光 / ~ sb. on the shoulder 拍某人肩膀 / ~ the table 拍桌子 / ~ the door 砰的一声把门关上 ②啪的一声放下, 猛掷, 漫不经心地扔: ~ the book down on the table 啪的一声把书丢在桌子上 ③任意涂; [喻]任意征(税), 轻率地课(罚金等); 强加 ④指责, 口头攻击; 侮辱 ❷ ***vi.*** ①用手猛拍(或打) ②拍, 打: Rain *slapped* at the window. 雨拍打窗户。**II *n.*** ①掴, 拍; 掌击 ②侮辱; 拒绝; (对自尊心等的)伤害 ③【机】松动(声): piston ~ 活塞松动 **III *ad.*** [口] ①突然地; 猛地里: come ~ up against sb. 突然遇到某人 ②直接地; 一直地: This path leads ~ to the playground. 这条小路直接通到运动场。‖***a ~ in the face*** (或 ***eye***) 一个耳光; [喻]突如其来的责备(或侮辱、拒绝) / ***~ around*** 打击; 粗暴地对待 / ***~ down*** ①粗暴地禁止(或阻止) ②镇压; 压制 / ***~ sb. on the back*** 见 **back** / ***~ together*** 草率地建造; 拼凑 ‖'**~-'bang** ***a.*** & ***ad.*** =~dash (*a.* & *ad.*) / '**~dash** ***a.*** & ***ad.*** [口]猛烈的(地); 卤莽的(地); 粗心的(地); 草率的(地) ***n.*** ①草率; 卤莽 ②粗制滥造的东西 ③打底子用的粗灰泥 ***vt.*** ①用粗灰泥涂(墙壁) ②草拟(计划等) / '**~ˌhappy** ***a.*** [俚] ①头昏眼花的; 因受击而头晕目眩的 ②轻率的; 莽撞的 ③愚笨的, 傻的 ④振奋的; (因成功等而)得意忘形的, 忘乎所以的 / '**~jack** ***n.*** [美] ①一种薄饼 ②一种纸牌戏 / '**~man** ***n.*** [美俚]便衣警官 / '**~stick** ***n.*** ①(旧时滑稽演员打人时能发出响声的)敲板 ②一种粗鲁的滑稽剧; 动作激烈所引起的笑闹 ***a.*** 粗鲁滑稽剧的 / '**~-up** ***a.*** [英口] ①上等的; 第一流的; 极好的 ②时髦的 ③彻底的

slash[1] [slæʃ] **I** ❶ ***vt.*** ①(用刀、剑等)猛砍, 乱砍, 劈刺; 砍伤, 割伤 ②挥(剑、鞭等); 鞭打 ③(作为装饰)开长缝于, 开叉于(衣服): ~*ed* sleeves 开叉的衣袖 ④(大幅度)削减, 减低(工资等), 减少(犯罪率等) ⑤【军】砍(树)成鹿砦 ⑥严厉地批评 ❷ ***vi.*** ①猛砍, 乱砍; 挥击(*at*) ②严厉地批评(*at*) **II *n.*** ①猛砍, 乱砍; 劈刺, 挥击; 砍痕, 深的切痕 ②(衣服上作装饰的)长缝, 衣叉 ③(大幅度的)削减, 减低, 减少 ④(树木砍伐后形成的)林中空地; (树木砍伐后留下的)枝桠, 废材 ‖**~er** ***n.*** ①猛砍者, 乱砍者; 乱砍树木者; 好殴斗者; 恃强欺弱的人 ②刀, 剑; 剃刀片; (泥工用)泥刀 ③圆材切段机; 浆纱机 ④[俚]过分用功的学生 ‖'**~-and-'burn** ***a.*** 刀耕火种的(指砍伐树木, 加以焚烧, 作为肥料, 就地下种的耕作法)

slash[2] [slæʃ] ***n.*** [美]长有灌木的低洼沼泽地

slat[1] [slæt] **I *n.*** ①(木头、金属等的)条板; (固定百页窗等的)板条, 狭板; (椅背的)梯级横木 ②[复][俚]屁股; 肋骨 **II** (slatted; slatting) ***vt.*** 用条板制造; 给…装条板 ‖***hit the ~s*** [美俚](躺下)睡觉

slat[2] [slæt] **I** (slatted; slatting) ❶ ***vi.*** (帆或索具等同桅杆等碰撞时)发劈啪声; (帆等在风中)猛烈拍动 ❷ ***vt.*** [英方] ①猛投, 猛掷 ②打, 击; 以拳连击 **II *n.*** [方]拍打; 猛烈的一击

slate[1] [sleit] **I *n.*** ①板岩; 石板瓦; (建筑用的)石板 ②(书写用的)石板 ③暗蓝灰色, 石板色 ④(操行等的)记录: have a clean ~ 历史清白 ⑤[美]候选人(提名)名单; 内定用人名单 **II *a.*** ①石板色的, 蓝灰色的 ②【地】含板岩的 **III *vt.*** ①用石板瓦盖(屋顶等); 给…铺石板 ②[美]提名…为候选人; 内定…任某职 ‖***clean the ~*** 勾销往事; 了结义务; 免除(或卸掉)义务 / ***have a ~ missing*** (或 ***loose***) 精神有点不正常 / ***start with a clean ~*** 改过自新; 重新开始; 言归于好 ‖**~r** ***n.*** ①石板瓦工; 铺石板者 ②【动】鼠妇(一种陆栖的等足类甲壳虫); 水栖的等足类动物 ‖**~ club** [英](成员每周缴少量钱的)互助会 / '**~-ˌcolo(u)red** ***a.*** 石板色的, 蓝灰色的 / **~ pencil** 石笔

slate[2] [sleit] ***vt.*** [口] ①(尤指评论中对作品或作者)严厉地批评 ②责骂 ③痛打; 鞭打; 拳打

slattern ['slætə(ː)n] **I *n.*** ①懒妇, 邋遢女人 ②妓女 **II *a.*** 不整洁的; 邋遢的 **III *vt.*** 浪费掉, 消磨掉(*away*): ~ *away* one's time in nothings 白白地浪费时间

slatternly ['slætə(ː)nli] ***a.*** & ***ad.*** 不整洁的(地); 邋遢的(地); 懒散的(地) ‖**slatternliness** ***n.***

slaty ['sleiti] ***a.*** ①板岩(质)的; 石板(状)的 ②石板色的, 蓝灰色的

slaughter ['slɔːtə] **I *n.*** ①屠宰 ②屠杀, 残杀 **II *vt.*** ①屠宰(牛羊等) ②屠杀, 杀戮 ③亏本出售(证券) ‖***~ of the innocents*** 见 **innocent** ‖**~er** ['slɔːtərə] ***n.*** ①屠夫 ②屠杀者, 刽子手 ‖'**~house** ***n.*** 屠宰场: ~*house* wool 屠宰场羊毛(即皮板毛)

slave [sleiv] **I *n.*** ①奴隶 ②奴隶般工作的人, 苦工 ③摆脱不了某种习惯(或影响)的人: a ~ to drink 酒鬼 / ~*s* of (或 to) fashion 拚命赶时髦的人们 ④[古]卑鄙的人 ⑤【动】奴隶蚁(=~ ant) ⑥【机】从动装置 **II** ❶ ***vi.*** ①作苦工; 奴隶般工作; 做牛马: ~ (away) at sth. 拚命地(或十分辛苦地)干某事 ②贩卖奴隶 ❷ ***vt.*** [古]奴役 ‖'**~-born** ***a.*** 出身奴隶家庭的 / **~ driver** 监管奴隶的人; 严厉的监工; 使人工作过度的老板(或当权者) / '**~ˌholder** ***n.*** 奴隶主 / '**~ˌholding** ***a.*** 占有奴隶的 ***n.*** 占有奴隶 / **~ labo(u)r** ①

奴隶劳动 ②强迫劳动 / **~ market** ①奴隶市场 ②[谑]职业介绍所; 职业介绍所所在的街道 (或地区) / **~ ship** 贩奴船 / **~ state** ①(美国南北战争前)实行奴隶制度的州 ②极权国家 / **~ station** (双曲线导航系统中受主台控制的)辅助电台 / **~ trade, ~ traffic** 贩卖奴隶(尤指过去的黑奴)

slaver[1] ['sleivə] *n.* ①奴隶贩子; 贩运奴隶的船 ②诱骗女子为娼者(=white ~)

slaver[2] ['slævə] **I** ❶ *vi.* ①垂涎, 淌口水 ②[喻]谄媚, 奉承 ❷ *vt.* 口水淌湿…; 流涎弄脏(衣服等) **II** *n.* ①唾液, 涎沫, 口水 ②[喻]谄媚, 奉承

slavery ['sleivəri] *n.* ①奴隶身分: be sold into ~ 被卖为奴隶 ②奴隶制度; 占有奴隶 ③苦役, 奴隶般的劳动 ④(对某种习惯或影响的)屈服

slavish ['sleiviʃ] *a.* ①奴隶(般)的; 奴性的, 卑屈的: ~ thinking 奴才思想 ②缺乏独创性的, 盲从的: a ~ imitation 依样画葫芦的模仿 ③[古]压迫的; 专横的 ‖**~ly** *ad.* / **~ness** *n.*

slay [slei] (slew [slu:], slain [slein]) ❶ *vt.* ①杀死, 杀害 ②[美俚]使(异性)爱慕自己; 给…以强烈的好印象; 使赞同; 使禁不住大笑 ❷ *vi.* 杀死; 谋杀; 引起死亡 ‖**~er** *n.* 杀人者, 凶手; 屠宰者

sled [sled] **I** *n.* ①(滑雪用的)小橇; (运载用的)雪橇 ②摘棉机(= cotton ~) **II** (sledded; sledding) ❶ *vt.* 用雪橇运送 ②用摘棉机摘: *sledded* cotton 机摘棉 ❷ *vi.* 乘雪橇 ‖**hard sledding** 费劲: The work was *hard sledding*. 这项工作很费劲。

sledge[1] [sledʒ] **I** *n.* (装运货物或旅客的)雪橇 **II** ❶ *vi.* 乘雪橇: go *sledging* 乘雪橇去 ❷ *vt.* 用雪橇运送

sledge[2] [sledʒ] *n., vt. & vi.* =sledgehammer (*n., vt. & vi.*)

sledgehammer ['sledʒ,hæmə] **I** *n.* (锻工等用的)大锤 **II** *vt. & vi.* ①(像)用大锤敲打; 猛击 ②锤炼 **III** *a.* (像)用大锤敲打的; 猛烈的, 重大的; 致命的: a ~ blow 重大的打击, 致命的打击 / a ~ argument 激烈的争论; 驳得对方哑口无言的议论

sleek [sli:k] **I** *a.* ①(毛发等)光滑的, 柔滑的 ②(动物)壮健的, 养得好的; (植物)茁壮的 ③圆滑的, 滑头的; 花言巧语的 ④雅致的; 时髦的; 阔气的, 豪华的 **II** ❶ *vt.* ①使光滑; 使柔滑发亮 ②掩饰, 掩盖(over) ❷ *vi.* ①打扮整洁; 扮扮漂亮(up) ②滑动 ‖**~ly** *ad.* / **~ness** *n.*

sleep [sli:p] **I** *n.* ①睡眠: He didn't get much ~. 他只睡了一会儿。 / have a good ~ 好好睡一觉 / a ~ of eight hours 八小时的睡眠 / He talks in his ~. 他说梦话。 / go to ~ 入睡; 睡着 / get to ~ 设法睡着; 入睡 / fall into a deep ~ 酣睡 / a broken ~ 断断续续的睡眠 ②昏迷状态; 麻木; 长眠, 死亡: My foot has gone to ~. 我的脚麻木了。 / the last ~ 长眠, 死亡 ③静寂: the ~ among the lonely hills 荒山中的沉寂 ④(动物的)冬眠, 蛰伏; (植物叶子、花瓣的)

夜间闭合 ⑤一夜: Ten ~s have passed since his return. 他回来后十个夜晚已经过去了。⑥一天的旅程: The mine was two ~s from the village. 从村子到矿山是两天的路程。 **II** (slept [slept]) ❶ *vi.* ①睡, 睡眠; 睡着: ~ well (badly) 睡得好(不好) / ~ late 睡懒觉; 迟起 / He *slept* eight hours. 他睡了八小时。 ②(象睡着似的)静止; 长眠, 被埋葬着: a ~*ing* volcano 静止的火山 ③过夜, 住宿 (*at, in*) ④发生性关系 (*with*) ⑤(动物)冬眠, 蛰伏; (植物叶子、花瓣)夜间闭合 ❷ *vt.* ①睡: ~ a sound sleep 睡得极甜 / ~ the sleep of the just [谑]安心地睡; 酣睡 / ~ the clock round 接连睡十二小时(以上) / ~ oneself sober 通过睡眠使自己清醒 ②以睡眠消除(或度过)(*off, away*): ~ off a headache 用睡眠治好头痛 / ~ off one's vexation 以睡眠消除烦恼 / ~ the afternoon *away* 以睡眠打发一个下午 ③[口]供…住宿; 可睡…人: This cabin will ~ four. 这间船舱可睡四人。‖**fall on ~** [古]入睡; 死亡 / **have one's beauty ~** 午夜前(酣)睡几小时; 睡头觉 / **have one's ~ out** 睡够, 睡足: Let him *have his* ~ *out*. 让他睡个够吧。 / **lay to ~** 使入睡; 埋葬 / **put sb. to ~** 使某人入睡 / **~ around** [俚]到处乱搞男女关系 / **~ in** ①住在雇主家里 ②迟起; 睡懒觉 ③睡过头 / **~ like a log** (或 **top**) 熟睡 / **~ on it** 把问题留到第二天解决 / **~ out** ①在户外睡觉 ②(佣工)住在自己家里 ③不在家里过夜 ④睡过整整(一段时间) / **~ over** [口] ①借宿别人处 ②忽视; 不注意(某事等) / **~ rough** 在公园(或车站等处)过夜(而不住在旅馆里) / **~ that knows not breaking** 长眠, 死亡 ‖**~-in** *a. & n.* 住在雇主家里的(佣工) / **~ing bag, ~ing sack** 睡袋(野外用) / **Sleeping Beauty** 睡美人(法国童话中因着魔而昏睡一百年的公主) / **~ing beauty, ~ing clover** 【植】白花酢浆草 / **~ing car, ~ing carriage** 卧车 / **~ing draught** 安眠药 / **~ing partner** (不参与经营的)隐名合伙人 / **~ing pill** 安眠药片 / **~ing rent** 固定的租金; 不依获利多寡而增减的租金 / **~ing sickness** (采采蝇引起的)昏睡病; 非洲睡眠病; 非洲锥虫病 / **~ing suit** 睡衣裤 / **'~-out** *a. & n.* 不住在雇主家里的(佣工) / **'~,walker** *n.* 梦游者 / **'~,walking** *n.* 梦游; 梦游病 / **'~wear** *n.* [总称]睡衣睡裤

sleeper ['sli:pə] *n.* ①睡眠者: a heavy ~ 不易醒的人 / a light ~ 睡不沉的人 ②(铁路)枕木; 【建】小搁栅; 【船】机座垫 ③卧车; 卧铺 ④眼看要输而意外取胜的赛马; 暂时未受赏识的商品 ⑤在耳上作了记号但尚未打烙印的小牛 ⑥[复]小孩睡衣裤

sleepless ['sli:p-lis] *a.* ①失眠的; 不眠的, 醒着的: a ~ night 不眠之夜 ②警觉的; 戒备不懈的 ③无休止的: the ~ wind 刮不停的风 ‖**~ly** *ad.* / **~ness** *n.*

sleet [sli:t] **I** *n.* ①冻雨; 雨夹雪, 霰 ②雨淞(冷雨

落在物体表面而成的冰状冻结物) **II** *vi.* 下冻雨;
下雨夹雪 ‖~**y** *a.*

sleeve [sli:v] **I** *n.* ①袖子;袖套 ②唱片套 ③【气】
风(向)袋 ④【机】套筒 **II** *vt.* 给…装袖子;给…
装套筒 ‖*hang on sb.'s* ~ 依赖某人 / *have
something up* (或 *in*) *one's* ~ 暗中已有应急
的打算(如计划等) / *laugh in* (或 *up*) *one's* ~
暗幕发笑,窃笑 / *roll* (或 *turn*) *up one's* ~s
卷起袖子;准备行动(或工作) / *wear one's heart
on* (或 *upon*) *one's* ~ 见 **heart** ‖~**d** *a.* [常
用以构成复合词]装有袖子的: short-~**d** 短袖
的 / ~*less* *a.* ①无袖的 ②徒然的,无益的: a
~*less* errand 徒劳的差使 / ~*let* ['sli:vlit] *n.*
袖套 ‖~ **button** 袖口钮 / ~ **emblem** (军队中
文职人员佩戴的)袖章 / '~-**fish** *n.* 【动】枪鲗,
鱿鱼 / ~ **link** 袖口钮 / ~ **nut** 【机】套筒螺
母 / ~ **target** (飞机在飞行中拖曳的)筒形拖靶
(作射靶练习用) / ~ **valve** 【机】套阀

sleigh [slei] **I** *n.* (尤指用马拉的)雪车;雪橇 **II** ❶
vi. 驾雪车;乘雪橇 ❷ *vt.* 用雪车运输(货物)

sleigh

sleight [slait] *n.* ①奸诈;诡计 ②熟练,灵巧 ‖(*a*)
~ *of hand* ①(变戏法等中)手法的熟练 ② 戏
法,魔术;花招: perform ~ *of hand* 变戏法; 耍
花招 / turn out to be a clumsy ~ *of hand* 戏法
不高明;弄巧成拙

slender ['slendə] *a.* ①细长的;苗条的;纤弱的: a
~ figure 细长的身材 / a ~ iris 【植】细叶鸢尾
② 微薄的;微少的;不足的: a ~ income 微薄的
收入 / a ~ hope 渺茫的希望 ③(声音)微弱的,
不洪亮的 ‖~**ly** *ad.* / ~**ness** *n.*

slept [slept] sleep 的过去式和过去分词

sleuth [slu:θ] **I** *n.* 警犬;[口]侦探 **II** *vi.* 做侦探
‖'~'**hound** *n.* =sleuth (*n.*)

slew¹ [slu:] slay 的过去式

slew² [slu:] **I** ❶ *vt.* 使旋转 (*around, round*): ~
one's head *around* 把头转过来 ❷ *vi.* ①旋转
(*around, round*): The crane ~ed round. 吊车转
了过来。②滑溜 **II** *n.* 回转,旋转;旋转后的位置

slew³ [slu:] *n.* [美]沼泽

slew⁴ [slu:] *n.* [美口]许多;大量: ~s (或 a ~) of
work (people) 很多工作(人)

slice [slais] **I** *n.* ①薄片,切片,片: a ~ of bread
一片面包 ②部分;份: a ~ of territory 一块

领土 / a ~ of life 人生的片段 / a ~ of good
luck 一份好运气 ③ 菜刀;锅铲;火铲 ④【建】泥
刀;【印】油墨铲 ⑤(高尔夫球中右手击球者的)右
曲球;(左手击球者的)左曲球 ⑥【无】限幅,削波
II ❶ *vt.* ①把…切成薄片: ~ up a loaf 把面包
切成片 ②切下;切开;割去 (*off, away, from*): ~
off a piece of meat 切下一块肉 / The plough
~*d* the land. 犁耕过地面。 / ~ *away* a tract
of territory 割去一块领土 ③ 把…分成部分(或
份) ④(用锅铲等)铲;(用泥刀等)铺 ⑤(高尔夫
球中)使(球)曲向右边(或左边) ❷ *vi.* ①切 ②
打右(或左)曲球 ‖~**r** *n.* ①切薄片的人 ②切片
刀;切片机 / '~-**of**-'**life** *a.* 栩栩如生地反映现
实生活的一个侧面的

slick [slik] **I** *a.* ①光滑的;滑溜溜的 ②熟练的;
灵巧的 ③聪明的;机智的 ④[口]圆滑的;花言巧
语的;狡猾的: a ~ alibi 圆滑的托词 ⑤[口](作
品等)华而不实的: a ~ book (style) 华而不实的
书(文体) ⑥陈腐的,老一套的;平凡的,无独创性
的: a story of the ~ variety 老一套的故事
⑦[俚]极好的;第一流的: a ~ meal 美餐 ⑧[俚]
讨人喜欢的;吸引人的 **II** *ad.* ①润滑地,自如
地,灵活地: go ~ 运转自如' ② 熟练地;巧妙地;
聪明地 ③ 径直地;恰好地: run ~ into sth. 迎
头撞在某物上 / hit sb. ~ in the eye 恰好打着
某人的眼睛 **III** ❶ *vt.* ①使光滑,使滑溜 ②[口]
使整洁,使漂亮 (*up*) ❷ *vi.* ①打扮整洁;打扮漂亮
(*up*) **IV** *n.* ①(有一层油膜的)平滑的水面;油膜
②修光工具;平滑器 ③[口]用上等有光纸印刷的
通俗杂志 ‖~**ly** *ad.* / ~**ness** *n.*

slide [slaid] **I** (过去式 slid [slid], 过去分词 slid 或
slidden ['slidn]) ❶ *vi.* ①滑;滑动: ~ on ice 溜
冰 / The drawers of this desk ~ in and out
easily. 这张桌子的抽屉容易拉进拉出。②滑落:
The pen *slid* from his hand. 笔从他的手中滑
落。③不知不觉地陷入 (*into*): ~ *into* bad habits
不知不觉地沾染上坏习惯 ④偷偷地走: ~ *into*
a room 偷偷地溜进房间 ⑤ 流;流逝: The years
~ past. 一年年悄悄地过去了。❷ *vt.* ①使滑动
②把…偷偷地放入 (*in, into*): ~ sth. *into* a
drawer 偷偷地把某物塞进抽屉 **II** *n.* ①滑(动)
②滑道;滑面;滑坡;滑梯 ③雪崩;山崩;土崩
④滑动的部分;【机】滑板;滑座 ⑤幻灯片 ⑥(显
微镜用)承物玻璃片 ⑦【地】断层 ⑧【音】滑音,延
音;长号的 U 字形伸缩管 ⑨(妇女保持头发整齐
的)发夹 (=hair~) ‖*let things* (或 *it*) ~ 让它
去; 听其自然 / ~ *over* 略过; 回避: ~ *over* a
ticklish question 略过棘手的问题 ‖~ **bar** 【机】
滑杆 / ~ **block** 【机】滑块 / ~ **carriage** 【军】滑
动炮架 / ~ **fastener** 拉链 / ~ **rule** 计算尺 /
~ **valve** 【机】滑阀 / '~**way** *n.* 滑路,滑斜面

sliding ['slaidiŋ] *a.* ①(根据具体情况而) 变化的;
可调整的 ②滑动的: a ~ door 拉门,滑门 ‖~
board (儿童游戏用的)滑梯 / ~ **scale** ①计算
尺 ②(按市场等情况变化调整工资、税收、价格等
的)比例相应增减(制): the ~ *scale* of medical

fees (根据个人收入等的变化)可调整的医药费比例 / ~ **seat** (赛艇等上划手所坐的)滑动座位

slight [slait] **I** a. ①细长的; 苗条的; 瘦小的: a ~ figure 瘦小的身材 ②脆弱的, 不结实的; a ~ framework 脆弱的骨架 ③轻微的; 微小的; 少量的: a ~ cold 轻微的伤风 / a ~ difference 微小的区别 / a ~ odour of gas 一点煤气味 / pay sb. ~ attention 不大注意(或尊重)某人 / There is not the ~est reason. 毫无理由。/ not in the ~est 一点不(=not at all) **II** vt. ①轻视; 藐视; 怠慢: feel ~ed 感觉受到轻蔑 ②玩忽: ~ one's work 玩忽职务 **III** n. 轻蔑; 怠慢: put a ~ on (或 upon) sb. 蔑视某人 / suffer ~s 受到怠慢 ‖~**ly** ad. a ~ly built child 身材瘦小的孩子 / ~**ness** n.

slim [slim] **I** (slimmer, slimmest) a. ①细长的; 苗条的, 纤细的: a ~ person 细长身材的人 ②微小的; 稀少的; 不充分的: a ~ possibility 微小的可能性 / a ~ excuse 站不住脚的借口 ③[方]狡猾的 ④低劣的, 无价值的 **II** (slimmed; slimming) **❶** vi. (用运动、减食等)减轻体重而变苗条 **❷** vt. 使变苗条 ‖~**ly** ad. / ~**ness** n. ‖'~-**jim** n. 瘦削的人

slime [slaim] **I** n. ①软泥; 粘土 ②粘质物; (动物分泌的)粘液 ③【矿】矿泥, 煤泥 ④[古]沥青 **II** **❶** vt. ①用粘泥(或粘液)涂抹 ②去除(鱼等)的粘液 ③把(矿石)研磨成矿泥 **❷** vi. ①变粘滑 ②[英俚]滑走, 用狡猾手段脱身溜掉 (through, away, past, out of) ‖~ **pit** ①产沥青的矿井 ②贮矿泥的坑

slimy ['slaimi] a. ①粘性的; 粘滑的 ②泥泞的 ③谄媚的; 讨厌的; 卑鄙的 ‖**slimily** ad. / **sliminess** n.

sling[1] [sliŋ] **I** n. ①投石器, 投石环索; (游戏用的)弹弓 (=~shot) ②抛, 投, 掷 ③吊索, 吊链, 吊带;【海】一吊货, 一关 ④【医】悬带 ⑤(枪)的背带 ⑥(吊货物用的)网兜 **II** (slung [slʌŋ]) vt. **❶** (用投石器或用力)投, 掷, 抛 ❷ 吊, 用索: a crate on board a ship 把一只木板箱吊到船上 / a schoolbag slung over one's shoulder 背在肩上的一只书包 / ~ arms【军】枪上肩 ‖~ a nasty foot 见 **foot** / ~ **ink** 见 **ink** / ~ **mud at** 见 **mud** / ~ **one's hook** 见 **hook** / ~ **over** 用力拥抱 / ~ **the hatchet** 见 **hatchet** ‖~**er** n. ①使用投石器者; 投掷者 ②吊装工 ‖~ **cart** 车轴上有吊链的运货车 / ~ **dogs** 吊钩 / '~**shot** n. ①弹弓 ②紧追在后的赛车的突然超前 ③驾驶员坐在后轮后方的一种赛车

sling[2] [sliŋ] n. [美]以酒、糖等混合后加柠檬汁制成的冷饮料(或加肉豆蔻粉制成的热饮料)

slink[1] [sliŋk] **I** (slunk [slʌŋk]) vi. 鬼鬼祟祟地走; 溜走 (off, away, by) **II** n. 鬼鬼祟祟的人

slink[2] [sliŋk] **I** (slunk [slʌŋk]) vt. & vi. (动物,尤指家畜)早产 **II** a. ①早产的, 不足月的 ②[主方]骨瘦如柴的 **III** n. ①早产所生的动物(尤指小牛); 早产小牛的肉(或皮) ②[主方]虚弱的人

slip[1] [slip] **I** (slipped; slipping) **❶** vi. ①滑动, 滑行: As the door closes the catch ~s into place. 门关上时弹簧锁就扣上了。/ The boat ~s through the water. 船在水上轻快地滑行。②滑跤, 失足: ~ in the mud 在泥泞中滑倒 / ~ on the stairs 在楼梯上失足 ③滑落, 滑掉; 松脱: The pen slipped from his hand. 钢笔从他手中滑落。/ The knot is so firm that it can't ~. 那么紧的结不会松开。④溜, 溜走; 悄悄走; (时间)不知不觉地过去: ~ out of the room 偷偷地溜出房间 / let an opportunity ~ 错过机会 / A mistake has slipped in. 不知不觉间出了差错。/ ~ off (或 away) 不告而别 / Time is slipping away (或 by). 时间悄悄过去了。⑤疏忽; 犯错误; 不经意讲出; 被遗忘: ~ in one's grammar 不经心地犯语法错误 / ~ into idealism 滑到唯心论方面去 / Not a word slipped from his mouth about his illness. 他只字不提自己的病。The name slipped from my memory (或 mind). 我一时想不起这个名字了。⑥(健康等方面)变坏; 下降: He has slipped badly since his last illness. 他上次生病以后, 身体越来越坏了。/ Sales ~ in some lines. 某些方面的商品销售量下降。⑦匆忙地穿(或脱): ~ into (out of) one's coat 匆忙穿上(脱去)上衣 ⑧【空】侧滑 **❷** vt. ①使滑动; 使滑行 ②滑过, 被…忽略: The appointment slipped my memory. 我把约会忘了。/ The point slipped my attention. 这点我未曾注意。③摆脱; 挣脱; 闪开(拳击等): ~ one's pursuers 摆脱追赶者 / The horse slipped its bridle. 马挣脱了笼头。④打开; 放掉(猎狗等); (编结中)滑漏; (动物)早产: ~ a lock 开锁 / ~ a knot 解开绳结 / ~ the anchor【海】斩断锚链 / ~ a stitch 滑漏一针 / The cow has slipped her calf. 这头母牛早产了。⑤匆忙地穿(或脱); 蜕(皮): ~ one's clothes on (off) 匆忙穿上(脱下)衣服 / The snake slipped its skin. 蛇蜕皮了。⑥塞入; 暗中塞(钱等); 把…塞给: ~ a marker between the pages 在书页中夹上书签 / ~ a letter into one's pocket 悄悄地把信放入口袋 ⑦使脱臼: ~ one's shoulder 使肩膀脱臼 **II** n. ①滑动; 滑跤; 失足; 下降: have a ~ on the ice 在冰上滑了一跤 / a ~ in stock prices 股票价格的下降 ②意外事故; 不幸事件 ③溜; 溜走; 不告而别 ④疏忽; 错误: a ~ of the pen (tongue) 笔(口)误 / make a ~ in spelling 犯拼写错误 ⑤[船]滑台, 滑路; 船台; 两码头间的水区 ⑥【机】滑程; 滑率; 滑动量; 空转; 转差 ⑦(牵狗等用的)皮带; 可突然松脱的装置 ⑧(儿童的)外衣, 围涎; 有背带的女式长衬衣; 枕套 ⑨[复]男子游泳裤 ⑩[地](岩层的)滑距 ⑪[复]舞台边门(供布景或演员出场前停留的地方) ⑫(板球)外场区; [~s][用作单]外场员防守的地区 ⑬[动]小比目鱼 ⑭【空】侧滑 ⑮滑润性 **III** a. ①滑动的; 滑移的; 可拆卸的, 活络的: a ~ scraper 滑行刮土机 / a ~ compartment 可拆卸的隔间 ②有活结的; 可立即松脱的: a ~ cord 打活结的绳索 / a ~

bolt 伸缩螺栓 ‖*give sb. the* ~ (或 *give the* ~ *to sb.*) 乘某人不备时溜掉 / ***let*** ~ 见 let[1] / ~ ***along*** [俚]飞快行进 / ~ ***into*** ①匆忙穿上 ②[俚]痛殴 ③大吃 ④滑到…方面去 / ~ ***one over on*** [口]欺骗… / ~ ***over*** 对…漫不经心 / ~ ***sth. over*** 用欺骗手段把某物塞给他人; 用欺骗手段胜过他人 / ~ ***up*** [口] ①滑跤,跌倒 ②犯错误;疏忽: ~ *up* in one's calculations 计算中出差错 ③遭到不幸 / ***There's many a*** ~ ***'twixt the cup and the lip.*** [谚]事情往往会功亏一篑。(或: 凡事都难以十拿九稳。) ‖~ **carriage,** ~ **coach** [英]滑脱车厢(火车不停即可卸落的车厢) / '~**case** ***n.*** 书套 / '~ˌ**cover** ***n.*** ①家具套;沙发套 ②书的封套 / ~ **galley** 长条排字盘 / ~ **hook**【机】滑脱环;活钩 / '~**knot** ***n.*** 活结 / ~ **noose** 有活结的套索 / '~-'**on** ***n.*** 套领衫;无扣手套;无带、扣的鞋子;套裙 ***a.*** 易于穿、脱的;套领的 / '~ˌ**over** ***n.*** 套领衫;套领运动衣 ***a.*** 易于穿、脱的;套领的 / ~ **ring**【机】滑动环;【电】集流环,汇电环 / ~ **road** 汽车道的支路;叉道 / ~ **rope**【船】回头缆,准备解脱的缆绳 / ~ **sheet** 薄衬纸 / '~-**sheet** ***vt.*** 用薄衬纸夹衬(印好的书页等) / '~**shod** ***a.*** ①穿着塌跟鞋的;破烂的 ②不整洁的;马虎的;潦草的: be ~*shod* in work 工作随便 / '~**slop** ***n.*** ①廉价酒;淡酒 ②肤浅的、不着边际的文章;废话 ③拍打的声音;啪嗒啪嗒的响声 / '~**stick** ***n.*** 计算尺 / ~ **stitch** (编结)跳针,漏针;【纺】暗缝 / '~**stream** ***n.***【空】滑流;(螺旋桨或喷气发动机形成的)向后气流 / '~**up** ***n.*** ①错误;疏忽 ②不幸事故 / '~**way** ***n.*** (船坞中的)滑台;滑路;船台

slip[2] [slip] **I** ***n.*** ①接枝;插枝;[喻]后裔: a bastard ~【植】吸枝;[喻]私生子 ②瘦长的青年人: a ~ of a girl 瘦长的姑娘 ③片条,板条;纸条;【印】长条校样: Give me a ~ of paper. 给我一张纸条。/ a rejection ~ 退稿单 / an order ~ 订货通知单 ④(教堂内)有靠背的狭长板凳 **II** (slipped; slipping) ***vt.*** 从(植物)取接枝(或插枝)

slip[3] [slip] ***n.*** (涂敷于陶器的)泥釉;粘土与水的混合物

slipper ['slipə] **I** ***n.*** ①[常用复]拖鞋;便鞋: a pair of ~*s* 一双拖鞋 / plastic ~*s* 塑料拖鞋 ②【机】滑动部分;滑屐 **II** ***vt.*** 用拖鞋打(孩子等) ‖~**ed** ***a.*** 穿着拖鞋的

slippery ['slipəri] ***a.*** ①滑的;使人滑跤的;[喻](问题等)要小心对待的: ~ roads 滑的路 / Be careful. It's ~. 当心滑跤。②易滑脱的 ③圆滑的;不老实的,不可靠的: a ~ customer 滑头,狡猾的家伙 ④(地位等)不稳固的;(言语等)含糊的,难以捉摸的: be on ~ ground 在不稳的立足点上;在不可靠的基础上 ‖~ ***as an eel*** 油滑的;不可靠的 ‖**slipperily** ***ad.*** / **slipperiness** ***n.***

slit [slit] **I** ***n.*** 狭长的切口;细长的裂口;裂缝: the ~ of a letter box 信箱的投信口 **II** (slit; slitting) ❶ ***vt.*** ①切开;撕开;割掉;切成长条: ~ an envelope open 撕开信封 / ~ a sheet of leather into thongs 把一块皮革切成皮条 ②使成狭缝: ~ one's eyes 眯眼睛 ❷ ***vi.*** 纵切;纵裂: The shirt has ~ down the back. 这件衬衫的背部已从上到下裂开了。‖**slitter** ***n.*** ①开切口的人 ②切开的器具,切刀 ‖~ **trench**【军】狭长掩壕

slither ['sliðə] ❶ ***vi.*** 不稳地滑动;蜿蜒地滑行 ❷ ***vt.*** 使滑动;使滑行

slobber ['slɔbə] **I** ❶ ***vi.*** ①流涎,淌口水 ②(说话等时)过度伤感;感情迸发 ❷ ***vt.*** ①用涎弄湿(衣服等) ②口齿不清地说(或唱) ③草率地做;搞坏(工作) **II** ***n.*** ①涎,口水 ②过分伤感的说话(或接吻等);口齿不清的话;语无伦次的话

slogan ['slougən] ***n.*** ①(尤指苏格兰或爱尔兰氏族的)战斗的呐喊;集合信号 ②口号;标语: shout ~*s* 呼口号 ③简短而吸引人的广告用语

sloop [slu:p] ***n.*** ①单桅小帆船 ②【军】海岸炮舰;(尤指第二次世界大战中担任反潜艇任务的)小型护航舰

slop[1] [slɔp] ***n.*** ①(宽松的)罩衣,外衣;工作服 ②[复]廉价的现成衣服;卖给水手的物品(如衣服、被褥等) ‖~ **chest** (船上)准备发给海员的贮备商品(指衣服与烟、酒等杂货,货款常从工资中扣除) / '~-**room** ***n.*** (船上为海员所设的)衣服被褥分发室 / '~ˌ**seller** ***n.*** 经售廉价现成衣服的商人 / '~**shop** ***n.*** 出售廉价现成衣服的商店

slop[2] [slɔp] **I** ***n.*** ①泥浆;半融雪 ②[复]污水,脏水;(用作饲料的)厨房下脚 ③[常用复]人体排泄物 ④[英][复](尤指供病人吃的)液体食物(如牛奶、粥等) ⑤[常用复]稀薄乏味的液体食物(或饮料);不含酒精的饮料 ⑥溅出的液体;溢出的液体 ⑦酿造过程中的釜馏物 **II** (slopped; slopping) ❶ ***vi.*** ①溅出;溢出 (*over, out*) ②在泥浆(或半融雪)中走 ③超出界限,越出范围 (*over*) ④感情迸发;极度伤感 (*over*) ❷ ***vt.*** ①使(液体)溅出,溢出 ②溅污,弄脏 ③使液汁等溢出地盛(或上)(菜等) ④咂咂地吃;贪婪地喝 ⑤用下脚喂(猪等) ‖***get slopped*** [美俚]喝醉 ‖~ **basin** [英](餐桌上)倒茶脚等残渣用的盆 / ~ **chute** 船后部的垃圾筒 / ~ **jar** 盛污水(或小便等)的大桶 / ~ **pail** 污水桶

slope [sloup] **I** ***n.*** ①倾斜;坡度;斜度;【数】斜率: a hill with a ~ of 1 in 5 有五分之一坡度的小山 / There is always a certain ~ in a ship's deck. 船的甲板总有几分倾斜。②斜面;斜坡: mountain ~*s* 山坡 ③掮枪的姿势: with one's rifle at the ~ 掮着枪 ④【矿】斜井 **II** ❶ ***vi.*** ①倾斜: The ground ~*s* down to the sea. 地势向海面倾斜。②[俚]逃走;离去 (*off*);闲荡 (*about*) ❷ ***vt.*** ①使倾斜;使有斜度: ~ a roof 使屋顶有斜度 ②掮(枪) **III** ***a.*** [诗]倾斜的

slot[1] [slɔt] **I** ***n.*** ①狭孔,缝;槽,狭槽: deliver mail through a ~ in a door 把信从门缝里塞进去 ②【空】翼缝 ③狭通道;狭窄的地位: a ~ between the two islands 两岛之间狭窄的通道 ④(在组织、名单、程序单等中所占的)位置;职位: a TV show in the six-o'clock ~ 排在六点钟的一次电

视节目 / fill a job ~ 填补职位,补缺 **II** (slotted; slotting) *vt.* 开槽于: *slotting* machine【机】插床 ‖~ **car** 一种电动玩具赛车(靠底下的轨槽供电)/ '~**-drill** *vt.* 铣(槽) / ~ **machine** 投入一枚硬币即自行开动的机器(如自动售货机及俗称吃角子老虎的一种赌具等) / ~ **man** 负责新闻编排的报纸编辑

slot² [slɔt] **I** [单复同] *n.* ①(尤指鹿的)足迹 ②轨迹 **II** (slotted; slotting) *vt.* 跟踪

sloth [slouθ] *n.* ①懒惰;懒散 ②【动】树懒(南美洲等产的一种哺乳动物,栖于森林,行动缓慢) ‖~**bear** (印度、斯里兰卡产的)懒熊

slouch [slautʃ] **I** *n.* ①没精打采的姿态;懒散的样子 ②(帽边等的)耷拉 ③萎靡不振的人;笨拙的人 ④[口][常与否定词连用]无能的人: He is no ~ at tennis. 他网球打得很不错。**II** ❶ *vi.* ①没精打采地走(或坐、站) ②(帽子等)耷拉着 ❷ *vt.* 使低垂: ~ a hat over one's eyes 把帽子拉得遮住眼睛 ‖~ **hat** 阔软边呢帽

slough¹ [slau] **I** *n.* ①泥沼;沼泽地,泥泞的地方 ②[喻]泥坑;绝望境地 ③[slu:][美]河湾,又沼泽(或潮浦)地中的小溪 **II** ❶ *vt.* ①使陷入泥沼;[喻]使陷入泥坑,使沉沦 ②[美俚]逮捕;监禁 (up, in) ❷ *vi.* 在泥浆中跋涉 ‖*the Slough of Despond* 绝望的深渊;极度沮丧状态

slough² [slʌf] **I** *n.* ①蛇(蜕)的皮;(动物身上)按时脱落的部分 ②【医】腐肉,死肉,腐痂 ③可丢弃的东西(指习惯、偏见、旧事物等) **II** ❶ *vi.* ①(蛇皮等)脱落;(蛇等)蜕皮;(痂等)脱落;(标点等)漏掉 ②(岩石、河岸等)崩塌 ❷ *vt.* ①脱落(皮等) ②抛弃,丢弃(off) : ~ (off) bad habits 戒除坏习惯 / ~ the unimportant verbiage 删除无关紧要的空话 ‖~ over 把⋯当作无关紧要;轻视: ~ over certain items of the project 认为计划中的某些项目无足轻重

sloven ['slʌvn] **I** *n.* ①邋遢人;不修边幅的人 ②(工作等)马马虎虎的人;懒散的人 **II** *a.* ① =slovenly (a.) ②未开垦的;未开发的

slovenly ['slʌvnli] *a.* & *ad.* ①邋遢;不整洁;不修边幅 ②懒散;马虎;潦草 ‖**slovenliness** *n.*

slow [slou] **I** *a.* ①慢的,缓慢的: a ~ train 慢车 / a ~ stream 缓慢的溪流 / a ~ march (军队、送葬行列等的)缓慢行进 ②(在时间方面)慢了的;慢于⋯的,晚于⋯的(on) : My watch is five minutes ~. 我的表慢了五分钟。/ Washington is several hours ~ on London. 华盛顿时间比伦敦时间晚几个小时。③迟钝的;冷漠的;不活跃的: a ~ learner 学得慢的人 / a ~ imagination 迟钝的想象力 / ~ of speech 嘴钝的,讷于言的 / be ~ to wrath 不轻易发怒 / a ship ~ to answer the helm 对船舵反应不灵敏的船 / a ~ audience 感动缓慢的观众 / He is absurdly ~ in giving me an answer. 他迟迟不给我回音,真不象话。/ ~ in action 行动缓慢 / ~ at accounts 不善于算帐 / a ~ season 淡季 / These articles were particularly ~. 这些商品特

别滞销。/ a ~ fire 文火 ④不精采的;乏味的: a ~ afternoon 沉闷的下午 ⑤落后的;落后于时代的: a ~ town 落后的城镇 ⑥(路面等)妨碍前进(或行动)的;使减低速度的: a ~ track 跑不快的松软跑道 ⑦作用缓慢的: a ~ poison 慢性毒药 / a ~ filter 慢滤器 ⑧(照相机镜头)孔径小的,曝光慢的 **II** *ad.* 缓慢地;慢慢地(一般用在 go, run, speak, read, burn 或 how 等之后): My watch goes ~. 我的表经常慢。/ Read ~-er. 读得慢一些。/ How ~ the time passes! 时间过得多慢呀! **III** ❶ *vt.* 使慢下来;使(市场等)变得呆滞(up, down) : ~ (up 或 down) a motorcar 放慢汽车速度 ❷ *vi.* 慢下来(up, down) : Slow up (或 down) before you reach the crossroads. 快开到十字路口时(车子)要减速。‖go ~ 见 go / ~ and steady (或 sure) 慢而稳;稳扎稳打 ‖~**ish** *a.* 比较慢的,有点儿慢的;有点迟钝的;有点沉闷的 / ~**ly** *ad.* / ~**ness** *n.* / ~**burn** [美俚]渐渐的发怒: do a ~ burn 渐渐地发起火来 / ~ **coach** 迟钝的人;慢性子的人;落后于时代的人 / '~**down** *n.* ①减速 ②减退: ③怠工: stage a ~down 举行怠工 / '~-**footed** *a.* 速度慢的,进展缓慢的 / '~**going** *a.* ①悠闲地进行的 ②不想有所作为的;劲儿不足的 / ~ **match** 缓燃引信 / ~ **motion** 慢动作: a ~ motion film 慢镜头电影 / a ~ motion camera (拍慢镜头的)快速度摄影机 / '~-'**moving** *a.* ①动作缓慢的 ②(商品、股票等)滞销的 / '~**poke** *n.* [美俚]行动迟缓的人 / '~-**up** *n.* 减速;减退 / '~-'**witted** *a.* 迟钝的;笨的 / ~**worm** *n.* 【动】蛇蜥

sludge [slʌdʒ] *n.* ①软泥;淤泥: carry ~ from the riverbed to be used as manure 罱河泥积肥 ②(锅炉等)泥状沉积物 ③细碎的浮冰 ④【矿】矿泥;煤泥;淤渣;钻泥 ⑤[油](油罐底)酸渣;碱渣

slug¹ [slʌg] **I** *n.* ①【动】蛞蝓(俗称鼻涕虫);蛞蝓型幼虫 ②懒汉;[古]动作迟缓的动物(或车辆) **II** (slugged; slugging) *vi.* ①捕杀蛞蝓 ②[口]偷懒: ~ in bed 睡懒觉

slug² [slʌg] **I** *n.* ①(滑膛枪的)弹丸;子弹 ②金属小块;(待加工的)金属片状毛坯 ③(用以开动自动售货机等的)代硬币的金属圆片;冒充的硬币 ④【物】斯勒格,斯(质量单位) ⑤【无】铁心;波导调配柱 ⑥[印]铅字条;嵌片 **II** (slugged; slugging) *vt.* 插嵌片于

slug³ [slʌg] [美] **I** *n.* =slog (n.) **II** (slugged; slugging) *vt.* & *vi.* =slog (vt. & vi.) ‖'~**fest** *n.* 相互猛击,大殴斗

sluggard ['slʌgəd] **I** *n.* 懒汉 **II** *a.* 懒惰的 ‖~**ly** *a.* 懒惰的 / ~**ness** *n.* 懒惰

sluggish ['slʌgiʃ] *a.* ①懒惰的,懒散的;不大想动的: Many freshwater fishes become ~ in winter. 很多淡水鱼在冬季变得不活动了。②缓慢的 ③迟钝的 ④呆滞的,萧条的: a ~ market 呆滞的市面 ‖~**ly** *ad.* / ~**ness** *n.*

sluice [slu:s] **I** *n.* ①水门,水闸: a ~ gate 水闸

(门) ②(调节水位的)渠道,水槽,水门沟 ③(被闸门门拦住的)蓄水;(从闸门流出的)泄水 ④(淘洗金矿用的)流矿槽;(放流木材等用的)斜水槽 **Ⅱ** **❶** *vt.* ①(开水闸)排泄 ②放流(木材) ③(用水流)淘洗;冲洗: ~ a pavement with a hose 用水龙带冲刷人行道 **❷** *vi.* 奔泻,奔流 ‖**open** (或 **let loose, free**) *the* ~**s** ①打开闸门让水奔流 ②打开话匣子;让压抑着的感情迸发(或奔放) ‖**sluicy** *a.* 奔泻的 ‖**~way** *n.* 人工水闸渠道

slum¹ [slʌm] **Ⅰ** *n.* ①贫民窟;贫民区;陋巷: the ~s 贫民区 / a ~ area (或 district) 贫民区 ②[美俚](碰运气的竞技等中)不值钱的奖品;(摊子上出售的)蹩脚货 **Ⅱ** (slummed; slumming) *vi.* (尤指有钱人为了猎奇或作乐等)访问贫民区: go *slumming* 去访问贫民区 ‖**slummer** *n.* ①贫民窟的居民 ②访问贫民区的人 ‖**~lord** *n.* 从出租贫民窟(或简陋)的房屋牟取暴利的房东

slum² [slʌm] *n.* 【油】润滑油渣

slum³ [slʌm] *n.* [美俚] ①燉肉 ②大锅菜

slumber ['slʌmbə] **Ⅰ** *n.* ①睡眠;微睡: fall into a ~ 入睡 / be lost in ~ 酣睡 / disturb sb.'s ~(s) 打扰某人的睡眠 ②[喻]沉睡状态;懈怠 **Ⅱ** **❶** *vi.* ①睡眠;微睡 ②处于静止状态;蛰伏,潜伏 **❷** *vt.* (用睡眠)消磨(时间)(*away*) ‖**~er** ['slʌmbərə] *n.* 睡眠者;微睡者 ‖**~-wear** *n.* (商店用语)睡衣类

slump [slʌmp] **Ⅰ** *n.* ①暴跌;下降;不景气 ②消沉,萎靡;衰退 **Ⅱ** *vi.* ①(物价等)暴跌;(市场等)萧条;衰退 ②陷入;掉入;颓然倒下: ~ into a chair 倒在椅子里 ③消沉,萎靡

slung [slʌŋ] sling¹ 的过去式和过去分词 ‖**~shot** *n.* 头上装有石块(或金属块)的软鞭(一种武器)

slunk [slʌŋk] slink 的过去式和过去分词

slur [slə:] **Ⅰ** (slurred; slurring ['slə:riŋ]) **❶** *vt.* ①忽视,略过 (*over*) ②含糊地发(音);含糊地发(词)的音;模糊不清地写 ③匆忙地做(功课等) ④[音]圆润地接连唱(或奏);给…标连线 ⑤【印】使印得糊涂(指字迹重复或网点变形等) ⑥诽谤,诋毁;玷污 ⑦掩盖(罪行等) **❷** *vi.* ①模糊不清地发音(或写) ②引起印刷糊涂 ③[英方]滑 ④拖沓着走 **Ⅱ** *n.* ①污点;污辱,毁谤: cast a ~ on sb.'s reputation 损害某人的名誉 / put a ~ upon sb. 诋毁某人 / keep one's reputation free from (all) ~s 使自己的名誉不受损害 ②含糊音 ③【印】印刷糊涂,字迹重复,网点变形 ④【音】连线

slush [slʌʃ] **Ⅰ** *n.* ①烂泥;淤泥 ②半融雪(或冰);雪水 ③(尤指船上的)伙房的废弃油脂 【机】抗蚀润滑脂 ⑤水泥砂浆;(造纸用的)粥浆 ⑥油灰,白铅白灰 ⑦(书报、电影等中的)废话,无聊话 ⑧[美] = ~ fund **Ⅱ** **❶** *vt.* ①溅湿;溅污 ②灌泥浆于…;嵌油灰于…;用水泥砂浆补 ③给…加润滑脂 **❷** *vi.* ①(在泥浆等中)跋涉 ②发出溅泼声 ‖**casting** ~ 【机】空壳铸件 ‖**~ fund** [美]①把船舰上的油脚废物卖掉后用来改善生活的资金 ②用于收买官员(或散播政治谣言等)的资金

slut [slʌt] *n.* ①邋遢女人;懒妇 ②荡妇;妓女 ③[谑]女郎;大胆孟浪的女子 ④母狗

sly [slai] *a.* ①狡猾的;狡诈的 ②躲躲闪闪的;偷偷摸摸的: a ~ answer 躲躲闪闪的回答 / a ~ glance 偷偷的一瞥 ③[方]灵巧的,巧妙的 ④淘气的;顽皮的 ‖*a* ~ *dog* 见 **dog** / *on the* ~ 秘密地;偷偷地: catch sb. *on the* ~ 冷不防地抓住某人(尤指抓住其小过失) ‖**~ly** *ad.* / **~ness** *n.* ‖**~boots** [复] *n.* [用作单]顽皮的家伙

smack¹ [smæk] **Ⅰ** *n.* ①滋味;风味: an orange with a bitter ~ 苦味的柑子 ②少量,一点点: add a ~ of pepper to a dish 菜里略放一些胡椒 / have a ~ of obstinacy in one's character 性格有点固执 **Ⅱ** *vi.* 微有(某)味;带有(某种)风味(*of*): The water ~s of sulphur. 这水有点硫磺味。/ His talk ~s of the sea. 他的言谈很有点海员味道(指常谈及海上生活)。‖*a wet* ~ 讨厌的人;使人扫兴的人

smack² [smæk] **Ⅰ** **❶** *vt.* ①(用掌)掴,拍,打: ~ the table 拍一下桌子 ②使劈啪作响: ~ a whip 打个响鞭子 ③咂;出声地吻: ~ one's lips 咂嘴 **❷** *vi.* ①咂嘴 ②发出拍击声: The snowball ~ed against the wall. 雪球啪的一声打在墙上。**Ⅱ** *n.* ①拍击(声);掌掴(声);鞭打(声): the ~ of a whip 鞭甩打声 ②咂嘴(声);出声的接吻: with a ~ of the lips 咂着嘴 ③猛击: give the ball a hard ~ 使劲击球 **Ⅲ** *ad.* ①啪地一声: hit sb. ~ in the face 啪地掴某人耳光 ②猛烈地;恰好地,不偏不倚地: run ~ into sth. 猛然直撞在某物上 ‖*get a* ~ *in the eye* [口]遭受挫折;失意;失望 / *have a* ~ *at sth.* [口]试做某事 / ~ *down* [美俚]①责骂 ②使丧失地位,使失去身分 ‖'~-'dab *ad.* [方]恰好地,不偏不倚地

smack³ [smæk] *n.* ①(尤指单桅的)小帆船 ②(设有养鱼舱的)小渔船

smack⁴ [smæk] *n.* [俚]海洛因

small [smɔ:l] **Ⅰ** *a.* ①(体积)小的;细小的;(数量)少的;小额的: a ~ letter 小写字母 / The boy is ~ for his age. 就年龄来说这男孩的个子小了些。/ a ~ audience 为数不多的观(或听)众 / a ~ sum of money 一笔小额的款子 / ~ circle mentality 小圈子主义 ②(规模、价值、重要性、程度等)小型的;琐细的;微不足道的: experiment on a ~ scale 小规模地搞试验 / a ~ shopkeeper 小业主 / a ~ matter 小事 / a ~ favour 小恩小惠 / a ~ fault 小错,小处的失检 / pay ~ heed to 对…不在意 / have ~ Latin and less Greek 拉丁语懂得不多,希腊语懂得少 / There was no ~ excitement about it. 这事引起的激动可真不小呢。③(出身、地位)低微的: people, great and ~ 上上下下各阶层的人 ④小气的,吝啬的;气量狭隘的;卑劣的: a ~ nature 小心眼 / It's ~ of him to say that. 他说这话,未免太小气了。⑤(雨)细微的;(声音)细弱的;(酒等)淡的 **Ⅱ** *ad.* ①些微地,细细地: slice sth. ~ 把某物切成小片 ②微弱地;轻轻地,小声地: speak ~ 轻声细语 ③小型地,小规模地: They planned to start ~. 他们计划开始时候小干干。 ④轻视地: think ~ of sb. 瞧不起某人 **III** *n.* ①(物体的)狭小部分: the ~ of the back 腰背部 ②[复][口]小尺寸的东西; (送去洗的)小件衣服 ③[复](牛津大学)文学士学位考试的第一场 ‖*and ~ wonder* 见 **wonder** / *a ~ and early* 来客不多、结束又早的社交晚会 / *by ~ and ~* 慢慢地、一点一点地 / *feel ~* 觉得渺小; 觉得无地自容 / *in a ~ way* 见 **way** / *look ~* 显得渺小; 自惭形秽 / *on the ~ side* 见 **side** / *the ~ hours* 见 **hour** / *the still ~ voice* 见 **voice** ‖**~ness** *n.* ‖~ **arms** ①轻兵器 ②个人武器 / '**~-'beer** *a.* 微不足道的, 无价值的 / '**~-bore** *a.* ①小口径的: ~*-bore* rifles 小口径步枪 ②思想狭窄的 / ~ **capital** 【印】小体大写字母 / ~ **change** ①零钱; 找头 ②无聊话; 无关紧要的东西 / '**~clothes** [复] *n.* ①(十八世纪的)紧身半长裤 ②小件衣服(尤指内衣) / '**~-fry** *a.* ①次要的, 不重要的 ②为儿童设计的; 供儿童用的 / ~ **holding** [英]出卖(或出租)的五十英亩以下的小农田 / '**~-'minded** *a.* 眼光狭小的; 小气的 / '**~pox** *n.* 天花 / '**~-'scale** *a.* ①小规模的: ~*-scale* peasant economy 小农经济 ②(地图)小比例尺的 / '**~-'screen** *n.* [口]电视的, 电视上的 / '**~shot** *n.* [俚]小人物 / ~ **talk** 闲聊, 谈家常 / '**~-time** *a.* [美]次等的; 无足轻重的 / '**~ware** *n.* [英]①(常用复)小商品 ②狭幅的衣料

smart [smɑːt] **I** *a.* ①(如针扎般)刺痛的; 厉害的; 剧烈的: a ~ blow 狠狠的一击 / a ~ frost 严霜 / bring the kettle to a ~ boil 使一壶水(或其他东西)开个透 ②轻快的, 敏捷的, 活泼的: at a ~ pace 步伐轻快地 / a ~ gust of wind 一阵疾风 ③巧妙的, 灵巧的; 伶俐的, 机警的; 精明的: a ~ retort 巧妙的反驳 / a ~ invention 灵巧的发明 / He is too ~ not to jump at the chance. 他这人很精明, 不会错过这个机会。 ④洒脱的, 潇洒的; 俏的, 漂亮的; 时髦的: make a ~ job of it 把这事干得漂亮出色 / a ~ yacht 漂亮的游艇 / You look very ~ today. 你今天真漂亮啊! / a ~ neighbourhood 时髦阶层聚居区 ⑤[方]相当的, 可观的: a ~ price 挺贵的价格 / a ~ few 相当多的一些 **II** *vi.* ①刺痛, 扎痛; 针扎似地作痛: Iodine ~*s* when it is put on a cut. 碘酒涂在伤口上使人感到刺痛。 / My finger ~*s* so. 我的手指扎得厉害呢。 / The gibe ~*ed* in his brain. 人家的嘲笑在他脑子里针扎似地作痛。 ②感痛苦; 懊恼, 伤心 (*under, with, from*): ~ *from* one's defeats 因失败而感到痛苦 ③吃苦头, 受罚 (*for*): He feared that he would ~ *for* this foolishness. 他担心为了这一愚蠢举动而吃苦头。 **III** *ad.* =~**ly** **IV** *n.* ①刺痛; 痛苦; 懊恼 ②要聪明(或时髦)的人 ‖*as ~ as a new pin* 非常潇洒(或漂亮) / *as ~ as a steel trap* [美俚](做生意等)非常精明泼辣 / *right ~* [美]极大(的), 许许多多(的) ‖**-ly** *ad.* ①轻快地 ②厉害地, 严厉地 ③灵巧地, 能干地; 精明地 ④整齐地; 精确地

⑤漂亮地; 时髦地 ⑥大大地 / **~ness** *n.* ‖~ **aleck**, **~-alec** ['smɑːt,ælik] [美俚]自作聪明的人, 自以为样样懂的人 / **~-aleckry** ['smɑːt,ælikri] *n.* 自作聪明的话(或作风) / **~-alecky** ['smɑːt,æliki], **~-aleck**, **~-alec** ['smɑːt,ælik] *a.* 自作聪明的 / "**~**" **bomb** 灵敏的炸弹(指装有激光制导器的炸弹) / ~ **money** ①罚款; 赔偿金 ②伤兵抚恤金 ③由于掌握内部情况而投下的赌注(或资金) / ~ **set** [总称]最时髦的人士; 最时髦的社团

smarten ['smɑːtn] **❶** *vt.* ①使漂亮潇洒(*up*) ②使轻快; 使活泼: ~ the pace 使步伐轻快矫健 ③使变得聪明(或精明) **❷** *vi.* ①变得漂亮潇洒(*up*) ②变强烈: a ~*ing* wind 越来越强的风

smash¹ [smæʃ] **I** **❶** *vt.* ①打碎, 打破; 粉碎: ~ a teacup 打碎茶杯 / ~ up the furniture 捣毁家具 / ~ a record 打破纪录 / ~ up a monopoly 打破垄断 / ~ the schemes for aggression by 生裂变 ②猛掷; 挥(拳等)/(网球等运动中)猛叩(球) **❷** *vi.* ①碎裂 ②猛撞; 猛冲: The car ~*ed* into a wall. 汽车猛撞在墙上。 / ~ *through* a thicket 冲出丛林 ③破产; 瓦解, 垮掉(*up*) ④叩球, 杀球 **II** *n.* ①打碎; 粉碎 ②猛撞; 猛击; 叩球, 杀球 ③器物破碎的声音; 撞碰声 ④破产; 瓦解, 垮掉 ⑤(压碎果子榨取的)果子露 ⑥(演出等的)成功 **III** *ad.* 轰隆一声: go ~ into a truck 轰隆一声与卡车相撞 **IV** *a.* 出色的, 非凡的: a ~ success 极大的成功 ‖*go* (或 *come*) *to ~* [口]破碎; 垮台, 完蛋 ‖**~ed** *a.* [俚]喝醉的 / **~er** *n.* ①打碎者; 善于叩球者 ②[俚]沉重的打击; 摔跟头: come a ~ 摔下跟头; 受到重大挫折 ③[俚]出色的人(或东西); 特大的东西 ④[俚]令人信服的议论 ‖'**~-and-'grab raid** [主英]打碎商店橱窗的抢劫 / ~ **hit** 非常受欢迎的书(或电影、演员等); 十分流行的歌曲 / '**~up** *n.* ①(汽车等的)猛撞; 撞车事故: a head-on ~*up* between two trucks 两辆卡车的迎头猛撞 ②崩溃, 瓦解, 垮掉: an unexpected ~*up* in health 健康的突然恶化 ③灾难

smash² [smæʃ] **I** *vt.* 使用(假硬币) **II** *n.* ①假硬币 ②硬币; [俚]钱 ‖**~er** *n.* ①使用假硬币(或假钞票)者 ②收买赃物者

smatter ['smætə] **I** *n.* 肤浅的知识 **II** **❶** *vt.* ①一知半解地谈论 ②涉猎, 肤浅地研究 **❷** *vi.* 一知半解地谈论, 瞎讲 ‖**~er** ['smætərə] *n.* 一知半解者 / **~ing** ['smætəriŋ] *n.* ①肤浅的知识, 片断的知识: have a ~*ing* of English 懂得一点点英语; 对英语一知半解 ②少数; 少量

smaze [smeiz] *n.* 烟霾

smear [smiə] **I** **❶** *vt.* ①涂; 敷; 抹: ~ machine parts with oil (或 ~ oil on machine parts) 把油涂在机器零件上 ②弄脏 ③诽谤; 玷污: ~ sb.'s reputation 毁坏某人名誉 ④涂去, 抹去; 使轮廓不清: ~ a word 涂掉一个字 / ~ a cigarette end on the ashtray 在烟灰缸里把香烟头捻熄 ⑤[美俚]挫败, 打垮; 杀死 ⑥[美俚]贿赂 **❷** *vi.* 被涂污, 被弄脏 **II** *n.* ①污点; 污迹 ②涂抹物;

【医】涂片 ③诽谤;污蔑 ‖~ **word** 污蔑性的字眼

smell [smel] *n.* ①嗅觉: a fine sense of ~ 良好的嗅觉 ②气味: the sweet, intense ~ of ripe fruit 熟了的水果的浓烈香味 ③臭味, 难闻的气味: What a ~! 多难闻的气味啊! ④嗅,闻: take a ~ at (或[主美] of) the milk 闻一闻牛奶的气味 ⑤气息;风味 **II** [smelt [smelt] 或 smelled) ❶ *vt.* ①嗅;嗅到: I am sure l ~ gas. 我肯定闻到了煤气味。②察觉;查察: ~ trouble 察觉有麻烦 ③发出…的气味: You ~ wine. 你身上全是酒气味。❷ *vi.* ①有嗅觉;嗅(at): Can (或 Does) a bee ~? 蜜蜂有嗅觉吗? / ~ at (或[主美] of) a bottle 对着瓶子嗅一嗅 ②散发气味;有…的气味(of): The flowers ~ sweet. 花朵散发芳香。/ This dish ~s of garlic. 这菜有大蒜味。/ His accounts seemed to me to ~ of truth. 他的叙述据我看来有点真实性。③发出臭气;令人作呕: This decaying fish ~s. 腐烂的鱼散发臭气。 ‖~ **about** (或 **round**) 到处嗅寻; [喻]到处寻找; 到处打听 / ~ **out** ①嗅出,凭嗅觉发现(猎物) ②[喻]查出;察觉: ~ out a secret 察觉秘密 / ~ **up** 使充满臭气;使臭气熏天 ‖~**er** *n.* ①嗅的人(或动物);用嗅觉测定食品质量的人 ②发出臭气的东西 ③触须;触角 ④[俚]鼻子 ‖'~**less** *a.* 无气味的人 ‖'~**-feast** *n.* ①逢人家请客便跑去大吃的人 ②食客 / ~**ing bottle** 嗅盐瓶(装有鼻盐,供嗅闻用) / ~**ing salts** 鼻盐,嗅盐,碳酸铵(常混有香料,治疗昏厥等用)

smelt[1] [smelt] smell 的过去式和过去分词

smelt[2] [smelt] ([复] smelt(s)) *n.* 【动】胡瓜鱼属的鱼;胡瓜鱼

smelt[3] [smelt] *vt.* 熔炼;精炼 ‖~**er** *n.* ①熔铸工,冶炼者 ②熔炉;冶炼厂;冶金厂

smile [smail] **I** ❶ *vi.* ①微笑: What are you *smiling* at? 你在笑什么? / ~ to see the children's frolics 看到孩子们嬉闹而笑了 ②冷笑,讥笑(at): She ~d at his threats. 她对于他的威胁一笑置之。③[诗](天地,景色等)开颜,呈喜色 ❷ *vt.* ①以微笑表示: ~ a forced smile 强作笑容 / She ~s her consent. 她笑着表示同意。②微笑着使…: ~ sb. into good humour 笑得某人高兴起来 / ~ sb. out of his misgivings 笑着使某人不再疑惧 / ~ away sb.'s embarrassment 以微笑解除某人的窘态 **II** *n.* 微笑, 笑容; 喜色: He was all ~s. 他满脸笑容。/ a bitter ~ 苦笑 ‖**come up smiling** 重振精神,迎接新的战斗 / **crack a** ~ 展颜微笑 / ~ **on** (或 **upon**) 对…赞许, 对…加以青睐; (运气等)向…开颜, 厚待… ‖~**less** *a.* 不笑的;严肃的

smiling ['smailiŋ] *a.* 微笑的;(风景等)明媚的,喜气洋洋的 ‖~**ly** *ad.*

smirch [smə:tʃ] **I** *vt.* ①弄脏 ②玷污(名誉) **II** *n.* 污迹;污点

smirk [smə:k] *vi. & n.* 傻笑;假笑

smite [smait] **I** (过去式 smote [smout] 或 [古]

smit [smit], 过去分词 smitten ['smitn] 或 smote 或[古] smit) ❶ *vt.* ①重击, 打: ~ sb. on the head 猛击某人头部 / ~ sb. dead 打死某人 / ~ cymbals together 击钹 ②击败; 毁灭; 惩罚; 杀死 ③(疾病等)侵袭; 袭击: be *smitten with* palsy on one side 患半身不遂病 / A strong smell *smote* our nostrils. 强烈的气味刺激着我们的鼻孔。④使极度不安,折磨;使神魂颠倒: be *smitten with* remorse 受悔恨的折磨 / be *smitten with* a desire to do sth. 极想做某事 ❷ *vi.* 重击,打: ~ on the door 砰砰地敲门 / The sound ~s upon the ear. 声音震耳。**II** *n.* [口]①重击,打 ②尝试 ‖~**r** *n.* 打击者

smith [smiθ] *n.* ①铁匠;锻工 ②[用以构成复合词]…的制造者: a gold~ 金匠 / a tune~ 作曲者

smithy ['smiði] *n.* ①铁匠工场;锻工车间 ②铁匠,锻工

smock [smɔk] **I** *n.* ①(工作时保护衣服的)罩衫,工作服; (儿童的)罩衣 ②[古]女式衬衣 **II** *vt.* ①给…穿上罩衫(或工作服) ②用正面刺绣针迹装饰 ‖~ **frock** (欧洲等地农民干活时穿的)罩衫

smoke [smouk] **I** *n.* ①烟;烟尘;烟柱: a cloud of ~ 一团烟 / The ~ is curling upward. 烟缕绕上升。②蒸气,水汽;雾 ③明显的证据,确证 ④无实体的东西;无意义的东西;昙花一现的东西 ⑤模糊视线的东西 ⑥抽烟;雪茄烟;香烟;[美俚]内含大麻毒品的香烟: Have a ~. 请抽烟。/ pass the ~s round 分发香烟 ⑦淡蓝色; 烟色 ⑧速度 ⑨[美](贬)黑人 ⑩[美]劣质酒 ⑪[美俚]铁路上的救火员 **II** ❶ *vi.* ①冒烟; 冒蒸气: That oil lamp ~s badly. 那油灯冒烟很厉害。/ *smoking* porridge 冒热气的粥 ②烟似地升起; (雾等)弥漫 ③抽烟; (烟斗、雪茄等)抽起来: Do you ~? 你抽烟吗? / The pipe ~s well. 这烟斗很好抽。④飞速行进,一溜烟地行进 ⑤[古]受罚;冒汗 ⑥[美俚]气得七窍生烟 ❷ *vt.* ①熏脏,熏黑;把…煮得带烟味;用烟熏,熏制(鱼、肉);用烟熏法驱(虫等): a sheet of ~d glass (用以观察太阳等用的)一块烟玻璃 / The porridge is ~d. 粥煮得带烟味了。/ ~ the plants in the greenhouse 用烟熏温室中的植物(以杀虫) / ~d ham 熏火腿 / ~ out mosquitoes 用烟熏出蚊子 ②抽(烟): ~ a cigarette (pipe) 抽香烟(烟斗) ③[~ oneself]抽烟抽得…: ~ oneself ill 抽烟抽得生病 ④[古]察觉,怀疑 ⑤[古]嘲笑,愚弄 ‖**end (up) in** ~ 一无结果,到头来一场空 / **from (the)** ~ **into (the) smother** 越来越糟,避坑落井 / **go up in** ~ ①被烧光 ②化为乌有 / **like** ~ [俚]一溜烟地; 顺当地,容易地 / **Put that in your pipe and** ~ **it.** 见 pipe / ~ **like a chimney** 烟瘾极大 / ~ **out** ①用烟熏出 ②查出 使…公诸于世 / **the big** ~ [俚]雾都(指伦敦);任何烟雾弥漫的大城市 / **There is no** ~ **without fire.** [谚]无风不起浪。/ **watch my** ~ [美俚]看我做得多快;看看我的本领 ‖~ **ball** ①烟幕弹; 发烟弹 ②(垒球等运动中)速度极快的飞

球 / ~ **bell** (煤油灯等的)烟罩 / ~ **black** 烟炱 / ~ **bomb** 烟幕弹, 发烟炸弹 / '~**box** *n.* (汽锅的)烟箱 / '~,**chaser** *n.* 森林灭火员 / ~ **consumer** 完全燃烧装置 / '~-**dried** *a.* (火腿、鱼等)烟熏的 / '~-**filled room** (旅馆中)政客们进行密商的小房间 / ~ **helmet** (救火时用的)防毒面具 / '~**house** *n.* 鱼肉熏制厂 / '~-**in** *n.* (资本主义社会的一种颓废现象) 集体吸服麻醉品; 吸服麻醉品的集会 / '~**jack** *n.* (借烟囱内气体上升之力, 推动铁签旋转的)烤鱼肉装置 / ~ **jumper** 空降森林灭火员 / '~-**oh** *n.* =smoko / '~**proof** *a.* 不透烟的,防烟的 / ~ **room** [主英] (旅馆、俱乐部等的)吸烟室 (=smoking room) / ~ **screen** 烟幕: put up a ~ *screen* 放烟幕 / **shell** 发烟炮弹 / '~**stack** *n.* (轮船、火车、工厂的)大烟囱 / '~**stone** *n.* 【矿】烟晶 / ~ **tree** 【植】黄栌属植物 / ~ **wag(g)on** [美俚] ① 手枪 ② 火车

smokeless ['sməuklis] *a.* 无烟的: ~ powder 无烟火药 / a ~ furnace 无烟炉 ‖~**ly** *ad.*

smoker ['smoukə] *n.* ① 吸烟者; 熏制(肉类等)者: a heavy ~ 烟瘾大的人 ② 冒烟的东西; 施放烟幕的船只(或飞机) ③ (火车上的)吸烟车厢 ④ 男子非正式的社交集会 ⑤ [美俚] 蒸汽火车头

smooth [smu:ð] **I** *a.* ① 平滑的, 光滑的; 平坦的: ~ paper 光滑的纸张 / a broad ~ highway 一条宽阔平坦的公路 / ~ to the touch 摸起来平滑的 / make things ~ for sb. 为某人排除困难 ② 平静的; 平稳的: in ~ water 在风平浪静的水面上 / [喻] (进过难关之后)处于顺境中 / a ~ flight 平稳的飞行 / The car came to a ~ stop. 汽车平稳地停住了。③ (文章、文体等)流畅的; (诗歌等)节奏和谐悦耳的 ④ (性情等)平和的; 和蔼的 ⑤ 圆滑的, 迎合讨好的; 油腔滑调的: ~ words 圆滑讨好的话 ⑥ (液体、浆糊等)调匀的; (酒)温和的: a ~ cocktail 温和的鸡尾酒 ⑦ 无毛的; 无胡须的: a ~ cheek 光洁、没有胡须的脸 ⑧ [美俚]绝妙的, 刮刮叫的; 吸引人的, 有趣的: a ~ dancer 刮刮叫的舞蹈演员 / have a ~ time 过得好快活 ⑨ 【语】不送气的 **II** ❶ *vt.* ① 使光滑, 使平滑; 把…弄平; 烫平: ~ the soil in a flower bed 整平花圃的泥土 / ~ the way for a treaty 为订立条约铺平道路 / ~ out a handker-chief 把一块手绢弄平 / ~ down one's hair 捋平头发 / ~ a rumpled bedsheet 烫平弄皱的被单 ② 使(文体、举止等)优雅; 使(脸部表情)平和下来 ③ 使(余年等)安乐 ④ 消除(障碍、困难、分歧等) (out, over, down, away) ⑤ 掩饰(过失等)(over) ❷ *vi.* ① 变光滑; 变平滑 ② 变平静, 变缓和(down): The sea gradually ~ed down. 海面逐渐平静下来。/ Affairs (或 Things) are ~ing down. 事态正在缓和下来。**III** *n.* ① 一段平地; 草坪 ② 一湾静水(或东西)的平滑部分; (事物的)顺意方面 ③ 光亮; 摸平: give one's hair a ~ 将一捋头发 ④ 修光(或磨平)的工具(如刨等) **IV** *ad.* =~ly: Things are running ~. 事情正在顺利进展。‖**a ~ article** 圆滑的人, 八面玲珑的人 / ~

things 见 thing[1] / *Smooth water runs deep.* 见 water / *take the rough with the ~* 见 rough ‖~**ly** *ad.* ① 光滑地, 平滑地 ② 平稳地 ③ 圆滑地 ④ 流畅地 ~**ness** *n.* ‖'~**bore** *n.* 滑膛枪 *a.* 滑膛的 / '~-**faced** *a.* ① 脸光光的, 没胡须的 ② (布匹等)面光滑的 ③ 假装和颜悦色的; 奉承讨好的 / ~**ing iron** 熨斗, 烙铁 / ~**ing plane** (木工用的)细刨 / '~-,**shaven** *a.* 脸刮得光光的 / '~-,**spoken** *a.* ① 言词流利的, 娓娓动听的 ② 用花言巧语讨好的 / '~-**tongued** *a.* 油嘴滑舌的, 用花言巧语讨好的

smother ['smʌðə] **I** ❶ *vt.* ① 使窒息, 使透不过气来; 把…闷死: be ~ed by thick smoke 被浓烟闷得透不过气来 / a child with kisses 吻得孩子透不过气 ② (用灰、黄砂等)闷熄; 闷住(火) ③ 忍住, 抑制(感情等); 把…掩盖起来: ~ a yawn 忍住呵欠 / ~ one's anger 抑制怒气 / ~ up a scandal 掩盖丑事 ④ 覆盖: be ~ed with (或 in) dust by passing cars 被汽车驶过时扬起的尘土所笼罩 / ~ a salad with oil 用油浇满色拉 ⑤ 扼杀(议案等); 一举消灭(敌军等) ⑥ 用文火煨 ❷ *vi.* ① 窒息; 闷死 ② [方]用文火闷烧 ③ 被闷住, 被抑制 **II** *n.* ① 浓烟; 浓雾; 令人窒息的一阵雪(或蒸气等) ② 窒息状态; 被抑制状态 ③ 杂乱的一大堆东西; 杂乱无章 ‖~**ed mate** (国际象棋中)用车马逼死对方的王的一着

smoulder ['smouldə] **I** *vi.* ① 用文火闷烧, 熏烧 ② (愤怒等)闷在心里, 郁积: Hatred ~ed in his heart. 他满腔愤恨。/ ~**ing** discontent 郁积着的不满 ③ 流露难以抑制的愤怒(或仇恨、妒忌): His eyes ~ed. 他的眼睛冒着怒火。**II** *n.* 闷烧; 闷火: The ~ became a blaze. 闷火变为烈焰。

smudge [smʌdʒ] **I** *n.* ① 污点; 污迹 ② 模糊不清的一堆 ③ 浓烟; (为驱虫或使作物免受霜冻而设在上风处的)产生滚滚浓烟的火堆 **II** ❶ *vt.* ① 弄脏; 涂污; 玷污 ② 涂去; 使模糊 ③ 用浓烟熏; 使(火)生出滚滚浓烟 ❷ *vi.* ① (墨水、油漆等)形成污迹 ② 被弄脏

smug [smʌg] **I** *a.* ① 整洁的; 体面的 ② 自满的; 沾沾自喜的: ~ calculations 如意算盘 **II** *n.* ① 自命不凡的人, 沾沾自喜的人 ② [英][学俚]不爱交际和体育活动的学生 ‖~**ly** *ad.* / ~**ness** *n.*

smuggle ['smʌgl] ❶ *vt.* ① 私运: ~ goods into (out of) a country 向(自)一国走私 ② 偷带: ~ a letter into a prison 把一封信偷偷地带进监狱 ❷ *vi.* 走私 ‖~**r** *n.* ① 走私者 ② 走私船 / **smuggling** *n.* 走私

smut [smʌt] **I** *n.* ① 煤炱, 黑烟灰片; 煤尘 ② 污点; 污迹 ③ 淫词秽语; 淫秽的东西 ④ 【植】黑穗病; 黑粉病 ⑤ (含大量泥质的)劣质软煤 **II** (smut-ted; smutting) ❶ *vt.* ① (用煤炱等)弄脏; 玷污 ② 使(农作物)患黑穗病 ❷ *vi.* 患黑穗病 ‖**brother** ~ [俚]你(狎昵的称呼) / *Ditto, brother* ~! 你也一样! (一种反击语, 指对方讲的话也同样是粗鄙的) ‖~ **ball** [微]马勃菌科的菌 / ~ **mill** (清除患黑穗病谷粒的)清谷机

smutty ['smʌti] *a.* ①给煤炱弄黑的 ②患黑穗病的 ③猥亵的 ‖**smuttily** *ad.* / **smuttiness** *n.*

Sn【化】元素锡 (tin) 的符号，由拉丁名 stannum 而来

snack [snæk] **I** *n.* ①小吃，快餐 ②一份 **II** *vi.* 小吃，吃快餐 ‖**go ~s** [口]均分，摊派 / *Snacks!* 均分吧! ‖**~ bar, ~ counter** 快餐柜，快餐部; 小吃店 / **~ table** 供单人用的小餐桌

snag [snæg] **I** *n.* ①残干；残根，根株；(妨碍航行的)水中隐树; 暗礁 ②断牙; 暴牙; 歪斜不齐的牙齿 ③(被根株等拉坏的)裂口 ④[喻]意外障碍; 隐伏的困难: strike (或 hit) a ~ 遇到意外困难 / run into ~s 碰钉子 **II** (snagged; snagging) *vt.* ①乱截(树枝等)使留下锯齿状的根株 ②绊住,阻碍;使(船)触礁: one's trousers on the barbed wire fence 被铁丝网钩住裤子 ③清除(水道等处)的根株 (或其他障碍物) ④迅速抓住 (或抢到): ~ a football pass from the opponent (足球运动中)截获对方传递中的球 ‖**snagged** *a.* ①=snaggy ②被根株钩住的; 被路树损坏的 / **snaggy** ['snægi] *a.* 多根株的;多隐树的

snail [sneil] **I** *n.* ①蜗牛: the doctrine of trailing behind at a ~'s pace 爬行主义 / salied ~s 咸泥螺 ②行动缓慢(或懒散)的人; 动作迟缓的动物 ③[美俚]蜗牛形肉桂面包卷 ④ = ~ wheel **II** ❶ *vt.* 清除(园圃等处)的蜗牛 ❷ *vi.* ①捉蜗牛 ②缓慢移动 ‖**~like** *a.* 象蜗牛的 ‖**~ clover, ~ trefoil**【植】苜蓿属植物;蜗牛苜蓿 / **~ fever** 血吸虫病 / **'~fish** *n.*【动】狮子鱼属的鱼 / **'~-paced,** *a.* **'~-slow** *a.* 蜗牛般慢行的,慢吞吞的 / **~ wheel** (时钟上确定敲击次数的)蜗形轮

snake [sneik] **I** *n.* ①蛇 ②冷酷阴险的人; 虚伪的人; 卑鄙的人 ③清除管道污垢用的铁丝 ④[美俚]劣质威士忌酒 ⑤[美俚]追求和欺骗少女的男子(一般指男青年),男阿飞 **II** ❶ *vi.* ①蛇般爬行; 蜿蜒前进,迂回前进: They planned a canal that would ~ around the mountains. 他们设计了一条绕山而行的渠道。②偷偷行进;偷偷溜走 ❷ *vt.* ①迂回地取(道): a train *snaking* its way along the slope 沿着山坡蜿蜒而行的一列火车 ②[美]拖,拉(木材等) ‖**a black ~** [美]长鞭子 / **a snake ~** 运猴火车 / **a ~ in sb.'s bosom** 对某人恩将仇报的人: warm (或 cherish) a ~ *in* one's *bosom* 姑息坏人; 养虎贻患 / **a ~ in the grass** 潜伏的危险; 潜伏的敌人 / **have ~s in one's boots** (或 **see ~s**) ①喝醉酒 ②患震颤性谵妄 / **raise** (或 **wake**) **~s** 引起骚动; 引起激烈的争吵 ‖**~like** *a.* 蛇形的;蛇般的 ‖**'~bird** *n.*【动】蛇鹈 / **'~bite** *n.* (毒)蛇的咬伤 / **~ charmer** (用音乐驱蛇的)玩蛇者,弄蛇人 / **'~-,charming** *n.* 玩蛇术 / **~ dance** ①(印度宗教仪式上的)蛇舞 ②蜿蜒前进的队伍 / **'~,eater** *n.*【动】①鹝②鹭鹰 / **~ eyes** [美俚](掷骰子中的)两点 / **~ fence** 蛇形栅栏 / **~ fly**【动】蛇蛉亚目的昆虫; 骆驼虫 / **~ gourd**【植】蛇瓜;蛇甜瓜 / **~ pit** ①蛇洞 ②精神病医院 ③乱七八糟的地方 /

'~root *n.* 能治蛇咬的植物 (或其根) / **'~'s=head** *n.* ①【植】白龟头花 ②【动】一种鳢 / **'~skin** *n.* 蛇皮制成的皮革 / **~weed** *n.*【植】拳参 / **'~wood** *n.*【植】① 蛇根木 ② 马钱子 (又名番木鳖)

snaky, snakey ['sneiki] *a.* ①有蛇缠住的 ②形状像蛇的;弯曲的 ③蛇性的;阴险的: ~ cunning 蛇一般的狡猾 ④多蛇的: a ~ forest 多蛇的森林

snap [snæp] **I** (snapped; snapping) ❶ *vt.* ①猛咬: The dog *snapped* his leg. 狗咬他的腿。②攫夺;争购(up): The wind *snapped* the scarf from her hand. 风吹掉了她手里的围巾。The new commemorative stamps were soon *snapped up.* 新的纪念邮票立即被购买一空。③ 突然折断;拉断: ~ off a twig 啪地一下折断树枝 / a piece of thread in two 把线绷成两段 ④使(鞭子、风帆等)发劈啪声;捻(手指)使劈啪作响;啪地关上(或打开、扣住): ~ a whip 打一个响鞭子 / ~ down the lid of a box 啪地一声关上箱盖 / ~ the top from a bottle 啪地一下打开瓶盖 / ~ the safety before putting the gun away 在把枪收起来前啪地扣住保险 ⑤ 厉声说, 急促地说(out); 怒气冲冲地顶(或打断): "Halt!" *snapped* the guard. "站住!"卫兵喝了一声。/ ~ out an order 大声发出命令 / ~ sb. a sharp reply 怒气冲冲地用话把某人顶回去 / ~ sb. short 怒气冲冲地打断某人的话 ⑥扣动(枪)的扳机; 急射, 乱射; 快速传 (球) ⑦用快照拍摄 ❷ *vi.* ①咬; 攫; 抓(at): A fish *snapped* at the bait. 鱼咬住饵了。/ ~ at a chance 抓住一个机会 ②劈啪地响;(盖子、门等)喀嗒一声关上: The fire is *snapping.* 火劈劈啪啪地响。/ The lock *snapped* shut. 锁喀嗒一声锁上了。/ The door *snapped* to. 门啪地一声关上了。/ The soldiers *snapped* to attention. 士兵喀嚓一声立正。③啪地一声折断; 绷断;(神经、抵抗等)突然坍垮: A branch *snapped* off the tree in the wind. 在大风中一条树枝啪地从树上断落。/ If a bow string is too taut, it will ~. 弓弦张得太紧就会绷断。④厉声说, 急促地说(at); (眼睛因愤怒而)闪烁: eyes *snapping* with fury 闪烁着怒火的眼睛 **II** *n.* ①猛咬; 猛扑; 攫夺; 攫取: the ~ of the scissors cut the string. 喀嚓一声,剪刀把绳子剪断了。②突然折断; 绷断 ③劈啪声; 厉声的申斥; 粗声暴气: the ~ of a twig 树枝的折断声 / a ~ of the fingers 一捻手指发出的劈啪声 / shut the book with a ~ 啪地一声把书合上 ④(天气的)一阵突变(尤指转寒): a cold ~ 寒潮 ⑤[美俚]迅速发财的机会; 有利可图的差使; 容易的工作(或问题等);易驾驭的人: The course was a ~ for him. 这课程对他来说太容易了。/ a soft ~ 轻松容易的工作 ⑥快照 ⑦快速传球 ⑧精力, 活力, 生气: a young man with plenty of ~ 精力充沛的小伙子 ⑨少量, 一点儿; 一小块: care not a ~ for sb.'s advice 对某人的劝告一点也不在意 ⑩小脆饼: ginger ~s 姜脆饼 ⑪揿钮, 按扣, 扣

扣;【无】揿钮接头: the ~s on a suitcase 衣箱上的扣襻 ⑫[戏]演员的临时雇用 **Ⅲ** *a.* ①突然的; 仓卒的: take a ~ vote 举行突然的表决 ②可咯嗒一声扣住的; 装扣子的 ③[美]极简单容易的: a ~ course 极容易的课程 **Ⅳ** *ad.* 啪地一声; 猛然: *Snap* went the oar. 桨啪地一声断了。 ‖*in a* ~ 立刻, 马上 / ~ *back* 很快恢复过来 / ~ *into it* [美俚]迅速地干起来; 打起精神干 / ~ *it up* [美俚]赶快 / ~ *out of it* [美俚]突然改变情绪(或习惯等);改变精神状态; 振作起来 / ~ *sb. up* 突然打断某人的话 ‖'~**back** *n.* ①(橄榄球运动中的)快速传球 ②很快的恢复 / ~ **bolt** 【建】自动门闩 / '~,**dragon** *n.* 【植】金鱼草属植物; 金鱼草 / ~ **fastener** 揿钮, 按扣 / ~ **hook**, ~ **link** (索、链等的)弹簧扣 / ~ **lock** 弹簧锁 / '~**-on** *a.* ①可咯嗒一声盖住的 ②(衣领等)可用揿钮缀上或取下的 / ~ **roll** [空](飞行特技的)快滚 / '~**shoot** *vt.* 快镜拍摄 / ~ **shot** 急射, 乱射 / '~**shot** *n.* 快照: take a ~*shot* of sb. 给某人拍张快照 *vt.* 快镜拍摄 (=~shoot)

snappy ['snæpi] *a.* ①(=snappish ②)做得飞快的; 敏捷的, 活泼的; 生动的: Make it ~! [口]直截了当地干! 干脆一点! / a short ~ article 一篇短小精悍的文章 ③(天气)冷但令人感到爽快的 ④时髦的; 漂亮的 ⑤发出劈啪声的 ‖**snappily** *ad.* / **snappiness** *n.*

snare [snɛə] **Ⅰ** *n.* ①圈套; 罗网; 陷阱: fall into a ~ 落入圈套 / lay a ~ 设罗网 ②[医]勒除器 (勒除肿瘤等用的金属丝圈) ③[复]绷在小鼓下方鼓面上的肠线, 响弦 **Ⅱ** *vt.* ①(用罗网等)诱捕 ②(用计谋)诱获; 陷害 ‖~**r** ['snɛərə] *n.* 设陷阱者; 设圈套者 ‖~ **drum** 下方鼓面上绷有响弦的小鼓

snarl[1] [snɑːl] **Ⅰ** *n.* ①缠结; 纠结 ②混乱; 无秩序; 错杂: the traffic ~s in a big city 大城市里的交通混乱状态 ③乱糟糟的一群 **Ⅱ** ❶ *vt.* ①使(线、发等)缠结 ②搞乱, 使错杂; 使(自己)处于乱糟糟的困难境地: ~ a once simple problem 把一个原来很简单的问题弄得复杂得很 ③在(金属层等)上敲出浮凸花纹 ❷ *vi.* 缠结

snarl[2] [snɑːl] **Ⅰ** ❶ *vi.* ①(狗等)吠, 嗥 ②(人)咆哮; 被粗暴地表达出来: His anger ~s forth in hot words. 他的怒气被愤怒的言词表达了出来。 ❷ *vt.* ①咆哮着说; 粗暴地表示 ②咆哮得使…: ~ oneself hoarse 咆哮得把嗓子都叫哑了 **Ⅱ** *n.* 吠, 嗥, 猖哮; 咆哮: answer with a ~ 咆哮着回答 ‖~**er** *n.* ①狂吠的动物 ②咆哮者

snatch [snætʃ] **Ⅰ** ❶ *vt.* ①攫取; 抓住; 夺得: He ~ed the letter *from* me. 他从我手里抢走了信。 / The wind ~ed his cap *off*. 风把他的帽子吹掉了。 / a victory out of defeat 转败为胜 / a few hours' rest 趁空休息几小时 / be ~ed *from* the jaws of death 侥幸得救 / be ~ed *away* by premature death 突然夭折 ②[美俚]拐走, 绑架 ❷ *vi.* 攫取; 抓取(*at*): ~ *at* a rope 抓绳 / We ~ *at* every chance to improve our work. 我们抓住一切机会改进我们的工作。

Ⅱ *n.* ①攫取; 抢夺: make a ~ *at* sth. 伸手去抓某物 ②(会话、诗歌等的)片段; 短时: overhear ~*es* of conversation 偶然听到谈话的若干片断 / work in (或 by) ~*es* 断断续续地工作 ③[美俚]拐骗, 绑架 ‖~**er** *n.* 攫夺者; 诱拐者, 绑架者 ‖~ **block** 【建】扣绳滑轮

snatchy ['snætʃi] *a.* 断断续续的; 不连贯的: a ~ conversation 断断续续的谈话 ‖**snatchily** *ad.*

sneak [sniːk] **Ⅰ** ❶ *vi.* ①偷偷摸摸地行动; 偷偷走, 潜行: ~ in (out) 偷偷地走进(走出) ②(行动)鬼鬼祟祟; (态度)卑躬屈节 ③[英][学俚](向教师)告密, 告发 ❷ *vt.* ①偷偷地做; ~ a smoke 偷偷地抽烟 / ~ a glance 偷看一眼 ②[口]偷窃 **Ⅱ** *n.* ①鬼鬼祟祟的人 ②[英][学俚](向教师)告密的学生 ③(乘人不注意时的)逃跑; 偷偷摸摸的行为 ④[常用复]帆布面橡胶底轻便运动鞋; 旅行鞋 **Ⅲ** *a.* 暗中进行的; 突如其来的: a ~ landing 偷渡登陆 / a ~ attack 突然袭击 ‖*on the* ~ 偷偷地; 秘密地 / ~ *out of* 偷偷地逃避(责任、工作等) ‖~**er** *n.* ①鬼鬼祟祟的人 ②[常用复]帆布面橡胶底轻便运动鞋; 旅行鞋 ‖~ **current** [电]潜行电流, 寄生电流 / ~ **preview** 不说明片名的新片预映(目的在于了解观众反应) / '~**-raid** *n.* 偷袭(轰炸) / ~ **thief** 顺手牵羊的小偷

sneer [sniə] **Ⅰ** ❶ *vi.* ①轻蔑地笑; 冷笑 ②嘲笑, 讥笑(*at*) ❷ *vt.* ①轻蔑地笑着说出: ~ a reply 冷笑着回答 ②嘲笑着使: ~ sb. out of countenance 嘲笑得使某人窘态毕露 / The proposal was ~*ed* down. 提议被一片嘲笑声否决。 **Ⅱ** *n.* 冷笑; 嘲笑, 讥笑 ‖~**er** ['sniərə] *n.* 嘲笑者, 讥笑者

sneering ['sniəriŋ] *a.* 嘲笑的; 讥笑的; 轻蔑的 ‖~**ly** *ad.*

sneeze [sniːz] **Ⅰ** *n.* 喷嚏(声); 打喷嚏 **Ⅱ** *vi.* 打喷嚏: Use a handkerchief when you ~. 打喷嚏时应用手帕捂住。 ‖*not to be* ~*d at* 不可轻视; 尚过得去; 值得考虑 / ~ *into a basket* 见 **basket** ‖**sneezy** *a.* 老打喷嚏的; 引起喷嚏的

sniff [snif] **Ⅰ** ❶ *vi.* ①(有声音地)以鼻吸气; 嗅 ②嗤之以鼻, 蔑视(*at*) ❷ *vt.* ①用力吸; 嗅, 闻 ②嗅出, 觉察出: ~ (out) danger 觉察有危险 **Ⅱ** *n.* ①吸气(声); 嗅: Take a ~ at everything and distinguish the good from the bad. 对于任何东西都要用鼻子嗅一嗅, 鉴别其好坏。 ②嗤之以鼻 ③从鼻子吸入的东西

sniffle ['snifl] **Ⅰ** *vi.* ①(一再)抽鼻子, 发声地吸气 ②抽着鼻子说话 **Ⅱ** *n.* 抽鼻子(声) ‖*the* ~*s* [口] ①感冒 ②抽噎

snip [snip] **Ⅰ** (snipped; snipping) ❶ *vt.* 剪; 剪断, 剪去: ~ cloth 剪布 / ~ a hole 剪一个洞 / ~ *off* the ends 剪去末端 ❷ *vi.* 剪 **Ⅱ** *n.* ①(一)剪; 剪净 ②剪下的小片; 片段 ③[复](剪金属薄片的)平头剪; 铁丝剪 ④傲慢无礼的人; 孟浪的女子 ⑤[英俚]一定会成功的事; 不吃亏的买卖 ⑥[俚]裁缝 ⑦[口]年轻人; 不足道的人

snipe [snaip] **Ⅰ** *n.* ①([复] snipe(s))【动】鹬; 沙锥鸟 ②狙击 ③可鄙的人 ④[美俚]香烟(或雪茄

烟)屁股 **II** ❶ *vt*. 狙击 ❷ *vi*. ①射鹬；猎鹬 ②狙击(*at*) ③诽谤；中伤

sniper ['snaipə] *n*. 狙击手 ‖~**scope** *n*. 红外线瞄准镜，夜装镜(狙击手夜间使用的瞄准镜，此镜利用红外线发现目标)

snippet ['snipit] *n*. ①(切下的)小片，小部分 ②[复](消息、新闻等的)片断；摘录 ③[美口]年青人；不足道的人

snivel ['snivl] **I** (snivel(l)ed; snivel(l)ing) *vi*. ①流鼻涕；抽鼻子 ②吸泣；哭诉 ③假哭；假作悲伤 **II** *n*. ①流鼻涕；抽鼻子 ②吸泣；哭诉 ③假哭；假作悲伤；假话 ④[古]鼻涕 ⑤[复][方]伤风 ‖**snivel(l)er** *n*. 假哭者；哭诉者

snob [snob] *n*. ①势利的人；谄上欺下的人 ②假内行: a musical ～ 自以为懂得音乐的人 ③[英方]鞋匠 ‖～ **appeal** 商品对势利顾客的吸引力(如高档、罕见、外国产)

snobbery ['snobəri] *n*. ①势利；谄上欺下 ②[复]势利行为；势利话

snobbish ['snobiʃ] *a*. 势利的；谄上欺下的 ‖～**ly** *ad*. / ～**ness** *n*.

snoop [snu:p] **I** *vi*. 探听；窥探 **II** *n*. =snooper

snooper ['snu:pə] *n*. 探听者；窥探者；管闲事者 ‖~**scope** *n*. (利用红外线原理的)夜望镜

snooze [snu:z] **I** ❶ *vi*. 打瞌睡；睡午觉，(白天)小睡 ❷ *vt*. 懒散地消磨(时间)(*away*) **II** *n*. 瞌睡；(白天的)小睡

snore [snɔ:] **I** ❶ *vi*. 打鼾 ❷ *vt*. 打着鼾度过(时间)(*away*) **II** *n*. 打鼾；鼾声 ‖～**r** ['snɔ:rə] *n*. 打鼾者

snort [snɔ:t] **I** ❶ *vi*. ①喷鼻息；鼓鼻 ②发哼声(表示轻蔑、愤怒、惊讶或不信): ～ with rage at sb. (sth.) 气愤地对某人(某事)发哼声 ③(蒸汽机等)发喷汽声: The train ～ed and stopped. 火车喷着汽停下来了。④[口]高声大笑 ❷ *vt*. ①哼着鼻子说(或表示) ②(喷鼻息般地)喷出 ③吸入(粉末状的麻醉毒品) **II** *n*. ①喷鼻息；鼻息声；喷汽声 ②[英]潜水艇的通气管 ③一口酒 ‖～**er** *n*. ①鼻息粗的人(或动物)；表示轻蔑(或愤怒等)的人 ②[口]不寻常的人(或事物)；令人咋舌的人(或事物): a real ～er at chess 下棋妙手 ③大风

snout [snaut] *n*. ①(动物的)口鼻部；猪嘴 ②[贬](人的)大鼻子 ③猪嘴状物；喷嘴；船首 ‖～**ed** *a*. [常用以构成复合词]有…鼻子的: long-～ed 长鼻的 ‖～ **beetle** 【动】象鼻虫

snow [snou] **I** *n*. ①雪；[复]积雪(地带): a heavy fall of ～ 一场大雪 / the high ～s 高原积雪(带) ②雪般的东西(尤指雪白的东西): the ～s of seventy years 七十高龄的苍苍白发 ③白布丁；[俚]可卡因 ④(电视、雷达屏幕图象上出现的)雪花形干扰，雪花效应 **II** ❶ *vi*. 下雪；雪一般地落下来: It ～ed two feet deep. 雪下了二呎深。/ Congratulations ～ed in. 贺电雪片似地飞来。❷ *vt*. ①使雪一般地落下来: After the rain the peach blossoms ～ed their petals. 雨

后桃花雪片般地落下了花瓣。②用雪覆盖；用雪困住 ③使象雪一样白: hair ～ed by age 苍苍白发 ④[美俚]花言巧语地蒙骗，使相信 ‖be ～ed **in** (或 **up**) 被雪封住，被雪困住 ‖[美俚]被毒品麻醉；被花言巧语蒙骗住 / ～ **under** ① 把…埋在雪里 ②[喻]压倒；以绝对优势票数击败: be ～ed under with work 工作忙不过来 / be ～ed under in the election 在选举中被彻底击败 ‖～**less** *a*. 无雪的 ‖～**ball** *n*. ①雪球 ②滚雪球式扩大(或增长)的事物 ③滚雪球式的募捐法 ④苹果馅的米布丁 ⑤荚蒾属植物 *vi*. ①扔雪球(*at*)，打雪仗 ②滚雪球以地增长(或扩大) *vt*. ①向…扔雪球 ②使滚雪球以地增长(或扩大): ～ball one's political influence 不断迅速扩大自己的政治影响 / ～**ball bush** 荚蒾属植物 / ～**bank** *n*. 雪堆，雪堤 / ～ **banner** 雪旗(从山顶向空中吹散成旗帜形的雪) / ～**bird** *n*. 【动】雪鹀 ②[美俚]有可卡因瘾者 ③[美俚]冬季到南方来打短工的流动工人 / ～**-blind** *a*. 雪盲的 / ～ **blindness** 雪盲(症) / ～**blink** *n*. 【气】雪照云光 / ～ **blower** [美]吹雪机，螺桨式除雪机 / ～**bound** *a*. 被雪困住(或封住)的 / ～**-broth** *n*. ①雪水；新融化的雪 ②冰镇酒类 / ～**cap** *n*. ①(山上的)雪顶 ②(产于中美洲，头部白色的)一种蜂鸟 / ～**-capped** *a*. 顶部被覆盖住的: ～capped mountains 山顶积雪的群山 / ～**-,covered** *a*. 被雪覆盖的 / ～ **devil** 被风扬起的雪尘柱 / ～**drift** *n*. ①(被风吹成的)雪堆；吹雪 ②【植】香雪球 / ～**drop** *n*. ①雪花莲属一种植物 ②[美俚]宪兵 / ～**fall** *n*. 下雪；雪量 / ～ **fence** 防雪栅栏 / ～**field** *n*. 雪原；雪野 / ～**flake** *n*. ①雪花 ②【植】雪片莲 / ～ **ga(u)ge** 量雪器 / ～ **goggles** (登山者防止雪盲的)墨片眼镜 / ～ **goose** 【动】雪雁 / ～ **grouse** 【动】雷鸟属鸟 / ～ **ice** 雪冰 / ～**-in-'summer** *n*. [俚]绒毛卷耳 / ～ **job** [俚](对新结识者、上司、顾主等)天花乱坠的自吹 / ～ **leopard**, ～ **panther** 【动】雪豹 / ～ **line** 雪线 / ～**man** *n*. ①雪堆成的人 ②[S-] 雪人(传说生存在喜马拉雅山上的一种动物，据信是熊；=Abominable Snowman) / ～**mobile** ['snəuməbi:l] *n*. 履带式雪上汽车 *vi*. 乘雪上汽车旅行 / ～**-on-the-'mountain** *n*. 【植】银边翠 / ～**pack** *n*. 积雪场(以融雪的水供灌溉或发电用) / ～ **plant** 【植】赤雪藻 / ～**-'plough**, ～**'plow** *n*. 雪梨，犁雪机，扫雪机 / ～ **plume** (由山顶等处吹下来的)雪缕 / ～**shoe** *n*. 雪鞋 *vi*. 穿着雪鞋走 / ～**-,shovel** *n*. 雪铲 / ～**slide**, ～**slip** *n*. 雪崩 / ～**storm** *n*. ①雪暴，暴风雪 ②[美俚]掼奶油 / ～**suit** *n*. 儿童风雪大衣 / ～ **sweeper** 扫雪机 / ～ **tire** [美](用特殊车胎花纹防滑的)雪地用汽车轮胎 / ～ **train** 开往冬季运动胜地的特别列车 / ～**-'white** *a*. 雪白的

snub [snʌb] **I** (snubbed; snubbing) *vt*. ①以斥责制止 ②冷落；怠慢；冷冰冰地拒绝 ③ 挽桩滞(缆等)；挽桩滞缆而刹住(船等)；止住: ～ a vibration

止住振动 ④压熄: ~ out a cigarette 压熄香烟
II *n.* 斥责; 冷落; 怠慢 **III** *a.* ①(缆索等)用来勒
住的 ②(鼻子)扁的: a ~ nose 狮子鼻 ‖**snubbing post** 系船柱; 滞缆桩 / '**~-nosed** *a.* 塌鼻
的, 狮子鼻的

snuff[1] [snʌf] **I** *n.* ①烛花, 灯花 ②[苏格兰]发怒
II ❶ *vt.* ①剪(烛)花: ~ a candle with a pistol
开枪打掉烛花而不使蜡烛熄灭 ②掐灭(蜡烛); 扼
杀, 消灭, 扑灭(叛乱、希望 等) (out) **❷** *vi.*
[俚]死去 (out) ‖**go off like the ~ of a candle**
突然死掉 / **~ it** [美俚]死

snuff[2] [snʌf] **I ❶** *vt.* ①用鼻子使劲吸: ~ the
fragrance of the clover 使劲闻三叶草的香味儿
②嗅出, 闻出(危险等) ③(动物)嗅, 闻: The dog
~ed him all over. 那狗把他全身嗅了一遍.
❷ *vi.* 抽鼻子; 嗅, 闻 (at) **II** *n.* ①以鼻吸气; 以鼻
吸气声; 闻, 嗅 ②气息; 气味 ③鼻烟; 【医】鼻吸
药, 鼻粉: take a pinch of ~ 吸一撮鼻烟 ④(鼻
烟的)一撮 ‖**give sb. ~** 严厉对待某人, 惩罚某
人 / **up to ~** [俚]①正常的; 符合标准的 ②精
明的, 机警的; 不易受骗的 ‖'**~-box** *n.* 鼻烟盒
②[俚]鼻子 / '**~-,colo(u)red** *a.* 鼻烟色的, 黄褐
色的 / **~ mill** ①[苏格兰]鼻烟盒 ②碾鼻烟器 /
'**~-,taker** *n.* 吸鼻烟者 / '**~-,taking** *n.* 吸鼻烟

snuffle ['snʌfl] **I ❶** *vi.* ①抽鼻子; 急促有声地
呼吸(如鼻子半塞时); 嗅, 闻 (at) ②用鼻音讲话
③[罕]用悲哀而伪善的声调讲话 **❷** *vt.* ①用鼻
音讲(out) ②抽着鼻子嗅; 嗅着去找 **II** *n.* ①抽
鼻子; 鼻塞声 ②鼻音 ③[罕]悲哀而伪善的话
④[the ~s] 鼻塞, 伤风 ‖**~r** *n.* ①抽鼻子者
②用悲哀而伪善的声调讲话者; snuffler

snug [snʌg] **I** (snugger, snuggest) *a.* ①不受风寒
侵袭的; 舒适的; 温暖的: sit in a ~ little parlour
坐在舒适温暖的小客厅里 ②小而安排适当的; 整
洁的: a ~ shop 整洁小巧的商店 ③ (收入等)尚
可的 ④(服装等)紧贴合身的 ⑤(船只)适于航海
的, 建造与保养良好的 ⑥隐藏的: The boy kept
~ behind the door. 那男孩躲在门后. **II**
(snugged; snugging) **❶** *vi.* [方]舒适地蜷伏; 偎依
❷ *vt.* ①使紧贴合身 ②使整洁; 使舒适温暖 ③隐
藏; 藏匿 ④[海]为(船)作好防备暴风来袭的准备
(down) **III** *ad.* =snugly **IV** *n.* [英]酒店中的私室
‖**as ~ as a bug in a rug** 非常舒适 ‖**~ness** *n.*

snuggle ['snʌgl] **❶** *vi.* 舒适地蜷伏; 偎依: The
child ~d up to its mother. 那孩子偎着母亲. /
~ down in bed 舒适地蜷伏在床上 **❷** *vt.* ①紧抱,
偎 ②使舒适温暖

so [sou; 弱 so, sə] **I** *ad.* ①[表示方式、方法、情况
等]这样, 那样: Hold your hoe ~. 把你的锄头
这样拿着. / Plough just ~. 就这样犁. / Is
that ~? 是那样的吗?
②[表示程度]这么, 那么, 如此地: ~ important
an event 这么重要的一件事 / He did not
notice us, ~ absorbed he was (或 was he) in his
work. 他那么专心于工作, 所以没有注意到我们.
③[代替上文中的形容词、名词或动词]同样, 也;
对, 不错: A: It's warmer today. B: So it is.

甲: 今天暖一些了. 乙: 是的. / You say he works
hard; ~ he does, and ~ do you. 你说他很努力,
对, 他确实很努力, 你也一样.
④[口]非常, 极, 很: It's ~ good of you! 你真
好!(或: 多谢你!) / I'm ~ glad that you've come!
你来了, 我真太高兴了! / We ~ want to see the
performance again. 我们真想再看一次这场表
演. / The article is wonderful; I like it ~.
这篇文章好极了, 我非常喜欢.
⑤因而, 所以: The witness is unbiased and ~
reliable. 那个证人没有偏见, 所以是可靠的.
⑥[口]的确, 确实: I did ~ tell the truth. 我的
确说了真话.
II *conj.* ①因而, 所以, 结果是: It was late, ~
we went home. 天晚了, 所以我们就回家去了. /
Everybody lent a hand, ~ the sowing was done
in time. 人人动手, 结果播种及时完成.
②为的是, 以便, 使得 (=~ that): Speak clearly,
~ they may understand you. 说得清楚些, 使
他们听懂你的意思.
③那么, 这样看来: So you fully agree. 那么, 你
完全同意了. / So here we are at last. 好了, 我
们终于到了. / So there you are! 喏, 情况就是
这样!
④[古]只要 (=provided that): So (that) it is
done, it matters not by whom. 只要做得好, 谁
做都行.
III *pron.* ①[用作 expect, hope, say 一类动词的
宾语]这样, 如此: I expect ~. 我看是这样. /
Well, I told you ~, didn't I? 我不正是这样对
你说的吗? / You don't say ~. 真是这样吗?
(或: 你不会是这个意思吧.)
②[用在 or 后]左右, 上下: I read only a page
or ~. 我只念了一页左右. / It will be warmer
in another month or ~. 再过一个月左右天气就
要转暖了.
IV *int.* 好; 就这样; 别动; 停住; 别吵: A little
more to the right, ~! 再靠右一点, 好了! / If
they agree, ~; if not, why, ~. 如果他们同意,
就这样; 如果不同意, 也这样.
‖**and ~ on** (或 **and ~ forth, and ~ on and
~ forth**) 等等 / **as ...,~ ...** 见 as / **ever ~**
见 ever / **How ~**? 见 how / **if ~** 见 if / **in ~
far as** 见 far / **not** (或 **without**) **~ much as**
见 much / **Quite ~**! 见 quite / **~ and ~**
only 只有这样(才): So and ~ only can it be
done. 只有这样做才行. / **~ as** 只要 / **~ as
to** ①为的是; 使得; 以便: unite the overwhelming
majority of people ~ as to isolate the handful
of enemies 团结绝大多数的人以孤立一小撮敌
人 / check the names carefully ~ as to
avoid mistakes 仔细地核对名字以免发生错误
②结果是; 以致: He struck the snake ~ as to
break its back. 他对蛇一击, 结果打断了它的背
脊. / **~ ... as to** 如此…以致: He was ~
angry *as to* be unable to speak. 他气得话都说
不出来. / Be ~ good *as to* lend us your

mower. 请把你们的割草机借给我们用一下。 / *So be it.* 就那样吧。(表示许可或听任) / ~ *far* 见 *far* / ~ *far from* 非但不…: *So far from relaxing, we redoubled our efforts.* 我们非但没有松劲,而且加倍努力。 / *So far, ~ good.* 见 *far* / *So long!* 见 **long**[1] / ~ *long as* 见 **long**[1] / ~ *many* 见 **many** / ~ *much* ~ *much* ... *that* 到这样程度以致…。 / ~ *much the* ...[后接形容词比较级]那就更…了: *If you join us,* ~ *much the better.* 要是你加入到我们中间来,那就更好了。 / ~ ~ [口]勉强过得去,一般: *He plays tennis only* ~ ~. 他网球打得不过如此。 / ~ *that* ① 为的是,目的是: *I'll give you all the facts* ~ *that you can judge for yourself.* 我把所有事实都告诉你,使你能自己作出判断。 ② 结果是,以致: *Everybody lent a hand,* ~ *that the work was finished ahead of schedule.* 人人动手,结果提前完成了任务。 ③[古]只要(表示条件) / ~ ... *that* ... 如此…以致…; 如此…使得…: *He was* ~ *excited that he could not speak.* 他兴奋得连话都说不出来了。 / *We have* ~ *arranged matters that* one of us is always on duty. 我们已作好安排使得每天总有我们中的一人在值班。 / *So that's that.* [口]就是这么一回事。(意即没什么别的可说的了) / ~ *to speak* (或 ~ *to say*) [作插入语]可以这么说; 打个譬喻说 ‖~-and-~ ['souənsou] *n.* ① 某某人, 某某事: *He told me to do* ~-*and*-~. 他叫我做某某事。 ② 讨厌的家伙,卑鄙的人; 坏蛋 *ad.* 如此这般地: *treat sb.* ~-*and*-~ 如此这般地对待某人 *a.* 可诅咒的,该死的 / '~-'called *a.* [贬]所谓的,号称的: *the* ~-*called* civilized world 所谓的"文明世界"

soak [souk] **I ❶** *vt.* ① 浸,泡,渍,使浸透: *Soak the clothes before washing.* 洗前把衣服浸湿。 / *bread* ~*ed in milk* 浸泡在牛奶中的面包 / ~*ed cartridges* 受潮的弹药 / *be* ~*ed to the skin* (或 *be* ~*ed through*) 浑身湿透 / ~ *oneself in the sunshine* 使自己沐浴在阳光里 / ~ *oneself in history* 攻读历史 / *a book* ~*ed in sentiment* 充满着感伤情调的书 ② 吸,吸收 (*in, up*): *Sponge* ~*s up water.* 海绵吸水。 / ~ *up the sunshine* 吸收阳光 / ~ *up surplus labour* 吸收多余劳动力 ③ 浸掉,浸出 (*out*): ~ *the dirt out* (*of the clothes*) 把污垢(从衣上)浸泡掉 ④[口]使(自己)喝醉 ⑤[俚]向…敲竹杠; 向…征重税 ⑥[俚]痛殴; 重罚 ⑦[俚]典当(东西) ⑧ 对(金属等)进行长时间热处理 **❷** *vi.* ① 浸泡: *Let the beans* ~ *overnight.* 让豆子浸泡过夜。 ② 渗透,印进: *The rain has* ~*ed into the ground.* 雨水已渗到土里去了。 / *Blood* ~*ed through the bandage.* 血渗透了绷带。 / *The fact* ~*ed into his head.* 那事实印进了他的头脑。 ③[口]狂饮 ④ 经受长时间热处理 **II** *n.* ① 浸泡,浸渍; 浸液 ②[俚]大雨 ③[俚]酒鬼; 狂饮闹宴 ④[俚]痛殴,猛击 ⑤[俚]典当: *in* ~ (东西)在典当中 ‖**~age** ['soukidʒ] *n.*

浸湿(性); 渗透(量) / ~*er* *n.* ①浸渍者 ②大雨 ③[俚]酒鬼 ④[复]婴儿用的尿布垫褥 ⑤[化]浸渍剂;(石油)裂化反应室 / ~*ing* *a.* 使人湿透的: *a* ~*ing* downpour 滂沱大雨 *ad.* 湿透地: ~*ing wet* 湿淋淋的 *n.* 浸,泡,渍

soap [soup] **I** *n.* ①肥皂,胰子: *a cake (bar) of* ~ 一块(条)肥皂 / *marine* ~ 海水皂, 船用肥皂 / *toilet* ~ 香皂 / *medicated* ~ 药皂 ②【化】脂肪酸盐 ③[美俚]钱(尤指贿赂) **II** *vt.* ①用肥皂擦洗; 上肥皂于: ~ *the clothes* 往衣服上擦肥皂 / ~ *oneself down* 用肥皂擦洗身子 ②[口]奉承,谄媚 ‖*no* ~ [美俚]不,不行; 不知道 / *soft* ~ ①软皂, 钾皂 ②奉承 / *wash one's hands with invisible* ~ *and imperceptible water* (由于尴尬,紧张等)搓手 ‖~*less* *a.* ①无肥皂的 ②未洗的; 肮脏的 ‖'~,**berry** *n.*【植】无患子 / '~-,**boiler** *n.* 煮皂工 / '~-,**boiling** *n.* 煮皂 / '~**box** *n.* ①肥皂盒;肥皂箱 ②(街头演说者所用的)临时演说台 *a.* 街头演说的: *a* ~*box* orator 街头演说者 / ~*box* politics 街头演说式的政治宣传 *vi.* 作街头演说 / ~ **bubble** ①肥皂泡 ②徒有其表的事物, 短暂而不实在的东西 / ~ **dish** 肥皂碟 / ~ **earth**【化】皂石 / ~ **flakes** (肥)皂片 / ~ **opera** [美口]日间无线电(或电视)节目里的连续广播剧(往往有关家事问题,因肥皂商常利用这种戏剧做广告,故名) / ~ **plant** 某部分可作肥皂用的植物 / ~ **powder** 皂粉 / '~**stone** *n.*【化】皂石 / '~-**suds** [复] *n.* 起泡沫的肥皂水; 肥皂水上的泡沫 / ~ **works** [作单或复]肥皂厂 / '~**wort** *n.*【植】皂草

soapy ['soupi] *a.* ① 涂着肥皂的 ② 含有肥皂的;肥皂般的; 多脂的; 滑腻腻的 ③[俚]满口奉承的,谄媚的;殷勤的;油滑的 ‖**soapily** *ad.* / **soapiness** *n.*

soar [sɔː] **I** *n.* ①高飞, 翱翔 ②高飞范围; 高涨程度;耸立高度 **II ❶** *vi.* ①(鹰等)高飞,翱翔;[空]滑翔 ②(思想等)向上; 昂扬,高涨: *Songs of victory* ~ *to the skies.* 凯歌直上云霄。 ③(山、建筑物等)高耸, 屹立 ④ (物价、失业人数等)猛增,剧增 **❷** *vt.* [诗]飞达,飞到 ‖~*er* ['sɔːrə] *n.* (高空)滑翔机

sob [sɔb] **I** (sobbed; sobbing) **❶** *vi.* ①啜泣,呜咽,抽噎 ②(风等)发呜咽声: *The wind* ~*s.* 风在鸣咽。 **❷** *vt.* ①哭诉, 呜咽地说 (*out*): ~ *out one's grievances* 诉苦 ②哭得使… : ~ *oneself to sleep* 哭得睡着了 **II** *n.* 啜泣(声), 呜咽(声) ‖~ **sister** [美俚] ①写伤感文章的女记者;演伤感角色的女演员 ②伤感而不实际的人 / ~ **story** [美俚]非常悲伤的故事 / ~ **stuff** [美俚]伤感的文章(或故事)

sober ['soubə] *a.* ① 清醒的,未喝醉的;饮酒有节制的;饮食有度的 ② 适度的,有节制的: *with* ~ *words* 用适度的话 ③严肃的,庄重的;认真的: *as* ~ *as a judge* 象法官一样严肃认真 / *be in* ~ *earnest* 非常严肃认真 ④不夸大的,不歪曲的;非想象的: *the* ~ *truth* 不加渲染的事实真相 / *in* ~ *fact* 完全就事实而言 ⑤有理智的, 合理的 ⑥

(衣服、色彩等)朴素的，朴实的，素静的 ⑦[古] 不慌不忙的，从容的 **II ❶ vt.** 使清醒；使严肃；使自制 **❷ vi.** 清醒起来 (*up, off*)；变严肃，变持重 (*down*): He apologized when he ~ed up. 他清醒过来后表示道歉。/ The excited spectators have ~ed down. 激动的观众们安静下来了。 **‖appeal from Philip drunk to Philip ~** 请求复审(因初审在某种影响下不够郑重，故请求再审) **‖-ly ad. ~ness n. ‖'~-'minded a.** 清醒的；严肃的 / **'~sides** [复] **n.** [用作单或复] [口]严肃庄重的人

sobriety [sou'braiəti] **n.** 清醒；节制，自制；严肃，庄重，冷静

soccer ['sɔkə] **n.** 英式足球(=association football)

sociable ['souʃəbl] **I a.** ① 好交际的；友善的，和蔼可亲的，表示友谊的 ② 增进交谊的 ③ 喜欢群居的 **II n.** ①对座四轮马车；双座三轮脚踏车；S 形双人坐椅 ②[美]社交会，联谊会，联欢会 **‖sociability** [,souʃə'biliti] **n.** / **sociably ad.**

social ['souʃəl] **I a.** ① 社会的: a ~ system 社会制度 / man's ~ being 人们的社会存在 / ~ contradictions 社会矛盾 / ~ consciousness 社会意识 / ~ practice 社会实践 / ~ investigations 社会调查 / ~ sciences 社会科学 ②社交的，交际的；喜欢交际的；有关社会福利的: ~ intercourse 社交 / a ~ gathering 社交集会 / a ~ nature 喜欢交际的性格 / ~ work 福利救济工作 ③ 一定社会阶层(或地位)的；上流社会的: a ~ climber 企图与权贵(或富人)交往者，向上爬的人 ④社会性的；【动】群居的: a ~ disease 性病；(肺病等)社会性疾病 / ~ insects 社会性昆虫，群居昆虫 **II n.** 联欢会 **‖-ly ad.** ①在社交方面；善于交际的 ②在社会地位上；在全社会中 **‖'~-'chauvinism n.** 社会沙文主义 / **'~-'chauvinist n.** 社会沙文主义者 **a.** 社会沙文主义的 / ~ **democrat** ①社会民主主义者 ② [S- D-] 社会民主党人 / **'~-'fascism n.** 社会法西斯主义 / **'~-'fascist n.** 社会法西斯主义者 **a.** 社会法西斯主义的 / **'~-im'perialism n.** 社会帝国主义 / **'~-im'perialist n.** 社会帝国主义者 **a.** 社会帝国主义的 / **'~-'minded a.** 关心社会的；热心于社会福利事业的 / ~ **secretary** 负责信件和社交约会的私人秘书 / ~ **service** 社会公益服务(尤指有组织的所谓慈善事业) / ~ **welfare** 社会福利；社会福利救济

socialism ['souʃəlizəm] **n.** 社会主义: scientific ~ 科学社会主义 / state ~ 国家社会主义 / Utopian ~ 空想社会主义，乌托邦社会主义

socialist ['souʃəlist] **I n.** ① 社会主义者 ② [S-] 社会党人 **II a.** ① 社会主义的 ② [S-] 社会党的 **‖'~-'minded a.** 有社会主义觉悟的

socialistic [,souʃə'listik] **a.** 社会主义的；趋向社会主义的

socialize ['souʃəlaiz] **❶ vt.** ① 使社会化；使社会主义化: ~d medicine 社会化的医疗制度，公费医疗制 ② 使适合社会需要；使适合于过社会生活

③组织学生集体参加(课堂练习等) **❷ vi.** [美口] 参加社交活动，发生社交往来 **‖socialization** [,souʃəlai'zeiʃən] **n.**

society [sə'saiəti] **n.** ① 社会: the new (old) ~ 新(旧)社会 / (a) socialist ~ 社会主义社会 / human ~ 人类社会 / newborn forces in ~ 社会新生力量 / pests of ~ 社会的蟊贼 ② 团体，会，社: the *Society* of *Friends*【基督教】公谊会 / a cooperative ~ 合作社 ③ 友谊；交往: enjoy sb.'s ~ 跟某人来往作伴觉得很愉快 / seek (avoid) the ~ of sb. 追求(避免)和某人交往 ④ 社交界；上流社会: be introduced to ~ 被介绍给社交界 / This is a busy week for ~. 这是社交界繁忙的一周。/ move in polite ~ 出入上流社会 / ~ people 上流社会人士 ⑤ 群栖，群集 **‖~ verse** 适合社交界口味的轻松风趣的诗

sociology [,sousi'ɔlədʒi] **n.** 社会学 **‖sociologist n.** 社会学家

sock¹ [sɔk] **I n.** ①([复] socks 或 sox [sɔks])短袜: a pair of nylon ~s 一双尼龙袜 ② 鞋内的衬垫 ③(古希腊、罗马喜剧演员穿的)轻软鞋；[喻]喜剧 ④[美俚]钱袋，银箱；钱财，存款；巨款 **II vt.** ①给…穿上短袜 ②[美俚]存(钱): ~ away money in the bank 把钱存进银行里 ③[美俚](企业、戏目等)赚(钱) **‖old ~s** [美俚](男子间的亲热称呼)老兄 / **Pull up your ~s!** [英口] 鼓起劲儿来! / **Put a ~ in** (或 **into**) **it!** [俚]住口! 别作声! / ~ **in** ①关闭…不许飞机起落 ②阻止…飞行

sock² [sɔk] [俚] **I ❶ vt.** ①猛投；抛掷(石头、球等)；用投掷物击中(某人): ~ a stone *at* sth. (sb.) 向某物(某人)掷石头 ②拳打；猛击: get ~ed to dreamland 被打昏过去 **❷ vi.** 殴打；猛撞 **II n.** ①拳打；重击；(棒球中的)一击: give sb. ~s 狠揍某人 / a knockout ~ 打得对方昏过去的一击 ②力量；劲儿: add new ~ to the army's firepower 给这支陆军部队增强火力 ③一举成功的人(或电影、戏剧等) **III ad.** 沉重地；正着地: hit sb. ~ in the eye 正打在某人的眼睛上 **‖~ it to sb.** [俚](用语言或行动)狠狠打击某人，给某人颜色看

sock³ [sɔk] [英] [学俚] **I n.** 零食 **II ❶ vt.** 请…吃零食；送(东西)给 **❷ vi.** 爱吃零食

sock⁴ [sɔk] **a.** [美俚] ① 非常成功的: a ~ show 非常成功的演出 ②大声的；有力的

socket ['sɔkit] **I n.** ①窝；穴；孔: the eye ~ 眼窝 / an inflamed tooth ~ 发炎的牙床 ②【机】承窝，座；套节 ③插座，插口: an electric bulb ~ 灯泡座 / put the flagpole in its ~ 把旗杆插进座孔内 **II vt.** ① 给…配插座(或承窝等)；使装入插座(或承窝) ② 用球棒的后跟击(高尔夫球)

sod¹ [sɔd] **I n.** ①(方块)草皮；草根泥；草地 ②故乡，本国 **II** (sodded; sodding) **vt.** 铺草皮于；用草泥覆盖 **‖the old ~** 故乡，本国 / *under the* ~ 被埋葬着，在墓中

sod² [sɔd] **n.** 鸡奸者(尤用作骂人语)

soda ['soudə] *n.* ①【化】碳酸钠,纯碱;碳酸氢钠,小苏打;氢氧化钠;氧化钠;(化合物中的)钠: caustic ~ 苛性钠,烧碱 / washing ~ 洗濯碱,晶碱 ②苏打水;汽水 ‖~ **ash**【化】纯碱,无水碳酸钠,苏打灰 / ~ **biscuit**, ~ **cracker** 苏打饼干 / ~ **fountain** (装有龙头的)汽水容器; 冷饮柜 / ~ **jerk**, ~ **jerker** 冷饮柜台的店员 / ~ **lime**【化】碱石灰 / ~ **water** 苏打水;汽水

sodden ['sɔdn] **I** *a.* ① 湿润的; 浸透了的: the ~ ground 湿润的地面 / ~ with rain 雨水浸透了的衣服 ②未煮透的;(面包等)未烘透的: ~ biscuits 未烘透的饼干 ③ (尤指因沉迷于酒而)呆头呆脑的,无表情的; 麻木的 **II** ❶ *vt.* ①浸湿: bread which has been ~ed in water 水里泡过的面包 ②使呆头呆脑; 使(头脑)麻木 ❷ *vi.* 被浸湿: The sands ~ as the waves move in. 浪潮打来时,沙滩浸湿了。‖~**ly** *ad.* / ~**ness** *n.*

sodium ['soudjəm] *n.*【化】钠 ‖~ **bicarbonate** 碳酸氢钠,小苏打 / ~ **carbonate** 碳酸钠,纯碱 / ~ **chloride** 氯化钠,食盐 / ~ **hydroxide** 氢氧化钠,苛性钠,烧碱 / ~ **nitrate** 硝酸钠,智利硝 / ~ **silicate** 硅酸钠,水玻璃 / '~-'vapo(u)r **lamp** (公路等照明用的)钠蒸气灯

soever [sou'evə] *ad.* ① 无论: how dark ~ the night may be 无论夜如何黑 ② 不论何种,任何: have no rest ~ 毫无休息

sofa ['soufə] *n.* 长沙发,沙发 ‖~ **bed** 坐卧两用沙发

soft [sɔft] **I** *a.* ①软的;硬度低的: ~ tissues 柔组织 / ~ tack (船员吃的)软面包(与 hard tack 相对) / ~ X rays 软性 X 射线 ② (皮肤、头发等)柔滑的;(色彩、光线、目光、声调等)柔和的 ③(轮廓、线条)模糊的;(睡眠)平静的,安稳的 ④(天气、风、雨)温和的;[英]下雨的;解冻的;潮湿的: a ~ breeze 和风 ⑤温柔的,和蔼的;宽厚的,好心肠的: ~ manners 温和的举动 / a ~ answer (对辱骂、责备等)温和的答复 / go ~ on sb. 以温和手段对待某人 ⑥ 软弱的,不坚强的; 吃不了苦的 ⑦ [俚]轻松的,舒服的: a ~ job 轻松的工作 / a ~ thing 工作轻松、报酬丰厚的职务; 容易挣钱的买卖 ⑧(水)无矿盐的;(饮料)不含酒精的: ~ water 软水 / ~ drinks 软饮料,不含酒精的饮料(尤指果汁) ⑨坡度小的;(山峰等)线条柔和的: a ~ slope 平坦的斜坡 ⑩【语】发咝音的(如 gin 中的 g 和 city 中的 c);(辅音)带声的,浊的;不送气的; 软音的 ⑪ 纸币的;(货币)黄金后盾不足的,不稳的; 难以兑换成外币的: ~ money 纸币 / ~ currency 软通货,软币(指在国际市场上不吃香的通货) ⑫(导弹发射场等)无掩蔽而易受攻击的 **II** *n.* ① 柔软的东西;柔软部分 ② 笨人,傻子 ③ [the ~][美俚]钱(尤指纸币) **III** *ad.* [常用比较级]柔软地;温柔地; 柔和地;温和地: Play ~er, please. 请弹得轻一些。**IV** *int.* [古]别作声! ‖~**ly** *ad.* / ~**ness** *n.* ‖'~**ball** *n.* 垒球(运动) / '~-'boiled *a.* ① (蛋)煮成溏心的 ②多愁善感的 / ~ **coal** 烟煤 / '~-'footed

a. 脚步轻盈的 / ~ **goods** ① [英] 纺织品,匹头 ②[美]不耐用的纺织品 / '~**head** *n.* 自己无主意的人,易受愚弄(或摆布)的人 / '~,headed *a.* 自己无判断力的 / '~-'hearted *a.* 心肠软的;好心肠的 / '~-**land** *vi.* & *vt.* (使)软着陆 / '~-,lander *n.* 软着陆装置 / ~ **landing** 软着陆 / ~ **line** 温和路线 / '~-,liner *n.* 实行温和路线者;温和路线支持(或主张)者 / ~ **palate** 软颚 / ~ **pedal** ①(用以减弱音量的)钢琴踏板 ②减弱效果的东西 / '~-'pedal *vt.* ①在演奏…时使用减音踏板 ②降低(意见、批评等)的调子 ③对…不予张扬,使…变得不显眼 / '~-'rayed *a.* (鱼鳍)有软条的 / ~ **rot** 菌类所引起的植物腐烂症 / ~ **sawder** 奉承,谄媚 / '~-'sawder *vt.* 奉承,谄媚 / ~ **sell** 使用诱劝等软办法的推销 / ~ **snap** 不需花费多少力气的事情 / ~ **soap** ① 软皂,半液体皂 ②奉承,谄媚 / '~-'soap *vt.* & *vi.* 奉承,谄媚 / '~-'soaper *n.* 奉承者,拍马者 / ~ **solder** 软焊料(用于易熔金属) / '~-,spoken *a.* 说话温柔的,中听的 / ~ **spot** ①(性格中)易受打动的一点; 弱点 ②软弱不振的企业(或经济部门) / ~ **steel** 软钢 / ~ **touch** ① 容易轻信上当的人 ②很容易作成的事 ③可轻易击败的对手 / '~**ware** *n.* ①【自】设计计算方法 ②(计算机的)软件; 程序设备 / '~-'witted *a.* 半痴半呆的 / '~**wood** *n.* ①软材;针叶树材 ②针叶树

soften ['sɔfn] ❶ *vt.* 弄软;使软化;使温和;使软弱使柔和: Heat ~s iron. 热使铁变软。/ ~ the light 把光线弄得柔和些 ❷ *vi.* 变软;软化; 变温和;变软弱;变柔和 ‖~ *up* ①(在进攻前用轰炸等)削弱(敌方)的抵抗力及士气 ②(用对肉体或精神的折磨)使软化 ‖~**er** *n.* 软化剂; 硬水软化器

soggy ['sɔgi] *a.* ①浸水的; 湿透的; 湿润的 ②未烘透的 ③ (文章、谈话等)沉闷的;没劲的 ‖**soggily** *ad.* / **sogginess** *n.*

soil[1] [sɔil] *n.* ①泥土,土壤;土地,地面: good (poor) ~ 沃(瘠)土 / a ~ rich in humus 一种多腐殖质的土壤 / ~ science 土壤学 / barren ~ 不毛之地 / prepare the ~ for seed 整理土地准备播种 / break the virgin ~ 开垦处女地 ②国土; 国家: one's native ~ 本国; 家乡 / on foreign ~ 在外国 ③[喻]温床,滋生地 ④农业生活;务农: a son of the ~ 务农的人 ‖*racy of the* ~ 见 **racy**[1] ‖~ **conservation** 土壤保持

soil[2] [sɔil] **I** ❶ *vt.* ① 弄脏,弄污: ~ one's hands 弄脏自己的手; 玷污自己的人格 / ~ed clothes 脏衣服 ②沾污; 败坏 ③[罕]施肥于 ❷ *vi.* 变脏: It ~s easily. 这东西容易弄脏。**II** *n.* ① 污物;污斑;污秽 ②粪便; 肥料: night ~ 粪便 ③(道德的)败坏,腐败 ‖~ **pipe** (厕所的)粪管,污水管

soil[3] [sɔil] *vt.* (在棚内)用青草(或青饲料)喂(牲畜);喂以青饲料使(牲畜)泻清肠中积粪

sojourn ['sɔdʒəːn] *vi.* & *n.* 旅居,逗留 ‖~**er** *n.* 旅居的人,逗留的人

solace ['sɔləs] **I** *n.* 安慰; 安慰物: find ~ in 在…中得到安慰 **II** *vt.* ① 安慰; 使快乐: ~ oneself with 用…来安慰自己 ②减轻(悲痛等)

solar ['soulə] *a.* 太阳的, 日光的; 利用太阳光的: the ~ calendar 阳历 / ~ energy 太阳能 / a ~ spectrum 太阳光谱 ‖~ **battery** 太阳电池 / **day** 【天】太阳日 / ~ **eclipse** 【天】日食 / **flare** 【天】日晕 / ~ **house** 采太阳光用于加热的玻璃房 / ~ **plexus** 【医】太阳神经丛, 太阳丛 / ~ **system** 【天】太阳系 / ~ **year** 【天】太阳年

sold [sould] sell 的过去式和过去分词

solder ['sɔldə] **I** *n.* ① (低温)焊料, 焊锡: hard ~ 硬焊料 / soft ~ 软焊料 / tin ~ 锡焊料 ②结合物, 联接因素 **II** *vt.* & *vi.* ①(锡)焊, 焊合, 焊接 ②(使)联结在一起 ‖~ing iron 焊铁, 烙铁

soldier ['souldʒə] **I** *n.* ① (陆军的)士兵; 军人: a foot ~ 步兵 / both officers and ~s 全体官兵 / a disabled ~ 残废军人 ② 军事指挥官; 军事家: the great ~s of history 历史上的名将 / be no ~ 没有军事才能 ③ 为某种事业而奋斗的人, 战士: a ~ in the cause of justice 维护正义的战士 ④【动】(社会性昆虫)兵(虫); 兵蚁; 寄居蟹 ⑤逃避工作的人; 懒汉 **II** *vi.* ① 从军, 当兵: go ~ing 从军 ② 担负起责任, 尽职: ~ on 不屈不挠地坚持下去 ③ 偷懒, 磨洋工 ‖**a common** (或 *private*) ~ 列兵; 二等兵 / **an old** ~ ① 老兵; 老将; 老手 ②[俚] 空酒瓶; 雪茄烟蒂 / **a** ~ **of fortune** 兵痞, 想通过当兵捞一把的人, 到军队里来寻欢作乐的冒险家 / **come the old** ~ **over** 对…摆老资格; 企图欺侮 ‖~**ly**, ~**like** *a.* ①军人(似)的 ②英勇的, 勇猛的, 英俊的 / ~**ship** *n.* ①军事才干 ②军事科学 ‖~ **ant** 【动】兵蚁 / **crab** 【动】寄居蟹 / ~**s' home** [美] 退伍军人收容所 / **Soldier's Medal** [美] 军人奖章(因作战以外的英勇事迹而被授予的奖章) / ~**'s wind** 【海】侧风

soldiery ['souldʒəri] *n.* ①[总称]军人; 军队 ② 军事训练; 军事科学; 军人的职业

sole¹ [soul] *a.* ① 单独的; 唯一的: the ~ agent 独家代理商 / have the ~ right of selling sth. 有独家经售某物的权利 / He did it on his own ~ responsibility. 他做这事全由他个人负责。/ the ~ heir 唯一的继承人 / the ~ reason 唯一的理由 ②【律】(常指女子)独身的, 未婚的 ③[古] 孤独的: go forth ~ 独自一人出去 ‖~**ly** *ad.*

sole² [soul] **I** *n.* ① 脚底; 鞋底; 袜底 ② (刨、货车、犁、高尔夫球棒等的)底部, 底面, 底板, 基底 **II** *vt.* ① 给(鞋等)配底(或换底): send a pair of shoes to be ~d and heeled 把一双鞋送去换底并打后掌 ②(击高尔夫球前的一种姿态)把(棒)底放到地面 ‖**from the** ~ **of the foot to the crown of the head** 从头到脚 ‖~**d** *a.* [常用以构成复合词] …底的: rubber-~d boots 橡皮底的靴 / thin-~d shoes 薄底鞋 ‖'~-,**channel** *n.* 鞋底缝线处的凹槽 / ~ **leather** 鞋底皮 / '~**plate** *n.* 【机】底板

sole³ [soul] *n.* 【动】鳎科的鱼; 箬鳎鱼, 舌鳎

solecism ['sɔlisizəm] *n.* ① 语法错误; 文理不通 ②失礼; 无礼 ③ 谬误; 不恰当 ‖**solecistic** [,sɔli'sistik] *a.*

solemn ['sɔləm] *a.* ① 庄严的; 严肃的: a ~ statement 庄严的声明 ② 隆重的; 庄重的 ③ 合仪式的, 按照仪式的; 正式的; 神圣的: a ~ oath 正式的誓言 / a ~ hymn 圣歌 ④一本正经的: put on a ~ face 板起面孔 ⑤ (颜色)暗黑的: a suit of ~ black 一套暗黑色的衣服 ‖~**ly** *ad.* / ~**ness** *n.*

solemnity [sə'lemniti] *n.* ①庄严; 严肃 ②隆重; 庄重 ③一本正经 ④庄重的仪式

solemnize ['sɔləmnaiz] *vt.* ① 隆重庆祝(或纪念); 为(婚礼)举行宗教仪式 ②使庄严; 使严肃 ‖**solemnization** ['sɔləmnai'zeiʃən] *n.*

solicit [sə'lisit] ❶ *vt.* ① 请求; 恳求; 恳求给予; 要求: ~ sb. for help 请求某人帮助 / ~ sb.'s support 请求某人支持 / The situation ~s the closest attention. 这情况须密切予以注意。② 征求: ~ contributions from sb. 向某人征稿(或募捐) ③诱惑; 勾引…做坏事; (妓女)拉(客) ④引发, 诱发: ~ a bowel movement with a laxative 服轻泻剂通大便 ❷ *vi.* ①请求; 恳求; 征求 (*for*): ~ for subscriptions 征求订户 ②(妓女)拉客 ‖~**ant** *n.* 请求者; 征求者

solicitor [sə'lisitə] *n.* ① [英] (初级)律师 ② [美] (政府部门或一城市中负责法律事务的)法务官 ③[美] 揽待; 游说者(如拉票者等); 募捐者 ④[军] 恳求者 ‖~ **general** ① [英] 副检察长; [美] 副司法部长 ②(美国若干州的)首席司法官

solicitous [sə'lisitəs] *a.* ①焦虑的; 挂念的, 担心的: be ~ about a friend's health 担心朋友的健康 / be ~ for sb.'s safety 牵挂某人的安全 ②渴望的: be ~ of sb.'s help 渴望着某人的帮助 / be ~ to do sth. 一心想做某事 ③非常讲究的, 十分注意的: be ~ in matters of dress 在穿着方面极为讲究 ‖~**ly** *ad.*

solicitude [sə'lisitju:d] *n.* ①焦虑; 挂念, 关心; 渴望 ②[复] 担心的事情

solid ['sɔlid] **I** *a.* ①固体的; (物质结构)紧密的; (看上去)浓密的: a ~ body 固体 / ~ fuels 固体燃料 / a ~ mass of rock 结构坚硬的岩石 / a ~ fog 浓雾 ② 坚固的, 坚牢的; 结实的: on ~ ground 在稳固的基础上 / a man of ~ build 结实的人 ③实心的; 无空隙的: a ~ ball 实心球 / a ~ tire 实心轮胎 ④立体的; 立方的: a ~ metre 一立方米 ⑤纯质的; (颜色或音调等)同一的, 单一的: ~ gold 赤金, 纯金 / ~ colour 单色 ⑥ 连续的; 完整的, 完全的: a ~ hour (day) 整整一小时(一天) / ~ satisfaction 心满意足 ⑦ 基础稳固的, 有根据的; 确实的; 可靠的; 稳健的: ~ learning 实在的学问 / ~ arguments (reasons) 有根据的论点(理由) / ~ support 可靠的支持 ⑧ 资金雄厚的, 殷实的: a ~ business firm 殷实的商号 / a ~ man 有钱人 ⑨ 一致的, 团结的: a ~ vote 全体一致的投票 / the *Solid* South 传统上一贯投民主党票的美国南部各州 ⑩慎重的; 严肃

的: ~ reading 严肃的读物 ⑪紧密连接的;【印】
(行间)密排的 ⑫[美俚](音乐)极好的,(表演)精
彩的 **II** n. ①固体 ②【数】立体 **III** ad. ①全体
一致地; 无异议地 ②全部地: The hotels were
booked ~. 所有旅馆全部客满。‖**go**(或 **be**)~
for 团结一致地赞成(或支持)… / ~ **ivory** [美
俚]头脑迟钝的人 ‖**~ly** ad. / **~ness** n. ‖**~
compound** 连写的复合词 (例如 seaport) /
'**~-drawn** a.【冶】整体拉伸的 / ~ **geometry**
立体几何 / '**~-hoofed** a. (有)单蹄的 / '**~-
horned** a. (有)实角的 / '**~-,looking** a. 看来
生活过得好的 / '**~-'state** a. 固态的: ~**-state**
physics 固态物理学 / a ~**-state** circuit 固体电路

solidarity [,soli'dæriti] n. ①团结(一致) ②休戚相
关

solidify [sə'lidifai] vt. & vi. ①(使)团结 ②(使)凝
固,(使)固化,(使)变硬 ③(使)结晶 ④充实,巩
固 ‖**solidification** [sə,lidifi'keiʃən] n.

solidity [sə'liditi] n. ①固体性,固态; 固体 ②坚固;
紧密; 硬度,强度 ③稳健,可靠;殷实 ④【数】体积
⑤完整性,连续性

soliloquize [sə'liləkwaiz] vi. & vt. ① 自言自语地
说 ②【戏】用独白说

soliloquy [sə'liləkwi] n. ① 自言自语 ②【戏】独白

soliped ['soliped] a. & n. 单蹄的(兽)

solitary ['solitəri] **I** a. ①独居的; 无伴的,单独:
a ~ life 独居生活 / a ~ walk 独个儿的散步
②荒凉的; 冷落的,偏僻的; 寂寞的: a ~ district
冷落的地区 ③单个的,唯一的: a ~ example 独
一无二的例子 ④【植】单生的 **II** n. ① 隐居者
②单独监禁 ‖**solitarily** ['solitərili; 美 ,soli'terili]
ad. / **solitariness** n. ‖~ **confinement** 单独
监禁

solitude ['solitju:d] n. ① 孤独;寂寞;隐居,与外界
隔绝 ②冷僻处;荒凉地(如沙漠)

solo ['soulou] **I** ([复] solos 或 soli ['souli:]) n. ①
独奏曲; 独唱曲; 独奏; 独唱: a piano ~ 钢琴独
奏曲 / play a ~ 独奏 ②单独表演;【空】单飞:
dance a ~ 跳单人舞 / fly a ~ 单飞 ③单人纸牌
戏; 一种惠斯特纸牌戏(由一人对抗三人) **II** a.
①独奏(曲)的; 独唱(曲)的 ②单独的; 单独表演
的 **III** ad. 单独地: fly ~ 单飞 **IV** vi. 单独表演;
单飞

solstice ['solstis] n.【天】至, 至点: the summer ~
夏至 / the winter ~ 冬至

soluble ['soljubl] a. ①可溶的;可乳化的: Sugar is
~ in water. 糖在水中会溶解。/ a ~ oil 油乳
胶 ②可以解决的;可解释的;【数】可解的: Such
problems are perfectly ~. 这样一些问题完全
可以解决。‖**solubility** [,solju'biliti] n. ①【化】
溶(解)度,溶(解)性;(可)溶性;(可)溶解性;可解
释性 ‖~ **glass**【化】溶性玻璃

solution [sə'lju:ʃən] n. ①解决(办法);解答;解释:
problems awaiting ~ 尚待解决的问题 / hit on
a ~ 想出了解决问题的办法 / work out a ~ for
(或 of, to) the problem 给问题找答案 ②【数】解

法,解式 ③溶解(作用);溶解状态; 溶液; 溶体:
chemical ~ 化学溶解(成分发生化学变化) / mechanical ~ 机械溶解(成分不发生化学变化) /
a saline ~ 盐水溶液 ④瓦解; 中断; 消散: a violent ~ of the continuity of a joint 关节的猛然
脱臼 / the gradual ~ of the clouds 云的逐渐消
散 ⑤橡胶水 (=rubber ~) **II** vt. 涂溶液于; 用
橡胶水胶粘 ‖**in** ~ ①在溶解状态中 ②(思想等)
在不断变化中,动摇不定

solve [solv] vt. ①解释; 解答; 解决: ~ a mathematical equation 解一项数学方程式 / ~ a
difficulty 解决困难 ②清偿(债务)

solvency ['solvənsi] n. ①【化】溶解本领 ② 偿付
能力

solvent ['solvənt] **I** a. ①有偿付能力的 ②溶解的;
有溶解力的: the ~ action of water 水的溶解作
用 / ~ fluids 溶液 ③(对传统、信仰等)具有削弱
作用的 **II** n. ①【化】溶剂; 溶媒 ② 具有削弱作
用的事物; (问题等)的解决办法

sombre, somber ['sombə] a. ①昏暗的; 阴沉的: a
~ sky 阴沉的天空 ② 忧郁的: a ~ countenance
忧郁的脸容 ③ 暗淡的;浅黑的: a ~ hue 暗淡的
颜色 ‖**~ly** ad. / **~ness** n.

some [强 sʌm; 弱 səm, sm] **I** a. ① [用于肯定句]
一些, 若干; 有些: I have ~ questions. 我有一
些问题。/ He has waited ~ time. 他等了一会
儿了。/ Give me ~ more. 再给我一些。/ Not
all wood is hard, ~ wood is soft. 木料不一定
都硬, 也有软的。②[用于疑问句,盼望得到肯定
的答复或表示建议、请求等]: Aren't there ~
envelopes in that drawer? 那个抽屉里不是
还有几只信封吗? / Would you have ~ tea?
您喝茶吗? ③ 某一: He is working at ~ place
in the north. 他在北方某地工作。/ Some person
at the door is asking to see you. 门口有人要见
你。④[sʌm][在美口语、英俚语中用来强调语气]
很大的, 惊人的, 了不起的: That was ~ storm!
那暴风雨可厉害呢! / I call that ~ picture.
我看那张画挺不错。**II** pron. ①一些, 若干: Some
of it is good. 其中一部分是好的。/ Some of
these books are quite useful. 这些书中有些是很
有用的。②[用作复]有些人; 有些东西: Some
answered yes and ~ (或 others) answered no.
有的回答"是", 有的回答"不是"。**III** ad. ①大约:
~ 40 tons 四十吨左右 / ~ few minutes 几分钟
②[口]几分, 稍微: He felt ~ better. 他觉得好
些了。/ The sea has gone down ~. 海浪平息了
一些。③[美俚]很; 非常好: That'll keep you ~
busy. 那要使你忙一番了。/ shoot ~ 枪打得很
准 / That's going ~. 那很不错。‖**and then ~**
见 **then** / **~ ... or other** (用以表示不肯定或
不精确之意)某一…: I shall be coming again ~
day or other. 我过几天还要再来。/ I've read
about it before in ~ magazine or other. 我以前
曾在某一本杂志里看到过。

somebody ['sʌmbədi] **I** pron. 某人, 有人: There

is ～ waiting for you. 有人在等你。/ That must be ～ from the Foreign Ministry. 那一定是从外交部来的人。/ ～ else('s) 别人(的) / ～ or other 不知是哪一个; 总有一个人 **II** *n.* 重要人物, 大人物: think oneself to be (a) ～ 自以为是一个要人

somehow ['sʌmhau] *ad.* ① 由于某种(未弄清的)原因, 不知怎么地, 莫其妙地: *Somehow (or other)* he again made a mistake in solving the mathematical problem. 不知怎么地, 他在解这道数学题时又算错了。②以某种方法, 以某种方式: We must get the work finished ～ (or other) by tomorrow morning. 我们必须设法在明天早上以前把工作做完。

someone ['sʌmwʌn] *pron.* 某人, 有人: *Someone* has been here. 有人到这儿来过了。

someplace ['sʌmpleis] *ad.* [美] =somewhere (*ad.*)

somersault ['sʌməsɔːlt] **I** *n.* ① 筋斗: turn (或 throw) a ～ 翻一个筋斗 ② (意见、政策等)一百八十度的转变 **II** *vi.* 翻筋斗

something ['sʌmθiŋ] **I** *pron.* ①某事, 某物, 某东西: I've ～ to tell you. 我有事要告诉你。/ The child wants ～ to eat. 这孩子要东西吃。/ There's ～ wrong with the machine. 这台机器什么地方出了毛病。②(表示模糊的概念) 什么: I caught the twelve ～ train. 我赶上了十二点几分的那班火车。/ He is a teacher or ～. 他大概是当教师的。/ *Something or other* prevented him from coming. 不知什么事使他不能来。③ 实有物(和 nothing 相对而言): *Something* is better than nothing. 有比没有好。④重要东西; 重要人物: There is ～ in what you say. 你所说的有些道理。/ That's ～. 这多少是一种安慰(或收获等)。/ I hope this advice will go for ～ with them. 我希望这一劝告对他们会发生些效果。/ think ～ of oneself (或 think oneself ～) 自以为了不起 **II** *ad.* ① 几分, 多少, 稍微: be ～ impatient 有点儿不耐烦 ② 很, 非常: It rained ～ awful last night. 昨天晚上雨下得很大。‖*have ～ to do with* 与…有点关系 / *make ～ of* ①从…中取利, 利用… ②[口] 为…而吵架 ③ 把…说得非常重要 / *see ～ of* 见到一些…: We hope to *see ～ of* you during the holidays. 我们希望在假期中能时而见到你。/ *see ～ of* the world 见一些世面 / ～ *damp* [美俚]酒 / ～ *else* ①另外的一些东西 ②[美俚]相当出色的人 (或物) / ～ *like* ①几分象: It is shaped ～ *like* a ball. 那东西有些象球。②大约: It must be ～ *like* seven o'clock. 该是七点钟左右了吧。③[口] 了不起的; 好透的: ～ *like* a day 大好的天气 / That's ～ *like!* 那真妙极了！/ ～ *of* 在某种意义(或程度)上: He is ～ *of* an athlete. 他几分运动员的才能。/ ～ *of the kind* 类似的事物 / ～ *on the hip* [美俚]酒 / ～ *to write home about* 值得大书特书的事情 / *take a drop of* ～ 喝一点酒

sometimes ['sʌmtaimz] *ad.* 不时, 有时: I have letters from him. (或 I have letters from him ～.) 我有时收到他的来信。/ It is ～ warm and ～ (或 at other times) cold. 天气时暖时冷。

someway(s) ['sʌmwei(z)] *ad.* 以某种方法, 以某种方式; 不知怎么地

somewhat ['sʌmhwɔt] **I** *pron.* ① 一点儿, 几分: He is ～ of a connoisseur. 他这人有点鉴赏家的味道。/ The machine has lost ～ of its speed. 这机器的速度有点儿慢了。/ neglect ～ of one's duty 有点失职 ②某事, 某物 ③重要东西; 重要人物 **II** *ad.* 有点, 稍微: ～ different 多少有点不同 / He was ～ encouraged by your words. 他听了你的话受到了一些鼓励。

somewhere ['sʌmhwɛə] **I** *ad.* ①在某处; 到某处: He lives ～ in this neighbourhood. 他住在附近某处。/ You'll find the passage ～ in the book. 你可以在本书某一地方找到这段文章。/ ～ out of town 到城外某地去 / ～ about 在附近; 前后, 大约 (about): ～ about the school 在学校附近 / ～ about nine o'clock 大约九点钟 **II** *n.* 某地: The troops have been sent to ～ at the front. 部队被派到前线某地去了。‖*see sb.* ～ 要某人滚蛋, 要某人见鬼去: I'll *see* you ～ (in hell) first! 滚你的蛋! 去你的!

somnolence ['sɔmnələns], **somnolency** ['sɔmnələnsi] *n.* ①思睡, 困倦 【医】嗜眠(症)

somnolent ['sɔmnələnt] *a.* ① 想睡的, 困倦的 ②催眠的 ‖～**ly** *ad.*

son [sʌn] *n.* ①儿子: He is his father's ～. 他酷似其父。② 女婿; 养子 ③[常用复]后裔, 子孙: the ～s of Abraham 亚伯拉罕的子孙, 犹太人 ④国民; 居民: a ～ of France 法国人 ⑤以某一地的人: a ～ of the Muses 诗人 / a ～ of toil 劳动者 ⑥(对男孩或青年人的爱称)小弟弟, 孩子 ‖a *favo(u)rite* ～ ①最喜爱的儿子, 宠儿 ②[美]本州代表们所支持的总统候选人 / a ～ *of a bitch* (或 *gun*) [俚](骂人语)畜生, 狗娘养的 ②(对伙伴的戏谑性称呼)家伙 / 不了的任务 / a ～ *of Bacchus* 酒鬼 / a ～ *of dripping* 厨子 / a ～ *of ebony* 黑人 / a ～ *of Momus* 爱嘲弄的人; 滑稽的人 / a ～ *of the morning* 趁早赶路的人 / a ～ *of the soil* 本地人; 农民 / *every mother's* ～ 人人, 所有的人 / *the Son* 或 *the Son of God* 或 *the Son of Man* 耶稣基督 / *the* ～s *of men* (或 *Adam*) 人类 ‖～**less** *a.* 无后嗣的 / ～**ly** *a.* 儿子般的; 尽孝道的 / ～**ship** *n.* 儿子身分 ‖'～-**in-law** ([复] ～s-in-law) *n.* 女婿

sonata [sə'nɑːtə] *n.* 【音】奏鸣曲

song [sɔŋ] *n.* ①歌唱; 声乐: break (或 burst forth) into ～ 唱起歌来 / deeds that move people to ～ and tears 可歌可泣的事迹 ②歌曲; 歌词; 歌曲集: popular ～s 流行歌曲 ③诗歌; 韵文: a hero honoured *in* ～ 诗歌中所歌颂的英雄 ④鸣声; 吵嚷: the ～ of the wind 风声 / the ～ of birds 鸟鸣声 / put up quite a ~ 大吵大闹 ⑤[美俚]自首;告密;胡说 ‖*a ~ and dance* [美] ① 歌舞表演: *a ~ and dance* ensemble 歌舞团 ②[口]不着边际的解释;遁词;废话 ③[俚]骗取同情的谎话;自我吹嘘 / *for a* ~ (或 *for an old* ~) 非常便宜地: buy sth. *for a* ~ 廉价买某物 / *nothing to make a ~ about* [口]不足道;不重要 / *sing another* ~ 改变调子(或方针、态度等);谦恭起来 / *sing the same* (或 *old*) ~ 唱老调 ‖~**ful** *a.* 旋律优美的,调子好听的 / ~**less** *a.* ①无歌唱的 ②不会唱的 ‖'~**bird** *n.* 鸣鸟, 鸣禽 / '~**book** *n.* 歌曲集; 歌本 / '~-,plugging *n.* 通过无线电反复广播等方式使歌曲流行 / '~**smith** *n.* 作曲家 / ~ **sparrow** (北美产)麻雀 / '~,writer *n.* 流行歌曲的作者

sonic ['sɔnik] *a.* ①【物】声音的;音速的;利用音波的: ~ speed 音速 / a ~ mine 音响水雷 ②能发出声音的 ‖~ **barrier** 【空】音障 / ~ **boom** 【空】声震 (以超音速飞行的飞机在降近地面时因机头冲击波受阻而发出的爆音) / ~ **depth finder** 回音测深仪

sonnet ['sɔnit] I *n.* 十四行诗;商籁体 II (sonnet(t)ed; sonnet(t)ing) *vi. & vt.* =sonnetize

sonorous [sə'nɔːrəs] *a.* ①响亮的,洪亮的 ②能发出(响亮)声音的 ‖~**ly** *ad.* / ~**ness** *n.*

soon [suːn] *ad.* ①不久: We shall ~ start. 我们不久就要出发了。/ We shall start very (或 quite) ~. 我们很快就要出发了。/ He arrived ~ after six. 六点刚过他就到了。②早;快: We reached the station one hour too ~. 我们早到车站一小时。/ How ~ can you be ready? 你什么时候能准备好? / The more help, the ~*er* done. 人手越多做事越快。③宁可, 宁愿 ‖*as* (或 *so*) ~ *as* ①……(就…): Come here *as* ~ *as* you finish the work. 工作一结束,你就到这里来一次。②如…一般早(或快): They didn't arrive *so* (或 *as*) ~ *as* we had expected. 他们到得不象我们期待的那么早。/ *as* ~ *as not* 再也乐意不过地: He would go *as* ~ *as not*. 他太乐意去了。/ *as* ~ *as possible* 尽快 / *no* ~*er than* ——……就…: I had *no* ~*er* (或 *No* ~*er* had I) reached home *than* it began to rain. 我刚到家天就下雨了。/ *No* ~*er* said *than* done. 说到做到。/ *~er or later* 迟早 / *The* ~*er the better.* 越快越好。(或: 愈早愈好。)

soot [sut] I *n.* 煤烟, 烟灰 II *vt.* 用煤烟弄脏;用烟炱覆盖

sooth [suːθ] I *a.* ①[古]真实的;真正的 ②[诗]镇静的; 抚慰的 ③[古]温柔的; 甜蜜的 II *n.* [古]真实 ‖*in* ~ [古]其实; 真实地 ‖~**ly** *ad.* ‖'~,sayer *n.* ①占卜者; 预言者 ②螳螂 / '~,saying *n.* 预言

soothe [suːð] ❶ *vt.* ①安慰,抚慰;使平静,使镇定: ~ a crying baby 哄哭着的婴孩 / ~ sb.'s anger 使某人息怒 ②使(痛苦、疼痛等)减轻, 缓和 ③奉承 ❷ *vi.* 起安慰作用;起镇静作用 ‖~**r** *n.* ①安

慰的人,抚慰的人;奉承拍马者 ② (哄婴儿的)橡皮假奶头

soothing ['suːðiŋ] *a.* ①安慰性的 ②起镇静作用的: ~ syrup 镇静糖浆 ‖~**ly** *ad.* / ~**ness** *n.*

sooty ['suti] *a.* ①煤烟的,烟灰的;生煤烟的 ②被煤烟弄脏的;被烟炱覆盖的 ③乌黑色的 ‖sooti-ness *n.* ‖~ **mo(u)ld** (结在植物上的)烟霉 / ~ **tern** 【动】乌燕鸥

sop [sɔp] I *n.* ①(泡在牛奶、肉汤等里的)面包片;湿透的东西: The ground is a mere ~. 地面湿透啦。② 打狗的肉包子(指抛给凶恶的东西吃的东西); (给刁难者等的)贿赂 ③懦夫, 柔弱的男子;[美俚]酒鬼 II (sopped; sopping) ❶ *vt.* ①浸, 泡(面包等); 浸湿: be *sopped* through (或 *to the skin*) 浑身湿透 ②吸(水等) (up): ~ *up* the water with a towel 用毛巾吸水 ③贿赂 ❷ *vi.* ①湿透: We are *sopping with* rain. 我们被雨淋湿了。②(液体)渗透 ‖*a ~ in the pan* 油煎面包;一口美味的东西 / *throw* (或 *give*) *a ~ to Cerberus* 贿赂看守(或官员、刁难者等)

sophism ['sɔfizəm] *n.* ①诡辩,似是而非的论点 ②诡辩法

sophist ['sɔfist] *n.* ①[常作 S-] 诡辩(学)者(指以诡辩出名的古希腊哲学、修辞学等教师): the *Sophists* 诡辩派 ②诡辩家 ③大智者,博学者

sophomore ['sɔfəmɔː] *n.* ①大学(或中学)二年级学生 ②在企业(或机关等)中工作第二年的人员 ③自以为样样都懂而实际上幼稚浅薄的人 ‖**sophomoric(al)** [,sɔfə'mɔrik(əl)] *a.* ①二年级学生的 ②自以为样样都懂而实际上幼稚浅薄的

soporific [,soupə'rifik] I *a.* ①引起酣睡的; 催眠的 ②酣睡的 II *n.* 安眠药

soppy ['sɔpi] *a.* ①湿透的; 浸湿的 ②多雨的 ③[英口]太伤感的

soprano [sə'prɑːnou] I ([复] sopranos 或 soprani [sə'prɑːniː]) *n.* ①女高音;高音部 ②女高音歌手;唱最高音者 II *n.* 女高音的;最高音的 ‖**so-pranist** [sə'prɑːnist] *n.* 女高音歌手;唱最高音者

sorcerer ['sɔːsərə] *n.* 男巫; 术士; 魔术师 ‖**sorceress** ['sɔːsəris] *n.* 女巫; 女术士; 女魔术师

sorcery ['sɔːsəri] *n.* 巫术, 妖术; 魔术

sordid ['sɔːdid] *a.* ①肮脏的,污秽的,破烂的;令人不舒服的: ~ surroundings 肮脏的环境 ②(人、行为等)卑鄙的,下贱的; 恶劣的; 利欲熏心的: ~ motives 卑鄙的动机 ③可怜的, 悲惨的: live in ~ poverty 过着可怜的贫困生活 ④色彩暗淡的; 泥色的 ‖~**ly** *ad.* / ~**ness** *n.*

sordino [sɔː'diːnou] ([复] sordini [sɔː'diːniː]) *n.* [意]【音】弱音器;弱音踏板

sore [sɔː] I *a.* ①痛的; 疼痛发炎的: 一碰就痛的: have a ~ arm 手臂痛 / My throat is ~: 我喉咙痛。② 使人痛苦的;易引起精神痛苦的: ~ news 使人痛心的消息 / a ~ subject 使人难堪的话题 ③恼火的;动辄要恼火的: get ~ over (或 about) sth. 因某事而恼火 / a ~ loser 一输就恼火的人,输不起的人 ④ 极度的, 剧烈的:

be in ~ need of help 极需帮助 **II** *n.* ①(身体上的)痛处;疮,溃疡: bed ~s 褥疮 / a running ~ 流脓的疮伤 ②(精神上的)痛处,恨事,伤心事: reopen old ~s 揭旧疮疤,旧恨重提 **III** *ad.* [古] =~ly ‖*be ~d up* [美俚]发怒 ‖*~ly ad.* ①痛苦地,悲痛地②严厉地;剧烈地: be ~ly oppressed 惨遭压迫 ③极,非常: feel ~ly inclined to do sth. 极想做某事 / **~ness** *n.* ‖'**~head** *n.* 动辄要恼火的人;老是发牢骚的人 *a.* 因失意而恼火的 / **~ throat** 咽喉炎

sorrow ['sɔrou] **I** *n.* ①悲痛,悲哀,悲伤;悲伤的表示: convert ~ into strength 化悲痛为力量 / feel ~ 感到悲伤 / cause much ~ to sb. 使某人大为伤心 / His ~ was loud and long. 他因为悲伤大哭了好久。 ② 悲哀的原因;不幸事,伤心事 ③懊悔,遗憾: express ~ for one's mistake 对错误表示遗憾 **II** *vi.* 感到悲伤;懊悔;遗憾 (*at, for, over*) ‖'**~-,stricken** *a.* 悲痛的,哀伤的

sorrowful ['sɔrəful] *a.* ①伤心的,悲伤的,悲痛的: feel ~ 感到悲伤 / ~ tears 悲伤的眼泪 ②使人伤心的: a ~ accident 悲惨的事故 ‖**~ly** *ad.* / **~ness** *n.*

sorry ['sɔri] *a.* ①难过的;惋惜的: We are ~ to hear that he has been seriously ill. 我们听说他生了重病觉得很难过。 / I feel ~ for you. 我为你感到惋惜。 ②懊悔的,后悔的: He is ~ for the mistake he has made. 他对他所犯的错误感到懊悔。 / You'll be ~ about this later. 对这件事你以后会后悔的。 ③对不起的,抱歉的,遗憾的: *Sorry!* 对不起! / I am very ~. 我很抱歉。 / I'm ~ to say (that) the work was not well done. 很遗憾,这件工作没有做好。 / I'm ~ for giving you so much trouble. 对不起,给你添了很多麻烦。 ④悲哀的,悲伤的: a ~ end 悲哀的结局 ⑤ 卑鄙的;可悲的,拙劣的;破烂的: make a ~ spectacle of oneself 出洋相 / cut a ~ figure 出丑 / in a ~ plight 处于可悲的境地 / in ~ clothes 穿着褴褛的衣服 ‖(*feel*) ~ *for oneself* [口]垂头丧气,灰溜溜

sort [sɔːt] **I** *n.* ①种类;类别: I'll never do this ~ of thing (或 these ~ of things 或 things of this ~). 我决不会干这种事。 / under all ~s of names 以种种各样的名义 / What ~ of book do you want? 你需要的是哪一种书? / people of every ~ and kind 各种各样的人 / He is not (of) my ~. 他那样的人我可合不来。 / That's your ~. 那是你的做法(或想法)。 / Nothing of the ~! 根本没有那回事! ② 样子;举止 ③ 品质,性质 ④ 一套;[常用复]一套铅字: The copy runs (或 is hard) on ~s. 这份稿件排式复杂。(指着各种花式的铅字) **II** ❶ *vt.* 把…分类,整理; 拣选: ~ letters 把信件分类 / ~ *out* enemies from friends 区分敌友 / ~ *out* those of the largest size 拣出其中最大的 / ~ *out* historical legacy 清理历史遗产 ❷ *vi.* ① 交往 (*with*)

② [古]一致,协调 (*with*) ‖*after* (或 *in*) a ~ 有几分,稍微 / a good ~ 好人;受人欢迎的人 / *in any* ~ 以各种方法,无论如何 / *in a* ~ *of way* 有些,略为 / *in some* ~ 稍微,多少 / *of a* ~ ①同一类的 ②勉强称得上的,较差的: tea *of a* ~ 蹩脚茶叶 / *of* ~*s* ①各种各样的;未经选择的 ②[口]勉强称得上的 / *out of* ~*s* ①不舒服的;不高兴的 ②【印】缺少某些铅字 / ~ *of* 有几分地: I ~ *of* expected it. 我有几分料到的。

sortie ['sɔːtiː] *n.* 【军】 ① 出击;突围;出港 ② 出击部队 ③ 出动架次(指一架飞机的一次出动): The two planes each made three ~s yesterday. 两架飞机昨天各出动了三次。 / fly 500 ~s in 100 groups 出动一百批共五百架次的飞机 / ~ rate 架次率

SOS ['es,ou'es] *n.* ①[无]国际通用的(船舶、飞机等的)呼救信号(………) ②[口][喻]求救;求助(如通过广播找人等)

sot [sɔt] **I** *n.* 酒鬼;酒糊涂 **II** (sotted; sotting) ❶ *vt.* 因嗜酒而浪费掉 (*away*) ❷ *vi.* 嗜酒;滥喝酒

sough [sau] **I** *n.* 飕飕声,飒飒声(如树间的风声) **II** *vi.* (风)飒飒作声

sought [sɔːt] seek 的过去式和过去分词

soul [soul] **I** *n.* ①灵魂;心灵 ② 精神;精力;气魄;热情: serve the people heart and ~ 全心全意地为人民服务 / put one's heart and ~ into the work 全神贯注地工作 / His paintings lack ~. 他的绘画没有气魄。 ③精髓,精华;中心人物: the ~ of a book 一本书的精髓 ④ 人: The ship was lost with 150 ~s. 那艘船沉没了,一百五十人遇难。 / Not a ~ to be seen. 一个人影也看不到。 / the greatest ~s of antiquity 古代最伟大的人物 / a cheery ~ 乐观的人 / a thirsty ~ 醉汉 ⑤ 化身,典型: the ~ of uprightness 正直的典型 ⑥鬼魂: All *Souls*' Day 【天主教】万灵节(十一月二日) ⑦(美国)黑人文化遗产的特征,(美国)黑人的种族自豪感 **II** *a.* (美国)黑人的 ‖*call one's ~ one's own* 自己支配自己 / *for the ~ of me* [用于否定句]不管怎样,无论如何: I can't remember *for the ~ of me.* 我怎么也想不起来。 / *in one's ~ of* ~*s* 在灵魂深处 / *poor* ~ [用作插入语]可怜的人儿啊 / *upon* (或 *'pon*) *my* ~ ①我敢发誓说 ②天哪(表示惊讶) ‖**~ed** *a.* ①有灵魂的;有感情的 ②[常用以构成复合词]灵魂…的: high-~ed 具有高尚灵魂的 ‖~ **brother** (美国)黑人男子 / '**~-des,troying** *a.* 毁灭灵魂的; 消磨精神的 / ~ **food** [美口]南方黑人吃的一般食物 / ~ **kiss** 深深的一吻 / ~ **mate** 性情相投的人;情人 / '**~-,searching** *n.* 良心上的自我反省 / '~**-,stirring** *a.* 使精神兴奋的

soulful ['soulful] *a.* 感情上的;充满热情的;深情的 ‖**~ly** *ad.* / **~ness** *n.*

soulless ['soullis] *a.* ①没有灵魂的;没有精神的 ②卑鄙的;无情的 ‖**~ly** *ad.* / **~ness** *n.*

sound¹ [saund] **I** *a.* ①健康的;健全的: a ~ constitution 强健的体质 / children of ~ mind and body 身心健康的孩子们 ②完好的: ~ fruit (timber) 完好的水果(木材) ③正确的;合理的;稳妥的: ~ advice 忠告 / ~ reasoning 正确的推理 / a ~ policy 明智稳妥的政策 ④坚固的;殷实的;可靠的: a building of ~ construction 结构牢固的建筑物 ⑤彻底的,充分的;严厉的: a ~ sleep 酣睡 / a ~ beating 一顿痛打 ⑥(人)有判断力的,见解正确的: Is he ~ on the problem? 他对这个问题的见解是否正确呢? ⑦忠实可靠的;道德高尚的 ⑧正统的 【律】有效的 **II** *ad.* 彻底地,充分地: be ~ asleep 酣睡着 / You'll sleep the ~er for it. 这么一来你可以睡得更畅些了。‖as ~ as a bell 十分健全的 / ~ in wind and limb [口] 身体健全的 ‖~ly ad. / ~ness n.

sound² [saund] **I** *n.* ①声音: the ~ of running water 流水声 / the ~ of voices 说话声 ②语音: a consonant (vowel) ~ 辅(元)音 / a breathed (voiced) ~ 清(浊)音 ③闹声,噪声: ~ and fury 大吵大闹 / the ~ nuisance 噪音危害 ④语调;笔调;含意: I don't like the ~ of this letter. 我不喜欢这封信的语气。⑤听力范围: within (out of) ~ of sb.'s voice 在听得到(听不到)某人声音的地方 ⑥(电影、唱片等的)录音 ⑦【物】声(音),声学 **II** ❶ *vi.* ①响,发声;回响;召唤: The bugle ~s to battle. 战斗号角吹响了。②听起来: A: How does this proposal ~ to you? B: It ~s quite all right. 甲: 你觉得这个提议怎样? 乙: 听上去挺不错。❷ *vt.* ①使发声;(用吹号等方式)通知;命令: ~ a bugle 吹号 / a gong 敲锣 / ~ an alarm 发出警报;敲起警钟 ②发…的音: The h in hour is not ~ed. 在 hour 这个词中 h 是不发音的。③宣告;传播: They ~ed her praises. 他们到处扬她。④听诊;触探: ~ the lungs 听诊肺音 ‖ ~ off [美] ①【军】奏序曲 ②呼行军口令(即"一,二,一!");依次报数 ③提高声音说话 ④(有力地)充分发表意见;呱啦呱啦乱说,吹牛 / ~ arrester 遮音装置 / ~ barrier 【无】音障,声障 / '~board n. 共鸣板,共振板 / ~ box 共鸣箱,共鸣器;吸声箱 / ~ camera 电影录音摄影机 / ~ detector 测音器;【无】伴音信号检波器 / ~ effects 音响效果 / ~ film ①有声电影 ②录音胶片,音膜 / ~ locator 【物】声波定位器 / ~ man 负责音响效果的人 / ~ motion picture 有声电影 / '~proof a. 隔音的 vt. 给…隔音 / ~ recording 录音 / ~ track 声迹;声带,声槽 / ~ truck (竞选、作广告等用的)广播车 / ~ wave ① [复]声波,音波 ②音色,音调

sound³ [saund] **I** *vt.* ①测…的深度;锤测(深度);探测(大气上层)的温度(或气压、湿度等): ~ the sea 测量海深 ②试探 (out): ~ sb. (out) on (或 about) a question 试探某人对一个问题的意见 ③【医】用探子检查(尿道等) ❷ *vi.* ①测

深 ②试探 ③(鲸鱼等)突然潜入海底 **II** *n.* 【医】探子,探条

sound⁴ [saund] *n.* ①海峡;海湾 ②(鱼类的)鳔

soundless¹ ['saundlis] *a.* 无声的,寂静的 ‖~ly ad.

soundless² ['saundlis] *a.* 深不可测的,无底的

soup¹ [su:p] *n.* ①汤: clear (thick) ~ 清(浓)汤 / sour-pepper ~ 酸辣汤 / eat (或 drink) ~ 喝汤 ②羹汤般稠浓的东西;[美俚]浓雾;硝化甘油,炸药;(照相)显影液 ③[英俚]【律】委托资历较浅律师承办的刑事起诉案件 ‖duck ~ [美俚]容易做的事情;好欺侮的人 / from ~ to nuts 从头至尾;一应俱全 / in the ~ [俚]在困境中 / ~ and fish [俚](男子)晚礼服 ‖ kitchen ①(救济贫困者的)施粥所,施济处 ②流动厨房 / ~ plate 汤盆 / ~ spoon 汤匙 / ~ ticket 施粥券

soup² [su:p] [美俚] **I** *vt.* 增加(发动机等)的马力(或效率) (up) **II** *n.* 马力;加大了的力量(或效率) ‖ '~ed-'up a. ①加强了马力(或效率)的 ②经过加工变得花哨的,弄得极吸引人的

sour ['sauə] **I** *a.* ①酸的,酸味的: The fruit is still green and eats ~. 果子还青,吃起来很酸。②酸腐的,酸臭的: This milk has turned ~. 这牛奶发酸了。/ a ~ smell 酸臭味 ③发酵的 ④脾气坏的,乖戾的;愠怒的;敌对的: a ~ temper 乖戾的脾气 / a ~ face 愠怒的面孔 / take a ~ view of things 对事物持阴郁的看法 ⑤讨厌的;乏味的: a ~ job 枯燥无味的工作 ⑥刺耳的;拙劣的: play a ~ note 奏出刺耳的音调 ⑦(土壤)酸性过强的;湿冷的 ⑧(汽油等)含硫的 **II** *vt.* ①使变酸;使变酸腐 ②使变得不愉快;使失望;使变得讨厌无趣: This experience has ~ed him for any further contact. 这一经历使他再也不愿有进一步的接触了。/ ~ sb. on sth. 使某人对某事失望 ③(尤指在漂白等时)用稀酸溶液处理 ❷ *vi.* ①变酸;变酸腐;发酵: Milk ~s quickly in heat. 牛奶受热易变酸。②(土壤)变成酸性,变得贫瘠 ③变得不愉快;厌烦 ④变坏 **III** *n.* ①酸味;酸性物质 ②酸味饮料;酸味鸡尾酒 ‖be ~ on [美口] 嫌恶…,讨厌… / go ~ ①变酸 ②(计划等)出岔;(建议等)不再受欢迎 ③对…不再抱幻想 (on) / in ~ [美俚]失宠;出事 / ~ grapes 见 grape ‖~ly ad. / ~ness n. ‖'~crout n.;'~krout n. 泡菜 / '~dough n. ①(留待下次发酵用的)含酵母的面团 ②[美]旧时加拿大西北部(或阿拉斯加)的探矿者;老居民 / '~puss n. [俚]坏脾气的人;面无笑容的人

source [sɔ:s] *n.* ①河的源头;水源 ②根源,来源: electric light ~s 各种电光源 ③提供消息者: informed ~s 消息灵通人士 ④出处;原始资料: historical ~s 史料 ‖ ~ book (有关历史、文艺、宗教等的)原始资料;原始资料集 / ~ language 被译语言

souse¹ [saus] **I** ❶ *vt.* ①腌 ②浸,泡;使湿透 ③[俚]灌醉 ❷ *vi.* ①泡在水里;被浸透 ②[俚]

喝醉 **II** *n.* ① 腌渍品(尤指腌猪头、腌猪脚、腌鱼等) ② 腌渍用的盐水 ③ 浸,泡;腌 ④[俚]醉汉 ⑤ 狂饮

souse² [saus] **I** [古] ❶ *vi.* (隼等)飞扑 ❷ *vt.* 猛地扑下而撞倒;向…飞扑 **II** *ad.* 飞扑地;扑通一声: *Souse* went the sheep into a pool. 羊扑通一声掉进了水塘。

south [sauθ] **I** *n.* ①南,南方: ~ by east 南偏东(即正南偏东 11°15′,写作 S 11°15′ E) / ~ by west 南偏西(即正南偏西 11°15′,写作 S 11°15′ W) ② [S-] (一国或一地区)南部 ③ [常作 S-] 地球的南部(尤指南极地区) ④ 南风 **II** *a.* ①南的,南方的 ②向南的: a room with a ~ aspect 窗户向南的房间 ③从南面来的: a ~ wind 南风 ④ [S-] (一国、一洲或一地区)南方的 **III** *ad.* 向南方;在南方;自南方: The wind blows ~. 刮南风。**IV** [sauθ] *vi.* ①转向南方 ②[天](日、月等)到达子午线,过南北线 ‖ *go* ~ *with sth.* [美俚]偷走某物;私占某物 ‖ **South Island** 南岛[新西兰两主岛之一] / '~**land** *n.* [诗]南国,南方 / '~**paw** *n.* [俚]惯用左手的运动员;(棒球)左手投手 *a.* [俚]用左手的 / **South Pole** 南极

souther ['sʌðə] *n.* 南风;来自南方的风暴

southerly ['sʌðəli] **I** *ad.* & *a.* ①在南方(的);向南方(的) ②来自南方(的) **II** *n.* 南风

southern ['sʌðən] **I** *a.* ①[常作 S-] (一国或一地区)南方的,南部的;南部方言的: the Southern States of the U.S.A. 美国南部各州 ②来自南方的 ③朝南的 ④有南方地区特征的 **II** *n.* ①=~er ②[常作 S-] 美国南部方言 ‖ ~er *n.* ①南方人;居住在南方的人 / ~**ly** *ad.* & *a.* =southerly (*ad.* & *a.*) ‖ **Southern Cross** [天]南十字;南十字(星)座 / ~ **hemisphere** 南半球 / ~ **lights** 南极光

southward ['sauθwəd] **I** *ad.* & *a.* 向南方(的) **II** *n.* 向南方向;南方地区 ‖ ~**ly** *ad.* & *a.* 向南方(的);来自南方的

southwards ['sauθwədz] *ad.* 向南方

southwester [sauθ'westə] *n.* ①西南大风(或风暴) ②海员用的防水帽

souvenir ['su:vəniə] *n.* 纪念礼物,纪念品 ‖ ~ **sheet** (印在纸片上的)纪念邮票

sou'wester [sau'westə] *n.* ①西南风,西南强风 ②海员用的防水帽 ③油布长雨衣(尤指在海上暴风雨时穿的)

sovereign ['sovrin] **I** *n.* ①君主,国王;统治者 ②[英]一金镑硬币(现不通用,面值一英镑) **II** *a.* ①最高的,无限的,无上的: ~ power 最高权力,绝对权力 / the ~ good (或 virtue) 至善 ②拥有最高权力的;独立自主的: a ~ state 主权国家 ③君主的,国王的 ④完全的,不折不扣的: in ~ contempt of danger 完全不顾危险地 ⑤极好的,有效的: a ~ remedy 特效药

sovereignty ['sovrənti] *n.* ①君权,统治权 ②主权

sow¹ [sou] (过去式 sowed,过去分词 sown [soun]

或 sowed) ❶ *vt.* ①播(种);播种于(土地等): ~ seeds in the field 在田里播种 / ~ a field with wheat 在田里播种小麦 ②散布,传播;惹起: ~ dissension (或 discord) 分化离间 / ~ suspicion 引起怀疑 ③使密布: a sky *sown* with stars 满天星斗 ❷ *vi.* 播种 ‖ *As a man ~s, so he shall reap.* (或 *You must reap what you have sown.*) 种瓜得瓜,种豆得豆。/ *reap as* (或 *what*) *one has sown* 自食其果 / *reap where one has not sown* 不劳而获 / *~ the wind and reap the whirlwind* 见 wind¹ ‖ ~er *n.* ①播种者 ②播种机 ③散布者,传播者;煽动者 ‖ '~**ing-ma'chine** *n.* 播种机

sow² [sau] *n.* ①大母猪;牝猪 ②[冶](高炉)铁水沟 (=~ channel);炉底结块: ~ iron 沟铁 ③【动】土鳖,地鳖(一种生于朽木、湿地等处的等足类甲壳动物) (=~ bug) ‖ *as drunk as a ~* 烂醉 / *get the wrong ~ by the ear* 弄错人(或事);得出错误的结论 / *One cannot make a silk purse out of a ~'s ear.* 见 purse ‖ '~**back** *n.* 山脊;沙丘 / '~,belly *n.* [口] 腌猪肉 / '~**bread** *n.*【植】仙客来 / ~ **thistle** 【植】苦苣菜

soy [soi] *n.* ①酱油 ②大豆,黄豆

soybean ['soi'bi:n] *n.* 大豆,黄豆: a ~ cake 豆饼

spa [spɑ:] *n.* ①矿泉;矿泉疗养地 ②(有闲阶级的)游乐胜地(或豪华旅馆)

space [speis] **I** *n.* ①空间;太空: time and ~ 时间和空间 / outer ~ 外层空间,宇宙空间 ②场地;空地;余地;篇幅: a floor ~ of 1,800 square metres 一千八百平方米的楼面面积 / the seating ~ of an auditorium 礼堂的座席面积 / This box occupies too much ~. 这只箱子占的地位太多了。/ There isn't much ~ left. 余地不多了。/ *Space* forbids. 篇幅不容许。③空白;距离,间隔: separate by a ~ of two metres 以两米的间隔分开 ④(一段)时间: in the ~ of three days 在三天之内 / after a short ~ 片刻后 / Let us rest a ~. 让我们休息一会儿。⑤(火车、轮船等预订的)座位,舱位 ⑥印刷(或书写)物的行间空白;打字稿一行的宽度: leave a ~ between lines 行与行之间留出空白 ⑦电台(或电视)为广告节目留出的时间 ⑧[印]空铅间隔 ⑨【音】(谱表的)线间空白,线间 ⑩【电】开键 **II** ❶ *vt.* 把…分隔开 (out): ~ out the lampposts 20 metres apart 把电线杆每根隔开二十米 ❷ *vi.* 留间隔 ‖ ~**less** *a.* ①无限的 ②不占地位的 / ~**ward** *ad.* 向太空 ‖ ~ **bar** (打字机上一按即跳格的)间隔棒 / ~ **cadet** ①响往星际旅行的青年人 ②[俚]好卖弄的飞行员 / ~ **charge** 【无】空间电荷 / '~**craft** *n.* 宇宙飞船 / ~ **fiction** 关于星际旅行的科学小说 / '~**flight** *n.* 外层空间飞行;小型供热器(装于室内,既不靠导管从室外热源采暖,也不通过规定排气) / ~ **heater** 宇宙飞行帽 / ~ **lattice** 【原】空间栅格;空间点阵 / '~**man** *n.* 宇宙飞行员;

宇宙科学工作者；太空人 / ～ **mark** 间隔符号(即 #) / ～ **medicine** 外层空间医学 / ～ **opera** 描写星际探险的幻想作品(尤指电视剧) / **'～port** *n.* 火箭、导弹和卫星的试验发射中心 / ～ **rocket** 宇宙火箭 / **'～,saving** *a.* 节省篇幅的 / ～ **science** 宇宙学 / **'～ship** *n.* 宇宙飞船 / ～ **shuttle** 【宇】航天飞行；航天飞机 / ～ **station,** ～ **platform** 空间站，宇宙站 / ～ **suit** 宇宙飞行服 / **'～time** *n.* 【物】【数】时空连续体；时空(关系) / ～ **travel** 宇宙飞行 / **'～walk** *n.* & *vi.* 空间行走，宇宙行走(指离开飞船外出活动) / ～ **writer** 照篇幅取稿费的撰稿人

spacious ['speiʃəs] *a.* 广阔的；宽敞的；广大的 ‖**～ly** *ad.* / **～ness** *n.*

spade[1] [speid] **I** *n.* ①铲；铁锹 ②铲形物；【军】驻锄(在炮架架尾的后端，插入地面，用以阻止炮架因后坐力而移动的锄形装置) **II** ❶ *vt.* 铲；用铁锹掘：～ up the vegetable patch 铲平菜园 ❷ *vi.* 铲 ‖*call a* ～ *a* ～ 是啥说啥,直言不讳 / **～ful** *n.* 一铲，一锹 / **～r** *n.* 铲人；(用铲子等)铲的人 ‖ **spading fork** (一种农具)叉(尤指四齿叉)

spade[2] [speid] *n.* ①(纸牌中的)黑桃牌；(一张)黑桃牌；[复]一副黑桃(牌) ②[美俚][贬]黑人 ‖*in ～s* [美俚] ① 肯定地；明确地；非常: Whether you realize it or not, you've made a mistake—*in ～s*. 不管你有没有意识到，你已肯定搞错了。②毫不迟疑地；坦率地；毫不留情地: She is going to criticize him, *in ～s*. 她将坦率地批评他。

spaghetti [spə'geti] *n.* [意] ① 细条实心面(与 macaroni 空心面相对) ②【电】漆布绝缘管, 绝缘套管

span[1] [spæn] **I** *n.* ①指距，一拃宽(手掌张开时, 大拇指和小指两端的距离, 通常为 9 吋或 23 厘米): measure by ～*s* 用指距来量 ② 全长；【空】翼展: the whole ～ of a bridge 桥的全长 ③ (桥墩间的)墩距；孔；跨距, 跨(度)；支点距: a bridge of four ～*s* 四孔桥 / the ～ of a crane 起重机臂伸距 / the ～ of an arch 拱跨 ④ 一段时间: in a short ～ of three years 在短短的三年之中 / the whole ～ of Roman history 罗马的全部历史 / lengthen the machine's life ～ 延长机器的使用寿命 ⑤(思想活动的)广度: widen the ～ of knowledge 扩大知识面 / the ～ of memory 记忆广度 ⑥【海】跨缆 ⑦ 双马；双骡; 共轭牛 **II** (spanned; spanning) ❶ *vt.* ①以指距量; 量: His eye *spanned* the intervening space. 他目测间隔距离。② 横跨；跨越;[喻]弥补: ～ a river with a bridge 在河上架桥 / Rails ～ mountains and rivers. 铁路跨山越水。 / It takes twenty minutes to ～ the bay. 越过海湾需二十分钟。③【海】缚住, 扎牢 ❷ *vi.* 尺蠖般地蠕动 ‖～ **dogs** 木材抓起机 / **'～-'new** *a.* 簇新的, 崭新的 / ～ **roof** 【建】等斜屋顶 / **'～worm** *n.* 【动】尺蠖

spangle ['spæŋgl] **I** *n.* ①(尤指衣服上用作装饰的)亮晶晶的金属片(或塑料片) ②亮晶晶的小东

西 **II** ❶ *vt.* 用发光的金属片装饰；使闪烁: The sky is ～*d* with stars. 天空闪烁着星星。 / the Star-*Spangled* Banner 星条旗(美国国旗);美国国歌 ❷ *vi.* 闪烁

spaniel ['spænjəl] *n.* ①一种长毛垂耳狗; 獚 ②马屁精

spank [spæŋk] **I** ❶ *vt.* ①(用手掌等)打…的屁股; 拍击 ②鞭策…前进 ③[美俚](在比赛中)击败 ❷ *vi.* (马等)飞跑; (船等)疾驶 **II** *n.* 一掴; 一巴掌 ‖**～er** *n.* ①急行的人; 飞跑的马 ②[口]出色的人(或东西) ③【船】后樯纵帆

spanking ['spæŋkiŋ] **I** *a.* ①疾行的; 快的 ②劲吹的; 强烈的: a ～ breeze 劲风 ③[口]第一流的; 极好的: have a ～ time 过得很痛快 **II** *ad.* 显著地; 突出地: a ～ new design 崭新的式样 **III** *n.* 打屁股; 拍击

spanner ['spænə] *n.* ①扳手, 扳头, 扳钳, 搬子: an adjustable (或 a monkey) ～ 活动扳手; 活搬子 ②【建】(桥梁的)交叉支撑, 横拉条 ③【动】尺蠖 ‖*throw a ～ into the works* 从中捣乱

spar[1] [spɑː] *n.* 【矿】晶石: calcareous ～ 重晶石 / fluor ～ 萤石, 氟石 / Iceland ～ 方解石, 冰洲石

spar[2] [spɑː] **I** *n.* ①圆材(如船舶的桅杆、帆桁等) ②【空】(翼)梁 **II** (sparred; sparring ['spɑːriŋ]) *vt.* ①装圆材于 ②用圆材使(船)脱离浅滩 ‖～ **buoy** 【海】杆状浮标 / ～ **deck** 【船】轻甲板

spar[3] [spɑː] **I** (sparred; sparring ['spɑːriŋ]) *vi.* ①(拳击中)用拳攻击与防卫; 拳斗 ②[喻]争论; 争吵 ③(鸡)用脚踢斗 **II** *n.* ①拳斗动作; 拳击比赛 ②争论 ③斗鸡 ‖**sparring-match** *n.* ①示范性拳赛 ②争论 / **sparring partner** 拳击练习的对手

spare [spɛə] **I** ❶ *vt.* ①节约, 省用; 吝惜: ～ no efforts (或 pains) 不遗余力 / ～ no expense 不惜工本 / We hope that readers will not ～ their comments. 我们希望读者不无保留地提出意见。②用不着; 省掉: We can ～ you for tomorrow. 明天我们可以不要你帮忙了。 / He could have ～*d* the explanation. 他本可不必解释。③抽出 (时间); 剩下; 出让, 让给: have no time to ～ 抽不出时间 / He caught the train with a few minutes to ～. 他赶上火车时还剩下几分钟。 / He said he could ～ me half an hour. 他说他能为我抽出半小时来。(或: 他说他能让我有半小时的自由活动时间。) / Can you ～ me this book for a while? 这本书你能让我看一会儿吗? ④饶恕, 赦免; 不伤害: ～ sb.'s life (或 ～ sb. his life) 饶某人一命 / ～ sb.'s feelings 不使某人难过 (或难堪) / *Spare* his blushes. 别叫他脸红了。 / He does not ～ himself. 他对自己要求很严。❷ *vi.* ①节约, 节俭 ②饶恕; 宽容 **II** *a.* ①多余的, 剩下的; 空闲的: ～ money 余款 / ～ time 余暇 ②备用的: a ～ room 备用房间(如客房) / a ～ tyre 备用轮胎 [美俚]多余的人; 讨厌的人 ③节约的; 少量的; 贫乏的: a ～ diet 简单的饮食 / He is ～ *of* speech. 他很少说话。④瘦的: a man of ～ frame 瘦小的男子 **III** *n.* ①(机器等的)备

件; 备用品; 备用轮胎 ②[美](十柱戏)头两个球
把十柱打得全倒 ‖(*enough*) *and to* ~ 很多, 大
量; 有余: We have grain (*enough*) *and to* ~. 我
们的粮食很宽裕。/ *if one is* ~d 如果活着 /
Spare the rod and spoil the child. 见 rod
‖~**able** ['speərəbl] *a.* 可节省的; 可让出的; 可
饶恕的 / ~**ly** *ad.* 节约地; 少量地; 贫乏地; 瘦
小地 / ~**ness** *n.* ‖~ **hand** 替班工人 / ~ **part**
(机器等的)备件 / '~**time** *a.* 业余的: a ~*time
school* 业余学校
spark¹ [spɑːk] I *n.* ①火花, 火星: A single ~ can
start a prairie fire. 星星之火, 可以燎原。/
Sparks flew from the furnace. 炉中射出火花。
②(宝石等的)闪光; [美]小宝石, 金刚钻 ③生气,
活力; (才智等的)焕发: the ~ of life 生气, 活
力 / strike ~s out of sb. 激发某人的才智 ④
[常用于否定句]丝毫, 一点点: He showed *not a*
~ *of interest.* 他丝毫不感兴趣。⑤【电】电花;
瞬态放电; 【机】(火花塞里的)控制放电装置 ⑥
[~s][用作呼]船上无线电操作员 II ❶ *vi.* ①
发火花, 飞火星; 发电花; 闪耀: Her eyes ~ed
with fury. 她眼冒怒火。②热烈赞同; 欣然同意:
~ to the idea of an early start 热烈赞成早一
点出发 ❷ *vt.* ①发动 / 激发(感情等); 鼓舞:
Our success ~ed us to fresh efforts. 我们的成
就鼓舞我们作进一步努力。‖*as the* ~*s fly
upward* 象自然规律那样确实无疑 ‖~**less** *a.*
不发火花(或电花)的 ‖~ **arrester** 火花避雷器;
防止火花外射的装置 / ~ **gap** 火花隙; 放电器,
避雷器 / ~ **plug** 火花塞; 电孔插头(=[英]
~**ing plug**) ②[美]积极的促进者, 中坚分子 /
'~**plug** *vt.* 发动, 激励
spark² [spɑːk] I *n.* ①翩翩少年; 花花公子 ②情
郎 II *vt.* & *vi.* (向…)求婚; (向…)求爱 ‖~**ish**
a. 翩翩少年似的; 情郎似的 / ②服饰华丽的
sparkle ['spɑːkl] I ❶ *vi.* ①发火花; 闪耀; (才智
等)焕发: Dewdrops ~ in the morning sun. 露
珠在早晨的阳光下闪闪发光。/ Her eyes ~d
with joy. 她的眼睛闪耀着喜悦的神情。/ The
dialogue ~s with wit. 这段对话妙趣横生。
②(香槟酒等)发泡 ❷ *vt.* ①使闪耀, 使闪光
②用眼神表示(喜悦等) II *n.* ①火花; 闪耀, 闪
光; 光彩 ②生气, 活力 ③发泡 ‖~**r** *n.* ①闪光
的东西; 钻石; 烟火, 花炮 ②才华焕发的人
sparrow ['spærou] *n.* ①麻雀 ②[美]个子小的人
‖~**bill** *n.* =sparable / '~**grass** *n.* [方]【植】
石刁柏, 芦笋 / '~**hawk** *n.* 【动】(食)雀鹰 /
'~**tongue** *n.* 【植】蔨蓄
sparse [spɑːs] *a.* 稀少的; 稀疏的: a ~ population 稀少的人口 / ~ hair 稀疏的头发 ‖~**ly**
ad. / ~**ness** *n.*
sparsity ['spɑːsiti] *n.* 稀少; 稀疏
spasm ['spæzəm] *n.* ①痉挛, 抽搐: a facial ~ 面
部痉挛 / a ~ of the stomach 胃痉挛 ②(动作,
感情等的)一阵发作: a ~ of coughing 一阵咳
嗽 / a ~ of excitement (pain) 一阵激动(痛苦)
spasmodic [spæz'mɔdik] *a.* ①痉挛的, 抽搐的; 由

痉挛引起的; 痉挛性的: ~ asthma 痉挛性气喘
②间歇的; 一阵阵的: ~ sobs 抽泣 / a ~ worker
做事忽冷忽热的人 ③易激动的 ‖~**ally** *ad.*
spat¹ [spæt] spit² 的过去式和过去分词
spat² [spæt] I ([复] spat(s)) *n.* 蠔卵, 牡蛎卵; 幼
蠔 II (spatted; spatting) *vi.* (蠔)产卵
spat³ [spæt] *n.* [常用复]鞋罩
spat⁴ [spæt] [美] I *n.* ①口角, 小争吵 ②[方]拍打
③(大雨点落下的)噼啪声 II (spatted; spatting)
❶ *vt.* [方]拍打 ❷ *vi.* ①争吵 ②雨点般溅落:
Bullets were *spatting* down. 子弹象雨点般落下。
spate [speit] *n.* ①大水, 洪水; (河水的)猛涨: The
river is in ~. 河水猛涨。②[苏格兰]倾盆大雨
③大量; 许多: a ~ of new books 大量新书 ④一
阵: a ~ of anger 一阵大怒
spatial ['speiʃəl] *a.* 空间的; 篇幅的; 存在(或发生)
于空间的; 占据空间的 ‖~**ly** *ad.*
spatter ['spætə] I ❶ *vt.* ①溅, 溅污; 洒: ~ the
floor with grease 把油污溅在地板上 / ~ mud
on sb.'s clothes 把污泥溅到某人的衣服上 ②污
蔑, 中伤: ~ sb. with slander 诽谤某人 ❷ *vi.*
滴下; 飞溅: The rain ~ed down on the roof. 雨
滴滴嗒嗒地落在屋顶上。II *n.* ①溅; 洒; 滴落;
飞溅: a ~ of rain 一阵雨 ②(雨等的)淅沥声;
飞溅声 ③泼溅的污迹: mud (grease) ~s 泥(油)
迹 ④少量; 点滴
spawn [spɔːn] I *n.* ①(鱼, 蛙等水生动物一次产
下的)卵, 子 ②[蔑]小子; 小畜生: You young
devil's ~! 你这小鬼! ③产物 ④(不良事物的)
根源 ⑤【植】(繁殖菌类植物的)菌丝 II ❶ *vt.*
①(鱼等)产(卵); 使(鱼)产卵 ②[贬](人)生育
③酿成, 引起 ④种菌丝于(苗床) ❷ *vi.* ①产卵
②大量生育
speak [spiːk] (过去式 spoke [spouk] 或[古]
spake [speik], 过去分词 spoken ['spoukən])
❶ *vi.* ①说话, 讲话: The baby is learning to
~. 这孩子在学习讲话了。/ Please ~ more
distinctly. 请你讲清楚些。/ He ~s in French.
他用法语讲话。②谈话: I'll ~ to him *about* the
matter. 这件事我要同他谈一谈。/ We have
heard him ~ *of* it. ·我们听到过他谈及此事。
③发言, 演说 ④表明; (用语言以外的方式)表达:
The portrait ~s. 这幅画像栩栩如生。⑤(枪
炮, 乐器等)发响声; (狗)吠: The big guns *spoke*
thunderously. 大炮轰鸣如雷。⑥作证 ❷ *vt.*
①说, 讲; 操(某种语言): He does not ~ English.
他不会讲英语。/ Is French *spoken* here? 这里
通用法语吗? / How many languages do you ~?
你会讲几种语言? ②讲出, 说出: He ~s the
sentiments of us all. 他讲出了我们大家的感
想。/ ~ the truth 说老实话 ③显示; 表达(情
感等): In this passage the writer is ~*ing* his
own convictions. 在这段文章里, 作者表达出他自
己的坚定信心。④用响声宣告: The tower clock
~s night. 塔楼大钟的钟声报着夜晚的来临。
⑤[古]证明: His conduct ~s him pure and
noble-minded. 他的行为表明了他的纯洁和高

尚。⑥朗诵(短文等) ⑦(航海时用旗语等方式)与…联络，招呼 ‖*Actions ~ louder than words.* 见 action / *frankly (generally, strictly) ~ing* [用作插入语]坦率(一般，严格)地说 / *not to ~ of* 更不用说: We defy death, *not to ~* of hardships and difficulties. 我们死都不怕，更不用说艰苦困难了。/ *so to ~* 见 so / *~ by the book* 见 book / *~ daggers to sb.* 见 dagger / *~ down to sb.* 以上司的口吻对某人说话 / *~ for* ①代表…讲话; 充当…的代言人; 为…辩护 ②要求得到: *~ for tea* 要求喝茶 ③订购: *for* the new products 订购新产品 / *~ for itself* 不言而喻 / *~ for oneself* ①为自己辩护 ②发表个人意见 ③谈自己的事 / *~ highly of* 赞扬 / *~ ill (well) of* 说…坏(好)话 / *~ like a book* 见 book / *~ out* ①大胆地说 ②清楚和响亮地说 / *~ sb. fair* 对某人彬彬有礼地说话 / *~ to* ①对…说话; 招呼; 对…演讲 ②说到; 针对…讲: I shall *~ to* that point later. 我在后面还要说到那一点。/ *~ to* the topic under discussion 针对讨论的题目讲 ③责备: *~ to* sb. *about* his slackness in work 责备某人工作松懈 ④证明: I can *~ to* his veracity. 我可以证明他说的是实话。/ *~ up* = out / *~ volumes for* 见 volume / *~ well for* 证明…很好: It *spoke well for* him that his every shot told. 他百发百中，这说明他很行。/ *to ~ of* [常用于否定句]值得一提的: It is nothing *to ~ of.* 那不值得一提。‖**~able** *a.* 可以交谈的; 可说出口的 ‖**~,easy** *a.* [美俚]非法酒店

speaker ['spi:kə] *n.* ①说话者; 演讲者; 演说家; 代言人 ②[S-] (英国下议院、美国众议院)议长 ③扬声器(=loudspeaker) ④[美]练习演讲用的范本 ‖**~ship** *n.* 议长的职位; 议长的任期 ‖**~phone** *n.* 扬声器电话(指由电话线连接的对讲装置，包括话筒和扬声器)

spear [spiə] **I** *n.* ①矛，枪，梭镖; 鱼叉 ②持矛的人; 持矛的士兵 ③(草的)叶片; 幼芽，幼苗 **II** ❶ *vt.* 用矛刺; 用鱼叉刺 ❷ *vi.* ①刺，戳 ②(植物)发芽成茎 **III** *a.* 父系的: the ~ side of the family 家族中的父系一方 ‖**~head** *n.* ①矛头; 枪尖: the ~*head* of struggle 斗争的矛头 ②先头突击部队 ③尖端; 先锋 *vt.* 领先突击; 当…的先锋: ~*head* the attack 当进攻的先锋 / **~man** ['spiəmən] *n.* 持矛的人; 持矛的士兵 / **~mint** *n.* 【植】绿薄荷，留兰香: ~*mint* oil 留兰香油

spear

special ['speʃəl] **I** *a.* ①特殊的，特别的: a ~ purpose 特殊目的 / be worthy of ~ mention 值得一提 / pay ~ attention to 特别注意… ②专门的，特设的: a ~ correspondent 特派记者 / ~ troops 【军】特种部队 / a ~ hospital 专门医院 / On holidays the railways put on ~ trains. 在节日铁路增开专车。/ a ~ administrative area (行政)专区 ③附加的，额外的: ~ treatment 额外待遇 / a ~ edition (of a newspaper) (报纸的)特刊，号外 ④特别亲密的; 主要的: He is not a ~ friend of mine. 他不是我的挚友。 **II** *n.* ①临时警察; 特别警卫员 ②特别的东西; 专车，临时列车; 特刊，号外; 特别考试; 特约稿; 特写稿(或通讯) ‖**~ism** *n.* (学科等方面的)特长; 专门学科; 专门化 / **~ist** *n.* ① 专家: a ~*ist in* geology (或 a geology ~*ist*) 地质学专家 ②[美] (陆军中)级别在下士与军事长之间的士兵 / **~ly** *ad.* 特别地; 尤其: I came here ~*ly* to see you. 我特地到这儿看你。/ **~ness** *n.* 特殊，专门 ‖**~, agent** ①特别经理人; 特别代理人 ②特务分子 / **~ area** [英]长期不景气的工业地区 / **~ constable** 临时警察 / **~ delivery** [美]邮件的快递 / **~ pleading** ①【律】间接答辩法(不直接答复对方，而提出新事实以抵销对方论点效果) ②(抓住对己有利的一点尽力发挥而对不利之处则回避的)诡辩法

speciality [,speʃi'æliti] *n.* ①特性，特质 ②专门研究; 专业; 特长: Physics is his ~. 物理学是他的专业(或专长)。/ make a ~ of English 专门研究英语 ③特制品，特产: Shell carvings are a ~ of the town. 贝雕是这座城的特产。/ Ink is a ~ of this factory. 这家工厂专造墨水。④【律】盖印契约(或契据) ⑤[复]特点，细节

specialize ['speʃəlaiz] ❶ *vt.* ①特加指明; 列举: ~ one's accusation 指明控诉 / ~ each item 逐项列举 ②把…用于专门目的; 限定…的范围; 使专门化: ~ one's studies 使研究专门化 ③在(票据)上作记明受款人的背书 ④[英]使特化，使专化 ❷ *vi.* ①成为专家; 专门研究; 专攻: He ~*s in* chemistry. 他专门研究化学。②逐条详述 ③【生】特化，专化 ‖**specialization** [,speʃəlai'zeiʃən] *n.* ①特殊化，专门化 ②【生】特化(作用); 专化性 / **~d** *a.* ①专门的; 专科的: ~*d* knowledge 专门知识 / a highly ~*d* reference library 高度专业化的参考图书馆 ②【生】特化的，专化的

specie ['spi:ʃi:] *n.* 硬币: ~ payments 硬币支付 ‖*in* ~ ①用硬币: be paid *in* ~ 被付给硬币 ②以同种类(或形式)

species ['spi:ʃi:z] [单复同] *n.* ①种类: feel a ~ of uneasiness 有一种不安的感觉 ②【生】[冠]种: The Origin of Species 《物种起源》(达尔文著) ③[原]核素 ④【律】式样，形式 ⑤[宗]圣餐物 ‖*the* (或 *our*) ~ 人类

specifiable ['spesifaiəbl] *a.* 能指定的; 能详细说明的; 能列举的

specific [spi'sifik] **I** *a.* ①特有的，特定的: a ~

style 独特的风格 ②具体的; 明确的: according to ~ circumstances 根据具体情况 / have no ~ aim 没有明确目标 ③【生】种的: the ~ name of an animal 动物的种名 ④【医】有特效的; 由特种病菌（或病毒）引起的: a ~ remedy 特效药 ⑤【物】比的: ~ gravity 比重 / ~ heat 比热 ⑥【商】从量的: a ~ duty 从量税 **II** *n.* ①特定用途的东西 ②【医】特效药: a ~ for (或against) dysentery 痢疾特效药 ③特性 ④细节; [复](计划、建议等的)详细说明书

specification [,spesifi'keiʃən] *n.* ①载明，详述 ②[常用复]规格,规范;明细单;计划书 ③(载有约定条件等的)说明书; 列入说明书的一个项目 ④对发明物申请专利的说明书 ⑤【律】用他人的原料加工制成新产品; 对来料加工制成新产品所取得的权利

specify ['spesifai] *vt.* ①指定; 详细说明: The contract *specifies* steel sashes for the windows. 合约指定用钢窗。/ The products have reached state-*specified* standards. 产品已达到国家规定的标准。/ as *specified* 按照说明 ②把…列入说明书(或清单)

specimen ['spesimin] *n.* ①样本; 标本; 样品; 抽样: collect insect ~*s* 收集昆虫标本 / pages of a book 书籍的样张 / send a ~ of sb.'s urine to the hospital for examination 把某人小便的抽样送交医院检验 ②供检查用的材料,试料: wool ~*s* for staple testing 供检验纤维长度用的羊毛试料 ③[口][贬]怪人; 怪事: an unsavoury ~ 讨厌的家伙 / What a ~! 真是个怪人!

speciology [,spi:ʃi'olədʒi] *n.* 【生】物种学 ‖**speciological** [,spi:ʃiə'lodʒikəl] *a.*

speciosity [,spi:ʃi'ositi] *n.* ①外表美观; 华而不实 ②似是而非; 貌似有理

specious ['spi:ʃəs] *a.* ①外表美观的; 华而不实的: a ~ person 华而不实的人 ②似是而非的; 貌似有理的: ~ reasoning 似是而非的推理 ‖**~ly** *ad.* / **~ness** *n.*

speck[1] [spek] **I** *n.* ①斑点; 污点; 缺点: a ~ on cloth 布上的污迹 / a character without a ~ 没有污点的人格 ②微粒, 小点; 一点点: a ~ of dust 一点灰尘 / a ~ in a vast ocean 沧海一粟 / a ~ of milk 一点儿牛奶 / arouse not a ~ of interest 引不起一点兴趣 ③(水果上的)烂斑, 疵伤 ④有斑点的东西; 有烂斑的水果; 有斑点的鱼 **II** *vt.* 使有斑点; 使弄上污点 ‖**~ed** *a.* 有斑点的; 有疵痕的 / **~less** *a.* 无斑点的

speck[2] [spek] *n.* (美国及南非用语)肥肉; (海豹、鲸等的)脂肪

speckle ['spekl] **I** *n.* 小斑点: a grey hen with white ~*s* 一只白斑灰色母鸡 **II** *vt.* 使弄上斑点; 使玷污: The pond is ~*d* with foam. 池塘里有一点一点的水泡。②点缀: a mountain slope ~*d* with houses 点缀着房屋的山坡 ‖**~d** *a.* 有斑点的

spectacle ['spektəkl] *n.* ①公开展示, 场面: The

ceremonial opening of the exhibition was a fine ~. 展览会的开幕式是一个壮观的场面。②光景, 景象; 奇观, 壮观 ③[复]眼镜; 护目镜: a pair of ~*s* 一副眼镜 / a man in ~*s* 一个戴眼镜的男子 / wear (take off) ~*s* 戴(摘下)眼镜 ④(铁路上红绿信号灯的)玻璃框 ‖**look through colo(u)red** ~*s* 戴着有色眼镜看 / **make a (sorry)** ~ **of oneself** 使自己出丑, 出洋相 / **see everything through rose-colo(u)red** ~*s* 凡事抱乐观态度 ‖**~d** *a.* ①戴眼镜的 ②有眼镜状斑纹的: a ~*d* cobra 眼镜蛇

spectacular [spek'tækjulə] **I** *a.* ①公开展示的; 场面富丽的; 壮观的, 洋洋大观的 ②引人注意的; 惊人的: a ~ achievement in science 科学上的一项惊人成就 **II** *n.* ①展览物; 壮观的景象 ②[美](长达一小时半以上的)场面富丽的电视表演 ③[美]引人注目的霓虹灯(或电灯)广告 ‖**~ity** [spek,tækju'læriti] *n.* 壮观; 惊人 / **~ly** *ad.*

spectator [spek'teitə; 美 'spekteitə] *n.* (比赛等的)观众; 旁观者

spectre, specter ['spektə] *n.* 鬼怪; 幽灵; 无法摆脱的忧惧

spectrum ['spektrəm] ([复] spectra ['spektrə] 或 spectrums) *n.* ①系列; 范围: a diverse ~ of political tendencies 一系列不同的政治倾向 / the whole ~ of industry 整个工业范围 ②【物】谱; 波谱; 光谱: atomic ~ 原子光谱 / solar ~ 太阳光谱 ③[无]射频频谱; 无线电(信号)频谱 ④【心】余象

speculate ['spekjuleit] *vi.* ①思索; 沉思; 推测 (on, upon, about): ~ upon the origin of the universe 推究宇宙的起源 ②投机: ~ in stocks 做股票投机

speculation [,spekju'leiʃən] *n.* ①思索; 沉思; 推测: I am sorry to disturb your ~*s*. 打扰了你的思考, 很抱歉。/ Much ~ is rife about this matter. 关于此事流行着种种推测。②投机; 投机事业, 投机买卖: engage in ~ 从事于投机 / buy sth. as a ~ 投机购买某物 ③一种纸牌戏

speculator ['spekjuleitə] *n.* ①思索者; 推理者; 抽象的理论家 ②投机者, 投机商

sped [sped] speed 的过去式和过去分词

speech [spi:tʃ] *n.* ①言语; 谈话, 说话; 说话方式(或能力等): express one's thoughts by ~ 用说话表达思想 / practise freedom of ~ (或 free ~) among the people 在人民内部实行言论自由 / the faculty of ~ 说话的能力 / find (lose) one's ~ 说得出(说不出)话 / clear (indistinct) ~ 说话清楚(不清楚) / a ~ organ 发音器官; 喉舌 ②演说; 发言; 讲话: an opening (a closing) ~ 开幕(闭幕)词 / a set ~ 经过准备的演说 / deliver (或 make) a ~ on current affairs 作关于当前形势的报告 / the King's (或 Queen's) (或 the ~ from the throne) 英国议会开幕时国王(或女王)所作(或委托宣读)的国情与施政演说 ③民族语言; 方言; 专门语言: a ~ community 使

用某种特有语言(或方言)的集团 / a musical ~ 音乐语言 ④[语]词(类);引语;用语: parts of ~ 词类 / the direct (indirect) ~ 直接(间接)引语 / a figure of ~ 一种修辞用法 ⑤(乐器)发声 ||*Speech is silver* (或 *silvern*), *silence is golden.* [谚]雄辩是银,沉默是金。||~ **amplifier** 【无】音(或声)频放大器 / ~ **centre** 言语中枢 / '~**craft** *n.* 口才,辞令 / ~ **day** [英](学校)一年一度的授奖典礼日 / '~,**maker** *n.* 演讲人,发言者 / '~,**prefix** *n.* (剧本)台词前注的人物姓名(常缩写) / '~,**reading** *n.* 视话法(聋哑人看别人嘴动而了解意义的方法) / '~**way** *n.* 某民族(或地区、集团)特有的言语方式

speechless ['spi:tʃlis] *a.* ①不会说话的,哑的 ②说不出话的: be ~ *with* (或 *from*) surprise 惊讶得说不出话来 ③无言的;非言语所能表达的: Her frown gave him a ~ message. 她的皱眉给了他一个暗示。/ ~ terror 说不出的恐惧 ④[俚]烂醉的 ||~**ly** *ad.* / ~**ness** *n.*

speed [spi:d] **I** *n.* ①快,迅速: a horse of ~ 快马 / move with great ~ 很快地移动 / It's dangerous to corner at ~. 高速转弯是危险的。②速率,速度: drive at full (或top) ~ 全速驾驶 / travel at a ~ of thirty kilometres an hour 以一小时三十公里的速度行驶 / put on ~ 加快速度 ③(胶片、照相纸等的)感光速率;(摄影机的)曝光速率 ④(汽车等的)速率排挡: first (second, third, fourth) ~ 头(二,三,四)档速率 ⑤[古]昌盛,成功: wish sb. good ~ 祝愿某人成功 **II** (sped [sped] 或 speeded) **❶** *vi.* ①迅速前进,快行: ~ through wind and waves 斩风劈浪向前猛进 / The boy *sped down* the street. 那孩子沿街飞奔而去。②(驾车者)以非法(或危险)的速度行驶 ③加速(up): The heart ~s up. 心跳加速。④[古]过日子;兴隆;成功: How have you *sped*? 您近来可好? **❷** *vt.* ①快速传送;发射: He *sped* the ball on its way. 他带球迅速前进。/ ~ an arrow 射箭 ②促进;使加速(前进);使赶快: ~ the process of digestion 促进消化作用 / ~ the construction pace 加快建设步伐 / ~ the wounded back to health 使伤员早日恢复健康 ③调整(机器)的速率;使定速运行 ④祝愿(某人)一路平安;祝愿(某人)运气好;[古]使成功,使兴隆: ~ the parting guests 祝愿客人一路顺风 / God ~ you. (基督教徒用语)愿上帝使你成功。||*at railway* ~ 飞快地 / *Full* ~ *ahead!* [海]全速前进! / ~ **up** (使)加快速度 ||~**er** *n.* ①[机]加速器;调速装置 ②违法超速驾驶者 ||'~**ball** *n.* ①一种类似足球但可用手接球和传球的运动 ②[俚]掺海洛因(或吗啡等)的可卡因 / '~**boat** *n.* 快速汽艇 / ~ **change gear** 【机】变速齿轮;变速装置 / ~ **cop** *n.* [俚]取缔汽车超速的骑摩托车的警察 / '~-**down** *n.* 减速 / '~**flash** *n.* =~**light** / ~ **indicator** 示速器,速度表,速度计 / '~**light** *n.* 闪光管,频闪放电管 / ~ **limit** 速度极限 / ~ **multiplier** 【机】

倍速器 / '~-,**reading** *n.* (掠过一些段落的)快速阅读 / ~ **scout** 【军】高速侦察机 / ~ **shop** 高速赛车部件商店 / '~-**track** *n.* =~way / ~ **trap** (汽车)速度监视所 / '~**up** *n.* ①增速,加速 ②(雇主对雇员提出的)增加产量(而不增加工资)的要求 / '~**way** *n.* ①高速车道,快车道,高速道路 ②(摩托车、汽车等的)赛车跑道 / '~**well** *n.* 【植】(药用)婆婆纳

speedometer [spi'dɔmitə] *n.* 【机】示速器,速度计;里程计

speedy ['spi:di] *a.* 快的;迅速的: a ~ reply 迅速的回答 ||**speedily** *ad.* / **speediness** *n.*

spell¹ [spel] (spelt [spelt] 或 spelled) **❶** *vt.* ①用字母拼;拼写: How do you ~ your name? 你的名字是怎样拼的? ②(字母)拼作,拼缀成: B-o-o-k ~s "book". ·b-o-o-k 拼缀成 "book"。③慢而费力地读懂 (*out, over*): ~ *out* a medieval manuscript 费力地读懂一部中世纪的手稿 ④认真研究出,琢磨;理解 (*out*): find it hard to ~ *out* sb.'s meaning 觉得很难理解某人的意思 ⑤招致;带来;意味: Delay ~s losses. 拖延招致损失。**❷** *vi.* 拼字: learn to ~ correctly 学会正确地拼写 ||~ **able** [美俚]有能力,干练 / ~ **backward** 倒拼;误解;曲解 / ~ **down** 在拼字比赛中胜过(某人) / ~ **out** 讲清楚;清楚地说明: These views will be further ~*ed out* in another article. 这些观点将在另一篇文章中进一步阐明。/ ~ **over** 思考;考虑 ||~**able** *n.* 可拼写的 / '~**er** *n.* ①拼字者 ②缀字课本 ||'~-**down** *n.* 拼字比赛

spell² [spel] **I** *n.* ①轮班,轮值;轮值时间: keep (或 take, have) one's regular ~ 按时换班 / take ~s at the oars 换班划船 ②(一段)工作时间: a ~ of carpentering 做木工的一段时间 / a ~ of service in the Foreign Ministry 在外交部服务的一段时间 ③[澳]休息时间: get a ~ 换班休息 ④发病时间;(疾病等的)一次发作: a ~ of coughing 一阵咳嗽 ⑤一段时间;(某种天气的)一段持续时间: rest for a ~ 休息片刻 / a ~ of cold weather (或 a cold ~) 一阵寒潮 / an exceptionally long ~ of drought 一段特别长的干旱期 ⑥[口]短距离 **II** *vt.* & *vi.* ①轮替 ②(使)换班休息 ||*by* ~ **s** 断断续续地: By ~s his stomach ached. 他的胃部一阵一阵地痛。

spell³ [spel] **I** *n.* ①符咒,咒语 ②吸引力,迷惑力,魅力 **II** *vt.* 使入迷: ~ one's audience 使听众入迷 ||*cast a* ~ *on* ①用符咒迷惑 ②迷住 / *under a* ~ ①被符咒镇住 ②被迷住,着迷 ||'~-**bind** *vt.* ①迷住,魅惑 ②用符咒镇住 / '~-,**binder** *n.* 能使听众入迷的演说者 / '~**bound** *a.* ①入迷的;出神的 ②被符咒镇住的

spelling ['speliŋ] *n.* 拼字;拼法,缀字法: This word has two ~s. 这字有两种拼法。|| ~ **bee** 拼字比赛 / ~ **book** 缀字课本 / ~ **pronunciation** 照拼法发音(指和不正确的发音,如 forehead,本应读作 ['fɔrid] 而照其拼法误读作 ['fɔ:hed])

spend [spend] (spent [spent]) ❶ ***vt.*** ①用(钱),花费: ~ money *on* books 花钱买书 / How much have you *spent*? 你花了多少钱? ②消耗; 用尽(弹药、气力等); 浪费: ~ all one's energies 竭尽全力; 耗尽精力 / The storm gradually *spent itself*. 暴风雨逐渐减弱。/ ~ a lot of care *on* sth. (in doing sth.) 在某事上(做某事时)费很多心血 ③消磨(时间); 度过, 过(日子): How do you ~ your spare time? 你怎样利用你的业余时间? ④献出(生命等); (船因风暴等)失去(桅杆) ❷ ***vi.*** ①花费; 浪费 ②(被)耗尽, 用尽: Candles ~ fast in draught. 风中之烛点得快。③(鱼等)产卵, 下子 ‖**~able** ***a.*** 可花费的 / **~er** ***n.*** 用钱(尤指浪费)的人: an extravagant *~er* 一个大肆挥霍的人 / **~ing** ***n.*** 经费, 开销: military *~ing* 军费 / *~ing* money [美]零用钱 ‖'**~all** ***n.*** 挥霍者, 浪费者

spendthrift ['spendθrift] **I** ***n.*** 挥霍者, 浪费者 **II** ***a.*** 挥霍的,浪费的

spent [spent] **I** spend 的过去式和过去分词 **II** ***a.*** ①用尽的; 精疲力竭的; 失去效能的: a ~ swimmer (horse) 精疲力竭的游泳者(马) / a ~ bullet 【军】乏弹(冲力已尽的子弹) ②(鱼等)产完卵的; 排完精的

sperm¹ [spəːm] ***n.*** ①鲸蜡, 鲸脑油 ②鲸油 ③巨头鲸,抹香鲸 ‖**~ oil** 鲸油 / **~ whale** 巨头鲸,抹香鲸

sperm² [spəːm] ***n.*** 精液; 精子

spew [spjuː] **I** ❶ ***vt.*** ①呕出 ②喷: a volcano *~ing* out lava 喷出熔岩的火山 ❷ ***vi.*** ①呕吐 ②涌出: a violently *~ing* flood 汹涌的洪水 ③渗出: Water *~ed* slowly from the soil. 水慢慢从土中渗出。**II** ***n.*** 呕吐物; 喷出物; 渗出物

sphere [sfiə] **I** ***n.*** ①球; 圆体; 球面; [美俚]棒球; 高尔夫球: geometry of *~s* 球面几何学 ②天体;星; 行星 ③地球仪; 天体仪 ④范围; 领域: a ~ of influence 势力范围 / the ideological ~ 意识形态领域 / in all *~s* of the superstructure 在上层建筑各个领域 ⑤地位,身分 ⑥[诗]天空; 天堂 **II** ***vt.*** ①使成球形 ②把…放在球内; 把…放在天体内 ③包围; 围住

spherical ['sferikəl] ***a.*** 球的; 球形的; 球面的; 天体的: a ~ valve 球形阀 / ~ aberration【物】球面像差 / ~ astronomy 球面天文学 / ~ geometry 球面几何学 / ~ sailing【海】球面航行(计算时考虑到地球的球面形状的航海法) ‖**~ly** ***ad.***

spheroid ['sfiərɔid] **I** ***n.*** 球(状)体; 扁球体; 椭球体 **II** ***a.*** =spheroidal

sphinx [sfiŋks] ([复] sphinxes 或 sphinges ['sfindʒiːz]) ***n.*** ① [S-]【希神】斯芬克斯(带翼狮身女怪。传说她常叫过路行人猜谜, 猜不出者即遭杀害): a *Sphinx's* riddle 怪谜; [喻]难题 ②(古埃及)狮身人面像, 狮身羊头(或鹰头)像: the *Sphinx* (埃及吉萨地方金字塔附近的)狮身人面巨像 ③[喻]谜样的人物 ④【动】天蛾; 一种西非狒狒

spice [spais] **I** ***n.*** ①香料, 调味品: a dealer in ~ 香料商人 / Pepper, ginger, nutmeg, etc. are *~s*. 胡椒、生姜、豆蔻等都是调味品。②香气, 香味 ③[喻]趣味, 风味: a story that lacks ~ 乏味的故事 / a ~ of humour 幽默风味 **II** ***vt.*** ①加香料于 ②使增添趣味 ‖'**~ˌberry** ***n.*** 香料作物(尤指白珠树属植物) / **~ box** 香料盒 / '**~bush** ***n.***【植】①黄果山胡椒 ②西美蜡梅

spider ['spaidə] ***n.*** ①蜘蛛 ②设圈套者: ~ and fly 设圈套者和入圈套者 ③三脚架 ④有柄带脚煎锅 ⑤【机】星形轮; 十字叉 ⑥(中耕机用的)泥土粉碎器 ⑦[美俚]缫丝工人 ‖**~like** ***a.*** 蜘蛛似的 ‖**~ crab**【动】尖头蟹 / **~ line** (光学仪器)交叉瞄准线,叉丝 / **~ monkey**【动】蛛猴 / **~ wasp**【动】(幼虫食蜘蛛的)黄蜂 / **~ web** ①蜘蛛网 ②蜘蛛网状的东西: a ~ *web* of railways 纵横交错的铁路线

spike¹ [spaik] **I** ***n.*** ①(墙头上的尖头向上、防人翻越的)尖铁 ②大钉;【交】道钉 ③[复]鞋底钉; 底部有钉的鞋 ④长而尖的东西; 幼鹿的单枝鹿角 ⑤【动】(长不满六吋的)幼鲐 ⑥(赛跑等用的)钉鞋; 女子高跟鞋 ⑦【无】尖峰信号; 测试信号 ⑧[美俚]皮下注射用的针尖 **II** ***vt.*** ①用大钉钉; 加鞋底钉于(鞋等)上: *~d* running shoes 赛跑用的钉鞋 ②用长而尖之物刺 ③塞住(大炮)火门 ④阻止; 抑制; 使(计划等)受挫折: ~ a rumour 制止谣言 ⑤加酒精(或烈酒)于(饮料); 增强…的效果, 使增添生气(或风味): *~d* beer 加了威士忌的啤酒 ⑥(在球类比赛中)用运动鞋的鞋底钉踩伤(对方) ⑦将(排球)猛扣至对方场地 ‖***hang up one's ~s*** [口]退出职业运动界; 退休 / ***~ sb.'s guns*** 见 **gun** ‖**~r** ***n.*** ①钉道钉的护路工 ②钉大钉者 ③排球队的扣杀员 ‖**~ heel** 女子皮鞋上的高后跟 / **~ team** 一匹在前两匹并列在后的拉车马队 / '**~-tooth harrow** 附有多排铁齿的碎土、整土耙

spike² [spaik] ***n.***【植】①(谷物的)穗 ②穗状花序 ‖**~d** ***a.*** 有穗的, 长有穗状花序的 / **~let** ['spaiklit] ***n.*** 小穗; 小穗状花序

spill¹ [spil] **I** (spilt [spilt] 或 spilled) ❶ ***vt.*** ①使溢出; 使溅出; 使散落: ~ ink on the desk 把墨水泼在书桌上 / fill one's cup without *~ing* a drop 一滴不泼出地把杯子斟满 / ~ the salt all over the floor 洒了一地的盐 / an aeroplane *~ing* leaflets 在空中散发传单的飞机 ②使(血)流出: ~ the blood of sb. 杀死某人 ③倾倒出: Birds were *~ing* their song over the quiet woods. 寂静的林子里到处是鸟儿的歌声。④使(帆)漏风; 减小(风)对帆的压力 ⑤使摔下,使跌下: be *spilt* from a horse (vehicle) 从马(车)上摔下 ⑥泄漏(秘密等) ❷ ***vi.*** ①溢出; 溅出; (人群等)涌流: Don't let the soup ~ on your clothes. 别让汤泼在你的衣服上。/ Light *~ed* out through the windows. 光从窗子泻出。/ The hall had already been full; the latecomers *~ed* over to adjacent rooms. 大厅已挤满了, 后来的人便往邻室拥

去。/ Article after article ~*ed* from his pen. 一篇又一篇的文章从他笔下奔泻而出。 ② 充满: The sidewalks were ~*ing* over with people. 人行道上满是人。③(马、马车等)倾覆;(人)摔下,跌下 ④泄密 **II** *n.* ①溢出;溅出;散落 ②(人口等的)涌出 ③溢出量;溢出的东西 ④ = ~way ⑤摔下,跌下: take a ~ at a turn 在转弯时跌下 ⑥(价格的)骤降,暴跌 ‖ ~ **one's guts** [美俚]把自己知道的一切原原本本地说出去;告密 / ~ **the beans** [美俚]说漏嘴,不慎泄密 ‖ **~age** ['spilidʒ] *n.* ①溢出;溅出;涌出 ②溢出量 ‖ **~,over** *n.* ①溢出;溢出量 ②(大城市等)容纳不下的人口,外流人口 ③因某种商品供应不足而引起的对其他有关商品的需求 / **~way** *n.* 溢水口;溢洪道

spill² [spil] *n.* ①木片;点火用的纸捻 ②小塞子 ③小金属棒;销子 ④(包东西用的)锥形(或圆筒形)纸包

spin [spin] **I** (spun [spʌn]; spinning) **❶** *vt.* ①纺: ~ cotton into yarn 把棉花纺成纱 / ~ wool (flax) 纺羊毛(麻) ②(蚕等)吐(丝),作(茧);(蜘蛛)结(网): Silkworms ~ cocoons. 蚕作茧。/ a spider *spinning* its web 在结网的蜘蛛 ③(用车床等)旋(金属碗、杯等) ④编造,撰写(故事等): ~ a yarn 讲故事 ⑤使旋转: ~ a top 抽陀螺 / ~ records 放唱片 / ~ the bottle 把瓶子横放在平面上旋转(一种游戏;瓶停转时瓶口朝向谁,谁就应受罚等) ⑥[英俚](通过考试)不录取(学生) ⑦(通过离心力作用)抛出,丢开(*off*) ⑧[美俚]欺骗 **❷** *vi.* ①纺纱;从事纺绩 ②(蚕等)吐丝,作茧;(蜘蛛)结网 ③旋转;向后转;[喻]眩晕;疾驰 ⑤[空]旋冲 ⑥[英俚]考试不及格 ⑦[美俚]跳舞 **II** *n.* ①旋转;自旋: atomic (electron, nuclear) ~ 原子(电子,核)自旋 ②眩晕;内心素乱 ③疾驶;兜一圈: go for a ~ in a car (on a bicycle) 乘汽车(骑自行车)去兜一圈 ④[空]旋冲;螺旋: flat ~ 平螺旋 / tail ~ 尾旋 ⑤[澳]运气 ‖ ~ **in** [美俚]上床;睡午觉 / ~ **out** ①消磨,度过 ②拉长;拖延: never ~ *out* the material for a sketch into a novel 决不把速写材料拉长成小说 / try to gain time by *spinning out* the negotiation 企图拖延谈判以争取时间 ③使(钱等)勉强够用一段时间 ④(驾车人)使汽车作回形滑行 ‖ **~-off** *n.* ①母公司收回子公司全部股本使之脱离的做法 ②有用的副产品

spinach, spinage ['spinidʒ] *n.* ①菠菜 ②[美]不需要(或虚假)的东西;胡说八道 ③[美]杂乱的蔓生物;未加修剪的胡子

spinal ['spainl] **I** *a.* ①脊骨的,脊柱的;脊髓的 ②[生]针的;刺的;棘状突起的 **II** *n.* [医] ~ anaesthesia 脊髓麻醉,脊椎麻醉;脊髓性感觉缺失 ‖ **~ly** *ad.* 在脊骨方面;沿着脊骨 ‖ ~ **anaesthesia** 脊髓麻醉,脊椎麻醉;脊髓性感觉缺失 / ~ **column** [解]脊骨,脊柱 / ~ **cord** [解]脊髓 / ~ **nerve** [解](脊)髓神经

spindle ['spindl] **I** *n.* ①锭子,纺锤,筳子: the ~s in operation 开工锭数 ②心轴;指轴: a boring ~ (镗床的)镗杆 / a lathe ~ 车床轴 / a valve ~ 阀轴 / a wheel ~ 轮轴 ③门锁的转柄 ④线的度量单位(棉纱等于15,120码,麻纱等于14,400码) ⑤瘦长的人;细长的东西 ⑥[生]纺锤体 ⑦(栏杆的)纺锤形立柱 ⑧螺旋扶梯的中柱 ⑨[海]杆状警标 **II** **❶** *vi.* ①长得细长 ②长成细长茎 **❷** *vt.* ①装锭子于;使成锭子 ②用纺锤形锉刺(或打眼于) **III** *a.* ①(象)锭子的: a ~ buoy 纺锤形浮标 ②[古](家族)母系的,母方的: the ~ side 母方,母系(与the spear side 父方,父系相对) ‖ **~-legged, ~-shanked** *a.* 腿细长的 / **~-legs, ~-shanks** [复] *n.* ①细长的腿 ②[作单用]腿细长的人 / ~ **oil** [机]锭子油;轴润滑油 / ~ **tree** [植]欧卫矛,卫矛

spine [spain] *n.* ①脊骨,脊柱 ②类似脊骨的东西;书脊;地面上隆起地带;[喻]中心;支持因素: He has ~ and starch. 他有骨气,有毅力。③[植]针,刺 ④[动]刺,壳针 ⑤[地]火山栓,熔岩塔 ⑥[美俚]铁路上货车的平顶

spineless ['spainlis] *a.* ①无脊骨的 ②[喻]无脊气的;没有勇气的;柔弱无力的 ③[生]无刺的 ‖ **~ly** *ad.* / **~ness** *n.*

spinster ['spinstə] *n.* ①[美]从事纺绩的女子 ②未婚女子;老处女 ‖ **~hood** *n.* 未婚女子的身分;老处女的身分

spiral ['spaiərəl] **I** *a.* 螺旋(形)的;螺线的;蜷线的;盘旋的;盘旋上升的 **II** *n.* ①螺旋(形);螺线;蜷线 ②螺旋形的东西(如弹簧等) ③[空]旋旋(足球的)旋球 ⑤(物价等)不断加剧的上升(或下降) **III** (spiral(l)ed; spiral(l)ing) **❶** *vi.* ①盘旋: The smoke *spiral(l)ed* up. 烟缕绕上升。②(物价等)螺旋形地上升(或下降),不断加剧地增加(或减少) **❷** *vt.* ①使成螺旋形 ②使作螺旋形上升(或下降) ‖ *a vicious* ~ 恶性螺旋上升,恶性循环 ‖ **~ly** *ad.*

spire¹ ['spaiə] **I** *n.* ①螺旋;螺线 ②[动]螺旋部;(软体动物的)螺塔 **II** *vi.* 螺旋形上升 ‖ **~d** *a.* 螺旋形的

spire² ['spaiə] **I** *n.* ①塔尖;尖顶;锥形体 ②[植]幼叶;幼苗 **II** **❶** *vt.* 给…加塔尖 **❷** *vi.* ①塔状矗立;耸立 ②发芽 ‖ **~d** *a.* ①有塔尖的 ②成锥形的

spirit ['spirit] **I** *n.* ①(与肉体相对而言的)精神,心灵;灵魂: body and ~ 肉体和精神 ②[只用单][喻](时代等的)潮流,精神,风气;(文件、法律等的)精神实质: the ~ of the age (或 times) 时代精神 / consider the ~ of the law, not the letter of it 考虑法律的精神,不死扣文字 ③[只用单]气魄,气概;志气: the fighting ~ 斗志 / go at it with ~ 斗志昂扬地干着 ④[只用单]态度: in a ~ of fun 以开玩笑的态度 ⑤[复]情绪,心情;兴致: in high (或 great) ~s 情绪高涨,兴高采烈 / in poor (或 low) ~s 情绪低落,意气消沉 ⑥(具有某种精神或品质的)人物: What a noble ~ he is! 他是个多么高尚的人! / one of the leading ~s 主要(或领导)人物之一 / a master ~ 杰出人才 ⑦神灵;幽灵;鬼怪,妖精: the (Holy) *Spirit*【宗】圣灵 ⑧[常用复]烈酒;酒精;精(指任何馏出的液体);【医】酊剂: abstain from ~s 戒酒 / ~(s) of camphor 樟脑精 / ~(s) of wine 酒精,乙醇 II *vt.* ① 使精神振作;鼓舞,鼓励(*up*) ② 迅速而神秘地带走;拐走;偷走(*away, off*) ‖*be down in ~s* 情绪低落 / *break sb.'s ~* 挫某人锐气;使某人垂头丧气 / *give up the ~* 死去 / *in royal ~s* 情绪极佳,极为高兴 / *in ~s* 兴致勃勃 / *in (the) ~* 在内心;在精神上: be vexed *in ~* 心中烦恼 / *We shall be with you in (the) ~.* 精神上我们将和你们在一起。 / *keep up one's ~s* 振作精神 / *lose one's ~s* 垂头丧气 / *out of ~s* 没精打采 / *take sth. in a wrong ~* 对某事生气;对某事生气 / *the poor in ~* 温顺谦和的人 ‖~ **blue**【化】醇溶青 / ~ **ga(u)ge** 酒精比重计 / ~ **gum** 粘上假发用的胶水 / ~ **lamp** 酒精灯 / ~ **level**【物】(气泡)酒精水准器 / ~ **rapper** 自称可通过敲击桌子与死者通信息的巫师 / ~ **room**【海】食品贮藏室 / ~ **stove** (烹饪用的)酒精炉 / ~ **writing** 被认为是在神鬼缠身时写出来的东西

spirited ['spiritid] *a.* ①精神饱满的,生气勃勃的,活泼的;勇敢的,猛烈的: a ~ attack 猛烈的攻击 ②[用以构成复合词]精神…的;情绪…的;心地…的: high-~ 勇敢的;兴奋的 / low-~ 沮丧的,精神不振的 / public-~ 热心公益的 ‖~**ly** *ad.* / ~**ness** *n.*

spiritism ['spiritizəm] *n.* 招魂论(相信死者的灵魂可通过诸如击桌等方式与活人通信息);招魂术

spiritless ['spirit-lis] *a.* ①没精打采的,垂头丧气的; 灰心的 ②无生命的,死的 ‖~**ly** *ad.* / ~**ness** *n.*

spiritual ['spiritjuəl] I *a.* ①精神(上)的,心灵的: one's ~ 精神生活 ②神的;神圣的;宗教的;高尚的;超越世俗的 / ~ songs 圣歌,赞美歌 / lords ~ [英]上议院中的主教及大主教 ③鬼的;招魂论的;唯灵论的 II *n.* ①[复]有关教会的事情 ②[美]黑人的圣歌 ‖~**ly** *ad.*

spiritualist ['spiritjuəlist] *n.* ①唯灵论者 ②迷信招魂术者;关亡术师,巫 ‖~**ic** [,spiritjuə'listik] *a.*

spirituous ['spiritjuəs] *a.* 含酒精的;酒精成分高的

spit¹ [spit] I *n.* ①烤肉铁叉,炙叉 ②岬,伸入海中的狭长陆地,沙嘴;狭长的暗礁 II (spitted; spitting) *vt.* ①以炙叉穿过(肉片等) ②(以刀、矛等)刺,戳

spit² [spit] I (spat [spæt] 或 spit; spitting) ❶ *vt.* ①吐(唾液等);霏霏地下(雨、雪等): ~ blood 咯血 咯血而出(或愤怒地)说: ~ (out) curses at sb. 尖刻地咒骂某人 ③点燃: ~ a fuse 点燃导火线 ❷ *vi.* ①吐唾沫;吐痰;唾弃,蔑视: No *spitting*! 不准随地吐痰! / ~ in sb.'s face 啐唾沫于某人脸上 ②(雨、雪)霏霏下降;(钢笔)漏墨水 ③(蜡烛等)爆出火花;(枪等)发出火舌;(猫

等) 呼噜呼噜怒叫; (发动机等) 劈啪作响 II *n.* ①吐,啐;唾液 ②微雨;小雪 ③【动】(树上某些昆虫的)泡沫状分泌物 ④[口]一模一样,肖像(*of*): He is the very (或 dead) ~ *of* his father. 他活象他的父亲。 ‖~ *and polish* 对整洁(或礼节、外观等)的极度注重 / (士兵等)对营房、装备等的擦洗打扫 / ~ *in the eye of* 藐视,蔑视 / *Spit it out!* ①大声些! ②爽快地讲出来! / ~ *on* (或 *upon, at*) 向…吐唾沫; 对…表示蔑视(或憎恶、侮辱) / *the ~ and image* (或 *the spitting image*) *of* [口]同…简直一模一样的人(或东西) ‖~**ball** *n.* ① 小孩用唾沫弄湿了来扔人的纸团 ②(棒球中)用唾沫、汗水把球弄湿后的一击 / '~**box** *n.* 痰盂 / '~**fire** *n.* 烈性子的人(尤指女子)

spit³ [spit] ([复] spit(s)) *n.* 一铲的深度: Dig the patch two ~(s) deep. 把这块地掘到两铲深。

spite [spait] I *n.* 恶意;怨恨: from (或 out of) ~ 出于恶意 / vent personal ~ 泄私愤 / have a ~ against sb. (或 owe sb. a ~) 对某人怀恨在心 II *vt.* 恶意对待;刁难;使恼怒 ‖*in ~ of* 不顾,不管: keep on fighting *in ~ of* all setbacks 百折不回地战斗下去 / *in ~ of oneself* 不由自主地: He laughed *in ~ of himself*. 他不禁笑起来。

spiteful ['spaitful] *a.* 怀恨的;恶意的 ‖~**ly** *ad.* / ~**ness** *n.*

splash [splæʃ] I ❶ *vt.* ①溅,泼,使飞溅;溅湿;溅污: ~ water over the floor 泼水于地板上 / Don't ~ your dress. 不要溅湿你的衣服。 / ~ a page with ink (或 ~ ink on a page) 把墨水溅在书页上 ②使溅起水花(或泥浆);溅着泥浆(或水)走(路): Stop ~ing your feet in the puddles. 别踩踏这些水坑。 / We ~ed our way through the mud. 我们溅着泥浆前进。 ③(溅水般地)洒;撒: The sunset colours were ~ed across the skies. 天空布满夕阳西斜时的种种色彩。④使成斑驳状: mountainsides ~ed with snow 白雪斑斑的山腰 ⑤[美俚]以显眼地位展示(或发表);鼓吹 ⑥[美俚]击落(敌机等) ⑦[美俚](钱财): ~ one's money about 大肆挥霍 ❷ *vi.* ①溅起水(或泥浆),泼水;(在液体中)溅泼着行进: a fish ~ing about in the water 溅起水花的鱼 ②飞溅: fountains ~ing in the park 公园里飞溅的喷泉 / The water ~ed out of the tub upon the floor. 水从桶里飞溅出来,落在地板上。 ③发出溅水声落下;劈劈啪啪地撞击: 咯吱咯吱地踏着泥浆(或水)行进: The boy ~ed into the lake. 那男孩扑通一声跳入湖中。 / Rain ~ed against the window. 雨劈劈啪啪地打在窗户上。 / We ~ed across the stream. 我们溅着水走过小溪。④[美俚]洗澡;游泳 II *n.* ①溅,泼,飞溅 ②短时间的游泳 ③溅泼声,飞溅声: He jumped into the swimming pool with a ~. 他扑通一声跳入了游泳池。 / The rain came down in a ~. 瓢泼大雨哗哗而下。④溅起的泥浆(或水等);溅污的斑

点: There are some ~*es* of mud on your stockings. 你的袜子上有点泥迹。⑤色斑(尤指动物皮毛的斑点) ⑥夸示，炫耀; (夸示或炫耀所产生的)生动印象; (报刊上)引人注目的报道: The story got a front-page ~. 这条新闻在头版醒目地位登出。⑦[英口](掺威士忌酒等用的)少量汽水 ⑧米粉制成的香粉 ⑨[美俚]被击落的飞机 ⑩[美俚]水,一杯水; 汤 ‖*make a* ~ ①发出溅泼声 ②[口]作惊人注目的夸示; 引起一时的轰动 / ~ *down* (宇宙飞船在海洋中)溅落 ‖~*er n.* ①溅起泥浆(或水)的人(或物); 溅洒器 ②挡泥板: a wheel ~*er* 轮挡 ③(盥洗盆后保护墙壁的)防护板 ④[俚]挥霍无度的人 ‖~*board n.* ①挡泥板,挡溅板 ②(水坝溢洪道或水闸的)挡水板 / '~*down n.* (宇宙飞船在海洋中的)溅落 / ~ *guard* (装在车子后轮上的)挡泥板 / ~ *headline* (报纸等)显眼的大字标题

splay [splei] **I** ❶ *vt.* ①展开,张开(手掌、足趾等) (*out*) ②[建]使斜削; 使成八字形 ❷ *vi.* ①伸展开 ②[建]倾斜; 成八字形 **II** *n.* ①展开 ②[建]斜削; 斜面(度) **III** *a.* ①向外张开的; 八字形的; 宽扁的 ②笨重的; 样子难看的 ‖'~*foot n. & a.* 八字脚(的); 平蹠外翻脚(的)

spleen [spli:n] *n.* ①[解]脾 ②坏脾气,怒气; 恶意,怨恨: in a fit of ~ 怒气冲冲 / vent one's ~ on sb. 向某人大发脾气 / bear a ~ against sb. 对某人怀恨 ③[古]忧郁; 意气消沉 ‖~*less a.* 脾切除了的

splendid ['splendid] *a.* ①有光彩的; 灿烂的: ~ jewellery 光彩夺目的珠宝 ②壮丽的; 辉煌的: a ~ scene 壮丽的景象 / a ~ victory (achievement) 辉煌的胜利(成就) ③显著的; 杰出的: a ~ figure in history 历史上杰出的人物 ④[口]极好的; 极令人满意的: a ~ idea 极好的主意 / What ~ weather! 多么好的天气! / That's ~! 那可太好了! ‖~*ly ad.* / ~*ness n.*

splendo(u)r ['splendə] *n.* ①光辉; 光彩: the ~ of the sun 太阳的光辉 ②壮丽; 壮观 ③显赫; 杰出

splice [splais] **I** *vt.* ①拼接,迭接(木板等); 绞接,捻接(绳子等) ②[俚]使结婚: get ~*d* 结婚 **II** *n.* ①拼接; 绞接; 接合处 ②[俚]结婚 ‖*sit on the* ~ [俚](板球戏中)小心地取守势 / ~ *the main brace* 见 **brace**

splint [splint] **I** *n.* ①(编织篮子等用的)藤条; 薄木条: match ~*s* 火柴梗 ②(制铠甲用的)薄金属片 ③[英口]裂片 ④[医]夹板,夹: plastic ~*s* 石膏夹板 ⑤[动](马等)炮骨上的瘤 ‖~ *bone* **II** *vt.* 用夹板夹 ‖~ *bone* ①(马等的)赘骨 ②[解]腓骨 / ~ *coal* [矿]硬烟煤

splinter ['splintə] **I** *n.* ①(木头、玻璃、炮弹等的)裂片,破片,尖片: bomb ~*s* 弹片 / run a ~ into one's finger 手上扎了一根刺 ②分裂出来的小派别 ③微不足道的事情; 微小的东西 **II** *vt. & vi.* ①(使)裂成碎片; (使)分裂瘦的人 **II** *vt. & vi.* ①(使)裂成碎片; (使)分裂 ‖~*less a.* (玻璃等)不会裂成碎片的 ‖~ *bar* (马车等上)支承弹簧的横木 / ~ *deck* 【军】防破

片甲板 / ~ *party* 分裂出来的小派别 / '~*proof a.* 防破片的; 防弹片的

split [split] **I** (split; splitting) ❶ *vt.* ①劈开; 切开; 割裂; 撕裂: ~ a log 劈木头 / ~ up a hill to let the water through 劈山引水 / The explosion ~ our ears. 爆炸声震耳欲聋。②使分裂; 使分离; (平)分 ❷ *vi.* ①被劈开; 裂开; 爆裂: My head is *splitting*. 我头痛欲裂。②分裂; 分离; 破裂; 决裂, 断绝关系: ~ up into several factions 分成几派 ③[口]均分负担(或所得) ④[俚]告密: ~ on an accomplice 告发同犯 ⑤疾走 **II** *n.* ①劈裂; 割裂; 直裂口, 裂缝: a ~ in a rock 岩石的裂口 ②分裂, 分化; (分裂出的)派系, 派别 ③裂片, 薄片; (横剖的一层)兽皮; (编织用)劈开的柳条(或藤条等) ④[英]告密者; 便衣警察 ⑤[口]半瓶汽水; 半杯酒 ⑥[复](舞蹈、体操中的)劈叉: do the ~*s* 劈一字腿 ⑦[美俚](赃物等的)一份 ⑧水果片、冰淇淋、糖浆等制成的甜食 **III** *a.* 分裂的; 分离的; 裂开的; 劈开的: ~ bamboo 开的竹子 / a ~ decision 比赛中裁判员意见分歧的裁判 / ~ gear 【机】拼合齿轮 / ~ pin 【机】开尾销 ‖(*at*) *full* ~ [俚]拼命, 以极高速度 / *run like* ~ 飞奔 / ~ *chums* 绝交 / ~ *fair* [俚]说真话 / ~ *hairs* (*over sth.*) 见 **hair** / ~ *off* (使)分裂; (使)分离 / ~ *the carbon dioxide off* 裂解二氧化碳 / ~ *off* from sb. 和某人决裂 / ~ *one's sides* (*with laughter*) 捧腹大笑 / *one's vote* 见 **vote** / ~ *the difference* 见 **difference** ‖'~-'*hair a.* 极其精确的; 过分琐细的 / ~ *infinitive* 【语】分离不定式(副词插在 to 和原形动词间的结构) / '~-,*level a.* 【建】错层式的 / '~-*off n.* ①分裂; 分裂出去的东西(或派别) ②母公司向子公司的部分股本转移 / ~ *pea* 干燥后裂开的豌豆 / ~ *personality* 分裂人格 / ~ *second* 一刹那 / ~ *shift* 工作时间分成间歇较长的两段(或几段)的班头(如上半班在早晨、下半班在傍晚) / ~ *ticket* [美]同时投几个党候选人的票 / '~-*up n.* ①分裂; (股本的)分散转移; 母公司向子公司的全部股本转移 ②[美俚]吵架; 离婚

spoil [spoil] **I** (spoilt [spoilt] 或 spoiled) ❶ *vt.* ①损坏; 糟踢; 搞糟: kill the insects that ~ the fruit in orchards 消灭果园中损害水果的害虫 / *spoilt* ballot papers 因未按规定圈选而无效的选票,废票 / ~ the pleasure (或 fun) 扫兴 ②宠坏,溺爱: a ~*ed* child 宠坏的孩子 ③[古](过去式和过去分词只用 spoiled)抢劫,掠夺 ④[俚]伤害,杀害,使完蛋 ❷ *vi.* ①(食物等)变坏,腐败 ②抢劫,掠夺 **II** *n.* ①掠夺物; 赃物: the ~*s* of war 战利品 / share (或 divide up) the ~(*s*) 分赃 ②抢劫,掠夺 ③[美][常用复]得胜政党分到的官职: the ~*s system* 政党分赃制(指将公职委派给获胜政党支持者的制度) ④(开掘、疏浚时)挖出的泥土和岩石 ⑤废品; 次品 ‖*be ~ing for* 一心想, 切望: be ~*ing for* a fight 摩拳擦掌, 极想打架 ‖~*er n.* ①掠夺者; 搞坏(事情、东西)的

人；宠坏(别人)的人 ②【空】扰流器 ‖'~sport **n.** 扫兴的人

spoke [spouk] **I n.** ①(轮)辐 ②【船】舵轮把柄 ③扶梯棍 ④(尤指下坡时)防止车轮旋转的煞车 **II vt.** ①给…装上辐 ②用煞车煞住(车轮) ‖***put a ~ in sb.'s wheel*** 破坏某人的计划 ‖'~**shave n.**【机】辐刨片

spoken ['spoukən] **I** speak 的过去分词 **II a.** ①口说的,口头的;口语的 ②[用以构成复合词]以…为说话特点的: plain~ 直言不讳的,坦率的 / soft-~ 说话温柔的;中听的

spokesman ['spouksmən] ([复] spokesmen) **n.** 发言人;代言人

sponge [spʌndʒ] **I n.** ①海绵 ②海绵状物;海绵状橡皮;多孔塑料;金属绵(疏松多孔的金属,如铂绵) ③【医】外科用纱布,棉球 ④炮刷 ⑤发了酵的面团;多孔布丁;蛋糕 ⑥一堆蟹子 ⑦(擦身用)海绵揩: have a ~ (down) 洗一个海绵擦身浴 ⑧[喻]寄生虫,依赖他人生活的人 ⑨酒量大的人 **II ❶ vt.** ①用海绵揩拭;用海绵润湿: ~ a wound 用海绵洗伤口 ②用海绵揩去;[喻]消除(债务等);忘却(往事等)(*out, off, away*) ③用海绵吸(水等)(*up*) ④[口]乞讨;骗取: ~ a fiver from an old acquaintance 从老相识那里讨来五元钱 / ~ a dinner 骗了一顿白食 **❷ vi.** ①采集海绵 ②海绵般吸收 ③[口]做寄生虫,依赖他人生活: ~ *upon* (或 *on*) one's friends 依赖朋友过日子 ‖***pass the ~ over*** 抹去;同意忘掉(嫌隙等) / ***throw*** (或 ***toss, chuck***) ***up*** (或 ***in***) ***the ~*** 承认失败;认输;投降 ‖~**r n.** ①采集海绵的人(或船);用海绵擦洗的人 ②[口]寄生虫,依赖他人生活的人 ‖~ **bath** 海绵擦身浴 / ~ **cake** 松糕 / ~ **cloth** ①【纺】海绵布 ②(熨衣服用的)润湿布 / ~ **gourd** 丝瓜 / ~ **rubber** 海绵状橡皮 / ~ **tree**【植】金合欢

spongy ['spʌndʒi] **a.** ①海绵质的;海绵状的 ②多孔的;有吸水性的 ③轻软而富有弹性的 ‖**spongily ad.** / **sponginess n.**

sponsor ['spɔnsə] **I n.** ①发起者;主办者;倡议者: a ~ country 提案国;发起国 ②保证人 ③【宗】教父,教母 ④出资用广播(或电视)节目做广告者 **II vt.** ①发起;主办;倡议 ②为…做保证人 ③做(广播或电视中商业广告节目)的出资者 ‖~**ial** [spɔn'sɔːriəl] **a.** / ~**ship n.** ①发起;主办;倡议: under the ~*ship* of 由…发起(或主办、倡议) ②保证人(或教父、教母)的地位

spontaneous [spɔn'teinjəs] **a.** ①自发的;一时冲动的: ~ struggle 自发斗争 ②出自自然的,不依赖人工的: ~ growth of willows 柳树的自然生长 ③本能的;自动的: ~ recovery from a disease 病的不药而愈 / a ~ offer of help 自动提出的帮助 ④(文体等)自然而优雅的 ‖~**ly ad.** / ~**ness n.** ‖~ **combustion** 自燃 / ~ **generation** 自然发生

spoof [spuːf] [俚] **I ❶ vt.** ①哄骗;戏弄: He has often been ~*ed*. 他常常受骗。②开…的玩笑;讽刺 **❷ vi.** 欺骗,哄骗;开玩笑 **II n.** ①哄骗;戏弄;玩笑 ②轻松幽默的讽刺诗文 ‖~**er n.** ①哄骗者 ②幽默讽刺诗文的作者 / ~**ing n.** 哄骗;【军】电子欺骗(指诱使敌人在己方通信联络已不使用的频率上进行电子干扰,并发出假电报供敌人截收等)

spook [spuːk] **I n.** ①鬼 ②[美俚]古怪的人;幽灵般的人;暗探 ③[美俚]代笔者 ④[美俚][贬]黑人 **II ❶ vt.** ①鬼怪般地出没于 ②惊吓: ~ a deer 把鹿吓得惊慌而逃 ③[美俚]代写 **❷ vi.** (因受惊而)逃窜

spool [spuːl] **I n.** ①【纺】(空心而两端有突缘的)有边筒子;线轴;(照相胶片、录音胶带、打字机色带等的)卷轴: ~ cotton 线团,木纱团 ②有边筒子(或卷轴)状物 ③绕于卷轴上的材料,所绕的数量: To record these speeches one ~ is enough. 把这几个讲话录下来,一盘胶带就够了。**II vt.** 把…绕于有边筒子(或卷轴)上;缠绕: The film is ~*ed* for use. 胶卷已卷入卷轴。‖~**er n.** ①【纺】络纱机,筒子车 ②绕卷轴工人,绕筒子工人 / ~**ing n.**【纺】络纱,络筒

spoon [spuːn] **I n.** ①[常用以构成复合词]匙,调羹: a table~ 餐匙,汤匙,大型匙(烹调中相当于三茶匙量) / a dessert~ 点心匙,中型匙 / a tea~ 茶匙,小型匙 ②一匙的量(=~ful): two ~*s* of sugar 两匙糖 ③匙状物;(钓鱼用的)匙状假饵(=~ bait);匙形桨 ④三号木高尔夫球棒 ⑤挖土机;泥铲(=~ shovel) ⑥[俚](指男子)傻瓜,笨蛋;痴恋者;轻佻的情人 **II ❶ vt.** ①用匙舀;舀取: She ~*ed* out bowls of porridge. 她用匙舀了几碗粥。/ The dredger ~*ed* up mud. 挖泥船把泥土挖起。②使成匙形,把…挖空成匙形 ③轻轻向上击(球) ④面对背地贴卧在…旁 ⑤[口](男子)向…求爱;对…动手动脚 **❷ vi.** ①用匙形假饵钓鱼 ②轻轻向上击球 ③面对背地贴卧(*up*) ④[口]谈情说爱;动手动脚 ‖***be ~s on*** (或 ***with***) [俚](男子)痴情地爱着 / ***born with a silver ~ in one's mouth*** 生在富贵人家 / ***He that sups with the devil must have a long ~.*** 见 **devil** / ***make a ~ or spoil the horn*** 非成功即失败,孤注一掷 / ***stick one's ~ in the wall*** [俚]死 / ***the wooden ~*** ①【史】英国剑桥大学给数学学位考试末名及格者的木匙;得木匙者 ②末位奖;得末位奖的人 ‖~**ful n.** 一匙(尤指一茶匙)的量 ‖'~**bill n.**【动】①篦鹭 ②阔嘴鸭 / ~ **bread** [美方](须用匙吃的)软质蛋奶面包 / '~**drift n.** =spindrift / '~-ˌ**fashion ad.** (象迭调羹似地)面对背地迭着: sleep ~-*fashion* 面对背地睡 / '~-ˌ**fashioned a.** 面对背地迭着的 / '~-**fed a.** ①用匙喂的 ②被过分宠爱的;被宠坏的 ③(学生)受填鸭式教育的;无独立思考(或行动)余地的 ④(工业等)受特惠待遇的(如奖励金、进口税保护等) / '~-**feed vt.** ①用匙喂 ②填鸭式灌输(知识等);对…进行填鸭式灌输 / ~ **meat** (半)流质食物;婴儿食物 / '~-**net n.** (垂钓人用于把鱼弄上岸的)捞网

spoony, spooney ['spuːni] **I a.** ①[主英]愚蠢的;多愁善感的 ②[口]痴情的,迷恋的(*over, on*)

II *n.* 蠢人，傻瓜；痴情者；轻佻的情人 ‖**spoonily** *ad.* / **spooniness** *n.*

spoor [spuə] I *n.* (野兽的) 脚迹，臭迹 II *vt. & vi.* 跟踪追赶 ‖**~er** ['spuərə] *n.* 跟踪者

sporadic [spə'rædik] *a.* 单个发生的，偶尔发生的；分散的，零星的: a ~ case of disease 个别病例 / ~ fighting 零星战斗 ‖**~ally** *ad.* / **~alness** *n.* ‖**~ E layer** 【无】分散 E 层

spore [spɔː] I *n.* ①【生】孢子 ②【喻】事物的根源，苗子 II *vi.* 长孢子 ‖**~ case** =sporangium

sport [spɔːt] I *n.* ①娱乐，消遣，游戏: Don't spend the evening in ~ and play only. 晚上的时间不要仅仅玩掉。/ What ~! 真好玩啊！/ find it great ~ to do sth. 认为做某事很好玩 ②运动: Swimming in rivers is a splendid ~. 在江河游泳是极好的运动。/ outdoor (indoor) ~s 室外(内)运动 / atheletic (aquatic) ~s 体育(水上)运动 / country ~s 野外运动(尤指打猎、骑马、钓鱼等) ③[复]运动会: the school ~s 学校运动会 / the interuniversity ~s 大学校际运动会 ④玩笑，戏谑；玩物，玩弄品；嘲弄对象，笑柄: say in ~ 说着开玩笑 / make ~ of sb. 开某人的玩笑，嘲弄某人 / The boat became the ~ of the raging wind. 小船为狂风所摆弄。⑤[口]有体育道德精神的人；运动员；讨人欢喜的人: a good ~ 堂堂正正的好汉(尤指具有公正、勇敢、不气馁等性格的);[俚]讨人喜欢的人 ⑥[美俚]赌徒；好酒色的人，爱享乐的人(打猎等时)漂亮时髦的人 ⑦[生]突变；变态(或畸形)的人(或动植物) II ❶ *vt.* ①[口]炫耀；夸示: ~ a new hat 炫耀新帽子 ②突变为；芽变出 ③[英]关(门);把(门)关着(通常表示无暇接待宾客) ❷ *vi.* ①游戏，玩耍；寻欢作乐: The children are ~ing on the meadow. 孩子们在草坪上玩耍。/ go ~ing 去寻欢作乐 ②参加运动 ③开玩笑；嘲弄 (with) ④突变；芽变 III [常作~s] *a.* 运动的；适用于运动的: mass ~(s) activities 群众性体育活动 / a ~s meet (或 meeting) 运动会 / a ~s field 运动场 / ~s goods (equipment) 体育用品 (用具) / ~(s) jackets (shoes) 运动衫(鞋) / a ~s fan 运动迷 ‖**have good ~** (打猎等时)满载而归 / **~ one's** (或 **the**) **oak** 见 **oak** / **the mitten ~** [美俚]拳击 / **the ~ of kings** ①赛马 ②打猎；放鹰行猎 ‖**~dom** *n.* [美]体育界 ‖**~(s) car** 比赛用汽车；双座轻型汽车 / '**~scast** *n.* 电台(或电视台)的体育节目 / '**~s,caster** *n.* 体育节目广播员 / **~(s) editor** 体育新闻编辑 / **~ shirt** 运动衫 / **~s page** (报纸的)体育版 / **~s section** (报纸的)体育栏 / '**~swear** *n.* 运动服装 / '**~s,writer** *n.* (报纸的)体育专栏作家

sporting ['spɔːtiŋ] *a.* ①运动的；有关体育运动的；喜爱运动的 ②有体育道德的；光明正大的；公平的: It's very ~ of you to give me such an advantage. 你给我这样的礼让，真有运动家的风格。/ ~ conduct 光明正大的行为 / a ~ chance (成败均有可能的)机会 ③放荡的；

嗜好赌博的 ④【生】突变的；芽变的 ‖**~ly** *ad.* ‖**~ editor** 体育新闻编辑 / **~ girl, ~ woman** 妓女 / **~ house** ①[美俚]妓院 ②[古]赌场 / **~ page** (报纸的)体育版

sportive ['spɔːtiv] *a.* ①嬉戏的，欢闹的；开玩笑的 ②运动的(尤指户外) ③好色的 ‖**~ly** *ad.* / **~ness** *n.*

sportsman ['spɔːtsmən] ([复] sportsmen) *n.* ①爱好运动(尤指钓鱼、打猎等)的人；运动员，运动家 ②具有运动家道德(指竞争中不对对方做小动作等)的人 ‖**~like, ~ly** *a.* 具有运动家道德的,具有运动家风格的 / **~ship** *n.* 运动家道德,运动家风格

sportswoman ['spɔːts,wumən] ([复] sportswomen ['spɔːts,wimin]) *n.* 女运动爱好者；女运动员,女运动家

spot [spɔt] I *n.* ①点；斑点；污点；疵点，缺点: add up the ~s on the dice 把骰子的点数加起来 / white calico with red ~s 白底红点花布 / grease (ink, mud) ~s on one's clothing 衣服上的油(墨水,泥)渍 / a ~ on one's reputation 名誉上的污点 / a bruised ~ on the pear 梨上的伤痕 ②(肺部等处的)阴影；(太阳等上的)黑点 ③地点，场所；[俚](在节目单、组织或节中所处的)地位，位置；职位；部位: a scenic (或 beauty) ~ 风景胜地 / a historic ~ 古迹；有历史意义的胜地 / a danger ~ 危险地点 / a hot ~ (易出事的)麻烦地点 / a picnic ~ 适于进行野餐的地点 / vice ~s 堕落场所(指妓院、赌窟等) / find a ~ as a typist 找到一个打字员的职位 / a sore ~ in the throat 喉头发痛部位 ④处境(尤指困境、窘境): You don't want to end up in his ~, do you? 你总不想落得个他那样的下场吧？⑤插在广播(或电视节目)间的简短通知(或广告) ⑥[口]少量，少许，少量酒: lie down for a ~ of rest 躺下略事休息 / There is not a ~ of room in the hall. 大厅里挤得水泄不通。/ Can you do with a few ~s? 你能少量喝点酒吗？⑦[复]现货 ⑧[美俚][常接在数词后构成复合词]小面额钞票: a five-~ 一张五元票 / a two-~ (或 deuce-~) 一张二元票 ⑨[美俚]酒吧间；夜总会 ⑩[美俚][常接在数词后构成复合词]短期徒刑: a one-~ 一年徒刑 ⑪[美俚](舞台)聚光灯 (=spotlight) ⑫【动】黄鲴 ⑬一种家鸽 ⑭[复][美俚]金钱豹 II (spotted; spotting) ❶ *vt.* ①点缀；把…弄脏；玷污: The night sky is spotted with stars. 夜晚的天空繁星点点。/ a notebook spotted with ink 沾上墨水渍的笔记本 ②在…上用点子作记号 ③[口]认出，发现；预先认准(比赛中的优胜者等);记认(惯犯、嫌疑犯等): ~ a mistake 发现错误 / He was the first to ~ the danger. 他是第一个发觉这危险的人。/ I couldn't ~ her in the crowd. 在人群中我认不出她。/ ~ sb. as the winner 赛开始前认准某人会得胜 ④准确地定出…的位置；使准确地击中目标 ⑤把…散置在各点上；把…置于指定(或需要)地点: ~ field telephones at strategic points 在各战略点上设置战地电话 ⑥ 使处于聚光灯光束下; 集中照射: His genial smile was *spotted* on everyone in turn. 他依次向每个人投来亲切的微笑。⑦ 把(节目等)排在特定的位置(或时间): His performance was *spotted* at nine o'clock. 他的演出被排在九点钟。⑧ 从…除去疵点(或污点) (out) ⑨ [口](比赛中) 给(对方) 以礼让(如下棋时先让一子): I *spotted* him two points. 我让他两分。❷ *vi.* ① 沾上污点, 变污; 弄污: This linen cloth ~s easily. 这麻布容易沾污。/ This liquid will not ~. 这液体不会把容器(或其他东西)弄污的。② [军](从空中)侦察敌军目标 ③ [口]下小雨: It is beginning to ~. (或 It is *spotting with* rain). 在下小雨了。III *a.* [只作定语] ① 现场的: ~ coverage of an international conference 国际会议的现场采访 / ~ regulation of traffic 现场交通管制 ② 现货; 现付的; 专做现货生意的: a ~ transaction 现货交易 / ~ wheat 现货小麦 / ~ cash (货到即付的) 现款, 现金 / a ~ broker 现货交易掮客 ③ 插在电台(或电视台)节目之间播送的; 地方性电台(或电视台)为全国性广告商所播送的 ④ 局限于某些项目(或地点)的; 任选的; 抽样的: a ~ survey 局限性调查 / ~ check 抽查 ||*a tender* ~ 提起即易伤感情的话题; 痛处 / *Can the leopard change his* ~*s?* 见 leopard / *hit the high* ~s [口]概述要点 / *hit the* ~ [口]满足要求;(食品、酒等)合口味 / *in a* ~ [口]在困难中, 处于劣境中 / *in* ~s [美]时时;在某几点上 / *knock (the)* ~s off (或 *out of*) [美俚]彻底打败… / *off the* ~ [美俚]不准确, 离题 / *on (或 upon) the* ~ ① 当场, 立即;在现场: decide the matter *on the* ~ 把这件事当场决定下来 ② [俚]在困难中, 在危险中(尤指被暗杀的危险): put sb. *on the* ~ 决定要杀害某人 ③ 完全有应付能力;处于良好的竞技状态 ④ 处于负责地位;处于必须行动(或作反应)的地位 / *put one's finger on sb.'s weak* ~ 指出某人(性格上)的弱点 / *touch sb.'s sore* ~ [口]触到某人的痛处 / ||~ *ball* (台球)置球点上的球, 有黑点的白球 / ||~-*check vt. & vi.* 抽查, 抽样 / ~ *lamp* =spotlight (n.) / ~ *news* 最新消息 / ~ *pass* 定点长传球(让球远落在球场某处的传递) / ~ *price* 现货价格 / ~ *test* 当场试测; 抽查, 抽样

spotless ['spɔtlis] *a.* ① 没有污点的, 纯洁的; 无瑕疵的 ② 极其清洁的: a ~ kitchen 极为干净的厨房 ||~**ly** *ad.* / ~**ness** *n.*

spotlight ['spɔt-lait] I *n.* ① (舞台)聚光灯; 聚光灯照明圈 ② 公众注意中心: seek the ~ 想出风头 / hold (或 be in) the political ~ 成为政治上注意的中心 ③ 灿烂的照明物; 使变得突出醒目的因素: throw a ~ into the dark corners of the problem 使问题阴暗不清的方面突然变得明朗 II *vt.* 聚光照明; 使突出醒目

spotty ['spɔti] *a.* ① 多斑点的; 尽是污点的 ② 质量

不一的; 不规则的: ~ attendance 时多时少的出席人数 ||**spottily** *ad.* / **spottiness** *n.*

spouse [spauz] I *n.* 配偶(指夫或妻) II *vt.* [古]和…结婚

spout [spaut] I *n.* ① 喷管; 喷口;(茶壶等的)嘴 ② 喷流; 水柱;【气】龙卷 ③ 水落管 ④ [冶]斜槽;(金属或炉渣的)流出槽 ⑤ [古]当铺 ⑥【动】(鲸类的)喷水孔 II ❶ *vt.* ① 喷出, 喷射: ~ water into the air 向天空喷水 ② 滔滔不绝地讲: ~ opinions 哇啦哇啦地发议论 ③ [古]典押 II ❷ *vi.* ① 喷出, 喷射: Blood was ~*ing* from the severed artery. 血从切断的动脉里喷出来。② 高谈阔论 ||*up the* ~ [俚] ① 在典押中 ② 在困难中; 已破落 ||~**er** *n.* ① 喷油井 ② 说话滔滔不绝的人 ③ 捕鲸船 ④ 照管流出槽的工人 / ~**less** *a.* 无喷嘴的

sprain [sprein] I *n.* 扭伤 II *vt.* 扭, 扭伤: ~ one's ankle and wrist 扭伤了足踝和手腕

sprang [spræŋ] spring[1] 的过去式

sprat [spræt] I *n.* ①【动】西鲱 ② 年青人; 瘦小个子; 小人物 II (spratted; spratting) *vi.* 捕西鲱 ||*Jack* ~ 矮子, 侏儒 / *throw* (或 *fling away*) *a* ~ *to catch a mackerel* (或 *herring, whale*) [喻]施小惠而得大利; 吃小亏占大便宜

sprawl [sprɔ:l] I ❶ *vi.* ① 伸开着手足躺(或坐): ~ on the sofa 懒散地伸着四肢躺在沙发上 / send sb. ~*ing* on the ground 把某人打翻在地 ② 笨拙地爬行: go ~*ing* 爬着前进 ③ (字体、队伍等)不整齐, 散漫 ④ (植物)蔓生, 蔓延;(建筑物等)无计划地扩展: a city that ~s *out into* the countryside 乱七八糟地向农村延伸的城市 ❷ *vt.* ① 懒散(或笨拙)地伸开(手、足): He ~ed *out* his legs. 他懒散地伸开双腿。② 使蔓生; 使散漫地伸展; 潦草地书写: He ~ed his signature over the paper. 他在纸上潦草地签了名。II *n.* ① 伸开四肢的躺卧姿势 ② 蔓生; 散乱: a ~ of log cabins 散乱的一簇木屋 ||【美方】毅力

spray[1] [sprei] I *n.* ① 浪花; 水花, 飞沫: the ~ of a waterfall 瀑布的水花飞溅 ② 喷雾 ③ 用作喷雾的液体 ④ 喷雾器 ⑤ 喷雾状物, 飞沫状物: a ~ of gunfire 散射的炮火 II ❶ *vt.* 喷; 向…喷射; 喷涂: ~ an insecticide upon plants 给植物喷一种杀虫剂 / ~ sb. with water 把水喷溅在某人身上 / ~ the furniture with paint 给家具喷漆 ❷ *vi.* 喷;(如浪花般)溅散 ||~**er** *n.* ① 喷雾者 ② 喷雾器; 喷布器; 洒水车 / ||~**board** *n.*【船】防溅船舷 / ~ *gun* 喷枪; 喷漆枪;(喷射农药的)药水枪 / ~ *nozzle* 喷雾嘴 / ~**-'paint** *vt.* 喷漆

spray[2] [sprei] *n.* ① 小树枝; 小花枝 ② 枝状饰; 枝状物 ||~ *drain* 以小树枝枝填在沟槽内上面覆土而形成的) 排水暗沟

spread [spred] I (spread) ❶ *vt.* ① 伸开, 展开; 铺开, 摆开: The bird ~ its wings. 鸟儿伸开翅膀。/ ~ *out* a map (newspaper) 摊开地图(报纸) / ~ the table for dinner 摆好餐桌准备开饭 ② 传播; 散布; 使扩大蔓延开去: ~ news (scientific knowledge) 传播消息(科学知识) / ~ diseases(rumours)散布疾病(谣言) ③涂,敷;撒;施: ~ jam on bread 在面包上涂果酱 / ~ the slice of bread with jelly 用果子冻涂在面包片上 / ~ manure over the vegetable plot 在菜田上施肥料 ④把…分期;使延长: ~ out the payments on the loan over eighteen months 把借款分十八个月摊还 ⑤展宽,延伸(金属等);敲平(铆钉头): ~ a plate 展宽金属板 ⑥展出,展示 ⑦详细记录;详述 ❷ vi. ①展开;扩大;伸展;伸长: A scene of prosperity ~s out before us 一幅欣欣向荣的景象展现在我们面前。 / This course ~s over one year. 这门课程一年时间学完。 ②传开;蔓延开;(水等)渗开: The fire (epidemic) ~s quickly. 火势(流行病)迅速蔓延。 / the tendency of a vine to ~ 葡萄藤的蔓延性 / ~ from mouth to mouth 众口流传 ③(金属等)展宽,延伸 II n. ①伸展;扩展: the ~ of a great metropolis 大都市的扩展 / a middle-age(d) ~ 中年发胖 ②传播;散布;蔓延: the ~ of education 教育的普及 ③(一片)广阔的土地(或水域);[美]大牧场: a giant ~ of land 一片辽阔的土地 ④报刊上占显著地位的登载;报刊上整页(或跨数栏)的文章(或广告等);(报纸上)横贯两版的篇幅 ⑤被单;桌布 ⑥涂抹食品(如果酱、黄油等);[口]丰盛的酒席,宴会 ⑦差距,脱节;【机】距;【商】制造成本和卖价间的差额: the wide ~ between theory and fact 理论和事实的严重脱节 / ~ of wheel【机】轮距 / ~ of wing【空】翼展 III a. [只作定语] ①扩大的;伸展的;广大的: a two-page ~ advertisement 占两版的大幅广告 ②(宝石)薄而无光泽的 ‖ ~ it on thick [美俚]夸大;奉承 / ~ like wildfire 象野火般迅速传播 / ~ oneself ①平直地舒展四肢 ②夸夸其谈;舞文弄墨 ③博取别人的好感;做得过分: ~ oneself to entertain sb. 过分殷勤地款待某人 / ~ oneself thin 试图同时干太多的工作: There aren't many of them and they ~ themselves pretty thin. 他们人数不多,但想干的工作却不少。 ‖ ~er n. ①散布者,传播者 ②涂黄油用的小刀 ③(肥料、碎石等的)撒布机 ④[纺]分纱器,分丝筘 (=~ing machine) ‖ ~ eagle ①张着翅膀的鹰(常作美国硬币上的图案等) ②溜冰鞋脚跟对脚跟成直线的溜冰花样 ③【海】伸开四肢缚在索具上受刑的人 / '~-,eagle vi. ①手脚伸展着站立(或爬行)②(溜冰时)作横一字型: The boy ~-eagled on the ice. 这个男孩在冰上作横一字型溜冰。 vt. 张开…的手脚,横跨 a. ①象张着翅膀的鹰 ②夸张的 /'~head n.(报纸上占两栏以上的)大标题/'~,over (system) [英]对工作时间根据特殊的工作需要而作调整的制度

spree [spri:] I n. ①狂欢,纵乐;狂饮: have a ~ 狂欢作乐 ②无节制的狂热行为: a buying ~ 狂购乱买 II vi. 狂欢,纵乐;狂饮 ‖ be on the ~ 在狂饮中;沉湎于欢闹中 / go on the ~ 行乐,狂饮狂闹一番

sprig [sprig] I n. ①小枝 ②小枝状饰物 ③[谑]子孙;后辈 ④[常作贬]年青人;小家伙 ⑤无头小钉 ⑥嵌玻璃针(锡或锌制的三角小针,用以固住窗玻璃) II (sprigged; sprigging) vt. ①用小枝(或枝状物)装饰: sprigged muslin 有枝叶花纹的薄棉布 ②使(草)蔓生 ③除去…的小枝: ~ a tree 除去树上小枝 ④把无头钉钉入 ‖'~tail n. 尖尾鸭

sprightly ['spraitli] ad. & a. 活泼地(的);生气勃勃地(的);轻快地(的) ‖ sprightliness n.

spring¹ [spriŋ] I (过去式 sprang [spræŋ] 或 sprung [sprʌŋ],过去分词 sprung) ❶ vi. ①跳,跃;弹跳: ~ to one's feet 一跃而起 / ~ out of bed 从床上跳起来 / ~ to action 突然行动起来 / ~ to sb.'s assistance 迅速赶去支援某人 / The ball sprang back and hit him. 球弹回打在他身上。 / The door sprang to. 门弹回关上。 ②涌出;涌上: Out of the sluice ~s an inexhaustible supply of water. 水从水闸中源源涌出。 / Blood sprang to his cheeks. 他面孔突然涨得通红。 ③(植物等)生长;发生,出现: The buds are ~ing. 正在抽芽。 / A breeze sprang up. 突然吹起一阵轻风。 / A great number of factories have sprung up. 新建了许多工厂。 / The error sprang from carelessness. 这个错误是由粗心造成的。 ④出身: He ~s (或 He is sprung) from a poor peasant's family. 他出身于贫农家庭。 ⑤(地雷等)炸开;(木材等)裂开;弯曲: My table-tennis bat has sprung. 我的乒乓球拍翘了。 ⑥高耸: The spire ~s high above the town. 尖塔高耸于城镇上空。 ⑦(拱等)升起 ❷ vt. ①使跳(或弹)起;惊起(猎物);跳过: ~ a mousetrap 触发捕鼠器 / ~ a wall 越墙而过 ②使爆炸;使破裂;把…弄弯: ~ a mine 使地雷爆炸 / I have sprung my tennis racket. 我把网球拍弄弯了。 / The boat sprang a leak. 小船突然出现漏缝。 ③突然提出(或宣布): ~ a new proposal on sb. 突然向某人提出新建议 / ~ a surprise on sb. 使某人大吃一惊 / When will you ~ that news? 你预备什么时候宣布那消息? ④扭伤(腿等),使跛 ⑤[美俚]解除对…的拘禁 II n. ①跳跃,跳起;弹回: The cat made a ~ at the mouse. 猫向老鼠扑去。 / the ~ of a bow 弓的弹回 ②弹性,弹力;活力: the ~ of rubber tyres (muscles) 橡胶轮胎(肌肉)的弹力 / There is a ~ in his steps. 他的步伐轻快有力。 ③弹簧,发条: a hair ~ 游丝;(头发)细(弹)簧 / a tension ~ 伸张弹簧 ④泉,源泉 ⑤[常用复]根源;原动力;动机: the ~s of conduct 行为的动机 / The custom had its ~ in another country. 这风俗起源于外国。 ⑥(桅杆等的)裂缝;裂开;【海】倒缆;【建】起拱点;起拱面 ⑦[复]大潮期 ‖ ~ up like mushrooms 见 mushroom ‖ ~er n. ①跳的人(或东西) ②快生产的母牛 ③【建】拱底石 / ~less a. 无弹性的;无弹簧的 /'~ balance 弹簧秤 / ~ /

bed 弹簧床;弹簧床垫 / ~ **binder** 弹簧活页夹 / '~**blade knife** 弹簧折合刀 / '~**board** n. ①跳板 ②出发点(*for, to*) / '~**bok** n. ①南非小羚羊 ②[英俚]南非足球队 / ~ **gun** 弹簧枪;伏击枪 / '~**halt** n. 马的跛行症 / '~**head** n. 源头;水源 / '~**house** n. [美](建造在泉水上供冷藏乳品肉类等的)冷藏所 / ~ **lock** 弹簧锁 / '~**mattress** 弹簧床垫 / ~ **steel** 弹簧钢 / '~**water** n. 泉水

spring² [spriŋ] n. 春天,春季;青春(期): in ~ 在春天 / ~ ploughing 春耕 / the ~ of life 青春(时代) ||~**like** a. 象春天的 ||~ **chicken** ①童子鸡 ②[美俚]年轻而无经验的人,年轻幼稚的女子 / ~-'**clean** vt. 彻底打扫(房屋等) n. [英]大扫除 / '~-'**cleaning** n. [美]大扫除 / ~ **fever** 春倦症 / '~**tide** n. ①(新月和满月时的)大潮;[喻]高潮 ②=~**time** / '~**time** n. ①春天,春季;青春(期) ②发展的早期;全盛期 / '~**wood** n. 早材,春材

sprinkle ['spriŋkl] I ❶ vt. ①洒,喷淋: ~ the floor with water 用水洒地 ②撒;撒布;使散布: ~ salt on meat 在肉上撒盐 / ~ sugar over berries 在浆果上撒糖 / a fish with pepper on 在鱼上撒胡椒 ③点缀: a wooded area ~d with lakes 有湖泊夹杂其间的林区 ❷ vi. ①洒,喷淋 ②下稀疏小雨 II n. ①洒;撒 ②小雨;间断雨 ③少量;散布着的东西: a ~ of houses 稀稀拉拉的一些房屋 ④[常用复]撒在面上的东西: be covered with chocolate ~s 上面盖有巧克力屑 ||~**r** n. ①洒水器;洒水车;喷水设备: a ~**r** system 洒水灭火系统(屋内的管道系统,通常在火灾时因温度激增而自动洒水或喷出其他灭火液) ②(洗衣作)喷水烫衣工

sprinkling ['spriŋkliŋ] n. ①洒,撒 ②少量,稀落,点滴: We have had a ~ of rain (snow). 我们这里下了一点点雨(雪)。/ He hasn't even a ~ of common sense. 他简直一点常识也没有。||~**can** (浇花用)喷水壶

sprint [sprint] I ❶ vi. 用全速奔跑,疾跑(尤指短距离): He ~ed to cover. 他全速跑去隐蔽起来。❷ vt. 用全速跑过 II n. ①全速疾跑;短(距离赛)跑 ②长距离赛跑中的冲刺;紧张活动中的一段短暂的时间: a ~ at the finish 近终点时的猛冲 ||~**er** n. 短程疾跑者;短跑选手,短跑运动员 ||~ **car** 短程泥路赛车

sprite [sprait] n. ①鬼怪;小妖精 ②调皮捣蛋的人

sprout [spraut] I ❶ vi. ①发芽;抽条: The rice seeds have ~ed. 稻种已发芽了。②很快地生长(或发展) ❷ vt. ①使萌发;使生长: Trees ~ed their new leaves. 树木长出新叶。/ The rain has ~ed the seeds overnight. 雨一夜就使种子发芽了。/ ~ horns 长角 / ~ a moustache 长胡髭 ②摘去…的芽: ~ potatoes 摘去马铃薯的芽 II n. ①新芽;籽苗;嫩枝 ②[复]【植】汤菜 ③幼苗状物;年青人;[美俚]后代

spruce¹ [spru:s] n. ①云杉属植物;云杉: ~ beer 云杉酒(用云杉的叶和枝加糖酿成) ②云杉木

spruce² [spru:s] I a. 整洁的;潇洒的: make oneself ~ 把自己打扮得整整齐齐 II vt. & vi. (把…)打扮整齐(*up*) ||~**ly** ad. / ~**ness** n.

sprue¹ [spru:] n. 【医】口炎性腹泻

sprue² [spru:] n. ①(铸型的)注入口 ②熔渣

sprung [sprʌŋ] spring¹ 的过去式和过去分词

spry [sprai] a. 充满生气的;敏捷的 ||Look ~! 赶快! ||~**ly** ad. / ~**ness** n.

spud [spʌd] I n. ①(除野草用的)小锄,草锄 ②(除树皮用的)铲凿 ③[口]马铃薯 ④短而粗的东西 II (spudded; spudding) vt. 用草锄锄(草等)(*up, out*)

spue [spju:] vt., vi. & n. =spew

spume [spju:m] I n. 泡沫;浮沫 II vi. & vt. (使)起泡沫

spun [spʌn] I spin 的过去式和过去分词 II a. 纺成的;象纺成的 ||~ **glass** 玻璃丝 / ~ **silk** 绢丝 / ~ **sugar** 棉花糖(一种煮融后拉长或揉成各种形状的糖) / ~ **yarn** ①精纺纱,细纱 ②【海】细油麻绳(由二至四根绳条捻成)

spur [spə:] I n. ①踢马刺,靴刺 ②刺激物,鼓励品;策励,鼓舞: This book is a ~ to the child's imagination. 这本书促进了那孩子的想象力。③【动】(鸟、虫等的)距;(斗鸡时加于鸡腿上的)距铁 ④(攀爬者靴鞋上装的)刺铁 ⑤【植】花距;短枝 ⑥山嘴,石嘴,尖坡,山鼻子 ⑦【建】凸壁,支撑物 II (spurred; spurring ['spə:riŋ]) ❶ vt. ①用踢马刺催促(马)②刺激;鼓舞;鞭策 ③给…装上踢马刺 ❷ vi. ①用踢马刺驱马前进 ②疾驰: ~ on (或 forward) to the destination 向目的地疾驰而去 ||need the ~ 需加鞭策才行(针对做事懒散) / on the ~ of the moment 一时冲动之下,不加思索地 / put (或 set) ~s to 对…加以刺激(或促进) / a willing horse 见 horse / whip and ~ 见 whip / win one's ~s (古时)因功被封为武士;[喻]立功成名 ||~**less** a. ①没有踢马刺的 ②没有花距的 / **spurred** a. ①靴上装有踢马刺的 ②有花距的 ||~ **gear** [机]正齿轮 / '~-**of-the-'moment** a. 一时冲动的;不假思索的;立即的 / ~ **track** 支路,短叉道 / ~ **wheel** =~ gear / '~**wort** n. 茜草属植物

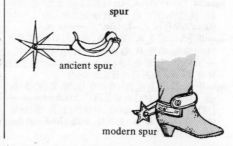

spur

ancient spur

modern spur

spurious ['spjuəriəs] *a.* ①假的；假造的：~ coins 伪币 / ~ fruit【植】假果 ②私生的 ③欺骗性的 ④（论证等）不合逻辑的，谬误的 ‖~**ly** *ad.* / ~**ness** *n.*

spurn [spə:n] I ❶ *vt.* ①践踏；一脚踢开 (*away*) ②轻蔑地拒绝，摒弃，唾弃 ❷ *vi.* 摒弃，藐视：~ *at* danger 藐视危险 II *n.* ①踢 ②摒弃，藐视

spurrier ['spəriə] *n.* 制造踢马刺者；制造距铁者

spurt [spə:t] I ❶ *vt.* 喷射：~ water 喷水 ❷ *vi.* ①喷出：Blood ~*ed* (*out*) from the wound. 血从伤口喷出。 ②突然拼命努力；（赛跑中）冲刺 ③突然迸发；突然兴隆：~ into popularity 突然走红 II *n.* ①突然的喷射 ②短促突然的爆发（或激增）；（怒气、精力等的）迸发 ③短时间，一时 ④（营业的）突然兴隆

spy [spai] I *n.* ①密探，侦探，间谍，特务：a police ~ 警局密探 / a military ~ 军事间谍 / a master ~ 间谍大王，特务头子 ②密探行为 II ❶ *vt.* ①暗中监视；侦察；探出，查出 ②察见，发现 ③仔细察看：~ all the exhibits at the fair 仔细察看展览会的全部陈列品 ❷ *vi.* ①做密探；做间谍；暗中监视；侦查：~ *on* (或 *upon*) sb. 暗中监视某人；侦查某人 / ~ *into* sth. 侦查某事 ②仔细察看 ‖~ *strangers.* 见 **stranger** ‖~**glass** *n.* 小望远镜 / '~-**hole** *n.* 探视孔，窥测孔

squabble ['skwɔbl] I ❶ *vi.* （为琐事）争吵，口角：~ *with* sb. 与某人争吵 / ~ *about* (或 *over*) sth. 为某事争吵 ❷ *vt.*【印】搞乱（排好的铅字）II *n.* 争吵，口角 ‖~**r** *n.* 吵架者，口角者

squad [skwɔd] I *n.* ①【军】班：a ~ leader 班长 / ~ drill 班教练 ②小组，小队：a football ~ 足球队 / a flying ~ （配备汽车的）警察追捕队 / a vice ~ [美]（取缔卖淫、赌博等的）警察缉捕队 / a goon ~ [美俚]打手队 / a beef ~ [美俚]大力士打手队 II *vt.* 把…编成班（或小组）‖*an awkward* ~ 训练不足的新兵团；[喻]乌合之众 ‖~ **car** （装有与总局联系的短波无线电话的）警备车 / ~ **room** ①【军】士兵寝室 ②（警察局点名或分配任务的）集合厅

squadron ['skwɔdrən] I *n.* ①（陆军的）骑兵中队；[英]（装甲兵、工兵、通信兵的）连 ②（海军的）中队 ③（空军的）中队；中队飞行队形 ④团体；一组，一群 II *vt.* 把…编成中队 ‖~ **leader** ①（空军）中队长 ②（英）空军少校

squalid ['skwɔlid] *a.* ①肮脏的，邋遢的 ②悲惨的；贫穷的；可怜的 ③道德品质卑劣的 ‖~**ity** [skwɔ'liditi] *n.* / ~**ly** *ad.* / ~**ness** *n.*

squall[1] [skwɔ:l] I *n.* （因疼痛、害怕而引起的）高声喊叫；嚎叫，啼哭 II ❶ *vi.* 尖声高叫；嚎叫，啼哭：~ in terror 恐怖地尖叫 / a ~*ing* baby 啼哭的婴孩 ❷ *vt.* 尖声高叫着发出 (*out*)

squall[2] [skwɔ:l] I *n.* ①（常伴有雨、雪、雹的）暴风，飑：arched ~【气】拱状云飑 / black (white) ~【气】乌云(无形)飑 ②[口]麻烦事；扰乱 ③（短暂的）动荡，骚动 II *vi.* 起风暴，刮飑 ‖*look out for* ~*s* [喻]提防危险

squander ['skwɔndə] I ❶ *vt.* ①浪费，滥用，乱花（时间、金钱等）：never ~ a single *fen* of the collective fund 决不乱花集体一分钱 ②使分散；驱散 ❷ *vi.* ①浪费 ②浪荡，漂泊 ③四散 II *n.* 浪费，挥霍 ‖~**er** ['skwɔndərə] *n.* 浪费者

square [skwɛə] I *n.* ①正方形；方形物：a ~ of glass 一块方玻璃 ②平方，二次幂：Nine is the ~ of three. 九是三的平方。 ③广场；四面有街的房屋区 ④直角尺，矩尺：a set ~ 三角板 ⑤棋盘上的方格；纵横字谜（每方格填入字母，使纵横都成相同的词） ⑥【军】方阵 ⑦一百平方呎（用于计算房屋面积） ⑧含苞未放的棉蕾 ⑨[俚]古板守旧的人 II *a.* ①正方形的；成直角的；矩形的：a ~ table 方桌 / a table with ~ corners 矩形桌 / a ~ bracket 方括号 / a ~ tower 方塔 ②平方的；二乘的：four ~ metres 四平方米 / the ~ root 平方根 ③宽阔而结实的：a ~ jaw (或 chin) 方下巴 / ~ shoulders 宽肩 ④适合的，正好的 ⑤公正的：a ~ deal (或 shake) 公平交易；公平待遇 / a ~ game 公平的比赛 ⑥结清的，两讫的；扯平的：get one's accounts ~ 结清帐目 ⑦干脆的，断然的：a ~ refusal 断然的拒绝 ⑧充实的，令人满意的：a ~ meal 一顿丰盛的饭菜 ⑨[俚]古板的，守旧的 ⑩（船）与龙骨和桅成直角的 III *ad.* ①成直角地；成方形地；面对面地；对准地：The path turned ~ to the left. 这条路成直角地向左转去。 ②正直地；公平地：play fair and ~ 表现得正大光明 ③坚定地；坚决不动地：look sb. ~ in the eye 直瞪瞪地逼视某人的眼睛 IV ❶ *vt.* ①把…弄成方形；把…弄成直角：~ a timber (或 log) 将木材锯方 ②检验…的平直度：~ the surface with a straightedge 用直尺检验表面的平均性 ③抬平（肩膀等）：stand with feet apart and elbows ~*d* 两脚叉开、两肘曲张地站着 ④使作平方自乘；求…的面积：Four ~*d* is sixteen. 四自乘等于十六。 ⑤调正，修正 ⑥结清（帐目）；清算；使（人）结清欠帐；拉平（球赛等）的比分；拉平(比分)：I have ~*d* accounts *with* him. 我已与他算清帐。(或：我已向他报复。) ⑦把（纸张等）划分成方格 (*off*) ⑧使符合，使一致：~ one's words with one's conduct 言行一致 ⑨贿赂，收买：be ~*d* to hold one's tongue 受贿不吐露真情；因受贿而默认坏事 ❷ *vi.* ①符合，一致：His statement does not ~ *with* the facts. 他所说的跟事实不符。②结清，付讫：~ *for* one's meal 付饭钱 / ~ *up* and go back 结清帐目而回 ③（拳击中）摆出架势 (*up, off*) ④（高尔夫球赛中）拉平比分 ‖*all* ~ 不分上下，势均力敌；比分相等 / a ~ *peg in a round hole* 见 **peg** / *by the* ~ 恰好地 / *call it* ~ 当作已了结，不必再提起 / *get* ~ *with* 和…清帐；向…报仇 / *on the* ~ ①成直角 ②正直的(地)，诚实的(地)；公平的(地)：expect sb. to act *on the* ~ 指望某人会诚实公平地行事 ③以平等条件 ④为共济会会员 / *out of* ~ ①不成直角 ②[口]不调和，不一致

没有次序; 不正确 / **~ away** ①【海】迎风扬帆 ②(拳击中)摆好架势 ③把…弄整齐(或准备好); 把一切弄整齐(或准备好) / **~ oneself** ①[口]道歉; 赔偿别人的损失 ②摆好架势 / **~ the circle** 见 **circle** / **~ up** ①清帐 ②摆好架势: **~ up to** sb. 摆好要与某人打架的架势 ③摆好姿势准备跳方形舞 ‖**~ly** *ad.* / **~ness** *n.* ‖**~-built** *a.* (身体)宽阔的 / **~ dance** 四对男女跳的方形舞 / **~d circle** 拳击台 / **~-face** *n.* 廉价烈酒 / **'~head** *n.* [美]在美国(或加拿大)的北欧人; [蔑]德国人 / **~ John** [美俚]守法良民; 无吸毒瘾的好人 / **~man** ['skwɛəmən] *n.* 石匠; 木匠 / **~ measure** 平方面积的 / **'~-rigged** *a.* 【海】横帆的 / **~ sail** 【海】横帆 / **~ shooter** 公正诚实的人 / **'~-'shouldered** *a.* 平肩的, 阔肩的 / **'~-'toed** *a.* ①(鞋)方头的 ②古板的, 守旧的 / **~ toes** 古板的人

squash[1] [skwɔʃ] I ❶ *vt.* ①把…压扁; 把…碾扁: **~** a hat 压扁帽子 / **~** a mosquito on the windowpane 在窗玻璃上揿死一只蚊子 ②镇压; 压制: **~** a revolt 镇压叛乱 ③[口](以压制手段)使沉默, 压服 ❷ *vi.* ① 被压扁; 被碾平: Ripe persimmons **~** easily. 熟柿子容易被压烂。②发溅泼声; 发咭吱声: **~** through a bog 咭吱咭吱地走过泥沼地 ③挤进, 挤入 (in, into): He managed to **~** into the car. 他设法挤入了车子。II *n.* ①易压碎(或压坯、压扁)的东西; 压得粉碎的一摊: The enemy tank was reduced to **~**. 敌人的坦克被打得稀巴烂。② (软物落下时的)啪声; (行走泥沼地或鞋内有水时的)咭吱声 ③[英](掺有汽水的)果子汁(尤指瓶装的冰镇饮料): lemon **~** 柠檬汽水 ④**~** hat ⑤[常用单]拥挤的人群 ⑥**~** rackets ⑦**~** tennis III *ad.* 啪地 ‖**~ hat** 软毡帽 / **~ rackets** [用作单或复] (在围墙内用小网拍玩的)小橡皮球戏 / **~ tennis** (在较大院子内用大网拍玩的)橡皮球戏

squash[2] [~ʃ] ([复] squash(es)) *n.* 【植】南瓜, 倭瓜; 笋瓜; 西葫芦

squat [skwɔt] I (squatted; squatting) ❶ *vi.* ①蹲; 蹲坐: He *squatted* down on the ground. 他蹲坐在地上。② [口]坐 (down, on); 坐下休息(或闲谈): Find somewhere to **~**. 找个地方坐坐。③ [美俚]登坑大便 ④ (动物)蹲伏; 踞伏 ⑤擅自占地, 非法占据空屋; 依法在政府公地上定居下来(以图获得对该地的所有权) ⑥【海】(船高速航行时)尾部下坐 ❷ *vt.* ① 使蹲坐; 使踞坐: He *squatted* himself *down*. 他蹲了下来。② 霸占, 侵占(土地等) II (squatter, squattest) *a.* ①蹲着的: a hare **~** on the hillside 山边蹲着的野兔 ②矮胖的: a **~** stove 一只矮墩墩的火炉 III *n.* ①蹲; 蹲坐 ②供蹲坐的地方(尤指小动物的窝) ③矮胖的人 ‖**~ hot** [美俚]坐电椅, 被电刑处死 / **take a ~** [美俚]登坑大便 / **the hot ~** [俚]电椅 ‖**squatty** *a.* ①蹲着的 ②矮胖的

squatter[1] ['skwɔtə] *n.* ①蹲坐着的人(或动物) ②擅自占地(或空屋)者; 依法在政府公地上定居以图获得对该地的所有权的人 ③(澳大利亚的)

牧羊场主 ‖**~ sovereignty** 【美史】人民主权论 (南北战争前一种政治上的主义, 主张各州人民有权处理其内政, 并决定是否容许奴隶制; ＝popular sovereignty)

squatter[2] ['skwɔtə] *vi.* 涉水而行; 涉水般而过

squaw [skwɔ:] *n.* ①美洲印第安女人 ②[贬]女人; 老婆 ③[贬]女子气的男人 ④ 跪跽人形靶 ‖**~ man** 娶印第安女人为妻的白人

squawk [skwɔ:k] I ❶ *vi.* ①(鹦鹉、鸡、鸭等受伤或受惊时)发出粗厉的叫声 ②(粗声或大声地)诉苦, 抗议 (about) ③[美俚]自首并告发别人 ❷ *vt.* 粗声叫出 II *n.* ① 粗厉的叫声 ② (粗声或大声的)诉苦, 抗议 ③【动】黑冠夜苍鹭 ‖**~er** *n.* ①发出粗厉叫声的玩具 ②仿鸭叫声的器具 ③老是爱抱怨的人 ④告密者 ‖**~ box** ＝**~ box** (供内部联系用的)扬声器, 通话盒 / **~ sheet** 飞行员关于飞机在飞行时各种缺点的报告

squeak [skwi:k] I *n.* ① 短促刺耳的声音; (老鼠)吱吱叫声; (未经滑润的铰链等的)轧轧声 ②机会: give sb. one more **~** 再给某人一个机会 II ❶ *vi.* ① 发出短促的尖声: These new shoes **~**. 新鞋子走起路来咯咯吱吱地响。② [俚]告密 ③非常勉强地通过; 非常侥幸地成功(或获胜): He managed to **~** by somehow. 他想了个什么办法总算对付过去了。❷ *vt.* 以短促尖声发出: The radio **~ed** five. 收音机吱吱地发出五点钟的报时信号。‖**a narrow (close, near) ~** 九死一生的脱险; 非常勉强的成功 ‖**~er** *n.* ①[俚]告密者 ②雏鸟(尤指雏鸽) ③[英]小猪 ④以微弱优势赢得的竞赛

squeal [skwi:l] I ❶ *vi.* ①(小孩、猪等)发出长声尖叫: The boy **~ed** with pain. 这男孩痛得直叫。②告密; 泄密: **~** on sb. 告发某人 ③抱怨, 激烈抗议 (against) ❷ *vt.* 用长而尖锐的声音说; 用长而尖的声音发出(或表示) II *n.* 长而尖的声音; 长而尖的叫声 ‖**make sb. ~** [俚]敲某人竹杠 ‖**~er** *n.* ①告密者 ②尖叫的动物 ③雏鸟 (尤指雏鸽)

squeamish ['skwi:miʃ] *a.* ①易呕吐的 ②易受惊的; 易生气的; 神经质的 ③吹毛求疵的; 过于拘谨的 ‖**~ly** *ad.* / **~ness** *n.*

squeeze [skwi:z] I ❶ *vt.* ①榨; 挤; 塞; 紧握: **~** juice from an orange 榨桔子汁 / **~** a lemon dry 榨干柠檬 / **~** a tear 挤出一滴眼泪 / **~** things into a trunk 把东西塞进箱子 / **~** oneself into a crowded bus 挤入拥挤的公共汽车 ②榨取; 压榨 ③使(利润等)缩减 ④勉强赢得(或赚得) ⑤压印(硬币等) ⑥(桥牌中)逼(对方)出牌; 以逼牌法赢得 ❷ *vi.* ①榨; 挤; 压: He **~d** through the crowd. 他挤过人群。/ Can you **~** in? 你挤得进去吗? ②压榨 ③勉强通过(或赢得): The measure **~d** through the parliament. 议案在议会勉强通过。II *n.* ①压榨; 压力; 挤; 紧紧握手(或拥抱): We all got in, but it was a (tight) **~**. 我们都进去了, 可是挤得很紧。/ give sb. a **~** of the hand 紧握一下某人的手 ②榨出的少量东西: a **~** of lemon (一点)柠檬汁 ③(密

集的)一群人: a ~ of people 密集的一群人 ④佣金; 回扣; [美俚]勒索 ⑤(桥牌中)被逼扔出的牌 ⑥(硬币等的)压印 ‖a ~d orange 见 orange / put a ~ on sb. 对某人施加压力; 压榨某人 / ~ off 扳枪机射击 / Squeeze one! [美俚]来一瓶桔子水! / ~ out 榨出; 挤出; 把…排挤出去 / ~ the shorts 轧空头,迫使卖空者用高价补进 ‖~ bottle (可用手挤出内装东西的)塑料挤瓶 / ~ play 压力; resort to ~ play 采取施加压力的办法

squelch [skweltʃ] I ❶ vt. ①压碎 ②镇压 ③压服;使不再作声 ④使咯吱咯吱作响 ❷ vi. ①咯吱咯吱作响: The water ~ed in my shoes. 水在我鞋子里咕咕咕咕作响。②涉水而行; (在泥沼地等处)咯吱咯吱地走 II n. ①咯吱声 ②镇压;压制 ③使对方不再作声的反驳(或回话、责备等) ④被压碎的一摊 ⑤[无]啸声抑制电路 (= ~ circuit)

squib [skwib] I n. ①爆竹; 甩炮 ②讽刺(或幽默)短文(或讲话) ③胡乱写成的短文 [美俚]简短的广告; (商品的)标签; 填补报上空白地位的滑稽短文(或通告) ④[军]电气导火管; 小型点火器 II (squibbed; squibbing) ❶ vi. ①放爆竹 ②发表讽刺短文(或演讲) ❷ vt. ①放(爆竹) ②作短文讽刺 ③信口讲; 随便地写

squint [skwint] I ❶ vi. ①斜着眼看; 眯眼看 (at, through) ②成斜视眼 ③偏离正确方向, 越轨 ④有间接关系(或意义) ❷ vt. 使斜视; 眯着(眼)看 II n. ①斜视眼 ②斜眼看; [口]一瞥, 一瞧: Let me have a ~ at it. 让我瞧一瞧。③倾向; 偏向 (to, towards) ④[建]斜孔小窗, 窥视窗 ⑤[无]斜倾, 偏斜(指天线方向性); 斜视角; 两波束轴间夹角 III a. ①斜视的; 眼睛斜视的 ‖~ eyes 斜视眼 / ~er n. 斜视的人; 眯着眼看的人 / ~ingly ad. / ~y a. ‖~-eyed a. ①有斜视眼的 ②斜看的 ③[喻]有恶意的; 不赞许的

squire [skwaiə] I n. ①[英]乡绅; (某一地区)最大的地主 ②[美]治安官; 律师; 法官 ③(骑士的)扈从 ④侍从; 护卫 ⑤殷勤待候妇女的人: a ~ of dames 对妇女献殷勤的男子 II vi. & vt. ①护卫; 侍从 ②殷勤待候(妇女) ‖~arch ['skwaiər-a:k] n. 地主 / ~archy ['skwaiərɑ:ki] n. ①地主阶级; 地主势力 ②地主政治 / ~let ['skwaiəlit] n. 小地主 / ~ling n. 小地主

squirm [skwə:m] I vi. ①蠕动; 蠢动 ②(因苦痛等而)辗转不安 II n. ①蠕动 ②[海](绳索的)扭曲

squirrel ['skwirəl] I ([复] squirrel(s) n. ①松鼠 ②松鼠毛皮 ③[美俚]威士忌酒 ④[美俚]疯子; 怪人 ⑤[美俚]心理学家; 精神病专家 ⑥[美俚]乱开车的人 ⑦[美俚]老是跟在一帮人后面想成为其中一分子的人 II ❶ vi. [美俚]把车开得东摇西晃 ❷ vt. 贮藏…以备后用 ‖~ cage ①关松鼠的笼子 ②老是作无意义重复的东西 / '~fish n. 鳂属的鱼 / ~ hawk 捕食松鼠的大鹰 / ~ monkey [动]鼠猴 / '~tail n. [植]瓶刷坦坦麦

squirrel(l)y ['skwirəli] a. [美俚]古怪的; 毫无意义的; 发疯的

squirt [skwə:t] I vt. & vi. 喷; 喷出; 喷湿 II n. ①喷; 细的喷流 ②喷射器; 水枪 ③年青人(尤指夜郎自大者) ④小个子; 无足轻重的人 ⑤[俚]喷气式飞机 ‖~ gun 喷射器; 水枪

Sr [化]元素锶 (strontium) 的符号

stab[1] [stæb] I (stabbed; stabbing) ❶ vt. ①刺, 戳; 刺入; 刺伤: ~ sb. with a dagger 用匕首刺某人 ②(在感情方面)刺痛, 使受创伤: The news stabbed him to the heart. 这消息刺伤了他的心。③[建]把(砖墙)凿粗糙(以备涂上灰泥) ❷ vi. 刺; 刺伤: ~ at sb. 向某人刺去 / The thought stabbed through her like a knife. 这念头就象刀一样刺痛了她。 II n. ①刺, 戳; 刺伤的伤口 ②一阵突然而强烈的感觉: have a sharp ~ of pain in the leg 在腿部觉得有刀刺般的剧痛 / a ~ of anxiety (joy, envy) 一阵焦急(快乐, 妒忌) ③企图, 尝试; 努力: have a ~ on (或 make a ~ at) sth. 试做某事, 在某事方面努力一下子 ‖a ~ in the back 伤人的暗箭, 诽谤

stab[2] [stæb] n. [英](印刷所的)周薪制, 时薪制(别于计件制): a ~ hand 周薪(或时薪)工人

stability [stə'biliti] n. ①稳定, 稳定性; 巩固: gravitational ~ 重力稳定性 / the ~ of an airplane (a ship) 飞机(船)的稳定性 ②坚定; 恒心 ③(罗马天主教)僧侣许身寺院的誓约

stabilize ['steibilaiz] ❶ vt. ①稳定, 安定: ~ the market 稳定市场 / ~d warfare [军]阵地战 / ~ a security 通过大量买进维持一种证券的最低价格 ②给(飞机、船只等)装稳定器 ❷ vi. 稳定, 安定: His blood pressure tended to ~. 他的血压趋向稳定。 ‖stabilization [,steibilai'zeiʃən] n. 稳定(作用); 安定(作用) / ~r n. 稳定器, 安定器; [空]安定面; [医]安定剂

stable[1] ['steibl] a. ①稳定的; 不变的; 坚固的: Commodity prices are ~ in our country. 我国物价稳定。/ ~ equilibrium [物]安定平衡, 稳定平衡 / ~ isotope [原]稳定同位素 / a ~ structure 坚固的结构 / ensure ~ peace 保障稳固和平 ②坚定的; 有恒心的: a man of ~ character 性格坚定的人 ‖~ness n.

stable[2] ['steibl] I n. ①厩; 马厩; 牛棚 ②[总称]属于同一马主的赛马, 厩中的马 ③[总称]赛马饲养训练人员 ④[总称]受同一经理人管的运动员(或赛跑车、出版物等) ⑤[复][军]马厩值班; 马厩值勤号 II ❶ vt. 把…拴进马厩(或牛棚等): Where can we ~ our horses? 我们的马拴到哪个马房里去? ❷ vi. 被关在马厩(或牛棚)里; (人)住在马厩般的地方 ‖lock (或 shut) the ~ door when (或 after) the horse is stolen 贼去关门 / smell of the ~ (一个人的言行)带有所从事职业的味道 ‖~r n. 厩主 ‖~boy n. 小马倌, 马僮 / '~com'panion n. ①同一马厩的马 ②[口]同学; 俱乐部同人 / '~man n. 马倌, 马夫 / ~mate n. ①同一马主的马 ②受雇于同一老板的拳击手 / ~ push [美俚]

幕新闻; 来自有影响人士的消息

staccato [stə'kɑ:tou] **I** *a. & ad.* ①【音】断奏的(地) ②断续的(地), 不连贯的(地) **II** *n.* ①【音】断奏; 断奏的一段音乐 ② 不连贯的东西(如说话方式、发动机的声音等)

stack [stæk] **I** *n.* ①(稻草、麦秆、谷物等的)堆, 垛; 整齐堆迭的一堆: a ~ of rice straw 稻草堆 / a ~ of paper boxes 一堆迭着的纸盒 ②[英]一堆(木材等的计量单位; 等于 108 立方呎); 木材堆 ③[口]大量, 许多: I have ~s (或 a whole ~) of work to get through. 我有一大堆工作要完成。/ There're ~s of places to stay. 可以暂住的地方极多。④[常用复]许多书架; 书库 ⑤(三支步枪架放的)叠状塔形)枪架 ⑥烟囱群; 烟囱(车、船的) 烟突, 烟道, 排气管; (高炉)炉身: a factory ~ 工厂的大烟囱 ⑦ (突出海面的)浪蚀岩柱, 石柱 ⑧(赌牌时的)一堆筹码 ⑨【无】迭式存储器 **II ❶** *vt.* ① 堆积; 堆起: Stack arms! (口令)架枪! / ~ the firewood in the back yard 把木柴堆在后院里 ②在…堆放, 堆满: The floor was ~ed high with bales of cotton. 地板上高高地堆放着许多包棉花。③【空】指令(飞机)作分层盘旋飞行等待着陆 ④[美俚]把(房间)弄得乱七八糟 ⑤洗(牌)作弊 **❷** *vi.* 堆起, 成堆 ‖*blow one's ~* [俚] 发脾气, 勃然大怒 / *the cards* 见 *card*[1] / *~ up* ①总起来, 加起来: This is how things ~ up today. 目前的情况总起来就是这样。② 较量, 比高低, 争胜负 *(against, with)*: The products of this small factory can ~ up *against* similar products of other large factories. 这家小厂的产品比得过对大厂的同类产品。‖*~ed a.* [俚](女子)体态漂亮的 / *~er n.* ① 堆垛者, 堆垛工 ② 可升降摄象机台 ‖*~,funnel n.* 烟囱内的尖塔形通风设备 / *~ room* 书库 / *'~stand n.* 干草堆的支撑架 / *'~up n.* 【空】(飞机等待依次着陆时)分层盘旋飞行

stacte ['stækti:] *n.* (古犹太人制香用的)香料

stactometer [stæk'tɔmitə] *n.* 滴量计

staddle ['stædl] *n.* ①草垛的底座 ②承架; 根底, 基础

stadholder ['stæd,houldə], **stadtholder** ['stæt,houldə] *n.*【史】荷兰的省长; 荷兰联合省的最高行政长官

stadia ['steidjə] *n.*【测】视距; 视距尺: ~ hairs (或 wires) 视距丝 / ~ rod 视距尺

stadium ['steidjəm] ([复] stadia ['steidjə] 或 stadiums) *n.* ① 古希腊长度单位; 古罗马长度单位 ②(古希腊)赛跑运动场; 跑道周围台阶式看台 ③[复数形式常用 stadiums](周围有看台的)露天大型运动场 ④【医】(疾病的)期 ⑤【动】龄期(尤指前后二次换羽或脱皮之间的)

staff[1] [stɑ:f] **I** ([复] staffs 或 staves [steivz]) *n.* ①(拐)杖; (棍)棒; (旗)杆; (梯子等的)横档: the beggar's ~ 讨饭棒 ②支柱: the ~ of life 生活必需品; 主食, 面包 / He is a ~ to the whole group. 他是全组的支柱。③ 权杖; (主教的)牧杖 ④【医】导引探子 ⑤【机】小轴杆 ⑥(铁路上

工作人员用的)路签 ⑦ (测量或造船用的)标尺 ⑧[复] staves 【音】五线谱 ⑨[复] staffs 全体)工作人员; (全体)职员: the teaching ~ of a school 学校的全体教师 / permanent ~ 永久编制人员 / a ~ member (或 a member of the ~)职员之一 / He is *on* the editorial ~ of the newspaper. 他是这家报纸的编辑部人员。⑩ ([复] staffs)【军】参谋, 参谋人员; 参谋机构: the Headquarters of the General *Staff* 总参谋部 / the Chief of General *Staff* 总参谋长 / a ~ college 参谋学院 **II** *vt.* 为…配备职员(或工作人员): ~ an institution 为某一机构配备工作人员 / a finely ~ed school 教员充实的学校 ‖*~er n.* 职员; 报刊的编辑(或采访)人员 ‖*~ officer* 参谋 / *~ sergeant* (英)陆军上士; (美)空军(或海军陆战队)参谋军士

staff[2] [stɑ:f] *n.*【建】纤维灰浆

stag [stæg] **I** *n.* ①牡鹿(尤指牡赤鹿) ②[苏格兰]小马 ③阉割过的雄畜 ④刚长大的雄家禽 ⑤不带女伴的舞客(或交际者); 只有男子的社交集会 ⑥[英](认购股票打算一遇有利机会即出售的)非真心投资的认股者 ⑦[英俚]非正规性的证券商 ⑧[英] 告密者 **II** (stagged; stagging) **❶** *vi.* ①[英]成为告密者 ②不带女伴参加舞会(或交际会) **❷** *vt.* ①[英]侦查 ② 截短(长裤) **III** *a.* ①全是男人, 男子集会用的: a ~ party (dinner)男子交际会(宴会) ②无异性伴侣的 ‖*go* ~ [口](不带女伴) 去参加联谊会 ‖*~ beetle* 【动】锹形甲虫, 鹿角甲虫 / *'~-,evil n.* 马的破伤风 / *'~hound n.*【动】鹿提(捕鹿的猎狗)

stage [steidʒ] **I** *n.* ① 舞台; [the ~] 戏剧, 戏剧艺术; 演剧: She left the ~ at 60. 她在六十岁的时候停止演戏了。②注意中心, 活动舞台, 场所: ③(进展的)阶段; 时期: a critical ~ 危险期 / at the initial ~ of a disease 在发病初期 ④ 站, 驿站; 二驿站间的距离, 行程; 公共马车; 公共汽车 ⑤(宝塔等的)层; 级; 脚手架; (地层的)阶; (地文的)期: a chroma amplifier ~ (彩色电视机的)彩色信号放大级 / a three-~ rocket 三级火箭 ⑥(显微镜)镜台 ⑦浮码头, 趸船 (=landing ~) **II ❶** *vt.* ①把…搬上舞台; 上演: The opera will be ~d with new scenery during the forthcoming festival. 那歌剧在即将来临的音乐节上演时将配以新的布景。② 筹划; 举行(示威) **❷** *vi.* ①(剧本)适于上演: ~ well (badly) (剧本)很(不)适于上演 ② 乘公共马车旅行 ‖*at this* ~ 眼下, 暂时 / *by easy* ~s 从容不迫地(指旅行、工作等) / *by* ~s 分(阶)段地 / *come upon the* ~ 进入社会(或政治舞台) / *go on* (或 *take to* 或 *tread*) *the* ~ 上舞台, 做演员 / *quit the* ~ 退出舞台 / *by* ~ 逐步地 ‖*~r n.* (常作 old ~r) 经验丰富的人, 老手; 识途老马 / *~y a.* =stagy ‖*~ box* (舞台幕前侧旁的)特别包厢 / *'~coach n.* 公共马车 / *'~craft n.* 演剧(或编剧、导演)技巧 / *~ direction* 剧本中(指导演员或关于布景等的)舞台指导说明 / *~ director* (戏剧)导演; 舞台监督 / *~ door* 后台入口 / *~

effect 舞台效果 / ~ **fever** (想做戏剧演员的)演员狂 / ~ **fright** (初上舞台的)怯场 / '~**hand** *n.* 管理舞台布景(或道具、灯光等)的工作人员 / '~-,**manage** *vt.* 为加强效果对(舞台)进行安排;为…做舞台监督;对…进行幕后安排与指挥 / ~ **manager** 舞台监督 / ~ **right** 上演权 / ~ **set** (某一场的)场景和道具布置 / '~-**struck** *a.* 一心想做戏剧演员的 / ~ **whisper** (舞台上)演员对观众的高声耳语;有意让别人能听见的耳语

stagger ['stægə] **I ❶** *vi.* ①摇晃;蹒跚: ~ to one's feet 摇摇摆摆地站立起来 / ~ along 摇摇晃晃地走 ②犹豫,动摇 ❷ *vt.* ①使摇晃 ②使犹豫,使动摇;使震惊: This unexpected blow did not ~ his resolution. 这个意外的打击并没有动摇他的决心。/ The question ~ed him. 这个问题使他不知所措。/ He was ~ed by the news. 这消息使他惊愕。③交错;错开: ~ work shifts 错开工作班 / ~ed rivet joint 【机】错列铆接 **II** *n.* ①摇晃;蹒跚 ②[复]家畜晕倒病,蹒跚病 (=blind ~s);眩晕 ③【空】(双翼机)斜翼,翼角: forward ~ 前斜翼,正斜翼 **III** *a.* 交错的,错开的 ||~**er** ['stægərə] *n.* ①蹒跚的人 ②犹豫的人 ③难事,难题

staggering ['stægəriŋ] *a.* ①摇晃的;蹒跚的 ②令人惊愕的;压倒的: The cost has soared to a ~ one million. 费用激增到令人惊愕的数字——一百万元。/ a ~ problem 一个难题 ||~**ly** *ad.*

staggy ['stægi] *a.* (雌畜或阉割过的雄畜)像成年雄畜的

stagnant ['stægnənt] *a.* ①停滞的,不流动的: ~ water 不流动的水 ②(水等因不流动而)污浊的: The long disuse of the room made the air ~. 房间长期不使用使室内空气变得污浊。③迟钝的,呆笨的: a ~ mind 迟钝的头脑 ④萧条的,不景气的: Business was ~. 生意萧条。 ||~**ly** *ad.*

stagnate ['stægneit] *vi. & vt.* ①(使)停滞,(使)不流动 ②(使)迟钝,(使)不活泼 ③(使)变萧条

staid [steid] *a.* ①固定的 ②沉着的;稳重的: ~ colours 庄重的色彩 ||~**ly** *ad.* / ~**ness** *n.*

stain [stein] **I ❶** *vt.* ①沾污,沾染;玷污: ~ one's fingers with ink 使手指沾上墨水 / clothes ~ed with grease 被油脂沾污的衣服 / ~ sb.'s name with slander 用毁谤的手段败坏某人的名声 ②(在制造过程中用化学方法等)给(木料、玻璃等)染色,着色;把(标本等)染色便于在显微镜下观察: ~ wood with acids 用酸使木材染上色 ③在(糊墙纸)上印上颜色 ❷ *vi.* 变脏,被沾污: White clothes ~ easily. 白色衣服容易弄脏。 **II** *n.* ①污点,瑕疵: an ink ~ 墨水渍 / a blood ~ 血迹 / a ~ on sb.'s reputation 某人名誉上的污点 ②色斑 ③着色剂,染(色)剂 ||~**able** *a.* 可染色的 / ~**ed** *a.* ①沾污的;褪色的: a ~ed and tattered jacket 一件褪色的破烂上装 ②着色的,染色的: ~ed glass 彩色玻璃;【商】冰屑玻

璃 / a bookcase ~ed and waxed 着色并上过蜡的书橱 / ~**er** *n.* ①(木材和皮革的)染色工 ②色料

stainless ['steinlis] *a.* ①没有污点的;纯洁的: a ~ character 纯洁的品格 ②不锈的: ~ steel 不锈钢 ||~**ly** *ad.*

stair [stɛə] **I** *n.* ①[常作 ~s][用作单或复]楼梯: a flight (或 pair) of ~s 一段楼梯 / come up (down) ~s 上(下)楼 / live up two pairs of ~s 住在再上去二层楼的地方 / a steep ~ 陡的楼梯 / ascend a ~s 登楼梯 ②梯级: the top (bottom) ~ 楼梯最上(最下)面的一级 ③[复]浮码头,趸船 **II** [~s] *ad.* 在(或向)楼上(=upstairs) ||**below** ~s 在地下室;在仆人所住的地方 ||'~-,**carpet** *n.* 铺在楼梯上的地毯 / '~-**case** *n.* 楼梯;楼梯间 / ~ **head** 【建】楼梯顶口 / ~ **rod** 【建】楼梯毯梗 / '~**way** *n.* 楼梯 / ~**well** *n.* 【建】楼梯井

stake [steik] **I** *n.* ①桩;标桩: tie the horse to a ~ 把马拴在桩上 ②桩砧;圆头砧 ③火刑柱;炮烙刑: be condemned to the ~ 被判处炮烙刑,被判以火刑处死 ④[常用复]赌本,赌注: play for high ~s 下大赌注赌钱 ⑤[常用复]奖品;奖金;有奖赛马: trial ~s 有奖赛马的预赛 ⑥利害关系: have a ~ in 与…利害攸关 / consider the immensity of the ~ 考虑到有重大利害关系 ⑦下在投机生意上的股本 ⑧平台车边上的栅柱;有栅柱的车 ⑨(以分享所获物为条件)对探矿者的资助 **II ❶** *vt.* ①系于桩上;用桩撑住: ~ vines 用桩支持葡萄藤 ②立桩标出(off): ~ off a site for a schoolhouse 立桩标出校舍地基 ③用桩围住(up, in) ④把…押下打赌: ~ one's future on the outcome of the competition 把自己的前途押在竞争的结果上 ⑤资助…做投机生意;(以分享所获为目的)资助(探矿者) ❷ *vi.* 打赌 ||at ~ 危若累卵;在危险中;存亡攸关: The life of the sick man is at ~. 病人的生命在危急中。/ **pull (up)** ~s 迁离;收摊子 / ~ **out** ①把…立桩标出 ②派遣(警察等)至某地区进行监视;把…置于警察监视下 / ~ **out** (或 **off**) **a claim** 见 claim / ~ **boat** 航标艇(赛船时用以表示起点或航路的)标艇 / ~ **body** 周围有插孔可装栅柱的平板车身 / '~-,**holder** *n.* 赌金保管者 / ~ **net** 挂在桩上的渔网 / '~**out** *n.* (警察对地区或犯罪对象的)监视;监视地区 / ~ **truck** 车身装有栅柱的卡车

stalactite ['stæləktait] *n.* ①【地】钟乳石 ②钟乳石状物

stalagmite ['stæləgmait] *n.* 【地】石笋

stale[1] [steil] **I** *a.* ①陈腐的,陈旧的: Running water never gets ~. 流水不腐。/ a ~ joke 听厌了的笑话 / ~ news 过时消息 ②走了气的;走了味的;不新鲜的,干瘪的: ~ beer 走了气的啤酒 / ~ bread 不新鲜的面包 ③停滞的,不流通的: ~ air 不流通的空气 / ~ water 死水 ④疲惫不堪的,(运动员)因过分劳而表现不佳的: He has gone ~. 他已疲惫不堪了。⑤【律】失时效的: a ~ cheque 过期已久的支票 / a ~ debt 失时效的债务 II *vt.* & *vi.* ①(使)变陈旧;(使)变得无味 ②(使)失时效 ‖~ly *ad.* / ~ness *n.*

stale[2] [steil] I *n.* (牛、马等的)尿 II *vi.* (牛、马、骆驼等)撒尿

stalemate ['steil'meit] I *n.* ①(国际象棋中的)僵局,王棋受困 ②僵持,对峙: a strategic ~ 战略上的相持 II *vt.* ①(国际象棋中)使成僵局,使王棋受困 ②使僵持,使相持不下

stalk[1] [stɔ:k] *n.* ①(草本植物的)主茎,轴;花梗,叶柄 ②(无脊椎动物的)肉柄,梗节 ③(工厂等的)高烟囱 ④【建】叶梗饰 ⑤酒杯脚

stalk[2] [stɔ:k] I *vi.* ①蹑手蹑脚地走近;潜近猎物 ②高视阔步地走,大踏步走: ~ out of the room 傲然阔步走出房去 ❷ *vt.* ①潜步追踪:②搜索(地区): ~ the woods for deer 在林中搜猎鹿 ③高视阔步地走过 II *n.* ①潜随 ②高视阔步 ‖~er *n.* 潜随猎物者

stall[1] [stɔ:l] I *n.* ①(畜舍内的)分隔栏,厩 ②汽车停车处 ③(教堂内置于高坛或唱诗班席位上的)牧师座位;牧师职位 ④(教堂内的)长排座椅 ⑤[英][常用复]戏院正厅前排座位;[复]前座观众 ⑥货摊;书摊;棚店: a butcher's ~ 肉摊 / a candy ~ 糖果摊 ⑦手指(或脚趾)护套 ⑧小分隔间: a shower ~ 淋浴分隔间 ⑨【空】失速,失举 ⑩【矿】矿坑,敞式矿砂焙烧炉 II ❶ *vt.* ①把(牲畜)关入厩中;[古]把(牲畜)置于厩中饲肥 ②使陷入泥潭或雪地等): The train got ~ed in a snowstorm. 火车陷于大风雪中。③使(机车等)停顿,使停止;阻塞: ~ed traffic 阻塞了的交通 / The enemy troops were ~ed by our heavy fire. 敌军为我们的猛烈炮火所阻。④【空】使失速 ❷ *vi.* ①(牲畜)被关在厩内 ②陷入泥(或雪)中 ③(机车等)停顿,停止: The car ~ed on a hill. 汽车在小山上抛锚了。④【空】失速,失举 ‖~feed *vt.* 把(牲畜)关禁养肥;用干饲料饲养 / '~in *n.* 阻塞交通示威(一种示威方式,将车开至交通要道,放出汽油,使后边车辆无法通行,形成交通阻塞) / '~keeper *n.* 摊贩

stall[2] [stɔ:l] I *n.* ①(使主犯作案时不受注意并助之逃脱的)扒手的同党 ②拖延;支吾;口实,遁词 II ❶ *vi.* ①做扒手的同党 ②拖延;支吾: ~ for time 拖延时间 / ~ing tactics 拖延战术,缓兵之计 ❷ *vt.* 拖延;敷衍;把…的注意力引开: try to ~ off one's creditors 试图用托词把债主们搪塞起来

stallion ['stæljən] *n.* 未阉割的雄马(尤指种马)

stalwart ['stɔ:lwət] I *a.* ①高大健壮的;结实的 ②坚定的,刚毅的,不屈不挠的: a ~ supporter 坚定的支持者 II *n.* ①高大健壮的人 ②忠于某一政党的人 ‖~ly *ad.* / ~ness *n.*

stamen ['steimen] ([复] stamens 或 stamina ['stæminə]) *n.*【植】雄蕊

stamina ['stæminə] I stamen 的复数 II *n.* 持久力,耐力;精力: physical ~ 好体力

stammer ['stæmə] I ❶ *vt.* 结结巴巴地说,口吃地说(out): He ~ed out his request. 他结结巴巴地说出他的要求。❷ *vi.* 结结巴巴地说,口吃地说话: He ~s badly. 他口吃得很厉害。II *n.* 口吃: He is troubled with ~. 他患口吃。‖~er ['stæmərə] *n.* 口吃者,结结巴巴地说话的人

stamp [stæmp] I *n.* ①戳子,印,图章;(印下的)戳记,标记: Our ~ is the certificate of quality. 我们的戳记是质量合格的证明。②邮票;印花: a set of commemoration (postage) ~s 一套纪念邮票 / affix revenue ~s to a document 在文件上贴印花 ③[常用单]标志;特征;痕迹 ④类型;种类 ⑤跺脚;重踩: with a ~ of impatience 不耐烦地一顿脚 ⑥压印机,捣击机,捣矿机;杵 II ❶ *vt.* ①盖章于;压印于;打上(标记);用印模冲压;[喻]铭刻: ~ the envelope *with* one's address 在信封上盖印自己的地址 / ~ patterns *on* cloth 在布上印花样 ②贴邮票于;贴印花于: a ~ed envelope 印有邮票的信封 ③标出,表示: These actions ~ him as a highly principled man. 这些行为说明他是个有高度原则的人。/ an art product ~ed *with* great beauty 一件非常优美的艺术品 ④(用杵等)捣槌,压碎: ~ ores 压碎矿石 ⑤跺(脚);用脚踩踏;扑灭(out): ~ one's feet with anger 气得直跺脚 / ~ the floor in anger 气得直跺地板 / ~ the grass flat 把草踩平 / ~ out a fire (an epidemic) 扑灭火灾(瘟疫) ❷ *vi.* ①捣碎 ②跺脚;重步走;踩(on);[喻]拒绝;扑灭,毁掉(on): ~ about the room 在房里跺着脚走来走去 / ~ on a cockroach 踩死一只蟑螂 / We told him our idea, but he just ~ed on it. 我们把主意告诉了他,但他贸然拒绝了。‖~er *n.* ①盖章者,打印人;邮票盖销员 ②模压工,冲压工 ③捣击机,捣矿机;压模,模子 ‖~-,album *n.* 集邮簿 / '~-col,lector *n.* 集邮者 / ~ duty 印花税 / ~ing ground [口]常到的地方,经常出没的处所;落脚处 / '~=ma,chine *n.* 邮票印刷机 / ~ mill 捣矿机;捣矿厂(也作 ~ing mill) / ~-,office *n.* 印花税务局 / ~ tax 印花税 (=~ duty)

stampede [stæm'pi:d] I *n.* ①(畜群的)惊跑,乱窜;(军队的)大溃退 ②(人群的)蜂拥;(选举中的)突然一面倒 II ❶ *vt.* ①使(畜群)惊跑;使溃散 ②使乱拥;使(投票人、代表等)一下子倒向某候选人;使(大群人)一下子冲动行事: be ~d into a wave of panic buying 被一下子卷入恐慌抢购的风潮中 ❷ *vi.* ①惊跑,乱窜;溃散 ②(人群)突然蜂拥;突然冲动行事

stanch [sta:ntʃ] *vt.* ①使(伤口)止血;止(血);止流;使不漏水 ②停止,止住 ‖~er *n.* 止血药

stanchion ['sta:nʃən] I *n.* ①支柱,柱子;标柱 ②(牲畜栏中)限制牲畜活动的枷 II *vt.* ①用支柱支撑;给…装柱子 ②用枷拴住(牲畜)

stand [stænd] I (stood [stud]) ❶ *vi.* ①站,立: The baby cannot ~ yet. 这小孩迄今还不会站立。/

~ at ease (at attention) 稍息(立正)着 / *Stand easy!* [英]稍息! / He ~s one metre and seventy. 他身高一米七十。 / make sb.'s hair ~ on end 使某人毛发耸然

②坐落,位于: A row of willows ~s on the riverside. 沿河长着一行柳树。 / The house ~s on a hill. 房屋坐落于小山上。 / a ladder ~*ing* against the wall 靠墙放着的梯子

③停住不动;停滞,滞留: ~ still 站着不动;停滞不前 / He was commanded to ~. 他被命令站住。 / The car *stood* waiting for the green light. 车停着等候绿灯。 / Let the wine ~ for a while so that the lees will settle. 把酒静止地搁一会儿, 让渣子沉淀下去。 / *rainwater ~ing* in stagnant pools 滞留在死水潭里的雨水 / Tears *stood* in her eyes. 她双眼噙着泪。

④ 处某种状态(或境地);取某种态度: Truth ~s in opposition to falsehood. 真理同谬误是对立的。/ ~ ready for battle 作好战斗准备/ ~ first on the honour list 在光荣榜上名列第一 / The thermometer *stood at* 26°C. 温度计读数是摄氏二十六度。 / The monthly average output ~s *at* 600,000 tons. 每月平均产量六十万吨。 / The matter ~s thus. 事情就是这样。 / as things ~ 按照现状来看 / ~ surety for sb. 为某人做保证人 / How does he ~ on this question? 他对这个问题抱什么态度?

⑤ 坚持; 维持原状; 继续有效: ~ firm (或 fast) 屹立不动; 不让步 / The house will ~ another century. 这幢房子还可维持一个世纪。/ Let the word ~. 让这字留着,别去改动它。/ The order issued last week still ~s. 上星期发布的命令仍然有效。/ The same remark ~s good. 这句话继续有效。

⑥[英]做候选人,参加竞选

⑦【海】取某一航向: ~ for the harbour 向港口航行 / ~ in for the shore 驶向海岸

⑧(雄马)可作种马

❷ *vt.* ① 使站立; 竖放: ~ a child on his feet 使孩子直立。in the corner by way of punishment 罚某人立壁角 / *Stand* the pole here. 把杆子竖在这里。 / ~ facts on their heads 颠倒事实

②忍受; 经受; 顶住; 接受: I can't ~ that fellow. 我不能容忍那个家伙。/ Can you ~ the pain? 你受得住这疼痛吗? / I cannot ~ waiting (或 [美] to wait) any longer. 再等下去我可受不了啦。 / ~ the test of time 经受时间的考验 / wear and tear 耐磨损 / ~ gunfire(a siege) 顶住炮火 / ~ trial 受审讯

③(吃饭等时)为…付帐,为…会钞: ~ sb. a dinner (或 ~ a dinner for sb.) 请某人吃饭 / ~ a bottle to the company 为全作伴的人们买一瓶酒 / Who is going to ~ treat? 谁会钞?

④有供…站立的地位: The bus ~s 40 people. 这辆公共汽车内可站立四十人。

⑤【军】排成(某种队形)

II *n.* ①站住; 停住: come (或 be brought) to a ~ 陷于停顿

②(在撤退途中的)停下反击,停下抵抗

③站立位置; 立场: take a ~ for (against) sth. 表示赞成(反对)某事

④ [美] 法院的证人席: be called to the (witness) ~ 被传到庭作证 / take the ~ 站在证人席上作证

⑤架; 台; 讲坛; 看台; [常用复]看台上的观众: an umbrella ~ 伞架 / a music ~ 乐谱架 / a launching ~ (火箭)发射台 / a band ~ 乐队演奏台 / a reviewing ~ 检阅台 / a roar of applause from the ~s 看台上的观众发出的一阵热烈掌声

⑥摊; 报摊; 停车处; (适合于营业的)地点: a fruit ~ 水果摊 / a good ~ for a hotel 一处开设旅馆的好地点

⑦旅行剧团的停留演出; 停留演出地: a one-night ~ 一夜的停留演出

⑧ (一片) 生长的植物 (尤指植物在一定面积的疏密度): a good ~ of wheat 一片生长良好的小麦 / timber thinned to a proper ~ 伐到适当密度的林木

⑨[澳]森林; (被视作商品的)森林木材

⑩[苏格兰] (衣服等的) 一套 / [英] (一个士兵的)全套武装: a ~ of arms 一副武装

|| *a ~ of colo(u)rs* 军旗; 团旗 / *at a ~* 在停顿中;陷入僵局 / *It ~s to reason that ....* …是合乎情理的。 / *make a ~* ①站住,立定 ②(在撤退途中)停住进行抵抗;对抗 ③全力拥护;为…而奋斗: *make a ~ for* justice 为维护正义而斗争 / ~ *a good (~ no) chance* 见 chance / *Stand and deliver!* [古] (拦路强盗用语)留下买路钱! / ~ *aside* ① 站开; 让开; 躲开, 避开 ②(候选人)自行退出竞选 / ~ *back* 退后, 靠后站; 位于(或坐落在)靠后一点的地方: *Stand back and let the car pass.* 靠后站, 让车通过。 / ~ *by* 与…站在一起; 支持…: ② 遵守 (诺言等) ③站在旁边; 袖手旁观: Don't just ~, can't you lend a hand? 别站在一旁旁观,你不能帮一下忙吗? ④作好准备,准备行动: ~ *by* to await further instructions 作好准备等候进一步的指示 ⑤【讯】(发报台)准备发送信号; (收报台)处于调谐状态 / ~ *clear* 站开; 让开: ~ *clear* to let the car pass 站开让出车子通过 / ~ *clear of* (或 *from*) the gunfire 避开炮火 / ~ *down* ① 离开法庭的证人席 ② 暂时辞退; [英]不在阵地值勤; 退出游戏 (或竞选等); 退出领导岗位 ③ 顺潮流航行 / ~ *for* ①代表,代替; 象征,意味着 ②支持; 主张 ③做…的候选人,参加…的竞选: ~ *for* Parliament 竞选议员 / [口] 容忍; 允许: He can't ~ *for* those who put on airs. 他不能容忍摆架子的人。⑤【海】向…航行 / ~ *in* ①(拍影片时在灯光等布置好以前) 代替演员站好位置 (*for*) ②使花费: It *stood* me *in* a lot of money. 这花掉我许多钱。 / ~ *in with* ① 同…分担: Let me ~ *in with* you if it's expensive. 如果贵的话,我来同你分担。②同…联合; 同…勾结 ③与

…的宠爱; 和…友好 / **~ off** ①疏远, 不亲近; 远离 ②驶离岸边 ③[英]暂时解雇 ④避开(债主、攻击者等); 挡开 / **~ off and on** 【海】航行时一忽儿驶近海岸一忽儿远离海岸 / **~ on** 【海】继续向同一的方向航行 / **~ on ceremony** 见 **ceremony** / **~ one's ground** 见 **ground**[1] / **~ on one's own legs** 见 **leg** / **~ on one's rights** 见 **right** / **~ or fall** 好歹; 无论成败 / **~ out** ①突出; 出色: Red ~s out against a white background. 白底衬着红色特别醒目。②坚持抵抗; 支撑住: The troops *stood out* against the enemy attacks. 部队一直坚持抵住敌人的进攻。/ **~ out a storm** 抵挡住暴风雨 ③【海】(离岸)驶去: ~ *out* from the shore 驶离海岸 / **~ over** ①延期; 延缓: Let the matter ~ *over* until the next meeting. 把这事搁到下次会议上去解决。②监督, 监视 / **~ pat** 见 **pat**[2] / **~ sb. in good stead** 见 **stead** / **~ the racket** 见 **racket**[2] / **~ to** ①遵守(诺言等): ~ *to* one's word 遵守诺言, 守约 ②固守; 坚持: ~ *to* one's post 坚守岗位 / ~ *to* one's principles 坚持原则 / ~ *to* one's guns [喻]坚持原则, 固守自己的决定 / We ~ *to* it that .... 我们坚决主张… ③进入阵地防备敌人攻击 / **~ to win (gain, lose)** 一定赢(得益, 失利) / **~ up** ①站起; 向上升起; (使)竖立: Stand up, please. 请起立。/ columns of smoke ~*ing up* to the sky 向天空上升的烟柱 ②站得住脚; 经得起磨损: a proof that would ~ *up* in court 在法庭上可站得住脚的证据 ③[美俚]不守同…订好的约会; 背弃同…的婚约; 不再和…谈恋爱 ④坚持; 拥护, 支持 (*for*): be ready at all times to ~ *up for* truth 随时准备坚持真理 ⑤勇敢地面对; 抵抗; (物料)经得起(磨损)等) (*to*): insulation materials that ~ *up to* very high voltages 能耐极高电压的绝缘材料 ⑥给…当婚礼傧相 (*with*): ~ *well with sb.* 得某人好感; 受某人宠爱

‖**'~a'way** *a.* (裙子等)不贴住身子的 / **'~by** *n.* ① 可依靠的人; 可靠的东西; 被喜爱的食品; 受欢迎的娱乐节目 ②备用品, 备用设备 ③【军】一等战斗准备 ④【讯】(呼叫信号)准备发报; 准备收报 / **~ camera** 放在三脚架上的摄影机 / **'~-down** *n.* ①休止, 暂时停止活动: a military ~-*down* 暂停军事行动 ②[工厂]停工; 暂时被解雇期 / **'~-'in** *n.* ① (拍影片时在灯光等布置好以前)代替演员站着的人; 替身 ②有利地位, 得宠地位: have a ~-*in* with sb. 得某人的宠爱 / **'~-off** *a.* ①冷淡的 ②有支座的, 有托脚的: a ~*off* insulator 支座绝缘子, 托脚隔电子 *n.* ①离岸驶去; 避开; 挡开 ②冷淡 ③[英]闲散, 停工 ④平衡; 抵销; 中和 ⑤(比赛等的)不分胜负, 和局 / **'~'offish** *a.* 有点冷淡的, 不亲近的 / **'~out** *n.* ①杰出的人(或物); [美俚](在比赛中)有获胜把握的选手 ②[口]拒绝附和赞同和同中多数人的意见者, 坚持己见者 *a.* 出色的, 杰出的 / **'~pat** *a.* 固执保守的 *n.* =~**patter** / **'~,patter** *n.* (特指政治上的)固执保守分子; 顽固地反对变革的人 /

'~pipe *n.* (稳定给水系统中水压用的)圆筒形水塔; 竖管; 储水管, 水鹤 / **'~point** *n.* 立场, 观点 / **'~still** *n.* 停止; 停顿; 停滞不前: come (或被 brought) to a ~*still* 停顿下来 / **'~to** *n.* [英] 【军】战斗准备 / **'~-up** *a.* ①[美俚]敢说敢干的; 坦率正直的 ②(衣领)直立的(与 turn-down 相对) ③站着的, 以直立姿势进行的: a ~-*up* buffet 供顾客站着吃的小餐室 / a ~-*up* meal 立餐 ④(打架)凭真功夫的, 不要手段的, 光明正大的

standard ['stændəd] **I** *n.* ①标准, 水准; 规格; 规范: the ~ of living (或 the living ~) 生活水平 / raise the ~ of the people's material and cultural life 提高人民的物质和文化生活水平 / conform to the ~s of society 合乎社会准则 / set a high ~ for one's work 对自己的工作提出高标准的要求 / be up to (below) the ~ 达到(低于)标准 ②旗; 军旗; (骑兵队或摩托化部队的)队旗; (王室的)旗标 ③ (货币制度的)本位: the gold-exchange ~ 金汇兑本位 ④金银货币中的纯金银与合金的法定比例 ⑤【植】中年木; 第一代上木, 保残木; (园艺中)嫁接于树干上的灌木 ⑥直立支柱; 灯台; 烛台; 电杆; 垂直的水管(或煤气管) ⑦ (英国小学的)年级 ⑧【植】旗瓣 **II** *a.* ①标准的: the ~ atmospheric pressure 标准大气压 / the ~ weights and measures 标准度量衡 ②公认为优秀的, 权威的: the ~ work on the subject 关于这个科目的权威著作 ③合规格的; 一般性的: the ~ model of an automobile 普通定型式的汽车 ④装支柱的: a ~ lamp (支柱能伸缩的)标地灯 ⑤不依附别物生长的: ~ fruit trees 独立生长的果树 ‖**~-bearer** *n.* 掌旗者, 旗手; [喻]杰出的倡导者, 领导者 / **~ candle** 标准烛光 / **~ deviation** 标准离差, 标准偏差 / **Standard English** 标准英语 / **~ error** 标准误差 / **~ ga(u)ge** 标准量规; 标准轨距 (= 1.435 米) / **~ time** 标准时间

standardize ['stændədaiz] *vt.* ①使与标准比较, 用标准校验: ~ a voltmeter 用标准校验一只伏特计 ②使合标准, 使标准化, 使统一: These machine parts have been ~*d.* 这些机件已标准化了。/ ~*d* products 标准化产品 ‖**standardization** [ˌstændədai'zeiʃən]

standing ['stændiŋ] **I** *a.* ①直立的; 站着的: ~ corn 未割的谷物 / a ~ shot 立射 / a ~ jump 立定跳远 / a ~ ovation 起立欢呼 / a ~ vote 起立表决 ②停滞的, 不流动的; 停着的, 不在运转的: pools of ~ water 死水潭 / a ~ factory (machine) 停工的工厂(停开的机器) ③持续的; 长期有效的; 标准的: a ~ dish 常备的菜 / a ~ joke (或 jest) 老笑话 / a ~ order 长期订单 / the ~ orders (议会的) 议事规则; 【军】标准作战规定 / ~ operating procedure 【军】标准作战规定; [美俚]标准操作规定, 标准做法 ④常备的, 常设的: a ~ army 常备军, 现役部队 / a ~ committee 常务委员会 ⑤固定的; 有垫脚的: a ~ washtub 固定的洗衣盆 / a ~ cup 高脚杯 ⑥已由法律(或

习惯)所确定的; 永久的 **II** *n.* ①站立; 站立处 ②身分,地位,名望: a man of (high) ~ 名望(或地位)高的人 / international ~ 国际地位 ③持续; 期间: an illness (a dispute) of long ~ 长期疾病(争论) / a worker of ten years' ~ 有十年工龄的工人 ‖~ **room** 站的地位(尤指戏院或公共车辆满座时站的地方): *Standing room only!* (戏院或车辆售票处用语)只有站票! / ~ **wave** 【物】驻波,定波

standish ['stændiʃ] *n.* 墨水台

stank [stæŋk] *n.* ①[英方]池塘;水沟 ②[英]坝,堰

stannum ['stænəm] *n.* [拉][化]锡

stanza ['stænzə] *n.* ①(诗的)节 ②[美俚](在一地的)演出期(尤指一星期): The play is to be held over for another ~. 这出戏将再继续上演一星期。 ③[美俚](体育比赛的)局, 盘, 场 ‖~**ic** [stæn'zeiik] *a.* 诗节的

staple[1] ['steipl] **I** *n.* ①U形钉, 肘钉; 订书钉 ②钩环, 锁环 ③[音](双簧管等放置簧片的)嘴套 **II** *vt.* 用肘钉(或订书钉)钉住 ‖'**stapling-ma-,chine** *n.* 订书机

staple[2] ['steipl] **I** *n.* ①大宗出产; 主要商品(或产品): Tea is one of our ~s. 茶叶是我们的主要产品之一。 ②销路稳定的商品; 常用品; 广泛采用的东西: Sugar and salt are ~s of a grocery store. 糖与盐是杂货铺销路稳定的商品。 / Fish is one of the ~s of the Japanese diet. 鱼是日本人常吃的食品之一。③原材料 ④主要成分;主题: the ~ of conversation 主要话题 ⑤(羊毛、棉、麻、化纤等的)纤维 (=~ fibre); 纤维(平均)长度: cotton of long (short) ~ 长(短)绒棉 ⑥来源(地);中心: the chief ~ of news 消息的主要来源 ⑦[古]贸易中心城镇 **II** *a.* ①主要的; 大宗生产的: Rice is our ~ food. 大米是我们的主食。 / ~ crops 主要农作物 ②经常需要的; 经常用的: ~ goods 大路货 ③常用的 ‖~ rayon 人造棉 **III** *vt.* (按纤维长短)把…分级;把…分类

star [stɑː] **I** *n.* ①星;【天】恒星: a fixed ~ 恒星 / a shooting (或 falling) ~ 流星 / the morning (evening) ~ 晨(昏)星 ②星状物; 星章; 星形勋章 ③[印]星号(即*) ④[常用复](占星术的)司命星;命运 ⑤(电影、戏剧等的)明星 ⑥(马等额上的)白斑 ⑦[动]海星 (=~fish) ⑧[英]初次坐牢的犯人 **II** (starred; starring) ['stɑːriŋ]) ❶ *vt.* ①[常用被动语态]用星(或星状物)装饰; 点缀 (*with*): a meadow *starred with* red flowers 星星点点地长着一些红花的草地 ②用星号标出, 用星号注明: ~ an item in a list 把单子上的一项目注上星号 ③使担任主角,使成为明星 ❷ *vi.* 扮演主角; 表演出色 **III** *a.* ①星的 ②名演员的, 明星的: play ~ roles 当主角 ③优越的;出众的: a ~ athlete 优秀运动员 / a ~ diplomat 出色的外交家 ‖*see* ~s [口]眼里冒金星,目眩: The pain made him *see* ~s. 痛得他眼里直冒金星。 / *thank one's* (*lucky*) ~s 谢天谢地, 额手称庆 / *the* ~ *of day* (或 *noon*) 太阳 / *the Stars and Stripes* 星条旗(美国国旗) / *this* ~ [诗]地球 / *with* ~s *in one's eyes* 自鸣得意地 ‖**~dom** *n.* ①明星的地位,明星界 ②一群明星 / **~less** *a.* 无星的 / **~let** ['stɑːlit] *n.* ①小星 ②[口]小女明星 / **~like** *a.* 象星那样明亮的;星形的 ‖**Star Chamber** 【英史】星法院(于 1641 年停闭; 以专断暴虐出名) / '~,**chamber** *a.* 秘密的; 专断的 / **cluster** 【天】星团 / '~-**crossed** *a.* 命运不佳的, 倒运的 / '~-**drift** *n.* 【天】星流 / '~**dust** *n.* ①[常作 ~ dust](大群小星的)星团; 宇宙尘 ②幻觉; 恍惚 / '~**fish** *n.* 【动】海星 / '~**flower** *n.* 【植】美洲七瓣莲; 虎眼万年青 / '~**gaze** *vi.* 凝视 / '~**gazer** *n.* ①占星家; [谑]天文学家 ②空想家 ③瞻星鱼 / '~,**gazing** *n.* 凝视; 心不在焉; 空想 / '~**light** *n.* 星光 *a.* 有星光的: a ~*light* night 星光之夜 / '~**lit** *a.* 星光照耀的 / **Star of David** 大卫王之星(犹太教的六芒星形标志,意为"大卫王的盾牌") / ~ **route** [美]星号邮线(指在乡间等偏僻地区由专门雇员递送邮件的路线) / ~ **shell** 照明弹 / '~-,**spangled** *a.* ①镶有星星的; 星光灿烂的: the *Star-Spangled* Banner 星条旗(美国国旗); 美国国歌 ②美国的; 美国公民的 / ~ **streaming** 【天】星流 / '~-,**studded** *a.* 星罗棋布的; 星星点缀着的: a ~-*studded* sky 布满星星的天空 / ~ **system** ①【天】银河系 ②(以一、二个明星作为台柱的)明星制度 / ~ **turn** [主英] ①(演出中的)主要节目 ②被广为宣传的人(或节目)

starboard ['stɑːbəd, 'stɑːbɔːd] **I** *n.* (船、飞机的)右舷: alter course to ~ 转向右(舷)航行 / sighted a steamer to ~. 我在右舷方向看见一艘轮船。 **II** *a.* 右舷的,右侧的: the ~ side 右舷 / the ~ tack 右抢(帆船右舷逼风) / on the ~ bow 在船头右舷 **III** *vt.* 把(舵)转向右: *Starboard* the helm! 右舵!

starch [stɑːtʃ] **I** *n.* ①【化】淀粉; [复]淀粉类食物: animal ~ 牲粉, 糖原 / ~ gum 淀粉胶, 糊精 / ~ iodide 碘化淀粉 ②古板,生硬,拘泥 ③[美俚]勇气,刚毅;精力 **II** *vt.* ①给(衣服等)上浆,浆硬 ②使古板; 使拘泥: a ~*ed* manner 拘泥的态度 ‖**~edly** ['stɑːtʃidli] *ad.* 古板地, 拘泥地 / '~-**ed-ness** ['stɑːtʃidnis] *n.* 古板, 拘泥

starchy ['stɑːtʃi] *a.* ①淀粉的; 似淀粉的; 含淀粉的: a ~ food 含淀粉的食物 ②上过浆似的; 浆硬的 ③古板的, 拘泥的; [美]高傲的, 不客气的 ‖**starchily** *ad.* / **starchiness** *n.*

stare [stɛə] **I** ❶ *vi.* ①盯, 凝视, 目不转睛地看: ~ *at* sb. 盯着某人 / ~ *into* the distance 凝视远方, 远瞩 / ~ *with* astonishment 惊讶地瞪着眼 ②(颜色等)惹眼, 显眼 ③(毛发等)竖立 ❷ *vt.* 盯, 凝视, 目不转睛地看得…: ~ sb. up and down 上下打量某人 / ~ sb. down 盯得某人不敢再对视下去 / ~ sb. out of countenance 盯得某人侷促不安 **II** *n.* 盯, 凝视: with a blank (或 empty, vacant) ~ 茫然凝视地 / with a ~ of horror (astonishment) 带着惊恐(惊愕)的眼神

give sb. a rude (frosty) ~ 无礼地(冷若冰霜地)盯某人一眼 ‖*make sb.* ~ 使某人惊愕 / ~ *sb. in the face* 见 **face**

staring ['steəriŋ] *a.* ① 目不转睛的, 凝视的: with ~ eyes 凝视地, 目不转睛地 ②(颜色等)惹眼的, 显眼的, 过于鲜艳的: a ~ green 太显眼的绿色 ③(毛发)竖立的 ‖*stark* ~ *mad* 完全发狂的 ‖~*ly ad.*

stark [stɑːk] Ⅰ *a.* ① 僵硬的; 严格的, 刻板的: lie stiff and ~ in death 直挺挺地躺着死了 / ~ discipline 严格的纪律 ② 完全的, 十足的: ~ denial 完全否认 / a ~ exposure 彻底的揭露 ③赤裸裸的; 十分明显的; 轮廓明显的: a ~ fact 极其明显的事实 ③荒凉的;光秃秃的,空的;贫瘠的 ⑤健壮的,结实的 Ⅱ *ad.* 完全: ~ poor 赤贫的 ‖~*ly ad.* 完全;分明地;赤裸裸地 ‖'~-'**naked** *a.* 一丝不挂的

starling[1] ['stɑːliŋ] *n.* 【动】欧椋鸟;椋鸟科的鸟

starling[2] ['stɑːliŋ] *n.* 【建】杀水桩,桥墩尖端

start [stɑːt] Ⅰ *vi.* ①跳起;惊起;吃惊: ~ *to* one's feet 蓦地站起 / ~ *at* the mere rustle of leaves in the wind 一有风吹草动就胆战心惊 ② 涌出; 突然出现: Blood ~ed from the wound. 血从伤口涌出。 / They forged ahead in spite of the great difficulties that had ~ed *up.* 尽管出现了巨大的困难,他们仍然奋勇前进。 / He was so excited that tears ~ed *to* his eyes. 他激动得热泪盈眶。 ③ 突起; 鼓出: with ~*ing* eyes 眼睛瞪得大大地 ④出发,起程 ⑤ 开动;开始,着手: The engine won't ~. 引擎发动不起来。 / Knowledge ~s with practice. 认识从实践开始。 ⑥ 松动, 脱落; (木料等)翘曲: A nail has ~ed. 一颗钉子松动了。 / The ship has ~ed at the seams. 船接缝处已松裂。 ⑦参加比赛 Ⅱ *vt.* ① 惊动; 使惊起; 惊出: ~ a fox from its lair 把狐狸惊出巢穴 ②开动,使起动,发动: ~ (*up*) a car 发动汽车 / ~ a press campaign 在报刊上发动一次宣传运动 / ~ a war 发动战争 ③引起;使开始;开动: The smoke ~ed him coughing. 烟呛得他发咳。 / His criticism ~ed me thinking seriously. 他的批评引起我认真思考。 / ~ a fire 点火, 引火 / ~ sb. in business 帮助某人开始经商 / ~ work (或 working) 开始工作 / It ~ed raining (或 to rain). 开始下雨了。 / She has ~ed a baby. [口]她已怀孕。 ④ 提出(题目等)供考虑(或讨论) ⑤创办,开设 ⑥使松动;使脱落;使翘曲: The collision ~ed a seam. 碰撞使一条接缝松了。 / The damp has ~ed the timbers. 潮湿已使木料弯翘了。 ⑦开始雇用(某人)【海】把(酒)从桶里倒出;开(桶)取酒 ⑨给(赛跑者)发起跑信号 ⑩ 使参加比赛 Ⅱ *n.* ① 跳起;惊起;吃惊: awake *with* a ~ 惊醒 ②出发;开始,开端;开始信号;起点;【体】起跑;起跑点: We made an early ~ as we had a long way to go. 因路远,我们一早就出发了。 / make (或 get) a good (bad) ~ 开端好(坏) / The ~ is fixed at 2 p.m. 定于下午二时出发。 ③ 有利条件,占先地位: give sb. a

10 metres (10 seconds) ~ 让某人先跑十米(早跑十秒) ④ 开始事业的机会: get a good ~ *in* life 得到一个好机缘而开始了自己的事业 ⑤(东西的)松动部分; 分裂;漏隙 ‖a *rum* ~ [口]惊人事件 / *at the very* ~ 一开始 / *by fits and* ~s 一阵一阵地, 间歇地 / *from* ~ *to finish* 自始至终;彻头彻尾 / *get* (或 *have*) *the* ~ *of sb.* 比某人居先, 比某人占优势 / ~ *after sb.* 开始追赶某人 / ~ *against sb.* 参加对某人的比赛(或竞争) / ~ *aside* 跳往一旁, 跳开 / ~ *back* 惊退, 畏缩 / ~ *from* (或 *at, on*) *scratch* 见 **scratch** / ~ *in* [口]开始: It ~ed *in* to rain. 下起雨来了。 / He ~ed *in* on the cake. 他吃起饼来。 / ~ *off* 出发, 动身; 开始: What shall we ~ *off with*? 我们从哪儿谈起好? / ~ *on* 开始(旅程等) / ~ *out* ①起程;出发 ②[口]着手进行: ~ *out* to write the history of a factory 着手写厂史 / ~ *something* 制造麻烦, 制造骚乱 / ~ *up* ① 突然站起, 惊起 ② 突然出现, 崛起 ③发动, 使开始运转 / *to* ~ *with* ①作为开始: Our group had five members to ~ *with.* 我们的小组开始时只有五个人。 ②首先, 第一点: *To* ~ *with*, we have the correct orientation. 首先,我们的方向是对头的。 ‖~**er** *n.* ①开端者 ②参加赛跑的人(或马) ③赛跑开始的发号员; (车辆等的)调度员 ④起动机;自动起动机;启动器 ⑤酵母 ‖'~-**up** *n.* 起动(学)

startle ['stɑːtl] Ⅰ ❶ *vt.* 使大吃一惊: be ~d to see … 看到…吃了一惊 / be ~d by (或 at) sth. 为某事所惊 / be ~d out of one's sleep 从睡梦中惊醒 ❷ *vi.* 惊起, 惊跳起来: babies who ~ easily 容易惊跳的婴儿 Ⅱ *n.* 吃惊;惊跳 ‖~**r** *n.* 令人吃惊者

starvation [stɑː'veiʃən] *n.* 饥饿; 饿死: die of ~ 活活饿死 / ~ wages 不足温饱的工资,饥饿工资 / a ~ diet 不足维持健康的食物

starve [stɑːv] ❶ *vi.* ①饿死 ②挨饿 ③[口]饿得慌: When will dinner be ready? We are simply *starving* (for food). 饭什么时候才能准备好? 我们简直饿坏了。 ④极需; 渴望 (*for*) ⑤[古]冻死; 挨冻 ❷ *vt.* ① 使饿死; 使挨饿: be ~d to death 饿死 ②[古]使冻死 ③[口]使饥饿迫使: try to ~ sb. *into* submission 企图以饥饿迫使某人屈服 ④ 以节食治疗: Feed a cold and ~ a fever. 伤风时宜吃,发烧时宜饿。

state[1] [steit] Ⅰ *n.* ① 状态, 状况, 情形: in a ~ of upheaval 处在动荡的状态 / the ~ of affairs 事态 / the ~ of war 战争状态 / the ~ of the art (电子计算机等发展中科学的) 工艺水平 / one's mental ~ 精神状态 / The building is in a bad ~ of repair. 那建筑物需大修。 / What a ~ you are in! 你竟弄成这副样子! ②[口]激动,兴奋; 过分紧张: He was in quite a ~ about the matter. 他对这事非常激动。 / Don't get into a ~. 不要激动(或担忧)! ③ 国家; 政府; 领土: a socialist ~ 社会主义国家 / a federal (neutral, sovereign) ~ 联邦(中立，主权)国家 / a non-nuclear (nuclear-poor) ~ 无核(少核)国家 / a head of ~ 国家元首 / Church and State 教会和政府；政教 ④[常作 S-] (美国等的)州: Kansas State (美国)堪萨斯州 / the Southern States 美国南方各州 / the United States (of America) 美利坚合众国 ⑤ 国务: Secretary of State (美国)国务卿；(英国)国务大臣 / the Department of State (或 the State Department) (美国)国务院 ⑥ [S-] (美国)国务院 ⑦ (尤指高的)社会地位，身分；社会阶层: persons in every ~ of life 各阶层的人们 ⑧ 尊严；堂皇，豪华: keep (one's) ~ 维持尊严，摆架子 / arrive in great ~ 威风凛凛地到达 **II** *a.* 国家的；国务的；州的: ~ machinery 国家机器 / ~ relations 国家关系 ② 礼仪用的；礼仪上的，仪式的: ~ apartments 举行隆重礼仪用的房间 / a ~ carriage 御用马车，礼车；贵宾室 / a ~ call [口]正式访问 ‖ *a ~ of siege* 戒严状态 / *be in a ~ of grace* 【宗】蒙受天恩 / *in a ~ of nature* ① 处于原始状态，处于未开化状态 ② 裸体 ③【宗】有罪 / *in ~* 正式地；庄严堂皇地；隆重地 / *lie in ~* (遗体)殡殓后任人凭吊，葬前供公众瞻仰 / *the States* [口]美国(美国国外的用法，美国国内不用) ‖~**hood** *n.* ① 国家的地位 ②[美]州一级，州的地位 / ~**less** *a.* ①无国家的 ②无国籍的 ③无公民权的 ‖ ~ **aid** [美]州政府用于地方公共事业的补助费 / ~ **bank** ①国家银行 ②[美]州立银行 / ~ **capitalism** 国家资本主义 / '~**craft** *n.* 管理国家事务的本领 / ~ **criminal** 政治犯 / **State flower** (代表美国某州的)州花 / '**Statehouse** *n.* [美]州议会大楼；州的首府 / ~ **medicine** 国家公费医疗 / ~ **prisoner** 政治犯人，重罪犯人 / '~**room** *n.* ①(宫殿等的)大厅 ②(轮船的)特别房舱，睡舱；(美国火车上的)特别包厢，卧室 / ~'**s evidence** [美] ①刑事案件中对同案犯的揭发证词 ②刑事案件中的证人 / **States General** (一七八九年前)法国的议会；(十五、十六世纪时)荷兰的国会 / '~**side** *a.* (不包括阿拉斯加州和夏威夷州)大陆美国的，美国国内的; *in* (或向、从) 大陆美国的 *ad.* 在大陆美国; 向(或从)大陆美国 / ~ **socialism** 国家社会主义 / **State(s') Rights** [美]州权 / ~ **trial** 由国家起诉的案件(尤指政治案件)的审问 / '~**wide** *a.* 全国范围的: a ~*wide* celebration 全国性的庆祝活动 *ad.* 在全国范围内

state² [steit] *vt.* ①陈述，说明，阐明，声明: ~ one's views 陈述自己的观点 / ~ the facts of a case 阐明案情的真相 ②规定(日期、价格等) ③【数】用符号表示(问题、关系等)

stated ['steitid] *a.* ① 规定的，固定的，定期的: at ~ intervals 每隔一定的时间 / ~ office hours 规定的办公时间 / *Stated* meetings are held every Thursday afternoon. 例会每星期四下午举行。 ②被宣称的；被宣明的: ~ exceptions 被宣明的例外 / ~ value [美](无票面值股票的)宣称价值 ③【数】用符号表示的；用代数式表示的

stately ['steitli] *a.* 庄严的，高贵的；堂皇的，雄伟的: a ~ pace 稳重庄严的步子 / a ~ building 雄伟的大厦 ‖**stateliness** *n.*

statement ['steitmənt] *n.* ① 陈述，声明；声明书；【律】供述: issue a ~ 发表声明 / an official ~ 正式声明 / make a ~ 陈述，供述 ② 财务报表；财务报告书: a bank ~ 银行报告，银行结单

statesman ['steitsmən] ([复] statesmen) *n.* ①政治家，国务活动家 ②[英](英国北部的)小自耕农 ‖*an elder ~* 政界元老 / ~**like**, ~**ly** *a.* 政治家的；有政治家才能的；有政治家风度的 / ~**ship** *n.* 治国之才；政治家的才能；政治家风度

static ['stætik] **I** *a.* ① 静的；静态的；静力的: a ~ load 静荷载，恒载 / ~ characteristic 【无】静态特性 ②【物】静电的: ~ electricity 静电；静电学 ③固定的；不活泼的，不生动的；变化小的 ④使安静的，使平稳的 **II** *n.* 【电】天电，静电；天电干扰，静电干扰: man-made ~s 人为静电干扰 ‖'~-**free** *a.* 不受天电干扰的 / ~ **line** [空]固定开伞索

station ['steiʃən] **I** *n.* ①站，台，所，局；车站；航空站: a pumping (power) ~ 抽水(发电)站 / a fire ~ 消防站 / a space ~ 宇宙站，空间站 / a police ~ 警察所，警察分局 / a postal ~ 邮政所 / a railway ~ 火车站 ② 驻地；停泊地；岗位；位置: a ~ hospital 【军】驻地医院 / a naval ~ 海军站，军港 / a battle ~ 战斗岗位 / One of the planes was out of ~. 一架飞机飞离了编队位置。 / the policemen at their ~s 站在自己岗位上的警察 ③身分，地位；职位: a woman of high ~ 贵妇人 ④电台；广播电台；电视台: a broadcasting ~ 广播电台 / a television ~ 电视台 ⑤科学考察站，研究所: an agricultural experiment ~ 农业试验站 ⑥【测】测站 ⑦【生】生境，栖所 ⑧[澳]牧场 ⑨军事基地；[总称]驻扎在基地的人员 ⑩[美]空军兵站 ⑪站位(姿态)，停留 ⑫【宗】十四幅耶稣受难像之一 **II** *vt.* 驻扎，安置: ~ the troops on a hill 把部队驻扎在小山上 / He ~ed himself at the exit. 他站(或坐定)在出口处。 ‖~*s of the cross* 【宗】① 十四幅耶稣受难像 ② 在耶稣受难前作的纪念默祷 ‖~ **agent** [美]火车站管理人员 / ~ **break** 电台间歇；间歇时间里所作的通知(或广告)；联播结束信号 / '~-**calendar** *n.* [英]火车离站时刻指示牌 / ~ **house** 站(尤指警察分局、消防站)上的建筑物 / '~-**master** *n.* 火车站站长 / ~ **pointer** 【测】三杆分度仪 / ~ **wag(g)on** 旅行汽车，小型客车，客货两用车

stationary ['steiʃəneri] **I** *a.* 不动的，静止的；不变的，固定的；停留的: ~ radiant 【天】不动辐射点 / a ~ temperature 不变的温度 / a ~ engine 固定式发动机 / ~ wave 【物】驻波，定波 / ~ air 静气(呼吸时留在肺部的空气) / ~ point 【天】留点 / ~ troops 驻军 **II** *n.* ①[复]驻军 ②固定物 ‖**stationariness** *n.*

stationer ['steiʃənə] *n.* ①文具商: go to the ~'s 到文具店去买文具 ②[古]书商;出版商

stationery ['steiʃənəri] *n.* ①[总称]文具 ②信笺(通常配有信封): hotel ~ 旅馆供应的信笺 ‖**Stationery Office** (英国)文书局(出版和发行政府文件、书籍等)

statist ['steitist] **I** *n.* ①主张中央集权下经济统制的人 ②统计学家;统计员 **II** *a.* 主张中央集权下经济统制的

statistic [stə'tistik] **I** *a.* = statistical **II** *n.* [只用单] ①统计资料中的一项 ②(对总体具有代表性的)典型统计量

statistical [stə'tistikəl] *a.* 统计的;统计学的: a ~ chart (table) 统计图(表) / ~ data 统计资料 / ~ figures 统计数字 ‖~ly *ad.*

statistician [,stætis'tiʃən] *n.* 统计学家;统计员

statistics [stə'tistiks] [复] *n.* ①统计;统计数字,统计资料: ~ of population 人口统计 / capital construction ~ 基本建设统计 / *Statistics* tell part of the story. 统计数字说明了部分问题。②[用作单]统计学

statue ['stætju:] **I** *n.* 雕像, 塑像, 铸像 **II** *vt.* ①以雕像装饰(道路、花园等) ②[古]为…作塑像 ‖*the Statue of Liberty* (美国纽约的)自由女神铜像 ‖~d *a.* 饰以雕像的

statuesque [,stætju'esk] *a.* 塑像般的;轮廓清晰的;庄严的,优美的 ‖~ly *ad.* / ~ness *n.*

statuette [,stætju'et] *n.* 小雕像,小塑像

stature ['stætʃə] *n.* ①身高, 身材: be short of ~ 身材矮小 / be of medium ~ (或 be medium in ~) 长着中等身材 ②(精神、道德等的)发展成长状况,高度: a figure of world ~ 世界性人物

status ['steitəs] *n.* ①情形, 状况: the ~ of affairs 事态,形势 / the alert ~【军】待机状态 ②地位,身分: class ~ 阶级成分 / political (social) ~ 政治(社会)地位 ③重要地位,要人身分: a ~ seeker 想往上爬的人 / a ~ symbol 表示人地位高的东西,地位高的人的表征 ‖*status quo* [kwou] [拉] 现状: seek to preserve the *status quo* 企图维持现状 / *status quo ante* ['ænti] [拉]原状,以前的状态

statute ['stætju:t] *n.*【律】法令, 法规, 成文律: public (private) ~ 公(私)法 / ~s at large 全文法令集 / the ~ law 成文法 ② (公司、学校等的)章程,条例: the ~s of a university 大学章程 ‖~ **book** 法令全书 / ~ **mile** 法定哩 (=5,280 呎)

statutory ['stætjutəri] *a.* ①法令的,有关法令的 ②法定的,依照法令的 ‖~ **rape**【律】强奸在法定承诺年龄之下女子的罪行,强奸幼女

staunch[1] ['stɔ:ntʃ, stɑ:ntʃ] *a.* ①坚定的, 忠诚的: a ~ ally 坚定可靠的同盟者 / a ~ defender of national independence 民族独立的忠诚捍卫者 ②壮健的 ③坚固的; 不透水的, 不透气的: a ~ ship 牢固的船 ‖~ly *ad.* / ~ness *n.*

stave [steiv] **I** *n.* ①狭板,桶板 ②梯子横木,梯级 ③棍,棒,杖 ④诗节;诗句 ⑤【音】五线谱表 **II** (staved 或 stove [stouv]) ❶ *vt.* ①击穿,弄破;凿孔于: ~ *in* a cask (boat) 在桶(船)上弄出一个洞 / The deckhouse has been ~*d in* by the tremendous seas. 甲板室已被巨浪打破。②压扁,打坏(帽子、盒子等);压牢(金属等) ③挡开;避开;延缓 (off): ~ *off* a blow 架开一击 / ~ *off* exposure 避免暴露 ④给…装上桶板 ❷ *vi.* ①穿孔, 破碎, 被打穿: The boat ~*d in* when it struck the rocks. 小船在触礁时撞破了。②快步走动

stay[1] [stei] **I** ❶ *vi.* ①停留; 保持下去: *Stay* here till I return. 在我回来之前别离开。/ ~ at home 呆在家里 / The weather ~*ed* fine for three days. 一连三天都是好天气。/ The patient's temperature ~*ed* around 40°C. 这病人的体温持续在摄氏四十度左右。②(暂)住;耽搁,逗留: ~ in a hotel 住在旅馆 / ~ in town 耽搁在城里 / ~ with friends 与朋友们暂住在一起 / Won't you ~ *for* (或 *to*) supper? 请留下吃晚饭好吗? ③站住,停住;中止,暂停: *Stay!* You have forgotten the umbrella. 等一等! 你把雨伞忘了。/ Get him to ~ a minute. 叫他停一下。④坚持;持久: ~ to the end of the race 坚持跑完全程 / ~*ing* power 持久力 ⑤并驾齐驱 (with): ~ *with* one's rival 与敌手并驾齐驱 ❷ *vt.* ①阻止,制止,抑制;平息;暂时平息…的饥渴: ~ the inroads of a disease 阻止疾病的侵入 / ~ one's stomach 充饥 ②延缓: ~ judgement (proceedings) 延缓审判(诉讼程序) ③坚持;停留到…完: ~ the course 坚持跑完全程;[喻]坚持(奋斗)到底 / He'll ~ the week (out). 他将呆过这个星期。④留等 **II** *n.* ①逗留;停留 ②制止,抑制,中止 ③延缓: ~ of execution【律】延期执行 ④[口]持久力,耐力 ‖**come** (或 **be here**) **to** ~ 留下不走;扎下根来: The new work style has come to ~. 新的工作作风已经扎下根了。/ ~ *away* 不在家,外出;离开 / ~ *in* 呆在家里,不外出;课后留在学校 / ~ *on* 继续停留 / ~ *one's* (*sb.'s*) *hand* 见 hand / ~ *out* ①呆在户外 ②呆到…的结束 / ~ *over* (*at sb.'s*) (在某人处)过夜 / ~ *put* [口]装牢;留在原处不动 / ~ *up* 不睡觉: He ~*ed up* all night. 他通宵未睡。‖~-**at-home** ['steiəthoum] *a.* & *n.* 不爱出门的(人);不爱离开本乡(或本国)的(人) / '~-**down strike** (矿工)留在矿井下的罢工;静坐罢工 / '~-**in strike** 留厂罢工;静坐罢工

stay[2] [stei] **I** *n.* ①【海】支索 ②支柱;赡养者 ③支撑物;撑条;拉条;牵条: a ~ tube 撑管 ④[复]女用束腹;紧身胸衣 **II** ❶ *vt.* ①【海】用支索固定;用支索使(桅)改变角度;使(船)转向上风 ②支持,支撑 ❷ *vi.*【海】转向上风: ~s 转向上风,在抢风 / slack in ~s (帆船)掉头时放慢速度的 / *miss* (或 *lose*)~s 抢风失败 ‖~ **bar**, ~ **rod** 撑杆 / ~ **lace** 女用束腹的带子 / '~**sail** *n.*【海】支索帆

stead [sted] **I** *n.* ①替代: If you can't come, send her *in* your ~. 如果你不能来,叫她代你来。

② 好处，用处；有利性 **II** *vt.* 对…有利；对…有用，对…有帮助 ‖*in (the)* ~ *of* 代替 (=instead of) / *stand sb. in good* ~ 给某人以好处，对某人有用

steadfast ['stedfəst] *a.* ① 固定的，不变的 ② 坚定的，不动摇的；坚信的: be ~ in the midst of difficulties 身在困难中坚决不动摇 / a ~ man 意志坚定的人 ‖~**ly** *ad.* / ~**ness** *n.*

steady ['stedi] **I** *a.* ① 稳固的，平稳的: a ~ foundation 稳固的基础 / a ~ hand 不颤抖的手；[喻] 果断的手段，坚强的领导 / not ~ on one's legs 步子不稳的 ② 稳定的；不变的: a ~ increase in output 产量的稳步增长 / a ~ pace 稳定的步伐 / Prices remain ~ all the time. 物价一直保持着稳定。 / ~ rain 连绵的雨 / make ~ progress 稳步前进 ③ 坚定的；扎实的，可靠的: be ~ in one's purpose 意志坚定 / a ~ young man 一个踏实的青年 / ~ work 扎实的工作 ④ 镇静的，沉着的，从容的: ~ as a rock 泰然，安如磐石 ⑤ (船) 不畏风浪依旧昂首前进的 **II ①** *vt.* ① 使稳定；使稳固: ~ a boat 使船只稳定 ② 使坚定；使沉着 **②** *vi.* 稳定；稳固: The boat soon *steadied* again. 船马上重新稳定下来。 **III** *n.* ① [美] (关系相当确定的) 情侣 ② [机] 固定中心架 **IV** *ad.* ① 稳固地；稳定地 ② [海] 按原定方向地，把定，照直走 ‖go ~ [美俚] 成为关系相当确定的情侣 / *Keep her* ~! 【海】(舵令) 把定! 照直走! / *Steady!* 别急! 镇定些! 留心! / *Steady on!* 停止! 沉着些! 沉着些! ‖**steadily** *ad.* / **steadiness** *n.* ‖'~-,**going** *a.* ① 稳定的；不变的 ② 稳重的，镇定的 / ~ **load** 【机】恒稳定载荷

steak [steik] *n.* ① 大块牛肉片；大块肉 (或鱼) 片: halibut ~ 大块比目鱼片，比目鱼排 ② 牛排；扒: fried ~ 炸牛排 / ham ~ 火腿扒 / four beef-~s 四块牛排 ‖~ **house** 专门供应牛排的饭馆 / ~ **knife** 顶端有锯齿的切牛排餐刀

steal [sti:l] **I** (stole [stəul], stolen ['stəulən]) **①** *vt.* ① 偷，窃取: have one's purse *stolen* 钱包被偷 / ~ sb. sth. 为某人偷窃某物 / ~ information 盗窃情报 ② 偷偷地夺取，巧取: ~ sb.'s heart 巧妙地博取某人的欢心 ③ 僭据；侵占: ~ the show (或 the limelight) (演出时) 不恰当地突出自己所扮演的角色，把观众等的注意力引过来；排挤掉别人以表现自己 ④ 偷偷地投射 (或进行)，偷偷地做: ~ a glance at sb. 偷看某人一眼 / ~ a visit 暗地里进行一次访问 ⑤ (棒球赛中) 偷进到 (前垒) **②** *vi.* ① 偷东西，做贼 ② 偷偷地行动；溜: ~ into a house 潜入一幢房屋 / ~ away 溜掉 / Mist *stole* over the valley. 雾悄悄地把整个山谷笼罩起来。③ (棒球中) 偷垒 **II** *n.* ① 偷窃；窃得物 ② 不正常的 (或可疑的) 政治交易 ③ 以极其低廉价格买得的东西 ④ (棒球的) 偷垒 ‖*a march on sb.* 见 march¹

stealth [stelθ] *n.* 秘密行动；秘密，鬼祟 ‖*by* ~ 偷偷地；在暗中: do good *by* ~ 暗中做好事

stealthy ['stelθi] *a.* 隐秘的，暗中的: a ~ glance 偷偷的一瞥 ‖**stealthily** *ad.* / **stealthiness** *n.*

steam [sti:m] **I** *n.* ① 蒸汽，水蒸气；水汽；蒸汽压力: dry (wet) ~ 干 (湿) 蒸汽 / saturated ~ 饱和蒸汽 / windows covered with ~ 凝结着水汽的窗子 / The engine is worked by ~ 这发动机用蒸汽推动。② [口] 精力；气力 ③ 轮船；乘轮船旅行: travel by ~ 乘轮船旅行 / a night and a day's ~ 一昼一夜的轮船旅行 **II ①** *vi.* ① 蒸发；冒热气: The vegetable soup ~ed. 菜汤冒热气。/ a cup of ~ing hot tea 一杯滚烫的茶 ② (火车，轮船) 行驶: The ship ~ed at twelve knots. 船以时速十二浬行驶。/ The train ~ed into the station. 火车喷着汽驶入车站。③ 发怒: He ~s easily. 他这人动辄发怒。**②** *vt.* ① 蒸，煮: ~ fish 蒸鱼 / a ~ed bun (roll) 馒头 (花卷) ② 散发 (蒸汽) ③ 用蒸汽开动: ~ a ship through the strait 把轮船开过海峡 ‖*at full* ~ 开足马力地；尽力地 / *blow* (或 *let*) *off* ~ ① 放掉多余的蒸汽 ② 花掉多余的精力；发泄强烈的感情，发脾气 / *Full* ~ (或 *speed*) *ahead*! 【海】全速前进! / ~ *gather* ① 积聚蒸汽 ② (政治运动等) 高涨 / *get up* (或 *raise*) ~ ① 加热锅炉，增高汽压 ② 振起精神 / *put on* ~ 使劲，加油 / ~ *up* ① (使) 有蒸汽 ② 给…动力，促进 ③ 使发怒，惹…发怒 ④ [美俚] 兴奋，热切 / *under* ~ (船) 在行驶中 / *work off* ~ 使劲干活以花掉多余的精力 (或发泄强烈的感情) ‖'~**boat** *n.* 汽船；轮船 / ~ *boiler* 蒸汽锅炉 / ~ *box* ① 蒸汽箱，汽柜 ② 汽蒸器；蒸笼 / ~ *brake* 汽闸 / ~ *chest* 汽柜 / ~ *coal* 蒸汽锅炉用煤 / '~-,**colo(u)r** *n.* 汽染色 / ~ *crane* 蒸汽起重机，蒸汽吊车 / ~ *cylinder* 汽缸 / ~ *dome* 汽室 / ~ *engine* 蒸汽机 / ~ *fiddle* [美俚] 发音乐声的汽笛 / ~ *fitter* 汽管装配工 / '~-*gas* *n.* 过热蒸汽 / ~ *ga(u)ge* 汽压计 / ~ *hammer* 汽锤 / ~ *heat* 汽热 / '~-,**heated** *a.* 用蒸汽加热的，蒸汽取暖的 / ~ *heater* 蒸汽加热器 / ~ *jacket* 汽套 / ~ *launch* 小火轮 / ~ *navvy* [英] ~ shovel / ~ *power* 汽力 / ~ *pressure* 汽压 (力) / ~ *rate* 耗汽率 / '~-*roll* *vt.* ① 用压路机碾压 ② 用高压压倒；粉碎 *vi.* 以不可抗拒之势前进 / '~-,**roller** *n.* ① 蒸汽压路机 ② 高压力量，高压手段 *vt. & vi.* = ~roll / '~**ship** *n.* 汽船；轮船 / ~ *shovel* 蒸汽挖掘机，蒸汽掘土机 / ~ *table* ① 蒸汽桌 (桌面有洞，放置用蒸汽或热水保暖的食品容器) ② 蒸汽表 / '~-*tight* *a.* 汽密的，蒸汽透平 / ~ *whistle* 汽笛 / ~ *winch* 蒸汽绞车，蒸汽起货机

steamer ['sti:mə] *n.* ① 汽船；轮船 ② 蒸汽车；蒸汽机 ③ 汽锅；汽蒸器；蒸笼 ④ 汽蒸者；汽蒸物 ‖~ *rug* 轮船上用的毛毯 / ~ *trunk* (适于放在轮船床铺下的) 浅皮箱

steamy ['sti:mi] *a.* 蒸汽的；似蒸汽的；多蒸汽的，水汽蒙蒙的 ‖**steamily** *ad.* / **steaminess** *n.*

steed [sti:d] *n.* ① 马 (尤指仗马或战马) ② [诗] 骏马

steel [sti:l] **I** *n.* ①钢,钢铁;(象钢铁般的)坚硬,坚固: alloy ~ 合金钢 / cast ~ 铸钢 / stainless ~ 不锈钢 / tool ~ 工具钢 / turn out a heat of ~ 炼出一炉钢 / muscles of ~ 坚硬的肌肉 / a heart of ~ 铁石心肠 ②钢制品(尤指刀、工具、武器等);(在燧石上打火的)打火镰: cold ~ 利器(指刀剑等) ③(用以撑开妇女紧身围腰或衬裙的)钢条 ④炼钢工业;[复]钢铁公司股票(或债券) **II** *a.* ① 钢的,钢制的: a ~ helmet (或 cap) 钢盔 / a ~ ingot 钢锭 ②钢铁业的: the ~ industry 钢铁工业 / a ~ complex 钢铁联合企业 ③钢铁般的,坚强的: ~. courage 百折不挠的勇气 **III** *vt.* ①钢化,给…包上钢,用钢作…的刀口: ~ a razor 把剃刀口钢化 ②使象钢;使坚强,使有决心,使经受锻炼: ~ oneself in labour 在劳动中锻炼自己 ③使冷酷: ~ oneself (或 one's heart) against pity 使自己变得心如铁石 / ~ oneself to do sth. 硬起心肠做某事 ④[美俚]用刀戳(某人) ‖*an enemy* (或 *a foe*) *worthy of sb.'s* ~ (值得某人与之一斗的)劲敌,强敌 / (*as*) *true as* ~ 见 true ‖**~like** *a.* 钢铁般的 ‖**~ ball** 钢珠 / **~ blue** 钢青色 / **~ casting** 铸钢件;铸钢 / **~ engraving** [印]①钢板雕刻(术)②钢板印刷(品) / **~ grey** 青灰色 / **~ guitar** 夏威夷吉他 / **Steel Helmets** (德国历史上的)钢盔团 / '**~,making** *n.* 炼钢 / **~ plate** 钢板 / **~ rule** 钢尺 / '**~-'trap** *a.* 极快的,直接的 / '**~-wire** *n.* 钢丝 / **~ wool** 钢丝绒(用来磨光和擦亮金属制品) / '**~,work** *n.* 钢铁工程;钢制品;钢结构 / '**~,worker** *n.* 炼钢工人 / '**~,works** [复] *n.* [用作单或复]炼钢厂 / '**~yard** *n.* 秤,提秤

steely ['sti:li] *a.* ①钢制的;含钢的;似钢的 ②(硬度、颜色、意志等)象钢的,钢铁般的: ~ fortitude 刚强不拔 / a ~ wind 刺骨的风 ③(羊毛)缺乏天然卷缩性(或弹性)的 ‖**steeliness** *n.*

steep¹ [sti:p] **I** *a.* ① 极高的(主要指海浪): The ship steamed into ~ head seas. 那条船迎着极高的顶头浪行驶。②险峻的,陡峭的: a ~ hill 陡峭的山 ③急剧下降的,急转直下的: a ~ rise in output 产量的激增 / ~ dive bombing 垂直俯冲轰炸 ④难以接受的,难以做到的,不合理的,过分的; 夸大了的: a ~ demand 过高的要求 / a ~ story 夸大了的故事 **II** *n.* 峭壁,悬崖 ‖**~ly** *ad.* / **~ness** *n.*

steep² [sti:p] **I** ❶ *vt.* 浸(渍),泡 / [喻]沉浸: ~ vegetables in brine 把蔬菜浸在盐水里 ❷ *vi.* 浸,泡 **II** *n.* 浸渍;浸 ‖**~er** *n.* 浸渍者;浸渍器

steeple ['sti:pl] *n.* (教堂建筑的)尖顶;尖塔 ‖**~d** *a.* 装有尖顶的;尖塔形的 ‖**~bush** *n.* [植]绒毛绣线菊 / '**~,chase** *n.* ①越野赛马;障碍赛马 ②越野赛跑;障碍赛跑 / '**~jack** *n.* 烟囱(或尖塔)修建工人,高空作业工人 / '**~,top** *n.* ①尖塔状顶部 ②北极鲸

steer¹ [stiə] **I** ❶ *vt.* ①驾驶,为(船等)掌舵;指导,筹划: ~ a satellite 操纵卫星飞行 / ~ a bill through the legislature 使一项议案在立法机构获得通过 / He ~ed our efforts in the correct direction. 他指导我们朝正确的方向努力。②沿着(某一航道)前进: The ship ~ed a steady course. 这艘船沿着航道稳稳前进。③[美俚]勾引…到赌场(或妓院)去 ❷ *vi.* ①驾驶,掌舵: ~ by the stars 凭星辰辨向驾驶 ②行驶;行进: The car ~ed north. 汽车朝北驶去。/ Where are you ~ing for? 你上哪儿去? ③被驾驶,驾驶起来: a ship that ~s well 好驾驶的船 ④[美俚]替赌场(或妓院)拉客 **II** *n.* ① 关于驾驶(或行路)的指示;[美俚]建议;劝告,忠告: He gave us a ~ toward that place. 他指点我们怎样到那个地方去。/ give sb. a friendly ~ 给某人一个友善的劝告 / a bum ~ 错误的指点 ②(车、船等的)驾驶设备 ‖**clear of** ~ 绕开;避开 ‖**~able** ['stiərəbl] *a.* (船、汽车等)易驾驶的,易操纵的;(天线等)易改变位置的 / **~er** ['stiərə] *n.* ①驾驶者,舵手 ②具有某种驾驶性能的车(或船等): a quick ~er 能开得飞快的车(或船等) ③[美俚]骗人去赌场(或妓院等坏地方)者; 骗人去上当者 ‖**~sman** ['stiəzmən] *n.* 舵手;撑筏者

steer² [stiə] *n.* 小公牛;阉牛;菜牛

steerage ['stiəridʒ] *n.* ①驾驶,掌舵;操纵 ②【海】舵效: The ship goes with easy ~. 这船容易操纵。③驾驶设备 ④下等客舱,统舱 ⑤(军舰的)下级军官室 ‖*go* (或 *travel*) ~ 坐下等舱旅行 ‖**~way** *n.* 【海】舵效速率(指使舵生效的船速)

stellar ['stelə] *a.* ①星的,星球的,恒星的: ~ interferometer 【天】恒星干涉仪 / ~ parallax 【天】恒星视差 ②星似的,星形的 ③(戏剧或电影)明星的,名演员的 ④主要的,显著的

stem¹ [stem] **I** *n.* ①茎,(树)干,(叶)梗 ②(工具的)柄,把,杆 ③高酒杯的脚,烟斗柄 ④[复][美俚]腿 ⑤(手表、怀表的)转柄;【无】电子管心柱;晶体管管座 ⑥【音】(乐谱上的)符尾 ⑦【海】艏柱;艏材;船头,艏 ⑧[语]词干 ⑨血统,家系 ⑩【动】羽轴 ⑪一串香蕉 ⑫[美俚](城市中的)大街 ⑬[美俚]鸦片烟枪 ‖**stemmed**; **stemming**) ❶ *vt.* ①抽去(或剔除)…的梗(或茎): ~ tobacco leaves 去烟叶梗 / a stemming machine (烟叶)抽梗机 ②给…装柄(或把、杆等),给(假花等)装梗 ❷ *vi.* [美]起源,导源;发生: cadres stemming from (或 out of) workers, peasants and soldiers 工农兵出身的干部 / an error stemming from miscalculation 计算的错误 ‖*from* ~ *to stern* ①从船头到船尾 ②从头到尾,完全 ‖**~less** *a.* 无茎的,无梗的 / **~let** ['stemlit] *n.* 小茎,小干,小梗 / **stemmy** *a.* 多梗的 / ‖**~ware** *n.* [总称]有脚的器皿(尤指酒杯) / **~-winder** ['stem,waində] *n.* ①转柄表(指拧转柄而上发条的手表、怀表) ②第一流人物(或东西) / **~-winding** ['stem,waindiŋ] *a.* (手表、怀表)拧转柄而上发条的

stem² [stem] **I** (stemmed; stemming) ❶ *vt.* ①堵住,塞住;挡住: ~ the flow of water 堵住水流 / ~ a hole 堵住一个洞 / ~ a vicious spiral 止住一个恶性循环 ②逆(流)而行,顶着…而上: ~ the tide 反潮流而行 ③(滑雪时)转动(滑雪屐)以停止滑行 ❷ vi. ① 堵住, 止住 ② 逆: Our ship *stemmed* on *against* the current. 我们的船逆流而行。③转动滑雪屐以停止滑行 II n. ①堵塞物; 坝; 止住 ② 转动滑雪屐以停止滑行 ‖~ **turn** (滑雪中的)停滑转动

stench [stentʃ] I n. 恶臭: a ~ bomb 恶臭炸弹 / a ~ trap (阴沟等的)防臭瓣, 存水弯 II vt. & vi. (使)发恶臭 ‖~**ful** a. 充满恶臭的 / ~**y** a. 恶臭的

stencil ['stensil] I n. ①(镂花)模板, 模绘板, 型板; (用模板或蜡纸印成的)图案, 文字 ②(油印用的)蜡纸: cut a ~ 刻蜡纸 / on the ~ 在蜡纸上打字 II (stencil(l)ed; stencil(l)ing) vt. 用模板印刷; 用蜡纸印 ‖**stencil(l)er** n. 用模板绘写者, 刻蜡纸者 ‖~ **paper** 蜡纸 / ~ **pen** (刻蜡纸用的)铁笔 / '~-**plate** n. (镂花)模板

stenochromy [ste'nɔkrəmi] n.【印】数色同时印刷术, 彩色一次印刷法

stenography [ste'nɔɡrəfi] n. 速记; 速记法; 速记学 ‖**stenographic(al)** [,stenə'ɡræfik(ə)l] a.

step [step] I n. ①(脚)步; 步态; 步幅: take a ~ forward (back) 前进(后退)一步 / walk with a fast ~ 快步走 / It is necessary to fight the force of habit every ~ of the way. 必须不断地跟习惯势力作斗争。/ It's but a ~ to the school. 这儿到学校没有几步路。/ This is a long ~ towards achieving our objective. 这朝着我们的目标迈进了一大步。②脚步声; 脚印, 足迹: know (或 recognize) sb.'s ~ 听出某人的脚步声 ③[复]进程, 前进的道路: direct one's ~s towards the river 向河边走去 ④ 步调, 步伐 ⑤ 步骤; 手段; 措施: What's the next ~? 下一步怎么办? / take ~s to meet the situation 采取步骤以适应局势 / a decisive (rash, prudent) ~ 决定性(轻率, 慎重)的步骤 ⑥踏板; 梯级; 台阶; (矿层等上凿出的)踏脚处: the ~ of a truck 卡车的踏板 / a ladder of twenty ~s 二十级的梯子 / run down the ~s 跑下台阶(或楼梯) ⑦ 一梯级的高度 ⑧ 等级; 升级: ~ in the social scale 社会等级 / get one's ~ 获得提升 / give sb. a ~ 提升某人 ⑨[复] = ~ladder ⑩[复]一段楼梯, 一段梯级 ⑪【海】桅座; 【机】轴瓦; 级, 档 ⑫[音]音级, 度 ⑬舞步: one-~ 单步舞 / two-~ 二步舞 II (stepped; stepping) ❶ vi. ①跨步; 走; 步行: *Step* this way, please. 请这边走。②跳舞; 轻快地行走 ③跨(入), 踏(进): ~ *into* a car 上车 / ~ *into* a new stage 进入新阶段 ④ 踩: ~ *on* a nail 踩在钉子上 ⑤踏(上), 走(上): ~ *on to* a new path 走上新路 ❷ vt. ①跨(步); 踏(脚); 散步于: ~ three paces 跨三步 / ~ foot on one's native land 踏上故土 / ~ a pavement 在人行道上散步 ②跳(舞) ③步测 (out, off): ~ out the length of a bridge 步测桥的长度 ④ 使成梯级; 使成梯级状: ~ the hill leading to one's house 在屋前的山坡上凿出台阶 ⑤【海】竖立(桅杆)于桅座上 ⑥逐步(或分

段)安排 ‖**break** ~ ①走乱步伐 ②【军】换便步走 / **change** ~ 【军】换步 / **follow** (或 **tread**) **in sb.'s** ~**s** 踏着某人的足迹; 效法某人的榜样 / **pick one's** ~ 小心地走路, 看一步走一步 / **rise a** ~ **in sb.'s opinion** (或 **estimation**) 变得较受某人重视, 使某人对自己的评价略有提高 / ~ **along** 走开, 动身离开: I must ~ *along* now. 我该走了。/ ~ **aside** 走到一边去; 避开; [喻]退让; (谈话中)离题 / ~ **by** 逐步地; 稳步地 / ~ **down** ①走下(车等)②逐步减低 ③降低(电流)的电压 ④ 辞职, 让位; 下台, 退出 / ~ **high** (马)高抬着脚走 / ~ **in** ①走进 ②插手, 干涉 ③作短时间的非正式访问 / ~ **into the shoes of sb.** 见 **shoe** / ~ **it** ① 跳舞 ②步行 / ~ **off** [美俚] ①结婚 ②死 / ~ **off the deep end** [美俚] ① 仓促上阵; 参与自己并不了解的事 ②死 / ~ **on it** ①[口]赶快 ②(踩加速器)加快摩托车速度 / ~ **on sb.'s toes** 见 **toe** / ~ **on the gas** 见 **gas** / ~ **out** ①离开, 走出(尤指短时间、短距离的离开) ②[口]出去娱乐; 过活跃的社交生活 ③健步走; 快走 ④死 ⑤(在爱情方面)不忠实于 (on) / ~ **up** ①走近来; 登上去 ②逐步增加③升高(电流)的电压 ④提升; 获得提升 / **take a false** ~ 走错一步, 失策 / **turn one's** ~**s to** 转向…走去; 转而做… / **watch one's** ~ 走路小心: *Watch your* ~! 留神脚下! (或: 当心!) ②讲话(或做事)谨慎小心 ‖**stepper** n. ①快与 ② 跳舞者 ③ [美俚]化很多时间参加社交活动的学生 / ~ **bearing** 【机】立式止推轴承 / ~ **block** 【机】级型垫铁 / '~-**by-** / a. 逐步的, 逐部的: a ~-*by*-development 逐步的发展 / '~-**cone** n. 【机】级塔轮, 宝塔轮 / ~ **dance** 踢踏舞 / '~= **down** n. ①下车 ②往下处的行走 ③下台 ④(逐渐的) 缩小, 减少: a ~-*down* in dosage 剂量的渐减 a. 降低电压的: a ~-*down* transformer 降压变压器 / '~-**in** a. (鞋等)伸腿穿入的 n. [复]①女内裤 ②船鞋 / '~,**ladder** n. 活梯, 凳 / ~,**motor** n. 步进电动机 / '~-**out** n. 【无】失调, 失步 / '**stepped-up** a. 加速的; 加强了的 / '**stepping-stone** n. ① (浅河中)供踏脚的石头; (上下马用的)踏脚台 ② 达成目的的手段; 进身之阶 ③(途中的)歇脚地 / ~ **rocket** 多级火箭 / '~**stone** n. 楼梯石级 / ~ **turn** (滑雪时的)侧向换步 / '~-**up** n. (体积、数量等的)逐渐增加 a. 促进的, 加强的;【电】增加电压的

stepbrother ['step,brʌðə] n. 继父与其前妻(或继母与其前夫)所生的儿子

stepchild ['steptʃaild] ([复] stepchildren ['step,tʃildrən]) n. 妻与前夫(或夫与前妻)所生的孩子

stepdaughter ['step,dɔ:tə] n. 妻与前夫(或夫与前妻)所生的女儿

stepfather ['step,fɑ:ðə] n. 继父

stepmother ['step,mʌðə] n. 继母

steppe [step] n. ①(尤指东南欧或西伯利亚地区的)无树林的大平原 ②(仅有旱生植物的)干旷草原

stepsister ['step,sistə] *n.* 继父与其前妻(或继母与其前夫)所生的女儿

stepson ['stepsʌn] *n.* 妻与前夫(或夫与前妻)所生的儿子

stereo ['stiəriou] **I** *n.* ① =stereotype (*n.*) ②体视术; 体视效应; 体视系统; (立)体视镜 ③立体照片, 体视照片 ④(收音设备等放出的)立体声; 立体声系统 **II** *a.* ① =stereotyped ② 立体的; 体视(镜)的 ③立体声的

stereoscope ['stiəriəskoup] *n.* (立)体视镜

stereoscopic(al) [,stiəriəs'kɔpik(əl)] *a.* 立体的; 体视(镜)的: a *stereoscopic* camera 立体摄像机 / *stereoscopic* television 立体电视 ‖**stereoscopically** *ad.*

stereotype ['stiəriətaip] **I** *n.* ①【印】铅版; 铅版制版法 ②陈规, 老套, 旧框框: break through the ~s 打破旧框框 **II** *vt.* ①浇铸…的铅版: ~ the pages of a newspaper 浇铸一份报纸的铅版 ②(用铅版)印刷 ③使成为刻板文章, 把…弄得一成不变 ④对…产生成见: ~d thinking 老一套的想法 / ~**r** *n.* ①浇铸铅版者, 铸版工人 ②盲人文字凸版印制机 / **stereotypist** *n.* 盲人文字凸版印制机工人

sterile ['sterail; 美 'steril] *a.* ①不生育的; 不结果实的: a ~ woman 不生育的妇女 / a ~ flower 不结果实的花; 雄花 ②贫瘠的: ~ land 不毛之地 ③无菌的, 消过毒的: a ~ gown (医生、护士等穿的)消毒白罩衣 ④缺乏独创性的, 枯燥无味的: ~ prose 乏味的散文 ⑤无效果的, 无结果的: ~ negotiations 无结果的谈判 ‖**sterility** [ste'riliti] *n.*

sterilization [,sterilai'zeiʃən] *n.* ①消毒, 灭菌 ②绝育

sterilize ['sterilaiz] *vt.* ①把…消毒, 使无菌: ~ the surgical instruments 把外科手术用具消毒 / ~d milk 消毒牛奶 ②使绝育 ③使成不毛之地 ④使不起作用; 封存(黄金) ‖~**r** *n.* ①消毒者 ②消毒器

sterling ['stə:liŋ] **I** *n.* ①英国货币 ②标准纯银; [总称]纯银制品: a set of ~ 一套银器 **II** *a.* ①英币的; 用英币支付(或计算)的: five pounds ~ (略作£5 stg.) 英币五镑 / a ~ bill 英币汇票 / ~ prices 以英币计算的价格 ②(金、银)标准成分的; 标准纯银的; 纯银制的: ~ of gold 以标准成分的黄金制成的 ③合最高标准的, 纯正的, 优秀的 ‖~**area** 英镑区 / ~**bloc** 英镑集团

stern¹ [stə:n] *a.* ①严厉的, 严格的; 严峻的; 苛刻的: a ~ rebuke 严厉的谴责 / be ~ to sb. 对某人严厉 / ~ discipline 严格的纪律 / a ~ face 铁板的面孔 / ~ treatment 苛刻的待遇 ②坚定的, 不动摇的: a ~ resolve 坚强的决心 ‖~**ly** *ad.* / ~**ness** *n.*

stern² [stə:n] *n.* ①船尾, 艇: a ~ anchor 艇锚 / a ~ light 艇灯 ②臀, 臀部 ③(尤指猎狐犬的)尾 ④(任何东西的)尾部, 后部 ‖**by the** ~ 船尾吃水

较深地: sink *by the* ~ 船尾向下地沉没 / *from stem to* ~ 见 stem¹ / *sit at the* ~ 管理公共事务 / ~ **on** 船尾向前地 ‖~**most** *a.* 在船尾最后部的 / ~**ward(s)** *ad.* & *a.* 在船尾(的); 向船尾(的) ‖~**chase** (后船对前船的)尾追 / ~**chaser** 舰尾炮 ‖~**fast**, ~**line** 艉缆 / ~'**foremost** *ad.* ①船尾向前地 ②笨拙地 / '~**post** *n.* 船尾柱 / ~**sheets** 小艇艉台, 艇尾部, 艇后座位部 / '~**way** *n.* (船的)后退, 倒驶 / '~-,**wheeler** *n.* 艉明轮船

stern(o)- [构词成分] 表示"胸"; "胸骨"; "胸骨和…"

stethoscope ['steθəskoup] **I** *n.* 【医】听诊器, 听筒 **II** *vt.* 用听诊器检查: ~ the patient's chest 用听诊器检查病员的胸部

stevedore ['sti:vidɔ:] **I** *n.* 码头装卸工人, 搬运工人 **II** ❶ *vt.* 装货上(船); 从(船)上卸货 ❷ *vi.* 装卸货物; 做码头工人

stew¹ [stju:; 美 stju:] **I** ❶ *vt.* ①炖, 煨, 焖: ~ chicken 煨鸡 / ~ beef 炖牛肉 ②[口]使焦急, 使烦恼: ~ oneself into an illness 烦恼得生起病来 ❷ *vi.* ①(食物)炖着; 被炖熟 ②(关在房中)受闷热, 热得发昏; [俚]用功读书 ③烦恼; 焦急 **II** *n.* ①炖过的食品(尤指炖肉或炖鱼) ②混杂物 ③烦躁拥挤的状况; [口]烦恼; 着急: in a ~ 很着急; 很烦恼 / ~ *in one's own juice* (或 *grease*) 自作自受 ‖'~**bum** *n.* 酒鬼 / '~**pan** *n.* (长柄)炖锅 / '~**pot** *n.* (双把)炖锅

stew² [stju:; 美 stju:] *n.* ①热浴; 热浴室 ②妓院, 窑子; [the ~s] 妓院区

stew³ [stju:; 美 stju:] *n.* [英]鱼塘; 养活鱼的桶; 人工养殖场

steward [stjuəd] **I** *n.* ①(轮船、飞机的)乘务员, 服务员 ②(学校、医院、旅馆等的)伙食管理员 ③管家; 财务管理员 ④(舞会、赛马、集会等的)干事 ⑤[美]车间(或部门)的工会代表 **II** ❶ *vt.* 做…的乘务员(或管家等), 管理 ❷ *vi.* 当乘务员(或管家等) ‖~**ess** *n.* 女乘务员(或女服务员等) / ~**ship** *n.* 乘务员(或服务员)的职位

stick [stik] **I** *n.* ①枝条; 枯枝; 柴枝: gather ~s to make a campfire 拾柴生营火
②棍, 棒, 杖; 手杖: a hockey ~ 曲棍球棒 / walk with a ~ 拄着手杖走路
③(草本植物的)茎, 梗: celery ~s 芹菜梗
④(细圆的)条状物: a ~ of chalk 一支粉笔 / a ~ of charcoal 一根木炭条
⑤(指炸弹等)连续投下的一批; 一批连续跳下的伞兵
⑥[口]木头木脑的人; 蹩脚演员
⑦(建筑物等的)一部分: The house was pulled down and *not* a ~ left standing. 这房子被一点也不留地拆毁了。
⑧混在饮料里的酒
⑨刺; 戳
⑩粘性
⑪【空】手柄; 操纵杆; (汽车的)变速杆, 换档杆;

【海】桅杆;桁;【音】指挥棒;【印】排字盘
⑫[the ~s][美口]小镇;郊区;乡间;边远森林地
⑬一件(家具): a few ~s of furniture 几件(简单的)家具

II (stuck [stʌk]) ❶ *vt.* ①刺;戳;刺死;刺猎: an awl through the leather 用锥子刺穿皮革 / ~ a pig (用屠刀刺入喉部)宰猪 / a wild boar (用枪标)刺杀野猪

②钉住;插牢;放置: ~ an insect specimen 钉住昆虫标本 / a coat *stuck* with medals 别着许多奖章的上衣 / a post in the ground 把杆插在地上 / The postman *stuck* the letter under the door. 邮递员把信从门底下塞入。/ He *stuck* the book back on its shelf. 他把书放回书架。

③伸;伸出: He *stuck* his arm out. 他伸出手臂。

④粘贴;张贴: ~ a stamp on a letter 在信上贴邮票 / *Stick* no bills! 请勿张贴! / ~ up a notice on a bulletin board 在布告栏上张贴通知

⑤使停止;阻塞: prevent the valve from being *stuck* 防止阀被阻塞 / The vessel has been *stuck* here for a week by bad weather. 由于天气恶劣,船只被阻在此已有一周。

⑥[口]难住;以…困住: He was *stuck* by this question. 他被这个问题难住了。/ John bought an old car and got *stuck* with it. 约翰购进了一辆旧汽车,无法脱手。

⑦[俚]容忍,忍受: I can't ~ it any longer. 我再也不能容忍了。

⑧迫使…偿付,敲(某人)竹杠;欺骗

⑨(过去式及过去分词用 sticked)用棒支撑;【印】在排字盘中排(字)

❷ *vi.* ①粘住;钉住: Several pages have *stuck* (together). 几页粘在一起了。/ friends that ~ together 经常在一起的要好朋友 / A thorn *stuck* in his finger. 他手指上扎了一根刺。/ The nickname *stuck* to him. 他这个绰号一直被人叫着。

②停留;坚持;固守: ~ at home 呆在家里 / through thick and thin 在任何情况下一直坚持下去 / ~ to a post 坚守一个岗位 / ~ to one's word 遵守诺言 / ~ to the point 紧扣要点

③梗塞;轧牢;陷住;被难住: Something has *stuck* in the water pipe. 水管里有东西塞住了。/ The gears *stuck*. 齿轮轧住了。/ The bill *stuck* in the Upper House. 这个议案在上院被搁置住了。

④伸出;突出: He had a bundle of handbills ~*ing* from his pocket. 他的口袋里露出一迭传单。

‖*be on the* ~ [美俚]警觉的;效率高的 / *be stuck on* 迷恋于,爱上 / *be tarred with the same* ~ 见 *tar¹* / *cut one's* ~ [俚]逃走,离去 / *give sb. the* ~ 杖责某人 / *go to* ~s *and staves* 碎掉;毁掉,变槽 / *hold a* ~ *to* (或 *hold* ~s *with*) 旗鼓相当地与…竞争 / *hop the* ~ 突然离去;死去 / *in a*

cleft ~ 在进退两难中 / ~ *around* [口]呆在附近; 逗留 / ~ *at* ①迟疑,犹像: Don't ~ *at* trifles. 琐碎小事,毋需迟疑。/ ~ *at* nothing 无所顾忌 ②坚持: ~ *at* one's work 坚持工作 / ~ *by* 忠于 / ~ *down* ①[口]放下: *Stick it down* in the storehouse. 把它放在仓库里。②[口]写下: ~ *down* new words in a notebook 把生词记在笔记本上 ③粘住: ~ *down* (the flap of) an envelope 封好信口 / ~ *for* ~ *and carrot for carrot* 以打对打,以拉对拉 / ~ *in* (或 *indoors*) 呆在家中,不出去 / ~ *it on* [俚]①索取高价 ②夸张其词 / ~ *it* (*out*) [俚]坚持到底 / ~ *like a bur* 打发不掉 / ~ *like a limpet* 缠住不放,纠缠不休 / ~ *on* ①保持在…之上: Can you ~ *on* a horse? 你能骑在马上不摔下来吗? ②贴上: ~ *on* a label 把标签贴上去 / ~ *out for* 坚持索取 / ~ *up* ①竖起;竖起: *Stick 'em up!* 把双手举起来! ②[俚]使惶惑: He is *stuck up.* 他楞住了。③[俚]抢劫(银行、邮车等) / ~ *up for* 维护,支持;为…辩护 / ~ *up to* 抵抗,抵制 / *the short* (或 *dirty*) *end of the* ~ 不公平的待遇;不利的处境 / *the* ~ *and the carrot* (或 ~ *and carrot*) 大棒与胡萝卜;软硬两手: a "~ *and carrot*" policy "大棒与胡萝卜"政策 / *the wrong end of the* ~ ①错误的认识(或说法): You have got hold of *the wrong end of the* ~. 你完全搞错了。②不公平的待遇;不利的处境

‖~*ful n.* [印]满满的一盘(排好的活字)
‖~*-at-itiveness* [sti'kætitivnis] *n.* 坚韧不拔 / ~ *insect* 竹节虫 / ~*-in-the-mud n.* [口]顽固保守者,墨守成规者;迟钝的人,木头木脑的人 *a.* 保守的;迟钝的 / '~*jaw n.* 粘牙的糖(或布丁等) / '~*on a.* 粘贴上去的: ~*-on* labels 粘贴上去的标签 / '~*pin n.* (用于领带等的)装饰别针 / '~*seed n.* 鹤蝨属植物 / '~*-to-itiveness* [stik'tu:itivnis] *n.* =~*-at-itiveness* / '~*up n.* ①竖起物;翘起物(如竖领) ②抢劫 ③粘贴印刷品;粘贴 *a.* ①竖起的;翘起的 ②(供)粘贴的 / '~*work n.* (打曲棍球等的)棒法

sticking ['stikiŋ] *n.* ①刺;戳 ②粘,贴;粘胶,粘料
‖~ *place* ①进到不能再进的地方,顶住点,顶点: Screw your courage to the ~ *place.* 鼓足你的勇气吧。②(猪颈上的)屠刀插入处 / ~ *plaster* 橡皮膏 / ~ *point* ①顶住点,顶点 ②(谈判等)症结

stickler ['stiklə] *n.* ①坚持要求一丝不苟者: a ~ *for* formality 拘泥形式的人 ②难题;费解的事物

stiff [stif] **I** *a.* ①硬的;挺的: a ~ collar 硬领 / stand straight and ~ 直挺挺地站着 ②(手足等)僵直的,僵硬的: be ~ with cold 冻僵 ③不易移动的,不灵活的: a ~ joint 就痛的 ~ a piston 粘牢的活塞 / ~ joints 不灵活的关节;不灵活的接头 / a ~ neck 硬脖子(指风湿性颈肌强直) ④(绳子等)拉紧的,绷紧的,张紧的: keep a ~ rein 勒紧

缰绳 ⑤拘谨的，生硬的，不自然的，呆板的；傲慢的: be ~ in manner 态度生硬 / keep a ~ face 板着面孔 ⑥刚强的，倔强的 ⑦强烈的；猛烈的；强有力的: a ~ drink 烈酒 / a ~ wind 狂风 / a ~ dose 一服高效的药 ⑧[美俚]喝醉的 ⑨(价格)坚挺的；昂贵的: a ~ price 昂贵的价格 ⑩粘的，胶粘的，稠的；(土质)紧密的: beat egg whites until ~ 把蛋白打稠 / ~ clay 紧密的粘土 ⑪艰难的；费劲的: a ~ task 费劲的工作 / a ~ climb 艰难的攀登 / a ~ slope 难登的坡，陡坡 ⑫严厉的: a ~ penalty 严厉的处罚 ⑬[口][只作表语]极度的，极点的: It bored me ~. 它烦死我了。/ He was scared ~. 他惊恐极了。⑭[海](船因稳性大)不易倾侧的 II n. [俚] ①死尸 ②[英]不可救药的人 ③[美]醉鬼；傲慢(或拘谨、讨厌)的人；游民；吝啬鬼 ④[美]普通工人；流动工人 ⑤流通(可转让的)票据；钞票，金钱 ⑥[美]不肯给小帐(或给小帐很吝啬)的人 ⑦[美俚]不肯给…小帐；让…空手而去 ‖as ~ as a poker 生硬，刻板(指姿态、态度) / a ~ 'un 见 'un¹ / cut up ~ 发脾气，发怒 / keep (或 carry, have) a ~ upper lip 见 lip ‖~ish a. 相当挺(或强劲、拘谨、昂贵等)的 / ~ly ad. / ~ness n. ‖~-arm vt. 伸直手把…推开 n. 伸直手推开 / '~-bit n. 马嚼子 / '~'necked a. 倔强的；傲慢的

stiffen ['stifn] ❶ vt. ①使硬；使挺 ②使僵硬 ③使绷紧 ④使生硬；使呆板 ⑤使强硬: ~ one's attitude 使态度变强硬 ⑥使胶粘；使稠 ⑦使(价格)坚挺 ⑧使(船)不易倾侧 ❷ vi. ①变硬；变挺: Mud ~s when it dries. 泥巴一干就变硬了。②变僵硬 ③变强劲；变坚强: a ~ing breeze 渐渐强劲的风 / Our resolution ~s. 我们的决心加强了。④变胶粘；变稠 ⑤(价格)变坚挺 ⑥变得费劲: The climb ~ed as we neared the top of the hill. 我们接近山顶攀登就费劲了。‖~er n. ①使变硬的人(或物)，加固物；【建】【机】支肋，加强板 ②增强(勇气、决心等)的事物 ③强壮剂，兴奋剂

stifle¹ ['staifl] ❶ vt. ①使窒息，使闷住；闷死 ②抑制；镇压，扑灭: ~ one's laughter 忍住笑声 / ~ a rebellion 镇压叛乱 ❷ vi. ①窒息，闷死；闷死: ~ in a hot kitchen 在热烘烘的厨房里闷得要死 ②受抑制

stifle² ['staifl] n. ①四足动物(如马等)后腿的膝盖关节(= ~ joint) ②(四足动物后腿的)膝盖关节病，膝盖骨病 ‖~ bone (马等的)膝盖骨

stigma ['stigmə] ([复] stigmas 或 stigmata ['stigmətə]) n. ①耻辱，污名；[古]烙印: No ~ rests on (或 attaches to) him. 他清白无瑕。②【植】柱头；眼点【动】气门；点斑；翅痣；眼点 ④【医】(病的)特征；小斑: a ~ of degeneracy 衰颓的特征 ‖~tic [stig'mætik] a.

stigmatize ['stígmətaiz] vt. ①[古]给…打上烙印 ②诬蔑，污辱: be ~d as a coward 被诬蔑为懦夫

stile¹ [stail] n. ①篱(或墙)两边的阶梯(供人越过用) ②旋转栅门(如公园入口处所设)

stile² [stail] n. 【建】窗桎；门桎；坚框

stiletto [sti'letou] I ([复] stiletto(e)s) n. ①短剑，匕首 ②打眼锥 II vt. 用短剑刺(或刺死)

still¹ [stil] I a. ①静止的，不动的；平静的，寂静的: keep (lie) ~ 保持(躺着)不动 / a ~ lake 平静的湖 / a ~ evening 寂静的夜晚 / in ~ meditation 在静思中 / All sounds are ~. 万籁俱寂。②(酒)不起泡的，不含气体的 ③【摄】静物摄影的；普通摄影的(与电影摄影相对) II n. ①[诗]寂静: in the ~ of the night 夜深人静时 ②(登在电视节目或报上的)剧照；电视室布景；静物摄影照片；[口]静物画 ③不用警报器而用电话(或口头)传送的火警警报 III ❶ vt. 使平静；使停止，止住: ~ a crying baby 使婴孩止哭 / one's hunger and thirst (the pain of a wound) 止住饥渴(伤口疼痛) ❷ vi. 静止；平静: The wind ~s down. 风息了。IV ad. ①还，仍旧: Will you ~ be here tomorrow? 明天你还会在这儿吗? ②[修饰比较级]还要，更: It was cold yesterday, but today it is ~ colder. 昨天很冷，但是今天更冷。③[作连词用](虽然…)还是，还是要: We have made some achievements, ~ we should be modest and prudent. 我们虽然取得了一些成绩,但还是要谦虚谨慎。‖ Still waters run deep. 见 water ‖~ness n. 寂静,无声 / '~birth n. 【医】胎死,死产 / '~born a. ①【医】死产的 ②不成功的,流产的: a ~born scheme 流产的计划 / '~,bugle n. [英]要求全体人员在第二次军号声前保持原地不动的海军军号声 / '~-fish vi. 抛锚停船捕鱼 / ~ hunt ①轻声的追击(或伏击)猎物 ②暗中的搜寻,暗中的追逐 / '~-hunt vi. & vt. 伏击,偷袭(猎物等) / ~ life ①静物 ②静物画

still² [stil] I n. ①蒸馏室；酿酒场 ②蒸馏器 II vt. & vi. 蒸馏 ‖~room n. [英] ①(饮料等的)储藏室 ②蒸馏室

stilt [stilt] I n. ①[常用复]高跷: walk on ~s 踏高跷 ②支撑物,支材 ③([复] stilt(s))[动]长脚鹬 II vt. ①使踏上高跷 ②使(文体等)夸张 ‖on ~s ①踏着高跷 ②趾高气扬 ③(文体等)夸张做作

stilt

stilted ['stiltid], **stilty** ['stilti] *a.* ①踏上高跷的；如踏上高跷的 ②(文体等)夸张的 ③呆板的；做作的，不自然的 ‖**stiltedly** *ad.* / **stiltedness** *n.* ‖**stilted arch** 【建】上心拱

stimulant ['stimjulənt] **I** *n.* 兴奋剂；刺激物；酒：He never takes ~s. 他从不喝酒。 **II** *a.* 使兴奋的；刺激性的

stimulate ['stimjuleit] ❶ *vt.* 刺激；激发，激励，促进：This medicine will help ~ the function of the patient's organs. 这种药有助于促进病人的器官功能。 / ~ sb. to further efforts (或 ~ sb. to make greater efforts)激励某人作更大的努力 ❷ *vi.* 起刺激作用 ‖**stimulating** *a.*

stimulus ['stimjuləs] ([复] stimuli ['stimjulai]) *n.* 刺激；刺激物；促进因素：under the ~ of this hope 在这个希望激励下

sting [stiŋ] **I** (stung [stʌŋ]) ❶ *vt.* ①刺，螫，叮：A wasp *stung* me on the finger. 黄蜂螫了我的手指。 ②刺痛，使感觉痛：Smoke began to ~ his eyes. 烟渐渐地刺痛他的眼睛。 / be *stung* by remorse 因悔恨而感痛苦 / ~*ing* words 刺人的话 ③刺激；激励：Pepper ~s the tongue. 胡椒刺激舌头。 / The insulting remarks *stung* him to a rage. 这些污辱性的话惹得他大怒起来。 / be *stung* with desire 受欲望驱使 ④[口][常用被动语态]骗；敲…竹杠：He was *stung* for ten dollars. 他被骗(或被敲)去十元。 ❷ *vi.* ①刺，叮：Not all nettles ~. 不是所有荨麻都会刺人。 ②刺痛，剧痛：My tooth ~s. 我牙痛得厉害。 **II** *n.* ①刺，叮：be hurt by a ~ 被刺伤 ②刺痛，刺伤：feel a sharp ~ 感到一阵剧烈的刺痛 / a face covered with ~s 满是刺伤的脸 / the ~(s) of conscience 良心的谴责 ③刺激；讽刺：His bowling has no ~ in it. 他(打板球时)的投球不厉害。 / His words carry a ~. 他话中有刺。 ④(昆虫的)螫针，刺；(植物的)刺，刺毛 ‖**ingly** *ad.* 有刺地；尖锐地，尖酸刻薄地 / ~**less** *a.* 无刺的 ‖'~**bull** *n.* 【动】锯鲉 / .'~**fish** *n.* =~-bull / '~**ray** *n.* 【动】虹，鳐鱼

stingy[1] ['stindʒi] *a.* ①吝啬的，小气的 ②缺乏的，不足的，极少的

stingy[2] ['stiŋi] *a.* 有刺的；会刺的

stink [stiŋk] **I** (过去式 stank [stæŋk] 或 stunk [stʌŋk],过去分词 stunk) ❶ *vi.* ①发恶臭：That fish ~s. 那鱼臭了。 / He *stank* of garlic. 他身上有股大蒜味。 / ~ with (或 of) money 钱多得发臭 ②讨人厌；名声臭；坏透：~ in sb.'s nostrils 惹某人讨厌 ❷ *vt.* ①用臭气赶出 (out)：~ sb. out 臭得使某人呆不住 ②[俚]闻出…的臭气：can ~ it a mile off 一哩之外也能闻出这臭味 **II** *n.* ①恶臭，臭气 ②[英][复][学俚]自然科学；化学 ③(对丑事的)张扬：make a big ~ over being shortchanged 因被少找了钱而大叫大嚷 ‖~**er** *n.* ①发恶臭的人(或动物) ②讨厌的人；卑鄙的人 ③极低劣的东西 ④[美俚]极难的事 ⑤[英俚]措词不客气的信 ‖'~**ball** *n.* (过去海

战中用的)臭弹 / ~.**bomb** 恶臭炸弹 / '~**bug** *n.* 臭虫；发臭气的昆虫 / '~**pot** *n.* ①盛臭物的容器 ②=~ball ③讨厌透顶的人 / '~**stone** *n.* 【地】臭灰岩 / ~ **trap** (阴沟的)防臭瓣 / '~-**wood** *n.* 臭木

stint[1] [stint] **I** ❶ *vt.* ①[古]停止 ②限制；节制；吝惜：~ sb. in (或 of) food 限制某人的食物 / ~ oneself 省吃俭用 / ~ money 吝惜金钱 ③分配任务给 ❷ *vi.* ①[古]停止 ②节约：~ on administrative expenses 节约行政费用 **II** *n.* ①吝惜；限制：without ~ 不吝惜地；不加限制地 ②定额工作；定量，限额：do one's daily ~ 做每天的定额工作 ‖~**ingly** *ad.* 吝惜地 / ~**less** *a.* 不停的；无限制的

stint[2] [stint] ([复] stint(s)) *n.* 【动】滨鹬

stipend ['staipend] *n.* ①(牧师、教师等的)俸给，薪金 ②(尤指学生的)定期生活津贴

stipple ['stipl] *vt. & n.* (指雕刻)点刻；(指绘画)点画 ‖~**r** *n.* 点刻者；点画家 / **stippling** *n.* 呈点画(或点刻)状 ‖'~-.**graver** *n.* 点刻工具

stipulate[1] ['stipjuleit] ❶ *vt.* ①订定，规定：The treaty ~d the return of all these islands. 条约规定归还所有这些岛屿。 / It was ~d that the payment should be made within a month. 订明一月内付款。 ②保证，约定：~ to dismantle these fortifications 保证拆除这些工事 ❷ *vi.* ①订定，规定 (for) ②坚持以…作为协议的条件 (for)：~ for the use of the best materials 坚持以使用最好的材料作为条件

stipulate[2] ['stipjulit] *a.* 【植】有托叶的

stipulation [,stipju'leiʃən] *n.* ①订定，规定 ②(条约、契约等的)条款，项目

stir[1] [stə:] **I** (stirred; stirring ['stə:riŋ]) ❶ *vt.* ①动；移动；摇动：~ one's lips 微微动了动嘴唇 / Not a breath *stirred* the lake. 没有一点风吹皱湖面。 / No one could ~ him *from* his resolve. 谁也不能动摇他的决心。 ②拨动；搅拌；搅起 (up)：~ the fire with a poker 用拨火棍拨火 / ~ the soup with a spoon 用匙搅汤 / ~ up the dust 扬起灰尘 ③激起；激动；煽动；鼓动，煽动：~ sb.'s wrath 激起某人的愤怒 / The news *stirred* the world. 这条新闻轰动了世界。 / be deeply *stirred* 深为激动 / He wants *stirring up*. 要激励他一下。 / ~ up strife (trouble, hatred) 挑起争端(纷扰，仇恨) / ~ up sb. to mischief 煽动某人胡闹 ❷ *vi.* ①动；走动；活动；[口]起床：*Stir* and I shoot. (你)动一动，我就开枪。 / ~ abroad 外出，出门 ②(消息)传布；流通；流行：There is no news *stirring*. 还没有什么消息。 ③受搅拌：This paste ~s easily. 这浆糊易于搅拌。 **II** *n.* ①微动；骚动；激动；轰动：not a ~ 没有动静，一片沉寂 / full of ~ and movement 一片熙熙攘攘的景象 / create (或 make) a ~ in scientific circles 在科学界引起轰动 ②拨动；搅拌：give the embers a ~ 拨一拨炉火的余烬 ‖*not* ~ *a finger* 不尽一举手之劳；一点忙都不帮 /

not ~ an eyelid 不眨眼; 不为所动; 处之泰然 / **~ oneself** 奋发, 振作 / **~ one's stumps** [口]赶快, 快走 ‖**~less** *a.* 不动的, 沉静的 ‖**~about** ['stə:rəbaut] *n.* ①麦片粥 ②骚乱 ③忙忙碌碌的人

stir² [stə:] *n.* [俚]监牢 ‖**~ bug** [俚](因坐牢而)精神失常的人 / **~ crazy** [俚](因坐牢或孤独而)精神失常的

stirrup ['stirəp] *n.* ①(马)镫 ②【建】镫筋, 箍筋; 【机】镫形物(如自行车的脚镫) ③【海】镫索 ‖**bar** 悬镫铁条; (镫的)横踏板 / **~ bone**【解】镫骨 / **~ cup** (送别登程骑者的)饯别酒 / **~ iron** 马镫(不连皮带) / **~ leather, ~ strap** 马镫皮带 / **'~-piece** *n.* (木工用的)镫形支架 / **~ pump** (放在水桶里用一脚踏在镫上使其固定的)一种手摇灭火泵

stitch¹ [stitʃ] **I** *n.* ①(缝纫或编织的)一针; 针脚, 缝线: put a few **~es** in a shirt 在衬衫上缝几针 / drop a **~** (编绒线时)漏针一针 / make small (long) **~es** 密(稀)缝 / put **~es** into a wound 缝合伤口 / take **~es** out of a wound 拆去伤口的缝线 ②针法, 缝法, 编法: buttonhole **~** 钮孔针迹, 圈针迹 ③[口]少许衣服; 一点, 少许: have not a **~** on (或 wear not a **~** of clothes) 一点儿衣服也没穿, 光着身子 / He hasn't done a **~** of work. 他一点工作都没做过. ④[只用单](胁部)突然剧痛: I feel a **~** in my side. 我感到胁部一阵剧痛. ⑤[英方]畦, 犁沟间的脊 **II** ❶ *vt.* ①缝; 缝合; 缝缀: **~** (up) a rent 缝(好)衣上的破绽 ②装订 ③[英方]把(耕地)弄成畦 ❷ *vi.* 缝, 缝纫 ‖*A ~ in time saves nine.* [谚]小洞不补, 大洞吃苦. (意指: 及时处理, 事半功倍.) / *in ~es* 忍不住大笑 ‖**~ing horse** (缝纫皮料用的)压脚, 压板 / **~ wheel** (缝纫皮料用的)穿孔齿锥 / **'~work** *n.* 刺绣; 缝纫 / **'~wort** *n.* 繁缕属植物; 刺草

stitch² [stitʃ] *n.* [英方]距离; [方]一段时间

stoat [stout] *n.*【动】鼬

stock [stɔk] **I** *n.* ①树干; 根株; 根状茎 ②苗木; 砧木 ③[古]木头, 木块 ④托盘; 托柄, 后把; 钻柄; 枪护木; 弩战炮架的长梁; 锚柄: the **~** of a fishing rod 钓鱼杆的柄 / the **~** of a plough 犁杨 / the **~** of a rifle 步枪枪托 ⑤祖先; 家系, 世系, 血统; 种族; 【语】语族; 语系: a woman of Irish **~** 一个爱尔兰血统的妇女 / come of Protestant (farming) **~** 出身新教徒世系(世代农家) / languages of Germanic **~** 日耳曼系的语言 ⑥原料, 材料; 备料: (炖鱼、肉等所得的)原汁, 汤料: paper **~** 造纸备料 ⑦(牌局开始时)没发完的牌, 发剩下来的牌 ⑧库存品, 存货; 贮存: This store keeps a large **~** of hardware. 这店里备有大批五金存货. / the gold **~** 黄金储备 / have a rich **~** of information 有很丰富的材料 ⑨[美](企业的)股份总额; 股本; 股票 (=[英] shares): The **~** is in 1,000 shares. 全部股份分为一千股. / common **~** 普通股 / preference (或 pre-

ferred) **~** 优先股 / watered **~** 搀水股(指价值不实的股份) ⑩[英]公债; 公债券 (=[美] bond): hold **~** 持有公债 / have £100 in the **~s** 拥有价值 100 英镑的公债券 ⑪[总称]家畜, 牲畜 (=livestock); 农具: fat **~** 食用家畜 / take over a farm with the **~** 连同牲畜买下农场 / dead **~** 农具 ⑫[复]足枷, 手枷(旧时的刑具) / (给马等钉蹄铁时用的)夹架 ⑬[复]【船】船底枕木; 造船台 ⑭【生】类族;【动】原种; 无性种; 一群蜜蜂 ⑮紫罗兰属植物(如紫罗兰、夜紫罗兰) ⑯估计, 估量; 信任, 相信: put little **~** in 不信任… ⑰固定在某一剧院演出轮换剧目的剧团; 固定剧院的剧目上演的轮换剧目 ⑱(十八世纪男子用的)宽大硬领巾 ⑲【机】台, 座; 刨台: **~** engine 座式发动机 ⑳【地】岩株 ㉑[英]高级窑砖 **II** *a.* ①库存的; 现有的; 常备的: **~** sizes in hats 常备的帽子尺寸 / a **~** model of an automobile(供出售的)现有型式的汽车 ②平凡的, 普通的; 陈腐的: a **~** joke 陈腐的笑话 / **~** arguments 老一套的论点 ③繁殖用的: a **~** mare 母种马 / a **~** bull 公种牛 ④饲养牲畜的; 供牲畜用的; 宜于饲养作食用的: a **~** farm 畜牧场 / a **~** train 运牲畜的火车 / **~** cattle 食用牛 ⑤证券的; 股票的 ⑥管理证券的: a **~** clerk 存货管理员 ⑦固定在某一剧院上演轮换剧目剧团的 **III** ❶ *vt.* ①给…装上把手(或柄、横档等) ②给(商店)办货; 供给(牧场)以牲畜; 贮备, 备有: a well **~ed** library 藏书丰富的图书馆 / His head is well **~ed** with ideas. 他脑袋里主意很多. / Most bookshops do not **~** encyclop(a)edias. 大部分书店都不备有百科全书. ③放牧, 在…放牧牲口: **~** livestock 放牧牲口 / a pasture 在草场上放牧牲口 ④使(雌畜)受孕 ⑤种牧草于: **~** the land 在土地上种植牧草 ⑥给(罪犯)上枷 ❷ *vi.* ①(截断的树干或根株)出新芽 ②办货 (up): **~** up for the busy season 为旺季办货 ‖*in ~* 在贮存中; 现有, 备有: goods *in ~* 现货, 存货 / have wool *in ~* 备有羊毛 / *lock, ~ and barrel* 见 lock¹ / *off the ~s* ①(船)下水了的 ②已完成的; 已发送的: a piece of work *off the ~s* 已完成的工作 / *on the ~s* (船等)在建造中; [喻]在准备中 / *out of ~* 已脱销; 已无在贮存中 / *~s and stones* 无生命之物, 木石; 偶像; [喻]迟钝的人们 / *take ~* 清查存货, 盘存 / *take ~ in* ①购买(公司等)的股票 ②[口]相信, 信任; 看重; 注意: He did not *take* much *~ in* what they said. 他很不相信他们的话. / *take ~ of* 估量; 观察: *take ~ of* the situation 估计形势 ‖**~less** *a.* 无柄的, 无把的; 无锚杆的 ‖**~ anchor** 有杆锚 ‖**~ account** ①[英]股份帐 ②存货帐 / **~ book** ①存货簿 ②有集邮袋的簿子 / **'~,breeder** *n.* 牲畜饲养人 / **'~,breeding** *n.* 饲养牲畜; 畜牧业 / **'~,broker** *n.* (代客买卖的)证券经纪人 / **'~,brokerage, '~,broking** *n.* 代客买卖证券业务 / **'~car** *n.* ①运牲口的火车车辆 ②常备的普通式样汽车 ③比赛用汽车: **~car** racing 汽车比赛 / **~ company** ①股份公司 ②固定在某

一剧院上演轮换剧目的剧团(尤指没有名演员的剧团) / **~ dividend** 以股票形式分发的红利;作为红利分发的股票 / **~ exchange** 证券交易所 / **~ farmer** 畜牧业者 / **'~-fish** *n.* (未加过盐的)鳕鱼干 / **'~-gang** *n.* (可把木料一次锯成木板的)框锯 / **'~,holder** *n.* ①股东 ②[古]牧主 / **'~-in-'trade** *n.* ①存货;(行业的)全部营业用具,生财 ②惯用手段 / **'~,jobber** *n.* ①[美]证券经纪人 ②[英]证券批发商(以证券经纪人为买卖的对象) / **'~,jobbing** *n.* 证券批发(营业) / **~ list** (证券交易所公布的)证券行市表 / **~ lock** 门外锁 / **'~man** ['stɔkmən] *n.* ①牧场主 ②牧场工人,饲养员 ③仓库管理员 / **~ market** ①证券市场;证券交易;证券行市 ②牲畜市场 / **'~pile** *n.* ①(堆在路边为修路用的)料堆 ②贮存,(准备应急用的)原料物资(或武器装备等)的全国贮存所;科研资料的积累: build up a ~*pile* of strategic metals 贮存战略性金属物资 *vt.* 贮存,堆积;积聚: ~*pile* manure 积肥 / ~*pile* nuclear weapons 储存核武器 *vi.* 贮存物资;积聚资料 / **'~,piling** *n.* 贮存,堆积;积聚 / **'~pot** *n.* ①(炖汤用的)汤锅 ②什锦锅;[喻](作家等的)材料库 / **~ power** 股票转让授权书 / **~ rail** (转辙器的)本轨 / **~ raising** 牲畜饲养(业) / **~ room** ①贮藏室 ②(旅馆中供旅行推销员用的)商品展览室 / **'~-'still** *a.* 静止的,不动的: stand ~-*still* 站着一动也不动 / **'~,taking** *n.* ①存货的盘点 ②估量;打量 / **~ ticker** 自动把证券行市记下来的收报机 / **~ whip** *n.* [英]短柄长鞭 / **'~work** *n.* [矿]网状脉 / **'~yard** *n.* ①牲畜围场(尤指屠宰或装运前临时关闭家畜用的围场) ②堆料场

stockade [stɔ'keid] **I** *n.* ①(一列)栅栏;(一列)围桩 ②由栅栏围起的一块地方 ③用铁丝网围住的监牢(尤指兵营监牢);俘房拘留营 ④防波围桩 **II** *vt.* 用栅栏围住;用栅栏防卫

stocking ['stɔkiŋ] *n.* ①长(统)袜;似长(统)袜的东西: a pair of ~s 一双长袜 / elastic ~s 【医】外科用橡皮袜子 ②与身体其他部分毛色不同的兽脚: a horse with white ~s 白脚马 \|*in one's* ~s (或 *in one's* ~s *feet*) 不穿鞋只穿袜: He is (或 stands) 1.7 metres *in his* ~s. 他不穿鞋时身高一米七十。 \|**~ed** *a.* 穿袜的 \| **~ cap** (冬季运动戴的、有绒球或穗的圆锥形)线绒帽,针织帽 / **~ frame, ~ loom, ~ machine** 织袜机

stocky ['stɔki] *a.* 矮胖的,粗壮的

stodgy ['stɔdʒi] *a.* ①(食物)不易消化的,厚腻的 ②身体笨重的;行走缓慢而吃力的 ③装得满满的,塞满的 ④(作品等)烦琐乏味的;(风格等)滞重无趣的 ⑤(人)迟钝的;庸俗的;平凡的,非常老派的 ⑥(色彩)暗淡的;(衣服等)不时髦的,式样难看的 \|**stodgily** *ad.* / **stodginess** *n.*

stoic ['stɔuik] **I** *a.* ①[S-]斯多葛派(公元前四世纪创立于雅典的哲学派别)的 ②禁欲主义的,不以苦乐为意的,淡泊的 **II** *n.* ①[S-]斯多葛学者,

画廊派的人 ②禁欲主义者 \|**~ism** ['stɔuisizəm] *n.* ①[S-]斯多葛哲学 ②禁欲主义;淡泊

stoical ['stɔuikəl] *a.* =stoic (*a.*) \|**~ly** *ad.*

stoke[1] [stɔuk] **❶** *vt.* ①给(炉子)添燃料,司(炉);烧(火);拨旺(火): ~ (up) the furnace 给炉子添燃料 / ~ the fire of sb.'s jealousy with lies 用谎言来煽旺某人的妒火 ②使大吃: ~ oneself 饱吃一顿 **❷** *vi.* ①司炉;烧火 ②大吃,狼吞虎咽 \|**~r** *n.* ①烧火工人,司炉 ②加煤机 \|**'~hold** *n.* 【海】生火间,锅炉舱;炉前 / **'~hole** *n.* 炉膛口;炉前;生火间

stoke[2] [stɔuk] *n.* 沲(动力粘度单位)

stole [stɔul] *n.* ①女用披肩 ②(牧师等在举行仪式时披的)圣带,长巾;圣衣 ③(古罗马的)妇女长外衣

stolid ['stɔlid] *a.* 不易激动的;感觉迟钝的;呆头呆脑的 \|**~ity** [stɔ'liditi] *n.* / **~ly** *ad.*

stomach ['stʌmək] **I** *n.* ①胃: the coat of the ~ 胃粘膜 / the coats of the ~ 胃壁,胃膜 / the ruminants' ~s 反刍动物的四只胃 / on a full (an empty) ~ 饱着(空着)肚子 / lie heavy on sb.'s ~ (食物)滞积在某人胃里 ②肚子,腹部: the pit of the ~ 躯体上胸骨下方凹进处,心窝 / have a pain in the ~ 肚子痛 / lie on one's ~ 伏卧 / What a ~ he has got! 他真是个大腹便便的人! ③食欲,胃口;欲望,志趣: have a good ~ for dinner 食欲旺盛 / It goes against my ~. 这不合我的胃口(或脾气)。/ have no ~ for doing sth. 不想做某事,对做某事无兴趣 **II** *vt.* ①津津有味地吃;消化 ②[常与否定词或疑问词连用]忍耐,忍受: He could not ~ such an insult. 他不能忍受这样的侮辱。 ③[古]对…发怒 \|**stay sb.'s ~** (暂时性地)解某人的饥 / **turn sb.'s ~** 使某人恶心欲吐 \|**~ful** *n.* 一满胃;满腹: have a ~*ful* of sb.'s abuse 受够了某人的辱骂 / **~less** *a.* 无胃的;没有胃口的 \|**'~ache** *n.* 胃痛;肚子痛 / **~ pump** 【医】胃唧筒 / **~ staggers** 家畜的刍料中毒 / **~ tooth** (幼儿的)下犬齿 / **~ tube** 【医】胃管

stone [stɔun] **I** *n.* ①石,石头;铺石;石料: Cornish ['kɔ:niʃ] ~ 瓷土石 / meteoric ~ 陨石 / a heart of ~ [喻]铁石心肠 ②宝石(也作 precious ~);(表中的)钻石: a ring set with five ~s 镶有五颗宝石的戒指 ③界碑;里程碑;纪念碑;墓碑 ④磨石;磨刀石,砥石 ⑤[印]排版用石台;调墨石台;石印石 ⑥【医】结石;结石病: a kidney ~ 肾结石 / undergo an operation for (the) ~ 开刀取结石 ⑦冰雹(常作 hail~) ⑧果核: the ~ of a peach 桃核 / ~s of apricots 杏仁 ⑨[古]睾丸 ⑩[单复同]呋(英国重量名,常用来表示体重,等于 14 磅;用于肉类等商品时等于 8 磅;用于干酪时等于 16 磅) **II** *a.* 石的;石制的: a ~ bridge 石桥 / ~ sculpture 石雕 **III** *vt.* ①向…扔石头;用石头掷向某人 ②用石头铺;用石(墙)围: ~ a well 在井的内壁砌上石块 ③去…的核: ~d raisins (dates) 去核

葡萄干(枣子) ④用磨刀石磨快; 用磨石磨光(皮革、金属等) ‖*A rolling ~ gathers no moss.* [谚]滚石不生苔, 转业不聚财。 / *break ~s* (为铺路)敲碎石子; [喻]做苦活; 陷于贫困 / *cast the first ~* 首先攻击, 首先谴责 / *give a ~ and a beating to* [俚](原系赛马用语)轻易胜过… / *give a ~ for bread* 帮忙是假愚弄是真 / *leave no ~ unturned* 千方百计, 想尽方法: The geologists *left no ~ unturned* to discover more oil fields. 为了发现更多的油田, 地质工作者们千方百计到处寻找。 / *mark sth. with a white ~* 标记某事以示喜庆 / *set ~ out* 将石块砌成层次突出状(指上边一块比下边一块稍稍突出, 依次排下) / *Stones will cry out.* 真是罪大恶极, 连石头也要说话了。 / *swim like a ~* [谑]沉下去 / *the ~ of Sisyphus* 徒劳无功的事摘 / *throw* (或 *cast*) *~s* (或 *a ~*) *at* 非难, 指摘 ‖**~less** *a.* (尤指水果)无核的 ‖**Stone Age** 石器时代 / **~ ax(e)** 石斧 / **'~-'blind** *a.* ①完全瞎的 ②[美俚]酩酊大醉的 / **~ blue** 灰蓝色 / **'~boat** *n.* (装载石块或重物的)平底橇 / **'~brash** *n.* 砂土 / **'~-,breaker** *n.* 敲碎石的人; 碎石机 / **'~-'broke** *a.* 一个钱也没有的, 赤贫的 / **'~-cast** *n.* =*~'s cast* / **'~-coal** 【动】黑喉石鹛 / **~ coal** 白煤, 块状无烟煤 / **'~-'cold** *a.* 完全冷了的, 冷透的 / **'~crop** *n.* 【植】景天(用作轻泻剂) / **~ curlew** 【动】石鸻 / **'~,cutter** *n.* 石工; 切石机 / **'~-'dead** *a.* 完全断了气的, 完全死了的 / **'~-'deaf** *a.* 完全聋的 / **~ fence** [美方]石围栏, 石墙 ②[美俚](威士忌、苹果酒等)混合饮料 / **~ fruit** 果 / **'~-'ground** *n.* 在磨石作坊内研磨的 / **'~-horse** *n.* [主方]种马 / **'~-jug** *n.* [俚]监狱 / **~ lily** 海百合纲动物化石 / **~man** ['stounmen] *n.* ①装版工人 ②石匠 ③(作界标等用的)圆锥形石堆, 石标 / **'~,mason** *n.* 石匠 / **~ mill** 磨石机; 切石机; 石粉工场 / **~ pine** 【植】意大利五针松 / **'~-pit** *n.* 石坑; 采石场 / **'~-race** *n.* 边赛跑边拾石头的一种游戏 / **~'s cast**, **~'s throw** 一投石之距离; 短距离: The post office is only a *~'s throw* away. 邮局就在近处。 / The house was within a *~'s throw* of the sea. 这座房屋离海不远。 / **~seed** *n.* 【植】紫草属植物(如多花紫草、药用紫草等) / **'~-'still** *a.* 非常寂静的, 一动也不动的: sit *~-still* for hours 一动也不动地坐了几小时 / **~ wall** [美方]石壁, 石墙 ②(在议事等进行中)难以逾越的障碍 / **~'wall** *vi.* ①(板球中)打守球(而不想得分) ②[主英](用辩论等拖延手段)阻碍议事进行 ③围以石墙 *vt.* [主英]妨碍(议事等) / **'~'waller** *n.* ①过分小心地打板球者 ②[英]阻碍(议事)者 / **'~'walling** *n.* ①(板球的)慎打 ②[英]阻碍议事 ③筑石墙; 石墙 / **'~ware** *n.* [总称]石制品, 缸器; 粗陶器 / **'~work** *n.* ①石造物; 建筑的石造部分 ②石方工程, 石细工 ③[复]石匠工场, 石铺 / **'~wort** *n.* 【植】轮藻

stony, stoney ['stouni] *a.* ①多石的; 石质的; 铺着石块的; 坚硬如石的: ~ soil 多石的土壤 / a ~ path 碎石路 ②冷酷的, 无情的; 没有表情的: a ~ heart 铁石心肠 / with a ~ face 板着面孔 ③[俚]一个钱也没有的 (=stone-broke) ④[古][诗]石造的, 石制的 ‖**stonily** *ad.* / **stoniness** *n.* ‖**'~-'broke** *a.* =stone-broke / **'~,hearted** *a.* 铁石心肠的, 冷酷无情的

stool [stu:l] **I** *n.* ①凳子 ②搁脚凳; 跪凳; 【建】内窗台 ③象征职权的座位; 酋长身分 ④厕所; 马桶; 大便, 粪便: go to ~ 去大便 / loose ~ 稀粪 ⑤根株; 生出新芽的根株 ⑥囮鸟的栖木 ⑦= ~ pigeon **II** ❶ *vi.* ①(根株)长芽 ②[美俚]作囮子; 充当密探 ③[古]去大便 ❷ *vt.* 诱捕(野禽); 引诱 ‖a ~ of repentance 【宗】悔罪席 / *fall between two ~s* 两头落空 ‖**'~ball** *n.* 旧时英国妇女玩的一种类似板球的球戏 / **~ pigeon** ①(用来诱捕野鸟的)囮鸽 ②用来引诱他人入圈套者, 囮子 ③密探, 警探 / **~ plate** 【机】垫板 / **~ shoot** 根株萌芽

stoop[1] [stu:p] **I** ❶ *vi.* ①俯身, 弯腰; 弯腰曲背地站立(或走路): ~ *down* to pick sth. up 弯腰拾某物 / ~ *over* a desk 伏案 / ~ *with* (old) age 因年老而弯腰曲背 ②降尊; 屈从; 堕落: ~ *to conquer* 降低自己的身分去求得 / ~ *to cheating*(flattery) 堕落到干欺骗勾当(谄媚)的地步 (鹰在捕猎时)下扑; [古]下降, 降落 ❷ *vt.* ①俯曲(头、肩、背等) ②辱没 **II** *n.* ①弯腰, 曲背: walk with a ~ 曲着背走路 ②降尊, 自贬; 屈从 ③(鹰的)下扑 ‖**~ingly** *ad.* ①佝偻地 ②屈尊地 ‖**~ labo(u)r** 弯腰的劳动(如采摘); 干弯腰活的劳动力

stoop[2] [stu:p] *n.* 门廊; 门户阶

stop [stop] **I** (stopped; stopping) ❶ *vt.* ①塞住; 阻塞; 堵塞; 填塞: ~ a wound 止住伤口出血 / ~ the blood 止血 / ~ a passage 堵塞通道 / ~ a loophole 堵塞漏洞 / ~ a (decayed) tooth 补(蛀)牙 / ~ a bottle with a cork 用软木塞塞住瓶子 ②阻止, 阻挡; 拦住; 截住, 使狼狈; 击败(对方); 击落, 击毙(飞鸟等): a blow 挡开一击 / ~ a letter 扣住信件 / *Stop thief!* 捉贼! / ~ a bullet [俚]中弹, 挂彩 / be *stopped* by a question 被一个问题所难倒 / ~ the opposing team by a wide margin 以悬殊的比分打败对方球队 / ~ a bird with a shot 一枪打落飞鸟 ③停止, 止住: I wonder what has *stopped* the clock. 我不知道这钟是怎么停的。 / ~ a machine 使机器停止运转 ④断绝; 止付; 扣留: ~ supplies 断绝供应 / ~ a cheque (或 payment on a cheque) 嘱咐银行止付支票 / payment (银行等) 宣告无力支付; (存户给银行的通知)止付已开出的支票 / All the expenses have been *stopped* out of my wages. 一切费用已从我的工资中扣除。 ⑤给…加标点: a badly *stopped* letter 标点错乱的信件 ⑥用手指压(乐器上的弦、孔等)以改变音调 ⑦[海]系紧(船缆等) ❷ *vi.* ①停止; 中止, 停下来: The rain has *stopped*. 雨已停了。 / The motor *stopped*. 马达停了。 / He *stopped to* talk with me. 他停下来跟我谈话。(试比较: He *stopped* talking. 他停止讲话。) / The long gown *stopped* at his ankles. 他的袍子长到脚踝。②踌躇: ~ at no sacrifices 不惜一切牺牲 / The greedy boss *stopped at nothing* to gain profit. 贪心不足的老板为了攫取利润而无所不为。②[口]逗留,停留; 歇宿; (偶然)过访: ~ in bed 不起床 / ~ at a hotel 住在旅馆里 / ~ with a relative 逗留在亲戚家里 ④被塞住 (*up*): The sink *stopped up.* 洗涤槽塞住了。⑤以手指压乐器的弦(或孔处)以改变音调 II *n.* ①停止; 中止; 终止; 停车: The car made a brief ~ to refuel. 车子暂时停了一下以便加油。②停车站; 停留场所: a bus ~ 公共汽车站 / a request ~ 招呼(停车)站 ③逗留,停留; 歇宿: make an overnight ~ 逗留一宵 ④塞住; 填塞; 阻碍; 障碍 ⑤[英]标点(特指句号): put in the ~s 加标点符号 / a full ~ 句号(美国称 period) ⑥【语】闭止音(指: [p], [t], [k], [g], [b], [d]) ⑦(以手指压乐器的弦、孔等的)调整音调; [喻]说法,语气,语调: put on (或 pull out) the sympathetic ~ 发出同情的调子 ⑧风琴的音栓; (六弦琴等的)柱,马 ⑨ = ~ order ⑩【海】掣,索定: a ~ rope 掣索 ⑪【机】掣子,挡,销; 断流阀;【建】门闩 ⑫【摄】光圈; 光圈数(即 f 数)刻度 III *a.* 停止的,用来使停止的,制动的: a ~ signal 停车信号 / a ~ line (汽车)停车线 ‖*come to a (full)* ~ 停(完全停)住 / *pull out all* ~*s* ①弹动风琴所有的音栓 ②全力以赴; 千方百计 / *put a* ~ *to sth.* (或 *bring sth. to a* ~) 使某事物停止下来 / *a gap* 见 gap / ~ *by* (或 *in*) [美](顺便)访问 / ~ *down* 【摄】缩小(镜头)的光圈 / ~ *off* ①[美](在旅程中)中途停留; 中途下车; 中途分道 ②用沙填满(模子的不用部分) / ~ *one's ears* 见 ear¹ / ~ *out* (在蚀刻过程中)覆盖…使其不受腐蚀 / ~ *over* = ~ off / ~ *sb.'s breath* 见 breath / ~ *sb.'s mouth* 见 mouth / ~ *short* (或 *dead*) 突然停住 / ~ *the show* 见 show / ~ *up* ①[口]不就寝,睡得迟 ②塞住 ‖~**block** *n.* 止轮楔 / '~**cock** *n.* 【机】管门; 活塞; 活栓 / '~-,**collar** *n.* 【机】限动环 / '~-,**cylinder press** 自动停滚式印刷机 / ~ **drill** (带有凸肩可限制钻头深度的)钻头 / '~**gap** *n.* ①权宜之计 ②补缺者; 临时代替的人(或物) *a.* 补缺的,暂时的: a ~*gap* measure 权宜措施,临时措施 / '~**key,** ~ **knob** *n.* 风琴音钮 / '~**light** *n.* ①(汽车车尾的)停车灯 ②交通指示灯 / '~-**loss order** = ~ order / '~-**off** *n.* (旅程)中途停留; 中途分道 / ~ **order** 指示经纪人在证券行情上涨(或下跌)到某一价格时立即买进的命令 / '~**,over** *n.* (旅程)中途停留; 中途停留地: a ~*over* station 中继站,中停站 / ~ **plate** 【机】止动片 / ~ **press** [主英]报纸付印时插入的最新消息栏 / '~= '**press** *a.* ①报纸付印时临时加入的: a ~*-press* correction (报纸付印时)临时加入的更正 ②最新的,截至最近的 / ~ **street** 车辆在进入直通干道前必须停车的街道 / ~ **valve** 【机】断流阀,

停汽阀,节流阀 / ~ **volley** (网球中的)吊短球(恰巧过网而对手无法接住的轻击) / '~**watch** *n.* (赛跑等用的)跑表,记秒表 / '~**work** *n.* ①防止钟表发条上得过紧的装置 ②[澳]停工,罢工

stoppage ['stɔpidʒ] *n.* ①停止; 中止 ②阻塞; 堵塞; 阻碍;【军】故障 ③停付, (工资等的)扣留,扣除 ④停工,罢工: an antiwar ~ 反战罢工

stopper ['stɔpə] I *n.* ①停止者; 制止者 ②阻塞物; (瓶等的)塞子;【机】制动器,限制器,闭锁装置 ③【海】掣(索) ④【矿】伸缩式凿岩机 II *vt.* (用塞子等)塞住 ‖*put a* ~ *on* 使停止; 制止 ‖~ **knot** 防止绳索穿过孔隙的结

storage ['stɔ:ridʒ] *n.* ①贮藏,保管: place the goods in ~ 把货物贮藏起来 / keep fish and meat in cold ~ 把鱼,肉冷藏起来 ②贮藏量,库存量 ③贮藏库,货栈,仓库: an oil ~ 贮油池 / a ~ room 库房 ④仓库费,栈租 ⑤【电】蓄电 ⑥【自】(电子计算机的)记忆,存储器 ‖~ **battery**, ~ **cell** 蓄电池 / ~ **life** 保存期限,贮存寿命 / ~ **tube** 电荷贮存管 / ~ **yard** 贮藏场,储料场

store [stɔ:] I *n.* ①贮藏,贮存; 许多,丰富: a ~ of goods (food)许多货物(食物) ②[复]贮存品,备用品,补给品: military ~*s* 军需品 / a ship's ~*s* 船用补给品 / marine ~*s* 船舶用具 ③[英]仓库,堆栈,货栈 (= [美] warehouse) ④ [~*s*] [用作单或复][英]百货商店 (= [美] department store): get things at the ~*s* 在百货商店里买东西 / a general ~*s* 乡村百货店,杂货店 ⑤[美]商店,店铺 (= [英] shop): a grocery ~ 杂货店 / a furniture ~ 家具商店 / a clothing ~ 服装商店 ⑥[主英]【自】(电子计算机中的)存储器 II *a.* ①[也作 ~*s*]贮藏的,贮存的; 用作贮藏处的: a ~ barge 补给船 ②从店里买来的; 现成的: ~ clothes 现成服装 / ~ teeth 假牙 III ❶ *vt.* ①贮藏,贮备: ~ *away* grain against famine 贮粮备荒 / ~ *up* a saying in one's heart 把一条格言记在心里 / conserve one's strength and ~ *up* one's energy 养精蓄锐 ②供应,供给; 装备: ~ a ship *with* provisions 给船只装备食物 / a well-~*d* memory 丰富的记忆 ③容纳,包含,容量: The shed will ~ 20 tons of coal. 这棚屋能容纳二十吨煤。④把…存入仓库; 把…交给栈房 ❷ *vi.* ①贮藏; 贮藏得不变质: These vegetables ~ well at temperatures below 20°C. 这些蔬菜在摄氏 20 度以下的温度中能够很好地贮藏。②装备补给品,贮藏供应品: The ships are *storing* in the harbour. 那些船只正在港口装补给品。‖*in* ~ ①贮藏着; 准备着: I have some good news *in* ~ *for* you. 我有一些好消息要告诉你。②必将发生; 就要来到: Defeat is *in* ~ *for* the aggressors. 侵略者必将遭到失败。/ *lay* ~ *by* (或 *on*) 重视… / *out of* ~ 耗尽; 售完 / *set* (*much, great, little, no*) ~ *by* (非常,极,简直不)重视 ‖~ **cattle** [英]准备养肥(或适合于养肥)的牛 / '~**front** *n.* ①商店(或仓库)的沿街正面,沿街铺面 ②沿街大楼; (沿街的)房间

(或套房) *a.* 占有沿街铺面的 / **'~house** *n.* ①仓库，堆栈，货栈 ②宝库: The sea is the world's greatest *~house* of raw materials. 海洋是世界上最大的原料宝库。/ He is a *~house* of information. 他是一个见闻广博的人。/ **'~keeper** *n.* ①仓库管理员; 军需品管理员 ②[美] 零售店店主 / **'~room** *n.* 贮藏室, 物料间; 商品陈列室 / **'~ship** *n.* 军需船 / **~(s)man** ['stɔ:(z)mən] *n.* ①零售店店主 ②仓库工人; 仓库管理员 / **'~wide** *a.* 包括店内全部(或大部分)商品的: a *~wide* sale 全部商品的减价出售, 全部商品的大减价

stor(e)y ['stɔ:ri] *n.* (英)(层)楼: a house of one ~ 平房 (=a single-~ house) / a building of ten storeys (或 stories) 十层大楼 (=a ten-~ building) ‖*the upper* ~ ①楼上 ②[喻]头脑: a little wrong in *the upper* ~ 神经不大正常 ‖**'~post** *n.* 【建】层柱

storied² ['stɔ:rid] *a.* ①用(历史)故事画装饰的: a ~ tapestry 历史(故事)画挂毯 ②历史上(或传说中)有名的: a ~ tower 历史上(或传说中)有名的塔 / the ~ greats 历史上的伟人; 传说中的伟人

stork [stɔ:k] *n.* 【动】鹳: a white ~ 白鹳 ‖*a King Stork* 暴君(源出《伊索寓言》) / *a visit from the* ~ 婴儿的诞生

storm [stɔ:m] *n.* ①风暴; 暴(风)雨; 暴(风)雪; 风雹; 【气】风暴, 十一级风: press ahead through wind and ~ 在大风大浪中前进 / a gathering ~ 酝酿中的风暴 / a cyclonic ~ 气旋风暴, 旋风 / an electric ~ 电暴(雷电交作的暴风雨, 常妨碍电讯) / a magnetic ~ 磁暴(地球磁场的骚动) / (政治, 社会等方面的)风暴, 大动荡, 风潮 ③(风暴般的)猛烈, 纷飞; (感情上的)激动, 爆发: a ~ of bullets 一阵弹雨 / a ~ of applause (cheers) 一阵暴风雨般的掌声(欢呼) / a ~ of protests (criticism) 一阵猛烈的抗议(抨击) ④(军事上的)猛攻, 攻占 ⑤[复]御风暴的外重窗 II ❶ *vi.* ①起风暴; 刮大风; 下暴雨; 下暴雪; 下雹: It ~ed all day. 风暴整天不息。②强攻; 猛冲, 横冲直撞: ~ ashore 强击登岸 / ~ towards a city 直捣一座城市 / ~ through the streets 猛冲过街道 / He ~ed into the office. 他气冲冲地闯入办公室。③震怒, 发雷霆; 怒骂 (at): ~ *at* the unexpected delay 因意外耽搁而大发雷霆 / ~ at sb. 怒骂某人 ❷ *vt.* ①猛攻, 直捣; 袭取; 狠狠抨击: ~ an enemy position 猛攻敌人阵地 / ~ the tiger's den 直捣虎穴 / ~ sb. with questions 猛烈质问某人 ②强烈感染, 使神魂颠倒 ‖*a feeding* ~ 越来越厉害的暴风雨 / *After a* ~ *(comes) a calm.* [谚]雨过天晴。/ *a* ~ *in a teacup* 小范围内的骚动; 小事引起的大风波, 小题大做, 大惊小怪 / *be in a* ~ [美俚]激动; 惶惑 / *bring a* ~ *about one's ears* 引起强烈反对, 惹起大乱子 / *ride out a* ~ ①安然渡过风暴 ②[喻]平安渡过困难 (或攻击等) / ~ *out* [美俚] ①(因暴怒等)猛冲而出 ②快走, 快驰 / *take by* ~ ①攻占, 强夺: take the enemy fortress *by* ~ 攻占敌人要塞 ②强烈感染; 使大吃一惊; 使神魂颠倒: *take the audience by* ~ 使观众大为倾倒 / *the Storm and Stress* 狂飙运动(指十八世纪后期德国资产阶级的文学运动) / *the* ~ *and stress* (政治、社会等方面的)大动荡, 风暴: in *the* ~ *and stress* of struggle 在斗争的风雨中间 ‖**~er** *n.* ①猛攻者 ②发怒者, 大发雷霆者 / **~less** *a.* 无风暴的 / ‖**'~-,beaten** *a.* 受风暴损坏的; 风吹雨打的; 饱经风霜的, 多经患难的 / **~ belt** *n.* 风暴地带 / **'~bird** *n.* =~ petrel / **~ boat** 强击登陆艇, 强击舟 / **'~bound** *a.* (船、旅客等)为风暴所阻的; (港口等)为风暴所困的 / **'~-card** *n.* (航行中用来推测风暴中心位置的)风暴图 / **~ centre, ~ center** 风暴中心; 骚乱的中心 / **~ cloud** 风暴云; 局面(或形势)动乱的预兆 / **'~-cone** *n.* (帆布制)锥形风暴信号 / **~ door** 御风暴(或御寒)的外重门 / **'~-drum** *n.* (加在锥形风暴信号上表示预测有特大风暴的)圆柱形风暴信号 / **'~-finch** *n.* [英] =~ petrel / **~ glass** 气候变化预测管 / **~ing party** [军]强击队 / **~ lantern, ~ lamp** [主英][海]汽风灯, 防风灯 / **~ petrel** (预兆风暴的)海燕 / **~proof** *a.* 耐风暴的, 御风暴的 / **~ sail** (风暴时使用的)较小而牢的帆 / **~ sash** 外重窗 (=~ window) / **~ sewer** 雨水管 / **~ signal** 风暴信号 / **~ tide** 风暴潮(因岸向风而产生的特大高潮) / **'~-tossed** *a.* 飘摇于风暴中的 / **~ track** (风暴中心)路径 / **~ trooper** ①[S- T-] 纳粹的冲锋队员 ②突击队员 / **~ troops** ①[S- T-] 纳粹的冲锋队 ②突击队, 强击部队 / **~ valve** (船)排水口止回阀 / **~ warning** 风暴警报 / **~ wind** 暴风, 狂风 / **~ window** ①御风暴(或御寒)的外重窗 ②(垂直)屋顶窗 / **'~-zone** *n.* 风暴带, 风暴区

stormy ['stɔ:mi] *a.* ①有暴风雨的; 多风暴的: a ~ night 暴风雨之夜 / a ~ autumn 一个多风暴的秋天 ②烈性子的, 暴躁的: a ~ temper 暴躁的脾气 ③激烈的; 多风波的: a ~ debate 激烈的辩论 / ~ applause 暴风雨般的掌声 / a ~ life 变动剧烈的生活, 惊涛骇浪的经历 ‖**stormily** *ad.* / **storminess** *n.* 【气】风暴度; 暴躁; 激烈 ‖**~ petrel** ① =storm petrel ②爱争吵的人, 制造纷争的人, 预示会发生骚乱的人

story¹ ['stɔ:ri] I *n.* ①故事; 小说; 传奇; 轶事; 传说; 传记; 史话; [古]历史 ②(对某事的)描述, 叙述: They all tell the same ~. 他们都这样说。/ according to sb.'s own ~ 据某人自述 / The man's ~ of the accident was not convincing. 这人关于那事故的叙述不足信。③经历, 阅历: write the ~ of one's life 写自己的生活经历 / His ~ is told. 他的一生到此为止了。④(小说、戏剧等的)情节, 本事: the ~ of a ballet 芭蕾舞剧情 ⑤内情, 真相: These figures gave only part of the ~. 这些数字只不过说明部分情况。⑥(新闻)记事,报道;值得报道的人物(或事实): a news ~ 新闻报道 / a feature ~ 特写 ⑦[儿语]假话,谎话;说谎者: It's a ~. (或 'Tis a ~.) 这是假话。/ Oh, you ~! 哦,你这说谎的家伙! **II** *vt.* ①[古]用故事描写,编成故事叙述 ❷ *vi.* 说假话: He *storied* about his age. 他隐瞒年龄。‖*as the ~ goes* 据说 / *But that is another ~.* 但那是一会事。(或: 那是题外的话了。)/ *It is quite another ~ now.* 现在情形完全不同了。/ *tell a ~* 说谎 / *tell its own ~* 不言而喻,自己表明 / *The ~ goes* (或 *runs*) *that* .... 据说…,传说… / *to make a long ~ short* 长话短说,简而言之 ‖'~*book* n. 故事书,小说书 /'~*,teller* n. ①讲故事的人,说书人;小说作者 ②[口]说谎的人 /'~*,writer* n. 小说作者,小说家

stout [staut] **I** *a.* ①结实的,牢固的: a ~ box 结实的箱子 / a ~ ship 牢固的船 / ~ boots 耐穿的靴子 ②勇敢的; 坚定的; 不妥协的 ③有力的,猛烈的,激烈的: a ~ attack 强有力的进攻 / a ~ wind 暴风 ④强壮的; 矮胖的; 胖的: a man of ~ build 身材矮胖的人 ⑤粗壮的; 厚的: ~ branches 粗大的树枝 / a ~ volume 一厚册 **II** *n.* ①矮胖子;大号的衣服尺寸 ②烈黑啤酒 ‖~*ish* *a.* 略胖的 / ~*ly* *ad.* / ~*ness* *n.* ‖'~*hearted* *a.* 勇敢的 / ~*heartedly* *ad.* 勇敢地 / '~*heartedness* *n.* 勇敢

stove [stouv] **I** *n.* ①(取暖或烹饪用的)炉,火炉,电炉,加热器 ②窑;烘房 [主英]温室 **II** *vt.* [主英]在温室内培育(植物) ‖~*pipe* *n.* ①火炉烟囱管;通至烟囱的烟筒 ②[美口]礼帽(一种高筒狭边男用丝绒帽)(= ~*pipe hat*) ③[美俚]流行的闲谈 ④[美俚]迫击炮;喷气式战斗机 / ~ *plant* 须在温室内培育的植物

stow [stou] *vt.* ①堆垛,堆装; 装载: ~ the hold with cargo (或 ~ *cargo in the hold*) 将货物堆装在船舱里 / *Stow away from boiler.* 切勿靠近锅炉。(货物外面的防热标志) ②贮藏,收藏: ~ the winter clothes away into a trunk 把冬衣收藏入箱 ③使暂留,使暂宿: The patient was ~*ed* in the hospital's emergency room. 那个病人被暂留在急诊间里。④[俚][常用祈使语气]停止: *Stow the chatter!* 别唠叨了! ⑤用…填喂 ‖~ *away* 做揩油乘客,偷乘船(或火车、飞机等) / *Stow it.* [美俚]停止! 别说了! ‖'~*away* *n.* ①揩油乘客,偷乘者 ②隐藏的地方,收藏处 / '~*wood* *n.* (船舱内垫圆桶的)楔木,垫木

straddle ['strædl] **I** ❶ *vi.* ①叉开腿,叉开腿坐;叉开腿站立;叉开腿走路;跨骑 ②杂乱地伸展: Branches ~*d* in every direction. 树枝杂乱地向四处伸展。③骑墙,观望 ④在一市场上买空在另一市场上卖空,一面做多头一面做空头 ❷ *vt.* ①叉开腿坐于;跨立: ~ a horse 跨在马上 / A bridge ~*s* the river. 一桥横越大江。②对…不表态,对…持观望态度: ~ an issue 对争端抱观

望态度 ③夹叉射击;夹叉轰炸 **II** *n.* ①叉腿,跨 ②观望态度,骑墙,暧昧 ③(证券交易中)使对方在一定期限内按某一价格收货(或交货)的权利;套利(同时在一种证券上做多头而在另一种证券上做空头的交易) ④夹叉弹;夹叉射击 ‖~ *trench* 【军】战地便坑

straggle ['strægl] **I** *vi.* ①迷路;掉队,落伍;流离 ②蔓延,蔓生;四散;散落出现: the grapevines *straggling* over the trellis 蔓延在棚架上的葡萄藤 / with hair *straggling* over one's shoulder 头发散披在肩上 / Hamlets ~ along both sides of the creek. 小村散布在小河两岸。**II** *n.* 散乱;man with a ~ of a beard 胡子蓬乱的人 ‖~*r* *n.* ①落伍士兵;掉队的飞机;迟到二十四小时归队(或归舰)的人员 ②蔓生的枝叶 ③走失的家畜

straight [streit] **I** *a.* ①直的,笔直的,挺直的: a ~ road 直路 / ~ timber 【建】笔直木材 / a ~ back 挺直的背 ②直接的;连续的: a ~*er* path to a place 到某处去的一条更直接的路 / the ~ sequence of events 事件的先后顺序 ③整齐的;端正的;有条理的: Put your room ~. 把你的房间整理好。/ put a picture ~ 把一幅画摆端正 / He is a ~ thinker. 他思路很有条理。④正直的,有品德的;坦率的: be ~ in one's dealings 待人接物正直老实 / keep sb. ~ 使某人端正自己的行为 / give a ~ answer 给与坦率的回答 ⑤[口]可靠的;正确的: a ~ tip (关于行情等的)第一手可靠消息 / The accounts are ~. 帐目正确无误。⑥(发动机)汽缸直排式的 ⑦[美]纯粹的,不掺杂的: ~ cement 纯水泥 / a whisky ~ 纯威士忌酒 / He writes ~ humour. 他写的东西都是地道的幽默。⑧(对政党、原则等)始终忠实的,彻底支持的: a ~ Democrat 顽固的民主党人 / a ~ ballot 彻底支持某政党所有候选人的一票 ⑨(不论多少)每份的: eggs seven cents ~ (不论顾客买多少)七分钱一只的鸡蛋 **II** *ad.* ①直: stand ~ 直立 ②直接地;一直地: come ~ home 直接回家 / make ~ for (或 go ~ to) the factory 直接到工厂去 / keep ~ on 一直走(或做)下去 / come ~ to the point 直入本题,开门见山 ③正直地;老实地;坦率地: talk ~ 直言不讳 / tell sb. ~ out 坦率地告诉某人 ④立刻,马上: Let's go to the meeting ~ away. 我们马上就会去吧。/ I can't tell you ~ off. 我不能一下子就告诉你。**III** *n.* [the ~] ①直;挺直: be out of the ~ 不平直,歪着,弯着 ②直线;(赛跑跑道近终点的) 直线部分 ③ (纸牌)五张顺子 ④[口]真相: Tell us the ~ of it. 告诉我们事情的真相吧。⑤ (赛马)第一名;(射击等的)连续命中 **IV** *vt.* [苏格兰] =straighten (*vt.*)‖*as ~ as a die* 见*die²* / a ~ *fight* 一对一的两人竞选 / a ~ *job* [美俚](无拖车的)载重汽车 / a ~ *race* 全力以赴的竞赛 / (*be*) *on the* ~ [口](指原来犯过事的人)老实做人;品行端正 / ~ *dry* ~ [口]结果很好;终于好转 / *get* ~ [美]了解,搞通;办好 / *go* ~ ①笔直走 ②正直做人 ③戒去

毒瘾 / *put things* ~ 整顿局面 / *see* ~ 看得清楚,看得对头 / *shoot* ~ 瞄准打;命中率高 / ~ *from the shoulder* 见 **shoulder** / ~ *goods* [美]真相,事实 / ~ *talk* [美]诚恳而又简明扼要的谈话 ‖ **-ness** *n*. ‖ **A** [美]成绩最优秀的: a ~ *A* student 成绩最优秀的学生 / ~ **accent** 【语】长音符 / ~ **angle** 【数】平角 / ~ **arch** 【建】平拱 / **'~-arm** *vt*. (橄榄球中)伸直手臂挡住(对手) *n*. 伸臂挡住对手的动作 / **~away** *n*. 直线跑道(指赛跑跑道近终点处的直线部分);陆路(或水路)上的直段 *a*. ①直线行进的: a plane in ~*away* flight 直线航行的飞机 ②(故事)顺序直述的 ③(作品)通俗易懂的 ④立刻的: make a ~*away* reply 立刻答复 *ad*. 立刻,马上 / **chain** 【化】直链 / **'~-cut** *a*. (烟叶)纵切的 / **'~edge** *n*. 直尺,标尺 *vt*. 把…的一边弄直 / 用直尺检验 / **'~-eight** *n*. (指汽车)八汽缸直排式,直八式 / ~ **eye** 能看出东西是否正(或直)的眼力 / ~ **face** 没有表情的脸;不露笑容的脸: keep a ~ *face* 板着面孔,不露笑容 / **'~jacket** *n*. & *vt*. =straitjacket / ~ **jet** (无螺旋桨的)喷气式飞机 / **'~laced** *a*. =straitlaced / **'~line** *a*. 直线的;直排式的 / ~ **man** 喜剧中丑角的助手 / **'~-out** *n*. (对某一政党或政策)支持到底的人 *a*. 坦率的;彻底的 / ~ **paper** 由个人签发(或背书)的流通票据 / ~ **razor** (一般理发室中使用的)折迭式剃刀 / ~ **ticket** [美]只选某一政党所有候选人的选票 / ~ **time** 正式工作时间,规定工时(不包括请假或加班的时间);正式工作时间的工资率 / **'~way** *ad*. 直接地;立刻,马上 *a*. 畅通无阻的。

straighten ['streitn] ❶ *vt*. ①把…弄直,使挺直: ~ a piece of wire 弄直一段铁丝 / ~ one's back 挺直背脊 ②整顿,清理;澄清 (out, up): ~ out the accounts 清理帐目 / ~ up the house 把屋子搞整洁 / ~ things *out* 弄清问题 / ~ *out* the confused thinking 澄清混乱的思想 ③使改正;使好转 (out): Discipline without education will not thoroughly ~ *out* anyone. 只有处分,不加教育,不能使人彻底改正错误。/ He is only tired; a cup of tea will ~ him out. 他只是疲乏了,喝杯茶精神就会好起来的。❷ *vi*. ①直起来;挺起来 (up) ②改正;好转 (out, up): These problems will ~ *out* in time. 这些问题总会解决的。

straightforward [streit'fɔ:wəd] I *a*. ①一直向前的;直接的 ②正直的;老实的;坦率的: a ~ reply 坦率的回答 ③易做的;易懂的: a ~ job 一项简单的工作 / a ~ problem in geometry 几何学中的一个简易题目 ④明确的,肯定的: Your responsibility is ~. 你的职责是明确的。II *ad*. 坦率地,直截了当地 ‖ **~ly** *ad*. / **~ness** *n*.

straightforwards [streit'fɔ:wədz] *ad*. 坦率地,直截了当地

strain[1] [strein] *n*. ①(人的)血缘,世系;种,族;(动植物的)系,品系;【微】菌株,小种: a high-

yielding ~ of winter wheat 高产冬小麦种 / a hybrid ~ 杂交种 / a horse of good ~ 良种马 / ~ selection 选种 / a ~ for making antibiotics 用来制造抗菌素的菌株 ②气质,(性格上的)倾向: There is a ~ of weakness in him. 他性格有点儿软弱。③[常用复]曲调,旋律;乐曲;诗,歌;诗节,歌节 ④口吻,语气;笔调;情调: He went on in another ~. 他换了语气再继续讲下去。/ talk in a lofty ~ 高谈阔论

strain[2] [strein] I ❶ *vt*. ①拉紧;拖紧;伸张: ~ the canvas over a frame 把帆布在架上张紧 ②使紧张;尽力使用(耳、目、嗓子等);使过劳(以致受损伤);扭伤: ~ every nerve 全力以赴,竭尽全力 / ~ one's eyes 尽力注视;用目过度而损伤视力 / ~ one's voice 尽力提高嗓子;喊哑嗓子 / ~ the wrist 扭伤手腕 ③滥用;(牵强地)曲解,歪曲: ~ one's authority 滥用职权 / ~ the meaning of a word 曲解词义 / ~ the law 歪曲法律 ④紧抱(一般只用于以下这类例证中): ~ a child *to one's breast* 把孩子紧抱在怀里 ⑤滤: ~ wine (coffee) 滤酒(咖啡) / ~ the gravy *free from* lumps 滤肉汁使不含肉块 / ~ the lumps *out of* the gravy 把肉汁里的肉块滤掉 ❷ *vi*. ①尽力,努力,使劲: His eyes ~ed to catch a glimpse of the sea. 他极目望去,想看到一点海景。/ plants ~*ing* upwards to the light 争向阳光的植物 / ~ *at* the oar 使劲划桨 / ~ *at* stool 用力大便 / ~ *under* a heavy burden 在重压之下苦撑苦度 ②紧拉;紧拖 (at): a ship ~*ing at* its anchor 紧拉着锚绳的船 ③不肯接受,以为不可: Anyone would ~ *at* such an interpretation. 这种解释谁都难以接受。④扭歪;弯曲 (因用力而)变形 ⑤被过滤;渗出: This liquid ~s readily. 这液体容易过滤。/ water ~*ing* through sandy soil 从沙土渗出的水 II *n*. ①拉紧;张力;【物】应变,胁变: the breaking ~ of a cable 钢索的断裂应变 / calculate the ~s and stresses of a bridge 计算桥梁的应变和应力 / ~ of flexure 挠曲应变 ②过度的使用,过房;极度紧张;费力之物;严峻的考验: the ~ of sleepless nights 连夜不眠的过度劳累 / be a ~ on sb.'s resources 对某人的财力是一项重负 ③扭伤: a ~ in the arm 手臂扭伤 / a back ~ 背扭伤 ④[古]曲解 ‖ **~ after** 勉力追求,拚命争取: ~ *after* originality 力求不落俗套,标新立异 / ~ *a point* 见 **point** ‖ **~ed** *a*. ①牵强附会的: a ~ed interpretation 牵强的解释 ②紧张的: ~ed relations 紧张的关系 ③勉强的,不自然的: a ~ed laugh 强笑 / ~ed manners 不自然的态度 / **~er** *n*. 滤器;滤网,筛网: a tea ~er 滤茶器 ‖ **ga(u)ge** 应变仪,应变计

strait[1] [streit] *a*. ①[古]狭窄的;紧的 ②[古]被束缚的;受限制的 ③[古]严格的,严密的 ④困难的;苦简的;窘迫的 ‖ **~ly** *ad*. / **~ness** *n*. ‖ **'~jacket** *n*. (给疯人或犯人穿的)拘束衣;[喻]约束物 *vt*. 用拘束衣拘束;束缚 / **'~laced** *a*.

①[古]束硬围腰的; 穿紧身衣的 ②(在举止、道德观念等方面)极端严谨的 / '~-'waistcoat n. [主英] =~jacket (n.)

strait² [streit] n. ①[古]狭窄的通道, 狭隘的地方 ②[与专有名词连用时常作 ~s][用作单]海峡: the Straits (旧时指)直布罗陀海峡; (现指)马六甲海峡 / the Strait(s) of Dover 多佛(尔)海峡(即加来海峡)[欧洲] / the Strait of Hormuz (或 Ormuz) 霍(尔)木兹海峡[亚洲] / the Soya Strait 宗谷海峡[亚洲] ③地峡 ④[常用复]困难; 窘迫: in financial ~s 处于经济困难中 / fall into hopeless ~s 陷入绝境 ⑤[解](狭)口: the upper (lower) ~ 骨盆上(下)口 ‖**Straits dollar** 叻币(马来西亚货币单位,马来西亚元的习称)

straiten ['streitn] vt. ①使紧窄, 使狭窄 ②限制; 使紧缩 ③[常用被动语态]使窘迫, 使困苦: in ~ed circumstances 处于贫困的境地 / be ~ed in time 时间紧迫 / be ~ed in room 缺乏余地

strand¹ [strænd] I n. 海滨, 海滩; 河岸; 湖滨 II ❶ vt. ①使搁浅: The ship remained ~ed. 那条船仍搁浅着。/ a ~ing harbour 浅水港 ②(由于资金等的缺乏)使处于困境; 使束手无策: be ~ed in a strange city 流落在陌生城市里一筹莫展 ③使掉队, 使落后 ❷ vi. 搁浅

strand² [strænd] I n. ①(绳、线等的)股; 缕; 绞: ~ wire 多股绞合金属线 / a rope of three ~s 三股的绳子 ②线; 绳 ③串 ④一组成部分 ⑤[电]导线束; 裸多心电缆 II vt. ①扯断(绳索)的一股(或多股) ②搓,绞(绳索等) ‖~er n. 绳缆搓绞机

strange [streindʒ] a. ①陌生的; 生疏的, 不熟悉的: a ~ face 陌生面孔 / The handwriting is ~ to me. 我不熟悉这笔迹。/ I am quite ~ here. 我在这里人地生疏。②奇怪的, 奇妙的, 不可思议的: a ~ dream 奇梦 / ~ clothes 奇装异服 / He is very ~ in his manner. 他的态度很怪。③生手的, 外行的, 没有经验的; 不习惯的: He was still ~ to the work. 他对这项工作还很生疏。/ be ~ at football 对足球是外行 ④疏远的; 冷淡的, 不亲热的 ⑤外地的, 异乡的; [古]外国的: in a ~ land 在异地; 在国外 ‖feel ~ 觉得不舒服, 觉得头昏眼花 / ~ to say 说也奇怪: Strange to say, he is still ignorant of it. 说也奇怪, 他还不知道这件事。‖~ly ad. / ~ness n. ‖~ woman 娼妓

stranger ['streindʒə] I n. ①陌生人: He is no ~ to me. 他对我来说并不陌生。/ You are quite a ~. [口]好久不见了。(或: 你真是个稀客。) ②新来者; 生客; 异乡人: the little ~ 新生婴儿 / I am a ~ in this town. 我在这个镇上人地生疏。③外行, 生手; 局外人; 不习惯于…的人 (to): We are no ~s to this kind of thing. 我们对于这类事是有亲身体会的。/ I am a complete ~ to city life. 我对城市生活很不习惯。④外国人 ⑤[律]非当事人, 第三者 ⑥[美]先生(在乡下

对陌生人用的招呼语, =sir) II a. 外国人的 ‖I spy (或 see) ~s. (英国下议院用语)请旁听者退场。/ make a (no) ~ of 冷淡地(亲热地)对待…

strangle ['stræŋgl] ❶ vt. ①扼死; 勒死; 绞死 ②扼住, 闷住, 使窒息 ③抑制, 压制 ❷ vi. ①被扼死; 被勒死; 被绞死 ②窒息而死 ‖~hold n. ①(摔角)勒颈 ②压制; 束缚: put a ~hold on sth. 对某事进行压制

strap [stræp] I n. ①带, 皮带; 布带; 铁带, 铁皮条: a shoe ~ 鞋的搭扣带 / a shoulder ~ 肩带 / an iron 条钢, 扁钢 ②(磨刀刀的)皮带, 革砥 ③搭扣鞋 (=~ shoe) ④(合拢伤口或粘牢绷带用的)橡皮膏 ⑤[the ~]鞭打 ⑥[英]信用 ⑦[爱尔兰语]轻佻的女子; 娼妓 ⑧[海]滑车带 II (strapped; strapping) vt. ①用皮带束住; 捆扎: ~ on a wristwatch 带上手表 / ~ up a suitcase 用皮带及搭扣束住手提皮箱 ②用皮带抽打 ③在皮条上磨(剃刀) ④绑扎(伤口等); 用橡皮膏粘贴 ‖~less a. 无带的(游泳衣、女式晚服等)无背带的 / strapped a. ①用带绑着的; 被抽打的 ②[美俚]没有分文的, 没有资金的 ‖~ brake 【机】带闸 / '~,hanger n. (公共车辆上)拉着吊带站立的乘客 / '~-laid a. 用两条三股绳平列缝合的 / '~-oil n. [俚]抽打 / '~work n. 【建】用窄带折迭(或交织)而成的装饰图案 / '~wort n. 【植】海滨蓬秋罗

strapping ['stræpiŋ] I a. 身体高大而匀称的, 魁梧的; 强壮的 II n. ①贴膏法; 橡皮膏 ②皮革材料

stratagem ['strætidʒəm] n. 计策, 计谋; 策略

strategy ['strætidʒi] n. ①战略, 战略学: ~ and tactics 战略与战术 ②策略, 计谋

stratosphere ['strætousfiə] n. ①【气】平流层, 同温层 ②最上层; 最高档; 最高部位 ③艰深的学科领域 ‖**stratospheric** [,strætou'sferik] a.

stratum ['strɑːtəm, 'streitəm] ([复] strata ['strɑːtə, 'streitə]) n. ①【地】地层: an oil-bearing ~ 地下油层 ②阶层: people of all social strata 社会上各阶层的人们 / the privileged ~ 特权阶层

stratus ['streitəs] ([复] strati ['streitai]) n. 【气】层云

straw [strɔː] I n. ①稻草; 麦秆; (喝汽水等用的)麦秆吸管: a heap of ~ 稻草堆; 麦秆堆 / made of ~ 稻草制的 / a house thatched with ~ 屋顶用稻草盖的房子,茅屋 / suck lemonade through a ~ 用麦管吸柠檬水 ②用稻草(或麦秆)做成的东西; 草帽: a man in a white ~ 戴白草帽的男子 ③无价值的东西; 无意义的事情; 一点点: not worth a ~ 毫无价值 / not care a ~ (或 two ~s, three ~s) 毫不在乎 / It doesn't matter a ~. 一点儿也没有关系。II a. ①稻草(或麦秆)的; 用稻草(或麦秆)做的: ~ sandals 草鞋 / a ~ mattress 草垫 ②稻草色的, 淡黄色的 ③无价值的, 无意义的, 琐碎的 ④(投票)仅为测验一下民意的, 假的; (关于)假投票结果的 ⑤稻草人

般的; (对手等)假想的; (在非法交易等中)被人推出来做挡箭牌的 **III** *vt.* [古] =strew ‖*a man of ~* 见 **man** / *A ~ shows which way the wind blows.* [谚]草动知风向。/ *catch* (或 *clutch, grasp*) *at a ~* (遭水淹的人) 捞救命稻草; 依靠完全靠不住的东西 / *draw ~s* (用不同长短的麦秆) 抽签 / *in the ~* [古] (产妇) 坐褥 / *make bricks without ~* 见 **brick** / *One's eyes draw* (或 *gather, pick*) *~s.* 昏昏欲睡。/ *split ~s* 为一些极细小的分歧而争吵 / *~s in the wind* 显示大动向的小事 / *throw a ~ against the wind* 扔草抵风, 螳臂挡车 ‖*~* **bail** [美]无资力的保人 / '*~board* *n.* 草纸板 / *~* **boss** [口]工头助手 / *~* **colo(u)r** 稻草色, 淡黄色 / '*~flower* *n.* 终年不谢的野花 / '*~hat theatre* 夏季剧院 / *~* **man** ① 假想的(易击败的)对手; 设想的(易驳倒的)的相反论点 ②(在非法交易等中)被用作挡箭牌的人 / *~* **plait** 草帽缏 / *~* **poll** [美] *~* vote / *~* **rope** 草绳 / *~* **stem** 一种细脚酒杯 / *~* **vote** [美]测验民意的假投票 / '*~worm* *n.* ①毛翅目昆虫的幼虫(水栖;用作鱼饵) ②膜翅目昆虫的幼虫(有害于麦类) / *~* **yellow** 淡黄色

strawberry ['strɔ:bəri] *n.* 【植】草莓 ‖*~* **leaf** 公爵爵位的象征 / *~* **mark** 红色胎记, 莓状痣(一种先天性血管瘤) / *~* **tree** 杨梅树; 莓实树(欧洲产的一种石南科小树)

stray [strei] **I** *vi.* ① 走离, 偏离; 迷路, 走失: *~ from* (或 *off*) *the right path* 偏离正道 / *Don't ~ from the point.* 不要离题乱扯。/ *They ~ed apart in the woods.* 他们在森林中失散了。②漫游; 流浪, 漂泊 **II** *a.* ①迷路的; 离群的: *a ~ child* 迷途的孩子 / *a ~ sheep* 迷途的羊 / *a bullet* 流弹 ②偶遇的; 零落的: *a few ~ hairs* 几根稀疏的毛发 / *a few ~ instances* 偶有的例子 **III** *n.* ①迷路者;流浪者;迷路的家畜 ② 因无人继承而归公的遗产 ③[常用复](干扰无线电接收的)天电 【地】(石油钻探中)偶然出现的间层, 杂层 ‖*waifs and ~s* 见 **waif** ‖*~er* *n.* 迷失者

streak [stri:k] **I** *n.* ① 条纹, 纹理; 色线: *red with green ~s* 夹有绿条的红色 / *the first grey ~s of dawn* 黎明时(天空中)最初出现的灰色条纹 / *~ of lightning* 一道电光 / *like a ~ (of lightning)* 闪电般地, 飞快地 / *the silver ~* 银带(英吉利海峡的别名) ②(性格上不太显著的)特色: *a nervous ~* 轻微的神经质 / *He has a ~ of humour in him.* 他略具幽默感。③ 条层: *The bacon has a ~ of lean (fat).* 这块咸肉中带有一层瘦(肥)肉。④[口]一连串, 一系列; (短暂的)一段时期: *a long ~ of winning* 一连串的胜利 / *a ~ of luck* 一段走运的时期 ⑤【矿】矿脉; 矿层; 矿物痕色, 矿物粉色 ⑥【微】划线, 条斑; *~ culture* 划线培养 **II** ❶ *vt.* 在…上加条纹 ❷ *vi.* ①形成条纹 ②飞跑, 疾驰 ‖*~ed* *a.* 有条纹的 /

~ing *n.* (美国颓废派在大街等处的)裸体飞跑

streaky ['stri:ki] *a.* ①有条纹的; 似条纹的: *pork* (肥瘦相间的)五花肉 ②忧愁的, 担心的: *be nervous and ~ about sth.* 对某事感到忧虑不安 ③(性质)不均匀的, 混杂的; 变化多端的, 不可靠的 ‖*streakily* *ad.* / *streakiness* *n.*

stream [stri:m] **I** *n.* ①(小)河;川; 溪流: *a mountain ~* 山涧 / *go up ~* 逆流而上 / *flow down ~* 顺流淌下 / *be situated up* (*down*) *~* 位于上(下)游 ②流;流出;流动;一连串: *a ~ of water* 一流细水 / *a ~ of lava* 熔岩流 / *a ~ of cold air* 一股冷空气 / *a ~ of light* 一缕光线 / *a ~ of cars* 一长串汽车 / *sun ~s* 太阳光线 / *Visitors entered the exhibition hall in a steady ~* (或 *in ~s*). 参观者川流不息地进入展览厅。③ 趋向, 趋势: *a ~ of thought* 思潮 / *~ of consciousness* 意识之流(美国实用主义者詹姆斯的哲学用语) ④[英]同一年级的学生按智力划分的小组 **II** ❶ *vi.* ①流; 流出; 流动; 涌: *Tears ~ed down her cheeks.* 热泪从她脸上流下。/ *~ing eyes* 泪汪汪的眼睛 / *a ~ing umbrella* 滴着水的雨伞 / *The students ~ed into the auditorium.* 学生们络绎不绝地进入礼堂。②飘扬, 招展: *A red flag ~ed* (*out*) *in the breeze.* 红旗迎着微风招展。/ *Her hair ~ed back.* 她的头发向后飘动。❷ *vt.* ①流; 流出: *The wounds ~ed blood.* 伤口流血。②展开(旗帜等) ③[英]把(学生)按智力划分 ‖*go* (或 *swim*) *against the ~* 不随波逐流, 反潮流; 逆潮流而行事 / *go* (或 *swim*) *with the ~* 随波逐流, 随大流 / *on ~* 进行生产; 投入生产: *The plant will go on ~ this year.* 这工厂将在今年投入生产。‖*~less* *a.* 无溪流的 / *~let* ['stri:mlit] *n.* 小溪 ‖ **anchor** 【海】中锚, 流锚 / '*~line* *n.* ①【物】流线 ②(飞机、汽车等的)流线型 *a.* 流线(型)的: *a ~line form* (或 *shape*) 流线型 / *a ~line boat* 流线型船 *vt.* ①把…设计(或制)成流线型 ②把…集为一个整体 ③使现代化; 使合理化; 精简…使效率更高: *The leadership ~lined the plant organization.* 工厂领导精简了机构。/ '*~lined* *a.* ①流线的, 流线型的: *~lined cars* 流线型汽车 ②集成一个整体的 ③ 现代化了的; 合理化了的; 精简了的: *the ~lined methods for fitting steel bars* 安装钢筋的合理化作业法 / *a ~lined course* 速成班 / '*~liner* *n.* 流线型物(特指流线型火车) / '*~of-'consciousness* *a.* 意识之流的

streamer ['stri:me] *n.* ①横幅; 长旗; 幡 ②下垂的饰带; 飘带; 旒 ③【气】光幕; [复]北极光; 【电】流光, 射光; 由电子雪崩产生的电子流 ④ 报纸上横贯全页的标题

street [stri:t] **I** *n.* ①街, 街道; 行车道, 马路: *a main ~* 大街 / *meet a friend in* (或[美] *on*) *the ~* 在街上碰到一个朋友 / *go down the ~* 顺着街走 / *Don't play in the ~.* 别在马路上玩耍。/ *Look about you before crossing the ~.* 穿马路前看清楚往车辆。②街区; 全街区的人: *live in a fashionable ~* 住在时髦阶层居住的街

上 / The whole ~ was stirred. 街坊全部动起来了。③ [the S-] [美]华尔街(纽约金融中心) (=Wall Street); [英]伦巴第大街(伦敦金融中心) (=Lombard Street); [英]舰队街(伦敦新闻业集中的街) (=Fleet Street); (一定上下文中特别提到的)某一大街 ④ [美俚]释放出狱,自由 **II** *a.* ①街道的,街上的: ~ combat (或 fighting) 巷战 / ~ cries 街上小贩的叫卖声 ②(女子服装)适合上街穿的,下摆不拖到地面的 ‖*a woman of the ~*(*s*) 娼妓 / *get* (或 *have*) *the key of the ~* 见 key¹ / *go on the ~s* 做妓女 / *go up King Street* 见 king / *in the ~* ①在街上;在户外 ②(证券交易)在交易所打烊后进行的 / *live in the ~* 老是在外头,老是不在家 / *live on the ~s* 以卖淫为生 / *milk the ~* [美俚]操纵有价证券从中取利 / *not in* (或 *up*) *sb.'s* ~ 非某人所关心的;非某人所长 / *not in the same ~ with* (或 *as*) [口](在能力等方面)难以和…相比 / *not the length of a ~* 很近的距离;些微的差别 / *on easy* ~ 生活优裕 / *put it on the ~* [美俚]泄漏秘密(或把张扬别人的隐私) / *the man in* (或 *on*) *the* ~ 见 man / *walk the ~s* 做妓女 ‖*~ward ad. & a.* 向街(的) ‖*~ Arab* 街头流浪儿 / *'~car n.* [美]市内有轨电车 / ~ **door** 临街大门 / ~ **girl** 妓女 / '~-map, '~-plan *n.* 街道图 / ~ **orderly** [英]街道清扫工 / ~ **price** (交易所)场外行情 / ~ **sweeper** ①扫街车,清道机 ②街道清扫工 / '~,walker *n.* 妓女 / '~,walking *n.* 卖淫

strength [streŋθ] *n.* ①力,力量,力气;实力: a man of great ~ 力气大的人 / fighting ~ 战斗力 / push with all one's ~ 用全力推 / Union is ~. 团结就是力量。/ the ~ of memory 记忆力 / the ~ of will 意志力 / too much for sb.'s ~ 非某人力所能及的 / the position of ~ 实力地位 ② 强度;(酒、茶、颜色等的)浓度: the ~ of a wire 金属丝的强度 / compressive ~ 抗压强度 / test the ~ of steel 试验钢的强度 / alcohol of different ~s 不同浓度的酒精 ③ 人数;兵员,兵力: the effective ~ 实际人数,实额;有生力量 / the establishment ~ 编制人员 / an army unit of a ~ of 6,000 一支六千人的军队 / below ~ 不足规定人数的,不足规定兵员的 / up to ~ 达到规定人数的,达到规定兵员的 / What is your ~? 你们一共有多少人? / Our army is in (great) ~. 我军兵力强大。/ They are here in full ~. 他们全体出动,都在这里了。/ The battalion is at full ~. 这个营的人员是足额的。④[美]股票市场价格上升(或稳定)的趋势 ⑤[美俚]利润(尤指可能得到的最大利润) ‖*be* (或 *be taken*) *on the* ~ 编在兵员名册上 / *by main* ~ 全靠力气 / *from* ~ *to* ~ 不断壮大,越来越强大 / *on the* ~ *of...* 受…的鼓励,依赖…,凭借…: I bought this dictionary *on the* ~ *of* your recommendation. 由于你的推荐,我买了这本词典。‖*~less a.* 无力量的

strengthen ['streŋθən] **❶** *vt.* ①加强,巩固;使坚强: ~ national defence 巩固国防 / ~ defence works 加强防御工事 / ~ unity 加强团结 / ~ discipline 加强纪律 ②增加…的艺术效果 **❷** *vi.* ①变强 ②(股票)价格上涨 ‖*~ sb.'s hand* 增加某人的资本;增强某人的实力 / *~ sb.'s hands* 使某人得以采取强有力的行动

strenuous ['strenjuəs] *a.* ①奋发的,使劲的: make ~ efforts 尽全力 ②紧张的: a long ~ march 艰苦的长途行军 / a ~ examination 紧张的考试 ③热烈的,狂热的 ‖**strenuosity** [,strenju-'ɔsiti] *n.* / *~ly ad.* / *~ness n.*

streptocin [strep'tousin] *n.* 【药】灰链丝菌素

stress [stres] **I** *n.* ①压力,重压;紧迫,紧张: in times of ~ 在艰难困苦之时; 在供不应求的旺季 / under ~ of weather (circumstances) 迫于恶劣的天气(环境) / driven by ~ of hunger 为饥饿所迫 ②重要,重点;强调 ③【语】重音,重读: the word (sentence) ~ 词(句)重音 / a primary (或 strong) ~ 主重音 / a secondary (或 light, weak) ~ 次重音 / The ~ is (或 falls) on the second syllable. 重音在第二个音节上。/ It is important to know where to place the ~es. 知道什么地方要重读是重要的。④【物】应力: a ~ diagram 应力图 / allowable ~ 许可应力 / alternate ~ 交变应力 / impact ~ 冲击应力 **II** *vt.* ①着重,强调: He ~ed the point that we should be punctual. 他强调的一点是我们必须准时。②用重音读,重读: a ~ed syllable 重读音节 / The word is ~ed on the first syllable. 这个词的第一个音节重读。③使受应力 ‖*lay* (或 *place, put*) ~ *on* (或 *upon*) 把重点放在…上;在…上用力: He *laid* special ~ *on* analysing the particularity of the contradiction. 他着重分析这一矛盾的特殊性。/ *Stress should be put on* the prevention of diseases. 疾病应以预防为主。/ Don't *lay* undue ~ *on* difficulties in our work. 不要不适当地强调我们工作中的困难。‖*~less a.* 没有重音的 / *'~-mark n.* 重音符号

stretch [stretʃ] **I** **❶** *vt.* ①伸展,伸张;展开,铺开;把…拉直,把…拉长: He ~ed out his arm to take the book. 他伸出手臂去拿书。/ ~ oneself 伸直身子;伸懒腰 / ~ one's legs (久坐后)伸伸腿 / ~ the carpet out to dry 铺晒地毯 / The rope must be ~ed tight. 必须把绳子拉紧。/ ~ a wire across the road 把电线拉到道路的对面 ②使过度伸展;使(精神、肌肉等)过度紧张: Transport was rather ~ed in the Spring Festival. 春节期间运输相当紧张。/ ~ every nerve to do sth. 全神贯注地做某事 ③曲解;滥用;[口]夸张: ~ the law 不恰当地引伸法律 / ~ one's powers 滥用权力 / ~ the facts 夸大事实,言过其实 ④[俚]打倒: ~ sb. on the ground 把某人打翻在地 ⑤[俚]绞死,吊死 ⑥[俚]为(尸体)作殡葬准备 **❷** *vi.* ①伸,展,延伸;延续;延绵: Rubber ~es easily. 橡胶容易延伸。/ This word will not ~ to cover that meaning. 这个词不能引伸作那个解释。② 伸肢体：He ~ed on the lawn and took a nap. 他伸手伸脚地躺在草坪上睡了个午觉。/ yawn and ~ 打呵欠伸懒腰 ③[口]夸大事实，吹牛 ④[俚]被绞死 ⑤[海]张帆航行 II n. ①伸展，伸长；延亘，连绵：make a ~ of the arm 伸出手臂 / give a ~ 伸懒腰 / a ~ of hills 连绵的群山 / vast ~es of paddyfields 大片大片的稻田 / a ~ of open country 一片旷野 ② 紧张；过度延伸：nerves on the ~ 紧张的神经 / a ~ of authority 超越权限 / a ~ of the imagination 一阵幻想，想入非非 / a ~ of the law 对法律的滥用，枉法行为 / by a ~ of language 用牵强附会的语言 ③ (消除疲劳的)散步 ④ 一段持续的时间；一段路程；【海】一次航程：a long ~ of time 一段长时间 / over a ~ of three months 三个月以来 / travel a hard ~ of road 走一段艰难路程 ⑤[俚]徒刑；服刑期 ⑥ (赛马终点线前的)直线部分；最后阶段 ⑦弹性 III a. 弹性的：~ hosiery [总称]弹力袜 ‖at a ~ 不休息地，一口气地：He worked four hours at a ~. 他不休息地连续工作四小时。/ at full ~ 非常紧张：The workers were at full ~. 工人们非常紧张地在干活。/ on (或 upon) the ~ 紧张着：with all one's mental faculties on the ~ 全神贯注地 / put (或 set) upon the full ~ 使极度紧张，使倾注全力 / a point 见 point / ~ out 伸手；开始大踏步走 ‖'~-out n. [美](不增加或略加工资，迫使工人负担额外劳动或管理更多的机器等的)增加劳动强度的工业管理制度

stretcher ['stretʃə] n. ① 延伸器，伸张器，展宽器；(撑开鞋帽等的)撑具 ②(绷面布的)框子 ③(桌椅等脚之间的)横木，横档；(框架的)横条 ④【建】顺(砌)砖，露侧石，顺(边)砖 ⑤(救生艇上的)脚蹬 ⑥[俚]夸张话；谎言 ‖'~-'bearer n. 担架兵，担架员 / ~ bond 【建】顺砖砌合 / '~-,party n. (营救死伤人员的)担架队

strew [stru:](过去式 strewed，过去分词 strewn [stru:n] 或 strewed) vt. ① 撒，播：~ seeds in the field 在田里播种 ② 点缀，铺盖

stricken ['strikən] I strike 的过去分词 II a. ①被打中的；被击伤的 ②[常用以构成复合词]受灾的，罹难的；患病的；衰老的：a ~ area 灾区 / panic-~ 受惊的，恐慌的 / poverty-~ 贫穷不堪的 / be ~ with fever 患热症，发烧 / a man ~ in age (或 years) 年老体衰的男人 ③被刮得与量器边缘齐平的：a ~ measure of rice 平平的一量器米 ‖~ field 战场 / ~ hour 整整的一小时

strict [strikt] a. ①严格的：maintain ~ discipline 保持严格的纪律 ②严谨的，严密的，精确的：in the ~ sense 严格说来；按精确的意义(指词等) / ~ secrecy 绝密 ③[古]紧的；紧密的 ④【植】笔直的 ‖~ly ad. ~ly speaking 严格说来 / ~ness n.

stricture ['striktʃə] n. ① [常用复]苛评，责难

pass ~s on (或 upon) sb. 责难某人 ②【医】狭窄 ③束缚(物)，限制(物) ‖~d a. 狭窄的，收窄的

stride [straid] I (过去式 strode [stroud]，过去分词 stridden ['stridn] 或 strid [strid]) ❶ vi. ① 大踏步走；迈进 ② 跨；跨过：~ over a fence 跨过篱笆 ❷ vt. ① 大步走过：They strode the street. 他们大步走过街道。② 跨，骑；跨过：~ a horse 骑马 / ~ a ditch 跨过沟 II n. ① 大步，阔步；一大步的距离；[常用复][喻]进展，进步：walk with vigorous (rapid) ~s 健(快)步走 / advance in (或 with) giant ~s 大踏步前进 ②[英][复]裤子 ‖get into (或 hit, strike) one's ~ 开始上轨道；开始紧张地工作起来 / take sth. in (one's) ~ 从容地对付某事，轻快地解决某事 / take every difficulty in their ~ 他们很快地克服一切困难。‖ ~ piano 左手在琴键上大幅度掠过的爵士乐钢琴奏法

strident ['straidnt] a. 轧轧响的，刺耳的 ‖~ly ad.

strife [straif] n. 竞争；冲突；争吵；斗争：be at ~ 不和 / a civil ~ 内乱

strike [straik] I (过去式 struck [strʌk]，过去分词 struck 或 stricken ['strikən]) ❶ vt. ①打；击；撞击；攻击；冲击：~ the nail with a hammer 用锤敲钉子 / He struck his head against the stove as he fell. 他倒下时，头撞在炉子上。②(用爪)抓伤；(用毒牙)咬伤：be struck by a snake 被蛇咬伤 ③(疾病)侵袭：The herds were struck by an epidemic. 畜群受疫病侵袭。/ He was struck with fever (paralysis, pestilence). 他发烧(瘫痪，感染时疫)了 ④(钟)敲响报(时)：The huge clock of the Customs House ~s the hours. 海关大钟报时。/ The clock is striking four. 钟在敲四点。⑤(船)触；(光)落在…上，照到；(声)使…听见：The ship struck a rock. 船触礁了。/ ~ a mine 触雷 / The lamplight struck him in the face. 灯光照在他的脸上。/ A loud whistle struck his ear. 响亮的哨声传入他的耳中。⑥擦打；铸；压出，冲制；印(纸币)；盖(章)：~ a match 擦火柴 / ~ a light 打火，擦火 / ~ fire (sparks) out of a flint 从火石打出火(火花) / ~ coins 铸硬币 / ~ a medal 冲压徽章 / ~ a handstamp 盖图章 ⑦勾销；取消：~ a word through 把一个词划掉 / ~ out a few paragraphs 划掉几个段落 / His name was struck off the list. 他的名字从单子上被勾销了。/ ~ an appropriation from the budget 从预算中取消一项拨款 ⑧拍(掌)定约；定下(交易、合同等)；结算：~ hands upon a bargain 拍掌成交 / ~ a bargain 成交，定约 / ~ a balance 结算余额，结帐 ⑨打动；感动；给…以印象：The result of the experiment struck me as most significant. 在我看来，实验的结果意义十分重大。/ He was struck dumb with stage fright. 他由于怯场而讲不出话。

⑩拆除;降下(帆、旗等);把(货物)放入船舱: ~ a stage set 拆除舞台布景道具 / ~ a tent 拆除帐篷 / ~ camp 拔营,开拔
⑪罢(工): ~ work 罢工
⑫刺透;穿透;使穿透,使深入
⑬扎(根),插(根);使(插枝等)生根: The young tree has *struck* root. 这幼树已经扎根了。
⑭到达;取···方向前进: We *struck* the main road after a short drive. 行驶了一段短距离后我们就上了大道。 / They *struck* their path across the fields. 他们取道田间走去。
⑮遇见,碰到;发现: He is the most obstinate person I ever *struck*. 他是我所遇见过的人中间最固执的一个。 / It is the best children's story I have ever *struck* in years. 这是我多年来读到的最好的一篇儿童故事。 / ~ a bed 发现煤层;发现矿层 / ~ a lead 找到矿脉 / ~ oil 钻井发现石油;[喻]暴发,忽获巨利
⑯取···姿态;装出: ~ an attitude 装腔作势
⑰弹奏: ~ a lyre 弹奏七弦琴 / ~ a few chords on the piano 在钢琴上弹几个和音
⑱用斗刮刮平(高出斛口的谷物等)
⑲猛拉钓索以钩住;(鱼)咬;咬住(钓饵): ~ a fish 猛拉钓索把鱼钩住
⑳触发(电弧)
㉑(昆虫)产卵于
㉒组成(陪审团)
❷ *vi.* ①打;击;撞;打击;攻击;冲击: ~ at a nail with a hammer 用锤敲钉子 / She *struck* against the stove as she fell. 她倒下时撞在炉子上。 / fast vessels that can ~ and get away 能够打了就走的快艇
②(蛇、兽等)咬;抓
③罢工;罢课;罢市: ~ for 为···而罢工 / ~ against 为反对···而罢工
④(心脏)搏动;(光)落下;(声)被听到;(船)触礁,搁浅,下帆;(蟛)贴附: His heart *struck* heavily as he thought of the coming interview. 想到即将来临的会见时,他的心激烈地跳动起来。 / The sunbeam *struck* full on his face. 阳光正好照在他脸上。 / The ship *struck* on a reef. 船触礁了。
⑤(时钟等)敲,响,鸣: The clock was *striking*. 钟在敲着。 / He returned after two o'clock had *struck*. 他是在敲过两点钟后回来的。
⑥擦(或打)火: ~ on a tinder 擦打火绒 / The damp match won't ~. 这潮湿的火柴擦不着。
⑦刺透;穿透: A chill *struck* into the marrow of his bones. 一股寒气直透他的骨髓。 / The sunrays have *struck* through the heavy fog. 阳光冲破了浓雾。
⑧突然想到;打动;给以印象: ~ on (或 upon) an idea 突然想到一个主意 / What ~s at a first reading is its vividness and terseness. 初读时它给人的印象是生动和简洁。
⑨开始;取某一方向;朝某一方向前进: You must ~ east from here. 你应由此向东前进。 / The

road *struck* down into sand hills. 道路转入沙丘之间。 / He *struck* out across the fields. 他迈步越过田野。 / ~ into a gallop (马)开始奔驰 / ~ into a subject 突然进入某一题目
⑩勾销;取消
⑪(截下的枝)扎根;(种子)发芽
⑫降旗(表示投降)
⑬(鱼)上钩,咬住钓饵;猛拉钓索钩住鱼
⑭触发电弧;(雷电)闪击: The lightning *struck* again. 雷电再次闪击。
⑮努力,力争
II *n.* ①打;击;(尤指飞机的)攻击,进攻;(一起出击的)机组,一支打击力量: air ~s on that bridge 对那座桥的空中打击 / In the afternoon a second ~ was flown off. 下午又飞出第二批轰炸机群。
②罢工;罢课;罢市: go (或 come out) on ~ 举行罢工 / a sympathetic (或 sympathy) ~ 同情罢工(指为了声援别的罢工工人而举行的罢工) / break up a ~ 破坏罢工
③(石油、煤等矿藏的)发现;意外成功;走运
④斗刮(用来刮平斛口谷物的器具)
⑤一次铸成的全部硬币(或冲压成的全部徽章等)
⑥(鱼的)上钩;猛拉钓索
⑦【地】走向: fault ~ 断层走向 / seam ~ 矿层走向
⑧(滚木球中)第一球将木柱全部打倒(或其所得的分数);(棒球中)对于投手所投球的迎击;(投手所投的)好球,正球
⑨不利,挫折
‖*be struck all of a heap* 见 **heap** / *have two ~s against one* [口]处于绝对不利的地位 / ~ *at the root of* 见 **root**[1] / ~ *back* 回击 / ~ *down* 击倒;杀死;[喻]打倒 / ~ *home* 击中要害;取得意想的结果: The explanation *struck home.* 这解释很中肯。 / ~ *in* 插嘴 / ~ *it rich* ①发现丰富的矿藏 ②发横财;走运 / ~ *of day* 破晓,黎明 / ~ *off* ①一击而使···分离,击断 ②勾销;取消 ③印刷: ~ *off* 10,000 copies of a book 一本书印一万册 ④轻易搞成,一蹴而就: ~ *off* a poem for the occasion 即席作诗应景 ⑤清楚正确地描绘 / ~ *out* ①打;击 ②敲出;冲压成 ③搞出;做成;产生;设计成: ~ *out* a plan 搞出一个计划 / ~ *out* a line for oneself 独树一帜;自行谋生 ④划掉,勾销 ⑤尽力游泳(或滑冰): ~ *out* for the midstream 中流击水 ⑥(棒球中)三击不中退场;使(击手)三击不中而退场 / ~ *up* ①开始演奏(或歌唱);开始敲响: The band *struck up* the strains of a welcome march. 乐队开始演奏迎宾曲。 / ~ *up* an old tune 重弹老调,使开始: ~ *up* an acquaintance with sb. 与某人结交朋友 ③在(金属等)上拷花;雕出(装饰图案等) / *Strike while the iron is hot.* [谚]趁热打铁。
‖~*-a-light* *n.* (用火石的)打火器 / '~**bound** *a.* 因罢工而停顿的 / '~**breaker** *n.* 罢工破坏者,工贼 / '~**breaking** *n.* 破坏罢工 / ~ **leader** 罢

工领导人 / '~,over n. (打字中的)两字母重叠 / ~ pay 工会在罢工期内给工人的津贴

striker ['straikə] n. ①打击者 ②罢工(或罢课、罢市)者 ③铁匠的打铁助手 ④钟锤;(枪的)撞针 ⑤叉鱼的人 ⑥(美军)陆军军官的勤务兵

striking ['straikiŋ] a. ①打击的;攻击的;突击的;鸣响的: a ~ clock 报时的钟 【军】突击部队(机动防御的主力) ②罢工(或罢市)的:~ workers 罢工工人 ③显著的,引人注目的;惊人的: a ~ proof (contrast) 显著的证明(对比) ||~ly ad. 显著地,引人注目地;惊人地 / ~ness n. 显著;惊人 || ~ distance 【军】攻击距离

string [striŋ] I n. ①线;细绳;带子;[美]鞋带(=shoe~): a (piece of) ~ 一根绳子 / a ball of ~ 一团线 / an apron ~ 围裙带 ②(穿珠、钱等的)串线,串珠;操纵木偶的线;一串,一行,一串: a ~ of cash 一贯钱 / a ~ of buses 一长串公共汽车 / a ~ of lies (excuses) 一连串谎话(借口) ③(植物的)纤维(尤指荚壳的接缝处),筋 ④(弓、乐器等的)弦: the ~s [总称]乐队的弦乐器(或弦乐部分) / touch the ~s 奏弦乐器 ⑤[复]附带条件: no ~s attached 不附带条件 / aid without ~s 无条件援助 ⑥【建】短梯级;束带层 (= ~course) ⑦属于一个马主的一群赛马 II (strung [strʌŋ] ❶ vt. ①(用线、绳)缚,扎,挂;(用线)穿,串起;使排成一列: ~ a parcel 扎包裹 / ~ shoes 缚鞋带 / ~ beads 串珠 / These houses were strung along the thoroughfare. 这些房子沿着大街排成一行。②上弦于(弓、乐器)上;调(乐器)的弦 ③抽去(豆荚等)的筋 ④伸展,拉直: ~ a cable 拉直电缆 ⑤使(精神等)紧张,使作好准备;使兴奋,使敏感(up): The athlete was strung up before the race. 运动员在赛跑前进入了竞技状态。/ a highly strung (或 a high-strung) person 神经过敏的人,易激动的人 ⑥[美口]戏弄,愚弄;欺骗(along) ❷ vi. 成线索状;连成一串;排成一行;排成一行前进 ||be in leading ~s 处于幼稚阶段;象幼孩一样受着管教 / harp on one (或 the same) ~ 反复说(或写)同一件事,老调重弹: You are always harping on the same ~. 你总是老调重弹。/ have a second ~ to one's bow 有别的手段,有后备 / have sb. on a ~ 操纵某人 / have two ~s to one's bow 有两手准备 / pull the ~s 在幕后拉线,在幕后操纵 / ~ along with 陪伴;与……一致;追随,忠于 / ~ sb. up [口]吊死某人 / the first (second) ~ 第一个(第二个)办法(或靠山) / touch a ~ 触动心弦 ||~ed a. ①有弦的;由弦所发出的:~ed instruments 弦乐器 / ~ed music 弦乐 ②用弦缚成的;用弦固住的 / ~er n. 【建】纵梁;楼梯基;(铁路的)纵向轨枕 ②(乐器等的)上弦工人;制造(或出售)弓弦的人 / ~less a. 无弦的 ||~ bag 网线袋 / ~ band 弦乐队 / '~bark n. =stringy-bark / ~ bean ①菜豆 ②[口]瘦长条子 / '~board n. 【建】楼基盖板 / '~course n. 【建】束带层 / ~ electrometer 【无】弦线式静电计

~halt n. (马的)跛行症 / '~piece n. 纵梁;楼梯基 / ~ quartet(te) 弦乐四重奏,弦乐四重奏曲

stringent ['strindʒənt] a. ①严格的,严厉的: make ~ rules 订严格的规则 ②(银根)紧的,(货币与信贷数量)缺少的: The money market is very ~. 货币市场上银根奇紧。③令人信服的,有说服力的 ||~ly ad. / ~ness n.

stringy ['striŋi] a. ①象线的(或绳的);纤维的;多筋的: ~ meat 多筋的肉 ②(液体)粘性的: ~ molasses 粘性的糖蜜 ||stringiness n. ||'~bark n. 一种澳洲桉树

strip [strip] I (stripped; stripping) ❶ vt. ①剥,剥去,剥光:~ the bark off (或 from) a tree 剥去树皮 / ~ paper from a wall 撕去墙上的纸 / ~ sb. to the skin 剥光某人的衣服 / ~ oneself to the waist 赤膊 ②夺去,剥夺(财产、荣誉、权力、职务等);掠夺;使赤贫 ③拆卸;完全除去…的附属物: ~ a room of furniture 搬光房间内的家具 / ~ a ship for action 清除舰上不必要的杂物准备投入战斗 / ~ a tree 砍去树枝(或削去树皮) / The locusts stripped the fields. 蝗虫吃光了田里的庄稼。④折断(齿轮)的牙;磨掉(螺钉、螺栓等)的螺纹;由于腔速过高擦去(子弹)的皮 ⑤挤掉(牛)的最后一滴奶:~ a cow 挤干牛的奶 ⑥去(烟叶等)的茎 ⑦从…中删除不必要的内容 ⑧【化】使去色;(通过蒸馏等)除去…中的挥发性成分 ⑨把…撕成带形;把…切成细条 ⑩撕纸条卷(拍纸簿的台边) ❷ vi. ①脱去衣服,脱光衣服:~ for a bath 脱衣洗澡 ②(子弹)不旋转地打出去,直脱,擦去弹皮 ③(螺丝钉)磨损螺纹 ④表演脱衣舞 II n. ①条,带;细长片: a ~ of paper (cloth, board) 纸(布,板)条 / a ~ of territory 狭长地带 ②条幅式侦察照片;(报纸等的)连环漫画 ③【空】简易机场(=air~或 landing ~) ④【冶】带钢 ⑤(集邮薄上的)一行(一列)邮票 ⑥(子弹)的直脱 ⑦【矿】露天开采;[英]捣矿机排矿沉淀槽 ⑧支板;(舞台等上排列安放四至六只灯泡的)插座条 ⑨[复]无茎及中肋的烟叶 ⑩脱衣舞 (=striptease) ||leave a ~ [美俚]突然停车,急刹车(形象化用语,指停车过快而擦下一块轮胎皮) / '~,car,toon n. 连环漫画 / ~ cropping 【农】带状播种(在坡地上轮流以带状种植两种不同植物,以减少土地的被侵蚀) / '~-leaf n. (去茎的)烟叶 / '~light n. (舞台照明用的)长条状灯 / ~ mine 露天矿 / ~ mining 露天采采(一种不爱护矿藏资源、一味追求利润的开采法)

stripe [straip] I n. ①条纹,条子: ~ weave 【纺】条纹组织 / the Stars and Stripes 星条旗(美国国旗) / the ~s of a tiger (zebra) 虎(斑马)纹 ②条纹布 ③【军】制服上表示等级的条纹,道道: get (lose) a ~ 升(降)一级 ④(人的)类型,类别 ⑤[复]犯人穿的横条服,囚衣 ⑥[复][口]虎(马戏团中用语) ⑦(一道)鞭痕;(一记)鞭挞;(一记)抽打;[复]鞭挞 II vt. 给…划上条纹;使

成条纹状 ‖*wear* (*the*) ～**s** [美俚](穿横条子囚衣)坐牢 ‖～**d** *a.* ①有条纹的: Do you like this ～**d** stuff? 你喜欢这种条子衣料(或衣服)吗? ②[美俚]喝醉的 ‖'～**d-pants** *a.* (在礼仪、社交活动等方面)过于注重形式的

stripling ['striplin] *n.* 年轻人,小伙子

strive [straiv] (过去式 strove [strouv] 或 strived, 过去分词 striven ['strivn] 或 strived) *vi.* ①努力,奋斗,力求: ～ *for* further progress 继续求进步 / ～ *after* a lofty ideal 为一个崇高的理想而奋斗 ②斗争;反抗: ～ *against* (或 *with*) difficulties(oppression)与困难(压迫)作斗争 ‖～**r** *n.* 奋斗者

stroke¹ [strouk] **I** *n.* ①打;击,敲: the ～ of a hammer 锤击 / He split the log with one ～ of the axe. 他一斧劈开了那木料。/ receive several ～s of the whip 被鞭打几下 ②(划船、游泳的)一划,划法;尾桨手,领桨;(网球、板球等的)一抽,一击,打法: row a fast (slow) ～ (划船)划得快(慢) / set the ～ 定下每分钟划桨的次数 / the breast (back, side) ～ 俯(仰,侧)泳 / swim with a fast ～ 游得快 / invent a new ～ in cricket 发明板球的一种新打法 ③(写字、绘画的)一笔,一划;笔触;(写作的)手法: dash off a picture with a few ～s 几笔就画成一张画 / He writes with firm ～s. 他笔力道劲。/ end up the story with a clever ～ 以灵巧的一笔结束了那故事 / You could do it with a ～ of the pen. 你大笔一挥就行了。④(钟的)敲声,鸣声: on the ～ of three 敲三点的时候 / He was here *on the* ～. 他准时到了这里。⑤突来的一击,闪击;(病)突然发作;中风,麻痹: a ～ of lightning 闪电一击 / What a ～ of luck (misfortune)! 真走运(倒霉)! / a ～ of paralysis (或 a paralytic ～) 突然瘫痪 / have a ～ 中风 ⑥一举,一着,一次努力;一次努力的成果: a great ～ of diplomacy 外交上重要的一着 / a good ～ of business 一桩赚钱的买卖(或合算的交易) / He has not done a ～ of work today. 他今天没做一点事。⑦(心脏的)跳动;脉搏;(鸟翼的)一拍 ⑧【机】冲程,行程 **II** *vt.* ①划短横于: ～ the t's 写 t 时划短横 ②划线勾销,删掉 (*out*): ～ *out* the superfluous words in the article 划掉文章里的多余词语 ③充当(划艇的)尾桨手 ④击,抽(球) ‖*a finishing* ～ 最后致命的一击;最后的一笔 / *a gallery* ～ (赛球或演戏时)卖弄技巧的表演,为博得喝采的表演 / *a* ～ *above* [口]比…高明一些,胜(人)一筹: He is a ～ *above* me. 他比我高明些。/ *at one* ～ 一笔,一举: write sth. off *at one* ～ 一笔勾销某事 / *keep* ～ 有节奏地划桨 / *Little* ～s *fell great oaks.* [谚]水滴石穿。‖～ **oar** [罕]尾桨;尾桨手

stroke² [strouk] **I** *vt.* (用手)抚,摩,捋: ～ a cat 抚猫 / ～ one's beard 捋胡子 / ～ the hair down 把头发掠平 **II** *n.* 抚,摩,捋 ‖～ **sb. down** 平息某人的怒气 / ～ **sb.** (或 *sb.'s hair*) *the wrong*

way 触怒某人,犯某人之忌 ‖～**r** *n.* 抚摩者;安抚者 / **strokingly** *ad.* 抚摩地;安抚地

stroll [stroul] **I** ❶ *vi.* ①散步,溜达,闲逛 ②(为找活干等)四处流浪;巡回演出: ～*ing* players 流浪艺人 ❷ *vt.* ①散步于,在…溜达 ②跋涉于;流浪于 **II** *n.* 散步,溜达: have (或 take, go for) a ～ 散步

strong [stron] **I** *a.* ①强壮的,强健的;坚固的,牢固的: a ～ constitution 强壮的体格 / ～ as a bull 力大如牛 / feel quite ～ again (病后)感到精力已经恢复 / ～ cloth 牢的布 / a ～ fortress 坚固的要塞 ②(性格)坚强的,坚定的;(态度、作风)坚决的;强烈的,猛烈的,强硬的: a ～ character 坚强的性格 / have ～ nerves 有胆量(指不易受惊吓) / a ～ faith (或 belief) 坚定的信仰 / be ～ *for* (*against*) sth. 坚决赞成(反对)某事物 / a ～ opinion 坚决的意见 / a ～ protest 强烈的抗议 / ～ measures 强硬措施 / a ～ contrast 强烈的对照 / a ～ situation (故事、戏剧等中)动人的场面 / a ～ literary style 泼辣的文风 ③(兵员、人数)达…的;(势力)强大的;资力雄厚的;强有力的: How many ～ are you? 你们有多少人员? / an army a million ～ 百万雄师 / a ten thousand ～ rally (也作 a ten-thousand-～ rally) 万人大会 / a ～ nation 强国 / a ～ bank 资力雄厚的银行 / a ～ cast of actors 演员的坚强阵容 / a ～ candidate 强有力的候选人 / a ～ argument (evidence) 有力的论点(证据) ④(能力)优良的,擅长的: one's ～ point 某人的长处,优点 / He is ～ *in* English. 他长于英语。⑤烈性的;浓厚的,冲鼻(难闻)的;难消化的: ～ drinks 烈性饮料(如酒等) / ～ tea 浓茶 / ～ cheese 浓味乳酪 / a ～ colour 强烈的色彩 / ～ breath 口臭 / ～ meat 难消化的肉;[喻]深奥的理论 ⑥坚挺的,价格稳步上升的: a ～ market 坚挺的市场价格,看涨的行情 ⑦【语】强变化的: a ～ verb 不规则动词 **II** *ad.* =～**ly** ‖*by the* ～ **arm** (或 **hand**) 强制地 / *come* (或 *go*) *it* ～ [俚] ①过分地做;做得过火 ②尽力干 ③夸大,过甚其词 / *come on* ～ [美俚]给人以强烈印象(常指带有盛气凌人的架势) / *come out* ～ [口]以坚决的姿态发言(或行动) / *go* ～ [俚](体力)强健的;(情况)良好,兴旺;有力地继续 / *go* ～ *on* 竭力主张 ‖～**ish** *a.* 有点儿强的 / ～**ly** *ad.* 强壮地;坚固地;强烈地 ‖～ **arm** 强制力;暴力;高压手段 / '～**-arm** *a.* 强暴的: ～*-arm* methods 强暴的方法 *vt.* 用暴力对付; 抢劫 / '～**-bodied** *a.* 体力强壮的 / '～**box** *n.* 保险箱 / '～**'hearted** *a.* 勇敢的 / '～**hold** *n.* 要塞,堡垒;[喻]据点,大本营 / ～ **language** 强硬措词;骂人话 / ～ **man** ①大力士 ②有才干的人,能担负责任的人 ③有实力者;实权派;铁腕人物 / '～**-'minded** *a.* 有独立见解(或主张)的;意志坚强的 / '～**point** *n.* 防守上的战术据点 / ～ **room** ①(贮藏金钱、宝物的)保险库 ②精神病人专用的保安房间 / ～ **suit** ① 一手同花色的

的长牌 ②拿手好戏,擅长的事物 / '~-'willed *a.*
意志坚强的

struck [strʌk] I strike 的过去式和过去分词 II *a.*
因罢工而关闭的,受到罢工影响的: a ~ factory
因罢工而关闭的工厂

structural ['strʌktʃərəl] *a.* 结构(上)的;构造的;
建筑上的;组织上的: ~ stability 结构稳定性 /
~ timber 建筑用的木材 / ~ unemployment 由
于社会经济结构所造成的失业 / ~ linguistics 结
构语言学 / ~ formula【化】结构式 ‖~ly *ad.*

structure ['strʌktʃə] I *n.* ①结构;构造;组织: soil
~ 土壤结构 / the ~ of the human body 人体构
造 / the ~ of a plant 一种植物的构造 / the ~
of society 社会结构 / economic ~ 经济组织,经
济结构 / simplify the administrative ~ 精简行
政机构 ②结构物;建筑物: a magnificent marble
~ 宏伟的大理石建筑物 / a temporary wooden
~ 临时性的木棚 ③【心】直接经验中显现的结构
性(或整体性);格式塔(指组织结构、式样或整体)
II *vt.* 构造;组织;建造 ‖~d *a.* 有结构的 /
~less *a.* 无结构的;无细胞结构的: a ~less
membrane 无细胞结构膜

struggle ['strʌgl] I *n.* ①斗争,奋斗: carry on
the fine tradition of hard ~ 发扬艰苦奋斗的优
良传统 / the ~ for existence 生存竞争 ②挣扎:
be in one's death-bed ~ 进行垂死挣扎 ③【哲】
斗争性 II *vi.* ①斗争;奋斗,努力: ~ against
(或 with) difficulties 与困难作斗争 / ~ for national independence 为民族独立而斗争 / ~ to
overcome one's shortcomings 努力克服自己的缺
点 ②奋力前进;挣扎: ~ through the snowstorm
冒着暴风雪前进 / The lamplight ~d out through
the fog. 灯光勉强透过迷雾照射出来。/ The
sick baby cried and ~d in its mother's arms.
病孩哭闹着,在母亲怀抱中挣扎。/ ~ for breath
困难地喘着气 ‖~r *n.* 斗争者; 奋斗者; 挣扎着
的人 / **struggling** *a.* 奋斗的(尤指为生计、名
声、地位等)

strum [strʌm] I (strummed; strumming) ❶ *vt.*
乱弹; 乱奏, 拙劣地弹奏: ~ a guitar 乱弹吉
他 / ~ a tune on the piano 在钢琴上拙劣地弹
一个曲子 ❷ *vi.* 在琴上乱弹, 乱奏 (on) II *n.* 乱
弹(声): the ~ of typewriters 打字机的嗒嗒声
‖**strummer** *n.* 乱弹琴的人

strung [strʌŋ] string 的过去式和过去分词

strut[1] [strʌt] I (strutted; strutting) ❶ *vi.* ①肿
胀, 鼓起 ②大摇大摆地走, 架子十足地走: ~ into
a room 神气活现地走进房间 ❷ *vt.* 炫耀(服装、
珠宝等) II *n.* 高视阔步 ‖~ one's stuff 见 stuff
‖**strutter** *n.* 高视阔步者 / **strutting** *a.* 肿胀
的;高视阔步的

strut[2] [strʌt] I *n.* 支柱, 撑杆; 压杆; 轨撑: inter-
plane ~s【空】(双翼机的)翼间支柱 II (strutted;
strutting) *vt.* 支撑; 撑开; 给⋯加撑杆 ‖'~beam
n.【建】支梁

stub [stʌb] I *n.* ①树桩, 残根, 残株 ②残余部分,

残端: the ~ of a cigar 雪茄烟烟蒂 / a pencil ~
(用剩的)铅笔头 ③用秃了的笔 ④[美]票根,存
根: the ~s of a checkbook 支票簿存根 II (stubbed; stubbing) *vt.* ①连根挖(或拔); 紧沿着树根
砍(或锯) ②清除(地)里的树根(或草根) ③碰踢:
~ one's toe and fall 绊了一跤 ④捻熄, 踩熄: ~
out a cigarette 捻熄(或踩熄)香烟 ‖**stubbed** *a.*
树根样的;似树桩的 ‖**mortise**【建】
短粗榫眼 / ~ **nail** 短而粗的铁钉; 破损的马掌
钉 / ~ **tenon**【建】短粗榫

stubble ['stʌbl] *n.* ①庄稼收割后余留的部分,茬
②=~ field ③短发; 短髭; 残梗状的东西
‖**stubbly** *a.* ①布满茬儿的 ②残梗状的 ‖~
field 收割后(布满茬儿)的田地

stubborn ['stʌbən] *a.* ①顽固的,执拗的,不听调动
的: as ~ as a mule 象骡子一样顽固 ②顽强的;
坚持的: ~ resistance 顽强的抵抗 ③难对付的,
棘手的: a ~ illness 顽疾 / ~ problems 棘手的
问题 ‖~ly *ad.* / ~ness *n.*

stubby ['stʌbi] *a.* ①多残株的 ②似残株的, 粗短
的, 矮胖的; 粗钝的: ~ fingers 粗而短的手指 /
an old ~ pencil 一枝用剩的短铅笔 ③短而密的:
~ bristles 短而密的猪鬃

stucco ['stʌkou] I ([复] stucco(e)s) *n.* ①拉毛水
泥, 灰墁 ②(拉)毛粉饰 II *vt.* (用灰泥)粉饰, 粉
刷 ‖'~work *n.* (拉)毛粉饰

stuck [stʌk] stick 的过去式和过去分词 ‖'~-'up
a. [口]势利的;自大的, 傲慢的

stud[1] [stʌd] I *n.* ①大头钉; (装饰在大门、盾牌或皮
件等表面的)饰钉 ②领扣; 衬衫前胸饰钮 ③【机】
双端螺栓, 柱(头)螺栓; 轴, 端轴颈, 销子; 中介轴
④【建】壁桩, 墙筋, 中间柱 ⑤房间净高度 ⑥链
档: a ~ link 有档链环 II (studded; studding)
vt. ①装饰钉于, 用大头钉装饰(或保护) ②散布;
密布;点缀: Rocks ~ the hillside. 岩石一块一
块突出在山边。/ a sea studded with islands 岛
屿密布的海面 ③给(房屋或墙壁)加壁骨(或柱
子) ‖'~work *n.*【建】壁骨工作物

stud[2] [stʌd] *n.* ①种马, 留种的雄畜; (为繁殖、赛
跑、打猎等而饲养的)马群 ②种畜畜牧场; 种马
饲养场 ‖*at* (或 *in*) ~ 供留种用(尤指雄畜)
‖'~book *n.* (犬、马等的)血统记录簿 / ~ **farm**
育马场; 种马饲养场; 配种站 / '~horse *n.* 种
马 / ~ **poker** [美]一种纸牌戏

studio ['stju:diou] *n.* ①(画家、雕刻师、摄影者、艺
术家等的)工作室: a photo graphic ~ 摄影
室 ②电影制片厂: a movie ~ 电影制片厂
③(无线电、电视)播音室, 演播室 ‖~ **apartment**
①一套小型公寓房间 (一般是一个房间, 外加浴
室和小厨房) ②工作室公寓(指公寓中有一间窗
户宽大、高平顶、类似艺术家工作室的房间) / ~
couch 三用沙发

studious ['stju:djəs] *a.* ①勤学的, 用功的 ②认真
的; 热心的: be ~ to do sth. 认真做某事 / be ~
of doing sth. 非常想做某事 ③刻意的, 故意的:
with ~ politeness 故作有礼地 ‖~ly *ad.* /
~ness *n.*

study ['stʌdi] **I** *n.* ①学习;研究;[常用复](在学校的)肄业: the ~ of a foreign language 外国语的学习 / investigation and ~ 调查研究 / make a ~ of history 研究历史 / intelligence ~ 【军】敌情研究 / pursue one's *studies* 求学,肄业 ②研究项目;(值得)研究的对象;学科;论文: Fluid dynamics is his chief ~. 流体动力学是他的主要研究项目。/ His face was a perfect ~. 他的脸真值得研究(或真有意思)。③试画,试作;习作;【音】练习曲: a ~ of a head 头像试画 ④[常与形容词连用]台词记得…的演员: a good (slow) ~ 台词背得好(慢)的演员 ⑤沉思,默想[现多用 brown ~]: There he sat for an hour *in a* ~. 他坐在那里沉思了一个小时(而不觉周围事情的发生)。⑥意图;努力;努力的对象: It is his constant ~ to serve the customers well. 他经常努力设法好好为顾客服务。⑦书房;(个人的)事务室: You will find him in his ~. 你在他的书房里可以找到他。**II ❶** *vt.* ①学,学习;研究: ~ law (French) 学习法律(法语) / In ~*ing* a problem, we must shun subjectivity, one-sidedness and superficiality. 研究问题,忌带主观性、片面性和表面性。②考虑,细想;细看,细察: We shall ~ your problem. 我们将考虑你的问题。③计划,企图 ④记熟,背诵(台词等) **❷** *vi.* ①学习 ②努力,力图: ~ to avoid making mistakes 力图不犯错误 ③[方]沉思,默想 / *be in a brown* ~ 沉思,默想,空想,幻想 / *out* ①研究出;解决: He has *studied* out the mystery. 他解开了这个神秘事件。/ ~ *out* a problem 解决一个问题 ②设计,计划出,拟定: ~ *out* a plan 拟出一个计划 / ~ *up* 用功预备考试(或其他工作) / ~ *up on* [美口]对…进行仔细的研究 ‖~ *hall* ①学生自修室 ②学生白天自修时间 / '~-in *n.* [美]听课抗议;听课示威(黑人学生或同情黑人的白人学生进入种族歧视的学校听课,以表示抗议)

stuff [stʌf] **I** *n.* ①材料,原料;木料;资料;东西: feeding ~s 饲料 / green (或 garden) ~ 蔬菜 / sweet ~ 饼,点心 / household ~ [古]家具 / doctor's ~ [口]药品 / inch ~ 一时厚的木板 / thick ~ 四时以上厚的木板 / ~ knots (造纸用)浆块 / collect the ~ for a report 搜集报告的资料 / This book is good (poor, sorry) ~. 这本书好(不好,蹩脚)。②素质,本质;要素: What ~ is he made of? 他是什么样的人?(或:他品质如何?) / He has good ~ in him. 他品质优良。③织品(尤指毛的);呢绒: ~ goods 毛织品 / a dress made of ~ 呢女衣 / a hat ~ 呢帽 / silk ~ 丝织品 ④废物;废话: Take that ~ away. 把那废物拿走。/ None of your ~! 别说废话! / *Stuff* and nonsense! 胡说八道!(或:废话!)⑤填充料;【船】(焦油、松节油和脂)的混合涂料(用作木船防腐剂)⑥枪弹,炮弹 ⑦[the ~][口]金钱,现钱;任何现成备用的东西 ⑧[美俚]毒品,麻醉剂 ⑨[美俚]赃物;走私货,走私威士忌酒 **II ❶** *vt.* ①装;把…装满;填,塞;把…塞进: The shops are ~*ed* full of goods. 商店里备货充足。/ a bag *with* things 把袋子装满东西 / ~ a child *with* food 喂饱孩子 / a ~*ed* pillow (以木棉或羽毛等)填制的枕头 / an article ~*ed with cliches* 充塞着陈词滥调的文章 / ~ *up* a hole 填洞 / My nose is ~*ed up.* 我鼻子塞住了。②(为制作标本)剥制: a ~*ed* tiger (bird) 剥制的老虎(鸟) ③[美俚]欺骗;愚弄;向…贩卖假货: Don't believe him — he's ~*ing* you. 别相信他,他在骗你。/ ~ sb. *with* lies 用谎话欺骗某人 ④[美]以假造的选票充塞(投票箱) **❷** *vi.* 饱食,吃得过多(或过快) ‖*cut the rough* [美俚]停止粗鲁的言行 / *Do your* ~! [美俚]①拿出你本领来吧!(或:显显你的身手吧!)②干你的事吧! / *know one's* ~ [俚]对本分的工作很内行,精通自己的业务 / *strut* (或 *do*) *one's* ~ [美俚]显身手,表演拿手杰作 / *That's the* ~ *to give 'em* (或 *the troops*). [俚]这真是个好主意。②(为制作标本)‖~*er* *n.* ①填塞工人 ②[俚]贩卖假货的人 / ~*ed shirt* ①自命不凡的顽固派;神气十足的讨厌鬼 ②[美俚]有钱的人,有地位的人 / ~ *gown* [英] ①(旧时)资历较浅的律师穿的毛质长袍 ②资历较浅的律师

stuffing ['stʌfiŋ] *n.* ①填塞 ②(枕、被、垫子等的)填塞料,(塞在鸡、鸭等肚子里的)填馅;填充剂;填料: metallic ~ 金属填料 ③(鸟兽的)剥制 ‖*knock the* ~ *out of sb.* ①挫败某人的傲气(或锐气)②(疾病等)使某人虚弱,使某人疲倦 ‖~ *box* 【机】填充函,填料函

stuffy ['stʌfi] *a.* ①不通气的,窒息的;闷热的: a ~ room 闷热的房间 ②(人或事物)呆滞的,乏味的 ③愠怒的,绷着脸的 ④固步自封的,自以为是的 ‖*stuffily ad. / stuffiness n.*

stull [stʌl] *n.* ①【矿】横梁,横撑 ②支柱

stultify ['stʌltifai] *vt.* ①使显得愚蠢,使显得荒谬可笑 ②使无效;使无价值: His present behaviour *stultifies* his previous efforts. 他目前的行为使他过去的努力全白费了。③【律】声明(某人)精神错乱因而不负法律责任: ~ oneself 自己声明精神错乱 ‖*stultification* [,stʌltifi'keiʃən] *n.*

stumble ['stʌmbl] **I ❶** *vi.* ①绊一下脚;绊跌,绊倒: ~ over (或 against) a stump 在树桩上绊了一下脚 ②犯错误;失足,走入迷路 ③蹒跚 ④结巴地说话;踌躇,迟疑: ~ through a recitation 结结巴巴地背诵 / ~ over one's words 结结巴巴地说话 / ~ at a step 对某一步骤踌躇不决 ⑤偶然碰见,偶尔发现 (upon, across): ~ upon an evidence in favour of one's theory 偶然得到了一个有利于自己的理论的证据 **❷** *vt.* ①使绊倒;使失足 ②使困惑: The problem ~s him. 这问题使他困惑不解。**II** *n.* ①绊倒 ②错误 ‖*stumblingly ad.* ‖'~*bum n.* [美俚]①笨手笨脚的人;无能力的人 ②喝醉酒的(或技巧低劣的)拳师 ③街头流浪汉,酗酒鬼 / *stumbling block* 障碍物,绊脚石

stump[1] [stʌmp] **I** ***n.*** ①树桩,根株 ②残余部分,残干: a cigarette ~ 香烟蒂头 / a pencil ~ (用剩的)铅笔头 / the ~ of a limb 残肢 ③(美国竞选时在野外演说的)树桩讲台 ④[口]挑战,考验 ⑤[复][谑]腿,脚 ⑥(板球)三柱门的一柱 **II** ❶ ***vt.*** ①截去(树)的干,使成根株 ②清除(田地)的树桩 ③向…挑战,干犯;使惶惑,难住: ~ the experts 难倒专家们 ④[美口]游历(某地区)作政治演说(尤指竞选时) ⑤以笨重的脚步走过(地方) ⑥碰踢: ~ one's toe on (或 against) sth. 把脚趾碰在某物上 ❷ ***vi.*** ①笨重地行走 ②[美口]游历各地作政治演说 ‖***be*** (或 ***go***) ***on the ~*** (或 ***take the ~***) [口]游历各地作政治演说 / ***on the ~s*** (或 ***on a row of ~s***) [口]在困难中,处于窘境 / ***stir one's ~s*** [口]赶快,快走 / ***~ up*** [英俚]付出所需要的钱;拿出(一笔钱) / ***up a ~*** [口]处境尴尬;茫然失措 ‖**'~-ˌjumper** ***n.*** [俚] ①=~ speaker ②农民 / **~ speaker, ~ orator** 树桩演说家 / **~ speaking, ~ oratory** 树桩演说(术) / **~ speech**(一次)树桩演说

stump[2] [stʌmp] **I** ***n.*** (用来给垩笔画或铅笔画画阴影的)皮(或纸)做的锥形擦笔 **II** ***vt.*** 用擦笔调整(垩笔画或铅笔画)的色调

stumpy ['stʌmpi] **I** ***a.*** ①多树桩的 ②桩状的,粗短的: a ~ man 矮胖人 / a ~ pencil 粗而短的铅笔 / a ~ tail 短而粗的尾巴 **II** ***n.*** ①矮胖的人 ②[英]钱 ‖**stumpily** ***ad.*** / **stumpiness** ***n.***

stun [stʌn] **I** (stunned; stunning) ***vt.*** ①把…打晕,使晕眩: be *stunned* by a blow 被打晕过去 ②使震聋 ③使大吃一惊,使不知所措 **II** ***n.*** ①晕眩 ②惊人的事物;猛击

stunt[1] [stʌnt] **I** ***vt.*** 阻碍…的发育(或成长): trees *~ed* in growth 矮树,生长受阻的树 / a *~ed* adult 发育不全的成年人 **II** ***n.*** ①发育迟缓 ②矮小的人;矮小的东西(如树木等)

stunt[2] [stʌnt] **I** ***n.*** ①[口]惊人的表演,绝技: an acrobatic ~ 杂技的绝招 / a ~ of agility 巧功夫 / a ~ of strength 硬功夫 / ~ flying 特技飞行 ②花招,噱头,手段,手腕: pull off a ~ 耍花招 / advertising *~s* 广告噱头 **II** ***vi.*** 作惊人表演,使绝招 ‖**~ man** 拍摄危险镜头时做电影演员替身的杂技演员

stupefy ['stju:pifai] ***vt.*** ①使麻木,使失感觉 ②使惊得发呆,使呆若木鸡 ‖**stupefier** ***n.*** 使惊呆者

stupendous [stju(:)'pendəs] ***a.*** 巨大的,惊人的,了不起的: a ~ achievement 伟大的成就 / a ~ error 大错 / a ~ structure 巨大的建筑物 ‖**~ly** ***ad.*** / **~ness** ***n.***

stupid ['stju:pid] **I** ***a.*** ①愚蠢的,笨的: a ~ person 笨蛋 / a ~ idea 笨主意 ②感觉迟钝的;麻痹的: ~ with sleep (drink) 睡(酒喝)得昏昏沉沉的 ③乏味的,无聊的: a ~ performance (book) 乏味的表演(书) **II** ***n.*** [口]傻瓜,笨蛋 ‖***as ~ as an owl*** 笨透了 ‖**~ly** ***ad.*** / **~ness** ***n.***

stupidity [stju(:)'piditi] ***n.*** ①愚蠢,愚笨 ②愚蠢的行为(或想法、话等)

stupor ['stju:pə] ***n.*** ①昏迷,恍惚,不省人事: fall into a drunken ~ 醉得不省人事 ②麻木,僵呆 ‖**~ous** ['stju:pərəs] ***a.***

sturdy[1] ['stə:di] ***a.*** ①强健的,茁壮的;坚实的: a ~ lad 强健的小伙子 / a ~ plant 茁壮的植物 / ~ cloth 牢的布料 / ~ knowledge 真才实学 / ~ common sense 健全的常识 ②坚定的,坚强的,刚毅不屈的: ~ resistance 坚强的抵抗 ‖**sturdily** ***ad.*** / **sturdiness** ***n.***

sturdy[2] ['stə:di] ***n.*** (羊的)晕倒病

stutter ['stʌtə] **I** ❶ ***vt.*** 结结巴巴地说出: ~ (out) sth. 结结巴巴地说某事 ❷ ***vi.*** 结结巴巴地说话,口吃地说话 **II** ***n.*** 口吃 ‖**~er** ['stʌtərə] ***n.*** 口吃者,说话结巴者 / **~ing** ['stʌtəriŋ] ***n.*** 口吃,结巴 / **~ingly** ['stʌtəriŋli] ***ad.*** (说话)结结巴巴地

sty[1] [stai] **I** ([复] sties 或 styes) ***n.*** ①猪圈,猪栏 ②[喻]肮脏的房子(或地方) **II** ❶ ***vt.*** 把…关在猪圈里(或猪圈似的地方) ❷ ***vi.*** 住在猪圈里

sty[2], **stye** [stai] ([复] sties 或 styes) ***n.*** 【医】睑腺炎,麦粒肿

style [stail] **I** ***n.*** ①风格,作风: a democratic ~ 民主作风 / keep to the ~ of hard struggle and plain living 保持艰苦奋斗的作风 ②文体;文风;语调: the epic (lyric, prose) ~ 史诗(抒情诗,散文)体 / a florid ~ with little content 缺乏内容的华丽文风 ③风度;时髦: do things in ~ 事情做得出色(或体面堂皇) / live in (grand) ~ 生活豪华 / be out of ~ 不合时式,不时髦 ④式样;类型;记时方式: hats in all sizes and *~s* 各种尺寸和式样的帽子 / the Old *Style* 西洋旧历(略作 O. S.) / the New *Style* 新历(即现在通用的阳历,略作 N. S.) ⑤称号,称呼 ⑥(古人在蜡板上写字用的)铁笔,尖笔;[诗]笔,铅笔;雕刻刀;唱机的唱针;日晷仪的时针 ⑦【动】尾片;铗下器;节芒;尾须;产卵器;【植】花柱 **II** ***vt.*** ①称呼;命名: They *~d* him poet. 他们称他为诗人。/ a self-*~d* authority 一个自命的权威 ②使符合时式;使成为时髦: ~ a manuscript 把文稿修改成流行的文体 ③设计: ~ new cars 设计新型汽车 ‖***cramp sb.'s ~*** [俚]使某人受拘束而不能正常发挥其平时的才能 / ***have enough of that ~ of thing*** 这种事已经受够了 / ***the (big) bowwow ~*** 武断的语调(或笔调) / ***The ~ is the man.*** [谚]文如其人。‖**'~book** ***n.*** 式样书,样本: a dress-maker's *~book* 服装式样本

stylish ['stailiʃ] ***a.*** 时髦的,时式的;漂亮的: ~ garments 式样新颖的服装 ‖**~ly** ***ad.*** / **~ness** ***n.***

stylist ['stailist] ***n.*** ①文体家;文体批评家 ②(服装、家具等的)设计师 ③以动作正确优美著称的运动员

stylistics [stai'listiks] [复] ***n.*** [用作单或复]文体学;风格学

stylus ['stailəs] ([复] styli ['stailai] 或 styluses) ***n.*** ①(古人在蜡板上写字用的)尖笔,铁笔 ②(誊写

用) 铁笔; (唱机) 唱针; 描画针; (日晷) 指时针 ③杆剂; 花柱; 针突; 生殖器鞘; 产卵管

suave [swɑ:v, sweiv] *a.* ①温和的, 和蔼的; 文雅的 ②(酒、药等)平和的 ③讨好人的, 巴结人的 ‖**~ly** *ad.* / **suavity** ['swæviti, 'sweiviti] *n.*

sub[1] [sʌb] *a.* 附属的, 次级的: a ~ post office 邮政支局

sub[2] [sʌb] I *n.* ①代替者; 代替物 (substitute 的缩略) ②[美俚](球队等的)候补队员 II (subbed; subbing) ❶ *vi.* [口] 做代替者, 做替工 (*for*) ❷ *vt.* [美俚]代替…进行比赛

sub[3] [sʌb] I *n.* 【摄】(促使感光乳剂固着于片基的) 胶层 (substratum 的缩略) II (subbed; subbing) *vt.* 涂胶层于(片基)

subaltern ['sʌbltən] I *a.* ① 下的, 副的, 次的 ②【哲】特称的, 非全称的: a ~ proposition 特称判断 II *n.* ①副官; 部下 ②[主英]陆军中(或少) 尉 ③【哲】特称判断(=~ proposition)

subconscious ['sʌb'kɔnʃəs] I *a.* ①下意识的, 潜意识的 ②模糊的意识的 II *n.* [the ~] 下意识, 潜意识 ‖**~ly** *ad.* / **~ness** *n.*

subcontinent ['sʌb'kɔntinənt] *n.* 次大陆(如南亚次大陆); 次洲 ‖**~al** ['sʌb,kɔnti'nentl] *a.*

subdivide ['sʌbdi'vaid] ❶ *vt.* ①把…再分, 把… 细分 ②把…分成几份(尤指把大片土地分成供建屋用或出卖的小块) ❷ *vi.* 再分, 细分

subdue [səb'dju:] *vt.* ①使屈服; 征服; 使驯服: an enemy 使敌人屈服 / ~ nature 征服自然 ②克制, 抑制(感情、欲望等): ~ one's anger 克制愤怒 ③使(色调、光线等)柔和; 放低(声音); 缓和, 减轻 ④开垦(土地)

subhead ['sʌbhed], **subheading** ['sʌb,hediŋ] *n.* (书中一章或报上一篇文章内的)小标题; 副标题

subject ['sʌbdʒikt] I *n.* ①(君主国)国民, 臣民, 臣下: a British ~ 英国国民 ②题目; 问题; 主题: a ~ for discussion 讨论的题目, 议题 / wander from the ~ 离开本题 / change the ~ 改变话题 / a vital ~ 极重要的问题 / the ~ of a poem (an essay) 诗(小品文)的主题 ③学科, 科目: the main ~ in our school curriculum 我们学校课程中的主要科目 ④受治疗者; 受实验者; 实验材料; 解剖用的尸体: a medical (surgical) ~ 内科(外科)病人 / the ~ of an experiment 实验的对象 ⑤原因; 理由: a ~ of dispute 争论的原因 / a ~ for complaint 抱怨的理由 / a ~ for congratulation 值得庆贺的事 ⑥【语】主语 ⑦【哲】(意识的)主体; 主观意识; 自我: ~ and object 主体和客体; 主观意识和客观事物 ⑧【音】主题, 主旋律 ⑨具有…气质的人: a hysterical ~ 有歇斯底里毛病的人 II *a.* ①隶属的, 从属的; 受支配的: a ~ state 属国 / ~ to the law of the land 受国家法律的管辖的 ②易受…的; 常遭… 的; 惯患…的(*to*): be ~ to damage 易受损伤 / be ~ to earthquakes 常发生地震 / be ~ to fits of passion 动辄发怒 / be ~ to fever (colds) 容

易发烧(感冒) ③有待于…的, 须经…的; 可以… 的(*to*): The treaty is ~ to ratification. 本条约须经批准方可生效。/ The schedule is ~ to change without notice. 本时间表可随时更改, 不另行通知。④ 有关本题的, 有关本学科的: in search of ~ books 搜寻有关本题的书籍 III *ad.* 在…条件下 (*to*): We shall go ahead, ~ to your approval. 你一批准, 我们就开始干。/ This can only be done ~ to his consent. 这只有在他同意的条件下才可以做。IV [səb'dʒekt] *vt.* ①使隶属; 使服从 (*to*) ②使受到; 使遭遇 (*to*) ③[罕]提出; 呈交: a plan ~ed for approval 呈请批准的计划 ‖**~less** *a.* 没题目的; 无主题(或主旨)的 ‖**~ index** 标题索引; 主题索引 / **~ matter** 题材; 题目; 论题; 话题

subjection [səb'dʒekʃən] *n.* ①征服; 镇压 ②隶属; 受支配; 屈从(地位); 服从: be in a state of ~ 处于被统治地位 / bring sb. under ~ 制服某人 / keep (或 hold)... in ~ 使…处于被统治地位

subjugate ['sʌbdʒugeit] *vt.* ①使屈服, 征服; 使服从: ~ a wild horse 制服野马 ②克制, 抑制(感情等): He had to ~ his own feeling. 他不得不克制他自己的情感。‖**subjugator** *n.* 征服者; 制服者

subjugation [,sʌbdʒu'geiʃən] *n.* ①征服 ②克制 ③被征服状态 ‖**~ist** *n.* 亡国论者

sublet ['sʌb'let] I (sublet; subletting) ❶ *vt.* ①转租, 分租(房屋或土地) ②把(工作)转包(或分包)出去 ❷ *vi.* 转租, 分租 II *n.* 转租(或分租)的房屋(或土地)

sublime [sə'blaim] I *a.* ①庄严的; 崇高的; 令人崇敬的; 卓越的; 雄伟的: a ~ thought 崇高的思想 / a ~ mountain 雄伟的山 / ~ scenery 壮丽的景色 ②极端的; 异常的: ~ conceit 极端的骄傲 / ~ indifference 异常的冷淡 / You ~ idiot! 你这个大傻瓜! ③[诗]傲慢的 II *n.* ① [the ~] 崇高; 庄严; 崇高的事物 ②极点, 顶点 III *vt.* & *vi.* ①【化】(使)升华 ②(使)变高尚; 提高; (使)纯化 ‖*the Sublime Porte* (帝制时代的)土耳其政府 ‖**~ly** *ad.* / **~r** *n.* 使升华的人; 升华器

submarine ['sʌbməri:n, ,sʌbmə'ri:n] I *a.* ①水下的; 水底的; 海底的: a ~ cable 水底电缆 / a ~ mine 水雷 II *n.* ①潜水艇: a missile-launching ~ 导弹潜水艇 / an atom-powered ~ 原子动力潜水艇 / a nuclear-powered ~ 核动力潜水艇 ②海底生物 III *vt.* 用潜水艇袭击(或击沉) ‖**~r** *n.* 潜水艇乘员 ‖**~ chaser** 猎潜舰艇 / **~ tender** 潜水艇供应船

submerge [səb'mə:dʒ] ❶ *vt.* 浸没, 淹没: The flood ~d the town. 洪水淹没了市镇。/ be ~d in the mighty torrent of history 为历史洪流所淹没 ❷ *vi.* 没入水中; 潜入水中, 潜下去

submission [səb'miʃən] *n.* ①屈服; 服从; 降服: give in one's ~ 归顺 / frighten sb. into ~ 把某人吓服 / unquestioning ~ to sb.'s will 绝对

服从某人的意志 ②谦逊,谦恭: with all due ~ 恭恭敬敬地 ③递呈; 提交; 提出;【律】提交公断; 提交物: the ~ of one's poem for the newspaper 把诗送交报纸发表 / the ~ of tenders【商】投标 / We have received more ~s than we can possibly publish. 我们收到的稿件超过我们所能发表的数量。④【律】意见,看法;建议: My ~ is that (或 In my ~,) …… 我认为…

submissive [səb'misiv] *a.* 服从的;顺从的;柔顺的;谦恭的: ~ to advice 听从忠告的 / ~ demeanour 谦恭的举止 ‖~ly *ad.* / ~ness *n.*

submit [səb'mit] (submitted; submitting) ❶ *vt.* ①使屈从;使受到 (to): ~ oneself *to* discipline 遵守纪律 ②呈送; 提交; 提出: ~ a plan (proposal) 提出计划(建议) / ~ a case *to* the court 向法院起诉 ③认为,以为: I ~ that this judgement was wrong. 我认为这判决是错误的。❷ *vi.* 服从;屈服;顺从;忍受;甘受 (to): refuse to ~ *to* an unjust decision 拒绝服从不公正的决定 / He has to ~ *to* an operation. 他必须动一次手术。

subnormal ['sʌb'nɔ:məl] I *a.* 低于正常的,逊常的: ~ temperature 亚正常温度 II *n.* ①(尤指智力上)逊常的人 ②【数】次法距;次法线 ‖~ity ['sʌbnɔ:'mæliti] *n.* / ~ly *ad.*

subordinate [sə'bɔ:dinit] I *a.* 下级的;次要的,从属的: a ~ unit 下级单位 / be in a ~ position 处于从属地位 / The minority is ~ *to* the majority. 少数服从多数。/ a ~ clause 【语】从句 / a ~ conjunction 【语】从属连接词 II *n.* 部属;部下;下级职员 III [sə'bɔ:dineit] *vt.* 把…列在下级;使列于次要地位;使服从 ‖~ly *ad.* / ~ness *n.* / **subordination** [sə,bɔ:di'neiʃən] *n.* / **subordinative** [sə'bɔ:dinətiv] *a.* 从属性的;表示从属关系的

subscribe [səb'skraib] ❶ *vt.* ①签署(文件);在(图画等)下方署名;题(词);签(名): ~ an act 签署法案 / ~ a motto 题词 / ~ a picture 在画的下方签名 / ~ one's name *to* a written statement of determination 在决心书上签名 ②捐助,认捐(款项): ~ £20 *to* the relief fund 认捐二十英镑救灾基金 ❷ *vi.* ①捐款: ~ liberally *to* the relief fund 为救灾基金慷慨捐款 ②预订;订阅 (for, to): ~ *for* a dictionary 预订词典 / ~ *to* a magazine 订阅杂志 ③认购: ~ *for* 200 shares 认购二百股 ④同意,赞成;赞助: ~ *to* an opinion (a doctrine, a proposal, a view) 同意(或赞成)某一意见(学说,建议,观点) ⑤在文件(或信件)上签名

subscriber [səb'skraibə] *n.* ①签署者 ②预订者;订阅者,订户: a ~ *for* a newspaper (magazine) 报纸(杂志)订户 ③电话用户 ④捐款者;赞助者 ⑤认购者;承购者: a ~ *to* a government loan 公债认购人

subscription [səb'skripʃən] *n.* ①签署;同意;赞助 ②亲笔签名;有亲笔签名的文件 ③预订;订购;订

阅费;预订费: the ~ rate 订(阅)费标准 ④认捐额;认缴额: sb.'s ~ *to* a fund 某人对某一基金的认捐(或认缴)额 / the ~ realized 所募得的总金额 ⑤【医】(处方上的)调剂注明

subsequent ['sʌbsikwənt] *a.* ①继…之后的,随后的,后来的: ~ events 后来发生的事件 / the period ~ *to* the war 战后时期 ②后成的,后起的: ~ river 【地】后成河,次成河 ‖~ly *ad.*

subservient [səb'sə:vjənt] *a.* ①辅助性的;从属的 ②有帮助的,有用的(尤指在从属地位上) ③屈从的;奉承的,谄媚的 ‖~ly *ad.*

subside [səb'said] *vi.* ①沉到底;沉淀 ②(土地、房屋等)沉降;(船只)下沉 ③(风雨、骚动、冲动等)平静下来,平息;(肿、热度等)减退: The sea ~s. 海浪平静下来了。④[口](慢吞吞地)坐下;躺下: He ~d into a chair. 他慢吞吞地坐到椅子里。‖~nce [səb'saidəns, 'sʌbsidəns] *n.* / ~r *n.* 【化】沉降槽

subsidiary [səb'sidjəri] I *a.* 辅助的;补助的;补充的;次要的;附属的: ~ agricultural products 农业副产品 / a ~ coin 硬辅币 / a ~ company (或 corporation) 子公司 / a ~ production 副业生产 / a ~ ledger 明细分类帐;辅助帐 II *n.* ①辅助者;辅助物 ②附属机构;子公司 ③【音】副主题

subsidize ['sʌbsidaiz] *vt.* 给…补助金;资助;津贴

subsidy ['sʌbsidi] *n.* 补助金;津贴: subsidies for health 保健费

subsist [səb'sist] ❶ *vi.* ①生存,维持生活 ②存在;继续存在 ③【哲】(逻辑上)可以理解;有效 ❷ *vt.* 供养: ~ the troops 供给部队粮食

subsistence [səb'sistəns] *n.* ①生存;生计;生活费;口粮;给养: means of ~ 生计 / ~ wages 维持生活的最低工资 ②存在;持续;内在性;【哲】存在物,实体 ③生活维持费;生活津贴;(军队)口粮代金 (= money, allowance)

substance ['sʌbstəns] *n.* ①物质: a mineral ~ 矿物 ②实质;实体;本质;本体: sacrifice (或 lose) the ~ for the shadow 舍本逐末 / a question of ~ 实质性问题 ③本旨,主旨;要义;真义: the ~ of a speech 讲话的要旨 ④财产,财物: a man of ~ 有财产的人 / waste one's ~ 浪费钱财 ⑤(质地的)坚实,牢固: a material of marked ~ 极为坚实的材料 ‖in ~ 本质上;基本上;大体上;实际上: I agree with you in ~. 我基本上同意你的意见。

substantial [səb'stænʃəl] I *a.* ①物质的;实质的;实体的;真实的,实际上的: ~ things 实际存在的东西 ②坚固的,结实的: a ~ building 坚固的大厦 / a man of ~ build 体格结实的人 ③多的;大的;大量的: a ~ victory 巨大的胜利 / a ~ increase in production 生产上的大幅度增长 / a ~ meal 丰盛的一餐 ④有重大价值的;内容充实的: a ~ argument 重要的论证 ⑤富裕的;多财的;殷实的: a ~ firm 殷实的商号 II *n.* [常用

复]①实质性的东西;实际存在物 ②有实际价值的东西 ③重要的东西;重要部分;要领 ‖~ity [səb,stænʃi'æliti] n. / ~ly ad. / ~ness n.

substantiate [səb'stænʃieit] vt. ①证实;证明(控诉、陈述、主张等)有根据 ②使具体化,使实体化

substitute ['sʌbstitjuːt] I n. ①代替人;代替物,代用品: use plastics as a ~ for wood 用塑料做木材的代用品 / a milk ~ prepared from soybeans 用大豆做的代乳品 ②【语】代用词;代用语(如 He writes better than I do. 这一句中的 do 是代用词) ③【矿】转接器,短节 II ❶ vt. 用…代替;代替(某人或某物): ~ A for B (或 ~ B by A, ~ B with A) 用甲来代乙 ❷ vi. ①作代替者;替代: He ~d for the typist during her absence. 打字员不在时由他代替。/ He ~s as our teacher of English. 他代任我们的英语教师。②【化】取代 III ❶ vt. 作为代用品的;使用代用品的: a ~ food 代用食物 / ~ feeding of infants 用代乳品喂婴儿

substitution [,sʌbsti'tjuːʃən] n. ①代,代替,替换: the ~ of tea for coffee 以茶代咖啡 ②【化】取代(作用);【数】代换,置换,代入 ‖~ary a.

subterfuge ['sʌbtəfjuːdʒ] n. 遁词,托词;巧妙的名目;狡猾的逃避手段: by various ~s 要尽花招;采用各种借口

subterranean [,sʌbtə'reinjən] I a. ①地下的: ~ water 地下水 ②隐蔽的;秘密的 II n. ①地下洞穴;地下室 ②在地下生活(或工作)的人 ‖~ly ad.

subtle ['sʌtl] a. ①稀薄的,不浓的: a ~ vapour 稀薄的水汽 / the ~ aroma of sandalwood 檀香木的幽香 ②精巧的,精妙的: a ~ device 精巧的设计 ③微妙的;微细的;难以捉摸的: a ~ distinction 极细微的区别 / a ~ diplomatic problem 微妙的外交问题 ④敏感的;敏锐的;有辨别力的: a ~ observer 敏锐的观察者 / ~ susceptibility 敏锐的感受性 ⑤阴险的;狡猾的: a ~ enemy 阴险的敌人 / a ~ rogue 狡猾的流氓 ‖~ness, ~ty n. / subtly ad.

subtract [səb'trækt] ❶ vt. 减,减去,去掉: ~ five from ten 十减五 ❷ vi. 作减法计算 ‖~er n. 作减法计算者;减法器 / ~ion [səb'trækʃən] n.

suburb ['sʌbəːb] n. ①[常用复]郊区,郊外;近郊 ②[复]边缘;近处: the ~s of destruction 灭亡的边缘

subversive [sʌb'vəːsiv] I a. 颠覆性的;起破坏作用的: ~ activities 颠覆活动 II n. 颠覆分子,搞颠覆阴谋的人 ‖~ly ad. / ~ness n.

subvert [sʌb'vəːt] vt. ①颠覆;暗中破坏 ②搅乱(人心等);败坏(道德等) ‖~er n. 颠覆者;破坏者

subway ['sʌbwei] I n. ①地(下)道 ②[美]地下铁道(英国称 underground) ③地下铁道列车 II vi. [美]乘地下铁道列车

succeed [sək'siːd] ❶ vt. 继…之后;接替;继承;接着…发生: ~ sb. as secretary 继某人任书记 /

~ oneself [美]重新当选;连任,留任 / Day ~s day. 日复一日。/ One event ~ed another. 事情一件接着一件发生。❷ vi. ①成功: ~ in (passing) an examination 考试及格 / ~ with the public 大受公众欢迎 ②继续;继任;继承;接着发生: Day ~s to day. 日复一日。/ ~ to the crown (或 throne) 继承王位 / ~ to a fortune 继承大笔遗产 / The vice-president ~s in case of the president's death. 如总统故世由副总统继任。/ All ~ing laws were null and void. 以后所制定的法律一律无效。‖*Nothing ~s like success.* 见 **nothing**

success [sək'ses] n. ①成功;成就;胜利: We must not become complacent over any ~. 我们决不能一见成绩就自满自足起来。/ We are sure of ~. 我们一定能成功。/ meet with ~ 获得成功 / Failure is the mother of ~. 失败是成功之母。/ His efforts were crowned with ~. 他的努力获得了成功。②成功的事;取得成就的人;考试及格的学生: The meeting was a ~. 会开得很成功。/ He is a great ~ as a teacher. 作为一个教师,他是很出色的。

successful [sək'sesful] a. ①成功的;结果良好的: a ~ experiment 成功的试验 / be ~ in fulfilling the plan ahead of time 成功地提前完成计划 ②有成就的 ‖~ly ad. / ~ness n.

succession [sək'seʃən] n. ①连续,接续: a ~ of gales 阵阵疾风 ②继任;继承;继承权;继承次序;有继承权者;后裔;后继者: be first in ~ to the throne 是王位的第一继承人 / be second in the ~ 是第二继承人 / It was left to him and his ~. 这被留给了他和他的后代。/ ~ duty [英] 遗产税,继承税(美国称 inheritance tax) / the *Succession* States 【史】奥匈帝国分裂后成立的各国 ③【生】演替 ‖in ~ 接连地: reap bumper harvests in ~ 连续获得丰收 / Reports of victory came in quick ~. 捷报频传。‖~al a.

successive [sək'sesiv] a. 连续的,接连的;相继的;逐次的: Steelworkers set ~ records. 钢铁工人连续创造记录。/ sb.'s fourth ~ victory 某人连续获得的第四次胜利 ‖~ly ad.

successor [sək'sesə] n. 继承人;继任者;后继者;接班人

succinct [sək'siŋkt] a. ①简明的;简洁的: be ~ in wording 用字简练 ②紧身的,贴身的 ‖~ly ad. / ~ness n.

succo(u)r ['sʌkə] I n. ①救济;援助 ②济急的东西;救助者 ③[复][古]援军 II vt. 救济;援助

succulence ['sʌkjuləns] n. ①多汁;【植】肉质性 ②青饲料

succulent ['sʌkjulənt] I a. ①多汁的: a ~ fruit 多汁果 ②【植】肉质的 ③活力充沛的;新鲜的;有趣的;引人入胜的 II n. 肉质植物(如仙人掌) ‖~ly ad.

succumb [sə'kʌm] vi. ①屈服;屈从 (to) ②死 (to): He ~ed to cancer. 他死于癌症。

such [强 sʌtʃ; 弱 sətʃ] I *a.* [无比较级和最高级] ① [遇不定冠词 a(n) 时，要放在该冠词之前；遇 all, no, one, few, several, some, any 等时，则放在其后]这样的，这种的；如此的: ~ a man 这样的一个人 / ~ an action 这种行为 / All ~ possibilities must be considered. 所有这种种可能性都必须考虑到。/ no ~ thing 没这种事情 / One ~ dictionary is enough. 有一本就够了。/ hats, gloves, and ~ objects 帽子、手套这一类东西 / He is not generous; he only seems ~. 他并不慷慨，只是看来这样罢了。/ Long may he continue ~. 但愿他永远如此。② [~ (...) as to; ~ (...) that] 如此的…(以致): We are not ~ fools as to believe him. 我们不是那样的蠢人，竟会相信他。/ His illness is not ~ as to cause anxiety. 他的病还没有严重到令人忧虑的地步。/ His excitement was ~ that he shouted. (=He shouted, ~ was his excitement.) 他兴奋得叫了起来。③[表示惊叹，或加强语气]这样，那样: We had ~ fun! 我们玩得开心极了! / Don't be in a hurry. 别这样急急忙忙。④上述的，该: He was instructed to inspect the cargo on the ship and detain ~ cargo if necessary. 他奉命去检查船上所载货物并于必要时扣留该项货物。⑤某某; 如此这般的;这样那样的: He told me to go to ~ a place on ~ a date. 他叫我于某日去某地。II *ad.* 那么: ~ tall buildings 那么高的建筑物 / a long time 那么长的时间 III *pron.* 这样的人(们); 这样的事物; 上述的事物(或人): ~ as have erred 犯过错误的那些人 / puppets and *all* ~ 傀儡和所有这种家伙 / *Such* was the result. 结果就是这样。/ We will not tolerate another ~. 再发生这种事，我们不答应了。∥*and* ~ [口] 等等: machines, tools, *and* ~ 机器、工具等等 / *as* ~ ① 照此; 就以这种资格(或身分): He was a guest and was treated *as* ~. 他是个客人，并确被作为客人来款待。② 本身: He did not oppose the scheme *as* ~. 就计划本身说，他并不反对。/ ~ *and* ~ 某某; 这种那种的: ~ a person 某某人 / *Such* and ~ results follow from ~ *and* ~ causes. 这样那样的原因就产生这样那样的结果。/ ~ *as* 象…这种的，诸如…之类的; 例如…: on occasions ~ *as* these 在此类场合下 / books of reference, ~ *as* dictionaries and handbooks 参考书，例如词典、手册之类 / ~ *as it is* 质量不过如此的(东西): The food, ~ *as it is*, is plentiful. 食物虽不精，但量是多的。/ You can use my bicycle, ~ *as it is*. 尽管我的自行车不怎么好，请就用吧。/ ~ *being the case* 事实既然如此: *Such being the case*, let's go ahead by ourselves. 情况既然如此，我们就自己干吧。

suck [sʌk] I ❶ *vt.* ① 吸，吮，嗽，嘬: ~ the breast 吮乳 / ~ the juice from a lemon 吮吸柠檬汁 / ~ an orange dry 把桔子吮吸干 / ~ a lollipop 吮食棒糖 ②吸收，吸取(水分、知识等); 获得(利益等): Blotting paper ~*s up* ink. 吸墨水纸吸墨水。/ ~ knowledge into one's mind 吸收知识 / ~ the blood of 吸取…的血; 榨取…的膏血 / ~ advantage out of 从…得到利益 ❷ *vi.* ①(婴儿)吸奶; 吸; 发吮吸似的声音: ~ at one's pipe 抽烟斗 / The pump ~ed. 尽泵是抽着空气(抽不上液体)。②[美]奉承，拍马 ③[美俚]使人极度反感 II *n.* ①吸，吮，嗽，嘬: give ~ to a baby 给婴儿喂奶 / a child at ~ 吃着奶的孩子 ②(一)吮，(一)口: a ~ of wine 一口酒 / take a ~ at one's pipe 吸一口烟 ③吮吸似的声音 ④(漩涡等的)吸力 ⑤[复][俚]糖果 ⑥[俚]欺骗; 失望; 失败 ⑦[英俚]酒 ∥*a ~ed orange* 见 **orange** / ~ *around* [美俚](为博取好感)老是围着…打转 / ~ *in* ① 吸收，吸取; ~ *in* knowledge 吸收知识 ②(漩涡等)把…吞没 ③[俚]欺骗 / ~ *off* [美俚]拍…马屁 / *Sucks!* =What a ~! / ~ *sb.'s brains* 见 **brain** / ~ *the monkey* 见 **monkey** / ~ *up to* 见 **What a** ~! 你瞧! 好! 真痛快! (看见很象有把握的对手失败时说) ∥'~-*fish* [动]鲫 / '~-*in* *n.* [英俚]欺骗; 失望; 失败 / '~-*up* *n.* [俚]拍马者，奉承者

sucker ['sʌkə] I *n.* ① 吮吸者; 乳儿; 乳兽(尤指猪或鲸) ②[动]吸盘 ③[动]膦脂鱼类 ④[植]根出条;(寄生性植物的)吸器，吸根 ⑤吸管;(泵或针筒的)活塞 ⑥[俚]容易受骗的人，傻瓜，笨蛋; 对某种事物(或某种人)容易着迷的人 (*for*) ⑦[口]棒糖: an ice ~ 棒冰，冰棍 II ❶ *vt.* ①(为了有利于植物生长)从…除去根出条(或根) ②[俚]欺骗 ❷ *vi.* [植]长出根出条; 形成吸根 ∥~ *list* [美俚]可游说拉拢的对象名单

suckle ['sʌkl] *vt.* ①给…喂奶，哺乳 ②养育，哺育 ③吮取; 吸取

suckling ['sʌkliŋ] *n.* ① 乳儿，乳兽 ② 乳臭未干的小伙子 ∥*babes and* ~*s* 见 **babe**

suction ['sʌkʃən] *n.* ① 吸，吸引，吸入，吸气引液 ②(排去空气后所产生的)吸力 ③ =~ pump ④[英]喝酒 ⑤[美俚]上司的青睐 ∥*in a* ~ [美俚]被恋爱弄得神魂颠倒 / ~ **chamber** [机]吸室 / ~ **dredge** 吸扬式挖泥船，吸泥机 / ~ **fan** 吸风机 / ~ **head** [机]吸引位差，吸升高度 / ~ **pipe** 吸入管，吸水管 / ~ **plate** ①[机]吸板 ②[医](托牙的)吸板，吸附假牙床 / ~ **pump** 空吸泵，空吸抽机，抽水机 / ~ **stroke** [机]吸入冲程，进气行程

sudden ['sʌdn] I *a.* ①突然的，忽然的，意外的: ~ attack 突然袭击 / be ~ in one's action 行动突然 ②[古]迅速的，即刻的; 即席作成的: He requested their ~ help. 他要求他们迅速帮助。II *n.* 突然发生的事[只用于下列习语] ∥*all of a* ~ (或 *on a* ~, *all on a* ~) 突然，冷不防 ∥~*ly* *ad.* / ~*ness* *n.* / ~ **death** ①暴死 ②[体]对胜负不分的比赛所增加的决赛时间

suds [sʌdz] I [复] *n.* ①肥皂溶液，浓肥皂水 ②泡

沫; 粘稠介质中的空气泡 ③[俚]啤酒 **II ❶** *vt.* 在起泡沫的浓肥皂水中洗 **❷** *vi.* 形成起泡沫的浓肥皂水 ‖**be in the ~** ①在洗涤中 ②[俚]陷入困境 ③情绪低落, 沮丧 ‖**~y** *a.* 多泡沫的; 象肥皂溶液的

sue [sju:, su:] **❶** *vt.* ①控告, 控诉: ~ sb. in a law-court 向法院控诉某人 / ~ sb. *for* damages 控诉某人要求赔偿损失 ②(为了…)向 … 请求: ~ the court *for* a writ of recovery 请求法院宣告恢复权利的裁定 / ~ sb. *for* mercy 求饶 **❷** *vi.* ①提出诉讼: ~ at (the) law 起诉 / ~ *for* a breach of promise 为违约提出控诉 / ~ *for* a divorce 诉请离婚 ②提出请求: ~ *to* sb. 请求某人 / ~ *for* a favour 求惠 / ~ *for* a woman's hand 向女子求婚 ‖**~ out** 【律】经向法院请求而得到(赦免、赔偿等): ~ out a pardon 求得宽赦

suède [sweid] *n.* 小山羊皮(里面刮起毛头或绒, 做鞋面、手套等用), 起毛皮革: ~ gloves 羊皮手套 / ~ fabric 仿麂皮织物(或针织品)

suet ['sju(:)it] *n.* (牛、羊等的)板油 ‖**~y** *a.* (含)板油的; 板油似的

suffer ['sʌfə] **❶** *vt.* ①遭受, 蒙受; 经历: ~ heavy casualties 遭到严重伤亡 / ~ hunger 挨饿 / no change in chemical structure 化学结构上没有经历变化 ②[常用于否定句]忍受, 耐住: He could not ~ criticism. 他受不了批评。/ These plants cannot ~ a cold winter. 这些植物耐不住寒冬。③容许, 允许; 容忍: ~ sb. to come near 允许某人走近 / How can you ~ his insolence? 你怎么能容忍他傲慢无礼? **❷** *vi.* ①受痛苦; 患病; 被处死刑: ~ *from* heart failure 患心力衰竭 / He was ~ed *for* his carelessness. 他因粗心而遭受恶果。/ He was to ~ the next morning. 他次晨将被处死刑。②受损失, 受损害; 受到妨碍: ~ *from* floods 遭受水灾 / Be careful, or our work will ~. 要细心, 否则我们的工作要受损失。

sufferance ['sʌfərəns] *n.* ①忍耐, 忍受; 忍耐力: It is beyond ~. 这无法忍受。②[古]痛苦, 苦难 ③默许, 容许, 容忍, 容忍 ‖**on** (或 **by, through**) ~ 经默许, 被容忍: He remains there *on* ~. 他勉强被容许留在那儿。

suffering ['sʌfəriŋ] **I** *n.* ①受苦, 遭难 ②痛苦, 疾苦; 苦难 **II** *a.* ①受难的, 受苦的 ②患病的

suffice [sə'fais] **❶** *vi.* ①足够: One word will ~. 一句话就够了。/ Suffice it to say that .... 只要说…就够了。②有能力 **❷** *vt.* 满足…的需要; 满足: That will ~ me. 那就能满足我的需要了。/ This ~s present needs. 这能满足眼下的需要。‖**sufficingly** *ad.* 足够地

sufficiency [sə'fiʃənsi] *n.* ①[常与不定冠词连用](财富、收入、能力等的)充足, 足量: a ~ of natural resources 足够的自然资源 ②自满, 自负

sufficient [sə'fiʃənt] **I** *a.* ①足够的, 充分的: be ~ for sb.'s needs 足够满足某人的需要 / He has

acquired ~ proficiency to read Chinese literary works. 他已获得足够能力阅读中国文学著作。②[古]能胜任的, 有充分能力的 **II** *n.* [俗]足够: Have you had ~? 你已经够了吗? ‖**not** ~ (银行用语)存款不足(常略作 N S) / *Sufficient for the day is the evil thereof.* 见 **evil** ‖**~ly** *ad.*

suffix **I** ['sʌfiks] *n.* ①后缀, 词尾 ②【数】下标; 添标, 尾标 **II** ['sʌfiks, sʌ'fiks] *vt.* 添加…作后缀

suffocate ['sʌfəkeit] **❶** *vt.* ①使窒息; 把…闷死: be ~d by (或 with) excitement 兴奋得透不过气来 ②闷熄: ~ the fire 将火闷熄 ③妨碍(或阻止)…的发展 **❷** *vi.* ①闷死, 窒息; 闷得难受 ②受阻, 不能发展 ‖**suffocatingly** *ad.*

suffocation [,sʌfə'keiʃən] *n.* 窒息

suffrage ['sʌfridʒ] *n.* ①投票; 所投的票(尤指赞成票): They gave their ~s for that policy. 他们对该政策投赞成票。②投票权, 选举权, 参政权: manhood (woman) ~ 成年男子(妇女)选举权 / universal ~ 普选权 ③【宗】代祷

suffuse [sə'fju:z] *vt.* (液体、光、色等)充满, 弥漫于: Her eyes were ~d with warm, excited tears. 她热泪盈眶。/ skies ~d with crimson 一片紫红色的天空

sugar ['ʃugə] **I** *n.* ①糖; 糖块: granulated ~ 粒状糖, 砂糖 / powdered ~ 糖粉, 棉白糖 / spun ~ 棉花糖 / block (或 cube, cut) ~ 方糖 / brown ~ 黄糖; raw (或 muscovado) ~ 粗糖, 混糖, 赤砂糖 / cane ~ 蔗糖 / a lump of ~ 一块方糖 / How many ~s do you want in your tea? 你的茶里要放几块糖? ②【化】有甜味的一种碳水化合物, 糖(如葡萄糖、乳糖、果糖等) ③(有盖和柄的)糖缸 (= ~ bowl) ④甜言蜜语; 阿谀, 奉承 ⑤[俚]钱; 贿金 ⑥[美俚]麻醉品(指海洛因、吗啡等) ⑦[美俚]心爱的人 **II** **❶** *vt.* ①加糖于, 撒糖于; 包糖衣于, 使甜: ~ a cake 在糕饼上加糖 / ~ed almonds 糖衣杏仁 ②使甜蜜, 使容易被接受; 粉饰, 美化 (up, over): ~ one's reproach with words of endearment 用亲热的话使责备不太逆耳 / ~ up reality 粉饰现实 ③[美俚]用钱收买, 贿赂 ④[俚][用被动语态]诅咒 **❷** *vi.* ①制成糖; 变成(糖似的)颗粒状 ②[英俚]工作不卖力, 偷懒 ‖**bring ~ in one's spade** [美]准备行贿 / **heavy ~** [美俚]①大量的钱(赌博等)一下子赢得的钱 ②有钱的人, 富翁 ③值钱的东西, 珍宝 / **~ and honey** [英俚]钱 / **~ the pill** 见 **pill¹** ‖**~less** *a.* 无糖的, 不含糖的 ‖**~ basin** [英] (= ~ bowl) / **~ bean** 一种菜豆(也叫四季豆、云豆) / **~ beet** (可制糖的)糖甜菜, 糖恭菜 / '**~bird** *n.* 吸花蜜的鸟 / **~ bowl** (有盖和柄的)糖缸 / **~ bush** 糖槭林 / **~ camp** [美方] (= ~ bush) / **~ candy** ①冰糖 ②甜蜜的东西, 悦人的东西 / '**~cane** *n.* 甘蔗 / '**~coat** *vt.* ①包糖衣于 ②使甜蜜, 使有吸引力 / **~ daddy** 在少女身上滥花钱的老色迷 / **~ gum** 产于澳洲的甜叶桉树 / **Sugar Hill** [美俚](纽约市)俯瞰哈莱姆区的富人居住区 / '**~house** *n.* 糖厂, 炼糖所 / '**~ing off** 把槭

树汁熬成糖；熬糖会 (熬糖时节的点心招待会) / **'~loaf** *n.* ① 圆锥形糖块 ② 塔形高丘，圆锥形高丘 / **~ maple** 【植】糖槭 / **'~-mill** *n.* 糖厂，糖作坊 / **~ mite** 生长于粗糖上的蛆 / **~ orchard** [美方] =~ bush / **'~plum** *n.* ① 小糖果 ② 甜言蜜语；贿赂；甜头 / **'~-re,finery** *n.* 炼糖厂 / **~ report** [美俚] (尤指寄给士兵的) 情书 / **~ tongs** 方糖钳子

suggest [sə'dʒest] *vt.* ① 建议，提出 (意见、计划、理论等): It is ~ed that .... 有人提议… / ~ a visit to the Industrial Exhibition 提议去参观工业展览会 / I ~ that you had an ulterior motive in doing this. 我认为你做这事是别有用心的。② 暗示；启发: a short story ~ed by an actual incident 受一件真事启发而写的一篇短篇小说 ③ 使人想起，使人联想到: a factory that ~s a small city 象一座小城市那样的工厂 / Her sun-tanned face ~s excellent health. 她那被太阳晒黑了的脸表明她身体非常健康。‖ ~ *itself to* 浮现在…的心中: An idea ~ed *itself to* me (或 *to* my mind). 我想起了一个念头。

suggestion [sə'dʒestʃən] *n.* ① 建议；意见: at (或 on) sb.'s ~ 根据某人的建议 / make a ~ 提出建议 ② 暗示；示意；启发 ③ 联想 ④ 微量，细微的迹象: There was a ~ of boredom in her tone. 她的语调中略露厌烦情绪。/ blue with a ~ of grey 微带灰色的蓝色

suggestive [sə'dʒestiv] *a.* ① 暗示的；示意的；启发的；引起联想的: a ~ lecture 有启发性的演讲 ② 挑动色情的，含有猥亵意味的 ‖ **~ly** *ad.* / **~ness** *n.*

suicidal [sjui'saidl] *a.* 自杀的；危及性命的；[喻] 自取灭亡的: with ~ intent 蓄意自杀地 / a ~ policy 自杀政策 ‖ **~ly** *ad.*

suicide ['sjuisaid] I *n.* ① 自杀；[喻] 自取灭亡: commit ~ 自杀 / political ~ 政治上的自取灭亡 / race ~ 种族因过度节育而逐渐消灭 ② 自杀事件 ③ 自杀者；企图自杀者 II ❶ *vi.* [口] 自杀 ❷ *vt.* [~ oneself] 自杀 III *a.* 自杀的；构成自杀的；自杀性的 ‖ **~ squad** 【军】敢死队

suit [sju:t, su:t] I *n.* ① 请求，恳求；求婚: make a ~ 请愿，乞求 / grant sb.'s ~ 答应某人的请求 / prosper (fail) in one's ~ 求婚成功 (失败) ② 起诉；诉讼，讼案: a civil (criminal) ~ 民事 (刑事) 诉讼 / bring a ~ against sb. 控告某人 ③ (一套) 衣服: a man's (woman's) ~ 一套男子 (妇女) 衣服 / a lounge ~ 男式普通西服 / a dress ~ 男式夜礼服 / a three-piece ~ 三件一套的西服 / a gym ~ 体操衣 ④ 套；副；组: a ~ of clothes (sails) 一套衣服 (篷帆) / a ~ of armour 一副甲胄 ⑤ 同花色的一组纸牌: a long ~ of spades 一手黑桃长牌 (有四张以上黑桃) ⑥ [古] 随从，扈从 II ❶ *vt.* ① 适合；中…的意: Any time will ~ me. 什么时候我都行。/ an arrangement that ~s sb. perfectly 某人最中意的安排 ② 使配合，使适应 (*to*): *Suit* your style of writing *to* the masses. 你的笔调应大众化。/ new types of tractors ~ed *to* different local conditions 适应不同地区条件的各种新型拖拉机 / He is best ~ed *to* do (或 *for* doing, *for*) this task. 他最适宜担任这项工作。③ [军] 给…穿衣；供给…衣服 ❷ *vi.* ① 合适，适当: Will that date ~? 那个日期合适吗? ② 相称；彼此协调 (*to*, *with*): His new job ~s well *with* his abilities. 他的新工作和他的能力很相称。‖ *follow* ~ 跟出同花色的牌；[喻] 跟着做，照着做 / *in one's birthday* ~ 赤身裸体，一丝不挂 / *one's strong* ~ 特长，优点 / *press* (或 *push*) *one's* ~ 苦苦哀求，迫切要求 / *put on the* ~ [美俚] 穿上军装当兵 / ~ *oneself* 随自己的意愿行事，自便 / ~ *sb.* (*down*) *to the ground* 见 ground[1] ‖ **~or** *n.* 起诉人；请愿者；请求者；求婚者

suitable ['sju:təbl] *a.* 合适的；适宜的；适当的；相对的 (*to*, *for*): words ~ *to* the occasion 适合该场合的言词 / books ~ *for* children 适合儿童阅读的书籍 ‖ **suitability** [,sju:tə'biliti] *n.* / **~ness** *n.* / **suitably** *ad.*

suitcase ['sju:tkeis] *n.* 小提箱，衣箱

suite [swi:t] *n.* ① (一批) 随从人员 ② 套，组；(一套) 房间；(一套) 家具: a ~ of rooms 一套房间 / a bedroom ~ 一套卧室用家具 ③ 【音】组曲 (由从前的舞蹈组曲发展而来)

sukey, sukie, suky ['sju:ki] *n.* [方] 水壶

sulk [sʌlk] I *vi.* 生气，愠怒 II *n.* ① [常用复] 生气，愠怒 ② 生气的人，含怒不语的人 ‖ *be in the* ~s 在生气，在发脾气，绷着脸 / *have* (*a fit of*) *the* ~s 发脾气，生气

sulky ['sʌlki] I *a.* ① 生气的，绷着脸的 ② (天气等) 阴沉的 ③ 单座两轮的 II *n.* 单座两轮马车 ‖ **sulkily** *ad.* / **sulkiness** *n.*

sulky

sullage ['sʌlidʒ] *n.* ① 污水，阴沟污物 ② (流水所沉淀的) 淤泥 ③ 【冶】勺内熔化金属上的渣

sullen ['sʌlən] *a.* ① 愠怒的，闷闷不乐的，绷着脸不高兴的: ~ looks 不高兴的脸色 ② (天气等) 阴沉的: a ~ sky 阴沉的天空 ③ (声音) 沉闷的；(色彩) 不鲜艳的 ④ 行动迟缓的；缓慢的: a ~ stream 缓慢的流水 ‖ **~ly** *ad.* / **~ness** *n.*

sully ['sʌli] I *vt.* 弄脏；玷污: ~ sb.'s reputation 玷污某人名誉 II *n.* [古] 污斑，污点

sulphur ['sʌlfə] **I** *n.*【化】硫(磺)，硫黄: ~ dyes (或 colours) 硫化染料(也作 sulphide dyes 或 sulphide colours) **II** *vt.* 用硫处理; 用硫黄烟熏; 用亚硫酸盐处理 ‖'~-,bottom (**whale**) *n.*【动】长须鲸 (=blue whale) / ~ **spring** 含有硫化物的泉水 / '~weed, '~wort *n.*【植】药用前胡

sultan ['sʌltən] *n.* ① 苏丹(某些伊斯兰教国家最高统治者的称号); [S-] 苏丹(旧时土耳其君主的称号) ② [常作 S-] 土耳其种小白鸡(脚及腿上有厚羽)

sultry ['sʌltri] *a.* ①闷热的; 酷热的 ②(性情等)易激动的, 狂暴的; (言语等)激烈的, 狂热的 ③(能)激起性欲的, 淫荡的 ‖**sultrily** *ad.* / **sultriness** *n.*

sum [sʌm] **I** *n.* ①总数, 总和;【数】和: the ~ total 总数 / the ~ of all one's wishes 某人的全部愿望 / That is the ~ of our experience. 那就是我们的全部经验。/ The ~ of five and four is nine. 五加四的和是九。 ②金额: a good (或 round, considerable) ~ 可观的金额 / a lump ~ 总额; 整笔付给的款子 ③算术题(的运算): do ~s 做算术 / do a rapid ~ in one's head 敏捷地心算 ④概要; 要点: the ~ of this book 这本书的要点 / the ~ and substance of sb.'s opinions 某人意见的主要内容 ⑤顶点, 极点 **II** (summed; summing) **❶** *vt.* ① 计算⋯的总数: ~ (*up*) the costs of sth. 计算某物的总成本费 ②总结; 概括; 概述 (*up*): It is necessary to ~ *up* experience conscientiously. 要认真总结经验。/ ~ *up* the situation at a glance 一眼就看清情况 / ~ sb. *up* 看清某人的性格 **❷** *vi.* 共计 (*to*, *into*) ‖*in* ~ 简言之, 一言以蔽之 / *to* ~ *up* 总结一下; 总而言之, 总之 ‖**~less** *a.* 无数的, 无限的; 不可估量的 ‖**'summing-'up** (复) summings-up) *n.* 总结; 【律】(讼案中法官对证据、辩论等的)总结, 概述 / **'~-up** *n.* 总结

summarize ['sʌməraiz] *vt. & vi.* 概括, 概述, 总结 ‖**summarization** [,sʌmərai'zeiʃən] *n.*

summary ['sʌməri] **I** *a.* ①概括的, 扼要的: a ~ ·account 概括的报道 ②即时的, 速决的, 简单(化)的: ~ justice (jurisdiction) 即决裁判(裁判权) / ~ punishment 即刻的处罚 **II** *n.* 摘要, 概要, 一览

summer¹ ['sʌmə] **I** *n.* ①夏, 夏季: this (last, next) ~ 今(去, 明)夏 / in (the) ~ 在夏季 / in the ~ of 1972 在一九七二年夏季 / ~ harvesting and planting 夏收夏种 / a ~ resort 避暑地 / the ~ vacation (或 holidays) 暑假 ②[喻]壮年; 最盛期, 兴旺时期: in the ~ of one's life 在壮年时期 ③[复][诗]岁: a lad of eighteen ~s 十八岁的小伙子 **II** **❶** *vi.* 过夏天, 避暑 **❷** *vt.* 夏季放牧(牲口) ‖ *St. Luke's* ~ [英]圣路加节出现的小阳春(在十月十八日左右) / *St. Martin's* ~ [英]圣马丁节出现的小阳春(在十一月内) / *and winter* ①经过整整一年 ②始终不渝地(保卫、爱护或忠于) ③[苏格兰]喋喋不休 ‖**~ly** *a.* 夏的; 如夏季的 ‖**~ house** [美]避暑别墅 /

'~house *n.* 凉亭 / ~ kitchen 夏季厨房(设在住房外的毗邻小屋里, 以免烹调给住房带来高温) / ~ lightning 夏夜在远处看到但听不到雷声的闪电, 热闪, 干闪 / ~ school 暑期学校, 暑期(补习)班 / '~tide, '~time *n.* 夏季 / ~ time [主英](将钟点拨快一小时的)夏令时(略作 S. T.) (=daylight saving (time) 经济时) / '~wood *n.* 晚材, 秋材; 大(木)材

summer² ['sʌmə] *n.*【建】大梁, 檩条; 楣; (托住拱或楣的)柱顶石 (=~ beam)

summer³ ['sʌmə] *n.*【自】加法器

summit ['sʌmit] **I** *n.* ① 顶点, 绝顶: the ~ of a mountain 山顶 ②极度, 极点: at the ~ of one's wrath 盛怒的时候 ③最高的官阶(尤指外交上所称政府首脑级): talks at the ~ 最高级会谈 ④最高级会议 **II** *a.* 政府首脑级的, 最高级的: a ~ conference (或 meeting) 最高级会议

summon ['sʌmən] *vt.* ① 召集; 传唤; 召唤; 号召: ~ Parliament (a conference) 召开国会(会议) / the defendant 传被告 be ~ed as a witness 被传唤作证 / ~ sb. to one's presence 把某人召来 / ~ a physician 请医生 / ~ sb. to be in readiness 号召某人作好准备 / ~ a garrison to surrender 向守军招降 ②鼓起(勇气等), 振作(精神); 唤起: ~ (*up*) one's courage for a task (to do sth.) 鼓起勇气干工作(做某事)

summons ['sʌmənz] **I** *n.* ①召唤, 命令 ②【律】传唤; 传票: issue a ~ 发出传票 / serve a ~ *on* (或 *upon*) sb. (或 serve sb. with a ~) 把传票送达某人 **II** *vt.* [口]把传票送达(某人), 用传票传唤

sump [sʌmp] *n.* ①池, 坑(尤指污水坑、化粪池); (内燃机润滑系统的)集油槽 ②[主英]【机】油盘; 曲柄箱 ③【矿】水仓, 水窝 ‖~ **pump**【矿】水仓泵, 水窝泵

sumptuous ['sʌmptjuəs] *a.* 豪华的; 奢侈的: a ~ banquet 豪华的宴会 ‖**~ly** *ad.* / **~ness** *n.*

sun [sʌn] **I** *n.* ① 太阳, 日: the earth's revolution about (或 around, round) the ~ 地球环绕太阳的运转 / the midnight ~ 北(或南)极的午夜太阳 ②日光, 阳光: bathe (或 bask) in the ~ 晒太阳, 沐日光浴 ③(有卫星的)恒星 ④[诗](一)日; (一年中)【古】日出; 日落 ⑤中心人物; 太阳状的东西 ⑥荣耀; 光耀; 权力 ⑦旧式(煤气)簇灯 **II** (sunned; sunning) **❶** *vt.* 晒, 曝: ~ oneself 晒太阳; [喻]受宠 **❷** *vi.* 晒太阳 ‖*against* (*with*) *the* ~ 朝着反(顺)时针方向 / *a place in the* ~ 好的境遇; 显要的地位 / *from* ~ *to* ~ 从日出到日落 / *hold a candle to the* ~ 见 **candle** / *in the* ~ ①在阳光下 ②无忧无虑 ③为大家所注目 / *One's* ~ *is set.* 全盛时期已经过去。 / *rise with the* ~ 早起 / *see the* ~ 活着 / *shoot the* ~ [俚]【海】中午时用六分仪测量太阳的高度(以确定船的位置等) / *soak up the* ~ 沐日光浴 / *take the* ~ ① 晒太阳 ②【海】=shoot the ~ / *the Sun of Righteousness*【宗】耶稣 / *the* ~'s *eyelashes* (或 *the* ~'s *backstays,* *the* ~

drawing water) 由云缝中漏出的阳光所照射出来的空中微尘的平行线现象 / *under the ~* ①天下，世界上 ②到底，究竟: Where *under the ~* did he go? 他到底上哪儿去了? ‖**~less** *a.* ①不见太阳的，阴暗的 ②忧郁的，情绪低落的 / **~like** *a.* 象太阳的 / **~ward** *ad.* & *a.* 向太阳(的) / **~wards** *ad.* 向太阳 / **~wise** *ad.* 顺着太阳; 以顺时针方向 ‖'**~baked** *a.* 日晒的; 被太阳晒得干而发硬的: *~baked* bricks 日晒砖 / '**~bath** *n.* 日光浴 / '**~bathe** *vi.* 沐日光浴 / '**~beam** *n.* ①(一道)日光，阳光 ②[口]活泼快乐的人(尤指孩子) / **~bird** *n.* 太阳鸟 / '**~blind** *n.* [主英](窗外的)遮篷，遮帘 / '**~bonnet** *n.* (女用)阔边遮太阳帽 / '**~bow** *n.* [诗]虹 / '**~burn** *n.* 日炙; 晒黑; 晒斑 *vt.* & *vi.* (使)晒黑，(使)晒焦; (使)晒得退色 / **~ burner** (旧式)煤气簧灯 / '**~burnt, '~burned** *a.* 晒黑的; 日炙的; 有晒斑的 / '**~burst** *n.* ①(破云而出的)阳光突现 ②嵌有宝石的旭日形饰针 / **crack** (泥土、树脂的)晒裂 / **~ -cured** *a.* (肉、鱼等)晒干的 / **~ dance** (北美印第安人的)夏至拜太阳舞 / **~ deck** ①[船]日光甲板 ②[建]太阳浴层面 / '**~dew** *n.* 【植】茅膏菜属植物(包括茅膏菜、毛毡苔、捕蝇草等) / '**~dial** *n.* 日规，日晷仪 / **~ dog** [气]幻日，假日 / '**~down** *n.* ①日落，日没 ②阔边女帽 / '**~downer** *n.* ①[澳](算好时间到牧场等处借宿的)无业游民 ②[英口]日落时喝的饮料 ③要求见习生在日落时就回舰的军官; [美俚]执行纪律严格者 / '**~dried** *a.* (水果等)晒干的 / '**~drops** [复] *n.* [用作单或复]【植】月见草属植物 / '**~fast** *a.* 耐晒的，不退色的 / **~fish** *n.* [动]翻车鱼 / '**,flower** *n.* 向日葵，葵花，向阳花 / '**,glasses** [复] *n.* 太阳眼镜，墨镜 / '**~glow** *n.* 朝霞; 晚霞; 太阳白冕 / '**~god** *n.* 日神，太阳神 / **~ hat** (男用)阔边太阳帽 / **~ helmet** (男用)硬壳太阳帽 / '**~lamp** *n.* (治疗用的)太阳灯 / '**~light** *n.* 日光，阳光 / '**~lit** *a.* 阳光照亮的，阳光普照的 / **~ parlo(u)r, ~ porch** =**~-room** / '**~proof** *a.* 不透日光的; 耐日晒的 / '**~pump** *n.* 【物】日光泵; 日光抽运 / '**~ray** *n.* ①太阳光线; [复]紫外线 ②(画面上的)光线 / '**~rise** *n.* 日出(时分): at *~rise* 黎明时 / '**~room** *n.* (用玻璃建造的)日光室 / '**~set** *n.* ①日落(时分) ②[喻]晚年: the *~set* of life 晚年 / '**~shade** *n.* ①(女用)阳伞 ②(橱窗等的)遮篷; 百页窗; 天棚 ③【物】物镜遮光罩 / '**~spot** *n.* ①太阳黑子(常见于太阳表面的黑斑) ②雀斑 / '**~stone** *n.* [地]日长石; 太阳石(琥珀); 猫睛石(金绿石) / '**~stroke** *n.* 日射病，中暑 / '**~struck** *a.* 中暑的 / '**~tan** *n.* [常用作定语]晒黑 / '**~-trap** *n.* 能晒到太阳而又免受冷风侵袭的花园(或露台) / '**~up** *n.* [口] =**~rise** / '**,worship** *n.* 太阳崇拜

Sunday ['sʌndi] **I** *n.* 星期日，(基督教徒的)礼拜日: last ~ (或 on ~ last) 在上星期日 / on ~ 在星期日 / on ~s 每逢星期日 / on ~ morning 在星期日上午 **II** *a.* ①星期日的; 礼拜日的 ②最好的: a ~ suit 最好的服装 ③业余的: ~ painters 业余画家 **III** *vi.* 度星期日: ~ with sb. in the country 与某人一起在乡下度星期日 ‖*a carless* ~ 无车星期日(指因能源危机而不准在星期日驾车耗油) / *a Hospital* ~ 医院的星期日募捐日(指在教堂内募捐的日子) / *a month* (或 *week*) *of ~s* 很长的时间，很久 / *in one's ~ best* 穿着节日的服装 / *~ run* 见 **run**[1] ‖**~s** *ad.* [美]每星期日，在任何星期日 ‖'**~-go-to-'meeting** *a.* [口](言语、举止等)适宜于礼拜日做礼拜用的; (衣服等)最好的 / **~ letter** 主日字母(以 A B C D E F G 七个字母分别代表一月的首七天。如一月一日是星期日，这一年的"主日字母"就是 A;如一月二日是星期日，这一年的"主日字母"就是 B; 余依此类推。又称 dominical letter) / **~ punch** [美](拳击中)旨在于打倒对方的一击 ②对付敌手最厉害的一着 / **~ school** 【宗】主日学校; 主日学校的全体师生

sundries ['sʌndriz] [复] *n.* 杂物; 杂项

sundry ['sʌndri] *a.* 各式各样的，杂的，各种的: ~ goods 杂货 / ~ revenue 杂项税收 / on ~ occasions 在各种不同的场合 ‖*all and ~* 全部; 所有的人: extend a welcome to *all and ~* 对来宾一一表示欢迎

sunk [sʌŋk] **I** sink 的过去分词和[罕]过去式 **II** *a.* [美] ① 凹陷的 (=sunken): ~ cheeks 凹陷的双颊 / a ~ basin 集水井 / ~ screw 【机】埋头螺丝，沉头螺丝 ②情绪低落的: She was rather ~ on hearing the news. 她听到这消息情绪有些低落。 ③完蛋了的 ‖~ **fence** (不遮住视线的)矮篱，矮墙

sunken ['sʌŋkən] **I** sink 的过去分词 **II** *a.* ① 沉没的; 水面下的: a ~ ship 沉船 / a ~ marsh 被水淹没的沼泽 ②下陷的; 凹陷的: a ~ rock 下陷的岩石 / ~ cheeks 凹陷的双颊 ③低于地面(或楼面)的: a ~ living room 低于楼面的起居室

super ['sju:pə] **I** *n.* ①[口]跑龙套的角色; [喻]无足轻重者 ②[口]特级品; 特大号商品 ③[口]监督人 ④(装订书脊用的)上浆网眼布 ⑤ =superfilm ⑥[美俚]表(尤指挂表) ⑦蜂房上层活动架 **II** *a.* ①特级的; 极好的; 顶呱呱的 ②特大的; 威力强大的: a ~ truck 特大号的卡车 ③十分的; 过分的: ~ secrecy 绝密 ④平方的: 50 ～ ft. 五十平方呎 **III** *ad.* 非常; 过分地 **IV** ❶ *vt.* 用上浆网眼布装(书脊) ❷ *vi.* 充当跑龙套角色

superannuate [,sju:pə'rænjueit] *vt.* ① 给养老金使退休; 因年老(或体弱)令…退职 ② (因太旧或过时而)淘汰，废弃 ③ 因超过一定年龄而成绩未达到标准令(学生)退学 ‖**~d** *a.* ① 年老(或体弱)退休的，领养老金的; 年老无能的 ②过时的，太旧的; 废弃的

superannuation [,sju:pə,rænju'eiʃən] *n.* ①年老(或体弱)退休，退职 ②淘汰，废弃 ③退休金

superb [sju(:)'pə:b] *a.* ①壮丽的; 华丽的: a ~

building 壮丽的建筑物 ②超等的，极好的: a ~ view 极好的景致 / ~ courage 极大的胆量 / That's ~! 好极啦! ||~ly *ad.* / ~ness *n.*

supercilious [ˌsjuːpəˈsiliəs] *a.* 目空一切的；傲慢的 ||~ly *ad.* / ~ness *n.*

supererogation [ˌsjuːpərˌerəˈgeiʃən] *n.* 职责以外的工作: works of ~ 【天主教】余功

superficial [ˌsjuːpəˈfiʃəl] *a.* ①表面的；表面性的: ~ resemblance 表面上的相似 / a ~ wound 表皮上的伤 ②肤浅的，浅薄的: ~ knowledge 浅薄的知识 ③平方的: a ~ metre 一平方米 ④快而粗略的，浮面的 ||~ity [ˌsjuːpəˌfiʃiˈæliti] *n.* ①表面性；肤浅，浅薄 ②表面性的事物 / ~ly *ad.*

superfine [ˈsjuːpəˈfain] *a.* ①过分精细的 ②(商品等)特级的

superfluous [sjuː(ː)ˈpəːfluəs] *a.* 过剩的；多余的，不必要的: a ~ remark 多余的话 ||~ly *ad.* / ~ness *n.*

superintend [ˌsjuːpərinˈtend] *vt. & vi.* 监督，主管，指挥(工作等)

superintendent [ˌsjuːpərinˈtendənt] I *n.* ①监督人，主管人，指挥者；(部门、机关、企业等的)负责人 ②警察长 II *a.* 监督的，管理的

superior [sjuː(ː)ˈpiəriə] I *a.* ①(指位置方面)在上的，较高的: ~ antenna 【动】上触角 / ~ ovary 【植】上位子房 ②(在职位、权力等方面)较高的，上级的: a ~ court 上级法院 / a ~ officer 上级军官 ③(在数量等方面)较大的，较多的: ~ limit 【数】上限 ④优越的，优良的: ~ alloy steel 高质合金钢 ⑤不为…所惑的，不屈服于…的(to): be ~ to temptation 不受引诱 / be ~ to hardship 不屈服于艰难困苦 ⑥高傲的，傲慢的: with a ~ air 态度傲慢地 ⑦包括范围更广的: A genus is ~ to a species. (生物学上的)属比种包括更多。⑧[印]位于上角的(如 xⁿ 中的 n)；比一行中其他字母高的 ⑨比地球离太阳更远的，在地球轨道以外的: a ~ planet 外行星 II *n.* ①上级；长官；长者 ②占优势者，优胜者: He has no ~ in this respect. 在这个方面没有人能胜过他。③修道院院长: the Father (Mother) Superior 男(女)修道院院长 ||rise ~ to 不受…的影响，不为…所动 ||~ly *ad.*

superiority [sjuː(ː)ˌpiəriˈɔriti] *n.* 优越(性)，优势: the ~ of your production facilities *to* ours 与我们相比你们在生产设备方面的优越性 / a sense of ~ 优越感 / the ~ *over* the enemy troops 对敌军的优势 / air (naval) ~ 空中(海上)优势 ||~ complex 【心】自尊情结

superjacent [ˌsjuːpəˈdʒeisənt] *a.* 盖在上面的，压在上面的

superjet [ˈsjuːpədʒet] *n.* 超音速喷气机

superlative [sjuː(ː)ˈpəːlətiv] I *a.* ①最高的；最好的: ~ wisdom 极高的智慧 ②过度的，被夸大了的 ③【语】(形容词、副词的)最高级的: the ~ degree 最高级 II *n.* ①最高的程度，极度；顶峰

②最好的物(或人) ③【语】最高级；最高级形式 ||*speak in* ~*s* 把话讲绝；讲得过分夸张 ||~ly *ad.* / ~ness *n.*

supermarket [ˈsjuːpəˌmɑːkit] *n.* 超级商场；自动售货商店

supernatural [ˌsjuːpəˈnætʃərəl] I *a.* 超自然的；神奇的，不可思议的 II *n.* ①超自然物；神奇的东西 ②[the ~]超自然现象 ||~ism *n.* 超自然性；超自然主义(认为自然及宇宙由某种超自然力控制) / ~ist *n.* 超自然主义者 *a.* 超自然主义的 / ~ly *ad.*

supersede [ˌsjuːpəˈsiːd] *vt.* ①代替；取代: The new ~s the old. 新的代替旧的。(或: 新陈代谢。) ②接替: ~ sb. as ambassador 接替某人当大使 ③废弃

supersonic [ˈsjuːpəˈsɔnik] I *a.* 超声(频)的；超声速的: a ~ plane 超音速飞机 II *n.* 超声波；超声频

superstition [ˌsjuːpəˈstiʃən] *n.* 迷信；迷信行为: Do away with all fetishes and ~s. 破除迷信。||*the thirteen* ~ (西方)以十三为不吉利的迷信

superstitious [ˌsjuːpəˈstiʃəs] *a.* 迷信的；由迷信引起的 ||~ly *ad.* / ~ness *n.*

superstructure [ˈsjuːpəˌstrʌktʃə] *n.* ①上层建筑: in the realm of the ~ 在上层建筑领域内 ②【建】上部结构；【船】(尤指战舰的)上层结构

supervene [ˌsjuːpəˈviːn] *vi.* 意外发生；伴随产生

supervise [ˈsjuːpəvaiz] *vt. & vi.* 监督，管理 ||supervision [ˌsjuːpəˈviʒən] *n.*

supervisor [ˈsjuːpəvaizə] *n.* ①监督(人)，管理人，主管人 ②督学(员) ||~ship *n.* 管理(或监督、主管)人的职位

supine¹ [sjuːˈpain] *a.* ①仰卧的；(手)掌心向上的；(手)掌心朝外的 ②懒散的；苟安的，因循的 ③[古]向后靠的 ||~ly *ad.* / ~ness *n.*

supine² [ˈsjuːpain] *n.* (拉丁语法中的)动名词

supper [ˈsʌpə] *n.* 晚饭，晚餐: have very little (a hearty) ~ 晚饭吃得很少(很丰盛) ||*the Last Supper* 【宗】耶稣及其十二门徒的最后晚餐 / *the Lord's Supper* 【宗】①圣餐(仪式) ②耶稣及其十二门徒的最后晚餐 ||~ club 高级夜总会

supplant [səˈplɑːnt] *vt.* ①把…排挤掉 ②代替；取代 ||~ation [ˌsʌplænˈteiʃən] *n.* / ~er *n.* 排挤者，取代者

supple [ˈsʌpl] I *a.* ①柔软的，易弯曲的: ~ leather 柔软的皮革 / the ~ body of a gymnast 体操运动员的柔软的身体 ②顺从的；巴结的 ③(思想等)易适应的，反应快的 ④轻快的；流畅的 II ❶ *vt.* 使柔软；使顺从；使驯服: ~ the rawhide 把生皮弄柔软 / a horse 驯马 ❷ *vi.* [古]变柔顺；变柔和 ||~ly *ad.* / ~ness *n.* ||~jack *n.* ①具有软韧树干的攀缘植物(尤指美国南部的一种藤) ②软韧(攀缘植物制成的)手杖

supplement I [ˈsʌplimənt] *n.* ①增补,补充 ②(书籍的)补遗;附录;(报刊等的)副刊,增刊: a ~ to a dictionary 词典的补编 ③【数】补角 **II** ['sʌpli-ment] *vt.* 增补,补充: ~ natural fertilizer with chemical fertilizer 用化肥补充天然肥料 ‖**-ation** [,sʌplimen'teiʃən] *n.*

supplementary [,sʌpli'mentəri] *a.* ① 补充的,增补的;追加的: ~ reading 辅助阅读(材料) / a ~ means 辅助手段 ②【数】(角)补成一百八十度的: ~ angle 补角

suppliant ['sʌpliənt] **I** *n.* 恳求者,哀求者 **II** *a.* (表示)恳求的,(表示)哀求的: ~ words 恳求的话 ‖**~ly** *ad.*

supplicate ['sʌplikeit] **❶** *vt.* 哀求,恳求;祈求: ~ (sb. for) pardon 求(向某人求)饶 / ~ sb. to help 恳求某人帮助 **❷** *vi.* 哀求;祈求: ~ for mercy 乞求怜悯,求饶 ‖**supplicatingly** *ad.* / **supplication** [,sʌpli'keiʃən] *n.* / **supplicatory** ['sʌplikətəri] *a.*

supply[1] [sə'plai] **I** **❶** *vt.* ①供给,供应,提供: ~ the market *with* new commodities 向市场供应新商品 / ~ sb. an answer 向某人提供答案 ②补充,填补: ~ a deficiency 弥补不足 / ~ a need (或 demand) 满足需要 ③代理,暂代: ~ an office 代理职务 **❷** *vi.* 代理,暂代 **II** *n.* ①供给(量);供应(量);补给: ~ and demand 供给与需要,供与求 / a good ~ of meat (fish, fruit) 肉类(鱼类,水果)的大量供应 / water ~ 供水 / a ~ depot (line, base) 补给仓库(线,基地) / the Committee of *Supply* (英国)下院的预算委员会 ②[常用复]供应品;生活用品;(储备)物资;补给品;存货: rush *supplies* to a place 赶运供应品至某地 / military *supplies* 军需品 / household (medical) *supplies* 家庭(医药)用品 ③[复](供给某人的)生活费用;议会对政府费用的拨款 ④代理牧师;代课教师 ‖*in short* ~ 供应不足 / *the place of* 见 place ‖**supplier** *n.* ①供应者,供应厂商 ②原料(或商品)供应国(或地区)

support [sə'pɔ:t] **I** *vt.* ①支撑,支承: a roof ~ed *by* arches 用拱支承的屋顶 / ~ oneself *with* a stick 拄着手杖 / be ~ed home 被扶着回家 ②支持;支援;赞助;拥护: ~ a resolution 赞成一项决议 / ~ a government statement 拥护政府声明 ③经受,忍受: ~ fatigue 忍受疲劳 / I can ~ such insolence no longer. 我不能再忍受这样的无礼。④供养,维持;资助: ~ a family 养家 / ~ oneself 养活自己 ⑤为…提供证据;证实: ~ an argument 为一论点提供证据 ⑥激励,使有勇气(或信心): 保持…进行下去: The discussion was not well ~ed. 这次讨论不是一直进行得很好。⑦【戏】替…当配角;演…角色;【音】伴奏 ⑧通过买进(或借贷)的方法维持(高的价格),维持(农产品等)的价格 **II** *n.* ①支持,支承 ②支持;援助;拥护: The proposal obtained much ~. 这个建议得到很多支持。/ A just cause enjoys abundant ~. 得道多助。/ a ~ line 【军】补给线,供应线 / a ~ trench 【军】支援堑壕 ③供养;生计: production by the army for its own 军

队的生产自给 / refuse to pay ~ 拒付赡养费 ④支持者;支撑物;支柱;支座 ⑤【军】支援部队 ⑥【戏】配角;【音】伴奏 ‖*in* ~ 【军】供支援用的,后备的: troops *in* ~ 后备部队 / *in* ~ *of* 支援;支持;拥护 / ~ *one's self* 见 self ‖**~less** *a.* 没有支撑的;没有支持的

suppose [sə'pəuz] **❶** *vt.* ①猜想,料想;想象: I ~ (that) he is not yet twenty. (或 I ~ him to be not yet twenty.) 我猜想他还不到二十岁。②假定: *Suppose* A equals B. 假定 A 等于 B。/ Let us ~ another planet with conditions similar to those on the earth. 让我们假定另外有一个具有和地球上相似条件的行星。/ *Suppose* (或 *Supposing*) he is absent, what shall we do? 假使他不在,我们怎么办? / *Suppose* (或 *Supposing*) it rained, we would still go. 假如下雨的话,我们还是要去。③[用于祈使语气]让: *Suppose* we start(ed) tomorrow. 我们明天动身吧。(用 started 时语气较婉转) ④必须先假定,需要以…作为条件,意味着: That ~s a machine without internal friction. 那就必须假定有一架内部不存在摩擦的机器。**❷** *vi.* 猜想,料想: The work will be finished tomorrow, I ~. 我想这件工作明天可以完成了。/ I ~ so. 我看是这样。/ I ~ not. 我看不见得。‖*be* ~*d to* ①被期望;应该: We *are* ~*d to* be here at seven. 我们应该七时到达这里。②[用于否定句][口]获准: You *are not* ~*d to* smoke on the bus. 你不可能在公共汽车上抽烟。

supposed [sə'pəuzd] *a.* 想象上的;假定的;被信以为真的: a ~ case 假定的场合 / sb.'s ~ kindness 某人那种被信以为真的好意

supposedly [sə'pəuzidli] *ad.* 想象上;按照推测;恐怕: a book ~ written by the same author 被猜想由同一作者写的一本书

supposition [,sʌpə'ziʃən] *n.* 想象;假定;推测: This is not based on mere ~. 这并不是仅仅根据推测。/ on the ~ that . . . 假定…

suppress [sə'pres] *vt.* ①压制: ~ criticism 压制批评 ②抑制,阻止…的生长: ~ a cough 忍住咳嗽 / ~ one's feelings 抑制情感 ③隐藏,隐瞒: ~ the truth (name) 隐瞒真相(名字) ④禁止(书刊等)发行;查禁: ~ news 封锁新闻 ‖**~ion** [sə'preʃən] *n.* / **~or** *n.* (干扰)抑制器;消除器;【无】抑制栅极

supreme [sju(:)'pri:m] *a.* ①最高的,至上的: the ~ ideal 最高理想 ②最大的,极度的;最重要的: a (或 the) ~ moment 决定性的时刻 / a ~ fool 大傻瓜 ‖*the Supreme* (*Being*) 【宗】上帝 / *the* ~ *end* 见 end ‖**~ly** *ad.* ‖**Supreme Court** (美国)联邦最高法院;州最高法院 / ~ **good** 至善 / **Supreme Soviet** (苏联)的最高苏维埃

surcharge ['sə:tʃɑ:dʒ] **I** *n.* ①超载;负荷过重;过度的负担 ②额外费;附加罚款(如对欠资信件的罚款);过高的索价: a sleeping car ~ 卧车增收费 ③(邮票等上的)更改票值的印记;盖有改值印记的邮票 ④指出对方在贷方漏记一笔帐 **II** *vt.*

①使载得过多,使负担过重; 使充满 ②对…索费过多; 向…收取额外费; 处(某人)以附加罚款 ③在(邮票)上加盖改值印记 ④指出对方在(帐)上漏记一笔贷方款项

sure [ʃuə] **I** *a.* ①[用作表语]确信的,有把握的; 一定的,必定的: Are you ~ (of it)? 你能肯定吗? / Do you feel ~ about it? 你对这有把握吗? / I am ~ (that) he will come. 我肯定他会来。/ be ~ of sb.'s sincerity 确信某人的诚意 / You are ~ of a cordial reception. 你肯定会受到热诚的接待。/ Well, I am ~! 啊,真的! (表示惊奇的用语) / I'm ~ I don't know. 我真的不知道。/ Be ~ not to forget it. 千万不要忘记呀! / It is ~ to rain. 一定会下雨。/ I'm not ~ whether I've met him before. 我不能确定以前是否见到过他。②确实的,稳当的; 可靠的; 万全的: ~ victory 必定无疑的胜利 / ~ evidence 确凿的证据 / a ~ foundation 稳固的基础 / a ~ remedy for colds 治感冒的良药 / the *surest* means to the end 达到此目的最有效的办法 / a ~ shot 百发百中的射手 / steady and ~ 踏实而稳妥 **II** *ad.* [美口]的确,一定: It ~ was a cold night. 的确是个寒冷的夜晚。/ A: Are you going? B: *Sure!* 甲:你去吗? 乙:当然啦! ‖*as ~ as a gun* (或 *as ~ as eggs is eggs*, *as ~ as death*, *as ~ as nails*, *as ~ as fate*, *as ~ as one lives*) [口]的确确,千真万确: It will happen, *as ~ as a gun.* 那是必定会发生的。/ *be ~ and* ... [口]千万要…,一定要…: *Be ~ and* remember what I told you. 千万要记住我对你讲的话。/ *be* (或 *feel*) *~ of oneself* 有自信心 / *for ~* 确实,毫无疑问地: I don't know it *for ~.* 这事我不确切知道。/ *make ~* ①查明,弄确实; 使确定: I think the quotation is from Volume IV, but you'd better make ~. 我想这段引文是摘自第四卷,但你最好核实一下。②确信/~ *enough* 果然,果真: We said things would turn out well, and ~ *enough* they did. 我们说情况会变好的,果然如此。/ ~ *thing* 见 *thing*¹ / *to be* ~ [口]①[用作插入语]诚然,固然: He is young, *to be ~*, but very experienced. 他固然还年轻,但已很有经验了。②[用于惊叹句]哎呀: So it is, *to be ~!* 啊! 真的是那样呀! ‖~*ness* *n.* ‖~-*enough* ['ʃuəri'naf] *a.* [美口]真正的,确实的 / '~*fire* *a.* [美口]一定会成功的; 可靠的: a ~*fire* winner 肯定会获胜的人 / '~*footed* *a.* ①脚步稳的, 不会摔倒的: a ~*footed* horse 脚步稳的马 ②稳当的,踏实的,不会出差错的: ~*footed* judgement 稳当的判断 / a ~*footed* driver 稳妥的驾驶员

surely ['ʃuəli] *ad.* ①确实,无疑,一定: This achievement is ~ unprecedented. 这成就确实是空前的。/ He knows full ~ that .... 他确实完全知道… / They will ~ succeed. 他们一定会成功。②稳当地,踏实地: He is working steadily and ~. 他在踏踏实实地工作。③[常放在句首或句尾,强调推断等]谅必,一定: *Surely* you don't believe that! 你谅必不会相信那个吧! / It cannot be true, ~. 那决不至于是真的。/ *Surely* I have met you before somewhere. 我记得一定在什么地方碰到过你的。④[主美][常用于问答句中]当然: A: Are you going with us? B: *Surely.* 甲:你和我们一起去吗? 乙:当然啦!

surety ['ʃuəti] *n.* ①[古]确实,肯定: of a ~ 的确,肯定地 ②保证,担保; 保证人; [罕]担保品: stand ~ for sb. 为某人作保 / find ~ (或 *sureties*) 具保 / ~**ship** *n.* 保人的地位(或资格、责任)

surf [sə:f] *n.* 拍岸浪; 拍岸浪花; 拍岸涛声 **II** *vi.* 乘冲浪板,作冲浪运动 ‖~**board** *n.* (冲浪运动用的)冲浪板(一种狭长的板,人站其上滑过浪顶向岸边冲去) / '~**boat** *n.* (牢固,具有高度浮力的)破浪艇 / ~**man** ['sə:fmən] *n.* 善于在浪中驾船的船夫(尤指美国海岸警卫队雇用的救生员) / '~-,**riding** *n.* 乘冲浪板,冲浪运动

surface ['sə:fis] **I** *n.* ①面,表面: the ~ of the earth 地球的表面 / A cube has six ~s. 立方体有六个面。/ a plane (curved) ~ 平(曲)面 ②水面: The submarine rose to the ~. 潜水艇浮出水面。③外表,外观: look below (或 beneath) the ~ of things 透过表面观察事物 / One never gets below the ~ with him. 人们无法看透他究竟是怎样一个人。④[空]翼面 **II** *a.* ①表面的,外观的,外表上的: ~ impressions 表面上的印象 / ~ tension [物]表面张力 ②水面上的; 地面上的: ~ craft (或 vessels) 水面舰船,普通船只(与潜水艇相对而言) / ~ mail (用车辆或船只递送的)普通邮件(与航空邮件相对而言) **III** ❶ *vt.* ①对…进行表面处理,使光滑,刨光; 在…上加表面: ~ a highway 给公路铺面 ②使(潜水艇等)浮出水面; 使露头,使出现 ❷ *vi.* ①在地面(或近地面)工作(如采矿)②浮出水面: The fish ~d and jumped. 鱼露出水面跳跃。③显露,呈现: The truth (grievances) began to ~. 真相(愤懑的情绪)开始显露了。‖*on the* (或 *of the*) ~ 表面上,外表上: His politeness is only *on the* ~. 他只是表面上客气。/ *scratch the* ~ *(of)* (对…)作肤浅的探讨,(对…)浅尝即止 ‖~**r** *n.* [机]平面刨床 / **surfacing** *n.* 铺面(材料) ‖~-,**active** *a.* [化]表面活性的 / ~ **car** [美]路面车辆(与地上及架空的车辆相对而言) / ~ **colo(u)r** 表面色,表面反射的颜料 ②表面色 / ~ **force** ①地面部队 ②水面部队; 水面舰艇 / ~-**man** ['sə:fismən] *n.* ①(铁路)护路工人 ②[矿]井上工人 / ~ **noise** 针头在唱片上的摩擦声 / ~ **plate** [机]平板(铸铁制成,检验作件平正度用) / ~ **printing** 凸板印刷 / '~-**to-air** *a.* (导弹)地对空的 / '~-**to-**,~ *a.* (导弹)地对地的 / ~ **water** 地表水; 淤水 / ~ **wave** (地震的)面波; [电]表面波,地表电波

surfeit ['sə:fit] **I** *n.* ①过量; 过度 (*of*): a ~ *of* complaints 过多的埋怨 ②饮食过度: die of a ~ 暴饮暴食而死 ③(饮食过度等引起的)恶心,不

适: feed oneself to ~ 吃得太多而不适 **II ❶** *vt.*
使饮食过度; 过多地供给; 使沉溺于 (with): ~
oneself *with* good eating 好东西吃得过多 / be
~ed *with* pleasure 放纵地享乐 **❷** *vi.* 饮食过度;
[古]沉溺,放纵

surge [sə:dʒ] **I** *n.* ①巨浪,波涛 ②汹涌,澎湃:
the ~ of the sea 海浪的奔腾 / ~s of enthusiasm
热情的洋溢 ③【电】电流急冲,电涌: ~ current
冲击电流,浪涌电流 ④【海】(绞盘急速松缆的)锥
形部; (缆绳的)滑脱(或放松) **II ❶** *vi.* ①汹涌
澎湃; 波动; 激动: The waves ~ high. 波涛汹
涌。/ *surging* crowds 蜂拥的人群 ②【电】电流急
冲, 电涌; 振荡 ③(绞盘上的绳或缆)滑脱, 放松
④(车轮)空转不前 **❷** *vt.* 急放(绳缆等)

surgeon [ˈsə:dʒən] *n.* ①外科医师: a dental ~ 口
腔科医师 ②军医 **‖~cy** *n.* [英]外科医师的职
位 **‖~ dentist** 口腔科医师 / **Surgeon General**
①(美国)军医局局长 ②(美国)卫生局医务主任
③[s- g-](英国陆军中的)军医 / **~'s knot** (绑
扎或缝合用的)外科结

surgery [ˈsə:dʒəri] *n.* ①外科; 外科学; 外科手术:
oral ~ 口腔外科 / clinical ~ 临证(或临床)外
科学 / plastic ~ 成形外科学 ②外科手术室; 外
科实验室 ③[英](开业医师的)诊所

surgical [ˈsə:dʒikəl] *a.* ①外科(术)的; 外科医师
的: a ~ operation 外科手术 / ~ skills 外科技
术 ②外科(手术)用的: ~ implements 外科用器
械 / ~ gloves 外科手术用手套 ③外科手术引起
的: ~ fevers 外科手术热 **‖~ly** *ad.*

surly [ˈsə:li] *a.* ①乖戾的; 阴郁的; 粗暴的,无礼的:
a ~ beggar (或 dog) 乖戾的人, 粗暴的人 ②(天
气等)阴沉的,阴霾的 **‖surlily** *ad.* / **surliness** *n.*

surmise **I** [sə:ˈmaiz] *vt.* & *vi.* 推测; 猜测, 臆测
II [ˈsə:maiz] *n.* 推测; 猜测, 臆测

surmount [sə:ˈmaunt] *vt.* ①克服; 越过; 登上: ~
every difficulty 排除万难 / ~ obstacles 克服(或
越过)障碍 / a temptation 不受诱惑 / ~ one
crag after another 登上一块又一块的巉岩 ②[常
用被动语态]在…顶上覆盖; 装在…顶上: a peak
~ed *with* snow 积雪的峰顶 / A weathercock ~s
the steeple. 塔尖上装着风标。**‖~able** *a.* 可
克服的; 可超越的

surname [ˈsə:neim] **I** *n.* ①姓 ②别号; 外号; 浑
名,绰号 **II** *vt.* ①给…起别号(或绰号) ②给…
取姓氏

surpass [sə:ˈpɑ:s] *vt.* 超越, 胜过: ~ advanced
world levels 超过世界先进水平 / The latecomers
~ the early starters. 后来居上。

surplice [ˈsə:pləs] *n.* (教士穿的)宽大白色法衣
‖~d *a.* 穿白色法衣的

surplus [ˈsə:pləs] **I** *n.* ①过剩; 剩余(物资); 剩余
额: war ~ 剩余作战物资 / have a ~ of tea for
sale 有剩余的茶叶待售 ②公积金; 盈余: foreign
trade ~ 对外贸易顺差(或出超) **II** *a.* 过剩的,
剩余的; 多余的: articles ~ *to* one's requirements
超过需要的物品 / an essay heavy with

~ phrasing 废话连篇的散文 **‖~ value** 剩余
价值

surprise [səˈpraiz] **I** *vt.* ①使惊奇,使诧异,使感
到意外: You ~ me! 你真使我惊奇! / I am
~d *at* you. 我对你的举动感到诧异。/ I was
~d *at* seeing (或 to see) him there. 我真想不到
会在那里见到他。/ We are ~d (to learn) that
he lost the game. 我们对他在比赛中的失败感
到惊奇。②突然袭击; 突然攻占; 出其不意地俘
获: ~ the enemy 奇袭敌人 ③乘对方不备时设
法得到; 乘其不备地使吐露真言; 出其不意地使
(某人)做某事(*into*): ~ an admission from sb.
在某人不备时使其作出承认 / ~ sb. *into* (giving)
consent 用出其不意的办法使某人同意 ④意外地
遇见, 撞见; 当场捉住: ~ a burglar breaking
into a store 撞见(或抓住)一个闯入商店正在作
案的夜盗 **II** *n.* ①惊奇, 诧异: *in* ~ 惊异地 /
To my (great) ~, he managed to accomplish the
task only in a few days. 使我(非常)惊奇的是,
他竟能在短短几天内完成了这个任务。②使人惊异
的事物: What a ~! 真是意想不到的事! /
I have a ~ *for* you. 我有一件你想不到的事
(或消息)告诉你。(或: 我有一样你想不到的礼物
送给你。) / The whole thing is a great ~ *to* us.
整个事情使我们感到十分惊奇。③出其不意, 突
然袭击: capture sb. *by* ~ 出其不意地俘获某
人 / a ~ visit 突然访问 / a ~ attack 奇袭 /
a ~ party 奇袭队 **‖ take by** ~ ①出奇兵攻占
②撞见; 冷不防地捉住 ③使吃惊, 使诧异: His
sudden departure *took* us quite *by* ~. 他的突
然离去使我们非常惊奇

surprising [səˈpraiziŋ] *a.* 使人惊奇的, 惊人的; 出
人意外的: with ~ rapidity 以惊人的速度 / a ~
success 出人意外的成功 **‖~ly** *ad.*

surrender [səˈrendə] **I ❶** *vt.* ①交出; 放弃:
Surrender your arms, or we'll shoot! 缴枪不
杀! / ~ a fortress 放弃要塞 / ~ one's privi-
leges 放弃金权特权 / ~ one's insurance policy 取得
退保金而将保险单交回保险公司 ②[~
oneself] 使投降; 使自首 ③[常用 ~ oneself]
听任, 使沉溺于 (to) **❷** *vi.* 投降; 自首: ~ *to*
one's bail (犯人)交保期满后自动归押 **II** *n.*
①交出; 放弃; 投降: demand the ~ of all
weapons 要求交出所有武器 / unconditional ~
无条件投降 ②【律】逃犯的引渡 ③(保释人)将罪
犯交回(司法机关)的行动 (= ~ by bail) ④专利
权的放弃; (为取得退保金额而作的)保险的放弃
‖~ at discretion 无条件投降 **‖~ value** (被保
险人中途放弃保险时)保险单的退保值, 退保金额

surreptitious [ˌsʌrəpˈtiʃəs] *a.* 鬼鬼祟祟的, 偷偷摸
摸的; 秘密的 **‖~ly** *ad.*

surround [səˈraund] **I** *vt.* 围, 围绕; 圈住; 包围:
A crowd ~ed him. 一群人围着他。/ The school
was ~ed *by* (或 *with*) a fence. 学校四周围着
篱笆。/ Complete secrecy ~ed the meeting.
会议在绝密中进行。**II** *n.* ①围绕物: the paved

~ of a swimming pool 游泳池四周的铺道 ②地毯周围与墙之间的地板; 地毯与墙之间的地板上的铺盖物: a linoleum ~ 铺在地毯四周的油地毡

surrounding [sə'raundiŋ] I n. [复]周围的事物; 环境: The guest house stands in picturesque ~s. 宾馆四周的环境优美如画。 II a. 周围的: the ~ country 近郊

surtax ['sə:tæks] I n. ①附加税 ②(对超过一定额的收入征收的)超额累进所得税 II vt. 对…征收附加税(或超额累进所得税)

survey [sə(:)'vei] I ❶ vt. ①俯瞰; 环视; 眺望: ~ the surrounding landscape 眺望周围的景色 ②检查; 调查; 概括地观察(或评述); 审视: ~ the equipment 检查设备 / ~ population growth 调查人口增长情况 / ~ the international situation 概括地评述国际形势 / ~ a stranger from head to toe 从头到脚打量陌生人 ③测量, 勘定: ~ the boundaries of a tract of land 勘定一片土地的边界 ❷ vi. 测量土地 II ['sə:vei, sə:'vei] n. ①俯瞰; 环视; 眺望 ②概观; 概括的研究, 全面的评述, 综论; 检查; 调查 ③测量, 查勘: geological ~ 地质调查, 地质勘测 ④被测量的地区; 测量图, 测量记录; 测量部 ||~ing n. ①环视; 概观; 检查 ②测量; 测量学, 测量术 / ~ course 概况课程

surveyor [sə(:)'veiə] n. ①测量员, 勘测员, 测地员 ②(海关等的)检查员, 检查官; 鉴定人 ||a ~ of the highways ①负责检查公路的官员 ②醉汉 / a ~ of the pavement 戴上颈手枷示众的犯人 ||~ general ①(某部门、某地区或某项任务的)总检查员, 总监督官 ②[美](某地区公地的)测量主任

survival [sə'vaivəl] n. ①幸存, 残存; 生存 ②幸存者; 残存物: a ~ from ancient times 古代遗物(或遗风) ||the ~ of the fittest 适者生存

survive [sə'vaiv] ❶ vt. ①比…活得长: She ~d her husband for ten years. 她比她的丈夫多活了十年。 ②幸免于, 从…中逃生: He ~d the shipwreck. 在这次船只沉没事件中他幸免于死。 / The house ~d the storm. 经过暴风雨袭击, 这所房屋并未倒塌。 / ~ one's usefulness 年老无用 ❷ vi. 活下来; 幸存; 残存

survivor [sə'vaivə] n. 幸存者, 生还者; 残存物: the ~s of an air raid 空袭后的幸存者 ||~ship n. ①幸存, 未死; 残存 ②[律](财产共有者中)生者对死者名下财产的享有权

susceptible [sə'septəbl] a. ①易受感动的, 易受影响的; 敏感的 (to): a ~ fellow 易动情感的人 / be ~ to cold 容易受凉 / be very~ to satire 对讽刺很敏感 ②能容许…的, 可被…的, 可受…影响的 (of, to): a theory ~ of proof 能证实的理论 / The problem is ~ to solution. 这问题是可以解决的。 / testimony ~ of error 不大可靠的证词 ||**susceptibility** [sə,septə'biliti] n. ①易感性, 易感性; 敏感性 ②[复]感情, 敏感之处 ③[物]磁化率, 磁化系数 / **susceptibly** ad.

suspect [səs'pekt] I ❶ vt. ①疑有, 猜想; 觉得: ~ danger (an ambush) 疑有危险(埋伏) / We

~ him to be ill (或 that he is ill). 我们猜想他病了。 ②怀疑, 不信任: ~ the authenticity of the evidence 怀疑那份证据的可靠性 ③怀疑(某人犯有过错): ~ sb. of giving false information 怀疑某人提供假情报 / be ~ed of a theft 有偷窃的嫌疑 / I ~ him to be a liar (或 that he is a liar). 我怀疑他是个说谎的家伙。 / a ~ed criminal 嫌疑犯 ❷ vi. 怀疑, 疑心; 猜疑: You don't care, I ~. 我想你大概不在乎吧。 II ['sʌspekt] n. 嫌疑犯; 可疑分子: a political ~ 政治嫌疑犯 III ['sʌspekt] a. [只作表语]可疑的: The testimony given by him is ~. 他所作的证词是可疑的。 ||~able a. 可疑的

suspend [səs'pend] ❶ vt. ①吊, 悬; 使悬浮: ~ a lamp from the ceiling 把灯从天花板挂下 / a balloon ~ed in mid air 悬在半空中的气球 / ~ed particles of dust 浮在空中的尘埃 ②使悬而不决; 推迟; 中止; 暂停: ~ judgement (sentence) 缓期宣判(处刑) / ~ publication 暂时停刊 / ~ talks 中止谈判 / ~ diplomatic relations 中止外交关系 / ~ one's indignation 暂息怒气 / ~ a bicycle license 暂时吊销自行车执照 / ~ed animation 【医】活状暂停, 不省人事 ③暂令…停职(或停学等): be ~ed from school (office) 被暂令停学(职) / ~ a football player 暂停一个足球队员的比赛权 ❷ vi. ①暂停; 中止 ②【商】无力支付, 宣布破产 ③悬, 挂; 悬浮: fine particles that ~ readily in water 很易浮在水中的细粒 ||~er n. ①吊的东西; 吊杆, 吊索 ②[美][复]吊裤带, 吊带; [英][复]吊袜带

suspense [səs'pens] n. ①悬而不决, 未定: Our next step is still in ~. 我们的下一个步骤尚未决定。 ②挂虑, 不安, 担心: keep sb. in ~ 使某人挂虑(或悬念) ③(权利等的)暂时停止; 中止 ||~ account 【会计】暂记帐

suspension [səs'penʃən] n. ①悬, 吊; 悬挂物; 【机】悬置(指车轴上利用弹簧等托住车身等); 【化】悬浮(液), 悬胶(体): droplets of oil in ~ in a gas 悬在气体中的小油滴 / spring ~ 弹簧悬置 ②暂停; 中止; 暂时停职, 暂时停学: ~ from school (office) 暂时停学(职) / the ~ of business 暂时停业 / the ~ of a meeting 会议的中止 / the ~ of a member of Parliament 暂停一个议员的职权 ③【商】停止(或无力)支付, 无力偿债 ④未决, 悬而不决 ⑤【音】悬留法, 悬留音 ⑥【语】(使读者等悬念下文的)宕笔法, 卖关子; 缩略(法) ||~ bridge 吊桥 / ~ points, ~ periods 省略号(即…)

suspicion [səs'piʃən] I n. ①怀疑, 疑心; 猜疑: have a ~ that... 怀疑… / a groundless ~ 无根据的怀疑 / There is a strong ~ against him. 对他有很大怀疑。 / The behaviour of the stranger aroused our ~. 那陌生人的行为引起了我们的怀疑。 / be above (under) ~ 无可(受到)怀疑 / with ~ 怀疑地 ②嫌疑: be examined on (the) ~ of being an enemy agent 因敌特

嫌疑而受审查 / lay oneself open to ~ 使自己遭到嫌疑 ③ [a ~] 一点儿 (of): without a ~ of humour 毫无幽默 II *vt.* [美口]怀疑 ||~less *a.* 不(表示)怀疑的

suspicious [səs'piʃəs] *a.* ①可疑的· a ~ character 可疑人物 / ~ actions 可疑的行为 ②猜疑的;疑心的;多疑的: a ~ glance 猜疑的一瞥 / be ~ of sb. (sth.) 对某人(某事)起疑心 / The rabbit is timid and ~. 兔子胆怯而多疑。||~ly *ad.* / ~ness *n.*

sustain [səs'tein] *vt.* ①支撑, 撑住, 承受住: The pillars ~ the roof. 几根柱子撑住屋顶。/ be ~ed by the faith in 在对…的信念的支持(或鼓舞)下 ②供养, 维持; 继续: ~ a family 赡养家庭 / food sufficient to ~ life 足够维持生命的食物 / ~ conversation for hours 使谈话持续数小时 / ~ a note 持续地唱(或奏)一个音符 / friendly relations 保持友好关系 ③蒙受, 遭受: ~ losses 蒙受损失 / ~ a defeat 遭到失败 ④忍受, 经受住: He could not ~ such a shock. 他受不住这样的震惊。/ It will not ~ comparison with another. 这东西经不起与另一个东西相比。⑤证实, 证明: These facts ~ the theory. 这些事实证实了这学说。⑥(法庭等)确认, 认可; 准许; 支持: ~ an applicant in his claim 确定申请人的要求合理 / ~ an objection 支持异议 ⑦恰当地扮演(角色): ~ the part of 恰当地扮演…的角色 ||~able *a.* 能支撑住的; 能忍受的; 可证实的

sustained [səs'teind] *a.* 持续的, 持久的; 持久不变的: ~ fire 持续的火力 / launch a ~ struggle 进行不懈的斗争 / make a ~ effort to practise economy 持久地厉行节约 / a ~ note 持续音(符)

sustenance ['sʌstinəns] *n.* ①生计 ②粮食, 食物; 营养 ③支持; 维持; 供养 ④支撑物

suzerain ['sju:zərein] *n.* ①封建主 ②宗主国

swab [swɔb] I *n.* ①(擦洗甲板、地板等用的)拖把 ②[医]拭子, 药签; (用拭子取下的)化验标本: a gauze ~ 纱布拭子 / a cotton ~ 棉花签 ③[军]枪炮刷 ④[俚]笨拙的人 ⑤[美俚](商船上的)水手 ⑥[英俚](海军军官的)肩章 II (swabbed; swabbing) *vt.* ①(用拖把)擦洗; (用拭子等)拭抹: ~ the deck 擦甲板 ②(用药签)敷药于: ~ the wound with mercurochrome 用药签在伤口上敷红药水 ||~ down ①擦甲板; 擦洗(甲板等) ②洗澡 ||**swabber** *n.* ①使用拖把(或拭子等)的人 ②水手 ③装管工 ④笨拙的人 ||~-downs [复] *n.* [海][俚]肩章

swag [swæg] I *n.* ①[澳](步行者或矿工等的)行李包, 包袱 ②摇晃; 倾侧 ③赃物 ④珍贵物; 钱财; 大量 ⑤一丛垂花(或垂枝); [建]垂花饰 ⑥洼地, 水潭 II (swagged; swagging) *vi.* ①摇晃; 倾侧 ②沉下; 垂下 ③[澳]背着行李旅行

swagger ['swægə] I ❶ *vi.* ①昂首阔步 (about, in, out) ②狂妄自大, 自鸣得意 ③吹牛皮, 说大话 (about): ~ about one's exploits 吹嘘自己的业绩

❷ *vt.* 恫吓, 吓唬: ~ sb. *into* concession 吓唬某人让步 / ~ sb. *out* of his money 诈诈某人的钱财 II *n.* ①昂首阔步 ②狂妄自大 ③虚张声势, 摆架子 III *a.* [口](衣服等)漂亮的, 时髦的 ||~er ['swægərə] *n.* 昂首阔步者; 狂妄自大者; 吹牛的家伙 / ~ingly ['swægəriŋli] *ad.* ||~ stick (军官等用的)轻便手杖

swallow¹ ['swɔlou] *n.* 燕子 ||*One ~ does not make a summer.* [谚](源自《伊索寓言》)一燕不成夏。(或: 轻率推论必成大错。或: 一关渡过并非万事大吉。) ||~ dive 燕式跳水 / ~ plover 燕鸻 / ~ shrike 燕鹀 / ~tail *n.* ①燕尾 ②燕尾服 ③[动]凤蝶 ④燕尾旗的末端 ⑤[建]燕尾榫; (城堡的)燕尾形外障 / '~-tailed *a.* 如燕尾的, 燕尾式的: a ~-tailed coat 燕尾服

swallow² ['swɔlou] I ❶ *vt.* ①吞下, 咽下: ~ sth. (down) 吞下某物 ②吞没, 淹没 (up): The fog ~ed up the whole city. 迷雾笼罩全城。/ The billows ~ed up the vessel. 巨浪吞没了船只。③耗尽, 用尽 (up): ~ one's earnings 耗尽了挣来的钱 ④[口]轻信; 轻易接受: ~ sb.'s words 轻信某人的话 / ~ an idea 轻易接受一种想法 ⑤忍受: ~ an insult 忍辱 ⑥压制, 抑制: ~ a laugh (sob) 忍住不笑(哭)出来 ⑦取消(前言等): ~ one's words 取消前言, 承认失言 ⑧把(字、音)发得含糊 ❷ *vi.* 吞下, 咽下: chew well and then ~ 嚼细后咽下 / hard ~ 忍气吞声; 抑制强烈的感情 II *n.* ①吞, 咽: eat sth. in one ~ 把某物一口吞下 ②一次吞咽之物: take a ~ of brandy 喝一口白兰地酒 ③咽喉, 食道 ④[海](滑车等的)通索孔 ⑤ =~-hole / ~ *a camel* 见 camel / ~ *the anchor* 见 anchor / ~ *the bait* 见 bait ||~able *a.* 可吞咽的; 宜于吞咽的 / ~er *n.* ①吞咽者 ②贪吃的人 ||'~-hole *n.* 【地】石灰坑, 斗淋

swamp [swɔmp] I *n.* ①沼泽; 沼泽地 ②[矿]煤层聚水道 II ❶ *vt.* ①使陷入沼泽; 淹没: This factory is ~ed *with* orders. 这家工厂的订货多得应接不暇。②击溃, 压倒 ③淹没(林中杂品等); 开辟(道路) ❷ *vi.* 陷入沼泽; 淹没; 沉没 ||~ buggy 沼泽地带用的车辆; 水陆牵引车; 用螺旋桨推进的平底船 / ~ fever ①疟疾; 感染性贫血 ②钩端螺体病, 细螺旋体病 / '~land *n.* 沼泽地

swampy ['swɔmpi] *a.* (多)沼泽的; 似沼泽的; 湿而松软的

swan¹ [swɔn] *n.* ①([复] swan(s)) 天鹅 ②天鹅般的人(或物); (卓越的)诗人, 歌手: the *Swan* of Avon ['eivən] (英国剧作家与诗人)莎士比亚的外号(莎士比亚的故乡位于 Avon 艾冯河畔) ③ [S-] 【天】天鹅座 ||*All your ~s are geese.* 你的一切美妙期望(或诺言)都成了泡影。||~like *a.* 天鹅似的; 天鹅般的长颈的; 优雅的; 弯曲的 ||~ boat (船首有天鹅模型的)小游艇 / ~ dive [美]燕式跳水 (=swallow dive) / ~ goose 中国鹅 / '~-neck *n.* (轨道、管子等的)鹅颈弯(头) /

~sdown ['swɔnzdaun] *n.* ①天鹅绒毛 ②天鹅绒女式呢(由羊毛与丝、棉等混纺织成);纬面起绒厚棉布 / **~ shot** (打野禽等用的)大号子弹 / **'~skin** *n.* ①(带有绒毛、羽毛的)天鹅皮 ②厚密法兰绒 / **~ song** (西方古代传说中)天鹅临死时发出的美妙歌声 ②(诗人等的)最后作品;最后的露面;最后的言行 / **'~-,upping** *n.* [英](为了标明所有者)在小天鹅嘴上刻标记;每年一次为标刻泰晤士河上的小天鹅而作的旅行

swan² [swɔn] (swanned; swanning) *vi.* ①闲荡,游逛 ②(车辆等)蜿蜒地行驶: an aeroplane *swanning* over a forest 在森林上空盘旋的飞机

swan³ [swɔn] (swanned; swanning) *vi.* [方]发誓;宣称

swank [swæŋk] [口] **I** *n.* ①出风头,炫耀 ②虚张声势;摆架子;吹牛 ③优雅;漂亮 **II** *a.* =swanky **III** *vi.* 出风头,炫耀;摆架子;说大话 ||**~er** *n.* [主英]摆架子的人;虚张声势者

swap [swɔp] **I** (swapped; swapping) ❶ *vt.* 交换;交流;用…作交易: ~ data 交换资料 / ~ experience 交流经验 / ~ rice *for* wheat 以大米换小麦 ❷ *vi.* 交换;做交易 **II** *n.* 交换;交易: stock ~ 证券交易 ||*Never ~ horses while crossing the stream.* 见 **horse** ||**~ meet** 旧货物物交换会

sward [swɔ:d] **I** *n.* 草地;草皮 **II** *vt. & vi.* (给…)铺上草皮 ||**~ed** *a.* 铺上草皮的

swarm¹ [swɔ:m] **I** *n.* ①(为建立新巢而跟随蜂王迁出的)蜂群 ②(蜂房中的)蜂群 ③(移动中的)一群昆虫: a ~ of ants 一群蚂蚁 ④[生]游动的单细胞生物群(如游动孢子) ⑤一大群: ~s of people 密密麻麻的人群 / ~s of stars 繁星 **II** ❶ *vi.* ①(蜜蜂)成群飞离蜂巢 ②密集,云集;涌往: People ~ed *into* the exhibition hall. 人群涌进展览馆。/ Customers ~ed before the counter. 柜台前挤满了顾客。③充满(with); 在周围徘徊: a pond ~ing *with* geese 满是鹅的池塘 / The boy was ~ing *around* me. 这男孩子围着我转来转去。④[生]成群裂出(如从孢子囊中);(细胞、生物)成群浮游 ❷ *vt.* 挤满: The garden was ~ed *with* bees. 蜜蜂在花园里成群地飞来飞去。||**~ cell, ~ spore** [生]游动孢子,游走细胞

swarm² [swɔ:m] ❶ *vt.* 爬(树等): ~ up a pole 爬杆 ❷ *vi.* 爬杆(或树等)

swarthy ['swɔ:ði] *a.* 黝黑的,黑皮肤的 ||**swarthily** *ad.* / **swarthiness** *n.*

swastika, swastica ['swæstikə, 'swɔstikə] *n.* ①卍字饰(相传为象征太阳、吉祥等的标志) ②卐字(德国纳粹党的党徽)

swat [swɔt] **I** (swatted; swatting) *vt.* 重拍,猛击: ~ a fly 拍苍蝇 **II** *n.* 重拍,猛击

swathe [sweið] **I** *vt.* ①绑;裹;缠 ②包围;封住 **II** *n.* 带子,绷带;用以包物的东西

sway [swei] **I** ❶ *vi.* ①摇动;摇摆: Branches ~ gently in the wind. 树枝在风中微微摆动。②歪,倾斜,偏向一边: The earthquake caused the wall to ~ to the right. 地震使墙向右边倾斜。③动摇;转向: His resolution never ~s. 他的决心从不动摇。④支配,统治: That was the motive that ~ed with him. 那就是支配他的动机。❷ *vt.* ①摇,摇动;使摇摆: Wind ~s trees and grass. 风吹动树木和草。②弄歪,使倾斜,使偏向一边 ③使动摇,使转向;影响: He was not ~ed by the speaker's eloquence. 他不为演说者的口才所动。/ ~ the minds of men 动摇人心 ④[古]挥动,挥舞(剑等);支配,统治: ~ a nation 统治一个国家 ⑤[海]扯起(帆桁)(up) **II** *n.* ①摇动,摇摆;倾斜 ②支配,统治;影响;势力,权势: hold ~ 支配 / under the ~ of 受…统治,被…支配 ||**~back** *n.* (牛、马等)由于负重过度而特别凹陷的背部 / **'~backed** *a.* 背部特别凹陷的

swear [swɛə] **I** (过去式 swore [swɔ:] 或[古] sware [swɛə], 过去分词 sworn [swɔ:n]) ❶ *vt.* ①宣(誓),立(誓),发(誓): ~ an oath 宣誓 宣誓表示;郑重保证,强调: ~ allegiance 宣誓效忠 / He *swore* to abide by this principle. 他郑重保证恪守这一原则。/ I ~ he's a swindler. 我肯定他是一个骗子。③使宣誓;使宣誓就职: (*in*) a witness 令证人宣誓 / ~ sb. to secrecy 令某人发誓必保密 / ~ the jury 使陪审员宣誓就职 ④诅咒得使: He *swore* himself hoarse. 他骂得嗓子都哑了。/ ~ sb. away 把某人骂走 ❷ *vi.* ①宣誓,发誓 ②诅咒,骂 **II** *n.* 誓言;一阵咒骂;诅咒,骂人话 ||*hard ~ing* [委婉语]伪证 / *not enough to ~ by* 仅仅一点点 / ~ *against* 起誓证实(某事)以反对(某人) / ~ a charge *against* sb. 控告某人并发誓该项控告属实 / ~ *at* ①诅咒,骂: ~ *at* sb. 咒骂某人 ②与…不协调: His cap *swore at* his coat. 他的帽子与上衣不相称。/ ~ *black is white* (帮人)颠倒黑白 / ~ *by* ①对…发誓: ~ *by* God 对着上帝起誓 ②极其信赖: ~ *by* one's doctor 深信自己的医生 / ~ *for* 保证: I'll ~ *for* his honesty. 我愿担保他是诚实的。/ ~ *in* 使宣誓就职: be *sworn in* to office 宣誓就职 / ~ *like a trooper* (或 *pirate*) 破口大骂 / ~ *off* [口]誓戒: ~ *off* smoking 立誓戒烟 / ~ *on* 凭…发誓: ~ *on* the Bible 把手搁在《圣经》上发誓 / ~ *out* 通过宣誓控告使法院发出(对被控告人的拘捕证) / ~ *the peace against* sb. 见 **peace** / ~ *to* 断言,坚决肯定: I *swore to* having met that man somewhere. 我肯定曾在某处见过那人。||**~er** ['swɛərə] *n.* 宣誓者;咒骂者 ||**~word** *n.* 诅咒,骂人话

sweat [swet] **I** *n.* ①汗: be dripping (wet) with ~ 汗水直淌(湿透) ②出汗;一身汗: A good ~ will cure a cold. 出一身大汗可以治好感冒。/ night(ly) ~s 盗汗 / a cold ~ 一身冷汗 ③(物体表面结的)水珠,湿气: ~ formed on the cold pitcher 凝结在冷水罐上的水珠 ④[口]辛苦的劳动;苦差使: We will take the ~. 我们愿意做这吃力的工作。/ What a ~! 好辛苦的活儿!

⑤[口]不安,焦躁: He was *in a* terrible ~. 他非常焦躁不安。 **II** (sweat 或 sweated) **❶** *vi.* ①出汗: We are not a bit afraid of bleeding and ~*ing*. 我们决不怕流血流汗。 / ~ **at night** 盗汗 ②[口]努力工作;干苦活儿: He ~*ed away at* his work with all his heart. 他全心全意、勤勤恳恳地埋头工作。 / Now machines do most of the ~*ing*. 现在大部分繁重的工作都由机器来做了。 ③(物体表面)结水珠,附上水汽: The glass is ~*ing*. 玻璃上正在结上水珠。 ④(烟叶等)发酵 ⑤焦虑,烦恼;懊恼: He shall ~ **for** it. 他一定会后悔的。 ⑥渗出 **❷** *vt.* ①使出汗;出汗弄湿: The doctor ~*ed* his patient. 医生设法使病人发汗。 / ~ **one's collar** 出汗弄湿了领子 ②(使)渗出,(使)流出;榨出 ③费力地操作(或搬动);努力生产: ~ **guns** up the hill 吃力地把炮运上山 / ~ **out** one novel after another 努力写出一部又一部的小说 ④使工作过度;榨取(工人等)的血汗 ⑤通过出汗而减轻(体重)(*away, off*) ⑥用不正当手段获得(硬币)以盗取金银粉末 ⑦[美俚]拷问 ⑧使(烟叶)发酵;使(原皮)潮湿发霉脱毛【冶】热析(金属中易熔成分);熔焊(金属制件)(*on, in*);熔化(焊料) ‖*all of a* ~ [口]一身大汗;焦急;惊吓 / *an old* ~ [主英]老兵;老手 / *by* (或 *in*) *the* ~ *of one's brow* (或 *face*) 靠自己辛苦劳动 / *in a* ~ 一身大汗 / [口]焦急;惊吓 / *no* ~ [美俚]不费力地,便当地 / ~ *blood* 见 **blood** / ~ *it* (或 *sth.*) *out* [美俚]束手无策地等待某事物 / ~ *out* ①出一身汗以去掉: ~ *out* a cold 出汗医伤风 ②吃力地干以求达到(目的等) ③忍受(或等待)到底 ‖~**ed** *a.* 血汗劳动制下生产的;残酷剥削的: ~*ed* goods 血汗产品 / ~*ed* labour 血汗劳动 ‖'~**band** *n.* (帽内或系在头上的)汗带 / '~**box** *n.* ①(使生皮等潮湿发霉的)发汗装置 ②处罚犯人的狭小囚室 / ~ **gland** 【解】汗腺 / '~**ing-bath** *n.* 汗浴 / ~**ing iron** 洗刷马汗和污垢的刮片(或棒) / ~**ing system** 血汗(劳动)制 / ~ **pants** 长运动裤 / ~ **shirt** 圆领长袖运动衫 / '~**shop** *n.* 血汗工厂(工资低、劳动条件恶劣、残酷剥削工人的小工厂)

sweater ['swetə] *n.* ①(过分)出汗者;发汗剂 ②榨取别人血汗的人 ③厚运动衫;毛线衫,卫生衫 ④[化]石蜡发汗室;(烟叶、生皮等的)发汗器

sweaty ['sweti] *a.* ①汗湿透的;发汗臭的 ②引起出汗的;吃力的: a ~ day 热得人直出汗的日子 / ~ work 吃力的工作 ‖**sweatily** *ad.* / **sweatiness** *n.*

sweep [swi:p] **I** (swept [swept]) **❶** *vt.* ①扫;打扫,扫除: ~ the floor 扫地 / ~ (*out*) the room 打扫房间 / ~ *away* (或 *off*) rubbish 扫去垃圾 / ~ *up* dead leaves 扫(拢)落叶 ②猛力移动,猛推,猛拉: ~ the curtains aside 哗地一声把帷布(或帘布)拉开 / ~ one's hand across 把手急速挥动了一下 ③扫荡;肃清,消灭: ~ all obstacles *from* one's path 扫除前进道路上的一

切障碍 ④(风等)刮起;(浪等)冲走,带走;席卷: The wind *swept* his hat *off*. 风吹去了他的帽子。 / be *swept along* in the crowd 被人群拥着向前走 / He *swept* his audience *along with* him. 他完全控制住了听众的思想感情。 ⑤环视,眺望;扫过,掠过,擦过: He (或 His eyes) *swept* the room. 他把室内扫视了一遍。 / He (或 His fingers) *swept* the keys of the piano. 他的手指在钢琴琴键上飞快地掠过去 / The train of her dress *swept* the ground as she walked. 走路时她的裙裾在地上拖曳。 ⑥【军】扫射;扫(雷) ⑦在…中获全胜,全盘赢得: ~ an election 在选举中获全胜 / ~ everything into one's net 囊括一切 ⑧[古](向某人)很快地行(礼) ⑨用网打捞 ⑩描绘…的轮廓 **❷** *vi.* ①扫;打扫,扫除 ②表志,(风等)刮起;席卷 ③环视;掠过;急速移动:Our jet fighters just *swept* past. 我们的喷气式战斗机刚从上空扫过。 / The music *swept* to a thrilling close. 乐声扣人心弦地戛然而停。 ④拖曳着衣裙走;堂皇地走动: She *swept* out of the room. 她仪态万方地走出房间。 ⑤连绵,延伸: The road ~*s* up the hill. 道路向山上延伸而去。 **II** *n.* ①扫;打扫,扫除: give the room a good (或 thorough) ~ 把房间彻底打扫一下 ②(风的)吹,刮;(浪的)冲激;(手等的)挥动;[喻]推进气势: the indignant ~ of arms 手臂的愤怒挥动 / revolutionary ~ 革命气概 / the onward ~ of history 前进着的历史潮流 ③肃清,清除 ④范围;视野: within (beyond) the ~ of 在…的范围内(外) ⑤连绵区域;一带坡地;弯曲(处): a ~ of mountain country 一片连绵起伏的山区 / The river makes a ~ to the left. 河道向左方弯曲过去。 ⑥绝对优势的胜利;全胜,全赢 ⑦[英]扫烟囱的人(=chimney ~);[英俚]下贱的人 ⑧井边的有支柱的杠杆式吊水设备;(风车的)风帆 ⑨长桨 ⑩[常用复]扫拢的垃圾 ⑪[口]=~-stake(s) ⑫(飞机、军舰等的)攻击;巡弋;搜索;扫雷 ‖*A new broom* ~*s clean.* 见 **broom** / *make a clean* ~ *of* 彻底扫除;全部撤换: make a clean ~ of superstitions 彻底破除迷信 / ~ *all before one* 全胜,得到彻底的成功 / ~ *down* 突然猛袭 / ~ *off* 拂去;扫去;大量清除: The epidemic *swept off* most of the villagers. 流行病在当时夺去了大部村民的生命。 / ~ *sb. off his feet* 使某人大为激动 / ~ *the board* 见 **board** / ~ *the seas* 见 **sea** / *swept and garnished* 打扫干净并布置一新的 ‖~**er** *n.* ①打扫者;扫除机;【军】扫雷舰 / a road (snow) ~*er* 扫路(扫雪)机 / '~**back** *n.* 【空】后掠形,箭形;后掠角 / ~ **circuit** 【电】扫描电路 / '~**for-ward** *n.* 【空】前掠 / ~ **hand** =~-second / ~ **mo(u)lding** 【冶】刮模 / ~ **net** (渔船用的)大拖网;(捕虫网) / '~-**,second** *n.* 长秒针;有长秒针的表(或钟) / ~ **seine** = net / '~**stake(s)** *n.* ①赌金独得的跑马比赛 ②竞赛,比赛 ③各种抽彩赌博法 / '~**up** *n.* 大扫除

sweeping ['swi:piŋ] **I** *a.* ①扫除的；扫荡的 ②连绵的，呈弯曲状的 ③范围广大的，一扫无遗的；彻底的；总括的: ~ reforms 彻底的改革 / ~ generalizations 总的归纳 **II** *n.* ①扫除；扫荡: give the room a good ~ 把房间彻底打扫一下 ②[复]扫拢的垃圾 ‖~**ly** *ad.* / ~**ness** *n.*

sweet [swi:t] **I** *a.* ①甜的，甜味的，滋味好的: wine 甜酒 / Sugar canes taste ~. 甘蔗味甜. / She likes her tea ~. 她喝茶时喜欢多放糖. ②[口]愉快的；惬意的，中意的: have a ~ sleep 睡一个好觉 ③悦耳的；漂亮的；可爱的；美妙的: a ~ voice (song) 悦耳的嗓音(歌曲) / a little baby 逗人喜欢的婴孩 / ~ colours 悦目的颜色 ④亲切的，和蔼的；温柔的: It's very ~ of you to come. 您来使我(们)感到非常高兴. / be ~ to sb. 对某人和蔼可亲 / a ~ temper 温和的性情 ⑤芳香的: the ~ smell of paddy (roses) 稻谷(玫瑰花)的芳香 ⑥新鲜的；淡的，不咸的: ~ milk 新鲜的牛奶 / ~ water 淡水，饮用水 / keep the assembly hall clean and ~ 保持礼堂整洁和空气清新 ⑦[口]亲爱的 ⑧轻快的；灵活的，轻便的，易驾驶的: ~ going 路平车稳的愉快旅行 / a ~ ship 轻便灵活的船 ⑨[用作反语]艰苦的，厉害的: I had a ~ time carrying a large basket of eggs. 带着这大筐蛋真够我受的了. / give sb. a ~ one on the ear 狠狠打某人一记耳光 ⑩【化】无过量腐蚀性(或酸性)物质的；脱硫的，低硫的；无有害气体和气味的 ⑪(土地)非酸性的，适宜耕种的 ⑫[用以加强语气]非常的，惊人的: a ~ inferiority feeling 极度的自卑感 **II** *n.* ①甜食；蜜饯；[英][常用复]糖果(=[美]candy)；[英](餐后的)一道甜食(如馅饼、蛋糕、布丁等) ②甜味；[常用复]芳香: flowers diffusing their ~s on the air 在空气中散发芳香的鲜花 ③[常用复]快乐,乐趣: the ~s and bitters (或 the ~ and the bitter) of life 人生的苦乐 / taste the ~s of success 尝到成功的乐趣 ④[口]亲爱的(称呼语) **III** *ad.* =~ly ‖*at one's own ~ will* 见 **will** / *be ~ on* (或 *upon*) [口]极喜欢；爱上 / *have a ~ tooth* 喜欢吃甜食 / *toil* 喜欢干的辛苦工作 ‖~**ly** *ad.* ①甜，甜甜蜜蜜地 ②惬意地 ③可爱地，亲切地 ④轻快地 ⑤[用以加强语气]十分，大大地 / ~**ness** *n.* ‖'~-**and-'sour** *a.* 用糖醋(或糖和柠檬汁)调味的 / '~**bread** *n.* (供食用的小牛等的)胰脏(或膵脏，胸腺) / '~'**briar**, '~'**brier** *n.* 【植】多花蔷薇 / ~ **clover** 草木犀属植物 / ~ **flag** 【植】菖蒲(又名白菖) / ~**heart** *n.* ①爱人；情人 ②[俚]非常让人欢喜的；佳品 *vi.* 恋爱，求爱. 向…求爱 / '~**heart contract** 黄色工会头目与资方勾结而搞出来的合同 / '~**meat** *n.* [常用复]糖果；甜食；蜜饯 / ~ **oil** 橄榄油；菜油(或类似的其他食用油) / ~ **pea** 香豌豆 / ~ **potato** 白薯，山芋 / '~**root** *n.* 【植】黄杨叶念珠藤；菖蒲(=~'**scented** *a.* 芳香的 / ~**shop** *n.* [英]糖果店(=[美]candy store) / ~ **sop** *n.* 【植】蕃荔枝 / ~ **sultan** 【植】香芙蓉 / '~-**talk** *vt.* & *vi.* 谄

媚，奉承；用甜蜜的话劝诱 / '~-'**tempered** *a.* 性情温和的，脾气好的 / ~ **violet** 【植】香堇菜 / ~ **William** 【植】美国石竹 / '~**wood** *n.* 【植】月桂树

sweeten ['swi:tn] ❶ *vt.* ①使变甜，加糖于；使变香 ②使(音调)悦耳 ③使温和，使温柔 ④减轻(痛苦)；使愉快 ⑤把…弄清洁；使新鲜；去…的臭味 ⑥[口]增加(担保品)；改善(证券发行)的条件；增加(扑克赌金) ❷ *vi.* 变甜；变香；变好听；变温和

sweetening ['swi:tniŋ] *n.* ①弄甜 ②使甜的东西

swell [swel] **I** (过去式 swelled, 过去分词 swollen ['swoulən] 或 swelled) ❶ *vi.* ①膨胀；肿胀: A tire ~s as it is filled with air. 打气时轮胎会鼓起来. / His injured wrist began to ~ (up). 他那受了伤的手腕开始肿起. ②(土地等)隆起；(河水等)上涨: The river has swollen with melted snow. 雪融河涨. ③增长；增大；壮大: The wind ~ed into a tempest. 风力渐增，终于形成一场暴风雨. / The enrolment of our school ~ed to 1,000 this year. 今年我们学校的入学人数增至一千人. ④(声音、音乐等)增强 ⑤骄傲，自负；夸大；装出得意的样子: Never ~ with pride when you make some contributions. 有了贡献不要沾沾自喜. ⑥(情绪等)高涨，增长: His emotion ~s and subsides. 他的情绪忽高忽低. ❷ *vt.* ①使膨胀；使(力量、数目等)增长；使壮大 ②使隆起；使上涨 ③使骄傲自大；使(情绪等)高涨: be swollen with indignation 满腔愤怒 ④提高(音调、声音等) **II** *n.* ①膨胀；肿胀；隆起；增长；增大 ②隆起处；(海底等的)隆起地 ③[只用单]浪涛，滚滚的浪潮 ④【音】渐强到渐弱；渐强到渐弱符号(<>) ⑤[口]衣着时髦的人；了不起的人；头面人物；极有才能的人: What a ~ you are! 你穿得多么漂亮啊! / a heavy ~ 穿得过于花哨(或时髦)的人 / a ~ at tennis 网球好手 **III** *a.* [口]①时髦的；漂亮的: ~ clothes 时髦的衣服 ②第一流的；了不起的；身分高的: a ~ pianist 第一流的钢琴家 ‖*come the heavy ~ over sb.* [俚]摆出一副显赫人物的架势对待某人 ‖~**ing** *n.* ①肿胀；肿大；隆起部 ②膨胀；增大 *a.* 肿大的；突起的 ‖~ **box** 【音】(风琴)的增减音器 / '~-'**butted** *a.* (树等)根部特别大的 / ~**ed head** 自负，自大: have (或 suffer from) ~**ed head** 自负，自大 / '~-'**headed** *a.* 自负的，自大的 / '~ **fish** *n.* 【动】河豚，东方鲀 / '~**head** *n.* 骄傲自大，自负 / ~ **mob** [英]绅士打扮的一群扒手 / '~-,**mobsman** *n.* [英]绅士打扮的扒手 / ~ **organ** 【音】管风琴装有增减音器的部分

swelter ['sweltə] **I** ❶ *vi.* 热得发昏，热得无力，中暑 ❷ *vt.* ①使闷热；使热得发昏，使中暑 ②[古]流出，渗出(毒液等) **II** *n.* ①闷热，酷热: work *in a* ~ 在酷热下工作 ②混乱 ③极度紧张的心情，满身大汗

swerve [swə:v] **I** ❶ *vi.* 突然转向；转弯；背离(*from*): The horse ~d suddenly. 马突然转

向。/ The road ~s to the left. 道路向左转弯。/ never ~ *from* one's duty 从不背离职守 ❷ *vt.* 使突然转向; 使转弯; 使背离 (*from*): ~ the car 急速使汽车转向 / Nothing can ~ him *from* his resolution. 什么也动摇不了他的决心。Ⅱ *n.* 转向; 弯曲; (球在空中行的)弧线形运动; 背离 ‖**~less** *a.* 不转向的; 坚定不移的

swift [swift] Ⅰ *a.* ①快的, 迅速的: the ~ flight of an arrow 箭的飞驰 / The river is too ~ to swim. 这条河水流太急不能游泳。/ be ~ *of* foot [书面语]能健步疾走 ②立刻的, 突然发生的: as ~ as thought 顷刻间 / a ~ change 突然的变化 ③反应快的, 思想敏捷的: have a ~ response 反应迅速 / be ~ to anger [书面语]动辄生气 Ⅱ *ad.* 快, 迅速地; 敏捷地 Ⅲ *n.* ①【纺】大滚筒; 纱筐, 绷架; 篗子 ②雨燕; 爬行快的蜥蜴 ‖**-let** ['swiftlit] *n.* 【动】东亚雨燕(产食用燕窝) / **~ly** *ad.* / **~ness** *n.* ‖**~-'footed** *a.* 跑得快的 / **~-'handed** *a.* 手快的 / **~-'winged** *a.* 飞得快的

swill [swil] Ⅰ ❶ *vt.* ①涮, 冲洗 (*out*): ~ *out* a dirty basin 把脏脸盆涮一下 ②大口喝, 痛饮 ③倒出(饮料等); 用(水等)涮容器: ~ a little hot water *round* in the pot before steeping the tea 泡茶前用一点热水把壶涮一下 ④用泔脚饲料喂(猪等) ❷ *vi.* ①大口喝, 痛饮 ②发激荡声 Ⅱ *n.* ①涮, 冲洗; (浪等的)激荡声 ②大喝; 痛饮酒 ③劣酒 ④泔脚; 猪食, 泔脚饲料; 剩饭残羹

swim [swim] Ⅰ (swam [swæm], swum [swʌm]; swimming) ❶ *vi.* ①游, 游泳: You cannot learn to ~ unless you go into the water. 要学会游泳, 就必须下水。/ ~ in big rivers and seas to temper oneself 在大江、大海里游泳锻炼 / Let's go *swimming*. 咱们游泳去。/ ~ *on* one's chest (back, side) 俯(仰, 侧)泳 / Fish ~ 鱼会游水。②浮, 漂浮; 滑行: Oil ~s *on* water. 油浮于水。/ A cloud swam slowly *across* the moon. 浮云慢慢飘过月亮。③浸, 泡; 覆盖; 充溢 (*with*, *in*): meat *swimming in* gravy 浸在浓汁中的肉 / When I heard the good news, my heart *swam with* joy. 我听到这好消息, 内心充满喜悦。④旋转, 摇晃; 眼花, 眩晕: The room swam before her eyes and she had to lie down again. 房间好象在她眼前旋转, 她只得再躺下。/ His head swam. 他头发晕。❷ *vt.* ①游过; 与…赛游泳 He can't ~ a stroke. 他一点也不会游泳。②使(马等)游水; 使浮起: ~ a horse *across* a river 使马渡河 / ~ wheat to select seed 浮麦选种 Ⅱ *n.* ①游泳: go for a ~ 去游泳 / have a ~ 游一会儿水 ②漂浮; 滑行 ③[the ~]潮流, 趋势 ④眩晕, 眼花: Her head was in a ~. 她感到头晕眼花。⑤多鱼的深水区 ‖in (out of) the ~ 积极参加(不积极参加)社交活动; 合(不合)时髦; 合(不合)潮流 / sink or ~ 见 sink / ~ to the bottom (或 ~ like a stone) [谑]沉下去 ‖swimmer *n.* 游泳者 ‖ bladder (鱼)鳔 /

pool 游泳池 / '**~suit** *n.* 游泳衣

swimmeret(te) ['swimərət] *n.* 【动】桡肢, 游泳足

swimming ['swimiŋ] Ⅰ *n.* ①游泳, 游水 ②眩晕: I have a ~ in my head. 我头晕。Ⅱ *a.* ①(适用于)游泳的 ②充溢的: ~ eyes 充满泪水的眼睛 ③眩晕的, 眼花的 ‖**~ bath** [英](一般指室内的)游泳池 / '**~-belt** *n.* 学游泳者用的救生圈 / **bladder** (鱼)鳔 / **costume** 游泳衣 / **~ pool** 游泳池 / **~ stone** 【地】浮蛋白石

swindle ['swindl] Ⅰ ❶ *vt.* 诈取, 骗取: ~ sb. out of his money (或 ~ money out of sb.) 骗某人钱财 ❷ *vi.* 诈取, 骗取 Ⅱ *n.* ①欺诈, 诈取 ②骗局; 骗人的东西: a peace talk ~ 和谈骗局 ‖**~r** *n.* 骗子, 诈骗犯 / **swindlingly** *ad.* 用诈骗手段

swine [swain] [单复同] *n.* ①猪 ②猪猡, 下流坯 ‖**~herd** *n.* 养猪人, 猪倌

swing [swiŋ] Ⅰ (swung [swʌŋ]) ❶ *vi.* ①摇摆, 摆动, 摇荡: The pendulum ~s. 钟摆摆动。②(手臂自由摆动着)轻松地走(或跑); 大摇大摆地行走 (*along*, *past*, *by*): He swung *out* of the room. 他大摇大摆地走出房间。③悬挂, 悬空 (*from*): Lanterns swung from the ceiling. 灯笼吊从天花板挂下。④(绕轴心、铰链等)回转, 旋转; (人等)转向, 转身: The door swung to (或 swung shut). 门关上了。/ The ship is ~ing round. 船在转身(或掉头)。/ He swung round and faced me. 他迅速转过身来面对着我。⑤演奏(或演唱)摇摆舞音乐 ⑥转变, 转向: ~ *against* sb. 转过来反对某人 ⑦挥动手臂击(中)某物 ⑧[口]被处绞刑 (*for*) ⑨精神饱满地立即开始: ~ *into* action 积极行动起来 ❷ *vt.* ①挥舞, 使摆动: ~ one's arms 挥舞手臂 / ~ a baby in the cradle 摇动摇篮里的婴孩 ②使(顺轴等)回转, 使旋转; 使(人等)转向 ③悬挂; 吊运: ~ a basket of seed *from* a hook 把一篮子种子挂在钩子上 / ~ a hammock 挂起吊床 / Huge cranes are ~ing cargo *up*. 巨大的起重机正在吊运货物。④[美口]操纵; (成功地)处理, 完成, 获取 ⑤演奏(或演唱)(摇摆舞音乐) Ⅱ *n.* ①摇摆, 摆动; 振幅, 摆幅: a ~ of one metre 一米的振幅 / the ~ of the tides 潮汐的涨落 ②[只用单](诗歌、音乐、舞蹈等的)韵律; 节奏; [美]摇摆舞音乐 (=~ music) ③(手臂的)挥舞; 轻松有节奏的步伐; 大摇大摆的走路姿势 ④(工作等的)进行, 开展 ⑤[美口](利率、物价、行情等的)涨落, 上落 ⑥[美](条件、形式、态度等的)周期性交替 ⑦秋千: play on the ~ 荡秋千 ⑧放任; 自由活动(范围) ⑨(摆动等的)冲力 ⑩(竞选等时的)巡回旅行 ⑪(滑雪中的)旋转 Ⅲ *a.* ①(绕轴心)旋转的; 悬挂的: a ~ lamp 挂灯 ②摇摆舞音乐的 ‖*a ~ around* (或 *round*) *the circle* (指政客)发表政见的巡回旅行 / *get into the ~ of one's work* (或 *get into one's ~*) 积极投入工作 / *go with a ~* (音乐、诗歌等)节奏轻快; [喻](表演、事件等)顺利进行 / *have* (或 *take*) *one's full* ~ 自由行动, 不

受拘束; 放荡不羁, 为所欲为 / *in full* 活跃; 正在全力进行 / *let it have its* ~ 听其自然 / ~ *in with* 加入… / *the* ~ *of the pendulum* ①钟摆的摆动 ②[喻]盛衰, 消长; 舆论从一个极端转到另一个极端; 政党间执政的交替 / *What you lose on the* ~*s you get back on the roundabouts.* [谚]失之东隅, 收之桑榆。 || '~'**boat** *n.* 船形秋千 / ~ **bridge** (平)旋桥, 平转桥 / '~'**by** *n.* 〖宇〗(利用中间行星或目的行星的重力场改变航道或轨道的)借力式飞行路线 / ~(**ing**) **door** 转门, 双动自止门 / ~ **jack** 横式起重器 / ~ **link** 摆杆 / ~ **music** 摇摆舞音乐 / ~ **room** [美](工厂工人等的)休息室, 吸烟室 / ~ **shift** 从下午四时到半夜的工作班, 中班; 全体中班工人

swipe [swaip] **I** *n.* ①[主英][方](泵等的)柄, 杆 ②[口]猛击 ③马夫 ④大口的喝 **II** ❶ *vt.* ①[口]猛击 ②[俚]偷, 扒 ❷ *vi.* ①[口]猛击 ②大口喝酒 ||~**r** *n.* ①猛击者 ②大口喝酒的人 ③偷窃者

swirl [swə:l] **I** ❶ *vi.* ①打漩; 旋动, 涡动 ②卷曲, 盘绕 ③(头)发晕 ❷ *vt.* 使打旋; 使涡动 **II** *n.* ①旋动; 漩涡 ②旋动物; 卷状(如毛皮、木头的纹理等) ③[美]弯曲, 围绕 ④纷乱, 混乱: a ~ of voices 人声嘈杂 / a ~ of events 纷乱的事情 ⑤鱼跃

swish [swiʃ] **I** ❶ *vt.* (鞭、马尾等)嗖地挥动; (衣裙等)作窸窣声: A car ~ed past. 一辆汽车嗖地驶了过去。 ❷ *vt.* ①嗖地挥动; 使作沙沙声: The horse ~ed its tail. 马嗖嗖地挥着尾巴。 / sip water and ~ it about in the mouth 喝了一点水在嘴里来回涮洗 ②嚓嚓地切割(或移动): ~ off the branches of a tree 嚓嚓地割下树枝 ③嗖地挥鞭毒打 **II** *n.* ①嗖嗖声; 飒飒声; 窸窣声: hear the ~ of drawing paper being unrolled 听到把制图纸摊开的窸窣声 the steady ~ of the sickle 镰刀的不断的嚓嚓声 ②发出嗖一声的动作 ③(打人用的)鞭子; (鞭等的)一击, 一挥 ④漂亮, 时髦 ⑤[美俚]搞同性关系的人 **III** *a.* 漂亮的, 时髦的 **IV** *ad.* 发嗖嗖(或窸窣、沙沙)声地 ||~**y** *a.* ①发咝嗖(或窸窣)声的, 作沙沙声的 ②[美俚]搞同性关系的 ||'~-'**swash** *n.* [英俚]啤酒

switch [switʃ] **I** *n.* ①开关, 电闸, 电键, 转换器: a two-way ~ 双向开关 ②(思想等)的骤变; 转换, 掉换; (铁路的)转辙器; 铁道侧线 ③(树木的)软枝条; (细软的)鞭子, 杖条; 鞭子的一击 ④(女人的)假发 ⑤动物尾巴上的毛簇 **II** ❶ *vt.* ①接通…的电流 (*on*); 切断…的电流 (*off*); 接通(电流) (*on*); 切断(电流) (*off*); 转换(电路): ~ the light on (*off*) 开(关)电灯 / ~ on (*off*) the radio 开(关)收音机 / ~ sb. on (*off*) 接通(挂断)与某人的电话通话 ③(使用铁路转辙器)转辙; 在终点站使(车辆)调头 ③转换, 改变(思路、话题等): ~ tactics 改换策略 / ~ sides 改变立场 / ~ the discussion *to* another topic 换一个讨论题目

④鞭打 ⑤摆动(尾巴等) ⑥突然夺去: ~ sth. *out of* sb.'s hand 从某人手中把某物突然抢去 ❷ *vi.* ①转换, 变换: ~ *over to* the counteroffensive 转入反攻 ②(尾巴等)摆动 ③(铁路)转辙 ||*asleep at the* ~ 错过机会 ||'~'**back** *n.* (山区的)之字形路线 / ~ **bar** 转辙杆 / '~(**blade**) **knife** 一种用弹簧开启的折刀 / '~'**board** *n.* ①配电盘, 配电板; 开关屏 ②(电话的)交换机, 交换台 / ~ **box** ①〖电〗转换开关盒, (电)闸盒 ②〖交〗转辙器柄座箱 / '~**gear** *n.* 开关齿轮 / '~-,**hitter** *n.* 〖美〗左右手均能击球的棒球球手 / ~ **lever** ①转辙杆 ②开关杆 / ~**man** ['switʃ-mən] *n.* (铁路)转辙员, 扳道工人 / '~,**over** *n.* 大转变 / '~-,**signal** *n.* (铁路)转辙器信号 / ~ **tower** 〖美〗(铁路)的信号塔 / '~'**yard** *n.* (铁路)调车场, 编组站

swivel ['swivl] **I** *n.* ①〖机〗(链的)转节, 转环; 旋轴; 旋转接头 ②=~ **gun** ③[俚]斜视 **II** (swivel(l)ed; swivel(l)ing) ❶ *vt.* ①使旋转 ②用转节固定住, 用转节支住 ❷ *vi.* (在转节上)旋转 ||~ **chain** 转动链 / ~ **chair** 转椅 / '~-**eye** *n.* 斜视 / '~-**eyed** *a.* 斜视的 / ~ **gun** 〖军〗回旋炮; 回旋枪 / ~ **hook** 转动钩 / ~ **table** 〖机〗(工具的)转台 / ~ **weaving** 〖纺〗挖花织造

swollen ['swoulən] **I** swell 的过去分词 **II** *a.* ①膨胀的; 肿起的; (河水)涨起的: a ~ ankle 肿踝 ②夸张的 ③骄傲的: be ~ with arrogance 趾高气扬, 气焰嚣张 ||'~-'**headed** *a.* 傲慢的, 自负的

swoon [swu:n] **I** *vi.* ①晕厥, 昏倒; 神魂颠倒: ~ *with* pain 痛得昏过去 / ~ *for* joy 狂喜 ②(乐声等)渐渐消失: The noise ~ed away. 闹声渐渐消失了。 **II** *n.* ①晕厥, 昏倒, 神魂颠倒: fall into a ~ 晕厥, 昏倒 / waken from a ~ 苏醒过来 ②渐渐的消失 ||~**ingly** *ad.*

swoop [swu:p] **I** ❶ *vt.* 攫取; [口]抢去 (*up*): The whirlwind's blast ~ed the haycocks off the lea. 旋风卷去草原上的干草堆。 ❷ *vi.* (鹰等向目的物)飞扑, 猛扑; 猝然攻击: The eagle ~ed *down on* a chicken. 鹰猛扑小鸡。 / ~ *down upon* the enemy 突击敌人 **II** *n.* 飞扑; 下攫 ||*at one (fell)* ~ 一下子, 一举

swop [swɔp] *n.*, (swopped; swopping) *vt.* & *vi.* =swap

sword [sɔ:d] **I** *n.* ①剑, 刀; 〖军俚〗刺刀: sharpen a ~ 磨刀 / a cavalry ~ 骑兵的军刀, 马刀 / a court (或 dress) ~ 礼服的佩剑 ②[the ~] 武力; 兵权, 军权; 君权; 战争; 杀戮, 屠杀: the ~ and the purse 武力和财力 / appeal to the ~ 诉诸武力 / the ~ of justice 司法权 ||cross ~s 交锋; 争论: cross verbal ~s 唇枪舌剑地交锋 / draw the ~ 开战 / put to the ~ 杀死…; (在战争中)屠杀… / put up the ~ 息干戈, 讲和 / the ~ of Damocles 临头的危险 / the ~ of State (或 honour) [英]国剑(大节日时在英王前

由人捧持的宝剑) / *the ~ of the spirit* 【宗】上帝的话 / *throw one's ~ into the scale* 用武力强求 / *wear the ~* 当兵 / *worry the ~* (击剑中)连续快速戳刺以乱对方阵脚 ‖*~less a.* 无刀剑的 / *~like a.* 似刀剑的 ‖ **~ arm** 右臂 / **~ bayonet** (枪上的)刺刀 / **~ bean** 刀豆 / '**~-,bearer** 捧(帝王等的)宝剑者 / '**~-belt** 剑带,刀带 / **~ cane** 内藏刀剑的手杖 / '**~-cut** *n.* 刀剑伤(疤) / **~ dance** 剑舞,剑架舞 / '**~-fish** *n.* 箭鱼(有剑状长上颚的大海鱼) / '**~-flag** *n.* 【植】黄菖蒲 / **~ grass** 具剑状(或齿状)叶的草 (如美洲珍珠茅等) / '**~-guard** *n.* (刀剑的)护手 / '**~-hand** *n.* 右手 / **~ knot** 系于剑柄的带结 / '**~-law** *n.* 武力统治 / **~ lily** =gladiolus / '**~-play** *n.* ①剑术,舞剑 ②[喻]激辩;巧答 / '**~-proof** *a.* 刀剑戳不穿的 / **~ stick** =~ cane

swordsman ['sɔːdzmən] ([复] swordsmen) *n.* ①剑手,剑客 ②[古]军士,武士 ‖**~ship** *n.* 剑术

swore [swɔː] swear 的过去式

sworn [swɔːn] I swear 的过去分词 II *a.* 盟誓的: ~ brothers 结义弟兄 / a ~ enemy 不共戴天的仇敌 / ~ evidence 发誓后提出的证词 / ~ friends 盟友

swot¹ [swɔt] *vt.* (swotted; swotting) & *n.* =swat

swot² [swɔt] [英][学俚] I (swotted; swotting) ❶ *vi.* 用功读书,死用功: ~ at a subject 拼命攻读一门功课 ❷ *vt.* 用功学: ~ *up* one's geometry (临时抱佛脚地)赶学几何 II *n.* ①用功读书;用功的学生,一心读书的人 ②吃力的工作: What a ~! 这事真吃力!

sycamore ['sikəmɔː] *n.* 【植】①(埃及和小亚细亚产的)埃及榕 ②美国梧桐 ③假挪威槭

sycophant ['sikəfənt] I *n.* 拍马者,谄媚者 II *a.* 拍马的,谄媚的 ‖**~ly** *ad.*

syllabic [si'læbik] I *a.* ①音节的,表示音节的 ②自成音节的: The sound [l] is ~ in the word "battle". 在 "battle" 这个单词中 [l] 音是成音节的。 ③各个音节有明晰发音的 ④(诗体)按每行音节数而不照韵(或重音)安排的 II *n.* 自成音节的声音,浊音;有声字 ‖**~ally** *ad.*

syllable ['siləbl] I *n.* ①音节: The accent is on the third ~. 重音在第三个音节上。②只言片语: Not a ~! 别说话! II *vt.* ①给…分音节 ②按音节发…的音 ③[诗]说出(名字、话) ‖**~d** *a.* [常用以构成复合词]有(若干)音节的: "Revolution" is a four-~d word. "revolution" 是一个四音节的词。

syllabus ['siləbəs] ([复] syllabi ['siləbai] 或 syllabuses) *n.* ①摘要,提纲;教学大纲,课程提纲 ②【律】判词前的说明

syllogism ['silədʒizəm] *n.* ①【逻】三段论法;演绎推理 ②诡辩

sylph [silf] *n.* ①(十五至十六世纪德国医学家巴拉赛尔苏斯 (Paracelsus) 学说中的)"气精" ②窈窕的妇女 ③一种长尾蜂鸟 ‖**~like** *a.* 窈窕的

symbol ['simbəl] I *n.* ①象征 ②符号;记号;

代号: chemical ~s 化学符号 / phonetic ~s 注音符号,音标 ③【宗】信经,信条 II (symbol(l)ed; symbol(l)ing) *vt.* & *vi.* =symbolize

symbolic(al) [sim'bɔlik(əl)] *a.* ①象征的,象征性的 ②符号的,用作符号的 ③使用符号的 ④(文学艺术上的)象征派的 ‖**symbolically** *ad.*

symbolize ['simbəlaiz] ❶ *vt.* ①象征,作为…的象征;代表: The dove ~s peace. 鸽子象征和平。/ The sign "+" ~s addition in arithmetic. 在算术中"+"号代加法。②用象征表示,用符号表示: How shall we ~ mineral deposits on this map? 在这张地图上我们应该怎样表示矿床? / Pride is ~d as a peacock. 骄傲是用孔雀来象征的。❷ *vi.* 采用象征; 使用符号 ‖**symbolization** [,simbəlai'zeiʃən] *n.*

symmetry ['simitri] *n.* 对称(性);对称美;匀称: the axis of ~ 对称轴 / mirror ~ 【物】镜面对称

sympathetic [,simpə'θetik] I *a.* ①同情的,表示同情的;有同情心的: a ~ person 富有同情心的人 / a ~ look 同情的目光 / ~ words 表示同情的言语 / be ~ *with* the patients 对病人抱同情态度 ②和谐的,合意的: in a ~ atmosphere 在和谐的气氛中 / live in ~ surroundings 住在合意的环境中 ③[口]有好感的,赞同的: be ~ *to* (或 *towards*) a project 对一项计划持赞同态度 ④惹人喜爱的,可爱的 ⑤【解】交感(神经系)的 ⑥【物】共振的,共鸣的: ~ resonance 共鸣 II *n.* ①交感神经系 ②(对催眠术等)易感受的人 ‖**~ally** *ad.* ‖**~ ink** 隐显墨水(起初无色,经热、光或药品等作用而显示) / **~ nerve** 交感神经 / **~ strike** 同情罢工(指为了声援别的罢工工人而举行的罢工) / **~ vibration** 共振

sympathize ['simpəθaiz] *vi.* ①同情,表示同情: ~ *with* sb. in his sufferings 对某人遭遇的苦难表示同情 ②同感,共鸣,一致;同意,赞成: ~ *with* sb. in his point of view (或 ~ *with* sb.'s point of view) 赞同某人的观点 ③吊唁,吊慰 (*with*) ‖**~r** *n.* 同情者;赞同者;支持者

sympathy ['simpəθi] *n.* ①同情,同情心: feel ~ *for* sb. 对某人抱着同情 / have ~ *with* the sick 对病人表示同情 / seek ~ *from* a friend 想得到朋友的同情 / Popular *sympathies* are on her side (或 are with her). 一般人的同情都在她这方面。②一致,同感;赞同: I have every ~ *with* you in your love of country life. 在爱好农村生活这点上我和你完全有同感。/ be in (out of) ~ *with* a plan 赞同(不赞同)某一计划 ③慰问;吊慰: a letter of ~ 慰问信 / express ~ *for* (或 *with*) sb. 对某人表示慰问 ④【物】共振,共鸣 ⑤(病症的)交感,共感 ‖**~ strike** 同情罢工(指为了声援别的罢工工人而举行的罢工)

symphony ['simfəni] *n.* ①交响曲,交响乐 ②交响乐队,交响乐团(=~ orchestra) ③[口]交响音乐会 ④谐音 ⑤(颜色、构图等的)调和 ‖**symphonist** *n.* 交响乐作曲家,交响乐作者

symposium [sim'pouzjəm] ([复] symposia [sim'pouzjə] 或 symposiums) *n.* ①(正式宴会后以音

乐及谈话为主的)酒会 ②座谈会;专题讨论会 ③(不同著作者对某一题目的)专题论丛,专题论文集

symptom ['simptəm] *n.* 症状; 征侯; 征兆: clinical ~s 临床症状 ‖~less *a.* 无症状的; 无征侯的

symptomatic [ˌsimptə'mætik] *a.* ①(有)症状的; 征侯的; 征兆的 (*of*): A persistent cough may be ~ *of* tuberculosis. 咳嗽不止可能是肺结核的症状。 ② 根据症状的: ~ treatment 症状疗法 ③ 有代表性的, 表明的 ‖~ally *ad.*

synagog(ue) ['sinəgɔg] *n.* ①犹太教堂 ②犹太教徒的集会 ‖**synagogical** [ˌsinə'gɔdʒikəl], **synagogal** ['sinəgɔgəl] *a.*

synchronize ['siŋkrənaiz] **❶** *vi.* 同时发生,同步: Action and sound must ~ perfectly. 动作与声音必须完全同步。 **❷** *vt.* ①使在时间上一致;【物】使同步,使整步: ~ two clocks 使两钟时间一致 / ~ troop movement and artillery fire 使部队的移动和炮火在时间上密切配合 / ~ the scanning electron beam in the television receiver with that in the studio 使电视接收机和电视演播室中的扫描电子射线完全同步 ②使(电影的台词、音响效果)与画面动作吻合 ③把…并列对照 ‖**synchronization** [ˌsiŋkrənai'zeiʃən] *n.* / ~**r** *n.* 同步器 ‖**d swimming** 配乐游泳表演(一种有音乐伴奏、做出各种花式动作的游泳表演)

syndicate I ['sindikit] *n.* ①【经】辛迪加,企业联合组织(一般为临时性的) ②报业辛迪加(包括向各报纸或杂志出售稿件供同时发表的企业及在统一经营管理下的一批报纸) ③(剑桥大学的)大学管理会特别委员会 ④罪犯集团的操纵组织,罪犯辛迪加 **II** ['sindikeit] **❶** *vt.* ①把…组成辛迪加,使处于联合管理下: ~ a number of newspapers 把好多家报纸组成报业辛迪加 ②通过报业辛迪加出售(文章、漫画等);通过报业辛迪加在多家报纸上同时发表(文章、漫画等) **❷** *vi.* 联合成辛迪加 ‖**syndication** [ˌsindi'keiʃən] *n.* / **syndicator** ['sindikeitə] *n.* 组织辛迪加者;参加辛迪加者;经营辛迪加者

synod ['sinəd] *n.* ①宗教会议;路德教派的组织 ②会议;讨论会 ③【天】会合 ‖~**al** *a.*

synonym ['sinənim] *n.* ①同义词 ②象征性的名称,使产生对另一名称联想的名称 ‖~**ic** [ˌsinə'nimik] *a.* / ~**ist** [si'nɔnimist] *n.* 同义词研究者

synonymous [si'nɔniməs] *a.* 同义的 (*with*) ‖~**ly** *ad.*

synopsis [si'nɔpsis] ([复] synopses [si'nɔpsi:z]) *n.* (书、剧本等的)提要, 概要, 梗概

syntax ['sintæks] *n.*【语】句法

synthesis ['sinθisis] ([复] syntheses ['sinθisi:z]) *n.* ①综合;综合物 ②【化】合成(法) ③【哲】【逻】综合(性) ④【医】接合 ‖~**t** *n.* 综合者;合成法使用者

synthetic [sin'θetik] **I** *a.* ①综合(性)的 ②合成的;人造的: ~ fabrics 合成纤维织物 / ~ leather 合成皮革,人造革 ③假想的,虚假的: ~ combat

mission 假想的战斗任务 / a ~ training device 摹拟的训练器材 / ~ enthusiasm 虚假的热情 ④(语言)综合性的,以借助词尾变化表示句法关系为特征的 **II** *n.* 化学合成物;合成纤维织物;合成剂 ‖**detergent** 合成洗涤剂 / **fibre** 合成纤维 / ~ **philosophy** (斯宾塞派的)综合哲学 / ~ **resin** 合成树脂 / ~ **rubber** 合成橡胶

syringe ['sirindʒ] **I** *n.* 注射器;灌肠器;洗涤器;喷水器: a hypodermic ~ 皮下注射器 **II** *vt.* (用注射器等)注射;灌洗;冲洗

syrup ['sirəp] *n.* ①糖浆,糖汁;果汁;浆: cough ~ 咳嗽糖浆 / fruit ~ 果味糖浆 / golden ~ 糖蜜、转化糖、玉米糖浆混合成的餐用糖浆 ②甜蜜的情感 ③〔英俚〕钱 ‖~**y** *a.* ①糖浆(状)的 ②(音乐等)甜蜜的,美妙的

system ['sistim, 'sistəm] *n.* ①系统;体系: the digestive ~ 消化系统 / an irrigation ~ 灌溉系统 / the solar ~ 太阳系 / a telegraph (telephone) ~ 电报(电话)网 / a radio broadcasting ~ 广播网 / a railway ~ 铁路网 / an ideological ~ 思想体系 / a ~ of philosophy 哲学体系 / a ~ of pulleys 一组滑轮 ②制度,体制; [the ~] 现存社会体制: a social ~ 社会制度 / the communist ~ 共产主义制度 / a ~ of government 政体 / a ~ of ownership 所有制 / abolish all ~s of exploitation of man by man 消灭一切人剥削人的制度 / the metric ~ 米制 ③方法,方式: a new ~ of teaching foreign languages 一套新的外语教学法 / a ~ of numbering (measuring) 计算(测量)法 / What ~ do you go on? 你根据什么方式(或方法)去进行呢? ④秩序,规律: He works with ~. 他工作有条理。/ have(lack) ~ in one's work 工作有(缺乏)条理 / arrangement without ~ 不规则排列 ⑤分类(法): the natural ~ 自然分类法 ⑥宇宙,世界: the great ~ 宇宙 ⑦身体,全身: Too much alcohol is bad for the ~. 过量的酒对身体有害。 ⑧【音】总乐谱表 ‖~**less** *a.* 无系统的;无秩序的,无规则的 ‖~**s analysis** (利用计算机计算等数学方法来研究问题并提出多种解决办法以供选择的)系统分析

systematic [ˌsisti'mætik] *a.* ①有系统的,成体系的;有秩序的,有规则的,有组织的: ~ investigation and study 系统的调查研究 / a ~ worker 工作有条不紊的人 ②【生】分类(上)的,分类学的: ~ botany (zoology) 植物(动物)分类学 / ~ entomology 昆虫分类学,系统昆虫学 / the ~ nomenclature 分类命名法 ③有计划的;非偶然的,故意的: ~ thieving 有计划的偷窃 / a ~ liar 一贯说谎的人 ‖~**al** *a.* / ~**ally** *ad.* / **systematist** ['sistimətist] *n.* ①订立制度(或系统)者;履行制度者;按照系统者 ②分类学者

systemic [sis'temik] *a.* ①全身的;影响全身的: a ~ disease 全身病 / ~ circulation 体循环 ②【生】内吸收的 ‖**insecticide** 内吸杀虫剂(注入动植物内无害但能杀死吮取吸汁或血的寄生虫)

tab 995 tabulate

T

tab [tæb] **I** *n.* ①供手拉(或悬挂等)用的短小突出部(如附在鞋口后部的拉襻、指引卡上的突出部等) ②(服装上装饰用的)垂片;鞋带末端的包头;帽子的护耳 ③[英]【军】参谋的领章 ④监督;记录 ⑤账单: pick up the ~ 付账,承担费用 ⑥【空】调整片: trimming ~ 平衡调整片;配平补翼 ⑦=tabloid (*n.*) ⑧=tabulator ⑨=tablet **II** (tabbed; tabbing) *vt.* ①为…加上短小突出部 ②选中,指定 ③把…列表 ‖*keep* ~ (或 *a* ~, ~*s*) *on* 记录;监视: keep a ~ on the expenses 记录(或监督)各项费用

table ['teibl] **I** *n.* ①桌子,台子: a dining ~ 餐桌 / a dressing (或 toilet) ~ 镜台,梳妆台 / at the conference ~ 在会议桌上 ②餐桌;[只用单]食物,酒菜;一桌人(指进餐者、玩牌者等): lay (或 set, spread) the ~ for ten 摆餐桌供十人进餐 / ~ plan 宴会座位安排 / sit down to ~ 坐下吃饭,入席 / keep a good ~ 经常备着好酒菜 / The whole ~ got excited at the happy news. 喜讯传来,举桌欢腾。③(机器的)放料盘;台;工作台: a ~ feeder 平板给料器 / a universal ~ 万能工作台 / an operating ~ 手术台 / a ~ planing machine 龙门刨床 ④木牌;石板;(碑、板上刻的)铭文,文献: the twelve ~s 罗马法典(公元前 451—450 年颁布) / the two ~s (或 the ~s of the law)【基督教】摩西十诫 ⑤【建】上楣(柱);花檐;装饰板,镶板;束带层 ⑥项目表,表格: a statistical ~ 统计表 / a ~ of weights and measures 度量衡表 / the multiplication ~ 乘法表 / the logarithmic (或 log) ~ 对数表 / a ~ of contents 目录 / compile (或 draw up) a ~ 制表,造表 ⑦【地】高原,台地(=~land);平地层: a ~ mountain 桌状山 / (头盖)骨板;手掌(尤指看手相的部分) ⑧(宝石顶部的)切平面;有切平面的宝石 **II** *vt.* ①[古]把…放在桌上 ②搁置(议案等): ~ a motion (bill) 搁置动议(议案) ③[英]把…列入议事日程;提出: The committee will ~ its report this week. 委员会将于本周提出报告。④嵌合(刻有凹凸槽的木材);~d fish plate 凹凸接板 ⑤(用阔边)加固(风帆) ⑥把…制成表格 ‖*a* ~ *of* (*prohibited*) *degrees* (禁止通婚的)直系近亲谱 / *at* ~ 在餐桌边,在进餐时: sit (down) *at* ~ 坐下吃饭 [注意: sit at a (或 the) ~ 意为"坐在桌子旁"] / He seldom talks *at* ~. 他吃饭时难得说话。/ *be sb.'s neighbour at* ~ 席间坐在某人身旁 / *lay on the* ~ 搁置(议案等) / *lie on the* ~ 被搁置 / *on the* ~ (摆)在桌面上,公开地 / *the Lord's* ~ 【基督教】圣餐台,神坛 / *turn the* ~(*s*) 转变形

势,扭转局面;转败为胜: turn the ~s on the attackers 反守为攻 / *under the* ~ ①酒醉;发呆: drink sb. *under the* ~ 把某人灌醉 ②秘密地,私下,悄悄: buy sth. *under the* ~ 私下买某物 / *upon the* ~ 尽人皆知的,已成为公开讨论之事的 / *wait at* ~ (或 [美] *wait* (*on*) ~) 伺候进餐 ‖**~-board** *n.* ①牌桌 ②(不供住宿的)包伙食 / **~ book** (尤指客厅桌上)供摆设的图书 / **'~-cloth** *n.* (餐桌用)白色台布;(一般用)彩色台布 / **'~-cut** *a.* (宝石等)顶面切平的 / **~-flap** *n.* (折迭式桌面的)折板 / **'~-hop** *vi.* (在宴会等上)周旋于餐桌之间(与人交谈) / **knife** 餐刀 / **'~land** *n.* 高原,台地 / **~ linen** 餐桌用布(指台布、餐巾等) / **~ money** ①(发给高级军官等的)请客津贴 ②(向俱乐部成员收的)就餐费 / **~ salt** (餐桌上用的)食盐 / **~ set** 成套餐具 / **'~spoon** *n.* 大汤匙;一大汤匙容量 / **'~spoon,ful** *n.* 一大汤匙容量 / **~ talk** 席间闲谈,餐桌漫谈 / **~ tennis** 乒乓球 / **'~top** *n.* ①桌面 ②桌上静物摄影(拍摄在桌上设置的小摆设或景物) / **~ tripod** (电影或电视摄影机的)矮三角架 / **~ vice, ~ vise** (机器)台虎钳 / **'~ware** *n.* [总称]餐具

tablet ['tæblit] *n.* ①[古]书板(木、石等制成的平板,供写刻文字用) ②(刻铭文的)碑,匾: a memorial ~ (常指嵌在墙上的)纪念碑 ③便笺簿;拍纸簿;报告纸簿 ④小块,小片: a ~ of soap 一块肥皂 / aspirin ~s 阿司匹林药片 / throat ~s 润喉片 ⑥【建】笠石 ‖**'~-arm chair, ~ chair** (课堂用)右边有阔扶手供书写用的椅子

taboo [tə'bu:] **I** *n.* ①(宗教迷信或社会习俗方面的)禁忌,忌讳,戒律: under ~ 属禁忌之列 / ~s and commandments 清规戒律 ②信奉禁忌 ③【语】禁忌语 **II** *a.* 禁忌的,忌讳的;禁止的 **III** *vt.* 把…列为禁忌;禁止

tabular ['tæbjulə] *a.* ①表格式的,列成表的;按表格计算的: data given in ~ form 列成表格状的资料 / ~ computations 表格计算 / a ~ statement 表格状报告书 ②平坦的;平板(状)的;薄层的,片状的: a ~ surface 平(坦)面 / a ~ structure【地】板状构造 ‖**~ly** *ad.* / **~ difference** 【数】表差 / **~ standard** (为保障债权人利益而按物价指数订定的)币值计算标准表

tabulate ['tæbjuleit] **I** *vt.* ①把…制成表,列表显示: ~ statistics (data) 把统计数字(数据)列表 / a ~d quotation 行情表 / a *tabulating* machine 制表机 ②使成平面 **II** *a.* ①板状的,平面的 ②薄片构成的 ‖**tabulation** [,tæbju'leiʃən] *n.* 制表,列表;表

tacit ['tæsit] *a.* ①缄默的: a ~ spectator 缄默的旁观者 ②心照不宣的,不言而喻的: ~ approval 默认 / ~ consent 默许 / a ~ agreement (或understanding) 默契 ③【律】由于法律的执行而产生的 ‖~ly *ad.*

taciturn ['tæsitə:n] *a.* 沉默寡言的 ‖~ity [,tæsi-'tə:niti] *n.* / ~ly *ad.*

tack¹ [tæk] I *n.* ①平头钉: a thumb ~ 图钉 / a ~ rivet 定位铆钉 ②[复](缝纫中的)粗缝,假缝 ③【海】(帆的)上下角;上下角索 ④【海】(帆船的)逆风换抢,抢风行驶; (指帆向而言的)航向; 航向不变所驶过的一段航程: sail on the port (starboard) ~ 左(右)舷抢风行驶 / ~ and ~ 接连地逆风抢 ⑤在陆上所作的Z字形移动: He got through the dense crowd in a series of ~s. 他不停地东弯西拐才穿过拥挤的人群。⑥行动步骤,方针: be on the right (wrong) ~ 方针正确(错误) / try another ~ 改换方针 ⑦[英]附加条款(在英国议院用语中尤指为保证通过起见而附于财政提案后的与该案无关的条款,因上院无权修正财政提案) ⑧(清漆等的)粘性 ⑨[用以构成复合词]食物,食品: hard~ (船上用语)硬饼干,硬面包; 粗劣食品 / soft~ (船上用语)软面包,普通面包; 精美食品 II ❶ *vt.* ①钉住; 暂时用粗针缝缝: ~ a notice on a bulletin board 把通知钉在布告板上 / ~ a ribbon on to sth. 用粗针脚把缎带缝在帽上 ②(在议会提案中)增加(附加条款); 附加,添加 ③使(船)抢风转变航向 ❷ *vi.* ①抢风转变航向: ~ with the wind 顺风转舵 ②Z字形地移动 ③突然改变行动步骤(或方针,政策) ‖*get* (或 *come*) *down to brass ~s* 讨论实质问题;讨论重要事情 ‖**~er** *n.* ①揪平头钉的人 ②用粗针脚缝的人 ③[英]试图采用附加条款的办法使议案通过的人 ‖**~ board** (软木制)布告板 / **claw** 平头钉拔除器 / **~ driver** 平头钉自动敲打机 / **~ hammer** 平头钉锤

tack² [tæk] *n.* [苏格兰] ①租借契约 ②租得的牧地

tackle ['tækl] I *n.* ①滑车,复滑车;【船】帆的滑车索具: block and ~ 滑车组 / hoisting ~ 起重滑车 ②用具,装备: fishing ~ 钓鱼用具 ③擒抱,阻挡(指橄榄球赛中抱住带球跑的对方队员) II ❶ *vt.* ①用滑车固定; 给(马)套上马具 ②抓住,揪住; (橄榄球中)抱住并摔倒(或挡住)(对方带球跑的球员): The wrestler ~d his opponent. 摔角运动员扭住了对手。③向…交涉: ~ sb. on a subject 为某一问题与某人交涉 / ~ sb. over (或about) a matter 为某事与某人打交道 ④着手处理,对付,解决: ~ a task 着手进行一项任务 / ~ a difficult problem 对付难题 ❷ *vi.* (橄榄球中)抱住并摔倒(或挡住)对方球员 ‖**~ to** [英口]劲头十足地开始工作

tact [tækt] *n.* ①[古]触觉 ②老练;机智;圆滑;得体

tactful ['tæktful] *a.* 老练的;机智的;圆滑的;得体的 ‖~ly *ad.*

tactical ['tæktikəl] *a.* ①战术的; 作战的; 与地面(或海上)作战直接配合进行的: ~ offensive (defensive) 战术攻势(防御) / ~ thinking 战术思想 / a ~ airfield 战术飞机场,作战飞机场 / ~ air operations 战术性空中作战(支援地面部队而进行的一切作战) / a ~ locality 战术据点 / the ~ use of atomic weapons 原子武器的战术运用 / a ~ exercise 战术演习 ②策略(上)的;善于机变的;巧妙设计的 ‖~ly *ad.* ‖**~ diameter** 【海】旋回初径 / **~ radius** 【军】战斗半径(飞机装载足够油量可以飞至目标并返回基地的距离) / **~ range** 【军】战斗航程 / **~ unit** 【军】战术单位;作战部队;空中支援部队

tactician [tæk'tiʃən] *n.* ①战术家,兵法家 ②策略家,策士

tactics ['tæktiks] [复] *n.* ①[用作单]战术;兵法: *Tactics* is subordinate to strategy. 战术是从属于战略的。/ grand (或 major) ~ 大兵团(作)战术 / the ~ of "wear and tear" "蘑菇"战术 ②[常用复]策略,手法: These ~ are unlikely to help you. 这些手法看来对你不会有帮助。/ counterrevolutionary dual ~ 反革命的两面派策略 ③[用作单或复]【语】法素学;序素学

tactless ['tæktlis] *a.* 不老练的,不机智的;不圆滑的;不得体的 ‖~ly *ad.* / **~ness** *n.*

tadpole ['tædpoul] *n.* ①【动】蝌蚪 ②[美俚]法国小孩

taffrail ['tæfreil] *n.* 船尾栏杆

tag [tæg] I *n.* ①(破衣裙等上)悬着的碎片; 松散(或破碎)的末尾部; (羊身上)蓬乱的一簇羊毛 ②(鞋带末端的)包头,箍; (动物的)尾,尾尖 ③(服装上的)挂襻;缀饰; (鞋口后部的)拉襻 ④(戏剧、演说等的)结束语,结束语; 歌曲末尾的迭句 ⑤陈词滥调;口头禅: "You see?" is his habitual ~. "你明白吗?"是他的口头禅。⑥为修辞目的或炫耀词藻而引用的简短引语 ⑦附加语: a question ~ 【语】附加疑问(如 You'll come, won't you? 中的 won't you) ⑧形象生动的称号,浑名 ⑨标签: a shipping ~ 货运标签 / a price ~ 价目标签 ⑩残片,残迹 ⑪儿童捉人游戏 II (tagged; tagging) ❶ *vt.* ①装包头于(鞋带、绳等);加标签于;在(违章的)车上贴违犯交通规则的条子: ~ every item in the store 给每一种商品加上标签 ②给…起浑名; 把…称为: ~ sb. as "Wild Horse" 给某人起了个绰号叫"野马" ③给(戏剧、文学作品等)加上终场词(或结束语) ④ 连接,结合并 (together); 把(一篇文章)并入(另一篇文章)(to, on to) ⑤替(诗句)押韵;串(韵脚) ⑥剪下(蓬乱的羊毛) ⑦(儿童捉人游戏中)追到,捉到 ⑧指责,指控 ⑨[口]紧紧地跟在…后面,尾随 ⑩【原】(用同位素)标记: isotopically *tagged* 同位素示踪的, 同位素标记的 ❷ *vi.* [口]紧紧地跟在后面 (along, after, behind) ‖**~, rag, and bobtail** 乌合之众; 下层人民; 下层社会 ‖**~along** (令人讨厌的)追随学样者 / **'~board** *n.* 作货运标签用的硬板纸 / **~ day** [美]街头募捐日(对捐

款者赠以小标签) / **~ end** ①末尾, 末端: at the ~ *end* of the nineteenth century 在十九世纪末 ②[常用复]零星杂乱的东西: ~ *ends* of memories 支离破碎的回忆 / **~ line** ①(剧本或笑话中起画龙点睛作用以增加效果的)收尾语 ②(人、团体等的)常用口号, 时髦用语 / '**~rag** *n.* 乌合之众 *a.* 褴褛的 / **~raggery** ['tægrægəri] *n.* (人或物)杂乱的混合

tail¹ [teil] **I** *n.* ①(动物的)尾巴; 尾状物; 发辫; (g, y 等字母)伸出在格子线下面的部分 ② 末尾部分, 后部, 底部; 较弱的部分; [俚]屁股: the ~ of a truck 卡车的尾部 / the ~ of the eye 眼梢 / the ~ of a stream 河流下游水势较缓的部分 / the ~ of a football team 足球队中较弱的队员 ③[天]彗(星)尾, 流星尾; [空]飞翼尾 ④(等候乘车、购物等的)长队, 长列; 随员, 扈从 ⑤(盯梢的)特务, 暗探; (逃犯的)踪迹 ⑥[复][口]燕尾服; 男子夜礼服 ⑦[史](土耳其高级官员表示品位的)马尾旌 ⑧[常用复]钱币背面: Heads or ~s? (通过掷硬币来决定某事物)你猜正面还是反面? ⑨[印]地脚 ⑩(屋瓦等的)外露部分; (半嵌在墙内砖、石的)嵌入部分 ⑪(诗律规定之外的)附加诗句 ⑫[音]符尾 **II** ❶ *vt.* ①为⋯装尾: ~ a kite 为风筝装尾巴 ②截短⋯的尾巴; 摘除(水果柄、梗) ③排在(行列等)后面; 位于⋯的后部(或末端)使尾部连结: ~ sth. *on to* another 把某物尾端连接在另一物上 ④把(木材、砖石的一端)嵌进; 使架住, 使搭牢 (*in, on*): ~ a timber *in* (或 *on*) a wall 把木料搭牢在墙上 ⑤尾随; 跟踪, 监视: ~ a suspect 跟踪嫌疑犯 ❷ *vi.* ①成为散乱的行列; 以散乱的行列行进 ②[口]尾随, 跟踪; 追随 (*after, behind*) ③(木材、砖石一端)嵌入, 搭上 ④船尾朝前停上浅滩, 船尾搁浅 (*aground*); (停泊中的船只)船尾朝着某一方向停住(或摆动): The ship ~ed down stream. 那船船尾朝下游停着. **III** *a.* ①尾部的, 后部的 ②后面来的: a ~ wind 顺风 ‖*drop a pinch of salt on the ~ of* 见 **salt** / *get ... on the ~* (或 *get on the ~ of ...*) [军俚](空战时)咬住⋯的尾巴, 从背后攻击⋯ / *make neither head nor ~ of sth.* 见 **head** / *~ off* (或 *away*) ①成为零零落落的一行落在后面 ②变少, 缩小; (讲话等)吞吞吐吐、不得要领地结束: His voice ~ed off into silence. 他话音愈来愈低, 终于哑然无声了. / *~s up* 兴致勃勃 / *~ to the tide* 见 **tide** / *The ~ wags the dog.* (社会或党派中)小人物掌权. / *tuck one's ~* 夹起尾巴; 感到羞耻 / *turn ~* 逃跑: Badly damaged, the enemy tanks turned ~. 敌人坦克受到重创后逃跑了. / *twist the lion's ~* (常用于指美国政客的言论等)触犯英国 / *with ~ in the water* [美俚]兴旺, 发达 / *with ~ between the legs* 夹着尾巴; 垂头丧气, 灰溜溜地: The enemy vessel fled *with its ~ between its legs.* 敌舰夹着尾巴逃跑了. ‖**~ed** *a.* ①[用以构成复合词]有⋯(状)尾的: bob~ed 截尾的 / long-

~ed 长尾的 ②去掉尾的 / **~er** *n.* 尾随者, 跟踪者; 侦探 / **~less** *a.* 无尾的 ‖'**~board** *n.* (手推车等后部可移动的)尾板, 后挡板 / '**~·coat** *n.* 燕尾服 / **~ cups** 【空】尾伞 / **~ dive, ~ drop** 【空】尾坠 / '**~·down** *a. & ad.* 【空】机朝下的 / '**~·end** 末端, 末尾, (队伍的)排尾; 结尾部; 结束时期; 屁股 / **~ fin** (鱼的)尾鳍 ②【空】直尾翼; 垂直安定面 / **~ lamp** = ~light / '**~light** *n.* (车辆的)尾灯, 后灯 / **~ margin** 【印】地脚 / '**~·piece** *n.* ①(在末尾的)附属物, 附加物 ②【建】半端梁 ③【机】尾端件 ④(提琴等的)系弦板 ⑤(书籍章节末尾的)补白花饰 / **~ pipe** (机动车辆、喷气引擎等的)排气尾管 / **~ plane** 【空】横尾翼, 水平安定面 / **~ race** *n.* (涡轮机或水车等运转处的)泄水道; 排表矿渣的水渠 / **~ skid** 【空】尾橇 / **~ slide, ~ slip** 【空】尾滑 / '**~·spin** *n.* ①【空】(飞机)尾旋, 螺旋 ②失去控制, 混乱; 困境: an economic ~*spin* 经济混乱 / *plunge* (或 *send*) *sth. into a* ~*spin* 把某事搞得乱糟糟 / '**~·stock** *n.* 【机】尾座 / **~ turret** 【空】机尾炮塔 / '**~·,wagging** *n.* (滑雪的)高速旋转, 平行旋转; 【空】(特技飞行的)摆尾

tail² [teil] **I** *n.* ①【律】限定所有权; 限定继承权: an heir *in* ~ 限定继承人 ②【律】限定继承的产业: a fee ~ 具有一定身分的人才能继承的土地 **II** *a.* 限定继承的

tailor ['teilə] **I** *n.* (尤指做外衣的)裁缝, 成衣工, 成衣商: go to the ~'s 到服装店做衣服 **II** ❶ *vi.* 做裁缝 ❷ *vt.* ① 裁制(衣服): a well-~ed coat 一件裁制合身的上衣 ②为(某人)做衣服 ③(为某一特定目的而)剪裁, 制作 ④ 按男装式样裁制(女服) ‖*ride like a ~* 不善骑马 / *The ~ makes the man.* [谚]人靠衣装. / **~ing** ['teilərin] *n.* ①裁缝业 ②做衣服, 成衣 ③(为某一特定目的的)剪裁, 制作 ‖'**~·bird** *n.* 【动】长尾缝叶莺 / '**~·,fashion** *ad.* 盘膝: sit ~*fashion* 盘膝而坐 / '**~·made** *a.* ①裁缝制的, 样式和裁制考究的; 似由高级裁缝制作的; (女式服装)线条简单、腰身服贴而少花饰的 ②(为某一目的)特制的 (香烟)机制的 / **~'s chair** (裁缝工作用)无脚有背的座椅 / **~'s chalk** 裁缝划线用的划粉, 粉片 / **~'s clippings** 裁剪碎料 / **~'s twist** 缝纫粗丝线

taint [teint] **I** ❶ *vt.* ①使感染, 使腐坏; 沾染: The meat was ~ed. 这肉腐坏了. / be ~ed with prejudices 受偏见的影响 ②使道德败坏, 腐蚀: Bad books will ~ the young mind. 坏书会毒害年轻人的思想. ❷ *vi.* [古]腐坏; 败坏 **II** *n.* ①污点; (名誉等的)玷污 ②感染; 腐坏 ‖**~less** *a.* 未玷污的; 未感染的; 纯洁的 ‖**~ed goods** 工会禁止受理的货物(因该货物是由非工会会员制造的或经手过的)

take [teik] **I** (took [tuk], taken ['teikən]) ❶ *vt.* ①拿, 取; 攻取: ~ (up) a book 拿(起)一本书 / ~ sb. by the hand 拉住某人的手 / ~ sth. on one's shoulder 掮某物 / ~ sth. up with a pair of pincers 用钳子钳起某物 / ~ hold of sth. 抓

住某物 / ～ two cities 攻克两座城市
②抓，捕；吸引：～ fish 捕鱼 / ～ sb. at a disadvantage 趁某人不备加以攻击；抓住某人的把柄
③拿走，取走；夺去(生命)；赢(牌)；吃掉(棋子)：Who has ～n my pen? 谁把我的笔拿走了? / ～ three from nine 九减三
④带去，带领：Take an umbrella with you. 带把伞去。/ ～ the students round (或 about) the factory 带领学生参观工厂 / Will this road ～ me to the station? 走这条路能到车站吗?
⑤取得，获得，得到：～ (the) first place 居首位，得第一 / This river ～s its rise from (或 in) a lake. 这条河发源于一个湖。/ ～ cold 感冒 / ～ a day off 请一天假 / ～ one's leave 告辞
⑥(疾病、不愉快的事情等)突然侵袭：be ～n with a fit of anger 勃然大怒 / The fire had been put down before it took the forest. 火在蔓延到森林前就被扑灭了。
⑦就(座、职等)；避入：Take a seat, please. 请坐。/ ～ office 就职 / ～ the chair 任会议主席；主持开会 / ～ the floor (在会上)起来发言 / ～ harbour 避入港湾
⑧接受；收(房客等)，娶(妻)；承担；容忍：～ sb.'s advice 接受某人的劝告 / He will not ～ a hint. 给他暗示他不会接受。/ You may ～ it from me (或 ～ my word for it). 你尽管相信我的话。/ ～ sb. into one's confidence 把某人当作知心人 / He took his dead younger brother's child. 他把已去世的弟弟的孩子领来抚养。/ ～ a class 负责一个班级 / ～ the blame 承担过错 / ～ things as they are 接受事物的现状，安于现状 / You must ～ us as you find us. 请你不要苛求。(或：请你多包涵。) / I'm not taking any. [口]我不要。(或：我不接受。) / We'll ～ no nonsense. 我们不允许胡闹。
⑨买下；租下；订阅(报刊等)；定(座等)：I'll ～ this cap. 我买这顶帽子。
⑩吃；喝；服(药等)；吸入(新鲜空气等)；吸收；容纳：Will you ～ a cup of tea? 你要喝杯茶吗? / ～ dinner about six 六时左右进正餐 / The medicine is to be ～n three times a day. 这药日服三次。/ go for a walk and ～ the air 散一下步并呼吸新鲜空气 / cloth that ～s dye well 着色性能好的布 / The shelf just ～s the books. 这架子正好可以装进这些书。
⑪选取，采取：～ action 采取行动
⑫利用，采用：Don't rush. Take your time. 别忙，慢慢来好了。/ ～ a chopper to the poisonous weeds 铲除毒草
⑬记录；摘录；量取(体温、尺寸等)；拍摄(照相等)；画下：～ notes 记笔记 / ～ a letter 记录口授函件 / ～ a photo 拍照 / ～ the children in their new clothes 给穿着新衣服的孩子拍照
⑭乘，搭(车、船等)：～ a bus to work 乘公共汽车上班

⑮需要，花费，占用：The work took us a week to finish. 我们花了一个星期完成这项工作。/ It ～s many men to build a house. 建造一幢房屋需要很多人。/ It ～s a lot of doing. 这要花很大气力。/ The box does not ～ (up) much room. 这箱子占的地方不多。
⑯理解，领会：How do you ～ this passage? 这段话你怎么理解? / if I ～ you correctly 如果我对你的意思理解得不错的话
⑰以为；把…看作；对待：I ～ him to be sincere. 我当他是诚恳的。/ I ～ it that he approves. 我想他是同意的。/ ～ sth. as settled 把某事看成已解决 / Strategically we despise difficulties, and tactically we ～ them seriously. 在战略上我们藐视困难，在战术上我们认真对待困难。
⑱生，产生：～ an interest in 对…发生兴趣 / ～ pity on 对…产生怜悯
⑲[俚]欺骗，使上当：Are you sure you're not being ～n? 你有把握没有被骗吗?
⑳越过(障碍)：～ a hurdle 跨栏
㉑打，击：～ sb. on the nose 朝着某人鼻子打一拳 / ～ sb. a smart box on the ear 打某人一记响亮的耳光
㉒以…为例 (=～ for example)：～ the 19th century 以十九世纪为例
㉓[表示做一次动作]：～ a bath 洗个澡 / ～ a look 看一看 / ～ a rest 休息一下 / ～ no notice 不注意

❷ vi. ①得，取，拿；【律】获得财产
②(鱼等)被捕捉：Fish ～ best after rain. 雨后最易捕鱼。
③(齿轮等)啮合；(植物等)生根，开始生长
④(计划、接种等)奏效；起作用；(染料等)被吸收：The smallpox vaccination took. 牛痘发了。/ Has the scheme any chance of taking? 那计划可能有效吗? / Dry fuel ～s readily. 干燥的燃料极易着火。
⑤(作品、产品等)受人欢迎：The novel didn't ～. 那小说不受欢迎。
⑥拍照片来：He does not ～ well. 他不上照。
⑦走，行走：～ across a field (over a hill) 越过田野(小山)
⑧ [～ and ...][方][用以加强后随动词语气]：He took and grabbed his hat and ran. 他拿起帽子就跑。
⑨变得，成为：～ ill (或 sick) 生病 / ～ pretty surly 变得十分乖戾

Ⅱ n. ①得，取，拿
②捕获量；收入：a large ～ of fish 捕到的很多鱼 / the yearly ～ from tourism 旅游事业的岁入 / pull in a ～ 获得一笔收入
③奏效的东西(如受到喜爱的戏剧、歌曲等)
④(植皮)愈合；(种牛痘)发痘
⑤反应
⑥(一次拍摄的)电影(或电视)镜头
⑦录音；一次录的音

⑧【印】一次排稿的量
‖*be able to* (或 *can*) ~ *it* 能经受得住(如刑罚、攻击、轰炸等) / *be ~n aback* 吃了一惊 / *be ~n ill* 得病 / *be ~n short* [口]突然觉得要大便 / *give and* ~ 见 *give* / *give or* ~ 见 *give* / ~ *after* ①(面貌、性格方面)象(自己的父母等) ②学…的样 / ~ *against* 反对…;不喜欢… / ~ *amiss* 曲解(某一行动);对…感到生气 / ~ *apart* 拆开(机器等);(机器等)可拆开: The gadget ~*s apart* for cleaning. 这个小机件是可以拆开来洗的。②剖析,抨击(论点等) ③粗暴对待,无情攻击 / ~ *away* ①拿走 ②夺去 ③使离去: What ~*s* you *away* so early? 为什么你这么早就走? / ~ *back* 拿回;收回 / ~ *back* one's words (表示认错、道歉等)收回自己的话 ②带回 / ~ *down* ①拿下;咽下 ②记下;(用机器)录下 ③拆卸(机器),拆掉(房屋等);能被拆卸 ④压下…的气焰 ⑤受打扰,病倒: ~ *down* with typhoid 患伤寒病倒 / ~ *five* 休息五分钟,小憩 / ~ *for* 认为,以为;误认为: What do you ~ me *for*? 你把我当作什么人来看? / ~ *from* 减少,减损,降低 / ~ *in* ①接受,接待;陪同(或挽引)(女宾)由客厅进入餐厅;收容;吸收 ②在家承接(活计等) ③改小(衣服);卷(帆): This coat needs to be ~*n in* a bit.这件上衣要改小些。④[主英]订阅(报刊) ⑤领会,理解:~ the situation *in* 认清形势(或处境) / ~ *in* the meaning of 理解…的含义 ⑥把…尽收眼底;注意到 ⑦包含,包括;将…排入旅程 ⑧轻信(假话等) ⑨欺骗: be ~*n in* by 被…所骗 ⑩观看: ~ *in* a movie (play) 看一场电影(一出戏) ⑪拘留 ⑫获有(土地、领土等);围垦;开垦 / ~ *it easy* 见 *easy* / ~ *it on the chin* 见 *chin*[1] / ~ *it or leave it* 要么接受要么舍弃,不容讨价还价 / ~ *it out in* 接受…为抵偿 / ~ *it out of* ①向(某人)报复,以…来出气 ②使(某人)疲乏 / ~ *it out on sb.* 向某人出气 / ~ ... *lying down* 见 *lie*[1] / ~*n* (或 *taking*) one with another 总的看来 / ~ *off* ①拿去,去掉,取消,脱(衣、帽等),夺去(生命等): The 5 a.m. train has long been ~*n off*. 凌晨五点的那班车早已取消了。 / ~ *off* a tax (the restrictions) 取消一种税(限制) ②带领,把…带往: ~ sb. *off* to (see) an exhibition 带某人去(看)展览会 ③从…中去掉;把(目光、思路等)从…移开;(风、潮水等)减弱: ~ ten percent *off* the nonproductive expenses 削减非生产性开支的百分之十 ④复制(副本等) ⑤(嘲弄地)学…的样 ⑥(飞机等)起飞,离地;离开 ⑦跳起来 ⑧叉开,岔开;(从…)产生,(以…)作为出发点 (*from*) / ~ *on* ①呈现(新面貌等);具有(特征等) ②雇用;增加(人手等);接纳(乘客);(火车等)把…载到目的地: I fell asleep in the bus and was ~*n on* to the terminal. 我在公共汽车里睡着了,错过了站一直乘到终点。③承担: be ready to ~ on heavy responsibilities 乐于挑重担 ④同(对手)较量,对付 ⑤[口](因发怒等)激动 ⑥(服装式样、歌曲等)风行,流行 ⑦盛气凌人 / ~ *oneself off* 走开,离去 / ~ *out* ①拿出,取出 ②去掉: ~ *out* stains from one's clothes 去掉衣服上的污渍 / ~ the conceit *out* of sb. 打掉某人的骄气 ③扣除,除去 ④带…出去 ⑤发泄 ⑥抵充: ~ part of the debt *out* in goods 以货物抵充部分债务 ⑦取得(专利权等);领取(执照等) ⑧出发,起始 ⑨(桥牌)另叫花色以使(搭档)改叫 / ~ *over* ①把…接过来,接收;接管;接任 ②盛行起来 / ~ (*sth.*) *for granted* 见 *grant* / ~ *sth. hard* 心里因某事而不快,对某事非常耿耿于怀 / ~ *sth. ill* 对某事感到生气;认为做某事并非出自好意 / ~ *ten* 休息十分钟,小憩 / ~ *to* ①开始,开始从事: ~ *to* studying English 开始学英语 ②喜欢,亲近(人) ③养成(…的习惯);沉湎于 ④走向,赴;委身于: ~ *to* flight 逃走 / ~ *to the* street (罢工队伍等)走上街头 / ~ *to* the life boats 登上救生艇 / ~ *up* ①拿起 ②着手处理;开始(从事于): ~ *up* the matter with 向…提出问题(要求处理、答复等) / When did you ~ *up* basketball? 你什么时候开始打篮球的? (指从事这一项运动) / ~ *up* a post 就职 ③继续: Let's ~ *up* the work where they've left off. 让我们接着他们干下去。④接纳(乘客);装载(货物) ⑤采纳(观点等);采取(某种态度) ⑥接受(挑战等) ⑦吸收(水分);溶解(固体) ⑧占去,占据(时间、地位、注意力等) ⑨把…当作被保护人;培植 ⑩拘捕(为表示异议等)打断…的话;责备 ⑫付清;承兑(汇票);认购(公债等);接受(抵押品);全部买去 ⑬扎住;补(漏针): ~ *up* an artery 夹住动脉(防止流血) ⑭使绷紧;绷紧;收缩 ⑮定(居): ~ *up* one's residence at 定居于… ⑯[口][方](天气)变晴朗 / ~ *upon* (或 *on*) oneself 承担: How can you ~ (it) *upon yourself* to say this? 你怎么可以这样说呢? / ~ *up with* ①与…亲密交往 ②对…发生兴趣,致力于
‖**~r** n. ①取者 ②捕者 ③接受者 ④收取者: a ticket ~r 收票员

‖'~**down** n. ①(机械等的)拆卸 ②[口]失面子,羞辱 a. (机械等)可拆卸的 / '~-**home pay** = ~-**home pay** / '~-**home pay** (扣除捐税等以后)实得的工资 / '~-'**in** n. [口]欺骗,欺诈 / '~**off** n. ①起飞;起跳(点);出发点 ②[口](嘲弄性的)学样 ③拿走 ④(所需材料等的)估计,估量 ⑤功率输出端 / '~**out** n. ①(桥牌中)示意搭档改叫的叫牌 ②取出的东西,取出的数量 ③把成品从模子取出的自动装置 ④. (桥牌中)用的"加倍")向搭档示意而非为惩罚对方的 ②(食物)供顾客带出外吃的 / '~-**over** n. 接收;接管;接任 / '~-**up** n. ①收缩;调整;吸水 ②【机】(缝纫机上拨线上升的)提升装置;松紧装置 ③【纺】织缩;卷取 ④【摄】卷片装置 / '~-**up spool** (电影放映机、录音机等的)卷片轴,卷带轴

taking ['teikiŋ] **I** n. ①拿;取得,获得;捕获物 ②[复]收入;利息;进款 ③[口]激动;兴奋;心烦意乱: be in a great ~ 极为心烦意乱 **II** a. ①引

人注目的，吸引人的；迷人的 ②传染的 ‖~ly *ad.* / ~ness *n.*

tale [teil] *n.* ①故事，传说；叙述: a fairy ~ 神仙故事；童话 / a nursery ~ 童话 / All this is now a ~. 所有这些全是往事了。/ tell the ~ of one's experiences 讲述自己的经历 / I prefer to tell my own ~. 我宁可由我自己来说明这件事。②坏话，流言蜚语；谎言: spin tall ~s 捏造骗人的鬼话 ③[古]计算；总数: The shepherd tells his ~. 牧羊人清点他的羊数。/ the ~ of dead and wounded 死伤者总数 ‖a ~ of a tub 无稽之谈 / a twice-told ~ 陈旧的故事；尽人皆知的事情 / old wives' ~s (无知老妇的)愚蠢之谈，荒诞故事 / tell its own ~ 不言自喻，显而易见 / tell ~s (out of school) 揭人隐私，搬弄是非，背后讲人坏话 / tell the ~ [俚](为引起同情)编讲悲惨的往事 / That tells a ~. 这很说明问题(或揭露了内情)。/ Thereby hangs a ~. 其中大有文章。‖'~,bearer *n.* 搬弄是非的人 / '~,bearing *n.* 搬弄是非 / '~,carrier *n.* =~bearer / '~,teller *n.* ①讲故事的人 ②(背后)讲人坏话的人，搬弄是非者 / '~,telling *n.* ①讲故事 ②(背后)讲人坏话，搬弄是非 ③[古]总数

talent ['tælənt] *n.* ①天才，天资 ②才能，才干: have a ~ for organization 有组织才能 ③有才能的人；人才，有才能的人们: athletic ~ 体育人才 ④[the ~][俚](赛马等场合非职业性的)赌客们 ⑤古希腊(或罗马、中东等)的重量及货币单位 ‖hide one's ~s in a napkin 埋没自己的才能 ‖~ed *a.* 天资高的；有才能的 / ~less *a.* 没有天赋的；无才能的 ‖~ scout (为某活动领域发掘并招收新手的)人才发掘者 / ~ show 业余能手演唱会

talisman ['tælizmən] ([复] talismans) *n.* ①护符，辟邪物，被认为会带来好运的东西(如小装饰物、戒指等) ②能产生奇异效果的东西，法宝 ‖~ic(al) [,tæliz'mænik(əb] *a.* 护符的；有护符般效力的

talk [tɔːk] I ❶ *vi.* ①讲话；谈话；演讲: What are you ~ing about? 你们在谈些什么? / They were ~ing to some foreign sailors through an interpreter. 他们通过译员在同外国海员们谈话。/ ~ before an audience (a meeting) 对听众(大会)讲话 / ~ of visiting sb. 谈到要去看望某人 / ~ over the telephone 在电话里谈话 ②(用信号等)通讯，通话: ~ by radio signals 用无线电信号通讯 / ~ by gestures 用手势交谈 ③(会)说话；有讲话能力；学人讲话: Many deaf-mutes began to ~ after acupuncture treatment. 许多聋哑人经过针刺治疗后开始能说话了。/ The baby is learning to ~. 婴儿咿咿呀呀学语。/ Some parrots can ~. 有些鹦鹉能学人讲话。④闲聊；说闲话，讲人坏话，揭人隐私；传播小道消息: ~ behind sb.'s back 背后议论某人 / People will ~. 人们要论长道短的。❷ *vt.* ①讲，说: He ~s

sense. 他说得有理。②用(某种语言、方言等)讲: ~ Chinese (English) 讲汉语(英语) / ~ slang 用俚语讲 ③谈论；讨论: ~ the day's news 谈论当天的新闻 / We ~ed the situation over. 我们讨论了这形势。/ ~ business 谈生意经；讲正经事 / never ~ personalities 从不飞短流长说人坏话 ④说得使…，讲得使…: ~ oneself hoarse (out of breath) 讲得声音嘶哑(喘不过气来) / a child to sleep (讲故事等)讲得孩子入睡 / sb.'s worries away 通过劝说使某人消除顾虑 II *n.* ①谈话；交谈；(正式)会谈，会议: a heart-to-heart ~ 谈心 / have cordial and friendly ~s with foreign friends 跟外国朋友们进行亲切、友好的交谈 / the Paris ~s 巴黎会谈 / hold ~s with 与…举行会谈 ②讲话；(非正式)的演讲，报告；讲课: He gave a ~ on "the Tradition of French Literature". 他作了题为"法国文学传统"的报告。③空谈；空论: He is all ~. 他这个人就是会说空话。/ It will end in ~. 只是空谈一阵，什么事也成不了。④谣言；流言蜚语；(小道)传说: We heard it in ~, but nobody believed it. 我们听到了这种传说，不过谁也不相信。⑤谈论的题材: become the ~ of the town 成为众人的话题 ⑥讲话方式，语言；方言；隐语 ‖big ~ 大话，牛皮 / idle ~ 闲扯，山海经 / make ~ ①闲谈，无话找话谈(以消磨时间) ②引起背后议论 / Money ~s. [美俚]金钱万能。/ Now you're ~ing. [俚]你这样说才合我意了(指建议语) / perfumed ~ [美]谄坏话，骂人话 / small ~ 闲聊，谈家常 / straight ~ [美俚]诚恳而又简明扼要的谈话 / against time 见 time / ~ . . . around 说得…同意自己，说服 / ~ at sb. 影射某人，指桑骂槐地讲某人 / ~ away ①不断地谈 ②在谈话中度过(一段时间): ~ the night away 谈了一夜 / ~ back 顶嘴，反驳 / ~ big 说大话，吹牛，自吹自擂 / ~ (cold) turkey [美口]直率地说；谈正经事 / ~ . . . down ①大声说着压倒，驳倒 ②以话语鄙薄 ③通过无线电通讯使降落: ~ a pilot (an aircraft) down (通过雷达观察并用无线电通讯)引导驾驶员(飞机)降落 / ~ down to sb. 高人一等地对某人讲话，(因轻视而)对某人讲得简单 / ~ horse 见 horse / ~ . . . in = ~ . . . down / ~ing of 谈到，至于(讲到): Talking of travel, have you ever been to London? 讲到旅行，你到过伦敦吗? / Talk of the devil and he will appear. 见 devil / ~ out ①把…谈透 ②通过商谈消除(分歧) ③响亮地说 ④[英]把讨论拖长到议会休会以使(议案等)搁置 / ~ over ①商量，讨论: Let's ~ it over. 咱们来商量一下。/ ~ over a plan 讨论计划 ②说得…同意自己，说服 / ~ round ①兜圈子谈(问题等) ②说得…同意自己，说服 / ~ sb. into (out of) sth. 说服某人做(不做)某事: ~ sb. into consent (或 agreeing) 说服某人同意 / ~ sb.'s head (或 arm, ear) off [俚]对某人说个不停，对某人唠叨

不休 / ~ *shop* 见 **shop** / ~ *tall* 说大话,吹牛,自吹自擂 / ~ *the hind leg off a donkey* (或 *dog, horse*) 见 **leg** / *through one's hat* [俚] 吹牛; 胡说八道 / ~ *through* (*the back of*) *one's neck* 吹牛, 讲蠢话 / ~ *to sb.* 找某人谈话;[口]责备某人: I'll ~ *to* him about his carelessness. 我要找他谈谈,批评他的粗心大意。/ ~ *to death* 见 **death** / ~ *up* ①大声讲,响亮地讲 ②大胆讲;鲁莽地讲 ③为引起兴趣而讨论;赞扬 / ~ *with* ①与…交谈,与…讨论 ②试图说服 / *tall* ~ 大话,牛皮 / You can't ~. [口]你没有资格讲。(意为: 你也一样坏。) ‖**~able** *a.* 可谈论的;善谈的,健谈的 / **'~-back** *n.* 【讯】(专线)工作联络电话 / **~fest** ['to:kfest] *n.* ①漫谈会,(非正式的)讨论会 ②冗长的讨论(或辩论)/ ~ **show** (广播、电视的)谈话节目(通常由知名人士进行讨论或回答问题)

tall [to:l] **I** *a.* ①身材高的,高的: a ~ man 高个子 / a ~ pine 高大的松树 / a ~ chimney (flagpole, mast) 高高的烟囱(旗杆,桅杆) / He is six feet ~. 他身高六呎。(现常用 high) ②[口]夸大的;过分的;难以相信的;夸口的: a ~ story 难以相信的故事 / ~ talk 大话,牛皮 / a ~ order 苛求,难办的差使 ③[口]巨大的;大量的: a ~ price 高价 / a ~ drink 一大杯酒 / a ~-water man (海员用语)远洋海员 **II** *ad.* [口]夸大地;趾高气扬地 ‖**~ish** *a.* 有些高的 / **~ness** *n.* ‖**'~boy** *n.* ①高脚柜 ②烟囱帽(烟囱的出口处) / ~ **money** [美俚]大宗财富 / ~ **oil** 妥尔油(蒸煮硫酸盐木浆时的副产品,可用于制造肥皂、清漆等) / ~ **timber** 偏僻地区,人烟稀少的地区

tallow ['tælou] **I** *n.* (做皂、烛等用的)牛脂,(动物)脂: a ~ candle 脂烛,蜡烛 **II** *vt.* ①涂动物脂于 ②把(牲畜)养肥 ‖~ **chandler** (牛)油烛制造人;油烛商 / **'~-faced** *a.* 脸色苍白的,脸色发黄的 / ~ **tree** 【植】乌桕

tally ['tæli] **I** *n.* ①符木(古时刻痕计数的木签,分作两半,借贷双方各执一半为凭);计数的签,筹码 ②账;记账;记录: keep a daily ~ of the water level fluctuations 记录每天水位变化情况 ③(比赛时的)比分,得分; 分: make a record ~ 获得创纪录的比分 / score a ~ 获得一分 ④簿记表格,簿记账页 ⑤手执计数器,计数板 ⑥(系在物件、树木等上的)标签,小牌 ⑦(供两相验合用的)对应物,验合用的凭据 ⑧符合,吻合 ⑨计算单位(具体可指一打、二十、一百等): buy goods by the ~ 按打数(或百数等)购买货物 / ... 8, 10, ~ (以一打计数时用语)…八,十,一打 / ... 96, 98, ~ (以百打计数时用语)…九十六,九十八,一百 ⑩【海】理货,点数 **II** ❶ *vt.* ①计算,数,清点(货物等): ~ the cargo 点货 ②up for and against 统计赞成票和反对票 ②记账,记(分) ③加标签(或标记)于 ④使(两物)符合,使吻合 ❷ *vi.* ①符合,吻合: What he says *tallies* with facts. 他的话符合事实。②记录;记

分 ‖*buy on* (或 *upon*) ~ 赊购 / *live* (on) ~ [英俚]非婚同居 ‖~ **clerk** 理货员 / ~ **company** 理货公司 / **~man** ['tælimən] *n.* ①[英]经管赊销商品的商人 ②带样品卖货的人 ③记账员;理货员 / ~ **sheet** 计数单;理货单 / ~ **shop** 赊销商店 / ~ **system,** ~ **trade** 赊卖

tallyho ['tæli'hou] **I** *n.* ①"嗬"声(猎人发现狐狸时的喊声) ②四匹马拉的马车 ③(英空军用语)发现目标 **II** *int.* 嗬! **III** ❶ *vi.* 发出"嗬"声 ❷ *vt.* 用"嗬"声驱策(猎狗)

talon ['tælən] *n.* ①[常用复]爪(尤指猛禽的) ②(如爪般的)手指;手;魔爪 ③爪状物;【建】爪饰 ④(牌戏中)发剩的牌 ⑤剑的刃根 ⑥(由钥匙顶住借以推动锁栓的)螺栓肩 ⑦【商】股息单掉换券

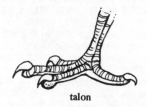

talon

talus ['teiləs] ([复] tali ['teilai]) *n.* ①【解】距骨 ②踝

tamarisk ['tæmərisk] *n.* 【植】柽柳属植物

tame [teim] **I** *a.* ①(动物)养服了的,驯服的: a ~ bear 驯服的熊 ②(土地)被开垦的;(植物)人工栽培的 ③顺从的,听话的 ④无精打采的,没有劲的;平淡的,沉闷的: a ~ book 一本平淡乏味的书 **II** ❶ *vt.* ①驯服,制服: a tiger 驯虎 / a trouble-making river 治好一条为害的河流 / ~ the atom 控制原子 ②使软化 ③使变得平淡 ❷ *vi.* 变得驯服 ‖**~less** *a.* 难驯服的;未经驯服的 / **~ly** *ad.* / **~ness** *n.* ‖**~r** *n.* 驯养人,驯服…的人(或物): a lion ~r 驯狮人 / troops of river ~rs 治河大军 ‖~ **cat** 极为顺从的人,甘愿受人摆布的人

tamper[1] ['tæmpə] *n.* ①捣棒;夯,夯具 ②填塞者;捣实者 ③【原】(中子)反射器;(中子)反射剂

tamper[2] ['tæmpə] ❶ *vi.* ①损害,削弱;窜改 (*with*): ~ *with* traditions 损害传统 / ~ *with* history (sb.'s teachings) 窜改历史(某人的学说) ②(用不正当手段)影响,左右;贿赂: ~ *with* voters 以不正当手段影响投票人; 收买投票人 ③瞎摸弄,瞎搞(*with*): ~ *with* a lock 撬锁 ❷ *vt.* 窜改

tan [tæn] **I** *n.* ①鞣料树皮(含有鞣酸的树皮,如橡树等);鞣料;(铺路用的)鞣料渣 ②鞣料的颜色,棕黄色 ③[复]棕黄色的皮鞋(或其他穿着用品) ④日晒后的肤色;棕褐色: get a good ~ 晒得黑黑的 ⑤[the ~] 马戏团;骑马学校的场地: kiss the ~ 从马上摔下来 **II** *a.* ①棕黄色的;棕褐色的: ~ leather shoes 棕黄色皮鞋 ②鞣料的;鞣皮的 **III** (tanned; tanning) ❶ *vt.* ①鞣(革),硝(皮) ②把…晒黑: He is well *tanned*. 他被晒得黑黑

的。③狠狠鞭打: ~ sb.'s hide 狠狠鞭打某人
❷ vi. ①鞣革;制成革 ②晒黑;晒成棕褐色: She
~s quickly. 她很容易晒黑。‖~ball n. (作燃
料用的) 球状鞣料渣 / '~,liquor, '~-ooze,
'~-,pickle n. 鞣酸溶液 / '~yard n. 制革工场

tandem ['tændəm] I n. ①两匹马前后成纵列拉的
双轮马车 ②两匹前后成纵列套在马车上的马 ③
两个(或两个以上) 前后排列同时使用 (或协调动
作) 的一组事物 ④ =~ bicycle ⑤ =~ aeroplane II ad. 一前一后地: horses driven ~ 排
成纵列驾驭的马 III a. 一前一后排列的,串联的:
a ~ arrangement of engine cylinders 发动机汽
缸的串联式排列 ‖in ~ ①一前一后地 ②相互
合作地,协力地 / ~ aeroplane 串翼型飞机 / ~
bicycle 两人(或两人以上)前后坐的自行车

tang[1] [tæn] I n. (刀、锉等的) 柄脚(指插入柄中的
部分) II vt. 在(刀、锉等)上做柄脚

tang[2] [tæn] I n. ①强烈的味道;特别浓烈的气味:
a dish with the ~ of garlic 带有强烈蒜味的菜 /
the ~ of new-mown grass 新割的草发出的浓郁
气味 ②特性 ③气息,意味: be seasoned with the
~ of humour 带有幽默的意味 II vt. 使具有气味

tang[3] [tæn] n. 【植】墨角藻(或其他海产草本植物)

tang[4] [tæn] I n. (击金属所发的) 当的一声;弦声
II ❶ vt. ① 使发出当的一声 ② 铿锵地说出
❷ vi. 发出当的一声

tangent ['tændʒənt] I n. ①【数】正切;切线 ②(铁
路或道路的) 直线区间 II a. ①【数】正切的;相切
的;切线的: ~ plane 切面 / ~ circle 相切圆 /
~ curve 切线曲面 ②离题的;背离原来途径的:
~ remarks 扯到题外的话 ‖fly (或 go) off at
a ~ (说话时)突然扯到题外;突然背离原来的途
径,突然改变行径

tangible ['tændʒəbl] I a. ①可触知的;有实质的;
有形的: ~ assets 有形资产 ②明确的,确实的:
~ results 确实的成效 / ~ proofs 明确的证据
II n. [复]有形资产 ‖**tangibility** [,tændʒi'biliti]
n.

tangle ['tæŋgl] I n. ①(头发、线、树枝等的) 缠结,
纠结: His hair is all in a ~. 他的头发乱成一
团。②纷乱;困惑: traffic ~s 混乱的交通情况 /
His mind was in a ~. 他的思想陷于困惑之中。
③争执,纠纷: a ~ with sb. 与某人的争执 ④采
集海底生物的装置 II ❶ vt. 使缠结;使纠缠;使
混乱: get ~d in a quarrel 被纠缠到一场争吵中
去 ❷ vi. 缠结;被纠缠;卷入争论;进行较量: They
~d heatedly over the question. 他们在这个问题
上激烈地争了起来。‖~d a. 纠缠的;紊乱的:
a ~d affair 错综复杂的事 / ~some ['tæŋglsəm]
a. 紊乱的,复杂的 / tangly a. 纠缠在一起的;
紊乱的 ‖'~foot n. [俚]烈酒,蹩脚的威士忌酒

tango ['tæŋgou] I n. ①探戈舞 ②探戈舞曲 II vi.
跳探戈舞

tank [tæŋk] I n. ①(盛液体或气体的)大容器;槽;
箱;柜;罐: an auxiliary fuel ~ (飞机上的)副油
箱 / a gasoline ~ 汽油箱,汽油桶 / a storage

~ 储油罐 ②储水池;游泳池;【船】船模试验池: a
~ race 游泳池中举行的游泳比赛 ③【船】液体
舱: ~ top (船的)内层底 ④坦克: a heavy
(medium, light) ~ 重(中,轻)型坦克 / an
amphibious ~ 水陆两用坦克 / a ~ carrier 坦

tank

克运输船 / a ~ destroyer 自行防坦克炮 / a ~
trap 坦克陷坑 / ~ mines 防坦克地雷 / ~ units
(或 forces) 坦克部队 ⑤混合牢房(尤指犯人初入
狱时被关押在内的) II vt. ①把…储在槽(或箱、
柜等容器)内 ②把…放在槽(或箱、柜等容器)中
处理 ‖~ up [口] ①(给…)灌满一油箱的油 ②
喝大量的酒 ‖~ed a. ①放在槽(或箱、柜等容
器)内的 ②[俚]喝醉的 ‖~er n. ①坦克手 ②油
船 ③空中加油飞机;运油飞机 ④油槽(或水槽)
汽车 ‖~ buster 防坦克飞机 / ~ car 铁路
油槽车;油槽汽车;洒水车 / ~ engine, ~
locomotive 带水柜机车 / ~ farm 油罐场 / ~
man ['tæŋkmən] n. ①坦克手 ②工业用罐场
管理工 / ~ ship n. 油船 / ~ town 火车停靠
加水的小镇;(不出名的)小城镇 / ~ trailer 油
槽(或水槽)拖车 / ~ truck 油槽(或水槽)汽车

tankard ['tæŋkəd] n. ①(银或锡镴制的、一般连盖
的)单柄大酒杯 ②一大酒杯的容量: a ~ of ale
一大杯啤酒

tantalize, tantalise ['tæntəlaiz] vt. (引起兴趣而
不给予满足地)逗弄,惹弄,使干着急: be ~d by
vain hopes 被徒然的希望所玩弄 ‖**tantalization**
[,tæntəlai'zeiʃən] n.

tantamount ['tæntəmaunt] a. 相等(于…)的,相
当(于…)的 (to): Not to give an answer is ~ to
a refusal (或 to saying no). 不答复等于拒绝。

tantrum ['tæntrəm] n. 发脾气: be in one's ~s
在发脾气 / go (或 fly) into a ~ 发脾气,动气 /
an outburst of ~ (发)一阵脾气

tap[1] [tæp] I (tapped; tapping) ❶ vt. ①(连续)轻
打,轻叩,轻拍: ~ sb. on the shoulder 拍拍某人
的肩膀 ②用…轻叩: He tapped a stick against
the window. 他用手杖轻轻敲窗。③敲出(out):
~ out a news story on the typewriter 用打字机
打一篇新闻报道 ④给(鞋)打掌子 ⑤选择,推
选 ❷ vi. ①轻叩,轻敲: ~ at the door 敲门,叩
门 ②轻声走 ③跳踢踏舞 II n. ①轻叩,轻拍;轻
敲声 ②鞋掌 ③鞋底(或鞋跟)上钉的铁皮 ④[~s]

[用作单](美军)熄灯号,熄灯鼓 ‖~ **dance** 踢踏舞 / '**~-dance** *vi.* 跳踢踏舞 / '~-' ~ *n.* 嗒嗒声 *vi.* 发出嗒嗒声 / '**~-off** *n.* (篮球比赛开始时的)跳球

tap² [tæp] **I** *n.* ①塞子 ②(自来水、煤气等的)旋塞,龙头;排出孔: turn on (off) the ~ 开(关)龙头 / Don't leave the ~ running. 别让龙头开着。~ water 自来水 ③龙头中流出的液体;熔炉中流出的熔液 ④抽液: a spinal ~ 脊椎抽液 ⑤【机】螺丝攻 ⑥【电】分接头,抽头;分支,支管 ⑦(在电话线路上搭线)窃听: put a ~ on sb.'s telephone 搭线窃听某人电话 ⑧[口]酒吧间 **II** (tapped; tapping) *vt.* ①在…上开一个孔(导出液体): ~ the abdomen 【医】放腹水 / ~ a blast furnace 出铁 / ~ a rubber tree 采橡胶 ②(开孔或去塞)使流出: ~ a heat of molten iron 出一炉铁 ③开发,发掘;召集(预备役人员等): ~ the natural resources 开发资源 / ~ the spring of happiness for the people 为人民开出幸福泉 / ~ the production potential 发掘生产潜力 ③分接(电流、自来水等);搭上(电话线路等)进行窃听: They *tapped* the water main to supply the new workers' residential quarters. 他们接通了总水管,为新建工人住宅区供水。/ ~ phones 窃听电话 ⑤在…的里面攻出螺纹 ⑥要求: ~ sb. for money 向某人要钱 / ~ sb. for information 要求某人透露消息 ‖**on** ~ ①(桶里的酒等)可以随时取用的: ale on ~ (桶装)龙头啤酒 ②有出水洞的;装有龙头的 ③就在手边的;需要时就能得到的: The newspapers are always **on** ~. 手边总有报纸。‖~ **bolt** 【机】螺基 / ~ **borer** 【机】螺孔钻 / ~ **drill** 【机】螺孔钻头 / '~**hole** *n.* 塞孔,(熔炉的)出铁口,出钢口,放出口 / ~-**room** *n.* 酒吧间 / '~**root** 【植】直根,主根

tape [teip] **I** *n.* ①狭带;线带,棉纱带 ②卷尺;带尺: a steel ~ 钢卷尺 ③磁带,录音带;(电报)纸带;胶布;【电】绝缘胶布: play a ~ 放一卷录音带 ④赛跑终点线的细绳: breast the ~ 冲线,跑第一 ⑤绦虫 ⑥[俚]烈酒 **II** *vt.* ①用带子捆扎;用狭带装订(书);用胶布把…粘牢 ②用卷尺(或带尺)量 ③用磁带为…录音: have a speech ~*d* 把一篇讲话录下音来 ‖**get**(或 **have**) **sth.** ~*d* ①把某物量好;彻底了解某事物 ②把某事安排好 / red ~ 官样文章,繁琐、拖拉的公事程序 / run a ~ over 进行全身健康检查 ‖~ **deck** 【机】磁带运转机械装置,(录音机的)走带机构 / ~磁带录音机的放音装置 / '~**line** *n.* = ~ measure / ~ **machine** ①自动收报机 ②磁带录音机 / ~ **measure** 卷尺;带尺 / ~ **player** 磁带录音机的放音装置 / '~-**re**'**cord** *vt.* 用磁带为…录音 / ~ **recorder** 磁带录音机 / ~ **recording** 磁带录音 / '~**worm** *n.* 绦虫

taper [teipə] **I** *n.* ①(为烛灯、烟斗等点火用的)涂蜡长烛芯;极细的蜡烛 ②微光 ③(形体、力量等的)逐渐缩减;逐渐减弱 ④锥形;圆锥;锥度;斜度 ⑤【机】拔梢 **II** ❶ *vi.* 逐渐变细;逐渐减少: One

end of the object ~*s off* to a point. 这物体的一头渐渐细下去,形成尖端。/ Nonproductive expenditures keep ~*ing* down. 非生产性开支一直在减少。❷ *vt.* 使逐渐变细;使逐渐减少 **III** *a.* ①一头逐渐变细的 ②分等级的: ~ freight rates 分等级的运费 ‖~ **off** ①(使)一头逐渐变细;(使)逐渐减少 ②逐渐停止 ‖~**ed** *a.* 锥形的,尖削的;渐缩的 / ~**ingly** ['teipəriŋli] *ad.* 逐渐缩减地;一头逐渐变细地 / ~**ness** *n.*

tapestry ['tæpistri] **I** *n.* ①花毯,挂毯 ②单面仿花毯的家具装饰用织物 ③绒绣;织毯 **II** *vt.* ①用花毯(或挂毯)装饰 ②把(图案等)编织进花毯里 ‖~ **carpet** 印经绒圈地毯 / ~ **satin** 织锦缎

tapioca [,tæpi'oukə] *n.* (食用)木薯淀粉

tar¹ [tɑ:] **I** *n.* ①焦油;焦油沥青,柏油: road ~ 筑路焦油沥青,筑路柏油 / ~ acid 焦油酸 ②[美俚]鸦片;清咖啡 **II** (tarred; tarring ['tɑ:riŋ]) *vt.* 涂(或浇)焦油(或柏油)于;[喻]弄污 **III** *a.* ①焦油(或柏油)的 ②涂有焦油(或柏油)的 ‖*be tarred with the same brush*(或 *stick*) 是一路货色,是一丘之貉 / *knock*(或 *beat*) *out of sb.* [美俚]痛揍某人 / ~ *and feather* 把(人)浑身涂柏油并粘上羽毛(作为刑罚) ‖'~-**board** *n.* 一种坚固的书皮硬纸板 / '~**brush** *n.* 柏油刷: a touch(或 dash)of the ~*brush* [蔑](有)黑人血统 / '~**mac** *n.* [主英]①一种冷铺柏油碎石路 ②浇路面用的焦油沥青结合料 / '~**ma'cadam** *n.* ①柏油碎石 ②柏油碎石路 / '~-**paved** *a.* (路面)铺柏油的 / '~-,**water** *n.* 含有焦油的冷浸剂(旧时当作万应药)

tar² [tɑ:] (tarred; tarring ['tɑ:riŋ]) *vt.* 怂恿,煽动(*on*): ~ sb. *on* 怂恿某人

tardily ['tɑ:dili] *ad.* ①缓慢地 ②迟 ③不情愿地;拖拉地

tardiness ['tɑ:dinis] *n.* ①缓慢 ②迟 ③不情愿;拖拉

tardy ['tɑ:di] *a.* ①慢的,行动缓慢的: make ~ progress 进展缓慢 ②迟的,迟到的: be ~ in one's payments 迟延付款 / be an hour ~ for supper 吃晚饭晚到了一小时 / make a ~ appearance 迟到,来得晚 ③勉强的,不情愿的;拖拉的: a ~ consent 勉强的答应

target ['tɑ:git] **I** *n.* ①靶,标的: hit (miss) the ~ 射中(未射中)靶子 / an ordinary ~ 【军】圈靶 / isotopic ~ 【原】同位素靶 ②目标;(批评或嘲笑

target

等的)对象: the ～ of criticism 批评的对象 / be made a ～ for attack 被当作攻击的目标, 成为众矢之的 ③指标: production ～s 生产指标 / set a ～ for production 为生产订一指标 ④(测量用的)靶板 ⑤铁路圆板形道岔日间信号标 ⑥【物】(X 射线管中的)对阴极 ⑦小羊的颈胸肉 ⑧[古]小圆盾 II **vt.** ①把…作为目标(或对象) ②为…订指标; 订定: Steel production was ～ed for 50,000 tons last month. 钢产量上月指标订为五万吨。 / reach ～ed levels 达到指标水平 ‖*be dead on the ～* 正中目标; 正对着目标 ‖～ **date** 预定(开始或结束的)日期 / ～ **language** 被译成的语言 / ～ **practice** 打靶; 射击练习(或演习) / ～ **seeker** 寻的武器(寻的炸弹、寻的火箭等); 寻的装置 / ～ **ship** 靶舰(作靶子用的废旧舰)

tariff ['tærif] I **n.** ① 关税表; 关税率; 关税: a preferential ～ 特惠(关)税率 / a retaliatory ～ 报复(关)税率 / a ～ wall 关税壁垒 / the policy of protective ～s 保护关税政策 / the ～ on cotton 棉花税 ②(旅馆或公用事业的)收费表, 价目表: a refreshment-room ～ [英]餐室价目表 / a postal ～ 邮费表 II **vt.** ①对…征收关税; 为…定税率 ②为…定收费标准 ‖ **reform** 关税改革(在美国历史上指要求削减进口税率, 摆脱保护主义; 在英国历史上指反对"自由贸易", 要求征收进口税)

tarry[1] ['tæri] I ❶ **vi.** ①逗留, 停留; 住 (*at, in*): ～ *at* an inn 在旅店里逗留 ②等候 (*for*): ～ *for* a person 等候一个人 ③耽搁, 迟延: We had no time to ～. 我们没有时间可耽搁。 ❷ **vt.** [古] 等候 II **n.** 逗留

tarry[2] ['tɑːri] **a.** 柏油的; 涂柏油的; 给柏油弄脏的

tart[1] [tɑːt] **a.** ①酸的; 辛辣的: ～ fruit 酸果 ②尖酸的, 刻薄的: a ～ answer 尖刻的回答 ‖～**ly** **ad.** / ～**ness n.**

tart[2] [tɑːt] **n.** ①[英]果馅饼: an apple ～ 苹果馅饼 ②(面上有水果或糖浆的)小烘饼

tart[3] [tɑːt] **n.** [俚]妓女; 举止轻佻的女子

tart[4] [tɑːt] **vt.** [主英]打扮; 把…装饰起来 (*up*)

tartan[1] ['tɑːtən] I **n.** ①(有不同颜色和宽度的条子的)格子花呢(尤指苏格兰高地人的衣料) ②格子织物: silk ～ 格子绸 ③(作为苏格兰氏族标志等的)格子图案 ④格子衣料的服装 II **a.** (象)格子花呢的

tartan[2] ['tɑːtən] **n.** (地中海沿岸的)单桅三角帆船

task [tɑːsk] I **n.** ①任务; 工作; 作业, 功课: fulfil a ～ 完成一项任务 / bend one's back to the ～ until one's dying day 鞠躬尽瘁, 死而后已 / set sb. a ～ 派某人做一项工作 / be at one's ～ 正在做着工作 / do one's home ～ 做课外作业 ②艰苦的事情, 困难的工作: quite a ～ 简直是一件难事(或艰巨的任务) II **vt.** ①派给…工作 ②使辛劳; 使过于劳累; 使做艰苦的工作: ～ one's mind 伤脑筋, 绞脑汁 / ～ one's energies 尽全力 ‖*take* (或 *call, bring*) *sb. to* ～ 责备某人, 申斥某人 ‖～ **force** [美] ①【军】特遣部队 ②(非军

事性的)特别工作组 / '～,master **n.** 工头, 监工 / '～**work n.** ①计件工作, 件工 ②重活

tassel ['tæsəl] I **n.** ①缨; 缝, 绥; 流苏; (一头固定在书脊上端作书签用的)丝带 ②流苏状物; 玉蜀黍的穗状雄花 ③【建】承梁木 II (tassel(l)ed; tassel(l)ing) ❶ **vt.** ①装缨于…; 装流苏于…: a red-*tassel*(l)ed spear 红缨枪 ②使成流苏状 ③(为使植物茁壮生长而)摘去(玉蜀黍等)的穗状雄花 ❷ **vi.** (玉蜀黍等)长出穗状雄花

taste [teist] I ❶ **vt.** ①尝, 辨(味); (少量地)吃, 喝: Please ～ the soup and see if it has enough salt. 请尝一口汤, 看盐够不够。 / The patient has not ～ed food for two days. 病人两天不吃东西了。 ②尝出…的味道: One can ～ nothing when one has a cold. 感冒时吃东西没有味道。 / ～ onion in the soup 吃出汤里有洋葱味 ③尝到, 感到; 体验 ❷ **vi.** ①尝起来, 吃起来; 辨味: It ～s sweet(fine) 这东西吃起来很甜(好吃)。 / Good medicine ～s bitter to the mouth. 良药苦口。 ②有某种味道(或气息) (*of*): It ～s too much *of* pepper. 胡椒味太浓了。 / a style tasting *of* the schools 带学究气的文体 ③尝到, 感到; 体验 (*of*): ～ *of* poverty 尝到贫困的滋味 II **n.** ①味觉: be sour to the ～ 吃起来有酸味 / A sick man has little (或 not much) ～ for food. 病人吃东西没什么味道。 ②味道, 滋味: the ～ of a pear 梨子的滋味 / a chocolate ～ 巧克力的味道 ③感受, 体验: This is his first ～ of sailing the sea. 这是他航海的初次体验。 ④ [a ～] 一口; 一点儿, 少量: Do have a ～ of this green tea. 请尝尝这种绿茶。 / give sb. a ～ of one's quality 向某人显示一点本领 ⑤爱好, 兴趣: He has a ～ for folk songs. 他喜欢民歌。 / She has no expensive ～s in dress. 她不爱穿奢侈的服装。 ⑥趣味, 情趣; 鉴赏(力), 审美(力); (举止等的)风雅, 大方; (行为、谈吐等的)得体, 有礼: oriental ～ 东方风味 / canons of literary ～ 文艺鉴赏的标准 / cultivate one's musical ～ 培养自己的音乐欣赏能力 / a man of ～ 风雅的人 ‖*in bad* (或 *poor*) ～ 趣味低级, 粗俗; 不得体; 不礼貌: That remark was *in bad* ～. 那句话不得体。 / *in good* (或 *excellent*) ～ 风雅的, 大方的; 得体的; 有礼的 / ～ =*in good* ～=good ～ / *leave a bad* (或 *nasty*) ～ *in the mouth* ①在嘴里留下恶心的味道 ②留下令人厌恶的印象 / *to* ～ 按口味; 合口味; 中意: add salt *to* ～ 按口味(或适量地)加盐 / This dish is *to* his ～. 这道菜合他口味。 / This kind of painting is not *to* my ～. 我不喜欢这种图画。 / *to the queen's* ～ 使十分挑剔的人满意地, 尽善尽美地 ‖～ **bud** 【解】味蕾 / '～,maker **n.** 时髦风尚的带头人

tasteful ['teistful] **a.** ①有鉴赏力的, 有审美力的 ②雅致的, 雅观的; 风雅的 ③[罕]美味的 ‖～**ly** **ad.** / ～**ness n.**

tasteless ['teistlis] **a.** ①不能辨味的 ②无味的; [喻]乏味的: ～ medicine 无味药品 / ～ food 无

味的(指不好吃的)食物 / the ~ ending of a story 一个故事的素然无味的结局 ③不雅观的; 庸俗的; 不得体的; 不礼貌的: ~ luxury 庸俗的奢华 ④无鉴赏力的、无审美力的 ‖~ly *ad.* / ~ness *n.*

tasty ['teisti] *a.* ①美味的, 可口的: ~ dishes 鲜美的菜肴 ②[俗](服装等)雅观的, 大方的 ‖**tastily** *ad.* / **tastiness** *n.*

tatter ['tætə] I *n.* ①(撕下的或悬挂着的)破布条, 碎纸片; 破布: tear to ~s 把…扯碎; 把…驳得体无完肤 ②[复]破衣服: be dressed in ~s 衣衫褴褛 II ❶ *vt.* 扯碎, 撕碎; 使破烂 ❷ *vi.* 变得破烂 ‖~ed *a.* (衣服等)破烂的; 衣衫褴褛的

tattle ['tætl] I ❶ *vi.* ①闲谈, 聊天; 饶舌 ②泄露别人的隐私 ❷ *vt.* 在闲谈中说出(或泄露出): ~ a secret 泄露秘密 II *n.* 空话; 闲谈; 饶舌 ‖~r *n.* ①闲谈者; 搬弄是非的人; 泄露秘密的人 ②【动】鹬科鸟(如红脚鹬等)

tattoo[1] [tə'tu:] *n.* (印度用英语)矮脚马, 小马

tattoo[2] [tə'tu:] I *n.* ①【军】归营号(指号声或鼓声), 熄灯号 ②军队夜间表演操(通常配以军乐作为表演节目) ③得得的连敲声: a loud ~ on the door 响而连续的敲门声 II *vt.* & *vi.* 得得地连续敲击 ‖the *devil's* ~ 手指(或脚)的不停的敲响: beat the *devil's* ~ (表示焦躁不安等)用手指得得地敲击桌子; 脚跟着地用脚尖敲出嗒嗒声

tattoo[3] [tə'tu:] I *n.* (皮肤上的)刺花纹, 文身, 黥墨 II *vt.* 刺花纹于…; 刺(花纹等): ~ the skin 在皮肤上刺花纹 / have a design ~ed on one's arm 在手臂上刺上花纹

taunt[1] [tɔ:nt] I *n.* ①嘲笑; 辱骂; 奚落人的话 ②[古]被嘲笑的人 II *vt.* ①嘲笑; 辱骂; 奚落 ②用嘲笑来刺激: ~ sb. into losing his temper 嘲笑得某人发脾气 ‖~ingly *ad.* 嘲笑地; 辱骂地

taunt[2] [tɔ:nt] *a.* 【海】(桅杆)很高的

taut [tɔ:t] *a.* ①(绳子等)拉紧的, 绷紧的 ②(神经等)紧张的 ③(船等)整洁的; 整齐的; 秩序井然的; 纪律严明的 ④严格的, 严峻的 ‖~ly *ad.* / ~ness *n.* ‖~ helm ① 船只顺风偏斜的倾向 ②稍稍偏向上风方向的船艏

tautology [tɔ:'tɔlədʒi] *n.* 同义反复; 重复, 赘述

tavern ['tævə(:)n] *n.* ①(供堂吃的)酒菜馆 ②小旅馆

taw[1] [tɔ:] *vt.* ①(用明矾和盐的溶液等而不用鞣酸)硝(生皮) ②[方]打, 鞭打

taw[2] [tɔ:] I *n.* ①石弹戏 ②石弹戏的基线 ③石弹 II *vi.* 发出石弹 ‖come (bring) to ~ [美口]到(使到)预定的位置; 站到(使站到)起跑线

tawdry ['tɔ:dri] I *a.* 俗气的, 俗丽的, 花哨而庸俗的: ~ garments 花哨俗气的衣服 II *n.* 俗丽的服饰 ‖**tawdrily** *ad.* / **tawdriness** *n.*

tawny ['tɔ:ni] *n.* & *a.* 黄褐色(的), 茶色(的)

tax [tæks] I *n.* ①税; 税款: levy a ~ on 对…征税 / free of ~ 免税 / ~ paid in kind 用实物缴纳的税 ②[只用单]负担; 压力(on, upon): a ~ on one's energy (health) 精力(健康)上的负担 /

It will be a heavy ~ on my time. 这要耗费我许多时间。③(会社、团体等的)会费 ④[口](酒菜馆等的)收费 ‖an additional ~ 附加税 / a business ~ 营业税 / a direct (an indirect) ~ 直接(间接)税 / a housing and land ~ 房地产税 / an import (export) ~ 进口(出口)税 / an income ~ 所得税 / a poll (或 capitation) ~ 人头税 / a progressive ~ 累进税 / a proportional ~ 比例税 II *vt.* ①对…征税: ~ tobacco (wine, luxuries) 征收烟草(酒,奢侈品)税 ②对…收会费 ③使负重担; 使受压力: ~ one's strength 费尽气力 / ~ one's memory 竭力回忆 ④指责, 责备, 谴责: ~ sb. with a fault 责备某人的过失 / ~ sb. with having neglected his work 指责某人工作不负责 ⑤[美口]要(人)支付; 开(价): What will you ~ me for this shirt? 这件衬衫多少钱? ⑥【律】评定(诉讼费等) ‖~ collector 收税官; 税务员 / '~-de'ductible *a.* 在计算所得税时可予以扣除的 / ~ dodger 偷税人, 逃税人 / ~ dodging 逃税,漏税 / ~ evasion 逃税 / ~= exempt ['tæksig'zempt] *a.* ①免税的 ②(债券)利息免税的 / ~ farmer 税款包收人, 包税商 / '~-'free *a.* 免税的,无税的 / ~ gatherer =~ collector / '~,payer ~ 纳税人 (在美国常作为"公民"的同义词)

taxable ['tæksəbl] *a.* 可征税的; 应纳税的

taxation [tæk'seiʃən] *n.* ①征税; 纳税; 税制: be subject to ~ 应纳税 / be exempt from ~ 免税 / the ~ bureau (office) 税务局 (署) / progressive ~ 累进税制,征收累进税 ②税,税款; 税收 ③估价征税

taxi ['tæksi] I *n.* 出租汽车: go by ~ 坐出租汽车去 / take a ~ to the airport 乘出租汽车到机场 II (单数第三人称现在式 taxis 或 taxies; 现在分词 taxiing 或 taxying) ❶ *vi.* ①乘出租汽车 ②(飞机在地面或水上)滑行; (驾驶员)驾驶飞机滑行: The plane came in and ~ed along the runway. 飞机降落,在跑道上滑行。❷ *vt.* ①用出租汽车送 ②使(飞机)滑行 ‖'~cab *n.* 出租汽车 / ~ dancer 舞女 / ~ flying 【空】滑走飞行 / ~man ['tæksimən] *n.* 出租汽车驾驶员 / '~,meter *n.* 车费计,计程器 / '~plane ~ 出租飞机 / '~= rank *n.* 出租汽车停车处 / ~ squad 租来的一群职业橄榄球球员(参加训练但不能参加正式比赛) / ~ stand =~-rank / '~way *n.* (飞机出入机库的)滑行道

taxidermy ['tæksidə:mi] *n.* 动物标本剥制术 ‖**taxidermal** [,tæksi'də:məl], **taxidermic** [,tæksi'də:mik] *a.* / **taxidermist** *n.* 动物标本剥制者

Tb 【化】元素铽 (terbium) 的符号

tea [ti:] I *n.* ①茶树 ②茶叶: black ~ 红茶 / green ~ 绿茶 / brick ~ 茶砖 / scented (或 jasmine) ~ 花茶 / gunpowder ~ 中国珠茶 / This ~ draws well. 这茶叶经得起多次冲泡。③茶;饮料: Have a cup of ~, please. 请喝一杯茶。/ make (the) ~ 沏茶, 泡茶 / the first infusion of

~ 头泡茶 / strong (weak) ~ 浓 (淡) 茶 / beef
~ 牛茶 (一种牛肉汁) / camomile ~ 甘菊茶
④茶点; 茶会: afternoon ~ 午后茶点 / high (或
meat) ~ [英](下午五至六时之间、有肉食冷盘
的) 正式茶点 / make thirty ~s 准备三十客茶点
⑤[美俚]大麻(叶);大麻香烟 II ❶ vt. 给…沏
茶; 以茶招待: ~ a guest 给客人喝茶 ❷ vi. 喝
茶; 吃茶点: They ~ at five. 他们在下午五时进
茶点。 ‖ a ~ hound 见 hound¹ / sb.'s cup of
~ 见 cup / ~ed up [美俚]中大麻毒的, 昏迷的
‖~ bag 茶叶袋(装茶叶后放在杯中泡茶用, 用布
或滤纸制) / ~ ball ①滤茶球(泡茶时用, 金属
制, 上有小孔, 内装茶叶) ②=~ bag / ~board
n. 茶盘 / ~ caddy 茶叶盒, 茶叶罐 / ~ cake
午后茶点中吃的点心 / ~ chest ① (出口用)茶
叶箱 ②=~ caddy / ~ cloth '(吃茶时用的)小
台布;茶盘盖布;茶具抹布 / ~ cosy, ~ cozy
(保暖用的)茶壶套 / '~cup n. 茶杯: ~cup and
saucer (描写中产阶级生活的)文雅的戏剧 / ~
dance (傍晚)有茶点的舞会, 茶舞 / '~-,dealer
n. 茶商 / ~ fight =~ party / ~ garden ①
茶叶种植场 ②有茶室的公园 / ~ gown (茶会时
穿的)宽松的女袍 / ~ green 茶绿色 / '~house
n. 茶馆, 茶室 / '~,kettle n. (烧水沏茶用的)
茶水壶 / ~ leaf ①[常用复](泡开的)茶叶; 茶
渣 ②[英俚]贼 / ~ party 茶会, 茶话会 / ~
plantation 茶叶种植场 / ~ pot 茶壶 / '~-
poy n. 茶几;三脚的小桌 / '~room n. 茶室 /
~ service (一套)茶具 / ~ set =~ service /
'~spoon n. 茶匙;一茶匙容量 / '~spoon,ful
n. 一茶匙容量 / '~-,strainer n. 滤茶器 /
table 茶桌, 茶几 / '~-things [复] n. 茶具 /
'~time n. 吃茶点的时间(一般在下午五时左
右) / ~ tray 茶盘 / ~ tree 茶树 / ~ trolley
=~ wag(g)on / '~-urn n. (煮或泡大量茶水
的)茶水壶 / ~ wag(g)on (有小脚轮的)茶具台

teach [ti:tʃ] (taught [tɔ:t]) ❶ vt. ①教, 讲授: the
principle of officers ~ing soldiers, soldiers
~ing officers and soldiers ~ing each other 官教
兵, 兵教官, 兵教兵的原则 / ~ the students
chemistry (或 ~ chemistry to the students) 教
学生化学 / ~ a child (how) to swim 教孩
子游泳 / ~ the piano 教钢琴 / He was
never taught painting. 他从未正式学过绘画。
② 教导; 教育: ~ children by example 用榜
样教育儿童 ③[口]教训, 告诫…不要(做某事):
I'll ~ him to be so careless. 我要告诫他别这么
粗心大意。 ❷ vi. ①教书;教学: She ~es
at a middle school. 她在中学教书。 / He has
been ~ing three periods this morning. 今天上
午他已教了三节课。②被讲授, 教起来: a book
that ~es easily 容易教的书 ‖~ school [美]教
书, 当教师 ‖'~-in n. [美](大学生对政府政
策, 尤其是外交政策, 进行讨论和辩论的)宣讲会

teacher ['ti:tʃə] n. ①教员, 教师, 老师, 先生: To
be a good ~, one must first be a good pupil. 要

作好先生, 首先要作好学生。 / a ~ of English
英语教师 / a ~ at a primary school 小学教师 /
a woman ~ 女教师 / a ~s college 师范学院 /
a ~ by negative example 反面教员 ②导师

teaching ['ti:tʃiŋ] I n. ① 教学, 讲授; 教学工
作: take up history ~ 担任历史教学 ②
[常用复] 教导; 学说, 主义 ③[常用复]【宗】
教义 II a. 教学的; 教导的: ~ material 教材
‖~ aid 教具 / ~ fellow 兼任教学(或实验室)
工作的研究生 / ~ hospital 教学医院 / ~
machine (装有电子计算机等以自动配合学生学
习进度的)教学机

teak [ti:k] n. ①柚木树 ②柚木

team [ti:m] I n. ①队;组: a production ~ 生产队 / a
mutual-aid ~ 互助组 / a football ~ 足球队 / Is
he on that ~? 他是那个队的成员吗? ②一窝小
动物 (尤指小鸭或小猪);一组好对的供展览的
动物 ③(一起拉车或拉犁的)一组马(或牛), 联畜
马(或牛)及其所拉的车, 兽拉的车 II a. 队的;
组的; 由一队人从事的: ~ spirit (组、队成员的)
协作精神 III ❶ vt. ①把(牛、马等)连在一个车
上 ②用联畜拖运 ③把(工作)包给承包人 ❷ vi.
①驾驭联畜运车;驾驶卡车 ②结成一队;协作, 合
作 (up): ~ up with sb. 与某人合作;与某人勾结
‖'~work n. 协力, 配合: have good ~work 配
合得好 / a ~work government 实行集体领导的
政府

tear¹ [tiə] I n. ①[常用复]眼泪, 泪珠: eyes filled
with ~s 充满泪水的眼睛 / move sb. to ~s 使
某人感动得流泪 / shed ~s for sb. 为同情某人
而流泪 / shed ~s of joy 流下高兴的眼泪 /
laugh till the ~s come 笑得把眼泪笑出 ②泪珠
物, 滴, 露; [美俚]珍珠: ~s of resin 树脂滴
II vi. 流泪; 含泪: eyes ~ing in the cold wind
寒风中被吹得流泪的眼睛 ‖crocodile ~s 见
crocodile / in ~s 流着泪; 含着泪; 哭着 /
reduce sb. to ~s 使某人流泪 / ~s of Eos
晨露 / ~s of strong wine 酒泪(指盛酒的杯内
由于酒精化气而结成的露珠) ‖~less a. ①无眼
泪的; 不流泪的 ②流不出泪的: ~less grief 欲
哭无泪的悲痛, 极度的悲痛 ‖~ bomb 催泪弹
(=~ gas bomb) / ~drop n. ①泪珠 ②泪珠
物; (耳环或项圈上)下垂的宝石 / ~ duct 泪腺,
泪管 / ~ gas 催泪性毒气: a ~ gas candle (pot)
催泪性毒气筒(瓶) / '~-'gas vt. 用催泪性毒气
袭击(或驱散) / '~,jerker n. [俚]使人流泪的
歌曲(或故事、戏剧、电影等) / ~ shell 催泪弹 /
'~-stained a. 泪水沾湿的: a ~-stained face
满满泪水的脸

tear² [tɛə] I (tore [tɔ:], torn [tɔ:n]) ❶ vt. ①撕开,
撕裂: ~ sth. to pieces (或 bits, shreds) 把某物
撕成碎片 / ~ a sheet of paper in two (或 in
half) 把一张纸撕成两半 ②扯破; 截破; 划破: A
nail tore a hole in his shirt. 钉子把他的衬衫戳
了个洞。 / The saw tore her hand. 锯子划破了
她的手。③拉掉; 拔掉; 撕掉: ~ up cotton stalks

by the roots 把棉花梗连根拔起 / ~ *out* a fuse 拔出信管 / ~ *down* a notice 撕下通告 / ~ a leaf *from* a calendar 从日历牌上撕下一页 / ~ sth. *away from* sb.'s hands 从某人手中夺走某物 ④ [常用被动语态] 使分裂; (疑虑等) 使精神不安; 使激动; 折磨: He was *torn* by rage (grief). 他愤怒 (悲伤) 之极。 ❷ *vi.* ①撕, 扯 (*at*): ~ *at* the cover of a parcel 扯包裹的封皮 ② 被撕裂, 被扯破: This paper ~*s* easily. 这种纸一撕就破。 / nylon fabrics that will not ~ 不易撕裂的尼龙织物 / The pocket *tore* when it caught on the nail. 口袋钩住钉子就撕破了。 ③ 飞跑, 狂奔, 猛闯: children ~*ing about* in the play ground 在游戏场上飞跑的孩子们 / ~ *up* the stairs two steps at a time 两级一跨地飞奔上楼 Ⅱ *n.* ①撕, 扯 ②裂缝; 扯破的洞; 撕裂处: a ~ in the coat 上衣的撕裂处 ③激怒, 发作 ④ [美俚] 狂饮大闹, 狂欢: go on a ~ 去寻欢作乐 ⑤ 飞奔, 猛闯; 匆忙: The train passed by at a ~. 火车疾驶而过。 / Why are you in such a ~ to go away? 你为什么这样急着要离开? ‖ ~ *down* ① 扯下; 拆毁; 拆卸: ~ *down* a dangerous wall 把危险墙壁拆除 / ~ *down* a machine 拆卸机器 ②逐条驳斥 (论点等) ③诋毁, 毁坏 (名誉) / ~ *into* 猛攻, 向…猛扑: ~ *into* a job like a young tiger 象小老虎一样投入工作 / ~ *it* [英俚] 使希望成泡影; 打破计划; 使不能继续下去: That's *torn* it! 那样一来它就完蛋了! / ~ *off* ①扯掉 ②迅速走掉, 匆匆写成: ~ *off* a letter home in five minutes 五分钟内匆匆写就一封家信 ④ 匆匆做成; 获得: ~ *off* some sleep 抓紧时间睡一会 / ~ *off* a piece of music 匆匆演奏一支曲子 / ~ *oneself away* 勉强使自己离开; 忍痛舍去: He could not ~ *himself away* from the book. 他看书看得不忍释手。 / ~ *one's hair* 见 hair ‖ ~ **away** ['tɛərəwei] *a.* 行动莽撞的 *n.* ①行动莽撞的人 ②流氓, 暴徒 / '~**down** *n.* 拆卸 / ~= **off** ['tɛər(ː)f] *n.* 可按虚线撕下的纸片 / ~ **strip** 罐头开口条 (用连着开口条的钥匙卷动一圈, 即可将罐头打开); 信封开口条 (或 ~ **tape** (一头露在外面便于拉开货物包装的撕条, 拉搭

tearful ['tiəful] *a.* 流泪的; 含泪的, 眼泪汪汪的: ~ eyes 泪眼 / ~ looks 眼泪汪汪的样子 ②使人流泪的, 悲哀的 ‖ ~**ly** *ad.* / ~**ness** *n.*

tease [tiːz] Ⅰ *vt.* ①取笑; 戏弄, 逗弄: Don't ~ others. 不要取笑别人。 ② 强求; 哄: She is *teasing* her mother *for* something (或 *to give* her something). 她缠着她妈妈要东西。③梳理 (羊毛、亚麻等); 使 (布等) 的表面起毛; 使起绒 Ⅱ *n.* ①戏弄, 逗弄 ②爱戏弄别人的人 ‖ ~**r** *n.* ①起绒工人; 起绒机 ②爱戏弄别人的人 ③ [口] 难题; 难处理的事情 / **teasingly** *ad.*

teat [tiːt] *n.* ①(人或动物的) 乳头 ②[英] (奶瓶上的) 橡皮奶头 ③(机械部件上的) 小突

technical ['teknikəl] *a.* ①技术的, 工艺的, 技能的; 专门性的: a ~ adviser 技术顾问 / ~ know-

how 技术知识 / a ~ school 技术学校 / ~ skill 专门技术 / a ~ term 专门名词, 术语 ②严格根据法律意义的; 根据法律的: a ~ assault 法律上认为的攻击 ③由于市场内部因素 (如投机、操纵等) 引起的 ④ (化工产品) 用工业方式生产的: ~ isooctane 工业异辛烷 ‖ ~**ly** *ad.* ‖ ~ **sergeant** (美) 空军 (或海军陆战队) 技术军士

technicality [ˌtekni'kæliti] *n.* ①技术性; 专门性 ②技术细节; 专门性事项 ③术语, 专门语

technique [tek'niːk] *n.* ①(工艺或艺术上的) 技术, 技巧: adopt advanced ~s 采用先进技术 / farming ~ 农业技术 ②技能 ③方法

technology [tek'nɔlədʒi] *n.* ①工艺学; 工艺, (工业) 技术: chemical ~ 化学工艺学 / space ~ 宇宙飞行技术, 空间技术 / science and ~ 科学和技术 ②[总称] 术语, 专门语 ‖**technologist** *n.* 工艺学家; 技术专家

tedious ['tiːdjəs] *a.* 冗长乏味的; 使人厌烦的; 沉闷的: a ~ story 冗长乏味的故事 ‖ ~**ly** *ad.* ‖ ~**ness** *n.*

tedium ['tiːdjəm] *n.* 冗长乏味; 沉闷; 单调

teem¹ [tiːm] ❶ *vi.* ①充满, 富于 (*with*): The article ~*s with* blunders. 这篇文章错误百出。 / This river ~*s with* fish. 这条河产鱼很多。②大量地出现, 涌现: Fish ~ in this river. 这条河产鱼很多。 / A score of plans were ~*ing* in his mind. 在他的脑子里涌现出许多计划。 ❷ *vt.* [古] 产, 生 ‖ ~**ingly** *ad.* 充满地, 丰富地; 多产地

teem² [tiːm] ❶ *vt.* ①[古] 把…倒空 ②倒出; 【冶】把 (钢水等) 注入模具 ❷ *vi.* (雨、水等) 倾注

teen-ager ['tiːnˌeidʒə] *n.* (十三至十九岁的) 青少年, 十几岁的少年

teens [tiːnz] [复] *n.* ①十多岁 (十三至十九岁): in one's ~ 在十多岁时, 在青少年时代 / in one's early ~ 在十三、四岁的年纪 / not yet out of one's ~ 还没有到二十岁 ②[总称] 十几岁的青少年们

teeth [tiːθ] tooth 的复数

teethe [tiːð] *vi.* 出乳牙; 生牙 ‖**teething troubles** 出牙期的病痛; [喻] 事情开始时暂时的困难

telegram ['teligræm] *n.* 电报: by ~ 用电报 / send an express ~ 发急电 / a ~ in cipher (plain language) 密码 (明文) 电报 Ⅱ (telegrammed; telegramming) *vt. & vi.* =telegraph (*vt. & vi.*) ‖**milk a ~** [俚] 窃取拍发给他人的电报

telegraph ['teligraːf] Ⅰ *n.* ①电报机; 信号机: a duplex (quadruple) ~ 双工 (四路多工) 电报机 ②【海】(驾驶台与机舱之间的) 传令钟 ③运动比赛得分等的) 揭示板 (=~ board) ④ 电报 (指通信方式): by ~ 用电报 / a ~ slip 电报纸条 / a ~ office 电报局 ⑤(一份) 电报 (=telegram) ⑥ [T-] [用于报刊名] 电讯报: The Daily Telegraph 《每日电讯报》 Ⅱ ❶ *vt.* ①用电报发送 (信息等); 打电报给 (某人): ~ a message to sb. (或 ~ sb.

a message) 打电报给某人 / I ~*ed* him the result. 我已把结果电告他了。②电汇 ③ 在揭示板上显示出(比分等) ④ 流露;(通过无意识的动作等)泄露: a look that ~*ed* good news 流露出有好消息的神情 / ~ a punch (通过眼光或臀部活动等)显示出要击出一拳的样子 ❷ *vi.* 打电报: ~ for sb. 电邀某人 / I ~*ed* to him to come. 我已发电报要他来。‖~**er** *n.* 报务员 / ~**ist** *n.* 报务员;【军】电信兵 ‖ ~ **board** (运动比赛得分等的)揭示板 / ~**cable** 电报电缆 / ~ **key** 电报电键 / ~ **line** 电报线路 / ~ **operator** 报务员 / ~ **plant**【植】舞草 / ~ **pole,** ~ **post** 电杆,电线柱 / ~ **receiver** 收报机 / ~ **repeater** 电报转发(或中继)器 / ~ **stamp** 电报费收讫章 / ~ **transmitter** 电报发送机,发报机

telegraphic [ˌteli'græfik] *a.* ①电报的;电送的: a ~ address 电报挂号;收电报用的地址 / a ~ money order 电汇 ② 电文体的;简洁的: a ~ style 电文体;简洁的文体 ③(目光等)从远处传来的 ‖~**ally** *ad.*

telegraphy [ti'legrəfi] *n.* ① 电报学;电报(术);通报: wireless ~ 无线电报(术)(=radiotelegraphy) / line ~ 有线电报(术) / facsimile (或 picture) ~ 传真电报(术) / submarine ~ 海底电缆电报(术) ②电报机装置(术)

telepathy [ti'lepəθi] *n.* 心灵感应,传心术

telephone ['telifoun] **I** *n.* 电话;电话机: by ~ 用电话 / call sb. to the ~ 叫某人听电话 / talk on (或 over) the ~ 通电话 / You are wanted on the ~. 请你去听电话。/ Is he on the ~? 他那里装有电话吗?(或:他正在通电话吗?) / The ~ rings. 电话铃响了。‖ *a public* ~ 公用电话 / a ~ *book* 电话(号码)簿 / a ~ *booth* [美](公用)电话间 / a ~ *box* [英](公用)电话间 / a ~ *directory* 电话(号码)簿 / a ~ *exchange* 电话局;电话交换机 / a ~ *operator* 电话接线员,话务员 / a ~ *receiver* 电话听筒,受话器 / a ~ *set* 电话机 / a ~ *subscriber* 电话用户 / a ~ *transmitter* 送话器 **II** ❶ *vi.* 打电话,通电话: ~ to sb. 打电话给某人 ❷ *vt.* 打电话告;用电话告知: ~ the editor 打电话给编者 / a ~ message to sb. 打电话告诉某人一项消息 / He ~*d* that he could not come. 他打电话来说他不能来了。

telescope ['teliskoup] **I** *n.* 望远镜;望远装置: an astronomical ~ 天文望远镜 / a binocular ~ 双筒望远镜 / a radio ~ 射电望远镜,无线电望远镜 / a reflecting ~ 反射式望远镜 / a refracting ~ 折射式望远镜 **II** ❶ *vi.* 套入,迭进;(由于碰撞而)直插进;缩短: As a result of the collision, the first two cars ~*d*. 由于碰撞的结果,头两节车厢迭嵌在一起了。 ❷ *vt.* 使套入,使迭进;使直插进;使缩短

telescopic [ˌtelis'kɔpik] *a.* ①望远镜的;用望远镜看的;只能在望远镜中看见的: ~ observation 望远镜观察 / ~ stars 用望远镜才能看到的星

②能看见远处的,远视的: a ~ sight (观测器、大炮等)望远镜瞄准具 ③ 套迭的;伸缩的: a ~ axle 套筒轴 / a ~ tube 伸缩管 / a ~ aerial 可伸缩天线 / a ~ word 合成词(指把一词的头几个字母与另一词的最后几个字母套迭而成的新词,如 motel) ‖~**ally** *ad.*

television ['teliˌviʒən] *n.* ①电视: watch ~ 看电视 / appear on ~ 在电视中出现 / black-and-white (或 monochrome) ~ 黑白电视 / colour (或 polychrome) ~ 彩色电视 / large-screen ~ 大屏幕电视,剧院电视 / stereoscopic ~ 立体电视 / a ~ camera 电视摄象机 / a ~ set 电视(接收)机 / a ~ talk 电视讲话 / a ~ broadcasting station 电视广播电台 ②电视(接收)机 ③电视学,电视术 ④电视广播事业 ‖~**ally** [ˌteli'viʒənəli] *ad.* / ~**ary** [ˌteli'viʒənəri] *a.*

tell [tel] **I** (told [tould]) ❶ *vt.* ①讲述,说;告诉 / ~ the truth (a lie) 说实话(谎话) / He *told* the happy news to everybody. 他把消息告诉了大家。/ *Tell* me where you live. 告诉我你住在哪儿。/ *Tell* me, is there anything else? [美口]告诉我,还有别的什么事吗? ②吩咐,命令: *Tell* him to wait. 叫他等着。/ We were *told* to stay where we were. 我们被通知留在原地。③[常与 can, could, be able to 连用]辨别,分辨: Can you ~ her *from* her twin sister? 你能分得出她和她的孪生姐妹吗? / I cannot ~ them *apart*. 我分不清他们。/ ~ true friends *from* false ones 辨别真假朋友 ④断定,知道,说出: Can you ~ who is over there? 你能看清那边的人是谁吗? / I can't ~ what to do. 我说不上来该怎么办。/ The child can already ~ the time. 那孩子已经会看钟了。⑤泄漏(机密等);吐露(真情等): Her face *told* her joy. 她脸上显出欢乐的神情。/ Fossils ~ much about the past. 化石很能说明过去的历史。⑥数: ~ one's beads 数念珠念经 / ~ over one's money 数钱 ❷ *vi.* ①讲述 (of, about): ~ of (或 about) 确定地说出来: Who can ~? 谁能说得上来? / I can't ~. 我说不上来。/ How can I ~? 我怎么知道呢? ③泄密;说坏话;告发 (on): I promised not to ~. 我保证不说出去。/ ~ on sb. 告发某人 ④产生效果,发生影响: Every shot told. 弹无虚发。(或:百发百中。)/ His age is beginning to ~ on him. 年纪开始显得衰老了。⑤作证;表明,说明 (*of*) **II** *n.* [方]话;传说: I have a ~ for (或 with) you. 我有话跟你说。/ according to sb.'s ~ 据某人说 ‖*all told* 总共,合计: a team of 12 *all told* 共计十二个人的一个队 / *Don't* ~ *me...!* (表示惊讶或惊恐)不至于…吧!: *Don't* ~ *me* it's too late! 不至于太晚吧! / *I can* ~ *you* (或 *I* ~ *you, let me* ~ *you*) 我可以肯定地说: *I (can)* ~ *you, it's not so easy.* 我可以肯定那不是那么容易的。/ *I'll* ~ *you what.* ①让我告诉你事情的真相。②让我告诉你该怎么

办。(或: 你听我说。) / *I'm ~ing you!* 不要你强辩,听我讲! / *Never ~ me!* (或 *Don't ~ me!*) 别瞎扯啦! (或: 我简直不相信了!) / *~ down* [苏格兰]付 (钱) / *~ it like it is* 实事求是地说; 坦率而诚实 / *~ noses* 数人数(尤指支持者的人数); 单凭人数决定问题 / *~ off* ①分派出 ②斥责, 责备: sb. *off* for being so rude 责备某人太粗暴 ③向…透露消息 / *sb. where to get off* [美俚]严厉斥责某人(一般指责其不要忘乎所以) / *~ the world* [俚]郑重宣布, 着重声明 / *there is no ~ing* 难以预料, 不可能知道: *There is no ~ing* when he will return. 说不清他什么时候会回来。 / *You are ~ing me!* 还要你告诉我! (或: 我早就知道了!)

teller ['telə] *n.* ①讲述者;讲故事的人 ②记数者;(议会等的)点票员 ③(银行等的)出纳员; a paying (receiving) ~ 付 (收)款员 ④【军】防空情报报告员 ‖**~ship** *n.* 点票员 (或出纳员等)的职位

telling ['teliŋ] *a.* ①有效的;有力的: History is the most ~ witness. 历史是最有力的见证人。/ a ~ argument (retort) 有力的论证(反驳) ②生动的;说明问题的: the most ~ passages in that novel 那部小说中最生动的一些段落 ‖**~ly** *ad.*

telltale ['tel-teil] **I** *n.* ①搬弄是非者;告密者;泄露真情的事物 ②指示器;警告悬条标(铁路用标志,表示前有低的旱桥) ③【海】舵位指示器;挂罗针仪 (= ~ compass): ~ disc 转盘 ④(能在考勤卡上记录职工上下班时间的)考勤钟 **II** *a.* ①搬弄是非的;泄露秘密的,暴露内情的 ②说明问题的: a ~ face 流露实情的脸容 / a ~ scar 泄露隐情的伤疤 ② (机械装置等)起警告作用的; 起监督(或记录)作用的

temerity [ti'meriti] *n.* 轻率,鲁莽,蛮勇

temper ['tempə] **I** ❶ *vt.* ①【冶】使回火;[喻]锻炼: a ~ing furnace 回火炉 / ~ oneself through manual labour 劳动锻炼 ②调合,揉和,捏(粘土等): ~ paints with oil 调油彩 ③搀和;使软化;使缓和,减轻: ~ wine with water 在酒里搀水 ④【音】(按平均律)为(钢琴等)调音 ⑤[军]使适合 (to) ❷ *vi.* (金属)经过回火后具有适当的韧度 **II** *n.* ①(钢等的)韧度;回火色;(影响钢硬度的)含碳量 ②(制合金,调灰泥等用的)调合物,混合物 ③ (皮革的)质地,坚韧性 ④ 心情,情绪;性情,脾气;怒气: be *in* a good (bad) ~ 心情好(不好) / be *of* a calm (或 an even) ~ 性情平和 / be *of* a quick (或 hot) ~ 脾气急躁 / a fit of ~ 一阵脾气 ⑤ 特征;倾向,趋势: the ~ of the times 时代特征(或倾向) / the ~ of modern French art 近代法国艺术的倾向 ⑥崇高精神;勇气 ⑦[古]适中,中庸 ‖*get* (或 *go*, *fly*) *into a ~* 发脾气 / *keep* (或 *control*) *one's ~* 忍住性子,不使脾气发作 / *lose one's ~* 发脾气 / *out of ~* (*with* sb.) (对某人)生气 / *show ~* 急躁,动怒 / *~ justice with mercy* 见 **justice** ‖**~er** ['tempərə] *n.* ①回火工人;鞣革工人 ②(灰泥,

油彩等的)调合人;调合机 ③缓和者,抚慰者

temperament ['tempərəmənt] *n.* ①气质,性情;性格: a nervous ~ 神经质 / an excitable ~ 易激动的性情 / a hot ~ 热烈 (或急躁)的性格 ②容易激动;喜怒无常;急躁: a display of ~ 发一阵脾气 ③ (中世纪生理学中所谓的) 质: the sanguine (phlegmatic, choleric, melancholic) ~ 多血(粘液,胆汁,忧郁)质 ④调和;调节;适中 ⑤【音】平均律

temperamental [,tempərə'mentl] *a.* ①气质的,性情的;性格的 ②敏感的;易激动的,冲动的;变幻无常的,多变的: ~ weather 变幻无常的气候 ‖**~ly** *ad.*

temperance ['tempərəns] *n.* ①节制,自我克制;节欲: practise ~ in eating and drinking 节制饮食 ②戒酒,禁酒: a ~ hotel 不卖酒的旅馆

temperate ['tempərit] *a.* ①有节制的 ②戒酒的,节酒的 ③不过分的,稳健的,适度的: be ~ in one's language 说话措词温和 ④ (气候等)温和的: the ~ zone 温带 / the north (south) ~ zone 北(南)温带 ‖**~ly** *ad.* / **~ness** *n.*

temperature ['tempəritʃə] *n.* ①温度: The ~ is high (low). 温度高(低)。/ absolute ~ 【物】绝对温度 / the atmospheric ~ 气温 / a ~ curve 温度曲线 ②体温;[口]寒热: take one's ~ 量体温 / have (或 run) a ~ 发烧

tempered ['tempəd] *a.* ①【冶】经过回火的;经过锻炼的: ~ steel 回火钢 / ~ glass 强化玻璃 / a well-~ sword 精炼的宝刀 (或剑) ②调合的,调和的;温和的,适中的 ③[用以构成复合词]脾气 (或性情)…的: ill-~ 脾气坏的 / short-~ 性子急的 / a sweet-~ (fiery-~) man 性情温和 (暴躁)的人 ‖**~ly** *ad.*

tempest ['tempist] **I** *n.* ①大风暴;暴风雨;暴风雪 ②骚动,风潮: a ~ of applause 暴风雨般的掌声 **II** *vt.* 使骚动,使激动 ‖a ~ *in a barrel* (或 *bucket*, *teapot*) 小事引起的大风波,大惊小怪 ‖'~-,beat-en *a.* 受暴风雨袭击的 / '~-tossed, '~-tost *a.* 被暴风雨震荡的;颠簸飘摇的,动荡不定的

tempestuous [tem'pestjuəs] *a.* ①大风暴的;暴风雨的;暴风雪的 ②剧烈的;骚动的 ‖**~ly** *ad.* / **~ness** *n.*

temple[1] ['templ] *n.* ①(古希腊人、罗马人和佛教徒等的)圣堂,神殿;庙宇,寺院 ②(基督教的)教堂,礼拜堂 (一般用 church 或 chapel) ③[常作T-] 古代耶路撒冷三个相继建立的犹太教圣殿之一 ④[喻]上帝所在的地方,圣灵所宿之处 ⑤(某些互助会的)地方分会 ⑥[美](专供某种活动之用的)场所: (movie) ~s 电影院 / *the Inner* (*Middle*) *Temple* 内 (中)殿法学协会(伦敦四所享有检定律师权力的法学协会中的两所)

temple[2] ['templ] *n.* 太阳穴,颞颥;鬓角

temple[3] ['templ] *n.* 【纺】边撑,伸幅器

tempo ['tempou] ([复] tempos 或 tempi ['tempi:]) *n.* [意] ①【音】速度 ②(局势、艺术作品等的)发展速度: keep pace with the swift ~ of the day

跟上时代的飞速步伐 ③(下棋时的)一着,一步

temporal¹ ['tempərəl] **I** *a.* ①暂存的, 短暂的, 非永恒的 ②世间的; 世俗的; 现世的 ③时间的(与 spatial 空间的相对) ④【语】(表示)时间的; 时态的: ~ conjunctions 时间连接词(如 when, while 等) **II** *n.* [常用复] ①暂存的事物; 世间的事物 ②教会财产 ∥~**ity** [,tempə'ræliti] *n.* ①暂存性, 短暂性 ②俗权(与 spiritual ~ 或 ecclesiastic power 教权相对) ③[常用复] 教会财产, 教会收入 / ~**ize** *vt.* ① 把…放在时间关系中(来确定) ②使世俗化 / ~**ty** *n.* [总称]俗人

temporal² ['tempərəl] **I** *a.* 太阳穴的, 颞颥的: ~ bone 【解】颞颥骨 **II** *n.* 颞颥部机体部分(如颞颥骨、颞颥肌或颞颥动脉等)

temporary ['tempərəri] **I** *a.* 暂时的; 临时的: ~ needs 暂时需要 / a ~ receipt 临时收据 / a ~ office 临时办公室 **II** *n.* 临时工 ∥**temporarily** ['tempərərili; 美 ,tempə'rerili] *ad.* / **temporariness** *n.*

temporize, temporise ['tempəraiz] *vi.* ①顺应时势, 迎合潮流: *temporizing* measures 权宜措施 ②(为争取时间)拖延, 应付 ③妥协: ~ *with* sb. 与某人妥协 / ~ *between* two parties 为两造谋求妥协 ∥**temporization** [,tempərai'zeiʃən] *n.* / ~**r** *n.* 顺应时势的人; 拖延应付的人

tempt [tempt] *vt.* ①引诱, 诱惑: never to be ~ed off the straight path 决不被引入歧途 / ~ sb. to wrong 诱人作恶 ② 吸引; 使发生兴趣; 诱导: Can't I ~ you to have another helping? 请再吃一点, 好不好? / I am ~ed to try it again. 我很想再试一下。③触犯; 冒…的风险: ~ the hardships of a strange land 不怕人地生疏的艰苦 ④[古]试探, 考验 ∥~ **fate** (或 **fortune**) 蔑视命运 ∥~**er** *n.* ① 引诱者, 诱惑者 ② [the T-] 撒旦, 魔鬼

temptation [temp'teiʃən] *n.* ①引诱, 诱惑: resist ~ 抵制诱惑, 不受诱惑 / yield (或 give way) to ~ 受诱惑 / fall into ~ 受诱惑 ②诱惑物

tempting ['temptiŋ] *a.* 引诱人的; 吸引人的, 使发生兴趣的: a ~ offer 吸引人的提议 / These peaches look very ~. 这些桃子看上去真诱人。∥~**ly** *ad.*

ten [ten] **I** *num.* 十; 十个(人或物); 第十(卷、章、页等)(用例参看 **eight**) **II** *n.* ①十英镑纸币 ②十美元纸币 ③十岁 ④十点钟•∥*take* ~ 休息十分钟, 小憩 / ~*s of thousands* 好几万 / ~ *times* 十倍; …得多: be ~ *times* as big as … 等于…的十倍(或好几倍); 比…大得多 / He is ~ *times* the man you are. 比你高明多了。/ I'd ~ *times* rather .... 我最好是… / ~ *to one* 十之八九, 很可能: *Ten* to one he has forgotten it. 他很可能已经忘记了。/ *the upper* ~ (*thousand*) 上流社会; 贵族阶层 ∥~**fold** *a.* & *ad.* 十倍; 十重 ∥'~'**cent store** 小烟杂店 ∥'~'**gallon hat** [美俚](牛仔戴的)宽边高顶帽 / '~'**minute man** [美俚](见利眼红的)个人奋斗者; 油嘴滑舌糊弄

人的人 / '~-**per-** '**center** *n.* [美俚]演员(或作家等)的代理人; 抽10%佣金的人 / '~**pins** [复] *n.* [用作单]十柱戏 / '~-**spot** *n.* ①十元一张的纸币 ②[美俚]十年的刑期 / '~-**strike** *n.* ①(十柱戏中的)十柱全倒 ②大胜利, 大成功 / '~-'**twenty-'thirty** *n.* ① 低级闹剧表演 ② 表演低级闹剧的剧场(或剧团)

tenable ['tenəbl] *a.* ①(阵地等)守得住的, 可防守的: a ~ position (fortress) 守得住的阵地(堡垒) ②(主张等)站得住脚的: a ~ theory 站得住脚的理论 ③可保持(某一段时间)的 (*for*): a ~ scholarship ~ *for* four years 为期四年的奖学金 ∥**tenability** [,tenə'biliti] / ~**ness** *n.*

tenacious [ti'neiʃəs] *a.* ①紧握的; 坚持的, 顽强的; 固执的:a ~ grip 紧握 / a ~ struggle 不屈不挠的斗争 / a ~ old man 生命力顽强的老头 / be ~ of purpose (opinion) 不轻易改变目标(意见) ②(记忆力等)强的: have a ~ memory 记忆力强 ③ 粘的, 粘着力强的; 坚韧的: ~ clay 粘土 / ~ wood 一种坚韧的木料 ∥~**ly** *ad.* / ~**ness** *n.*

tenacity [ti'næsiti] *n.* ①紧握; 坚持, 顽强; 固执 ②坚韧, 韧性; 粘性

tenancy ['tenənsi] *n.* ① (土地的)租佃; (房屋的)租赁; 租用 ②租地(或租屋等) ③租期 ④(职位、处所等的)占据, 据有

tenant ['tenənt] **I** *n.* ①承租人, 租户; 佃户; 房客: a ~ at will (不必提前通知)可随时令其退租的租赁者 ②【律】不动产占有人; 不动产诉讼的被告 ③居住者, 占用者: ~s of the woods 树林的居住者, 鸟类 **II** *vt.* [常用被动语态]租借, 租用: houses ~ed by workers 工人租用的房屋 ∥~**able** *a.* 可租赁的 / ~**less** *a.* 无人租赁的 / ~**ry** *n.* ① [总称]承租人 ② 租出的财产 ③ 租赁 ∥~ **farmer** 佃农; 租地自行经营的农民 / '~-,**peasant** *n.* 佃农 / ~ **right** [英]租户权利(租户于租约期满时有权继续租赁, 被迫迁出时得要求赔偿)

tend¹ [tend] ❶ *vt.* ①照管, 照料; 护理; 管理: ~ sheep 看羊 / ~ the sick 护理病人 / ~ a store (machine) 照料商店(机器) ②【海】照料(缆绳、锚链) ❷ *vi.* ①服侍, 招待 (*on, upon*) ②注意, 留心 (*to*): ~ to one's affairs 照料事务 ∥~ *shop* 当伙计, 招待顾客

tend² [tend] *vi.* ①走向; 趋向 (*to, towards*): ~ *towards* the shore 向着岸边走(或航行) / ~ downwards 降下 / ~ upwards 升高 / ~ *to* the same conclusion 趋于同一结论 ②倾向: a style that ~s *to* elaboration 倾向于雕琢的风格 / ~ *to* be optimistic 倾向乐观 ③有助于: measures ~*ing* to improve working conditions 有助于改善劳动条件的措施

tendency ['tendənsi] *n.* ①趋向, 趋势, 倾向: a ~ *towards* simpler administration 精简机构的趋势 / show a ~ *to* improve 显示改善的倾向 ②脾性; 癖好 ③ (文学作品等的)旨趣, 意向, 倾向(性): writers with radical *tendencies* 有激进

倾向的作家 / ～ drama (novel) 倾向性戏剧(小说)

tender[1] ['tendə] **I** *a.* ① 嫩的; 柔软的: ～ green 嫩绿, 新绿 / a ～ beefsteak 嫩牛排 ②脆弱的, 纤弱的; 幼弱的, 未成熟的: extremely ～ eggs 壳很脆的卵 / a person of ～ age (或 years) 幼弱未成熟的人 ③敏感的; 一触即痛的: touch sb. on a ～ spot 触及某人的弱点, 打中某人的痛处 ④温柔的, 亲切的, 体贴的: ～ looks 温柔的神情 / a ～ heart 软心肠 ⑤微妙的, 棘手的, 难对付的: a ～ subject 需要小心处理以免伤人感情的问题 ⑥ 担心的 (*of*); 不轻易给予的 (*of*): be ～ *of* hurting other people's feelings 生怕伤害别人的感情 / be ～ *of* one's praise 慎于赞许,不随便称赞 ⑦【海】易倾斜的, 稳性小的 **II** ❶ *vt.* ① 使变软软; 使变脆弱 ②[古] 温柔地对待 ❷ *vi.* 变柔软; 变脆弱 ‖~ly *ad.* / ～ness *n.* ‖-eyed ['tendər'aid] *a.* 目光和善的; 目力弱的 / '～foot ([复] ～feet 或 ～foots) *n.* [美俚]艰苦地区的新来者; 新手 / '～'hearted *a.* 软心肠的 / '～loin *n.* ①(牛、猪等的)腰部嫩肉 ②[美][T-]纽约市的娱乐区 ③[美俚]城市中罪恶活动集中区; 贪官污吏敲榨勒索的好地方 / '～-,minded *a.* 空想的, 脱离实际的

tender[2] ['tendə] **I** ❶ *vt.* ①(正式)提出, 提供: ～ one's advice (protest) 提出意见(抗议) / ～ one's services to 表示愿为…效劳, 向…自荐 / ～ one's resignation 提出辞职(书) ② 清偿, 偿付: ～ the amount of rent 偿付租费 / ～ money in payment of a debt 付款还债 ❷ *vi.* 投标 (*for*): ～ *for* the construction of a new bridge 投标承建一座新桥 **II** *n.* ① 提出, 提供 ② 清偿, 偿付 ③投标: call for ～s 招标 / put in (或 make) a ～ *for* sth. 投标承办某事物 ④偿付债务的手段; 货币: legal ～ 合法货币; 偿付债务时债主必须接受的货币 ‖-er ['tendərə] *n.* 提出者; 投标者

tender[3] ['tendə] *n.* ①看管人, 照料人 ②(铁路)煤水车 ③供应船, 补给船; 交通船; 小船; 汽艇

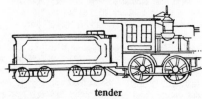

tender

tendon ['tendən] *n.* [解]腱

tendril ['tendril] *n.* [植]卷须

tenebrific [,teni'brifik] *a.* ① 阴沉的 ② 产生阴暗的, 造成黑暗的

tenebrous ['tenibrəs] *a.* ① 黑暗的; 阴沉的: a ～ cave 黑暗的洞穴 ② 难以理解的, 晦涩的: a ～ theory 难懂的理论 ‖～ness *n.*

tenement ['tenimənt] *n.* ①地产;【律】保有物, 享有物 (指受于他人而在一定期间或终身享有的土

地、房屋、爵位、特权等) ②住屋; 一套房间 ③分租房屋, 经济公寓 (一般指几户合住, 条件较差的住房) (=～ house) ‖-al [,teni'mentl] *a.* ①地产的; 住屋的 ②出租的 / ～ary [,teni'mentəri] *a.* ① 地产的, 住屋的 ② 供出租的, 供分租的

tenet ['ti:net] *n.* 信条, 宗旨; 原则: basic ～s 基本原则

tennis ['tenis] *n.* ①(旧时在室内场地进行并利用围墙等设备的)室内网球(运动) (=court ～) ②网球(运动) (=lawn ～), 包括草地网球、硬地网球): ～ played on a grass (hard) court 草地(硬地)网球 ‖～ arm, ～ elbow 网球员肘病 / ～ ball 网球 / ～ court 网球场 / ～ shoes 网球鞋, 跑鞋

tenon ['tenən] **I** *n.* (木工的)雄榫, 榫舌, 凸榫: a ～ and mortise 雌雄榫 **II** *vt.* ①在…上制榫 ②用榫接合 ‖～er *n.* 接榫者; 制榫机 / '～-saw *n.* 手锯, 榫锯

tenor[1] ['tenə] *n.* ① (生活等的)一般趋向, 进程 ②要旨, 大意: the ～ of a speech 讲话的大意 ③(文件等) 精确的抄本; 誊本 ④ (支票的) 期限 ⑤【矿】(矿石) 金属含量品位: ～ of ore 矿石金属含量, 矿石品位

tenor[2] ['tenə] 【音】 **I** *n.* ①男高音; 男高音歌手; 次中音部; 次中音乐器; 适于男高音(或次中音)的乐曲 (一组钟中)最低音的钟 **II** *a.* ①男高音的; 次中音部的: ～ voice 男高音 / ～ saxophone 次中音萨克斯管 ②(一组钟中)最低音的

tense[1] [tens] *n.* 【语】(动词的)时态, 时: the present (past, future) ～ 现在(过去, 将来)时 / the progressive (或 continuous) ～ 进行时 / the perfect (imperfect) ～ 完成(未完成)时 ‖at prime ～ 起先, 起初; 立即 ‖～less *a.* 没有时态的

tense[2] [tens] **I** *a.* ①拉紧的, 绷紧的; 紧张的: ～ nerves 紧张的神经 / a ～ game 紧张的比赛 / a face ～ with anxiety 因焦虑而显得紧张的脸色 / ～ excitement 非常激动 / a ～ atmosphere 紧张的气氛 ②【语】(语音)紧的: a ～ (lax) vowel 紧(松)元音 **II** *vt. & vi.* (使)拉紧; (使)紧张 ‖～ly *ad.* / ～ness *n.*

tensile ['tensail] *a.* ①张力的, 拉力的; 抗张的: ～ force 【物】张力 / ～ strain 【物】张应变 / ～ strength 【物】抗张强度 / ～ stress 【物】张胁强, 张应力 ②能伸长的; 能拉长的 ‖**tensility** [ten-'siliti] *n.*

tension ['tenʃən] **I** *n.* ①拉紧, 绷紧 ②紧张(指心理状态、形势等): muscular ～ 肌(肉)紧张 / create (ease) international ～ 制造(缓和)国际紧张局势 / racial ～(s) 种族间的紧张关系 ③【物】张力, 拉力, 牵力; (蒸汽等的)膨胀力, 压力; 电压: surface ～ 表面张力 / vapour ～ 汽压 / high ～ wire 【电】高压线 **II** *vt.* 拉紧, 绷紧; 使紧张 ‖～al *a.*

tensity ['tensiti] *n.* 紧张; 紧张度

tent[1] [tent] **I** *n.* ①帐篷,帐棚;(医疗等中用的)帐状物: a bell ~ (正中有一根支柱的)圆形帐篷 / pitch (strike) a ~ 搭(拆)帐篷 / rig up a ~ 赶搭帐篷 / an oxygen ~ 氧气帐(一种为病人提供辅助氧气的小帐篷) ②住处,寓所 ③【摄】(户外用的)携带暗室 (=dark ~) **II ❶** *vi.* ①住帐篷;宿营: We ~ed in a village for a week. 我们在一个村子里宿营一星期。②暂时居住 **❷** *vt.* ①用帐篷(或帐篷状的东西)遮盖 ②使在帐篷里宿营 ‖**~less** *a.* 无帐篷的 / **~ bed** 行军床,帐篷式卧床 / **~ fly** 帐篷盖 / '**~,maker** *n.* 造帐篷的人 / **~ peg** 帐篷桩 / **~ pegging** 挑桩(源于印度的一种运动,骑者奔驰时以枪尖挑起打在地上的桩) / **~ stitch** (刺绣)斜向平行的针脚

tent[2] [tent] *n.* 【医】塞条,塞子: sponge ~ 海绵塞条 **II** *vt.*【医】将塞条等嵌进(伤口)

tent[3] [tent] *vt.* [苏格兰]①注意②看护,照料③观察

tent[4] [tent] *n.* 深红色葡萄酒(西班牙产,尤用于圣餐)

tentacle ['tentəkl] *n.* ①【动】触手;触角;触须;触器;【植】触毛②[喻]似触手的东西 ‖**~d** *a.* 有触手(或触角等)的 / **tentacular** [ten'tækjulə] *a.* 触手的;触手状的

tentative ['tentətiv] **I** *a.* ①试验(性)的,尝试的;暂定的,暂时的: a ~ plan 试验性的计划 / make a ~ conclusion 作出暂时的结论②踌躇的,不明确的: a ~ smile 勉强的微笑 **II** *n.* 试验;试验性提议 ‖**~ly** *ad.* / **~ness** *n.*

tenterhook ['tentəhuk] *n.*【纺】拉幅钩,张布钩 ‖**be on ~s** 提心吊胆;焦虑不安;如坐针毡

tenth [tenθ] **I** *num.* ①第十(个)②十分之一(的): a ~ part 十分之一 **II** *n.* ①【音】十度音程;第十音②【英史】什一税③(月的)第十日 ‖**nine ~s** 十之八九;几乎全部 / **the submerged ~** 社会的最底层;最穷困的阶层 ‖**~ly** *ad.* 第十(列举条目等时用) ‖**~-'rate** *a.* 最劣等的

tenuis ['tenjuis] ([复] **tenues** ['tenjui:z]) *n.*【语】(旧称)清爆破音(如 [k], [p], [t] 等)

tenuous ['tenjuəs] *a.* ①纤细的;单薄的: a ~ nylon rope 纤细的尼龙绳②稀薄的③脆弱的,无力的: the ~ character of one's physical strength 体力的虚弱④精细的,微妙的: a ~ distinction 精细的区别 ‖**~ly** *ad.* / **~ness** *n.*

tenure ['tenjuə] *n.* (财产、职位等的)占有;占有权;占有期;占有条件;(土地的)使用;使用权;使用期: during one's ~ of office 在任职期间 / hold one's life on a precarious ~ 过朝不保夕的生活 / security of ~ 租地使用权的保障;职位(或地位)的稳固(或保证) / military ~ 【史】由于服兵役而获得的土地所有权 ‖**tenurial** [te-'njuəriəl] *a.*

tepid ['tepid] *a.* ①微温的;温热的: a ~ bath 温水浴②[喻]不太热烈的,不冷不热的: ~ praise 不热烈的赞扬 / a ~ reception 不冷不热的接待 / have only a ~ interest in 对…兴趣不大

‖**~ity** [te'piditi] *n.* / **~ly** *ad.* / **~ness** *n.*

tercentenary [,tə:sen'ti:nəri] *n.* & *a.* 三百年(的);三百年纪念日(的);三百年纪念日的庆祝(的)

term [tə:m] **I** *n.* ①期,期限: serve one's ~ of service 服规定年限的兵役;服役 / the ~ of an insurance policy 保险契约有效期 / get a ~ of ten years in prison 被判十年徒刑②学期: the spring (autumn) ~ 春(秋)季学期 / during ~ (或 ~time) 在学期(的过程)中 / a mid-~ test 期中测验③任期: during one's ~ of office 在任职期间 / When does his ~ as President expire? 他当总统什么时候期满? / run for a second ~ 竞选连任④限期;结帐期(尤指法定季度结帐日,=quarter day);(租赁等的)终止期⑤【律】开庭期;地产租用期;限期租用的地产;偿债期⑥(正常的)分娩期: be born at full ~ 足月生⑦[复](契约、谈判等的)条件;条款;费用,价钱: What are your sales ~s? 你们的售货条件是什么? / Terms cash. 须用现金支付。/ the ~s of an agreement 协议条款 / inclusive ~s (付给旅馆等的)一应在内的费用⑧[复]关系,交谊;地位: be on good (bad) ~s with sb. 同某人关系好(不好) / They are on familiar (intimate) ~s. 他们彼此很熟悉(亲密)。/ be on first-name ~s with sb. 同某人称名不称姓;同某人很熟 / meet sb. on equal ~s 以平等地位与某人相见⑨(有特定意义的)词,词语;专门名词,术语;措词,话: a derogatory ~ 贬义词 / a set ~ 固定词语 / technical ~s 专门名词,术语 / a medical (legal) ~ 医学(法律)术语 / in plain (concise) ~s 以简明(简练)的措词⑩【逻】项,名词: the major (middle, minor) ~ 大(中,小)项 ⑪【数】【物】项;条: ~ value 项值 / extreme ~ 外项 / ~-by-~ integration 逐项积分法⑫界石,界标;【建】胸像柱⑬[古]界限;极限;终点,终止 **II** *vt.* 把…称为,把…叫做: be officially ~ed … 被正式称作… / ~ it sheer robbery 把这称为十足的抢劫 / ~ oneself an authority 自封为"权威" ‖**at ~** 期终时;到期 / **be on speaking ~s** ①关系好,友好: I'm not on speaking ~s with him at the present time. (由于争吵过等)现在我同他的关系不好(或同他不交谈)。②只是泛泛之交,仅仅相识而已③相适应: Solid food and myself are not on speaking ~s just now. 目前我还吃不下较硬的食物。/ **bring sb. to ~s** 迫使某人同意(或接受条件);迫使某人屈服 / **come to ~s** 达成协议;妥协;让步;屈服 / **eat one's ~s** [英]学法律 / in ~s of ①用…的话,以…的措词: speak of sth. in ~s of praise 以赞美的话谈某事②按,照;用…的思想方法: consider problems in ~s of the people's interests 从人民利益出发考虑问题 / think in ~s of materialist dialectics 按照唯物辩证法进行思考③在…方面,从…方面(说来): in ~s of manpower 在人力方面 / in

~s of theory 在理论上 / *keep ón good ~s* *(with sb.)* (同某人)保持友好关系 / *keep ~s with sb.* 同某人交往;同某人友好 / *make ~s* 达成协议 / *not on any ~s* (或 *on no ~s*)无论如何不 / *not on borrowing ~s* 不友好;没有交情(尤指邻居之间) / *on easy ~s* 以宽厚的条件;(商业用语)以分期付款方式 / *on one's own ~s* ①根据自己的主张;根据自己的条件 ② 按照自己的定价 / *set a ~ to* 给…定限期;给…定限度;对…加以限制 / *~s of reference* (委员会等的)受权调查范围: This question is within our ~s *of reference.* 这个问题是在我们受权调查范围内的。/ *~s of trade* 进出口交换比率(指进出口货价之间的比率) ‖**~ less** *a.* ①无穷的,无限的 ②无条件的 ‖ **~ day** ①(租金等)支付日;[苏格兰]法定季度结帐日 ②【律】开庭日 ③(科学工作者规定的观察气象等的)观察日 / *~* **paper** 学期论文 / *~* **policy** 定期财产保险契约 / **'~time** *n.* ①学期 ②[苏格兰](租金或利息的)法定支付期 (=legal *~*)

terminable ['təːminəbl] *a.* 可终止的;有限期的: a *~* contract (annuity) 有限期的合同(年金或养老金) ‖**terminability** [,təːminə'biliti] *n.* 可终止性;有限期性 / **~ness** *n.* **terminably** *ad.*

terminal ['təːminl] **I** *a.* ①末端的;终点的;结尾的;极限的: a *~* station 终点站 / a *~* syllable 结尾的音节 / *~* velocity (射弹的)落速,末速;极限速度,临界速度 / a *~* nose dive (飞机)极限垂直俯冲 / *~* charges (铁道等的)装卸费 ②【植】顶生的;【动】端的;末梢的: *~* flower (bud) 顶生花(芽) / *~* spine 端刺 ③每期的;定期的;学期的: a *~* subscription 定期订费 / a *~* examination 学期考试,大考 ④末期的,晚期的: a *~* cancer ward 晚期癌症病房 **II** *n.* ①末端;终点;极限 ②【电】【自】端子;线接头;接线柱 ③(铁路、公共汽车等的)终点(站);总站;(通讯)端末站: an air *~* (城市里的)航空集散站(去机场或来自机场的旅客集散地);航空终点站 ④【语】词尾(结尾的字母、音素、音节等);结尾的词 ⑤【建】端饰: a *~* pedestal 胸像台 ‖**~ly** *ad.* ‖**~ leave** [美](军人退役前的)末次假期(包括以前积累的未度过的假期) / *~* **market** (农产品)集散的中心市场

terminate ['təːmineit] **I** ❶ *vt.* (时间上)使停止,使结束;(空间上)使终止,使结尾: *~* a contract (pact) 解除契约(条约) / the syllable *terminating* a word 词的结尾音节 / The corridor is ~d with a staircase. 走廊末端是楼梯。❷ *vi.* 结束;终止: The mass rally ~d at 5 p.m. 群众大会在下午五时结束。/ The road *~s* in a forest. 路的尽头是森林。/ nouns *terminating* in -ness 以"-ness"结尾的名词 **II** *a.* 终止的;有界限的

termination [,təːmi'neiʃən] *n.* ①结束;结局;终止;终点: the *~* of a treaty 条约的满期 / *~* of life 寿终,死 / put a *~* to sth. (或 bring sth. to a *~*) 结束某事 / a friendly *~* of dispute 争论

的和好的结局 / a *~* slip [美]解雇通知单 / the *~* of a journey 旅程的终点 ②【语】词尾(尤指词尾变化或派生结构) ‖**~al** *a.*

terminology [,təːmi'nɔlədʒi] *n.* 术语学;术语,专门名词: scientific (linguistic) *~* 科学(语言学)术语 ‖**terminologist** *n.* 术语学家

terminus ['təːminəs] ([复] termini ['təːminai] 或 terminuses) *n.* ①终点;目标 ②(铁路、汽车、航空等的)终点站;[主英]终点城镇 ③界标,界牌,界石;胸像台 ④[T-]【罗神】护界神 ⑤[军]界限,极限

termite ['təːmait] *n.* 白蚁

terrace ['terəs] **I** *n.* ①倾斜的平地;台地;阶地;梯田 ②露台,平台,阳台 ③(西班牙式或东方式的)平台屋顶;有列柱的游廊 ④ 斜坡上(或高于街道地面)的一排房屋 ⑤斜坡上房屋前的街巷 ⑥(马路中央的)狭长形小园地;地坪 **II** *vt.* 使成阶地;把…筑成坛;使成梯田: We built ~d fields on the mountain sides. 我们在山腰上筑了梯田。/ a ~d roof 平台屋顶

terrace

terra-cotta ['terə'kɔtə] *n.* ①(制陶器等或建筑用的,上釉或无釉的)赤土,赤陶: a *~* vase 赤陶花瓶 ②赤褐色 ③一种带褐色的柑子

terrain ['terein] *n.* ①(作一定用途的)地面;地域,地带;【军】地形: a difficult *~* for tanks 不利于使用坦克的地形 / a strategically important *~* 战略上的重要地势 ②【地】地体;岩层 ③(知识的)领域;(行动的)场所,范围: the whole *~* of economics 经济学的整个领域

terrapin ['terəpin] *n.* 【动】龟鳖类爬行动物(如泥龟、鳖)

terrazzo [te'rɑːtsou] *n.* [意]水磨石

terrestrial [ti'restriəl] **I** *a.* ①地球(上)的: the *~* globe (或 ball) 地球 / a *~* globe 地球仪 / *~* gravitation 地球引力 / *~* magnetism 地磁 ②陆(地)的,陆上的;(动物)陆栖的;(植物)陆生的: *~* transportation 陆上运输 / the *~* parts of the world 世界的陆地部分 ③人间的;世俗的: *~* aims (或 interests) 名利心 **II** *n.* 地球上的居民;陆栖动物;陆生植物 ‖**~ly** *ad.*

terrible ['terəbl] *a.* ①可怕的,可怖的,骇人的;令人敬畏的: a *~* storm 可怕的风暴;极其猛烈的风暴 ②极度的;厉害的: a *~* headache 剧烈的

头痛 / a ～ heat 酷暑 / a ～ responsibility 极其重大的责任 ③[口]极坏的,很糟的: a ～ performance 很糟糕的演出 ④[美俚]极妙的,了不起的 ‖**~ness** n. / **terribly** ad.

terrier[1] ['teriə] n. ①㹴(一种狗) ②[英口](由义勇兵组成、保卫英国本土的)本土军士兵

terrier[2] ['teriə] n. 地产册,地籍册

terrific [tə'rifik] a. ①可怕的,可怖的,骇人的: a ～ hurricane 可怕的飓风 ②[口]极大的; 极度的;非常的: at a ～ speed 以极高速度 ③[美俚]极妙的,了不起的: a ～ view all the way to the scenic spot 到那风景区途中一路上奇妙的景色 ‖**~ally** ad.

terrify ['terifai] vt. 使恐惧,使惊吓;恐吓: You ～ me! 你吓了我一跳。 / be terrified at (或 with) 被…吓一跳 / be terrified out of one's senses (或 wits) 吓得魂不附体 / ～ sb. into doing sth. 恐吓某人做某事 / be terrified of 对…感到惊恐

territorial [,teri'tɔːriəl] I a. ①领土的: ～ integrity 领土完整 / ～ sovereignty 领土主权 / ～ sea (或 waters) 领海 / ～ air (或 sky) 领空 / ～ boundaries 边界 / have ～ claims against a country 对一个国家提出领土要求 ②土地的: ～ property 地产 ③区域(性)的,地方(性)的: a ～ commander 地区司令 / a ～ industry 地方工业 ④[T-] 美国领土(或领地)的; 美国的准州的: Territorial laws 美国领地的法律 ⑤[常作 T-] [英](保卫)本土的: the Territorial Army (由义勇兵组成、保卫英国本土的)本土军 II n. [英]本土军士兵 ‖**~ly** ad. ‖**~ department** (美国)海外领土部(负责组织与协调美国海外领土范围内的军事行动) / ～ **system** (地方)政府权力高于教会的制度

territory ['teritəri] n. ①领土,版图;领地 ②地区; (按某种目的划定的)区域(尤指商业推销区): the most fertile ～ 最肥沃的地区 ③[T-](美国)准州(指尚未正式成为州但有本地立法机构的地区) ④(行动、知识等)的领域,范围

terror ['terə] n. ①恐怖,惊骇: run away in ～ 十分惊慌地逃走 / have a ～ of sth. 对某事感到恐怖 ②引起恐惧的事物: be a ～ to sb. 使某人恐惧 ③[常作 T-] 恐怖统治: the white ～ 白色恐怖 ④[口]极讨厌的人: a holy (或 perfect) ～ 实在讨厌的家伙(常指小孩) ‖**strike ～ into sb.'s heart** 使某人心惊胆战 / **the King of Terrors** 死神 / **the Reign of Terror** 见 **reign** ‖**~ism** ['terərizəm] n. 恐怖主义;恐怖行为 / **~ist** ['terərist] n. 恐怖主义者;恐怖分子 a. 恐怖主义的;恐怖行为的

terse [təːs] a. (话语、文笔等)精练的,简洁的,扼要的 ‖**~ly** ad. / **~ness** n.

tervalent [təː'veilənt] a. 【化】三价的

test[1] [test] I n. ①(物质、性质、效能等)试验: an endurance (efficiency) ～ 耐力(效能)试验 / an underground nuclear ～ 地下核试验 / a ～ flight (飞机)试飞 ②化验;化验法;化验剂: a blood ～ 验血 / a ～ for tuberculosis 结核病检查 ③化验的阳性结果 ④检验;检验标准: Practice is the only reliable ～ of a theory. 实践是对理论的唯一可靠的检验。 ⑤测验;考查;小考: an intelligence ～ 智力测验 / a ～ in mathematics 数学考查 / give (take) a ～ 举行(参加)测验 ⑥考验: be subjected to severe ～s 经受严峻考验 ⑦[主英] 【冶】烤钵,灰皿,提银盘 (=cupel) ⑧[口] =～ match II ❶ vt. ①测验;试验;检验: ～ sb.'s ability 测验某人的能力 / a ～ product 检验产品 / I'll have my eyesight ~ed. 我要检查一下视力。 / be ~ed against reality 受客观实际检查 ②化验: ～ ore for iron 化验矿石中的含铁量 ③考验;考查 ④【冶】在烤钵中精炼 ❷ vi. ①受试验;受测验 ②测得结果: Our eyesight ~ed the same. 测验证明,我们的视力相同。 ③(为鉴定而)进行测验 (for): use different methods to ～ for allergies 用不同的方法来测定变态反应性 ‖**put to the ～** 使受试验;使受检验;使受考验 / **stand the ～** 经受住考验(或检验等) ‖**~ed** a. ①经过试验的; 经受过考验的: a ～ed veteran sailor 久经磨练的老海员 / time-~ed principles 久经考验的原则 ②经鉴定的;检验无病的: tuberculin-~ed cattle 用结核菌素检验过的牛 ‖**~ ban** 禁止核试验协定 / '**~-bed** n. 试验机器等用的支架,试验台,试验床 / '**~-fire** vt. 试射: ~-fire a machine gun 试射机枪 / ～ **glass** 试(验)杯 / ～ **match** (板球和橄榄球等)各国家队间的决赛阶段的比赛 / ～ **paper** ①试纸 ②测验题目纸;测验的试卷 ③[美]供检定笔迹的文件 / ～ **pattern** (电视的)测试图 / ～ **pilot** (飞机)试飞员 / ～ **tube** 试(验)管 / '**~-tube** a. ①在试管中发展(或生长)的 ②由人工授精而生产的: a ～-tube baby 用人工授精而生产的婴儿 / ～ **type** 视力测验表上的字型,试验标型

test[2] [test] n. (蟹、蛤等的)甲壳,介壳

testament ['testəmənt] n. ①[T-](基督教)圣约书(《旧约全书》或《新约全书》): The Old Testament 《旧约全书》/ The New Testament 《新约全书》 ②[T-][口]《新约全书》 ③【律】遗嘱,遗言: make one's ～ 立遗嘱 ④确实的证明,实证 ⑤信仰的声明

testify ['testifai] ❶ vi. 证明,证实,作(见)证: to sb.'s innocence 证明某人无罪 / ～ against sb. 作不利于某人的证明 / ～ on behalf of sb. (或 on sb.'s behalf) 为某人作证;作有利于某人的证明 ❷ vt. 证明,证实;表明,声明: ～ one's regret 表示歉意 / Acts ～ intent. 行动表明动机。 / ～ under oath that ... 发誓声明(或证明)…

testimonial [,testi'məunjəl] I n. ①(能力、资格、品德等的)证明书,介绍信;鉴定书 ②奖品,奖金;奖状;书面的感谢(或表扬等);纪念品 II a. ①

(有关)证明书(或鉴定书等)的 ②表扬的,褒奖的

testimony ['testimeni] *n.* ①证据,证明;【律】(宣誓) 证言: call sb. in ~ 传某人作证 / produce ~ to (或 of) 提出…的证据 / bear ~ to 证明…;证实…/ the ~ of history 历史的证明 / the ~ of witness【律】人证 / give false ~ 作伪证明 ②声明;陈述;公开的承认 ③表示,表明: His smile was ~ of his approval. 他的微笑表明他赞同了。④【基督教】(刻在两块石碑上的)摩西十诫;[复](基督教《圣经》中)上帝的箴言

testy ['testi] *a.* ①(人)易怒的,暴躁的 ②(话等)恼火的,烦躁的: a ~ remark 生气的话

tête-à-tête ['teita'teit] [法] **I** *n.* ①(两人之间的)私下谈话(或会见);促膝谈心: have a ~ with sb. 与某人密谈 ②(面对面式的)双人沙发 **II** *a.* 面对面的;两人私下的: have a ~ talk 密谈 **III** *ad.* 面对面地;两人私下地: dine ~ with sb. 同某人(私下)一起进餐

tether ['teðə] **I** *n.* ①(拴牛、马等的)系绳,系链 ②(力量、权力等的)限度,范围: beyond sb.'s ~ 为某人力所不及;在某人权限外 **II** *vt.* ①(用绳、链等)拴: ~ a horse to a tree 把马拴在树上 ②束缚;限制,限定(计划的范围等) ‖*at the end of one's ~* 山穷水尽;智穷力竭

text [tekst] *n.* ①原文,本文;正文: the full ~ 全文 / a corrupt ~ 同原文有出入的文本 (可能由于抄firstly错误) ②课文;课本,教科书: a ~ in chemistry 化学课本 ③版本 ④(讨论等的)题目,主题;(演说等中引自权威方面的)引语: stick to one's ~ (谈话时)不离正题 ⑤(基督教《圣经》的)经文,经句(引作布道的题目等) ⑥谱成曲子的诗(或经文,民间故事等);(刊印的)乐谱 ⑦一种铅字: German ~ 德文式黑体字 / 碑铭上刻的黑体字 ‖'~**book** *n.* 课本,教科书: a ~*book* example 范例;极好的例子 / '~**,bookish** *a.* 教科书式的;[喻]呆板乏味的 / ~ **edition** 供教学用的版本 / ~ **hand** 粗体正楷

textile ['tekstail] **I** *n.* 纺织品;纺织原料 **II** *a.* 纺织的: ~ fibres 纺织纤维 / a ~ fabric 纺织品,织物 / ~ machinery 纺织机器 / the ~ industry 纺织工业

texture ['tekstʃə] **I** *n.* ①(织物的)组织,结构,质地: a cloth with a close (loose) ~ 质地紧密(稀松)的布 / ~ effect (起绒织物的)结构效应 ②织品,织物 / ~ 结构(文艺作品等的)结构,组织 ④(材料等的)构造,构成;(岩石等的)纹理;(皮肤的)肌理 ⑤本质,实质;特征: the ~ of an ancient culture 一种古代文化的特征 **II** *vt.* 使具有某种结构(或特征): ~*d* worsted 花式组织精纺呢 ‖~**less** *a.* 无明显结构的;无定形的

than [强 ðæn; 弱 ðən, ðn] **I** *conj.* ①[用于形容词、副词的比较级之后]比: He is taller ~ his brother. 他比他的兄弟长得高。/ She is healthier ~ (she has) ever (been). 她比以前任何时候都更健康。/ Easier said ~ done. [谚]说来容易做来难。/ I know better ~ to believe such a man.

我不至于会去相信这样一个人的。/ I know you better ~ she (does). 我比她更了解他。/ I know you better ~ (I know) her. 我对你比对她更了解。[注意:句中用不及物动词时,than 后的代词可用宾格或宾格,意义并无区别,如: She draws better ~ I (或 me). 她画得比我好。若代词后接 all 时,代词一般用宾格,如: She draws better ~ us all. 她画得比我们大家都好。上述两句中代词用宾格时, than 用作前置词。] ②[用于 else, other 等之后]除…(外): What he did was nothing else ~ a practical joke. 他干的事简直是恶作剧。③[用于 rather, sooner 之后]与其…(宁愿…) ④[用于 scarcely, hardly 之后,表示时间]就: We had scarcely arrived there ~ (或 when) it began to rain. 我们刚到那里就下雨了。 **II** *prep.* [用于 ~ whom, ~ which 两个词组和某些用不及物动词的句中(参看本词条的 **I** 末)]比: No man ~ *whom* no one is more fit for this job 最适宜做这件事的人 ‖*no more ~* 仅仅,只是: It is *no more* ~ a beginning. 这仅仅是个开端。/ *no other* ~ [加强语气用]①除…外没有;只有 ②正是,就是: It was *no* (或 none) *other* ~ my mother. 这(不是别人)正是我的母亲。

thank [θæŋk] **I** *vt.* ①谢谢,感谢: *Thank* you. 谢谢(你)。/ No, ~ you. 不,谢谢(你)。(表示婉拒)/ No more, ~ you. 够了,谢谢(你)。/ *Thank* you in anticipation. 遇事先致谢。②[用于 will 或 'll 后,表示客气的请求;现常用作反语,含有责备的意思]感谢,请: I will ~ you to shut the door. 请你把门带上,好吗? / I'll ~ you to leave my affairs alone (或 to mind your own business). 请你别管闲事。③[用作反语]要…负责;责怪: He can be ~*ed* for this setback. 这个挫折要怪他。 **II** *n.* [复]感谢,谢忱,谢意: *Thanks!* 谢谢! [注意: 此句语气轻于 Thank you.] / Many ~*s*. (或 *Thanks* a lot.) 多谢。/ express one's heartfelt ~*s* 表示衷心感谢 / A thousand ~*s* for your kindness. 非常感谢你的好意。/ No, ~*s*. 不,谢谢(你)。‖*bow one's* ~*s* 鞠躬致谢 / *get small* ~*s for it* 白做了;并不讨好 / *have only oneself to* ~ (*for that*) 只能怪自己;自作自受 / *no* ~*s to* 并非由于 / ~ *God* 见 *god* / ~*s to* 幸亏;由于: *Thanks to* your help, we accomplished the task ahead of schedule. 多亏你们的帮助,我们提前完成了任务。/ *Thank you for nothing.* (表示蔑视的拒绝)得了,别瞎起劲。 ‖~**er** *n.* 感谢者 ‖~**ee**, ~**y**. ['θæŋki:], ~**ye** ['θæŋkji] *int.* 谢谢 / ~ **offering** [宗]感恩的供品;谢恩的捐献 / '~**,worthy** *a.* 值得感谢的;应感激的

thankful ['θæŋkful] *a.* ①感谢的,感激的: I am ~ to you for all this help. 我感谢你的这一切帮助。②欣慰的: You should be ~ that you have caught the train. 你应该为你赶上火车感到高兴。 ‖~**ly** *ad.* / ~**ness** *n.*

thankless ['θæŋklis] *a.* ①不感激的; 负义的 ②不使人感激的; 徒劳的: a ～ job 吃力不讨好的工作 ‖～ly *ad.* / ～ness *n.*

thanksgiving ['θæŋks,giviŋ] *n.* ① 感谢, 感恩; 【宗】感恩祈祷 ②[T-] =Thanksgiving Day ‖**Thanksgiving Day【基督教】**感恩节(例假日, 在美国是十一月的最后一个星期四, 在加拿大是十月的第二个星期一)

that [ðæt] **I** *a.* [后接复数名词时用 those] ①那, 那个: (on) ～ day 在那天 / (in) those days 那时, 当时 / This street is broader than ～ one. 这条街比那一条宽阔。/ ～ child of his 他的那个孩子 / That George! 乔治那个家伙! / unforgettable ten days in Albania 在阿尔巴尼亚(度过的)那难忘的十天[注意: 把"十天"视作整体, 故用 ～; 也可用 those]
②那样的, 如此的(现常用 such, such a 等): He had ～ confidence in himself (that) he did not consult anybody. 他是那样的自信, 以致跟任何人都没有商量过。

II ❶ ([复] those [ðouz]) *demonstrative pron.*
①那, 那个: What (Who) is ～? 那是什么(谁)? / Is ～ you, John? (用于打电话或其他听得见而看不到的场合) 是你吗, 约翰? / Are those your schoolmates? 那些是你的同学吗? / This tastes better than ～. 这个比那个好吃。/ Don't grin like ～. 别那样咧着嘴(傻)笑。/ How to do it better and faster, ～ is the question. 问题在于怎样才能做得更好更快。/ He's trying to fool you, ～'s all ～ is. 他是想骗你, 就是那么回事。
②(刚提到的) 那时; (刚提到的) 那事: After ～ he left. 随着他就离开了。
③前者(指上文已提到的两点中的前一点, 其后一点用 this 表示)
④[用作关系代词的先行词; 关系代词为宾格时常省略]那, 那个: What was ～ (which) he said? 他说了些什么? / Those (whom) we met were young workers. 我们碰到的那些人是青年工人。/ unite with all those who can be united 团结一切可以团结的人们 / Those may try it who choose. (或 Those who choose may try it.) 想试的人可以试一下。

❷ [强 ðæt; 弱 ðət] [单复同] *relative pron.* [引导限制性定语从句, 前面不用逗号] ①[在从句中作主语时相当于 who 或 which; 但在 it is (或 was) … 句型中, 以及最高级形容词或 all, any, little, much, no, only 等词后比 who 或 which 常用]: This is the best article ～ has been written on the subject. 在有关这个题目的文章中, 这一篇是最好的。/ He is the only one among us ～ knows German. 我们中间只有他懂德语。/ This book contains much (little) ～ is useful. 这本书中有很多(没有多少)有用的东西。/ It's not everybody (～) can draw so well. 不是每个人都能画得这样好的。/ Mrs.

Brown, Jane Smith ～ was. . . . . [口]布朗夫人, 就是(结婚前的)简·史密斯, …
②[在从句中作宾语或前置词宾语等时, 常省略; 相当于 whom 或 which; 与动词搭配的前置词常在从句的结尾]: Do the best (～) you can (do). (你要)尽力而为。[注意: 这里不可用 which 代替～] / Is this the pen (～) you were looking for? 你要找的钢笔是这一枝吗? / The man (～) you got the news from is a friend of mine. 告诉你这个消息的人是我的朋友。
③[用来代替表示时间的词时, 常省略; 相当于 when]: the year (～ 或 when) he was born 他诞生的(那)一年 / We left the day (～ 或 when) he arrived. 他来的(那)一天我们就离开了。
④[用来代替主句中的名词及其前置词]: I like the place for the very reason ～ (=for which) you dislike it. 我喜欢那地方的原因恰恰是你不喜欢它的原因。/ He doesn't see things the way (～) we see them. 他看问题跟我们不一样。(这句中的 the way =in the way, 所以 ～ =in which)
⑤[在从句中用于不加冠词的、表示某种特性的名词后, 作表语]如此, 尽管, 虽然: Fool ～ I was, I took his word for it. 我真傻, 竟然相信了他的话。/ Child ～ he was, he knew what was the right thing to do. 尽管他是个孩子, 他却懂得应该做什么。

III *conj.* ①[引导名词性从句]: They said (～) they could do it ahead of schedule. 他们说他们能够提前完成。[注意: 在及物动词后, ～ 常可省略] / See (to it) ～ everyone is fully prepared. 务必使每个人都充分准备好。/ The trouble is ～ you couldn't come. 麻烦就在于你不能来。
②[引导状语从句, 表明原因或理由]因为, 由于: We are glad (～) we have reaped another bumper harvest. 我们都感到高兴, 因为又获得了丰收。/ It is rather ～ he was ill then. 主要是由于他当时在生病。/ Not ～ I'm unwilling to go with you, but ～ I'm busy now. 并不是我不愿意跟你一起去, 而是我现在很忙。
③[引导状语从句, 表明目的或结果]为了; 以至于: Speak louder (so) ～ everybody may hear what you say. 讲得响一些, 让每个人都能听清楚你的话。/ The performance was such ～ the audience were deeply moved. 演出那么精采, 观众深受感动。/ What have I done ～ he should be angry with me? 我究竟干了些什么, 他要对我生气呢?
④[引导表示愿望、感叹等的从句; 主句常可省略]: That (或 How I wish ～) I could go to France with you! 我多么想同你一起到法国去呀! / That he should do such a thing! (真想不到) 他竟会干出这种事来! / Oh, ～ I should live to see this. 真没想到我会遇上这样的事。

IV *ad.* 那样, 那么: a dam about ～ high 大约那

样高的堤坝 / The weather isn't (all) ~ hot. 天气(根本) 没有那么热。 / I know only ~ much. 我只知道那么多。 / Can you walk ~ far? 你能走得那么远吗?

‖**and all** / 诸如此类 / **and** ~ [加强语气用] 而且: They finished the work, *and* ~ in only a few days. 他们完成了那工作, 而且只用了几天的工夫。 / **at** ~ ①就那样, 就这样; 到此为止: They left it *at* ~. 他们就这样把那事搁下了。 (或: 他们谈到那里为止。) ②[加强语气用] 而且: The workers produced more steel, and all of fine quality *at* ~. 工人们生产了更多的钢, 而且都是优质钢。 ③但是, 然而; 要说起来: We might have done still better *at* ~. 然而我们本来还可做得更好些。 / **Come out of** ~! [俚]走开! / **for all** ~ 尽管如此 / **in** ~ [书面语] 既然; 因为: Criticism and self-criticism is necessary *in* ~ it helps us to correct our mistakes. 批评与自我批评是必要的, 因为能帮助我们改正错误。 / **not** ~ 见 **not** / **now** ~ 既然, 由于: You ought to write *now* ~ you know the address. 你既然已知道地址, 就该写信了。 / ~ **is** [作插入语]那就是; [때]常略作 i.e.: a week later. ~ *is*, March 1 一星期后, 即三月一日 / ~ **is to say** 见 **say** / **That's a dear!** [口]这才乖呢! 这才是好孩子! / ~'**s it** [口] ① 对啦 (= ~'s right) ②就这样; 完了 (= ~'s all) / ~'**s** (或 **so** ~'**s** ~) [口][加强语气用] (表示决心、结束争论、讲完故事等时用语)就是这样; 就是那么回事; 再没什么可说的了: We will finish the task in two days, and ~'s ~. 我们一定要在两天内完成任务, 就是这样。 / **That will do.** ①(那样)够了。 (或: 不用继续下去了。) ②(那样)行。 / **this and** ~ 见 **this** / **this, ~, and** (或 **or**) **the other** 见 **this** / **upon** ~ 于是(立刻) / **with** ~ 接着就

thatch [θætʃ] **I** *n.* ①盖屋顶的材料(指稻草、茅草、棕榈等) ②茅屋顶 ③[口]头发, 粗密的头发 **II** *vt.* 用茅草等盖(屋顶); 象茅草屋顶一样地覆盖 ‖~**er** *n.* 盖屋顶者 / ~**ing** *n.* ①盖屋顶 ②盖屋顶的材料 / ~**y** *a.* 茅屋顶的; 象茅屋顶的

thatch

thaumaturge ['θɔ:mətə:dʒ] *n.* 演奇术者, 魔术师, 术士 ‖**thaumaturgic(al)** [,θɔ:mə'tə:dʒik(əl)] *a.* 奇术的, 魔术的 / **thaumaturgist** *n.* =thaumaturge / **thaumaturgy** *n.* 奇术, 魔术

thaw [θɔ:] **I** ❶ *vi.* (冰、雪等)融化, 融解, 融冻; (在态度、感情等方面)趋于和缓: It is ~ing. 解冻了。 / The snow has ~ed. 雪已融化了。 / The ground has ~ed out. 地面解冻了。 / a "~ing" of the relations between the two countries 两国关系的"解冻" / He ~ed perceptibly. 他的态度明显地缓和下来了。 ❷ *vt.* 使融化; 使缓和: make a fire to ~ (out) the frozen earth 点火以融化冻土 / ~ out the frozen assets 解除对资产的冻结 / ~ sb. (out) 使某人的态度缓和下来 **II** *n.* ①融化, 解冻; (在态度、感情等方面的)和缓 ②(足以解冻的)温暖气候: A ~ has set in. 暖流来了。 ‖~**less** *a.* (永)不融化的 / ~**y** *a.* 解冻的, 融化的

the [强 ði:; 弱 (元音前) ði, (辅音前) ðə, ð] **I** *art.* [定冠词] [释义 ①—㉓] 用于名词或名词性词组前, 表示: 已被确认、提到、遇到、正在谈到、熟悉的、实际存在的或独一无二的人或事物, 意义相当于"这(些)"、"那(些)", 以区别于 a, an "一个"、"某个" ①[指特定的人或事物]: ~ river 这条(或那条)河 [区别于 *a* river 一条河] / ~ old worker 这个(或那个)老工人 [区别于 *an* old worker 一个老工人] / ~ year 1949 一九四九年 ②[指已提到或正谈到的人或事物]: Who was ~ visitor? 来访者是谁? / What is the title of ~ book? 这本书名叫什么?

③[指谈话双方能体会到的人或事物]: Close ~ window, please. 请把窗关上。 / When will you go to ~ market? 你什么时候到市场去?

④[指独一无二的事物]: ~ sun 太阳 / ~ moon 月亮 / ~ earth 地球 / ~ world 世界 / ~ universe 宇宙 / ~ east (west) 东(西)方

⑤[用于表示自然界现象等的名词如 sky, sea, wind 等之前(特别当这些名词前不带形容词时)]: There was no cloud in ~ sky. 天空中没有云。 / *The* sea was calm. 海上风平浪静。 / *The* wind was blowing. 风在吹着。 [注意: sea, wind 等名词如有形容词修饰, 可用不定冠词, 如: a blue sky 蓝天 / a strong wind 劲风]

⑥[用于被限制性短语或从句修饰的名词前]: ~ cover of that book 那本书的封面 / ~ books on the shelf 书架上的书 / ~ main trend in the world today 当前世界的主要倾向 / ~ man you talked to 你跟他谈过话的那人

⑦[用来加强特指意义, 即表达"恰恰(是)"、"最适合的"、"最典型的"等意思(这种用法的 the 须强读, 印刷中常用斜体)]: Quinine is *the* medicine for malaria. 奎宁是治疟良药。 / This is *the* word to be used. 这是最恰当的字眼。

⑧[与表示计算单位的名词连用, 含"每", "每一"的意思(=a, per, each 等)]: This car does 10 kilome tres to ~ litre. 这汽车用一公升汽油能驶十公里。 / be paid by ~ hour (piece) 计时(件)取酬

⑨[代替所有格代词, 指已提到过的人的身体或衣着的一部分]: hit sb. in ~ face 打某人的脸 /

grasp sb. by ～ collar 抓住某人的衣领 / How's ～ arm today? 你的手臂今天好点了吗?

⑩[旧时用于病名前,现在除口语及俚语中在复数形式的名词前尚保留外,其余通常省略]: (～) gout 痛风 / (～) toothache 牙痛 / (～) measles 麻疹 / ～ creeps 毛骨悚然的感觉 / ～ fidgets 坐立不安 / ～ dumps 忧郁 / have ～ blues 闷闷不乐 / ～ horrors 惊恐 / ～ drink [俗]酒癖

⑪[用于乐器名称前]: play ～ piano 弹钢琴 / play ～ violin 拉小提琴[比较: 球类及游戏名称前不用冠词,如 play basketball (football, billiards, chess, cards)打篮球(踢足球,打台球,下棋,打牌)]

⑫[用于可数名词的单数前,统指类别]: The horse is a useful animal. 马是有用的动物。[注意: 在口语中通常用不带定冠词的名词复数形式: Horses are useful animals.]

⑬[用于表示发明物的单数名词前]: The compass was invented by the Chinese. 指南针是中国人发明的。

⑭[用于具体名词的单数形式前,指其属性、功能等,使具抽象性]: This colour is pleasant to ～ eye. 这颜色好看。/ He is at home in ～ saddle. 他精通骑术。/ Have you ～ nerve to do it? 你敢做这件事吗? / There is still much of ～ schoolboy in him. 他还带有很多学生气。

⑮[用于集合名词前,指一个整体]: ～ people 人民 / ～ public 公众

⑯[用于复数名词前,指全体,以别于个体]: ～ Chinese 中国人[比较: a (four) Chinese 一个(四个)中国人] / ～ Albanians 阿尔巴尼亚人 / ～ masses 群众

⑰[用于姓的复数前,指全家人或全家中的一些人]: The Wangs have moved into the newly built workers' residential area. 王家已搬进新建的工人住宅区。

⑱[用于河、运河、海、洋的名称前]: ～ Yangtse (River) 长江 / ～ Yellow River 黄河 / ～ Rhine 来因河 / ～ Suez (Canal) 苏伊士运河 / ～ East China Sea 东海 / ～ Pacific (Ocean) 太平洋

⑲[用于山脉名称或复数形式的地名前]: ～ Tien Shan 天山山脉 / ～ Himalayas 喜马拉雅山脉 / ～ Alps 阿尔卑斯山(脉) / ～ Philippines 菲律宾 / ～ Netherlands 荷兰 / ～ British Isles 不列颠群岛

⑳[用于某些国名、地名前]: ～ Argentine 阿根廷 / The Hague 海牙 / ～ Crimea 克里米亚 / ～ Sahara 撒哈拉(沙漠) / ～ Ukraine 乌克兰

㉑[人名或不用冠词的地名,常加定冠词时,常加定语修饰时]: ～ late Mr. Brown 已故的布朗先生 / ～ Venice of the East 东方的威尼斯

㉒[船只名称和旅馆、剧院、建筑物的名称前,常加定冠词]: at ～ Capital 在首都剧院

㉓[用于某些著作、报刊、乐曲的名称前]: The Times (英国)《泰晤士报》

[注意: a)两个或两个以上名词连用时(包括一些

短语),可不用冠词: Boy and girl came up to me together. 男孩和女孩一起走到我跟前。/ Both rider and horse fell. 人和马都跌倒在地。/ a musical piece for violin and piano 供小提琴和钢琴合奏的乐曲 / night and day 日日夜夜 / from head to foot 从头到脚

b)在一些惯用的短语中不用冠词: at home 在家 / in bed 在床上 / in question 讨论中的 / on foot 步行 / on purpose 故意 / go to bed 上床睡觉 / go to school 上学 (比较: go to the school 到学校去)

c)报刊、书籍的标题中,广告、商业文件中,电报、日记、注解、定义等中,常省略定冠词: (The) Conference Opens 会议召开了(用于报刊标题中) / Write for (～) free catalogue (免费)目录函索即寄(用于广告中) / see (～) next page 见下页(用于注解中)

d)职务名称、家人称呼、各餐名称前常不用冠词: He was editor of the local newspaper. 他当过本地报纸的编辑。/ Father (Mother, Uncle) has come. 爸爸(妈妈,叔叔)来了。/ Lunch is ready. 午饭准备好了。

e)街道名称前不用冠词: in Nanking Road 在南京路(注意: 街道若某地并以某地命名的道路有些要用定冠词,如英国通往 Dover 多佛的 ～ Dover Road)

f)基数词用在名词后起序数词作用时所构成的词组不用冠词: Lesson One 第一课 / World War II 第二次世界大战

g)由同一个可数名词构成两个并列词组时,定冠词用法如下: ～ first and ～ second chapter 第一和第二章 / ～ first and second chapters 第一和第二章]

㉔[用于形容词前,使成为表示抽象或具体事物的名词] / ～ true and ～ false 真与假 / The unexpected has happened. 意料不到的事发生了。

㉕[用于形容词、分词前,指一类人]: ～ old and ～ young 老年和青年 / ～ dead (全体)死者 [注意: 有时也指一类中的一个,如: ～ deceased (一个)死者 / ～ accused (一个)被告]

㉖[用于形容词、副词最高级前,有时也用于形容词比较级前]: The best way is to mobilize the masses first. 先去发动群众是最好的方法。/ ～ elder of the two brothers 两兄弟中年纪大的一个[注意: a)形容词最高级单独作表语时,不加定冠词: It is best to mobilize the masses first. 最好首先发动群众。b) most 作"非常"解时,不用定冠词: That story is most interesting. 那故事非常有趣。]

㉗[用于逢十的数词的复数形式前,指世纪中的特定年代或人的约略年岁]: in ～ seventies of the twentieth century 在二十世纪七十年代中 / a man somewhere in ～ fifties 一个五十多岁的人

II ad. ①[用于形容词、副词比较级前]: So much ～ better. 那就更好了。/ That will make it all ~ worse. 那反而会把它搞得更糟。 ②[~ ... ~ ...][用于形容词、副词比较级前]: *The* greater the danger ~ more must we drive ahead. 越是艰险越向前。/ ~ sooner ~ better 越快越好 ③[用于副词最高级前]: Among them, he works ~ hardest. 他们中间他工作最努力。

theatre, theater ['θiətə] *n.* ①戏院,剧场;电影院;(古希腊、罗马的)露天剧场;全体观众: go to the ~ 去看戏 ② [the ~] 剧,戏剧;戏剧文学: the modern ~ 现代戏剧 / the ~ of Bernard Shaw [总称]肖伯纳剧作 ③戏剧效果;表现手法: The play was good ~. 这戏有好的舞台效果。④ (阶梯式的)讲堂,教室;(科学方面的)示范室: an operating ~ 手术示范室 ⑤活动场所;(发生重要事件的)场所;【军】战区,战场: the ~ of war 战争领域;战区 / the ~ of operations 战区 ⑥剧团 ||*the living* ~ 舞台剧(与电影及电视相对而言) ||'~-,goer *n.* 经常看戏的人,爱看戏的人 / '~-,going *n.* 看戏 / '~-in-the-'round *n.* 表演场设在观众座席中央的剧院

theatre, theatre

theatrical [θi'ætrikəl] **I** *a.* ①剧场的;戏剧的: ~ performances 舞台演出 ②戏剧性的;演戏似的;夸张的: ~ gestures 戏剧性的姿势 **II** *n.* ①[复]戏剧演出(尤指业余性的) ②[复]舞台表演艺术 ③职业演员 ||~ism *n.* 舞台作风;夸耀作风 / ~ity [θi,ætri'kæliti] *n.* 戏剧性 / ~ly *ad.*

thee [ði:] *pron.* ①[古][thou 的宾格]你,汝 ②[古]你自己(=thyself) ③[公谊会教徒之间用作主格,并接第三人称动词]你: Thee speaks harshly. 你说话太粗。

theft [θeft] *n.* 偷窃;盗窃

their [ðeə; 弱(元音前) ðər] *pron.* ①[they 的所有格]他(她、它)们的 ②[泛指;用以代替不确定的单数先行词]他的,她的 (=his, her): anyone in ~ senses 凡有神智健全的人

theirs [ðeəz] *pron.* ①[物主代词]他(她)们的东西;他(她)们的家属(或有关的人): These tools are not ~. 这些工具不是他们的(东西)。/ *Theirs* is a big school. 他们的学校规模很大。/ It's a habit of ~. 这是他们的一个习惯。②[泛指;

用以代替不确定的单数先行词]他(她)的东西,他(她)的(=his, hers)

theism[1] ['θi:izəm] *n.* 有神论;一神论 ||**theist** *n.* 有神论者;一神论者

theism[2] ['θi:izəm] *n.* 茶(碱)中毒

them [强 ðem; 弱 ðəm] *pron.* [they 的宾格] ①[用作宾语]他们,她们;它们: I know both of ~. 他们(或她们)两人我都认识。/ Give ~ to me. 把它们给我。/ It was very kind of ~. 多谢他们。②[口][用作表语]他们,她们;它们(=they): That's ~. 就是他们。

theme [θi:m] *n.* ①(谈话、讨论、文章等的)题目;主题 ②学生的作文;作文题 ③【语】词干 ④【音】主题,主旋律 ⑤ =song ⑥【史】(东罗马帝国的)省 ||~ song ①主题歌 ②(表示某广播节目开始或完毕的)信号曲,信号调 ③(某人的)老套话(指常提到的主张、抱怨等)

then [ðen] **I** *ad.* ①(指过去)当时;(指将来)到那时: We shall have left school ~. 到那时我们将已毕业离校了。② 然后;接着;于是: We, ~, made this decision. 于是,我们做出了这个决定。③[常用于句首或句尾]那么: Then, let's begin. 那么,咱们就开始吧。/ Alright ~, you may go now. 那么好吧,你可以走啦。/ Do as you think fit, ~. 那么,你就看着办吧。④而且,另外;还有,再者: And ~ there are other things to be taken into account. 而且还有其它需要考虑的事情呢。/ Then, don't forget to write me on your arrival. 再者,到了那里不要忘记给我写信。⑤[与 now, sometimes 等连用](一会儿…)一会儿又…: Now the weather is fine, ~ nasty. 天气一会儿好,一会儿坏。**II** *a.* [用作定语]当时的: the ~ mayor 当时的市长 **III** *n.* [常用于前置词后]那时: by ~ 到那时 / from ~ on 从那时起 / since ~ 从那时以来 / till ~ 到那时为止 ||*and* ~ *some* 而且还远不止此;至少: That would need all his courage *and* ~ *some*. 那将至少需要他拿出全部勇气。/ *but* ~ 见 but[1] / (*every*) *now and* ~ 见 now / *now* ~ *now* / ~ *and there* (或 *there and* ~) 当时当地: We turned down their proposal ~ *and there*. 我们在当时当场就拒绝了他们的建议。/ *what* ~ (或 ~ *what*)(下一步)怎么办? 又怎么样呢: After you have finished this process, *what* ~ (或 ~ *what*)? 你做完这一步后,接下去怎么办?

thence [ðens] *ad.* [现罕用于口语] ①从那里起 ②从那时起(或以后) ③由此,因此: It ~ appears that .... 由此看来… / Thence a new trend results. 于是形成了一种新的倾向。 ||~'forth *ad.* 从那时起(或以后) / '~-'forward(s) *ad.* 从那时起(或以后);从那里起(或再往前)

theology [θi'ɔlədʒi] *n.* 神学

theorem ['θiərəm] *n.* ①定理 ②原理;原则 ||~atic [,θiərə'mætik] *a.*

theory ['θiəri] *n.* ①理论; 学理, 原理: integrate ~ with practice 理论联系实际 / Without practice there would be no ~. 没有实践就没有理论. / Your plan is good in ~, but does it work in practice? 你的计划在理论上是不错的, 但实行起来能行吗? ②学说; 论说; ~论 ③意见; 推测, 揣度: My ~ is that .... 我的意见是… ④分析: the ~ of games (商业、军事等方面) 从衡量利弊得失角度出发的形势分析

there [ðeə; 弱 ðe] **I** *ad.* ①在那里; 往那里: Have you ever been ~? 你到过那里吗? / I go ~ every year. 我每年到那里去. ②在那点上, 在那个方面: I disagree with you ~. 在那一点上我不同意你的意见. ③[用以引起注意、加强语气等; 除主语为人称代词外, 须主谓倒装]: There comes the bus. 公共汽车来了. / There you go again. 你又来这一套了. / There's a good boy! 真是个好孩子! / Turn to the left and ~ you are. 向左转弯就到了. ④[常读作 ðe][与动词 to be 连用, 表示"有"的意思]: There is contradiction in everything. 一切事物都包含矛盾. / Are ~ enough tools to go round? 工具够大家用吗? / There is no holding back the wheel of history. 历史车轮不可阻挡. / There being nobody else at hand, I had to do it by myself. 由于附近没有旁人, 我只得独自干了. ⑤[与 seem, appear 等动词连用]: There seems (to be) something wrong about it. 好象有点不大对头. / There appeared to be no better way. 看来没有更好的办法了. **II** *int.* [表示安慰、引起注意、加强语气、进行挑衅等]: There, ~, never mind. 好啦, 好啦, 不要紧的! / There, the work's done. 瞧, 事情做好啦. / There now! What did I tell you? 你看, 我怎么跟你说来着? / You ~! 喂! / I'm not sorry I said it, so ~. 我这么说并不感到后悔, 就是这样. (意指: 你敢怎么样?) **III** *n.* 那个地方: from ~ 从那里 / live somewhere near ~ 住在那地方附近 ‖*all* ~ 见 **all** / *Are you* ~? (打电话时用) 喂, 你听着吗? / *be in* ~ ... 坚持 (进行斗争等), 不懈地从事…: They *are in* ~ busily harvesting. 他们正在忙于收割. / *have been* ~ (*before*) [俚] 全都知道; 直接了解; 亲眼看到 / *over* ~ 在那里 (指较远处) / ~ *and back* 到那里再回来: We have time to go ~ *and back* before lunch. 我们到那里去一次, 回来吃午饭还来得及. / ~ *and then* (或 *then and* ~) 当时当地 / ~ *or thereabouts* (表示时间、数量等) 大约 / *You had him* ~. 这下你把他治住了.

thereabout(s) ['ðeərəbaut(s)] *ad.* ①在那附近: ②(表示数目、数量、时间、程度等) 大约, 左右, 上下: in two hours or ~ 两小时左右 / twenty or ~ 二十左右

thereafter [ðeər'ɑːftə] *ad.* ①[书面语] 此后, 以后 ②[古] 据此

thereby ['ðeə'bai] *ad.* ①因此, 由此, 从而: I gave him my advice; I hope he may profit ~. 我已给他劝告了, 希望他可以由此得到益处. ②[苏格兰] =thereabout(s) ‖*Thereby hangs a tale.* 其中大有文章.

therefore ['ðeəfɔː] *ad.* 因此, 所以: It rained; ~ the football match was postponed. 天下雨, 所以足球比赛延期了.

thereupon ['ðeərə'pɔn] *ad.* ①在其上; 关于那 ②随即; 因此

therm [θəːm] *n.* 【物】①克卡 (公制中的热单位, 即小卡) ②千卡 (公制中的热单位, 即大卡) ③一种煤气热量单位 (在英国等于 100,000 Btu, 在美国等于 1,000 千卡)

thermal ['θəːml] **I** *a.* ①热的, 热量的; 由热造成的: ~ conductivity 导热性; 导热系数 / a ~ unit 热量单位 / a ~ power station 火力发电站 ②温泉的: a ~ spring 温泉 / a ~ region 温泉区 **II** *n.* 上升暖气流 ‖~ly *ad.* ‖~ barrier 【空】热障 (=heat barrier)

thermometer [θə'mɔmitə] *n.* 温度计; 寒暑表: a clinical ~ 体温计 / a centigrade (或 Celsius) ~ 摄氏温度计 / a Fahrenheit ~ 华氏温度计 / a Reaumur ~ 列氏温度计

these [ðiːz] this 的复数

thesis ['θiːsis] ([复] theses ['θiːsiːz]) *n.* ①论题, 命题; 论点 ②论文; 毕业 (或学位) 论文; (学生的) 作文 ③ ['θesis] (古希腊、罗马诗韵中的) 扬音节; (现代诗韵中的) 抑音节 ④【音】强声部 ‖~ novel 主题小说 (提出并阐述某一鲜明主题的小说, 也称 tendentious novel)

thew [θjuː] *n.* [复] ①肌 (肉), 筋 (肉) ②筋力; 体力; 力量 ③[古] 精神 (或道德) 的素质 ‖~less *a.* [苏格兰] ①肌肉不发达的, 体力虚弱的 ②没有精神的, 无活力的; 懒惰的

they [ðei; 弱 ðe] *pron.* [主格] ①他们, 她们; 它们 ②人们: They say it's so. 据说是这样.

thick [θik] **I** *a.* ①厚的; 粗的; 粗壮的; 【印】粗体的: a ~ book 一本厚书 / a plank four inches ~ 四吋厚的木板 / a ~ rod 粗竿 / a ~ man 身材粗壮的人 / a ~ type 粗体 (铅) 字 / ~ print 粗体字 ②密; 茂密的; 密集的; 密布的, 充满的; 闷塞的: a ~ head of hair 一头浓密的头发 / ~ woods 密林 / trees ~ with leaves 叶子茂密的树 / The crowd grew ~er. 人群愈来愈密集. / The air was ~ with the fumes of gunpowder. 空中硝烟弥漫. ③浓; 粘稠的: ~ soup 浓汤 / a fog ~ syrup 粘稠的糖浆 ④混浊的; 阴霾的, 多雾的; 看不清的: a ~ puddle 混浊的泥潭 / ~ weather 阴霾天气 / ~ darkness 漆黑 ⑤口齿不清的; (声音) 浊的, 沙哑的; (口音) 重的: ~ speech 口齿不清的讲话 / speak with a ~ local accent 说话带着很重的乡土音 ⑥理解力差的; 愚钝的, 笨的 ⑦[口] 亲密的; 友好的: be ~ with sb. 与某人非常亲密 ⑧非常的, 过分的: lay one's flattery on ~ 拼命恭维 / ~ silence 沉寂 **II** *n.*

①最厚（或密、浓）的部分；最激烈处；（人群等）最密集处；最活跃的部分: the ~ of the forest 森林的最密处 / the ~ of winter 隆冬 / go into the ~ of the struggle 深入斗争 ②[口]笨蛋 **III** *ad.* 厚；密；浓；强烈地: The snow is falling ~. 雪下得正密。/ My heart beats ~. 我的心跳得厉害。‖**a bit ~**（或 **rather ~** 或 **a little too ~**）[口]太过分，过度: I think it *a bit* ~ to do it that way. 我认为那样的做法太过分了。/ **(as) ~ as hail** 密如雨点；纷至沓来 / **(as) ~ as thieves** 亲密无间 / **give sb. a ~ ear** 把某人的耳朵打肿 / **in the ~ of ...** 在…的最激烈的时刻，在…的最激烈处；处在…的中心 / **in the ~ of battle** 在酣战中 / **lay it on ~** [俚]拚命恭维；过分责备 / **~ and fast** 大量而急速地；频频、密集地 / **through ~ and thin** 不顾艰难险阻，在任何情况下: We'll stand by you *through ~ and thin*. 在任何艰难情况下我们将一直支持你们。‖**~ish** *a.* 相当厚（或粗、密、浓等）的 / **~ly** *ad.* ‖**'~-and-'thin** *a.* 不顾艰难险阻的；忠贞不渝的: ~-*and-thin* supporters 坚决的支持者，共患难的支持者 / **'~head** *n.* 傻瓜 / **'~headed** *a.* 笨的 / **'~set** *a.* ①稠密的，密植的: a ~*set* wood 密林 / a ~*set* hedge 紧密的篱笆 ②体格结实的, *n.* ① 紧密的篱笆 ②结实的粗斜纹布 / **'~-'skinned** *a.* 厚皮的；感觉迟钝的；不知羞耻的 / **'~-'skulled, '~-'witted** *a.* 迟钝的，笨的

thicken ['θikən] **❶** *vt.* ①使变厚（或粗、密、浓）；使更厚（或更粗、更密、更浓）②加强；加深: All this may help to ~ other proofs. 这一切可以加强其他的证据。③使（话等）讲不清晰，使模糊 **❷** *vi.* ① 变厚（或粗、密、浓）: The mist is ~*ing*. 雾变浓了。②变得不清晰；(天气)变得阴暗 ③变复杂: The plot ~s. 情节变复杂了。‖**~er** *n.* 增稠器；增稠剂 / **~ing** *n.* ① 增厚（或粗、密、浓）；稠化；增稠过程，稠化过程 ② 增稠剂 ③ 被加厚（或加粗）的东西（或部分）

thicket ['θikit] *n.* ①灌木丛 ②丛状物，密集的东西 ③[植]植丛，丛薄

thickness ['θiknis] *n.* ①厚(度)；粗; length, width, and ~ 长、阔、厚 ②密(度)，稠密；浓(度)，粘稠: the relative ~ of population in an area 一个地区的人口相对密度 ③混浊；多雾，多烟 ④迟钝，笨 ⑤最厚（或粗、密、浓等）处 ⑥(一)层: two ~*es* of cardboard 两层纸板

thief [θi:f] ([复] thieves [θi:vz]) *n.* ①窃贼，小偷；偷窃犯: the trick of a ~ crying "Stop ~" 贼喊捉贼的伎俩 / *thieves*' Latin 盗贼的黑话 ②(使蜡烛外淌的)烛芯突出部分 ‖**Set a ~ to catch a ~.** [谚]以贼捉贼。（或: 以毒攻毒。）

thigh [θai] *n.* ①股，大腿 ②[动](昆虫的)股节 ‖**smite hip and ~** 见 **hip**[1] ‖**'~bone** *n.* 股骨

thimble ['θimbl] *n.* ①(缝纫用的)顶针，针箍;嵌环 ②[机]套筒;套管 / ~ coupling 套筒联轴节

thimbleful ['θimbl,ful] *n.* (酒等的)极少量；些微: a ~ of brandy 极少量的白兰地酒 / a ~ of

insight 一点儿洞察力

thin [θin] **I** (thinner, thinnest) *a.* ① 薄的；细的；瘦的；[印]细体的: ~ ice 薄冰 / ~ thread 细线 / I want some *thinner* paper. 我要薄一点的纸。/ ~ fingers 纤细的手指 / She's getting ~. 她瘦下来了。/ You look rather ~ after illness. 你病后显得瘦多了。② 稀薄的，淡薄的；淡的；弱的: ~ air 稀薄的空气 / ~ gruel 薄粥 / ~ green 淡(或浅)绿 / ~ wine 淡酒 / a ~ voice (light) 微弱的嗓音(光) ③ 稀少的；稀疏的；缺乏的: ~ population 稀少的人口 / ~ hair 稀疏的头发 / a ~ house (指戏院演出)观众稀少的一场 / a ~ attendance at the meeting 不多的到会人数 / a ~ market 交易不旺的市场 ④ 空洞的；缺乏重要成分的；浅薄的；显而易见的；易看破的: a ~ story 内容空洞的故事 / a ~ argument 难以使人信服的论据 / That's too ~. [口]那太明显了。/ a ~ excuse 勉强的借口 / a ~ disguise 易于察破的伪装 ⑤将要垮掉的；守不住的: His patience was wearing ~. 他将耐不住了。⑥[俚]不舒服的，不愉快的；[美俚]一钱没有的: have a ~ time 过得很不愉快 ⑦[摄](照片或底片)衬度弱的，不够浓的 **II** (thinner, thinnest) *ad.* [常用以构成复合词]薄；细；稀；疏；微 **III** *n.* 细小部分；稀薄部分 **IV** (thinned; thinning) **❶** *vt.* 使薄；使细；使瘦；使稀薄；使淡；使稀疏: ~ wine with water 用水冲淡酒 / ~ out the seedlings 间苗，拔除过多的苗 **❷** *vi.* 变薄；变细；变瘦；变稀薄；变淡；变稀疏: Toward the city limits the houses begin to ~ out. 靠近城市尽头的地方房屋渐渐稀少。/ The stream had *thinned* down to a mere trickle. 这条小河变成细流了。/ wait until the fog ~s 等候雾散 / At last the crowd thinned. 最后，人群散开了。‖**as ~ as a lath** 骨瘦如柴 / **as ~ as a wafer** 极薄 / **spread oneself ~** 试图同时干太多的工作 / **through thick and ~** 见 **thick** ‖**~ly** *ad.* / **~ness** *n.* ‖**'~-clad** *a.* 穿得单薄的, *n.* 赛跑运动员 / **'~-'skinned** *a.* 脸皮薄的；(对批评等)敏感的；易怒的

thine [ðain] *pron.* [古] ①[物主代词]你的东西；你的家属(或有关的人) ②[thou 的所有格, 用在以元音或 h 开始的词前]你的: ~ eyes 你的眼睛 / ~ heart 你的心

thing[1] [θiŋ] *n.* ①物，东西；事物: What's the ~ in your right hand? 你右手拿的是什么东西? / living ~*s* 有生命的东西 / spiritual ~*s* 精神方面的事物 / every ~ in the universe 宇宙间的每一事物 ②[复](个人的)所有物；用品，用具；财产: Have you packed your ~*s* for the camping trip? 你把你野营时要用的东西打好包没有? / tea ~*s* 茶具 / ~*s* personal [律]动产 ③事，事情，事件: have a lot of ~*s* to do 有许多事要做 / take ~*s* too seriously 把事情看得太严重 / That fire was a terrible ~. 那场火灾是一个可怕的事件。④局面；情况；消息；[复]形势: look at this

~ another way 从另一角度看这局面 / How are ~s going at your school? 你们学校情况如何? / cannot get a ~ out of sb. 从某人那里弄不到一点消息 / Things are getting better. 形势(或情况)越来越好。⑤事业; 行为; 成就, 成果: accomplish great ~s 完成大事业 / do good ~s for the people 为人民做好事 ⑥举动, 行动; (努力的)目标: What's the next ~ to do? 下一步做什么? / The ~ now is to devise a better method. 现在要做的就是设计出一个更好的方法。/ put first ~s first 最重要的事最先做 ⑦题目, 主题: speak of many ~s 讲了好几个问题 / There is another ~ I want to ask you about. 我还有一件事要问你。⑧细节; 要点: check every little ~ 检查每一细微处 / Not a ~ is to be overlooked. 不可忽视每一个细节。⑨衣服: Wait a moment. Let me put on my ~s. 等一等, 让我把衣服穿上。/ have not a ~ to wear 没有衣服穿 ⑩家伙, 东西(指人或动物, 带有怜悯、爱或轻蔑等感情色彩): a poor little ~ 可怜的小家伙 / an old ~ 老朋友; 老家伙 / You selfish ~! 你这个自私鬼! ⑪[the ~]最适合的东西(或样式、状况等): That's not at all the ~ to do. 那样做很不恰当。/ These two books are just the ~ for me. 这两本书正合我的需要。/ the latest ~ in transistor radios 最新式的晶体管收音机 ⑫[复][后接形容词]…样的事物; 文物: ~s artistic 艺术品 / a close ~ [口]侥幸的脱险 / a general (或 usual) ~ 惯例 / all ~s considered 见 consider / among other ~s 除了别的以外(还): He, among other ~s, talked about the excellent situation at home and abroad. 除了旁的一些话, 他还谈到国内外大好形势。/ a near ~ 极险的事, 死里逃生 / an understood ~ 已经商妥的事; 心照不宣的事 / as ~s are (或 stand) 照目前情况, 在目前形势下 / a ~ of naught 无价值的东西, 无用之物 / be up to a ~ or two =know a ~ or two / come (或 amount) to the same ~ 仍旧一样, 结果相同 / do one's (own) ~ 以自己独特的方式(或专长)表现自己的个性 / do the handsome ~ by 宽厚地对待 / dumb ~s 牲畜 / feel (look) not quite (或 not at all) the ~ 感到(看上去)身体不适 / for one ~ 首先; 一则, 举个例说(表示作为其中一点理由): I can't go. For one ~, I've no time. 我不能去。理由之一是我没有时间。/ for one ~ ...; for another ... 首先...; 再者... For one ~, I have seen the film; for another I have an important meeting to attend tonight. 一则我已看过这部影片, 二则今晚我有一个重要会议。/ have a ~ about [口]对…有一种病态的惧怕 / It is a good ~ that .... …是好事情(或好买卖、妙语、好吃的东西): / know a ~ or two 明白事理; 很有经验, 精明能干 / let ~s go hang [口]不去管它, 对事情不关心 / let ~s

slide (或 rip) 让它去; 听其自然 / make a good ~ of 从…中获得很大好处(或很多利润) / make ~s warm for sb. 使某人为难; 惩罚某人 / of all ~s 首要, 第一 / one of those ~s 不可避免的事; 无可挽回的事 / other ~s being equal 在其他各点都相同的条件下 / pretty much the same ~ 差不多一样 / put ~s straight 整顿局面 / quite the ~ 很时髦 / see ~s [俚]产生幻觉: Oh, you're seeing ~s. 啊, 你在见鬼了。/ smooth ~s (虚伪的) 恭维话 / soft ~ [俚]既轻松而薪俸又高的工作 / sure ~ 确实(性); 当然, 一定: A: Are you coming? B: Sure ~! 甲: 你来吗? 乙: 当然来! / take one ~ with another 考虑各种情况 / tell sb. a ~ or two 教训教训某人 / (the) first ~ 立即; 作为第一件要做的事: I'll do it first ~ in the morning. 早上我将首先来做这件事。/ the ~ is 问题是: The ~ is, can we finish the work in time? 问题是, 我们能不能及时完成这工作? / Things are in good train. 事情很顺利。/ Well, of all ~s! 哼, 竟然如此! (表示惊讶、愤怒等) / whoop ~s up 见 whoop ‖~ness n. 物体属性(或状态); 客观现实 ‖,~-in-it'self ([复] ~s-in-themselves) n. 【哲】自在之物, 物自体

thing[2] [θiŋ] n. (斯堪的纳维亚各国的)立法(或司法)机构

think [θiŋk] I (thought [θɔːt]) ❶ vt. ①想, 思索: I was ~ing (to myself) how strange it was. 我(自个儿)在想那件事多么奇怪。②想出; 想起: I can't ~ how you did it (what you are driving at). 我想不出你怎样做这事的(你是什么意思)。/ He thought his way out of the dilemma. 他动脑筋想办法, 摆脱了困境。/ I did not ~ to ask him what to buy. 我没有想起问一问他要买什么。③使想; 想得: ~ oneself silly 想得傻了 / ~ oneself into a dilemma 想得无所适从 ④想要, 打算; 考虑后决定…: He thought to set off early. 他原来打算早点动身。/ I ~ I'll try. 我想试一试。/ ~ what to do next 考虑下一步做什么 ⑤认为; 以为: I ~ (that) he must have arrived there by now. 我想他现在一定已经到达那里了。/ Do you ~ it possible to finish the work this week? 你认为有可能在本周内完成这项工作吗? / His suggestion was thought (to be) valuable. 他的建议被认为很宝贵。⑥料想; 揣测, 猜想; 想象: I never thought to see you here! 我真想不到会在这儿见到你! / You can't ~ how magnificent the scene was. 你想象不出那场面是多么雄伟。/ I thought to find him home. 我原来猜想他会在家的。/ Who would have thought that such a serious illness could be cured. 谁会想到如此重的病能被治好? ⑦感到: ~ no harm in doing sth. 感到做某事没有害处 / ~ shame to be so careless 因这样粗枝大叶而感到惭愧 ❷ vi. ①想, 思考: Let me ~

a moment. 让我想一想。/ Please ~ more (again). 请多(再)想想。/ *Think before you act.* 考虑后再行动。/ learn to ~ 学会思考 / ~ in English 用英语思维 ②认为;料想: I don't ~ so (或 I ~ not). 我不认为如此。/ I'm not sure, but I rather ~ so. 我没有什么把握,但认为很可能如此。/ Do as you ~ best. 你认为怎样好就怎么去做。/ The plan may prove better than you ~. 这个计划可能比你料想的要好。/ I *thought* as much. 果然不出我所料。II *n.* 想;想法: You had better have another ~. 你最好再想一想。/ make up one's mind in a deep hard ~ 经过苦思作出决心 / Let's exchange ~s. 咱们来交换交换想法吧。III *a.* 思想(方面)的;供思考的: a ~ film 引人思索的影片 ‖~ *about* ①考虑: ~ *about* a plan 考虑一项计划 ②回想: ~ *aloud* (或 ~ *out loud*) 边想边说出声;自言自语 / ~ *better of* ①对…有更高的评价: I ~ much *better of* him after I have found out his true motive. 我发觉他的真实动机后,对他的评价高得多了。②重新考虑后决定不做(或放弃): I hope you'll ~ *better of* this matter and change your mind. 我希望你再考虑一下这事情,改变你的打算。/ ~ *fit* (或 *good*) (to do sth.) 甘愿(做某事),宁愿(做某事)(尤指做蠢事、无理的事等) / ~ *long* [英方] 渴望,切望 (*for, after*) / ~ *of* ①考虑;关心: What are you ~*ing of*? 你在想些什么? / have many things to ~ *of* 有许多事要考虑 / always ~ *of* other people first 总是先想到别人 ②想起;记得: I *thought of* my hometown when I saw the beautiful scenery. 看见这美丽的景色,我想起了我的家乡。/ Who first *thought of* that idea? 谁先想到那个主意? / I can't ~ *of* his name right now. 我一下子记不起他的名字。③想一想;想象: *Think of* the past and you'll see what a happy life we are leading now. 只要想一想过去,你就会感到我们现在的生活是多么幸福。/ To ~ *of* his having heard nothing of the news! 想想看,他对这消息竟一无所闻! ④[常与 could, should, never 连用]有…的看法(或想法): He *would never* ~ *of* giving up this project. 他是决不会想到放弃这一计划的。⑤[常与副词或副词短语连用]对…有某种看法: What do you ~ *of* it? 你认为这事怎么样? / ~ well (ill) *of* 认为…好(不好) / ~ much (little) *of* 认为…很不错(没有什么了不起) / ~ no end (或 no small beer) *of* 极端看重… ⑥把…看作 (*as*);考虑…是否适合…(*for*): ~ *of* oneself *as* a common soldier 把自己看作普通一兵 / ~ *of* sb. *for* group leader 考虑某人是否适于担任组长 / ~ *on* 思考,思量 / ~ *out* ①彻底地想一想 ②(通过思维)设计出,发现,解决: ~ *out* a plan 想出一个计划 / ~ *over* 仔细考虑: Let me ~ it *over*. 让我(好好)想一想。/ ~ *through* 思考…直到得出结论(或解决办法) / ~ *twice* 重新考虑 / ~ *up* [口] 想

出;设计出,发明 ‖~**er** *n.* 思想家;思考者: a great ~*er* 伟大的思想家 / a superficial ~*er* 思想肤浅的人 ‖~ **columnist** [美]内幕新闻专栏作家 / ~ **piece** [美](带有分析和评论的)内幕新闻报道 / '~**-so** *n.* 未经证实的想法;得不到支持的意见 ‖~ **tank**, ~ **factory** 智囊班子,智囊机构(尤指配备电子计算机或其他复杂仪器的一群人)

third [θə:d] I *num.* ①第三(个): every ~ day 每隔两天 ②三分之一(的): one ~ of a ton 三分之一吨 / two ~s 三分之二 / the three ~s system (三方面各占三分之一的)三三制 II *n.* ①(时间或角度的)六十分之一秒 ②(汽车的)第三速率,第三档 ③【音】三度音程;三度和音;第三音 ④[复][律]归寡妇所有的亡夫遗产的三分之一 ⑤(月的)第三日 ‖~**ly** *ad.* 第三(列举条目等时用) ‖~ **base** [体](棒球)第三垒 / ~ **class** ①三等,三级;三等品;三等舱 ②[美]三类邮件(指书籍,广告信等) / '~**-'class** *a.* 三等的: a ~*-class* ticket 三等票 / ~*-class* matter 三类邮件 ②平庸的,低劣的 *ad.* 乘坐三等车(或舱): go ~*-class* 乘三等车(或舱)去 / ~ **degree** [美](警察的)逼供,拷问;疲劳讯问 / ~ **dimension** ①第三维,第三度(指厚度或深度) ②使栩栩如生的因素,产生真实感的素质 / ~ **ear** [美俚]告密者 / ~ **estate** 平民阶级(区别于僧侣、贵族而言) / ~ **floor** [英]四楼;[美]三楼 / ~ **force** 第三种力量 / ~ **house** [美](国会的)第三院,院外活动集团 / ~ **party** 第三者,第三方;(两党制政体的)第三党 / ~ **person** 【语】第三人称 / ~ **rail** ①电动机车的输电轨 ②[美俚]烈酒 ③[美俚]扒手 / '~**-'rate** *a.* 三等的;三流的;低劣的,下等的 / '~**-'rater** *n.* 低劣的人(或物) / ~ **reading** 议案的第三次(表决前最后一次)宣读 / **Third Republic** 【史】法兰西第三共和国 (1870—1940) / ~ **sex** [总称]搞同性关系的人 / ~ **stor(e)y** =~ floor / ~ **ventricle** 【解】第三脑室 / **Third World** 第三世界

thirst [θə:st] I *n.* ①渴,口渴: quench (或 slake, relieve) one's ~ 止渴 ②渴望,热望: a ~ for knowledge 对知识的渴望 ③[口]酒瘾 II *vi.* ①感到口渴 ②渴望,热望: ~ to learn 渴望学习 / ~ for (或 after) knowledge 渴望求知 ‖~**less** *a.* 不渴的

thirsty ['θə:sti] *a.* ①渴的: I am (或 feel) ~. 我感到口渴。②爱喝酒的: a ~ soul 酒徒 ③渴望的: be ~ for knowledge 渴望知识 ④(土地等)干燥的;干旱的;有高度吸收性的: a ~ land 干旱的土地 / a ~ towel 吸水性强的毛巾 ⑤致渴的: ~ work (food) 使人口渴的工作(食物) ‖ **thirstily** *ad.* / **thirstiness** *n.*

thirteen ['θə:'ti:n] I *num.* 十三;十三个(人或物);第十三(卷、章、页等)(用例参看 **eight**) II *n.* ①十三岁 ②十三点钟(即下午一点) ‖the ~ **superstition** (西方)以十三为不吉利的迷信 ‖~**th** *num.* 第十三(个) ②十三分之一(的) *n.* (月的)第十三日

thirtieth ['θə:tiiθ] **I** *num.* ①第三十(个) ②三十分之一(的) **II** *n.* (月的)第三十日

thirty ['θə:ti] **I** *num.* 三十;三十个(人或物);第三十(卷、章、页等)(用例参看 **eight**) **II** *n.* ①[复](世纪的)三十年代: during the *thirties* of the twentieth century 在二十世纪三十年代 ②三十岁; [复]三十到三十九岁的时期: a man in his *thirties* 三十多岁的男子 ③[美](新闻通讯中使用的符号)完、终;结束 ④(网球)得两分时的称呼 ⑤口径为 30 的机枪(常写作 .30) ‖**~ish** *a.* 近三十岁的;三十岁左右的 ‖**~-twomo** ['θə:ti'tu:mou] *n.* 三十二开(指纸张、书页);三十二开本(常写作 32 mo)

·this [ðis] **I** *a.* [后接复数名词时用 these] ①这: ~ house 这幢房子 / Who is ~ man? 这个人是谁? / Are *these* books yours? 这些书是你的吗? / ~ bicycle of mine (yours, his) 我的(你的,他的)这辆自行车 / Come ~ way please. 请这边走。 / ~ time 这时候;这一次 / at ~ time tomorrow 在明天这个时候 ②今,本: ~ morning (evening) 今晨(晚) / ~ week (month) 本周(月) / I shall be in Peking ~ day week (month). 下星期(月)的今天我将在北京了。 ③[与表示时间的词组连用]刚过去的;即将来到的: Supper has been waiting ~ half an hour. 晚饭已经准备好半个小时了。 / We have been discussing the plan ~ (或 *these*) ten days. 近十天来我们都在讨论这计划。 ④某,(方向等)一定的: run ~ way and that 东奔西跑 **II** ([复] these [ði:z]) *pron.*①这,这个: *This* is Mr.Brown speaking.(打电话用语)我是布朗。 / What is all ~ about? 这是怎么回事? / Are *these* your books? 这些是你的书吗? / Do it like ~. 照这样做。②以下(或上)所述: The reason is ~. 理由如下。 / *This* is the news of the past twenty-four hours. 以下是过去二十四小时的新闻。 / There is ~ to be noted about it. 关于此事还有以下这点要注意。③这时;这里: before ~ 在这以前 / by ~ 到这时 / on (或 upon) ~ 于是 / Get out of ~! 滚出去! ④后者(指上文已提到的两点中的后一点,其前一点用 that 表示): Of the two possibilities, ~ is more likely than that. 两个可能中,后者比前者更可能。 **III** *ad.* 达到这样的程度,这样地,这么: They didn't expect to wait ~ long. 他们没有料到要等这么久。 / Can you give me ~ much? 你能给我这么些吗? / I know ~ much, that he will come sometime next week. 我所知道的只是他在下星期里要到达。 ‖**at ~** =with ~ / **for all ~** 尽管如此 / **these days** 见 **day** / **~ and that** 又是这个…又是那个;各种各样的(东西): He went to ~ place *and that* (或 ~ and that place). 他到处奔走。 / put ~ *and that* together 把各种事实凑合起来 / **many a day** 见 **day** / **~**, that (或 **or**) **the other** 形形色色,诸如此类: talk about ~, that, and the other 谈论种种事情 / ~, that, or

the other business 种种事务 / **with ~** 说完这个(就);这样说着(就): With ~, he went out. 他说完就走出去了。

thistle ['θisl] *n.* 蓟;蓟属植物 ‖*grasp the* *~ firmly* 毅然处理困难局面 ‖**thistly** *a.* 多蓟的;像蓟一般的;有刺的;刺人的 ‖'**~down** *n.* 蓟花的冠毛: as light as ~*down* 轻如飞絮,极轻 / **~finch** 金翅雀

thither ['ðiðə] **I** *ad.* 那里;向那里;到那里 **II** *a.* 那边的;在远处的,更遥远的: the ~ bank of the river 河对岸 ‖*hither and* ~ 到处;向各处;忽此忽彼 / **on the ~ side of** 见 **side** / **~ward(s)** *ad.* =thither (*ad.*)

thong [θɔŋ] **I** *n.* 皮带,皮条;皮鞭,鞭梢 **II** *vt.* 给…装上皮带;用皮带捆;用皮鞭打

thorax ['θɔ:ræks] ([复] thoraxes 或 thoraces ['θɔ:rəsi:z]) *n.* ①【解】胸,胸郭;胸腔 ②【动】胸,胸部(昆虫体三部分的中间部分)

thorn [θɔ:n] *n.* ①刺,棘 ②荆棘,蒺藜 ③使人生气(或苦恼)的事物 ④【动】壳针 ‖*a ~ in sb.'s flesh* (或 *side*) 不断使某人生气(或苦恼)的事物(或人);某人的肉中刺(或眼中钉) / **be** (或 **sit**) **on ~s** 如坐针毡;焦虑不安 ‖**~less** *a.* 无刺的 / **~like** *a.* 象刺一样的

thorny ['θɔ:ni] *a.* ①多刺的;有棘刺的;刺一般的 ②棘手的;多障碍的,多困难的;引起争论的: tread a ~ path 走艰险的道路 / a ~ problem 难题

thorough ['θʌrə] **I** *a.* ①彻底的: a ~ investigation 彻底的调查 / give the room a ~ cleaning 把房间彻底打扫一下 ②详尽的;透彻的;全面掌握的;完善的: a ~ description 详尽的描写(或说明) / have a ~ understanding of sth. 对某事物有透彻的了解 / a ~ musician 熟练的音乐家 ③非常精确的,(对细节)不厌其烦的: be ~ in one's work 工作毫不马虎 / a ~ person 一丝不苟的人 ④彻头彻尾的,绝对的: a ~ rascal 彻头彻尾的坏蛋 **II** *n.* [常作 T-]彻底的专横的政策(如英王查理一世时期所施行的);彻底的行动 ‖**~ly** *ad.* / **~ness** *n.* ‖**~ bass** 【音】通奏音;通奏低音记谱法;(泛指)和音作品 / **~ brace** 勒在马车车身下起弹簧作用的皮带 / '**~fare** *n.* 通道;通衢,大道;通行: No ~*fare*! 禁止通行! / '**~,going** *a.* 彻底的,十足的: a ~*going* materialist 彻底的唯物主义者 / in a ~*going* way 彻底地 / '**~-paced** *a.* ①(原指马的步伐)受过完善训练的 ②彻底的,完全的 / '**~pin** *n.* (马的)跗关节肿

thoroughbred ['θʌrə-bred] **I** *a.* ①受过严格训练的;有良好教养的 ②(马、犬等)良种的,纯种的;[T-](英国赛马)良种马的 ③优美的,有勇气的;第一流的 **II** *n.* ①良种动物;[T-]英国赛马用的良种马 ②受过严格训练的人;有良好教养的人;有勇气的人 ③第一流的车子

thou [ðau] **I** *pron.* [古]汝,尔,你 **II** *vt. & vi.* 用"汝"称呼(对方)

though [ðou] **I** *conj.* ① 虽然，尽管: Though the task was difficult (或 Difficult ~ the task was), they managed to accomplish it in time. 虽然任务艰巨，他们还是设法及时完成。/ The article is very important ~ (it is) short. 那篇文章虽短，但很重要。/ ~ he was a child (或 child ~ he was) 虽然他是个小孩 ②即使: He will never do such a thing ~ he (should) be forced to. 他即使被迫，也决不会做这样的事。③ [用于主句后，引接补充说明]可是，不过，然而: He will come back for supper, ~ you never know. 他要回来吃晚饭的，可是谁也说不定。**II** *ad.* 可是，不过，然而: I've a bit of a cold. It's nothing much, ~. 我有点感冒，不过并不严重。/ Make haste, ~; we haven't time to lose. 可是得赶快，我们时间很紧。/ That wasn't all, ~. 还不单是这样呢! ‖*as* ~ 好象，仿佛 / *even* ~ 即使，纵然 / *what* ~ 尽管…不为什么关系: What ~ the way is long? 路远又有什么关系呢?

thought[1] [θɔ:t] think 的过去式和过去分词

thought[2] [θɔ:t] *n.* ① 思想: the central ~ of this paragraph 这一段的中心思想 / a great and noble ~ 伟大崇高的思想 ②思维，思考; 推理能力;思想活动: be deep in ~ 在沉思 / after much ~ 经仔细考虑后/beyond ~ 想象不到 ④思潮;思想方式: modern scientific ~ 近代科学思潮 ④想法，意图;观念: present one's ~s clearly 清楚地表达自己的想法 / keep one's ~s to oneself 把想法闷在自己肚里 / Please let me have your ~s on the matter. 请告诉我你对此事的意见。/ have no ~ of doing that 没有打算做那事 ⑤关心，顾虑，挂念: He never gave a ~ to his own illness. 他从来不把自己的病放在心上。/ Don't waste your ~s on that matter. 你不必为那件事花费心思。/ You are much in my ~s. 我常常想念你。⑥ [a ~] 稍许，一点点，少量: Please be a ~ more careful. 请稍许仔仔细细。‖*A penny for your ~s!* 见 penny / *(as) quick as* ~ 极快地，一闪而过地 / *at first* ~ 乍一想 / *at the (bare)* ~ *of* 一想起…(就) / *on second* ~s 进一步考虑后 / *Perish the* ~! 死了心吧! / *Second* ~s *are best.* [谚]再思而后行。/ *take* ~ *for* 对…担心;对…挂念 / *think ...* ~s 具有…的想法 / *without a moment's* ~ 不加考虑地，立刻 ‖'~-*'out* a. 慎重考虑后产生的 / '~-*pro*,*voking* a. 令人深思的，发人深省的 / '~-,*reading* n.【心】测心术 / ~ *transference* 【心】思想传授 / '~*way* n. 思想方法

thoughtful ['θɔ:tful] *a.* ①沉思的，思考的: He was quiet and ~ for a while. 他静下来沉思了一会儿。/ ~ looks 沉思的表情 ②表达思想的;富有思想的;经认真推敲的: a ~ book 一本富有思想内容的书 ③体贴的;考虑周到的: It was very ~ *of* you to make all the necessary arrangements for us. 你们考虑得真周到，为我们作好了一切必要的安排。/ a ~ man 体贴别人的人 ‖~*ly* *ad.* / ~*ness* *n.*

thoughtless ['θɔ:tlis] *a.* ① 无思想的 ② 缺少考虑的，轻率的，粗心的: a ~ person 粗心大意的人 ③ 自私的，不顾及他人的 ④ 迟钝的，笨的 ‖~*ly* *ad.* / ~*ness* *n.*

thousand ['θauzənd] **I** *num.* 千;千个(人或物): a (或 one) ~ men 一千个人 / two ~ two hundred (and) twenty two units 两千两百二十二个单位 (hundred 后面的 and 在美国常略) / in the year of one ~ nine hundred (and) seventy-four (常略作 nineteen seventy-four) 在一九七四年 / several ~(s) of (或 several ~) visitors 几千个来访者 / some ~ books 一千本左右的书 / some ~s of books 几千本书 / ten ~ 一万 / a hundred ~ 十万 **II** *n.* ①一千个(人或物)一组 ②[复]许许多多，无数: ~s of times 几千遍，千遍万遍，无数次;千万倍 **III** *a.* 许许多多，无数的: a ~ times easier than 比…容易千万倍 / A ~ thanks for your kindness. 对你的好意万分感谢。‖*(a)* ~ *and one* 一千零一，许许多多: The Thousand and One Nights《一千零一夜》(旧译《天方夜谭》，古代阿拉伯的民间故事) / *in a* ~ *and one ways* 千方百计地 / *a* ~ *to one* 千对一，几乎绝对的 / *by the* ~(s) (或 *by* ~s) 数以千计，大批大批地 / *one in a* ~ 千中之一;难得的(美好的)人(或物) / *the upper ten* ~ 上流社会;贵族阶层 / ~s *upon* ~s 成千上万 ‖~-*fold* a. & ad. 千倍;千重 / ~*th* *num.* ①第一千(个) ②千分之一(的)

thrall [θrɔ:l] **I** *n.* ① 奴隶;奴仆，农奴: be ~ *to* one's passions 成为感情的俘虏;感情用事 ② 奴隶状态;奴役: in ~ 受奴役;处于奴隶状态 / in ~ *to* 被…束缚着 **II** *a.* [古]使成奴隶;迷惑，吸引住 **III** *a.* [古]被奴役的,被束缚的;变成奴隶的

thral(l)dom ['θrɔ:ldəm] *n.* 奴隶的身分;奴役;束缚: hold ... in ~ 使…受奴役;束缚…

thrash [θræʃ] **I ❶** *vt.* ①打(谷) ②(用棍、鞭等)痛打 ③打败: ~ the blue team 战胜蓝队 ④多次地做，反复地做;推敲，研讨: ~ the matter over without reaching a conclusion 对这件事进行了多次探讨而无结果 ⑤猛烈摆动，使颠簸: ~ one's arms 挥动手臂 ⑥ 使(船)迎风破浪前进 ❷ *vi.* ①打谷 ②(用棍、鞭等)打，击 ③猛烈摆动，颠簸;翻来复去: ~ in bed with fever 发烧在床上翻来覆去 ④(船)迎风破浪前进 **II** *n.* 打，击;(自由泳或仰泳中腿的)打水，拍水 ‖~ *out* 研讨解决;通过讨论获得: ~ *out* a problem 经过研究讨论解决问题 / ~ *out* a plan 经过研究讨论订出计划 / ~ *out* the rights and wrongs of the case 弄清案件的是非 ‖~*er* *n.* ①打谷者;打谷机，脱粒机 ②一种美洲长尾鸣禽

thrashing ['θræʃiŋ] *n.* ①打谷 ②鞭打，痛打 ‖~ *floor* 打谷场 / ~ *machine* 打谷机,脱粒机

thread [θred] **I** *n.* ①线: cotton (silk, flax) ~ 纱(丝,麻)线 / a reel of ~ 一团线,一卷线 / pass a

~ through the eye of a needle 把线穿过针眼 / a length (或 piece) of ~ 一段线，一根线 ②丝，丝状体: the ~s of a spider web 蛛网丝 ③细细的一条: a ~ of water (light) 细细的一条流水(光线) / a ~ of yellow colour 黄色的细条 / a ~ of hope 一线希望 ④螺纹 ⑤头绪,思路;贯穿着的东西: lose the ~ of one's discourse (argument) 讲话(争辩)时乱了头绪 / pick up (或 resume) the ~s 接着讲下去 / the ~ of life (命定的)生活历程,命数 ⑥细矿脉 **II ❶** *vt.* ①穿线于…;装胶片于…: ~ a needle 穿针 / ~ a camera 为照相机装胶片 ②穿(珍珠、小珠子等);把…穿成一串;使穿入: ~ a film 把胶片装入放映机(以待放映) ③通,通过;穿过: ~ a pipe with wire 用铅丝通烟斗 / ~ narrow alleys 穿过小巷 / ~ one's way through a crowd 从人群中挤过去 ④使交织: dark hair ~ed with silver 花白的头发 ⑤刻螺纹于… **❷** *vi.* ①通过;穿透过(through) ②(糖浆等)滴下成丝状 ‖*gather up the* ~*s* 综合分别处理的问题(或部分) / *hang by* (或 *depend on*) *a* ~ 千钧一发;岌岌可危;摇摇欲坠 / *have not a dry* ~ *on one* 浑身湿透 / ~ *and thrum* 玉石混杂地,好坏不分地 ‖**~less** *a.* 无线的;无螺纹的 / **~like** *a.* 线状的,象线一般的 ‖**~bare** *a.* ①(衣服等)绒毛磨光露出织纹的,穿旧的 ②衣着褴褛的 ③(笑话、说教等)俗套的,乏味的 / ~ **lace** 线织花边 / ~ **mark** (钞票纸中的)彩色丝纹 / **~-,needle** *n. & vi.* (做)穿针游戏(玩者相继从举起的双臂下通过);(跳)穿针游戏式舞蹈 / ~ **paper** ①裹线束的纸条 ②细长条的人(或物) / **~worm** *n.* 蛲虫

threat [θret] **I** *n.* 威胁,恐吓;造成威胁的事物;凶兆,坏兆头: a ~ against sb.'s life 对于某人生命的威胁 / relieve the ~ of flood 解除洪水的威胁 / There was a ~ of typhoon. 有刮台风的(坏)兆头。 **II** *vt. & vi.* [古] =threaten

threaten ['θretn] **❶** *vt.* ①威胁,恐吓,恫吓: ~ peace 威胁和平 / ~ to do sth. 威胁要做某事 / ~ sb. with death 用死来恐吓某人 ②预示…的凶兆;有…的危险: The dark clouds ~ed a big storm. 乌云预示暴风雨来临。/ It ~s to rain. 天象要下雨。 **❷** *vi.* ①威胁,恐吓,恫吓 ②似将发生,可能来临: If danger ~s, it is all the more important to keep an unmoved mind. 如果危险来临,思想更应坚定。 ‖**~ingly** *ad.*

three [θri:] **I** *num.* 三;三个(人或物);第三(卷、章、页等)(用例参看 **eight**) **II** *n.* ③ 3 字形溜冰花式 ②三个(人或物)一组 ③一组(或一系列)中的第三个 ④三岁 ⑤三点钟 ‖ *sheets in* (或 *to*) *the wind* 见 **sheet** / ~ *times* 三次三次呼: give sb. ~ *times* ~ 给某人反复三次三次呼 ‖**~fold** *a. & ad.* 三倍;三重 / **~some** ['θri:səm] *a.* 三人的,三人共事的 *n.* 三人游戏;三人一组 / **~-'bagger** *n.* (棒球中)击球后可顺利跑到三垒的一击 (=~-base hit) / **~-,colo(u)r** *a.* 三色的: ~-*colo(u)r process*【印】三色版(法)/

'**~-'cornered** *a.* ①三角的 ②由三个竞争者形成的 / **~-D, 3-D** [θri:'di:] *n. & a.* 三维(的);三度(的) / '**~-'decker** *n.* ①(旧时)上、中、下三层甲板都装有炮的军舰;三层甲板船 ②三片面包两层夹心的三明治 ③分成三册的书(尤指小说) ④(教堂内)有三层平台的布道坛 / '**~-di-'mensional** *a.* 三维的;三度的;立体的: ~*-dimensional printing* 立体印刷 / ~*-dimensional space* (立体)空间 / ~*-dimensional warfare* 立体战争(包括海、陆、空) ②有立体感的;[喻]真实的 / '**~-'handed** *a.* (游戏)三人玩的 / ~ **handkerchief** [美俚](引人挥泪不止的)伤感剧 / '**~-in-'one** *n.* 三结合 ③【宗】三位一体 / '**~-'legged** *a.* 三腿的: a ~*-legged stool* 三脚凳 / a ~*-legged race* 两人三腿赛跑(每组两人,把一人的左腿和另一人的右腿缚在一起) / '**~-'master** *n.* 三桅船 / '**~-mile limit** 沿岸三浬的领海界限 / **~pence** ['θrepəns] *n.* 三便士;三便士硬币 / **~penny** ['θrepəni] *a.* ①三便士的 ②微不足道的 / '**~-phase** *a.*【电】三相的: ~*-phase current* 三相电流 / '**~-piece** *a.* (衣服等)三件成一套的 / '**~-ply** *a.* 三层的;三重的;(线等)三股头的 *n.* 三夹板 / '**~-point landing** (飞机)三点着陆(主轮与尾轮同时着地) / '**~-,quarter** *n.* ①【摄】大半身像;展示脸的四分之三的像片 ②(橄榄球的)中后卫 (=three-quarter back) / '**~-'quarter(s)** *a.* 四分之三的;【摄】(拍到大腿部的)大半身的;(正面与侧面之间)展示脸的四分之三的 / '**~-'score** *n. & a.* 六十: ~*score and ten* 七十岁 / '**~-'square** *a.* (指锉刀)截面成等边三角形的 / '**~-'star** *a.* (美军官)三星级的: a ~*-star general* 中将 / '**~-'wheeler** *n.* (机动)三轮车;带边车的摩托车

thresh [θreʃ] **❶** *vt.* ①打(谷)多次地做,反复地做;推敲,研讨 ③反复打,反复击 **❷** *vi.* ①打谷 ②(用棍、鞭等)打,击 ③猛烈摆动,颠簸;翻来复去 ‖ ~ *out* = thrash out (见 **thrash**) ‖**~er** *n.* ①打谷者;打谷机,脱粒机 ②【动】长尾鲨

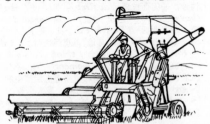

thresher

threshold ['θreʃhould] *n.* ①门槛;门: cross the ~ 跨过门槛 ②入门;开端,开始:on the ~ of a great change 在大变革的开始 ③界限,限度;终点;跑道的尽头 ④【物】阈;临界值;【心】阈限: photo-electric ~【物】光电阈 / ~ of consciousness【心】识阈

threw [θru:] throw 的过去式

thrice [θrais] *ad.* ①三次；三倍 ②非常，十分: a ~ empty phrase 十足的空谈 / ~-blessed (或 ~-happy, ~-favo(u)red) 极幸福的，非常幸运的

thrift [θrift] *n.* ①节俭，节约 ②健壮，(植物的)繁茂 ③[苏格兰] (有利可得的)职业；兴旺之道 ④【植】海石竹 ‖~ **shop** [美]旧货店(尤指为"慈善"目的的搜来旧货出售的商店)

thrill [θril] I *n.* ①一阵激动；一阵毛骨悚然的感觉: a ~ of joy 一阵欢乐 / a ~ of horror 一阵恐怖 / give sb. a ~ 使某人激动(或毛骨悚然) ②(电影、小说等的)刺激性，紧张感 ③颤动，抖动；【医】(心脏的)震颤音 ④[俚]惊险小说；恐怖小说 II ❶ *vt.* ①使激动，使毛骨悚然 ②使颤动，使抖动；使震颤: The earthquake ~ed the land. 地震使大地颤动。❷ *vi.* ① 激动；毛骨悚然: ~ with horror 恐怖得毛骨悚然 ②颤动,抖动;震颤: Her voice ~ed with joy. 她高兴得声音发抖了。 ③ (感情等)穿过, 闪过 (through, over, along): Fear ~ed through his veins. 他感到一阵害怕。 ‖~**er** *n.* ① 引起激动的人(或物)；使人毛骨悚然的人(或物) ②惊险小说(或电影等)；恐怖小说(或电影等)

thrive [θraiv] (过去式 throve [θrouv] 或 thrived, 过去分词 thriven ['θrivn] 或 thrived) *vi.* ①兴旺，繁荣；旺盛: Markets are thriving and prices are stable. 市场繁荣，物价稳定。②茁壮成长: Grafted saplings ~ best in hot weather. 嫁接的树苗在热天容易成活。‖**He that will ~ must rise at five.** [谚]五更起床，百事兴旺。

throat [θrout] I *n.* ①咽喉，喉咙；喉头；颈前: have a sore ~ 喉咙痛 / clear one's ~ (开始说话前)清清喉咙 ②咽喉状的部分；入口；窄路: the ~ of a chimney 烟囱口 ③嗓音，嗓门 ④ 网球拍的柄与拍之间的部分 II *vt.* ①用喉音说(或唱)；声音沙哑地说(或唱): ~ one's words huskily 嘎声地说话 ②开沟于，开槽于 ‖a clergyman's sore ~ 慢性喉炎 / a lump in the (或 one's) ~ 见 lump¹ / cram (或 ram, thrust) sth. down sb.'s ~ 把某人硬塞给某人吃下去；(填鸭式地)反复对某人灌输某事 / cut one another's ~s [口]相互残杀 / cut one's own ~ 割喉自杀 [口]自取灭亡 / cut the ~ of 消灭，扼杀 / fly at sb.'s ~ ①(狗等)扑向某人 ②攻击，袭击 / give sb. the lie in his ~ 指责某人撒谎 / have a bone in one's ~ 难于启齿 / jump down sb.'s ~ [口]突然粗暴地回答(或打断)某人，使某人哑口无言 / lie in one's ~ 撒大谎 / relaxed ~ 一种喉咙炎 / stick in sb.'s ~ ①使某人无法吞下 ②使某人难以接受 ③使某人说不出口；使某人耿耿于怀 / take by the ~ 掐住…的脖子；扼杀，掐死

throaty ['θrouti] *a.* ① (声音等)喉部发出的 ②喉音的；沙哑的 ‖**throatily** *ad.* / **throatiness** *n.*

throb [θrob] I (throbbed; throbbing) *vi.* ①(心脏、

脉搏等)跳动,悸动: The pulse throbbed steadily. 脉搏稳定地跳动。 / My heart throbbed with excitement. 我的心兴奋得直跳。② 抽动；(有规律地)颤动，震动: His finger throbbed from the cut. 他的手指因划破而阵阵抽痛。 / The engine is throbbing quietly. 发动机轻轻地颤动着。 II *n.* ① 跳动,悸动 ② 抽动；颤动,震动: a ~ of pain 抽痛

throe [θrou] I *n.* ①[复] (分娩时的)阵痛；临死的苦痛，垂死的挣扎 ②剧痛 ③[常用复]痛苦,苦闷；艰苦的奋斗: be in the ~s of ... 处在…的痛苦中 II *vi.* 受痛苦

throne [θroun] I *n.* ①宝座,御座 ②[the ~] 王位,帝位；王权,君权: come to (或 mount) the ~ 即王位 ③君王,皇上 ④[复]九级天使中的第三级 II *vt.* & *vi.* (使)登王位,(使)即位 ‖~**room** ①(设有御座的)觐见室 ②权势集中的地方

throng [θroŋ] I *n.* ① 群，人群: a ~ of people 一群人 ②群集；事务繁迫 ③ 众多，大量 II ❶ *vt.* 挤满，壅塞；挤拥: The street is ~ed with people. 街上挤满了人。❷ *vi.* 群集；蜂拥: ~ around sb. 拥在某人周围 / People ~ed towards the entrance. 人们拥向入口处。

throttle ['θrotl] I ❶ *vt.* ① 掐住…的脖子；掐死(某人)；使窒息 ② 扼杀；压制: ~ freedom 扼杀自由 / ~ trade 抑制贸易 ③【机】使节流，调节；使减速 ❷ *vi.* 闷住,窒息 ②【机】节流，减速 II *n.* ①【机】节流阀(或杆)，风门(杆) ②[无]节流圈，扼流圈 ③[军]喉咙,气管 ‖at full ~ 以最高速度，开足马力 ‖~**hold** *n.* 扼杀，压制 / ~ **valve** 【机】节气阀,节流阀,风门

through [θru:] I *prep.* ① (指空间)穿过，通过: The train passed ~ a tunnel. 列车穿过隧道。 / The river flows ~ the city from west to east. 那条河从西到东流过城市。 / drive ~ a red light (驾驶车辆时)穿红灯 ②(指时间)从头到尾经过;[美]直到(某一时刻): work ~ the night 通宵工作 / ~ the ages 古往今来 / sit ~ a lecture 听完一堂课 / from September ~ November [美]从九月到十一月(包括十一月在内) / I'll be there (from) Monday ~ Thursday. 星期一到星期四我都将在那里。③ (指方法、手段等)经由，以…: learn warfare ~ warfare 从战争学习战争 / build up our country ~ diligence and frugality 勤俭建国 ④(指原因、理由)由于，因为: mistakes made ~ carelessness 由于粗心大意而造成的错误 / That was all done ~ friendship 那样做完全是出于友爱。⑤(做)完…；(耗)尽…: get ~ a book 看完一本书 / go ~ a bottle of wine 喝完一瓶酒 / go ~ a fortune 耗尽财产 II *ad.* ①对穿；穿过；通过: pierce sth. ~ 穿透某物 / let sb. (pass) ~ 让某人通过 ②从头到尾；自始至终；到底: read a book ~ 把书从头到尾读一遍 / sleep the night ~ 一觉睡到天亮 / Let's hear him ~. 让我们听他讲完

吧。/ We'll see it ～. 我们会照料把这件事办好。③透，彻底: be wet ～ 浑身湿透 ④出来: break ～ 冲破;突围出来 III **a.** ① 对穿的;(道路等)可通行的: a ～ bolt 贯穿螺栓 / a ～ street 直通街道,干道 ②直达的;过境的: a ～ train 直达列车 / a ～ ticket 通票,联票 / ～ transport by land and water 水陆联运 / ～ traffic 过境交通;联运 ③穿了的,有洞的: The child's trousers are ～ at the knees. 孩子的裤子膝盖处破了。④(电话用语) [英]接通;[美]通话完毕,打完: You are ～. [英]你要的电话接通了。/ Are you ～? [美]你的电话打完了吗。‖ **all ～** 一直,从来就 / **be ～ (with)** ① 完成,做好: When will you be ～ with your work? 你的工作什么时候能做好? ②弃绝,嫌弃;完蛋: be ～ with sb. 与某人断绝关系 / be ～ with drinking (smoking) 不再喝酒(吸烟) / He is ～. 他完蛋了。/ **～ and ～** 彻头彻尾地;从头至尾地: look sb. ～ and ～ 仔细地打量某人 ②反复;穿透: read the book ～ and ～ 一遍又一遍地重读那本书 / The rain drenched him ～ and ～. 雨淋得他浑身湿透。/ **～ to** 直到 ‖**～put n.** ①生产量,生产能力,生产率 ②通过量 ③容许能力 / **～ stone【建】系石** / **'～way n.** ①直通街道 ②快速道路

throughout [θru(ː)'aut] **I prep.** 遍及;贯穿: people ～ China and the world 全中国和全世界人民 / ～ the day 整天 / ～ history 在整个历史上 / one's life 终生 **II ad.** 到处;始终;彻头彻尾: be painted green ～ 全部漆成绿色 / Prices remain stable ～. 物价始终保持稳定。/ The timber is rotten ～. 这块木料已整个腐烂。

throve [θrouv] thrive 的过去式

throw [θrou] **I** (threw [θruː], thrown [θroun]) **❶ vt.** ①投,掷,抛,扔: He threw the grenade 50 metres. 他把手榴弹投出五十米。/ Please ～ me the matches. 请把火柴扔给我。/ ～ rubbish into a dustbin 把垃圾扔进垃圾箱 / ～ a glance at 对…看一眼 / ～ one's eyes to the ground 眼睛朝下看地上 ②发射,射;喷射: ～ bullets 发射子弹 / ～ a satellite into space 把卫星射入空间 / water thrown by a hose 水龙带喷出的水 ③摔倒,摔下: ～ sb. to the ground 把某人摔倒在地 / be thrown by a horse 被马摔下来 ④匆匆穿上;匆匆脱下: ～ on (off) a coat 匆匆穿上(脱下)上衣 / ～ a shawl over one's shoulders 把披巾匆匆往肩上一披 ⑤伸(四肢),挺(胸),仰(首);挥(拳): ～ one's chest out 挺起胸膛 / ～ one's head back with laughter 仰首大笑 ⑥抛弃,放弃;摆脱: The fish tried to ～ the hook. 鱼挣扎着想要脱钩。⑦投射(光线、阴影等): ～ light on sth. 把光射在某物上;[喻]有助于理解某事物 ⑧施加(影响): ～ one's influence on sb.'s side 利用自己的影响帮助某人 ⑨产(崽、谷等);蜕(壳);脱落(马蹄铁) ⑩制(圆形陶坯) ⑪掷(骰子);掷出(某一点数) ⑫把…拈成线 ⑬

[美]故意输掉(比赛等) ⑭[俚]举行(宴会等) ⑮开关(离合器等);推动(离合器等的杠杆) **❷ vi.** 投,掷,抛,扔: He ～s well. 他能投掷得很远。**II n.** ①投掷;投掷的距离: make a nice ～ 投得好 / a record ～ with the hammer 创纪录的链球掷远 ②掷骰子;掷出的点数 ③冒险,孤注一掷 ④床罩 ⑤女用围巾;薄披巾 ⑥【地】落差,断层垂直位移 ⑦【机】行程;摆度 ⑧【体】(摔角中的)摔倒;摔倒对方的方法 ‖ **～ about** ① 到处扔;舞动(手脚等): ～ one's money about 乱花钱 / one's arms about 乱舞双臂 ② 转向航行 / **～ away** ①扔掉 ②(牌戏中)填(闲牌) ③浪费掉(金钱等);放过(机会等) ④轻轻带过(台词等) / **～ back** ①掷还;把…向后掷;使(头、肩等)向后: with shoulders thrown back 挺着胸 ②阻止,阻碍 ③使重新依靠(on, upon) ④反射(光线等) ⑤【生】呈返祖现象 / **～ by** 把…扔在一起;扔掉(无用之物) / **～ down** ① 扔下,扔掉: ～ down tools 放下工具;罢工 ②使倒下;推翻;摧毁: ～ oneself down 平躺下 ③[俚]拒绝 / **～ in** ①扔进;增添;免费添加: ～ in a word or two 插进一两句话 ② 把(排好的铅字等)拆开归还原处 ③使(离合器)接合;使(齿轮)啮合 ④入伙,参加合伙经营 / **～ off** ①扔开,扔掉: ～ off one's airs 放下架子 ②匆匆脱掉(衣服) ③摆脱掉;甩掉: cannot ～ off one's cold 感冒老是不好 / ～ off a pursuer 摆脱追踪者 ④发出,放出 ⑤轻易地作出,即席作出: ～ off a poem (tune) 即席作出一首诗(一支曲子) ⑥使形成偏差;使犯错误,使产生错觉: His composure threw the man off. 他的镇静使那人上了当。⑦开始出猎;开始讲话(或表演等) ⑧说坏话: ～ off on sb. 说某人的坏话 / **～ oneself at** 拼命讨好 / **～ oneself into** 投身于,积极从事: ～ oneself into work 投身工作 / **～ oneself on** (或 **upon**) 委身于,依赖 / **～ open** 见 **open** / **～ out** ①伸(四肢),挺(胸) ②抛出;扔掉(无用之物) ③说出: ～ out a suggestion 提出建议 ④撵走;解雇 ⑤不予考虑,拒绝(提议等) ⑥显示,展示: The signal has been thrown out. 信号已经发出。⑦把…甩在后面 ⑧发出,放出: The apple trees threw out a nice scent. 苹果树发出好闻的香味。⑨派出 ⑩使延伸;添建;建造(伸展或突出的建筑物): ～ out a wing 添建一翼 / ～ out a pier 建造凸式码头 ⑪打扰,打乱: The accident threw the whole schedule out. 事故打乱了整个日程安排。⑫使突出,使显眼 ⑬(棒球中)使出局 ⑭使(离合器)分离 / **～ over** ①抛弃(计划等);遗弃 ②拒绝,拒绝接受 / **～ together** ①匆匆拼凑成 ②使偶然相遇 / **～ up** ①抛起,举起;把…迅速地向上推: ～ up one's hands 举起双手;[喻]认输 / **～ up** one's eyes 惊呆 ②放弃(职位等) ③匆匆建造 ④呕出(食物);呕吐;产生;指出(人才): information thrown up by investigation 由调查所得来的情况 ⑥把…衬托出来,使显眼 ⑦唠唠叨叨地说(责备话) (to) / **within a stone's ～ (of)** 在(…的)附

近, (离…)一箭之远: live *within a stone's* ~ *of the factory* 住在工厂附近 ‖**-er** *n.* ①投掷者 ②发射器,喷射器: a flame ~er 火焰喷射器 ③制陶坯的工人 ④ 拈丝工 (=throwster) ‖**'~away** *n.* 免费散发的传单(或小册子、纸张等) / **'~back** *n.* ①【生】返祖现象;[喻]大倒退 ② =flashback / **'~-off** *n.* 开始出猎 / **'~-out** *n.* 被遗弃的人; 被抛弃的东西 / **'~-,over** *n.* 【无】① 转换, 转接, 换向 ②换速

thrum[1] [θrʌm] **I** *n.* ① 纱头, 线头; [复]【纺】了机回丝; 接头纱 ② 碎屑 ③【植】花丝; 花药 ④ [复]【海】绳屑 **II** (thrummed; thrumming) *vt.* ① 加缨于 ②【海】把绳屑嵌入(帆布等)(用以防擦或堵漏) ‖*not to care a* ~ 一点也不介意 / *thread and* ~ 见 thread ‖**thrummy** *a.* 用纱头做的; 表面粗糙的

thrum[2] [θrʌm] **I** (thrummed; thrumming) ❶ *vt.* ① 乱弹(弦乐器), 轻松随便地弹: ~ a guitar 漫弹吉他 / ~ a few preliminary chords 轻松随便地弹曲子开始的几个和弦 ② 用单调的声音朗诵 ③(用指头不断地)轻敲, 弹: ~ a table (用指头)轻敲桌子 ❷ *vi.* ① 乱弹, 随便弹 ②单调地作响 ③(用指头不断地)轻敲, 弹 **II** *n.* ① 乱弹; 轻敲 ②乱弹声, (指头)得得的敲击声

thrush[1] [θrʌʃ] *n.*【动】鸫属的鸟; 鸫

thrush[2] [θrʌʃ] *n.* ①【医】霉菌性口炎, 鹅口疮 ②(马的)蹄叉腐疽

thrust [θrʌst] **I** (thrust) ❶ *vt.* ①插; 塞; 刺; 戳: ~ a letter into one's pocket 把一封信塞入口袋 ②猛推; 冲: ~ a chair forward 把椅子猛然向前推去 / ~ one's fist into sb.'s face 用拳头猛击某人面部 / ~ one's way through a crowd 挤过人群 ③突然提出;不恰当地插进: He ~ in a question occasionally. 他不时地插嘴提问题。 ④将…强加于: ~ sth. upon sb. 将某事强加于某人 ⑤挺伸; 延伸: ~ one's head out of a window 将头伸出窗外 / The tree ~s its roots far and wide. 这棵树的根延伸得很远很广。❷ *vi.* ①插入; 刺; 戳: ~ at sb. with a knife 用刀戳某人 ②强行推进, 强行进入: ~ ashore 强行登岸 ③挺伸; 延伸: a rock ~ing fifty metres above water 伸出水面五十米的一块岩石 / New railroads are rapidly ~ing into the hilly regions. 新的铁路线迅速向山区延伸。**II** *n.* ①插; 刺; 戳: make a ~ with a sword 用剑猛刺 ②猛推; 挺伸 ③(辩论等时的)口头攻击; 讥刺: a shrewd (home) ~ 锐利(中要害)的一击 ④【机】推力,侧向压力 ⑤【矿】煤柱压裂 ⑥【地】冲断层, 逆断层 ‖~ *oneself in* 探听; 干涉 / ~ *sth. down sb.'s throat* 见 throat ‖**~er** *n.* ①向上钻营的人 ②推冲器, 起飞加速器 ‖**~ hoe** 推锄 / ~ **point** 【军】推力点 / ~ **stage** ③三面对着观众的舞台 ②向戏场内伸出很远的舞台前台

thud [θʌd] **I** *n.* 重击声, 砰的一声: fall with a ~ 砰地落下(或倒下) **II** (thudded; thudding) *vi.* 砰地落下; 发出重击声

thug [θʌg] *n.* 恶棍, 暴徒; 刺客, 凶手 ‖**thuggery** ['θʌgəri] *n.* 谋财害命 / **thuggish** *a.*

thumb [θʌm] **I** *n.* ① (大)拇指; (手套的)(大)拇指部分 ②【建】馒形饰 **II** *vt.* ①(用拇指)弄坏, 弄脏: The pages were badly ~ed. 书页翻得一塌糊涂。 ② 翻阅; 翻查: I shall prize the book and continue to ~ it. 我将珍视这本书并继续翻阅它。 / ~ a billfold 翻查票据夹 ③(用拇指)摸, 揿, 压 ④拙劣地弹(钢琴、乐曲等) ⑤(竖起拇指)向过路汽车作手势要求搭车: 搭车赶(路) ‖*be all* ~ 笨拙的, 笨手笨脚的 / *bite the* ~*s at* 对…嗤之以鼻, 蔑视… / *count one's* ~s [美俚] 消磨时间, 打发时间 / *rule of* ~ 见 rule / ~ *a lift* 见 lift / ~ *one's nose* (*at*) 见 nose / *Thumbs down!* 槽糕! (或: 差劲!) / *Thumbs up!* 刮刮叫! / ~ *through* 把(书等)一翻而过; 翻查: ~ *through* the records of 翻…的老帐 / *turn down the* ~ 表示反对; 贬低 / *turn up the* ~ 表示赞成; 称赞 / *twiddle* (或 *twirl*) *one's* ~s 抚弄大拇指; 闲得无聊 / *under sb.'s* ~ 在某人的支配下, 在某人的势力下 / *weigh the* ~ [美俚]骗秤头(指称东西时作弊、克扣分量) ‖**~ blue** *n.* (洗衣时上蓝用的)靛蓝 / **'~hole** *n.* 供塞入拇指的孔; 管乐器上的拇指孔 / ~ **index** 书边标目 / **,index** *vt.* 给(词典等)挖制书边标目 / ~ **latch** (门窗的)插销 / **'~mark** *n.* (留在书页上的)拇指痕,手垢 / **'~nail** *n.* ①拇指甲 ②略图; 短文 *a.* 拇指甲大小的; 小型的; 简略的: a ~nail sketch 简略的速写(或特写) / ~ **pin** 图钉, 揿钉 / **'~-print** *n.* (手指的)拇指纹;[美俚]个人性格上的特征 / **~screw** *n.* ①【机】指旋螺丝; 翼形螺钉 ②(古时的刑具)拇指夹 / **'~s-down** *n.* [美]责备, 不赞成 / **'~stall** *n.* 拇指套 / **'~tack** *n.* =~ pin / **'~-up** *n.* 翘拇指(满意或赞同的表示): give the ~-up sign to praise sb. 翘拇指赞扬某人

thump [θʌmp] **I** *n.* ①重击, 捶击 ②重击声, 砰然声 ③【无】键击噪声; 低音噪音; (电话中)的电报噪音 **II** ❶ *vt.* 重击, 捶击; 砰然地击: ~ the desk with one's fist 用拳头敲桌子 / ~ a big drum 擂大鼓 / ~ a glass on the table 把玻璃杯砰地放在桌上 ❷ *vi.* 重击, 捶击; 砰然地响: ~ on the door 捶门 / His heart ~ed with excitement. 他兴奋得心头怦怦直跳。 ‖**~er** *n.* ①捶击的人(或物) ②重击 ③庞然大物

thunder ['θʌndə] **I** *n.* ①雷, 雷声: a loud crash of ~ 震耳的雷声 / a long roll of ~ 隆隆的雷声 ②似雷的响声, 轰隆声: a ~ (或 ~s) of applause 雷鸣般的掌声 / the ~ of guns 隆隆的炮声 ③怒喝; 威吓, 恐吓 ④ [古]雷电, 霹雳 ❶ *vi.* ①打雷: It is ~ing. 打雷了。②发出雷鸣般的响声, 轰隆地响: Someone is ~ing at the door. 有人在砰砰地擂门。 / Tanks ~ed down the road. 坦克轰隆轰隆地沿路开过去。③怒喝; 恐吓 (*against*)

❷ vt. ①轰隆地发出: Guns ~ed out a salute. 礼炮轰响。 / ~ blows upon 轰击… ②大声发出; 吼叫: ~ threats at sb. 大声恐吓某人 ‖**By ~!** [口]哎! 真的! 岂有此理! / **steal sb.'s ~** 抢先讲某人要讲的事; 窃取某人的发明而抢先利用 ‖**~er** [ˈθʌndərə] n. ①大声说话的人; 怒喝的人 ②[the T-][罗神]朱庇特 / **~y** [ˈθʌndəri] a. ①雷声似的, 轰隆轰隆的 ②有雷的, 要打雷的 ‖**'~-and-'lightning** a. (服饰等)由截然相反的色彩配在一起的; 颜色夺目的 / **'~bird** n. (神话中)引起雷雨的巨鸟 int. [美俚]妙哉! / **'~bolt** n. ①雷电, 霹雳 ②[喻]意外的事件, 晴天霹雳: This information was a ~bolt to her. 这消息对她是一个晴天霹雳。③怒喝; 恐吓 ④雷石; 黄铁矿团块 / **'~clap** n. 雷声, 霹雳; 晴天霹雳似的消息(或事件) / **'~cloud** n. 雷云, 产生雷电的云 / **'~-gust** n. 伴有大风的雷暴雨 / **'~head** n. 【气】(雷暴前常见的)雷暴云砧, 雷雨云砧 / **'~₁shower** n. 雷阵雨 / **'~storm** n. 雷暴雨 / **'~struck** a. 遭雷击的; 吓坏了的, 大吃一惊的

Thursday [ˈθəːzdi] n. 星期四 ‖**Holy ~** [基督教]①升天节(复活节后四十天的星期四) ②复活节前三天的星期四 (=Maundy [ˈmɔːndi] ~) ‖**~s** ad. [美]每星期四; 在任何星期四

thus [ðʌs] ad. ①如此, 这样; 到如此程度: He spoke ~. 他是这样说的。/ Only ~ can we fulfil the task. 只有这样我们才能完成任务。/ Why ~ excited? 为什么这样激动? ②因而, 从而: The bus was held up by the snowstorm, ~ causing the delay. 公共汽车被大风雪所阻, 因而耽搁了。③例如 ‖**~ and ~** (或 so) 如此这般 / **~ far** 到此为止; 迄今 / **~ much** 这些; 到此: Thus much at least is clear. 至少这些是明白的。

thwart [θwɔːt] I vt. ①反对, 阻挠; 使受挫折; 挫败: be ~ed in one's plans 计划遭到挫折 ②横过, 穿过 II a. 横放的; 横着的 III ad. & prep. 横过, 横跨 IV n. (划艇中横贯船体的)座板 ‖**~ly** ad. / **~wise** ad. & a. 横着的(的)

thy [ðai] pron. [古][thou 的所有格]你的

thyme [taim] n. 【植】百里香属植物; 百里香, 麝香草

tiara [tiˈɑːrə] n. ①古波斯人的头巾; 罗马教皇的三重冕 ②罗马教皇的职权 ③妇女的冕状头饰

tick¹ [tik] I n. ①(钟表等的)滴答声 ②[主英][口]滴答的一瞬间, 一刹那: We'll be ready in a couple of ~s. 我们再过一会儿就准备好了。/ Half a ~! 稍等一会儿! ③(核对帐目等用的)记号 (✓, / 等) II ❶ vi. ①(钟表等)滴答滴答响 ②(象钟表般)持续活动: He kept ~ing along fine on one kidney. 他虽然只剩一只腰子, 依然活得很好。❷ vt. ①滴答滴答地记录(时间); 滴答滴答地发出: The clock ~ed away (或 off) the time. 时钟滴答滴答地响, 表示时间过去了。/ The

telegraph ~ed out a message. 发报机滴滴答答地发出电报。② 对…标以记号: ~ off an item on a list 把表格上一个项目用记号标出 ‖**~ off** ①用记号勾出; 指出, 列举(项目) ②[英俚]责备, 斥责; [俚]激怒 ③ 简短地描述 / ~ over (内燃机等)慢车转动着松开传动装置; [喻]接近停滞, 踌躇, 吞吞吐吐 / **to** (或 on) the ~ 极为准时地: arrive at one's destination at six on the ~ 六时正到达目的地

tick² [tik] n. 【动】(寄生吸血的)扁虱, 蜱, 壁虱 ‖**~ fever** 【医】蜱热

tick³ [tik] n. ①褥子的外皮; (弹簧椅等的)面子; 枕心套; 褥子 ②[口](做褥子外皮等用的)坚固条纹棉布(或亚麻布) (=ticking) ‖**tight as a ~** 见 **tight**

tick⁴ [tik] [口] I n. 信用; 赊欠: buy goods on ~ 赊购货物 II ❶ vi. 赊销, 赊购 ❷ vt. ①赊销(货物); 赊给(某人) ②赊购(货物)

ticket [ˈtikit] I n. ①票, 券; 车票; 入场券: a theatre ~ 戏票 / a platform ~ [英]月台票 / a lottery ~ 彩票 / a single (或 [美]one-way) ~ 单程票 / a return (或 [美]round-trip) ~ 来回票 / a season ~ [英]月季票, 定期票, 长期票(用于乘车, 观剧等, 期限可为一个月, 一季度, 半年等) / a through ~ 通票, 联票 / Admission by ~ only. 凭票入场。/ buy (book) a ~ 买(订)票 ②(货物上的)票签, 标签; (记录金额或记事用的)便签; (放在出租房屋窗口的)召租牌 ③证明书, 许可证; (商船船长或飞行员的)执照 ④[某一政党在一次选举中所提出的]候选人名单; [喻](政党的)纲领, 政见; (事业等的)计划, 规划 ⑤[口](给违反交通规则者等的)传票 ⑥ [the ~][口]合适的东西: That's the ~. 那正合适。/ be not quite the ~ 不太合适 ⑦[英][军俚]开除: get one's ~ 被开除 II a. ①加票签于 ②…购票; 对…发出传票 ‖**cut a ~** [美]涂掉选票上候选人的名字; 投反对票 / **vote the split ~** [美]兼投一党以上的候选人的票 / **vote the straight ~** [美]只投某一政党全部候选人的票 / **write one's own ~** 自订计划, 自行决定 ‖**agency** (车, 船, 飞机或戏院等的)售票代理处 / **~ agent** (车, 船, 飞机或戏院等)售票代理人 / **~ day** [主英](交易所)交割日的前一天 / **inspector** 查票员 / **~ office** 票房, 售票处 / **'~-of-'leave** n. [英][律](囚犯的)假释许可证: be on ~-of-leave 获准假释在外 / a ~-of-leave man 假释犯 / **~ porter** (伦敦市的)有执照车站搬运工

tickle [ˈtikl] I ❶ vt. ①使觉得痒: ~ sb. with a feather 用羽毛逗某人发痒 / It ~d my nose. 这东西扰我的鼻子搞得痒痒的。②逗乐, 使高兴; 激起: The jest ~d him immensely. 那笑话把他逗得乐极了。/ be ~d to death 高兴极了 / sb.'s palate 合某人胃口, 合某人嗜好 / ~ sb.'s vanity 使某人扬扬得意 ③用手抓(鱼等) ❷ vi. ①觉得痒: My foot ~s. 我的脚痒。②使人觉得

痒: The blanket ~s. 这毯子使人发痒。**II** *n.*
①使人发痒; 痒 ②使人发痒的东西; 使人高兴的
事物 ‖~ **sb. pink** [美俚]使某人非常高兴

ticklish ['tikliʃ] *a.* ① 怕呵痒的, 怕痒的 ② 不稳定
的; 易变的; 易怒的 ③需要小心从事的; 难对付
的, 棘手的: a ~ situation 难处理的局面 ‖~**ly**
ad. / ~**ness** *n.*

tidal ['taidl] *a.* ① 潮汐的; 定时涨落的: a ~ river
潮(水)河 / a ~ harbour 潮港 ② 根据潮汐涨落
而定班次的: a ~ steamer 根据潮汐定班次的轮
船 ‖~**ly** *ad.* ‖~ **air** 一次呼吸进出肺部的空气 /
~ **current** 潮流 / ~ **wave** ① 潮汐波, 潮浪; 海
啸 ②[喻]浪潮(指感情的迸发、投票时压倒的多
数等): a *wave* of protest 抗议的浪潮

tide [taid] **I** *n.* ① 潮, 潮汐; 潮水: The ~ is coming in(going out).涨(退)潮了。②潮流, 趋势; 形势:
the ~ of history 历史潮流 / the ~ of public
opinion 舆论的趋势 / go with the ~ 随大流, 赶
潮流 / go against the ~ 反潮流 ③涨潮; 高潮:
The ship departed on the ~. 这条船于涨潮时离
去。④时机 ⑤[古]一段时间; 时刻 ⑥[古][用以
构成复合词]时节, 宗教节期: Christmas ~ 圣诞
节节期 ‖*ebb* ~ 落潮 / *flood* ~ 涨潮 / *meteoro-
logical* ~ 气象潮 / *neap* ~ 小潮 / *spring* ~ 大
潮, 春潮 **II** ❶ *vi.* ①潮水般地奔流 ②(船只进港
或离港时)顺潮行驶 ❷ *vt.* 使随潮水漂浮: The
sea ~d the debris ashore. 潮水将碎片杂物冲上
海滩。/ ~ one's way 顺潮势行驶 ‖*at high
(low)* ~ 处于高(低)潮中 / *roll back the* ~
of war 击退侵略 / *save the* ~ 趁涨潮进出港
口 / *swim with the* ~ 随波逐流; 随大流 /
tail to the ~ (船只停泊中)随潮起伏 / *The* ~
turns. 潮流是会变的。/ ~ *over* 渡过, 克服
(困难等) / *Time and* ~ *wait(s) for no man.*
见 *time* / *work double* ~s 昼夜工作 ‖~
ga(u)ge 验潮器 / '~**land** 潮淹区(指涨潮时
为水所淹的地带) / '~**lock** 潮闸 / '~**mark** *n.*
① 潮标 ② 涨潮点 / ~ **rip** 潮水(或水流)冲突时
引起的波浪 / ~ **table** 潮汐表 / '~,**waiter** *n.*
登上进港船只检查的海关工作人员 / '~,**water**
n. ① 潮水 ② 水位受潮汐影响的沿海低洼地区 /
'~**way** *n.* ①潮路 ②河流受潮汐影响的部分, 潮
(水)河 ③潮流

tidily ['taidili] *ad.* 整洁地, 整齐地

tidiness ['taidinis] *n.* 整洁, 整齐

tidings ['taidiŋz] [复] *n.* [用作单或复][书面语]
消息, 音信: glad ~ about the successes in our
industrial production 我国工业生产胜利的喜讯 /
evil ~ 恶讯 / The ~ come(s) too late. 消息来
得太晚了。

tidy ['taidi] **I** *a.* ① 整洁的, 整齐的; 有条不紊的:
a ~ person 整洁的人 / a ~ room 整洁的房间 /
a ~ handwriting 工整的笔迹 / a ~ mind 严谨
的头脑 ② [口]相当健康的: He is feeling
pretty ~. 他感到身体很好。③ [口]相当好的,
令人满意的 ④ [口]相当大的, 相当多的: a ~

sum of money 相当大的一笔钱 / a ~ penny 很
多钱 **II** ❶ *vt.* 使整洁, 整理 (up): I have to ~
myself (up) a bit. 我得梳理一下。/ ~ up the
room 整理房间 ❷ *vi.* 收拾, 整理 (up): ~ up
after dinner 饭后收拾餐具 **III** *n.* ①(沙发靠背、
扶手等上的)小垫布, 罩布 ②装零碎东西的容器:
a street ~ 马路旁的杂物箱

tie [tai] **I** *n.* ① (结物等用的)带子, 线, 绳; 鞋带
② 领带; 领结: knot one's ~ 打领带 ③ 联系; 关
系; 纽带: trade ~s between countries 国家
间的贸易关系 / ~s of blood 血缘关系 / ~s
of friendship 友情 ④ 系绳(或打结)的方法;
打法, 系法 ⑤束缚; 牵累: be bound by legal ~s
受法律约束 ⑥(投票等的)同数;(比赛等的)同分;
平局: The game ended in a ~. 比赛打成平局。
⑦【建】连系杆; [美]铁路枕木, 轨枕 ⑧【音】连结
符号 ⑨ [美] [常用复] 低帮系带皮鞋 **II** (tied;
tying 或 tieing) ❶ *vt.* ①(用带、绳、线等)系, 拴,
扎, 束紧: ~ a horse to a tree 把马拴在树上 /
~ off an artery 结扎动脉 / ~ up a parcel 把包
裹扎起来 ② 把(带子等)打结; 打(结): ~ one's
shoelaces 结鞋带 / ~ one's tie 打领带 / ~ the
ribbon in a bow 把丝带打成蝴蝶结 / ~ a knot
in a piece of string 在绳子上打一个结 / ~ a
wreath 扎花圈 ③ 束缚, 约束, 限制: ~ sb.'s
tongue 封住某人的口 / be ~d to one's bed 卧病
不起 / a ~d house (专销某酒厂产品的)特约酒
店 ④连接(两个供电系统);【音】用连结符号连接
(音符) ⑤把(轨道)固定在枕木上; 给(铁路线)铺
设枕木 ⑥ 使结成夫妇 ⑦ 与…打成平局; 与…势
均力敌: ~ the visiting team 与客队打成平局
❷ *vi.* ① 结合; 结住 ② 打结; 能打结: This rope
won't ~. 这根绳子打不起结。③ 得同样分数, 不
分胜负: They ~d for first place in the high
jump. 他们在跳高比赛中并列第一名。‖*hit the
~s* [美]沿铁路徒步旅行 / *play* (或 *shoot, run*)
off a ~ 平局后再赛以决胜负 / *ride and* ~ 见
ride / *the old school* ~ 校友戴的领带; [喻]
同学情谊 / ~ *down* 束缚: ~ sb. *down* to a contract 使某人受合同约束 / ~ *in* ①(使)结合成一
整体; (使)相配: ~ a generating station *in with*
a power system 把发电站与供电系统连接起来 /
The illustrations are cleverly ~d *in with* the
text. 插图与本文配合得很巧妙。② 最后连接:
~ *in* a pipe line 把管道最后接通 / ~ *into* [美]
①猛烈进攻; 严厉责骂 ②狼吞虎咽地吃 ③猛击
(棒球) ④把…弄到手 / ~ *one on* [美俚]喝醉 /
~ *to* 依靠, 依赖(某人) / ~ *up* ① 束紧, 缚牢
② 包扎 ③ 停泊; 靠码头: We ~d *up* at the
riverside. 我们把船停泊在河边。④ 阻碍; 使处
于停顿状态: a port ~d *up* by the dockers'
strike 因码头工人罢工而陷于瘫痪的港口 ⑤ 使
(资金等)专作某种用途而不能随便动用; 使(财产
等)受法律束缚而不能随意变卖 ⑥(与…)密切联
系; 合伙: This ~s *up* with what you were told
before. 这和你以前被告知的事有密切关系。⑦

使无空闲; 占用: be ~d up in conference all day 开了一整天会 / ~ up a phone for an hour 占用电话一小时 ‖ '~back n. ①(装饰性的)窗帘钩 ②[常用复]用钩子挂起的窗帘(与用滑轮拉开的相别) / ~ bar【建】系杆, 拉杆 / ~ beam【建】系梁, 小屋梁 / '~-in a. 必须有搭卖品才出售的: a ~-in sale 必须有搭卖品的出售 n. 相配物 (如相互配合的广告); 关连; 必须有搭卖品的货物(或购货权) / ~ pin n. 领带扣针, 领结别针 / ~ plate【建】系板, 垫板 / ~ silk 领带绸 / '~=up n. ①用来束缚的东西; 被扎束的东西 ②船只停泊处 ③ 牛棚 ④(由罢工等引起的)交通停顿, 停业; 停止活动: a transportation ~-up 交通停顿 / a ~-up in negotiations 谈判中的僵局 ⑤联系; 联合: the organic ~-up between ... and ... ...与...之间的有机联系 / refuse to admit any ~-up with sb. 拒绝承认与某人有任何瓜葛

tier[1] ['tai-ə] n. ①包扎的人(或工具); 包扎工 ②[美](用带子结住的)围涎

tier[2] [tiə] I n. ①(一)排, (一)层: a ~ of seats 一排座位 / ~s of terraced fields 层层梯田 / a ~ of fire【军】重层射击 ② (衣服等上的)一行褶裥 ③【电】定向天线元 ④ 等级: the lowest ~ of society 社会的最底层 II ❶ vt. 层层排列 (up) ❷ vi. 层层上升 ‖ ~ building 多层房屋 / ~ table 宝塔桌(有两张或两张以上相互重叠的圆桌面的小桌)

tiff[1] [tif] I n. (朋友或熟人间的)口角, 争执; 生气: have a ~ with one's pal 和好朋友发生小争执 II vi. 口角, 争执; 生气

tiff[2] [tif] I n. ① 酒; 淡酒 ② 一口酒; 小饮 II vt. 喝; 饮

tiff[3] [tif] vi. (印度用英语)吃午餐

tiffin ['tifin] (印度用英语) I n. 午餐 II vi. 吃午餐

tiger ['taigə] n. ① 虎: How can you catch ~ cubs without entering the ~'s lair? 不入虎穴, 焉得虎子? / work like a ~ 生龙活虎地干活 / a paper ~ 纸老虎 / an American ~ 美洲豹 (= jaguar) ②(作为某一组织标志的)虎的图象; [T-]以虎为标志的组织 ③凶恶的人, 虎狼之徒; 凶性, 残性 ④[英](穿制服的)马夫 ⑤[口](比赛的)劲敌 ⑥[美](欢呼三声之后的)高呼声(一般即呼 ~) ‖~ish ['taigəriʃ] a. 虎的; 虎一般的; 残忍的, 凶暴的; 嗜血的 / ~like a. 似虎的 ‖~ beetle【动】虎甲科的甲虫 / ~ cat【动】豹猫; 薮猫 / ~eye ['taigərai] n. 虎眼石(一种宝石) / ~ lilly【植】卷丹 / '~-moth n.【动】灯蛾 / '~'s-eye n. =~eye

tight [tait] I a. ① 紧的, 不松动的; 牢固的: a ~ knot 打得紧紧的结 ②拉紧的, 绷紧的: a ~ rope 绷紧的绳索 / a ~ smile 不自然的笑 ③紧身的, 紧贴的: painfully ~ shoes 紧得脚痛的鞋子 ④密封的; 不漏的, 透不过的: water-~ compartments (船的)密封舱 / air-~ 密封的, 不漏气的 / a ~ cask 不漏的桶 ⑤装紧的, 挤满的; 密集的: a ~ bale of cotton 扎得结结实实的一包棉花 ⑥

严厉的, 严格的: ~ discipline 严格的纪律 ⑦麻烦的, 棘手的, 困难的, 尴尬的: a ~ squeeze 困难 / be in a ~ place (或 corner, spot) 处境困难 ⑧(比赛等)势力均敌的: a ~ table-tennis match 势均力敌的乒乓球赛 ⑨(文字、作品等)紧凑的, 简洁的, 精练的; 排得紧的: a ~ literary style 精练的文风 / a ~ line of print 排得满满的一行字 ⑩整洁的; 整齐的, 安排得当的: a ~ little room 整洁的小房间 ⑪吝啬的, 小气的 ⑫[商]商品难得到的; 银根紧的: a ~ market 供不应求的市场 / a ~ money market 银根紧的金融市场 ⑬有能力的; 机警的 ⑭[俚]醉醺醺的 II n. [复] (运动员或舞蹈演员的)紧身衣裤 III ad. ①紧, 紧紧地: The door was shut ~. 门关得紧紧的。②[方]酣畅地: fall asleep 酣睡 ‖sit ~ 见 sit / ~ as a tick [美俚]喝得烂醉的 ‖~ly ad. / ~ness n. ‖'~'fisted a. 吝啬的, 小气的 / '~-lipped a. 嘴唇紧闭的; 寡言的, 沉默的 / '~-mouthed a. 守口如瓶的 / ~rope n. (供走索用的)绷索: ~rope dancing 在绷索上跳舞; [喻]在危险的形势中艰难地对付 / '~wad n. [俚]吝啬鬼, 守财奴 / '~wire n. 钢制的绷索, 钢索

tighten ['taitn] ❶ vt. 使变紧; 使绷紧: ~ the ropes 绷紧绳索 ❷ vi. 变紧; 绷紧 ‖~ one's belt 见 belt ‖~er n. 使收紧的人(或物);【机】紧带轮

tile [tail] I n. ①【建】瓦片; 瓷砖, 花砖; (软木、橡胶等制成用于铺地面的)弹性砖片: Dutch ~ 饰瓦; 彩砖, 荷兰砖 / plain ~ 无楞瓦 / roofing ~ 屋顶瓦 / ~ floor 砖地 ②【建】贴砖, 铺瓦; 瓦面 ③ (排水的)瓦管, 瓦筒; 瓦沟 ④[口]丝质高礼帽 ⑤(一张)麻将牌 II vt. ① 用瓦盖, 铺瓦于; 贴砖于; 装瓦管于; 铺瓦沟于 ②(共济会用语)派人看守(会所等); 使保守秘密 ‖be (out) on the ~s [俚]寻欢作乐, 花天酒地 / fly a ~ [俚]把帽子打掉 / have a ~ loose [俚]有点疯 / ~ in 用砖片盖没 ‖~r n. 砖瓦匠, 制砖瓦者; 铺瓦者, 贴砖者 ②(共济会等)秘密会所的看门人 (=tyler) / ~ry ['tailəri] n. ① 制瓦厂, 烧瓦场 ②装饰性砖瓦铺贴术 ‖~stone n.【建】瓦石, 石板 / ~ tea 茶砖

till[1] [til] [till 基本上与 until 相同, 但句首一般不用 till, 而用 until] I prep. ①直到…为止: fight on ~ one's last breath 战斗到最后一息 / from morning ~ night 从早到晚 / ~ now (then) 直到目前(那时) ②[用在否定句中]在…以前, 直到…(才): Don't wake him ~ midnight. 午夜前不要叫醒他。/ He did not finish the work ~ yesterday. 他直到昨天才结束那工作。③[苏格兰]=to[1] (prep.) II conj. ①直到…为止: I lived in that city ~ I was fifteen. 我在那城市里一直住到十五岁。/ Wait here ~ he arrives. 在这里等到他来。②[用于否定式的主句后]在…以前, 直到…(才): Don't go away ~ I come back. 我回来前不要走开。/ You cannot learn anything ~ you rid yourself of complacency. 去掉自满，你才能真正学到一点东西。‖~ **all is blue** 见 **blue** / ~ **the cows come home** 见 **cow**[1]

till[2] [til] **vt.** 耕种，耕作：~ the land for the revolution 为革命种田 ‖**~able** *a.* 可耕种的，可耕作的 / **~age** ['tilidʒ] *n.* ①耕种，耕作 ②耕地；耕地上的作物

till[3] [til] *n.* ① (帐台中) 放钱的抽屉；(橱柜中) 放置贵重物品的格子 (或抽屉) ②备用现金

till[4] [til] *n.* 【地】冰碛，冰碛物

tiller[1] ['tilə] *n.* 耕种者；农夫 (=farmer)

tiller[2] ['tilə] **I** *n.* 【植】分蘖 **II** *vi.* 分蘖，长新芽

tiller[3] ['tilə] *n.* 【船】舵柄 ‖**~-chain** *n.* 转舵链 / **~-rope** *n.* 转舵索

tilt[1] [tilt] **I** ❶ *vt.* ①使倾斜，使歪斜；使翘起：Don't ~ the chair. 不要把椅子翘起来。/ He ~ed the cart (*up*) to empty it. 他把小车侧倒空。②斜持 (矛)，投 (矛)；向 (敌人) 冲刺 ③用跳动锤打钉 ❷ *vi.* ①倾斜，歪斜；翘起：The tree ~s to the south. 树向南倾斜。/ be apt to ~ over 容易倾倒 / ~ing strata 【地】倾斜地层 ②骑马持矛冲刺；[喻]抨击，攻击 (*at*)：~ at an opponent 向敌手冲刺；抨击对手 **II** *n.* ①骑马持矛冲刺，马上比枪；[喻]激烈的竞争，争论 ②倾斜，歪斜；翘起 ③斜坡 ④跷跷板 ⑤跳动锤，落锤 ‖ (*at*) *full* ~ 全速地；用力地，猛地：run *full* ~ into sb. 与某人撞个满怀 / *have a* ~ *at* sb. 攻击某人；奚落某人 / ~**ed** *a.* 倾斜的；翘起的 / ~**er** *n.* ①(旧时) 骑马的比武者 ②使用跳动锤者 ③倾倒者 ‖ **hammer** 跳动锤，落锤

tilt[2] [tilt] **I** *n.* (小舟、车辆、地摊等的) 帐篷，遮阳 **II** *vt.* 用帐篷遮盖，为…搭帐篷

timber ['timbə] **I** *n.* ①木材，木料 ②(可作木材的) 树木，树林：put the hillside under ~ 在山坡上造林 / fell ~ 伐木 ③栋木；【船】船骨，肋材 ④ [美] (人的) 素质，气质：a man of his ~ 他这种素质的人 ⑤ (猎狐时用的) 木栅栏，木门 **II** *vt.* 用木材建造；用木材支撑 **III** *int.* (伐木工在树木倒下前的呼喊声) 倒啦！成啦！‖**Shiver my ~s!** [俚] 真见鬼！‖**~ed** *a.* ①木造的；装有木料的 ②长满树木的建筑物的树木的；多树林的 / **~ing** ['timbəriŋ] **I** *n.* [总称]木材 ②结构材，木结构；【矿】支架 ‖ **hitch** 【海】圆材结 (一种捆扎圆木材的绳结) / **~jack** *n.* 伐木工 / **~land** *n.* 森林，林地 / **~line** *n.* 树木线 / ~ **right** (在无地产权的土地上的) 伐木权 / ~ **toe** 木头假腿 / **~work** *n.* 结构材，木结构 (尤指屋架、栋梁和船身制作等) / **~yard** *n.* 木材堆置场，贮木场

timbrel ['timbrəl] *n.* 铃鼓；小手鼓

time [taim] **I** *n.* ①时间；【天】时：The new method saves both ~ and labour. 新方法既省时间又省劳力。/ ~ and space 时间和空间 / It's only a matter of ~. 那只是时间早晚而已。/ be pressed for ~ 时间紧迫 / spend (waste) ~ 花掉 (浪费) 时间 / have no ~ to do sth. 没有时间做某事 / have no ~ for reading

(sport) 没有读书 (运动) 的时间 / fix a ~ for doing sth. 规定时间做某事 / The job takes ~. 这工作要费时间。/ stand the test of ~ 经受时间的考验 / Time is up. 时间到了。(指限定的时间已到，必须结束) / standard ~ 标准时间 / summer ~ 夏令时间 / Greenwich ~ 格林威治时间，国际标准时间 / civil ~ 【天】民用时 ②时候；时刻：What is the ~? (或 What ~ is it?) 现在什么时候啦？/ Now is the ~ to get in the wheat. 现在是收割小麦的时候了。/ It's ~ for lunch. 午饭时候到了。/ It's ~ for us to start. (或 It is ~ we started.) 我们该动身了。/ The trains leave at stated ~s. 列车按规定时刻开出。③时机，机会：lose no ~ in doing sth. 不失时机地做某事 / Now is your ~. 现在你的机会来了。④[常用复]时代；时势；境况；[the ~]当代：The ~s are different. 时代不同了。/ in ancient (modern) ~s 在古 (近) 代 / What wonderful ~s we live in! 我们生活在多么了不起的时代啊！/ hard ~s 艰难时世 / What a ~ you'll have doing that! 干那个可够你受的了。/ one of the most important issues of the ~ 当代最重大的问题之一 ⑤时期；时令：in ~ of war 在战时 / in ~ of peace 在和平时期 / holiday ~ 假期 / close ~ [英]禁期；禁猎期 / at flowering ~ 在开花时节 ⑥生活期；死期；学徒期；服役期；产期；刑期：I've never come across such an experience in my ~. 我一生中从没有经历过这样的事情。/ His ~ is close at hand. 他快死了。/ She is near her ~. 她快分娩了。/ be serving one's ~ 正在当学徒 (或服刑) ⑦次，回：several ~s 数次 / for the first (last) ~ 第一 (最后一) 次 / this (last, next) ~ 这 (上、下) 次 / Each ~ I called on him, he was busy with his work. 每次我去看他，他总是在忙着工作。⑧倍 (用来表示倍数或乘法)：four ~s as long as … 是…的四倍长；比…长三倍 / three ~s the size of 等于…三倍大 / ten ~s easier (或 as easy) 十倍地容易 / Five ~s six is (或 are) thirty. 五 (乘) 六得三十。⑨进行速度，节奏；【音】拍子，速度，节拍：go at double ~ 用加倍的速度进行；跑步前进 / beat ~ 打拍子 / keep ~ 合着拍子唱 (或跳) / common ~ 普通拍子 (指二或四拍) / waltz (march) ~ 圆舞曲 (进行曲) 节拍 ⑩ [Times] [用于报刊名]时报：*The New York Times* 《纽约时报》(美国) / *The Times* 《泰晤士报》(英国) ⑪(规定的) 工作时间；占用时间，所需时间：make up ~ 补足工作时间 / The runner's ~ was 11 seconds. 这位赛跑运动员的成绩是十一秒。

⑫计时工资率;按计时工资率领取的工资;最后一次工资: ask for one's ~ 要求领取应得工资(或最后一次的工资)

⑬【体】(一场或一局等的)比赛时限;暂停: The umpire called ~. 裁判员叫暂停。(或: 裁判员宣布时间到了。)

II ❶ vt. ①安排…的时间;为…选择时机: The train is ~d to leave at 3 p.m. 火车定于下午三点开出。/ ~ the assault 选择攻击时间 / a well-~d action 时机恰当的行动

②测定…的时间,记录…的时间;测定…完成某一过程的最终时刻: ~ a race (horse) 测定赛跑(马跑)的时间

③安排…的速度(或节拍);使合拍子: The conductor ~d the performance admirably. 乐队指挥把演奏的速度处理得非常出色。/ ~ one's steps to the music 按乐曲踏步(或跳舞)

④拨准(钟、表)的快慢;调整好(机件)的速度

❷ vi. [罕]合拍;打拍子;和谐

III a. ①时间(方面)的: ~ coordination 时间上的协同

②记录时间的: a ~ register 记时器

③定时发火的,定时爆炸的: a ~ fuze 定时引信

④定期的: a ~ bill【商】期票

⑤分期(付款)的: a ~ payment 分期付款,被分成若干次的支付 / a ~ purchase 分期付款购买

‖abreast of the ~s 符合时代的;时新的,新式的;对新事物有了解的: keep abreast of the ~s 与时代并进 / against ~ 争分夺秒地,尽快地;力争及时完成地: work against ~ 抢时间完成工作 / ahead of (或 born before) one's ~(s) (想法等)比之所处时代先进得过分的 / ahead of ~ 在原定时间以前;提早 / all the ~ 一直;始终: Conditions are changing all the ~. 情况在不断地变化着。/ as ~ goes on 随着时间的推移 / at all ~s 无论何时,一直 / (at) any ~ 在任何时候 / at a ~ ①每次,一次: Pass me the bricks two at a ~. 把砖头递给我,每次两块。②在某个时刻,一度 / at no ~ 在任何时候都不,决不 / at one ~ ①同时 ②从前有个时期,曾经: At one ~ we met frequently. 有一个时期我们常常见面。/ at other ~s 在另外的一些场合中 / at that ~ 在那时 / at the best of ~s 在情况最好的时候 / at the same ~ ①同时,一齐 ②但,然而: This is a difficult problem, at the same ~ it is extremely interesting. 这是个困难的问题,但却极为有趣。/ at the ~ of 在…的时候 / at this ~ of day 直到这时候(才…),这么迟才… / at no ~ 在任何时候不 / before one's ~ ①提前;过早: He came here before his ~. 他提前到这儿来了。②在某人出世前 ③不足月(而生);过早(衰坏或死亡) / before the ~s 在时代前头 / behind the ~s 落在时代后面(思想等)过时 / behind ~ 在原定时间以后;迟,晚: The train is ten minutes behind ~. 火车

晚点十分钟。/ be behind ~ in payment 拖延付款 / between ~s 有时候,偶尔,间或 / bide one's ~ 等待时机 / buy ~ (用拖延等手法)赢得时间,争取时间 / by the ~ … 到…的时候 / by this ~ 到此刻,到现在 / come to ~ 履行义务 / do ~ 服徒刑 / every ~ ①每次,总是: That team wins every ~. 那球队每战皆捷。②每当 / for a ~ 暂时;一度 / for the being 暂时,眼下 / from ~ to ~ 有时,不时 / gain ~ ①(钟、表等)走得快 ②(用拖延等手法)赢得时间 / give sb. ~ 给某人放宽(偿还欠账等)的时间 / give the ~ of day 问好,说"早安"(或"晚安"等) / go with the ~s 随大流,赶时髦 / half the ~ ①一半时间: We fulfilled the plan in half the ~. 我们只用了一半时间就完成了计划。②长时间地;(几乎)经常 / have a good ~ 过得快活,过得愉快 / have a rough ~ 吃苦,受难 / have a royal ~ 过得愉快 / Have I ~ to (do) ...? 我来得及(做)…吗? / have ~ to burn 有用不完的时间 / in good ~ 及时地;迅速地: sum up experience in good ~ 及时总结经验 / in jig ~ [口]极快地 / in no ~ 立刻;很快: You'll be all right in no ~. 你很快就会好的。/ in one's own good ~ 在方便的时候 / in sb.'s ~ ①在某人一生中 ②当某人在某处工作(或学习等)的期间: He was no longer head of the college in my ~. 当我在那学院的时候,他已不当院长了。/ in (the) course of ~ 最后;经过一定的时间 / in the nick of ~ nick / in ~ ①及时;还早: We were just in ~ for (或 to catch) the bus. 我们正好赶上那班公共汽车。②总有一天;最后,终于: If you keep on, you will succeed in ~. 如果坚持下去,你们总有一天会成功的。③合拍子 / in ~s to come 在将来 / keep good (bad) ~ (钟、表等)走得准(不准) / kill ~ 消磨时间 / know the ~ of day ①消息灵通;有经验 ②处事机智;能见机行事 / lose ~ ①(钟、表等)走得慢 ②耽误时间 / make ~ ①腾出时间;加速以弥补失去的时间: Could you make ~ to copy it for me? 你能抽空帮我把它抄一下吗? ②(以某种速度)进行;(快速)行驶: We made good (poor) ~ this morning. 今天早上我们走得很快(慢)。/ many a ~ (或 many ~s) 多次,常常 / many a ~ and oft (或 many and many a ~) [诗]许多次 / mark ~ ①【军】【体】踏步 ②停顿不前,暂缓进行 / ninety-nine ~s out of a hundred (或 nine ~s out of ten) 几乎每次,十之八九,常常 / not give sb. the ~ of day [美口]不理睬某人,讨厌某人 / off ~ (言语等)不合时宜 / of the ~ ①当时的;当代的,当今的 ②当代人 / once upon a ~ (常用于故事开头)从前 / one ~ with another 前后合起来: He was principal of the school one ~ with another for nine years. 他在该校前后一共当了九年校长。/ on one's own ~ 在规定工时以外的时间,在非工作时间 / on *short* ~ 开工时间不足，以部分时间开工（或做工）/ **on** ~ ① 按时，准时：于指定时间：The train pulled in *on* ~. 火车准时进站。②[美] 分期付款方式 / *out of* ~ ① 不合时宜 ② 不合拍 / *pass the* ~ *of day* (*with sb.*) （与某人）打招呼（如说"你早"等）/ *play for* ~ 为争取时间而拖延 / *sack* ~ [美俚]睡觉时间 / *serve the* ~ 随波逐流；趋炎附势 / *some* ~ *or other* 总有一天，迟早 / *So that's the* ~ *of day!* [俚]情况原来如此！（或：原来是你耍的小花招！）/ *straight* ~ （一周或其他时间内）正规的工作时间(不包括请假或加班的时间) / *take* (*one's*) ~ 从容进行 / *take sb. all his* ~ [口]花费某人全部精力 / *take* ~ *by the forelock* 抓住时机 / *take* ~ *out* (或 *off*) *to* (do) 暂停下来(做) / *talk against* ~ ①在规定时间内尽快讲完 ②用谈话（或讨论）消磨时间(如为阻挠议案等的通过) / *ten* ~*s* 见 *ten* / *the good old* ~*s* 往昔 / *There are* ~*s when* .... 有时常会… / *There is a* ~ *for everything*. 做事要当其时。/ *the* ~ *of day* (钟表上的)时刻 / *the* ~ *of one's life* [口] 一生中最愉快的一段时期：have *the* ~ *of one's life* 过得非常愉快 / give sb. *the* ~ *of his life* 使某人过得极其愉快 / *Those were* (*fine*) ~*s!* 好快活的岁月啊！ / ~ *about* [苏格兰]轮流 / ~ *after* ~ (或 ~ *and again*) 多次，反复地；不断地 / ~ *and a half* [美] 超过原工资标准一倍的加班工资 / *Time and tide wait*(*s*) *for no man*. [谚]岁月不待人。/ ~ *enough* [口]还早，来得及：We got there ~ *enough* to see the match start. 我们到达那儿时间还早，来得及看到比赛开始。/ *Time hangs heavy on sb.'s hands*. 某人感到时间过得沉闷。/ *Time is money*. [谚]一寸光阴一寸金。/ ~ *of life* 年龄：You ought to know better at your ~ *of life*. 在你这样的年龄该懂事些了。/ ~ *out of mind* (或 ~ *immemorial*) 太古时代，很久以前 / ~*s without* (或 *out of*) *number* 屡次，无数次；反复地 / *Time was when* .... 事情发生在从前…的时候。/ *to the end of* ~ 永远 / *up to* ~ [英]准时 / *watch one's* ~ 等待时机，窥伺时间 / *what* ~ [诗]当…时候

‖~ **ball** 报时球 / ~ **base** 【无】时基，扫描；时间坐标 / ~ **bill** 定期汇票 / ~ **bomb** ①定时炸弹 ②[喻]潜在的爆炸性因素 / ~ **book** 工作时间记录簿 / ~ **capsule** 存放现代历史资料和文物的储放器(埋藏起来供后人了解现代情况之用) / ~ **card** 工作时间记录卡片 / ~ **clock** ①特制的上下班记时钟，生产记录钟 ②【无】时钟脉冲 / '~-con,suming *a*. ①花费大量时间的 ②拖延时间的 / ~ **copy** (报刊的)已排好字的待用稿件 / ~ **deposit** 定期存款 / ~ **difference** 时差 / ~ **discount** 【商】贴现 / ~ **draft** 【商】定期汇票 / '~-ex,pired *a*. 满了服役期的 / ~ **exposure** (拍照时)长时间(一般指超过半秒)的

曝光；长时间曝光拍摄的照片 / '~-,hono(u)red *a*. 古老而受到敬仰的；历史悠久的；由来已久的：the ~-*hono(u)red* friendly relations between the two peoples 两国人民之间历史悠久的友好关系 / '~,keeper *n*. ①时计(指钟、表) ②(比赛中的)计时员；(记雇员工作时间的)记时员 ③打拍子的人 / ~ **killer** ①消磨时间的人 ②消遣物 / ~ **lag** 时间上的间隔；【物】时滞 / '~-lapse *a*. (如表现花开过程等)慢转速拍摄后用普通转速放映的 / ~ **limit** 期限；限期 / ~ **loan**, ~ **money** 定期贷款 / ~ **lock** 定时锁(用机件控制不到固定时间打不开的锁) / '~-'out *n*. (比赛等过程中的)暂停，暂休 / '~piece *n*. 时计(指钟、表) / '~-,saver *n*. 节省时间的事物(或因素) / '~,saving *n*. 节省时间的 / '~-,server *n*. 随波逐流的人；趋炎附势者 / '~-,serving *n*. & *a*. 随波逐流(的)；趋炎附势(的) / ~ **sharing** 【自】分时，时间划分 / ~ **sheet** =~ card / ~ **shell** 【军】(装有引信，于预定时间在空中爆炸的)空炸炮弹 / ~ **signal** 报时信号 / ~ **slot** (电视台、广播电台等为插入的节目留出的)时间空档 / ~ **spirit** 时代精神 / ~ **switch** 自动按时启闭的电动开关 / '~,table *n*. 时间表，时刻表 / '~-,tested *a*. 经受过时间考验的 / '~work *n*. 计时(或计日)的工作 / '~worn *a*. ①用得陈旧了的；陈腐的：a ~*worn* expression 陈词滥调 ②古老的 / ~ **zone** 【天】时区

timeless ['taimlis] *a*. ①无时间限制的；无日期的；长期有效的 ②永恒的，无始无终的 ③[古]过早的，不合时宜的 ‖~**ly** *ad*. / ~**ness** *n*.

timely ['taimli] **I** *a*. ① 及时的：~ medical treatment 及时的医疗 ②适时的；合时势的：a ~ remark 适时的话 **II** *ad*. 及时地 ‖**timeliness** *n*.

timer ['taime] *n*. ①计时员；记时员 ②时计；(比赛中测时用的)跑表 ③定时器，自动按时操作装置；【机】(内燃机的)发火定时器 ④[用以构成复合词]化…时间工作(或学习)的人；…辈的人；第…次来某机构服务的人：a half-~ [英]以一半时间上课，一半时间做工糊口的学龄儿童 / an old-~ 老资格的人；上了年纪的人；守旧的人 / a first ~ in the office 初次来该机构工作的人

timid ['timid] *a*. 胆怯的，易受惊的；羞怯的，缺乏自信力的：as ~ as a hare 胆小如鼠 / be ~ of dogs 怕狗 / a ~ reply 战战兢兢的答复 ‖~**ly** *ad*. / ~**ness** *n*.

timidity [ti'miditi] *n*. 胆怯；羞怯

timorous ['timeres] *a*. 胆小的；易受惊的，畏怯的：a ~ bearing 怯生生的样子 ‖~**ly** *ad*. / ~**ness** *n*.

tin [tin] **I** *n*. ①锡(化学符号 Sn)：~ solder 锡焊料 ②马口铁，镀锡铁皮 (=~plate) ③马口铁器皿；[英](保藏食物的)罐头，听头 (=[美] can)：a ~ of cigarettes 一听香烟 ④[俚]金钱 ⑤[美俚]警察的徽章；警察，警探 **II** (tinned; tinning) *vt*. ①在…上镀锡(或包锡、包马口铁) ②[英]

把(食品等)装罐 **III** *a*. 锡制的; 马口铁制的 ②蹩脚的; 假冒的: a ~ beard 假胡须 ‖a (*little*) ~ **god** 见 **god** ‖~ **can** ① 锡杯, 锡罐 ②[美俚]小驱逐舰; 潜艇; 深水炸弹 ③[美俚]老式汽车 / '~-**clad** *n*. [谑]装甲舰 / ~ **cow** [美俚]罐头牛奶 / ~ **ear** [美俚]①听觉不灵的耳朵, 聋耳朵 ②(受伤后)畸形的耳朵 ③不懂音乐的人, 无音乐感的人 / ~ **fish** [美俚]鱼雷 / '~'**foil** *n*. 锡箔, 锡纸 / ~ **hat** [军俚]钢盔 / ~ **horn** *n*. [美俚]吹牛的人; 赌金少的赌徒 / '~-'**lined pipe** 衬锡管 / ~ **liquor** 【化】二氯化锡液(一种媒染剂) / ~ **Lizzie**, ~ **lizzie** 老式小汽车; 价钱便宜的汽车(或飞机) / ~**man** ['tinmən] *n*. =~smith / ~ **opener** [英]开听刀 / **Tin Pan Alley** [美俚]流行歌曲作曲家和发行人的集中地; [总称]流行歌曲作曲家和发行人; 流行歌曲 / ~ **pants** [美俚](石蜡处理过的)防水帆布裤 / '~**plate** *n*. 马口铁, 镀锡铁皮 / '~-**plate** *vt*. 在…上包马口铁, 在…上镀锡 / ~ **pot** ① 锡罐, 锡壶; 马口铁罐 ②(镀锡时用的)熔锡盛器 / '~-**pot** *a*. 低劣的, 不足道的 / ~**smith** *n*. 白铁工 / ~ **star** [美俚]私家侦探 / ~**stone** *n*. 【矿】锡石 / '~**ware** *n*. [总称]马口铁器皿 / '~**work** *n*. ①锡工, 锡制品 ②[~works][用作单或复]锡工场

tincture ['tiŋktʃə] **I** *n*. ①色泽; 色调; 染料, 颜料: all the ~s of the rainbow 虹的各种色调 / with a ~ of red 带点儿红色 ②气息, 特征, 迹象(*of*): a faint ~ of tobacco 轻微的烟草气味 / a word with a derogative ~ 有贬义色彩的词 ③酊(剂): 药酒: ~ of iodine 【药】碘酊, 碘酒 **II** *vt*. ①着色于, 染 ②使有气息, 使带风味; 使充满: The heavy traffic ~s the air with carbon monoxide. 繁忙的交通使空气里充满一氧化碳。 / a remark ~d with prejudice 带有偏见的言论

tinder ['tində] *n*. 引火物, 火绒, 火种 ‖~**y** ['tindəri] *a*. 火绒似的; 易燃的 ‖~**box** *n*. ①(金属)火绒盒, 取火盒 ②高度燃烧物, 易燃建筑物; 易燃烧的地方 ③容易激动的人

tinge [tindʒ] **I** *n*. ①(较淡的)色调, 色彩: the ~s of spring 春天的色彩 / a literary ~ 文学色彩 ②气息, 味道; 风味: a ~ of irony 一点讽刺的味道 **II** *vt*. ①(较淡地)着色于, 染: be ~d with red 染成淡红色 ②使带气息(或味道、风味): The pines ~d the air with their fragrance. 松树使空气带上一股清香味。 / be ~d with liberalism 带自由主义色彩

tingle ['tiŋgl] **I** ❶ *vi*. ①感到刺痛: His fingers ~d with the cold. 他的手指冻得刺痛。 ②(耳等)鸣响; 发出丁当声: My ears are *tingling*. 我耳鸣。 ③震颤, 抖动; [喻]激动: They were all *tingling* with excitement. 他们都兴奋得激动起来。 ❷ *vt*. 使感刺痛 **II** *n*. ①刺痛: have a ~ in one's toes 脚趾有刺痛的感觉 ②(耳等)的鸣响 ③震颤; 激动

tinker ['tiŋkə] **I** *n*. ① (流动的)补锅工人; 白铁工

人; 能作各种小修小补的人 ②拙劣的修补工; 粗劣的修补 ③[美]小鲆鱼 **II** ❶ *vi*. ①做白铁工 ②作拙劣的修补 ❷ *vt*. 粗修, 修补 (*up*); 调整: ~ (*up*) a clock 把钟随便修一下 ‖*not care a ~'s damn* (或 *cuss*) 毫不介意 ‖~**ly** *a*. 补锅工人似的; 粗笨的, 拙劣的

tinkle ['tiŋkl] **I** *n*. ①丁丁声, 丁当声 ②[美俚]电话 **II** ❶ *vt*. ①使发丁丁(或丁当)声 ②丁丁地发出; 丁当地报出(时间) ❷ *vi*. ①丁丁(或丁当)作响 ‖~**r** *n*. 发丁丁(或丁当)声的东西

tinsel ['tinsəl] **I** *n*. ①金属箔, 金属丝 ②金银丝的交织物 ③华美而不值钱的东西; 华而不实 **II** *a*. ①金银丝(或箔)制的; 饰有金银丝(或箔)的 ②虚饰的, 华而不实的 **III** (tinsel(l)ed; tinsel(l)ing) *vt*. ①用金属丝(或箔)修饰 ②虚饰

tint [tint] **I** *n*. ①色泽, 色彩; 颜色的浓淡; 【物】色辉: the ~s of early morning 晨曦的各种色彩 / autumn ~s 秋色; 红叶 / in all ~s of green 用深浅不一的各种绿色 / red of (或 with) a blue ~ 红里透蓝 ②浅色; 【印】淡色 ③(雕刻中的)线晕 ④不很明显的性质(或特征): have no ~ of fear 一点也不害怕 / show a ~ of jealousy 微露妒意 ⑤染发剂 **II** *vt*. 给…着色, 给…染色 ‖*flat* ~ 制服 ‖~**er** *n*. ①着色者, 染色者; 着色器, 染色器 ②(作衬底的)素色幻灯片 / ~**less** *a*. 无色的

tiny ['taini] *a*. 极小的; 微小的: a ~ minority 极少数 / a little ~ (或 ~ little) boy 小得可怜的男孩

tip[1] [tip] **I** *n*. ①梢, 末端; 尖, 尖端: the ~ of a toe (finger) 脚趾(手指)尖 / the ~ of a hill 山顶 / at the southern ~ of an island 在岛的最南端 ②(鸟或飞机的)翼尖, 翼梢 ③顶端附加的小件(或套子); 鞋尖: pencils with rubber ~s 有橡皮头的铅笔 / filter ~s (香烟的)过滤嘴; 有过滤嘴的香烟 ④镀金用的刷子 **II** (tipped; tipping) *vt*. ①在…的顶端装附加物: filter-*tipped* cigarettes 过滤嘴香烟 ②覆盖(或装饰)…的尖端 (*with*); 作为…的尖端 ③去掉(生长物)的尖端 ④(在书页间装订处)粘附(插页) ⑤为(毛皮)尖端上色 ‖*have sth. at the ~s of one's fingers* 手头就有某物, 有某物随时可供应用 / *have sth. on* (或 *at*) *the ~ of one's tongue* 差点说出某事, 差一点就能想起某事; 某事就在嘴边: I had his name *on the ~ of my tongue*. 他的名字就在我嘴边。(意指一时想不起) / *to the ~s of one's fingers* 彻底地, 彻头彻尾地 ‖~**staff** *n*. [古]装有金属头的杖(法警的标志); 法警 / '~-**tilted** *a*. (鼻子等)尖端翘起的 / '~'**top** *n*. 绝顶, 最高点 ②[口]出色的, 第一流的: a ~*top* hotel 第一流旅馆 *ad*. [口]非常好地: You have done ~*top*. 你干得好极了。

tip[2] [tip] **I** (tipped; tipping) ❶ *vt*. ①使倾斜: He sat with his chair *tipped* up. 他翘起椅子坐着。 / ~ one's head to one side 把头歪向一边 / ~ the balance of power in favour of 使力

量对比有利于… ②使翻倒, 使倾覆: The typhoon nearly *tipped over* the house. 台风几乎把屋子刮倒。 / be *tipped* into a ditch 被摔进沟里 ③[英]倒, 倾泻: ～ water out of a pail 把水从水桶中倒出 / ～ cinders into a dustbin 把炉灰倒人垃圾箱 ❷ *vi.* ①倾斜 ②翻倒, 倾覆 **II** *n.* ①倾斜: have a slight ～ to the south 稍稍向南倾斜 ②(垃圾等的)弃置场 ‖～ *over* 倒翻 ②[美俚]抢劫; 搜查 ③[美俚]死 / ～ *the scale(s)* 见 scale² ‖～cart *n.* 倾卸车, 翻斗车 / ～ lorry, ～ truck 自动倾卸车, 翻斗卡车 / '～-up seat (戏院等的)翻椅

tip³ [tip] **I** (tipped; tipping) ❶ *vt.* ① 轻击; 轻触: ～ the ball with one's bat 用球拍轻轻击球 / The sword *tipped* his arm. 剑轻轻触到他的手臂。 / ～ one's hat 轻触帽沿(表示敬意) ②给; 递送: ～ sb. a song (yarn) 给某人唱歌(讲故事) / ～ sb. a signal 给某人一个信号, 向某人示意 / ～ sb. the wink 向某人眨眼示意 ③给(侍者等)小费 ④向(某人)泄露消息, 泄露关于(某事)的消息; 暗示; 告诫: be *tipped* (*off*) to flee in time 接到消息(或被告诫)及时逃走 / ～ the plot 泄露阴谋 ⑤提示…作为可能的优胜者(或有利可图的投资对象) ❷ *vi.* ①踮着脚走 ②给小费 **II** *n.* ①小费 ②告诫; 提示: Take my ～ and don't run the risk. 听我的告诫, 不要冒这险。/ give sb. the ～ to do sth. 提示某人做某事 ③(关于行情等的)秘密消息; 预测: give sb. the straight ～ 把可靠消息透露给某人 ④轻推; 轻击 ‖*miss one's* ～ 失算, 打错主意 / ～ *off* ①向…泄露消息; 告诫 ②[俚]杀死 / *one's hand* 见 hand / ～ *sb.'s mit(t)* [美俚]泄露某人的秘密 ‖'～-and-'run *a.* 打了就跑的: a ～-*and-run* raid 打了就跑的袭击 / '～-off *n.* ①告诫; 提示 ②(篮球比赛开始时的)跳球 / ～ *sheet* (股票买卖、赛马等的)内情通报

tipple¹ ['tipl] **I** ❶ *vt.* 一点一点地连续饮 (烈酒) ❷ *vi.* 饮烈酒; 惯饮烈酒, 酗酒 **II** *n.* 致醉的饮料; 烈酒 ‖～r *n.* 惯饮烈酒者; 酒徒

tipple² ['tipl] *n.* ① (运货卡车上的) 自动倾卸装置 ②倒煤场; 筛煤场

tipster ['tipstə] *n.* 提供赛马情报(或股票行情等)的人; 告密者

tipsy ['tipsi] *a.* ①喝醉的, 微醉的 ②步履不稳的, 摇摇晃晃的 ③歪斜的: a ～ fence 歪斜的篱笆 ‖*tipsily ad.* / *tipsiness n.*

tiptoe ['tiptou] **I** *n.* 脚趾尖; 脚尖 **II** *ad.* 踮着脚 **III** *a.* ①踮着脚走(或站)的 ②小心翼翼的; 偷偷摸摸的 **IV** *vi.* ①踮起脚 ②踮着脚走; 蹑手蹑脚地行进 ‖*be on (the)* ～ *of expectation* 翘首以待, 殷切期待 / *on* ～ 踮着脚

tirade [tai'reid] *n.* 长篇的激烈演说(尤指指责性的)

tire¹ ['taiə] ❶ *vi.* ①疲劳, 累: The patient ～s very soon if he exerts himself. 病人一用力气就感到疲劳。/ He seemed to be *tiring*. 他看上

去累了。 ②厌倦, 厌烦 (*of*): He never ～s of helping others. 对帮助别人他从不厌倦。❷ *vt.* ① 使疲倦, 使累: The long walk ～d the child. 走了一长段路孩子累了。 ②使厌倦, 使厌烦: He ～d the audience *with* his long speeches. 他的冗长发言使听众不耐烦了。‖～ *out* 使十分疲劳

tire² ['taiə] [美] *n.* & *vt.* = tyre¹ ‖*peel* ～*s* [美俚](驾车时)突然加大油门

tire³ ['taiə] **I** *n.* ① (女用) 头发, 头饰; [古]服装 **II** *vt.* ① [古]打扮, 装饰 ②梳理(头发) ‖'～-,woman *n.* 贵妇人的女侍 / 'tiring-house *n.* (剧院的)化装间 / 'tiring-room *n.* 化装室(尤指剧院内的)

tired ['taiəd] *a.* ①疲劳的, 累的: Are you ～? 你累了吗? / He was a ～ man when the long race was over. 当他跑完长跑后, 他疲乏极了。/ Go to bed. You look ～ *out*. 去睡觉吧, 你看上去疲倦极了。 ②厌倦; 厌烦 (*of*): be ～ *of* (doing) sth. 厌烦(做)某事 ③破旧的; 陈腐的, 陈旧的: a ～ chair 破旧的椅子 / a ～ joke 老得没牙的笑话 ‖～ly *ad.* / ～ness *n.*

tireless ['taiəlis] *a.* ①不疲劳的, 不累的; 不厌倦的: a ～ worker 工作起来孜孜不倦的人 / be ～ in teaching 海人不倦 ②坚韧的, 不停的, 持久的: ～ energy 持久的精力 ‖～ly *ad.*

tiresome ['taiəsəm] *a.* 使人疲劳的; 令人厌倦的; 讨厌的: a ～ piece of work 一项累人的工作 / a ～ lecture 使人不耐烦的演讲 ‖～ly *ad.*

tissue ['tisju:] *n.* ①薄绢; 纱; 织物 ②薄纸, 棉纸: toilet ～ 卫生纸 / face ～s 化妆纸 ③[生]组织: connective ～ 结缔组织 / nervous ～ 神经组织 ④[喻](罗织成章的)一套; 连篇: a ～ of lies 连篇谎言 ‖～d 金银线织的, 织锦的 ‖～ *paper* 薄纸, 纱纸

tit¹ [tit] *n.*【动】山雀

tit² [tit] *n.* 轻打 ‖～ *for tat* 针锋相对: give (或 pay) ～ *for tat* 针锋相对

tit³ [tit] *n.* ① [古]小马, 劣马 ②[俚][贬]小女孩, 女人

tit⁴ [tit] *n.* 奶头

titanic [tai'tænik] *a.*【化】钛的, 四价钛的: ～ acid 钛酸

titbit ['titbit] *n.* 少量吸引人的东西 (如精美的食物、新闻等); 珍品; 珍闻

tithe [taið] **I** *n.* ① [常用复] (向教会交纳的)农产品什一税 ②十分之一; 小部分; 一点点: I cannot remember a ～ of it. 这事我一点点儿也想不起来。 ③ 杂税 **II** ❶ *vt.* 向…征收什一税; 把(农产品等)的十分之一缴纳 ❷ *vi.* 缴纳什一税 ‖*tithable a.* 可征收什一税的; 应缴什一税的 ‖～ *barn* 储放什一税农产品的仓库

title ['taitl] **I** *n.* ① (书籍、诗歌、乐曲等的)标题, 题目; 书名, 篇名 ② (书刊的)扉页 ③称号; 衔头 (如爵位、官衔、学衔等); 有衔头的人 (尤指贵族) ④权利, 资格; 所有权; 所有权凭证: have

~ **to do sth.** 有权做某事 ⑤【宗】(英国国教的)就任圣职须具备的资格; (天主教的)教区 ⑥【体】锦标,冠军: win the man's singles ~ 获得男子单打冠军 ⑦(电影或电视的)字幕: credit ~s (电影或电视中映出的)制作人员名单 ⑧(以"开"数表示的金的)成色 II *vt.* ①加标题于 ②授予…称号;用衔头称呼 ||quiet ~【律】判决产权属谁 / *regal* ~ 王的称号 ||~**d** *a.* 有爵位的,有贵族头衔的 / **titlist** *n.* (体育运动项目的)冠军保持者或扡 / **~deed**【律】地契 / **~holder** *n.* 拥有称号者;【体】冠军 / **match** 锦标赛 / **page** (书刊的)扉页,书名页 / ~ **role** (戏剧或电影中其名被用作剧名或片名的)剧名角色,片名角色

titter ['titə] I *n.* 窃笑; 傻笑 II *vi.* 窃笑; 傻笑; 嗤嗤地笑

tit(t)ivate ['titiveit] *vt.* & *vi.* 打扮, 装饰 ||**tit(t)ivation** [,titi'veiʃən] *n.*

tittle ['titl] *n.* ①(书写或印刷中的) 小点, 符号 ②一点点, 微量: There is *not one jot or* ~ of evidence against him. 没有丝毫证据说明他错了(或有罪)。||**to a** ~ 丝毫不差地

tittle-tattle ['titl,tætl] *n.* & *vi.* 闲聊, 漫谈

titular ['titjulə] I *a.* ①享有所有权的, 有权持有的: ~ possessions 有权持有的财产 ②有名无实的; 挂名的, 空衔的 ③有称号的; 有衔头的 ④题名的; (小说、戏剧中的人物) 被用作标题(或片名、剧名)的: a ~ role 剧名角色 II *n.* 有称号(或衔头)的人(尤指挂名不做事的人) ||**~ly** *ad.*

Tl【化】元素铊 (thallium) 的符号

to¹ I [强 tu:; 弱 tu, tə] *prep.* ①[表示方向、距离]到, 向, 往: go ~ the countryside 到农村去 / from top ~ bottom 从上到下;完完全全 / turn ~ the left 向左转 / ten kilometres ~ the station 离车站十公里
②[表示状态的变化]趋于, 倾向: grow ~ manhood 长大成人 / be slow ~ anger 不易生气 / a tendency ~ improvement 改善的趋势 / stand ~ attention 立正 / To arms!【军】武装紧急集合!
③[表示时间]直至…为止, 在…之前: stay ~ the end of the month 呆到月底 / from Monday ~ Saturday 从星期一到星期六 / from morning ~ night 从早到晚 / ten minutes ~ nine 九点差十分
④[表示程度]到, 达到: ~ the best of one's ability 竭尽所能 / exert oneself ~ the utmost 使出全部力量 / to a certain extént (或 degree) 到达某种程度,在某种程度上 / The answer was ~ the point. 回答得很中肯。
⑤[表示对应]对…: be opposed ~ sth. 与某事物相对立,反对某事物
⑥[表示间接关系]给…,于…: To whom did you send the message? 你把信儿捎给谁啦? / address a letter ~ sb. 把信写给某人 / a field planted

corn 种玉米的田
⑦[表示归属]归于
⑧[表示比较]比: The score was 6 ~ 2. 比分是六比二。/ He is quite strong now ~ what he used to be. 与过去的情况相比他现在是很强壮了。/ This machine is far superior ~ that one. 这台机器比那台好得多。/ prefer death ~ surrender 宁死不投降
⑨[表示数量与单位的关系]每: 50 pieces ~ the box 每箱五十件 / 200 persons ~ the square kilometre 每平方公里二百人
⑩[表示目的]为了: ~ that end 为了那个目的 / come ~ sb.'s aid 前来帮助某人 / with a view ~ improving one's work 为了改进工作 / drink ~ sb.'s health 为某人的健康干杯
⑪[表示关连、联系]对于,至于,关于: the right answer ~ the question 对那问题的正确答复 / What do you say ~ that? 你对那有什么意见? / Water is ~ fish what air is ~ man. 水对鱼的关系正如空气对人的关系一样。/ an appendix ~ a dictionary 词典的附录 / secretary ~ the premier 总理的秘书 / be open ~ the public 向公众开放 / hold ~ one's opinions 坚持己见 / That's all there is ~ it. 那就是有关这点的一切。(或: 如此而已。)
⑫[表示适应、遵照]按, 按照; 随同, 伴随: add salt ~ taste 按照口味加盐 / ~ sb.'s knowledge 据某人所知 / The map was drawn ~ scale. 这地图是按比例绘制的。/ sing ~ the piano 钢琴伴唱
⑬[表示结果、效果]致, 致使: all ~ no purpose 毫无结果 / To our great surprise, he didn't turn up. 使我们很奇怪的是他竟然没有露面。
⑭[~ oneself] 专为…单独所有(或所用); 专对: have the room ~ *oneself* 独住一间 / This problem gets a chapter ~ *itself*. 这一问题有专门一章加以讨论。/ keep oneself ~ *oneself* 不与人来往 / think ~ *oneself* 自忖 / talk ~ *oneself* 自言自语
⑮[表示原因]由于: fall ~ one's opponent's blows 受到对手的打击而倒下
II [tu:] *ad.* ①向前: put on one's hat wrong side ~ 前后颠倒地戴上帽子
②(指门窗等)关上; 虚掩着: The door snapped ~. 门砰地一声关上了。/ The door is ~. 门虚掩着。/ leave the door ~ 让门虚掩着
③着手(干): It's time we turned ~. 我们该动手干了。/ fall ~ 着手干; 开始进食
④在近旁: We were close ~ when it happened. 那事发生时我们就在近旁。
⑤(用)上: set ~ one's seal 盖印 / put the horses ~ 套上马
⑥苏醒过来: The wounded has come ~. 伤者已苏醒。/ bring sb. ~ 使某人苏醒过来
||~ **and fro** 往复地,来回地: Trucks shuttled

~ *and fro* on the highways. 公路上载重汽车穿梭似地来来往往。
‖ **~-and-fro** ['tu(ː)ən'frou] *a.* 来来往往的，往复的: *~-and-fro* motion 往复运动 *n.* 来来往往，往复；动摇

to² [强 tuː; 弱 tu, tə] **I** [与原形动词一起构成动词不定式；动词不定式用法如下] ① [用作主语或表语]: *To* see is ~ believe. 百闻不如一见。② [用作宾语]: propose ~ stay 建议留下 / want ~ know 想要知道 / begin ~ read 开始读 ③ [用作定语]: a house ~ let 供出租的房屋 / in days ~ come 在未来的日子里 / He was the last person ~ leave the room. 他是最后一个离开房间的人。④ [用作状语]: They came ~ see us. 他们来看我们 / He lived ~ be ninety. 他活到九十岁。/ We rejoice ~ hear of your success. 听到你们的成就，我们很高兴。/ be ready ~ help 乐于帮助 / The tea is too hot ~ drink. 茶太烫了不能喝。⑤ [用作插入语]: *To* tell the truth, I know nothing about it. 老实说，我对此一无所知。**II** [用来代替动词不定式或不定式短语，避免重复]: You may go if you want ~. 你要去可以去。/ I meant to tell you, but forgot ~. 我本想告诉你，但是忘了。

toad [toud] *n.* ① [动] 蟾蜍，癞蛤蟆 ② (物) 讨厌的人 ‖ *a ~ under a hammer* 经常受压迫(或迫害)的人 / *eat sb.'s ~s* 拍某人的马屁 / *the biggest ~ in the puddle* [俚] (在政治方面或其他集团中) 众所公认的头子，要人 ‖ **~,eater** *n.* 谄媚者，马屁精 / **~,eating** *n.* 谄媚，拍马 / **'~fish** *n.* 蟾鱼科的鱼 / **'~flax** *n.* 【植】柳穿鱼属植物，蟾蜍 / **'~-in-the-'hole** *n.* 面拖烤肉 / **'~stone** *n.* 【地】蟾蜍岩 / **'~stool** *n.* 【植】伞菌科的菌；牛肝菌科的菌；毒蕈；毒菌

toady ['toudi] **I** *n.* 谄媚者，马屁精 **II** *vt. & vi.* 奉承，谄媚 ‖ **~ism** *n.* 奉承，谄媚

toast¹ [toust] **I** *n.* ① 烤面包(片)，吐司: two slices of ~ 两片烤面包 ② 烤面包做的食物 **II** ❶ *vt.* ① 烤，烘(面包等): the bread very dark 把面包烤得很焦黄 ② 使暖和: ~ oneself before a fire 烤火取暖 ❷ *vi.* 烤，烘；烘热: ~ in the sun 在阳光下取暖 ‖ *as warm as a* ~ 暖烘烘的 / *have sb. on* ~ [俚] 任意摆布某人 ‖ **~ing-fork** *n.* 长柄烤面包铁叉 (又作 ~ing-iron) / **~ rack** (餐桌上用的)面包架 / **~ water** 泡过烤面包的水(一种清凉饮料)

toast² [toust] **I** *n.* ① 祝酒，干杯: propose a ~ to the health of the guests 提议为来宾的健康干杯 / drink a ~ 干杯 / respond (或 reply) to the ~ 答谢祝酒，回敬 ② 祝酒词 ③ 受祝酒的人 (或事物)；受到高度敬仰的人: the ~ of the town 城里最受敬仰的人 **II** *vt.* 为…举杯祝酒 ‖ **~ee** [tous'tiː] *n.* 被祝酒的人 / **~er** *n.* 祝酒人 ‖ **~ list** 敬酒名单 / **'~,master** *n.* 宴会主持人 / **'~,mistress** *n.* 宴会女主持人

tobacco [tə'bækou] *n.* ① 烟草；烟叶: smoking ~ 板烟丝 / roasted ~ 烤烟 ② 烟草制品(如香烟、雪茄、鼻烟等): users of ~ 抽烟者，烟客 ③ 抽烟: swear off ~ 戒烟 ‖ **'~-,curing** *n.* 烟的生产,制烟 / **~ cutter** ① 切烟机,切烟刀 ② 切烟人 / **~ heart** 【医】烟毒心,烟毒性心脏 / **~ pipe** 烟斗 / **~ pouch** 烟(丝)袋

toboggan [tə'bɒgən] **I** *n.* ① 平底雪橇 ② 突然的下降 **II** *vi.* ① 坐雪橇滑行 ② (价格等)突然下降

tocsin ['tɒksin] *n.* ① 警钟；警报 ② 警讯信号

today, to-day [tə'dei, tu'dei] **I** *ad.* ① 在今天,在今日: I saw (shall see) him ~. 我今天看到过(将要看到)他。/ It is warm ~. 今天天气很暖(或热)。/ They are coming here ~ week (或 a week ~). 他们将于下星期的今天到这里来。/ I went there five years ago ~. 我是在五年前的今天到那里去的。② 现在,现今;当代 **II** *n.* ①今天, 今日: *Today* is Monday. 今天是星期一。/ ~'s newspaper 今天的报纸 ② 现在,现今;当代: science of ~ 现代科学

toddle ['tɒdl] **I** *n.* ① (小孩等的)蹒跚行走；[口] 信步 ② [口] 学步的小孩 **II** *vi.* (小孩在学步等时) 蹒跚行走；[口] 信步走: ~ round to see a friend 信步走着去看朋友 ‖ **~r** *n.* 蹒跚行走的人；学步的小孩；[口] 信步走的人

toddy ['tɒdi] *n.* ① 棕榈汁；棕榈酒 ② 加热水的烈酒；加热水的酒类饮料

to-do [tə'duː] *n.* [口] 骚扰；骚动；喧闹: What a ~! 多么吵闹啊! / make a terrible ~ about sth. 对某事大惊小怪,就某事喧嚷不休

toe [tou] **I** *n.* ① 脚趾；足尖；[口] 脚；(动物的)趾: the big (little) ~ 大(小)脚趾 ② (鞋、袜)的足尖部 ③ 脚趾状物；【建】坡脚；(木工)斜钉；【机】轴踵；(高尔夫球的)球棒尖 **II** ❶ *vt.* ① 用脚趾踢(或触)；用脚趾伸九: ~ the cigarette out 把香烟踩灭 / ~ sb. out 把某人踢出去 ② 装(鞋、袜等)的尖；修补(鞋、袜等)的尖: She ~d the stockings. 她给袜子装袜顶。③ 斜敲(或钉)(钉子等),斜敲钉子使…固定 ❷ *vi.* 动脚尖;用足尖立(或走): ~ in (out) 足尖朝内 (外) 走路 ‖ *from top to* ~ 完完全全 / *keep off sb.'s* ~ 由某人去自行其是 / *on one's* ~s [口] 警觉的；准备行动的 / *the light fantastic* ~ [谑] 跳舞 / *~ and heel (it)* [美] 跳舞 / *~ the line* 见 line¹ / *~ the mark* 见 mark¹ / *~ the scratch* 见 scratch / *tread* (或 *step*) *on sb.'s* ~s 踩某人的脚尖 ② 触怒某人, 得罪某人 / *turn one's* ~*s in* (*out*) (走路时)脚尖朝内(外) / *turn up one's* ~*s* [俚]死 ‖ **~less** *a.* ① 无趾的 ② (鞋子)无鞋尖的,鞋尖部镂空的 ‖ **~ cap** 鞋尖装饰,鞋尖饰皮；鞋头 / **~ dance** 足尖舞 / **'~hold** *n.* ① (攀登悬崖等时)不稳的小立足点 ② 克服困难的办法 ③ 初步的地位,微小的优势 / **'~-in** *n.* 车轮内向(汽车轮前部朝里倾斜) / **'~nail** *n.* ① 脚趾甲 ② (木工用的)斜钉

vt. 用斜钉钉牢 / **~ shoe, ~ slipper** 芭蕾舞鞋

toff [tɔf] *n.* [主英] 纨袴子弟, 花花公子; 时髦人物

toffee, toffy ['tɔfi] *n.* [英]奶脂糖, 太妃糖(=[美] taffy) ‖*not for* ~ [俚]绝不 / *not to be able to do sth. for* ~ [俚]对某事完全不胜任 ‖'**toffee= 'nosed** *a.* [英俚]势利的; 摆阔的

together [tə'geðə] *ad.* ①共同, 一起; 一致地: live ~ in the same house 同住在一所房子里 / fight ~ 一起战斗 / These colours go well ~. 这些颜色很相配。②集合起; 集拢地; 总合地: tie the two sticks ~ 把两根棍子绑在一起 / The two countries are held ~ by a common cause. 共同的事业把这两个国家联合在一起。/ The company leader called the fighters ~. 连长把战士们召集起来。/ All ~, there are 15 items. 总共有十五个项目。/ These facts, taken ~, explain the matter. 这些事实放在一起看就说明了问题。③[常用以加强语气]相互, 彼此: join ~ 彼此结合 / add ~ 相加 / They were not on good terms ~. 他们彼此间关系不和。④同时; 连续, 一连: events that happened ~ 同时发生的事 / talk for hours ~ 一连谈了好几个小时 ⑤ 头脑清楚而镇定 ‖*get* ~ 见 **get** / *go* ~ 见 **go** / *put two and two* ~ 见 **two** / ~ *with* 和; 加之; 连同: I am sending you the book, ~ *with* all the available comments on it. 我把这本书寄给你, 随同附上所能得到的一切有关评论。‖**~ness** *n.*

toil[1] [tɔil] **I** *n.* ①辛苦, 劳累 ②苦工, 苦活; 难事: Some books are a ~ to read. 有些书读起来真费劲。**II ❶** *vi.* ①苦干, 辛劳地从事(于)(*at, on, through*): ~ at one's task 辛苦工作 ②艰苦地行动; 跋涉: ~ along the road 艰苦地沿路行进 / ~ up hill 使劲爬上山 ❷ *vt.* [古]①使过分操劳 ②费劲地做, 费劲地完成 ‖*sweet* ~ 喜欢干的辛苦工作 / ~ *and moil* 辛辛苦苦地工作 ‖**~er** *n.* 辛勤工作的人, 劳苦者; 勤劳者 / **~ful** *a.* 辛苦的, 劳苦的 / **~less** *a.* 不费力的, 容易的 ‖'**~worn** *a.* 疲劳的, 工作疲乏的, 劳累了的

toil[2] [tɔil] *n.* [常用复]网, 罗网; 圈套, 陷阱: enmesh sb. in the ~s of the law 使某人陷入法网 ‖*be taken in the* ~**s** ①落网 ②被迷惑住

toilet ['tɔilit] **I** *n.* ①梳妆, 打扮: make one's ~ 梳理打扮 / ~ articles 梳妆用具 / spend a few minutes on one's ~ 花几分钟进行梳洗 ②[古]梳妆台 ③ 女式服装; 服饰: an elaborate ~ 盛服; 艳妆 ④ 盥洗室, 浴室; 厕所; 便池, 抽水马桶 ⑤【医】(手术前后的)洗涤 **II ❶** *vi.* ①梳妆, 打扮 ②上盥洗室; 上厕所 ❷ *vt.* ①给…穿衣; 给…梳妆打扮 ②照料(孩子)上厕所 ‖**~ry** *n.* 化妆用品, 梳妆用具 ‖**~ bowl** 抽水马桶 / ~ **cover** 梳妆台布 / ~ **glass** 梳妆镜 / ~ **paper** 卫生纸, 草纸 / ~ **powder** 扑粉, 爽身粉 / '**~-roll** *n.* 卫生卷纸 / ~ **seat** 马桶座圈 / ~ **set** 梳妆用具 / ~ **soap** 香皂 / ~ **table** 梳妆台 / ~ **water** 花露水

token ['toukən] **I** *n.* ①表示; 标志, 象征; 记号, 【语】语言符号: He did that as a ~ of good faith. 他那样做是为了表示诚意。② 特征; 证明; 信物 ③ 纪念品: give sb. a book as a going-away ~ 送某人一本书作为临别纪念 ④【英史】民铸货币, 代币 ⑤辅币, 代价券: a bus ~ 公共汽车专用辅币 **II** *a.* ①作为标志的, 表意的: a ~ gesture 表意的姿势 / 象征性的, 装门面的: a ~ attack (或 resistance) 象征性的攻击(或抵抗) ‖*as a* ~ *of* 作为…的标志(或象征) / *by the same* ~ 由于同样原因 / *by this* ~ 由此看来, 照此说来 / *in* ~ *of*=as a ~ of / *more by* ~ [古]=by the same ~ ‖**~ism** *n.* 装门面, 表面文章 / ~ **money** 【英史】(商人自铸、价值较低但可兑换标准货币的)代币 / ~ **payment** 象征性偿付(偿付所欠的一小部分, 作为承认该债务的象征) / ~ **vote** 议会象征性的拨款(意为同意政府支用较大金额而无须再行讨论或表决)

told [tould] tell 的过去式和过去分词

tolerable ['tɔlərəbl] *a.* ①(苦痛等)可忍受的; (错误等)可容忍的, 可宽恕的: The pain was severe but ~. 痛得很厉害, 但是还忍得住。②尚好的, 尚可的; 过得去的: The food was ~. 食物质量还可以。③[口](身体)还算健康的 ‖**tolerability** [,tɔlərə'biliti] *n.* 可忍性; 尚可 / **tolerably** *ad.* 过得去地, 还算不错地: be tolerably well 还算健康

tolerance ['tɔlərəns] *n.* ①忍受; 容忍, 宽恕; [罕]耐性, 坚韧性: show ~ towards sb. 容忍某人, 宽恕某人 ②【机】(配合)公差; 【物】容限 ③ (食物中)残存杀虫剂的法定容许量 ④【医】耐(药)量, 耐受性

tolerant ['tɔlərənt] *a.* ①忍受的; 容忍的, 宽恕的: be ~ of opinions different from one's own (能)容忍不同意见 / be ~ toward sb. 宽容某人 ②有耐药力的 ‖**~ly** *ad.*

tolerate ['tɔləreit] *vt.* ① 忍受; 容忍, 宽恕; 默认; ② 有耐(药)力

toleration [,tɔlə'reiʃən] *n.* ① 忍受; 容忍, 宽恕; 默认 ②信仰自由 ③(食物中)残存杀虫剂的法定容许量

toll[1] [toul] **I** *n.* ①(道路、桥梁、港口、市场等的)捐税; 通行费, 通过税: levy ~ on sb. 向某人征收捐税 / ~s on the canal 运河通行费 ② 服务费用; 运费; 长途电话费: a telegraphic ~ 电报费 ③[英](磨谷物时)磨坊作为费用抽取的部分谷物 ④(通行税等的)征收权 ⑤重大的代价; 损失; (事故等的)伤亡人数: death ~ 死亡人数 / road ~ 车祸伤亡 **II ❶** *vi.* 征收捐税 ❷ *vt.* ①抽取…的部分作为费用; 作为捐税征收 ②向(某人)征收捐税 ‖*take* ~ *of* ①抽取…的一部分 ②夺去; 使遭受伤亡 ‖~ **bar** =~**gate** / ~ **bridge** 征税卡, 收费桥 / ~ **call** 收费的长途电话 / '**~gate** *n.* 收费门, 收(通行)税卡口 / '**~house** *n.* 征税所, 收税处 / ~ **line** 长途电话线 / ~ **man** ['toulmən] *n.* 收税人 / ~ **thorough** [英]道

路税; 过桥费 / **~ traverse** [英]私有地通行
税 / **~ turn** [英]牲畜市场税

toll² [toul] **I ❶** *vt.* ① 鸣(钟), 敲(钟): **~** the
death knell for sb. 为某人敲响丧钟 ② 鸣钟报
告(时辰、噩耗等); 鸣钟召唤(人等): **~** the hour
of day 鸣钟报时 ❷ *vi.* ① 鸣钟, 敲钟 ②缓慢而
有规律地响 **II** *n.* 钟声

toll³ [toul] *vt.* ①引诱, 勾引 ②引诱(猎物)接近;
用诱饵引(鱼); 把(家畜)引到目的地

tomahawk ['tɔməhɔːk] **I** *n.* (北美印第安人用的)
石斧; 战斧, 钺 **II** *vt.* ① 用斧劈(或斩);用战斧
砍杀 ②苛评(文学作品等) ‖**bury** (或 **lay aside**)
the ~ 停战;讲和 / **dig up** (或 **raise, take up**)
the ~ 宣战

tomato [tə'mɑːtou; 美 tə'meitou] ([复] tomatoes)
n. ①番茄, 西红柿: **~** paste 番茄酱 / currant
~ [植]醋栗番茄 ②[俚]脸; 头 ③[俚]美貌女子
④[俚]蹩脚的拳击手

tomb [tuːm] **I** *n.* ① 坟, 冢; 墓碑 ②[the **~**] [喻]
死亡 **II** *vt.* 埋葬; 把…葬入坟墓 ‖**'~stone** *n.*
墓碑, 墓石

tome [toum] *n.* ①册, 卷 ②大册书; (学术巨著的)
大本书

tomorrow, to-morrow [tə'mɔrou, tu'mɔrou] **I** *ad.*
在明天, 在明日: I'll see you **~**. (或 See you
~.) 明天见。 **II** *n.* ① 明天, 明日: *Tomorrow*
will be (或 is) Saturday. 明天是星期六。 / **~'s**
newspaper 明天的报纸 / the day after **~** 后
天 / **~** morning (afternoon, evening) 明天上午
(下午, 晚上) / **~** week 下星期的明天 ② 来日,
未来: the world's **~** 世界的未来 ‖**Don't put**
off till ~ what should be done today. [谚]
今日事今日毕。 / **Tomorrow never comes.**
[谚]切莫依赖明天。‖**~er** *n.* 做事拖延的人

tom-tom ['tɔmtɔm] **I** *n.* ①(狭长的)印度手鼓; 锣
②单调的敲打; 单调的节拍 **II** (tom-tommed;
tom-tomming) *vi.* 打鼓

ton [tʌn] ([复] ton(s)) *n.* ①(重量单位)吨; 公吨:
a long (或 gross) **~** 英吨 (=2240 磅) / a short
~ 美吨 (=2000 磅) / a metric **~** 公吨 (=1000
公斤或 2204.6 磅) / three **~**(s) of coal 三吨煤
②货物容积单位 (如木材等一般为 40 立方呎; 石
料为 16 立方呎; 盐为 42 蒲式耳; 小麦为 20
蒲式耳; 焦炭为 28 蒲式耳) ③ 商船登记的容
积单位; 船只装载单位 ④ 船只的排水吨 (=
displacement **~**, 相当于海水 35 立方呎) ⑤[常
用复][口]大量: **~s** of people 许许多多的人 /
have asked sb. **~s** of times 问过某人无数次 ⑥
[俚]每小时一百哩的速度: a **~**-up boy 以每小
时一百哩速度飞驰的摩托车驾驶者 ‖**hit like a**
~ of bricks [美俚]极打动人; 使人惊愕

ton [tɔ̃ːŋ] *n.* [法]时髦, 时式, 流行 ‖**in the ~** 在
风行

tone [toun] **I** *n.* ①音, 乐音; 音质; 音调, 调子: a
voice with a full, clear **~** 洪亮的嗓音 / heart

~s [医]心音 / fundamental **~** [音]基音 / the
sweet **~s** of a violin 小提琴奏出的悦耳调子
②腔调, 语气: speak in a commanding **~** 用命
令的口吻说 / take a high **~** 口气傲慢 / reiterate
in most emphatic **~s** 十分强调地重申 / The
letter had a friendly **~**. 这封信语气友好。 /
read with a **~** 装腔作势地念 ③声调; 语调: the
four **~s** of Chinese characters 汉字的四声 / the
rising (falling) **~** 升(降)调 ④ 色调; 光度: red
with a purplish **~** 带紫的红色 / a photograph
in warm **~s** 暖色调的照片 ⑤[只用单]风气; 气
氛: the **~** of a school 校风 / the moral **~** 道德
风气 / His speech altered the **~** of the meeting.
他的讲话改变了会议的气氛。⑥身体及其各部分
的健康状况: lose (recover) **~** 失去(恢复)健康
⑦正常的弹性(或伸缩性): This wood has lost its
~. 这块木材失去了弹性。⑧(市场的)供销(或
价格)情况: The **~** of the stock market is not
steady. 股票市场价格不稳定。⑨思想状态; 心
情, 心境: be in a philosophical **~** 处于哲理性的
思想状态中 ⑩[音]全音; 全音程: whole-**~** scale
全音音阶 **II ❶** *vt.* ①用某种调子说; 装腔作势
地说(或念) ②给…定调子; 使变调子; 给(乐器)
定音调; 给(画面)决定色调: Excitement **~d** his
voice. 激动使他声调变了。③增强(机体): The
medicine **~d** up his system. 药物使他身体恢复
正常。④[摄]给…上色, 给…着色 ⑤调节(乐器
部件)使产生一定音质效果 ❷ *vi.* ①呈现悦目色
调 ②颜色调和(或和谐): The building **~s** (*in*)
well *with* the surroundings. 这建筑物和周围环
境颜色很调和。‖**Gregorian ~s** (基督教)赞美
诗传统唱法所用的调子 / **~ down** (使)降低;
(使)柔和; (使)缓和: **~ down** the colours of a
picture 使图画的色调柔和 / **~ down** sb.'s anger
缓和某人的怒气 / **~ in with** 与…相配合 / **~**
up 给…以更高(或更强)的调子; 增强, 增益:
~ up a picture 使图画的色调更明亮 / Tone up
a little here. 这儿的调子要略为提高一些。‖**~**
arm (唱机的)拾音器支臂 / **~ colo(u)r** 音色 /
'~-deaf *a.* 不善于辨别音高的 / **~ language**
声调语言 / **~ poem** 取材于文学的管弦乐曲; 色
调象诗一般和谐的绘画

toned [tound] *a.* ①[常用以构成复合词]具有…音
质的: a full-**~** voice 洪亮的嗓音 ②(语言)有声
调的 ③(纸张等)年久变色的

toneless ['tounlis] *a.* ① 缺乏声调(或色调)的
②单调的, 平板的, 沉闷的: recite a poem in
a **~** voice 用平板的声调朗诵诗 ‖**~ly** *ad.* /
~ness *n.*

tong¹ [tɔŋ] **I** *n.* [**~s**][用作单或复]钳, 镊, 夹子: a
pair of **~s** 一把钳子 / coal **~s** 火钳, 煤镊 **II** *vt.*
& *vi.* 用钳夹取(或夹住); 用钳收集 ‖**be** (或 **go**)
at it hammer and ~s 见 **hammer** / **hammer**
and ~s 见 **hammer**

tong² [tɔŋ] *n.* 堂 (在美国的中国侨民的兄弟会等帮
会组织)

tongue [tʌŋ] **I** *n.* ①舌,舌头: put out one's ~ 伸出舌头 (做鬼脸或给医生诊察) / coated (或 furred) ~【医】有苔舌 / a smoked ~ 熏舌肉 (作菜用) ② 说话能力(或方式);口才: have a loose ~ 惯于随口乱讲,饶舌 / have a rough ~ 说话粗鲁 / have a ready ~ 有敏捷的口才 / have a bitter ~ 嘴刻薄 / a silver ~ 流利的口才 / a slip of the ~ 失言,口误 ③语言;方言,方言,土语: one's mother ~ 祖国语言 / the Spanish ~ 西班牙语言 / speak a common ~ with ... 和…有共同的语言,和…说同样的话 ④ 舌状物;鞋舌;铃舌;环扣的针;车的辕杆;管乐器的簧片;秤的指针: ~s of fire 火舌 ⑤ 伸入海(或河、湖)中的狭长陆地;岬 ⑥【电】衔铁,舌簧,(继电器的)舌片 ⑦【建】雄榫 ⑧(铁路的)尖轨 ⑨【美俚】律师 **II ❶** *vt.* ①舔 ②用舌吹(管乐器) ③发(音): ~ the notes as instructed 按指导发音 ④【古】责骂;说,讲 ⑤在(木板等)上做舌榫;用雌雄榫连接(木板) **❷** *vi.* ①吹管乐器使发出音调 ②【罕】说话;饶舌 ③(地等)呈舌形突出 ‖*a ~ not understood of the people* 外国语 / *bite the ~* 保持缄默 / *find one's ~* (吓得或羞得说不出话之后) 能说话了,能开口了 / *give* (或 *throw*) ~ (猎狗发现猎物) 狂吠 / *have lost one's ~* 吓得 (或羞怯得) 说不出话来,开不出口 / *have sth. on* (或 *at*) *the tip of one's ~* 见 tip¹ / *hold one's ~* 不开口,缄默 / *keep a civil ~ in one's head* 措辞谨慎 / *oil one's ~* 说奉承话,谄媚 / *on the ~s of men* (或 *on everyone's ~*) 被众人谈论着 / *smite with the ~* 血口喷人;谴责 / *the gift of ~s* 说外语的能力 / *wag one's ~* 唠叨不停 / *with one's ~ in one's cheek* 假心假意地,说话无诚意地;说话带挖苦地 ‖*~less a.* 没有舌头的;不开口的,缄默的,哑的 ‖*~ster* ['tʌŋstə] *n.* 健谈的人;饶舌的人 ‖*~ bone* 舌骨 / '*~-lash vt.* 申斥,责骂;谴责 / '*~-,lashing n.* 申斥,责骂;谴责 / '*~-shy a.* 羞怯得说不出话来的;结结巴巴的 / '*~-tie n.* 短舌头 *vt.* 使发音不清;使说不出话 / '*~-tied a.* ①舌头短的;(由于为难等)开不出口的,结结巴巴的 / ~ **twister** 拗口令 (如 She sells sea shells by the seashore.)

tongued [tʌŋd] *a.* ①[常用以构成复合词] 有…舌头的;有…说话派头 (或方式) 的: loose-~ 饶舌的,随口乱说的 / a silver-~ orator 能言善辩的演说家 ②有舌头的

tonic ['tɔnik] **I** *a.* ① 滋补的,强身的: a ~ medicine 补药,强身剂 ② 使精神振作的,有兴奋作用的 ③【音】主音的 ④【语】声调的;声调语的;(音节)有重音的: ~ accent 声调重音 ⑤【医】强直的: ~ spasm 强直性痉挛 **II** *n.* ①补药,补剂: a hematic ~ 补血药 / a stomachic ~ 健胃药 ②有兴奋作用的东西;激励物: The good news acted as a ~ on us all. 这个好消息使我们大家感到振奋。③【音】主音 ④【语】浊音;重读音节 ‖~ **sol-fa** 首调唱法 (以字音,如 sol, fa, doh, 表示音符的教唱法) / ~ **water** 奎宁水

tonight, to-night [tə'nait, tu'nait] **I** *ad.* 在今夜,在今晚: the guests ~ 今晚的客人 **II** *n.* 今夜,今晚: ~'s radio news 今晚的广播新闻

tonkin [tɔn'kin] *n.* 越南产的一种竹(可作滑雪杖、钓鱼竿等)

tonnage ['tʌnidʒ] *n.* ①登记吨,登记吨位 (衡量船舶容积的单位);船舶的吨位 (或吨数): The ship has a ~ of 20,000. 这艘船载重两万吨。②(一国或一港口的)船舶总吨数 ③军舰的排水量 ④航运(或采掘等)的总吨数 ⑤每吨货物的运输费;船舶吨税 ‖*gross* ~ 总吨位 (或吨数) / *net* ~ 净吨位 / *register*(*ed*) ~ 登记吨位 (或吨数) / *dues* ~ 船舶吨税

tonsil ['tɔnsl] *n.*【解】扁桃体,扁桃腺 ‖**tonsil**(**l**)**ar** *a.*

tonsure ['tɔnʃə] **I** *n.* ①(当教士或入修道院时的)削发;削发仪式: give the ~ to 给…剃光头顶 / take the ~ 削发为僧,出家 ②僧侣头顶的剃光部分;(指头)光顶,秃顶 **II** *vt.* 为…削发;给…举行削发仪式 ‖*~d a.* 象教士 (或修道士) 那样剃光头顶的;削发出家的;头顶光秃的

too [tu:] *ad.* ①[用于肯定句]也, 还(否定句用 either): I'll go there ~. 我也要到那儿去。/ You, ~, may have a try. 你也可试一试。/ *Too*, the reader will find in this book many interesting illustrations. 读者还能在书中看到许多有趣的插图。②[用于肯定词组后]而且,还(否定词组后用 either): They got the work done quickly, and well ~. 他们迅速地把工作做完,而且做得很好。③[加强语气时用,无具体意义]: I will ~ go! 我要去的! ④太,过分: Don't read ~ fast. 不要念得太快。/ The shirt is ~ large (much ~ large, a little ~ large) for me. 衬衫我穿起来太大 (实在太大,稍大一些)。/ make ~ long a speech (或 a ~ long speech) 讲话讲得太长 / You have given me two copies ~ many (few). 你多(少)给了我两本。/ That's ~ much. 那太过分了。/ That's ~ bad. 太糟糕了。(或:太不幸了。) / go ~ far 走得过远;讲话(或行动)太过分 ⑤非常,很: He is not ~ well these days. 这几天他身体不太好。/ How ~ terrible! 多么可怕呀! ‖*all* ~ 太: *all* ~ quickly 太快 / *cannot* (或 *can never*) ... ~ ... 怎么…也不会过分: You *cannot* praise the play ~ highly. 这出戏你无论怎样称赞都不会过分。/ One can never be ~ careful in one's work. 工作越过细越好。/ *none* ~ 一点也不: *none* ~ soon 一点也不早 / *one* ~ *many* 见 one / *one* ~ *many* (或 *much*) *for* 见 one / *only* ~ 见 only / *quite* ~ 简直太 / *Too* (*bloody*) *Irish* (或 *right*)! 当然! / ~ ... *by half* [贬]可太…啦: ~ clever *by half* 可太聪明啦 / ~ *far north* 精明的,不会受骗的 / ~ *much* 见 much / ~ *much of a good thing* 见 much / ~ ... *to* ... 太…以致不能…: The child is ~ young *to* go to school. 那孩子还没到上学年龄。/ Instances are ~ numerous *to* list.

例子多得举不胜举。/ He is ~ careful not to have noticed it. 他那么细心，不会不注意到这一点的。/ ～ ～ 简直太

took [tuk] take 的过去式

tool [tu:l] I n. ①工具,器具,用具;刀具;器械;机床,工作母机: carpenter's ~s 木工工具 / farm ~s 农具 / a high speed turning ~ 高速车刀 / a machine ~ 机床,工作母机 ②爪牙;傀儡;走狗;[俚]扒手 ③(压印书籍封面文字或图案的)压印器 II ❶ vt. ①用工具给…加工(或成形);用凿刀修整(石块);压印图案于(书籍封面) ②用机床(或器械等)装备(工厂) (up) ③赶(马车);用车载(人) ❷ vi. ①使用工具 ②用机床(或器械等)装备工厂 ③赶车;乘车 ‖'~box n. 工具箱 / '~holder n. 【机】刀夹 / '~house n. 工具房 / '~maker n. 制造、维修、校准机床的机工 / ~ post, ~ rest 【机】刀架 / '~room n. 工具间 / ~ subject 工具课程(为具备学习其他课程所需要的技能而学的课程)

toot¹ [tu:t] I n. (喇叭、号角、笛等的)短而尖锐的声音;嘟嘟声 II ❶ vt. 使发嘟嘟声;吹奏出: ~ a horn 按(或吹)喇叭;吹号角 / The bugle ~ed advance. 号角吹出进军令。❷ vi. 吹喇叭(或号角等);发出嘟嘟声 ‖~er n. ①吹管乐器者 ②发出嘟嘟声的东西

toot² [tu:t] n. 酒宴;痛饮

tooth [tu:θ] I ([复] teeth [ti:θ]) n. ①牙齿: clean one's teeth 刷牙 / have a ~ out (或 pulled) 拔牙 / have all one's own teeth 牙齿全部完好无缺 ②齿状物;(齿轮、锯、梳、树叶等的)齿: a saw ~ 锯齿 / the teeth of a rake 耙齿 ③(用机器或手工制成的)粗糙面 ④嗜好;胃口: have a ~ for candy 喜欢吃糖果 ⑤起损害(或折磨、毁坏)作用的东西;强迫(或惩罚等)的有效手段 ‖a false (或 artificial) ~ 假牙 / canine ~ 【解】犬牙, 犬齿 / incisor ~ 【解】切牙, 门齿 / milk ~ 【解】乳牙, 乳齿 / molar ~ 【解】磨牙, 臼齿 / wisdom ~ 【解】智牙, 第三磨牙 II ❶ vt. ①给…装齿;使成锯齿状 ②给…如锯子锉齿 ③使…的表面粗糙 ❷ vi. (齿轮等)相咬, 啮合 ‖be armed to the teeth 武装到牙齿 / between the teeth 低声地 / cast (或 throw, fling) sth. in sb.'s teeth 用某事来面斥(或嘲骂)某人 / cut a ~ (或 one's teeth) 牙齿透(牙)肉而出: That child is cutting its teeth. 那幼孩在长新牙。/ cut one's wisdom teeth (或 eyeteeth) 开始懂事;开始识世故 / draw (或 pull) sb.'s teeth 使某人不能作恶;解除某人的武装;除去某人的爪牙 / escape by (或 with) the skin of one's teeth [口]幸免于难 / fly in the teeth of 悍然不顾…;公然违抗… / from one's teeth 怀恨地;无诚意地 / from the teeth outwards (或 forwards) 在表面上;无诚意地 / grind one's teeth 磨牙;咬牙切齿 / have a sweet ~ 喜欢吃甜食 / in spite of sb.'s teeth 不顾某人的反对 / in

the teeth ①直接反对, 对面冲突 ②当面;公然 / in the teeth of 抵挡着…的全部力量;对抗;面对;不顾: in the teeth of the wind 【海】逆着风 / lie in one's teeth 撒大谎 / long in the ~ 年纪大(原指马因年纪大而齿跟萎缩) / put teeth in (或 into)强制执行: put teeth in a law 强制执行一项法律 / set one's teeth 咬紧牙关; [喻]下决心对付困难(或苦恼等) / set sb.'s teeth on edge 使某人感到牙齿不舒服 / show one's teeth 作威胁姿态, 发怒 / sow dragon's teeth 挑动纠纷, 引起战争 / ~ and nail 竭尽全力地: fight ~ and nail 奋力作战, 拼命打 / to the teeth 当面, 公然 ‖~ed a. 有齿的, 装齿的;齿状物的 / ~less a. 没有牙齿的 / ~let ['tu:θlit] n. 小齿 / ~some ['tu:θsəm] a. 美味的, 可口的 ‖'~ache n. 牙痛 / '~brush n. 牙刷 / '~comb n. 细齿梳;篦子 / ~ ornament 【建】齿饰 / '~paste n. 牙膏 / '~pick n. ①牙签 ②[美俚]小刀: an Arkansas ~pick [美俚]有鞘的刀;猎刀, 匕首 / ~ powder 牙粉

top¹ [top] I n. ①顶, 顶部, 顶端: at the ~ of the hill 在山顶 / a gilt ~ 烫金的书顶 ②(物的)上面, 上边, 上部, 上端: the ~ of a table 桌面 / the ~ of a shoe 鞋面 / The submarine came to the ~. 潜水艇浮出水面。/ line 9 from the ~ 正数第九行 ③盖, 顶盖;篷: a smokestack ~ 烟囱盖 / a bottle ~ 瓶盖 / a carriage without a ~ 无篷的马车 ④最高职位(或成就);首位;居首位的人: take the ~ of the table 就上座, 坐在首席 / the government ~s 政府高级官员 ⑤顶点;最高度: The output of steel has reached the all-time ~. 钢产量达到了历史上最高点。/ shout at the ~ of one's voice 高声叫喊 ⑥精华: the ~ of the crop 收成中最好的一部分 ⑦戏院最高票价 ⑧[常用复](植物)长出地面的部分; (根菜类的)叶: turnip ~s 芜菁叶 ⑨开端: the ~ of the year 年初 / the ~ of a lake 湖泊接近进水源的部分 ⑩(一)束: (一磅半,常用作毛条、纤维等的计量单位) ⑪【纺】毛条;化纤条 ⑪(油)蒸出的轻馏份 ⑫【船】桅楼 ⑬正面镀过的金属钮扣 ⑭使球向前旋转的一击;向前旋转的球 ⑮[复](牌戏中)稳拿分的两张大牌 II (topped; topping) ❶ vt. ①盖;给…加盖(或顶): a mountain topped with snow 峰顶盖着雪的山 ②【农】截去(植物等)的顶端, 为…打尖; beets 剪去甜菜的叶子 ③到达…的顶部;上升到…的顶点, 高达: They topped the hill at 4 p. m. 他们于下午四时到达山顶。/ ~ the list 名列前茅;领衔 / He ~s 1.80 m. 他身高一米八十。④高于;超过;胜过;越过;出色地扮演(或完成): Production in many factories topped the highest level in history. 许多工厂的生产超过了历史上最高水平。/ He ~s us all at table tennis. 他的乒乓球比我们都打得好。/ ~ a barrier 越过障碍 / ~ one's part 出色地扮演所担任的角色; 出色地完成所担任的工作 ⑤用分馏法提炼

⑥给…涂上保护层;【纺】套染,套色染…;用颜料染(毛条等) ⑦【海】使(桅桁等)倾斜 ⑧击(球)使向前旋转 ⑨[美俚]绞死,杀死 ❷ vi. ①结束,完成 (off, out, up) ②胜过某人(或某物) Ⅲ a. 顶的;顶上的;最高的;头等的: the ~ floor 顶层 / in ~ form (或 shape) 很健康;竞技状态极好 / ~ officials 最高级官员 / ~ talks 最高级会谈 / ~ honours 最高荣誉 / at ~ speed 用全速 / ~ priority 绝对优先 / the ~ news 头条新闻 ‖at the ~ of one's lungs 用尽量大的声音 / at the ~ of the tree (或 ladder) 在本行业中居登峰造极的地位 见 dog / blow one's ~ [俚]发脾气,勃然大怒 / come out (at the) ~ 名列前茅 / come to the ~ 出名;成功 / from ~ to toe (或 bottom) 从头到脚;完完全全: survey sb. from ~ to toe 从头到脚打量某人 / go over the ~ ①(进攻时)跳出战壕 ②采取断然步骤 ③超过限额(或指标) / in ~ [英]用高速档,全速地: a car running in ~ 全速前进的汽车 / off one's ~ 神经失常 / on ~ ①在上面 ②成功 ③领先: He went on ~ in the last lap. 他跑到最后一圈时领先了。 ④(指飞行)在云层上面 ⑤ =in ~ / on ~ of ①驾驭;熟练掌握: a man on ~ of his job 胜任工作的人 / persons on ~ of the situation 通晓情况(或掌握局面)的人们 ②在…之上;除…之外,另加,还有: put this book on ~ of others 把这本书放在其他书的上面 / He writes for the newspaper on ~ of his regular job. 他除了日常工作外,还为报纸写稿。 ③在…左近;紧接着…: When I turned the corner, I was right on ~ of the post office. 转过弯,邮局就在我眼前。 / Victories come on ~ of each other. 胜利一个接着一个。 / on ~ of the world [口]幸福到极点,对一切都感到满意 / talk off the ~ of one's head ①作即席谈话 ②假充内行谈论自己不熟悉的题目 / the big ~ 马戏团的大帐篷 / the ~ of the morning (to you) [爱尔兰]早晨好 / (the) ~s [用作表语][俚]最好的,最能干的,最受欢迎的 / ~ off 结束,完成 / ~ up ①装满,加满 ② =~ off / to the ~ of one's bent 尽情地 / to ~ it all [常用作插入语]更有甚者,更奇怪(或糟糕)的是 ‖~ful a. 满的,满到边的 / ~less a. 无顶的,无盖的,无篷的 / ~most a. 最高的,最上面的 ‖~ banana [美俚]①主要演员(尤指喜剧主角) ②最重要人物 / ~ billing [美]演员表上最显著的地位;特等广告 / ~ boots 一种长筒马靴 / ~ brass [美][总称]要员 / '~'coat n. 轻便大衣 / '~-dog a. 居支配地位的,有最高权威的 / '~-'down a. 组织、控制、管理严密的 / ~ drawer 社会最上层;最高权威阶层 / '~-'drawer a. 最高级别的;头等重要的;社会最上层的 / ~-drawer socialites 社交界知名人士 / '~-'dress vt. 给(土地)施表肥;表面处治(路面等) / '~-'dressing n. 土表追肥,顶肥;表面处治 / '~flight a. [口]第一流的,最好的,最高级

的 / '~gallant n. 【船】上桅;上桅帆 a. 上桅(或上桅帆)的;隆起的,高起的 / '~-,hamper n. 【船】高处的索具及其它笨重物件;多余碍事的东西 / ~ hat 大礼帽 / '~-'heavy a. 头重脚轻的;上层机构臃肿的;投资过多的 / [英]高级的;头等的 / '~hole n. ①顶髻;头饰 ②(鸟的)冠毛 / '~-'level a. 最高级的: a ~-level conference 最高级会议 / ~ light, ~ lantern 旗舰后桅楼的灯 / '~line n. 动物身体上部从头至尾的外形线 / '~-'line a. 头条新闻的: ~-line news 头条新闻 / '~,liner n. [主英] 头条新闻中的人物(或事件) / '~'lofty a. 在上手的锯工 ②地面上工作的矿工 ③地面上做杂务的建筑工人 ④操作拔顶蒸馏器的工人 / '~mast n.【船】中桅 / '~'notch n. 顶点 / '~-'notch a. [口]最高质量的;第一流的 / topped crude 【油】拔顶原油 / '~-,ranking a. 最高级的 / ~sail ['tɒpsl, 'tɒpseil] n. 【船】中桅帆 / '~sawyer 在上手的锯工 / [喻]居高位者,地位优越者 / '~-'secret a. 绝密的 / '~'side n. ①[复]【船】顶边,舷侧 ②[总称]最高级人员 ad. ①在甲板上(又作 ~sides) ②到顶;到面上 ③处于权威地位 / ~sman ['tɒpsmən] n. [英]在桅楼执行任务者 / ~soil n. 表土层,土层;土壤耕种层 vt. ①用表土铺盖 ②去掉(地面)的表土 / '~work vt. 剪顶枝嫁接(果树等)

top² [tɒp] n. 陀螺: The ~ sleeps (或 is asleep). 陀螺转得很稳。 ‖old ~ [俚](称呼)老兄,老朋友 / sleep like a ~ 熟睡

topaz ['toupæz] n. ①【矿】黄玉 ②南美的蜂鸟

topic ['tɒpik] Ⅰ n. ①(文章、讲演的)题目,论题,话题;(节、段的)主题: a ~ sentence 说明段落主题的句子 ②(提纲、大纲的)标题,细目 Ⅱ a.【医】局部的 ‖~ book [英]一组丛书中的一本

topical ['tɒpikəl] a. ①题目的;主题的;论题的,话题的 ②有关时事的 ③某一地方的;【医】局部的: a ~ anaesthetic 局部麻醉剂 ‖~ly ad.

topographic(al) [,tɒpə'græfik(əl)] a. 地形的;地形学的;地形测量的: ~ features 地貌,地形情况 / a ~ map 地形图 / ~ surveying 地形测量 / ~ troops 【军】测绘部队 ‖**topographically** ad.

topography [tə'pɒgrəfi] n. ①地志 ②地形;地形学;地形测量学 ③局部解剖学,局部解剖图

topple ['tɒpl] ❶ vt. 使倒塌;推翻,颠覆 (down, over) ❷ vi. ①倒塌,倒下 (down, over) ②摇摇欲坠

topsy-turvy ['tɒpsi'tə:vi] Ⅰ ad. & a. 颠倒地(的);乱七八糟地(的) Ⅱ n. 颠倒;混乱 Ⅲ vt. 使颠倒;使乱七八糟 ‖~dom n. ①颠倒(或混乱)状态 ②混乱世界

torch [tɔ:tʃ] n. ①火炬,火把 ②【机】喷灯,气炬,吹管: welding ~ 吹管焊接 ③[主英]手电筒 ④[俚]手枪 ‖carry a (或 the) ~ ①开战,奋斗 ②单恋 / hand on the ~ 把知识(或文化、智慧

等) 的火把传给后代 / **the ~ of Hymen** 爱情 ‖**'~,bearer** *n.* ①持火把者, 执炬者 ②启蒙者, 启发者 / **~ fishing** 灯光捉鱼法 / **'~light** *n.* ①火炬: a ~*light* parade 火炬游行 ②火炬光 / **~ race** (古希腊) 火炬接力赛跑 / **~ singer** 专唱感伤恋歌的女歌手 / **~ song** (常以单恋为主题的) 感伤的流行歌曲

tore [tɔ:] tear[2] 的过去式

torment I ['tɔ:ment] *n.* ①痛苦; 苦恼; 折磨: be in ~ 在痛苦中, 受折磨 / suffer ~(s) from an aching tooth 因牙痛而受苦 ②使人痛苦 (或烦恼) 的东西; 折磨者 **II** [tɔ:'ment] *vt.* ①使痛苦; 折磨 ②使烦恼; 烦扰 ③搅动, 搅起: ~ed seas 波涛汹涌的海洋 ④曲解, 歪曲

tormentor, tormenter [tɔ:'mentə] *n.* ①使人痛苦的人 (或事物); 折磨者 ②舞台两翼的固定幕 ③(摄制影片时的) 回声防止幕 ④(海船上厨师用的) 长肉叉 ⑤【农】轮耙

tornado [tɔ:'neidou] ([复] tornado(e)s) *n.* ①龙卷风, 旋风; 【气】陆龙卷 ②(非洲的) 随雷阵雨而来的狂风 ‖**tornadic** [tɔ:'nædik] *a.*

torpedo [tɔ:'pi:dou] **I** ([复] torpedoes) *n.* ①鱼雷; 水雷 ②油井爆破药筒; (铁路用) 信号雷管; ③掼炮 (一种掷地爆裂发声的爆竹) ④[俚] (被雇用的) 刺客, 打手, 保镖 ⑤【动】电鳐 ‖*an aerial* ~ 空投鱼雷 / a *diving* ~ 深水炸弹 / a *ground* ~ 海底水雷 **II** *vt.* ①用鱼雷进攻, 用鱼雷袭击 (或击沉) (船、舰) ②破坏, 废弃: ~ a plan 破坏计划 ‖ ~ **artificer** 鱼雷机械兵 / ~ **boat** 鱼雷 (快) 艇 / **tor'pedo-boat destroyer** 舰队驱逐舰 (旧称) / ~ **bomber** 鱼雷轰炸机 / ~ **director** 鱼雷定向盘 / **tor'pedoman** *n.* 鱼雷兵 / ~ **net** 防鱼雷网 / ~ **tube** 鱼雷发射管

torpid ['tɔ:pid] *a.* ①麻痹的; 麻木的 ②呆钝的, 迟钝的, 不活泼的 ③(动物等) 蛰伏的 ‖**~ity** [tɔ:'piditi] *n.* / **~ly** *ad.*

torpor ['tɔ:pə] *n.* 麻痹; 麻木; 迟钝; 蛰伏

torrent ['tɔrənt] **I** *n.* ①(水、熔岩等的) 奔流, 激流, 急流; 洪流: mountain ~s 山洪 ②[复] 倾注: ~s of rain 倾盆大雨, 骤雨 / It rains in ~s. 大雨倾盆. ③(谩骂、质问等的) 连发; (感情等的) 迸发; 狂潮: a ~ of eloquence 滔滔不绝的口才 / a ~ of speculative buying (投机市场) 抢购狂潮 **II** *a.* =torrential ‖*stem the ~ of* 抵制; 反对; 阻止

torrential [tɔ'renʃəl] *a.* ①奔流的, 急流的: a ~ rain 骤雨 ②急流所造成的: the ~ gravel 急流冲来的砂砾 ③奔流的; [喻] 奔放的, 激烈的 ‖**~ly** *ad.*

torrid ['tɔrid] *a.* ①晒热的; 烘热的: ~ sands 晒得滚热的沙地 ②发出强烈热气的, 灼热的 ③热情的, 热烈的 ‖ ~ **zone** 热带

torso ['tɔ:sou] *n.* ①(人体的) 躯干 ②(无头和四肢的) 裸体躯干雕像 ③未完成 (或残缺) 的东西

tortoise ['tɔ:təs] *n.* ①龟, 乌龟 ②缓慢 (或落后) 的人 (或物) ‖**~shell** ['tɔ:təʃel] *n.* 龟甲, 龟板; 玳瑁壳 *a.* (像) 龟甲的; (像) 玳瑁壳的

tortuous ['tɔ:tjuəs] *a.* ① 曲折的; 弯弯曲曲的: a ~ path 弯曲的小道 / a protracted, ~ struggle 长期的曲折的斗争 ②转弯抹角的 ③居心叵测的; 欺骗的, 不正当的 ‖**tortuosity** [,tɔ:tju'ɔsiti] *n.* 曲折, 弯扭 / **~ly** *ad.*

torture ['tɔ:tʃə] **I** *n.* ①拷问, 拷打; 严刑: put sb. to (the) ~ 拷问某人 / instruments of ~ 刑具 ②折磨; 痛苦; 苦恼; 使人痛苦 (或苦恼) 的事物: be in ~ 处境痛苦 ③(意义、论点等的) 歪曲, 曲解 **II** *vt.* ①拷打, 拷问; 虐待 ②折磨, 使痛苦: be ~d with a disease 受疾病的折磨 ③使翘曲; 使弯曲 ④歪曲, 曲解 ‖**~r** ['tɔ:tʃərə] *n.* 拷问者; 虐待者

tosh [tɔʃ] *n.* ①[俚] 胡说, 废话; 冗长乏味的话 ②(板球、网球中的) 旋转球, 发旋转球

toss [tɔs] **I** (tossed 或[古][诗] tost [tɔst]) ❶ *vt.* ①扔, 抛, 掷: ~ a ball to sb. 把球扔给某人 / The horse ~ed its rider. 马将骑手摔下来. / ~ (up) a coin 掷钱币猜其落地时是正面还是反面 (以决定某事) / ~ sth. aside 把某物抛在一边 ②突然举起, 突然抬起: ~ one's head angrily 愤怒地把头往后一仰 (表示轻蔑或不耐烦) ③使摇摆, 使颠簸, 使动荡: The waves ~ed the boat. 浪打得船只颠簸不停. ④使不安; 扰乱; 扰乱 ⑤(轻轻地) 拌: ~ a salad 拌色拉 ⑥使 (杯等) 猛然倾斜 (如喝酒时干杯的动作): ~ one's glass 举杯一饮而尽 ❷ *vi.* ①摇摆, 颠簸: The branches were ~*ing* in the wind. 树枝在风中摇曳. ②翻来复去: ~ all night long 整夜辗转不能入睡 ③掷钱币 (看其正反) 决定某事 **II** *n.* ①扔, 抛, 掷 ②猛举, 猛抬, 猛顿 ③摇摆, 颠簸 ④掷钱币决定某事; 由掷钱币决定的事 ‖ ~ **for sth.** 掷钱币以决定某事 / ~ **oars** 举桨致敬 / ~ **off** ①一饮而尽 ②轻而易举地完成 (或处理) / ~ **up** ①匆忙准备 (饭菜) ②掷钱币 / **win (lose) the** ~ 掷钱币猜赢 (猜输) ‖**~-up** *n.* 掷钱币决定某事; 碰运气的事; 输赢各半的打赌: It is quite a ~-up whether he comes or not. 他来不来很难说.

tot[1] [tɔt] *n.* ①小孩: a tiny ~ 小娃娃 ②(酒的) 一小杯; 少量酒; 少量

tot[2] [tɔt] **I** (totted; totting) ❶ *vt.* 加: ~ *up* this column of figures 把这一栏的数字加起来 ❷ *vi.* 合计 **II** *n.* [主英] ①合计; 总数 ②加法演算

total ['toutl] **I** *a.* ①总的, 总括的, 全体的: the ~ amount 总额, 总量 / the sum ~ 总数 / ~ industrial output value 工业总产值 / ~ heat 【物】总热量; 热函, 焓 ②完全的; 绝对的: a ~ failure 彻底的失败 / ~ silence 一片沉寂 ③总体的; 全面发动的: a war of ~ resistance 全面抗战 / a ~ war 总体战 / ~ diplomacy 总体外交 / ~ strength 总兵力 **II** *n.* 总数, 合计; 全体 / a grand ~ 总计 **III** (total(l)ed; total-d)ing) **❶** *vt.* ①计算⋯的总数; 总数达: ~ all the expenditures 计算全部支出 / The visitors total(l)ed 8,000. 来访者总数达八千人。②[美俚]把⋯完全毁掉 **❷** *vi.* 合计; 计算总数 **IV** *ad.* 统统, 完全 ‖**~ism** *n.* 极权主义 **~ity** [tou'tæliti] *n.* ①全体; 总数; 总额: view things in their *~ity* 看事物的全部 ②[天]全食; 全食的时间 / **~ly** *ad.* 统统; 完全: be ~*ly* blind 完全瞎的 ‖**~ eclipse** [天](日或月)全食

totalitarian [ˌtoutæli'tɛəriən] **I** *n.* 极权主义者 **II** *a.* 极权主义的 ‖**~ism** *n.* 极权主义

totalizator, totalisator ['toutəlaizeitə] *n.* (赛马、赛狗的)赌金计算器

tote[1] [tout] **I** *vt.* ①(手)提, (背)负; 携带 ②搬运; 拖, 拉, 牵引 **II** *n.* 负担, 装载; 携带(或装运)物

tote[2] [tout] **I** **❶** *vt.* 加, 计算⋯的总数 **❷** *vi.* 合计 **II** *n.* ①[英方]总数 ② =totalizator

totem ['toutəm] *n.* ①图腾(原始社会作为种族或氏族血统的标志并当作祖先来崇拜的动物或植物等);图腾形象: A ~ was carved on the pole. 柱上刻有图腾形象。②有共同图腾形象的氏族 ③标识, 徽章; 崇敬的对象 ‖**~ic** [tou'temik] *a.* 图腾的 / **~ism** *n.* 图腾崇拜, 图腾制度 / **~ist** *n.* 图腾制氏族成员; 图腾的研究者 / **~istic** [ˌtoutə'mistik] *a.* 图腾制度的, 图腾崇拜的 ‖**~ pole** ①图腾柱 ②等级

totem

totipotency [tou'tipətensi] *n.* [生]全能性

totter ['totə] **I** *vi.* ①蹒跚, 跟跄: ~ along the road 在路上蹒跚 ②摇摇欲坠, 动摇 **II** *n.* 蹒跚的步子 ‖**~y** ['totəri] *a.* 蹒跚的; 摇摇欲坠的

touch [tʌtʃ] **I** **❶** *vt.* ①触摸; 接触, 碰到: Please don't ~ the exhibits. 请勿触摸展品。/ The branches of the willow ~ed the water. 柳枝碰到水面。/ Can you ~ the top of the blackboard? 你能碰得到黑板的上边吗? / ~ one's hat to sb. 轻触帽沿向某人致意 ②轻击, 轻按: He ~ed the horse with the whip. 他用鞭子轻轻打马。/ Someone ~ed me on the shoulder. 有人在我肩上轻轻拍了一下。/ ~ the bell 按电铃 ③[古]在乐器上奏(曲调等); 弹拨(琴、弦) ④使接触, 使

相碰: ~ a lighted match to the kindling 用擦着的火柴点引火物 / ~ glasses 碰杯(祝酒) / I just ~ed the eggs together and they cracked. 我只不过把鸡蛋碰了一下, 它们就碎了。⑤[主要用于否定意义的句中]对(某事)插一手; 对(食物)尝一口: He would not ~ the matter. 他不愿插手这事。/ He never ~es alcoholic drinks. 他不喝酒。/ I can't ~ anything today. 我今天什么也吃不下。⑥达到; [主要用于否定意义的句中]比得上: The thermometer ~ed 38°C. 温度计升到摄氏三十八度。/ No one can ~ him in this role. 演这角色没人能赶上他。/ There is nothing to ~ swimming for exercise in summer. 夏季没有比游泳更好的锻炼了。⑦触动, 感动: ~ (sb. to) the heart 触动(某人)的心弦 ⑧触痛, 触犯: ~ sb. home (或 to the quick, on a tender place) 触到某人痛处; 触犯某人 ⑨涉及; (简略地)论及, 提到: an issue that ~es the collective interests 涉及集体利益的事情 / They ~ed many questions of mutual concern in their talks. 他们在会谈中谈到了许多双方关心的问题。⑩影响到;损及: The crops were not ~ed by the early frost. 庄稼未受早寒的影响。⑪使带上轻微色彩 (或情调等); 点缀: clouds ~ed with pink 带浅红色的云彩 / a remark ~ed with irony 带有讽刺意味的话 ⑫用轻巧的笔法画出 ⑬[常用于否定意义的句中]对付, 起作用于: Nothing will ~ these ink spots. 什么东西都去不掉这些墨水迹。/ I couldn't ~ these mathematical problems. 这几道数学题我一点也答不出。⑭[俚]向⋯商借, 向⋯乞讨 (for); 偷窃: ~ sb. for £5 向某人商借五英镑 ⑮试(金); 在(检验过的金银)上打印记 ⑯[数]与⋯相切 ⑰触诊(病人) **❷** *vi.* ①触摸 ②接近, 近乎 (on): Such actions ~ on betrayal. 这种行为近乎叛变。③与⋯有关, 涉及 (on, upon) ④(简略地)论及, 提到 (on, upon): centre on the main problem and ~ upon others 集中谈主要问题, 同时提到其他问题 ⑤短暂停靠, 靠岸 (at) ⑥触诊 **II** *n.* ①触; 碰; 轻击: 按: give sb. a ~ on the arm 碰一下某人的手臂 ②触觉, 触感: Fur is soft to the ~. 毛皮摸起来很软。/ Silk fabrics have a cool ~. 丝织品摸起来很凉爽。③机灵, 机敏: have a steady ~ in dealing with difficult situations 善于沉着应付困难的情况 ④(画笔等的)轻触; 笔触; 润色: This painting lacks the finishing ~es. 这幅画尚欠润色。⑤格调, 风格; 特点: the characteristic ~ of a writer 某一作家特有的格调 ⑥少许, 一点(尤指痕迹、风味、色调、病痛等): The soup wants a ~ of salt. 汤里少了些盐。/ a ~ of spring 春意 / have not the slightest ~ of self-interest 一点私心也没有 / have a ~ of fever (rheumatism) 有一点热度(风湿痛) / have a ~ of the sun 有点中暑 ⑦缺点, 缺陷: a ~ in one's wits 智力上的缺陷 ⑧(琴键或打字机字键的)弹性, 弹力; (按键的)指触: a piano (typewriter) with a stiff

~ 键子不灵活的钢琴(打字机) / a pianist with a firm ~ 指触有力的钢琴家 ⑨接触,联系: keep in ~ with sb. 与某人保持接触 / keep in ~ with the current situation 关心当前形势 / get in (或 into) ~ with sb. by phone 用电话与某人联系 / lose (或 be out of) ~ with sb. 与某人失去联系 ⑩ [俚] 乞讨,恳借; 讨到的东西,借到的钱: a beggar making his ~ 向人讨钱的乞丐 ⑪试金石;试金;(金银等)的验定纯度;验讫合格的印记 ⑫试验,测验 ⑬【物】接触磁化 ⑭【医】触诊 ⑮(足球场的)边线区域 ‖ **a near** ~ 侥幸的脱险,九死一生 / **at a** ~ 一触(就…) / **give sb. a** ~ **of the rope's end** 给某人以体罚 / **put** (或 **bring**) **sth. to the** ~ 检验某事物 / **the Nelson** ['nelsn] ~ (象英国海军上将纳尔逊的)临机果断的本领 / ~ **at** 短暂停靠,靠岸 / ~ **bottom** 见 **bottom** / ~ **down** ①(橄榄球中)底线得分;挽球 ②降落: The plane ~ed down at 15:45. 飞机在十五时四十五分降落。 / ~ **off** ①开(炮等);使炸裂 ②触发,激起: ~ off a storm of protest 激起抗议的浪潮 ③(用几笔)勾划出;传神地描绘出: With a few strokes, the artist ~ed off her profile. 画家用几笔就勾划出她的侧面像来。④挂断电话 / ~ **up** ①润色(图画、文章等) ②(用鞭)击(马);引起(回忆等) / ~ **within** (或 **in**) ~ ①在能接触到之处 ②能达到的 ③在…的附近 (of) ‖~**able** a. ①可触知的 ②可食用的 / ~**ed** a. ①情绪激动的 ②有些疯癫的 / ~**less** a. 无触觉的 ‖ ~ **and go** ①(从一点到另一点)快速的行动;轻率从事的行动 ②一触即发的形势;高度的不安定性 / '~-**and-'go** a. ①(从一点到另一点)快速行动的 ②一触即发的;高度不安定的: a ~-and-go situation 一触即发的形势 / ~ **body**, ~ **corpuscle** 【解】触觉体 / '~**down** n. ①(橄榄球)的底线得分 ②(飞机的)降落;降落时间 / ~ **football** 非正式)的触身法橄榄球赛(防守方用双手触及持球人身体代替正式橄榄球赛中的扭摔动作) / '~**hole** n. (旧式炮)的火门 / '~**line** n. (足球或橄榄球场的)边线 / '~-me,**not** n. ①【植】凤仙花属植物;凤仙花;苍白凤仙花 ②【植】喷瓜 ③ 高傲自持的人(尤指冷若冰霜的女人) / ~ **paper** (导火用的)火硝纸 / '~**stone** n. ①试金石 ②检验标准;检验 / '~**system** 打字的指法 / '~-**type** vt. & vi. (打字中)按指法打 / '~**wood** n. ①(作火绒用的)朽木 ②(被捉者触及树、木即不能再捉的)一种捉人游戏

touching ['tʌtʃiŋ] I a. 动人的; 使人感伤的: a ~ story 动人的故事 II n. 触摸; 触觉 III prep. [古] [书面语]关于,至于 (=as ~) ‖~**ly** ad.

touchy ['tʌtʃi] a. ①易因小事生气的 ②(身体的部分)敏感的,易受刺激的 ③易燃的, 有爆炸性的 ④须小心对待的,棘手的: a ~ situation 棘手的局面 ‖**touchily** ad. / **touchiness** n.

tough [tʌf] I a. ①坚韧的; 不易磨损的; 咬不动的: a beefsteak as ~ as leather 老得像皮革的牛排 ②健壮的; 坚强的,能吃苦耐劳的: ~ sailors 能吃苦耐劳的海员 ③强硬的;不屈的,顽强的;倔强的,顽固的: a ~ policy 强硬的政策 / get ~ with sb. 对某人强硬起来 / a ~ antagonist 顽强的对手 ④粗暴的,强横的;铁石心肠的: a ~ customer [口] 莽汉 / a ~ guy 硬汉 ⑤ 难对付的;费力的: a ~ job (problem) 棘手的工作(问题) ⑥猛烈的: a ~ contest 激烈的比赛 ⑦[口](命运等)困苦的;严峻的;不愉快的 ⑧(泥灰等)粘的,稠的: ~ putty 很粘的油灰 ⑨[美俚]顶好的,了不起的 II n. [美]流氓,恶棍 ‖~**ish** a. 有点儿强硬(或粗暴等)的 / ~**ly** ad. / ~**ness** n. / '~-**minded** a. 意志坚强的;固执的;讲究实际的,现实的

toughen ['tʌfn] vt. & vi. ①(使)变坚韧 ②(使)变健壮; (使)变坚强 ③(使)变强硬; (使)变顽固 ④(使)变困难

tour [tue] I n. ①旅行,游历; 观光,参观; 巡视: make a round-the-world ~ 作环球旅行 / go on an inspection ~ 出去视察 / a conducted ~ 有向导的团体旅行 / a ~ of observation 考察 ②(轮值的)班;【军】在海外陆(或海)军基地的任职期; 海外服务期: three ~s a day 每日三班 / a ~ of duty 【军】值班,值日勤务 ③巡回; 巡回演出,访问演出;巡回医疗: The theatrical troupe is on ~ in the rural areas. 剧团正在农村巡回演出。 II vi. ①旅行,游历; 观光 ②巡回 ③vt. ①旅行,周游; 观光: ~ the world 周游世界 ②使(剧团、剧目等)巡回演出; 在…作巡回演出(或巡回医疗): a medical team ~ing the countryside 农村巡回医疗队 / The play will ~ the countryside in the autumn. 这出戏将于今秋在农村巡回演出。 ‖**the grand** ~ 【英史】欧洲大陆的旅行(旧时上流社会的子弟作为学业的最后一部分) ‖~**er** ['tuere] n. 游览车 / ~**ing** ['tueriŋ] n. 游览。 ~ing car 游览车

tourist ['tuerist] I n. 旅行者,游览者,观光者 II a. 旅行的,游览的,观光的: a ~ agency 旅行社 / a ~ party 观光团 ‖~**ry** n. 旅游; [总称]旅行者,观光者 / ~**y** a. 游览者的;游览者喜欢的 ‖~ **attraction** 旅游胜地; 吸引游客的东西 / ~ **car**, ~ **coach** ①游览车 ②(火车的)二等卧车 / ~ **card** (有期限的)游览护照 / ~ **class** (轮船的)二等舱,(火车、飞机的)经济座 / ~ **court** =motel / ~ **home** 旅客住宿所 / ~ **ticket** (火车等的)游览优待票 / ~ **trap** 敲游客竹杠的旅馆(或餐馆、商店等)

tournament ['tuenement, 'te:nement] n. ①锦标赛,联赛; 比赛: Asian-African-Latin American Table Tennis Friendship Invitational *Tournament* 亚非拉乒乓球友好邀请赛 ⑦(中古时代的)马上比武(大会)

tourney ['tueni] I n. =tournament II vi. 参加比赛;参加(中古时代的)马上比武

tourniquet ['tuenikei] n. 【医】压脉器,止血带

tousle ['tauzl] I vt. 弄乱(头发等); 弄皱(衣服)

II *n.* ①蓬乱的头发 ②乱七八糟的一团 ③[苏格兰]嬉戏;扭打

tousy ['tauzi] *a.* ①蓬松的;弄乱的 ②简陋的,不讲究的

tout [taut] **I** ❶ *vi.* ①招徕顾客;拉生意: ~ for votes 拉选票 ②[主英]为下赌注而探听赛马情况,暗通赛马情报;招徕赛马看客下赌注 ❷ *vt.* ①招徕;兜售 ②[口]高度赞颂,吹捧 ③侦查,暗查 ④[主英]探听有关…的消息,暗通(赛马)的情报;招徕赛马看客赌(赛马) **II** *n.* ①招徕顾客者;兜售者 ②侦查者 ③[主英]探听或暗通赛马情报者;招徕赛马看客下赌注者

tow[1] [tou] **I** *vt.* 拖,拉;牵引: ~ a damaged ship into port 把坏了的船拖进港口 / ~ sb. along 拖着某人走 / a boat ~ed by horses on the bank 由岸上的马匹拉纤前进的船 / ~ed artillery【军】牵引炮;牵引炮兵 **II** *n.* ①拖,拉;牵引 ②被拖(或拉)的东西(如拖船,拖车) ③拖缆;纤;[英方]绳子 ‖*in* ~ ①拖着,拉着;牵引着: take a boat *in* ~ 拖一艘船 ②在身边,在一起: have one's family *in* ~ 带着一家人一起生活 ③在指导(或保护)之下: take sb. *in* ~ 照管某人 ‖**~boat** *n.* 拖轮 / ~(ing) **line** 拖缆;纤 / ~(ing) **net** (采集用的)拖网 / ~(ing) **path** 拖船路;纤路 / ~(ing) **rope** =~(ing) line / ~ **truck** [美](拖走抛锚或违反停车规则车辆的)拖曳车

tow[2] [tou] *n.* 【纺】落纤;短麻屑;亚麻短纤维;丝束,纤维束 ‖~ **linen** 短亚麻织物 / ~ **sack**[方]麻袋,麻包

toward(s)[1] [tə'wɔ:d(z), twɔːd(z)] *prep.* ①向,朝: walk ~ the town 向镇上走去 / march ~ the enemy 向敌挺进 / The house faces ~ the south. 这幢房子朝南。 / a step ~ the realization of one's aim 实现目标的步骤 ②对于: a correct attitude ~ one's work 对工作的正确态度 ③接近,将近: They left ~ ten o'clock. 他们离去时将近十点了。 / There were ~ 200 of them. 他们将近有二百人。④为;有助于;用于: I'll do all I can ~ getting things ready. 我将尽力帮助做好准备。 / save money ~ the repair of the equipment 省下款项以供修理设备之用 ‖**go far** ~ 大有助于: The statement *goes far* ~ clarifying the case. 那声明大有助于澄清问题。

toward(s)[2] ['touəd(z)] *a.* ①即将来到的;在准备中的 ②进行中的 ③[常作 toward]有利的;吉利的: a *toward* breeze 顺风

towel ['tauəl] **I** *n.* 毛巾,手巾;[美]擦手纸,擦脸纸(=paper ~) **II** (towel(l)ed; towel(l)ing) ❶ *vt.* ①用毛巾擦: ~ oneself 用毛巾擦身 ②[英俚]鞭打 ❷ *vi.* 用毛巾擦(或擦干)(*off*) ‖*a lead* ~ [古][俚]子弹 / *an oaken* ~ [古][俚]木棍 / *throw* (或 *toss*) *in the* ~ (拳击中)承认被击败;[喻]认输 ‖**towel(l)ing** *n.* 制毛巾的布料 ‖~ **gourd** 丝瓜 / ~ **horse**, ~ **rack** (木制的)毛巾架 / ~ **rail** 挂毛巾的横档

tower ['tauə] **I** *n.* ①塔,塔状建筑; 高楼; 城楼: a water ~ 水塔 / an observation ~ 了望塔 /

tower

an airdrome control ~ 机场指挥塔台 ②堡垒;监狱堡 **II** *vi.* ①屹立; 高耸: ~ over the plain 高耸在平原上 / Ancient trees ~ed to the skies. 古木参天。②翱翔,高飞 ‖*a* ~ *of strength* (危急、困难时)可信赖的人;中流砥柱 / *the* ~ *of ivory* (或 *the ivory* ~) 象牙塔 / *the Tower* (*of London*) 伦敦塔(伦敦古堡,曾作监狱,现作文物保存处) / ~ *above* (或 *over*) 高出;[喻]胜过: ~ *above* the rest in vigour and height of intellect 精力过人、智力超群 ‖~**ed** *a.* ①有塔的 ②高耸云霄的 / ~**ing** ['tauəriŋ] *a.* ①屹立的,高耸的;巨大的: ~*ing* trees 参天的树木 / ~*ing* crimes 滔天罪行 ②激烈的;过分的: ~*ing* rage 狂怒 / ~**y** ['tauəri] *a.* ①有塔的 ②高的,高耸云霄的 ‖~ **clock** 屋顶钟,楼钟 / ~ **house** 中世纪的城堡 / '~**man**, ~ **operator** *n.* [美]信号员

town [taun] *n.* ①镇,市镇,城镇: a market ~ 集镇 ②城市,都市;市区,商业中心区: narrow down the difference between ~ and countryside 缩小城乡差别 / go down ~ 到市中心区去 ③[the ~][总称]镇民,市民: The whole ~ knows of it. 满镇上都知道这件事。 / It is the talk of the ~. 这已是街头巷尾谈论的事了。 ‖*a man about* ~ 见 **man** / *a woman of the* ~ 见 **woman** / *be in* ~ 在城里;[英]在伦敦 / *be out of* ~ 不在城里;[英]不在伦敦 / *come to* ~ 到城里来 ②到场,露面 / *go to* ~ ①上城里去 ②寻欢作乐;(言论、行为上)放肆无忌 ③顺利进行;飞黄腾达 / *go up to* ~ 上城里去;[英]上伦敦去 / *on the* ~ ①靠城镇慈善机关救济 ②[美俚]在城里寻欢作乐 ③过男盗女娼的生活 / *paint the* ~ *red* [俚]狂欢,痛饮,胡闹 / ~ *and gown* (英国牛津和剑桥的)城镇居民和大学里的人 ‖~**ee** [tau'ni:] *n.* ① =~**sman** ②[英俚]大学城市的居民 ③[贬]不懂农活的城里人 / ~**less** *a.* 无城镇的 / ~**let** ['taunlit] *n.* 小镇 / ~**ship** *n.* ①(美国、加拿大等的)区,乡;(美国土地测量中)六哩见方的地区 ②(南非)黑人居住区 ③(澳洲)城市规划区 / ~**ward** *a.* 往城里的 *ad.* =

~wards / **~wards** *ad.* 往城里 / **~y** *n.* = ~sman *a.* 城里的;城市生活的 ‖~ **council** 镇议会 / ~ **crier** (巡行街道)大声宣读公告的人 / ~ **hall** 镇公所,市政厅 ①(尤指主要住在乡间者的)市内住所 ②[常作~house]镇公所,市政厅 / ~ **planning** 城镇规划 / ~sfolk ['taunzfouk] [复] *n.* 镇民,市民 / **~sman** ['taunzmən] *n.* ①镇民,市民;城里人 ②同镇人,同市人;同乡 / ~**s,people** [复] *n.* ①镇民,市民 ②城里生长的人 / ~ **talk** 街谈巷议 / '~wear *n.* (办公等时穿的)深色正式服装

toxic ['tɔksik] *a.* ①有毒的,有毒性的: ~ smoke (gases)毒烟(气) / ~ emissions 毒性发射物 / ~ efficacy【医】毒的效能 ②中毒的: ~ symptoms 中毒症候

toy [tɔi] **I** *n.* ①玩具,玩物 ②游戏,消遣;消遣性的短文(或小调) ③矮小的人;小动物 ④不值钱的东西;小装饰品 **II** *a.* ①玩具似的;小如玩具的 ②作为玩具的: a ~ truck 玩具卡车 / a ~ soldier (铅等制成的)玩具士兵 **III** *vi.* ①调情 ②玩弄,戏耍(with): ~ with a pencil 把铅笔弄着玩 ③不认真地对待;做着玩: ~ with the idea of doing sth. 不很认真地考虑做某事 ‖**make a ~ of sth.** 把某物当作玩具;以某事自娱 / **~er** *n.* 玩弄者 ‖~ **box** 玩具匣 / ~ **dog** (供玩耍的)小狗 / **~man** ['tɔimən] *n.* 玩具商;玩具制造者 / '**~shop** *n.* 玩具店

trace[1] [treis] **I** *n.* ①痕迹;踪迹;足迹;遗迹: Age has left its ~s on his face. 岁月在他脸上留下了痕迹。 / Traces of Darwinism are clearly discernible in these works. 在这些著作中可以明显地看出达尔文主义的影响。/ We have lost all ~ of him. 我们完全不知道他现在在哪里。/ ~s of an ancient civilization 古代文化遗迹 ②[古]小径,道路 ③丝毫;微量;【化】痕量: a mere ~ of a smile 一丝笑意 / The soup needs just a ~ more salt. 汤里还需再放一点儿盐。/ ~ elements【化】痕量元素 ④描绘;描绘图;【军】经始线 ⑤记录器的图录(示波器上的)扫描(行程),扫迹 ⑥【心】记忆痕 ⑦(几何学上的)交点,交线 **II** ❶ *vt.* ①跟踪,追踪: ~ a fox to its den 追踪到狐狸的洞穴 ②查出;找出;探索: ~ a rumour to its source 追查谣言的根源 / I can't ~ any letter of that date. 我查不出曾收到过注有这个日期的信件。/ His satisfaction can be ~d between the lines. 从字里行间可以看出他很满意。/ ~ the former course of a river 探索河流的早期河道 ③追溯 ④描绘;勾出…的轮廓;【军】绘出(军事设施)的经始线 ⑤(out) the plan of a construction site 描绘工地平面图 / ~ (out) a policy 草拟一项政策 ⑤(根据衬在下面的图样等)摹写,映描;复写 ⑥(费力、细心地)写(字) ⑦【建】给…装以线状花饰 ❷ *vi.* ①沿着路(或路线)走 ②上溯

trace[2] [treis] *n.* ①挽绳,缰绳 ②【机】连动杆 ③【植】(脉)迹 ‖**in the ~s** 被套着挽具;[喻]受

驾驭 / **jump the ~s** 挣脱挽绳;[喻]摆脱约束 / **kick over the ~s** 不服驾驭,不受约束;表示反抗

tracery ['treisəri] *n.*【建】窗花格

track [træk] **I** *n.* ①行踪;轨迹;航迹;[常用复]足迹: follow sb.'s ~ 跟踪某人;追随某人 / the ~ of a ship 船只(驶过后)的浪迹 / ~s in the snow 雪地上的足迹 ②路,径,小道: a ~ through a forest 林中小道 ③轨道;(录音磁带的)音轨: a single (double) ~ 单(双)轨 / leave the ~ 出轨 ④【体】跑道;径赛运动;田径运动: a cinder ~ 煤屑跑道 / ~ events 径赛项目 ⑤历程,行程;行动路线,思路: the ~ of a typhoon 台风的路线 / the ~ of a bullet 弹道 / interrupt the ~ of sb.'s thoughts 打断某人的思路 ⑥【机】跨距;(车辆的)轮距 ⑦(坦克、拖拉机的)履带 **II** ❶ *vt.* ①跟踪;追踪: ~ a hare 追猎野兔 / ~ planes with searchlights 用探照灯跟踪飞机 ②沿着(道路)走;根据(线索等)探索 ③走过,通过: ~ a grassland 通过一片大草地 ④在…上留下印迹;脚上带(泥)留下印迹: Don't ~ up the floor. 别把地板踩脏了。/ ~ mud all over the room 把脚上的泥弄得满屋都是 ⑤为…铺轨 ❷ *vi.* ①追踪 ②留下足迹 ③走: ~ about 走来走去 ④(车轮等)保持跨距;(车轮等)跨距与轨距相符;(车辆的后轮)与前轮在同一轮迹上转动 ‖**a beaten ~** 踏出来的路;[喻]常规,惯例,陈套 / **across the ~s** 在贫民区 / **be on the ~ of sb.** (或 be on sb.'s ~) ①追踪着某人 ②掌握着某人行为(或企图等)的线索 / **born on the wrong side of the ~s** [美]出身贫苦的 / **clear the ~** 扫清道路;开道 / **cover up one's ~s** 隐匿行踪 / **in one's ~s** [俚]当时当地 / **keep ~ of** ①记录: keep ~ of every cent one spends 记录花掉的每一分钱 ②掌握…的线索;保持对…的联系: keep ~ of current events 随时关心时事动态 / **lose ~ of** 失去…的线索;失掉对…的联系 / **make ~s** [口]匆匆奔去;逃跑 / **make ~s for** [口]朝…而去;追踪 / **off the beaten ~** 偏僻的(地);不落俗套的(地) / **off the ~** ①出轨;离题,离开目标;搞错的 ②(猎狗)失去臭迹 / **on the ~** 在轨道上;未离题(或目标);对头的 / **on the wallaby ~** 在流浪,失业 / **put sb. on the ~** 使某人尾随…;使某人能找到… / **the inside ~** ①内圈跑道 ②(竞争时的)有利地位,好机会 / **~ down** 追捕(到);对…追查到底 / **~ out** 根据(遗迹等)探索出 ‖**~ed** *a.* 有履带的: ~ed vehicles 履带式车辆 / **~less** *a.* ①无路的 ②不留踪迹的;无人迹的 ③无轨的: a ~less trolley (bus) 无轨电车 / '**~-and-field** *a.* 田径运动的 / **~,clearer** *n.* (火车车头部的)排障器 / ~ **ga(u)ge** 轨距(规) / **~ing station** [宇]【军】跟踪站 / '**~,layer** *n.* 铺轨工人;铺轨机;履带式车辆;履带式拖拉机 / **~man** ['trækmən] *n.* [美]铁道护路员 / ~ **man** 田径运动员 / ~ **shoe** (赛跑用的)钉鞋 / '**~,walker** *n.* [美] ① = ~-

man ②(铁路的)轨道巡视员

tract[1] [trækt] *n.* ①(土地、森林等的)一片;一片土地;地带: a great ~ of sea (sand) 一片汪洋大海 (大沙漠) / a wooded ~ 一片森林地带 ②[古] (时间的)一段 ③【解】系统,道;束: digestive ~ 消化道 / respiratory ~ 呼吸道 / optic ~ 视(神经)束

tract[2] [trækt] *n.* (政治或宗教宣传的)短文,传单;小册子 ‖~ **society** 宗教小册子出版会

tractable ['træktəbl] *a.* ①易管教的;易控制的;温顺的, 驯服的: a ~ child 听话的孩子 / a ~ horse 驯服的马 ②易处理的;易加工的 ‖**tractability** [,træktə'biliti] *n.* / **tractably** *ad.*

traction ['trækʃən] *n.* ①拖,牵引;牵引(动)力: steam ~ 蒸汽牵引 ②附着摩擦力 ③【医】(肌肉等的)牵引: skeletal ~ 骨骼牵引 ④[喻]吸引力 ⑤公共运输事业 ‖~**al** *a.* / ~ **engine** 牵引机 / ~ **wheel** (火车机车的)动轮

tractor ['træktə] *n.* ①拖拉机: an all-purpose (或 a multi-purpose) ~ 万能拖拉机 / a walking ~ 手扶拖拉机 / an agricultural (或 a farm) ~ 农用拖拉机 / a ~ driver 拖拉机手 ②牵引式飞机 ③牵引车 ④【医】牵引器 ‖~ **aeroplane** 牵引式飞机 / ~ **propeller** 牵引式螺旋桨 / ~ **truck** 牵引车

trade [treid] **I** *n.* ①贸易, 商业; 交易; 生意: foreign (international) ~ 对外(国际)贸易 / domestic (或 home) ~ 国内贸易 / free ~ 自由贸易 / the balance of ~ 贸易平衡 / develop ~ relations between the two nations 发展两国间的贸易关系 / engage (或 be) in ~ 开铺子, 做买卖;当零售商 / barter ~ 实物交易;易货贸易 / a trick of the ~ 做生意的诀窍 / do a large ~ in tea 做大宗茶叶生意 / be in the silk ~ 做丝绸生意 ②职业; 行业; 手工艺: He is a carpenter by ~. 他是做木工的。/ learn a ~ 学一门手艺 ③[总称](从事某行业的)同人,同行; 同业: the news ~ 新闻界 ④[总称](某店的)顾客, 主顾: solicit ~ 招徕顾客 ⑤[美]政治上的交易: deals and ~s at the polls 选举投票上的交易 ⑥[the ~][口]酒商, 酿酒商 ⑦[英][the ~][军俚]英海军潜艇部队 ⑧ [the ~s]【气】贸易风, 信风 **II** ❶ *vi.* ①交易; 经商: ~ *in* industrial and agricultural products *with* many countries 与许多国家进行工农业产品方面的贸易 / vessels *trading to* Latin America 到拉丁美洲进行贸易的商船 ②对换: He wanted to change his days off and got a fellow worker to ~ *with* him. 他想调休, 找到一位同事和他对换。③购物: He usually ~s at the No. One Department Store. 他通常在第一百货商店买东西。④(政治上)交易 ⑤(禽鸟)来回飞翔 ❷ *vt.* ①用…进行交换: ~ space *for* time 以空间换取时间 / ~ seats *with* sb. 和某人对换座位 ②经营(股票等)的交易 ‖**blow** ~ (风)不改方向

地吹 / *sheltered* ~s [英] 不受外国竞争影响的行业 (如建筑、国内运输等) / *shepherd's* ~ ①作田园诗 ②【宗】耶稣的业绩 / ~ *in* ... *for* ... 以(旧物)折价换取(同类新物): ~ *in* an old bicycle *for* a new one 把旧自行车折价换新的 / ~ *off* ①交替换位: ~ *off* with each other several years for first place in the tennis tournament 多年来彼此轮流取得网球赛的冠军称号 ② 交替使用: ~ *off* large and small brushes for rough and fine work 交替使用大小刷子来做粗工和精工 ③通过交换(或买卖)抛弃,换掉;卖掉 / ~ *on* (或 *upon*)(为自私的目的)利用: ~ *on* one's social standing 利用自己的社会地位 / ~ *on* sb.'s generosity (credulity) 利用某人的慷慨大度(轻信) / ~ *out* 出卖: ~ sth. *out* to sb. 把某物出卖给某人 / ~ *up* ①买更高价的东西: A homeowner wanted to move or ~ up. 一个房主想搬家或买入更高价的房子。②劝…买更高价的东西: try to ~ the customers *up* 想说服顾客购买更贵的物品 ③使熟悉某一行: ~ *up* the youth in industrial arts 使青年得到工艺的训练 / *Two of a* ~ *never agree.* [谚] 同行是冤家。‖~**r** *n.* ①商人 ②商船 ‖~ **acceptance** 商业承兑汇票 / ~ **agreement** ①国际贸易协定 ② (行业性的)劳资协议 / ~ **association** 同业公会 / **Trade Board** [英]劳资协商会 / ~ **book** ①普及版的书 ②~ **edition** / ~ **cycle** [英]商业盛衰的周期性 (=business cycle) / ~ **discount** 商业折扣, 批发折扣 / ~ **edition** 普及版 / '~-**in** *n.* 折价物 / **journal** 行业杂志 / '~-**last** *n.* (要对方把听来的恭维自己的话先说出后才说出的)自己所听到的恭维对方的话 / '~**mark** *n.* 商标 *vt.* ①注册(商品)的商标;以…作为商标 ②给(商品)标上商标 / ~ **name** ①商号, 店名 ②(某商品在)行业中的俗名;商标名称,商品名 / '~-**off** *n.* ①(对不能同时兼顾的因素的)权衡 ②物物交换 / ~ **price** 批发价 / ~ **route** 商队的路线,商船的航线 / ~ **school** 中等专业学校 / '~**sfolk** ['treidzfouk] *n.* =~speople / ~ **show** (新电影的)内部预映 / '~**sman** ['treidzmən] *n.* ①商人, 店主;零售商 ②手工工人,手艺人 / '~**s,people** [复] *n.* [总称]商人;商界 / '~**s,woman** *n.* 女商人,女店主;女零售商 / ~ **union**, ~s union 工会 / ~ **unionism** 工联主义 / ~ **unionist** ①工联主义者 ②工会会员 / ~ **wind**【气】贸易风,信风

tradition [trə'diʃən] *n.* ①传统; 惯例; 因袭: a keep up the fine ~ of plain living and hard work 保持艰苦奋斗的优良传统 / by force of long ~ 因为多年遗留下来的习惯 ②口传;传说: *Tradition* says (或 runs) that .... 据传说说 ... / The story is based mainly on ~(s). 这故事主要是根据传说。/ true to ~ 名不虚传 ③【宗】口头流传下来的教义 ④【律】交付, 引渡 ‖*by* ~ ①根据传统 ②根据口传

traditional [trə'diʃənl] *a.* ①传统的;惯例的;因袭的: ~ friendship 传统的友谊 / ~ Chinese medicine 中药 ②口传的;传说的 ‖~ly *ad.*

traduce [trə'dju:s] *vt.* ①诽谤,中伤,诋毁 ②违反;背叛 ‖~ment *n.* / ~r *n.* 诽谤者

traffic ['træfik] I *n.* ①交通;通行,往来: ~ regulations 交通规则 / a ~ police box 交通警岗亭 / The new bridge was opened to (或 for) ~ ahead of schedule. 新建的大桥提前通车了。/ ~ deaths 交通事故引起的死亡 ②运输;客运及货运业务: goods ~ 货运 / international air ~ 国际航空 ③交通量;运输量: There is little ~ on these roads. 这些道路上行人车辆很少。④贸易,买卖;交易: the ~ in furs 毛皮贸易 / the illegal drug ~ 非法的毒品买卖 ⑤(人与人间的)交往;(精神或思想上的)交流 ⑥[讯]电信;通信业务;通信量: telephone ~ 电话业务,话务 / telegraph ~ 电报业务,报务 / radio ~ 无线电通讯 II (trafficked; trafficking) ❶ *vi.* 做买卖,做非法买卖,做肮脏交易: ~ *in* wheat (*with* sb.) (同某人)做小麦生意 ❷ *vt.* ①用…进行交换;以…作交易 ②在…上通行: the most heavily *trafficked* highway in the country 全国交通最繁忙的公路 ‖the ~ *will bear* 现有情况所许可的: get all that the ~ *will bear* 取得现有情况所许可的一切 / ~ *away* 通过交易断送… ‖**trafficker** *n.* [常贬]商人,做买卖者;掮客 ‖~less *a.* 无交通往来的;无通信的 ‖**block** [英] =~ jam / ~ **circle** 【交】环形交叉口,环形交叉枢纽 / ~ **cop** [美]交通警察 / ~ **court** 交通法庭 / ~ **department** 交通局,交通局 / ~ **engineering** 交通运输工程,交通工程(学) / ~ **island** (道路中间分快慢车道的)交通岛 / ~ **jam** 交通拥挤,交通阻塞 / ~ **light** 交通管理色灯(俗称红绿灯) / ~ **police** 交通警察 / ~ **returns** 运输统计报告(表) / ~ **sign** 交通标志 / ~ **signal** 交通信号(即交通管理色灯)

tragedy ['trædʒidi] *n.* ①悲剧;悲剧作品;悲剧体裁 ②惨事,惨案;灾难,不幸 ③悲惨;悲剧性 ‖~ **queen** 悲剧女演员

tragic ['trædʒik] *a.* ①悲剧的: a ~ actor 悲剧演员 / ~ drama 悲剧 ②悲剧性的;悲惨的,灾难性的: a ~ tale (scene) 悲惨的故事(景象) / a ~ event 灾难性的事件 ‖the ~ (文艺作品或生活中的)悲剧因素

tragical ['trædʒikəl] *a.* =tragic ‖~ly *ad.* / ~ness *n.*

trail [treil] I *n.* ①痕迹;足迹;臭迹;残迹: the ~ of a meteor 流星余迹 / vapour ~s (飞机在高空飞行时产生的)雾化尾迹 ②一串;(后果等的)一系列: a ~ of smoke 一缕烟 / leave a ~ of trouble and difficulty behind 留下一系列麻烦和困难 ③拖曳物,尾部;拖裾,裙裾;蔓;(炮架的)架尾: Ivy has sent ~s up the wall. 常青藤顺着墙向上蔓延。④(荒野山区中的)小径,(踩出的)小道;标出的山路: tortuous mountain ~s 曲

折崎岖的山路 / a one-man ~ 只能走一个人的小道 ⑤【军】持枪姿势(右手紧握枪,枪托底板微离地,枪与人成一角度): be at the ~ 做持枪姿势 II ❶ *vt.* ①跟踪;追猎: ~ a suspect 追踪嫌疑犯 / ~ the beast to its lair 追捕野兽直到兽穴 ②拖,曳: ~ a log up a slope 拖木头上坡 / ~ one's feet along 拖着腿走 ③拖带: Don't ~ mud into the house. 别把污泥带进屋里。/ He came to see me and ~ed a stranger. 他来看我,还带了一个陌生人来。④ 落后于: ~ one's classmates 落后于班上同学 ⑤踩出(路);标出(路): ~ the grass 在草地上踩出一条路 / ~ a path 踩出一条小路 ⑥【军】持(枪): *Trail* arms! (口令)持枪! ❷ *vi.* ①拖曳;拖着;垂下: a cable ~*ing* along the ground 在地上拖动着的缆绳 / The tablecloth ~*s* on the floor. 桌布一直垂到地板上。②拖沓行走;落后;跟在后面走: Thoroughly criticize the doctrine of ~*ing* behind a snail's pace. 彻底批判爬行主义。/ ~ along after sb. 慢吞吞地跟在某人后头走 ③(缓慢地)飘出,流出: Smoke ~ed from the chimney. 烟从烟囱里飘出来。④ 伸展开;蔓生 ⑤(猎犬等)追踪猎物: spend days ~*ing* over the desert 花好几天在沙漠上追踪猎物 ⑥减弱,变小 (*off, away*): a voice ~*ing off* 逐渐低下去的声音 ‖*be hot on sb.'s* ~ 紧紧追赶着某人 / *blaze a* ~ ①在树上刻标指示林中路径 ②开辟道路;带头 / *in* ~ 成一列纵队: march *in* ~ 成一列纵队行进 / *off the* ~ 失去臭迹,找不到踪迹;[喻]出轨;离题 / *a pike* ~ 见 pike¹ / ~ *one's coat* (或 *coattails*) 见 coat ‖~blazer, '~breaker *n.* 开路先锋 / ~car 拖车,挂车 / ~ing edge (飞机机翼的)后缘 / ~ing wheel 后轮 / ~ net (捕鱼的)拖网 / ~rope 拖绳

trailer ['treilə] I *n.* ①拖曳者;拖曳的牲口(或东西) ②追踪者;追猎者 ③拖车,挂车 ④汽车拖的活动住屋(或野外工作室) ⑤ 蔓生植物 ⑥ (广告性的)电影预告片 II *vt.* ①用拖车运(游艇等) ❷ *vi.* ①住在用汽车拖的活动住屋内 ②可用拖车运 ‖~ camp, ~ court, ~ park 活动住屋集中地

train [trein] I ❶ *vt.* ①培养,训练: ~ sb. *in* medicine 培养某人学医 / ~ sb. *as a* "barefoot doctor" 培养某人当赤脚医生 / be specially ~ed *for* a kind of work 受某种工作的专门训练 / Not the slightest error in pronunciation escapes his ~ed ear. 再小的发音错误也逃不过他的训练有素的耳朵。/ ~ a horse to do farm work 训练马做农活 ②使(植物)沿着一定方向生长: ~ the vines over the porch 使葡萄藤爬在门廊上 ③把(枪炮、摄影机、灯光等)对准,瞄准: ~ one's gun on the enemy 把枪口瞄向敌人 ④[罕]引诱;吸引 (*away*) ⑤[罕]拖,拉(重物) ⑥[口]训练(小孩、小狗等)不随地大小便 ❷ *vi.* ①接受训练;锻炼: He ~s on a special diet. 他经常吃特定的食物以保持健康。②[口]乘火车旅行 II *n.*

①列车,火车: a passenger (goods) ~ 客(货)车 / a through ~ 直达列车 /.au up(a down) ~ 上(下)行列车 / an armoured ~ 装甲列车 / a wild ~ 不按行车时间表开出的列车 / a *de luxe* 高级豪华列车,花车 / The ~ is in. 火车正在站上。/ go by ~ 乘火车去 / miss (catch) one's ~ 误了(赶上)火车 ②(行进中的)长列,队列;系列: a long ~ of visitors before the monument 纪念碑前的一长列参观者 / a ~ of loaded mules 一队运货的骡子 / a ~ of ideas (thoughts) 一系列的主意(想法) / a ~ of events 一连串的事件 ③[总称]随行人员 ④伴随而来的事物;后果: the production cut which comes *in the* ~ *of* an economic crisis 随着经济危机而来的生产缩减 ⑤顺序,秩序: Things proceeded in this ~ for several days. 一连几天事情就这样进行着。⑥后拖物;拖裾,裙裾;(禽类的)长尾 ⑦导火线 ⑧【军】辎重队 ⑨【机】(传动)轮系,齿轮系: ~ of wheels 轮系 / ~ of mechanism 机构系 ⑩挂有拖车的牵引车 ‖*in* (*good*) ~ 准备就绪 / *jump a* ~ 违章搭乘运货列车 / *ride the gravy* ~ [美俚]获得容易赚钱的机会;干不费劲的差事 / ~ *down* 从事锻炼使体重减轻 / ~ *fine* (把…)锻炼得处于良好的状态 / ~ *it* [口]坐火车去: We'll ~ *it* all the way. 我们整个路都要坐火车。/ ~ *off* ①锻炼过分以致精力减退 ②(子弹)打歪,没打中 / ~ *on* 锻炼得有所改善 / ~ *with* [美俚]与…有往来,结交 ‖~ *dispatcher* 列车调度员 / ~ *ferry* 火车轮渡 / '~*load* *n.* 列车载重;(一)列车的装载量: a ~*load of* building materials 一列车建筑材料 / ~*man* ['treinmən] *n.* 乘务员;制动手 / '~*mile* *n.* 列车哩 / ~ *oil* 海产动物油;鲸油 / '~*sick* *a.* (乘火车)晕车的 / ~ *sickness* (乘火车)晕车

trainee [trei'ni:] *n.* 受训练人

trainer ['treinə] *n.* ①训练人;(体育运动的)教练员 ②驯兽人 ③训练器材,练习器 ④[空]教练机 ⑤【军】(火炮方向角的)瞄准手 ⑥受训练人

training ['treiniŋ] *n.* ①训练,锻炼;培养: flight ~ 飞行训练 / be in (out of) ~ (运动员等)锻炼得好(不好) / go into ~ 从事锻炼 / give attention to the ~ of medical workers 注意培养医务工作者 ②使植物向一定方向生长的栽培法 ③(枪炮、摄影机、灯光等的)对准,瞄准 ‖~*bit* *n.* (驯马用的)马衔 / ~ *college* [英]师范学院 / ~ *school* ①师范学校;职业学校 ②少年罪犯教养所 / ~ *ship* 教练舰,教练船 / ~ *table* 体育锻炼人员的伙食

trait [trei, treit] *n.* ①品质;特性;性格: national ~*s* 民族性 / marked English ~*s* 英国人的显著特点 ②一笔,一划;一触 ③一点点,少许,微量: a ~ of humour 一点幽默

traitor ['treitə] *n.* 叛徒;卖国贼: turn ~ 成为叛徒 / a hidden ~ 内奸 / a ~ *to* one's country 叛国分子 ‖~*ism* ['treitərizəm] *n.* 卖国主义;叛

变行为

traitorous ['treitərəs] *a.* ①叛徒的;卖国贼的: a ~ clique 叛徒集团;卖国集团 ②叛变的;卖国的: ~ action 叛变行为;卖国行为 ③奸诈的,不忠的: a ~ scheme 奸计 ‖~*ly* *ad.* / ~*ness* *n.*

traitress ['treitris] *n.* 女叛徒;女卖国贼

trajectory ['trædʒiktəri] *n.* 【物】(射体)轨道,弹道,流线;【数】轨线

tram[1] [træm] **I** *n.* ①[英](有轨)电车 (=[美] streetcar 或 trolley): go by ~ 乘电车去 ②[英]电车轨道;[复]电车行驶路线 ③煤车;矿车;吊车 **II** (trammed; tramming) ❶ *vt.* 用煤车(或吊车等)运载 ❷ *vi.* 乘电车;开电车;调度电车 ‖'~*car* *n.* ①[英](有轨)电车 ②煤车;矿车 / '~*line* *n.* [英]有轨电车路线 / ~ *rail* ①电车轨道 ②(吊车的)索道 / ~ *road* 电车道;矿车轨道 / ~ *service* (有轨)电车交通 / ~ *stop* 电车站 / '~*way* *n.* ①=~ road ②有轨电车路线;(有轨)电车 ③(吊车的)索道

tram[2] [træm] *n.* 一种丝线(用作上等天鹅绒和丝织品的纬线)

tram[3] [træm] **I** *n.* ①椭圆规脚 ②指针 ③正确的调整 **II** (trammed; tramming) *vt.* & *vi.* 用椭圆规调准

trammel ['træməl] **I** *n.* ①(一种捕鸟、鱼等的)网 (=~ net) ②马桀 ③[常用复](习惯、礼节等的)拘束,束缚;妨碍 ④锅钩 ⑤[复]椭圆规;横木规;梁规 **II** (trammel(l)ed; trammel(l)ing) *vt.* ①使陷入网内 ②束缚;妨碍;遏制

tramp [træmp] **I** ❶ *vi.* ①用沉重的脚步走: ~ about 用沉重的脚步走来走去 ②步行;徒步旅行: ~ ten kilometres in the heat 在大热天徒步走了十公里 ③流浪,漂泊 ④踏,踩: ~ upon sb.'s toes 踩着某人的脚趾 ❷ *vt.* ①走,跋涉: We missed the train and had to ~ it. 我们没有赶上火车,因此不得不步行。/ ~ the whole country 徒步走遍全国 ②踩;揉洗(衣服等) **II** *n.* ①步行;徒步旅行;步行者;徒步旅行者: on the ~ 在流浪 在跑码头 ②游民;流浪者;流浪乞丐: look like a ~ 样子邋遢,服装不整洁 ③妓女;荡妇 ④[只用单]脚步声;重步声: the ~ of marching feet 行军的脚步声 ⑤保护鞋底的铁片;(在冰上防滑的)鞋底钉 ⑥不定期货船 (=~ ship 或 ~ steamer): an ocean ~ 远洋不定期货船 ‖'~*pick* *n.* 掘土撬杆

trample ['træmpl] **I** ❶ *vt.* 踩;践踏;蹂躏,轻蔑(或粗暴)地对待: ~ down the grass 把草踏倒 / ~ out the fire 把火踏灭 / ~ all difficulties underfoot 压倒一切困难 ❷ *vi.* 踩;践踏;蹂躏,轻蔑(或粗暴)地对待 (on, upon, over): Don't ~ on grass. 勿踏草地。

trampolin(e) ['træmpəlin] *n.* (杂技表演中翻筋斗用的)蹦床

trance [trɑ:ns] **I** *n.* ①恍惚,出神;发呆: in a ~ 恍惚地 ②昏睡状态,【医】迷睡 ③(佛教的)入定;

（降神术所谓的）阴魂附身 **II** *vt.* 使恍惚；使发呆；使迷睡

tranquil ['træŋkwil] *a.* ①平静的，安静的，安宁的：the ～ surface of the water 平静的水面 / preserve a ～ mind 保持安宁的心情 ②平稳的，稳定的 ‖**tranquil(l)ity** [træŋ'kwiliti] *n.* 平静，安静，安宁

transact [træn'zækt] ❶ *vt.* 办理，处理；执行：～ business 处理事务；做交易 / ～ negotiations 进行谈判 ❷ *vi.* ①做交易；谈判 ②在原则上让步，进行调和折中 ‖～**or** *n.* 办理（或处理）人

transaction [træn'zækʃən] *n.* ①办理，处理；执行：leave the ～ of the matter to sb. 把这件事的处理交托某人 ②（一笔）交易；（具体）事务：a credit ～ 赊购交易 / conclude a ～ 达成交易 / cash ～s 现金交易 / be engaged in various ～s 忙于种种事务 ③[复]议事录；会报，学报 ④[律]和解

transcend [træn'send] ❶ *vt.* ①超出，超过（经验、理性、信念等范围）②【哲】【宗】超越（宇宙、物质世界等）：～ sb.'s comprehension 超出某人的理解力 / ～ description 无法形容 ②胜过 ❷ *vi.* 超越；胜过

transcendent [træn'sendənt] **I** *a.* ①卓越的，超常的，出类拔萃的 ②【哲】超验的 ③【宗】超越宇宙（或物质世界）的 **II** *n.* 卓越的人；超绝物

transcribe [træns'kraib] *vt.* ①抄写，誊写；用打字机打出…的复本 ②译，意译；把（速记符号）译成文字；把（资料）改录成另一种形式 ③写下，录下；用音标记录 ④预录（广播节目）；录音播送 ⑤[音]改编，改作 ‖～**r** *n.* ①抄写者，誊写员 ②抄录器；读数器；信息转换器

transcript ['trænskript] *n.* ①抄本，誊本；副本 ②正式文本；肄业证书 ③（经历等的）以文艺形式的再现

transcription [træns'kripʃən] *n.* ①抄写，誊写：errors in ～ 抄写错误 ②（速记符号记录等的）翻译；按速记稿在打字机上打出文字 ③抄本，誊本；副本；以某种特殊符号写成的东西：phonetic ～s 用语音符号写成的字（或文句）；音标 ④（乐曲的）改编 ⑤录音，录制；录音广播；（广播用的）唱片（或磁带等）‖～**al** *a.*

transept ['trænsept] *n.* 【建】（教堂的）交叉甬道，十字形耳堂

transfer I [træns'fə:] (transferred; transferring [træns'fə:riŋ]) ❶ *vt.* ①转移；传递，传输：The passengers were *transferred* to a ferry at the bus terminus. 在公共汽车终点站乘客转入渡轮。～ motion 传动 ②调动 ③改变，转变；变换：～ wasteland into fertile fields 把荒地改变为良田 ④转让，让与（财产等）⑤（从一平面到另一平面）转印，转写；摹绘 ❷ *vi.* ①转移；转职，转学，转系(to)：～ from the army to the navy 从陆军转到海军 / ～ to another college (department) 转到另一学院（系）②换车；换船：～ from a bus *to* a tram 从公共汽车换乘电车 / ～ at Chengchow 在郑州换车 **II** ['trænsfə(:)] *n.* ①转移，传递，传

输；职务调动；调任（或转学）证书；变换 ②（权利、财产等的）转让，让与；让与证书 ③（股票等的）过户；过户凭单 ④汇划，汇兑；电汇：telegraphic ～（略作 T/T）电汇 / mail ～（略作 M/T）信汇 ⑤（供）转印的图画（或图案等）⑥[主英]转入其他部队的士兵；转学生 ⑦转换处；车辆或火车的）摆渡处；（车辆或火车的）渡轮 ⑧转车证 ‖～ **book**（股票等的）过户帐 / ～ **company** 转运公司 / ～ **days** 过户日（英格兰银行免费办理公债等过户的日子，指星期一至星期五）/ ～ **ink**【印】转写墨 / ～ **paper**【印】贴花纸用的纸基 / ～ **payments** [美]用于失业救济等公共事业方面的开支

transfigure [træns'figə] *vt.* ①使变形；使改观 ②美化，理想化 ‖**transfiguration** [ˌtrænsfigju-'reiʃən] *n.*

transfix [træns'fiks] *vt.* ①戳穿，刺穿；钉住：～ a tiger with a spear 用矛刺穿老虎 ②使呆着不动；使麻木：He stood ～*ed* with horror. 他站在那里吓得呆若木鸡。‖～**ion** [træns'fikʃən] *n.* 戳穿，刺穿；钉住；【医】贯穿术

transform I [træns'fɔ:m] ❶ *vt.* ①改变，转变；使变态：～ arid land *into* irrigated fields 变旱地为灌溉地 / ～ one form of energy *into* another 把一种能转变成另一种能 / ～ passivity *into* initiative 化被动为主动 ②改造，改革：a gigantic battle to ～ nature 改造自然的巨大战斗 / ～ the old educational system 改革旧的教育制度 / ～ one's world outlook 改造世界观 ③【电】变换，转换；变压 ④【数】变换 ❷ *vi.* 改变，转化；变换；变形，变态：～ from a backward agricultural country *into* an advanced industrial country 从落后的农业国转变为先进的工业国 **II** ['trænsfɔ:m] *n.* ①【数】变换式 ②【化】反式

transformation [ˌtrænsfə'meiʃən] *n.* ①变化；变形，【生】变态；转化 ②改造，改革：social ～ 社会改革 / socialist ～ 社会主义改造 / the ～ of one's world outlook 世界观的改造 ③转变，转化；【数】变换：the ～ of the two contradictory aspects within a thing 事物内部矛盾着的两方面的相互转化 ④【电】变压；【化】蜕变（原子的品种、结构或内部配置的变化）⑤（女人用的）假发 ‖～**ist** *n.* =transformist

transformer [træns'fɔ:mə] *n.* ①促使变化的人（或物）②【电】变压器；变换器：high frequency (intermediate frequency, audio) ～ 高频（中频、音频）变压器 / bell ringing ～ 电铃变压器 / frequency ～ 变频器，频率变换器 / ～ amplifier 变压器耦合放大器 / ～ core 变压器铁心

transfuse [træns'fju:z] *vt.* ①移注；倾注；渗入；灌输 ②【医】输（血），给…输血；注…入血管 ‖**transfusion** [træns'fju:ʒən] *n.* 移注；倾注；渗入；输血；输血法 / **transfusive** [træns'fju:siv] *a.*

transgress [træns'gres] ❶ *vt.* ①侵越，越过（限度、范围等）②违反，违背（规则、法律等）❷ *vi.* ①越界 ②违法；犯罪 ‖～**ion** [træns'greʃən] *n.*

①侵越；违反；犯法，犯罪 ②【地】海进，海侵 / ~or n. 犯法者；违背者；(宗教、道德上的)罪人

transient ['trænziənt] **I** a. ①短暂的，易逝的，倏忽的；无常的: a ~ gleam of hope 倏忽的一线希望 ②路过的，留片刻就走的: a ~ guest 暂住的客人 / a ~ stay 暂住，短留 ③【物】瞬变的: ~ current 瞬变电流 / ~ plasma 瞬间等离子体 ④【音】经过的: a ~ note 经过音 **II** n. ①[美] 暂时寄住的旅客，过客；流浪者 ②候鸟 ③【物】暂态值，瞬变值 ④【无】瞬变现象，过渡现象，瞬变过程，瞬态

transistor [træn'sistə] n. 【无】①晶体管: a ~ set 晶体管收音机 / diffused base ~ 扩散基极晶体管 / epitaxial mesa ~ 外延台面晶体管 / junction (planar) ~ 面结合型(平面型)晶体管 / point contact ~ 点接触型晶体管 / field-effect ~ 场效应晶体管 ②晶体管收音机，半导体收音机

transit ['trænsit] **I** n. ①通过，经过；通行，运行: the ~ of radio signals from the earth to the moon and back 无线电信号从地球到月球再回到地球的往返 / We were allowed two days for the ~ of the lake. 我们被准许在两天之内通过该湖。②运输，运送；通路，运输线；公共交通系统: air ~ 航空转运 / a means of ~ 一种运输工具 / in ~ 在运输中 / the ~ workers 运输(交通)工人 / the overland ~ 陆上运输线 ③(外贸)过境运输 ④转变，过渡: the ~ of autumn to winter 由秋季过渡到冬季 ⑤【天】中天；凌日；中星仪；经纬仪: ~ of Mercury (Venus) 水星(金星)凌日 **II** ❶ vt. ①通过；运送过: ~ the canal 通过这条运河 ②(天体)经过 ❷ vi. 通过 ‖~ camp 过境部队宿营地 / ~ circle 【天】子午仪 / ~ company 转运公司 / ~ compass 转镜仪，转镜经纬仪 / ~ duty, ~ dues (货物的)通过税，通行税 / ~ instrument 【天】中星仪

transition [træn'siʒən] n. ①过渡；过渡时期 ②转变，变迁: a ~ from cold to warm weather 由寒冷到温暖的天气转变 / the ~ from ape to man 从猿到人的转变 ③【物】跃迁: allowable ~ 容许跃迁 / energy ~ 转变能，跃迁能 ④【音】变调，转调 ⑤转移论锋；(文章等中的)转折；【语】语次转变 ‖~al a.

transitive ['trænsitiv] **I** a. ①【语】及物的: a ~ verb 及物动词 ②有转移力的 ③过渡的 **II** n. 【语】及物动词 ‖~ly ad.

transitory ['trænsitəri] a. 暂时的；短暂的；瞬息的；昙花一现的 ‖**transitorily** ['trænsitərili; 美 ˌtrænsi'tɔːrili] ad. / **transitoriness** n.

translate [træns'leit] ❶ vt. ①翻译，译；转写，给(诗等)译出: ~ English into Chinese 把英语译成汉语 / This story is ~d from (the) French. 这篇故事译自法语。/ an article into braille 把一篇文章译成盲文 ②解释；说明: ~ one's impressions accurately 准确地说明自己的印象 / ~ sb.'s silence as a protest 把某人的沉默解释

为抗议 ③转化，化；使以另一形式表现: ~ an ideal *into* reality 把理想变为现实 / ~ an instruction (a policy) *into* action 使指示(政策)化为行动 ④使转移；调动: be ~d to the countryside (the Ministry) 被调到乡下(部里)工作 ⑤[英]把(旧衣、旧鞋等)翻新 ⑥(基督教《圣经》中用语)使肉身不死而升天 ⑦[宗]调任(主教)至其他教区；移葬(圣徒遗骸等) ⑧[罕]使狂喜 ⑨【机】使作直线运动，使平移 ⑩【讯】自动转拍(电报) ❷ vi. ①翻译 ②能译出: Not every idiom ~s with such ease. 不是每个习语都能这样容易地译出来。‖**Kindly** ~. 请你简单明了地说明你的意思。

translation [træns'leiʃən] n. ①翻译，译: ~ of a report *from* Chinese *into* English 一个报告的汉译英 / have experience in ~ 有翻译经验 / free ~ 意译 / literal ~ 直译 / close ~ 忠实的翻译 ②译文，译本 ③转化，化: the ~ of the scientific knowledge into practical instruments 科学知识的转化为实用工具 ④转移；调任: one's ~ to another place 被调至他处 ⑤(基督教《圣经》)肉身升天；(主教的)调任 ⑥[英](旧鞋等的)翻新 ⑦【机】直线运动，平动，平移 (=~al motion) ⑧【讯】电报的自动转拍 ‖~al a.

translucent [trænz'ljuːsnt] a. ①半透明的；半透彻的 ②[罕]透明的

transmission [trænz'miʃən] n. ①传送；传达 ②【机】传动；传递；变速器；联动机件 ③【无】【讯】发射；播送；通话；传输；【物】透射 ④【医】遗传；传染 ‖~ bands 传输频带，通频带 / ~ case 传动箱 / ~ line 传输线；馈电线；谐振线；波导线 / ~ shaft 传动轴

transmit [trænz'mit] (transmitted; transmitting) ❶ vt. ①传送；传达: ~ a letter by hand 派专人递送信件 / ~ an order to sb. 把命令传达给某人 ②使(光、热、声等)透过；传导；传动: Glass ~s light. 玻璃能透光。/ Water will ~ sound. 水会传声。/ The power developed by the engine is *transmitted* to the wheels by some essential parts. 引擎发出的动力通过某些主要部件传动轮子。③留传；遗传 ④发射；播送: ~ news by radio 由无线电发送消息 ⑤传播；传染: Anopheles mosquitos ~ malaria. 疟蚊传播疟疾。❷ vi. 播送(或发射)信号；发报 ‖**transmitting set** 发射机；发报机 / **transmitting station** 发射台；发报台

transmitter [trænz'mitə] n. ①传送者；传达者 ②【无】【讯】发射机，发报机；送话器，话筒: insert ~ 插入式话筒 / pulse ~ 脉冲发射机，脉冲发送机 / television ~ 电视发射机 ‖**trans'mitter-re'ceiver** n. 收发两用机

transparence [træns'pɛərəns] n. 透明；透明性；透明度；透光度

transparency [træns'pɛərənsi] n. ①透明；透明性，透彻性；透明度 ②透明物；印有图画(或图

案、照片等)的玻璃(或薄布、瓷器等);背后装灯的透明画(常作广告用); 幻灯片 ‖*his* (或 *your*) *Transparency* [谑]阁下(间接提及时用 his, 直接称呼时用 your)

transparent [træns'pɛərənt] *a.* ①透明的;可为某种辐射(如 X 光)所透射的: This plastic is ~. 这种塑料是透明的。 / ~ colours (绘画)透明颜料 ②半透明的: a ~ soap 半透明肥皂 / ~ muslin 半透明薄纱 ③(托辞等)易识破的;(动机等)显而易见的: a ~ lie 明显的谎言 / a ~ attempt 显而易见的意图 ④(性格等)坦率的,明朗的 ⑤(文体)清楚的,明白的 ‖~**ly** *ad.* / ~**ness** *n.*

transpire [træns'paiə] ❶ *vi.* ①蒸发;发散;排出 ②泄露;显露,被人知道 ③发生 ❷ *vt.* 使蒸发;使发散;使排出 ‖**transpiration** [,trænspi'reiʃən] *n.* ①蒸发;发散;排出 ②【物】渗漏 ③【植】蒸腾作用 ④【医】不自觉性出汗

transplant [træns'plɑːnt] I ❶ *vt.* ①移植,移种: ~ rice seedlings (或 shoots) 插秧 ②迁移;移民 ❷ *vi.* ①移植,移种 ②适宜移植(或移种): Some plants do not ~ well. 有些植物不宜移植。 II *n.* ①移植;被移植物,移植片 ②移居者 ‖~**ation** [,trænsplɑː'neiʃən] *n.* 移植,移种;移植法 / ~**er** *n.* 移植者;移植机: a rice ~er 插秧机

transport [træns'pɔːt] I *vt.* ①运输,运送;输送;搬运 ②流放,放逐(罪犯);把…驱逐出境 ③[用被动语态]使万分激动: be ~ed with joy 欣喜若狂 II ['trænspɔːt] *n.* ①运输: a ~ network 运输网 / a ~ corps 运输队 / ~ charges 运输费 / rush ~ 抢运 / through ~ by land and water 经水陆联运 ②运输工具;运输船;运输飞机 ③激动;狂喜: in a ~ of rage 大发雷霆 / in ~s 狂喜 ④流放犯 ‖~**er** *n.* 运输者;转运装置;转运机

transportation [,trænspɔː'teiʃən] *n.* ①运输,运送;客运,货运;搬运: ~ troops【军】运输部队 / water and land ~ 水陆运输 / railroad ~ 铁路运输 ②运输工具: Their ~ was camel. 骆驼是他们的运输工具。③运费 ④放逐,流放: be sentenced to ~ for life 被判为终身流放

transpose [træns'pɔuz] ❶ *vt.* ①使互换位置,调换,变换 ②【数】移(项) ③【音】使换调,使变调: be ~d from G to B 从 G 调变为 B 调 ❷ *vi.* ①进行变换 ②【音】变调作曲;变调演奏

transposition [,trænspə'ziʃən] *n.* ①互换位置,调换,变换 ②【语】词序的变换 ③【数】易位,对换,移项: ~ of terms of an equation 方程的移项 ④【音】换调,变调;变调曲 ⑤【电】导线交叉

trans-sonic [træns'sɔnik] *a.* 超声的,超声速的;跨音速的

transverse ['trænzvəːs] I *a.* 横向的;横切的,横断的,横截的: ~ nerve【医】横神经 / ~ strain【机】横应变 / ~ wave【物】横波 / ~ axis【数】贯轴 / a ~ section 横断面 II *n.* ①横轴;横骨;横墙 ②【解】横肌 (= ~ muscle) ‖~**ly** *ad.*

trap¹ [træp] I *n.* ①(捕动物的)陷阱,罗网,夹子,捕捉机;(陷人的)圈套,诡计;埋伏: set a ~ 设陷阱;设圈套 / be caught in a ~ (或 fall into a ~) 坠入陷阱;落入圈套 / a mouse-~ 捕鼠机,鼠夹 ②存水弯;汽水阀;防(臭)气阀;放泄弯管: an air ~ 防气阀 / a drain ~ 放泄弯管 ③【字】(固体火箭发动机)火药柱挡板;吸尘罩;陷波电路: wave ~ 陷波器,陷波电路 ④装抛球门于(练习射击用的)泥鸽投射器;(射球戏用的)鞋形投球器 ⑥双轮轻便马车 ⑦[美俚]嘴;[英]侦探,警察 ⑧[复]打击乐器 II (trapped 或 [古] trapt; trapping) ❶ *vt.* ①设陷阱捕,诱捕;设陷阱于(某处);使堕入圈套,使陷于困境;使受限制 ②止住;抓住 ③使(水与气体等)分离 ④装活板门于(舞台等) ⑤装存水弯于(排水管等);用防气阀堵住(臭气);使(蒸汽)密封于管内 ❷ *vi.* 设陷阱,装捕捉机;设圈套 ‖*be up to* ~ 奸滑,诡诡 / *understand* ~ 聪明,机警 ‖~**ball** *n.* 射球戏 / ~ **cellar** 舞台下有活板门的小房间 / '~**-door** *n.* (舞台等的)地板口,活板门;(房顶的)活动天窗;(矿的)调节风门 / ~ **mine**【军】地雷 / '~-**,shooting** *n.* 飞靶射击(投射泥鸽于空中练习射击)

trap² [træp] *n.*【矿】暗色岩

trap³ [træp] (trapped; trapping) *vt.* ①替(马)装马饰 ②装饰

trapeze [trə'piːz] *n.* ①(健身或杂技表演用的)吊架,高秋千: a ~ acrobat (杂技)空中飞人 ②[英]梯形;[美]不规则四边形 (=trapezium)

trapeze

trapezium [trə'piːzjəm] ([复] trapəziums 或 trapezia [trə'piːzjə]) *n.* ①[英]梯形;[美]不规则四边形 ②【解】大多角骨

trapper ['træpə] *n.* ①设陷阱捕兽者 ②【矿】看门工

trappings ['træpiŋz] [复] *n.* ①马饰 ②(尤指作为官职标志的)服饰;装饰品;礼服 ③外部标志

trash [træʃ] I *n.* ①废物,垃圾;(修剪下来的)断枝;落叶;甘蔗渣,甘蔗枯叶 ②劣货;拙劣的文学作品;糟粕;废话 ③无用的人;[美]贫穷的白人;[总称]人类渣滓 II *vt.* ①修剪(树等)的枯枝残叶;去除(甘蔗)的叶子 ②把…视为废物;废弃 ③捣毁(尤指为表示抗议) ‖~ **can** 金属制垃圾箱 / ~ **ice** 混有水的碎冰

trashy ['træʃi] *a.* 废物似的,垃圾似的;毫无价值的 ‖**trashiness** *n.*

travail ['træveil] I *n.* ①艰苦的努力; 工作, 劳动; 苦功 ②分娩: a woman in ～ 临产的妇女 ③痛苦, 剧痛 II *vi.* ①辛勤劳动; 艰苦努力 ②感受阵痛

travel ['trævl] I (travel(l)ed; travel(l)ing) ❶ *vi.* ①旅行: ～ through the whole country 旅行全国 / ～ to Africa 旅行到非洲去 / ～ first class 乘头等车(或舱)旅行 / ～ light 轻装旅行 ②作旅行推销: a salesman travel(l)ing abroad for his firm 一个在国外为他的商号兜生意的推销员 / ～ in office appliances 旅行推销办公用具 ③[口]快速前进, 飞驰; [方]步行: The car can really ～. 这汽车开起来可轻快啦. ④行进; 被传播; 被运送: Light ～s faster than sound. 光比声音传得快. / The good news travel(l)ed quickly. 喜讯迅速传开. / a conception that didn't ～ well 一个未被普遍接受的想法 / goods which ～ in lorries 用卡车运送的货物 / This fish ～s poorly. 这种鱼经不起运输. (指容易死) ⑤移动: a phonograph needle travel(l)ing in a groove 沿着唱片纹路移动的唱针 / His eyes travel(l)ed about the room. 他的眼睛在室内到处巡视着. / My mind travel(l)ed back to that happy moment. 我的思想回到了那幸福的时刻. ⑥交往: ～ with bad elements 与坏人交往 ⑦(打篮球等时)带球走 ❷ *vt.* ①旅行: ～ Europe (the whole world) 旅行欧洲(全世界) / ～ long distances 作长途旅行 ②循…行走, 通行于: This bill travel(l)ed an arduous road. 这议案好不容易才获得通过. ③跑(某地)做生意, 以旅行推销员身份旅行(某地区) ④使移动; 赶, 运送(牲畜等) II *n.* ①旅行: be fond of ～ 喜欢旅行 / come home from one's ～s 旅行结束回到家里 ②[复]旅行笔记, 游记: read ～s 读游记 ③运动, 移动;【机】行程: crank ～ 曲柄行程 ④(在一固定地点)通过的车辆行人数: Travel is very heavy here on holidays. 在假日这儿的交通非常拥挤. ‖ *along* [口]步行; 快步行走 / ～ *out of the record* 扯到题外; 离开议题 / ～ *s in the blue* 沉思, 冥想 / ～ *agency, ～ bureau* 旅行社 / ～ *agent* 旅行代理人 / '～*-soiled,* '～*-stained* *a.* 仆仆风尘的, 旅行中弄脏的 / '～*-worn* *a.* 旅行得疲乏的; 旅行中用旧的

travel(l)er ['trævlə] *n.* ①旅行者; 旅客 ②旅行推销员 ③移动式起重机, 行车; 活动起重架 ④[船]铁杆(或绳索等)上的活动铁环; 甲板上有活动铁环的铁杆 ⑤(待顾客选购完毕后合并结算用的)临时记帐单 ‖ *tip sb. the ～* 欺骗某人 ‖ ～'s cheque, ～'s check 旅行支票 / '～'s-joy *n.* 葡萄叶铁线莲 / '～'s tale 无稽之谈 / '～'s-tree *n.* 旅人蕉(叶柄中含水, 可供旅客饮用)

travel(l)ing ['trævliŋ] *a.* ①旅行的; 旅行用的: a ～ allowance 旅行津贴 / a ～ companion 旅伴 ②移动的 ‖～ bag 旅行手提包 / ～ case 旅行衣箱 / ～ clock 旅行钟 / ～ crane 移动式起重机, 行车 / ～ fellow 享受旅行奖学金(或出国奖学金)的人 / ～ fellowship 旅行奖学金, 出国奖

学金 / ～ salesman 旅行推销员 / ～ wave 【无】行波

traverse ['trævə(:)s] I ❶ *vt.* ①横越, 横切; 横向穿过; 经过: A bridge ～s the rivulet. 一座桥横跨小溪. / The railway ～s the country. 这条铁路横贯全国. ②[喻]全面研究; 详细讨论(问题); 详细考察 ③反对(计划、意见等);【律】否认, 反驳 ④旋转(炮口等); 横刨(木料) ⑤在…上来回移动, 沿…来回移动 ⑥对…作导线测量 ❷ *vi.* ①横越; 横断, 横切 ②(横向)往返移动 ③(磁针等)横转, 旋转; (马等)横走; (爬山时)作Z字形攀登 ④导线测量 II *n.* ①横越; 横断; 横向 ②横断物;【建】横梁; (与对面建筑物相通的)通廊; (城墙、壕沟的)护墙 ③障碍, 障碍物 ④(炮口等的)旋转;【海】(逆风时的)曲线航行; (登山)Z字形攀登 ⑤【律】否认, 反驳 ⑥【数】横截线 ⑦(测量)导线 III *a.* 横断的; 横过的; 横的: ～ sailing 航行 ‖～r *n.* ①横过者; 横断物 ②(铁路的)转盘, 移车台 ③【律】否认者, 反驳者 ‖～ table (铁路的)转盘, 移车台; (测量用的)小平板

travesty ['trævisti] I *n.* (对人或文学作品等的)滑稽模仿; 歪曲; 效颦 II *vt.* 滑稽地模仿(或描述); 歪曲

trawl [trɔːl] I *n.* 拖网; [美](捕海鱼的)排钩 II *vi. & vt.* 用拖网捕(鱼) ‖～er *n.* 拖网渔船; 用拖网捕鱼者 ‖'～boat *n.* 拖网渔船 / '～net *n.* 拖网

tray [trei] *n.* ①(浅)盘, 托盘; 碟: a tea ～ 盘 ②(放在书桌上的)公文格: an in-～ 来函(或其他待办事项的)文件格 / an out-～ 待发文件格 ③(衣箱内的)隔底盘 ④【无】发射箱, 发射架 ‖～ful *n.* 满盘, 一盘子

treacherous ['tretʃərəs] *a.* ①背叛的; 背信弃义的; 奸诈的: ～ acts 背叛行为 ②不可靠的; 不实在的; 有暗藏的危险的: a ～ memory 不可靠的记忆 / ～ quicksand 不坚实的流沙 / ～ ice 仅仅表面坚实的冰 / ～ weather 变化莫测的天气 ‖～ly *ad.* / ～ness *n.*

treachery ['tretʃəri] *n.* ①背叛, 变节; 背信弃义 ②背叛行为, 变节行为

treacle ['triːkl] *n.* ①[英]糖浆, 糖蜜; [喻]甜言 ②(古时的)解毒舐剂 ‖**treacly** *a.* 糖蜜似的; 甜蜜的

tread [tred] I (过去式 trod [trɔd], 过去分词 trodden ['trɔdn] 或 trod) ❶ *vi.* ①踩, 踏; 走: Don't ～ on the crops. 不要踩踏庄稼. / ～ warily on a slippery ground 在滑的地上小心行走 ②(雄鸟)交尾(with) ❷ *vt.* ①踩, 踏; 在…上走: ～ a dozen hurried paces 急促地走了十几步 / ～ the deck 上船, 当水手 / ～ the path of life 踏上人生的道路 ②跳: ～ a measure 合着拍子跳舞 ③踏成, 踩出: Woodmen trod a path on the mountainside. 伐木工人在山麓上踩出了一条小路. ④践踏, 蹂躏: ～ sb.'s rights underfoot 践踏某人的权利 ⑤(雄鸟)与…交尾 II *n.* ①踩, 踏; 步法, 步态; 足音: with a heavy ～ 脚步沉重

地 ②(雄鸟的)交尾 ③(楼梯等的)踏板,踏面,级宽;(轮胎的)着地面,胎面;胎 / ~ caterpillar 履带 / ~ pattern 车胎花纹 ④鞋底 ⑤(汽车左右两轮的)轮距;自行车两踏脚间的距离 ⑥【医】(马蹄的)践伤 ⑦【动】(卵的)胚点,卵(黄系)带 ‖ (as) on eggs 如履薄冰,瞻前顾后,战战兢兢 / ~ awry 失败,出差错 / ~ down ①踏实,踩碎 ②抑制(感情);压迫,压服 / ~ in 用脚把…踩入(地里) / ~ lightly 轻轻走着;[喻] 小心处理 / ~ on air 洋洋得意 / ~ on sb.'s toes ①踩某人的脚尖 ②触怒某人,得罪某人 / ~ on the heels of 紧随…之后 / ~ on the neck of 骑在…头上,压迫 / ~ out 踩灭(火等);扑灭(叛乱等);踩榨出(葡萄汁等);踩出(谷物的)谷粒 / ~ the boards (或 stage) 上舞台,做演员 / ~ water (游泳时)踩水 ‖ ~mill n. (古时罚囚犯踩踏的)踏车;[喻] 单调的工作

treadle ['tredl] **I** n. (自行车、缝纫机等的)踏板 **II** vi. 踏动踏板 ‖ ~r n. 踏踏板的人 ‖ '~-ma,chine, '~-press n. 脚踏印刷机

treason ['tri:zn] n. ①叛逆,谋反;通敌;叛国罪: a case of ~ 叛国案 ②不忠;背信 ‖ felony [英]叛逆罪

treasonable ['tri:znəbl], **treasonous** ['tri:zənəs] a. 叛逆的,谋反的;犯叛国罪的,涉及叛国罪的

treasure ['treʒə] **I** n. ①金银财宝,财富 ②珍宝,珍品: priceless art ~s 无价的艺术珍品 ③[口]不可多得的人材;宝贝儿(尤指孩子) **II** vt. ①珍藏,秘藏 (up);[喻]铭记 (up): ~ up stamps 珍藏邮票(指集邮) / sth. up in one's memory 铭记某事 ②珍重,珍惜 ‖ ~ manpower and material resources 爱惜人力物力 ‖ '~-house n. 宝库 / ~ trove = trove

treasurer ['treʒərə] n. 司库,掌管财务的人 ‖ Lord High Treasurer 【英史】财政大臣 / Treasurer of the Household [英]王室财务主管 ‖ ~ship n. 司库的职位

treasury ['treʒəri] n. ①宝库;宝藏 ②库房;金库;国库;库存 ③[T-]财政部 ④[T-](由财政部发行的)国库券,债券 ⑤被视为知识宝库的人(或典籍);文库,诗集;艺术品集: a ~ of verse 诗集 / The book is a ~ of information. 这本书有极丰富的资料。 ‖ First Lord of the Treasury [英]第一财政大臣 / the Treasury [英]财政部 / Treasury bench [英]下院政府大臣席 / Treasury Board (=Lords (或 Commissioners) of the Treasury) [英]财政委员会(通常由首相、财政大臣及其他五人组成) / Treasury Department [美]财政部 ‖ ~ bill [英](为筹款由财政部发行的)国库债券 / ~ note [英]国库券(由财政部发行,值一镑,现由英国银行的纸币代替);[美]财政部发行的一种证券 / ~ stock 【商】库存股份

treat [tri:t] **I** ❶ vt. ①对待,看待,把…看作: ~ sb. as a distinguished guest 把某人待如上宾 / ~ sb. with consideration 对某人很体贴 / No errors are to be ~ed lightly. 对于错误,不能等

闲视之。 ②处理;论述;探讨: The theme of the play is skilfully ~ed. 这剧本的主题处理得很好。 ③医治,治疗: ~ sb. for influenza 给某人医治流行性感冒 / ~ a fracture of the bone 治疗骨折 ④款待,请(客);(竞选时)请客拉拢(投票人): ~ sb. to an ice-cream (a theatre) 请某人吃冰淇淋(看戏) / I'll ~ myself to a sunbath. 我要好好地享受一次日光浴。 ⑤【化】处理;为…涂上保护层: ~ a substance with sulphuric acid 用硫酸处理某物 ❷ vi. ①交涉,谈判;商议: ~ with sb. on equal terms 在平等基础上与某人谈判 ②作东,请客 **II** n. ①款待,请客: This is my ~. 这次由我请客。 ②难得的乐事: The performance is a great ~ to us. 演出使我们高兴极了。 / It is a ~ to see you. 看见你真高兴。 ‖ a children's (或 a school) ~ (尤指教会所办的)主日学堂的)儿童远足 / stand ~ 作东,请客 / ~ of 是关于,论及: This article ~s of the use of chemical fertilizers. 这篇文章讲的是化肥的使用。 ‖ ~able a. (人)好对付的;能处理的;能治疗的: a ~able disease 能治疗的疾病 / ~er n. ①谈判者 ②用化学药品处理物品者;【化】处理器;提纯器

treatise ['tri:tiz] n. (专题)论文: a ~ on traditional Chinese medicine 一篇有关中医的论文

treatment ['tri:tmənt] n. ①待遇: preferential ~ 优待 / receive good ~ from sb. 受到某人良好的待遇 / give lenient ~ to prisoners of war 宽待战俘 ②处理;论述: heat ~ 【冶】热处理 / an exhaustive ~ of a question 对问题的详尽论述 ③治疗;疗法;疗程: be under (medical) ~ 在治疗中 / free ~ 免费治疗 / a new ~ for cancer 癌症新疗法

treaty ['tri:ti] n. ①(国家之间的)条约: a peace ~ 和平条约 / conclude a ~ 订立条约 / enter into a ~ with 与…缔结条约 ②(人与人之间的)协议,协定;协商;谈判: be in ~ with sb. for sth. 与某人谈判某事 / private ~ 产业交易中买卖双方私人之间的协定 ‖ ~ port (条约规定的)通商口岸

treble ['trebl] **I** a. ①三倍的;三重的: ~ figures 三倍的数字 / The production is ~ what it was. 生产比过去增加两倍(或是过去的三倍)。②【音】最高音部的;唱(或奏)最高音部的 ③尖锐刺耳声的;高音的: ~ frequencies 高音频率 **II** n. ①三倍;三重 ②【音】最高音部;唱最高音部的人;奏最高音部用的乐器 ③尖锐刺耳声 **III** ❶ vt. 使成三倍,使增加两倍: We have ~d our output. 我们把产量提高到原来的三倍。❷ vi. 成为三倍,增加两倍: The number of livestock has ~d. 牲畜增加了两倍。 ‖ **trebly** ad. 三倍地;三重地

tree [tri:] **I** n. ①树;乔木;树状灌木: a deciduous ~ 落叶树 / a rose ~ 玫瑰树 ②木料;木制构件 ③树状物;【数】树(形);【化】树状晶体 ④世系图: a family ~ 家族世系图;家谱 ⑤棺椁 ⑥圣诞树(=Christmas ~) ⑦[古]绞台;绞架 ⑧[古]

(钉耶稣的)十字架 **II** *vt.* ①赶(人、兽等)上树躲避;［口］使处于困境: The dog ~d the cat. 狗赶猫上树。②用鞋楦植(鞋) ‖*at the top of the ~* 见 **top**[1] / *bark up the wrong* ~ 攻击错了目标;把精力花在不该花的地方 / *in the dry* (*green*) ~ 处于劣(佳)境 / *shake the pagoda* ~ (在印度)暴发致富 / ~ *of Buddha*【植】菩提树 / ~ *of knowledge of good and evil* (基督教《圣经》)伊甸园中知善恶的树,开知识的树(亚当与夏娃违背上帝禁令而食其果) / ~ *of life* ① 金钟柏属植物 ②(基督教《圣经》)伊甸园中的生命树(据说食其果能长生) / *up a gum* ~ 进退两难,骑虎难下 / *up a* ~［口］进退两难 ②处于冷眼旁观地位 ‖*~less a.* 无树木的 ‖~ **agate** (有树枝状花纹的)苔纹玛瑙 / ~ **calf** (经化学处理后)有木纹的小牛皮 / ~ **creeper**【动】旋木雀科的鸟,旋木雀 / ~ **farm** 林场 / ~ **fern**【植】灰白水龙骨(一种高大如树的蕨类植物) / ~ **house** 建造在树上的巢屋 / ~ **milk** 树乳(一种印度尼西亚藤类植物的可供食用的树液) / '~**nail** *n.* 木栓 / ~ **peony**【植】牡丹 / ~ **ring** (树木的)年轮 / ~ **toad**【动】雨蛙 / '~**top** *n.* ① 树顶 ②［复］(树林的)树顶高度(线)

trek [trek] **I** (trekked; trekking) ❶ *vi.* ①(南非用英语)(牛)拉车;(牛)担负重荷;坐牛车旅行;乘牛车迁徙 ②缓慢地行进;艰苦跋涉: Our medical workers *trekked* through high mountains to collect valuable medicinal herbs. 我们的医务人员踏遍高山峻岭采集珍贵药材。❷ *vt.* (南非用英语)(牛)拉(车) **II** *n.* ①(南非用英语)牛车旅行;牛车旅行中的一段旅程 ②艰苦的跋涉;一段旅程 ③集体迁徙

trellis ['trelis] **I** *n.* ①【建】格构,格子结构;(葡萄等的)棚,架: cucumber ~*es* 黄瓜棚 ②棚架式拱道,格构拱道;格构凉亭;格构遮板;格子遮板 **II** *vt.* ①为…建棚架; 使(藤)在棚架上攀缘: a ~*ed* verandah 格构廊庑 ②使交织成格状 ‖'~**work** *n.* 格构: a ~*work* bridge 桁梁桥,格构桥

tremble ['trembl] **I** *vi.* ①发抖,哆嗦;震颤: His voice ~*d* with excitement. 他兴奋得声音发抖。/ ~ with cold (fright) 冷得(吓得)发抖 ②焦虑,担忧: ~ for sb.'s safety 为某人的安全担忧 / ~ to think ... 一想到…就不寒而栗 ③摇晃,摇动: The leaves ~*d* in the breeze. 树叶在微风中摇动。**II** *n.* ①颤抖;［有时用复］一阵哆嗦 ②［复］马霉颤病;乳(毒)病 ‖*be all of a* ~［口］浑身发抖 / *Hear and* ~! 好好听着,牢牢记住! / ~ *in the balance* 见 **balance** ‖*~r n.* ①发抖的人;震颤的东西 ②【电】自动振动器;电铃;断续器;蜂鸣器 ③【机】震颤片

tremendous [tri'mendəs] *a.* ①可怕的 ②极大的,非常的;惊人的: a ~ difference 极大的差别 / ~ efforts 巨大的努力 / a ~ eater 食量极大的人 / a ~ talker 非常健谈的人 / at a ~ speed 以惊人的速度 ‖*~ly ad.* / *~ness n.*

tremor ['tremə] *n.* ①震颤;发抖: intention ~

【医】动作震颤 ②震动;微动: earth ~s 地动 / the ~ of a leaf 树叶的抖动 ③战栗;激烈的情感;激动: face danger without a ~ 临危不惧 ④颤抖的声音

tremulous ['tremjuləs] *a.* ①震颤的;发抖的: in a ~ voice 以颤抖的声音 ②胆小的;动摇的 ③歪斜的;不稳定的: a ~ handwriting 歪歪斜斜的笔迹 ④过分敏感的 ‖*~ly ad.* / *~ness n.*

trench [trentʃ] **I** ❶ *vt.* ①挖战壕于…;掘沟于…: ~ a field 在地里挖沟 ②刻,挖;［英］刻槽于(木材等) ③用战壕围住;用战壕防御 ❷ *vi.* ①挖沟;掘战壕 ②接近,近似 (on, upon): ~ upon plagiarism 近近剽窃 ③侵占,侵占 (on, upon): ~ upon sb.'s rights 侵犯某人的权利 / ~ on sb.'s time 侵占某人的时间 **II** *n.* ①深沟;地沟: dig ~es for drainage 挖排水沟 ②【军】堑壕,壕沟: open the ~es 开始挖壕沟 / mount the ~es 在堑壕里守卫 / a communication ~ 交通壕 ‖~ **cart** (战壕用)矮轮手推车 / ~ **coat** 军用胶布夹(或棉)雨衣 / ~ **fever**【医】战壕热,五日热 / ~ **foot**【医】战壕足病 / ~ **knife** (近战用的)两刃短刀 / ~ **mortar** 迫击炮 / ~ **mouth**【医】战壕口炎 / ~ **plough** 深耕犁 / ~ **warfare** 堑壕战

trenchant ['trentʃənt] *a.* ①犀利的,锋利的,锐利的: ~ words 锋利的语言 / a ~ weapon 锐利的武器 ②有力的: a ~ argument 有力的论据 ③分明的,清晰的: a ~ pattern 清晰的图案 ‖**trenchancy** *n.* / *~ly ad.*

trend [trend] **I** *vi.* ①伸向;折向,转向: The river ~s (towards the) east. 这条河向东流。②倾向,趋向: His opinion ~ed towards yours. 他倾向于你的意见。**II** *n.* ① (海岸、河流等的)走向: The ~ of the coastline is to the south. 海岸线向南延展。②倾向,趋势,动向: the general ~ of history 历史的总趋向 / a ~ of thought (或 an ideological ~) 思潮 ‖*~y a.* 随潮流的;时髦的

trepidation [ˌtrepi'deiʃən] *n.* ①发抖;震颤 ②惊惶;慌张

trespass ['trespəs] **I** *vi.* ①未经许可进入私人土地;非法侵入,侵犯 (on, upon): ~ upon sb.'s property 非法侵入某人的土地 / No ~*ing*! (告示用语)不准入内! ②叨扰;打扰,妨碍 (on, upon): ~ on sb.'s hospitality 叨扰某人 / ~ upon sb.'s time 占去某人的时间 ③冒犯;违规 (against): ~ against sb. 冒犯某人 **II** *n.* ①侵入私人土地;侵占;侵犯 ②冒犯;罪过 ‖*~er n.* 侵犯者;侵犯他人土地者

tress [tres] *n.* ①一绺头发;一束头发;发辫 ②［复］(尤指长而未束的)女人头发

trestle ['tresl] *n.* ①支架;搁凳 ②【建】栈桥,高架桥 (=~ bridge); 栈架 ‖~ **table** 支架上搁桌面而成的桌子,搁板桌 / ~**tree**【船】桅顶纵桁 / '~**work** *n.* 栈架结构

trial ['traiəl] *n.* ①试;试用;试验: make a ~ 试一下;进行试验 / give sb. a ~ 让某人试一试,试用

某人 / an air ~ 飞行试验;试飞 / put the new machine to ~ 试验新机器 ②考验;磨炼;艰苦;痛苦: a period of ~ 一段考验的时间 / stand the ~s of hardships 经得起艰苦的考验 / the ~s of a long march 长途行军的磨炼 ③讨厌的人;麻烦的事物: That child of his is a great ~. 他的那个孩子真叫人受不了。④审问,审判: bring sb. to (或 up for) ~ 审问某人 / conduct a public ~ 举行公审 / grant a new ~ 允予复审 / ~ by jury 由陪审团进行的审讯 ⑤【体】选拔赛;预赛 ⑥尝试;努力 II a. 尝试的;试验性的;试制的: a ~ trip 试航 /【喻】flight 试飞 / ~ production 产品试制 / on a ~ basis 在试验的基础上;试验性地 / ~ subscription (杂志等的)试订 ‖on ~ ①在试用中;试验性地;经试验后: This new method is on ~. 这个新方法正在试用。/ This method was found on ~ to be practicable. 经过试验发现这种方法是可行的。②在受审: be on (one's) ~ for theft 因盗窃而受审 / stand (或 undergo) (one's) ~ for 因…而受审 / ~ and error 反复试验;不断摸索: learn technical skills through (或 by) ~ and error 通过不断摸索掌握技能 ‖~ balance 【会计】试算表 / ~ balloon 【军】测验风速(或气流)的气球 ②试探舆论的行动(或声明等) / ~ eights 参加选拔赛的(八人一队的)两队划船手 / ~ horse 被安排与对手对阵的练习对手 / ~ jury 审讯案件的陪审团;小陪审团 / '~-,manu'facture vt. & n. 试制 / '~-pro'duce vt. 试制(产品等) / ~ run 试航;试车;试验

triangle ['traiæŋgl] n. ①【数】三角(形): solution by a ~ 三角形解法 / ~ of force 力的三角形 ②三角板 ③【音】三角铁(一种打击乐器) ④三角关系(尤指男女间的) ⑤[T-]【天】三角座 ‖equilateral ~ 等边三角形 / isosceles ~ 等腰三角形 / right-angled ~ 直角三角形 / obtuse ~ 钝角三角形 / scalene ~ 不规则三角形

triangular [trai'æŋgjulə] a. ①三角(形)的: ~ numbers 【数】三角形数 / ~ thread 【机】三角螺纹 ②有三角形底的: a ~ prism 三棱柱 / a ~ pyramid 三棱锥 ③三人间的;三者间的;【军】三制的: a ~ treaty 三边条约 / a ~ division 三制师,三团制师 ‖~ity [trai,æŋgju'læriti] n. / ~ly ad.

tribal ['traibəl] a. 部落的;宗族的 ‖~ism n. 部落制;部落文化

tribe [traib] n. ①部落;宗族: the Indian ~s of America 美洲的印第安人部落 ②[贬](一)帮,(一)伙,(一)批: the ~ of parasites 那批寄生虫 / the scribbling ~ 动动笔头的一伙 ③【生】族(动植物分类单位): cat ~ 猫族 ‖~sman ['traibzmən] n. 部落的一员;同宗族的人

tribulation [,tribju'leiʃən] n. ①苦难;患难;忧伤 ②引起苦难的事物;磨难

tribunal [trai'bju:nl, tri'bju:nl] n. ①审判员席,法官席 ②法庭(常指特种法庭或作比喻用): a

military ~ 军事法庭 / stand before the ~ of public opinion 受到公众舆论的制裁

tributary ['tribjutəri] I a. ①进贡的,纳贡的;附庸的,从属的: a ~ state 进贡国;附庸国,属国 ②辅助的 ③(河)支流的 II n. ①进贡国;附庸国,属国 ②进贡者(指附庸国的统治者等) ③支流

tribute ['tribju:t] n. ①贡金;贡物: pay ~ to 向…进贡 ②为交纳贡金而收的税 ③纳贡的地位,臣属的地位;纳贡的义务 ④勒索的款额 ⑤礼物;颂词,称赞;殷勤: one's ~ of praise 颂词,称赞的话 / floral ~s 用以表示敬意的鲜花,敬献的鲜花 ‖lay under ~ 强使进贡;使处从属地位 / pay (a) ~ to 称赞,歌颂

trice¹ [trais] vt. 拉起;拉起并缚住;缚住 (up)

trice² [trais] n. 一刹那 ‖in a ~ 转眼之间,瞬息间: fall asleep in a ~ 转眼就睡着了

trick [trik] I n. ①诡计,奸计;骗局;谋略: Don't try any ~s! 别耍花招! / a dirty (或 a mean, a shabby, an underhand) ~ 卑鄙手段 / a double-dealing ~ 两面派手法 ②恶作剧: play a ~ on sb. 捉弄某人 ③轻率愚蠢的行为: It's fool's ~ to trust his words. 信他的话才蠢呢! ④(行为、举止等方面的)习惯,癖好: He has a ~ of repeating himself. 他有讲话重复的习惯。/ a ~ of archaism 爱用古语的癖好 ⑤窍门;[常贬](迅速获得成功的)诀窍: learn (或 get) the ~ of sailing a boat 学会行船的窍门 / learn the ~s of the trade 学这一行生意的诀窍 ⑥戏法,把戏: a conjurer's ~s 魔术家的戏法 / card ~s 用纸牌变的戏法 / a mere ~ of the light (魔术中)仅靠灯光造成的幻觉 ⑦舵手的一班(通常为二小时);(指值班时间)一班;(雇员等)的出差,公出 ⑧(牌戏中各家所出牌集合而成的)一叠牌: take (或 win) a ~ 赢一墩牌 / the odd ~ 决定胜负的最后一墩牌 ⑨[口]逗人的孩子;俏姑娘 ⑩[美俚]犯罪行为;抢劫;刑期 ⑪(廉价的)小物件,小玩意儿 II a. ①有诀窍的;特技的;花巧的: ~ photography 特技摄影 / a ~ shot (电影)特技镜头 / ~ cycling 车技 ②欺诈的,弄虚作假的 ③漂亮的,潇洒的,有效的;能干的 ④靠不住的;(关节等)会突然撑不住的: a ~ lock that doesn't always catch 不是经常锁得住的蹩脚锁 / a ~ knee resulting from an injury 因受过损伤而会突然支撑不住的膝关节 III ❶ vt. ①哄骗: ~ sb. into consent 哄骗某人应允 / ~ sb. into doing sth. 哄骗某人去干某事 / ~ sb. out of his money 骗取某人的钱 ②装饰,打扮 (out, up, off): be ~ed out in gaudy dress 用过分艳丽的服装打扮起来 ❷ vi. ①哄骗 ②恶作剧;戏弄 (with) ‖do (或 turn) the ~ [俚]达到预期目的;获得成功 / know a ~ or two (或 be up to a ~ or two) 相当机灵;精明 / know a ~ worth two of that [口]知道更好的方法;有更妙的办法 ‖~er n. 耍诡计的人;骗子 ‖~ cyclist 特技自行车手;[俚]精神病学家;精神病医生

trickery ['trikəri] n. 欺骗;哄骗;诡计;圈套

trickle ['trikl] I ❶ *vi.* ①滴; 淌; 细流; 流出液体: Blood ~*d* down his arm. 血从他臂上一滴滴流下。/ The tears ~*d* from her eyes. 泪珠从她的眼中流出。 ②慢慢地移动: The information ~*d* out. 消息慢慢透露出来。/ The crowd began to ~ away. 人群开始慢慢地散去。 ❷ *vt.* 使滴; 使淌; 使细流: He ~*d* oil into the gear. 他把油滴入传动装置。 II *n.* 滴; 涓滴; 细流 ‖~**t** ['triklit] *n.* 细流 / **trickly** *a.* 一滴一滴流的 ‖~ **charger**【电】点滴式充电(法), 连续补充充电(法)

trickster ['trikstə] *n.* 骗子; 魔术师; 恶作剧的精灵

tricky ['triki] *a.* ①狡猾的; 要花招的 ②(工作等)复杂的; 微妙的; 棘手的 ③靠不住的; (关节等)会突然撑不住的

tricolo(u)r ['trikələ, 'trai,kʌlə] I *a.* ①(有)三色的 ②三色国旗的; 有三色国旗的国家的(常指法国的) II *n.* 三色旗(尤指法国国旗) ‖~**ed** *a.* (有)三色的

tricycle ['traisikl] I *n.* 三轮脚踏车; 三轮手摇车; 三轮摩托车 II *vi.* 骑三轮脚踏车(或三轮摩托车) ‖**tricyclist** ['traisiklist] *n.* 骑三轮脚踏车(或三轮摩托车)的人

trident ['traidənt] I *n.* ①(希腊、罗马神话中海神的)三叉戟 ②有三个叉头的鱼叉 ③制海权的象征 ④[T-]三叉戟式飞机 II *a.* 三叉的

triennial [trai'enjəl] I *a.* ①每三年一次的: a ~ election 三年一次的选举 ②持续三年的: ~ plants 三年生植物 II *n.* ①三年生植物 ②每三年发生一次的事件 ③三周年纪念 ④【天主教】三年间为死者每天举行的弥撒 ‖~**ly** *ad.*

trifle ['traifl] I *n.* ①小事儿; 琐事; 细故; 无价值的东西: quarrel over ~*s* 为小事争吵 / waste time on ~*s* 为琐事浪费时间 ②少许, 少量; 一点钱: a ~ of sugar 少量食糖 / cost sb. only a ~ 仅要某人花费很少的钱 ③一种用蛋白、奶油、果酱、糕饼等做成的甜食; 蛋糕; 松糕 ④白镴(锡基合金); [复]白镴制品 II ❶ *vi.* ①开玩笑; 嘲弄; 轻视 (*with*): The matter is not to be ~*d with*. 这事可不能闹着玩的。②玩弄 (*with*): ~ *with* sb.'s affections 玩弄某人的感情 ③闲混: ~ through one's youth 虚度青春 ❷ *vt.* 浪费(时间、精力、钱等) (*away*): ~ the hours *away* 浪费时间 ‖*a* ~ 有点儿, 稍微: be *a* ~ alarmed 稍感惊慌 ‖~**r** *n.* 闹着玩的人; 吊儿郎当的人

trifling ['traifliŋ] *a.* ①不重要的; 微不足道的; 无聊的: a ~ error 小错误 / a ~ gift 薄礼 / ~ value 价值很小的 / It's no ~ matter. 这不是小事。/ ~ talk 无聊的谈话 ②轻薄的; 情意不专的 ③[方]懒散的, 不求上进的: a ~ fellow 一个懒散的人 ‖~**ly** *ad.* / ~**ness** *n.*

trigger ['trigə] I *n.* ①【军】扳机; 触发器: have one's finger on the ~ 手指放在扳机上; 准备射击 / a ~ for an H-bomb 氢弹的起爆器 ②【电】起动线路; 起动装置; 【机】扳柄; 闸柄 ③能引起反应的刺激物: The odour of food may be a ~ for

salivation. 食物的香味可能会引起唾液分泌。 II ❶ *vt.* ①扣扳机开(枪等); 发射: ~ a rifle 开枪 / ~ a missile 发射导弹 ②激发起, 引起 (*off*): ~ (*off*) an armed clash 引起武装冲突 / ~ (*off*) a chain reaction 引起连锁反应 ❷ *vi.* 松开扳柄(或闸柄等) ‖**quick on the ~** [口]动不动就开枪的; 行动迅速的; 机灵的 ‖~**-'happy** *a.* 乱开枪的; 嗜杀的; 冒战争危险的; 好战的 / ~**man** ['trigəmən] *n.* ①开枪行凶的人; 刺客; 匪徒 ②保镖 ③拉动扳柄使船下水的人

trigonometry [,trigə'nɔmitri] *n.* 【数】三角(学) ①三角学 ②三角学论文; 三角学教科书

trilateral ['trai'lætərəl] I *a.* 三边的: a ~ figure 三边形 / a ~ agreement 三边协定 II *n.* 三角形; 三边形 ‖~**ity** ['trai,lætə'ræliti] *n.* / ~**ly** *ad.*

trill [tril] I *n.* ①(音乐演奏和发音时的)颤动 ②【音】【语】颤音 ③(鸟的)啭鸣 II ❶ *vt.* 以颤声发出; 以颤声奏(或唱等) ❷ *vi.* 发出颤声

trillion ['triljən] I *num.* ①(英、德)百万的三次幂(或乘方)(在 1 后加 18 个零所得的数) ②(美、法)百万的二次幂(或乘方)(在 1 后加 12 个零所得的数), 万亿 II *n.* 大量, 无数

trilogy ['trilədʒi] *n.* ①(音乐、戏剧、小说等的)三部曲 ②(古希腊)连续演出的三部悲剧

trim [trim] I (trimmer, trimmest) *a.* ①整齐的; 整洁的; 漂亮的: ~ houses 整齐的房屋 ②[古]适当调整的; 准备就绪的 II (trimmed; trimming) ❶ *vt.* ①使整齐, 整理; 修剪: ~ one's nails (beard) 修剪指甲(胡子) / ~ dead branches off a tree 剪掉树上的枯枝 / ~ oneself up 打扮, 修饰 / ~ a budget 削减预算 ②装饰, 点缀; 布置(商店橱窗): ~ an arch in celebration of National Day 装饰牌楼庆祝国庆 / ~ a dress with lace 给衣服饰花边 ③装稳(船只);【空】使(飞机)配平: ~ a vessel (指将货物散装)平舱 ④调整(船帆)以适应风向: ~ the sails 随风使帆 ⑤刨平和修整(木料) ⑥【口】骂; 训斥; 殴打; 击败; 诈骗(钱财) ❷ *vi.* ①(政治上)两面讨好, 骑墙; 走中间路线; 见风使舵 ②(船)保持平衡; 顺风使帆 III *n.* ①整理; 修剪; 调整;【无】微调, 垫整 ②整顿; 准备; 齐备: in fighting ~ 处于战备状态 / get into good ~ 准备就绪 / be out of ~ 未准备好 ③(华丽的)服装, 外表 ④装饰(物);【建】贴脸; 门框(或窗框)的细木工; 汽车内部的装潢 ⑤(船等的)平衡;【海】吃水差;【军】潜艇的浮力;【空】配平 ⑥修剪下来的东西 IV *ad.* = ~**ly** ‖~ sb.'s jacket 毆打某人 ‖~**ly** *ad.* 整齐地; 整洁地 / ~**ness** *n.* 整齐; 整洁 ‖~ **size** 实际尺寸(如在装订过程中, 书页的多余部分已切除后所余的面积)

trimming ['trimiŋ] *n.* ①整理, 修饰; 修剪; 装饰品, 装饰物 ②[复](主菜之外的)花色配菜: turkey with all ~*s* 有各色配菜的火鸡 ③[复]修剪下来的东西 ④[口]责骂; 殴打; 击败; 诈骗

trinity ['triniti] *n.* ①三个(人或物组成的)一组，三位一体 ②[the T-]【宗】(圣父、圣子、圣灵)三位一体；三位一体的艺术象征 ③[T-]【宗】三一节，复活主日(=Trinity Sunday)

trinket ['triŋkit] *n.* ①小件饰物 ②无价值的琐碎东西，小玩意儿 ‖**~ry** *n.* [集合名词]小件饰物

trio ['tri(:)ou] *n.* ①【音】三重奏；三重唱；三部合奏(或合唱)曲 ②用复三段式写作的乐曲的中段 ③三重唱(或三重奏、三人舞)演出小组；三人一组；三件一套

trip [trip] I (tripped; tripping) ❶ *vi.* ①轻快地走(或跑)；轻快地跳舞：The children *tripped* into the classroom. 孩子们轻快地跑进教室。②绊；绊倒：~ and fall 跌跤 / He *tripped* over a stone. 他给一块石头绊了一下。③失足；犯错误，出差错 ④说话结结巴巴：He stammered and *tripped*. 他结结巴巴地说话。⑤旅行，远足 ⑥(表等)擒纵机构转动 ❷ *vt.* ①绊；绊倒；使失足；使犯错误；使受挫，使失败：The wrestler *tripped (up)* his opponent. 摔角运动员摔倒了他的对手。②找出(某人)的过错；挑剔(up): Wrongdoing inevitably ~s up itself. 做坏事必然会暴露。③[古]轻快地跳(舞)：~ a measure 轻快地跳舞 ④【海】起(锚)；竖直(帆桁) ⑤【机】松开棘爪而开动 II *n.* ①(摔角中)摔倒对手的动作；绊；绊倒 ②失足；过失，错误：A ~ in one point would have spoiled all. 走错一着，全盘皆输。③支吾，结结巴巴；失言 ④(车辆较短距离的)行驶；往返 ⑤旅行，远足；一次来回：a ~ to the seaside 去海滨的远足 / a ~ around the world 环球旅行 / make a ~ to the dentist 去看一次牙医生 / The postal carriers make two ~s a day. 邮递员每日送两次信。⑥行程，旅程：a round ~ 往返的旅程 / The other village was two hours' motor ~ further west. 另一个村庄在汽车朝西再开两小时的地方。⑦轻快的步伐 ⑧渔船航行一次的捕获量 ⑨【机】【电】解扣，跳闸：overload ~ 过载跳闸 ⑩生活方式 ⑪吸麻醉毒品者的幻觉 ‖*catch sb. tripping* 抓住某人的差错；抓住某人的把柄 / ~ *the light fantastic* [美]跳舞 ‖~ **flare** 绊索照明弹 / '~-**hammer** *n.*【机】杵锤 / ~ **wire** ①绊网 ②地雷拉发线

tripartite ['trai'pɑ:tait] *a.* ①分成三部分的；三部分组成的；三重的 ②一式三份的：a ~ indenture 三联合同 ③三方面之间的：a ~ treaty (conference) 三方条约(会议) ④【植】(叶子)三深裂的 ‖~**ly** *ad.*

tripe [traip] *n.* ①(牛等的)肚(供食用)：a dish of stewed ~ 一盘焖牛肚 ②[常用复]内脏 ③[俚]废物；废话；讨厌的东西：Stop talking ~! 不要说废话!

triple ['tripl] I *a.* 三倍的；三重的；三层的；三部分的：~ thread【机】三线螺纹 / ~ point【物】三态点，三相点 / the *Triple* Alliance【史】英国、瑞典、荷兰的三国同盟(1668)；英国、法国、荷兰的三国同盟(1717)；德国、奥地利、意大利的三国同盟 (1882—1883) / the ~ crown 罗马教皇的三重皇冠 II *n.* ①三倍数；三倍量；三个一组 ②(棒球的)三垒打(即可连跑三垒的一击) III ❶ *vt.* 三倍于，使增至三倍：~ the output 使产量增加两倍(即增至三倍) / one's efforts 作出三倍的努力 ❷ *vi.* 增至三倍 ‖~ **counterpoint**【音】三重对位 / ~ **jump** 三级跳远 / ~ **measure** = ~ time / '~-'**nerved** *a.*【植】离基三出脉的 / ~ **play** (棒球)攻方三个球员出局的一场比赛 / '~-'**space** *vt.* (打字时)每空两行打(文件等)・*vi.* 每空两行打字 / ~ **threat** 能奔、能踢、能传球的足球能手 / ~ **time**【音】三拍子

triplet ['triplit] *n.* ①三个一组；三件一套 ②押韵的三行诗 ③【音】三连音符 ④三胞胎中的一个；[复]三胞胎

triplicate ['triplikit] I *a.* ①一式三份的；重复三次的：a ~ agreement 一式三份的协议 ②(一式几份中)第三份的：file the ~ copy 把第三副本归档 II *n.* 三个相同物中的第三个；一式三份中的一份 III ['triplikeit] *vt.* ①把…作成一式三份 ②使增至三倍 ‖*in* ~ 一式三份：type a report *in* ~ (用打字机)把报告打成一式三份 ‖**triplication** [,tripli'keiʃən] *n.*

tripod ['traipod] *n.* ①三脚桌；三脚凳；鼎；三脚支撑物：~ landing gear【空】三轮起落架 ②(照相机等的)三脚架 ③(古希腊 Delphi 特尔斐城内的)青铜三脚祭坛；三脚祭坛的模拟品(古希腊用作在特尔斐举行的运动会的奖品) ‖~**al** ['tripədəl] *a.* 有三脚的

trisect [trai'sekt] *vt.* ①把…分成三份；把…截成三段 ②【数】三等分 ‖~**ion** [trai'sekʃən] *n.*

trite [trait] *a.* ①用坏了的 ②(言词、引语、观念、意见等)陈腐的；平凡的；老一套的 ‖~**ly** *ad.* / ~**ness** *n.*

triumph ['traiəmf] I *n.* ①(古罗马)凯旋仪式 ②凯旋；胜利；成功；成就：win a ~ over one's opponent 击败敌手 / return home in ~ 凯旋 / the ~s of science 科学的成就 ③(胜利或成功时的)狂欢，喜悦：detect ~ in sb.'s eye 在某人的目光中看出胜利的喜悦 II *vi.* ①获胜；成功；击败(over) ②热烈庆祝胜利；(胜利而)狂欢

triumphal [trai'ʌmfəl] *a.* 凯旋(式)的；庆贺胜利的；胜利的；成功的：a ~ arch 凯旋门 / a ~ feast 庆功宴

triumphant [trai'ʌmfənt] *a.* ①胜利的；成功的 ②(因胜利而)狂欢的，喜悦的；得意洋洋的 ‖~**ly** *ad.*

trivial ['triviəl] *a.* ①琐细的；轻微的；不重要的；价值不大的：~ matters 琐事 / ~ formalities 繁文缛节 / a ~ loss 轻微的损失 / put the ~ above the important 轻重倒置 ②平常的，平凡的；(名称)通俗的：the ~ round of daily life 平凡的日常生活 / a ~ name 俗名 ③(人)浅薄的；轻浮的；无能的；缺德的 ‖~**ly** *ad.* / ~**ness** *n.*

triviality [,trivi'æliti] *n.* ①琐事；琐碎；平凡：talk

(write) *trivialities* 讲(写)琐碎的事情 ②(人的)浅薄;轻浮

trodden ['trɔdn] tread 的过去分词

troglodyte ['trɔglədait] *n.* ①史前穴居人 ②[喻]隐居者,遁世者 ③[动]类人猿

trolley ['trɔli] I *n.* ①[英]手推车;(医院用)装有四轮的担架;(用以送食物、书籍等的)装有脚轮的小台,台车;(铁路)手摇车,(铁路)道渣车;(铁路)倾卸式货车皮;矿车 ②空中吊篮车 ③[美]有轨电车(= [英] tram) ④(电车与架空电线接触的)触轮 II ❶ *vt.* 用手推车(或有轨电车等)载运 ❷ *vi.* 乘有轨电车(或手摇车等) ‖*off one's* ~ [美俚]丧失理智,疯疯癫癫 ‖'~**bus** *n.* 无轨电车(也称 ~ coach) / ~ **car** [美](触轮式)电车,有轨电车 / ~**man** ['trɔlimən] *n.* (电车)司机,售票员(= [英] tram) ③[美]这种电车上的司机 / ~ **pole** 触轮杆 / '~-,**table** *n.* 装有脚轮的小台,台车 / ~ **wheel** 触轮 / ~ **wire** (电车的)架空线

trombone [trɔm'boun] *n.* [音]长号,拉管

trona ['trounə] *n.* [化]天然碱

troop [tru:p] I *n.* ①[常用复]军队,部队: better ~s and simpler administration 精兵简政 / regular (regional) ~s 正规(地方)军 / a thousand ~s 一千士兵 / despatch (station, withdraw) ~s 派(驻,撤)军 ②骑兵队(相当于一个步兵连,由上尉指挥) ③一群;大量,许多: a ~ of schoolchildren 一群小学生 / a ~ of antelope(s) 一群羚羊 / be surrounded by ~s of welcomers 被许多欢迎者围绕着 ④十六(或三十二)人一队的童子军 ⑤[古]剧团,戏班 ⑥进军鼓 II *vi.* ①群集,集合 (up, together) ②成群结队地走: The children ~ed out of school. 孩子们成群结队地从学校出来。③匆匆走掉: The crowd ~ed away. 人群匆匆散去。‖*get one's* ~ 晋升为上尉 / *household* ~s 王室禁卫军 / ~*ing the colour(s)* [英]行军旗敬礼分列式 ‖~ **carrier** 部队运输机;部队运输船 / '~**ship** *n.* 部队运输船

trooper ['tru:pə] *n.* ①骑兵;伞兵 ②骑兵的马 ③骑警 ④[美口]州警察 ⑤[主英]部队运输船 ‖*swear like a* ~ 破口大骂

trophy ['troufi] I *n.* ①(古希腊、罗马在战场或公共场所树立的)胜利纪念碑 ②(作纪念品保存的)战利品;纪念品 ③勋章上的战利品图案 ④(体育比赛等的)奖品,银杯 ⑤[建]战利品(装)饰 ⑥陈列的猎获物(如狮皮、鹿头等) II *vt.* 用战利品装饰;授予战利品

tropic ['trɔpik] I *n.* [天]回归线 ②[复]热带地区: the ~s 热带(也作 the *Tropics*) ‖*the Tropic of Cancer* 北回归线 / *the Tropic of Capricorn* 南回归线 II *a.* 热带的

tropical ['trɔpikəl] *a.* ①热带的;位于热带的;用于热带的: a ~ climate 热带气候 / ~ crops 热带作物 / the ~ zone 热带 ②炎热的;酷热的 ③热烈的;热情的 ④转义的;比喻的 ‖~**ize** *vt.* 使热带化;使适应热带气候 / ~**ly** *ad.* ‖~ **aquarium**

(养热带鱼等用的)恒温鱼缸 / ~ **cyclone** [气]热带气旋 / ~ **fish** 热带鱼 / ~ **month** [天]分主月 / ~ **revolution** [天]分主周 / ~ **storm** [气]热带风暴 / ~ **year** [天]回归年

trot [trɔt] I (trotted; trotting) ❶ *vi.* ①(马)小跑;驾马小跑,骑马小跑;(人)小步跑;快步走;匆忙走 ②[口]走: You ~ away! 走开! ❷ *vt.* 使小跑;使快步走 II *n.* ①(马)的小跑;骑马 ②(人的)小跑步;快步,疾走;卖力的活动;忙碌: proceed at a ~ 快步前进 / keep sb. on the ~ 使某人忙碌 ③小跑的蹄声 ④[早]摇摇晃晃学走路的小孩 ⑤[贬]老太婆 ⑤[美俚](帮助学生读外文作品的)逐字译本: read Dante without a ~ 不靠逐字译本阅读但丁的作品 ⑥[复][俗]拉痢 ‖~ *out* ①(马的)小跑;骑马 ②炫耀: ~ out one's knowledge 炫耀自己的知识 ③提出…供考虑(或批准) / ~ *sb. off his legs* 使某人得精疲力竭 / ~ *sb. round* [口]领某人到处走走(如逛商店等)

troth [trouθ, trɔθ] I *n.* [古]①忠诚 ②真实 ③誓言 ④订婚 II *vt.* [古]发誓保证;同…订婚 ‖*by* (或 *upon*) *my* ~ (表示断定)我保证,请相信我 / *in* ~ 实在,的确 / *plight one's* ~ 盟誓(尤指订婚)

troubadour ['tru:bəduə] *n.* ①(十一到十三世纪主要在法国南部及意大利北部的)抒情诗人,行吟诗人 ②民谣歌手(或乐师)

trouble ['trʌbl] I *n.* ①烦恼,苦恼;忧虑: His ~s are over now. 他现在再也没有烦恼了。(有时指人已去世) ②困难;困境: I have some ~ in reading her handwriting. 我认她的笔迹感到有些困难。/ The ~ is that …. 困难在于… ③烦劳,麻烦;辛劳,辛苦: I am sorry to put you to so much ~. 我这样麻烦你真太对不起。/ No ~ (at all). 不费事。(或: 没什么。) / save (give) sb. ~ 给某人省(添)麻烦 / a great deal of ~ (或 a lot of ~s) 很多麻烦 / He took the ~ to gather the materials for us. 他不辞辛劳地为我们收集材料。/ She went to the ~ of compiling a handbook for the students. 她不辞劳苦替学生编了一本手册。④讨厌的事(或人): It's a great ~ to carry these breakables. 带这些易碎品可真是件麻烦事。/ I don't want to be a ~ to you. 我不愿成为你的负担。⑤(政治、社会方面的)动乱,纠纷,风潮: stir up ~ 兴风作浪 / lead to ~ 出乱子;导致纠纷 ⑥疾病;(机器等的)故障: stomach (eye) ~ 胃(眼)病 / engine ~ 发动机故障 / What's the ~ with the machine? 这机器出了什么毛病? ⑦[英方]分娩;非婚怀孕 ⑧[地]断层 II ❶ *vt.* ①使烦恼,使苦恼;使忧虑: Don't ~ yourself about (或 with) such a trifle. 不要为这样的小事而烦恼。/ What ~s me is …. 使我不安的是… ②[常用被动语态]扰乱;使激动: The waters were ~. 水面上波涛起伏。③(表示客气时)麻烦: May I ~ you for the ashtray? 麻烦你把烟灰缸递给我好吗? /

May I ~ you to call him up? 劳驾给他打个电话好吗? ④(病痛)折磨; 使不舒服, 使疼痛: His wound ~s him a good deal. 伤口把他折磨得厉害。/ I am much ~d by gout. 痛风折磨得我很厉害。❷ vi. [常用于否定句和疑问句]烦恼, 苦恼; 费心, 费神: Don't ~ about it. 别为此而苦恼(或费心)。/ Oh, don't ~, thanks. 啊, 别麻烦啦, 谢谢。/ Don't ~ to come out, please. 请留步, 别出来啦。‖ask (或 look) for ~ 自找麻烦, 自讨苦吃 / borrow ~ [俚]自找麻烦 / get into ~ 招致不幸; 引起指责; 招致责备; 陷入困境; 被捕, 入狱 / get sb. into (out of) ~ 使某人陷入(摆脱)困境 / have ~ with ❶同…闹纠纷 ❷有…病痛: She is having ~ with her teeth. 她牙齿正有病。/ in ~ ①处于不幸(或苦恼、困境)中 ②在监禁中 ③未结婚而怀孕的 / make ~ 闹事, 捣乱; 捣蛋 / meet ~ halfway 自寻烦恼, 杞人忧天 / Never ~ till ~s you. [谚]麻烦没有来找你, 别去自找麻烦。/ teething ~s 出牙期的病痛; [喻]事情开始时暂时的困难 ‖'~maker n. 惹事生非者; 闹事者, 捣乱者 / ~ man (机器等的)故障检修员 / '~shooter n. ①(机器等的)故障检修员 ②(政治、外交、商业等方面)解决麻烦问题的能手 / ~ spot ①纠纷地区; 可能产生纠纷的地区 ②(容易)出故障处

troublesome ['trʌblsəm] a. ①令人烦恼的, 讨厌的: a ~ child 惹烦恼的孩子 / The cough is quite ~. 这咳嗽真讨厌。②麻烦的, 困难的; 累赘的: a ~ problem 难题 ③[古]骚乱的; 痛苦的 ‖~ly ad. / ~ness n.

trough [trɔ(:)f] n. ①槽; 水槽; 饲料槽; 木盆; (面包作坊用的)长形揉面槽 ②檐槽; 管道 ③【物】(波)谷 ④【气】低压槽, 槽形低压 ⑤[地]深海槽 ⑥商业周期的低潮 ‖feed at the public ~ [美] ① 拿干薪 ② 占据清闲的高薪职位 / walk up to the ~, fodder or no fodder [美] ①安于自己的命运 ②负起自己的责任

trounce [trauns] vt. ①痛打 ②严责, 呵斥 ③[口]打败 ‖trouncing n.

troupe [tru:p] I n. ①剧团, 戏班; 杂技团; 马戏团: a ballet ~ 芭蕾舞剧团 / a chorus ~ 合唱团 ②[美俚]一群扒手(或在街上结伙闹事的青少年) II vi. (作为剧团成员)巡回演出; 演出 ‖~r n. ①(剧团、杂技团等的)演员, 团员 ②[口]有经验的演员

trouser ['trauzə] a. 裤子的: ~ pockets 裤袋 / ~ legs 裤脚

trousseau ['tru:sou] ([复] trousseaux ['tru:souz] 或 trousseaus) n. 嫁妆, 妆奁

trout [traut] I ([复] trout(s)) n. ①鳟属鱼类的鱼, 红点鲑属鱼类的鱼, 真鳟 ②似真鳟的鱼 II vi. 捕鳟鱼, 捕鳟鱼 ‖~let ['trautlit] n. 小鳟鱼; 小鳟鱼 / ~y a. 有许多鳟鱼(或鳟鱼)的 / '~=colo(u)red a. (马)白毛黑花(或红棕色花)的

trowel ['trauəl] I n. ①泥刀, 修平刀, 镘刀 ②泥铲 II (trowel(l)ed; trowel(l)ing) vt. 用泥刀涂抹(或修平、拌和等) ‖lay it on with a ~ 竭力恭维, 过分夸奖

troy [trɔi] I n. 金衡制(金、银、宝石的衡量制度, 一磅等于十二盎司) (= ~ weight): weigh 2 lb. 4 oz. ~ 计重金衡制两磅四盎司 II a. 用金衡制表示的

truant ['tru(:)ənt] I n. ①逃避责任者, 玩忽职守者 ②逃学者, 旷课者 II a. 逃学的; 闲荡的, 懒散的 III vi. 逃避责任; 逃学, 旷课 ‖play ~ 逃学; 偷懒; 逃避责任 / ~ly ad.

truce [tru:s] I n. ①休战, 停战; 休战协定: a ~ agreement 停战协定 / a negotiation 停战谈判 / a flag of ~ 白旗, 停战旗 ②(尤指苦痛、烦恼等的)中止, 暂停 II ❶ vi. 休战 ❷ vt. 以休战结束… ‖a ~ to 别再…了: A ~ to folly (nonsense)! 别再胡闹(胡说)了!

truck¹ [trʌk] I n. ①[美]卡车, 载重汽车, 运货车(英国通常用 lorry): a tip ~ 自动倾卸车 / a crane ~ 汽车(式)起重机 / a tank service ~ 加油车 / a flat ~ 平板车 / a ~ trailer 载重拖车 ②[英](铁路)敞车, 无盖货车 ③(车站上推行李的)手推车 ④【机】转向架 ⑤旗杆(或桅杆)顶端穿绳索的小木冠 ⑥无胎小轮(尤指炮车上的) II ❶ vt. 用货车装运 ❷ vi. ①以驾驶卡车为职业 ②驾驶货车; 以货车运货 ‖~age ['trʌkidʒ] n. 货车运费; 货车运输 / ~er n. 卡车驾驶员; 从事货车运输业者 ‖'~=bolster n. 车架承梁 / '~load n. ①货车荷载 ②(计算运费规定的)最低起运量 / ~man ['trʌkmən] n. ①卡车驾驶员 ②(消防队的)梯车驾驶员

truck² [trʌk] I ❶ vt. 交换; 以实物换取 ❷ vi. ①以物易物 ②(秘密地)打交道 II n. ①以物易物 ②打交道, 来往: have no ~ with . . . 不与…打交道; 不与…来往; 同…毫无关系 ③适于以物易物(或小额贸易)的商品 ④ 实物工资 ⑤[美]供应市场的蔬菜 ⑥ 不值钱的杂物; 废物; 废话 ‖~er n. ①以物易物者; [苏格兰]小贩 ②[美]以蔬菜供应市场的菜农 ‖~ farm, ~ garden [美]蔬菜农场 / ~ system 实物工资制

truckle ['trʌkl] I n. ①小轮, 滑轮 ② = ~ bed II ❶ vi. ①靠小脚轮移动 ② 屈从, 讨好, 谄媚 (to) ❷ vt. 用小脚轮使移动 ‖~r n. 屈从者, 谄媚者 ‖~ bed 有脚轮的矮床(不用时可推入另一床下)

truculence ['trʌkjuləns], **truculency** ['trʌkjulənsi] n. ①好战, 好斗; 凶猛; 残忍 ②致命性, 毁灭性 ③粗暴, 刻毒(尤指说话与文字)

truculent ['trʌkjulənt] a. ①好战的, 好斗的; 凶猛的; 残忍的 ②致命的, 毁灭性的 ③(说话等)粗暴的, 刻毒的 ‖~ly ad.

trudge [trʌdʒ] I ❶ vi. 跋涉, 步履艰难地走 ❷ vt. 沿着…跋涉; 艰难地走过… II n. 长途跋涉

true [tru:] I a. ①真的; 真实的, 确实的: a ~ pearl 真的珍珠 / This picture is ~ to nature

(或 life). 这幅画很逼真。/ Is it ～ that she has returned? 她真的回来了吗?/ That's only too ～. 千真万确。/ It's too good to be ～. 这太好了。(或: 这简直好得叫人难以相信) / *True, it would be too late.* 确实, 那就太晚了。② 忠实的, 忠诚的; 坚定的; 可靠的: a ～ friend 真朋友 / a translation ～ to the original 忠实于原文的译文 / be ～ to one's word (或 be ～ in word) 讲话靠得住; 遵守诺言 ③ 正确的; 准确的: a ～ judgement 正确的判断 / a ～ copy of a document 一份文件的准确的抄本 / make a ～ estimate of the situation 对形势作正确的估计 ④(指安装、调整、部位、形状等)正的, 准的; 平衡的; 挺直的: Is the beam ～? 这根梁正吗?/ The wheel is ～. 这个轮子装得很准。⑤ 纯粹的; 纯种的: ～ grass(es)【植】真禾本科 ⑥ 正式的, 合法的: a ～ heir 合法继承人 ⑦ 限定的, 确切的; 严格的: in the ～ sense of the word 按照这个词的确切意义 ⑧ 根据地极(而不是根据磁极)确定的: ～ north 真北 ⑨[古]老实的 **II** *n.* ①[the ～]真实, 真理: tell the ～ from the false 分辨真伪 ②(指安装、调整等)正, 准, 精确(用于 in ～, out of ～): The post is *in* ～. 柱子很正。/ The axle is *out of* ～. 轴装得不准。**III** *ad.* [仅与某些动词连用]真实地; 确实地; 准确地; 纯粹地: Tell me ～. 照实说吧。/ aim ～ 瞄准 / breed ～ (动物)生育纯种 **IV** (trued; truing 或 trueing) *vt.* (指安装、调整等)摆正; 装准, 配准; 校准 (up): ～ up a fixture 把夹具装准 ‖as ～ as a die ①绝对真实; 绝对可靠 ②非常老实 / (as) ～ as steel (或 flint, touch) 极其真实(或忠实); 绝对可靠 / be ～ of 符合于…, 对…适用: The same is ～ of all other cases. 对于其他各例而言, 也是如此。/ come ～ ①(希望、理想等)实现, 达到: a dream that has *come* ～ 已成为事实的梦想 ②(籽苗)不变种地生长 / *hold* ～ 适用; 有效 / ～ to type 见 **type** ‖~ness *n.* ‖～ bill 【律】大陪审团认为证据充分而准予受理的起诉书 / ～ blue ①不褪色的蓝色染料 ②(十七世纪苏格兰的)长老会教徒 ③赤胆忠心; 忠心耿耿的人 / '～-'blue *a.* (对党派等)非常忠诚的, 坚定的 *n.* 忠实的人, 可靠的人 / '～-born *a.* 嫡出的; 地道的, 十足的: a ～born New Yorker 地道的纽约人 / '～-bred *a.* ①纯种的 ②有教养的 / '～'hearted *a.* 忠实的, 忠诚的 / '～-life *a.* (作品等)忠实于现实生活的 / '～-love *n.* (忠实的)恋人, 爱人: a ～love knot (象征忠贞的爱情的)同心结 / '～,penny *n.* [古]老实人, 可信任的人

truly ['tru:li] *ad.* ①真正地; 确实地, 事实上: *Truly*, he is a brave man. 他真是个勇敢的人。/ We can ～ say (that) it's a miracle. 我们确实可以说这是个奇迹。/ Why, ～, I cannot say. 我实在说不上呀。②忠实地, 忠诚地: Yours ～ (或 *Truly* yours) 您的忠实的(信末署名前的客套语) ③正当地; 正确地; 有理地

trump[1] [trʌmp] **I** *n.* ①(牌戏的)王牌, 将牌; 最后手段; [复]一套王牌: put sb. to his ～s 逼某人打出王牌; 逼某人使出最后一着 ②[口]好人, 可靠的人, 勇敢的人, 慷慨的人 **II** ❶ *vt.* ①出王牌赢(牌) ②超过, 胜过, 打赢 ❷ *vi.* 出王牌; 出王牌获胜 ‖～ up 捏造, 假造: ～ up a charge against sb. 捏造某人的罪名 / ～ up a story 捏造故事(或情节) / ～ up excuses 制造借口 / **turn up** ～s ①(出乎意料地)令人满意; 对人有帮助 ②交好运 ‖～ card 王牌, 将牌; 翻引来定王牌的牌; play one's ～ card 打出王牌; 拿出最后一手 / '～ed-up *a.* 捏造的: a ～ed-up charge 捏造的罪名 / a ～ed-up case 诬告的案件

trump[2] [trʌmp] *n.* [古][诗]喇叭; 喇叭声, 号声: the last ～ (或 the ～ of doom)【基督教】最后审判日的号声

trumpery ['trʌmpəri] **I** *n.* ①中看不中用的东西 ②废物; 废话 **II** *a.* 虚有其表的; 无用的; 浅薄的: ～ furniture 华丽而不适用的家具 / a ～ argument 肤浅的论据

trumpet ['trʌmpit] **I** *n.* ①喇叭; 【音】小号 ②喇叭似的声音(尤指象的吼声) ③喇叭形的东西; [复]有喇叭形叶子的植物 ④(乐队)小号吹奏者; 喇叭手 ⑤(风琴的)小号音栓 **II** ❶ *vi.* ①吹喇叭, 吹号 ②发出喇叭似的声音 ❷ *vt.* ①用小号吹出 ②以喇叭似的声音说出 ③鼓吹 ‖*a flourish of* ～s (重要事情开始前的)大肆宣扬 / *blow one's own* ～ 自吹自擂 / *the feast of* ～s 犹太人的新年 ‖～ call 号声; 紧急的召唤 / ～ conch, ～ shell 海螺; 海螺壳 / ～ creeper 【植】美洲凌霄花, 紫葳 / '～-leaf *n.* 有喇叭状叶子的植物 / ～ major (骑兵团的)号兵长

truncate ['trʌŋkeit] **I** *vt.* ①截去…的顶端(或末端); 把…截短; [喻]缩短(冗长的引语等) ②截去(晶体的棱或角)使成平面 **II** *a.* 截短的; 【动】【植】(羽、叶)平截的, 平截的, 平头的: ～ leaf 【植】截形叶 ‖～d *a.* 截短的; 好象截短过的; 截棱成平面的; 缩短了的: ～d cone 【数】截头圆锥体 / a ～d quotation 缩短了的引语 / ～ly *ad.* / truncation [trʌŋ'keiʃən] *n.*

truncheon ['trʌntʃən] **I** *n.* ①粗短的棍棒; 警棍 ②作权威标志的杖(或棍棒) ③[古]矛柄 **II** *vt.* 用警棍(或短棒)打

trundle ['trʌndl] **I** *n.* ①阔而小的轮子; (可推动的床、椅等脚上装的)小脚轮 ②矮轮手推车 ③=～ bed ④【机】灯笼式小齿轮 ⑤滚动; 滚动声 **II** ❶ *vt.* 使滚动; 使旋转: ～ a hoop along the sidewalk 沿人行道滚铁环 / ～ a barrow 推手推车 ❷ *vi.* 滚动着前进; 旋转, 转动 ‖～ bed 有脚轮的矮床(不用时可推入另一床下)

trunk [trʌŋk] **I** *n.* ①树干; (人体、动物的)躯干; 昆虫的胸部 ②大血管, 神经干 ③(铁路、运河、电话线等的)干线 ④象鼻; (鸟、虫等的)长嘴 ⑤(旅行用的)大衣箱, 皮箱; 汽车车尾的行李箱 ⑥[复]男用运动裤 ⑦【建】柱身 ⑧【讯】中继线 ⑨[船]半显舱室; 凸起舱口; 围壁洞道: access ～ 【船】

便门 ⑩【矿】洗矿槽 ⑪ =～ engine **II** *vt.* 槽内洗选(矿砂) **III** *a.* ①树干的;躯干的 ②(铁路、运河、电话线等)干线的 ③箱形的 ④有筒管的 ||～**ful** *n.* ①一满箱 ②许多 / ～**less** *a.* 没有树干的;无躯干的 ||～ **call** [英]长途电话 / ～ **engine**【机】筒状活塞发动机 / ～ **line** (铁路、运河、天然气等)干线;干线;(电话)中继线 / ',**maker** *n.* ①制造箱的人 ②[古]滞销书的堆放处(由于旧时以滞销书纸张作为箱子的衬里而有此义) / '～-**nail** *n.* (皮箱等用的)饰钉 / ～ **road** 干道

truss [trʌs] **I** *vt.* ①扎;捆:～ hay 捆干草 ②烹烤前将(鸡、鸭等或鸡、鸭等的翅膀)扎紧;将(人)的双手捆绑在身旁(*up*) ③用桁架(或构架)支撑(桥、屋顶等) ④[古]把…处绞刑(*up*) **II** *n.* ①捆、束 ②一捆干草;一捆麦秸 ③桁架;构架 ④【植】花束(指茎端的一簇花) ⑤【医】疝气带;托带 ⑥纪念碑的翅托 ||～ **bridge**【建】桁架桥

trust [trʌst] **I** *n.* ①信任,信赖:enjoy the ～ of the people 得到人民的信任 / put no ～ in sb. 不信任某人 ②可信任的人(或事物):be sb.'s ～ 是某人所信任的人 ③职责,职守;(因受信用而被托付的)责任:fulfil one's ～ 尽责 / hold (或 be in) a position of great ～ 担任职责重大的工作 ④信心;希望:have ～ in the future 对未来有信心 ⑤托管,信托:a child committed to sb.'s ～ 托给某人管养的孩子 ⑥【律】托管财产的所有权;信托财产,信托物 ⑦【经】托拉斯 ⑧【商】信用;赊帐 ⑨[罕]可靠,忠诚 **II** ❶ *vt.* ①相信,信任,信赖:We have always ～ed him. 我们一直信任他。/ We ～ his words. 我们相信他的话。/ I ～ed my child to do it all by itself. 我放手让孩子自己去干。②把…委托给,委托;存放(*with*, *in*):～ this matter to sb. (或 ～ sb. with this matter)把此事委托给某人办理 / ～ sth. *with* sb. 把某物存放在某人处 / ～ sth. *in* a place 把某物放在某处 / I ～ed him *with* my bike. 我把自行车交给他(保管使用)。③希望,盼望:I ～ to hear better news from you. 我盼望从你处听到更好的消息。/ I ～ (that) you are in good health. 我希望你身体健康。④ 赊卖给:～ sb. *for* a typewriter 把打字机赊卖给某人 ❷ *vi.* ①相信,信赖;倚靠:～ *in* sb. 相信某人 / ～ *to* one's memory 凭记忆 / Don't ～ *to* chance (或 luck)! 不要靠碰运气! ②希望:We'll see you soon, I ～. 希望不久就能见到你。③赊售 ||*in* ～ 被托管 / *on* ～ ①不加深究地,不加考察地:take a statement *on* ～ 不深究地相信一番话 ②赊帐:buy (sell) *on* ～ 赊购(售) ||'～,**buster** *n.* 设法解散托拉斯的人(尤指根据反托拉斯法令对托拉斯起诉的美国联邦政府官员) / ～ **company** 信托公司 / ～ **deed** 信托书,委托书 / ～ **money** 托管金,委托金 / ～ **territory** 托管地,托管领土

trustee [trʌs'ti:] **I** *n.* ①(财产、业务等)受托管理人 ②(社团、医院、学校等的)理事,评议员

③托管国(受托管理托管领土的国家) **II** ❶ *vt.* ①移交(财产或管理权)给受托人 ②【律】扣押(债户财产、工资等)以偿欠款 ❷ *vi.* 履行受托人职责

trusteeship [trʌs'ti:-ʃip] *n.* ①托管人的职责 ②(托管国对被托管地的)受托管理;托管制度

trustful ['trʌstful] *a.* 深不疑的,信任他人的 ||～**ly** *ad.* / ～**ness** *n.*

trusting ['trʌstiŋ] *a.* 深信不疑的,信任他人的 ||～**ly** *ad.*

trustworthy ['trʌst,wə:ði] *a.* 值得信任的,可信赖的,可靠的 ||**trustworthily** *ad.* / **trustworthiness** *n.*

trusty ['trʌsti] **I** *a.* ①可信赖的,可靠的 ②[罕]深信不疑的,信任人的 **II** *n.* ①受到信任的人 ②(因表现好而)享有特权的犯人

truth [tru:θ] ([复] truths [tru:ðz, tru:θs]) *n.* ①真理:The sum total of innumerable relative ～s constitutes absolute ～. 无数相对的真理之总和,就是绝对的真理。/ seek ～ from facts 实事求是 / uphold the ～ 坚持真理 ②真实;真相,实际情况:the hard ～ of facts 铁一般的事实真相 / the naked ～ 赤裸裸的事实,未加渲染的真相 / stand ～ on its head 颠倒是非 / The ～ is that he didn't come. 其实他没有来。/ tell (或 speak) the ～ 说实话 / There is not a word of ～ in what he says. 他完全在撒谎。③[主英](指安装、调整等)正,精确:The wheel is out of ～. 轮子装得不准。④(艺术作品等的)真实性,忠实性 ⑤[古]忠实,忠诚 ⑥[T-](基督教信仰疗法派用语)上帝 ||*a home* ～ ①使人难堪的事实,令人不愉快的真实情况;逆耳的老实话 ②老生常谈 / *God's* ～ 天经地义的事,千真万确的事 / *in* (*all*) ～ 事实上;的确 / *of a* ～ [古]事实上;的确 / *the* ～, *the whole* ～, *and nothing but the* ～ 【律】(证人在法庭上的誓言)所说全是事实,决无谎言 / *to tell the* ～ (或 ～ *to tell*) [用作插入语]老实说:*To tell the* ～, I don't agree with you. 老实说,我不同意你的意见。||～ **serum, drug** 据称能使人吐露真情的麻醉药

truthful ['tru:θful] *a.* ①说真话的,诚实的(讲话、作品等)真实的,如实的 ||～**ly** *ad.* / ～**ness** *n.*

try [trai] **I** ❶ *vt.* ①试,尝试;试用;试验:～ a new medicine 试用一种新药 / ～ sb. for a job 让某人试做某项工作;试用某人 / ～ using another method 试用另一种方法 / Do ～ more. 请再尝一点。(指饮食等) / Try our red wine. 请试试我们的红葡萄酒。/ ～ one's hand at painting 试学绘画 / Each instrument is *tried* before it is packed. 每一件仪器包装前都经过试用检验。/ ～ one's best to do sth. 竭尽所能做某事 ②考验,磨炼;使艰苦(或痛苦):sb.'s courage (will) 考验某人的勇气(意志) / Small print *tries* the eyes. 小号字很费目力。③ 审问,审判:be *tried* for a crime 因犯罪而受审 / be *tried* on a charge of murder 被控谋杀而受审 / ~ a case 审讯一个案件 ④(通过试验或调查)解决(问题、争论等); (通过角斗)解决(争执等) ⑤提炼(金属、油脂等)(out): ~ out whale oil 提炼鲸油 ⑥校准; 为…最后加工(尤指刨光木板等)(up): ~ up a right angle with a square 用直角尺校准直角 ❷ vi. 尝试; 试验; 试图, 努力: Try again (或 once more). 再试一遍。 / ~ at a somersault 试翻筋斗 / ~ to solve a problem 试图解决问题 / Try and finish the work in a week. 要争取在一星期内完成这工作。[注意: 这里的 try and =try to; 这一结构常用于口语的祈使句中] Ⅱ n. ①尝试; 试验; 试图: Let me have a ~ at (或 for) it. 让我试一下。 ②(橄榄球赛中)在对方球门线上(或后面)带球触地(可得三分, 并获得再试行射门的权利, 射中时可再得两分) ‖~ a fall (with) 见 fall / ~ back ①(猎犬)回老路找嗅迹 ②重新回到(原来的话题) / ~ conclusions with 见 conclusion / ~ for 谋求, 争取: ~ for a job 谋职业 / ~ it on the (或 a) dog 见 dog / ~ ①试穿: ~ on a coat 试穿一件上衣 ②试用; 试验 ③[英](为愚弄人而)耍弄, 玩弄(花招等)(with): It is no use ~ing such tricks on with us. 对我们耍这种花招是没有用的。 / ~ out ①(彻底)试验: ~ out a new farming method 试验新的耕作法 / ~ out an idea 试验一种设想 ②参加选拔赛: ~ out for the football team 参加足球队员的选拔赛 / ~ out for the male lead 参加选拔男主角的表演 ‖~'on n. ①试穿 ②试用; 试验 ③[英]耍花招, 欺骗 / '~'out n. ①试用; 试验; 示范性的试验 ②(戏剧等的)试演; 预演: give the play a ~out 预演一出戏 ③(选拔运动员、演员等的)选拔赛, 选拔表演; gymnastic ~outs 体操选拔赛 / '~sail n. 【船】斜桁纵帆(风暴时用) / ~ square 验方角尺, 直角尺, 矩尺 / '~works [复] n. 安放鲸油提炼锅的砖炉; 提炼鲸油的设备

trying ['traiiŋ] a. 难受的, 难堪的; 费劲的; 恼人的: a ~ situation 尴尬的局面, 难处的境况 / a ~ person to deal with 一个难以对付的人 / Small print is ~ to the eyes. 小号字很费目力。

tryst [traist, trist] I n. ①幽会, 约会: keep (break) ~ with sb. 遵守(不遵守)与某人的约会 ②幽会处, 约会处(=~ing place) ③[苏格兰]市场, 市集(尤指每年定期举行的牛市集) Ⅱ [苏格兰] ❶ vt. 和…约会 ❷ vi. 约会; 守约

tsetse ['tsetsi, 'tetsi] n. 【动】舌蝇, 采采蝇(=~ fly)

tsunami [tsu'nɑ:mi] n. 海震, 海啸

T-time ['ti:'taim] n. 试验发射时刻 (=time for test-firing)

tub [tʌb] I n. ①桶, 盆; 浴盆, 浴缸: a rain-water ~ 盛雨水的桶 / a dung ~ 粪桶 ②一桶(或一盆)的容量: a ~ of water 一桶水 ③[口](在浴缸里的)沐浴; 洗澡: have a cold ~ 洗个冷水澡 / take one's ~ 洗澡 / prefer a ~ to a shower 喜欢盆浴胜过淋浴 ④【矿】(指运输或提取煤、矿砂

等)矿车, 吊桶 ⑤[贬]行驶缓慢的船; 练习用的赛艇 ⑥[美俚]大胖子 (=~-of-guts, ~ of lard) Ⅱ (tubbed; tubbing) ❶ vt. ①(在浴缸里)为…洗澡; 把(衣物等)放在桶里洗 ②把(植物)种植在桶里: tubbed pines 种在桶里的松树 ③把…放(或贮藏)在桶里: ~ vegetables in brine 腌在放有盐水的桶里 ❷ vi. ①洗盆浴 ②被放在桶里洗 ‖a tale of a ~ 见 tale / in the ~ [美俚]破产 / Let every ~ stand on its own bottom. [谚]各人管各人自己。/ throw out a ~ to the whale 转移对方视线(以便乘机摆脱危险) / '~ful n. 一桶的容量 ‖'~-eight n. 八个划手的练习赛艇 / '~-pair n. 两个划手的练习赛艇 / '~-,thumper n. ①慷慨激昂的讲话者(或讲道者); 叫嚣者 ②[美俚](政府机构等的)发言人, 代言人 ③[美俚]鼓手 / '~-,thumping n. & a. 慷慨激昂的讲话(或讲道)(的); 大肆宣扬(的) / ~ wheel (洗发用的)鼓轮

tubby ['tʌbi] a. ①桶状的, 肥圆的; 矮胖的 ②(乐器等)发钝音的, 缺少回响的

tube [tju:b] I n. ①管; 软管: a test ~ 试管 / a seamless steel ~ 无缝钢管 / a ~ of toothpaste 一管牙膏 / ~ of force 【物】力管 / ~ of magnetic induction 【物】磁感应管 ②[美]电子管, 真空管 (=[英] valve); (电视)显象管 ③(轮胎的)内胎 ④【解】管: bronchial ~ 支气管 / Fallopian ~s 输卵管 ⑤地下铁道的隧道; [主英][口]地下铁道: go by ~ 乘地下铁道列车 ⑥[古]望远镜 Ⅱ ❶ vt. ①把…装管 ②把…做成管状 ③使通过管子 ❷ vi. [主英]乘地下铁道列车 ‖the ~ [美口]电视 ‖~ culture (微生物)试管培养 / '~-train n. 地下铁道的列车 / ~ well 管井

tuber ['tju:bə] n. ①【植】块茎: ~ crops 块茎作物, 薯类作物 ②【解】结节

tubercular [tju(:)'bə:kjulə] I a. ①结节(状)的, 有结节的; 瘤状的 ②结核病的; 患结核的; 结核性的 Ⅱ n. 结核病患者

tuberculosis [tju(:),bə:kju'lousis] n. 结核(病); 肺结核(略作 TB): pulmonary (intestinal) ~ 肺(肠)结核

tuberculous [tju(:)'bə:kjuləs] a. ①结核(病)的; 感染结核病的; 结核性的 ②结节的; 结核状的

tuck¹ [tʌk] I ❶ vt. ①折短, 卷起; 在(衣服)上打横褶(up): ~ up one's shirt sleeves 卷起衬衫袖子 / ~ up one's robe 把袍子提起束住 ②塞: ~ in one's shirt 把衬衫下摆塞进裤中 / She ~ed her hair into her cap. 她把头发塞进帽子里。/ ~ a handkerchief into one's pocket 把手帕塞进口袋 / ~ a blanket around the child 把小孩盖的毯子塞紧 ③使盖好被子安睡(up, in): The mother is ~ing in the child. 母亲正在把孩子安顿在床上睡觉。/ ~ oneself up in bed 上床安睡 ④使隐藏(away); 使蜷曲: a small village ~ed away in the hill 隐藏在山中的小村庄 / be ~ed away in a corner 被藏在角落里 / The bird ~ed its head under its wing. 鸟把头缩在翅膀

下。/ ～ the legs to the chest 把两腿拳曲在胸前 ⑤[英俚]大吃(in, away, into) ⑥用网兜把(鱼)从大网捞出 ⑦[俚]绞死,吊死(up) ❷ vi. 折成褶子;缩拢 II n. ①(衣裤等的)缝褶,横褶 ②船底后端 ③[英俚]食物(尤指糖果、糕点) ④被塞进(或折进)的东西 ⑤(跳水等时)大腿贴近胸前两手抱住小腿的姿式 ‖～ one's tail 夹起尾巴;感到羞耻 ‖～-in n. [主英]丰盛的一餐 / ～ net (从大网中捞鱼的)小网兜 / '～-out n. [主英]=～-in / '～-,pointing n. 凸嵌(一种嵌砖缝的方法) / ～ seine =～ net / '～-shop n. [英]食品店,糖果店(尤指学校附近的)

tuck² [tʌk] n. ①鼓声;击鼓般的声音 ②[古]号角;喇叭声

tuck³ [tʌk] n. 活力,精力

Tuesday ['tju:zdi] n. 星期二 ‖～s ad. [美]每星期二;在任何星期二

tuft [tʌft] I n. ①(头发、羽毛、草等的)一簇,一束 ②丛生植物,丛树 ③(钉牢被、褥垫心的)线束;(用线束牵牢的)床垫扣结 ④[解](细血管)丛 ⑤髭 ⑥土丘 II ❶ vt. ①用丛毛装饰 ②(为固定垫心,每隔一定距离)用线束钉住(被、褥) ❷ vi. 丛生;形成一簇 ‖～ed a. ①从毛的;②簇状的,丛生的 ‖'～,hunter n. 逢迎权贵的人;势利的人

tug [tʌg] I (tugged; tugging) ❶ vi. ①用力拖,使劲拉(at) ②苦干;挣扎 ❷ vt. ①用力拖(或扯、拉) ②吃力地搬运 ③用拖轮拖曳 II n. ①猛拉,拖,牵引: give the rope a ～ 猛然拉一下绳索 ②苦干,努力,挣扎: have a great ～ to persuade sb. 费尽口舌说服某人 ③(对立双方的)争执,较量 ④(拖、拉、牵引用的)绳索,链条;(马车的)挽革 ⑤拖船 ⑥[英俚](伊顿公学的)公费生 ⑦[矿]装有滑车的铁钩 ‖'～boat n. 拖船 / '～-of-'war n. 拔河(游戏);激烈的竞争

tuition [tju(:)'iʃən] n. ①教,教诲,讲授: receive careful ～ from sb. 受到某人的细心教诲 ②学费 ‖～al, ～ary a.

tulip ['tju:lip] n. 【植】郁金香属植物;郁金香(花或球茎),山慈姑 ‖～ root 燕麦等的一种病(引起茎部膨胀等) / ～ tree 【植】鹅掌楸属树木; 美国鹅掌楸

tumble ['tʌmbl] I ❶ vi. ①摔倒,跌倒: ～ off a bicycle 从自行车上摔下来 / ～ over a stone 在石头上绊一交 / ～ in (或 into) a stream 跌入小河 ②倒坍;(证券价格等)下跌 ③翻腾,打滚: Thoughts were tumbling about in her mind. 各种思想在她脑海里翻腾。/ He ～d in his sleep. 他睡着时身子翻来复去。④翻筋斗;作杂技表演 ⑤仓促地行动;匆匆忙忙地倾倒出来: He came tumbling along. 他莽莽撞撞地走来。/ ～ into (out of) bed 匆匆地上(起)床 / ～ down (up) the stairs 跌跌撞撞地下(上)楼 / Words ～d eagerly from his lips. 话从他的嘴里急促地倾吐出来。⑥[俚]终于明白,恍然大悟(to): ～ to sb.'s intention 终于明白某人的意图 ⑦偶然遇见

(into, upon): ～ upon a rare book 偶然发现一部珍本 ❷ vt. ①使翻倒;使滚翻: A sudden braking ～d him down. 急然车使他摔倒了。②弄乱,搞乱(床单、衣服、头发等) ③使(工作件、材料等)在滚筒里转动;把…放在扫荡圆筒里扫洗 ④射落(飞禽);击倒(野兔等) II n. ①摔交;跌落: have a nasty (slight) ～ 重重(轻轻)地跌一交 ②翻滚;翻筋斗: the ～ of the waves 波涛滚滚 / take a number of ～s 翻几个筋斗 ③混乱;杂乱的一堆: be all in a ～ 乱作一团 ‖take a ～ [美俚]恍然大悟 / ～ down the sink (大口地)饮 / ～ home【海】(船舷大幅度)内倾 / ～ in ①嵌入,镶上(木料) ②[俚]上床睡觉 ‖'～bug n.【动】金龟子科甲虫,金龟子 / '～down a. 摇摇欲坠的 / '～weed n.【植】风滚草;丝石竹;苋属植物,广布苋

tumbler ['tʌmblə] n. ①翻筋斗者;杂技演员 ②平底无脚酒杯 ③(机枪的)机心 ④锁的制栓 ⑤【机】转臂;转筒;摆动换向齿轮;转向轮 ⑥(衣服)干燥机 ⑦不驯翁(玩具) ⑧翻头鸽;一种翻兔的狗 ⑨[英方]粪车,肥料车 ‖～ful n. (一)满杯

tumbrel ['tʌmbrəl], **tumbril** ['tʌmbril] n. ①(农村用)倾卸式两轮车;粪车,肥料车 ②(1789年法国大革命时)死刑犯押送车 ③(英国旧时运输弹药和工具等用的)军用二轮车

tummy ['tʌmi] n. [儿语]肚子

tumo(u)r ['tju:mə] n. 肿大,肿块;(肿)瘤;赘生物: a fatty ～ 脂(肪)瘤 / a benign (malignant) ～ 良(恶)性瘤 ‖～like a. 像肿瘤的 / **tumorous** ['tju:mərəs] a. 肿瘤的;像肿瘤的

tumult ['tju:mʌlt] n. ①吵闹,喧哗;骚动 ②(思想感情等的)激动,混乱: Her mind was in a ～. 她心烦意乱。③一阵发作: a ～ of rejoicing (weeping) 一阵欢乐(哭泣)

tumultuous [tju(:)'mʌltjuəs] a. ①吵闹的;喧哗的 ②骚动的 ③激动的;混乱的 ‖～ly ad. / ～ness n.

tundra ['tʌndrə] n. (北极及北极附近地区的)冻原,苔原,冻土带

tune [tju:n] I n. ①调子,曲调;主题: a popular ～ 流行的曲调 ②正确的音高;协调,一致: sing (play) in ～ 唱(奏)得合调 / The violin is out of ～. 小提琴走调了。/ be in ～ with the times 适合时代潮流 / be out of ～ with one's company 与同伴们格格不入 ③声调,语调,语气;态度: In face of these facts he altered his ～. 在这些事实面前他改变了态度。④程度;数量: change sth. to such a ～ as to make it look entirely different 使某事物彻底改变项目 ⑤[古]心情,情绪: be in ～ for 感到想要(做某事) ⑥[古]音质 II ❶ vt. ①为…调音: ～ a piano (violin) 调准钢琴(小提琴)的音 ②[古]唱,唱出: The bird is tuning its song. 鸟儿在唱歌。③调谐,调整(收音机等)的频率;收听: ～ in the news programme 收听新闻节目 / a ～d amplifier 调谐放大器 / a ～d circuit 调谐电路 ④用无线电与…取得联系: ～

in a directional beacon 用无线电同定向信标台联络 ⑤使和谐,使一致;调整,调节: The colours are perfectly ~*d* to each other. 颜色很协调。/ The machine has just been ~*d*. 机器刚调整过。❷ *vi.* ①合调;协调 ②调谐;收听: ~ *about* for the latest news 转动收音机旋钮找最新消息听 / ~ *in on* a radio station 收听一个电台 ‖*call the* ~ 定调子;发号施令;操纵 / *change one's* ~ 改变调子;转变态度(如前倨后恭等) / *dance to another* ~ 改弦易辙 / *dance to sb.'s* ~ 跟着某人亦步亦趋 / *play down one's* ~ 降低调子 / *sing another* (或 *a different*) ~ =change one's ~ / *the* ~ *the* (*old*) *cow died of* [俚] ①刺耳声;嘈杂的怪声 ②陈腔,老调 / *to the* ~ *of* [口]达到…数量;价格达…: be fined *to the* ~ *of* 1,000 dollars 被罚款达一千美元 / ~ *out* 关掉(收音机等) / ~ *up* ①(尤指乐队)调弦,定弦;调音;[口]奏起来;唱起来;[谑](孩子)哭起来;嚷起来 ②调整,调节(机器等)(使发挥最大效力): ~ *up* a generator 调整发电机 ③(比赛前)做准备动作 ‖**~less** *a.* ①不合调的;不协调的,不和谐的 ②无音调的;无声的,(乐器)不在演奏的 / **~r** *n.* ①调音者;调弦者 ②(收音机上的)调谐器 ‖'**~d-in** *a.* 对时髦事物极敏感的,好赶时髦的 / '**~,pattern** *n.* (京剧等的)腔调 / '**~smith** *n.* (尤指流行歌曲的)作曲者 / '**~-up** *n.* ①(为使机器等发挥最大效力所作的)调整,调节 ②(运动前的)准备动作 (= warm-up)

tuneful ['tju:nful] *a.* ①曲调优美的,悦耳的;和谐的 ②[古]发出音调的;好唱歌的 ‖**~ly** *ad.* / **~ness** *n.*

tungstic ['tʌŋstik] *a.* ①六价钨的;(正)钨的 ②五价钨的

tunic ['tju:nik] *n.* ①(古希腊、古罗马)长达膝盖的短袖束腰外衣 ②(妇女、女孩的)束腰外衣 ③[主英](警察、士兵的)紧身短上衣 ④=tunicle ⑤[植]鳞茎皮;膜被;原套;[动]膜;被囊;[解]膜,层

tunic

tunicle ['tju:nikl] *n.* (天主教主教、助祭穿的)法衣,祭服

tunnel ['tʌnl] **I** *n.* ①隧道,坑道;地道;隧洞: Dig ~*s* deep, store grain everywhere, and never

seek hegemony. 深挖洞,广积粮,不称霸。/ a railway ~ 铁路隧道 / ~ *warfare* 地道战 ②[矿]石巷,平峒 ③烟道,烟囱;风洞 **II** (tunnel(l)ed; tunnel(l)ing) ❶ *vt.* ①掘地道(或凿地道)穿过: ~ one's way through the hill 凿隧道通过小山 ②在…开隧道: ~ a hill 凿山开隧道 ❷ *vi.* ①掘地道,凿隧道 ②通过地道(*through*);进地道(*into*) ‖**tunnel(l)er** *n.* ①挖掘隧道的人 ②隧道掘进机 / **~like** *a.* 象地道的,象坑道的 ‖ **~ borer** 隧道掘进机 / ~ **diode** [无]隧道二极管 / ~ **net** 宽口窄底的渔网 / ~ **vision** ①[军]坑道视界 ②井蛙之见

tuppence ['tʌpəns] *n.* 两便士 (=twopence)

turban ['tə:bən] *n.* ①穆斯林的头巾 ②(某些亚洲国家)男用头巾 ③(妇女或儿童)头巾式无沿帽 ④(单贝壳)螺旋,涡纹 ‖**~ed** *a.* 戴头巾(或头巾式帽子)的 ‖ **~ shell** 蝶螺科软体动物(的壳) / ~ **stone** 顶端刻有头巾的伊斯兰教墓碑 / '**~top** *n.* 一种可食用的菌类植物

turbid ['tə:bid] *a.* ①混浊的,污浊的: ~ waters 浊水 ②烟雾腾腾的;雾重的 ③混乱的: ~ thoughts 混乱的思想 ‖**~ity** [tə:'biditi] *n.* / **~ly** *ad.* / **~ness** *n.*

turbine ['tə:bin, 'tə:bain] *n.* 透平(机),叶轮机,汽轮机,涡轮(机): a hydraulic ~ 水轮机

turbot ['tə:bət] ([复] turbot(s)) *n.* [动]大菱鲆(比目鱼的一种)

turbulence ['tə:bjuləns] *n.* ①骚动;骚乱 ②(水流的)汹涌;(风势的)狂暴 ③[气]湍流

turbulent ['tə:bjulent] *a.* ①骚动的;骚乱的 ②好骚动的 ③汹涌的;狂暴的;湍流的: a ~ flow 紊流,湍流 ‖**~ly** *ad.*

tureen [tə'ri:n,tju'ri:n] *n.* ①大而深的盖碗(盛汤、菜用) ②(烧菜和上菜用的)焙盘,蒸锅

turf [tə:f] **I** ([复] turfs 或[古] turves [tə:vz]) *n.* ①草根土;草皮 ②灰炭;泥炭 ③[the ~] 赛马场;赛马 ④(流氓等黑势力的)地盘 **II** *vt.* ①用草皮铺盖 ②[俚]抛出(东西),赶走(人)(*out*) ‖*the* ~ ①以赛马为业 ②[美俚]卖淫 ③[美俚]穷极无聊,不名一文 ‖~ **accountant** [英]赛马场的赌注登记人 / '**~-bound** *a.* 长满草皮的 / ~ **drain** 水道上铺有草皮的排水沟

turgid ['tə:dʒid] *a.* ①肿胀的,浮肿的;饱满的: ~ limbs 浮肿的四肢 / Healthy living cells are ~. 健康的活细胞是饱满的。 ②(文体等)浮夸的,华而不实的 ‖**~ity** [tə:'dʒiditi] *n.* / **~ly** *ad.* / **~ness** *n.*

Turkey ['tə:ki] *n.* 土耳其[亚洲]

turkey ['tə:ki] *n.* ①[动]吐绶鸡,火鸡 ②(食用)火鸡肉 ③[美俚](装个人用品的)帆布袋,箱子 ④[美俚]无能的人(或物);不受欢迎的人(或东西) ⑤[美俚]廉价菜肴;劣等戏;劣等货;失败的作品 ‖*have a* ~ *on one's back* [美俚]酒醉;吸毒成瘾 / *say* ~ *to one and buzzard to another* [美俚]厚此薄彼 / *talk* (*cold*) ~ [美

口]直率地说; 谈正经事 / **walk** ~ [美俚](船)前后左右颠簸 ‖~ **buzzard** 【动】兀鹰 / '~-**cock** **n.** ① 雄吐绶鸡, 雄火鸡: be as red as a ~-cock (因生气而)满面通红 ② 妄自尊大的人 / '~= **poult** **n.** 小吐绶鸡, 小火鸡 / ~ **vulture** =~ buzzard

turmoil ['tə:moil] **n.** 骚动; 混乱; 喧嚷: be in a ~ 处于混乱之中

turn [tə:n] **I ❶ vt.** ①转, 转动, 旋转: The wheel of history cannot be ~ed back. 历史的车轮不能倒转。 / The crank ~s the wheel. 曲柄使轮子转动。 / ~ a key in the lock 在锁眼中转动钥匙 / ~ the water tap *on* (*off*) 旋开(关上)自来水龙头 / ~ *on* (*off*) the light (gas, water) 开(关)灯(煤气, 自来水) / ~ the gaslight low 把煤气灯关小 / ~ a screw tight 拧紧螺丝 ②扭; 扭曲; 使弯曲; 折(书页等); 使(刀口)卷起; 使变钝: ~ one's ankle 扭伤脚踝 / ~ a lead pipe 弯铅管 / ~ the edge of a remark 磨去一句话的锋芒 ③ 使转向; 使转变思想, 劝说: ~ one's steps homewards 转身回家 / ~ one's head away 把头掉开 / ~ sb. to correct views 说服某人接受正确观点 ④ 把(注意力等)转向; 把…用于; 把…对准: ~ one's attention to important matters 把注意力转向重大的事情 / ~ one's thoughts elsewhere 把思想转向别处 / ~ one's hand to writing 致力于写作 ⑤动: not ~ a finger to help 不肯以一举手之劳来进行帮助 / not ~ a hair 不动声色 ⑥挡开; 使偏斜: He ~ed the blow. 他挡开了那一击。 / ~ a bullet 挡住(或挡开)子弹 ⑦ 驱使, 撵: ~ cows to pasture 放牛吃草 / ~ sb. out of the house 把某人赶出门 ⑧驱散; 击退 ⑨翻, 翻转: ~ (over) the pages of a book 翻书页 / ~ (over) a phonograph record 把唱片翻过来 / ~ the soil 翻土 / ~ somersaults 翻筋斗 / ~ a collar (dress) 把领子(衣服)翻新 ⑩使颠倒; 倾倒: ~ a bottle of milk into the pot 把一瓶牛奶倒进锅里 / ~ the contents of one's bag out on to the table 把袋里的东西倒在桌上 ⑪使回击; 使作对: His own words were ~ed against him. 别人用他自己的话来攻击他。 / ~ sb. against another 使某人与另一人作对 ⑫绕过; 改变: ~ a street corner 沿街角拐弯 ⑬转变; 改变: ~ sterile land into high-yield fields 变不毛之地为高产田 / ~ grief into strength 化悲痛为力量 / ~ defeat into victory 转败为胜 ⑭使变酸, 使变质: The hot weather has ~ed the milk. 天热使牛奶变质(发酸)了。 ⑮使(树叶等)变色 ⑯使遭受, 使受到(*to*): ~ sb.'s remarks *to* ridicule 使某人所说的话显得滑稽可笑

⑰兑换; 翻译; 改写: ~ coins into paper money 把硬币换成纸币 / Can you ~ this passage into English? 你能把这一段译成英语吗? / ~ verse into prose 把诗改写成散文 ⑱搅乱(心智), 使(心神)不安: His mind was ~ed by grief. 他因悲哀而心神不宁。 / Don't let success ~ your head. 不要让成绩冲昏头脑。 ⑲反(胃): The rotten fish ~ed my stomach. 臭鱼使我恶心。 ⑳(时刻等)超过, 逾: He has ~ed forty. 他已过四十岁了。 / It has just ~ed twelve. 刚过十二点钟。 ㉑【机】旋, 车; 为…车床圆外; [喻]使成圆形: ~ a machine part 车机器部件 / ~ the heel of a sock 结袜子后跟(使成圆形) ㉒使具有优美形式: a well ~ed phrase 漂亮的词句 / can ~ a compliment 会说恭维话 / well ~ed wrists 优美的腕部 ㉓使(钱、货等)流通, 周转; 出清(存货); 赚, 挣(钱等): ~ a quick profit 迅速牟利 / ~ a penny 赚一些钱 ㉔【印】倒植; 倒排: a ~ed comma 一个倒排的逗号(指" ")

❷ vi. ①转动; 旋转: The wheels were ~ing swiftly. 轮子飞快转动着。 / This tap won't ~. 这龙头旋不动。 ②朝向; 转向: ~ to the sun 转朝太阳 / ~ (to the) left 向左转 / The wind ~ed and the sky cleared. 风转天晴。 / The road ~s sharp right. 路向右急转。 / scarcely know where (或 which way) to ~ 不知往哪里走; [喻]不知所措; 不知往哪里求援 ③致力: She has ~ed to (away from) music. 她在搞(不搞)音乐了。 ④求教; 求助: We often ~ to this handbook for information on transistors. 我们常从这本手册查阅有关晶体管的资料。 ⑤转向; 回转; 转身: The tide has ~ed. 潮转了。(或: [喻]潮流变了。) / The stock market ~ed sharply. 股票市场情况急转。 / He ~ed when I called him. 我叫他, 他就回过头来。 ⑥翻, 翻转: toss and ~ in one's bed 在床上翻来翻去 / ~ to page 84 翻到第八十四页 ⑦ 转而反对(*against*); (对…) 发怒, 攻击(*on*, *upon*): ~ against sb. 转而反对某人 ⑧改变信仰; 变节 ⑨变弯; 变钝: The edge of the knife has ~ed. 刀口钝了。 ⑩变成; (树叶等)变色; 变酸, 变质; 变化无常; 神经失常: a worker ~ed engineer 工人出身的工程师 / Both sisters ~ed musician(s). 姊妹两人都成了音乐家。 / His hair has ~ed grey. 他的头发白了。 / Her voice ~ed hoarse. 她的声音哑了。 / The leaves are ~ing. 叶子正在变颜色。 / The milk has ~ed. 牛奶变质了。 ⑪【机】(被)旋, (被)车; 在车床上操作: a metal that ~s easily 容易车的金属

⑫晕眩;作呕: My head (stomach) is ~ing. 我头晕(恶心)。

⑬(商品)转手,易手

II *n.* ①转动;旋转: a ~ of the wheel 轮子的一次转动

②(舞蹈时的)旋转;【体】(杠上运动的)小滚翻;(花式溜冰的)曲线转折

③转向;转弯;转角;曲线部: Left (Right) ~! 向左(右)转! / About ~! 向后转! / take a ~ to the right 向右转弯 / a path full of twists and ~s 蜿蜒曲折的小道;艰难曲折的道路

④(纸牌等的)翻转;翻开: the ~ of a sheet 一张纸的翻转

⑤转变;变化;转折(点): leave the port before the ~ of the tide 在潮转前离港 / a nasty ~ in the weather 天气的突然变坏 / give a new ~ to the argument 把辩论引到一个新的方面 / The event took an explosive ~. 事态起了爆炸性的变化。/ His illness took a favourable ~. 他的病情有了好转。/ a ~ for the better 好转 / the ~ of the century 世纪初;世纪末 / the ~ of the centuries 两个世纪交替之时

⑥(一)圈;(一)阵;(一)回: a coil of 1,000 ~s 一千匝的线圈 / take a ~ in a park (on a bicycle) 在公园里(骑自行车)兜一圈 / take a ~ at the oars 划一会儿(桨) / take a ~ of work 做一会儿工作 / a ~ of rage (dizziness) 一阵盛怒(晕眩)

⑦(杂耍或广播、电视杂剧中的)项目,剧目

⑧(帮助或损害别人的)举动,行为: do sb. a good (bad) ~ 做一件有利(损)于某人的事

⑨(依次轮流的)名分;(顺)次: Wait your ~. 等着轮到你吧。/ It's your ~ to keep guard. 轮到你放哨了。

⑩班: on the afternoon ~ 值下午班 / add a second ~ (除原有一班外)另加一班

⑪倾向;性格;性情;才能: an optimistic ~ of mind 乐观的性格 / have a ~ for music 有音乐才能

⑫(语言等的)特色;措词;措词特征: the ~ of a language 一种语言的特色 / I don't like the ~ of the sentence. 我可不喜欢这句话的措词。/ one's ~s of speech 说话的措词特征 / have a quaint ~ to one's dress 穿着古怪

⑬(对原作的)阐述;改动: give the old yarn a new ~ 用新的讲法讲旧故事

⑭形状;样子: the ~ of one's shoulders 肩部形状

⑮[口]惊吓: It gave me quite a ~. 可把我吓了一跳。

⑯(包括买进和卖出的)一笔证券交易;一笔证券交易的获利;(商品批售补进的)一个周转

⑰【机】车床;有旋转把柄的橱门闩

⑱【印】(无本字时暂用的)倒头铅字,倒植的铅字

⑲【音】回音

⑳[复]月经

㉑[古]计谋,计策

‖*at every* ~ 事事;处处;经常: think of the collective *at every* ~ 事事想到集体 / *A worm will* ~. 见 **worm** / *be* ~*ed* (*of*) 年在…以上,年逾: He *was* ~*ed of* sixty. 他已年逾六十。/ *by* ~*s* 轮流,交替: wash dishes *by* ~*s* 轮流洗碗碟 / She went hot and cold *by* ~*s*. 她一阵发热一阵发冷。/ *call the* ~ 定调子;发号施令;操纵 / *give sb. another* ~ *of the screw* 见 **screw** / *in one's* ~ [常用作插入语]轮到某人也(做某事),也: They, *in their* ~, made a proposal. 他们接着也提出了一个建议。/ *in the* ~ *of a hand* 顷刻,转瞬间 / *in* ~ 依次,轮流: speak *in* ~ 依次发言 / Theory is based on practice and *in* ~ serves practice. 理论的基础是实践,又转过来为实践服务。/ *make sb. in his grave* 使某人纵在九泉也不得安宁 / *not do a hand's* ~ 不动手;不帮忙 / *One good* ~ *deserves another.* [谚]善良的行为必须用善良的行为来报答。/ *on the* ~ 正在转变中;(牛奶)正在变酸: The tide is now *on the* ~. 潮在转。/ *out of* ~ ①不依顺序地 ②不合时宜地;轻率地,鲁莽地 / *serve sb.'s* ~ 合某人之用,有助于达到某人所要达到的目的: This hoe will *serve* my ~. 这把锄头我用着合适。/ *serve the* ~ 合用,管用 / *take* ~*s* 依次,轮流: *take* ~*s* to watch (或 at watching) the dyke 轮流守堤 / *the* ~ *of life* 【医】绝经期,更年期 / *the* ~ *of the wheel* 命运的转变 / *to a* ~ 正好,恰好: The meat is done to a ~. 肉烧得恰到好处。/ *to the* ~ *of a hair* 丝毫不差地 / ~ *about* ①转身;(使)转向: He ~*ed about* and faced me. 他转过身来,脸朝着我。② =~ *and* ~ *about* ③反复思考: He was still ~*ing* the idea *about* when he fell asleep. 当他入睡时,他还是在反复考虑这个主意。/ ~ *a* (或 *the*) *cold shoulder to sb.* 见 **shoulder** / ~ *a deaf ear to* 见 **ear**[1] / ~ *and rend* 攻击(朋友) / ~ *and* ~ *about* 依次,轮流(尤指两者相互交替地) / ~ *aside* ①闪开,避开;转过脸去 ②撇开,撇掉;使转变方向: ~ *aside* a decision 把一个决议搁置一边 / ~ *aside* a bullet 把子弹挡开 ③偏离;叉开: ~ *aside from* the intended course 离开原定的途径 / ~ *away* ①走开,离开 ②转过脸去;把(脸)转过去 ③把…打发走;解雇 ④避免,防止(灾祸等) / ~ (*away*) *from* 对…感到厌恶: The child is ill and ~*s* (*away*) *from* his food. 孩子病了,不想吃东西。/ ~ *back* ①停止前进;往回走,折回: Then we decided to ~ *back*. 接着我们决定往回走。②翻回到;重新提到 (*to*): ~ *back to* p. 10 翻回到第十页 ③折转: ~ *back* the bedclothes 把盖被翻开 ④挡住;使折回: be ~*ed back* at the gate 在大门口被挡回 / ~ *back the clock* 见 **clock**[1] / ~ *colo(u)r* 见 **colo(u)r** / ~ *down* ①(能被)翻下;(能被)向下折转: ~ *down* the collar 翻下衣领 / The collar ~*s down*. 衣领能翻下。/

~ *down* the corner of a page 向下折转书角 ②
关小,调低: ~ *down* the gas 把煤气关得小一点
③ 拒绝,摒斥: ~ *down* a suggestion 拒绝考虑
一项建议 ④使(纸牌等)面朝下 / ~ *in* ①转身
进入;拐入: He saw them ~ *in* at the entrance.
他看到他们从入口处进去。 ② 上床睡觉 ③ (趾
等)内倾 ④交出,上缴: ~ *in* public grain (to the
state) (向国家) 缴公粮 / *Turn in* everything
captured. 一切缴获要归公。⑤把…向里折: *Turn
in* the raw edge before you sew the seam. 缝合
前先把毛边折进。⑥告发;出卖: ~ oneself *in* 自
首 ⑦作出: ~ *in* a good job (a fine performance) 作出良好成绩(精采表演) / ~ *inside out*
翻出: ~ one's pocket *inside out* 把口袋翻出来 /
~ *into* ①进入: ~ *into* a narrow lane 进入小
巷 ②使成为;使变成: ~ *into* waste land *into* paddy
fields 变荒地为稻田 / ~ the article *into* English
把文章译成英语 ③变成 / ~ *loose* ①释放,放
掉 ②使不受拘束,放纵(感情等) ③发射(子弹
等);开(枪等);开火 ④不停地讲话;无拘束地讲
话 / ~ *off* ①关(水源、煤气、电灯等): *Turn off*
the light when you leave the room. 离开房间,
随手关灯。② 撇开,避开(问题等) / 使转变方向
③解雇 ④生产,制造;完成 ⑤处理;出售 ⑥把…
绞死 ⑦(用车床)旋掉,车掉;车成,车出 ⑧使厌
烦,使不感兴趣 ⑨(行人等)拐弯;(路)叉开: He
~ed *off* into a side street. 他拐入一条横街。
⑩[英]变坏,变质 ⑪使变冷: The evening had ~ed
off cool. 夜晚天气转凉了。/ ~ *on* ①开,旋开
(电灯、自来水、无线电等): ~ *on* the radio 开收
音机 ②以…为指向,把…对准: ~ the hose *on* the
fire 把消防水管对准火 ③对…发怒;反对;攻击:
He ~ed *on* his brother, who, he thought,
had deceived him. 他对他兄弟翻脸,认为后者
欺骗了他。/ The dog ~ed *on* me and bit me in
the leg. 那条狗向我扑来,在我腿上咬了一口。
④依靠,依赖,取决于: The trip ~s *on* whether
it will be fine tomorrow. 这次旅行取决于明天
是否天晴。⑤(服麻醉药后)(使)产生幻觉;变得
兴奋 ⑥刺激,使生快感 / ~ one's *back on* (或
upon) / ~ *back* / ~ one's *coat* 见 *coat* / ~
out ①(为打扫而)出清;打扫 ②驱逐,把…赶走
③使(趾等)外倾 ④生产,制造;培养,训练:
~ *out* high-precision instruments 制造精密仪器 /
~ *out* cadres 培养干部 ⑤赶出(牛羊等)进行放
牧: The sheep are ~ed *out* to grass. 羊被放出吃
草。⑥翻出: ~ one's pocket 把口袋翻
出来 ⑦关,旋熄(灯、煤气等) ⑧…叫出来
集合整队 ⑨装饰,打扮 ⑩(应召)出来,出动
⑪起床 ⑫结果(是),原来(是),证明(是): It
~ed *out* (to be) a fine day. 结果,那天是一个晴
天。/ ~ *out* well 终于证明很不错;结果获得成
功 ⑬教…学时髦(如教唆吸毒) / ~ *over*
(使)打翻,(使)倾倒: The lamp was ~ed *over*.
灯给打翻了。②营业额达,做(一定数额)的买卖:
~ *over* 5,000 dollars a month 每月营业额为五

千元 ③ 周转(一定数额的商品) ④ 移交,交给
⑤把…逐件翻查 ⑥翻阅(书籍) ⑦反复考
虑: ~ a matter *over* in one's mind 心中反
复考虑一件事 ⑧翻身,折腾: ~ *over* in bed 在
床上翻身 ⑨(胃)翻动;(心脏)惊悸 ⑩(机器等)
转动 ⑪把(词、文章)接转到下一行(或栏、页) /
~ *round* ①转身 ②转变;改变意见;采取新政
策 / ~ *sb. adrift* 见 *adrift* / ~ *sb. round*
one's *finger* 见 *finger* / ~ *tail* 见 *tail*[1] / ~
the *corner* / ~ the *scale(s)* 见 *scale*[2] /
~ the *table(s)* 见 *table* / ~ *to* ①转向;变成
②求教于,求助于: ~ *to* sb. for help 求某人帮
助 ③致力于,着手: ~ *to* a task 着手工作 ④开
始工作;积极行动: They ~ed *to* at once. 他们
立即就干了起来。/ ~ *turtle* 见 *turtle* / ~ *up*
①找到,发现;发掘出 ②出现,被找到;突然发
生: Something unexpected ~ed *up*. 发生了
没有意料到的事情。③证明是 (=~ out to be):
~ *up* missing at roll call 点名时被发现缺席
④[英]参考,查阅(书籍);寻找,查(词等) ⑤把…
翻转过来;翻掘: ~ *up* the soil 翻土 ⑥翘起;卷
起;折起: ~ *up* one's toes 跷起足趾;[喻]死去 /
~ *up* the sleeves 卷起衣袖;[喻]准备行动(或工
作) / ~ *up* the ends of one's trousers 卷起裤腿
⑦来到,到达: I wonder when they will ~ *up*.
真不知道他们什么时候才能来。⑧旋大(灯火等);
开大(煤气等) ⑨拐入,弯入(街道);转身登上(山
道等) ⑩使取仰卧姿势;使(纸牌等)面朝上 ⑪杀
死 ⑫转速达到 ⑬(帆船)逆风换抢 / ~ *up one's*
nose at 见 nose / ~ *upside down* 把…完全颠
倒: ~ the facts *upside down* 颠倒事实 / ~ *up*
trumps 见 *trump*[1]
∥'~**about** n. ① 转身,转向;向后转 ②(方针、
倾向等的) 转变 ③ 转到另一边;变节 ④ 叛徒
⑤ (娱乐场的) 转马 ⑥ 正反面都能穿的衣服 /
'~**around** n. ①供车辆回旋的空地,回车场;回
车道 ②飞机卸货、加油、检修及再装货所需的时
间 ③(立场、方针等的)转变 / '~**bench** n. (可
携带的)钟表工人用的车床 / '~**buckle** n.
【机】松紧螺纽扣 / '~**cap** n. (烟囱顶的)旋转
帽 / '~**coat** n. 变节者,叛徒 / '~**cock** n. 水
龙头管理员 / '~**down** a. (衣领等)可翻折的,
穿时翻下的 / '~**ed-'on** a. 对时髦事物极敏感的,好赶时
髦的 / '~**-in** n. 折进物(如书籍封面沿硬纸板边
折进的部分) / '~**key** n. 监狱看守 / '~**off** n.
①岔开;避开 ②岔道,支路(尤指从高速公路岔出
的坡道) ③成品 / '~**out** n. ①出动 ②(为某种
目的)出动的人群;集合的人群 ③[英]罢工;罢
工的工人 / 【交】避车道,分道;岔道 ⑤产品;产
额 ⑥出清;扫除 ⑦设备,装备 ⑧一辆马车的全套
配备、马匹和人员 ⑨穿着方式 / '~**,over** n. ①
翻倒;翻转 ②翻倒物;翻转物 ③倒转;转向反面;
转向对方 ④半圆形卷饼 ⑤营业额,成交量;证券
交易额 ⑥流动,流通,吞吐 ⑦(在特定时间内雇佣
的)补缺工人数;补缺工人所占比例 ⑧人员调整

⑨[英](报纸上)从第一版末转入第二版的时事小品 *a.* (衣领等)翻转的 / **'~pike** *n.* ①(旧时的)收税栅 ②收税路;收货高速公路 ③(泛指)公路,大道 / **'~-round** *n.* ①船只进港、卸货、装货、离境的全部过程 ②转身地;回车场 ③正反面都能穿的衣服 / **'~-screw** *n.* 旋凿;(旋转螺丝钉的)起子 / **'~-sole** *n.* 向阳性植物(向向日葵等) / **'~stile** *n.* (入口处等的)旋转式栅门;绕杆 / **'~stone** *n.* 【动】翻石鹬属的鸟 / **~ story** 从一页底部转入次页头上的新闻报道 / **~,table** *n.* ①(转换机车等方向的)转(车)台,旋车盘 ②(唱机的)转盘 ③(餐桌上用的)旋盘 ④(广播用)录音转播机 / **'~up** *n.* ①翻起物;衣服的卷起部分;[主英]裤腿的卷边 ②[英]吵闹,吵架;打架 ③面朝上翻开的牌 *a.* (可)翻起的,(可)卷起的,(可)翘起的: a ~up collar 可翻起的衣领 / a ~up nose 翘鼻子

turner[1] ['tə:nə] *n.* ①旋转者;翻拌者 ②旋转器;翻拌器 ③车工,旋工 ④[英]一种翻筋斗的鸽子

turner[2] ['tə:nə] *n.* [美]体育俱乐部会员;体育家

turning ['tə:niŋ] *n.* ①旋转;翻转;弯曲 ②变向,转向 ③转弯处: stop at the next ~ 在下一个拐弯处停下来 ④车工工艺;车削工作: rough ~ 粗车(削) / finish ~ 光车(削),精车(削) ‖ **~ point** 转折点: a ~ *point* in history 历史转折点

turnip ['tə:nip] *n.* ①【植】芜菁,萝卜 ②[俚]大挂表 ‖ **~y** *a.* 芜菁味的;芜菁状的 ‖ **~ radish** (圆)萝卜 / **~ tops** 芜菁嫩叶

turpentine ['tə:pəntain] I *n.* ①松油;松脂 ②松节油 (=~ oil) ③松木油 (=wood ~) II ❶ *vt.* ①涂松节油于… ②从(松树)中采松油 ❷ *vi.* 制松节油;采集松脂

turpitude ['tə:pitju:d] *n.* 卑鄙,堕落;卑鄙的行为

turquois(e) ['tə:kwɑ:z] I *n.* ①【矿】绿松石 ②绿松石色,青绿色 (=~ blue) II *a.* 青绿色的

turret ['tʌrit] *n.* ①【建】塔楼;角塔 ②【机】(六角)转台: ~ lathe 六角车床,转塔车床 ③(战舰、坦克、飞机等的)炮塔 ④(装在摄影机或电视摄影机上的)透镜旋转台 ‖ **~ed** *a.* ①有角塔(或六角转台等)的 ②角塔状的 ③(软体动物的)壳有锥形螺旋状壳阶的 ‖ **~ gun** 炮塔炮;炮塔内旋回式机枪 / **~ ship** 装有炮塔炮的军舰

turtle ['tə:tl] I *n.* ①【动】海龟;蠵龟;玳瑁;甲鱼 ②(食用)海龟肉,甲鱼肉 II *vi.* 捉海龟(尤指作为职业) ‖ **turn ~** ①(使)倾覆 ②变得无能为力;逃跑;退缩,畏缩 ‖ **~r** *n.* ①捉海龟者;拾海龟蛋者 ②海龟商 ‖ **'~-dove** *n.* ①【动】斑鸠;雉鸠 ②情人 / **'~-neck** *n.* 高而紧的衣领;高领绒衣 / **~ shell** 海龟甲;玳瑁壳

turves [tə:vz] [古] turf 的复数

tusk [tʌsk] I *n.* ①(象、野猪等的)长牙;獠牙 ②(耙等的)齿状物;(多牙榫的)牙 II *vt.* 用长牙抵(或掘) ‖ **~ed, ~y** *a.* 有獠牙的,有长牙的 ‖ **~ tenon** 多牙榫

tussle ['tʌsl] *n.* & *vi.* 扭打,扭斗;争论;奋斗 (*with*)

tutor ['tju:tə] I *n.* ①家庭教师,私人教师 ②[英](大学、学院中的)指导教师,导师 ③(美国某些大学或学院中的)助教 ④[律](未成年者及其财产的)监护人 II ❶ *vt.* ①当…的教师;当…的监护人 ②(常指个别地)教;指导 ③约束,克制: ~ oneself 自我克制 / ~ one's passions 抑制激情 ❷ *vi.* ①当家庭教师;当指导教师 ②受家庭教师的教导 ‖ **~age** ['tju:təridʒ] *n.* 家庭教师(或指导教师等)的职位(或工作、职责)

tutorial [tju:(ˈ)tɔ:riəl] I *a.* 家庭教师的;指导教师的 II *n.* ①大学导师的指导期;个别指导期 ②由指导导师个别指导(或主持讨论)的班级(或研究班): attend a ~ 上指导教师的课 ‖ **~ly** *ad.* ‖ **~ system** 导师制

twaddle ['twɔdl] I *n.* ①废话,蠢话;无聊话 ②讲(或写)废话的人 II *vi.* 讲(或写)废话 ‖ **~r** *n.* 讲(或写)废话的人

twain [twein] [古] I *n.* 二,两;一对,一双: cut in ~ 一切为二 II *num.* 二,两

twang[1] [twæŋ] I *n.* ①拨弦声 ②鼻声,鼻音: speak with a ~ 说话带鼻音 ③土音,口音: a cockney ~ 伦敦土音 ④内疚,痛苦 ⑤拨动 II ❶ *vi.* ①发拨弦声 ②发鼻音,带鼻音讲话 ③(箭)嗖地一声射出 ④(由于痛苦、紧张等而)颤动,抽动 ❷ *vt.* ①使发拨弦声: ~ a banjo 弹班卓琴 ②带鼻音讲(或读) ③嗖地一声射出(箭)

twang[2] [twæŋ] *n.* ①长久附着不散掉的气味 ②意味,味儿

tweak [twi:k] I *n.* ①拧,捏,扭 ②焦急,苦恼 II *vt.* ①拧,捏,扭(鼻子、耳朵等) ②捏…的鼻子 ‖ **~er** *n.* [英俚](儿童玩的)弹弓

tweed [twi:d] I *n.* ①(粗)花呢 ②[复]一套花呢的衣服 ‖ **~y** *a.* ①穿花呢服的;穿着漂亮的 ②松散悠闲的 ③男子气概的

tweezers ['twi:zəz] [复] *n.* 镊子,小钳子: a pair of ~ 一把镊子

twelfth [twelfθ] I *num.* ①第十二(个) ②十二分之一(的) II *n.* (月的)第十二日 ‖ **the ~** 八月十二日(英国松鸡猎期开始日) ‖ **~ly** *ad.* 第十二(列举条目等时用) ‖ **Twelfth day, ~ day** 【宗】主显节(基督教圣诞节后的第十二天) / **Twelfth night, ~ night** 【宗】①主显节的前夕 ②主显节之夜

twelve [twelv] I *num.* 十二;十二个(人或物);第十二(卷、章、页等)(用例参看 eight) II *n.* ①十二岁 ②十二点钟 ‖ **in ~s** 【印】十二开 / **strike ~** 达到最高目标,获得大成功 / **the Twelve** 【宗】耶稣的十二门徒 ‖ **'~-tone** *a.* 【音】十二音体系的

twentieth ['twentiiθ] I *num.* ①第二十(个) ②二十分之一(的) II *n.* (月的)第二十日

twenty ['twenti] I *num.* 二十;二十个(人或物);第二十(卷、章、页等)(用例参看 eight) II *n.* ①[复](世纪的)二十年代 ②二十岁;[复]二十到二十九岁的时期 ③二十英镑(或美元)票面的纸币 ④二十点钟(即下午八点) III *a.* 许多的: ~ and

~ 许许多多 / I have told you ~ times. 我对你讲过多少遍了。‖**~-'fourmo, 24 mo** *n.* 二十四开 (的书) / **'~mo, 20 mo** *n.* 二十开 (的书) / **'~-'~, 20/20** *a.* 视力正常的

twice [twais] *ad.* 两次;两倍: be absent ~ 缺席两次 / *Twice* two is four. 二二得四。/ be worth ~ as much 价值达两倍之多 / This room is ~ as large as that one. 这间屋子比那间大一倍。/ have ~ the strength 力量大一倍 / He is ~ the man he was. 他比过去强健了一倍。‖*at* ~ ①分两次(做某事) ②在第二次时: They succeeded *at* ~. 第二次他们成功了。/ *in* ~ 分两次(做某事) / *think* ~ 重新考虑 ‖**~-'told** *a.* ①讲过两次的 ②讲过多次的,陈旧的: a *~-told* tale 陈旧的故事

twiddle ['twidl] Ⅰ ❶ *vt.* 捻弄,旋弄 ❷ *vi.* ①玩弄 (*with*): ~ *with* one's moustaches 抚弄胡须 ②忙于琐事 ③旋转着移动 Ⅱ *n.* 捻,旋 ‖*one's thumbs* 见 **thumb**

twig[1] [twig] *n.* ①细枝,嫩枝 ②纤细的动脉(或神经) ‖*hop the* ~ [口] ①死去 ②躲开债主 ③突然离去 ‖**twigged** *a.* 有细枝(或嫩枝)的 / **twiggy** *a.* ①象细枝的;苗条的 ②多细枝的 / **~less** *a.* 无细枝(或嫩枝)的

twig[2] [twig] (twigged; twigging) *vt. & vi.* [口] ①观察;注意 ②懂得,了解

twilight ['twailait] Ⅰ *n.* ①黄昏时的光线;曙光; 【天】晨昏蒙影,曙暮光 ②黄昏;黎明 ③微弱的光 ④洪荒时代;没落时代 Ⅱ *a.* 曙暮光的,微明的,昏暗的 ‖**~ sleep** 【医】半麻醉(主要用于分娩) / **~ zone** ①[无]半阴影区,微明区 ②边缘地区;(难于明确划界的)过渡区

twin [twin] Ⅰ *a.* ①孪生的,双胞胎的;双胞胎之一的: ~ girls 孪生女孩 / a ~ sister 孪生的姐姐(或妹妹) ②两个相似(或相关)部分组成的;成对的;一双之一的: ~ triode 【无】双三极管 / ~ crystal 【物】孪晶 Ⅱ *n.* ①孪生儿之一 [复] 孪生儿,双胎: Siamese ~s 【医】暹罗双胎,剑突联胎(指人或动物身体连接的双胎) ②两个相象的人(或物)之一;[复]两个相象的人(或物) ③[Twins]【天】双子座;双子宫【结晶学】双晶: swallowtail ~ 石膏双晶,燕尾双晶 / ~ axis 双晶轴 Ⅲ (twinned; twinning) ❶ *vi.* ①生双胞胎 ②(与…)成对(*with*) ③形成双晶 ❷ *vt.* ①孪生 ②给…提供配对物 ③使成对,使相联 ‖**'~-born** *a.* 双生的,孪生的

twine [twain] Ⅰ *n.* ①二股(或二股以上)的线;麻线;细绳 ②捻,搓;盘绕,缠绕 ③缠绕物 Ⅱ ❶ *vt.* ①捻,搓;使交织;编: ~ a wreath of flowers 编花圈 ②围住,盘绕 ③使缠绕,使怀抱: The mother ~d her arms around her child. 母亲搂抱着她的孩子。❷ *vi.* ①捻,搓;交织;编 ②缠绕,盘绕: a vine has ~s about the tree trunk 缠绕树干的藤 ③蜿蜒: A snake ~d over the ground. 蛇在地上蜿蜒爬行。‖**~r** *n.* ①缠绕物 ②缠绕植物(如牵牛花)

twinge [twind3] Ⅰ *vt. & vi.* 刺痛 Ⅱ *n.* ①刺痛,剧痛: a ~ of toothache 一阵牙痛 ②(精神或良心上的)痛苦: a ~ of remorse 悔恨所引起的一阵痛苦,内疚

twinkle ['twiŋkl] Ⅰ ❶ *vi.* ①闪烁,闪耀: Stars ~d in the sky. 星星在天空闪烁。②(眼睛因愉快、欢乐而)闪闪发光 (*at*): His eyes ~d *at* the good news. 听到好消息,他眼里闪烁着喜悦的光芒。③(双腿)快速移动;(眼睑)迅速开合 ❷ *vt.* ①使闪闪发亮 ②闪出(光芒) Ⅱ *n.* ①闪烁;(眼睛的)发光: a merry ~ in one's eyes 喜悦的眼光 ②眨眼 ③一刹那,转瞬之间: in a ~ 转瞬之间 ④快速的移动 ‖**~r** *n.* 发光体

twinkling ['twiŋkliŋ] *n.* [只用单]闪烁;眨眼;一眨眼的瞬间,瞬间: in a ~ (或 in the ~ of an eye, in the ~ of a bed post) 一刹那,转瞬之间

twirl [twə:l] Ⅰ ❶ *vt.* ①使快速转动;使快速旋转: ~ a brace drill 转动曲柄钻 ②捻弄,拈(须) ③(棒球中)投(球) ❷ *vi.* ①快速转动 ②[罕](蛇般)扭动;蟠绕 ③(棒球中)投球 Ⅱ *n.* ①转动;旋转 ②旋转的东西;螺旋形的东西;(装饰花体字的)曲线 ③[美俚]复制的钥匙;万能钥匙 ‖*one's thumbs* 见 **thumb**

twist [twist] Ⅰ ❶ *vt.* ①捻,搓,拈: ~ threads together 把纱线捻在一起 / ~ pieces of straw into a rope 把稻草搓成绳子 ②编织;使交织: ~ flowers into a garland 把花编成花圈 / a plot with (或 in with) another 使两个情节交织在一起 ③使扭转,使呈螺旋形;拧,扭,绞: a wet towel 拧干毛巾 / ~ the cap off a fountain pen 拧开自来水笔的套子 ④ 缠绕,盘绕: ~ a rope round the post 把绳索绕在柱子上 ⑤弯弯曲曲地走过: ~ one's way through a crowd 在人群中曲折穿行 ⑥扭曲;扭歪;扭伤: ~ one's face into a grin 龇牙咧嘴地笑 / He fell and ~ed his ankle. 他摔了一跤,扭伤了足踝。⑦歪曲;曲解: ~ sb.'s words 曲解别人的话 ⑧ 使转动: ~ one's rocking chair to the left 把摇椅转向左方 ⑨使苦恼,折磨: 使混乱,使慌乱: I'm all ~ed. 我简直搞糊涂了。⑩使(球)旋转 ❷ *vi.* ①扭弯;扭曲;扭伤: Wire ~s easily. 铁丝很容易扭曲。/ His face ~ed with pain. 他痛得脸都扭歪了。/ The child's ankle ~ed. 孩子的足踝扭伤了。②缠绕,盘绕;盘旋: The snake ~ed around a branch. 蛇缠绕在树枝上。/ The highway ~s up on the mountainside. 公路沿山腰盘旋而上。③曲折穿行: a stream ~ing through valleys 蜿蜒地流过山谷的河流 ④扭动:呈螺旋形 ⑤转身 (*around, about*): He ~ed *around* to see what was happening. 他转过身去看发生了什么事。⑥(球)作曲线转动,旋转 ⑦跳扭摆舞 Ⅱ *n.* ①(一)捻,(一)搓,(一)拈: Give the rope a few more ~s. 把绳索再搓几下。②(一)拧,(一)扭,(一)绞;扭转 ③捻成的线;经纱;缝纫丝线 ④烟草卷;面包卷 ⑤扭弯;扭歪;扭曲 ⑥卷曲;曲折: a rope full of ~s 纠结很多的绳

子 / a ～ in a stream 河流的曲折 ⑦(对意义、内容等的)歪曲,曲解: give the fact a ～ 对事实加以歪曲 ⑧(机器等的)螺旋运动; 旋转: give a ～ to a ball 打转球 ⑨古怪,怪僻 ⑩螺旋状; 缠度 (弹丸在膛内回转一周前进的距离) ⑪ 意想不到的转折: The author gives an unusual ～ to his story. 作者使故事起了一个不寻常的转折。⑫手法,办法; (新)花样: the usual ～s of oratory 演讲术中的常用手法 ⑬扭摆舞 ⑭[美俚](轻浮的)女郎,女人 ⑮[英]混合酒; [英口]胃口: have a tremendous ～ 胃口很大 ⑯[英](末端拧紧而成的)纸包 (=～ of paper) ‖*a ～ in one's tongue* 口齿不清 / ～ *off* 拧断; 扭断: ～ *off* a twig 拧断一根树枝 / ～*s and turns* 迂回曲折: While the prospects are bright, the road has ～*s and turns.* 前途是光明的,道路是曲折的。/ ～ *sb. round* (或 *around) one's finger* 左右某人; 任意摆布某人 / ～ *sb.'s arm* 倒扭某人的手臂; [喻]向某人施加压力; 强迫某人 / ～ *up* 把(纸等)卷成螺旋形

twister ['twistə] *n.* ①扭曲者,扭卷者; 缠绕者; 【纺】拈接工 ②缠绕物; 盘绕物;【纺】拈线机 ③旋转球 ④[气]陆龙卷; 水龙卷; 沙柱; 尘旋 ⑤[口]不可靠的人,奸诈的人 ④难题,棘手的事; 拗口令 (=tongue ～) ⑦(杂技演员)在空中扭身的筋斗

twit [twit] **I** (twitted; twitting) *vt.* 责备; 挖苦,揶揄: ～ sb. with his fault 以某人的错误来挖苦某人 **II** *n.* 责备; 挖苦,揶揄 ‖**twittingly** *ad.*

twitch [twitʃ] **I ❶** *vt.* ①骤然一抽,急扯; 攫取: He ～ed the photo out of my hand. 他骤然从我手中把照片夺去。② 抽动: The dog ～ed its ears. 狗抽动耳朵。**❷** *vi.* ①急速拉动 (at): ～ at sb.'s sleeve 拉一拉某人的袖子(以引起注意) ②(肌肉等)颤动,抽搐: His left cheek ～ed. 他的左颊抽搐着。③抽痛,阵痛 **II** *n.* ①急拉 ②颤动,抽搐 ③抽痛,阵痛

twitter ['twitə] **I ❶** *vi.* ①(鸟)吱吱地叫,鸣啭 ②(因兴奋、紧张而)喊喊喳喳地讲; 吃吃地笑 ③(因激动而)颤抖 **❷** *vt.* ①喊喊喳喳地讲; 抖动 **II** *n.* ①鸣啭; 喊喊喳喳声 ②(由激动引起的)颤抖: in a ～ 颤抖着 ‖**ation** [,twitə'reiʃən] *n.* (由激动引起的)颤抖,紧张

two [tu:, tu] **I** *num.* 二; 两个(人或物); 第二(卷、章、页等)(用例参看 **eight**) **II** *n.* ①两个(人或物)一组 ②两元票面的纸币 ③两岁 ④两点钟 ‖*by ～s and threes* 三个三个一次; 三三两两 / *in ～ ～s* [口]在极短时间里,立刻 / *one or ～* ①一或两 ②几个,少许 / *put ～ and ～ together* 根据事实推断,推理 / *Two can play at that game.* [谚]你有一手,我也有一手。(意为: 受害要报复。) / *Two heads are better than one.* 见 **head** / *Two of a trade never agree.* [谚]同行是冤家。/ *Two's company, three's none.* [谚]两人成伴,三人不欢。‖**～fold** *a. & ad.* 两倍; 双重 / **～ness** *n.* ‖*～-and-,one-'half*

striper [美]海军少校 / '～-'bit *a.* [美俚]①价值两角五分美金的 ②便宜的,无价值的 / ～ **bits** [美俚]两角五分美金 / **～-by-four** ['tu:bə'fɔ:] *a.* ① 2 吋 (或呎等)×4 吋(或呎等)的 ② 小的,微不足道的 / '～-'cleft *a.*【植】二半裂的 / '～= di'mensional *a.*【数】两维的,两度的 / '～= 'edged *a.* (刀)双刃的; 有双重意义的 / '～= 'faced *a.* ①两面的 ②两面派的,伪君子的,奸诈的: expose the ～-*faced* tactics of the renegades 揭露叛徒的两面派手法 / '～-'fisted *a.* 强有力的,雄赳赳的 / '～-'handed *a.* ① 有两只手的 ②两手都会使用的 ③(剑等)需要双手拿的; (锯等)需要两人操作的 / '～-'handled *a.* 有两个捏手的,双柄的 / '～-'legged *a.* 有两条腿的 / '～-line *a.*【印】(铅字等)比普通型大一倍的 / '～-'masted *a.* 双桅的 / '～-'pair front [英]三楼前房 / '～-,party line 两户合用电话线 / '～= ,party system 两党制 / ～pence ['tʌpəns] *n.* 两便士 / 两便士银币: want ～*pence* in the shilling 脑子不灵; 精神失常 / ～penny ['tʌpəni] *a.* ①两便士的 ②廉价的,无价值的 *n.* ①两便士银币 ②一丁点儿: I don't care a ～*penny*. 我一点儿也不在意。/ ～penny-halfpenny ['tʌpəni-'heipəni] *a.* ①两便士半的 ②不足道的,不重要的 / '～-'petal(l)ed *a.*【植】双花瓣的 / '～-'piece *a.* (服装)上下身成套的 / '～-ply *a.* 两层的,双重的,双股的 / '～-'seater *n.* 双座汽车 (或飞机) / '～-shot *n.* 双人特写镜头 / '～-'sided *a.* ①两边的,两方面的 ②两面派的 / '～-speed *a.*【机】双速的 / '～-star *a.* (美军)二星级(少将级)的; 中等的 / '～-tier *a.* 双重的: a ～-*tier* foreign exchange system 双重汇率制 / '～-'time *vt.* 欺骗,对(爱人)不忠 / '～-time loser ① 两次坐牢的人 ② 做某事失败过两次的人; 两次离婚者; 两度破产者 / '～-'tongued *a.* 说假话的,骗人的 / '～-'way *a.* ①双向的; 双通的; 两路的; 两方面的: a ～-*way* radio 收发两用无线电设备 / ～-*way* traffic 双向交通 / ～-*way* television 双向电视 / a ～-*way* switch 双向开关,双路开关 / ②(衣服)两面可穿的,可反穿的

type [taip] **I** *n.* ①型,类型,式: a new ～ (of) aeroplane 新型飞机 / various blood ～s 各种血型 / men of that ～ 那种类型的人 / meat ～ poultry 食用家禽 ②典型; 榜样,模范; 样本,样板: ～ reaction【化】典型反应 ③标志; 代表; 象征; 记号,符号: Water may serve as a ～ of instability. 水可以作为不稳定性的象征。④【神学中所谓的】预示 ⑤[总称]也可用作可数名词,指一个【印】铅字,活字: Wooden ～s are (或 Wooden ～ is) now used only for posters. 木刻活字现仅用于印刷招贴。/ be printed *in* large ～ (*in various* ～s) 用大号铅字(各种铅字)排印 / set (up) ～ 排字,排版 / set ... *in* ～ 把...排版,把...付排 (印出的)字体: Very small ～ is hard to read. 很小的字体读起来费力。⑦【生】模式标本: vertebrate ～ 脊椎动物型 / genus 模式属 ⑧(奖

章、硬币等的) 图案 ⑨ [美俚] 打字机 ‖*black-letter* ~ (或 *boldface* ~) 黑体字,粗体字 / *gothic* (或 *Gothic*) ~ 粗黑体字,哥特体活字 / *italic* ~ 斜体活字 / *movable* ~ 活字 / *pearl* (*agate*, *nonpareil*, *minion*, …) ~ 5 (5½, 6, 7, …) 点铅字 / *roman* ~ 正体活字,罗马活字 **Ⅱ ❶** *vt.* ①作为…的典型(或代表) ②测定(血等)的类型 ③分配(演员)扮演某一类型的角色: ~ an actor as a negative character 分派某演员扮演反面角色 ④(常指宗教人物或事件)典型地预示 ⑤用打字机打 (=typewrite): ~ a document 打一份文件 / a ~d letter 一封打字的信 ⑥铸,浇(铅字等) ❷ *vi.* 打字 (=typewrite) ‖*be in* ~ 排好字(的): This article *is* now *in* ~. 这篇文章已排好字(待印)了。 / *true to* ~ 典型地(地);合乎本性的(地);纯种的,与原种相同的: Plants grown from seed are sometimes not *true to* ~. 由籽苗生长的植物有时并不和原种相同。 ‖'~bar *n.* ①(打字机上)装有铅字的连动杆 ②铸成条的一列铅字 / ~ **case** 铅字盘 / '~cast *vt.* ①浇铸(铅字等) ②为(演员)分配角色;经常为(演员)分配同一类型的角色 / '~,casting *n.* 铸字,浇铸 / ~ **cutter** 刻(铸字用)铜模的工人 / '~face *n.* ①铅字面;铅字印出的字样 ②[总称](某种字体的)全部铅字 / '~,founder *n.* 铸字工人 / '~,founding *n.* 铸字;铸字业 / '~foundry *n.* 铸字工场 / '~-'high *a.* (木刻版等)与铅字标准高度 (0.9186 吋) 一样高的 / ~ **metal** 活字金属,字铅 / '~-script *n.* 打字稿,打字文件 / '~set *vt.* 把…排版 / '~,setter *n.* ①排字工人 ②排字机(有时兼可铸字) / '~,setting *n.* 排字 *a.* 排字(用)的: a ~*setting* machine (有时兼可铸字的)自动排字机 / ~ **wheel** (某些打字机、电报机等上的)活字轮

typewrite ['taip-rait] (typewrote ['taip-rout], typewritten ['taip,ritn]) ❶ *vt.* 用打字机打 ❷ *vi.* 打字 ‖**typewriting** *n.* ①打字; 打字术; 打字工作 ②打字稿,打字文件 ③[美俚]机枪火力

typewriter ['taip,raitə] *n.* ①打字机; [罕]打字员 ②[英俚]格斗者; 拳击手 ③[美俚]机枪(尤指小型的)

typhoid ['taifɔid] **Ⅰ** *a.* 伤寒的 **Ⅱ** *n.* 伤寒 (=~ fever) ‖~**al** [tai'fɔidl] *a.* 伤寒的; 类伤寒的

typhoon [tai'fu:n] *n.* 台风 ‖**typhonic** [tai'fɔnik] *a.* 台风的; 台风性的

typhus ['taifəs] *n.* 斑疹伤寒 (=~ fever) ‖**typhous** ['taifəs] *a.* 斑疹伤寒的; 斑疹伤寒性的

typical ['tipikəl] *a.* 典型的,代表性的; 象征性的: a ~ character 典型人物 / grasp ~ cases 抓典型 / The book is ~ of its kind. 这本书在同类书籍中有典型性。 / It is ~ of him to take hard jobs. 抢挑重担是他的特点。 ‖~**ity** [,tipi'kæliti] *n.* 典型性; 特征 / ~**ly** *ad.* / ~**ness** *n.*

typify ['tipifai] *vt.* ①作为…的典型,代表; 具有…的特征 ②象征; (宗教人物或事件)预示 ‖**typification** [,tipifi'keiʃən] *n.* 典型化 / **typifier** *n.* 典型代表者; 代表性事物

typist ['taipist] *n.* 打字者; 打字员

typography [tai'pɔgrəfi] *n.* ①(活版)印刷术 ②排印 ③(书籍等的)印刷格式,印刷工艺 ‖**typographer** *n.* ①排印工人 ②精通印刷术的人 ③印刷商

Tyr [tiə] *n.* (北欧神话中的)战神

tyrannic(al) [ti'rænik(əl)] *a.*° 暴君的; 专制的,专横的; 暴虐的; 残酷的 (现常用 tyrannical) ‖**tyrannically** *ad.* / **tyrannicalness** *n.*

tyrannize ['tirənaiz] ❶ *vi.* ①施暴政; 实行极权统治 ②横行霸道 ❷ *vt.* [罕]对…施暴政; 压迫

tyrannous ['tirənəs] *a.* 暴政的; 暴虐的; 专横的; 严酷的 ‖~**ly** *ad.*

tyranny ['tirəni] *n.* ①暴政,苛政; 专制 ②暴虐,专横; 暴行 ③严峻,严酷 ④(古希腊城邦国家等的)僭主政治

tyrant ['taiərənt] *n.* ①(古希腊等的)专制统治者,僭主 ②暴君 ③恶霸: local ~s 土豪,恶霸 ④专横的权势; 使人痛苦的事物: that ~, time 不饶人的岁月

tyre[1] ['taiə] [英] **Ⅰ** *n.* ①轮箍 ②轮胎,车胎(尤指外胎): a pneumatic ~ 气胎 / a synthetic rubber ~ 合成橡胶轮胎 **Ⅱ** *vt.* 装轮胎在…上

tyre[2] ['taiə] *n.* (印度用英语)凝乳

tyro ['taiərou] *n.* 初学者,新手,生手

U

ubiety [ju(:)'baieti] *n.* 所在,位置; 位置关系

ubiquitous [ju(:)'bikwitəs] *a.* (同时)普遍存在的,无处不在的: The struggle between opposites is ~. 对立面的斗争是普遍存在的。 ‖~**ly** *ad.* / ~**ness** *n.*

ubiquity [ju(:)'bikwiti] *n.* (同时的)普遍存在,无处不在

U-boat ['ju:bout] *n.* 德国潜水艇; 潜水艇

udder ['ʌdə] *n.* (牛、羊等的)乳房; 乳腺 ‖~**ed** *a.* [常用以构成复合词](牛、羊等)乳房…的,有…乳

房的: large-～ed 乳房大的 / two-～ed 有两个
乳房的 / ～less a. ①无乳房的 ②失去母乳的;
无母的: an ～less lamb 失去母羊的羔羊

ugly ['ʌgli] **I** a. ①丑陋的, 难看的: an ～ scar 难
看的伤疤 / Don't make ～ faces. 别做怪脸。②
可怕的; 可憎的; 讨厌的: an ～ wound 吓人的伤
口 / an ～ sound (smell) 讨厌的声音(气味) ③
道德败坏的, 邪恶的; 丑恶的: the ～ fact of life
人间丑事; 生活中的阴暗面 / ～ rumours 不堪
入耳的谣言 ④ 险恶的; (天气)阴沉的; 不祥.
an ～ situation 险恶的形势 / The sky has an ～
look. 天空显得阴沉沉的。/ The news is ～. 消
息不祥。⑤[口]暴躁的; 乖戾的; 好吵架的: an ～
temper 暴躁的脾气 / an ～ customer 难对付的
家伙 **II** n. 丑陋的人(或动物、东西) ‖*cut up*
发脾气, 发怒 ‖**uglily** ad. / **ugliness** n. ‖～
duckling ①(安徒生童话中变成天鹅的)丑小鸭
②[喻] 小时难看长大后好看的人; 先遭轻视后受
赞美的人(或物)

ukulele [ˌjuːkəˈleili] n. 尤克里里琴(一种象吉他的
四弦琴, 流行于夏威夷等地)

ukulele

ulcer ['ʌlsə] **I** n. ①【医】溃疡: gastric ⟨duodenal⟩
～ 胃(十二指肠)溃疡 / mycotic (warty) ～ 霉
菌性(疣状)溃疡 ②[喻]腐烂的事物; 腐败的根
源

ulster ['ʌlstə] n. 有带的宽大长外套

ulterior [ʌlˈtiəriə] a. ①在那边的; 较远的: on the
～ side of the river 在河的那一边 ②日后的, 将
来的; 进一步的: the ～ consequences 后果 /
take ～ steps 采取进一步的步骤 ③隐蔽的, 秘而
不宣的: with ～ motives 别有用心地 ‖～**ly** ad.

ultimate ['ʌltimit] **I** a. ①最远的: the ～ ends of
the earth 天涯海角 ②最后的, 最终的 ③基本
的, 根本的; 首要的; 不能再分解(或分析)的: ～
principles 基本原理 / the ～ cause 【哲】终极因
④最大的, 极限的: ～ strain 极限应变 / ～
stress 极限应力 **II** n. ①终极的; 极限; 顶点: the
～ of one's desires 最终的愿望 / an absurdity
carried to its ～ 极端的荒谬 ②基本原理 ‖～**ly**
ad. / ～**ness** n. ‖～ **analysis** 【化】元素分析 /
Ultimate Reality 主宰一切的最高权力(宗教中
指上帝)

ultimatum [ˌʌltiˈmeitəm] ([复] ultimatums 或
ultimata [ˌʌltiˈmeitə]) n. ①最后通牒, 哀的美敦
书 ②最后的结论 ③基本原理

ultra ['ʌltrə] **I** a. 过激的; 极端的 **II** n. 过激派;
走极端的人 ‖～**ism** n. 过激论; 极端主义 /
～**ist** n. & a. 极端主义者(的)

ultramarine[1] [ˌʌltrəməˈriːn] a. 在海那边的, 在海
外的

ultramarine[2] [ˌʌltrəməˈriːn] **I** n. ①【化】佛青, 群
青(一种合成的蓝色颜料): yellow ～ 黄佛青 /
synthetic ～ 合成佛青 ②深蓝色 **II** a. 佛青的;
深蓝色的

umbrage ['ʌmbridʒ] n. ①树荫; (成荫的)簇叶;
[诗]荫影 ②生气, 不愉快: give ～ 惹怒, 使生气 /
take ～ at a remark 为一句话而生气 ③细微的
迹象: His opinion carries no ～ of reason. 他的
意见一点道理也没有。④怀疑

umbrella [ʌmˈbrelə] **I** n. ①雨伞; [罕] (女用)阳
伞: open (shut) an ～ 张 (收)雨伞 ②伞形物;
[喻] (政治等方面的)保护, 保护伞: under the ～
of 在…的保护下 / a nuclear ～ 核保护伞 ③
【军】(战斗机形成的)掩护幕; (阻击敌机的)火力
网: an air ～ 空中掩护幕 / an ～ barrage 防空
火网 ④【动】(水母等的)伞膜 ⑤[船]烟囱顶罩
II a. (似)伞的; (组织等)机构庞大的, 包含无遗
的 **III** vt. 用伞遮盖; 以战斗机队掩护幕保护; 以
保护伞保护 ‖～ **arch** 【建】道口拱 / ～ **stand**
伞架 / ～ **tree** 木兰树(尤指三瓣木兰); 伞形树

umpire ['ʌmpaiə] **I** n. ①公断人, 仲裁人; 【律】裁
决者(指仲裁人之间意见不一致时参加公断的第
三者) ②(棒球、板球等的)裁判员; 【军】演习裁判
(指演习中担任裁判和讲评的军官) ③决定性的
事物 **II** ❶ vt. 仲裁; 裁判 ❷ vi. 任公断人; 当
裁判: ～ in a dispute 在争论中任公断人 ‖～-
ship n. =umpirage

un , 'un [ʌn] pron. [口]家伙, 人; 东西: He's a
tough ～. 他是个厉害的家伙。‖*a good* ～ [口]
①优秀人物; 好人 ②极好的东西; 非伪造的东西
③巧妙的谎言; 有趣的故事 / *a red* ～ [俚]金
币; 金表 / *a stiff* ～ ①[口]老运动员 ②[俚]
(赛马中)一定要输的马 ③[俚]尸体 / *a wrong*
～ [俚] ①坏人 ②伪造的货币

unabated ['ʌnəˈbeitid] a. (风暴等)不减弱的; 不
衰退的: Thunderous cheers continued ～ for a
long time. 欢呼声雷动, 经久不息。‖～**ly** ad.

unaccountable ['ʌnəˈkauntəbl] a. ①无法解释的;
不可理解的 ②无责任的 ‖**unaccountability**
['ʌnəˌkauntə'biliti] n. / **unaccountably** ad.

unanimity [ˌjuːnəˈnimiti] n. (全体)一致; 一致同
意: achieve ～ through consultation 通过协商
达到一致 / reach ～ of views on some problems
在某些问题上取得一致意见

unanimous [juⁿˈnæniməs] a. (全体)一致的; 一
致同意的; 无异议的: The meeting was ～ in
support of the decision. 与会者一致拥护这个
决议。/ be elected by a ～ vote 以全票当选
‖～**ly** ad.

unassuming ['ʌnəˈsjuːmiŋ] a. 不摆架子的; 不装
腔作势的; 不傲慢的, 谦逊的

unawares [ˌʌnə'wɛəz] *ad.* ① 冷不防地，出其不意地，突然地: be caught ~ 措手不及地被抓住(或被发觉) ②不知不觉地;无意中: You must have dropped it ~. 你一定是不留神时把它丢了。

unbalance [ˈʌn'bæləns] **I** *vt.* ① 使失去平衡; 使不均衡 ②使(精神)错乱, 使紊乱 **II** *n.* 不均衡; 失衡; 错乱, 紊乱 ‖~**d** *a.* ①不均衡的; 失衡的 ②精神失常的, 错乱的; 不稳定的; (判断等)不可靠的 ③未决算的; 借贷不平衡的, 收支不平衡的

unbend [ˈʌn'bend] (unbent [ˈʌn'bent]) ❶ *vt.* ①弄直; 伸直; 放直 ②放松; 使松懈: ~ a bow 放松弓弦 / ~ one's mind 散心 ③解开(绳索等); 卸下(帆等): ~ a cable 解开锚索 ❷ *vi.* ①变直 ②松弛; 变得随意, 变得不一本正经; 变得和蔼

unbosom [ʌn'buzəm] *vt. & vi.* 吐露(心事), 暴露(思想); 说出(秘密) ‖~ **oneself** 吐露心事, 表明心迹; 暴露思想

unbridle [ˈʌn'braidl] *vt.* ① 去掉(马)的辔头, 放松(马)的缰绳 ②[喻]对…不加拘束; 放纵: ~ the tongue 信口开河 ‖~**d** *a.* ①(马等)脱缰的, 无约束的 ②[喻]放纵的, 放肆的; 激烈的: ~d passions 放纵的情欲 / ~d behaviour 放纵的行为

unburden [ʌn'bə:dn] *vt.* ①卸去…的负担 ②[喻](卸去精神负担似地)表白; 吐露: ~ one's resentment against sb. 发泄(或表明)对某人的不满 / ~ oneself (或 one's heart) to sb. 向某人倾诉衷情 / ~ oneself of a secret 讲出秘密

uncanny [ʌn'kæni] *a.* ①怪模怪样的, 可怕的 ②离奇的; 神秘的; 不可思议的 ③[方]危险的 ④[方](打击)猛烈的; (创伤)严重的

uncared-for [ʌn'kɛədfɔ:] *a.* 没人照顾的; 没人注意的; 被忽视的: an ~ garden 弃园

uncle [ʌŋkl] *n.* ① 伯父; 叔父; 舅父; 姑丈; 姨丈 ②[口](对年长者的称呼)叔叔, 伯伯 ③ 援助者, 忠告者, 鼓励者: He played ~ to the movement. 他赞助这项运动。④ [俚] 开当铺者 ⑤ [U-] = Uncle Sam ‖my ~ [俚] 开当铺者 / my ~'s [俚] 当铺 / 厕所 / say (或 cry) ~ 认输, 承认失败 / talk to sb. like a Dutch ~ 严厉地告诫某人 / your ~ [俚](自称)我, 咱, 老子 ‖Uncle Sam [口]山姆大叔(美国, 美国政府或美国人的绰号) / Uncle Sam's action [美俚] 征召入伍 / Uncle Tom 汤姆叔叔(美国女作家斯陀一八五二年发表的长篇小说《汤姆叔叔的小屋》中的主人公); [喻]逆来顺受的黑人 / Uncle Tomism (黑人的)逆来顺受主义

unconformable [ˈʌn-kən'fɔ:məbl] *a.* ①不顺从的, 不服从的 ②不适合的; 不一致的 ③【地】不整合的

unconscionable [ʌn'kɔnʃənəbl] *a.* ①非由良心引导的, 不受良心节制的; 肆无忌惮的 ②过度的; 不合理的; 极不公正的; 骇人的

uncouth [ʌn'ku:θ] *a.* ① (人, 动作等)笨拙的; 粗野的; (言语)粗鲁的 ②(生活)不文明的, 不舒适的;

③[书面语](地方)人迹稀少的, 荒凉的 ④[古]不知道的; 陌生的 ‖~**ly** *ad.* / ~**ness** *n.*

unction [ʌŋkʃən] *n.* ①涂油; [宗]涂油礼: extreme ~ (天主教和东正教的)临终涂油礼 ②油, 油膏; 软膏 ③ 使人感到安慰的话(或环境等) ④ (宗教性的)热忱 ⑤假情假意; 甜言蜜语 ⑥浓厚的兴趣;津津有味: tell a story with much ~ 津津有味地讲故事

unctuous [ʌŋktjuəs] *a.* ①. 油的; 油膏的; 含油脂的 ②油似的; 腻滑的 ③松软肥沃的: ~ soil 松软肥沃的土壤 ④ 塑性的: fine ~ clay 细的重粘土 ⑤油滑的; 甜言蜜语的; 假殷勤的

under [ʌndə] **I** *prep.* ①[表示位置]在…下面; 在…底下; 在…之中, 在…之内: every place ~ the sun 普天之下 / a field ~ corn 种玉米的田, 玉米地 / swim ~ the water 在水下潜泳 / ~ the skin 皮下 / stand ~ the wall 站在墙脚下 / The child ran out from ~ the tree. 孩子从树下跑出来。/ wear a sweater ~ one's jacket 在外套里面穿着运动衫 / send a catalogue ~ separate cover 将目录另封寄发 ②[表示级别, 数量, 标准等]低于…; 少于…; 在…以下: officers ~ a colonel 上校以下的军官 / children ~ twelve years of age 十二岁以下的儿童 / Under fifty people were there. 在那里的人不足五十。/ run a hundred metres in ~ eleven seconds 在十一秒内跑完一百米 / sell sth. ~ five dollars 在五元以下出售某物 ③[表示从属关系]在…之下; 在…指引下; 在…指导下: democracy ~ centralized guidance 集中指导下的民主 / study the piano ~ sb. 在某人指导下学弹钢琴 / serve ~ a colonel 在上校手下任职 ④[表示负荷, 条件等]在…之下: ~ a heavy load 在重担之下 / ~ attack 受到攻击 / ~ the circumstances 在这些情况下 / the district ~ martial law 戒严地区 / ~ this heading 在这个标题下 ⑤[表示名义, 假托等]在…之下: ~ sb.'s signature (或 hand) 经某人签名 / ~ the pretext of 以…为借口 / ~ a false name 用假名 ⑥[表示过程]在…中; 在…期间: the road ~ repair 修理中的道路 / the question ~ discussion 讨论中的问题 / the patient ~ treatment 治疗中的病人 / land ~ cultivation 耕地 / ~ way 在进行中 / ~ the Third French Republic 在法兰西第三共和国时期 **II** *a.* 下面的; 次一级的, 从属的; 标准以下的: the ~ layer 下面的一层 / an ~ dose of medicine 低剂量的药 **III** *ad.* 在下; 从属地; 少于: A cloth should be spread ~. 下面该铺一块布。

undercurrent [ˈʌndəˌkʌrənt] *n.* ① 潜流, 底流 ②[喻](舆论, 感情等的)暗流; 掩盖着的倾向; 潜在势力 ③[电]电流不足 ④[矿]宽平的分支洗金槽

undercut I [ˈʌndəkʌt] *n.* ①底切; 底切部 ②(伐树)砍口 ③[英](牛)软腰肉 ④(拳击中)的上击; (网球等的)下旋球 **II** [ˌʌndə'kʌt] (undercut; undercutting) ❶ *vt.* ①从下面切开; 底切 ②掘(矿层)的下部 ③雕出(花样), 浮雕(花样) ④削

低(商品价格)，削价与…抢生意；愿拿较低工资与
…抢饭碗(指职位) ⑤【体】用下旋手法击(球等)
❷ *vi.* 切去下部；底切

underdog ['ʌndədɔg] *n.* ① 斗输了的狗 ② 竞争失
败的人；处于劣势的一方 ③ 受迫害者；倒霉的人

underdone ['ʌndə'dʌn] I underdo 的过去分词
II *a.* (尤指肉)不太熟的；煮得嫩的；半生不熟的:
The beef is ～. 牛肉未煮透。

undergird ['ʌndə'gə:d] *vt.* ① 从底层加固，从底层
支持 ②支持；加强

undergo [,ʌndə'gou] (underwent [,ʌndə'went],
undergone [,ʌndə'gɔn]) *vt.* 经历，经受；忍受:
～ a long process of tempering 经过长期的磨练 /
～ a surgical operation 经受外科手术

undergraduate [,ʌndə'grædjuit] I *n.* 大学肄业
生,(尚未取得学位的)大学生 II *a.* 大学生的；大
学生身分的: ～ studies 大学生的研究科目

underground ['ʌndə'graund] I *a.* ①地下的,地面
下的: an ～ railway 地下铁道 / an ～ nuclear
test 地下核试验 ②秘密的；隐蔽的；不公开的:
the ～ movement 秘密抵抗运动 / engage in ～
work 做地下工作 ③(报刊或电影)在本机构之外
出版(或制作)的；反现存体制的；先锋派的，先锋
派出版(或制作)的；标新立异的II [,ʌndə'graund]
ad. ①在地下 ②秘密地；隐蔽地: go ～ 转入地
下 III *n.* ①地面下层 ②地下空间；地道 ③[英]
地下铁道(美国称 subway) ④ 秘密活动；地下组
织,秘密团体 ⑤先锋派运动(或团体) ‖～er *n.*
①在地面下工作的人 ②秘密组织成员 ③地下铁
道乘客 ‖ ～ railroad ①[英]地下铁道 ②[U- R-]
【美史】(反对奴隶制者)帮助南方奴隶潜逃到北方
(或加拿大)的秘密组织

undergrowth ['ʌndə-grouθ] *n.* ①(长在大树下的)
下层林丛，下木 ② (动物长毛下面的)浓密绒毛
③发育不全

underhand ['ʌndəhænd] *a.* & *ad.* ① 秘密的(地)；
欺诈的(地)；阴险的(地) ②(打球时)手不过肩(或
肘)的(地) ③(射箭中)瞄准时目标见于左手下方
的(地)

underlie [,ʌndə'lai] (underlay [,ʌndə'lei], under-
lain [,ʌndə'lein]; underlying [,ʌndə'laiiŋ]) *vt.*
①位于…的下面,放在…的下面 ②支承；构成(理
论、政策、行为等)的基础 ③屈服于: a ～
challenge 不敢应战 ④[商](权利、索赔等)优先于

underline¹ I [,ʌndə'lain] *vt.* ①划线于…之下:
a sentence 在句子下划线 ②[喻]强调；使突出 ③
预告: The book is ～d for publication next
month. 预告这本书将在下月出版。 II ['ʌndə-
lain] *n.* ① 划在下面的线 ② (在戏单下面的)下
期节目预告；插图下面的说明 ③动物下体的轮廓

underline² [,ʌndə'lain] *vt.* 作…的衬里: a collar
～d with white 用白色布作衬里的衣领

underling ['ʌndəliŋ] *n.* [贬]下属；下手；走卒

undermine [,ʌndə'main] *vt.* ① 在…下挖坑道；削
弱…的基础: ～ a wall 挖墙脚 / Streams ～ the

rocks. 流水侵蚀岩石的基础。②暗中破坏；逐渐
损害: ～ sb.'s reputation 暗中破坏某人的名誉 /
～ sb.'s health 损害某人健康 ‖～r *n.* ①挖坑道
者 ②暗中破坏者

underneath [,ʌndə'ni:θ] I *ad.* ①在下面,在底下:
a mansion with a solid foundation ～ 下面有坚
实地基的大厦 ②在下部,在下层 II *prep.* ①在
…下面,在…之下: ～ the address. 把日期写在地址下面。②在
…的形式下；在…的乔装下: treachery lying ～ a
mask of friendliness 口蜜腹剑；笑里藏刀 ③隶属
于；在…的支配下: ～ the tyranny of 在…的暴
虐统治下 III *a.* 下面的；底层的 IV *n.* 下部；下
面: the ～ of a pot 壶底

underpin [,ʌndə'pin] (underpinned; underpinning) *vt.* ① 在…的下面加基础；加强…的基础:
～ a sagging building 在下陷的建筑物下加固基
础 ② [喻]支持；巩固: a hopeless attempt to ～
the tottering colonial rule 枉费心机地支持摇摇
欲坠的殖民统治的企图 / ～ a thesis with
evidence 用证据支持一论点 ‖**underpinning** *n.*
①基础材料,基础结构 ②[常用复](学说、理论等
的)基础 ③[常用复](人的)腿

underprivileged ['ʌndə'priviliʤd] *a.* ①(阶级、阶
层、民族等)被剥夺基本社会权利的；贫困的 ②社
会地位低下的；下层社会的: the ～ 下层社会

undersell ['ʌndə'sel] (undersold ['ʌndə'sould]) *vt.*
① 售价比…低 ② 廉价出卖(商品)

undersign [,ʌndə'sain] *vt.* 签名于(信、文件)的末
尾 ‖～ed *a.* 在下面(或文件末尾)签名的 *n.*
['ʌndəsaind] [the ～ed] [用作单或复](下面的或
文件末尾的)签名者,签名人

understand [,ʌndə'stænd] (过去式 understood
[,ʌndə'stud], 过去分词 understood 或[古] un-
derstanded) ❶ *vt.* ①懂；理解；熟悉；通晓:
Do you ～ English? 你懂英语吗? / His behaviour is hard to ～. 他的行为难以理解。 / ～ the
masses 了解群众 / Everything that exists objec-
tively can be *understood*. 客观存在的事物都是能
够了解的。 / This old peasant ～s rice planting
as nobody else can. 这位老农民对种稻比谁都熟
悉。 / It is *understood* that …. 不用说…(或:
…是不言而喻的。) ② 获悉；听说: We ～ from
an authoritative source that …. 我们从权威
方面获悉… / So I ～. 我听说是如此。③推断,
认为: What did you ～ him to say? 你认为他说
的是什么意思呢? / Am I to ～ that you refuse?
我可以认为你是拒绝了吗? ④[常用被动语态](因
含意自明而) 省略: In this case the verb may be
either expressed or *understood*. 在这种情况下动
词可用可不用。 ❷ *vi.* ①懂得,取得理解: Even-
tually he will ～. 他终究会理解的。 ②[用作插
入语]据说；认为: He is ～, no longer here. 据
说,他离开这里了。 ③给予同情(或谅解等): rely
on sb. to ～ and sympathize 依赖某人的谅解和
同情 ‖***a tongue not ～ed of the people*** 外国

语 / **give sb. to ~** 使某人领会；通知某人: He *gave* me *to* ~ that the meetng would take place. 从他的话里我了解会是要开的。/ ***make oneself understood*** 表达自己的意思，使旁人理解自己的意思: Can you *make yourself understood* in English? 你能用英语表达自己的意思吗? / **Now, ~ me!** 喂，听着! (表示警告或恐吓) / **~ one another** 相互了解；明了彼此的看法(或情绪、意图等): They have not reached an agreement yet, but at least they ~ *one another*. 他们还没达成协议，但至少了解了彼此的看法。‖**~able** *a.* 可懂的; 可了解的

understanding [ˌʌndə'stændiŋ] **I** *n.* ①了解；理解；领会；认识: This is my ~ of the matter. 这是我对这事的理解(或认识)。/ subjective ~ 主观认识 ②理解力；判断力: lack ~ 缺乏理解力 ③同情心，同感; 友好的关系，融洽 ④[常与不定冠词连用，罕用复数](非正式的)协定; 协议; 谅解: a tacit ~ 默契 / reach (或 come to, arrive at) an ~ (with sb. about sth.) (与某人对某事)达成非正式的协议 / mutual ~ 互相谅解 ⑤(德国古典哲学中用语)知性 (reason 理性之对) ⑥[复][俚]脚; 腿; 鞋 **II** *a.* ①了解的; 有理解力的; 聪明的: an ~ smile 会心的微笑 ②能谅解的，宽容的 ‖**on the ~ that** 以…为条件; 如果… / **with** (或 **on**) **this** ~ 根据这个条件，在此条件下

understudy ['ʌndəˌstʌdi] **I** *n.* ①[戏]预备演员，替角 ②熟悉某工作以便接替的人 **II** ❶ *vt.* ①学习(某角色)以便当替角; 练习代演(某角色) ②通过观察(或实习)掌握(某工作) ❷ *vi.* 练习当替角

undertake [ˌʌndə'teik] (undertook [ˌʌndə'tuk], undertaken [ˌʌndə'teikən]) ❶ *vt.* ①着手做；进行，从事: ~ self-criticism 作自我批评 / ~ a journey 去旅行 / ~ detailed and comprehensive investigations 从事细致和全面的调查 ②承担; 接受; 同意: ~ responsibility 承担责任 / ~ a patient 接受病人 / He *undertook* to be (或 to act as) our guide. 他同意做我们的向导。③保证: I will ~ that all the cattle shall (或 will) grow well. 我保证所有的牲畜都能养好。❷ *vi.* ①[古]担保; 负责 (for): ~ for sb.'s security 担保某人的安全 ②[口]承办丧葬事宜 ‖**~r** *n.* ①承担者，承办人 ②企业家 ③['ʌndəˌteikə] 承办丧葬者，殡仪员

undertaking [ˌʌndə'teikiŋ] *n.* ①任务; 事业; 企业: a difficult but glorious ~ 一项艰苦而光荣的任务 / a mass ~ 群众性的事业 ②承担; 许诺，保证 ③['ʌndəˌteikiŋ] 丧葬事宜，殡仪业

undertone ['ʌndətoun] *n.* ①低音; 小声: talk in ~s 低声说话 ②淡色; 底彩 ③(言行中的)含意; 市场的潜在倾向: an ~ of doubt 怀疑的口气

undertow ['ʌndətou] *n.* ①回头浪 ②【地】底流

underwear ['ʌndəwɛə] *n.* [总称]衬衣，内衣

underworld ['ʌndəwə:ld] *n.* ①[古]地球，大地 ②阴间，地狱 ③对跖点(地球上某一点的相对点)

④下流社会; 以卖淫、盗窃等为生的人们 ⑤下层社会，底层社会

underwrite ['ʌndərait] (underwrote ['ʌndərout], underwritten ['ʌndəˌritn]) ❶ *vt.* ①写在…下面(或末尾) ②签名于(保险单等); 给…保险 ③签名同意负担…费用 ④认购(证券、公债等); 认捐 ⑤赞同 ❷ *vi.* 经营(海上)保险业 ‖**~r** *n.* 担保人; 保险商(尤指水险商); (证券、公债等的)认购者 / **underwriting** *n.* (海上)保险业

undies ['ʌndiz] [复] *n.* [口]内衣(尤指妇女的内衣)

undo [ʌn'du:] (undid [ʌn'did], undone [ʌn'dʌn]; 第三人称单数现在式 undoes ['ʌn'dʌz]) ❶ *vt.* ①解开，打开; 使松开; 脱去(衣服等): ~ a knot (button) 解开结子(钮扣) / ~ a parcel 打开包裹 ②取消，消除; 使失效; 使复旧: What's done cannot be *undone*. [谚]事已定局，无可挽回。(或: 覆水难收。) ③破坏，败坏(成果、名誉等); 使败落; 毁灭 ④扰乱，使不安 ⑤勾引，引诱 ❷ *vi.* 开，松开 ‖**~er** *n.* 破坏者; 勾引者 / **~ing** *n.* ①解开，打开 ②取消; 复旧 ③破坏; 毁灭; 毁灭的原因，祸根

undomesticated ['ʌn-də'mestikeitid] *a.* ①(动物)未驯服的: an ~ horse 未驯服的马 ②不适应家庭生活的; 不喜欢家庭的; 不善于(或不爱)做家务的

undue [ʌn'dju:] *a.* ①过度的，过分的; 不适当的: lay ~ emphasis on sth. 过分强调某事 / treat the matter with ~ haste 过急地处理这事 ②不正当的，非法的: ~ influence 【律】威胁手段 ③【商】未到(支付)期的

undulate ['ʌndjuleit] **I** ❶ *vi.* ①(水面等)波动，起浪; (地形、声音等)起伏 ②呈波浪形; 形成波浪; 成波浪形前进 ❷ *vt.* ①使波动; 使起伏 ②使成波浪形 **II** *a.* 波浪形的; 起伏的 ‖**undulation** [ˌʌndju'leiʃən] *n.*

unduly [ʌn'dju:li] *ad.* ①过度地，过分地; 不适当地 ②不正当地

unearth [ʌn'ə:θ] *vt.* ①(从地下)发掘，掘出: ~ relics of early civilization 发掘早期文化的遗迹 ②揭露; 发现: ~ a plot 揭露阴谋 / ~ new facts 发现新事实 ③从洞中赶出(狐等)

unearthly [ʌn'ə:θli] *a.* ①不属于现世的; 非尘世的; 超自然的 ②精神的，理想的 ③神秘的; 鬼怪的; 可怕的 ④[口]不合理的，荒谬的; 不可思议的

uneasy [ʌn'i:zi] **I** *a.* ①心神不安的，忧虑的，担心的: feel ~ about sth. 为某事感到不安 ②拘束的，不自在的: ~ manners 拘束的态度 ③不稳定的; 不宁静的; 汹涌的: an ~ coalition cabinet 不稳定的联合内阁 / ~ waters 汹涌的水流 ④[古]不舒服的，不适意的 ⑤[古]不容易的，困难的; 难行的 **II** *ad.* 心神不安; 不自在地; 不稳地

unerring [ʌn'ə:riŋ] *a.* 没有偏差的，准确的; 没有过错的: fire with ~ aim 准确地射击 / be ~ in judgement 判断正确 ‖**~ly** *ad.*

unexampled [ˌʌnig'zɑ:mpld] *a.* 无先例的，空前

的; 绝无仅有的

unfailing [ʌn'feiliŋ] *a.* ①无穷无尽的; 经久不衰的; 永恒的: an ～ supply of water 源源不断的水的供应 / a subject of ～ interest 引人经久感兴趣的题目 ②可靠的, 永不辜负期望的: an ～ test 准确可靠的试验 / an ～ defender 忠实可靠的保卫者 ‖～ly *ad.* / ～ness *n.*

unfold¹ [ʌn'fould] ❶ *vt.* ①展开, 摊开; 打开: ～ a map 摊开地图 / ～ a parcel 打开包裹 ②开展(运动等): ～ a mass movement 开展群众运动 ③逐渐表露; 阐明: ～ one's thought 逐渐敞开自己的思想 ❷ *vi.* ①伸展; 开花 ②(运动等)展开, 发展 ③显露, 呈现: The landscape ～ed before us. 风景展现在我们眼前。

unfold² [ʌn'fould] *vt.* 放(羊)出栏

unfounded ['ʌn'faundid] *a.* ①没有事实根据的, 没有理由的; 虚幻的: These slanders are absolutely ～. 这些诽谤是毫无事实根据的。/ an ～ talk 无稽之谈 ②未建立的

unfrock ['ʌn'frɔk] *vt.* ①脱去…的法衣; 免去…的圣职 ②剥夺…的职权

ungainly [ʌn'geinli] *a. & ad.* ①笨拙的(地); 笨重的(地) ②难看的(地); 不雅的(地) ‖**ungainliness** *n.*

ungovernable [ʌn'gʌvənəbl] *a.* ①难统治的; 难抑制的 ②放肆的, 任性的; 野性难驯的 ‖**ungovernably** *ad.*

unguarded ['ʌn'gɑ:did] *a.* ①没有防备的; 易受攻击的: an ～ gate 没人看守的门 ②不留神的, 大意的; 不慎重的, 轻率的: In an ～ moment he gave away the secret. 他一时没留神泄漏了秘密。‖～ly *ad.*

unheard-of [ʌn'hə:dɔv] *a.* 前所未闻的; 没有前例的; 空前的

unhinge [ʌn'hindʒ] *vt.* ①把…从铰链上取下; 把铰链从…上拆下: ～ an old barn door 把旧谷仓的门从铰链上取下 ②使移走, 使分开, 使裂开 ③使动摇; 使错乱, 使失常

unicorn ['ju:nikɔ:n] *n.* ①(传说中)身体似马的独角兽; (指纹章)有山羊胡子和狮尾的独角兽标记; (基督教《圣经》中)似牛的双角兽 ②【动】一角(齿鲸的一种) ③一匹在前两匹并列在后的一组马

unicorn

uniform ['ju:nifɔ:m] **I** *a.* ①(与其他)一样的, 相同的, 一致的: of ～ size and shape 大小和形状

一样的 / present a ～ appearance 呈现相同的外表 / be ～ with the other volumes 与其他各卷大小一律 ②一直不变的; 始终如一的; 一贯的: keep a room at a ～ temperature 使房间保持恒温 ③均质的, 均匀的: ～ load【机】均匀负载 / ～ motion 匀速运动, 等速运动 / ～ acceleration 匀加速度, 等加速度 **II** *n.* 制服; 军服: a nurse's ～ 护士制服 / a school ～ 学生制服 / in full ～ 穿着全套军礼服 / out of ～ 穿着便服 / a dress ～ 军礼服 / an undress ～ 军便服 **III** *vt.* ①使一样, 使一律化 ②使穿制服(或军服) ‖～ise, ～ize *vt.* 使成一样, 使一致 / ～ly *ad.*

uniformity [ˌju:ni'fɔ:miti] *n.* ①一样, 一式; 一律; 一致(性): variety and ～ 多样性和一致性 ②均一, 均匀(性)

unify ['ju:nifai] *vt.* 统一, 使成一体; 使一致, 使一元化: ～ the thinking of 统一……的思想 / distribute in a *unified* way 统一分配 / a *unified* command 联合指挥部

unimpeachable [ˌʌnim'pi:tʃəbl] *a.* 无可指摘的; 无懈可击的; 无可怀疑的: an ～ reputation 清白的名声 / news from an ～ source 来源可靠的消息 ‖**unimpeachably** *ad.*

union ['ju:njən] *n.* ①联合; 合并: effect a ～ 实现联合 ②团结; 一致; 融洽: in (perfect) ～ (完全)一致地; (十分)融洽地 / Union is (或 gives) strength. 团结就是力量。③联邦; 联盟: the *Union* of Soviet Socialist Republics 苏维埃社会主义共和国联盟(简称 the Soviet *Union* 苏联) / the Universal Postal *Union* 万国邮政联盟(联合国) ④协会; 联合会; 公会; 工会: a labour ～ 工会 ⑤[英]【宗】教区间的救济联合组织; 教区间联合组织的救济院 ⑥国旗上象征政治统一的图案(位于旗的内上角或全旗); 旗帜的内上角: hoist an ensign ～ down (船遇险求救时)升起倒挂旗 ⑦结婚; 性交: a happy ～ 美满的婚姻 ⑧连接; 结合; 【机】联管节, 管(子)接头 (=pipe ～); 【医】愈合: ～ link 联结环 / ～ nut 联管螺母 / ～ by first intention 第一期愈合 ⑨【纺】交织织物; 混纺织物 ‖*the Union* ①[英史]一七〇六年英格兰和苏格兰的合并 / 一八〇一年大不列颠和爱尔兰的合并 ②美利坚合众国: the President's address to *the Union* 美国总统对全国的演讲 ③大学学生俱乐部(或其会所): the debate of *the* Oxford *Union* 牛津大学学生俱乐部举行的辩论会 ‖～crat *n.* 工会迷; 工联主义者 ‖～-'busting *n.* & *a.* 打击工会(的) / ～ card 工会会员证 / **Union Jack, Union flag** 英国国旗 / ～ shop [美]资方与工会订约规定雇用的非工会成员必须在一定时期内加入工会的工商企业 / ～ suit 连衫裤

unionist ['ju:njənist] *n.* ①联合主义者 ②工会会员 ③工会主义者; 工联主义者 ④[U-](美国南北战争时期的)联邦主义者, 联邦政府的支持者 ⑤[U-]【史】爱尔兰自由邦成立前反对爱尔兰自治的英国人; 爱尔兰自由邦成立前的英国保守党党员 ‖～ic [ˌju:njə'nistik] *a.*

unique [juː'niːk] **I** *a.* ①唯一的,独一无二的;无比的,无可匹敌的;独特的: an almost ~ experience 可算是独特的经历 / The problem is by no means ~ to this region. 这问题决不是这个地区所独有的。②[口]珍奇的,罕有的;不平凡的;极好的: a ~ opportunity 极难得的机会 / ~ ability 罕见的才能 ③【物】单值的 **II** *n.* 独一无二的事物 ‖~ly *ad.* / ~ness *n.*

unison ['juːnizn] **I** *n.* ①一致;调和 ②【音】同度,同音; 齐唱,齐奏: sing in ~ 齐声歌唱 **II** *a.* 【音】同度的,同音的

unit ['juːnit] **I** *n.* ①单位(指构成整体的人、物、团体、机构等): a productive ~ 生产单位 / an administrative ~ 行政单位 / The clause is a larger ~ than the phrase in the sentence. 在句子中从句是比词组更大的单位。②【军】小队, 分队;部队: a mechanized ~ 机械化部队 ③(计数或计量的)单位;单元: a C. G. S. ~ 厘米克秒制单位 / Each gram contains 5,000 international ~s of penicillin. 每克含青霉素五千国际单位。/ an arithmetic ~ 运算单元 ④(机械等的)部件,元件;装置,组: a plug-in ~ 插入部件 / a ~ of structure 构件 / a tuner (或 tuning) ~ 调谐装置,调谐器 / a power ~ 动力组;电源设置 ⑤(教学学分的)学习量(通常根据上课时数来决定);教学单元 ⑥最小整数,一,基数 ⑦一套用具: a kitchen ~ 一套厨房用具(如污水槽、碗橱等) **II** *a.* 单位的;单元的;一套的: ~ area 单位面积 / a ~ price 单价 / ~ furniture 成套家具 ‖be a ~ [美]一致: They *are* not yet *a* ~ on the question. 在这个问题上意见还没一致。‖~ **character** 【生】单位性状 / ~ **rule** [美]单位投票法(以代表团为单位,根据本团多数意见,作为一个单位向大会投票) / ~ **train** 运送单一商品的火车

unite [juː'nait] **❶** *vi.* ①联合;团结 ②粘合;混合: Oil will not ~ *with* water. 油水不相融。③联合行动;一致行动 **❷** *vt.* ①使联合;统一;使团结: be ~*d* as one 团结一致 ②使粘合;使混合: ~ the parts with cement 用水泥把各部分连接起来 ③兼备(各种特性) ④使结婚

united [juː'naitid] *a.* ①联合的;统一的 ②团结的,一致的;和睦的: make a ~ effort 同心协力 / a ~ family 和睦的家庭 ‖a ~ front 统一战线,联合阵线;人民阵线 / the United *Kingdom* (大不列颠和北爱尔兰)联合王国;【英史】(1801—1922 的大不列颠和爱尔兰)联合王国 / the United Nations 联合国 / United Nations Day 联合国建立纪念日(十月二十四日) / the United Nations General Assembly 联合国大会 / the United Nations Organization 联合国组织 / the United Nations Security Council 联合国安全理事会 / United Press International 合众国际社(美国) / the United States (of America) 美利坚合众国,美国 ‖~ly *ad.* ‖United-Statesian [juː'naitid'steitsiən] *n.* 美国人 *a.* 美国的

unity ['juːniti] *n.* ①单一;个体;整体 ②统一(性);一致(性);协调(性);统一体: the ~ of opposites 对立的统一 / the ~ of motive and effect 动机和效果的统一 / bring about the ~ of a country 实现国家的统一 / live in (或 at) ~ 和睦相处 / the ~ of a painting 画面的协调 / ~ in variety 多样化中的统一性(一种美学原理) ③团结;联合: Unity is strength, ~ is victory. 团结就是力量,团结就是胜利。④(目的、行动等的)一贯性,不变性 ⑤【数】单位元素;一 ⑥【律】共同租地权 ‖the dramatic unities (或 the unities of action, time, and place) 三一律(十七世纪欧洲古典主义戏剧创作原则,规定剧本必须在情节、时间、地点上一致)

universal [ˌjuːni'vəːsəl] **I** *a.* ①宇宙的;全世界的: ~ gravitation 万有引力 ②普遍的;普通的,一般的;全体的;影响全体的: a ~ rule 众人的法则 / a ~ affirmative 全体一致的肯定 ③通用的,广用的;万能的;多才多艺的: a ~ milling machine 万能铣床 / a ~ motor 交直流两用电动机 / a ~ meter 通用电表 / a ~ instrument 万能仪 / a ~ provider 百货商 ④【逻】全称的: a ~ proposition 全称命题 **II** *n.* ①【逻】全称命题 ②【哲】一般概念 ③带有普遍性的生活方式(一定社会的)成年人普遍具有的文化特征 ‖~ly *ad.* ‖~ **agent** 全权代理人 / ~ **chuck** 【机】万能夹头,万能夹具 / ~ **compass** 万能两脚规 / ~ **coupling**, ~ **joint** 【机】万向(联轴)节 / ~ **language** 世界通用语 / ~ **successor**, **legatee** 全财产继承人 / ~ **suffrage** 普选权 / ~ **time** 世界时,格林威治时

universe ['juːnivəːs] *n.* ①宇宙;世界;天地万物;万象;全人类 ②【逻】整体;(思想、学科等自成体系的)领域: the ~ of discourse 论域 ③【天】银河系,恒星与星辰系

university [ˌjuːni'vəːsiti] *n.* ① 综合性大学;大学: go to (the) ~ 上大学 ②[总称]大学人员(包括学生、教职员等) ③【体】大学选手(队)‖~ **college** 附属于大学的学院 / ~ **extension** 大学的附设部分(如夜校、函授部等)

unkempt ['ʌn'kempt] *a.* ①(头发)未梳的,蓬乱的;不整洁的,邋遢的: an ~ appearance 不修边幅的外貌 ②(言语等)粗野的,修辞粗糙的

unless [ən'les, ʌn'les] **I** *conj.* 如果不;除非: I will not go ~ I hear from him. 如果他不通知我,我就不去。/ I shall go there ~ it rains. 如果不下雨,我将到那里去。/ We shall not call the meeting ~ absolutely necessary. 除非绝对必要,我们将不召开会议。**II** *prep.* 除…之外 ‖~ *and until* 直到…才 (=until)

unlettered ['ʌn'letəd] *a.* ① 未受教育的;文盲的,不识字的 ② 无学问的,无学识的 ③ 无字的: an ~ tombstone 无字的墓碑

unlooked-for [ʌn'luktfɔː] *a.* 非寻求来的;意外的,

没有预料到的: an ~ guest 一位不期而来的客人,不速之客

unman ['ʌn'mæn] (unmanned; unmanning) *vt.* ① 使失去男子汉气概; 使懦弱; 使泄气 ②阉割 ③撤去(船只或舰队)的人员

unmatched [ʌn'mætʃt] *a.* ① 无敌的, 无比的 ②(颜色、设计等)不相配的

unmeaning [ʌn'miːniŋ] *a.* ① 无表情的, 呆板的: an ~ facial expression 呆板的面部表情 ② 无意义的; 索然无味的

unmentionable [ʌn'menʃənəbl] **I** *a.* 说不出口的; 不宜在社交场合提到的 **II** *n.* [复] 不宜说出来(或议论)的东西; [谑] 裤子; 内衣

unmistakable ['ʌnmis'teikəbl] *a.* 不会弄错的; 不会被误解的; 清楚明白的 ‖**unmistakably** *ad.*

unmitigated [ʌn'mitigeitid] *a.* ① 未缓和的, 未减轻的: The heat is ~. 热未减退。 ② 纯粹的, 十足的, 完完全全的: an ~ lie 纯粹的谎话 / an ~ blackguard 十足的无赖 ‖~ly *ad.*

unnerve [ʌn'nəːv] *vt.* ①使气馁, 使丧失勇气 ②使失常; 使烦恼不安

unparliamentary ['ʌn,pɑːlə'mentəri] *a.* 违反议会法的; 议会所不允许的; (言、行)不符议会惯例的: ~ language 辱骂性的言辞

unpleasant [ʌn'pleznt] *a.* 使人不愉快的, 不合意的; 讨厌的 ‖~ly *ad.* / ~ness *n.* ①不愉快; 煞风景 ②不愉快事件, 争执: have a slight ~ness with sb. 同某人发生小冲突

unprecedented [ʌn'presidəntid] *a.* ① 无前例的, 空前的, 前所未有的: on an ~ scale 以空前的规模 / soar to ~ heights 空前高涨 ②崭新的, 新奇的 ‖~ly *ad.*

unpretending ['ʌn-pri'tendiŋ] *a.* 不装模作样的; 不骄傲的, 谦逊的; 质朴的 ‖~ly *ad.* / ~ness *n.*

unpretentious ['ʌn-pri'tenʃəs] *a.* 不铺张招摇的; 不装模作样的; 谦逊的 ‖~ly *ad.* / ~ness *n.*

unprincipled [ʌn'prinsəpld] *a.* ① 不道德的, 肆无忌惮的; 无耻的 ②无原则的: ~ disputes 无原则纠纷

unprofessional ['ʌn-prə'feʃənl] *a.* ① 违反行业习惯(或道德)的 ②非职业性的, 非专业的, 外行的 ‖~ly *ad.*

unprovoked ['ʌn-prə'voukt] *a.* 非因触犯而发生的, 无缘无故的: an ~ assault 无缘无故的打人 ‖~ly ['ʌn-prə'voukidli] *ad.* / ~ness *n.*

unravel [ʌn'rævəl] (unravel(l)ed; unravel(l)ing) ❶ *vt.* ①解开, 拆散: ~ the threads of a tangled skein 将一团乱丝线解开 / ~ the knitting 拆散编结物 ②解释, 阐明, 澄清; 解决: ~ a mystery 阐明一件奥秘的事 / ~ a difficulty 解决一件难事 ❷ *vi.* 散开: The rope had frayed and unravel(l)ed. 绳子磨损并散开了。

unreconstructed ['ʌn,riːkən'strʌktid] *a.* 不顺从时势变化的, 坚持过时观点的, 顽固守旧的

unrelieved ['ʌnri'liːvd] *a.* ① 未受救济的 ② 未被减轻的; 未经解除的; 未得缓和的 ③无变化的; 单调的

unremitting [,ʌnri'mitiŋ] *a.* 不间断的, 持续的; 不停的; 不懈的 ‖~ly *ad.*

unrequited ['ʌnri'kwaitid] *a.* 无报答的; 无报酬的; 有仇未报的: ~ affection (或 love) 单恋, 单相思 ‖*Wickedness does not go altogether ~.* [谚]恶有恶报。

unrest ['ʌn'rest] *n.* 不宁, 不安; 动乱, 骚动 ‖~ful *a.*

unruly [ʌn'ruːli] *a.* 难驾驭的, 难控制的; 不守秩序的, 不守规矩的 ‖**unruliness** *n.*

unsavo(u)ry [ʌn'seivəri] *a.* ① 没有味道的, 没有香味的; 难吃的, 难闻的 ②(品德上)令人讨厌的, 令人不快的: a man with an ~ reputation 声名狼藉的人

unscrupulous [ʌn'skruːpjuləs] *a.* 不审慎的; 不讲道德的; 无耻的; 肆无忌惮的 ‖~ly *ad.* / ~ness *n.*

unseat ['ʌn'siːt] *vt.* ①剥夺…的席位; 使失去资格; 使退位, 使退职 ②使从座位上摔下; 使从马上摔下

unseen ['ʌn'siːn] **I** *a.* ① 未看见的; 未受注意的; 未被觉察的; 未被发现的 ② 看不见的 ③ 未经预习的; 不用参考书的; 即席的: an ~ translation 即席翻译 **II** *n.* ① [the ~] [宗]幽冥, 灵魂世界 ②即席翻译; 即席翻译的章节: He is doing an ~. 他正在即席翻译一篇东西。 / Spanish ~s 当场要译的几段西班牙文

unsettle ['ʌn'setl] ❶ *vt.* ①使不稳定; 使移动; 使松动 ②扰乱, 使不安定; 动摇, 使不确定: Nothing can ~ his resolution. 什么也不能动摇他的决心。 ❷ *vi.* 离开固定的位置; 动乱不定 ‖**unsettling** *a.* 扰乱的; 使人不安的: *unsettling* news 使人不安的消息

unsightly [ʌn'saitli] *a.* 不悦目的, 难看的, 不雅观的

unsound ['ʌn'saund] *a.* ①不健全的, 不健康的, 有病的: have an ~ heart 心脏不健全 / a man of ~ mind 精神不健全的人 / an ~ horse 羸马 ②腐烂的, 烂的: ~ fruit (timber) 烂水果(木材) ③谬误的; 无根据的: ~ arguments 谬论 ④不安全的; 不稳固的, 不可靠的 ⑤(睡眠)不沉的, 不酣的 ‖~ly *ad.* / ~ness *n.*

unspeakable [ʌn'spiːkəbl] *a.* ①说不出的, 不能以言语表达的, 无法形容的: ~ delight 说不出的高兴 ②恶劣得难以形容的: His manners are ~. 他的态度真是坏得无话可说。 ③ 说不出口的; 不可以说出来的 ‖**unspeakably** *ad.*

unstrung ['ʌn'strʌŋ] **I** unstring 的过去式和过去分词 **II** *a.* ①(弓等)解去弦线的; 弦线放松的 ②神经衰弱的; 心烦不安的

unstudied ['ʌn'stʌdid] *a.* ①未学得的; 不通晓的: be ~ in mathematics 不懂数学 ②不故意做作的, 自然的: have a simple ~ charm 具有简朴自

然之美 ③即席而成的，随便的

unthinkable [ʌn'θiŋkəbl] *a.* ①难以想象的；非常的：~ joy 难以想象的高兴 ②不可思议的；不可理解的；难以置信的：It seems ~ that .... …似乎是难以置信的。③不必加以考虑的；毫无可能的

unthinking ['ʌn'θiŋkiŋ] *a.* ①无思想的；不动脑筋的；心不在焉的 ②未加思考的，不注意的；疏忽的；不体贴的 ③无思考能力的 ‖~**ly** *ad.*

until [ən'til, ʌn'til] **I** *prep.* ①直到…为止：I shall stay here ~ twelve o'clock. 我将留在这里一直到十二点钟。/ Until the last minute of the match we kept on playing energetically. 直到比赛的最后一分钟,我们仍然坚持奋战。②[用在否定句中] 在…以前,不到…(不)：He did not come ~ late in the evening. 他直到晚上很迟才回来。/ His absence remained unnoticed ~ morning. 直到早上才发觉他不在了。/ Until then, I knew nothing at all about it. 在那以前,我对此一无所知。/ Not ~ midnight did it stop raining. 直到午夜,雨才停止。③[苏格兰] =to¹ (*prep.*) ④[苏格兰] =unto **II** *conj.* ①直到…为止：They kept on working ~ it became completely dark. 他们一直工作到天完全暗下。/ Go straight on ~ you come to a bridge. 一直前,直到你走到一座桥为止。/ He ran ~ he was breathless. 他一直跑到喘不过气来为止。②[用于否定句]在…以前,不到…(不)：He didn't arrive ~ the game had begun. 直到比赛开始他才来到。/ Until you told me I had no idea of it. 在你告诉我之前,我对此一无所知。‖**unless and ~** 见 **unless**

untimely [ʌn'taimli] **I** *a.* ①过早的：an ~ death 天折 ②不适时的；不合时宜的：an ~ joke 不合时宜的笑话 / an ~ frost 不合时令的霜冻 **II** *ad.* 过早地；不合时宜地 ‖**come to an ~ end** 过早死亡,天折

unto ['ʌntu, 'ʌntu:, 'ʌntə] *prep.* [古][诗] ①到；对：Do ~ him as he does ~ others. 以其人之道,还治其人之身。②直到；到…为止

untold ['ʌn'tould] *a.* ①未说过的,未加叙述的；未透露的 ②数不清的,无数的；不可计量的,无限的：~ wealth 大量财富 / ~ sufferings 极端的痛苦 / ~ damage 极大的损害

untoward [ʌn'touəd] *a.* ①倔强的；刚愎的；难对付的 ②不幸的；不愉快的；麻烦的；不利的 ③不适当的；不合宜的 ‖~**ly** *ad.* / ~**ness** *n.*

unutterable [ʌn'ʌtərəbl] *a.* ①说不出的；难以形容的：with ~ longing 难以形容地渴望着 ②坏透的；彻头彻尾的,十足的：an ~ scoundrel 一个十足的流氓 ③不能发音的 ‖**unutterably** *ad.*

unvarnished *a.* ①['ʌn'vɑ:niʃt] 未油漆的：an ~ floor 没油漆过的地板 ②[ʌn'vɑ:niʃt] 不加掩饰的；质朴的；天真的,坦率的：give an ~ account of what happened 对所发生的事情不加掩饰的

叙述 / We appreciate ~ discourse. 我们赞成说话就直截了当地说。

unwary [ʌn'wɛəri] *a.* 不注意的,粗心大意的；不警惕的；易受欺的

unwieldy [ʌn'wi:ldi] *a.* ①笨拙的；不灵巧的 ②难操纵的；难控制的 ③不实用的,使用不便的 ④笨重的,庞大的

unwitting [ʌn'witiŋ] *a.* 不知情的；无意的；不是故意的；不知不觉的 ‖~**ly** *ad.*

up [ʌp] **I** (最高级 uppermost) *ad.* ①向上；在上面；在(较)高处；在地(或水)平线上；露出(或离开)地面：go ~ to the top of the mountain 攀上山顶 / The airplane flew high ~ in the sky. 飞机在高空飞行。/ The sun is ~. 太阳升起了。/ The corn is ~. 玉米长出来了。/ pull ~ a plant 把植物拔起 / Show him ~. 把他带上楼去。/ He lives three floors ~. 他住在这儿上去三层的楼上。②趋向(或处于)直立姿势；起床,起来：spring ~ from one's seat 从座位上跳起来 / Up! 起来! (是祈使句 "Get (或 Stand) ~!" 的省略) / Up with you! 站起来! (或: 起床!) / Down with the old and ~ with the new. 破旧立新。/ I was ~ early this morning. 今天我一早就起来了。/ Is he ~ yet? 他起床了没有? / He was ~ late last night. 他昨晚很迟才睡。③(在程度、地位、声音、价值等方面)由小变大；高涨起来；由少到多：The wind is ~. 风大起来了。/ The river is ~. 河水涨了。/ Speak ~! 大声点说! / The temperature has gone ~. 温度上升了。/ The fire is mounting ~. 火势正在增强。/ A plant grows ~ from a seed. 植物是从种子长成的。/ bring ~ a child 把孩子抚育大 / The atten dance is ~. 出席人数增加了。④(从边远地区、农村、南方、下游、海边等被看作下方的地方往首都、城市、北方、上游、大学等地)往上方；在上方；往较重要处；【海】向上风；【戏】向(或在)舞台后方：go ~ from the country 从乡下到城里去 / What are you ~ for? 你上首都(或城里)去有什么事? / follow ~ the river to its source 沿上游而去直至河的发源地 / go ~ to Oxford 上牛津大学 / be (或 stay)~ during the vacation 假期中留在大学里不回家 / The case was brought ~ before a higher court. 案件已呈交上级法院。⑤向目的地,向说话者所在处：She went straight ~ to the door. 她一直走到门口。/ He came ~ (to me) and asked me for a light. 他走到我跟前向我要火。⑥(情绪上)高昂起来,激动起来；(事情)发生,出现；(论题)提出：His spirits went ~. 他的精神振奋起来了。/ His blood (或 anger) is ~. 他怒火上升。/ Screw ~ your courage. 鼓起勇气

来。/ He was wrought ~ by the news. 他很为这消息所激动。/ All the town is ~. 全城沸腾了。/ There's something ~. 一定出了什么事了。/ What's ~ (with you)? (你)怎么了？(或：出了什么事?) / The question came ~ for discussion. 问题已提出来讨论了。/ The lost book has turned ~. 遗失的书找到了。

⑦ (在空间、时间、程度等方面)赶上；达到；及；一直到；在…以上：catch ~ in the race 在赛跑中赶上去 / keep ~ with the times 赶上时代 / Can you get ~ to that note? 你能唱得到那么高吗?/ from one's childhood ~ 从童年时代起(直到现在)/from third grade ~ 三年级以上

⑧ [与动词连用，表示完全、彻底]…完，…光：eat everything ~ 把所有的东西都吃光 / finish ~ the job 把工作结束掉 / burn ~ 烧尽 / Time's ~. (或 The time is ~.) 时间到了。/ When is your leave ~? 你的假期什么时候结束? / The jig is ~. 一切都完蛋了。/ Parliament is ~. [主英]议会闭会了。

⑨ 贮藏起；封起；监禁：lay ~ grain against war and natural disasters 贮粮备战备荒 / tie ~ a package 打包 / Button ~ your coat. 把你的大衣钮子扣上。/ lock ~ a house 把房子锁起 / Jack went ~ in 1920 for twenty years. 杰克于一九二〇年被判刑监禁二十年。

⑩ [与动词连用用以加强语气]：light ~ a cigarette 点着一支香烟 / write ~ a story 写成一篇故事 / clean ~ the house 把房子打扫得干干净净

⑪【体】超过；双方平：He is one ~ on his opponent. 他胜过他的对手一分。/ The score is 15 ~. 比分为十五平。

II *prep.* ① 向(高处)；在(高处)；向(或在)…上面：go ~ a hill 登山 / climb ~ a ladder 登上楼梯 / Smoke goes ~ the chimney. 烟由烟囱冒出。② 向(或在)…的上游；逆着…的方向：sail ~ a river 向上游驶去 / ~ (the) wind 顶着风 ③ 向(或在)…的内地；向(或在)离…更远的地点：travel ~ country 往内地旅行 / walk ~ the road 沿着路走去

III (比较级 upper，最高级 upmost 或 uppermost) *a.* 向上的：an ~ line (铁路)上行线 / an ~ platform 上行列车用的月台 / an ~ train (铁路)上行列车

IV *n.* ① 居高位者；处于有利地位的人 ② 向上的坡 ③ 繁荣，全盛 ④ 上行列车；上行公共汽车 ⑤ [复] [美俚]刺激性毒品

V (upped; upping) ❶ *vi.* [口] ① (站)起来，突然做某事(或讲话)：He ~s and says. 他起来讲话。② 举起，拿起(with)：~ with one's hammer 举起锤子 ❷ *vt.* [口] ① 举起，拿起：an *upped* sail 扬起的帆

② 提高(价格、生产、地位等)：prices that are being *upped* by 20% 上涨百分之二十的价格 / ~ one's status 抬高地位 ③ 增加(赌注)：~ the ante 增加扑克赌注

‖*all* ~ 见 **all** / *on the ~and-~* ① 光明磊落的；诚实的，正当的 ② 走上坡路的，越来越好的 / *~ against* [口]面临：~ *against* difficulties 面临困难 / *~ against it* [口]面临极大的困难(尤指经济困难) / *~ and about* (病人)已起床走动 / *~ and doing* 活泼，敏捷；忙碌 / *~ and down* ① 上上下下 ② 前前后后 ③ 来来往往 ④ 处处：I have looked *for* it *~ and down.* 我到处都找过了。/ *~ for* ① 在(选举等)中被提名供考虑 ② 在法庭受(审) / *~ hill and down dale* 见 **hill** / *~ on* (或 *in*) 熟悉；精通：He is well ~ *in* English. 他精通英语。/ *~s and downs* 盛衰，浮沉 / *~ there* 在那里；[美俚]在天上 / *~ to* ① 从事于；忙于：What is he ~ *to*? 他在做什么?(或：他居心何在?) ② 胜任，适于：be ~ *to* standard 符合标准 / He is not ~ *to* his work. 他不胜任他的工作。/ be not ~ *to* much 不是怎样了不起，蹩脚 ③ 该由…；轮到：It is ~ *to* us to give them all the help we can. 我们有责任全力帮助他们。④ 直到：~ *to* now (then) 直到现在(那时) / be ~ *to* one's neck(或 ears) in 深陷于…；沉溺于…

‖*'~-and-'coming a.* [口](人在事业上)进取的；有希望的 / *'~-and-'down a.* 上上下下的；来来往往的；起伏的；变动的 / *'~-and-'~ n.* ① 光明磊落的行动；诚实的行为 ② 越来越好：Business was on the *~-and-~.* 生意越做越大。/ *'~-to-'date a.* [通常作定语用]直到最近的；现代的，新式的，时新的 / *'~-to-the-'minute a.* 很现代化的；最近的

upbraid [ʌp'breid] *vt.* 责备，谴责；申斥：~ sb. *with* a fault (*for* doing sth.) 责备某人犯错误(做某事) ‖*~er n.* 责备者；申斥者 / *~ing n. & a.* 责备(的)；申斥(的)

upbringing ['ʌp,briŋiŋ] *n.* 抚育，养育；教养；培养

upheaval [ʌp'hi:vəl] *n.* ① 胀起，鼓起；举起；(地壳)隆起 ② 激变，剧变；动乱：social ~s 社会的大变动

uphill ['ʌp'hil] **I** *n.* 登高；上升；上坡 **II** *a.* ① 位于高处的 ② 上升的，向上的；上坡的：an ~ road 上坡路 ③ 艰难的，费力的：an ~ task 艰难的任务 **III** *ad.* ① 往上坡，往山上：run ~ 往上坡跑 ② 费力地，迎着困难地

uphold [ʌp'hould] (upheld [ʌp'held]) *vt.* ① 举起，高举 ② 支撑，支持；维持；坚持；鼓励：These columns ~ the roof. 这些柱子支撑着屋顶。/ ~ principle (unity) 坚持原则(团结) ③ 赞成，拥护；确认：~ a decision 拥护一个决议 / ~ a verdict 确认一个判决 ‖*~er n.* 支持者，赞成者，拥护者；支撑物

upholster [ʌp'houlstə] *vt.* ①为(沙发、椅子等)装上垫子(或套子、弹簧): ～ a chair *in* (或 *with*) tapestry 给椅子装上花毯面子 ②(用挂毡、地毯、家具等)布置(房间);装潢 ‖～**er** [ʌp'houlstərə] *n.* 室内装潢商,家具商

upholstery [ʌp'houlstəri] *n.* ①室内装潢 ②室内装潢业

upkeep ['ʌpkiːp] *n.* ①(房屋、设备等的)保养,维修 ②维修费,养护费

upland ['ʌplənd] **I** *n.* 高地;山地 **II** *a.* 高地的;山地的: an ～ field 高地田 / ～ rice 旱地稻

uplift **I** [ʌp'lift] ❶ *vt.* ①高举; 使(地面)隆起 ②(指道德等方面)促进,提高; 振奋(精神): Their spirits were ～ed by the news. 他们的精神被这个消息振奋起来。❷ *vi.* 上升,升起 **II** ['ʌplift] *n.* ①举起; 抬起 ②情绪高涨; 社会进步; 道德提高; 提高道德和文化水平的社会运动: an ～ worker 社会事业家 ③(地壳的)隆起 ④胸罩

upon [强 ə'pɔn; 弱 əpən] *prep.* =on (prep.) [upon 和 on 一般可通用,但有下列区别: ①表示日期时一般只用 on, 不用 upon, 如: on Sunday, *on* the fifth of April ②在某些习语中, upon 与 on 不能互相调换, 如: *upon* my word, once *upon* a time, *on* no account ③在句末或分句末的动词不定式后往往用 upon, 而不用 on, 如: nothing to depend *upon*, not enough to live *upon* ④on 比 upon 通俗, 口语中用 on 较多]

upper ['ʌpə] **I** *a.* [up 的比较级] ①上(面)的;上首的; (河的)上流的: the ～ lip 上唇 / the ～ deck 上甲板 / the ～ seats (或 circle) (剧院的)花楼 / the ～ end of the table (宴会等的)上座(主人的席位) / the ～ keyboard (钢琴、打字机等的)键盘右侧 / the ～ end of a hall 大厅最里面的一头 / the ～ course of a river 河的上游 ②地位(或等级、权力等)较高的: the ～ servants [总称]管家; (管理膳食的)领班 ③(议会)上院的: the *Upper* House 上议院 ④穿在外面的: ～ clothes 外衣 / [U-] 地后期的: *Upper* Carboniferous period 后期石炭纪 ⑥较早的 ⑦北部的: ～ Manhattan (美国纽约市的)曼哈顿北部 **II** *n.* ①鞋帮 ②腰带; [复]绑腿, 腿套 ③(一颗)上齿; 上排牙齿; 上排假牙 ④[口]上铺(=～ berth) ⑤刺激性药物(尤指安非他明) ‖**be (down) on one's ～s** 穿着破旧的鞋子; 一贫如洗,处于困境 / *have* (*get*) *the* ～ *hand of* 占着(占)…的上风 / *the Upper Bench* 见 **bench** / *the* ～ *stor(e)y* 见 **stor(e)y** / *the* ～ *ten* (*thousand*) 见 **ten** ‖**Upper Austria** 上奥地利(奥地利北部一省) / '～-'**bracket** *a.* 高级的,到顶的: ～-*bracket* taxpayers 高额纳税人 / ～ **case** [印]大写字母盒 / '～'**case** *a.* 大写的,n. 大写字母 *vt.* 用大写字母排印 / ～ **crust** ①面包表层的皮 ②[口]贵族阶级,上流阶层; (某一社会阶级的)最上层 / ～ **dead centre** 【机】上死点 / **Upper Volta** ['vɔltə] 上沃尔特[非洲] / ～ **works** 【海】水线以上的船体

uppermost ['ʌpəmoust] **I** *a.* [up 的最高级]至上的; 最高的; 最主要的 **II** *ad.* [up 的最高级]至上; 最高; 最初: He said whatever came ～. 最先想到什么他就说什么。

upright ['ʌp-rait] **I** *a.* ①垂直的, 笔直的; 直立的; 竖式的: an ～ tree 笔直的树木 / an ～ engine 立式发动机 / an ～ piano 竖式钢琴 ②正直的; 诚实的: an ～ man 正直的人 **II** *a.* 笔直; 竖立着: stand ～ 笔挺地立着 / set sth. ～ 把某物竖直 **III** *n.* ①垂直; 竖立: be out of ～ 偏斜, 歪 ②笔直的东西; 【机】柱: the ～ of **a** boring machine 镗床柱 ③【音】竖式钢琴 ④[复]球门柱(尤指美式足球中的) ‖**bolt** ～ 笔直竖直 ‖～**ly** *ad.* / ～**ness** *n.*

uprising [ʌp'raiziŋ] *n.* ①上升; 起立; 起床 ②上升的斜坡 ③起义,暴动: the peasant ～s 农民起义

uproar ['ʌp,rɔː] *n.* ①扰乱; 骚动 ②吵闹声; 喧嚣; 鼎沸: be *in an* ～ 吵吵闹闹

uproarious [ʌp'rɔːriəs] *a.* ①骚动的; 喧嚣的; 吵闹的: burst into ～ laughter 哄然大笑 ②引人捧腹大笑的,非常可笑的: an ～ comedy 令人捧腹大笑的喜剧 ‖～**ly** *ad.* / ～**ness** *n.*

uproot [ʌp'ruːt] ❶ *vt.* ①连根拔; 根除; 灭绝: ～ colonialism 根除殖民主义 ②赶走,把…赶出家园 ❷ *vi.* 迁离; 改变生活方式

upset [ʌp'set] **I** (upset; upsetting) ❶ *vt.* ①弄翻,打翻,倾覆: ～ a bottle of ink 打翻一瓶墨水 ②打乱,搅乱 ③(体育比赛或政党竞争时)意外地击败(对方) ④使心烦意乱: The news quite ～ him. 这消息使他心烦意乱。 / ～ one's stomach 使胃不舒服 ⑤【机】顿锻,缩锻,镦粗 ❷ *vi.* 翻倒,倾复: The boat ～. 船翻了。 **II** *n.* ①翻倒,倾覆 ②混乱,搅乱 ③心烦意乱; (肠胃等)不适 ④(尤指意外的)击败 ⑤【机】(缩锻用)陷型模; 缩锻钢条的粗大末端 ‖～ ['ʌpset] **price** (拍卖时起喊的)开拍价格; (公卖时所定的)最低价格

upshot ['ʌpʃɔt] *n.* [只用单数并与定冠词连用] ①结果,结局: in the ～ 最后,终于 / The ～ of the matter was that .... 事情的结局是… ②(分析或议论的)结论; 要点: the ～ of these paragraphs 这些段落的要点

upside ['ʌpsaid] *n.* 上边; 上面; 上部 ‖～ **down** ①颠倒; 倒转: turn **a** table ～ *down* 把桌子弄翻倒 ②乱七八糟,混乱: turn everything in the room ～ *down* 把室内的一切弄得乱七八糟 ‖'～-'**down** *a.* 颠倒的; 乱七八糟的: ～-*down* logic 颠倒的逻辑

upstairs ['ʌp'stɛəz] **I** *ad.* ①在楼上; 往楼上: sleep ～ 睡在楼上 / go ～ 上楼 ②处于更高地位; 往更高地位(尤指明升暗降): ostensibly move sb. ～ to board chairman 表面上把某人提升为董事会会长 ③在高空; 往高处: take a new plane ～ 乘新飞机往高空飞 ④[美俚]在头脑里: He is all vacant ～. 他头脑里空空如也。 **II** *a.* ①楼上的,在楼上的: an ～ room 一间楼上的房间 ②高

水平的,上层的 **III** *n.* 楼上; [美俚]【宗】天堂 ||*kick* ~ [口][喻]把…明升暗降

upstream ['ʌp'stri:m] *ad. & a.* 在上游(的); 向上游(的); 逆流(的)

uptake ['ʌpteik] *n.* ①举起; 拿起 ②领会; 理解(力) ③上升烟道;【矿】上风井,上风口 ④(生物机体的)吸收 ||*be quick in* (或 *on*) *the* ~ 理解很快

upward ['ʌpwəd] **I** *a.* ①向上的; 上升的: an ~ glance 向上的一瞥 / an ~ tendency 向上的趋势 ②(声调)升高的 **II** *ad.* =upwards ||~**ly** *ad.* / ~**ness** *n.* ||~ **mobility** 升入较高社会阶层的流动性

upwards ['ʌpwədz] *ad.* ①向上; (数量、程度、质量、职位、比率方面)趋向上升: The jet plane roared ~. 这架喷气式飞机呼啸着向上飞去。/ shoot ~ 向上射去 / Our production goes steadily ~. 我们的生产稳步上升。②向上游; 向内地: move ~ from the river mouth 从河口向上游移动 ③在更高处; 在上部; 朝头部: The swelling spread from his legs ~. 肿胀从他的腿部向上扩展。④以上: We have notebooks from five cents ~. 本店有五分和五分以上的笔记本。/ boys of ten years and ~ 十岁和十岁以上的男孩 ⑤进入往后的岁月: from one's youth ~ 从青年时代起 ||~ *of* …以上,多于…: *Upwards of* 8,000 persons joined the rally. 八千多人参加了集会。/ They have turned out ~ *of* 300 water pumps. 他们生产出三百多台水泵。

uranium [juə'reinjəm] *n.*【化】铀

urban ['ə:bən] *a.* 城市的,都市的: ~ districts 市区 / ~ inhabitants 城市居民 / the ~ poor 城市贫民 ||~**ism** *n.* ①城市居民的生活方式 ②都市社会物质需求的研究 ③都市化 / ~**ist** *n.* 城市规划专家

urbane [ə:'bein] *a.* 有礼貌的; 温文有礼的; 文雅的 ||~**ly** *ad.*

urbanity [ə:'bæniti] *n.* ①温文有礼; 文雅 ②[复]文雅的举止

urchin ['ə:tʃin] *n.* ①小淘气, 顽童 ②【动】(刺)猬 ③【动】海胆

urge [ə:dʒ] **I** ❶ *vt.* ①推进; 驱策: ~ a horse on 策马前进 ②极力主张; 强烈要求: ~ upon sb. the importance of a matter 向某人力陈某事的重要性 / He ~*d* that we (should) take these steps. 他们极力主张我们采取这些步骤 ③催促; 力劝; 激励; 怂恿: ~ sb. *to do* (或 *into doing*) sth. 怂恿某人做某事 / ~ sb. *to* a task 催促某人去完成一项任务 ④使劲干: ~ one's oars 用力划桨 ❷ *vi.* 极力主张; 强烈要求: ~ against the adoption of the measure 极力反对采纳这项措施 **II** *n.* ①[常用单]强烈的欲望; 冲动;迫切的要求; ② 推动力

urgency ['ə:dʒənsi] *n.* ①紧急; 迫切: a matter of great ~ 非常紧急的事情 ②强求, 催促; 坚持

③紧急的事

urgent ['ə:dʒənt] *a.* ①紧急的, 急迫的: be in ~ need 急需 / an ~ appeal 紧急的呼吁 ②强求的; 催促的: He was ~ *with* me for (或 to disclose) further particulars. 他硬要我讲得更详细点。/ She was ~ for the doctor to come. 她急切地催促医生来。||~**ly** *ad.*

urine ['juərin] *n.* 尿: diabetic ~ 糖尿病性尿, 糖尿 / pass (或 discharge) (one's) ~ 解小便, 撒尿

urn [ə:n] *n.* ①瓮; 缸 ②骨灰瓮; [喻]坟墓 ③茶水壶: a coffee ~ 咖啡壶 ④【植】蒴壶

urn

us [强 ʌs; 弱 əs, s] *pron.* [we的宾格] ①[用作宾语]我们: Let ~ go. 我们走吧。②[口][用作表语]我们 (=we): It's ~ (或 we). 就是我们。

usage ['ju:zidʒ] *n.* ①使用; 对待; 用法: broken by long, rough ~ 由于长期不小心的使用而破损的 / the increasing ~ of plastics 塑料制品的日益广泛的使用 / a person who met with harsh ~ 受到虐待的人 ②习惯; 惯例;【语】惯用法;【律】习惯法: an ill-bred ~ 由于缺乏教养而形成的习惯 / social ~(s) 社会习俗 / ~s of war 战时惯例 /. sanctified *by* ~ 约定俗成的 / That phrase has come into (gone out of) ~. 那短语已为(已不再为)大家所惯用。/ modern English ~ 现代英语惯用法 ③利益, 好处: put these things to sb.'s ~ 把这些东西供某人利用

use [ju:s] **I** ❶ [ju:z] *vt.* ①用; 使用; 应用: May I ~ your bicycle? 我可以用一下你的自行车吗? / ~ the dialectical-materialist viewpoint in looking at problems 用辩证唯物主义的观点看问题 / learn to ~ a dictionary 学会使用词典 ②发挥, 使出; 行使; 运用: ~ all one's efforts 作出一切努力 / ~ one's brains 用脑筋, 想 / ~ judgement 运用判断力 / ~ one's legs 用双腿走路 ③耗费, 消费; 耗尽 (*up*) He has ~*d up* all his energy. 他已筋疲力尽。④经常服用 (饮料或药品等); 吸(烟), 嚼(烟叶): Do you ~ sugar in your coffee? 你喝咖啡常放糖吗? ⑤对待: ~ sb. well (ill) 待某人好(不好) ⑥利用; [口]自私地利用(某人): ~ every opportunity 利用一切机会 / He was being ~*d* and manipulated. 他受人操纵利用。❷ *vi.* 惯常(现主要用过去式, 见 **used**[1]) **II** *n.* ①用;

使用; 应用; 运用; 利用: For ~ only in case of fire! 只供火警时用! / the plan for the ~ of land 土地利用的规划 ②运用能力; 使用权: regain the ~ of one's arm 恢复手臂功能 / give sb. the ~ of one's camera 让某人使用自己的照相机 ③用法: learn the ~ of various kinds of agricultural tools 学习各种农具的使用法 ④用途; 价值; 效用; 益处: an electronic device with many ~s 具有多种用途的电子仪器 / find a ~ for sth. 设法对某物加以利用 / What's the ~ of complaining? (或 Is there any ~ in complaining?) 抱怨有什么用呢? ⑤习惯; 惯例: according to an ancient ~ 按照古老的习惯 / It is his ~ to take a walk every morning. 他有每天早晨散步的习惯。 ⑥【律】(对委托他人管理的不动产的) 收益权 ⑦(教堂或主教管区的) 特有的礼拜仪式 ‖come into ~ 开始被使用: Electronic computers have come into wide ~. 电子计算机已开始被广泛使用。 / go (或 fall) out of ~ 不再被使用, 被废弃 / have no ~ for ①不需要 ②[喻]对…不耐烦; 厌恶, 不喜欢: I have no ~ for novels like that. 我不喜欢象那样的小说。 / in ~ 在使用着 / make ~ of 利用: make the best ~ of everything 使物尽其用 / (of) no ~ 没用: This medicine is (of) no ~ to me. 此药对我不起效用。 / It is (of) no ~ talking (或 to talk). 说也没用。 / of ~ 有用: It is of great ~ for our work. 这对我们的工作非常有用。 / out of ~ 不在使用着; 废弃 / put to ~ 使用; 利用: put it to a good ~ 好好利用它 / ~ and wont 习惯; 惯例

used[1] [ju:st] (use vi. 的过去式) (否定式 ~ not 可缩写为 usedn't 或 usen't, 读音均为 ['ju:snt]) 过去常常, 过去惯常: I do not swim so often as I ~ (to). 我不象过去那样常游泳了。 / You ~ to go there, ~n't you (或[口]didn't you)? 你过去经常到那儿去, 不是吗? / There ~ to be a bookshelf in this room. 这房间里, 过去一直有一个书架。 / It ~ to be said that .... 过去常说… / He ~n't (或[口] didn't use) to come. 他过去不常来。 / Used he (或[口] Did he use) to come by bus? 他过去常乘公共汽车来吗?

used[2] a. ①[ju:zd][美]旧的; 用旧了的: ~ books 旧书 ②[ju:st][作表语]习惯于…的 (to): He is ~ to hard work. 他习惯于艰苦工作。/ You will soon get (或 become) ~ to it. 你很快会对它习惯的。 ‖~ up [口]筋疲力尽的: He is ~ up. 他筋疲力尽了。

useful ['ju:sful] a. ①有用的; 有益的; 实用的; 有帮助的: all sorts of ~ implements 各种有用的工具 / absorb whatever experience is ~ to us 吸取对我们有益的经验 / ~ load [空] 有效负载 / ~ life 有效寿命 / ~ hints 有启发的暗示 / a ~ book for beginners in French 一本有助于初学法文者的书 / He makes himself generally ~. 他能干各式各样的工作。②[俚]值得高度赞

扬的; 对…很熟练的 (at): pretty ~ performance 相当好的表演 / be very ~ at mathematics 精通数学

useless ['ju:slis] a. ①无用的; 无效的; 无价值的; 无益的 ②[俚]身体不适的; 没精打采的: I am feeling ~. 我觉得很不舒服。 ‖~ly ad. / ~ness n.

user ['ju:zə] n. ①使用者, 用户; 使用物 ②【律】权利的实际享有 (或行使) ③[美俚]吸毒成瘾者

usher ['ʌʃə] I n. ①(戏院、教堂等公共场所的) 招待员, 引座员 ②(法院等的) 门房; 传达员 ③(给显贵人物) 领路的人, 前驱 ④[英][贬]助理教员, 助教 II ❶ vt. ①引, 领; 招待: He ~ed me into the reception room. 他把我引进会客室。/ ~ sb. to his seat 领某人入座 ②迎接 (in) ③引进; 宣告, 展示 (in) ❷ vi. 作招待员 ‖~ette[,ʌʃə'ret] n. (戏院) 女引座员 / ~- ship n. 招待员 (或引座员, 传达员等) 的职务

usual ['ju:ʒuəl] a. 通常的, 平常的; 惯常的, 惯例的: arrive earlier than ~ 到得比平常早 / follow the ~ method 采用通常方法 / It is ~ with him to go to the office on foot. 他惯常步行去办公。 ‖as per ~ [谑]=as ~ 或 ~ as ~ 象往常一样, 照例: As ~, he got up very early. 他象平常一样很早就起身了。 ‖~ly ad. / ~ness n.

usurp [ju(:)'zə:p] ❶ vt. 篡夺; 夺取; 侵占: ~ the name of 盗用…的名义 ❷ vi. ①篡夺; 篡位; 篡权 ②侵占 (on, upon) ‖~er n.

usury ['ju:ʒuri] n. ①高利贷, 高利剥削 ②高利 (尤指超出法定利率); [喻]利益

utensil [ju(:)'tensl] n. 器皿 (尤指家庭厨房用具): household ~s 家用器具 / kitchen ~s 厨房用具 / cooking ~s 烹饪用具 / farming ~s 农具

utility [ju(:)'tiliti] I n. ①效用, 有用, 实用, 功利: marginal ~【经】边际效用, 限界效用 ②有用的东西 ③ 公用事业 (=public ~) ④ 公用事业公司, 公用事业设备; [复]公用事业公司股票 ⑤演配角的演员 II a. ①有多种用途的; 各种工作都会做的: a ~ aircraft 通用飞机 / a ~ knife 有多种用途的小刀 ② 实用的, 经济实惠的: ~ furniture 经济实用的家具 ③ (牲畜) 为获得经济价值而饲养的 (与用来供欣赏用的相对而言) ④ 公用事业的; 公用事业公司股票价格的 ‖~ man 演各种配角的演员; 杂务工 / ~ room 杂用室

utilize, utilise ['ju:tilaiz] vt. 利用: ~ every opportunity 利用一切机会 / ~ straw as fodder 利用稻草作饲料 / ~ waterfalls for producing electric power 利用瀑布发电 ‖utilizable ['ju:ti-laizəbl] a. 可利用的 / utilization [,ju:tilai-'zeiʃən] n. 利用: comprehensive utilization 综合利用

utmost ['ʌtmoust] I a. 最远的; 极度的, 最大的: the ~ limits 极限 / to the ~ ends of the earth 到天涯海角 / with the ~ pleasure 极其高兴

地 / of the ～ importance 极重要的 **II** *n.* 极限; 极度, 最大可能: That is the ～ that I can do. 这就是我尽全力所能做到的。 ‖ *at the* ～ 至多 / *do one's* ～ 竭力, 尽全力 / *to the* ～ 尽力

Utopia [juː'toupjə] *n.* ①乌托邦 ②[常作 u-] 理想的完美境界; 空想的社会改良计划

Utopian [juː'toupjən] **I** *a.* ①乌托邦的, 象乌托邦的 ②[常作 u-] 空想的: a *utopian* scheme 空想的计划 **II** *n.* ①乌托邦的居民 ②[常作 u-] 空想家; 空想社会主义者 ‖～**ism** *n.* 乌托邦思想; 乌托邦理论 ‖ **utopian communism** 空想共产主义 / **utopian socialism** 空想社会主义

utter¹ ['ʌtə] *a.* ①完全的, 彻底的, 十足的: ～ ignorance 完全无知 / be at an ～ loss what to do 完全不知道怎么办 ②无条件的; 绝对的: an ～ denial (refusal) 绝对否认(拒绝) ‖～**ly** *ad.* ‖～ **barrister** [英]【律】外席律师

utter² ['ʌtə] *vt.* ①发出(声音等); 说, 讲; 表达: ～ a groan 发出呻吟 / Not a sound was ～ed. 一声不吭。 / ～ one's feelings (thoughts) 用言词表达情感(思想) / ～ a libel 公然发表诽谤言论 ②流通, 行使(货币, 尤指伪币) ③发射, 喷射: The fountain ～ed glittering streams of water. 喷泉喷射出晶莹的水流。

utterance¹ ['ʌtərəns] *n.* ①发声; 表达: give ～ to one's rage 用言词表达自己的愤怒 ②[只用单]口才; 说法; 语调; 发音: a clear ～ 发音清楚 / a defective ～ 有缺陷的发音 ③言词, 言论; 意见

utterance² ['ʌtərəns] *n.* [书面语]终极; 死: fight to the ～ 战斗到底

uttermost ['ʌtəmoust] **I** *a.* ①最远的: the ～ parts of the earth 天涯海角 ②最大的, 极度的: ～ efforts 最大的努力 **II** *n.* 最大限度, 极端: exert oneself to the ～ 作出极大的努力

V

vacancy ['veikənsi] *n.* ①空; 空白; 空处; 空地; 空房间: three *vacancies* in this apartment house 这所公寓的三间空房间 ②(心灵)空虚; 失神 ③清闲; 空闲 ④空缺, 空额

vacant ['veikənt] *a.* ①空的; 空白的: gaze into the immense ～ space 凝视浩瀚的太空 ②未被占用的; (广告用语)可使用的: ～ possession (广告用语)空屋出卖 / a ～ seats in a bus 公共汽车上的空座 / a ～ room 空房间 ③(心灵)空虚的; 心不在焉的; 无表情的; 愚蠢的: a ～ mind 茫然的心情 / a ～ look 发呆的样子 ④清闲的; 空闲的: ～ hours 空闲时间 ⑤(职位)空缺的 ‖～**ly** *ad.* 空虚地; 心不在焉地; 无表情地

vacate [və'keit; 美 'veikeit] ❶ *vt.* ①使空出; 腾出, 搬出: ～ a room 腾出房间 ②解除(职位); 退(位), 辞(职); 撤离(阵地)【律】取消, 使作废 ❷ *vi.* ①腾出空房(或空地) ②辞职 ③[美口] 离去, 走开

vacation [və'keiʃən; 美 vei'keiʃən] **I** *n.* ①假期; 休假; (法院的)休庭期: the long ～ [主英](学校、法院的)暑假 / be on ～ 在度假期 ②(房屋等的)腾出, 搬出; (职位的)辞去 **II** *vi.* [美]度假期; 休假 ‖～**ist** *n.* 休假者, 度假日者(尤指假日旅行者) ‖ **va'cationland** *n.* 度假胜地

vaccinate ['væksineit] **I** ❶ *vt.* ①给…种牛痘: be ～d against smallpox 种牛痘以防天花 ②给…接种疫苗 ❷ *vi.* 施种牛痘, 进行预防接种 **II** *n.* 被接种牛痘者, 被接种疫苗者

vaccination [ˌvæksi'neiʃən] *n.* 【医】种痘; 接种 ②牛痘疤 ‖～**ist** *n.* 主张(强迫)种痘者

vaccine ['væksiːn] **I** *a.* 牛痘的, 痘苗的; 疫苗的 **II** *n.* 牛痘苗; 疫苗, 菌苗

vacillate ['væsileit] *vi.* ①摇摆; 振荡; 波动 ②犹豫, 踌躇: ～ between two courses of action 在两种办法间举棋不定

vacillation [ˌvæsi'leiʃən] *n.* ①摇摆; 振荡; 波动 ②犹豫不决, 踌躇

vacuous ['vækjuəs] *a.* ①空的, 空洞的 ②(精神上)空虚的; 内容贫乏的; 无意义的 ③愚蠢的; 茫然若失的: a ～ stare 呆视 / a ～ look 茫然若失的神情 ④(生活)无聊的; 无所事事的 ‖～**ly** *ad.* / ～**ness** *n.*

vacuum ['vækjuəm] **I** ([复] vacuums 或 vacua ['vækjuə]) *n.* ①真空; 真空度; 真空般状态: create a power ～ 制造一个权力真空状态 ②真空装置; 真空吸尘器 (=～ cleaner) ③空虚: feel a ～ in the lower regions 感到饥饿 **II** *a.* ①真空的 ②用以产生真空的; 利用真空的: ～ distillation 真空蒸馏 **III** *vt.* [口]用真空吸尘器打扫 ‖～ **bottle**, ～ **flask** 保温瓶, 热水瓶 / ～ **brake** 【机】真空闸 / ～ **cleaner** 真空吸尘器; [美俚](人)肺 / ～ **ga(u)ge** 真空计 / '～-'**packed** *a.* 真空包装的(密封前抽去大量空气的) / ～ **pump** 【机】真空泵 / ～ **tube** [美]真空管, 电子管 / ～ **valve** [英] =～ tube

vagabond ['vægəbɔnd, 'vægəbənd] **I** *a.* ①流浪的, 漂泊的: live a ～ life 过着流浪生活 / ～ elements 游民分子 ②流浪者的 ③浪荡的; 懒散的 **II** *n.* 流浪者; 流浪乞丐; 浪子; 懒汉; 流氓 **III** *vi.* 到处流浪 ‖～**age** ['vægəbɔndidʒ] *n.* ①流

浪；流浪生活；流浪习惯 ②［总称］流浪者 /
~ish *a.* 流浪者的 / **~ism** *n.* =**~age** /
~ize *vi.* 流浪

vagary ['veigəri, və'gɛəri] *n.* ①奇想；异想天开
②古怪的行为；反复无常的行为；难以预测的变
化：be independent of the *vagaries* of the
international market 不受变化莫测的国际市场
的制约

vagrancy ['veigrənsi] *n.* ①(思想、说话的)游移
不定，离题 ②流浪；漂泊；【律】流浪罪

vagrant ['veigrənt] **I** *n.* 流浪者，漂泊者；游民
II *a.* ①流浪的；漂泊不定的：a ~ life 流浪生活
②(思想等)游移不定的；(风等)无定向的；(植物)
蔓生的 ‖**~ly** *ad.*

vague [veig] *a.* ①含糊的；模糊的；不明确的：a ~
answer 含糊的回答 / a ~ idea 模糊的思想 / I
haven't the ~st notion what he means. 我一
点也不懂他的意思。②无表情的：~ eyes 发呆
的眼睛 ‖**~ly** *ad.* / **~ness** *n.*

vain [vein] *a.* ①徒劳的；徒然的：a ~ attempt 徒
劳的尝试 ②空虚的；虚浮的：~ boasts 空洞的大
话 / ~ titles 空衔 ③自负的；自视过高的；爱虚
荣的：be ~ of one's learning 对自己的学问很
自负 / a ~ man 爱虚荣的人 ④愚蠢的 ‖*in* ~
①徒劳，白辛苦：Our efforts were not *in* ~. 我
们的气力没有白费。/ try *in* ~ to do sth. 枉
费心机地试做某事 ②轻慢，不尊敬：take sb.'s
name *in* ~ 轻慢地谈论某人(尤指亵渎上帝的名)
‖**~ly** *ad.* / **~ness** *n.*

vainglorious [vein'glɔ:riəs] *a.* 自负的；极度虚荣的
‖**~ly** *ad.*

vainglory [vein'glɔ:ri] *n.* 自负；极度的虚荣心

vale[1] [veil] *n.* 谷；溪谷(用于诗和地名中)

vale[2] ['veili, 'vælei] *int. & n.* 再见，再会

valiant ['væljənt] **I** *a.* 勇敢的，英勇的：the ~
fighting spirit 勇敢的战斗精神 **II** *n.* 勇敢的人
‖**~ly** *ad.* / **~ness** *n.*

valid ['vælid] *a.* ①【律】有效的；经过正当手续的：
a ~ contract 有效的契约 / be ~ for three
months 有效期三个月 ②正当的；正确的；有根据
的：a ~ reason 正当的理由 / a ~ argument 正
确的论点 / ~ evidence 确凿的证据 ③[罕]强壮
的，健康的 ‖**~ly** *ad.* .

validate ['vælideit] *vt.* ①【律】使生效；使合法化；
批准；宣布(某人)当选：~ a treaty 使条约生
效 / ~ an election 使选举合法化 ②证实：~
a theory 证实一种理论 ‖**validation** [,væli-
'deiʃən] *n.*

validity [və'liditi] *n.* ①【律】有效；效力；合法性：
the term of ~ 有效期 ②正当；正确；确实

valise [və'li:z] *n.* 旅行袋，旅行小皮包；兵士的
背囊

valley ['væli] *n.* ①(山)谷；溪谷 ②流域 ③凹
陷处，凹地 ④【建】屋谷，屋面天沟 ‖*the ~ of
the shadow of death* 死荫的幽谷(源出基督教
《圣经》)；临死的痛苦时刻

---

valorous ['vælərəs] *a.* 勇猛的，英勇的；无畏的：
~ soldier 勇猛的战士 / ~ deeds 英勇的事迹

valour ['vælə] *n.* 勇猛，英勇

valuable ['væljuəbl] **I** *a.* ①值钱的，贵重的 ②有
价值的，有用的；宝贵的：~ assistance 宝贵的援
助 / a ~ discovery 有价值的发现 ③可估价的：
a service not ~ in money 不能以金钱估价的贡
献 **II** *n.* [常用复]贵重物品，财宝 ‖**~ness** *n.* /
valuably *ad.* ‖~ **consideration** 与受益价值
相等的酬报

valuation [,vælju'eiʃən] *n.* ①估价；估定的价值(或
价格)，定价：be disposed of at a low ~ 廉价出
售 ②评价：set too high a ~ on sb.'s abilities
对某人的能力评价过高

value ['vælju:] **I** *n.* ①价值：gross output ~ of
industry and agriculture 工农业总产值 / face
~ 票面价值 / surplus ~ 剩余价值 ②价格；交
换力；购买力：The market ~ of this property
has declined. 这地产的市价下跌了。/ The ~
of our currency is stable. 我们的币值是稳定的。
③益处；重要性；有用性：a man who is of ~ to
the people 对人民有益的人 / the ~ of sunlight
to health 阳光对健康的重要性 / These data will
be of great (some) ~ to us in our research work.
这些资料对我们的研究工作将有很大 (一些) 帮
助。④ 等值；公平的代价：We got good ~ for
our money. 我们的钱花得很值得。/ pay full
~ for sth. 以实足的代价取得某物 ⑤估价；评
价：set a high ~ on one's time 珍惜时间 ⑥(邮
票等的)面值 ⑦ 涵义，意义：the precise ~ of a
word 一个词的确切涵义 ⑧【数】值；【语】音值；
【生】(分类上的)等级；【音】音的长短；(绘画中)明
暗的配合 ~ out of ~ 明暗不调和的 ⑨[复]对价值
的看法，标准；社会准则 **II** *vt.* ①估…的价；把…
作价为 ②评价；尊重，重视 ‖~ **oneself on** (或
upon) 自夸 ‖**~less** *a.* 无价值的，没有用的

valve [vælv] **I** *n.* ①【机】阀，活门：clack ~ 瓣阀 /
rotary (或 rotating) ~ 回转阀 / sliding (或
slide) ~ 滑阀 / poppet ~ 提升阀 / safety ~
安全阀 ②【解】瓣，瓣膜；【植】(藻的)瓣，(果实的)
裂片：the tricuspid ~ 三尖瓣 ③[英]电子管，真
空管：a ~ detector 电子管检波器 ④【音】(管
乐器用以改变音调的)栓塞 ⑤【动】贝壳；阴门
II *vt. & vi.* 装阀(于)；用阀调节(液体)的流量
‖**~d** *a.* 装有阀的 / **~less** *a.* 无阀的

van[1] [væn] *n.* ①【军】前卫；先头部队(或舰队)
②[喻](社会政治运动的)前驱，先锋，领导者：be
in the ~ of a movement 站在运动的前列

van[2] [væn] **I** *n.* ①大篷货车；运货车，搬运车：a
furniture ~ 家具搬运车 / a livestock ~ 运牲
畜车 ②[英]有棚盖的铁路货车；行李车：a luggage ~ 行李车 ③(吉卜赛人等所住的)篷车
II (vanned; vanning) *vt.* 用车搬运 ‖~ **line**
[美]长途搬运公司

van[3] [væn] *n.* ①[英方]簸(谷)器 ②【矿】洗矿铲；
[英方]铲头洗矿 ③[诗](鸟、昆虫的)翼

Vandal ['vændəl] **I** *n.* ①汪达尔人(属日耳曼民族,公元四至五世纪进入高卢、西班牙、北非等地,并曾攻占罗马) ②[v-]摧残文化、艺术者;破坏他人(或公共)财产者 **II** *a.* ①汪达尔人的 ②[v-]破坏性的 ‖~ic [væn'dælik] *a.* ①汪达尔人的 ②[v-]破坏性的;野蛮的 / **vandalism** *n.* 故意破坏文化、艺术的行为;破坏他人(或公共)财产的行为

vane [vein] *n.* ①【气】风向标;[喻]反复无常的人,变化不定的事物 ②(风车、螺旋桨等的)翼;叶片;轮叶 ③【测】瞄准板,觇板 ④(罗盘等的)照准器 ⑤(鸟的)羽片,翀 ‖~d *a.*

vanguard ['vænɡɑ:d] *n.* ①【军】前卫;先头部队;尖兵: ~ action 前卫战 ②[喻](社会政治运动的)先锋(队),领导者: play a ~ role 起先锋作用

vanish ['væniʃ] **I** *vi.* ①突然不见;逐渐消散;消失;消灭: ~ from sight 消失不见 / ~ into the void 化为乌有 ②【数】成为零 **II** *n.*【语】弱化音 ‖~ing cream 雪花膏 / ~ing point ①没影点(透视画中平行线条的会聚点) ②(事物的)尽头: cut down the incidence of tuberculosis to the ~ing point 消灭结核病

vanity ['væniti] *n.* ①虚夸,虚荣心: do sth. out of ~ 出于虚荣做某事 ②自负,自大 ③空虚;无益,无用;无价值的东西 ④(妇女手提包中用的)小粉盒;(女用)手袋,手提包 ⑤梳妆台 ‖~ **bag,** ~ **box,** ~ **case** (女用)小手袋,小手提包 / **Vanity Fair** 浮华虚荣的社会,名利场 / ~ **press,** ~ **publisher** 出版由作者自己出钱印刷的书的出版社

vanquish ['væŋkwiʃ] *vt.* 征服,战胜,击败;克服,抑制(感情等) ‖~**able** *a.* 可征服的,能战胜的 / ~**er** *n.* 征服者,战胜者

vapid ['væpid] *a.* ①乏味的,无滋味的: ~ beer 淡而无味的啤酒 ②无趣味的,枯燥乏味的;无生气的: a ~ speech 枯燥乏味的演说 ‖~**ly** *ad.* / ~**ness** *n.*

vapidity [væ'piditi] *n.* ①乏味;无滋味 ②无趣味;枯燥乏味;无生气 ③[复]无趣味的话

vaporize, vaporise ['veipəraiz] *vt.* & *vi.* (使)蒸发;(使)汽化 ‖**vaporizable** *a.* 可汽化的;可蒸发的 / **vaporization** [,veipərai'zeiʃən] *n.* / ~**r** *n.* 汽化器;喷雾器;蒸馏器

vapo(u)r ['veipə] **I** *n.* ①蒸气;汽;雾;烟雾: water ~ 水蒸气 ②无实质之物;空想的东西;愚蠢的想法,幻想 ③[the ~s] 忧郁(症) ④【药】吸入剂 **II** ① *vi.* ①蒸发;变成蒸气;散发蒸气 ②自夸,说废话 ❷ *vt.* ①使蒸发;使汽化 ②[古]使患忧郁症 ‖~**er** ['veipərə] *n.* 吹牛者;夸夸其谈者 / ~**ing** ['veipəriŋ] *n.* [常用复]大话;自夸 *a.* ①蒸发的 ②自夸的 ‖~ **bath** ①蒸汽浴 ②蒸汽浴浴室 / ~ **trail** 【空】(飞机在高空飞行时产生的)雾化尾迹

variable ['vɛəriəbl] **I** *a.* ①易变的;常变的;反复不定的: a ~ mood (temper) 反复无常的情绪(脾

气) / ~ winds 方向不定的风 ②可变的: a ~ gear 变速齿轮 / a ~ period of 5 to 10 days 五天到十天的可变更期限 / a word of ~ construction 可作多种不同解释的词 ③【数】变量的 ④(星)亮度变化的: a ~ star 变星 ⑤【生】变异的;变型的;畸变的 **II** *n.* ①可变物 ②【海】(方向或风力不定的)变风,不定风 ③【天】变星 ④【数】变量;变数;变元;变项 ⑤[the ~s](东北与东南信风带之间的)变风区 ‖**variability** [,vɛəriə'biliti] *n.* 变化性;易变;【生】变异性 / ~**ness** *n.* / **variably** *ad.*

variance ['vɛəriəns] *n.* ①变化;变动;变异: ~ of temperature 温度的变化 ②(意见等的)不一致,分歧;争论;不和: the ~ between two weather reports 两个气象报告间的差异 / I once had a slight ~ with him. 我和他有过小争论。③【律】(诉状和供词等之间的)不符 ④ (对某种行为的)特殊许可 ⑤(统计学中的)方差 ‖at ~ (人和人间)有分歧;不和;(事物间)不符: On that point we are at ~ (among ourselves). 在那点上我们(自己)意见不一致。/ His conduct is at ~ with his words. 他言行不一。/ set at ~ 使不和,离间

variant ['vɛəriənt] **I** *a.* 不同的;变异的;差别的: ~ spellings of a word 一个词的不同拼法 / ~ interpretations 不同的解释 / ~ types of pigeon 鸽子的各种变种 / a ~ reading (稿本的)异文 / ~ editions 不同的版本 **II** *n.* ①变体;变种;变形 ②异体,异体字;异文;(同一词的)异读 ③(统计学中的)变式;【生】变异体

variation [,vɛəri'eiʃən] *n.* ①变化;变动;变更: ~s in speed 速度的变化 / These prices are subject to ~. 这些价格可能变更。②变化的程度 ③【数】变分;【生】变异;变种;【天】变差;(月的)二均差;【物】磁差;【语】词尾变化;【音】变奏(曲) ④(古典芭蕾舞中的)一种独人舞;(现代芭蕾舞中)重复出现而有所变化的一组动作 ‖~**al** *a.*

varied ['vɛərid] *a.* ①多变化的;各种各样的;不相同的: a ~ career 变动多的经历 / a ~ economy 多种经营的经济 / ~ opinions 各种不同的意见 ②改变了的: a ~ form of a word 字的异体 ③杂色的;斑驳的 ‖~**ly** *ad.*

variegated ['vɛərigeitid] *a.* ①杂色的;斑驳的: ~ copper (ore) 斑铜矿 / ~ leaves 【植】斑叶 ②多样化的

variety [və'raiəti] *n.* ①多样化;变化: give ~ to the programme 使节目丰富多采 / His writing lacks ~. 他的文体缺乏变化。②种类: a choice ~ of black tea 特级红茶 / varieties of cloth 各种布匹 ③[a ~]种种: Iron has a ~ of uses. 铁有种种用处。/ for a ~ of reasons 由于种种原因 ④【生】变种;品种;【语】异体: a new ~ of apples 苹果的新品种 ⑤(音乐、舞蹈、杂耍等的)联合演出: a ~ entertainment (或 show) 杂耍演出 / a ~ theatre 杂耍剧场 / ~ artists 杂耍艺人 ‖~ **meat** 牛(或羊、猪)什(包括心、肝、腰子、

舌等) / **～ shop, ～ store** 杂货铺

various ['vɛəriəs] *a.* ①各种各样的,不同的;种种的: at ～ times 在不同的时代 / ～ opinions 不同的意见 / for ～ reasons 为了种种的原因 ②多方面的;多才多艺的;具有各种不同特征的: ～ branches of knowledge 多方面的知识 ③几个的,许多的 ④(一团体内)各个的,个别的: distribute the pamphlets to the ～ group members 把小册子发给小组内各成员 ⑤杂色的,彩色的: birds of ～ plumage 有杂色羽毛的鸟 ⑥[复][口][作代词用]好几个:I questioned ～ of them. 我问过他们中间好几个人。‖**～ly** *ad.* / **～ness** *n.*

varnish ['vɑːniʃ] **I** *n.* ①清漆,罩光漆,凡立水,釉子;印刷调墨油 ②(人工或天然的)光泽,(瓷器等的)光泽面 ③[喻]虚饰;文饰: with a ～ of good manners 装着有礼貌的样子 ④[主英]指甲油 ⑤[复][美俚]～ed car **II** *vt.* ①涂清漆;使有光泽;给…上釉 ②粉饰,文饰 ③装饰,修饰 ‖**～ed car** [美俚](火车的)客车;卧车;特别快车 / **～ing day** ①画展开幕前作者修饰作品的一天 ②艺术展览会开幕日 / **～ remover** [美俚]①浓咖啡 ②威士忌酒(尤指廉价的劣酒)

vary ['vɛəri] ❶ *vt.* ①改变;变更;修改: ～ one's method of work 改变工作方法 / ～ one's plans 变更计划 / ～ the speed 改变速度 ②使多样化;使有变化: ～ a programme to avoid monotony 使节目多样化以免单调 / ～ one's reading 泛阅多样化的读物 ③[音]变奏(曲调或主题) ❷ *vi.* ①变化;不同: The weather *varies* from hour to hour in some mountain districts. 在某些山区天气时刻变化。/ Opinions ～ on that point. 在那一点上意见各不相同。/ in ～ing degrees 在不同程度上 / ～ in size (weight) 大小(重量)不同 ②违反;偏离: ～ from the law of nature 违反自然规律 ③[生]变异 ④[数](按正比或反比)改变,变化: ～ directly (inversely) *as* . . . 和…成正(反)比 ‖**～ with** 随…而变化: prices that ～ *with* the quality 随质量不同而不同的价格

vas [væs] ([复]vasa ['veisə]) *n.* [拉][生][解]管;血管;脉管 ‖**～ deferens** ['defərenz] 输精管

vase [vɑːz; 美 veis] *n.* ①(装饰用的)瓶;花瓶: a flower ～ 花瓶 ②[建]瓶饰

vassal ['væsəl] **I** *n.* ①(封建时代的)诸侯,封臣;陪臣 ②附庸,奴仆;奴隶: troops from ～ **II** *a.* ①臣的,为臣的 ②奴仆的,为奴仆的;奴隶的: a ～ state 仆从国

vassalage ['væsəlidʒ] *n.* ①诸侯(或封臣等)的身分;臣属 ②忠顺,效忠 ③采地,领地 ④附庸的地位

vast [vɑːst] **I** *a.* ①巨大的,庞大的: a ～ building 巨大的建筑物 / a ～ improvement 巨大的进步 / sb.'s ～ frame 某人庞大的体格 / a ～ scheme 庞大的计划 ②大量的,巨额的;浩瀚的: a ～ multitude 一大群人 / a ～ sum of money 一笔巨款 ③广阔的;深远的: a ～ expanse of water

一片汪洋 / in those ～ areas of Asia, Africa and Latin America 在亚洲、非洲和拉丁美洲的广大地区 / accumulate a ～ knowledge 积累渊博的知识 ④[口]非常的;莫大的: make a ～ difference 形成天渊之别 / give sb. ～ satisfaction 使某人心满意足 **II** *n.* [诗]茫茫,无边无际的空间: the ～ of heaven 万里长空 ‖**～ly** *ad.* / **～ness** *n.*

vat [væt] **I** *n.* ①(染色、酿造等用的)大桶;大盆;瓮,缸: a dye ～ 染瓮 / a water ～ 水缸 ②瓮(染料)还原物 **II** (vatted; vatting) *vt.* 把…盛入大桶;在大桶里染(或处理) ‖**～ful** *n.* 满满一大桶,一大桶的量 ‖**～ dye, ～ colo(u)r** 瓮染料,还原染料 / **'～-'dyed** *a.* 用一种(或多种)瓮染料染的

vaudeville ['voudəvi(ː)l] *n.* ①轻歌舞剧 ②歌舞杂耍表演 ‖**vaudevillian** [,voudə'vi(ː)liən] *n.* 轻歌舞剧编剧者;轻歌舞剧(或歌舞杂耍表演)的演员

vault¹ [vɔːlt] **I** *n.* ①[建]拱顶;穹窿状覆盖物: a barrel ～ 筒形拱顶 / the ～ of heaven 天穹,苍穹 ②拱顶室;地下室;地窖: a wine ～ 酒窖 ③(教堂下的)墓穴;(金属或水泥的)棺椁 ④(银行等的)保管库(贵重物品储藏处) ⑤[解]穹窿 **II** ❶ *vt.* ①给…盖以拱顶 ②使作成穹形 ❷ *vi.* 成穹状弯曲 ‖**～ed** *a.* 盖有拱顶的;拱状的

vault

vault² [vɔːlt] **I** ❶ *vi.* 跳跃(尤指以手撑物跳跃或撑竿跳跃): ～ on to a horse 跃上马(背) / ～ into the saddle 跃登马鞍 / ～ over a ditch 跳过沟 ❷ *vt.* 以手撑物跃过;撑竿跃过: ～ a fence 跳过篱笆 **II** *n.* 跳跃;撑物跳跃;撑竿跳;(马的)腾跃 ‖**～er** *n.* 撑物跳跃者;撑竿跳者

vaunt [vɔːnt] **I** *vt.* & *vi.* 自夸 **II** *n.* 自吹自擂;夸张自负的话 ‖**～er** *n.* 自吹自擂的人

veal [viːl] **I** *n.* (食用的)小牛肉;幼小的菜牛 **II** *vt.* 宰(小牛)

veer¹ [viə] **I** ❶ *vi.* ①改变方向,转向: The wind ～ed round to the east. 风向转东。②[气](风向)顺(时针)转 ③[海](帆船)顺风换抢,调转船尾向上风 ④[喻]改变 (*from*) ❷ *vt.* ①使改变方向 ②[海]使顺风,使(船)改变航向(船尾转向上风) **II** *n.* 方向的改变 ‖**～ingly** ['viəriŋli] *ad.*

veer² [viə] *vt.* [海]放出(绳索、锚等) (*out*) ‖**～ and haul** [海](把绳索等)一放一收

vegetable ['vedʒitəbl] **I** *n.* ① 植物 ② 蔬菜: pickled ~s 咸菜 ③[喻]生活呆板单调的人 **II** *a.* ①植物的; 植物性的; 由植物得来的; 关于植物的: ~ matter 植物质 / ~ fat 植物油脂 / anatomy 植物解剖学 ②蔬菜的: a ~ diet 素食 / ~ soup 菜汤 ③[喻]生活呆板单调的 ‖**vegetably** *ad.* 呆板单调地 ‖~ **butter** (食用)植物脂 / ~ **kingdom** 植物界 / ~ **oil** 植物油 / ~ **plate** (西餐中作为主菜用的)蔬菜什锦 / ~ **silk** 植物丝, 丝状植物纤维 / ~ **sponge** 丝瓜筋 / ~ **tallow** (制肥皂、烛等用的)植物脂 / ~ **wax** 植物蜡

vegetal ['vedʒitl] **I** *a.* ①植物的; 植物性的 ② 有关植物生长和营养机能的 ③动植物共通的 **II** *n.* ①植物 ②蔬菜

vegetarian [,vedʒi'tɛəriən] **I** *n.* ①吃素的人; 素食主义者 ② 食草动物 **II** *a.* ①素食的; 素食者的; 素食主义的: ~ principles 素食主义 / go ~ 吃素 ② 光是蔬菜的, 素菜的: a ~ diet 素食 ‖~**ism** *n.* 素食主义

vegetation [,vedʒi'teiʃən] *n.* ①【植】植被; 营养体生长 ②[总称]植物, 草木 ③ 呆板单调的生活 ④【医】赘生物, 增殖体 ‖~**al** *a.*

vehemence ['vi:iməns] *n.* 热烈, 热心; 强烈; 猛烈; 激烈

vehement ['vi:imənt] *a.* ①感情激烈的; 热烈的: a man of ~ character 感情激烈的人 / a ~ desire 热烈的愿望 ② 强烈的; 猛烈的; 激烈的: a ~ protest 强烈的抗议 / a ~ onset 猛烈的攻击; (疾病等)猛烈的开始 / a ~ wind 一阵猛烈的风 ‖~**ly** *ad.*

vehicle ['vi:ikl] *n.* ①运载工具; 车辆, 机动车; 机械器具; 推进装置; 飞行器: The launch ~ lifts the satellite into the orbit. 运载火箭把人造卫星送入运行轨道。 / tractors and farm ~s 拖拉机及农业机械器具 / an unmanned ~ 无人驾驶飞行器 / a hypersonic test ~ 高超音速两极试验火箭 ②传达思想感情的工具; 媒介物: Language is a ~ of human thought. 语言是人类表达思想的一种工具。 / a ~ of disease 疾病的媒介物 ③【药】赋形剂 ④【化】展色料, 载色剂

vehicular [vi'hikjulə] *a.* ①车(辆)的; 用车辆运载的; 供车辆通过的: The road is closed to ~ traffic. 此路不准车辆通过。 / a ~ tunnel 供车辆通过的隧道 ②作为媒介的

veil [veil] **I** *n.* ①面纱, 面罩: She raised (dropped) her ~. 她揭起(放下)面罩。 ② 幕; 帐, 幔 ③ [喻]遮蔽物; 掩饰物; 借口; 假托: a ~ of mist 一层雾 / a ~ of silence 一片肃静 / under the ~ of religion 在宗教的外衣下 ④修女的头巾; 修女生活: take the ~ 去当修女 ⑤声音微哑 ⑥【动】【植】膜, 缘膜; 菌幕; 【解】(胎儿的)胎膜 **II** *vt.* ①以面纱遮掩: These women are ~ed. 这些妇女蒙着面纱。 ② 遮盖; 掩饰; 隐蔽: ~ one's distrust of sth. 把自己对某事的怀疑掩盖起来 ❷ *vi.* 蒙上面纱 ‖**beyond the ~** 在死后的无知

境界 / **draw a ~ over sth.** 把某事掩盖起来; 避而不谈某事

vein [vein] **I** *n.* ① 静脉; [俗]血管 ②【地】【矿】脉; 矿脉; 岩脉; (地层或冰层中的)水脉: a ~ of coal 煤层 / a ~ of ore 矿脉 ③【动】翅脉; 【植】叶脉 ④纹理; 木纹; 石理 ⑤性情; 气质; 才干; 语调, 风格; 意向; 情绪: a man of an imaginative ~ 爱好想象的人 / He had no comedy ~ in his youth. 在青年时代他并没有演喜剧的才干。 / other remarks in the same ~ 同一腔调的其他评论 / He speaks in a humorous ~. 他说话富有风趣。 / in a merry (humorous, melancholic) ~ 带着愉快(幽默, 忧郁)的情绪 / I am not in (the) ~ just now. 我目前没有这种兴致。 **II** *vt.* [常用被动语态] ① 使成脉络(或纹理): The backs of her hands are ~ed. 她的手背脉络暴露。 ② 象脉络(或纹理)般分布于: be ~ed by railroads 布满四通八达的铁路线 ‖~**al** *a.* 静脉的; 脉的 / ~ed *a.* 有纹理的; 有叶脉的; 显出纹理的; 显出静脉的: ~ed marble 有纹理的大理石 / a ~ed leaf 有叶脉的叶子 / ~**ing** *n.* 叶脉(或纹理等)的形成(或排列)

veld(t) [velt] *n.* (南非洲的)草原

vellum ['veləm] **I** *n.* ① 精制犊皮纸; 精制羔皮纸 (书写或装帧用) ② 犊皮纸手抄稿 ③ 仿羊皮纸 (= ~ paper) **II** *a.* 犊皮纸的; 羔皮纸的; 仿羊皮纸的 ‖~**y** *a.*

velocity [vi'lɔsiti] *n.* ①速度; 速率: the ~ of sound 音速 / uniform ~ 匀速度 / initial ~ 初速度 / muzzle ~ 腔口速度(射弹离开炮口瞬间的速度) / instantaneous ~ 瞬时速度 / ~ of escape (=escape ~) 逃逸速度, 克服地球吸力的速度, 第二宇宙速度 ②迅速, 快速: dart off with the ~ of a bird 像鸟一样迅速地掠过 ③周转率: ~ of money 资金周转率

velvet ['velvit] **I** *n.* ① 天鹅绒, 丝绒, 立绒, 经绒 ② 天鹅绒似的东西; 柔软; 光滑 ③ 鹿茸的嫩皮 ④(赌博中)赢得的钱; 意外的盈利 **II** *a.* ①天鹅绒制的; 用天鹅绒覆盖的 ②天鹅绒般的; 柔软的; 光滑的 ‖**a (或 the) ~ glove** 内里强硬表面温和的东西, 表面的温和 / **a ~ paw** 见 **paw** / **on ~** 在有利的(或兴盛的)地位, (赌博、投机等时)在稳赚钱的地位 / **with an iron hand in a ~ glove** 见 **hand**

venal ['vi:nl] *a.* ①可以利诱的, 可以收买的, 贪污的: ~ officials 贪官污吏 ②(行为)受贿赂影响的; 可用金钱得到的, 为钱而做的: ~ practices 贿赂(或受贿)行为 ‖~**ity** [vi(:)'næliti] *n.* / ~**ly** *ad.*

vend [vend] ❶ *vt.* ①(主要为法律用语)出售 ②贩卖, 叫卖(尤指小商品) ③公开发表(意见) ❷ *vi.* 出售货物; 从事贩卖 ‖~**er** *n.* =vendor ‖~**ing machine** 自动售货机(出售香烟等小商品)

vendetta [ven'detə] *n.* ①族间血仇(尤指意大利某些地区和科西嘉等地的族间仇杀) ②深仇, 长年

的争斗 ‖**vendettist** [ven'detist] *n.* 卷入族间仇杀的人; 复仇者

vendor ['vendɔ:] *n.* ①(主要为法律用语)卖主 ②小贩: a news ~ 报贩 ③自动售货机

veneer [vi'niə] **I** *n.* ① 镶饰表面的薄板;胶合板;三夹板 ② (墙壁上的)饰面; 护面(如砖、石等) ③(掩盖真情的)外表; 虚饰: a ~ of fair-mindedness 貌似公正 **II** *vt.* ①镶盖;镶饰;砌面: ~ a pine desk with mahogany 用桃花心木薄板镶于松木桌上 ②胶合(薄片) ③虚饰

venenate ['venineit] **❶** *vt.* 使中毒;把毒注入… **❷** *vi.* (虫等在吮血时) 放出毒液 ‖**venenation** [,veni'neiʃən] *n.*

venerable ['venərəbl] *a.* ① 可尊敬的, 可崇敬的; 年高德劭的: a ~ old worker 可尊敬的老工人 ② 历史悠久的; 令人肃然起敬的; 古老的: a ~ monument 历史悠久的纪念碑 / ~ pines 古松 / a ~ age 高龄 / a ~ beard 长髯 ③(英国国教)副主教的尊称;【天主教】被列入圣徒的人的头衔 ‖**venerability** [,venərə'biliti] *n.* / **venerably** *ad.*

venerate ['venəreit] *vt.* 尊敬; 崇拜: a man to be ~d for uprightness 由于正直而受尊敬的人 ‖**venerator** *n.* 尊敬(他人)者; 崇拜者

veneration [,venə'reiʃən] *n.* 尊敬; 崇拜: be filled with ~ for 对…充满崇敬的心情

venereal [vi'niəriəl] *a.* ①性交的; 因性交引起的 ②性病的, 花柳病的: ~ diseases 性病, 花柳病 / ~ remedies 治性病的药

vengeance ['vendʒəns] *n.* 报仇, 报复: exact a ~ from sb. for 为…向某人报仇 / take (或 inflict, wreak) ~ on sb. for 为…向某人报仇 / lay oneself open to the ~ of sb. 使自己陷于受某人报复的危险 / seek ~ upon sb. 找机会向某人报复 / *Heaven's ~ is slow but sure.* [谚] 天网恢恢, 疏而不漏。 / *with a ~* [口]猛烈地; 彻底地; 极度地; 过度地: The rain came down *with a ~*. 大雨滂沱。 / *This is punctuality with a ~.* 这样刻板地遵守时间未免过分。

vengeful ['vendʒful] *a.* ① 有报仇心理的; 谋报复的 ②(利于)报复的 ‖**~ly** *ad.* / **~ness** *n.*

venial ['vi:njəl] *a.* 可原谅的; 可宽恕的; (错误)轻微的: a ~ fault 小错误 ‖**~ly** *ad.* / **~ness** *n.* ‖**~ sin**【天主教】(可用祈祷等赎的)小罪

venison ['venizn] *n.* ①野味 ②鹿肉

venom ['venəm] **I** *n.* ①(毒蛇等的) 毒液; (一般)毒物: a ~ duct (fang, gland) 毒管(牙, 腺) ②恶意;恶毒的话(或行为) **II** *vt.* 放毒; 使恶毒: ~ed remarks 恶毒的话

venomous ['venəməs] *a.* ①有毒的; 分泌毒液的; 有毒腺的: ~ snakes 毒蛇 ②恶意的;恶毒的, 狠毒的: a ~ attack 恶毒的攻击 / a ~ scheme 毒计 ‖**~ly** *ad.* / **~ness** *n.*

vent[1] [vent] **I** *n.* ①出口, 出路; 漏孔 ②通风孔, 出烟孔; 排气道; [苏格兰]烟囱(管) ③(管乐器的)指孔 ④(旧式枪、炮的)火门 ⑤火山口 ⑥(鸟、虫、鱼等的)肛门 ⑦[只用单](感情等的)发泄, 吐露: give ~ to one's anger 泄怒, 出气 / The news has taken ~. 消息给泄漏了。 **II** *vt.* ①给…开孔; 给…一个出口: ~ a cask 开桶 / Chimneys ~ smoke. 烟囱出烟。 ②放出; 排出 ③发泄感情: ~ one's spite upon sb. 向某人泄愤, 在某人身上出气 ‖**~less** *a.* 无孔的; 无出口的 ‖**~hole** *n.* 通风孔; 排气口; 排气管 (桶等的)通气孔塞 / '**~-pipe** *n.* 通风管; 排气管 / '**~-plug** *n.* ①通风孔塞 ②(枪炮的)火门塞

vent[2] [vent] *n.* (上衣背部或裙子等的)叉口, 开叉

ventiduct ['ventidʌkt] *n.*【建】(尤指地下的)通风管, 通风道

ventilate ['ventileit] *vt.* ①使通风, 使通气; 使换气;给…装置通风设备: ~ the galleries of a coal mine 使煤矿坑道通风 ②宣布, 公开; 自由讨论(问题、意见等): ~ one's views 发表自己的看法 ③【医】使(血液)吸收氧气 ‖**ventilative** *a.* / **ventilator** *n.* 通风装置; 排气风扇; 送风机; 通气孔

ventilation [,venti'leiʃən] *n.* ①通风; 流通空气: ~ facilities 通风设备 / a room with good ~ 通风良好的房间 ②通风设备;通气法 ③公开讨论

ventriloquism [ven'triləkwizəm], **ventriloquy** [ven'triləkwi] *n.* 口技 ‖**ventriloquist** *n.* 口技表演者

venture ['ventʃə] **I** *n.* ①冒险,冒险行动: He declined to risk his life in any ~. 他拒绝了任何冒险行动。/ be ready for any ~ 准备冒任何危险 ②冒险事业;商业冒险, 投机: fail in one's ~s 投机失败 ③用于投机事业的商船(或货物); 赌注 **II** **❶** *vt.* ①冒…的危险: He ~d his life to rescue the drowning child. 他冒着生命危险抢救快要淹死的孩子。②拿…进行投机: ~ one's money on the stocks 拿股票来投机 / ~ a fortune on a single chance 拿大宗财产作孤注一掷 ③敢于; 大胆表示(或提出): ~ an objection (姑且)大胆提出反对意见 / I ~ to say that .... 我敢(冒昧地)说… / I ~ to differ from you. 对不起, 我跟你意见不同。**❷** *vi.* 冒险; 敢于; 鼓起勇气前进 (on, upon): ~ on (或 upon) a stormy sea 冒着风浪出海 / Will you ~ on a slice of my home-made cake? 你愿意尝一尝我家自制的饼吗? ‖*at a ~* 冒险地, 碰运气地 / 胡乱地, 随便地 / *Nothing ~, nothing have.* [谚]不入虎穴, 焉得虎子? ‖**~r** ['ventʃərə] *n.* 冒险者;投机者

venturesome ['ventʃəsəm] *a.* ①好冒险的; 大胆的 ②危险的, 有危险的: a ~ journey 艰险的旅程 ‖**~ly** *ad.* / **~ness** *n.*

veracious [ve'reiʃəs] *a.* ①讲实话的; 诚实的 ②准确的;真实的 ‖**~ly** *ad.* / **~ness** *n.*

veracity [ve'ræsiti] *n.* ①讲实话; 诚实 ②真实(性); 确实 ③(感觉、衡量等的)准确(性), 精确(性)

veranda(h) [vəˈrændə] *n.* 游廊; 走廊; 阳台

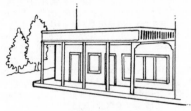

veranda(h)

verb [vəːb] **I** *n.* 【语】动词: a regular (an irregular) ~ 规则 (不规则) 动词 / a transitive (an intransitive) ~ 及物 (不及物) 动词 / an auxiliary ~ 助动词 / a modal ~ 情态动词 / a link (或 linking) ~ 连系动词 / take a plural ~ (需) 用动词复数形式 **II** *a.* 动词的; 动词性质的; 有动词作用的

verbal [ˈvəːbəl] **I** *a.* ①词语的, 言语的, 字句的; 关于词语的: a ~ image 用词语描写的形象 / a ~ error 用词的错误 / have a good ~ memory 善于记忆字句 ②口头的,非书面的: ~ confession 口供 / a ~ contract 口头约定 / a ~ message 口信 ③逐字的,照字面的: ~ translation 逐字翻译,直译 ④【语】动词的; 动词性质的; 由动词形成的; 用以构成动词的: ~ inflexions 动词的变化 / a ~ suffix 构成动词的后缀 **II** *n.* 【语】动词的非谓语形式(指不定式、分词和动名词) ‖**~ism** *n.* ①言语表达 ②拘泥文字 ③赘语,冗词 / **~ist** *n.* 善用词藻者; 咬文嚼字者 / **~ly** *ad.*

auxiliary 【语】助动词 / ~ note (外交上) 不签字的备忘录(述及非紧要的但不能忽视的事情) / ~ noun 【语】(名词化的)动名词

verbatim [vəːˈbeitim] **I** *ad.* (照原文或原本)逐字地; (完全)照字面地: copy it ~ 逐字地抄录 / report a speech ~ 逐字地报道一篇演说 **II** *a.* 逐字的; 照字面的: a ~ reprint 毫无改动的再版

verbose [vəːˈbous] *a.* 唠叨的; 累赘的; 冗长的 ‖**~ly** *ad.* / **verbosity** [vəːˈbɔsiti] *n.*

verdant [ˈvəːdənt] *a.* ①青翠的, 嫩绿的: ~ grass 青草 / ~ fields 青翠的田野 ②生疏的; 不老练的; 无经验的: a ~ youth 缺乏经验的青年

verdict [ˈvəːdikt] *n.* ①【律】(陪审团的)裁决,评决: The jury brought in a ~ of guilty (not guilty). 陪审团裁决有罪(无罪)。/ a ~ for the plaintiff 有利于原告的裁决 ②定论; 判断; 意见: a final ~ 定论 / a ~ of history 历史的结论 / reverse the ~ 翻案 / pass one's ~ upon 对…下判断 / a popular ~ 公众的意见 / My ~s differ from yours in this matter. 在这个问题上我的意见和你不同。‖**an open ~** 死因未详的裁决 / **a partial ~** 部分有罪的裁决 / **a privy** (或 **sealed**) **~** 密封的裁决书(指法官退席后,陪审团

交给法院书吏的初步的书面裁决) / **a special ~** 特别裁决(陪审团只提供已证实的事实,由法庭据此进行判决)

verdigris [ˈvəːdigris] *n.* ①(铜器等面上的)铜绿 ②碱性碳酸铜; 碱性醋酸铜

verge [vəːdʒ] **I** *n.* ①边缘; 边界,界限: the ~ of a forest 森林的边缘 / the ~ of the sea 海边 ②【建】山墙檐边瓦; 花坛的围边草 ③(钟表)摆轮的心轴 ④(标志主教等职权的)杖,节 ⑤【英史】王室司法官的辖区 **II** *vi.* ①接近; 濒于: a path *verging* on the edge of a precipice 沿着崖边的一条小路 / Such a remark ~s on impertinence. 这种话近于无礼。/ ~ on total collapse 濒于全面崩溃 / They seemed to be *verging* toward a quarrel. 他们似乎要吵起来了。②(太阳等)下沉; 趋向,斜向; (山脉等)延伸: The hill ~s to the north. 小山向北延伸。‖**bring sb. to the ~ of** 使某人濒于: bring sb. to the ~ of tears 使某人快要哭出来 / **on the ~ of** 接近于; 濒于: She is *on the* ~ *of* ninety. 她年近九十了。/ The child was *on the* ~ *of* laughing. 孩子差点笑出来。/ *on the* ~ *of* extinction 将近灭亡 ‖**board** 【建】挡风板,山头封檐板

verger [ˈvəːdʒə] *n.* ①[英](行列中为主教、大学副校长等)持权标的人员 ②管理教堂内部事务者; 堂守

verifiable [ˈverifai-əbl] *a.* 可证实的; 可检验的; 可考证的;可核实的 ‖**verifiability** [ˌverifai-əˈbiliti] *n.* / **~ness** *n.*

verification [ˌverifiˈkeiʃən] *n.* ①证实, 证明; 证据; 检验; 核实 ②【律】诉状(或答辩状)结尾的举证声明

verify [ˈverifai] *vt.* ①证实; 查证; 检验; 核实: Truth can only be *verified* through practice. 只有通过实践,才能检验真理。/ ~ the figures of a report 核实一个报告里的数字 ②【律】(宣誓)证明; 把举证声明写入(诉状或答辩状)的末尾

verily [ˈverili] *ad.* ①真正地; 毫无疑问地; 肯定地 ②忠实地; 确信地; 真实地

verisimilitude [ˌverisiˈmilitjuːd] *n.* ①逼真, 貌似真实: the ~ of the tale 故事的逼真 / *Verisimilitude* is not proof. 貌似真实不足为据。②逼真的事物; 貌似真实的事物; 似乎真实的话

veritable [ˈveritəbl] *a.* 确实的; 真正的; 名符其实的: a ~ blackguard 十足的无赖 ‖**~ness** *n.* / **veritably** *ad.*

verity [ˈveriti] *n.* ①真实性: doubt the ~ of sb.'s statement 怀疑某人陈述的真实性 ②真理; 事实;确实存在的事物 ③诚实可靠: a man of unquestioned ~ 绝对可靠的人

vermil(l)ion [vəˈmiljən] **I** *n.* ①银硃,辰砂,硃砂; 硫化汞 ②朱红色 **II** *a.* 朱红色的 **III** *vt.* 涂朱红色于

vermin [ˈvəːmin] ⌊单复同⌋ *n.* ①害虫(指虱等)寄生虫; 害兽; 害鸟 ②[喻]害人虫; 歹徒

verminous ['vəːminəs] *a.* ① 害虫的; 似害虫的 ② 长有(虱等)害虫的; 有害的 ③ 引起害虫孳生的, 污秽的: ~ garbage 肮脏的垃圾 ④ 由害虫引起的: ~ diseases 由害虫引起的疾病 ‖~ly *ad.*

vernacular [vəˈnækjulə] I *n.* ①本国语; 本地话, 土话, 方言; 白话: the English ~ of Ireland 爱尔兰的英语方言 / written in the ~ 用白话文写的 ②行话 ③动植物的俗名 II *a.* ①用本国语(写)的; 用方言(写)的; 本地话的, 方言的; 白话的: a ~ poet 方言诗人 / a ~ idiom 本地话的习惯用语 / the ~ style of writing 白话文体 ②本国的; 本地的, 乡土的: a ~ disease 地方病 / the ~ arts of Fukien 福建的地方工艺 ③动植物俗名的 ‖~ism [vəˈnækjulərizəm] *n.* 方言的词语; 方言的习惯用法; 方言的运用 / ~ize [vəˈnækjuləraiz] *vt.* 使方言化; 用方言表达 / ~ly *ad.*

vernal ['vəːnl] *a.* ①春天的; 春天发生的: the ~ sunshine 春天的阳光 / ~ flowers (breezes) 春花(风) ②春天似的; 和煦的; 清新的; 青春的: the ~ freshness of youth 青春的朝气 ‖~ly *ad.* ‖~ equinox 春分点

versatile ['vəːsətail] *a.* ①多方面的, 多才多艺的: a ~ man (或 worker) 多面手 ②万用的, 通用的, 多方面适用的: ~ weapons 有多方面用途的武器 ③活动的, 万向的: a ~ spindle 万向轴 ④(鸟趾、昆虫触角、附着于花丝的花药等)能转动的 ⑤[罕]易变的, 反复无常的 ‖~ly *ad.* / **versatility** [,vəːsəˈtiliti] *n.* (才能、用途等的) 多面性

verse [vəːs] I *n.* ①诗句, 诗行; 诗节: quote a few ~s from sb. 引用某人的几句诗 / a poem of five ~s 一首有五个诗节的诗 ②诗; 诗体; 韵文: written in ~ 以诗体写成的 / prose and ~ 散文与韵文 / blank (free) ~ 无韵(自由)诗 / an elegiac ~ 挽歌, 哀歌 / an iambic ~ 抑扬格的诗 ③(基督教《圣经》中的)节, 短句(《圣歌等的)独唱部 II ❶ *vt.* ①用诗表达 ②把…改写成诗 ❷ *vi.* 作诗 ‖*give chapter and ~ for* 见 **chapter** ‖~let ['vəːslit] *n.* 小诗 / ~r *n.* = versifier ‖~man ['vəːsmən] *n.* =versifier

versed [vəːst] *a.* 通晓的, 精通的; 熟练的: be (well) ~ in mathematics 精通数学 ‖~ sine【数】正矢

version ['vəːʃən] *n.* ①译文, 译本; 翻译 ②(根据个人观点对事件等的)描述; 说法, 看法: There are three different ~s of what happened. 对所发生的事情有三种不同的说法。 ③[常作 V-] 基督教《圣经》的译本: the Authorized *Version* 基督教《圣经》的钦定译本 ④改写本; 经改编的乐曲: a stage ~ of the novel 根据小说所改编的剧本 / a ~ of symphony arranged as a ballet suite 为芭蕾舞配乐而改编的交响曲 ⑤表演: His ~ of the role has matured. 他演这角色已经熟练了。 ⑥版本; 形式; 变形, 变体 ⑦【医】胎位倒转; 倒转术

versus ['vəːsəs] *prep.* ①(诉讼、比赛等中)对 (= against; 常略作 v. 或 vs.): James ~ Smith (指诉讼)詹姆斯对史密斯 ②与…相对: restriction ~ opposition to restriction 限制与反限制

vertebrate ['vəːtibrit] I *n.* 脊椎动物 II *a.* ①有椎骨的, 有脊椎的; 脊椎动物的 ②(作品等)结构严密的 ‖~d ['vəːtibreitid] *a.* ① =vertebrate (*a.*) ②由椎骨组成的 / **vertebration** [,vəːti-ˈbreiʃən] *n.* ①脊椎形成 ②结构的严密性: the solid *vertebration* of sb.'s logic 某人严密的逻辑性

vertical ['vəːtikəl] I *a.* ①垂直的; 直立的; 竖式的; 垂直航空照片的: a ~ cliff 陡直的峭壁 / a ~ lathe 立式车床 / ~ dive (飞机)垂直俯冲 / a ~ takeoff aircraft 垂直起飞的飞机 ②顶点的, 至高点的, 绝顶的 ③【解】头顶的 ④【植】纵长的, 直上的: ~ leaves 直上叶, 直生叶 ⑤(企业)统管生产和销售全部过程的 II *n.* ①垂直线; 垂直(平)面 ②竖向 ③【建】竖杆 ④垂直航空照片(= ~ aerial photograph) ‖*out of the* ~ 不垂直的 ‖~ly *ad.* / ~ness *n.* ‖~ **angles**【数】对等角 / ~ **circle**【天】平经圈 / ~ **envelopment** (空降部队等的)垂直包围 / ~ **file** 直立式档案箱; (图书馆等中)供迅速查阅的资料(指小册子、剪报等) / ~ **fin** ①【动】竖鳍(指脊鳍、臀鳍或尾鳍) ②(飞机的)垂直尾翼, 垂直安定面 / ~ **fire** 高角射击 / ~ **line** 垂直线 / ~ **plane** 垂直面 / ~ **union** 同一工业内跨行业的职工工会 (=industrial union) / ~ horizontal union 不同工业内同行业的职工工会相对)

vertigo ['vəːtigou] ([复] vertigoes 或 vertigines [vəːˈtidʒiniːz]) *n.* 眩晕; 头晕; 晕头转向

verve [vəəv] *n.* ①[古]特殊才能 ②(文艺作品的)气势; 神韵 ③活力; 生命力; 热情

very ['veri] I *ad.* ①[用于修饰形容词、副词或分词]很, 甚, 极为, 非常: a ~ cold day 很冷的一天 / ~ happy (useful) 很幸福(有用) / a ~ interesting book 非常有趣的书 / ~ quickly 极快地 / ~ high (low) frequency【无】甚高(低)频 / We were ~ (much) pleased at the news. 听到这消息我们都感到极其高兴。 / a ~ puzzled (surprised) expression 非常疑惑(惊讶)的表情 ②[常用于形容词最高级前]最大程度地; 完全, 充分; 真正地: I'll do my ~ utmost (或 do the ~ best I can) to serve the people. 我要尽最大努力为人民服务。 / the ~ best quality 最好的质量 / the ~ first to arrive 最早到达者 / nine o'clock at the ~ latest 最迟到九点钟 / That is the ~ last thing I expected. 这完全出乎我意料之外。 ③[not ~][表示语气的委婉]不很, 不大, 不: It is not ~ warm today. 今天不很热。 / It is not of ~ much use. 这没有多大用处。 / I am not ~ keen on going there. 我不大想到那里去。 / He does not talk ~ much. 他不大讲话。 II *a.* ①真的, 真正的, 真实的: sb.'s ~ daughter 某人的亲生女儿 / in ~ truth (或

deed)真正地;事实上 / *Very God of* ~ *God*【宗】神中之神,真神 ②[与the, this 或 my, your 等连用,以加强语气]正是那个;正是所要的;恰好的;甚至于,连; 同一的; 极其: You are the ~ man I am looking for. 你正是我要寻找的人。/ A dictionary is the ~ thing (for our purpose). 词典正是我们想要的东西。/ the ~ heart of the city 市区的最中心 / at the ~ moment 恰恰在那个时刻 / He knows our ~ thoughts. 他甚至了解我们内心(深处)的思想。/ The ~ rafters shook. 甚至屋椽都震动了。/ be caught in the ~ act 当场被抓住 ③十足的, 绝对的, 完全的: a ~ rascal 十足的流氓 / the ~ reverse 完全相反 / That's the ~ shame of it. 这事之可耻就在于此。④仅仅的, 只: The ~ thought encouraged him. 只要想到这点,他就受到鼓舞。/ The ~ idea of going there delighted her. 她一想起要到那里去就感到高兴。⑤特别的, 特殊的 [*my* (*your*, *his* 等) ~ *own* 完全属我 (你, 他等) 所有: You may keep the pamphlet for *your* ~ *own*. 这本小册子你完全可以保留着自己使用。/ ~ *fine* 好极了, 好啊(常用作反语) / ~ *good* (表示同意、赞许等)很好 (较客气的用语) / ~ *well* 好吧(常带点勉强的口吻): *Very well, if* you insist. 如果你坚持你的话, 就这样吧。/ *That's all* ~ *well, but* . . . . 这(听起来)都很好,不过…

vesper ['vespə] **I** *n.* ①[诗]薄暮 ②[复]【宗】晚祷; 晚课; 晚祷曲 ③晚祷钟 (=~ bell) ④ [V-]【天】长庚星,金星 **II** *a.* ①夜晚的 ②晚祷的

vessel ['vesl] *n.* ①容器, 器皿 (尤指盛液体的,如桶、壶、瓶、碗、杯等) ②船; 飞船; 飞机 (尤指水上飞机): a coasting ~ 沿海商船 / a composite ~ 混合构造船 / a sailing ~ 帆船 / an escort ~ 护卫舰 ③【解】管; 脉管; 【植】导管 ④【宗】人 (指被看作一种容器来接受某种精神或影响者): a ~ of wrath 遭受天谴的人 / a chosen ~ 被(上帝) 选中的人 / the weaker ~ [总称]妇女,女性

vest [vest] **I** *n.* ①[英]汗衫 ②[美]背心, 马甲 (=[英] waistcoat); (作战等时穿的)防护衣: a bullet-proof ~ 防弹背心 ③内衣,衬衣 ④女子服装前面的 V 字形装饰布 ⑤[古]外衣; 法衣; 长袍; 衣服 **II** ❶ *vt.* ①使穿衣服; 给穿上 (尤指法衣、祭服等) ②授予, 赋予, 给予: ~ sb. *with* authority (或 ~ authority *in* sb.) 授权给某人 / ~ *in* sb. the power to do sth. 授予某人做某事的权力 ❷ *vi.* ①穿衣服; 穿祭服 ②(财产、权力等)属,归属 (*in*) ‖*play close to the* ~ 把…保守秘密 / *pull down one's* ~ [美俚]多管自己(别管闲事) ‖*-like a.* 背心似的 ‖*~-'pocket a.* 适合装入内衣口袋的; 袖珍的, 小的: a ~-*pocket* edition 袖珍版本 / a ~-*pocket* park 城市小公园

vestibule ['vestibju:l] **I** *n.* ①门厅, 前厅 ②[美] (火车车厢末端的)连廊, 通廊: a ~ train [美]

(各车厢相通的) 连廊列车 ③【解】【动】前庭; (昆虫的) 外生殖腔, 气门室; ~ of ear 耳前庭 **II** *vt.* ①为…设置门廊 ②以通廊连接 ‖~**d a.** 有门厅的, 有前厅的 ‖~ **school** (工厂的)技工学校, 新工人培训学校

vestige ['vestidʒ] *n.* ①痕迹; 遗迹; 残余; [罕]足迹: the ~s of an ancient civilization 一种古代文明的遗迹 / wipe out all pernicious ~s of feudalism 肃清封建余毒 / find no ~ of sb.'s presence 不见某人的踪迹 ②【生】退化器官 ③[常用于否定形式]一点儿, 丝毫: He has not a ~ of evidence for this assertion. 他对这个论断提不出一点证据。/ without a ~ of clothing 一丝不挂 ‖**vestigial** [ves'tidʒiəl] *a.* 发育不全的; 退化器官的

vestment ['vestmənt] *n.* ①外衣; 制服 ②法衣,祭服 ③[复]衣服 ④祭坛布 ‖~**al** [vest'mentl] *a.*

vestry ['vestri] *n.* ①教堂的法衣室 (置放法衣、圣器等) ②教堂的附属室 (用作主日学教室、祈祷室等) ③教区会; 教区委员会 ‖~**man** ['vestrimən] *n.* 教区会成员; 教区委员

vet [vet] [口] **I** *n.* 兽医 **II** (vetted; vetting) ❶ *vt.* ①诊治(人或牲畜); 给…作体格检查 ②检审(稿件等) ❷ *vi.* 当兽医

veteran ['vetərən] **I** *n.* ①老兵, 老战士; 老手, 富有经验的人: a ~ in battle 身经百战的老战士 ②[美] 退役军人: *Veterans*(') Day (美国)退伍军人节(十一月十一日) ③(常指齐胸处直径超过两呎的)老树 **II** *a.* 老战士的; 老练的; 经验丰富的: a ~ worker 富有经验的工人, 老工人 / ~ troops 有作战经验的部队 ‖**Veterans' Administration** (美国)退役军人管理局 (主要负责退伍军人的福利事宜) / ~**s' preference** (美国)对退伍军人的优待 (尤指文职官员选拔考试时的优先录取)

veterinary ['vetərinəri] **I** *a.* 兽医的: ~ medicine (或 science) 兽医学 / a ~ centre (college) 兽医站(学院) **II** *n.* 兽医 ‖~ **surgeon** [主英]兽医

veto ['vi:tou] **I** ([复] vetoes) *n.* 否决; 禁止; 否决权: put a (或 one's) ~ on a proposal 否决一项提案 / the No. 1 ~ man 专投反对票的人; 头号反对派 / the power of ~ (议案的) 相对否决权 / exercise the ~ 行使否决权 **II** *vt.* 否决; 禁止: ~ a bill 否决议案 / His parents ~ed his plan to buy a new bike. 他的父母不同意他买一辆新自行车的计划。‖~**er** *n.* 否决者

vex [veks] *vt.* ①使烦恼, 使苦恼, 使伤脑筋; 使恼火: be ~ed at sth. 为某事恼火 / be ~ed about sth. 为着某事恼火 / be ~ed at one's failure 因失败而苦恼 / be ~ed at sb.'s idleness (或 be ~ed with sb. *for* his idleness) 为某人的懒惰而恼火 ②[罕](疾病)折磨: be ~ed with a disease 闹病 ③[诗]使汹涌, 使激荡: a sea ~ed by storms 因暴风雨而汹涌澎湃的海面

vexation [vek'seiʃən] *n.* ①烦恼, 苦恼, 伤脑筋 ②

恼火；着急 ③苦恼的原因；使人恼火的事情

vexatious [vek'seiʃəs] ***a.*** ①使人烦恼的，伤脑筋的；使人恼火的；使人焦急的：a ~ child 使人烦恼的孩子 ②麻烦的；多难的；不安的：a ~ period in one's life 一生中麻烦事很多的一段时期 ③(诉讼)无根据的，旨在使对方为难的 ‖**~ly** ***ad.*** / **~ness** ***n.***

via ['vaiə] ***prep.*** ①经过，经由；取道 ②通过(某种手段或某人)：~ blitz attack 通过闪电战(或突然袭击)

via ['vaiə] ***n.*** [拉]道路：*Via Lactea* ['lǽktiə]【天】银河 / ~ *media* ['mi:diə] 中间道路

viaduct ['vaiədʌkt] ***n.*** ①高架桥；跨线桥；旱桥 ②高架铁路(或道路)；栈道

vibrant ['vaibrənt] ***a.*** ①颤动的；振动的 ②振动作响的；响亮的：a ~ baritone voice 响亮的男中音 ③有活力的；活跃的；激动的：the ~ atmosphere of a new age 新时代的蓬勃的气氛 / a ~ personality 充满活力的性格 / ~ streets 熙熙攘攘的街道 ④【语】声带振动的

vibration [vai'breiʃən] ***n.*** ①颤动；振动；震动：forty ~*s* per second 每秒振动四十次 / forced (free) ~【物】受迫(自由)振动 / ~ period【物】振动周期 / a tractor-drawn ~ plough 用拖拉机牵引的振动犁 ②摆动，摇摆 ③激动 ④犹豫 ‖**~al** ***a.*** ①颤动的；振动的；震动的：~*al* energy 振动能(量) ②摆动的，摇摆的

vicar ['vikə] ***n.*** ①(英国国教)教区牧师 ②【天主教】代理主教，副主教：a cardinal ~ (作为教皇代理人的)罗马教区主教 ③代理人，代表者 ‖***the ~ of Bray*** 看风使舵的人，两面派 / ***the Vicar of Christ***【天主教】教皇 ‖**~ship** ***n.*** 教区牧师的职权(或职位) ‖**~ apostolic**【天主教】(在传道地区代表教皇的)名誉主教 / **'~-'general** ***n.*** (英国国教)(在诉讼等方面协助大主教或主教的)代理监督；【天主教】(教区的)代理主教

vicarage ['vikəridʒ] ***n.*** [英]教区牧师的住宅(或俸禄、职权)

vicarious [vai'kɛəriəs] ***a.*** ①代理的，代理人的：~ authority 代理的职权 ②替代别人的；(想象别人的苦乐等而)产生同感(或共鸣)的：a ~ punishment 代(别人)受的惩罚 / a ~ pleasure 由于共鸣而感到的愉快 ③【医】替代(性)的：~ menstruation 替代性行经，倒经 ‖**~ly** ***ad.*** / **~ness** ***n.***

vice[1] [vais] ***n.*** ①罪恶，坏事；不道德行为 ②恶习；堕落，腐化 ③(文体、性格上的)缺点，瑕疵 ④(生理上的)缺陷(或畸形等) ⑤(马、犬等)牲口的恶癖：This horse is free from ~ (或 has no ~*s*). 这匹马没有恶癖。⑥[V-](旧时英国说教剧中)象征罪恶的角色；丑角 ⑦卖淫 ‖**~ squad** [美](取缔卖淫、赌博等的)警察缉捕队

vice[2] [vais] [主英] **I** ***n.*** (老)虎钳：grip like a ~ 钳住(或攫住)不放 **II** ***vt.*** 钳住，夹紧

vice[3] [vais] ***n.*** [口]副总统(或大学副校长、副队长等)

vice[4] ['vaisi] ***prep.*** 代替；接替

viceroy ['vais-rɔi] ***n.*** ①(代表国王管辖行省或殖民地的)总督 ②(美洲产)一种黑红色蝴蝶 ‖**~ship** ***n.*** 总督的职权(或任期、管辖区)

vice versa ['vaisi 'vəːsə] [拉]反过来(也是这样)：Students should learn from teachers and *vice versa*. 学生应当向教师学习，教师也应当向学生学习。

vicinity [vi'siniti] ***n.*** ①附近；邻近：The workers' residential district is in close ~ to the factory. 工人住宅区靠近工厂。②附近地区；近处，近邻：There are two primary schools in our ~. 我们附近有两所小学。‖***in the ~ of*** ①在…附近 ②在…上下，在…左右

vicious ['viʃəs] ***a.*** ①邪恶的；堕落的：~ habits 恶习 / a ~ person 恶人；腐化堕落的人 ②恶意的；恶毒的；凶恶的：a ~ glance 恶意的眼光 / a ~ remark 恶毒的话 ③恶性的；险恶的；烈性的 ④有错误的，有毛病的：a ~ argument (逻辑上)有错误的论点 / a notoriously ~ manuscript 错误百出的稿本 / ~ pronunciation 不正确的发音 ‖**~ly** ***ad.*** / **~ness** ***n.*** ‖**~ circle** ①恶性循环 ②【逻】循环论证 / **~ spiral** 恶性螺旋上升，恶性循环

vicissitude [vi'sisitjuːd] ***n.*** 变化；变迁；盛衰，兴败；[古][诗]代谢，交替：the ~*s* of life 人生的浮沉 / the ~*s* of the seasons 四季的变迁

victim ['viktim] ***n.*** ①受害者；牺牲者；受骗者：a ~ of infantile paralysis 患小儿麻痹症的残疾者 / fall a ~ *to* one's own avarice 成为贪婪的牺牲品，由于贪婪而自食其果 ②牺牲(品)；献祭用的人(或牲畜)

victimize ['viktimaiz] ***vt.*** 使牺牲；使受害；欺骗：be ~*d* by swindlers 受到骗子的欺骗 ‖**victimization** [ˌviktimai'zeiʃən] ***n.***

victor ['viktə] ***n.*** & ***a.*** 胜利者(的)，战胜者(的)；得胜者(的)

victorious [vik'tɔːriəs] ***a.*** 胜利的，战胜的；得胜的 ‖**~ly** ***ad.*** / **~ness** ***n.***

victory ['viktəri] ***n.*** ①胜利，战胜；克服：a major ~ 大捷 / Perseverance means ~. 坚持就是胜利。/ win a (或 the) ~ over 战胜，击败 / a moral ~ 精神上的胜利 ②[V-]【罗神】胜利女神(的塑像)

victual ['vitl] **I** ***n.*** [复]食物，饮料，食品，粮食 **II** (victual(l)ed; victual(l)ing) ❶ ***vt.*** 给…供应储备食物：~ a ship 给一艘船供应储备食物 ❷ ***vi.*** ①吃 ②(船只)装贮食物 ‖**victual(l)er** ***n.*** ①[英]客栈老板 ②(专为船或部队)供应食物者 ③补给船

vie [vai] (vying) ❶ ***vi.*** 争；竞争：~ *with* each other 互相竞争 / ~ *with* sb. *for* sth. 为某事与某人竞争 / ~ *with* sb. *in* doing sth. 与某人竞争做某事 ❷ ***vt.*** ①下(赌注)；冒…危险：~ money on the turn of a card 把赌金压在翻一张牌(的点数)上 ② 使竞争; 使针锋相对: ～ accusation against accusation 以非难对非难 ‖～r n. 竞争者

view [vju:] I n. ① 看, 眺望; 观察: command an extensive ～ 一望无际 / a private ～ (正式展览前的)预展 ② 视力; 视域; 眼界: pass from one's ～ 从眼前消逝 / The speaker stood in full ～ of the crowd. 演讲者站在大家都能看得到的地方。/ people or objects within ～ 在视线内的人或物体 ③ 看见的东西; 风景, 景色; 风景画(或照): an' album of ～s 风景画集 ④ 观点, 见解, 意见: fall in with sb.'s ～ on that subject 在那个问题上与某人的观点一致 / May I have your ～s on the question? 可以让我知道您对这个问题的看法吗? / take long (short) ～s 目光远大(短浅) / take a dim ～ of 对…抱悲观的看法 / take a poor ～ of sb.'s behaviour 不赞成某人的行为 ⑤目的, 意图; 希望, 期待, 展望: Will this meet your ～s? 这符合你的意图吗? ⑥思量, 考虑; 估量 ⑦(制图用语)图, 视图: a back ～ 后视图 / an end ～ 侧视图 / a front ～ 前视图 ⑧【律】(陪审团对有关财物、尸体、现场等的)查验: take a ～ of the scene 视察现场 ⑨概观; 梗概: The author gave a brief ～ of his book. 作者对他的书作了简短的概述。 II vt. ① 看: ～ the pictures 看图 ②仔细观察, 视察; 检查: ～ records 仔细检查记录 ③考虑, 估计; 期待, 展望: ～ things in their totality 看事物的全部 / ～ the matter in the right light 正确估量这件事 ④【律】查验: ～ the body 验尸 ‖**a point of** ～ 观点; 着眼点 / **at first** ～ 初看; 一见(就…) / **in** ～ ①在看得见的地方: Then we came in ～ of a lake. 接着我们看见了一个湖泊。/ Victory is in ～. 胜利在望。 ②被考虑; 被记住: have a plan in ～ 在考虑一项计划 / keep the whole world in ～ 放眼全球 ③被期待, 被指望 / **in** ～ **of** 鉴于…, 考虑到; 由于: in ～ of these facts 考虑到这些事实 / **on** ～ 展览着; 上映中: The exhibits are on ～ from 9 a.m. to 6 p.m. 展品从上午九时至下午六时展出。/ **to the** ～ 公开 / **with a** ～ **to** ①以…目的: He studies hard with a ～ to serving the people better in future. 他为了今后能更好地为人民服务而努力学习。②着眼于; 觊觎着 ③[俗]鉴于…, 考虑到; 由于 / **with the** (或 a) ～ **of** 以…为目的 ‖～**er** n. 观察者; 看电视者; 【律】视察员; 【物】观察器 / ～**less** a. [诗]看不见的; [美]不表示意见的; 无景色的 ‖'～**finder** n. 【物】探视器; 【摄】取景器 / '～**point** n. 观察点, 视点; 观点, 看法, 见解: the mass ～**point** 群众观点

vigil ['vidʒil] n. ①守夜, 值夜; 警戒; 监视: keep ～ 守夜 / sick-room ～s 病房的夜班 / keep ～ over a sick person 不眠地看护病人 ② [常用复]【宗】斋戒的前夜; (节日前夜的)守夜; (节日前夜的)祝祷仪式

vigilance ['vidʒiləns] n. ①警戒, 警惕(性): exer-

cise ～ 防范, 戒备; 守夜 / relax ～ 放松警惕 ②警醒症, 失眠症 ‖～ **committee** (美国)治安维持会 (一种民间组织)

vigilant ['vidʒilənt] a. 警备着的, 警惕着的; 警醒的: a ～ sentry 一个警惕的哨兵 / ～ attention 警惕 ‖～**ly** ad.

vigorous ['vigərəs] a. ①朝气蓬勃的, 精力充沛的; 壮健的, 茁壮的: a ～ youth 精力旺盛的青年 / ～ plant 茁壮的植物 ②强有力的: a ～ style 刚健的风格 / be ～ in action 行动有魄力 / ～ enforcement of laws 执法如山 ‖～**ly** ad.

vigo(u)r ['vigə] n. ① 活力, 精力: the ～ of youth 青春的活力 / full of ～ and vitality 朝气蓬勃的 ② 壮健, 茁壮: a plant that grows with ～ 茁壮成长的植物 ③ 力量; 气势; 魄力: the ～ of an argument 论证的有力 / command troops with ～ 有魄力地指挥部队 ④(法律上的)效力: laws that are still in ～ 仍然有效的法律 ‖～**less** a. 没有活力的; 不健壮的; 萎靡不振的, 软弱的

vile [vail] a. ①卑鄙的; 可耻的; 邪恶的; 令人作呕的, 讨厌的: ～ practices 无耻行径 / a ～ tendency 恶劣倾向 ②坏透的: ～ weather 恶劣的天气 ③不足道的, 无价值的 ‖～**ly** ad. / ～**ness** n.

vilify ['vilifai] vt. 诬蔑, 中伤, 诽谤; 辱骂 ②贬低 ‖**vilification** [,vilifi'keiʃən] n. 诬蔑, 中伤, 诽谤 / **vilifier** ['vilifaiə] n. 诬蔑者, 中伤者, 诽谤者

villa ['vilə] n. ①别墅 ②[英]城郊小屋

village ['vilidʒ] I n. ① 乡村, 村庄: go out to the ～s 下乡 ②[the ～][总称] 村民: the whole ～ 全村的人 ③ (动物的)群落 II a. 村的, 村庄的, 乡下的: ～ people 村民, 乡下人 / ～ industry 农村工业 ‖～**r** n. 村民, 乡下人 ‖～ **community** n. 【史】(土地公有的)村社, 农村公社

villain ['vilən] n. ① 坏人, 恶棍; (戏剧、小说等中的)反派角色, 反面人物: play the ～ 演反派角色 ② [口][谑]家伙; 小淘气: You little ～! 你这个小淘气! ③ ['vilin] =villein ④[古]巴佬, 粗汉 ‖**the** ～ **of the piece** ①剧中的反面人物 ②首恶者, 为害者 ‖～**ess** n. ①坏女人, 女恶棍 ②女的反派角色(或反面人物)

villainous ['vilənəs] a. ①坏人的, 恶棍的; 恶棍似的 ②腐化堕落的; 罪恶的; 卑鄙可耻的 ③[口]坏透的; 讨厌的: ～ weather 恶劣的天气 ‖～**ly** ad. / ～**ness** n.

villainy ['viləni] n. ①邪恶, 腐化堕落, 道德败坏 ②[复]邪恶的行为; 犯罪的行为

vim [vim] n. 活力, 精力: full of ～ and vigour 精力充沛的

vindicate ['vindikeit] vt. ①维护: ～ one's rights 维护自己的权利 ②为…辩护; 为…辩白: ～ sb. from a charge 辩明某人没犯某罪 ③证明…正确: Subsequent events ～d the policy. 后来的事实证明了那政策是对的。④[古]为…报仇 ‖**vindication** [,vindi'keiʃən] n.

vindictive [vin'diktiv] *a.* ① 志在报复的，复仇的: ~ punishment 报复性的惩罚 / a ~ action 报复行为 ②恶意的，怀恨的 ③惩罚性的: ~ damages 惩罚性的损害赔偿费

vine [vain] **I** *n.* ① 葡萄树 ② 藤本植物; 蔓, 藤: two melons growing on the same ~ 生在一根藤上的两个瓜 **II** *vi.* 形成(或长成)蔓藤 ‖*a clinging* ~ 惯于依赖男子的孤立无助的女子 / *die on the* ~ (计划等)未能实现, 中途天折 / *under one's* ~ *and fig tree* 平安在家 ‖~ *borer* 葡萄树上的钻蛀虫 / '~,dresser *n.* 栽培和修剪葡萄树的人 / ~yard ['vinjəd] *n.* 葡萄园

vinegar ['vinigə] **I** *n.* ①醋 ② (言语、性格或态度所表示的)尖酸味; 不愉快: ~ in sb.'s speech (countenance) 某人说话中(面上)流露的不愉快 ③充沛的精力 **II** *vt.* 加醋于; 使酸溜溜 ‖~**ish** ['vinigəriʃ] *a.* 不愉快的; 尖酸的, 乖戾的 / ~**y** ['vinigəri] *a.* ①醋似的, 酸溜溜的 ②不愉快的; 尖酸的, 乖戾的 ‖~ **eel** 醋鳗

vintage ['vintidʒ] **I** *n.* ① 收葡萄; 葡萄收获期 ② 酿酒; 酿酒期 ③ (一地一季的)葡萄收获量(或酿酒量) ④ 酒; (特指某葡萄名产地、某丰收年所酿造并标明年分窖藏的)佳酿酒 ⑤同年代的一批产品; 同一批产生的人物: a book of the 1970 ~ 1970 年出版的一本书 / a drama of prewar ~ 一个战前的剧本 ⑥ 制造的时期, 开始存在的时期; 寿命 **II** ❶ *vt.* 为酿酒而收(葡萄) ❷ *vi.* 收葡萄 **III** *a.* ① 古老而有声誉的; 古典的: a ~ tune 一支古老的曲调 ②旧式的, 老式的; 过时的: a ~ aircraft 一架老式飞机 / a ~ novel of no merit whatever 一本没有任何价值的过时的小说 ③[常用于专有名词前]最好的, 最典型的: ~ Lu Hsun 鲁迅的代表作 ‖~**r** *n.* 摘葡萄者 ‖~ **wine** 佳酿酒 / ~ **year** ① 佳酿酒酿成的年分 ②有卓越成就的一年

viola¹ [vi'oulə] *n.* 中提琴

viola

viola² ['vaiələ] *n.* 【植】堇菜属植物

violate ['vai-əleit] *vt.* ① 违犯, 违背, 违反: ~ the law 犯法 ②侵犯; 妨碍; 扰乱: ~ a nation's territory and sovereignty 侵犯一个国家的领土和主权 / ~ sb.'s privacy 惊扰某人(如闯进某人私室等) ③亵渎(神圣); 玷污, 污辱 ④强奸 ‖**violator** *n.* ①违犯者, 违背者 ②侵犯者; 亵渎者; 妨碍者 ③强奸者

violation [,vai-ə'leiʃən] *n.* ①违犯, 违背, 违反: act in ~ of the stipulations 违反条款 / ~s of the law and breaches of discipline 违法乱纪行为 ②侵犯, 侵害; 亵渎; 妨碍, 妨害 ③【体】违例 ④强奸

violence ['vaiələns] *n.* ① 猛烈, 激烈; 强烈: the ~ of the wind and waves 风浪的凶猛 / with ~ 猛烈地 ②暴力; 暴力行为: an act of ~ 暴力行为 / an apparatus of ~ 暴力机器 / take by ~ 强夺 ③侵犯; 亵渎, 不敬 ④狂热性; 狂热的行为 ⑤(对文字的)篡改 ‖*do* ~ *to* ①向…行凶; 强暴对待 ②歪曲(事实真相等)

violent ['vaiələnt] *a.* ① 猛烈的; 激烈的; 强烈的: ~ language 激烈的言语 / a ~ storm 猛烈的风暴 / a ~ attack 猛攻 ② 极端的, 极度的: a ~ dislike 极端厌恶 ③ 狂暴的, 凶暴的: become ~ after an insult 受到侮辱暴跳如雷 / lay hands on 行凶, 向…下毒手 / resort to ~ means 采用凶暴手段 ④ 由暴力引起的: a ~ death 横死 ⑤歪曲的, 曲解的: a ~ interpretation 歪曲的解释 ‖~**ly** *ad.*

violet ['vaiəlit] **I** *n.* ①堇菜科植物; 紫罗兰: sweet ~ 香堇菜, 香紫罗兰 ② 紫罗兰色, 紫色 ③ 紫色小蝴蝶 ④【动】紫罗兰色的 ‖~ **ray** 紫外线

violin [,vaiə'lin] *n.* ① 小提琴: play the ~ 拉小提琴 ② 小提琴手: He is first (second) ~ of an orchestra. 他是管弦乐队的第一(第二)小提琴手。 ‖*play first* ~ ①担任第一小提琴手 ②居首要职位, 当第一把手 ‖~**ist** ['vaiəlinist] *n.* 小提琴手

violoncello [,vaiələn'tʃelou] *n.* 大提琴 (=cello)

viper ['vaipə] *n.* ①【动】蝰蛇 ②毒蛇 ③阴险恶毒的人, 奸诈者 ④[美俚]毒品贩子

virgin ['və:dʒin] **I** *n.* ① 处女 ②[the V-]【宗】圣母玛利亚 (=the Blessed Virgin Mary) ③ 贞女;【宗】修女 ④[罕]童男 ⑤【动】单性生殖雌虫; 未交配过的雌动物 ⑥[V-]【天】室女座; 室女宫 (=Virgo) **II** *a.* ①处女(般)的, 贞洁的; (昆虫)未受精而产卵的: a ~ queen 未受精的蜂王 / the Virgin Queen (英国)伊丽莎白女王一世 ② 未开发的; 未经利用的: a ~ forest 原始林, 未开发的森林 / a ~ peak 没有人攀登过的山峰 / ~ soil 处女地, 未开垦的土地 ③ 纯洁的, 未玷污的: ~ whiteness 纯白 ④首次的, 创始的: a ~ voyage 处女航 ⑤ 纯粹的; 未掺杂的: ~ silver 纯银 / ~ gold 纯金 ⑥【化】(植物油)初榨的; 直馏的;【冶】由矿石直接提炼的 ‖**Virgin Birth** 圣灵感孕 (认为耶稣由童贞女玛利亚神奇地怀孕的唯心说法) / **Virgin Islands** 维尔京群岛[拉丁美洲] / **Virgin Mary** 【宗】圣母玛利亚 / ~ **wool** 未加工的羊毛

virginal ['və:dʒinl] **I** *a.* ① 处女(般)的, 有处女特点的: ~ membrane 【解】处女膜 ②纯洁的, 没有玷污的 ③【动】未受精的 **II** *n.* [常用复](十六、十七世纪的)一种方形无脚的古钢琴类乐器(又称 a pair of ~s) ‖~**ly** *ad.*

virginity [vəˈdʒiniti] *n.* ① 童贞, 处女性; 纯洁 ② 未婚女子的独身生活

virile [ˈvirail] *a.* ① 男性的; 有男性生殖力的 ② 男的, 男子的 ③ 有男子气概的; 精力充沛的; 强有力的; 雄浑的: a ~ government 有魄力的政府 / a ~ voice 雄壮的声音 / a ~ literary style 雄浑的文学风格

virility [viˈriliti] *n.* ① (男子的) 成年; 男生殖能 ② 男子气概; 精力充沛; 刚强有力; 雄浑

virtual [ˈvəːtjuəl] *a.* ① 实质上的, 实际上的, 事实上的: The reply is a ~ acceptance of our offer. 这个回答实质上是接受了我们的建议。 / a ~ agreement 实际上的同意 / He is a ~ stranger, although we've met. 我们虽曾见过面, 但他对我来说实在还是个陌生人。 ②【物】虚的: ~ displacement 虚位移 / ~ focus 虚焦点 / ~ work 虚功 / ~ phonon 虚声子 ③【物】有效的: ~ height 有效高度 / ~ value 有效值 ‖**~ly** *ad.* 实质上, 实际上, 事实上

virtue [ˈvəːtjuː] *n.* ① 善, 德: ~ and vice 善与恶 ② 美德, 德行, 贞操: a woman of ~ 贞淑的女人 ③ 优点, 长处: Brevity is one of the ~s of this essay. 简洁是这篇文章的优点之一。 ④ 功效, 效能, 效力: the ~ of herbs to heal sickness 药草治病的效能 ⑤ (男子的) 力; 英勇; 刚毅 ‖**by** (或 **in**) ~ **of** 依靠…(的力量), 凭借; 由于, 因为 / **make a** ~ **of necessity** 把非做不可的事装成出于好心才做的 ‖**~less** *a.* 没有道德的; 没有长处的; 没有效力的

virtuous [ˈvəːtjuəs] *a.* ① 有道德的, 有德行的; 善良的 ② 正直的, 公正的 ③ 贞节的 ④ 有效力的, 有效验的 ‖**~ly** *ad.* / **~ness** *n.*

virulence [ˈvirjuləns] *n.* ① 毒力, 毒性; 致命性 ② 刻毒, 恶毒 ③【医】病毒性, 致病力

virulent [ˈvirjulənt] *a.* ① 剧毒的; 致命的: a ~ poison 一种致命的毒质 ② 刻毒的, 恶毒的: ~ abuse 毒骂 ③ (疾病) 恶性的; (微生物) 致病力强的, 易传染的 ④【医】有病毒的, 因病毒而引起的: ~ ulcer 因病毒而引起的溃疡 ‖**~ly** *ad.*

virus [ˈvaiərəs] *n.* ①【微】病毒; 传染毒; 滤过性病原体: smallpox ~【医】天花病毒 / filtrable ~【医】滤过性病毒 ② (精神, 道德方面的) 毒素; 毒害: remove the ~ of prejudice 去除偏见的毒害 ③ 恶意, 恶毒

visage [ˈvizidʒ] *n.* [书面语] 脸; 面容; 外表: stern (agreeable) in ~ 面容严峻 (愉快) 的 / be fierce of ~ and faint of heart 外强中干

vis-à-vis [ˈviːzɑːviː] I [单复同] *n.* ① 对面的人 (如对坐的, 对舞的): speak to one's ~ 和对面的人讲话 ② 坐位相对的马车, 两人对坐的 S 形长椅 (或沙发) ③ (职位上的) 对等人物; 对手 ④ (西方女子赴社交场所的) 陪伴者; (男女相互约会的) 对方 ⑤ 面对面的谈话, 密谈 II *prep.* ① 和…面对面 ② 和…相对; 同…相比 ③ 关于, 对于: one's attitude ~ sb. (sth.) 对某人 (某事) 的态度 III

ad. 面对面; 在一起: sit ~ in a train 在火车上相对而坐

viscose [ˈviskous] I *n.*【化】粘胶液; 粘胶纤维: filament yarn 粘胶长丝 / ~ staple fibre 粘胶纤维 II *a.* ① 粘滞的, 粘性的 ② (含) 粘胶的; 粘胶制的

viscount [ˈvaikaunt] *n.* (英国的) 子爵 ‖**~cy, ~ship** *n.* 子爵的头衔 (或地位等)

visible [ˈvizəbl] I *a.* ① 看得见的; 可见的: ~ stars 看得见的星星 / ~ to the naked eyes 肉眼所看得到的 / be ~ with a microscope 可用显微镜看见 / a house barely ~ on the horizon 在地平线上隐约可见的一所房子 / receive sb. with ~ pleasure 喜形于色地接待某人 ② 在望的; 可得到的: the total of ~ wheat 眼望可得到的小麦总产量 ③ 明显的; 显然的: serve no ~ purpose 看不出有什么好处, 显然无用 ④ 可会见到的, 接见客人的: He is ~ only on Thursdays. 他只在星期四接见客人。 ⑤ (为便于查阅, 设计时使档案、记录等) 显露部分内容 (或摘要) 的; 显露式的: a ~ file 显露式档案夹子 II *n.* ① 可见物; 直观教具 ② [美] 白人商店为装点门面而雇用的黑人 (= ~ Negro) ‖**visibility** [ˌviziˈbiliti] *n.* ① 可见性; 明显度; 清晰程度 ② 可见度, 能见度; 视见度; 视程, 能见距离: visibility good 能见度良好 / horizontal (vertical) visibility【空】水平 (垂直) 能见度 ③ 看得见的东西 / **~ness** *n.* / **visibly** *ad.* 明显地, 显而易见地: The spectators were visibly moved. 观众显然受了感动。 ‖**~ spectrum**【物】可见光谱 / **~ speech**【物】可见语言

vision [ˈviʒən] I *n.* ① 视, 视力, 视觉: beyond sb.'s ~ 在某人视力以外 / colour ~ 色视觉 / defects of ~ 视觉上的缺点 / the field of ~ 视野 ② 眼光, 远见; 想象力: the ~ of a poet 诗人的想象力 / a man without ~ 没有远见的人 ③ 梦幻, 幻想; 梦幻 (或想象) 中所见的物; 幻象;【宗】显圣 ④ 极美的人 (尤指幻女); 绝妙的物 II *vt.* ① 幻见, 梦见; 想象 ② 显示 ‖**have ~s of** 想象到 / **see ~s** 见幻象; 能预卜未来, 做先知

visionary [ˈviʒənəri] I *a.* ① 梦幻的; 幻觉的; 想象的; 非实有的: a ~ state of things 空幻境界 ② 耽于空想的, 好梦想的; 不实际的: a ~ enthusiast 不实际的热心家 ③ 出于空想的; 不可实行的: a ~ scheme 空想的计划 II *n.* ① 见幻象 (或有幻觉) 的人 ② 好幻想的人, 空想家

visit [ˈvizit] I ❶ *vt.* ① 访问, 拜访; 探望; 参观, 游览: ~ a friend 访问朋友 / ~ a sick person 探望病人 ② 在…处逗留作客; 常去…作短期逗留: ~ a colleague for a week at his home 在一同事家作客住一个星期 / Many migratory birds ~ this lake annually. 许多候鸟每年到这个湖上作短期逗留。 ③ 去 (某处); 去 (某人) 处: ~ the library every night 每晚去图书馆 / The doctor ~s his patients at their homes at regular intervals. 那医生定期到病从家出诊。 ④ 视察, 巡视

⑤(灾害、疾病等)侵袭,降临 ⑥(基督教《圣经》用语)惩罚(某人),惩治(某罪);施加: ~ everlasting grief *upon* sb. 使某人悲痛不已 ❷ *vi.* ①访问;参观;逗留,逗留作客: spend the whole afternoon ~*ing* 花整个下午的时间进行访问 ②[美]叙谈,闲谈 (*with*): Let's sit here and ~ together for a while. 让我们在这儿坐下谈一会儿。/ ~ *with* a friend on the telephone 和一个朋友在电话中交谈 Ⅱ *n.* ①访问;参观,游览;(作客)逗留: pay (或 make) a ~ to sb. 拜访某人 / return a ~ 回访 / a ~ of a week 历时一周的访问 / a state (friendly) ~ 国事(友好)访问 / pay a ~ to an exhibition 参观展览会 / a place worthy of a ~ 值得一游的地方 / I don't live here; I'm only on a ~. 我不住在这儿,我是在这儿作客逗留的。②视察;调查;出差 ③出诊;就诊 ④(战时)海军人员对中立国船只的检查 ⑤[美]叙谈,闲谈 ‖*a ~ from the stork* 婴儿的诞生

visitation [ˌviziˈteiʃən] *n.* ①访问;探望 ②视察,巡视 ③(战时)海军人员对中立国船只的检查: the right of ~ (或 visit) 对中立国船只的检查权 ④[宗]天罚,天祸;天赐 ⑤[V-]【宗】圣母访问节(七月二日) ⑥[口]逗留得过久的探望(或拜访) ⑦(鸟兽等)反常的大批迁移 ‖~ *of Providence* 天灾 ‖~*al a.*

visitor [ˈvizitə] *n.* ①访问者;来宾: We have had quite a number of ~s lately. 最近我们有许多来访者。②游客;参观者: a ~s' book (旅馆、游览处等的)旅客登记簿,来客签名簿 / *Visitors* not admitted. 游客止步。(或: 谢绝参观。) ③视察者,检查者,[英](大学等的)视察员

vista [ˈvistə] *n.* ①(从两排树木或房屋等中间看出去的)狭长的景色,(树、屋等)排成长列的景色;深景,远景: a ~ of the pagoda at the end of a street 街道远端的宝塔的景色 ②(对往事)一连串的追忆;(对前景)一系列的展望: look back through the ~s of bygone days 追忆一连串的往事

visual [ˈvizjuəl] *a.* ①看的;视觉的,视力的: ~ art 供观赏的艺术(指电影、电视等) ②看得见的;凭视力的: ~ reconnaissance【军】目视侦察 ③光学的: the ~ focus of a lens 透镜的光学焦点 ④形象化的;栩栩如生的: His narratives are extremely ~. 他的记叙文写得非常生动。‖~**ly** *ad.* ‖~ **acuity** 视觉敏锐度 / ~ **aids** 直观教具 (如图片、电影等) / ~ **angle** 视角 / '~-'**aural** (**radio**) **range**【无】可见可听式无线电航向信标,声影显示无线电航向信标 / ~ **field** 视野,视界 / ~ **purple**【化】【医】视紫质 / ~ **ray**【物】维生射线 / ~ **yellow**【化】【医】视黄质

visualize, visualise [ˈvizjuəlaiz] ❶ *vt.* ①使可见,使具形象,使具体化 ②设想,想象: I can easily ~ the scene. 这个景象我是不难想象的。❷ *vi.* ①想象 ②(尤指通过窥镜等身体内部器官或情况)显现 ‖**visualization** [ˌvizjuəlaiˈzeiʃən] *n.* ①形象;形象化;想象 ②(身体内部器官的)显现 /

~**r** *n.* 想象者;观察仪

vita [ˈwiːtɑː, ˈvaitə] ([复] vitae [ˈwiːtai, ˈvaitiː]) *n.* (博士论文等内所附的)个人简历

vital [ˈvaitl] *a.* ①生命的,生机的;维持生命所必需的: ~ energies 生命力 / ~ functions 生命机能 / ~ power (维持生命的)生活力 / ~ centre 【医】生命中枢 ②有生命力的;充满活力的,生气勃勃的,生动的: ~ in every part 各部分都充满着活力的 ③致命的;生死存亡的,生命攸关的: a ~ wound 致命伤 / a ~ question 生死攸关的问题 ④极其重要的,必不可少的: ~ communication lines 交通要道 / be ~ to 对…极端重要 / of ~ importance 极其重要的 ‖~**ism** *n.* ①生机论,生机说 ②活力论 / ~**ist** *n.* 主张生机论者;活力论者 / ~**ly** *ad.* ‖~ **capacity**【医】肺活量 / ~ **force,** ~ **principle** 生命力,生机 / ~ **signs** 脉搏、呼吸、体温、血压数字 ① 人口统计 ②[口]妇女腰身(或胸围等)的尺寸

vitality [vaiˈtæliti] *n.* ①生命力;生气,活力: the ~ of an idiom 习语的生命力 / be full of ~ 充满生气 ②生动性: the ~ of sb.'s reasoning 某人说理的生动有力

vitalize, vitalise [ˈvaitəlaiz] *vt.* ①给与…生命力 ②使有生气,使增添活力;激发: ~ a dull story 使一个枯燥的故事变得生动 / ~ the patriotic spirit 激发爱国热情 ‖**vitalization** [ˌvaitəlaiˈzeiʃən] *n.*

vitamin(e) [ˈvitəmin, ˈvaitəmin] *n.* 维生素,维他命: ~ tablets 维生素片 ‖~ **A** 维生素 A,抗干眼醇 / ~ **B complex** 复合维生素 B / ~ **B₁** 维生素 B₁,硫胺 / ~ **B₂** 维生素 B₂,核黄素 / ~ **B₆** 维生素 B₆,吡多醇 / ~ **B₁₂** 维生素 B₁₂,钴维生素 / ~ **C** 维生素 C,抗坏血酸 / ~ **D** 维生素 D / ~ **E** 维生素 E / ~ **G** 维生素 G / ~ **K** 维生素 K,凝血萘醌 / ~ **P** 维生素 P,柠檬素 / ~ **PP** 维生素 PP,抗蜀黍红斑维生素(如烟酰胺、烟酸)

vitiate [ˈviʃieit] *vt.* ①使腐败,污染;使有缺陷: ~ the air 使空气污浊 / ~*d* blood 污血 / a ~*d* judgement 错误的判断 ②使堕落,败坏(道德等): a ~*d* mind 卑劣的心地 ③使(契约等)无效;使失效: ~ a contract (will) 使契约(遗嘱)无效 ‖**vitiation** [ˌviʃiˈeiʃən] *n.* / **vitiator** *n.* 败坏者(或物);使无效者(或物)

vitriol [ˈvitriəl] Ⅰ *n.* ①【化】硫酸盐;矾;硫酸: blue ~ 胆矾,硫酸铜 / green ~ 绿矾,硫酸亚铁 / oil of ~ 矾油,(浓)硫酸 / red ~ 红矾,一种天然的硫酸亚钴 / white ~ 皓矾,硫酸锌 ②[喻]尖刻的话(或批评);刻薄,讽刺: put plenty of ~ in one's talk 在讲话中插入许多尖刻的话 Ⅱ *vt.* 浸…于稀硫酸中,用硫酸处理 ‖*throw* ~ *over* (或 *at*) 浇硫酸于…以毁其容貌(一种嫉妒泄忿的犯罪行为) ‖'~-,**throwing** *n.* 浇硫酸毁人容貌以报私仇

vitriolic [ˌvitriˈɔlik] *a.* ①硫酸的,由硫酸得来的 ②[喻]尖刻的,辛辣的,讽刺的: ~ criticism 辛

辣的批评 / launch a ~ attack on sth.(sb.) 对某事(某人)发动辛辣的攻击

vituperate [vi'tju:pəreit] *vt.* 漫骂，咒骂，辱骂 ‖**~ration** [vi,tju:pə'reiʃən] *n.* / **vitupera-tive** [vi'tju:pərətiv] *a.* / **vituperator** *n.* 漫骂者，咒骂者，辱骂者

vivacious [vi'veiʃəs] *a.* ① 活泼的；快活的；有生气的；轻松愉快的: a bright ~ strain 明快活泼的曲调 / a ~ pupil 活泼的小学生 ②[古]长命的；难杀死的，难毁坏的 ③【植】多年生的；耐冬的 ‖**~ly** *ad.*

vivacity [vi'væsiti] *n.* 活泼；快活，高兴；有生气；轻松愉快

vivid ['vivid] *a.* ① (色彩、光线等)鲜艳的；鲜明的；强烈的: ~ green 鲜绿色，嫩绿色 / a ~ flash of lightning 电光强烈的一闪 ②活泼的；有生气的: the exuberant ~ young people 活力充沛的青年人 / be ~ with life 生气勃勃 / a ~ imagination 活跃的想象力 ③ 生动的；逼真的；清晰的: a ~ description 生动的描写 / It is still ~ in my memory. 这事我还记得清清楚楚。‖**~ly** *ad.* / **~ness** *n.*

vivisect [,vivi'sekt] ❶ *vt.* 解剖(动物活体) ❷ *vi.* 进行动物活体解剖 ‖**~or** *n.* 活体解剖者

vivisection [,vivi'sekʃən] *n.* 活体解剖；动物解剖实验 ‖**~al** *a.* / **~ist** *n.* 活体解剖者；活体解剖论者

vixen ['viksn] *n.* ①雌狐 ②悍妇，泼妇，刁妇

vizi(e)r [vi'ziə] *n.* (伊斯兰国家的)高官；大臣

vocabulary [və'kæbjuləri] *n.* ①(通常按词序排列并注有释义等的)词汇表；词汇汇编；词典 ②(某种语言、某人、某行业或某知识领域所使用的)词汇，语汇；词汇量: a language with a large ~ 词汇丰富的语言 / enlarge (enrich) one's ~ 扩大(丰富)自己的词汇量 / an ever-increasing ~ of scientific and technical terms 不断增加的科技词汇 ‖**~ entry** (词汇表、词汇汇编、词典中的)词条

vocal ['voukəl] I *a.* ①有声的，发嗓音的，使用嗓音的；歌唱的: ~ cords 声带 / ~ organs 发音器官 / ~ music 声乐 / a ~ solo 独唱 ②用语言表达的，口述的: a ~ communication 口头传话 ③畅所欲言的；畅言无忌的: a ~ critic 畅言无忌的批评者 ④充满嗓音的；富于声响的 ⑤【语】元音的；属于元音性质的；浊音的，响音的 ⑥[诗](流水、树木等)被赋予声音的，仿佛能说话的 II *n.* ①【语】元音 ②声乐作品；声乐演唱 ③(天主教会用语)有投票权的人 ‖**give with (the) ~s** [美俚]表演歌唱节目 ‖**~ly** *ad.*

vocalist ['voukəlist] *n.* 歌唱者；歌唱家；声乐家

vocation [vou'keiʃən] *n.* ①神召，天命；天职，使命 ②(对于某种职业的)禀性，倾向，才能 (for) ③行业，职业；从事某一行业的人们

vocational [vou'keiʃənl] *a.* 行业的，职业的，业务的: a ~ school 职业学校 / ~ education 职业教

育 / ~ work 业务工作 / ~ study 业务学习 ‖**~ism** *n.* 强调职业教育的主张 / **~ly** *ad.*

vodka ['vɔdkə] *n.* [俄]伏特加(一种用麦酿制的烈性烧酒)

vogue [voug] I *n.* ①时尚；流行物，时髦的事物；时髦的人物: the ~ of the day 风行一时的事物 / the ~s of the last century 上一世纪的风尚 ②流行，风行，时髦: come into (go out of) ~ 开始(已不)流行 / This style of writing has had a great ~. 这种写作风格曾经大为流行过。 II *a.* 流行的，时髦的: a ~ word 时髦的词 ‖**all the ~** 到处受欢迎；最新流行品 / **(be) in ~** 正在流行；行时

voice [vois] I *n.* ①说话声，嗓声，嗓子；禽鸣声；虫鸣声: We recognized his ~ at once. 我们立刻听出了他的嗓音。 / speak in a loud (soft, sweet) ~ 大声 (轻声, 悦耳) 地说 / He is not in (good) ~. 他目前嗓子不好。 / lose one's ~ 倒嗓，嗓子哑 / the ~ of the cuckoo 杜鹃的叫声 ②(类似或比喻作说话声的)声音: the ~ of the sea 大海的波涛声 / the ~ of conscience 良心的呼声 ③(公开或正式表达出的)意见，愿望；发言权；投票权: We have no ~ in the matter. 对这件事我们没有发言权。 / I count on your ~. 我期望你的(口头或书面的)声援。④表达；表露: give ~ to one's opinion (indignation) 表示意见(义愤) / find ~ in song 用唱歌来表达 ⑤喉舌，代言人 ⑥(唱歌、演讲时的)嗓子运用法: study (teach) ~ 学习(教授)嗓子运用法 ⑦【语】语态；声带振动，浊音特性: the active (passive) ~ 主动(被动)语态 ⑧【音】声部；歌唱的才能 ⑨歌唱家 II *vt.* ①(用言语)表达，吐露: ~ one's opinions 发表意见 ②【音】调整(管风琴管子等)的音 ③【语】使发成浊音 ‖**a ~ in the wilderness** ①荒野里的呼声 ②无人理睬的改革主张 / **find one's ~** (吓得或羞得说不出话之后)能说话了，能开口了 / **lift up one's ~** 高声叫喊；大声疾呼 / **the still small ~** 良心的呼声 / **with one ~** 异口同声地；一致地 ‖**~ful** *a.* 有声的；高声的；声音嘈杂的 / **~less** *a.* 无声的，沉默的 ②无发言(或投票)权的 ③【语】清音的: ~less consonants 清辅音 ‖**~ box** 喉 / **'~-'over** *n.* (电视等的)画外音 / **~ part** 【音】声部 / **'~print** *n.* (用仪器描录因人而异的)声波纹 / **~ vote** 呼声表决(法)(参加表决者叫喊"同意"或"不同意"，按呼声更响亮的一方议定表决事项)

void [void] I *a.* ①空的，空无所有的: a ~ space 空无所有的空间 ②(房屋、土地等)没人住的；无人占用的 ③(职位等)无人担任的: The bishopric fell ~. 主教职位出缺。④空闲的: ~ hours 空闲的时刻 ⑤没有的，缺乏的: His style is ~ of affectation. 他的文风毫不矫揉造作。/ be ~ of common sense 缺乏常识 / a hand ~ of spades 没有黑桃花色的一手牌 ⑥无用的；无效的，作废的；可作废的: be null and ~ 无效 / a ~ ballot

无效票, 废票 **II** *n.* ①空处; 空间; 真空; 空虚; 空位: emerge out of the ~ 凭空出现 / vanish into the ~ 消失得无影无踪 ②空虚感; 寂寞的心情: an aching ~ 痛苦的寂寞心情 ③空隙; 空隙率: a ~ test 空隙测定 ④ (纸牌戏中) 缺一门花色的一手牌 **III** *vt.* ①排泄; 放出 ②使 (契约等) 无效; 把…作废, 取消 ③使空出; 退出; 离开 ‖~ness *n.*

volatile ['vɔlətail] **I** *a.* ①飞行的; 能飞的 ②(液体等) 易挥发的, 易发散的: ~ matter 挥发物 / ~ oil 挥发油 ③轻快的, 快活的; 易激动的, 易发作的; 爆炸性的 ④易变的; 反复无常的; 短暂的: a ~ disposition 反复无常的脾气 / a ~ market 不稳定的行情 **II** *n.* ①有翅的动物 ②挥发物 ‖~ness *n.*

volcanic [vɔl'kænik] **I** *a.* ①火山 (性) 的, 由火山作用所引起的: ~ activity 火山活动 / eruption 火山爆发 / ~ glass 火山玻璃 / ~ rocks 火山岩 ②有火山的; 由火山构成的 ③火山似的; 猛烈的, 猛烈的: a ~ character 暴烈的性格 **II** *n.* 火山岩 ‖~ally *ad.* 火山似地; 暴烈地, 猛烈地

volcano [vɔl'keinou] ([复] volcano(e)s) *n.* 火山: an active ~ 活火山 / a dormant ~ 休眠火山 / an extinct ~ 死火山 / [喻] 丧失活力的人 / a submarine ~ 海底火山 / a ~ bursting into eruption 在爆发中的火山 / sit on a ~ 坐在火山上; [喻] 处境危险

volition [vou'liʃən] *n.* 意志; 意志力; 决断: of one's own ~ 出于自己的意志 ‖~al *a.*

volley ['vɔli] **I** *n.* ①(枪炮、弓箭等的) 群射; 排枪射击 (指一队步枪兵所发射的敬礼枪): fire a ~ (或 fire by ~s) 齐射 / ~ bombing 【军】齐投轰炸 ②群射出的子弹 (或箭等) ③(质问、咒骂等的) 连发; 迸发: a ~ of laughter 一阵哄笑 / a ~ of curses 一阵咒骂 / a ~ of questions 一连串的问题 ④(球着地前的) 运行; 截击, 截踢 (指球落地前即回击或回踢): a half ~ 半截击, 半截踢 (球刚落地即行回击或回踢) **II** ❶ *vt.* ①齐发, 群射 (子弹等) ②连声发出 (咒骂等) ③截击, 截踢 (球) ❷ *vi.* ①进行群射; (枪炮) 齐鸣 ②(子弹等) 被群射出 ③(球戏中) 截击, 截踢 (或 on) the ~ ①不经意地; 顺便地 ②(球) 在运行中, 在运动中 ‖~ball *n.* 排球; 排球运动 / ~ fire 【军】群射 / ~ gun 速射榴弹炮 (旧称)

volt[1] [voult] *n.* 【电】伏特, 伏 ‖~-'ampere *n.* 伏安, 伏特安培

volt[2] [volt] *n.* ①(马术中的) 环行成圈的步法; 环行所成之圈; 环行的场地 ②(剑术中的) 闪避

voltage ['voultidʒ] *n.* 【电】电压, 伏特数: puncture ~ 击穿电压 / ~ amplifier 电压放大器 / divider 分压器

voltmeter ['voult,mi:tə] *n.* 【电】伏特计, 电压表: electronic ~ 电子管伏特计 / graphic recording ~ 自动记录电压表

voluble ['vɔljubl] *a.* ①(言词、文章) 流利的; 健谈的; 滔滔不绝的 ②易旋转的 ③【植】缠绕的 ‖vol-

ubility [,vɔlju'biliti] ~ness *n.* / volubly *ad.* 流利地; 滔滔不绝地

volume ['vɔlju(:)m] **I** *n.* ①卷; 册; 书籍 (略作vol.): a novel in three ~s 一部三卷本的小说 / a library of 100,000 ~s 藏书十万卷的图书馆 ②容积, 容量; 体积: the ~ of a container 容器的容积; 容器的体积 / the ~ of beer in a cask 桶里的啤酒量 / ~ expansion 【物】体积膨胀 ③大量, 许多; [复] (烟、蒸汽等的) 大团: a great ~ of water 大量水 / ~s of smoke 成团成团的烟 ④份量; 量: increase the ~ of transport 增加运输量 / trade ~ 贸易量 ⑤音量; 响度: a voice of great ~ 洪亮的声音 / ~ control 【无】音量控制 / ~ level 【物】强 (或响) 度级 ⑥【史】(用埃及纸、纸草纸等写的) 书卷, 卷轴 ⑦(音乐唱片集的) 一册; (录音带的) 一卷 **II** ❶ *vi.* (烟、蒸汽等) 成团升起, 成团卷起 ❷ *vt.* ①把…收集成卷; 把…装订成册 ②成团地散发出 **III** *a.* 大量的: ~ production of cotton piece goods 棉布的大量生产 ‖a great ~ of sound 一阵风; 疾风 / gather ~ 增大 / speak ~s 很有意义; 含义很深 / speak ~s for 充分说明; 为…提供有力证据 ‖~-'pro'duce *vt.* 大量生产

voluminous [və'lju:minəs] *a.* ①多卷的; 长篇的: a ~ work 大部头的著作 / a ~ report 长篇报告 ②著作多的; 话多的: a ~ writer 多产的作家 ③体积大的; 庞大的; 宽大的; 很多的; 丰满的: a ~ man 身材粗壮的人 / ~ correspondence 大量的通信 ④盘绕的 ‖~ly *ad.* / ~ness *n.*

voluntary ['vɔləntəri] **I** *a.* ①自愿的, 志愿的: a ~ action 自愿的行动 / a ~ army 志愿军, 义勇军 / ~ enlistment 志愿兵制 / on a ~ basis 在自愿的基础上 / ~ labour 义务劳动 ②有意的, 故意的: ~ manslaughter 故意杀人 / a ~ misstatement 故意误述 / ~ waste [英] 对租得的不动产的蓄意破坏 ③靠自由捐助维持的; 非官办的: a ~ school [英] 民办小学 (通常为教会办的) / a ~ hospital 私人医院 / ~ churches 不受国家资助的教堂 ④由主观意志所控制的; 随意的, 任意的; 有自由意志的: ~ muscles 【解】随意肌 / ~ movement 随意运动 ⑤自发的: ~ enthusiasm 自发的积极性 ⑥【律】自动的, 自动完成的; 无偿的: make a ~ confession 自动招供 / ~ conveyance 无偿让与 / a ~ grantee 无偿受让人 **II** *n.* ①【音】(教堂礼拜式中或礼拜式前后的) 风琴独奏; 即兴演奏; (演奏比赛中) 比赛者自选的节目 ②主张教会 (或教育) 不受国家资助而由民间捐助维持者 ③自愿的行动; 志愿者

volunteer [,vɔlən'tiə] **I** *n.* ①自愿参加者, 志愿者: Any ~s? 有谁自愿做这件事吗? ②志愿兵, 义勇兵 ③自生植物 **II** *a.* ①自愿参加的, 志愿的: ~ donors of blood 志愿献血者 ②【植】自生自长的 **III** ❶ *vt.* 自愿 (做、提供、参加等): ~ to do sth. 自愿做某事 / ~ one's services 自愿提供服务 / ~ a donation 自愿捐赠 ❷ *vi.* ①自愿; 当志愿军: ~ for service 自愿参

军 / ～ for the work 自愿做这工作 ②【植】自生自长

voluptuous [vəˈlʌptjuəs] *a.* ①骄奢淫逸的，贪图酒色的 ②妖娆的，色情的，激起情欲的 ‖**～ly** *ad.* / **～ness** *n.*

vomit [ˈvɔmit] I *n.* 呕吐；呕吐物；催吐剂 II ❶ *vt.* ①呕吐；(火山、烟囱等)喷出；吐出(恶语等)：blood 吐血 / The guns ～ed fire. 炮火猛发。/ A volcano ～s lava. 火山喷出熔岩。/ ～ abuses 辱骂 ②[古] 使呕吐 ❷ *vi.* 呕吐；(火山、烟囱等)喷出：make one feel like ～ing 令人作呕 ‖**～er** *n.* 呕吐的人 / **～ing** *n.* 呕吐：cyclic ～ing 周期(轮发性)呕吐 / ～ing of pregnancy 妊娠呕吐 / ～ing gas【军】呕吐性毒气

voracious [vəˈreiʃəs] *a.* ①狼吞虎咽的，贪吃的：a ～ appetite 大胃口 ②贪婪的，贪得无厌的：a ～ blood sucker 贪得无厌的吸血鬼 / a ～ reader 求知欲很强的读者 ‖**～ly** *ad.* / **～ness** *n.*

voracity [vɔ(ː)ˈræsiti] *n.* 贪食，暴食；贪婪，贪得无厌

vortex [ˈvɔːteks] ([复] vortices [ˈvɔːtisiːz] 或 vortexes) *n.* ①旋涡；旋风(尤指旋风中心)；[喻](动乱、争论等的)中心：be drawn (或 sucked) into the ～ of 被卷入…的旋涡 ②【空】涡流：wing tip ～ 翼梢涡流 / bound ～ 附体涡流 ③【物】涡旋：～ line 涡(旋)线 / ～ tube 涡管 ‖**～-free** *a.* 无旋的 / **'～-ring** *n.* 涡(旋)环

vote [vout] I *n.* ①选举；投票；表决；票；选票：give one's ～ to (或 for) 投赞成…的票 / put a question to the ～ 把问题交付表决 / Shall we take a ～ on the question? 这个问题我们要不要付表决？/ The chairman proposed a ～ of thanks to the speaker. 会议主席建议大家向演说者鼓掌表示感谢。/ an open (a secret) ～ 记名(无记名)投票 / a spoilt ～ 废票 / an affirmative (a negative) ～ 赞成(反对)票 / cast a ～ 投票 / The motion was carried by 15 ～s with 2 abstentions. 动议以十五票赞成二票弃权通过。②选举权；投票权；表决权 ③投票总数；得票数：the Labour ～ 工党的得票数 / The ～ was light. 投票数不多。④议决的事项；议决的金额(或拨款)：pass a ～ of confidence (nonconfidence) 通过信任(不信任)案 / the army ～ 通过的军事拨款 ⑤投票过程；投票方法 ⑥投票人；(属于同一派别的)一群投票者 ⑦[V-] 英国下(议)院日常会议录 II ❶ *vi.* 投票；表决；发表意见：～ for (against) sb. 投票选(不选)某人 / ～ for (against) a measure 投票赞成(反对)一项措施 / ～ by open ballot 记名投票 / ～ by a show of hands 举手表决 ❷ *vt.* ①投票决定；投票通过；投票选举：～ a sum of money for 投票通过关于…的拨款 ②由会议决定；[口]公认：He was ～d a good member. 大家一致认为他是一个好会员。③[口]建议 ④[美]使投票；按他人意图投票(票) ‖**split one's** ～ 兼投一党以上的候选人的票 / ～ **down** 否决 / ～ **in** 选出；选举 / ～

out [美] 选举中击败(原任者) / ～ **the split ticket** 见 ticket / ～ **the straight ticket** 见 ticket / ～ **through** 表决通过；投票同意；a bill *through* 使议案表决通过；投票通过一项议案 ‖**～able** *a.* =votable / **～less** *a.* 无投票权的；无选举权的 / **～r** *n.* 选举人；投票人；有投票权者

vouch [vautʃ] ❶ *vi.* ①担保，保证；证明，作证(*for*)：～ *for* sb. 替某人担保 / ～ *for* sb.'s honesty 保证某人的诚实 ②确定，确定地说：I can't ～ for it that he is in town. 我不能说他一定在城里。❷ *vt.* ①担保；证明，证实：Will you ～ him honest? 你愿意保证他诚实吗？/ ～ one's words with one's deeds 用自己的行动来证明自己的言词 ②断定；明言 ③[传](某人)出庭作证 ‖**～ee** [vautʃˈiː] *n.* 被担保者 / **～er** *n.* ①担保人，保证人；证人，证明者 ②证件；证书；收据；凭证：an excess luggage ～*er* 超重行李运货收据 / a summarized ～*er* 汇总凭证 / a hotel ～*er* 预订旅馆的凭单 *vt.* ①证实…的可靠性 ②为…准备凭证

vouchsafe [vautʃˈseif] *vt.* ①赐予，给予：He ～*d* me no reply. 他没有给我答复。/ *Vouchsafe* me a visit. 请光临 ②俯允，允诺：～ to do sth. 应允某事

vow[1] [vau] I *n.* 誓；誓约；誓言；许愿：take (或 make) a ～ 立誓，起誓 / break a ～ 违反誓约 / be under a ～ to drink no more wine 发过誓不再喝酒 II ❶ *vt.* ①立誓，起誓：～ to dedicate one's life to 宣誓献身于… ②立誓奉献；立誓要：～ obedience 立誓表示服从 ③[古] 起(誓) ❷ *vi.* 发誓；许愿 ‖**～er** *n.* 发誓者；宣誓者

vow[2] [vau] *vt.* & *vi.* 承认；公开宣布

vowel [ˈvauəl] I *n.*【语】元音；元音字母：front (central, back) ～*s* 前(中，后)元音 / rounded ～*s* 圆唇元音 II *a.* 元音的 III (vowel(l)ed; vowel(l)ing) *vt.* 加元音符号于 ‖**～less** *a.* 无元音的 / **～like** *a.* 象元音的 ‖**～ mark, ～ point** 元音符号 / ～ **system** 元音系统

voyage [ˈvɔidʒ, ˈvɔiidʒ] I *n.* ①航海；航空；航行；航程：go on a ～ 航海去 / on the ～ out (home) 在出(归)航途中 / on the outward (homeward) ～ 在出(归)航途中 / a broken ～ (捕鲸)没有渔获的航行 / a rocket ～ to the moon 到月球去的火箭航行 / the earth in its annual ～ round the sun 环绕太阳作周年运行的地球 ②旅行 ③航海记 II ❶ *vi.* 航海；航空；航行；旅行：～ through the oceans 在各大洋航行 ❷ *vt.* 渡过；飞过 ‖**～able** *a.* 可航行的 / **～r** [ˈvɔiidʒə] *n.* 航海者；航海探险者；航行者；旅行者 ‖**～ charter** 【海】航次租赁 / ～ **policy** 【海】航次保险

vulcanize, vulcanise [ˈvʌlkənaiz] *vt.* & *vi.* (使)硫化；(使)硬化 ‖**vulcanization** [ˌvʌlkənaiˈzeiʃən] *n.*

vulgar [ˈvʌlgə] *a.* ①粗俗的；粗陋的；庸俗的；卑

下的: ~ interests (或 tastes) 低级趣味 / a ~ style 庸俗作风 / ~ evolutionism 庸俗进化论 / ~ materialism 庸俗唯物主义 ②普通的, 一般的; 通俗的: ~ superstitions 一般的迷信 / ~ errors 一般的错误 ③(语言)本土的, 非拉丁的: the ~ languages of Europe 欧洲各国的本民族语言 ④世俗的, 非基督教的 ‖~ly ad.

vulnerable ['vʌlnərəbl] a. ①易受伤的; 脆弱的: a ~ point 弱点 ②易受攻击的, 易受责难的: a

~ statement 易招致抨击的话 / be ~ to criticism 易受到批评; 非无懈可击 / be ~ to fraud 易受骗 ③易受武力袭击的: a ~ outpost 易受袭击的哨所 ④(打桥牌的一方)已成局的, 打不到合约数时罚分要增加的 ‖**vulnerability** [,vʌlnərə-'biliti], ~**ness** n. / **vulnerably** ad.

vulture ['vʌltʃə] n. ①【动】秃鹫, 坐山雕, 狗头雕 ②贪得无厌的人; 劫掠成性的人

vying ['vaiiŋ] I vie 的现在分词 II a. 竞争的

W

wad [wɔd] I n. ①软物的小块; 软填料(如棉花、破纸等); 【军】炮塞 ②(文件、钞票等的)一卷, 一迭; (嚼烟等的)一小块 ; [英方](稻草等的)一捆 ③[美俚]一迭钞票; 金钱 ④[常用复]很可观的数目; 大量: get ~s of publicity 被广为鼓吹(或宣传) II (wadded; wadding) vt. ①把…卷为一卷; 把…压成一迭: 把…搓成小块 ②(用填料)填塞; 填塞住; 填衬: wadded clothes 棉衣 / be well wadded with conceit 妄自尊大, 自命不凡 ‖*shoot one's* ~ [美俚] ①孤注一掷 ②说出想说的话 ③因过多而大倒胃口; 完蛋 ·

wadding ['wɔdiŋ] n. 软填料, 纤维填料; 衬料; 棉胎

waddle ['wɔdl] I vi. (鸭、鹅或矮胖子等)摇摇摆摆地走 II n. 摇摇摆摆的步子; 蹒跚 ‖**waddlingly** ad.

wade [weid] I ❶ vi. ①蹚, 跋涉: ~ across a river 蹚水过河 / ~ through the marshland 涉过沼泽地 / a wading bird 涉禽 ②费力地前进; 困难地通过: ~ through a dull book 啃完一本枯燥乏味的书 / ~ through thick and thin 克服一切困难障碍 / ~ through slaughter (或 blood) to 通过血腥手段达到… ❷ vt. 蹚(河), 涉(泥地、沙滩等) II n. ①蹚, 跋涉 ②可涉水而过的地方; 浅滩 ‖~ *in* ①猛烈进攻 ②插手, 介入 ③[口] 精神饱满地开始工作 / ~ *into* ①猛烈进攻(人、事物) ②[口]精神饱满地开始(工作、讨论等) ‖~**able** a. ~wadable ~r n. ①跋涉者, 蹚水者 ②涉水禽鸟(如鹤、鹭等) ③[英][复](涉水捕鱼用的)高统防水靴 ‖**wading pool** (供孩子蹚水玩乐的)浅水池

wadi, wady ['wɔdi] [复] wadi(e)s n. ①(阿拉伯和北非仅在雨季有水的)干涸河道(或溪谷); 【地】旱谷 ②流经干涸河道的水流 ③(沙漠中的)绿洲

wafer ['weifə] I n. ①薄脆饼; 圆片糖果 ②【宗】圣饼(圣餐时的未发酵的圆面包片) ③(封信或文件等用的)干胶片, 封缄纸 ④[无]薄片, 圆片, 晶片: ~ socket 【无】饼形管座 ⑤包药干糊片(俗称糯米纸) II vt. 用干胶片封(信件等) ‖*as thin as a*

~ 极薄 ‖~**y** ['weifəri] a. 象薄脆饼似的; 极薄的

waft [wɑːft] I ❶ vt. 吹送, 飘送; 使飘荡: A distant song was ~ed to our ears by the breeze. 远处的歌声随风飘送到我们耳中。 ❷ vi. 飘荡 II n. ①吹送; 飘荡 ②(风、气味、声音等的)一阵; (鸟翼的)一搧 ③(和平、喜悦等的)短暂的感觉, 一时的感觉 ④波浪; 波动, 浮动 ⑤【海】(表示风向、遇险等的)信号旗; (用旗等表示的)信号; 求救信号 ‖~**er** n. 转盘风扇

wag[1] [wæg] (wagged; wagging) ❶ vt. ①(向左右或上下)摇; 摇摆, 摇动: The dog wagged its tail. 狗摇动着尾巴。/ ~ one's finger at sb. 向某人摇手指(表示指责) ②饶(舌): ~ one's tongue (或 jaws) 喋喋不休 ❷ vi. ①(向左右或上下)摇; 摆动; 颤动: The dog's tail wagged. 狗尾巴摆动着。②[古](时势等)推移, 变迁: So the world ~s. 人世变迁就是这样。/ How ~s the world (with you)? (你)近况如何? ③喋喋不休: The tongues (或 jaws, beards, chins) are wagging. 大家谈个没完。/ Your tongue ~s too freely. 你说话太随便了。④[古]离开, 动身; 游荡 ⑤(动物)摇尾巴 II n. 摇摆, 摆动 ‖*The tail* ~s *the dog.* (社会或党派中)小人物掌权。/ ~ *the feather* 见 **feather**

wag[2] [wæg] n. ①爱说笑打趣的人; 小丑 ②[英俚]逃学: play (the) ~ 逃学

wage[1] [weidʒ] I n. ①[常用复]工资, 工钱: His ~s are £3 a week. 他的工资每周三英镑。/ get good ~s 拿优厚的工资 / nominal (real) ~s 名义(实际)工资 / a living ~ 能满足生活需要的工资 / ~ labour 雇佣劳动(力) / work at a ~ (或 at ~s) of £12 a month 每月拿十二英镑的工资工作 ②[~s][用作单或复]报应, 报答 ③[~s][用作单或复]年产额(或国家纯利)中作为劳动工资的部分 II vt. [方]雇用 ‖~ **earner** 靠工资为生的人, 雇佣劳动者 / ~ **freeze** 工资冻结 / ~ **scale** 工资等级(表) / '~(s)-**fund** n.

工资基金（一定时期一定社会的总资本中用于支付工资的部分）/ ~ **slave** 工资奴隶，雇佣劳动者 / '~**worker** *n.* earner

wage² [weidʒ] ❶ *vt.* 开展(运动)；进行(斗争)；作(战) ❷ *vi.* 在开展中；在进行中：The controversy ~d for months. 论战进行了好几个月。

wager ['weidʒə] Ⅰ *n.* 赌注，赌物；赌博：lay (或 make) a ~ with sb. 与某人打赌 / take up (或 accept) a ~ 接受打赌 Ⅱ ❶ *vt.* 以…打赌(赌注)；同…打赌 ②保证，担保 ❷ *vi.* 打赌 ‖ ~ **of battle** 【史】决斗断讼法 / ~ **of law** 【史】宣誓断讼法

waggle ['wægl] *vt., vi. & n.* 来回摇动，来回摇摆 ‖**waggly** *a.*

wag(g)on ['wægən] Ⅰ *n.* ① 四轮运货马车(或牛车)；运货车 ②[英](铁路)货车(=[美] freight car) ③小型手推(送货)车；(餐室中用的)流动服务车 ④旅行(汽)车；小型客车 ⑤[矿]矿车 ⑥[the ~] [美口]囚车 ⑦[W-]【天】北斗七星 ⑧[美俚]左轮手枪；战舰 Ⅱ ❶ *vi.* 用运货马车(或牛车等)运输货物；乘运货车旅行 ❷ *vt.* 用运货马车(或牛车等)运输(货物) ‖ **fix sb.'s** [美俚]伤害某人以为报复 / **hitch one's ~ to a star** 立雄心；志大才疏 / **off the ~** [美俚]不再戒酒 / **on the (water) ~** [美俚]戒酒 ‖~**age** ['wægənidʒ] *n.* ①运货(马)车运输(费) ②[总称]运货(马)车 / ~**er** *n.* ①赶大车的人 ②[W-]【天】御夫座；北斗七星 / ~**ette** [,wægə-'net] *n.* (有两排相对座位的)四轮游览轻便马车 ‖ ~ **soldier** [美俚]野战炮兵 / ~ **train** 【军】车辆纵列

waif [weif] *n.* ①无主失物；漂流物 ②迷路的人(或动物)；无家可归者，流浪儿 ③[复]【律】窃贼逃跑时丢弃的赃物 ④【海】信号旗；(用旗表示的)信号 ‖~**s and strays** ①流浪儿；遗弃的孩子 ②零碎东西

wail [weil] Ⅰ ❶ *vi.* ①恸哭，嚎咷 ②(风等)呼啸；(警报器)尖啸 ③哀诉，悲叹，呜咽 ❷ *vt.* [古]哀悼(某人的死亡)；悲痛(某人的惨遇) Ⅱ *n.* ①恸哭(声)，嚎咷(声) ②呼啸(声)；尖啸(声) ③哀诉，悲叹，呜咽 ‖~**ful** *a.* 悲恸的；(像)悲号声的 ‖~**ingly** *ad.* ‖~**ing wall** ①[W-W-]哭墙(指耶路撒冷古城中一所犹太教庙宇的残壁，该庙相传在公元七十年左右被罗马人灭犹太国时所毁) ②安慰物，慰藉物

waist [weist] *n.* ①腰，腰部：a large (small) ~ 粗(细)腰 / have a long (short) ~ 上身长(短) / He has no ~. 他胖得看不出腰身。 / a ~ shot 【摄】(至腰部为止的)上身镜头 ②衣服的上身(或腰身)部分；背心，紧身胸衣，乳褡；儿童内衣 ③(提琴、鞋等)中间细的部分 ④【船】上甲板中部；船腰、(帆船)主桅与前桅间的中部 ⑤飞机机身中部 ‖~**ed** *a.* ①[常用以构成复合词]有…腰身的：wasp-~**ed** 细腰的；束腰的；紧胸的 ②腰状的 ‖~**band** *n.* 腰带，裤带，裙带 / '~-**belt** *n.* 腰带，裤带 / '~**cloth** *n.* (围)腰布 / ~**coat**

['weiskəut] *n.* [英]背心，马甲 / '~-'**deep**, '~=**high** *a. & ad.* 齐腰深(或高) / '~**line** *n.* 腰身，腰身部分

wait [weit] Ⅰ ❶ *vi.* ①等，等候，等待：Wait a minute. 等一等! / Don't ~ (for me) if I am late. 万一我晚到了，不要等我。 / ~ for sb.'s reply (或 ~ for sb. to reply) 等候某人答复 / We shall ~ till (或 until) he comes. 我们要等到他来。 / keep sb. ~**ing** 使某人等着 ②准备好，在手边：The car is ~**ing** for us. 汽车准备好了，就等我们了。 / A letter is ~**ing** for you on the table. 桌上有你的一封信(等着你去拿)。③伺候进餐：~ at (或 on) table 伺候进餐 ④耽搁，暂缓：That work will have to ~. 那项工作暂时搁一下。 ❷ *vt.* ①等待，期待；听候：~ one's chance (或 opportunity, time, hour) 等待时机 / ~ one's turn 等轮到自己 / ~ sb.'s convenience 等候某人的方便 / ~ orders 听候命令 ②[口](为等候而)推迟(饭餐、茶点等)：Don't ~ dinner for me. 别等我吃饭。 ③伺候(进餐)：~ table 伺候进餐 Ⅱ ❶ *n.* ①等待；等待的时间：have a long ~ for the train 等火车等了很久 / a four-hour ~ 四小时的等待 ②埋伏 ③[the ~s] (圣诞节时)沿街唱颂诗的人们 ‖**lie in ~** (或 **lay**) **for** 埋伏着等待… / ~ **on** (或 **upon**) ①服侍(某人) ②招待(顾客) ③晋谒，拜访(某人)；陪伴(来宾等) ④随着…而产生：May good luck ~ **upon** you. 望你交好运。 ⑤(赛跑中)故意尾随(对手) ⑥焦急地等待… / ~ **out** 到…结束：~ **out** a storm 等到风暴过去 / ~ **up (for)** (为…而)等候着不睡 ‖~**er** *n.* ①等候者 ②侍者，服务员：a ~**er upon** Providence 不可靠的酒肉朋友；趋炎附势的人；等待时机(而下决心)者 ③(端菜具等用的)托盘 / ~**ress** ['weitris] *n.* 女侍者，女服务员 ‖'~-**a-bit** *n.* 有钩刺的灌木 / '~-**and-'see** *a.* 等着瞧的，观望的：a ~**-and-see** attitude (policy) 观望态度(政策) / '~**list** *vt.* 把…登入申请人名单

waive [weiv] *vt.* ①放弃，不坚持(权利、要求等)：~ one's claim 放弃要求 ②推迟考虑；延期进行 ③挥手打发走：~ sb. off 把某人打发走 / ~ sth. aside 把某事撇开不管 ④丢弃(所偷赃物) ‖~**r** *n.* 【律】①自动放弃，弃权 ②弃权声明书

wake¹ [weik] Ⅰ (过去式 waked 或 woke [wouk], 过去分词 waked 或 woken ['woukən] 或 woke) ❶ *vi.* ①醒，醒来；醒着：Has he ~d (up) yet? 他醒了没有? / He woke to find himself in the hospital. 他醒来发现自己在医院里。②觉醒，觉悟 ③警觉，认识(到)(to)：~ (up) to the importance of 认识到…的重要性 / ~ (up) to the fact that … 认识到…的事实 ④ 变活跃；振奋：The scene suddenly woke into life. 场面突然活跃起来。⑤[古][方]守夜；守灵 ❷ *vt.* ①唤醒，弄醒：Please ~ me (up) at five. 请在五点钟叫醒我。/ Don't ~ the baby. 别弄醒孩子。②使觉悟；激发，引起：The event may ~ him up. 这件事可

能使他醒悟。/ This bowl ~d memories of his childhood. 这只碗引起了他对童年的回忆。/ ~ echoes 引起回响 ③[古][方]为…守夜;为…守灵 **II** *n.* ①醒,不眠 ②(葬礼前的)守夜;守灵 ③[英]每年一度纪念教堂守护神的节日;(教堂守护神节前夕的)守夜;[常用复]教区的节庆 ④[常用复](英国北部一些工业城市的)每年一度的假日 ‖**~-ful** *a.* ①觉醒的 ②警觉的,戒备的 ③不眠的;失眠的: a ~*ful* night 不眠之夜 / **~less** *a.* 酣(睡)的 / **waking** *a.* 醒着的: in one's *waking* hours 在醒着的时候 ‖**~-,robin** *n.* 【植】海芋属植物;斑叶阿若母;延龄草

wake² [weik] *n.* (船的)尾波,航迹;(飞机的)尾流;(人、车等经过的)痕迹: A truck passed, and a ~ of dust floated toward us. 卡车驶过,一股尘埃迎面飘来。/ the ~ of a meteor (typhoon) 流星(台风)尾巴 ‖*in the ~ of* ①尾随(船): steer *in the ~ of* another vessel 尾随着另一船只驶行 ②紧跟…,随着…而来: problems which follow *in the ~ of* a flood 随着水灾之后而来的一些问题 ③追随…之后,仿效…

walk [wɔ:k] **I ❶** *vi.* ①走,步行;散步;(马等)慢步走: ~ into a room 走进房间 / ~ backwards (sideways) 倒退着(横着)走 / ~ one hour a day 一天步行一小时 / ~ about 踱来踱去;散步 / go ~*ing* in the park 上公园去逛逛 ②(物体)行走似地移动;步步延伸: pylons ~*ing* across the valley 穿过山谷的一行高压输电塔 ③处世,行事;生活: ~ warily 谨慎行事 ④(鬼魂等)行走,出现 ⑤【体】(篮球赛中违例)带球走,走步 **❷** *vt.* ①走遍;走过;…上走,沿着…走: ~ the floor (the deck) 在房间里(甲板上)踱步 / ~ a tightrope 走绳索,走钢丝 / 徒步执行(或查看、测量): ~ guard 巡逻 / ~ the (picket) line (罢工等时)当纠察 / ~ tracks 查修路轨 / ~ a boundary 用脚步测量界线 ③使走: ~ sb. to exhaustion 使某人走得筋疲力尽 / ~ a horse 遛马 / ~ sb. into jail 把某人押进监牢 / ~ pigs to market 把猪赶到市集 / ~ a bicycle 推着自行车走 / ~ a patient 扶着病人走 / I'll ~ you to the bus stop. 我陪你走到汽车站。④同…竞走: No one could ~ him. 谁也走不过他。⑤使(物体)行走似地移动: ~ one's fingers 把手指前后交替地移动 / ~ a heavy box into the house (on its corners) (以使箱角轮流着地的方法)把沉重的箱子挪进屋子 ⑥【体】(篮球赛中违例)带(球)走 ⑦慢步跳(舞) **II** *n.* ①走,步行;散步;(马等的)慢步走;【体】竞走: He started at a ~ but soon broke into a run. 他开始时慢慢走着,但一会儿就奔跑起来。/ take (或 go for) a ~ 去散步 ②走步的姿势: I can know him at once by his ~. 我能从他走路的样子一下子认出他。③走的路程;(邮递员、巡逻兵等)走的固定路线: The town is an hour's ~ from here. 从这儿走到城里有一小时的路程。④常走之处; 散步场所;(屋

顶的)平台;走道,人行道;(制造绳索用的)狭长走道: sb.'s favourite ~ 某人爱去散步的地方 ⑤(禽、畜等的)活动场地,放牧场;(栽植成行的)种植园;(英国护林人的)管区 ⑥极慢的速度: slow down production to a ~ 使生产降低到极慢速度 ⑦阶层;行业;生活方式;行为: people of (或 in, from) all ~s of life 各界人士 / one's ~ of life 职业 ⑧[英](庄严的)行列,仪仗队 ‖*in a ~* 轻而易举地: win in a ~ 轻易取胜 / ~ *away from* ①从…旁边走开 ②(比赛中)轻易地胜过… ③从…平安地脱身 / ~ *away with sth.* 顺手牵羊地拿走某物: Someone has ~*ed away with* my umbrella. 有人把我的伞拿走了。/ ~ *down* ①通过散步消化(食物等) ②在步行速度和距离方面胜过… / ~ *heavy* [美俚]神气活现 / ~ *into* ①走进(屋子等) ②[口]狼吞虎咽地吃(食物);很快地用完(东西) ③[口]痛骂,严斥(某人);攻击(某人) / ~ *off* ①(突然)离开: ~ *off* the job 离开工作(岗位);罢工 ②带走: The policeman ~*ed* him *off*. 警察把他带走了。③用走路来消除: ~ *off* one's headache 散散步解除头痛 / ~ *off with* ①偷走;顺手拿走 ②轻易赢得 / ~ *out* ①走出;把(某人)带出 ②[口]罢工 ③退席(表示抗议) / ~ °*out on sb.* [美口](正当某人需要帮助的时候)离开某人,遗弃某人 / ~ *out with sb.* [口]同某人恋爱 / ~ *over sb.* ①无视某人的愿望(或感情),轻蔑地对待某人 ②轻易胜过某人 / ~ *over the course* 见 **course** / ~ *sb. off his legs* 见 **leg** / ~ *the plank* 见 **plank** / ~ *through* ①走过场似地表演: ~ *through* a play 马虎地排一出戏 ②敷衍了事地做完: ~ *through* a test 草草地做完测验 / ~ *up* ①请进(在马戏团等门外招呼观众用语) ②沿…走 ③走上(山、楼等): ~ *up* a hill 登上山丘 / ~ *up to* 走近,走向: ~ *up to* sb. 走近(或向)某人 ‖**~able** *a.* 适于步行的;可以步行的: a ~*able* path 适宜步行的小路 / a ~*able* distance 步行可以到达的距离 / **~er** *n.* ①步行者;常散步的人;参加竞走者;徒步叫卖的小贩: He is not much of a ~*er*. 他不善于走路。②(帮助小孩、病弱者学走路用的)扶车;轻便鞋 ③【动】走禽 ‖**~-about** *n.* ①(澳洲土著的)短期丛林流浪生活 ②徒步旅行 / '**~away** *n.* ①轻易取胜的比赛;轻易取得的胜利 ②轻易完成的事情 / '**~-in** *a.* ①(壁橱等)大得能走进去的 ②(房间等)能不经过穿廊直接进去的 ③未经预约而来的 *n.* ①人进得去的冰箱(或冷藏室) ②轻易获得的竞选胜利 ③未经预约而来的人 / '**~-on** *n.* (戏剧的)跑龙套角色 / '**~-out** *n.* ①罢工(者);罢课(者) ②(表示抗议的)退席;退出组织 / '**~over** *n.* ①只有一匹马参加的比赛 ②对手不强的比赛;不经比赛就取得的胜利,轻易取得的胜利 / '**~-through** *n.* ①(戏剧、电视剧等的)初排 ②地下步行道 / '**~-up** *n.* 无电梯的大楼;无电梯大楼的楼上房间 *a.* ①(公寓房屋等)无电梯的 ②(房间)在无电梯大楼楼上的 / '**~way** *n.* 走道

wall¹ [wɔːl] **I** *n.* ①墙,壁;围墙;城墙;[常用复]壁垒: a party (或 partition) ~ 隔墙,通墙 / a blank ~ 无门窗(或装饰等)的墙,平壁 / within four ~s 在室内 ②间隔层;内壁:cell ~【生】细胞壁,细胞膜 / the ~s of the chest【解】胸壁 / ~ of a container 容器壁 / foot【矿】底帮,底壁,下盘 / hanging ~【矿】上盘,悬帮 ③(形状或作用如墙的)分界物;屏障: a mountain ~ 山屏;峭壁 / a ~ of partition [喻]鸿沟,分界线 / a tariff ~ 关税壁垒 / a ~ of secrecy 包住秘密的屏障 ④(路的)靠墙的一边 **II** *a.* 墙(或壁)的;墙上的;靠墙的;爬墙的: ~ cabinets 壁橱 / a (telephone) set 墙式电话机,墙机 / ~ plants 爬墙植物 **III** *vt.* ①用墙围住(或分隔,防护): a ~ed city 有城墙的城市 / a lake ~ed in by peaks 群山环绕的湖泊 / ~ off half the house 用墙把屋子一隔为两 ②堵塞(门、窗等);禁闭: ~ up the window 堵塞窗户 / ~ up the danger 杜绝危险 ‖*drive* (或 *push*) *sb. to the* ~ 逼某人至绝境 / *give sb. the* ~ 把好走的路让给某人 / *go over the* ~ [美俚]越狱 / *go to the* ~ (因弱小或无助)被推开在一旁;失败,败北 / *run into a blank* ~ 碰壁 / *run one's head against a* ~ 试图干不可能的事,碰壁 / *see through a brick* ~ 有敏锐的眼光,有惊人的洞察力 / *take the* ~ *of sb.* 不把好走的路让给某人;[喻]占某人的上风 / *up against the* ~ 在非常困难的境地,碰壁 / *Walls have ears.* [谚]隔墙有耳。/ *with one's back to the* ~ 见 **back** ‖**-less** *a.* 无墙壁的 / **~-like** *a.* 似墙的 ‖'**~board** *n.* 墙板 / '**~,flower** *n.* ①常生在墙上的一种黄色草花;开橙色(或棕色)芳香花簇的春季园艺植物 ②[口]舞会中没有舞伴而坐着看的女子 / **~newspaper(s)** 墙报 / **~ painting** 壁画 / '**~,paper** *n.* 糊墙纸 *vt.* & *vi.* 糊墙纸(于) / **~ plate**【建】承梁板 / '**~,washer** *n.*【建】撑墙支架板

wall² [wɔːl] *vt.* & *vi.* 演戏般地转动(眼睛)

wallaby ['wɔləbi] *n.* ①[动]鼩(袋鼠科中的小兽) ②[复][口]澳大利亚人 ‖*on the* ~ (*track*) 在流浪,失业

wallet ['wɔlit] *n.* ①(放钞票等的)皮夹子 ②皮制小工具袋;钓鱼袋 ③[古](香客等的)行囊,旅行袋

wallow ['wɔlou] **I** *vi.* ①(猪等在泥、脏水等中)打滚: ~ in the mire 在泥沼中打滚 ②[喻]沉迷;纵乐(*in*): ~ *in* luxury (vice) 沉迷于奢侈(罪恶)生活 ③(船等)颠簸,摇摆;笨重地驶行 ④(烟、焰等)冒起 **II** *n.* ①打滚,翻滚 ②(水牛等经常打滚的)泥沼,水坑;(动物打滚造成的)洼地,坑 ③[喻]堕落 ‖*in money* 见 **money**

walnut ['wɔːlnʌt] *n.* ①胡桃属植物;胡桃;胡桃树 ②胡桃木 ‖*over the* ~s *and the wine* 在餐后吃水果、喝葡萄酒的时候

walrus ['wɔːlrəs] **I** ([复] walrus(es)) *n.* ①[动]海象 ②[美俚]矮胖子 **II** *a.* ①海象的 ②海象似的(尤指末端下垂的长胡须)

walrus

waltz [wɔːls, wɔːlts] **I** *n.* 华尔兹舞;圆舞曲 **II** *a.* 华尔兹舞的;圆舞曲的 **III** ❶ *vi.* ①跳华尔兹舞 ②轻快地走动;旋转: ~ in and out of the room 翩跹地进出房间 ③轻快顺利地前进: ~ *through* a contest 轻而易举地通过比赛 ❷ *vt.* ①与…跳华尔兹舞 ②硬拉,硬拖: ~ sb. upstairs 把某人硬拖上楼

wan [wɔn] **I** *a.* ①苍白的,无血色的: a ~ complexion 苍白的面色 ②病态的;有倦容的;有愁容的: a ~ smile 惨淡的笑容 ③暗淡的;微弱的: ~ stars 暗淡的星星 **II** (wanned; wanning) *vi.* & *vt.* (使)变苍白;(使)呈病态 ‖**~ly** *ad.* / **~ness** *n.*

wand [wɔnd] *n.* ①棒,棍,竿,杖 ②魔杖;【音】指挥棒 ③(表示官职的)权杖,权标 ④(柳树等幼树的)嫩枝 ⑤[美]箭靶

wander ['wɔndə] ❶ *vi.* ①漫游;闲逛;漫步;徘徊,彷徨: ~ *about* (或 *over, through*) the world 漫游世界 / ~ *about* (或 *up and down*) the street 在街上徘徊 ②迷路: The travellers ~ed for some time in the fog. 旅行者在雾中迷了一会路。③离开正道;离题;错乱: ~ *from* proper conduct 行为不正派 / ~ *from* the subject (或 point) 离题 / His mind (或 thoughts) ~ed back to his school days. 他回想到他的学生时代。/ He ~s in his talk. 他说话东拉西扯。④(河流等)蜿蜒,曲折地流 ❷ *vt.* 漫游: ~ the world 漫游世界 ‖**~er** ['wɔndərə] *n.* 漫游者;流浪汉;彷徨者;迷路的动物

wandering ['wɔndəriŋ] **I** *a.* ①漫游的;闲逛的: a ~ minstrel (中世纪)周游四方的行吟诗人;江湖艺人 ②(部落)游牧的 ③(河流等)曲折的,蜿蜒的 ④(精神)恍惚的;错乱的 ⑤(植物)有长藤的,有卷须的,攀绕的 **II** *n.* [常用复] ①漫游;闲逛 ②离开正道;离题 ③神志恍惚;精神错乱;胡言乱语 ‖~ **cell** 游走细胞 / **the W- J-** [W- J-] 流浪的犹太人(据传说因他嘲弄了受难的耶稣,被罚永世流浪) ②漫游各国者;流浪者 ③攀绕植物(尤指吊竹梅或白花紫露草)

wane [wein] **I** *vi.* ①(月)亏,缺: the *waning* moon 下弦月 ②变暗淡;变小;减少 ③衰落,衰退;没落;消逝: His strength is *waning*. 他的精力在衰退。/ *waning* influence (popularity) 衰落中的影响(声望) / The day ~s. 一天快过去了。(或:近

黄昏了。) / ～ to the close 接近末尾,将完结 ④退潮 **Ⅱ** *n.* ①月亏;月亏期 ②衰退;衰退期 ③(木材的)缺损 ‖on the ～ 日益衰落,逐渐败落 / *wax and* ～ 见 **wax²**

wangle ['wæŋgl] **Ⅰ ❶** *vi.* ①(从人群中)扭身挤出;(从困境中)设法脱身 ②使用诡计(或花言巧语等): ～ to forestall payment of a debt 用尽诡计赖债 **❷** *vt.* ①扭身挤出: ～ one's way through a crowd 从人群中扭身挤出一条路 ②用诡计获得;哄骗: ～ votes 拉选票 / ～ sb. into loaning money 哄骗某人答应借钱 / ～ sth. out of sb. 从某人处骗出某物 ③虚饰;假造: ～ accounts 造假帐 **Ⅱ** *n.* ①巧计获得;哄骗;骗得的东西 ②虚饰;假造

want [wɒnt] **Ⅰ ❶** *vt.* ①要,想要: ～ (sb.) to do sth. 要(某人)做某事 / ～ sth. done 要别人把某事做好 / I don't ～ there to be any misunderstanding. 我不希望发生什么误会。/ The salesman asked me what I ～ed. 营业员问我要买什么。②要…来,要…去: The teacher ～s you in the classroom. 老师在教室里要你去。/ You won't be ～ed this afternoon. 今天下午(没你的事)你不必来了。③需要;应该;必须: The sick child ～s somebody to look after it. 病孩需要有人照顾。/The house ～s repairs (或 repairing, to be repaired, to undergo repairs). 这屋子需要修理了。/ That sort of thing ～s some doing.[口]那种事情得花些工夫(或有点本领)才做得好。/ You don't ～ to be rude. 你不该(或不必)粗鲁。④欠缺,缺少: It ～s three minutes to twelve. 十二点差三分钟。/ The picture ～s something of perfection. 这幅画有些美中不足。/ ～ neither food nor clothes 不愁吃穿 ⑤[常用被动语态]征求;通缉: *Wanted, a typist.* (报刊广告等用语)招聘:打字员一名。 be ～ed by the police 被警察局通缉 / a ～ed list (poster) 通缉名单(告示) **❷** *vi.* 需要,缺少 (for, in); 生活困难;贫困: We shall not ～ for food. 我们不会缺少食物了。/ ～ for nothing 不缺乏任何生活必需品,丰衣足食 / ～ in judgement 缺乏判断力 **Ⅱ** *n.* ①需要;[常用复]需求,必需品: be in ～ of repair 需要整修 / meet a long-felt ～ 满足长期以来的需要 / We can supply all your ～s. 我们能供给你所需要的一切。②缺乏,缺少: The plant drooped from (或 for) ～ of water. 这株植物因缺水而枯萎。/ Your work shows ～ of care. 你的工作显示出你不细心。/ There is a ～ of confidence in him. 人们对他缺乏信心。③匮乏,贫困: live in ～ 生活困苦 ④缺点;过失 ‖~ *in (out, off)* [口][方]想要进来 (出去, 走掉): The child ～s *out.* 这孩子想到外面去。‖~*age* ['wɒntidʒ] *n.* 缺少;缺少量 / ～*less* *a.* 无所需求的 ‖~ *ad* (报刊等的)征求(或招聘)广告

wanting ['wɒntiŋ] **Ⅰ** *a.* ①缺少的;没有的: A few pages of this book are ～. 这本书缺了几页。/

a coat with some buttons ～ 缺少几个钮扣的外套 / be ～ in courtesy 无礼 / Fresh water fish is totally ～ there. 那儿完全没有淡水鱼。②不够格的;迟钝的: be ～ to one's duty 不称职 / try sth. and find it (to be) ～ 试用某物发现它不够标准 / be a little ～ 有点笨 **Ⅱ** *prep.* 缺,无: a month ～ two days 一个月缺二天 / *Wanting* mutual support, victory is impossible. 没有互相支援就不可能胜利。

wanton ['wɒntən] **Ⅰ** *a.* ①爱玩的,嬉闹的;任性的,不负责任的;变化无常的: a ～ child 嬉闹(或顽皮)的孩子 / a ～ breeze 飘忽不定的微风 ②(草木等)繁茂的;(语言、想象力等)夸张的,奔放的 ③(侵略、破坏、侮辱等)蛮横的;胡乱的;放肆的: ～ aggression 蛮横的(或肆无忌惮的)侵略 / ～ bombing 狂轰滥炸 ④(人、思想、书等)淫乱的 **Ⅱ** *n.* ①嬉闹的孩子(或动物) ②宠坏的人(或动物) ③着乡享乐的人 ④淫乱的人(尤指荡妇) **Ⅲ ❶** *vi.* ①任性;反复无常;嬉戏 ②生活奢侈;放肆;淫荡 **❷** *vt.* 挥霍(钱财) ‖~*ly ad.* / ～*ness n.*

war [wɔː] **Ⅰ** *n.* ①战争;战争状态;战术: be prepared against ～ 备战 / a ～ of aggression 侵略战争 / a prisoner of ～ 战俘 / annals of ～ 战争史 / a protracted ～ 持久战 / a ～ of attrition 消耗战 ②军事学 the principles of ～ 军事原则 / the art of ～ 战略和战术 ③冲突,斗争;竞争: a private ～ (个人或家族间的)私斗,械斗 / 一国国民未经政府同意对别国发动的武装袭击 / a ～ of the elements 暴风雨;自然灾害,天灾 / a ～ against disease 同疾病所作的斗争 ‖a civil ～ 内战,国内战争 / cold ～ 冷战 / a conventional ～ 常规战争 / the First (Second, Third) Revolutionary Civil War 第一 (二, 三) 次国内革命战争 / the First (Second) World War (或 World War I (II)) 第一(二)次世界大战 / a limited ～ 有限战争 / a nuclear ～ 核战争 / a shooting ～ 热战 / a special ～ 特种战争 / a total ～ 总体战 / the War between the States (或 the Civil War, the War of Secession)【美史】南北战争 (1861—1865) / the War of Nations 第一次世界大战 (1914—1918) / a war of nerves 神经战 / the War of Resistance against Japanese Aggression 抗日战争 (1937—1945) / the Wars of the Roses【英史】玫瑰 (或蔷薇) 战争 (1455—1485) / a white ～ 不流血的战争;经济竞争 **Ⅱ** (warred; warring ['wɔːriŋ]) **❶** *vi.* ①进行战争;战斗: ～ for national independence 进行民族独立战争 ②斗争;竞争 **❷** *vt.* [苏格兰]击败 **Ⅲ** *a.* 战争的;战时的;战争中用的;战争引起的: a cabinet 战时内阁 / a ～ *communiqué* 战报 / ～ escalation 战争升级 / ～ industry 军事工业 / ～ material 军需物资 / a ～ theatre 战场,战区 / ～ production 军工生产 ②[苏格兰]更坏的,更差的 ‖*be at* ～ *(with)* (同…)处于交战状态;(同…)进行竞争 / *carry the* ～ *into* the enemy's camp (或country) 向敌方反击; 反驳 / declare ~ on (或 upon) 向…宣战; 向…发动进攻; 表示反对… / drift into ~ 卷入战争 (或斗争) / go to the ~(s) 当兵, 从军; 开始作战; (战时) 参军 / have been in the ~s 在战争中负过伤; [口]吃过苦头, 受过创伤 / make (或 wage) ~ upon 对…进行战争, 向…开战 / roll back the tide of ~ 击退侵略 / ~ in the third dimension 空中作战 / ~ to the knife 你死我活的搏斗; 拼死的斗争 ‖~ baby ①战时诞生的孩子(尤指士兵的私生子) ②由于战时需要而大大发展的工业(或产品) ③因战争状态而价值激增的证券(或股份) / '~bird n. [美俚]作战飞机 / ~ chest ①战争基金 ②(为竞选等)筹措的资金 / ~ cloud(s) 战云, 可能引起战争的紧张局势 / ~ correspondent 军事记者, 战地记者 / '~craft n. ①军用飞机; 军舰 ②战略和战术, 兵法 / ~ crime(s) 战争罪(如种族灭绝、虐待战俘等) / ~ criminal 战犯 / ~ cry ①作战时的呐喊 ②(政党竞选时提出的)口号, 标语 ③(斗争中)发动群众的口号 / ~ dance (原始部落)作战前的舞蹈; 摹仿作战的舞蹈 / ~ game ①摹拟实际战争的教练演习(如图上作业、沙盘作业) ②军事演习, 实地演习 / ~ hawk 主战分子, 战争叫嚣者 / ~ head n. 弹头: a missile ~head 导弹弹头 / '~-horse n. ①战马, 军马 ②老兵; 老练的政客; 经验丰富的人 ③牢记过去功业(或争论)的人 ④(乐曲等中的)陈腔, 老调 / '~lord n. 军阀 / '~,lordism n. 军阀主义; 军阀作风 / ~-monger 战争贩子 / ~ paint ①(原始部落)出战前涂在身上的颜料 ②[俚]盛装; 礼服 ③(妇女的)化妆(品) / ~ party 主战派 / '~path n. (美洲印第安人的)征途; 敌对行动, 敌对情绪: be on the ~path 准备作战(或争吵); 正在作战(或争吵) / '~plane n. 军用飞机 / ~ potential 战争潜力 / '~ship n. 军舰 / '~time n. 战时: ~time rationing 战时配给(制) / ~ vessel 军舰 / '~,weariness n. 厌战情绪 / '~-,weary a. ①厌战的 ②(战斗机)破损不堪的 / '~worn a. 由于战争而筋疲力尽的; 遭受战争创伤的; 被战争毁坏的 / ~ zone 交战地带, 战区(尤指公海上的)

warble[1] ['wɔːbl] I **❶** vi. ①(鸟)啭鸣 ②用柔和的颤音唱歌 ③发出音乐般的声音: The brook ~d. 溪声潺潺。 **❷** vt. ①(鸟)啭鸣着唱 ②用柔和的颤音唱 ③鸟啭似地讲(或朗诵等) II n. ①啭鸣; 颤声的歌唱 ②颤音 ③歌曲; 颂歌 ‖~r n. 鸣禽; 歌手

warble[2] ['wɔːbl] n. ①(马鞍磨出来的)马背的硬瘤 ②由牛蝇幼虫寄生而形成的)动物皮下的肿块 ③牛蝇幼虫; 牛蝇 (=~ fly)

ward [wɔːd] I n. ①保卫; 保护; 看护; 监护: To whom is the child in ~? 谁是这孩子的监护人? ②监禁, 拘留; 监督, 监视: put sb. in ~ 监禁(或监视)某人 / be under ~ 被监禁; 被监督 / keep watch and ~ 不断监视; 日夜警卫 ③[古]守卫

队; 卫兵 ④受(法院或监护人)监护的未成年者(或疯人等); 受政府保护(或训导)的人(或集团) ⑤病房, 病室: a medical (surgical) ~ 内科(外科)病房 / an isolation ~ 隔离病房 / an emergency ~ 急诊病房 ⑥牢房: a condemned ~ 死刑犯人牢房 ⑦(慈善机关、养老院等的)收容室 ⑧行政区; 选区; (英格兰北部和苏格兰的)分区(相当一百户) ⑨(城堡、要塞内的)空旷场地 ⑩防卫设施 ⑪[复]锁孔; (钥匙的)榫槽 ⑫(剑术等的)防卫姿势 II vt. ①保护; 守卫 ②避开; 防止; 挡住 (off): ~ off an attack (a blow, a danger) 避开攻击(打击, 危险) ③使入病房 ‖~er n. ①看门人, 门警 ②[英]管理人; 监狱看守人; 狱吏 ③[古](国王或司令官用来标志权力的)节, 杖 / ~ress ['wɔːdris] n. 监狱的女看守人 / ~ship n. ①监护; 保护 ②(封建制度下)对佃户的幼年子女及其财产的监督权 ‖ heeler [美俚][贬](政治团体或选区委员会中的)小人物; (竞选时)在选区游说、拉票的小政客; 政客的走卒 / '~room n. (军舰上除舰长外的)军官起居室(尤指餐室)

warden[1] ['wɔːdn] n. ①看守人; 保管员; 管理员; 监察人: a game ~ 比赛中协助裁判者(如巡边员) ②[美]镇长; 区长; 要塞的长官 ③[英](第二次世界大战时的)民防队员: an air-raid ~ 空袭时的民防队员 ④[英](某些大学的)院长; 校长; 训导长 ⑤[英]高级官员的称号(尤指总督, 大臣, 港务局长、市场主管等) ⑥[英]同业公会会长; 医院院长; 理事 ⑦[美]监狱长, 看守长 ⑧[宗](圣公会的)教区委员。‖~ship n. 看守人(或保管员等)的职务(或职权)

warden[2], **Warden** ['wɔːdn] n. (供煮食的)一种冬梨

wardrobe ['wɔːdroub] n. ①衣柜, 衣橱; 藏衣室; (剧场的)戏装保藏室 ②(个人的)全部服装; (为某个季节或某种活动用的)全套服装; (剧团的)全部戏装, 行头: a spring ~ 春装 ③(可挂衣服的)大衣箱 (= ~ trunk) ④(皇族或显贵宅邸中的)保管库(保藏衣服、珠宝等) ‖~ dealer 旧衣商 / ~ mistress 戏装的女保管员

ware[1] [wɛə] n. ①[常用复]商品, 货物: This shop sells a great variety of ~s. 这家店铺出售许多不同的商品。 / heavy ~s 重型物件(如机械、车辆等) / a popular ~ 热门货 ②[总称][可用以构成复合词]物品; 器皿: household ~ 家用物品 / lacquer ~ 漆器 / glass ~ 玻璃器皿 / enamel ~ 搪瓷器皿 / china ~ 瓷器 ③陶器: a ~ with mottle glaze 有斑点釉面的陶器 ‖'~house n. 货栈, 仓库 vt. 把…(暂时)放在货栈中, 使落栈 / '~room n. 商品陈列室; 商品储藏室

ware[2] [wɛə] I vt. [用于祈使句] ①当心: Ware wire! 当心铁丝网! / Ware hounds! 当心猎狗! ②[口]避免 II a. ①知道的, 意识到的 (of) ②[古]留神的, 警惕的

warm [wɔːm] I a. ①暖和的, 温暖的, 暖热的; 保暖的: The weather is getting ~. 天气暖和起来了。 / ~ tea 不太热的茶 / ~ clothes 保暖的

衣服 / ～ exercise 使身体暖和的活动;【体】准备动作 / a ～ water port 不冻港 / Red, yellow and orange are called ～ colours. 红、黄、橙称为暖色。 ② 热烈的, 热情的; 富于同情心的: ～ applause (welcome) 热烈的掌声(欢迎) / encouragement 热情的鼓励 / a ～ friend 热心的朋友 / He has a ～ heart. 他很热心。③兴奋的, 激动的; 激烈的: be ～ with wine 喝酒后兴奋起来 / The dispute grew ～. 争论激烈起来。④多情的; 色情的: a man with a ～ temperament 好色之徒 / ～ descriptions 色情的描写 ⑤(处境等)为难的, 危险的 ⑥(嗅迹等)新鲜的, 强烈的;(游戏中)快要发现的, 即将猜中的: You're getting ～. 你就要找到(或猜中)了。⑦(官员等)已做惯的, 地位稳定的: be ～ in office 职位稳固 ⑧[口]富裕的: a ～ existence 优裕的生活 **II ❶ vt.** ①使暖和, 使温暖, 使暖热: ～ oneself at (或 by) the fire 烤火取暖 / The sight of the happy children ～ed his heart. 看到幸福的孩子们他心中感到热呼呼的。②使兴奋, 使激动; 使有生气; 使热烈 ③使做准备动作 (up) ④把(食物)重新煮热 (up, over): Please ～ (up) the dish over the stove. 请把菜放在炉子上热一下。⑤ [方]打, 鞭打 **❷ vi.** ①变暖和, 变温暖, 变暖热 (up): The room is ～ing up. 房子里暖和起来了。/ The milk is ～ing up on the stove. 牛奶正在炉上温热。②兴奋, 激动; 变得激烈 (up): He ～ed up as he expounded his views. 他在阐明自己的意见时兴奋起来了。③同情, 爱好 (to, towards): My heart ～s to him. 我对他生了好感。/ He is beginning to ～ to his work. 他对工作开始爱好起来。④(比赛前)做准备动作 (up) **III n.** ①[口]暖, 变暖: Come to the fire and have a ～. 到炉边来暖和一下。②保暖的东西; [英]军用短大衣(也作 British ～) ‖**as ～ as a toast** 暖烘烘的 / **a ～ corner** 困境; **corner / make things** (或 **it**) **～ for sb.** 使某人为难; 惩罚某人 / **～ sb.** (或 **～ sb.'s jacket**) 打某人, 辱骂某人 / **～ work** 见 **work** ‖**~er n.** 取暖器, 保暖器: a foot **~er** 脚炉 / **~ly ad.** ‖**~ blood** 热血动物/'**~-,blooded** a. ①(动物)热血的,②热情的 ③(性情)易变的, 易趋极端的 / '**~ed-'over** a. ①(菜等)重新热过的 ②(主意等)重新提出来的; 陈腐的 / **～ front** 【气】暖锋 / '**~'hearted** a. 热烈的, 热情的; 富于同情心的 / **~-up** n. ①【体】准备动作: a **~-up** suit 做准备动作时穿的运动衣 ②(马达、收音机等的)预热

warmth [wɔːmθ] **n.** ①暖和, 温暖, 暖热 ②热情, 多情 ③激动; 生气: He spoke with some ～. 他说话时有点激动。

warn [wɔːn] **❶ vt.** ①警告; 告诫: He was ～ed of the danger. 他被警告有危险。/ The doctor ～ed the patient against smoking (或 not to smoke). 医生告诫病人不要抽烟。/ ～ sb. against false friends 要某人提防假朋友 ②预先

通知: The weather station ～ed that a storm was coming. 气象台预报即将有暴风雨来临。**❷ vi.** 发出警告; 发出预告 ‖**~er n.** 警告者; 告诫者; 预告者

warning [ˈwɔːniŋ] **I n.** ①警告; 告诫; 前车之鉴, 鉴诫, 前兆: sound a serious ～ 发出严重警告 / take ～ from an accident 把一次事故引为鉴诫 / typhoon (air-raid) ～s 台风(空袭)警报 / Palpitation is a ～ of heart trouble. 心悸是心脏病的预兆。②(解雇、辞职等的)预先通知: The boss gave John a week's ～ without reason. 老板毫无理由地通知约翰一星期后离职。**II a.** 警告的; 告诫的; 引为鉴诫的: give sb. a ～ look 向某人使一个警告的眼色 / ～ colouration 警戒色 / a national ～ system 全国警报系统 ‖**~ly ad.**

warp [wɔːp] **I ❶ vt.** ①使翘起; 弄歪; 弄歪: The hot sun ～ed the boards. 强烈的阳光把木板晒得翘曲了。②使(性格等)不正常, 使乖戾, 使有偏见: ～ed judgement (私心、偏见等造成的)不公正的判断 ③歪曲(历史、记载等): a ～ed account 歪曲真相的叙述 ④把(线、纱)排列成经: ～ing machine 【纺】整经机 ⑤【海】用绞船索曳(船) ⑥ 引潮水入(低洼地)(指利用沉积物来肥田) **❷ vi.** ①变成翘曲; 变弯; 变歪: Seasoned timber does not ～. 晒干的木材不会翘曲。②(海)(船)被绞船索曳动; 用绞船索曳动 **II n.** ①弯曲; 歪斜: There is a ～ in the board. 这块板有些弯曲。②(思想、判断、行动等的)偏差, 偏见; (性情等的)乖戾, 不正常 ③【海】绞船索 ④【纺】经: ～ and woof 经和纬 ⑤(浊水的)沉积物, 冲积土 ⑥ 基础: the ～ of the economic structure 经济结构的基础 ‖**~er n.** 【纺】整经机; 整经工

warrant [ˈwɔrənt] **I n.** ①(正当)理由, 根据; 证明, 保证: He said so without ～ (或 He had no ～ for saying so). 他这样说是没有理由的。②授权; 批准; 授权证; 许可证; 逮捕状; 搜查令: a ～ of attorney 给诉讼代理人(或律师)的委托书 / a ～ of attachment 扣压状 / A ～ was out against him. 对他发出了逮捕状。③【军】准升委任状 ④付款凭单, 收款凭单 ⑤(公司发出的)认股证书 ⑥[英]栈单 ‖**a chief ～ officer** (美) 陆军(或空军)一级准尉 / **a commissioned ～ officer** (美)海军(或海军陆战队)一级准尉 / **a ～ officer** (美)海军(或海军陆战队)二级准尉 / **a Warrant Officer (Class I)** (英)一级准尉 / **a Warrant Officer (Class II)** (英)二级准尉 / **a Warrant Officer, Junior Grade** (美)陆军(或空军)二级准尉 **II vt.** ①使有(正当)理由, 成为…的根据: That does not ～ your doing so (或 ～ you in doing so). 那并不等于你有理由这样做。/ This state of affairs ～s our attention. 这种事态值得我们注意。②授权给; 批准 ③向(某人)保证, 保证(货物)的质量; 担保: I ～ you he is telling the truth. 我向你保证他说的是真话。/ The material is ～ed (to be) pure steel. 这种材料保证是纯钢。/ I ～ he won't be late. 我有

把握他一定不会迟到。‖**~able** *a.* 可保证的; 可认为正当的; 可批准的 / **~ee** [,wɔrən'tiː] *n.* 被保证人 / **~or** ['ɔrəntɔː, 'wɔrəntə], **~er** *n.* 保证人

warren ['wɔrin] *n.* ①小猎物(如野兔、野鸡)繁殖的围地; 在小猎物繁殖围地狩猎的特权 ②养兔场; 养兔场的兔子 ③[喻]拥挤的地区(或房屋) ‖*like* (或 *as thick as*) *rabbits in a ~* 挤得水泄不通

warrior ['wɔriə] *n.* ①[书面语]武士, 勇士; (老)战士; (原始部落等的)斗士: the Unknown *Warrior* (遗体被选来代表所有阵亡士兵接受国葬的)无名战士 ②鼓吹战争的人: a cold (psychological) ~ 冷战(心理战)专家 ③战斗; 尚武: a ~ ant 兵蚁

wart [wɔːt] *n.* ①[医]疣, 肉赘 ②[植]树瘤 ‖**~y** *a.* ①有疣的; 疣似的 ②有树瘤的; 多树瘤的; 树瘤似的 ‖**'~hog** *n.* (非洲产)一种野猪(脸部有肉赘), 疣猪

wary ['wɛəri] *a.* ①谨慎的, 小心翼翼的; 警惕的: ~ tactics 审慎的策略 / keep a ~ eye on sb. 密切注意某人 / ~ movements 小心翼翼的动作 ②谨防的; 唯恐的 (*of*): be ~ of flatterers 提防拍马的人 / be ~ of giving offence 唯恐得罪人

wash [wɔʃ] **I** ❶ *vt.* ①洗, 洗涤; 【矿】洗(矿); 洗刷(罪过等): ~ clothes (dishes) 洗衣服(碟子) / ~ oneself 洗澡 / That soap will ~ silks. 那种肥皂能洗丝织物。/ ~ *off* (或 *out*) stains 洗去污点 ②冲, 冲(成): an empty boat ~ed away by the tide 被潮水冲走的空船 / The rain has ~ed channels in the sand. 雨水在砂土上冲出一条条的沟。③(海水等)拍打; 流过; 弄湿: The waves ~ed the seashore. 波浪拍打海岸。④弄湿, 浸透; 漫过: sunflowers ~ed with dew 被露水湿润的葵花 ⑤粉刷, 涂水彩于; 镀金(或银等)于: ~ the walls with white 把墙刷白 / a silver-~ed tablespoon 镀银的汤匙 ❷ *vi.* ①洗涤; 洗衣; 洗脸, 洗手; 洗澡: ~ before each meal 饭前洗手 / The stain ~ed out. 污点洗掉了。②耐洗; [英口](论点等)经得住考验: The cloth ~es well. / That argument won't ~. 那论点站不住脚。③被冲(蚀) (*out, away*); (浪涛等)拍打, 溅泼 (*over, against, along*): The bridge had ~ed out. 那座桥已被冲掉了。/ Breakers ~ed over the deck. 浪花溅泼在甲板上。④漂浮, 漂流; 流过, 掠过: cakes of ice ~ing *along* the river 漂流在河上的冰块 / A breeze ~ed *against* his face. 微风拂过他的脸孔。**II** *n.* ①洗, 洗涤; 冲洗; 刷, 泼溅: go and have a ~ 去洗一洗 / give the car a ~ (或 ~-down) 把汽车冲洗一下 / The material stands ~. 这衣料耐洗。/ dry ~ 干洗 / ore ~ 【矿】洗矿 ②洗的衣物; 洗衣店: I have a large ~ this Sunday. 这星期天我有一大堆东西要洗。/ hang out the ~ 晾洗好的衣服 / Send the shirts to the ~. 把这些衬衫送去洗衣店去。

③洗涤剂; 洗药; 生发油, 香水; (水彩或金属)涂层: a hair ~ 洗发水 ④[the ~] 拍打(声); (螺旋桨等在空气中引起的)激荡: the ~ of waves 波涛的拍打声 ⑤稀淡饮料(或食物); 已发酵待蒸馏的酒; [口](饮烈酒后喝的)淡饮料; [喻]内容贫乏的作品(或讲话): This tea (soup) is a mere ~. 这茶(汤)淡得象水一样。⑥(水流的)冲积物; 沖脚; [喻]废话 ⑦洼地, 沼泽; 浅水池(或湾) ⑧(水流)冲出的沟槽; (美国西部的)干河床 (=dry ~) ⑨(水彩颜料等的)薄涂层 ⑩【矿】含矿土 ⑪【地】冲蚀 ‖*come out in the ~* [俚]暴露; 真相大白 / ~ *and wear* 洗后不烫就平的 / ~ *down* ①冲洗: ~ down a car 冲洗汽车 ②(用开水等)吞, 咽下: ~ down a pill with water 用开水吞服药丸 / ~ *out* [口] ①破产, 失败 ②(飞机因故障)降落 ③淘汰 / ~ *up* (餐后)洗餐具 ‖**~able** *a.* 可洗的; 耐洗的 ‖**'~,basin** *n.* 脸盆 / **'~board** *n.* 洗衣板; 【建】壁脚板; 【船】防波板 / **'~bottle** *n.* (气体)洗涤瓶 / **'~bowl** *n.* 脸盆 / **'~cloth** *n.* 浴巾; 洗碗布 / **'~day** *n.* (家庭中固定的)洗衣日 / ~ *drawing* 淡水彩画 / **'~house** *n.* 洗衣房 / **'~in** *n.* (飞机的)加梢角 / **'~,leather** *n.* (擦拭玻璃窗等用的)软皮 / **~man** [wɔʃmən] *n.* 男洗衣工 / **'~out** *n.* ①(道路或铁路的)冲坏部分 ②[口]大败, 惨败; 破产, 完蛋 ③[口]失败者, (在训练或学习中)被淘汰者 ④[口]无用的家伙 ⑤(飞机的)减梢角 / **'~rag** *n.* [美] =~cloth / **'~room** *n.* [美]盥洗室; 厕所 / ~ *sale* [美](股票市场为维持买卖兴旺的假象而进行的)虚抛, 虚卖 / **'~stand** *n.* ①脸盆架 ②盥洗盆 / **'~tub** *n.* 洗衣盆 / **'~,woman** *n.* 洗衣女工

washed-out ['wɔʃt'aut] *a.* ①褪色的; (照片等)模糊的 ②[口]筋疲力尽的; 面容苍白的; 没精打采的 ③被(水等)冲蚀的

washer ['wɔʃə] *n.* ①洗涤器, 洗衣机 ②洗衣人 ③【机】垫圈 ④[美俚]酒馆 ‖**~-,drier** *n.* 附有脱水机的洗衣机 / **~man** [wɔʃəmən] *n.* 男洗衣工 / **'~,woman** *n.* 洗衣女工

washer

washing ['wɔʃiŋ] *n.* ①洗, 洗涤; 洗的衣物; 洗下的污垢; [复]洗涤剂 ②浸; 冲(蚀); 冲走的东西 ③涂刷; 涂上的薄层 ④洗出的矿物; (洗出矿物的)产矿地 ‖**'~-day** *n.* =washday / ~ *machine* 洗衣机 / ~ *soda* 洗衣石碱 / ~ *stand* =washstand / **'~up** *n.* (餐后碗碟等的)洗涤

washy ['wɔʃi] *a.* ①(食物等)稀薄的 ②(颜色等)褪了的, 淡的; 苍白的 ③(文章等)贫乏的, 乏味的, 空洞的; (感情等)脆弱的, 无力的 ④[罕](气候等)湿润的, 有雨意的

wasp [wɔsp] *n.* ①黄蜂, 蚂蜂: a waist like a ~'s 蜂腰, 细腰 ②易动怒的人, 暴躁的人; 刻毒的人 ‖~-,**waisted** *a.* 细腰的; 束腰的; 紧胸的

waste [weist] **I** *n.* ① 浪费, 滥用: combat extravagance and ~ 反对铺张浪费 / wilful ~ 任意挥霍 / His idle talk is just ~ of time. 他的空谈简直是浪费时间。②损耗, 消耗; 【律】(对房产等的) 损坏: ~ and repair 损耗和修复 / the ~ of vigour 精力的消耗 ③一片荒凉(或空旷); [常用复]荒地, 未开垦地; 沙漠; 海洋: a ~ of tumbled walls 一大片断垣残壁 / a ~ of waters 一片汪洋 / the ~s of the Sahara 撒哈拉沙漠 / the seething Pacific ~s 怒涛汹涌的太平洋 ④废(弃)物; 废料; 废棉纱头: convert ~s into useful materials 废物利用 ⑤ 垃圾; 污水; [复]粪便 ⑥【地】(水流冲走的)地面风化物: Rock ~ continues to stream away. 地面的岩屑不断流走。**II** ❶ *vt.* ①浪费; 未充分利用; 【律】(因使用不当而)损坏(房屋): Don't ~ money on trash. 不要浪费钱去买无用的东西。/ ~d efforts 徒劳 / a good opportunity 失去良机 ②消耗; 使消瘦: His body was ~d by long illness. 他的身体因久病而消瘦了。③使(土地等)荒芜; 使荒废 ④[美俚]杀害, 消灭; 打伤 ❷ *vi.* ①浪费: Turn the tap off—the water is *wasting*. 把水龙头关上——水在白白流掉了。② 消耗: The oil resources in some countries are rapidly *wasting*. 有些国家的石油资源正在迅速消耗。/ Day ~s. 日暮。③消瘦 (*away*): He is *wasting away* from disease. 他病得消瘦了。**III** *a.* ①(土地等)荒芜的; 荒废的; 未开垦的; 不毛的; (城市等)成为废墟的 ②废弃的, 无用的; 多余的, 剩余的; (体内)排泄的: a ~ product 废品 / ~ water 废水 / ~ work 【机】耗功 / ~ heat 【机】余热, 废热 ③排除废物的, 盛放废物的 ④[喻]贫乏的; 单调的: the ~ periods of history 历史上的平凡时期 ‖*lay* ~ 损毁, 蹂躏 / *lie* ~ (土地等)荒芜 / *go* (或 *run*) *to* ~ ①浪费掉: Don't let the gas *go to* ~. 别让煤气浪费掉。②[喻](慈爱等感情)白费, 付诸东流 / *Waste not, want not.* [谚]不浪费, 不愁缺。/ ~ *one's words* (或 *breath*) 白费口舌 ‖**wastage** ['weistidʒ] *n.* ①浪费(量); 损耗(量); 漏失(量) ②废物, 废料 ③【地】(冰、雪等的)消融 / ~**less** *a.* 用不尽的, 无穷的; a ~*less* source of energy 无穷的力量的源泉; 无穷的能源 / ~**r** *n.* ①造成浪费(或耗费、损坏)的人(或物): a procedure that is a ~*r* of time 浪费时间的程序 ②挥霍者, 浪子; [口]饭桶, 无用的人 ③废品, 次品 ‖~,**basket** [美] *n.* 废纸篓 *vt.* 把…放入废纸篓 / '~**bin** *n.* 废物箱, 垃圾桶 / '~-**butt** *n.* ①客栈(或酒馆)的老板 ②[谑]小饭店 / ~**land** *n.* ①荒地, 荒原; 未垦地; 废墟: reclaim ~*land* 开荒 / a ~*land* of burned houses (被烧毁的房屋留下的)瓦砾废墟 ②(生活等的)贫乏, 单调 / '~,**paper** *n.* 废纸; 废纸般的东西(如欺骗性的证券等) / ~ **paper**

① (书籍卷首卷尾的)衬页 ② =~paper / '~-'**paper basket** [英] =~basket / ~ **pipe** 污水管, 废水管

wasteful ['weistful] *a.* 浪费的; 挥霍的; 耗费的: ~ expenditure 浪费的开支 / ~ habits 挥霍的习惯 / a boiler ~ of fuel 费燃料的锅炉 ‖~**ly** *ad.* / ~**ness** *n.*

wastrel ['weistrəl] *n.* ①浪费者, 挥霍者 ②无用的人, 饭桶 ③废品 ④流浪的儿童; 流浪汉, 浪荡子

watch [wɔtʃ] **I** ❶ *vt.* ①观看, 注视: ~ television 看电视 / ~ a football game 观看足球赛 / *Watch* how I do it. 看着我怎么做。/ ~ sb. do sth. 注视某人做某事 ②看守, 守卫; 守护, 照看; 监视; 注意: ~ a flock of sheep 看守羊群 / a house ~ed by guards 由警卫员守卫着的房屋 / ~ a patient 护理病人 / ~ sb.'s diet 照料某人的饮食 / ~ the situation 注意形势 / If you don't ~ it, ... 要是你不注意的话, … ③守候, 等待: ~ one's opportunity 等候机会, 伺机 ❷ *vi.* ① 观看, 注视: Are you going to play or only ~? 你将参加比赛是只去看看? / He ~ed to see what would happen. 他注视着看会发生什么事。② 看守, 守卫; 监视; 注意: There's a policeman ~ing outside the house. 有一名警察在屋外监视着。/ ~ *for* symptoms of a disease 注意症状 ③守候 (*for*): ~ *for* a hare to come out of the burrow 守着野兔出洞来 / ~ *for* a chance 等候机会, 伺机 ④ 整夜守护(或照管); 【宗】守夜(指行一种礼拜仪式): ~ *with* the sick 通宵看护病人 **II** *n.* ①手表; 挂表; 【海】船上天文钟: What time is it by your ~? 你的表上几点钟? / set one's ~ 把表拨准 / a stop~ (赛跑等用的)秒表 ②看守, 守卫; 守护, 照管; 监视; 注意: keep (a) ~ 守望; 值班; 放哨 / keep ~ by sb.'s bed 在床边护理某人 / be under close ~ 被严密监视着 / be on the ~ (for ...) (对…)留神着; (对…)戒备着 / keep ~ and ward 不断监视; 日夜警卫 ③值班人(员), 值夜人(员); 看守人(员); 哨兵, 警卫(队); [the ~][古](夜间的)巡逻队, 更夫 ④(值班的)一班, 一岗; 【海】(值员的)值班时间(每班二或四小时); 值班的海员(通常为全船人员的一半): on (off) ~ 在(不在)值班 / the first ~ 【海】头班(下午八时至午夜) / the middle ~ 【海】中班(午夜至凌晨四时) / ~ and ~ 【海】(海员分两班的)轮值 / port (starboard) ~ 【海】床位在左(右)舷的海员的值班 / the dog-~es 【海】每班两小时的轮值(下午四时至六时, 或六时至八时) ⑤(旧时夜晚的时刻)更: the first (或 evening) ~ 一更 / the fourth (或 morning) ~ 四更 ⑥[常用复][罕]夜间醒时: in the still ~es of the night 夜深人静不眠时 ‖*A* ~*ed pot never boils.* 见 *pot* / *pass as a* ~ *in the night* 很快被忘掉 / ~ *one's step* 见 *step* / ~ *one's time* 等待时机, 窥伺时机 / ~ *out* (*for*) 密切注意; 戒备, 提防: *Watch out for* these pictures. (广告用语)注意这些影片的

上映 (时间)。/ ～ out for careerists and conspirators 警惕野心家和阴谋家 / ～ over 看守,守卫; 监视 ‖～able a. 值得注意 (或注视) 的 / ～er n. ①看守人;守夜者,值夜者;【军】哨兵,岗哨 ②(夜间对病人的)护理者;守灵者 ③观察者,视察者;(代表政党或候选人的)投票监察员 ‖'～band n. 手表带 / '～case n. 表壳;表盒; ～ chain 表链 / Watch Committee [英](管理公安、灯火等事宜的)市镇委员会 / '～dog n. ① 看门狗 ② 监察人 vt. 为…看门(或守卫); 监督 / ～ fire 营火 / '～guard 挂表链,挂表带 / '～house n. ①哨房 ②拘留所 / ～ key 开旧式挂表发条的钥匙 / '～maker n. 钟表制造(或修理)人 / ～man ['wɔtʃmən] n. ①看守人;警卫员 ②(旧时的)更夫 / ～ meeting【宗】除夕礼拜 / ～ night ①除夕 ②=～ meeting / ～ pocket (背心、裤腰上的)表袋 / ～ spring 表的发条 / '～tower n. 岗楼,了望塔 / '～word n. ①暗语,暗号;【军】口令 ②口号,标语;格言

watchful ['wɔtʃful] a. ①警惕的,戒备的;注意的: be ～ against temptation 提防诱惑 / be ～ of one's step 提防走路摔跤; [喻]行事谨慎 ②[古]醒的,不眠的 ‖～ly ad. / ～ness n.

water ['wɔːtə] I n. ①水;[常用复]矿泉水: salt (fresh and sweet) ～ 咸(淡)水 / hard (soft, heavy) ～【化】硬(软,重)水 / ammonia (soda, rose) ～ 氨(苏打,玫瑰香)水 / conservancy works 水利工程 / shed blood like ～ 血流如注 / holy 【宗】圣水 / table ～s 进餐时饮的(瓶装)矿泉水 / drink (或 take) the ～s for rheumatism 饮用矿泉水治风湿病 ②水深;水位;水面;水路: The boat draws six feet of ～. 这船吃水六呎(深)。/ High (Low) ～ will be at six o'clock. 六点钟将有高(低)潮。/ be under ～ 淹在水中 ③[常用复]大片的水;水体(指江、湖、池、海等);海域,近海: the ～s of the lake 湖中的水 / cross the ～s [诗]渡过海洋,跨海 / be in from blue 从海上来 / a ship for service in home ～s 在领海内航行的船 ④(生物体内的)流体,分泌液(尤指尿、泪、口水、胃液、胰液、羊水等): pass ～ 小便 / red (或 bloody) ～ 血尿 ⑤水彩颜料;水彩画(=～colo(u)r) ⑥(宝石的)透明度,光泽度;优质度;(品质或类型的)程度: a diamond of the first ～ 最好的(或第一水的)钻石 / an artist of the purest ～ 第一流的艺术家 / a fool of the purest ～ 大傻瓜 ⑦(织物或金属面的)光泽,波纹 ⑧【商】超过实际资产的估值(或股额),清水股 II ❶ vt. ①使湿;在…上洒(或浇)水,灌溉: ～ the streets 在街上洒水 ②供给…饮水;使(牛马等)饮水;给(锅炉等)加水 ③在…中搀水,冲淡: ～ the wine (milk) 在酒(牛奶)中搀水 ④把(布等)轧波纹 ⑤【商】不增资而增(股额等)(down)

❷ vi. ①流泪;淌口水: The smoke made my eyes ～. 烟熏得我流泪。②(船等)加水;(动物等)饮水 III a. ①水的;用水的 ②水中的,水上的: ～ sports 水上运动 ③水生的;生长水边的: ～ plants 水生植物 ④含水的,含液体的 ‖above ～ 脱离困境(或麻烦);摆脱债务 / a cup of cold ～ 见 cup / back ～ ①倒划桨(使船向后) ②[美]从原有立场倒退回去,退缩 / be in (get into) hot ～ (由于言行失检等)处于(陷入)困境 / between wind and ～ 见 wind[1] / bring the ～ to sb.'s mouth 使某人垂涎 / cast (或 throw) one's bread upon the ～(s) 不期望报答地做好事;行善 / Don't cast out the foul ～ till you bring in the clean. (或 Don't throw out your dirty ～ before you get in fresh.) [谚]清水未来,莫泼脏水。/ draw ～ to one's mill 有利皆因 / draw ～ with a sieve (或 pour ～ into a sieve) [谚]竹篮子打水一场空 / fish in troubled ～s 混水摸鱼 / go through fire and ～ 赴汤蹈火 / hold ～ ①(容器等)盛得住水 ②(论点等)站得住脚;说得通: What you said doesn't hold ～. 你的话站不住脚。③(划船时)稳住桨使船停 / in deep ～(s) 陷入困境的 / in low ～ 缺钱,拮据 / in rough (或 troubled) ～ 很困难 / in smooth ～ (渡过难关后)处于顺境中 / keep oneself (或 one's head) above ～ ①免遭灭顶 ②不背债 / like a fish out of ～ 如鱼离水,感到生疏,不适应 / like ～ off a duck's back 不发生作用的,毫无影响的 (船在浅水航行中) / make foul ～ (船只)漏水: The ship is making ～ in No. 1 Hold. 这船的第一舱在漏水。/ Much ～ runs by the mill that the miller knows not of. [谚]我们眼前所发生的事情,有许多是我们所不知道的。/ on the ～ ①在水上 ②在船上: Let's go on the ～ this afternoon. 今天下午我们划船去吧。/ pour oil on the (troubled) ～s 见 oil / spend money like ～ 挥金如土 / Still ～s run deep. (或 Smooth ～ runs deep.) [谚]①静水流深。(或: 外表淡漠然而内心深情。)②沉默者深谋。(或: 大智若愚。) / strong ～ [古]烈酒,烧酒 / take (the) ～ ①(游泳者、水禽、船只等)下水;上船 ②[美俚]退却,打退堂鼓 / throw (或 pour) cold ～ on 对…泼冷水 / Too much ～ drowned the miller. [谚]太多反有害。/ tread ～ (游泳时)踩水 / ～ bewitched [口]淡茶;淡饮料 / ～ of life ①(基督教《圣经》用语)生命之水;使人长生之水;精神上的启示;超度 ②白兰地(或威士忌等)酒 / ～ on the brain 脑积水,水脑 / ～ on the knee 膝关节水肿 / ～s of forgetfulness ①[希神]遗忘之河,忘川;忘却 ②死亡 / ～ (sth.) down (在某物中)搀水,冲淡(某物);(把某物)打折扣: The story has been ～ed *down.* 故事的生动性已被冲淡了。 / according to statistical figures ~*ed down* 根据已打了折扣的统计数字 / *We never know the worth of ~ till the well is dry.* 〔谚〕井干方知水可贵。 / *whoopee ~* 〔美俚〕酒(尤指香槟) / *wring* (或 *get*) *~ from a flint* 击燧取水(指做不可能的事) / *written in ~* (名声、成就等)转瞬即逝的, 昙花一现的

‖~-age ['wɔːtəridʒ] *n.* 〔英〕(货物的)水运(费) / ~ed *a.* ①洒了水的; 用水的; 搀了水的 ②有水的; 有河流的; 用水灌溉了的 ③(织物等)有波纹的; (金属等)有光泽的: ~ed silk 波纹绸 ④【商】(股票等)不增资而发行的, 滥发的 / ~ish ['wɔːtəriʃ] *a.* =watery / ~less *a.* ①无水的, 干的 ②(冷却、烹调等)不用水的

‖~ back 火炉上的把水加热的装置 / ~ bag ①(盛饮用水的)水袋 ②(骆驼等)有储水囊的蜂窠胃 / ~ bailiff 【英史】海关官员; (泰晤士河等处的)渔业管理员; (防止偷捕鱼的)水上警察 / ~ ballet (一群游泳者同时进行的)一系列向前的花式动作 / ~ bed (附有电热装置的乙烯基的)充水床垫 / ~ bird 水鸟, 水禽 / ~ biscuit 一种薄薄的硬饼干 / ~ blister 水疱 / ~ boatman 【动】(两腿似桨的)水虫 / '~borne *a.* ①由水浮起的; 水上的 ②水运的: ~*borne* traffic 水上交通 ③(疾病)饮水传染的 / ~ bottle (玻璃)水瓶, 水袋; (军用)水壶 (=canteen) / '~bound *a.* ①受洪水所困的 ②【建】水结的 / ~ boy ①供应饮水的人 ②〔美俚〕俯首听命的人 / brash 【医】泛酸; 胃灼热 / '~buck *n.* 非洲产的大羚羊 / ~ buffalo 水牛; 〔军俚〕登陆牵引车 / ~ butt 盛(雨)水的大桶 / ~ cannon 水炮(装甲车等的喷水炮形装置) / ~ carriage 水运(工具) / ~ cart *n.* 运水车; 卖水车; 洒水车 / chestnut 欧菱; 荸荠 / ~ chute (驾舟自高而下作游水游戏用的)滑漕 / ~ circulation 【机】冷水环流 / ~ clock 水钟, 滴漏 / ~ closet 盥洗室, 厕所; 抽水马桶 / ~ cock 【动】凫翁 / '~‚colo(u)r *n.* 水彩颜料; 水彩画: an exhibition of ~*colo(u)rs* 水彩画展 / '~‚colo(u)rist *n.* 水彩画作者, 水彩画家 / '~con‚trol *n.* 治水 / '~-cool *vt.* 用水冷却 / '~-cooled *a.* 水冷式的: a ~*cooled* engine 水冷式发动机 / '~course *n.* 水道; 河道, 渠道 / ~craft *n.* ①驾舟技术; 水性 ②〔集合名词〕水运工具; 船, 轮, 筏; 船舶: The harbour was crowded with ~*craft.* 港里停满了船舶。 / '~cress *n.* 【植】水田芥 / cure ①(饮)水疗法 ②灌水的刑罚 / ~ cycle 靠脚踏推进的船 / ~ dog ①喜水的狗; 会泅水的猎狗 ②水性好的人, 老练的水手(或海员) ③【动】水獭 ④【动】蝾螈; 泥狗 (=mud puppy) ⑤(下雨前的)小云层 / '~‚drinker *n.* ①喜爱(或习惯)饮水(尤其是矿泉水)的人 ②不喝酒的人 / ~ed-'down *a.* (液体等)冲淡了的; (数字等)打了折扣的 / ~ equivalent 【化】水当量 / '~fall *n.* ①瀑布 ②〔美俚〕披垂的长卷发 /

'~-fast *a.* 不溶于水的: a ~-*fast* dye 水洗不褪色的染料 / ~ feed(er) 供水器 / '~fowl *n.* 水鸟; [复]水禽 / '~front *n.* ①〔常作定语〕水边, 滩; (城市中的)滨水区 ②(炉灶上)热水箱的管组 / ~ gap 水峡, 溪涧流过的峡谷 / ~ gas 水煤气 / ~ gate 水闸, 闸口 / ga(u)ge 水标, 水(位)尺 / ~ glass ①盛水的玻璃容器; 玻璃(酒)杯 ②玻璃水标尺; (观察水底用的)玻璃筒镜 ③(古代计时用的)滴漏 ④【化】水玻璃, 硅酸钠 / ~ hammer 【物】水击作用 / ~ hardening 【冶】水淬硬化 / '~head *n.* ①(江河的)水源 ②(用拦水坝)拦住的水; 拦住的水的水位(或水量) ③【医】脑积水, 水脑 / ~ hen 【动】鹟 / ~ hole ①水坑(尤指干涸河床上的) ②冰层下的洞穴 ③〔美俚〕巢穴 ④〔美俚〕小镇 / ~ ice 糖水冰糕; 冰果子露 ②(非雪压成的)水冻冰块 / '~-inch ['wɔːtər'intʃ] *n.* (旧时的)一种放水量单位(一吋径的圆孔管在二十四小时中所放水量) / ~ jacket 【机】水套 / ~ joint 水密接头, 防水接头 / '~=laid *a.* (绳子)(左拈的)三股绞成的 / ~ level ①水平面, 水位 ②(船的)吃水线 ③水准器 / ~ lily 【植】睡莲 / ~ line *n.* ①(船的)吃水线: the loading (light) ~*line* 重船(空船)吃水线 ②(纸张上的)水印横格线 / '~locked *a.* 环水的 / '~locks [复] *n.* 水闸 / '~log *vt.* 使(船等)浸满水; 使浸透水(而不能浮动等) / '~logged *a.* ①(船等)浸满水的, 浮动迟缓的, 不易航行的 ②(木材等)浸透水的 ③(土地等)涝的 / '~‚logging *n.* 淹, 涝; 水浸 / main 总水管 / ~man ['wɔːtəmən] *n.* ①船工; 船夫, 船家 ②划手: a good (bad) ~*man* 技巧好(差)的划手 ③运水人 / ~manship ['wɔːtəmənʃip] *n.* ①水上职业; 驾船技术; 水性 / '~mark *n.* ①水位标记 ②(纸张上的)水印图案 *vt.* 在(纸张)上印水印图案; 把(图案)水印 / ~ meadow (利用水涝保持肥沃的)低平草地 / '~‚melon *n.* 西瓜 / ~ meter 水表 / ~ mill 水车, 水力磨 / ~ moccasin ①(美国南部产的)一种蝮蛇 ②一种游蛇, 水蛇 / '~‚monkey *n.* (热带用的口狭、有气孔的)陶制水壶 / ~ motor 水(力效)动机 / ~ nymph 水中女仙 / ~ ox = buffalo / pipe ①水管 ②水烟筒 / ~ pistol (玩具)喷水手枪 / ~ plane ①【海】(船舶的)水线平面 ②水上飞机 / ~ polo 【体】水球 / ~‚power *n.* ①水力, 水能 ②水力发电 ③磨坊的水力使用权 / ~ press 水压机 / '~proof *a.* 不透水的, 防水的: ~*proof* material 防水材料 ②不透水的织物, 防水布; 〔英〕雨衣 *vt.* 使不透水, 使防水; 把…上胶 / '~‚proofer *n.* ①防水布; 防水材料 ②使(某物)不透水的工人; 雨衣上胶工人 / ~ rat ①水老鼠; 水鼷; 〔美〕麝香鼠 ②〔俚〕水滨小偷; 水滨游民 / ~ rate 〔英〕(自来)水费 ②【机】(蒸汽机等的)耗水率, 耗汽率 / ~re'sistant *a.* 抗水的(但不完全防水的) / ~ right 用水权(如用来灌溉); 河(或湖)的使用权 / ~ seal 【机】水封闭 / '~shed *n.* ①流域 ②分水岭; 分界线 / ~

shield 【植】莼菜; 水盾草属植物 / '~-sick *a.* 水浇灌得过多的; 受涝的 / '~side *n. & a.* 水边(的); 河滨(的); 湖滨(的); 海滨(的) / '~,sider *n.* [澳]码头工人 / ~ **ski** (由快艇拖曳的)滑水橇 / '~-ski *vi.* 用滑水橇滑行 / '~-skin *n.* 革制的水袋 / ~ **snake** 水蛇 / '~-soak *vt.* 用水浸湿 / ~ **softener** 【化】①软水剂 ②软水器 / '~-,solu'bility *n.* 水溶性 / '**Water-,splashing Festival** 泼水节 / ~ **spot** (水果)浸水造成的烂斑(或腐烂) / '~spout *n.* ① 水落管, 排水口 ② 龙卷风卷起的水柱, 海龙卷 / ~ **sprite** 水妖, 水精; 水中仙女 / ~ **supply** ①(地区用水的)水源; 给水; 自来水 ②蓄水与供水系统(如蓄水池、水库等) / ~ **system** ①水系 =~ supply / ~ **table** ①地下水位 ②【建】承雨线脚 / '~**tight** *a.* ①不漏水的, 水密的: ~*tight* boots 不漏水的靴子 / a ~*tight* joint 水密接缝 ②(计划, 措词等)严密的, 无懈可击的, 天衣无缝的: ~*tight* block-ade 严密的封锁 / ~*tight* block-ade 严密的封锁 / ~ **tower** ①(自来)水塔 ②(救火用的)高喷水塔 / '~-,vascular **system** 【动】水管系 / ~ **wag(g)on** 运水车; 卖水车; 洒水车: on the ~ wag(g)on 戒酒 / ~ **wave** 水烫(一种理发方式或式样) / '~**way** *n.* ①水路, 航道: an inland ~way 内河(航道) ②排水道, (船上的)舷侧排水沟 / ~**wheel** *n.* ①(水力推动的)水轮, 水车 ②(汲水用的)辘轳 / ~ **wings** (学游泳时用的)浮圈, 浮袋 / ~ **witch** ①自称能用测水杖等发现地下水源的人 ②【动】(一种游禽)鹛鹛, 水鹙 / '~**works** [复] *n.* ①(城市等的)供水系统 ②[用作单或复]自来水厂 ③喷水装置 ④[俚]眼泪: turn on the ~*works* 哭起来 / '~**worn** *a.* (岩石等)水冲蚀的

watering ['wɔ:təriŋ] **I** *n.* ①洒水, 浇水; 供水; 搀水, 冲淡 ②灌溉; 排水渠 ③(牛马等的)饮水 ④(织物等的)光泽; (轧)波纹 **II** *a.* ①洒水(用)的, 浇水(用)的; 供水的: a ~ bucket 水桶 ②有水的[英]有矿泉的 / ~ **can, ~ pot** 洒水壶, 浇水筒 / ~ **cart** 洒水车 / ~ **hole** 卖酒处(如夜总会、酒吧间等); 人们聚谈的社交场所 / ~ **place** ①供应水的地方; 水坑; (牛马等的)饮水处 ②[英]矿泉, 温泉 ③海滨胜地(或疗养地、浴场等) ③卖酒处(如夜总会、酒吧间等)

watt [wɔt] *n.* 【电】瓦(特) ‖~,**meter** *n.* 瓦特计

wattle ['wɔtl] **I** *n.* ①枝, 枝条; 篱笆条; [英方]手杖 ②篱笆; ~ and daub 【建】泥笆墙 ③[复](支撑茅屋顶的)枝条构架 ④【动】(火鸡等的)垂肉 ⑤【动】(鱼的)触须 ⑥【植】金合欢树(枝可编篱笆, 皮可鞣革) **II** *a.* 用枝条编的; 用枝条做屋顶的 **III** *vt.* ①编(枝条)成篱笆(或屋顶等) ②以枝条作(篱笆、屋顶等) ‖~d *a.* ①用枝条做的: ~d walls 篱笆墙 ②有垂肉的

wave [weiv] **I** *n.* ①波, 波浪, 波涛; [the ~(s)][诗]海, 水: *Waves* urge ~s. 后浪推前浪。/ The ~s rolled on. 波涛滚滚(向前)。/ surge forward ~ *upon* ~ 一浪高一浪地向前推进 ②【物】(光、声等的)波: burst ~ 爆破波 / ultra-short

sound ~ 超声波 / long (medium, short) ~ 长(中, 短)波 ③波浪形, 起伏; 波状物; (头发的)鬈曲; (织物的)波纹: golden ~s of wheat in the field 田野里金黄色的麦浪 / a natural ~ 天然鬈曲 / a permanent ~ 烫成的鬈曲 ④(情绪等的)波动; 高涨, 高潮; (人群的)潮涌, 运动: a ~ of anger 一阵愤怒 / a ~ of enthusiasm 热情的高涨 ⑤浪潮似的移动; (一群同类动物的)蜂涌; (人口)激增; 【军】攻击波, 批: attack in ~s 作波浪式的进攻 / fly 100 sorties in 10 ~s (飞机)作十批一百架次的飞行 ⑥(用手等挥动的)示意, 致意; 信号: with a ~ of one's hand 把手一挥 ⑦(天气)的突变, 浪潮似的一阵: a cold ~ 寒潮 / a heat ~ 热浪 ⑧示波图 **II ❶** *vi.* ①波动; 飘动, 飘扬 ②起伏; 成波浪形: Seen from an airplane, the terrain curves and ~s. 从飞机上看下去, 地形蜿蜒起伏。③挥手示意(或致意); 挥动旗(或灯等)示意 **❷** *vt.* ①使波动, 使起伏; 使飘扬 ②挥舞; 晃动: ~ a sword threateningly 挥臂胁地挥舞刀(或剑) ③挥手表示(致敬、告别等); 向…挥手(或旗等)示意: ~ farewell 挥手告别 / ~ sb. to come 招手要某人来 / ~ sb. a greeting 挥手向某人致意 / ~ sb. on (away) 挥手叫某人前进(走开) ④使成波浪形; 使鬈曲; 使(织物)成波纹 ‖~ *aside* 对…置之不理, 对…不屑一顾; 把…丢在一边: ~ *aside* sb.'s sugges-tions 对某人的建议置之不理 ‖~d *a.* 波浪形的, 起伏的; (织物)有波纹的; 飘动的 / ~**less** *a.* 无波浪的; 平静的 / ~**let** ['weivlit] *n.* 【物】子波 / ~**like** *ad. & a.* 波浪般地(的), 波状地(的) ‖~ **band** [无]波段 / ~ **detector** [无]检波器 / ~ **front** 【物】波阵面, 波前 / ~ **guide** [物]波导; [无]波导管, 波导管 / '~-,hopping *n. & a.* 贴近地面(或水面)飞行(的) / '~**length** *n.* 【无】【物】波长 / ~ **mechanics** 【物】波动力学 / '~-,meter *n.* 【物】波长计 / ~ **motion** 波状运动 / ~ **train** [物]波列 / ~ **velocity** [无]波速度

waver[1] ['weivə] *n.* ①挥动者; 挥手(示意)者 ②鬈发用具; 专门烫发的理发员 ③[无]波段开关, 波形转换器

waver[2] ['weivə] **I** *vi.* ①摇摆; 摇晃; 摇曳: He ~s a little as he walks. 他走路时有些摇晃。/ The feather ~ed to the floor. 羽毛飘摇落地。/ A thin grey smoke ~ed up. 一缕灰色的烟袅袅上升。②(声音)颤抖; (光亮)闪烁: Her voice ~ed with strain. 她的声音紧张得颤抖。/ The candle flames ~ed. 烛光闪烁。③犹豫不决; 动摇: ~ *between* two choices 对两种选择犹豫不决 / ~ in one's faith 信仰动摇 **II** *n.* 摇摆, 摇晃; 抖动; 犹豫; 动摇 ‖~**er** ['weivərə] *n.* 摇晃的人; 犹豫不决的人, 动摇不定的人 / ~**ing** ['wei-vəriŋ] *a.* ①摇摆的, 摇曳的; 抖动的 ②犹豫不决的; 动摇的

wax[1] [wæks] **I** *n.* ①蜡; 蜂蜡; 蜡状物: cobbler's ~ (制鞋用的)线蜡 ②耳垢 ③[美]唱片 **II** *vt.* ①给(家具、地板等)上蜡 ②[美]把…录成唱片

‖*mo(u)ld sb. like* ~ 按照自己的意向塑造某人性格；任意地支配某人 ‖~ **candle** 蜡烛 / '~=,**chandler** *n.* 蜡烛商 / ~ **cloth** ①蜡布 ②油布 / ~ **doll** 蜡人；美貌但缺少感情的女人 / ~**(ed) paper** （包装用）蜡纸 / ~ **insect** 白蜡虫 / ~ **light** 蜡烛 / ~ **tree** 野漆树 / '~**work** *n.* ①蜡制品；蜡像 ②[~works][用作单或复]蜡像陈列馆

wax² [wæks] **I** *vi.* ①(月亮)渐圆，渐满；增加，变大 ②(渐渐)变成，转为：~ merry 高兴起来 **II** *n.* ①增加，变大 ②由新月至满月的时期 ‖~ *and wane* (月的)盈亏，圆缺；[喻]盛衰

wax³ [wæks] *n.* [俚]一阵发怒：be in a ~ 发怒 / get into a ~ 发起怒来 / put sb. in a ~ 使某人发怒

waxen ['wæksən] *a.* ①蜡制的；涂蜡的 ②蜡似的；苍白的；柔软的；光滑的：a ~ complexion 蜡黄的面色 ③[古](心肠)软的，柔顺的

way [wei] **I** *n.* ①路，道路：the ~ to the station 到车站的路 / ask the (或 one's) ~ 问路 / the ~ in (out) 进(出)路 / He squeezed his ~ out. 他挤了出去。②路线；路途；路程：He is on the (或 his) ~ home. 他在回家途中。/ They sang songs to cheer the ~. 他们唱着歌活跃旅途。/ The school is a long ~ off. 学校离这儿很远。/ His work is still a long ~ off perfection. 他的工作还远远不够完美。③方向；[只用单][口]附近：He went that ~. 他往那边去了。/ This ~, please. 请这边走。/ The crops are looking very well our ~. 我们这儿的庄稼长势很好。④方法；手段；方式：the best ~ to do (或 of doing) sth. 做某事的最好方法 / in every possible ~ 千方百计地 / speak in a careless ~ 漫不经心地说话 ⑤情形，状况；规模；程度：The ~ things are pleases us tremendously. 形势使我们十分高兴。/ do an experiment in a small ~ 进行小规模的试验 ⑥习惯；作风：break down the old ~s 破除旧习惯 / English ~s of living 英国人的生活方式 / It's not his ~ to shun responsibilities. 他一向不推诿责任。/ It is outrageous the ~ the aggressors behave. 侵略者的行径凶暴透顶。⑦行业；(经历或活动的)范围：He is in the grocery ~. 他是经营杂货业的。/ Football is not in my ~ (或 is out of my ~). 足球我不内行。/ I'll buy a few things in the stationery ~. 我要买一些文具用品。/ This never came (或 fell) my ~. 这种事我从来没经历过。⑧方面；(某)点：In some ~s you are right. 你有些地方是对的。/ They are no ~ similar. 他们无一处相似。/ What have we in the ~ of food? 我们家里有些什么可以吃的? (或：我们下一顿吃什么呢?)

⑨【律】通行权；[复]【船】船台，下水台；【机】(车床等的)导轨 **II** *ad.* [美]远远地；大大地；非常：He is ~ ahead (behind). 他远远地在前领先(落在后面)。/ He was notified of the meeting ~ in advance. 这会议老早就预先通知他了。/ be ~ beyond expectation 大大出乎意料之外 ‖*a lion in the* ~ 见 **lion** / *all the* ~ ①从远道：come *all the* ~ from Canada 从加拿大远道而来 ②从头至尾，自始至终：stay in the game *all the* ~ 自始至终参加了比赛(指未中途淘汰) / *all the* ~ *from the grass-roots to the higher leading bodies* 从基层一直到高级领导机关 / be estimated *all the* ~ from five to eight tons 估计有五到八吨重 ③一路上 / *any* ~ 不管怎样，无论如何 / *a right of* ~ 见 **right** / *beat one's* ~ [美俚]无票乘车，偷搭车 / *be in a bad* ~ 病情严重；处于困境 / *be in a (great)* ~ [英口]激动 / *both* ~s ①在两方面 ②=each ~ / *by a long* ~ 远远地，大大地 / *by the* ~ ①在途中；在路旁 ②顺便说；附带说明 / *by ~ of* ①经由 ②通过…方法 (或形式等)：learn reading *by* ~ *of* pictures 看图识字 ③当作，作为：say a few words *by* ~ *of* introduction 讲几句开场白 / *by* ~ *of* exception 作为例外 ④以求，为了：make inquiries *by* ~ *of* discovering the truth 进行调查以了解真相 ⑤处于…状态 (或地位)；做出…的样子：He is *by* ~ *of* being a musician. 他也算是个音乐家。/ He is *by* ~ *of* paying particular attention. 他做出特别注意的样子。⑥[英口]快要，行将：He is *by* ~ *of* going to Peking. 他快要去北京了。/ *carve out one's* (或 *a*) ~ 开辟道路 / *clear the* ~ *(for)* (为…) 扫清道路；(为…)让路 / *cut both* ~s (议论、行动等)对双方都起作用，两面都说得通；模棱两可，两边倒 / *devour the* ~ [诗](马等)兼程急进 / *each* ~ [英](赛马)得胜，获前三名之一 / *every which* ~ [口]①四面八方 ②非常混乱地 / *feel one's* ~ ①(黑暗中)摸索着走 ②想一步走一步，谨慎行事 / *fetch* ~ (因船只颠簸而)滑离原处 / *fight one's* ~ 打出道路；奋斗前进：*fight one's* ~ out 向外打出一条路，杀出生路 / *find a* ~ *out* 找(到)出路 / *find one's* ~ *to* (或 *into*) 设法到达；到达 / *from* ~ *back* ①从远处；从穷乡僻壤 ②从很久以前；由来已久；彻底，完全：a friend *from* ~ *back* 老朋友 / an artist *from* ~ *back* 内行的艺术家 / *gather* ~ (船等)加速 / *get under* ~ (船)开动；开始进行：A battle to conquer nature *got under* ~. 一场征服自然的战斗打响了。/ *give* ~ ①撤退 ②让路；让步；退让；让位；屈服：The barren land has *given* ~ to green vegetation. 不毛之地已盖满葱绿的作物。/ Don't *give* ~ *to* grief. 不要过度悲伤。③坍陷，倒塌；(身体)垮掉 ④(股票)跌价 ⑤划起来；用力划 / *go a little* ~ ①不大有作用 ②走一点点路 / *go all the* ~

①完全一致 ②[美俚]性交 / *go a long* (或 *good, great*) ~ ①大有帮助,大有作用;(钱)可以买许多东西;(食物等)可以维持很久: Meat *goes a long* ~ *towards* meeting the body's requirements of the necessary nutrients. 在满足人体内必需的养料方面,肉类能提供很多的东西。 / This will *go a long* ~ *in* overcoming the difficulty. 这对克服困难很有帮助。②走了一大段路;[喻](谈判时为迁就对方) 采取主动: *go a long* ~ *to meet* sb. 走了一大截路去迎接某人;采取主动态度与某人谈判;/ go (或 *take*) *one's own* ~ 独自行动;一意孤行 / *go one's* ~(s) 出发,动身 / *go out of the* (或 *one's*) ~ ①特地,不怕麻烦: They *went out of their* ~ to help us. 他们不怕麻烦地来帮助我们。② 故意 / *go the* ~ *of all flesh* (或 *of all the earth* 或 *of nature*) 死 / *have it both* ~s (参加双方争论时) 忽左忽右,见风使舵 / *Have it your own* ~! (不再继续争辩时用语)随你的便吧! / *have* (或 *get*) *one's own* ~ 自主行事;为所欲为,随心所欲 / *have* ~ *on* (船)航行着 / *in a big* ~ 强调地;彻底地;大规模地;热情地 / *in a family* ~ ①象一家人一样地,不拘礼节地 ②[美]怀孕 / *in a general* ~ 一般地 / *in a small* ~ 小规模的(地);俭朴的(地): a printer *in a small* ~ 小本经营的印刷业者 / live *in a small* ~ 生活简朴 / *in a tin-pot* ~ 蹩脚地,低劣地 / *in a* (或 *one*) ~ ①在某点上,在某种程度上: The work is well done *in a* ~. 从某方面来讲,工作做得很好。②有几分,稍微 / *in no* ~ 一点也不;决不: Teaching in school can *in no* ~ be separated from practice. 学校教学决不能脱离实践。/ *in the family* ~ [英]怀孕 / *in the* ~ ①挡道的;妨碍人的;使人不便的: Don't stand *in the* ~. 不要挡住路。(或: 不要妨碍人。)②[英]近在咫尺;在场 / (*in*) *the worst* ~ [俚]十分,非常,强烈地 / *labo(u)r one's* ~ 吃力地前进 / *lead the* ~ 带路;引路;示范 / *learn sth. the hard* ~ 通过艰难困苦而学到某事 / *look one* ~ *and row another* 声东击西 / *look the other* ~ 故意朝另一边看 / *lose one's* (或 *the*) ~ 迷路 / *lose* ~ (船等)减速 / *make one's own* ~ 成功,发迹 / *make one's* ~ ①前进,行进: *make one's* ~ *home* 回家去 ②成功,发迹 / *make the best of one's* ~ 尽快走 / *make* ~ ①前进;进展 ②让路给 (*for*) / *mend one's* ~s 改过 / *oar one's* ~ 划桨前进 / *once in a* ~ 见 *once* / *one's* ~ *around* (或 *about*) 必须熟悉的业务知识: know *one's* ~ *around* 熟谙业务 / *on the* ~ *out* [口]即将过时,行将消亡 / *out of harm's* ~ 在安全的地方: a loudspeaker set high *out of harm's* ~ 装在高处免遭损坏的扩音喇叭 / *out of the* ~ ①不挡道;不碍人;靠边: Get *out of the* ~! 滚开! / get sth. *out of the* ~ 处理掉某事物 ②不恰当: say something *out of the* ~ 说一些不当的话 ③异常;奇特: see nothing *out of the* ~ 没有看到什么异常的东西 ④偏僻 / *pave the* ~ *for* (或 *to*) 为…铺平道路 /

pay one's ~ ①支付应承担的费用,支付生活费 ②勉强维持,不负债 / *pick one's* ~ 择路而行,行路谨慎 / *put oneself out of the* ~ (为了别人)使自己受累,不辞劳累 / *put sb. in the* ~ *of* 给某人以…的机会 / *put sb. out of the* ~ 搞掉某人(指监禁或杀死某人等) / *rub sb. the right* ~ 讨好某人;抚慰某人 / *rub sb.* (或 *rough sb. up*) *the wrong* ~ 触犯某人,惹怒某人 / *see one's* ~ (*clear*) *to do* (或 *to doing*) sth. 有可能(或有意)做某事: I hope you can *see your* ~ (*clear*) *to* settle (或 *to* settling) the matter. 我希望你能设法解决这件事。/ We cannot *see our* ~ (*clear*) *to* grant your request. 我们恐怕不能满足你的要求。/ *see which* ~ *the cat jumps* 见 *cat* / *shoot one's* ~ 用战争(或战争威胁)来达到目的,用武力(或威胁)来达到目的 / *show sb. the* ~ (用言语或手势等)给某人指路;给某人带路,给某人引路;为某人作示范,为某人作指点 / *six* ~*s to* (或 *for*) *Sunday* [美俚]在许多方面;在各方面;完全;彻底 / *take one's* ~ *to* (或 *toward*) 向…走去 / *the broad* ~ ①逍遥作乐之路,堕落之路 ②宽路 / *The farthest* ~ *about is the nearest* ~ *home.* [谚]遥程路反近,捷径常误人。/ *the Great White Way* [美](纽约)百老汇娱乐区 / *the Milky Way* 银河 / *the narrow* ~ 见 *narrow* / *the other* ~ *round* 相反地;从相反方向;用相反方式: do it *the other* ~ *round* 倒过来做 / *the permanent* ~ [英]铁轨,铁道全长 / *the right* ~ ①正道,正路 ②最正确(或恰当、有效)的方法 ③真相,事实 ④[用作状语]方向正确地;恰当地,有效地 / *the six-foot* ~ [英]一对铁轨与另一对铁轨之间的距离 / *the* ~ ①用这样的方式: He does not bother about trifles *the* ~ his elder brother does. 他不象他哥哥常为琐事而奔忙。②从…样子看来: The ~ *you work,* you must be a master carpenter. 看你干活的手法,你一定是个技术熟练的木匠师傅。/ *the Way of the Cross* 【基督教】十字架之路(教堂内或附近描绘耶稣去受难地的一组图画或雕刻) / *the* ~ *of the world* 世道常情 / *the whole* ~ =all the ~ / *to my* ~ *of thinking* 我认为,在我看来 / *under* ~ ①前进着;进行中: Preparations for spring ploughing are well *under* ~. 春耕的准备工作正在扎实地进行着。②(船)在行进 / *Way enough!* 【海】停划! / ~*s and means* ①(尤指筹款的)方法,办法 ② [Ways and Means] 赋税方法;(议会中的)赋税委员会 / *wedge one's* ~ 用力挤过去: *wedge one's* ~ *into* the crowd 用力挤入人群 / *Where there is a will, there is a* ~. [谚]有志者事竟成。/ *win one's* ~ 奋力前进

‖~**less** *a.* 无路的
‖'~**bill** *n.* 运货单;乘客单 / ~ *car* ①[美]守车(货物列车末尾工作人员乘坐的车厢) ② 开到铁路小站的零担货物列车 / '~**farer** *n.* (徒步)旅行者 / '~**faring** *a.* (徒步)旅行的 / '~**going** *n.* [苏格兰]出发,动身 / ~'**lay** *vt.* 伏击;拦路

抢劫;拦住…问讯 / '~leave n. (矿主租借的)道路通行权 / '~-'out a. ①遥远的 ②[口]不同于众的, 非寻常的; 试验性的 / ~ shaft【机】摇臂轴 / '~side n. 路边 a. 路边的: ~side flowers 路边花 / ~side inns 路旁客栈 / ~ station (铁路)小站 / ~ train 普通客车,慢车 / '~worn a. 旅途劳累的

wayward ['weiwəd] a. ①任性的,刚愎的,倔强的: a child with a ~ disposition 性格倔强的孩子 ②难捉摸的, 反复无常的 ③违意的, 不如意的 ‖~ly ad. / ~ness n.

we [wi:; 弱 wi] pron. [主格] ①我们: We have stood up. 我们已经站起来了。②(报刊编者等用语)本报, 本刊; 笔者,本人; 我(们) ③(泛指)人们: We have shortcomings as well as good points. 人总是既有优点, 也有缺点。④[口](表示亲切或关心)你(们): We don't want to wake daddy, do ~? (哄孩子安静的用语)咱们总不想吵醒爸爸吧? / How are ~ feeling today? (对病人的问话)今天感觉怎么样? ⑤(帝王在正式场合用来代替 I)朕,寡人

weak [wi:k] a. ①弱的, 虚弱的; 衰弱的: a ~ constitution 虚弱的体格 / ~ features 病容 / a ~ point(或 side)弱点 / a ~ voice 微弱的声音 ②软弱的; 懦弱的; (论证等)不充分的, 无力的: a ~ character 意志薄弱的人 / a ~ argument 没有说服力的论点 / a ~ evidence 不充分的证据 / be outwardly strong but inwardly ~ 外强中干 ③缺乏战斗力的; 易破的; 不耐用的; 易弯的: a ~ fortification 易攻破的要塞 / a ~ bridge 不能受重载的桥梁 ④差的, 薄弱的; 淡薄的: be ~ in pronunciation (hearing) 发音(听觉)差 / ~ tea 淡茶 ⑤(文体)无活力的; 散漫的; 不简练的 ⑥【商】疲软的; (股票市价等)低落的: a ~ market 疲软的市场 ⑦【语】有规则变化的, 弱变化的: a ~ verb 变化规则的动词 ⑧【语】轻音的, 不重读的 ‖as ~ as water (或 as ~ as a cat) 身体虚弱; 意志薄弱 / the ~er sex 女性 / The ~est goes to the wall. [谚](在竞争等中)强胜弱败。‖~ish a. 有些弱的; 淡薄的 / ~ly a. & ad. 虚弱的(地); 软弱的(地); 有病的(地) / ~ness n. ①虚弱; 软弱; 薄弱 ②缺点, 弱点 ③嗜好, 癖好: She has a ~ness for candy. (或 Candy is her ~ness.) 她特别喜欢吃糖果。‖'~-'eyed a. 视力差的 / '~-'headed a. ①易头晕的; 易醉的 ②=~-minded / '~-kneed a. 易屈服的, 不坚定的; 缺乏决断(力)的 / '~-'minded a. ①优柔寡断的, 意志薄弱的 ②低能的, 笨拙的 / ~ sister [美俚](常指男人)不可靠的人; 胆怯的人; (一群人中的)弱者, 不起作用的人 / '~-'spirited a. 缺乏勇气和自主力的 / ~ vessel 不可靠的人 / '~-'willed a. 意志薄弱的 ·n. 意志薄弱者

weaken ['wi:kən] ❶ vt. ①削弱,减弱: We never ~ our efforts in face of difficulties. 我们在困难面前从不松劲。②使稀薄,使淡薄 ❷ vi. ①变

弱,变衰弱 ②变软弱,变得优柔寡断

weal[1] [wi:l] n. 福利; 幸福; 好运道 ‖for the public (或 general) ~ 为了社会福利 / ~ and (或 or) woe 祸福; 幸或不幸: share ~ and woe 同甘共苦

weal[2] [wi:l] n. 鞭痕, (棒打的)伤痕

wealth [welθ] n. ①财富; 财产; 资源; 富有: the ~ of the oceans 海洋资源 / a man of ~ 富人 ②丰富,大量: accumulate a ~ of experience 积累丰富经验 / a ~ of data 大量资料

wealthy ['welθi] a. 富的,富裕的; 丰富的: a ~ family 富裕的家庭 / ~ in resources 资源丰富的 ‖wealthily ad. / wealthiness n.

wean[1] [wi:n] vt. ①使断奶: ~ a baby from the breast (或 its mother) 给婴孩断奶 ②使断绝; 使放弃; 使戒掉: ~ oneself from drinking (smoking) 戒酒(烟) ‖~er n. ① (牲畜的)断奶器 ②断了奶的幼畜

wean[2] [wi:n] n. [苏格兰]婴儿,小孩

weapon ['wepən] I n. ①武器,兵器: a nuclear ~ 核武器 / a chemical (bacteriological) ~ 化学(细菌)武器 / conventional ~s 常规武器 ②斗争工具(或手段) II vt. 武装 ‖~less a. 无武器的, 没有武装的

wear[1] [wɛə] I (wore [wɔ:], worn [wɔ:n]) ❶ vt. ①穿着; 戴; (为表示身分等)佩带着; 蓄留着(须、发); 使(身体某部)成一定的姿态: He ~s a military uniform. 他穿着军装。/ ~ an overcoat today. 他今天穿着大衣。/ ~ red 穿红色衣服 / ~ serge 穿哔叽衣服 / Which size do you ~? 你穿(或戴)哪一号尺寸? / ~ glasses (或 spectacles) 戴眼镜 / ~ diamonds 戴钻石首饰 / ~ one's hair short 留着短发 / ~ a long beard 蓄长须 / ~ one's head high 头昂得高高的 / a style that is much worn 很流行的式样 ②(脸色等)呈现, 显出; (船)升,挂(旗): ~ a happy smile 带着幸福的笑容 / This building wore a dilapidated look. 这座建筑物显出倾圮的样子。③耗损, 磨损, 磨破; 用旧; 磨成, 擦成(to, into): The dripping water wore a hole in the stone. 滴水穿石。/ The coat is much worn. 这件外衣穿得很旧了。/ The socks were worn into holes. 袜子穿破了。/ ~ one's clothes to rags 把衣服穿得破烂不堪 / be worn to a shadow with care 因忧愁而消瘦得不成样子 ④使疲乏; 使厌烦 (out, down) ⑤消磨(时间) (away, out) ❷ vi. ①磨损; 变旧; 穿破; 用坏: The child's trousers have worn through at the knees. 孩子的裤子膝盖处磨破了。/ The tablecloth will soon ~. 这块桌布很快就要破了。②耐久; 耐穿; 磨: This material ~s well (won't ~). 这种材料耐久(不耐久)。/ The veteran worker is ~ing well. 这位老工人并不见老。③逐渐变得: The stock of that fund began to ~ low. 那笔基金逐渐变得少起来。④(时间等)逐渐消逝 (on, away); 消失 (off): As the night wore on, it grew colder.

随着夜深,天气冷起来了。/ Her fever is ~ing off. 她的热度在退了。**II** *n.* ①穿; 佩; 戴; 使用: clothes for everyday ~ 日常穿的衣服 / the best material for working ~ 最适合劳动时穿的衣料 / the coat sb. has in ~ 某人常穿的上衣 / show signs of ~ 显得 (穿) 旧了 ②衣服,服装; (商业用语)[常用以构成复合词]特殊场合穿的服装; 时装; 流行的样式: children's ~ 童装 / foot~[总称]鞋; 袜 / under~ 内衣 ③磨损, 损耗; 损耗量: The bedcover is showing ~. 这块床罩已用得破旧了。/ normal ~ 正常损耗 / a ~-resistant surface 耐磨(表)面 ④耐久性; 耐用性: There's plenty of ~ in this cloth. 这种布很牢。/ not much ~ left in it 穿(或用)不了多久了 ‖**be in general** ~ (服式等)流行一时, 人人爱穿 / **be the worse for** ~ 被用坏; 被穿破 / **better** ~ **out than rust out** 与其锈掉不如用坏; 与其闲散不如忙碌; 应老当益壮才好 / ~ **and tear** ①损耗, 磨损: Our products must stand ~ *and tear*. 我们的产品必须经久耐用。/ the tactics of "~ *and tear*" "蘑菇"战术 ②折磨: the ~ *and tear* of life 生活的折磨 / ~ *away* ①(使)磨损, (使)磨坏: The waterfall is ~ing *away* the rocks. 瀑布不断地冲蚀着岩石。②(印象、时间等)消逝; (人)衰退: The year is ~ing *away*. 一年快过去了。③消磨(时间); 虚度: ~ *away* one's youth (in trifles) 虚度青春 / ~ *black* 穿丧服 / ~ *down* ①(使)磨损, (使)损耗; (使)磨薄, (使)磨短, (使)磨穿: The heels of my shoes have (been) *worn down*. 我的鞋跟给磨损了。②使筋疲力尽; 使厌倦 ③(以坚韧意志)克服: We hope your persuasion will ~ *down* his opposition. 我们希望你能说服他不再反对。/ ~ *hollow* 使 hollow / ~ *off* ①逐渐减弱; (印象等)消失; 消逝: The novelty has *worn off*. 这种新奇的感觉已消失了。②(使)磨去; (使)耗损; (使)擦去: The nap of the coat has (been) *worn off*. 外衣的绒毛磨损得几乎没有了。/ ~ *on* ①(时间)消逝 ②使恼火; 骚扰 / ~ *one's heart on* (或 *upon*) *one's sleeve* 见 heart / ~ *out* ①消瘦 ②(把)穿破, (把)用坏; 用旧; 耗损: I have *worn out* my overall. 我把工作服穿破了。③(使)疲乏; (使)耗尽: feel *worn out* 感到困乏 / My patience wore (或 was *worn*) *out*. 我已忍耐不住了。/ ~ *out* one's welcome 因去得太频繁(或呆得太久)而不再受欢迎 / be *worn out* with age 衰老 ④(以坚韧意志)克服: ~ *out* a storm 度过风暴 / ~ *sb.* (*sth.*) *in one's heart* 忠于某人(某事) / ~ *the breeches* 掌权当家(指妇女) / ~ *the crown* 见 crown / ~ *the gown* 见 gown / ~ *the pants* 见 pants / ~ (*the*) *stripes* 见 stripe / ~ *the sword* 见 sword / ~ *the trousers* 掌权当家(指妇女) / ~ *the willow* 见 willow[1] / ~ *thin* 逐渐消失: His argument is ~ing *thin*. 他的论点正在失去说服力。/ His patience wore *thin*.

他逐渐变得不耐烦了。/ ~ *through the day* 好歹捱过一天 / ~ *to one's shape* 见 shape / ~ *well* 经久耐用; 使(高龄)不显于容貌: He ~s his years *well*. 他一点不见老。‖~able ['weərəbl] *a.* 可穿戴的; 适宜穿戴的 *n.* [复]衣服, 服装 / ~er ['weərə] *n.* 穿戴者; 佩带者

wear[2] [weə] (wore [wɔ:], worn [wɔ:n]) [海] **①** *vt.* 把(船)的尾部转向风 **②** *vi.* (船)尾部转向风

weary ['wiəri] **I** *a.* ①疲倦的, 困乏的; 消沉的, 萎靡的: feel ~ 感到困乏 / a ~ face 显得疲倦的脸 ②厌倦的; 不耐烦的(*of*): be ~ *of* waiting 等得不耐烦 ③令人厌倦的; 令人厌烦的: a long and ~ journey 令人厌倦的长途旅程 **II ①** *vt.* 使疲乏; 使厌烦: The child *wearied* him *with* endless questions. 孩子不断地问长问短使他感到不耐烦。**②** *vi.* ①疲乏; 厌倦; 不耐烦: ~ *with* talking 讲累了 / ~ *of* countless restrictions and fetters 对种种清规戒律感到很厌烦 ②不耐烦地等待; 渴望: ~ *for* the boat to get around 焦躁地等着船开过来 ‖~ *out* ①使筋疲力尽, 使困乏 ②(单调地或厌倦地)度过(时间) / ~ *Willie* [俚]经常萎靡不振的人; 流浪汉 ‖**weariful** *a.* 使人疲倦(或厌倦)的 / **weariless** *a.* (使人)不倦的; 不厌烦的 / **wearily** *ad.* / **weariness** *n.* / **wearisome** ['wiərisəm] *a.* 使人疲倦的; 令人厌烦的: a *wearisome* babbler 令人厌烦的唠叨者 / a *wearisome* article 令人生厌的文章

weasel ['wi:zl] **I** *n.* ①鼬鼠, 黄鼠狼 ②狡猾的人, 奸刁的人 ③[美俚]告密者 ④鬼鬼祟祟的; 马屁精; 卑微的人; 矮小的男子 ④[美]含糊的话, 模棱两可的话 ⑤水陆两用自动车 ⑥[军]小型登陆车辆 ⑥[美][常作 W-]美国南卡罗来纳州人的别名 **II** *vi.* ①躲避; 躲闪: ~ *out of* a hard situation 从困境中脱身 / ~ *from* an obligation 逃避责任 ②[美]含糊其词 ③[美俚]告密 ‖*catch a* ~ *asleep* 欺骗精明的人, 乘人麻痹不备 / ~ *out* [美口](从团体中)退出; 逃避义务; 背弃诺言 ‖~-**faced** *a.* 瘦长脸的 / ~ *word*(*s*) [美]含糊的话, 遁辞

weather ['weðə] **I** *n.* ①天气: fine (或 fair) ~ 好天气, 晴天 / bad (或 foul) ~ 坏天气 / cloudy (wet) ~ 阴(雨)天 / *for all* ~s 各种天气都适用的 / *in* most ~s 在大多数天气条件下 / The ~ has changed. 天气变了。/ *Weather* permitting, I'll come. 天气好的话, 我就来。/ a ~ bureau 气象局 ②恶劣天气: We are expecting some ~. 我们预计天气要变坏。/ for protection against the ~ 为了防备坏天气 ③处境, 境遇: run into rough ~ 陷入困境 / dark ~ of grim resolution 狠下决心对付的逆境 **II** *a.* 【海】上风的, 迎风的: ~ helm 偏向上风的舵 **III ①** *vt.* ①使经受风吹雨打, 使经受日晒夜露; 使褪色; 侵蚀; 风干; 【地】使风化: ~ed limestone 风化石灰岩 ②度过(暴风雨, 困难等), 经受住: ~ the storm 战胜暴风雨 / [喻]克服困难 / The little tree has ~ed many bitter winters. 这棵小树经受了好几个严

冬。③【海】航行到…的上风: ～ another ship 驶
到另一条船的上风 ④使(屋顶等)倾斜(以便雨水
流泻) ❷ vi. ①(因风吹雨打而)褪色, 受侵
蚀;风化: The walls ～ed to silvery grey.　由于
日晒风吹雨打, 墙变成银灰色了。/ The rock has
～ed away into soil.　岩石风化成土了。②经受
风雨。‖April ～ (四月的天气)乍雨乍晴; [喻]一会
儿哭一会儿笑 / be (或 feel) under the ～ [口]
① 不舒服, 有点小病: Just a bit under the ～,
nothing to fret about.　只是有点儿不舒服, 不必
担心。② 微醉 / broken ～ 阴晴不定的天气 /
in all ～s 不论天气如何, 风雨无阻: I'll come in
all ～s.　不管天气怎样, 我准来。/ keep the ～
占上风; 操大权 / King's (或 Queen's 或 royal)
～ 庆典时的晴朗天气 / make good (bad) ～
【海】碰到好(坏)天气 / make heavy ～ of sth.
对某事考虑过多, 对某事小题大做; 发现某事棘
手 / merry ～ 快活的时候 / under stress of ～
迫于恶劣的天气: The ship didn't sail under
stress of ～.　因天气恶劣, 船没有开。‖～ability
[ˌweðərə'biliti] n. 耐气候性, 经得住风吹雨打 /
～ed a. ① 风化的 ② 倾斜(以便雨水流泻)的 /
～ing ['weðəriŋ] n. ① 风化(作用);风蚀 ②【建】
泻水用的倾斜装置 / ～ly a. 能抢风航行的 ‖'～-
,beaten a. ① 饱经风霜的, (脸等)晒黑的 ② 风
雨剥蚀(或损耗)的 / '～board n.【建】檐板
②【海】上风舷 vt. 给…装檐板 / '～,boarding n.
①[集合名词]【建】檐板, 墙面板 ② (给屋顶等)装
檐板(或墙面板) / '～-bound a. (船、飞机等)因
恶劣天气受阻的 / ～ box 晴雨指示箱 / '～
breeder 孕育着暴风雨的晴天, 暴风雨前的沉静 /
～ chart, ～ map 天气图 / '～cock n.　风标;
[喻]易变的人(或物), 随风倒的人 / ～ deck 露
天甲板, 干舷甲板 / ～ eye ① 善于观测天气的眼
睛 ② 警惕: keep one's ～ eye open 留心看着;
注意; 保持警惕 / keep a ～ eye on a touchy
situation 严密注视着带爆炸性的局势 / '～fore-
cast 天气预报 / ～ ga(u)ge 天气器 / '～glass
n. 晴雨计 / '～man n. [口]预报天气者(尤指气
象局人员), 气象员 / ～ mo(u)lding 【建】泻水
线条 / '～proof a. 防风雨(或日晒等)的;抗风化
的;不受气候影响的 vt. 使防风雨(或日晒等) /
～ service 气象服务(站) / ～ ship 气象观测船 /
～ side 上风舷 / '～-stained a. 因日晒风吹雨
打而斑驳变色的 / ～ station 气象站, 天气图 /
～ strip (门、窗的)挡风雨条, 塞眼片 / '～'tight
a. 防风雨的 / ～ vane 风标 / '～-wise a. ①善

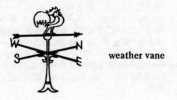

weather vane

于预测天气的 ② [喻]善于预测舆论(或意见、感
情等)变化的 / '～worn a. 风雨剥蚀(或损耗)的

weave[1] [wiːv] I (wove [wouv], woven ['wouvən])
❶ vt. ①织; 编(制): It is woven of silk.　这是
用丝织成的。/ ～ osiers into a basket 把柳条
编成篮子 / a garland 编花环 ② (蜘蛛等)结
(网) ③ 构成;编排: ～ a plot 编排情节 / ～ a
story around the incident 围绕这一事件编一个
故事 ④使迂回行进: ～ one's way (或 one's
person) through a crowd 在人群中曲折穿行 ❷
vi. ① 纺织;织布 ② 迂回行进 ③[英][空军俚]闪
避: The road ～s through the valleys.　道路
曲折地通过山谷。II n. ①织法, 编法; 编织式样:
loose (tight, coarse, plain) ～ 松(紧, 粗, 平)织 ②
织物

weave[2] [wiːv] vi. 摇晃

weaver ['wiːvə] n. ① 织布工; 编织者, 织补者
②[动] =～bird ‖'～bird n.【动】(文鸟科中的)
一种织巢鸟 / ～'s knot, ～'s hitch 织布结

web [web] I n. ① (蜘蛛等的)网; 丝; 网状物; 网状
组织;【纺】棉网, 毛网: a ～ of railways 铁路网
②织物; (织物的)一匹 ③ (阴谋等的)一套; 圈套:
the ～ of intrigue 阴谋圈套 ④ (印报纸的)卷筒
纸; (卷筒纸的)一卷, 一筒 ⑤ (蛙、水禽、蝙蝠等
的)蹼; (鸟翮上的)短毛 ⑥【机】连接板, 金属薄条
片(如刀叶、锯片等): joint ～ 连板接 ⑦【建】腹
板, 梁腹 II (webbed; webbing) ❶ vt. ① (蜘蛛
等)在…上结丝网; 丝网般密布在…上 ② 用丝网
绊住; 使落入圈套 ❷ vi. ① 织丝网 ② 成丝网状
‖a Penelope's ～ 永远完不成的工作 ‖'～webbed
a. ① 有蹼的 ② 多蜘蛛网的; 给蜘蛛网遮住的 /
webbing n. (做吊带、挽具等用的)带子; 结实的
带状织物 / ～like a. 似网的 ‖'～-eye n. 眼翳
病, 蹼状眼 / '～-eyed a. 患眼翳病的, 蹼状眼
的 / '～-,fingered a. 蹼指的 / '～foot n. ①蹼
足 ② 蹼足动物 ③[美][常作 W-] 俄勒冈州人的
别名(也作 Webfooter) / '～-,footed a. 蹼足
的 / ～ member【建】腹杆 / ～ press 卷筒纸轮
转印刷机 / ～ spinner =～worm / '～-'toed a.
蹼趾的 / '～-wheel n. (钟表等的)板轮 / '～-
worm n. 略有群居性的结网毛虫

wed [wed] (wed(ded); wedding) ❶ vt. ① 娶; 嫁;
与…结婚 ②使结合: ～ simplicity to (或 with 或
and) elegance 既朴素又雅致 ❷ vi. 结婚

wedding ['wediŋ] n. ① 婚礼; 结婚; 结婚纪念:
attend a ～ 参加婚礼 / a silver (golden, diamond) ～ 结婚二十五(五十, 六十或七十五)周年
纪念 ②结合 ‖a penny ～ [英]用客人送的钱举
行的婚礼 ‖～ breakfast 喜宴(在婚礼后蜜月旅
行前举行) / ～ cake 结婚蛋糕 / ～ day 婚礼
日; 结婚纪念日 / ～ march 婚礼进行曲 / ～
ring 结婚戒指

wedge [wedʒ] I n. ① 楔; 劈: force sth. apart
with a ～ 用楔把某物劈开 ② 使分裂的东西 ③
楔形, 楔形物: a ～ of cake 楔形的糕 / ～ for-

mation【军】楔形队形 ④起因,引起某种行动(或发展)的事物 Ⅱ ❶ vt. ①楔入;劈开;分裂 ②把…楔住,把…楔牢 ③挤入,插入 (in): be ~d (in) between two persons 挤在两人中间 / ~ oneself into the crowd 挤入人群 ❷ vi. 楔入;挤进 ‖drive a ~ into 在…中打进楔子;破坏… / knock out the ~s 诱导上当后冷眼旁观 / the thin end of the ~ 得寸进尺的开端;可能有重大后果的小事 ‖~d a. 楔形的 / ~wise ad. 成楔形

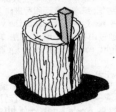

wedge

Wednesday ['wenzdi] n. 星期三 ‖~s ad. [美] 每星期三;在任何星期三

wee [wi:] Ⅰ a. ①极小的,很少的: a ~ bit tedious 有些乏味 / a ~ drop of wine 极少量酒 ②很早的: the ~ hours 半夜一、二、三点钟 Ⅱ n. [苏格兰]一点点;一会儿: bide a ~ 等一会儿 ‖~folk [总称]小仙人,仙人们

weed [wi:d] Ⅰ n. ①杂草;野草;莠草: distinguish fragrant flowers from poisonous ~s 区别香花与毒草 ②水生植物(尤指海藻) ③[the ~]烟草;[美俚]大麻烟;香烟;劣等雪茄烟: the soothing ~ 烟草 ④[俚]瘦高个子,纤弱的人(或马) ⑤多余讨厌的东西(或人),赘疣 ⑥[the ~s]美俚]流浪工人的帐篷;丛林 Ⅱ ❶ vi. 除草;除害 ❷ vt. ①除去…的草: ~ a garden 除去花园内的杂草 ②剔出,清除(out): ~ out weeds 除去杂草‖grow like a ~ 杂草般地蔓延,生长迅速 / Ill ~s grow apace. ①莠草易长。(对长得很快的孩子的戏言) ②[喻]恶习易染。‖~ed a. ①铲除了野草的 ②野草丛生的 / ~er n. ①除草者 ②除草工具,除草机 / ~less a. 无杂草的 ‖~= grown a. =weedy / ~ killer =weedicide

weeds [wi:dz] [复] n. ①丧服(尤指寡妇所穿的): widow's ~ 寡妇的丧服 ②(表示哀悼的)黑纱带

weedy ['wi:di] a. ①杂草丛生的 ②蔓延的;长得快的 ③(人或动物)瘦长的,瘦弱的;丑陋的 ‖**weediness** n.

week [wi:k] n. ①星期,周;(从任何时候算起的)连续七天: What day of the ~ is it? 今天星期几? / this (last, next) ~ 本(上,下)星期 / the ~ of the 6th 六号开始的一星期 / I haven't seen you for ~s. 我好几星期没见到你了。/ a two ~s' visit 为期两周的访问 / Traffic Safety Week 交通安全周 / an officer of the ~ 值星官 ②工作周(指一周中除例假日外的工作日): a

six-day, eight-hour a day ~ 每周六天、每天八小时的工作周 / He spends the ~ at the factory and goes home on Sundays. 他平时在工厂,星期天回家。③ 从某日起算七天前(或后)的一天: He was here this day ~ (或 today ~). 上星期的今天他在这里。/ School begins this day ~ (或 today ~). 下星期的今天开学。/ yesterday ~ 上(或下)星期的昨天(即:八天前的那天,或六天后的那天) / tomorrow ~ 上(或下)星期的明天(即:六天前的那天,或八天后的那天) / Sunday (Monday, Tuesday, etc.) ~ 最近过去的(或倒数上去的)第二个星期日(一,二等);以后的(或接次下去的)第二个星期日(一,二等) ‖an old home ~ ①居住区邀请昔日居民团聚的联欢周 ②旧友联欢会 / a ~ of Sundays 很长的时间,很久 / knock (或 send) sb. into the middle of next ~ 打得某人抱头鼠窜 / ~ about 每隔一周(= every other ~) / ~ in, ~ out 一星期又一星期地;接连好多星期 ‖~day n. 星期天(或星期六和星期日)以外的日子,周日,工作日: go to school on ~days 平时天天上学 / '~days ad. [美]在每个周日,在平时每天: go to work ~days 平时天天上班 / '~end n. 周末;周末假期 vi. 过周末 / '~end bag, '~end case 过周末假期用的旅行袋 / '~ender n. ①过周末假期的人 ② =~end bag 过周末假期的人 ‖~ends ad. [美]在每周末

weekly ['wi:kli] Ⅰ a. 一星期的;每周的;一周一次的;按周计算的: a ~ magazine 周刊 / a ~ rental 按周计算的租金 / a ~ visit 每周一次的访问 Ⅱ ad. 每周;每周一次: be published ~ 每周出版一次 Ⅲ n. 周刊,周报

weeny ['wi:ni], **weensy** ['wi:nsi] a. 极小的

weep [wi:p] Ⅰ (wept [wept]) ❶ vi. ①哭泣,流泪: ~ at the painful news 听到悲痛的消息而哭泣 / ~ for (或 with) joy 由于高兴而落泪 ②悲叹,哀悼: ~ over sb.'s untimely death 悲叹某人过早去世 / ~ for the deceased 哀悼死者 ③(液体)缓慢地流;滴下 ④渗出液体 ⑤(柳树等)弯垂 ❷ vt. ①流(泪),哭着使…: ~ tears of joy 流出快乐的眼泪 / ~ oneself to sleep 哭得睡着 ②悲叹,哀悼: ~ one's misfortune 悲叹自己的不幸 ③渗出(液体) Ⅱ n. ①[常用复](一阵)哭泣;[美俚]眼泪 ②(水珠)的渗出,滴下 ‖~ away 在哭泣中度过: ~ away a whole hour 哭了整整一小时 / ~ Irish (假装同情)流泪,假哭 / ~ oneself out (或 ~ one's heart out) 哭得死去活来 / ~ out 边哭边说出 ‖~er n. ①哭泣(或悲叹)的人 ②(丧礼时雇用的)哭丧者 ③丧事的标记(如围于袖上的黑纱等) ④[美俚]使人哭泣的小说(或戏剧、电影等)

weeping ['wi:piŋ] Ⅰ n. 哭泣,流泪 Ⅱ a. ①哭泣的;泪汪汪的;滴水的: a ~ pipe (每隔一定时间滴水的)滴水管 ②下雨的,多雨的: a ~ day 雨天 ③垂枝的: a ~ willow 垂柳 ‖**Weeping Cross** 【宗】立于路旁为忏悔者祈祷所用的十字架: come home by the Weeping Cross 后悔自己的行为;受挫败

weevil ['wi:vil] *n.* 【动】象鼻虫,姑螬 ‖**weevil(l)ed,**
weevil(l)y *a.* 长满象鼻虫的

weft[1] [weft] *n.* ①【纺】纬;纬纱 ②织物

weft[2] [weft] *n.* 【海】(表示风向、遇险等的)信号旗;
(用旗表示的)信号,求救信号

weigh[1] [wei] **I ❶** *vt.* ①称…的重量,掂估…的分
量: ~ cotton in the scales 在磅秤上称棉花 / ~
sth. in one's hand(s) 用手掂估某物的分量 / ~
oneself 称体重 ②掂量,考虑;权衡: ~ one's
words 斟酌词句 / ~ one plan *against* another
权衡一个计划与另一个计划的优劣 / ~ the pros
and cons 考虑正反两面意见 / ~ the advantages
and disadvantages 权衡利弊 ③重压,把…压倒;
使下垂;使不平衡: The fruit ~ed the branches
down. 果实把树枝压弯了。/ be ~ed *down* with
cares 被忧虑压得心情沉重 / 【海】起(锚),拔
(锚): ~ anchor 起锚,启航 **❷** *vi.* ① 重若干;
称分量: ~ heavy(light)(称起来)分量重(轻) /
When did you ~ last? 你上次是什么时候称体
重的? ②有分量,有意义,有影响: His remarks
~ heavily *with* me. 他的话对我很有影响。/
Evidence will ~ *against* him. 证据将对他不利。
③重压(on, upon): The news ~ed on his mind.
消息使他心情沉重。④【海】起锚,启航 **II** *n.* 称
分量,上秤,过秤 ‖~ *in* ①参加,介入 ②称分
量,称体重(尤指骑师、拳击手或摔角手比赛前称
体重) / ~ *in with* (在讨论中)成功地提出(论
点等) / ~ *out* ① 称出,量出: ~ *out* a catty of
flour 称出一斤面粉 ②(骑师等)比赛前称体重 /
~ *the thumb* [美俚]骗秤头(指称东西时作
弊、克扣分量) / ~ *up* ①估量: ~ *up* the
situation 估量形势 ②称出 ③重得使…翘起来:
The bucket was ~ed *up* by the mass of iron at
the other end of the lever. 吊桶在杠杆另一端
的铁块的压力下翘了上来。‖~**er** *n.* ①过磅员,
称货员 ②衡器,称物机 ‖~**beam** *n.* 秤杆 /
'~**bridge** *n.* (称车、马重量的)台秤,桥秤 /
'~**house** *n.* 过磅处,计量所 / ~**ing machine**
称量机,衡器 / '~**lock** *n.* 船闸(运河中称船重
的水闸) / ~**man** ['weimən] *n.* 过磅员,称货
员 / '~**shaft** *n.* 【机】摇臂轴

weigh[2] [wei] *n.* [仅用于以下习语中] ‖*under* ~
在进行中

weight [weit] **I** *n.* ①重,重量;分量;体重: gross
(net) ~ 毛(净)重 / a ~ of 100 kilogrammes 一
百公斤的重量 / five pounds ~ of tin 五磅锡 /
The two bags are (of) the same ~. 两只包一
样重。/ What is your ~? 你体重多少? ②趋
向吸引中心的力: the ~s of the planets 行星受
太阳吸引的引力 ③重量单位;衡量(制): ~s and
measures 度量衡 / troy ~ 金衡 / avoirdupois ~
常衡 ④砝码,秤砣: a pound ~ 一磅重的砝码
⑤重体(如铅球、铁饼、钟锤等): a paper ~ 镇纸,
压纸器 ⑥重担,负荷,重压(如责任或忧虑): a ~
on the mind 精神负担 ⑦重要(性);重大: a

matter of great ~ 重大事件 ⑧影响;力量;权
力,势力: What he said has great ~ with us.
他所说的对我们很有影响。/ a man of ~ 有影
响(或有权力)的人物 ⑨[常用以构成复合词](适
宜于某一季节穿的)衣服的质地(指厚薄、轻重):
dress ~ 衣服的厚薄 ⑩(拳击、摔角等)运动员的
体重级别 ⑪(统计学中的)权 **II** *vt.* ①加重量
于;Don't ~ the boat too heavily. 别把船装得太
重。②重压,压迫 ③用金属盐增加(线、纤维)的重量:
~ed silk 【纺】加重丝绸,加量丝绸 ④(统计学中)
使加权: a ~ed average 加权平均数 ⑤称…的重
量,掂估…的分量 ‖*by* ~ 按重量计算 / *carry* ~
重要,有影响: opinions that *carry* ~ 有分量的
意见 / *gain* (*lose*) ~ 体重增加(减轻) / *lumping*
~ 足重,十足重量 / *over* ~ 过重 / *pull* one's
~ ①划船时有效利用自己的重量 ②喻努力做
好自己分内的工作 / *put on* ~ 体重增加,长胖 /
throw one's ~ *about* [口]滥用权势,仗势欺人 /
under ~ 重量不足 / *whip* one's ~ *in wild*
cats [美口]非常凶猛而出色地战斗 ‖~ **lifter** 举
重者 / ~ **lifting** 举重 / ~ **man** 掷重(如铁饼、
铅球)运动员

weighty ['weiti] *a.* ①重的,沉重的 ②繁重的;累
人的 ③重大的,重要的;有影响的;有分量的: ~
matters of state 国家的重大事情 / a ~
personage 重要人物 / ~ arguments 有力的论据
④肥大的 ‖**weightily** *ad.* / **weightiness** *n.*

weir [wiə] *n.* ①堰,低坝,导流坝 ②(用小木桩或
小枝编成的篱笆于河中捕鱼的)鱼梁

weird [wiəd] **I** *a.* ①[古]命运的;命运三女神的
②超自然的 ③似鬼的;怪诞的;神秘的 ④[口]离
奇的,古怪的;不可思议的: a ~ tale 离奇的故
事 / ~ dress 奇装异服 **II** *n.* [苏格兰]①命运
(尤指坏运气) ②[W-](神话中的)命运三女神之
一 ③预言 ④占卜者,预言者;符咒 ‖~**ly** *ad.* /
~**ness** *n.* ‖**Weird Sisters** [复](神话中的)命运
三女神

welcome ['welkəm] **I** *a.* ①受欢迎的: a ~ guest
受欢迎的客人 / Orders are ~. 欢迎订购。
②可喜的,来得正好的: ~ news 好消息 / a ~
opportunity 好机会 / Your suggestion is most
~ (to us). 你的建议提得好。③[作表语用]被
允许的;可随意使用…的;不必感谢的: You are
~ to (use) any instrument here. 这儿的任何
仪器你尽管使用好了。/ You are ~. (回答
对方道谢时的常用语)不用谢。**II** *int.* 欢迎:
Welcome home! 欢迎你(们)回来! **III** *n.* ①欢
迎: We gave the delegation a warm ~. 我们
热烈欢迎代表团。/ the heartiest of ~s 最热闹
的欢迎 / We shook hands with the visitors *in*
~. 我们和来访者握手,表示欢迎。②(某种姿态
的)迎接: We gave the intruders a hot ~. 我
们给入侵者以猛烈的迎击 / a cool ~ 冷淡的迎
接 **IV** *vt.* 欢迎,欢欢喜喜地迎接: We ~ criticism. 我们欢迎批评。/ ~ in a new year 迎
来新的一年 ‖*and* ~ 而且是欢迎的: You may

take my book *and* ～. 你尽管把我的书拿去好了。/ **bid** (或 **make**) sb. ～ 向某人表示欢迎 / **outstay** (或 **overstay**) one's ～ 因呆得太久而不再受欢迎 / **wear out** one's ～ 因去得太频繁 (或呆得太久)而不再受欢迎 ‖**～ly** *ad.* / **～ness** *n.* / **～r** *n.* 欢迎者 ‖ **mat** [美]门口的擦鞋垫(尤指迎客时铺在门前的): put (或 roll) out the ～ mat 热烈欢迎

weld¹ [weld] **I ❶** *vt.* ①焊接,熔接②锻接②(紧密)团结,结合;使连成整体 (*into*) **❷** *vi.* 焊牢;能被焊接 **II** *n.* 焊接,熔接;锻接;焊接点,接头 ‖**～er** *n.* ①焊工②焊机 / **～ing** *a.* 焊的: a ～*ing* rod 焊条 / a ～*ing* helmet 焊工帽罩 *n.* 焊接,熔接;锻接: electrical arc ～*ing* 电弧焊 / gas ～*ing* 气焊 / **～less** *a.* 无焊缝的 / **～ment** *n.* 焊(成)件 / **～or** *n.* 焊工

weld² [weld] *n.* ①【植】(淡)黄木犀草②用黄木犀草制的黄色植物染料

welfare ['welfeə] **I** *n.* ①幸福;福利;康乐: care for the ～ of children 关心孩子们的幸福 / public ～ 公共福利 / ～ facilities 福利设施 / national ～ and people's livelihood 国计民生②福利事业 **II** *a.* ①福利(事业)的②接受福利救济的 ‖**welfarism**['welfeərizəm] *n.*福利主义 ‖ **fund** 福利基金 / ～ **state** 福利国家 / ～ **work** 福利事业

well¹ [wel] **I** *n.* ①井: sink (或 drive) a ～ 凿井 / ～ water 井水 / an oil ～ 油井②泉水;泉,池③源泉: He is indeed a ～ of information. 他知道的东西真多。④深坑③【建】井孔,通风竖井;(房屋中央的)楼梯井;升降机井道⑥[英](法庭上设有围栏的)律师席⑦[海](船舱中)保护水泵的井状围栏⑧(渔船上的)养鱼舱⑨盛放液体的容器 (如墨水池等) **II ❶** *vi.* 涌出: Water ～s from a spring beneath the rock. 水从岩石下的泉中涌出。/ Joy ～ed up in his heart. 欢乐涌上他的心头。**❷** *vt.* 涌出 ‖**～ deck** 井形甲板 / **'～head** *n.*泉源;水源 / ～ **sinker** 凿井工 / 油井钻工 / **'～spring** *n.* =～head / ～ **tube** (钻井) 套管

well² [wel] **I** (better ['betə], best [best]) *ad.* ①好;妥善地;令人满意地: Well done (said)! 干(说)得好! / act one's part ～ 演得好 / live ～ 生活得好 / It was ～ done of you (或 You did ～) to arrive in time. 你及时来到,很好。/ The affair ended ～. 这事圆满结束。/ Do these two colours go ～ together? 这两种颜色是否协调?②好意地,关心地;优待地;赞扬地: treat sb. ～ 待某人好 / think (speak) ～ of sb. 认为(说)某人好 / This speaks ～ for his sense of discipline. 这足以说明他的纪律性。③有理由地;恰当地: He may ～ be praised. 他很值得表扬。/ They were confident, as they ～ might, that the experiment would be a success. 他们相信,并且也确有理由相信,这次实验一定成

功。/ I cannot ～ refuse. 我难以拒绝。/ He took the news ～. 他对此消息处之泰然。④完全地;充分地;彻底地: Shake the bottle ～ before you take the medicine. 服药前将瓶充分摇动。/ You know perfectly ～ that he was there. 你非常清楚地知道他当时是在那里的。⑤很;很可能: It's ～ worth trying. 这很值得一试。/ His name is ～ up in the list. 他的名字排在名单的很前面。/ He must be ～ past (或 over) forty. 他肯定大大超过四十岁了。/ be ～ advanced in years 已有相当年纪 / a struggle that may ～ last many decades 很可能持续好几十年的斗争

II (better ['betə], best [best]) *a.* ①健康的;治愈的: You don't look ～. 你的脸色不好。/ the ～ and the unwell [罕][主英]健康的人和有病的人 / I am not feeling very ～. 我觉得身体不太舒服。/ I'm quite ～, thank you. 谢谢你,我很好。/ The wound is nearly ～. 伤快要好了。②恰当的,可取的; 幸运的: It might be ～ for you to see a doctor. 你还是去看看医生的好。/ It's ～ that this has happened. 幸亏这事发生了。③令人满意的, 良好的: We are very ～ where we are. 我们目前的处境(或位置)很好。/ Things are ～ with us. 我们事情很顺利。/ be ～ with sb. 与某人相处得好 / The building looks ～. 这座楼房看上去很不错。④富有的;有钱的

III *int.* ①[表示惊讶]咳;嗯;唷: *Well*, who would have thought it? 咳, 谁会想到这样呢?②[表示快慰]好啦: *Well*, here we are at last. 好啦,终于到了。③[表示无可奈何]嗯;唉: *Well*, it can't be helped. 嗯,只好如此。④[表示同意、期望、让步等]好吧; 喂: Very ～, then, we'll talk it over again tomorrow. 好吧,那么我们明天再谈吧。/ *Well*, then? 后来怎样呢? / *Well*, what's the matter with you? 喂,你怎么啦? / *Well*, you may be right. 好吧,也许你是对的。⑤(用于重新开始说话时)喔,噢,这个: *Well*, as I was saying, ... 这个,我刚才在说…

IV *n.* 好,美满;令人满意的事物: I wish you ～. 愿你称心如意。

‖***All's ～ that ends ～.*** [谚]结果好就一切都好。/ **as ～** (*as*) 也,又;He is a worker, and a militiaman *as ～*. 他是工人,也是民兵。/ He knows German *as ～*. 他也懂德文。/ The child is lively *as ～ as* healthy. 这孩子既健康又活泼。/ **be ～ out of** *sth.* 安然摆脱某事: You are ～ *out of* it. 你幸亏没参与这事。/ **do oneself ～** 见 **do¹** / **do** ～ 见 **do¹** / **It's all very ～,** but .... (表示不赞成、不满意的反语)…好倒是好,可是…: It's all very ～ for you to suggest taking a few days' rest, but how can we stop our work? 你建议休息几天,好倒

是好,可是我们怎能把工作停下来呢? / (*just*) *as* ~ 还是…好;不妨: You may *just as* ~ tell me the truth. 你还是对我说实话的好。/ It's *just as* ~. 这样也不妨。/ We may ~ begin at once. 我们还是立即开始的好。/ *let* ~ *alone* 不要画蛇添足; 对已经满意的事不要再多管 / *pretty* ~ 几乎: You are *pretty* ~ the only person willing to stay. 你几乎是唯一愿意留下的人。/ ~ *and good* (表示可接受)也好: If that's the case, ~ *and good*. 如果情况是这样,那也好。/ ~ *and truly* ①周密而准确地 ②确实地 / ~ *as a storm* (或 *as snow in harvest* 或 *as water into a ship*) 不合时宜的,不受欢迎的 / *Well begun is half done.* [谚]开始好就等于一半成功。/ ~ *enough* 见 *enough* / *Well fed, well bred.* [谚]吃得饱,懂礼貌。/ *Well met!* 幸会,幸会! / ~ *off* 富裕的;处境好的

‖'~-ad'vised *a.* 明智的;谨慎的;经周密考虑的: a ~-*advised* plan 经周密考虑的计划 / '~-ap-'pointed *a.* 设备完善的: ~-*appointed* residence 设备完善的住宅 / '~-'balanced *a.* 匀称的,均衡的;神志健全的;明智的 / '~-be'haved *a.* 品行端正的;有礼貌的 / '~-'being *n.* 健康;幸福;福利: have a sense of ~-*being* 觉得身体健康 / be concerned with the ~-*being* of the masses 关心群众生活 / '~-be'loved *a.* 深受热爱的;(用于称呼前)尊敬的 *n.* 亲爱的人 / '~-'born *a.* 出身高贵的,出身名门的 / '~-'bred *a.* ①教养良好的 ②良种的: ~-*bred* swine 良种猪 / '~-'chosen *a.* 精选的;恰当的: ~-*chosen* phrase 选择得当的词语 / '~-con'ditioned *a.* ①性情好的,品行好的 ②强壮的,健全的 / '~-con'ducted *a.* 品行端正的 / '~-con'nected *a.* 出身名门的;与权贵有关系的 / '~-con'tent(ed) *a.* 十分满意的 / '~-dis'posed *a.* 怀好意的,乐于助人的: be ~-*disposed towards* sb. 对某人怀好意 / '~-'doer *n.* 做好事的人,善人 / '~-'done *a.* ①干得好的,做得好的: a ~-*done* job 完成得很好的工作 ②煮得透的 / '~-'dressed *a.* 穿得很体面的 / '~-'earned *a.* 劳动所得的,正当的;应得的: a ~-*earned* punishment 罪有应得的惩罚 / '~-'favo(u)red *a.* 漂亮的,好看的 / '~-'fed *a.* 营养充足的,吃得很好的 / '~-'fixed *a.* 富裕的,有钱的 / '~-'found *a.* 装备完善的: a ~-*found* ship 装备完善的轮船 / '~-'founded *a.* ①基础牢固的: a ~-*founded* building 基础牢固的建筑物 ②有充分根据的,理由充足的: a ~-*founded* argument 理由充足的论点 / '~-'groomed *a.* 穿着考究的,十分整洁的 / '~-'grounded *a.* =~-*founded* / '~-in'formed *a.* 见识广博的;消息灵通的 / '~-in'tentioned *a.* 善意的,好心的 / '~-'judged *a.* 判断正确的;适时的: a ~-*judged* reply 中肯的答复 / '~-'knit *a.* ①结实的,健壮的: a ~-*knit* athlete 强壮的运动员 ②组织严密的: a ~-*knit* argument 严密的论点 / a ~-*knit* composition 构思严密的文章 / '~-'known *a.* ①出名的,众所周知的: a ~-*known* drama critic 有名的戏剧评论家 ②熟知的: a ~-*known* voice 熟悉的嗓音 / '~-'lined *a.* (钱包)放满钱的 / '~-'looking *a.* 漂亮的 / '~-'made *a.* 样子好的,匀称的;做工考究的,(剧本等)情节安排得很好的 / '~-'marked *a.* 明确的,明显的: ~-*marked* differences 明显的分歧 / '~-'meaning *a.* 本意良好的(往往指结果不好的) / '~-'nigh *ad.* 几乎: be ~-*nigh* perfect 几乎是完美无缺的 / '~-'off *a.* ①富裕的 ②处于有利地位的 ③供应充裕的 / '~-'oiled *a.* 谄媚的; [口]微醉的 / '~-'ordered *a.* 安排得很好的 / '~-'paid *a.* 高工资的;报酬优厚的 / '~-pre'served *a.* 保养得很好的 / '~-pro'portioned *a.* 很均匀的,匀称的 / '~-'read ['wel'red] *a.* 博览群书的;博学的 / '~-'regulated *a.* 管理得好的;纪律严明的 / '~-re'membered *a.* 被牢记的 / '~-re'puted *a.* 得好评的,名声好的 / '~-'rounded *a.* ①丰满的 ②经过周密计划的,各方面安排得很好的 ③有多方面兴趣(或能力)的 / '~-'seeming *a.* 看上去令人满意的 / '~-'set *a.* ①安放恰当的;牢固安置的 ②结实的,强健的 / '~-'set-'up *a.* 身材长得好的 / '~-'spent *a.* (时间、劳力等)使用得当的 / '~-'spoken *a.* ①谈吐优雅的,善于词令的 ②讲得体的,有分寸的: ~-*spoken* words 有分寸的话 / '~-'tempered *a.* ①脾气好的 ②经过锻炼的 / '~-'thought-of *a.* =~-*reputed* / '~-'timbered *a.* ①用木材撑牢(或加固)的: a ~-*timbered* house 用木材结实地建造的房屋 ②强壮的: a ~-*timbered* horse 强壮的马 ③树木繁茂的 / '~-'timed *a.* ①时机选得好的: a ~-*timed* move 时机选择得好的行动 ②有节拍的 ③准时的: a ~-*timed* crew 行动准时的全体船员 / a ~-*timed* chronometer 准时的航海时计 / '~-'to-'do *a.* 富有的: the ~-*to-do* middle peasants 富裕中农 / '~-'tried *a.* 经反复试验证明的 / '~-'trod(den) *a.* (人迹)常到的;用旧了的,陈腐的 / '~-'turned *a.* ①匀称的 ②讲得恰当的: a ~-*turned* phrase 恰当的词语 / '~-'weighed *a.* 经斟酌的,经慎重考虑的 / '~-'wired *a.* [美]在政界和商界多熟人的 / '~-'wisher *n.* 表示良好祝愿的人 / '~-'wishing *n.* 良好的祝愿 / '~-'worn *a.* ①用旧了的 ②老生常谈的,陈腐的 ③佩戴得适当的

welt [welt] **I** *n.* ①(皮鞋鞋面和鞋面接缝间的)贴边,革条 ②(衣服的)贴边,滚条 ③鞭痕,条痕;猛击,殴打 **II** *vt.* ①给(皮鞋等)加贴边 ②鞭打;痛打

welter[1] ['weltə] **I** *vi.* ①滚,打滚,翻滚: The hog ~*ed* in the mire. 猪在泥中打滚。②[喻]沉溺,沉迷: ~ *in pleasures* 沉迷于享乐之中 ③浸;浸湿;染污: ~ *in blood* 浸于血泊之中 ④颠簸,起落: ~ *in the sea* 在海洋中颠簸 ⑤扰乱 **II** *n.*

①混乱；杂乱无章 ②(波涛等的)起伏，翻腾

welter² ['weltə] *n.* ① 重骑师(指体重较重的骑师) ②次中量级拳击手(或摔角手) ③[口]重击 ④[口]巨大的人(或物) ‖**~-race** *n.* 重骑师赛马 / '**~weight** *n.* ①重骑师 ②(在跳栏赛马时)加在马上的特别重量(一般为二十八磅) ③次中量级拳击手(或摔角手) *a.* 重骑师的；次中量级拳击手的

wench [wentʃ] **I** *n.* ① 少妇；[方]女孩子，少女 ②乡村姑娘；女佣 ③荡妇；妓女 **II** *vi.* ①[方]献殷勤；求爱 ②嫖妓；私通

wend [wend] ❶ *vi.* 行，走 ❷ *vt.* 走；赴，往：~ one's way 赴，往

went [went] go 的过去式

wept [wept] weep¹ 的过去式

west [west] **I** *n.* ①西；西部 ②[the W-]西洋，西方，欧美；美国西部；【史】西罗马帝国 ③西风 **II** *a.* ①西方的；西部的；朝西的：the ~ coast 西海岸 / the ~ central 西中央区 (伦敦邮政区之一) / the West End 伦敦西区(住宅区) / the ~ longitude 西经 / West Africa 西非 ②从西方来的：a ~ wind 西风 **III** *ad.* 在西方；向西方：sail due ~ 向正西方向航行 / lie east and ~ (道路等)东西横亘 ‖**go** ~ [谑]上西天，死；完蛋 / (to the) ~ of 在…以西：Korea lies (to the) ~ of Japan. 朝鲜在日本以西。‖**West Point** (美国)西点军校 / **West Pointer** (美国)西点军校学员(或毕业生)

wester ['westə] **I** *vi.* 转向西面 **II** *n.* 西风；从西面来的暴风雨

westerly ['westəli] **I** *a.* ①西的；向西方的：take a ~ course 向西行进 ②从西面来的：a ~ wind 西风 **II** *ad.* ①向西方：steer away ~ 向西方驶去 ②从西方：The wind blew ~. 风从西方吹来。**III** *n.* 西风；[复]西风带

western ['westən] **I** *a.* ① 西的；[常作 W-]西方的；西部的：the Western Hemisphere 西半球 ②朝西的 ③(罕)(风)从西吹来的 **II** *n.* ①西部(尤指美国西部)的产品；具有美国西部特征的产品 ②[常作 W-](取材于十九世纪下半叶美国西部生活的)西部电影(或小说，广播) ‖**~er** *n.* [常作 W-]①西方人；西洋人 ②美国西部人 ③(尤指十九世纪俄国的)主张采用西欧文化的人

westernize ['westənaiz] *vt.* & *vi.* (使)西洋化，(使)欧化 ‖**westernization** [,westənai'zeiʃən] *n.*

westward ['westwəd] **I** *a.* 向西的：go in a ~ direction 向西走 **II** *ad.* 向西 **III** *n.* 西方；西部：sail to the ~ 向西航行 / lie to the ~ 位于西面 ‖**~ly** *ad.* & *a.* 向西(的)

westwards ['westwədz] *ad.* 向西：march ~ 向西行军

wet [wet] **I** (wetter, wettest) *a.* ① 湿的，潮的：~ clothes 湿衣服 / Wet Paint! 油漆未干! / be ~ through 浑身湿透 / cheeks ~ with happy

tears 淌着快乐的泪水的面颊 ②下雨的，多雨的：a ~ day 雨天 / the wettest summer for the recent years 近几年来雨水最多的夏季 ③(用糖、酒精等)浸渍(保存)的 ④用水(或其他液体)处理的：~ process【化】湿法 / ~ distillation 水蒸气蒸馏 ⑤ (鱼)未经加工(或晒干)的 ⑥ (天然气)含大量石油气的 ⑦[美] 允许制酒(或卖酒)的；反对禁酒的：a ~ State 不禁酒的州 / a ~ candidate 主张不禁酒的候选人 ⑧弄错了的，搞错的：He is all ~. 他完全弄错了。⑨[俚]喝醉的 ⑩[俚]不讨人喜欢的；蠢的；无价值的 ⑪极易伤感的 **II** *n.* ①湿气；潮湿；水分，液体：wring the ~ out 把水绞出来 ② [the ~] 雨；雨天：Come in out of the ~. 进来，免得淋雨。/ We went outside in the ~ as usual to transplant rice shoots. 天下雨时我们照常出去插秧。③[美]反对禁酒的人 **III** (wetted 或 [美] wet; wetting) ❶ *vt.* ①把…弄湿；把…尿湿：a ~ sponge 蘸海棉 / The baby has wetted the bed again. 婴儿又尿床湿了。②为(某事)喝酒庆祝 ❷ *vi.* 变湿；尿湿 ‖a ~ hen [美俚]讨厌的人；泼妇 / row ~ 水花飞溅地划桨 / ~ down 洒水使湿 ‖**~ly** *ad.* / **~ness** *n.* ‖'**~-back** *n.* 未经合法手续进入美国的墨西哥流动工人 / '**~ bargain** 饮酒成交 / ~ **blanket** ①(灭火等用的)弄湿的毯子 ②扫兴的人；败兴的事(或物) / '**~-'blanket** *vt.* 用湿毯子扑灭；使扫兴 / '**~-'bulb thermometer** 湿球温度计 / ~ **dock** 系船船坞，湿坞 / ~ **dream** 梦中遗精 / ~ **goods** 酒；液体物质(如油漆、油等) / '**~-land** *n.* 潮湿的土壤 / '**~-nose** *a.* [美俚]年轻无经验的，生手的 / ~ **nurse** 奶妈，乳母 / '**~-nurse** *vt.* ①做…的奶妈 ②给…以过分的照顾 / ~ **plate** (照相的)湿板 / ~ **smack** [美俚]讨厌的人；使人扫兴的人 / ~ **wash** [总称]洗好而未烫过的潮湿衣服

wether ['weðə] *n.* 阉羊

whack [hwæk] **I** ❶ *vt.* ① 使劲打，(用棍子等)重打：~ the desk with a ruler 用尺重敲桌子 ②砍，劈：~ a considerable amount from the proposed budget 从被提出的预算中削减一大笔金额 ③[主英]反对；击败：You are ~ed today. 你今天被击败了。④[俚]按份儿分 (up) ⑤匆忙做好，赶紧凑成 (up, out) ⑥催赶(牲口) (up) ❷ *vi.* 重击，用力打 **II** *n.* ①重击；重击声：hear the ~ of the boat on the waves 听到浪拍船的声音 ②一份，份儿：get one's ~ 得到自己的一份 ③尝试；机会：have a ~ at a job 试作某事 ④正常工作情况：The motor is out of ~. 发动机运转失常了。⑤一次：borrow 500 dollars all at one ~ 一下子借五百元 ‖**It's** (或 That's) a ~. [美口]一言为定。‖**~er** *n.* 异常巨大的东西(或人)；特大的谎言 / '**~ing** *n.* 重打 *a.* 巨大的，极大的 *ad.* 非常，极：a ~ing great lie 弥天大谎

whale¹ [hweil] **I** ([复] whale(s)) *n.* ① 鲸：a bull (cow) ~ 雄(雌)鲸 / a finback (right, sperm) ~ 鳁(露脊，抹香)鲸 ②巨大的人(或物)；极好的人

（或物）**II** *vi.* 捕鲸: go *whaling* 去捕鲸 ‖*a ~ at*（或 *for, on*）善于…的人;热心于…的人: *a ~ at* table tennis 乒乓球打得很出色的人 / *a ~ for* work 工作劲头很大的人 / *a ~ on* sports 运动迷 / *a ~ of a* ...［口］极大的;极好的,了不起的: *a ~ of a* difference 天壤之别 / *a ~ of a* story 极妙的故事 / have *a ~ of a* good time 玩得很愉快 / *very like a ~*（对谬论的讽刺性赞同语）的确 ‖*~r n.* 捕鲸者;捕鲸船 ‖**~back** *n.* ①鲸背状的山（或浪等）②鲸背甲板船 / **'~boat** *n.*①捕鲸船②捕鲸船式捕鲸船 / **'~bone** *n.*①鲸须,鲸骨②用鲸骨制成的东西 / **~ calf** 幼鲸 / **~ catcher, ~ chaser** 捕鲸船 / **~ fin** 鲸须 / **~ fishery** ①捕鲸业②捕鲸区 / **~ line, ~ rope**（捕鲸用的）叉索 / **~man** ['hweilmən] *n.* 捕鲸者;捕鲸船 / **~ oil** 鲸油

whale² [hweil]［美口］❶ *vt.* ①揍;猛击②使遭惨败: ~ one's rival 11 to 1 以十一比一击败对手 ❷ *vi.* 进行猛烈攻击

wharf [hwɔ:f] **I**（[复] wharves [hwɔ:vz] 或 wharfs）*n.* 码头,停泊处 **II** ❶ *vt.* ①使（船）靠码头②把（货物）卸在码头上③为…设立码头 ❷ *vi.* 入坞 ‖**~age** ['hwɔ:fidʒ] *n.* ①码头,码头设备②码头费③码头上货物的运输和储藏 ‖**'~,master** *n.* 码头老板;码头管理人

what [hwɔt] **I** *pron.* ①［疑问代词］什么: *What* do you want? 你要什么? / I don't know ~ you mean. 我不知道你是什么意思。/ *What* is the price? 价钱多少? / A: *What* is he? B: He is a worker. 甲: 他是干什么的?乙: 他是个工人。[试比较: A: *Who* is he? B: He is my younger brother. 甲: 他是谁?乙: 他是我的弟弟。] / He did not know ~ to do. 他不知道怎么办才好。/ *What* did you do that for? 你为什么做那事? / *What* is he like? 他是什么样子的(人)? ②［用于感叹句中］多少: *What* these ancient walls could tell us! 这些古老的城墙能告诉我们多少事情啊! ③［关系代词］所…的事物（或人）(=that which 或 those which): Show me ~ you have written. 把你所写的给我看。/ *What* was once regarded as impossible has now become a reality. 过去认为不可能的事现在已成为现实。/ He is not ~ he was a few years ago. 他不是几年前的他了。④［关系代词］凡是…的事物(=whatever): You may say ~ you will. 你要怎么说就怎么说。**II** *a.* ①［表示疑问］什么: *What* commodities do we export? 我们出口什么商品? / *What* size do you want? 你要什么尺寸? / *What* news? 有什么消息? ②［表示感叹］多么,何等: *What* happy children! 多么幸福的孩子们! ③［关系形容词］所…的,尽可能多的: Lend me ~ reference books you have on the subject. 把你所有的关于这题目的参考书都借给我。/ I will

give you ~ help I can. 我当尽我的能力帮助你。**III** *ad.* 在哪一方面;到什么程度: *What* does it benefit him? 这对他有什么好处? / *What* does it matter? 这有什么关系? **IV** *int.* ①［表示惊讶、气愤等］什么: *What,* do you really mean it? 什么,你真是这个意思吗? ②［英口］［常用于句尾］是不是,不是吗: It's a good film, ~? 这是部好电影,是不是?

‖**and ~ not** 诸如此类,等等: paper clips, pins, *and ~ not* 回形针、大头针等等 / **but ~**［用于否定词或疑问词之后,相当于 that not］而不…: Not a day comes *but ~* makes a change. 每天都有些变化。/ **come ~ may**（或 *will*）见 come / **I know ~.** 我有一个主意。/ **I'll tell you ~.** ①让我告诉你事情的真相。②让我告诉你该怎么办。/ **not but ~** 见 not / **or ~**［用在问句末尾］还是其他的什么: Is it raining, or snowing, or ~? 是在下雨,还是下雪,还是别的什么呢? / **So ~?**［口］那又怎么样呢?(表示不感兴趣,或认为不重要) / **What about ... ?**（征求意见或问消息时用）…怎么样?: The girl students will pick cotton. *What about* the boys? 女同学去摘棉花。男同学怎么样? / *What about* having a game of table tennis? 咱们打一盘乒乓球怎么样? / **What can I do for you?** 见 do¹ / **~ for** ①为何目的;为什么 ②［主方］哪一种(=~ kind of): *What for* tobacco are you smoking? 你抽哪一种烟? ③［也作 ~-for］［俚］惩罚,责备: give the boy *~-for* 把男孩责备一顿 / **~ have you**［美俚］诸如此类: cups, bowls, dishes, or *have you* 杯子、碗、碟子等等 / **~ ho!**（打招呼用语）喂! / **~ if** 倘使…将会怎样;即使…又有什么要紧: *What if* they do not come? 如果他们不来,怎么办呢?(或: 即使他们不来,又有什么关系呢?) / **~ is called** 所谓 / **~ is more** 而且: He is a tractor driver and, *~ is more,* a good sportsman. 他是一个拖拉机手,而且是一个好运动员。/ **~ it takes**［美俚］成功（或出名、完成某事）的必要条件(如金钱、美貌、才智) / **What next?** 见 next / **~ of** ①…的情况怎样 ②…有什么重要性: *What of* it? 那又怎么样呢?(或: 那又有什么了不起呢?) / **What's done cannot be undone.**［谚］事已定局,无可挽回。(或: 覆水难收。) / **What's happening?**［美口］(用作熟人间的招呼语)怎么样? 你好吗? / **~'s ~**［口］事情的真相: find out ~'s ~ 了解事情真相 / know ~'s ~ 有常识,懂事;有鉴别能力 / **~ though** 尽管…有什么关系: *What though* it's raining? 下雨又有什么关系呢? / **~ with ... and (~ with)** 半因…半因…;一部因由于…一方面由于…: *What with* overwork *and ~ with* hunger, John fell ill. 一半由于工作过度,一半由于饥饿,约翰病倒了。/ *What with* reaping *and* sowing, the time passed quickly. 一方面收割,一方面播种,时间过得很快。

‖**'~-d'you-'call-him(-her, -it, -'em)** *n.* 某某

（忘记姓名、名称时说）: Mr. ~-d'you-call-him 那位某某先生

whatever [hwɔt'evə] **I** *pron.* ①[关系代词] 无论什么,不管什么,凡是…的事物:Take ~ you want. 你要什么就拿什么吧。②[连接代词]无论什么:We are determined to fulfil the task, ~ happens. 不管发生什么事,我们决心完成任务。/ The peasants have decided to build a reservoir, ~ the difficulties (may be). 农民们决心建造一个水库, 不管有多少困难。③诸如此类: buffalo or rhinoceros or ~ 水牛或犀牛, 或诸如此类 ④[口]究竟什么: *Whatever* do you mean by that? 你说这话究竟是什么意思? **II** *a.* ①[关系形容词]无论什么样的: You can take ~ farm tools you need. 你们需要什么农具,都可以拿。②[连接形容词]不管什么样的: *Whatever* dictionary you have, lend it to me. 不管你有什么词典,借给我。③[用在含有否定词或 any 的句中,放在名词后面] 任何的 (=at all): There is *no* doubt ~ about it. 关于这一点, 没有任何疑问。/ Is there *any* chance ~? 有一点儿可能性吗? / cannot see *any* one ~ 看不见任何人

wheat [hwi:t] *n.* ①小麦: spring (winter) ~ 春(冬)小麦 / raise (reap) ~ 种(割)小麦 ②[美俚]朴实的人;天真无邪的青年; 乡下人 ‖~ **bread** 用精白面粉和未去麸的粗面粉混合做成的面包 / ~ **cake** 面粉做成的烤饼 / '~**grass** *n.* 【植】冰草属植物;窗匐冰草 / ~ **rust** ①小麦锈病 ②形成小麦锈病的菌(如杆锈菌)

wheaten ['hwi:tn] *a.* ①小麦的; 小麦粉制成的: ~ bread 小麦粉制成的面包 ②小麦色的, 灰黄色的

wheedle ['hwi:dl] ❶ *vt.* 哄, 骗;(用谄媚、阿谀等)骗取: ~ sb. *into* doing sth. 哄骗某人干某事 / ~ sth. *from* (或 *out of*) sb. 骗取某人的某物 / ~ one's way into favour 骗取欢心 ❷ *vi.* 哄, 骗

wheel [hwi:l] **I** *n.* ①轮, 车轮; 机轮; 轮状物: the ~ of history 历史车轮 / a water ~ 水车, 水轮 / idle ~ 【机】空转轮 / ~ and axle 【机】差动滑轮 ②舵轮; 转向轮, 驾驶盘 ③自行车;[罕](儿童)三轮脚踏车;纺车;[史](分裂肢体的)刑车 ④旋转; 旋转运动(尤指军队、船队等的方向变换) ⑤机构, 机关;(一个机构的)重要人物, 有权人士: the ~s of government 行政机关 / a big ~ 大人物 ⑥轮转烟火 ⑦体育联合团体;(轮流交换演出节目的)联营剧场(或娱乐场) ⑧(歌曲末尾的)重唱句, 叠句 ⑨[美俚]一元银币 ⑩[复][美俚]腿;汽车 **II** ❶ *vi.* ①旋转; 转弯: ~ round 旋转 / Left (Right) ~! (口令)左(右)转弯走! / ~ about (或 around) to the other extreme 转向另一极端 ②盘旋: The eagle ~ed in the sky. 鹰在空中盘旋。③骑自行车; 驾(或乘)车前进;[美俚]高速驾车 ❷ *vt.* ①滚动, 转动; 推动: ~ a barrow 推独轮车 ②用车运(货等) ③使交换方向;使旋转: ~ one's horse about 拨转马头 ④给…装轮子 ⑤[美俚]高速驾(车) ‖a *fly on the* ~ 见 **fly**² / *break a butterfly* on the ~ 见 **butterfly** / *break a fly* on the ~ 见 **fly**² / *break sb. on the* ~ 【史】用刑车处死某人 / *Fortune's* ~ 命运; 人生的变迁 / *go*(或 *run*) *on* ~s 顺利进行 / *grease the* ~ 使事情顺利进行; 贿赂 / *have* ~s *in one's head* [美俚]发疯 / *oil the* ~s ①给轮子(或机器)加油 ②用圆滑手段使事情顺利进行 / *put a spoke in sb.'s* ~ 见 **spoke**¹ / *put* (或 *set*) *one's shoulder to the* ~ 见 **shoulder** / *the fifth* ~ *of a coach* 多余的东西 / *the man at the* ~ ①舵手; 驾驶员 ②负责人 / *the turn of the* ~ 命运的转变 / *the* ~s *of life* 人体器官的机能(作用) / ~ *and deal* ①独立行动; 一意孤行 ②当头子, 做负责人 / ~s *within* ~s 复杂的结构; 错综复杂的事情; 间接而秘密的力量 ‖~**ed** *a.* ①装有轮的: a ~ed scraper 轮式铲运机, 轮式刮土机 ②靠车轮行动(或作用)的: ~ed traffic 车辆交通 / ~**er** *n.* ①推车工人; 车轮制造人 ②[常用以构成复合词]有…轮的东西: a side-~er 明轮船 ③(马车的)后马, (紧靠车身的)辕马 ④[美俚]骑摩托车的警察 / ~**ing** *n.* ①旋转 ②车运;骑自行车 ③道路的好坏, 道路行车鉴定: It is good ~ing. 这条路好走(指车辆而言)。 / ~**less** *a.* ①无轮的 ②(人)无车辆的 ‖'~**barrow** *n.* 独轮小车, 手推车 *vt.* 用手推车运送 / '~**base** *n.* 轴距; (机车的)轮组定距 / '~**box** *n.* 【机】轮箱 / '~**chair** *n.* (病人等用的)轮椅 / '~**er-'dealer** *n.* [美俚]独立行动者; 一意孤行的人 ②机灵诡诈的人 ③从事多种商业(或社会活动)的人 / ~**horse** *n.* ①(马车的)后马, (紧靠车身的)辕马 ②(政党、团体中)勤勉而听话的人 / '~**house** *n.* 操舵室 / ~**man** ['hwi:lmən] *n.* ①舵手 ②骑自行车的人; 汽车驾驶员 / '~**-seat** *n.* 【机】轮座 / ~**sman** ['hwi:lzmən] *n.* 舵手 / '~**-tread** *n.* 【机】轮(辙)距; 轮胎花纹 / '~**work** *n.* (机器中的)轮动装置 / '~**wright** *n.* 修造轮子(或车辆)的人

wheeze [hwi:z] **I** ❶ *vi.* ①喘, 喘息 ②呼哧呼哧响: This old organ ~d. 这架旧风琴呼哧呼哧响。❷ *vt.* 喘息地说(out) **II** *n.* ①喘气声, 喘息声 ②喘气 ③[俚]俏皮话, 笑话(尤指舞台常用的插科打诨) ④[俚]诡计;巧妙的主意

whelp [hwelp] **I** *n.* ①小狗 ②(食肉动物的)幼兽(如幼虎、幼熊、幼狼等) ③[贬]崽子(指男或女孩) ④可鄙的人; 被人瞧不起的人 ⑤[机](链轮的)扣链齿 ⑥[常用复]【船】绞盘的肋骨 **II** ❶ *vt.* (尤指母狗)下(崽);[贬](女人)生育 ❷ *vi.* 下崽, 生幼兽

when [hwen] **I** *ad.* ①[疑问副词]什么时候, 何时: *When* did the ship leave? 船什么时候开走的? / I don't know ~ the ship left. 我不知道船什么时候开走的。②[关系副词, 引导定语从句]当…时: He came at a time ~ we needed help. 他在我们需要人帮忙的时候来到了。 **II** *conj.* ①当…时:It was snowing ~ he arrived at the construction site. 他到达工地时, 正在下雪。/ He was fond of swimming ~ (he was) yet a child. 他还是一个孩子的时候，就喜欢游泳。②—…(就…):We'll start ~ the team leader comes. 队长一来，我们就出发。③如果: Turn off the switch ~ anything goes wrong with the machine. 如果机器发生故障，就把电门关上。④虽然; (然)而: He usually walks ~ he might ride. 虽然有车可坐，他通常总是步行。/ They had only three rakes ~ they needed five. 他们需要五把耙子，可是只有三把。⑤既然; 考虑到: Why use metal ~ you can use plastic? 既然能用塑料，为什么要用金属呢？/ How could you, ~ you knew that this might damage the apparatus? 既然你知道这样会损坏仪器，你怎么能这样做呢？⑥在那时; 然后: We'll go to the countryside at the beginning of June, ~ the summer harvest will start. 我们六月初下乡去，那时夏收开始了。/ I stayed till noon, ~ I went home. 我呆到中午，然后就回家了。**III pron.** ①[疑问代词]什么时候: Till ~ can you stay? 你能呆到什么时候？/ From ~? 从什么时候起？②[关系代词]那时: We came back on Tuesday; since ~ we have been working in the repair shop. 我们星期二回来，从那时起就一直在修配间工作。**IV n.** (事件发生的)时间: Tell me the ~ and (the) how of it. 请把这事的时间和原委告诉我。/ the ~ and (the) where of the traffic accident 交通事故发生的时间和地点

whence [hwens] [书面语] **I ad.** ①[疑问副词]从何处; 出于什么原因: He inquired ~ the sound came. 他问声音是从哪里来的。/ *Whence* comes it that …? 这怎么会…? / *Whence* (come) the differences? 分歧从何而来? ②[关系副词]从那里，从那个; 由此 ③[连接副词](到)…的地方:Return ~ you came. 从哪里来，就回到哪里去。**II pron.** ①[疑问代词]何处: From ~ is it? 这是从哪里来的? ②[关系代词]那里: the source from ~ it springs 这事发生的根源 **III n.** 来处,根源:know neither one's ~ nor one's whither 不知从何处来也不知往何处去

whenever [hwen'evə] **I conj.** 每当，无论何时: *Whenever* we met with difficulties, they came to help us. 每当我们遇到困难时，他们总来帮助我们。/ Come to see us ~ you can. 你什么时候有空，就过来看看我们。**II ad.** 究竟何时: *Whenever* (通常作 *When ever*) did I make such a promise? 我究竟何时许过这样的诺言?

where [hweə] **I ad.** ①[疑问副词]在哪里; 往哪里; 从哪里; 在哪一点上: *Where* does he live? 他住在哪里? / *Where* are you going? 你上哪儿去? / *Where* did you get the information? 你这消息从哪来的? / *Where* does it concern us? 这在哪一点上和我们有关系? / I don't know ~ I can find him (或 ~ to find him). 我不知道上哪儿去找他。②[关系副词]在那里; 往那里 ③[连接副词]在…的地方;到…的地方;…的地方: This

is ~ I live. 我就住在这里。/ That's ~ it is. [口]这才说到节骨眼上。(或: 问题就在这里。) **II pron.** 哪里: *Where* do you come *from*? 你是哪里人? / *Where* have you come *to*? 你刚从哪里来? **III n.** 地点: the when and (the) ~ of the event 事件发生的时间和地点 / The ~s and whens are important. 地点和时间是重要的。‖ *Where from?* 打哪儿来? / ~ *it's at* 事情(或形势)的核心所在 / ~ *sb. is at* 某人的本质所在 / *Where to?* 上哪儿去?

whereabout ['hwesərə'baut] **ad. & n.** [罕] = whereabouts

whereabouts I ['hwesərə'bauts] **ad.** [疑问副词]在哪里，靠近哪里: *Whereabouts* did you put it? 你把它放在哪里了? / We must first know ~ the line should be drawn. 我们首先要知道这条界线应划在哪里。**II** ['hwesərə'bauts] [复] [用作单或复] 下落，行踪; 所在: His present ~ is (或 are) unknown. 他目前行止不明。

whereas [hweər'æz] **conj.** ① (公文用语) 有鉴于: *Whereas* the following incidents have occurred …. 有鉴于下列事件已经发生… ② 而，却; 反之: He is ill, ~ I am only a little tired. 他生病了，而我只不过稍觉疲倦罢了

wherefore ['hweəfɔ:] **I ad.** ①[关系副词]为此: the reason ~ sb. went there 某人去那里的原因 ②[古][疑问副词]为什么: *Wherefore* did you go? 你为什么去? **II conj.** 因此: We ran out of kerosene, ~ we used coal. 煤油用完了，因此我们用煤。**III n.** 理由，原因: Never mind the why(s) and ~(s). 不用管什么原因。

whereupon [,hwesərə'pon] **ad.** ①[疑问副词]在什么上面; 在谁身上 ②[关系副词]因此，于是: He did not understand the point, ~ I had to explain further. 他不理解这一点，因此，我只得进一步作了解释。

wherever [hwesər'evə] **ad.** ① 究竟在哪里; 究竟到哪里: *Wherever* did you see such a thing? 你究竟在哪里看到过这样的东西? ② 在任何地方; 到任何地方: explore northward or ~ 朝北或到任何地方勘探 ③[连接副词]无论在哪里; 无论到哪里

wherewith [hwesə'wiθ] **I ad.** ①[关系副词]用以: metal tools ~ to break ground 用来破土的金属工具 ②[古][疑问副词]用什么 **II pron.** 用以…的东西(后接不定式)

wherewithal I [,hwesəwi'ðɔ:l] **ad. & pron.** [古] =wherewith **II** ['hwesəwiðɔ:l] **n.** 必要的资力; 钱财

whet [hwet] **I** (whetted; whetting) **vt.** ①磨，磨快: ~ a knife 把刀磨快 ②刺激，促进; 增强(食欲、欲望等): It'll ~ the appetite. 它会增强食欲。/ His words *whetted* my curiosity. 他的话激起了我的好奇心。**II n.** ①磨 ②开胃物(如酒等); 刺激物 ③[方]时间;一会儿: a long ~ 好久 ‖ '~**stone** n. 磨刀石, 【机】油石

whether ['hweðə] **I** *conj.* 是否: I don't know ～ he will be able to come. 我不知道他是否来得来。/ I wonder ～ I'll catch the last bus (or not). 我不知道是否赶得上末班公共汽车。/ *Whether* it is true remains a question. 到底是真是假还是一个问题。/ He asked ～ I would attend the meeting. 他问我是否将参加那个会。**II** *pron.* [古] ①[疑问代词](两个中的)哪一个 ②[关系代词](两个中的)任何一个 ‖～ … or … ① 是…还是…: It is uncertain ～ he will succeed *or* fail. 他成功还是失败, 还不能肯定。/ Please tell us ～ to go *or* stay. 请告诉我们是去还是留下。②或者…或者…; 不是…就是…: He did it ～ by accident *or* design. 他不知是偶然还是有意做了这事。③不管…还是…: *Whether* he drives *or* (～ he) takes the train, he'll be here on time. 不管他开汽车来还是乘火车来, 他总会准时到达的。/ ～ **or no** 不管怎样, 无论如何: We must stick to our promise ～ *or no*. 不管怎样, 我们必须遵守诺言。

whey [hwei] *n.* 乳清 ‖～**ey** ['hweii] *a.* 似乳清的; 含乳清的 ‖'～**-face** *n.* ①苍白的脸(常指因惊吓引起的)②脸色苍白的人 / '～**-faced** *a.* 脸色苍白的, 失色的

which [hwitʃ] **I** *pron.* ①[疑问代词]哪一个; 哪一些: *Which* of them swims the fastest? 他们之中谁游得最快? / *Which* is heavier, iron or copper? 铁和铜哪一种重? / Tell me ～ is better. 告诉我哪一个较好。/ *Which* of you wish to go with me? 你们中间哪些人想和我一起去? ②[关系代词]那一个; 那一些: Take the sickle ～ is lying on the grindstone. 把磨刀石上的那把镰刀拿去。/ This is the factory of ～ I was speaking. 这就是我所说的那个工厂。/ Strive to keep the fruits of victory ～ the people have won. 努力保卫人民赢得的胜利果实。**II** *a.* ①[疑问形容词]哪一个, 哪一些: *Which* foreign language have you studied? 你学过哪一种外语? ②[关系形容词]这个; 这些: We told him to consult a doctor, ～ advice he took. 我们叫他去看医生, 他接受了这个意见。③[连接形容词]无论哪个; 无论哪些 [一般多用 whichever]

whichever [hwitʃ'evə] **I** *pron.* [关系代词] 无论哪个; 无论哪些: You may choose ～ you want. 你要哪一个, 你就挑哪一个。/ *Whichever* of us fulfils his task first will lend a helping hand to others. 我们之中无论谁先做完自己的工作, 就去帮助别人。**II** *a.* ①[关系形容词]无论哪个; 无论哪些: Take ～ seat you like. 你喜欢哪一个座位, 就挑哪一个。②[连接形容词]无论哪个; 无论哪些: *Whichever* book you borrow, you must return it in a week. 你无论借哪本书, 都必须在一周内归还。

whiff[1] [hwif] **I** *n.* ① (空气、香烟等的)一吸; (风、烟等的)一吹, 一喷: want a ～ of fresh air 需要吸一点新鲜空气 / go off at the first ～ of ether 经醚一喷就失去了知觉 / take a ～ or two 抽几口烟 ②一阵(微弱)的气味: a ～ of garlic 一股大蒜气味 ③轻吹声, 轻喷声 ④[口]小雪茄烟 ⑤[英](一人划的)敞篷小艇 ⑥一点点: There is a ～ of sarcasm in it. 这里面带有一点点讥刺的味道。**II** ❶ *vt.* ①吹送, 吹起: The storm ～*ed* dust into their faces. 风暴把灰尘吹到他们的脸上。②喷出(烟雾等)③吸(烟), 抽(烟)④(棒球中)使(击球员)三次失球而出局 ❷ *vi.* ① 轻吹, 轻拂, 发轻吹声: The wind ～*ed* through the trees. 风轻轻地吹过树林。②喷烟, 喷气 ③(用鼻)嗅气味 ④(棒球击球员)三次失球而退出

whiff[2] [hwif] *n.* 一种比目鱼

whiff[3] [hwif] *vi.* 垂饵于水面钓鱼

while [hwail] **I** *n.* 一会儿, 一段时间: wait (for) a ～ 等一会儿 / rest (for) a ～ 休息一会儿 / after a ～ 过了一会儿 / a short (或 little) ～ ago 方才 / I haven't seen him for a long (或 good) ～. 我好久没有看见他了。/ Where have you been all this ～? 这一阵子你在哪里? **II** *conj.* ①当…的时候, 和…同时: Strike ～ the iron is hot. [谚]打铁趁热。/ be pupils ～ serving as teachers 一面当先生, 一面当学生 ②而, 然而: Motion is absolute ～ stagnation is relative. 运动是绝对的, 而静止是相对的。③虽然; 尽管: *While* I admit his good points, I can see his shortcomings. 尽管我承认他的优点, 我还是看到他的缺点的。④只要 **III** *prep.* [古]到…时候为止, 直到… **IV** *vt.* 消磨 (*away*): ～ the time *away* 消磨时间 ‖ **all the** ～ 一直, 始终 / **at** ～**s** 有时, 间或 / **between** ～**s** 时时, 时常 / **make it worth sb.'s** ～ 酬谢某人; [贬]贿赂某人 / **once in a** ～ 见 **once** / **the** ～ 其时, 当时, (与此)同时: We rowed the boat and sang the ～. 我们一面划船一面唱歌。/ **worth** (**sb.'s**) ～ 值得(某人)(花时间、精力等)的: It isn't *worth* (*your*) ～ going there. (你)到那儿去是不值得的。

whim [hwim] *n.* ①狂想, 幻想, 怪想: be full of ～s and fancies 充满着怪念头 ②突然的念头, 一时的兴致: a passing ～ 一时的兴致所在 / take a ～ for doing sth. 忽然想起要做某事 ③[矿]绞盘, (提升用的)绞绳滚筒: a horse ～ 马拉绞盘 ‖ '～**-wham** *n.* ①古怪的小装饰品(或服装)②奇想, 怪念头 ③[复]发酒狂; 精神不安

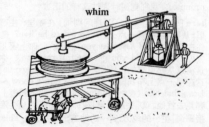

whim

whimper ['hwimpə] I ❶ *vi.* ①吸泣,呜咽 ②发抱怨声 ❷ *vt.* 吸泣地说,呜咽地说 II *n.* ①吸泣声,呜咽声 ②牢骚,怨声 ‖~**er** ['hwimpərə] *n.* 吸泣者,呜咽者;抱怨者 / ~**ingly** ['hwimpəriŋli] *ad.*

whimsy ['hwimzi] *n.* ① 奇想,怪念头 ②(尤指写作或艺术上的)古怪的手法;奇趣 ‖~**-whamsy** ['hwimzi,hwæmzi] *n.* 奇想,怪念头

whine [hwain] I ❶ *vi.* ①(狗等)发哀鸣声;(汽笛、飞行中的炮弹等)发鸣鸣声 ②哀诉 ③嘀咕,发牢骚 (*about*) ❷ *vt.* 哀诉;嘀咕地说 (*out*) ‖ *n.* ①哀鸣声;鸣鸣声 ②哀诉;牢骚 ‖~**r** *n.* 哀鸣者;哀诉者;嘀咕者 / **whiningly** *ad.* 哀鸣地;嘀咕地

whinny ['hwini] I ❶ *vi.* (马)嘶(指表示高兴的一种低微和缓的嘶声) ❷ *vt.* 带嘶声地说 II *n.* 马嘶;嘶声

whip [hwip] I (whipped; whipping) ❶ *vt.* ①鞭笞抽打;(似鞭子般地)打击: ~ a horse on 策马前进 / ~ a top 抽陀螺 / The rain was *whipping* the pavement. 雨打着人行道。②搅打,把…打起泡沫: ~ eggs 打蛋 / *whipped* cream 搅奶油 ③激起;煽动: The storm *whipped up* powerful waves. 暴风雨激起巨浪。④(为求统一步调等)集合,纠合(团体的成员) ⑤(以尖锐的语言)攻击 ⑥用细绳缠绕加固(绳子或钓竿);紧绕(绳等)于某物上;包缝(布边等) ⑦反复投钓丝于(河)中钓鱼 ⑧突然拿取(或移动): ~ *off* one's sweater 一下子把绒衫脱掉 / ~ *out* a knife 突然拔出刀来 ⑨ 仓促制成;[口] 很快地烧煮(食物) (*up*): ~ *up* a sketch 匆匆完成一幅速写 ⑩[俚]胜过,击败 ⑪【海】(用绳通过小滑轮)将…曳起 ❷ *vi.* ①抽打;拍击: Flags are *whipping* in the wind. 旗在风中拍拍作响。②急走,急移;突然行动: ~ down the stairs 急急地跑下楼梯 / ~ away to a certain place 突然去某地 ③急速地投竿钓鱼 II *n.* ①鞭子: wield a ~ 挥鞭 ②执鞭者;赶马车者;帮猎人赶猎狗的人(也作 whipper-in) ③抽打;一挥: with a ~ of one's left hand 左手一挥 ④(厨房中用的)搅拌器 ⑤用搅奶油(或其他搅打成的食品)制成的餐后甜食 ⑥[英]政党的组织秘书(有维持纪律及要求该党议员出席议会讨论及表决之权): the ministerial (或 government) ~ 执政党议员首领 / the opposition ~ 在野党议员首领 ⑦[英][常作 W-]组织秘书发给本党议员要求出席辩论和投票的命令: a three-line *Whip* 要求出席议会的紧急命令;要求支持的紧急呼吁 ⑧迅速转动的机件;风车翼 ⑨小滑轮吊车 ⑩(似鞭子一样的)易弯性,柔韧性 ‖~ *a fault out of sb.* 见 **fault** / ~ *and spur* 快马加鞭,以最快的速度,火急地 / ~ ①用鞭驱赶(猎犬)使不散去 ② 集合(议员等)赴会 / ~ *off* ①用鞭驱赶(猎犬)使散去 ②匆忙地带领…而去 / ~ *the devil round the stump* (或 *post*) 见 **devil** / ~ *together* ①用鞭驱(猎犬)使集拢 ②纠集(议会中的同党) ‖~**like** *a.* 鞭子似的 ‖~**-and-'derry** *n.* (滑轮)简易起重机 / '~**cord** *n.* ①鞭绳 ②马裤呢 ③一种肠线 / '~**crack** *n.* 抽响鞭;抽鞭声 / '~**-,cracker** *n.* 抽响鞭的人,马戏团驯兽人;[喻]有权威的人 / ~ **crane** 动臂起重机 / '~**gin** *n.* 简易起重机的滑轮 / ~ **hand** ①拿鞭子的手 ②优势;主动地位: have the ~ **hand** 占优势,处于支配地位 / '~**lash** *n.* ①鞭子顶端的短绳 ②鞭打;(鞭笞般的)击打 ③(乘坐汽车被撞引起的)头部受伤 (=~lash injury) / '~**round** *n.* [主英]捐款呼吁书;募捐 / '~**saw** *n.* ①狭边(钩齿)粗木锯 ②双人横切锯 / ~ **saw** *vt.* ①用狭边钩齿粗木锯(或双人横切锯)锯 ②(扑克赌博中两人串通着)击败,欺骗 / ~ **snake** (产于亚洲及南美洲的)一种无毒的蛇 / ~ **stall** 【空】(由于垂直上升太快操纵杆后拉过多形成完全失速而引起的)机头急坠失速/ '~**stitch** *vt.* 包缝(布边等) *n.* ①包缝针迹,锁缝针迹 ②一会儿,一瞬息

whipping ['hwipiŋ] *n.* ①鞭打;严惩 ②用来缚扎(或抽打)的绳索 ③包缝,锁缝 ④搅打 ‖~ **boy** ①(旧时)陪王子读书时代他受罚的少年 ②代人受罪者 / ~ **post** 绑缚受鞭笞者的柱子 / ~ **top** 用鞭抽的陀螺

whir [hwə:] I (whirred; whirring ['hwə:riŋ]) ❶ *vi.* 呼呼作声地飞(或转);作呼呼声: A bird *whirred* past. 一只鸟呼地一声飞过。❷ *vt.* 使呼呼地飞(或转);带走: The car *whirred* him away. 汽车呼地一声把他载走。II *n.* ①(疾飞或急转而产生的)呼呼声,飕飕声: the ~ of wheels (propellers) 车轮(螺旋桨)的呼呼声 ②匆忙;纷乱;熙攘

whirl [hwə:l] I ❶ *vt.* ① 使回旋;使旋转;使急转 ②卷走;旋风似地急速带走: The car ~ed him down the bridge. 汽车载着他疾驰下桥。❷ *vi.* ①回旋;急转;急转: The leaves ~ed in the wind. 树叶在风中回旋。/ ~ about to the door 急忙转向门去 ②急走;飞跑: The car ~ed out of sight. 汽车很快地开得不见了。③发晕;变混乱: My head is ~ing. 我的头在发晕。II *n.* ①回旋旋转;急转 ②旋转物 ③接连的活动;繁忙: in a ~ of business 事务繁忙时 ④眩晕;混乱: His brain was in a ~. 他的头脑一片混乱。⑤尝试,小试: take a ~ at that kind of life 试一试那种生活 ‖*the ~ of society* 社交界的忙碌应酬 ‖~**about** *n.* 旋转;盘旋 / '~**pool** *n.* ①旋涡;(旋涡般的)强烈运动: be drawn into a ~pool 被卷入旋涡 ②混乱,纷乱

whirlwind ['hwə:lwind] *n.* ①旋风;旋流 ②猛烈的势力;破坏性的事物 ‖*ride the ~* (天使)驾御旋风;[喻]叱咤风云 / *sow the wind and reap the ~* 见 **wind**¹

whisk [hwisk] I ❶ *vt.* ①掸,拂: ~ away the dust 掸去灰尘 / ~ off the crumbs 拂去面包屑 ②挥动: The cow ~ed her tail. 母牛挥动它的尾巴。③[英]搅;打(蛋、乳酪等)成泡沫 ④ 突然移动;急送;突然带走: ~ a book off 突然拿走一本书

❷ *vi.* 飞奔,疾过: ～ upstairs 飞步上楼 / The mouse ～ed into its hole. 老鼠飞窜入洞。 **II** *n.* ①撑,拂 ②小笤帚,掸帚 ③飞奔;急取 ④打蛋器 ‖～ **broom** 小笤帚,掸帚

whisker ['hwiskə] *n.* ①扫拂者; 疾行者; 掸帚 ②(一根)须,(动物的)须 ③[复]连鬓胡子,颊须,髯;[古]小胡子 ④细丝,似须物 ⑤[复][美俚]腮帮子,颚,下巴颏 ⑥[复][美俚]上了年纪的人 ⑦[Whiskers][美俚]美国政府; 美国政府的法律执行官员

whisky ['hwiski] *n.* 一种轻便马车

whisper ['hwispə] **I** *vi.* ①低语,耳语,私语: ～ about sth. 密谈某事 / ～ to sb. 对某人窃窃耳语 ②(树木等)发沙沙声; (风)发飒飒声 ❷ *vt.* 低声地讲; 私下说: ～ a story 低声讲故事 / It is ～ed that.... 有人私下说…(或:据人暗中传说…) **II** *n.* ①低语,耳语; 私语: speak in a ～ (或 in ～s) 低声说话 ②谣传; 暗示; 秘密话 ③沙沙声; 飒飒声 ‖*in a pig's ～* [俚]低声地; 顷刻间 ‖～**er** ['hwispərə] *n.* 低语者,窃窃私语的人; 传播谣言的人

whist[1] [hwist] **I** *int.* 嘘! 静! **II** *a.* 静的,不作声的

whist[2] [hwist] *n.* 惠斯特(类似桥牌的一种牌戏)

whistle ['hwisl] **I** *n.* ①口哨,笛;汽笛;哨子: blow a ～ 吹口哨 / a penny ～ 六孔小锡笛 / a police ～ 警笛 ②口哨声; 笛声;汽笛声;哨子声 ③(兽)啸叫声; (鸟)啭鸣声; 风啸声 ④吹响(或吹笛)发出的信号 ⑤喉[只用于习语 wet one's (或 the) ～ 中] **II** ❶ *vi.* ①吹口哨; 鸣笛; 吹哨子: The train ～d. 火车鸣笛。 ②(兽)啸叫; (鸟)啭鸣; (风)啸; (子弹)发嗖嗖声: The wind ～d past. 风嗖嗖吹过。 ③吹口哨(或笛)召唤(或通知): ～ to a dog 吹口哨唤狗 / ～ for a taxi 吹口哨召出租汽车 ❷ *vt.* ①吹口哨(或笛)召唤(或通知): ～ a dog back 吹口哨叫狗回来 ②用口哨吹奏(曲调等) ③使嗖啸声行进: ～ a shot over sb.'s head 使子弹在某人头上呼啸而过 ‖*as clean as a ～* 洁净; 光滑 / *blow the ～ (on)* [美俚] ①告发(…); 揭发(…) ②(使)停下来 / *let sb. go ～* 不顾某人的愿望 / *may ～ for it* 空想, 徒然希望 / *pay (dear) for one's ～* 出高价买无价值的小东西; 由于一时兴致而付很大的代价; 得不偿失 / *wet one's (或 the) ～* 润喉; 喝酒 / *～ down the wind* 见 wind[1] / *～ for a wind* 见 wind[1] / *～ in the dark* 给自己壮胆 / *worth the ～* 值得邀请的; 值得注意的 ‖～**able** *a.* 可口吹的: a ～**able** tune 可用口哨吹奏的曲子 / ～**r** *n.* ①吹哨(或笛)的人; 发啸声的东西(或动物) ②喘气的马 ③[动]白颊兔; 北美大土拨鼠 ④[无](由于闪电造成的)啸声干扰 ‖'**~,blower** *n.* [美](大公司等内部)起来揭发腐败内幕的雇员 / '**~-stop** *n.* ①(火车站,言号之停站的铁路沿线的)小镇, 小村落 ②[美](尤指候选人作竞选旅行时在列车站台上的)短暂逗留 *vi.* 旅行(尤指竞选中向各小村镇作多次短暂的逗留)

whit [hwit] *n.* [多用于否定句中]一点点; 丝毫: not care a ～ 毫不介意 / There's not a (或 no) ～ of truth in the statement. 这声明里没有丝毫的真实性。

white [hwait] **I** *a.* ①白的; 苍白的: a ～ shirt 白衬衫 / ～ pigment 白色颜料 / a dress ～ from many washings 由于洗得多而发白的衣服 / lips (a face) ～ with terror 吓得发白的嘴唇(脸色) ②白种(人)的: a ～ man 白(种)人 ③(政治上)白色的,反革命的: the ～ terror 白色恐怖 / a ～ area 白区 / the ～ army 白军 ④空白的, 没有写过字(或印刷过)的 ⑤清白的, 纯洁的; 善意的 ⑥[俚]正直的,公正的; 诚实的, 可靠的 ⑦幸运的,吉利的: a ～ day 吉日 ‖～ *alkali* 【化】白苏打 / a ～ *alloy* 假银 / a ～ *ant* 白蚁 / ～ *arsenic* 【化】砒霜,三氧化二砷 / ～ *(blood) cell* 【解】白血球, 白(血)细胞 / a ～ *book* 白皮书(某些国家政府发表的有关政治、外交问题的文件) / a ～ *Christmas* 有雪的圣诞节 / ～ *coal* 水力 / ～ *coffee* 加牛奶的咖啡 / ～ *corpuscle* =～ (blood) cell / ～ *crops* 白谷(指成熟后变白的大麦、小麦等) / ～ *dwarf* 【天】白矮星 / a ～ *ensign* 英国皇家海军旗 / a ～ *flag* (用于表示投降的)白旗, 休战旗 / ～ *hands* (不从事劳动的)雪白的手; 洁白,诚实 / a ～ *hope* [美](有足够把握赢得冠军的)白种拳击选手; 足以为某一团体(或城镇)带来荣誉的人 / ～ *horse* 白马 / a ～ *mule* [美] ～ *horses* 白帽浪(波峰有白色泡沫的海浪) / ～ *iron* 白铁,马口铁 / a ～ *lie* 无恶意的谎言 / ～ *light* 【物】白光; 公正无私的裁判 / ～ *lime* 熟石灰 / ～ *magic* 戏法,魔术 / ～ *meat* 白肉(指禽类的胸部和翅膀等处的肉) / a ～ *metal* 白色金属; 白铜(以铅、锑)为基的合金; 假银 / ～ *money* [美俚]银币 / ～ *mule* [美俚]酒 / a ～ *night* 白夜; 不眠之夜 / a ～ *paper* [英]白皮书(在重要性和完整性方面略低于 ～ book 或 blue book) / ～ *plague* (肺)结核病 / ～ *rage* 震怒 / ～ *rent* 锡矿工人所纳的税[用银币支付的租金 / *White Russia* 白俄罗斯[苏联](=Byelorussia) / *White Russians* 白俄罗斯人[苏联](=Byelorussia) / a ～ *sale* 白布的销售 / a ～ *slave* [美俚]被迫(或被骗)为娼者 / ～ *squall* 【气】无形飑 / a ～ *war* 不流血的战争; 经济竞争 / ～ *wax* 白蜡 / the ～ *way* 白光大街(城市里灯光灿烂的商业区或剧场区) / ～ *wine* 白葡萄酒 / a ～ *witch* 做善事的女巫 **II** *n.* ①白色; 洁白: be dressed in ～ 身穿白衣 ②白种人 ③眼白 ④蛋白 ⑤精白面粉; 白酒; 白色颜料 ⑥白毛动物(如白马或白猪) ⑦[复]【医】白带 ⑧(书写或印刷留下的)空白处 ⑨白蝶 ‖a ～ *elephant* 见 elephant / *bleed ～* 见 bleed / *call ～ black* (或 *call black ～*) 颠倒黑白 / *days marked with a ～ stone* 幸福的日子 / *put on* (或 *stand in*) a ～ *sheet* 见 sheet / ～ *as a sheet* 苍白如纸 ‖～**d** *a.* 刷白的; 弄白的; 漂白的 / ～**ness** *n.* 白; 苍白; 洁白 ‖～ *alert* (空袭)解除警报 / '～**bait** *n.* 欧洲小鲱鱼 / '～**cap** *n.* ①[复]白帽浪(波峰有白色

泡沫的海浪) ②[W-](美国种族主义分子的暴力组织)白帽队队员 / ～ **chip** ①(扑克牌戏中的)白色筹码 ②价值微小的东西(或数量) / '～,**collar** *a.* 白领阶层的(指一般不从事体力劳动的教师、机关职员等): ～-*collar* workers 脑力工作者 / ～-*collar* jobs 脑力工作,文职 / ～ **goods** ①日用漂白织物(指被褥内衣等) ②大型家庭用具(指冰箱、火炉等) / '**White'hall** *n.* 白厅(伦敦的一条街道,英国政府机关所在地); 英国政府 / '～-**'handed** *a.* ①两手雪白的; 不从事劳动的 ②清白的,老实的 / '～**'headed** *a.* ①白发的; 淡黄色头发的 ②[爱尔兰]得宠的: the ～*headed* boy 宠儿 / ～ **heat** ①[物]白热 ②(感情、行动上)高度紧张的状态 / '～-'**hot** *a.* 白热的; 极热烈的 / **White House** 白宫; 美国政府 / ～ **leather** ①白革,矾鞣革 ②[解]项韧带 / '～-**lipped** *a.* (吓得)嘴唇发白的 / ～ **list** "白名单"(指守法人士,合法机构、可上演节目等的名单,系 black list 黑名单之对) / '～-,**livered** *a.* 懦弱的,胆小的 / '～**out** *n.* ①[气]乳白天空 ②(画家等为反对画展当局等不公平待遇而进行的)用白布遮盖本人作品的抗议 / ～ **room**(制造精密机械等时用的)绝尘室 / '～**smith** *n.* 锡匠; 银匠; 镀银匠 / '～-**thorn** *n.* 【植】山楂 [总称][贬]穷苦白人 / '～**wall** *n.* 侧壁有白圈的汽车轮胎 / '～-**wash** *n.* ①白涂料,刷白用的粉水 ②香粉,雪花膏,油脂 ③粉饰,美化,掩盖真相 *vt.* ①刷白灰水于…,涂白,粉刷 ②粉饰,美化,掩饰 ③彻底击败(对手) / '～**wing** *n.* (穿白色制服的)街道清洁工 / '～**wood** *n.* 白木(如椴属、三角叶杨等的木材)

whither ['hwiðə] **I** *ad.* [古] [现在一般用 where 代替]往何处,向哪里; 无论到哪里: *Whither* did they go? 他们往何处去? / I see ～ your question tends. 我明白你的问题用意何在。 / the place ～ sb. went 某人所去的地方 / Let him go ～ he pleases. 他喜欢到哪里,就让他到哪里。 **II** *n.* 去处: sb.'s whence and ～ 某人的来处和去处 / no ～ [古]没有去处

Whitsun ['hwitsn] *a.* 【宗】降灵节的; 降灵节时期的

whittle ['hwitl] **I ❶** *vt.* ①切,削; 削成 ②削减; 削弱: ～ *down* expenses 削减费用 / ～ *away* a fortune 耗费资财 **❷** *vi.* ①削木头; 削成形 ②(由于烦恼、忧愁等)弄坏身体 **II** *n.* 大刀,屠刀 ‖～**r** *n.* 削者; 削木者

whiz(z) [hwiz] **I** (whizzed; whizzing) *vt. & vi.* ①(使)发飕飕声,(使)飞鸣 ②[美俚]横冲直撞地开(汽车) ③[美俚]扒窃 **II** *n.* ①飕飕声,嘘嘘声 ②[美俚]熟手,能手; 极出色的人(或东西): a ～ at football 足球能手 / a ～ of a camera 极出色的照相机 ③[美俚]合同,契约 ④[美俚]庆祝,庆祝会 ⑤[美俚]扒窃集团的成员 ⑥[美俚](学校的)小测验 ⑦[美俚]力量,精力 ‖～**bang** [美俚] *n.* ①小口径高速度炮的炮弹; 一种速爆烟火 ②自动操纵的飞弹 ③杰出的人; 出色的事

物 ④笑话 *a.* 杰出的,出色的 / ～ **kid** [美俚]神童

who [hu:] *pron.* [主格] ①[疑问代词]谁: *Who* is he (are they)? 他(他们)是谁? / Halt! *Who* goes there? 站住!谁? / I wonder ～ will play in the basketball match. 我不知道这场篮球比赛将上场。 / *Who* (或 Whom) else did you see? 你还见到了谁? / *Who* (或 Whom) are you looking for? 你在找谁? [注意: 本例句和上一例句在口语中常用 who 代替 whom] ②[限制性的关系代词]…的人(有时也用于动物): a man ～ is of value to the people 一个有益于人民的人 / unite with all those ～ can be united 团结一切可以团结的人 / There is somebody (～) wants to see you. 有人找你。 [注意: 在口语中,句中的 ～ 常省略] ③[非限制性的关系代词]他(她); 他(她)们 ④[古][省略先行词的关系代词]…的人: *Who* breaks pays. 损坏者需作赔偿。 ‖ *as* ～ *should say* [古]可谓,可以这样说 ‖～'**s** ① 社团领袖,有影响人士,名人 ②[W-W-]名人录; 人名词典

whoever [hu:(:)'evə] (宾格 whomever; 所有格 whosoever)*pron.* ①[引导名词从句]谁: We wrote a letter of thanks to ～ had helped us. 凡是帮助过我们的,我们都去了谢谢信。 ②[引导副词从句,表示让步]无论谁,不管什么人: *Whoever* did it, I didn't. 不管这事是谁干的,反正不是我干的。 ③ 到底是谁,究竟是谁: *Whoever* told you that? 到底是谁告诉你的?

whole [houl] **I** *a.* ①完整的,齐全的; 无缺的,无损的: a ～ set of *Lu Hsun's Complete Works* 完整的一套《鲁迅全集》 / The dish is still ～ for all the shocks. 尽管受了很多震动,盘子依然无损。 / get off with a ～ skin 安然逃脱 ②整个的; 未经分割的: swallow a date ～ 囫囵吞枣 / a ～ roast duck 烤全鸭 ③纯粹的; 未经减缩(或冲淡)的: ～ milk powder 全脂奶粉 ④[加定冠词 the,或加代词所有格 his 等,修饰单数名词]: 全部的; 全体的; 所有的: the ～ city 全市; 全市人民 / the ～ nation in arms 全民皆兵 / do sth. with one's ～ heart (attention) 全心全意地(专心致志地)做某事 / That's the ～ truth about it. 这就是事情的全部真相。 / the ～ aim of present strategy 当前战略的总目标 / the ～ time 全部时间,自始至终 / the ～ lot 全部(人或物) ⑤[修饰复数名词; 修饰单数名词时,加不定冠词 a]整的,不少于…的;【数】整(数)的,不含分数的: Forty is a ～ number. 四十是整数。 ⑥同父母的: ～ brothers (sisters) 同胞兄弟(姊妹) ⑦[古]健康的,无恙的; (伤)治愈了的,复原了的: They that are ～ need not a physician. 健康的人不需要医生。 **II** *n.* ①全部,全数; 全体; 整个 (*of*) ②整体,(有机的)统一体; 综合: part of the ～ 整体的一部分 / Nature is a ～. 自然界是一个统一体。 ‖ *as a* ～ 总体上: view the situation *as a* ~ 从总体上看形势 / *on the* ~ 总的看来; 大体上, 基本上: Our opinions are *on the* ~ the same. 我们的意见大体上是一样的。/ Not bad *on the* ~. 一般说来还不算坏。‖'~**-ness** *n.* ‖'~**-,colo(u)red** *a.* [主英]纯色的,单色的/ **gale** 狂风 / '~**-'hearted** *a.* 全心全意的 / '~**-'heartedly** *ad.* 全心全意地; 全神贯注地: Serve the people ~*heartedly*. 全心全意地为人民服务。/ '~**-'heartedness** *n.* 全心全意; 全神贯注 / ~ **hog** [俚] ①全部 ②全部地, 彻底地 / '~**-'hogger** *n.* 极端派 / '~**-length** *a.* 全长的; 全身的: a ~*-length* statue 全身塑像 *n.* 全身像 / ~ **meal** (没有去麸的)粗面粉: ~ *meal* bread 粗面粉面包 / ~ **note** [音]全音符(四拍) / ~ **number** [数]整数 / ~ **wheat** 用保存全部营养成分的面粉制的; 保麸的: ~ *wheat* bread 全营养面包 / ~ *wheat* flour 保麸面粉

wholesale ['houlseil] **I** *n.* 批发, 趸售 **II** *a.* ①批发的; 成批售出的: a ~ dealer 批发商 / at ~ prices 按批发价格 ②大批的, 大规模的; 无选择的; 全部的: a ~ slaughter 大屠杀 / "~ westernization" "全盘西化" **III** *ad.* ①以批发方式: sell (buy) ~ 批发售出(购进) ②大批地, 大规模地; 无选择地; 全部地 **IV** ❶ *vi.* ①经营批发业 ②成批售出 ❷ *vt.* 批发(货物), 趸售(货物) ‖*by* ~ ①以批发方式 ②成批地, 大规模地; 无选择地; 全部地: kill off the pests *by* ~ 大规模地消灭害虫 ‖~**r** *n.* 批发商

wholesome ['houlsəm] *a.* ①适合卫生的, 促进健康的: a ~ climate 有益于健康的气候 / ~ food 卫生的食品 ②(道德上)健康的; 有益的: a ~ thought 健康的思想 / ~ advice 忠告 / ~ reading 有益的读物 / a ~ motion picture for children 对儿童有教育意义的电影 ③强健的; 有生气的; 显示身心健康的: a ~ youth 精神饱满的青年 / There was something ~ about his smile. 从他的微笑看来, 他身心很健康。④审慎的; 安全的: It wouldn't be ~ to go there. 到那里去似乎不够安全。‖~**ly** *ad.* / ~**ness** *n.*

wholly ['houlli, 'houli] *ad.* 完全地; 全部, 统统: devote oneself ~ to a task 尽力从事某一工作 / I ~ agree with you. 我完全同意你。/ This place is used ~ for raising livestock. 这地方全部用来养家畜。

whom [hu:m] *pron.* (who 的宾格) ①[疑问代词]谁: *Whom* (或 Who) did you give the letter to? 你把信交给谁了? / *Whom* (或 Who) do you think I met in the street this morning? 你猜我今天早晨在街上遇见了谁? [注意: 在口语中常用 who 代替 whom] ②[关系代词]那些人; 他(她); 他(她)们 ③[古][省略先行词的关系代词]…的人: *Whom*(=Those *whom*)the gods love die young. [谚] 神爱者去世早。(或: 聪明者不长寿。)

whoop [hu:p] **I** *n.* ①(激动、欢乐时的)高喊, 高呼; (战斗中或追击时的)呐喊: ~*s of joy* 欢呼 ②(猫头鹰等的)鸣声 [医]哮喘声; 喘息声 ③小

块, 一点点: not care a ~ 毫不在乎 ④[动]戴胜 (产于欧、亚及北非的羽毛美丽的鸟) **II** ❶ *vi.* ①高喊; 呐喊 ②作枭鸣 ③发喘息声; (百日咳似地)咳嗽 ④大叫大嚷地走过 ❷ *vt.* ①高声说: ~ a welcome 高喊欢迎 ②大声呐喊着追赶 ③哄抬(价格等) **III** *int.* 呵! [表示欢乐、激动等] ‖*not worth a* ~ [口]一文不值, 毫无价值 / *the ~s and jingles* [美俚](过度饮酒后的)震战性谵妄; 极度的神经紧张 / ~ *it* (或 *things*) *up* [美俚] ①欢闹庆祝 ②(为某事或某人)大事宣扬, 捧场 (*for*) ‖~**-de-do(o)** ['hu:pdi'du:] *n.* ①喧闹; 轰动 ②激烈的公开辩论 / ~ **swan** 疣鼻天鹅

whooping ['hu:piŋ] *a.* 高喊声的; (百日咳)咳嗽声似的 ‖~ **cough** [医]百日咳 / ~ **crane** 美洲鹤 (=whooper) / ~ **swan** 疣鼻天鹅

whose [hu:z] *pron.* (who 或 which 的所有格) ①[疑问代词]谁的: *Whose* pen is that? 那是谁的钢笔? / I wonder ~ notebook that is. 我不知道那是谁的笔记本。②[关系代词]那个人的, 那些人的; 他(她)的; 他们(她们)的: Is there anyone here ~ name is Wang Hong? 这儿有叫王红的人吗? / My aunt, ~ photo I showed you yesterday, will come to see us this evening. 我姨妈今晚要来看我们, 她的照片我昨天给你看过。③[关系代词]它的; 它们的(=of which): The building ~ roof (=the roof of which) we can see from here is a hotel. 在我们这儿望得见屋顶的那座房子是一个旅馆。/ a dictionary ~ cover (=the cover of which) has come off 一本封面脱落的词典

why [hwai] **I** *ad.* ①[疑问副词]为什么: *Why* did he go? 他为什么去? / I don't know ~ the meeting was postponed. 我不知道会议为什么延期。/ *Why* turn off the gas? 为什么要把煤气关掉? / *Why* not try again? 为什么不再试一下? / Tell me ~. 告诉我为什么。/ *Why* not? 为什么不? / *Why* so? 为什么这样? ②[关系副词]为什么: The reason ~ he changed his mind is not clear. 他改变主意的原因不清楚。/ This is ~ we started so early. 这是我们那么早出发的原因。**II** *n.* ①原因, 理由: the ~(s) and wherefore(s) 原由 ②难解的问题, 谜 **III** *int.* [表示惊奇、不耐烦、抗议、赞成、犹豫等]: *Why*, what a bruise you have got! 啊唷,你怎么弄了这块青紫伤痕! / *Why*, even a child knows that! 哎呀, 这连小孩子都知道! / *Why*, what's the harm? 嗨, 这有什么害处呢? / *Why*, of course, I'll do it. 噢, 当然罗, 我要做的。/ *Why*, yes, I think so. 对——对的, 我是这样想的。‖*Every* ~ *has a* (或 *its*) *wherefore*. [谚]凡事均有因。

wick[1] [wik] *n.* ①灯芯, 灯带; 烛芯 ②[机](吸)油绳: ~ lubricator 油绳滑润器 ③[医](塞入伤口吸干用的)纱布条

wick[2] [wik] *n.* [常用以构成地名及其他复合词]镇, 村, 区

wicked['wikid] *a.* ①坏的;邪恶的 ②(尤指动物)性情凶恶的: a ～ horse 烈马 ③怀恶意的,刻毒的:have a ～ tongue 说话刻毒 ④令人厌恶的;恶劣的: a ～ odour 恶臭 / ～ winter weather 冬季恶劣的天气 / a ～ headache 剧烈的头痛 ⑤捣蛋的,淘气的: a ～ urchin 顽童 ⑥[美俚]显示高超技艺的: He plays a ～ game of table tennis. 他乒乓打得好极了。‖**~ly** *ad.* **~ness** *n. Wickedness* does not go altogether unrequited. [谚]恶有恶报。

wicker ['wikə] **I** *n.* ①枝条;柳条 ②柳条制品 **II** *a.* ①柳条编制的: a ～ basket 柳条篮 ②装在柳条编织物里的: a ～ flask 装在柳条编织物里的长颈瓶 ‖**~work** *n.* ①编制在一起的柳条 ②柳条制品

wicket ['wikit] *n.* ①(装在正门上或正门边上的)小门;边门;腰门 ②(售票处等的)窗口 ③旋转栅门 ④水闸门 ⑤(板球的)三柱机;两个三柱机之间的球场 ‖*be on a good (sticky)* ～ 处于有利(不利)地位 ‖～ **door, ~ gate** 小门;边门;腰门

wide [waid] **I** *a.* ①宽阔的;宽松的: a ～ river 宽阔的河流 / a highway ten metres ～ 十米宽的公路 / a ～ blouse 宽松的短衫 ②广阔的,广大的;广泛的;(教育等)一般的,非专门化的: be of ～ distribution 分布广 / a ～ difference 很大的差异 / a ～ variety 品种繁多 / a man with ～ interests 兴趣广泛的人 / a ～ hazard a ～ guess 随便猜测 ③充分张开的,开得很大的: stare with ～ eyes 睁大了眼睛注视 ④离目标远的,差得远的: His guess was ～ of the mark. 他猜得完全离了谱。⑤【语】(元音)开的,松的 ⑥[英俚]狡猾的,机警的 **II** *ad.* ①广大地,广阔地:travel far and ～ 到处旅行 ②全部地,充分地;张得很大地: Open your mouth ～. 把嘴张大。/ He stands with legs ～ apart. 他两腿分开站着。③离目标很远地,偏斜地: The arrow fell ～. 箭没有射中。 **III** *n.* [the ～] 广大的世界 ‖*a ～ place in the road* 见 **place** / *be broke to the ～* [俚]一个钱也没有,穷到极点 / ～ **open** ①[口]没有保护的;容易受到攻击(或遭到失败等)的 ②(城市、地区等对非法活动)开绿灯的,取缔不严的 ‖**~ly** *ad.* 广,广泛;远;大大地: be ～*ly* known 名气很大 / differ ～*ly* 大不相同 ‖**'~a'wake** *a.* 完全清醒的;[喻]机警的,警惕的: **'~-'screen** *a.* 宽银幕的: a ～*-screen* film 宽银幕影片 / **'~spread** *a.* 分布广的,流传广的;普遍的

widen ['waidn] ❶ *vt.* 加宽,放宽;扩大: ～ a road 加宽路面 / not ～ the scope of the attack 不扩大打击面 ❷ *vi.* 变宽,变阔;扩大: His interests ～*ed.* 他的兴趣面扩大了。

widow ['widou] **I** *n.* ①寡妇 ②[印](一页开头或末尾)未排足的行 ③(某种牌戏中发在桌面上的)额外一副牌 ④[the ～][俚]香槟酒 **II** *vt.* ①使成寡妇(或鳏夫),使丧偶: a ～*ed* father (mother) 失去了配偶的父亲(母亲) ②[诗]使失去亲密朋友(或爱物) ③[罕]成为…的寡妇 ‖**~hood** *n.* 守寡,居孀 ‖**~ bird** (非洲产的)一种黑色鸟(雄的有长尾) / **~ lady** 寡妇 / **~'s mite** 少而可贵的捐献 / **~'s peak** 额前的 V 形发尖(旧时迷信要早寡) / **~ woman** =～ lady

widower ['widouə] *n.* 鳏夫

width [widθ] *n.* ①宽度,广阔;广博;宽大: a road of great ～ 宽阔的道路 / ～ of views 见识的广博 ②宽度,阔度 ③(某宽度的)一块料子: join two ～s 把两幅料子拼起来 / a ～ of calico 一幅布料

wield [wi:ld] *vt.* ① 挥动 (武器等);使用: ～ a scythe 挥镰 / ～ a facile pen 文笔流畅 ②行使;运用: ～ power 行使权力 / ～ influence (control) 施加影响(控制) ③[方]处理 ‖～ *the sceptre* 见 **sceptre** ‖**~y** *a.* ①易挥动的,易使用的 ②有挥动能力的,有使用能力的

wife [waif] (复 wives [waivz]) *n.* ①妻;已婚妇女: husband and ～ 夫妻 / have a ～ 已娶妻 / one's lawful (或 wedded) ～ 正妻,元配 / a book for young *wives* 给年轻已婚妇女们看的书 ②妇人(尤指没有文化的老妇人) ③[用以构成复合词]…妇,…婆: a house～ 主妇 ‖*old wives' tales* 见 **tale** / *take* (或 *have*) *sb. to* ～ 娶某人为妻 ‖**~hood** *n.* 妻子的身分 / **~less** *a.* 没有妻子的 / **~like, ~ly** *a.* 妻子(般)的;(适于)已婚妇女的

wig [wig] **I** *n.* ①假发 ②骂,叱责 ③[美俚]头发;头;头脑 ④[美俚]知识分子 **II** (wigged; wigging) ❶ *vt.* ①给…装假发 ②[英口]骂,叱责 ③使烦恼;激怒 ④[美俚]使激动;使发狂 (out) ❷ *vi.* [美俚]激动;发狂 (out) ‖*pull* ～*s* 扭打;吵架 / ～*s on the green* ①打架 ②激烈的公开争辩 ‖**wigged** *a.* 戴假发的 / **wigging** *n.* 骂,叱责

wiggle ['wigl] **I** ❶ *vt.* ①摆动;扭动: ～ one's toes 扭动脚趾 ②[英](在船尾用单桨)划 (船) ❷ *vi.* 摆动;扭动 **II** *n.* ①摆动;扭动 ②奶油青豆烧鱼(或蛤蜊) ‖*get a* ～ *on* [美俚]快,赶紧: Better *get a* ～ *on* or we'll be late. 最好快一点,不然我们要迟到了。‖**~r** *n.* ①摆动者;扭动者 ②【动】孑孓 (=wriggler) / **wiggly** *a.* 摆动的;扭动的

wilco ['wilkou] *int.* (无线电通信用语或信号; = will comply) 照办;来电收到即将照办

wild [waild] **I** *a.* ①野生的,野的;不驯服的: a ～ plant 野生植物 / ～ animals 野兽 ②(马、野禽等)易受惊的,难接近的: The deer are rather ～. 鹿是容易受惊的。③(人、部落等)野蛮的,未开化的,原始的 ④荒芜的,荒凉的;无人烟的:cultivate ～ mountain regions 开垦荒芜的山区 / ～ scenery 荒凉的景色 ⑤失去控制的,放荡的,任性的: ～ price fluctuations 行市的狂涨暴跌 / ～ work 不法行为 / a ～ fellow 放荡的家伙 ⑥暴风雨的;狂暴的: a ～ night 暴风雨夜 / a ～ sea 激涛怒海 / ～ cheers 暴风雨般的欢呼 ⑦杂乱的,无秩序的;不切实际的,轻率的;未中目标的:

~ hair 乱蓬蓬的头发 / in ~ disorder 杂乱无章 / ~ times 乱世 / a ~ scheme 轻率的计划 / a ~ guess 乱猜 ⑧狂热的；发怒的；疯狂的；急切的：be ~ with joy 欣喜若狂 / ~ rage 狂怒 / drive sb. ~ 激得某人狂怒 / be ~ about sports 热衷于体育运动 / be ~ to do sth. 渴望做某事 ⑨(牌戏中)百搭的 **II ad.** ①狂暴地；胡乱地；无控制地：shoot ~ 乱射 **III n.** ①荒地，荒野，旷野：turn the ~ into fertile land 把荒地变为良田 ②[the ~s] 未开发的地方：go out into the ~s 到未开发的地方去 ‖**run** ~ 变野蛮；放肆起来 / **the** ~ **men** 见 **man** / **and woolly** [美]粗野的 ‖**~ly** ad. / **~ness** n. ‖~ **duck** 野鸭 / '**~-eyed** a. ①显得暴怒的，狂暴的 ②激进的 / '**~,fire** n. ①(毁灭性的)大火灾；制服不住的野火：spread like ~fire 象野火般迅速传播 / sell like ~fire 销售得很快 ②(旧时海战中用的)燃烧剂 ③鬼火，磷火 ④(无雷的)闪电，电光 ⑤[英俚]极易燃的东西 / ~ **flower** 野花 / '**~fowl** n. 猎鸟(尤指野鸭、野雁等) / ~ **goose** 雁 / ~ **man** ①未开化的人 ②粗野的男子 ③政治上的极端分子 / '**~wood** n. 自然林，原始森林

wilderness ['wildənis] n. ①荒地，荒野，荒芜的地方；(园中)荒芜的一角 ②茫茫一片；大量，无数 (of)：a ~ of waters 一片汪洋 ③混乱的一群，杂乱的一团 ‖**a voice in the** ~ ①荒野里的呼声 ②无人理睬的改革主张 / **wandering in the** ~ (政党)在野的 ‖**~ area** (政府划定为科研或游览用的)保留自然环境面貌的地区

wile [wail] **I** n. [常用复] ①诡计，奸计；骗人的把戏 ②欺骗，欺诈 **II** vt. ①欺骗，诱惑：~ sb. into doing sth. 诱骗某人做某事 ②[while 的误用]消磨，消遣 (away)：~ away the time 消磨时间

wilful ['wilful] a. ①任性的，固执的：a ~ fellow 固执的家伙 ②故意的，存心的：~ distortion of the facts 对事实的故意歪曲 / ~ murder 蓄意的谋杀 ‖**~ly** ad. / **~ness** n.

will [强 wil; 弱 l, wəl, əl] **I** ❶(过去式 would [强 wud; 弱 wəd, əd, d]) (will not 的缩写为 won't [wount]) v. aux. ①[表示单纯的将来，用于第二、三人称。第一人称的单纯将来，英国人用 shall，美国人常用 will 代替。口语中可缩写为 'll] 将要；会：He ~ come back soon. 他很快就将回来了。/ There ~ be another bumper harvest this year. 今年又将获得丰收。/ Press the button and the wheel ~ turn. 按一下电钮，轮子就会转动。/ Will they (you) be here tomorrow? 他们(你们)明天到这儿来吗？/ I won't be back for supper. [美]我不回来吃晚饭了。②[表示意志、意愿、建议]愿，要：We ~ fight on until final victory is won. 我们一定要战斗到赢得最后胜利。/ I have made up my mind to go and go I ~. 我已决定要走就一定要走。/ I ~

do my best to help you. 我愿尽力帮助你。/ She ~ not shove the heavy load on to others. 她不愿把重担子推给别人。/ Will you join our discussion? 你愿参加我们的讨论吗？/ I won't do so. 我不愿这样做。/ Come whenever you ~. 你愿什么时候来就什么时候来。③[表示功能]能，行：This ~ do if there is nothing better. 如果没有更好的，这个也行。/ Each bench ~ seat four persons. 每条凳子能坐四个人。/ The door won't open. 这门打不开。/ A: I want someone to copy it for me. B: Will I do? 甲：我要人帮我把它抄一下。乙：我行吗？④[表示推测]可能，该是：That ~ be the postman at the door, I suppose. 我想门外可能是邮递员。/ He ~ have got home by now. 现在他该到家了。⑤[表示习惯、经常性、倾向性]惯于，总是：He ~ sit for hours reading. 他常常接连坐上几小时看书。/ Boys ~ be boys. 男孩子究竟是男孩子。/ Sometimes the screw ~ work loose. 这只螺钉有时要松开。⑥[表示命令、指示]务必，必须，应：You ~ please do so. 请你照这样办吧。/ You ~ do as I say, at once. 你马上照我的话去做。

❷ (willed; willing) vt. ①意欲，决心要：The work has been finished as he ~ed it. 工作已照他打算的那样完成了。②用意志力使，主观促成：~ oneself to keep awake (或 into keeping awake) 努力使自己醒着 / ~ one's countenance back to composure 尽力使面色恢复镇静 ③立遗嘱言明；遗赠：He ~ed all his books to the city library. 他把所有的书都遗赠给市图书馆。❸ (willed; willing) vi. ①行使意志力；下决心 ②愿意

II n. ①意志，意志力；决心：the ~ of the people 人民的意志 / a man of iron ~ 钢铁般意志的人 / heighten one's ~ to fight 增强战斗意志 / an objective law independent of man's ~ 不以人们意志为转移的客观规律 ②意愿；旨意；目的：good (ill) ~ 好(恶)意 / What is your ~? 你需要什么？(一般用 What do you want?) ③干劲，热情：work with a ~ 起劲地干 / have a ~ that surmounts all difficulties 有克服一切困难的劲头 ④遗嘱：make a ~ 立遗嘱 / leave sb. sth. in one's ~ 在遗嘱中将某物遗赠某人 ‖**against one's** ~ 违背意愿地，违心地：He fell ill and left the construction site against his ~. 他得了病，不得已而离开工地。/ **at one's own sweet** ~ =at ~ / **at** ~ 任意，随意：fire at ~ 【军】自由射击 / **do the** ~ **of** 服从…的意志(或指挥) / **have one's** ~ 达到自己的愿望；自行其是 / **if you** ~ 如果你愿意

那样说的话 / ***of one's (own) free ~*** 出于自愿 / ***one's last ~ and testament*** 【律】遗嘱 / ***take the ~ for the deed*** 事虽未成但仍领其心意 / ***Where there is a ~, there is a way.*** [谚]有志者事竟成。/ ***~ I (he, ye), nill I (he, ye)*** 不管我(他,你)是否愿意; 强迫地 / ***work one's ~ upon sb.*** 把自己的意志强加于某人 ‖**~-less** *a.* ①无意志的, 缺乏毅力的 ②非出于本意的 ③未留下遗嘱的 ‖**'~-'call** *n.* & *a.* (大商店)预订零售部(的) / **'~ˌpower** *n.* 意志力 / **~ to power** ①【哲】(尼采唯心主义哲学的)权力意志 ②支配别人的欲望

willing ['wiliŋ] *a.* 愿意的; 心甘情愿的; 乐意的: be ~ to help others 乐于帮助别人 ‖**~ly** *ad.* / **~ness** *n.*

will-o'-the-wisp ['wiləðwisp] *n.* ①鬼火, 磷火 ②捉摸不定的东西(或人); 迷惑人的事物

willow[1] ['wilou] **I** *n.* ①柳, 柳树; 柳木: a weeping ~ 垂柳 ②柳木制品; 板球(或棒球)的球棒: handle the ~ 用球棒打球 **II** *a.* ①柳(树)的; 长满柳树的 ②柳木制的 ‖***wear the ~*** 服丧, 戴孝; 痛失心爱的人, 悲悼爱人的逝世(昔时佩柳叶花圈以示哀悼) ‖**~y** *a.* ①柳树多的 ②柳树似的; 易弯的; 苗条的 ‖**~ pattern** (中国瓷器的)白底蓝色柳树图案 / **'~ware** *n.* [总称]白底蓝色柳树图案的瓷器餐具

willow[2] ['wilou] **I** *vt.* 【纺】(用威罗机)清理(棉花等纤维材料) **II** *n.* 威罗机

willy-nilly ['wili'nili] **I** *ad.* 不管愿不愿意, 强迫地 **II** *a.* ①不管愿不愿意的, 强迫的 ②犹豫不决的

willy-willy ['wiliˌwili] *n.* 【气】畏来风(见于澳大利亚西部)

wilt [wilt] **I** *vi.* & *vt.* ①(使)枯萎, (使)雕残 ②(使)衰弱, (使)憔悴 ③(使)畏缩 **II** *n.* ①枯萎, 雕残 ②衰弱, 憔悴 ③【植】萎蔫病

wily ['waili] *a.* 诡计多端的; 狡猾的

win[1] [win] **I** (won [wʌn]; winning) ❶ *vi.* ①获胜, 赢: We've *won*! 我们胜利了! / ~ by a length 以一马(或艇)身长的距离获胜 ②(经过努力)成功, 成为, 达到: ~ through all difficulties 克服了种种困难取得成功 / ~ free (或 clear) 挣脱; 摆脱困境 / ~ to shore 终于抵岸 ③(逐渐)吸引, 影响 (*on, upon*): ~ *upon* sb. by degrees 逐渐影响某人 ❷ *vt.* ①赢得; 获得; 博得: ~ victory 赢得胜利 / ~ a prize 获奖 / ~ a race 在赛跑中获胜 / ~ a fortress 夺得要塞 / ~ honour for . . . 为…争光 / ~ sympathy and support 博得同情和支持 / ~ £5 *of* (或[口] *off*) sb. 从某人那里赢得五英镑 ②打胜, 打赢 ③(经努力)到达, 达到: ~ the shore 终于抵岸 / ~ the summit 攀上高峰 ④争取; 说服: You have *won* me. 你把我说服了。/ ~ *over* the masses 争取群众 / We have *won* him (*over*) to our side. 我们把他争取过来了。/ ~ sb. to consent 说服某人同意 ⑤【矿】采(矿); 从矿石中提炼(金属); 为采矿而准备(竖井等) **II** *n.* ①胜利, 赢: have three ~*s* and no defeats 三战三胜 / another ~ 又一次得胜 ②赢得物, 收益 ‖***~ one's spurs*** 见 **spur** / ***~ one's way*** 见 **way** / ***~ the day*** 打胜 / ***~ the field*** 见 **field** / ***~ the toss*** 见 **toss** / ***~ up*** 上马; 攀登; 起立

win[2] [win] *vt.* [英方]把(草等)吹干(或烘干)

wince [wins] *vi.* & *n.* (因疼痛等)畏缩, 退缩

winch [wintʃ] **I** *n.* 绞车, 起货机; 曲柄 **II** *vt.* 用绞车提升(或拖); 用起货机吊起(货物等) ‖**~man** ['wintʃmən] *n.* 绞车手

wind[1] [wind] **I** *n.* ①风: a gust of ~ 一阵风 / a constant (variable) ~ 风向稳定(不定)的风 / fair (contrary) ~*s* 顺(逆)风 / There is much ~ today. 今天风很大。/ The ~ is rising (falling). 风刮起来(平息下去)了。/ advance against the ~*s* and the waves 迎着风浪前进 ②气息; 呼吸; 胸口, 心窝: stop to recover (或 get back) one's ~ 停下来喘一口气 ③气味; [喻]风声, 传说: take (或 get) ~ 被谣传 ④破坏性的力量(或影响); 时尚, 趋势: the ~*s* of popular opinion 公众舆论的影响 ⑤[复](四个)基本方位; 风吹来的方向: from the four ~*s* 从四面八方 ⑥空话, 空谈; 虚无的东西; 自负: be puffed up with ~ 自高自大 ⑦肠气(指屁) ⑧压缩空气(或气体) ⑨[the ~]管乐器; [复]管乐器演奏者 **II** ❶ *vt.* ①使通风; 使吹干 ②嗅出: The hounds ~*ed* the fox. 猎狗嗅出了狐狸。③使喘气: The run ~*ed* him. 这阵跑步使他喘气。④使(马等)休息一下喘口气: The soldiers stopped to ~ their horses. 士兵们停止前进, 让马匹休息一下。⑤调整(管乐器)的进气 ❷ *vi.* ①嗅出猎物 ②[方]休息一下喘口气 ‖***a free ~*** 顺风 / ***before the ~*** 顺风 / ***between ~ and water*** ①在船的水线处 ②[喻]在最易受打击的地方, 在要害处 / ***break ~*** 放屁 / ***broken ~*** (指马等的)喘气 / ***burn the ~*** 飞速前进 / ***cast*** (或 ***fling, throw***) ***. . . to the ~s*** 不再考虑…, 完全不顾… / ***down (the) ~*** 顺着风 / ***eat the ~ out of*** 【海】占(他船)的上风 / ***find out*** (或 ***see***) ***how the ~ blows*** (或 ***lies***) 看风向; 观望形势 / ***get*** (或 ***have***) ***the ~ up*** [俚]受惊吓; 担心害怕 / ***get ~ of*** 得到…的风声; 获得…的线索 / ***go like the ~*** 飞驰 / ***haul upon the ~*** 【海】抢风驶船 / ***have a good (bad) ~*** 气长(短) / ***have . . . in the ~*** 得到…的线索 / ***have one's ~ taken*** 被打中胸口而瘫倒 / ***have*** (或 ***gain***) ***the ~ of*** 【海】占(他船)的上风; 对…占优势地位; 得到…的线索 / ***head ~*** 顶风 / ***high ~*** 疾风 / ***in the teeth of the ~*** (或 ***in the ~'s eye*** 或 ***in the eye of the ~***) 【海】逆着风 / ***in the ~*** 将要发生; (秘密地)在进行: There's something *in the* ~. 好象有什么事情要发生了。/ ***into the ~*** 迎风 / ***It's an ill ~ that blows nobody (any) good.*** [谚]使人人遭殃的风才是恶风。(指此失则彼得, 没有使所有的人都受害的坏事) / ***kick the ~*** 被绞死 / ***let***

sth. go down the ~ 抛弃某物 / *lose one's* ~ 喘气 / *off the* ~ [海]背着风;顺着风 / *on the* ~ 几乎顶风 / *put the* ~ *up sb.* [俚]使某人害怕 / *raise the* ~ [喻]筹款 / *run before the* ~ 【海】顺风行驶 / *sail against the* ~ ①几乎顶风地航行 ②在困难情况下工作 / *sail before the* ~ ①顺风航行 ②取得成功;发迹 / *sail near* (或 *close to*) *the* ~ ①迎风行航行 ②几乎犯法;几乎行动失检 / *second* ~ 喘气后恢复正常的呼吸 / *Sits the* ~ *there?* 形势是这样吗? / *slip one's* ~ 断气,死 / *sound in* ~ *and limb* [口]身体健全的 / *sow the* ~ *and reap the whirlwind* 干坏事必将遭到加倍报应,恶有恶报 / *take* (或 *get*) *the* ~ *of* 占(他人)的上风 / *take the* ~ *out of sb.'s sails* 抢先说(或做)以阻止某人说(或做);先发制人地占某人的上风;突然夺去某人的优势 / *temper the* ~ *to the shorn lamb* 以温和手段对待弱者;体谅不幸者 / *three sheets in* (或 *to*) *the* ~ 见 *sheet* / *touch the* ~ 【海】顺风行航行 / *under the* ~ 在背风处 / *up the* ~ 顶着风 / *whistle down the* ~ ①放弃 ②白费唇舌 ③诽谤 / *whistle for a* ~ 吹口哨求风(过去水手的一种迷信) ‖**~less** *a.* 无风的,平静的 ‖**~bag** *n.* 空谈者,夸夸其谈者;[复][美俚]肺 / '**~,baggary** *n.* 空谈,夸夸其谈 / '**~-borne** *a.* (花粉等)风传送的 / '**~bound** *a.* 【海】因逆风(或疾风)不能航行的 / '**~break** *n.* 防风林;防风篱 / ,**breaker** *n.* (源自商标名)(皮或呢制)防风外衣 / '**~-,broken** *a.* (马等)呼吸器官有病的;喘气的 / '**~,cheater** *n.* [英]防风上衣 / ~ **colic** 肠气胀痛 / ~ **cone** =~ sock / ~ **egg** 未受精的蛋 / '**~fall** *n.* ①被风吹落的果实(或刮倒的树木) ②[喻]意外的收获,横财 / '**~,flower** *n.* 银莲花属植物 / ~ **furnace** 【冶】风炉 / '**~gall** *n.* (马脚踝的)关节软瘤 / ~ **gap** 【地】风口,风坳 / **ga(u)ge** 风速器 / '**~,hover** *n.* [英]【动】茶隼 / ~ **instrument** 管乐器 / '**~,jammer** *n.* 帆船;帆船船员;[俚]吹牛的人 / '**~mill** *n.* ①风车

windmill

[美俚]直升飞机 ②假想的对手;假想的邪恶: fight (或 tilt at) ~*mills* 与假想的对手作战;企图战胜想象中的邪恶 / '**~pipe** *n.* 气管 / '**~-,pollinated** *a.* 【植】风媒传粉的 / '**~proof** *a.* 防风的 / '**~row** *n.* 摊成行吹干的谷物(或草等) ②风吹拢的一行灰土(或树叶等) ③堆积在路旁的一长列筑路材料;堆 ④种甘蔗时在田里挖

的深沟;畦 *vt.* ①(风等)把…吹堆成行 ②在深沟里种(甘蔗) / '**~sail** *n.* (船)帆布通风筒 / ~ **scale** 【气】风级 / '**~screen** *n.* [英](汽车等的)挡风玻璃(屏) / '**~,shaken** *a.* (木头等)被狂风吹裂的 / '**~shield** *n.* [美] =~screen / ~ **sleeve** =~ sock / ~ **sock** 风(向)袋 / '**~spout** *n.* 旋风 / '**~storm** *n.* 风暴 / '**~swept** *a.* 当风的;(山坡等)被强风吹光的 / ~ **tee** 【气】风向齿 / ~ **tight** *a.* 不透风的,不通风的 / ~ **tunnel** 【空】风洞 / ~ **vane** 风向标

wind² [waind] (winded 或 wound [waund]) ❶ *vt.* 吹(号角等);用号角发出(信号等)· ~ a horn 吹号角 ❷ *vi.* 吹响号角

wind³ [waind] I (wound [waund] 或 winded) ❶ *vt.* ①绕,缠绕,卷绕: ~ (up) wool into a ball 把毛线绕成一团 ②包,裹;抱: He wound a heavy scarf around his neck. 他用一条厚围巾裹着头颈。/ She wound the child in her arms. 她抱着孩子。③(用绞车等)绞起,吊起;用绞车拖(船等): ~ up ore from a mine 用绞车从矿里吊出矿石 ④上紧…的发条: ~ a clock (watch) 上钟(表) / ~ down the car window 把汽车的窗子摇下 ⑤绕…而曲前进;使(船)转向(或掉头): The river ~s the valley. 这条河蜿蜒流过山谷。⑥使弯曲;使弯曲前进;通过巧妙手法使…: ~ oneself (或 one's way) *into* sb.'s confidence 用巧妙的手法获得某人的信任 ❷ *vi.* ①弯曲前进,迂回 ②卷曲;缠绕: A snake ~s round a branch. 蛇缠绕在树枝上。③(船停泊时)掉转方向 II *n.* ①缠绕装置;绞车 ②弯曲;卷绕;卷法,绕法 ③一圈,一盘,一转 ‖~ **off** 卷开,缠开 / ~ **sb. round one's** (little) **finger** 见 **finger** / ~ **up** ①卷紧,卷拢 ②上紧…的发条 ③[常用被动语态]使振奋起来;使紧张: be wound up into a high pitch of excitement 变得极度兴奋 ④结束;【商】(公司等)结业 ⑤(棒球中)掷球前挥舞(手臂) ‖**~er** *n.* ①【纺】络纱工;络筒机;络纱机 ②开发条的钥匙 ③【建】(楼梯)的斜级

windage ['windidʒ] *n.* ①游隙(炮管内径和炮弹外径的差率);炮孔直径与炮弹直径的差率 ②[军]风力影响;风力修正量 ③(子弹等飞过而引起的)气流 ④船身的对风面

winding ['waindiŋ] I *n.* ①卷绕着的线(或绳索等);【电】绕组,线圈 ②(卷绕着的)一圈,一转 ③绕,卷绕;卷法,绕法: shunt ~ 【电】并激绕法 ④弯曲,卷曲;弯曲的路(或路线): a board in ~ 卷曲的板 ⑤迂回曲折的方法(或行为) ⑥【矿】提升,卷扬 II *a.* ①卷绕的;弯曲的;曲折的;迂回的: a ~ staircase 盘旋式楼梯 ‖**~ly** *ad.* ‖**~ engine** 卷扬机 / '**~-sheet** *n.* 裹尸布 / '**~-'up** *n.* 【商】(公司等的)结业

windlass ['windləs] I *n.* 起锚机;卷扬机 II *vt.* (用起锚机等)吊起

window ['windou] I *n.* ①窗子,窗户,窗口;窗孔;窗玻璃;橱窗: The ~ looks out towards the river. 窗子临河。/ look out of the ~ 从窗口

看出去 / display goods in the ~s 把商品放在橱窗里陈列 ②窗状开口; (开窗信封上的)透明纸窗: ~ of tube【无】荧光屏 ③[复][美俚]眼镜 ④【无】(反雷达的)金属干扰带; 触发脉冲 ⑤(为完成特定任务而发射火箭或宇宙飞船时的)发射时限 ⑥(宇宙飞船重返大气层时必须通过的)大气层边缘通过区 ‖a bay (或 window) / a blank (或 blind, dead, false) ~ 假窗, 盲窗 / a casement ~ 竖铰链窗 / a dormer ~ 屋顶窗, 老虎窗 / a French ~ 落地长窗 / a lattice ~ 格构窗, 花格窗 / an oriel ~ 凸肚窗 / a sash ~ 框格窗 II vt. 给…开(或装)窗 ‖have all one's goods in the ~ 见 goods / out (of) the ~ [美俚] ①失去了的; 毁灭了的; 名誉扫地的; 彻底破产了的 ②(商品)一陈列出去就被抢购一空的 ‖~ed a. 有窗的 / ~less a.无窗的 ‖~ bar 窗门 / ~ blind 遮光帘 / '~-box n.【建】窗锤箱 ②窗槛花箱 / ~ curtain 窗帘 / ~ dressing ①(商店的)橱窗布置 ②摆阔, 粉饰门面; 炫耀自己 / ~ envelope 开窗信封(信封正面有透明纸框可看见收信人地址) / ~ frame 窗框 / '~pane n. 窗玻璃 / ~ sash 窗框; 上下开关的窗扇 / ~ screen 纱窗 / ~ shade 遮光帘 / '~-shop vi. (在街上)溜达着看橱窗 / '~-,shopper n. 溜达着看橱窗的人 / '~sill n. 窗槛;【建】窗盘

windy ['windi] a. ①有风的, 风大的: a ~ day 风大的日子 / a ~ downpour 狂风暴雨 / the ~ side of the house 屋子向风的一面 ②狂风似的; 猛烈的, 狂暴的: ~ anger 狂怒 ③由风(或压缩空气)产生的 ④生肠气的; 腹胀的, 气胀的 ⑤空谈的, 吹牛的, 夸夸其谈的: a ~ speaker 夸夸其谈的人 ⑥虚无的, 无形的 ⑦[俚]被吓唬的, 受惊的 ‖on the ~ side of 在…的势力所不及的地方 ‖windily ad. / windiness n. ‖Windy City 风城(美国芝加哥市的别名)

wine [wain] I n. ① 葡萄酒; 果子酒; 酒; 药酒: drink a glass (drop) of ~ 喝一杯(少量)酒 / strong(mild)~ 烈(淡)酒/dry(sweet)~ 无甜味的(有甜味的)酒/yellow rice ~ 黄酒/Chinese ~ 各种中国酒 / ~ of Scotland 威士忌酒 / green ~ (不到一年的)新酒 / old ~ 陈酒 / ~ brewing industry 酿酒工业 ②深红色, 紫红色 ③使人振作的东西; 使人沉醉的东西 ④(英国大学中的)饭后酒会 II vt. & vi. (请…)喝酒 ‖Adam's ~ 水 / (be) in ~ 喝醉; 喝得兴高采烈 / Good ~ needs no bush. [谚]酒好客自来。/ new ~ in old bottles 旧瓶装新酒; [喻]旧形式不能适应新内容 / take ~ with 与…相互祝酒 / ~ and dine (款待…)吃喝 ‖'~bag n. ① =~-skin ②酒鬼 / '~,bibber n. 酒鬼 / '~,bottle n. ①酒瓶 ② =~-skin / '~,bowl n. ①酒杯, 酒碗 ②酒癖 / ~ cellar ①酒窖, 酒的贮藏室 ②一批贮藏的酒 / ~ cooler 冰酒器, 凉酒器 / '~glass n. ①酒杯 ② [也作 ~glassful] 一酒杯的量 (相当于四汤匙的计量单位) / '~,grower

n. 种葡萄酿酒的人 / '~press n. (榨取酿酒用的葡萄汁的)榨汁机 / 'Winesap n. 一种冬季产的美国红苹果 / '~shop n. 酒馆 / '~skin n. (整张皮制的)酒囊 / ~ stone【化】酒石; 葡萄子 / ~ taster ①品酒人 ②品酒用的小酒杯 / '~vault n. ①酒窖 ②酒店, 酒吧间

wing [wiŋ] I n. ①翼, 翅膀, 翅: The ~s of a crow can never cover up the sun. 乌鸦的翅膀决不能遮住太阳。②机翼: the ~s of an aeroplane 飞机机翼 ③【建】侧厅, 边房; (舞台的)侧面布置; [复]舞台两侧 ④(政党等的左、右)翼, 派别 ⑤【军】(侧)翼; (足球运动中的)翼, 边锋 ⑥【军】空军联队; [复]空军徽章 ⑦翼状物; 风向标;【植】翼瓣;(汽车的)挡泥板 ⑧[口][谑]手臂 ⑨飞行 II vt. ①飞过: The plane ~ed its way through the clouds. 飞机穿过云层。②在…上装翼; 造主房 ③使飞, 使加速: ~ an arrow at the mark 放箭射靶 / Anxiety ~ed her feet. 忧虑使她飞也似地奔跑起来。④空运 ⑤伤(鸟)翼; 伤(人)臂 ❷ vi. 飞行; 飞速行进(或传播): The good news ~ed to all corners of the country. 好消息迅速传遍全国。‖clip sb.'s ~s 使某人无技可施; 扼杀某人的雄心; 限制某人的活动(或开支等) / give ~ (或 ~s) to 使添翼高飞 / His ~s are sprouting. 他的道德高超(好比神话中生翅膀的天使)。/ in the ~s ① 在观众视线之外的舞台两侧 ②在后方; 在左近 / lend (或 add) ~s to 加快…的速度 / on the ~ 在飞行(或旅行、行动)中 / on the ~s of the wind 飞快地 / on ~s 飞一般地; 无忧无虑; 飘飘然 / singe one's ~s ① 损害自己的名誉 ② (由于某种举动而)使自己遭受损失 / take to itself ~s 消失; (钱等)迅速花掉 / take ~ 起飞; 逃走 / under the ~(s) of 在…的庇护下 / ~ it 不按剧本表演, 即兴表演 ‖~less a. 没有翼的, 没有翅的 / ~let ['wiŋlit] n. 小翼, 小翅 ‖'~beat n. 飞行时翅膀的拍击 / ~ case【动】鞘翅, 翅芽 / ~ chair (可以挡风、靠头的)高背椅 / ~ commander【军】空军联队指挥官, (英)空军中校 / '~footed a. 步履轻捷的, 健步如飞的 / ~ gun 机翼固定机枪 / ~man ['wiŋmən] n. ①僚机驾驶员 ②僚机 / '~manship ['wiŋmənʃip] n. 飞行技术 / '~over n.【空】横转, 翻转 / ~ plane 僚机 / ~ rail (铁道的)翼轨 / ~ sheath =~ case / ~ skid (飞机的)翼梢橇 / '~span, '~spread n. 翼展 / '~stroke n. =~beat / ~ tank 机翼油箱 / ~ tip 翼梢

wink [wiŋk] I ❶ vi. ①眨眼 ②使眼色, 眨眼示意: ~ at sb 向某人使眼色 ③假装不见, 故意忽视(at): We must not ~ at this error. 我们对于这种错误决不能视而不见。④(灯光、星等)闪烁, 闪耀 ⑤突然终止, 完结; 熄灭(out) ⑥(用灯光)打信号 ❷ vt. ①眨(眼) ②眨(眼): one's eyes (at sb.) (对某人)眨眼睛 ③眨掉(眼泪): The little girl ~ed back her tears. 小女孩眨眨眼忍住了眼泪。II n. ①眨眼; 眨眼示意 ②小睡,

打盹: get a ～ of sleep 打一会儿盹 / not sleep a ～ all night 整夜没有合眼 ③霎时, 瞬息: in a ～ 瞬息之间 ‖*A nod is as good as a ～ to a blind horse.* 见 nod / forty ～s [口]小睡, 盹儿(尤指白天打盹); [美口]一会儿 / *like ～ing* [俚]转瞬间, 很快地; 有劲地 / *tip sb. the ～* [俚]向某人使眼色, 向某人眨眼暗示 ‖～er n. ①眨眼的人; 闪烁的灯 ②马眼罩 ③[口]眼睛; 睫毛 ④[美俚](汽车的)方向指示灯

winnow ['winou] I ❶ vt. ①扬, 簸(谷物): ～ grain 扬谷 / ～ wheat 簸小麦 ②扬掉, 筛去; 使分离: ～ the chaff away (或 out) 筛掉谷壳 / ～ the chaff from the grain 扬去谷壳 / ～ truth from falsehood 去伪存真, 辨明真伪 ③吹掉; 吹散; 吹乱: The wind ～ed the leaves. 风吹散了树叶。④[诗](用翼)扇动(空气等); 振(翼) ❷ vi. ①扬谷, 簸谷 ②分出好坏 ③鼓翼而飞; 飞行 II n. ①簸扬; 扬谷 ②扬谷器 ‖～er n. ①扬谷者 ②扬谷器, 风选机

winter ['wintə] I n. ①冬, 冬季; 冬天: a hard (mild) ～ 一个严寒(温暖)的冬天 ②[诗]年, 岁: fifty ～s ago 五十年前 / a man of sixty ～s 六十岁的人 ③萧条期, 衰落期, 不顺利时期 II a. ①冬天的; 冬天用的: ～ sports 冬季运动 ②可贮藏过冬的: ～ apples 可贮藏过冬的苹果 ③冬天播种的: ～ wheat 冬小麦 III ❶ vt. 对(动、植物)进行冬天保护; 对…进行冬天饲养; 对…进行冬天管理: ～ cattle on straw 用稻草喂牛过冬 ❷ vi. 过冬: ～ in the south 在南方过冬 / ～ on straw 靠吃稻草过冬 ‖～less a. 没有冬天的; 不象冬天的 / ～ly a. 冬天似的;忧郁的 ‖'～bourne n. 冬天才有水的小溪 / '～clad a. 穿得可以御冬的, 穿冬服的 / '～feed vt. 冬天饲养(动物) / '～green n. 【植】白珠树; 冬青; 【化】冬青油 / '～kill vt. 使(植物)冻死: The young tree was ～-killed. 那棵小树冻死了。vi. (植物)冻死 / ～ melon 可保藏过冬的一种甜瓜 / ～ quarters 冬营地 / ～ sleep (动物)冬眠 / solstice 冬至 / '～tide n. [诗]冬季 / '～time n. 冬天 / '～-weight a. (衣服)厚得足以御冬的

wipe [waip] I ❶ vt. ①揩, 擦; 擦净; 揩干: ～ the table 擦桌子 / ～ one's hand on a towel 在手巾上揩手 / ～ one's eyes 揩干眼泪 ②用…揩, …擦: He ～d his hand across his forehead. 他用手揩额。③擦去; 去除; 消灭: ～ (away) one's tears 擦去眼泪 / ～ out a stain 擦去污点 / ～ off a debt 了结债务 ④抹上, 涂上(油等): ～ grease over the surface of a machine 在机器表面涂上一层油脂 ⑤【机】拭接(铅管的接头) ❷ vi. [俚]打(at) II n. ①擦, 揩: give the blackboard a ～ 把黑板揩一擦 ②揩擦的人; 揩擦的东西; [俚]手帕 ③[俚]打: fetch a ～ at sb. (或 fetch sb. a ～)打某人 ‖～ one's boots on sb. 见 **boot¹** / ～ out ①擦洗…的内部: ～ out the bath 把浴盆擦洗干净 ②去除; 洗雪: ～ out illiteracy 扫除文盲 / ～ out a disgrace 雪耻 ③消灭, 歼灭

(敌人等) ④[常用被动语态][美俚]使飘飘然, 使醉倒 / ～ sb.'s eye 见 **eye** / ～ the floor with sb. 见 **floor** / ～ up ①擦干净: ～ up slops 把污水揩掉 ②消灭, 歼灭 ‖～r n. ①揩擦的人; 擦拭的东西 ②滑水片; (汽车挡风玻璃上的)刮水器; 【电】接触电刷; 电位计游标 ‖～out n. ①(在乘冲浪板进行游戏时的)被浪打翻 ②失败, 大丢丑

wire [waiə] I n. ①金属丝, 金属线(如钢丝、铜丝、铜线等); (乐器的)金属弦线; 金属丝状物: copper (或 bronze) ～ 铜线 / barbed ～ 有刺铁丝 / piano ～ 钢琴弦 ②电缆, 电线;【电】线路: insulated ～ 绝缘线 / a private ～ 专用电报(或电话)线 / a party ～ 电话合用线 / lay a telephone ～ 架设电话线 ③[复](木偶戏的)牵线;[喻]背后操纵的势力 ④金属丝制品; 金属丝网(如铁丝网等) ⑤电信;[口]电报;[美]电报(或电话)系统: report by ～ 用电报报告 / send off a ～ 发电报 ⑥(赛马的)终点线 II ❶ vt. ①用金属丝缚(或串、联接、加固等): ～ pearls 用金属丝串珠子 / ～ a fence 用铁丝扎篱笆 ②给…装电线: a house for electricity 给房子安装电线 ③(用铁丝笼)诱捕(鸟、兔等) ④[口]用电报发送; 打电报给: ～ a message of congratulation to sb. 打电报祝贺某人 / He ～d me that …. 他打电报对我说… / Please ～ me the result. 结果如何请打电报告诉我。❷ vi. ①打电报: Please ～ (to me) as soon as you hear. 接信后速来电。/ ～ for sb. 打电报要某人来 / ～ back 回回电 ②[口]劲力干(in): Let's ～ in and finish the job. 让我们加把劲把工作赶完吧。‖a live ～ ①通电电线 ②生龙活虎的人 / be on ～s 极度兴奋, 紧张 / lay ～s for 为…作好准备 / pull (the) ～s ①(木偶戏中)牵线 ②幕后操纵 / under the ～ ①在终点线(的): the third horse under the ～ 第三名到达终点线的马 ②在最后期限前(的): return books just under the ～ 快到期时才还书 / under ～ 用有刺铁丝拦住的 ‖～ agency 新闻电讯社 / ～ cloth (过滤用的)金属丝布, 丝布, 铜丝布 / '～-,cutter n. 钢丝(轧断)钳 / '～,dancer n. 走钢丝演员 / '～draw vt. ①(金属)拉成丝 ②猛力拉; 使延长; 使过分细致 / '～drawn a. 过分细致的: a ～drawn comparison 过分细微的比较 / ～ edge (凿和剃刀的)磨得过薄时所形成的)卷口; 硬币的丝状边口 / ～ entanglement【军】铁丝网 / ～ ga(u)ge【机】金属丝规, 线规 / ～ gauze 金属丝网 / ～ glass 嵌丝玻璃, 铁丝网玻璃 / '～haired a. (狗)有硬毛的 / '～man ['waiəmən] n. 架线工; 线路工; (电路)检修工;【军】架线兵 / ～ netting 金属网, 金属栅栏 / '～,photo n. 有线传真; 有线传真收发装置; 有线传真照片 vt. 用有线传真发送(图片) / '～-pull vi. 牵线, 幕后操纵 / '～,pulier n. 牵线者, 幕后操纵者 / ～ recorder 钢丝录音机 / ～ recording 钢丝录音 / ～ service (用专线电报发稿的)通讯社 / '～tap vt., vi. & n. 从电话(或电报)线路上窃取(情报) a. 从电话(或

电报)线路上窃取的 / '~,**tapper** *n.* ①从电话(或电报)上窃取情报者 ②以窃取的情报进行诈骗者 / '~**way** *n.* 钢丝绳道,提升绳道; 电线槽金属线导管 / '~**work** *n.* ①金属丝制品;金属丝网 ②(杂技演员的)走钢丝 [~**works**][用作单或复]金属丝厂,金属丝制品厂 / '~**worm** *n.*【动】(对植物有害的)切根虫;线虫

wireless ['waiəlis] **I** *a.* 不用电线的,无线的; [主英] 无线电的,无线电报(或电话)的: ~ telegraphy 无线电报法 / ~ telephone 无线电话 / ~ communications 无线电通讯 **II** *n.* [主英] 无线电,无线电收音机: a ~ set 无线电收音机 / listen to the news over the ~ 从无线电中收听新闻 ②无线电报;无线电话: a ~ message 无线电讯 **III** *vt.* & *vi.* 用无线电发送(消息等);用无线电报(同…)联系

wiring ['waiəriŋ] *n.* ①装设金属线,接线,布线 ②【电】配线,接线 ③用金属丝架置动物标本 ④【医】(骨折的)镍缝术 ‖~ **diagram** 接线图

wiry ['waiəri] *a.* ①金属线制的,金属丝制的 ②金属丝般的; 坚硬的; 韧的 ③(人体等)瘦长而结实的 ④(声音)金属弦发出的; 金属弦声似的 ‖**wirily** *ad.* / **wiriness** *n.*

wisdom ['wizdəm] *n.* ①智慧,才智; 明智 ②知识,学问; 常识 ③(古人的)名言,教训 ④贤人,哲士: all the wit and ~ of the place 该地所有的贤人哲士 ‖~ **tooth** 【解】智牙,第三磨牙: cut one's ~ teeth [喻]开始懂事;开始识世故

wise[1] [waiz] **I** *a.* ①有智慧的,聪明的: a ~ saying 名言 / be ~ after the event 事后聪明,做事后诸葛亮 ②英明的,贤明的: ~ leadership 英明的领导 ③谨慎的,考虑周到的;明智的: He was ~ not to go. 他没有去是明智的。 ④博学的,有见识的 ⑤明白的,了解的: He seems to be none the ~r after all this. 经过这一切后他看来还是那样糊里糊涂。 / reply with a ~ shake of the head 很知情地摇着头回答说 ⑥狡猾的,诡诈的;机灵的 ⑦[俚]自作聪明的;自高自大的;卤莽的 **II** ❶ *vt.* [俚]告诉;教会(up): I'll ~ you. 我将告诉你。 ❷ *vi.* 知道,了解(up): You can ~ up on details by reading the newspaper. 读了报纸你就知道详情了。 ‖**be**(或 **get**)~ **to** [俚]知道,了解: If he gets ~ to what you are up to, he is sure to be angry. 假使他知道了你干的事一定会生气的。 / **crack** ~ [美俚]说俏皮话 / **put sb.** ~ [美俚]使某人事先心中有数,使某人知情 ‖~**ly** *ad.* / ~**ness** *n.* ‖~**acre** ['waiz-,eikə] *n.* 自作聪明的人 / '~**crack** *n.* 妙语;俏皮话 *vi.* 说俏皮话 / ~ **guy** 自作聪明的人,自以为是的人 / ~ **hook** [美俚]邮寄订购目录 / ~ **man** ①圣人,贤人 ②术士,男巫 / '~,**woman** *n.* ①女巫 ②助产士,产婆

wise[2] [waiz] *n.* 方法,方式 ‖*in any* ~ 无论如何 / *in like* ~ 同样地 / *in no* ~ 一点也不,决不: His explanation differed *in no* ~ from yours. 他的解释与你的完全一样。 / *in this* ~ 这样地

wise[3] [waiz] *vt.* [苏格兰] ①引导;劝导: ~ sb. to go 劝某人走 ②迫使;遣送

wish [wiʃ] **I** ❶ *vt.* ①祝,祝愿: ~ sb. success (或 ~ success to sb.) 祝某人成功 / I ~ you a happy New Year (a good journey). 祝你新年快乐(一路平安)。 ②想要,需要;希望,愿望,渴望: I ~ the work (to be) finished this week. 我希望本周内能完成这项工作。 / I ~ you away. 我要你走开。 / I ~ to inform you that…. (书信用语)兹通知… / We sincerely ~ him happy. 我们衷心希望他快乐。 / ~ sb. well (ill) 希望某人走运(倒霉) / I ~ I may live to see it. 我希望还能够活着看见这件事。 / It is to be ~ed that the dispute will soon be settled. 希望这争议不久即解决。 ③向…致(问候语): ~ sb. good morning 向某人道早安 / He ~ed me good-bye. 他向我告别。 ④[后接表示虚拟语气的从句]但愿: I ~ (that) I were young again. 要是我能返老还童多好喽。 / We ~ (that) he could come. 他要能来就好了。 / He ~ed (that) he had stayed at home. 他想那时要是留在家里就好了。 ⑤把…强加于,把…硬塞给 (on): ~ a task on sb. 强要某人接受一项工作 ❷ *vi.* 希望,想要: The weather is all one could ~ for. 天气再好也没有了。 / ~ : May I smoke? B: Just as you ~ . 甲: 我可以抽烟吗? 乙: 请自便。 **II** *n.* ①希望;愿望: the needs and ~es of the masses 群众的需要和愿望 / grant (go against) sb.'s ~ 满足(违背)某人的愿望 / He got his ~es. 他如愿以偿了。 / have a (no) ~ to do sth. 想(不想)做某事 ②命令;请求: It is her ~ that you enter. 她要你进去。 ③[复]祝愿,好意: With best ~es. (信末结束语)祝好 / give (或 send) one's best ~es to sb. 向某人致意 ‖*If ~es were horses, beggars might ride.* [谚] 要是愿望等于事实,乞丐也早就发财了。 / *The ~ is father to the thought.* [谚] 愿望是思想之父。 (或: 主观上希望什么是真的就对什么产生信念。) / ~ **sb. further** (或 **at the devil**) 希望某人离得远些 ‖~**er** *n.* 祝愿者,希望者 ‖'~**bone**, ~**ing bone** *n.* (鸟胸的)叉骨,如愿骨(西方迷信说两人同扯此骨时,扯到长的一段的人可以有求必应) / ~ **fulfil(l)ment** 【心】愿望满足

wishful ['wiʃful] *a.* 怀有希望的; 表示愿望的; 愿望的: be ~ to do sth. 想做某事 / be ~ for sth. 想得某事物 / with ~ eyes 望眼欲穿地 ‖~**ly** *ad.* / ~**ness** *n.* ‖~ **thinking** 如意算盘,痴心妄想

wisp [wisp] **I** *n.* ①小捆,小把,小束: a ~ of straw 一小捆草 ②(纸等捻成的)一条,一片: light a fire with a ~ of paper 用一条纸捻点火 ③(烟、气等的)一缕 ④(鸟的)一群 ⑤纤弱的人;细微的东西: a ~ of a girl 娇弱的女孩 / a ~ of a smile 一丝笑意 ⑥鬼火,磷火;迷惑人的

东西 ⑦小扫帚,掸帚 **II** *vt.* 把…卷成一捆(或一束等);把…捻成一条 ‖**~y** *a.* ①小捆(或小束)似的 ②纤弱的;细微的 ③飘渺的,模糊的

wistful ['wistful] *a.* ①渴望的;想望的;欲望得不到满足似的: ~ eyes (looks) 渴望的眼睛(神色) ②沉思的,若有所思的;愁闷的 ③引起怀念的 ‖**~ly** *ad.* / **~ness** *n.*

wit[1] [wit] *n.* ①智力;才智,智能;机智: A fall into the pit, a gain in your ~. 吃一堑,长一智。/ have quick ~s 有急智 / have not the ~(s) (或 ~ enough) to see sth. 无明辨某事的能力 ②[常用复] 理智,(清醒的)头脑: lose one's ~s 丧失理智 ③措辞巧妙的能力;妙语,打趣话,戏谑话: be full of ~ 情趣横溢 ④富于机智的人,才子 ‖**at one's ~s' end** 智穷计尽;不知所措 / **have** (或 **keep**) **one's ~s about one** 警觉,保持机警 / **live by one's ~s** 靠施展小聪明过日子 / **out of one's ~s** 不知所措;精神错乱;发疯: be scared *out of one's ~s* 被吓昏了头脑,吓得惊慌失措 / **set one's ~s to sb.'s** 同某人争辩 / **set one's ~s to sth.** 设法解决某事 / *Wit once bought is worth twice taught.* [谚] 一次的亲身经验抵过两次的老师教导。/ *woman's ~* 女人凭直觉的洞察力(或机智)

wit[2] [wit] (一般现在式第一、第三人称单数 wot [wɔt] 过去式和过去分词 wist [wist] 现在分词 witting) *vt. & vi.* [古]知道 ‖**to** 即,就是

witch [witʃ] **I** *n.* ①女巫;[英方] 巫 ②老巫妇,恶婆 ③[口]迷人的女子,美女;[美俚]姑娘,女人 **II** *vt.* ①迷惑,蛊惑 ②用魔法迷住 ‖**~ing** *n.* 行使巫术 *a.* 有魔力的;迷人的 ‖'**~craft** *n.* ①巫术,魔法 ②魅力 / ~ **doctor** 巫医 / '**~- hunt** *n.* ①对行巫者的搜捕 ②对政治可疑分子的调查;政治迫害: launch a ~-hunt against sb. 对某人进行政治迫害 / '**~-,hunter** *n.* 进行政治迫害者 / '**~-,hunting** *n.* 政治迫害

witchery ['witʃəri] *n.* ①巫术;魔法 ②魅力

with [wið] *prep.* ①和…一起,跟…一起;和…,跟…: eat, live and work together ~ the poor and lower-middle peasants 和贫下中农同吃、同住、同劳动 / learn farming ~ an old peasant 跟老农学种田 / cooperate ~ sb. 同某人合作 / fight (quarrel, argue) ~ sb. 跟某人打架(争吵,辩论) ②在…一边,与…一致;拥护,有利于: I'm ~ you. 我站在你一边。(或:我同意你。)/ I agree ~ you there. 在那一点上我和你意见一致。/ John voted ~ the Tories. 约翰投票支持保守党。/ The tide is ~ us. 我们是顺水行舟。(或:时势有利于我们。) ③具有;带有;加上;包括…在内: a cup ~ a handle 有柄的杯子 / a man ~ a good nose 嗅觉灵敏的人 / come ~ good news 带来好消息 / cost 500 dollars ~ tax 连税在内价值五百元 ④在…身上,在…身边: Have you some money

~ you? 你(身上)带钱吗? / Take an umbrella ~ you. 随身带把伞去。 ⑤由…负责(或处理): Leave the patient ~ me. 把病人交给我。/ The decision rests ~ you. 这要由你决定。/ The deal is ~ you. 轮到你发牌了。 ⑥[表示同时或同一方向]随着: change ~ the temperature 随着温度而变化 / be up ~ the dawn 黎明即起 / *With* these words he left the room. 他说完这些话就离开了房间。/ sail ~ the wind 顺风航行 ⑦[表示使用的工具、手段等]用: dig ~ a pick 用镐挖掘 / pave a road ~ stone 用石铺路 / a ship loaded ~ cargo 装着货物的船 / fields covered ~ snow 积雪的田野 / Let's begin ~ this question. 让我们首先谈这个问题。 ⑧[表示行为方式]以…,带着: serve the people ~ one's whole heart 全心全意地为人民服务 / fight ~ courage 勇敢作战 / Handle ~ care! 小心轻放! ⑨[后面加复合宾语,说明附带情况]: sleep ~ the windows open 开着窗睡觉 ⑩由于,因: jump ~ joy 高兴得跳起来 / shiver ~ cold 冷得发抖 / be down ~ fever 发热病倒 ⑪对…;就…说来;关于: be angry ~ sb. 对某人生气 / What do you want ~ me? 你找我干什么? / It is the custom ~ the Chinese. 这是中国人的风俗。/ a dictionary popular ~ students 为学生所欢迎的词典 / Things go well ~ us. 我们事事顺利 / How are you getting along ~ your work? 你的工作进行得怎样? ⑫虽有,尽管: *With* all his achievements he remains modest and prudent. 他虽有很多成就,但还是谦虚、谨慎。 ⑬[与副词连用,构成祈使句]: On ~ your shoes! 穿上鞋子! / Out ~ it! 说出来! ‖**be in ~ sb.** 见 **in** / (**heavy**) ~ **child** 见 **child** / **In ~ it!** 见 **in** / **what ~ . . . and** (**what ~**) **. . .** 见 **what** / ~ **God** 见 **god** / ~ **that** 见 **that** / ~ **this** 见 **this** / ~ **young** 见 **young**

withdraw [wið'drɔ:] (withdrew [wið'dru:], withdrawn [wið'drɔ:n]) **❶** *vt.* ①收回;取回;提取: ~ one's hand 把手缩回 / ~ money from the bank 向银行提取款子 ②使撤退;撤回;撤消;使退出: ~ troops from 把军队从…撤回 / ~ a bill (demand) 撤消议案(要求) ③拉开,拉下: ~ a curtain 拉开窗帘(或幕布) / ~ one's eyes from 把眼睛从…移开(指不再看) **❷** *vi.* 撤退;离开;退出: ~ *from* a meeting 离会,退席

withdrawal [wið'drɔ:əl] *n.* ①收回;撤回;撤消;撤退: troop ~ 撤军 ②退居,退隐 ③停止服药 ④【商】退股,提款

wither ['wiðə] **❶** *vi.* ①枯萎,干枯;雕谢: Flowers ~ 花总要雕谢。/ Her hopes ~ed. 她的希望

破灭了。②消亡;衰弱;失去生气 ❷ *vt.* ①使枯萎;使雕谢: The summer heat ~ed (up) certain plants. 盛夏炎热使某些植物枯萎了。②使消亡;使衰弱 ③使畏缩;使目瞪口呆;使感到羞惭(或迷惑): ~ sb. with a look 恶狠狠地朝某人看一眼使他畏缩

withhold [wið'hould] (withheld [wið'held]) ❶ *vt.* ①抑制;制止,阻止: ~ one's hand [古]住手不干 ②扣留;不给;拒绝: ~ one's consent 不同意,不许可 / ~ one's support 不支持,不援助 / He *withheld* the news from us. 他对我们隐瞒消息。❷ *vi.* 抑制;忍住: ~ from doing sth. 忍着不做某事 ‖**~er** *n.* 抑制者;抑制因素 ‖**~ing tax** 预扣赋税(雇主发工资时替政府预扣的所得税)

within [wi'ðin] I *prep.* ①在…里面,在…内部: ~ doors 在屋内 ②在…范围以内;不超过: do what is ~ one's power 尽自己的力量去做 / ~ an hour(three days, a year)在一小时(三天,一年)之内 / She lives ~ five minutes' walk. 她住的地方走五分钟就到。/ The department store is ~ ten metres of the bus stop. 百货店离公共汽车站不到十米。/ wait ~ call (hearing, sight) 在叫得应(听得到,看得见)的地方等着 / live ~ one's income 量入为出 / keep a dictionary ~ one's reach 把词典放在手边 II *ad.* ①在里面,在内部: be clean ~ and with out 里里外外都干净 / whitewash the walls ~ and without 把屋子内外的墙壁粉刷一新 / be strong without but feeble ~ 外强中干 ②户内: For details, inquire ~. 欲知详情,请入内询问。③在内心: be pure ~ 心地纯洁 III *n.* 里面,内部: The easiest way to capture a fortress is from ~. 堡垒是最容易从内部攻破的。‖**~ an ace of** 离…只差一点儿

without [wi'ðaut] I *prep.* ①无,没有;不: a country ~ internal and external debts 一个既无内债又无外债的国家 / be ~ fear in face of danger 临危不惧 / Can you manage ~ help? 没人帮忙你能对付吗? / I will come to see you ~ fail 我一定来看你。/ go out ~ a cap 不戴帽子外出 / *Without* doubt, the news is true 无疑,这消息是真的。/ not ~ reason 不无理由 / That goes ~ saying. 那不消说。/ look ~ seeing 视而不见 ②在…外面,在…外部: wait ~ the door 在门外等候 ③在…范围以外,超过: ~ sb.'s reach 在某人所及的范围之外 II *ad.* ①在外面,外表上: A persimmon is red within and ~. 柿子里外都红。②户外: The air is fresh ~. 户外空气新鲜。③在没有(或缺少)的情况下: Never mind, we can manage ~. 不要紧,没有也行。III *n.* 外面;外部: help from ~ 外援 / as seen from ~ 从外面看来 IV *conj.* [方]除非,如果不(=unless): You will never succeed ~ you work hard. 你如果不努力,决不能成功。

withstand [wið'stænd] (withstood [wið'stud]) ❶ *vt.* 抵挡,反抗;顶得住,经受住: ~ the storm 顶

住暴风雨 / ~ severe tests 经得起严峻的考验 / shoes that will ~ hard wear 耐穿的鞋 ❷ *vi.* [诗]反抗

witness ['witnis] I *n.* ①证据;证明;证言: History is the most telling ~. 历史是最好的见证。/ These facts are a ~ to his ignorance. 这些事实证明了他的无知。/ call sb. to ~ 叫某人作证 / give ~ in a law court 在法庭上作证 ②【律】证人;连署人: swear a ~ 使证人宣誓 / a perjured ~ 伪证人 ③目击者: a ~ of an incident 事件的目击者 II ❶ *vt.* ①目睹,目击: He ~ed the battle. 他亲眼目睹了那场战斗。②作(协议、遗嘱等)的连署人: ~ a document 在文件上连署 / ~ sb.'s signature 在某人的签字旁连署 ③表明,表示,说明: His flushed face ~ed the great excitement he felt. 他通红的脸表明他很激动。④作证实;证明: None could ~ that he was present. 没有人能证明他是在场的。⑤(年代、地点等)目睹;经历 ❷ *vi.* 作证人;成为证据:~ against the accused 证明被告有罪 / ~ to a fact 为事实作证 ‖*bear*(或 *stand*)~ 证明,作证:He will *bear* ~ that I have done so. 他将证明我是这样做的。/ *bear* false ~ against 作对…不利的伪证 / *give* ~ *on behalf of sb.* 为某人作证 / *(stand) in* ~ *of* 作为…的证据(或证人) / *with a* ~ [古]明确无疑 / *Witness Heaven!* [古]让老天作证吧! ‖**~-box** *n.* [英]证人席 / **~ stand** 证人席: take the ~ *stand* 出庭作证

witticism ['witisizəm] *n.* 妙语;打趣话,戏谑话

witting ['witiŋ] I *a.* 知道的;有意的,故意的 II *n.* [方]①知道,察觉 ②消息,新闻 ‖**~ly** *ad.*

witty ['witi] *a.* ①机智的;[方]聪明的,有才智的 ②措辞巧妙的;情趣横溢的;诙谐的: a ~ remark 妙语 ‖**wittily** *ad.* / **wittiness** *n.*

wizard ['wizəd] I *n.* ①男巫;术士 ②[口]奇才: a math ~ 数学奇才 / a financial ~ 生财有道者 II *a.* ①有魔力的 ②巫术的;着魔的 ③[主英]极好的,绝妙的 ‖**~ly** *ad.* / **~ry** *n.* 巫术;魔力

wizened ['wiznd] *a.* 枯萎的,雕谢的: a ~ man 形容枯槁的人 / a ~ face 干瘪的脸 / ~ apples 干枯的苹果

wobble ['wɔbl] I ❶ *vi.* ①摇晃,晃动;(声音等)颤动,颤抖: This table ~s. 这桌子晃动不稳。②[喻]犹豫不决;反复无常: ~ between two opinions 在两种意见之间摇摆不定 ❷ *vt.* 使摇摆,使晃动;使颤动,使颤抖 II *n.* ①摇摆,晃动 ②犹豫;波动 ③(声音的)变量,变度 ‖**~r** *n.* 摇摆不定的人(或物) / **wobbly** *a.* 摇摆的,不稳定的;颤动的 ‖**~ pump** *n.*【空】手摇泵

woe [wou] I *int.* [表示悲伤、懊悔、惋惜]咳! 唉呀! II *n.* ①悲哀;苦恼: a tale of ~ 悲哀的故事 / a face of ~ 愁眉苦脸 ②[常用复]不幸的事故;灾难: tell all one's ~s 说难诉苦 ‖*weal* *and* ~ 见 **weal**[1] / ~ *be to sb.* (或 ~ *betide sb.*) (咀咒语)愿某人受难 / *Woe is me!* 我真不幸啊! (或: 哀哉!) / ~ *worth the day* 今天真倒霉 ‖~**be,gone** *a.* 愁眉苦脸的: a ~*begone* appearance 愁眉苦脸的样子

woeful ['wouful] *a.* ①悲哀的, 悲痛的: a ~ cry 悲哀的叫声 / a ~ sight 悲惨的景象 ②不幸的; 令人遗憾的; 可悲的: ~ ignorance 可悲的无知 ‖~**ly** *ad.* / ~**ness** *n.*

wold [would] *n.* (无树的)山地, 高原

wolf [wulf] **I** ([复] wolves [wulvz]) *n.* ①狼; 狼皮 ②残暴成性的人; 阴险狡猾的人; 贪婪的人 ③追逐女性的人, 色鬼 ④起腐蚀(或破坏)作用的东西 ⑤极端的贫困 ⑥损害谷物的)小甲虫的幼虫, 牛蝇的蛆 ⑦【音】不协调音; 粗厉音 **II** *vt.* 狼吞虎咽地吃 (*down*) ‖*a lone* ~ 不喜欢与人来往的人; 独居单干的人 / a ~ *in sheep's clothing* (或 a ~ *in lamb's skin*) 披着羊皮的豺狼 / *cry* ~ 喊叫"狼来了", 发假警报 / *have* (或 *hold*) a ~ *by the ears* 骑虎难下, 进退两难 / *keep the* ~ *from the door* 免于饥饿, 勉强度日 / *see a* ~ 张口结舌, 说不出话来 / *the big bad* ~ 大坏蛋 / *wake a sleeping* ~ 自找麻烦 ‖~**er** *n.* 猎狼者 ‖~**like** *a.* 狼似的 ‖~**ling** *n.* 狼崽, 小狼 ‖~ **call** 色鬼调戏妇女时的怪叫 / ~ **child** 狼孩(据信由狼喂养大的孩子) / ~ **cub** ①狼崽 ②[英]小童子军 / ~ **dog** ①(保护羊群的)猎狗的狗 ②狼狗; 似狼的狗 / '~**fish** *n.* 【动】狼鱼(一种凶猛的食肉鱼) / ~ **pack** ①【军】群狼战术的作战单位(协同攻击的潜水艇群或战斗机群) ②[美俚]追逐妇女的流氓集团 / '~**sbane** *n.* 【植】乌头属植物(尤指狼毒乌头) / ~**'s claws** 【植】石松; 卷柏

woman ['wumən] **I** ([复] women ['wimin]) *n.* ①成年女子, 妇女; [不用冠词][总称]女人, 女性: *women* on all fronts 各条战线的妇女 / International Labour *Women's* Day 国际劳动妇女节 / equality between men and *women* 男女平等 ②[the ~] 女子气质, 女子感情 ③女子气的男人 ④妻子; 爱人; 情妇 ⑤女仆 **II** *a.* 妇女的; 女性的: a ~ doctor (teacher) 女医生(教师) **III** *vt.* ①使成女人腔(如使哭哭啼啼等) ②贬称(某人)为"女人", 称"…为"女人" ‖*all the old women of both sexes* 婆婆妈妈的男女们 / *a man born of* ~ 见 **man** / *a single* ~ 单身女子, 老处女 / *a* ~ *of letters* 女作家, 女文人; 女学者 / *a* ~ *of the street*(s) (或 *town*) 娼妓 / *a* ~ *of the world* 深通世故的女人 / *a* ~ *with a past* 有一段丑史的女人 / *make an honest* ~ *of* ... 与诱奸过的…正式结婚 / *one's* (或 *the*) *old* [美俚]妻子, 老婆 / *play the* ~ 作女儿态; 撒娇气(如啼哭, 显得胆小等) / *The old* ~ *is plucking her geese.* [儿语]下雪了。 / *There's a* ~ *in it.* (用于解释男子莫名其妙的行为)这事有女人在捣鬼。 / *the scarlet* ~ [宗] 未信奉基督时的罗马; [贬]教皇统治的罗马; 世俗

精神 / ~*'s wit* 见 **wit**[1] ‖~**hood** *n.* ①(女子的)成年身分(或资格); (女子)成年期: grow into ~**hood** (女子)成年 ②女子气质, 女子特性 ③[总称]女子 / ~**like** *a.* ①象女人的, 女子似的 ②有女子气质的 *ad.* 女子般地 ‖'~**folk** *n.* (一家庭或团体的)妇女们, 女子们 (=~**kind**) / ~ **hater** 厌恶女子的人 / '~**kind** *n.* [用作单或复]①女子, 女性 ②(一家庭或团体的)妇女们, 女子们: sb.'s ~**kind** 某人家的女眷 / '~**power** *n.* 妇女力量 / ~**'s rights** ①妇女权利 ②妇女权运动 / ~ **suffrage** 妇女选举权; 妇女参政权

womanly ['wumənli] **I** *a.* ①有女子气质的 ②适合女子的 **II** *ad.* 女子般地 ‖**womanliness** *n.*

womb [wu:m] *n.* ①【解】子宫: falling of the ~ 【医】子宫脱垂 ②发源地; 孕育处 ‖*from the* ~ *to the tomb* 从生到死; 一生 / *in the* ~ *of time* 在酝酿中; 尚未发生 / *the fruit of the* ~ 子女; 儿童

won [wʌn] win[1] 的过去式和过去分词

wonder ['wʌndə] **I** *n.* ①惊异; 惊奇; 惊叹; 惊讶: a look of ~ 惊异的神情 / be filled with ~ 非常惊奇 / be lost in ~ 惊奇得出神 / look at sb. in silent ~ 惊讶得默不作声地看着某人 ②奇迹, 奇观; 奇事; 奇才: do (或 perform, work) ~s 创造奇迹; 取得惊人的成就 / The ivory work is a ~ of delicate workmanship. 这件象牙雕刻是手艺精巧的珍品。 / a ~ drug 特效药 ③疑惑不定 **II** ❶ *vi.* ①感到惊异; 感到惊讶; 惊叹: I ~ at his doing that. 我对他那样干感到惊讶。 / It's not to be ~ed at. 这是不足为奇的。 / They ~ed to hear the news. 他们听到这消息感到惊奇。 ②感到奇怪, 感到疑惑: What are you ~*ing about*? 你对什么感到疑惑呀? ❷ *vt.* 对…感到奇怪, 对…感到怀疑; 想知道: I ~ who he is, where he came from and why he came. 我很想知道他是谁, 从哪里来, 来干什么。 / She ~ed what the child was doing. 她感到纳闷, 孩子究竟在干什么。 / I ~ whether (或 if) you would mind helping me. 不知你是否能帮帮我的忙。 / Can you ~ he refused? 难道你对他的拒绝会感到奇怪吗? ‖*and no* (或 *small*) ~ 不足为奇 / *a nine days* ~ 轰动一时(便被遗忘)的事物 / *for a* ~ 说来奇怪; 意想不到地: You are punctual *for a* ~. 你居然准时到, 好难得! / *It is a* ~ *that* ... 奇怪的是… / *I* ~ *at you.* (用于对小孩子说) 你怎么搞的? (或: 你真使我吃惊。) / *No* (或 *Little, Small*) ~ (*that*) .... 难怪…; …不足为奇: He had made a thorough investigation. *No* ~ he knew so much about it. 他进行了彻底的调查。 无怪他对此事了解很多。 / *seven* ~s *of the world* (古代)世界七大奇迹 / *signs and* ~s 见 **sign** / *What a* ~! 好奇怪呀! / *What* ~ *that* ...! …有什么奇怪呢! ‖~**ment** *n.* ①惊奇, 惊讶 ②奇观; 奇事 ③好奇心 ‖~ **boy** 事业发达的青年男子; 深得人心的交际家 / ~ **child** 神童 / '~**land** *n.* (童话里的)仙境; 奇境: a scenic

~land 风景胜地 / '~-struck, '~-,stricken a. 惊讶不已的 / '~work n. 奇迹; 奇异的事物, 惊人的东西 / '~,worker n. 创造奇迹的人 / '~-,working a. 创造奇迹的

wonderful ['wʌndəful] a. ①惊人的; 奇妙的; 精彩的: ~ courage 惊人的勇气 / a ~ sight (invention) 奇妙的景象(发明) / a ~ performance 精彩的演奏 ②[口]极好的: The weather has been ~! 近来天气好极了! / It's simply ~. 简直妙极了! / That's a ~ idea. 那可是个好主意。/ have a ~ time 玩得快活极了 ‖~ly ad. / ~ness n.

wondrous ['wʌndrəs] [诗] I a. =wonderful II ad. [只用于修饰形容词]惊人地; 出奇地; 异常地: ~ brave 异常地勇敢 ‖~ly ad. / ~ness n.

wont [wount; 美 wont, wount] I a. [用作表语] ①惯常于, 惯于: He was ~ to rise early. 他惯常起得很早。②倾向于, 易于 II n. [只用单]惯常做法, 习惯: It is his ~ to do physical exercises in the early morning. 他惯于在清晨做早操。/ She came home later than was her ~. 她比平常回家晚了些。III (过去式 wont, 过去分词 wont或 wonted) ❶ vi. 习惯, 惯常: ~ to do sth. 惯于做某事 ❷ vt. 使习惯于: ~ oneself with the new environment 使自己习惯于新环境 ‖*according to one's* ~ 按照自己的常规 / *use and* ~ 习惯; 惯例 ‖~ed a. 习惯的, 惯常的: leave home for work at one's ~ed hour 按惯常的时间离家去上班 / He heard me out with his ~ed patience. 他象平时一样耐心地听我把话说完。

won't [wount] =will not

woo [wuː] ❶ vt. ①向⋯求爱, 向⋯求婚 ②追求; 想得到: ~ fame and fortune 追求名利 ③恳求, 劝诱: ~ sb. to do sth. 恳求某人做某事 / ~ sb. to compliance 劝说某人同意 ④(非存心地)招致: ~ defeat 自招失败 ❷ vi. ①求爱, 求婚 ②恳求 ‖~er n. 求爱者, 求婚者

wood [wud] I n. ①[常作 ~s][用作单或复]树林, 森林; 林地: a ~ of larches 落叶松林 / ride through the ~(s) 骑马穿过树林 / live in a nearby ~s 住在附近的林子里 ②木头; 木材; 木柴: a suitcase made of ~ 木制提箱 / chop ~ for the fire 劈柴生火 ③木制酒桶: wine in the ~ 桶装的酒 / beer drawn from the ~ 从桶里放出的啤酒 ④【音】木制管乐器 ⑤木制的东西(如印花用的木模、木球、打高尔夫球的木制球棒等) II ❶ vt. ①供木材(尤指木柴)给: ~ the stove 给炉子添柴 ②植树于 ❷ vi. 收集木材(或木柴); 得到木材(或木柴)供应 ‖*cannot see the ~ for the trees* 见树不见林 / *in the green ~* 处于佳境 / *knock on* ~ [美] =touch ~ / *out of the* ~(s) ①出森林 ②[喻]脱离险境(或困境): Do not halloo until you are *out of the* ~(s). [谚]未出危险境, 切莫先高兴。/ *saw* ~ [美俚]

①一心只管干自己的事; 不管闲事 ②打鼾; 睡觉 / *take to the* ~s ①逃进树林 ②[喻]逃避责任; 弃权 / *touch* ~ (迷信认为在夸说好运气后)用手碰木头以免好运气跑掉 ‖~ed a. 长满树木的; 多树木的 / ~less a. 没有树木的 ‖~ alcohol 【化】甲醇, 木醇 / '~bind, '~bine n. 【植】开淡黄色花的一种忍冬(产于欧洲); 五叶地锦 / ~ block ①【印】铺木; 版木 ② =~cut / ~ carving 木雕(术) / '~,chopper n. 伐木者 / '~chuck n. 【动】土拨鼠 / ~ coal 木炭; 褐煤 / '~cock n. 【动】丘鹬(别名山鹬) / '~craft n. ①木工技术 ②森林知识(尤指林中识路、打猎等) / '~cut n. 木刻, 木版画 / '~,cutter n. ①樵夫; 伐木工人 ②木刻家 / ~ engraving 木刻(术); 木版画 / ~ fibre 木质纤维 / ~ gas 【化】木(煤)气 / ~land ['wudlənd] n. 树林, 林地 / ~ louse 【动】土鳖, 地鳖 / '~man ['wudmən] n. ① =~sman ②樵夫 / '~note n. ①林中鸟叫声 ②自然朴素的诗歌 / ~ oil 桐油 / ~ paper 木制纸 / '~,pecker n. 啄木鸟 / ~ pigeon 【动】斑尾林鸽; 美国西部野鸽 / '~print n. 木版画 / '~ pulp 木(浆)浆 / '~ruff n. 【植】香车叶草 / '~shed n. 柴间; 木料间 vi. 练习吹奏(或演奏)乐器 / ~sman ['wudzmən] n. ①在森林中居住的人; 熟悉林业知识的人 ②在森林中工作的人; 伐木管理人; 猎人 / ~ sorrel 【植】酢浆草 / ~ spirit ①甲醇, 木精 ②森林中的精灵 / ~ tar 木焦油, 木柏油, 木溶 / '~wind n. 木制管乐器 / '~wool n. 细刨花, 木毛, 木丝 / '~work n. ①木制品; 房屋内部的木建部分(如门、梯等) ②木工活 / '~yard n. 堆木场

wooden ['wudn] ①木制的: a ~ shelf 木架 ②呆板的, 毫无表情的; 笨拙的: a ~ face 呆板的脸 / a ~ stare 呆望 / ~ motions 笨拙的动作 ‖~ly ad. / ~ness n. ‖'~-head n. 愚笨的人, 木头脑袋 / '~-,headed a. 愚笨的, 木头脑的 / ~ horse 木马; 特洛伊木马 / ~ walls 古时防御用的军舰 / '~ware n. [总称]木器 / ~ wedding (西方风俗)木婚, 结婚五周年纪念

woody ['wudi] a. ①树木茂密的: a ~ hill 树木葱茏的山丘 ②木质的; 木本的: the ~ parts of a plant 植物的木质部分 / a ~ plant 木本植物 ③木头似的: a ~ taste 木头般的味道 ‖wood-iness n.

wool [wul] n. ①羊毛: carding (或 short) ~ 粗梳羊毛; 短毛(二吋以下) / combing (或 long) ~ 精梳羊毛; 长毛(二吋以上) ②毛线, 绒线; 呢绒; 毛织物; 毛料衣服: Berlin ~ 柏林绒线(四股或八股) / wear ~ 穿毛料衣服 ③羊毛状物; (动、植物上)绵状毛; 厚的短卷发: cotton ~ 原棉; 脱脂棉, 药棉 / mineral ~ 渣绒 ④蒙蔽性事物, 妨碍了解的事物 ‖*all* ~ *and a yard wide* 优质的; 货真价实的 / *dyed in the* ~ ①原毛(加工前)染色的 ②[喻]彻头彻尾的, 彻底的 / *go for* ~ *and come home shorn* 偷鸡不着蚀把米; 弄

巧成拙 / *lose one's* ~ [俚] 发怒 / *much cry and little* ~ 见 *cry* / *pull the* ~ *over sb.'s eyes* 蒙蔽某人 ‖~ *fat*, ~ *grease*, ~ *oil* 羊毛脂 / '~fell *n.* [英]羊毛皮 / '~,gather *vi.* 心不在焉; 胡思乱想 / '~,gatherer *n.* 心不在焉(或胡思乱想)的人 / '~,gathering *n.* & *a.* 心不在焉(的); 胡思乱想(的) / '~,grower *n.* [主英]养羊售毛业者 / ~*man* ['wulmən] 羊毛商 / '~pack *n.* ①(用黄麻制的)羊毛打包布 ②羊毛包(每包 240 磅) ③【气】卷毛云 / '~sack *n.* ①装羊毛的袋 ②英国上院议长(兼大法官)席位的坐垫(内塞羊毛): reach the ~*sack* 成为上院议长 / take seat on the ~*sack* (在上院)宣布开会 / '~skin *n.* [美]羊毛皮 / ~ **stapler** 把羊毛整理分类的人; 羊毛商 / ~ **top** [纺]毛条 / '~work *n.* 绒绣

wool(l)en ['wulin] **I** *a.* ①羊毛制的; 毛线的: ~ fabrics 毛织品, 粗纺毛织物 / a ~ blanket 毛毯 ②生产(或经营)毛织品的: à ~ mill (粗梳)毛纺厂 / ~ workers 毛纺工人 / a ~ draper 毛织品零售商(店) **II** *n.* [常用复]毛织品, 羊毛织物; 毛料衣服

wool(l)y ['wuli] **I** *a.* ①长满羊毛的; 羊毛(制)的: the ~ flock 羊群 / a ~ coat 羊毛外衣 ②羊毛状的; (动、植物)绵状的, 毛茸茸的, 长满鬈发的: ~ hair 蓬松的鬈发; 【动】胎毛 ③模糊的, 不鲜明的; (声音)嘶哑的: a ~ painting (轮廓、色彩等)不鲜明的图画 / vague and ~ ideas 含糊不清的想法 / the ~ sound of a worn record 旧唱片的嘎声 ④[美]粗犷的(指具有早期美国西部生活特色的): wild and ~ 粗野的 **II** *n.* ①[常用复]毛线衣; 羊毛内衣 ②[美方][澳]羊 ‖**woolliness** *n.* ‖~ **bear** 【动】多毛的毛虫(尤指灯蛾科的幼虫) / '~,headed *a.* ①有鬈发(尤指浓密的鬈发)的 ②头脑糊涂的

word [wə:d] **I** *n.* ①词, 单词: a new ~ 生词; 新词 / a ~ list 词表 / coin ~s (生)造新词 / What does this ~ mean? 这个词是什么意思? / not to breathe a ~ about sth. 对某事只字不提 / "Good" is not the ~ for it. You ought to have said "sublime". "好"这字眼在这儿用得不恰当, 你应说"崇高"。②言词, 言语; 歌词: a ~ of advice 劝告的话 / put one's thoughts into ~s 把自己的想法用言语表达出来 / Our excitement was beyond ~s when we heard the good news. 我们听到这好消息时的激动心情是无法用语言表达的。/ Words failed him. 他找不出话表达自己的思想感情。/ His ~s betrayed his anxiety. 他的话流露出焦急的心情。/ honeyed ~s 甜言蜜语 / She didn't say a ~. 她一言不发。/ a man of few (many) ~s 沉默寡言(话多)的人 / too beautiful for ~s 美丽得难以用语言形容的 ③谈话; [复]口角: Can I have a ~ with you? 我可以和你谈一下吗? / have ~s with sb. 与某人吵嘴 ④消息, 信息; 谣言, 传说: I have had no ~

from him since he left. 他走了以后我没有得到他的信息。/ I have received ~ of his coming. 我得到了他来的消息。/ I just got ~ that he is not coming this evening. 我刚听说他今晚不来了。⑤诺言; 保证: I hope you will always respect your ~. 我希望你能始终遵守自己的诺言。/ a man of his ~ 有信用的人 / go back on one's ~s 推翻诺言, 食言 / His ~ is as good as his bond. 他的诺言可以信得过。⑥命令; 口令: The commander gave the ~ to fire. 指挥员下令开火。/ You must give the ~ before you can pass. 你必须说出口令才能通行。/ ~s of command [军](尤指对操练的士兵们发出的)口令 ⑦[自]代码, 字码: machine ~ 计算机语, 计算机信息元 ⑧[古]格言 ⑨[the W-][宗]圣经 (= Word of God 或 God's Word) **II** *vt.* 用言词表达: I should ~ it rather differently. 我倒想用个不同的说法。/ a strongly ~ed statement 措词强烈的声明 ‖*a bad* ~ 亵渎的词语; 淫猥话 / *a household* ~ 家喻户晓的词(或用语) / *a play upon* ~s 双关语, 俏皮话 / *at a* ~ ①(对请求、建议或命令等)反应迅速地, 立即 ②简言之 / *a* ~ *and a blow* 一言不合就动手打 / *a* ~ *in (out) of season* 合 (不合) 时宜的话; 受 (不受) 欢迎的忠告 / *A* ~ *in your ears.* (附耳过来)跟你说句私房话。/ *a* ~ *to the wise* 智者一言已足 / *be as good as one's* ~ 守信 / *believe sb.'s bare* ~ (或 *believe sb. on his bare* ~) 轻信某人的 (毫无根据的) 话 / *big* ~s 大话, 夸张之词 / *break one's* ~ 失信, 食言 / *burning* ~s 热情洋溢的话 / *by* ~ *of mouth* 口头地: I have informed him *by* ~ *of mouth*. 我已口头通知他了。/ *eat one's* ~s 收回前言, 认错道歉 / *fair* (或 *good*) ~s 恭维话 / *from the* ~ *go* 从一开始 / *get a* ~ *in edgeways* (或 *edgewise*) (趁健谈的人讲话的间隙)插嘴 / *give one's* ~ 保证, 允诺 / *give one's* ~ *of hono(u)r* 用名誉担保 / *give sb. one's good* ~ 推荐某人 / *give* (或 *pledge, pass*) *sb. one's* ~ ①对某人许下诺言 ②[罕] 对某人说 / *hang on sb.'s* ~s 热切地听着某人的话 / *Hard* ~s *break no bones, fine* ~s *butter no parsnips.* [谚]粗话无害, 甘言无益。(或: 空话不如行动。) / *have no* ~s *for sth.* 无法形容某物 / *high* (或 *hard, warm, hot, sharp*) ~s 忿怒的话, 激烈的话 / *holiday* ~s 奉承话; 客套语 / *I give you my* ~ *for it.* 我向你保证确是这样。/ *in a* (或 *one*) ~ 简言之, 总之, 一句话 / *in other* ~s 也就是说, 换句话说 / *in so many* ~s 明确地, 直截了当地 / *in* ~ *and (in) deed* 真正, 不只是口头上 / *keep one's* ~ 遵守诺言 / *leave* ~ 留言: Please·*leave* ~ (for me) with my child if I'm not at home. 如果我不在家, 请留个信叫我孩子转达。/ *multiply* ~s 废话连篇 / *Mum's the* ~! 见 **mum**[1] / *my* ~ *upon it* 我向你保证确是这样 / *not have a* ~ *to throw at a dog* (因孤僻或高傲而)不和别人说话 / *not to mince* one's ~s 见 **mince** / *on one's* ~ *of hono(u)r* 以名誉担保 / *proceed from* ~*s to blows* 吵着吵着就打起来了 / *put* ~*s into sb.'s mouth* 教某人怎样讲；认为某人说过某些话 / *say a few* ~*s* (即席)说几句: *say* (或 *put in*) *a good* ~ *for sb.* 为某人说好话；为某人说情 / *say the* ~ 发命令 / *send* ~ 捎信；(间接)通知；转告: Please *send* me ~ of your safe arrival. 请把你平安到达的消息告诉我。/ *Sharp's the* ~. 见 **sharp**. / *suit the action to the* ~ 见 **action** / *take my* ~ *for it* 相信我的话 / *take sb. at his* ~*s* 相信某人的话 / *take the* ~*s out of sb.'s mouth* 抢先讲出某人要讲的话 / *the last* ~ ①最后一句话；最后决定权；决定性的说明；定论 ②(同类事物中)最新型式，最新品种 / *the last* ~*s* 临终的话，遗言 / *upon my* ~ ① =my ~ upon it [也作 my ~] 哎呀: *My* ~, the road's pretty bumpy just here. 嗳呀，这儿的路真不平。/ *waste* (或 *spend*) *one's* ~*s* 白费口舌 / *weigh one's* ~ 斟酌字句 / *wild and whirling* ~*s* 考虑欠周到的话 / ~ *for* ~ 逐字地；一字不变地: translate ~ *for* ~ 逐字翻译 / repeat ~ *for* ~ 逐字复述(或背诵) / ~*s of one syllable* 简单明了的语言 / *Words pay no debts.* [谚]空话还不了债。(或: 空言无补。) ‖~**ing** n. [只用单] 措词，用词，表达法: a relevent (an irrelevent) ~*ing* 得当的 (不得当的) 用词 / A different ~*ing* will make the meaning clearer. 换一个说法将使意义更清楚。/ ~**less** a. ①未用文字表达的 ②沉默的，没话的 ‖~**-blind** a. 患失读症的 / **blindness** 【医】无读字能(力)，失读症 / '~**book** n. ①词典；词汇表 ②歌剧剧本；诗歌集 / '~**-,building,** '~**-for,mation** n. 构词法 / ~ **deafness** 【医】无听言能(力) / '~**-for-'** a. 逐字的: ~*-for-*~ translation 逐字翻译，直译 / '~**-hoard** n. 词汇表 / '~**,monger** n. 卖文为生者；舞文弄墨者 / '~**-of-'mouth** a. 口头表达的 / ~ **order** 【语】词序 / '~**-,painter** n. 能用文字生动描述者 / '~**-'perfect** a. 一字不错地熟记的 / '~**picture** 生动的文字描述 / '~**play** n. ①敏捷巧妙的对话 ②双关语；俏皮话 / '~**,spinning** n. 用冗长夸张的文字 / '~**-,splitting** n. 过分精细地区分词义，咬文嚼字；诡辩 / ~ **square** 四方联词 (即将字母排成四方形，无论横直都可读出相同的词。见右) / ~ **stress** 【语】词重音 / ~ **time** 【自】取字时间，出字时间

```
DATE
ACID
TING
EDGE
```

wordy ['wə:di] a. ①多言的，唠叨的；冗长的: a ~ speaker 说话唠叨的人 / a ~ style 冗长的文风 ②文字的；口头的: ~ warfare 笔战；舌战 ‖**wordily** ad. / **wordiness** n.

wore [wɔ:] ① wear¹ 的过去式 ② wear² 的过去式和过去分词

work [wə:k] **1** n. ①工作；劳动；(要做的)事情；作业: be hard at ~ 正在努力工作 / He has done a good day's ~. 他干了整整一天的活。/ go to ~ 上班 / They stop ~ at five. 他们五点钟下班(或放工)。/ They had pretty hard ~ getting the roof of the storehouse repaired before the rain came. 他们费了很大的劲在下雨前把仓库屋顶修好。/ I have a lot of ~ to do this evening. 今晚我有许多事要做。

②职业；业务: be in regular ~ 有固定工作 / look for ~ 找工作，找职业

③ 行为；作用；【物】功: The medicine has begun to do its ~. 药物已开始起作用了。/ convert heat into ~ 变热为功 / mechanical ~ 机械功

④[常用复，有时作 a ~] 著作；作品: ~*s* of literature and art 文艺作品 / a new ~ on acupuncture 一本关于针刺疗法的新书

⑤成果，产品；工艺品；针线活；刺绣品: This book is the ~ of many hands. 这本书是许多人的劳动成果。/ a ~ of art 一件艺术品(如诗、画、建筑物等) / carved ~ 雕刻品 / moulded ~ 模塑品 / fine porcelain ~ in many styles 各种各样的精美瓷器 / What a beautiful piece of ~! 多美的一件工艺品啊!

⑥[复](建筑等)工程；【军】工事；[~s][用作单或复]工厂: public ~*s* 公共建筑工程，市政工程 / the Ministry of *Works* 建筑工程部 / defensive ~(s) 防御工事 / a cement ~*s* 水泥厂 / an iron and steel ~*s* 钢铁厂

⑦工件，工作物；[复]活动的机件: Bring your ~ downstairs. 把你的活儿(或课本等)带到楼下来。/ There's something wrong with the ~*s*. 机件有毛病了。/ clean the ~*s* of a clock 擦洗钟的机件

⑧工作质量；做工；工艺

⑨(发酵产生的)泡沫

⑩[复](神学用语)善行，德行

‖*brain* ~ 脑力劳动 / *economic* ~ 经济工作 / *political* ~ 政治工作 / *progress of* ~ 工作进程 / *a report on* ~ 工作报告 / *shock* ~ 突击工作 / ~ *clothes* 工作服 / ~ *experience* 工作经验 / ~ *hours* 工时 / ~ *policy* 工作方针 / *shoes* 工作鞋 / ~ *style* 工作作风 / *a* ~ *team* 工作队，工作组

II (worked 或 wrought [rɔ:t]) **❶** vi. ①工作，劳动，干活；做 (at): ~ in the interests of the people 为人民的利益服务 / ~ at a difficult problem in mathematics 做一道数学难题

②从事某种职业: ~ as a bus driver 当公共汽车司机

③(机器、器官等)运转，活动: The machine ~*s* smoothly. 机器运转正常。/ My brain doesn't seem to be ~*ing* well today. 我的脑筋今天好象不大灵活。

④起作用，产生影响；行得通: The medicine ~*ed*. 药物奏效了。/ The appeal ~*ed* powerfully upon him. 呼吁对他起了强烈作用。/ ～ like a charm 产生奇效 / A utopian plan just won't ～. 空想的计划是行不通的。

⑤缓慢而费力地前进; (由于运动、使用 等)逐渐变动: We ～ed south through the forest. 我们费力地通过森林向南前进。/ The root ～ed down between the stones. 树根在石缝间钻下去。/ The knot ～ed loose. 结头松掉了。/ The screw has ～ed out of the joint. 螺钉从接合处脱出来了。

⑥抽搐, 牵动; 激动, 不平静: His face ～ed with emotion. 他激动得面部抽搐。/ Thoughts are ～ing within me. 我心潮澎湃。/ Waves ～ed to and fro. 波浪翻腾。

⑦做细活; 做针线活, 绣花

⑧发酵: The yeast began to ～. 酵母开始发酵。

⑨被加工, 被揉: This wood ～s easily. 这木料很容易加工。/ This putty ～s easily. 这油灰很好揉。

❷ vt. ①使工作, 使干活: ～ oneself too much 操劳过度

②使转动, 开动; 使用, 操作: ～ a machine 开机器 / ～ an abacus 打算盘 / a pump ～ed by hand 手摇泵

③经营, 管理; 主管(某部门或地区)的工作(或活动): ～ a farm 办农场 / This mine is no longer being ～ed. 这矿现在已不开采了。

④[过去式和过去分词常用 wrought]影响; 说服; 劝诱: ～ sb. to one's own way of thinking 说服某人使他和自己想法一样

⑤使缓慢前进; 使逐渐变动: He patiently ～ed the stone slab into position. 他耐心地把那块石板放好。/ ～ the manure deep into the soil 使肥料深入土壤 / Vibration has ～ed the screw loose. 震动使螺钉松脱了。

⑥通过努力取得; 靠做工取得: ～ one's way through a crowd 挤过人群 / ～ one's way through college 靠做工来读完大学 / ～ one's passage to Europe 用做工挣得旅费的办法到达欧洲

⑦[过去式和过去分词常用 wrought]造成, 引起; 激起: ～ wonders (或 miracles) 创造奇迹 / So the frost wrought no havoc with the crop. 这么说, 严霜并没有损害庄稼。/ ～ the audience into enthusiasm 使听众情绪热烈起来 / ～ oneself into a rage 动怒

⑧精工细做; 织, 纺, 绣; 绘制, 雕刻(肖像); 切削, 铸造, 锤炼(金属): a vase cunningly wrought 制作精巧的花瓶 / ～ a pattern on linen 在亚麻布上绣花样 / ～ a sweater 织毛线衫

⑨揉(面团); 搅(黄油); 使(面团等)发酵

⑩计算; 算出: ～ (out) a mathematical problem 算出一道数学题 / ～ calculations in one's head 心算

⑪[口]利用; 哄骗: ～ one's connections 利用私人关系

⑫耕作; 使芽接, 嫁接 (on): ～ the fields 耕种田地 / Apples ～ed on seedling stocks are often especially vigorous. 芽接在实生苗上的苹果往往特别丰硕。

‖All ～ and no play makes Jack a dull boy. [谚]只工作不玩耍, 聪明孩子也变傻。/ a nasty piece of ～ ①[口]讨厌的家伙, 下流坯 ②恶意行为, 阴谋 / at ～ ①(人)在工作; (机器)在运转; (因素等)在起作用 ②从事于, 忙于 (on, upon): They are at ～ on a new dictionary. 他们正在编一本新词典。/ a ～ of longue haleine 需要长期努力的工作(尤指长篇著作) / be all in the day's ～ 无非是日常生活的一部分; 不足为奇; 合乎常情 / dlrty ～ ①苦活; 吃力不讨好的工作 ②卑鄙的勾当 / get the ～s [俚] ①吃苦头; 受折磨 ②被杀害 / give sb. the ～s [俚] ①(恶意地或开玩笑地)给某人吃苦头, 折磨某人 ②杀害某人 / have one's ～ cut out for one 工作已经排定; 十分忙碌 / in ～ ①在业, 有工作 ②正在完成之中: The studio has three films in ～ right now. 制片厂目前正在摄制三部影片。/ make sad ～ of it 做坏, 搞糟 / make short (或 quick) ～ of sth. ①迅速做某事; 迅速处理某事; 迅速解决某事 ②除掉某物 / mighty ～s 奇迹 / oil the ～s ①给机器加油 ②运用圆滑手段使事情顺当 / out of ～ ①失业 ②(机器)有毛病 / rough ～ ①粗活 ②暴力 ③制作粗糙的东西 / set (或 go) about one's ～ 着手工作 / set to ～ 见 set / shoot the ～s [俚] ①孤注一掷 ②作最大努力 / the ～ of a moment 易如反掌的事 / the ～s of God 宇宙万物, 大自然 / warm ～ ①使人体热的工作 ②费劲(或危险)的工作; 激战 / ～ against time 抢时间完成工作 / ～ away 不停地继续工作: He is still ～ing away at his homework. 他还在做课外作业。/ ～ double tides 见 tide / ～ in ①插进, 引进: ～ in a few jokes in the speech 在讲话里插进些笑话 ②配合 (with): Their plan ～s in with ours. 他们的计划和我们的计划相互配合。/ ～ it [俚]完成; 做好: I'll ～ it if I can. 只要我能做的话, 我一定完成。/ ～ off ①排除; 清理; 偿清: ～ off impurities 排除杂质 / ～ off arrears 清理积压的工作 / ～ off a debt (做工)偿清债务 ②卖掉, 售出: ～ off 3,000 copies 售出三千册 ③发泄: ～ off one's bad temper on sb. 把气出在某人身上 / ～ on ①继续工作, 不断工作 ②做(某人)工作, 设法说服, 影响: ～ on those who have erred and help them do right 对犯了错误的人做工作以帮助他们改正 / ～ one's will upon sb. 见 will / ～ out ①作出; 设计出; 制订出: ～ out a plan 制订计划 / ～ out one's own salvation 自救 ②算出: What does that ～ out at? 算下来是多少钱? ③消耗完(精力等); 采掘完(矿): He never seems to be ～ed out. 他好象永远不会疲乏似的。④做工抵偿 / ～ over ①检查; 研究 ②重做 ③殴打 / ～

to rule 见 **rule** / ～ *up* ①逐步建立起(事业等) ② 逐步引起 (或激起): be ～ed up 激动起来; 被激怒 / ～ *up* sb.'s feelings 激起某人的情绪 / in a highly *wrought-up* state 情绪异常激动 ③综合加工, 整理: ～ *up* the data into an article 把资料整理成文 ④逐步发展: ～ *up* the plot of a novel 逐步发展小说的情节 / ～ *up* to a climax 逐步发展到高潮

‖～**ed** *a.* 经过加工 (或制作等)的: newly ～ed fields 刚耕种过的田地 / ～**less** *a.* 失业的: the ～less [总称]失业者

‖'～**bag** *n.* 针线袋; 工具袋 / '～**basket** *n.* 针线筐 / '～**bench** *n.* 【机】工作台 / '～**boat** *n.* 工作船(指非航海等用的) / '～**book** *n.* ①(教科书的)辅助练习册 ②工作规程书 ③工作记事簿, 工作手册, 笔记本 / '～**box** *n.* 针线盒; 工具箱 / ～ **camp** ①囚犯劳动营 ②(宗教组织等的)义务劳动所 / '～**day** *n.* 工作日 / '～**fare** *n.* 工作福利(指用物质福利刺激人们工作的计划) / ～ **farm** (轻罪罪犯)劳教农场 / '～**folk(s)** [复] *n.* [总称]劳动者(尤指农场的) / ～ **force** 劳动大军, 劳动力 / '～**hand** *n.* (受雇用的)人手 / '～**horse** *n.* ①载重马 ②做重活的人 ③载重量大的车(或船、机器) / '～**house** *n.* ①[英]贫民习艺所; 济贫院 ②[美]感化院, 教养所 / '～**-in** *n.* [美]工作斗争(指美国学生假期到工厂做工与工人一起进行抗暴、反战等的斗争) / ～ **load** 工作负担, (规定期限的)工作量 / '～**mate** *n.* 共同工作者, 同事 / '～**out** *n.* ①(体育)锻炼, (体育)测验 ②(工作)能力测验 / '～**-out** *a.* (市场)疲软的 / '～**people** [复] *n.* [英]工人们, 劳工们 / '～**piece** *n.* 工(作)件 / '～**place** *n.* 工作场所; 车间; 工厂 / '～**point** *n.* 工分: appraise ～points 评工分 / '～**room** *n.* 工场间 / ～ **council** (私营企业主在本企业中组成的)劳资协议会 / '～**shop** *n.* ①车间, 工场; 作坊: a ～shop committee 车间委员会 / a ～shop director 车间主任 ②(文学、艺术的)创作室; 创作法 ③(研究、写作等的)实习班, 实验班: a summer ～shop in short-story writing 短篇小说的暑期写作班 ④专题讨论会 / '～**-shy** *a.* 懒于工作的, 不愿工作的 *n.* 懒汉 / '～**site** *n.* 工地 / '～**-soiled** *a.* 由于工作而弄脏的: rough ～soiled hands 粗黑的手 / ～ **song** 劳动号子 / ～ **stoppage** (工人的)停工斗争 / '～**study** *n.* 工作效率的研究 / '～**table** *n.* (做针线等用的有抽屉的)工作台 / ～ **ticket** 工票 / '～**-up** *n.* ①病情的检查: a cardiac ～up 心脏检查 ②[印](印刷物表面的)污迹 / '～**week** *n.* 工作周, 一周的总工时: a 6-day ～week 六天的工作周

workable ['wə:kəbl] *a.* ①(工具、机器等)可使用的, 可操作的, 可运转的; (矿山等)可经营的; 中用的: ～ soil 可耕种的土壤 ②切实可行的: a ～ programme 一个切实可行的规划 ③易加工的; 可塑的: Waxes, plastics, etc. are highly ～. 蜡类、塑料等都是高度可塑的。 ‖**workability**

[,wə:kə'biliti] *n.* / ～**ness** *n.* / **workably** *ad.*

workaday ['wə:kədei] *a.* ①工作日的; 日常的 ② 普通的; 平凡的, 乏味的

worker ['wə:kə] *n.* ①工人, 劳动者; 无产者: an industrial ～ 产业工人 / a model ～ 劳动模范 / a veteran ～ 老工人 / a manual (mental) ～ 体力(脑力)劳动者 / a skilled ～ 熟练工人 / a ～s' propaganda team 工人宣传队 ②工作者; 人员: scientific and technological ～s 科技工作者 / an office ～ 科室人员 / a health ～ 卫生工作者 / kitchen and service ～s 炊事员和服务员 / a fast ～ 精明、油滑、善于图利的人 / a wonder ～ 奇迹创造者; 魔术师 ③【动】职虫(工蜂或工蚁) ④【印】电铸版 ‖～**-cadre** *n.* 工人干部 / '～**engi,neer** *n.* 工人工程师 / '～**-peasant** *a.* 工人和农民的, 工农的: the ～-*peasant* alliance 工农联盟 / '～**-peasant-'soldier** *a.* 工农兵的: '～**-student** *n.* 工人学员 *a.* 工人和学生的 / '～**-teacher** *n.* 工人教师 / '～**-tech,nician** *n.* 工人技术员

working ['wə:kiŋ] **I** *a.* ①工作的, 劳动的: ～ personnel 工作人员 / the ～ masses 劳动群众 / ～ age 工龄 / ～ hours 工时 / ～ conditions 工作条件, 生产条件 / ～ clothes 工作服 ②运转的, 转动的, 在使用的: a ～ rule 操作惯例, 工作规律; 通例 ③经营的, 营业上的: ～ expenses 经营费, 工作费用 / a ～ partner 经营合伙人 / ～ miles (铁路等的)营业哩数 ④足以成事的: a ～ majority (议会票数等)足以成事的大多数 ⑤施工用的; 【物】资用的: a ～ drawing 施工(详)图, 工作图 / a ～ plan 工作规划 ⑥(面部等)抽搐的, 抽动的 **II** *n.* ①工作, 劳动, 作业 ②运转, 转动; 操作 ③费力缓慢的前进 ④活动方式; 作用: the ～s of the human mind 人脑的活动 ⑤ (面部等)抽搐 ⑥[常用复]矿内巷道, 矿内工作区: abandoned ～s 废巷道, 采空区 / active ～s 生产工作区, 生产巷道 ‖～ **asset** 【商】运用资产 / ～ **capital** 流动资本, 运用资本 / ～ **class** 工人阶级: ～**-classization** ['wə:kiŋ,klɑ:sai'zeiʃən] *n.* 工人阶级化 / ～**-classize** ['wə:kiŋ,klɑ:saiz] *vt.* 使工人阶级化 / ～ **day** 工作日(=workday) / ～ **load** 【机】资用荷载, 工作荷载, 活荷载, 作用荷载 / '～**man**, ～ **man** *n.* 工人 / ～ **order** (机器等的)正常运转状态 / '～**-out** *n.* 计算; 算出; 制订: the ～-*out* of a plan 计划的制订 / ～ **paper** (会计核算用的)工作底稿 / ～ **papers** (未成年者的)雇用证书 / ～ **party** ①[英]经营效率提高委员会; (政府指定的)专题调查委员会 ②(军队中被派出从事非本职工作的)作业队 / ～ **people** 劳动人民 / ～ **stress** 【物】资用应力, 工作应力 / ～ **substance** 【机】工质(如发动机的燃油及冷凝机中的致冷气体) / '～**woman** *n.* 女工

workman ['wə:kmən] ([复] workmen) *n.* 工人, 劳动者; 工作者; 工匠 ‖*Bad workmen quarrel with* (或 *often blame*) *their tools.* (或 *An ill*

~ quarrels with his tools.）［谚］拙匠常怪工具差。‖*~like a.* 工作熟练的; 有技巧的; 精巧的: The book is a *~like* job. 这本书不愧为独具匠心的作品。/ **~ship n.** ①手艺, 工艺; 工作质量, 做工: a vase of exquisite (poor) *~ship* 做工精细(粗劣)的花瓶 ②工艺品; 作品: a splendid piece of *~ship* 一件绝妙的工艺品

world [wə:ld] **n.** ①世界, 天下; 地球; 宇宙, 万物: people all over the *~* (或 people the *~ over*)全世界人民/ an event that shook the *~* 震撼世界的事件/ the objective(subjective) *~* 客观(主观)世界/ the Third *World* 第三世界/ the Old *World* 东半球(与美洲大陆相对而言; 尤指欧洲) / the New *World* 西半球; 美洲/ a voyage around the *~* 环球航行 ②世人, 众人: All the *~* (或 The whole *~*) knows .... 人人都知道…/ What will the *~* say? 人家会怎么说? ③世间, 人间; 物质生活: this *~* 此生, 今世/ the other (或 next, future) *~* 阴间, 来世/ the *~ to come* 来世/ bring a child into the *~* 生孩子/ be not long for this *~* 即将死去/ forsake the *~* 厌世; 厌弃物质生活 ④界, 领域: the newspaper (academic, educational) *~* 新闻(学术, 教育)界/ the *~* of literature and art 文艺界/ the sporting (或 sports) *~* 体育界/ the *~* of animals (minerals, vegetables) 动物(矿物, 植物)界/ the English-speaking *~* 讲英语的国家和地区 ⑤人世生活, 世事; 世情; 世面; 世故: How goes the *~* with you? 你近况如何? / see much of the *~* 见过不少世面/ a man of the *~* 老于世故的人 ⑥(个人)身世, 经历; 眼界: His *~* is narrow. 他眼界狭窄。⑦社会生活, 交际界; 上流社会: withdraw from the *~* 退隐, 隐居/ the great (fashionable) *~* 上流(时髦)社会/ live out of the *~* 深居简出 ⑧大量, 无数: a *~* of waters 一片汪洋/ The criticism did me a *~* of good. 那批评对我有很大好处。/ have *~s* to say 有很多话要讲/ The two things are *~s* apart (或 away). 这两者有天壤之别。/ It makes a *~* of difference whether precautions are taken or not. 有没有预防措施是大不一样的。/ a *~* too big 远远太大/ There is a *~* of meaning in his remark. 他的话含意无穷。⑨(类似地球的)天体, 星球 ‖*a ~ language* 世界通用的语言/ *a ~ outlook* 世界观/ *a ~ record* 世界纪录/ *a ~ tendency* 世界潮流, 世界趋势 ‖*all the ~ to sb.* 对某人说来是最重要的事/ *be beforehand with the ~* 手头有钱/ *be broke to the ~* ［俚］一个钱也没有, 穷到极点/ *before the ~* 在全世界面前, 公然地/ *begin the ~* 开始自己谋生/ *carry the ~ before one* 迅速全面地成功/ *come down in the ~* 落魄/ *come into the ~* 出世, 诞生: (著作)问世/ *for all the ~* ①完全, 一点不差地: He looks *for all the ~* like his father. 他和他父亲简直一模一样。②［常用于否定句］无论如何(也作 for *~s*): I wouldn't do it *for all the*

~. 我决不会这样做。/ *get the ~ off one's back* 卸下重担/ *give to the ~* 出版, 发表/ *go out of this ~* 去世, 死/ *go to the better ~* 死, 去世/ *in the ~* ［加强语气用]天下; 到底: the best *in the ~* 天下第一/ Where *in the ~* did you go? 你到底哪里去了? / *make a noise in the ~* 名噪一时/ *make the best of both ~s* 企图生前享福死后极乐; 两全其美/ *out of this* (或 the) *~* ［俚］十全十美的; 极其动人的; 无比优秀的: The performance was simply *out of this ~*. 那演出简直再好没有了。/ *renounce the ~* (或 *retire from the ~*) 退隐/ *rise in the ~* 飞黄腾达/ *set the ~ on fire* ［美］非常成功; 大大出名/ *So the ~ wags.* 人世变迁就是这样。/ *tell the ~* ［俚］郑重宣布, 着重声明/ *the lower ~* 地狱/ *the outer ~* 外界; 外部世界/ *The ~ is but a little place, after all.* 我们又遇见了。(或: 天涯原咫尺, 此地又逢君。) / *the ~'s end* 天涯海角: We'll go to the *~'s end* to find that out. 我们一定要把那事弄个水落石出。/ *think* (all) *the ~ of* 极其看重(或渴望, 热爱)…/ *to the ~* ［俚］极度地; 完全地: be tired *to the ~* 疲乏得要命/ *~ without end* 永远, 永久/ *would give the ~* (或 *give ~s*) *to know sth.* 为了知道某事愿付出一切代价 ‖*~-beater n.* 举世无双的人(或事物)/ *'~-class a.* 世界第一流水平的/ **World Court** 国际法庭/ *'~-'famous a.* 世界闻名的: the *~-famous* Long March 世界闻名的长征/ **World Island** 世界岛(地缘政治学家认为征服世界所必先占有的地方, 指欧、亚、非大陆)/ *'~-old a.* 极其古老的/ *'~-power* 世界强国/ *'~-,shaking a.* 震撼世界的, 惊天动地的/ *~ war* 世界大战/ *'~-'weariness n.* 厌世/ *'~-'weary a.* 厌世的/ *'~-wide a.* 遍及全球的, 世界范围的: *~wide* influence 世界性的影响 **ad.** 在世界范围内

worldly ['wə:ldli] **a.** ①世间的; 尘世的: *~* affairs 俗务/ *~* goods 财产/ *~* wisdom 处世本领, 世故 ②俗气的; 市侩气的 ③老于世故的, 善于处世的 ‖**worldliness n.** 世俗的/ *'~-minded a.* 世俗的; 汲汲于名利的/ *'~-'wise a.* 老于世故的, 善于处世的

worm [wə:m] **I n.** ①虫, 蠕虫; 蚯蚓; 蛆; 肠虫, 寄生虫; 蛇蜥 (=blindworm); 凿船虫 (=shipworm): The child has *~s*. 这孩子肠子里有虫。②小人物; 可怜的家伙; 可怜虫 ③【机】螺纹; 蜗杆; 蛇管, 旋管; 螺旋升水器 ④(狗舌下的)韧带 **II ❶ vt.** ①使蠕行; 小心缓慢(或狡猾)地行(路): The drill *~ed* its long tongue into the solid rock. 钻子的长钻头钻入了坚硬的岩石。/ *~* one's way through the bushes (慢慢地) 爬过灌木林 ②慢慢探得: *~* a secret out of sb.* 从某人处渐渐探出秘密 ③给…驱肠虫; 给(花坛等)除虫 ④在(电缆、粗绳等)的外面绕线 ⑤给(狗)割去舌下韧带 ❷ **vi.** 蠕行; 小心缓慢(或狡猾)地行进: *~*

through the snow 蠕行穿过雪地 / ～ out of difficulties 逐渐摆脱困难 ‖*A ～ will turn.* [谚] 如被逼太甚，最温顺者也会反抗。/ *be food for ～s* 死 / *I am a ～ today.* 我今天一点精神也没有。/ *the ～ of conscience* 折磨人的内疚，悔恨 ‖*~like a.* 像虫一样的 ‖'~cast n. 蚯蚓粪 / '~-,eaten a.* ①虫蛀的 ②过时的,陈旧的 / ～ fence 曲折栅栏(又称 snake fence 蛇形栅栏) / ～ gear 【机】蜗轮 / ～ gearing

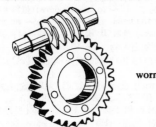

worm gear

【机】蜗轮传动装置 / '~hole n. 虫孔，蛀洞 / '~holed a. 多蛀孔的；虫蚀的 / ～ pipe 【机】蜗形管 / '~seed n. 【植】山道年；美洲土荆芥 / ～ wheel 【机】蜗轮 / '~wood n. ①蒿属植物 (尤指洋艾) ②苦艾 ③苦恼；苦恼的原因

worn [wɔːn] **I** *wear*[1] 的过去分词 **II** *a.* ①用旧的；穿坏的，穿旧的: ～ garments 旧衣服 ②焦虑不堪的: a ～ and haggard face 焦虑憔悴的面容 ③筋疲力尽的；耗尽的；变得衰弱的 ‖'~-'out a. ①用坏的，穿破的，不能再用的: a ~out coat 一件穿破了的上衣 / a ~out automobile 一辆破旧的汽车 ②筋疲力尽的；变得衰弱的；耗尽的: ~out soils 贫瘠的土壤 ③陈腐的: ~out figures of speech 陈腐的修辞手段

worry ['wʌri] **I** ❶ *vt.* ①使烦恼，使焦虑，使担忧: What's ~ing you? 什么事使你烦恼? ②困扰，折磨: ～ sb. for sth. 缠着某人要某物 / ～ sb. to do sth. 缠着某人要他做某事 ③撕咬，咬碎: The dog is ~ing an old shoe. 狗撕咬着一只旧鞋。④反复推(或拉等)；使改变位置 ⑤[英方]塞住，闷死 ❷ *vi.* ①烦恼，担心，发愁: Tell them not to ~. 告诉他们别担心。You don't have to ~ about that. 你不必为那事操心。/ ～ over sb.'s health 为某人的健康担心 ②撕咬，咬碎(at) ③努力移动；挣扎着前进 ④[英方]塞住，闷死 **II** *n.* ①烦恼，焦虑，担忧；[常用复]烦恼事: show signs of ～ 显出焦虑的样子 / family worries 家里的烦恼事 / What a ～ that child is! 那孩子真令人心烦啊! ②猎狗撕咬猎物 ‖*I should ～.* [美口]我一点儿也不在乎。/ ～ along (或 through) 不顾困难设法进行，熬过 / ～ down 好容易吞下 / ～ oneself 自寻烦恼: She will ～ herself to death. 她会愁出病来的。/ ～ out 绞尽脑汁解决(或想出): ～ out a problem 绞尽脑汁解决问题 / ～ out ways to speed up a job 千方百计设法加快工作进程 / ～ the sword 见 sword

‖**worried** *a.* 烦恼的；焦虑的: a worried look 担心的神色 / **worrier** *n.* 使人烦恼的人(或事物) / **worriless** *a.* 无忧虑的 / **worriment** *n.* 烦恼；焦虑 ‖'~wart n. 自寻烦恼的人

worse [wəːs] **I** *a.* ①[bad 的比较级]更坏的，更差的，更恶化的: to make the matter ～ (或 and what is ～, 或 ～ than all) [常用作插入语]更糟的是 / My shoes are the ～ for wear. 我的鞋子穿得更不堪了。②[ill 的比较级](病情)更重的: The patient is (getting) ～ this morning. 今天早晨病人的病势加重了。**II** *ad.* [badly, ill 的比较级] ①更坏，更糟；(病)更重: I slept ～ in hot weather. 我在热天更加睡不好。/ She has been taken ～. 她病情更重了。②更猛烈，更厉害: It was raining ～ than ever. 雨越下越大。**III** *n.* ①更坏的事: I have ～ to tell. 我还有更坏的事要说。/ a change for the ～ 向更坏方向的转化 / Worse cannot happen. 事情不可能更坏了。②[the ～] 失败的地位；输 ‖*for better for ～* (或 *for better or ～*) 见 **better**[1] / *go from bad to ～* 见 **bad** / *none the ～* 并不更差；仍然，还是: He fell into the river but is none the ～. 他掉在河里，但是并没有怎么样。/ like sb. *none the ～* for being outspoken 并不因某人讲话直爽而讨厌他 / think *none the ～* of sb. 仍然尊重某人 / *put sb. to the ～* 打败某人 / *so much the ～* 更加不妙(或糟糕) / *~ and ～* 越来越坏，每况愈下 / *~ off* 情况更坏；恶化；处境更糟

worsen ['wəːsn] ❶ *vt.* 使变得更坏；使恶化；损害: Heavy storms ~ed the fuel shortage. 暴风雨使燃料不足的情况更加严重了。❷ *vi.* 变得更坏；恶化: His health rapidly ~ed. 他的健康状况迅速恶化。‖~ing *n.* 恶化

worship ['wəːʃip] **I** *n.* ①[宗]礼拜: a place of ～ 礼拜堂，教堂 / the hours of ～ 礼拜时间 ②崇拜；敬仰，敬慕: an object of ～ 崇拜对象 / book ～ 书本崇拜,本本主义 / hero ～ 英雄崇拜 / ～ of the dollar 金元崇拜 / win (have) ～ 得到(享有)别人的敬仰 / with ～ in one's eyes 以敬慕的眼光 ③[主英][W-] 阁下(对地方长官的尊称): your (或 his) Worship the Mayor of Manchester 曼彻斯特市长阁下(直接称呼时用 your, 间接提及时用 his) **II** (worship(p)ed; worship(p)ing) ❶ *vt.* 崇拜；尊敬: ～ the ground sb. treads on 拜倒在某人脚下 / the slavish ideas of worship(p)ing everything foreign 崇洋的奴隶思想 ❷ *vi.* 做礼拜: Where does he ～? 他在哪个教堂做礼拜? ‖**worship(p)er** *n.* 礼拜者；崇拜者；爱慕者

worst [wəːst] **I** *a.* [bad, ill 的最高级；常加定冠词 the] ①最坏的，最差的: the ～ land of the tract 这一片地当中最贫瘠的土地 ②最恶劣的；最有害的: the ～ enemy 最险恶的敌人 / the ～ villain 罪大恶极的坏蛋 ③最不利的；最痛苦的；最不适合的；错误最多的；效能最低的: the ～ flood for these hundred years 百年来最大的洪水 / conquer the ~ difficulties 克服最严重的困难 **II ad.** [bad, badly; ill, illy 的最高级]最坏地; 最恶劣地; 最有害地; 最不利地: There were many who played tennis badly, but I played ~. 很多人网球打得不好, 而我是打得最差的。 **III n.** 最坏者; 最坏的部分; 最坏的情况(如事件、结果等): be prepared for the ~ 作最坏的打算 / when things are at their ~ 当情况最恶劣的时候 / Do your ~. (挑战语)你有什么狠处尽管拿出来。 **IV vt.** 击败; 胜过: ~ one's opponent 击败对手 ‖ *at ~* 在最坏(或不利)的情况下 / *give sb. the ~ of it* 击败(或胜过)某人 / *if ~ comes to ~* 如果最坏的事发生 / *(in) the ~ way* [俚]十分, 非常, 强烈地: want to be an opera singer *the ~ way* 极想做一个歌剧演员 / *make the ~ of* 对…作最坏打算

worsted ['wustid] **I n.** 毛线, 绒线, 精纺毛纱; 精纺毛织物 **II a.** 毛线的, 绒线的; 精纺的: ~ socks 毛线袜 / a ~ carding machine 精梳毛纺梳毛机

worth [wə:θ] **I a.** [用作表语, 后接宾语] ①值…的, 相当于…的价值的: This precision instrument is ~ 10,000 dollars. 这台精密仪器值一万元。 / What is it ~? (或 How much is it ~?) 这值多少钱? / be not ~ a straw 比草还贱 / The rarer it is, the more it is ~. 物以希为贵。 ②值得…的, 有…的价值的: be ~ a rap (或 a damn) 毫无价值 / be ~ notice 值得注意 / be not ~ refuting 不值一驳 / be ~ the trouble 麻烦一点也值得 / The research work is ~ our while (或 [口] ~ it). 我们在这项研究工作上花了精力是值得的。 / It is ~ while discussing (或 to discuss) the question again. 这问题值得再讨论一下。 ③拥有…价值的财产的 **II n.** ①价值; 货币价值; 物质价值; 精神价值: a jewel of great ~ 一颗价值昂贵的宝石 / transform wastes of little ~ into valuable industrial products 把没有价值的废物变成宝贵的工业品 / His selfless service to the people proves his superior ~. 他忘我地为人民服务, 说明他具有优秀的品质。 ②[发音常作 wəθ]值一定金额的数量; (折合较高币值的)货币数量: twenty dollars' ~ of sugar 二十元钱的糖 / two dollars' ~ of coins 两元钱的硬币 **III vt.** [古] 发生, 落到…上(=befall): Woe ~ the day! 今天真倒霉! ‖ *A bird in the hand is ~ two in the bush.* 见 **bird** / *for all one is ~* 尽力, 拼命: He is working *for all he is ~*. 他在拼命干。 / *for what it is ~* 不论真伪: take the story (the news) *for what it is ~* 不管传说(消息)是真是假姑妄听之 / *get one's money's ~* 花钱划得来 / *put in one's two cents ~* 发表意见; 发言 / *one's salt* 见 **salt** ‖ **~ful a.** ①有极大功劳的; 荣誉的 ②有价值的; 可贵的 / **'~'while a.** 值得花时间(或精力)的: These results were not ~*while*. 这些结果并不合算。

worthily ['wə:ðili] **ad.** 值得地, 配得上地

worthless ['wə:θlis] **a.** ①无价值的; 无用的: turn the once ~ desert into fertile land 把曾是毫无用处的沙漠变为良田 ②不足道的, 不可取的; 卑微的; 卑郲的 ‖ **~ly ad.** / **~ness n.**

worthy ['wə:ði] **I a.** ①有价值的; 可尊敬的: a ~ man 高尚的人 / a ~ cause 正义的事业 / a ~ son of the people 人民的好儿子 ②[常作表语]值得的, 配得上的, 相称的: something ~ of note 值得注意的事 / ~ to be considered 值得考虑的 / ~ of the name 名符其实的 / a ~ enemy (或 adversary) 劲敌 **II n.** ①(一国或一时代的)知名人士; 杰出人物: an Elizabethan ~ (英国)伊丽莎白(女王)时代的名人 ②[谑][讽]大人物

would [强 wud; 弱 wəd, əd, d] (will 的过去式) **v. aux.** ①[表示过去将来时, 用于第二、三人称; 美国也用于第一人称]将 ②[表示意志]愿, 要; 偏要: He ~ not leave before he finished his work. 他在完成工作以前不愿离开。 / I promised that I ~ do my best. 我答应过要尽力而为。 / I told him not to go, but he ~ not listen to me. 我叫他别去, 可他偏不听。 / The wound ~ not heal. 伤口老不肯好。 ③[表示习惯性]总是, 总会: On Sundays he ~ come to our production team and work with us. 星期天他总是到我们生产队来和我们一起劳动。 ④[表示推测]大概: That ~ be in spring 1964. 那大概是一九六四年春天的事情。 / I ~ be about ten when my brother left home. 我哥哥离家时, 我大概十岁光景。 / That ~ be the book you are looking for. 那该是你在寻找的那本书吧。 ⑤[表示设想的意志]愿意, 要: I could do so if I ~. 要是我愿意, 我能够这样做。 / If you ~ do this for me, I should be grateful indeed. 假使你愿意为我做这事, 我将万分感激。 ⑥[表示虚拟、假设、条件等, 用于第二、三人称; 美国也用于第一人称]要, 将要; 会, 会是: What ~ you say to him if he should come? 要是他来的话, 你将怎么跟他说呢? / If you had come earlier, you ~ have seen him. 假使你早来一些, 就会看到他了。 / It ~ be better to adopt the new method. 采用新方法更好。 ⑦[表示请求或个人的想法、看法, 使语气婉转]愿; 倒: *Would* you take a seat? 请坐! / Reach me that book, ~ you? 请把那本书递给我好吗? / I ~ like to join your discussion. 我想参加你们的讨论。 / It ~ seem (或 One ~ think) that he was right. 看来他倒是对的。 ⑧[表示愿望]但愿, 要是…多好 ⑨能, 能够(=could): The barrel ~ hold 100 litres. 这桶能装一百升。 ⑩[表示愿望、请求、劝告等]会, 要: We wish that he ~ come again. 我们但愿他会再来。 / We prefer that you ~ not go. 我们希望你不要去。 ‖ *~ rather* (或 *sooner*)宁愿, 宁可: The soldiers ~ *rather* (或 *sooner*) die than surrender. 士兵

们宁死不降。

wound¹ [wu:nd] **I** *n.* ①创伤,伤;伤口;伤疤: a bullet ~ 枪伤 / a contused ~ 打伤, 挫伤 / an incised ~ 割伤 / a mortal ~ 致命伤 / dress a ~ 包扎伤口 ②(名誉等的)损伤;(感情上的)痛苦: a ~ to sb.'s pride 对某人自尊心的伤害 **II ❶** *vt.* ①使受伤,伤害: The bullet ~ed him in the shoulder. 枪弹打伤了他的肩膀。/ Although he was seriously ~ed, he went on fighting heroically. 他虽受重伤,但仍继续英勇战斗。②(在感情等方面)伤害: ~ sb. by sarcasm 用讽刺伤害某人感情 **❷** *vi.* 打伤, 伤害: intend only to ~, not to kill 只想要打伤,不是要打死 ‖*willing to* ~ 怀恨的, 带有恶意的 ‖~**ed** *a.* 受伤的: a ~ed soldier 伤兵,伤员 *n.* [the ~ed] 受伤的人们,受伤者: transport the ~ed 运送伤员 / treatment of the ~ed 对受伤者的治疗 / ~**less** *a.* 没有受伤的;[古]不会受伤的

wound² [waund] wind² 和 wind³ 的过去式和过去分词

wove [wouv] **I** weave¹ 的过去式 **II** *a.* 布纹的: ~ paper 布纹纸

woven ['wouvən] weave¹ 的过去分词

wrangle ['ræŋgl] **I ❶** *vi.* 争论, 争辩; 口角, 争吵: ~ with sb. over (或 about) sth. 为某事与某人争吵 **❷** *vt.* ①把…辩得 (*into, out of*) ②放牧; 赶拢(牲口等) **II** *n.* 口角, 吵嘴 ‖~**r** *n.* ①辩论者; 争吵者 ②照料乘骑用马匹的牧场助手; (美国西部)骑马牧者 ③(英国剑桥大学)数学学位考试一等及格者

wrap [ræp] **I** (wrapped 或 [罕] wrapt [ræpt]; wrapping) **❶** *vt.* ①裹; 包; 捆; 缠, 环绕: ~ oneself in a blanket 把毯子裹在身上 / ~ a book in a newspaper 把书包在报纸里 / She *wrapped* her shawl closer about her. 她把围巾围得紧一些。②覆盖; 遮蔽: The mountain top is *wrapped* in mist. 迷雾笼罩山顶。③隐藏; 掩饰, 伪装: ~ oneself in reserve 用沉默寡言的办法隐藏自己的真面目 / The affair is *wrapped* (*up*) in mystery. 这件事情真相未明。/ ~ *up* the meaning in an allegory 把意义包含在譬喻中 / ~ *up* a censure in a polite formula 在一句客套话中暗含指责 ④使全神贯注 (*up*) **❷** *vi.* ①缠绕; 盘绕; 互叠, 重叠: The edges should ~. 边须对齐互叠。②穿外衣; 围好围巾 (*up*): Mind you ~ *up* well if you go out. 你出外的话要围好围巾。③包起来 (*up*): ~ *up* into a small package 被包成小包 **II** *n.* ①包裹(物); 覆盖(物) ②[常用复]外衣; 围巾; 披肩; 毯子; 手帕; 头巾 ③封面内保护书籍的空页 ④(包裹物的)一层; (环绕物的)一圈 ⑤[复]限制; 约束; 秘密; (对书刊等的)检查: The plan was kept under ~s. 这计划被保密。‖*be* *wrapped up in* ①被包藏于…中; 埋头于, 全神贯注于 ②与…有关系; 被牵涉 (或连累) 在一切 ‖'~-**up** *n.* [美口]总结性的新闻摘要报导 ②[美俚]不费事的快速推销 *a.* [美口]总结性的; 最后的

wrapper ['ræpə] *n.* ①包裹者, 包装者 ②包装物; 覆盖物; (雪茄烟的)外包烟叶; (邮寄报纸、刊物、书籍的)包纸; 书的封皮 ③轻便晨衣, 妇女晨衣

wrapping ['ræpiŋ] *n.* [常用复]用于包裹的材料: ~ paper 包装纸(用来包物的厚纸)

wrath [rɔ:θ] *n.* ①愤怒, 激怒, 狂怒; 愤慨: rouse sb.'s ~ 激起某人的愤怒 ②出于愤怒的行为(尤指报仇、惩罚) ③【宗】神谴, 天罚: vessels (或 children) of ~ 遭天罚的人们 ‖*be slow to* ~ 不轻易动怒 ‖~**less** *a.* 没有怒气的, 不动怒的

wreak [ri:k] *vt.* ①泄(怒); 露出(恶意); 发(脾气): ~ one's anger on 泄怒于… ②报(仇); 施加

wreath [ri:θ] ([复] wreaths [ri:ðz]) *n.* ①花圈; 花环; 花冠: place (或 lay) a ~ at (或 on) the tomb of revolutionary martyrs 向革命烈士墓献上花圈 ②圈状物, 环状物, 螺旋形物: ~s of smoke 缭绕的烟圈 ③[诗]围舞的人们; 围观的人群 ④【天】南冕座

wreathe [ri:ð] **❶** *vt.* ①将…扎成圈 (或环、冠); 做成(花圈等); 用花圈装饰…: ~ flowers into a garland 将花扎成花圈 ②盘绕, 缠住; 扭, 拧: a column ~d with vines 藤蔓缠绕的柱子 / Clouds ~d the mountains. 云雾萦绕群山。③覆盖, 包围: a face ~d in smiles (wrinkles) 含笑(布满皱纹)的脸 ④使交织 **❷** *vi.* ①扭动; 扭皱 ②(烟等)成圈; 缭绕; 旋卷

wreck [rek] **I** *n.* ①(船只等)失事, 遭难: save a ship from ~ 营救遇难的船只 / The storm caused many ~s. 暴风雨使许多船失事。②失事的船(或飞机等); (漂到岸上的)失事船中的货物; (失事船或飞机等的)残骸 ③健康极度受损的人(或动物); 遭到严重破坏的建筑物(或车辆): be but a(或 the) ~ of one's former self 身体大不如前; 瘦得不成样子 / The building is a ~. 建筑物已一片破败。 **II ❶** *vt.* ①使(船、火车等)失事, 使遭难 ②拆毁(建筑物等)使瓦解;破坏;损害;阻挠 ④ 摧残(身体健康等) **❷** *vi.* ①(船只等)失事; 遭受破坏, 毁灭: ~ on a rock 触礁失事 ②营救失事的船只; 抢劫失事的船只 ‖*go to* ~ 遭到毁灭 ‖~ **master** 捞获的失事船货物的指定管理人

wreckage ['rekidʒ] *n.* ①(船只等的)失事, 遭难, 毁坏 ②(被毁物的)残骸, 残余 ③[总称] 被遗弃的底层人物

wrecker ['rekə] *n.* ①寻觅失事船只者; 为行动而使船只失事者 ②拆卸旧建筑物者 ③破坏分子 ④打捞(沉船或货物)者; 打捞船; 营救船 ⑤(清除失事火车、修理路基等的)救援火车; (抢救失事或抛锚汽车的)救险车 ⑥购买旧汽车以拆卸其零件者 ⑦救援火车(或救险车)的司机

wren [ren] *n.* 【动】鹪鹩

wrench [rentʃ] *n.* ①扳手, 扳头, 扳钳, 搬子: an adjustable (或 a monkey) ~ 活动扳手, 活搬子 / a pipe ~ 管扳手, 管搬子, 管子钳 / a solid

~ 呆扳手,死搬子 / a socket ~ 套筒扳手,套筒搬子 ②猛扭,突然一扭,一拧;一扳: He gave a ~ at the door-handle. 他猛扭一下门的把手. ③扭伤: He gave a ~ to his ankle (shoulder). 他把踝骨(肩部)扭伤了. ④ 歪曲,曲解 ⑤(离别等场合的)突然的一阵悲痛 II ❶ vt. ① 猛扭(或拧,扳): ~ a door open 用力扭开门 / ~ the horse's head round 猛然勒转马头 / ~ a screw (cap, nut) off 拧去螺钉(盖子,螺帽) ②扭伤: one's ankle (back, shoulder) 扭伤踝(背,肩) ③ 曲解,歪曲(事实,意义等): ~ the meaning 歪曲意义 ④抢;攫取 ⑤使受痛苦;折磨 ❷ vi. ①猛力扭动,拧;扳 ②绞: Of a sudden her heart ~ed. 刹时间她心痛如绞. ||throw a (monkey) ~ into 阻碍,破坏

wrest [rest] I n. ①扭,拧 ②【音】(校准弦音的)扭钥,校音钥 II vt. ①扭,拧(尤指用力拧拔、拧拉) ②夺取,强夺: ~ political power 夺取政权 / ~ initiative (victory) 夺取主动权(胜利) ③费力取得: They ~ed high yields even from the barren land. 他们甚至在贫瘠的土地上也夺得了高产. / ~ from Nature her secrets 探索自然界奥秘 ④歪曲,曲解: ~ facts 歪曲事实 / ~ the sense of a passage 曲解一段文章的含义 / ~ the law to suit oneself 曲解法律以营私

wrestle ['resl] I n. ①【体】摔角,角力 ②斗争,搏斗 II ❶ vi. ①摔角,角力: ~ with sb. 与某人角力 ②斗争,搏斗;全力对付: ~ with a difficulty 与困难作斗争 / ~ with (或 against) temptation 抵制引诱 / ~ with a mass of correspondence 努力处理一大堆信件 ③深思,斟酌: ~ with a technical problem 仔细地考虑一个技术问题 ❷ vt. ①摔(角): ~ a bout 摔一个回合 / a match 作一次摔角比赛 ②(以角力或类似的方式)与…搏斗: ~ a bear 与熊搏斗 ③(使动)搬动,移动 ④ [美]为打烙印把(小牛等)摔倒 ||with God (或 in prayer) 热忱祈祷 ||~r n. 摔角运动员;扭斗者,搏斗者

wretch [retʃ] n. ①可怜的人,不幸的人 ②卑鄙的人,可耻的人 ③[谑](小)坏蛋

wretched ['retʃid] a. ①可怜的;悲惨的,不幸的,感到沮丧的: the ~ sufferers 可怜的受苦者;不幸的人 / feel ~ 感到痛苦;感到倒霉 ②使人很不舒服的,讨厌的;肮脏的;恶劣的: What a ~ place it was! 多么肮脏破败的地方! / ~ weather 恶劣的气候 / ~ health 极差的健康状况 ③质量差的;可鄙的,不足道的: a ~ poet 一个不足道的诗人 ④(用于含贬义的事物)极大的;过度的;严重的: ~ insufficiency (stupidity) 非常不足(愚蠢) ||~ly ad. / ~ness n.

wriggle ['rigl] I ❶ vi. ①蠕动;扭动;蜿蜒而行: ~ up to a ridge 蜿蜒而上山脊 ②摆脱;溜掉;混入: ~ out of a difficulty 千方百计摆脱困难 ❷ vt. 使扭动;挣: ~ oneself free 挣脱束缚 / ~ one's way 蜿蜒前进 II n. ①蠕动;扭动 ②蜿蜒;起伏 ||~r n. ①扭动的人(或物) ②【动】孑孓

wring [riŋ] I (wrung [rʌŋ] 或 [罕] wringed) ❶ vt. ①绞,拧,挤,榨,扭: ~ (out) wet clothes 把湿衣服拧干 / ~ water from (或 out of) a towel 把毛巾的水绞出来 / ~ sb.'s hand 热情地紧握某人的手 / ~ one's hands 绞手,扭手(表示失望、悲哀) ②榨取;勒索;强求: ~ high profits 榨取高额利润 / ~ money from (或 out of) sb. 勒索某人的钱财 / ~ a consent from (或 out of) sb. 迫使某人同意 ③使苦恼;折磨;使悲痛: ~ sb.'s heart 使某人悲痛 ④把…拧得变形;扭紧,拧入 ❷ vi. ①蠕动,扭动 ②(用力)绞,拧,挤,榨,扭 II n. 绞,拧,挤,榨,扭: give wet clothes a ~ 把湿衣服拧一拧 ||~ water from a flint 见 **water** / ~er n. ①绞扭者;勒索者,敲榨者 ②榨干机;绞衣机 ③造成艰难困苦的事件(或过程): put sb. through the ~er [美俚] 对某人严加审问 ||'~ing-wet a. 湿得可拧出水来的,湿得需要拧的

wrinkle[1] ['riŋkl] I n. ①皱,皱纹: ~s round one's eyes 眼角周围的皱纹 / ~s in a face 脸上的皱纹 / iron out ~s in the dress 烫平衣服的皱褶 ②[美俚]情人的母亲 ③缺点;错误 II ❶ vt. 使起皱纹: ~ (up) one's forehead 皱起额头(表示迷惑) ❷ vi. 起皱纹;皱起来: ~ with age 老得脸上起皱

wrinkle[2] ['riŋkl] n. ①妙计,好主意;消息: be full of ~s 足智多谋 / give sb. a ~ 给某人一条妙计 / put sb. up to a ~ or two 给某人一二妙策 ②方法;技巧;(设备、方法、技术等的)革新,创新

wrist [rist] n. ①腕;腕关节: sprain one's ~ 扭伤手腕 ②腕部技巧: That was all ~. 这全凭手腕功夫. ③(袖子、手套等的)腕部 ④【机】肘节: ~ pin 肘节销 ||slap sb.'s ~ [美俚]轻罚某人;斥责某人 ||'~band n. (衬衫等的)袖口 / ~ drop 【医】腕垂病 / ~ joint 【解】腕关节 / '~watch n. 手表

wristlet ['ristlit] n. ①(保暖的)腕带;表带 ②手镯 ③[俚]手铐 ||~ watch [英]手表(=wrist-watch)

writ[1] [rit] n. ①[古]书写物;文书 ②(法院等的)命令,令状: a ~ for the arrest of sb. 逮捕某人的令状(或拘票) / serve a ~ on sb. 将传票送交给某人 / a ~ of attachment 扣押令,拘留状 / a ~ of execution 执行令状 / a ~ of privilege (对特权人物因民事诉讼而被拘留时的)释放令状 ||a ~ of error 【律】(推翻错误原判的)再审令 / Holy (或 Sacred) Writ 基督教《圣经》 / The ~ runs. 法令有效.

writ[2] [rit] [古] write 的过去式和过去分词

write [rait] (wrote [rout] 或 [古] writ [rit], written ['ritn] 或 [古] writ) ❶ vt. ①书写,写下: ~ one's name 写自己的名字 / can ~ one's alphabet 会写字母 / ~ the letters separate 把字母分开写 / a good hand 写得一手好字 / He ~s German with ease. 他德文写得很流畅. ②写(书信、报告等),编写(乐曲等): ~ a novel

写小说 / ～ a letter 写信 / ～ a report 写报告 / ～ a will 写遗嘱 ③把…写得；把…写入(into): ～ oneself into fame 著书出名 / ～ sb. into fiction 把某人写进小说 ④写信给；写信说, 函告: Please ～ me promptly on arrival. 请你一到就写信给我。/ Write us the result. 把结果函告我们。/ He wrote (me) that he was working in a factory. 他(给我)来信说他在工厂里工作。⑤填写；写满: ～ a cheque 开支票 / ～ an application for 填写…申请书 / ～ four sheets 写满四张纸 ⑥把…描写成；称…为 ⑦[常用被动语态]显露；使留下印记: happiness written on the faces of these old peasants 老农们脸上显露的欢乐 / Her heroic image is written on our hearts. 她的英雄形象永远铭记在我们心中。⑧签署契约承担；签署订货单认购; 承保: ～ life insurance 承保人寿险 ⑨命中注定 ❷ vi. ①写；写字: ～ on both sides of the paper 在纸的两面写 / ～ in English 用英语写 / You may ～ in ink or pencil. 你用钢笔或铅笔写都可以。/ The pen ～s smoothly. 这支笔书写流畅。/ He ～s legibly. 他的字写得很清楚。/ He can read and ～. 他能够读书写字。②写信: He ～s home once a week. 他每星期给家里写一封信。③写作；作曲: ～ for the workers, peasants and soldiers 为工农兵写作 / ～ for (或 in) the newspapers 为报纸写稿 / ～ for a living 靠写作过活 ‖*be written in the book of life* 见 **book** / *nothing (something) to ～ home about* 不值得(值得)大书特书的事情 / *What I have written I have written.* 既已写了就坚决不改。/ *～ down* ① 写下, 记下: *Write down* the address before you forget it. 把地址写下来, 免得忘记。②把…描写成; 使成文章: ～ sb. *down* a drunkard 把某人描写成一个酒鬼 / ～ oneself *down* a bore 使自己被人认为讨厌 ③写文章贬损 ④减低(资产、货物等)的帐面价值;贬低(地位、重要性等) ⑤(降低身分)写较低级的作品 / ～ *in* ①把…写入: ～ *in* an amendment to a law 把修正案写入法律条文 / 向中心站(或供应点)打报告提出(要求等) ③在选票上写人(非原定候选人的名字); 投 (非原定候选人的票) / ～ *off* ① 容易地写成(文章等); 一口气写成: ～ *off* an account of one's trip 一口气把旅行见闻写下来 ②写信寄出: ～ *off* for a fresh supply of penicillin 写信要求再供应一批青霉素 ③ 注销, 取消(债款等); 勾销: ～ *off* a bad debt 注销一笔坏帐, 划去已无法收到的帐 / ～ *off* uncollectibles 销除收不回的帐目 / ～ *off* a question with one stroke 一笔勾销某问题 ④[美俚] 毁掉; 杀掉; 结束掉 / ～ oneself *out* (作家等)写到头脑枯竭 / ～ one's own ticket 见 **ticket** / ～ *out* 写出; 全部写出: ～ *out* an agreement 缮写契约 / ～ *out* a prescription 开药方 / ～ *out* fair 誊清 / ～ *up* 补写…到最近日期: ～ *up* one's diary 补写日记 ②把…写成文; 详细描写; 把(报道等)写得有吸引力: ～

up a news story 把一篇新闻报道写得有声有色 ③写文章赞扬 ④抬高(资产、货物等)的帐面价值 ⑤[美]写传票传唤 / *writ* (或 *written*) *large* 以鲜明的(或放大了的)形式表示的 / *writ small* 以缩小了的形式表示的 ‖'*～-down* n. (资产等)帐面价值的有意减低 / '*～-in* n. ①在选票上被写入的非原定候选人的名字 ②对非原定候选人所投的选票 / '*～-off* n. 销帐, 删除帐面值; 帐面价值的削减; 被勾销的项目 / '*～-up* n. ①捧场文章 ②(资产等)帐面价值的提高

writer ['raitə] *n.* ①作者; 作家, 文学家; 记者; 撰稿者: the ～ of a report 报告的作者 / an African ～ 非洲作家 / a ～ of novels 小说家 ②抄写员; 文书; 办事员 ③写作手册: a ～ 书信写作手册, 尺牍 ④[苏格兰]律师 ‖*a ～ to the signet* [英]苏格兰律师 / ‖*～'s cramp*, *～'s palsy* 【医】指痉挛, 书写痉挛(由于书写过多而引起)

writhe [raið] **I** ❶ *vt.* ①扭曲; 扭歪 ②(因剧痛、苦恼等)翻滚, 扭动(身体等) ③缠结, 缠绕 ❷ *vi.* ①蠕动, 蜿蜒翻动 ②翻滚, 扭动: ～ in agony 病苦地扭动 ③苦恼, 不安: ～ at (或 under) an insult 因受侮辱而感到苦恼 / ～ with shame 因怕羞而忸怩不安 **II** *n.* 扭动, 翻滚

writing ['raitiŋ] *n.* ① 书写; 写; 写作; 书面形式: reading and ～ 读与写 / a ～ group 写作小组 / put ... in ～ 把…写下来 ②书法; 笔迹; 文体: His ～ is easy to read. 他的字迹清楚易认。③著作;文学作品: sb.'s ～s on electronics 某人关于电子学的著作 ④文字; 文件; 信件; 铭 ⑤作家职业 ‖*commit sth. to ～* 见 **commit** / *the ～* (或 *handwriting*) *on the wall* 凶事的预兆 ‖*case ～* 文具盒 / ～ *chair* 写字椅(一边有作写字板用的椅臂) / ～ *desk* ①(桌面斜的)写字台, 书桌 ②(箱面可用作写字板的)文具箱 / ～ *ink* 墨水 / ～ *paper* 写字纸; 信纸 / ～ *table* 写字台

wrong [rɔŋ] **I** *a.* ①错误的, 不正确的: a ～ answer (decision) 错误的答案 (决定) / I was (My opinions were) ～. 我(我的看法)错了。/ It would be ～ for you to refuse. 你如果拒绝就错了。/ It was ～ of him (或 He was ～) to make such a promise. 他作了这样的诺言是错误的。/ He took the ～ street. 他走错了街道。/ We got into the ～ room. 我们走错了房间。/ We have come the ～ way. 我们走错路了。②不适当的: That was the ～ thing to say. 那个话不该说。③不正常的, 不好的, 不健全的: be ～ in the head 神志不正常 / Something is ～ with him (the machine). 他(那机器)有点毛病。/ What's ～ with that? 那有什么不对呢? ④不道德的; 犯罪的; 邪恶的: ～ conduct 不道德的行为 ⑤反(面)的: the ～ side of the cloth 布的反面 **II** *ad.* 错, 不对: guess (answer) ～ 猜(答)错 / lead sb. ～ 带某人走错路(或走上歧路) / The camera has gone ～. 照相机不灵了。/ He told me ～. 他对我讲的是错的。/ You've got it ～.

你搞错了。(指算错、理解错等)**III** *n.* ①错误; 坏事; 邪恶: Two ~s do not make a right. 两个错误不等于一个正确。(或: 别人错了不等于你就对了。) / know the difference between right and ~ 辨是非, 明善恶 ②不公正, 冤屈: right a ~ 矫枉, 雪冤 / suffer ~ 受冤屈 / complain of one's ~s 诉自己所受的冤屈 ③不道德; 违法, 犯罪 【律】侵犯权利 **IV** *vt.* ①冤枉, 委屈: You ~ed him when you said that he was dishonest. 你说他不诚实是冤枉他了。②无礼地对待, 虐待; 诈骗: We will not tolerate his ~ing her any more. 我们决不能再容忍他虐待她了。/ ~ sb. out of a thing 夺去某人的东西 ③勾引, 玷污(女子) ④中伤; 侮辱 ‖be in the ~ 错, 理亏; 谬误: He admitted that he was in the ~. 他承认是他的不是。/ do sb. ~ (或 do ~ to sb.) 对待某人不公平; 冤屈某人, 委屈某人 / do ~ 做错; 作恶, 犯罪 / get (或 have) hold of the ~ end of the stick 见 hold / get in ~ with sb. [美口] 惹得某人讨厌 / get sb. in ~ [美口] 使某人失去众望; 使某人失宠(或受冷淡) / get up on the ~ side of (the) bed 见 side / go ~ 见 go / in the ~ box 见 box¹ / on the ~ side of 已过…岁 / put sb. in the ~ 冤枉某人, 委屈某人 ‖~ly *ad.* ①错误地, 不正当地 ②不正直地, 不公正地 / ~ness *n.* ①谬误(性); 不当 ②不正直, 不公正 ‖'~'doer *n.* 做坏事的人 / '~'doing *n.* 不道德的行为, 坏事: admit one's ~doings 承认所干的坏事 / ~ font 大小(或式样)不合的铅字 ‖'~'headed *a.* 坚持错误的, 刚愎自用的, 固执的

wrongful ['rɔŋful] *a.* ①恶劣的; 不公允的; 不义的 ②违法的, 非法的; 不正当的: a ~ heir 非法继承人 / ~ dismissal 非法解雇 ‖~ly *ad.* / ~ness *n.*

wroth [rouθ, rɔ(:)θ] *a.* 极愤怒的, 怒气冲冲的

wrought [rɔ:t] **I** work 的过去式和过去分词 **II** *a.* ①制造的; 形成的 ②(金属)锻的, 用锤敲击成的: ~ iron 熟铁, 锻铁 ③精心作成的; 精炼的 ④装饰的 ⑤激动的, 兴奋的: get ~ up 激动起来; 被激怒

wry [rai] **I** *vi.* & *vt.* 扭曲, 扭歪 **II** *a.* ①扭歪的; 歪斜的: a ~ nose 歪鼻子 ②(表示厌恶、不满等)面部肌肉扭曲的: a ~ smile 苦笑 / make a ~ face 做鬼脸 ③坚持错误的, 荒谬的; 曲解的 ④讽刺性幽默的, 作弄(人)的 ‖~ly *ad.* / ~ness *n.* ‖~-mouthed ['raimauðd] *a.* ①歪嘴的 ②讽刺地恭维的 / '~neck *n.* ①歪扭颈, 斜颈 ②歪头颈的人 ③【动】歪脖(一种啄木鸟) / '~-necked *a.* 歪头颈的

wud [wud] *a.* [苏格兰]发疯的, 疯狂的

wulfenite ['wulfənait] *n.* 【矿】钼铅矿

wurst [wə:st] *n.* 香肠

Wusuli River ['wu:,su:'li: 'rivə] 乌苏里江[黑龙江支流]

wychelm ['witʃ'elm] *n.* ①【植】无毛榆 ②榆木

wychhazel ['witʃ'heizəl] *n.* ① =wychelm ②【植】美洲金缕梅

wye [wai] *n.* ①(英语字母) Y, y ② Y 形的东西

wyliecoat ['wailikout] *n.* [苏格兰] ① 保暖的内衣 ② =petticoat (*n.*)

X

X chromosome ['eks 'krouməsoum] 【生】X 染色体

xenogenesis [,zenou'dʒenisis], **xenogeny** [zi(:)-'nɔdʒini] *n.* 【生】①(认为有生命物起自无生命物的)无生源说 ②异型有性世代交替 ③异种生殖(生出与母体完全不同的机体的假想)

xenon ['zenɔn] *n.* 【化】氙: a long-arc ~ lamp 长弧氙灯

xenophobe ['zenəfoub] *n.* 畏惧和憎恨外国人 (或外国事物)的人

xenophobia [,zenə'foubjə] *n.* 对外国人 (或外国事物)的畏惧和憎恨

xenophobic [,zenə'foubik] *a.* 畏惧和憎恨外国人 (或外国事物)的

xerography [zi'rɔgrəfi] *n.* 【印】静电印刷术 ‖**xerographic** [,ziərou'græfik] *a.*

xeroradiography [,ziərəreidi'ɔgrəfi] *n.* 干放射性照相术

Xerox ['ziərɔks] *vt.* & *vi.* 用静电印刷术复制

Xmas ['krisməs, 'eksməs] *n.* =Christmas

X particle ['eks 'pɑ:tikl] 【原】X 粒子, 介子

X-radiation ['eks,reidi'eiʃən] *n.* 【物】X 射线; X 射线辐射

X-ray ['eks'rei] **I** *a.* X 射线的, X 光的: ~ therapy X 光治疗 / an ~ photograph X 光照片 **II** *vt.* 用 X 光检查(或处理、摄影、治疗等)

xylem ['zailem] *n.* 【植】木(质)部

xylograph ['zailəgrɑ:f] *n.* 木刻; 木版印画 ‖~er [zai'lɔgrəfə] *n.* 木刻者 / ~ic(al) [,zaile'græfik-(əl)] *a.* 木刻的; 木版画的; 木版(印刷)的 / ~y [zai'lɔgrəfi] *n.* 木刻术; 木版(印刷)术; 木版画印画法

Y

yacht [jɔt] **I** *n.* 快艇;游艇: a racing ～ 竞赛用快艇 **II** *vi.* 驾快艇;赛快艇;乘游艇: go ～ing 乘快艇(或游艇)游玩 ‖～ing *n.* 驾驶快艇;快艇游航 ‖～ **club** 游艇总会,游艇俱乐部 / ～ **rope** 用软质马尼拉麻制成的优质绳 / ～**sman** ['jɔtsmən] *n.* 驾驶快艇的人;快艇主人

yak¹ [jæk] (【复】 yak⒮) *n.*【动】牦牛(主要产于中国西藏)

yak² [jæk] **I** *n.* ①长而无聊的谈话,废话 ②高声大笑 ③(演出中)引起哄堂大笑的滑稽小插曲 **II** (yakked; yakking) *vi.* 喋喋不休地讲;瞎扯,瞎谈

yam [jæm] *n.* 薯蓣属植物(如山药、甘薯): the Chinese ～ 薯蓣,山药

yap [jæp] **I** (yapped; yapping) *vi.* ①(狗)狂吠 ②哇啦哇啦乱讲;[美俚]瞎讲 **II** *n.* ①(狗的)狂吠声 ②[美俚]喧闹的傻话 ③[美俚](看作说话工具的)嘴 ④[美俚]无赖汉,阿飞 ⑤[美俚]乡下人 ‖**open one's** ～ 开口,说话

yard¹ [jɑːd] **I** *n.* ①院子,围场;[美]庭院: a front ～ 前院 ②[常用以构成复合词](作一定用途的)场地;(露天)工场;堆置场;贮藏处;(家畜、家禽)圈栏: a dock～ (或 ship～)造船厂,造船所 / a railway (或 marshalling) ～ (铁路)调车场,编车场 / a cattle ～ 放置牲畜的仓前空场;(车站等旁的)牲畜栏 ③ [the Y-] 伦敦警察厅;伦敦警察厅刑事部 (＝the Scotland Yard) ④(鹿等)冬天林中集居处 **II** ❶ *vt.* ①把(家畜、家禽)赶进围栏 ②把…放入场地 ❷ *vi.* (鹿等冬天在林中)集居 (up) ‖～**age** ['jɑːdidʒ] *n.* 车站旁牲畜栏的使用;牲畜栏使用费 ‖～**bird** *n.* ①入伍新兵;[美俚]步兵 ②罚做杂务(或只准在某一范围内活动)的士兵 / ～**man** ['jɑːdmən] *n.* 场地工作人员;(铁路)车场工作人员 / '～-**,master** *n.* (铁路)车场场长

yard² [jɑːd] *n.* ①码(英美长度单位;＝3 呎,略作 yd.): five ～s of cloth 五码布 / a square (cubic) ～ 一平方(立方)码 ②(沙、土等的)一立方码 ③【海】(帆)桁 ④[美俚]一百元;一百元的钞票;一千元;一千元的钞票 ‖a ～ of clay 陶制长烟管 / man the ～s 【海】行登桁仪式 / ～**age** ['jɑːdidʒ] *n.* ①以码测量的长度;码数 ②方码数(指以立方码为单位的体积) ‖'～**arm** *n.*【海】(帆)桁端 / ～ **goods** 按码出售的织物 / ～ **measure** 码尺(指直尺或卷尺) / ～ **rope** 【海】(帆)桁索(指升降帆桁的缆索) / '～**stick** *n.* 码尺(指直尺);[喻]衡量的标准,尺度: The ～*stick* of truth is practice. 检验真理的标准是实践。 / '～**wand** *n.* 码尺(指直尺)

yarn [jɑːn] **I** *n.* ①纱,纱线: cotton ～ 棉纱 / woollen ～ 粗纺毛纱 ②[口]故事;奇谈: spin a ～ 讲故事 **II** *vi.* [口]讲故事 ‖'～-**beam**, '～-**roll** *n.*【纺】卷经线的木轴 / '～-**dye** *vt.* (在编或织前)染,把…原纱染色 / ～ **number** 纱线支数 / '～**smith** *n.* 编故事的人;作家

yawn [jɔːn] **I** ❶ *vi.* ①打呵欠: make sb. ～ 使某人困倦 ②张开口;裂开 ❷ *vt.* 打着呵欠说 **II** *n.* ①呵欠: with a ～ 打着呵欠 ②裂口,裂缝;陷窟 ‖～**ful** *a.* 使人无聊得打呵欠的

ye¹ [jiː] *pron.* ①[古]你们,汝等 ②[古][方]你: What d'～ think? 你看怎么样?

ye² [jiː] *art.* [定冠词][古]＝the (*art.*) (现今在一些商号中仍用此词,以示该店历史悠久)

yea [jei] **I** *ad.* [古]①是(现除口头表决时使用外已为 yes 所代替) ②而且,甚至可说: ～ and 更有甚者 / ready, ～ eager 准备好了,甚至可说很急切 **II** *n.* ①肯定,赞成 ②赞成票;投赞成票者: the ～s and nays 赞成票和反对票 ‖**Let your** ～ **be** ～ **and your nay be nay.** 赞成你就说赞成,不赞成你就说不赞成。 / ～ **and nay** 犹豫不决;优柔寡断 ‖'～-,**sayer** *n.* ①(对人生或事物)肯定者 ②唯唯诺诺的人 / '～-,**saying** *a.* (对人生或事物)抱积极态度的,肯定的

year [jəː, jiə] *n.* ①年: a solar ～ 太阳年 / a tropical ～ 回归年 / a sidereal ～ 恒星年 / a lunar ～ 太阴年 / a calendar ～ 历年 / a civil (legal) ～ 民用(法定)年 / a common ～ 平年 / a leap ～ 闰年 / this ～ 今年 / last ～ 去年 / next ～ 明年 / the next ～ 翌年,第二年 / the ～ before last 前年 / the ～ after next 后年 / in the ～ 1974 在一九七四年 / this day ～ 去年今日;明年今日 ②年度: the school (或 academic) ～ 学年 / the fiscal (或 financial) ～ 财政年度,会计年度 ③[复]年纪,岁数: He is twenty ～s old (或 twenty ～s of age). 他二十岁。 / be old (young) for one's ～s 比年龄显得老(年轻) / He is already advanced in ～s. 他已年老。 ④[复]多年,长久: ～s ago 多年前 / It is ～s since we last met. 我们已经多年不见了。 ⑤[美俚]一元 ‖**all the** ～ **round** 一年到头 / **a** ～ **and a day** 【律】满一年,一整年 / **from** ～ **to** ～ 年年,每年 / **in the** ～ **one** 在公元一年;[喻]很久以前,早年 / **in** ～**s** 年老的 / **of late** ～**s** 近年来 / **over the** ～**s** 在这(或那)几年中 / **the** ～ **of grace ...** (或 **the ...th** ～ **of** grace 或 **the** ～ **of our Lord ...** 或 **the** ～ **of our redemption ...**) 耶稣纪元…年,公元…年 / **three score** ～**s and**

ten 人生七十年，一辈子，一般人的寿命 / ～ *after* ～ (或 ～ *by* ～) 年年，每年 / ～ *in* ～ *out* 年复一年地，不断地，始终 ‖～ly *a.* 每年的；一年一次的；一年间的；按年的 *ad.* 每年；一年一度；年年；按年 ‖～book *n.* 年鉴，年刊 / ～-end ['jə:rend] *n.* & *a.* 年终(的) / '～'long *a.* 持续一年的，整整一年的 / '～-round *a.* 一年到头的，整年的

yearling ['jə:liŋ, 'jiəliŋ] I *n.* ①一岁崽，一周岁至两周岁之间的动物 ②出生后第二年的赛马(指出生后第二年一月一日至第三年一月一日之间的马) ③[美俚](西点军校的)二年级学员 II *a.* ①一岁的，一龄的 ②满一周年而还未满两周岁的

yearn [jə:n] *vi.* 想念，怀念；思慕，向往；渴望；极想：～ *to* (或 *towards*) sb. 向往某人 / ～ *for* (或 *after*) 渴望

yearning ['jə:niŋ] I *n.* 怀念；思慕，向往；渴望 II *a.* 怀念的；思慕的，向往的；渴望的 ‖～ly *ad.*

yeast [ji:st] I *n.* ①酵母 ②麯子，鲜酵母块，酵母片 ③泡沫 ④激动；激动的起因 II *vi.* [罕]发酵；起泡沫 ‖～ *cake* 面面饼，鲜酵母块 / ～ *powder* 发酵粉(酵母的代用品)

yell [jel] I ❶ *vi.* 叫喊；叫嚷；忍不住大笑：～ *for* help 大声呼救 / ～ *with* fury (pain, delight) 发怒(痛得，乐得)大叫 ❷ *vt.* ①叫着说：～ *a* warning 高声警告 / ～ *out an oath* 破口咒骂 ②用喊声鼓励：～ *the* team *to victory* 用喊声鼓励运动队取胜 II *n.* [美](鼓励运动员的)喊声，拉拉队有节奏的叫喊声

yellow ['jeləu] I *a.* ①黄(色)的；黄皮肤的：the ～ races 黄色人种 ②(因病等)发黄的；(因陈旧)泛黄的 ③(报刊等)采用耸人听闻手法的，作低级渲染的 ④[口]胆怯的；卑鄙的；靠不住的 ⑤(脸色、心情等)妒忌的，猜疑的 II *n.* ①黄(色) ②黄色颜料(或染料) ③蛋黄 ④黄种人 ⑤[医]黄疸；【植】黄化病 ⑥[口]胆怯 ⑦[古]妒忌 III ❶ *vi.* 变黄，发黄：the ～*ing* leaves 变黄的叶子 ❷ *vt.* 使变黄，使发黄：Time has ～*ed* the wallpaper. 时间使糊墙纸发黄了。‖～ish, ～y *a.* 淡黄色的，带黄色的 / ～ness *n.* ‖～ *alert* (空袭)预备警报 / '～-back *n.* 十九世纪流行的黄封面的廉价通俗小说；法国廉价小说 / '～-,belly *n.* 可鄙的胆小鬼 / ～ *book* 黄皮书(法国等政府或议会发表的报告书) / ～ *dog* ①杂种狗 ②卑鄙的人 / '～-'dog *a.* ①卑鄙的，可耻的 ②反对工会的：a ～-dog contract 以受雇工人不加入工会为条件的雇用契约 / ～ *fever* 【医】黄热病 / ～ *jack* ① = ～ fever ②(检疫中的船上所悬挂的)黄旗 / ～ *jacket* ①鲜黄色胡蜂 ②(清代权贵穿的)黄马褂 ③[美俚]盛麻醉品的黄色胶囊 / ～ *journalism* 黄色新闻编辑作风(指不择手段地夸张、渲染以招揽或影响读者) / ～ *metal* 一种黄铜(含铜60%，锌40%) ②黄金 / ～ *peril* 黄祸(指所谓的黄种人带给西方的威胁) / ～ *press* [总称]黄色报刊 / ～ *spot* 【解】(视网膜上的)黄斑 / ～ *streak* 胆怯，懦怯

yelp [jelp] I ❶ *vi.* (狗)吠，猛跳；(因痛而)叫喊 ❷ *vt.* 叫喊着说 II *n.* (短促而尖锐的)吠声(或叫喊声)

yeoman ['jəumən] ([复] yeomen) *n.* ①【英史】自由民；(国王或贵族的)侍者，仆人 ②[英]自耕农 ③(英国国王的)仪仗卫士 ④[美](海军)文书军士 ⑤义勇骑兵 ‖*do* ～('s) *service* (一旦有事时)给予有效的援助 ‖～ly *a.* ①象自由民的；义勇骑兵的；卫士的 ②勇敢的；刚毅的；忠实的 *ad.* 勇敢地；刚毅地；忠实地

yeomanry ['jəumənri] *n.* ①[总称]自由民；自耕农 ②[英]义勇骑兵队

yes [jes, jə:s] I *ad.* ①是，是的：A: Are you ready? B: *Yes*, I am (ready). 甲：你准备好了吗？乙：是，准备好了。[注意：回答反面提问时，Yes 和 No 的用法和汉语习惯不同：A: Don't you like it? B: *Yes*, I do. (不说 No, I do.) 甲：你不喜欢这个吗？乙：不，我喜欢。/ A: Isn't this book yours? B: No, it isn't. (不说 Yes, it isn't.) 甲：这本书不是你的吗？乙：是的，这本书不是我的。] ②[用升调，表示疑问或鼓励对方进一步讲述]是吗，真的吗：A: The boy can run 100 metres in eleven seconds. B: *Yes*? 甲：这个男孩一百米只跑十一秒。乙：真的吗？/ A: Just then a heavy rain poured down. B: *Yes*? 甲：正在那个时候，忽然大雨倾盆。乙：是吗？(或：那末后来怎么样呢？) ③[用升调，征求对方意见]是不是：We can definitely finish it today, ～? 我们今天一定可以完成，(你说)是不是？ ④[应答呼唤]是，嗳，我在这儿 ⑤[加强语气用]是的，说真的：He has read, ～, and studied the article carefully. 他不但阅读，而且仔细研究了那篇文章。II ([复] yeses ['jesiz]) *n.* ①是，同意，赞成：answer ～ or no 明确回答"是"还是"不是"(或同意还是不同意) ②赞成票；投赞成票的人 (yessed; yessing) *vt.* & *vi.* (对…)说"是"，同意，赞成 ‖*say* ～ (*to*) 同意(…)，允诺(…) ‖～-man *n.* 唯唯诺诺的人

yesterday ['jestədi] I *n.* ①昨天，昨日：*Yesterday* was Monday. 昨天是星期一。/ the day before ～ 前天 / ～'s newspaper 昨天的报纸 / on ～ [美](在)昨天 / ～ morning (afternoon, evening) 昨天早晨(下午，晚上) / ～ week 上星期的昨天(即八天前)；下星期的昨天(即六天后) ②近来，最近：a thing of ～ 最近的事 ③[常用复]过去的日子，往昔 II *ad.* ①昨天，昨日：He arrived ～. 他昨天到达。②最近：I was not born ～. 我不是最近才出生的。(意指：你不要认为我一无所知。)

yet [jet] I *ad.* ①还，尚；仍然：They have not started ～. 他们还没有出发(或开始)。/ a ～ unfinished task 尚未完成的任务 / A: Have they arrived? B: Not ～. 甲：他们到了吗？乙：还没有(到)。/ Much ～ remains (或 remains ～) to be done. 还有许多事要做。/ The best is ～ to come. 最好的还在后头。/ He will win ~. 他还是会胜利的。②已经: Is everything ready ~? 一切都准备好了吗? / Need you go ~? 你现在就得走了吗? ③[与比较级连用]比…还要, 更; [与 once, again 等连用]再: a ~ easier (~ more difficult) task 更容易(更困难)的工作 / ~ once (more) 再一次 / ~ again 再一次 / another and ~ another 一个又一个, 接二连三 ④[与最高级连用]到目前(或当时)为止(最…): This is the biggest underground lake ~ discovered. 这是迄今已发现的最大的地下湖。⑤也: He did not come, nor ~ write. 他人不来, 信也不写。⑥而, 而又, 然而: This article, which seems a little loose in construction, is ~ quite inspiring. 这篇文章虽然结构似乎松弛些, 却是很有启发的。**II** conj. 而, 而又; 然而: a glorious ~ difficult task 一项光荣而艰巨的任务 / We have won great victories, ~ more serious struggles are still ahead of us. 我们取得了伟大的胜利, 然而我们前面还有更严重的斗争。‖and ~ 而, 然而: It is strange, and ~ it is true. 这很奇怪, 但却是真的。/ as ~ 到目前为止; 到当时为止: As ~ we haven't heard from him. 我们到目前为止还没有收到他的来信。

yew [juː] n. 紫杉属树木(尤指浆果紫杉)

yield [jiːld] **I ❶** vt. ①出产, 生长出(作物等), 结出(果实); 产生(效果、收益等): Grapes ~ wine. 葡萄可以酿酒。/an investment that ~s 10 percent 产生 10% 利润的投资 / Practice ~s genuine knowledge. 实践出真知。②让与, 给与; 同意: A difficult situation ~ed place to a favourable one. 困难的局面让位于顺利的局面。/ They must ~ the point. 他们(在辩论中)必须在这点上让步。/ ~ precedence to 让…居先 / He ~ed his consent. 他同意了。/ ~ submission 服从, 屈服 ③被迫放弃; [~ oneself] 放纵 (up): ~ up the ghost (或 life, soul, breath, spirit) 死 / ~ oneself up to pleasure 沉湎于逸乐 **❷** vi. ①出产: This land ~s well (poorly). 这块土地产量高(低)。②服从; 屈服; 投降 (to): ~ to persuasion 听从劝告 / ~ to despair 陷于悲观 / The disease ~ed to treatment. 疾病经过医疗有所好转(或给治好了)。/ The door ~ed to a strong push. 猛烈一推, 门开了。**II** n. 产量, 收获量; 收益: a large ~ of wheat 小麦的丰收 / The ~s have increased this year. 今年产量增长了。‖~ oneself prisoner 投降做俘虏 / ~ the palm to sb. 见 palm²

yielding [ˈjiːldiŋ] a. ①出产的: a wheat that is high ~ 一种高产小麦 ②易变形的; 易弯曲的 ③柔顺的; 依从的, 屈从的 ‖~ly ad.

yoke [jouk] **I** n. ①牛轭; 轭 ②[单复同](同轭的)一对牛(或马等): three ~ of oxen 三对同轭牛 ③轭状扁担; 吊钟的横木 ④轭状物;【史】架在被俘人员脖子上的轭状枷锁; 轭门(举牛轭或架三矛而成的拱门, 令战俘在其下面通过以示服从): pass (或 come) under the ~ 认输; 承认失败; 屈从, 屈服 ⑤[喻]束缚; 压力; 支配, 管辖: the heavy ~ of public opinion 舆论的沉重压力 / shake (或 throw) off the ~ 拒绝服从, 摆脱枷锁 ⑥[喻](联结夫妇等的)情义: the ~ of brotherhood 不可分的兄弟关系, 手足之情 ⑦【船】横舵柄 ⑧【空】飞机操纵杆 ⑨【物】轭铁 ⑩【无】轭, 架, 座; 偏转线圈 ⑪【交】护轨夹 ⑫【建】窗头板 ⑬【动】翅轭 ⑭(女服)上衣的抵肩; 裙子的腰 ⑮[古]一对牛一天耕的土地 **II ❶** vt. ①给…上轭; 用轭连起 ②把牛套到(犁等)之上 ③结合; 接合; 连接 ④使成配偶: be ~d in marriage 被婚姻结合在一起 ⑤[罕]束缚, 奴役 **❷** vi. 结合; 连合; 配合 ‖~ bone 颧骨 / '~ fellow, '~ mate n. 同事; 配偶; 伙伴; 搭档 / '~ lines, '~ ropes [复] n. 【船】横舵柄索

yoke

yokel [ˈjoukəl] n. [贬]乡下佬, 土包子

yolk [jouk] n. ①蛋黄, 卵黄 ②羊毛油脂 ‖'~y ①蛋黄的; 似蛋黄的; 充满蛋黄的 ②有羊毛脂的 ‖~ bag, ~ sac【生】卵黄囊

yon [jɔn] **I** ad. & a. [古][方]=yonder (ad. & a.) **II** pron. [古]在那儿的东西(或人)

yonder [ˈjɔndə] **I** ad. 那边; 在远处: Yonder stands an oak. 那里有一棵树。**II** a. 那边的; 远处的: on the ~ side 在远处那一边 **III** pron. 那边, 远处; 那边(或远处)的东西

yore [jɔː] n. 昔时, 往昔(现只用于 of ~ 一语中): of ~ 从前的, 往昔 / in days of ~ 昔时

you [juː; 弱 ju] [单数、复数、主格、宾格形式均同] pron. ①你; 你们: You are our friend. 你是我们的朋友。/ You are our friends. 你们是我们的朋友。/ Shall I pour ~ a cup of tea? 要给你倒杯茶吗? / These two spades are for ~ and me. 这两把铲子是给你和我(用)的。②[呼唤、祈使、感叹用]: What's your name? 喂, 你叫什么名字? / Begin ~ (=You begin)! 你开始! (或: 你开头儿!) / You naughty boy! 你这个顽皮孩子啊! ③(泛指)一个人, 任何人: You never can (或 can never) tell! 谁也没法预料! ④[古]你(们)自己 ‖between ~ and me 你我两人之间讲的话, 不足为外人道 ‖~-'all pron. [美俚]你们大家; [美俚]你 / '~-know-'what n. [俚]那个东西(指不必明言或不便明言的东西)

young [jʌŋ] **I** (younger ['jʌŋgə], youngest ['jʌŋgist]) *a.* ① 年轻的; 幼小的; 青春时期的: The ~ people are the most active and vital force in society. 青年是整个社会力量中的一部分最积极最有生气的力量。/ a ~ man 青年男子 / Now, ~ man! 喂, 小子! / a ~ child 幼童 / a ~ family (一家人中的) 幼小子女 / a ~ animal (tree) 幼小的动物(树) / in one's days 在年轻时候 ②象青年的, 有青春活力的, 朝气蓬勃的: a ~ state 年轻的国家 / be ~ in spirit 朝气蓬勃 / be ~ for one's age (或 years) 比年龄显得年轻 ③[Y-] (政党、运动等) 新(兴)的, 青年的: the Young Turks (一八八九年至一九二六年间的)青年土耳其党; (泛指)激进派 ④初期的, 开始不久的: The century (year, night) is still ~. 这个世纪(年头, 夜晚)还刚开始不久。⑤ 没有经验的, 初出茅庐的, 未成熟的: be ~ in the trade (at the work) 对这行业(工作)还是新手 ⑥(父子、兄弟等之间)年龄较小的; 年轻时代的: ~ Jones 小琼斯(尤指儿子); 年轻的琼斯 / the ~ Joneses 年轻时代的琼斯 / the ~ Joneses 琼斯家的孩子们 ⑦【地】幼年的, 受侵蚀尚少的 **II** [单复同] *n.* ① [the ~]青年们: books for the ~ 青年读物 ②崽, 仔, 雏: The cow took good care of her ~. 母牛很当心它的小牛。‖~ and old 老老少少, 不分老幼 / with ~ 怀胎: The mare is with ~. 母马怀着胎。‖**~ish** *a.* 还年轻的, 还幼小的 ‖**~ blood** ①[总称]青年 ②青春活力, 青年的思想行动 ③新鲜血液; [总称]新接纳的成员 ④[总称]时髦人

youngster ['jʌŋstə] *n.* ①年轻人, 小伙子; 小孩 ②美国海军学校的二年级学生 ③(培育的)幼小动物; 幼苗

your [jɔ:, juə; 弱 jo, je] *pron.* ① [you 的所有格]你的; 你们的: Open ~ books. 把书打开。/ by (或 with) ~ leave 在你的许可下 / Do ~ best. 尽力去干。②(泛指)一个人的, 任何人的: When you face the south, the east is at ~ left. 面朝南的时候, 左边是东方。③ [后接 Excellency, Honour 等, 构成对贵族、官员等的尊称, 直接呼时用]: Your Majesty 陛下 / Your Excellency 阁下 ④ [古] (今用于口语, 含贬意)你(们)那种

…; 你(们)所谓的…: So that's ~ philanthropy! 你们所谓的慈善原来如此!

yours [jɔ:z] *pron.* ①[物主代词]你的(东西); 你们的(东西): This pen is ~. 这支笔是你的。/ Yours is a good suggestion indeed. 你的建议确实很好。/ a friend of ~ 你的一位朋友 ②你(们)的家属: Best regards to you and ~. 向你和你的家属致意。③你(们)的来信: ~ of the 10th inst. 本月十日来信 / Yours is to hand. 来信收到。④[在信尾具名前, 与 truly, faithfully, sincerely 等连用, 作为客套语]: Yours truly (或 Truly ~) 你的忠实的 ‖**What's ~?** [口]你要喝什么酒? / ~ **truly** (或 **sincerely**) [谑]鄙人, 我

yourself [jɔ:'self] *pron.* ① [反身代词]你自己: Take care not to hurt ~. 当心别弄伤了自己。/ Help ~. (主人招待客人时用语)请吃。②[用以加强语气]你亲自, 你本人: You ~ said so. 你自己这样说的。③ [用于 be, come to 等之后]你的正常情况(指健康、情绪等): You are not quite ~ today. 你今天好象精神不好(或有点不高兴)。‖**(all) by ~** ①你独自地: Why are you sitting here by ~? 你干吗一个人坐在这儿? ②你独力地, 全靠(你)自己: Can you do it by ~? 你一个人干得了吗? / **Be ~!** [口]振作起来! (或: 不要没精打采!) / **How's ~?** [俚]你自己好吗?(用以应答对方 "How are you?" 的客套话)

youth [ju:θ] (['复] youths [ju:ðz]) *n.* ①青春; 青年时期; 初期: full of ~ and vigour 充满青春活力 / in (the days of) one's ~ 在年轻的时候 / the ~ of the world 世界的初期, 太古, 古代 ②青年们: The ~ of our country have lofty ideals. 我国的青年有崇高的理想。③ (男)青年, 小伙子: a ~ of twenty 一个二十岁的青年 ‖**~ hostel** (为徒步或骑自行车旅行者所设的)青年招待所

youthful ['ju:θful] *a.* ①年轻的; 青年的: a ~ cadre 年轻的干部 / ~ days 青年时期 ②富于青春活力的, 朝气蓬勃的 ③【地】幼年的, 受侵蚀尚少的: a ~ river 幼年河 ‖**~ly** *ad.* / **~ness** *n.*

yule [ju:l] *n.* [常作 Y-] 【基督教】圣诞节; 圣诞节期: the Yule block (或 clog, log)圣诞前夜放入炉中焚烧的大木 ‖**~tide** *n.* [常作 Y-] 圣诞节期

Z

zeal [zi:l] *n.* 热心, 热情, 热忱: a man of ~ 热心人 / with extraordinary ~ 非常热忱地

zealot ['zelət] *n.* ①热心者; 狂热者; 坚持党派观念的人 ②[Z-]【史】(公元六年至七〇年间反抗罗马统治的)犹太某一教派中的热情的信徒

zealous ['zeləs] *a.* 热心的, 热情的; 积极的: be ~ in one's work 热心工作 / be ~ for progress 积极争取进步 ‖**~ly** *ad.*

zebra ['zi:brə, 'zebrə] *n.* 【动】斑马 ‖**~ crossing** (英国)斑马线 (指马路上涂有黑白相间颜色的人

行横道线)

zein ['zi:in] *n.* 【生化】玉米朊; 玉蜀黍醇溶朊

zenith ['zeniθ, 'zi:niθ] *n.* ①【天】天顶 ②(幸运、繁荣、权力等的)顶点, 顶峰 ‖~al *a.* ‖~ distance 【天】天顶距 / ~ telescope 【天】天顶仪

zephyr ['zefə] *n.* ①西风 ②和风, 微风 ③轻薄织物(或衣着等); 轻罗 ④轻飘的东西

zero ['ziərou] **I** (复] zero(e)s) *n.* ①【数】零 ②零号(即 0); 零点, 零位; (温度计的)零度; 【空】零高度: absolute ~ 绝对零度 / fly at ~ 【空】在一千呎高度以下飞行, 超低空飞行 / ~ point 零点; 致死临界温度 / ~ position 零位 ③最低点; 无, 乌有: Their hopes were reduced to ~. 他们的希望化为乌有。/ His chances of success sank to ~. 他的成功机会降到了最低点。④无足轻重的人; 没价值的东西 ⑤【天】天底 **II** *a.* ①零的 ②【语】无屈折的; 无词尾变化的; 零形态的: ~ plural 无词尾变化的复数 ③【气】(云幕高度)小于五十呎的; (能见度)小于一百六十五呎的 **III** *vt.* ①把(机械等)的调节器调整归零 ②把…减少(或减低)到零位 ‖~ in ①把(枪炮等)调整归零 ②把(枪炮、抨击的火力等)对准目标; 对…集中火力(on): Artillery and mortars were ~ed in on all avenues of approach. 大炮和迫击炮对着所有的来路瞄准着。‖~ beat 【无】零差, 零拍 / ~ count 发射制导弹等计算时间的最后时间(从十倒数到零即行发射) / ~ G, ~ gravity 【物】零重量, 无重量, 失重 / ~ hour ①【军】进攻发起的时刻; 零时 ②[喻]决定性的时刻, 紧急关头 / '~-'sum *a.* 一方得益引起另一方相应损失的 / '~-'~ *a.* 【气】云幕高度和能见度等于零的; 视程零的: ~-~ weather 咫尺莫辨的恶劣天气 / a ~-~ fog 能见度等于零的浓雾

zest [zest] **I** *n.* ①(辛辣的)滋味; 风味; 香味; 风趣; 兴趣: add (或 give) ~ to 给…增添风趣 ②热心, 热情: enter into a piece of work with ~ 热情地开始工作 ③[罕]香橙皮; 柠檬皮(用作香料) **II** *vt.* ①给…加香味; 给…调味 ②给…添风趣; 给…增添 ‖~y *a.*

Zeus [zju:s] *n.* 【希神】宙斯(希腊神话中的主神)

zigzag ['zigzæg] **I** *n.* ①之字形, Z 字形; 锯齿形 ②之字形的线条(或道路、壕沟、装饰等): walk in ~s 作之字形行走 ③蜿蜒曲折, 盘旋弯曲 ④【无】变压器中的一种绕组连接方式 **II** *a.* ①之字形的; 锯齿形的: ~ connection 【无】交错连接, 曲折连接 / ~ line【建】之字形线, Z 字形线; 锯齿形曲线 / ~ pattern【建】Z 形图案 / ~ riveted joint【机】交错铆接 ②盘旋的; 弯弯曲曲的, 蜿蜒的: a ~ path (弯曲的)羊肠小道 / ~ crack【建】不规则裂缝 / ~ route【建】之字路, Z 形路; 蜿蜒路; 回头线 **III** *ad.* ①盘旋地; 弯弯曲曲地: The path runs ~. 小径向山顶蜿蜒盘旋。②成之字形地; 成锯齿形地 **IV** (zigzagged; zigzagging) ❶ *vt.* 把…作成之字形地; 使成锯齿形; 使曲折盘旋: ~ the rivets 把铆钉铆

成错纵状 ❷ *vi.* 成之字形; 作之字形进行; 弯弯曲曲地走路: The climbers *zigzagged* up the mountain. 登山运动员盘旋上山。

zinc [zink] **I** *n.* 【化】锌 **II** (zincked 或 zinced; zincking 或 zincing) *vt.* 在…上镀锌; 用锌处理 ‖~ blende 【矿】闪锌矿 / ~ bloom 【矿】水锌矿 / ~ white 【化】锌华, 氧化锌

zip[1] [zip] **I** *n.* ①(子弹的)尖啸声; (布匹的)撕裂声 ②[口]精力, 活力 **II** (zipped; zipping) ❶ *vt.* ①给…速度(或力量) ②使增加热情(或兴趣、生命力)(up) ❷ *vi.* ①嘶嘶地响; 嘶嘶地飞 ②[口]精力充沛地干

zip[2] [zip] (zipped; zipping) ❶ *vt.* ①拉开(或扣上)…的拉链 ②拉开(拉链); 扣上(拉链) ❷ *vi.* 拉开(或扣上)拉链 ‖*Zip your lips*! [美俚]别开口! ‖~-,fastener *n.* [英]拉链

zipper ['zipə] **I** *n.* 拉链 **II** *vt.* & *vi.* (被)用拉链扣上 ‖~ed *a.* 装有拉链的; 拉链式的

zodiac ['zoudiæk] *n.* 【天】黄道带 ‖~al [zou'daiekəl] *a.* ~al circle 黄道圈 / ~al light 黄道光 / ~al signs 黄道十二宫 (=signs of the ~)

zonal ['zounəl] *a.* ①带的; 成带的; 带状的: ~ structure 【矿】带状构造, 环带构造 ②形成地带的; 分区的; 地区性的

zone [zoun] **I** *n.* ①[古][诗]带子; 腰带; 环状带 ②【地】地带; 地带; (结晶的)晶带: frigid (temperate, torrid) ~ 寒(温, 热)带 / ~ axis 【矿】晶带轴 / a ~ in depth 【军】纵深地带 / a forecast ~ (气象)预报地带 ③地区; (城市、运动场等的)区; 区域; 范围; 界: a cotton ~ 产棉区 / a business (residence) ~ 商业(住宅)区 / a danger ~ 危险地区 / a mined ~ 布雷区 / a demilitarized ~ 非军事区 / a guerrilla ~ 游击区 / a time ~ 区时, 地方时间 / a ~ of communication 战区后勤地带 / a ~ of fire 射界 / a ~ of influence 势力范围 / tolerance ~ 【机】公差范围 / ~ purification 【化】逐区提纯 / ~ refining 【化】逐区精炼 / open up the "forbidden ~" of curing deaf-mutes 打开治愈聋哑的"禁区" / incubation ~ 【医】潜伏区 ④ (包裹邮资分区计算的)邮区 (=parcel post ~); [美](大城市中的)邮区; (铁路运费等分区计算的)区, 段 ⑤层; 圈, 环带: ~ of fracture 【地】断裂带; 破裂带 / melting ~ 熔化层 / annual ~【植】年轮 / spherical ~【数】球面带 **II** ❶ *vt.* ①用带子围绕; 环绕 ②将…分区; 使分成地带 ❷ *vi.* 分成区; 分成地带 ‖*loose the maiden ~ of* 破坏…的童贞

zoo [zu:] *n.* ①[口]动物园; [the Z-]伦敦动物园 ②[美俚](铁路货车末尾工作人员乘的)守车

zoological [,zouə'lɔdʒikəl] *a.* 动物学的: a ~ garden 动物园 ‖~ly *ad.*

zoology [zou'ɔlədʒi] *n.* ①动物学 ②[总称](某地区的)动物 ③动物学论文 ④[总称]某种动物(或动物类型)的特性(或特征) ‖**zoologist** *n.* 动物学家

APPENDIX I 附录一

A List of Irregular Verbs
不 规 则 动 词 表

Infinitive 不 定 式	*Past Tense* 过 去 式	*Past Participle* 过 去 分 词
abide	abode, abided	abode, abided
arise	arose	arisen
awake	awoke	awoke, awaked
be (am, are, is; are)	was; were	been
bear	bore	borne, born
beat	beat	beaten
become	became	become
befall	befell	befallen
beget	begot	begotten, begot
begin	began	begun
behold	beheld	beheld
bend	bent	bent
bereave	bereaved, bereft	bereaved, bereft
beseech	besought, beseeched	besought, beseeched
beset	beset	beset
bestride	bestrode	bestridden, bestrid, bestrode
bet	bet, betted	bet, betted
betake	betook	betaken
bid	bade, bid	bidden, bid
bide	bode, bided	bided
bind	bound	bound
bite	bit	bitten, bit
bleed	bled	bled
blend	blended, blent	blended, blent
bless	blessed, blest	blessed, blest
blow	blew	blown
break	broke	broken
breed	bred	bred
bring	brought	brought
broadcast	broadcast, broadcasted	broadcast, broadcasted
browbeat	browbeat	browbeaten
build	built	built
burn	burnt, burned	burnt, burned
burst	burst	burst
buy	bought	bought
cast	cast	cast
catch	caught	caught
chide	chid, chided	chid, chidden, chided
choose	chose	chosen
cleave[1]	cleaved, cleft, clove	cleaved, cleft, cloven
cleave[2]	cleaved, clave	cleaved
cling	clung	clung
clothe	clothed, clad	clothed, clad

Infinitive 不 定 式	*Past Tense* 过 去 式	*Past Participle* 过 去 分 词
come	came	come
cost	cost	cost
creep	crept	crept
crow	crowed, crew	crowed
cut	cut	cut
deal	dealt	dealt
dig	dug	dug
do	did	done
draw	drew	drawn
dream	dreamed, dreamt	dreamed, dreamt
drink	drank	drunk
drive	drove	driven
dwell	dwelt, dwelled	dwelt, dwelled
eat	ate	eaten
fall	fell	fallen
feed	fed	fed
feel	felt	felt
fight	fought	fought
find	found	found
flee	fled	fled
fling	flung	flung
fly	flew	flown
forbear	forbore	forborne
forbid	forbade, forbad	forbidden
forecast	forecast, forecasted	forecast, forecasted
forego	forewent	foregone
foresee	foresaw	foreseen
foretell	foretold	foretold
forget	forgot	forgotten, forgot
forgive	forgave	forgiven
forsake	forsook	forsaken
forswear	forswore	forsworn
freeze	froze	frozen
gainsay	gainsaid	gainsaid
get	got	got, gotten
gild	gilded, gilt	gilded
gird	girded, girt	girded, girt
give	gave	given
go	went	gone
grave	graved	graven, graved
grind	ground	ground
grow	grew	grown
hamstring	hamstringed, hamstrung	hamstringed, hamstrung
hang	hung, hanged	hung, hanged
have (has)	had	had
hear	heard	heard
heave	heaved, hove	heaved, hove
hew	hewed	hewed, hewn
hide	hid	hidden, hid
hit	hit	hit
hold	held	held
hurt	hurt	hurt
inlay	inlaid	inlaid
keep	kept	kept

Infinitive 不 定 式	*Past Tense* 过 去 式	*Past Participle* 过 去 分 词
kneel	knelt, kneeled	knelt, kneeled
knit	knitted, knit	knitted, knit
know	knew	known
lade	laded	laded, laden
lay	laid	laid
lead	led	led
lean	leaned, leant	leaned, leant
leap	leapt, leaped	leapt, leaped
learn	learnt, learned	learnt, learned
leave	left	left
lend	lent	lent
let	let	let
lie	lay	lain
light	lit, lighted	lit, lighted
lose	lost	lost
make	made	made
mean	meant	meant
meet	met	met
melt	melted	melted, molten
misdeal	misdealt	misdealt
misgive	misgave	misgiven
mislay	mislaid	mislaid
mislead	misled	misled
mistake	mistook	mistaken
misunderstand	misunderstood	misunderstood
mow	mowed	mowed, mown
outbid	outbade, outbid	outbidden, outbid
outdo	outdid	outdone
outgrow	outgrew	outgrown
outlay	outlaid	outlaid
overbear	overbore	overborne
overcome	overcame	overcome
overdo	overdid	overdone
overdraw	overdrew	overdrawn
overgrow	overgrew	overgrown
overhang	overhung	overhung
overhear	overheard	overheard
overlay	overlaid	overlaid
override	overrode	overridden
overrun	overran	overrun
oversee	oversaw	overseen
overtake	overtook	overtaken
overthrow	overthrew	overthrown
partake	partook	partaken
pay	paid	paid
prove	proved	proved, proven
put	put	put
quit	quitted, quit	quitted, quit
read	read [red]	read [red]
recast	recast	recast
relay	relaid	relaid
rend	rent	rent
repay	repaid	repaid

Infinitive 不 定 式	_Past Tense_ 过 去 式	_Past Participle_ 过 去 分 词
rid	rid, ridded	rid, ridded
ride	rode	ridden
ring	rang	rung
rive	rived	riven, rived
run	ran	run
saw	sawed	sawn, sawed
say	said	said
see	saw	seen
seek	sought	sought
sell	sold	sold
send	sent	sent
set	set	set
sew	sewed	sewn, sewed
shake	shook	shaken
shave	shaved	shaved, shaven
shear	sheared	shorn, sheared
shed	shed	shed
shine	shone, shined	shone, shined
shoe	shod, shoed	shod, shoed
shoot	shot	shot
show	showed	shown, showed
shred	shredded, shred	shredded, shred
shrink	shrank, shrunk	shrunk, shrunken
shrive	shrove, shrived	shriven, shrived
shut	shut	shut
sing	sang, sung	sung
sink	sank, sunk	sunk, sunken
sit	sat	sat
slay	slew	slain
sleep	slept	slept
slide	slid	slid, slidden
sling	slung	slung
slink	slunk	slunk
slit	slit	slit
smell	smelt, smelled	smelt, smelled
smite	smote	smitten, smote
sow	sowed	sown, sowed
speak	spoke	spoken
speed	sped, speeded	sped, speeded
spell	spelt, spelled	spelt. spelled
spend	spent	spent
spill	spilt, spilled	spilt, spilled
spin	spun	spun
spit	spat, spit	spat, spit
split	split	split
spoil	spoilt, spoiled	spoilt, spoiled
spread	spread	spread
spring	sprang, sprung	sprung
stand	stood	stood
steal	stole	stolen
stick	stuck	stuck
sting	stung	stung
stink	stank, stunk	stunk

Infinitive 不定式	Past Tense 过去式	Past Participle 过去分词
strew	strewed	strewn, strewed
stride	strode	stridden, strid
strike	struck	struck, stricken
string	strung	strung
strive	strove, strived	striven, strived
swear	swore	sworn
sweat	sweat, sweated	sweat, sweated
sweep	swept	swept
swell	swelled	swollen, swelled
swim	swam	swum
swing	swung	swung
take	took	taken
teach	taught	taught
tear	tore	torn
tell	told	told
think	thought	thought
thrive	throve, thrived	thriven, thrived
throw	threw	thrown
thrust	thrust	thrust
tread	trod	trodden, trod
unbend	unbent	unbent
undercut	undercut	undercut
undergo	underwent	undergone
underlay	underlaid	underlaid
underlie	underlay	underlain
undersell	undersold	undersold
understand	understood	understood
undertake	undertook	undertaken
underwrite	underwrote	underwritten
undo	undid	undone
upset	upset	upset
unstring	unstrung	unstrung
uphold	upheld	upheld
wake	waked, woke	waked, woken, woke
wear	wore	worn
weave	wove	woven
wed	wedded, wed	wedded, wed
weep	wept	wept
wet	wetted, wet	wetted, wet
win	won	won
wind	winded, wound	winded, wound
wit (wot)	wist	wist
withdraw	withdrew	withdrawn
withhold	withheld	withheld
work	worked, wrought	worked, wrought
wring	wrung	wrung
write	wrote	written

注: 本表只收列不规则动词的一般变化形式, 有些属于罕用或古体的变化形式表内未予收列, 可从词典本文的有关词条中查得。

APPENDIX II 附录二

Common Marks and Symbols
常 用 符 号

1. Punctuation Marks 标点符号

Mark 符 号	English Name 英 语 名 称	Chinese Name 汉 语 名 称
.	period (或 full stop, full point)	句 号
,	comma	逗 号
;	semicolon	分 号
:	colon	冒 号
?	question mark (或 interrogation point)	问 号
!	exclamation mark (或 exclamation point)	感叹号(或感情号,惊叹号)
" " (或 " ")	(double) quotation marks	引 号
' ' (或 ' ')	single quotation marks	单 引 号
——	dash	破 折 号
-	hyphen	连 字 号
' (或 ')	apostrophe	撇号; 省字号
…	ellipsis (或 suspension points)	省 略 号
( )	parentheses (或 curves)	(圆) 括 号
[ ]	square brackets	方 括 号
〖 〗	double brackets	双 方 括 号
⟨ ⟩	angle brackets	角 括 号
{ }	braces	大 括 号
~	swung dash (或 tilde)	代 字 号
∧	caret	脱 字 号
/	virgule (或 slant)	斜 线 号
*	asterisk	星 号
†	dagger	剑 号
‡	double dagger	双 剑 号
¶ (或 ¶, ‖)	paragraph	段 落 号
§	section (或 numbered clause)	分 节 号
‖	parallels	平 行 号
☞	index (或 fist)	参 见 号
⟶	arrow	箭 号

2. Commercial Symbols 商业符号

Symbol 符 号	English Reading or Name 英 语 读 法 或 名 称	Chinese Reading or Name 汉 语 读 法 或 名 称
@	at; each	单价
%	percent	百分之…
‰	per thousand	千分之…
#	① number (before a figure): as, track #3	①…号(在数字前表示数目, 如 track #3 即 3 号轨道)
	② pound(s) (after a figure): as, 5#	②…磅(在数字后表示磅, 如 5# 即 5 磅)
¥	① Renminbi yuan	①人民币元
	② yen	②日元
£	pound(s) sterling	(英)镑
$ (或 $)	dollar(s)	(美)元
/	shilling(s)	先令
¢	cent(s)	分
®	registered trademark	注册商标
©	copyrighted	版权所有

APPENDIX III 附录三

Tables of Measures and Weights

度 量 衡 表

The Metric System 公制

Classification 类别	English Name 英语名称	Abbreviation or Symbol 缩写或符号	Chinese Name 汉语名称	Ratio to the Primary Unit 对主单位的比	Approximate Chinese Equivalent 折合市制
Length 长 度	millimicron	mμ	毫微米	1/1,000,000,000	
	micron	μ	微米	1/1,000,000	
	centimillimetre	cmm.	忽米	1/100,000	
	decimillimetre	dmm.	丝米	1/10,000	
	millimetre	mm.	毫米	1/1,000	
	centimetre	cm.	厘米	1/100	
	decimetre	dm.	分米	1/10	
	metre	m.	米	Primary Unit 主单位	=3 市尺
	decametre	dam.	十米	10	
	hectometre	hm.	百米	100	
	kilometre	km.	公里	1,000	=2 市里
Area 面积及地积	**square metre**	sq. m.	平方米	Primary Unit 主单位	=9 平方市尺
	are	a.	公亩	100	=0.15 市亩
	hectare	ha.	公顷	10,000	=15 市亩
	square kilometre	sq. km.	平方公里	1,000,000	=4 平方市里
Weight and Mass 重量和质量	milligram(me)	mg.	毫克	1/1,000,000	
	centigram(me)	cg.	厘克	1/100,000	
	decigram(me)	dg.	分克	1/10,000	
	gram(me)	g.	克	1/1,000	
	decagram(me)	dag.	十克	1/100	
	hectogram(me)	hg.	百克	1/10	
	kilogram(me)	kg.	公斤	Primary Unit 主单位	=2 市斤
	quintal	q.	公担	100	=200 市斤
	metric ton	MT (或 t.)	公吨	1,000	=2,000 市斤
Capacity 容 量	microlitre	μl.	微升	1/1,000,000	
	millilitre	ml.	毫升	1/1,000	
	centilitre	cl.	厘升	1/100	
	decilitre	dl.	分升	1/10	
	litre	l.	升	Primary Unit 主单位	=1 市升
	decalitre	dal.	十升	10	
	hectolitre	hl.	百升	100	
	kilolitre	kl.	千升	1,000	

APPENDIX IV   附录四

The Greek Alphabet

希 腊 字 母 表

Letter 字 母		Name 名 称	Pronunciation 读 音
A	α	alpha	['ælfə]
B	β	beta	['biːtə, 'beitə]
Γ	γ	gamma	['gæmə]
Δ	δ	delta	['deltə]
E	ε	epsilon	[ep'sailən, 'epsilən]
Z	ζ	zeta	['ziːtə]
H	η	eta	['iːtə, 'eitə]
Θ	θ	theta	['θiːtə]
I	ι	iota	[ai'outə]
K	κ	kappa	['kæpə]
Λ	λ	lambda	['læmdə]
M	μ	mu	[mjuː]
N	ν	nu	[njuː]
Ξ	ξ	xi	[gzai, ksai, zai]
O	o	omicron	[ou'maikrən]
Π	π	pi	[pai]
P	ρ	rho	[rou]
Σ	σ	sigma	['sigmə]
T	τ	tau	[tɔː]
Υ	υ	upsilon	[juːp'sailən, 'juːpsilən]
Φ	φ	phi	[fai]
X	χ	chi	[kai]
Ψ	ψ	psi	[psai]
Ω	ω	omega	['oumigə]